15th International Conference on Autonomous Agents and Multiagent Systems (AAMAS 2016)

Singapore
9-13 May 2016

Volume 1 of 2

ISBN: 978-1-5108-5508-3

Printed from e-media with permission by:

Curran Associates, Inc.
57 Morehouse Lane
Red Hook, NY 12571

Some format issues inherent in the e-media version may also appear in this print version.

Printed by Curran Associates, Inc. (2017)

Additional copies of this publication are available from:

Curran Associates, Inc.
57 Morehouse Lane
Red Hook, NY 12571 USA
Phone: 845-758-0400
Fax: 845-758-2633
Email: curran@proceedings.com
Web: www.proceedings.com

Table of Contents

Invited Talks

Game Theory I

Game Theory II

Game Theory III

Game Theory IV

Social Choice I

Social Choice II

Social Choice III

Social Choice IV

Learning I

Learning II

Learning III

Learning IV

Trust & Cooperation

Logic I

Logic II

Bargaining & Negotiation

Applications I

Applications II

Applications III

Virtual Agents II

Robotics I

Robotics II

Robotics III

Agent Societies

Planning

Verification

Demonstrations

Doctoral Mentoring Abstracts

9–13 May 2016

AAMAS 2016

Singapore

International Conference on *Autonomous Agents and Multiagent Systems*

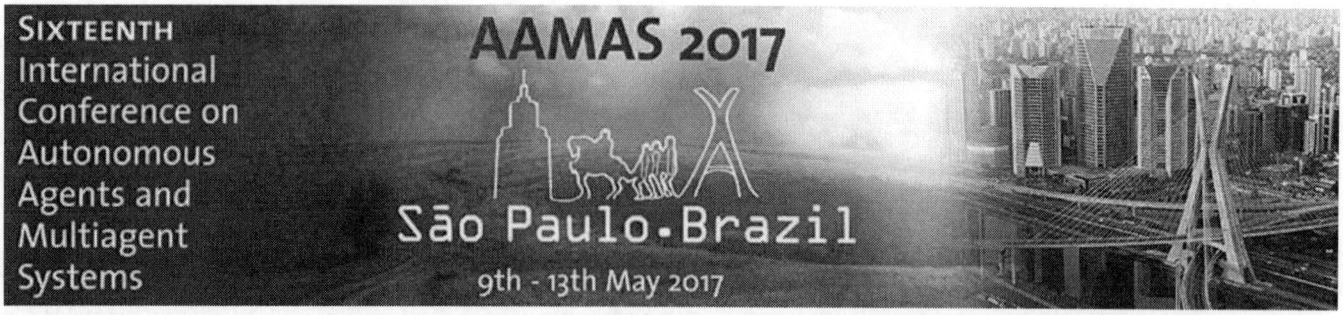

Important Dates:

Abstract Submission: 11th of November 2016 (23:59 UTC-12)
Full Paper Submission: 15th of November, 2016 (23:59 UTC-12)
Rebuttal Phase: 9th – 10th of January, 2017 (23:59 UTC-12)
Author Notification: 24th of January, 2017

About AAMAS:

AAMAS is the leading scientific conference for research in autonomous agents and multiagent systems. The AAMAS conference series was initiated in 2002 by merging three highly respected meetings: the International Conference on Multi-Agent Systems (ICMAS); the International Workshop on Agent Theories, Architectures, and Languages (ATAL); and the International Conference on Autonomous Agents (AA). The aim of the joint conference is to provide a single, high-profile, internationally respected archival forum for scientific research in the theory and practice of autonomous agents and multiagent systems.

AAMAS 2017, the sixteenth conference in the AAMAS series, seeks the submission of high-quality papers limited to 8 pages in length, with any additional pages containing only bibliographic references. Reviews will be double blind; authors must avoid including anything that can be used to identify them. Please note that submitting an abstract is required to submit a full paper. However, the abstracts will not be reviewed and full papers must be submitted for the review process to begin. All work must be original, i.e., it must not have appeared in a conference proceedings, book, or journal and may not be under review for another archival conference. In addition to submissions in the main track, AAMAS 2017 will be soliciting papers in special tracks. The review process for the special tracks will be similar to the main track, but with program committee members specially selected for each track. All accepted papers for the special tracks will be included in the proceedings.

AAMAS 2017 General Chairs: Kate Larson (University of Waterloo, Canada)
Michael Winikoff (University of Otago, New Zealand)
Program Chairs: Sanmay Das (Washington University in St. Louis, USA)
Edmund H. Durfee (University of Michigan, USA)
Local Chair: Jaime Simão Sichman (University of São Paulo, Brazil)

The full AAMAS 2017 Call for Papers, along with descriptions of the special tracks and all topics of interest, can be found at:

http://www.aamas2017.org

Introduction

The Autonomous Agents and MultiAgent Systems (AAMAS) conference series brings together researchers from around the world to share the latest advances in the field. It is the premier forum for research in the theory and practice of autonomous agents and multi-agent systems. AAMAS 2002, the first of the series, was held in Bologna, followed by Melbourne (2003), New York (2004), Utrecht (2005), Hakodate (2006), Honolulu (2007), Estoril (2008), Budapest (2009), Toronto (2010), Taipei (2011), Valencia (2012), Saint Paul (2013), Paris (2014), and Istanbul (2015). This volume constitutes the proceedings of AAMAS 2016, the fifteenth conference in the series, held in Singapore in May 2016.

In line with previous editions, AAMAS 2016 attracted submissions for a general track and five special tracks: Innovative Applications, Robotics, Embodied Virtual Agents and Human-Agent Interaction, Blue Sky Ideas track, and the JAAMAS presentation track. The special tracks were chaired by leading researchers in their corresponding fields: Onn Shehory and Noa Agmon chaired the Innovative Applications track, Francesco Amigoni and Roderich Gross the Robotics track, Tim Bickmore and Hannes Vilhjálmsson the Embodied Virtual Agents and Human-Agent Interaction track, and Frank Dignum the Blue Sky Ideas track. As a new initiative, the chairs of AAMAS 2016 also solicited articles published in the Journal of Autonomous Agents and Multiagent Systems for the *JAAMAS Presentation Track*. Only papers that have appeared in the Journal of Autonomous Agents and Multi-agent Systems (JAAMAS) in the 12 months period preceding the AAMAS notification date were eligible. This new track was chaired by Peter Stone.

Jointly with the PC chairs the special track chairs were responsible for appointing the Programme Committee (PC) members and the Senior Programme Committee members (SPC) for their tracks, and they made acceptance/rejection recommendations for their tracks in consultation with Programme Chairs based on input provided by the track PC, SPC, and Area Experts. This year the PC chairs introduced the new role of Area Experts, i.e., SPC members with additional responsibilities, to assist with selecting SPC members for specific research areas, identifying appropriate keywords, and assisting in potential issues during discussion phase. This new role was a success and increased the quality of our SPC and PC, and also the reviewing process in general.

Full paper submissions (8 pages plus bibliographic references) and Blue Sky Ideas paper submissions (4 pages plus references) were solicited for AAMAS 2016. Some of the full paper submissions were accepted as extended abstracts (2 pages). The papers were selected by means of a thorough review and discussion process, which included an opportunity for authors to respond to reviewer comments during a rebuttal phase. All SPC members, Area Experts, and Track Chairs followed and contributed to the technical discussions on the papers they were overseeing. The JAAMAS presentation Track submissions published as extended abstracts were handled by the track chair.

AAMAS 2016 attracted a good number of high-quality submissions; the result of the reviewing process is summarised by the following table:

Track	*Reviewed*	*Accepted as full paper*		*Accepted as Extended Abstract*	
Main	411	109	27%	97	24%
Innovative Applications	38	10	26%	12	31%
Robotics	46	10	22%	14	30%
Embodied Virtual Agents and Human-Agent Interaction	42	7	17%	8	19%
Blue Sky Ideas	13	1	8%	0	0%
JAAMAS Presentation	16	16	100%	-	-

Overall, out of 550 submissions, 137 (25%) were accepted as full papers and 143 (26%) were accepted as extended abstracts. Additionally, all 16 JAAMAS track submissions were accepted.

The acceptance rates by a paper's primary high-level keyword from the conference topics of interest (not including JAAMAS Presentation Track) are as follows:

Topic	*Reviewed*	*Accepted as full paper*		*Accepted as Extended Abstract*	
Agent Theories and Models	50	11	22%	7	14%
Communication and Argumentation	16	6	37%	2	12%
Cooperation	48	5	10%	14	29%
Agent Societies and Societal Issues	34	4	12%	12	35%
Knowledge Representation and Reasoning	28	4	14%	10	36%
Learning and Adaptation	49	16	33%	13	26%
Economic Paradigms	127	43	34%	30	24%
Social simulation	19	3	16%	7	37%
Engineering Multi-Agent Systems	14	3	21%	3	21%
Agents & Mainstream Computing	4	0	-	0	-
Verification and Validation of Agent-Based Systems	12	5	42%	3	25%
Robotics	56	12	21%	13	23%
Blue Sky	4	1	25%	0	-
Innovative Applications	40	13	32%	9	22%
Virtual Agents and Humans	49	10	20%	10	20%

Full papers were presented orally in 20 minute slots; all extended abstracts and, optionally, full papers were presented as posters during the conference.

Out of the 550 submissions, 351 (64%) had a student as the primary author, 82 of these were accepted as full papers (23%), and a further 90 (26%) were accepted as extended abstracts.

The proceedings also contain 17 Demonstration papers, 13 Doctoral Consortium papers, as well as abstracts of the invited talks and details of some of the awards given.

We would like to thank the authors in our and nearby communities for submitting a large number of top quality papers and the PC, SPC members, Area Experts and Track Chairs for their dedication in reviewing the submissions and for engaging in all the technical discussions held during the reviewing process. We'd like to express our gratitude to Dave Shield for assisting us with Confmaster throughout the entire process. We also thank Jie Zhang for arranging the conference proceedings and Pradeep Varakantham and all the members of the local committee for organizing the venue, the website of the conference, as well as the social program.

John Thangarajah and Karl Tuyls
AAMAS 2016 Program Co-Chairs

Catholijn Jonker and Stacy Marsella
AAMAS 2016 General Co-Chairs

AAMAS 2016 Organizing Committee

General co-Chairs	Catholijn M. Jonker, TU Delft, Netherlands Stacy Marsella, University of Southern California, USA
Program co-Chairs	John Thangarajah, RMIT University. Australia Karl Tuyls, University of Liverpool, UK
Robotics Track Chairs	Francesco Amigoni, Politecnico di Milano, Italy Roderich Gross, University of Sheffield, UK
Virtual Agents Track Chairs	Tim Bickmore, Northeastern University, USA Hannes Högni Vilhjálmsson, Reykjavík University, Iceland
Innovative Applications Chairs	Onn Shehory, IBM Haifa Labs, Israel Noa Agmon, Bar-Ilan University, Israel
Blue Sky Ideas, Challenges & Visions	Frank Dignum, Utrecht University, Netherlands
Finance Chair	Christopher Kiekintveld, University of Texas at El Paso, USA
Publicity Chair	Adrian Pearce, University of Melbourne, Australia
Publications Chair	Jie Zhang, Nanyang Technological University, Singapore
Tutorials Chairs	David Pynadath, University of Southern California, USA Sebastian Sardina, RMIT University. Australia
Workshops Chairs	Carles Sierra, Spanish Research Council - CISC, Spain Nardine Osman, Spanish Research Council - CISC, Spain
Exhibitions Chair	Bo An, Nanyang Technological University, Singapore
Demonstrations Chairs	Ann Nowe, Vrije Universiteit Brussel, Belgium Shih-Fen Cheng, Singapore Management University, Singapore
Scholarships Co-Chairs	Matthew Taylor, Washington State University, USA Koen V. Hindriks, TU Delft, Netherlands Katsuhide Fujita, Nagoya Institute of Technology, Japan
Doctoral Consortium Co-Chairs	Gita Sukthankar, University of Central Florida, USA Maria Gini, University of Minnesota, USA

Sponsorship Co-Chairs

Americas	Janus Marecki, Google Deep Mind, UK
Asia/Oceania	Bryan Low, National University of Singapore, Singapore
Europe	Amit Chopra, Lancaster University, UK
Local Arrangements Chair	Pradeep Varakantham, Singapore Management University, Singapore
Local Arrangements Committee	Akshat Kumar, Singapore Management University, Singapore Bo An, Nanyang Technological University, Singapore Bryan Low, National University of Singapore, Singapore Lau Hoong Chuin, Singapore Management University, Singapore Jie Zhang, Nanyang Technological University, Singapore Somchaya Liemhetcharat, Uber Advanced Technologies Center, USA

AAMAS'16 Senior Program Committee

Thomas Ågotnes, University of Bergen
Natasha Alechina, University of Nottingham
Christopher Amato, University of New Hampshire
Bo An, Nanyang Technological University
Yoram Bachrach, Microsoft Research Cambridge
Matteo Baldoni, Dip. di Informatica, Univ. di Torino
Ana Bazzan, UFRGS, Area Expert
Lars Braubach, University of Hamburg
Nils Bulling, Delft University of Technology
Massimo Cossentino, ICAR - CNR
Jacob Crandall, Masdar Institute
Stephen Cranefield, University of Otago
Marina De Vos, University of Bath
Mathijs de Weerdt, Delft University of Technology
Frank Dignum, Utrecht University
Virginia Dignum, Delft University of Technology, Area Expert
James Edmondson, Carnegie Mellon University
Amal El Fallah Seghrouchni, LIP6 - UPMC, Area Expert
Edith Elkind, University of Oxford, Area Expert
Kobi Gal, BGU
Enrico Gerding, University of Southampton
Paolo Giorgini, University of Trento, Italy
Stephen Guy, University of Minnesota
Daniel Hennes, DFKI Robotics Innovation Center
Wiebe van der Hoek, University of Liverpool, Area Expert
Tom Holvoet, Katholieke Universiteit Leuven, Area Expert
Wojciech Jamroga, Polish Academy of Sciences
Ece Kamar, MSR
Christopher Kiekintveld, University of Texas at Elpaso
Alexander Kleiner, iRobot
Franziska Klugl, Orebro University
Matthias Klusch, DFKI
Fernando Koch, Samsung Research Institute Brazil
Andreas Kolling, University of Sheffield
Sarit Kraus, Bar Ilan University, BIU
Daniel Kudenko, University of York
Han La Poutre, CWI Amsterdam
Jerome Lang, University Paris Dauphine
Kate Larson, University of Waterloo
James Lester, North Carolina State University
Kevin Leyton-Brown, University of British Columbia, Area Expert

Brian Logan, University of Nottingham, Area Expert
Nicolas Maudet, LIP6, Univ. Pierre et Marie Curie
Peter McBurney, King's College London, Area Expert
Francisco Melo, INESC-ID/Instituto Superior Técnico
Joerg Mueller, Department of Informatics
Yukiko Nakano, Seikei University
Frans Oliehoek, Liverpool
Julian Padget, University of Bath, Area Expert
Lin Padgham, RMIT University, Area Expert
Simon Parsons, King's College London, Area Expert
Terry Payne, University of Liverpool, Area Expert
Tao Qin, Microsoft Research Asia
Scott Sanner, Oregon State University
Paul Scerri, Carnegie Mellon University, Area Expert
Sandip Sen, University of Tulsa, Area Expert
Munindar Singh, North Carolina State University
Matthijs Spaan, Delft University of Technology, Area Expert
Mohan Sridharan, The University of Auckland
Milind Tambe, University of Southern California, Area Expert
Kagan Tumer, Oregon State University, Area Expert
Wamberto Vasconcelos, University of Aberdeen, Area Expert
Gerhard Weiss, University of Maastricht
Shimon Whiteson, University of Oxford
Michael Winikoff, University of Otago, Area Expert
Michael Wooldridge, University of Oxford, Area Expert
Makoto Yokoo, Kyushu University
Pinar Yolum, Bogazici University

AAMAS'16 Program Committee

Sherief Abdallah, British University in Dubai
Carole Adam, University of Grenoble - UJF - LIG
Aamir Ahmad, Max Planck Institute
Stephane Airiau, Université Paris-Dauphine
Stefano Albrecht, The University of Texas at Austin
Huib Aldewereld, Delft University of Technology
Leila Amgoud, CNRS
Edouard Amouroux, RMIT University Vietnam
Luis Antunes, University of Lisbon
Katie Atkinson, University of Liverpool
Tsz-Chiu Au, Ulsan National Institute of Science and Technology
Priscilla Avegliano, IBM Research
Robert Axtell, George Mason University
Reyhan Aydogan, Ozyegin University
Amos Azaria, Carnegie Mellon University, CMU
Haris Aziz, NICTA
Tim Baarslag, University of Southampton
Dirk Bade, University of Hamburg
Tina Balke, University of Surrey
Cristina Baroglio, University of Torino
Johan Barthelemy, University of Wollongong
Nicola Basilico, University of Milan
Dorothea Baumeister, Heinrich Heine University
Christian Becker-Asano, BOSCH Research
Sven Behnke, University of Bonn
Francesco Belardinelli, University of Évry Val d'Essonne
Vaishak Belle, University of Toronto
Itzhak Benenson, Tel Aviv University
Jamal Bentahar, Concordia University
Carole Bernon, University of Toulouse
Aurélie Beynier, LIP6, University Pierre
Reinaldo Bianchi, FEI
Daan Bloembergen, University of Liverpool
Thomas Bolander, Technical University of Denmark
Rafael Bordini, FACIN-PUCRS
Daniel Borrajo, Universidad Carlos III de Madrid
Branislav Bosansky, Czech Technical University
Tibor Bosse, VU University Amsterdam
Vicent Botti, Polytechnic University of Valencia
Sylvain Bouveret, University of Grenoble
Simina Brânzei, Aarhus University

Felix Brandt, Technische Universität München
Jean-Pierre Briot, LIP6
Joost Broekens, Delft University of Technology
Matthew Brown, University of Southern California
Olivier Buffet, INRIA
Neil Burch, University of Alberta
Jesus Capitan, University of Seville
Carlos Cardonha, IBM Research
Marc Cavazza, University of Teesside
Lawrence Cavedon, RMIT University
Federico Cerutti, Cardiff University
Nilanjan Chakraborty, Stony Brook University
Wei Chen, Microsoft Research
Yingke Chen, Sichuan University
Shih-Fen Cheng, Singapore Management University
Sonia Chernova, Georgia Institute of Technology
Amit Chopra, Lancaster University
Jen Jen Chung, Oregon State University
Helder Coelho, Universidade de Lisboa
Robin Cohen, University of Waterloo
Mitchell Colby, Oregon State University
Rem Collier, University College Dublin
Natalia Criado, Liverpool John Moores University
Bruno da Silva, UFRGS
Fabiano Dalpiaz, Utrecht University
Hoa Dam, University of Wollongong
Mehdi Dastani, Utrecht University
Bart de Keijzer, Sapienza University of Rome
Lavindra de Silva, University of Nottingham
Keith Decker, University of Delaware
Karina Valdivia Delgado, University of Sao Paulo
Louise Dennis, University of Liverpool
Sam Devlin, York Centre for Complex Systems Analysis
Marcos Dias de Assuncao, French Institute for Research in Computer Science
Jilles Dibangoye, INSA
Frank Dignum, Utrecht University
Virginia Dignum, Delft University of Technology
Catalin Dima, Université Paris Est Créteil
Sylvie Doutre, Université Toulouse 1 Capitole - IRIT
Adam Eck, University of Nebraska-Lincoln
Stefan Edelkamp, University of Bremen
Kyriakos Efthymiadis, AI Lab, Vrije Universiteit Brussel
Edith Elkind, University of Oxford
Rick Evertsz, RMIT University, Australia

Piotr Faliszewski, AGH University of Science and Technology
Shaheen Fatima, Loughborough University
Klaus Fischer, DFKI
Nicoletta Fornara, Università della Svizzera Italiana
Giancarlo Fortino, Università della Calabria
Martin Gairing, University of Liverpool
Stéphane Galland, Université Bourgogne Franche-Comté
Sam Ganzfried, Ganzfried Research
Nicola Gatti, Politecnico di Milano
Amineh Ghorbani, Faculty of Technology, Policy and Management
Aditya Ghose, Wollongong University
Massimiliano Giacomin, University of Brescia
Joseph Giampapa, Carnegie Mellon University
Maria Gini, University of Minnesota
Marie-Pierre Gleizes, IRIT Toulouse
Jorge Gomez-Sanz, Universidad Complutense de Madrid
Ricardo Gonçalves, Universidade Nova de Lisboa
Juan Carlos González Moreno, University of Vigo
Guido Governatori, NICTA
Umberto Grandi, University of Toulouse
Gianluigi Greco, University of Calabria, Italy
Nathan Griffiths, University of Warwick
Francisco Grimaldo, Universitat de València
Davide Grossi, University of Liverpool
Zahia Guessoum, Universite de Paris 6
Akin Gunay, Nanyang Technological University
Mingyu Guo, University of Adelaide
Julian Gutierrez, University of Oxford
Musad Haque, Vanderbilt University
Maaike Harbers, Delft University of Technology
James Harland, RMIT University
Paul Harrenstein, University of Oxford
Brent Harrison, The Georgia Institute of Technology
William Haskell, National University of Singapore
Di He, Microsoft Research Asia
Andreas Herzig, University of Toulouse - CNRS - IRIT
Vincent Hilaire, UTBM
Jesse Hoey, University of Waterloo
Martin Homola, Comenius University
Enda Howley, National University of Ireland, Galway
Hung-Hsuan Huang, College of Information Science & Engineering
Jomi Hubner, Federal University of Santa Catarina
Atsushi Iwasaki, University of Electro-Communications
Yichuan Jiang, Southeast University

Ozgur Kafali, Department of Computer Science
Michael Kaisers, Centrum Wiskunde & Informatica, Amsterdam
Ioannis Karamouzas, University of Minnesota
Ian Kash, Microsoft Research
Michael Kirley, Senior Lecturer, The University of Melbourne
Matthias Knorr, NOVA LINCS, Universidade Nova de Lisboa
Martin Kollingbaum, University of Aberdeen
Sebastien Konieczny, CRIL-CNRS
Stefan Kopp, Bielefeld University
Hatice Kose, Istanbul Technical University
Ryszard Kowalczyk, Swinburne University of Technology
Louwe B. Kuijer, University of Liverpool
Akshat Kumar, Singapore Management University
Marco Lützenberger, Technische Universität Berlin
Bruno Lacerda, University of Birmingham, UK
Marc Lanctot, Google Deepmind
Jeehang Lee, University of bath
Jimmy Lee, The Chinese University of Hong Kong
Matteo Leonetti, University of Texas at Austin
Julien Lesca, Paris Dauphine University
Yves Lespérance, York University
Boyang Li, Disney Research
Christopher Lin, University of Washington
Raz Lin, Bar-Ilan University
Viliam Lisy, University of Alberta
Michael Littman, Brown University
Alessio Lomuscio, Imperial College London
Manuel Lopes, INRIA
Henrique Lopes Cardoso, Universidade do Porto
Maite Lopez-Sanchez, University of Barcelona
Emiliano Lorini, IRIT-CNRS
Steven Loscalzo, US Air Force Research Laboratory
Bryan Kian Hsiang Low, National University of Singapore
Michael Luck, King's College London
Weidong Ma, Microsoft Research Asia
Kleanthis Malialis, University College London
Andrew Mao, Microsoft Research
Toshihiro Matsui, Nagoya Institute of Technology
Nicholas Mattei, DATA 61, NICTA
Reshef Meir, Harvard University
Felipe Meneguzzi, PUCRS
Cetin Mericli, Carnegie Mellon University
Fabrizio Messina, University of Catania
Roberto Micalizio, Università degli Studi di Torino

Mihail Mihaylov, Vrije Universiteit Brussel
Tim Miller, The University of Melbourne
Fabio Mogavero, University of Oxford
Marco Montali, Free University of Bozen-Bolzano, Italy
Enrique Munoz de Cote, INAOE
Aniello Murano, University of Napoli Federico II
Karen Myers, SRI
Nina Narodytska, Samsung Research America
Michael Neff, UC Davis
Thanh Nguyen, University of Southern California
Jinzhong Niu, City University of New York
Itsuki Noda, Human Information Research Institute
Emma Norling, Manchester Metropolitan University
Timothy Norman, University of Aberdeen
Ingrid Nunes, UFRGS
Eduardo Oliveira, The University of Melbourne
Eva Onaindia, Universitat Politecnica de Valencia
Santi Ontanon, Drexel University
Nir Oren, University of Aberdeen
Sascha Ossowski, University Rey Juan Carlos
Lin Padgham, RMIT University
Maurice Pagnucco, The University of New South Wales
Praveen Paruchuri, IIIT Hyderabad
Adrian Pearce, University of Melbourne
Truls Pedersen, University of Bergen
Tomislav Pejsa, University of Wisconsin-Madison
Wojciech Penczek, IPI PAN Warsaw
Giuseppe Perelli, University of Oxford
pascal perez, University of Wollongong
Max Pfingsthorn, Jacobs University Bremen
Steve Phelps, CCFEA, CSEE, University of Essex
Alexander Pokahr, University of Hamburg
Ronald Poppe, University of Utrecht
Daniele Porello, LOA, ISTC-CNR, Italy
Rui Prada, Instituto Superior Tecnico
Henry Prakken, Utrecht University
Hongyang Qu, University of Sheffield
Zinovi Rabinovich, Mobileye Vision Technologies Ltd.
Franco Raimondi, Middlesex University
Anita Raja, The Cooper Union
Subramanian Ramamoorthy, The University of Edinburgh
Patrizia Ribino, ICAR - Consiglio Nazionale delle Ricerche
Alessandro Ricci, University of Bologna
Deborah Richards, Macquarie University, Australia

Ariella Richardson, Lev Academic Center
Valentin Robu, Heriot-Watt University, Edinburgh
Antônio Carlos Rocha Costa, UFRGS-FURG
Sebastian Rodriguez, GITIA - FRT - Univ. Tecnologica Nacional
Nicole Ronald, Swinburne University of Technology
Nico Roos, Maastricht University
Jeffrey Rosenschein, Hebrew University of Jerusalem
Joerg Rothe, Heinrich-Heine-Universitaet Duesseldorf
Michael Rovatsos, University of Edinburgh
Jordi Sabater-Mir, IIIA-CSIC
Luca Sabatucci, Icar Institute, National Research Council
Joshua Sack, California State University Long Beach
Abdallah Saffidine, University of New South Wales
Yuko Sakurai, Kyushu University
Sanem Sariel, Istanbul Technical University
Rahul Savani, University of Liverpool
Bastin Tony Roy Savarimuthu, Department of Information Science
Guido Schaefer, CWI
Stefan Scherer, University of Southern California
Michael Ignaz Schomacher, UAS Western Switzerland, HES-SO
Valeria Seidita, Università degli Studi di Palermo, Italy
Murat Sensoy, Ozyegin University
Pedro Sequeira, INESC-ID / Instituto Superior Tecnico
Paulo Shakarian, Arizona State University
Alexei Sharpanskykh, Delft University of Technology
Onn Shehory, IBM Research
Jivko Sinapov, University of Texas at Austin
Dhirendra Singh, RMIT University
Arunesh Sinha, University of Southern California
Oskar Skibski, University of Warsaw
Marija Slavkovik, University of Bergen
Leen-Kiat Soh, Department of Computer Science & Engineering
Leandro Soriano Marcolino, University of Southern California
Sebastian Stein, University of Southampton
Roni Stern, Ben Gurion University of the Negev
Gita Sukthankar, University of Central Florida
Katia Sycara, Carnegie Mellon University
Yuqing Tang, Carnegie Mellon University, US
Matthias Thimm, University of Koblenz-Landau
Ingo Timm, University of Trier
Taiki Todo, Department of Informatics, Kyushu University
Viviane Torres da Silva, IBM Research - Brazil
Stojan Trajanovski, Delft University of Technology
Paolo Turrini, Imperial College London

Leendert van der Torre, University of Luxembourg
Leo van Moergestel, HU University of applied sciences Utrecht
Salvatore Venticinque, Second University of Naples
Giuseppe Vizzari, University of Milano-Bicocca
Quoc Bao Vo, Swinburne University of Technology
Yevgeniy Vorobeychik, Vanderbilt University
Peter Vrancx, Vrije Universiteit Brussel
Thomas J. Walsh, Kronos Incorporated
Changjun Wang, BI-SEC, Beijing University of Technology
Yi Wang, Zhejiang University
Yonghong Wang, Apple Inc
Nigel Ward, University of Texas, El Paso
Martijn Warnier, Delft University of Technology
Rym Wenkstern, University of Texas at Dallas
Danny Weyns, Linnaeus University, Sweden
Michael Winikoff, University of Otago
Feng Wu, University of Science and Technology of China
Lirong Xia, RPI
Yang Xu, UESTC
Nitin Yadav, RMIT University
Bo Yang, Jilin University
William Yeoh, New Mexico State University
Logan Yliniemi, University of Nevada, Reno
Neil Yorke-Smith, American University of Beirut
Fabio Zambetta, School of CSIT, RMIT University
Chongjie Zhang, Massachusetts Institute of Technology
Jie Zhang, Nanyang Technological University
Shiqi Zhang, The University of Texas at Austin
Yingqian Zhang, Erasmus University Rotterdam
Yair Zick, Carnegie Mellon University
Roie Zivan, Ben Gurion University of the Negev
Aviv Zohar, Hebrew University Jerusalem Israel
Inon Zuckerman, Ariel University Center of Samaria

AAMAS'16 Additional Reviewers

Sierra Adibi
Ashkan Aleali
B. Alfonso
Shaull Almagor
Mohammed Basil Almukaynizi
Faisal Al-Saqqar
Hamidreza Alvari
Alba Amato
Merlinda Andoni
James Archbold
João Balsa
Luis Botelho
Florian Brandl
Simon Busard
Zhigang Cao
Rafael Cardoso
Bobby Davis
Argyrios Deligkas
Ahmad Diab
Sjur Dyrkolbotn
Jan van Eijck
Mohamed El-Menshawy
Sebastian Enqvist
Hui Fang
Giovani Farias
Ferdinando Fioretto
Scott Forer
Dimitris Fotakis
Julio Godoy
Hiromitsu Hattori
Khoi Dai Hoang
Trong Nghia Hoang
Johannes Hofbauer
Hadi Hosseini
Athirai A. Irissappane
Astrid Jackson
Siwei Jiang
Debarun Kar
Bilal Kartal
Piotr Kazmierczak
Warda El Kholy
Michal Knapik
Tobias Küster
Nicholas Lawrance
Bo Li
Somchaya Liemhetcharat
Yuan Liu
Dominique Lonin
Jian Lou
Marin Lujak
Nuno Magessi
Ericsson Santana Marin
Nils Masuch
Mohamad Mehdi
Luis Moniz
Oscar Morales
Larry Moss
Ayan Mukhopadhyay
Tim Muller
Peter Náther
Daniel Neugebauer
Nhan-Tam Nguyen
Quoc Phong Nguyen
Davide Nunes
Ernesto Nunes
Svetlana Obraztsova
Swetasudha Panda
Alison Panisson
Dominik Peters
Gleb Polevoy
José Carlos Pulido
David Rajaratnam
Anja Rey
Lisa Rey
Thiago R.P.M. Rúbio
Soumajyoti Sarkar
Lena Schend
Ann-Kathrin Selker
Elham Shaabani
Nick Sohre
Thane Somers
Gita Sukthankar
Khalid Sultan
Jesse Thomason
Carmine Ventre
E. Vivancos
Omar Abdel Wahab
Dongxia Wang
Zhanhao Xiao
Haifeng Xu
Amulya Yadav
Tomohisa Yamashita
Jie Zhang

International Foundation for Autonomous Agents and Multiagent Systems

Artificial Intelligence journal

ACM Special Interest Group on Artificial Intelligence

Sumitomo Electric

Panasonic

Panasonic R&D Center Singapore

National Science Foundation

Springer

Unicen

Living Analytics Research Center

Awards

ACM SIGART Autonomous Agents Research Award

The ACM SIGART Autonomous Agents Research Award is an annual award for excellence in research in the area of autonomous agents. The award is intended to recognize researchers in autonomous agents whose current work is an important influence on the field. The award is an official ACM award, funded by an endowment created by ACM SIGART from the proceeds of previous Autonomous Agents conferences. Candidates for the award are nominated through an open nomination process. Previous winners of the SIGART Autonomous Research Award were Catherine Pelachaud (2015), Michael Wellman (2014), Jeffrey S. Rosenschein (2013), Moshe Tennenholtz (2012), Joe Halpern (2011), Jonathan Gratch and Stacy Marsella (2010), Manuela Veloso (2009), Yoav Shoham (2008), Sarit Kraus (2007), Michael Wooldridge (2006), Milind Tambe (2005), Makoto Yokoo (2004), Nick Jennings (2003), Katia Sycara (2002), and Tuomas Sandholm (2001).

The selection committee for the ACM/SIGAI Autonomous Agents Research Award is pleased to announce that Prof. Peter Stone of the University of Texas at Austin is the recipient of the 2016 award. Prof. Stone's work is exceptional in both its breadth and depth in multiagent systems. Some of his most influential work has been in reinforcement learning and multiagent learning as applied to robot soccer, autonomous traffic management, and trading agents. His contributions are ongoing, as evidenced by the growing influence of one of his recent innovations, the formulation of ad hoc teamwork as a new research area. In addition to the impact of his research, his teams' successes in international competitions, including RoboCup and the Trading Agent Competition, are particularly notable. Prof. Stone has also served the multiagent systems, AI, and RoboCup communities in various leadership roles.

IFAAMAS Victor Lesser Distinguished Dissertation Award

This award was started for dissertations defended in 2006 and is named for Professor Victor Lesser, a long standing member of the AAMAS community who has graduated a large number of outstanding PhD students in the area. To be eligible for the 2014 award, a dissertation had to have been written as part of a PhD defended during the year 2014, and had to be nominated by the supervisor with three supporting references.

Selection is based on originality, depth, impact and written quality, supported by quality publications. Previous winners of this award were Yair Zick (2014), Manish Jain (2013), Birgit Endrass (2012), Daniel Villatoro (2011), Bo An (2010), Andrew Gilpin (2009), Ariel Procaccia (2008), Radu Jurca (2007), and Vincent Conitzer (2006).

The 2015 IFAAMAS Victor Lesser Distinguished Dissertation Award recipient is Dr. Amos Azaria, whose thesis titled "Agents for Automated Human Persuasion" was supervised by Prof. Sarit Kraus and Prof. Yonatan Aumann. The committee also wanted to recognize Dr. Piotr Skowron, whose thesis titled "Resource Allocation in Selfish and Cooperative Distributed Systems" was supervised by Prof. Piotr Faliszewski and Prof. Krzysztof Rzadca.

IFAAMAS Influential Paper Award

The International Foundation for Autonomous Agents and Multi-Agent Systems set up an influential paper award in 2006 to recognize publications that have made seminal contributions to the field. Such papers represent the best and most influential work in the area of autonomous agents and multi-agent systems. These papers might, therefore, have proved a key result, led to the development of a new sub-field, demonstrated a significant new application or system, or simply presented a new way of thinking about a topic that has proved influential. The award is open to any paper that was published at least 10 years before the award is made. The paper can have been published in any journal, conference, or workshop. The award is sponsored by the Agent Theories, Architectures and Languages foundation.

The winner of the 2016 IFAAMAS Influential Paper Award:

Munindar P. Singh (1998)
Agent Communication Languages: Rethinking the Principles
IEEE Computer, vol. 31, no. 12, December 1998, pp. 40-47.

Deep Learning: What's Next

Dr. Andrew Ng
Baidu, Inc.
Computer Science Department, Stanford University
ang@cs.stanford.edu

ABSTRACT

Deep Learning has transformed many important tasks, including speech and image recognition. Deep Learning systems scale well by absorbing huge amounts of data to create accurate models. However, as Deep Learning has become more mainstream, it has generated some hype, and has been linked to everything from world peace to evil killer robots. In this talk, Dr. Ng will help separate hype from reality, and discuss potential ways that Deep Learning technologies can benefit society in the short and long term.

Appears in: *Proceedings of the 15th International Conference on Autonomous Agents and Multiagent Systems (AAMAS 2016), J. Thangarajah, K. Tuyls, C. Jonker, S. Marsella (eds.), May 9–13, 2016, Singapore.*

Short Bio

Andrew Ng is Chief Scientist at Baidu. He leads Baidu Research, which includes the Silicon Valley AI Lab, the Institute of Deep Learning and the Big Data Lab. The organization brings together global research talent to work on fundamental technologies in areas such as image recognition and image-based search, speech recognition, natural language processing and semantic intelligence. In addition to his role at Baidu, Dr. Ng is a faculty member in Stanford University's Computer Science Department, and Chairman of Coursera, an online education platform that he co-founded. Dr. Ng is the author or co-author of over 100 published papers in machine learning, robotics and related fields. He holds degrees from Carnegie Mellon University, MIT and the University of California, Berkeley.

Autonomous Learning Agents: Layered Learning and Ad Hoc Teamwork

Professor Peter Stone
Department of Computer Science
The University of Texas at Austin
pstone@cs.utexas.edu

ABSTRACT

In order to achieve long-term autonomy in the real world, fully autonomous agents need to be able to learn, both to improve their behaviors in a complex, dynamically changing world, and to enable interaction with previously unfamiliar agents. This talk begins by presenting layered learning, a hierarchical machine learning paradigm that enables learning of complex behaviors by incrementally learning a series of sub-behaviors. Layered learning was the key deciding factor in UT Austin Villa's recent RoboCup 3D simulation league championship. The talk then introduces ad hoc teamwork as an emerging multiagent learning challenge. Ad hoc teamwork is based on the premise that as autonomous agents become capable of long-term autonomy, they will increasingly need to band together for cooperative activities with previously unfamiliar teammates. In such "ad hoc" team settings, team strategies cannot be developed a priori. Rather, an agent must learn to cooperate with new teammates on the fly. This talk reports on both theoretical and empirical ad hoc teamwork results, including from recent "pick up" RoboCup robot soccer competitions.

CCS Concepts

•Computing methodologies → Multi-agent systems; Multi-agent reinforcement learning; •Computer systems organization → Robotic control;

Keywords

Autonomous agents; multiagent systems; layered learning; ad hoc teamwork; reinforcement learning; RoboCup soccer

Appears in: *Proceedings of the 15th International Conference on Autonomous Agents and Multiagent Systems (AAMAS 2016), J. Thangarajah, K. Tuyls, C. Jonker, S. Marsella (eds.), May 9–13, 2016, Singapore.*

Short Bio

Peter Stone is the David Bruton, Jr. Centennial Professor of Computer Science at the University of Texas at Austin. In 2013 he was awarded the University of Texas System Regents' Outstanding Teaching Award and in 2014 he was inducted into the UT Austin Academy of Distinguished Teachers, earning him the title of University Distinguished Teaching Professor. Professor Stone's research interests in Artificial Intelligence include machine learning (especially reinforcement learning), multiagent systems, robotics, and e-commerce. Professor Stone received his Ph.D in Computer Science in 1998 from Carnegie Mellon University. From 1999 to 2002 he was a Senior Technical Staff Member in the Artificial Intelligence Principles Research Department at AT&T Labs - Research. He is an Alfred P. Sloan Research Fellow, Guggenheim Fellow, AAAI Fellow, Fulbright Scholar, and 2004 ONR Young Investigator. In 2003, he won an NSF CAREER award for his proposed long term research on learning agents in dynamic, collaborative, and adversarial multiagent environments, and in 2007 he received the prestigious IJCAI Computers and Thought Award, given biannually to the top AI researcher under the age of 35.

Discrete Optimization for Agents

Professor Peter J. Stuckey
Data 61 and University of Melbourne, 3010, Australia
pstuckey@unimelb.edu.au

ABSTRACT

Many an agent needs to make a decision of what do to given a limited amount of resources. This is a discrete optimization problem. Recent advances in discrete optimization modelling technology have made it easier than ever before to model difficult ad hoc optimization problems, and apply off the shelf solving technology rapidly and efficiently, while rapid advances in discrete optimization solving technology have made it faster than ever before to solve such problems. In this talk I will illustrate how

- modern languages allow us to capture the combinatorial substructure of discrete optimization problems thus allowing solving to be much more rapid;
- how nogood learning can exponentially improve our ability to solve these problems;
- and how these combine to allow us to rapidly resolve problems that are slowly changing, a case that seems particularly relevant to agents readjusting their plans in a changing environment

My hope is that the agent community will be inspired to learn and use more of the tools and techniques developed by the discrete optimization community.

CCS Concepts

•Mathematics of computing → Discrete optimization; •Theory of computation → Constraint and logic programming; •Hardware → *Theorem proving and SAT solving;*

Keywords

Discrete optimization; nogood learning; lifelong learning

Appears in: *Proceedings of the 15th International Conference on Autonomous Agents and Multiagent Systems (AAMAS 2016), J. Thangarajah, K. Tuyls, C. Jonker, S. Marsella (eds.), May 9–13, 2016, Singapore.*

Short Bio

Peter J. Stuckey is a Professor in the Department of Computing and Information Systems at the University of Melbourne, and project leader at NICTA and Data61. Peter Stuckey is a pioneer in constraint programming, the science of modelling and solving complex combinatorial problems. His research interests include: constraint programming; programming languages, in particular declarative programing languages; constraint solving algorithms; bioinformatics; and constraint-based graphics. He enjoys problem solving in any area, having publications in e.g. databases, timetabling, and system security.

Peter Stuckey received a B.Sc and Ph.D both in Computer Science from Monash University in 1985 and 1988 respectively. In 2009 he was recognized as an ACM Distinguished Scientist. In 2010 he was awarded the Google Australia Eureka Prize for Innovation in Computer Science for his work on lazy clause generation. He was awarded the 2010 University of Melbourne Woodward Medal for most outstanding publication in Science and Technology across the university.

Am I bovvered? Fifteen years of Empathic Agents

Professor Ruth Aylett
School of Mathematical & Computer Sciences
Heriot-Watt University, Edinburgh, Scotland
r.s.aylett@hw.ac.uk

ABSTRACT

In 2001, the EU-funded project VICTEC pioneered the concept of an Empathic Agent. This was reported at AAMAS in 2004 in a well-cited paper 'Caring for Agents and Agents that Care: Building Empathic Relations with Synthetic Agents' (Paiva, Dias, Sobral, Aylett, Sobreperez, Woods, Zoll, Hall). It advanced two goals for embodied empathic agents: characters that, by their actions and behaviours, are able to show empathy (or not) for other characters; and characters that, by their appearance, situation, and behaviour, are able to trigger empathic reactions in the user.

In this talk we discuss how far Embodied Empathic Agents - whether graphical or robotic - are succeeding; what we can now do, and what open research questions remain. What are the key theoretical and technological advances already made and which are still needed? What applications are Empathic Agents 'good' for, and how do we know they are? And how do they relate to the broader field of social agents?

CCS Concepts

•**Computing methodologies** → **Cognitive science; Intelligent agents;** *Discourse, dialogue and pragmatics; Cognitive robotics; Theory of mind;* •**Human-centered computing** → *Collaborative interaction;*

Keywords

Empathic agents; social agents; intelligent graphical agents; affective computing; human-robot interaction

Short Bio

Ruth Aylett is a Professor of Computer Science at Heriot-Watt University in Edinburgh, UK. She researches affective and social agents, human-robot interaction and digital story-telling and has more then 250 refereed publications in these areas. She has coordinated three large EU projects developing intelligent graphical agents and has also acted as a PI in the EU LIREC project investigating long-lived robot companions, and the EU EMOTE project, researching empathic robot tutors. She was a founder of the international conference Intelligent Virtual Agents and a member of the Humaine network on affective computing.

Appears in: *Proceedings of the 15th International Conference on Autonomous Agents and Multiagent Systems (AAMAS 2016), J. Thangarajah, K. Tuyls, C. Jonker, S. Marsella (eds.), May 9–13, 2016, Singapore.*

Complexity and Algorithms of K-implementation

Yuan Deng
Dept. of Computer Science
Duke University
ericdy@cs.duke.edu

Pingzhong Tang
Institute of interdisciplinary information sciences
Tsinghua University, China
kenshinping@gmail.com

Shuran Zheng
Institute of interdisciplinary information sciences
Tsinghua University, China
sherry.zhengshuran@gmail.com

ABSTRACT

This paper settles the complexity of *K-implementation*, a ten-year open problem in AI. The problem is for a designer to modify an existing normal-form game, in a cost-optimal way, so as to ensure the solutions of the modified game fall into a given set of outcomes. We first prove that the problem is NP-COMPLETE for general games with respect to dominance by pure strategies, and then provide an alternative proof showing that the problem is NP-COMPLETE even for two-player games with respect to dominance by mixed strategies. We then consider a related but different objective, show its hardness and develop computationally efficient algorithms for a class of well-known games called *supermodular games*. For this objective, we are able to provide an optimal algorithm based on mixed-integer linear program. Interestingly, this algorithm also provides a lower-bound approximation guarantee for the original K-implementation problem and approximates the optimal solution well in experiments.

General Terms

Algorithms; Economics; Theory;

Keywords

K-implementation; Complexity; Algorithm;

1. INTRODUCTION

Using monetary payment to incentivize agents' behaviors has now become a standard approach in artificial intelligence, multi-agent systems and electronic commerces. The foundations of this approach date back to the pioneer works of *mechanism design theory* [2, 8, 11, 15, 20], where payments are used to design incentive compatible institutions and to circumvent impossibility results [7, 16].

Building upon these seminal works is an interesting line of research [4, 5, 6, 13, 14], rooted in the AI and MAS community, that looks at a different type of implementation problems, where there exists an incumbent game and the designer wants to subsidize the payoffs of the incumbent game, in a cost-minimum way, so as to ensure the solutions of the revised game fall into a pre-specified set of outcomes.

Appears in: *Proceedings of the 15th International Conference on Autonomous Agents and Multiagent Systems (AAMAS 2016), J. Thangarajah, K. Tuyls, C. Jonker, S. Marsella (eds.), May 9–13, 2016, Singapore.*

For example, consider taxation in the U.S. [10] where policy makers do not have full flexibility in designing a new taxation policy and can only modify the current system to some minimum extent. Similar is the case of redesign salary for government employees in China.

Monderer and Tennenholtz [13] initiate the first problem of this sort, called *K-implementation*, where the solution concept is *one-round dominance*, namely, whether one can distribute a positive[1] payment K to the incumbent game payoffs such that, by applying one round elimination of dominated strategies in the modified game, the remaining outcomes belong to a predefined sets. Clearly, the solution of *K-implementation* also provides a feasible solution if the solution concept is replaced by *iterated dominance*, since the outcomes survive iterated dominance can only be a subset of that of one-round dominance. They further show that the general problem is NP-HARD and study the cases where the predefined sets are restricted to singletons or the incumbent games are the VCG mechanisms.

This particular work generates fairly considerable interests, both within and outside the AI community, leads to a number of extensions. For instance, Ashlagi et al. [1] generalized to incomplete information setting and applied their new theories to position auctions and Zhang et al. [21] considered the case where an interested party aims to influence an agent's decisions by making limited changes to the agent's environment. Furthermore, the concept is applicable in dynamic mechanism design settings where, as time goes by, the designer needs to adaptively modify an existing game without flexibility to design a new games [9].

Unfortunately, the hardness proof from 3-SAT by Monderer and Tennenholtz is incorrect. As pointed out by [5], "while there indeed exists a 2-implementation for every satisfiable formula, it can be shown that 2-implementations also exist for non-satisfiable formulas", showing the incorrectness of the original proof. The complexity of K-IMPLEMENTATION has been open since [5, 6, 13].

In the first part of the paper, we pin down the correct proofs of the *K-implementation* problem. More specifically, we prove the following two results.

- We first show that K-IMPLEMENTATION is NP-COMPLETE, by reducing the 3-SAT problem to an instance of K-IMPLEMENTATION in a 6-player game.
- We then come up with a different proof that reduces the 3-SAT problem to a K-IMPLEMENTATION instance in a 2-player game only.

[1]There always exists a $-\infty$ solution to this problem.

The reason that we have two separate proofs is that the 6-player proof works under both dominance by pure strategies and dominance by mixed-strategies, while the 2-player works only under the notion of dominance by mix-strategies.

These results confirm that, even in the simplest game-theoretical setting with only two players[2], K-IMPLEMENTATION is computationally hard.

In the second part of the paper, we look for practical algorithms to solve a variation of K-IMPLEMENTATION problem with approximation guarantee, called INDIVIDUAL K-IMPLEMENTATION problem. Our results are two algorithms, one based on mixed-integer linear programming for the general INDIVIDUAL K-IMPLEMENTATION problem, the other is a polynomial time algorithm for a certain subclass of games. Finally, through experiments, we show that the optimal solution for INDIVIDUAL K-IMPLEMENTATION problem approximates K-IMPLEMENTATION well in practice.

2. PRELIMINARIES

Let $G = \langle N, S, U\rangle$ be a normal form game, where N is the set of n player, $S = S_1 \times \cdots \times S_n$ is the set of strategy profiles and $U = (U_1, \cdots, U_n)$ is the set of utility functions for each player. As usual, denote $s = (s_i, s_{-i}) \in S$ where $s_i \in S_i$ and $s_{-i} \in S_{-i}$ represents the strategies played by players other than player i.

A strategy $s_i \in S_i$ is weakly dominated by pure strategies if there exists $s'_i \in S_i$ such that for all $s_{-i} \in S_{-i}$, $U_i(s_i, s_{-i}) \leq U_i(s'_i, s_{-i})$. A strategy $s_i \in S_i$ is weakly dominated by mixed strategies if there exists $\sigma_i \in \Delta(S_i)$ such that for all $s_{-i} \in S_{-i}$, $U_i(s_i, s_{-i}) \leq U_i(\sigma_i, s_{-i})$, where $\Delta(S_i)$ is the set of mixed strategies on S_i.

The designer has a set of desirable strategy profiles $O \subseteq S$, and players are rational in the sense that they do not adopt a strategy that is weakly dominated[3] by another, *possibly mixed*, strategy.

A non-negative vector of payoff functions $V = (V_1, \cdots, V_n)$ implements O in game G if in the new game $\langle N, S, U + V\rangle$, the set of strategies $X = \{X_1 \times X_2 \times \cdots \times X_n\}$, satisfies

1. for all i, $S_i \setminus X_i$ is weakly dominated;
2. $\emptyset \subset X \subseteq O$.

Such a V is called a k-implementation of O in game G, if $\sum_{i=1}^{n} V_i(x) \leq k, \forall x \in X$. Denote $\langle G, O, k\rangle$ as the set of non-negative vector of payoff functions V such that V is a k-implementation of O in game G. Moreover, if k is the minimum cost such that $\langle G, O, k\rangle$ is not empty, we say the *implementation value (cost)* of G w.r.t O is k.

In order to prove the NP-COMPLETENESS of checking whether set $\langle G, O, k\rangle$ is empty or not, it suffices to consider only the case, where the desirable set O can be expressed as a Cartesian product of individual sets: $O = \prod_{i=1}^{n} O_i$ with $O_i \subseteq S_i$.

Moreover, to develop a practically efficient algorithm, we consider a variant, called INDIVIDUAL K-IMPLEMENTATION. V is an individual k-implementation of O in game G, if $V_i(x) \leq k, \forall x \in X, i \in N$. In other words, we measure the largest cost spent on an individual player[4].

While our investigation of individual K-implementation is of independent interests, we are also interested in the connections between the two problems: it turns out the INDIVIDUAL K-IMPLEMENTATION admits a compact mixed integer linear programming formation and its optimal solution also provides an approximately good solution to the original problem. Furthermore, the new problem can be solved efficiently on certain subclasses of games. We show this by developing an efficient algorithm for INDIVIDUAL K-IMPLEMENTATION in supermodular games [12, 18, 19].

3. THE COMPLEXITY OF K-IMPLEMENTATION

We develop two reductions, both from 3-SAT, to show NP-COMPLETENESS for K-IMPLEMENTATION, one for 6 players and the other for 2 players.

3.1 NP-COMPLETENESS for 6-player games

THEOREM 1. *It is* NP-COMPLETE *to decide whether* $\langle G, O, k\rangle$ *is empty in* 6*-player games.*

It is clear that the problem is in NP, since given a V vector, one can check whether $V \in \langle G, O, k\rangle$ in polynomial time w.r.t the input size [3].

To prove completeness, we reduce from 3-SAT. 3-SAT is the most famous NP-COMPLETE problem. An instance of 3-SAT is a Boolean formula in conjunctive normal form, which is "AND" operations over clauses, each of which is "OR" operations over exactly three ground literals (ground variables and their negations). The problem is to decide whether there exists an assignment of truth values to the variables such that the value of the formula is true.

Let $\phi = c_1 \wedge c_2 \wedge \cdots \wedge c_m$ be an instance of 3-SAT, where the ith clause $c_i = (l_i^1 \vee l_i^2 \vee l_i^3)$ and $l_i^j = +x_k$ or $-x_k$, where x_k is a ground variable from $\{x_1, \cdots, x_n\}$.

We now construct a K-IMPLEMENTATION instance $\langle G(\phi), O, \delta\rangle$, where δ is a real such that $0 < \delta \ll 1$, $G(\phi)$ is a 6-player game $\langle\{1, 2, 3, 4, 5, 6\}, S, U\rangle$. The strategy sets of the players are defined as follows:

- $S_1 = S_2 = S_3 = \bigcup_{i=1}^{n}\{+x_i\} \cup \bigcup_{i=1}^{n}\{-x_i\} \cup \{\epsilon\}$;
- $S_4 = \bigcup_{i=1}^{m}\{c_i\} \cup \{\epsilon\}$, $S_5 = S_6 = \bigcup_{i=1}^{n}\{+x_i\}$;

We now define the utility function for each player. In following definitions, we use $*_i$ to denote an arbitrary strategy of player i. The undefined utility entries are 0.

- Players 5 and 6 only care about each other, $\forall x_i$:
  - $U_5(*_1, *_2, *_3, *_4, +x_i, +x_i) = 1$
  - $U_6(*_1, *_2, *_3, *_4, +x_i, +x_{(i+1) \bmod n}) = 1$
- Player 1 only cares about player 6, $\forall x_i$:
  - $U_1(+x_i, *_2, *_3, *_4, *_5, +x_i) = 1$
  - $U_1(-x_i, *_2, *_3, *_4, *_5, +x_i) = 1$

[2]1-agent K-IMPLEMENTATION is computationally easy.

[3]Strict and weak dominance are the same w.r.t K-implementation, since one can turn a solution of weak dominance into a strict one by adding an infinitely small cost to each outcome without changing the cost. For the same reason, our definition of *weak dominance* is also the same as the standard definition of weak dominance that requires at least one strict inequality.

[4]Our techniques can be extended to the case where the requirements are $V_i(x) \leq k_i, \forall x \in X, i \in N$ and the goal is to minimize $\sum_i k_i$. For simplicity, we only consider the special case with $k = k_i$ for all i.

- Player 2, 3 care about player 1, $\forall l$:
  - $U_2(l, l, *_3, *_4, *_5, *_6) = 1$
  - $U_3(l, *_2, l, *_4, *_5, *_6) = 1$
  - $U_2(*_1, \epsilon, *_3, *_4, *_5, *_6) = 0.1$
  - $U_3(*_1, *_2, \epsilon, *_4, *_5, *_6) = 0.1$
- Player 4 care about players 1, 2, 3, $\forall c_i = (l_i^1 \vee l_i^2 \vee l_i^3)$:
  - $U_4(l_i^1, l_i^2, l_i^3, c_i, *_5, *_6) = 1$
  - $U_4(*_1, *_2, *_3, \epsilon, *_5, *_6) = 0.1$

The set of desirable outcomes are defined by:

$$O_4 = \{\epsilon\} \text{ and for all } k \neq 4, O_k = S_k$$

We complete the reduction by showing that ϕ is satisfiable if and only if $\langle G(\phi), O, \delta\rangle \neq \emptyset$. The easier direction is proved in the following lemma.

Lemma 1. *If ϕ is satisfiable, then $\langle G(\phi), O, \delta\rangle \neq \emptyset$.*

Proof. Let literals $(l_1', \cdots, l_n')$ be a feasible assignment that satisfies ϕ. We show that the following V is in $\langle G(\phi), O, \delta\rangle$. (the undefined entries are 0)

- $V_1(-l_i', *_2, *_3, *_4, *_5, *_6) = \delta, \forall 0 \le i < n$;
- $V_2(l_i', \epsilon, *_3, *_4, *_5, *_6) = 1, \forall 0 \le i < n$;
- $V_3(l_i', *_2, \epsilon, *_4, *_5, *_6) = 1, \forall 0 \le i < n$;
- $V_4(l_j^1, l_j^2, l_j^3, \epsilon, *_5, *_6) = 1, \forall c_j = (l_j^1 \vee l_j^2 \vee l_j^3)$;

We can verify the following,

- By our construction of U_5 and U_6, no action of player 5 or 6 is weakly dominated, thus $X_5 = O_5$, $X_6 = O_6$.
- By our construction of V_1 and U_1, for player 1, l_i' is strictly dominated by $-l_i'$ since we now add δ to playing $-l_i'$. Therefore $X_1 = \bigcup_i \{-l_i'\}$.
- By our construction of V_2, V_3, for both players 2 and 3, l_i' is now strictly dominated by ϵ, therefore $X_2 = X_3 = \bigcup_i \{-l_i'\} \cup \{\epsilon\}$. In other words, all the literals that are *true* in the satisfying assignment are eleminated.
- For player 4, c_i is strictly dominated by ϵ, $X_4 = \{\epsilon\}$.

Clearly, for each i, we have $X_i \subseteq O_i$, therefore $X \subseteq O$, as required by K-implementation.

Finally, we prove that $k = \max_{x \in X} \sum_i V_i(x) = \delta$. Since $l_i' \notin X_1$, $(l_i', *_2, *_3, *_4, *_5, *_6) \notin X$, i.e., V_2 or V_3 do not contribute to the implementation cost $\max_{x \in X} \sum_i V_i(x)$.

In addition, since $(l_1', \cdots, l_n')$ satisfies ϕ, we have for all j, at least one of l_j^1, l_j^2, l_j^3 is *true*. Notice that X_1, X_2 and X_3 only contain negations of l_i''s, then $(l_j^1, l_j^2, l_j^3, \epsilon, *_5, *_6) \notin X$. In other words, V_4 does not contribute to the implementation cost either.

It then follows that the implementation k is at most the maximum cost resulting from $V_1(\cdot)$, which is exactly δ. In other words, V is in $\langle G(\phi), O, \delta\rangle$. □

To establish the other direction, we have:

Lemma 2. *If $\langle G(\phi), O, \delta\rangle \neq \emptyset$, then ϕ is satisfiable.*

Proof. Let such a δ-implementation be V and set a literal l to be true if and only if $l \notin X_1$ or $l \notin X_2$ or $l \notin X_3$. We prove this is a satisfying assignment for ϕ.

Claim 1. *$X_5 = O_5$, $X_6 = O_6$.*

Proof. Notice that the payoffs of player 5 and player 6 is independent of the actions played by the other players, and thus, one can think of a 2-player game between player 5 and player 6 and compute X_5 and X_6 in this 2-player game.

Since S_5 and S_6 only contain positive variables and the fact that both X_5 and X_6 are nonempty, it is with loss of generality to assume that there exists $+x_k \in X_6$. We then have $+x_k \in X_5$ as well, since otherwise, in order to eliminate $+x_k$ from X_5 given $+x_k \in X_6$, there must exist a $j \neq k$, $+x_j \in X_5$ such that $V_5(*_1, *_2, *_3, *_4, +x_j, +x_k) \geq 1 > \delta$, which contradicts to our assumption that largest cost is less than or equal to δ. Similarly, suppose $+x_k \in X_5$, we must have $+x_{(k+1) \bmod n} \in X_6$ as well by similar arguments.

Therefore, if $+x_k \in X_6$, $+x_k \in X_5$, $+x_{(k+1) \bmod n} \in X_6$ and $+x_{(k+1) \bmod n} \in X_5$... By repeating this argument, we conclude that $X_5 = O_5$ and $X_6 = O_6$. □

The intuition of the lemma above should be clear: elimination of any actions of player 5 and player 6 is costly.

The next claim guarantees that the constructed assignment is well-defined in the sense that it never simultaneously assigns *true* to a variable and its negation.

Claim 2. *$\forall i$, either we have $+x_i \in X_1$ and $+x_i \in X_2$ and $+x_i \in X_3$ hold simultaneously; or we have $-x_i \in X_1$ and $-x_i \in X_2$ and $-x_i \in X_3$ hold simultaneously.*

Proof. First of all, by Claim 1, for player 1, $+x_i$ and $-x_i$ cannot be both strictly dominated, i.e., at least one of $+x_i$ and $-x_i$ is in X_1; since otherwise, there must exist $x' \in X_1$ such that $x' \neq +x_i, -x_i$ and $V_1(x', *_2, *_3, *_4, *_5, +x_i) \geq 1 > \delta$, which again contradicts to δ-implementation.

For player 2, we must have $l \in X_2$ if $l \in X_1$; since otherwise, there must exist $l' \in X_2$ such that $V_2(l, l', *_3, *_4, *_5, *_6) \geq 1 > \delta$, a contradiction; or $V_2(l, \varepsilon, *_3, *_4, *_5, *_6) \geq 1 - 0.1 = 0.9 > \delta$, also a contradiction to δ-implementation.

For player 3, we can apply the same argument to conclude that $l \in X_3$ if $l \in X_1$. □

To complete the proof of the lemma, we need to prove that for any clause $c_i = (l_i^1 \vee l_i^2 \vee l_i^3)$, at least one of l_i^1, l_i^2, l_i^3 is assigned true. According to our construction at the beginning of the proof, it is equivalent to that $\exists j, l_i^j \notin X_j$. Suppose otherwise that $l_i^1 \in X_1, l_i^2 \in X_2, l_i^3 \in X_3$, we must have $c_i \in X_4$; since otherwise, there exists $c' \in X_4$ such that $V_4(l_i^1, l_i^2, l_i^3, c', *_5, *_6) \geq 1 > \delta$ or $V_4(l_i^1, l_i^2, l_i^3, \epsilon, *_5, *_6) \geq 0.9 > \delta$. In other words, we need to cost at least 0.9 to eliminate c_i in S_4 in presence of $l_i^1 \in X_1, l_i^2 \in X_2, l_i^3 \in X_3$. Note that however, $c_i \in X_4$ is unacceptable since we need $X_4 = \{\epsilon\}$. We therefore conclude that $l_i^1 \in X_1, l_i^2 \in X_2, l_i^3 \in X_3$ cannot hold simultaneously, that is, at least one of l_i^1, l_i^2, l_i^3 is assigned true in any clause, i.e., the assignment we constructed is indeed a satisfying assignment. □

Combining Lemma 1 and Lemma 2, we show ϕ is satisfiable if and only if $\langle G(\phi), O, \delta\rangle \neq \emptyset$, completing the proof.

Remark 1. *The K-implementation defined by [13] is w.r.t dominance by pure strategies. The above proof is general in the sense that it applies to either dominance by pure strategies or mixed strategies.*

$U_1 \setminus U_2$	x_1	x_2	x_3	$+x_1$	$-x_1$	$+x_2$	$-x_2$	$+x_3$	$-x_3$	c_1	c_2
$(+x_1, c_1)$	$(0,\varepsilon_b)$	$(r_{x_2}^{+x_1,c_1},0)$	$(r_{x_3}^{+x_1,c_1},0)$	(0,1)	(0,0)	(0,0)	(0,0)	(0,0)	(0,0)	$(0,\varepsilon_a)$	(0,0)
$(+x_2, c_1)$	$(r_{x_1}^{+x_2,c_1},0)$	$(0,\varepsilon_b)$	$(r_{x_3}^{+x_2,c_1},0)$	(0,0)	(0,0)	(0,1)	(0,0)	(0,0)	(0,0)	$(0,\varepsilon_a)$	(0,0)
$(+x_3, c_1)$	$(r_{x_1}^{+x_3,c_1},0)$	$(r_{x_3}^{+x_3,c_1},0)$	$(0,\varepsilon_b)$	(0,0)	(0,0)	(0,0)	(0,0)	(0,1)	(0,0)	$(0,\varepsilon_a)$	(0,0)
$(-x_1, c_2)$	$(0,\varepsilon_b)$	$(r_{x_2}^{-x_1,c_2},0)$	$(r_{x_3}^{-x_1,c_2},0)$	(0,0)	(0,1)	(0,0)	(0,0)	(0,0)	(0,0)	(0,0)	$(0,\varepsilon_a)$
$(-x_2, c_2)$	$(r_{x_1}^{-x_2,c_2},0)$	$(0,\varepsilon_b)$	$(r_{x_3}^{-x_2,c_2},0)$	(0,0)	(0,0)	(0,0)	(0,1)	(0,0)	(0,0)	(0,0)	$(0,\varepsilon_a)$
$(+x_3, c_2)$	$(r_{x_1}^{+x_3,c_2},0)$	$(r_{x_2}^{+x_3,c_2},0)$	$(0,\varepsilon_b)$	(0,0)	(0,0)	(0,0)	(0,0)	(0,1)	(0,0)	(0,0)	$(0,\varepsilon_a)$
x_{1+}	(0,1)	(0,1)	(0,1)	(2,0)	(0,0)	(0,0)	(0,0)	(0,0)	(0,0)	(0,0)	(0,0)
x_{1-}	(0,1)	(0,1)	(0,1)	(0,0)	(2,0)	(0,0)	(0,0)	(0,0)	(0,0)	(0,0)	(0,0)
x_{1*}	(0,0)	(0,0)	(0,0)	(1.5,0)	(1.5,0)	(0,0)	(0,0)	(0,0)	(0,0)	(0,0)	(0,0)
x_{2+}	(0,1)	(0,1)	(0,1)	(0,0)	(0,0)	(2,0)	(0,0)	(0,0)	(0,0)	(0,0)	(0,0)
x_{2-}	(0,1)	(0,1)	(0,1)	(0,0)	(0,0)	(0,0)	(2,0)	(0,0)	(0,0)	(0,0)	(0,0)
x_{2*}	(0,0)	(0,0)	(0,0)	(0,0)	(0,0)	(1.5,0)	(1.5,0)	(0,0)	(0,0)	(0,0)	(0,0)
x_{3+}	(0,1)	(0,1)	(0,1)	(0,0)	(0,0)	(0,0)	(0,0)	(2,0)	(0,0)	(0,0)	(0,0)
x_{3-}	(0,1)	(0,1)	(0,1)	(0,0)	(0,0)	(0,0)	(0,0)	(0,0)	(2,0)	(0,0)	(0,0)
x_{3*}	(0,0)	(0,0)	(0,0)	(0,0)	(0,0)	(0,0)	(0,0)	(1.5,0)	(1.5,0)	(0,0)	(0,0)

Table 1: $G_{\varepsilon,\delta}(\phi)$ **for** $A = \{x_1, x_2, x_3\}$ **and** $c_1 = (+x_1 \vee +x_2 \vee +x_3)$, $c_2 = (-x_1 \vee -x_2 \vee +x_3)$.

3.2 NP-COMPLETENESS for 2-player games

THEOREM 2. *It is* NP-COMPLETE *to decide whether* $\langle G, O, k\rangle$ *is empty in 2-player games.*

Let ϕ be an instance of 3-SAT. Let A be the set of its variables $x_1, \cdots, x_n$, L be the corresponding literals and C be the set of clauses. Moreover, let L^+ be the set of positive literals and L^- be the set of negative ones. Define function $v : L \to A$ to return the corresponding variable of a literal, that is, $v(+x_i) = v(-x_i) = x_i$. We construct $G_{\varepsilon,\delta}(\phi)$ with $0 < \varepsilon \ll \delta \ll 1$ to be the following 2-player game, with an example shown in Table 1.

In $G_{\varepsilon,\delta}(\phi)$, the action set of the column player is $S_2 = A \cup L \cup C$. As for the row player, define a product set $B = \{(l, c) \in L \times C | l \in c\}$, and the action set of the row player is $S_1 = B \cup (A \times \{-, +, *\})$. For convenience, denote by $s_{l,c}$ a strategy in B, and v_-, v_+ v_* for elements in $(A \times \{-, +, *\})$. Let the desirable sets be $O_1 = B \cup (A \times \{-, +\}) \subseteq S_1$ and $O_2 = A \cup L \subseteq S_2$. Payoff functions U is defined as follows,

- $U_2(s_{l,c}, l) = 1$, $U_2(s_{l,c}, c) = \varepsilon_a$, $\forall (l, c) \in B$;
- $U_2(s_{l,c}, v) = \varepsilon_b$, $\forall (l, c) \in B, v \in A$ with $v(l) = v$;
- $U_1(v_-, l) = 2$, $\forall l \in L^-, v \in A$ with $v(l) = v$;
- $U_1(v_+, l) = 2$, $\forall l \in L^+, v \in A$ with $v(l) = v$;
- $U_1(v_*, l) = 1.5$ $\forall l \in L, v \in A$ with $v(l) = v$;
- $U_2(v_+, v') = 1, U_2(v_-, v') = 1$ $\forall v, v' \in A$;
- For each $s_{l,c} \in B$, set $U_1(s_{l,c}, v) = r_v^{l,c}$ for $v \in A$. The vector $r^{l,c}$ satisfies that
  - $r_{v(l)}^{l,c} = 0$;
  - Let $r'^{l,c}$ as a $(|A| - 1)$-dimension vector by removing the $v(l)$-th element from $r^{l,c}$, we require $\|r'^{l,c}\|_2 = 1$ and $\|r'^{l,c} - \frac{1}{\sqrt{|A|-1}}\mathbf{1}\|_2 = \delta$,

    (where $\mathbf{1}$ is a vector with 1s);
  - [5]For all possible pairs (l', c'), (l, c) with $l' \neq l$ but $v(l') = v(l)$, $r^{l',c'} \neq r^{l,c}$;

where $\varepsilon_b = 1 - \frac{1}{2}\varepsilon$, ε_a is a number that satisfies $\frac{1}{3}\varepsilon_b + \varepsilon < \varepsilon_a < \frac{\varepsilon_b}{2+\varepsilon_b} + \varepsilon$,[6] and undefined payoff entries are 0. Choose ε according to δ by the following lemma.

LEMMA 3. *Given* $0 < \delta \ll 1$, *there exists a sufficiently small* ε *with* $0 < \varepsilon \ll \delta$ *such that given any non-negative vector of payoff functions* V, *if a row strategy* $b \in B$ *but* $b \notin X_1$, *then there exists* $v \in A, d \in X_1$ *such that* $V_1(d, v) > \varepsilon$.[7]

We complete the reduction by showing that ϕ is satisfiable if and only if $\langle G_{\varepsilon,\delta}(\phi), O, \varepsilon\rangle \neq \emptyset$. The "only if" direction is relatively straightforward (Lemma 4): if ϕ is satisfiable, one can directly construct V matrices that guarantee a ε-implementation. The "if" direction is more involved.

To prove the "if" direction, we show that, given any $V \in \langle G_{\varepsilon,\delta}(\phi), O, \varepsilon\rangle$ and its X_1, X_2, assigning truth to literals in $X_2 \cap L$ forms a satisfying assignment. To verify this claim, we show that our construction enjoys two properties:

1. For all $v \in A$, $+v$ and $-v$ cannot be in X_2 simultaneously, which guarantees that the assignment induced by $X_2 \cap L$ is well-defined (Claim 3).
2. For each clause $c = (l_1 \vee l_2 \vee l_3) \in C$, at least one $l_j \in X_2$ for $j \in \{1, 2, 3\}$. This property is achieved by first showing that $B \subseteq X_1$ (Claim 4). Together with property 1 above, we are able to conclude if none of l_j is in X_2, we must have c is in X_2, contradicting to our definition of O_2.

LEMMA 4. *If* ϕ *is satisfiable, then* $\langle G_{\varepsilon,\delta}(\phi), O, \varepsilon\rangle \neq \emptyset$.

PROOF. Suppose the literals $(l'_1, \cdots, l'_n)$ is a satisfying assignment for ϕ. We show that the following V is in $\langle G_{\varepsilon,\delta}(\phi), O, \varepsilon\rangle$ (the undefined entries are simply 0)

- $V_2(s_{l,c}, l'_i) = \varepsilon$, $\forall i, (l, c) \in B$;
- $V_2(s_{l,c}, v) = \varepsilon$, $\forall (l, c) \in B, v \in A$;
- $V_1(v_b, -l'_i) = 2$, $\forall i, v(l'_i) = v, l'_i \notin L^b$;

First, we prove that the constructed V implements O.

[5]This requirement ensures that for all pairs (l, c), their corresponding $r^{l,c}$ are distinct.

[6]Such an ε_a always exists cause $\frac{1}{3}\varepsilon_b < \frac{\varepsilon_b}{2+\varepsilon_b}$ when $0 < \varepsilon_b < 1$

[7]Missing proofs are deferred to the full version.

- $C \cap X_2 = \emptyset$: For each clause $c = (l_1 \vee l_2 \vee l_3) \in C$, since $(l'_1, \cdots, l'_n)$ satisfies ϕ, at least one $l'_j \in c_i$. Without loss of generality, suppose l_1 is assigned true. We claim that the column strategy c is dominated by the convex combination of the column strategy $l_1, v(l_2), v(l_3)$ with probability $(p, \frac{1-p}{2}, \frac{1-p}{2})$, where $p = \frac{\varepsilon_b}{\varepsilon_b+2}$. Notice that in utility matrix $U_2 + V_2$, column c only has three non-zero entries with value ε_a in rows $s_{l_1,c}, s_{l_2,c}, s_{l_3,c}$ and the utilities of $l_1, v(l_2), v(l_3)$ in these three rows are $(1+\varepsilon, \varepsilon, \varepsilon), (\varepsilon, \varepsilon+\varepsilon_b, \varepsilon), (\varepsilon, \varepsilon, \varepsilon+\varepsilon_b)$.

$$p(1+\varepsilon,\varepsilon,\varepsilon) + \frac{1-p}{2}(\varepsilon,\varepsilon+\varepsilon_b,\varepsilon) + \frac{1-p}{2}(\varepsilon,\varepsilon,\varepsilon+\varepsilon_b)$$
$$= (p+\varepsilon, p+\varepsilon, p+\varepsilon) \geq (\varepsilon_a, \varepsilon_a, \varepsilon_a),$$

since $\frac{1-p}{2} \cdot \varepsilon_b = p$ and $\varepsilon_a < \varepsilon + p$.

- $A \times \{*\} \cap X_1 = \emptyset$: Either v_+ or v_- can dominate v_*.

Next, we show that V has implementation cost ε. Note that each column $-l'_i$ is dominated by column $v(-l'_i)$, since $\varepsilon_b + \varepsilon > 1$, implying V_1 does not contribute to the implementation cost. Thus, the implementation cost is ε. □

LEMMA 5. *If $\langle G_{\varepsilon,\delta}(\phi), O, \varepsilon\rangle \neq \emptyset$, then ϕ is satisfiable.*

PROOF. Suppose $V \in \langle G_{\varepsilon,\delta}(\phi), O, \varepsilon\rangle$. We prove that giving truth to literals in $X_2 \cap L$ forms a satisfying assignment for ϕ. First, we show that such assignment is well-defined.

CLAIM 3. *For all $v \in A$, $\{+v, -v\} \nsubseteq X_2$.*

PROOF. Suppose not, then the row player's utility on rows v_+, v_-, v_* on column $+v$ and $-v$ forms a gadget $v_+ : (2,0)$, $v_- : (0,2)$, $v_* : (1.5, 1.5)$. In order to dominate v_*, the implementation cost is at least $0.5 > \varepsilon$ such that v_+ changes to $(2.5, 0.5)$, v_- changes to $(0.5, 2.5)$ and thus, $(\frac{1}{2}v_+ + \frac{1}{2}v_-)$ weakly dominates v_*. □

CLAIM 4. *$B \subseteq X_1$.*

Finally, we prove that at least one literal is assigned true in each clause. Suppose not, and there exists $c = (l_1 \vee l_2 \vee l_3)$ such that $l_j \notin X_2$ for all $j \in \{1,2,3\}$. Since V implements O, we have $c \notin X_2$, which means that there exists a convex combination of strategies in X_2 that can weakly dominate c. Notice that in utility matrix U_2, column c only has three non-zero entries $(\varepsilon_a, \varepsilon_a, \varepsilon_a)$ in rows $s_{l_1,c}, s_{l_2,c}, s_{l_3,c}$. Given that $l_j \notin X_2$ for all j, the only strategies in X_2 that have non-zero entries in these three rows are $v(l_1), v(l_2), v(l_3)$, with utilities $(\varepsilon_b, 0, 0), (0, \varepsilon_b, 0), (0, 0, \varepsilon_b)$ respectively. Based on $\{s_{l_1,c}, s_{l_2,c}, s_{l_3,c}\} \subseteq B \subseteq X_1$ and $\frac{\varepsilon_b}{3} + \varepsilon < \varepsilon_a$, it is impossible to dominate c with implementation cost ε. □

Based on a similar construction (let $U_1(v_*, c_i) = 1$, for all $c_i \in C$ to enforce $C \cap X_2 = \emptyset$), we conclude

COROLLARY 1. *It is* NP-COMPLETE *to decide whether $\langle G, O, k\rangle$ is empty in 2-player case even if $O_1 = S_1$.*

Moreover, the construction still holds if we apply iterative elimination of dominated strategies. In fact, we remark without proof that the two notions of dominance are equivalent with respect to K-implementation.

COROLLARY 2. *It is* NP-COMPLETE *to decide whether $\langle G, O, k\rangle$ is empty even in the 2-player case, under iteratively elimination of strictly dominated strategies.*

4. INDIVIDUAL K-IMPLEMENTATION

We now turn to the INDIVIDUAL K-IMPLEMENTATION problem. As mentioned, while this problem is of independent interest, it turns out that one can also connect the two problems, by using an exact algorithm of INDIVIDUAL K-IMPLEMENTATION to return approximately optimal solutions to the original problem. A polynomial time algorithm is further developed for a special subclass of games. With the same proof as that of Theorem 1, we have,

THEOREM 3. *It is* NP-COMPLETE *to decide whether $\langle G, O, k\rangle$ is empty for* INDIVIDUAL K-IMPLEMENTATION.

The following proposition establishes the approximation guarantee for K-IMPLEMENTATION problem via solving INDIVIDUAL K-IMPLEMENTATION.

PROPOSITION 1. *Given n-player games, the optimal* INDIVIDUAL K-IMPLEMENTATION *solution is an n-approximation solution of* K-IMPLEMENTATION.

4.1 A mixed-integer linear program

We propose an exact algorithm via mixed-integer linear program (MILP), starting with the following observation.

OBSERVATION 1. *For* INDIVIDUAL K-IMPLEMENTATION, *if $V \in \langle G, O, \varepsilon\rangle$, then let $V' = V$ except $V'_i(x) = \varepsilon$ for all $1 \leq i \leq n$ and $x \in X$, we still have $V' \in \langle G, O, \varepsilon\rangle$.*

The above observation states that for every $x \in X$, we can increase $V_i(x)$ to ε without violating implementability.

4.1.1 Two-player, product desirable set

For ease of presentation, we first consider two player normal-form game with product desirable set $O = O_1 \times O_2$. Let the strategy sets be $S_1 = [n]$ and $S_2 = [m]$ while $O_1 \subseteq S_1$, $O_2 \subseteq S_2$, respectively. Moreover, let the payoff matrix be A for row player and B for column player. That is, $U_1(i,j) = A_{i,j}$ and $U_2(i,j) = B_{i,j}$.

Without loss of generality, suppose all utilities are positive and let M be the largest utility. Divide each utility by M to normalize the utility so that no utility is greater than 1.

To formulate MILP, we first introduce an indicator vector $\mathbf{r} \in \{0,1\}^n$ to indicate whether row player actions are in X or not. Formally, $\mathbf{r}_i = 1$ if and only if action $i \in X_1$. Similarly, we define such a indicator vector $\mathbf{c} \in \{0,1\}^n$ for column actions and $\mathbf{c}_j = 1$ if and only if action $j \in X_2$.

We must ensure that, row player action i is indeed weakly dominated if and only if $\mathbf{r}_i = 0$. This step is done by a well-known linear program by Conitzer and Sandholm [3] and restated in [17]. For each row player action k, define a vector of probability variables $\mathbf{p}^k \in [0,1]^n$, where $\mathbf{p}^k_i$ represents the probability assigned to row strategy i. One can check weak dominance for row strategy k by following linear program,

$$\begin{aligned} \min \quad & 0 \\ s.t. \quad & A^T \mathbf{p}^k \geq A^T_{:,k} \\ & \mathbf{p}^k \geq 0, |\mathbf{p}^k|_1 = 1 \end{aligned}$$

Here, $A^T_{:,k}$ denotes the k-th column of matrix A^T. To extend this linear programming to INDIVIDUAL K-IMPLEMENTATION setting, we first need to ensure that if $\mathbf{r}_i = 0$, then $\mathbf{p}^k_i = 0$ and if $\mathbf{r}_i = 1$, $\mathbf{p}^k_i \in [0,1]$. In other words, if an action is dominated, it cannot appear as support in any mixed strategy for the purpose of checking dominance. The constraints can be conveniently presented as follows:

$$0 \le \mathbf{p}_i^k \le \mathbf{r}_i \quad 1 \le i, k \le n$$

Moreover, for indicator $\mathbf{r}_i$, if $i \notin O_1$, $\mathbf{r}_i$ must be 0. Thus, the integer constraints are

$$\begin{array}{ll} \mathbf{r}_i \in \{0,1\} & 1 \le i \le n \\ \mathbf{r}_i = 0 & \forall i \notin X_1 \end{array}$$

To put the Conizter-Sandholm LP framework under the context of ε-implementation, and further incorporate Observation 1, the constraints for the row players become:

$$(A^T + V_\varepsilon)\mathbf{p}^k \ge A^T_{:,k}$$

where V_ε is a matrix with ε in all entries, equivalent to

$$A^T\mathbf{p}^k \ge A^T_{:,k} - \varepsilon\mathbf{1}$$

where $\mathbf{1}$ is a vector with all 1's.

The constraint above is otherwise correct with one important exception. If a column strategy $j \notin X_2$, since we only count the implementation cost for action profiles in X in individual implementation, there is no implementation cost to dominate row player action k on the j-th column, since one can set sufficient large value of V_1 on column j without worrying about the objective value. Due to normalization, 1 is sufficiently large for this purpose and can be conveniently represented as $1 - c_j$ if this case happens (i.e., $c_j = 0$). Thus, the correct constraints for the row players are

$$A^T\mathbf{p}^k + (\mathbf{1} - \mathbf{c}) \ge A^T_{:,k} - \varepsilon\mathbf{1}$$

Similarly, the linear constraints on columns are

$$B\mathbf{q}^l + (\mathbf{1} - \mathbf{r}) \ge B_{:,l} - \varepsilon\mathbf{1}$$

To sum up, the MILP is described as follows:

$$\begin{array}{lll} \min & \varepsilon & \\ s.t. & A^T\mathbf{p}^k + (\mathbf{1} - \mathbf{c}) \ge A^T_{:,k} - \varepsilon\mathbf{1} & 1 \le k \le n \\ & B\mathbf{q}^l + (\mathbf{1} - \mathbf{r}) \ge B_{:,l} - \varepsilon\mathbf{1} & 1 \le l \le m \\ & & \\ & 0 \le \mathbf{p}_i^k \le \mathbf{r}_i, 0 \le \mathbf{q}_j^l \le \mathbf{c}_j & 1 \le i,k \le n, 1 \le j,l \le m \\ & |\mathbf{p}^k|_1 = 1, |\mathbf{q}^l|_1 = 1 & 1 \le k \le n, 1 \le l \le m \\ & \mathbf{r}_i, \mathbf{c}_j \in \{0,1\} & 1 \le i \le n, 1 \le j \le m \\ & \mathbf{r}_i = 0, \mathbf{c}_j = 0 & \forall\, i \notin X_1, \forall\, j \notin X_2 \end{array} \tag{1}$$

The implementation cost to INDIVIDUAL K-IMPLEMENTATION is $\varepsilon^* M$, where ε^* is the optimal value of the above program and M is largest utility in the original payoff matrices.

THEOREM 4. *The MILP(1) correctly computes the optimal solution of* INDIVIDUAL K-IMPLEMENTATION *in two-player, product desirable set setting.*

4.1.2 Multi-player, general desirable set

In a n-player normal-form game, player k's strategy set is $S_k = [m_k]$ and his utility in strategy profile $s = (s_k, s_{-k})$ is $A^k(s_{-k}, s_k)$, where A^k is a matrix with size $(\prod_{i \ne k} m_i) \times m_k$, and the desirable set is $O \subseteq S = \prod_1^n S_i$. Without loss of generality, suppose all utilities are positive and let M be the largest utility. Divide each utility by M to normalize the utility so that no utility is greater than 1.

- $\mathbf{g}^k \in \{0,1\}^{m_k}$ is a indicator vector that indicates whether player k's strategies are in X or not. Formally, $g_i^k = 1$ if and only if action $i \in X_k$;

- $\mathbf{p}^{k,l}$ is the probability assigned to player k's strategies for the purpose of checking dominance of player k's l-th strategy;

Similar to two-player games, constraints on $\mathbf{p}_i^{k,l}$ are,

$$0 \le \mathbf{p}_i^{k,l} \le \mathbf{g}_i^k \quad \forall k, 1 \le i, l \le m_k$$

Moreover, note that a strategy profile $s \notin X$ if and only if $\neg(\forall k, s_k \in X_k)$. Thus, the desirable set requirements can be presented by indicator vectors $\mathbf{g}^k$ as follows:

$$\sum_k \mathbf{g}^k_{s_k} \le n - 1 \quad \forall s \notin O$$

Finally, when consider player k, if $s_{-k} \notin X_{-k}$, there is no implementation value and one can set a sufficiently large value without worrying about the objective value. Due to normalization, 1 is enough and

$$\mathbf{z}^k_{s_{-k}} := \sum_{j \ne k}(1 - \mathbf{g}^j_{s_{-k_j}}) \ge 1 \quad \forall k, s_{-k} \in S_{-k}$$

if and only if $s_{-k} \notin X_{-k}$ holds[8]. To sum up, the MILP for multi-player general cases can be described as follows:

$$\begin{array}{lll} \min & \varepsilon & \\ s.t. & A^k\mathbf{p}^{k,l} + \mathbf{z}^k \ge A^k_{:,l} - \varepsilon\mathbf{1} & \forall k, 1 \le l \le m_k \\ & \mathbf{z}^k_{s_{-k}} = \sum_{j \ne k}(1 - \mathbf{g}^j_{s_{-k_j}}) & \forall k, s_{-k} \in S_{-k} \\ & 0 \le \mathbf{p}_i^{k,l} \le \mathbf{g}_i^k, \quad |\mathbf{p}^{k,l}|_1 = 1 & \forall k, 1 \le i, l \le m_k \\ & \sum_k \mathbf{g}^k_{s_k} \le n - 1 & \forall s \notin O \\ & \mathbf{g}_i^k \in \{0,1\} & \forall k, 1 \le i \le m_k \end{array} \tag{2}$$

THEOREM 5. *The MILP(2) correctly computes the optimal solution of* INDIVIDUAL K-IMPLEMENTATION *in multi-player, general desirable set setting.*

4.2 Supermodular games

In this subsection, we show that in finite *supermodular games* [12, 18, 19], INDIVIDUAL K-IMPLEMENTATION with a consecutive product desirable set can be solved efficiently.

DEFINITION 1. *A n-player finite game with player i's strategy set $S_i = [m]$ is supermodular if for all i, player i's utility function A^i has increasing difference, i.e., $\forall s, s' \in S$ and $s \ge s'$ (that is, $\forall j$, $s_j \ge s'_j$),*

$$A^i(s_{-i}, s_i) - A^i(s_{-i}, s'_i) \ge A^i(s'_{-i}, s_i) - A^i(s'_{-i}, s'_i).$$

We say a product outcome set $O = \prod O_i$ is consecutive if it is in the form of $O_i = \{l_i, l_i + 1, \cdots, r_i\} \subseteq S_i$. Without loss of generality, assume for all $s \in S$, $0 \le A^i(s) \le 1$.

Note that, we can compute the cost of INDIVIDUAL K-IMPLEMENTATION by enumerating all $X \subseteq O$ and solving the following variation of MILP(2) to exactly implement X (that

---

[8]In the formula, we abuse the notation and use s_{-k_j} to represent player j's strategy in strategy profile s_{-k}.

is, for all i, any strategy in $S_i \setminus X_i$ is weakly dominated):

$$\begin{array}{lll} \min & \varepsilon & \\ s.t. & A^k \mathbf{p}^{k,l} + \mathbf{z}^k \geq A^k_{:,l} - \varepsilon \mathbf{1} & \forall k, 1 \leq l \leq m_k \\ & \mathbf{z}^k_{s_{-k}} = \sum_{j \neq k}(1 - \mathbf{g}^j_{s_{-k_j}}) & \forall k, s_{-k} \in S_{-k} \\ & 0 \leq \mathbf{p}^{k,l}_i \leq \mathbf{g}^k_i, \quad |\mathbf{p}^{k,l}|_1 = 1 & \forall k, 1 \leq i, l \leq m_k \\ & \mathbf{g}^k_i = 0 & \forall k, i \notin X_k \\ & \mathbf{g}^k_i = 1 & \forall k, i \in X_k \end{array} \quad (3)$$

Suppose the optimal solution of MILP(3) w.r.t $X \subseteq O$ is $OPT(X)$. Then, the optimal implementation value ε_* for O can be computed by $\varepsilon_* = \min_{X \subseteq O} OPT(X)$.

The next lemma states that we can compute the cost of INDIVIDUAL K-IMPLEMENTATION in finite supermodular games with a consecutive product desirable set by *only* enumerating all possible consecutive product outcome sets $X \subseteq O$.

LEMMA 6. *If $X = \prod X_i \subseteq O$ and $X' = \prod X'_i$ where $X'_i = \{\min X_i, \min X_i + 1, \cdots, \max X_i\}$, $OPT(X') \leq OPT(X)$.*

PROOF. We prove this lemma via MILP(3). Our idea is to show that if ε^* is the optimal solution for MILP(3) w.r.t X and its corresponding variables are $(\varepsilon^*, \mathbf{p}, \mathbf{z}, \mathbf{g})$, then one can construct a feasible solution $(\varepsilon^*, \mathbf{p}', \mathbf{z}', \mathbf{g}')$ of MILP(3) w.r.t X'. It immediately follows that $OPT(X') \leq OPT(X)$. The variables $\mathbf{p}'$ are constructed from $\mathbf{p}$ as follows:

- $\mathbf{p}' = \mathbf{p}$, except when $l \in X'_k$:
  $\mathbf{p}'^{k,l}_l = 1$ and $\forall i \neq l$, $\mathbf{p}'^{k,l}_i = 0$;

Notice that the indicator vectors $\mathbf{g}$ and $\mathbf{g}'$ are determined by X and X', respectively. We need to show that in our construction of $\mathbf{p}'$, the constraints $0 \leq \mathbf{p}'^{k,l}_i \leq \mathbf{g}'^k_i$ still hold. Notice that, according to our construction, $X \subseteq X'$, so we have $\mathbf{g}'^k_i \neq \mathbf{g}^k_i$ if and only if strategy $i \in X'_k \setminus X_k$ and thus, when $\mathbf{g}'^k_i \neq \mathbf{g}^k_i$, it is certain that $\mathbf{g}'^k_i = 1$ and $\mathbf{g}^k_i = 0$. Thus, for all k and $l \notin X'_k$, $0 \leq \mathbf{p}'^{k,l}_i \leq \mathbf{g}^k_i \leq \mathbf{g}'^k_i$. As for the case $l \in X'_k$, since $\mathbf{g}'^k_l = 1$, we conclude $1 = \mathbf{p}'^{k,l}_l \leq \mathbf{g}'^k_l = 1$ and $\forall i \neq l$, $\mathbf{0} = p'^{k,l}_i \leq \mathbf{g}'^k_i$.

Moreover, the vector $\mathbf{z}'$ are determined by $\mathbf{g}'$. Thus, the only remaining constraints needed to check are

$$A^k \mathbf{p}'^{k,l} + \mathbf{z}'^k \geq A^k_{:,l} - \varepsilon' \mathbf{1} \quad \forall k, 1 \leq l \leq m_k$$

Note that when $l \notin X'_k$, it does not hold only if for some s_{-k}, $0 = \mathbf{z}'^k_{s_{-k}} < \mathbf{z}^k_{s_{-k}}$, that is $s_{-k} \in X'_{-k}$ while $s_{-k} \notin X_{-k}$.

Suppose there exists player $k = k^*$ and strategy $l = l^*$ in which the assignments $\varepsilon' = \varepsilon^*$ and our construction of $(\mathbf{p}', \mathbf{g}', \mathbf{z}')$ violate the above constraint.

- *Case 1*: $\min X'_k \leq l^* \leq \max X'_k$. In this case, according to our construction of X', strategy $l^* \in X'_{k^*}$. Thus, strategy l^* can weakly dominate itself on its own and actually, in our construction, $p'^{k^*,l^*}_{l^*} = 1$ if $l^* \in X'_{k^*}$;

Intuitively, in Case 2 and 3, we argue that for player k^*, the optimal cost only depends on the weak dominance of $s^{\min}_{-k^*} = \min X_{-k^*}$ or $s^{\max}_{-k^*} = \max X_{-k^*}$.

- *Case 2*: $l^* < \min X'_{k^*}$. In this case, $l^* \notin X'_{k^*}$ and thus, according to our construction, $\mathbf{p}'^{k^*,l^*} = \mathbf{p}^{k^*,l^*}$. Consider $s^{\min}_{-k^*} = \min X'_{-k^*}$, i.e. $s_{-k^*j} = \min X_j$. Since $(\varepsilon^*, \mathbf{p}, \mathbf{z}, \mathbf{g})$ is a feasible solution for MILP(3) w.r.t X and $s^{\min}_{-k^*} \in X_{-k^*}$, it is true that,

$$A^{k^*} \mathbf{p}^{k^*,l^*} + \mathbf{z}^{k^*} \geq A^{k^*}_{:,l^*} - \varepsilon^* \mathbf{1}.$$

Henceforth, for a specific $s^{\min}_{-k^*}$, we have

$$A^{k^*}_{s^{\min}_{-k^*},:} \mathbf{p}^{k^*,l^*} + \mathbf{z}^{k^*}_{s^{\min}_{-k^*}} \geq A^{k^*}_{s^{\min}_{-k^*},l^*} - \varepsilon^*$$

which is equivalent to

$$\sum_{i \in X_{k^*}} (A^{k^*}_{s^{\min}_{-k^*},i} - A^{k^*}_{s^{\min}_{-k^*},l^*}) \mathbf{p}^{k^*,l^*}_i \geq -\varepsilon^*$$

since $\sum_{i \in X_{k^*}} \mathbf{p}^{k^*,l^*}_i = 1$ and because of $s^{\min}_{-k^*} \in X_{-k^*}$, $\mathbf{z}^{k^*}_{s^{\min}_{-k^*}} = 0$. Notice that, what we want to prove is, for all s_{-k^*}, the following inequality holds

$$A^{k^*}_{s_{-k^*},:} \mathbf{p}^{k^*,l^*} + \mathbf{z}'^{k^*}_{s_{-k^*}} \geq A^{k^*}_{s_{-k^*},l^*} - \varepsilon^*$$

Recall that the constraint is violated only if $\mathbf{z}'^{k^*}_{s_{-k^*}} = 0$. Therefore, the above constraint is equivalent to,

$$\sum_{i \in X_{k^*}} (A^k_{s_{-k^*},i} - A^{k^*}_{s_{-k^*},l^*}) \mathbf{p}^{k^*,l^*}_i \geq -\varepsilon^*$$

and in additional, we have $s_{-k^*} \in X'_{-k^*}$ and thus, $s^{\min}_{-k^*} \leq s_{-k^*}$. Applying the definition of supermodularity, we can conclude this case by

$$\begin{aligned} & \sum_{i \in X_{k^*}} (A^{k^*}_{s_{-k^*},i} - A^{k^*}_{s_{-k^*},l^*}) \mathbf{p}^{k^*,l^*}_i \\ \geq & \sum_{i \in X_{k^*}} (A^{k^*}_{s^{\min}_{-k^*},i} - A^{k^*}_{s^{\min}_{-k^*},l^*}) \mathbf{p}^{k^*,l^*}_i \geq -\varepsilon^* \end{aligned}$$

- *Case 3*: $l^* > \max X'_{k^*}$. Consider $s^{\max}_{-k^*} = \max X'_{-k^*} \in X_{-k^*}$ and the proof is similar to the one in Case 2.

Therefore, our construction of $(\mathbf{p}', \mathbf{z}', \mathbf{g}')$ along with ε^* is a feasible solution to MILP(2) w.r.t X'. □

With Lemma 6, one can reduce computing the optimal implementation cost of O to computing $OPT(X)$ for all consecutive outcome sets $X \subseteq O$, which can be done in polynomial time. Note $\{X \mid X \text{ is a consecutive outcome set}, X \subseteq O\} = O(m^{2n})$, a polynomial w.r.t. the size of game $O(m^n)$.

THEOREM 6. *In supermodular games with consecutive product desirable sets, the cost of* INDIVIDUAL K-IMPLEMENTATION *can be computed in polynomial time, precisely, $O(m^{2n}n)$.*

5. EXPERIMENTS

We implement our MILP algorithm proposed in the previous section. We measure the time efficiency and optimality of our MILP algorithms, by comparing it to the algorithm implemented in [5, 6], called BRUTE-FORCE-PURE.

The BRUTE-FORCE-PURE is a double-exponential algorithm that computes general K-IMPLEMENTATION under dominance by pure-strategies, by exhaustively enumerating all possible $X \subseteq O$ (which could be exponentially many) and using an exponential algorithm to compute the cost of exact K-implementation w.r.t each X.

5.1 Experiments Setup

All our experiments are performed on a PC with 2.6 GHz Intel Core i5 processor, and 8 GB 1600 MHz DDR3 memory. We use MATLAB 2014b to serve as MILP solver. We focus on 2-player normal-form games with product desirable sets.

We implemented two versions of MILP(1) that corresponds to INDIVIDUAL K-IMPLEMENTATION problem w.r.t dominance

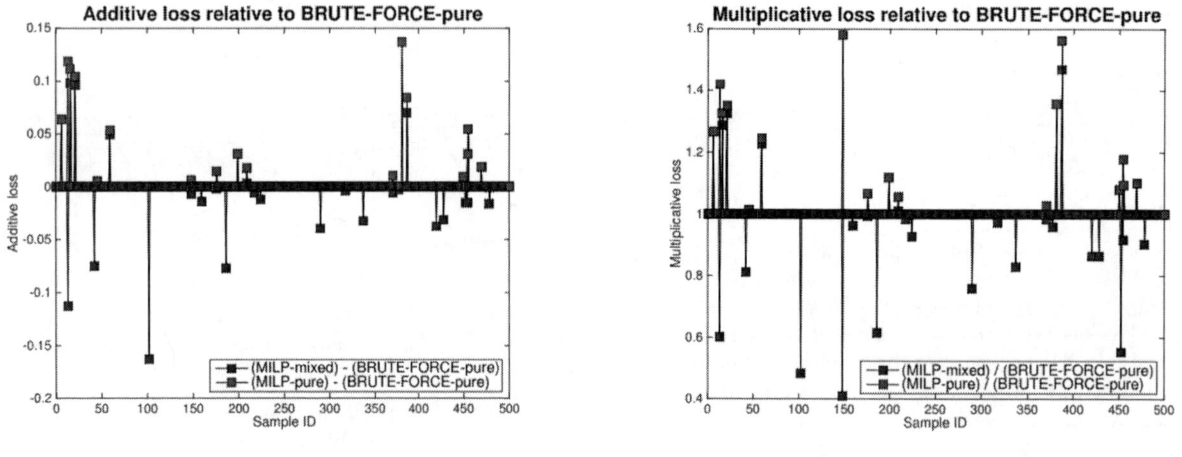

Figure 1: Additive/multiplicative losses of MILP-MIXED **and** MILP-PURE **compared to** BRUTE-FORCE-PURE

by pure strategies and mixed strategies respectively. To better approximate the original K-IMPLEMENTATION, the INDIVIDUAL K-IMPLEMENTATION we implement here is a more general, player-specific version in the sense that we impose individual implementation cost upper bound $V_i(x) \le k_i, \forall x \in X, i \in \{1,2\}$ and measure the sum of individual cost $k_1 + k_2$ as objective. The MILP for this more general problem can also be straightforwardly adjusted from MILP(1).

To measure the time efficiency of our MILP, we randomly generate 20 cases of $N \times N$ 2-player normal-form games with every utility uniformly drawn from $[0,1]$, while the probability that a strategy j is in the desirable set is $1/2$. We measure the running time as a function of N.

To measure the optimality of our MILP, due to the running time of BRUTE-FORCE-PURE, we can only repeat the experiments w.r.t a relatively small game size. In particular, we general 500 cases of 2-player normal-form games with $N = 10$ with same utility distribution as before. Moreover, we randomly generate O satisfying $1 \le |O_1|, |O_2| \le 5$. To sum up, we compare the following:

1. MILP algorithm with respect to dominance by mixed strategies, called MILP-MIXED,
2. MILP algorithm with respect to dominance by pure strategies, called MILP-PURE,
3. BRUTE-FORCE-PURE. This algorithm serves as baseline for the following loss calibrations.

5.2 Experimental Results

The average running time of our MILP according to N is shown in Table 2. For time efficiency, our MILP runs considerably fast when N is small and reasonably fast as N increases up to 70, while the base-line algorithm finished in 580s on average for $N = 9$.

Size	10	20	30	40
Time(s)	0.0879	0.3391	1.7455	9.6937
Size	50	60	70	···
Time(s)	33.4201	89.4129	216.3254	···

Table 2: Running time of MILP

As for the comparison of implementation cost, the results are shown in Figure 1 with two calibrations of loss,

- Additive: (Algorithm) - (Baseline);
- Multiplicative: (Algorithm) / (Baseline);

Moreover, the average additive loss and multiplicative loss between MILP-MIXED and BRUTE-FORCE-PURE are -5.1397×10^{-5} and 0.9975, while between MILP-PURE and BRUTE-FORCE-PURE are 0.0017 and 1.0077. One can see that, in randomly generated cases under the notion of dominance by pure strategies, optimal solution INDIVIDUAL K-IMPLEMENTATION approximates K-IMPLEMENTATION pretty well while MILP-MIXED can sometimes perform better than BRUTE-FORCE-PURE due to that dominance by mixed strategies is allowed in the MILP. By the experimental results between MILP-PURE and BRUTE-FORCE-PURE, we expect that MILP-MIXED approximates K-IMPLEMENTATION reasonably well.

6. CONCLUSION

In this paper, we pin down the correct hardness proofs to show that K-IMPLEMENTATION problem is indeed NP-complete. In addition, we study a variation of K-IMPLEMENTION problem called INDIVIDUAL K-IMPLEMENTATION problem, which provides an approximation guarantee to K-IMPLEMENTION problem and enjoys a mixed-integer linear programming for general INDIVIDUAL K-IMPLEMENTATION problem and a polynomial time runnable algorithm for supermodular games with a consecutive product desirable set. Finally, our experiments confirm that the optimal solution with respect to INDIVIDUAL K-IMPLEMENTATION problem approximates K-IMPLEMENTATION problem well in practice.

Acknowledgments

This work was supported by the National Basic Research Program of China Grant 2011CBA00300, 2011CBA00301, the Natural Science Foundation of China Grant 61033001, 61361136003, 61303077, 61561146398, a Tsinghua Initiative Scientific Research Grant and a China Youth 1000-talent program.

REFERENCES

[1] I. Ashlagi, D. Monderer, and M. Tennenholtz. Mediators in position auctions. In *Proceedings of the 8th ACM conference on Electronic commerce*, pages 279–287. ACM, 2007.

[2] E. H. Clarke. Multipart pricing of public goods. *Public Choice*, 2:19–33, 1971.

[3] V. Conitzer and T. Sandholm. Complexity of (iterated) dominance. In *Proceedings 6th ACM Conference on Electronic Commerce (EC-2005), Vancouver, BC, Canada, June 5-8, 2005*, pages 88–97, 2005.

[4] R. Eidenbenz, Y. A. Oswald, S. Schmid, and R. Wattenhofer. Manipulation in games. In *Algorithms and Computation*, pages 365–376. Springer, 2007.

[5] R. Eidenbenz, Y. A. Oswald, S. Schmid, and R. Wattenhofer. Mechanism design by creditability. In *Combinatorial Optimization and Applications*, pages 208–219. Springer, 2007.

[6] R. Eidenbenz, Y. A. Pignolet, S. Schmid, and R. Wattenhofer. Cost and complexity of harnessing games with payments. *International Game Theory Review*, 13(01):13–44, 2011.

[7] A. Gibbard. Manipulation of voting schemes: A general result. *Econometrica*, 41(4):587–601, July 1973.

[8] T. Groves. Incentives in Teams. *Econometrica*, 41:617–631, 1973.

[9] J. M. Kleinberg and S. Oren. Time-inconsistent planning: a computational problem in behavioral economics. In *ACM Conference on Economics and Computation, EC '14, Stanford , CA, USA, June 8-12, 2014*, pages 547–564, 2014.

[10] N. G. Mankiw, M. Weinzierl, and D. Yagan. Optimal taxation in theory and practice. Technical report, National Bureau of Economic Research, 2009.

[11] E. Maskin and T. Sjostrom. *Implementation theory*, volume 1 of *Handbook of Social Choice and Welfare*. Elsevier, March 2002.

[12] P. Milgrom and J. Roberts. Rationalizability, Learning, and Equilibrium in Games with Strategic Complementarities. *Econometrica*, 58(6):1255–77, November 1990.

[13] D. Monderer and M. Tennenholtz. K-implementation. *J. Artif. Intell. Res. (JAIR)*, 21:37–62, 2004.

[14] T. Moscibroda and S. Schmid. On mechanism design without payments for throughput maximization. In *INFOCOM 2009, IEEE*, pages 972–980. IEEE, 2009.

[15] R. B. Myerson. Optimal auction design. *Mathematics of Operations Research*, 6(1):58–73, 1981.

[16] M. A. Satterthwaite. Strategy-proofness and arrow's conditions: Existence and correspondence theorems for voting procedures and social welfare functions. *Journal of Economic Theory*, 10(2):187–217, April 1975.

[17] Y. Shoham and K. Leyton-Brown. *Multiagent Systems: Algorithmic, Game theoretic and Logical Fundations*. Cambridge Uni. Press, 2009.

[18] P. Tang and F. Lin. Two equivalence results for two-person strict games. *Games and Economic Behavior*, 71(2):479–486, 2011.

[19] D. Topkis. *Supermodularity and Complementarity*. Frontiers of Economic Research. Princeton University Press, 2011.

[20] W. Vickrey. Counterspeculation, Auctions and Competitive Sealed Tenders. *Journal of Finance*, pages 8–37, 1961.

[21] H. Zhang, Y. Chen, and D. C. Parkes. A general approach to environment design with one agent. In *IJCAI 2009*, pages 2002–2014, 2009.

On the Power of Dominated Players in Team Competitions *

Kai Jin
Institute for Interdisciplinary Information Sciences
Tsinghua University
Beijing, China
cscjjk@gmail.com

Pingzhong Tang
Institute for Interdisciplinary Information Sciences
Tsinghua University
Beijing, China
kenshinping@gmail.com

Shiteng Chen
Institute for Interdisciplinary Information Sciences
Tsinghua University
Beijing, China
cst100@gmail.com

ABSTRACT

We investigate multi-round team competitions between two teams, where each team selects one of its players simultaneously in each round and each player can play at most once. The competition defines an extensive-form game with perfect recall and can be solved efficiently by standard methods. We are interested in the properties of the subgame perfect equilibria of this game.

We first show that uniformly random strategy is a subgame perfect equilibrium strategy for both teams when there are no redundant players (i.e., the number of players in each team equals to the number of rounds of the competition). Secondly, a team can safely abandon its weak players if it has redundant players and the strength of players is transitive.

We then focus on the more interesting case where there are redundant players and the strength of players is not transitive. In this case, we obtain several counterintuitive results. First of all, a player might help improve the payoff of its team, even if it is dominated by the entire other team. We give a necessary condition for a dominated player to be useful. We also study the extent to which the dominated players can increase the payoff.

These results bring insights into playing and designing general team competitions.

General Terms

Algorithms, Economics, Theory

Keywords

Team competition, dominated players, subgame perfect equilibrium

*This work was supported by the National Basic Research Program of China Grant 2011CBA00300, 2011CBA00301, the Natural Science Foundation of China Grant 61033001, 61361136003, 61303077, 61561146398, a Tsinghua Initiative Scientific Research Grant and a China Youth 1000-talent program.

Appears in: *Proceedings of the 15th International Conference on Autonomous Agents and Multiagent Systems (AAMAS 2016), J. Thangarajah, K. Tuyls, C. Jonker, S. Marsella (eds.), May 9–13, 2016, Singapore.*

1. INTRODUCTION

We investigate a type of *team competitions* where there are two teams, each with a number of players, competing against each other. The competition proceeds in a fixed number of rounds. In each round, each team simultaneously sends out a player to a match. The result of the match is then revealed according to a probabilistic strength matrix between players. The selected players cannot compete in the subsequent rounds. The competition proceeds to the next round if there is one; or terminated otherwise. The format of the competition and the strength matrix are common knowledge to both teams. The final payoff of each team is the number of matches it wins. We also consider another commonly seen form where each team gets payoff 1 if it wins strictly more matches than the other team, 0 if ties, and -1 if it wins less matches. Clearly, the competition defines a standard *extensive-form game*, or more precisely, a *stacked matrix game* ([6]). We are interested in the sub-game perfect equilibria of the game, i.e., a strategy profile that specifies for each team which player to play at each round.

We are particularly interested in a situation where at least one team has more players than the number of rounds in the competition. As a result, some players will never have chance to participate in any match. The main agenda of this paper is to understand to what extent can the presence of additional players affect the payoff of both teams. In particular, we ask the following questions: 1. Can the presence of additional weakest teammate, a teammate whose row in the strength matrix is strictly dominated by any other row, help increase the payoff of the team? 2. Can the presence of additional dominated teammate, a teammate that always loses to any player in the opponent team, help increase the payoff of the team?

It might appear intuitive that the answers to both questions are negative. For the first question, it seems that the weakest teammate will never have a chance to participate in any match since one can always replace him by a better teammate and increase payoff. For the second question, it might seem more obvious since the dominated teammate will lose any matches thus must be replaced by a better teammate. To our surprise, we find that the answers to both questions are affirmative.

1.1 Our contributions

We first show that uniformly random strategy is a subgame perfect equilibrium strategy for both teams when there are no redundant players (i.e., the number of players in each team equals to the number of rounds of the competition). The uniformly random strategy always picks the unmatched player uniformly at random in each round.

Then, we consider the general case where at least one team has redundant players. We first study the case where the strength of players is transitive, which means that the players can be rearranged in a queue so that each of them is weaker than its successor. We prove that, a team can safely abandon its weak players if it has redundant players and the strength of players is transitive. Therefore, this case reduces to the case where there are no redundant players.

Finally, we focus on the case where there are redundant players and the strength of players is not transitive. In this case, we obtain a number of counterintuitive results. Most importantly, a player might help improve its team's payoff, even if it is dominated by the entire opposing team. We give a necessary condition for a dominated player to be useful, which alternatively suggest that a particular utility function (named U_E below) is more reasonable in team competition. Our results imply that a team can increase its utility by recruiting additional dominated players. We further show that, the optimal number of dominated players to recruit can scale with the number of rounds. More precisely, this number can be $\Theta(T)$ if there are T rounds. Last but not least, we study the limitation of dominated players.

1.2 Motivations

Our model is first motivated by the Chinese horse race story described in [11] (see also [15]). It represents one of the most popular forms of horse races where each team ranks its horses to match sequentially. Moreover, the Swaythling Cup, as known as World Table Tennis Championships, follows the same model described in our paper: each team adaptively selects a ranking of three players and brings two additional substitutes. In fact, this has been one of the most popular formats of team competition in table tennis. In addition, the card game Goofspeil ([6, 14]) also falls into nearly the same model as described in our paper.

1.3 Related works

Tang, Shoham and Lin [11, 12] study a team competition setting where the number of players equals the number of rounds and both teams must determine the ordering of players upfront, before the competition starts. They put forward competition rules that are truthful while satisfy other desirable properties. The main difference between their work and ours is that we do not design new mechanisms but study game theoretical properties of commonly used competition rules. The differences also lie in that the strategies are adaptive in our setting and each team can have more players than the number of matches.

The strategic aspects of team competition have also been under scrutiny of computer scientists due to a recent Olympic scandal in badminton, where several teams deliberately throw matches in order to avoid a strong opponent in the next round. The phenomenon has been discussed in depth in a series of algorithmic game theory blogposts by Kleinberg [3] and Procaccia [8].

A parallel literature has been concerned with the strategic aspect of tournament seeding [2, 9, 4, 10, 13, 1]. It is well known that there are cases where by strategic seeding and structuring, any player can be winner in knockout tournament. Various game theoretical questions, such as player-optimal seeding, complexity of manipulation and incentives to guarantee strategyproofness, have been investigated in this literature.

2. THE MODEL

Team 1 has a set of m players $\{A_1, \ldots, A_m\}$. Team 2 has a set of n players $\{B_1, \ldots, B_n\}$. A competition between team 1 and 2 is a tuple $G(T, P, U)$ where,

1. T is the number of rounds.
2. In each round, each team simultaneously selects one of its players that have not been selected yet.
3. P is a probabilistic matrix that describes the relative strength between players, with $P_{i,j}$ denoting the probability that A_i wins against B_j and $1 - P_{i,j}$ the probability for A_i to lose to B_j.
4. $U : [T] \to R$ denotes the utility function of each team. The utility function only depends on the number of rounds t each team wins, i.e., it can be represented by $U(t)$. This also implies that both teams have the same utility functions.
5. The parameters n, m, T, P, U are common knowledge to both teams, and historical plays are perfectly observable. It is assured that $P_{i,j} \in [0, 1]$ for all i, j and that $m \geq T$ and $n \geq T$ so that there are enough players to complete the competition.

The following utility functions U_E and U_M are two commonly seen ones:

$$U_E(t) = t - T/2. \quad U_M(t) = \begin{cases} 1 & t > T/2 \\ 0 & t = T/2 \\ -1 & t < T/2 \end{cases}. \qquad (1)$$

In other words, U_E describes a competition where a team's utility is exactly the number of rounds it wins (minus some constant $T/2$); while $U_M(t)$ describes a competition where a team's utility is whether it wins more than its opponent. Notice that, when $U = U_E$ or $U = U_M$, we have $U(t) + U(T - t) = 0$, hence both utility functions define a zero-sum game. In this paper we always assume that $U(T) + U(T - t) = 0$.

2.1 Example: simultaneous card games

The models above formulates the standard team competitions as commonly seen under the context of sports, but shall not be limited to sports. The following is an instance of card games that fall into our framework.

Suppose that Alice and Bob each has a deck of three cards. In each deck one card is in suit ♡ and two cards are in suit ♠. They play three rounds; in each round Alice and Bob select one card and they reveal the cards simultaneously. If they select cards in same suit (both in ♡ or both in ♠), Alice wins this round; otherwise Bob wins this round. The one who wins two or three rounds gets utility 1; the other one wins zero or one rounds and it gets utility -1.

This game can be conveniently represented in our model using the following parameters:

$$m = n = T = 3, P = \begin{pmatrix} 1 & 0 & 0 \\ 0 & 1 & 1 \\ 0 & 1 & 1 \end{pmatrix}, U = U_M.$$

For this game, according to our first theorem, a (subgame perfect) equilibrium strategy for both players exists, and it is to just to play uniformly random. It follows that Alice has expected utility $-1/3$ and Bob has $+1/3$.

2.2 Extensive-form game with perfect recall

Any particular instance $G(T, P, U)$ of our team competition is an extensive-form game. In this game, a history can be described by a tuple $(k, \mathbf{a}, \mathbf{b}, \mathbf{c})$ where:

- k indicates the number of rounds that has been played;
- $\mathbf{a}$ is a k-dimensional vector which stores the players selected by Team 1 in the past k rounds;
- $\mathbf{b}$ stores the players selected by Team 2;
- $\mathbf{c}$ is a k-dimensional $0-1$ vector which stores the results in the first k rounds, where 0 corresponds to a lose by Team 1 and 1 corresponds to a win by Team 1.

A behavioral strategy in this game is a mapping from every history to a probability distribution over actions. That is, at each history, the strategy of each team is to pick the next player according to a probability distribution. By Kuhn' Theorem ([7, 5]), there is a subgame perfect equilibrium (SPE), in which both teams use behavioral strategies. According to the SPE, a value $V(H)$ can be defined for each history H, which indicates the expected utility that Team 1 would get at the end of the game if it is now at history H. Note that each history is the root of a subgame and so the value of a history is the same as the value of the subgame.

2.3 Computing SPE

By backward induction, one can easily get

LEMMA 1. *Two histories have the same value if they have selected the same players to play (but may be in different orders) and Team 1 won the same number of rounds.*

Based on the above lemma, the histories can be partitioned to equivalence classes, such that each equivalence class corresponds to a four-tuple (k, X, Y, w): k is a number in $[T]$ which denotes the number of past rounds; X is a subset of A of size k; Y is a subset of B of size k; X, Y denote the players that have played; w is a number in $[k]$ which denotes how many rounds Team 1 has won so far.

In the following, we show in detail how to compute the value of each equivalence class via dynamic programming.

Let $V[k, X, Y, w]$ denote the expected utility of Team 1 when the history belongs to class (k, X, Y, w).

Clearly, we have $V[k, X, Y, w] = U(w)$ when $k = T$.

When $k < T$, computing $V[k, X, Y, w]$ reduces to computing the value of the matrix game $M(k, X, Y, w)$ where the matrix $M(k, X, Y, w)$ is defined as follows.

It consists of $m-k$ rows and $n-k$ columns. Each row corresponds to a player in $A-X$, and each column corresponds to a player in $B-Y$. The cell corresponding to A_i, B_j equals to the expect utility of Team 1 when Team 1 and Team 2 respectively make action A_i and B_j on the current state (k, X, Y, w), which equals

$$V[k+1, X+\{A_i\}, Y+\{B_j\}, w+1] \cdot P_{i,j} + V[k+1, X+\{A_i\}, Y+\{B_j\}, w] \cdot (1-P_{i,j}).$$

The reason behind the above definition of $M(k, X, Y, w)$ is as follows. If the two teams select A_i, B_j in this round, Team 1 has probability $P_{i,j}$ to win this round and hence the history becomes $(k+1, X+\{A_i\}, Y+\{B_j\}, w+1)$; besides, Team 1 has probability $(1-P_{i,j})$ to lose this round and hence the history becomes $(k+1, X+\{A_i\}, Y+\{B_j\}, w)$.

We can compute the value of all equivalent classes of histories according to the above induction. In fact, by computing these values, we also find a subgame perfect behaviorial strategy for both players. To see this, suppose that (k, X, Y, w) is a non-terminal equivalent class of history. On solving the matrix game $M[k, X, Y, w]$ we find the strategies for all the histories in the history class (k, X, Y, w).

3. UNIFORMLY RANDOM STRATEGIES

The next theorem states that, if there are no redundant players, uniformly random is an equilibrium strategy for the teams. It holds for arbitrary utility function including U_E and U_M.

Definition 1. The *uniformly random strategy* is a behavioral strategy, in which a team always selects from the remaining players uniformly at random in each round.

THEOREM 1. *When both teams have no redundant players (i.e. $n = m = T$), then it is a SPE when both teams apply the uniformly random strategy.* [1]

We apply the following lemma for proving Theorem 1.

LEMMA 2. *Suppose that there are no redundant players. Let $\mathbb{S}$ denote the set of all matchings between $\{A_1, \ldots, A_T\}$ and $\{B_1, \ldots, B_T\}$. If Team 1* **or** *Team 2 applies the uniformly random strategy, then the probability that the competition ends with any fixed matching in $\mathbb{S}$ is exactly $1/(T!)$.*

PROOF OF LEMMA 2. First, suppose that Team 1 applies the uniformly random strategy while Team 2 applies an arbitrary pure strategy. In this case, we claim that the probability that competition ends with any fixed matching is exactly $1/(T!)$. This can be proved by induction on the number of players as the following. Assume that Team 2 selects B_i in the first stage, then the probability that it meets A_j is $1/T$ for any j. By induction hypothesis, any matching has equal probability to appear. Then, since that any mixed strategy is a linear combination of the pure strategies, the above claim implies the statement given in Lemma 2. □

PROOF OF THEOREM 1. Let $\mathbb{S}$ denote the same set as in Lemma 2. Since there are no redundant players, a game will always end with some matching in $\mathbb{S}$. For a matching $s \in \mathbb{S}$, let Z_s denote the event that the game ends with this matching. According to the lemma, if Team 1 applies the uniformly random strategy, it will get expected utility

$$\sum_{s \in \mathbb{S}} E(\text{the utility of Team 1} \mid Z_s)/(T!)$$

Similarly, if Team 2 applies the uniformly random strategy, it will get

$$\sum_{s \in \mathbb{S}} E(\text{the utility of Team 2} \mid Z_s)/(T!)$$
$$= \sum_{s \in \mathbb{S}} -E(\text{the utility of Team 1} \mid Z_s)/(T!)$$

[1] Note that there could be other SPEs. For example, when players in Team 1 always lose, any strategies for the two teams form a SPE.

Therefore, it is a Nash Equilibrium if both teams apply the uniformly random strategy. The argument can be similarly extended to show that it is SPE. □

In the remainder of this paper, we focus on the case where there are redundant players.

CLAIM 1. *If there are redundant players, then the uniformly random strategy may* not *be a SPE strategy.*

This claim is obvious for a team with redundant players; but less obvious for a team without redundant players. Here we give an example in which the uniformly random strategy is not a SPE strategy for a team with no redundant players.

Example 1. Let $m = T = 2, n = 3$, $U = U_E = U_M$ (note that $U_E = U_M$ when $T = 2$), $P = \begin{pmatrix} 0 & 0 & 1 \\ 1 & 1 & 0 \end{pmatrix}$.

According to method given in Subsection 2.3, we can compute that $M(0, \varnothing, \varnothing, 0) = \begin{pmatrix} -1 & -1 & 1 \\ 0 & 0 & -1 \end{pmatrix}$. Therefore, in the SPE, the behavior for Team 1 on the initial state should be select A_1 with probability 1/3 and select A_2 with probability 2/3. This guarantees (expected) utility −1/3. If to the contrary that Team 1 adopts the uniformly random strategy, it should select A_1, A_2 with probability 1/2, which would only guarantees (expected) utility −1/2.

3.1 Transitive strength

Definition 2. Player A_i is *weaker* than its teammate A_j, denoted by $A_i \preceq A_j$, if for any opponent B_k, the probability of "A_i wins against B_k" is less than or equal to the probability of "A_j wins against B_k". Similar for Team 2.

Team 1 $\{A_1, \dots, A_m\}$ are *transitive* if there is a permutation π of $1, \dots, m$, such that $A_{\pi(1)} \preceq \dots \preceq A_{\pi(m)}$. Similar for Team 2.

Definition 3. A utility function U is *monotone* if $U(t+1) \geq U(t)$ for $t \in 0, \dots T-1$.

THEOREM 2. *Assume the utility function is monotone. We have that, (1) If $A_m \preceq \dots \preceq A_1$, Team 1 has a SPE strategy which only selects $A_1, \dots, A_T$. (2) Symmetrically, if $B_n \preceq \dots \preceq B_1$, Team 2 has a SPE strategy which only selects $B_1, \dots, B_T$.*

By combining Theorem 1 and Theorem 2, we can immediately get the following

COROLLARY 1. *When players in each team are transitive and U is monotone, there is a simple SPE strategy for both teams as follows. Assume that $A_m \preceq \dots \preceq A_1$ and $B_n \preceq \dots \preceq B_1$. Then, the SPE strategy for Team 1 is to select an unused player in $A_1, \dots, A_T$ uniformly random in each round; a SPE strategy for Team 2 is to select an unused player in $B_1, \dots, B_T$ uniformly random in each round.*

Theorem 2 and Corollary 1 have many applications. In the real word, the utility function is monotone and moreover, in many situations such as in board games or some sport games, it is indeed the case that the players are transitive.

We prove Theorem 2 (1) in the next; the claim (2) is symmetric.

We first provide two basic terminologies which are necessary for understanding the subsequent proof. Suppose that $A_m \preceq \dots \preceq A_1$ and that A' is a subset of A and $A' = (A_{i[1]}, \dots A_{i[|A'|]})$, where $i[1] < \dots < i[|A'|]$. Then, for any $0 \leq C \leq |A'|$, the top C players of A' refers to $\{A_{i[1]}, \dots, A_{i[C]}\}$, and the rank C player of A' refers to $A_{i[C]}$.

LEMMA 3. *Suppose that $U()$ is monotone.*

1. *Consider a pair of history classes $H_1 = (k, X_1, Y, w_1)$ and $H_2 = (k, X_2, Y, w_2)$. We claim that, if the top $T-k$ players of $A - X_1$ and the top $T-k$ players of $A - X_2$ are the same and $w_1 \geq w_2$, then $V(H_1) \geq V(H_2)$.*
2. *Let $H = (k, X, Y, w)$ be a non-terminal history class. Let A_u be the rank $T-k$ player in $A - X$, and let A_v be any player in $A - X$ that is not a top $T-k$ player. Then, the row in $M(k, X, Y, w)$ that corresponds to A_u dominates the row that corresponds to A_v. It further implies that, there is an equilibrium strategy at history H (for Team 1) which only selects the top $T-k$ unmatched players to play.*

PROOF. We prove it by backward induction. When $k = T$, Claim 1 holds according to the monotone property of $U()$; and Claim 2 naturally holds since it is a terminal history.

Now, we argue that, for $0 \leq k < T$, if the lemma holds for $k+1$, it also holds for k.

First, we prove Claim 2. Let us compare the two rows corresponding to A_u and A_v. Let us fix a column, say the one corresponding to B_r. The cell corresponding to (A_u, B_r) is

$$M[u,r] = \underbrace{V(k+1, X+\{A_u\}, Y+\{B_r\}, w+1)}_{a} \cdot P_{u,r} + \underbrace{V(k+1, X+\{A_u\}, Y+\{B_r\}, w)}_{b} \cdot (1 - P_{u,r})$$

The cell corresponding to (A_v, B_r) is

$$M[v,r] = \underbrace{V(k+1, X+\{A_v\}, Y+\{B_r\}, w+1)}_{a'} \cdot P_{v,r} + \underbrace{V(k+1, X+\{A_u\}, Y+\{B_r\}, w)}_{b'} \cdot (1 - P_{v,r})$$

Notice that the top $T-k-1$ players in $A - X - \{A_u\}$ and $A - X - \{A_v\}$ are the same. So, from the induction hypothesis, $a' \geq a \geq a' \geq b \geq b' \geq b$, i.e. $a = a' \geq b = b'$.

Since that A_u is the top $T-k$ player while A_v is not, player A_v is weaker than A_u, which means that $P_{u,r} \geq P_{v,r}$.

Combining the above arguments, we get that

$$M[u,r] - M[v,r] = (a-b) \cdot (P_{u,r} - P_{v,r}) \geq 0.$$

Therefore, $M[u,r] \geq M[v,r]$, and thus Claim 2 holds.

Then, we prove Claim 1. Let M_1 denote $M(k, X_1, Y, w_1)$ and M_2 denote $M(k, X_2, Y, w_2)$ for short. Suppose that A_u is a top $T-k$ player in $A - X_1$ (which is also a top $T-k$ player in $A - X_2$) and that B_r is any player in $B - Y$.

We know

$$\begin{aligned} M_1[u,r] =& V(k+1, X_1+\{A_u\}, Y+\{B_r\}, w_1+1) \cdot P_{u,r} + \\ & V(k+1, X_1+\{A_u\}, Y+\{B_r\}, w_1) \cdot (1-P_{u,r}) \\ M_2[u,r] =& V(k+1, X_2+\{A_u\}, Y+\{B_r\}, w_2+1) \cdot P_{u,r} + \\ & V(k+1, X_2+\{A_u\}, Y+\{B_r\}, w_2) \cdot (1-P_{u,r}) \end{aligned}$$

By induction hypothesis, it follows that $M_1[u,r] \geq M_2[u,r]$.

Now, let σ denote the equilibrium strategy at H_2 that only selects the top $T-k$ unmatched players to play. (Such a strategy exists according to Claim 2.) Note that σ is also a legal strategy at H_1. Let $\mu(H_1,\sigma)$ and $\mu(H_2,\sigma)$ respectively denote the utility of Team 1 when it applies strategy σ on H_1 and H_2. Then,

$$\mu(H_1,\sigma) = \min_{r:B_r\in Y} \sum_{u:A_u\in A-X_1} \sigma(A_u)\cdot M_1(u,r),$$

$$\mu(H_2,\sigma) = \min_{r:B_r\in Y} \sum_{u:A_u\in A-X_2} \sigma(A_u)\cdot M_2(u,r).$$

From the inequality $M_1(u,r) \geq M_2(u,r)$, we get $\mu(H_1,\sigma) \geq \mu(H_2,\sigma)$. Moreover, we also have $V(H_1) \geq \mu(H_1,\sigma)$ and $V(H_2) = \mu(H_2,\sigma)$ (the equality is since that σ is the equilibrium strategy on H_2). Together, $V(H_1) \geq V(H_2)$. □

Finally, Claim 2 of Lemma 3 implies Theorem 2 (1).

4. NONTRANSITIVE STRENGTH

Definition 4. A player is said to be *weakest*, if it is weaker than all its teammates; and is said to be *dominated*, if it has 0 probability to win against any player in the opponent team.

Assume that the utility function is monotone. In the previous section, we show that if there are redundant players in Team 1 and if these players are transitive, then there is a SPE strategy for Team 1 which does not select the weakest player. In other words, Team 1 can abandon the weakest one without decreasing its utility. In this section, we show that the transitivity is essential for this to hold. We start by the following claim.

CLAIM 2. *Suppose that Team 1 has redundant players and one of them is the weakest. If the players in Team 1 are not transitive, Team 1 might decrease its utility by abandoning the weakest player.*

This is somewhat counterintuitive; it might be intuitive that the weakest player has no chance to participate in any match since one can always replace him by a better teammate and increase utility. Perhaps even more surprisingly, we have the following claim:

CLAIM 3. *Suppose that Team 1 has redundant players and one of them is dominated by the other team (i.e., has no chance to win at all). If the players in Team 1 are not transitive, Team 1 might decrease its utility by abandoning the dominated player.*

The above claims confirms that, the weakest player or even dominated player could help its team.

We would now like to state the organization of the remainder of the section. In Subsection 4.1, we give examples that verify Claim 3, and we briefly explain the reason why we need dominated players. In Subsection 4.2, we identify a special case where the weakest player can be abandoned without changing the utility. In Subsection 4.3, we consider the optimal number of dominated players that we may need to achieve maximum utility. In Subsection 4.4, we discuss the limitations of the dominated players.

4.1 Dominated teammates can be helpful

Let $V(T,P,U)$ denote the value of game $G(T,P,U)$. Let P^* denote the sub-matrix of P by deleting the last row (thus $G(T,P^*,U)$ is the game where Team 1 has abandoned A_m).

Example 2. Let $n=m=3, T=2$, $U=U_E$ (recall that $U_E(t)=t-T/2$), and let $P=\begin{pmatrix}1&0&0\\0&1&0\\0&0&0\end{pmatrix}$.

In Example 2, there are redundant players and the players in each team are not transitive. Besides, A_3 is a dominated player. We argue the follows: (I) If A_3 is abandoned, Team 2 can win both rounds and hence $V(T,P^*,U)=-1$. (II) If A_3 is in the team, Team 2 cannot win both rounds with certainty and that means $V(T,P,U)>-1$. Combining (I) and (II), we get $V(T,P,U)>V(T,P^*,U)$, which implies Claim 3.

PROOF OF (I). If A_3 is abandoned, Team 2 can play as follows. It chooses B_3 to win the first round. If B_3 defeated A_1, it chooses B_1 in the second round to beat A_2; otherwise, it chooses B_2 in the second round to beat A_1. □

PROOF OF (II). If Team 2 wants to win with certainty in both rounds, it must select B_3 to play the first round. However, if Team 1 selects the dominated player A_3 to play the first round, Team 2 cannot win the second round with certainty anymore. □

From this example, we see why a dominated player might be helpful for its team. The reason behind is similar to the horse race story described at the beginning of [12].

In the next, we give one more example. It gives, to our best knowledge, the largest decrease of utility by abandoning a dominated player.

Example 3. Let $m=4, n=T=3$. Let $U=U_E$ or $U=U_M$. Let $P=\begin{pmatrix}1&0&0\\0&1&0\\0&0&1\\0&0&0\end{pmatrix}$.

According the method shown in Subsection 2.3, we can compute that [2]

$$V(T,P,U_M)=0; \qquad V(T,P^*,U_M)=-2/3;$$
$$V(T,P,U_E)=-1/2; \qquad V(T,P^*,U_E)=-1/2.$$

So, for the game $G(T,P,U_M)$, we will lose utility as much as 2/3 if we abandon the dominated player.

In the following we explicitly state a SPE strategy for Team 1. In the first round it selects the dominated player A_4. Without loss of generality, assume that it loses to B_1. In the second round, it selects A_2, A_3 uniformly random. So, there is 1/2 chance that Team 1 wins this round. Furthermore, if Team 1 wins the second round (say A_2 beats B_2) it can also wins the next (let A_3 beat B_3) and thus gets utility 1. By this strategy, there is 1/2 chance to get utility 1 and 1/2 chance to get utility -1, so the expected utility is 0.

However, for the game (T,P,U_E), we do not lose any utility by abandoning the dominated player. This is not a coincidence. In fact, this example belongs to a special case where the weakest player can indeed be abandoned. We show this in the next theorem.

[2]Note that the value of $G(T,P^*,U_M)$ and $G(T,P^*,U_M)$ can be simply computed according to Theorem 1 since there are no redundant players in these games.

4.2 A case where the weakest player can be abandoned

We have seen that the weakest redundant player is useless when the players are transitive (as proved in Theorem 2) but might be useful when the players are not transitive (as shown in the previous subsection). So, the next question is:

Question 1. If the players are not transitive, on what cases the weakest player can be abandoned?

We get the following result.

THEOREM 3. *Suppose that Team 1 has redundant players but Team 2 does not. So, $m > T$ and $n = T$. Suppose that each player in $A_{T+1}, \ldots, A_m$ is weaker than each player in $A_1..A_T$. Let $U = U_E$. Then, Team 1 can abandon all the players in $A_{T+1}, \ldots, A_m$ without losing its utility.*

Before we give the proof, we make two remarks.
1. The condition $m > n = T$ is important for Theorem 3. If both team got redundant players, then the claim in this theorem does not hold anymore.
2. From Example 3, we see that the claim in this theorem fails when $U = U_M$. Therefore, as a comparison, by recruiting extra dominated players, a team can gain more utility when $U = U_M$, but cannot when $U = U_E$. This may suggest that U_E is more reasonable than U_M in team competition.

We need the following lemma on proving Theorem 3. It is a technical statement of probability theory. Proof omitted.

LEMMA 4. *Assume that $n = T$ and A_i, B_j are any pair of players from the two teams. Let $Q^{\sigma}_{i,j}$ denote the probability that A_i meets B_j in the game when Team 2 applies the uniformly random strategy and Team 1 applies some strategy σ. Then,*

$$Q^{\sigma}_{i,j} \leq 1/T. \tag{2}$$

PROOF OF THEOREM 3. We call $A_{T+1}, \ldots, A_m$ the weak players. When the weak players are abandoned, there are T remaining players for each team. By Theorem 1, the uniformly random strategy is a SPE strategy for Team 2. To prove Theorem 3, the key idea is to show that even if Team 1 is allowed to select the weak player, it will not gain more utility if Team 2 keep using the uniformly random strategy. On the other hand, it is obvious that Team 2 can't gain more utility. Therefore, the value of game does not change when the weak players are allowed to play.

When Team 1 abandons its weak players, its maximum utility is

$$U^* = (\sum_{j=1..T} \sum_{i=1..T} \frac{1}{T} P_{i,j}) - \frac{T}{2}.$$

Let $Q^{\sigma}(i,j)$ be defined as Lemma 4. The utility of Team 1 when it applies strategy σ against the uniformly random strategy of Team 2 is

$$U^{\sigma} = (\sum_{j=1..T} \sum_{i=1..m} Q^{\sigma}_{i,j} P_{i,j}) - \frac{T}{2}$$

We need to prove that $U^{\sigma} \leq U^*$, and it reduces to show that for any fixed j in $1..T$,

$$\sum_{i=1..m} P_{i,j} Q^{\sigma}_{i,j} \leq \sum_{i=1..T} \frac{1}{T} P_{i,j} \tag{3}$$

To prove (3), consider the following optimization problem:

$$\begin{cases} \texttt{Variables:} & x = (x_1, \ldots, x_m) \\ \texttt{Parameters:} & c = (c_1, \ldots, c_m) \\ \texttt{Guarantee:} & c_i \geq c'_i (\forall (i,i') \text{ such that } i \leq T < i') \\ \texttt{Constrant 1:} & 0 \leq x_i \leq \frac{1}{T} (\forall 1 \leq i \leq m) \\ \texttt{Constrant 2:} & \sum_{i=1}^{m} x_i = 1 \\ \texttt{Objective:} & \max f(x) = \sum_{i=1}^{m} c_i x_i \end{cases}$$

Clearly, $f(x)$ is maximized at x^*, where $x^*_i = \begin{cases} \frac{1}{T} & i \leq T \\ 0 & i > T \end{cases}$.

Noticing the following facts, we see that inequality (3) is just an application of the above problem.

$$\begin{array}{rl} Q^{\sigma}_{i,j} \leq \frac{1}{T} & \text{(Applying Lemma 4)} \\ \sum_{i=1}^{m} Q^{\sigma}_{i,j} = 1 & \text{(According to the definition)} \\ \forall i \leq T < i', P_{i,j} \geq P_{i',j} & \text{(Since } A_{i'} \text{ is weaker than } A_i) \end{array}$$

□

4.3 Optimal number of dominated players

Here we study the power of dominated players in another direction. As we see in Subsection 4.1, by abandoning a redundant dominated player, Team 1 may decrease its utility. In other words, it states that Team 1 may increase its utility by recruiting more dominated players. Note that the utility of Team 1 will not decrease by recruiting more dominated players. However, it is unclear that the utility will strictly increase by doing so. For example, it is clear that recruiting T dominated players is the same as recruiting $T-1$ players — in any case, if any team uses T dominated players in a competition, it gets the lowest utility!

So, a natural question is,

Question 2. In order to get the maximum utility, how many dominated players should we recruit at least? Is it possible that we need as many as $\Theta(T)$ such players?

The theorem below answers this question.

THEOREM 4.

1. *Suppose $U = U_E$. Recruiting $T-1$ dominated players can be better than $T-2$, but recruiting T dominated players is the same as $T-1$. So, to achieve optimal utility, one may require $T-1$ dominated players. This number is tight.*
2. *Suppose $U = U_M$. Recruiting $\lfloor T/2 \rfloor$ dominated players can be better than $\lfloor T/2 \rfloor - 1$, but recruiting $\lfloor T/2 \rfloor + 1$ dominated players cannot be better than $\lfloor T/2 \rfloor$. So, to achieve optimal utility, one may require $\lfloor T/2 \rfloor$ dominated players, and this number is tight as well.*

One direction in these claims are rather trivial; we should never use T dominated players when $U = U_E$ or $\lfloor T/2 \rfloor + 1$ players when $U = U_M$. To prove the other direction, we need to construct some examples in which recruiting $T-1$ (resp. $\lfloor T/2 \rfloor$) could be better than $T-2$ (resp. $\lfloor T/2 \rfloor - 1$) when $U = U_E$ (resp. $U = U_M$). To construct such examples, an intuition is that we should make the current players in Team 1 as weak as possible. Our construction is as follows.

Example 4.

$$T \geq 1, m = T, n = T + (T-1),$$

$$U = U_E, P_{i,j} = \begin{cases} 1 & i = j \\ 0 & i \neq j \end{cases}$$

Example 5.

$$T \geq 1, m = T, n = T + \lfloor T/2 \rfloor,$$
$$U = U_M, P_{i,j} = \begin{cases} 1 & i = j \\ 0 & i \neq j \end{cases}$$

The following claims together prove Theorem 4.

C1. In Example 4, if Team 1 only recruit $T-2$ dominated players, it can win no rounds and thus can get utility $-T/2$.

C2. In Example 4, if Team 1 recruit $T-1$ dominated players, it can win a positive number of rounds in expected and thus gain utility more than $-T/2$.

C3. In Example 5, if Team 1 only recruit $\lfloor T/2 \rfloor - 1$ dominated players, it will always lose at least $\lfloor T/2 \rfloor + 1$ rounds and thus can only get utility -1.

C4. In Example 5, if Team 1 recruit $\lfloor T/2 \rfloor$ dominated players, it can sometimes win at least $\lceil T/2 \rceil$ rounds and thus can gain utility more than -1.

PROOF OF C1. In this case Team 2 can win all the rounds by playing as follows. In the first $T-1$ rounds, it selects the players $B_{T+1}, \ldots, B_{2T-1}$ to play; and they all win. Then, since Team 1 only has $T-2$ dominated players, at least one player in $A_1, \ldots, A_T$ has already played, denote it by A_i. In the last round, Team 2 select B_i and it definitely wins. □

PROOF OF C3. In this case, by applying a strategy similar to C1, Team 2 can win all the first $\lfloor T/2 \rfloor + 1$ rounds.[3] □

PROOF OF C2. For convenience, we denote the $T-1$ dominated players by $A_{T+1}, \ldots, A_{2T-1}$. We argue that, if Team 1 applies the uniform random strategy (that is, select one unused player in $A_1, \ldots, A_{2T-1}$ uniformly random in each round), then, Team 2 has no strategy to win all rounds all the time. Suppose to the contrary that Team 2 can do it, it must select a player from $B_{T+1} \ldots, B_{2T-1}$ to play in the first round; otherwise there is a chance that it loses the first round. Note that, since Team 1 apply the uniform random strategy, there is a chance that Team 1 select a dominated player in the first round. If this happens, Team 2 must again select a player from $B_{T+1} \ldots, B_{2T-1}$ to play in the second round. Once again, Team 1 might still select a dominated player in the second round. By induction, there is chance that Team 1 select all the dominated players in the first $T-1$ rounds while Team 2 consumes all its $T-1$ invincible players in $B_{T+1} \ldots, B_{2T-1}$. Then, Team 2 cannot win with certainty in the last round. □

The claim C4 is the most nontrivial. To prove it we first state the following lemma.

Definition 5. For integers a, b, C such that

$$C \geq 1, 0 \leq a \leq \lceil C/2 \rceil, 0 \leq b \leq \lfloor C/2 \rfloor, \tag{4}$$

let $\Gamma^C_{a,b}$ denote the following instance of team competition:

$$m = n = (C-a) + (\lfloor C/2 \rfloor - b),$$
$$T = C - a - b, P_{i,j} = \begin{cases} 1 & i = j \leq C - a \\ 0 & \textit{otherwise} \end{cases}.$$

[3]In this case Team 2 can actually win all the T rounds.

The utility is as follows.[4] If Team 1 wins at least $\lceil C/2 \rceil - a$ rounds, it gets utility 1 and Team 2 gets -1; otherwise, Team 1 gets utility -1 and Team 2 gets 1.

LEMMA 5. *For integers a, b, C satisfying condition (4), Team 1 can win utility larger than -1 in the game $\Gamma^C_{a,b}$.*

PROOF. Consider three cases.

Case 1 $a = \lceil C/2 \rceil$.
In this case, Team 1 always get utility 1, and so $\Gamma^C_{a,b}$ has value 1, which is larger than -1.

Case 2 $b = \lfloor C/2 \rfloor$.
The game $\Gamma^C_{a,b}$ can be restated as follows.

- $m = n = C - a$, $T = \lceil C/2 \rceil - a$.
  Player A_i can only defeat B_i for i in $1..m$.
  Team 1 gets utility 1 if it wins all the rounds; and -1 otherwise.

We argue that the uniformly random strategy guarantees Team 1 an expected utility larger than -1. Equivalently speaking, by applying the uniformly random strategy, Team 1 has a chance to win all the rounds. The proof is as follows. In the first round, there is a positive chance that A_i meets B_i for some i. Then, in the second round, same thing happens with a positive chance. This could happen for each round. When these coincidences happen, Team 1 wins all the rounds.

Case 3 $a < \lceil C/2 \rceil$ and $b < \lfloor C/2 \rfloor$.
We use induction. Assume that $\Gamma^C_{a+1,b}$ and $\Gamma^C_{a,b+1}$ both have value larger than -1, we argue that so does $\Gamma^C_{a,b}$.

The following facts follow from the definition of $\Gamma^C_{a,b}$.

Fact 1. If the two teams select A_i and B_i for $i \leq C-a$ in the first round, it becomes a subgame that is equivalent to $\Gamma^C_{a+1,b}$.

Fact 2. If the two teams select A_i and B_i for $i > C-a$ in the first round, it becomes a subgame that is equivalent to $\Gamma^C_{a,b+1}$.

Combining them with the induction hypothesis, we get

Fact 3. If the two teams select players under the same index, it becomes a subgame whose value is larger than -1.

We know that the value of $\Gamma^C_{a,b}$ is equal to the value of the matrix game M, where $M(i,j)$ indicate the value of the subgame when Team 1 select A_i and Team 2 select B_j in the first round. Fact 3 implies that all the utilities on the diagonal of matrix M are larger than -1. Therefore, by using uniformly random strategy over its players, Team 1 can win a utility larger than -1. Therefore, $\Gamma^C_{a,b}$ has value larger than -1.

□

[4]Here the utility functions for two teams are not identical. However, since it is still a zero-sum game, SPE strategies for the teams exists as before. The requirement that the utility functions are identical is not necessary in our model.

Proof of C4. Let G denote the revised game of Example 5, in which Team 1 has recruited $\lfloor T/2 \rfloor$ dominated players. We could observe that game G is almost the same as $\Gamma^T_{0,0}$. To be more specific, when T is odd, G is exactly $\Gamma^T_{0,0}$; when T is even, the parameters m, n, T, P in G and $\Gamma^T_{0,0}$ are the same; but the utility U is slightly different.

Suppose that the value of G is -1. Then, Team 2 has a strategy which guarantees a expected utility -1. It means that Team 2 has a strategy which can always win $\lfloor \frac{T}{2} \rfloor + 1$ or more rounds. When Team 2 applies this strategy, Team 1 can never win $\lceil \frac{T}{2} \rceil$ rounds. It further implies that the value of $\Gamma^T_{0,0}$ is also -1. However, this contradicts with Lemma 5. Therefore, the value of G must be larger than -1. □

4.4 Limitations of the dominated players

Although the presences of dominated players can affect the value of the game, we conjecture that it will not be too much. A question is then,

Question 3. By abandoning a dominated player, how much utility might be lost in the worst case? In other words, how much can a team gain by recruiting dominated players?

According to our simulations, we have the following conjecture that we cannot prove at the moment.

Conjecture 1. *If $U = U_M$, we can gain at most 2/3 extra utility by recruiting arbitrary number of dominated players. If $U = U_E$, we can gain at most 1 extra utility by recruiting arbitrary number of dominated players.*

5. THROWING A MATCH AND DISCARDING A PLAYER

Recall the card game between Alice and Bob in Subsection 2.1. We shall point out that, recruiting a dominated player in this context can be thought of applying a cheating action, which is to *throw a match* by not placing any card in that round. In the mentioned card game, if Alice and Bob are not allowed to throw a match, Alice can get expected utility $-1/3$; if Alice is allowed to throw a match, she can get expected utility $1/3$. This can be computed according to the method shown in Subsection 2.3. Therefore, throwing a match is profitable if permitted.

It may seem unnatural to let a team throw a match like this. The following alternative cheating action called *discarding*, which may seem more natural, is still profitable for the team.

Discarding is defined as follows. Alice (Team 1) is allowed to discard one of its cards and agrees to lose in that round; however the discarded card is never revealed to Bob (Team 2). By discarding, Alice do not gain one more card at hand, unlike the case of throwing a match.

However, if discarding is allowed, it may still be beneficial. We give an instance in which one may gain extra utility by discarding. Formally, we have the following theorem.

Theorem 5. *There exists a game G such that $V_K(G) > V_{K-1}(G)$, where $V_K(G)$ denotes the value of game G in which Team 1 is allowed to discard at most K players.*

Example 6.

$$m = K + 1, n = 2K + 1, T = K + 1,$$

$$U = U_E, P = \begin{cases} 1 & i = j \\ 0 & i \neq j \end{cases}$$

The following claims together imply Theorem 5.

C5 In Example 6, if Team 1 is only allowed to discard $K - 1$ times, it cannot win in any round.

C6 In Example 6, if Team 1 is allowed to discard K times, it can win some rounds in expectation.

Proof of C5. Suppose that Team 1 is only allowed to use discarding $K - 1$ times. Observer that, for any i in $1..m$, after A_i has played and revealed by Team 1, player B_i becomes invincible that he would win with certainty if he plays in the next rounds. Notice that there are K invincible players at beginning (which are $B_{K+1} \dots B_{2k+1}$) and Team 1 has only $K - 1$ chances to hide a player by discarding. So, in any round, Team 2 has an invincible player at hand. Therefore, Team 2 can win all the rounds. □

Proof of C6. Consider the following strategy for Team 1. First, Team 1 randomly chooses an order of the players (say, each order with possibility $1/m!$), and then it randomly chooses exactly K of its players so that these players will be discarded while playing. We argue that this strategy guarantees Team 1 to win positive rounds in expected. It reduces to prove that no strategy of Team 2 can win all the rounds against this strategy. Suppose that Team 2 can do so. In the first round, it must select an invincible player (i.e. a player in $B_{T+1} \dots B_{T+k}$). Otherwise, there is a chance that it loses the first round. And then, we know that there is a chance Team 1 discards in the first round. If this happens, Team 2 must also select an invincible player in the second round. Again, it is possible that Team 1 still discards in this round. Continuing this process we see that, it could happen that, in the first K rounds Team 2 use all its K invincible players, while on the other hand Team 1 uses discarding K times. Then, Team 2 could lose in the $K + 1$-th round. □

Note that, when discarding is allowed, the value of the game cannot be computed easily, because the competition becomes an extensive-game with imperfect information.

6. CONCLUSIONS

In this paper, we study a novel game-theoretic model of situations where two teams make sequential decisions about which of a set of exhaustible actions to select in each round. These actions can be interpreted as team members, cards in a hand, etc. We present a simple SPE for the case where there are no redundant players or the strength of players is transitive. For the other case, we exhibit evidence that the redundant dominated players cannot be easily discounted in their contribution to team performance, which may appear counterintuitive. We investigate the power of the dominated players in three directions: 1. When do they influence the value of the competition? 2. If additional dominated players can be recruited, how many should be required to attain the maximum utility? 3. How much utility might be lost at most if we abandon them? We obtain several nontrivial results that fully or partially answer these questions. We believe that our results are of particular interests to both designers and players of team competitions.

REFERENCES

[1] A. Altman, A. D. Procaccia, and M. Tennenholtz. Nonmanipulable selections from a tournament. In C. Boutilier, editor, *IJCAI*, pages 27–32, 2009.

[2] F. K. Hwang. New concepts in seeding knockout tournaments. *American Mathematics Monthly*, 89(4):235–239, 1982.

[3] R. Kleinberg. Olympic badminton is not incentive compatible, turing's invisible hand. Technical report, 2012.

[4] D. E. Knuth. A random knockout tournament. *American Mathematics Monthly*, 93:127–129, 1987.

[5] H. W. Kuhn. *Extensive games and the problem of information.* Princeton University Press, 1953.

[6] M. Lanctot, V. Lisý, and M. Winands. Monte carlo tree search in simultaneous move games with applications to goofspiel. In *Computer Games*, volume 408 of *Communications in Computer and Information Science*, pages 28–43. 2014.

[7] M. J. Osborne and A. Rubinstein. *A Course in Game Theory.* MIT Press, 1994.

[8] A. Procaccia. Olympic badminton is not incentive compatible – revisited, turing's invisible hand. Technical report, 2013.

[9] S. Rosen. Prizes and incentives in elimination tournaments. *American Economic Review*, 76, 1986.

[10] A. J. Schwenk. What is the correct way to seed a knockout tournament? *American Mathematics Monthly*, 107(2):140–150, 2000.

[11] P. Tang, Y. Shoham, and F. Lin. Team competition. In *Proceedings of AAMAS,*, 2009.

[12] P. Tang, Y. Shoham, and F. Lin. Designing competitions between teams of individuals. *Artif. Intell.*, 174(11):749–766, 2010.

[13] T. Vu, A. Altman, and Y. Shoham. On the complexity of schedule control problems for knockout tournaments. In *AAMAS '09*, pages 225–232, 2009.

[14] Wikipedia. Goofspiel. Technical report, 2015.

[15] Wikipedia. Sun bin. Technical report, 2015.

Network Pollution Games*

Eleftherios Anastasiadis
University of Liverpool
Liverpool, UK
e.anastasiadis@liv.ac.uk

Xiaotie Deng
Shanghai Jiao Tong University
Shanghai, China
deng-xt@cs.sjtu.edu.cn

Piotr Krysta
University of Liverpool
Liverpool, UK
p.krysta@liverpool.ac.uk

Minming Li
City University of Hong Kong
Hong Kong, China
minming.li@cityu.edu.hk

Han Qiao
University of Chinese
Academy of Sciences
China
qiaohan@ucas.ac.cn

Jinshan Zhang
University of Liverpool
Liverpool, UK
jinshan.zhang@liverpool.ac.uk

ABSTRACT

We introduce a new network model of the pollution control problem and present two applications of this model. On a high level, our model comprises a graph whose nodes represent the agents, that could be thought of as sources of pollution, and edges between agents represent the effect of spread of pollution. The government as the regulator is responsible to maximize the social welfare while setting bounds on the levels of emitted pollution both locally and globally. Our model is inspired by the existing literature in environmental economics that applies game theoretical methodology to control pollution. We study the social welfare maximization problem in our model. Our main results include hardness results for the problem, and in complement, a constant approximation algorithm on planar graphs. Our approximation algorithm leads to a truthful in expectation mechanism, and it is obtained by a novel decomposition technique of planar graphs to deal with constraints on vertices. We note that no known planar decomposition techniques can be used here and our technique can be of independent interest.

Keywords

Algorithmic mechanism design; approximation algorithms; planar graphs; pollution control

1. INTRODUCTION

Technology advance and commercial freedom have fused and accelerated the development process in an unprecedented scale. Environmental degradation however has accompanied this progress, resulting in global water and air pollution. In many developing countries, this has caused wide public concerns. As an example, in 2012, China discharged 68.5 billion tons of industrial wastewater, and the SO_2 emissions reached 21.2 million tons (National Bureau of Statistics of China, 2013). China has become one of the most polluted countries in the world, with industrial emissions as the main source of its pollution. The recent annual State of the Air report of the American Lung Association finds 47% of Americans live in counties with frequently unhealthy levels of either ozone or particulate pollution, see [4]. The latest assessment of air quality, by the European Environment Agency, finds that around 90% of city inhabitants in the European Union are exposed to one of the most damaging air pollutants at harmful levels, see [1]. It is the role of regulatory authorities to make efficient environmental policies in balancing economic growth and environment protection.

Our model and motivation. Pollution control regulations are inspired by the managerial approaches in environment policies, where models based on game theory are proposed and analysed. Kwerel [25] proposed a mechanism where firms, potential polluters, report their clean-up cost information to the regulator. The regulator sells a fixed number of pollution licences at a fixed price per licence and offers a subsidy for those licences which firms hold in excess of emission, based on the cost information provided by firms. In Kwerel's mechanism truth-telling by all firms implies a Nash equilibrium. Kwerel's scheme maintains a mild level of pollution by optimizing the social welfare (sum of the global clean-up cost and damage cost of emitted pollution).

From a different viewpoint, Dasgupta, Hammond and Maskin [11] focus on minimizing the sum of pollution damages, abatement costs and individual rationality for consumers. Spulber [36] develops a market model of environmental regulation with interdependent production, pollution abatement costs and heterogeneous firms who have private information about costs and pursue Bayes-Nash strategies in communication with the regulator. Their paper illustrates that the full information optimum cannot be attained unless gains from trade in the product market net of external damages exceed the information rents earned by firms, and aggregate output and externality levels are lower at the regulated equilibrium than at the full information social optimum.

Pollution has a diffusion nature: emitted at one source, it will have an effect on its neighbours at some diminish-

*Xiaotie Deng was supported by the National Science Foundation of China (Grant No. 61173011) and a Project 985 grant of Shanghai Jiaotong University. Piotr Krysta and Jinshan Zhang were supported by the Engineering and Physical Sciences Research Council under grant EP/K01000X/1. Minming Li was partly supported by a grant from the Research Grants Council of the Hong Kong Special Administrative Region, China (Project No. CityU 117913). Han Qiao was supported by the National Science Foundation of China (Grant No. 71373262).

Appears in: *Proceedings of the 15th International Conference on Autonomous Agents and Multiagent Systems (AAMAS 2016), J. Thangarajah, K. Tuyls, C. Jonker, S. Marsella (eds.), May 9–13, 2016, Singapore.*

ing level. We consider two applications using a network model. In the first application, the vertices represent pollution sources and edges are routes of pollution transition from one source to another similar to Belitskaya [9]. Our model measures the pollution diminishing transition by arbitrary weights on the edges, which is also present in the model by Montgomery [28]. The polluters' privately known clean-up cost and damage of the emitted pollution in our model are inspired by Kwerel. In the second application, the vertices represent mayors of cities and edges the roads between cities. The percentage of cars moving from one city to another is represented by the weight of the corresponding edge.

Our model covers both aforementioned applications with details given in section 3. The government as the regulator can decide to either shut down or keep open a pollution source taking into account the diffusion nature of pollution. It sets bounds on global and local levels of pollution, while trying to optimize the social welfare. The emissions that exceed the licences, if any, must be cleaned-up (hence, agent's clean-up cost). Furthermore our model allows the regulator to auction pollution licences for cars to mayors. In this case, the pollution level of an agent (mayor), i.e., the number of allocated licences, is set by the regulator together with the prices that the agent pays to get them.

Finding an optimal social welfare maximizing solution to our problem, which we call Pollution Game (PG), is NP-hard, that is why we study polynomial time approximation algorithms which can lead to incentive compatible (truthful) mechanisms. We study linear cost and damage functions, and derive approximation algorithms and truthful mechanisms focusing on planar network topologies. In contrast, Belitskaya assumes quadratic cost functions and linear damage functions and derives optimal social welfare and Nash equilibria solutions by explicit analytic formulas. We focus our study on planar network topologies which model realistic scenarios.

Most of the cited economics papers derive equilibria by closed analytic formulas. Some of these papers provide computational mechanisms without investigating polynomial running time. Our approach is algorithmic and focuses on efficiently computing these solutions. We also analyse the computational complexity/hardness, of computing the social optimum in our model. To the best of our knowledge, our work is the first attempt to algorithmically analyze pollution control from the perspective of regulators by a network game model with information asymmetry between regulators and polluters.

Technical contributions. Our main algorithmic contributions are for linear objective functions on planar graphs. Baker's shifting and tree-width decomposition techniques, see, e.g., [6, 21], are used for designing PTASs [1] for various problems on planar graphs. It seems impossible to design a PTAS for PG with binary variables on planar graphs by adapting these techniques. That is because they deal with constraints on edges (e.g., for the independent set problem), but PG's constraints are imposed on vertices from its neighbouring vertices. More precisely, given two optimal solutions on two subgraphs (with common boundary vertices) of the planar graph, combining them together may not result in a feasible solution for PG on the whole graph.This is due to the possible infeasibility of local constraints of the boundary vertices of these two subgraphs. We overcome this major difficulty by introducing a new decomposition technique of planar graphs, an (α, β)-decomposition. This new technique is of independent interest and it may have further applications for the problems with constraints on vertices rather than on edges.

Even when polluters' cost functions are linear with a single parameter, simple monotonicity is not sufficient to turn our algorithms into truthful mechanisms (see e.g. Chapter 11 in [29]). This is because polluters' utility functions have externalities – they are affected by their neighbours. Thus, we need to use general techniques to obtain truthful mechanisms: maximal in range mechanisms (for deterministic truthfulness) and maximal in distributional range mechanisms (for truthfulness in expectation).

Organization. In Section 2 we present a general overview of literature on game theoretic approaches to pollution control. The reader can skip this section during first reading with no harm to further reading. Section 3 contains definitions, the problem formulation and two applications of our model. In Section 4 we present the hardness results for the pollution game and in Section 5 we present our technique to get a constant approximation algorithm and a truthful in expectation mechanism for planar graphs. We conclude in Section 6 with a few open problems.

2. LITERATURE OVERVIEW

An invaluable source of pollution control regulations comes from the managerial approaches in environment policies. The majority of literature in this field dealt with symmetric information. This problem however shows a fundamental asymmetry between the regulatory bodies and pollutants. The research contributions considering environmental policy with asymmetric information and the diffusion nature of pollution have been limited until recently.

In order to control pollution, an incentive mechanism that is environmentally friendly and resource efficient needs to be designed and deployed by regulatory authorities. However, it is not obvious how to design such a mechanism in presence of asymmetric information; just as Hurwicz [18] put it: the firms know that information will be used by the regulator to design a policy which will affect their profits. Hence, they have an incentive to manipulate reported information in order to influence the content of the policy. In this context, Farell [15] discusses the relevance of the Coase Theorem. This theorem basically asserts that bargaining will lead to an efficient outcome regardless of the initial allocation of property if negotiation and trade in presence of externality are possible and the transaction costs are sufficiently low. Considering the problems of incomplete information, this paper shows that voluntary negotiation does not lead to the first-best outcome that maximizes joint surplus in the presence of two-sided private information. That is to say, centralised economic institutions such as government control and intervention, and decentralised institutions such as bargaining and ownership rights, should be viewed as complementary to each other. Therefore, a necessary condition for the government when designing an optimal pollution control plan is the truthful information about firms.

Kwerel [25], Dasgupta et al. [11] and Spulber [36] have

[1]Polynomial Time Approximation Schemes

proposed mechanisms that implement truth telling by firms to maintain a mild level of pollution. Under the assumption that firms can communicate with the regulator but not with one another, In Kwerel's scheme [25] firms are informed in advance that their messages will be translated into pollution taxes. The regulator issues a fixed number of transferable pollution licences and offers a subsidy for those licences which firms hold in excess of emission. Both the number of licences to be issued and the subsidy rate offered are calculated on the basis of the cost information provided by firms.

Kim and Chang [22] constructed an optimal incentive tax/subsidy scheme in an oligopoly market with pollution and suggested a differential damages mechanism, which leads to an optimal emission level. McKitrick [27] proposes a Cournot Mechanism for pollution control under asymmetric information, in which Nash Equilibrium exists, is stable, and can be reached by iterative computations. Because firms may attempt to manipulate the pollution level allocation to their own advantage, the adjustment rule is exogenous and depends on the actions of the firms. An approach in Karp and Livernois [20] is related to that in Conrad and Wang [10] who examine the steady-state properties of a tax adjustment mechanism in situations where the government has no information about firms' abatement costs.

These prior studies provide an overall framework in the administrative approach to control pollution. However, those models are only a first level of approximation in characterizing the reality. Although, there is some literature studying an economics environment consisting of firms or countries with geographical distinction, few of them take the diffusion nature of air and water pollution into consideration. For instance, Petrosjan and Zaccour [30] study the problem of allocation over time of total cost incurred by countries in a cooperative game of pollution reduction. Segerson [34] develops a general incentive scheme for controlling nonpoint source pollution[2] that considers the diffusion nature, in which rewards for environmental quality above a given standard are combined with penalties for substandard quality. Based on the work of Petrosjan and Zaccour [30], Belitskaya [9] develops an n-person network game model of emission reduction. Dorner et al. [14] create a multi-objective modeling system using Bayesian probability networks to study nonpoint source pollution. Both the work of Belitskaya and Dorner et al. are different from the setting of this paper, in either model assumption or function settings. In addition to these works built on network framework, Dong et al. [13] models the water pollution problem as a cost sharing problem on a tree network. However, none of the literature mentioned above takes into account the role of governments in pollution abatement, more specifically how to make policies assuming information asymmetry. A model that adequately takes both factors into account is what we need to tackle such problems in reality.

Few other papers have studied air pollution in relation to network models. Singh and Datta [35] use artificial neural network method to identify unknown pollution sources in the groundwater. Gianessi et al. [17] analyze the national water pollution control policies. And, finally, Trujillo and Hugh [39] study multi-objective air pollution monitoring network design. These papers use networks in a very different context than ours.

Turning into current practice, emissions trading is a market-based approach used to control pollution by providing economic incentives for achieving reductions in the emissions of pollutants. Various countries have adopted emission trading systems as one of the strategies for mitigating climate-change by addressing international greenhouse-gas emission [38].

A central authority (usually a governmental body) sets a limit or cap on the amount of a pollutant that may be emitted. The limit or cap is allocated and/or sold by the central authority to firms in the form of emissions permits which represent the right to emit or discharge a specific volume of the specified pollutant [37]. Permits (and possibly also derivatives of permits) can then be traded on secondary markets. For example, the European Union Emissions Trading Scheme (EU ETS) trades primarily in European Union Allowances (EUAs), the Californian scheme in California Carbon Allowances, the New Zealand scheme in New Zealand Units and the Australian scheme in Australian Units [2]. Firms are required to hold a number of permits (or allowances or carbon credits) equivalent to their emissions. The total number of permits cannot exceed the cap, limiting total emissions to that level. Firms that need to increase their volume of emissions must buy permits from those who require fewer permits [37, 38]. Currently a simple auction mechanism for selling EUAs is adopted in Europe, see, e.g., [3]. Furthermore in order to limit the automobile pollution, governments use policies of car taxation [19], [16]. A radical transport policy introduced in the UK and first applied in Central London resulted in 19% reduction of CO_2 emissions (see table 2 in [7]).

3. PRELIMINARIES

3.1 Model and applications

We introduce our model in context of our first application where given an area of pollution sources (e.g. factories) each one owned by an agent, the goal of the government as a regulator is to optimize the social welfare while restricting the levels of emitted pollution. More formally, given a weighted digraph $G = (V, E)$, where V is the set of n pollution sources (players, agents) and edge $(u, v) \in E$ represents the fact that u and v are geographic neighbours i.e. $(u, v) \in E$ if and only if the pollution emitted by u affects v (No geometric assumptions are made.) For each $(u, v) \in E$ weight $w_{(u,v)} = w_{uv}$ denotes a discount factor of the pollution discharged by player u affecting its neighbour v. Without loss of generality, we may suppose $w_{uv} \in (0, 1]$, $\forall (u, v) \in E$.

The government sets the total pollution quota discharged to the environment (by the number of pollution sources that remain open) to be $p \geq \sum_{v \in V} x_v$, where $x_v \in \{0, 1\}$ denotes whether pollution source $v \in V$ will be shut down or not. Each agent v has a non-decreasing benefit function $b_v : \mathbb{R}_{\geq 0} \longrightarrow \mathbb{R}_{\geq 0}$, where $b_v(x_v)$ is a concave increasing function (economic diminishing marginal utility phenomenon) with $b_v(0) = 0$ which represents the benefit incurred by v. Each v has a non-decreasing damage function $d_v : \mathbb{R}_{\geq 0} \longrightarrow \mathbb{R}_{\geq 0}$, and b_v is concave increasing (the damaging effect of more

[2]Nonpoint source (NPS) pollution refers to both water and air pollution from diffuse sources, that is sources without a specified fixed location. For instance, nonpoint source water pollution affects a water body from sources such as polluted runoff from agricultural areas draining into a river, or wind-borne debris blowing out to sea. Our paper deals mainly with point source pollution.

emitted pollution is accelerating),[3] $b_v(0) = 0$ and d_v is convex increasing [25]. Player v's total welfare r_v is v's benefit minus his damage cost: $b_v(x_v) - d_v\left(x_v + \sum_{u\in\delta_G^-(v)} w_{uv}x_u\right)$, where, $\delta_G^-(v) = \{u \in V : (u,v) \in E\}$, $\delta_G^+(v) = \{u \in V : (v,u) \in E\}$. Thus, player v is affected via the damage function by his own discharged pollution if $x_v = 1$ and by the total discounted pollution of his neighbours. This models that pollution spreads along the edges of G. We assume that the government decides on the allowable local level of pollution p_v, for every $v \in V$. This imposes the following constraints for every player $v \in V$: $x_v \le q_v$, $x_v + \sum_{u\in\delta_G^-(v)} w_{uv}x_u \le p_v$. Our first application assumes $x_v \in \{0,1\}$ and $q_v = 1$, $\forall v \in V$. In the second application $x_v \in \{0,1,\ldots,q_v\}$ and $q_v \in \mathbb{N}$.

The problem of social welfare maximization can be formulated in the general form by the following integer program:

$$\max\ R(x) = \sum_{v\in V}\left(b_v(x_v) - d_v\left(x_v + \sum_{u\in\delta_G^-(v)} w_{uv}x_u\right)\right) \quad (1)$$

$$\text{s.t.} \quad \sum_{v\in V} x_v \le p \quad (2)$$

$$x_v + \sum_{u\in\delta_G^-(v)} w_{uv}x_u \le p_v,\ \forall v \in V \quad (3)$$

$$x_v \in \{0,1,\ldots,q_v\},\ \forall v \in V \quad (4)$$

where (2) is called global constraint and (3) are local constraints. We call $x_v + \sum_{u\in\delta_G^-(v)} w_{uv}x_u$ the local level of pollution of v. The bound q_v is decided by the government and for this application has value of 1. The above convex integer program is called a pollution game (PG) on G. We call this problem PG with integer variables (if $x_v \in \mathbb{Z}$) or with binary variables (if $x_v \in \{0,1\}$). For an instance I of PG, $|I|$ denotes the number of bits to encode I, and if $q \in poly(|I|)$, where $q = \max_{v\in V}\{q_v\}+1$, we call this problem PG with polynomial size integer variables.

In our second application formulated by the above convex program we consider an area of n cities each one administered by its mayor (agent) where there are available observations of car traffic patterns. More precisely we consider a network represented by a weighted digraph $G = (V,E,w)$, where V is the set of n agents (mayors of the cities), E is the set of roads connecting cities s.t. $(u,v) \in E$ if and only if u and v are neighbouring cities, and $w : E \to \mathbb{R}$ represents the percentage of cars entering a city from a neighboring one i.e. w_{uv} denotes the percentage of cars driving from u to v in some time interval measured by observations. The duty of the regulator is to allocate a number of licences to the agents (mayors) such that the total welfare is maximized while fulfilling a number of constraints. We denote by x_u the number of licences allocated to agent u. The agent with x_u licences gains a benefit of $b_u(x_u)$ which is a monetary income coming from selling these x_u licences to car drivers (our model does not model this explicitly but just assumes for simplicity that all x_u licences are sold). The pollution damage caused in the area of agent u is given by $d_u(x_u + \sum_{v\in\delta_G^-(u)} w_{vu}x_v)$. The total welfare that the regulator aims to maximize is: $\sum_{u\in V} b_u(x_u) - d_u(x_u + \sum_{v\in\delta_G^-(u)} w_{vu}x_v)$.

The total number of licences is bounded by a number p given in the input of the problem. Naturally a percentage of cars with licences from city u remains in u and the rest is split and drives into the neighboring cities. We denote by w_u the percentage of cars remaining in u and w'_{vu} the percentage of cars entering u from neighbouring city v. The maximum number of cars (maximum number of licences) allowed at any moment in city u is bounded by p'_u also given in the input. This is represented by the local constraint: $w_u x_u + \sum_{v\in\delta(u)} w'_{vu}x_v \le p'_u$. If $w_u \ne 0$ the last inequality can equivalently be written as $x_u + \sum_{v\in\delta(u)} w_{vu}x_v \le p_u$, where $w_{vu} = w'_{vu}/w_u$ and $p_u = p'_u/w_u$. There is also a bound q_u on the number of licences issued in city $u, \forall u \in V$, thus we can model this second application as (1) – (4).

Planar graphs are close to real applications, and it is natural to study our second application on planar networks [40]. Imagine a collection of cities (each being a contiguous geographic area) and roads connecting them. This defines a planar map where we only consider edges (roads) between neighbouring cities, which implies a planar graph. We disregard other roads and we consider only frequent driving patterns in a time interval measured by observations. They correspond to frequent commuters, e.g., between house and work, which typically are neighbouring cities.

In the following sections we assume that b_v and d_v are both linear functions with slopes s_v^0 and s_v^1 respectively, i.e. $b_v(x) = s_v^0 x$ and $d_v(y) = s_v^1 y$, for any $v \in V$. The social welfare function is $R(x) = \sum_{v\in V} \omega_v x_v$, where $\omega_v = s_v^0 - s_v^1 - \sum_{u\in\delta_G^+(v)} s_u^1 w_{vu}$ $(R(x) = \sum_{v\in V} b_v(x_v) - d_v(x_v + \sum_{u\in\delta_G^-(v)} w_{uv}x_u) = \sum_{v\in V} s_v^0 x_v - s_v^1(x_v + \sum_{u\in\delta_G^-(v)} w_{uv}x_u) = \sum_{v\in V}\omega_v x_v)$.

3.2 Basic definitions

Let $I = (G,\mathbf{b},\mathbf{d},\mathbf{p},\mathbf{q})$ be an instance of PG, where $\mathbf{b} = (b_v)_{v\in V}$, $\mathbf{d} = (d_v)_{v\in V}$, $\mathbf{p} = (p_v)_{v\in V}$ and $\mathbf{q} = (q_v)_{v\in V}$ (b_v is assumed private information of v and other parameters are public). Let $\mathcal{I}$ be the set of all instances, and $\mathcal{X}$ the set of feasible allocations. Given a digraph $G = (V,E)$, $G^{un} = (V, E^{un})$, where $E^{un} = \{(u,v) : (u,v) \in E \text{ or } (v,u) \in E\}$. A mechanism $\phi = (X,P)$ consists of an allocation $X : \mathcal{I} \to \mathcal{X}$ and payment function $P : \mathcal{I} \to \mathbb{R}_{\ge 0}^{|V|}$ ($X(I)$ satisfies (2)–(4)). For any vector x, x_{-u} denotes vector x without its u-th component. Note, $r_v(X(I)) = b_v(X_v(I)) - d_v(X_v(I) + \sum_{u\in\delta_G^-(v)} w_{uv}X_u(I))$ is the welfare of player v under $X(I)$. A mechanism $\phi = (X,P)$ is truthful, if for any b_{-v}, b_v and b'_v, $r_v(X(b_v,b_{-v})) - P_v(b_v,b_{-v}) \ge r_v(X(b'_v,b_{-v})) - P_v(b'_v,b_{-v})$. A randomized mechanism is truthful in expectation if for any b_{-v}, b_v and b'_v, $\mathbb{E}(r_v(X(b_v,b_{-v})) - P_v(b_v,b_{-v})) \ge \mathbb{E}(r_v(X(b'_v,b_{-v})) - P_v(b'_v,b_{-v}))$, where $\mathbb{E}(\cdot)$ is over the algorithm's random bits. $OPT_G^{fr}(PG)$ ($OPT_G^{in}(PG)$, resp.) denotes the value of the optimal fractional (integral, resp.) solution of PG on G. A mechanism is individually rational if each agent v has non-negative utility when he declares b_v, regardless of the other agents' declarations. The integrality gap of PG on G is defined as $\frac{OPT_G^{fr}(PG)}{OPT_G^{in}(PG)}$. The approximation ratio of an algorithm $\mathcal{A}$ w.r.t. $OPT_G^{in}(PG)$

[3] [25] uses cost function rather than benefit function, which can be viewed as $M_v - b_v(x_v)$, with M_v a large constant for any $v \in V$. The author assumes that cost function is convex decreasing and it is equivalent to $b_v(x_v)$ being a concave increasing function. We use benefit function rather than cost function for ease of analysis.

(resp. $OPT_G^{fr}(PG)$) is $\eta^{in}(\mathcal{A}) = \frac{OPT_G^{in}(PG)}{R(\mathcal{A})}$ ($\eta^{fr}(\mathcal{A}) = \frac{OPT_G^{fr}(PG)}{R(\mathcal{A})}$), where $R(\mathcal{A})$ is the objective value of the $\mathcal{A}$'s solution. If unspecified, the approximation ratio refers to η^{in}. An FPTAS (PTAS, EPTAS, resp.) [4] for a problem $\mathcal{P}$ is an algorithm $\mathcal{A}$ that for any $\epsilon > 0$ and any instance I of $\mathcal{P}$, outputs a solution with the objective value at least $(1 - \epsilon)OPT_I^{in}(\mathcal{P})$ and terminates in time $poly(\frac{1}{\epsilon}, |I|)$ ($(\frac{1}{\epsilon}|I|)^{g(\frac{1}{\epsilon})}$ and $g(\frac{1}{\epsilon})poly(|I|)$, resp.), where g is a function independent from I. Let $\gamma_k = \min\{2k^2+2, 8k, \frac{k}{(1-\frac{1}{k}(1+(\frac{2}{k})^{\frac{1}{3}}))^k}\} = (e+o(1))k = O(k)$, and $[n] = \{1, \ldots, n\}$.

Algorithms for packing problems. A linear constraint $ax \leq b$ with $x \in \mathbb{N}^n_{\geq 0}$ an integer vector, and $a, b \in \mathbb{R}^n_{\geq 0}$ are vectors, is called a packing constraint. A linear (resp. convex) maximization programming problem with packing constraints is called a linear (resp. convex) packing programming problem. A k-column-sparse packing integer program is one in which each variable j participates in at most k constraints.

Proposition 1 ([8],[31]). *There is a polynomial time deterministic algorithm for k column sparse linear packing programming problem with binary variables, achieving the approximation ratio $\eta^{fr} = \gamma_k$.*

Proposition 2 ([26]). *For any linear packing programming problem, if there is a polynomial deterministic algorithm with the approximation ratio η^{fr} for this problem, then there is a polynomial, randomized, individually rational, η^{fr}-approximation mechanism for the same problem that is truthful in expectation.*

4. HARDNESS

PG is weakly NP-hard even on trees without global constraint. Suppose that the underlying graph is a star. We observe that we can reduce to PG the knapsack problem, where the weights w_{uv} are the sizes of the items.

We also note that inequality (2) can also be written as equality

$$\sum_{u \in V} x_u = p \qquad (2')$$

since the upper limit of the total amount of the pollution is controlled by the government. If $\sum_{v \in V} x_v < p$ in the final allocation, then the government can simply set p equal to $\sum_{v \in V} x_v$ without any changes. However, for computational issues, these two representations lead to different computational complexity. If inequality (2) is replaced by (2′), then even finding a feasible solution of PG is NP-complete. Therefore, unless stated otherwise, we always suppose inequality (2) as a constraint of PG.

Theorem 1. *Finding a feasible solution which satisfies constraints (2′) and (3) to PG when $p_v = 1\ \forall v \in V$ and $w_{uv} > 0$ for any $(u, v) \in E$ is NP-complete.*

Proof. It is straight forward that the problem is in NP. Consider now a formula of monotone 1-in-3 SAT where an instance of this problem consists of n Boolean variables and m clauses. A YES instance is one in which an assignment to its Boolean variables is such that exactly one literal from each clause is true. The problem is known to be NP-Complete even when there are no negations [33]. The following proof is inspired by the reduction of 3-SAT to Independent Set (p. 248 [12]).

Let us represent a clause, say $(x \vee y \vee z)$, by a triangle with vertices labeled x, y, z. Repeat this construction for all clauses. Next consider one of the literals, say x, which appears in k clauses $C_{i_1}, \ldots, C_{i_k}$. Let $Tr_{i_1}, \ldots, Tr_{i_k}$ be the triangles of the clauses $C_{i_1}, \ldots, C_{i_k}$ respectively. Then connect x of Tr_{i_1} with all the vertices of $Tr_{i_2}, \ldots, Tr_{i_k}$ except those labeled with x. Repeat this construction for x in all these triangles and for all literals. For example consider the formula $\Phi = (x_1 \vee x_2 \vee x_3)(x_1 \vee x_4 \vee x_5)$ (see Figure 1). First construct the triangles labeled x_1, x_2, x_3 and x_1, x_4, x_5 for the two clauses respectively. Then connect vertex x_1 of the first clause with the vertices x_4 and x_5 of the second clause. In the same way connect vertex x_1 of the second clause with the vertices x_2 and x_3 of the first clause.

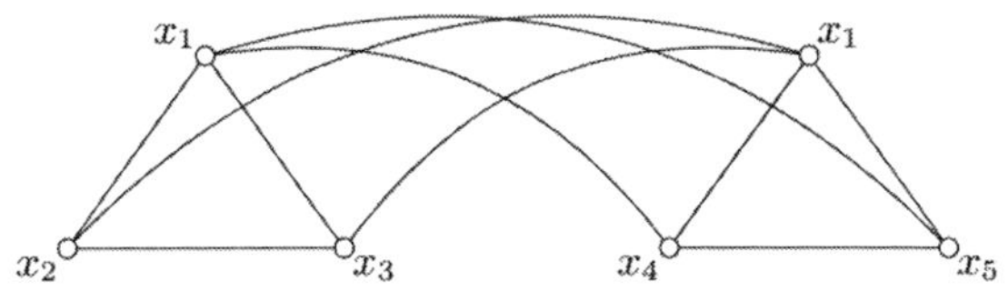

Figure 1: A gadget of reduction

Consider now an instance of 1-in-3 SAT which is true and let $G = (V, E)$ be the corresponding graph constructed as above. Furthermore for every vertex $u \in V$, let $p_u = 1$ and $p = m$. Suppose that we have a truth assignment which satisfies all the clauses. Then this means we choose p vertices in G without violating any of the constraints. Indeed if two vertices have the same label then they are not connected. If they have different labels, say x from clause C_1 and y from clause C_2 and they are connected, this is because their corresponding clauses have a common literal, either x or y. Thus if one of them has value true, the other will have value false for the formula to be satisfiable. Finally if two vertices belong to the same clause, only one of them will have the value true.

Suppose now that we can decide in polynomial time whether there is a solution in an instance of a graph constructed by a formula as described above with $p = m$ vertices when $p_v = 1$, $\forall v \in V$. Then setting the literal in the set $\{v : x_v = 1\}$ is a solution of 1-in-3 SAT. The argument is as follows, in each triangle, there is exactly one vertex such that its value is one since at most one vertex in each triangle can be selected and there are m triangles and $p = m$. By the construction of G, these vertices consist of a solution of 1-in-3 SAT. Thus exactly one literal in every clause has the value true in the formula. □

Theorem 2. *There is no EPTAS for PG with binary variables on the directed planar graph $G = (V, E)$ when b_v and d_v are both linear functions, for any $v \in V$.*

Proof. Consider PG on the following simple planar graph. There are $n+2$ vertices labeled as $\{o_1, o_2, 1, 2, ..., n\}$ and the edge set $E = \{(i, o_j), i \in [n], j \in [2]\}$. Weights w_{io_j},

[4] Fully Polynomial Time Approximation Scheme, Polynomial Time Approximation Scheme and Efficient Polynomial Time Approximation Scheme respectively

$i \in [n], j \in [2]$. For any two dimensional knapsack problem, there exists an instance of PG with binary variables without the global constraint on such a simple graph exactly corresponding to this two dimensional knapsack problem. According to [24], there is no EPTAS for two dimensional knapsack. Hence, there is no EPTAS for PG on this simple planar graph. □

5. CONSTANT APPROXIMATION ON PLANAR GRAPHS

5.1 Algorithms for (α, β)-decomposition

Given a digraph $G = (V, E)$ and a subset $U \subset V$, we call significant neighbours of U, $SN_G(U)$, all the vertices in $V \backslash U$ with at least two neighbours in U (see figure 2). Consider a partition $\{V^i\}_{i=1}^{\alpha}$ of V. Now let $SN_{G^{un}}(V^i) = \{u \notin V^i \mid \exists v \in V^i$, s.t. u is a significant neighbour of v w.r.t. $V^i\}$ denote the significant neighbours of V^i in G^{un}. Let G^i be the induced subgraph of $V^i \cup SN_{G^{un}}(V^i)$ in G^{un}. A partition $\{V^i\}_{i=1}^{\alpha}$ of V is called an (α, β)-partition (or (α, β)-decomposition) of G if for any $i \in [\alpha]$ and $v \in V^i$, $|\delta_{G^i(v)}| \leq \beta$, where α, β are two given positive integers.

According to the following Lemma 1, we can obtain a constant approximation for PG with integer variables for any graph with (α, β)-decomposition. Such a decomposition of planar graphs will be presented later.

LEMMA 1. *If a directed graph G has an (α, β)-decomposition, then there is a deterministic ($\eta^{fr} = \alpha\gamma_{\beta+2} + 1$)-approximation algorithm for PG with integer variables, and, a truthful in expectation mechanism for the same problem with the same approximation.*

PROOF. If there is an η^{fr}-approximation algorithm for a linear packing problem with binary variables, then there is an $(\eta^{fr} + 1)$-approximation algorithm for the same problem with integer variables [8]. Hence, it is sufficient to show that there is an $(\eta^{fr} = \alpha\gamma_{\beta+2})$-approximation algorithm for PG with binary variables. Now we consider PG with binary variables. Let $\{V^i\}_{i=1}^{\alpha}$ be an (α, β)-decomposition of graph G. Let x^* be the optimal fractional solution of PG with binary variables. Then $R(x^*) \leq \alpha \max_{i \in [\alpha]}\{R(x^*_{V^i})\}$, where $x^*_{V^i}$ is a fractional solution such that its value is equal to x^*_v, for any $v \in V^i$ and 0 otherwise. Let PG_i denote the PG on G by setting $x_v = 0$, for any $v \notin V^i$. Note that $x^*_{V^i}$ is a feasible solution for PG_i, which gives $R(x^*_{V^i}) \leq OPT^{fr}(PG_i)$. W.l.o.g. we suppose $w_{uv} \leq p_v$, for any $(u, v) \in E$ and $v \in V$ (otherwise $x_v \equiv 0$ for PG). Observe that in PG_i, only x_v, $v \in V^i$ are variables. Now for any $v \in V^i$, let us see how many constraints in PG_i contain x_v. Suppose $u \in V \backslash V^i$ is a neighbour of v in G^{un}. If u is not a significant neighbour of v, since $w_{vu} \leq p_u$, we can remove the constraint $w_{vu}x_v \leq p_v$ in PG_i. Hence, only the local constraints of the significant neighbours of v remain containing variable x_v. As $\{V^i\}_{i=1}^{\alpha}$ is an (α, β)-decomposition of graph G, there are at most $\beta + 1$ local constraints containing variable x_v (which includes the local constraint of vertex v itself). Together with the global constraint, we know x_v appears in at most $\beta + 2$ constraints in PG_i, for any $v \in V^i$, which means PG_i is $\beta + 2$ column sparse. Therefore, by Proposition 1, there is a polynomial deterministic algorithm for PG_i with binary variables, finding an integer solution y_i for PG_i such that $\gamma_{\beta+2}R(y_i) \geq OPT^{fr}(PG_i)$, for any $i \in [\alpha]$. Then $\alpha\gamma_{\beta+2} \max_{i \in [\alpha]}\{R(y_i)\} \geq \alpha \max_{i \in [\alpha]}\{OPT^{fr}(PG_i)\} \geq \alpha \max_{i \in [\alpha]}\{R(x^*_{V^i})\} \geq R(x^*) = OPT^{fr}(PG)$. A truthful in expectation mechanism with the same approximation ratio is guaranteed by Proposition 2. □

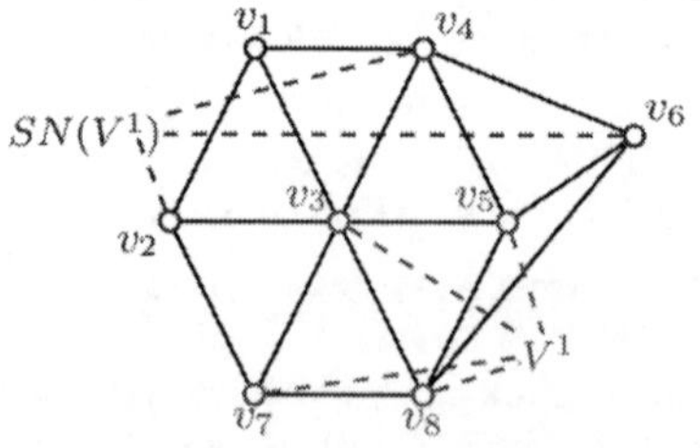

Figure 2: Significant neighbours $SN(V^1) = \{v_2, v_4, v_6\}$ of $V^1 = \{v_3, v_5, v_7, v_8\}$ in the graph of solid black lines.

Planar graphs. The integrality gap of PG on planar graphs is at least 4 as shown by a complete graph with four vertices. For a small $\epsilon > 0$, let $w_{uv} = \epsilon$, for any $(u, v) \in E$, and $p_v = \omega_v = 1$, for any $v \in V$. There is no global constraint. The optimal integer solution of PG on this graph is $x_v = 1$ for some $v \in V$ and $x_u = 0$ for all $u \neq v$, implying the optimal objective value 1. However, setting $x_v = 1 - 4\epsilon$, for any $v \in V$ provides a feasible fractional solution, which gives the objective value $4 - 16\epsilon$. Therefore, the integrality gap is at least 4, meaning that our LP relaxation cannot lead to better than 4 (e.g., PTAS) approximations.

We provide an (α, β)-decomposition of any planar graph, with $\alpha = 18$, $\beta = 6$ or $\alpha = 54$, $\beta = 4$. We did not attempt to optimize these two parameters.

THEOREM 3. *There is an (α, β)-decomposition of a directed planar graph $G = (V, E)$, where $(\alpha, \beta) = (18, 6)$ or $(54, 4)$.*

PROOF. Let $G' = G^{un}$. Suppose G' is connected, otherwise we can run the algorithm on each connected component respectively. Define the sequence of vertex sets $\{N_i\}_i$ of G' as follows. Fix an arbitrary vertex $v_0 \in V$, and let $N_1 = \{v_0\}$, and N_i is defined recursively as

$$N_{i+1} = \{v \in V \backslash \bigcup_{j=1}^{i} N_j \mid (v, u) \in G', \text{ for some } u \in N_i\},$$

for $i = 1, 2, ..., |V|$. By this definition, for any $v \in N_i$ and $u \in N_j$, if $|i - j| \geq 2$, then $(u, v) \notin E'$. We also observe that N_i is the set of vertices with distance $i - 1$ to v_0 in G' (i.e., the shortest path distance with respect to the number of edges). Suppose the length of the sequence $\{N_i\}_i$ is K. Let $S_i = \{j \equiv i \pmod 3) \mid j \in [K]\}$, $i \in [3]$. Let also $S_0 = S_3$, and $V^i = \bigcup_{j \in S_i} N_j$, $i \in [3]$. We will now need the following Lemmas 2, 3 and 4.

LEMMA 2. *For each $v \in N_j$, the number of significant neighbours of v in N_{j-1} w.r.t. N_j is at most two.*

PROOF. Suppose there exists $v_1 \neq v_2 \neq v_3 \in N_{j-1} \cap \delta_{G'}(v)$ and $v \neq u_1, u_2, u_3 \in N_j$ such that $(u_i, v_i) \in G'$, $i \in [3]$ (see Figure 3). By the definition of N_j, there is a path from v_0 to v_i, $i \in [3]$, and $(v, v_i) \in G'$, $i \in [3]$. W.l.o.g. suppose v_2 is inside the circle constructed from the path of v_0 to v_1, v_3 and edges (v, v_1) and (v, v_3) in the planar embedding. Then (u_2, v_2) will intersect this circle, which contradicts that G' is planar. □

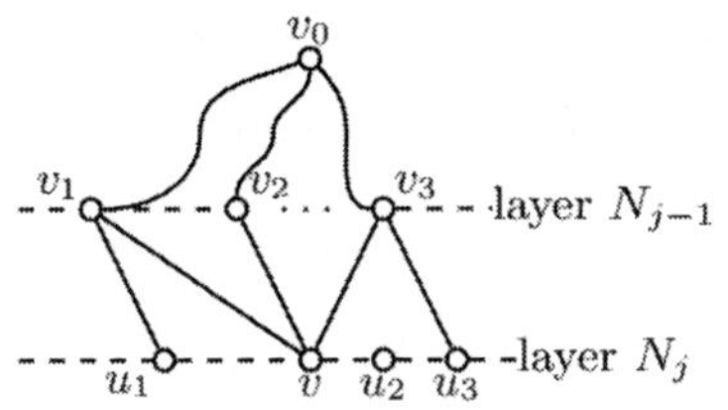

Figure 3: An illustration of relations between N_j and N_{j-1}.

Next, we partition N_j into two sets N_j^1 and N_j^2 such that each vertex in N_j^i has at most two significant neighbours in N_{j+1} w.r.t. N_j^i, $i \in [2]$. We say two vertices $v, u \in N_j$ are connected by a zigzag path if there exists a path $(v, v_1, v_2, v_3, .., v_s, u)$ in G' such that v_i and v_{i+1} alternatively belong to N_{j+1} and N_j, i.e., $v_1 \in N_{j+1}$ and $v_2 \in N_j$. Note that s must be odd. We define the zigzag length of this zigzag path as $\frac{s+1}{2}$. The zigzag distance between v and u, denoted d^z_{uv}, is defined as the zigzag length of the shortest zigzag path between v and u if there exists one and ∞ otherwise. Note that the zigzag distance of v to itself is zero. The partition algorithm PA_1 works as follows (see Algorithm 1). Let $N_j^1 = A_1$ and $N_j^2 = A_2$, where A_1, A_2 is output of PA_1. (Note that PA_1 is run for each $j \in [K]$.)

Algorithm 1: (PA_1)

```
Input: A1, A2 ← ∅, B ← N_j
Output: A1, A2
while B ≠ ∅ do
    Select a vertex v ∈ B;
    Find B1, B2 below by BFS.
    B1 ← {u ∈ N_j | d^z_uv is odd};
    B2 ← {u ∈ N_j | d^z_uv is even};
    A1 ← A1 ∪ B1; A2 ← A2 ∪ B2;
    B ← B\(B1 ∪ B2);
```

Algorithm 2: (PA_2)

```
Input: A1, A2, A3 ← ∅, B ← N_j^i
Output: A1, A2, A3
while B ≠ ∅ do
    Select a vertex v ∈ B;
    Find B_k's below by BFS.
    for k ← 1 to 3 do
        B_k ← {u ∈ N_j^i | d^{N_j}_uv ≡ k(mod 3)}
        A_k ← A_k ∪ B_k;
    B ← B\(B1 ∪ B2 ∪ B3);
```

LEMMA 3. *For each $v \in N_j^i$, v has at most two significant neighbours in N_{j+1} w.r.t. N_j^i, $i \in [2]$.*

PROOF. First, note that if v and u are selected in different iterations of the while loop in Algorithm 1, there is no zigzag path between them. Therefore, for a single iteration of the while loop, suppose $v \in B$ is selected. We only need to show that for any $u \in B_i$, u has at most two significant neighbours in N_{j+1} w.r.t. B_i, $i \in [2]$. First, note that $v \in B_2$ (its zigzag distance to itself is 0). Since all the other vertices in B_2 have zigzag distance to v at least two, v has no significant neighbours w.r.t. B_2 in N_{j+1}. Now fix $i \in [2]$. Consider any two vertices $u_1, u_2 \in B_i$, u_1 and u_2 connect to the same vertex in N_{j+1} only if they have the same zigzag distance to v. Suppose there exists three different vertices v_1, v_2, $v_3 \in N_{j+1}$, such that they are significant neighbours of u_1 w.r.t. B_i (see Fig. 4). By similar arguments as above, there exists zigzag paths from v to v_i, $i \in [3]$. Also note that edges $(u_1, v_i) \in G'$, $i \in [3]$. W.l.o.g. suppose v_2 is in the circle constructed from the zigzag paths v to v_1, v_3 and edges (u_1, v_1) and (u_1, v_3). Since the graph G' is planar, there exists no edge between v_2 and another vertex in B_i with the same zigzag distance as u_1. Therefore, u_1 has at most two significant neighbours w.r.t. B_i in N_{j+1}. □

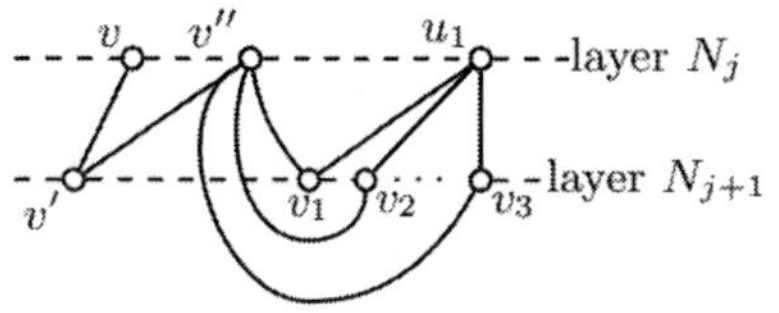

Figure 4: Relations between N_j and N_{j+1}

Next we will partition each set N_j^i, $i \in [2]$, $j \in [K]$ into a constant number of sets $\{N_j^{ik}\}_k$ such that each vertex in N_j^{ik} has at most a constant number of significant neighbours w.r.t. N_j^{ik} in N_j. We provide two partition algorithms. Both algorithms in spirit are similar to Algorithm 1. For any two vertices v, $u \in N_j^i$, we say they are connected by a N_j-path if there exists a path $(v, v_1, v_2, \cdots, v_s, u)$ in G' such that $v_\ell \in N_j$, $\forall \ell \in [s]$. N_j-distance of two vertices v, $u \in N_j^i$, denoted $d^{N_j}_{uv}$, is defined as the number of edges of the shortest N_j-path between v and u if there exists one and ∞ otherwise. The process works as PA_2 (Algorithm 2). Note that $v \in B_3$, because the N_j-distance from v to itself is zero. Let $N_j^{ik} = A_k$, $k \in [3]$ (where A_1, A_2, A_3 are a partition of N_j^i output by PA_2).

LEMMA 4. *For any $k \in [3]$, and each $v \in N_j^{ik}$, v has at most 2 neighbours in N_j, or has no neighbours in N_j^{ik} nor significant neighbours w.r.t. N_j^{ik} in $N_j \backslash N_j^{ik}$.*

PROOF. First, note that if v and u are selected in different iterations of while loop in Algorithm 2, there is no N_j-path between them. Therefore, for a single iteration of the while loop, suppose $v \in B$ is selected. Since $v \in B_3$ (N_j distance to itself is 0), v has no neighbours in B_3 nor significant neighbours w.r.t. B_3 in $N_j \backslash B_3$ by PA_2. Now fix $k \in [3]$. Consider any two vertices $u_1, u_2 \in B_k$, u_1 and u_2 connect to the same vertex in N_j only if they have the same N_j-distance to v. Next we will show for any $u_1 \neq v$ and $u_1 \in B_k$, for any k, u_1 has at most two neighbours in N_j. Suppose there exist three different vertices u_1, u_2, $u_3 \in N_j$, such that $(u_1, u_2) \in G'$ and $(u_1, u_3) \in G'$. By similar arguments as above, there exists N_j-paths from v to u_i, $i \in [3]$. Since $u_i \in N_j$, $i \in [3]$, there exist paths in G' from v_0 to u_i, $i \in [3]$. We observe that it is only possible that u_1 is in the circle constructed from the N_j paths v to u_2, u_3 and paths from v_0 to u_2 and u_3 (the case where u_2 or u_3 is in the circle constructed by the other two vertices with v and v_0 will violate the planarity of G') (see Fig. 5). Since graph G' is planar, there exists no edge between u_1 and another vertex

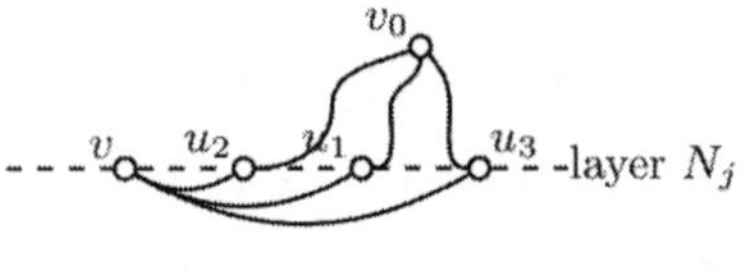

Figure 5: Relations between N_j and N_j.

in N_j (due to that such a vertex will have a path to v and v_0 respectively). Therefore, u_1 has at most two neighbours in N_j. □

Combining Lemmas 2, 3 and 4, $\{N_j^{ik}\}_{ijk}$ is an (α, β)- decomposition of G with $(\alpha, \beta) = (18, 6)$. The second partition procedure is based on Algorithm 2 and we just sketch it here. We can partition N_j^{ik} into another three sets, e.g. $N_j^{ik\ell}$, $\ell \in [3]$ by the same arguments as above by just partitioning it according to the length of path (mod 3) such that each vertex in $N_j^{ik\ell}$ will not have any neighbours in $N_j^{ik\ell}$. This procedure is exactly the same as Algorithm 2 where N_j^i is replaced with N_j^{ik}. Thus $\{N_j^{ik\ell}\}_{ijk\ell}$ is a $(54, 4)$-decomposition of G, which finishes the proof of Theorem 3.

By Theorem 3 and Lemma 1, and observing that $18 \min\{\gamma_8, 3\gamma_6\} = 18\gamma_8 = O(1)$, we have

THEOREM 4. *There is a randomized, individually rational and truthful in expectation* $(18\gamma_8 + 1)$*-approximation mechanism for PG on planar graphs with integer variables.*

5.2 Better approximation under some mild condition

We will use the 4-color theorem for planar graphs to present an improved $(6 + \epsilon)$-approximate truthful in expectation mechanism for PG under the following natural (and mild) assumption:

$$\sum_{u \in \delta_G^-(v)} w_{uv} \leq p_v \tag{5}$$

This constraint means that if each of v's neighbours emits only one unit amount of pollution, the level of pollution in v will not exceed v's local level of pollution. Let x^1 be the optimal fractional solution of PG with binary variables without global constraint on planar graph G.

THEOREM 5. *Suppose condition (5) holds and* $R(x^1) \geq 1$. *There is a randomized, individually rational,* $(\eta^{fr} = 6 + \epsilon)$*-approximation mechanism that is truthful in expectation for PG on planar graphs with integer variables, terminating in time* $poly(|I|, \log(\frac{1}{\epsilon}))$.

PROOF. Note that if condition (5) holds, then every independent set is a feasible solution for PG with binary variables without global constraint. By 4-color theorem [5, 32] for planar graphs, there is an independent set $S \subset V$ such that $4R(z_S) \geq R(x^1)$ where z_S is defined by $z_v = 1$ if $v \in S$ and $z_v = 0$ otherwise. Further there is an $O(|V|^2)$ algorithm finding z_S [32]. By theorem 3 of [23] and $R(x^1) \geq 1$, there is a deterministic $(\eta^{fr} = 5 + \epsilon)$-approximation algorithm for PG with binary variables, running in $poly(|I|, \log(\frac{1}{\epsilon}))$ time. Then there is a deterministic $(\eta^{fr} = 6 + \epsilon)$-approximation algorithm for PG with integer variables, running in time $poly(|I|, \log(\frac{1}{\epsilon}))$ [8]. By Proposition 2, this $(\eta^{fr} = 6 + \epsilon)$-approximation mechanism is truthful in expectation for PG with integer variables. □

6. CONCLUSION AND DISCUSSION

We present a new network model for the pollution control problem which is studied on planar networks. These networks can be applied to model air pollution from diffuse sources. Our results include computational hardness results, a constant approximation algorithm and truthful in expectation mechanisms. We obtain these results by introducing novel algorithmic techniques for planar graphs which are of independent interest. Many interesting open problems arise:

1. Determine whether PG with binary variables on planar graphs admits a PTAS or is APX-hard.
2. What about lower bounds on truthful (deterministic, universal, truthful in expectation) mechanisms for PG? Can externality be used to obtain such lower bounds?
3. How to generalize our results to other graphs, e.g., Euclidean graphs?

REFERENCES

[1] Air quality in Europe - 2014 Report. European Environment Agency Report No. 5/2014 `http://www.eea.europa.eu/publications/air-quality-in-europe-2014`.

[2] Emissions trading schemes around the world. `http://parlinfo.aph.gov.au/parlInfo/download/library/prspub/2501441/upload_binary/2501441.pdf`, 2013.

[3] Emissions auctions. `https://www.theice.com/emissions/auctions`, 2014.

[4] State of the Air 2014 Report. *American Lung Association*, 30 April, 2014. `http://www.stateoftheair.org/2014/key-findings/`.

[5] K. I. Appel and W. Haken. *Every planar map is four colorable*, volume 98. American mathematical society Providence, RI, 1989.

[6] B. S. Baker. Approximation algorithms for NP-complete problems on planar graphs. *J. of the ACM*, 41(1):153–180, 1994.

[7] D. Banister. The sustainable mobility paradigm. *Transport policy*, 15(2):73–80, 2008.

[8] N. Bansal, N. Korula, V. Nagarajan, and A. Srinivasan. Solving packing integer programs via randomized rounding with alterations. *Theory of Computing*, 8(1):533–565, 2012.

[9] A. Belitskaya. Network Game of Pollution Cost Reduction. *Contributions to Game Theory and Management*, 6(0):24–34, 2013.

[10] K. Conrad and J. Wang. On the design of incentive mechanisms in environmental policy. *Environmental and Resource Economics*, 3(3):245–262, 1993.

[11] P. Dasgupta, P. Hammond, and E. Maskin. On imperfect information and optimal pollution control. *The Review of Economic Studies*, pages 857–860, 1980.

[12] S. Dasgupta, C. H. Papadimitriou, and U. Vazirani. *Algorithms*. McGraw-Hill, Inc., 2006.

[13] B. Dong, D. Ni, and Y. Wang. Sharing a polluted river network. *Environmental and Resource Economics*, 53(3), 2012.

[14] S. Dorner, J. Shi, and D. Swayne. Multi-objective modelling and decision support using a bayesian

network approximation to a non-point source pollution model. *Environmental Modelling & Software*, 22(2):211–222, 2007.

[15] J. Farrell. Information and the coase theorem. *The Journal of Economic Perspectives*, 1(2):113–129, 1987.

[16] D. Fullerton and S. E. West. Can taxes on cars and on gasoline mimic an unavailable tax on emissions? *Journal of Environmental Economics and Management*, 43(1):135–157, 2002.

[17] L. P. Gianessi, H. M. Peskin, and G. K. Young. Analysis of national water pollution control policies: 1. a national network model. *Water Resources Research*, 17(4):796–802, 1981.

[18] L. Hurwicz. The design of mechanisms for resource allocation. *The American Economic Review*, pages 1–30, 1973.

[19] R. Innes. Regulating automobile pollution under certainty, competition, and imperfect information. *Journal of Environmental Economics and Management*, 31(2):219–239, 1996.

[20] L. Karp and J. Livernois. Using automatic tax changes to control pollution emissions. *Journal of Environmental Economics and Management*, 27(1):38–48, 1994.

[21] S. Khanna and R. Motwani. Towards a syntactic characterization of ptas. In *Proc. of the 28th STOC*, pages 329–337. ACM, 1996.

[22] J. Kim and K. Chang. An optimal tax/subsidy for output and pollution control under asymmetric information in oligopoly markets. *Journal of Regulatory Economics*, 5(2):183–197, 1993.

[23] A. Kulik and H. Shachnai. On lagrangian relaxation and subset selection problems. In *Approximation and Online Algorithms*, pages 160–173. Springer, 2009.

[24] A. Kulik and H. Shachnai. There is no eptas for two-dimensional knapsack. *Information Processing Letters*, 110(16):707–710, 2010.

[25] E. Kwerel. To tell the truth: Imperfect information and optimal pollution control. *The Review of Economic Studies*, pages 595–601, 1977.

[26] R. Lavi and C. Swamy. Truthful and near-optimal mechanism design via linear programming. *Journal of the ACM (JACM)*, 58(6):25, 2011.

[27] R. McKitrick. A cournot mechanism for pollution control under asymmetric information. *Environmental and Resource Economics*, 14(3):353–363, 1999.

[28] D. W. Montgomery. Markets in licenses and efficient pollution control programs. *J. of economic theory*, 5(3):395–418, 1972.

[29] N. Nisan, T. Roughgarden, E. Tardos, and V. V. Vazirani. *Algorithmic game theory*, volume 1. Cambridge University Press Cambridge, 2007.

[30] L. Petrosjan and G. Zaccour. Time-consistent shapley value allocation of pollution cost reduction. *Journal of Economic Dynamics and Control*, 27(3):381–398, 2003.

[31] D. Pritchard and D. Chakrabarty. Approximability of sparse integer programs. *Algorithmica*, 61(1):75–93, 2011.

[32] N. Robertson, D. Sanders, P. Seymour, and R. Thomas. A new proof of the four-colour theorem. *Electronic Research Announcements of the American Mathematical Society*, 2(1):17–25, 1996.

[33] T. J. Schaefer. The complexity of satisfiability problems. In *Proceedings of the tenth ACM STOC*, pages 216–226. ACM, 1978.

[34] K. Segerson. Uncertainty and incentives for nonpoint pollution control. *Journal of environmental economics and management*, 15(1):87–98, 1988.

[35] R. M. Singh and B. Datta. Artificial neural network modeling for identification of unknown pollution sources in groundwater with partially missing concentration observation data. *Water resources management*, 21(3):557–572, 2007.

[36] D. F. Spulber. Optimal environmental regulation under asymmetric information. *Journal of Public Economics*, 35(2):163–181, 1988.

[37] R. N. Stavins. Policy instruments for climate change: how can national governments address a global problem. *University of Chicago Law School*, page 293, 1997. Discussion Paper 97-11.

[38] R. N. Stavins. Experience with market-based environmental policy instruments. *Handbook of environmental economics*, 1:355–435, 2003.

[39] A. Trujillo-Ventura and J. Hugh E. Multiobjective air pollution monitoring network design. *Atmospheric Environment. Part A. General Topics*, 25(2):469–479, 1991.

[40] M. P. Viana, E. Strano, P. Bordin, and M. Barthelemy. The simplicity of planar networks. *Scientific reports*, 3, Article number 3495, 2013.

Manipulating Citation Indices in a Social Context

Chrystalla Pavlou
University of Edinburgh
Edinburgh, United Kingdom
C.Pavlou@sms.ed.ac.uk

Edith Elkind
University of Oxford
Oxford, United Kingdom
elkind@cs.ox.ac.uk

ABSTRACT

The h-index [6] is a popular measure of a researcher's publication activity: a researcher's h-index is the largest number x such that she has at least x papers that have received at least x citations each. It has been observed that one can manipulate her h-index by strategically merging one or more articles, and the complexity of finding a successful/optimal manipulation has been investigated for a variety of models [3, 11]. In this paper, we extend this line of research to two other popular citation indices, namely, the g-index [4] and the i10-index, and show that these indices are somewhat easier to manipulate than the h-index. We then consider settings where the manipulator would like to take into account the impact of her actions on other researchers (she may want to make sure that her manipulation does not harm her friends or that it hurts her competitors) or a group of researchers manipulate their indices simultaneously. We analyze the complexity of these problems, both in the worst-case and in the parameterized framework.

Keywords

h-index; g-index; i10-index; manipulation by merging

1. INTRODUCTION

Measuring a researcher's productivity is a notoriously difficult task: typically, hiring and promotion decisions are made based on a multitude of factors. However, many large organizations employ simple one-dimensional numerical measures of productivity as a primary filter. The perils of using the number of publications in this context are evident, and it has been argued that the total number of citations is not a good measure either, as it can be skewed by surveys and popular textbooks. Motivated by these considerations, Hirsch [6] proposed in 2005 a new citation index, which became known as the h-index: the h-index of a researcher is the largest number x such that she has at least x articles that receive at least x citations each. For instance, if Alice has 9 articles, cited by, respectively, $32, 25, 13, 8, 6, 3, 3, 2, 1$ other articles, then her h-index is 5.

This index has become very well known, and is reported by major bibliometric engines, including Google Scholar. It was covered in popular press [1], is widely discussed on blogs (see, e.g., [2, 8, 9] for a sample), and has been analyzed from an axiomatic perspective [13]. However, as it is becoming popular with administrators at universities and funding agencies, it is now evident that one needs to understand whether this index can be abused. Indeed, one of Hirsch's original motivations for proposing the h-index was that it is less susceptible to manipulation by self-citations than the total citation count: in the example above, if Alice were to write a new article that cites all of her previous articles, this would increase her citation count by 9, but her h-index would remain the same.

However, there exists a tool that is intended for legitimate purposes, yet can be quite efficient in increasing one's h-index: merging articles. Specifically, Google Scholar enables the authors to merge two or more articles into a single article. The reason for this is that Google Scholar identifies one's publications automatically by crawling the web, so if Alice's article has been posted on arXiv, appeared in a couple of workshops, was published in a conference and finally in a journal, Google Scholar would list this article several times. Alice can then merge all these entries of her Google Scholar profile and designate the representative version of her article, so that other researchers who are looking for it can identify the definitive version of her work. The citations of the merged article are computed from the citations received by its component articles (a naive approach is just to add up the citations counts of all versions; more sophisticated approaches discussed below take into account that another article may cite more than one of the component articles, and the component articles themselves may cite each other), and it is possible that the merge increases Alice's h-index. In our running example, if the citation count is updated naively, Alice can merge the two articles with 3 citations each to increase her h-index to 6.

Therefore, Alice may be tempted to merge several unrelated articles in order to increase her h-index. Google Scholar does not prevent her from doing so: she can merge articles with very different titles and groups of authors (provided she is an author on each of them). There is a good reason for this policy: for instance, if two groups of authors write two independent papers on a related topic, and then join forces for a journal version, they may want to merge all three articles on Google Scholar even though the two conference papers appear unrelated (in this case, the authors would have to proceed in two steps). There is also no limit on the number of articles one can merge, and, as argued above, it is not unusual for a paper to have 5 or 6 versions. Thus, there is very little to prevent a dishonest researcher from trying to find an optimal way of partitioning her articles into a few highly cited "super-articles"—except perhaps the sheer complexity of this task.

Indeed, recently de Keijzer and Apt [3] have demonstrated that, in the naive model, there is a polynomial-time algorithm for determining if one can increase their h-index by merging articles, but maximizing one's h-index in this way is NP-hard. In a follow-up paper, van Bevern et al. [11] consider the same questions in a

Appears in: *Proceedings of the 15th International Conference on Autonomous Agents and Multiagent Systems (AAMAS 2016), J. Thangarajah, K. Tuyls, C. Jonker, S. Marsella (eds.), May 9–13, 2016, Singapore.*

richer and more realistic model. Specifically, they work with a directed graph whose vertices are articles and whose arcs represent citations, and consider three ways of calculating the number of citations to a merged article, which they call sumCite, unionCite, and fusionCite. Briefly, sumCite computes the sum of indegrees of the articles within a merged article (i.e., this is exactly the naive measure discussed above), unionCite counts the number of distinct articles citing the components of the merged article (this is the measure currently used by Google Scholar), and fusionCite is derived by modifying unionCite so as not to double-count the citations by component articles of a merged article (see Section 2 for formal definitions). Van Bevern et al. also model the fact that a researcher may want to hide her manipulation and avoid merging obviously unrelated articles. To this end, they introduce the notion of a *compatibility graph* G, which indicates which articles can be merged, and require that each merged article corresponds to a clique in this graph. They then study the complexity of increasing/maximizing one's h-index under each of their citation measures (i.e., sumCite, unionCite, and fusionCite), both for general compatibility graphs and for the case where G is a clique. In addition to considering the worst-case complexity of these problems, they explore their parameterized complexity with respect to several natural parameters.

1.1 Our Contribution

Against this background, the contribution of our paper is twofold.

First, following the suggestion of van Bevern et al. [11], we extend the study of manipulation by merging to two other popular impact indices: the g-index and the i10-index. The g-index is the largest number x such that the researcher has at least x papers that in total receive at least x^2 citations. This index was proposed by Egghe [4] in 2006; subsequently, Woeginger [12] proposed an axiomatization for this index. The g-index behaves similarly to the h-index, but is more flexible in that it rewards a researcher both for producing a significant number of reasonably well-cited articles (as the h-index does) and for producing a small number of very highly cited articles and then remaining active in research. The i10-index is simply the number of articles with at least 10 citations; it is computed by Google Scholar, and can be seen as a very crude, but simple measure of one's impact.

We show that both of these indices are somewhat easier to manipulate than the h-index: all computational questions that are easy for the h-index remain easy for the g-index and the i10-index, and some problems that were NP-hard for the h-index become easy for the g-index and the i10-index. This provides an argument in favor of the h-index, as resistance to manipulation is a desirable quality.

Second, we investigate the settings where the manipulating researcher has to take into account the impact of her actions on other researchers. We observe that when Alice merges some of her articles, this may change Bob's citation index, either because Bob has written joint articles with Alice, or because his work is cited by Alice. (Our model assumes that when Alice merges two articles that she co-authored with Bob, these articles are automatically merged in Bob's profile. While this is currently not the case in Google Scholar, we believe that for non-strategic researchers, who probably constitute the overwhelming majority of authors, this would be a desirable feature: when Alice merges two articles, she thereby indicates that they are closely related, and this valuable information should be propagated through the system). The index of Bob may go up or down. If Bob is a friend of Alice, then Alice may decide not to merge her articles if the impact on Bob is negative: for instance, if Bob is a PhD student of Alice who is about to graduate, Alice may choose to postpone a legitimate merge, so as not to hurt Bob's chances in the job market. In contrast, if Alice and Bob are competing for the same position or award, Alice may try to maliciously merge her papers so as to lower Bob's index as much as possible (without lowering her own index). If an entire group of researchers is evaluated (as in, for instance, UK's Research Excellence Framework or Italy's Research Assessment Program), the researchers in the group may attempt to manipulate their indices simultaneously, with every researcher trying to achieve a value that is appropriate for his or her career stage. Thus, we consider the complexity of manipulating citation indices in a *social context*. Our results indicate that having to account for friends or enemies makes the manipulator's task harder: we get NP-hardness results even for very simple settings. However, some of our polynomial-time and FPT algorithms can be extended to this model.

2. PRELIMINARIES

We start by formally defining the citation indices that will be discussed in this paper. For readability, the definitions below are formulated in terms of articles and citations; however, they treat each article simply as a number, so all three indices can be defined for any multiset of non-negative integers.

DEFINITION 1. *A researcher's* h-index *is the largest natural number x such that she has at least x articles that were cited by at least x articles each. Her* g-index *is the largest natural number x such that she has x articles that in total receive at least x^2 citations. Her i10-index is simply the number of her articles that are cited at least* 10 *times.*

The value 10 in the definition of the i10-index can be replaced by any other natural number θ; we will refer to the resulting index as the *iθ-index*. For $I \in \{h, g, i10\}$, we denote the I-index of a researcher with the set of articles W by $I(W)$.

In what follows, we will mostly use the model of van Bevern et al. [11]. In this model, citations are represented by a directed acyclic graph $D = (V, A)$, where the vertices are articles and there is an arc (u, v) if article u cites article v. For each $v \in V$ and a subset of vertices $S \subseteq V$, we set $N_S^{\text{in}}(v) = \{u \mid u \in S, (u, v) \in A\}$ and $\deg_S^{\text{in}}(v) = |N_S^{\text{in}}(v)|$. The articles of each researcher correspond to a subset W of V, and the researcher can manipulate her citation indices by merging arbitrary subsets of articles in W. The result of a merge operation is a partition $\mathcal{P}$ of W, where a *merged article* is a part with cardinality at least 2. We will sometimes refer to articles in V as *atomic articles*, and, given a merged article $P \in \mathcal{P}$, we will refer to elements of P as *component articles* of P. Van Bevern et al. [11] consider three methods to compute the number of citations to a merged article P in a partition $\mathcal{P}$ of W:

- *sumCite*: the number of citations to a merged article P is set to be equal to the sum of citation counts of its component articles:

$$\mathsf{sCite}(P) = \sum_{v \in P} \deg_D^{\text{in}}(v).$$

- *unionCite*: the number of citations to a merged article P is set to be equal to the number of distinct articles that cite at least one of its component articles:

$$\mathsf{uCite}(P) = \left| \bigcup_{v \in P} N_D^{in}(v) \right|.$$

- *fusionCite*: the number of citations to a merged article P is set to be equal to the sum of two quantities: (1) the number of distinct articles in $V \setminus W$ that cite at least one component article of P and (2) the number of merged articles in $\mathcal{P}$ whose component articles cite P. Formally, for each $P' \in \mathcal{P} \setminus \{P\}$ we set $\delta(P', P) = 1$ if there exist some $v \in P'$, $w \in P$ such that $(v, w) \in A$ and $\delta(P', P) = 0$ otherwise, and let

$$\mathsf{fCite}(P) = |\bigcup_{v \in P} N^{in}_{V \setminus W}(v)| + \sum_{P' \in \mathcal{P}, P' \neq P} \delta(P', P).$$

Intuitively, these three citation measures correspond to different ways of treating parallel edges in the citation graph that arises after the merge, with sCite being the most generous and fCite being the stingiest. This is illustrated by the following example.

EXAMPLE 1. Consider the citation graph in the figure on the right. Suppose that a researcher decides to merge article 1 with article 2, and article 4 with article 5. It can be verified that for the merged article $P = \{4, 5\}$ we have $\mathsf{sCite}(P) = 4$, $\mathsf{uCite}(P) = 3$, $\mathsf{fCite}(P) = 2$. By scaling up this example appropriately, we can make the gap between sCite and uCite and between uCite and fCite arbitrarily large.

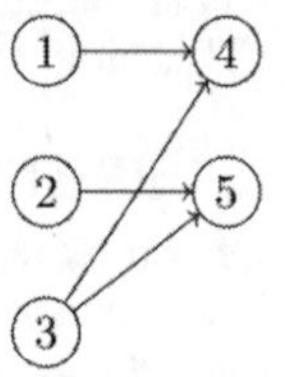

We note that, while the formal definition of fCite may appear to be complex, this is arguably the most intuitive citation measure: effectively, it recomputes the citation graph treating each merged article as a singleton.

To compute an I-index, $I \in \{h, g, i10\}$, of a partition $\mathcal{P}$ with respect to a measure $\mu \in \{\mathsf{sCite}, \mathsf{uCite}, \mathsf{fCite}\}$, we apply the usual procedure for computing this index to the multiset of non-negative integers $\{\mu(P) \mid P \in \mathcal{P}\}$; we denote the result by $I(\mathcal{P}, \mu)$.

In practice, a researcher who wants her manipulative actions to remain undetected may avoid merging obviously unrelated articles. To capture this, van Bevern et al. [11] introduce another graph on V, which they call the *compatibility graph*. This is an undirected graph $G = (V, E)$; an edge $\{u, v\} \in E$ indicates that u and v can be merged. This graph constrains the space of possible partitions of W: a partition $\mathcal{P}$ *complies with* G if each merged article $P \in \mathcal{P}$ is a clique in G. The case where arbitrary merges are allowed corresponds to G being a complete graph.

When considering an arbitrary graph H, we write $V(H)$ to denote the set of vertices of H and $E(H)$ to denote the set of edges of H.

3. COMPUTATIONAL PROBLEMS

We will now state the computational problems that will be studied in this paper. In what follows, for brevity we identify a researcher with her set of articles, i.e., instead of saying "the citation index of a researcher with the set of articles W", we say "the citation index of the set of articles W".

The most basic question one can ask in this framework is whether a researcher can improve her citation index at all; more ambitiously, one can ask whether a certain value of the index can be achieved. These questions can be asked for each $I \in \{h, g, i10\}$ and each $\mu \in \{\mathsf{sCite}, \mathsf{uCite}, \mathsf{fCite}\}$, and are captured by the following two families of problems.

(μ, I)-INDEXIMP
Input: A citation graph $D = (V, A)$, a compatibility graph $G = (V, E)$ and a set $W \subseteq V$ of articles.
Question: Is there a partition $\mathcal{P}$ of W that complies with G and satisfies $I(\mathcal{P}, \mu) > I(W)$?

(μ, I)-INDEXACH
Input: A citation graph $D = (V, A)$, a compatibility graph $G = (V, E)$, a set $W \subseteq V$ of articles and a non-negative integer t.
Question: Is there a partition $\mathcal{P}$ of W that complies with G and satisfies $I(\mathcal{P}, \mu) \geq t$?

For the h-index, these problems have been studied in previous work. Specifically, de Keijzer and Apt [3] considered the case $\mu = \mathsf{sCite}$ under the assumption that G is a complete graph, and van Bevern et al. [11] considered all three citation measures and general compatibility graphs. Thus, in what follows, we will only analyze them for $I \in \{g, i10\}$.

REMARK 1. Note that the only information about the citation graph D that is used to compute $I(\mathcal{P}, \mathsf{sCite})$, $I \in \{h, g, i10\}$, is the indegree of the nodes in W. Thus, for $\mu = \mathsf{sCite}$ we can represent the input by omitting the graph D and listing the citation counts of each article in W. When V is exponentially larger than W, this representation (which is used by de Keijzer and Apt [3]) is exponentially more succinct. Thus, a polynomial-time algorithm for the graph-based representation that needs to look at each article citing a given article is only a pseudopolynomial-time algorithm for the list-based representation. Conversely, a weak NP-hardness result for the list-based representation (e.g., one obtained by a reduction from PARTITION [5]) would not imply a hardness result for the graph-based representation. Fortunately, this distinction turns out to be immaterial: the efficient algorithms in our and previous work run in polynomial time given the list-based representation, and the hardness results are strong NP-hardness results for the list-based representation (and hence imply that the respective problems remain NP-hard under the graph-based representation).

The next type of computational problems we consider deals with maximizing one's citation index without lowering the index of another researcher (a friend), or jointly maximizing the indices of a group of friends.

(μ, I)-INDEXIMPFRIEND
Input: A citation graph $D = (V, A)$, a compatibility graph $G = (V, E)$ and two sets of articles $W_1 \subseteq V$, $W_2 \subseteq V$.
Question: Is there a partition $\mathcal{P}$ of W_1 that complies with G such that $I(\mathcal{P}, \mu) > I(W_1)$ and merging the articles according to $\mathcal{P}$ does not lower the I-index of W_2 with respect to μ?

(μ, I)-INDEXACHFRIEND
Input: A citation graph $D = (V, A)$, a compatibility graph $G = (V, E)$, two sets of articles $W_1 \subseteq V$, $W_2 \subseteq V$ and a nonnegative integer t.
Question: Is there a partition $\mathcal{P}$ of W_1 that complies with G such that $I(\mathcal{P}, \mu) \geq t$ and merging the articles according to $\mathcal{P}$ does not lower the I-index of W_2 with respect to μ?

We note that, in general, the manipulator is allowed to merge an article in $W_1 \cap W_2$ with an article in $W_1 \setminus W_2$; the discussion in the introduction suggests that merges of this form may be legitimate, and if they are not, we expect this information to be captured by G.

To model multiple researchers manipulating their citation indices simultaneously, we need a precise definition of what merges are legal. To illustrate the difficulty, consider the situation where Alice and Bob each have a single-author paper as well as a joint paper. In Google Scholar they are allowed to merge all three papers (indeed, the joint paper may be based on combining two related single-author conference papers into a journal paper): first, Alice merges her single-author paper with the joint paper, and then Bob merges his paper with this combined paper. However, this means that a merge can no longer be described as a partition of one's papers, and in particular a paper where Alice is not a co-author may contribute to her citation index.

To handle this, we propose the following formalism. Given a set of articles V and k subsets of articles $W_1 \subseteq V, \ldots, W_k \subseteq V$

we define the *mergeability graph* $M = (V, L)$, where $\{u, v\} \in L$ if and only if $u, v \in W_i$ for some $i = 1, \ldots, k$. We say that a partition $\mathcal{P}$ of $W_1 \cup \ldots \cup W_k$ is *admissible* if each part of $\mathcal{P}$ is connected in M. For $i = 1, \ldots, k$, let $I(i, \mathcal{P}, \mu)$ be the I-index of the set of non-negative integers $\{\mu(P) \mid P \in \mathcal{P}, P \cap W_i \neq \emptyset\}$. We can now define our computational problem.

(μ, I, k)-INDEXMACH
Input: A citation graph $D = (V, A)$, a compatibility graph $G = (V, E)$, k sets of articles $W_1 \subseteq V, \ldots, W_k \subseteq V$ and nonnegative integers $t_1, \ldots, t_k$.
Question: Is there an admissible partition $\mathcal{P}$ of $W_1 \cup \ldots \cup W_k$ that complies with G and satisfies $I(i, \mathcal{P}, \mu) \geq t_i$ for $i = 1, \ldots, k$?

Conversely, a researcher may want to manipulate her citation index in the presence of a competitor. Then her goal may be to increase/maximize her index while not increasing the index of another researcher, or, alternatively, to lower the competitor's index without lowering her own.

(μ, I)-INDEXIMPENEMY
Input: A citation graph $D = (V, A)$, a compatibility graph $G = (V, E)$ and two sets of articles $W_1 \subseteq V, W_2 \subseteq V$.
Question: Is there a partition $\mathcal{P}$ of W_1 that complies with G such that $I(\mathcal{P}, \mu) > I(W_1)$ and merging the articles according to $\mathcal{P}$ does not increase the I-index of W_2 with respect to μ?

(μ, I)-INDEXACHENEMY
Input: A citation graph $D = (V, A)$, a compatibility graph $G = (V, E)$, two sets of articles $W_1 \subseteq V, W_2 \subseteq V$ and a nonnegative integer t.
Question: Is there a partition $\mathcal{P}$ of W_1 that complies with G such that $I(\mathcal{P}, \mu) \geq t$ and merging the articles according to $\mathcal{P}$ does not increase the I-index of W_2 with respect to μ?

(μ, I)-INDEXHARMENEMY
Input: A citation graph $D = (V, A)$, a compatibility graph $G = (V, E)$ and two sets of articles $W_1 \subseteq V, W_2 \subseteq V$.
Question: Is there a partition $\mathcal{P}$ of W_1 that complies with G such that $I(\mathcal{P}, \mu) \geq I(W_1)$ and merging the articles according to $\mathcal{P}$ lowers the I-index of W_2 with respect to μ?

REMARK 2. Some of the computational problems introduced so far are related to each other. In particular, the improvement problem (with or without the social context) is a special case of the respective achievability problem that corresponds to setting $t = I(W) + 1$. By the same argument, INDEXMACH is at least as hard as INDEXACHFRIEND. Furthermore, it can be checked that all our hardness proofs for $\mu =$ sCite can be adapted to show hardness for $\mu =$ uCite and hardness proofs for $\mu =$ uCite can be adapted to show hardness for $\mu =$ fCite. Also, if a problem is hard for a single researcher, it clearly remains hard in a social context (note, however, that INDEXHARMENEMY is *not* a generalization of any of our single-researcher problems). Therefore, in what follows, once we prove a hardness result for an "easier" problem, we do not discuss the "harder" problems separately. Conversely, once we obtain an algorithm for a "harder" problem, we do not discuss the "easier" problems.

All of the problems listed above are in NP, so, in what follows, to prove that any of them is NP-complete, it is sufficient to show that it is NP-hard. To prove our hardness results, we will use reductions from the following well-known NP-hard problems.

CLIQUE [5]
Input: An n-vertex graph H and a positive integer k with $k \leq n$.
Question: Does H contain a clique of size at least k?

INDEPENDENT SET [5]
Input: An n-vertex graph H and a positive integer $k \leq n$.
Question: Does H have an independent set of size at least k?

3D MATCHING [5]
Input: A tuple (X, Y, Z, M), where X, Y and Z are disjoint sets of size n each and $M \subset X \times Y \times Z$.
Question: Does M contain a subset Q of size n such that for every pair of triples $(x, y, z), (x', y', z') \in Q$ it holds that $x \neq x'$ and $y \neq y'$ and $z \neq z'$?

SPECIAL 3-PARTITION [5, 3]
Input: Positive integers m and b, where b is bounded by a polynomial in m, $p(m)$, and a multiset S of $3m$ positive integers in $(\frac{b}{4}, \frac{b}{2})$ with $\sum_{x \in S} x = mb$.
Question: Is there a partition of S into m submultisets of cardinality 3 each such that the numbers in each submultiset sum up to exactly b?

4. MANIPULATION OF THE G-INDEX: ONE RESEARCHER

Interestingly, the g-index turns out to be more susceptible to manipulation than the h-index: we can show that (sCite, g)-INDEXACH is polynomial-time solvable as long as G is a clique; in contrast, (sCite, h)-INDEXACH is known to be NP-hard in this case [3].

PROPOSITION 1. (sCite, g)-INDEXACH *is solvable in polynomial time if the compatibility graph G is a clique.*

PROOF. Fix an instance (D, G, W, t) of (sCite, g)-INDEXACH. Suppose that $|W| = w$ and the total number of citations to articles in W is s. If $w < t$ or $s < t^2$ then clearly it is not possible to improve the researcher's g-index to t. Otherwise, pick some $w - t + 1$ articles in W, and merge them into a single article. After the merge, the researcher has exactly t articles, and his total number of citations is $s \geq t^2$. □

However, we obtain hardness results even for INDEXIMP if G is not a clique or if we use more sophisticated citation measures.

THEOREM 2. (sCite, g)-INDEXIMP *is* NP-*complete.*

PROOF. We give a reduction from CLIQUE. Given an instance (H, k) of CLIQUE, we build an instance (D, G, W) of (sCite, g)-INDEXIMP as follows. We set $W_1 = V(H)$, let W_2 consist of $k-1$ new articles, and set $W = W_1 \cup W_2$. To create the citation graph D, for each article $w \in W_2$ we add k articles that cite w and no other article, and for each article $w \in W_1$ we add one article that cites w and no other article. The compatibility graph G is created from H by adding each article in W_2 as an isolated vertex. We now show that (D, G, W) is a yes-instance of (sCite, g)-INDEXIMP if and only if (H, k) is a yes-instance of CLIQUE.

Suppose that (H, k) is a yes-instance of CLIQUE. Then H contains a clique T of size at least k. Merging the articles in $T \subseteq W_1$ complies with G, and hence we obtain a merged article with k citations. Together, with the $k - 1$ articles in W_2, this results in k articles with k citations, i.e., a partition with g-index k.

On the other hand, let (D, G, W) be a yes-instance of (sCite, g)-INDEXIMP. If $\mathcal{P}$ is an improving partition of W, it has at least one merged article P with at least k citations. As only articles in W_1 can be merged and the merge has to comply with G, it follows that $G[P] = H[P]$ is a clique. Since each vertex in W_1 has only one citation, we have $|P| \geq k$, and the proof is complete. □

THEOREM 3. (uCite, g)-INDEXIMP *is* NP-*complete even if the compatibility graph G is a clique.*

PROOF. We give a reduction from INDEPENDENT SET. Given an instance (H, k) of INDEPENDENT SET, we assume without loss of generality that $|V(H)| < |E(H)|$ and let $m = |E(H)|$, and construct an instance (D, G, W) of (uCite, g)-INDEXIMP as follows. We set $W = W_1 \cup W_2 \cup W_3$, where $W_1 = V(H)$, W_2 consists of $m - k$ (without loss of generality we assume $m > k$) new articles and W_3 consists of k new articles. To create the citation graph D, we add a new article w that cites all articles in W_1 and W_2. Then, for each edge $\{u, v\}$ in $E(H)$, we add a new article $e_{\{u,v\}}$ that cites u and v as well as all articles in W_2 and W_3. As a result, in W_2 we have $m - k$ articles with the same $m + 1$ citations, and in W_3 we have k articles with the same m citations; the articles in W_1 have at most m citations each. Finally, we set G to be a clique. We observe that the g-index of W is m, so the aim is to improve it to at least $m + 1$. We now show that (D, G, W) is a yes-instance of (uCite, g)-INDEXIMP if and only if (H, k) is a yes-instance of INDEPENDENT SET.

Suppose that (H, k) is a yes-instance of INDEPENDENT SET. Then H contains an independent set T of size k. As T is an independent set, $W_1 \setminus T$ is a vertex cover of H. Thus, by merging the articles in $W_1 \setminus T$, we get a merged article with $m + 1$ citations. Then, by pairing up articles in T and W_3 and merging the articles in each pair, we get k articles with $m + 1$ citations each. Together with the $m - k$ articles in W_2, we have $m + 1$ articles with $m + 1$ citations each. Hence, we have a partition with g-index $m + 1$.

On the other hand, suppose that (D, G, W) is a yes-instance of (uCite, g)-INDEXIMP. That is, we have $m+1$ articles with at least $(m + 1)^2$ total citations in an improving partition $\mathcal{P}$. Since there are $m + 1$ distinct articles citing articles in W, no merged article can obtain more than $m + 1$ citations. Consequently, in $\mathcal{P}$ there are $m + 1$ articles that get exactly $m + 1$ citations each. Since each article in W_2 gets $m + 1$ citations, we can assume that every such article is a singleton in $\mathcal{P}$. Further, since $|W_2| + |W_3| = m$, there has to be at least one merged article P with $P \subseteq W_1$. For P to get $m + 1$ citations, it must correspond to a vertex cover of H, so its complement $W_1 \setminus P$ is an independent set. Now, suppose that $|W_1 \setminus P| < k$, and hence $|W_3| + |W_1 \setminus P| < 2k$. But then any partition of $W_3 \cup (W_1 \setminus P)$ into at least k parts would contain fewer than k non-singleton parts, and every singleton part of this partition receives at most m citations. Thus, altogether we would have at most $|W_2|+1+(k-1) < m+1$ parts with $m+1$ citations, a contradiction. Hence, $W_1 \setminus P$ is an independent set of size at least k, and the proof is complete. □

5. MANIPULATION OF THE I10-INDEX: ONE RESEARCHER

Both the h-index and the g-index are hard to manipulate when there are constraints on which articles can be merged (i.e., G is not a clique). In contrast, for the i10-index we can obtain some easiness results even for this case.

PROPOSITION 4. $(\mu, i10)$-INDEXIMP *is solvable in polynomial time for* $\mu \in \{\mathsf{sCite}, \mathsf{uCite}\}$.

PROOF. We can safely ignore all articles with 0 citations, and there is no reason to touch articles that already receive 10 or more citations. Now, let W' be the set of all articles in W that have between 1 and 9 citations. We can enumerate all subsets of W' of size at most 10 in time polynomial in $|W|$. For each subset P, we check whether it corresponds to a clique in G and whether $\mu(P) \geq 10$. If so, we can merge the articles in P to improve the researcher's i10-index. The correctness of this algorithm follows from the fact that there is no need to use more than 10 articles to get 10 citations (to see why this is the case for uCite, consider starting with a set $S \subseteq W$ with $\mu(S) \geq 10$, $|S| > 10$, moving articles from S to P one by one, and discarding an article if it does not contribute to P's citation count). □

The algorithm described in Proposition 4 does not work for fCite: under this measure, merging "small" articles may lower the citation count of "large" articles. Indeed, the following theorem shows that $(\mathsf{fCite}, i10)$-INDEXIMP is NP-hard.

THEOREM 5. $(\mathsf{fCite}, i10)$-INDEXIMP *is* NP-*complete.*

PROOF. We give a reduction from 3D MATCHING. Given an instance (X, Y, Z, M) of 3D MATCHING with $|X| = |Y| = |Z| = n$, we build an instance (D, G, W) of $(\mathsf{fCite}, i10)$-INDEXIMP as follows. Let $W_1 = X \cup Y \cup Z$, let W_2 consist of four new articles, let W_3 consist of n new articles, and set $W = W_1 \cup W_2 \cup W_3$. To create the citation graph D, for each article $w \in W_1$ we add one article that cites w and no other article, and for each article $w \in W_2$ we add three articles that cite w and no other article. For each article w in W_3 we introduce six articles that cite w and no other article, and we also add citations from each article in W_2 to w. Thus, each article in W_3 has 10 citations, so the i10-index of W is n. The compatibility graph G contains edges (x, y), (y, z) and (x, z) for each triple $(x, y, z) \in M$, as well as the edges between all pairs of articles in W_2 and the edges $\{x, y \mid x \in W_3, y \in W_1\}$. We now show that (D, G, W) is a yes-instance of $(\mathsf{fCite}, i10)$-INDEXIMP if and only if (X, Y, Z, M) is a yes-instance of 3D MATCHING.

Suppose that (X, Y, Z, M) is a yes-instance of 3D MATCHING. Let Q be a certificate for that, so Q is a set of n disjoint triples. Then, merging the articles in each triple complies with G and creates n merged articles with three citations each. Next, we merge the four articles in W_2 to get a new merged article with 12 citations. However, this reduces the citations of each article in W_3 to 7. To fix this, we merge each article in W_3 with one merged article from W_1. These merges also comply with G. Thus, we obtain $n + 1$ articles with at least 10 citations each.

On the other hand, suppose that (D, G, W) is a yes-instance of $(\mathsf{fCite}, i10)$-INDEXIMP. Let $\mathcal{P}$ be a partition of W with i10-index $n+1$. Since $G[W_1]$ is a tripartite graph, each article in W_1 has only one citation, and articles in W_1 and W_2 are incompatible, the only way to create a new article with at least 10 citations is to merge the articles in W_2. Thus, we have $W_2 \in \mathcal{P}$. However, as argued above, merging the articles in W_2 reduces the citations of the articles in W_3. Since $\mathcal{P}$ contains $n+1$ articles with at least 10 citations each, it has to contain n merged articles each containing one of the articles in W_3. Since $\mathcal{P}$ has to comply with G, any of these merged articles consists of an article in W_3 and some articles in W_1. As each article in W_1 contributes just one citation and $|W_1| = 3n$, each article in $\mathcal{P} \setminus W_2$ contains exactly three atomic articles from W_1. Now, since these articles have to form a triangle in G, they also form a triple in M, so we obtain n disjoint triples. □

We now move to the study of INDEXACH. Our first result is a polynomial-time algorithm for $(\mathsf{sCite}, i10)$-INDEXACH when there are no restrictions on available merges.

THEOREM 6. $(\mathsf{sCite}, i10)$-INDEXACH *is solvable in polynomial time if G is a clique.*

PROOF. We will show that this problem can be captured by an integer linear program with a constant number of variables; by the classic result of Lenstra [7] optimal solutions of such programs can be found in polynomial time. For compactness, we present our argument for i3 rather than i10; extending it to i10 is straightforward.

Similarly to the proof of Proposition 4, it suffices to focus on articles with 1 or 2 citations. Suppose we have n_1 articles with one citation each and n_2 articles with 2 citations each. There are three ways to merge such articles to get an article with at least 3 citations: we can take (a) three articles with one citation each, (b) one article with one citation and one article with two citations, or (c) two articles with two citations each. Let x_{111}, x_{12}, and x_{22} denote the number of merged articles of type (a), (b), and (c) respectively. Let n_3 be the number of papers with three of more citations; then our task is captured by the following integer linear constraints:

$$\begin{aligned} x_{111} + x_{12} + x_{22} &\geq t - n_3 \\ 3x_{111} + x_{12} &\leq n_1 \\ x_{12} + 2x_{22} &\leq n_2 \\ x_{111}, x_{12}, x_{22} &\geq 0 \end{aligned}$$

For i10 the number of variables is bounded by the total number of partitions of numbers $10, \dots, 18$, which is 1500[1]. □

In contrast, if G can be arbitrary, (sCite, $i10$)-INDEXACH becomes NP-hard. The proof is by reduction from PARTITION INTO TRIANGLES [5]; we omit it due to space constraints.

THEOREM 7. (sCite, $i10$)-INDEXACH *is* NP-*complete.*

To summarize, we have fully characterized the worst-case complexity of (μ, $i10$)-INDEXIMP and (μ, $i10$)-INDEXACH, for $\mu \in$ {sCite, uCite, fCite}. When all merges are allowed, we have some positive results, but the complexity of (uCite, $i10$)-INDEXACH, (fCite, $i10$)-INDEXIMP and (fCite, $i10$)-INDEXACH remains unknown. We can show that the first of these problems becomes easy if we consider i2 instead of i10: (uCite, $i2$)-INDEXACH reduces to finding a maximum matching in a certain graph. However, it is not clear how to generalize this result even to i3.

6. COOPERATIVE FRAMEWORK

We now consider the problem of manipulating citation indices in the presence of friends. For each citation index we will limit ourselves to scenarios that are easy in the absence of social context (e.g., for the h-index this means considering sCite and assuming that the compatibility graph is a clique).

6.1 h-Index

For the h-index, taking care of a friend complicates the manipulator's task considerably: even for the least computationally demanding citation measure sCite and even if the compatibility graph is a clique, checking if a manipulator can improve her h-index by 1 without harming her friend becomes computationally hard.

THEOREM 8. (sCite, h)-INDEXIMPFRIEND *is* NP-*complete, even if the compatibility graph G is a clique.*

PROOF. Following Remark 1, we assume that the input is given by three multisets of numbers: S_{12} for the articles co-authored by both researchers, S_1 for the articles of the first researcher not co-authored by the second researcher, and S_2 for the articles of the second researcher not co-authored by the first researcher.

We provide a reduction from SPECIAL 3-PARTITION; importantly, this problem is strongly NP-hard [5, 3]. Given an instance (S, m, b) of SPECIAL 3-PARTITION, we construct an instance of (S_{12}, S_1, S_2) of (sCite, h)-INDEXIMPFRIEND as follows. First, we obtain S' from S by adding m to each number in S. We observe that (S, m, b) is a yes-instance of SPECIAL 3-PARTITION if and only if (S', m, k), where $k = b + 3m$, is a yes-instance of SPECIAL 3-PARTITION. Note also that $k - m = b + 2m > 0$. We let S_{12} contain $m - 1$ copies of $k - 1$. Then S_1 is obtained from S' by adding $k - m$ copies of k, and S_2 contains $k - m$ copies of $k - 1$. We will show that (S_{12}, S_1, S_2) is a yes-instance of (sCite, h)-INDEXIMPFRIEND if and only if (S', m, k) is a yes-instance of SPECIAL 3-PARTITION.

Suppose first that (S', m, k) is a yes-instance of SPECIAL 3-PARTITION, and let T be a certificate for that. Then T is a partition of S' into m parts such that the sum of the numbers in each part is k. Now, if we merge articles in S_1 according to T, we get m merged articles with k citations each, $k - m$ singleton articles with k citations each, and further $m - 1$ articles with $k - 1$ citations each. This partition improves the h-index of the first researcher to k, while the articles in S_{12} remain in singletons, so the second researcher is not affected.

On the other hand, suppose that (S_{12}, S_1, S_2) is a yes-instance of (sCite, h)-INDEXIMPFRIEND, and let $\mathcal{P}$ be a certificate for that. We can assume without loss of generality that all articles with k citations appear as singletons in $\mathcal{P}$: indeed, if a merged article contains a component article with k citations, the latter can be split off without lowering the h-index. Further, since the second researcher has $k - 1$ articles, and each of them gets $k - 1$ citations, none of his articles can be merged. Thus, $\mathcal{P}$ contains at least m merged articles whose component articles correspond to elements of S', and each of these merged articles receives at least k citations. Since $\sum_{x \in S'} x = mk$, each of these merged articles gets exactly k citations, so we have obtained a desired partition of S'.

Since our reduction is from a strongly NP-hard problem, our problem remains hard for the graph-based representation. □

6.2 g-Index

We have seen (Section 4) that for a single researcher the g-index is more susceptible to manipulation than the h-index. This is also the case in the cooperative setting: the next theorem describes a polynomial-time algorithm for (sCite, g)-INDEXACHFRIEND, under the assumption that arbitrary merges are allowed.

THEOREM 9. (sCite, g)-INDEXACHFRIEND *can be solved in polynomial time if the compatibility graph G is a clique.*

PROOF. We use the same input representation as in Theorem 8. Set $S_1' = S_1 \cup S_{12}$, $S_2' = S_2 \cup S_{12}$.

Let g_1 and g_2 be the g-indices of S_1' and S_2', respectively. Suppose that $|S_2'| = g_2 + x$, where x is a non-negative integer. As researcher 2 has to have at least g_2 articles after the merge, the top t parts of an improving partition of S_1' may contain at most $x + t$ articles from S_{12}. We consider the following cases:

$|S_{12}| \geq x + t$: Let S^* be the set of $x + t$ most cited articles in S_{12}. Then, if $\sum_{z \in S_1 \cup S^*} z \geq t^2$, we create a single merged article that contains $x + 1$ articles from S^* as well as all articles in S_1; the remaining articles in S_{12} remain singletons. The merged article and the remaining $t - 1$ articles in S^* contribute to the g-index of the first researcher, so his g-index becomes at least t; the second researcher is not affected. If $\sum_{z \in S_1 \cup S^*} z < t^2$, we have a no-instance of our problem: if we were to use more articles from S_{12}, we would decrease the g-index of S_2'.

$|S_{12}| = y < t$: If $|S_1| < t - y$ or $\sum_{z \in S_1'} z < t^2$, then there is no improving partition. Otherwise, we partition articles in S_1 into $t - y$ groups and merge the articles in each group; this improves the g-index of the first researcher to t without touching the articles of the second researcher.

[1]see the On-Line Encyclopedia of Integer Sequences at `https://oeis.org/A000041`

$|S_{12}| = y, t \leq y < x + t$: If $\sum_{x \in S_1'} x < t^2$, there is no improving partition. Otherwise, we create a merged article that contains some $y - t + 1$ articles of S_{12} and all articles of S_1; the remaining $t - 1$ articles in S_{12} remain singletons. This partition of S_1' has t parts and receives at least t^2 citations; on the other hand, the second researcher still has at least g_2 papers. □

However, this is the only easy case: the results of Section 4 imply that (μ, g)-INDEXACHFRIEND is NP-hard if $\mu =$ sCite, but G can be arbitrary, or if $\mu \in \{$uCite, fCite$\}$ (even if G is a clique).

6.3 i10-Index

For the i10-index, we observe that when citations to merged articles are computed according to sCite or uCite, a manipulator need not worry about her friends: as along as she is not merging articles that already have 10 or more citations (and she has no reason to do so), she is not harming other researchers. Moreover, the integer linear program from the proof of Theorem 6 can be modified to capture the setting where we want to increase the i10-indices of several researchers simultaneously (note that the number of researchers k is treated as a constant in our model; the number of variables in our ILP is exponential in k, as we need to keep track of mergeable articles). We obtain the following results.

THEOREM 10. *$(\mu, i10)$-INDEXIMPFRIEND is solvable in polynomial time for $\mu \in \{$sCite, uCite$\}$. Furthermore, (sCite, $i10$)-INDEXACHFRIEND and (sCite, $i10, k$)-INDEXMACH are solvable in polynomial time if G is a clique.*

For most of the remaining problems for the i10-index in the cooperative setting, we obtain NP-completeness results as corollaries of results of Section 5; the three open problems of Section 5 translate into open problems for the cooperative setting.

7. ADVERSARIAL FRAMEWORK

We will now consider the complexity of manipulation in the presence of adversaries. Again, we focus on scenarios where this problem is easy for a single researcher.

7.1 h-Index

For the h-index, the presence of enemies has the same computational cost as the presence of friends: manipulation becomes hard even for $\mu =$ sCite and even if G is a clique.

THEOREM 11. *(sCite, h)-INDEXIMPENEMY and (sCite, h)-INDEXHARMENEMY are NP-complete even if G is a clique.*

Just as in the cooperative case, the proofs proceed by reductions from SPECIAL 3-PARTITION, and establish strong NP-hardness for the list-based representation.

7.2 g-Index

Interestingly, for the g-index merging one's papers so as to harm a competitor (without harming oneself) turns out to be easier than maximizing one's own citation index without helping the competitor. Specifically, for $\mu =$ sCite we obtain the following results.

THEOREM 12. *(sCite, g)-INDEXIMPENEMY is NP-complete even when the compatibility graph G is a clique.*

The proof proceeds by reduction from SPECIAL 3-PARTITION and is omitted due to space constraints.

THEOREM 13. *(sCite, g)-INDEXHARMENEMY is solvable in polynomial time when the compatibility graph G is a clique.*

PROOF. We use the same notation as in Theorem 9.

Let g_1 and g_2 be the g-indices of S_1' and S_2' respectively. The first researcher can reduce the g-index of S_2' if and only if $|S_{12}| \geq |S_2'| - g_2 + 2$. Assume that this is the case. Now, if $|S_1'| - |S_2'| + g_2 - 1 \geq g_1$, the first researcher can achieve his goal by merging $|S_2'| - g_2 + 2$ articles in S_{12} into a single article, and not performing any other merges. if this condition does not hold, any partition that harms the second researcher would also harm the first researcher. □

However, (sCite, g)-INDEXHARMENEMY becomes NP-hard if G can be an arbitrary graph; we omit the proof, which is based on a reduction from 3D MATCHING.

THEOREM 14. *(sCite, g)-INDEXHARMENEMY is NP-complete.*

Moreover, for uCite this problem is hard even if arbitrary merges are allowed.

THEOREM 15. *(uCite, g)-INDEXHARMENEMY is NP-complete even if G is a clique.*

PROOF. We reduce from the restricted version of (uCite, g)-INDEXIMP where the compatibility graph is a clique; this problem is NP-hard by Theorem 3.

Suppose that we are given an instance (D', G', W) of (uCite, g)-INDEXIMP where $D' = (V', A')$ and G' is a clique. Let g be the g-index of W, and let $n = |V'|$. Suppose that the g most cited articles in W receive $s \geq g^2$ citations.

We construct an instance (D, G, W_1, W_2) of (uCite, g)-INDEXHARMENEMY as follows. Let $W_1 = W \cup \{w_1, w_2\}$, $W_2 = \{w_1, w_2, \ldots, w_n\}$. To construct D, we start with D', and add the following articles and citations: $n + 6$ articles that cite w_n only, $n + 2$ articles that cite w_i only for each $i = 3, \ldots, n - 1$, and $2g + 3$ articles that cite w_1. Now, we pick $x = \max\{0, (g + 2)^2 - (2g + 3) - s\} \leq 2g + 1$ among these $2g + 3$ articles, and add a citation from each of these x articles to w_2. The set W_1 contains $g + 2$ articles, which receive at least $s + 2g + 3 + x \geq (g + 2)^2$ citations, so its g-index is $g + 2$; the g-index of W_2 is n. Finally, let G be a clique.

Now, suppose W admits a partition $\mathcal{P}$ with g-index at least $g+1$. Then $\mathcal{P}' = \mathcal{P} \cup \{w_1, w_2\}$ is a partition of W_1 with g-index at least $g + 2$, and the g-index of W_2 drops to $n - 1$.

Conversely, as we have $W_1 \cap W_2 = \{w_1, w_2\}$, the only way for the first researcher to lower the g-index of the second researcher is to merge w_1 and w_2. But then to ensure that her own g-index does not go down, she needs to find a partition of W where the top $g + 1$ articles get at least $(g + 2)^2 - (2g + 3) \geq (g + 1)^2$ citations, i.e., an improving partition of W. This completes the proof. □

7.3 i10-Index

For i10, all easiness results from Section 5 remain true in the presence of enemies.

THEOREM 16. *The problems $(\mu, i10)$-INDEXIMPENEMY and $(\mu, i10)$-INDEXHARMENEMY are solvable in polynomial time for $\mu \in \{$sCite, uCite$\}$. Also, (sCite, $i10$)-INDEXACHENEMY is solvable in polynomial time if the compatibility graph G is a clique.*

PROOF. If Alice wants to improve her i10-index without helping Bob, she can use the algorithm from Proposition 4 with one modification: when going over subsets of her articles, she should discard the subsets that contain any of her joint articles with Bob. Similarly, to maximize her i10-index without helping Bob, she can discard her joint papers with Bob and then use the ILP from the proof of Theorem 6.

		IndexImp		IndexAch	
		G clique	G any	G clique	G any
h	sCite	P [3]	NPc [10]	NPc [3]	NPc
	uCite	NPc [10]	NPc	NPc	NPc
	fCite	NPc	NPc	NPc	NPc
g	sCite	P (Pr.1)	NPc (Th.2)	P (Pr.1)	NPc
	uCite	NPc (Th.3)	NPc	NPc	NPc
	fCite	NPc	NPc	NPc	NPc
i10	sCite	P	P (Pr.4)	P (Th.6)	NPc
	uCite	P	P (Pr.4)	?	NPc
	fCite	?	NPc (Th.5)	?	NPc

Table 1: Complexity results for citation indices. 'P' stands for 'polynomial-time solvable', 'NPc' stands for 'NP-complete'; '?' indicates that the problem is open. The number of the respective theorem/proposition is given in parentheses; when no reference is given, the result follows by Remark 2.

Finally, the only way for Alice to lower the i10-index of Bob is to merge two of her joint articles with Bob that receive at least 10 citations each. To ensure that this does not lower her i10-index, she should consider the set of her articles that receive between 1 and 9 citations each, go over all subsets of that set that contain at most 10 articles, and check if any such subset (a) complies with G, (b) receives at least 10 citations in total under μ (for $\mu \in \{\text{sCite}, \text{uCite}\}$), and (c) does not contain an article by Bob. □

In contrast, for (fCite, $i10$)-IndexHarmEnemy we get a hardness result by a reduction from (fCite, $i10$)-IndexImp; we omit the proof.

Theorem 17. *The problem* (fCite, $i10$)-IndexHarmEnemy *is* NP-*complete.*

8. PARAMETERIZED COMPLEXITY

Many of the computational problems considered so far turned out to be NP-hard. It is therefore natural to ask if they become easier when natural parameters of the input are small. This research agenda was initiated by van Bevern et al. [11], who have considered the following parameters: (i) the size c of the largest connected component of G; (ii) the target citation index t; (iii) the maximum allowed number of merges K. Indeed, it seems plausible that in realistic scenarios these parameters will be fairly small; in particular, a cautious manipulator woud not want to perform more than a few merges so as not to raise suspicions.

Van Bevern et al. obtain a number of fixed-parameter tractability results for these parameters. In particular, they establish that (μ, h)-IndexAch is FPT with respect to c for $\mu \in \{\text{sCite}, \text{uCite}\}$. Their algorithm proceeds by considering and evaluating all possible partitions of each connected component of G, and then finding an optimal way to combine these partitions by means of dynamic programming. This approach turns out to work for many of the problems we consider. Specifically, we obtain the following results (for compactness, the theorem below is stated so that it subsumes the results of van Bevern et al. and includes some problems that are known to be polynomial-time solvable).

Theorem 18. *For each* $\mu \in \{\text{sCite}, \text{uCite}\}$ *and each* $I \in \{g, h, i10\}$ *the following problems are fixed-parameter tractable with respect to the size of the largest connected component of G:*

- (μ, I)-IndexAch;
- (μ, I)-IndexAchFriend *and* (μ, I, k)-IndexMAch;
- (μ, I)-IndexAchEnemy *and* (μ, I)-IndexHarmEnemy.

ImpFriend	(sCite, g)* (Th.9), (sCite/uCite, $i10$) (Th.10)
AchFriend	(sCite, g)* (Th.9), (sCite, $i10$)* (Th.10)
MAch	(sCite, $i10$)* (Th.10)
ImpEnemy	(sCite/uCite, $i10$) (Th.16)
AchEnemy	(sCite, $i10$)* (Th.16)
HarmEnemy	(sCite, g)* (Th.13), (sCite/uCite, $i10$) (Th.16)

Table 2: Easiness results for manipulation in social context. For compactness, we omit the word Index from the left column. For each problem, we list combinations of citation measures and indices for which it is polynomial-time solvable. * indicates that the result holds only if the compatibility graph is complete.

Observe that Theorem 18 does not contain any results for fCite. Indeed, van Bevern et al. [11] show that (fCite, h)-IndexAch is NP-hard even for $c = 2$. We obtain similar hardness results for fCite with $c = 2$ for several other problems, for all three indices.

Theorem 19. *For each* $I \in \{h, g, i10\}$ *the following problems are* NP-*complete even if the size of the largest connected component of G is 2:*

- (fCite, I)-IndexAch
- (fCite, I)-IndexAchFriend *and* (fCite, I)-IndexMAch
- (fCite, I)-IndexAchEnemy.

A number of other results on the parameterized complexity of the problems considered in this paper can be found in the master's thesis of the first author [10].

9. CONCLUSIONS

We have investigated the complexity of manipulating one's citation indices, both for a researcher who only cares about her own performance and in the setting where one is interested in the performance of her colleagues and competitors. Our results are summarized in Tables 1 and 2. While we do not yet have a complete picture of the complexity of all problems we defined, it emerges that the h-index is harder to manipulate than the g-index and the i10-index.

While we phrased our results in terms of strategic merging of unrelated papers, many of them also apply in the setting where a researcher has to decide whether she can afford to merge several versions of her paper without lowering her (or possibly her students') citation indices; while a reputable researcher is unlikely to merge unrelated papers, *not* merging related papers is a less repugnant transaction.

Finally, we would like to emphasise that we do not want our results to be interpreted as an endorsement of the practice of relying on citation indices (or any other single-dimensional numeric measures) when making funding, hiring and promotion decisions; if anything, our results indicate that such measures can be gamed by dishonest researchers.

Acknowledgements

This work was done while the first author was an MSc student at Oxford, and she gratefully acknowledges financial support from HEFCE. The second author was partially supported by ERC StG 639945 and by Horizon 2020 OpenDreamKit project.

REFERENCES

[1] P. Ball. The h-index, or the academic equivalent of the stag's antlers. *Guardian*, January 6, 2012.

[2] A. Bateman. Why I love the h-index. *PLOS Biologue Community Blog*, 2012. `http://blogs.plos.org/biologue/2012/10/19/why-i-love-the-h-index/`.

[3] B. de Keijzer and K. R. Apt. The h-index can be easily manipulated. *Bulletin of the EATCS*, 110:79–85, 2013.

[4] L. Egghe. Theory and practise of the g-index. *Scientometrics*, 69(1):131–152, 2006.

[5] M. Garey and D. Johnson. *Computers and Intractability: A Guide to the Theory of NP-Completeness*. W. H. Freeman and Company, 1979.

[6] J. E. Hirsch. An index to quantify an individual's scientific research output. *Proceedings of the National Academy of Sciences*, 109(46):16569–16572, 2005.

[7] H. W. Lenstra Jr. Integer programming with a fixed number of variables. *Mathematics of Operations Research*, 8(4):538–548, 1983.

[8] O. Mryglod, R. Kenna, Y. Holovatch, and B. Berche. Predicting the results of the REF using departmental h-index: A look at biology, chemistry, physics, and sociology. *LSE: The impact blog*, 2014. `http://blogs.lse.ac.uk/impactofsocialsciences/2014/12/16/predicting-the-results-of-the-ref/`.

[9] J. Ollerton. How does a scientist's h-index change over time? *Jeff Ollerton's Biodiversity Blog*, 2015. `https://jeffollerton.wordpress.com/2015/05/10/how-does-a-scientists-h-index-change-over-time/`.

[10] C. Pavlou. Manipulation of popular scientific impact indices by merging articles. Master's thesis, University of Oxford, 2015.

[11] R. van Bevern, C. Komusiewicz, R. Niedermeier, M. Sorge, and T. Walsh. H-index manipulation by merging articles: Models, theory, and experiments. In *Proceedings of the 24th International Joint Conference on Artificial Intelligence, IJCAI'15, 2015*, pages 808–814, 2015.

[12] G. J. Woeginger. An axiomatic analysis of Egghe's g-index. *J. Informetrics*, 2(4):364–368, 2008.

[13] G. J. Woeginger. An axiomatic characterization of the Hirsch-index. *Mathematical Social Sciences*, 56(2):224–232, 2008.

Efficient Stabilization of Cooperative Matching Games

Takehiro Ito[*]
Tohoku University
takehiro@ecei.tohoku.ac.jp

Naonori Kakimura[†]
University of Tokyo
kakimura@global.c.u-tokyo.ac.jp

Naoyuki Kamiyama[‡]
Kyushu University
kamiyama@imi.kyushu-u.ac.jp

Yusuke Kobayashi[§]
University of Tsukuba
kobayashi@sk.tsukuba.ac.jp

Yoshio Okamoto[¶]
University of Electro-Communications
okamotoy@uec.ac.jp

ABSTRACT

Cooperative matching games have drawn much interest partly because of the connection with bargaining solutions in the networking environment. However, it is not always guaranteed that a network under investigation gives rise to a stable bargaining outcome. To address this issue, we consider a modification process, called stabilization, that yields a network with stable outcomes, where the modification should be as small as possible. Therefore, the problem is cast to a combinatorial-optimization problem in a graph. Recently, the stabilization by edge removal was shown to be **NP**-hard. On the contrary, in this paper, we show that other possible ways of stabilization, namely, edge addition, vertex removal and vertex addition, are all polynomial-time solvable. Thus, we obtain a complete complexity-theoretic classification of the natural four variants of the network stabilization problem. We further study weighted variants and prove that the variants for edge addition and vertex removal are **NP**-hard.

1. INTRODUCTION

Matching markets play a central role in economics and game theory, and much work has been done. Among them, we concentrate on cooperative games with transferable utility derived from matchings in a network, called matching games, which are also known as stable roommate problems with side payments (when it is modeled as a cooperative game). The following example was given by Eriksson and Karlander [12] to motivate such games.

> In the professional tennis circuit, there are parallel singles and doubles tournaments. Although the prize money in the doubles is not as generous as in the singles, the sums are still impressive. The players are free to form pairs for the doubles as they choose. It is not necessarily so that the two best single players make the best team; the strength of a pair is a more complex function of the players abilities.
>
> The players know each others' strengths and weaknesses, and can make good estimates of the expected prize money for each possible constellation. In the process of forming pairs, the players negotiate how to distribute the expected income within the pair. (At least, this is what rational tennis players should do.) The objective of each player in this process is to maximize his own expected prize money.

As a cooperative game with transferable utility, in a *matching game*, we are given a network (or an undirected graph), and each vertex of the graph corresponds to a player of the game. A *matching* is a set of pairs of players such that every player is involved in at most one pair, and a pair can be formed only if there is an edge between two players. The graph is often associated with edge weights so that the utility of forming a pair can be incorporated. The characteristic function value of a coalition is defined as the maximum possible total utility of a matching over the coalition.

Matching games have attracted researchers, and solution concepts for matching games have been studied through the algorithmic lens [13, 7, 6, 18, 17, 9, 2]. In particular, there is a polynomial-time algorithm to test whether a given matching game has a non-empty core [10], where the *core* is defined as the set of payoff vectors such that no coalition has a characteristic function value larger than the total payoff allocated to the players of the coalition. Thus, a "stable" payoff exists in a game with a non-empty core. We here note

[*]Supported by JSPS KAKENHI Grant Numbers 25330003, 15H00849.

[†]Supported by JST, ERATO, Kawarabayashi Large Graph Project, and by JSPS KAKENHI Grant Numbers 25730001, 24106002.

[‡]Supported by JST, PRESTO.

[§]Supported by JST, ERATO, Kawarabayashi Large Graph Project, and by JSPS KAKENHI Grant Numbers 24106002, 24700004.

[¶]Supported by JSPS KAKENHI Grant Numbers 24106005, 24700008, 24220003, 15K00009.

Appears in: *Proceedings of the 15th International Conference on Autonomous Agents and Multiagent Systems (AAMAS 2016), J. Thangarajah, K. Tuyls, C. Jonker, S. Marsella (eds.), May 9–13, 2016, Singapore.*

Table 1: The summary of our results. The mark * depicts the results in this paper.

Unweighted	Edge	Vertex
Removal	**NP**-hard [8]	Poly-time [*]
Addition	Poly-time [*]	Poly-time [*]

Weighted	Edge	Vertex
Removal	**NP**-hard [6]	**NP**-hard [*]
Addition	**NP**-hard [*]	—

that if the underlying network is bipartite, then the game is called an *assignment game*, which is also well studied in the literature [26].

On the other hand, if the core of a game is empty, then no payoff is stable. Therefore, we often modify the game itself to achieve the core non-emptiness. The literature offers options of taxation [22, 28], cost of stability [3], and least cores [18]. In this paper, we consider a structural modification of the underlying network, which better fits another motivation from network bargaining as explained later. The modification should be as small as possible so that the games themselves do not differ much.

There are several possible ways of modification. We consider the following four processes.

Edge removal: We remove a set of edges from the network. In this case, we want to remove as few edges as possible.

Edge addition: We add a set of edges to the network. In this case, we want to add as few edges as possible.

Vertex removal: We remove a set of vertices from the network. When we remove a vertex, all the edges incident to the vertex are removed too. In this case, we want to remove as few vertices as possible.

Vertex addition: We add a set of vertices to the network. When we add a vertex, we may also add edges from the new vertex to any of the existing vertices. In this case, we want to add as few vertices as possible.

The literature only studied edge removal. Namely, the problem was to find a smallest subset of edges whose removal resulted in a network with non-empty core. Biró et al. [6] proved that the problem is **NP**-hard for the weighted case. Later, Bock et al. [8] proved that the problem is still **NP**-hard for the unweighted case (as introduced above), and hard to approximate within factor less than two assuming the unique games conjecture [19]. Some approximation algorithms have been proposed [8, 21], but the existence of a constant-factor approximation algorithm is left open.

Our Results.

We study the remaining three options, namely, edge addition, vertex removal, and vertex addition. For all of them, we prove that the problems can be solved in polynomial time (Sections 3, 4, and 5, respectively). In this way, we obtain the complete complexity classification of the problem variants, and reveal that edge removal studied in the literature is the only hard case.

Those polynomial-time algorithms are obtained by a thorough treatment of the so-called Gallai–Edmonds decompositions that possess useful information on the structure of maximum matchings in a graph. We also utilize the theory of linear programming, as explained later, to connect our problems with fractional matchings of a graph.

One may think that in vertex addition, we may add a lot of edges at the same time even though we add only one vertex. However, as it turns out, our algorithm finds a solution which adds as few edges as possible among all the possible solutions for the vertex addition variant.

We also consider a weighted variant. In the edge addition variant, each possible edge is associated with a non-negative real number. In the vertex removal variant, each vertex is associated with a non-negative real number. Those numbers represent costs of addition or removal. That models a more realistic situation where each possible modification operation is not equivalently manageable. With this setup, we prove that for the edge addition and the vertex removal, the problem is **NP**-hard (Section 6).

The results are summarized in Table 1.

Simultaneously with us, Ahmadian, Sanita, and Hosseinzadeh [1] consider the vertex removal variant, and prove its polynomial-time solvability and the **NP**-hardness of the weighted variant. Furthermore, they propose approximation algorithms for the weighted variant.

Relation to Network Bargaining.

Bateni et al. [4] related the core non-emptiness of matching games with a desirable property in network bargaining by Kleinberg and Tardos [20]. We briefly look at the relationship here.

In their seminal paper, Kleinberg and Tardos [20] gave a theoretical and mathematical foundation for network bargaining. Their model assumes that each vertex of a network corresponds to a player, each edge corresponds to a possible unit-value deal between two players, and each player can be engaged in at most one deal with one of its neighbors in the network. Then, outcome consists of a matching of the network and a value obtained by each player. If a player is matched with another player, then a unit payoff is split to those two players as their values, and if a player is not matched to any other player, then the value of the player is zero. The classical two-player situation studied by Nash [24] corresponds to the two-vertex network with one edge.

Given an outcome, we may consider a deviation of a player from the current matching. Namely, a player A has an incentive to be matched with another player B if B is a neighbor of A in the network and the value of A is smaller than the value that can be obtained by a deal with B while the value of B stays the same. If no player has such an incentive, then the outcome is called stable. On the other hand, the outcome is called balanced if two players joined by an edge of the matching receive the values as Nash's bargaining solution. A main result of Kleinberg and Tardos [20] stated that a stable outcome exists if and only if a balanced outcome exists. Bateni et al. [4] proved that this is also equivalent to the property that the matching game on the same network has a non-empty core.

With this equivalence, following Bock et al. [8], we call the modification process to turn a given network into one with non-empty core *stabilization*, and if a graph yields a matching game with non-empty core, we call the graph *stable*.

We here emphasize that our structural modification is better suited than modification processes when we consider least cores or cost of stability. The modification for the latter two does not maintain the structure of characteristic functions as they arise from matching games, and thus does not give any implication to network bargaining.

Relation to Linear Programming.

It is known that theory of linear programming is a key to study the core non-emptiness of cooperative games arising from graphs and combinatorics. For a matching game, this translates to the relation of the matching number and the fractional matching number of a graph.

A matching of a graph can be seen as an assignment of zero or one to each edge of the graph so that for every vertex of the graph, the sum of the assigned values to the edges incident to that vertex is at most one. A *fractional matching* of a graph is defined as an assignment of non-negative real number to each edge of the graph so that for every vertex of the graph, the sum of the assigned values to the edges incident to that vertex is at most one. The *matching number* is defined as the maximum size of a matching in the graph, which can be seen as the maximum sum of the values assigned to the edges of the graph when the assignment corresponds to a matching. Similarly, the *fractional matching number* is defined as the maximum sum of the values assigned to the edges of the graph in a fractional matching.

The computation of the matching number can naturally be formulated as a 0/1 integer linear program, while the computation of the fractional matching number can be formulated as a linear program without integrality constraint.

By definition, the fractional matching number is always at least as large as the matching number. A result by Deng et al. [10] stated that those two are equal if and only if the matching game has a non-empty core. Moreover, if the core is non-empty, then it is exactly the set of optimal solutions to the dual of the linear program formulating the computation of the fractional matching number. The special case of bipartite graphs (i.e., assignment game) was already proved by Shapley and Shubik [26].

In the terminology of optimization, the difference of the fractional matching number and the matching number is called *integrality gap*, which is relevant in developing optimization algorithms, both exact and approximate. Our results are concerned with smallest modifications to input graphs such that the integrality gaps will be zero, and we use this view in designing our algorithms.

2. PRELIMINARIES

Matching Number and Stable Graphs.

In this paper, we are given a simple undirected graph G with a vertex set V and an edge set E, i.e., $G = (V, E)$. We denote by $\{u, v\}$ the edge between a pair of vertices u, v in V. For each subset X of V, we define $E(X) := \{\{u,v\} \in E \mid u, v \in X\}$. For each subset X of V, the subgraph of G induced by X is denoted by $G[X]$, i.e., $G[X] = (X, E(X))$. For each vertex v in V, we denote by $\delta(v)$ the set of edges incident to v. For each subset X of V, we define $\delta(X) := \bigcup_{v\in X} \delta(v) \setminus E(X)$, i.e., $\delta(X)$ represents the set of edges leaving from X. For each subset X of V, we define the *neighborhood* $N(X)$ as the set of vertices v in $V \setminus X$ such that there is a vertex u in X with $\{u, v\} \in E$. We denote by $\binom{V}{2}$ the family of subsets X of V such that $|X| = 2$. For each subset F of $\binom{V}{2} \setminus E$, we denote by $G + F$ the graph obtained from G by adding edges in F to G, i.e., $G + F = (V, E \cup F)$. For each subset X of V, we denote by $G - X$ the graph obtained from G by removing vertices in X from G, i.e., $G - X = (V \setminus X, E \setminus \bigcup_{v\in X} \delta(v))$. For each edge e in $\binom{V}{2} \setminus E$ (resp., each vertex v in V), we define $G + e := G + \{e\}$ (resp., $G - v := G - \{v\}$). A subset M of E is called a *matching* in G, if no two edges in M share a common vertex incident to them. The *matching number* of G, denoted by $\nu(G)$, is the maximum size of a matching in G. A matching in G is *perfect* if $|M| = |V|/2$.

Finding a maximum-size matching in G can be formulated by the following integer programming problem IP(G):

$$\nu(G) = \max\left\{\sum_{e\in E} x(e) \;\middle|\; \begin{array}{l}\sum_{e\in\delta(v)} x(e) \le 1 \ (v \in V),\\ x \in \{0,1\}^E\end{array}\right\}.$$

Consider the linear programming relaxation of IP(G), denoted by LP(G):

$$\nu_f(G) := \max\left\{\sum_{e\in E} x(e) \;\middle|\; \begin{array}{l}\sum_{e\in\delta(v)} x(e) \le 1 \ (v \in V),\\ x \in \mathbb{R}_+^E\end{array}\right\},$$

where $\mathbb{R}_+$ is the set of non-negative real numbers. The optimal value $\nu_f(G)$ of LP(G) is called the *fractional matching number of G*. Then $\nu_f(G) \ge \nu(G)$ holds. The dual problem DP(G) of LP(G) is

$$\tau_f(G) := \min\left\{\sum_{v\in V} y(v) \;\middle|\; \begin{array}{l}y(u) + y(v) \ge 1 \ (\{u,v\} \in E),\\ y \in \mathbb{R}_+^V\end{array}\right\}.$$

By the strong duality theorem in linear programming, $\nu_f(G) = \tau_f(G)$. Remark that the problem DP(G) is the linear programming relaxation of the problem of finding a minimum-size vertex cover in G, where a *vertex cover* is a subset X of V such that every edge of G has an incident vertex in X. The minimum size of a vertex cover is denoted by $\tau(G)$.

Recall that a graph G is called stable if the network bargaining on G has a stable outcome, equivalently, the matching game on G has a non-empty core. As mentioned before, the stability of a graph G can be characterized as follows.

PROPOSITION 1 ([10]). *A graph G is stable if and only if $\nu_f(G) = \nu(G)$.*

Therefore, stabilization of a graph G can be seen as the problem of modifying G so that the resulting graph G' satisfies $\nu_f(G') = \nu(G')$. For example, in the edge addition variant, we aim to find a minimum-size subset F of $\binom{V}{2} \setminus E$ such that $\nu_f(G + F) = \nu(G + F)$.

Gallai–Edmonds Decomposition.

For each subset M of E, we denote by ∂M the set of end vertices of M, i.e., $\partial M = \bigcup_{e\in M} e$. We say that a vertex v is *covered by* M if $v \in \partial M$, and *exposed* by M if $v \notin \partial M$. A vertex v in V is said to be *essential* if v is covered by every maximum-size matching in G, and *inessential* otherwise, i.e., if some maximum-size matching in G does not cover v.

Definition 1. (Gallai-Edmonds Decomposition [11, 14, 15]) Define a partition (B, A, D) of V as follows:

- B is the set of the inessential vertices;
- $A = N(B)$, i.e., A is the neighborhood of B;
- $D = V \setminus (B \cup A)$.

The partition (B, A, D) is called the *Gallai–Edmonds decomposition* of G.

It is known that the Gallai–Edmonds decomposition (B, A, D) of G uniquely exists and can be found in polynomial time (see e.g., [23]). By definition, every vertex in $A \cup D$ is covered by a maximum-size matching M in G, and vertices exposed by M are contained only in B.

Furthermore, the well-known Tutte–Berge formula can be written in terms of the Gallai–Edmonds decomposition.

PROPOSITION 2. (Tutte–Berge Formula [5, 27]) *We have*

$$\nu(G) = \frac{1}{2}\left(|V| - \mathrm{comp}(G[B]) + |A|\right),$$

where comp$(G[B])$ *is the number of connected components in* $G[B]$.

Bock et al. [8] characterize the difference $\nu_f(G) - \nu(G)$ using the Gallai–Edmonds decomposition to bound the size of an edge-removal stabilizer from below. In the rest of this section, we provide explicit optimal solutions for LP(G) and DP(G) using the Gallai–Edmonds decomposition (Proposition 4). This will be used to obtain a minimum-size stabilizer for the other variants. Note that the case of LP(G) was given in [25]. For the purpose, we first summarize fundamental properties of the Gallai–Edmonds decomposition (see e.g., [23]):

(a) Each connected component H in $G[B]$ is factor-critical, where a graph G' is *factor-critical* if there is a perfect matching in $G' - v$ for every vertex v of G'. Thus H has odd number of vertices.

(b) For a maximum-size matching M, each connected component H in $G[B]$ satisfies either (i) H has one vertex exposed by M and no edge in M leaving from H, or (ii) H has no vertex exposed by M and one edge in M leaving from H.

Let B_1 be the vertex set of singleton components in $G[B]$. Let $B_3 = B \setminus B_1$ be the vertex set of the other *non-trivial* connected components (i.e., connected components with size at least three) in $G[B]$. In this paper, we sometimes call the partition (B_1, B_3, A, D) the Gallai–Edmonds decomposition.

For each maximum-size matching M in G, an *M-alternating* cycle C is a cycle such that edges of M appear alternately in C (except for one vertex if the length is odd). An *M-alternating* path is defined similarly. From the structure of the Gallai–Edmonds decomposition, we have the following lemma.

LEMMA 1. *If a connected component H in $G[B_3]$ has a vertex v exposed by M, then H contains an M-alternating cycle of odd length through v.*

Let $G[B_1, A]$ be the bipartite graph induced by edges between B_1 and A. A maximum-size matching in G is said to be *B_1-optimal*, if $|\partial M \cap B_1| = \nu(G[B_1, A])$, i.e., the number of edges of M connected to B_1 is maximized. By an augmenting-type algorithm for finding a maximum-size matching, we can find a B_1-optimal matching in polynomial time.

PROPOSITION 3. *A B_1-optimal matching in G always exists, and can be found in polynomial time.*

With help of a B_1-optimal matching, we can give optimal solutions of LP(G) and DP(G).

PROPOSITION 4. *Assume that M is a B_1-optimal matching in G, and $v_1, v_2, \ldots, v_p$ are the vertices exposed by M in $G[B_3]$.*

1. *Let $C_1, C_2, \ldots, C_p$ be pairwise vertex-disjoint odd M-alternating cycles such that C_i has v_i for every $i = 1, 2, \ldots, p$. Then, the vector x in $\mathbb{R}_+^E$ defined by*

$$x(e) = \begin{cases} 1 & \text{if } e \in M \setminus \bigcup_{i=1}^p EC_i, \\ 1/2 & \text{if } e \in \bigcup_{i=1}^p EC_i, \\ 0 & \text{otherwise} \end{cases}$$

is an optimal solution for LP(G), *where EC_i is the edge set of C_i for each $i = 1, 2, \ldots, p$.*

2. *Let Y be a minimum vertex cover in $G[B_1, A]$. Then, the vector y in $\mathbb{R}_+^V$ defined by*

$$y(v) = \begin{cases} 1 & \text{if } v \in A \cap Y, \\ 0 & \text{if } v \in B_1 \setminus Y, \\ 1/2 & \text{otherwise} \end{cases}$$

is an optimal solution for DP(G).

3. *The optimal values of* LP(G) *and* DP(G) *are equal to*

$$\frac{1}{2}\big(|V \setminus B_1| + \nu(G[B_1, A])\big). \tag{1}$$

PROOF. We will show that x and y defined in the statements are feasible solutions for LP(G) and DP(G), respectively, with the same objective value (1).

It is clear that x is feasible for LP(G) since $\sum_{e \in \delta(v)} x(e) \in \{0, 1\}$ for every vertex v in V. Since $\sum_{e \in \delta(v)} x(e) = 0$ if and only if $v \in B_1 \setminus \partial M$, the objective value of x is

$$\sum_{e \in E} x(e) = \frac{1}{2} \sum_{v \in V} \sum_{e \in \delta(v)} x(e) = \frac{1}{2}\big(|D| + |A| + |B_3| + |B_1 \cap \partial M|\big).$$

Thus, since $|V| = |D| + |A| + |B_3| + |B_1|$ and $|B_1 \cap \partial M| = \nu(G[B_1, A])$, it is equal to (1).

On the other hand, the vector y is feasible for DP(G). Indeed, if an edge has an end vertex $v \in B_1 \setminus Y$ with $y(v) = 0$, the other end vertex u is in $A \cap Y$, since Y is a vertex cover in $G[B_1, A]$, and hence $y(u) = 1$. Thus, every edge $\{u, v\}$ satisfies $y(u) + y(v) \geq 1$. The objective value of y is

$$\sum_{v \in V} y(v) = \frac{|D|}{2} + \frac{|A \setminus Y|}{2} + |A \cap Y| + \frac{|B_1 \cap Y|}{2} + \frac{|B_3|}{2} = \frac{1}{2}\big(|D| + |A| + \nu(G[B_1, A]) + |B_3|\big),$$

where the last equality holds by $|A \cap Y| + |B_1 \cap Y| = |Y| = \nu(G[B_1, A])$. Hence the objective value is equal to (1).

Thus they are equal to (1), which means that they are optimal by the duality theorem of linear programming. □

Denote the difference between $\nu_f(G)$ and $\nu(G)$ by

$$d(G) := \nu_f(G) - \nu(G).$$

Combining Propositions 2 and 4, we can express $d(G)$ by the Gallai–Edmonds decomposition.

PROPOSITION 5. *It holds that*

$$d(G) = \frac{1}{2}\big(\mathrm{comp}(G[B_3]) - |A| + \nu(G[B_1, A])\big). \quad (2)$$

Bock et al. [8] showed that $2d(G)$ is equal to the number of components having exposed vertices in $G[B_3]$ for a B_1-optimal matching. By Proposition 5, it is equal to $\mathrm{comp}(G[B_3]) - |A| + \nu(G[B_1, A])$.

3. EDGE ADDITION

A subset F of $\binom{V}{2} \setminus E$ is called an *edge-addition stabilizer*, if $\nu(G+F) = \nu_f(G+F)$. In this section, we discuss the problem of deciding whether there exists an edge-addition stabilizer, and find a minimum-size edge-addition stabilizer if one exists.

We first describe a necessary condition that G has an edge-addition stabilizer.

THEOREM 1. *If $|V|$ is odd and $\nu(G[B_1, A]) = |B_1|$, then G has no edge-addition stabilizer.*

PROOF. Since $\nu(G[B_1, A]) = |B_1|$, the optimal value (1) in Proposition 4 is equal to $n/2$, where $n = |V|$. Hence, for every subset F of $\binom{V}{2} \setminus E$,

$$\nu_f(G+F) \geq \nu_f(G) = \frac{n}{2}.$$

On the other hand, since n is odd,

$$\nu(G+F) \leq \left\lfloor \frac{n}{2} \right\rfloor = \frac{n-1}{2}$$

for every subset F of $\binom{V}{2} \setminus E$. Thus, G does not have an edge-addition stabilizer. □

We next show that, if G does not satisfy the conditions in Theorem 1, then the minimum size of an edge-addition stabilizer is determined by $d(G)$.

THEOREM 2. *If $|V|$ is even or $\nu(G[B_1, A]) < |B_1|$, then G has an edge-addition stabilizer, and the minimum size of an edge-addition stabilizer is equal to $\lceil d(G) \rceil$.*

For the proof, we first consider adding one edge to a given graph in the following lemma, and the proof of Theorem 2 follows.

LEMMA 2. *For every edge e in $\binom{V}{2} \setminus E$,*

$$d(G) - d(G+e) \leq 1.$$

PROOF. It holds that

$$\nu(G+e) \leq \nu(G) + 1, \quad (3)$$

since otherwise a maximum-size matching in $G+e$ would yield a matching of size at least $\nu(G+e) - 1 > \nu(G)$ in G. On the other hand, since a feasible solution x of $\mathrm{LP}(G)$ is feasible for $\mathrm{LP}(G+e)$ by setting $x(e) = 0$,

$$\nu_f(G+e) \geq \nu_f(G). \quad (4)$$

Therefore, it follows from (3) and (4) that

$$\begin{aligned} &d(G) - d(G+e) \\ &\quad = (\nu_f(G) - \nu_f(G+e)) - (\nu(G) - \nu(G+e)) \leq 1. \end{aligned}$$

This completes the proof. □

PROOF OF THEOREM 2. We first prove that it is necessary to add at least $\lceil d(G) \rceil$ edges. Let $F = \{e_1, e_2, \ldots, e_p\}$ be an edge-addition stabilizer of size p. Furthermore, define $F_i := \{e_1, e_2, \ldots, e_i\}$ for each $i = 1, 2, \ldots, p$, and $F_0 := \emptyset$. Then, by applying Lemma 2 repeatedly,

$$d(G) - d(G+F) = \sum_{i=1}^{p} (d(G+F_{i-1}) - d(G+F_i)) \leq p.$$

Since $d(G+F) = 0$ and p is an integer, we see $\lceil d(G) \rceil \leq p$. Thus, the minimum size of an edge-addition stabilizer is at least $\lceil d(G) \rceil$.

Let M be a B_1-optimal matching in G. Then, $G[B_3]$ has $2d(G)$ vertices exposed by M (see the end of Section 2). We will find an edge-addition stabilizer of size $\lceil d(G) \rceil$ by considering the following two cases.

First suppose that $2d(G)$ is even. We make $d(G)$ disjoint pairs of exposed vertices in $G[B_3]$ arbitrarily, and denote the set of the pairs by F^*. The size of F^* is $d(G)$. Since $M \cup F^*$ is a matching of size $\nu(G) + |F^*|$ in $G + F^*$, we observe that

$$\nu(G+F^*) \geq \nu(G) + |F^*|. \quad (5)$$

Define a half-integral optimal dual solution y of $\mathrm{DP}(G)$ as in Proposition 4. Since the end vertices of each pair in F^* have value $1/2$, the vector y is feasible also for $\mathrm{DP}(G+F^*)$. Thus, $\tau_f(G+F^*) \leq \tau_f(G)$, and by the duality theorem in linear programming, we have

$$\nu_f(G+F^*) \leq \nu_f(G). \quad (6)$$

Therefore, it follows from (5), (6), and $|F^*| = d(G)$ that

$$\begin{aligned} d(G+F^*) &= \nu_f(G+F^*) - \nu(G+F^*) \\ &\leq \nu_f(G) - (\nu(G) + |F^*|) = 0. \end{aligned}$$

Thus, F^* is an edge-addition stabilizer.

Next suppose that $2d(G)$ is odd. In this case,

$$\nu(G[B_1, A]) < |B_1|,$$

since otherwise $|V|$ has to be even by the assumption but $|V| = 2|M| + 2d(G)$, which is a contradiction. We make $d(G)$ arbitrary pairs using the exposed vertices in $G[B_3]$ and one exposed vertex s in B_1, and the set of the pairs is denoted by F^*. The size of F^* is equal to $(2d(G)+1)/2 = \lceil d(G) \rceil$. Similarly to the first case, since $M \cup F^*$ is a matching in $G + F^*$, we observe that

$$\nu(G+F^*) \geq \nu(G) + |F^*|. \quad (7)$$

Moreover, define a half-integral optimal dual solution y of $\mathrm{DP}(G)$ as in Proposition 4. By increasing the value $y(s)$ by $1/2$, the vector becomes feasible for $\mathrm{DP}(G+F^*)$. Hence

$$\begin{aligned} \nu_f(G+F^*) &= \tau_f(G+F^*) \\ &\leq \tau_f(G) + 1/2 = \nu_f(G) + 1/2. \end{aligned} \quad (8)$$

Therefore, (7) and (8) imply that

$$\begin{aligned} d(G+F^*) &= \nu_f(G+F^*) - \nu(G+F^*) \\ &\leq (\nu_f(G) + 1/2) - (\nu(G) + |F^*|) = 0, \end{aligned}$$

since $|F^*| = d(G) + 1/2$. Thus, F^* is an edge-addition stabilizer.

Therefore, F^* is an edge-addition stabilizer of size $\lceil d(G) \rceil$ in either case, which is minimum. □

Theorems 1 and 2 lead to a polynomial-time algorithm for finding a minimum-size edge-addition stabilizer.

Algorithm for finding an edge-addition stabilizer

Step 0. Find the Gallai–Edmonds decomposition (B_1, B_3, A, D) of G.

Step 1. Find a maximum-size matching M^* in $G[B_1, A]$. If $|V|$ is odd and $\nu(G[B_1, A]) = |B_1|$, then return that "G has no edge-addition stabilizer." Otherwise, go to Step 2.

Step 2. Find a B_1-optimal matching M.

Step 3. Return $\lceil d(G) \rceil$ pairs of vertices from the exposed vertices in B_3 and one exposed vertex in B_1 (if $2d(G)$ is odd).

The Gallai–Edmonds decomposition and a maximum-size matching M^* in $G[B_1, A]$ can be found in polynomial time. Moreover, by Proposition 3, a B_1-optimal matching M in Step 2 can be obtained in polynomial time. Since Step 3 is easy, we obtain the following theorem.

THEOREM 3. *We can decide whether an edge-addition stabilizer exists, and find a minimum-size edge-addition stabilizer if one exists, in polynomial time.* □

4. VERTEX REMOVAL

A subset X of V is called *a vertex-removal stabilizer*, if $\nu(G - X) = \nu_f(G - X)$. Note that since $\nu(G - V) = 0 = \nu_f(G - V)$, a vertex-removal stabilizer always exists. In this section, we discuss the problem of finding a minimum-size vertex-removal stabilizer.

The main theorem in this section is the following.

THEOREM 4. *The minimum size of a vertex-removal stabilizer is equal to* $2d(G)$.

To prove Theorem 4, we first consider removing one vertex from a graph. Let (B_1, B_3, A, D) be the Gallai–Edmonds decomposition of G, and $B = B_1 \cup B_3$.

LEMMA 3. *For every vertex v in V,*

$$d(G) - d(G - v) \leq \begin{cases} 0 & \text{if } v \in V \setminus B, \\ 1/2 & \text{if } v \in B, \end{cases}$$

PROOF. The case when $v \in V \setminus B$ is not difficult to see by the definition of the Gallai–Edmonds decomposition. We here prove only when $v \in B$.

Since v is inessential, it follows that

$$\nu(G - v) = \nu(G). \tag{9}$$

We will show that

$$\nu_f(G - v) \geq \nu_f(G) - \frac{1}{2}. \tag{10}$$

If (10) is true, together with (9), we have $d(G) - d(G - v) = (\nu_f(G) - \nu_f(G - v)) - (\nu(G) - \nu(G - v)) \leq 1/2$, which completes the proof.

It remains to show (10). Let M be a B_1-optimal matching in G. Define a half-integral optimal solution x of LP(G) as in Proposition 4. Note that $\sum_{e \in \delta(u)} x(e) \in \{0, 1\}$ for every $u \in V$. If $\sum_{e \in \delta(v)} x(e) = 0$, then restricting x to $E \setminus \delta(v)$ implies a feasible solution of LP($G - v$), whose objective value is equal to $\nu_f(G)$. Hence $\nu_f(G - v) \geq \nu_f(G)$, and thus we can assume that $\sum_{e \in \delta(v)} x(e) = 1$. Then v has either two incident edges e, f with $x(e) = x(f) = 1/2$ or exactly one edge e in M such that $x(e) = 1$. We shall consider both cases separately.

First assume that v has two incident edges e, f with $x(e) = x(f) = 1/2$. By the structure of x, the vertex v is contained in some odd M-alternating cycle C such that $x(e) = 1/2$ for every edge e in EC, where EC is the edge set of C. The cycle C has a matching M_C of size $(|EC| - 1)/2$ that exposes v. Define a vector x' in $\mathbb{R}^E_+$ by

$$x'(e) = \begin{cases} 1 & \text{if } e \in EC \cap M_C, \\ 0 & \text{if } e \in EC \setminus M_C, \\ x(e) & \text{otherwise.} \end{cases}$$

Then, x' is feasible for LP(G), and $\sum_{e \in E} x'(e) = \nu_f(G) - 1/2$. Since restricting x' to $E \setminus \delta(v)$ implies a feasible solution of LP($G - v$) and $\sum_{e \in \delta(v)} x'(e) = 0$, the objective value with respect to LP($G - v$) is $\nu_f(G) - 1/2$. Thus, we have $\nu_f(G - v) \geq \nu_f(G) - 1/2$.

The remaining case is when v has exactly one edge e in M such that $x(e) = 1$. Since $v \in B$, there is a maximum-size matching M_v that exposes v in G. The symmetric difference $M \Delta M_v$ has an M-alternating path P of even length from v to a vertex $w \notin \partial M$. Let $C_1, \ldots, C_p$ be the M-alternating cycles as defined in Proposition 4. Recall that $x(e) = 1/2$ if and only if e is contained in some C_i.

First suppose that P intersects with no C_i's. Then $x(e) \in \{0, 1\}$ for each $e \in EP$, where EP is the edge set of P. Define a vector x' in $\mathbb{R}^E_+$ by

$$x'(e) = \begin{cases} 0 & \text{if } e \in EP \cap M, \\ 1 & \text{if } e \in EP \setminus M, \\ x(e) & \text{otherwise.} \end{cases} \tag{11}$$

Then, x' is a feasible solution for LP(G). Moreover, since P is of even length, $\sum_{e \in E} x'(e) = \sum_{e \in E} x(e) = \nu_f(G)$. Since restricting x' to $E \setminus \delta(v)$ implies a feasible solution of LP($G - v$) and $\sum_{e \in \delta(v)} x'(e) = 0$, the objective value with respect to LP($G - v$) is $\nu_f(G)$. Thus, we have $\nu_f(G - v) \geq \nu_f(G)$.

Next suppose that P intersects with some of C_i's. We may assume that P intersects with exactly one of C_i's, say C. Indeed, suppose that we traverse P from v and consider when P intersects with some C_i for the first time. Then the union of C_i and the subpath P from v to C_i contains an M-alternating path of even length from v to the exposed vertex in C_i, and we may replace P with the path. Define a vector x' in $\mathbb{R}^E_+$ by

$$x'(e) = \begin{cases} 0 & \text{if } e \in (EP \cap M) \cup (EC' \setminus M), \\ 1 & \text{if } e \in (EP \setminus M) \cup (EC' \cap M), \\ x(e) & \text{otherwise,} \end{cases} \tag{12}$$

where EC is the edge set in C and $EC' = EC \setminus EP$. Then, x' is a feasible solution for LP(G). Moreover, since $\sum_{e \in EP \cup EC} x'(e) = \sum_{e \in EP \cup EC} x(e) - 1/2$, it holds that $\sum_{e \in E} x'(e) = \nu_f(G) - 1/2$. Since restricting x' to $E \setminus \delta(v)$

implies a feasible solution of LP$(G-v)$ and $\sum_{e\in\delta(v)} x'(e) = 0$, the objective value with respect to LP$(G-v)$ is $\nu_f(G) - 1/2$. Thus, we have $\nu_f(G-v) \geq \nu_f(G) - 1/2$. Therefore, in either case, it holds that $\nu_f(G-v) \geq \nu_f(G) - 1/2$. □

PROOF OF THEOREM 4. We first claim that it is necessary to remove at least $d(G)$ vertices. Assume that we are given a vertex-removal stabilizer $X = \{x_1, x_2, \dots, x_p\}$ of size p. Define $X_i := \{x_1, x_2, \dots, x_i\}$ for each $i = 1, 2, \dots, p$ and $X_0 := \emptyset$. Then, by Lemma 3, $d(G) - d(G-X) = \sum_{i=1}^{p} (d(G-X_{i-1}) - d(G-X_i)) \leq p/2$. Since $d(G-X) = 0$, we have $p \geq 2d(G)$.

Let M be a B_1-optimal matching in G. Then $G[B_3]$ has $2d(G)$ vertices exposed by M, the set of which is denoted by X^*. The size of X^* is $2d(G)$, and $\nu(G-X^*) = \nu(G)$. We will claim that X^* is a vertex-removal stabilizer.

By Proposition 4, DP(G) has a half-integral dual optimal solution y satisfying that $y(v) = 1/2$ for every vertex v in B_3. The vector obtained by restricting y to $V \setminus X^*$ is a feasible solution for DP$(G-X^*)$, whose objective value is

$$\tau_f(G) - \frac{1}{2}|X^*| = \nu_f(G) - \frac{1}{2}|X^*| = \nu_f(G) - d(G).$$

Hence, we have $\tau_f(G-X^*) \leq \nu_f(G) - d(G)$. Since $\nu_f(G-X^*) = \tau_f(G-X^*)$, it holds that $d(G-X^*) = \nu_f(G-X^*) - \nu(G-X^*) \leq (\nu_f(G) - d(G)) - \nu(G) = 0$. This means that X^* is a vertex-removal stabilizer of size $d(G)$, and thus it is minimum. □

Theorem 4 naturally leads to a polynomial-time algorithm for finding a minimum-size vertex-removal stabilizer. The algorithm finds a B_1-optimal matching M in G, and return the set of vertices in $G[B_3]$ exposed by M. By Proposition 3, a B_1-optimal matching in G can be found in polynomial time. Therefore, we have the following theorem.

THEOREM 5. *We can find a minimum-size vertex-removal stabilizer in polynomial time.* □

5. VERTEX ADDITION

For each set X of vertices, we denote by $G+X$ the graph obtained from G by adding X with some edges from X. Note that $G+X$ is not uniquely determined, but the arguments below hold for any graph obtained by the vertex addition. When $X = \{v\}$ we denote $G+v$ for simplicity. A *vertex-addition stabilizer* is a set X of vertices such that the graph obtained by adding X with some edges from X is stable.

Similarly to Sections 3 and 4, we have the following lemma for adding one vertex. We omit the proof due to space limitation.

LEMMA 4. *For every vertex v, $d(G) - d(G+v) \leq 1/2$.*

With Lemma 4, we obtain a proposition similar to Theorem 4, which shows that the size of a vertex-addition stabilizer is at least $2d(G)$. Furthermore, a vertex-addition stabilizer of size $2d(G)$ can be found as follows: Look at the set X of $2d(G)$ vertices in $G[B_3]$ exposed by a B_1-optimal matching in G as in Theorem 4, and we add $2d(G)$ new vertices and connect each to a different vertex of X with a single edge. Then the resulting graph turns out to be stable.

THEOREM 6. *The minimum size of a vertex-addition stabilizer is equal to $2d(G)$. Moreover, we can find a minimum-size vertex-addition stabilizer in polynomial time.* □

It should be noted that our algorithm adds $2d(G)$ edges, which is optimal even when we aim to minimize the total number of appended vertices and edges.

6. HARDNESS FOR WEIGHTED CASES

6.1 Edge addition

In this section we consider the weighted variant of finding an edge-addition stabilizer. Precisely speaking, in this problem, we are given a weight function $w\colon \binom{V}{2}\setminus E \to \mathbb{R}_+$, and we aim to find a minimum-weight edge-addition stabilizer, i.e., an edge-addition stabilizer F minimizing $\sum_{e\in F} w(e)$ among all edge-addition stabilizers.

THEOREM 7. *The problem of finding a minimum-weight edge-addition stabilizer is* **NP**-*hard.*

PROOF. We reduce an **NP**-hard problem called EXACT COVER BY 3-SETS (X3C for short) to the problem of finding a minimum-weight edge-addition stabilizer. The problem X3C is defined as follows (see [16]).

Input. A set X with $|X| = 3n$ and a collection $\mathcal{C}$ of 3-element subsets of X.

Goal. Determine whether there is a subcollection $\mathcal{C}' \subseteq \mathcal{C}$ of size n such that every element of X occurs in exactly one member of $\mathcal{C}'$

Suppose we are given an instance of the X3C, i.e., we are given a set X and a collection $\mathcal{C}$ of 3-element subsets of X. In what follows, we construct an instance of the problem of finding a minimum-weight edge-addition stabilizer that is equivalent to the original instance of the X3C. For each element x in X, we introduce three vertices $v(x,0), v(x,1)$, and $v(x,2)$ and three edges between each pair of them. For each member $C = \{x_1, x_2, x_3\}$ in $\mathcal{C}$, we introduce nine vertices $v(C, x_i)$ for each $i = 1,2,3$ and $v(C, x_i, x_j)$ for each pair of $i, j = 1,2,3$ with $i \neq j$ and six edges between $v(C, x_i)$ and $v(C, x_i, x_j)$ for each $i, j = 1,2,3$ with $i \neq j$. The obtained graph is denoted by $G = (V, E)$. We define a weight function $w\colon \binom{V}{2} \setminus E \to \mathbb{R}_+$ as follows. For each member C in $\mathcal{C}$ and each element x in C, set $w(v(x,0), v(C,x)) = 3n + 1 (=: L)$. For each member C in $\mathcal{C}$ and each pair of elements x, y in C, set $w(v(C,x,y), v(C,y,x)) = 1$. We define the weight of the other pairs as a sufficiently large number (e.g., $nL + 3n + 1$).

We now show that there is an edge-addition stabilizer F such that $\sum_{e\in F} w(e) \leq nL + 3n$ if and only if the original instance of the X3C has a solution.

First, assume that the original instance of the X3C has a solution $\mathcal{C}' \subseteq \mathcal{C}$. Then,

$$F := \{\{v(x,0), v(C,x)\} \mid x \in C \in \mathcal{C}'\} \\ \cup \{\{v(C,x,y), v(C,y,x)\} \mid x, y \in C \in \mathcal{C}'\}$$

satisfies that $\nu(G+F) = \nu_f(G+F)$ and $\sum_{e\in F} w(e) = nL + 3n$, which shows the sufficiency of the claim.

Next, to show the necessity, assume that there is an edge-addition stabilizer F such that $\sum_{e\in F} w(e) \leq nL + 3n$. For every element x in X, since $v(x,0), v(x,1)$, and $v(x,2)$ form a triangle in G, which is not stable, at least one edge in F is incident to $v(x,0)$. Furthermore, since $\sum_{e\in F} w(e) \leq nL + 3n$, for every element x in X, there is a unique member $C = \{x, y, z\}$ in $\mathcal{C}$ such that $\{v(x,0), v(C,x)\} \in F$. Consider the connected component of $G+F$ that contains $v(x,0), v(x,1), v(x,2), v(C,x), v(C,x,y)$ and $v(C,x,z)$, where $C = \{x, y, z\} \in \mathcal{C}$ and $\{v(x,0), v(C,x)\} \in F$. Since this component has to be stable, we can easily check that F contains all of the edges in

$$E_C := \{\{v(C,x,y), v(C,y,x)\},\\ \{v(C,x,z), v(C,z,x)\}, \{v(C,y,z), v(C,z,y)\}\}.$$

This shows that $\mathcal{C}' := \{C \in \mathcal{C} \mid E_C \subseteq F\}$ covers X in the original instance of the X3C. On the other hand, since $\sum_{e \in F} w(e) \leq nL + 3n$ and F contains n edges of weight L, we have $|\mathcal{C}'| = |\{C \in \mathcal{C} \mid E_C \subseteq F\}| \leq 3n/3 = n$. Thus, each element of X occurs in exactly one member of $\mathcal{C}'$, which means that $\mathcal{C}'$ is a solution of the the original instance of the X3C.

Therefore, we can reduce the X3C to the problem of finding a minimum-weight edge-addition stabilizer, which completes the proof. □

6.2 Vertex removal

In this section we consider the weighted variant of finding a vertex-removal stabilizer. Precisely speaking, in this problem, we are given a weight function $w\colon V \to \mathbb{R}_+$, and we aim to find a minimum-weight vertex-removal stabilizer, i.e., a vertex-removal stabilizer X minimizing $\sum_{v \in X} w(v)$ among all vertex-removal stabilizers. We show that the problem of finding a minimum-weight vertex-removal stabilizer is also **NP**-hard.

THEOREM 8. *The problem of finding a minimum-weight vertex-removal stabilizer is* **NP***-hard.*

We reduce the clique problem (CLIQUE), which is defined as follows.

Input. A graph G' and a positive integer p.

Goal. Determine whether there exists a set F of $p(p-1)/2$ edges of G' such that $|\partial F|$ is at most p.

CLIQUE is known to be **NP**-hard [16]. A set of p vertices covered by $p(p-1)/2$ edges is called a *clique* of size p.

For a bipartite graph $H = (U_1, U_2; F)$ with $|U_1| \geq |U_2|$, a *U_2-perfect matching* is a matching of size $|U_2|$. That is, it is a matching covering all the vertices of U_2.

LEMMA 5. *The following problem is* **NP***-complete.*

Input. *A bipartite graph $H = (U_1, U_2; F)$ that has a U_2-perfect matching, and two positive integers p, q.*

Goal. *Determine whether there exists a set $X \subseteq U_1$ of size at most p such that $\nu(G - X) \leq |U_2| - q$.*

PROOF. Suppose that we are given an instance of CLIQUE, a graph $G' = (V', E')$ and a positive integer p. We construct a bipartite graph H as follows. Define $U_1' := V'$ and $U_2 := E'$, and there is an edge between a vertex v in U_1' and a vertex e in U_2 if and only if v is an end vertex of e in G' (i.e., $v \in e$). Furthermore, defining $S_e := \{s_e^1, \ldots, s_e^L\}$ for each edge e in E', where $L > |V'|$, we connect a vertex e of U_2 to each of S_e with L edges. In summary, the resulting graph $H = (U_1, U_2; F)$ is defined by

$$U_1 := U_1' \cup \bigcup_{e \in E} S_e, \qquad U_2 := E',$$

$$F := \{\{v, e\} \mid v \in e\} \cup \{\{s_e^j, e\} \mid j = 1, \ldots, L, e \in E'\}.$$

Set $q := p(p-1)/2$. We will show that H has a desired vertex set of size at most $Lp(p-1)/2 + p$ if and only if G' has a clique of size p.

Suppose that G' has a clique K of size p. Then we delete $X = VK \cup \bigcup_{e \in EK} S_e$ from U_1, where VK (resp., EK) is the vertex set (resp., the edge set) of K. The number of the deleted vertices is $Lp(p-1)/2 + p$. Since each vertex in U_2 corresponding to one in EK has no neighbor in $G' - X$, $G' - X$ has no matching of size greater than $|U_2| - |EK| = |U_2| - q$. Thus X is a solution of the problem.

Conversely, suppose that H has a solution set X of size at most $Lp(p-1)/2 + p$. We may assume that X is minimal. Then we see by the minimality that, in $H - X$, each vertex e in U_2 has either no single edges to S_e or all the single edges remaining. Hence exactly $p(p-1)/2$ vertices of U_2's have no neighbor to S_e's in $H - X$. The edge subset corresponding to these vertices is denoted by J. Since a vertex e in $U_2 \setminus J$ has an edge to S_e, $H - X$ has a matching of size at least $|E'| - p(p-1)/2$. Therefore, a vertex in J has to have no edge to U_1' in $H - X$. Hence $N(J) \cap U_1' \subseteq X$ holds, which implies that $|N(J) \cap U_1'| \leq p$. Since $|N(J) \cap U_1'| \geq p$ as $|J| = p(p-1)/2$, the number is exactly equal to p. This means that J forms a clique of size p in G'. □

PROOF OF THEOREM 8. We reduce the problem in Lemma 5. Suppose that we are given an instance of the problem, a bipartite graph $H = (U_1, U_2; F)$ and two positive integers p, q.

We prepare q triangles, $T_1, T_2, \ldots, T_q$, and append T_i to all the vertices of U_2, that is, $N(T_i) = U_2$. The resulting graph is denoted by $G = (V, E)$. Note that the Gallai–Edmonds decomposition of G is represented by $B_1 = U_1$, $B_3 = \bigcup_{i=1}^q VT_i$, $A = U_2$, and $D = \emptyset$, where VT_i is the vertex set of T_i. Since H has a U_2-perfect matching, G has a B_1-optimal matching that exposes all the triangles.

We define the weight function $w\colon V \to \mathbb{R}_+$ by $w(v) = 1$ if $v \in U_1$, and $w(v) = \infty$ otherwise (i.e., $w(v) \geq |V|$).

It is observed that G has a vertex-removal stabilizer of finite weight if and only if H has a solution of size p. Thus the statement holds. □

REFERENCES

[1] S. Ahmadian, L. Sanita, and H. Hosseinzadeh. Stabilizing network bargaining games by blocking players. In *Integer Programming and Combinatorial Optimization - 18th International Conference, IPCO 2016, Liége, Belgium, June 1-3, 2016. Proceedings*, 2016. to appear.

[2] H. Aziz and B. de Keijzer. Shapley meets shapley. In E. W. Mayr and N. Portier, editors, *31st International Symposium on Theoretical Aspects of Computer Science (STACS 2014), STACS 2014, March 5-8, 2014, Lyon, France*, volume 25 of *LIPIcs*, pages 99–111. Schloss Dagstuhl - Leibniz-Zentrum fuer Informatik, 2014.

[3] Y. Bachrach, E. Elkind, R. Meir, D. V. Pasechnik, M. Zuckerman, J. Rothe, and J. S. Rosenschein. The cost of stability in coalitional games. In M. Mavronicolas and V. G. Papadopoulou, editors, *Algorithmic Game Theory, Second International Symposium, SAGT 2009, Paphos, Cyprus, October 18-20, 2009. Proceedings*, volume 5814 of *Lecture*

Notes in Computer Science, pages 122–134. Springer, 2009.

[4] M. Bateni, M. Hajiaghayi, N. Immorlica, and H. Mahini. The cooperative game theory foundations of network bargaining games. In S. Abramsky, C. Gavoille, C. Kirchner, F. M. auf der Heide, and P. G. Spirakis, editors, *Automata, Languages and Programming, 37th International Colloquium, ICALP 2010, Bordeaux, France, July 6-10, 2010, Proceedings, Part I*, volume 6198 of *Lecture Notes in Computer Science*, pages 67–78. Springer, 2010.

[5] C. Berge. Sur le couplage maximum d'un graphe. *Comptes Rendus Hebdomadaires des Séances de l'Académie des Sciences [Paris]*, 247:258–259, 1958.

[6] P. Biró, M. Bomhoff, P. A. Golovach, W. Kern, and D. Paulusma. Solutions for the stable roommates problem with payments. *Theoretical Computer Science*, 540:53–61, 2014.

[7] P. Biró, W. Kern, and D. Paulusma. Computing solutions for matching games. *International Journal of Game Theory*, 41(1):75–90, 2012.

[8] A. Bock, K. Chandrasekaran, J. Könemann, B. Peis, and L. Sanità. Finding small stabilizers for unstable graphs. *Mathematical Programming, Series B*, 154(1-2):173–196, 2015.

[9] N. Chen, P. Lu, and H. Zhang. Computing the nucleolus of matching, cover and clique games. In J. Hoffmann and B. Selman, editors, *Proceedings of the Twenty-Sixth AAAI Conference on Artificial Intelligence, July 22-26, 2012, Toronto, Ontario, Canada*. AAAI Press, 2012.

[10] X. Deng, T. Ibaraki, and H. Nagamochi. Algorithmic aspects of the core of combinatorial optimization games. *Mathematics of Operations Research*, 24(3):751–766, 1999.

[11] J. Edmonds. Paths, trees, and flowers. *Canadian Journal of Mathematics*, 17:449–467, 1965.

[12] K. Eriksson and J. Karlander. Stable outcomes of the roommate game with transferable utility. *International Journal of Game Theory*, 29(4):555–569, 2001.

[13] U. Faigle, W. Kern, S. P. Fekete, and W. Hochstättler. The nucleon of cooperative games and an algorithm for matching games. *Mathematical Programming*, 83:195–211, 1998.

[14] T. Gallai. Kritische graphen II. *A Magyar Tudományos Akadémia – Matematikai Kutató Intézetének Közleményei*, 8:373–395, 1963.

[15] T. Gallai. Maximale systeme unabhänginger kanten. *A Magyar Tudományos Akadémia – Matematikai Kutató Intézetének Közleményei*, 9:401–413, 1964.

[16] M. R. Garey and D. S. Johnson. *Computers and Intractability; A Guide to the Theory of NP-Completeness*. W. H. Freeman & Co., New York, NY, USA, 1979.

[17] W. Hochstättler, H. Jin, and R. Nickel. Note on an auction procedure for a matching game in polynomial time. In S. Cheng and C. K. Poon, editors, *Algorithmic Aspects in Information and Management, Second International Conference, AAIM 2006, Hong Kong, China, June 20-22, 2006, Proceedings*, volume 4041 of *Lecture Notes in Computer Science*, pages 387–394. Springer, 2006.

[18] W. Kern and D. Paulusma. Matching games: The least core and the nucleolus. *Mathematics of Operations Research*, 28(2):294–308, 2003.

[19] S. Khot. On the power of unique 2-prover 1-round games. In J. H. Reif, editor, *Proceedings on 34th Annual ACM Symposium on Theory of Computing, May 19-21, 2002, Montréal, Québec, Canada*, pages 767–775. ACM, 2002.

[20] J. M. Kleinberg and É. Tardos. Balanced outcomes in social exchange networks. In C. Dwork, editor, *Proceedings of the 40th Annual ACM Symposium on Theory of Computing, Victoria, British Columbia, Canada, May 17-20, 2008*, pages 295–304. ACM, 2008.

[21] J. Könemann, K. Larson, and D. Steiner. Network bargaining: Using approximate blocking sets to stabilize unstable instances. *Theory of Computing Systems*, 57(3):655–672, 2015.

[22] Y. K. Kwon and P. L. Yu. Stabilization through taxation in n-person games. *Journal of Optimization Theory and Applications*, 23(2):277–284, 1977.

[23] L. Lovász and M. D. Plummer. *Matching Theory*, volume 29 of *Annals of Discrete Mathematics*. North-Holland, Amsterdam, 1986.

[24] J. F. Nash. The bargaining problem. *Econometrica*, 18(2):155–162, 1950.

[25] W. Pulleyblank. Fractional matchings and the Edmonds-Gallai theorem. *Discrete Applied Mathematics*, 16(1):51 – 58, 1987.

[26] L. Shapley and M. Shubik. The assignment game I: The core. *International Journal of Game Theory*, 1(1):111–130, 1971.

[27] W. T. Tutte. The factorization of linear graphs. *The Journal of the London Mathematical Society*, 22:107–111, 1947.

[28] Y. Zick, M. Polukarov, and N. R. Jennings. Taxation and stability in cooperative games. In M. L. Gini, O. Shehory, T. Ito, and C. M. Jonker, editors, *International conference on Autonomous Agents and Multi-Agent Systems, AAMAS 2013, Saint Paul, MN, USA, May 6-10, 2013*, pages 523–530. IFAAMAS, 2013.

An Agent-Based Model of Competition Between Financial Exchanges: Can Frequent Call Mechanisms Drive Trade Away from CDAs?

Zhuoshu Li
Washington University in St. Louis
zhuoshuli@wustl.edu

Sanmay Das
Washington University in St. Louis
sanmay@wustl.edu

ABSTRACT

In the debate over high frequency trading, the frequent call (Call) mechanism has recently received considerable attention as a proposal for replacing the continuous double auction (CDA) mechanisms that currently run most financial markets. One natural question, which has begun to spur the development of new models, is the effect of competition between platforms that use these two different mechanisms when agents can strategize over platform choice. In this paper we contribute to this nascent literature by developing an agent-based model of competition between a Call market and a CDA market. Our model incorporates patient informed traders (both high-frequency and not) who are willing to wait for order execution at their preferred price and impatient background traders who demand immediate execution. We show that there is a strong tendency for the Call market to absorb a significant fraction of trade under most equilibrium and approximate-equilibrium conditions. These equilibria typically lead to significantly higher welfare for the background traders, an important measure of social value, than the operation of an isolated CDA market.

Keywords

Competing platforms; agent-based modeling; market microstructure

1. INTRODUCTION

Most modern financial exchanges operate using the continuous double auction (CDA) mechanism, which in principle allows for trading in continuous time, at least to within our measurement and implementation capabilities. With companies investing in faster infrastructure for trading and events like the "flash crash" of May 2010, high frequency trading (HFT) has become an increasingly debated topic in both the media and policy spheres [15]. Proponents claim that high-frequency trading improves liquidity and price discovery. Improved liquidity means lower transaction costs for average investors, while better price discovery serves the social information aggregation and dissemination role of market prices [2,16]. However, there is increasing evidence that at least one form of high frequency trading, namely latency arbitrage, has reached a point of socially diminishing returns. Budish et al demonstrate this both empirically and through a simple model: empirically, they show that correlations between virtually identical assets being traded in different markets break down at very small timescales, while they are essentially perfect at larger timescales [3]. This can almost be thought of as a law of physics – there is no natural force tying the assets or markets together, so there is no way to make them actually move simultaneously. What is problematic is the "arms race" this creates to extract the maximum profit from squeezing this reaction time down as much as possible. Budish et al show that this is not only socially inefficient, it can actually create thinner markets. Along similar lines, Wah and Wellman build a model where an asset is traded on two markets, and there is an infinitely fast latency arbitrageur present. They show how the presence of the arbitrageur can hurt social welfare [22]. Both sets of authors recommend frequent batch auctions as a market structure that could replace CDAs, since the minimum time period between trades is specified, and there is no benefit to being faster than that.

An important question for the possible use of frequent batch (or call) auctions is how they would work in the presence of existing CDA markets. Competition between exchanges or platforms that try to attract trade is a vast topic, and there is evidence in many domains that platforms with better welfare properties *assuming that there is only one platform available* may not be able to capture enough of the market for these properties to become evident when they face competition from other platforms. For example, in living-donor paired kidney exchange, even though exchanges that wait to build thickness may be socially preferable, exchanges that match greedily can make them nonviable [6]. Therefore, even though they may have desirable welfare properties, could call auction based markets actually take volume away from CDA markets if both existed simultaneously? Wah et al have engaged this question using empirical game theoretic analysis [21]. They develop a model where the environment is populated by fast (HFT) and slow (non-HFT) traders. They argue that a frequent call market in the wild could attract sufficient volume for viability from two perspectives: first, in equilibrium, welfare of slow traders is generally higher in the call market, where they are relatively protected from sniping and adverse selection, and second, fast traders are willing to follow the slow traders to either market, including to the call market, so it could serve as a basin of attraction. Wah et al's model does not consider traders who have a preference for immediacy, and

Appears in: *Proceedings of the 15th International Conference on Autonomous Agents and Multiagent Systems (AAMAS 2016), J. Thangarajah, K. Tuyls, C. Jonker, S. Marsella (eds.), May 9–13, 2016, Singapore.*

they also restrict traders to choose a single market and then do not allow traders to move. While their results are quite promising, we seek to build a richer model that combines aspects of classic financial market microstructure models and agent-based models that are known to replicate important properties of order books.

Another line of literature relates to the TAC Market Design Competition (CAT) [17]. In this competition, participants aim to design better mechanisms to maximize a score (a combination of profit, market share and transaction success rate) when traders are drawn from a known population of different types. CAT gives a general view of competition among different markets, but our paper focuses on a comparison of two more specific market mechanisms and how they influence the social welfare of traders.

1.1 Overview and Contributions

In this paper, we build an agent-based model to analyze platform competition between financial exchanges. Agent-based modeling seeks to fill the hole in simple stylized models which may not represent agent behavior in sufficiently complex manners to really capture the essence of the important phenomena. The last two decades have seen substantial work on agent-based modeling of financial markets, using both sophisticated [4, 7, 9, 18] and simple [8, 12, 14] trader models in the population. Our model is as parsimonious as possible while attempting to capture the essential relevant behaviors that are important to understanding the behavior of these markets. As such, it follows the basic structure of classic models of market microstructure such as those of Glosten and Milgrom [11] and of Kyle [13], in which there are informed traders, who possess superior information and trade in search of profit, liquidity (or background) traders, who trade for exogenous reasons (e.g. retirement funds that receive cash and need to track indices, or investors liquidating portfolios in retirement or in order to buy a house, say) and demand immediacy, and market makers, who may be employed in order to facilitate price discovery and trade execution.

Our key measure of welfare is the price of immediacy – the expected loss suffered by background traders. This measures the cost that the "average trader" pays in order to execute transactions. This is a different measure than that of Wah and Wellman [23] or Wah et al [21], who use surplus. These are both reasonable measures, but surplus is most meaningful in private value models, where some meaning can be attributed to different agents having different valuations for an asset. Our model follows in a tradition of common value models, where the asset has a true underlying value, and different traders may have different estimates of that true value. The existence of background traders in our model provides a useful proxy for estimating the cost of trading. It is worth noting that this doesn't mean that background traders are necessarily losing money – typically such traders would stay in the market for much longer, and under reasonable models of price appreciation, these "losses" can be thought of as transaction costs for buy-and-hold type investors.

First, we look at simple models of individual markets and confirm that our model satisfies the basic intuitions one would expect. Namely, informed traders (in particular, low latency traders) make more profit (and background traders are consequently made worse off) in CDA markets than in frequent call markets. A zero-profit market maker (with no specialized information) can greatly improve the position of background traders, taking away most of the profit opportunities from informed traders in CDA markets. Next, we model competition between a CDA market and a frequent call market when informed traders pick which market to place their orders in based simply on which market is more mispriced with respect to their current belief. We show that the informed traders do better overall when they choose to place orders in the market that is more mispriced from their perspective. We show that, when informed traders are all using this strategy, a majority of orders flows to the call market, and background traders are better off than in a single CDA market.

Note that all of the above analysis is not in an equilibrium setting – we assume that all informed traders use the same strategy. We can use the insights developed in these models to begin analyzing strategic market choice. We do so by introducing a learning framework, where informed traders learn a parametric form for the expected profit of choosing to place an order in a market (and a non-parametric probability of order execution) given the distance of that market's "current price" from the trader's estimate of the true value of a stock. We show that, when all agents use this learning approach, they converge to an approximate equilibrium where a majority of trades again flow to the frequent call market.

2. MARKET MODEL

2.1 The CDA and Call Markets

Our model of competing markets consists of two markets, one employing a *continuous double auction* (CDA) mechanism and the other one employing a *frequent call* (CALL) mechanism. We begin by describing the details of each individual market, which will serve as the foundation for our model of competing markets.

Each market is running in the continuous-time interval [0,T]. A single security is traded in the market. There is an underlying "true value" process. The initial true value of the security v_0 is drawn from a Gaussian distribution with mean v_{initial} and standard deviation σ_{initial}. Then, the true value jumps according to a Poisson process with rate parameter λ_{jump}. If the true value jumps, the new true value v_t is generated from $v_t \sim \mathcal{N}(v_{t-dt}, \sigma_j)$, where v_{t-dt} is the price instantaneously before the jump (we restrict $v_t \geq 0$, so all values are truncated at 0).

In the CDA market, outstanding orders are maintained in two priority queues: one for bids (the buy orderbook) and one for asks (the sell orderbook). Bids and asks are prioritized by price first and time second. When a new order comes in, it is added to the corresponding order book. A trade is executed if the highest bid exceeds or is equal to the lowest ask. The execution involves the orders at the top of the bid and ask queues, at the price of the older of the two orders involved.

The CALL market is similar to that described by Budish et al [3]. It clears in fixed intervals of time τ (the *call interval*). At each clearing time, the market collates all of the orders and computes the aggregate demand and supply functions of all bids and asks, respectively. The market clears where supply equals demand, with all executions occurring at the same price, called the market-clearing price. None of the orders are visible to any traders during the call interval. The market announces the market-clearing price after each clearing (*market announcement*). When no order was executed at the last clearing time, if both the buy and sell orderbooks are not empty, the market announcement will be the mid-point of the highest bid and lowest ask, otherwise it will be the most recent available market-clearing price. All untraded orders roll into the next call.

2.2 Valuation model

Each trader has a private valuation for the security (or equivalently for our purposes, a private signal of the true value). We have two types of traders, informed (IF) traders and background (BG) traders. Each informed trader IF_i receives a private signal of the security value, $w_{i,t} \sim \mathcal{N}(v_{\hat{t}}, \sigma_{\text{trader}})$, where $v_{\hat{t}}$ is the underlying true value of the security at some time $\hat{t}$, where $\hat{t} \leq t$, and σ_{trader} is a noise parameter. We define two types of informed traders, namely, low latency (LL) traders and high latency (HL) traders. High latency traders have staler information, i.e., $w_{i,t} \sim \mathcal{N}(v_{t-\delta}, \sigma_{\text{trader}})$, and low latency traders observe information with no delay, thus $w_{i,t} \sim \mathcal{N}(v_t, \sigma_{\text{trader}})$. Background traders do not have any private information; each arriving background trader wishes to either buy or sell one unit (with equal probability). They demand immediacy, that is, they want to get their orders executed as soon as possible, so they are willing to take any market price.

2.3 Agent arrival process

There are a fixed number of traders of each type. Informed traders and background traders both arrive at the market according to separate Poisson processes, with informed traders arriving with rate λ_{IF} and background traders' arriving with rate λ_{BG}. In the event that an informed trader arrival occurs, a specific IF trader is selected uniformly at random from all the IF traders to place/replace an order; similarly, if a background trader arrival occurs, a specific BG trader is selected uniformly at random from all the BG traders to place/replace an order.

2.4 Agent strategies in individual markets

Each of the informed traders and background traders is only allowed to maintain a single unit order in the market. When informed and background traders reenter the market, they can replace existing orders that have not yet been executed. We model informed traders as using limit orders and background traders as using market orders exclusively.

Informed traders' strategy: $S_{\text{individual}}$.

We consider trading strategies in the *Zero Intelligence* (ZI) family for informed traders. There is a large literature involving ZI strategies, including some controversy, which we will not rehash here [4, 19]. While ZI strategies are clearly not the "best" trading strategies in isolation, it is also generally believed that they model order arrival processes well, and they are a standard method for choosing prices in complex agent-based market simulations [9, 18]. We first define, in the CDA market,

$$p^*_{t,\text{CDA}} = \begin{cases} \dfrac{(BID_t.p) + (ASK_t.p)}{2}, \text{if } BID_t \text{ and } ASK_t \text{ exist,} \\ \text{the most recent execution price, if any order} \\ \qquad\qquad\qquad\qquad\qquad \text{book is empty,} \end{cases}$$

where $(BID_t.p)$ and $(ASK_t.p)$ refer to the price of BID_t and ASK_t respectively. And in the CALL market,

$$p^*_{t,\text{CALL}} = \text{the most recent } \textit{market announcement.}$$

When an informed trader IF_i places an order, a limit price is generated from

$$p_{i,t} \sim \mathcal{N}(p^*_{t,\text{market}}, \sigma_{\text{price}}),$$

where market $\in$ {CDA, CALL}. Based on $p_{i,t}$ and $w_{i,t}$, the informed trader IF_i's strategy at time t is as follows,

$$p_{i,t} \begin{cases} > w_{i,t}, \text{places a unit sell order,} \\ < w_{i,t}, \text{places a unit buy order,} \\ = w_{i,t}, \text{uniformly at random places a unit buy or sell order.} \end{cases}$$

Note that $p_{i,t} = w_{i,t}$ is a zero probability event. If $p_{i,t} > (ASK_t.p)$ and the order is a buy order, then it executes immediately and therefore effectively functions as a market order. Similarly if $p_{i,t} < (BID_t.p)$ and the order is a sell order. We call the strategy above $S_{\text{individual}}$.

Background traders' strategy.

The background traders choose whether they want to buy or sell a unit uniformly at random. Once the direction is decided, the order is routed to the market and handled in a special manner as a market order through a "waiting" mechanism. The market is aware of the direction of a market order and the fact that this indicates the trader would like to execute the order at any available market price. However, market orders are not visible to any other traders in both the CDA and CALL markets, since they may need to wait for execution if there is no corresponding limit order on the other side in the CDA market, and at least until the next call in the CALL market.

Market maker's strategy.

In the CDA market, we also incorporate a market maker in some of our experiments. To increase the liquidity of the market, the market maker maintains a unit buy order and a unit sell order at all times. This market maker is implemented using the Bayesian market making algorithm (BMM) of Brahma et al [1], with parameters tuned to maintain near zero-profit. BMM is a learning algorithm that learns from the current bid and ask prices and the direction of incoming trades, augmented with jump prediction and a technique to widen its spread in times of uncertainty. BMM updates its own belief whenever there is an execution, and it immediately replaces its orders. Our implementation closely follows that of Brahma et al, except that we only need to use it for unit orders in our model.

2.5 CDA and CALL market operation

CDA market operation.

In the CDA market, BID_t and ASK_t are based only on orders from informed traders (and also possibly the market maker). If the order book only has market orders that are waiting from background traders, the market shows the order book as empty. The scenario that we want to simulate is that background traders are waiting in the market to buy or sell; as soon as an unfilled corresponding order becomes available, they will immediately take the other side of that order. We need to specify the execution priority in the situation where one side of the market has both market orders and limit orders from informed traders. In this case it must be that the other side of the market is empty (note that this never happens with a market maker present), otherwise the market orders on the first side would have executed. In this situation, we prioritize by time. Procedure 1 illustrates the operation of a CDA market when a new buy order arrives (a sell order arrival is similar).

Procedure 1 CDA market operation when a new buy order arrives

Input: buy orderbook, sell orderbook

A new buy order OD_1 arrives, $(OD_1.p)$ is the price of OD_1
if not empty(sell orderbook) **then**
  if OD_1 is a limit order **then**
    if $(OD_1.p) \geq (ASK_t.p)$ and ASK_t comes earlier than any market order **then**
      Execution(ASK_t, OD_1) at $(ASK_t.p)$
      (in which case, OD_1 is the highest bid and sell orderbook has limit orders from IF traders or BMM)
    else
      if sell orderbook contains market orders **then**
        Execution(the oldest market ask, OD_1) at $(BID_t.p)$
        (in which case, OD_1 is the highest bid)
      end if
    end if
  else {OD_1 is a market order}
    if ASK_t is available and comes earlier than any market order **then**
      Execution(ASK_t, OD_1) at $(ASK_t.p)$
    else
      Execution(the oldest market ask, OD_1) at *the most recent execution price*
    end if
  end if
end if

CALL market operation.

The main difference from a standard aggregation mechanism in our implementation involves the background traders. Background traders would like to buy or sell at any price, so all the market orders are always at the top of both the sell orderbook and the buy orderbook in the CALL market. All the market orders in each orderbook are prioritized by submission time, with earlier submissions having higher priority. At each clearing time, the market collates all of the orders and computes the aggregate demand and supply functions of all bids and asks, respectively. The market clears where supply equals demand, with all executions occurring at the same price, the market-clearing price. If the market only clears market orders, the market-clearing price is the most recent market announcement. If only market orders clear on one side of the market, while some limit orders clear on the other side, the market-clearing price is determined by the side that has limit orders being cleared. More specifically, if cleared buy orders consist of only market orders and cleared sell orders include limit orders, the clearing price will be the highest ask of all the cleared limit orders; if cleared sell orders consist of only market orders and cleared buy orders include limit orders, the clearing price will be the lowest bid of all the cleared limit orders. When some limit orders clear on both sides of the market, the clearing price is the midpoint of the highest ask and lowest bid of all cleared limit orders.

3. COMPETING MARKETS

In the competing markets model, we assume that one CDA market and one CALL market run simultaneously. A single security is traded in both markets. Thus, there is only one underlying "true value" process, but the CDA and CALL markets can price the security differently. The traders choose to place orders in only one market at a time, although they can switch markets each time they re-enter. Each market is running in the same manner as when there is an individual market and each trader can maintain only one unit order in the whole system.

3.1 Agent strategies in competing markets

Informed traders' strategy.

On what basis should a trader choose which market to place an order in? One important factor is the distance between the trader's belief and $p^*_{t,\text{market}}$,

$$d^{\text{market}}_{i,t} = |w_{i,t} - p^*_{t,\text{market}}|, \tag{1}$$

where market $\in \{\text{CDA}, \text{CALL}\}$. We call this the *belief distance.* Comparing $d^{\text{CDA}}_{i,t}$ with $d^{\text{CALL}}_{i,t}$, the informed trader IF_i can choose one of two strategies. One is to place the order in the market that has larger $d^{\text{market}}_{i,t}$, S_{LARGE}, and the other is to place the order in the market that has smaller $d^{\text{market}}_{i,t}$, S_{SMALL}. The tradeoff here is that IF_i gets lower probability of execution but higher profit if she places the order in the market that has larger $d^{\text{market}}_{i,t}$. We will discuss the effects of these two different strategies in Section 4. Strategy 1 shows a summary of IF_i's strategy in the competing markets. After IF_i decides in which market to place the limit order, she follows $S_{\text{individual}}$ to decide the direction and price of the order in the selected market.

Strategy 1 IF_i's strategy in the competing markets at time t

if following S_{LARGE} **then**

$$d^{\text{CDA}}_{i,t} \begin{cases} > d^{\text{CALL}}_{i,t}, & \text{places an order at CDA market following } S_{\text{individual}} \\ < d^{\text{CALL}}_{i,t}, & \text{places an order at CALL market following } S_{\text{individual}} \end{cases}$$

else {following S_{SMALL}}

$$d^{\text{CDA}}_{i,t} \begin{cases} < d^{\text{CALL}}_{i,t}, & \text{places an order at CDA market following } S_{\text{individual}} \\ > d^{\text{CALL}}_{i,t}, & \text{places an order at CALL market following } S_{\text{individual}} \end{cases}$$

end if

Background traders' strategy.

When a background trader enters the market to place or replace a new order, she first compares the price in both markets. For instance, if she wants to buy, she will compare

ASK_t and $p^*_{t,\mathrm{CALL}}$ (if they are available), and select the market which has the lower price to place a market order there. If ASK_t is not available, that is the sell orderbook in the CDA market shows as empty, she will place the order in the CALL market. She follows a similar process for sell orders.

After every market clearing in the CALL market, the background traders check whether their orders have been executed. If not, and the corresponding order books in the CDA market are not empty, that is the sell orderbook is not empty if a BG trader wants to buy and the buy orderbook is not empty if a BG trader wants to sell (here empty means the order books do not have orders from informed traders – market orders from background traders are not visible to any trader), the background traders move their existing orders from the CALL market to the CDA market. In the implementation, the background traders with orders that did not execute are randomly permuted. Each of them moves their order to the CDA market in this random order, until there are no corresponding limit orders on the other side of the market in the CDA. This process is atomic in time.

Strategy 2 shows the overall framework for implementing buy orders for background traders in the competing markets model. The sell strategies are similar.

Strategy 2 The overall framework for implementing the buy orders for background (BG) traders in the competing markets model

$t = 0$
while $t \leq T$ **do**
  An event happens afterΔ t
  $t = t + \Delta t$
  if A BG trader arrives in the market **then**
    BG_i is selected from all BG traders uniformly at random
    if ASK_t is available **then**
      if $ASK_t <= p^*_{t,\mathrm{CALL}}$ **then**
        BG_i places a market order in CDA market
      else
        BG_i places a market order in CALL market
      end if
    else {sell orderbook in CDA market shows as empty}
      BG_i places a market order in CALL market
    end if
  end if
  if CALL market clear **then**
    After each market clearing
    A = {All the BG traders who have buy orders in CALL market}
    while A is not empty and ASK_t is available **do**
      Select BG_i uniformly at random from A
      $A = A - \{\mathrm{BG}_i\}$
      BG_i moves her order to the buy orderbook in CDA market, the new order age is re-generated from the age counter.
      CDA market clears
    end while
  end if
end while

4. SIMULATION RESULTS

In this section, we simulate four different environments, namely CDA vs CALL competing markets (competing markets), an individual CDA market (i-CDA market), an individual CALL market (i-CALL market) and an individual CDA market with BMM (i-CDA-BMM market). The parameters are set as follows. Each simulation run lasts $T = 100,000$ units of time. The initial true value of the security v_0 is drawn from $\mathcal{N}(v_{\mathrm{initial}} = 50, \sigma_{\mathrm{initial}} = 4)$. The true value jump parameter $\sigma_j = 4.0$ and the rate parameter for the jump is $\lambda_{\mathrm{jump}} = 0.0001$, which means there is a jump every 10000 units of time on average. We have 20 informed traders, 10 high latency traders and 10 low latency traders, and 20 background traders. Reentry rates are fixed across the environments, with informed traders arriving in the market at rate $\lambda_{\mathrm{IF}} = 2$, and background traders entering at rate $\lambda_{\mathrm{BG}} = 1$. In all settings, CALL markets clear every 1 unit of time, $\tau = 1$. The standard deviation of informed traders' belief is $\sigma_{\mathrm{trader}} = 2.0$, and the high latency traders' information delay is $\delta = 1000$ units of time. The time between jumps is 10000 units of time on average, so high latency traders have information with no delay a significant fraction of the time, as $v_{t-\delta} = v_t$. Following a jump, high latency traders receive staler information for the next 1000 units of time. The standard deviation of the distribution from which informed traders draw ZI prices is $\sigma_{\mathrm{price}} = 4.0$. We simulate both $\mathrm{S}_{\mathrm{LARGE}}$ and $\mathrm{S}_{\mathrm{SMALL}}$ strategies for informed traders.

Across our experiments, we are interested in the total profit, expected per-order profit and order execution percentage for each trader type. At time T, all shares held by traders are liquidated at price v_T. Unfilled orders are abandoned. The expected per-order profit of each trader type is total profit divided by the total number of executed and replaced untraded orders. In the environment with competing markets, we also calculate the total and expected per-order profit in CDA market and CALL market separately.

Figure 1 shows that the informed traders make higher profit in both per-order and in total when using $\mathrm{S}_{\mathrm{LARGE}}$. The difference are small but statistically significant. Therefore, we would expect the informed traders to choose $\mathrm{S}_{\mathrm{LARGE}}$ if given these two options (if they had to choose one as a group), confirming our intuition that traders gravitate to markets in which they perceive more mispricing. Because of this, for the rest of our analysis, we use $\mathrm{S}_{\mathrm{LARGE}}$ as the strategy for informed traders in the competing markets.

As mentioned in the introduction, one measure of social welfare is the "price of immediacy" which is the loss suffered by background traders. Figure 2 shows that, for the non-competing settings, background traders perform better in the i-CALL market than the i-CDA market in terms of both the expected per-order (left figure) and total (right figure) profit (consequently, informed traders have lower profit in the i-CALL market than the i-CDA market). The i-CDA-BMM market has much higher social welfare, as measured by background trader losses, than both i-CALL and i-CDA markets. This confirms some of the results of Wah and Wellman [23] in a completely different model and setting. One possible solution to the problems resulting from HFT may then be to have market-making agents who are regulated and deployed to perform this specific role in CDAs. They could be compensated separately for this role. However, (1) there are additional risks associated with this role [5] and (2) markets have been moving away from having designated

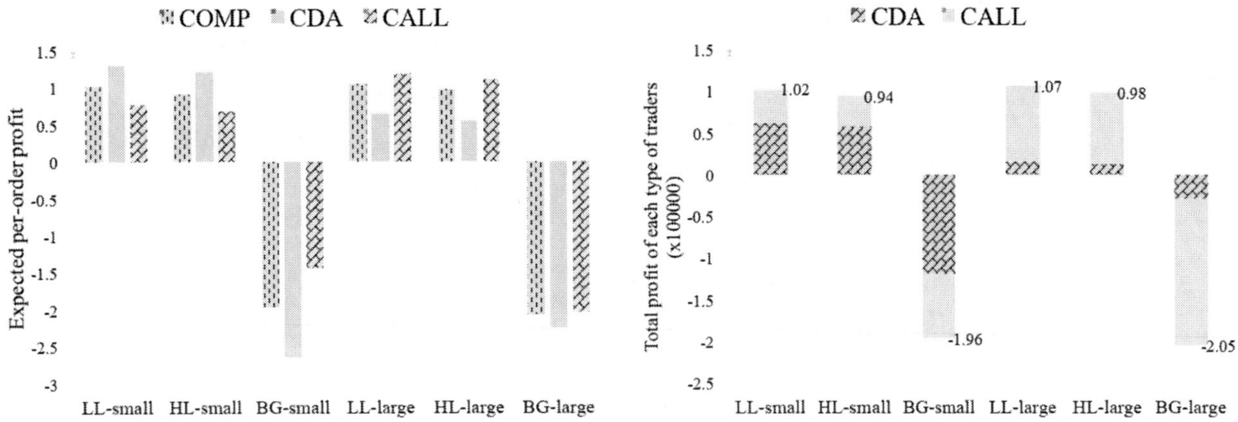

Figure 1: Comparison of expected per-order (left) and total (right) profit in the competing markets under the small distance (SSMALL) and large distance strategies (SLARGE). LL-*, HL-* and BG-* represent low latency, high latency, and background traders respectively. On the left, the first bar in each group shows the expected per-order profit in the whole competing system, while the second and third show the contributions of the CDA and CALL markets to that total. On the right, the stacked bars show total profit, with contributions from each of CDA and CALL shown within in different shades.

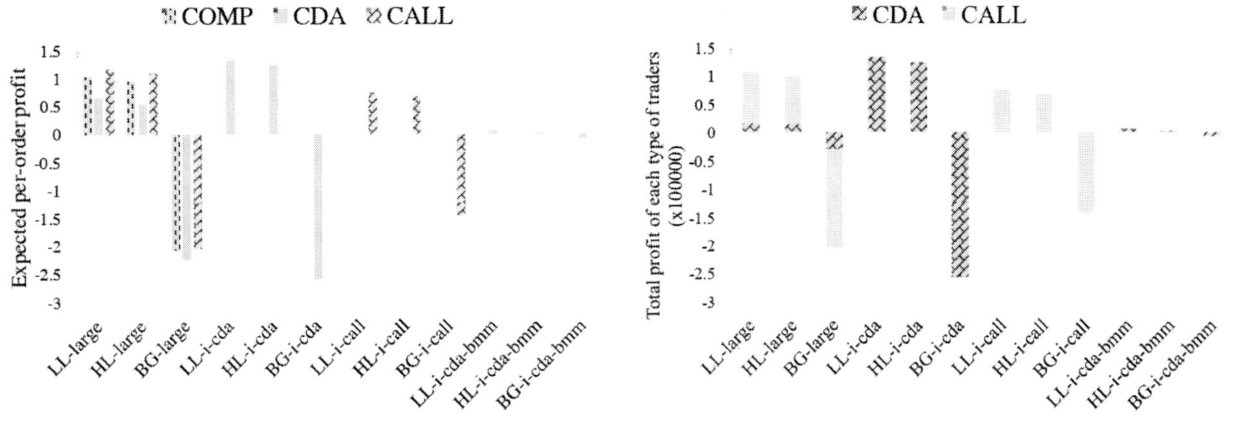

Figure 2: The expected per-order (left) and total profit (right) of different types of traders in the competing markets (*-large), the i-CDA market (*-i-cda), the i-CALL market (*-i-call) and the i-CDA-BMM market (*-i-cda-bmm).

specialists and allowing HFTs and others to fulfil the role of market-makers. Given these practical realities, it is important to understand how markets can function without them, so we focus on comparing situations with no market maker.

In the competing markets (first 3 panels of Figure 2), we analyze the expected per-order and total profit in the whole system, and also in the CDA market and CALL market separately. Similar to running an individual market, the order execution percentage is close to 100 for background traders in the competing markets (shown in Figure 3), and so background traders are not losing out in terms of order execution. Considering expected per-order profit, background traders do better in the CALL market than the CDA market in the competing markets (see left figure of Figure 2, *-large). Overall, they are doing worse in the CALL market than the CDA market in the competing system (shown on the right of Figure 2, *-large), but this is because a vast majority of orders are going to the CALL market (see Figure 4), and they lose more money there. In sum, they are doing slightly better in the competing markets than they do in the i-CDA market in terms of both the expected per-order and total profit. The better news is that the CALL is absorbing a large fraction of the orders, driving trade away from the CDA (see Figure 4). This is promising, because if the CALL could absorb all the trades, the BG traders would be better off, as the system would reduce to the i-CALL market. We note that these results are robust for a wide range of strategy parameters, information delay and arrival rates.

5. LEARNING TRADERS

The analysis above shows that frequent call markets absorb a large fraction of trade when we assume that all informed traders use the same strategy. We now use the insights developed in these models to analyze strategic market choice. In this section, we introduce a learning framework where informed traders learn a parametric form for the expected profit of choosing to place an order in a market, and also a non-parametric probability of order execution given

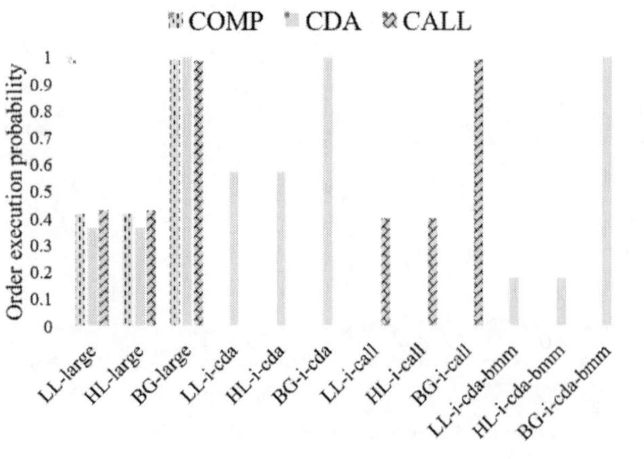

Figure 3: Order execution percentage in the competing markets (*-large), the i-CDA market (*-i-cda), the i-CALL market (*-i-call) and the i-CDA-BMM (*-i-wmm).

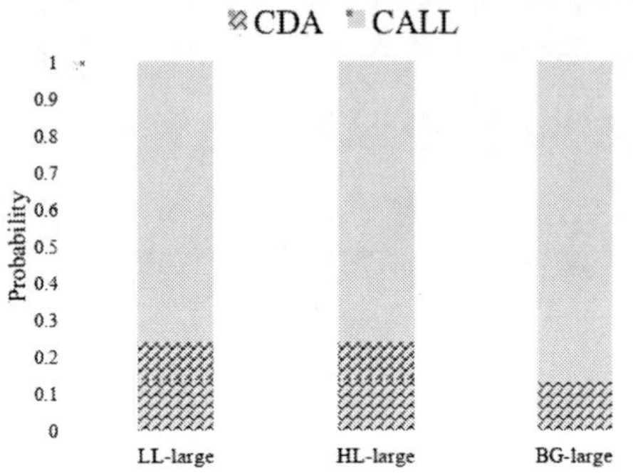

Figure 4: Illustration of proportion of orders entering CDA market vs. CALL market in the competing markets under S_{LARGE}.

the distance between that market's price and the trader's belief (the *belief distance* defined previously). We then analyze the behavior of the system with these learning traders.

5.1 Learning algorithm

The expected profit π_t of an order placed at time t, contingent on its execution, according to a trader's belief, is

$$\pi_t = \begin{cases} w_t - \text{execution price, if buy} \\ \text{execution price } - w_t, \text{if sell} \end{cases} \tag{2}$$

where w_t is the trader's belief about the true value at time t. The trader computes expected profit assuming her belief is correct. The main idea here is to predict the expected profit if the order is placed in a particular market. Traders must learn an estimate of this as a function of the belief distance. In this paper, we allow all the traders to learn an expected profit function that is quadratic in the belief distance. Each learning trader LIF_i uses an online regression algorithm for reinforcement learning based on one developed by Walsh et al [24]. The form of the learning model is:

$$y_{i,t}^{\text{market}} = \mathbf{D}_{i,t}^{\text{market}} \mathbf{Q}_i^{\text{market}}, \tag{3}$$

where $y_{i,t}^{\text{market}}$ predicts the expected per-order profit contingent on execution, market = $\{\text{CDA}, \text{CALL}\}$, $\mathbf{D}_{i,t}^{\text{market}} = [(d_{i,t}^{\text{market}})^2, d_{i,t}^{\text{market}}, 1]$ and $\mathbf{Q}_i^{\text{market}}$ contains the weight parameters of the model for market = $\{\text{CDA}, \text{CALL}\}$. Thus, the predicted expected per-order profit not contingent on execution is given by

$$\mathbb{E}(y_{i,t}^{\text{market}}) = \Pr(\text{exe}|d_{i,t}^{\text{market}}) \mathbf{D}_{i,t}^{\text{market}} \mathbf{Q}_i^{\text{market}} \tag{4}$$

The probability of execution $\Pr(\text{exe}|d_{i,t}^{\text{market}})$ is learned nonparametrically by counting successful and unsuccessful executions in bins of the belief distance.

The trader uses an ϵ-greedy algorithm to select a market to trade in along the learning path. Whenever the trader makes a decision, with probability $1-\epsilon$, she places an order in the market with higher predicted expected profit, and with probability ϵ, she randomly picks one market to place the order ($\epsilon = 0.1$ in our case). After market selection, the trader chooses a price based on the ZI strategy $S_{\text{individual}}$.

5.2 Results

Our goal is to use this model of learning traders to investigate two questions: (1) If all the informed traders use the same learning algorithm, do they converge to (approximate) equilibrium strategies? (2) Can we characterize any equilibria of the competing markets system?[1] We use an experimental framework similar to Section 4. A CALL market and a CDA market run simultaneously from $[0, T]$, $T = 100,000$. The CALL interval $\tau = 1$. There are 20 learning informed traders (LIF). These are all low latency traders who observe information with no delay; therefore $w_{i,t} \sim \mathcal{N}(v_t, \sigma_{\text{trader}})$, where v_t is the underlying true value of the security at time t, and σ_{trader} is the noise parameter. The reentry rate of learning informed traders is $\lambda_{\text{LIF}} = 2$. There are 20 background traders (with reentry rate $\lambda_{\text{BG}} = 1$) following Strategy 2. In addition, we also simulate the existence of a pool of *fixed* informed traders (FIF) who are committed to a particular market, either CDA or CALL. This is to ensure that there is some flow of trade in each market – otherwise there are degenerate equilibrium paths where all traders start off by going to one of the markets, and there is never incentive to deviate to the other. There are 5 fixed (low-latency) informed traders in each market who place orders following $S_{\text{individual}}$. The reentry rate of fixed informed traders is defined as λ_{FIF}. We vary the reentry rate of fixed informed traders $\lambda_{\text{FIF}} = \{1, 0.1, 0.0005\}$.

Outcomes of the learning process.

The first question is whether the learning process followed by the informed traders converges, and, if so, whether the learned representations are a good approximation to the true profit function. Empirically, we find that the estimates of $\mathbf{Q}_i^{\text{CDA}}, \mathbf{Q}_i^{\text{CALL}}$ under different λ_{FIF} settings all do converge. Further, each trader's parameters converge to very similar ranges (see Figure 5). We check whether these parameters are a good approximation by fixing the parameters of all

[1]Note that traders only choose which market to place an order in (albeit as a function of the belief distances to both markets, so this can be a complex decision space). Once the market is determined, the choice of price is according to the ZI strategy. The problem becomes exponentially more complex if traders can strategize over both market choice and price. Over time, traders should learn the expected profit of the ZI strategy in a market, a useful proxy for the profit potential of that market. It could be interesting to interact this learning problem with different pricing strategies, but some restriction will always be necessary to gain any traction.

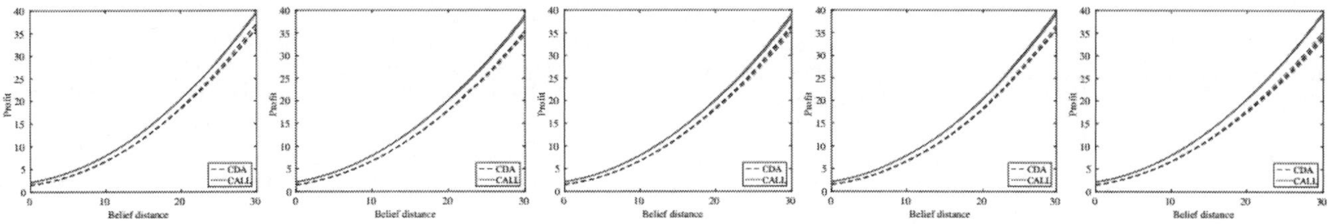

Figure 5: Five example plots of the curves traders learn for profits in the CDA and CALL markets. Each graph shows the learned curves of 5 traders in one instantiated learning simulation.

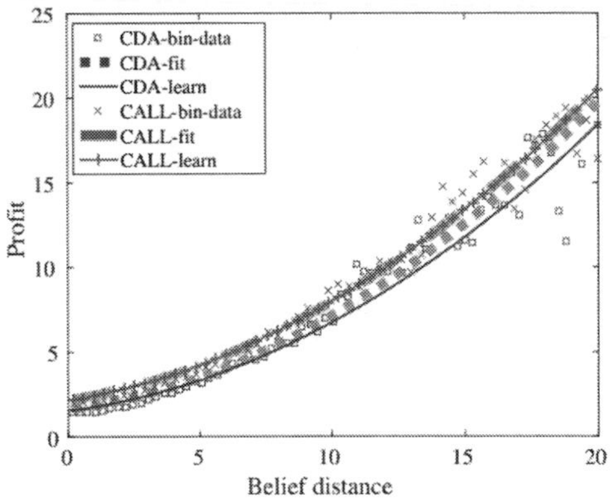

Figure 6: The learned curve vs. the best fit to realized after-the-fact data for profit as a function of belief distance in CDA and CALL markets.

the traders except one and having them play strategies using those parameters. For the remaining trader, we flip a coin to determine the choice of market, and test whether the profit achieved is well-fit by the curve given by the learned parameters. Figure 6 shows that the learning curves of the trader for each market are very close to the polynomial curves that are best-fit to the profits achieved using the randomized strategy, confirming both that the quadratic space is a good fit and that the learned parameters are correct for the environment.

Equilibrium.

As mentioned above, there are two main questions we would like to engage. First, since all the traders are converging to a particular set of learned parameters, do these parameters constitute an equilibrium or an approximate equilibrium (under the specified space of strategies – i.e., where the strategy is a mapping from d^{CALL} and d^{CDA} to one of the two markets, which can be specified by the quadratic form of the expected profit function and the nonparametric probability of execution model)? Is there a profitable deviation (some other set of parameters that one of the traders could use and increase her profits)?

To find deviations, we search the parameter space (holding the execution probability model constant) for this trader using Bayesian Optimization (BO), a powerful framework for optimization of a black-box function or expensive objective function that uses very few function evaluations [20]. Here, the objective function is the expected profit of a trading strategy that uses the parameters $\mathbf{Q}_i^{\mathrm{CDA}}, \mathbf{Q}_i^{\mathrm{CALL}}$ when the other traders are using their learned strategies. Market selection is determined by $y_{i,t}^{\mathrm{CDA}}$ and $y_{i,t}^{\mathrm{CALL}}$ based on Equation (4), so the actual values of $\mathbf{Q}_i^{\mathrm{CDA}}$ and $\mathbf{Q}_i^{\mathrm{CALL}}$ are not important in themselves. The important thing is how they decide the relation between $y_{i,t}^{\mathrm{CDA}}$ and $y_{i,t}^{\mathrm{CALL}}$ at each prediction. Therefore, based on the value of parameters of the learned curves from Figure 5, we constrain our search space from $[\mathbf{-10}, \mathbf{10}]$, as this is enough to represent the relation between predicted profit in these two markets. We utilize an existing code base for BO [10] to search the space.

Our results show that the learned parameters yield an approximate equilibrium, achieving between 90-95% (0.91, 0.95, 0.95 for $\lambda_{\mathrm{FIF}} = .0005, 0.1, 1$ respectively) of the profit of the best response strategy found by BO. In the learned approximate equilibrium, typically above 90% of orders are placed in the CALL market. Interestingly, the best response strategy found by BO always resulted in the deviating trader placing *every single order* in the call market. So we then asked whether all informed traders placing all their orders in the call market is an equilibrium, and found that, except under exceptional conditions, it is (that is, BO returned a set of parameters for the remaining trader that resulted in that trader placing all its orders in the CALL market as well). The only condition which we found under which it is not an equilibrium is when there is very little liquidity from FIF traders in the CDA market, but still some background traders – in this case the deviating informed trader can essentially become a price setter and trade with the background traders at whatever prices it chooses.

6. CONCLUSION

We have developed an agent-based model in the tradition of classic microstructure models to engage the question of whether frequent call markets can drive liquidity away from CDA markets. If they could do so, this would have the potential to increase welfare both by reducing transaction costs for average market participants and by reducing the incentive for firms to engage in the latency "arms race." Our results are promising. Even in the presence of impatient background traders who primarily demand immediacy and are willing to pay for it, we show in both a simple zero-intelligence model, and more sophisticated learning and equilibrium settings, that call markets have the potential to attract a large fraction of the order flow. In addition to the policy implications, we believe the modeling approach taken in this paper constitutes a useful bridge between classic financial microstructure models and more complex agent-based models, preserving intuition from the former, while allowing us to examine richer environments and questions.

Acknowledgments

We thank Elaine Wah and Michael Wellman for useful discussions. This research is supported by US National Science Foundation awards 1527037 and 1414452.

REFERENCES

[1] A. Brahma, M. Chakraborty, S. Das, A. Lavoie, and M. Magdon-Ismail. A Bayesian market maker. In *Proceedings of the 13th ACM Conference on Electronic Commerce*, EC '12, pages 215–232, New York, NY, USA, 2012. ACM.

[2] J. Brogaard, T. Hendershott, and R. Riordan. High-frequency trading and price discovery. *Review of Financial Studies*, 27(8):2267–2306, 2014.

[3] E. B. Budish, P. Cramton, and J. J. Shim. The high-frequency trading arms race: Frequent batch auctions as a market design response. *Quarterly Journal of Economics*, pages 1547–1621, 2015.

[4] D. Cliff, J. Bruten, et al. Zero not enough: On the lower limit of agent intelligence for continuous double auction markets. *HP Laboratories Technical Report HPL*, 1997.

[5] S. Das. The effects of market-making on price dynamics. In *Proceedings of the International Joint Conference on Autonomous Agents and Multi-Agent Systems*, pages 887–894, Estoril, Portugal, May 2008.

[6] S. Das, J. P. Dickerson, Z. Li, and T. Sandholm. Competing dynamic matching markets. In *Proceedings of the Conference on Auctions, Market Mechanisms and Their Applications (AMMA)*, 2015. To appear.

[7] L. Epstein, A. Levin, J. Mestre, and D. Segev. Improved approximation guarantees for weighted matching in the semi-streaming model. *SIAM Journal on Discrete Mathematics*, 25(3):1251–1265, 2011.

[8] J. D. Farmer and D. Foley. The economy needs agent-based modelling. *Nature*, 460(7256):685–686, 2009.

[9] J. D. Farmer, P. Patelli, and I. I. Zovko. The predictive power of zero intelligence in financial markets. *Proceedings of the National Academy of Sciences of the United States of America*, 102(6):2254–2259, 2005.

[10] J. Gardner, M. Kusner, K. Q. Weinberger, J. Cunningham, and Z. Xu. Bayesian optimization with inequality constraints. In *Proceedings of the 31st International Conference on Machine Learning (ICML-14)*, pages 937–945, 2014.

[11] L. R. Glosten and P. R. Milgrom. Bid, ask and transaction prices in a specialist market with heterogeneously informed traders. *Journal of Financial Economics*, 14(1):71–100, 1985.

[12] A. A. Kirilenko, A. S. Kyle, M. Samadi, and T. Tuzun. The flash crash: The impact of high frequency trading on an electronic market. *working paper*, 2014.

[13] A. S. Kyle. Continuous auctions and insider trading. *Econometrica: Journal of the Econometric Society*, pages 1315–1335, 1985.

[14] B. LeBaron, W. B. Arthur, and R. Palmer. Time series properties of an artificial stock market. *Journal of Economic Dynamics and Control*, 23(9):1487–1516, 1999.

[15] M. Lewis. *Flash Boys: A Wall Street Revolt*. WW Norton & Company, 2014.

[16] A. J. Menkveld. High frequency trading and the new market makers. *Journal of Financial Markets*, 16(4):712–740, 2013.

[17] J. Niu, K. Cai, S. Parsons, P. McBurney, and E. H. Gerding. What the 2007 TAC market design game tells us about effective auction mechanisms. *Autonomous Agents and Multi-Agent Systems*, 21(2):172–203, 2010.

[18] A. Othman. Zero-intelligence agents in prediction markets. In *Proceedings of the 7th International Joint Conference on Autonomous Agents and Multiagent Systems*, pages 879–886, 2008.

[19] I. Palit, S. Phelps, and W. L. Ng. Can a zero-intelligence plus model explain the stylized facts of financial time series data? In *Proceedings of the 11th International Conference on Autonomous Agents and Multiagent Systems*, pages 653–660. International Foundation for Autonomous Agents and Multiagent Systems, 2012.

[20] J. Snoek, H. Larochelle, and R. P. Adams. Practical Bayesian optimization of machine learning algorithms. In *Advances in Neural Information Processing Systems*, pages 2951–2959, 2012.

[21] E. Wah, D. R. Hurd, and M. P. Wellman. Strategic market choice: Frequent call markets vs. continuous double auctions for fast and slow traders. In *Proceedings of the Conference on Auctions, Market Mechanisms and Their Applications (AMMA)*, 2015. To appear.

[22] E. Wah and M. P. Wellman. Latency arbitrage, market fragmentation, and efficiency: A two-market model. In *Proceedings of the Fourteenth ACM Conference on Electronic Commerce*, pages 855–872. ACM, 2013.

[23] E. Wah and M. P. Wellman. Welfare effects of market making in continuous double auctions. In *Proceedings of the 2015 International Conference on Autonomous Agents and Multiagent Systems*, pages 57–66. International Foundation for Autonomous Agents and Multiagent Systems, 2015.

[24] T. J. Walsh, I. Szita, C. Diuk, and M. L. Littman. Exploring compact reinforcement-learning representations with linear regression. In *Proceedings of the Twenty-Fifth Conference on Uncertainty in Artificial Intelligence*, pages 591–598. AUAI Press, 2009.

Pareto Efficient Strategy-proof School Choice Mechanism with Minimum Quotas and Initial Endowments*

Ryoji Kurata, Naoto Hamada, Chia-Ling Hsu, Takamasa Suzuki,
Suguru Ueda, and Makoto Yokoo
Kyushu University
Motooka 744, Fukuoka, Japan
{kurata@agent.,nhamada@agent.,chialinghsu@,tsuzuki@,ueda@,yokoo@}inf.kyushu-u.ac.jp

ABSTRACT

This paper develops a strategy-proof and Pareto efficient mechanism for a school choice program called Top Trading Cycles among Representatives with Supplementary Seats (TTCR-SS). We consider a setting where minimum quotas are imposed for each school, i.e., a school is required to be assigned at least a certain number of students to operate, and the obtained matching must respect initial endowments, i.e., each student must be assigned to a school that is at least as good as her initial endowment school. Although minimum quotas are relevant in school choice programs and strategy-proofness is important to many policymakers, few existing mechanisms achieve both of them simultaneously. Furthermore, existing mechanisms require that all students consider all schools acceptable to obtain a feasible matching that respects minimum quotas and cannot guarantee Pareto efficiency. TTCR-SS is based on Top Trading Cycles (TTC) mechanism, while it is significantly extended to handle the supplementary seats of schools while respecting minimum quotas. Our simulation results show TTCR-SS is significantly better than an existing TTC-based mechanism in terms of students' welfare.

Keywords

Mechanism design; School choice; Resource allocation; Top trading cycles

1. INTRODUCTION

Traditionally, a student is assigned to a public school based on where she lives. School choice programs are implemented to give students/parents an opportunity to choose public schools. A seminal work [3] introduces the idea of using a mechanism design approach for this issue by formalizing it as a problem of allocating indivisible objects with multiple supplies (e.g., schools with seats) to agents (e.g., students).

In this paper, we consider the case where minimum quotas are imposed, i.e., a school is required to be assigned at least a certain number of students to operate. Also, we assume each student has a default school (that she would have attended without the school choice program), which we call her **initial endowment**. We also assume the initial endowments satisfy all minimum quotas and require that a student be allocated to a school that is at least as good as her initial endowment school. This requirement is natural since a student would not want to attend a public school located remotely away from her residence unless it offers some very appealing characteristics.

Although minimum quotas are relevant in school choice programs and strategy-proofness (i.e., no student ever has any incentive to misreport her preference, regardless of other students' reports) is important to many policymakers, there is a lack of strategy-proof mechanisms that consider them. A notable exception [10] develops strategy-proof mechanisms based on the Deferred Acceptance mechanism [11] that can handle minimum quotas. However, there are two limitations for applying their mechanisms in our setting. First, to guarantee that their mechanisms obtain feasible matchings (which respect minimum quotas), students must consider all of the schools **acceptable**. This requirement is unrealistic in our setting. The school choice program is intended to provide more choices to students/parents. However, with this requirement, students/parents are not allowed to declare that some schools are unacceptable. Second, their mechanisms cannot guarantee Pareto efficiency, which is a standard efficiency criterion in economics.

Our newly developed mechanism is based on Top Trading Cycles (TTC) mechanism [26], which is a standard way to improve students' welfare with initial endowments. In our setting, a school may have supplementary/empty seats, i.e., it can accept more students than the initial endowment students. By allocating supplementary seats, the welfare of students can be improved. To the best of our knowledge, there exists no TTC-based mechanism that can handle both initial endowments and supplementary seats while respecting minimum quotas.

Our mechanism is general enough to be applied to any allocation problem of indivisible objects with multiple supplies, where each agent has her initial endowment and minimum quotas are imposed on the number of supplies for each object. One possible application domain of our mechanism is reallocation in a student-laboratory assignment problem. In many universities in Japan, an undergraduate engineering student must be assigned to a laboratory to conduct a project. However, it is difficult for a student to choose an appropriate laboratory since her knowledge is limited. One

*This work was partially supported by JSPS KAKENHI Grant Number 24220003 and 15K16058.

Appears in: *Proceedings of the 15th International Conference on Autonomous Agents and Multiagent Systems (AAMAS 2016), J. Thangarajah, K. Tuyls, C. Jonker, S. Marsella (eds.), May 9–13, 2016, Singapore.*

possible remedy is to apply the following three-step procedure: (i) students are assigned to laboratories using some mechanism (e.g., [10]), (ii) students experience a certain trial period, and (iii) each student has a chance to apply to another laboratory if her interest changes or her current laboratory fails to meet her expectations. Our new mechanism can be used in Step (iii). It is natural to require that no student is reallocated to a laboratory that is worse than her current assignment. Also, it is natural to assume the current allocation is feasible.

The rest of this paper is organized as follows. We show a more detailed literature review in the rest of this section. Then we introduce a formal model of our problem setting (Section 2). Next we show a simple mechanism based on TTC (Section 3), introduce our newly developed mechanism (Section 4), and show its theoretical properties (Section 5). Finally, we evaluate our mechanism by computer simulation (Section 6).

1.1 Related literature

The problem of allocating objects to agents, when objects are initially owned by agents who have strict preferences over objects, is formulated as a housing market problem [26]. In the paper, they introduce TTC due to David Gale, to show that the core is nonempty. Roth and Postlewaite [25] further show that the core is a singleton for strict preferences. For the incentive property, Roth [23] shows that TTC is strategy-proof. Ma [19] shows that a trading mechanism is individual rational, Pareto efficient and strategy-proof if and only if it is TTC. Later, TTC is generalized to the hierarchical exchange mechanism [21] and to trading cycles mechanism [22]. Abdulkadiroğlu and Sönmez [2] consider a setting that resembles ours. In their setting, some houses are initially owned by tenants while others are not. They modify TTC to this setting. The differences between [2] and our work are that we consider the setting where multiple copies of objects (seats of schools) exist and minimum quotas are imposed. Erdil and Ergin [9] consider a setting in which priorities are not strict. They also modify TTC to this setting and develop the stable improvement cycles mechanism. This mechanism is stable, but not strategy-proof.

School choice programs are identified as an important application domain of TTC [3]. This work formulates a school choice problem, in which the seats of schools are allocated to students. Here, a school can have multiple seats, and each school can have an idiosyncratic priority among students. They also introduce a modified version of the original TTC that is specific to a school choice problem, and the mechanism is Pareto efficient and strategy-proof. Since then, TTC in the setting of a school choice problem has drawn independent research interest, and there are many directions of research. One direction of research is to design the priority structure of students for a given mechanism [13, 15]. Another direction of research is using an axiomatic approach to characterize TTC [1, 6, 20].

In our paper, we consider a new kind of institutional constraint: minimum quotas. The scenario applies to the situation where for a group, institute, or school to be operational, some minimum number of agents must be assigned to that group, institute, or school. An example is Hungary's college admission [4].

In the context of school choice, minimum quotas are often imposed on different **types** of students (e.g., gender, socioeconomic status) [5, 7, 8, 14, 16, 18, 27]. The crucial difference between our setting and these works is that we assume minimum quotas are hard constraints that must be satisfied by any matching, while they treat minimum quotas as "soft" constraints that may or may not actually be satisfied.

Ehlers et al. [8] show that if the constraints are interpreted as hard constraints, no mechanism that is fair and satisfies a definition that they call constrained nonwastefulness can simultaneously be strategy-proof. Due to this impossibility result, Fragiadakis et al. [10] develop two strategy-proof mechanisms that renounce fairness or nonwastefulness. Based on their work, Goto et al. [12] develop a strategy-proof mechanism that can handle hierarchical minimum quotas. We cannot use these mechanisms in our setting since they do not respect initial endowments. Furthermore, they are not Pareto efficient (note that Pareto efficiency implies nonwastefulness but not vice versa).

For school choice programs, fairness is another important criterion, and there exists a trade-off between fairness and efficiency. If the welfare of students is the primary concern, a policymaker should use a Pareto efficient mechanism. For example, a school choice program in New Orleans uses TTC [24]. The uniqueness of our work is that we consider a situation where students are initially endowed with some schools and a trading mechanism is used to achieve Pareto efficiency, while minimum quotas need to be satisfied.

2. MODEL

A market is a tuple $(S, C, X, q_C, p_C, \omega, \succ_S)$.

- $S = \{s_1, \ldots, s_n\}$ is a finite set of students.
- $C = \{c_1, \ldots, c_m\}$ is a finite set of schools.
- $X = S \times C$ is a finite set of contracts. Contract $x = (s, c) \in X$ represents that student s is assigned to school c. For any $X' \subseteq X$, let X'_s denote $\{(s, c) \in X' \mid c \in C\}$, i.e., the sets of contracts related to student s who is involved in X', and let X'_c denote $\{(s, c) \in X' \mid s \in S\}$, i.e., the sets of contracts related to school c involved in X'.
- $q_C = (q_c)_{c \in C}$ is a vector of the schools' maximum quotas.
- $p_C = (p_c)_{c \in C}$ is a vector of the schools' minimum quotas.
- ω: $S \to C$ is an initial endowment function. $\omega(s)$ returns $c \in C$, which is s's initial endowment. When $\omega(s) = c$, we say school c is student s's initial endowment school, and student s is school c's initial endowment student. Let X^* denote $\bigcup_{s \in S}\{(s, \omega(s))\}$, i.e., X^* is the set of contracts, where each element is a contract between a student and her initial endowment school.
- $\succ_S = (\succ_s)_{s \in S}$ is a profile of the students' preferences. For each student s, $\succ_s$ represents the preference of s over X_s. We assume $\succ_s$ is strict for each s. We say (s, c) is **acceptable** for s if $(s, c) \succ_s (s, \omega(s))$ or $c = \omega(s)$ holds. We sometimes use such notations as $c \succ_s c'$ instead of $(s, c) \succ_s (s, c')$.

We assume $\sum_{c \in C} p_c \leq n \leq \sum_{c \in C} q_c$ holds. Also, we assume X^* satisfies minimum/maximum quotas, i.e., for all $c \in C$, $p_c \leq |X^*_c| \leq q_c$ holds.

With a slight abuse of notation, for two sets of contracts, X' and X'', we denote $X'_s \succ_s X''_s$ if either (i) $X'_s = \{x'\}$, $X''_s = \{x''\}$, and $x' \succ_s x''$ for some $x', x'' \in X_s$ that are acceptable for s, or (ii) $X'_s = \{x'\}$ for some $x' \in X_s$ that is acceptable for s and $X''_s = \emptyset$. We denote $X'_s \succeq_s X''_s$ if either $X'_s \succ_s X''_s$ or $X'_s = X''_s$. Also, for $X'_s \subseteq X_s$, we say X'_s is acceptable for s if $X'_s = \{x\}$ and x is acceptable for s.

DEFINITION 1 (FEASIBILITY). *$X' \subseteq X$ is **student-feasible** if for all $s \in S$, X'_s is acceptable for s. X' is **school-feasible** if for all $c \in C, p_c \leq |X'_c| \leq q_c$ holds. X' is **feasible** if it is student- and school-feasible.*

We call a feasible set of contracts a **matching**. Note that by definition, any matching is individually rational, i.e., every student is matched with a school that is at least as good as her initial endowment school. Also note that X^* is school-feasible and therefore a matching.

A **mechanism** is a function that takes a profile of students' preferences as input and returns a matching.

DEFINITION 2 (STRATEGY-PROOFNESS). *A mechanism is **strategy-proof** if no student ever has any incentive to misreport her preference, regardless of other students' reports.*

DEFINITION 3 (PARETO EFFICIENCY). *Matching X' **Pareto dominates** another matching X'' if $\forall s \in S, X'_s \succeq_s X''_s$ and $\exists s \in S, X'_s \succ_s X''_s$ hold, i.e., compared with X'', X' makes all students weakly better off and at least one student strictly better off. A matching is **Pareto efficient** if there is no other matching that Pareto dominates it. A mechanism is Pareto efficient if it always selects a Pareto efficient matching.*

Directed graph G is a pair (V, E) where V is a set of vertices and $E \subseteq \{(i, j) \mid i, j \in V\}$ is a collection of ordered pairs of vertices in V. An ordered pair (i, j), where $i, j \in V$, is called a **directed edge** from i to j.

In a directed graph (V, E), a sequence of vertices $(i_1, \ldots, i_k)$, $k \geq 2$, is a **directed path** from vertex i_1 to vertex i_k if $(i_h, i_{h+1}) \in E$ for $h = 1, \ldots, k-1$. If $i_1 = i_k$, then we call this directed path a **cycle**. In particular, (i, i), where $(i, i) \in E$, is called a **self-loop** cycle.

3. TOP TRADING CYCLES AMONG REPRESENTATIVES

Before introducing our new mechanism, let us introduce a simpler mechanism based on TTC, which we call Top Trading Cycles among Representatives (TTCR). Since a student is indifferent between multiple seats within the same school, we cannot directly apply the standard TTC mechanism. TTCR is a special case of Algorithm III in [15].

TTCR utilizes $\succ_{ML}$, which is a strict common priority ordering among students called **master list (ML)**. Without loss of generality, we assume $\succ_{ML}$ is defined as follows: $s_1 \succ_{ML} s_2 \succ_{ML} \ldots \succ_{ML} s_n$.

This mechanism repeats several rounds. At Round k, Y^{k-1} represents the set of remaining initial endowment contracts and Z represents the set of contracts that have already been finalized. TTCR is defined in Mechanism 1.

Mechanism 1 Top Trading Cycles among Representatives (TTCR)

Initialize $Y^0 = X^*, Z = \emptyset, k = 1$

Round k

Step 1 Create directed graph $G^k = (V^k, E^k)$ as follows:

- V^k is a set of contracts, each of which is selected from each school. More specifically, for each school $c \in C$ s.t. $Y^{k-1}_c \neq \emptyset$, select (s, c) where s has the highest priority among students in Y^{k-1}_c according to the ML.
- E^k is the set of directed edges between contracts in V^k. There exists a directed edge $((s, c), (s', c')) \in E^k$ if c' is the most preferred school according to $\succ_s$ within schools in V^k.

Step 2 Let $\mathscr{C}^k$ denote a set of contracts, each of which is included in a cycle within G^k.

Step 3 For each contract $(s, c) \in \mathscr{C}^k$, let $((s, c), (s', c'))$ denote the direct edge from (s, c). Add (s, c') to Z. $Y^k \leftarrow Y^{k-1} \setminus \mathscr{C}^k$.

Step 4 If $Y^k = \emptyset$, then return Z. Otherwise, $k \leftarrow k + 1$ and go to the next round.

Intuitively, we can assume in TTCR, each school chooses one representative student from its initial endowment students based on ML. Then, within these representative students, the standard TTC mechanism is applied. By choosing one representative for each school, we can ignore the fact that a student is indifferent between multiple seats within the same school. Since a student considers her initial endowment school acceptable, there always exists at least one cycle. TTCR can be considered one instance of Algorithm III in [15]. In the algorithm, each school has its own priority ordering among students. Student s, who has the highest priority in school c's ordering, obtains all the seats of c. Then the standard TTC mechanism is applied among the students who own seats. When a student is involved in a cycle and obtains her desired seat, she returns the remaining seats to each school. Then the mechanism repeats the same procedure for the remaining students. If we assume the number of seats available for a school equals the number of its initial endowment students, and school c gives the highest priority to student s according to ML within her initial endowment students, this algorithm becomes identical to the above mechanism.

The obtained matching of TTCR satisfies all minimum/maximum quotas, since for the obtained matching Z, $|Z_c| = |X^*_c|$ holds for all $c \in C$. However, this mechanism is not Pareto efficient, as shown in the following example:

EXAMPLE 1. *Assume $S = \{s_1, s_2, s_3, s_4, s_5, s_6, s_7\}, C = \{c_1, c_2, c_3\}$, where $\omega(s_1) = \omega(s_2) = \omega(s_3) = c_1$, $\omega(s_4) = \omega(s_5) = \omega(s_6) = c_2$, and $\omega(s_7) = c_3$. $q_c = 3$ for all $c \in C$. $p_{c_1} = 2$ and $p_{c_2} = p_{c_3} = 0$.*

The preferences of students are given as follows:

$$\succ_{s_1}: \; c_2 \;\; c_1,$$
$$\succ_{s_2}, \succ_{s_3}: \; c_3 \;\; c_1,$$
$$\succ_{s_4}, \succ_{s_5}, \succ_{s_6}: \; c_3 \;\; c_2,$$
$$\succ_{s_7}: \; c_1 \;\; c_3.$$

First, Y^0 is determined: $\{(s_1, c_1), (s_2, c_1), (s_3, c_1), (s_4, c_2), (s_5, c_2), (s_6, c_2), (s_7, c_3)\}$.

At Step 1 of Round 1, since $Y^0_c \neq \emptyset$ for all $c \in C$, the mechanism selects each (s, c) where s has the highest priority according to ML within students in Y^0_c for all $c \in C$ and adds (s_1, c_1),(s_4, c_2), and (s_7, c_3) to V^1. Then each selected student points to her most preferred school according to $\succ_s$ within schools in V^1; s_1, s_4, and s_7 point to c_2, c_3, and c_1, respectively. Therefore, G^1 is determined as follows:

$$\begin{aligned} V^1 &= \{(s_1, c_1), (s_4, c_2), (s_7, c_3)\}, \\ E^1 &= \{((s_1, c_1), (s_4, c_2)), ((s_4, c_2), (s_7, c_3)), ((s_7, c_3), \\ &\quad (s_1, c_1))\}. \end{aligned}$$

There exists one cycle: $((s_1, c_1), (s_4, c_2), (s_7, c_3), (s_1, c_1))$. At Step 2, $\mathscr{C}^1$ is $\{(s_1, c_1), (s_4, c_2), (s_7, c_3)\}$. At Step 3, (s_1, c_2), (s_4, c_3), and (s_7, c_1) are added to Z and the contracts in $\mathscr{C}^1$ are removed from Y^0. Therefore, Z and Y^1 are determined as follows:

$$\begin{aligned} Z &= \{(s_1, c_2), (s_4, c_3), (s_7, c_1)\}, \\ Y^1 &= \{(s_2, c_1), (s_3, c_1), (s_5, c_2), (s_6, c_2)\}. \end{aligned}$$

At Step 4, go to Round 2 because $Y^1 \neq \emptyset$.

At Step 1 of Round 2, since $Y^1_{c_3} = \emptyset$, there is no representative student from c_3. The mechanism selects (s_2, c_1) and (s_5, c_2) according to ML and adds them to V^2. Then each selected student points to her most preferred school according to $\succ_s$ within schools in V^2. Therefore, G^2 is determined as follows:

$$\begin{aligned} V^2 &= \{(s_2, c_1), (s_5, c_2)\}, \\ E^2 &= \{((s_2, c_1), (s_2, c_1)), ((s_5, c_2), (s_5, c_2))\}. \end{aligned}$$

There are two self-loop cycles. At Step 2, $\mathscr{C}^2$ is $\{(s_2, c_1), (s_5, c_2)\}$. Therefore, at Step 3, Z and Y^2 are given as follows:

$$\begin{aligned} Z &= \{(s_1, c_2), (s_4, c_3), (s_7, c_1), (s_2, c_1), (s_5, c_2)\}, \\ Y^2 &= \{(s_3, c_1), (s_6, c_2)\}. \end{aligned}$$

At Step 4, go to Round 3 because $Y^2 \neq \emptyset$.

At Step 1 of Round 3, G^3 is determined as follows:

$$\begin{aligned} V^3 &= \{(s_3, c_1), (s_6, c_2)\}, \\ E^3 &= \{((s_3, c_1), (s_3, c_1)), ((s_6, c_2), (s_6, c_2))\}. \end{aligned}$$

There are two self-loop cycles. At Step 2, $\mathscr{C}^2$ is $\{(s_3, c_1), (s_6, c_2)\}$. Therefore, at Step 3, Z and Y^3 are given as follows:

$$\begin{aligned} Z &= \{(s_1, c_2), (s_4, c_3), (s_7, c_1), (s_2, c_1), (s_5, c_2), \\ &\quad (s_3, c_1), (s_6, c_2)\}, \\ Y^3 &= \emptyset. \end{aligned}$$

At Step 4, return Z because $Y^3 = \emptyset$.

In the end, obtained matching Z becomes:

$$\begin{aligned} Z &= \{(s_1, c_2), (s_2, c_1), (s_3, c_1), (s_4, c_3), (s_5, c_2), \\ &\quad (s_6, c_2), (s_7, c_1)\}. \end{aligned}$$

Consider another matching Z':

$$\begin{aligned} Z' &= \{(s_1, c_2), (s_2, c_3), (s_3, c_1), (s_4, c_3), (s_5, c_3), \\ &\quad (s_6, c_2), (s_7, c_1)\}. \end{aligned}$$

We can find that $Z'_s \succeq_s Z_s$ for all $s \in S$ and $Z'_s \succ_s Z_s$ for $s \in \{s_2, s_5\}$ hold. Therefore, Z is not Pareto efficient. Also, $|Z_c| = |X^*_c|$ for all $c \in C$.

4. TOP TRADING CYCLES AMONG REPRESENTATIVES WITH SUPPLEMENTARY SEATS

TTCR's limitation is that it cannot allocate supplementary seats, as shown in the previous example. However, if we allocate supplementary seats too generously, minimum quotas can be violated. In this section, we develop a new Pareto efficient mechanism called Top Trading Cycles among Representatives with Supplementary Seats (TTCR-SS), which utilizes the notion of a dummy student to control supplementary seats at each school. In TTCR-SS, if a school has already "consumed" its initial endowment students and has supplementary seats, it selects a dummy student as its representative.

TTCR-SS repeats several rounds like TTCR. We divide each school c at Round k into the following four categories:

minimum: $|Y^{k-1}_c| > 0$ and $|Z_c| + |Y^{k-1}_c| = p_c$, i.e., c has the remaining initial endowment contracts and the total number of students in the finalized contracts and the initial endowment contracts equals the minimum quota. Thus, a student in its initial endowment contracts cannot move to another school without violating the minimum quota.

decrementable: $|Y^{k-1}_c| > 0$ and $|Z_c| + |Y^{k-1}_c| > p_c$, i.e., c has the remaining initial endowment contracts and a student in its initial endowment contracts can move to another school.

maximum: $|Y^{k-1}_c| = 0$ and $|Z_c| = q_c$, i.e., c has no remaining initial endowment contracts and it has already accepted students up to its maximum quota.

incrementable: $|Y^{k-1}_c| = 0$ and $|Z_c| < q_c$, i.e., c has no remaining initial endowment contract and can accept another student without violating its maximum quota.

Let $C^k_{\min}$, C^k_{dec}, $C^k_{\max}$, and C^k_{inc} represent the sets of schools in each of the above categories, respectively.

TTCR-SS resembles TTCR, but if school c has exhausted its initial endowment students (i.e., $Y^{k-1}_c = \emptyset$ holds), while it has a supplementary seat (i.e., $|Z_c| < q_c$), the school is incrementable and can send dummy student s_d as its representative. If a dummy student points to (s, c) and obtains c's seat, in reality, it means that the number of assigned students in c is decremented by one. To ensure that the obtained matching respects minimum quotas, we carefully design the "preference" of each dummy student. If $|Y^{k-1}_c| + |Z_c| = p_c$ holds for school c, i.e., if c is minimum, then c cannot afford to "accept" a dummy student. Thus, each dummy student points to the contract, in which the student has the highest priority among students whose initial endowment schools are decrementable. Note that all dummy students point to the same contract. Thus, there exists at most one cycle that includes a dummy student. TTCR-SS is defined in Mechanism 2.

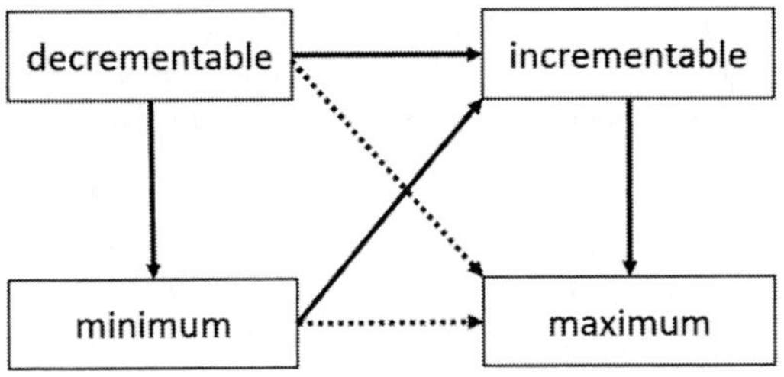

Figure 1: Transition of school categories

Mechanism 2 Top Trading Cycles among Representatives with Supplementary Seats (TTCR-SS)

Initialize $Y^0 = X^*, Z = \emptyset, k = 1$

Round k

Step 1 Create directed graph $G^k = (V^k, E^k)$ as follows:

- V^k is a set of contracts, each of which is selected from each school. More specifically, for each school $c \in C^k_{\text{min}} \cup C^k_{\text{dec}}$, select (s, c) where s has the highest priority among students in Y^{k-1}_c according to ML. Also, for each school $c \in C^k_{\text{inc}}$, select (s_d, c), where s_d is a dummy student, as long as $C^k_{\text{dec}} \neq \emptyset$.
- E^k is the set of directed edges among contracts. There exists a directed edge $((s, c), (s', c')) \in E^k$ if c' is the most preferred school according to $\succ_s$ within schools in V^k. For each contract related to a dummy student (s_d, c), there exists a directed edge $((s_d, c), (s, c')) \in E^k$, where s has the highest priority according to ML within students in V^k and $c' \in C^k_{\text{dec}}$.

Step 2 Let $\mathscr{C}^k$ denote a set of contracts, each of which is included in a cycle within G^k.

Step 3 For each contract $(s, c) \in \mathscr{C}^k$, let $((s, c), (s', c'))$ denote the direct edge from (s, c). Add (s, c') to Z when s is not a dummy student. $Y^k \leftarrow Y^{k-1} \setminus \mathscr{C}^k$.

Step 4 If $Y^k = \emptyset$, then return Z. Otherwise, $k \leftarrow k + 1$ and go to the next round.

Figure 1 shows the possible transition of school categories. Typically, school c is initially decrementable. If $|X^*_c| = p_c$, c is initially minimum. Also, if $|X^*_c| = 0$, c is initially incrementable. As long as all schools are decrementable or minimum, no dummy student is introduced. Thus, for each contract in a cycle, the related school is either decrementable or minimum. Then at some Round k, Y^k_c eventually becomes $\emptyset$ for some school c. c typically becomes incrementable, and a dummy student is introduced. After a dummy student is introduced, for each contract in a cycle, the related school can be incrementable, decrementable, or minimum, and a student whose initial endowment school is decrementable can obtain a seat of an incrementable school from a dummy student. A decrementable school can become minimum, and an incrementable school can become maximum. As an exceptional case (represented by a dotted line in Fig. 1), if for school c, the number of initial endowment students exactly equals q_c, and no student whose initial endowment is c gives a seat to a dummy student, then c becomes maximum when Y^k_c becomes $\emptyset$. As another exceptional case (represented by a dotted line in Fig. 1), if $p_c = q_c$ holds for school c, then c is initially minimum and directly moves to maximum when Y^k_c becomes $\emptyset$. The assignment of maximum schools becomes fixed. When there exits no decrementable school, no dummy student is introduced. Thus, for each contract in a cycle, the related school is minimum. Once this happens, there will be no decrementable school in the later rounds. Thus, no dummy student will be introduced at any later round.

Let us describe how TTCR-SS works.

Example 2. *Consider the same instance as Example 1. Y^0 is the same as Example 1.*

The mechanism behaves exactly the same as the previous example until a dummy student is introduced. The following is the result of Round 1:

$$Z = \{(s_1, c_2), (s_4, c_3), (s_7, c_1)\},$$
$$Y^1 = \{(s_2, c_1), (s_3, c_1), (s_5, c_2), (s_6, c_2)\}.$$

At Step 1 of Round 2, c_1 and c_2 are decrementable, and c_3 is incrementable. Schools c_1 and c_2 select their representative students s_2 and s_5, and (s_2, c_1) and (s_5, c_2) are added to V^2. Since there exist decrementable schools, c_3 sends a dummy student and (s_d, c_3) is added to V^2. Then each selected student points to her most preferred school according to $\succ_s$ within schools in V^2; s_2 and s_5 point to c_3. On the other hand, dummy student s_d points to the school whose initial endowment student has the highest priority according to ML within C^2_{dec}; s_d of c_3 points to c_1. Therefore, G^2 is given as follows:

$$V^2 = \{(s_2, c_1), (s_5, c_2), (s_d, c_3)\},$$
$$E^2 = \{((s_2, c_1), (s_d, c_3)), ((s_5, c_2), (s_d, c_3)), ((s_d, c_3), (s_2, c_1))\}.$$

There is one cycle $((s_2, c_1), (s_d, c_3), (s_2, c_1))$. At Step 2, $\mathscr{C}^2$ is $\{(s_2, c_1), (s_d, c_3)\}$. Therefore, at Step 3, Z and Y^3 are given as follows:

$$Z = \{(s_1, c_2), (s_4, c_3), (s_7, c_1), (s_2, c_3)\},$$
$$Y^2 = \{(s_3, c_1), (s_5, c_2), (s_6, c_2)\}.$$

At Step 1 of Round 3, c_1 is minimum, c_2 is decrementable, and c_3 is incrementable. Thus, the mechanism adds (s_3, c_1), (s_5, c_2), and (s_d, c_3) to V^3. Then, s_3 and s_5 point to c_3. Here, although s_3 has higher priority than s_5 according to the ML, since s_3's initial endowment school c_1 is minimum, s_d points to c_2 instead of c_1. Therefore, G^3 is given as follows:

$$V^3 = \{(s_3, c_1), (s_5, c_2), (s_d, c_3)\},$$
$$E^3 = \{((s_3, c_1), (s_d, c_3)), ((s_5, c_2), (s_d, c_3)), ((s_d, c_3), (s_5, c_2))\}.$$

There is one cycle $((s_5, c_2), (s_d, c_3), (s_5, c_2))$. At Step 2, $\mathscr{C}^3$ is $\{(s_5, c_2), (s_d, c_3)\}$. Z and Y^3 are given as follows:

$$Z = \{(s_1, c_2), (s_4, c_3), (s_7, c_1), (s_2, c_3), (s_5, c_3)\},$$
$$Y^3 = \{(s_3, c_1), (s_6, c_2)\}.$$

At Step 1 of Round 4, c_1 is minimum, c_2 is decrementable, and c_3 is maximum. Then the mechanism adds (s_3, c_1) and (s_6, c_2) to V^4. Since c_3 is maximum, it cannot send its representative. Thus, no dummy student is added. Therefore, G^4 is given as follows:

$$V^4 = \{(s_3, c_1), (s_6, c_2)\},$$
$$E^4 = \{((s_3, c_1), (s_3, c_1)), ((s_6, c_2), (s_6, c_2))\}.$$

There are two self-loop cycles. At Step 2, $\mathscr{C}^4$ is $\{(s_3, c_1), (s_6, c_2)\}$. Z and Y^4 are determined as follows:

$$\begin{aligned} Z &= \{(s_1, c_2), (s_4, c_3), (s_7, c_1), (s_2, c_3), (s_5, c_3), \\ &\quad (s_3, c_1), (s_6, c_2)\}, \\ Y^4 &= \emptyset. \end{aligned}$$

At Step 4, since $Y^4 = \emptyset$, the mechanism returns Z.

The obtained matching is identical to Z' in Example 1.

5. THEORETICAL PROPERTIES

In this section, we clarify the theoretical properties of TTCR-SS. We first show its feasibility. Note that there exists at most one cycle that includes a dummy student.

THEOREM 1. *TTCR-SS always produces a feasible matching.*

PROOF. It is clear that the outcome is student-feasible since a student never selects a contract that is related to her unacceptable school.

As for the school-feasibility of Z, we show that $\{Y^k \cup Z\}$ is school-feasible for any k by induction. For $k = 0$, it is clear that $\{Y^0 \cup Z\}$ is school-feasible because $Y^0 = X^*$ is school-feasible and $Z = \emptyset$. Suppose $\{Y^k \cup Z\}$ is school-feasible for some k. The induction completes if we show that for any $c \in C$ it holds that $p_c \leq |Y_c^{k+1}| + |Z_c| \leq q_c$ after Round $k+1$. If a contract related to c is not included in $\mathscr{C}^{k+1}$, the assignment related to c never changes. Thus, assume (s, c) is included in $\mathscr{C}^{k+1}$. Then, it is clear that c is not maximum. If c is incrementable, $Y_c^k = Y_c^{k+1} = \emptyset$, and $p_c \leq |Z_c| < q_c$ holds at the beginning of Round $k+1$. Z_c is incremented by one. Thus, $p_c \leq |Z_c| \leq q_c$ holds at the end of Round $k+1$. If c is decrementable, $p_c < |Y_c^k| + |Z_c| \leq q_c$ holds at the beginning of Round $k+1$. Also, $|Y_c^k| - 1 = |Y_c^{k+1}|$ holds, and Z_c does not change if a dummy student obtains the seat of c or is incremented by one if a non-dummy student obtains the seat of c. In either case, $p_c \leq |Y_c^{k+1}| + |Z_c| \leq q_c$ holds at the end of Round $k+1$. If c is minimum, $p_c = |Y_c^k| + |Z_c| \leq q_c$ holds at the beginning of Round $k+1$. $|Y_c^k| - 1 = |Y_c^{k+1}|$ holds, and Z_c is always incremented by one since a dummy student never obtains a seat of c. Thus, $p_c = |Y_c^{k+1}| + |Z_c| \leq q_c$ holds at the end of Round $k+1$. □

School c is **available** at Round k if either $C_{\text{dec}}^k \neq \emptyset$ and $c \in C \setminus C_{\max}^k$ or $C_{\text{dec}}^k = \emptyset$ and $c \in C_{\min}^k$ hold. Let C_{ava}^k denote the set of all available schools. It is clear that at Round k, a contract related to school c is included in V^k if and only if c is available at Round k.

It is obvious that the following lemma holds from the category transition of schools and the definition of C_{ava}^k.

LEMMA 1. *For any two rounds k and k' with $k < k'$, $C_{dec}^k \supseteq C_{dec}^{k'}$ and $C_{ava}^k \supseteq C_{ava}^{k'}$ hold.*

Intuitively, this lemma means that the possible choices for a student weakly monotonically shrinks in the later rounds. As a result, the following lemma says the choice of a student is the best within all schools that are available in the later rounds.

LEMMA 2. *Suppose TTCR-SS obtains X'. For any k and any $c \in C_{ava}^k$, and any student s who is included in $\mathscr{C}^{k'}$, i.e., a cycle at Round $k' \leq k$, $X'_s \succeq_s \{(s, c)\}$ holds.*

PROOF. From Lemma 1, $C_{\text{ava}}^k \subseteq C_{\text{ava}}^{k'}$ holds. Also, the fact that s is included in $\mathscr{C}^{k'}$ means that $\{(s, c')\} = X'_s$ and c' is the most preferred school for s within $C_{\text{ava}}^{k'}$. Thus, $X'_s \succeq_s \{(s, c)\}$ holds. □

The following lemma implies if there exists a directed path toward a contract at some round, the path remains in the later rounds unless the contract is removed by being included in a cycle. Thus, if a student can obtain a seat of a particular school in a round (either by truth-telling or by manipulation), she can also obtain the seat in the later rounds.

LEMMA 3. *Suppose there is a directed path from a contract (s, c) to (s', c') in G^k, and suppose $(s', c') \in V^{k'}$ for some $k' > k$. Then exactly the same directed path from (s, c) to (s', c') exists in $E^{k'}$.*

PROOF. It is sufficient to show that $((s, c), (s', c')) \in E^k$ and $(s', c') \in V^{k+1}$ imply $((s, c), (s', c')) \in E^{k+1}$, since a directed path is a sequence of directed edges. First, suppose $s \neq s_d$. From Lemma 1, $C_{\text{ava}}^{k+1} \subseteq C_{\text{ava}}^k$ holds. Since c' is the most preferred school for s within C_{ava}^k, if $c' \in C_{\text{ava}}^{k+1}$, c' remains the most preferred school for s within C_{ava}^{k+1}. Thus, $((s, c), (s', c')) \in E^{k+1}$ holds. Second, suppose $s = s_d$. The fact that $((s_d, c), (s', c')) \in E^k$ implies that c' is decrementable and that s' has the highest priority in ML within all the remaining students in all the decrementable schools. According to Lemma 1, the set of decrementable schools never expands. As long as (s', c') remains in V^{k+1}, c' remains decrementable and s' still has the highest priority in ML within all the remaining students in all the decrementable schools at Round $k+1$. Thus, $((s, c), (s', c')) \in E^{k+1}$ holds. □

The following lemma means that the declared preference of a student does not affect the outcome of the rounds before she is included in a cycle.

LEMMA 4. *Fix the reported preferences of all students except s at $\succ_{-s} = (\succ_{s'})_{s' \in S \setminus \{s\}}$. Suppose that $(s, \omega(s)) \in \mathscr{C}^k$ if she reports $\succ_s$ and $(s, \omega(s)) \in \mathscr{C}^{k'}$ if she reports $\succ'_s$, where $k \leq k'$. Then C_*^k, where "$*$" can be either "max", "min", "inc", "dec", or "ava", does not change regardless of whether student s reports $\succ_s$ or $\succ'_s$.*

PROOF. Since $(s, \omega(s)) \notin \mathscr{C}^{\hat{k}}$ holds for any $\hat{k} < k$, the same contracts form cycles before Round k whether student s reports $\succ_s$ or $\succ'_s$. Then in both cases, the same contracts remain in Y^{k-1} and the same contracts are added to Z, which implies C_*^k does not change. □

Now, we are ready to prove that TTCR-SS is strategy-proof and Pareto efficient.

THEOREM 2. *TTCR-SS is strategy-proof.*

PROOF. Fix the reported preferences of all students except s at $\succ_{-s} = (\succ_{s'})_{s' \in S \setminus \{s\}}$ and denote $\succ = (\succ_{-s}, \succ_s)$ and $\succ' = (\succ_{-s}, \succ'_s)$, where $\succ_s$ is her true preference and $\succ'_s$ is a fake preference. For some Round k, explicitly write $V^k(\succ)$, $G^k(\succ)$, $E^k(\succ)$, and $\mathscr{C}^k(\succ)$ to denote V^k, G^k, E^k, and $\mathscr{C}^k$ when the reported preference profile is $\succ$ and so on. Explicitly write $C_*^k(\succ)$ to denote C_*^k when the reported preference profile is $\succ$ and so on. Suppose that $(s, \omega(s)) \in \mathscr{C}^k(\succ)$, i.e., if s reports her true preference $\succ_s$, she belongs to a cycle at

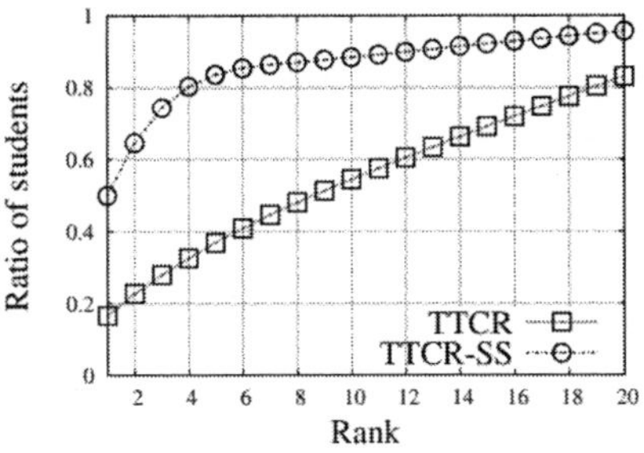

Figure 2: CDFs of students' welfare ($\alpha = 0.6$)

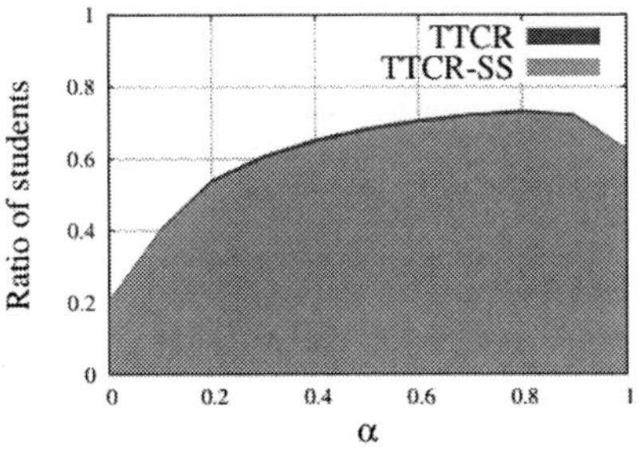

Figure 3: Ratio of students who prefer TTCR-SS/TTCR

Round k, and $(s, \omega(s)) \in \mathscr{C}^{k'}(\succ')$, i.e., if she reports some other preference $\succ'_s$, she belongs to a cycle at Round k'.

First, assume $k \le k'$. Since $(s, \omega(s)) \in \mathscr{C}^k(\succ)$, s must be matched with her most preferred school within $C^k_{\text{ava}}(\succ)$. Also, $(s, \omega(s)) \in \mathscr{C}^{k'}(\succ')$ means that s is matched with a school within $C^{k'}_{\text{ava}}(\succ')$. Therefore, it is sufficient to show that $C^{k'}_{\text{ava}}(\succ') \subseteq C^k_{\text{ava}}(\succ)$ holds. Since $k \le k'$, it follows from Lemma 4 that $C^k_{\text{ava}}(\succ') = C^k_{\text{ava}}(\succ)$ holds. Also, from Lemma 1, it follows that $C^{k'}_{\text{ava}}(\succ') \subseteq C^k_{\text{ava}}(\succ')$. Combining these results, we have $C^{k'}_{\text{ava}}(\succ') \subseteq C^k_{\text{ava}}(\succ)$.

Next, assume $k > k'$. Since $(s, \omega(s)) \in \mathscr{C}^{k'}(\succ')$, there exists a directed path from (s', c') to $(s, \omega(s))$ in $G^{k'}(\succ')$, where $((s, \omega(s)), (s', c')) \in E^{k'}(\succ')$. From Lemma 4, $C^{k'}_{\text{ava}}(\succ') = C^{k'}_{\text{ava}}(\succ)$ holds. Thus, there exists the same directed path from (s', c') to $(s, \omega(s))$ in $G^{k'}(\succ)$. The fact that $(s, \omega(s)) \in \mathscr{C}^k(\succ)$ implies $(s, \omega(s)) \in V^k(\succ)$, and thus from Lemma 3 there exists the same directed path from (s', c') to $(s, \omega(s))$ in $G^k(\succ)$. Then s's assignment under $\succ$ is at least as good as c', which is the assignment under $\succ'$. Thus, s cannot be better off by reporting $\succ'_s$. $\square$

THEOREM 3. *TTCR-SS is Pareto efficient.*

PROOF. Let X' denote the matching produced by TTCR-SS and suppose for contradiction that X' can be Pareto improved, i.e., there exists another matching X'' that Pareto dominates X'. Let S' denote the set of students such that $s \in S'$ if and only if $X''_s \succ_s X'_s$ holds, i.e., students whose assignments are strictly improved in X''.

Among the students in S', let $\widehat{s}_1$ be a student who is lastly allocated under the mechanism when generating X', i.e., $(\widehat{s}_1, \omega(\widehat{s}_1)) \in \mathscr{C}^{k_1}$ for some k_1 and there exists no $s' \in S'$ such that $(s', \omega(s')) \in \mathscr{C}^{k'}$ with $k' > k_1$. Since $\widehat{s}_1 \in S'$, it follows that $k_1 > 1$. If $k_1 = 1$ holds, $X'_{\widehat{s}_1}$ is the contract between $\widehat{s}_1$ and her most preferred school in C, and therefore no contract can improve $\widehat{s}_1$ from $X'_{\widehat{s}_1}$, which contradicts that $\widehat{s}_1 \in S'$.

Let $\widehat{c}_1$ be the school to which $\widehat{s}_1$ is assigned under X', i.e., $\{(\widehat{s}_1, \widehat{c}_1)\} = X'_{\widehat{s}_1}$. Since $\widehat{c}_1 \in C^{k_1}_{\text{ava}}$, Lemma 2 implies that for all $s \in S'$, it holds that $X'_s \succeq_s \{(s, \widehat{c}_1)\}$. Therefore, $X''_s \neq \{(s, \widehat{c}_1)\}$ for all $s \in S'$, and together with the fact that $X'_{\widehat{s}_1} = \{(\widehat{s}_1, \widehat{c}_1)\} \not\subseteq X''$, it holds that $X''_{\widehat{c}_1} \subsetneq X'_{\widehat{c}_1}$. Since X'' is feasible and thus $p_{\widehat{c}_1} \le |X''_{\widehat{c}_1}|$, it holds that $p_{\widehat{c}_1} < |X'_{\widehat{c}_1}|$.

Let $\widehat{c}_2$ be the school to which $\widehat{s}_1$ is assigned under X'', i.e., $\{(\widehat{s}_1, \widehat{c}_2)\} = X''_{\widehat{s}_1}$. By the definition of X'', it must hold that $\widehat{c}_2 \succ_{\widehat{s}_1} \widehat{c}_1$. Since $\{(\widehat{s}_1, \widehat{c}_1)\} = X'_{\widehat{s}_1}$ and $(\widehat{s}_1, \omega(\widehat{s}_1)) \in \mathscr{C}^{k_1}$, there exists a directed edge $((\widehat{s}_1, \omega(\widehat{s}_1)), (s, \widehat{c}_1)) \in E^{k_1}$. The fact that $\widehat{s}_1$ points to $\widehat{c}_1$ even though she prefers $\widehat{c}_2$ over $\widehat{c}_1$ implies either (i) $\widehat{c}_2$ is maximum at Round k_1 holds or (ii) $\widehat{c}_2$ is incrementable and there exists no decrementable school at Round k_1 holds. However, in this case, (ii) cannot hold; if it holds, all the contracts in V^{k_1} are related to minimum schools, but $\widehat{c}_1$ is not minimum. Thus, $\widehat{c}_2$ must be maximum at Round k_1. Then $|X'_{\widehat{c}_2}| = q_{\widehat{c}_2}$ holds. Since X'' is feasible and $(\widehat{s}_1, \widehat{c}_2) \notin X'$ but $(\widehat{s}_1, \widehat{c}_2) \in X''$, there must exist student $\widehat{s}_2$ who is matched with $\widehat{c}_2$ in X' and her assignment is changed in X'', i.e., $\widehat{s}_2 \in S'$ and $(\widehat{s}_2, \widehat{c}_2) \in X'$, and suppose $(\widehat{s}_2, \omega(\widehat{s}_2)) \in \mathscr{C}^{k_2}$ for some k_2, i.e., $\widehat{s}_2$ belongs to a cycle and is matched to $\widehat{c}_2$ at Round k_2. Then $\widehat{c}_2 \in C^{k_2}_{\text{ava}}$ must hold and Lemma 1 implies that $k_1 > k_2$.

Let $\widehat{c}_3$ be the school to which $\widehat{s}_2$ is assigned under X'', i.e., $\{(\widehat{s}_2, \widehat{c}_3)\} = X''_{\widehat{s}_2}$. Then by the definition of X'', it holds that $\widehat{c}_3 \succ_{\widehat{s}_2} \widehat{c}_2$. Since $\{(\widehat{s}_2, \widehat{c}_2)\} = X'_{\widehat{s}_2}$, A directed edge exists $((\widehat{s}_2, \omega(\widehat{s}_2)), (s, \widehat{c}_2)) \in E^{k_2}$. The fact that $\widehat{s}_2$ points to $\widehat{c}_2$ even though she prefers $\widehat{c}_3$ over $\widehat{c}_2$ implies that either $\widehat{c}_3$ is maximum or no decrementable schools exist. Using the similar argument as $\widehat{s}_1$, we can derive that $\widehat{c}_3$ is maximum and $|X'_{\widehat{c}_3}| = q_{\widehat{c}_3}$ holds. Since X'' is feasible and $(\widehat{s}_2, \widehat{c}_3) \notin X'$ but $(\widehat{s}_2, \widehat{c}_3) \in X''$, there must exist a student who is matched with $\widehat{c}_3$ in X' and her assignment is changed in X''. Let $\widehat{s}_3$ be such a student, i.e., $(\widehat{s}_3, \widehat{c}_3) \in X'$ and $\widehat{s}_3 \in S'$, and suppose $(\widehat{s}_3, \omega(\widehat{s}_3)) \in \mathscr{C}^{k_3}$ for some k_3, i.e., $\widehat{s}_3$ belongs to a cycle and is matched to $\widehat{c}_3$ at Round k_3. Then, by the same argument showing $k_1 > k_2$, it holds that $k_2 > k_3$.

We can continue this argument until we find a student $\widehat{s}_* \in S'$ with $(\widehat{s}_*, \omega(\widehat{s}_*)) \in \mathscr{C}^1$, i.e., a student who belongs to a cycle at Round 1 and whose assignment is strictly improved under X''. However, $\widehat{s}_*$ is matched with her most preferred school in C under X' and there is no contract for $\widehat{s}_*$ that is strictly better than $X'_{\widehat{s}_*}$, which contradicts that $\widehat{s}_* \in S'$ and thus no such X'' exists. $\square$

The fact that TTCR-SS is Pareto efficient, while TTCR is not, does not imply that all students weakly prefer the matching of TTCR-SS over that of TTCR. This is because there can be multiple Pareto efficient matchings. Let us show a simple example. Assume there are two students, s_1 and s_2, and three schools, c_1, c_2, and c_3. The minimum quota of c_1 is 1, and the minimum quotas of c_2 and c_3 are 0. The maximum quotas of all the schools are 1. The initial endowment schools of s_1 and s_2 are c_1 and c_2, respectively. The preference of s_1 is $c_2 \succ_{s_1} c_1$, and the preference of s_2 is $c_3 \succ_{s_2} c_1 \succ_{s_2} c_2$. In TTCR-SS, the dummy student of c_3 and s_2 swap their seats, and s_1 cannot move to c_2. Thus, the obtained matching is $\{(s_1, c_1), (s_2, c_3)\}$. On the other hand, in TTCR, no dummy student is introduced and s_1 and s_2 swap their seats. The obtained matching is

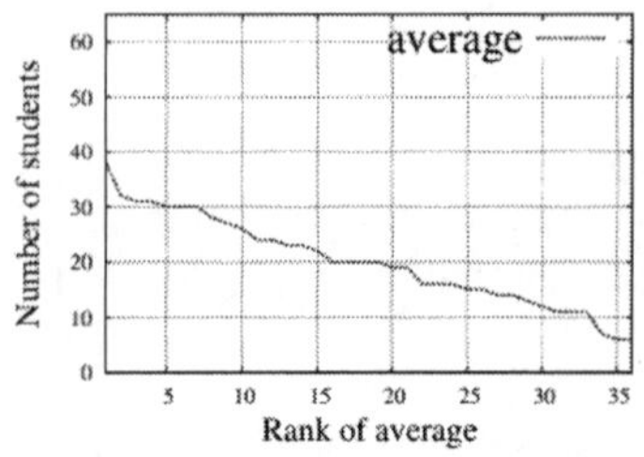

Figure 4: Difference of number of assigned students ($\alpha = 0$)

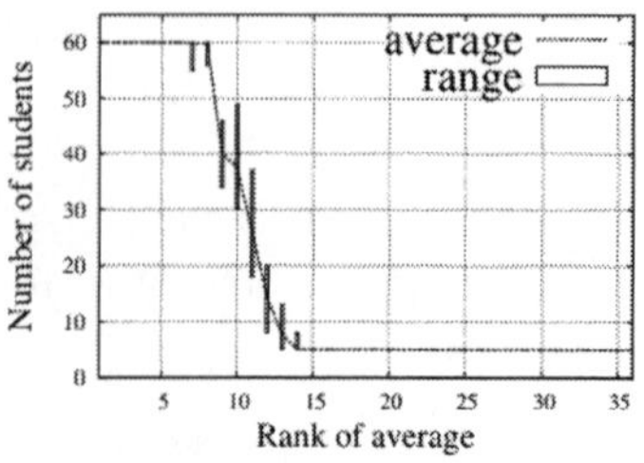

Figure 5: Difference of number of assigned students ($\alpha = 0.6$)

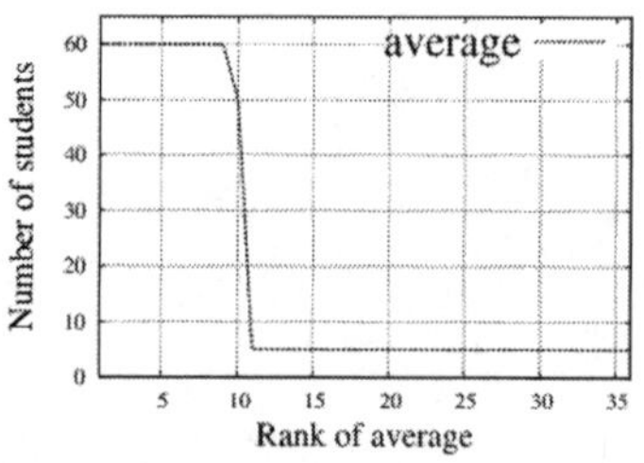

Figure 6: Difference of number of assigned students ($\alpha = 1$)

$\{(s_1, c_2), (s_2, c_1)\}$. Here, s_1 prefers the matching of TTCR. In the next section, we experimentally show that the overwhelming majority of students prefer the matching obtained by TTCR-SS.

Finally, we show that TTCR-SS can be done in polynomial time in $|S|$ and $|C|$.

THEOREM 4. *The time complexity of TTCR-SS is* $O(|S| \cdot |C|)$.

PROOF. At each round, there exists at least one cycle. A cycle must contain at least one student $s \in S$, and the assignment of s is fixed. Thus, the number of rounds required for TTCR-SS is at most $|S|$. Also, for each round, there are at most $|C|$ contracts, and finding cycles can be done in $O(|C|)$. Therefore, the time complexity of TTCR-SS is $O(|S| \cdot |C|)$. □

6. EVALUATION

This section evaluates TTCR-SS. We consider a market with $n = 720$ students and $m = 36$ schools. Each school has 20 initial endowment students. The minimum and maximum quotas of each school are 5 and 60, respectively. We generate students' preferences as follows. We draw one common vector v of the cardinal utilities from set $[0, 1]^m$ uniformly at random. We then randomly draw private vector u_s of the cardinal utilities from the same set, again uniformly at random. Next, we construct cardinal utilities over all m schools for student s as $\alpha v + (1 - \alpha)u_s$ for some $\alpha \in [0, 1]$. We convert these cardinal utilities into an ordinal preference relation for each student. The higher the value of α is, the more correlated the student preferences are.

6.1 Comparison with TTCR

We compare the welfare of the students for TTCR and TTCR-SS. We generate 100 problem instances. ML is set to $s_1, \ldots, s_n$. Figure 2 shows the Cumulative Distribution Functions (CDFs) of the average number of students matched with their k-th or higher ranked school under each mechanism when α is 0.6. Hence, a steep upper trend line is desirable. 50% of the students obtain their first choices, and 65% obtain their first or second choices in TTCR-SS, while in TTCR, only 16% of students obtain their most preferred contracts, and 23% obtain their most or second preferred contracts. Thus, the average student welfare of TTCR-SS clearly outperforms that of TTCR.

Next, we show the average ratio of students who strictly prefer the matching of one mechanism over that of the other mechanism (Fig. 3). Here, the gray area shows the ratio of students who prefer the matching of TTCR-SS, while the black area shows the ratio of students who prefer the matching of TTCR (note that the area is very narrow and it looks like a line). The white area shows the ratio of students whose assignments are the same. For example, when $\alpha = 0.6$, only 1% of the students prefer the matching of TTCR, while 70% prefer the matching of TTCR-SS; the overwhelming majority of students prefer the matching obtained by TTCR-SS.

6.2 Effect of choice of master list

ML must be chosen exogenously by the mechanism. If the obtained matching can vary significantly according to the choice of the ML, say, the number of students assigned to each school changes significantly, how to determine ML can be controversial. Here, we fix one problem instance and compare the results of TTCR-SS for 100 randomly generated different MLs. Figures 4, 5, and 6 show differences of the number of assigned students under the cases of $\alpha = 0$, 0.6, and 1, respectively. We show the average, minimum, and maximum of the number of allocated students for each school. The x-axis represents schools that are sorted in decreasing order of their average. When $\alpha = 0$, the preference of students are independent and there is virtually no competition among them. Then the choice of ML does not affect the outcome very much; the average, minimum, and maximum are almost the same (Fig. 4). When $\alpha = 1$, the preferences of the students are the same and they all compete for the seats of the same popular schools. Thus, the choice of ML affects who will be assigned to the popular schools, but it does not affect the number of students assigned to them. Thus, the average, minimum, and maximum are identical (Fig. 6). When $\alpha = 0.6$, the number of allocated students can vary according to the choice of ML. However, Figure 5 shows that the numbers of students allocated to popular/unpopular schools are almost the same, and it varies in the schools that are in the middle of popular/unpopular schools. Thus, we conjecture that the choice of ML is not too controversial; the choice does not affect the popularity of schools very much.

7. CONCLUSIONS

In this paper, we developed TTCR-SS for a school choice program, where the obtained matching must respect minimum quotas and initial endowments. We proved that TTCR-SS is strategy-proof and Pareto efficient. Our simulation results showed that it is significantly better than TTCR, which cannot allocate supplementary seats.

Our immediate future work is to extend our mechanism to handle different types of distributional constraints besides minimum quotas [17].

REFERENCES

[1] A. Abdulkadiroğlu and Y.-K. Che. The role of priorities in assigning indivisible objects: A characterization of top trading cycles. Working Paper, 2010.

[2] A. Abdulkadiroğlu and T. Sönmez. House allocation with existing tenants. *Journal of Economic Theory*, 88:233–260, 1999.

[3] A. Abdulkadiroğlu and T. Sönmez. School choice: A mechanism design approach. *American Economic Review*, 93(3):729–747, 2003.

[4] P. Biró, T. Fleiner, R. W. Irving, and D. F. Manlove. The college admission problem with lower and common quotas. *Theoretical Computer Science*, 411:3136 – 3153, 2010.

[5] S. Braun, N. Dwenger, D. Kübler, and A. Westkamp. Implementing quotas in university admissions: An experimental analysis. *Games and Economic Behavior*, 85:232–251, 2014.

[6] U. M. Dur. A characterization of the top trading cycles mechanism for school choice problem. Working Paper, 2013.

[7] U. M. Dur and M. U. Ünver. Two-sided matching via balanced exchange: Tuition and worker exchanges. Working Paper, 2015.

[8] L. Ehlers, I. E. Hafalir, M. B. Yenmez, and M. A. Yildirim. School choice with controlled choice constraints: Hard bounds versus soft bounds. *Journal of Economic Theory*, 153:648–683, 2014.

[9] A. Erdil and H. Ergin. What's the matter with tie-breaking? improving efficiency in school choice. *The American Economic Review*, 98(3):669–689, 2008.

[10] D. Fragiadakis, A. Iwasaki, P. Troyan, S. Ueda, and M. Yokoo. Strategyproof matching with minimum quotas. *ACM Transactions on Economics and Computation*, 4(1):6:1–6:40, 2015.

[11] D. Gale and L. S. Shapley. College admissions and the stability of marriage. *The American Mathematical Monthly*, 69(1):9–15, 1962.

[12] M. Goto, N. Hashimoto, A. Iwasaki, Y. Kawasaki, S. Ueda, Y. Yasuda, and M. Yokoo. Strategy-proof matching with regional minimum quotas. In *Proceedings of Thirteenth International Conference on Autonomous Agents and Multiagent Systems (AAMAS-2014)*, pages 1225–1232, 2014.

[13] G. Haeringer and F. Klijn. Constrained school choice. *Journal of Economic Theory*, 144:1921 – 1947, 2009.

[14] I. E. Hafalir, M. B. Yenmez, and M. A. Yildirim. Effective affirmative action in school choice. *Theoretical Economics*, 8(2):325–363, 2013.

[15] O. Kesten. On two competing mechanisms for priority-based allocation problems. *Journal of Economic Theory*, 127:155 – 171, 2006.

[16] F. Kojima. School choice: Impossibilities for affirmative action. *Games and Economic Behavior*, 75(2):685–693, 2012.

[17] F. Kojima, A. Tamura, and M. Yokoo. Designing matching mechanisms under constraints: An approach from discrete convex analysis. In *Proceedings of the Seventh International Symposium on Algorithmic Game Theory (SAGT-2014)*, 2014. the full version is available at http://mpra.ub.uni-muenchen.de/62226).

[18] R. Kurata, M. Goto, A. Iwasaki, and M. Yokoo. Controlled school choice with soft bounds and overlapping types. In *Proceedings of the Twenty-Ninth AAAI Conference on Artificial Intelligence (AAAI-2015)*, pages 951–957, 2015.

[19] J. Ma. Strategy-proofness and the strict core in a market with indivisibilities. *International Journal of Game Theory*, 23:75 – 83, 1994.

[20] T. Morrill. An alternative characterization of top trading cycles. *Economic Theory*, 54:181 – 197, 2013.

[21] S. Pápai. Strategyproof assignment by hierarchical exchange. *Econometrica*, 68(6):1403–1433, 2000.

[22] M. Pycia and M. U. Ünver. Incentive compatible allocation and exchange of discrete resources. *Theoretical Economics*, 2016. Forthcoming.

[23] A. E. Roth. Incentive compatibility in a market with indivisible goods. *Economics Letters*, 9:127 – 132, 1982.

[24] A. E. Roth. School choice in New Orleans with top trading cycles, April 17 2012. http://marketdesigner.blogspot.jp/2012/04/school-choice-in-new-orleans-with-top.html.

[25] A. E. Roth and A. Postlewaite. Weak versus strong domination in a market with indivisible goods. *Journal of Mathematical Economics*, 4:131 – 137, 1977.

[26] L. Shapley and H. Scarf. On cores and indivisibility. *Journal of Mathematical Economics*, 1:23 – 37, 1974.

[27] A. Westkamp. An analysis of the German university admissions system. *Economic Theory*, 53:561–589, 2013.

What to Verify for Optimal Truthful Mechanisms without Money

Diodato Ferraioli*
University of Salerno
dferraioli@unisa.it

Paolo Serafino
Teesside University
p.serafino@tees.ac.uk

Carmine Ventre†
Teesside University
c.ventre@tees.ac.uk

ABSTRACT

We aim at identifying a minimal set of conditions under which algorithms with good approximation guarantees are truthful without money. In line with recent literature, we wish to express such a set via verification assumptions, i.e., kind of agents' misbehavior that can be made impossible by the designer.

We initiate this research endeavour for the paradigmatic problem in approximate mechanism design without money, facility location. It is known how truthfulness imposes (even severe) losses and how certain notions of verification are unhelpful in this setting; one is thus left powerless to solve this problem satisfactorily in presence of selfish agents. We here address this issue and characterize the minimal set of verification assumptions needed for the truthfulness of optimal algorithms, for both social cost and max cost objective functions. En route, we give a host of novel conceptual and technical contributions ranging from topological notions of verification to a lower bounding technique for truthful mechanisms that connects methods to *test* truthfulness (i.e., cycle monotonicity) with *approximation guarantee*.

1. INTRODUCTION

How good an approximate solution can a truthful (or strategyproof (SP)) mechanism return for the optimization problem at hand? This question is an important line of investigation in mechanism design with monetary transfers [12, 1, 2] and without [15, 6, 23]. For the latter class of mechanisms, more appropriate to digital settings where there is no currency readily available, the tradeoff between incentives and approximation is at the heart of approximate mechanism design without money research agenda [21]. The paradigmatic problem in this area is K-facility location: n selfish agents are located on the real line; we want to place K facilities on input the n bids of the agents for their locations on the line. Each agent's objective is to minimize their connection cost, defined as the distance between their true location and the nearest facility. The designer's objective is to minimize the social cost (i.e., the sum of the connection costs of all the agents). It is known that the best deterministic SP mechanism can only return an $(n-2)$-approximation of the optimum, even for $K = 2$ [21, 6]. (A different version of the problem looks at the minimization of the maximum cost – the bound for $K = 2$ is, in this case, constant.)

This research leaves little hope to the mechanism designer facing this problem in presence of selfish agents. In fact, the designer cannot use computation time as a way out since practically all (few exceptions are known in the setting with money, e.g., [2]) the lower bounds to the approximation of SP mechanisms hold unconditionally, i.e., independently from the running time of algorithms. The designer could use randomization but with scarce results. For one, truthful in expectation mechanisms are vulnerable to different risk attitude of agents (indeed, SP is guaranteed only as long as agents are risk neutral). Secondly, mechanisms are suboptimal – a constant upper bound is known for $K = 2$ [15].

In this work, we want to propose a way forward to the mechanism designer in despair. On one hand, we want to focus on deterministic mechanisms, so as to avoid to make assumptions about agents' attitude to uncertainty. On the other hand, we wish to provide a small (ideally, minimum) set of conditions under which algorithms with "good" approximation guarantees are SP. This would inform the designer about the (minimum) investment in resources (e.g., policies, infrastructures, legislation) needed to prevent the lies that make the algorithms of interest not SP. The idea to restrict the way agents lie is well established in economics [10, 9] and computer science [20, 24, 13, 11, 3, 4, 7]. Therein, this assumption is dubbed *verification* to express that certain lies can be somehow verified and made impossible. Our novelty is the aim of "minimizing" the verification assumptions needed for the truthfulness of "good" algorithms, rather than showing that a particular verification leads to the truthfulness of a specific (class of) algorithm(s).

Our contribution

We initiate this line of enquiry and individuate a minimal set of verification assumptions for which optimum algorithms for K-facility location are SP.

The assumptions needed for a truthful optimum differ accordingly to the objective function of interest, social cost or maximum cost. The first ingredient, common to both scenarios, is a 'return to the origin' in verification literature. As in [17] the actual cost of the agents are bound to an insincere declaration (specifically, an agent overreporting their cost ends up paying this augmented cost), so here a lying agent

*This author was supported by the "GNCS – INdAM".
†This author was supported by EPSRC, through grant EP/M018113/1.

Appears in: *Proceedings of the 15th International Conference on Autonomous Agents and Multiagent Systems (AAMAS 2016), J. Thangarajah, K. Tuyls, C. Jonker, S. Marsella (eds.), May 9–13, 2016, Singapore.*

is forced to use the facility closest to her reported location (rather than closest to her actual location). This notion, named *cluster imposing* and first used in [19], generalizes winner imposing mechanisms considered by [5] and is easy to implement by defining, e.g., 'catchment areas' for facilities (much like, the system in place for public schooling in many countries). The second ingredient, common to social and maximum cost, is a *no-underbidding* assumption whereby agents cannot say to be closer to the cluster-imposed facility than they actually are. This concept rephrases the main assumption made in related literature (see [20, 13] and references therein) for problems like combinatorial auctions and scheduling; it can be readily imposed by the designer whenever it is possible to measure/prove the distance the agent covers to reach the facility (in which case, it is, in fact, possible to simulate longer trips but not shorter ones).

The third ingredient for the result on social cost is a conceptual novelty. Verification is commonly defined only in relation to (true/reported) costs. We here define a topological restriction for the access to facilities: agents located to the left (right) of the facility are not allowed to access it from the right (left). This assumption, called *direction imposing*, further restricts the way agents can misbehave as an agent with true location t cannot declare b whenever the algorithm locates the facility closest to b in between t and b. Direction imposing can be realized whenever it is feasible to implement a 'left/right door' infrastructure for the facilities. For instance, when facilities are routers relaying voice/data and the area code of source address cannot be spoofed, the direction (subnetwork) voice/data have been transmitted from can be checked.

The third ingredient for the result on max cost (which, incidentally, holds only for $K = 2$) falls again in the class of cost-only verification. We here need to also prevent agents from reporting to be farther from the cluster-imposed facility than they actually are. Together with no-underbidding, this gives rise to a *no-cost forging* verification that is adequate in settings in which expense proofs must be provided.

We prove that relaxing any of the assumptions above leads to suboptimal outcomes (even when the other notions are strengthened) for both objective functions, already for $K = 2$. This shows that our (set of) verification(s) is *necessary* in the sense that it individuates the incentive-compatibility (IC) constraints that make optimal algorithms vulnerable to misreports. Furthermore, our guarantee about minimal sets of assumptions is, in a sense, the best one can hope for in this setting. The difficulty here is about "weighing" an assumption in the set. If all were equally heavy then our results would actually prove that ours is a minimum set of assumptions, as we prove that relaxing either of those leads to suboptimal outcomes already for $K = 2$. However, one could also weigh an assumption with the number of IC constraints that a verification assumption removes (i.e., by how much an assumption restricts the possible declarations available to agents). From this perspective, though, it becomes very hard (if possible, at all) to give a compact, useful-to-the-mechanism-designer characterization of maximum (or, even, maximal in fact) set of IC constraints according to which algorithm f is SP. Firstly, any such characterization would need to list somehow IC constraints that f satisfies. Secondly, the mechanism designer has no way to distinguish feasible IC constraints from infeasible ones. For example, the no-underbidding verification would not be needed for f and a pair of declarations t, b whenever an agent positioned at t would not gain by underbidding the distance from the location in which f places the facility closest to b. But since the mechanism only knows b, there is no way the designer can avoid verifying the pair t, b (there might in fact be a location c for which c would indeed gain by underbidding the distance from the facility closest to b).

Discussion on verification

Our verification notions are *ex-post* as in all – [10] being an exception – aforementioned related literature, i.e., the actual outcome of the algorithm (the location of the facilities) is used to define restricted misbehavior. A different approach is *ex-ante* verification, where the set of restricted strategies is defined upon the type (location) of each agent. So, for example, in the ϵ-verification of [8] an agent with true location t can only declare locations in $[t - \epsilon, t + \epsilon]$ – this 'symmetric' verification is, however, ineffective as any truthful mechanism with verification is truthful without [8]. Our contribution can be cast in that framework as the study of (the "minimal") 'asymmetric' verification that truthfully implements optimum algorithms.

As discussed above, our assumptions are necessary: no optimal truthful algorithm for K-facility location exists without. When for the application of interest those assumptions cannot be implemented then one must content oneself with suboptimal solutions. Our results should then be read in the negative whenever our verification concepts cannot be enforced. Note, however, that in principle different definitions of verification could remove the exact same set of IC constraints we prove to break truthfulness. Nevertheless, the study of the best way to express those IC constraints depends on the setting at hand and is outside the scope of this work. (We stress that facility location is rather general and thus encodes many different real-life applications.)

More technical contributions

We believe that our results only scratch the surface as we conjecture that our assumptions are minimal not just for optimal algorithms but for all "simple" algorithms with constant approximation guarantee to the optimal social cost. By simple here we mean algorithms that only place the facilities at K of the locations declared by the agents. These algorithms are the most natural (e.g., no algorithm has better approximation guarantee) especially in the case of deterministic algorithms (cf. known upper bounds); our conjecture (if proved) suggests to look for 'unnatural' algorithms in order to get a good approximation truthfully.

We give some preliminary results towards settling this conjecture. Among the verification notions needed for a SP optimum, we drop direction-imposing (arguably, the most controversial and somewhat less practical of the concepts) and study the extent to which cost-only verification can be helpful in this context. We adopt the cycle-monotonicity technique to dig deeper into the structure of SP algorithms. This technique features a weighed graph encoding all the IC constraints. We begin by proving a surprising parallel between mechanisms with money and no verification, and mechanisms without money and no-underbidding verification (for any problem). A mechanism in the former category is SP iff all the cycles of the graph have non-negative weight [25]. We show that a mechanism in the latter category is SP iff all the cycles are comprised of edges weighing 0. We essentially complement this characterization by showing that there must be no 0-weight edges outside cycles for good approximations. Specifically, we prove that a class of truthful algorithms can have approximation better than roughly $0.29n$ if and only if they do not have 0-weight edges outside cycles of the IC graph, even if we equip the mechanism with cluster-imposing and no-cost-forging verification. This result showcases a promising and novel approach, being the first known connection between cycle monotonicity and approximation.

We complement this lower bound with a mechanism for $K = 2$, MEDIANFURTHEST, truthful with cluster-imposing no-underbidding verification and with approximation guarantee $0.75n$. We further observe that MEDIANFURTHEST can be seen as a composition of two "basic" algorithms (i.e., MEDIANLEFTMOST and MEDIANRIGHTMOST) and prove that no algorithm with better approximation guarantee exists unless more than two algorithms are composed.

2. MODEL AND PRELIMINARIES

In abstract, we have a set $\mathcal{O}$ of feasible solutions and n selfish agents, each of them having a *cost* (or *type*) $t_i \in D_i$, D_i being the *domain* of agent i. For $t_i \in D_i$, $t_i(X)$ is the cost paid by agent i to implement outcome $X \in \mathcal{O}$. The type t_i is *private knowledge* of agent i. A *mechanism* f takes in input the types *reported* by each agent, that is, the *bids* $\mathbf{b} = (b_1, \dots, b_n)$, $b_i \in D_i$ being the type reported by agent i, and returns a feasible solution $f(\mathbf{b}) \in \mathcal{O}$. We interchangeably use below the term mechanism and algorithm.

DEFINITION 1. *We say that f is a truthful mechanism if for any bidder i, $b_i \in D_i$ and $\mathbf{b}_{-i}$, the declarations of the bidders other than i, we have: $t_i(f(t_i, \mathbf{b}_{-i})) \leq t_i(f(\mathbf{b}))$.*

In certain contexts, some $b_i \in D_i$ can be "forgotten" when defining truthfulness.

DEFINITION 2. *A mechanism f with verification V defines a set of allowed lies $M_{f,V}(t_i, \mathbf{b}_{-i})$ for agent i of type t_i. Agent i can report b_i iff $b_i \in M_{f,V}(t_i, \mathbf{b}_{-i})$. If $b_i \notin M_{f,V}(t_i, \mathbf{b}_{-i})$ then i is* caught lying *and punished by f.*

We assume that being caught lying is a very undesirable behavior for the bidder (e.g., in such a case the bidder loses prestige and the possibility to participate in future mechanisms – for simplicity, we assume that in such a case the bidder will have to pay a fine of infinite value). This way truthfulness is satisfied directly when $b_i \notin M_{f,V}(t_i, \mathbf{b}_{-i})$.

Cycle monotonicity

We set up a weighted graph for each bidder i depending on f, D_i, verification paradigm V, and the declarations $\mathbf{b}_{-i}$. Non-existence of negative-weight edges in this graph guarantees the truthfulness of f.

More formally, fix mechanism f, bidder i and declarations $\mathbf{b}_{-i}$. Let V denote the verification paradigm at hand. The *declaration graph* with verification V associated to f has a vertex for each possible declaration in the domain D_i and an arc between t_i and b_i in D_i whenever $b_i \in M_{f,V}(t_i, \mathbf{b}_{-i})$. The weight of the edge (t_i, b_i) is defined as $-t_i(f(t_i, \mathbf{b}_{-i})) + t_i(f(b_i, \mathbf{b}_{-i}))$ and thus encodes the loss that a bidder whose type is t_i incurs into by declaring b_i.

PROPOSITION 1. *Each declaration graph with verification V associated to f does not have negative-weight edges iff f is a truthful mechanism with verification V.*

The proposition above is adapted from [22, 25] to the verification setting V as in [24]. A corollary of this proposition is the following algorithmic characterization of truthfulness.

COROLLARY 1. *Algorithm f is truthful with verification V iff for all $t_i, b_i \in D_i$ and $\mathbf{b}_{-i}$, $b_i \in M_{f,V}(t_i, \mathbf{b}_{-i})$ implies $t_i(f(t_i, \mathbf{b}_{-i})) \leq t_i(f(b_i, \mathbf{b}_{-i}))$.*

K-facility location

In the K-facility location problem, the set of feasible solutions $\mathcal{O}$ is comprised of all the K-tuples of possible allocations of the facilities whilst the domain of each agent is the real line. For a given mechanism f and $t_i \in D_i$, $t_i(f(t_i, \mathbf{b}_{-i})) = |t_i - f_{t_i}(t_i, \mathbf{b}_{-i})|$, where $f_{t_i}(t_i, \mathbf{b}_{-i})$ denotes the location of the facility output by $f(t_i, \mathbf{b}_{-i})$ closer to location t_i (whenever, t_i is equidistant to two facilities, ties are broken arbitrarily). In other words, $t_i(f(t_i, \mathbf{b}_{-i}))$ denotes the distance between t_i and the location of $f_{t_i}(t_i, \mathbf{b}_{-i})$ also denoted $d(t_i, f_{t_i}(t_i, \mathbf{b}_{-i}))$ below.

We focus on mechanisms f^* optimizing either the *social cost*, i.e., $f^*(\mathbf{b}) \in \arg\min_{X \in \mathcal{O}} cost(X, \mathbf{b})$, $cost(X, \mathbf{b}) = \sum_{i=1}^{n} b_i(X)$ or the *max cost*, i.e., $f^*(\mathbf{b}) \in \arg\min_{X \in \mathcal{O}} mc(X, \mathbf{b})$, $mc(X, \mathbf{b}) = \max_{i=1,\dots,n} b_i(X)$. We say that f is α-approximate for either objective if it returns a solution a factor α away from the corresponding optimum.

Our verification assumptions

We are now ready to formally define the verification assumptions discussed in the introduction in relation to K-facility location.

We say that a mechanism f is *cluster-imposing* if for every i of type t_i, for all $\mathbf{b}_{-i}$ and for all $b_i \in M_{V,f}(t_i, \mathbf{b}_{-i})$, $t_i(f(b_i, \mathbf{b}_{-i})) = |t_i - f_{b_i}(b_i, \mathbf{b}_{-i})| = d(t_i, f_{b_i}(b_i, \mathbf{b}_{-i}))$, that is, the facility *assigned* to i is the one computed by $f(b_i, \mathbf{b}_{-i})$ that is closer to her declaration b_i.

For a mechanism f with *no-underbidding* (*no-overbidding*, resp.) verification, $t_i(f(\mathbf{b})) \leq b_i(f(\mathbf{b}))$ ($t_i(f(\mathbf{b})) \geq b_i(f(\mathbf{b}))$, resp.) for every i of type t_i, for all $\mathbf{b}_{-i}$ and for all $b_i \in M_{V,f}(t_i, \mathbf{b}_{-i})$, i.e., agent i of type t cannot underreport (overreport, resp.) her distance from $f_{b_i}(b_i, \mathbf{b}_{-i})$. A mechanism f with *no-cost-forging verification* is a mechanism with no-underbidding *and* no-overbidding verification, i.e., for all $b_i \in M_{V,f}(t_i, \mathbf{b}_{-i})$, $t_i(f(\mathbf{b})) = b_i(f(\mathbf{b}))$.

We say that a mechanism has *direction-imposing* verification if $t_i, b_i < f_{b_i}(b_i, \mathbf{b}_{-i})$ or $t_i, b_i > f_{b_i}(b_i, \mathbf{b}_{-i})$ or $b_i = f_{b_i}(b_i, \mathbf{b}_{-i})$ or $t_i = f_{b_i}(b_i, \mathbf{b}_{-i})$, that is, t_i and b_i are on the same side of $f_{b_i}(b_i, \mathbf{b}_{-i})$.

2.1 Strengthening Proposition 1

Given that, like for K-facility location, it may be difficult to work with the algorithmic characterization of Corollary 1, we next give a more detailed graph-theoretic characterization of truthfulness with no-underbidding verification. Such a characterization holds not only for the facility location problem, but for any general setting that uses this notion of verification (and thus applies to all the aforementioned papers on ex-post verification).

THEOREM 1. *A mechanism f is truthful with no-underbidding verification iff in each declaration graph associated* *to f the cycles are comprised of 0-weight edges while the edges not belonging to any cycle have non-negative weight.*

PROOF. One direction easily follows from Proposition 1.

For the opposite direction, fix i and $\mathbf{b}_{-i}$ and consider a cycle $C = t_i^0 \to \cdots \to t_i^k = t_i^0$ in the declaration graph with no-underbidding verification associated to f. By definition, the weight of the cycle is

$$\sum_{j=0}^{k-1} -t_i^j(f(t_i^j, \mathbf{b}_{-i})) + t_i^j(f(t_i^{j+1}, \mathbf{b}_{-i})).$$

The existence of edge (t_i^j, t_i^{j+1}) yields

$$t_i^j(f(t_i^{j+1}, \mathbf{b}_{-i})) \le t_i^{j+1}(f(t_i^{j+1}, \mathbf{b}_{-i})).$$

Since f is truthful, then $t_i^j(f(t_i^j, \mathbf{b}_{-i})) \le t_i^j(f(t_i^{j+1}, \mathbf{b}_{-i}))$, for all j. Summing these inequalities, we have

$$t_i^j(f(t_i^j, \mathbf{b}_{-i})) = t_i^j(f(t_i^{j+1}, \mathbf{b}_{-i}))$$

for all j thus proving the theorem. □

3. SOCIAL COST

We call f^* the optimal algorithm for K-facility location that uses a *fixed tie-breaking rule*, i.e., for every i, $\mathbf{b}_{-i}$ and $t_i, b_i \in D_i$, if

$$cost(f^*(\mathbf{t}), \mathbf{b}) = cost(f^*(\mathbf{b}), \mathbf{b}) \quad (1)$$

and

$$cost(f^*(\mathbf{t}), \mathbf{t}) = cost(f^*(\mathbf{b}), \mathbf{t}), \quad (2)$$

then $f^*(\mathbf{b}) = f^*(t_i, \mathbf{b}_{-i})$. (Handling ties consistently is a rather standard assumption in mechanism design, see, e.g., [14].) It is easy to check that an optimal algorithm with fixed tie-breaking always exists. For example, the rule that chooses the lexicographically minimal allocation among all optimal allocations satisfies the property above.

THEOREM 2. *f^* is a truthful mechanism with cluster-imposing, no-underbidding and direction-imposing verification.*

PROOF. Suppose, by contradiction, that there is an agent i of type t_i, a declaration $b_i \neq t_i$ and $\mathbf{b}_{-i}$ such that

$$d(t_i, f_{t_i}^*) > d(t_i, f_{b_i}^*), \quad (3)$$

where $f_{t_i}^* = f_{t_i}^*(\mathbf{t})$ and $f_{b_i}^* = f_{b_i}^*(\mathbf{b})$, with $\mathbf{t} = (t_i, \mathbf{b}_{-i})$. Since the mechanism has no-underbidding verification

$$d(t_i, f_{b_i}^*) \le d(b_i, f_{b_i}^*). \quad (4)$$

By direction-imposing verification instead we have that,

$$\begin{array}{ll} t_i > f_{b_i}^* \Rightarrow b_i \ge f_{b_i}^*; & t_i < f_{b_i}^* \Rightarrow b_i \le f_{b_i}^*; \\ b_i > f_{b_i}^* \Rightarrow t_i \ge f_{b_i}^*; & b_i < f_{b_i}^* \Rightarrow t_i \le f_{b_i}^*. \end{array} \quad (5)$$

We then distinguish four possible cases.

Case 1. if $t_i \ge f_{t_i}^*$ and $t_i > f_{b_i}^*$ or $b_i \ge f_{b_i}^* = t_i$, then, from (3), it follows $t_i - f_{t_i}^* > t_i - f_{b_i}^*$ and thus $f_{t_i}^* < f_{b_i}^*$, and, from (5), we get $b_i \ge f_{b_i}^*$. The latter implies, along with (4), $t_i - f_{b_i}^* \le b_i - f_{b_i}^*$ and thus $t_i < b_i$. We conclude $f_{t_i}^* < f_{b_i}^* \le t_i < b_i$.

Case 2. if $t_i \le f_{t_i}^*$ and $t_i < f_{b_i}^*$ or $b_i \le f_{b_i}^* = t_i$, then, by the same arguments as above, we have that $b_i < t_i \le f_{b_i}^* < f_{t_i}^*$.

Case 3. if $t_i \ge f_{t_i}^*$ and $t_i < f_{b_i}^*$ or $b_i \le f_{b_i}^* = t_i$, then from (5), it follows that $b_i \le f_{b_i}^*$. The latter implies, along with (4), that $f_{b_i}^* - t_i \le f_{b_i}^* - b_i$ and thus $t_i > b_i$. Thus we have that $b_i < t_i \le f_{b_i}^*$, $f_{t_i}^* < t_i$ and $d(t_i, f_{t_i}^*) > d(t_i, f_{b_i}^*)$.

Case 4. if $t_i \le f_{t_i}^*$ and $t_i > f_{b_i}^*$ or $b_i \ge f_{b_i}^* = t_i$, then, by the same arguments, we have $f_{b_i}^* \le t_i < b_i$, $f_{t_i}^* > t_i$ and $d(t_i, f_{t_i}^*) > d(t_i, f_{b_i}^*)$.

We will show that these cases can never arise if the facilities are placed by f^*. Consider Case 1: since $b_i > t_i \ge f_{b_i}^*$, then $d(b_i, f_{b_i}^*) = d(t_i, f_{b_i}^*) + d(b_i, t_i)$. Hence,

$$\begin{aligned} cost(f^*(\mathbf{b}), \mathbf{b}) &= \sum_{j \neq i} b_j(f^*(\mathbf{b})) + d(t_i, f_{b_i}^*) + d(b_i, t_i) \\ &\ge \sum_{j \neq i} b_j(f^*(\mathbf{t})) + d(t_i, f_{t_i}^*) + d(b_i, t_i) \\ &= cost(f^*(\mathbf{t}), \mathbf{b}), \end{aligned}$$

where the inequality follows from $f^*(\mathbf{t})$ being the optimal facility location on input $\mathbf{t}$ and from the fact that $b_i > t_i > f_{t_i}^*$, so that $d(b_i, f_{t_i}^*) = d(t_i, f_{t_i}^*) + d(b_i, t_i)$. However, since $f^*(\mathbf{b})$ is optimal for $\mathbf{b}$ then $cost(f^*(\mathbf{b}), \mathbf{b}) \le cost(f^*(\mathbf{t}), \mathbf{b})$. Thus (1) holds. The same argument can be adopted for proving that (2) also holds. Hence, since f^* has a fixed tie-breaking, $f^*(\mathbf{b}) = f^*(\mathbf{t})$, contradicting the hypothesis that $f_{b_i}^* \neq f_{t_i}^*$. Observe that the Case 2 is symmetrical and thus the exact same arguments can be used.

Let us now consider Case 3. If $b_i \le f_{t_i}^* < t_i$, then $d(b_i, f_{t_i}^*) < d(b_i, f_{b_i}^*)$. Hence, $cost(f^*(\mathbf{b}), \mathbf{b})$ equals

$$\begin{aligned} &\sum_{j \neq i} b_j(f^*(\mathbf{b})) + d(t_i, f_{b_i}^*) + d(b_i, f_{b_i}^*) - d(t_i, f_{b_i}^*) \\ &> \sum_{j \neq i} b_j(f^*(\mathbf{t})) + d(t_i, f_{t_i}^*) + d(b_i, f_{t_i}^*) - d(t_i, f_{t_i}^*) \end{aligned}$$

where the inequality uses that $f^*(\mathbf{t})$ is optimal for $\mathbf{t}$. Observe that the latter quantity is $cost(f^*(\mathbf{t}), \mathbf{b})$, and so we get a contradiction with the optimality of $f^*(\mathbf{b})$. If instead $f_{t_i}^* < b_i < t_i$, then $d(b_i, f_{t_i}^*) = d(t_i, f_{t_i}^*) - d(b_i, t_i)$. Moreover, $b_i < t_i \le f_{b_i}^*$ yields $d(b_i, f_{b_i}^*) = d(t_i, f_{b_i}^*) + d(b_i, t_i)$. Hence,

$$\begin{aligned} cost(f^*(\mathbf{b}), \mathbf{b}) &= \sum_{j \neq i} b_j(f^*(\mathbf{b})) + d(t_i, f_{b_i}^*) + d(b_i, t_i) \\ &> \sum_{j \neq i} b_j(f^*(\mathbf{t})) + d(t_i, f_{t_i}^*) - d(b_i, t_i) \\ &= cost(f^*(\mathbf{t}), \mathbf{b}), \end{aligned}$$

where the inequality uses optimality of $f^*(\mathbf{t})$ and $d(b_i, t_i) > 0$. However, this contradicts the optimality of f^*. Finally, Case 4 is symmetrical to Case 3 and the same arguments prove that also this case is impossible. □

We next show that it is not possible to prove Theorem 2 by relaxing some verification notions or its hypothesis.

THEOREM 3. *The assumptions of Theorem 2 are necessary, even for $K = 2$.*

PROOF. We begin by proving that if the mechanism is not cluster-imposing, then the optimal algorithm is not truthful even if the mechanism uses no-cost-forging and direction-imposing verification. Note that the definition of direction-imposing verification given above makes sense only if we assume that the mechanism is also cluster-imposing. However, we can still define some weaker (and somewhat less natural) forms of direction-imposing verification in its absence. We say that the mechanism has a *weak direction-imposing* verification if $t_i \ge f_{t_i}(b_i, \mathbf{b}_{-i})$ iff $b_i \ge f_{b_i}(b_i, \mathbf{b}_{-i})$

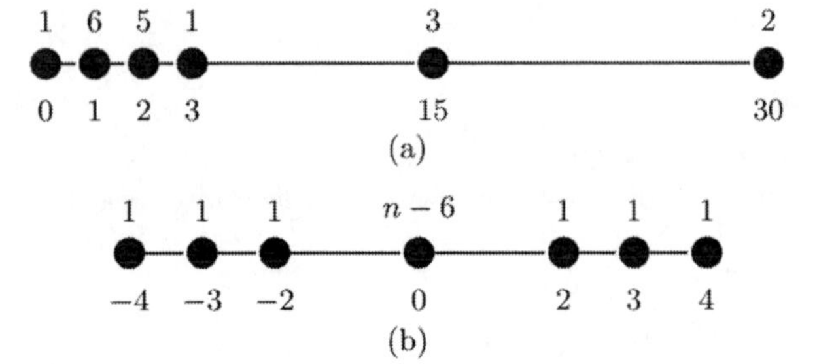

Figure 1: Instances used in the proof of Theorem 3

and $t_i \leq f_{t_i}(b_i, \mathbf{b}_{-i})$ iff $b_i \leq f_{b_i}(b_i, \mathbf{b}_{-i})$ (that is, both the real and the declared position of agent i are on the same side of their closest facilities); instead, we say that the mechanism has *ex-post direction-imposing* verification if $t_i \geq f_{t_i}(b_i, \mathbf{b}_{-i})$ iff $b_i \geq f_{t_i}(b_i, \mathbf{b}_{-i})$ and $t_i \leq f_{t_i}(b_i, \mathbf{b}_{-i})$ iff $b_i \leq f_{t_i}(b_i, \mathbf{b}_{-i})$ (i.e., both the real and the declared position of agent i are on the same side of the facility closest to t_i).

LEMMA 1. *Every optimal algorithm for K-facility location is not truthful, even if $K = 2$, the mechanism has no-cost-forging, weak direction-imposing and ex-post direction-imposing verification.*

PROOF. Consider the truthful instance described in Figure 1(a) where numbers below (above) the vertex represent its location (number of players on it). By inspection, the optimal algorithm places the facilities at 1 and 15. Let i be the agent at 3; her cost when she is truthful is 2. If she declares 31, then the optimal algorithm places a facility at 2 and the other at 30. Thus, she decreases her cost from 2 to 1, and is not caught lying by any kind of verification.

The instance can be generalized for any n, by having $\lceil (n-7)/2 \rceil$ in 1, $\lfloor (n-7)/2 \rfloor$ in 2 and moving the two leftmost positions from 15 and 30 to l and r, respectively where $r/2 + 2/3 > l > \min\{2r/5 + 4/5, (n+102)/10\}$. □

We now prove that if the mechanism has not the direction-imposing verification, then the optimum is not truthful even if the mechanism is cluster-imposing and has no-cost-forging verification. Consider the truthful instance described in Figure 1(b). The optimal algorithm places a facility in 0 and the second facility either in −3 or in 3. Suppose, w.l.o.g., that the optimum chooses −3 and consider agent i with truthful position 2. The cost of i when she truthfully declares her position is 2. If she declares location 4, then the optimal algorithm places a facility in 0 and the second in 3. Regardless from the mechanism being cluster-imposing or not, agent i is assigned to the facility in position 3, decreases her cost from 2 to 1, and is not caught lying by the no-cost-forging verification, since the distance from her real position and the facility is exactly the same as the distance from her declared position and the facility.

It is not too hard to use the instance in Figure 1(b) to prove the necessities of no-underbidding verification, and fixed tie-breaking rule. We omit the details. □

3.1 Simplicity and cost-only verification

Let us now focus on *simple algorithms* f, i.e., algorithms such that $f(\mathbf{b}) \subseteq \{b_1, \ldots, b_n\}$ for all $\mathbf{b}$. Moreover, let us consider mechanisms that do not use direction imposing, but only cluster-imposing, and no-underbidding or no-cost-forging verification. Next results highlight how hard it is to design a truthful deterministic mechanism with sub-linear approximation that uses only non-topological notions of verification.

A linear lower bound

We first prove a lower bound that holds for a large class of mechanisms even if we equip them with no-cost-forging verification along with cluster imposing.

DEFINITION 3. *A cluster-imposing algorithm f is 0-edged if for all $\mathbf{b}_{-i}$, the declaration graph with no-cost forging verification associated to f has a 0-edge that is not in a cycle.*

Roughly speaking, truthful 0-edged algorithms are not strictly truthful (i.e., truthtelling is not the only dominant strategy) for all the instances. These algorithms have a technical interest since they permit an "easy" connection between cycle monotonicity and approximation lower bounds (see Section 5 for obstacles and possible approaches to deal with more general classes of algorithms).

THEOREM 4. *No 0-edged simple algorithm f has approximation guarantee better than $2n/7$.*

PROOF. Let $\mathbf{b}_{-i}$ be the vector in which $\frac{5}{7}n - 1$ players are located at −1, $\frac{2}{7}n - 1$ at 0 and one at 1. Since f is simple, $f(\mathbf{b}) \subset \{-1, 0, 1, b_i\}$. The proof has two steps. We first show that no matter where player i is located, if f is 0-edged and is better than $2n/7$-approximate (absurdum hypothesis) then no facility can be placed at 0. We then observe that there is a bid b_i of player i for which $f(\mathbf{b})$ cannot return better than $2n/7$-approximate solutions – a contradiction.
<u>First step.</u> Since f is 0-edged then the declaration graph associated to f for the given $\mathbf{b}_{-i}$ must have a 0-weight edge that does not belong to a cycle. We next show this is not the case (i.e., the graph does not have such a 0-weight edge) when one of the facility is located at 0 and f is better than $2n/7$-approximate. Below, we drop $\mathbf{b}_{-i}$ from the notation.

For the declaration graph associated to f to have a 0-weight edge that is not part of a cycle, we need to provide two declarations of agent i, t_i and b_i, such that for some $\delta > 0$ one of the following must be true

$$f_{t_i}(t_i) = t_i - \delta < t_i < t_i + \delta = f_{b_i}(b_i) = b_i - \delta < b_i; \quad (6)$$

$$b_i < f_{b_i}(b_i) = b_i + \delta = t_i - \delta < t_i < f_{t_i}(t_i) = t_i + \delta, \quad (7)$$

while for $x, y \in \{t_i, b_i\}$, $x \neq y$, and $\delta > 0$, it must *not* be

$$x < f_x(x) = x + \delta = f_y(y) = y - \delta < y. \quad (8)$$

Indeed, since the graph has a 0-edge, then we need that there is an agent i, and two different declarations t_i and b_i, such that the following two properties occur: (i) agent i has the same cost when she declares her true type t_i and when she declares b_i, i.e., $t_i(f^*(\mathbf{b})) = t_i(f^*(\mathbf{t})) = d(t_i, f^*_{t_i})$ (let us denote with δ this value); (ii) agent i is not captured lying by the verification, i.e., by cluster-imposing verification, $t_i(f^*(\mathbf{b})) = d(t_i, f^*_{b_i})$, and, by no-cost-forging verification we require that $t_i(f^*(\mathbf{b})) = b_i(f^*(\mathbf{b})) = d(b_i, f^*_{b_i})$. Hence, we have that $d(t_i, f^*_{t_i}) = d(t_i, f^*_{b_i}) = d(b_i, f^*_{b_i}) = \delta$. There are only three ways of placing these four points (t_i, $f^*_{t_i}$, b_i, $f^*_{b_i}$) on a line so that they satisfy this condition, and they are exactly the ones described by equations (6)–(8). However, by definition, the 0-edge must not belong to a cycle. But in (8), if agent i, whose true type is b_i, declares t_i then she is not caught lying and therefore (b_i, t_i) is an edge of the graph. In particular, $t_i \to b_i \to t_i$ is a cycle. It is easy to check that this does not happen in (6) and (7).

We differentiate a number of cases according to the value of t_i and show that neither (6) nor (7) are possible without (8). Before, however, assume by contradiction that f is better than $2n/7$-approximate and note that $f(t_i, \mathbf{b}_{-i}) \subset \{-1, 0, t_i\}$ for each value of t_i.

Let us first consider the case in which $t_i \leq -1$ ($t_i > 0$, resp.). Since $f_{t_i}(t_i) \neq t_i$ for either (6) or (7) to be true, we have that f places the second facility at -1 and, consequently, that $f_{t_i}(t_i) = -1$ ($f_{t_i}(t_i) = 0$, resp.). Thus, we cannot have a situation like (6) ((7), resp.) since $f_{t_i}(t_i)$ is at the right (left, resp.) of t_i. We cannot have situation (7) ((6), resp.) either since when agent i goes to left (right, resp.) of t_i when declaring b_i there are not two locations on which $f_{b_i}(b_i)$ and b_i can be (recall that $f_{b_i}(b_i) \neq b_i$ and $1 \notin f(b_i, \mathbf{b}_{-i})$, since the approximation is better than $2n/7$).

We now deal with the case $t_i \in (-1, -1/2)$. Using the same argument as above we conclude that $f_{t_i}(t_i) = -1$. Here, we cannot have a situation like (7) given the relative order of $f_{t_i}(t_i)$ and t_i. Concerning situation (6), we note that when agent i goes to the right by declaring b_i the only possible locations for $f_{b_i}(b_i)$ are either 0 or 1: in both cases $d(t_i, f_{t_i}(t_i)) \neq d(t_i, f_{b_i}(b_i))$ as we would instead need.

Consider now the case $t_i = -1/2$. Here, t_i is equidistant from the locations of the two facilities (i.e., -1 and 0 – again, $f_{t_i}(t_i)$ must be different from t_i for otherwise no 0-weight edge (t_i, b_i) exists). We show that no matter the value of $f_{t_i}(t_i)$ if a 0-weight edge (t_i, b_i) exists according to either (6) or (7) then also (b_i, t_i) belongs to the graph; this shows the existence of a cycle, a contradiction with the fact that f is 0-edged. Specifically, if $f_{t_i}(t_i)$ is defined as -1 then $b_i = 1/2$ is a 0-weight edge as from (6) whilst if $f_{t_i}(t_i) = 0$ then $b_i = -3/2$ realizes the situation (7). However, in both scenarios the edge (b_i, t_i) also belongs to the graph.

Finally, take $t_i \in (-1/2, 0]$. Here, $f_{t_i}(t_i) = 0$ and we cannot have situation (6). As for (7), we note that when agent i goes to the left by declaring b_i the only possible location for $f_{b_i}(b_i)$ is -1, but then $d(t_i, f_{t_i}(t_i)) \neq d(t_i, f_{b_i}(b_i))$.

Second step. Let $b_i = 0$. By the argument above we know that $f(\mathbf{b})$ will locate one facility at -1 and the other at 1 for a cost of $\frac{2n}{7}$. The optimum, however, would only cost 1 by placing one facility at -1 and the other at 0. □

A linear upper bound

For $K = 2$, MEDIANFURTHEST locates one facility at the median location of the instance and the other at the furthest point from the median. Formally, given an instance $\mathbf{b}$, let b_M be the median location of $\mathbf{b}$. If $|\mathbf{b}|$ is even we take b_M to be the lower of the two middle values of $\mathbf{b}$. Let $\Delta_L = b_M - b_L$, where $b_L = \min_i b_i$, and $\Delta_R = b_R - b_M$, with $b_R = \max_i b_i$, be the distance of b_M from the leftmost and rightmost location of $\mathbf{b}$, respectively. Algorithm MEDIANFURTHEST on input $\mathbf{b}$ returns $\mathcal{F} = (b_M, b_L)$ if $\Delta_L > \Delta_R$, whereas it returns $\mathcal{F} = (b_M, b_R)$ if $\Delta_L \leq \Delta_R$. First we prove that this algorithm does not require a very demanding set of assumptions to be truthful (in particular, Theorem 2 does not apply since MEDIANFURTHEST is not optimal).

THEOREM 5. MEDIANFURTHEST *is truthful with cluster-imposing and no-underbidding verification.*

PROOF. Let us assume w.l.o.g. that the output of MEDIANFURTHEST on input $\mathbf{b}$ is $\mathcal{F} = (b_M, b_R)$ (the case when $\mathcal{F} = (b_M, b_L)$ is symmetric). Let i be the agent misreporting her location. It is easy to check that $t_i \notin \{b_M, b_R\}$, as in this case $d(\mathcal{F}, t_i) = 0$ and agent i cannot lower her cost any further. We will denote as b'_M and b'_R, respectively, the median and rightmost location of the instance $(b'_i, \mathbf{b}_{-i})$, and the output of MEDIANFURTHEST on such instance as $\mathcal{F}'$.

Let us first suppose that $t_i \in (b_M, b_R)$. If $b'_i < b_M$ and $b'_M - b'_i \leq b_R - b'_M$, then MEDIANFURTHEST would return allocation $\mathcal{F}' = (b'_M, b_R)$, with $b'_M < b_M$, and then $t_i(\mathcal{F}) \leq t_i(\mathcal{F}')$. If $b'_M - b'_i > b_R - b'_M$ the algorithm returns allocation $\mathcal{F}' = (b'_M, b'_i)$ and the misreport is detected by the verification step as $b'_i \in \mathcal{F}'$. If $b'_i > b_R$ then $\mathcal{F}' = (b_M, b'_i)$ and therefore $t_i(\mathcal{F}) \leq t_i(\mathcal{F}')$. Finally, if $b'_i \in (b_M, b_R)$, then the facility location does not change.

Let us now suppose that $t_i \in [b_L, b_M)$. Agent i can alter the output of the algorithm only if either (i) $b'_i > b_M$ or (ii) $b'_i < b_L$ and $b_M - b'_i > \Delta_R$ (note that in this case b_M does not change). If case (i) occurs, then $b'_i \geq b'_M > b_M$. Two sub-cases can occur: $b'_R - b'_M \geq b'_M - b_L$ and $b'_R - b'_M < b'_M - b_L$. If $b'_R - b'_M \geq b'_M - b_L$, then $\mathcal{F}' = (b'_M, b'_R)$ and $t_i(\mathcal{F}') > t_i(\mathcal{F})$ (in particular, if $b'_R \neq b_R$ it must be that $b'_R = b'_i$ and the misreport is detected by the verification step as $b'_i \in \mathcal{F}'$). If $b'_R - b'_M < b'_M - b_L$, then $\mathcal{F}' = (b'_M, b_L)$. We observe that since $b_L \leq b'_M \leq b'_i$, agent i must connect to the facility located at b'_M and since $b'_M \geq b_M > t_i$ then $d(t_i, b'_M) \geq d(b'_i, b_M)$. In case ($ii$) $b'_i < b_L$ and $b_M - b'_i > \Delta_R$, then $\mathcal{F}' = (b_M, b'_i)$. (Note that if $b_M - b'_i \leq \Delta_R$, MEDIANFURTHEST returns $\mathcal{F} = (b_M, b_R)$.) We note that in this case the verification step is capable of detecting the misreport by agent i, since $t_i(\mathcal{F}') = d(t_i, b'_i) > 0 = d(b'_i, b'_i) = b'_i(\mathcal{F}')$. □

This algorithm is not 0-edged (this is not too hard to see) yet it has approximation ratio $\frac{3}{4}n$. (The proof is only sketched due to lack of space.)

THEOREM 6. MEDIANFURTHEST *is* $\frac{3}{4}n$*-approximate.*

PROOF IDEA. Let us denote by $\mathcal{F} = (b_M, b_R)$ the output of MEDIANFURTHEST on input $\mathbf{b}$ (i.e., we assume w.l.o.g. that $\Delta_R \geq \Delta_L$, the case $\Delta_R < \Delta_L$ being symmetric). Let $L_{\mathbf{b}} = \{i : b_i \leq b_M, M \neq i\}$ and $R_{\mathbf{b}} = \{i : b_i \geq b_M, M \neq i\}$ denote, respectively, the set of agents to the left and to the right of b_M. We can express the cost of allocation $\mathcal{F}$ as $cost(\mathcal{F}, \mathbf{b}) = cost(\mathcal{F}, L_{\mathbf{b}}) + cost(\mathcal{F}, R_{\mathbf{b}})$ where $cost(\mathcal{F}, L_{\mathbf{b}}) = \sum_{i \in L_{\mathbf{b}}} (b_M - b_i)$ denotes the cost incurred by the agents to the left of b_M whereas $cost(\mathcal{F}, R_{\mathbf{b}}) = \sum_{i \in R_{\mathbf{b}}} \min\{b_R - b_i, b_i - b_M\}$ denotes the cost incurred by the agents to the right of b_M. By definition of b_M it follows that $|L_{\mathbf{b}}| \leq \frac{n-1}{2}$ and $|R_{\mathbf{b}}| \leq \frac{n}{2}$. The maximum cost incurred by an agent in $L_{\mathbf{b}}$ is Δ_L, hence it follows that $cost(\mathcal{F}, L_{\mathbf{b}}) \leq \Delta_L \cdot \frac{n-1}{2}$. Likewise, the maximum cost incurred by an agent in $R_{\mathbf{b}}$ is $\frac{\Delta_R}{2}$, so $cost(\mathcal{F}, R_{\mathbf{b}}) \leq \frac{\Delta_R}{2} \cdot \frac{n}{2}$. Let us first notice that we need to consider instances where agents are located at more than 2 different locations, as otherwise MEDIANFURTHEST is optimal. Since, by hypothesis, $\Delta_R \geq \Delta_L$, two cases can occur: $\Delta_L = 0$ and $\Delta_L > 0$. We prove that in both cases the social cost of the facility location returned by MEDIANFURTHEST $\frac{3n}{4}$-approximates the optimal allocation. □

Composition of basic algorithms

For $1 \leq k < \ell \leq n$, a (k, ℓ)-algorithm f, in input $\mathbf{b}$, places the facilities at the k-th and ℓ-th smallest positions in $\mathbf{b}$. TWOEXTREMES [21] is a $(1, n)$-algorithm and has approximation $n-2$. MEDIANFURTHEST can be seen as a composition of two such basic algorithms: $(1, \lfloor n/2 \rfloor)$ and $(\lfloor n/2 \rfloor, n)$. Here, by *composition* we mean that the two basic algorithms are run and a test chooses which one of their outcomes is returned (e.g., the better). (Note that MEDIANFURTHEST does not choose the best of the outcomes computed by MEDIANLEFTMOST and MEDIANRIGHTMOST in terms of social cost.) This way of composing algorithms is widely considered in literature [16] and it is a quite natural and successful algorithmic techniques. For example, the optimal algorithm itself can be seen as a composition of a linear number of (k, ℓ)-algorithms. Hence, by composing sufficiently many of these basic algorithms we can achieve a good approximation of the social welfare. But can a ratio better than linear be achieved with two algorithms?

We next show that MEDIANFURTHEST is asymptotically optimal in this class no matter the test used to choose between the outcomes the two algorithms and the truthfulness of the composition. Let the two algorithms be (k, ℓ) and (k', ℓ'). We distinguish several cases. First assume that $\ell^+ = \max\{\ell, \ell'\} < n$; consider the instance wherein ℓ^+ agents are in position 0 and $n - \ell^+$ are in 1. Both algorithms place both facilities in 0 and, hence, the composition does to. The approximation ratio of the composition is then unbounded. Suppose now that $k^- = \min\{k, k'\} > 1$; consider the instance in which $k^- - 1$ agents are in 0 and $n + 1 - k^-$ in 1. Here the composition is unbounded as well. Consider now that $\ell^+ = n$ and $k^- = 1$. We set $\ell^- = \min\{\ell, \ell'\}$ and $k^+ = \max\{k, k'\}$. Let us first assume that $q = \max\{k^+, \ell^-\} \leq n/2$. Then consider the following instance: q agents in 0, $n - q - 1$ in 1, and 1 agent in 2. One algorithm will place a facility in 0 and the second in 2, whereas the other algorithm will place both facilities in 0. Hence, the composition has a cost of at least $\frac{n}{2} - 1$ while the optimum costs 1. The approximation ratio of the composition is then $\frac{n}{2} - 1$. If $p = \min\{k^+, \ell^-\} \geq n/2 + 1$, then similar arguments hold for the instance in which 1 agent is in 0, $p - 2$ in 1, and $n - p + 1$ in 2. We are left with the case that $p \leq n/2 < q$. We can distinguishing each of the possible realizations of k, k', ℓ, ℓ' satisfying these conditions and give the instance establishing the lower bound (in what follows we will assume w.l.o.g. that $k^- = k$).

Case $k = 1, \ell = p, k' = q, \ell' = n$: $n/2$ agents in 0 and $n/2$ in 1. No algorithm (and then their composition) places the facilities in two different locations. The approximation ratio of the composition is then unbounded.

Case $k = 1, \ell = q, k' = p, \ell' = n$: 1 agent in 0, $n/2 - 1$ in 1, $n/2 - 1$ in 2, and 1 in 3. Here, one algorithm locates the facilities in 0 and 2, whereas the other places them in 1 and 3. So, the composition costs $n/2$ while the optimum costs 2. The approximation ratio of the composition is then $n/4$.

Case $k = 1, \ell = n, k' = p, \ell' = q$: 1 agent in 0, $n - 2$ in $1/n$, and 1 in 1. Here, one algorithm locates the facilities in 0 and 1, whereas the other places them both in $1/n$. The composition costs at least $\frac{n-2}{n}$ while the optimum costs $1/n$.

It is not hard to see that the proof above can be adapted to work even if we assume that no algorithm places two facilities in the same position. In fact, we can assume that any set of $c > 1$ agents assigned to the same position actually corresponds to c agents assigned to different positions that are very close to each other (e.g., at distance at most $1/2^n$ from each other). Moreover, the bound is purely algorithmic and holds regardless of the truthfulness of the composition.

4. MAX COST

We now consider $K = 2$. The algorithm OPTMINMAX returns an optimal allocation (f^0, f^1), $f^0 < f^1$, minimizing the maximum cost with a particular tie-breaking rule that we are going to define next.

Given an allocation (f^0, f^1), let $S_j \subseteq N$ be the set of agents that are closer to facility f^j than to facility $f^{|j-1|}$. Let $\Delta(S_j) = \max_{l_1, l_2 \in S_j} |b_{l_1} - b_{l_2}|$ denote the maximum distance between two elements of S_j. Whenever there is more than one solution minimizing the max cost, OPTMINMAX will choose the solution that minimizes $\Delta(S_0)$ and $\Delta(S_1)$, breaking any further tie in favor of minimizing $\Delta(S_0)$. It is easy to see that in this last case, i.e., there is a tie and $\Delta(S_0) = \Delta(S_1)$, one of the following two assertions must be true: either (i) $\Delta(S_j) = 2 \cdot mc(f(\mathbf{b}), \mathbf{b})$ $\forall j \in \{0, 1\}$, or (ii) $\Delta(S_0) < 2 \cdot mc(f(\mathbf{b}), \mathbf{b})$. Hereinafter, we will denote as $L(S_j) = \min S_j$ and $R(S_j) = \max S_j$. The tie breaking rule is such that in all cases the facility is allocated at the central point of the interval $[L(S_j), R(S_j)]$, namely, $f^j = \frac{L(S_j)+R(S_j)}{2}$, $j \in \{0, 1\}$. Fixed $\mathbf{b}_{-i}$, we let S'_j be the set S_j when agent i reports b_i instead of her true type t_i; we also let, as above, f_{t_i} and f_{b_i} be shorthands for OPTMINMAX$_{t_i}(t_i, \mathbf{b}_{-i})$ and OPTMINMAX$_{b_i}(b_i, \mathbf{b}_{-i})$, respectively. Next lemma assumes that the mechanism uses cluster-imposing no-cost-forging verification.

LEMMA 2. *Let b_i be a misreport by agent i located at t_i. Let $j \in \{0, 1\}$ be such that $f^j = f_{b_i}$. If $f_{t_i} \neq f_{b_i}$, then either $b_i \in \{L(S'_j), R(S'_j)\}$ or $t_i \notin [L(S'_j), R(S'_j)]$.*

PROOF. Two cases can occur: (i) $t_i \in (L(S_\ell), R(S_\ell))$ or (ii) $t_i \in \{L(S_\ell), R(S_\ell)\}$ for some $\ell \in \{0, 1\}$.

Let us consider case (i) first. We notice that if either $b_i \in [L(S_0), R(S_0)]$ or $b_i \in [L(S_1), R(S_1)]$, then $\Delta(S_0) = \Delta(S'_0)$ and $\Delta(S_1) = \Delta(S'_1)$ and hence $f_{t_i} = f_{b_i}$. Let us assume then that $b_i \notin [L(S_0), R(S_0)]$ and $b_i \notin [L(S_1), R(S_1)]$. Three cases can occur: $b_i < L(S_0)$, $R(S_0) < b_i < L(S_1)$ or $b_i > R(S_1)$. In all three cases it is immediately evident that $b_i \in \{L(S'_j), R(S'_j)\}$.

As for case (ii), we can assume that there is no $s \neq i$ such that $t_s = t_i$, as otherwise the same argument as case (i) applies (i.e., intervals cannot shrink). It is easy to check that if $b_i > R(S_1)$ or $b_i < L(S_0)$ then $b_i \in \{R(S'_1), L(S'_0)\}$. Let us consider the case when $t_i \in \{L(S_0), R(S_0)\}$ (the case when $t_i \in \{L(S_1), R(S_1)\}$ is symmetric). If $t_i = L(S_0)$ and $L(S_0) < b_i \leq R(S_0)$, the thesis holds. Likewise, if $t_i = R(S_0)$ and $L(S_0) \leq b_i < R(S_0)$ the thesis holds. If $R(S_0) < b_i < L(S_1)$, either $b_i \in \{R(S'_0), L(S'_1)\}$ (if $t_i = R(S_0)$) or $t_i \notin S'_0$ (if $t_i = L(S_0)$). If $L(S_1) \leq b_i \leq R(S_1)$ and $t_i = L(S_0)$ then $t_i \notin [L(S'_j), R(S'_j)]$. If $L(S_1) \leq b_i \leq R(S_1)$ and $t_i = R(S_0)$, it can either be $b_i = R(S'_0)$, for which the thesis holds, or $L(S'_1) \leq b_i$, in which case the thesis holds since $t_i \notin [L(S'_j), R(S'_j)]$. □

THEOREM 7. *OPTMINMAX is SP with cluster-imposing no-cost-forging verification.*

PROOF. Let us consider the case when agent i lies declaring b_i instead of her true type t_i. For the sake of contradiction, let us assume that OPTMINMAX is not SP with cluster-imposing no-cost-forging verification, i.e., $d(t_i, f_{t_i}) > d(t_i, f_{b_i})$. Let us suppose w.l.o.g. that $b_i \in S'_j$. We note that the misreport by agent i is not detected by the verification step only if $|f_{b_i} - b_i| = |f_{b_i} - t_i|$, which can happen only if $f_{b_i} - b_i = -(f_{b_i} - t_i)$, which implies that $f_{b_i} = \frac{t_i+b_i}{2}$. By Lemma 2, either (i) $t_i \notin [L(S'_j), R(S'_j)]$ or (ii) $b_i \in \{L(S'_j), R(S'_j)\}$. In case (i) we notice that the misreport is always detected by the verification step as $f_{b_i} = \frac{R(S'_j)+L(S'_j)}{2} \neq \frac{t_i+b_i}{2}$, since $t_i \notin [L(S'_j), R(S'_j)]$ and $b_i \in [L(S'_j), R(S'_j)]$. Hence we can assume $b_i \in \{L(S'_j), R(S'_j)\}$. By construction of the algorithm and by the verification step, this also implies that $t_i \in \{L(S'_j), R(S'_j)\}$, i.e. t_i and b_i are the extremal point of S'_j. We need to consider 4 cases.

$t_i \in S_j \wedge \Delta(S'_j) > \Delta(S_j)$. By construction of the algorithm we also have that $t_i \in \{L(S'_j), R(S'_j)\}$ and then

$$d(t_i, f_{b_i}) = \Delta(S'_j)/2 > \Delta(S_j)/2 \geq d(t_i, f_{t_i})$$

where: $t_i \in \{L(S'_j), R(S'_j)\}$ implies $d(t_i, f_{b_i}) = \Delta(S'_j)/2$, $\Delta(S'_j)/2 > \Delta(S_j)/2$ by hypothesis and $\Delta(S_j)/2 \geq d(t_i, f_{t_i})$ by construction.

$t_i \in S_j \wedge \Delta(S'_j) < \Delta(S_j)$. Here $t_i \in \{L(S_j),\ R(S_j)\}$. As above, agent i is not caught by verification only if $f_{b_i} = \frac{b_i+t_i}{2}$ and $S'_j = [\min\{t_i, b_i\}, \max\{t_i, b_i\}]$. We note that agent i is indeed always caught by the verification step as $\Delta(S'_j) < \Delta(S_j)$ implies that $t_i \notin S'_j$.

$t_i \in S_{|j-1|} \wedge \Delta(S'_j) > \Delta(S_j)$. By construction, $\Delta(S'_j) = |t_i - b_i|$ and $\frac{\Delta(S_{|j-1|})}{2} \geq |t_i - f^{|j-1|}| = d(t_i, f_{t_i})$. The following holds by the hypothesis that OptMinMax is not SP: $\frac{\Delta(S_{|j-1|})}{2} \geq |t_i - f^{|j-1|}| = d(t_i, f_{t_i}) > d(t_i, f_{b_i}) = \frac{|t_i-b_i|}{2}$. Let us define intervals $T_j = S'_j$, and $T_{|j-1|} = S_{|j-1|} \backslash S'_j$. We will first prove that the max cost of allocation (f^0, f^1) is $\frac{\Delta(S_{|j-1|})}{2}$. To this aim, we need to prove that $\Delta(S_{|j-1|}) \geq \Delta(S_j)$. By contradiction, let us suppose $\Delta(S_j) > \Delta(S_{|j-1|})$. From the latter, we get

$$\begin{aligned} d(t_i, f_{b_i}) = & \frac{|t_i - b_i|}{2} = \frac{\Delta(S'_j)}{2} > \frac{\Delta(S_j)}{2} > \\ > & \frac{\Delta(S_{|j-1|})}{2} \geq |t_i - f^{|j-1|}| = d(t_i, f_{t_i}) \end{aligned}$$

where $\Delta(S'_j)/2 > \Delta(S_j)/2$ follows by hypothesis, thus contradicting the hypothesis that OptMinMax is not SP.

We will now prove that allocating the facilities in the middle points of $T_{|j-1|}$ and T_j has a lower cost than $\frac{\Delta(S_{|j-1|})}{2}$, contradicting the optimality of (f^0, f^1). By construction $\Delta(T_{|j-1|}) < \Delta(S_{|j-1|})$. Furthermore, by hypothesis, it follows:

$$\frac{\Delta(T_j)}{2} = \frac{|t_i - b_i|}{2} < |t_i - f^{|j-1|}| \leq \frac{\Delta(S_{|j-1|})}{2}$$

which implies $\Delta(T_j) < \Delta(S_{|j-1|})$.

$t_i \in S_{|j-1|} \wedge \Delta(S'_j) < \Delta(S_j)$. The misreport of agent i is not detected by the verification step if and only if $f_{b_i} = \frac{t_i+b_i}{2}$, which means that $S'_j \subseteq [\min\{t_i, b_i\}, \max\{t_i, b_i\}]$. Let us define intervals $T_j = S'_j$ and $T_{|j-1|} = S_{|j-1|} \backslash S'_j$. Since $\Delta(T_{|j-1|}) < \Delta(S_{|j-1|})$ (by construction, as $t_i \in S'_j \cap S_{|j-1|}$) and $\Delta(T_j) = \Delta(S'_j) < \Delta(S_j)$ (by hypothesis), we obtain the absurd that allocating the facilities in the middle nodes of intervals T_j and $T_{|j-1|}$ has a lower max cost. □

THEOREM 8. *The assumptions of Theorem 7 are necessary.*

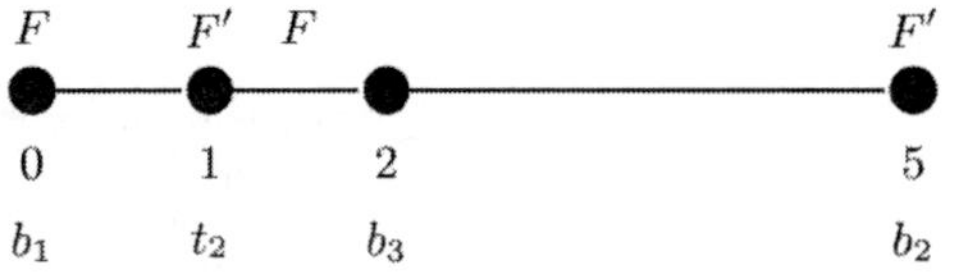

Figure 2: Instance used in Theorem 8

PROOF. Let us drop cluster-imposition and consider a 3-agent instance, where $b_1 = 0$, $t_2 = 1$ and $b_3 = 2$. The instance is depicted in Figure 2. The output of OptMinMax is $(f^0 = 0, f^1 = 1.5)$, and the cost for agent 2 is 0.5. When agent 2 lies declaring $b_2 = 5$ instead of her true type, then the allocation is $(f^0 = 1, f^1 = 5)$, and her cost becomes 0. The lie is not detected by the verification step as $d(b_2, f(b_2, \mathbf{b}_{-2})) = d(t_2, f(b_2, \mathbf{b}_{-2})) = 0$.

Let us now maintain cluster-imposition and relax no-cost-forging to no-underbidding. Consider the instance with 4 agents: $b_1 = 0$, $b_2 = 1$, $b_3 = \Delta + 1$, $t_4 = \Delta + 2$, for $\Delta \geq 2$. OptMinMax allocates one facility on 0.5 and the other on $\Delta + 1.5$; the cost for agent 4 is 0.5. If agent 4 declares $b_4 = \Delta + 2 + \epsilon$, $0 < \epsilon < 0.5$, OptMinMax allocates the second facility on $\Delta + 1.5 + \frac{\epsilon}{2}$, yielding a lower cost for agent 4. It is easy to check that this misreport is caught neither by no-underbidding nor cluster-imposing verification.

It is not hard to use similar ideas to find a counterexample for cluster-imposition and no-overbidding verification. □

5. CONCLUSIONS

We have shown what lies make the computation of optimal solutions for facility location vulnerable to selfish misreports. The set of verification assumptions are shown to be minimal and hence necessary. The parameters of the instances given in the proofs of Theorems 3 and 8 to prove this minimality can in fact be optimized to prove constant lower bounds. However, we conjecture that minimality can be extended to cover not just optimal algorithms, but all (simple) algorithms with constant (or even sublinear) approximation guarantees. We have focused on cost-only verification and given some results towards proving the conjecture, including the first use of cycle-monotonicity to establish approximation lower bounds, cf. Theorem 4. To strengthen this claim, one would need a property for $\mathbf{b}_{-i}$ which allows the construction of the right instance for a larger class of algorithms. This could be complemented by a better understanding of constant-approximation algorithms for the social cost (via, e.g., a deeper look at compositions of basic algorithms).

We leave a number of interesting, challenging open questions starting from the conjecture above. A first step could be to focus on Maximal-In-Range (MIR) algorithms [18] – indeed, it is not too difficult to check that Theorem 2 holds for any MIR algorithm.

Generalizing our results to different problems or settings without single-peaked preferences is clearly an interesting open problem and a further step in the research agenda we suggest. A first issue one would run into is represented by the "translation" of direction-imposing verification to diverse settings. This topological notion exploits the structure of facility location on the line and might be difficult to apply to different scenarios. A possible approach could be to look into different ways to express such a notion (see "Discussion on verification" paragraph in Section 2).

REFERENCES

[1] G. Christodoulou, E. Koutsoupias, and A. Kovács. Mechanism design for fractional scheduling on unrelated machines. In *ICALP*, pages 40–52, 2007.

[2] A. Daniely, M. Schapira, and S. Gal. Inapproximability of truthful mechanisms via generalizations of the VC dimension. In *STOC*, 2015.

[3] D. Fotakis, P. Krysta, and C. Ventre. Combinatorial auctions without money. In *AAMAS*, pages 1029–1036, 2014.

[4] D. Fotakis, P. Krysta, and C. Ventre. The power of verification for greedy mechanism design. In *AAMAS*, pages 307–315, 2015.

[5] D. Fotakis and C. Tzamos. Winner-imposing strategyproof mechanisms for multiple Facility Location games. *Theoretical Computer Science*, 472:90–103, 2013.

[6] D. Fotakis and C. Tzamos. On the power of deterministic mechanisms for facility location games. *ACM Trans. Economics and Comput.*, 2(4):15:1–15:37, 2014.

[7] D. Fotakis, C. Tzamos, and E. Zampetakis. Who to trust for truthfully maximizing welfare? *CoRR*, abs/1507.02301, 2015.

[8] D. Fotakis and E. Zampetakis. Truthfulness flooded domains and the power of verification for mechanism design. *ACM Trans. Economics and Comput.*, 3(4):20, 2015.

[9] C. Gorkem. Mechanism design with weaker incentive compatibility constraints. *Games and Economic Behavior*, 56(1):37–44, 2006.

[10] J. R. Green and J. Laffont. Partially Verifiable Information and Mechanism Design. *The Review of Economic Studies*, 53:447–456, 1986.

[11] E. Koutsoupias. Scheduling without payments. *Theory Comput. Syst.*, 54(3):375–387, 2014.

[12] E. Koutsoupias and A. Vidali. A lower bound of 1+Φ for truthful scheduling mechanisms. *Algorithmica*, 66(1):211–223, 2013.

[13] P. Krysta and C. Ventre. Combinatorial auctions with verification are tractable. *Theoretical Computer Science*, 571:21–35, 2015.

[14] D. J. Lehmann, L. O'Callaghan, and Y. Shoham. Truth revelation in approximately efficient combinatorial auctions. *J. ACM*, 49(5):577–602, 2002.

[15] P. Lu, X. Sun, Y. Wang, and Z. Zhu. Asymptotically Optimal Strategy-Proof Mechanisms for Two-Facility Games. In *EC*, pages 315–324, 2010.

[16] A. Mu'alem and N. Nisan. Truthful approximation mechanisms for restricted combinatorial auctions. *Games and Economic Behavior*, 64(2):612–631, 2008.

[17] N. Nisan and A. Ronen. Algorithmic Mechanism Design. *Games and Economic Behavior*, 35:166–196, 2001.

[18] N. Nisan and A. Ronen. Computationally feasible VCG mechanisms. *J. Artif. Intell. Res. (JAIR)*, 29:19–47, 2007.

[19] K. Nissim, R. Smorodinsky, and M. Tennenholtz. Approximately optimal mechanism design via Differential Privacy. In *ITCS*, pages 203–213, 2012.

[20] P. Penna and C. Ventre. Optimal collusion-resistant mechanisms with verification. *Games and Economic Behavior*, 86:491–509, 2014.

[21] A. D. Procaccia and M. Tennenholtz. Approximate mechanism design without money. *ACM Trans. Economics and Comput.*, 1(4):18, 2013.

[22] J. Rochet. A Condition for Rationalizability in a Quasi-Linear Context. *Journal of Mathematical Economics*, 16:191–200, 1987.

[23] P. Serafino and C. Ventre. Truthful mechanisms without money for non-utilitarian heterogeneous facility location. In *AAAI*, pages 1029–1035, 2015.

[24] C. Ventre. Truthful optimization using mechanisms with verification. *Theoretical Computer Science*, 518:64–79, 2014.

[25] R. Vohra. *Mechanism Design: A Linear Programming Approach.* Cambridge University Press, 2011.

Generalized Agent-mediated Procurement Auctions

Piero A. Bonatti Marco Faella Clemente Galdi Luigi Sauro
Dept. of Electrical Engineering and Information Technologies
University of Naples "Federico II", Italy
{pab,m.faella,clemente.galdi,luigi.sauro}@unina.it

ABSTRACT

Procurement auctions (where the auctioneer needs a service and bidders offer it at their own conditions) are an appealing method for on-line service selection. They can improve service features and cost by exploiting the competition between different service providers. Software agents, acting on behalf of human users and organizations, are essential in making such auctions practical and usable. Since conveying user preferences to the agents in a faithful and complete way is virtually impossible, we advocate an approximate approach, where only partial preferences are formalized, and users pick their choice from a short list of options selected by the agents by means of those partial preferences. Another peculiarity of our scenarios is that there may be no contracts with null utility for a given bidder. These features affect the classical, desirable properties of standard auction mechanisms. We prove some impossibility results concerning truthfulness and (a qualitative analogue of) revenue. Then, we investigate a novel auction mechanism that is *almost* truthful in the sense that any strategic deviation from truthfulness has limited impact on the auctioneer's revenue.

Categories and Subject Descriptors

Theory of Computation [**Theory and Algorithms for application domains**]: Algorithmic game theory and mechanism design—*Computational pricing and auctions*

General Terms

Economics, Human Factors, Theory

Keywords

Auctions, partial orders, preference relations

1. INTRODUCTION

In recent years, an intense cross-fertilization between Multiagent Systems and economic paradigms has determined a fruitful area of research. Here we are particularly interested in *auction mechanisms*, with particular regard to *procurement auctions*, that can be used for selecting on-line services in a way that improves the corresponding contracts by exploiting the competition between different service providers. Such scenarios differ from classical auction settings in a few aspects that determine significant changes in the underlying theoretical properties (especially the strategic behavior of participating agents), as discussed in the following.

When we *import* an economic paradigm (e.g. Game Theory and Social Mechanism Design) into our field, we are implicitly importing its model of what an agent is and how it acts proactively. In this respect, Decision Theory and its agent preference axiomatizations play a fundamental role.

In Decision Theory, one of the very basic properties of a preference relation $\preceq$ is its totality: given two potential outcomes a and b, either $a \preceq b$ or $b \preceq a$. From the theory's very start, such an assumption raised some criticisms[1].

Somewhat surprisingly, the founders themselves of Decision Theory considered this point as debatable:

> "It is conceivable and may even in a way be more realistic to allow for cases where the individual is neither able to state which of two alternatives he prefers nor that they are equally desirable. How real this possibility is, both for individuals and for organizations, seems to be an extremely interesting question, but it is a question of fact. It certainly deserves further study." [12].

Several domains would advocate the foregoing considerations. Preferences often result from complex trade-offs between different attributes (functionalities, cost, Quality of Service, information disclosure risks, etc.); in this case possible lack of knowledge as well as introspective sensations of vacillation would naturally move towards a relaxation of the totality property, admitting that some pairs of outcomes may be incomparable.

In this work we support and develop this perspective in the context of procurement auctions. However, before undertaking our study, a preliminarily step requires to deeply understand why decision theorists have substantially preserved totality so far. We clarify this point with an example. Assume to be in a restaurant which offers exotic foods. To make it simple, you can only choose between two dishes, say *pipi cruschi* and *stigghiola*, you do not have any idea of. If someone asks *do you like them the same?* you would probably reply *How can I know?* This seems to suggest that, from an introspective viewpoint, you do not judge them as equivalent. However, if you are starving and we only look at how

[1]In particular, Simon's kicked off a problem-solving perspective which was very influential in AI [11].

Appears in: *Proceedings of the 15th International Conference on Autonomous Agents and Multiagent Systems (AAMAS 2016), J. Thangarajah, K. Tuyls, C. Jonker, S. Marsella (eds.), May 9–13, 2016, Singapore.*

you actually behave, in this situation you would not mind delegating to coin flipping, which is just the same behavior you adopt in case of equivalence. Shortly, Decision Theory does not claim to look inside your mind, it only aims at justifying your behavior *at the moment* a decision is made.

However, unlike Decision Theory where decision makers *own* their preferences, in MAS we have to consider another fundamental aspect: software agents generally act *on behalf of* real users. For instance, in an electronic market, a software agent may apply an auction mechanism on behalf of a consumer, to filter the offers of the providers. This clearly raises the issue of how user preferences can be effectively transferred to software agents, considering that on the web offers can be plenty and diversified. If the delegated agent admits total preferences only, a user would be forced to disambiguate up front all (possibly unexpected) offers, and we have seen that one is introspectively reluctant to identify indecisions – either due to lack of knowledge or trembling desires – with indifference. Furthermore, even if the user had no indecisions and conformed with a classical economic man, her preference relation could be so voluminous and lacking of regularities that it could not be entirely and efficiently injected into the software agent – albeit ceteris paribus techniques could be adopted [4].

The foregoing arguments end up with the following consideration: if Decision Theory considers sufficient three possible options (choose a, choose b, and flip a coin), we propose a fourth one for the delegated agent, namely, deferring the decision and asking the user again. This involves distinguishing between indifference and incomparability.

Preference incompleteness is not the only source of differences between classical auction settings and our scenarios. Traditional settings enjoy the property that it is always possible to make a bid with null utility, by bidding exactly the value v attributed to the auction item. However, not all of our reference scenarios involve payments, and the space of bids may consist of contracts belonging to a discrete domain. In similar settings, it is well possible that no contract has exactly null utility for the bidder. We will show that due to this apparently minor difference, the tie-breaking rules traditionally used to select a winner when multiple bidders submit the same optimal choice make auctions *not truthful*. Recovering truthfulness (at least in part) requires invasive changes to the auction mechanism.

In the following section, we describe a detailed motivating scenario with the above features. Then, Section 3 lays the formal basis for our investigation, by defining auctions and their main desirable properties. In Section 4, we draw a comparison between our framework – characterized by partial preference relations and discrete contract spaces – and the classical one, where preferences are total orders and contracts are monetary and hence continuous. We show that the obvious adaptations of classical truthful auctions to our setting violate one or more of the desirable properties of auctions.

Next, in Section 5, we focus on single-item auctions. After proving that *no* such auction can possibly give strong guarantees on truthfulness and revenue at the same time, we introduce a *relatively optimal* auction and discuss its properties. Roughly speaking, a relatively optimal mechanism is one in which the outcome is guaranteed to be maximally preferred by the auctioneer. Then, by our negative result, this mechanism is necessarily not truthful. In particular, we prove that bidders may have an interest to offer contracts that are not actually convenient to them. However, the mechanism still manages to filter out those over-bids and select an outcome that is convenient to the winning bidder and maximally preferred by the auctioneer. Section 6 shows that multi-item auctions are much less problematic. We define a multi-item mechanism that is both truthful and weakly optimal. Finally, we discuss some related work in Section 7 and draw our conclusions in Section 8.

2. MOTIVATING SCENARIO

Consider the following scenario: Alice is organizing a trip and has to choose a portal for booking tickets and hotels. There is a long list of portals that provide such services, and a first polling shows that the options (across all portals) are: (*i*) traveling time between 8 and 24 hours; (*ii*) only ticket booking, only hotel booking, or complete bookings; (*iii*) prices between €1000 and €2500.

The software agent accepts constraints such as maximum cost and travel time, restrictions on transport means (e.g. no planes), hotel category, portal usability (e.g. no ads), privacy preferences (e.g. no contacts for marketing purposes are allowed), etc. Then, according to the specified preference relation, the agent filters a winning deal. If this is done through an electronic procurement auction, then the competition between the different booking services pushes them to improve their offers.

Clearly, Alice's desires are influenced by many of the above features. For instance, she favors 3 star hotels, prefers fast travels and flights, hates ads and being contacted for marketing purposes. Of course, ceteris paribus, she prefers cheaper solutions. Unfortunately, such preferences do not yield a total order over the options, as Alice cannot establish any fixed priority between the features. For instance, she prefers a package comprising an 8 hours long flight and 3 star hotel to another package comprising a 12 hours long flight and a 5 star hotel, when the latter costs more than €150/night; otherwise she prefers the latter option. Among two packages with the same hotel and similar prices (differing less than €20), Alice prefers the one with the shortest travel time. Alice soon realizes that providing a total order to the software agent is frustrating and requires about the same effort as comparing all the offers by herself.

On the contrary, by using partial preferences, we allow the software agent to use an approximate representation of Alice's desires and return a restricted list of choices from which Alice can select the preferred one. In other words, Alice has the ability to balance between the filtering power and the usability of the software agent. As a further advantage, Alice retains the ability to apply unforeseen, situation-specific preferences that could not be formalized in advance.

Note that the typical portals, in this scenario, are "free"; their revenues come from advertisement and the user's personal information, that can be sold to third parties for marketing purposes. Thus, the parameters that determine the portals' behavior and the quality of their suggestions (kind of trip, cost, duration, hotel category and price, value of advertisement and personal data, etc.) are not under the control of the provider, and it may well be the case that none of the possible options has null utility for the provider. If this is the case, then being selected by the user is never indifferent to not being selected, for any option.

3. PRELIMINARIES

The agents involved in our framework are an auctioneer a and a finite set $N = \{1, \ldots, n\}$ of bidders. We denote by A the set of possible contracts that the auctioneer can stipulate with a bidder. Typically, in procurement auctions – which are our primary reference domain – the auctioneer is a customer asking for a certain service, bidders are the providers of that service and a contract states all relevant properties of the service, such as functionality, quality of service, costs, terms of rescission, etc.

Clearly, the auctioneer may judge some contracts more profitable than others. Let $\leq_a$ be the auctioneer's preference relation. In standard auctions, which are founded on classical decision theory, $\leq_a$ is defined as a weak order, i.e. a total and transitive relation. On the contrary, we assume that two contracts may be incomparable for the auctioneer. Intuitively, two contracts being incomparable means that the auctioneer is not currently able to weigh them up against each other, but she does not want to demand the decision to coin flipping. Formally, we relinquish the totality property and assume $\leq_a$ to be a preorder, that is a reflexive and transitive relation over A. Clearly, weak orders can be viewed as a special class of preorders.

As usual, we write $b <_a b'$ and $b \sim_a b'$ in case b' is *strictly* preferred to b (i.e. $b \leq_a b'$ and $b' \not\leq_a b$) and b is equivalent to b' ($b \leq_a b'$ and $b' \leq_a b$), respectively. With $b \bowtie_a b'$ we mean that b and b' are incomparable ($b \not\leq_a b'$ and $b' \not\leq_a b$). Similarly, for each bidder i, $\leq_i$ is her partial preference relation. The only assumption we make on these preferences is the following: some contracts in A can be considered by some agent as inadmissible. A contract is inadmissible if by stipulating that contract the agent incurs a loss; in standard utility-based auctions inadmissible contracts are associated with negative values. We denote with $A_a \subseteq A$ (resp. $A_i \subseteq A$) the set of contracts that are admissible for the auctioneer (resp. for the bidder i). Then, any contract which does not incur a loss is strictly preferred to a contract that incurs a loss. Formally, for each $b \in A \setminus A_a$ and $b' \in A_a$ (resp. $b \in A \setminus A_i$ and $b' \in A_i$), $b <_a b'$ (resp. $b <_i b'$).

Note that in standard auctions it is generally assumed that the preference of the auctioneer are the inverse of the bidders' preferences. On the contrary, here we do not make any assumption on how preferences are related with each other. In particular this means that for some pairs of contracts, say b_1 and b_2, the preference of the auctioneer could be aligned with the preference of some bidder i, i.e. $b_1 \leq_a b_2$ and $b_1 \leq_i b_2$. This makes sense in several domains, for example in the context of cloud service providing, where *ceteris paribus* both the customer and providers may prefer to use a secure transport layer instead of unsafe protocols. Given a set $B \subseteq A$, we denote by $\max_a B$ (resp., $\max_i B$) the subset of B containing the elements b such that for all other elements $c \in B$, it holds that $b \not<_a c$ (resp., $b \not<_i c$).

At the end of the auction, the user must make a final decision. So, we assume that the auctioneer also has a *choice function* $choice_a : \wp(A) \to A$ which refines her partial preference $\leq_a$. Formally, for all $B \subseteq A$, $choice_a(B) \in \max_a B$. The objective of the following sections is to provide auctions that, using the partial preference $\leq_a$, filter the set of contracts offered by the providers, giving to the user a restricted list of contracts, from which she can choose the final outcome using function $choice_a$.

A *bid vector* is a vector $\langle B_1, \ldots, B_n \rangle$, where $B_i \subseteq A$ is the bid of bidder i. Hereafter, given a bid vector $\mathbf{B} = \langle B_1, \ldots, B_n \rangle$ and a bidder i, we also consider the corresponding *masked* vectors $\mathbf{B}_{-i} = \langle B_1, \ldots, B_{i-1}, ?, B_{i+1}, \ldots, B_n \rangle$, obtained by replacing B_i with the special distinguished symbol "?". As usual, by $(B, \mathbf{B}_{-i})$ we denote the bid vector obtained by replacing '?' with B, hence $(B_i, \mathbf{B}_{-i}) = \mathbf{B}$.

DEFINITION 3.1. *A multi-item A-auction is a function $\mathbf{A}$ from bid vectors to pairs $(\mathbf{x}, \mathbf{c})$, where $\mathbf{x}$ is a boolean allocation vector ($x_i = 1$ iff i is a winner) and $\mathbf{c}$ is the vector of contracts stipulated by each bidder: $\mathbf{c} \in (A \cup \{\bot\})^n$, where $\bot \notin A$ is the null contract.*

A *single-item* A-auction identifies a single winner and a single winning contract, i.e., for all $\mathbf{B}$ there exists at most one i such that $x_i = 1$, where $\mathbf{A}(\mathbf{B}) = (\mathbf{x}, \mathbf{c})$, and for all $j \neq i$, $c_j = \bot$. For simplicity, in case of a single winner i we write $\mathbf{A}(\mathbf{B}) = (i, c_i)$.

To reason about the expected behavior of a bidder, we need to lift her preference $\leq_i$ over contracts to a preference $\preceq_i$ over all possible outcomes $(\mathbf{x}, \mathbf{c})$ of the auction. We assume that $\preceq_i$ satisfies the following natural properties:

- bidders are indifferent losers (in the economic jargon, there are *no externalities*): if $x_i = x'_i = 0$ then $(\mathbf{x}, \mathbf{c}) \preceq_i (\mathbf{x}', \mathbf{c}')$ and $(\mathbf{x}', \mathbf{c}') \preceq_i (\mathbf{x}, \mathbf{c})$;
- preference between outcomes is consistent with preference between contracts: if $x_i = x'_i = 1$ then
$$c_i \leq_i c'_i \Leftrightarrow (\mathbf{x}, \mathbf{c}) \preceq_i (\mathbf{x}', \mathbf{c}');$$
- winning the auction with an admissible contract is at least as good as not winning: if $x_i > x'_i$ and $c_i \in A_i$, then $(\mathbf{x}', \mathbf{c}') \preceq_i (\mathbf{x}, \mathbf{c})$;
- bidders strictly prefer not to win rather than winning with an inadmissible contract: if $x_i > x'_i$ and $c_i \notin A_i$, then $(\mathbf{x}, \mathbf{c}) \prec_i (\mathbf{x}', \mathbf{c}')$.

In general, $\preceq_i$ may satisfy additional properties (i.e. it is not necessarily the least relation satisfying the above properties). Moreover, in general, $\preceq_i$ can be a partial relation as well. This leads to the following two notions of dominance.

DEFINITION 3.2 (DOMINANCE). *Let B_i and B'_i be two bids of provider i. We say that B'_i* dominates *B_i iff for all $\mathbf{B}_{-i}$: $\mathbf{A}(B_i, \mathbf{B}_{-i}) \preceq_i \mathbf{A}(B'_i, \mathbf{B}_{-i})$. Moreover, B'_i is a* dominant strategy *iff it dominates all other bids B_i. We say that a bid vector $\mathbf{B}'$ is a* dominant strategy equilibrium (DSE) *if for all i, B'_i is a dominant strategy.*

DEFINITION 3.3 (WEAK DOMINANCE). *Let B_i and B'_i be two bids of provider i. We say that B'_i* weakly dominates *B_i iff for all $\mathbf{B}_{-i}$: $\mathbf{A}(B'_i, \mathbf{B}_{-i}) \not\prec_i \mathbf{A}(B_i, \mathbf{B}_{-i})$. Moreover, B'_i is a* weakly dominant strategy *iff it weakly dominates all other bids B_i. We say that a bid vector $\mathbf{B}'$ is a* weakly dominant strategy equilibrium (WDSE) *if for all i, B'_i is a weakly dominant strategy.*

Definition 3.3 weakens Definition 3.2 since $\mathbf{A}(B'_i, \mathbf{B}_{-i}) \not\prec_i \mathbf{A}(B_i, \mathbf{B}_{-i})$ means that either $\mathbf{A}(B_i, \mathbf{B}_{-i}) \preceq_i \mathbf{A}(B'_i, \mathbf{B}_{-i})$ or $\mathbf{A}(B_i, \mathbf{B}_{-i})$ and $\mathbf{A}(B'_i, \mathbf{B}_{-i})$ are incomparable.

We can now state several desirable properties of an auction. For all bid vectors $\mathbf{B}$, let $\mathbf{A}(\mathbf{B}) = (\mathbf{x}, \mathbf{c})$:

- *no positive transfer*: for all bidders i, if $x_i = 1$ then $c_i \in B_i$;

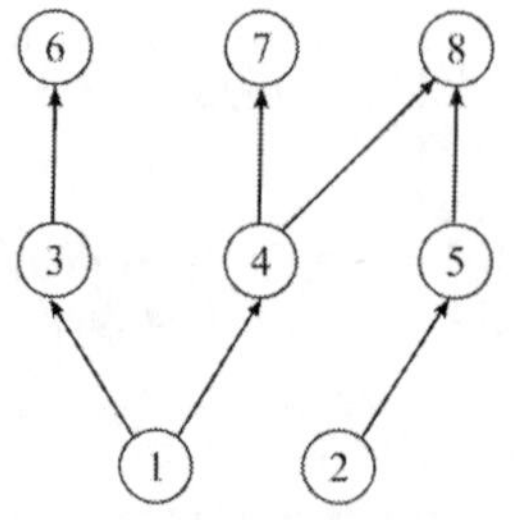

Figure 1: A graph representation of $\leq_a$ in Example 5.1.

- *relative optimality*: for all bidders i, j with $i \neq j$ and $b \in B_j$, if $x_i = 1$ then $c_i \not<_a b$; relative optimality, roughly speaking, is a sort of qualitative revenue maximization guarantee;
- *voluntary participation*: for all i, if $x_i = 0$ then $c_i = \bot$;
- *no failure*: if there exists at least one bidder i such that $B_i \cap A_a \neq \emptyset$ then there exists at least one j such that $x_j = 1$ and for all j such that $x_j = 1$ it holds that $c_j \in A_a$;
- *truthfulness*: the vector $\hat{\mathbf{B}} = \langle A_1, \ldots, A_n \rangle$ is a DSE;
- *weak truthfulness*: $\hat{\mathbf{B}}$ is a WDSE.

We say that an auction satisfies one of the above properties if it does so for all auctioneer preferences, bidder preferences, and bid vectors. Clearly, a single-item auction satisfies voluntary participation by definition.

4. A COMPARISON WITH CLASSICAL AUCTION SETTINGS

In this section we show that the standard properties of auctions do not hold in our reference scenarios.

4.1 Reduction to classical Vickrey auctions

It is tempting to obtain a truthful auction mechanism for agents with partial preferences by reducing the problem to standard second-price auctions, e.g.:

1. Let $\leq$ be any linearization of $\leq_a$ (the preference relation of the auctioneer);
2. Run a second-price auction using $\leq$ to order the bids.

This mechanism violates one of the standard desiderata for auctions: the property of *no positive transfer*. In particular, the second best bid might not be admissible for the winner, which may happen when another bidder makes an offer that is incomparable with i's bid.

EXAMPLE 4.1. *Let A_a be a set of 8 possible contracts and $\leq_a$ be the preference relation depicted in Figure 1, where an edge between two contracts c_i and c_j means that $c_i <_a c_j$. Moreover, we have three bidders that offer $B_1 = \{c_3, c_4, c_6\}$, $B_2 = \{c_1, c_2, c_7\}$, and $B_3 = \{c_5, c_8\}$, respectively.*

Assume the following linearization of $\leq_a$: $c_h \leq c_k$ iff $h \leq k$. Then, a second-price auction assigns the contract c_7 to bidder 3. However, c_7 is not included in B_3 which means that it is not an admissible option for 3.

It is not hard to see that adopting as $\leq$ the linearization of the preferences of any of the bidders yields similar problems. The details are left to the reader.

4.2 Bid-independent and truthful auctions

It is well-known that in classical price-based auctions, where bid vectors consist of tuples $\langle b_1, \ldots, b_n \rangle \in \mathbb{R}^n$, truthfulness is completely characterized by *bid-independent auctions*.

DEFINITION 4.1. *A* bid-independent *auction consists of a threshold function f from masked bid vectors to $\mathbb{R} \cup \{\infty\}$. For all given bid vectors $\mathbf{B}$, a bidder i is a winner iff $b_i \geq f(\mathbf{B}_{-i})$. All winners get a copy of the item and pay $f(\mathbf{B}_{-i})$.*

PROPOSITION 4.1 ([5]). *An auction mechanism is truthful iff it is equivalent to a bid-independent auction.*

Vickrey's single-item, second-price auctions are usually mentioned as an example of bid-independent auction that, by setting $f(\mathbf{B}_{-i}) = \max\{b_j \mid j \in N, j \neq i\}$, satisfies all the desiderata mentioned in Section 3. However, this is correct only if we assume that one bidder makes an offer that is strictly better than all the other bids, otherwise there would more than one winner and the auction would not be single-item.

Should this happen, the bid independent auction can be refined with a tie-breaking rule to select one winner among the bidders that submit the best offer. Strictly speaking, this is not a bid-independent auction anymore, so in general there is no truthfulness guarantee. However, in Vickrey's auctions, any tie-breaking criterion preserves truthfulness, because in case of multiple best offers the price paid by a truthful winner i is exactly $b_i = v_i$, (the value attributed to the item), therefore winning and not winning are indifferent to i, as $v_i - b_i = 0$ and there is no incentive to *overbid* (i.e. bid some $b_i > v_i$).

Unfortunately, in our scenarios, the space of bids is not continuous, and it is possible (even likely) that winning and not winning are *not* indifferent, for any contract (as if it were only possible to bid $b_i \neq v_i$).[2] Then each "almost truthful" bidder j who bids the maximal possible offer $b_j < v_j$ and is excluded by the tie breaking rule has an incentive to overbid. Indeed, if the bid were replaced by some $b'_j > b_j$, then j would become the only winner, and the price paid would still be $b_j < v_j$.

REMARK 4.1. *This proves that* if the bid space does not contain the private value v_i *(for some bidder i)*, then Vickrey auctions are not truthful.

REMARK 4.2. *Bid vectors with multiple optimal offers are often considered unlikely in the classical settings. However, when preferences are partial, it is not so unlikely to incur in multiple, mutually incomparable optimal offers, therefore fixing this problem is essential in our framework.*

Non-numeric bids require a slight generalization of the notion of bid-independent auction.

DEFINITION 4.2. *A* bid-independent A-auction *consists of a generalized threshold function f from masked vectors of contract sets to $A \cup \{\bot\}$. For all given bid vectors $\mathbf{B}$, a bidder i is a winner iff $f(\mathbf{B}_{-i}) \in B_i$. Each winner stipulates the contract $f(\mathbf{B}_{-i})$ with the auctioneer.*

[2]This happens when the provided service's utility is always nonzero, for all possible contracts.

Note that classical bid-independent auctions are essentially a special case of the above definition, in effect if i is willing to provide the good at the price b_i, it will also accept to give it at a higher price. This means that b_i is just a shorthand for $B_i = \{b \mid b \geq b_i\}$ and hence the condition $b_i \geq f(\mathbf{B}_{-i})$ in Definition 4.1 reduces to $f(\mathbf{B}_{-i}) \in B_i$.

It would be nice to use bid-independent A-auctions to reconstruct in the generalized framework the nice properties of Vickrey's auctions. Unfortunately, in so far as single-item auctions are concerned, relative optimality cannot be achieved at reasonable conditions.

PROPOSITION 4.2. *Assume that A has at least three contracts. Then, no single-item, bid-independent A-auction satisfies both relative optimality and no failure.*

PROOF. Let $N = \{1, 2\}$, $A = \{c, \top_1, \top_2\}$, and let $\leq_a = \{(\top_1, c), (\top_2, c)\}$. Suppose that f induces a single-item, bid-independent A-auction satisfying no-failure and relative optimality; we shall derive a contradiction.

Consider $\mathbf{B} = \langle\{c\}, \{c\}\rangle$. Assume without loss of generality that 1 wins (the other case is symmetrical). Then 2 shall not win as the auction is single-item, and hence

$$f(\mathbf{B}_{-2}) = d \in \{\top_1, \top_2, \bot\}. \tag{1}$$

Case $d = \top_1$. Let $\mathbf{B}' = \langle\{c\}, \{\top_2\}\rangle$. By relative optimality, 1 shall lose. Moreover, $\mathbf{B}'_{-2} = \mathbf{B}_{-2}$ so $f(\mathbf{B}'_{-2}) = f(\mathbf{B}_{-2}) = d = \top_1$ (by (1)). But then $f(\mathbf{B}'_{-2}) \notin b'_2$, therefore 2 loses and f violates the no-failure property (a contradiction).

Case $d = \top_2$. Symmetrical (swap $\top_1$ and $\top_2$ in the above proof).

Case $d = \bot$. Similar to the first case (replace $\top_1$ with $\bot$). □

In the light of the above result, we will focus on single-item auction mechanisms that are not bid-independent.

5. SINGLE-ITEM AUCTIONS

In classical price-based settings, Vickrey's auctions satisfy all the desiderata listed in Section 3. Therefore, a natural question is: can we in principle design generalized single-item auctions which reproduce the same good properties of Vickrey's auctions? Unfortunately, the following proposition shows that this is not possible.

PROPOSITION 5.1. *For some A and $\leq^a$, no single-item auction satisfies the properties no positive transfer, relative optimality, and weak truthfulness.*

PROOF. Suppose that $\mathbf{A}$ is always weakly optimal, weakly truthful, and satisfies the no positive transfer property too; we shall derive a contradiction.

Consider any $A \supseteq \{c_1, c_2\}$ such that $c_1 <^a c_2$. Let $\mathbf{B} = \langle\{c_1\}, \ldots, \{c_1\}\rangle$ and $\mathbf{A}(\mathbf{B}) = (w, c_1)$. Finally, suppose that none of c_1 and c_2 has null value for w, so that winning with outcome c_1 or c_2 is preferable to not winning.

Claim 1: $\mathbf{A}((\{c_1, c_2\}, \mathbf{B}_{-w})) = \mathbf{A}(\mathbf{B}) = (w, c_1)$.

First, only two different alternatives make the property of no positive transfer satisfied: $\mathbf{A}((\{c_1, c_2\}, \mathbf{B}_{-w})) = (i, c_1)$ and $\mathbf{A}((\{c_1, c_2\}, \mathbf{B}_{-w})) = (w, c_2)$.

If $\mathbf{A}((\{c_1, c_2\}, \mathbf{B}_{-w})) = (i, c_1)$, with $i \neq w$, then w would have an incentive to underbid when $A_w = \{c_1, c_2\}$ (because w is the winner in $\mathbf{B}$), so $\mathbf{A}$ would not be weakly truthful. Conversely, if $\mathbf{A}((\{c_1, c_2\}, \mathbf{B}_{-w})) = (w, c_2)$, then w would have an incentive to underbid whenever $c_2 <^w c_1$.

Claim 2: $\mathbf{A}((\{c_2\}, \mathbf{B}_{-w})) = (w, c_2)$.

Indeed, by weak optimality, w must be the winner (because $c_1 <^a c_2$). Then, according to the no positive transfer property, c_2 is the only possible contract.

But then, by Claim 1 and Claim 2, whenever $A_w = \{c_1, c_2\}$ and $c_1 <^w c_2$, w has an incentive to underbid, so $\mathbf{A}$ cannot be weakly truthful. □

Concerning the no positive transfer property, it is likely that a bidder is not willing to accept a contract not included in her bid. So, mechanisms not satisfying this property will not be taken into account.

The remaining options are either preserving weak truthfulness or preserving relative optimality. The first option is achieved by a simple mechanism that depends on two parameters: *(i)* the set A_a of contracts that are admissible for the auctioneer, and *(ii)* a linear priority ordering among bidders, which is used as a tie-breaking rule. The mechanism works according to the following definition.

DEFINITION 5.1. *Each bidder i submits a bid B_i. The winner w is the highest priority bidder i such that $A_a \cap B_i \neq \emptyset$; w selects an element b in $A_a \cap B_w$. The output is (w, b).*

Note that the previous definition is nothing but a form of dictatorship: the tie-breaking rule chooses a priori a winner w which can freely select any of her offers in $A_a \cap B_w$. Thus, w is incentivated to maximize the set of admissible choices, which means that A_w is her best strategy, and all the other bidders $j \neq w$ are indifferent to any strategy – indeed, they lose no matter what they offer. Consequently, Definition 5.1 is surely truthful. Moreover, it is equally clear that the mechanism is not relative optimal; more precisely, from the auctioneer's side the substantial lack of competition merely guarantees that the resulting contract is admissible.

So far, it is still an open question whether there exists a (weakly) truthful auction different from a dictatorship.

5.1 A relatively optimal mechanism

In this section we specify a relatively optimal mechanism for partial preferences. Such mechanism depends on the following parameters: *(i)* the set A_a of contracts that are admissible for the auctioneer; *(ii)* the preference relation $\leq_a$; *(iii)* a linear priority ordering among bidders, which is used as a tie-breaking rule. For simplicity, here we assume that i has higher priority than j iff $i < j$. Then, the mechanism works according to the following definition.

DEFINITION 5.2. *Each bidder i submits a bid B_i, giving rise to the bid vector $\mathbf{B} = \langle B_1, \ldots, B_n\rangle$. The auction proceeds as follows:*

1. *For each provider i, let $filter(i, \mathbf{B})$ be the set of contracts offered by i that are admissible for the auctioneer and such that no other bidder has made a strictly preferable offer. Formally,*

$$filter(i, \mathbf{B}) = \{b \in B_i \cap A_a \mid \forall j \neq i, \forall c \in B_j, b \not<_a c\}.$$

2. *The mechanism first selects those who submitted one of the top offers, that is, the members of*

$$cw(\mathbf{B}) = \{i \mid filter(i, \mathbf{B}) \neq \emptyset\},$$

(cw stands for candidate winners*). Then, by the tie-breaking rule, the winner w is the highest priority element in* $cw(\mathbf{B})$.

3. *The mechanism transmits to w the set* $filter(w, \mathbf{B})$.
4. *The winner replies with a non-empty subset* $B'_w \subseteq filter(w, \mathbf{B})$.
5. *The mechanism transmits to the auctioneer the set* B'_w.
6. *The auctioneer replies with the contract* $b = choice_a(B'_w)$.
7. *The output of the auction is* (w, b) *and the other bidders are assigned the null contract* $\perp$.

REMARK 5.1. *Note that the mechanism aims at using minimal information to select a contract. In particular, the bidders do not provide their preferences to the mechanism as the final selection is made privately (steps 3 and 4). This is a valuable desideratum in concrete applications where service providers, public companies or other kinds of enterprises, are scarcely inclined to disclose any information about their own profit model.*

EXAMPLE 5.1. *Consider the same preference* $\leq_a$ *and bid vector described in Example 4.1. By applying Definition 5.2, in step 1, the resulting filters are:*

$$\begin{aligned} filter(1, \mathbf{B}) &= \{c_3, c_6\} \\ filter(2, \mathbf{B}) &= \{c_7\} \\ filter(3, \mathbf{B}) &= \{c_5, c_8\}. \end{aligned}$$

Therefore, all the bidders are candidate winners. Then, according to the tie-breaking rule, bidder 1 is the final winner. In step 3 the mechanism transmits to bidder 1 the filter $\{c_3, c_6\}$. *Assume that she is indifferent between these two possible contracts and replies in step 4 with the same set* $\{c_3, c_6\}$. *Then, the mechanism returns the contracts* c_3 *and* c_6 *to the auctioneer that, according to her preferences, chooses* c_6.

Differently, if the preferences of bidder 1 were inverted w.r.t. Figure 1, then in step 4 she would return the single contract c_3 *which would be also the final outcome.*

The following proposition shows that, apart from truthfulness, Definition 5.2 fulfills all the desiderata mentioned in Section 3.

PROPOSITION 5.2. *The auction in Definition 5.2 satisfies the properties no failure, no positive transfer, relative optimality, and voluntary participation.*

PROOF. Assume that at least one bidder submits a contract which is admissible for the auctioneer, as the other case is trivial. Let $M = \max_a \bigcup_{i=1}^{n} B_i$. Clearly, there exists a bidder j such that $M \cap B_j \neq \emptyset$. By construction, $M \cap B_j \subseteq filter(B_j, \mathbf{B}_{-j})$. Hence, $cw(\mathbf{B}) \neq \emptyset$ and hence the auction returns an output (w, b) with $b \in A_a$ (no failure) and all other bidders receive the null contract (voluntary participation). Note that $b \in filter(B_w, \mathbf{B}_{-w})$ which means that $b \in B_w$ (no positive transfer) and for all $j \neq w$ and $c \in B_j$, $b \not<_a c$ (relative optimality). □

Finally, note that when offers are represented by monetary values, the presented mechanism *collapses* to standard second-price auctions. Keeping procurement auctions as our reference scenario, the auctioneer aims at minimizing prices, that is $b \leq_a c$ iff $c \leq b$. Conversely, for each bidder i, we have that $b \leq_i c$ iff $b \leq c$. The auctioneer fixes a maximum price p_a she is willing to pay, hence the set of admissible offers is $A_a = \{b \in A \mid b \leq p_a\}$. Each bidder i makes an offer b_i, which implicitly stands for the bid $B_i = \{b \in A \mid b \geq b_i\}$. Once the mechanism has collected all the bids, it computes the corresponding filters. Since prices are totally ordered, we have that $filter(i, \mathbf{B}) = \{b \in B_i \mid b \leq p_a \text{ and } \forall j \neq i, \forall c \in B_j, b \leq c\}$. Notice that if a bidder makes an offer b_i that is higher than p_a, his filter will be empty. For the sake of simplicity, assume that there exists only one candidate winner i_1 (the bidder offering the lowest price) and let i_2 the bidder offering the second lowest price. By definition, it holds that

$$filter(i_1, \mathbf{B}) = \{b \in B_{i_1} \mid b_{i_1} \leq b \leq b_{i_2}\}.$$

Consequently, once the mechanism returns $filter(i_1, \mathbf{B})$ in Step 4, i_1 will select her best possible choice which is indeed the second price b_{i_2}.

5.2 Strategic Analysis

In this section we look at an auction as a game where bidders act strategically.

First of all, in Step 3 the winning bidder w has to select a subset of her filter. Since no other bidder can influence the outcome and the auction satisfies no failure and no positive transfer, it is convenient for w to select the maximal elements of her filter, i.e.,

$$\max_w filter(w, \mathbf{B}).$$

The following proposition shows that, differently from classical Vickrey auctions, partial preferences make Definition 5.2 not weakly truthful.

PROPOSITION 5.3. *The auction in Definition 5.2 is not weakly truthful.*

PROOF. Consider the following counterexample: the set of admissible contracts for the auctioneer is $A_a = \{b, c, d\}$, where $c <_a b$, $d <_a b$, and $c \bowtie_a d$. We also have two bidders such that $A_1 = B_1 = \{c\}$ and $A_2 = \{d\}$. If 2 plays truthfully, i.e. $B_2 = \{d\}$, since $c \bowtie_a d$, both 1 and 2 are candidate winners. According to the tie-breaking rule, 2 loses the auction and the output is $(1, c)$. On the contrary, if 2 offers $B'_2 = \{b, d\}$, she is the only candidate winner and her filter is B'_2 itself. Then, in step 4 bidder 2 can select the set $\{d\}$, which means that the output is $(2, d)$. Now, assuming that d is better than losing, we have that $(1, c) \prec_2 (2, d)$. Therefore, playing truthfully is not a weakly dominant strategy for 2. □

Even if the mechanism is not (weakly) truthful, some valuable dominances between bids hold. In particular, each bid of i is dominated by the one obtained by adding to it all contracts that are admissible for i.

PROPOSITION 5.4. *For each bid* B_i *of bidder* i, $B_i \cup A_i$ *dominates* B_i.

PROOF. The thesis is trivially true in case $A_i \subseteq B_i$. Therefore, assume that there exists $c \in A_i$ such that $c \notin B_i$. Clearly, $B'_i = B_i \cup A_i$ is an overbid and contains c.

Let $\mathbf{B}_{-i}$ be a bid vector of the other providers. We denote with $\mathbf{B}$ and $\mathbf{B}'$ the bid vectors $(B_i, \mathbf{B}_{-i})$ and $(B'_i, \mathbf{B}_{-i})$, respectively. If $\mathit{filter}(i, \mathbf{B}') \cap A_i = \emptyset$, then $\mathit{filter}(i, \mathbf{B}) = \mathit{filter}(i, \mathbf{B}')$. Moreover, for all j it also holds $\mathit{filter}(j, \mathbf{B}) = \mathit{filter}(j, \mathbf{B}')$, and consequently $\mathbf{A}(\mathbf{B}) = \mathbf{A}(\mathbf{B}')$ and the conclusion follows.

Next suppose that $\mathit{filter}(i, \mathbf{B}') \cap A_i \neq \emptyset$. Since $B_i \subset B_i'$, by construction it follows that $\mathit{filter}(i, \mathbf{B}) \subseteq \mathit{filter}(i, \mathbf{B}')$. Therefore B_i' can only add better optimal offers (w.r.t. $\leq_a$), or leave them unchanged in the worst case. Consequently, B_i' may cause i to enter the set of candidate winners and other bidders to exit from it. We distinguish two cases: if i is the winner in $\mathbf{B}$, according to step 2 of the auction he is also the winner in $\mathbf{B}'$. Since $\mathit{filter}(i, \mathbf{B}) \subseteq \mathit{filter}(i, \mathbf{B}')$, for all $b \in \max_i \mathit{filter}(i, \mathbf{B})$ there exists $b' \in \max_i \mathit{filter}(i, \mathbf{B}')$ such that $b \leq_i b'$. Let $\mathbf{A}(\mathbf{B}) = (i, b)$ and $\mathbf{A}(\mathbf{B}') = (i, b')$. Assume by contradiction that $b' <_i b$ and let $c' \in \max_i \mathit{filter}(i, \mathbf{B}')$ be such that $b \leq_i c'$. By transitivity, $b' <_i c'$, which implies $b' \notin \max_i \mathit{filter}(i, \mathbf{B}')$, a contradiction.

Otherwise, i is not the winner in $\mathbf{B}$. If i is not the winner in $\mathbf{B}'$, then clearly i is indifferent between $\mathbf{B}$ and $\mathbf{B}'$ (indifferent loser assumption) and we are done. If instead i is also the winner in $\mathbf{B}'$, let $\mathbf{A}(\mathbf{B}') = (i, b)$. We have that $\max_i \mathit{filter}(i, \mathbf{B})$ is contained in A_i, because $\mathit{filter}(i, \mathbf{B}') \cap A_i \neq \emptyset$. Consequently, $b \in A_i$ and the thesis follows.

Finally, since we have proved that $\mathbf{A}(\mathbf{B}) \preceq_i \mathbf{A}(\mathbf{B}')$ no matter which $\mathbf{B}_{-i}$ is chosen, B_i' dominates B_i. $\square$

The previous theorem provides a uniform way to improve any bid B_i with a dominant extension that can possibly be an over-bid, namely $B_i \cup A_i$.[3] Therefore, i can safely reduce her space of possible moves to the bids $B \supseteq A_i$ only.

In the rest of this section we give a closer look at the strategic relations between the truthful bid A_i and a generic over-bid s $B \supseteq A_i$ from the points of view of the bidders and the auctioneer. The next theorem shows that if a bidder wins with the truthful bid, then over-bidding does not yield any advantage.

PROPOSITION 5.5. *Let* $\mathbf{B} = (A_i, \mathbf{B}_{-i})$ *and* $\mathbf{B}' = (B_i', \mathbf{B}_{-i})$, *where* $A_i \subset B_i'$ *and* $\mathbf{B}_{-i}$ *is any bid vector. If* $\mathbf{A}(\mathbf{B}) = (i, p)$, *then* $\mathbf{A}(\mathbf{B}') = (i, p)$.

PROOF. First, from $A_i \subset B_i'$, it is easy to verify that (1) $\mathit{filter}(j, \mathbf{B}') \subseteq \mathit{filter}(j, \mathbf{B})$ for all $j \neq i$, and (2) $\mathit{filter}(i, \mathbf{B}') = \mathit{filter}(i, \mathbf{B}) \cup C$ where C consists of non-admissible contracts only, i.e., for all $c \in C$ and $b \in \mathit{filter}(i, \mathbf{B})$ it holds that $c <_i b$. Since $\mathbf{A}(\mathbf{B}) = (i, p)$, we have that $\mathit{filter}(i, \mathbf{B}) \neq \emptyset$. From (2) and (1), it follows that $i \in cw(\mathbf{B}')$ and $cw(\mathbf{B}') \subseteq cw(\mathbf{B})$. So, the tie-breaking rule selects i as the winner in $\mathbf{B}'$ too.

Moreover, (2) implies that $\max_i \mathit{filter}(i, \mathbf{B}')$ does not contain any element in C and hence

$$\max_i \mathit{filter}(i, \mathbf{B}') = \max_i \mathit{filter}(i, \mathbf{B}) \triangleq D.$$

Consequently, in both $\mathbf{B}$ and $\mathbf{B}'$ the auction sends to the auctioneer the same set D of contracts at Step 5. The auctioneer then replies with the same contract $p = \mathit{choice}_a(D)$. $\square$

Somewhat dually, if a truthful bidder is not a candidate winner, then over-bidding is counterproductive.

PROPOSITION 5.6. *Let* $\mathbf{B} = (A_i, \mathbf{B}_{-i})$ *and* $\mathbf{B}' = (B_i', \mathbf{B}_{-i})$, *where* $A_i \subset B_i'$ *and* $\mathbf{B}_{-i}$ *is any bid vector. If* $i \notin cw(\mathbf{B})$, *then* $\mathbf{B}$ *dominates* $\mathbf{B}'$.

[3]In other words over-bids, taken *as a whole*, can be seen as a dominant set of strategies.

PROOF. Let $\mathbf{A}(\mathbf{B}) = (h, p)$ and $\mathbf{A}(\mathbf{B}') = (k, p')$. Clearly, $i \notin cw(\mathbf{B})$ implies that $h \neq i$. Now, if $k \neq i$, since i is an indifferent loser, she is indifferent between $\mathbf{B}$ and $\mathbf{B}'$, $(h, p) \sim_i (k, p')$. Then, assume that i wins the auction in the context $\mathbf{B}'$, i.e., $k = i$. Since all admissible contracts are discarded when i plays truthfully, i.e., $\mathit{filter}(i, \mathbf{B}) = \emptyset$, then $\mathit{filter}(i, \mathbf{B}')$ consists of non-admissible contracts only. This implies that $p' \notin A_i$ and hence $(i, p') \prec_i (h, p)$. $\square$

REMARK 5.2. *In the proof of Proposition 5.3 we have shown a case where over-bidding "hacks" the tie-breaking rule in favor of a certain bidder. Propositions 5.5 and 5.6 show that this is the only way a bidder can use over-bidding for her own advantage.*

Finally, we show that from the point of view of the auctioneer the effects of over-bidding on the outcome are limited. In particular, at least at the level of granularity of the partial preference $\leq_a$ provided to the mechanism, the auctioneer has no reason to complain because of an over-bid, as it cannot yield a strictly less preferable contract.

PROPOSITION 5.7. *Let* $\mathbf{B} = (A_i, \mathbf{B}_{-i})$ *and* $\mathbf{B}' = (B_i', \mathbf{B}_{-i})$, *where* $A_i \subseteq B_i'$ *and* $\mathbf{B}_{-i}$ *is any bid vector. Let* $\mathbf{A}(\mathbf{B}) = (k, q)$ *and* $\mathbf{A}(\mathbf{B}') = (j, p)$. *It holds that* $p \not<_a q$.

PROOF. First, assume $k = i$, i.e., i is the winner in $\mathbf{B}$. By Proposition 5.5, $j = i$ and $p = q$, which implies the thesis. In the following, we assume $k \neq i$ and distinguish three cases.

Case 1. $j = k$, i.e., the winner in $\mathbf{B}$ and $\mathbf{B}'$ is the same (different from i). When moving from $\mathbf{B}$ to $\mathbf{B}'$, some contracts from the filter of j are lost, because they are dominated by some "new" contract in $B_i' \setminus A_i$. The remaining contracts cannot be worse (for the auctioneer) than those that were removed, otherwise they would have been removed as well. Formally, for all $b \in \mathit{filter}(j, \mathbf{B}')$ and $c \in \mathit{filter}(j, \mathbf{B}) \setminus \mathit{filter}(j, \mathbf{B}')$ we have that $b \not\leq_a c$. If $q \notin \mathit{filter}(j, \mathbf{B}')$, since $p \in \mathit{filter}(j, \mathbf{B}')$, by the above observation we have that $p \not\leq_a q$ and in particular $p \not<_a q$. Otherwise, $q \in \mathit{filter}(j, \mathbf{B}')$. Since $\mathit{filter}(j, \mathbf{B}') \subseteq \mathit{filter}(j, \mathbf{B})$ and q is a maximal element of $\mathit{filter}(j, \mathbf{B})$ w.r.t. $\leq_j$, q is a maximal element of $\mathit{filter}(j, \mathbf{B}')$ as well. Formally, $q \in D$, where $D = \max_j \mathit{filter}(j, \mathbf{B}')$. Now, since $p = \mathit{choice}_a(D)$ and choice_a refines $\leq_a$, $p \in \max_a D$ which means that $p \not<_a q$.

Case 2. $j \neq k$ and $j \neq i$, that is the winners in $\mathbf{B}$ and $\mathbf{B}'$ are different from each other and i. First, since $j \neq i$, it holds that $\mathit{filter}(j, \mathbf{B}') \subseteq \mathit{filter}(j, \mathbf{B})$. Now, assume $p <_a q$. By definition, $p \notin \mathit{filter}(j, \mathbf{B})$ and hence $p \notin \mathit{filter}(j, \mathbf{B}')$. This is in contradiction with the hypothesis $\mathbf{A}(\mathbf{B}') = (j, p)$; subsequently, $p \not<_a q$.

Case 3. $j \neq k$ and $j = i$, i.e., i is the winner in $\mathbf{B}'$ but not in $\mathbf{B}$. Assume again that $p <_a q$. Now, since q belongs to B_k and $k \neq i$, p is not relative optimal in $\mathbf{B}'$ and hence it is discarded. As before, $p \notin \mathit{filter}(j, \mathbf{B}')$ clearly leads to a contradiction. $\square$

6. MULTI-ITEM AUCTIONS

Sometimes the auctioneer may be looking for multiple goods or services and then she is disposed to acknowledge multiple contracts. The bid-independent auctions defined in Def. 4.2 are naturally multi-item, as every agent i such that $f(\mathbf{B}_{-i}) \in B_i$ is a winner. Relative optimality is not precluded a priori (Prop. 4.2 refers to single-item auctions only). Nevertheless, Def. 4.2 presents another critical point:

there is no way to assure that $f(\mathbf{B}_{-i}) \in B_i$ holds for at least one bidder. Consequently, the following proposition holds.

PROPOSITION 6.1. *Generalized bid-independent auctions do not satisfy the no-failure property.*

PROOF. Assume there are two possible contracts c_1 and c_2 and two bidders. Since $\mathbf{B}_{-1} = B_2$ and $\mathbf{B}_{-2} = B_1$, f is a mapping from $\{c_1\}$, $\{c_2\}$, and $\{c_1, c_2\}$ into either c_1 or c_2.

Consider the restriction of f to singletons. If such a restriction is not surjective, e.g. $f(\{c_1\}) = f(\{c_2\}) = c_1$, then in case $B_1 = B_2 = \{c_2\}$ no winner is selected. If $f(\{c_1\}) = c_1$ and $f(\{c_2\}) = c_2$, then the mechanism fails when, for instance, $B_1 = \{c_1\}$ and $B_2 = \{c_2\}$. Finally, if $f(\{c_1\}) = c_2$ and $f(\{c_2\}) = c_2$, failure occurs when $B_1 = B_2 = \{c_1\}$.

Consequently, no function f can guarantee the no-failure property. □

To avoid failures, we consider a multi-item variant of the mechanism presented in Definition 5.2. Roughly speaking, for a given bid vector $\mathbf{B}$, the mechanism assigns a contract to *each* candidate winner in $cw(\mathbf{B})$. More formally, the mechanism is defined as follows.

DEFINITION 6.1. *Given an input bid-vector* $\mathbf{B}$, *for each bidder* i, *filter*$(i, \mathbf{B})$ *and* $cw(\mathbf{B})$ *are computed as in steps* 1 *and* 2 *in Definition 5.2. Steps* $3-6$ *are executed for each* $i \in cw(\mathbf{B})$, *that is, the mechanism (a) sends filter*$(i, \mathbf{B})$ *to bidder* i, *(b) gets* $B'_i \subseteq$ *filter*$(i, \mathbf{B})$ *back from* i *(c) sends* B'_i *to the auctioneer, (d) receives* $b_i = choice_a(B'_i)$. *Finally the mechanism outputs* $(\mathbf{x}, \mathbf{c})$, *where for each* $i \in cw(\mathbf{B}), x_i = 1$ *and* $c_i = b_i$ *while for each* $i \notin cw(\mathbf{B}), x_i = 0$ *and* $c_i = \perp$.

This mechanism is obviously relatively optimal, by definition of filters. On the strategy side, it is easy to verify that Propositions 5.4 and 5.6 still hold for the new mechanism. Similarly, it is possible to rephrase Proposition 5.5 as:

PROPOSITION 6.2. *Let* $\mathbf{B} = (A_i, \mathbf{B}_{-i})$ *and* $\mathbf{B}' = (B'_i, \mathbf{B}_{-i})$, *where* $A_i \subset B'_i$ *and* $\mathbf{B}_{-i}$ *is any bid vector. Furthermore, denote by* $\mathbf{A}(\mathbf{B}) = (\mathbf{x}, \mathbf{c})$ *and* $\mathbf{A}(\mathbf{B}') = (\mathbf{x}', \mathbf{c}')$. *If* $x_i = 1$ *then* $x'_i = 1$ *and* $c'_i = c_i$.

On the one hand Proposition 5.6 states that if bidder i is not a candidate winner by playing truthfully, then no over-bid B_i may lead to win the auction with an admissible contract. On the other hand, Proposition 6.2 states that if bidder i is a candidate winner by playing truthfully, then no overbid will improve her revenue. Therefore we can prove the following:

PROPOSITION 6.3. *Definition 6.1 satisfies truthfulness.*

PROOF. Assume that $\mathbf{B} = (A_i, \mathbf{B}_{-i})$, $\mathbf{B}' = (B'_i, \mathbf{B}_{-i})$, and $\mathbf{A}(\mathbf{B}') \npreceq_i \mathbf{A}(\mathbf{B})$.

Now, if $i \notin cw(\mathbf{B})$, then according to Proposition 5.6 $\mathbf{A}(\mathbf{B}') \preceq_i \mathbf{A}(\mathbf{B})$. Conversely, if $i \in cw(\mathbf{B})$, by Propositions 5.4 and 6.2 we have that

$$\mathbf{A}(\mathbf{B}') \preceq_i \mathbf{A}((A_i \cup B'_i, \mathbf{B}_{-i})) \sim_i \mathbf{A}(\mathbf{B}) .$$

Hence, $\mathbf{A}(\mathbf{B}') \preceq_i \mathbf{A}(\mathbf{B})$. In both the cases we have a contradiction. □

7. RELATED WORK

Traditionally, preferences are essentially linear orders, induced by underlying utility functions (e.g. [1, 6]). Partial preferences are dealt with in mechanisms without money, where most results on incentive compatibility are negative, [9, 10]. In [8] a generic model for matching with contracts (using a doctor-hospital metaphor) is introduced. Definitions and results rely on the assumption that preferences are total orders, if not, then truthfulness does not hold.

Vickrey auctions without payments and qualitative preference relations are dealt with in [7]. Auctioneers and bidders have independent preferences, as in our framework. However, the preference relation of the auctioneer is restricted to *total* preorders (actually, linear orders in the finite case). The tie-breaking over multiple maximal offers is dealt with by assuming the auctioneer's preferences to be *equipeaked* (all local maxima are also global maxima). Our framework supports unrestricted partial preferences, instead.

Bonatti et al. [3] introduce two mechanisms for unrestricted partial preferences and contracts with non-null utility. Among the main differences between [3] and this paper we mention: (i) the mechanisms of [3] are probabilistic; (ii) the theoretical properties of those two mechanisms need additional assumptions about agent preferences (that must be so-called superweak orders, or satisfy 5 axioms that extend some classical decision theory properties, respectively); the theoretical guarantees of the second mechanism of [3] concern the bidders rather than the auctioneer. We are more interested in the auctioneer, according to the applications to privacy enhancement such as those illustrated in [2].

Finally, to the best of our knowledge, Prop. 4.2 is the first negative result on the extension to partial preferences of the traditional techniques for achieving truthfulness.

8. CONCLUSIONS AND FUTURE WORK

In our reference scenarios, preferences are partial and the bid space is discrete, so all bids may have nonzero utility. These two features affect the theoretical properties of classical auctions: We showed that (i) a naive reduction to Vickrey's auctions violates the analogue of the "no positive transfer" principle; (ii) the tie-breaking rules for selecting a winner among multiple candidate winners affect truthfulness; (iii) bid-independent auctions in general violate either robustness (there may be no winner) or relative optimality.

We proved that single-item auctions cannot be both truthful and relatively optimal (the latter is a qualitative revenue guarantee). On the one hand, there exist dictatorial truthful mechanisms. On the other hand, relative optimality is preserved by a mechanism that admits over-bidding. However, from the auctioneer's perspective, overbidding can never make the outcome worse than the outcome of a truthful bid. Interestingly, from a bidder's perspective, overbidding can possibly be advantageous only in case of tie-breaking; otherwise it may yield an equivalent outcome or even cause a loss. This mechanism admits human user intervention in the final phases, when the space of possible outcomes has been restricted to a restricted list by user agents.

Two interesting open questions are whether dictatorship is the only truthful single-item mechanism in our scenarios, and whether some (possibly relaxed) form of truthfulness is compatible with relative optimality.

Acknowledgements

This work has been supported by the Italian PRIN project *Security Horizons* and the CINI project *PiattaformaMobilità*.

REFERENCES

[1] Robert J. Aumann. Utility theory without the completeness axiom. Econometric Res. Prog. Research memorandum n.26, Princeton University, 3 Apr. 1961.

[2] P. A. Bonatti, M. Faella, C. Galdi, and L. Sauro. Towards a mechanism for incentivating privacy. In *Proc. of the 16th European Symposium on Research in Computer Security,ESORICS11, Leuven, Belgium, September 12-14, 2011.*, 2011.

[3] P.A. Bonatti, M. Faella, C. Galdi, and L. Sauro. Auctions for partial heterogeneous preferences. In *Proc. of Mathematical Foundations of Computer Science, 38th Int. Symposium (MFCS 2013), Klosterneuburg, Austria, August 26-30, 2013*, 2013.

[4] C. Boutilier, R. I. Brafman, C. Domshlak, and H. H. Hoos. Cp-nets: A tool for representing and reasoning with conditional ceteris paribus preference statements. *Journal of Artificial Intelligence Research*, 21:135–191, 2004.

[5] Amos Fiat, Andrew V. Goldberg, Jason D. Hartline, and Anna R. Karlin. Competitive generalized auctions. In John H. Reif, editor, *Proceedings on 34th Annual ACM Symposium on Theory of Computing, May 19-21, 2002, Montréal, Québec, Canada*, pages 72–81. ACM, 2002.

[6] P.C. Fishburn. *Utility Theory for Decision Making.* Wiley, New York, 1970.

[7] Paul Harrenstein, Mathijs de Weerdt, and Vincent Conitzer. A qualitative Vickrey auction. In John Chuang, Lance Fortnow, and Pearl Pu, editors, *ACM Conference on Electronic Commerce*, pages 197–206. ACM, 2009.

[8] John William Hatfield and Paul R Milgrom. Matching with contracts. *American Economic Review*, pages 913–935, 2005.

[9] Noam Nisan, Tim Roughgarden, Eva Tardos, and Vijay V. Vazirani. *Algorithmic Game Theory.* Cambridge University Press, New York, NY, USA, 2007.

[10] Alexander Reffgen. Generalizing the Gibbard-Satterthwaite theorem: partial preferences, the degree of manipulation, and multi-valuedness. *Social Choice and Welfare*, 37(1):39–59, 2011.

[11] Herbert Simon. A behavioral model of rational choice. *The Quarterly Journal of Economics*, 69(1):99–118, 1955.

[12] J. van Neumann and O. Morgenstern. *Theory of Games and Economic Behavior.* Princeton University Press, 1944.

A Deterministic MAB Mechanism for Crowdsourcing with Logarithmic Regret and Immediate Payments

Shweta Jain
Indian Institute of Science
Bangalore, India
jainshweta@csa.iisc.ernet.in

Ganesh Ghalme
Indian Institute of Science
Bangalore, India
ganeshghalme@gmail.com

Satyanath Bhat
Indian Institute of Science
Bangalore, India
satya.bhat@gmail.com

Sujit Gujar*
Indian Institute of Science
Bangalore, India
sujit.gujar@gmail.com

Y. Narahari
Indian Institute of Science
Bangalore, India
hari@csa.iisc.ernet.in

ABSTRACT

We consider a general crowdsourcing setting with strategic workers whose qualities are unknown and design a multi-armed bandit (MAB) mechanism, CrowdUCB, which is deterministic, regret minimizing, and offers immediate payments to the workers. The problem involves sequentially selecting workers to process tasks in order to maximize the social welfare while learning the qualities of the strategic workers (strategic about their costs). Existing MAB mechanisms are either: (a) deterministic which potentially cause significant loss in social welfare, or (b) randomized which typically lead to high variance in payments. CrowdUCB completely addresses the above problems with the following features: (i) offers deterministic payments, (ii) achieves logarithmic regret in social welfare, (iii) renders allocations more effective by allocating blocks of tasks to a worker instead of a single task, and (iv) offers payment to a worker immediately upon completion of an assigned block of tasks. CrowdUCB is a mechanism with learning that learns the qualities of the workers while eliciting their true costs, irrespective of whether or not the workers know their own qualities. We show that CrowdUCB is ex-post individually rational (EPIR) and ex-post incentive compatible (EPIC) when the workers do not know their own qualities and when they update their beliefs in sync with the requester. When the workers know their own qualities, CrowdUCB is EPIR and ε−EPIC where ε is sub-linear in terms of the number of tasks.

Categories and Subject Descriptors

I.2.11 [**Distributed Artificial Intelligence**]: Intelligent agents; I.2.6 [**Learning**]: Parameter learning

*This work was done when the author was a post doctoral fellow at LIA, EPFL, Lausanne, Switzerland.

Appears in: *Proceedings of the 15th International Conference on Autonomous Agents and Multiagent Systems (AAMAS 2016), J. Thangarajah, K. Tuyls, C. Jonker, S. Marsella (eds.), May 9–13, 2016, Singapore.*

General Terms

Algorithms, Economics

Keywords

Crowdsourcing, Multi-armed bandit, Mechanism design

1. INTRODUCTION

Crowdsourcing is emerging as a powerful sourcing alternative to organizations for the execution of tasks in a timely, scalable, and cost-effective manner. The availability of a large worker pool enables crowdsourcing to be used widely to collect labels for large scale learning problems, like collecting a ground dataset for supervised learning algorithms. The rise in the number of crowdsourcing platforms in recent times indicates the usefulness of crowdsourcing in various real world applications.

On a crowdsourcing platform, a requester (one who is seeking the tasks to be performed) naturally seeks high quality and low cost workers. We focus our attention on crowdsourcing platforms where the number of tasks is large and individual tasks are simple, common, low cost tasks such as image labeling. Due to diverse, heterogeneous demographics of crowd workers and a rich variety of tasks available on a crowdsourcing platform, the quality of a worker is typically unknown to the requester and sometimes even to the worker as well. We allow workers to bid their costs for a particular task (for example, rent-a-coder.com). When there are low cost tasks at hand and auction overheads are involved, it is preferable to allocate a block of tasks to a worker rather than allocate a single task. The problem of choosing an optimal worker becomes a challenging one when these costs need to be elicited and qualities need to be learned via a suitable learning algorithm. This problem can be posed as a *multi-armed bandit* (MAB) mechanism design problem [5, 10], where, while eliciting the true costs, the requester needs to either explore the workers (modeled as arms) to learn their qualities or exploit the best worker identified so far.

There are two types of MAB mechanisms available in the literature: (a) deterministic mechanisms [5, 10, 7] which are known to incur high regret in social welfare (for example, as high as, $O(T^{2/3})$ where T is the number of tasks) but with zero variance in payments, and (b) randomized mechanisms [4, 6] where optimal (logarithmic) regret is achieved but with a high variance in payments. In this work, we propose a mechanism that (a) offers deterministic payments, (b) achieves minimal regret (logarithmic in the number of tasks), (c) allows allocation of blocks of tasks to workers, and (d) offers immediate payments. Moreover, the proposed mechanism allows workers the flexibility of modifying their bids in successive rounds. Following are the two key features that differentiate our work from extant work in the literature.

Deterministic MAB Mechanism with Logarithmic Regret

The lower bound characterization results for deterministic MAB mechanisms with dominant strategy incentive compatibility (DSIC) notion assumes that the manipulating worker has the power to know all the future events, leading to high regret [5, 10]. While such an approach is theoretically appealing, in practice, however, a worker is not sure about his own quality and thus cannot manipulate based on the knowledge of future events. Recent works [11, 13] argue against the approach of providing worst case guarantees for large games and recommend instead, simpler yet optimal strategies with pragmatic assumptions. For crowdsourcing, this approach is more suitable due to the large population of global workforce and the diversity in the nature of tasks posted by requesters.

To achieve logarithmic regret, we use the notion of *ex-post incentive compatibility* (EPIC). EPIC ensures that even after considering the future events, for every task, it is best for any worker to bid his cost truthfully when the other workers bid truthfully. Though EPIC is a weaker notion than DSIC, it is much stronger than Bayesian incentive compatibility that is often used in mechanism design [14]. Further, we make no assumptions about workers' knowledge of success realization (which future tasks will be successfully completed) and about the number of tasks requester wants to execute.

Block Allocations, Dynamic Bids, and Immediate Payments

In the context of learning of qualities, the algorithms in the literature usually allocate a single task at a time and make the next allocation following evaluation of the performance of the previous tasks. With low cost tasks, this could cause significant overheads and the workers may quit the crowdsourcing platform. Our mechanism has the enhanced feature of allocating blocks of tasks to the workers. The block sizes are dynamically updated based on the learned qualities and the bids of the workers. Our mechanism further allows the workers to bid different costs in different rounds as the time progresses and offers immediate payments to the workers.

Contributions

We propose two variants of our mechanism: (a) qualities are unknown to the workers and (b) qualities are private information of the workers. Following are the specific contributions:

- We design a MAB mechanism, *CrowdUCB* which is deterministic, regret optimal, makes block allocations, and offers immediate payments (Section 4).
- We theoretically prove that CrowdUCB suffers minimal regret that matches the lower bound in the space of stochastic MAB problems (Theorem 3).
- When workers are unaware of their qualities and learn these qualities as the mechanism progresses, we prove that CrowdUCB is ex-post individually rational (EPIR) and ex-post incentive compatible (EPIC)(Section 5).
- When workers know their qualities, we prove that CrowdUCB is $\varepsilon-$EPIC where ε is sub-linear in the number of tasks T, making CrowdUCB asymptotically EPIC in this setting (Section 6).
- We experimentally show that: (a) existing randomized mechanisms suffer from high variance as opposed to CrowdUCB and (b) the constants hidden within the regret are reasonable enough (Section 7).

2. RELATED WORK

While the MAB problem is a well studied area in machine learning community, designing MAB mechanisms is still a relatively unexplored area. Though there are optimal regret guarantees in MAB problems [8], strategic versions of the problem fail to achieve such guarantees [5, 10]. The lower bound proof in [5, 10] for any deterministic MAB mechanism makes a crucial assumption that a worker is fully aware of the complete success realization, thus giving more manipulative power to the worker. Our mechanism is more practical where we relax the above assumption and achieve logarithmic regret. In the literature, the high regret issue is alleviated via a randomized mechanism [3, 21] and it turns out that standard MAB algorithms like UCB1 [2] can be transformed into a truthful randomized mechanism. However, the payment scheme in such mechanisms involves a trade-off between the revenue obtained and the variance in the payment. It is then shown that this trade-off is necessary to achieve truthfulness [21]. In our work, we provide a mechanism that circumvents this trade-off in the specific context of crowdsourcing via realistic assumptions.

The concept of MAB based algorithms and MAB mechanisms is not new to crowdsourcing [18]. When the costs are fixed and known and qualities are unknown, the crowdsourcing setting can be formulated as a variation of a MAB problem with crowd workers acting as the arms [19, 20, 1, 12]. In another setting, When the costs of the workers are not known, but the qualities are homogeneous among workers, the problem of designing a posted price mechanism is formulated using a MAB algorithm with various prices as the arms of the bandit [3, 17]. When workers arrive online, designing a truthful mechanism for eliciting the bids from the workers is considered in [16] but the work assumes that the workers are homogeneous in terms of their qualities. With an offline worker pool, designing truthful MAB mechanisms in crowdsourcing setting for eliciting true costs and learning qualities at the same time is also considered by many authors. Authors in [7] considered an exploration separated mechanism to the budgeted crowdsourcing setting that is deterministic but incurs a high regret ($O(T^{2/3})$ with T being the number of tasks). On the other hand, [6] proposes a UCB1 [2] based algorithm for the allocation and provides a randomized mechanism similar to [4] to compute the payments which suffer high variation in payments. In this work, we design a deterministic MAB mechanism that achieves optimal regret similar to that of UCB1 with zero variance.

3. THE MODEL

There is a requester who seeks to allocate T homogeneous tasks among K crowd workers. Worker i ($i = 1, \dots, K$) has a fixed quality $q_i \in [0, 1]$ which is the probability with which worker i executes the task successfully. Due to heterogeneity among the tasks available at crowdsourcing platforms, the quality of a worker on a particular type of task is unknown to the requester and sometimes to the worker as well. A worker i incurs a cost $c_i \in [c_{\min}, c_{\max}]$ for completing the task and c_i is a private information of worker i. We assume that the qualities and costs do not change over time for homogeneous tasks that a requester seeks to get executed.

K	Number of crowd workers
T	Number of homogeneous tasks
$t \in \{1, \dots, T\}$	Running index of tasks
M	Reward to the requester for every successfully completed task
$q_i \in [0, 1]$	Quality of worker i
$c_i \in [c_{\min}, c_{\max}]$	Cost per task of worker i
c_{-i}	Cost vector of all workers other than i
$b_{i,t}$	Cost bid by worker i for task t
$b_{-i,t}$	Cost bid by workers other than i for task t
b_t	Cost bid vector of all the workers for task t
I_t	Worker allocated for task t
$\tau_t + 1$	Number of tasks allocated as a block to a worker from tasks t to $t + \tau_t$
$N_{i,t}$	Number of tasks allocated to worker i till tasks t
$S_{i,t}$	Number of tasks successfully completed by worker i till tasks t
h^t	History till tasks t of allocations and observed success i.e. $\{I_1, S_{I_1,1}, \dots, I_{t-1}, S_{I_{t-1},t-1}\}$
$p_{i,t}(b_t; h^t)$	Payment to worker i for task t with history h^t and cost bid vector b_t
$u_{i,t}(b_{i,t}, b_{-i,t}; h^t; c_i)$	Utility to worker i for task t with cost bid vector $(b_{i,t}, b_{-i,t})$, history h^t, and true cost c_i

Table 1: Notation Table

For each successfully completed task, the requester derives a reward of M, hence the expected reward of the requester is given by Mq_i, when the worker i is allocated a task. The requester would like to allocate the tasks so as to maximize the total expected reward. Since the qualities are unknown, in order to learn the qualities, the requester can allocate the tasks sequentially and can observe the qualities of the workers over the allocated tasks. Based on the learnt qualities over the previous tasks, the requester can compute allocations and payments for the future.

As the costs per task are private to the workers, we propose to use an auction for allocating tasks. Though the private cost of a worker does not change over time, his beliefs about his quality get updated. Therefore, a worker can update his bid to a different value for a task if he thinks it would give him better utility. Note that, inviting bids for every task t gives more flexibility to the workers. Let c_{-i} denote the private cost vector of all the workers other than i. Let $b_{i,t}$ be the bid by a worker i for a task t and $b_{-i,t}$ is the bid vector by the workers other than i. On completion of the task, the requester pays to the worker i, an amount $p_{i,t}$, if i is selected for the task t. The utility of a worker i for a task t with bid vector b_t and true valuation c_i is given as $u_{i,t}(b_t; h^t; c_i) = \mathbb{1}\{I_t(b_t; h^t) = i\}(p_{i,t}(b_t; h^t) - c_i)$. Here, I_t represents the index of the worker allocated the task t and h^t represents the history of all the allocations and the corresponding performances of the allocated workers in the past. Let $S_{i,t}$ denotes the reward of the worker i if he is allocated task t, then the history at task t is given as $h^t = \{(I_1, S_{I_1,1}), \dots, (I_{t-1}, S_{I_{t-1},t-1})\}$ and depends on the inherent quality of the workers.

A requester would like to update his beliefs about the qualities of the workers after completion of every task and select a worker for the next task based on updated beliefs. However, single task allocations followed by belief updates and invitation for bids involve considerable time overheads, moreover, the workers prefer receiving multiple tasks at a time. Our mechanism allows the requester to allocate a block of tasks without losing on optimality in learning. Let $0 \leq \tau_t \leq T - t$ denote the additional number of tasks allocated as a block starting from task t to $t + \tau_t$ (thus giving $\tau_t + 1$ tasks to the worker). If worker I_t is allocated a block of tasks from t to $t + \tau_t$, bids are not sought for next τ_t tasks. Thus, $b_{i,t'} = b_{i,t}$ $\forall i$, $\forall t' \in \{t, \dots, t + \tau_t\}$. After $\tau_t + 1$ tasks, empirical quality of the worker i is updated. Notations are provided in Table 1. We make the following key deviations from existing settings:

- Most of the literature in this space [5, 4] assumes that a strategic worker is fully aware of the future successes. This assumption leads to either higher regret or variance in the payments. In this work, a strategic worker is not cognizant of the future and has knowledge of only past allocations. However, the workers are aware of how a requester is learning and can manipulate their bids to maximize their utility with this information.
- Due to anonymity in crowdsourcing platforms, a worker does not have the knowledge of total number of tasks T available. Hence, he would not like to lose the allocations in the current rounds if the allocations result in positive utility.

We now define some properties that CrowdUCB satisfies in the settings considered.

Definition 1 ***Ex-Post Individual Rationality (EPIR):*** *A mechanism is said to be ex-post individually rational if each worker receives a non-negative utility for each task, irrespective of the history prior to this task and irrespective of the bids of other workers. That is,* $\forall i$, $\forall t$, $\forall h^t$, $\forall b_{-i,t}$,
$$u_{i,t}(c_i, b_{-i,t}; h^t; c_i) \geq 0, \ \forall c_i.$$

Definition 2 ***Ex-Post Incentive Compatibility (EPIC):*** *A mechanism is EPIC if for any worker i, bidding truthfully in all the rounds results in higher total utility as compared to non-truthful bidding in any round when the other workers are assumed to bid truthfully, i.e.* $\forall i$, $\forall c_{-i}$, $\forall c_i$, $\forall h^t$, $\forall b_{i,t}$,
$$\sum_{t=1}^{T} u_{i,t}(c_i, c_{-i}; h^t; c_i) \geq \sum_{t=1}^{T} u_{i,t}(b_{i,t}, c_{-i}; h^t; c_i).$$

Note that EPIC is a weaker notion than dominant strategy incentive compatibility where the other workers can bid different values in different rounds but it is stronger than Bayesian Nash incentive compatibility where a worker is truthful with respect to the expectation of other workers' valuations.

Let $u_{i,t}(b_{i,t}, c_{-i}; h^t; c_i; q_i)$ be the utility of worker i with bid $b_{i,t}$ for task t when he knows his true quality q_i. We will show that when workers' qualities are private knowledge then CrowdUCB is $\varepsilon-$EPIC which we define as follows:

Definition 3 ***$\varepsilon-$EPIC:***
A mechanism is said to be $\varepsilon-$EPIC if by misreporting bids in any round(s), no worker can gain more than ε in his total utility that he would have obtained by bidding truthfully in all the rounds when the other workers are assumed to bid truthfully. i.e. $\forall i$, $\forall c_{-i}$, $\forall c_i$, $\forall h^t$ and $\forall b_{i,t}$,

$$\mathbb{E}\left[\sum_{t=1}^{T} u_{i,t}(c_i, c_{-i}; h^t; c_i; q_i)\right] + \varepsilon \geq \mathbb{E}\left[\sum_{t=1}^{T} u_{i,t}(b_{i,t}, c_{-i}; h^t; c_i; q_i)\right].$$

Here, expectation is taken over success realizations given true qualities.

Definition 4 ***Asymptotically EPIC:***
We say that a mechanism is asymptotically EPIC when per round utility gain over truthful bidding for every worker i goes to zero with number of rounds to infinity when other workers report truthfully, i.e. $\forall i$, $\forall c_{-i}$, $\forall c_i$, $\forall h^t$, $\forall b_{i,t}$.

$$\lim_{T\to\infty} \frac{1}{T}\mathbb{E}\left[\sum_{t=1}^{T} \left(u_{i,t}(b_{i,t}, c_{-i}; h^t; c_i) - u_{i,t}(c_i, c_{-i}; h^t; c_i)\right)\right] = 0.$$

Definition 5 ***Regret in Social Welfare:*** *Social welfare is given by the sum of the valuation of all the workers and the requester. The valuation of the requester and a worker i is given by Mq_i and $-c_i$ respectively, if the worker i is given the task t. The regret in social welfare of an algorithm A is defined as the difference in the social welfare achieved by an optimal algorithm that knows the true qualities and the social welfare by the algorithm A that is learning the qualities. When the workers bid truthfully,*

$$R(A) = T(Mq_{i^*} - c_{i^*}) - \sum_{t=1}^{T}\sum_{i=1}^{K} \mathbb{1}\{I_t = i\}(Mq_i - c_i),$$

where, $i^* \in \arg\max_i (Mq_i - c_i)$.

Here, $\mathbb{1}\{I_t = i\}$, is an indicator variable which is 1 if $I_t = i$ and 0 otherwise. For the rest of the paper, whenever we talk about regret, we will be referring to regret in social welfare. Social welfare is helpful for many socially desirable outcomes, for example, a government procuring work from crowd for creating job opportunities or government seeking help from the volunteers through crowdsourcing of disaster relief. Moreover, for revenue maximization, it is shown that the revenue of social welfare maximizing mechanism approaches to that of revenue maximizing mechanism with large number of bidders [9]. Further, mechanisms with social welfare maximization are simple and more intuitive. We say that an algorithm A has *sub-linear* regret if the regret of the algorithm is sub-linear in the number of tasks i.e. $R(A) = o(T)$. We now propose our mechanism CrowdUCB that has sub-linear regret of $O(\ln T)$. CrowdUCB is EPIR and EPIC when workers are unaware of their qualities. Further, when workers know their qualities but the mechanism still learns the qualities of the workers, CrowdUCB is EPIR and $\varepsilon-$EPIC where ε is sub-linear in the number of tasks T hence is asymptotically EPIC.

4. PROPOSED MECHANISM: CROWDUCB

A deterministic mechanism, $\mathcal{M}_t(b_t; h^t) = \langle I_t, \tau_t, p_{I_t}\rangle$, at any time t, allocates $\tau_t + 1$ number of tasks to a worker I_t, and pays an amount $p_{I_t} = \sum_{s=t}^{s=t+\tau_t} p_{I_t,s}$. The allocated worker I_t, the number of tasks $\tau_t + 1$ and the payment p_{I_t} depend on the bid vector b_t and history h^t obtained so far. In the rest of the paper, we will not show this dependence explicitly if it is clear from the context. The next auction happens after $\tau_t + 1$ tasks are completed and thus, $b_{i,s} = b_{i,t}$, $\forall i$, $\forall s$, s.t. $t \leq s \leq \tau_t + t$. A new bid vector $b_{t+\tau_t+1}$ is obtained from the workers for task $t + \tau_t + 1$. *CrowdUCB* uses some learning bounds on qualites to make allocations and payments for the current task. These bounds are shown in Table 2.

$\hat{q}_{i,t} = \frac{S_{i,t}}{N_{i,t}}$	Estimate of quality q_i till tasks t
$\hat{q}^{+}_{i,t} = \hat{q}_{i,t} + \sqrt{\frac{2\ln(t)}{N_{i,t}}}$	Upper confidence bound (UCB) on the quality of the worker i till tasks t.
$\hat{q}^{+\bar{\rightarrow}\tau}_{i,t} = \frac{S_{i,t}}{N_{i,t+\tau}} + \sqrt{\frac{2\ln(t+\tau)}{N_{i,t+\tau}}}$	UCB on the quality of worker i if he fails on all the tasks from $t, t+1, \ldots, t+\tau$
$\hat{q}^{+\rightarrow\tau}_{i,t} = \frac{S_{i,t}}{N_{i,t}} + \sqrt{\frac{2\ln(t+\tau)}{N_{i,t}}}$	UCB on the quality of worker i when he does not get any task from t to $t+\tau$
$\hat{q}^{+\tilde{\rightarrow}\tau}_{i,t} = \frac{S_{i,t}}{N_{i,t}} + \sqrt{\frac{2\ln(t+\tau)}{N_{i,t+\tau}}}$	UCB on the quality of worker i when he gets tasks from t to $t+\tau$ and he performs the tasks with same empirical estimate as at time t

Table 2: Learning Bounds on Qualities

4.1 Allocation Rule

For a task t, the allocation rule selects a worker I_t and the number of additional tasks, τ_t, to be allocated to him. The allocation rule is designed keeping in view of the following two important yet conflicting objectives.

Learning: Let, $\hat{q}^{+}_{i,t} = \hat{q}_{i,t} + \sqrt{\frac{2\ln(t)}{N_{i,t}}}$ be the upper confidence bound (UCB) on the quality of the worker i. Here, $N_{i,t}$ is the number of tasks allocated to the worker i till task t and $\hat{q}_{i,t}$ is the empirical estimate of q_i. A worker I_t for the task t is selected as:

$$I_t \in \arg\max_i (M\hat{q}^{+}_{i,t} - b_{i,t}), \tag{1}$$

We refer, $M\hat{q}^{+}_{i,t} - b_{i,t}$ as the UCB index of the worker i. Note that for the fixed values of M and c_i, UCB index on $Mq_i - c_i$ can be computed by upper bounding q_i which is the only stochastic parameter. Hence, UCB index is defined accordingly. Thus, the allocation rule selects a worker I_t having the highest UCB index. The above strategy of optimism in the face of uncertainty is crucial for learning.

Block allocations: As already stated, though it is beneficial for the requester to allocate one task at a time, in this work, we propose the block allocation of tasks to reduce auction overheads. We propose a block size of $\tau_t + 1$ while allocating the task t. Here, $\tau_t + 1$ is the smallest block of tasks such that the worker I_t remains optimal even when he fails on every task in this block. Let $S_{i,t}$ denote the number of successfully completed tasks till task t (This implies, $\hat{q}_{i,t} = \frac{S_{i,t}}{N_{i,t}}$). Let $\hat{q}^{+\bar{\rightarrow}\tau}_{i,t} = \frac{S_{i,t}}{N_{i,t+\tau}} + \sqrt{\frac{2\ln(t+\tau)}{N_{i,t+\tau}}}$, denote UCB

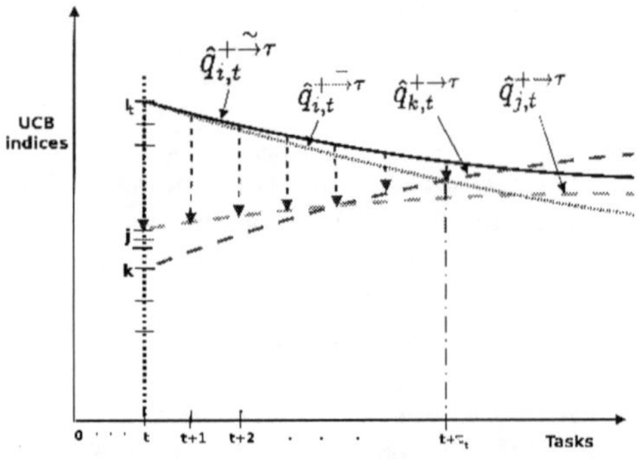

Figure 1: Allocation block given to the worker I_t from tasks t to $t+\tau_t$. The dotted arrows represent the utility to worker I_t from tasks t to $t+\tau_t$.

on quality of a worker i if he fails on all the tasks from $t, t+1, \ldots, t+\tau$. Similarly, let $\hat{q}_{i,t}^{+\rightarrow\tau} = \frac{S_{i,t}}{N_{i,t}} + \sqrt{\frac{2\ln(t+\tau)}{N_{i,t}}}$ denote UCB on quality of a worker i when he does not get any task from t to $t+\tau$. Then τ_t, the block size at the allocation of the task t is defined as:

$$\tau_t = \underset{0 \leq \tau \leq T-t}{\arg\max} \left\{ \begin{array}{l} M\hat{q}_{i,t}^{+\rightarrow\tau} - b_{i,t} \leq M\hat{q}_{I_t,t}^{+\bar{\rightarrow}\tau} - b_{I_t,t}, \\ \forall i \neq I_t \end{array} \right\}. \quad (2)$$

Thus, τ_t represents the maximum number of additional tasks that can be given to worker I_t even if he fails to successfully complete the tasks in the future while UCB indices on qualities of other workers evolve according to $\hat{q}_{i,t}^{+\rightarrow\tau}$. Figure 1 demonstrate this scheme pictorially.

4.2 Properties of the Allocation Rule

We first make the following observation.

Observation 1: $\forall t > e,\ t \geq n \geq 0, \tau \geq 0,\ \frac{\ln(t)}{n} \geq \frac{\ln(t+\tau)}{n+\tau}$.

PROOF. $t \geq n$ and $\ln(t) \geq 1 \implies \tau\frac{\ln(t)}{n} \geq \frac{\tau}{n} \geq \frac{\tau}{t}$. Using, $\forall x > -1,\ x \geq \ln(1+x)$, we get $\frac{\tau}{t} \geq \ln(1+\frac{\tau}{t})$. Thus,

$$\frac{\tau\ln(t)}{n} \geq \ln(1+\frac{\tau}{t}) \geq \ln(t+\tau) - \ln(t)$$

$$\implies \ln(t)(1+\frac{\tau}{n}) \geq \ln(t+\tau) \implies \frac{\ln(t)}{n} \geq \frac{\ln(t+\tau)}{n+\tau}. \square$$

Let, $\Gamma^j_{i,t,b_t}(\tau) = M\hat{q}_{j,t}^{+\rightarrow\tau} - b_{j,t} - M\hat{q}_{i,t}^{+\bar{\rightarrow}\tau} + b_{i,t}$. Intuitively, this term captures minimum loss in social welfare if the mechanism allocates next $\tau+1$ tasks to a worker j instead of i with the bid vector b_t. We will drop b_t from the notation if it clear from the context. From Equation (2), $\Gamma^j_{I_t,t}(\tau) \leq 0,\ \forall j \neq I_t,\ \forall \tau,\ 0 \leq \tau \leq \tau_t$. The following Lemma shows that $\forall j,\ \Gamma^j_{I_t,t}(\tau)$ increases monotonically with τ.

Lemma 1 *The term $\Gamma^j_{I_t,t}(\tau)$ increases with τ, $\forall j \neq I_t$. That is, $\Gamma^j_{I_t,t}(\tau+s) \geq \Gamma^j_{I_t,t}(\tau)$, $\forall j \neq I_t$, $\forall s \geq 0$.*

PROOF. From the definition of $\hat{q}_{i,t}^{+\rightarrow\tau}$, $\forall i$,

$$\hat{q}_{i,t}^{+\rightarrow\tau+s} \geq \hat{q}_{i,t}^{+\rightarrow\tau}. \quad (3)$$

Applying Observation 1, $\sqrt{\frac{2\ln(t+\tau+s)}{N_{I_t,t+\tau+s}}} \leq \sqrt{\frac{2\ln(t+\tau)}{N_{I_t,t+\tau}}}$ and since $\frac{S_{I_t,t}}{N_{I_t,t+\tau+s}} \leq \frac{S_{I_t,t}}{N_{I_t,t+\tau}}$,

$$\hat{q}_{I_t,t}^{+\bar{\rightarrow}\tau+s} \leq \hat{q}_{I_t,t}^{+\bar{\rightarrow}\tau}. \quad (4)$$

Using the above two inequalities,

$$\Gamma^j_{I_t,t}(\tau+s) = M\hat{q}_{j,t}^{+\rightarrow\tau+s} - b_{j,t} - M\hat{q}_{I_t,t}^{+\bar{\rightarrow}\tau+s} + b_{I_t,t}$$
$$\geq M\hat{q}_{j,t}^{+\rightarrow\tau} - b_{j,t} - M\hat{q}_{I_t,t}^{+\bar{\rightarrow}\tau} + b_{I_t,t} \geq \Gamma^j_{I_t,t}(\tau). \square$$

Thus, $\forall \tau, s,\ \Gamma^j_{I_t,t}(\tau) > 0 \implies \Gamma^j_{I_t,t}(\tau+s) > 0$. Therefore, for deciding a block size τ_t, it is enough to take the first value of τ such that $\Gamma^j_{I_t,t}(\tau+1) > 0$ for some worker j.

To achieve incentive compatibility, it is important that the allocation rule satisfies monotonicity condition with respect to the cost [15]. The following Lemma ensures this property:

Lemma 2 *The number of allocated tasks to any worker i for any task t, monotonically decreases with his reported cost if the costs of the other workers are fixed.*

PROOF. Consider two bids by a worker i, $b^+_{i,t} > b_{i,t}$ and the corresponding bid vectors be b^+_t and b_t respectively. From Equation (1), $I_t(b_t) \neq i \implies I_t(b^+_t) \neq i$, thus, satisfying monotonicity condition trivially. If $I_t(b_t) = i$ but $I_t(b^+_t) \neq i$, then there is nothing to prove. Let k and k' denote the additional number of tasks, worker i gets with bid $b_{i,t}$ and $b^+_{i,t}$ respectively. From Equation (2),

$$k = \underset{0 \leq \tau \leq T-t}{\arg\max} \left\{ \Gamma^j_{i,t,b_t}(\tau) \leq 0, \forall j \neq i \right\},$$
$$\implies \Gamma^j_{i,t,b_t}(k+1) > 0 \text{ for some } j \neq i.$$

Note that for a fixed τ and j, $\Gamma^j_{i,t,b_t}(\tau)$ monotonically increases with $b_{i,t}$ when all the other bids are fixed. Thus, $\Gamma^j_{i,t,b^+_t}(k+1) \geq \Gamma^j_{i,t,b_t}(k+1) > 0 \implies k' \leq k$. $\square$

4.3 Payment Scheme

We use externality based payment which also accounts for the loss of learning the qualities of the other workers. Let $j^\tau \in \arg\max_{j \neq I_t}(M\hat{q}_{j,t}^{+\rightarrow\tau} - b_{j,t})$, be the second best worker with the current beliefs about the qualities and the reported bids. Let, $\hat{q}_{I_t,t}^{+\tilde{\rightarrow}\tau} = \frac{S_{i,t}}{N_{i,t}} + \sqrt{\frac{2\ln(t+\tau)}{N_{i,t+\tau}}}$ be the UCB on the quality of worker i when he gets tasks from t to $t+\tau$ and he performs the tasks with same empirical estimate as at time t. Then, the payment to the worker I_t is the bid required by him to match the utility of the requester by assigning the task $t+\tau$ to the worker j^τ by performing the future tasks with the same quality. The payment for task $t+\tau$, with, $0 \leq \tau \leq \tau_t$ is given as:

$$p_{I_t,t+\tau}(b_{i,t}, b_{-i,t}; h^t) = M\hat{q}_{I_t,t}^{+\tilde{\rightarrow}\tau} - \left(M\hat{q}_{j^\tau,t}^{+\rightarrow\tau} - b_{j^\tau,t}\right). \quad (5)$$

To avoid notation clutter, we will use index j instead of j^τ, but it should be clear from the context that this index depends on the value of τ. We make an implicit assumption that each worker genuinely submits an assigned task and honestly performs the task. So, CrowdUCB offers a payment to a worker for each allocated task even if the submission is not successful. Not performing the task honestly, may affect the learning of the algorithm and hence more sophisticated analysis may be needed. Moreover, since we are interested in low cost tasks this assumption holds true in many practical situations. The mechanism can be easily modified to the case where a payment is not offered to a worker in the event the worker fails to submit the task successfully.

5. PROPERTIES OF CrowdUCB: UNKNOWN QUALITY SETTING

When the workers are unaware of their true qualities and learn their qualities as the mechanism progresses, we show that CrowdUCB is EPIR (Theorem 1), EPIC (Theorem 2), and achieves logarithmic regret (Theorem 3).

Theorem 1 *CrowdUCB is EPIR.*

PROOF. We need to prove that $\forall i$, $\forall t$, $\forall h^t$, $\forall b_{-i,t}$, $u_{i,t}(c_i, b_{-i,t}; h^t; c_i) \geq 0$. If $I_t \neq i$, $u_{i,t}(c_i, b_{-i,t}; h^t; c_i) = 0$ and hence nothing to prove. If $I_t = i$, $u_{i,t}(c_i, b_{-i,t}; h^t; c_i) = -c_i + p_{i,t}(c_i, b_{-i,t}; h^t)$. Hence it is enough to prove that,

$$p_{I_t,t+\tau}(c_{I_t}, b_{-I_t,t}; h^t) - c_{I_t} \geq 0 \ , \forall \tau, \ 0 \leq \tau \leq \tau_t.$$

CrowdUCB allocation rule is designed such that, $\forall j \neq I_t, \forall \tau \in \{0, 1, 2, \ldots, \tau_t\}, \forall b_{j,t}, \ \Gamma^j_{I_t,t,b_t}(\tau) \leq 0$. This leads to the following inequalities: $\forall\, j \neq I_t, \forall\, \tau \in \{0, 1, \ldots, \tau_t\}$,

$$M\hat{q}^{+\to\tau}_{j,t} - b_{j,t} - M\hat{q}^{+\overset{-}{\to}\tau}_{I_t,t} + c_{I_t} \leq 0$$

$$\implies c_{I_t} \leq M\hat{q}^{+\overset{-}{\to}\tau}_{I_t,t} + b_{j,t} - M\hat{q}^{+\to\tau}_{j,t}$$

$$\implies c_{I_t} \leq M\hat{q}^{+\overset{\sim}{\to}\tau}_{I_t,t} + b_{j,t} - M\hat{q}^{+\to\tau}_{j,t}$$

$$(\text{As, } \hat{q}^{+\overset{\sim}{\to}\tau}_{I_t,t} = \tfrac{S_{I_t}}{N_{I_t}} + \sqrt{\tfrac{2\ln(t+\tau)}{N_{I_t}+\tau}} \geq \tfrac{S_{I_t}}{N_{I_t}+\tau} + \sqrt{\tfrac{2\ln(t+\tau)}{N_{I_t}+\tau}} = \hat{q}^{+\overset{-}{\to}\tau}_{I_t,t})$$

$$\implies c_{I_t} \leq p_{I_t,t+\tau}(c_{I_t}, b_{-i,t}; h^t) \qquad \text{(From Equation (5)).}$$

□

We first make following observation before proving that CrowdUCB is EPIC.

Observation 2: If tasks t to $t + k_t$ are allocated to worker i, then $\forall j \neq i$, $\forall \tau$, $0 \leq \tau \leq k_t$ following holds: $\hat{q}^{+\to k_t}_{j,t} = \hat{q}^{+\to k_t-\tau}_{j,t+\tau}$

PROOF. Since tasks t to $t + k_t$ are given to worker i and not to worker j, $S_{j,t} = S_{j,t+\tau}$ and $N_{j,t} = N_{j,t+\tau}$. Thus, the observation is immediate from the definition of $\hat{q}^{+\to\tau}_{j,t}$. □

Theorem 2 *CrowdUCB is EPIC when the workers have the same beliefs about their qualities as the requester and do not know the value of T.*

PROOF. We need to prove that $\forall i$, $\forall c_{-i}$, $\forall c_i$, $\forall h^t$, $\forall b_{i,t}$

$$\sum_{t=1}^{T} u_{i,t}(c_i, c_{-i}; h^t; c_i) \geq \sum_{t=1}^{T} u_{i,t}(b_{i,t}, c_{-i}; h^t; c_i). \qquad (6)$$

We will show that for any task t, it is not beneficial for a worker to underbid or overbid even after considering the future utility gains. For a task t, there are two possibilities of manipulation for the worker i,

(I) *underbidding:* $b_{i,t} < c_i$

(II) *overbidding:* $b_{i,t} > c_i$.

Let $k_t, k'_t \geq 0$ denote the number of tasks allocated to the worker i with bids c_i and $b_{i,t}$ respectively. We will prove that non-truthful bidding results in lesser utility for all tasks from t to $\max(t+k_t-1, t+k'_t-1)$, thus proving Equation (6).

Underbidding

For this case, $k'_t \geq k_t$ from Lemma 2.

Case 1: $\mathbf{k_t = 0}$: That is $I_t \neq i$ if everybody bids truthfully. If $k'_t = 0$, there is nothing to prove. If $k'_t > 0$, $\forall\tau$, s.t, $0 \leq \tau \leq k'_t - 1$: $u_{i,t+\tau}(b_{i,t}, c_{-i}; h^t; c_i) = -c_i + M\hat{q}^{+\overset{\sim}{\to}\tau}_{i,t} - M\hat{q}^{+\to\tau}_{j,t} + c_j$, with $j = \arg\max_{j\neq i} M\hat{q}^{+\to\tau}_{j,t} - c_j$. Moreover, since $k_t = 0$, $\exists l$ s.t. $M\hat{q}^{+}_{i,t} - c_i \leq M\hat{q}^{+}_{l,t} - c_l \leq M\hat{q}^{+\to\tau}_{l,t} - c_l \leq M\hat{q}^{+\to\tau}_{j,t} - c_j$. From Observation 1, $\hat{q}^{+\overset{\sim}{\to}\tau}_{i,t} \leq \hat{q}^{+}_{i,t} \implies u_{i,t+\tau}(b_{i,t}, c{-}i; h^t; c_i) \leq 0 \leq u_{i,t+\tau}(c_i, c_{-i}; h^t; c_i)$. The later inequality follows from the EPIR property.

Case 2: $\mathbf{k_t > 0}$: Since the payment to the worker i is independent of his bid, $\forall\tau$, with $0 \leq \tau \leq k_t - 1$: $u_{i,t+\tau}(b_{i,t}, c_{-i}; h^t; c_i) = u_{i,t+\tau}(c_i, c_{-i}; h^t; c_i)$. If $k'_t = k_t$, Equation (6) holds true. Let $k = k'_t - k_t > 0$. In this case, we will prove that $\forall\tau$, $0 \leq \tau \leq k-1$, $u_{i,t+k_t+\tau}(b_{i,t}, c_{-i}; h^t; c_i) = u_{i,t+k_t+\tau}(c_i, c_{-i}; h^{t+k_t}; c_i)$ if worker i beliefs over his quality is same as that of the requester. Let, $s^{k_t} = \hat{q}_{i,t} * k_t$ denotes the belief of a worker i about the number of successes he will get in alloted k_t tasks. If truthful bidding again at $t + k_t$ results positive number of allocations for worker i then,

$$
\begin{aligned}
&u_{i,t+k_t+\tau}(b_{i,t}, c_{-i}; h^t; c_i)\\
&= -c_i + M\hat{q}^{+\overset{\sim}{\to}k_t+\tau}_{i,t} - M\hat{q}^{+\to k_t+\tau}_{j,t} + c_j\\
&= -c_i + M\left(\frac{S_{i,t}}{N_{i,t}} + \sqrt{\frac{2\ln(t+k_t+\tau)}{N_{i,t}+k_t+\tau}}\right) - M\hat{q}^{+\to k_t+\tau}_{j,t} + c_j\\
&= -c_i + M\left(\frac{S_{i,t}+s^{k_t}}{N_{i,t}+k_t} + \sqrt{\frac{2\ln(t+k_t+\tau)}{N_{i,t}+k_t+\tau}}\right) - M\hat{q}^{+\to k_t+\tau}_{j,t} + c_j
\end{aligned}
$$

Since worker i believes that his estimated quality will remain the same as t i.e. $\hat{q}_{i,t} = \hat{q}_{i,t+k_t}$, thus:

$$
\begin{aligned}
u_{i,t+k_t+\tau}(b_{i,t}, c_{-i}; h^t; c_i) &= -c_i + M\hat{q}^{+\overset{\sim}{\to}\tau}_{i,t+k_t} - M\hat{q}^{+\to k_t+\tau}_{j,t} + c_j\\
&= -c_i + M\hat{q}^{+\overset{\sim}{\to}\tau}_{i,t+k_t} - M\hat{q}^{+\to\tau}_{j,t+k_t} + c_j\\
&\qquad\qquad \text{(From Observation 2)}\\
&= u_{i,t+k_t+\tau}(c_i, c_{-i}; h^{t+k_t}; c_i).
\end{aligned}
$$

However, if truthful bidding again at $t + k_t$ results in zero number of allocations for worker i then the arguments go similar to case 1.

Overbidding

For this case, $k'_t \leq k_t$ from Lemma 2.

Case 1: $\mathbf{k_t = 0}$: This implies $k'_t = 0$ and there is nothing to prove.

Case 2: $\mathbf{k_t > 0}$: If $k'_t = 0$, then from Theorem 1, $u_{i,t+\tau}(c_i, c_{-i}; h^t; c_i) \geq 0 \ \forall\tau$, $0 \leq \tau \leq k_t - 1$. However, it may happen that by overbidding, the worker i loses initial allocations which goes to another worker say j, thus decreasing the UCB index of worker j. In this case, if the payment made to the worker i when he gets allocation for later tasks depends on the UCB index of worker j then the utility of the worker i for those tasks can increase. However, since the worker i is unaware of the number of remaining tasks, he will prefer not to lose the confirmed allocations with positive utility for small gain in utility for future tasks which may not happen. Thus, overbidding does not benefit the worker. If $k'_t = k_t$, then $u_{i,t+\tau}(c_i, c_{-i}; h^t; c_i) = u_{i,t+\tau}(b_{i,t}, c_{-i}; h^t; c_i)$ $\forall\tau$, $0 \leq \tau \leq k_t - 1$, as the payment does not depend on the bid of the worker i. If $k'_t < k_t$, then $\forall\tau$, $0 \leq \tau \leq k - 1$, $u_{i,t+k_t+\tau}(b_{i,t+k_t}, c_{-i}; h^{t+k_t}; c_i) = u_{i,t+k_t+\tau}(c_i, c_{-i}; h^t; c_i)$ from Case 2 of Underbidding using similar arguments. □

Theorem 3 *The allocation induced by CrowdUCB is same as the allocation induced by UCB1. This leads to the social welfare regret of CrowdUCB to be $O(\ln T)$.*

PROOF. Since, CrowdUCB is EPIC, we assume that all the workers bid truthfully for every task. Using induction, we will prove that for any task t, an agent I_t is selected by CrowdUCB if and only if he is selected by UCB1. For task $t = 1$, the condition is trivially satisfied as both UCB1 and CrowdUCB allocates in round robin fashion to get first estimates. By induction hypothesis, workers selected by CrowdUCB and UCB1 till tasks $t-1$ are same. For task t, UCB1 selects the worker I_t with highest UCB index. Since the workers selected by UCB1 and CrowdUCB for previous tasks were same, UCB indices of all the workers at t remain same. If bidding happens for task t then CrowdUCB will also select worker with highest UCB index i.e. I_t. If bidding does not happen at task t and CrowdUCB selects agent $j \neq I_t$ then for some previous task s, we have: $M\hat{q}_{j,s}^{+\rightarrow t-s} - c_j \geq M\hat{q}_{I_t,s}^{+\rightarrow t-s} - c_{I_t}$. But, this would mean $M\hat{q}_{j,t}^{+} - c_j \geq M\hat{q}_{I_t,t}^{+} - c_{I_t}$ (assuming there exists a single agent with highest UCB otherwise we would break the ties in similar way for both the algorithms) thus contradicting the fact that I_t has the highest UCB index at t. Thus, $j = I_t$ and the allocation induced by CrowdUCB is same as UCB1. Hence, CrowdUCB and UCB1 achieve same regret. □

6. PROPERTIES OF CrowdUCB: KNOWN QUALITY SETTING

We now show that when the workers are aware of their own qualities but do not know qualities of other workers then they can manipulate the learning of the requester by non-truthful bidding. However, when the workers do not know the number of tasks a requester has, then CrowdUCB is ε−EPIC under the assumption that at any round t, maximum block size τ_t does not exceed some constant B. The parameter ε depends on the total number of tasks and and is sub-linear in T. As a corollary, we get that CrowdUCB is asymptotically EPIC.

Theorem 4 *CrowdUCB is ε−EPIC with $\varepsilon = \sqrt{2}MB(\ln(T))^{\frac{3}{2}}$.*

PROOF. Let, worker i gets $k_t^{'}, k_t$ tasks with bid $b_{i,t}$ and c_i respectively. We look at underbidding ($b_{i,t} < c_i$) and overbidding ($b_{i,t} > c_i$) cases separately and first bound the gain in utility $\varepsilon_{i,t}$ by non-truthful bidding.

Underbidding($k_t^{'} \geq k_t$)

Case 1:$k_t = 0$ **:** If $k_t^{'} = 0$ then $i \neq I_t$ in both the cases, hence utility in both the cases is zero. If $k_t^{'} > 0$ then from Theorem 2 case 1 of underbidding, worker i will get negative utility for tasks t to $t + k_t^{'} - 1$ as the utility of a worker for any task depends only on the learnt quality by the requester and not on his true quality. However, he may improve his learning by getting negative utility in initial rounds so as to increase his future utility. Since, the worker is unaware of the total number of tasks, he would not risk to incur loss in immediate utility.

Case 2:$k_t > 0$**:** If $k_t = k_t^{'}$, then the utility from tasks t to $t+k_t-1$ is same in both cases. If $k_t^{'} > k_t$, at task $t+k_t$ there would be one more auction with truthful bidding. As worker i knows his true quality, his belief over quality about task $t+k_t$ would be $\frac{S_{i,t}+q_i k_t}{N_{i,t}+k_t}$. In this case the belief of a worker i about his utility for task $(t+k_t+\tau)$ $\forall\tau,\ 0 \leq \tau \leq k_t^{'} - k_t$ is given as:

$$
\begin{aligned}
&u_{i,t+k_t+\tau}(c_i, c_{-i}; h^t; c_i; q_i) \\
&= M\Big(\frac{S_{i,t}+q_i k_t}{N_{i,t}+k_t} + \sqrt{\frac{2ln(t+k_t+\tau)}{N_{i,t}+k_t+\tau}}\Big) - c_i - M\hat{q}_{j,t+k_t}^{+\rightarrow\tau} - c_j.
\end{aligned}
$$

Whereas, with bid $b_{i,t}$, the utility for task $(t+k_t+\tau)$ $\forall\tau,\ 0 \leq \tau \leq k_t^{'} - k_t$ is given as:

$$
\begin{aligned}
&u_{i,t+k_t+\tau}(b_{i,t}, c_{-i}; h^t; c_i; q_i) \\
&= M\Big(\frac{S_{i,t}}{N_{i,t}} + \sqrt{\frac{2ln(t+k_t+\tau)}{N_{i,t}+k_t+\tau}}\Big) - c_i - M\hat{q}_{j,t}^{+\rightarrow k_t+\tau} - c_j
\end{aligned}
$$

Thus, gain in utility is given by:

$$
\begin{aligned}
&u_{i,t+k_t+\tau}(b_{i,t}, c_{-i}; h^t; c_i; q_i) - u_{i,t+k_t+\tau}(c_i, c_{-i}; h^t; c_i; q_i) \\
&= M\Big(\frac{S_{i,t}}{N_{i,t}} - \frac{S_{i,t}+q_i k_t}{N_{i,t}+k_t}\Big) \qquad \text{(From Observation 2)} \\
&= Mk_t\Big(\frac{S_{i,t} - q_i N_{i,t}}{N_{i,t}(N_{i,t}+k_t)}\Big)
\end{aligned}
$$

From Hoeffding's inequality, i.e., w.p. $\geq 1 - t^{-4}$ we have, $\frac{S_{i,t}}{N_{i,t}} - \sqrt{\frac{2\ln(t)}{N_{i,t}}} \leq q_i \leq \frac{S_{i,t}}{N_{i,t}} + \sqrt{\frac{2\ln(t)}{N_{i,t}}}$. Thus,

$$
\begin{aligned}
&u_{i,t+k_t+\tau}(b_{i,t}, c_{-i}; h^t; c_i; q_i) - u_{i,t+k_t+\tau}(c_i, c_{-i}; h^t; c_i; q_i) \\
&\leq Mk_t\left(\frac{S_{i,t} - \left(\frac{S_{i,t}}{N_{i,t}} - \sqrt{\frac{2\ln(t)}{N_{i,t}}}\right)N_{i,t}}{N_{i,t}(N_{i,t}+k_t)}\right) \qquad (\text{w.p. } \geq 1 - t^{-4}) \\
&= Mk_t\left(\frac{\sqrt{2\ln(t)}}{\sqrt{N_{i,t}}(N_{i,t}+k_t)}\right) \leq Mk_t\left(\frac{\sqrt{2\ln(T)}}{N_{i,t}^{\frac{3}{2}}}\right) \\
&\leq MB\left(\frac{\sqrt{2\ln(T)}}{N_{i,t}^{\frac{3}{2}}}\right). \qquad (\text{As, } k_t \leq B)
\end{aligned}
$$

Overbidding($k_t^{'} \leq k_t$)

Case 1: $k_t^{'} = k_t = 0$**:** Nothing to prove.

Case 2: $k_t^{'} < k_t$**:** If $k_t^{'} = 0$, then worker i loses initial allocations but can increase his future utility by affecting the learning of other workers. However, since the number of tasks is unknown to the worker, he will not risk to lose the immediate positive utility. When $k_t^{'} > 0$, utility of worker i from t to $t + k_t^{'} - 1$ is same. At task $t + k_t^{'}$, there would be one more auction in overbidding case. With known true quality q_i, worker i's belief about his quality at the end of $t+k_t^{'}$ tasks will be, $\frac{S_{i,t}+q_i k_t^{'}}{N_{i,t}+k_t^{'}}$. Thus, his belief over his utility from tasks $t + k_t^{'} + \tau\ \forall\ \tau\ s.t\ 0 < \tau < k_t - k_t^{'}$ by overbidding is given by:

$$
\begin{aligned}
&u_{i,t+k_t^{'}+\tau}(b_{i,t}, c_{-i}; h^t; c_i; q_i) \\
&= M\left(\frac{S_{i,t}+q_i k_t^{'}}{N_{i,t}+k_t^{'}} + \sqrt{\frac{2\ln(t+k_t^{'}+\tau)}{N_{i,t}+k_t^{'}+\tau}}\right) - c_i - M\hat{q}_{j,t+k_t^{'}}^{+\rightarrow\tau} - c_j
\end{aligned}
$$

With truthful bidding his utility is given by:

$$
\begin{aligned}
&u_{i,t+k_t^{'}+\tau}(c_i, c_{-i}; h^t; c_i; q_i) \\
&= M\left(\frac{S_{i,t}}{N_{i,t}} + \sqrt{\frac{2\ln(t+k_t^{'}+\tau)}{N_{i,t}+k_t^{'}+\tau}}\right) - c_i - M\hat{q}_{j,t}^{+\rightarrow\tau+k_t^{'}} - c_j
\end{aligned}
$$

Thus, the gain in utility is given by:

$$
\begin{aligned}
&u_{i,t+k_t^{'}+\tau}(b_{i,t}, c_{-i}; h^t; c_i; q_i) - u_{i,t+k_t^{'}+\tau}(c_i, c_{-i}; h^t; c_i; q_i) \\
&= M\left(\frac{S_{i,t}+q_i k_t^{'}}{N_{i,t}+k_t^{'}} - \frac{S_{i,t}}{N_{i,t}}\right) \\
&\qquad \text{(From Observation 2)}
\end{aligned}
$$

$$\le Mk_t' \left(\frac{\sqrt{2\ln(T)}}{N_{i,t}^{\frac{3}{2}}}\right) \qquad (\text{w.p. } \ge 1 - t^{-4})$$

$$\le MB\left(\frac{\sqrt{2\ln(T)}}{N_{i,t}^{\frac{3}{2}}}\right) \qquad (\text{As, } k_t' \le B)$$

Here, second last inequality follows from similar arguments presented in case 2 of underbidding and using other side of Hoeffding's inequality. Note that maximum gain in utility for any task t by a worker i is given by $M\hat{q}_{i,t}^{+\tilde{\to}\tau} - c_i - (M\hat{q}_{j,t}^{+\to\tau} - c_j) \le M + c_{\max}$. As qualities are bounded above by 1 and c_j by $c_{\max}$. We now bound the expected gain in utilities over time horizon T i.e.

$$\mathbb{E}\left[\sum_{t=1}^{T}(u_{i,t}(c_i, c_{-i}; h^t; c_i; q_i) - u_{i,t}(b_i, c_{-i}; h^t; c_i; q_i))\right]$$

$$\le MB\sqrt{2\ln(T)}\left(\sum_{t=1}^{T}\frac{1}{N_{i,t}^{\frac{3}{2}}}(1 - t^{-4})\right) + \sum_{t=1}^{T} t^{-4}(M + c_{\max})$$

$$\le MB\left(\sqrt{2\ln(T)}\ln(N_{i,t})\right) + \left(\frac{1}{3} + \frac{1}{3T^3}\right)(M + c_{\max})$$

$$\le \sqrt{2}MB\ln(T)^{\frac{3}{2}} + \left(\frac{1}{3} + \frac{1}{3T^3}\right)(M + c_{\max}) \qquad (N_{i,t} \le T,\ \forall\ t)$$

□

Since ε is sub-linear in T, we get the following Corollary:

Corollary 1 *CrowdUCB is asymptotically EPIC under known quality setting.*

Note that CrowdUCB remains to be EPIR in this setting since the proof of Theorem 1 for worker i uses his true cost and not the bid that may change based on the knowledge of true quality.

7. SIMULATIONS

In this section, we show via simulations that CrowdUCB achieves logarithmic regret with constants matching the regret of the UCB1 algorithm [2]. Further, randomized mechanisms such as in [4] lead to very high variance in payments.

For the simulations, we fix the number of workers K to be 10. For each worker i, a fixed quality q_i and a fixed cost c_i are drawn independently and uniformly from the interval $[0, 1]$. For each successfully completed task, the requester receives a reward of $M = 2$. Figure 2 shows the regret of CrowdUCB and UCB1 with the number of tasks taken on a logarithmic scale along the X-axis. As can be seen from the figure, regrets of CrowdUCB and UCB1 match exactly and show logarithmic behavior.

As an example of a randomized mechanism, we have implemented the mechanism in [4] by modifying the mechanism for a crowdsourcing setting with the value of resampling parameter μ as 0.1. For a fixed cost vector and fixed quality vector, we first generate an instance (that is, success realization) by fixing a $K \times T$ table, where each entry (i, t) represents the reward by the worker i if the worker had been allocated task t. The entries of success realization are filled by obtaining Bernoulli rewards, that is, the entry (i, t) is 1 with probability q_i and 0 with probability $(1 - q_i)$. Figure 3 shows that, for a fixed success realization, the randomized mechanism incurs high variance in the payments whereas CrowdUCB being a deterministic mechanism yields the same payment when the mechanism is invoked several times for a fixed instance. The total payment given to the workers is plotted over 1000 calls to the mechanisms for a fixed instance and the shaded area represents the payment between maximum and minimum payments given by the randomized mechanism.

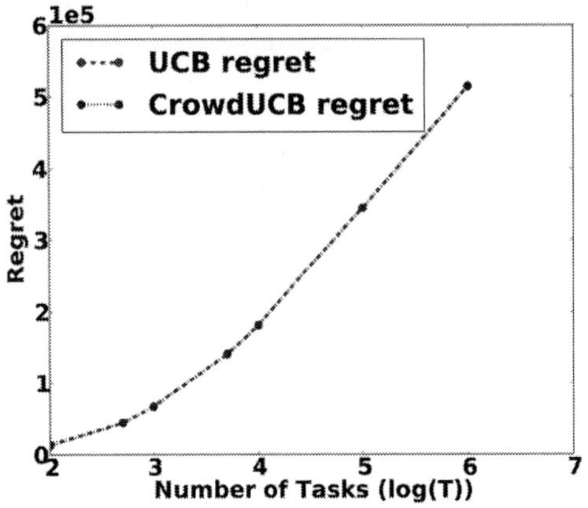

Figure 2: Regret of UCB1 and CrowdUCB on log scale of number of tasks.

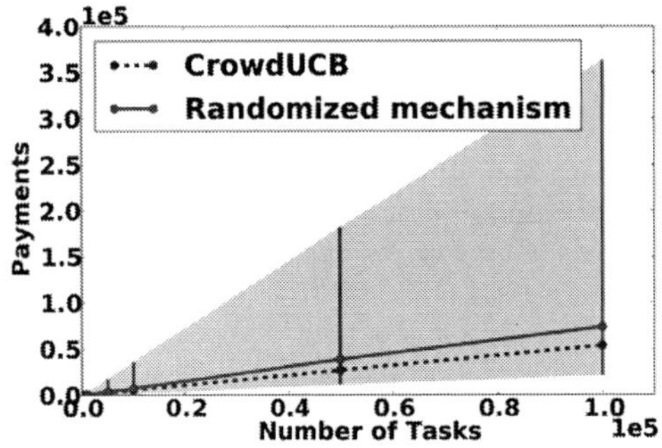

Figure 3: High variance in payments by a randomized mechanism for a fixed instance.

8. SUMMARY AND FUTURE DIRECTIONS

In this paper, we proposed a deterministic, ex-post individually rational and ex-post incentive compatible MAB mechanism that allows block allocations, and permits the workers to change their bids as the time progresses. This work is an important step towards designing a regret minimizing, deterministic MAB mechanisms for crowdsourcing and other general procurement settings. The work can be extended to a setting where workers' valuations also change over time. In this case, the optimal worker will change and hence one has to invoke contextual bandits. The other extension could be to design a deterministic mechanism with low regret that satisfies a stronger notion of truthfulness like dominant strategy incentive compatibility.

REFERENCES

[1] I. Abraham, O. Alonso, V. Kandylas, and A. Slivkins. Adaptive crowdsourcing algorithms for the bandit

survey problem. In *Conference On Learning Theory*, volume 30 of *JMLR Proceedings*, pages 882–910. JMLR.org, 2013.

[2] P. Auer, N. Cesa-Bianchi, and P. Fischer. Finite-time analysis of the multiarmed bandit problem. *Machine Learning*, 47(2-3):235–256, May 2002.

[3] M. Babaioff, S. Dughmi, R. Kleinberg, and A. Slivkins. Dynamic pricing with limited supply. In *Thirteenth ACM Conference on Electronic Commerce*, pages 74–91. ACM, 2012.

[4] M. Babaioff, R. D. Kleinberg, and A. Slivkins. Truthful mechanisms with implicit payment computation. In *Eleventh ACM Conference on Electronic Commerce*, pages 43–52. ACM, 2010.

[5] M. Babaioff, Y. Sharma, and A. Slivkins. Characterizing truthful multi-armed bandit mechanisms: extended abstract. In *Tenth ACM Conference on Electronic Commerce*, pages 79–88. ACM, 2009.

[6] S. Bhat, S. Jain, S. Gujar, and Y. Narahari. An optimal bidimensional multi-armed bandit auction for multi-unit procurement. In *Fourteenth International Conference on Autonomous Agents and Multiagent Systems*, pages 1789–1790, 2015.

[7] A. Biswas, S. Jain, D. Mandal, and Y. Narahari. A truthful budget feasible multi-armed bandit mechanism for crowdsourcing time critical tasks. In *Fourteenth International Conference on Autonomous Agents and Multiagent Systems*, pages 1101–1109, 2015.

[8] S. Bubeck and N. Cesa-Bianchi. Regret analysis of stochastic and nonstochastic multi-armed bandit problems. *Foundations and Trends in Machine Learning*, 5(1):1–122, 2012.

[9] J. Bulow and P. Klemperer. Auctions versus negotiations. *The American Economic Review*, 86(1):180–194, 1996.

[10] N. Devanur and S. Kakade. The price of truthfulness for pay-per-click auctions. In *Tenth ACM Conference on Electronic Commerce*, pages 99–106, 2009.

[11] M. Feldman, N. Immorlica, B. Lucier, T. Roughgarden, and V. Syrgkanis. The price of anarchy in large games. *CoRR*, abs/1503.04755, 2015.

[12] C. J. Ho, S. Jabbari, and J. W. Vaughan. Adaptive task assignment for crowdsourced classification. In *International Conference on Machine Learning*, volume 28, pages 534–542, 2013.

[13] S. Li, M. Mahdian, and R. P. McAfee. Value of learning in sponsored search auctions. In *Internet and Network Economics - 6th International Workshop, WINE 2010, Stanford, CA, USA, December 13-17, 2010. Proceedings*, pages 294–305, 2010.

[14] A. Mas-Colell, M. D. Whinston, and J. R. Green. *Microeconomic Theory*. Oxford University Press, 1995.

[15] R. B. Myerson. Optimal auction design. *Mathematics of Operations Research*, 6(1):pp. 58–73, 1981.

[16] Y. Singer and M. Mittal. Pricing mechanisms for crowdsourcing markets. In *Twenty Second Internation World Wide Web Conference*, pages 1157–1166, 2013.

[17] A. Singla and A. Krause. Truthful incentives in crowdsourcing tasks using regret minimization mechanisms. In *Twenty Second International World Wide Web Conference*, pages 1167–1178, 2013.

[18] A. Slivkins and J. W. Vaughan. Online decision making in crowdsourcing markets: Theoretical challenges. *SIGecom Exchanges*, 12(2), December 2013. Position paper and survey.

[19] L. Tran-Thanh, A. C. Chapman, A. Rogers, and N. R. Jennings. Knapsack based optimal policies for budget-limited multi-armed bandits. In *Twenty-Sixth Conference on Artificial Intelligence*, pages 1134–1140, 2012.

[20] L. Tran-Thanh, M. Venanzi, A. Rogers, and N. R. Jennings. Efficient budget allocation with accuracy guarantees for crowdsourcing classification tasks. In *Twelfth International Conference on Autonomous Agents and Multiagent Systems*, pages 901–908, May 2013.

[21] C. A. Wilkens and B. Sivan. Single-call mechanisms. In *Proceedings of the 13th ACM Conference on Electronic Commerce*, pages 946–963, New York, NY, USA, 2012. ACM.

Budgetary Effects on Pricing Equilibrium in Online Markets

Allan Borodin
University of Toronto
Toronto, Canada
bor@cs.toronto.edu

Omer Lev
University of Toronto
Toronto, Canada
omerl@cs.toronto.edu

Tyrone Strangway
University of Toronto
Toronto, Canada
tyrone@cs.toronto.edu

ABSTRACT

Following the work of Babaioff et al [4], we consider the pricing game with strategic vendors and a single buyer, modeling a scenario in which multiple competing vendors have very good knowledge of a buyer, as is common in online markets. We add to this model the realistic assumption that the buyer has a fixed budget and does not have unlimited funds. When the buyer's valuation function is additive, we are able to completely characterize the different possible pure Nash Equilibria (PNE) and in particular obtain a necessary and sufficient condition for uniqueness. Furthermore, we characterize the market clearing (or Walresian) equilibria for all submodular valuations.

Surprisingly, for certain monotone submodular function valuations, we show that the pure NE can exhibit some counterintuitive phenomena; namely, there is a valuation such that the pricing will be market clearing and within budget if the buyer does not reveal the budget but will result in a smaller set of allocated items (and higher prices for items) if the buyer does reveal the budget. It is also the case that the conditions that guarantee market clearing in Babaioff et al [4] for submodular functions are not necessarily market clearing when there is a budget. Furthermore, with respect to social welfare, while without budgets all equilibria are optimal (i.e. POA = POS = 1), we show that with budgets the worst equilibrium may only achieve $\frac{1}{n-2}$ of the best equilibrium.

Keywords

pricing, price of anarchy, budget, Nash equilibrium

1. INTRODUCTION

The question of how to price items in a market has existed for millennia, ever since people began trading with one another. Market pricing is clearly a central area of study in Economics. One of the most important aspects of these studies is market clearing (Walrasian) equilibria, initiated by Walras in 1874-1877 (See translation by Willam Jaffe [13]). The advent of online markets has changed pricing in many respects, both to the vendors benefit and to their detriment. On the one hand, vendors can gain vast information about their customers, and can tailor their prices to each particular customer. On the other hand, the instant availability of a large amount of competitors allows customers to pick and choose among the items they want. The speed and size of online markets necessitates having simple rules for setting prices and understanding the nature of pricing equilibria.

This world, where vendors compete with each other in online marketplaces (e.g., Amazon or E-Bay), and are able to adapt their prices to their customer, inspired a recent line of research [4, 12], utilizing a game theoretical toolbox to address these scenarios. Here self interested agents (the vendors) post prices for their wares and a buyer consumes a subset of the items based on their valuation for the items and the posted prices. The vendors aim is to maximize their individual profits (we assume no transaction or production costs) and they will post prices as high as possible. If a vendor does not wish to participate in the market they may price their items at infinity. How vendors best position themselves in the market relative to other vendors – and the valuation of the buyer – creates interesting and non trivial scenarios. While we use buyer - seller terminology, this problem is applicable to other allocation scenarios that may arise in a multi-agent environment.

We add to the setting of [4, 12] the vital component of budgets. Previous work assumed the buyer had unlimited purchasing power, their decision limited only by the valuations. Now we cannot assume the buyer will purchase any bundle at a price lower than its value. The buyer will consume the set of items with highest utility (i.e., net value, taking prices into account), that is within their budget, while the strategies of the vendors is determining the prices of the items they offer.

This brings about a departure from the previous results, as we show how the buyer's valuation and budget influence the market. Not only are some previous results now rendered impossible as they exceed the budget, but this more realistic assumption materially changes the structure of pricing from the intuitions formed in earlier research, as a more complex strategic behaviour needs to considered.

1.1 Our Contributions

We begin by studying additive buyer valuation functions. In the non budgeted world of Babaioff et al. [4] and Lev et al. [12] this is an uninteresting case where there is a simple and unique equilibrium in which every item is sold. We show, naturally, that a budgeted buyer can no longer necessarily purchase all of the items for sale. We identify a condition on the valuation function and the budget which is sufficient to ensure a market clearing equilibrium exists.

Appears in: *Proceedings of the 15th International Conference on Autonomous Agents and Multiagent Systems (AAMAS 2016), J. Thangarajah, K. Tuyls, C. Jonker, S. Marsella (eds.), May 9–13, 2016, Singapore.*

This equilibrium is interesting since each item is priced to provide identical utility to the buyer. We prove that under this condition the market clearing equilibrium is unique. We next examine what happens when the uniqueness condition does not hold in the additive case. We provide a method to identify a subset of the sellers whose existence in some sense generalizes the condition for uniqueness and thereby allows for a partial characterization of all PNE. We finally prove our condition for market clearance is necessary.

We then extend our equilibrium analysis to the case of monotone submodular valuation functions. We extend the notion of our conditions in the additive case to submodular valuations proving that a similar market clearing equilibrium exists. We also prove that the condition is again necessary to ensure market clearance. We next provide an example which shows a rather surprising consequence of the budget. We show that at certain equilibrium a buyer who has no budget can pay less and receive more items than their budgeted counterparts. We also show that our notion of generalizing the condition on the valuation and budget to reach an equal-utility equilibrium does not work for XOS valuations.

Finally, we explore the budget effects on social welfare. We show that while it is known [4] that without a budget the price of anarchy is 1, with a budget the price of anarchy can be arbitrarily high.

1.2 Previous work

As already mentioned, the study of market pricing and equilibria is one of the most classical areas of Economics. In particular, the study of Walrasian equilibria considers the question of which markets have market clearing equilibria; that is, an assignment of prices to items such that when all agents take their preferred allocation in this pricing (i.e. an allocation in their demand set), all items are sold. We are interested especially in settings where there are distinct sellers and buyers, which are termed Fisher markets [6, 9]. A lot of work has gone into examining this when all items are divisible (e.g., commodities, such as oil, grains, etc.), but we focus on the case of indivisible items, which is how most items are sold in say online markets.

One of the foundational "modern" papers in this regard is that of Gul and Stacchetti [10] who show that for indivisible items the class of Gross Substitutes, a strict subfamily of submodular functions, is the largest class of functions containing unit demand buyers that always possess a Walrasian equilibrium. There have been several papers that follow this work [9, 8, 2, 3, 1, 7]. The basic emphasis in these papers is the existence and convergence to such equilibria without explicit representation of a pricing function. Moreover, while budgets are mentioned in some of these papers, the usual assumption is that the budgets are sufficiently large.

Recently, as the ability of vendors to analyze individual buyers and personalize their prices in online markets has increased [14], research in analyzing competitive pricing analysis in this scenario has increased. The model of Babaioff et al. [4] is most similar to ours, with many strategic vendors each holding a single item, and a single buyer. The main difference from their work is that while they consider buyers with unlimited purchasing power, we limit ourselves to budget constrained buyers. They prove that in any game with monotone buyer valuations there always exists a pure Nash equilibrium that clears the market and maximizes social welfare. Furthermore, they show that for buyers with submodular valuations there is a unique equilibrium that maximizes social welfare, and that the price of anarchy (and hence price of stability) is 1.

While we do not apply the budgetary constraint to their setting, Lev et al. [12] generalized [4] by allowing sellers to sell multiple items, and letting them choose which items to offer and for what price. They prove that an equilibrium is not guaranteed to exist for submodular valuations. When an equilibrium does exist the price of anarchy and price of stability are roughly $\log n$ where n is the number of items offered.

2. PRELIMINARIES

Our setting has a set of vendors N ($|N| = n$) in which vendor i sells a single distinct item i. A strategy profile of the vendors is a price vector $\mathbf{p} = (p_1, \ldots, p_n) \in \mathbb{R}^n_{\geq 0}$ where item i is priced at p_i ($p_i \geq 0$). We use $p(S) = \sum_{i \in S} p_i$ to represent the cost to the buyer for purchasing a set $S \subseteq N$. We write p_{-i} to represent the set of prices excluding p_i, we write (p_i, p_{-i}) to represent the full set of prices $\mathbf{p}$. Opposite the vendors we have a single buyer, represented by a valuation function $v()$, who faced with price vector $\mathbf{p}$ consumes a set of items which maximises his utility.

2.1 The Buyer

The buyer will be represented by a valuation function and a budget. The valuation function $v : 2^N \to \mathbb{R}_{\geq 0}$ gives non negative value to each subset of N. We assume the function is normalized and monotone; that is, $v(\emptyset) = 0$ and $v(S) \leq v(T)$ for $S \subseteq T \subseteq N$. The budget $B \in \mathbb{R}_{>0}$ is simply the maximum capital the buyer has available to purchase items; the budget cannot be exceeded.

We shall discuss 3 types of valuation functions:

Additive This function is defined by a vector of per item valuations $v = (v_1, \ldots, v_n)$ and for any $S \subseteq N$ the valuation is $v(S) = \sum_{i \in S} v_i$.

Submodular This function is characterized by the idea of decreasing marginal utilities. That is, for a submodular function we have $v(S) - v(S \setminus \{a\}) \geq v(T) - v(T \setminus \{a\})$ for $S \subseteq T \subseteq N$ and $a \in S$.

XOS An XOS (Exclusive Or of Singletons) function is defined by a finite set of additive functions $F = \{f_1, \ldots, f_k\}$ such that $v(S) = max_{f_i \in F} f_i(S)$ for every $S \subseteq N$.

The set of additive functions is a strict subset of the set of monotone submodular functions which in turn is a strict subset of the set of XOS functions. It should be noted all of these sets of functions are strictly contained in the set of subadditive functions which are defined as: $v(S) + v(T) \geq V(S \cup T)$ for $S, T \subseteq N$. For a more in depth look at these functions see [11].

We assume the buyer has a budget bounded quasi-linear utility function. That is, for some bundle $S \subseteq N$ and pricing vector $\mathbf{p}$ we have:

$$u_b(S, \mathbf{p}) = \begin{cases} v(S) - p(S) & \text{if } p(S) \leq B \\ -\infty & \text{otherwise} \end{cases}$$

To ease reading and notation, we will write $u_b(i, \mathbf{p})$ in place of $u_b(\{i\}, \mathbf{p})$ and omit the $\mathbf{p}$ if it is unambiguous. Following notation in [4], the demand correspondence of a buyer with valuation function v facing pricing vector $\mathbf{p}$ is the family of sets that maximize the buyer's utility:

$$D(v, \mathbf{p}) = \{S \subseteq N : u_b(S) \geq u_b(T) \ \ \forall T \subseteq N\}$$

The buyer will consume a set $X(v, \mathbf{p}) \in D(v, \mathbf{p})$. We assume the buyer has access to a demand oracle which allows the buyer to find $X(v, \mathbf{p})$. For ease of notation we usually write $X(v, \mathbf{p})$ as $X_\mathbf{p}$ Often we will find $|D(v, \mathbf{p})| = 1$ in the cases we study. A common assumption [4] in cases where $|D(v, \mathbf{p})| > 1$ is that the buyer will opt for a set $S \subseteq N$ with the largest size. We call such a buyer maximal.

2.2 Vendor Utility and Equilibrium

As mentioned before, the utility of the vendors is simply the payment they receive for their items. That is, if the buyer consumes $X(v, \mathbf{p})$ when presented with prices $\mathbf{p}$ the utility to vendor i is:

$$u_i(X(v, \mathbf{p})) = \begin{cases} p_i & \text{if } i \in X(v, \mathbf{p}) \\ 0 & \text{otherwise} \end{cases}$$

In a slight abuse of notation we will often omit the $X(v, \mathbf{p})$ from $u_i(X(v, \mathbf{p}))$ instead we write $u_i(\mathbf{p})$ implicitly assuming the $X(\cdot)$ and v are in place. A pricing vector $\mathbf{p}$ is defined to be a pure Nash equilibrium (PNE) if there does not exist any agents that can improve their utility by unilaterally modifying their price. That is, $\nexists i \in N$ such that $u_i(p'_i, p_{-i}) > u_i(p_i, p_{-i}) = u_i(\mathbf{p})$ for some $p'_i \neq p_i$. We note that the sellers also have access to the demand oracle and are able to determine what $X(v, \mathbf{p})$ is.

We say a price vector $\mathbf{p}$ is *market clearing* if $X(v, \mathbf{p}) = N$ and $\min_i p_i > 0$. That is every item is bought and each vendor receives positive utility.

The game as described is entirely parametrized by the budget B and valuation profile $v()$. The agents will price themselves presenting a $\mathbf{p}$ that maximizes their individual utility. We are interested in studying the properties of stable pricing schemes, i.e., prices that are a PNE. In particular, when are the PNE unique, how must agents price their items, and what is consumed by the buyer. Note this is a game of full information: the agents are assumed to know B and v and can see the prices $\mathbf{p}$ posted by each of the agents.

3. ADDITIVE VALUATIONS

We begin our study with a very simple class of buyer valuations, additive functions. Recall $v(\cdot)$ is additive if there exists a set of item values $(v_1, ..., v_n)$ and $v(S) = \sum_{i \in S} v_i$ for $S \subseteq N$. As mentioned earlier, previous work [4, 12] does not explicitly study the additive case, as there is a very simple and unique solution in their setting: assuming a maximal non budgeted buyer, the seller holding item k should simply price the item at v_k. Hence, the maximal buyer will purchase the universe of items and social welfare is maximized. Since each item is being consumed, none have an incentive to lower their price. If $p_k < v_k$ then the agent holding k should be able to increase p_k to v_k and still be consumed by the maximal buyer. Now consider the following instance of our budgeted game ($B = 1, (v_1, v_2) = (2, \frac{1}{2})$). It is easy to verify that the only PNE are of the form: $\mathbf{p} = (1, x)$, for $x \in \mathbb{R}_{\geq 0}$, and $X_\mathbf{p} = v_1$. The budget has enabled the vendor with the more valuable item to demand the entire budget excluding the other vendor from participating in the game.

3.1 A Unique PNE

We now provide a sufficient condition (later, in Theorem 2, to be shown necessary) on the buyer's valuation to ensure a unique market clearing PNE in which each vendor participates in the game. More specifically we show that under this condition there is a unique PNE that clears the market providing each vendor with positive utility. Throughout this section we assume $V(N) > B$, otherwise this setting reduces to the setting of [4].

DEFINITION 1. *The* relative valuation constraint *for set $S \subseteq N$, valuations $(v_1, \ldots, v_n)$ and budget B is that for each $v_i \in S$, $v_i > \frac{\sum_{v_j \in S \setminus \{i\}} v_j - B}{|S|-1}$*

When considering the constraint on the full set of items (N) this is equivalent to stating it as a constraint on the budget: for every $i \in N$, $B > \sum_{j \neq i}(v_j - v_i)$.

We can see that this constraint does not imply that the valuation is a gross substitutes valuation. Namely, the additive function $v(S) = \sum_{i \in S} v_i$ for 3 items (v_1, v_2, v_3) with the values $(2, 2, 2)$ correspondingly and a budget of 1. The function satisfies the relative valuation constraint and is not gross substitutes: the pricing $(0.2, 0.4, 0.4)$ allows the buyer to buy all items, while the pricing $(0.3, 0.4, 0.4)$ forces the buyer to give up v_2 or v_3 despite their prices staying the same, hence not gross substitute[1].

THEOREM 1. *Given an additive valuation profile $(v_1, ..., v_n)$, where $\sum_i v_i > B$ and the valuations for N follow the relative valuation constraint for all items, there is a unique PNE $\mathbf{p}$ where $\min_i(p_i) > 0$, $\sum_i p_i = B$, $\forall (i, j), v_i - p_i = v_j - p_j$ and $X(v, \mathbf{p}) = N$.*

Before we prove Theorem 1 we will find the following lemma useful:

LEMMA 1. *Given an additive valuation profile $(v_1, ..., v_n)$ with budget B and sets A and U where $A \subset U \subseteq N$. If for $i \in U$, $v_i > \frac{\sum_{j \in U \setminus \{i\}} v_j - B}{|U|-1}$ then $v_i > \frac{\sum_{j \in A} v_j - B}{|A|}$.*

PROOF. Let $i = \arg\min_{j \in U \setminus A} v_j$, let $D = U \setminus (A \cup \{i\})$. From the condition on v_i:

$$\begin{aligned} v_i &> \frac{\sum_{j \in U \setminus \{i\}} v_j - B}{|U| - 1} \\ &= \frac{\sum_{j \in D} v_j + \sum_{j \in A} v_j - B}{|U| - 1} \end{aligned}$$

$$\implies (|U| - 1)v_i - \sum_{j \in D} v_j > \sum_{j \in A} v_j - B$$

$$((|U| - 1) - |D|)v_i \geq (|U| - 1)v_i - \sum_{j \in D} v_j > \sum_{j \in A} v_j - B$$

[1]A different example, shown in Lehmann et al. [11], is a budget-additive function $v(S) = \min\{B, \sum_{i \in S} v_i\}$ for 3 items $(v_1, v_2, v_3) = (1, 1, 2)$ and a budget $B = 2$, which satisfies the relative valuation constraint and is not gross substitutes: the prices $(0, \frac{1}{2}, 1)$, in which v_1 and v_2 are purchased, in comparison to prices $(1, \frac{1}{2}, 1)$ in which only v_3 would be bought.

Where the last line is because v_i was chosen to be the smallest value amongst those in $U \setminus A$. So now we have that:

$$((|U|-1)-|D|)v_i > \sum_{j\in A} v_j - B$$
$$\implies v_i > \frac{\sum_{j\in A} v_j - B}{(|U|-1)-|D|}$$
$$= \frac{\sum_{j\in A} v_j - B}{|A|}$$

□

Now we are ready to prove Theorem 1:

PROOF. We will divide the proof into two parts. First we will define a PNE $\mathbf{p}$ which meets our criteria. We then will show that this $\mathbf{p}$ is the only possible PNE when N satisfies the *relative valuation constraint.*

Existence of PNE p: Let $p_i = \frac{B+(n-1)v_i - \sum_{j\neq i} v_j}{n}$. First we note since $v_i > \frac{\sum_{j\neq i} v_j - B}{n-1}$ we get that $p_i > 0$. It is also easy to see that $\sum_i p_i = B$.

We now argue $v_i - p_i = v_j - p_j$ for any pair of vendors i and j. Fix some vendor k:

$$v_k - p_k = v_k - \frac{B+(n-1)v_k - \sum_{j\neq k} v_j}{n}$$
$$= \frac{nv_k - B - (n-1)v_k + \sum_{j\neq k} v_j}{n}$$
$$= \frac{\sum_i v_i - B}{n}$$
$$= \frac{v(N) - p(N)}{n}$$

That is, each seller i is providing exactly $\frac{1}{n}$ of $v(N) - p(N)$, so each item is priced so they provide identical utility to the buyer.

Next we show $v_i > p_i$ for each item i. Suppose for contradiction there is some i where $p_i \geq v_i$. Since $v_i - p_i = v_j - p_j$ for any item j it must be that $p_j \geq v_j$. Thus we get $p(N) \geq v(N) > B$, which contradicts $p(N) = B$ by construction.

Now we can prove $\mathbf{p}$ is a PNE:

Because $\sum_i p_i = B$ and $0 < p_i < v_i$ each seller has their item chosen. Thus none have an incentive to lower their price. Say seller i increases their price by of $\epsilon > 0$. Since $(p_i + \epsilon) + \sum_{j\neq i} p_j > B$ the buyer will consume at most $n-1$ items. Since $v_i - p_i = v_j - p_j$ for any pair of items i and j we get $v_i - (p_i + \epsilon) < v_j - p_j$, so item i is not consumed leaving its seller with 0 utility. So i should not increase its price. Thus $\mathbf{p}$ is a PNE.

Uniqueness of PNE p: Given that the relative valuation constraint holds for N, we now argue that $\mathbf{p}$ is the only PNE. Assume we have another PNE $\mathbf{p}' = (p'_1, \ldots, p'_n)$. First we show $\sum_i p'_i = B$:

Suppose $\sum_i p'_i < B$, then clearly $X_{\mathbf{p}'} = N$ since $\mathbf{p}'$ is a PNE. Since $\sum_i v_i > B$ it must be that $p'_j < v_j$ for some item j. Let $0 < \epsilon \leq \min\{B - (\sum_i p'_i), \frac{v_j - p'_j}{2}\}$. It is easy to see $(p'_j + \epsilon, p'_{-j})$ is a better solution for seller j. By the first term in the min the new pricing vector is not over budget by the second term $v_j < p'_j$ so the buyer still receives positive utility from item j. Thus item j is still consumed and we see that seller j should increase their price by ϵ.

Suppose $\sum_i p'_i > B$, then under this pricing scheme there is an agent i, $i \notin X(v, \mathbf{p}')$. We now argue i is able to offer a positive price where this item will be picked. For the remainder of this section when referring to $X_{\mathbf{p}'}$ we exclude items which are priced at zero. We can assume that $\sum_{j\in X_{\mathbf{p}'}} p'_j = B$, if this were not the case seller i could offer a positive price and still be consumed.

Let $s = \arg\min_{j\in X_{\mathbf{p}'}} u_b(j)$, that is s is the seller providing the least amount of utility amongst those who are picked. If $v_i > u_b(s)$ seller i can offer a price of $\min\{\frac{v_i - u_b(s)}{2}, \frac{B - \sum_{j\in X_{\mathbf{p}'}\setminus s} p'_j}{2}\}$. The first term in the min ensures that the buyer gets more utility from i than s, the second term ensures the buyer can afford the current chosen set when s will be replaced by i. Thus vendor i can replace vendor s in the chosen set.

We now prove $v_i > u_b(s)$. We know that $u_b(s)$ is at most the average utility provided by a seller in $X_{\mathbf{p}'}$. That is $u_b(s) \leq \frac{\sum_{j\in X_{\mathbf{p}'}} v_j - B}{|X_{\mathbf{p}'}|}$. So we must show show $v_i > \frac{\sum_{j\in X_{\mathbf{p}'}} v_j - B}{|X_{\mathbf{p}'}|}$. This is simply a direct result of Lemma 1, where we take the sets $X(v, \mathbf{p}')$ and N to be A and U in the lemma respectively.

Thus at any PNE $\mathbf{p}'$ each seller offers a positive price is bought and the budget is consumed.

We finally argue $u_b(i) = u_b(j)$ for all sellers i and j at any PNE $\mathbf{p}'$. Let $i = \arg\max_k u_b(k)$ and $j = \arg\min_k u_b(k)$. Assume, for contradiction, $u_b(i) > u_b(j)$. Let $0 < \epsilon \leq \min\{\frac{B - \sum_{k\neq j} v_k}{2}, \frac{u_b(i) - u_b(j)}{2}\}$ and consider the point $(p'_i + \epsilon, p'_{-i})$. Since $\mathbf{p}'$ is a PNE, $\sum_i p'_i = B$ so under $(p'_i + \epsilon, p'_{-i})$ at least one item will not be consumed. By the first term in the min, $p'_i + \epsilon + \sum_{k\neq i,j} p'_k < B$, so the buyer can afford all of the items except for j. By the second term in the min, $v_i - (p'_i + \epsilon) = u_b(i) - \epsilon > u_b(j)$ so the buyer gets more utility from seller i than from seller j. Since seller j is still providing the least utility, it will be the one left out of the chosen set. Thus we see that seller i should increase the price by ϵ and that $\mathbf{p}'$ is not a PNE. Thus it must be that $u_b(i) = u_b(j)$ for all sellers i and j.

Thus when the *relative valuation constraint* holds for N we get that all PNE must take the form of $\mathbf{p}$ as defined above. □

3.2 Non Market Clearing PNE and a Complete Characterization of Market Clearing PNE

In this section we will explore what happens when the *relative valuation constraint* does not hold for N. Without loss of generality, let the elements of N be in decreasing order of valuations; i.e. if $i < j$ then $v_i \geq v_j$.

DEFINITION 2. *A* PNE base set *is a set $L \subseteq N$, which is constructed by ordering the elements of N in non-increasing order of valuations. Starting with the first (most valuable) element of N iteratively add the next element to L until reaching an element i s.t. $v_i \leq \frac{\sum_{j\in L} v_j - B}{|L|}$.*

Note we are not counting v_i in the above sum nor the size of L.

In a sense L is a maximal set of the largest items. We note that a non-empty L must exist since $L = \{1\}$ certainly satisfies the definition. Furthermore, note that for several equal valued items, if one of them is in L, then all of them are in L.

We now prove some additional useful facts about L:

LEMMA 2. $\sum_{i \in L} v_i > B$

PROOF. If $L = N$ then since we assumed $\sum_i v_i > B$ we are done.

Let us suppose $L \neq N$ then there must be an element s s.t. $v_s \leq \frac{\sum_{j \in L} v_j - B}{|L|}$. Rearranging we get that $|L| v_s \leq \sum_{j \in L} v_j - B$, and since $v_s > 0$ we get that $\sum_{j \in L} v_j - B > 0$. Thus we see that L contains strictly more value than the budget. □

LEMMA 3. $\forall j \in L, v_j > \frac{\sum_{k \in L \setminus j} v_k - B}{|L|-1}$

PROOF. Let i be the last element added to L, that is v_i is the smallest value amongst items in L. When we added i to L it was because $v_i > \frac{\sum_{j \in L'} v_j - B}{|L'|}$ where L' is $L \setminus \{i\}$. Since $|L| - 1 = |L'|$ we get $v_i > \frac{\sum_{j \in L \setminus i} v_j - B}{|L|-1}$. Now trade v_i with any element in the sum; the value on the left of the inequality can't decrease since v_i was minimal and the value on the right can't increase since we are swapping in v_i for some larger element v_j. Thus the inequality still holds. □

It is easy to see that L as defined above is the unique maximal set such that $\forall i \in L, v_i > \frac{\sum_{j \in L \setminus i} v_j - B}{|L|-1}$. If this was not the case and some set M existed s.t. $\forall i \in M, v_i > \frac{\sum_{j \in M \setminus i} v_j - B}{|M|-1}$ and $L \subsetneq M$. Lemma 1, where L and M take the place of A and U in the lemma, implies that for each $i \in M$ $v_i > \frac{\sum_{j \in L} v_j - B}{|L|}$. Thus when constructing L and considering element $(|L| + 1) \in M$ we should have added it to L. Thus L is the largest set for which the *relative valuation constraint* holds.

LEMMA 4. *There is always a PNE* $\mathbf{p}$ *where* $X_p = L$ *and* $v_i - p_i = v_j - p_j$ *for all pairs of elements in* L.

PROOF. Let $\mathbf{p} = (p_1, ..., p_{|L|}, 0..., 0)$ where $p_i = \frac{B + (|L|-1)v_i - \sum_{j \in L \setminus i} v_j}{|L|}$.

By Lemma 3 we know $p_i > 0$. By the construction of each p_i, $\sum_i p_i = B$ and $v_i - p_i = v_j - p_j = \frac{\sum_{j \in L} v_j - B}{|L|}$ for all pairs $i, j \in L$. As in Theorem 1 no one agent in L has an incentive to lower their price since they are being sold. Furthermore, if one of the agents in L were to increase their price, they would be removed from $X_\mathbf{p}$ as they now provide the least utility in L, and prices are now over budget. Finally combining Lemma 2 and a similar argument found in Theorem 1 we get that $p_i \leq v_i$ for each $i \in L$.

Now we argue that none of the agents in $N \setminus L$ have an incentive to increase their price. Let v_s be the largest value amongst the agents in $N \setminus L$. By the construction of L, $v_s \leq \frac{\sum_{j \in L} v_j - B}{|L|}$. If agent s were to offer a price $p_s > 0$ it would not be chosen since $v_s - p_s < \frac{\sum_{j \in L} v_j - B}{|L|}$. Since we are now over budget and the utility provided by s is lower than the utility provided by any of the agents in L, s is not chosen. Since v_s was the largest value amongst the agents not in $X_\mathbf{p}$ none of the agents outside of $X_\mathbf{p}$ have a sufficient valuation to be chosen. □

Unfortunately we do not get a nice generalisation of Theorem 1 where at all PNE $v_i - p_i = v_j - p_j$ for each pair $i, j \in L$.

EXAMPLE 1. *Let the budget* $B = 1$, *the valuations* $\boldsymbol{v} = (2, 1.5, 0.6, 0.6)$ *and finally the prices* $\mathbf{p} = (0.6, 0.4, 0.3, 0.3)$. *The utility gained from each agent is simply* $\boldsymbol{u} = (1.4, 1.1, 0.3, 0.3)$. *It is easy to see that* $L = \{1, 2\}$ *and this is a non market clearing PNE where* $X = L$. *If the first agent increased their price the new consumed set would be* $\{2, 3, 4\}$. *If the second agent increased their price the new consumed set would be* $\{1, 3\}$ *or* $\{1, 4\}$. *And if the third or fourth agent dropped their price to any positive value the consumed set would still be* $L = \{1, 2\}$.

We can, however, obtain a partial characterization showing that at any PNE $\mathbf{p}$ the base set L must be a part of $X_\mathbf{p}$.

LEMMA 5. *Let* $\mathbf{p}$ *be some PNE and* $X_\mathbf{p}$ *be the set consumed (not including those selling for free) it must be that* $L \subseteq X_\mathbf{p}$.

PROOF. Assume for contradiction that $L \not\subseteq X_\mathbf{p}$ at some PNE $\mathbf{p}$ We break this into two cases.

Case 1 ($X_\mathbf{p} \cap (N \setminus L) \neq \emptyset$):

That is, there are elements of $N \setminus L$ in $X_\mathbf{p}$. Let s be the element of $X_\mathbf{p} \cap (N \setminus L)$ providing the least utility to the buyer. Let i be some element of $L \setminus X_\mathbf{p}$. Since L contained the largest valued elements of N it must be that $v_i > v_s$. The inequality must be strict for if $v_i = v_s$, s would be a member of L. Letting $p_i = p_s$, at this price agent i provides strictly more utility than agent s, who is providing the least, so the buyer will replace s with i in the consumed set. So $\mathbf{p}$ is not a PNE.

Case 2 ($X_\mathbf{p} \cap (N \setminus L) = \emptyset$):

That is, $X_\mathbf{p}$ is a strict subset of L. By making an argument similar to the one in Theorem 1 using Lemma 1, with $X_\mathbf{p}$ and L replacing A and U in the lemma, we get $\mathbf{p}$ is not a PNE. □

It is, however, possible that at a PNE $\mathbf{p}$, $X_\mathbf{p} \neq L$.

EXAMPLE 2. *Let the budget* $B = 1$, *the valuations* $\boldsymbol{v} = (2.5, 1.5, 1.4)$ *and the prices* $\mathbf{p} = (0.9, 0.1, 0.9)$. *The per agent utility is* $\boldsymbol{u} = (1.6, 1.4, 0.5)$. *Obviously* $L = \{1\}$ *and* $X_p = \{1, 2\} \neq L$. *If agent 1 raises the price the new consumed set will be* $\{2, 3\}$, *if agent 2 increases the price the new set will be* $\{1\}$ *and finally if agent 3 drops the price the consumed set will remain* $\{1, 2\}$. *Thus* $\mathbf{p}$ *is a PNE with* $L \neq X_p$.

We conclude our discussion of additive valuations by proving that having a market clearing PNE requires that the relative valuation constraint holds for N and hence the PNE is unique and must be of the form described in Theorem 1.

THEOREM 2. *Consider an additive valuation function* $\boldsymbol{v}$ *and budget* B *for the buyer. Let* $\mathbf{p}$ *be some market clearing PNE, such that is* $X_p = N$ *and* $\min_i p_i > 0$. *It must be that* relative valuation constraint *holds for* $\boldsymbol{v}$ *and* B; *equivalently, the PNE base set* $L = N$.

PROOF. Assume, for contradiction, $L \neq N$. Let s be the element providing the least utility to the buyer under the pricing $\mathbf{p}$.

Since $L \subsetneq X_p$ there must be an element $i \in L$ where $v_i - p_i > \frac{\sum_{j \in L} v_j - B}{|L|}$. This is because when the consumed set is only L the average utility provided by an agent in L is $\frac{\sum_{j \in L} v_j - B}{|L|}$. Now we have agents outside of L receiving utility, to accommodate them at least one agent in L must offer a lower price providing more utility. By the construction of L each element of $N \setminus L$ has value at most $\frac{\sum_{j \in L} v_j - B}{|L|}$. Since s is providing the least utility over all agents, and no agent outside of L can provide at most $\frac{\sum_{j \in L} v_j - B}{|L|}$ utility, $v_s - p_s < \frac{\sum_{j \in L} v_j - B}{|L|}$. So we get $v_i - p_i > v_s - p_s$. Thus we see that agent i can increase the price by $\min\{\frac{(v_i - p_i) - (v_s - p_s)}{2}, B - \sum_{j \in N \setminus s} p_j\}$. The first term ensures agent i still provides more utility than agent s while the second ensures $N \setminus s$ is budget feasible. Under the new pricing scheme at most $n-1$ items will be bought. Since s is still providing the least utility we get that $N \setminus s$ is the new consumed set. Thus $\mathbf{p}$ was not a PNE, a contradiction. □

This theorem, alongside Example 1, means that the Babaioff et al. [4] result showing that there is always a market clearing equilibrium for *all* montone valuation is not true when introducing budgets to the model and even fails for some additive valuations.

From Theorem 2 we conclude that any market clearing PNE $\mathbf{p}$ must be of the form of the one described in Theorem 1. That is:

COROLLARY 1. *If a PNE $\mathbf{p}$ is market clearing, then it is unique, and for all pairs (i, j) $v_i - p_i = v_j - p_j$ and $\sum_i p_i = B$.*

4. MONOTONE SUBMODULAR VALUATION FUNCTIONS

We now focus on submodular valuation functions. Recall submodular valuations are characterized by diminishing marginal values, that is for $S \subseteq T$ and $x \notin T$ we have $v(S \cup \{x\}) - v(S) \geq v(T \cup \{x\}) - v(T)$.

Define $v_T(S) = v(T) - v(T \setminus S)$ for $S \subseteq T \subseteq N$, that is the marginal value of set S for completing set T. To simplify reading, for a set S with single item s, we will use the notation $v_T(s)$ to denote $v_T(\{s\})$. We also define $u_b^i(S) = v_S(i) - p_i$, that is the seller i's marginal contribution to the buyers utility for completing set S. We will find the following lemmas regarding submodular and monotone functions useful in this section:

LEMMA 6. *For a submodular valuation v and pricing scheme $\mathbf{p}$, if for all vendors i, $p_i \leq v_D(i)$ then $v(D) - p(D) \geq v(C) - p(C)$ for sets $C \subseteq D$.*

PROOF. Consider some seller $j \in D \setminus C$. Since v is submodular and $p_j \leq v_D(j)$ we get $p_j \leq v_{C \cup \{j\}}(j)$, so $v(C \cup \{j\}) - p(C \cup \{j\}) \geq v(C) - p(C)$. Since $C \cup \{j\} \subseteq D$ we can take another seller $j' \in C \cup \{j\} \setminus D$ and again conclude due to $p'_j \leq v_D(j')$ and the submodularity of v $v(C \cup \{j, j'\}) - p(C \cup \{j, j'\}) \geq v(C) - p(C)$. We can repeat this process for the rest of the elements in $C \setminus D$ concluding $v(D) - p(D) \geq v(C) - p(C)$ for sets $C \subseteq D$. □

LEMMA 7. *For a monotone valuation v and pricing scheme $\mathbf{p}$, if for vendors a and c $v_N(a) - p_a = v_N(c) - p_c$ then $v(N \setminus c) - p(N \setminus c) = v(N \setminus a) - p(N \setminus a)$.*

PROOF. Assuming $v_N(a) - p_a = v_N(c) - p_c$:

$$\begin{aligned}
&v_N(a) - p_a = v_N(c) - p_c \\
\implies &v(N) - v(N \setminus a) - p_a = v(N) - v(N \setminus c) - p_c \\
\implies &v(N \setminus c) - p_a = v(N \setminus a) - p_c \\
\implies &v(N \setminus c) - p_a - \sum_{k \neq a,c} p_k = v(N \setminus a) - p_c - \sum_{k \neq a,c} p_k \\
\implies &v(N \setminus c) - \sum_{i \neq c} p_i = v(N \setminus a) - \sum_{i \neq a} p_i
\end{aligned}$$

□

THEOREM 3. *Given a submodular valuation function v where $\forall i \in N, v_N(i) > \frac{\sum_{j \neq i} v_N(j) - B}{n-1}$ there is a market clearing PNE $\mathbf{p}$ where $\sum_i p_i = B$ and $v_N(i) - p_i = v_N(j) - p_j$ for all pairs of vendors i and j.*

PROOF. Let $p_i = \frac{B + (n-1)v_N(i) - \sum_{j \neq i} v_N(j)}{n}$, this value is positive because of the condition on $v_N(i)$. As in the proof of Theorem 1 it is easy to see $v_N(i) - p_i = \frac{\sum_{j \in N} v_N(j) - B}{n}$ so $v_N(i) - p_i$ is the same for each vendor i. It is also easy to see $\sum_i p_i = B$. Combining these two facts we see that as in the proof of Theorem 1 $p_i < v_N(i)$. Using these facts and applying Lemma 6 to N we see each agent must be chosen and none have an incentive to lower their price.

Suppose $\mathbf{p}$ is not a PNE It must be that some agent has an incentive to increase their price, call this agent a. If a increases its price by $\epsilon > 0$, since $\sum_i p_i = B$ at least one of the agents must not be chosen under the new pricing scheme. Call this other agent c. Let $\mathbf{p}'$ be the new pricing scheme where a increases its price.

First we argue that $v(N \setminus c) - \sum_{i \neq c} p_i > v(X_{\mathbf{p}'}) - \sum_{i \in X_{\mathbf{p}'}} p_i - \epsilon$. Note $v(X_{\mathbf{p}'}) - \sum_{i \in X_{\mathbf{p}'}} p_i - \epsilon < v(X_{\mathbf{p}'}) - \sum_{i \in X_{\mathbf{p}'}} p_i$. This is now a simple application of Lemma 6 where C and D in the lemma are replaced with $X_{\mathbf{p}'}$ and $N \setminus c$ respectively. Thus we get $v(N \setminus c) - \sum_{i \neq c} p_i \geq v(X_{\mathbf{p}'}) - \sum_{i \in X_{\mathbf{p}'}} p_i > v(X_{\mathbf{p}'}) - \sum_{i \in X_{\mathbf{p}'}} p_i - \epsilon$.

Next we get directly from Lemma 7 $v(N \setminus c) - \sum_{i \neq c} p_i = v(N \setminus a) - \sum_{i \neq a} p_i$. Thus we get $v(N \setminus a) - \sum_{i \neq a} p_i = v(N \setminus c) - \sum_{i \neq c} p_i > v(X_{\mathbf{p}'}) - \sum_{i \in X_{\mathbf{p}'}} p_i - \epsilon$. Since $\sum_{i \neq a} p_i < B$ we see that the new consumed set will be all agents except a; thus it should not increase the price. So we see $\mathbf{p}$ was a indeed an equilibrium. □

Similar to Theorem 2 from the additive case we show that in the submodular case the only market clearing PNE are of the equal marginal utility kind. That is the all market clearing PNE must be of the form of the one described in Theorem 3

THEOREM 4. *For a submodular valuation v given any PNE $\mathbf{p}$ where $X(v, \mathbf{p}) = N$ and $u_i > 0$ for all vendors i, it must be that $v_N(k) - p_k = v_N(j) - p_j$ for any pair of vendors k and j.*

PROOF. Suppose at PNE $\mathbf{p}$ $X_{\mathbf{p}} = N$. Let $a = argmax_{i \in N} v_N(i) - p_i$, that is, a is providing the most marginal utility, so $v_N(a) - p_a \geq v_N(i) - p_i$ for every other vendor i. Assume for contradiction, that in at least one case this inequality is strict. Let vendor $c = \arg\min_i v_N(i) - p_i$ so $v_N(a) - p_a > v_N(c) - p_c$.

We now argue a has an incentive to increase its price by $\epsilon < \min\{\frac{u_b^a(N)}{2}, \frac{u_b^a(N)-u_b^c(N)}{2}, \min_{j\neq a} B - p(N \setminus j)\}$ (recall $u_b^i(N) = v_N(i) - p_i$). The first term is positive since since $v_N(c) - p_c \geq 0$ thus $v_N(a) - p_a > 0$ so $v_N(a) > p_a$. The second positive since $v_N(a) - p_a > v_N(c) - p_c$. The third is positive because $\sum_i p_i \leq B$. Let $(p_a + \epsilon, p_{-a}) = \mathbf{p}'$.

Since $X_{\mathbf{p}} = N$ we know that $p_i \leq v_N(i)$ for each vendor i and because of the first term in the above min, $p_i' \leq v_N(i)$. We can apply lemma 6 taking set D in the lemma to be any $K \subset N$ where $|K| = |N| - 1$ getting $v(K) - p'(K) \geq v(J) - p'(J)$ for $J \subseteq K$. So we see under $\mathbf{p}'$ the buyer will consume a set of size $|N| - 1$, assuming it is under budget.

By the second term in the min, $v_N(a) - p_a - \epsilon > v_N(c) - p_c$. Using this we can modify the proof of Lemma 7, replacing the equalities with inequalities, getting $v(N \setminus a) - \sum_{i\neq a} p_i < v(N \setminus c) - \sum_{i\neq c} p_i - \epsilon$. Thus the buyer will prefer to exclude c instead of a from $X_{\mathbf{p}'}$, assuming the chosen set with a is under budget. The third term in the min ensures any set of size $|N| - 1$ that a is a part of will remain under budget.

Thus we see a can raise its price by ϵ and $\mathbf{p}$ can't be a PNE. □

We note that we cannot extend the idea of the PNE base set to the submodular case in the same way – while a maximal set of items that adhere to the condition can be found, as shown in Example 3, the set is not unique, and hence not all equilibria are an extension of the same set.

EXAMPLE 3. *We have a set of 4 items* $N = \{a, b, c, d\}$. $v(a) = v(b) = 1$; $v(c) = v(d) = \frac{1}{2}$. $v(\{a, b\}) = \frac{3}{2}$, $v(\{c, d\}) = 1$, $v(\{a, c\}) = \frac{3}{2}$. $v(\{a, b, c\}) = \frac{7}{4}$, $v(\{a, c, d\}) = 1.52$ *and* $v(\{a, b, c, d\}) = 1.76$. *The values for the rest of the sets are defined by this as a and c can be replaced with b and d, respectively (if they were not in the original set). The budget is* 0.3.

Both sets $\{a, b, c\}$ *and* $\{a, b, d\}$ *conform to the relative valuation constraint (their marginal values with respect to the set are equal). However,* a, b, c, d *does not.*

4.1 When the Sum of Marginal Values is Below the Budget

When the sum of marginal values of items is below the budget, the equilibrium shown in [4] is both market clearing and lets the buyer keep some of their money. However, that equilibrium is unique only when the budget is not known to the sellers. When it is known, other equilibria arise, and some of them provide less utility to the buyer than the market clearing one, and reduces the social welfare. This shows buyers are worse off announcing their budget, as Example 4 shows.

EXAMPLE 4. *We have a set of 4 items* $N = \{a, b, c, d\}$. $v(a) = v(b) = 1$; $v(c) = v(d) = \frac{1}{4}$. $v(\{a, b\}) = \frac{7}{4}$, $v(\{c, d\}) = \frac{1}{2}$, $v(\{a, c\}) = \frac{9}{8}$. $v(\{a, b, c\}) = 1.76$, $v(\{a, c, d\}) = 1.135$ *and* $v(\{a, b, c, d\}) = 1.77$. *The values for the rest of the sets are defined by this as a and c can be replaced with b and d, respectively (if they were not in the original set). The budget is* 1.

The marginal values (in N) of a and b are 0.27, *of c and d* 0.1, *so pricing the items with these values is both under budget and an equilibrium, as [4] claim, and will result in all items being purchased by the seller. However, another equilibrium is pricing a and b at* $\frac{1}{2}$ *each, and c and d at* $\frac{1}{4}$. *Under these prices, the buyer will only buy items a and b (as they exhaust the budget). This is an equilibrium, as neither a nor b can raise their prices, as that precludes buying both of them, and buying the one that didn't raise its price with c and d is more beneficial for the buyer. Items c and d can't lower their prices to anything above* 0, *as there is no budget to purchase them, and even with only one of a or b, they still do not provide as much utility as purchasing both a and b.*

Finally, as Example 5 shows, unlike submodular valuation functions, we cannot always guarantee equal utility equilibria for XOS functions even when the valuations adhere to the relative valuation constraint:

EXAMPLE 5. *We have a set of 3 items* $N = \{a, b, c\}$. *The XOS valuation function is defined using 2 additive valuations: The first is* $(2, 1, 1)$ *respectively for* (a, b, c), *and the second is* $(3, 0, 0)$. *The budget is* 1.5. *The marginal value of item a is* 2, *and b and c have marginal value* 1, *so they comply with the relative valuation constraint.*

An equal marginal utility contribution would mean pricing item a at $\frac{7}{6}$ *and items b and c at* $\frac{1}{6}$ *each. However, in this case item a can increase its price to* $\frac{4}{3}$, *as without it, by buying only b and c the buyer has a utility of* $\frac{5}{3}$, *but by buying a and b, the buyer gets a utility of* 2.5, *being obviously better off, so this is not an equilibrium.*

5. SOCIAL WELFARE

While we have shown price equilibria in various settings, we have yet to investigate the value of the sold set to the buyer. As the sellers get the money from the buyer, this is equivalent to analyzing the social welfare – the amount of utility "created" in the equilibrium.

The common measures of the impact of equilibrium on the welfare are price of anarchy (PoA), and, to a lesser extent, price of stability (PoS), which are, respectively, ratio of the social welfare in the worst (respectively, the best) equilibria and the optimal welfare . However, the optimal welfare is, of course, that all items are given to the buyer for free, and therefore, the social welfare is the value of the whole set, namely $v(N)$.

In [4] the authors show that for monotone submodular valuations the PoA is always 1. Furthermore they show for any monotone function the PoS is 1, although the PoA can be infinite. In the multi item setting of [12] the authors show when PNE do exist for monotone submodular valuations both the PoA and PoS are approximately $log(m)$ where m is the number of items.

The usage of PoA is intended to aid us in understanding the effects of an equilibrium compared to the optimal state. Assuming sellers get nothing is not only unrealistic, it also does not let us consider the effect of an equilibrium under the budget constraints (as the budget plays no role). Therefore, we would like to have some measure that takes into account the existence of a budget, as well as the desire of sellers to be paid.

To deal with this problem we use a somewhat different metric: $\frac{PoA}{PoS}$, i.e., the ratio between the social welfare in the worst equilibrium and the social welfare in the best equilibrium. In order to avoid items being "given away" and artificially adding to the utility, we do not count the social welfare garnered from items priced at 0. Our measure shows the differences between different equilibria under the same budgetary constraint, and is, therefore, an indicator of how bad equilibria can become. Surprisingly. and in contrast to the results in [4], which showed that without a budget the PoA is 1, we discover the PoA can be arbitrarily bad for submodular functions. Moreover, with budgets, even in the additive case, the PoS can be greater than 1, as is shown by Theorem 2, and examples such as Example 1. Therefore, we can have $PoA > \frac{PoA}{PoS} \geq PoS > 1$.

THEOREM 5. *The $\frac{PoA}{PoS}$ (and hence the PoA) can be unbounded and approaching $n-2$ even for additive valuation functions. A corresponding upper bound is n, even for submodular functions.*

PROOF. We first show that the ratio is unbounded for the additive case and approaching $n-2$, and then show the upper bound of n for submodular functions.

Let v be an additive function. Let the value of item 1 be 2, the value of item $n-1$ and n be 0.55, and all the rest of the items (from 2 to $n-2$) have a value of 1. The budget is 1. It is easy to see the set L only contains the first item, and therefore there is an equilibrium in which all the budget goes to this item, and all others items priced at 0. Hence the utility of this equilibrium is 2 (note that as any equilibrium must include L, this is the worst possible equilibrium).

Now consider the following pricing: item 1 is priced at $\frac{1}{2}$, items valued at 1 have a price of $\frac{1}{2(n-3)}$, and the final two items are priced at 0.25 each. This is a Nash equilibrium in which all items but the last two are sold. None of the items valued at 1 can increase their price (as then they will be the item providing the least utility and be thrown out), and neither can the items valued at 0.55 lower their price to be purchased, as even then they provide too little utility. If item 1 tries to raise its price (which necessitates throwing out one of the items valued at 1), it is better for the buyer not to purchase item 1, and instead add both items $n-1$ and n to the purchases set. The value of this equilibrium is $2+(n-3)$. Thanks to Theorem 2, we know there is no market clearing equilibrium, and as is shown in the next paragraph, there can be no equilibrium with $n-1$ items. Hence $\frac{PoA}{PoS} = \frac{2+(n-3)}{2}$, which is unbounded.

Notice that replacing the valuation of the top item to any $k \in \mathbb{N}$ and the next $n-3$ items to $k-1$, does not change the existence of both equilibria, and $\frac{PoA}{PoS} \geq \frac{k(n-2)-0.1}{k+1} \xrightarrow[k\to\infty]{} n-2$

Looking at an upper bound, note that $\frac{PoA}{PoS}$ is actually $\frac{\text{value of best NE}}{\text{value of worst NE}}$. The best equilibrium is, at most, the value of the whole set, $v(N)$, and thanks to submodularity, $v(N) \leq n \cdot \max_{i\in N} v(\{i\})$. Furthermore, in any equilibrium, the buyer gets at least a value$\geq \max_{i\in N} v(\{i\})$. If not, suppose i' is the value maximizing $v(\{i\})$, and there is an equilibrium where the buyer purchases a set $S \subsetneq (N \setminus \{i'\})$ at price $b \leq B$, and $v(S) < v(\{i'\})$. Vendor i' can improve its situation (a utility of 0), by changing its price to b, and being bought instead of set S, proving that buying set S for a price of b is not an equilibrium. Hence the utility of the worst equilibrium is at least $\max_{i\in N} v(\{i\})$. Therefore, $\frac{PoA}{PoS} \leq n$. □

6. CONCLUSION AND FUTURE WORK

The addition of budgets to the work of [4] introduces interesting and strategic behaviour amongst agents. We identify the *relative valuation constraint* and prove it is both sufficient and necessary to ensure market clearance with submodular valuations, and in the additive case, we show the market clearing equilibrium is unique. This market clearing equilibrium is conceptually interesting, as in it each vendor provides equal marginal utility to the buyer for completing the universe of items. We also show how the constraint does not extend to XOS valuations where an equal marginal utility equilibrium is no longer guaranteed to exist. Furthermore we generalize the *relative valuation constraint* to subsets of the vendors for the additive case, and using this generalization, we identify a maximal base set of items (values) that can form an equilibrium similar to the market clearing one excluding other sellers. Finally we provide examples illustrating how the budget can influence the game in unexpected ways. Perhaps most striking of which is example 4 which can be interpreted as showing that a buyer announcing their budget may induce new and inferior equilibrium where they pay more and receive less compared to not announcing the budget at all.

Generalizing our model to many items per seller, as in [12], would be a likely logical extension to our work. When sellers hold many items the problem domain is significantly more complex. It is unknown even with simple additive valuations what Nash equilibrium this setting permits. It would also be interesting to see if with a budgeted and submodular buyer we also encounter the issue of no equilibria. Also, while [4, 12] are able to avoid the issue of item cost, due to the lack of budget, this issue becomes more interesting in our setting, and is yet to be explored.

Another direction that requires more attention is the multi buyer setting. The simplicity of our model where there is one idealized buyer lends itself to simple analysis. It is known [10] that with multiple buyers there is no Walrasian equilibrium unless the valuation class is essentially the class of Gross Substitutes [10, 5]. However, there may still be interesting results for a bounded, small number of buyers. Another open problem is whether the budgeted model may preclude any Nash equilibria (not just market clearing ones) in certain settings.

We suspect our results for the *relative valuation constraint* should generalize to XOS valuations. While the PNE would not be an equal marginal utility one, as our example shows is impossible, we do believe it is a necessary and sufficient condition for market clearance. Beyond this it would be interesting to study more general valuation functions, even ones that exhibit complements.

All of these directions are reasonable intermediate steps towards the most general pricing model with sellers holding many items and many buyers with complex valuations and differing budgets.

7. ACKNOWLEDGEMENTS

The authors thank Brendan Lucier for his insightful comments and clarifications. This work was supported by NSERC grant 482671.

REFERENCES

[1] N. Avigdor-Elgrabli and Y. Rabani. Convergence of tâtonnement in fisher markets. *CoRR*, 2014.

[2] Y. Azar, N. Buchbinder, and K. Jain. How to allocate goods in an online market? In *Algorithms - ESA 2010, 18th Annual European Symposium, Liverpool, UK, September 6-8, 2010. Proceedings, Part II*, pages 51–62, 2010.

[3] M. Babaioff, B. Lucier, N. Nisan, and R. P. Leme. On the efficiency of the walrasian mechanism. In *ACM Conference on Economics and Computation, EC '14, Stanford , CA, USA, June 8-12, 2014*, pages 783–800, 2014.

[4] M. Babaioff, N. Nisan, and R. P. Leme. Price competition in online combinatorial markets. In *Proceedings of the 23rd international conference on World Wide Web (WWW)*, pages 711–722, Seoul, Korea, April 2014.

[5] O. Ben-Zwi, R. Lavi, and I. Newman. Ascending auctions and walrasian equilibrium. *CoRR*, 2013.

[6] W. C. Brainard and H. E. Scarf. How to compute equilibrium prices in 1891. *American Journal of Economics and Sociology*, 64(1):57–83, January 2005.

[7] S. Brânzei, Y. Chen, X. Deng, A. Filos-Ratsikas, S. K. S. Frederiksen, and J. Zhang. The fisher market game: Equilibrium and welfare. In *Proceedings of the Twenty-Eighth AAAI Conference on Artificial Intelligence, July 27 -31, 2014, Québec City, Québec, Canada.*, pages 587–593, 2014.

[8] R. Cole and A. Rastogi. Indivisible markets with good approximate equilibriumprices. *Electronic Colloquium on Computational Complexity (ECCC)*, 14(017), 2007.

[9] D. Garg, K. Jain, K. Talwar, and V. V. Vazirani. A primal-dual algorithm for computing fisher equilibrium in the absence of gross substitutability property. *Theoretical Computer Science*, 378(2):143–152, June 2007.

[10] F. Gul and E. Stacchetti. Walrasian equilibrium with gross substitutes. *Journal of Economic Theory*, 87(1):95–124, July 1999.

[11] B. Lehmann, D. J. Lehmann, and N. Nisan. Combinatorial auctions with decreasing marginal utilities. *Games and Economic Behavior*, 55(2):270–296, 2006.

[12] O. Lev, J. Oren, C. Boutilier, and J. S. Rosenschein. The pricing war continues: On competitive multi-item pricing. In *Proceedings of the 29th AAAI Conference on Artificial Intelligence (AAAI)*, pages 972–978, Austin, Texas, January 2015.

[13] L. Walras (Translation by William Jaffe). *Elements of Pure Economics, Or the Theory of Social Wealth.* Taylor and Francis, 2003.

[14] R. M. Weiss and A. K. Mehorta. Online dynamic pricing: Efficiency, equity and the future of e-commerce. *Virgina Journal of Law and Technology*, 6(2), 2001.

Playing Repeated Security Games with No Prior Knowledge*

Haifeng Xu
University of Southern California
haifengx@usc.edu

Long Tran-Thanh
University of Southampton
l.tran-thanh@soton.ac.uk

Nicholas R. Jennings
University of Southampton
nrj@ecs.soton.ac.uk

ABSTRACT

This paper investigates repeated security games with *unknown* (to the defender) game payoffs and attacker behaviors. As existing work assumes prior knowledge about either the game payoffs or the attacker's behaviors, they are not suitable for tackling our problem. Given this, we propose the first efficient defender strategy, based on an adversarial online learning framework, that can provably achieve good performance guarantees without any prior knowledge. In particular, we prove that our algorithm can achieve low performance loss against the best *fixed* strategy on hindsight (i.e., having full knowledge of the attacker's moves). In addition, we prove that our algorithm can achieve an efficient competitive ratio against the optimal adaptive defender strategy. We also show that for zero-sum security games, our algorithm achieves efficient results in approximating a number of solution concepts, such as algorithmic equilibria and the minimax value. Finally, our extensive numerical results demonstrate that, without having any prior information, our algorithm still achieves good performance, compared to state-of-the-art algorithms from the literature on security games, such as SUQR [19], which require significant amount of prior knowledge.

General Terms

Game theory; Security; Theory

Keywords

Repeated Security Games; No-regret Learning; Adaptive Strategy

1. INTRODUCTION

In the recent years, security games have been widely used in many areas of artificial intelligence [24]. These games typically consist of a Stackelberg model in which the defender allocates a limited number of resources to protect a set of targets based on a randomized strategy, while the attacker, upon learning the strategy, chooses an optimal subset of targets to attack. Motivated by anti-terrorist patrolling, earlier work on security games typically focuses on one-shot game models, e.g., [22, 12]. However, recently, there has been a surge of interests in addressing various security domains involving *repeated* interactions between the defender and a *bounded-rational* attacker. These repeated security game models are motivated by many important real-world problems such as wildlife patrolling [26] and illegal fishing monitoring [11]. Due to the repeated manner of the games, one-shot models are not suitable to tackle these problems, since they do not take into account the learning and adaptive behaviour of the attackers. As such, new solutions are required to address this challenge within the repeated security games. In the literature on security games, such solutions typically assume a specific bounded-rationality attacker behavior model (e.g., the Quantal Response (QR) model) in order to predict the future behaviour of the attacker. However, as pointed out by Kar et al. [14], these bounded-rationality models suffer from a number of limitations. Particularly, they fall short in capturing adaptive attackers, who can adversarially change their attacking strategy over time based on the defender's past actions. Unfortunately, attackers are typically adaptive in real scenarios, making such approaches unsuitable to tackle real problems.

Although Kar et al. [14] refined the attacker behavior model and took into account the adaptive behaviour of attackers, such type of approaches still has a number of shortcomings, namely: (i) it assumes that the attacker's behaviour model, along with *all* the features/patterns that affect the model, is known a priori; (ii) it assumes that the attacker payoffs are known by the defender in advance; and (iii) it is computationally intractable and only local optimal strategy can be computed, therefore no theoretical performance guarantee can be provided. However in real-scenarios, attackers are not necessarily following a particular model and it is very hard to predict their behaviors. Moreover, it is widely recognized that the defender usually does not know the attacker's payoffs (Kiekintveld et al. [15], Blum et al. [3]). In fact, the defender may *even* not precisely know her own payoffs due to uncertainties in some domains. For example, in wildlife poaching or illegal fishing domains, the payoff of a target (i.e., a subarea) at each round depends on the *amount* and *types* of species showing up, which is random and difficult to estimate due to too much uncertainty in nature.

To overcome these issues, we propose a novel defender strategy for repeated security games, namely Follow the Perturbed Leader with Uniform Exploration (or **FPL-UE** for short), which is a variant of the celebrated Follow the Perturbed Leader (FPL) algorithm, a state-of-the-art method from the online learning theory literature [13]. In particular, we show that the defender's patrolling problem in repeated security games can be formulated as a combinatorial adversarial online learning problem, where at each round, an opponent (i.e., the attacker) adversarially sets a multidimensional vector of positive rewards, and the learner (i.e., the defender) can only choose to see a *subset* of entries of this vector (i.e., targets to protect), while the rest remains *unrevealed*. The learner's reward is the sum of the revealed entries, and her goal is to efficiently

*First two authors contribute equally.

Appears in: *Proceedings of the 15th International Conference on Autonomous Agents and Multiagent Systems (AAMAS 2016), J. Thangarajah, K. Tuyls, C. Jonker, S. Marsella (eds.), May 9–13, 2016, Singapore.*

maximise the total rewards against this adaptive and adversarial opponent (for more details, see, e.g., [6]). The current state of the art of the literature is the method proposed by Neu and Bartok [19].[1] However, their algorithm works only when the learner suffers *loss* (i.e., the goal is loss minimisation), while in our case, as we will show in Section 2, the learner collects *rewards* (i.e., the goal is reward maximisation). As Neu and Bartok noted *explicitly* in the paper, their algorithm, in particular, a key lemma in proving the regret guarantee, *cannot* be directly adapted for the reward scenario to guarantee fast regret convergence. As such, the FPL algorithm of Neu and Bartok cannot be directly applied to our setting. Against this background, we propose a new analysis for the reward maximisation scenario. In particular, we show that FPL-UE, which augments the algorithm in [19] with more ingredient of exploration and exploits the structures of security games, can provide efficient and provable performance guarantees for the defender in a repeated security game. Our numerical evaluation based on simulations also show the advantage of our algorithm and the failure of convergence of the algorithm in [19] when dealing with reward maximization cases.

Furthermore, our approach also enjoys the following advantages: (i) it does not require any prior knowledge about attacker's behaviour, and thus, is suitable for handling any types of attackers; (ii) it does not require any prior knowledge about the game payoffs either, and thus, can deal with payoff uncertainty; and (iii) it has efficient theoretical performance guarantees. In particular, the algorithm assumes an arbitrary attacker, and puts no assumptions on their behaviour. It then efficiently balances between exploration (i.e., learn which strategy is the best against the particular attacker) and exploitation (maximises the total utility over time). To do so, at each round, our algorithm calculates a mixed strategy that is a careful combination of uniform random distribution (for exploration) and a distribution derived from solving an optimisation problem (for exploitation) with perturbed values (i.e., with some artificially added noise). By doing so, we show that FPL-UE can provably achieve low-regret (i.e., performance loss) bounds, compared to that of the best fixed strategy on hindsight.

In particular, we show that the regret bound of FPL-UE is at most $O(\sqrt{T})$ in total within T time steps. This sub-linear regret implies that the average regret per time step is converging to 0 as T tends to infinity. Thus, the behaviour of FPL-UE converges to the best fixed strategy (i.e., the best response to the attacker's strategy) on hindsight, with a convergence rate of $O(\frac{1}{\sqrt{T}})$. We further show that within zero-sum security games (which are well-motivated by many real-world applications [11]), if both the defender and attacker use FPL-UE to make their actions, they can achieve an approximate (algorithmic) equilibrium. We also show that the minimax value, which is a powerful solution concept of the zero-sum games, can also be approximated with provable approximation guarantees, by using FPL-UE against a simulated user, who also uses FPL-UE to make decisions. As such, our work contributes to the state of the art in the following aspects:

- We provide a novel approach, based on online combinatorial optimisation, for designing efficient defender strategies in repeated security games. Our approach does not require additional prior knowledge about the attacker and the environment, and can be applied against adaptive attackers. Our approach is the first defender strategy for repeated security games that enjoys provable theoretical performance guarantees.
- We also show that for an important sub-class of repeated security games, namely the zero-sum games, we can approximate the algorithmic equilibrium and the minimax value of the game by applying our strategy for both sides.
- Finally, by using extensive numerical evaluations, we demonstrate that our algorithm, while it does not require any prior knowledge, can still achieve competitive performance, compared to the defender strategy generated using the Subjective Utility Quantal Response (**SUQR**) model [21], a state-of-the-art attacker behavior model that has been tested in real-world repeated security games for protecting wildlife and fishery [4, 7], which heavily relies on the existence of prior knowledge. We also show that the additional uniform exploration step in our algorithm is essential, as it significantly outperform the existing version of Neu and Bartok [19] in practice.

[1] We refer the reader to [6, 20] for a more detailed survey of the combinatorial online learning literature.

1.1 Additional Related Work

Our work is potentially related to two lines of research in security games. One line of work deals with uncertainties in security games, including payoff uncertainties, attacker surveillance and behavior uncertainties [23, 15, 1, 21]. These works either require strong model assumptions (e.g., the Quantal Response assumption) or are too conservative (e.g., the robust optimization approach). Moreover, the models are typically computationally hard and few theoretical guarantees can be given. In contrast, our approach requires no prior knowledge and is efficient. Another line of work is the recent research on learning in security games, but they are all different from ours. [3] considers the setting with unknown attacker payoffs and studies the defender's problem of learning the Stackelberg mixed strategy by attacker-best-response queries. Their setting, goal and approach are different from ours. [2] considers repeated security games with varying attacker types captured by different payoff matrices and uses the online learning approach, but they assume full knowledge of the game payoffs and perfect rationality of the attackers. Also, their algorithm is not computationally efficient. (Klima et al [16, 17]) consider repeated border patrolling with an online learning approach. They experimentally applied several known learning algorithms, but with no theoretical analysis.

2. PROBLEM FORMULATION

In this section, we first describe the repeated security game setting and discuss the assumption of information available to the defender. We then show how to formulate the repeated security game as an adversarial online combinatorial optimisation.

The Game: We consider a repeated security game played between a defender and an attacker. The defender has k security resources and needs to protect n (with $n >> k$) targets, while the attacker also has *multiple* attack resources and can attack at most m targets at the same time. We use $[n]$ to denote the set of all targets. A defender pure strategy is a subset of $[n]$, with cardinality *at most* k, indicating the set of protected targets in the pure strategy. Alternatively, we may use a *binary* vector $v \in \{0,1\}^n$ to denote a generic defender pure strategy, where entry i is 1 if and only if target i is protected in this pure strategy. Throughout this paper, we will use an n-dimensional binary vector to denote a pure strategy, and $\mathcal{V} \subseteq \{0,1\}^n$ to denote the set of all defender pure strategies. Therefore, $||v||_1 \leq k$ for any $v \in \mathcal{V}$. However, set $\mathcal{V}$ needs *not* to be the set of all v's satisfying $||v||_1 \leq k$ due to possible scheduling constraints in practice (see [12] for examples). Naturally, we assume that any target can be protected by at least some $v \in \mathcal{V}$. A defender mixed strategy is simply a distribution over $\mathcal{V}$. Similarly, we use $a \in \{0,1\}^n$ to denote a generic attacker pure strategy and

For all t = 1,2,...,T, repeat
1. The defender computes a mixed strategy from which she samples a pure strategy $v_t \in \mathcal{V}$ to play.
2. The attacker plays a pure strategy $a_t \in \mathcal{A}$;
3. The defender gets a utility depending on both v_t, a_t and potential uncertainties of U_i^u, U_i^c for all $i \in [n]$.
4. The defender observes feedbacks from the targets she visited in the pure strategy v_t;

Figure 1: The Repeated Security Game Procedure

set $\mathcal{A}$ to denote the set of all attacker pure strategies. Naturally, $||a||_1 \le m$ for any $a \in \mathcal{A}$. Given that target i is attacked, the defender gets utility $U_i^c \in [-0.5, 0.5]$ if target i is *covered* and gets $U_i^u \in [-0.5, 0.5]$ if i is *uncovered*.[2] As a standard assumption, we assume $U_i^c > U_i^u$, i.e., covering a target is strictly better for the defender than uncovering it. We allow *uncertainties* of U_i^c and U_i^u, since they can be random, potentially depending on environmental factors. The game is played for T rounds (see Figure 1).

One might wonder why repeated security games can be viewed as an online *reward* maximization problem since at the first glance, security games seem a loss minimization problem, i.e., the defender wants to minimize the loss from attack. Some thoughts reveal that this is actually *not* true, because the defender actively seeks to catch attackers in security games. In particular, at each round, the attacker attacks several targets. Then the defender's task is precisely to find these attacked targets and convert their states from "unprotected" to "protected", by which her utility converts from U_i^u to U_i^c, or equivalently, gains a reward $U_i^c - U_i^u (> 0)$. As shown later, our mathematical formulation formalizes this intuition.

Information and Behaviour Assumptions: The amount of information (or knowledge) players possess in a game has a profound influence on their equilibrium behaviour. Previous work in security games mostly assumes plenty knowledge for the defender and attacker. They know the payoff structures of the game, or at least the *range* of payoffs in some uncertain settings; And they know each other's actions or behavior models. However, as we mentioned above, in some important domains like wildlife poaching or illegal fishing, the value of a target at each round is unknown a priori and depends on random environmental factors. Moreover, even given the payoffs, it is still hard to predict the attackers' behaviours. This is due to at least two reasons: (i) the attacker may have different knowledge and constraints from what the defender thought; (ii) the attacker may be irrational to any extent.

Instead, our model adopts a completely different perspective – we do not require the defender to have any knowledge regarding the payoffs in advance. More practically, we assume the defender can only observe the real-time utilities at those targets where a patroller is sent. On the other hand, the only requirement for the attacker is that, he *cannot* observe the defender's move at current round, i.e., players move simultaneously at each round. This is reasonable because each round models a single-shot game. Furthermore, we assume that the defender is an expected utility maximiser. Finally, our algorithm requires no behaviour model for the attacker. Put differently, the attacker could be a utility maximiser or be irrational to any extent; could know the payoff structure or may be uncertain about the game to any level; could be totally adversarial, or could be a random player.

Utility Model and Problem Formulation: Given any defender and attacker pure strategy v_t and a_t at time t, the defender's utility is:

$$u(v_t, a_t) = \sum_{i\in[n]} v_{t,i} a_{t,i} U_i^c + \sum_{i\in[n]} (1 - v_{t,i}) a_{t,i} U_i^u$$

[2]Here, "0.5" is for normalization reason.

where the first [second] term is the utility from protected [unprotected] targets. We rewrite the utility as follows:

$$\begin{aligned} u(v_t, a_t) &= \sum_{i\in[n]} v_{t,i} a_{t,i} [U_i^c - U_i^u] + \sum_{i\in[n]} a_{t,i} U_i^u \\ &= v_t \cdot r_t(a_t) + C(a_t) \end{aligned} \quad (1)$$

where $r_t(a_t) \in R^n$ satisfying $r_{t,i} = a_{t,i}[U_i^c - U_i^u] \in [0, 1]$ (since $0.5 \ge U_i^c > U_i^u \ge -0.5$) and $C(a_t) = \sum_{i\in[n]} a_{t,i} U_i^u$ both depend *only* on the attacker strategy a_t. Here " $\cdot$ " denotes vector inner product, as will be used throughout the paper.

Eq. (1) provides another view of a repeated security game. That is, given the attacker's strategy at any round, the defender's task is to "collect" positive reward using k resources. This naturally connects to combinatorial adversarial online learning settings [6]. Note that if r_t is drawn independently from the same distribution for any t, then r_t is stochastic and this case admits efficient and regret-tight algorithms [10, 18].

In this paper, however, we consider that $r_t(a_t)$ is chosen adversarially. This is due to the following reasons. First, it is consistent with the nature of defender-attacker interactions especially when the attacker is adaptive. Second, due to irrationality and defender's incomplete knowledge of the attacker as well as uncontrollable environmental factors affecting payoffs, it is very difficult to estimate a distribution for r_t. Therefore, we take the worse-case analysis and assume that the reward is chosen adversarially. Let $\mathcal{F}_t$ denote the history information of the game by time t (inclusive), and $\mathcal{F}_0$ denote no history information at all. We allow r_t to depend on $\mathcal{F}_{t-1}$ but *not* v_t, i.e., the defender's play at round t. Given $a_1, ..., a_T$, we are interested in finding an *online* policy $v_1(\mathcal{F}_0), ..., v_T(\mathcal{F}_{T-1})$ (possibly randomized) that maximizes the defender's expected utility $\mathbb{E}\left[\sum_{t=1}^T u(v_t, a_t)\right]$ where the expectation is taken over the randomness of the policy and environment. Alternatively, we aim at minimizing the defender's *regret*, defined as:

$$\begin{aligned} R_T &= \max_{v\in\mathcal{V}} \sum_{t=1}^T u(v, a_t) - \mathbb{E}\left[\sum_{t=1}^T u(v_t, a_t)\right] \\ &= \max_{v\in\mathcal{V}} \sum_{t=1}^T r_t \cdot v - \mathbb{E}\left[\sum_{t=1}^T r_t \cdot v_t\right], \end{aligned} \quad (2)$$

where the first term $\max_{v\in\mathcal{V}} \sum_{t=1}^T r_t \cdot v$ is the utility of the optimal hindsight pure strategy,[3] and serves as a benchmark. Therefore, this gives a regret minimization formulation with linear *reward* function $r_t \cdot v_t$ where $r_t \in [0, 1]^n$ may be adversarially chosen.

This type of regret notion with optimal fixed strategy is common within the online learning theory literature [5, 6]. The underlying reason is that it is typically impossible to learn the optimal (adaptive) strategy (see [5, 6, 13]). In fact, as the attacker can arbitrarily (and adversarially) change his choice of a_t at each t, the optimal strategy at round t against that a_t can be independent from the history. As such, there is simply no way to predict a_t from the previous observations, and thus, the optimal adaptive strategy cannot be learned.

On the other hand, the best fixed strategy on hindsight can be efficiently learned with access to previous observations. A key intuition behind this is that as we play more and more rounds, no matter how adversarial the attacker will be in the next round, his choice of a_t for that particular round will have less effect on the performance of the best fixed strategy on hindsight, compared to the many previously played rounds.

[3]Notice that there always exists an optimal hindsight pure strategy even we optimize over the set of mixed strategies.

It is worthwhile to note that while the best fixed strategy (on hindsight) is more efficiently learnable, its performance can be arbitrarily bad, compared to that of the optimal adaptive strategy. However, we will show that it is not in our case. Particularly, in the next section we will propose a defender strategy that can achieve both low regret against the best fixed strategy, and provable convergence to a near-optimal adaptive strategy.

3. A LOW-REGRET DEFENCE STRATEGY

In this section, we propose FPL-UE, an FPL-based online learning algorithm for efficiently determining a low-regret defence strategy. To do so, we first brief the main concept of FPL. We then detail the modifications Neu and Bartok introduced to make FPL suitable for combinatorial online learning problems. Finally, we describe FPL-UE. Note that while FPL-UE inherits the main design spirit from FPL, our main contribution is to provide the theoretical guarantee for our setting. In fact, FPL has become an algorithm design concept in online learning literature and there is a family of FPL-based algorithms, which all share similar concept. The key challenges for designing these algorithms lie at the convergence analysis of the algorithm for different settings (which is also the case here).

The FPL algorithm: This type of online learning approach maintains a reward estimate $\widehat{r}_{t,i}$ for each target i and round t, with $\widehat{r}_{1,i} = 0$. Let $\widehat{r}_t$ be the vector of these estimates at round t, and let $z = (z_1, ..., z_n)$ be a random vector such that each $z_i \sim \exp(\eta)$ is independently drawn from the exponential distribution $\exp(\eta)$ with parameter η to be specified. At each round, the algorithm chooses a defender pure strategy v_t

$$v_t = \arg\max_{v \in \mathcal{V}} \{v \cdot (\widehat{r}_t + z)\}, \tag{3}$$

which collects the maximum estimated reward perturbed by the noise vector z. Since z is random, we will view v_t as a random vector as well. After observing the reward $r_{t,i}$ at any chosen target i, the corresponding reward estimates of the chosen target at round $t+1$ can be updated as follows:

$$\widehat{r}_{t+1,i} = \widehat{r}_{t,i} + \frac{r_{t,i}}{p_{t,i}} \mathbb{I}(t,i)$$

where $\mathbb{I}(t,i)$ is an indicator function indicating whether target i was chosen at round t, and $p_{t,i}$ is the probability that target i was chosen within that round. Note that the term $\frac{r_{t,i}}{p_{t,i}} \mathbb{I}(t,i)$ is an unbiased estimator of $r_{t,i}$ (since $\mathbb{E}[\frac{r_{t,i}}{p_{t,i}} \mathbb{I}(t,i)] = r_{t,i}$), and it is more preferred in the online learning literature, compared to the directly observed reward value $r_{t,i}$. This is due to convenience of theoretical analysis. However, while $\mathbb{I}(t,i)$ is fully observable (i.e., we either choose target i or not), $p_{t,i}$ cannot be computed efficiently, as it cannot be expressed in a closed form. To overcome this issue, Neu and Bartok proposed a method, called Geometric Re-sampling (GR), to estimate the value of $1/p_{t,i}$, and can be described as follows (see Algorithm 1):

The GR algorithm: The algorithm is based on the following observation: at round t, $v_{t,i}$ takes value 1 with probability $p_{t,i}$, therefore if we *simulate* strategy v_t, denoted as $\widetilde{v}$ in Algorithm 1, for enough trails, the number of trails needed for $\widetilde{v}_i$ to hit value 1 for the first time is a geometric distribution with mean $1/p_{t,i}$. The GR algorithm precisely follows this observation and estimates $1/p_{t,i}$ by simulating enough trails of $\widetilde{v}$ until $\widetilde{v}_i$ hits 1. However, since there is a positive probability that $\widetilde{v}_i = 1$ will never happen, GR might not ever stop in the worse case, making the algorithm computationally inefficient. To overcome this issue, GR truncates the number

---

Algorithm 1 The GR Algorithm

Input: $\eta \in \mathbb{R}^+, M \in \mathbb{Z}^+, \widehat{r} \in \mathbb{R}^n, t \in \mathbb{N}$;
Output: $K(t) := \{K(t,1), \dots, K(t,n)\} \in \mathbb{Z}^n$
1: Initialize $\forall i \in [n] : K(t,i) = 0, k = 1$;
2: **for** k=1,2,...,M **do**
3: Repeat step 4 $\sim$ 10 in Algorithm 2 once just to produce $\widetilde{v}$ as a simulation of v_t.
4: **for all** $i \in [n]$ **do**
5: **if** $k < M$ **and** $\widetilde{v}_i = 1$ **and** $K(t,i) = 0$ **then**
6: Set $K(t,i) = k$;
7: **else if** $k = M$ **and** $K(t,i) = 0$ **then**
8: Set $K(t,i) = M$;
9: **end if**
10: **end for**
11: **if** $K(t,i) > 0$ for all $i \in [n]$, **then** break;
12: **end for**

Algorithm 2 The FPL-UE Algorithm

Parameter: $\eta \in \mathbb{R}^+, M \in \mathbb{Z}^+, \gamma \in [0,1]$;
1: Initialize the estimated reward $\widehat{r} = \mathbf{0} \in R^n$;
2: Pick the set of exploration strategies $E = \{v_1, ..., v_n\}$ such that target i is protected in pure strategy v_i.
3: **for** t=1,...,T **do**
4: Sample $flag \in \{0,1\}$ such that $flag = 0$ with prob. γ;
5: **if** $flag = 0$ **then**
6: Let v_t be a uniform randomly sampled strategy from E;
7: **else**
8: Draw $z_i \sim \exp(\eta)$ independently for $i \in [n]$ and let $z = (z_1, ..., z_n)$;
9: Let $v_t = \arg\max_{v \in \mathcal{V}} \{v \cdot (\widehat{r} + z)\}$;
10: **end if**
11: Adversary picks $r_t \in [0,1]^n$ and defender plays v_t.
12: Run GR$(\eta, M, \widehat{r}, t)$: estimate $\frac{1}{p_{t,i}}$ as $K(t,i)$;
13: Update $\widehat{r}(i) \leftarrow \widehat{r}(i) + K(t,i) r_{t,i} \mathbb{I}(t,i)$; where $\mathbb{I}(t,i) = 1$ for i satisfying $v_{t,i} = 1$; $\mathbb{I}(t,i) = 0$ otherwise;
14: **end for**

---

of trials with a finite value M, and all the $K(t,i)$ in Algorithm 1, that have not been set yet, will be set to be M (steps 7, 8). This truncation introduces a bias for the estimation of $1/p_{t,i}$. However, the bias can be properly handled (see Lemma 5 in Section 7).

The FPL-UE algorithm: As mentioned earlier, it is not possible to directly apply FPL and GR to our settings. A key reason behind this is that the value of $p_{t,i}$ can be arbitrarily small. While this is not a problem for loss minimisation, it turns out to be a major challenge within our setting. As such, we overcome this issue by introducing additional fraction of uniform exploration to the algorithm. In particular, instead of solely relying on Eq. (3) to determine the defender pure strategy, we uniformly randomly choose a vector v_t from some pre-specified set E with carefully chosen probability $\gamma > 0$, while sets v_t to be the solution of Eq. (3) only with probability $(1-\gamma)$. This seemingly "arbitrary" modification actually allows us to provide effective theoretical analysis of convergence, and interestingly, our extensive simulations also show the necessity of the uniform exploration component – our algorithm outperforms, and in some cases significantly outperforms, the algorithm of Neu and Bartok in the repeated security game setting (see Section 4 and 6 for more details).

Given all these, the FPL-UE algorithm (Algorithm 2) can be described as follows. At each round t, our algorithm either does a uniform random exploration with probability γ (step 6) or plays an FPL strategy with probability $1-\gamma$ (steps 8, 9). Then the algorithm estimates the reward of round t by GR *after* playing the strategy v_t and observing reward (step $11-13$). Notice that, when updating $\widehat{r}$

(step 13), the i'th entry is updated only when $v_{t,i} = 1$, i.e., target i is visited. Otherwise, it keeps unchanged.

4. PERFORMANCE ANALYSIS

Given the description of FPL-UE, we now investigate the theoretical properties of the algorithm. In particular, our main theoretical result is the following guarantee of both computational efficiency and regret bound for FPL-UE.

THEOREM 1. *FPL-UE runs in $poly(n, k, T)$ time if the defender can best respond to any reward vector in $poly(n, k)$ time*[4]. *The regret R_T of FPL-UE is upper bounded as:*

$$R_T \leq \gamma mT + 2Tke^{-M\frac{\gamma}{n}} + \frac{k(\log n + 1)}{\eta} + \eta mT \min(m, k).$$

In particular, with $\eta = \sqrt{\frac{k(\log n+1)}{mT\min\{m,k\}}}$, $\gamma = \frac{\sqrt{k}}{\sqrt{mT}}$ *and* $M = n\sqrt{\frac{mT}{k}}\log(Tk)$, *$R_T$ is at most* $\mathcal{O}\left(\sqrt{kmT\min\{m,k\}\log n}\right)$.

The constant of the polynomial is approximately 2. We note that the convergence ratio depends on parameters that are *specific* to security games, for example, the number of attacker resources m. This translates to the upper bound of the sum of the reward vector. Our analysis explores such structure and provides better convergence ratio for security game settings than state-of-the-art algorithms (see Section 6 for more details). As a special case, when $m = n$, this is the general combinatorial adversarial online learning problem for *reward* maximisation with semi-bandit feedback, and for such general settings, FPL-UE achieves regret upper bound $\mathcal{O}\left(k\sqrt{nT\log n}\right)$, which matches the bound for the *loss* case in the state-of-the-art work [19]. We defer the detailed proof to Section 7.

We now investigate the performance of FPL-UE, compared to that of the optimal (adaptive) strategy on hindsight. This is the *best possible* defending strategy one can hope – at each round, the defender can first observe the attacker's move and then play a best response. Let $A = \{a_1, \ldots, a_T\}$ denote any attacker strategy over T rounds. Recall that $a_t \in \{0,1\}^n$ is the attacker's strategy at round t with $||a_t||_1 \leq m$. Let $OPT(A)$ denote the total *rewards* of the optimal (adaptive) defender strategy on hindsight against A, and let $FPL_(A)$ denote the expected total *rewards* of the defender by applying FPL-UE.[5] As we explained at the end of Section 2, it is generally not possible to provide any theoretical guarantee for $FPL(A)$, when compared with $OPT(A)$. Interestingly, we show that FPL-UE can gain an "almost" $\frac{k}{n}$ fraction of $OPT(A)$ in repeated security game settings.

PROPOSITION 2. *Assuming no schedule constraints, we have*

$$FPL(A) \geq \frac{k}{n}OPT(A) - \mathcal{O}\left(\sqrt{Tmk\min\{k,m\}\log n}\right).$$

Generally, $FPL(A)$ and $OPT(A)$ are of order T, so the term $\mathcal{O}\left(\sqrt{Tmk\min\{k,m\}\log n}\right)$ is relatively negligible. Due to space limitations, all the proofs, *except* for the proof of Theorem 1, are deferred to the online appendix of the paper. In what follows, we will detail a number of implications of these theoretical results, from a game theoretic perspective.

[4]This holds widely in security games.

[5]Note that reward $\neq$ defender utility, due to the extra, uncontrollable and generally negative, term $C(a_t)$ (see Equation 1). We compare the algorithm performance using *rewards*, due to two reasons: 1. $C(a_t)$ is uncontrollable by any algorithm; 2. reward is positive, thus the ratio in Proposition 2 is meaningful.

5. ZERO-SUM SECURITY GAMES

In this section, we consider *zero-sum* security games. Such games can be found in many real-world scenarios, e.g., the illegal fishing monitoring [11]. We first start with the estimation of an approximate algorithmic equilibrium in repeated zero-sum security games. We then investigate how to estimate the minimax value of the game.

Let $V = \{v_1, \ldots, v_T\}$ denote a strategy of the defender over T rounds. Suppose for now that the attacker is also a utility maximiser. Now, consider a pair of defender-attacker strategies (V, A). Let $U_D(V, A)$ denote the expected performance (i.e., the total utility) of the defender strategy V against the attacker strategy A. Note that the expected performance of attacker strategy A against V is $-U_D(V, A)$.

Approximate Algorithmic Equilibrium: A direct implication of Proposition 2 is the estimation of an approximate algorithmic (or program) equilibrium, which is the approximate version of the program equilibrium introduced by Tennenholtz [25]. It can be defined as follows:

DEFINITION 1. *For any $\varepsilon > 0$, the strategy profile (V, A) is a* ε-approximate algorithmic equilibrium *of the game if and only if for any V' and A', we have $U_D(V', A) \leq U_D(V, A) + \varepsilon$ and $U_D(V, A) \leq U_D(V, A') + \varepsilon$.*

Consider the case when both the defender and the attacker applies FPL-UE to choose their actions. Let

$$\varepsilon = \frac{n-k}{n}mT + 3\sqrt{kmT\min\{m,k\}\log n} \tag{4}$$

COROLLARY 3. *Assume* $\min\{k, m\}\log n \geq 3$ *and no schedule constraints. The strategy profile* (FPL-UE, FPL-UE) *(i.e., both players use FPL-UE) is an ε-approximate algorithmic equilibrium of the repeated zero-sum security game, where ε is defined as in Eq.* (4).

Minimax Value of the Game: In zero-sum games, the minimax (or maxmin) value of the game is a powerful solution concept, which provides a guarantee we can achieve even in the worst case scenario, and it is well known that the minimax value exists and can be efficiently computed, e.g., by linear programming [9]. In particular, let **v**/**a** denote a defender/attacker *mixed* strategy, and $\mathbf{u}^*$ denote the minimax value of the zero-sum security game. From von Neumann's Minimax Theorem, we have $\mathbf{u}^* = \max_{\mathbf{v}}\min_{\mathbf{a}} u(\mathbf{v}, \mathbf{a}) = \min_{\mathbf{a}}\max_{\mathbf{v}} u(\mathbf{v}, \mathbf{a})$. However, the minimax value *cannot* be calculated without having the full knowledge of the game, which unfortunately is indeed the case in our setting. Nevertheless, we can approximate this value by the FPL-UE strategy.

COROLLARY 4. *Assume* $\min\{k, m\}\log n \geq 3$. *Suppose that both the defender and attacker apply FPL-UE to make their actions. We have:*

$$\left|\mathbf{u}^* - \frac{U_D(\text{FPL},\text{FPL})}{T}\right| \leq 3\sqrt{\frac{km\min\{m,k\}(\log n+1)}{T}}$$

where $U_D(\text{FPL}, \text{FPL})$ *denotes the utility of the defender applying FPL-UE against a FPL-UE attacker.*

That is, to estimate the mimimax value of the game, we just need to simulate a game against an FPL-UE attacker and consider the average utility. Indeed, as T tends to infinity, the approximation gap converges to 0. Note that since the simulated attacker is not a real one, we still do not need to have any prior knowledge about real attackers. In fact, we only consider a simulated attacker, whose actions can be fully simulated. On the other hand, we require the knowledge of the payoff matrix (i.e., what is the payoff of each action pairs of the players) to calculate the minimax value of the game. This assumption, however, is reasonable, as in the zero-sum games, the payoff of the attacker is negative version of the defender's payoff. Thus, this assumption does not require prior knowledge about the attacker either.

6. NUMERICAL EVALUATIONS

We run our algorithm against a number of commonly seen attacker models with simulations. In our simulations, the payoffs U_i^c's and U_i^u's are randomly generated. In particular, for any target $i \in [n]$, we first drawn two numbers $a, b \in [-0.5, 0.5]$ uniformly at random, and then set $U_i^c = \max(a, b)$ and $U_i^u = \min(a, b)$, thus the condition $U_i^c \geq U_i^u$ is satisfied. Note that the defender has no a-priori knowledge about these payoffs.

We test our algorithm against different types of attackers, which together represent the majority of typical attacking models. Purely for the purpose of modeling the attacker's reaction to our algorithm, we also generate the attacker's payoffs in a similar fashion as the defender's payoffs, except that the attacker's payoff is higher if a target is *uncovered*. We consider 5 different types of attackers:[6]

- **Uniform**: an attacker with a uniformly random *mixed* strategy;
- **Adversarial**: an attacker with the maximin *mixed* strategy. That is, the attacker is fully adversarial – he only cares about minimizing the defender's utility;
- **Stackelberg**: the attacker always plays the optimal follower *pure* strategy of the Strong Stackelberg Equilibrium;
- **BestResponse**: at round t, the attacker best responds to the mixed strategy $\sum_{i=1}^{t-1} v_i/(t-1)$, i.e., the empirical defender mixed strategy in history;
- **QuantalResponse (QR)**: the attacker also responds to the empirical defender mixed strategy, but by a QR model [21].

Note that some attacker types are informationally very powerful, e.g., the *BestResponse* type knows all the payoffs as well as all the defender's past actions, while some may have very little knowledge (e.g., the *Uniform* type); Some types play mixed strategies (e.g., *Adversarial* type) while some play pure strategies (e.g., *Stackelberg* type); Some types are rational while some are not. Also note that our algorithm does not know which type of attackers we are facing. The simulation aims to test the "robustness" of the algorithm against varied types of attackers.

Baselines: We choose two algorithms as baselines. The first is the **FPL** algorithm of Neu and Bartok [19], a *state-of-the-art algorithm* for combinatorial adversarial online learning. As Neu and Bartok pointed out, the regret bound for their FPL algorithm can only be proved in the cost minimization scenario. Nevertheless, we use it as a baseline to see how it compares to FPL-UE and how it performs in repeated security games where the goal is to maximize reward. Another baseline is the Subjective Utility Quantal Response (**SUQR**) attacker behavior model [21], a *state-of-the-art human behavior model* in security games that captures the attacker's bounded rationality. SUQR model has been tested in several human behavior experiments of security games in Amazon Mechanical Turk (AMT), and is shown to outperform the strong Stackelberg equilibrium strategy and maximin strategy when playing against real-world humans [21, 8, 14]. In our simulation, at each round T, the SUQR model first looks at all the attack records from the past $T-1$ rounds and then learns the attacker's behavior model based on these *history records* and the *attacker's payoffs*. As a result, the SUQR model will be refined each round with more history records. After learning the attacker's SUQR behavior model, the defender then computes an optimal mixed strategy against the behavior model and samples a pure strategy to play.

We note that it is *not* completely fair to compare FPL-UE with SUQR because SUQR requires much more defender prior knowledge (e.g., past attack records and attacker payoffs) than FPL-UE. Nevertheless, we aim to examine how competitive FPL-UE is when compared with SUQR.

We set $n = 100$ and $k = 10$ in all our simulations, and test the convergence of the *average regret* (i.e., regret divided by T) for various m. We translate the defender utility of SUQR to regret (See Equation (2)). Figures 2, 3 and 4 show the case for $m = 1$, $m = 5$, and $m = 15$ respectively, within 1000 rounds. Note that average regret is upper-bounded by m. All these figures are the convergence plots for *one* randomly generated game instance, however we do emphasize that the general convergence trend is almost the same across the simulated instances except that the initial rounds in the figures may vary among different instances. Since the absolute value of regret at a fixed round T differs across different game instances, so averaging the regret over games destroys the convergence lines. So we only present one randomly chosen instance here. As an interesting side note, when $m = 15$, the defender has less resources than the attacker. To our knowledge, experiments for such cases have not been done before. We use it as a burden test for the robustness of our algorithm.

From the figures we know that FPL-UE converges in all these cases, while FPL fails to converge (at least within 1000 rounds) when played against *Stackelberg* type and *BestResponse* type. These figures clearly show that FPL-UE outperforms FPL. One interesting phenomenon is that FPL-UE always significantly outperforms FPL when playing against *Stackelberg* type and *BestResponse* type in all the instances we generated. Notice that these two cases are the "difficult" cases for online learning algorithms. The *Stackelberg* type always plays the same *pure* strategy over the whole game, therefore the best hindsight strategy is to protect the most valuable attacked targets, achieving a very high reward. Thus the algorithm takes longer time to converge, mainly due to the compensation for the big loss at the initial rounds where exploration happens mostly. While for the *BestResponse* type, the attacker is always adaptive to the algorithm. The comparison on these "difficult" types shows the advantage of FPL-UE over FPL.

One surprising observation is that, though requiring much more defender prior knowledge, SUQR does not obviously outperform FPL-UE. In fact, SUQR only weakly outperforms FPL-UE when playing against the *Uniform* type and *QuantalResponse* type. This is natural because these two types exactly lie at the realm of the SUQR model. For all the other three types, SUQR does not exhibit obvious advantage. In fact, when the attacker is totally adaptive, i.e., the *BestResponse* type, FPL-UE actually shows some weak advantage. We attribute this to the carefully designed adaptivity nature of the FPL-UE algorithm.

Finally, we observe that the regret against the *BestResponse* or *Stackelberg* type (the two difficult cases) with $m = 15$ is about 1.2 which approximates the regret upper bound ($\frac{m\sqrt{kT\log n}}{T} \approx 1.8$). Interestingly, this empirically shows that the algorithm approximates the upper bound regret when played in these hard cases. To summarize, depending on the rationality level, attacker strategy type and the amount of information the attacker has about the past games, the algorithm can converge at different rates, but will

[6]In the following description, if the attacker plays a *mixed* strategy, our simulation samples a *pure* strategy each round from the described mixed strategy to play.

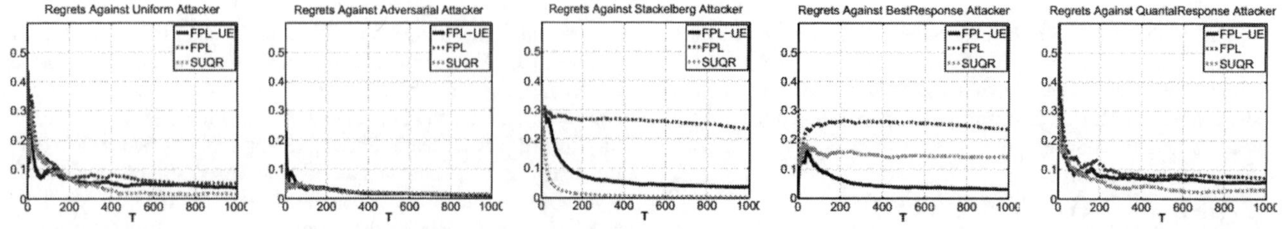

(a) Uniform (b) Adversarial (c) Stackelberg (d) BestResponse (e) QuantalResponse (QR)

Figure 2: Average regret (y-axis) against 5 attacker types after T rounds; Parameters: $n = 100, k = 10, \mathbf{m} = \mathbf{1}, \lambda = 2$ for *QR*.

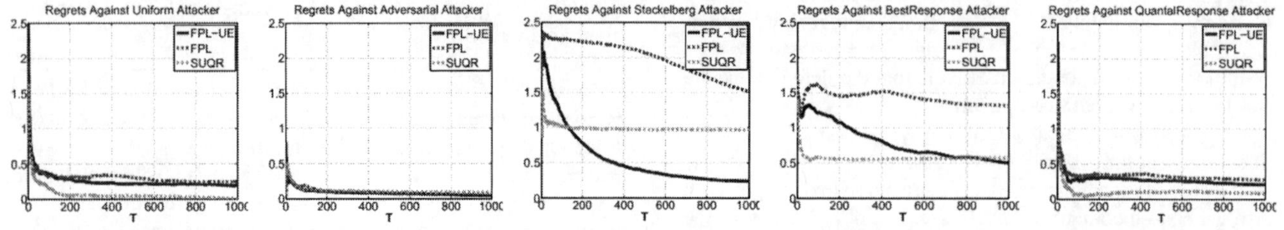

(a) Uniform (b) Adversarial (c) Stackelberg (d) BestResponse (e) QuantalResponse (QR)

Figure 3: Average regret (y-axis) against 5 attacker types after T rounds; Parameters: $n = 100, k = 10, \mathbf{m} = \mathbf{5}, \lambda = 2$ for *QR*.

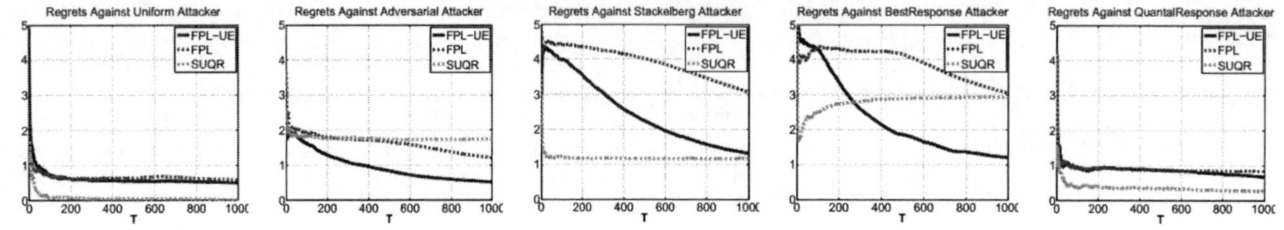

(a) Uniform (b) Adversarial (c) Stackelberg (d) BestResponse (e) QuantalResponse (QR)

Figure 4: Average regret (y-axis) against 5 attacker types after T rounds; Parameters: $n = 100, k = 10, \mathbf{m} = \mathbf{15}, \lambda = 2$ for *QR*.

always be upper bounded by the regret bound.

7. PROOF OF THEOREM 1

We now turn to prove Theorem 1. To do so, we first describe the following lemmas. Lemma 5, as proved in [19], captures the estimation bias of Geometric Re-sampling.

LEMMA 5. *[19]* $\mathbb{E}(\widehat{r}_{t,j}|\mathcal{F}_{t-1}) = (1 - (1 - p_{t,j})^M) r_{t,j}$.

In addition, the following lemma is a simple observation about the reward vector r_t of round t.

LEMMA 6. $||r_t||_1 \leq m$ *for any* t.

PROOF. Since $r_{t,i} \geq 0$, we have

$$||r_t||_1 = \sum_{i\in[n]} r_{t,i} = \sum_{i\in[n]} a_{t,i}[U_i^c - U_i^u] \leq \sum_{i\in[n]} a_{t,i} \leq m.$$

□

To analyse the algorithm, we first describe some notations. Let $\widehat{r}_t$, where $\widehat{r}_{t,i} = K(t,i) r_{t,i} \mathbb{I}(t,i) = K(t,i) r_{t,i} v_{t,i}$, denote the estimation of the reward at round t. Let

$$v_t^{FPL} = \arg\max_{v\in\mathcal{V}} v \cdot (\sum_{j=1}^{t-1} \widehat{r}_j + z), \tag{5}$$

denote the FPL strategy played *before* estimating $\widehat{r}_t$ (Step 9 in Algorithm 1). For the purpose of analysis, define the following *hindsight strategy* (imagine the defender can get the estimation $\widehat{r}_t$ *before* she plays a strategy at round t)

$$\widetilde{v}_t^{FPL} = \arg\max_{v\in\mathcal{V}} v \cdot (\sum_{j=1}^{t} \widehat{r}_j + z). \tag{6}$$

Therefore, we have $v_{t+1}^{FPL} \stackrel{st}{=} \widetilde{v}_t^{FPL}$ where "$\stackrel{st}{=}$" means stochastically equal due to the randomness of z.[7] Let $q_{t,i} = \mathbb{E}(v_{t,i}^{FPL})$ be the probability that target i is protected in strategy v_t^{FPL}, and $\widetilde{q}_{t,i} = \mathbb{E}(\widetilde{v}_{t,i}^{FPL})$ be the probability that target i is protected in strategy $\widetilde{v}_t^{FPL}$. Therefore $q_{t+1,i} = \widetilde{q}_{t,i}$. Notice that v_t^{FPL} is not the only possible strategy played at round t – with probability γ, the defender plays a uniformly randomly sampled pure strategy from set E. Let $p_{t,i} = \mathbb{E}(v_{t,i})$ denote the probability that target i is protected at time t in Algorithm 1. Due to the γ fraction of uniform exploration, we have $p_{t,i} \geq \frac{\gamma}{n}$ for any t, i since each target is protected by at least one pure strategy in E.

Now, we are ready to prove the regret upper bound of Algorithm 1. As observed, the algorithm does exploration with probability γ and exploitation with probability $1 - \gamma$. We start from analyzing the exploitation part. Using the "be-the-leader" lemma [5] to sequence $(\widehat{r}_1 + z, \widehat{r}_2, ..., \widehat{r}_T)$, we obtain

$$\sum_{t=1}^{T} \widehat{r}_t \cdot \widetilde{v}_t^{FPL} + z \cdot \widetilde{v}_1^{FPL} \geq \sum_{t=1}^{T} \widehat{r}_t \cdot v + z \cdot v, \forall v \in \mathcal{V}, \tag{7}$$

where $\widetilde{v}_t^{FPL}$ is defined in Equation (6). By rearranging Inequality

[7]Recall that, two random variable A, B are stochastically equal if $\mathbb{P}(A = x) = \mathbb{P}(B = x)$ for any x in the event set.

(7), we have

$$\begin{aligned}\mathbb{E}\left[\sum_{t=1}^{T}\widehat{r}_t\cdot(v-\widetilde{v}_t^{FPL})\right] &\le \mathbb{E}\left[z\cdot(\widetilde{v}_1^{FPL}-v)\right]\\ &\le \mathbb{E}\left[z\cdot\widetilde{v}_1^{FPL}\right]\\ &\le k\mathbb{E}(\max_{i\in[n]} z_i)\\ &\le \frac{k(\log n+1)}{\eta} \qquad (8)\end{aligned}$$

where the second last "$\le$" uses the inequality $\sum_{i\in[n]}\widetilde{v}_{1,i}^{FPL}\le k$; the last "$\le$" uses the fact that $\mathbb{E}(\max_{i\in[n]} z_i)\le\frac{\log n+1}{\eta}$.

The rest of the proof lies on the following basic intuitions. First, the played strategy v_t^{FPL} should not be too "far" from the hindsight strategy $\widetilde{v}_t^{FPL}$ since the reward estimations they used are only slightly different (compare Equation (5) and (6)). Second, the estimated reward $\widehat{r}_t$ hopefully is "close" to the real reward r_t. Therefore, Inequality (8) also roughly conveys that the played strategy sequence v_t^{FPL} is not too "bad" compared with *any* pure strategy v in the scenario of real reward r_t.

We first lower bound $q_{t,i}$ using $\widetilde{q}_{t,i}$ as follows.

$$\begin{aligned}q_{t,i} &= \int_{z\in[0,\infty]^n} v_{t,i}^{FPL}(z)f(z)dz\\ &= e^{-\eta\|\widehat{r}_t\|_1}\int_{z\in[0,\infty]^n} v_{t,i}^{FPL}(z)f(z-\widehat{r}_t)dz\\ &= e^{-\eta\|\widehat{r}_t\|_1}\int\cdots\int_{z_i\in[-\widehat{r}_{t,i},\infty]} v_{t,i}^{FPL}(z+\widehat{r}_t)f(z)dz\\ &= e^{-\eta\|\widehat{r}_t\|_1}\int\cdots\int_{z_i\in[-\widehat{r}_{t,i},\infty]} \widetilde{v}_{t,i}^{FPL}(z)f(z)dz\\ &\ge e^{-\eta\|\widehat{r}_t\|_1}\int\cdots\int_{z_i\in[0,\infty]} \widetilde{v}_{t,i}^{FPL}(z)f(z)dz\\ &= e^{-\eta\|\widehat{r}_t\|_1}\widetilde{q}_{t,i}\\ &\ge (1-\eta m)\widetilde{q}_{t,i}\end{aligned}$$

where the last inequality uses Lemma 6: $\|\widehat{r}_t\|_1\le m$ for any t. Now we bound the difference between $\mathbb{E}\left[\widehat{r}_t\cdot v_t^{FPL}\right]$ and $\mathbb{E}\left[\widehat{r}_t\cdot\widetilde{v}_t^{FPL}\right]$.

$$\begin{aligned}\mathbb{E}\left[\widehat{r}_t\cdot v_t^{FPL}|\mathcal{F}_t\right] &= \sum_{i\in[n]}\widehat{r}_{t,i}q_{t,i}\\ &\ge \sum_{i\in[n]}\widehat{r}_{t,i}\widetilde{q}_{t,i}-\eta m\sum_{i\in[n]}\widehat{r}_{t,i}\widetilde{q}_{t,i}\\ &\ge \mathbb{E}\left[\widehat{r}_t\cdot\widetilde{v}_t^{FPL}|\mathcal{F}_t\right]-\eta m\min(m,k)\end{aligned}$$

where we used the fact that $\widehat{r}_t$ and $\widehat{r}_{t-1}$ are fixed given $\mathcal{F}_t$, therefore the randomness of v_t^{FPL} and $\widetilde{v}_t^{FPL}$ only comes from z. Taking expectation over $\mathcal{F}_t$, we have

$$\mathbb{E}\left[\widehat{r}_t\cdot v_t^{FPL}\right]\ge\mathbb{E}\left[\widehat{r}_t\cdot\widetilde{v}_t^{FPL}\right]-\eta m\min(m,k) \qquad (9)$$

Now we can upper bound the loss from substituting $\widetilde{v}_t^{FPL}$ in Inequality (8) by v_t^{FPL}.

$$\begin{aligned}&\mathbb{E}\left[\sum_{t=1}^{T}\widehat{r}_t\cdot(v-v_t^{FPL})\right]\\ =\ &\mathbb{E}\left[\sum_{t=1}^{T}\widehat{r}_t\cdot(v-\widetilde{v}_t^{FPL})\right]+\mathbb{E}\left[\sum_{t=1}^{T}\widehat{r}_t\cdot(\widetilde{v}_t^{FPL}-v_t^{FPL})\right]\\ \le\ &\frac{k(\log n+1)}{\eta}+\eta mT\min(m,k),\end{aligned}$$

where the "$\le$" is due to the Inequality (8) and (9). Putting all these together, we can upper bound the regret from the exploitation part:

$$\begin{aligned}&\mathbb{E}\left[\sum_{t=1}^{T}r_t\cdot(v-v_t^{FPL})\right]\\ \le\ &\mathbb{E}\left[\sum_{t=1}^{T}(r_t-\widehat{r}_t)\cdot(v-v_t^{FPL})\right]+\mathbb{E}\left[\sum_{t=1}^{T}\widehat{r}_t\cdot(v-v_t^{FPL})\right]\\ \le\ &2Tk(1-\frac{\gamma}{n})^M+\frac{k(\log n+1)}{\eta}+\eta mT\min(m,k)\end{aligned}$$

Now configuring the regret from exploration, which is trivially upper bounded by m and happens with probability γ, we can upper-bound the total regret as

$$\begin{aligned}R_T &\le \gamma mT+(1-\gamma)\Big[2Tk(1-\frac{\gamma}{n})^M\\ &\quad+\frac{k(\log n+1)}{\eta}+\eta mT\min(m,k)\Big]\\ &\le \gamma mT+2Tke^{-M\frac{\gamma}{n}}\\ &\quad+\frac{k(\log n+1)}{\eta}+\eta mT\min(m,k)\end{aligned}$$

By taking $\eta=\sqrt{\frac{k(\log n+1)}{mT\min\{m,k\}}}$, $\gamma=\frac{\sqrt{k}}{\sqrt{mT}}$ and $M=n\sqrt{\frac{mT}{k}}\log(Tk)$, we obtain the upper bound $\mathcal{O}\left(\sqrt{kmT\min\{m,k\}\log n}\right)$.

8. CONCLUSIONS

In this paper we proposed FPL-UE, the first defender strategy for repeated security games assuming no prior knowledge about the attacker. We proved that our algorithm enjoys a number of compelling theoretical properties. In particular, we showed that FPL-UE can provably achieve low regret bounds, against both the best fixed strategy on hindsight, and the optimal adaptive strategy. In addition, we proved that our main theoretical results have a number of game theoretic implications, such as the efficient estimation of algorithmic equilibria and the minimax value of the game (for zero-sum security games). Our numerical evaluations demonstrated that FPL-UE is indeed efficient against typical attacker profiles. We also demonstrated that FPL-UE indeed outperforms the FPL version of Neu and Bartok. This justifies the usage of the additional uniform exploration steps. Furthermore, its performance is comparable to that of SUQR, a state of the art of the repeated security games literature. This result is surprising and significant, as our algorithm does not require any prior knowledge of the attacker, while SUQR relies much on the existence of such prior information. This implies that, our algorithm is very useful in real-world situations where the attacker behaviour model is not available at the beginning, or the attacker does not fully follow some rational behaviour model. Given this, we argue that our algorithm is more generic, compared to the state of the art, and thus, can be applied in many realistic scenarios of repeated security games.

Acknowledgement:

Xu is supported by MURI grant W911NF-11-1-0332 and NSF grant CCF- 1350900. Tran-Thanh and Jennings gratefully acknowledge funding from the UK Research Council for project "ORCHID", grant EP/I011587/1.

REFERENCES

[1] B. An, D. Kempe, C. Kiekintveld, E. Shieh, S. Singh, M. Tambe, and Y. Vorobeychik. Security games with limited surveillance. In *Conference on Artificial Intelligence (AAAI 2012)*, 2012.

[2] M.-F. Balcan, A. Blum, N. Haghtalab, and A. D. Procaccia. Commitment without regrets: Online learning in stackelberg security games. In *Proceedings of the Sixteenth ACM Conference on Economics and Computation*, EC 2015, pages 61–78, New York, NY, USA, 2015. ACM.

[3] A. Blum, N. Haghtalab, and A. D. Procaccia. Learning optimal commitment to overcome insecurity. In Z. Ghahramani, M. Welling, C. Cortes, N. Lawrence, and K. Weinberger, editors, *Advances in Neural Information Processing Systems 27*, pages 1826–1834. Curran Associates, Inc., 2014.

[4] M. Brown, W. B. Haskell, and M. Tambe. Addressing scalability and robustness in security games with multiple boundedly rational adversaries. In *Conference on Decision and Game Theory for Security (GameSec)*, 2014.

[5] N. Cesa-Bianchi and G. Lugosi. *Prediction, Learning, and Games*. Cambridge University Press, New York, NY, USA, 2006.

[6] N. Cesa-Bianchi and G. Lugosi. Combinatorial bandits. *Journal of Computer and System Sciences*, 78(5):1404–1422, 2012.

[7] F. Fang, P. Stone, and M. Tambe. When security games go green: Designing defender strategies to prevent poaching and illegal fishing. In *International Joint Conference on Artificial Intelligence (IJCAI 2015)*, 2015.

[8] B. Ford, T. Nguyen, M. Tambe, N. Sintov, and F. D. Fave. Beware the soothsayer: From attack prediction accuracy to predictive reliability in security games. In *Conference on Decision and Game Theory for Security*, 2015.

[9] D. Fudenberg and J. Tirole. *Game Theory*. MIT Press, 1991.

[10] Y. Gai, B. Krishnamachari, and R. Jain. Combinatorial network optimization with unknown variables: Multi-armed bandits with linear rewards and individual observations. *IEEE ACM Trans. Netw.*, 20 (5):1466–1478, 2012.

[11] W. B. Haskell, D. Kar, F. Fang, M. Tambe, S. Cheung, and E. Denicola. Robust protection of fisheries with compass. In *Proceedings of the Twenty-Eighth AAAI Conference on Artificial Intelligence, July 27 -31, 2014, Québec City, Québec, Canada.*, pages 2978–2983, 2014.

[12] M. Jain, J. Tsai, J. Pita, C. Kiekintveld, S. Rathi, M. Tambe, and F. Ordóñez. Software assistants for randomized patrol planning for the lax airport police and the federal air marshal service. *Interfaces*, 40(4):267–290, July 2010.

[13] A. Kalai and S. Vempala. Efficient algorithms for online decision problems. *J. Comput. Syst. Sci.*, 71(3):291–307, Oct. 2005.

[14] D. Kar, F. Fang, F. D. Fave, N. Sintov, and M. Tambe. Şa game of thronesŤ: When human behavior models compete in repeated stackelberg security games. In *International Conference on Autonomous Agents and Multiagent Systems (AAMAS 2015)*, 2015.

[15] C. Kiekintveld, J. Marecki, and M. Tambe. Approximation methods for infinite bayesian stackelberg games: Modeling distributional payoff uncertainty. In *The 10th International Conference on Autonomous Agents and Multiagent Systems - Volume 3*, AAMAS 2011, pages 1005–1012, Richland, SC, 2011. International Foundation for Autonomous Agents and Multiagent Systems.

[16] R. Klima, C. Kiekintveld, and V. Lisy. Online learning methods for border patrol resource allocation. In *GameSec*, 2014.

[17] R. Klima, V. Lisy, and C. Kiekintveld. Combining online learning and equilibrium computation in security games. In *GameSec*, 2015.

[18] B. Kveton, Z. Wen, A. Ashkan, and C. Szepesvári. Tight regret bounds for stochastic combinatorial semi-bandits. *AISTAT*, 2015.

[19] G. Neu and G. Bartók. An efficient algorithm for learning with semi-bandit feedback. *ALT*, pages 234–248, 2013.

[20] G. Neu and G. Bartók. Importance weighting without importance weights: An efficient algorithm for combinatorial semi-bandits. *CoRR*, abs/1503.05087, 2015.

[21] T. H. Nguyen, R. Yang, A. Azaria, S. Kraus, and M. Tambe. Analyzing the effectiveness of adversary modeling in security games. In *In Conf. on Artificial Intelligence (AAAI 2013)*, 2013.

[22] J. Pita, M. Jain, J. Marecki, F. Ordóñez, C. Portway, M. Tambe, C. Western, P. Paruchuri, and S. Kraus. Deployed armor protection: The application of a game theoretic model for security at the los angeles international airport. In *Proceedings of the 7th International Joint Conference on Autonomous Agents and Multiagent Systems: Industrial Track*, AAMAS 2008, pages 125–132, Richland, SC, 2008. International Foundation for Autonomous Agents and Multiagent Systems.

[23] J. Pita, M. Jain, M. Tambe, F. Ordóñez, and S. Kraus. Robust solutions to stackelberg games: Addressing bounded rationality and limited observations in human cognition. *Artificial Intelligence*, 174(15):1142 – 1171, 2010.

[24] M. Tambe. *Security and Game Theory: Algorithms, Deployed Systems, Lessons Learned*. Cambridge University Press, New York, NY, USA, 1st edition, 2011.

[25] M. Tennenholtz. Program equilibrium. *Games and Economic Behavior*, 49(2):363–373, 2004.

[26] R. Yang, B. Ford, M. Tambe, and A. Lemieux. Adaptive resource allocation for wildlife protection against illegal poachers. In *International Conference on Autonomous Agents and Multiagent Systems (AAMAS 2014)*, 2014.

Budget Feasible Mechanisms for Dealers

Hau Chan
Department of Computer Science
Trinity University
San Antonio, TX 78212
hchan@trinity.edu

Jing Chen
Department of Computer Science
Stony Brook University
Stony Brook, NY 11794
jingchen@cs.stonybrook.edu

ABSTRACT

We consider the problem of designing budget feasible mechanisms for a dealer, who aims to maximize revenue by buying items from a seller market and selling them to a buyer market that consists of unit-demand buyers. Different from the related literature, the dealer's "value" for a set of items that he purchased from the seller market is not directly given as a number but it is defined to be the maximum revenue the dealer can obtain from selling the items to the buyers.

We aim to design mechanisms that are dominant-strategy truthful for the sellers to report their costs and envy-free for the buyers to purchase their most preferred items (given their prices) in the final outcome, such that the total payment to the sellers does not exceed the dealer's budget and the dealer's revenue is (approximately) maximized.

First, to understand the structure of the optimal mechanisms, we show that the maximum (envy-free) revenue obtainable by the dealer as a function of the set of purchased items is monotone and subadditive. Thus, existing results on subadditive optimization problems are potentially applicable in solving the mechanism design problem for the dealer.

However, a crucial assumption adopted by all previous studies on subadditive functions is that the mechanism or algorithm has access to the value oracle and/or the demand oracle. In the dealer's problem, instead, we show that (1) the demand oracle can be efficiently simulated by the value oracle and (2) both have efficient $O(\log n)$-approximation algorithms, where n is the number of buyers. This is particularly interesting given the literature, since, in general, the demand oracle can always efficiently simulate the value oracle, and there are cases where the demand oracle is strictly more powerful. Our results show that, for the dealer's problem, the two oracles are as powerful as each other.

Finally, we construct a polynomial-time budget feasible mechanism for the dealer that doesn't use any oracle and provides an $O((\log^2 n)(\log^2 m))$-approximation of the optimal revenue, where m is the number of sellers.

Keywords

budget feasible mechanism; subadditive function; envy-free pricing; revenue; implementing value and demand oracles

Appears in: *Proceedings of the 15th International Conference on Autonomous Agents and Multiagent Systems (AAMAS 2016), J. Thangarajah, K. Tuyls, C. Jonker, S. Marsella (eds.), May 9–13, 2016, Singapore.*

1. INTRODUCTION

The goal of retailers or dealers is to sell products (or items) to consumers to make as much revenue as possible. But first, the dealers must *obtain* items from other sources such as wholesalers and manufacturers. Given the obtained items, the dealers then set the *item prices* so as to maximize the revenue from selling the items to the consumers. It is clear that the dealers often have some budget constraints limiting the amount of money that they can spend in their procurements. For instance, in ancient time, western merchants sailed to Asia and Africa to buy spices to sell in their home market. Their budgets, at that time, are the amount of gold they brought with them to Asia and Africa. In modern time, although electronic transactions have greatly sped up the money flow, the dealer still has a finite amount of money that he can spend at the time of the procurement, say the credit limit of his credit card or other forms of loans he can get. Thus, the dealer's goal can be described more precisely as *to maximize his revenue subject to his budget constraint.*

In hindsight, the dealers can perform the procurement part and the pricing part independently. However, a dealer's revenue not only depends on the consumers' demands/values of all possible items that he could potentially obtain, but also on the set of items that he can obtain under his budget. Hence, in order to make optimal or nearly optimal revenue, a dealer should decide *simultaneously* (1) what items to buy from the suppliers (and how much to pay them) and (2) what are the prices of the purchased items that will maximize revenue from selling them to the consumers.

The literature of mechanism design mainly treats the buying part and the selling part separately, and a lot of progress has been made in designing procurement mechanisms for buying items and auctions for selling the items. In this paper, we are interested in synthesizing these two parts and designing mechanisms for dealers, which allow them to simultaneously decide how to buy and sell the items.

1.1 In a Nutshell: Our Setting and Our Goal

Consider a dealer with a budget B. There is a market of m sellers and m items, where the dealer can purchase item j from seller j. Each seller j has a cost c_j for his item. There is also a market of n unit-demand buyers where the dealer can sell the (purchased) items. Each buyer i has a value v_{ij} for each item j. Ideally, the dealer wants to buy a set of items such that the total cost of the items is no more than the budget, and set the item prices to maximize revenue by selling them to the consumers, where his revenue is the sum of the prices of the sold items.

The sellers and the buyers are *strategic*, but in different ways. Each seller's cost is his private information, and the dealer has to give the sellers incentives to truthfully reveal their costs. On the other hand, the buyers' values are known to the dealer, but each buyer has "free choice" and only buys the item that maximizes his utility (i.e., his value minus the item price) from the dealer—that is, the buyers must be *envy-free* [22] in the final outcome. Intuitively, the buyers are from the "home market" of the dealer, which he knows well, and the sellers are from some "alien market" that the dealer just starts to explore.

Accordingly, a dealer mechanism asks each seller to report a cost, and returns an outcome that specifies

(1) dealer's set of items (i.e., the items he buys from the sellers),

(2) dealer's payment to each seller,

(3) dealer's price for each of his items, and

(4) the allocation of dealer's items to the buyers.

Indeed, this will be the input-output structure of our mechanism M_D constructed in Section 5.

In terms of the desirable properties of our mechanisms, we are interested in mechanisms that are

(a) computationally efficient,

(b) budget feasible (i.e., the total payment made by the dealer does not exceed his budget),

(c) dominant strategy truthful (DST) for the sellers,

(d) producing an envy-free pricing and allocation for the buyers, and

(e) producing an outcome that (approximately) maximizes the dealer's revenue.

When a mechanism is randomized, we require that it is a convex combination of deterministic mechanisms that satisfy the above requirements. Indeed, our mechanism, M_D, will be such a randomized mechanism, as will be shown by Theorem 3 and Corollary 2.

Different Solution Concepts for Sellers and Buyers.

Notice that in our model, the dealer's information about the sellers and the buyers are asymmetric. Therefore, we use different solution concepts to analyze the sellers' and the buyers' incentives. Of course, one can consider a worse scenario for the dealer, where both the sellers' costs and the buyers' values are private information, and ask for mechanisms that are truthful on both sides. However, it is well known that DST mechanisms (e.g., VCG [14, 21, 32]) cannot provide any meaningful revenue guarantee in multi-item multi-buyer auctions. One can consider the Bayesian setting and assume that the buyers' values are drawn from some joint distribution; yet, even in the simplest case of unit-demand single-buyer setting (without the sellers), truthful pricing schemes that approximate the optimal revenue is not well understood (see, e.g., [12] and [8] for recent studies on this topic). Given the literature, we consider the asymmetric "home-alien" market model to be a better starting point for the study of dealer mechanisms.

1.2 Main Contribution

Towards constructing approximately optimal mechanisms for the dealer, we start by identifying important structures of the problem, as shown in Theorems 1 and 2.

Our first result is a characterization of the dealer's revenue under the optimal envy-free pricing and allocation, which is defined as a function of the purchased items.

Theorem 1 (restated) *The dealer's revenue function is monotone and subadditive.*

To the best of our knowledge, this is the first characterization on the structure of the dealer's revenue function and it places the dealer's problem in the literature of mechanism design and optimization based on subadditive functions. In particular, [4, 7, 16] have designed budget feasible mechanisms for subadditive functions, and, assuming access to value and demand oracles (as defined later), their results immediately apply to the dealer's problem.

Our second result is about a crucial assumption widely adopted in mechanism design based on subadditive functions —the existence of oracles. Indeed, since a general subadditive function needs exponentially many numbers to describe, it can only be accessed via certain oracles. All budget feasible mechanisms mentioned above rely on the value oracle and/or the demand oracle, formally defined in Section 4. However, since oracles in general do not have efficient real-life implementations[1], it is unclear how these mechanisms can be implemented. It is important to understand when one can design efficient mechanisms that do not rely on any oracle. Our second theorem shows that the demand oracle for the dealer can be approximated by the value oracle.

Theorem 2 (restated) *Given any polynomial time algorithm that is an α-approximation for the dealer's value oracle, there is a polynomial time algorithm that is an α-approximation for the dealer's demand oracle.*

This result has two important implications. First, following [22], the dealer's value oracle can be efficiently approximated within a logarithmic factor; thus we immediately have that the dealer's demand oracle can also be approximated to the same degree. It eventually leads us to a mechanism for the dealer that runs in polynomial time *without accessing any oracle.* Second, in the literature, it is well known that the demand oracle is more powerful than the value oracle: following [29], a value oracle query can always be simulated by polynomially many demand oracle queries, but there are cases where one needs exponentially many value oracle queries to simulate a single demand oracle query. Our theorem shows that, in the case of the dealer's revenue function, the value oracle is *as powerful as* the demand oracle, and any approximation algorithm for the former can be converted to an approximation algorithm for the latter with the same approximation ratio.

Finally, our third result exploits these structures of the dealer's revenue function and replaces oracle queries in budget feasible mechanisms with approximation algorithms. It is well known that many classic mechanisms (e.g., the VCG mechanism) cease to be truthful when the required computation is only approximated. Accordingly, it is unclear upfront whether existing budget feasible mechanisms are still

[1]In particular, following [22] the dealer's revenue function is APX-hard to compute, and thus both oracles are hard to compute.

truthful when the oracles are replaced by approximation algorithms. We show that this is indeed the case for the mechanism in [31]: it can be revised to use approximation algorithms for the oracles such that the resulting mechanism is still truthful. We emphasize that (1) this is a black-box replacement of the oracles, although other parts of the mechanism need to be changed accordingly; and (2) the revised mechanism works with any approximation algorithm, thus in order to design mechanisms for the dealer, one can focus on designing approximation algorithms for the value oracle. More specifically, we have the following.

Theorem 3 (restated) *Given any polynomial time algorithm that is an α-approximation for the dealer's value oracle, there is a universally truthful, budget feasible, and polynomial time dealer mechanism that gives an $O((\log^2 m)\alpha^2)$-approximation to the optimal revenue.*

Following [22], there is an $O(\log n)$-approximation for the dealer's value oracle, thus we immediately have:

Corollary 2 (restated) *There is a universally truthful, budget feasible, and polynomial-time mechanism that gives an $O((\log^2 m)(\log^2 n))$-approximation to the optimal revenue.*

1.3 Open Problems

It is natural to generalize our model and consider the case where each seller has multiple units of his item for sale (as in [7]). It is easy to see that our results on the monotonicity and subadditivity of the revenue function (Theorem 1) and the approximability of the demand oracle (Theorem 2) hold for the multiple-unit settings. However, we do not know how to generalize our dealer mechanism to the multi-unit settings, and this would be an interesting open problem for future study.

In terms of approximating oracle queries, it is not hard to see that the mechanisms in [4, 31] for single-unit budget feasible procurement and those in [7] for multi-unit procurement remain truthful if the demand oracle is replaced by an ϵ-approximation where ϵ is a small constant. However, it is unknown whether such an approximation algorithm exists for the dealer's revenue function. Also, it is unclear whether these mechanisms are still truthful when the approximation ratio increases (to, say, $\log n$).

In most studies on mechanism design with budgets, the budget is treated as a hard constraint. However, it is conceivable that, in real life, obtaining additional liquidity may be feasible, although at an increasing marginal cost. Modeling and handling such a flexible liquidity will be a very interesting problem for future study.

Moreover, currently we do not have a matching lower bound for our mechanism's approximation ratio. However, even for budget feasible procurements with subadditive valuations, only poly-logarithmic approximations are known. It would be interesting to show matching lower bounds for both the dealer's problem and the procurement problem. Finally, generalizing our model to allow multiple dealers to compete in a market is another important direction worth investigating.

1.4 Additional Prior Work

There is a large amount of literature on the problem of finding the optimal envy-free pricing and allocation that maximizes revenue. The problem was first introduced and considered by [22] where the authors showed that the problem is APX-hard and there is an $O(\log n)$-approximation algorithm for it. Since then, many works have studied different variants of the problem. For example, when there is a single buyer whose values for the items are drawn from independent distributions [8, 12, 15], when the buyers' values have special structures [3, 9, 10], when the buyers have budgets [5, 19, 24], and when the items can only be sold in some special ways [6, 13, 17, 18, 20, 23]. In particular, [12] showed that the pricing problem with a single buyer is NP-complete even when the value distributions all have support size 3. Moreover, [8] showed that when the buyer's value distributions are either discrete or continuous with bounded supports (with proper oracle accesses), and when the distributions satisfy the monotone hazard rate (MHR) condition, there is an algorithm that is a constant approximation for the problem and runs in polynomial time with respect to the size of the largest support (when the distribution is discrete) or the ratio between the upper bound and the lower bound of the supports (when the distribution is continuous).

Budget feasible procurement mechanisms were first introduced by [31]. [31] and [11] provide constant approximation mechanisms for submodular functions, and [16] and [4] respectively provide $O(\log^2 m)$ and $O(\frac{\log^2 m}{\log\log m})$ approximation mechanisms for subadditive functions. All of them study the setting where each seller has a single item. Recently, [7] generalizes the setting to where each seller has multiple units of his item, and gives an $O(\log m)$ approximation for additive functions and an $O(\frac{\log^2 m}{\log\log m})$ approximation for subadditive functions. In [1], the authors study budget feasible mechanisms for additive functions, when each seller's cost is much smaller than the budget.

Another related line of research is double auctions [27, 28, 29]. In a double auction, buyers and sellers submit their private values and costs, respectively, to an intermediary. The goal of the latter is to construct mechanisms that are individually rational and truthful. While a double auction also deals with a two-sided market, the setting and goal are different from ours. Indeed, the goal there is to maximize social welfare and clear the market, instead of maximizing the intermediary's revenue. Also, double auctions treat sellers and buyers symmetrically, using the same solution concept; while we consider an asymmetric setting. Moreover, the intermediary in double auctions has no budget constraint.

Finally, a recent work [30] considers a dealer who has no budget constraint and wants to maximize his revenue minus the total payment to the sellers. However, the settings they consider are highly constrained compared with ours.

2. MODEL: DEFINITIONS AND NOTATIONS

Consider a *dealer* who is buying items from one market and selling them to another market. The market where he is buying is an "alien" market to him, that is, he does not know the sellers' true costs for the items that they sell on that market. The market where he is selling is his "home" market, that is, he knows the buyers' values for the items in that market. The dealer has a budget $B > 0$ specifying the most amount of money he can spend in the alien market.

More specifically, we have the following model. There are m sellers, indexed by $j \in [m] = \{1, 2, ..., m\}$. Each seller $j \in [m]$ has one unit of item j for sale, whose true cost is $c_j > 0$. The cost c_j is the private information of seller j. If the dealer buys item j from seller j with a payment q_j, then the *utility* of seller j, u_j^s, is $q_j - c_j$; and u_j^s is 0 if the dealer does not buy his item and does not pay him.

There are n buyers, indexed by $i \in [n] = \{1, 2, ..., n\}$. Each buyer i has a value v_{ij} for each item $j \in [m]$. Let $V = (v_{ij})_{i\in[n],j\in[m]}$ be the valuation matrix. The dealer knows the buyers' values. Let $\perp$ denote a dummy item such that $v_{i\perp} = 0$ for each $i \in [n]$. When the set of items bought by the dealer is $S \subseteq [m]$, an *assignment* for the buyers consists of a pair (p_S, A_S) where $p_S = (p_j)_{j\in S}$ is the *pricing* vector and $A_S : [n] \to S \cup \{\perp\}$ is the *allocation*, with each item $j \in S$ being allocated to at most one buyer (that is, $|A_S^{-1}(j)| \leq 1$ for each $j \in S$). The price of the dummy item is always $p_\perp = 0$. The *utility* of buyer i, u_i^b, is $v_{iA_S(i)} - p_{A_S(i)}$.

An assignment (p_S, A_S) is *envy-free* if $v_{iA_S(i)} - p_{A_S(i)} \geq v_{ij} - p_j$ for each $i \in [n]$ and $j \in S \cup \{\perp\}$. The *revenue* of an assignment is $Rev(p_S, A_S) = \sum_{i=1}^n p_{A_S(i)}$.

For each $S \subseteq [m]$, the *optimal assignment under* S is an envy-free assignment $(\hat{p}_S, \hat{A}_S)$ such that $(\hat{p}_S, \hat{A}_S) \in \text{argmax}_{(p'_S, A'_S) \text{ is envy-free}} Rev(p'_S, A'_S)$. The dealer's *revenue from* S is the maximum revenue that he can get from any envy-free assignment under S, that is, $R(S) = Rev(\hat{p}_S, \hat{A}_S)$. The *optimal procurement* of the dealer is a subset of items S^* such that $S^* \in \text{argmax}_{S\subseteq[m],\ \sum_{j\in S} c_j \leq B} R(S)$. Notice that $R(S^*) = Rev(\hat{p}_{S^*}, \hat{A}_{S^*})$. Moreover, we will refer R to the *revenue function* of the dealer.

REMARK 1. *We have two revenue functions: Rev is the revenue of a particular assignment, and R is the maximum revenue among all assignments for a given set of items.*

The solution concept.

A *dealer mechanism* M asks each seller j to report a cost $c'_j \geq 0$. Given the cost profile $c' = (c'_1, ..., c'_m)$, the mechanism outputs a subset of items $S \subseteq [m]$, a payment profile $q = (q_1, ..., q_m)$, and an envy-free assignment (p_S, A_S), such that $q_j = 0$ for all $j \in [m]\backslash S$. That is $M(c') = (S, q, p_S, A_S)$. The utility of each seller j under the strategy profile c' is $u_j^s(c') = q_j - c_j$ if $j \in S$, and $u_j^s(c') = 0$ otherwise.

A deterministic mechanism M is *truthful* if for each seller j, c'_j, and c'_{-j}, $u_j^s(c_j, c'_{-j}) \geq u_j^s(c'_j, c'_{-j})$. Let $M(c) = (S, q, p_S, A_S)$. Mechanism M is *individually rational* if for each seller j, $u_j^s(c) \geq 0$; and M is *budget feasible* if the dealer's total payment is no more than the budget, that is, $\sum_{j=1}^m q_j \leq B$. A randomized mechanism is *universally truthful* (respectively, *individually rational* and *budget feasible*) if it is a convex combination of deterministic truthful mechanisms (respectively, *individually rational*, and *budget feasible*).

DEFINITION 1. *Let $f(n) > 0$. A universally truthful dealer mechanism M is an $f(n)$-approximation to the value of the optimal procurement if the mechanism is individually rational and budget feasible, and the revenue under the true cost profile c, $Rev(p_S, A_S)$, has expected value at least $\frac{R(S^*)}{f(n)}$.*

3. PROPERTIES OF THE DEALER'S REVENUE FUNCTION

The structure of the dealer's revenue function R has never been studied. In this section, we show, for the first time, that R is subadditive, that is, $R(S \cup T) \leq R(S) + R(T)$ for any subsets of items S and T. Thus, existing techniques on subadditive optimization could potentially be applied to compute/approximate it. We first show the following lemma.

LEMMA 1. *The dealer's revenue function R is monotone. That is, for any two subsets S and T such that $S \subseteq T \subseteq [m]$, $R(S) \leq R(T)$.*

PROOF. Let $(\hat{p}_S, \hat{A}_S)$ be the optimal assignment under the set S. We define an assignment (p_T, A_T) for T as follows. Let $p_j = \hat{p}_j$ for $j \in S$, $p_j = \infty$ for $j \in T \setminus S$ and $A_T = A_S$. For any $i \in [n]$ and $j \in S \cup \{\perp\}$, we have $u_i^b(p_T, A_T) = u_i^b(\hat{p}_S, \hat{A}_S) = v_{i\hat{A}_S(i)} - \hat{p}_{\hat{A}_S(i)} \geq v_{ij} - \hat{p}_j = v_{ij} - p_j$, where the inequality is because of the envy-freeness of $(\hat{p}_S, \hat{A}_S)$. For any $i \in [n]$ and $j \in T \setminus S$, $u_i^b(p_T, A_T) \geq v_{ij} - p_j$ as $p_j = \infty$. Thus the assignment (p_T, A_T) is envy-free. Moreover, by definition, $R(S) = Rev(\hat{p}_S, \hat{A}_S) = \sum_{i=1}^n \hat{p}_{\hat{A}_S(i)} = \sum_{i=1}^n \hat{p}_{A_T(i)} = \sum_{i=1}^n p_{A_T(i)} = Rev(p_T, A_T)$. Since $Rev(p_T, A_T) \leq R(T)$ by definition, we have $R(S) \leq R(T)$. □

We have the following theorem.

THEOREM 1. *The function R is subadditive.*

Before proving Theorem 1, we recall the following notations, definitions, and results that we will use. Given a valuation matrix V, when the set of available items is S, we let V_S be the sub-matrix of V that contains only the items in S. Given the set of available items S, and a vector $r = (r_j)_{j\in S}$ of non-negative real numbers, a *Walrasian equilibrium with reserve prices* r [22] is an envy-free assignment (p_S, A_S) such that (1) $p_j \geq r_j$ for all $j \in S$, (2) if item j is not assigned to any buyer, then $p_j = r_j$, and (3) if item j is a most-preferred item of buyer i and j is not assigned, then buyer i is assigned an item. In [22], the authors constructed a polynomial time algorithm, MaxWEQ$_r$, that computes a Walrasian equilibrium with reserve prices, see the following lemma.

LEMMA 2. *[22] Given any inputs S, V_S, and r, the algorithm MaxWEQ$_r$ outputs a Walrasian equilibrium (p_S, A_S) with reserve prices r in polynomial time.*

Below we prove a key step in proving Theorem 1.

LEMMA 3. *For any set of items $S \subseteq [m]$, any envy-free assignment (p_S, A_S), and any subset $T \subseteq S \cap A_S([n])$, we have $\sum_{j\in T} p_j \leq R(T)$.*

PROOF. Given (p_S, A_S), we construct an envy-free assignment under T, whose revenue is at least $\sum_{j\in T} p_j$. To do so, we run the following algorithm Alg$_{Assign}$ with inputs S, V_S, (p_S, A_S), and T.

Notice that for each $j \in T$, the price output by MaxWEQ$_r$ in step 1 is $\bar{p}_j \geq r_j = p_j$, by Lemma 2. However, under $(\bar{p}_T, \bar{A}_T)$, some items in T might not be assigned to any buyer. Therefore, $Rev(\bar{p}_T, \bar{A}_T)$ may be strictly less than $\sum_{j\in T} \bar{p}_j$. That is why we augment $\bar{A}_T$ to A_T^* which assigns all items in T. More precisely, we have the following claim.

CLAIM 1. Alg$_{Assign}$ *returns an envy-free assignment $(\bar{p}_T, A_T^*)$ that assigns all items in T.*

PROOF. Notice that, when the algorithm terminates, A_T^* allocates all items in T. Thus, we need to show that the algorithm will not loop forever in step 3. To see why this

Algorithm 1: Alg$_{Assign}$ - An Algorithm to Produce an Envy-Free Assignment where All Items Are Sold

Input : A set of items S, a valuation matrix V_S, an envy-free assignment (p_S, A_S), and a set $T \subseteq S \cap A_S([n])$.

Output: An envy-free assignment $(\bar{p}_T, A^*_T)$

1 Run MaxWEQ$_r$ on inputs T, V_T, and reserve prices $r = (p_j)_{j \in T}$ and denote the outcome by $(\bar{p}_T, \bar{A}_T)$.
2 Initialize $A^*_T = \bar{A}_T$.
3 **while** *there exists an unassigned item j in T according to A^*_T* **do**
4   Let $i \in [n]$ be such that $A_S(i) = j$, and set $A^*_T(i) = j$.
5 **end while**
6 **return** $(\bar{p}_T, A^*_T)$

is true, notice that for each buyer $i \in [n]$, there is at most one item $j \in T$ such that $A_S(i) = j$. Accordingly, buyer i gets reassigned in A^*_T at step 3 for at most once. Since in each execution of step 3, one buyer gets reassigned, and since there are only n buyers, step 3 is executed at most n times and the algorithm will not loop forever.

Next, we show that after each execution of step 3, (1) $(\bar{p}_T, A^*_T)$ is envy-free and (2) for each item j that is not assigned by the current A^*_T, $\bar{p}_j = p_j$. To see why this is true, notice that the initial $(\bar{p}_T, A^*_T)$ satisfies (1) and (2) by the definition of Walrasian equilibrium with reserve prices. Accordingly, if item j is not assigned and $A_S(i) = j$, we have $v_{iA^*_T(i)} - \bar{p}_{A^*_T(i)} \geq v_{ij} - \bar{p}_j = v_{ij} - p_j$ and $v_{ij} - p_j \geq v_{iA^*_T(i)} - p_{A^*_T(i)}$, where the first inequality is because (1) and (2), and the second is because (p_S, A_S) is envy-free. Since $\bar{p}_{A^*_T(i)} \geq r_{A^*_T(i)} \geq p_{A^*_T(i)}$, we have $v_{ij} - p_j \geq v_{iA^*_T(i)} - p_{A^*_T(i)} \geq v_{iA^*_T(i)} - \bar{p}_{A^*_T(i)} \geq v_{ij} - \bar{p}_j = v_{ij} - p_j$, which implies $v_{ij} - \bar{p}_j = v_{ij} - p_j = v_{iA^*_T(i)} - p_{A^*_T(i)} = v_{iA^*_T(i)} - \bar{p}_{A^*_T(i)}$. Thus, item j maximizes i's utility under $\bar{p}_T$ and $p_{A^*_T(i)} = \bar{p}_{A^*_T(i)}$.

Notice that after the execution of step 3, buyer i is the only buyer whose assigned item changes, and the original item $A^*_T(i)$ is the only item that changed from assigned to unassigned. Accordingly, the new assignment $(\bar{p}_T, A^*_T)$ is still envy-free and any unassigned item $j' \in T$ has price $\bar{p}_{j'} = p_{j'}$. That is, $(\bar{p}_T, A^*_T)$ still satisfies (1) and (2) after the first execution of step 3. By induction, $(\bar{p}_T, A^*_T)$ satisfies (1) and (2) after each execution of step 3, as desired.

In sum, the final assignment $(\bar{p}_T, A^*_T)$ returned by Alg$_{Assign}$ is envy-free and assigns all items in T, and Claim 1 holds. □

By the construction of Alg$_{Assign}$ and Claim 1, $Rev(\bar{p}_T, A^*_T) = \sum_{j \in T} \bar{p}_j \geq \sum_{j \in T} r_j = \sum_{j \in T} p_j$, which implies $\sum_{j \in T} p_j \leq R(T)$. Thus, Lemma 3 holds.

Now we are ready to prove Theorem 1.

Proof of Theorem 1. For any subsets of items S and T, let $(\hat{p}_{S \cup T}, \hat{A}_{S \cup T})$ be the optimal assignment under $S \cup T$ and let $W = \hat{A}_{S \cup T}([n])$ be the set of assigned items under $\hat{A}_{S \cup T}$. We have $R(S \cup T) = Rev(\hat{p}_{S \cup T}, \hat{A}_{S \cup T}) = \sum_{i=1}^{n} \hat{p}_{A_{S \cup T}(i)} = \sum_{j \in W} \hat{p}_j \leq \sum_{j \in S \cap W} \hat{p}_j + \sum_{j \in T \cap W} \hat{p}_j$, where the first two equalities are by the definitions of functions R and Rev; the third equality is because the total revenue collected from the players is the same as the total revenue obtained by selling the items; and the inequality is because $W \setminus \{\perp\} \subseteq (S \cap W) \cup (T \cap W)$.

Since $\sum_{j \in S \cap W} \hat{p}_j \leq R(S \cap W)$ by Lemma 3 and $R(S \cap W) \leq R(S)$ by Lemma 1, we have $\sum_{j \in S \cap W} \hat{p}_j \leq R(S)$. Similarly, $\sum_{j \in T \cap W} \hat{p}_j \leq R(T)$. Therefore, we have $R(S \cup T) \leq R(S) + R(T)$, and Theorem 1 holds. □

Remark 2. *A function $f : 2^{[m]} \to \mathbb{R}$ is submodular if for any subsets of items S and T, $f(S \cup T) + f(S \cap T) \leq f(S) + f(T)$. It is unknown whether R is submodular or not.*

4. APPROXIMATING THE DEMAND ORACLE FOR THE DEALER

Mechanism design for the dealer requires optimization over his revenue function. In general, optimization over subadditive functions is NP-hard [25, 26] [2], and oracles of various forms are used to help solving the mechanism design problem. In particular, two oracles have been widely considered — the *value* oracle and the *demand* oracle [4, 7, 11, 16, 29, 31]. In our setting, the value oracle takes as input a subset $S \subseteq [m]$ and returns $R(S)$; and the demand oracle takes as input a cost vector $\bar{c} = (\bar{c}_1, ..., \bar{c}_m)$ and returns $S^*_{\bar{c}} \in \text{argmax}_{T \subseteq [m]} R(T) - \sum_{j \in T} \bar{c}_j$. For any subset $T \subseteq [m]$, the quantity $R(T) - \sum_{j \in T} \bar{c}_j$ is referred to as the *net revenue* of T given $\bar{c}$, denoted by $NR(T, \bar{c})$.

Given access to the value and demand oracles, the mechanism design problem for the dealer can be solved under the framework of budget feasible mechanisms for subadditive valuation functions [4, 7, 16]. However, how can a polynomial-time dealer answer oracle queries? There is little literature about oracle implementation, and most mechanisms over subadditive functions rely on oracle queries and thus do not have polynomial-time implementations.

As part of our main contribution, we show that the demand oracle for the dealer can be efficiently approximated. Using this approximation, in Section 5, we provide a polynomial time mechanism for the dealer *without oracle assesses.*

Our approximation algorithm of the demand oracle uses an approximation algorithm of the value oracle. More specifically, we say that an algorithm Alg$_{value}$ is an α-approximation of the value oracle with $\alpha \geq 1$ if it takes as inputs a set S and a valuation matrix V_S, and returns an envy-free assignment (p_S, A_S) such that $Rev(p_S, A_S) \geq \frac{R(S)}{\alpha}$. We say that an algorithm Alg$_{demand}$ is an α-approximation of the demand oracle with $\alpha \geq 1$ if it takes as inputs a cost profile $\bar{c}$ and a valuation matrix V, and returns a set $S_{\bar{c}}$ and an envy-free assignment $(p_{S_{\bar{c}}}, A_{S_{\bar{c}}})$ such that $Rev(p_{S_{\bar{c}}}, A_{S_{\bar{c}}}) - \sum_{j \in S_{\bar{c}}} \bar{c}_j \geq \frac{NR(S^*_{\bar{c}}, \bar{c})}{\alpha}$. We have the following theorem.

Theorem 2. *Given any polynomial time algorithm that is an α-approximation for the value oracle, there is a polynomial time algorithm that is an α-approximation for the demand oracle.*

As shown in [22], the value oracle is APX-hard to compute, and there is a polynomial-time $O(\log n)$-approximation for it. Thus, we immediately have the following corollary.

Corollary 1. *There exists a polynomial-time $O(\log n)$-approximation algorithm for the demand oracle.*

[2]Since submodular functions belong in the class of subadditive functions, and optimization over submodular is NP-hard in general, we have that optimization over subadditive functions is also NP-hard.

Interestingly, the demand oracle is in general more powerful and computationally harder than the value oracle. In [29], the authors show that a value query can be simulated by polynomially many demand queries, but an exponential number of value queries may be required for simulating a single demand query. Theorem 2 shows that this is not the case for the mechanism design problem for the dealer: here, the two oracles are as powerful as each other. The remaining part of this section is devoted to proving Theorem 2.

Let Alg_{value} be an arbitrary polynomial time algorithm that is an α-approximation of the value oracle, with $\alpha \geq 1$. Our algorithm Alg_{demand} is defined as follows.

Algorithm 2: Alg_{demand} - An Algorithm to Approximate the Demand Oracle

---

Input : A valuation matrix V and a cost profile $\bar{c}$.
Output: A set S and an envy-free assignment $(\tilde{p}_S, A_S)$.

```
Let V' be a valuation matrix such that
    v'_{ij} = v_{ij} - c̄_j for each i ∈ [n] and j ∈ [m].
Run Alg_value with inputs [m] and V', and let (p, A)
    be the output.
Let S = A([n]) \ {⊥} and Ã_S = A.
Let p̃_S = (p̃_j)_{j∈S} where p̃_j = p_j + c̄_j for j ∈ S.
return S and (p̃_S, Ã_S).
```

Below, we show that Alg_{demand} is an α-approximation of the demand oracle. Because we deal with two valuation matrices V and V', we use $f(\cdot; V')$ to denote a function f evaluated when the valuation matrix is V'. If no valuation matrix is specified, then the computation is always with respect to V. Recall that $S^*_{\bar{c}}$ is the output of the demand oracle given inputs V and $\bar{c}$. Let $(\hat{p}_{S^*_{\bar{c}}}, \hat{A}_{S^*_{\bar{c}}})$ be the envy-free assignment that gives the highest net revenue with respect to $S^*_{\bar{c}}$. We want to show that $(\hat{p}_{S^*_{\bar{c}}}, \hat{A}_{S^*_{\bar{c}}})$ is also an (not necessarily optimal) envy-free assignment for the buyers whose values for the items are according to the valuation matrix V' when the set of available items is $[m]$. We begin by showing some properties of $(\hat{p}_{S^*_{\bar{c}}}, \hat{A}_{S^*_{\bar{c}}})$.

LEMMA 4. *$\hat{A}_{S^*_{\bar{c}}}([n]) = S^*_{\bar{c}}$ or $\hat{A}_{S^*_{\bar{c}}}([n]) = S^*_{\bar{c}} \cup \{\perp\}$.*

PROOF. For ease of notations, let $S = S^*_{\bar{c}}$, $\hat{p}_S = \hat{p}_{S^*_{\bar{c}}}$, and $\hat{A}_S = \hat{A}_{S^*_{\bar{c}}}$. First notice that all of the available items are in S. Since $\hat{A}_S$ does not assign buyers to any item that is not in S, $\hat{A}_S([n]) \subseteq S \cup \{\perp\}$. Let $U = S \cup \{\perp\} - \hat{A}_S([n])$ be the set of unassigned items in S. To prove the lemma, it is suffice to show that U is either empty or contains only $\perp$. For the sake of contradiction, suppose U contains some item that is not $\perp$. The net revenue of the set S is

$$\begin{aligned} NR(S, \bar{c}) &= R(S) - \sum_{j \in S} \bar{c}_j = \sum_{i=1}^{n} \hat{p}_{\hat{A}_S(i)} - \sum_{j \in S} \bar{c}_j \\ &\geq NR(\bar{S}, \bar{c}), \end{aligned} \tag{1}$$

for any $\bar{S} \subseteq [m]$. Letting $\bar{S} = S - U$, $\bar{p}_{\bar{S}} = (\bar{p}_i)_{i \in \bar{S}}$ such that $\bar{p}_i = \hat{p}_i$ for $i \in \bar{S}$, and $\bar{A}_{\bar{S}} = \hat{A}_S$. It is easy to see that the assignment $(\bar{p}_{\bar{S}}, \bar{A}_{\bar{S}})$ is envy-free when the set of available items is $\bar{S}$, that is, $v_{i\bar{A}_{\bar{S}}(i)} - p_{\bar{A}_{\bar{S}}(i)} = v_{i\hat{A}_S(i)} - \hat{p}_{\hat{A}_S(i)} \geq v_{ij} - \hat{p}_j = v_{ij} - \bar{p}_j$ for all buyers $i \in [n]$ and all items $j \in \bar{S}$. It follows that $NR(\bar{S}, \bar{c}) = R(\bar{S}) - \sum_{j \in \bar{S}} \bar{c}_j \geq Rev(\bar{p}_{\bar{S}}, \bar{A}_{\bar{S}}) - \sum_{j \in \bar{S}} \bar{c}_j = \sum_{i=1}^{n} \bar{p}_{\bar{A}_{\bar{S}}(i)} - \sum_{j \in \bar{S}} \bar{c}_j = \sum_{i=1}^{n} \hat{p}_{\hat{A}_S(i)} - \sum_{j \in \bar{S}} \bar{c}_j > \sum_{i=1}^{n} \hat{p}_{\hat{A}_S(i)} - \sum_{j \in \bar{S} \cup U} \bar{c}_j = \sum_{i=1}^{n} \hat{p}_{\hat{A}_S(i)} - \sum_{j \in S} \bar{c}_j = NR(S, \bar{c})$, which is a contradiction to Equation 1. □

The above proof relies on the fact that the costs of the items are strictly greater than zero. If we allow the items' costs to be zero and if $\hat{A}_{S^*_{\bar{c}}}$ has some unallocated items with cost zero, then removing those items, we obtain another envy-free assignment with the (same) optimal net revenue that satisfies Lemma 4. Next, we show that the price of each item in $S^*_{\bar{c}}$ is at least its cost.

LEMMA 5. *For any $j \in S^*_{\bar{c}}$, $\hat{p}_j - \bar{c}_j \geq 0$.*

PROOF. Again for ease of notations, let $S = S^*_{\bar{c}}$, $\hat{p}_S = \hat{p}_{S^*_{\bar{c}}}$, and $\hat{A}_S = \hat{A}_{S^*_{\bar{c}}}$. Let $N = \{j \in S | \hat{p}_j - \bar{c}_j < 0\}$ be the set of items with prices less than costs. Assume $N \neq \emptyset$ and let $\bar{S} = S - N$. We show that $NR(\bar{S}, \bar{c}) > NR(S, \bar{c})$, which contradicts the optimality of S.

To do so, we run Alg_{Assign} with inputs S, V_S, $(\hat{p}_S, \hat{A}_S)$, and $\bar{S} = S - N$. Let $(\bar{p}_{\bar{S}}, \bar{A}_{\bar{S}})$ be the output. We have $NR(\bar{S}, \bar{c}) = R(\bar{S}) - \sum_{j \in \bar{S}} \bar{c}_j \geq Rev(\bar{p}_{\bar{S}}, \bar{A}_{\bar{S}}) - \sum_{j \in \bar{S}} \bar{c}_j = \sum_{i=1}^{n} \bar{p}_{\bar{A}_{\bar{S}}(i)} - \sum_{j \in \bar{S}} \bar{c}_j = \sum_{j \in \bar{S}} \bar{p}_j - \bar{c}_j > \sum_{j \in \bar{S}} \bar{p}_j - \bar{c}_j + \sum_{j \in N} \hat{p}_j - \bar{c}_j \geq \sum_{j \in \bar{S}} \hat{p}_j - \bar{c}_j + \sum_{j \in N} \hat{p}_j - \bar{c}_j = \sum_{j \in S} \hat{p}_j - \bar{c}_j = \sum_{i=1}^{n} \hat{p}_{\hat{A}_S(i)} - \sum_{j \in S} \bar{c}_j = NR(S, \bar{c})$, where the first inequality is because $R(\bar{S}) \geq Rev(\bar{p}_{\bar{S}}, \bar{A}_{\bar{S}})$, the third equality is because all items in $\bar{S}$ are sold according to $\bar{A}_{\bar{S}}$ (Claim 1), the second inequality is because $\hat{p}_j - \bar{c}_j < 0 \, \forall j \in N$, the third inequality is because $\bar{p}_j \geq \hat{p}_j \, \forall j \in \bar{S}$ (by the construction of Alg_{Assign}), and the fifth equality is because all items in S are sold according to $\hat{A}_S$ (Lemma 4). □

Next, we show that there is an assignment which is envy-free with respect to the valuation matrix V' and has revenue equals to $NR(S^*_{\bar{c}}, \bar{c})$. More precisely, let $\bar{p} = (\bar{p}_j)_{j \in S^*_{\bar{c}}}$ be such that $\bar{p}_j = \hat{p}_j - \bar{c}_j$ for all $j \in S^*_{\bar{c}}$ and $\bar{p}_j = \infty$ for all $j \in [m] \setminus S^*_{\bar{c}}$, and let $\bar{A} = \hat{A}_{S^*_{\bar{c}}}$. By Lemma 5, $\bar{p}_j \geq 0$ for each $j \in [m]$ and $\bar{p}$ is a well-defined price profile. We have the following two lemmas.

LEMMA 6. *$Rev(\bar{p}, \bar{A}; V') = NR(S^*_{\bar{c}}, \bar{c})$.*

PROOF. $Rev(\bar{p}, \bar{A}; V') = \sum_{i=1}^{n} \bar{p}_{\bar{A}(i)} = \sum_{i=1}^{n} \hat{p}_{\bar{A}(i)} - \bar{c}_{\bar{A}(i)} = \sum_{i=1}^{n} \hat{p}_{\hat{A}_{S^*_{\bar{c}}}(i)} - \bar{c}_{\hat{A}_{S^*_{\bar{c}}}(i)} = \sum_{i=1}^{n} \hat{p}_{\hat{A}_{S^*_{\bar{c}}}(i)} - \sum_{j \in S^*_{\bar{c}}} \bar{c}_j = NR(S^*_{\bar{c}}, \bar{c})$, where the first, second, and last equalities are by definition, the third is because $\bar{A} = \hat{A}_{S^*_{\bar{c}}}$, and the fourth is because all items in $S^*_{\bar{c}}$ are sold according to $\hat{A}_{S^*_{\bar{c}}}$ (by Lemma 4). □

LEMMA 7. *$(\bar{p}, \bar{A})$ is envy-free with respect to V'.*

PROOF. Recall the value of buyer i for item j with respect to V' is $v'_{ij} = v_{ij} - \bar{c}_j$. First, notice that for each buyer i, $u^b_i(\bar{p}, \bar{A}; V') = (v_{i\bar{A}(i)} - \bar{c}_{\bar{A}(i)}) - \bar{p}_{\bar{A}(i)} = (v_{i\bar{A}(i)} - \bar{c}_{\bar{A}(i)}) - (\hat{p}_{\bar{A}(i)} - \bar{c}_{\bar{A}(i)}) = v_{i\bar{A}(i)} - \hat{p}_{\bar{A}(i)} = v_{i\hat{A}_{S^*_{\bar{c}}}(i)} - \hat{p}_{\hat{A}_{S^*_{\bar{c}}}(i)} \geq 0$, where the last inequality is because $(\hat{p}_{S^*_{\bar{c}}}, \hat{A}_{S^*_{\bar{c}}})$ is envy-free under valuation matrix V. (Surely, since $\bar{p}_j \geq 0$ for each $j \in [m]$, we have $v_{i\bar{A}(i)} - \bar{c}_{\bar{A}(i)} \geq 0$ for each buyer $i \in [n]$.)

Moreover, for each buyer $i \in [n]$ and each item $j \in [m]$, $u^b_i(\bar{p}, \bar{A}; V') = v_{i\hat{A}_{S^*_{\bar{c}}}(i)} - \hat{p}_{\hat{A}_{S^*_{\bar{c}}}(i)} \geq v_{ij} - \hat{p}_j = (v_{ij} - \bar{c}_j) - (\hat{p}_j - \bar{c}_i) = (v_{ij} - \bar{c}_j) - \bar{p}_j = v'_{ij} - \bar{p}_j$, where the inequality is again because $(\hat{p}_{S^*_{\bar{c}}}, \hat{A}_{S^*_{\bar{c}}})$ is envy-free under V.

In sum, $(\bar{p}, \bar{A})$ is envy-free with respect to V'. □

Similarly, we have the following lemma for $(\tilde{p}_S, \tilde{A}_S)$, the assignment output by Alg_{demand}. Recall that (p, A) is the assignment output by Alg_{value} with inputs $[m]$ and V'.

LEMMA 8. *$Rev(\tilde{p}_S, \tilde{A}_S) - \sum_{j\in S} \bar{c}_j = Rev(p, A; V')$, and $(\tilde{p}_S, \tilde{A}_S)$ is envy-free with respect to V.*

PROOF. First of all, $Rev(\tilde{p}_S, \tilde{A}_S) - \sum_{j\in S} \bar{c}_j = \sum_{i=1}^n \tilde{p}_{\tilde{A}_S(i)} - \sum_{j\in S} \bar{c}_j = \sum_{i=1}^n (p_{\tilde{A}_S(i)} + \bar{c}_{\tilde{A}_S(i)}) - \sum_{j\in S} \bar{c}_j = \sum_{i=1}^n p_{A(i)} + \sum_{i=1}^n \bar{c}_{A(i)} - \sum_{j\in S} \bar{c}_j = \sum_{i=1}^n p_{A(i)} = Rev(p, A; V')$, where the fourth equality is because $S = A([n]) \setminus \{\perp\}$ and all the others are by definition.

Second, to show $(\tilde{p}_S, \tilde{A}_S)$ is envy-free, notice that for each buyer $i \in [n]$ and for each item $j \in S$, $u_i^b(\tilde{p}_S, \tilde{A}_S) = v_{i\tilde{A}_S(i)} - \tilde{p}_{\tilde{A}_S(i)} = v_{i\tilde{A}_S(i)} - (p_{\tilde{A}_S(i)} + \bar{c}_{\tilde{A}_S(i)}) = (v_{i\tilde{A}_S(i)} - \bar{c}_{\tilde{A}_S(i)}) - p_{\tilde{A}_S(i)} = (v_{iA(i)} - \bar{c}_{A(i)}) - p_{A(i)} \geq (v_{ij} - \bar{c}_j) - p_j = v_{ij} - (p_j + \bar{c}_j) = v_{ij} - \tilde{p}_j$, where the inequality is because (p, A) is envy-free with respect to V'. □

We are now ready to prove the main theorem.

PROOF OF THEOREM 2. Notice that $Rev(\tilde{p}_S, \tilde{A}_S) - \sum_{j\in S} \bar{c}_j = Rev(p, A; V') \geq \frac{R([m];V')}{\alpha} \geq \frac{Rev(\bar{p}, \bar{A}; V')}{\alpha} = \frac{NR(S^*_{\bar{c}}, \bar{c})}{\alpha}$, where the first equality is due to Lemma 8, the first inequality is because Alg_{value} is an α-approximation of the value oracle for the dealer, the second inequality is due to Lemma 7, and the second equality is due to Lemma 6. Therefore, Alg_{demand} is an α-approximation for the dealer and Theorem 2 holds. □

5. BUDGET FEASIBLE MECHANISMS FOR DEALERS

Recall that our main goal is to design individually rational, truthful, and budget feasible mechanisms for a dealer. Moreover, we want the mechanisms to return envy-free assignments that maximize the dealer's revenue (i.e., $R(S^*)$).

As shown earlier, the dealer's revenue function is subadditive. Previous work on designing budget feasible mechanisms for subadditive functions have relied on value and demand oracle queries. However, for envy-free revenue maximization, the existence of those oracles is questionable, as the optimal revenue is hard to compute. Thus, we are interested in mechanisms that do not access any oracle.

Given an α-approximation algorithm, Alg_{value}, of the revenue function R (i.e., the dealer's value oracle) and our α-approximation algorithm, Alg_{demand}, of the optimal net revenue (i.e., the demand oracle), we construct a truthful mechanism for the dealer, which is a variant of the one in [16].

For simplicity, let $R^\alpha(S, V_S) = Rev(Alg_{value}(S, V_S))$. When the valuation matrix is clear from the context, we write $R^\alpha(S)$ instead of $R^\alpha(S, V_S)$. Let $Val = \{1, 2, ..., 2^{\log(\alpha R^\alpha([m]))}\}$. As in [16], we assume without loss of generality that the smallest non-zero value of the revenue function R is 1, and we start with an algorithm, Alg_t, for finding a set of items of size t whose revenue is approximately optimal. Here, we only need to run Alg_{demand} a polynomial number of times.

CLAIM 2. *Let S and $(\tilde{p}_S, \tilde{A}_S)$ be the output of Alg_{demand} with inputs V and a cost vector $\bar{c}$ such that $\bar{c}_1 = \bar{c}_2 = \cdots = \bar{c}_m$. For any $S' \subseteq S$, we have $Rev(\bar{p}_{S'}, \bar{A}_{S'}) \geq |S'|\bar{c}_1$, where $(\bar{p}_{S'}, \bar{A}_{S'})$ is the envy-free assignment output by Alg_{Assign} given S, V_S, $(\tilde{p}_S, \tilde{A}_S)$, and S'.*

Algorithm 3: Alg_t - Finding a Set of Items of Size t with Approximately Optimal Revenue

Input : A positive integer t.
Output: A value $v \in Val$, a set S_v, and an envy-free assignment $(\bar{p}_{S_v}, A_{S_v})$.

```
1  Let S̄ = (S_v)_{v∈Val}.
2  for v ∈ Val do
3      Let c̄ = (c̄_j)_{j=1}^m where c̄_j = v/(2t) for all j ∈ [m]
       and run Alg_demand with V and c̄ to obtain a
       subset of items S ⊆ [m] and an envy-free
       assignment (p̃_S, Ã_S).
4      Let S_v = ∅.
5      if Rev(p̃_S, Ã_S) − |S| v/(2t) ≥ v/(2α) then
6          Let S_v = S.
7          if |S| > t then
8              Let S_v be some set of items of size t
               such that S_v ⊆ S.
9          end if
10     end if
11 end for
12 Run Alg_Assign with inputs S, V_S, (p̃_S, Ã_S), and
   S_v and let (p̄_{S_v}, Ā_{S_v}) be the output.
13 return (v, S_v, p̄_{S_v}, Ā_{S_v}) for the maximum
   v ∈ Val such that S_v is not empty from S̄
```

PROOF. We have $Rev(\bar{p}_{S'}, \bar{A}_{S'}) - |S'|\bar{c}_1 = \sum_{j\in S'} \bar{p}_j - |S'|\bar{c}_1 = \sum_{j\in S'} (\bar{p}_j - \bar{c}_1) \geq \sum_{j\in S'} (\tilde{p}_j - \bar{c}_1) \geq 0$, where the first equality is because all items in S' are sold according to Alg_{Assign}, the first inequality is because $\bar{p}_j \geq \tilde{p}_j$ for all $j \in S'$ according to Alg_{Assign}, and the second inequality is because $\tilde{p}_j \geq \bar{c}$ for all $i \in S$ by Alg_{demand}. Thus, $Rev(\bar{p}_{S'}, \bar{A}_{S'}) \geq |S'|\bar{c}$ and Claim 2 holds. □

LEMMA 9. *Let $S^* \in \text{argmax}_{|S|=t} R(S)$. The algorithm Alg_t finds a subset S_v such that $Rev(\bar{p}_{S_v}, \bar{A}_{S_v}) \geq \frac{R(S^*)}{4\alpha}$.*

PROOF. From the definition of Val, the value $v \in Val$ is such that either $v \leq R(S^*)$ or $v > R(S^*)$. We first consider the case where $v \leq R(S^*)$. Given V and a cost $\bar{c}_j = \frac{v}{2t}$ for all items $j \in [m]$, Alg_{demand} returns an item-set S and an envy-free assignment $(\tilde{p}_S, \tilde{A}_S)$. Recall that $S^*_{\bar{c}}$ is the output of the dealer's demand oracle. We have $Rev(\tilde{p}_S, \tilde{A}_S) - |S|\bar{c}_1 \geq \frac{NR(S^*_{\bar{c}}, \bar{c})}{\alpha} = \frac{R(S^*_{\bar{c}}) - |S^*_{\bar{c}}|\bar{c}_1}{\alpha} \geq \frac{R(S^*) - |S^*|\bar{c}_1}{\alpha} = \frac{R(S^*) - t\frac{v}{2t}}{\alpha} = \frac{R(S^*) - \frac{v}{2}}{\alpha} \geq \frac{R(S^*) - \frac{R(S^*)}{2}}{\alpha} = \frac{R(S^*)}{2\alpha} \geq \frac{v}{2\alpha}$, where the first inequality is by Theorem 2, the second inequality is because $S^*_{\bar{c}}$ is the output of the dealer's demand oracle, and the third and last inequalities are because $v \leq R(S^*)$. Therefore, $S_v \neq \emptyset$ and $Rev(\tilde{p}_S, \tilde{A}_S) \geq \frac{R(S^*)}{2\alpha}$.

If $|S| \leq t$, then $S_v = S$ and $Rev(\bar{p}_{S_v}, \bar{A}_{S_v}) \geq Rev(\tilde{p}_{S_v}, \tilde{A}_{S_v})$; thus $Rev(\bar{p}_{S_v}, \bar{A}_{S_v}) \geq \frac{R(S^*)}{2\alpha} \geq \frac{R(S^*)}{4\alpha}$, as desired. If $|S| > t$, then $Rev(\bar{p}_{S_v}, \bar{A}_{S_v}) \geq |S_v|\bar{c}_1 = t\frac{v}{2t} = \frac{v}{2}$ by Claim 2. Since v is the maximal $v \in Val$ such that $v \leq R(S^*)$, we have that $v \geq \frac{R(S^*)}{2}$, therefore $Rev(\bar{p}_{S_v}, \bar{A}_{S_v}) \geq \frac{R(S^*)}{4} \geq \frac{R(S^*)}{4\alpha}$.

Now consider the case of $v > R(S^*)$. When step b is passed, if $|S| \leq t$, then $S_v = S$ and $Rev(\bar{p}_{S_v}, \bar{A}_{S_v}) \geq Rev(\tilde{p}_{S_v}, \tilde{A}_{S_v}) = Rev(\tilde{p}_S, \tilde{A}_S) \geq \frac{v}{2\alpha} \geq \frac{R(S^*)}{2\alpha} \geq \frac{R(S^*)}{4\alpha}$; if $|S| > t$, by Claim 2, $Rev(\bar{p}_{S_v}, \bar{A}_{S_v}) \geq |S_v|\bar{c}_1 = t\frac{v}{2t} = \frac{v}{2} \geq \frac{R(S^*)}{2} \geq \frac{R(S^*)}{4\alpha}$. In sum, Lemma 9 holds. □

Using algorithm Alg_t, we construct a mechanism M_D for the dealer. Let $\beta = 2\lceil \log m \rceil$ and let $j^* \in [m]$ such that $j^* \in \text{argmax}_{j \in [m]} R(\{j\})$. It is relatively easy to compute j^*: look at the item that has the highest value among all buyers and assign that item to the buyer with the highest value and charge the buyer that value and set the price of all other items to be sufficiently high so that nobody will be assigned to any other item. Let (p_j^*, A_j^*) be the optimal envy-free assignment of $\{j^*\}$.

Mechanism 1: M_D - A Randomized Budget Feasible Mechanism for a Dealer

Input : Each seller $j \in [m]$ reports a cost $c_j > 0$.
Output: $(S, (q_j)_{j \in S}, \bar{p}_S, \bar{A}_S)$ or $(j^*, q_{j^*}, p_{j^*}^*, A_{j^*}^*)$

1 Let $T = \{1, 2, ..., 2^{\lceil \log m \rceil}\}$.
2 **for** $t \in T$ *in decreasing order* **do**
3 Let N' be the set of items with cost at most $B/(\beta t)$ that are different from j^*.
4 Using the algorithm Alg_t with input t, find $(v_t, S_t, \bar{p}_{S_t}, \bar{A}_{S_t})$ among items in N'. Let $S = \cup_t S_t$, and let $(\bar{p}_S, \bar{A}_S)$ be the output of Alg_{value} on S.
5 **for** $j \in S$ **do**
6 let q_j be the threshold for seller j: that is, the highest cost j can announce so that he is still selected, given c_{-j}.
7 **end for**
8 **end for**
9 Flip a fair coin.
10 **if** *coin = heads* **then**
11 The dealer buys items in S, pays q_j to each seller $j \in S$, pays 0 to each seller $j \notin S$, and sells the items to the buyers according to $(\bar{p}_S, \bar{A}_S)$.
12 **else**
13 The dealer buys item j^*, pays B to seller j^*, and sells the item according to $(p_{j^*}^*, A_{j^*}^*)$.
14 **end if**

THEOREM 3. *The mechanism M_D is universally truthful, budget feasible, and is an $O((\log^2 m)\alpha^2)$-approximation to the optimal procurement.*

PROOF. To show truthfulness of M_D, we note that in single-parameter settings, a mechanism is truthful if and only if it satisfies monotonicity and threshold payment (see [2] for the definition). Monotonicity comes from steps 2-3 of M_D and threshold payment is explicitly required in steps 5-6. Finally, it can be shown that the total payment is budget feasible in expectation. The analysis of the universal truthfulness and budget feasibility of M_D follows from the same reasoning as in [16] and thus is omitted. Below, we prove the claimed approximation ratio.

Recall the optimal procurement of the dealer is a subset of items S^* such that $S^* \in \text{argmax}_{S \subseteq [m], \sum_{j \in S} c_j \le B} R(S)$. Let $(\hat{p}_{S^*}, \hat{A}_{S^*})$ be the optimal envy-free assignment such that $R(S^*) = Rev(\hat{p}_{S^*}, \hat{A}_{S^*})$. Let $\bar{S}^* = \{i | i \in S^*, c_i > \frac{B}{\beta}\}$, and $\underline{S}^* = S^* - \bar{S}^*$. By Theorem 1, R is subadditve and $R(S^*) \le R(\bar{S}^*) + R(\underline{S}^*)$. Thus, $R(\bar{S}^*) \ge \frac{R(S^*)}{2}$ or $R(\underline{S}^*) \ge \frac{R(S^*)}{2}$.

We first consider the case that $R(\bar{S}^*) \ge \frac{R(S^*)}{2}$. Because the costs of the items in $\bar{S}^*$ is at least $\frac{B}{\beta}$, the payment for each of the items in $\bar{S}^*$ is at least $\frac{B}{\beta}$. Thus, $B \ge |\bar{S}^*| \frac{B}{\beta}$ and $\beta \ge |\bar{S}^*|$. By subaddtivity, we have $\sum_{j \in \bar{S}^*} R(\{j\}) \ge R(\bar{S}^*)$. Let $\bar{j} \in \text{argmax}_{j \in \bar{S}^*} R(\{j\})$, we have $R(\{\bar{j}\}) \ge \frac{R(\bar{S}^*)}{\beta}$. Moreover, $R(\{j^*\}) \ge R(\{\bar{j}\}) \ge \frac{R(\bar{S}^*)}{\beta} \ge \frac{R(S^*)}{2\beta}$. Since $Rev(p_j^*, A_j^*) = R(\{j^*\})$, with probability 1/2, j^* will be selected and we have a $O(\log m)$-approximation.

Now we consider the second case that $R(\underline{S}^*) \ge \frac{R(S^*)}{2}$. If $R(\{j^*\}) \ge \frac{R(\underline{S}^*)}{2} \ge \frac{R(S^*)}{4}$, then with probability 1/2, we have $R(\{j^*\}) \ge \frac{R(S^*)}{8}$ and we are done. Otherwise, let $\underline{S}^{*\prime} = \underline{S}^* \setminus \{j^*\}$. It follows that, by subadditivity, $R(\underline{S}^{*\prime}) + R(\{j^*\}) \ge R(\underline{S}^*)$, that is, $R(\underline{S}^{*\prime}) \ge R(\underline{S}^*) - R(\{j^*\})$, which implies $R(\underline{S}^{*\prime}) \ge R(\underline{S}^*) - \frac{R(\underline{S}^*)}{2} \ge \frac{R(\underline{S}^*)}{2} \ge \frac{R(S^*)}{4}$.

In what follows, we partition the items in $\underline{S}^{*\prime}$ based on their costs into $O(\log m)$ bins. Let $\text{Bin}(i) = \{j \in \underline{S}^{*\prime} \mid B/(\beta 2^{i+1}) < c_j \le B/(\beta 2^i)\}$ for $i \in \{0, 1, ..., \lceil \log m \rceil - 1\}$ and $\text{Bin}(\lceil \log m \rceil) = \{j \in \underline{S}^{*\prime} \mid 0 < c_j \le B/(\beta 2^{\lceil \log m \rceil})\}$. By subadditivity, there is a bin k such that $R(\text{Bin}(k)) \ge R(\text{Bin}(i))$ for all $i \in \{0, 1, ..., \lceil \log m \rceil\}$ and $R(\text{Bin}(k)) \ge \frac{R(\underline{S}^{*\prime})}{O(\log m)} = \frac{R(\underline{S}^*)}{O(\log m)}$, that is, the optimal revenue of the items in $\text{Bin}(k)$ is at least $O(\log m)$-fraction of $R(\underline{S}^*)$. By construction, $\text{Bin}(k)$ has at most $\beta 2^{k+1}$ items, it follows that the optimal solution of size $\beta 2^{k+1}$ of items with cost at most $B/(\beta 2^k)$ has revenue at least $\frac{R(\underline{S}^*)}{O(\log m)}$. Consider the iteration at $t = 2^k$, algorithm Alg_t with $t = 2^k$ gives us a set S_t that is a 4α-approximation to the optimal revenue of 2^k items (Lemma 9). Notice that by subadditivity, the optimal revenue of 2^k items is an 2β-approximation to the optimal revenue of $\beta 2^{k+1}$ items. It follows that $R(S_t)$ is an $8\alpha\beta$-approximation to the optimal solution of size $\beta 2^{k+1}$ with cost at most $B/(\beta 2^k)$. Thus, $R(S_t) \ge \frac{R(\underline{S}^*)}{O(\alpha\beta \log m)}$, and, by monotonicity, $R(\cup_t S_t) \ge R(S_t) \ge \frac{R(\underline{S}^*)}{O(\alpha \log^2 m)} \ge \frac{R(S^*)}{O(\alpha \log^2 m)}$. However, we do not know $R(\cup_t S_t)$, and we run Alg_{value} to get a α-approximation of it. Therefore, with probability $\frac{1}{2}$, we have the desired $O((\log^2 m)\alpha^2)$-approximation. □

REMARK 3. *Notice that the dealer will buy all items in S, but Alg_{value} may not sell all of them, thus the dealer's revenue may be less than his payment to the sellers. This has to be the case because the requirement of truthfulness. Indeed, if the dealer only buys items that are actually sold by Alg_{value}, the mechanism is not monotone and thus is not truthful. How to design truthful mechanisms where the dealer always sells all his purchased items is an interesting open problem.*

From Corollary 1, there is $O(\log n)$-approximation for the demand oracle. Thus, we have the following result.

COROLLARY 2. *There is a mechanism that is universally truthful, budget feasible, and is an $O((\log^2 m)\ (\log^2 n))$- approximation to the optimal procurement.*

Acknowledgments

We thank several anonymous reviewers for their comments.

REFERENCES

[1] N. Anari, G. Goel, and A. Nikzad. Mechanism design for crowdsourcing: An optimal 1-1/e competitive budget-feasible mechanism for large markets. In *Proceedings of the 2014 IEEE 55th Annual Symposium on Foundations of Computer Science*, FOCS '14, pages 266–275, 2014.

[2] A. Archer and É. Tardos. Truthful mechanisms for one-parameter agents. In *Proceedings of the 42nd IEEE Symposium on Foundations of Computer Science (FOCS'01)*, pages 482–491, 2001.

[3] M.-F. Balcan, A. Blum, and Y. Mansour. Item pricing for revenue maximization. In *Proceedings of the 9th ACM Conference on Electronic Commerce*, EC '08, pages 50–59, 2008.

[4] X. Bei, N. Chen, N. Gravin, and P. Lu. Budget feasible mechanism design: From prior-free to Bayesian. In *Proceedings of the Forty-fourth Annual ACM Symposium on Theory of Computing*, STOC '12, pages 449–458, 2012.

[5] P. Briest. Uniform budgets and the envy-free pricing problem. In *the 35th International Colloquium on Automata, Languages and Programming, Part I*, ICALP '08, pages 808–819, 2008.

[6] P. Briest and H. Röglin. The power of uncertainty: Bundle-pricing for unit-demand customers. In *Proceedings of the 8th International Conference on Approximation and Online Algorithms*, WAOA'10, pages 47–58, 2011.

[7] H. Chan and J. Chen. Truthful multi-unit procurements with budgets. In T.-Y. Liu, Q. Qi, and Y. Ye, editors, *Web and Internet Economics*, volume 8877, pages 89–105. Springer, 2014.

[8] S. Chawla, J. D. Hartline, and R. Kleinberg. Algorithmic pricing via virtual valuations. In *Proceedings of the 8th ACM Conference on Electronic Commerce*, EC '07, pages 243–251, 2007.

[9] N. Chen and X. Deng. Envy-free pricing in multi-item markets. *ACM Trans. Algorithms*, 10(2):7:1–7:15, Feb. 2014.

[10] N. Chen, A. Ghosh, and S. Vassilvitskii. Optimal envy-free pricing with metric substitutability. In *Proceedings of the 9th ACM Conference on Electronic Commerce*, EC '08, pages 60–69, 2008.

[11] N. Chen, N. Gravin, and P. Lu. On the approximability of budget feasible mechanisms. In *the 22nd Annual ACM-SIAM Symposium on Discrete Algorithms*, SODA '11, pages 685–699, 2011.

[12] X. Chen, I. Diakonikolas, D. Paparas, X. Sun, and M. Yannakakis. The complexity of optimal multidimensional pricing. In *Proceedings of the 25th Annual ACM-SIAM Symposium on Discrete Algorithms*, SODA '14, pages 1319–1328, 2014.

[13] M. Cheung and C. Swamy. Approximation algorithms for single-minded envy-free profit-maximization problems with limited supply. In *Proceedings of the 2008 49th Annual IEEE Symposium on Foundations of Computer Science*, FOCS '08, pages 35–44, 2008.

[14] E. H. Clarke. Multipart pricing of public goods. *Public Choice*, 11:pp. 17–33, 1971.

[15] C. Daskalakis, A. Deckelbaum, and C. Tzamos. Optimal pricing is hard. In *Proceedings of the 8th International Conference on Internet and Network Economics*, WINE'12, pages 298–308, 2012.

[16] S. Dobzinski, C. H. Papadimitriou, and Y. Singer. Mechanisms for complement-free procurement. In *Proceedings of the 12th ACM Conference on Electronic Commerce*, EC '11, pages 273–282, 2011.

[17] K. Elbassioni. A QPTAS for ϵ-envy-free profit-maximizing pricing on line graphs. In *Proceedings of the 39th International Colloquium Conference on Automata, Languages, and Programming - Volume Part II*, ICALP'12, pages 513–524, 2012.

[18] K. Elbassioni, R. Raman, S. Ray, and R. Sitters. On profit-maximizing pricing for the highway and tollbooth problems. In *Proceedings of the 2Nd International Symposium on Algorithmic Game Theory*, SAGT '09, pages 275–286, 2009.

[19] M. Feldman, A. Fiat, S. Leonardi, and P. Sankowski. Revenue maximizing envy-free multi-unit auctions with budgets. In *the 13th ACM Conference on Electronic Commerce*, EC '12, pages 532–549, 2012.

[20] A. Grigoriev, J. van Loon, R. Sitters, and M. Uetz. How to sell a graph: Guidelines for graph retailers. In *Proceedings of the 32nd International Conference on Graph-Theoretic Concepts in Computer Science*, WG'06, pages 125–136, 2006.

[21] T. Groves. Incentives in teams. *Econometrica*, 41(4):617–31, July 1973.

[22] V. Guruswami, J. D. Hartline, A. R. Karlin, D. Kempe, C. Kenyon, and F. McSherry. On profit-maximizing envy-free pricing. In *Proceedings of the 16th Annual ACM-SIAM Symposium on Discrete Algorithms*, SODA '05, pages 1164–1173, 2005.

[23] S. Im, P. Lu, and Y. Wang. Envy-free pricing with general supply constraints. In *Proceedings of the 6th International Conference on Internet and Network Economics*, WINE'10, pages 483–491, 2010.

[24] D. Kempe, A. Mu'Alem, and M. Salek. Envy-free allocations for budgeted bidders. In *Proceedings of the 5th International Workshop on Internet and Network Economics*, WINE '09, pages 537–544, 2009.

[25] S. Khuller, A. Moss, and J. S. Naor. The budgeted maximum coverage problem. *Inf. Process. Lett.*, 70(1):39–45, Apr. 1999.

[26] A. Krause and C. Guestrin. A note on the budgeted maximization of submodular functions. Technical report, CMU-CALD-05-103, 2005.

[27] P. McAfee. A dominant strategy double auction. *J. of Economic Theory*, 56(2):434–450, April 1992.

[28] R. Myerson and M. Satterthwaite. Efficient mechanisms for bilateral trading. *J. of Economic Theory*, 29(2):265–281, April 1983.

[29] N. Nisan, T. Roughgarden, É. Tardos, and V. V. Vazirani. *Algorithmic Game Theory*. Cambridge University Press, New York, NY, USA, 2007.

[30] A. Ray, D. Mandal, and Y. Narahari. Profit maximizing prior-free multi-unit procurement auctions with capacitated sellers. In *the 14th International Conference on Autonomous Agents and Multiagent Systems*, AAMAS '15, pages 1753–1754, 2015.

[31] Y. Singer. Budget feasible mechanisms. In *Proceedings of the 51st IEEE Annual Symposium on Foundations of Computer Science*, FOCS '10, pages 765–774, 2010.

[32] W. Vickrey. Counterspeculation, auctions, and competitive sealed tenders. *Journal of Finance*, 16(1):8–37, 03 1961.

Restless Poachers: Handling Exploration-Exploitation Tradeoffs in Security Domains

Yundi Qian, Chao Zhang, Bhaskar Krishnamachari, Milind Tambe
University of Southern California, Los Angeles, CA, 90089
{yundi.qian, zhan661, bkrishna, tambe}@usc.edu

ABSTRACT

The success of Stackelberg Security Games (SSGs) in counter-terrorism domains has inspired researchers' interest in applying game-theoretic models to other security domains with frequent interactions between defenders and attackers, e.g., wildlife protection. Previous research optimizes defenders' strategies by modeling this problem as a repeated Stackelberg game, capturing the special property in this domain — frequent interactions between defenders and attackers. However, this research fails to handle exploration-exploitation tradeoff in this domain caused by the fact that defenders only have knowledge of attack activities at targets they protect. This paper addresses this shortcoming and provides the following contributions: (i) We formulate the problem as a restless multi-armed bandit (RMAB) model to address this challenge. (ii) To use Whittle index policy to plan for patrol strategies in the RMAB, we provide two sufficient conditions for indexability and an algorithm to numerically evaluate indexability. (iii) Given indexability, we propose a binary search based algorithm to find Whittle index policy efficiently.

Categories and Subject Descriptors

I.2.11 [**Artificial Intelligence**]: Distributed Artificial Intelligence

General Terms

Security, Algorithms, Performance

Keywords

Exploration-exploitation tradeoff, Restless multi-armed bandit, Whittle index policy, POMDP

1. INTRODUCTION

Given the increasing need for security around the globe, optimizing the allocation of a limited number of security resources remains a crucial challenge. The successful applications of Stackelberg Security Games (SSGs) for security resource allocation in counter-terrorism domains [16] have inspired researchers' interest in applying game-theoretic models to new "frequent interaction" security domains with repeated interactions between defenders and attackers, e.g., wildlife protection domain. However, these two domains are different. In wildlife protection domain, attack (poaching) happens frequently so that it gives defenders (patrollers) the opportunity to learn attackers' (poachers') behavioral patterns from their previous actions and then to plan patrol strategies accordingly; while this learning opportunity does not arise in the counter-terrorism domain. Previous research [19, 5] has taken advantage of this opportunity and has modeled the wildlife protection domain as a repeated Stackelberg game. However, this work assumes that defenders have knowledge of all poaching activities throughout the wildlife protected area (we will discuss more about this related work in Section 7). Unfortunately, given vast geographic areas for wildlife protection, defenders do not have knowledge of poaching activities in areas they do not protect. Thus, defenders are faced with the exploration-exploitation tradeoff — whether to protect the targets that are already known to have a lot of poaching activities or to explore the targets that haven't been protected for a long time.

The exploration-exploitation tradeoff here is different from that in the non-Bayesian stochastic multi-armed bandit problem [2]. In stochastic multi-armed bandit problems, the rewards of every arm are random variables with a stationary unknown distribution. However, in our problem, patrol affects attack activities — more patrol is likely to decrease attack activities and less patrol is likely to increase attack activities. Thus, the random variable distribution is changing depending on player's choice — more selection (patrol) leads to lower reward (less attack activities) and less selection (patrol) leads to higher reward (more attack activities). On the other hand, adversarial multi-armed bandit problem [3] is also not an appropriate model for this domain. In adversarial multi-armed bandit problems, the reward can arbitrarily change while the attack activities in our problem are unlikely to change rapidly in a short period. This makes the adversarial multi-armed bandit model inappropriate for our domain.

In reality, how patrol affects attack activities would be reasonably assumed to follow a consistent pattern that can be learned from historical data (defenders' historical observations). We model this pattern as a Markov process and provide the following contributions in this paper. First, we formulate the problem into a restless multi-armed bandit (RMAB) model to handle the limited observability challenge — defenders do not have observations for arms they do not activate (targets they do not protect). Second, we propose an EM based learning algorithm to learn the RMAB model from defenders' historical observations. Third, we use the solution concept of Whittle index policy to solve the RMAB model to plan for defenders' patrol strategies. However, indexability is required for the existence of Whittle index, so we provide two sufficient conditions for indexability and an algorithm to numerically evaluate indexability. Fourth, we propose a binary search based algorithm to find the Whittle index policy efficiently.

Appears in: *Proceedings of the 15th International Conference on Autonomous Agents and Multiagent Systems (AAMAS 2016), J. Thangarajah, K. Tuyls, C. Jonker, S. Marsella (eds.), May 9–13, 2016, Singapore.*

2. MODEL

2.1 Motivating Domains and their Properties

Our work is mainly motivated by the domain of wildlife protection such as protecting endangered animals and fish stocks [14, 19, 5]. Other motivating domains include police patrol to catch fare-evaders in a barrier-free transit system [21], border patrol [7, 8], etc. The model we will describe in this paper is based on the following assumptions about the nature of interactions between defenders and attackers in these domains. Except the frequent interactions between defenders (patrollers/police) and attackers (poachers/fare-evaders/smugglers), these domains share another two important properties: (i) patrol affects attacking activities (poaching/fare evasion/smuggling); (ii) limited/partial observability. We will next use the wildlife protection domain as the example to illustrate these two properties.

Poaching activity is a dynamic process affected by patrol. If patrollers patrol in a certain location frequently, it is very likely that the poachers poaching in this location will switch to other locations for poaching. On the other hand, if a location hasn't been patrolled for a long time, poachers may gradually notice that and switch to this location for poaching.

In the wildlife protection domain, both patrollers and poachers do not have perfect observation of their opponents' actions. This observation imperfection lies in two aspects: (i) limited observability — patrollers/poachers do not know what happens at locations they do not patrol/poach; (ii) partial observability — patrollers/poachers do not have perfect observation even at locations they patrol/poach — the location might be large (e.g., a $2km \times 2km$ area) so that it is possible that patrollers and poachers do not see each other even if they are at the same location.

These two properties make it extremely difficult for defenders to optimally plan their patrol strategies. For example, defenders may find a target with a large number of attack activities at the beginning so they may start to protect this target frequently. After a period of time, attack activities at this target may start to decrease due to the frequent patrol. At this time, defenders have to decide whether to keep protecting this target (exploitation) or to switch to other targets (exploration). However, defenders do not have knowledge of attack activities at other targets at that moment, which makes this decision making extremely difficult for defenders.

Fortunately, the frequent interactions between defenders and attackers make it possible for defenders to learn the effect of patrol on attackers from the historical data. With this learned effect, defenders are able to estimate attack activities at targets they do not protect. Based on this concept, we model these domains as a restless multi-armed bandit problem and use the solution concept of Whittle index policy to plan for defenders' strategies.

2.2 Formal Model

We now formalize the story in Section 2.1 into a mathematical model that can be formulated as a restless multi-armed bandit problem. There are n targets that are indexed by $\mathbb{N} \triangleq \{1, \dots, n\}$. Defenders have k patrol resources that can be deployed to these n targets. At every round, defenders choose k targets to protect. After that, defenders will have an observation of the number of attack activities for targets they protect, and no information for targets they do not protect. The objective for defenders is to decide which k targets to protect at every round to catch as many attackers as possible.

Due to the partial observability on defenders' side — defenders' observation of attack activities is not perfect even for targets they protect, we introduce a hidden variable attack intensity, which represents the true degree of attack intensity at a certain target. Clearly, this hidden variable attack intensity cannot directly be observed by defenders. Instead, defenders' observation is a random variable conditioned on this hidden variable attack intensity, and the larger the attack intensity is, the more likely it is for defenders to observe more attack activities during their patrol.

We discretize the hidden variable attack intensity into n_s levels, denoted by $\mathbf{S} = \{0, 1, \dots, n_s - 1\}$. Lower i represents lower attack intensity. For a certain target, its attack intensity transitions after every round. If this target is protected, attack intensity transitions according to a $n_s \times n_s$ transition matrix T^1; if this target is not protected, attack intensity transitions according to another $n_s \times n_s$ transition matrix T^0. The transition matrix represents how patrol affects attack intensity — T^1 tends to reduce attack intensity and T^0 tends to increase attack intensity. The randomness in the transition matrix models attackers' partial observability discussed in Section 2.1. Note that different targets may have different transition matrices because some targets may be more attractive to attackers (for example, some locations may have more animal resources in the wildlife protection domain) so that it is more difficult for attack intensity to go down and easier for attack intensity to go up.

We also discretize defenders' observations of attack activities into n_o levels, denoted by $\mathbf{O} = \{0, 1, \dots, n_o - 1\}$. Lower i represents less attack activities defenders observe. Note that defenders will only have observation for targets they protect. A $n_s \times n_o$ observation matrix O determines how the observation depends on the hidden variable attack intensity. Generally, the larger the attack intensity is, the more likely it is for defenders to observe more attack activities during their patrol. Similar to transition matrices, different target may have different observation matrices.

While defenders get observations of attack activities during their patrol, they also receive rewards for that — arresting poachers/fare-evaders/smugglers bring benefit. Clearly, the reward defenders receive depends on their observation and we thus define the reward function $R(o), o \in \mathbf{O}$ — larger i leads to higher reward $R(i)$. For example, if $o = 0$ represents finding no attack activity and $o = 1$ represents finding attack activities, then $R(0) = 0$, $R(1) = 1$. Note that defenders only get rewards for targets they protect.

To summarize, for the targets defenders protect, defenders get an observation depending on its current attack intensity, get the reward associated with the observation, and then the attack intensity transitions according to T^1; for the targets defenders do not protect, defenders do not have any observation, get reward 0 and the attack intensity transitions according to T^0. Figure 1 demonstrates this process. In this model, the state discretization level n_s, observation discretization level n_o and reward function $R(o)$ are pre-specified by defenders; the transition matrices T^1 and T^0, observation matrix O and initial belief π can be learned from defenders' previous observations. We will briefly discuss the learning algorithm in Section 2.3. After those parameters are learned, this model is formulated into a restless multi-armed bandit model to plan for defenders' strategies.

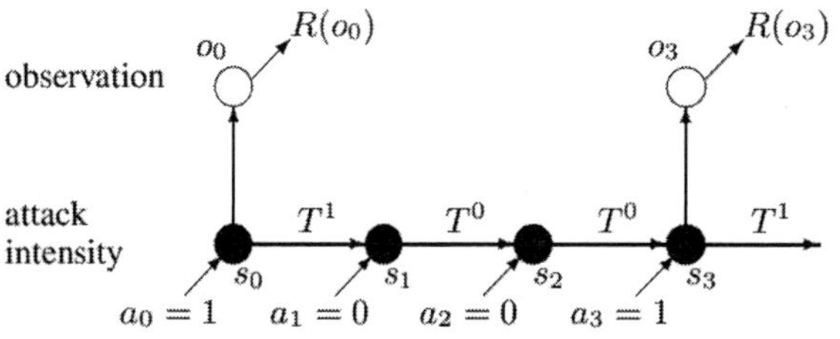

Figure 1: Model Illustration

2.3 Learning Model From Defenders' Previous Observations

Given defenders' action history $\{a_i\}$ and observation history $\{o_i\}$, our objective is to learn the transition matrices T^1 and T^0, observation matrix O and initial belief π. Due to the existence of hidden variables $\{s_i\}$, expectation-maximization (EM) algorithm is used for learning. We show the update steps here and the details are in the online appendix[1].

$$\pi_i^{(d+1)} = P(s_1 = i|x;\theta^d)$$

$$T_{ij}^{1(d+1)} = \frac{\sum_{t=1:a_t=1}^{T-1} P(s_t = i, s_{t+1} = j|x;\theta^d)}{\sum_{t=1:a_t=1}^{T-1} P(s_t = i|x;\theta^d)}$$

$$T_{ij}^{0(d+1)} = \frac{\sum_{t=1:a_t=0}^{T-1} P(s_t = i, s_{t+1} = j|x;\theta^d)}{\sum_{t=1:a_t=0}^{T-1} P(s_t = i|x;\theta^d)}$$

$$O_{ij}^{(d+1)} = \frac{\sum_{t=1:a_t=1}^{T} P(s_t = i|x;\theta^d)I(o_t = j)}{\sum_{t=1:a_t=1}^{T} P(s_t = i|x;\theta^d)}$$

where θ^d is the π, T^1, T^0, O last step and $P(s_t = i|x;\theta^d)$ and $P(s_t = i, s_{t+1} = j|x;\theta^d)$ are computed through forward-backward algorithm.

3. RESTLESS BANDIT FOR PLANNING

In this section, we will formulate the model discussed in Section 2.2 as a restless multi-armed bandit problem and plan defenders' strategies using the solution concept of Whittle index policy.

3.1 Restless Multi-armed Bandit Problems

In this section, we will briefly introduce the restless multi-armed bandit problems (RMABs) and their main solution concept Whittle index policy. In RMABs, each arm represents an independent Markov machine. At every round, the player chooses k out of n arms ($k < n$) to activate and receives the reward determined by the state of the activated arms. After that, the states of *all* arms will transition to new states according to certain Markov transition probabilities. The problem is called "restless" because the states of passive arms will also transition like active arms. The aim of the player is to maximize his cumulative reward by choosing which arms to activate at every round. It has shown by Papadimitriou and Tsitsiklis that it is PSPACE-hard to find the optimal strategy to general RMABs [13].

An index policy assigns an index to each state of each arm to measure how rewarding it is to activate an arm at a particular state. At every round, the index policy chooses to pick the k arms whose current states have the highest indices. Since the index of an arm only depends on the properties of this arm, index policy reduces an n-dimensional problem to n 1-dimensional problems so that the complexity is reduced from exponential with n to linear with n.

Whittle proposed a heuristic index policy for RMABs by considering the Lagrangian relaxation of the problem [18]. It has been shown that Whittle index policy is asymptotically optimal under certain conditions as k and n tend to ∞ with k/n fixed [17]. When k and n are finite, extensive empirical studies have also demonstrated the near-optimal performance of Whittle index policy [1, 6]. Whittle index measures how attractive it is to activate an arm based on the concept of subsidy for passivity. It gives the subsidy m to passive action (not activate) and the smallest m that would make passive action optimal for the current state is defined to be the Whittle index for this arm at this state. Whittle index policy chooses to activate the k arms with the highest Whittle indices. Intuitively, the larger the m is, the larger the gap is between active action (activate) and passive action, the more attractive it is for the player to activate this arm. Mathematically, denote $V_m(x; a = 0)$ ($V_m(x; a = 1)$) to be the maximum cumulative reward the player can achieve until the end if he takes passive (active) action at the first round at the state x with subsidy m. Whittle index $I(x)$ of state x is then defined to be:

$$I(x) \triangleq \inf_m\{m : V_m(x; a = 0) \geq V_m(x : a = 1)\}$$

However, Whittle index only exists and Whittle index policy can only be used when the problem satisfies a property known as indexability, which we define below. Define $\Phi(m)$ to be the set of states for which passive action is the optimal action given subsidy m:

$$\Phi(m) \triangleq \{x : V_m(x; a = 0) \geq V_m(x : a = 1)\}$$

DEFINITION 1. *An arm is indexable if $\Phi(m)$ monotonically increases from $\emptyset$ to the whole state space as m increases from $-\infty$ to $+\infty$. An RMAB is indexable if every arm is indexable.*

Intuitively, indexability requires that for a given state, its optimal action can never switch from passive action to active action with the increase of m. The indexability of an RMAB is often difficult to establish and computing Whittle index can be complex.

3.2 Restless Bandit Formulation

It is straightforward to formulation the model discussed in Section 2.2 into a restless multi-armed bandit problem. Every target is viewed as an arm and defenders choose k arms to activate (k targets to protect) at every round. Consider a single arm (target), it is associated with n_s (hidden) states, n_o observations, $n_s \times n_s$ transition matrices T^1 and T^0, $n_s \times n_o$ observation matrix O and reward function $R(o), o \in \mathbf{O}$ as is described in Section 2.2. For the arm defenders activate, defenders get an observation, get reward associated with the observation, and the state transitions according to T^1. Note that defenders' observation is not the state. Instead, it is a random variable conditioned on the state, and reveals some information about the state. For the arms defenders do not activate, defenders do not have any observation, get reward 0 and the state transitions according to T^0.

Since defenders can not directly observe the state, defenders maintain a belief b of the states for each target, based on which defenders make decisions. The belief is updated according to the Bayesian rules. The following equation shows the belief update when defenders protect this target ($a = 1$) and get observation o or defenders do not protect this target ($a = 0$).

$$b'(s') = \begin{cases} \eta \sum_{s\in\mathbf{S}} b(s)O_{so}T_{ss'}^1, & a = 1 \\ \sum_{s\in\mathbf{S}} b(s)T_{ss'}^0, & a = 0, \end{cases} \tag{1}$$

where η is the normalization factor. When defenders do not protect this target ($a = 0$), defenders do not have any observation, so their belief is updated according to the state transition rule; When defenders protect this target ($a = 1$), their belief is firstly updated according to their observation o ($b_{new}(s) = \eta b(s)O_{so}$ according to Bayes' rule), and then the new belief is then updated according to the state transition rule: $b'(s') = \sum_{s\in\mathbf{S}} b_{new}(s)T_{ss'}^1 = \sum_{s\in\mathbf{S}} \eta b(s)O_{so}T_{ss'}^1 = \eta \sum_{s\in\mathbf{S}} b(s)O_{so}T_{ss'}^1$

We now present the mathematical definition of Whittle index for our problem. Denote $V_m(b)$ to be the value function for belief state b with subsidy m; $V_m(b; a = 0)$ to be the value function for belief state b with subsidy m and defenders take passive action;

[1] http://teamcore.usc.edu/people/yundiqia/web%20page/papers/AAMAS2016Appendix.pdf

$V_m(b; a=1)$ to be the value function for belief state b with subsidy m and defenders take active action. The following equations show these value functions:

$$V_m(b; a=0) = m + \beta V_m(b_{a=0})$$
$$V_m(b; a=1) = \sum_{s \in \mathbf{S}} b(s) \sum_{o \in \mathbf{O}} O_{so} R(o) + \beta \sum_{o \in \mathbf{O}} \sum_{s \in \mathbf{S}} b(s) O_{so} V_m(b^o_{a=1})$$
$$V_m(b) = \max\{V_m(b; a=0), V_m(b; a=1)\}$$

When defenders take passive action, they get the immediate reward m and the β-discounted future reward — value function at new belief $b_{a=0}$, which is updated from b according to the case $a=0$ in Equation 1. When defenders take active action, they get the expected immediate reward $\sum_{s \in \mathbf{S}} b(s) \sum_{o \in \mathbf{O}} O_{so} R(o)$ and the β-discounted future reward. The future reward is composed of different observation cases — $\sum_{s \in \mathbf{S}} b(s) O_{so}$ is defenders' probability to have observation o at belief state b, and $V_m(b^o_{a=1})$ is the value function at new belief $b^o_{a=1}$ that is updated from b according to the case $a=1$ with observation o in Equation 1. The value function $V_m(b)$ is the maximum of $V_m(b; a=0)$ and $V_m(b; a=1)$. Whittle index $I(b)$ of belief state b is then defined to be :

$$I(b) \triangleq \inf_m \{m : V_m(b; a=0) \geq V_m(b : a=1)\}$$

The passive action set $\Phi(m)$, which is the set of belief states for which passive action is the optimal action given subsidy m is then defined to be:

$$\Phi(m) \triangleq \{b : V_m(b; a=0) \geq V_m(b : a=1)\}$$

3.3 Sufficient Conditions for Indexability

In this section, we provide two sufficient conditions for indexability when $n_o = 2$ and $n_s = 2$. Denote the transition matrices to be T^0 and T^1, observation matrix to be O. Clearly in our problem, $O_{11} > O_{01}$, $O_{00} > O_{10}$ (higher attack intensity leads to higher probability to see attack activities when patrolling); $T^1_{11} > T^1_{01}$, $T^1_{00} > T^1_{10}$; $T^0_{11} > T^0_{01}$, $T^0_{00} > T^0_{10}$ (positively correlated arms).

Define $\alpha \triangleq \max\{T^0_{11} - T^0_{01}, T^1_{11} - T^1_{01}\}$. Since it is a two-state problem with $\mathbf{S} = \{0, 1\}$, we use one variable x to represent the belief state: $x \triangleq b(s=1)$, which is the probability of being in state 1.

Define $\Gamma_1(x) = xT^1_{11} + (1-x)T^1_{01}$, which is the belief for the next round if the belief for the current round is x and the active action is taken. Similarly, $\Gamma_0(x) = xT^0_{11} + (1-x)T^0_{01}$, which is the belief for the next round if the belief for the current round is x and the passive action is taken.

We present below two theorems demonstrating two sufficient conditions for indexability. The proof is in the online appendix.

THEOREM 1. *When $\beta \leq 0.5$, the process is indexable, i.e., for any belief x, if $V_m(x; a=0) \geq V_m(x; a=1)$, then $V_{m'}(x; a=0) \geq V_{m'}(x; a=1)$, $\forall m' \geq m$*

THEOREM 2. *When $\alpha\beta \leq 0.5$ and $\Gamma_1(1) \leq \Gamma_0(0)$, the process is indexable, i.e., for any belief x, if $V_m(x; a=0) \geq V_m(x; a=1)$, then $V_{m'}(x; a=0) \geq V_{m'}(x; a=1)$, $\forall m' \geq m$*

3.4 Numerical Evaluation of Indexability

For problems other than those that have been proved to be indexable in Section 3.3, we can numerically evaluate their indexability. We first provide the following proposition.

PROPOSITION 1. *If $m < R(0) - \beta\frac{R(n_o-1)-R(0)}{1-\beta}$, $\Phi(m) = \emptyset$; if $m > R(n_o - 1)$, $\Phi(m)$ is the whole belief state space.*

PROOF. If $m < R(0) - \beta\frac{R(n_o-1)-R(0)}{1-\beta}$, denote $V_m(b; a=0) = m + \beta W_0$; $V_m(b; a=1) = R(o) + \beta W_1$, where W_1 and W_0 represent the maximum future reward. Since $W_0 \leq \frac{R(n_o-1)}{1-\beta}$ (achieving reward $R(n_o-1)$ at every round), $W_1 \geq \frac{R(0)}{1-\beta}$ (achieving reward $R(0)$ at every round), $R(o) \geq R(0)$, we have $V_m(b; a=1) - V_m(b; a=0) = R(o) - m + \beta(W_1 - W_0) \geq R(0) - m + \beta\frac{R(0)-R(n_o-1)}{1-\beta} > 0$. Thus, being active is always the optimal action for any state so that $\Phi(m) = \emptyset$.

If $m > R(n_o - 1)$, then the strategy of always being passive dominates other strategies so $\Phi(m)$ is the whole belief state space. □

Thus, we only need to determine whether the set $\Phi(m)$ monotonically increases for $m \subseteq [R(0) - \beta\frac{R(n_o-1)-R(0)}{1-\beta}, R(n_o-1)]$. Numerically, we can discretize this limited m range and then evaluate if $\Phi(m)$ monotonically increases with the increase of discretized m. Given the subsidy m, $\Phi(m)$ can be determined by solving a special POMDP model whose conditional observation probability is dependent on start state and action. We will discuss the algorithm in detail in Section 4. This algorithm returns a set D which contains n_s-length vectors $d_1, d_2, \ldots, d_{|D|}$. Every vector d_i is associated with an optimal action e_i. Given the belief b, the optimal action is determined by $a^{opt} = e_i$, $i = \arg\max_j b^T d_j$. Thus, $\Phi(m) = \bigcup_{i:e_i=0}\{b : b^T d_i \geq b^T d_j, \forall j\}$.

Given $m_0 < m_1$, our aim is to check whether $\Phi(m_0) \subseteq \Phi(m_1)$. Use the superscript 0 or 1 for set D, vector d, action e to distinguish between the returned solutions with subsidy m_0 and m_1. The following mixed-integer linear program (MILP) can be used to determine whether $\Phi(m_0) \subseteq \Phi(m_1)$.

$$\min_{b, z^0, z^1, \xi^0, \xi^1} \sum_{i=1}^{|D^0|} z^0_i e^0_i - \sum_{i=1}^{|D^1|} z^1_i e^1_i$$
$$s.t. \quad b_i \in [0,1], \forall i \in \mathbf{S}, \qquad \sum_{i \in \mathbf{S}} b_i = 1$$
$$z^0_i \in \{0,1\}, \forall i \in \{1, 2, \ldots, |D^0|\}, \qquad \sum_i z^0_i = 1$$
$$b^T d^0_i \leq \xi^0, \forall i \in \{1, 2, \ldots, |D^0|\}$$
$$\xi^0 \leq b^T d^0_i + M(1 - z^0_i), \forall i \in \{1, 2, \ldots, |D^0|\}$$
$$z^1_i \in \{0,1\}, \forall i \in \{1, 2, \ldots, |D^1|\} \qquad \sum_i z^1_i = 1$$
$$b^T d^1_i \leq \xi^1, \forall i \in \{1, 2, \ldots, |D^1|\}$$
$$\xi^1 \leq b^T d^1_i + M(1 - z^1_i), \forall i \in \{1, 2, \ldots, |D^1|\}$$

If the result of the above MILP is 0 or 1, $\Phi(m_0) \subseteq \Phi(m_1)$. In the MILP, M is a given large number, b is the belief state, $z^{0/1}_i$ is a binary variable that indicates whether $b^T d^{0/1}_i \geq b^T d^{0/1}_j, \forall j$ (1 indicates yes and 0 indicates no), $\xi^{0/1}$ is an auxiliary variable that equals $\max_i b^T d^{0/1}_i$, $\sum_{i=1}^{|D^{0/1}|} z^{0/1}_i e^{0/1}_i$ is the optimal action for the problem with subsidy $m_{0/1}$. If the result of this MILP is 0 or 1, it means that there does not exist a belief b under which the optimal action for the problem with subsidy m_0 is passive (0) and the optimal action for the problem with subsidy m_1 is active (1). This means $\Phi(m_0) \subseteq \Phi(m_1)$. On the other hand, if the result of the above MILP is -1, $\Phi(m_0) \nsubseteq \Phi(m_1)$.

3.5 Computation of Whittle Index Policy

Given the indexability, Whittle index can be found by doing a binary search within the range $m \subseteq [R(0)-\beta\frac{R(n_o-1)-R(0)}{1-\beta}, R(n_o-1)]$. Given the upper bound ub and lower bound lb, the problem with middle point $\frac{lb+ub}{2}$ as passive subsidy is sent to the special POMDP solver to find the optimal action for the current belief. If the optimal action is active, then the Whittle index is greater than the middle point so $lb \leftarrow \frac{lb+ub}{2}$; or else $ub \leftarrow \frac{lb+ub}{2}$. This binary search algorithm can find Whittle index with arbitrary precision. Naively, we can compute the Whittle index policy by computing the ε-precision indices of all arms and then picking the k arms with the highest indices.

However, since we are actually only interested in which k arms have the highest Whittle index and we do not care what exactly their indices are, we can do better than this naive method, which is demonstrated in Algorithm 1.

Algorithm 1 Algorithm to Compute Whittle Index Policy

```
1: function FINDWHITTLEINDEXPOLICY
2:     lb ← R(0) − β (R(n_o−1)−R(0))/(1−β), ub ← R(n_o − 1)
3:     A ← ∅, S ← {1, 2, ..., n}
4:     while |A| < k do
5:         S_1 ← ∅, S_0 ← ∅
6:         for i ∈ S do
7:             a^opt ← POMDPSOLVE(P_i, (lb+ub)/2)
8:             if a^opt = 1 then
9:                 S_1 ← S_1 ⋃ {i}
10:            else
11:                S_0 ← S_0 ⋃ {i}
12:            end if
13:        end for
14:        if |S_1| ≤ k − |A| then
15:            A ← A ⋃ S_1, S ← S − S_1
16:            ub ← (lb+ub)/2
17:        else
18:            S ← S − S_0
19:            lb ← (lb+ub)/2
20:        end if
21:    end while
22:    return A
23: end function
```

In Algorithm 1, A is Whittle index policy to be returned and is set to be $\emptyset$ at the beginning. S is the set of arms that we have not known whether belong to A or not and is set to be the whole set of arms at the beginning. Before it finds top-k arms (the loop between Line 4 and Line 21), it tests all the arms in S about their optimal action with subsidy $\frac{ub+lb}{2}$. If the optimal action is 1, it means this arm's index is higher than $\frac{ub+lb}{2}$ and we add it to S_1; if the optimal action is 0, it means this arm's index is lower than $\frac{ub+lb}{2}$ and we add it to S_0 (Lines $6-13$). At this moment, we know that all arms in S_1 have higher indices than all arms in S_0. If there is enough space in A to include all arms in S_1, we add S_1 to A, remove them from S and set the upper bound to be $\frac{ub+lb}{2}$ because we already know that S_1 belongs to Whittle index policy set and all the rest arms have the index lower than $\frac{ub+lb}{2}$ (Lines $14-16$). If there is not enough space in A, we remove S_0 from S and set the lower bound to be $\frac{ub+lb}{2}$ because we already know that S_0 does not belong to Whittle index policy set and all the rest arms have the index higher than $\frac{ub+lb}{2}$ (Lines $17-19$)

4. COMPUTATION OF PASSIVE ACTION SET

In this section, we will discuss the algorithm to compute the passive action set $\Phi(m)$ with the subsidy m. This problem can be viewed as solving a special POMDP model whose conditional observation probability is dependent on start state and action while the conditional observation probability is dependent on end state and action in standard POMDPs. Figure 2 demonstrates the difference. The left figure represents special POMDPs and the right figure represents standard POMDPs. In both cases, the original state is s, the agent takes action a, and the state transitions to s' according to $P(s'|s,a)$. However, the observation o the agent get during this process is dependent on s and a in our special POMDPs; while it depends on s' and a in standard POMDPs.

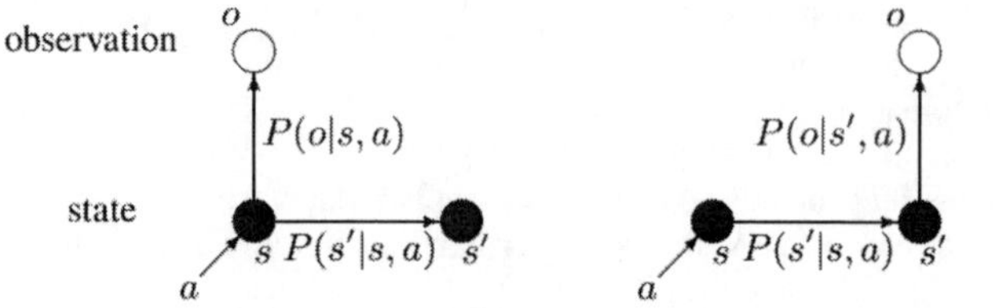

Figure 2: Special POMDPs vs Standard POMDPs

Despite this difference, the solution concept of value iteration algorithm in standard POMDPs can be used to solve our special POMDP formulations with appropriate modifications. We will discuss the special POMDP formulation for our problem in Section 4.1 and present the modified value iteration algorithm in Section 4.2.

4.1 Special POMDP Formulation

The special POMDP formulation for our problem is straightforward.

state space The state space is $\mathbf{S} = \{0, 1, \ldots, n_s - 1\}$.

action space The action space is $\mathbf{A} = \{0, 1\}$, where $a = 0$ represents passive action (do not protect) and $a = 1$ represents active action (protect).

observation space The observation space is $\mathbf{O} = \{-1, 0, 1, \ldots, n_o - 1\}$. It adds a "fake" observation $o = -1$ to represent no observation when taking action $a = 0$. It's called "fake" because defenders have probability 1 to observe $o = -1$ no matter what the state is when they take action $a = 0$, so this observation does not provide any information. When defenders take action $a = 1$, they may observe observations $\mathbf{O}\backslash\{-1\}$.

conditional transition probability The conditional transition probability $P(s'|s,a)$ is defined to be: $P(s' = j|s = i, a = 1) = T^1_{ij}$ and $P(s' = j|s = i, a = 0) = T^0_{ij}$.

conditional observation probability The conditional observation probability $P(o|s,a)$ is defined to be $P(o = -1|s, a = 0) = 1, \forall s \in \mathbf{S}$; $P(o = j|s = i, a = 1) = O_{ij}$. Note that the conditional observation probability here is dependent on the start state s and action a, while it depends on end state s' and action a in standard POMDP models. Intuitively, defenders' observation of attack activities today depends on the attack intensity today, not the transitioned attack intensity tomorrow.

reward function The reward function R is

$$R(s, s', a, o) = \begin{cases} 0, & a = 0, \\ R(o), & a = 1. \end{cases}$$

With the transition probability and observation probability, $R(s,a)$

can be computed. Note that this formulation is also slightly different due to the different definition of observation probability.

$$R(s,a) = \sum_{s' \in \mathbf{S}} P(s'|s,a) \sum_{o \in \mathbf{O}} P(o|s,a) R(s,s',a,o)$$

4.2 Value Iteration for Our Special POMDP

Different from standard POMDP formulation, the belief update in the special POMDP formulation is

$$b'(s') = \frac{\sum_{s \in \mathbf{S}} b(s) P(o|s,a) P(s'|s,a)}{P(o|b,a)} \tag{2}$$

where

$$P(o|b,a) = \sum_{s' \in \mathbf{S}} \sum_{s \in \mathbf{S}} b(s) P(o|s,a) P(s'|s,a) = \sum_{s \in \mathbf{S}} b(s) P(o|s,a)$$

Note that the belief update process is also consistent with that in Equation 1. Similar to standard POMDP formulation, we have the value function

$$V'(b) = \max_{a \in \mathbf{A}} \left(\sum_{s \in \mathbf{S}} b(s) R(s,a) + \beta \sum_{o \in \mathbf{O}} P(o|b,a) V(b_a^o) \right)$$

which can be broken up to simpler combinations of other value functions:

$$V'(b) = \max_{a \in \mathbf{A}} V_a(b)$$

$$V_a(b) = \sum_{o \in \mathbf{O}} V_a^o(b)$$

$$V_a^o(b) = \frac{\sum_{s \in \mathbf{S}} b(s) R(s,a)}{|\mathbf{O}|} + \beta P(o|b,a) V(b_a^o)$$

All the value functions can be represented as $V(b) = \max_{\alpha \in \mathbf{D}} b \cdot \alpha$ since the update process maintains this property, so we only need to update the set D when updating the value function. The set D is updated according to the following process:

$$D' = \text{purge}\left(\bigcup_{a \in \mathbf{A}} D_a \right)$$

$$D_a = \text{purge}\left(\bigoplus_{o \in \mathbf{O}} D_a^o \right)$$

$$D_a^o = \text{purge}\left(\{ \tau(\alpha, a, o) | \alpha \in D \} \right)$$

where $\tau(\alpha, a, o)$ is the $|D|$-vector given by

$$\tau(\alpha,a,o)(s) = (1/|\mathbf{O}|) R(s,a) + \beta P(o|s,a) \sum_{s' \in \mathbf{S}} \alpha(s') P(s'|s,a)$$

and purge($\cdot$) takes a set of vectors and reduces it to its unique minimum form (remove redundant vectors that are dominated by other vectors in the set). $\bigoplus$ represents the cross sum of two sets of vectors: $A \bigoplus B = \{\alpha + \beta | \alpha \in A, \beta \in B\}$.

The update of D' and D_a is intuitive, so we briefly explain the update of D_a^o[2] here:

$$P(o|b,a)V(b_a^o) = P(o|b,a) \max_{\alpha \in D} \sum_{s' \in \mathbf{S}} \alpha(s') P(s'|b,a,o)$$

$$= P(o|b,a) \max_{\alpha \in D} \sum_{s' \in \mathbf{S}} \alpha(s') \frac{\sum_{s \in \mathbf{S}} b(s) P(o|s,a) P(s'|s,a)}{P(o|b,a)}$$

$$= \max_{\alpha \in D} \sum_{s' \in \mathbf{S}} \alpha(s') \sum_{s \in \mathbf{S}} b(s) P(o|s,a) P(s'|s,a)$$

$$= \max_{\alpha \in D} \sum_{s \in \mathbf{S}} b(s) \cdot \left(P(o|s,a) \sum_{s' \in \mathbf{S}} \alpha(s') P(s'|s,a) \right)$$

Here, $P(s'|b,a,o)$ is the belief of state s' in the next round when the belief in the current round is b, the agent takes action a and get the observation o, which is the $b(s')$ in Equation 2.

5. PLANNING FROM POMDP VIEW

We have discussed in Section 4.1 that every single target can be modeled as a special POMDP model. Given that, we can combine these POMDP models at all targets to form a special POMDP model that describe the whole problem, and solving this special POMDP model leads to defenders' *exact* optimal strategy. Use the superscript i to denote target i. Generally, the POMDP model for the whole problem is the cross product of the single-target POMDP models at all targets with the constraint that only k targets are protected at every round.

state space The state space is $\mathbf{S} = \mathbf{S^1} \times \mathbf{S^2} \times \ldots \times \mathbf{S^n}$. Denote $s = (s^1, s^2, \ldots, s^n)$

action space The action space is $\mathbf{A} = \{(a^1, a^2, \ldots, a^n) | a^j \in \{0,1\}, \forall j \in \mathbb{N}, \sum_{j \in \mathbb{N}} a^j = k\}$, which represents that only k targets can be protected at a round. Denote $a = (a^1, a^2, \ldots, a^n)$

observation space The observation space is $\mathbf{O} = \mathbf{O^1} \times \mathbf{O^2} \times \ldots \times \mathbf{O^n}$. Denote $o = (o^1, o^2, \ldots, o^n)$

conditional transition probability The conditional transition probability is $P(s'|s,a) = \prod_{j \in \mathbb{N}} P^j(s'^j | s^j, a^j)$.

conditional observation probability The conditional observation probability is $P(o|s,a) = \prod_{j \in \mathbb{N}} P^j(o^j | s^j, a^j)$.

reward function The reward function is $R(s,s',a,o) = \sum_{j \in \mathbb{N}} R(s^j, s'^j, a^j, o^j)$

Naively, the modified value iteration algorithm discussed in Section 4.2 can be used to solve this special POMDP formulation. However, this POMDP formulation suffers from curse of dimensionality — the problem size increases exponentially with the number of targets. Thus, the computational cost of value iteration algorithm will soon become unaffordable as the problem size grows.

Silver and Veness [15] have proposed POMCP algorithm, which provides high quality solutions and is scalable to large POMDPs. The POMCP algorithm only requires a simulator of the problem so it also applies to our special POMDPs. At a high level, the POMCP algorithm is composed of two parts: (i) it uses a particle filter to maintain an approximation of the belief state; (ii) it draw state samples from the particle filter and then use MCTS to simulate what will happen next to find the best action. It uses a particle filter to approximate the belief state because it is even computationally impossible in many problems to update belief state due to the extreme large size of the state space. However, in our problem, the all-target POMDP model is the cross product of the single-target POMDP models at all targets. The single-state POMDP model is

[2] Actually the only difference of value iteration algorithm for the special POMDP formulation compared with that for the standard POMDP formulation is the different update of D_a^o.

small so that it is computationally inexpensive to maintain its belief state. Thus, we can easily sample the state s^i at target i from its belief state and then compose them together to get the state sample $s = (s^1, s^2, \dots, s^n)$ for the all-target POMDP model.

The details of MCTS in POMDP are available in [15] so we omit it here. Although the POMCP algorithm shows better scalability than the exact POMDP algorithm, its scalability is also limited because the action space and observation space are also exponential with k in our problem. Consider the problem instance of $n = 10$, $k = 3$ and $n_o = 2$, the number of actions is $\binom{10}{3} = \frac{10*9*8}{1*2*3} = 120$ and the number of observations is $\binom{10}{3} * 2^3 = 960$. Since actions and observations are the branches in the MCTS, the tree size will soon become extremely large when planning more rounds ahead. This leads to two problems: (i) it will soon run out of memory when planning more rounds ahead; (ii) a huge number of state samples is needed to establish the convergence. Thus, the POMCP algorithm only applies to problem instances with small k. Our experimental evaluation shows that the POMCP algorithm is unable to plan 3 horizons forward (runs out of memory) for the problem instance of $n = 10$, $k = 3$ and $n_o = 2$. It means that for large problem instances, the POMCP algorithm is reduced to myopic policy (only look one round ahead when planning).

6. EXPERIMENTAL EVALUATION

In this section, we will firstly evaluate the Whittle Index Policy in Section 6.1 and then evaluate the RMAB model in Section 6.2. The performance is evaluated in terms of the cumulative reward received within the first 20 rounds with discounting factor $\beta = 0.9$. All results are averaged over 500 simulation runs.

6.1 Evaluation of Whittle Index Policy

We will compare the Whittle Index policy with four baseline algorithms:

Random: The defenders randomly choose k targets to protect at every round.

Myopic: The defenders choose k targets with the highest immediate reward to protect at every round.

Exact POMDP: The defenders uses the modified value iteration algorithm to solve the special POMDP problem discussed in Section 5 to plan for patrol strategies at every round. Note that it only works for small-scale problems and is the *exact* optimal patrol strategy defenders may take

POMCP: The defenders uses POMCP algorithm to solve the special POMDP problem discussed in Section 5 to plan for patrol strategies at every round.

The computation of Whittle Index policy and exact POMDP algorithm involve solving special POMDPs using the modified value iteration algorithm as is discussed in Section 4.2. We implement the modified value iteration algorithm by modifying the POMDP solver written by Anthony R. Cassandra[3]. The detailed algorithm we use for value iteration is the incremental pruning algorithm [4].

There are two parameters in the POMCP algorithm: the number of state samples and the depth of the tree, i.e., the number of rounds we look ahead when planning. With the increase of the number of state samples, the performance of the POMCP algorithm improves; while the runtime also increases at the same time. Thus, for a fair comparison, during our experiment, we choose the number of state samples so that its runtime is similar to that of Whittle index policy. For the depth of the tree, we choose the one with the largest cumulative reward.

[3]http://pomdp.org/code/

Small Scale: Compare with Exact POMDP Algorithm We then evaluate these five planning algorithms in a small problem instance with $n = 2$, $k = 1$, $n_s = 2$ and $n_o = 2$. The result is shown in Table 1. From the table, we can see that our Whittle index policy and POMCP algorithm perform very close to the optimal Exact POMDP solution and are much better than the myopic optimal policy and random policy, demonstrating their high solution quality.

Table 1: Planning Algorithm Evaluation in Solution Quality for Small-scale Problem Instances

Random	Myopic Optimal	POMCP	Exact POMDP	Whittle Index
2.6534	3.1384	3.1694	3.1798	3.1740

Large Scale: We then evaluate our planning algorithms in a larger problem instance with $n = 10$. Figure 3(a) shows the solution quality comparison when $n_s = 2$ and $n_o = 2$. The x-axis shows the number of defenders (k) and the y-axis shows the cumulative reward. From this figure, we can see that Whittle index policy performs better than the POMCP algorithm and myopic optimal policy, and all of these three algorithms perform much better than the random policy. One thing to note is that the POMCP algorithm shows poor scalability with regard to k — it is unable to plan 3 horizons forward (runs out of memory) with $k = 3$. Figure 3(b) shows the solution quality comparison when $n_s = 3$ and $n_o = 3$, and demonstrates similar patterns as Figure 3(a).

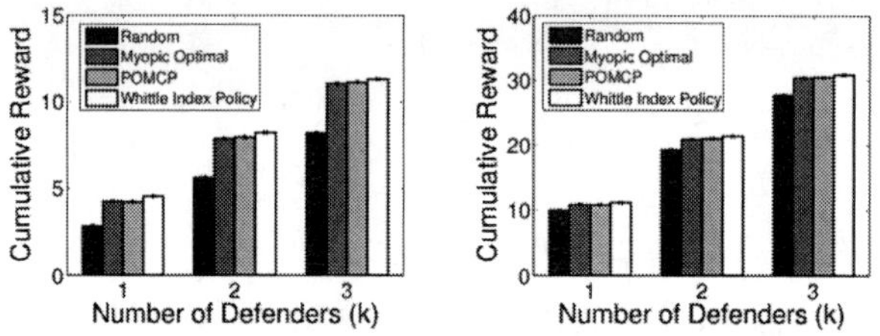

(a) $n_s = 2, n_o = 2$ (b) $n_s = 3, n_o = 3$

Figure 3: Planning Algorithm Evaluation in Solution Quality for Large-scale Problem Instances

An Example When Myopic Policy Fails We can see from Figures 3(a) and 3(b) that the myopic policy performs only slightly worse compared with the Whittle index policy. Here we provide an example where the myopic policy performs significantly worse. Consider the case with 2 targets and 1 defender.

For target 0:

$$T^0 = \begin{bmatrix} 0.95 & 0.05 \\ 0.05 & 0.95 \end{bmatrix} T^1 = \begin{bmatrix} 0.99 & 0.01 \\ 0.1 & 0.9 \end{bmatrix} O = \begin{bmatrix} 0.9 & 0.1 \\ 0.2 & 0.8 \end{bmatrix}$$

For target 1:

$$T^0 = \begin{bmatrix} 0.4 & 0.6 \\ 0.1 & 0.9 \end{bmatrix} \quad T^1 = \begin{bmatrix} 0.7 & 0.3 \\ 0.4 & 0.6 \end{bmatrix} \quad O = \begin{bmatrix} 0.7 & 0.3 \\ 0.3 & 0.7 \end{bmatrix}$$

Figure 4 shows the performance of different algorithms. In this case, the myopic policy performs similar to the random policy, and is much worse compared with Whittle Index policy.

Runtime Analysis of Whittle Index Policy: Figure 5 analyzes the runtime of Whittle index policy. The x-axis shows the number of targets (n) and the y-axis shows the average runtime. From the figure, we can see that the runtime increases linearly with the number of targets. This is because Whittle index policy reduces an n-dimensional problem to n 1-dimensional problems so that the complexity is linear with n. Another observation is that the number of defenders (k) does not affect the runtime a lot for a given n.

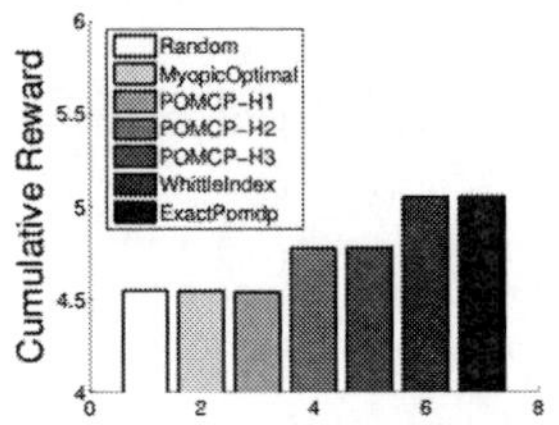

Figure 4: Example when Myopic Policy Fails

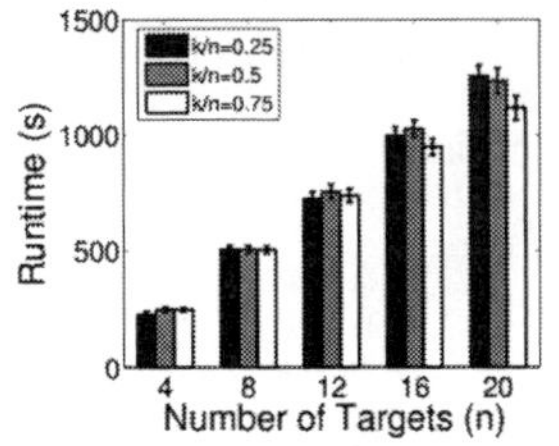

Figure 5: Runtime Analysis of Whittle Index Policy: $n_s = 2, n_o = 2$

6.2 Evaluation of RMAB Modeling

In this section, we will compare our RMAB model with the algorithms (UCB, SWUCB, EXP3) used in [7] with a group of simulated attackers. The performance is evaluated in terms of the cumulative reward received within the first 20 rounds after several rounds learning ($\beta = 0.9$).

Figure 6(a) demonstrates how the performance changes with different learning rounds and $n_s(n_o)$. It shows that when learning rounds is smaller (100), the model with $n_s = n_o = 2$ performs the best. This is because the model with higher $n_s(n_o)$ suffers overfitting with limited data at this time. When the data is relatively abundant (learning rounds = 1000), the model with higher $n_s(n_o)$ performs better. However, we noticed that the difference is not significantly large.

Figure 6(b) shows that comparison of our RMAB model with the Random/UCB/SWUCB/EXP3 algorithms. When learning rounds is smaller (100), our RMAB model performs similar to UCB algorithm, and is better than other algorithms. When learning rounds becomes larger, our RMAB model shows significant advantage over other algorithms.

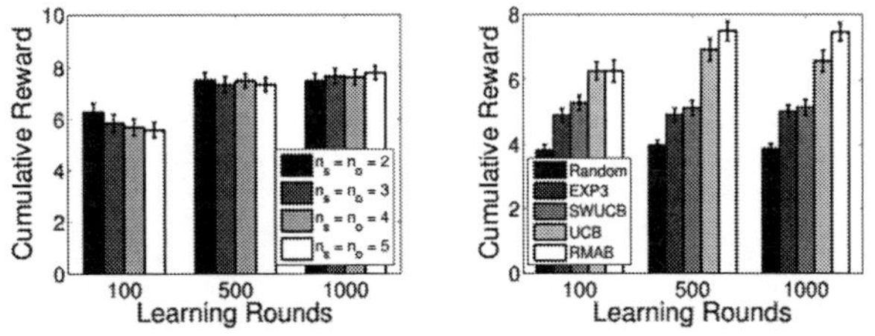

(a) RMAB (b) $n_s = 2, n_o = 2$

Figure 6: Evaluation of RMAB Modeling

7. RELATED WORK

Previous research in Green Security Games [19, 5, 14] suffers from two major limitations. First, this research fails to capture the defender's *lack of observation of attacks* — in the real world, given a large area to patrol, the defender only has observations of attacks on the limited set of targets she patrolled in any given round. She does not have full knowledge of all of attackers' actions as assumed in [19, 5, 14], leading to an unaddressed exploration-exploitation tradeoff for defenders: informally, should the defender allocate resources to protect targets that have already been visited and have been observed to have suffered a lot of attacks or should she allocate resources to protect targets that have not visited for a long time and hence where there are no observations of attacks. Second, while significant work in security games has focused on uncertainty over attackers' observations of defender actions [20], the reverse problem has received little attention. Specifically, given frequent interactions with multiple attackers, the defender herself faces *observation uncertainty* in observing all of the attacker actions *even in the targets she does patrol.* Addressing this uncertainty in the defender's observation is important when estimating attacks on targets and addressing the exploration-exploitation tradeoff.

The limited observability property and exploration-exploitation tradeoff is also noticed by Klíma in the domain of border patrol where the border is large area [7, 8]. They model the problem as a stochastic/adversarial multi-armed bandit problem and use (sliding-window) UCB algorithm [2]/EXP3 algorithm [3] to plan for patrollers' strategies. However, the stochastic bandit formulation fails to model patrol's effect on attackers' actions while the adversarial bandit formulation fails to capture attackers' behavioral pattern.

Zhang et al. [22] focus on deterring crimes in urban areas by police patrol. They use Dynamic Bayesian Network (DBN) to model criminals' response to police patrol. They learn the DBN model from real-world crime data and then plan police patrol according to the DBN model. Their work does not deal with the exploration-exploitation tradeoff since victims would mostly report crimes to police so the police does not suffer from limited/partial observability issue in this domain.

There is a rich literature on indexability of restless multi-armed bandit problem. Glazebrook et al. [6] provide some indexable families of restless multi-armed bandit problems. Nino-Mora [11] propose PCL-indexability and GCL-indexability and show that they are sufficient conditions for indexability. Liu and Zhao [9] apply the concept of RMABs in dynamic multichannel access. In their model, every arm is a two-state Markov chain and the player only knows the state of the arm he chooses to activate. They prove the indexability of their problem and find the closed-form solution for the Whittle index. In [12], Ny et al. also consider the same class of RMABs but motivated by the application of UAV routing. This problem shares some similarity with our problem but our problem is more difficult in the following aspects: (i) we cannot directly observe the states (POMDP vs. MDP); (ii) different actions lead to different transition matrices in our model; (iii) we allow for more states and observations. A further extension to this work discusses the case with probing errors where the player's observation about the state might be incorrect [10]. This concept is similar to what we assume in our model, but the detailed settings are different.

8. CONCLUSION

This paper presents a new solution framework for security domains with frequent interactions and limited/partial observability. The motivating domains include wildlife protection domain, police patrol to catch fare-evaders, border patrol, etc. We model these domains as an RMAB to handle the limited/partial observability challenge. We provide an EM based learning algorithm to learn the RMAB model and use the solution concept of Whittle index policy to solve the RMAB model for planning optimal patrol strategies.

9. ACKNOWLEDGEMENT

This research is supported by the MURI grant W911NF-11-1-0332.

REFERENCES

[1] P. Ansell, K. D. Glazebrook, J. Niño-Mora, and M. O'Keeffe. Whittle's index policy for a multi-class queueing system with convex holding costs. *Mathematical Methods of Operations Research*, 2003.

[2] P. Auer, N. Cesa-Bianchi, and P. Fischer. Finite-time analysis of the multiarmed bandit problem. *Machine learning*, 2002.

[3] P. Auer, N. Cesa-Bianchi, Y. Freund, and R. E. Schapire. Gambling in a rigged casino: The adversarial multi-armed bandit problem. In *Foundations of Computer Science, 1995. Proceedings., 36th Annual Symposium on*. IEEE, 1995.

[4] A. Cassandra, M. L. Littman, and N. L. Zhang. Incremental pruning: A simple, fast, exact method for partially observable markov decision processes. In *UAI*, 1997.

[5] F. Fang, P. Stone, and M. Tambe. When security games go green: Designing defender strategies to prevent poaching and illegal fishing. In *IJCAI*, 2015.

[6] K. Glazebrook, D. Ruiz-Hernandez, and C. Kirkbride. Some indexable families of restless bandit problems. *Advances in Applied Probability*, 2006.

[7] R. Klíma, C. Kiekintveld, and V. Lisý. Online learning methods for border patrol resource allocation. In *Decision and Game Theory for Security*. Springer, 2014.

[8] R. Klıma, V. Lisỳ, and C. Kiekintveld. Combining online learning and equilibrium computation in security games. 2015.

[9] K. Liu and Q. Zhao. Indexability of restless bandit problems and optimality of whittle index for dynamic multichannel access. *Information Theory, IEEE Transactions on*, 2010.

[10] K. Liu, Q. Zhao, and B. Krishnamachari. Dynamic multichannel access with imperfect channel state detection. *Signal Processing, IEEE Transactions on*, 2010.

[11] J. Nino-Mora. Restless bandits, partial conservation laws and indexability. *Advances in Applied Probability*, 2001.

[12] J. L. Ny, M. Dahleh, and E. Feron. Multi-uav dynamic routing with partial observations using restless bandit allocation indices. In *American Control Conference*. IEEE, 2008.

[13] C. H. Papadimitriou and J. N. Tsitsiklis. The complexity of optimal queuing network control. *Mathematics of Operations Research*, 1999.

[14] Y. Qian, W. B. Haskell, A. X. Jiang, and M. Tambe. Online planning for optimal protector strategies in resource conservation games. In *AAMAS*, 2014.

[15] D. Silver and J. Veness. Monte-carlo planning in large pomdps. In *NIPS*, 2010.

[16] M. Tambe. *Security and game theory: algorithms, deployed systems, lessons learned*. Cambridge University Press, 2011.

[17] R. R. Weber and G. Weiss. On an index policy for restless bandits. *Journal of Applied Probability*, 1990.

[18] P. Whittle. Restless bandits: Activity allocation in a changing world. *Journal of applied probability*, 1988.

[19] R. Yang, B. Ford, M. Tambe, and A. Lemieux. Adaptive resource allocation for wildlife protection against illegal poachers. In *AAMAS*, 2014.

[20] Z. Yin, M. Jain, M. Tambe, and F. Ordonez. Risk-averse strategies for security games with execution and observational uncertainty. In *Conference on Artificial Intelligence (AAAI)*, 2011.

[21] Z. Yin, A. Jiang, M. Johnson, M. Tambe, C. Kiekintveld, K. Leyton-Brown, T. Sandholm, and J. Sullivan. Trusts: Scheduling randomized patrols for fare inspection in transit systems. In *IAAI*, 2012.

[22] C. Zhang, A. Sinha, and M. Tambe. Keeping pace with criminals: Designing patrol allocation against adaptive opportunistic criminals. In *AAMAS*, 2015.

Strategy-Proofness in the Stable Matching Problem with Couples

Andrew Perrault, Joanna Drummond, and Fahiem Bacchus
Department of Computer Science
University of Toronto, Toronto, CANADA
{perrault, jdrummond, fbacchus}@cs.toronto.edu

ABSTRACT

Stable matching problems (SMPs) arising in real-world markets often have extra complementarities in the participants' preferences. These complementarities break many of the theoretical properties of SMP and make it computationally hard to find a stable matching. A common complementarity is the introduction of couples in labor markets, which gives rise to the stable matching problem with couples (SMP-C). A major concern in markets is strategy-proofness since markets that are easily manipulated often unravel. In this paper we provide some key insights into the issue of strategy-proofness in SMP-C. We provide theoretical results that relate the set of resident Pareto optimal stable matchings ($\mathcal{RP}_{opt}$) admitted by an SMP-C instance to the ability of the residents to manipulate. We show that a mechanism returning an $\mathcal{RP}_{opt}$ matching is, in certain cases, strategy-proof against residents attempting to manipulate by truncating their preference lists. We provide an algorithm for finding an $\mathcal{RP}_{opt}$ matching when one exists. And finally, we study empirically the frequency of multiple stable and multiple $\mathcal{RP}_{opt}$ matchings as the market sizes grows, and under different proportions of couples in the market. Our empirical results indicate that SMP-C becomes less susceptible to manipulation as both the size of the market grows and the fraction of couples in the market shrinks.

General Terms

Economics, Algorithms, Theory

Keywords

Stable Matching; Complementarities; Strategy-proofness; SAT

1. INTRODUCTION

The Stable Matching Problem (SMP), in which two groups wish to be matched with each other, is one of the most widely-studied problems in economics [11, 7]. A number of real-world applications can be cast as SMP, with residency matching being one the most well-known [18, 22, 1]. The National Resident Matching Program (NRMP) in the US, and the Scottish Foundation Allocation Scheme (SFAS) in Scotland, are two real-world instantiations of such matching markets [17, 9]. The SMP framework however does not allow for complementarities between the participants' preferences. In resident matching an important complementarity arises from couples among the residents: a resident's preferences can depend on the match received by their partner. To address this need for couples to coordinate their placement, residency matching markets (including the NRMP and SFAS) began allowing couples to express their preferences over residency programs jointly. This extension to SMP is called the Stable Matching Problem with Couples.

As in SMP, the goal of SMP-C is to find a match such that no pair (one from each side of the market) has an incentive to defect from their assignment. A matching with this property is said to be *stable*. In standard SMP, there always exists a resident-optimal stable matching ($\mathcal{R}_{opt}$) in which every resident is as least as well off as in any other stable matching; and the simple Deferred Acceptance (DA) algorithm [6] can find this $\mathcal{R}_{opt}$ matching in polynomial time. These properties no longer hold for SMP-C. Finding a stable matching in SMP-C becomes NP-complete [20]; a stable matching is not guaranteed to exist; and even when one does exist, an $\mathcal{R}_{opt}$ matching might not exist.

While there are many strategy-proofness results for SMP, little work has investigated strategy-proofness in SMP-C. For SMP, it is known that no stable matching mechanism is strategy-proof for both sides of the market [21]. There are, however, mechanisms that are approximately stable and approximately strategy-proof where the approximation becomes better as the market size grows [10]. Furthermore, in SMP an $\mathcal{R}_{opt}$ matching always exists and a mechanism returning it is known to be strategy-proof against manipulation by the residents [6].

Since SMP-C extends SMP there also can be no stable mechanism for SMP-C that is strategy-proof for both sides of the market. Furthermore, the limit results of [8, 10] are not known to hold for SMP-C. To the authors' knowledge, no investigation of strategy-proofness against residents in SMP-C has been published. This is a gap in the literature since strategy-proofness on one side of the market is frequently cited as an important property for real world matching mechanisms; e.g., there is evidence that mechanisms lacking this property are often abandoned in favor of strategy-proof ones [2].

In this paper we investigate the question of strategy-proofness against residents in SMP-C. We show that in general, no resident strategy-proof mechanism exists for SMP-C, but that there is a mechanism that is resident strategy-proof with respect to truncations when the SMP-C instance has

Appears in: *Proceedings of the 15th International Conference on Autonomous Agents and Multiagent Systems (AAMAS 2016), J. Thangarajah, K. Tuyls, C. Jonker, S. Marsella (eds.), May 9–13, 2016, Singapore.*

an $\mathcal{R}_{opt}$ matching. Furthermore, we provide an algorithm for implementing this mechanism. When no $\mathcal{R}_{opt}$ matching exists this mechanism will return a resident Pareto optimal ($\mathcal{RP}_{opt}$) matching (as long as the instance has at least one stable matching). We show that residents who have a unique match among the set of $\mathcal{RP}_{opt}$ matchings cannot manipulate this mechanism by truncating their preferences. We also show, however, that no stable mechanism can be strategy-proof when the residents can use the more general manipulation of reordering their preferences, even in the setting where a unique stable matching exists.

We empirically evaluate the set of stable and $\mathcal{RP}_{opt}$ matchings in instances drawn from two different synthetic markets (previously developed by Kojima et al. and Biró et al. [13, 15]). For problem instances of similar size and percentage of couples as the NRMP data investigated by Roth and Peranson [23], we find that nearly all problem instances admit an $\mathcal{R}_{opt}$ matching, and the DA-style algorithm presented by Roth and Peranson almost always finds that $\mathcal{R}_{opt}$ matching. Thus, in conjunction with our theoretical work, we provide an alternate hypothesis for behaviour seen by Roth and Peranson [23]: any mechanism that returns a $\mathcal{R}_{opt}$ matching will be resident strategy-proof with respect to truncations. We additionally find that the theoretical result of Immorlica and Mahdian [8] for large markets appears to hold for SMP-C, even though that result was only proved for SMP.

Section 2 formally defines SMP-C and $\mathcal{RP}_{opt}$ matches. Section 3 discusses strategy-proofness in SMP-C and provides some theoretical results for this question. Section 4 describes our algorithms for finding $\mathcal{RP}_{opt}$ matchings in SMP-C. These algorithms are extensions of a prior SAT based algorithm for SMP-C [5]. Section 5 provides our empirical results, investigating properties of the set of $\mathcal{RP}_{opt}$ matchings as the size and percentage of couples in the market varies. We conclude in Section 6.

2. BACKGROUND

The stable matching problem with couples (SMP-C) can be formalized in terms of the residency matching problem [23]. In this problem doctors wish to be matched with a hospital residency program,[1] and programs wish to accept some number of residents. Both doctors and programs have preferences over who they are matched with, expressed as ranked order lists (ROLs). Some doctors are members of a couple, and these couples provide a joint ROL.[2] Both doctors' and programs' ROLs can be incomplete: any alternative not listed in their ROL is considered to be unacceptable. That is, they would rather not be matched at all than be matched to an alternative not on their ROL. The SMP-C problem is to find a *stable* matching, such that no doctor-program pair has an incentive to defect from the assigned matching.

2.1 SMP-C

More formally, let D be a set of doctors and P be a set of programs. Since there is a preference to be unmatched over an unacceptable match, we use *nil* to denote this alternative: matching a program p to *nil* indicates that p has an unfilled slot while matching a doctor d to *nil* indicates that d was not placed into any program. Let D^+ and P^+ denote the sets $D \cup \{nil\}$ and $P \cup \{nil\}$ respectively.

The doctors are partitioned into two subsets, $S \subseteq D$ and $D \setminus S$. S is the set of single doctors and $D \setminus S$ is the set of doctors who are in couple relationships. Couples are specified by a set of pairs $C \subseteq (D \setminus S) \times (D \setminus S)$. If $(d_1, d_2) \in C$ we say that d_1 and d_2 are each other's partner. We require that every doctor who is not single (i.e., every doctor in $D \setminus S$) have one and only one partner in C. Each program $p \in P$ has an integer capacity $cap_p > 0$ specifying the maximum number of doctors p can accept.

Everyone participating in the matching market has preferences over their possible matches. Each participant a specifies their preferences in a ROL, rol_a, which lists a's preferred matches from most preferred to least preferred. The ROLs of single doctors $d \in S$ contain programs from P^+; the ROLs of couples $c \in C$ contain pairs of programs from $P^+ \times P^+$; and the ROLs of programs $p \in P$ contain doctors from D^+. Every ROL is terminated by *nil* (couple ROLs are terminated by (*nil*, *nil*)) since being unmatched is always the least preferred option, but is preferred to any option not on the ROL.

The order of items on a's ROL defines a partial ordering relation where $x \succeq_a y$ indicates that a prefers x to y (x appears before y on a's ROL) or $x = y$. We define $\succ_a$, $\preceq_a$, and $\succ_a$ in terms of $\succeq_a$ and equality in the standard way. We say that x is *acceptable* to a if $x \succeq_a nil$. (Note that unacceptable matches are not ordered by $\succeq_a$ and that *nil* is always acceptable.)

We define a choice function $Ch_p()$ for programs $p \in P$. Given a set of doctors R, $Ch_p(R)$ returns the subset of R that p would prefer to accept. In our setting $Ch_p(R)$ returns the maximal subset of R such that for all $d \in Ch_p(R)$, $d \succ_p nil$, for all $d' \in R - Ch_p(R)$, $d \succ_p d'$, and $|Ch_p(R)| \leq cap_p$. That is, all doctors in $Ch_p(R)$ are acceptable, are strictly preferred to all doctors not chosen, and p's capacity is not violated. It is also convenient to give the null program a choice function as well: $Ch_{nil}(O) = O$, i.e., *nil* will accept any and all matches.

We use the notation $ranked(a)$ to denote the set of options that a could potentially be matched with. For single doctors d and programs p this is simply the ROLs of d (rol_d) and p (rol_p). For a doctor that is part of a couple (d_1, d_2), $ranked(d_1) = \{p_1 | \exists p_2.(p_1, p_2) \in rol_{(d_1,d_2)}\}$ and similarly for d_2. Note we always have that $nil \in ranked(a)$.

Finally, we will sometimes use rol_a as an indexable vector (zero-based). We define the function $rank_a(x)$ to find the index i of x in a's rol: $rank_a(x) = i$ iff $rol_a[i] = x$. When $x \notin rol_a$ we let $rank_a(x) = |rol_a|$ (an out of bounds index).

2.2 Stable Matchings

Definition 1. A **matching** μ is a mapping from D to P^+. We say that a doctor d is matched to a program p under μ if $\mu(d) = p$, and that p is matched to d if $d \in \mu^{-1}(p)$.

We want to find a **stable** matching where no doctor-program pair has an incentive to defect. We call the pairs that do have an incentive to defect blocking pairs. First we define the condition $willAccept(p, R, S)$ to mean that given the set of doctors $R \cup S$, p will accept a set that includes R: $willAccept(p, R, S) \equiv R \subseteq Ch_p(S \cup R)$.

Definition 2. Let μ be a matching.

[1]Each residency program is in a specific medical speciality.
[2]Members of a couple often pursue different specializations and so must apply to different programs.

1. A single doctor $d \in S$ and a program $p \in P$ is a **blocking pair** for μ if $p \succ_d \mu(d)$ and $willAccept(p, \{d\}, \mu^{-1}(p))$.
2. A couple $c = (d_1, d_2) \in C$ and a program pair $(p_1, p_2) \in P^+ \times P^+$ with $p_1 \neq p_2$ is a **blocking pair** for μ if and only if $(p_1, p_2) \succ_{(d_1,d_2)} (\mu(d_1), \mu(d_2))$, $willAccept(p_1, \{d_1\}, \mu^{-1}(p_1))$, and $willAccept(p_2, \{d_2\}, \mu^{-1}(p_2))$.
3. A couple $c = (d_1, d_2)$ and a program $p \in P$ is a **blocking pair** for μ if $(p, p) \succ_{(d_1,d_2)} (\mu(d_1), \mu(d_2))$ and $willAccept(p, \{d_1, d_2\}, \mu^{-1}(p))$.

Definition 3. A matching μ is **individually rational** if (a) for all $d \in S$, $\mu(d) \succeq_d nil$, (b) for all $c = (d_1, d_2) \in C$, $(\mu(d_1), \mu(d_2)) \succeq_c (nil, nil)$, (c) for all $d \in \mu^{-1}(p)$, $d \succeq_p nil$, and (d) for all $p \in P$, $|\mu^{-1}(p)| \leq cap_p$.

Definition 4. A matching μ is **stable** if it is individually rational and no blocking pairs for μ exist.

2.3 Resident Preferred Matchings

The set of stable matchings can be quite large. In SMP (where there are no couples) this set is always non-empty [6] and has a nice structure: it forms a lattice under the partial order $\succeq_{\mathcal{R}}$ defined as follows.

Definition 5. A matching μ_1 is **resident preferred** to another matching μ_2 [11], denoted by $\mu_1 \succeq_{\mathcal{R}} \mu_2$, if for all $a \in S \cup C$ we have that $\mu_1(a) \succeq_a \mu_2(a)$. We also define $\succ_{\mathcal{R}}$, $\prec_{\mathcal{R}}$, and $\preceq_{\mathcal{R}}$ in terms of $\succeq_{\mathcal{R}}$ and equality in the standard way. In particular, $\mu_1 \succ_{\mathcal{R}} \mu_2$ whenever $\mu_1 \succeq_{\mathcal{R}} \mu_2$ and for at least one $a \in S \cup C$ we have that a strictly prefers μ_1 to μ_2 ($\mu_1(a) \succ_a \mu_2(a)$). When $\mu_1 \succ_{\mathcal{R}} \mu_2$ we say that μ_1 **dominates** μ_2.

Definition 6. We say that a matching μ is **resident optimal**, written $\mathcal{R}_{opt}(\mu)$ if μ is stable and it dominates all other stable matches. That is, for all stable matches μ' not equal to μ we have that $\mu \succ_{\mathcal{R}} \mu'$.

Note that we restrict the resident-optimal matching to be stable. It can be observed that when a matching μ is resident optimal ($\mathcal{R}_{opt}(\mu)$) then for any $a \in S \cup C$, $\mu(a)$ is the best match for a offered by *any* stable matching.

Resident optimality is generally cited as an important property for stable matching algorithms (e.g., [6, 23]). In SMP the fact that the stable matchings form a lattice under $\succeq_{\mathcal{R}}$ implies that a resident-optimal matching always exists. In the presence of couples however, stable matchings may not exist and even when they do an $\mathcal{R}_{opt}$ matching might not exist. However, the $\succeq_{\mathcal{R}}$ relation is still well defined, and for SMP-C leads to potentially multiple *resident Pareto-optimal* matchings.

Definition 7. We say that a matching μ is **resident Pareto optimal**, written $\mathcal{RP}_{opt}(\mu)$, if μ is stable and there does not exist another stable matching μ' such that $\mu' \succ_{\mathcal{R}} \mu$.

It is easy to see that in SMP-C every stable matching μ is either an $\mathcal{RP}_{opt}$ or is dominated by an $\mathcal{RP}_{opt}$ matching. This also means that an SMP-C instance has an $\mathcal{R}_{opt}$ matching if and only if it has a unique $\mathcal{RP}_{opt}$ matching.

2.4 Mechanisms and Strategy-Proofness

Definition 8. A **mechanism** for SMP-C is any algorithm that takes an SMP-C instance as input and returns a matching. A **stable mechanism** is a mechanism that always returns a stable matching if one exists and otherwise returns the empty matching (i.e., everyone is matched to *nil*).[3] A $\mathcal{P}$ **mechanism** is one that always returns a matching satisfying property $\mathcal{P}$ if one exists and the empty matching otherwise.

Definition 9. Let rol^*_α be the complete, true preferences of resident or couple α. rol^*_α consists of a number of programs or program pairs, then the *nil* program, and then the remaining programs or program pairs. α is **truthful** if their reported rol_α is the same as rol^*_α up to and including the *nil* program. α **manipulates** if they are not truthful. Any manipulation is a **reordering** of rol^*_α. A manipulation is a **truncation at rank i** if the reported rol_α is the first i elements of rol^*_α followed by *nil*.

Definition 10. A mechanism m for SMP-C is **resident strategy-proof** when for every SMP-C instance being truthful is a dominant strategy for every resident and couple. That is, no resident or couple in any SMP instance can improve their matching under m by manipulating. When no resident or couple can improve their matching using only truncation manipulations, we say that m is **resident strategy-proof against truncation**.

Definition 11. Let α be a resident (couple) in an SMP-C instance I. A program p (pair of programs) is a $\mathcal{P}$ **program** for α in I if there exists a matching μ for I such that μ satisfies property $\mathcal{P}$ and $p = \mu(\alpha)$.

3. STRATEGY-PROOFNESS IN SMP-C

The current NRMP mechanism was developed partly in response to concerns that the previous mechanism could be manipulated by residents by misreporting their ranking of programs [23]. In SMP, it is possible to achieve *strategy-proofness* for either side of the market by using a mechanism that returns the resident or program-optimal matching[4] [25]. The administrators of the NRMP perceived that residents had a much higher average difference in utility between adjacent elements on their *rol*; thus, the NRMP decided that they wanted a mechanism that was as close to resident strategy-proof as possible.

Roth and Peranson hypothesized that since there is a relatively small fraction of couples in the NRMP (4% in their historical data), the resident strategy-proof mechanism for SMP that returns the $\mathcal{R}_{opt}$ matching could be generalized to SMP-C and the result would be similar [23]. Although their mechanism was not in fact an $\mathcal{R}_{opt}$ mechanism it was quite successful empirically—less than 10 residents (out of 30,000) had an incentive to manipulate via truncation. While not all manipulations are truncations, they tested for truncations for several reasons: i) any outcome that can be achieved by manipulation in SMP can be achieved by a truncation [26] ii) profitable truncations are computationally inexpensive to check for, and iii) truncations are the kind of manipulations that can be potentially identified with the least information about others' preferences [24].

To our knowledge, no theoretical strategy-proofness results exist for SMP-C. We hypothesized that if we restricted

[3]An SMP-C instance might have no stable matchings, so we cannot define a stable mechanism to be one that **always** returns a stable matching as in [21].

[4]Strategy-proofness for both sides of the market is only possible for a small number of instances of SMP [21].

our attention to SMP-C instances in which an $\mathcal{R}_{opt}$ matching exists, then an $\mathcal{R}_{opt}$ mechanism would be resident strategy-proof. As shown in Theorem 2 below, we found that this is not the case. We did find, however, that such a mechanism is resident strategy-proof against truncations. This is useful in practice. In particular, as we will show in Sec. 5, an $\mathcal{R}_{opt}$ matching frequently exists in SMP-C instances that have a low proportion of couples. Furthermore, truncations are an attractive way to manipulate because of the computational and informational properties mentioned above. Hence, an $\mathcal{R}_{opt}$ mechanism can at least block this simpler form of manipulation in many practical cases.

We begin with a lemma that establishes a limit on the ability of truncating agents to benefit from manipulation.

LEMMA 1. *Let α be an agent who truncates their preferences at rank i in an SMP-C instance $\mathcal{I}$. Let Ω be the set of stable matchings before the truncation and let Ω' be the set of stable matchings after the truncation. For any $\mu \in \Omega'$, either i) $\mu \in \Omega$ or ii) $\mu(\alpha) = nil$.*

PROOF. Let μ' be a matching in Ω' where α is not matched to nil. It must be the case that $\mu'(\alpha)$ is ranked above i; otherwise $\mu'(\alpha)$ would be unacceptable to α and μ' would be unstable. Since rol_α is the same as rol^*_α above rank i and the rank order lists of all of the other agents and programs in the instance are the same, μ' must also be stable before α truncates. Thus $\mu' \in \Omega$. □

THEOREM 1. *Let α be a resident or couple in an SMP-C instance $\mathcal{I}$. For any property $\mathcal{P}$, if α has a unique $\mathcal{P}$ program in $\mathcal{I}$, then for any $\mathcal{P}$ mechanism $y_{\mathcal{P}}$, α cannot improve its matching under $y_{\mathcal{P}}$ using only truncation manipulations (α has no incentive to manipulate under $y_{\mathcal{P}}$).*

PROOF. The theorem says that there exists a program (or pair of programs) p such that for all $\mathcal{P}$ matchings μ we have that $\mu(\alpha) = p$, so before truncation $y_{\mathcal{P}}$ returns p as α's match. After truncation, by Lemma 1, $y_{\mathcal{P}}$ must return either p or nil as α's match. Neither of these improve α's match. □

A corollary is that in an instance of SMP-C that has an $\mathcal{R}_{opt}$ matching, a $\mathcal{R}_{opt}$ mechanism is resident strategy-proof against truncation. However, such mechanisms are not resident strategy-proof, as reordering manipulations can still be beneficial.

THEOREM 2. *Let $y_{\mathcal{R}_{opt}}$ be an $\mathcal{R}_{opt}$ mechanism for SMP-C. Then $y_{\mathcal{R}_{opt}}$ is strategy-proof against residents who manipulate via truncation. However, $y_{\mathcal{R}_{opt}}$ is not strategy-proof against residents who manipulate via reordering.*

PROOF. Part I: For any SMP-C instance $\mathcal{I}$, if $\mathcal{I}$ has an $\mathcal{R}_{opt}$ matching then every resident has a unique $\mathcal{R}_{opt}$ program. Then by Theorem 1 no resident has an incentive to manipulate $y_{\mathcal{R}_{opt}}$ using truncation. Otherwise $y_{\mathcal{R}_{opt}}$ always returns the empty match, and again no resident has an incentive to manipulate.

Part II: Reordering is not strategy-proof. We provide a counterexample in Figure 1. The preferences provided show residents' and programs' true preferences. Couples are identified by their resident-resident pair, and give joint preferences as expected. Given these true preferences, only one stable matching exists: $\mu(r_0) = c$, $\mu((r_1, r_2)) = (b, e)$, and

Resident preferences	Program preferences
$r_0 : a \succ b \succ c \succ d$	$a : r_3 \succ r_0 \succ r_1$
$(r_1, r_2) : (b, e) \succ (a, d)$	$b : r_1 \succ r_0$
$(r_3, r_4) : (a, d) \succ (c, e)$	$c : r_3 \succ r_0$
	$d : r_0 \succ r_2 \succ r_4$
	$e : r_4 \succ r_2$

Figure 1: An instance that is manipulable by r_0 using reordering under any mechanism. Each program has capacity 1.

Resident preferences	Program preferences
$(r_0, r_1) : (d, b) \succ (a, c)$	$a : r_0 \succ r_2 \succ r_4$
$(r_2, r_3) : (e, c) \succ (b, d) \succ (a, c)$	$b : r_2 \succ r_1$
$(r_4, r_5) : (a, c) \succ (e, nil)$	$c : r_1 \succ r_3 \succ r_5$
	$d : r_0 \succ r_3$
	$e : r_4 \succ r_2$

Figure 2: An instance that is manipulable for truncating residents under any stable mechanism. Each program has capacity 1.

$\mu((r_3, r_4)) = (a, d)$. However, even though only one stable matching exists (and thus this matching is $\mathcal{R}_{opt}$), the single resident r_0 has an incentive to manipulate via reordering. Instead of reporting $a \succ b \succ c \succ d$ (r_0's true preferences) r_0 can be matched to b instead of c by reporting $b \succ d \succ c \succ a$. (All other participants in the market report their true preferences.) The resulting matching is $\mu'(r_0) = b$, $\mu'((r_1, r_2)) = (a, d)$, and $\mu'((r_3, r_4)) = (c, e)$. μ' was not stable under the original preferences, and single resident r_0 is better off than when they reported their true preferences. □

We can strengthen the latter result of Theorem 2. Using the same instance from that proof, we can show that:

THEOREM 3. *No stable mechanism for SMP-C is resident strategy-proof.*

PROOF. Since the instance of Figure 1 has only one stable matching before and after r_0 reorders, any stable mechanism is manipulable by r_0. □

Thus, reorderings are a powerful way of manipulating in SMP-C. Reorderings can remove old stable matchings and create new ones allowing great scope for beneficial manipulations. In fact, for SMP-C, strategy-proofness is a very strong requirement due to diversity of instances. Hence, we can further strengthen Theorem 3 to show that even less general manipulations by truncations suffice to foil strategy-proofness for stable mechanisms.

THEOREM 4. *No stable mechanism for SMP-C is resident strategy-proof against truncations.*

PROOF. Figure 2 shows an instance that can be manipulated by couple (r_0, r_1) or couple (r_2, r_3). This instance has two stable matchings, μ and μ':

$$\mu((r_0, r_1)) = (a, c), \mu((r_2, r_3)) = (b, d), \mu((r_4, r_5)) = (e, nil)$$
$$\mu'((r_0, r_1)) = (d, b), \mu'((r_2, r_3)) = (a, c), \mu'((r_4, r_5)) = (e, nil)$$

Resident preferences	Program preferences
$(r_0, r_1) : (d, b) \succ (a, c) \succ (g, h)$	$a : r_0 \succ r_2$
$(r_2, r_3) : (a, f) \succ (b, e)$	$b : r_8 \succ r_2 \succ r_2 \succ r_7 \succ r_1$
$(r_4, r_5) : (c, e) \succ (d, f)$	$c : r_1 \succ r_4$
$(r_6, r_7) : (d, b) \succ (g, h)$	$d : r_4 \succ r_0 \succ r_6$
$(r_8, r_9) : (b, g)$	$e : r_3 \succ r_5$
	$f : r_5 \succ r_3$
	$g : r_0 \succ r_6 \succ r_9$
	$h : r_7 \succ r_1$

Figure 3: An instance where the $\mathcal{RP}_{opt}$ mechanism is weak to truncations. (r_0, r_1) manipulates and each program has capacity 1.

(r_0, r_1) prefers μ' to μ and (r_2, r_3) prefers μ to μ'. By truncating their rank-order list at rank 1, each couple can guarantee that their preferred stable matching is selected by the mechanism. Thus, any stable mechanism is manipulable by at least one of the two couples. □

In this situation it is unclear what mechanism to use for SMP-C when an $\mathcal{R}_{opt}$ matching does not exist. By extending the analogy with SMP, it would be intuitive for $\mathcal{RP}_{opt}$ mechanisms to be harder to manipulate via truncations than other stable mechanisms. However, Lemma 1 states that a truncating agent a may create new stable matchings where they are matched to *nil*. A stable mechanism might return one of these matching. Therefore, a might have a disincentive to manipulate by truncation because the mechanism might now return a matching in which a is unmatched. However, these new matches of a to *nil* might not be $\mathcal{RP}_{opt}$. In this case they would not be returned by an $\mathcal{RP}_{opt}$ mechanism. Hence, with an $\mathcal{RP}_{opt}$ mechanism a might no longer have a disincentive to manipulate. Figure 3 shows an instance where this occurs. Initially, there are four stable matchings and two $\mathcal{RP}_{opt}$ matchings (not shown in the figure). By truncating, (r_0, r_1) can eliminate one of the $\mathcal{RP}_{opt}$ matchings while also creating a new stable matching μ where they are matched to (*nil*, *nil*). However, μ is not $\mathcal{RP}_{opt}$, and so (r_0, r_1) can freely manipulate an $\mathcal{RP}_{opt}$-mechanism without fear of being matched to (*nil*, *nil*). Hence there are stable mechanisms that are strategy-proof against truncations for this instance, but some $\mathcal{RP}_{opt}$ mechanisms are not.

Despite this difficulty in comparing the strategy-proofness of $\mathcal{RP}_{opt}$ mechanisms with other stable mechanisms, we will show in Sec. 5 that empirically Theorem 1 can be used to show that often a larger number of residents will have no incentive to manipulate an $\mathcal{RP}_{opt}$ mechanism than a stable mechanisms.

4. ALGORITHMS FOR SMP-C

The standard approach to finding a stable matching in SMP-C has been to extend the deferred acceptance algorithm so that it can handle couples (e.g., [23, 12, 3]). However, these extensions are incomplete: they are unable to determine whether or not a stable matching exists, and even when a stable matching does exist they might not be able to find one.

Since SMP-C is known to be NP-Complete [20] it is also possible to encode it as another NP-Complete problem. For example, it can be encoded as a SAT (satisfiability) problem or as IP (integer program) problem [5, 4]. The advantage of doing this is that SAT and IP solvers have become very advanced and are routinely able to solve large practical problems. Another advantage of these solvers is that when given an instance for which no stable matching exists, they are often able to prove this.

4.1 DA-Style Algorithms for SMP-C

The basic principle of DA algorithms [6] is that members of one side of the market propose down their ROLs while the other side either rejects those proposals or holds them until they see a better proposal: once all proposals have been made the non-rejected proposals are accepted forming a match.

Roth and Peranson develop a DA algorithm, **RP99**, capable of dealing with couples [23]. This algorithm has been used with considerable success in practice, including most famously for finding matches for the NRMP which typically involves about 30,000 doctors [16]. RP99 employs an iterative scheme. After computing a stable matching for all single doctors, couples are added one at a time and a new stable matching computed after each addition. The algorithm uses DA at each stage to find these stable matchings. Matching a couple can make previously made matches unstable and in redoing these matches the algorithm might start to cycle. Hence, cycle checking (or a timeout) is sometimes needed to terminate the algorithm.

Kojima et al. develop a simple "sequential couples algorithm," which they use to show that the probability of a stable matchings existing goes to one under certain assumptions [12]. However, this simple algorithm is not useful in practice as it declares failure under very simple conditions. Kojima et al. also provide a more practical DA algorithm, **KPR**, that they use in their experiments. The main difference between KPR and RP99 is that KPR deals with all couples at the same time—it does not attempt to compute intermediate stable matchings. Drummond et al. found that KPR was much more efficient than RP99 [5].

Finally, Ashlagi et al. extend the analysis of Kojima et al., developing a more sophisticated "Sorted Deferred Acceptance Algorithm" and analyzing its behaviour [3]. This algorithm is designed mainly to be amenable to theoretical analysis rather than for practical application.

4.2 Solving SMP-C via SAT

Drummond et al. developed SAT-E, an effective encoding of SMP-C into SAT, and evaluated its performance on synthesized SMP-C problem instances [5]. They found that their encoding, used in conjunction with a state-of-the art SAT solver, scaled well, outperformed an IP encoding they also developed, and could find solutions to problem instances that the DA-style algorithms could not.

Given an SMP-C instance $\langle D, C, P, ROLs \rangle$, where $ROLs$ is the set of all participant ROLs, SAT-E($\langle D, C, P, ROLs \rangle$) can be viewed as a function that returns a SAT encoding in CNF (conjunctive normal form), which is the input format taken by modern SAT solvers.

We highlight three important things about SAT-E:

1. For any SMP-C instance $\mathcal{I} = \langle D, C, P, ROLs \rangle$, the satisfying models of SAT-E stand in a one-to-one correspondence with the stable models of $\mathcal{I}$.
2. SAT-E includes the set of propositional variables $m_d[p]$.

ALGORITHM 1: SAT-$\mathcal{RP}_{opt}$. Given an SMP-C instance return a $\mathcal{RP}_{opt}$ matching or the empty match if none exists.

Input: $\mathcal{I} = \langle D, C, P, ROLs \rangle$ an **SMP-C** instance.
Output: An $\mathcal{RP}_{opt}$ matching for $\mathcal{I}$.

CNF $\leftarrow$ SAT-E($\mathcal{I}$)
$\mu \leftarrow \emptyset$
while *true* **do**
  (sat?,π) $\leftarrow$ SatSolve(CNF)
  /* *SatSolve returns the status (sat or unsat) and a satisfying model π if sat* */
  if *not sat?* **then**
    return μ // *Return last match found.*
  $\mu \leftarrow$ stable matching corresponding to π
  $c \leftarrow \{\neg m_d[p] \mid \mu(d) = p\}$ // *Block this match*
  CNF $\leftarrow$ CNF $\cup \{c\}$
  for $d \in S$ **do**   //d must get an equally good match
    $c_d \leftarrow \{m_d[p] \mid p \succeq_d \mu(d)\}$
    CNF $\leftarrow$ CNF $\cup \{c_d\}$
  for $c \in C$ **do**   //c must get an equally good match
    $c_c \leftarrow \{m_c[i] \mid i = rank_c(\mu(c))\}$
    CNF $\leftarrow$ CNF $\cup \{c_c\}$

In any satisfying model, π, $m_d[p]$ is true if and only if $\mu(d) = p$ in the stable matching μ corresponding to π.

3. SAT-E also includes the set of propositional variables $m_c[i]$. In any satisfying model, π, $m_c[i]$ is true if and only if in μ, the stable matching corresponding to π, c is matched to a program pair they rank i or above in their ROL.

4.3 Finding $\mathcal{RP}_{opt}$ matchings

To implement an $\mathcal{RP}_{opt}$ mechanism we need to find an $\mathcal{RP}_{opt}$ matching. Using SAT-E and the above three facts, we provide SAT-$\mathcal{RP}_{opt}$ for finding an $\mathcal{RP}_{opt}$ matching. This algorithm will also return an $\mathcal{R}_{opt}$ matching if one exists (as an $\mathcal{R}_{opt}$ matching exists if and only if there is there is only one $\mathcal{RP}_{opt}$ matching).

SAT-$\mathcal{RP}_{opt}$ takes an SMP-C instance as input and constructs the SAT-E encoding for that instance. It finds a stable matching μ and then tries to find a new matching that dominates μ. This is accomplished by adding a *blocking clause* c to the SAT encoding. This clause c is a disjunction that says that no future solution is allowed to return the same stable model (one of the mappings $\mu(d) = p$ of all future solutions must be different, i.e., one of the variables $m_d[p]$ made true by μ must be false in every future matching). Along with the blocking clause, other clauses are added to ensure that in the next matching no doctor or couple receives a worse matching. For single doctors d a clause is added that says that d must be matched to a program it ranks at least as high as $\mu(d)$, and for every couple c a (unit) clause that says that c must be matched to a pair of programs it ranks at least as highly as $\mu(c)$. This causes the new match to be $\succeq_{\mathcal{R}} \mu$, and since the new match cannot be equal it must be $\succ_{\mathcal{R}} \mu$. That is, the new match must dominate μ. If no dominating match can be found, the current match is $\mathcal{RP}_{opt}$ and we return it. Note that an instance has no $\mathcal{RP}_{opt}$ matching if and only if it has no stable matching. So if the very first SAT call fails, there is no $\mathcal{RP}_{opt}$ matching and the empty matching will be returned.

ALGORITHM 2: SAT-ENUM. Find all stable models of an inputted SMP-C instance

Input: $\mathcal{I} = \langle D, C, P, ROLs \rangle$ an **SMP-C** instance
Output: Find all stable models of $\mathcal{I}$

CNF $\leftarrow$ SAT-E($\mathcal{I}$)
while *true* **do**
  (sat?,π) $\leftarrow$ SatSolve(CNF)
  if *sat?* **then**
    $\mu \leftarrow$ stable matching corresponding to π
    output(μ)
    $c \leftarrow \{\neg m_d[p] \mid \mu(d) = p\}$
    CNF $\leftarrow$ CNF $\cup \{c\}$ // *Block* μ
  else
    return   // *All stable matchings found.*

In our experiments (Sec. 5) we also need to find all the stable matchings of an instance. This can be accomplished with SAT-ENUM. SAT-ENUM uses a sequence of SAT calls each one returning a stable match. After each stable match is found we ensure that no future stable match is the same by adding a blocking clause to the SAT encoding as described for Algorithm 1.

5. EMPIRICAL RESULTS

We use SAT-ENUM to find all stable matchings for two distributions of synthetic data, which we call: i) impartial culture with geography (IC-GEOG), and ii) SFAS-tuned with geography (SFAS-GEOG). IC-GEOG generates heterogeneous preference profiles; each resident has an equal chance of drawing any program as her first choice. SFAS-GEOG generates more homogeneous profiles; certain programs are much more likely to be in a given resident's top 10. The models have slightly different procedures for generating couples preferences, but both models assign each program a geographic region and require that, for any program pair in a couple's ROL, the programs are in the same region. We describe the models in detail below. We then evaluate how frequently these instances admit $\mathcal{R}_{opt}$ and unique stable matchings for various parameters of the markets.

5.1 Statistical Models of SMP-C Instances

IC-GEOG is the model presented Kojima et al. [12, 13]. It draws residents' and programs' preferences from the impartial culture model (i.e., i.i.d. uniform). All residents draw i.i.d. an ROL of size 10. For singles, this is their final ROL after appending *nil*. To generate a couple's joint ROL, all 11^2 pairs are scored via a Borda-like scoring function, breaking ties according to an arbitrarily chosen member of the couple's preferences. However, as a couple's preferences are constrained by geography, a pair of programs is only added to the joint ROL if both programs are in the same geographic region (or one is *nil*). Each program is randomly assigned one of 5 regions. Each program ranks each resident that ranks them, again with preferences i.i.d. uniform.

SFAS-GEOG is a variant of the model presented by Biró et al. to mimic SFAS [15]. All residents draw i.i.d. a ROL of size 10 from a Plackett-Luce model [19, 14], where the most popular program (resp., resident) is five times more popular than the least popular program (resp., resident) as seen in the SFAS market. All other programs' popularity are linearly interpolated between the most and least popu-

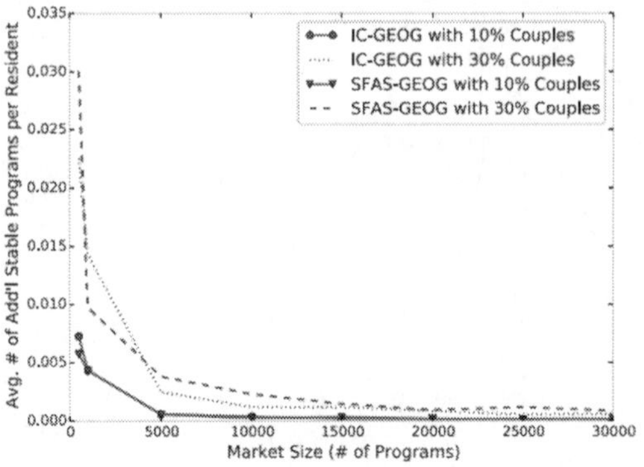

Figure 4: Average number of additional stable programs per resident as market size increases, only including satisfiable instances.

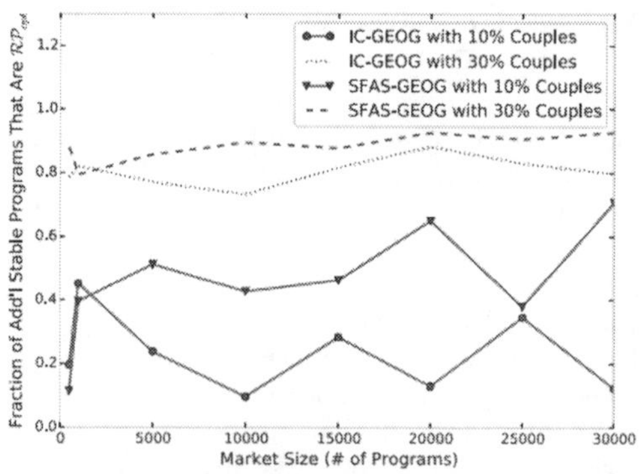

Figure 5: Average number of additional $\mathcal{RP}_{opt}$ matchings per resident divided by average number of additional stable matchings per resident as market size increases, only including satisfiable instances.

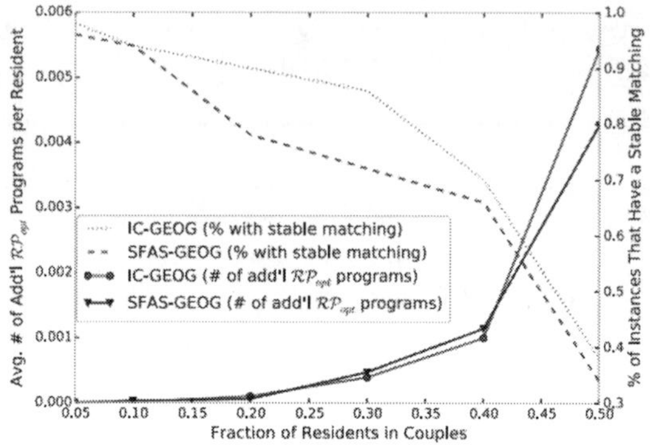

Figure 6: Average number of additional $\mathcal{RP}_{opt}$ programs per resident, and overall percentage of satisfiable instances, as fraction of residents in couples increases. 20,000 programs.

lar programs. Formally, given a reference ranking over all programs (resp., residents), the value of the ith element in the corresponding scoring vector is $m + 4i$, where m is the number of programs (resp., residents) in the match. For singles, this is their final ROL. For couples, all program-program pairs in the same geographic region are ranked in reverse lexicographic ordering, with arbitrary tie-breaking. Each program is randomly assigned one of 5 regions.

In order to ensure that the underlying preference distribution was responsible for any variance shown in the experiments, SFAS-GEOG is modified from Biró et al.'s original description to mirror IC-GEOG in the following ways: i) we fix all residents' ROL to be length 10; ii) we allow programs to rank all residents who rank them (again, drawing from a Plackett-Luce model with the scoring vector as described above); and iii) we impose the same geographical restriction on couples' joint ROLs as Kojima et al. do for IC-GEOG. In addition to being more directly comparable to IC-GEOG, imposing the geographical restriction on the Biró et al. model allows us to better capture couples' real-world preferences in larger markets. (The SFAS market has roughly 800 program positions; we test up to 30,000 program positions.)

In both models, we set the number of positions as 87% of the number of residents to match the 2015 NRMP data [17]. Each data point represents the average of 50 instances.

5.2 Results and Discussion

We begin by investigating the ability of residents to benefit by truncating their preferences in SMP-C as the size of the market gets large. Roth and Peranson found that, when using RP99 on historical NRMP data, very few residents had an incentive to truncate [23]. They conjectured that this was due to two reasons: i) as market size grows large relative to ROL length, the size of the set of all stable matches gets smaller, and ii) as in SMP, residents have no incentive to manipulate when a market has a unique stable matching. In Theorem 2, we prove the latter point for truncations, but show that it is false for reorderings. Immorlica and Mahdian proved the former point for SMP [8], and we address it empirically for SMP-C in this section.

Figure 4 shows the average number of *additional* stable programs per resident (i.e., in excess of one) for 10% and 30% residents in couples in IC-GEOG and SFAS-GEOG models as the market size increases.[5] Note that every resident has at least one stable program because we restrict our attention to SMP-C instances that are satisfiable. The models with a larger percentage of couples have more stable programs per resident, but the differences between IC-GEOG and SFAS-GEOG are small. We see that the average number of stable programs per resident drops rapidly as the market size increases, irrespective of model, which shows that an analog of Immorlica and Mahdian's result may apply in this setting.

In addition, we find that the residents' ability to truncate is even more strongly curtailed under an $\mathcal{RP}_{opt}$ mechanism. Figure 5 shows the average number of additional $\mathcal{RP}_{opt}$ programs per resident relative to the average number of additional stable programs per resident. We see that generally residents have much fewer additional $\mathcal{RP}_{opt}$ programs than additional stable programs. Since Figure 4 shows that the average number of additional stable programs is well below 1, this means that many residents have a unique stable program and even more will have a unique stable $\mathcal{RP}_{opt}$ program. Hence, by Theorem 1 there will be more residents with no incentive to manipulate an $\mathcal{RP}_{opt}$ mechanism than there are residents with no incentive to manipulate a stable mechanism.

Figure 6 provides a more detailed picture of what happens

[5]Standard error in this graph is 0.003-0.005% for the 30% couples models with market size under 1000 programs and less than 0.001% otherwise.

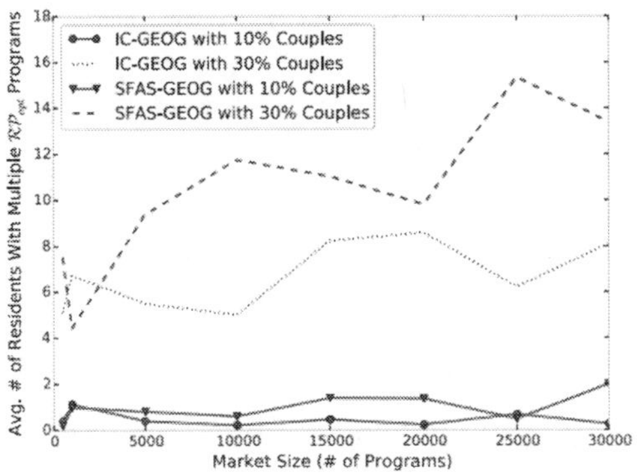

Figure 7: Average number of residents with multiple $\mathcal{RP}_{opt}$ programs as market size increases, only including satisfiable instances.

to the number of additional $\mathcal{RP}_{opt}$ programs per resident as the fraction of residents in couples increases for a fixed market size of 20,000. We see that the two models behave similarly, showing a superlinear growth. On the other axis, we see that although the average number of $\mathcal{RP}_{opt}$ programs per resident increases rapidly as the fraction of couples increases, the percentage of instances with a stable matching decreases. With 5% couples, almost all instances had at least one stable matching for IC-GEOG and SFAS-GEOG, while with 50% couples, fewer than 40% do. Thus, mechanism designers in environments with a high fraction of couples will have to contend with both the lack of existence of stable matchings and high incentives to truncate among residents.

We can conclude from Figure 5 that, under an $\mathcal{RP}_{opt}$ mechanism, residents will have substantially fewer programs they can potentially be matched to as the result of a truncation. Combining this result with Figure 6, this effect is particularly strong for low percentages of couples in the market. We find that both RP99 and KPR behave like $\mathcal{RP}_{opt}$ mechanisms in instances with a fraction of couples similar to that found in the NRMP in the 1990s (4% [23]). In particular, for instances with 20,000 programs and 5% couples and multiple stable matchings, KPR found an $\mathcal{RP}_{opt}$ matching 100% of the time and RP99 found an $\mathcal{RP}_{opt}$ matching more than 93% of the time.[6] Thus, i) RP99 is nearly an $\mathcal{RP}_{opt}$ mechanism, ii) $\mathcal{RP}_{opt}$ mechanisms can rarely be manipulated by resident truncations on markets with a low percentage of couples, and iii) when they can, only an extremely small number of residents can benefit. We thus hypothesize that the number of residents who could benefit by truncating observed by Roth and Peranson was made lower by their exploitation of $\mathcal{RP}_{opt}$ matchings rather than a small number of stable matchings as they conjectured.

However, there is a peculiar caveat to these results: the number of residents per instance with multiple stable or $\mathcal{RP}_{opt}$ programs does not seem to be affected by market size. Figure 7 shows the average number of residents with multiple $\mathcal{RP}_{opt}$ programs for 10% and 30% residents in couples in IC-GEOG and SFAS-GEOG models as the market size increases.[7] We see that the number of residents with multiple $\mathcal{RP}_{opt}$ programs does not decrease as market size increases. We observed similar behaviour for the number of residents with multiple stable matchings. Comparing IC-GEOG and SFAS-GEOG, we see that SFAS-GEOG has more residents with multiple $\mathcal{RP}_{opt}$ programs, which is consistent with the higher fraction of $\mathcal{RP}_{opt}$ programs in SFAS-GEOG that we previously observed. Unsurprisingly, the number of residents with multiple stable or $\mathcal{RP}_{opt}$ programs is higher when the fraction of couples is increased, since an instance with a higher fraction of couples tends to have a larger number of stable and $\mathcal{RP}_{opt}$ matchings.

Since it only requires a single resident with multiple $\mathcal{RP}_{opt}$ programs to prevent the existence of a $\mathcal{R}_{opt}$ matching, we likewise find that the frequency of instances that have $\mathcal{R}_{opt}$ matchings is not affected by market size. $\mathcal{R}_{opt}$ matchings exist 94.2% and 70.1% of the time for IC-GEOG with 10% and 30% couples and 91.1% and 62.9% of time for SFAS-GEOG with 10% and 30% couples.

These results suggest that Roth and Peranson's observation that few residents could benefit by truncating, was not affected by the size of the market, further suggesting their observation was only dependent on the percentage of residents in couples. While there may be some residents that can benefit from truncating irrespective of market size, we expect the fact that the number of them is so small to be a strong disincentive to truncating in practice. It requires considerable effort (e.g., learning the preferences of others) to be able to truncate effectively, and these efforts will be very unlikely to yield any benefit in sufficiently large instances. In addition, truncating carries the risk that a resident will become unmatched even under an $\mathcal{RP}_{opt}$ mechanism.

6. CONCLUSIONS

In this paper we examined strategy-proofness for SMP-C, showing that in general, no resident strategy-proof stable mechanism exists. We do show that, for certain problem instances, a stable matching mechanism that always returns an $\mathcal{RP}_{opt}$ matching is strategy-proof w.r.t. residents truncating their preferences, and we extend a previously developed SAT encoding to provide an $\mathcal{RP}_{opt}$ mechanism. We empirically show, on two very different preference distributions based on real-world markets, that when a low percentage of couples exist in the market, the $\mathcal{RP}_{opt}$ mechanism is frequently resistant to truncations, suggesting a new hypothesis for why there is little incentive for residents to truncate their preferences in the NRMP.

Furthermore, our empirical results suggest new avenues for theoretical research: we hypothesize that an analogous SMP-C result exists for the Immorlica and Mahdian large markets result for SMP [8]; we additionally hypothesize that if the percentage of couples in the market grows slower than the size of the market, an $\mathcal{R}_{opt}$ matching exists with high probability (an analogous result to the Ashlagi et al. large markets result [3]). We also wish to further use our extension to SAT-E to allow us to empirically explore different properties of SMP-C, providing further insight into possible theoretical results.

Acknowledgements

We acknowledge the support of NSERC. Drummond and Perrault were supported by OGS. We thank the reviewers for helpful suggestions.

[6]There was a problem instance where an $\mathcal{R}_{opt}$ matching existed, and RP99 did not find it.

[7]Standard error in this graph is 0.3-0.5 for the 10% couples models and 2.5-3.5 for the 30% couples models.

REFERENCES

[1] A. Abdulkadiroglu, P. Pathak, A. E. Roth, and T. Sönmez. The Boston public school match. *American Economic Review*, 95(2):368–371, 2005.

[2] A. Abdulkadiroglu, P. Pathak, A. E. Roth, and T. Sonmez. Changing the Boston school choice mechanism. Technical report, National Bureau of Economic Research, 2006.

[3] I. Ashlagi, M. Braverman, and A. Hassidim. Stability in large matching markets with complementarities. *Operations Research*, 62(4):713–732, 2014.

[4] P. Biró, D. F. Manlove, and I. McBride. The hospitals/residents problem with couples: Complexity and integer programming models. In *Experimental Algorithms*, pages 10–21. Springer, 2014.

[5] J. Drummond, A. Perrault, and F. Bacchus. SAT is an effective and complete method for solving stable matching problems with couples. In *Proceedings of the Twenty-Fourth International Joint Conference on Artificial Intelligence (IJCAI-15)*, 2015.

[6] D. Gale and L. S. Shapley. College admissions and the stability of marriage. *American Mathematical Monthly*, 69(1):9–15, 1962.

[7] D. Gusfield and R. W. Irvine. *The stable marriage problem: structure and algorithms*. Foundations of Computing Series. The MIT Press, 1989.

[8] N. Immorlica and M. Mahdian. Marriage, honesty, and stability. In *Proceedings of the Sixteenth Annual ACM-SIAM Symposium on Discrete Algorithms*, pages 53–62, 2005.

[9] R. Irving. Matching practices for entry-labor markets - scotland. 2011. Accessed: 2015-11-14.

[10] S. Kannan, J. Morgenstern, A. Roth, and Z. S. Wu. Approximately stable, school optimal, and student-truthful many-to-one matchings (via differential privacy). In *Proceedings of the Twenty-Sixth Annual ACM-SIAM Symposium on Discrete Algorithms*, pages 1890–1903, 2015.

[11] D. E. Knuth. *Marriages stables*. Les Presses de l'Universite de Montreal, 1976.

[12] F. Kojima, P. Pathak, and A. E. Roth. Matching with couples: Stability and incentives in large markets. *Quarterly Journal of Economics*, 128(4):1585–1632, 2013.

[13] F. Kojima, P. Pathak, and A. E. Roth. Online appendix matching with couples: Stability and incentives in large markets. *Quarterly Journal of Economics*, 128(4), 2013.

[14] R. D. Luce. *Individual Choice Behavior: A Theoretical Analysis*. Wiley, 1959.

[15] I. McBride and D. F. Manlove. The hospitals / residents problem with couples: Complexity and integer programming models. *CoRR*, abs/1308.4534, 2013.

[16] National Resident Matching Program. National resident matching program, results and data: 2013 main residency match®, 2013.

[17] National Resident Matching Program. National resident matching program, results and data: 2015 main residency match®. 2015.

[18] M. Niederle, A. E. Roth, and T. Sonmez. Matching and market design. In S. N. Durlauf and L. E. Blume, editors, *The New Palgrave Dictionary of Economics (2nd Ed.)*, volume 5, pages 436–445. Palgrave Macmillan, Cambridge, 2008.

[19] R. Plackett. The analysis of permutations. *Applied Statistics*, 24:193–202, 1975.

[20] E. Ronn. NP-complete stable matching problems. *Journal of Algorithms*, 11(2):285–304, 1990.

[21] A. E. Roth. The economics of matching: Stability and incentives. *Mathematics of Operations Research*, 7(4):617–628, 1982.

[22] A. E. Roth. The evolution of the labor market for medical interns and residents: A case study in game theory. *Journal of Political Economy*, 92(6):991–1016, 1984.

[23] A. E. Roth and E. Peranson. The redesign of the matching market for American physicians: Some engineering aspects of economic design. *The American Economic Review*, 89(1):748–780, September 1999.

[24] A. E. Roth and U. G. Rothblum. Truncation strategies in matching markets—in search of advice for participants. *Econometrica*, 67(1):21–43, 1999.

[25] A. E. Roth and M. Sotomayor. Chapter 16. two-sided matching. In R. J. Aumann and S. Hart, editors, *Handbook of Game Theory Volume 1*, pages 485–541. Elsevier, 1992.

[26] A. E. Roth and J. H. Vande Vate. Random paths to stability in two-sided matching. *Econometrica*, 58(6):1475–1480, 1990.

Manipulations in Two-Agent Sequential Allocation with Random Sequences

Yuto Tominaga, Taiki Todo, and Makoto Yokoo
Kyushu University, Motooka 744, Fukuoka, Japan
{ tominaga@agent., todo@, yokoo@ } inf.kyushu-u.ac.jp

ABSTRACT

Sequential allocation is one of the most fundamental models for allocating indivisible items to agents in a decentralized manner, in which agents sequentially pick their favorite items among the remainder based on a pre-defined priority ordering of agents (a sequence). In recent years, algorithmic issues about agents' manipulations have also been investigated, such as the computational complexity of verifying whether a given bundle of items is achievable and maximizing one's utility under a given additive utility function. In this paper we consider a slightly modified model, where the selection process is divided into rounds, each agent obtains exactly one item in each round, and the sequence per round is determined uniformly at random. It is natural to expect that finding a profitable manipulation is difficult even for the case of two agents, since a manipulator must consider exponentially many possible sequences with respect to the number of rounds due to randomization. To our surprise, however, an optimal manipulation can be computed without any exploration for exponentially decaying utilities. Furthermore, for general additive utilities, although some exploration is required, it can still be done in polynomial time with respect to the number of rounds.

CCS Concepts

•Computing methodologies → Multi-agent systems;
•Applied computing → *Economics;*

Keywords

Distributed Resource Allocation; Item Picking; Sequential Allocation; Uncertainty

1. INTRODUCTION

Sequential allocation, which is one of the most common research topics in the field of social science and economics [12], simply models the situation of allocating indivisible items to agents in a decentralized manner. In a traditional sequential allocation model, there is a set of indivisible items, a set of agents, and a fixed priority ordering (known as a *sequence*) over the set of agents, according to which they pick items one-by-one. Considering fairness among agents, the sequences used in practice are commonly 'balanced,' such that at every moment of the selection process the difference of the numbers of items already selected is bounded by one. This traditional model can represent several practical situations, including the draft system in many worldwide professional sports associations, such as the National Basketball Association in the US.

Sequential allocation has also been attracting a huge amount of attention from researchers in the fields of multi-agent systems, algorithmic game theory, and computational social choice, and several research issues related to these fields have been investigated. Bouveret and Lang [4] considers the problem of finding the optimal sequence in which social welfare, i.e., the sum of agents' utilities, is maximized, which was followed and extended by Kalinowski et al. [10]. Furthermore, Kalinowski et al. [11] addresses the problem from the viewpoint of sequential form games and studies the subgame-perfect equilibrium in a game defined by sequential allocation. Aziz et al. [2] investigates the computational complexity of verifying whether a given bundle is possible or necessary.

From the perspective of an agent who is willing to maximize her own utility, a natural algorithmic question asks whether she can obtain a specific bundle of items, as initiated by Bouveret and Lang [5]. Assuming that the utility of such an agent (a *manipulator*) is additive and that every other agent adopts the 'sincere' picking strategy, i.e., picking her most favorite item among the remainder at every moment of her action, they show that maximizing the manipulator's utility is solvable in polynomial time with respect to the number of items. They also conclude that the effect of such optimal manipulation on social welfare, specifically the loss of social welfare by manipulation, is not very large.

Although all of these research issues address sequential allocation with fixed sequences, some practical situations related to sequential allocation do not have such fixed sequences, including the draft system in Japan's professional baseball league. For such situations, it is natural to consider random tie-breaking in the sequential allocation problem, which is the issue we study in this paper. One of the simplest processes with random tie-breaking can be described as follows. In each round, each agent chooses one item. If there is a conflict among agents' choices, then a lottery is used to decide which agent among those having the conflict obtains the item. All of those who cannot obtain the item choose other items among the remaining ones, and the same process is repeated until every agent obtains exactly one in

Appears in: *Proceedings of the 15th International Conference on Autonomous Agents and Multiagent Systems (AAMAS 2016), J. Thangarajah, K. Tuyls, C. Jonker, S. Marsella (eds.), May 9–13, 2016, Singapore.*

the round. Then go to the next round and repeat the process until every item is given to an agent.

For simplicity, in this paper we consider a slightly different model and focus on the case of two agents (nevertheless, our results can still be applied to the above original model with two agents, as we discuss in Section 6). In our model, there exist $2m$ items and two agents, A and B, where m is a positive integer. The selection process is divided into m rounds, in each of which one agent obtains one item. At the beginning of each round, a coin flip determines which agent picks first; the sequence in a round is chosen uniformly at random between AB and BA, where AB means that agent A picks first followed by agent B. Here, an agent, say A, faces the problem of choosing between 'risk-taking' and a 'sure-thing.' Consider four items $\{1, 2, 3, 4\}$, where the indices indicate agent A's preference so that she prefers the lower-indexed one, agent B has preference (binary relation over the set of items) $\rhd_B$ such that $2 \rhd_B 3 \rhd_B 1 \rhd_B 4$ and plays a 'sincere' picking strategy, and the sequence in the first round is chosen as AB. By picking 2 first and deferring 1 to the next round, agent A takes a risk of losing 1 depending on the coin flip in the next round. On the other hand, by picking 1 first, she is guaranteed to obtain 1 but cannot obtain 2.

We focus on three specific computation problems, Bundle-Possibility, Bundle-Certainty and Max-Expected-Utility. Bundle-Possibility (respectively, Bundle-Certainty) defines the computation problem of verifying whether agent A can obtain a given bundle under some (resp. any) realizable sequence. On the other hand, Max-Expected-Utility defines the computation problem of finding the maximum value of her expected utility, where expectation is taken for the randomized realization of sequences. It is natural to expect that Max-Expected-Utility is not solvable in polynomial time, i.e., finding a profitable manipulation in the model with random sequences becomes much harder than in the model with deterministic sequences, since a manipulator must consider exponentially many possible sequences with respect to the number of rounds due to randomization. To our surprise, however, an optimal manipulation can be computed without any exploration in the exponentially decaying utility case. Furthermore, even in the general additive utility case, although some exploration is required to find an optimal manipulation, it can be done in polynomial time with respect to the number of rounds.

Let us introduce how we can interpret our technical results. From the viewpoint of a mechanism designer who organizes a sequential allocation with random sequences, those results have negative implications. If an agent wants to maximize her utility, finding the best manipulation is easy, and she will not use the sincere picking strategy. This means that introducing randomization in tie-breaking does not help the mechanism designer provide agents incentive to behave sincerely, at least for the case of two agents. However, our analysis is just a first step; considering more than two agents in the model and discussing other criteria such as social welfare and fairness remain an open and interesting future direction.

The paper is organized as follows. Section 2 compares our model and its contributions with previous works. Section 3 introduces our model and explains several terms used in the technical parts. Section 4 defines four decision problems, Bundle-Possibility, Bundle-Certainty, Find-Best-Possible and Find-Best-Certain, and shows that all can be solved in polynomial time. Section 5 defines the Max-Expected-Utility problem and shows that it can also be solved in polynomial time. Particularly, for the case of exponentially decaying utilities, we show that the problem can be solved much faster, without any exploration. Section 6 shows an application of our results to the model with random tie-breaking. Section 7 discusses related existing works and raises possible future research questions. Finally, Section 8 concludes the paper.

2. RELATED WORKS

Some prior works have dealt with the decentralized allocation of indivisible items with randomization. The contested pile methods, proposed by Vetschera and Kilgour [14] and followed by Brams et al. [6], create a decentralized allocation model, in which a conflict over an item is solved by putting it into a place called a *contested pile* and deciding its allocation after the picking sequence is completed. The parallel elicitation-free protocol, proposed by Huang et al. [9] is another class of decentralized procedures, in which every agent has the same probability to get each item. Both randomizations in these models differ from ours, and thus their results have no direct implication for our model.

In the literature of social choice and mechanism design, some researches also deal with the randomized allocation of indivisible items and focus on centralized allocation mechanisms. Budish and Cantillon [7] analyzes the random serial dictatorship mechanism, which is a well-known type of scheme for allocating indivisible items in a centralized manner. Bogomolnaia and Moulin [3] analyzes the probabilistic serial rule, which is another centralized mechanism that will be explained in more detail in Section 7. Analyzing manipulation complexity is also common in the fields of artificial intelligence and multi-agent systems, even for the problem of allocating indivisible items [1, 8, 13].

3. MODEL

We first introduce the model of sequential allocation with random sequence dealt with in this paper. There is a set $\mathcal{O}$ of $2m$ items, which are indivisible and distinct, and a set of two agents, A and B.

The sequential allocation we consider is described as follows. In each *round*, the rule flips a fair coin to determine which agent picks an item first. If 'heads' appears, the sequence in the round (or the *partial sequence*) is set to AB, where agent A first picks an item among the remaining ones, followed by agent B. If 'tails' appears, the sequence is set to BA, where agent B first picks, followed by agent A. Then go to the next round and repeat this process as long as items remain. Note that by definition, there are exactly m rounds and each agent has exactly one turn to pick an item in each round, and thus both agents finally obtain m items. Let $\pi \in \Pi_{\mathcal{B}} = \{\text{AB}, \text{BA}\}^m$ indicate a sequence of the realizations of 'heads' and 'tails' by coin flips in each of m rounds. Here $\Pi_{\mathcal{B}}$ corresponds to the set of possible 'recursively balanced' sequences [2].

Next let us introduce several terms that will be used to define the problems investigated in this paper. Consider agent A a manipulator, assuming that B plays a 'deterministic, simple picking' strategy [5], which is referred to as a *sincere strategy* in this paper. Let $\rhd_B$ indicate a strict ordering of all items $\mathcal{O}$, representing the *preference* of agent

B. Agent B picks, in each of her turns, her most favorite item among those remaining, and agent A knows this fact. Let $u_A : \mathcal{O} \to \mathbb{R}_+$ be a utility function of agent A. We assume, in this entire paper, that agent A's utility is *additive*, meaning that for given utility function u_A of agent A and bundle $X \subseteq \mathcal{O}$, $u_A(X) := \sum_{i \in X} u_A(i)$. We usually describe the items by indices $1, \ldots, 2m$ based on agent A's preference so that A prefers a lower-indexed one, i.e., for any $i, j \in \mathcal{O}$, $u_A(i) > u_A(j)$ if and only if $i < j$. We also say that utility function u_A is *exponentially decaying* if $u_A(i) > u_A(j) \to u_A(i) \geq 2u_A(j)$ for every $i, j \in \mathcal{O}$ Sometimes we refer to such a exponentially decaying utility function as v. Furthermore, for given utility function u_A and probability distribution function F associated with mass function f over $2^{\mathcal{O}}$, expected utility $u_A(F)$ of agent A is defined as $\mathbb{E}_{X \sim F}[u_A(X)] = \sum_{X \in 2^{\mathcal{O}}} u_A(X) \cdot f(X)$. We write $\rhd_B$ and u_A as $\rhd$ and u, respectively, if they are clear from the context.

Now we are ready to introduce some additional terms and notions related to agent A's strategy in our model of sequential allocation. For given bundle X of items and preference $\rhd$, let $L_{X,\rhd}$ be the list of the items in X that are ordered based on $\rhd$. Particularly, for given $\rhd$, let L^{init} be the sorted list of all the items in $\mathcal{O}$, where $L^{init} := L_{\mathcal{O},\rhd}$, which we sometimes denote as $L^{init} = (o_1, o_2, \ldots, o_{2m-1}, o_{2m})$. We omit both subscripts X and $\rhd$ for simplicity and write L whenever they are clear from the context. Furthermore, for notation simplicity, let $u(L_{X,\rhd}) := u(X)$.

A (standard) *plan* δ with length $k \leq m$ specifies, for given list L of remaining items and partial sequence $s \in \{\text{AB}, \text{BA}\}$ realized by a coin flip in the current round, a sequence of k choices for subsequent k rounds. Plan δ is represented as a binary tree, where each node corresponds to an item, the root node indicates the item that agent A is going to pick in the current round, and the left (resp. right) child indicates the item that A will pick when the partial sequence in the next round is AB (resp. BA). We say plan δ with length k is *feasible* for given list L of the remaining items and partial sequence s in the current round if for any possible sequence of k partial sequences that will be realized by coin flips in subsequent k rounds, agent A can pick the item indicated by the corresponding node. In other words, the item remains at the turn of A's choice. A *secure plan* is a special form of plans, which indicates, for each round, the selection of the same item regardless of the partial sequence. Hence, a secure plan can also be represented as a list, where the first (second, and so on) element of the list indicates the item A picks in the first (second, and so on) round.

Although a plan has a sufficient power of representation, it has $O(2^k)$ nodes that cannot be efficiently described. Therefore we introduce a compact representation of the plans called a *strategy*. Strategy σ is a function that returns an item, $\sigma(s, L)$, that agent A should pick for given partial sequence s and list L of the remaining items with even length. For given strategy σ and list L, let $E(L, \sigma)$ represent agent A's expected utility when she uses strategy σ for list L of items. Assume that $E(L, \sigma) = 0$ whenever L is empty list (). Analogously, let $E_{\text{AB}}(L, \sigma)$ (resp. $E_{\text{BA}}(L, \sigma)$) represent A's expected utility under the condition that the partial sequence in the current round is AB (resp. BA), i.e., $E_{\text{AB}}(L, \sigma) := u(i) + E(L', \sigma)$, where i is the item that σ indicates to pick at the current round under sequence AB, i.e., $i = \sigma(\text{AB}, L)$ and L' is the list of remaining items at the beginning of the next round. By the assumption that we focus on a fair coin, $E(L, \sigma) = 0.5 \cdot E_{\text{AB}}(L, \sigma) + 0.5 \cdot E_{\text{BA}}(L, \sigma)$. Let Σ be the set of all strategies of agent A for the problem. Furthermore, let $E^*(L)$ be A's optimal expected utility achieved using one of the optimal strategies for L. Formally, $E^*(L) = \max_{\sigma \in \Sigma} E(L, \sigma)$. As is the case with E, let $E^*_{\text{AB}}(L)$ (resp. $E^*_{\text{BA}}(L)$) represent A's optimal expected utility under the condition that the partial sequence in the current round is AB (resp. BA). By definition, $E^*(L) = 0.5 \cdot E^*_{\text{AB}}(L) + 0.5 \cdot E^*_{\text{BA}}(L)$.

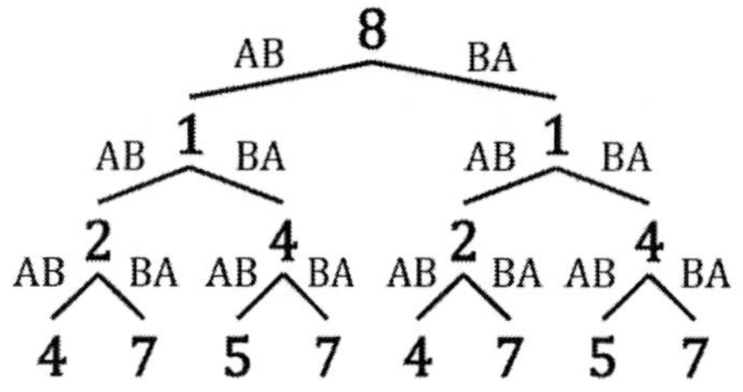

Figure 1: A plan is represented as a binary tree.

The following example explains how these terms work for a given problem instance.

EXAMPLE 1. *Consider two agents, A and B, and eight items $\mathcal{O} = \{1, 2, \cdots, 8\}$ (i.e., $m = 4$). Assume that B has preference $\rhd$ such that $3 \rhd 8 \rhd 6 \rhd 2 \rhd 1 \rhd 5 \rhd 4 \rhd 7$ over them. Furthermore, we consider two utility functions, u and v, that can be held by agent A. We assume that $u(i) = 9 - i$ for any $i \in \mathcal{O}$, i.e., u is the Borda scoring function, and $v(i) = 2^{8-i}$ for any $i \in \mathcal{O}$, i.e., v is exponentially decaying.*

Plan δ with length 4 of agent A is presented as a binary tree in Fig. 1. This plan is feasible for $L^{init} = (3, 8, 6, 2, 1, 5, 4, 7)$ and both $s = AB$ and $s = BA$. However, it is not secure, because for some list L of the remaining items, say $L = (2, 5, 4, 7)$ at the rightmost node with label 1, it chooses a different item based on the realized partial subsequence, explaining why this plan cannot be represented as a list.

As a compact representation, we define a strategy σ based on this plan δ. Strategy σ is a function such that $\sigma(AB, (2, 5, 4, 7)) = 2$, $\sigma(BA, (2, 5, 4, 7)) = 4$, etc. Under above utility function u, expected utility $E(L^{init}, \sigma)$ achieved by strategy σ is 18.25. Similarly, under v, the expected utility achieved by the strategy is 176.

4. POSSIBLE AND CERTAIN BUNDLES

In this section we consider the computation problem of verifying whether agent A can obtain a given bundle. As an analogy from the possible and necessary winner problems in the literature of computational social choice, we define two variants of the problem for our model of sequential allocation with random sequences.

DEFINITION 1 (BEST POSSIBLE (CERTAIN) BUNDLE). *For given $\rhd$ and current partial sequence s, bundle $X \subset \mathcal{O}$ is said to be* possible *(resp.* certain*) under $\rhd$ and s if for some (resp. any) sequence $\pi \in \Pi_B$ of realizations that begins with s, there exists feasible plan δ that achieves X. Furthermore, for given $\rhd$, s, and u, the* best possible *(resp.* best certain*) bundle is the possible (resp. certain) bundle X that maximizes $u(X)$ among all the possible (resp. certain) bundles under $\rhd$ and s.*

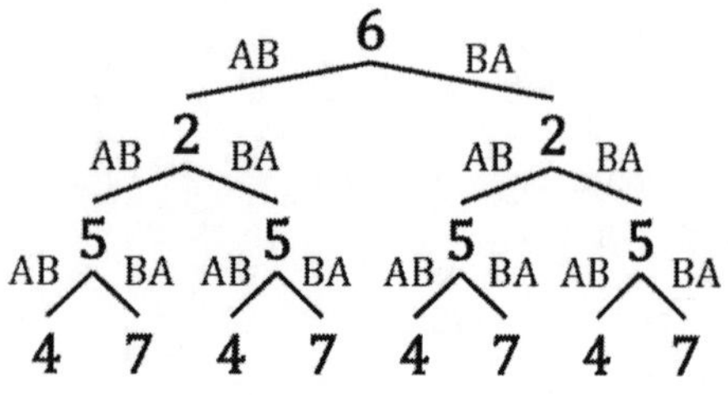

Figure 2: A feasible plan that achieves $(6,2,5,4)$ under the most optimistic sequence.

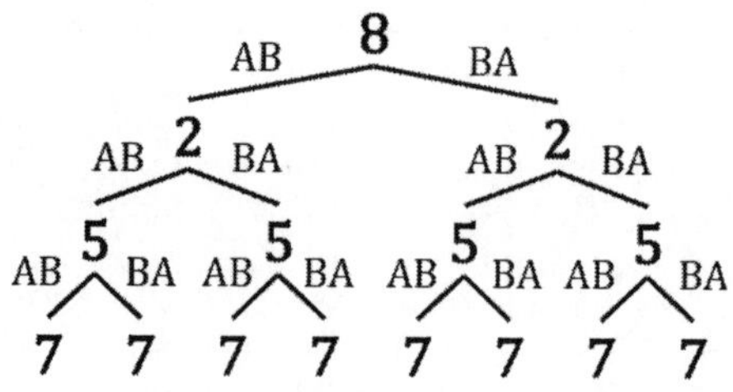

Figure 3: A feasible secure plan that achieves $(8,2,5,7)$ under the most pessimistic sequence.

DEFINITION 2 (BUNDLE-POSSIBILITY (-CERTAINTY)). *For given $\rhd$, s, and $X \subset \mathcal{O}$, is X possible (resp. certain) under $\rhd$ and s ?*

The following theorem shows that both problems can be efficiently solved by agent A, which has a negative implication that agent A will behave insincerely even if her computation power is bounded. These results can be considered as a generalization of the results in Bouveret and Lang [5].

THEOREM 1. *For any given $\rhd$, s, and $X \subset \mathcal{O}$, both* BUNDLE-POSSIBILITY *and* BUNDLE-CERTAINTY *can be solved in polynomial time with respect to m.*

PROOF. By Lemma 4 (resp. Lemma 5) that we will provide in Appendix, it suffices to verify whether X can be achieved under $\rhd$ and specific realization $\overline{\pi} = s\text{ABAB}\dots\text{AB}$ (resp. $\underline{\pi} = s\text{BABA}\dots\text{BA}$). Bouveret and Lang [4] proved that for any given $\rhd$ and any given sequence π, such a verification can be solved in polynomial time with respect to the number of items, $2m$ in our model. Therefore it is also solved in polynomial time with respect to m. □

The next problem of finding the best possible (resp. certain) bundle is also related to the above problem. Actually it can also be solved efficiently.

DEFINITION 3 (FIND-BEST-POSSIBLE(-CERTAIN)). *For given $\rhd$, s, and u, return the best possible (resp. best certain) bundle $X \subset \mathcal{O}$ under $\rhd$, s and u.*

THEOREM 2. *For any given $\rhd$, s, and u, both* FIND-BEST-POSSIBLE *and* FIND-BEST-CERTAIN *can be solved in polynomial time with respect to m.*

PROOF. By Lemma 4 (resp. Lemma 5), it suffices to return bundle X that maximizes $u(X)$ among all the bundles that can be achieved under $\rhd, \overline{\pi}$ (resp. $\underline{\pi}$). Bouveret and Lang [5] proved that for any given $\rhd$, any given s, and any given additive utility function u, such a bundle can be uniquely found in polynomial time with respect to the number of items, which is given as $2m$ in our model. Therefore it can still be found in polynomial time with respect to m. □

EXAMPLE 2. *Consider again the same problem with Example 1. For example, bundle $(6,2,5,4)$ is possible under $s = AB$ since it can be achieved by a feasible plan under $\rhd$ and $\overline{\pi} = ABABAB\dots$, e.g., by the one described in Fig. 2, while it is not certain since it cannot be achieved by any feasible plan under $\rhd$ and $\underline{\pi} = ABBABA\dots$. On the other hand, bundle $(8,2,5,7)$ is possible and certain under $s = AB$ since it can be achieved by a feasible secure plan under $\underline{\pi}$, e.g., by the one described in Fig. 3. By a similar argument (shown in the proof of Theorem 2), we can confirm that under both utility functions, u and v, $(3,2,1,4)$ and $(2,1,4,7)$ are the best possible and best certain bundle under $s = AB$, respectively.*

5. MAXIMIZING EXPECTED UTILITY

Another important question from the manipulator's viewpoint is how much expected utility she can get upon the uncertainty of the realization of subsequent sequences. First we formally define the problem.

DEFINITION 4 (MAX-EXPECTED-UTILITY). *For given $\rhd$, s, and u, return the maximum expected utility $E_s^*(L^{init}) = \max_{\sigma \in \Sigma} E_s(L^{init}, \sigma)$.*

To describe the main theorems in this section, we introduce an additional term called *critical depth*, which is related to agent A's strategy and is useful for the proof. Let L be the list of remaining items and X be the best possible bundle for L and current partial sequence s. Then the critical depth is integer $d \in \mathbb{N}$ such that A first fails to pick the d-th item in $L_{X,\rhd}$ under $\underline{\pi} = s\text{BABA}\cdots\text{BA}$ by picking from the top of list $L_{X,\rhd}$. When A does not fail until the end, i.e., when X is certain under $\rhd$ and s, critical depth d is defined by $|X|+1$, i.e., the number of remaining rounds (including the current one) plus one. Letting d be the critical depth, we observe that $d \geq 2$. Furthermore, letting x_d be the d-th top item in $L_{X,\rhd}$, we observe that x_d is always at an odd-numbered position in L, because (i) under the above strategy of A and the sincere strategy of B, exactly $2d-2$ items in total that appear before x_d in L^{init} will be picked before round d, and (ii) x_d is on the top of the list of remaining items at the beginning of round d, since x_d will be picked by agent B when $s = \text{BA}$ by definition.

We introduce another technical term called an *admissible secure plan*, which is a refinement of secure plans. Let $X_d = \{i \in X \mid i \rhd x_d \vee i = x_d\}$, i.e., the set of items in X that appears before x_d (including x_d). $|X_d| = d$ clearly holds. Then an admissible secure plan is a secure plan of length $d-1$ that picks the $d-1$ items among X_d in the first $d-1$ rounds in the order specified by $\rhd$. Thus, d admissible secure plans usually exist. When d is defined by the number of remaining rounds plus one, then the admissible secure plan just picks the items of X_d in the order specified by $\rhd$. In this case, only one admissible secure plan exists. Note that any admissible secure plan is feasible, because any bundle Z that satisfies $Z \subset X_d, |Z| = d-1$ is certain under s and $\rhd$.

Also, for given utility u, we call the admissible secure plan, which takes $d-1$ items among X_d except for $j' =$

$\arg\min_{j \in X_d} u(i)$, i.e., the least preferred item, a *prudent admissible secure plan.*

5.1 Exponentially Decaying Utilities

We first focus on a specific form of utility functions and show that the problem can be solved quite easily, in the sense that we do not need any exploration technique. More specifically, when the utility of agent A is restricted to exponentially decaying ones, we can solve the maximization problem without any exploration or comparison of the expected utilities during the whole search process.

THEOREM 3. *For any given $\rhd$, s, and A's utility function v that is exponentially decaying,* MAX-EXPECTED-UTILITY *can be solved in polynomial time with respect to m.*

PROOF SKETCH. Let us show the optimality of the following strategy $\widehat{\sigma} \in \Sigma$ of agent A: pick the item specified by the prudent admissible secure plan. Such strategy $\widehat{\sigma}$ is obviously feasible and also runs in polynomial time because of its 'greedy' nature, i.e., it just follow a particular secure plan and does not compare expected utilities that may happen in the future from the current state. Thus, $E_s(L, \widehat{\sigma})$ can be computed in polynomial time.

Now we show an intuition of why $\widehat{\sigma}$ achieves the optimal expected utility. Let v be the exponentially decaying utility function. Here, assume for the sake of contradiction that another strategy σ' achieves an optimal expected utility that is strictly better than that of $\widehat{\sigma}$. Then, during the first $d-1$ rounds in a possible partial sequence, it picks either (a) $d-1$ items among X_d that are different from those that $\widehat{\sigma}$ picks or (b) $d-1$ items some of which does not belong to X_d; otherwise σ' coincides with $\widehat{\sigma}$ by applying the same argument until the end.

For case (a), σ' assuredly obtains item $j' = \arg\min_{j \in X_d} v(i)$, by taking a risk that she cannot obtain another item that she prefers to j' among X_d with probability that exceeds $1/2$. Since v is exponentially decaying, the expected utility of such strategy σ' cannot dominate that of $\widehat{\sigma}$.

Case (b) is more complicated. σ' obtains bundle $Y \not\subseteq X_d$, which satisfies $|Y| = d-1$ and is possible under s and $\rhd$, during the first $d-1$ rounds. In this case, we can construct another strategy that dominates σ' by obtaining $d-1$ items from X_d during the first $d-1$ rounds and then assuredly obtaining those items $(Y \cap X) \setminus X_d$ during the later rounds, violating the assumption of the optimality of σ'. □

Theorem 3 is part of Theorem 4, which we present in the next subsection. However, the following example demonstrates that the optimal strategy for the case of exponentially decaying utilities runs without any exploration and thus is much faster than a strategy that can be applied to general additive utilities.

EXAMPLE 3. *Consider again the same problem with Example 1, and focus on utility function v that is exponentially decaying. When $s = AB$ in the first round, the (sorted) best possible bundle is $(3, 2, 1, 4)$ and the critical depth is 3. Then the strategy mentioned in the above proof suggests picking 2 in the first round (and 1 in the second round).*

At the beginning of the third round, the list of remaining items is $(6, 5, 4, 7)$. In this round, the best possible bundle is $(5, 4)$ and the critical depth is 2, regardless of s. Then the strategy suggests picking 4. In the final round, the strategy suggests picking the best remaining item. Thus, the strategy absolutaly takes $1, 2, 4$, and 5 or 7 with probability 0.5. The expected utility is 213.

When $s = BA$ in the first round, the plan suggests picking exactly the same items in the case where $s = AB$. Thus, the expected utility is 213.

5.2 General Additive Utilities

Unlike the case of exponentially decaying utility functions, the maximization problem seems much more difficult when utility functions are general. An intuition of the difficulty is that, to calculate the maximized expected utility, agent A needs to explore its future by comparing all admissible secure plans, appropriately choose one, and repeat this procedure until the best possible bundle at the moment becomes certain. However, the following theorem shows that the problem can still be solved in polynomial time. One main reason is that, although the whole procedure looks complicated, the number of states at which she needs to explore its future is bounded by a polynomial with respect to the number of items $2m$.

The following lemma implies that we can restrict our attention to plans/strategies that are based on admissible secure plans without losing optimality. Note that this is a generalization of case (b) in the proof of Theorem 3 for general additive utility functions.

LEMMA 1. *For any L of even length and s, there exists admissible secure plan L' such that $E^*_s(L) = u(L') + E^*(L'')$ holds, where L'' is the list of remaining items after executing L'.*

PROOF SKETCH. Let X be the best possible bundle under s and $\rhd$, let d be the critical depth under the current partial sequence s and the ordering $\rhd$, $X_d := \{i \in X \mid i \rhd x_d \vee i = x_d\}$, and let Y be an arbitrary bundle that is possible under s and $\rhd$ and satisfies both $|Y| = d-1$ and $Y \not\subset X_d$. Then we can construct $Z \subset X_d$ that satisfies $|Z| = d-1$ and $u(Z) + E^*(L'_Z) \geq u(Y) + E^*(L'_Y)$, where L'_Z (or L'_Y) is the list of remaining items after A takes items in Z (or Y) and B takes items based on $\rhd$ from L.

Now let Z^* be the optimal bundle among those Z that satisfies the above conditions. Such an optimal Z^* is certain under s and $\rhd$, and thus the optimal strategy must pick Z^* during the first $d-1$ rounds in the order specified by $\rhd$. This coincides with a strategy based on the admissible secure plan represented by $L_{Z^*,\rhd}$, which concludes the proof. □

THEOREM 4. *For any given $\rhd$, s, and u,* MAX-EXPECTED-UTILITY *can be solved in polynomial time with respect to m.*

To prove the statement, we first introduce the following specific form of schemes that we call *strategies based on admissible secure plans* (SASP). This is obviously a generalization of the strategy we mentioned in the proof of Theorem 3.

DEFINITION 5 (SASP). *The* strategy based on admissible secure plans $\sigma^*(s, L)$ *is defined as follows:*

1. *Enumerate all admissible secure plans.*
2. *For each admissible secure plan L', let L'' denote the list of remaining items after executing L'. If $E(L'', \sigma^*)$ was not calculated before, then recursively run*

$\sigma^*(AB, L'')$ and $\sigma^*(BA, L'')$ to obtain $E_{AB}(L'', \sigma^*)$ and $E_{BA}(L'', \sigma^*)$, respectively. Then set $E(L'', \sigma^*)$ to their average.

3. *Choose L' that maximizes $u(L')+E(L'', \sigma^*)$ and return the first item in L' and $u(L') + E(L'', \sigma^*)$.*

In the following we prove Theorem 4 by separately showing that (i) SASP is optimal (in Proposition 1) and that (ii) SASP runs in polynomial time in m (in Proposition 2).

PROPOSITION 1 (OPTIMALITY). *For any L, $E(L, \sigma^*) = E^*(L)$ holds. Hence, σ^* is an optimal strategy.*

PROOF. We prove the statement by mathematical induction with respect to the length of list L. Note again that the length of L is always even since we are focusing on recursively balanced sequences. For the base case, in which $L = ()$ holds, the statement is obviously true by definition. Now let us move to the induction step.

Assuming that $E(L, \sigma^*) = E^*(L)$ holds for any list L s.t. $|L| \leq 2n$ (where $n = 0, 1, \ldots$), we consider arbitrary list L s.t. $|L| = 2n+2$. First we focus on the case where the partial sequence in the current round is AB.

If the critical depth is $n + 2$, i.e., if the best possible bundle X can be achieved even under subsequence ABBABA...BA, then there exist a unique admissible secure plan that achieves the best possible bundle, and thus it holds that $E_{\text{AB}}(L, \sigma^*) = u(L_{X,\rhd}) + E((), \sigma^*) = E^*(L)$.

On the other hand, if the critical depth does not equal $n+2$, then from Lemma 1, there exists admissible secure plan L' such that $E^*_{\text{AB}}(L) = u(L') + E^*(L'')$, where L'' is the list of remaining items after executing L'. Since it is the case that $|L''| \leq 2n$, by the assumption, $E^*(L'') = E(L'', \sigma^*)$ holds.

Therefore, it holds that $E_{\text{AB}}(L, \sigma^*) \geq E^*_{\text{AB}}(L)$. By definition of E^*_{AB}, this implies that $E_{\text{AB}}(L, \sigma^*) = E^*_{\text{AB}}(L)$. By a similar argument, it also holds that $E_{\text{BA}}(L, \sigma^*) = E^*_{\text{BA}}(L)$. Thus, $E(L, \sigma^*) = E^*(L)$ holds. □

We then show that SASP can be calculated in polynomial time. First, we introduce an additional concept of *reachability* for bundles. Let $\mathcal{L}$ be a series of sorted lists defined below, each of which can be obtained by eliminating all but one element in the first $2t-1$ elements, for each $t \in 1, \ldots, m$:

$$\begin{aligned}
\mathcal{L} = \{&(o_1, o_2, \ldots, o_{2m}), \\
&(o_1, o_4, \ldots, o_{2m}), (o_2, o_4, \ldots, o_{2m}), (o_3, o_4, \ldots, o_{2m}), \\
&(o_1, o_6, \ldots, o_{2m}), (o_2, o_6, \ldots, o_{2m}), \ldots, (o_5, o_6, \ldots, o_{2m}), \\
&\vdots \\
&(o_1, o_{2t}, \ldots, o_{2m}), \ldots, (o_{2t-1}, o_{2t}, \ldots, o_{2m}), \\
&\vdots \\
&(o_1, o_{2m}), (o_2, o_{2m}), \ldots, (o_{2m-1}, o_{2m})\}.
\end{aligned}$$

Note that $|\mathcal{L}| = 1 + 3 + \cdots + (2m-1) = m^2$. List L is said to be *reachable* from L^{init} (by admissible secure plans) if there exists a series of partial sequences and an admissible secure plan such that after the execution of the admissible secure plan for the series of partial sequences, the list of remaining items becomes L.

The following lemma helps us to show the polynomial time computability, which implies that the number of lists of remaining items possible after any sequence of applications of an admissible secure plan is at most $|\mathcal{L}| = m^2$.

LEMMA 2. *If L is reachable from L^{init}, $L \in \mathcal{L} \cup \{()\}$ holds.*

PROOF. We prove the statement by mathematical induction with respect to k the number of times that an admissible secure plan is applied. For the base case in which $k = 0$, such a reachable list that is obtained without applying an admissible secure plan must be L^{init}, which is in set $\mathcal{L}$ by its definition.

Now we show the induction step. Assuming that any list that is reachable by applying an admissible secure plan k' times is in set $\mathcal{L}$, consider arbitrary list L that is reachable by applying an admissible secure plan $k' + 1$ times. At the moment of the $k' + 1$-st application of an admissible secure plan, remaining list $\widehat{L}$ is in $\mathcal{L}$, because of the fact that it is reachable by applying an admissible secure plan k' times and the assumption.

Here let d and L' be the critical depth and the sorted list of the items in the best possible bundle at the moment, respectively. If $d = |L'| + 1$, i.e., if all the remaining items in the best possible bundles can be obtained, then L is $()$. On the other hand, if it is not the case, then such list L is obtained by eliminating the top $2d-2$ items among the top $2d-1$ items in $\widehat{L}$ by the definition of the admissible secure plan and the sincere strategy of B, which results in a list belonging to $\mathcal{L}$. □

PROPOSITION 2 (POLY-TIME). *For any L that is reachable from L^{init} and any $s \in \{AB, BA\}$, $\sigma^*(s, L)$ is calculated in polynomial time with respect to m.*

PROOF. Strategy σ^* is applied only for each list that is reachable from L^{init}, which takes at most m^2 applications by Lemma 2. In each application of σ^*, the number of admissible secure plans is $O(m)$. Any admissible secure plan just needs operations (e.g., calculating the best possible bundle) that only take polynomial runtime. As a result, strategy σ^* can be calculated in polynomial time with respect to m. □

EXAMPLE 4. *Consider again the same problem with Example 1 with Borda scoring function u. When $s = AB$ in the first round, the (sorted) best possible bundle is $(3, 2, 1, 4)$, and the critical depth is 3. Then strategy σ^* considers obtaining two out of the three top items in $(3, 2, 1, 4)$ without taking any risk.*

Obtain $(3, 1)$**:** *After taking them, the remaining items at the beginning of the third round will be $(2, 5, 4, 7)$. When $s = AB$ in the third round, the best possible bundle is $(2, 4)$, and the critical depth is 2. Then the strategy next considers obtaining one out of the two items $(2, 4)$ without taking any risk.*

  Obtain (2)**:** *After taking item 2, the remaining items at the beginning of the fourth round will be $(4, 7)$. When $s = AB$ in the fourth round, the best possible bundle is (4), which is certain. When $s = BA$, the best possible bundle is (7), which is also certain. As a result, strategy σ^* returns an expected utility of $(u(4) + u(7))/2$.*

  Obtain (4)**:** *After taking item 4, the remaining items at the beginning of the fourth round will be $(5, 7)$. By a similar argument, it returns an expected utility of $(u(5) + u(7))/2$.*

Comparing $u(2) + (u(4) + u(7))/2$ and $u(4) + (u(5) + u(7))/2$, it suggests picking 2 when $s = AB$. By a *similar argument, it suggests picking* 4 *when* $s = BA$. *As a result, it returns an expected utility of*

$$u(3) + u(1) + \frac{(u(2) + \frac{u(4)+u(7)}{2}) + (u(4) + \frac{u(5)+u(7)}{2})}{2}.$$

Obtain $(3, 2)$: *By a similar argument, it returns*

$$u(3) + u(2) + \frac{(u(1) + \frac{u(4)+u(7)}{2}) + (u(4) + \frac{u(5)+u(7)}{2})}{2}.$$

Obtain $(2, 1)$: *it returns*

$$u(2) + u(1) + u(4) + \frac{u(5) + u(7)}{2}.$$

Comparing the expected utilities based on u, *it suggests picking* 3 *in the first round when* $s = AB$. *By a similar argument, it suggests picking* 2 *in the first round when* $s = BA$.

6. APPLYING TO RANDOM TIE-BREAKING

As an application of the results presented in the previous sections, we now show the original model of sequential allocation with random tie-breaking that was already mentioned in the introduction. Since the discussion in the previous sections is focused on the case of two agents, here we continune to focus on the case of two agents: A and B.

The process of sequential allocation with random tie-breaking is described as follows. In each round, each agent bids on an item that still exists. If there is no conflict, each gets the item on which she bids. If there is a conflict, the 'winner' is decided by flipping a fair coin. The other agent picks another item that is still present. The process is repeated until all the items are picked.

In this model we also assume that agent B just uses the sincere picking strategy based on her preference $\rhd$. Although the model with random tie-breaking is slightly different from random sequences, some strategies in the random sequence model remain valid for this random tie-breaking. More precisely, there exists a bijection between the set of all possible strategies in the model with random tie-breaking and a certain set of strategies in the random sequence model, such that corresponding strategies give the same expected utility for the random sequence model and the random tie-breaking model. Furthermore, SASP is actually in the set. Therefore, the following statement holds.

THEOREM 5. *Given any* $\rhd$ *and* u, *the maximum expected utility in sequential allocation with random tie-breaking can be calculated in polynomial time with respect to* m.

Due to space limitations, we omit the formal proof. Instead, we demonstrate how SASP works for this model.

EXAMPLE 5. *Consider again the same problem with Example 1 with Borda scoring function* u. *Agent* A *first computes SASP* σ^* *to determine the item on which she first bids, by assuming the random sequence model and that* $s = AB$ *in the first round. As we already observed in Example 4,* σ^* *returns item* 3.

Since B *also bids on* 3 *first based on the sincere picking strategy, there will be a coin flip. If* A *wins, she gets* 3. *Then in the next round she bids on* 1 *as* σ^* *suggests. After this,* A *computes* σ^* *again for the remaining items, and so on.*

On the other hand, if A *loses in the first round, she then computes* σ^* *again by assuming that the first partial sequence in the random sequence model is* BA, *which suggests picking* 2 *in the first round,* 1 *in the second round, and* 4 *in the third round, which ensures that no conflict occurs within the three rounds. Then* A *computes* σ^* *again for the remaining items.*

7. DISCUSSIONS

One possible question about our sequential allocation model with random sequences is how it differs from the well-known probabilistic serial rule [3]. Here we show an example that results in different outcomes under these two rules with sincere strategies chosen by both agents. Consider a situation with two agents, A and B, where B's preference $\rhd$ is such that $1 \rhd 4 \rhd 2 \rhd 3$, and both A and B choose the sincere picking strategy (not alike our analysis where A seeks the optimal strategy). Under the probabilistic serial rule, both first start to 'eat' item 1, and then after finishing 1, agent A eats 2 while B eats 4. Finally, both come to item 3 at identical timing, which results in a utility of $0.5 \cdot u(1) + u(2) + 0.5 \cdot u(3)$. On the other hand, under sequential allocation with random sequence, agent A's utility is $0.5 \cdot u(1) + 0.75 \cdot u(2) + 0.75 \cdot u(3)$. Note again that this utility is under A's sincere strategy. Verifying whether they still differ in equilibrium is an open question.

Another possible question is how the coincidence result presented in Section 6 could be applied to cases with more than two agents. We observed that sequential allocations with random sequences and random tie-breaking do not coincide when there are more than two agents. To demonstrate the intuition, consider the following three agents: agent A who is willing to pick bundle $(1, 2, 3)$ in this order, agent B who picks items sincerely with her preference $\rhd_B : (1, 3, 2)$, and agent C who also picks items sincerely with her preference $\rhd_C : (3, 2, 1)$. Under our model with random sequences, it is possible that partial sequence ABC is realized, which results in an allocation such that A, B, and C obtain 1, 3, and 2, respectively. On the other hand, in sequential allocation with random tie-breaking, agent C solely bids on 3 in the first round, while both A and B bid on 1. Therefore, regardless of the result of the coin flip for tie-breaking between A and B, C obtains 3, which cannot occur in the random sequence model.

From the perspective of fair allocation, perhaps constantly flipping a fair coin is not natural. This actually makes sense; when the 'heads' side appears in the first round, it seems fairer to use a biased coin so that it is likely to be 'tails' in the next round. However, to the best of our knowledge, no such discussion exists about the optimal (fairest) probability distribution of coin flips. In this sense, our contribution is a first step toward a new research direction on optimizing random sequences with respect to some fairness criteria, such as envy-freeness and/or proportionality.

8. CONCLUSIONS

In this paper we consider a new model of sequential allocation with random sequences. We focus on the case of two agents and additive utilities of a manipulator and show that BUNDLE-POSSIBILITY, BUNDLE-CERTAINTY, FIND-BEST-POSSIBLE, FIND-BEST-CERTAIN, and MAX-EXPECTED-UTILITY can be solved in polynomial time with respect to the number m of rounds. When the manipulator's utility is further restricted to be exponentially decaying, MAX-EXPECTED-UTILITY can be solved much faster than the general case. As an application of MAX-EXPECTED-UTILITY, we show that for a different model of sequential allocation with random tie-breaking, MAX-EXPECTED-UTILITY can also be solved in polynomial time. Besides the questions raised in Section 7, several related future research issues remain. Considering more than two agents in our model is one obvious future direction. Also discussing how such a selfish manipulation affects social welfare is another, as Bouveret and Lang [5] do for a model with deterministic sequences.

Acknowledgments

This work was partially supported by JSPS KAKENHI Grants Number 24220003, 26540118, and 26730005.

We thank Haris Aziz, Jérôme Lang, and anonymous referee for their helpful comments and suggestions. All errors are our own.

APPENDIX

Here we give supplementary materials used for the theorems in Section 4. We first introduce some additional notation for the proof.

First, for standard plan δ of length k defined for partial sequence s, list L, and sequence $\pi \in s\{AB, BA\}^{k-1}$, let $\delta(\pi)$ denote the list of items taken by δ when the realized sequence is π, i.e., $\delta(\pi)$ is one particular path in the tree represented by δ. We call $\delta(\pi)$ an induced plan of δ in π. Let X denote the set of items in $\delta(\pi)$. We say $\delta(\pi)$ is *regular*, if $\delta(\pi) = L_{X,\rhd}$, i.e., the induced plan takes the items in X in the order of $\rhd$.

Let $sb(\rhd, i) = |\{j \in \mathcal{O} \mid j \rhd i\}|$ be the number of items in $\mathcal{O}$ that are strictly better than item i under given ordering $\rhd$. Also, let $blk(\rhd, X, i) = sb(\rhd, i) - |\{j \in X \mid j \rhd i\}|$ be the number of "blanks" before item i, which means that when agent A is going to obtain X, agent B does not pick i in any round before $blk(\rhd, X, i)$. When it is clear from the context, we write $blk(i)$ instead of $blk(\rhd, X, i)$. Also, given π and $r \in \{1, \ldots, m\}$, let π_r indicate the partial sequence in π for round r. Then define $\rho(\pi_r)$ such that $\rho(\pi_r) = 1$ if π_r = AB and $\rho(\pi_r) = 0$ otherwise.

The following corollary is derived from Proposition 8 in Bouveret and Lang [5].

COROLLARY 1. *Given $\rhd$ and sequence π, X can be achieved under $\rhd$ and π if and only if there exists feasible plan δ such that its induced plan $\delta(\pi)$ is regular and achieves X under $\rhd$.*

PROPOSITION 3. *For given $\rhd$, π, and $X \subseteq \mathcal{O}$, a regular induced plan $\delta(\pi)$ achieves X under $\rhd$ if and only if $blk(x_r) \geq a(\pi, r)$ holds for any $r \in \{1, \ldots, |X|\}$, where $a(\pi, r) = r + \rho(\pi_r) - 1$, representing the number of actions (equally the number of items) B has already taken prior to A's r-th action.*

PROOF. The "if" part is obvious, because from the meaning of blk, x_r is still available for A during the first $blk(x_r)$ rounds from the current state. Therefore it suffices to show the "only if" part. Assuming that the regular induced plan $\delta(\pi)$ achieves X, we show the conclusion by mathematical induction for r.

As the base case, consider $r = 1$; we show that $blk(x_1) \geq a(\pi, 1) = \rho(\pi_1)$. Note again that there are $blk(x_1)$ items before x_1. If $blk(x_1) < a(\pi, 1)$ holds, then B obtains x_1 at her $blk(x_1) + 1$-st action, which violates the assumption that A can obtain X containing x_1 by $\delta(\pi)$.

As the induction step, assuming that the statement holds for $r = t$, we consider the case of $r = t + 1$. If $blk(x_{t+1}) < a(\pi, t + 1)$ holds, then there are $blk(x_{t+1})$ items, as well as $x_1, \ldots, x_t$, before x_{t+1}. From the assumption that $a(\pi, t) \leq blk(x_t)$, A obtains $x_1, \ldots, x_t$ before B's $blk(x_{t+1}) + 1$-st action. Thus, B obtains x_{t+1} by her $blk(x_{t+1}) + 1$-st action, which violates the assumption that $\delta(\pi)$ achieves X. □

Using this result, we can show the following lemma, which is an essential component in the proofs of Lemmas 4 and 5.

LEMMA 3. *Consider any ordering $\rhd$ and any sequence π. Assume that there exists feasible plan δ that achieves bundle X under π and $\rhd$. Then, for any $r' \in \{1, \ldots, m\}$, there also exists feasible plan δ' that achieves X under $\rhd$ and π s.t. for all $r \in \{1, \ldots, m\}$:*

$$\pi'_r = \begin{cases} AB & \text{if } r = r' \\ \pi_r & \text{otherwise.} \end{cases} \tag{1}$$

PROOF. Obviously we can focus on r' such that $r' \leq |X|$. From Corollary 1 and the assumption that there exists $\delta(\pi)$ that achieves X under $\rhd$, a regular induced plan that corresponds to $L_{X,\rhd}$ also achieves X under $\rhd$ and π. From Proposition 3, it holds that for any $r' \in \{1, \ldots, |X|\}$,

$$blk(x_r) \geq r + \rho(\pi_r) - 1.$$

Also, by the definitions of ρ and π', it holds that for any $r \in \{1, \ldots, |X|\}$,

$$r + \rho(\pi_r) - 1 \geq r + \rho(\pi'_r) - 1.$$

By summing them up, we have

$$blk(x_r) \geq r + \rho(\pi'_r) - 1$$

for all $r \in \{1, \ldots, |X|\}$, which coincides with the condition described in Proposition 3. □

LEMMA 4. *Given $\rhd$ and $X \subset \mathcal{O}$, X is possible under $\rhd$ if and only if X can be achieved under $\rhd$ and $\bar{\pi} = sAB \ldots AB$.*

PROOF. The "if" part is obvious. Let us focus on showing the "only if" part. Assume that feasible plan δ achieves X under $\rhd$ for at least one specific sequence π. X can be achieved under $\rhd$ and π. Here, by repeatedly applying a modification described in Eq. 1 to π, we can reach $\bar{\pi}$. Thus, from Corollary 1 and Lemma 3, X can be achieved under $\rhd$ and $\bar{\pi}$. □

LEMMA 5. *Given $\rhd$ and $X \subset \mathcal{O}$, X is certain under $\rhd$ if and only if X can be achieved under $\rhd$ and $\underline{\pi} = sBA \ldots BA$.*

PROOF. The "only if" part is obvious by the definition of certainty of bundle X, Now we turn to show the "if" part. Consider arbitrary bundle X that can be achieved under $\rhd$ and $\underline{\pi}$. From Corollary 1, a regular induced plan $\delta(\underline{\pi})$ achieves X under $\rhd$. From a similar argument with the proof of Lemma 4, X can be achieved by a regular induced plan $\delta'(\pi)$ under $\rhd$, where π is any possible sequence, which guarantees that X is certain under $\rhd$. □

REFERENCES

[1] H. Aziz, S. Gaspers, S. Mackenzie, N. Mattei, N. Narodytska, and T. Walsh. Manipulating the probabilistic serial rule. In *Proceedings of the Fourteenth International Conference on Autonomous Agents and Multiagent Systems (AAMAS-15)*, pages 1451–1459, 2015.

[2] H. Aziz, T. Walsh, and L. Xia. Possible and necessary allocations via sequential mechanisms. In *Proceedings of the Twenty-Fourth International Joint Conference on Artificial Intelligence (IJCAI-15)*, pages 468–474, 2015.

[3] A. Bogomolnaia and H. Moulin. A new solution to the random assignment problem. *Journal of Economic Theory*, 100(2):295–328, 2001.

[4] S. Bouveret and J. Lang. A general elicitation-free protocol for allocating indivisible goods. In *Proceedings of the Twenty-Second International Joint Conference on Artificial Intelligence (IJCAI-11)*, pages 73–78, 2011.

[5] S. Bouveret and J. Lang. Manipulating picking sequences. In *Proceedings of the Twenty-First European Conference on Artificial Intelligence (ECAI-14)*, pages 141–146, 2014.

[6] S. J. Brams, M. Kilgour, and C. Klamler. Two-person fair division of indivisible items: An efficient, envy-free algorithm. *Notices of the AMS*, 61(2):130–141, 2014.

[7] E. B. Budish and E. Cantillon. The multi-unit assignment problem: Theory and evidence from course allocation at harvard. *American Economic Review*, 102(5):2237–71, 2012.

[8] E. Fujita, J. Lesca, A. Sonoda, T. Todo, and M. Yokoo. A complexity approach for core-selecting exchange with multiple indivisible goods under lexicographic preferences. In *Proceedings of the Twenty-Ninth AAAI Conference on Artificial Intelligence (AAAI-15)*, pages 907–913, 2015.

[9] W. Huang, J. Lou, and Z. Wen. A parallel elicitation-free protocol for allocating indivisible goods. In *Seventh Multidisciplinary Workshop on Advances in Preference Handling (MPREF-13)*, 2013.

[10] T. Kalinowski, N. Narodytska, and T. Walsh. A social welfare optimal sequential allocation procedure. In *Proceedings of the Twenty-Third international joint conference on Artificial Intelligence (IJCAI-13)*, pages 227–233, 2013.

[11] T. Kalinowski, N. Narodytska, T. Walsh, and L. Xia. Strategic behavior when allocating indivisible goods sequentially. In *Proceedings of the Twenty-Seventh AAAI Conference on Artificial Intelligence (AAAI-13)*, pages 452–458, 2013.

[12] D. A. Kohler and R. Chandrasekaran. A class of sequential games. *Operations Research*, 19(2):270–277, 1971.

[13] M. S. Pini, F. Rossi, K. B. Venable, and T. Walsh. Manipulation complexity and gender neutrality in stable marriage procedures. *Autonomous Agents and Multi-Agent Systems*, 22(1):183–199, 2011.

[14] R. Vetschera and D. M. Kilgour. Fair division of indivisible items between two players: design parameters for contested pile methods. *Theory and Decision*, 76(4):547–572, 2014.

Signaling in Bayesian Stackelberg Games

Haifeng Xu
U. of Southern California
haifengx@usc.edu

Rupert Freeman
Duke University
rupert@cs.duke.edu

Vincent Conitzer
Duke University
conitzer@cs.duke.edu

Shaddin Dughmi
U. of Southern California
shaddin@usc.edu

Milind Tambe
U. of Southern California
tambe@usc.edu

ABSTRACT

Algorithms for solving Stackelberg games are used in an ever-growing variety of real-world domains. Previous work has extended this framework to allow the leader to commit not only to a distribution over actions, but also to a scheme for stochastically signaling information about these actions to the follower. This can result in higher utility for the leader. In this paper, we extend this methodology to Bayesian games, in which either the leader or the follower has payoff-relevant private information or both. This leads to novel variants of the model, for example by imposing an incentive compatibility constraint for each type to listen to the signal intended for it. We show that, in contrast to previous hardness results for the case without signaling [5, 16], we can solve unrestricted games in time polynomial in their natural representation. For security games, we obtain hardness results as well as efficient algorithms, depending on the settings. We show the benefits of our approach in experimental evaluations of our algorithms.

Keywords

Bayesian Stackelberg Games, Algorithms, Signaling, Security Games

1. INTRODUCTION

In the algorithmic game theory community, and especially the multiagent systems part of that community, there has been rapidly increasing interest in Stackelberg models where the leader can commit to a mixed strategy. This interest is driven in part by a number of high-impact deployed security applications [25]. One of the advantages of this framework—as opposed to, say, computing a Nash equilibrium of the simultaneous-move game—is that it sidesteps issues of equilibrium selection. Another is that in two-player normal-form games, an optimal mixed strategy to commit to can be found in polynomial time [5]. There are limits to this computational advantage, however; once we extend to three-player games or Bayesian games, the computational problem becomes hard again [5]. (In a Bayesian game, some of the players have private information that is relevant to the payoffs; their private information is encoded by their *type*.)

As has previously been observed [4, 28, 23], the leader may be able to do more than commit to a mixed strategy. The leader may additionally be able to commit to send signals to the follower(s) that are correlated with the action she has chosen. This ability can of course never hurt the leader: she always has the choice of sending an uninformative signal. In a two-player normal-form game, it turns out that no benefit can be had from sending an informative signal. This is because the expected leader utility conditioned on each signal, which corresponds to a posterior belief of the leader's action, is weakly dominated by the expected leader utility of committing to the optimal mixed strategy [4]. But this is no longer true in games with three or more players. Moreover, intriguingly, the enriched problem with signaling can still be solved in polynomial time in these games [4]. The idea of adding signals has also already been explored in security games [28], however these games were not Bayesian (but with richer game structure).

In this paper, we extend this line of work to Bayesian Stackelberg Games (**BSG**s). We suppose that, when the follower has multiple possible types, the leader is able to send a separate signal to each of these types, without learning what the type is. For example, consider a security game on a rail network in which we aim to catch ticketless travelers (or, better yet, give them incentives to buy a ticket). Here, the attacker's type could encode at which location he starts his journey. Then, by making a separate announcement at each station, we send a separate signal to each type. As another example, we may send different signals over different (say) radio frequencies. In this case, each follower type receives a separate signal depending on the frequency to which he is listening. In this latter example (unlike the former), we also require an *incentive compatibility (IC)* constraint: no type should find it beneficial to switch over to a different frequency, since we have no way of forcing a type to listen to a particular frequency.

Besides considering the case of multiple follower types, we also consider the case of multiple leader types. Here, the signal sent by the leader can be correlated with her type as well as her action. Among other examples, this allows us to capture models where the leader is a seller of some item, and the type of the leader corresponds to knowledge about, for example, the quality of the item. She can then send an informative (but perhaps not *completely* informative) signal about this quality to the buyer. Such models are sometimes studied in the auction design literature [8, 18, 12], but here our interest is in generally applicable algorithms.

Our Contributions: We consider signaling in different models of Bayesian Stackelberg games, and essentially pin down the computational complexity in each. For the case with multiple follower types (but a single leader type), we show that the optimal combinations of mixed strategies and signaling schemes can be computed in polynomial time using linear programming.[1] This is the case

[1]One may wonder whether this just follows from the fact that we can model Bayesian games by representing each type as a single player, thereby reducing it to a multiplayer game. But this does not work, because the corresponding normal form of the game would

Appears in: *Proceedings of the 15th International Conference on Autonomous Agents and Multiagent Systems (AAMAS 2016), J. Thangarajah, K. Tuyls, C. Jonker, S. Marsella (eds.), May 9–13, 2016, Singapore.*

	$F_\emptyset$	F_1	F_2
$L_\emptyset$	0	2	$-\infty$
L_1	0	-1	$-\infty$
L_2	0	2	$-\infty$

type $\theta_1, p = 0.55$

	$F_\emptyset$	F_1	F_2
$L_\emptyset$	0	$-\infty$	1
L_1	0	$-\infty$	1
L_2	0	$-\infty$	-1

type $\theta_2, p = 0.45$

Figure 1: Payoff Matrices for Followers of Different Types

whether an incentive compatibility constraint applies or not. However, for security games, we show that the problem is NP-hard, though we do identify a special case that can be solved efficiently. We also provide hardness evidence that this special case is almost the best one can hope in terms of polynomial computability.

For the case with multiple leader types (but a single follower type), we show that the optimal combinations of mixed strategies and signaling schemes can also be computed in polynomial time. Moreover, the polynomial-time solvability extends to security games in this setting. We note that our results (both hardness and polynomial-time solvability) can be easily generalized to the case with *both* multiple leader and follower types, thus we will not discuss it explicitly in the paper. We conclude with an experimental evaluation of our approach.

2. AN EXAMPLE OF STACKELBERG COMPETITION

The Stackelberg model was originally introduced to capture market competition between a *leader* (e.g., a leading firm in some area) and a *follower* (e.g., an emerging start-up). The leader has an advantage of committing to a strategy (or equivalently, moving first) before the follower makes decisions. Here we consider a Bayesian case of Stackelberg competition where the leader does not have full information about the follower.

For example, consider a market with two firms, a leader and a follower. The leader specializes in two products, product 1 and product 2. The follower is a new start-up which focuses on only *one* product. It is publicly known that the follower will focus on product 1 with probability 0.55 (call him a follower of type θ_1 in this case), and product 2 with probability 0.45 (call him a follower of type θ_2). But the realization is only known to the follower. The leader has a research team, and must decide which product to devote this (indivisible) team to, or to send them on vacation. On the other hand, the follower has two options: either entering the market and developing the product he focuses on, or leaving the market.

Naturally, the follower wants to avoid competition with the leader's research team. In particular, depending on the type of the follower, the leader's decision may drive the follower out of the market or leave the follower with a chance to gain substantial market share. This can be modeled as a Bayesian Stackelberg Game (BSG) where the leader has one type and the follower has two possible types. To be concrete, we specify the payoff matrices for different types of follower in Figure 1, where the leader's action L_i simply denotes the leader's decision to devote the team to product i for $i \in \{1, 2, \emptyset\}$; $\emptyset$ means a team vacation. Similarly, the follower's action F_i means the follower focuses on products $i \in \{1, 2, \emptyset\}$ where $\emptyset$ means leaving the market. Notice that the payoff matrices force the follower to only produce the product that is consistent with his type, otherwise he gets utility $-\infty$. The utility for the leader is relatively simple: the leader gets utility 1 only if the follower (of any type) takes action $F_\emptyset$, i.e., leaving the market, and gets utility 0 otherwise. In other words, the leader wants to drive the follower out of the market.

have size exponential in the number of types.

Possessing a first-mover advantage, the leader can commit to a *randomized* strategy to assign her research team so that it maximizes her utility in expectation over the randomness of her mixed strategy and the follower types. Unfortunately, finding the optimal mixed strategy to commit to turns out to be NP-hard for BSGs in general [5]. Nevertheless, by exploiting the special structure in this example, it is easy to show that any mixed strategy that puts at least $2/3$ probability on L_1 is optimal for the leader to commit to. This is because to drive a follower of type θ_1 out of the market, the leader has to take L_1 with probability at least $2/3$. Likewise, to drive a follower of type θ_2 out of the market, the leader has to take L_2 with probability at least $1/2$. Since $2/3 + 1/2 > 1$, the leader cannot achieve both, so the optimal choice is to drive the follower of type θ_1 (occurring with a higher probability) out of the market so that the leader gets utility 0.55 in expectation.

Notice that the leader commits to the strategy without knowing the realization of the follower's type. This is reasonable because the follower, as a start-up, can keep information confidential from the leader firm at the initial stage of the competition. However, as time goes on, the leader will gradually learn the type of the follower. Nevertheless, the leader firm cannot change her chosen action at that point because, for example, there is insufficient time to switch to another product. Can the leader still do something strategic at this point? In particular, we study whether the leader can benefit by partially revealing her action to the follower after observing the follower's type. To be concrete, consider the following leader policy. Before observing the follower's type, the leader commits to choose action L_1 and L_2 uniformly at random, each with probability $1/2$. Meanwhile, the leader also commits to the following *signaling scheme*. If the follower has type θ_1, the leader will send a signal $\sigma_\emptyset$ to the follower when the leader takes action L_1, and will send either $\sigma_\emptyset$ or σ_1 uniformly at random when the leader takes action L_2. Mathematically, the signaling scheme for the follower of type θ_1 is captured by the following probabilities.

$$\mathbf{Pr}(\sigma_\emptyset | L_1, \theta_1) = 1 \quad \mathbf{Pr}(\sigma_1 | L_1, \theta_1) = 0;$$
$$\mathbf{Pr}(\sigma_\emptyset | L_2, \theta_1) = \tfrac{1}{2} \quad \mathbf{Pr}(\sigma_1 | L_2, \theta_1) = \tfrac{1}{2}.$$

On the other hand, if the follower has type θ_2, the leader will always send $\sigma_\emptyset$ regardless of what action she has taken.

When a follower of type θ_1 receives signal $\sigma_\emptyset$ (occurring with probability $3/4$), he infers the posterior belief of the leader's strategy as $\mathbf{Pr}(L_1|\sigma_\emptyset, \theta_1) = 2/3$ and $\mathbf{Pr}(L_2|\sigma_\emptyset, \theta_1) = 1/3$, thus deriving an expected utility of 0 from taking action F_1. Assuming the follower breaks ties in favor of the leader,[2] he will then choose action $F_\emptyset$, leaving the market. On the other hand, if the follower receives σ_1 (occurring with probability $1/4$), he knows that the leader has taken action L_2 for sure; thus the follower will take action F_1, achieving utility 2. In other words, the signals $\sigma_\emptyset$ and σ_1 can be viewed as recommendations to the follower to leave the market ($\sigma_\emptyset$) or develop the product (σ_1), though we emphasize that a signal has no meaning beyond the posterior distribution on leader's actions that it induces. As a result, the leader drives the follower out of the market $3/4$ of the time. On the other hand, if the follower has type θ_2, since the leader reveals no information, the follower derives expected utility 0 from taking F_2, and thus will choose F_0 in favor of the leader. In expectation, the leader gets utility $\frac{3}{4} \times \frac{1}{2} + \frac{1}{2} = 0.875 (> 0.55)$. Thus, the leader achieves better utility by signaling.

The design of the signaling scheme above depends crucially on the fact that the leader can distinguish different follower types be-

[2]This is without loss of generality because the leader can always slightly tune the probability mass to make the follower slightly prefer $F_\emptyset$.

fore sending the signals and will signal differently to different follower types. This fits the setting where the leader can observe the follower's type after the leader takes her action and then signals accordingly. However, in many cases, the leader is *not* able to observe the follower's type. Interestingly, it turns out that the leader can in some cases design a signaling scheme which incentivizes the follower to *truthfully* report his type to the leader and still benefit from signaling. Note that the signaling scheme above does not satisfy the follower's incentive compatibility constraints – if the follower is asked to report his type, a follower of type θ_2 would be better off to report his type as θ_1. This follows from some simple calculation, but an intuitive reason is that a follower of type θ_2 will not get any information if he truthfully reports θ_2, but will receive a more informative signal, thus benefit himself, by reporting θ_1.

Now let us consider another leader policy. The leader commits to the mixed strategy $(L_\emptyset, L_1, L_2) = (1/11, 6/11, 4/11)$. Interestingly, this involves sometimes sending the research team on vacation! Meanwhile, the leader also commits to the following more sophisticated signaling scheme. If the follower reports type θ_1, the leader will send signal $\sigma_\emptyset$ whenever L_1 is taken as well as $\frac{3}{4}$ of the time that L_2 is taken; otherwise the leader sends signal σ_1. If the follower reports type θ_2, the leader sends signal $\sigma_\emptyset$ whenever L_2 is taken as well as $\frac{2}{3}$ of the time that L_1 is taken; otherwise the leader sends signal σ_2. It turns out that this policy is incentive compatible – truthfully reporting the type is in the follower's best interests – and achieves the maximum expected leader utility $\frac{17}{22} \approx 0.773 \in (0.55, 0.875)$ among all such policies.

Justification of Commitment: The assumption of commitment to strategies is well motivated, and has been justified, in many applications, e.g., market competition [9] and security [25]. This is usually due to the leader's first-mover advantage. The assumption of commitment to signaling schemes is justified on the grounds of games that are played repeatedly (e.g., a leading firm plays repeatedly with start-ups that can show up and fade away), so the follower can learn the signaling scheme - how the signals correlate with leader actions taken. On the other hand, to balance the short term utility and long-term credibility, the leader has incentives to follow the signaling scheme in order to build a reputation about her strategy of disclosing information. We refer the reader to [24] for more thorough discussions of this phenomenon.

Remark: This example shows that the additional ability of committing to a signaling scheme can profoundly affect both players' strategies. We study how such additional commitment changes the game as well as the computation of the leader's optimal policy. The rest of this paper is organized as follows. In Section 3 we generalize the above example to BSGs, and also examine its application to Bayesian Stackelberg *Security Games*, a model of growing interest in modeling various security challenges. Note that the above example only concerned the case where the *follower* has multiple types. In Section 4, we consider a variant of the model where the *leader* has multiple types (but the follower has only one type), and seek to compute the optimal leader policy. We show simulation results in Section 5 and conclude in Section 6.

3. SINGLE LEADER TYPE, MULTIPLE FOLLOWER TYPES

3.1 The Model

In this section, we generalize the example in Section 2 and consider how the leader's additional ability of committing to a signaling scheme changes the game and the computation. We start with a Bayesian Stackelberg Game (**BSG**) with one *leader* type and multiple *follower* types. Let Θ denote the set of all the follower types. An instance of such a BSG is given by a set of tuples $\{(A^\theta, B^\theta, \lambda_\theta)\}_{\theta \in \Theta}$ where $A^\theta, B^\theta \in \mathbb{R}^{m \times n}$ are the payoff matrices of the leader (row player) and the follower (column player) respectively when the follower has type θ, which occurs with probability λ_θ. We use $[m]$ and $[n]$ to denote the leader's and follower's pure strategy set respectively. For convenience, we assume that every follower type has the same number of actions (i.e., n) in the above notation. This is without loss of generality since we can always add "dummy" actions with payoff $-\infty$ to both players. We use a^θ_{ij} $[b^\theta_{ij}]$ to denote a generic entry of A^θ $[B^\theta]$. If $A^\theta = -B^\theta$ for all $\theta \in \Theta$, we say that the BSG is *zero-sum*. Following the standard assumption of Stackelberg games, we assume that the leader can commit to a mixed strategy. Such a leader strategy is *optimal* if it results in maximal leader utility in expectation over the randomness of the strategy and follower types, assuming each follower type best responds to the leader's mixed strategy.[3] It is known that computing the optimal mixed strategy, also known as the Bayesian Strong Stackelberg Equilibrium (**BSSE**) strategy, to commit to is NP-hard in such a BSG [5]. A later result strengthened the hardness to approximation – no polynomial time algorithm can give a non-trivial approximation ratio in general unless P=NP [16].

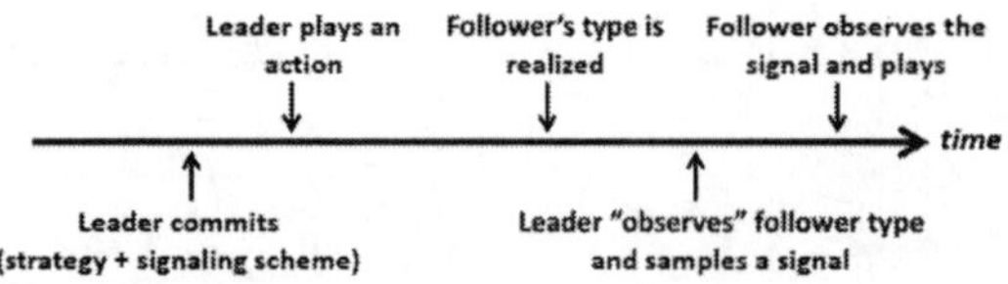

Figure 2: Timeline of the BSG with Multiple Follower Types.

We consider a richer model where the defender can commit not only to a mixed strategy but also to a scheme, often known as a *signaling scheme*, of partially releasing information regarding the action she is currently playing i.e., the sample from the leader's committed mixed strategy. Formally, the leader commits to a mixed strategy $\mathbf{x} \in \Delta_m$, where Δ_m is the m-dimensional simplex, and a signaling scheme φ which is a *stochastic* map from $\Theta \times [m]$ to a set of signals Σ. In other words, the sender randomly chooses a signal to send based on the action she currently plays and the follower type she observes. We call the pair

$$(\mathbf{x}, \varphi) \text{ where } \mathbf{x} \in \Delta_m;\ \varphi : \Theta \times [m] \xrightarrow{rnd} \Sigma \qquad (1)$$

a *leader policy*. After the commitment, the leader samples an action to play. Then the follower's type is realized, and the leader observes the follower's type and samples a signal. We assume that the follower has full knowledge of the leader policy. Upon receiving a signal, the follower updates his belief about the leader's action and takes a best response. Figure 2 illustrates the timeline of the game.

We note that if the leader cannot distinguish different follower types and has to send the same signal to all different follower types, then signaling does not benefit the leader (for the same reason as the non-Bayesian setting). In this case, she should simply commit to the optimal mixed strategy. The leader only benefits when she can target different follower types with different signals. In many cases, like the example in Section 2, the leader gets to observe the follower's type when it is realized (but after her action is completed) and can therefore choose to signal differently to different follower types. Moreover, in practice it is sometimes natural for the leader to send different signals to different follower types even without gen-

[3]Note that the follower cannot observe the leader's realized action, which is a standard assumption in Stackelberg games.

uinely learning their types, e.g., the follower's type may be defined by their location, in which case we can send signals using location-specific devices such as physical signs or radio transmission – this fits our model just as well. We will elaborate one such example when discussing security games.

3.2 Commitment to Optimal Leader Policy

We first consider the case where the leader can explicitly observe the follower's type, and thus can signal differently to different follower types, but this would also fit the location based model. We start with a simple observation.

OBSERVATION 3.1 (SEE, E.G., [15]). *There exists an optimal signaling scheme using at most n signals with signal σ_j recommending action $j \in [n]$ to the follower.*

Observation 3.1 follows simply from the fact that if two signals result in the same follower best-response action, we can merge these signals, resulting in a new signal without changing the follower's best response action and the leader's utility. As a result, for the rest of the paper we assume that $\Sigma = \{\sigma_j\}_{j\in[n]}$.

THEOREM 3.2. *The optimal leader policy can be computed in $poly(m, n, |\Theta|)$ time by linear programming.*

PROOF. Let $\mathbf{x} = (x_1, ..., x_m) \in \Delta_m$ be the leader's mixed strategy to commit to. As a result of Observation 3.1, the signaling scheme φ can be characterized by $\varphi(j|i,\theta)$ which is the probability of sending signal σ_j conditioned on the leader's (pure) action i and the follower's type θ. Then, $p^{\theta}_{ij} = x_i \cdot \varphi(j|i,\theta)$ is the *joint probability* that the leader plays pure strategy i and sends signal σ_j, conditioned on observing the follower of type θ. Then the following linear program computes the optimal leader policy captured by variables $\{x_i\}_{i\in[m]}$ and $\{p^{\theta}_{ij}\}_{i\in[m],j\in[n],\theta\in\Theta}$.

$$\begin{array}{lll} \text{maximize} & \sum_{\theta\in\Theta} \lambda_\theta \sum_{ij} p^{\theta}_{ij} a^{\theta}_{ij} & \\ \text{subject to} & \sum_{j=1}^{n} p^{\theta}_{ij} = x_i, & \text{for } i \in [m], \theta \in \Theta. \\ & \sum_{i=1}^{m} p^{\theta}_{ij} b^{\theta}_{ij} \geq \sum_{i=1}^{m} p^{\theta}_{ij} b^{\theta}_{ij'}, & \text{for } \theta, j \neq j'. \\ & \sum_{i=1}^{m} x_i = 1 & \\ & p^{\theta}_{ij} \geq 0, & \text{for all } i, j, \theta. \end{array} \tag{2}$$

The first set of constraints mean that the summation of probability mass p^{θ}_{ij} – the joint probability of playing pure strategy i and sending signal σ_j conditioned on follower type θ – over j should equal the probability of playing action i for any type θ. The second set of constraints are to guarantee that the recommended action j by signal σ_j is indeed the follower's best response.[4] □

Given any game G, let $U_{sig}(G)$ be the leader's expected utility by taking the optimal leader policy computed by LP (2). Moreover, let $U_{BSSE}(G)$ be the leader's utility in the BSSE, i.e., the expected leader utility by committing to (only) the optimal mixed strategy.

PROPOSITION 3.3. *If G is a zero-sum BSG, then $U_{sig}(G) = U_{BSSE}(G)$. That is, the leader does not benefit from signaling in zero-sum BSGs.*

The intuition underlying Proposition 3.3 is that, in a situation of pure competition, any information volunteered to the follower will be used to "harm" the leader. In other words, signaling is only helpful when the game exhibits some "cooperative components". We omit the detailed proof here due to space limitations. Note that all the omitted proofs can be found in the full version of this paper.

[4]This is often called "obedience".

Remark: Notice that computing the optimal mixed strategy (assuming no signaling) to commit to is NP-hard in general for the setting above (even NP-hard to approximate within any non-trivial ratio), as shown in [5, 16]. Interestingly, it turns out that when we consider a richer model with signaling, the problem becomes easy! Intuitively, this is because the signaling scheme "relaxes" the game by introducing correlation between the leader's and follower's action (via the signal). Such correlation allows more efficient computation. Similar intuition can be seen in the literature on computing Nash equilibria (hard for two players [6, 3]) and correlated equilibria (easy in fairly general settings [20, 14]).

3.3 Incentivizing the Follower Type

In many situations, it is not realistic to expect that the leader can observe the follower's type. For example, the follower's type may be whether he has a high or low value for an object, which is not directly observable. In such cases, the leader can ask the follower to report his type. However, it is not always in the follower's best interests to *truthfully* report his own type since the signal that is intended for a different follower type might be more beneficial to the follower (recall the example in Section 2). In this section, we consider how to compute an optimal *incentive compatible* (**IC**) leader policy that incentivizes the follower to truthfully report his type, and meanwhile benefits the leader.

We note that Observation 3.1 still holds in this setting. To see this, consider a follower of type θ that receives more than one signal, each resulting in the same follower best response. Then, as before, we can merge these signals without harming the follower of type θ. But if a follower of type $\beta \neq \theta$ misreports his type as θ, receiving the merged signal provides less information than receiving one of the unmerged signals. Therefore, if the follower of type β had no incentive to misreport type θ before the signals were merged, he has no incentive to misreport after the signals are merged. So any signaling scheme with more than n signals can be reduced to an equivalent scheme with exactly n signals.

THEOREM 3.4. *The optimal* incentive compatible *(***IC***) leader policy can be computed in $poly(m, n, |\Theta|)$ time by linear programming, assuming the leader does* not *observe the follower's type.*

PROOF. Similar to Section 3.2, we still use variables $\mathbf{x} \in \Delta_m$ and $\{p^{\theta}_{ij}\}_{i\in[m],j\in[n],\theta\in\Theta}$ to capture the leader's policy. Then $\alpha^{\theta}_j = \sum_{i=1}^{m} p^{\theta}_{ij}$ is the probability of sending signal j when the follower has type θ. Now consider the case where the follower reports type β, but has true type θ. When the leader recommends action j (assuming a follower of type β), which now is *not* necessarily the follower's best response due to the follower's misreport, the follower's utility for any action j' is $\frac{1}{\alpha^{\beta}_j} \sum_{i=1}^{m} p^{\beta}_{ij} b^{\theta}_{ij'}$. Therefore, the follower's action will be $\arg\max_{j'} \frac{1}{\alpha^{\beta}_j} \sum_{i=1}^{m} p^{\beta}_{ij} b^{\theta}_{ij'}$ with expected utility $\max_{j'} \frac{1}{\alpha^{\beta}_j} \sum_{i=1}^{m} p^{\beta}_{ij} b^{\theta}_{ij'}$. As a result, the expected utility for the follower of type θ, but misreporting type β, is

$$U(\beta;\theta) = \sum_{j=1}^{n} \left[\alpha^{\beta}_j \times \max_{j'} \frac{1}{\alpha^{\beta}_j} \sum_{i=1}^{m} p^{\beta}_{ij} b^{\theta}_{ij'} \right] = \sum_{j=1}^{n} \left[\max_{j'} \sum_{i=1}^{m} p^{\beta}_{ij} b^{\theta}_{ij'} \right]$$

Therefore, to incentivize the follower to truthfully report his type, we only need to add the incentive compatibility constraints $U(\theta;\theta) \geq U(\beta;\theta)$. Using the condition $\max_{j'} \sum_{i=1}^{m} p^{\theta}_{ij} b^{\theta}_{ij'} = \sum_{i=1}^{m} p^{\theta}_{ij} b^{\theta}_{ij}$, i.e., the recommended action j by σ_j is indeed the follower's best response when the follower has type θ, we have

$$U(\theta;\theta) = \sum_{j=1}^{n} \left[\max_{j'} \sum_{i=1}^{m} p^{\theta}_{ij} b^{\theta}_{ij'} \right] = \sum_{j=1}^{n} \sum_{i=1}^{m} p^{\theta}_{ij} b^{\theta}_{ij}$$

Therefore, incorporating the above constraints to LP (2) gives the following optimization program which computes an optimal incentive compatible leader policy.

$$\begin{aligned}
\text{maximize} \quad & \textstyle\sum_{\theta\in\Theta} \lambda_\theta \sum_{ij} p^\theta_{ij} a^\theta_{ij} & \\
\text{subject to} \quad & \textstyle\sum_{j=1}^n p^\theta_{ij} = x_i, & \text{for all } i, \theta. \\
& \textstyle\sum_{i=1}^m p^\theta_{ij} b^\theta_{ij} \geq \sum_{i=1}^m p^\theta_{ij} b^\theta_{ij'}, & \text{for } j \neq j'. \\
& \textstyle\sum_{j=1}^n \sum_{i=1}^m p^\theta_{ij} b^\theta_{ij} \geq & \\
& \qquad \textstyle\sum_{j=1}^n \left[\max_{j'} \sum_{i=1}^m p^\beta_{ij} b^\theta_{ij'}\right], & \text{for } \beta \neq \theta. \\
& \textstyle\sum_{i=1}^m x_i = 1 & \\
& p^\theta_{ij} \geq 0, & \text{for all } i, j, \theta.
\end{aligned} \tag{3}$$

Notice that $\sum_{j=1}^n \left[\max_{j'} \sum_{i=1}^m p^\beta_{ij} b^\theta_{ij'}\right]$ is a convex function, therefore the above is a convex program. By standard tricks, the convex constraint can be converted to a set of polynomially many linear constraints (see, e.g., [2]). □

Given any BSG G, let $U_{IC}(G)$ be the expected leader utility by playing an optimal incentive compatible leader policy computed by Convex Program (3). The following theorem captures the utility ranking of the different models.

PROPOSITION 3.5 (UTILITY RANKING).

$$U_{sig}(G) \geq U_{IC}(G) \geq U_{BSSE}(G).$$

PROOF. The first inequality holds because any feasible solution to Program (3) must also be feasible to LP (2). The second inequality follows from the fact that the BSSE is an incentive compatible leader policy where the signaling scheme simply reveals no information to any follower. This scheme is trivially incentive compatible because it is indifferent to the follower's report. □

Relation to Other Models. Our model in this section relates to the model of Persuasion with Privately Informed Receivers ("followers" in our terminology) by Kolotilin et al. [1]. Though in a different context, the model of Kolotilin et al. is essentially a BSG played between a leader and a follower of type only known to himself. In our model, players' payoffs are affected by the leader's action, thus the leader first commits to a mixed strategy and then signals her sampled action to the follower with incentive compatibility constraints. In [1], the leader does not have actions. Instead, the payoffs are determined by some random state of nature, which the leader can privately observe but does not have control over. The follower only has a prior belief about the state of nature, analogous to the follower knowing the leader's mixed strategy in our model. Kolotilin et al. study how the leader can signal such exogenously given information to the follower with incentive compatibility constraints. Mathematically, this corresponds to the case where $\mathbf{x}$ in Program (3) is given *a-priori* instead of being designed.

3.4 Security Games

In this section we consider the Bayesian *Security Games* played between a defender (leader) and an attacker (follower). Our results here are generally *negative* – the optimal leader policy becomes hard to compute even in the simplest of the security games. In particular, we consider a security game with n targets and k $(< n)$ *identical unconstrained* security resources. Each resource can be assigned to at most one target; a target with a resource assigned is called *covered*, otherwise it is *uncovered*. Therefore, the defender pure strategies are subsets of targets (to be protected) of cardinality k. On the other hand, the attacker has n actions – attack any one of the n targets. The attacker has a private type θ which is drawn from finite set Θ with probability λ_θ. The attacker is privy to his own type, but the defender only knows the distribution $\{\lambda_\theta\}_{\theta\in\Theta}$. This captures many natural security settings. For example, in airport patrolling, the attacker could either be a terrorist or a regular policy violator as modeled in [22]. In wildlife patrolling, the type of an attacker could be the species the attacker is interested in [10]. If the attacker chooses to attack target $i \in [n]$, players' utilities depend not only on whether target i is covered or not, but also on the attacker's type θ. We use $U^{d/a}_{c/u}(i|\theta)$ to denote the defender/attacker (d/a) utility when target i is covered/uncovered (c/u) and an attacker of type θ attacks target i.

Notice that the leader now has $\binom{n}{k}$ pure strategies, thus the natural LP has exponential size. Nevertheless, in security games we can sometimes solve the game efficiently by exploiting compact representations of the defender's strategies. Unfortunately, we show this is not possible here. Interestingly, it turns out that the hardness of the problem depends on how many targets an attacker is interested in. In particular, we say that an attacker of type θ is *not interested* in attacking target i if there exists j such that $U^a_u(i|\theta) < U^a_c(j|\theta)$. That is, even when target i is totally uncovered and target j is fully covered, the attacker still prefers attacking target j – thus target i will never be attacked by an attacker of type θ. Otherwise we say that an attacker of type θ is *interested* in attacking target i. One might imagine that if an attacker is only interested in a small number of targets, this should simplify the computation. Interestingly, it turns out that this is *not* the case.

PROPOSITION 3.6. *Computing the optimal defender policy in a Bayesian Stackelberg security game (both with and without type-reporting IC constraints) is NP-hard, even when the defender payoff does not depend on the attacker's type and when each type of attacker is interested in attacking at most four targets.*

The proof of Proposition 3.6 requires a slight modification of a similar proof in [17], and is omitted here. Our next proposition shows that we are able to compute the optimal defender policy in a restricted setting. This setting is motivated by fare evasion deterrence [29] where each attacker (i.e., a passenger) is only interested in attacking (i.e., stealing a ride from) *one* specific target (i.e., the metro station nearby), or choosing to not attack (e.g., buying a ticket) in which case both players get utility 0. Formally, we model this as a setting where each attacker type is interested in two targets: one *type-specific* target and one *common* target $t_\emptyset$ (corresponding to the option of not attacking). If $t_\emptyset$ is attacked, each player gets utility 0 regardless of whether $t_\emptyset$ is protected or not – we call $t_\emptyset$ *coverage-invariant* for this reason.[5]

PROPOSITION 3.7. *Suppose each attacker type is interested in two targets: the* common coverage-invariant *target $t_\emptyset$ and a* type-specific *target. Then the defender's optimal policy (without type-reporting IC constraints) can be computed in poly($m, n, |\Theta|$) time.*

The proof of Proposition 3.7 crucially exploits the fact that each player's utility is "coverage-invariant" on target $t_\emptyset$. As a result, the defender will not cover $t_\emptyset$ at optimality. Therefore, for any attacker of type θ who is interested in target i and $t_\emptyset$, the defender only needs to signal information about the protection of target i. This allows us to write a linear program. The proof is deferred to the full version. Note that when we take incentive compatibility constraints into account, the situation becomes more intricate. It could be the case that an attacker is not interested in attacking a target, but would still like to receive an informative signal regarding its coverage status in order to infer some information about the distribution of resources. This is reminiscent of information leakage as

[5]The utility 0 is not essential so long as $t_\emptyset$ is coverage-invariant.

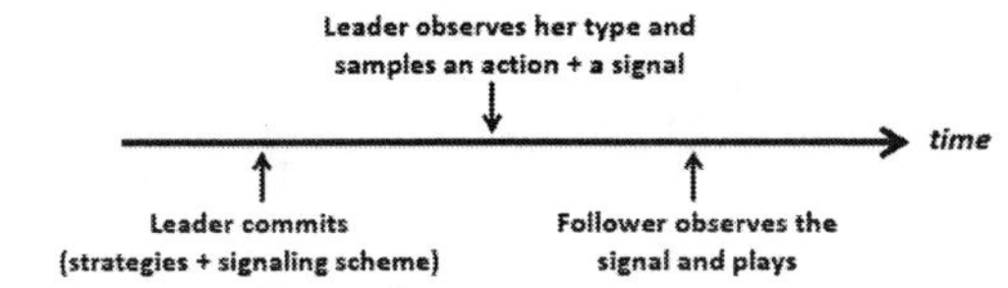

Figure 3: Timeline of the BSG With Multiple Leader Types

described by Xu et al. [27], and our proof does not naturally extend to this setting.

Interestingly, our next result shows that the restriction in Proposition 3.7 is almost necessary for efficient computation, as evidence of computational hardness manifests when we slightly go beyond the condition there.

PROPOSITION 3.8. *The defender oracle problem* [6] *is NP-hard (both with and without type-reporting IC constraints), even when each type of attacker is interested in two targets.*

4. MULTIPLE LEADER TYPES, SINGLE FOLLOWER TYPE

4.1 The Model

Similarly to Section 3, we still start with the normal-form Bayesian Stackelberg Game, but with multiple *leader* types and a single *follower* type. Following the notations in Section 3, an instance of such a BSG is also given by a set of tuples $\{(A^\theta, B^\theta, \lambda_\theta)\}_{\theta\in\Theta}$ where $A^\theta, B^\theta \in \mathbb{R}^{m\times n}$ are the payoff matrices of the leader (row player) and the follower (column player) respectively. However, Θ now is the set of leader types and λ_θ is the probability that the leader has type θ. Among its many applications, one key motivation of this model is from security domains. In security games, the follower, i.e., the attacker, usually does not have full information regarding the importance and vulnerability of the targets for attack, while the leader, i.e., the defender, possesses much better knowledge. This can be modeled as a BSG where the leader has multiple types and the single-type follower has a prior belief regarding the leader's types.

It is known that in this case, a set of linear programs suffices to compute the optimal mixed strategy to commit to [5]. We consider a richer model where the leader can additionally commit to a policy, namely a *signaling scheme*, of partially releasing her *type* and *action*. Formally, the leader commits to a mixed strategy $\mathbf{x}^\theta$ for each realized type θ and a signaling scheme φ which is a *stochastic* map from $\Theta \times [m]$ to Σ. We call the pair

$$(\{\mathbf{x}^\theta\}_{\theta\in\Theta}, \varphi) \text{ where } \mathbf{x}^\theta \in \Delta_m;\ \varphi: \Theta\times[m] \xrightarrow{rnd} \Sigma \quad (4)$$

a *leader policy* in this setting. The game starts with the leader's commitment. Afterwards, the leader observes her own type, and then samples an action and a signal accordingly. The follower observes the signal and best responds. Figure 3 illustrates the timeline of the game.

4.2 Commitment to Optimal Leader Policy

Similarly to Observation 3.1, it is easy to see there exists an optimal leader policy with n signals where each signal recommends an action to the follower. Therefore, without loss of generality, we assume $\Sigma = \{\sigma_1, ..., \sigma_n\}$ where σ_j is a signal recommending action j to the follower.

[6]The optimal policy can be computed by an LP with exponential size. The defender oracle is essentially the dual of the LP. See the Appendix for a derivation of the defender oracle and proof of the hardness.

THEOREM 4.1. *The optimal* leader policy *defined in Formula* (4) *can be computed in poly*$(m, n, |\Theta|)$ *time by linear programming.*

PROOF. To represent the signaling scheme φ, let $\varphi(j|i,\theta)$ be the probability of sending signal σ_j, conditioned on the realized leader type θ and pure strategy i. Then $p^\theta_{ij} = \varphi(j|i,\theta)\cdot x^\theta(i)$ is the *joint* probability for the leader to take (pure) action i and send signal σ_j, conditioned on a realized leader type θ. The following linear program computes the optimal $\{p^\theta_{ij}\}_{i\in[m],j\in[n],\theta\in\Theta}$.[7]

$$\begin{array}{lll} \text{maximize} & \sum_{\theta\in\Theta}\lambda_\theta\sum_{ij}p^\theta_{ij}a^\theta_{ij} & \\ \text{subject to} & \sum_{i=1}^m\sum_{j=1}^n p^\theta_{ij} = 1, & \text{for } \theta\in\Theta. \\ & \sum_{i,\theta}\lambda_\theta p^\theta_{ij}b^\theta_{ij} \geq \sum_{i,\theta}\lambda_\theta p^\theta_{ij}b^\theta_{ij'}, & \text{for } j\neq j'. \\ & p^\theta_{ij}\geq 0, & \text{for all } i,j,\theta. \end{array} \quad (5)$$

By letting $x^\theta(i) = \sum_{j=1}^n p^\theta_{ij}$ and $\varphi(j|i,\theta) = p^\theta_{ij}/x^\theta(i)$, we can recover the optimal defender policy $(\{\mathbf{x}^\theta\}_{\theta\in\Theta}, \varphi)$. □

4.3 Security Games

We now again consider the security game setting. We have shown in Section 3 that, when there are multiple follower types, the polynomial-time solvability of BSGs does not extend to even the simplest security game setting. Interestingly, it turns out that when the leader has multiple types, the optimal leader strategy and signaling scheme can be efficiently computed in fairly general settings, as we will show in this section.

Continuing the setup in Section 3.4, we first introduce a few more preliminaries. Note that θ is now the defender's type. In security games, any defender pure strategy, denoted as $\mathbf{e}$, is a subset of targets that are protected by this pure strategy. We will view $\mathbf{e}$ as a *binary* vector from $\{0,1\}^n$ with each entry specifying whether the corresponding target is protected or not in this pure strategy. Let $E = \{\mathbf{e}_1, ..., \mathbf{e}_L\}$ be the set of all pure strategies. Therefore, the *convex hull* of E

$$\mathcal{D} = Conv\{\mathbf{e}_1, ..., \mathbf{e}_L\} \quad (6)$$

corresponds to the set of all *mixed strategies*, where a mixed strategy is summarized by the *marginal* coverage probabilities of each target. In security games, L is usually exponentially large in the natural representation, but $\mathcal{D}$ usually has compact representations, and moreover, both the defender's and attacker's utilities can be compactly represented using marginal probabilities. For example, with k identical unconstrained defending resources and n targets, $L = C^k_n = \mathcal{O}(n^k)$, the number of subsets of cardinality k, however $\mathcal{D}$ has a compact representation $\{\mathbf{x}\in\mathbb{R}^n : \sum_j x_j = k;\ x_j \in [0,1]\,\forall j\}$. But in many cases, security resources have scheduling constraints and $\mathcal{D}$ becomes more complicated. It can be shown that if the defender best response problem can be solved in polynomial time, then the Strong Stackelberg equilibrium can also be computed in polynomial time [13, 26]. We now establish an analogous result for BSG with signaling.

THEOREM 4.2. *The optimal defender policy can be computed in poly*$(n, |\Theta|)$ *time if the defender's best response problem (i.e., defender oracle) admits a poly*(n) *time algorithm.*

PROOF. First, observe that LP (5) does not obviously extend to security game settings because the number of leader pure strategies

[7]Interestingly, when $|\Theta| = 1$, the game degenerates to a Stackelberg game without uncertainty of player types, and LP (5) degenerates to a linear program that computes the Strong Stackelberg equilibrium [4].

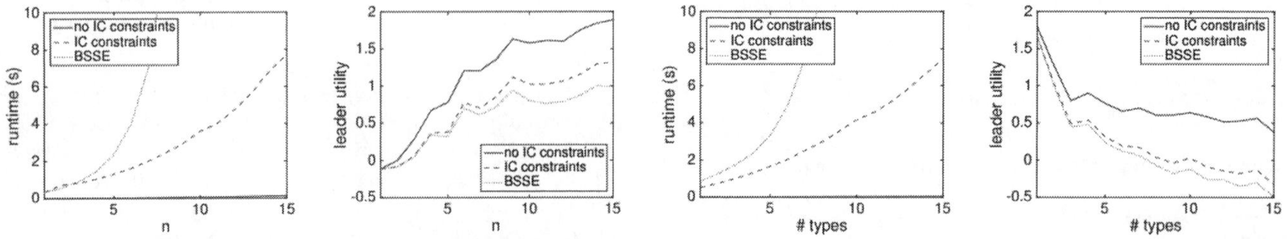

(a) Running time, $|\Theta|$ constant (b) Leader utility, $|\Theta|$ constant (c) Running time, n constant (d) Leader utility, n constant

Figure 4: Simulation results showing the effect of varying number of actions, n, and number of types, $|\theta|$, on the runtime and utility of the three different models in the case of multiple follower types.

is exponentially large here and so is the LP formulation. Therefore, like classic security game algorithms, it is crucial to exploit a compact representation of the leader's policy space. For this, we need an equivalent but slightly different view of the leader policy. That is, the leader policy can be *equivalently* viewed as follows: the leader observes her type θ and then randomly chooses a signal σ_j (occurring with probability $\sum_{i=1}^m p_{ij}^\theta$ in LP (5)), and finally picks a mixed strategy that depends on both θ and σ_j (i.e., the vector $(p_{1j}^\theta, p_{2j}^\theta, ..., p_{mj}^\theta)$ normalized by the factor $\sum_{i=1}^m p_{ij}^\theta$ in LP (5)).

The different view of leader policy above allows us to write a quadratic program for computing the optimal leader policy. In particular, let p_j^θ be the probability that the leader sends signal j conditioned on the realized leader type θ, and let $\mathbf{x}_j^\theta$ be the leader's (marginal) mixed strategy conditioned on observing θ and sending signal σ_j. Then, upon receiving signal σ_j, a rational Bayesian attacker will updates his belief, and compute the expected utility for attacking target j' as

$$\sum_\theta \left(\frac{\lambda_\theta p_j^\theta}{\alpha_j} \cdot \left[\mathbf{x}_j^\theta(j') U_c^a(j'|\theta) + \left(1 - \mathbf{x}_j^\theta(j')\right) U_u^a(j'|\theta) \right] \right) \quad (7)$$

where the normalization factor $\alpha_j = \sum_\theta \lambda_\theta p_j^\theta$ is the probability of sending signal σ_j. Define $AttU(j,j')$ to be the attacker utility by attacking target j' conditioned on receiving signal σ_j, multiplied by the probability α_j of receiving signal j. Formally,

$$\begin{aligned} & AttU(j,j') \\ = \ & \alpha_j \times \text{Equation (7)} \\ = \ & \textstyle\sum_\theta \left(\lambda_\theta p_j^\theta \mathbf{x}_j^\theta(j') U_c^a(j'|\theta) + \left[\lambda_\theta p_j^\theta - \lambda_\theta p_j^\theta \mathbf{x}_j^\theta(j') \right] U_u^a(j'|\theta) \right) \end{aligned}$$

Similarly, we can also define $DefU(j,j')$, the leader's expected utility of sending signal σ_j with target j' being attacked, scaled by the probability of sending σ_j. The attacker's incentive compatibility constraints are then $AttU(j,j) \geq AttU(j,j')$ for any $j' \neq j$. Then the leader's problem can be expressed as the following quadratic program with variables $\{\mathbf{x}_j^\theta\}_{j\in[n],\theta\in\Theta}$ and $\{p_j^\theta\}_{j\in[n],\theta\in\Theta}$.

$$\begin{array}{lll} \text{maximize} & \sum_j DefU(j,j) & \\ \text{subject to} & AttU(j,j) \geq AttU(j,j'), & \text{for } j \neq j'. \\ & \sum_j p_j^\theta = 1, & \text{for } \theta \in \Theta. \\ & \mathbf{x}_j^\theta \in \mathcal{D}, & \text{for } j, \theta. \\ & p_j^\theta \geq 0, & \text{for } j, \theta. \end{array} \quad (8)$$

The optimization program (8) is quadratic because $AttU(j,j')$ and $DefU(j,j')$ are quadratic in the variables. Notably, these two functions are *linear* in p_j^θ and the term $p_j^\theta \mathbf{x}_j^\theta$. Therefore, we define variables $\mathbf{y}_j^\theta = p_j^\theta \mathbf{x}_j^\theta \in \mathbb{R}^n$. Then, both $AttU(j,j')$ and $DefU(j,j')$ are linear in p_j^θ and $\mathbf{y}_j^\theta$. The only problematic constraint in program (8) is $\mathbf{x}_j^\theta \in \mathcal{D}$, which now becomes $\mathbf{y}_j^\theta \in p_j^\theta \mathcal{D}$ where both p_j^θ and $\mathbf{y}_j^\theta$ are variables. Here $p\mathcal{D}$ denotes the polytope $\{px : x \in \mathcal{D}\}$ for any given p. It turns out that this is still a convex constraint, and behaves nicely as long as the polytope $\mathcal{D}$ behaves nicely.

LEMMA 4.3. *Let $\mathcal{D} \subseteq \mathbb{R}^n$ be any* bounded *convex set. Then the following hold:*

1. The extended set $\widetilde{\mathcal{D}} = \{(\mathbf{x}, p) : \mathbf{x} \in p\mathcal{D}, p \geq 0\}$ is convex;

2. If $\mathcal{D}$ is a polytope expressed by constraints $A\mathbf{x} \leq \mathbf{b}$, then $\widetilde{\mathcal{D}}$ is also a polytope, given by $\{(\mathbf{x}, p) : A\mathbf{x} \leq p\mathbf{b}, p \geq 0\}$;

3. If $\mathcal{D}$ admits a $poly(n)$ time separation oracle, *so does $\widetilde{\mathcal{D}}$.*[8]

The proof of Lemma 4.3 is standard, and we defer it to the full version. We note that the restriction that $\mathcal{D}$ is bounded is important, otherwise some conclusions do not hold, e.g., Property 2. Fortunately, the polytope $\mathcal{D}$ of mixed strategies is bounded. Therefore, using Lemma 4.3, we can rewrite Quadratic Program (8) as the following linear program.

$$\begin{array}{lll} \text{maximize} & \sum_j DefU(j,j) & \\ \text{subject to} & AttU(j,j) \geq AttU(j,j'), & \text{for } j \neq j'. \\ & \sum_j p_j^\theta = 1, & \text{for } \theta \in \Theta. \\ & (\mathbf{y}_j^\theta, p_j^\theta) \in \widetilde{\mathcal{D}}, & \text{for } j, \theta. \\ & p_j^\theta \geq 0, & \text{for } j, \theta. \end{array} \quad (9)$$

Program (9) is linear because $AttU(j,j')$ and $DefU(j,j)$ are linear in p_j^θ and $\mathbf{y}_j^\theta$, and moreover, $(\mathbf{y}_j^\theta, p_j^\theta) \in \widetilde{\mathcal{D}}$ are essentially linear constraints due to Lemma 4.3 and the fact that $\mathcal{D}$ is a polytope in security games. Furthermore, LP (9) has a compact representation as long as the polytope of realizable mixed strategies $\mathcal{D}$ has one. In this case, LP (9) can be solved explicitly. More generally, by standard techniques from convex programing, we can show that the separation oracle for $\mathcal{D}$ easily reduces to the defender's best response problem. Thus if the defender oracle admits a $poly(n)$ time algorithm, then a separation oracle for $\mathcal{D}$ can be found in $poly(n)$ time. By Lemma 4.3, $\widetilde{\mathcal{D}}$ then admits a $poly(n)$ time separation oracle, so LP (9) can solved in $poly(n, |\Theta|)$ time. The proof is not particularly insightful and a similar argument can be found in [26]. So we omit the details here. □

4.4 Relation to Other Models

We note that our model in this section is related to several models from the literature on both information economics and security games. In particular, when the leader does not have actions

[8] A separation oracle for a convex set $\mathcal{D} \subseteq \mathbb{R}^n$ is an algorithm, which, given any $\mathbf{x_0} \in \mathbb{R}^n$, either correctly asserts $\mathbf{x_0} \in \mathcal{D}$ or asserts $\mathbf{x_0} \notin \mathcal{D}$ and find a hyperplane $\mathbf{a} \cdot \mathbf{x} = b$ separating x_0 from $\mathcal{D}$ in the following sense: $\mathbf{a} \cdot \mathbf{x_0} > b$ but $\mathbf{a} \cdot \mathbf{x} \leq b$ for any $\mathbf{x} \in \mathcal{D}$. It is well-known that the convex program $\max\ \mathbf{a} \cdot \mathbf{x}$ subject to $\mathbf{x} \in \mathcal{D}$ can be solved in $poly(n)$ time for any $\mathbf{a} \in \mathbb{R}^n$ if $\mathcal{D}$ has a $poly(n)$ time separation oracle [11].

and only privately observes her type, our model degenerates to the *Bayesian Persuasion* (BP) model of [15]. The BP model is a two-player game played between a *sender* (leader in our case) and a *receiver* (follower in our case). The receiver must take one of a number of actions with a-priori *unknown* payoff, and the sender has *no* actions but possesses additional information regarding the payoff of various receiver actions (i.e., the leader observes her type). The BP model studies how the sender can signal her additional information to persuade the receiver to take an action that is more favorable to the sender. Variants of the BP model have been applied to varied domains including auctions, advertising, voting, multi-armed bandits, medical research and financial regulation. For additional references, see [7]. Our model generalizes the BP model to the case where sender has both actions and additional private information, and our results show that this generalized model can be solved in fairly general settings.

The security game setting in this section also relates to the model of Rabinovich et al. [23]. Rabinovich et al. considered a similar security setting where the defender can partially signal her strategy and extra knowledge about targets' states to the attacker in order to achieve better defender utility. This is essentially a BSG with multiple leader types and a single follower type. Rabinovich et al. [23] were able to efficiently solve for the case with unconstrained identical security resources. Our Theorem 4.2 shows that this model can actually be efficiently solved in much more general security settings allowing complicated real-world scheduling constraints, as long as the defender oracle problem can be solved efficiently.

5. SIMULATIONS

We will mainly present the comparison of the models discussed in Section 3 in terms of both the leader's optimal utility and the runtime required to compute the leader's optimal policy. We focus primarily on the setting with one leader type and multiple follower types, for two reasons. First, this is the case in which it is NP-hard to compute the optimal leader strategy without allowing the leader to signal (i.e., to compute the BSSE strategy), while our models of signaling permit a polynomial time solution. Second, some interesting phenomena in our simulations for the case of multiple leader types also show up in the case of multiple follower types.

We generate random instances using a modification of the covariant game model [19]. In particular, for given values of m, n, and Θ, we independently set a^{θ}_{ij} equal to a random integer in the range $[-5, 5]$ for each i, j, θ. Probabilities $\{\lambda_\theta\}_{\theta\in\Theta}$ were generated randomly. For some value of $\alpha \in [0, 1]$, we then set $B = \alpha(B') + (1-\alpha)(-A)$, where B' is a random matrix generated in the same fashion as A. So in the case that $\alpha = 0$ the game is zero-sum, while $\alpha = 1$ means independent and uniform random leader and follower payoffs. For every set of parameter values, we averaged over 50 instances generated in this manner to obtain the utility/runtime values we report.

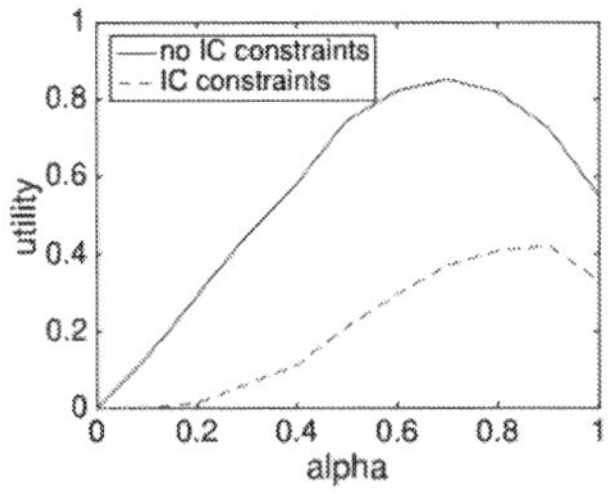

Figure 5: Extra utility gained by the leader from signaling.

We first consider the value of signaling for different values of α chosen from the set $\{0, 0.1, 0.2, ..., 1\}$. For these simulations, we fixed $m = n = 10$ and $|\Theta| = 5$. Figure 5 shows the *absolute* increase in leader utility from signaling (both with and without the type-reporting IC constraints), compared with the utility from BSSE (the $y = 0$ baseline). Note that when $\alpha = 0$ there is no gain from signaling, from Proposition 3.3. Interestingly, the gain from signaling is non-monotone, peaking at around $\alpha = 0.7$. Intuitively, large α means low correlation between the payoff matrices of the leader and follower, therefore there is a high probability that some entries will induce high payoff to both players. The leader can therefore extract high utility from commitment alone, thus derives little gain from signaling. However, as we decrease α and the game becomes more competitive, commitment alone is not as powerful for the leader and she has more to gain from being able to signal.

We next investigate the relation between the size of the BSG and the leader's utility, as well as runtime, for the three different models. In Figures 4(a) and 4(b), we hold the number of follower types constant ($|\Theta| = 5$) and vary $m = n$ between 1 and 15. In Figures 4(c) and 4(d) we fix $m = n = 5$ and vary $|\Theta|$ between 1 and 15. In all cases we set $\alpha = 0.5$ for generating random instances.

Not surprisingly, allowing signaling (both with and without the IC constraints) provides a significant speed-up over computing the BSSE.[9] On the other hand, the additional constraints in the model with IC constraints also increase the running time over the model without those constraints. Indeed, the time to compute the leader's optimal policy without the IC constraints appears as a flat line in Figures 4(a) and 4(c).

In both figures of leader utility, the differences of the leader's utility among the models are as indicated by Proposition 3.5. Observe that in all models the leader's utility increases with the number of actions, but decreases with the number of types. One explanation is that the former effect is due to the increased probability that the payoff matrices for a given follower type contain 'cooperative' entries where both players achieve high utility. However, as the number of follower types increases, it becomes less likely that the leader's strategy (which does not depend on the follower type) can "cooperate" with a majority of follower types simultaneously. Thus there is an increased chance that the leader's strategy results in low utilities when playing against a reasonable fraction of follower types, which accounts for the latter effect.

In the case of multiple leader types, allowing the leader to signal actually results in a small computational speed up compared to the case without signaling. We hypothesize that this is because we only need to solve one LP to compute the optimal policy, rather than the multiple LPs required to solve without signaling [5]. Unsurprisingly, we also see an increase in the leader's utility. The utility trends are similar to the case of multiple follower types, so we do not present them in detail.

6. CONCLUSIONS AND DISCUSSIONS

In this paper, we studied the effect of signaling in Bayesian Stackelberg games. We show that the leader's power of commitment to a signaling scheme not only achieves higher utility, but also computational speed-ups. Some of the polynomial-time solvability results extend to security games, an important application domain of Stackelberg games, while others cease to hold. There are many interesting directions for future work. What if different follower types can share information with each other? For a Bayesian leader, what if her signaling scheme cannot be correlated with her mixed strategy, but only carries information about her type? Can we apply these ideas to other domains, e.g., mechanism design where the mechanism designer implicitly serves as the leader?

[9]To compute the BSSE, we implement the state-of-art algorithm DOBBS, a mixed integer linear program as formulated in [21].

Acknowledgments: This research is supported by NSF grant CCF-1350900 and MURI grant W911NF-11-1-0332. Part of this research was done while the authors were visiting the Simons Institute for the Theory of Computing.

REFERENCES

[1] T. M. Anton Kolotilin, Ming Li and A. Zapechelnyuk. Persuasion of a privately informed receiver. *Working Paper*, 2015.

[2] S. Boyd and L. Vandenberghe. *Convex Optimization*. Cambridge University Press, New York, NY, USA, 2004.

[3] X. Chen, X. Deng, and S.-H. Teng. Settling the complexity of computing two-player Nash Equilibria. *J. ACM*, 56(3):14:1–14:57, May 2009.

[4] V. Conitzer and D. Korzhyk. Commitment to correlated strategies. In *Proceedings of the 25th AAAI Conference on Artificial Intelligence (AAAI)*, 2011.

[5] V. Conitzer and T. Sandholm. Computing the optimal strategy to commit to. In *Proceedings of the 7th ACM conference on Electronic commerce*, pages 82–90. ACM, 2006.

[6] C. Daskalakis, P. W. Goldberg, and C. H. Papadimitriou. The complexity of computing a Nash Equilibrium. In *Proceedings of the Thirty-eighth Annual ACM Symposium on Theory of Computing*, STOC '06, pages 71–78, New York, NY, USA, 2006. ACM.

[7] S. Dughmi and H. Xu. Algorithmic Bayesian persuasion. In *Proceedings of the Forty-eighth Annual ACM Symposium on Theory of Computing*, STOC '16, 2016.

[8] Y. Emek, M. Feldman, I. Gamzu, R. Paes Leme, and M. Tennenholtz. Signaling schemes for revenue maximization. In *Proceedings of the 13th ACM Conference on Electronic Commerce*, EC '12, pages 514–531, New York, NY, USA, 2012. ACM.

[9] F. Etro. Stackelberg, heinrich von: Market structure and equilibrium. *Journal of Economics*, 109(1):89–92, 2013.

[10] F. Fang, P. Stone, and M. Tambe. When security games go green: Designing defender strategies to prevent poaching and illegal fishing. In *International Joint Conference on Artificial Intelligence (IJCAI)*, 2015.

[11] M. Grötschel, L. Lovász, and A. Schrijver. *Geometric Algorithms and Combinatorial Optimization*, volume 2 of *Algorithms and Combinatorics*. Springer, 1988.

[12] M. Guo and A. Deligkas. Revenue maximization via hiding item attributes. *CoRR*, abs/1302.5332, 2013.

[13] M. Jain, E. Kardes, C. Kiekintveld, F. Ordóñez, and M. Tambe. Security games with arbitrary schedules: A branch and price approach. In M. Fox and D. Poole, editors, *Proceedings of the 24th AAAI Conference on Artificial Intelligence (AAAI)*. AAAI Press, 2010.

[14] A. X. Jiang and K. Leyton-Brown. Polynomial-time computation of exact correlated equilibrium in compact games. In *Proceedings of the Twelfth ACM Electronic Commerce Conference (ACM-EC)*, 2011.

[15] E. Kamenica and M. Gentzkow. Bayesian persuasion. *American Economic Review*, 101(6):2590–2615, 2011.

[16] J. Letchford, V. Conitzer, and K. Munagala. Learning and approximating the optimal strategy to commit to. In M. Mavronicolas and V. G. Papadopoulou, editors, *SAGT*, volume 5814 of *Lecture Notes in Computer Science*, pages 250–262. Springer, 2009.

[17] Y. Li, V. Conitzer, and D. Korzhyk. Catcher-evader games. *arXiv:1602.01896*.

[18] P. B. Miltersen and O. Sheffet. Send mixed signals: earn more, work less. In B. Faltings, K. Leyton-Brown, and P. Ipeirotis, editors, *EC*, pages 234–247. ACM, 2012.

[19] E. Nudelman, J. Wortman, Y. Shoham, and K. Leyton-Brown. Run the GAMUT: A comprehensive approach to evaluating game-theoretic algorithms. In *Proceedings of the Third International Joint Conference on Autonomous Agents and Multiagent Systems-Volume 2*, pages 880–887. IEEE Computer Society, 2004.

[20] C. H. Papadimitriou and T. Roughgarden. Computing correlated equilibria in multi-player games. *J. ACM*, 55(3):14:1–14:29, Aug. 2008.

[21] P. Paruchuri, J. P. Pearce, J. Marecki, M. Tambe, F. Ordonez, and S. Kraus. Efficient algorithms to solve Bayesian Stackelberg games for security applications. In *Proceedings of the 23rd AAAI Conference on Artificial Intelligence (AAAI)*, pages 1559–1562, 2008.

[22] J. Pita, M. Jain, J. Marecki, F. Ordóñez, C. Portway, M. Tambe, C. Western, P. Paruchuri, and S. Kraus. Deployed armor protection: the application of a game theoretic model for security at the Los Angeles international airport. In *Proceedings of the 7th international joint conference on Autonomous agents and multiagent systems: industrial track*, pages 125–132. International Foundation for Autonomous Agents and Multiagent Systems, 2008.

[23] Z. Rabinovich, A. X. Jiang, M. Jain, and H. Xu. Information disclosure as a means to security. In *Proceedings of the 2015 International Conference on Autonomous Agents and Multiagent Systems, AAMAS 2015, Istanbul, Turkey, May 4-8, 2015*, pages 645–653, 2015.

[24] L. Rayo and I. Segal. Optimal information disclosure. *Journal of Political Economy*, 118(5):949 – 987, 2010.

[25] M. Tambe. *Security and Game Theory: Algorithms, Deployed Systems, Lessons Learned*. Cambridge University Press, New York, NY, USA, 1st edition, 2011.

[26] H. Xu, F. Fang, A. X. Jiang, V. Conitzer, S. Dughmi, and M. Tambe. Solving zero-sum security games in discretized spatio-temporal domains. In *Proceedings of the 28th Conference on Artificial Intelligence (AAAI 2014), Québec, Canada*, 2014.

[27] H. Xu, A. X. Jiang, A. Sinha, Z. Rabinovich, S. Dughmi, and M. Tambe. Security games with information leakage: Modeling and computation. In *Proceedings of the Twenty-Fourth International Joint Conference on Artificial Intelligence, IJCAI 2015, Buenos Aires, Argentina, July 25-31, 2015*, pages 674–680, 2015.

[28] H. Xu, Z. Rabinovich, S. Dughmi, and M. Tambe. Exploring information asymmetry in two-stage security games. In *Proceedings of the 29th AAAI Conference on Artificial Intelligence (AAAI)*, 2015.

[29] Z. Yin, A. Jiang, M. Johnson, M. Tambe, C. Kiekintveld, K. Leyton-Brown, T. Sandholm, and J. Sullivan. TRUSTS: Scheduling randomized patrols for fare inspection in transit systems. In *Proceedings of the Conference on Innovative Applications of Artificial Intelligence (IAAI)*, 2012.

Coalitional Security Games

Qingyu Guo[1], Bo An[2], Yevgeniy Vorobeychik[3], Long Tran-Thanh[4], Jiarui Gan[2], Chunyan Miao[2]
[1]Joint NTU-UBC Research Centre of Excellence in Active Living for the Elderly, NTU, Singapore
[2]School of Computer Engineering, Nanyang Technological University, Singapore
[3]Electrical Engineering and Computer Science, Vanderbilt University, Nashville, TN
[4]Electronics and Computer Science, University of Southampton, UK
[1,2]{qguo005,boan,jrgan,ascymiao}@ntu.edu.sg,[3]yevgeniy.vorobeychik@vanderbilt.edu,[4]ltt08r@ecs.soton.ac.uk

ABSTRACT

Game theoretic models of security, and associated computational methods, have emerged as critical components of security posture across a broad array of domains, including airport security and coast guard. These approaches consider terrorists as motivated but independent entities. There is, however, increasing evidence that attackers, be it terrorists or cyber attackers, communicate extensively and form coalitions that can dramatically increase their ability to achieve malicious goals. To date, such cooperative decision making among attackers has been ignored in the security games literature. To address the issue of cooperation among attackers, we introduce a novel *coalitional security game (CSG)* model. A CSG consists of a set of attackers connected by a (communication or trust) network who can form coalitions as connected subgraphs of this network so as to attack a collection of targets. A defender in a CSG can delete a set of edges, incurring a cost for deleting each edge, with the goal of optimally limiting the attackers' ability to form effective coalitions (in terms of successfully attacking high value targets). We first show that a CSG is, in general, hard to approximate. Nevertheless, we develop a novel branch and price algorithm, leveraging a combination of column generation, relaxation, greedy approximation, and stabilization methods to enable scalable high-quality approximations of CSG solutions on realistic problem instances.

Keywords

Game Theory; Security; Optimization; Stackelberg Games

1. INTRODUCTION

Recent decades have seen a number of major terrorist attacks, such as WTC 9/11 attack, Jemaah Islamiyahs Bali bombing, and 7/7 London bombing, that have killed thousands of lives and caused significant economic losses. An important reason for the increasing threat of terrorism is cooperation between terrorist groups [22]. For example, three terrorist groups in Africa have been reported to share funds, training, and explosive materials with each other [27], and Chechen terrorists were reported to obtain weapons from terrorist organizations in the Middle East [19]. Such sharing of skills and resources among terrorist groups is common because it significantly increases their capability of achieving malicious goals, such as attacking high-value targets.

An important way to prevent individual terrorist groups from forming powerful coalitions is to cut off connections between them. This can be done by blocking their bank accounts, increasing surveillance of strategic exchange points, setting sentries in arterial roads, etc. However, since it is impractical to block all possible ways attackers can communicate, a central decision problem is to choose a subset of such connections to block so as to minimize expected efficacy of formed coalitions and resulting attacks. Addressing this problem entails several challenges: i) the set of possible combinations of edges to cut is exponential in the number of connections among attackers; ii) the number of possible coalitions to account for is exponential in the number of attackers; iii) coalition stability is an important consideration in assessing which coalitions will form, and it significantly increases problem difficulty; iv) the decision space of attackers includes the choice of targets to attack, which must also be accounted for by the defender.

While there is existing research on terrorist networks, it has been limited in scope to either social network analysis of terrorist groups [13, 29, 21, 12], or using cooperative game theory as a means for identifying key members of terrorist networks [17, 18]. The related research in security games, on the other hand, tends to model attackers as independent actors (indeed, only a single attack by a single attacker or group is typically considered) [30, 11, 31, 15, 32, 35, 10, 34, 33]. The ability and proclivity of attackers to form coalitions is thus largely ignored within the security games research.

To address the problem of optimally inhibiting formation of attack coalitions, we introduce a formal Coalitional Security Game (CSG) model. We show that the associated problem is MAX SNP-hard for the defender, indicating no polynomial time approximation scheme unless P=NP, and the decision problem is NP-hard for the attackers. To overcome the computational challenges, we develop a sophisticated branch and price algorithm, involving a novel combination of column generation and linear programming relaxation. Since the slave problem of column generation is formulated as a bilevel mixed-integer linear program (BMILP), we further improve the performance of the algorithm by using a novel linear relaxation approximation to reformulate the slave problem as an easily solvable single level MILP with formal constant factor approximation guarantee. Furthermore, we provide an interior-point stabilization to improve convergence properties of column generation by generating

Appears in: *Proceedings of the 15th International Conference on Autonomous Agents and Multiagent Systems (AAMAS 2016), J. Thangarajah, K. Tuyls, S. Marsella, C. Jonker (eds.), May 9–13, 2016, Singapore.*

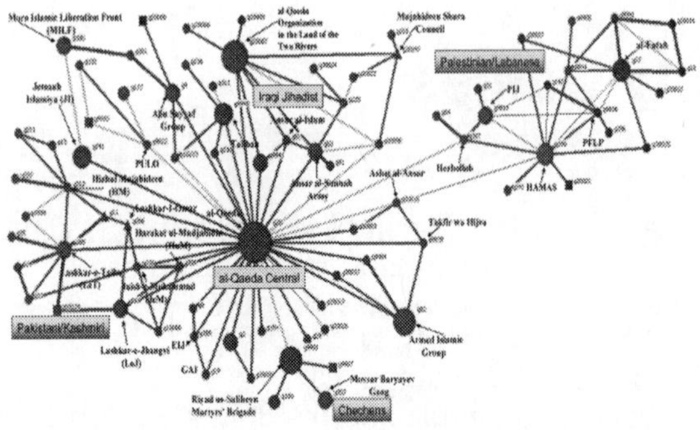

Figure 1: Mideast Terrorist Network [1].

an interior dual optimal solution of the master problem, and novel heuristics for generating multiple columns in each iteration to support the linear relaxation approximation and further speed up the column generation. Extensive experimental results show that our algorithms 1) provide orders of magnitude improvement in speed over the exact integer programming solution; 2) enable scalable high-quality approximation solutions of realistic CSG problem instances, outperforming existing classic heuristic search algorithms significantly; and 3) are remarkably robust against uncertainties of attackers' payoffs.

2. MOTIVATING DOMAIN

Cooperation among terrorist groups is common and necessary for their survival. During the past few decades, almost half of terrorist groups have had an ally [22]. Various kinds of cooperation are found among them, including transferring funds, weapons support, training, and other sharing of critical skills and resources. For example, the Al-Taqwa banking system financed the activities of multiple terrorist organizations, including Hamas [16]. Levitt [16] pointed out that there is significant overlap and cooperation between Palestinian terrorist groups like Hamas and other groups, such as al-Qaeda in the area of terrorist financing and logistical support. In 2000, Al-Qaeda held training camps which served as open universities, educating terrorists from a wide array of local and international terrorist groups [24]. Terrorist groups also cooperate with each other to coordinate attacks. For example, the Popular Resistance Committee (PRC) is a conglomeration of members of Islamic Jihad, Hamas and the various terrorist groups, and has conducted several infamous terrorist attacks, including the roadside bombing attack in February 14, 2002 [4].

Since cooperation among terrorist groups is achieved through communication channels, such as front companies, charities for transferring funds [16], and transportation hubs including roadways, ports, and rivers for weapon supply, training, and coordinated attacks, an important measure for preventing terrorist groups from forming coalitions is to cut off connections among them. For example, in 2003, FBI Assistant Director John Pistole testified to Congress that investigations into the financial activities of terrorist supporters in the United States helped prevent four different terrorist attacks abroad [23]. Moreover, the US strategy for combating terrorism asserts that *"The interconnected nature of terrorist organizations necessitates that we pursue them across the geographic spectrum to ensure that all linkages between the strong and the weak organizations are broken, leaving each of them isolated, exposed, and vulnerable to defeat"* [6].

In order to cut connections among terrorist groups, security agencies can shut down the front companies and charities, which are providing and transferring money for terrorist groups, to stem the flow of funds between terrorist groups [16]. Besides, blocking critical transportation hubs can significantly reduce efficiency of coordination attempts such as weapon support and terrorist training. Nevertheless, activities aimed at inhibiting communication among attackers, such as blocking roadways by setting sentries are costly, and it is infeasible to cut all the connections among terrorist groups. This motivates our investigation of optimal allocation of security resources to block attacker linkages, taking into account the associated costs, as well as the nature of coalitions that would form as a result.

3. COALITIONAL SECURITY GAMES

A *coalitional security game* (CSG) is modeled based on the *coalitional skill game* [2], and consists of T types of targets, each with a large number of copies, which is reasonable since there is a large pool of potential targets of terrorism around the world. There is a set N of terrorists (individuals or groups) who want to attack these targets. Each terrorist i has a set S_i of skills, and attacking a target of type $t \in T$ requires a set $S(t)$ of skills. Let $S = \bigcup_{i \in N} S_i$. We assume $S(t) \subseteq S$ for all $t \in T$ without loss of generality. Each type $t \in T$ has a value $p_t > 0$ for the terrorists. Typically, each terrorist i has a capacity $m_{is} \in \mathbb{N}$ for each of his skills $s \in S_i$, so that he can use s in at most m_{is} attacks. For example, a terrorist can provide weapons for a certain number of terrorist attacks.

The terrorists form coalitions to share skills to launch more attacks. Similar to existing work [18], we use a graph $G = (N, E)$ to represent the cooperation network of terrorists, where N is the set of terrorists and E is the set of edges representing connections between pairs of terrorists. We denote by (i, j) an edge connecting terrorists i and j. A set $C \subseteq N$ of terrorists can form into a coalition only when the *induced subgraph* $G_C = (C, E(C))$ is connected, where $E(C) = \{(i,j) \in E | i \in C, j \in C\}$. We use the set C to represent the coalition formed.

A terrorist coalition can choose multiple targets to attack simultaneously, so long as it possesses sufficient required skills and resources. For example, in 2008, a group of terrorists carried out a series of twelve coordinated shooting and bombing attacks in Mumbai [14], and in the September 11 attack, 4 airplanes were hijacked to attack several targets in 3 different cities. We model these types of threats through the definition of the value of a coalition. Formally, let $\mathbf{a} = \langle a_t \rangle$ be an attacking plan of a coalition C, where a_t is the number of targets of type t that coalition C plans to attack. An attacking plan $\mathbf{a}$ is feasible if

$$\sum\nolimits_{t \in T,\, s \in S(t)} a_t \leq \sum\nolimits_{i \in C,\, s \in S_i} m_{is}, \ \forall s \in S, \qquad (1)$$

The payoff $u(\mathbf{a})$ for an attacking plan $\mathbf{a}$ is the sum of values of all targets attacked, i.e., $u(\mathbf{a}) = \sum_t a_t p_t$. We assume that terrorists are utility-maximizers. Thus, once a coalition is formed, they choose an attack plan which maximizes payoff over all feasible plans.

$$v(C) = \max\nolimits_{\mathbf{a}:\ \text{satisfying Eq.(1)}} u(\mathbf{a}). \qquad (2)$$

The value $v(C)$ of a coalition C is defined as the maximum achievable payoff in Eq.(2). We use a payoff vector $\mathbf{y} = \langle y_i \rangle \geq \mathbf{0}$ to denote the payoff for each terrorist i. A payoff vector represents how the value of every coalition is divided among their members, so that for a coalition structure CS (i.e., a partition of N into disjoint coalitions) we require $\sum_{i \in C} y_i \leq v(C)$ for any $C \in CS$. The pair $(CS, \mathbf{y})$ is called an *outcome* of a coalitional game.

3.1 Stable Coalition Structure

Since the terrorists are self-interested and profit driven, we assume that a coalition structure CS formed by attackers must be stable in the sense that any subset of attackers has no (or little) incentive to break off into another coalition for higher payoff. To enforce coalition structure stability, we adopt the widely-used solution concept of ϵ-*core* [7].

DEFINITION 1 (**ϵ-core**). *The ϵ-core, for $\epsilon > 0$, is the set of all outcomes $(CS, \mathbf{y})$ such that for any coalition $C \subseteq N$, $\sum_{i \in C} y_i \geq v(C) - \epsilon$.*

Attackers always prefer the outcome in ϵ-core with as lower ϵ value as possible, and the minimal value ϵ^* for which the ϵ-core is non-empty is called the *least-core value* of the game, with the corresponding ϵ^*-core called the *least-core*. For a coalition structure CS, if there exists an outcome $(CS, \mathbf{y})$ in the least-core, we call CS a *stable coalition structure*. Although computing the least-core is extremely hard for general coalitional games [7], given the coalition value function v defined in Eq.(2), the coalitional game turns out to be *superadditive* (LEMMA 1). In this case, the attackers are willing to form as large coalitions as they can, and the coalition structure CS^*, whose induced subgraphs are all connected components, is a stable coalition structure (LEMMA 2).

LEMMA 1. *Given the value function defined in Eq.(2), the terrorists' coalitional game $G = (N, v)$ is superadditive, i.e., $v(C \cup D) \geq v(C) + v(D)$ for every pair of disjoint coalitions $C, D \subseteq N$.*

PROOF. For any pair of disjoint coalitions $C, D \subseteq N$, let $\mathbf{a}^C$ and $\mathbf{a}^D$ be the corresponding optimal attacking plans, and $v(C) = \sum_t a_t^C p_t$ and $v(D) = \sum_t a_t^D p_t$. For coalition $C \cup D$, the attacking plan $\mathbf{a}^{C \cup D}$, where $a_t^{C \cup D} = a_t^C + a_t^D$, is feasible since $\sum_{t \in T, s \in S(t)} (a_t^C + a_t^D) \leq \sum_{i \in C \cup D, s \in S_i} m_{is}$ $\forall s \in S$. Therefore, $v(C \cup D) \geq v(C) + v(D)$. $\square$

LEMMA 2. *The coalition structure consisting of all coalitions whose induced subgraphs are connected components of graph $G(N, E)$ is a stable coalition structure, and it has the maximum total value among all coalition structures.*

PROOF. Since a coalition cannot be formed by terrorists in different connected components of G, we can consider each connected component independently.

Let $G' = (N', E')$ be a connected component of G. Let $(CS, \mathbf{y})$ be an outcome of G' in the least-core. Now if all terrorists in G' forms into one coalition N' (i.e., the grand coalition whose induced subgraph is G'), we have $v(N') \geq \sum_{C \in CS} v(C)$ due to superadditivity. Therefore, we obtain a new outcome $(CS^*, \mathbf{y}^*) = (\{N'\}, \mathbf{y} + \frac{v(N') - \sum_{C \in CS} v(C)}{|N'|})$, such that $\mathbf{y}^* \succeq \mathbf{y}$ and $\sum_{i \in C} y_i^* \geq \sum_{i \in C} y_i \geq v(C) - \epsilon^* > 0$ for all $C \subseteq N'$. This means $(CS^*, \mathbf{y}^*)$ is in the least-core of G'. Obviously, CS^* has the maximum value since $v(N') \geq \sum_{C \in CS} v(C)$ holds for arbitrary CS. Applying the result to all connected components, we can obtain a stable coalition structure consisting of all coalitions whose induced subgraphs are connected components of G. $\square$

3.2 Defender Strategy

The defender's goal is to optimally cut off connections within terrorists to minimize threat due to attacks by formed coalitions. We use a symmetric matrix $\mathbf{B} = \langle B_{ij} \rangle$ to represent the defender's strategy, such that $B_{ij} = 1$ if edge (i, j) is blocked and $B_{ij} = 0$ otherwise. We let $B_{ii} = 0$ for all $i \in N$. Blocking an edge (i, j) incurs a cost, λ_{ij}. When the defender adopts strategy $\mathbf{B}$, the blocked edges are removed from the network, resulting in a new network $G(\mathbf{B}) = (N, E(\mathbf{B}))$ where $E(\mathbf{B}) = E \backslash \{(i, j) \in E | B_{ij} = 1\}$. Given $\mathbf{B}$, the attackers play a coalitional skill game on the induced graph $G(\mathbf{B}) = (N, E(\mathbf{B}))$, and form a coalition structure $CS^*(\mathbf{B})$ consisting of all coalitions whose induced subgraphs are connected components of $G(\mathbf{B})$. The defender's utility is then

$$U_d(\mathbf{B}) = -\sum_{C \in CS^*(\mathbf{B})} v(C) - \sum_{(i,j) \in E} B_{ij} \lambda_{ij}$$

4. COMPLEXITY ANALYSIS

We first investigate the computational complexity of finding the optimal strategies for both the defender and the attackers, and show that the defender's and the attackers' decision-making problems are MAX SNP-hard and NP-hard respectively.

4.1 Defender's Decision-Making Problem

We reduce the *k-TERMINAL CUT* problem [8], whose MAX SNP-hardness has been proved for any fixed $k \geq 3$, to the defender's decision-making problem by a *linear reduction* which preserves the approximation property (MAX SNP-hardness) [20]. The following definitions will be useful to introduce our key result (THEOREM 1).

DEFINITION 2 (**k-TERMINAL CUT**). *Given a graph $G = (N, E)$, a set $H = \{h_1, \cdots, h_k\}$ of k specified vertices or terminals, and a positive weight w_{ij} for each edge $(i, j) \in E$, find a minimum weight set of edges $E^* \subseteq E$ such that the removal of E^* from E disconnects each terminal from all the other terminals.*

DEFINITION 3 (**Linear reduction**). *Let A and B be two optimization problems (either maximization or minimization). We say that A linearly reduces to B if there are two polynomial time algorithms f and g and constants α, $\beta > 0$ such that:*

1. *Given an instance a of A, algorithm f produces an instance $b = f(a)$ of B such that the cost (objective value) of an optimal solution for b, opt(b), is at most $\alpha \cdot$ opt(a).*

2. *Given a, $b = f(a)$, and any solution y of b, algorithm g produces a solution x of a such that $|cost(x) - opt(a)| \leq \beta |cost(y) - opt(b)|$, where $cost(x)$ and $cost(y)$ refer to the objective values of x and y.*

THEOREM 1. *Finding an optimal defender strategy for a coalitional security game is MAX SNP-hard.*

PROOF. W.l.o.g, we apply linear reduction to reduce 3-TERMINAL CUT problem to the defender's decision-making problem. Let a and b be instances of 3-TERMINAL

CUT and defender's decision-making problem respectively. Let E' and $\mathbf{B}$ be solutions for a and b correspondingly, and $opt(a)$, $opt(b)$ are costs of the optimal solutions for a and b respectively, i.e., the costs of optimal cuts E^* and optimal defender strategy $\mathbf{B}^*$. We first present a polynomial time algorithm f to reduce 3-TERMINAL CUT to defender's decision-making problem. Here for any input instance $a = \langle G, H, w\rangle$, f outputs an instance b of defender's decision-making problem with the following components.

1. G as the cooperation network, and N (nodes of G) as the set of terrorists. The blocking cost λ_{ij} of edge $(i,j) \in E$ equals to w_{ij}.

2. $S = \{s_1, s_2, s_3, s_4\}$ as the skill set; $S_{h_1} = \{s_1, s_4\}$, $S_{h_2} = \{s_2, s_4\}$ and $S_{h_3} = \{s_3, s_4\}$ as skills for terrorists h_1, h_2 and h_3 who are referred to as the *terminal attackers*; $S_i = \{s_4\}$ as skill for all the other terrorists $i \notin \{h_1, h_2, h_3\}$; and $m_{is} = 1$ for all $i \in N$, $s \in S$.

3. A set T of four target types $\{t_1, t_2, t_3, t_4\}$ with $S(t_1) = \{s_1, s_2, s_4\}$, $S(t_2) = \{s_1, s_3, s_4\}$, $S(t_3) = \{s_2, s_3, s_4\}$ and $S(t_4) = \{s_1, s_2, s_3, s_4\}$; $p_1 = p_2 = p_3 = M > W_{max} \cdot |E|$ and $p_4 = 2M$ where $W_{max} = \max_{(i,j)\in E} \lambda_{ij}$.

Obviously, f reduces a to b in polynomial time. For a given defender strategy $\mathbf{B}$, the cost (defender's total loss) is $cost(\mathbf{B}) = \sum_{(i,j)\in E} w_{ij} B_{ij} + \widetilde{F}_{\mathbf{B}}$, where $\widetilde{F}_{\mathbf{B}} = 0$ if any pair of terminal attackers are not connected under $\mathbf{B}$, $\widetilde{F}_{\mathbf{B}} = M$ if any two terminal attackers are connected while the rest one is disconnected to both of them, and $\widetilde{F}_{\mathbf{B}} = 2M$ if all three terminals are connected. Then we can have a polynomial time algorithm g, which simply constructs a solution $E' = \{(i,j) | B_{ij} = 1\}$ for a from the solution $\mathbf{B}$ of $b = f(a)$.

Next, we will show that there exists a constant α such that $opt(b)$, is at most $\alpha \cdot opt(a)$. Let the optimal solution of a be E^*, i.e., $opt(a) = \sum_{(i,j)\in E^*} w_{ij}$. Let $\mathbf{B}^*$ be a solution of b, such that $B^*_{ij} = 1$ if $(i,j) \in E^*$, and $B^*_{ij} = 0$ otherwise. We show by contradiction that $\mathbf{B}^*$ is optimal for b.

Suppose the optimal defender strategy is another one $\mathbf{B}$. We have $cost(\mathbf{B}^*) - cost(\mathbf{B}) = \sum_{(i,j)\in E} w_{ij}(B^*_{ij} - B_{ij}) - \widetilde{F}_{\mathbf{B}}$ since $\widetilde{F}_{\mathbf{B}^*} = 0$. If $\widetilde{F}_{\mathbf{B}} = 0$, which means that any two terminals are not connected under $\mathbf{B}$, then according to the fact that E^* is the minimum weight set of edges such that the removal of them disconnects each terminal from all the others, we have $cost(\mathbf{B}^*) - cost(\mathbf{B}) = \sum_{(i,j)\in E} w_{ij}(B^*_{ij} - B_{ij}) \leq 0$, which means that $\mathbf{B}^*$ is optimal. Otherwise, $\widetilde{F}_{\mathbf{B}} \neq 0$, we have $\widetilde{F}_{\mathbf{B}} \geq M > W_{max} \cdot |E|$. It follows that $cost(\mathbf{B}^*) - cost(\mathbf{B}) < \sum_{(i,j)\in E} w_{ij} B^*_{ij} - W_{max} \cdot |E| \leq 0$, which contradicts that $\mathbf{B}$ is optimal. We conclude that $\mathbf{B}^*$ is optimal to b. Therefore, $\alpha = 1$ is a satisfying constant.

Finally, when $\beta = 1$, $|cost(E') - opt(a)| \leq |cost(E') + \widetilde{F}_{\mathbf{B}} - opt(a)| = \beta |cost(\mathbf{B}) - opt(b)|$ holds for any $\mathbf{B}$. We conclude that the transformation is a linear reduction, and the defender's decision-making problem is MAX SNP-hard. □

Theorem 1 indicates that computing an optimal defender strategy does not admit a polynomial time approximation scheme unless P=NP. Indeed, what makes the defender's problem particularly challenging is the fact that the attacker's problem is hard as well, as we will demonstrate later.

4.2 Attackers' Decision-Making Problem

For a given coalition C, the attackers' decision-making problem of choosing the optimal attacking plan $\mathbf{a}$ is NP-hard, as the following theorem asserts.

THEOREM 2. *Computing the attackers' optimal attacking plan is NP-hard.*

PROOF. We reduce EXACT-COVER, an NP-complete problem, to coalition's decision-making problem. The EXACT-COVER is defined as follows: Given a finite set Q and a collection CQ of subsets of Q, does CQ contain an exact cover for Q, i.e., a subcollection $CQ' \subseteq CQ$ such that every element in Q occurs in exactly one member of CQ'?

The reduction can be done as follows. First, let the set of skills $S = Q$, and the number of attackers $|C| = |Q|$. For each attacker i, let $S_i = \{s_i\}$. For each member $Q_j \in CQ$, we assign a target t_j into T with $S(t_j) = \{s_i | q_i \in Q_j\}$, where q_i is the i-th element of Q, with value $p_j = |S(t_j)|$. Let $m_{is} = 1$ for any attacker i and skill s.

Next, we show that the optimal attacking plan $\mathbf{a}$ satisfies $u(\mathbf{a}) \geq |Q|$ iff EXACT-COVER has a "yes" solution.

If direction: If there exists a "yes" solution to EXACT-COVER and CQ^* is the corresponding exact cover of Q, then the attacking plan $\mathbf{a}$, where $a_j = 1$ when $Q_j \in CQ^*$, and $a_j = 0$ otherwise, satisfies $u(\mathbf{a}) \geq |Q|$ since $u(\mathbf{a}) = \sum_j a_j p_j = \sum_{Q_j \in CQ^*} |S(t_j)| = |Q|$.

Only if direction: The attacker has an optimal attacking plan $\mathbf{a}$ satisfying $u(\mathbf{a}) \geq |Q|$ only if EXACT-COVER has a "yes" solution. According to Eq.(1), any attacking plan $\mathbf{a}$ attacking two targets t', t'' such that $S(t') \cap S(t'') \neq \emptyset$ is not feasible since $a_{t'} + a_{t''} > \sum_{i\in C, s\in S_i} m_{is} = 1$ for $s \in S(t')$ and $s \in S(t'')$. Thus $u(\mathbf{a}) < |Q|$ holds for any feasible attacking plan if CQ has no exact cover for Q.

Therefore, we conclude that computing the optimal plan $\mathbf{a}$ for attackers is NP-hard. □

Despite these rather negative results, we nevertheless undertake the task of devising a method for computing optimal CSG solutions, showing the challenges can be overcome for realistic problem instances, even if not in the worst case.

5. SOLUTION APPROACH

We now turn to the computational issues in CSGs. We first propose an *integer program* (IP) to solve it exactly. Because the IP has an exponentially many variables, we propose a *branch and price* algorithm to tackle it.

5.1 Coalition Enumeration Approach

We start with the IP computing the optimal solution. Suppose $\mathcal{C}$ is the set of all coalitions for which the induced subgraphs on $G = (N, E)$ are connected, and $C_k \in \mathcal{C}$ is the kth coalition in $\mathcal{C}$ with coalition value denoted by v_k. Let $\alpha_{ki} = 1$ if $i \in C_k$ and $\alpha_{ki} = 0$ otherwise. Let the binary variables $\mathbf{x}$ represent the attackers' strategy of forming a coalition structure CS, such that $x_k = 1$ iff $C_k \in CS$. If we suppose that all coalitions in $\mathcal{C}$ as well as their associated values have been precomputed, the defender's optimization problem can be formulated as the following integer program, with the objective of minimizing the defender's loss and Eqs.(3b)–(3c) restricting the stable coalition structure:

$$\min_{\mathbf{x},\mathbf{B}} \quad \sum\nolimits_{C_k\in\mathcal{C}} v_k x_k + \sum\nolimits_{(i,j)\in E} B_{ij}\lambda_{ij} \qquad (3a)$$

$$\text{s.t.} \quad \sum_{C_k \in \mathcal{C}} \alpha_{ki} x_k = 1 \qquad i \in N \qquad (3b)$$

$$\sum_{C_k \in \mathcal{C}} \alpha_{ki}\alpha_{kj} x_k \geq 1 - B_{ij} \quad (i,j) \in E \quad (3c)$$

$$\mathbf{x} \in \{0,1\}^{|\mathcal{C}|}, \mathbf{B} \in \{0,1\}^{|N| \times |N|} \qquad (3d)$$

Eq.(3b) ensures that each attacker is in exactly one coalition, so that CS denoted by $\mathbf{x}$ is a partition of N. Eq.(3c) means that once an edge $(i,j) \in E$ is not blocked by the defender, i.e., $B_{ij} = 0$, then i and j must be in the same coalition of CS. Let $\mathcal{C}_{\mathbf{B}}$ be the set of coalitions whose induced subgraphs are connected components of $G(\mathbf{B})$. According to Eqs.(3b)–(3c), for a feasible solution $\mathbf{x}$, $x_k = 1$ if and only if $C_k \in \mathcal{C}_{\mathbf{B}}$ or C_k is a superset of several coalitions in $\mathcal{C}_{\mathbf{B}}$. With the superadditive coalition's value and the minimizing objective, the solution $\mathbf{x}$ with $x_k = 1$ for $C_k \in \mathcal{C}_{\mathbf{B}}$ is always optimal for a fixed defender strategy $\mathbf{B}$, corresponding with LEMMA 2. Although IP (3) can obtain the optimal defender strategy $\mathbf{B}^*$, it has exponentially many ($|\mathcal{C}| + |E|$) variables, which makes it impossible to scale up to large game instances with standard *branch and cut* method adopted by popular commercial solvers, such as CPLEX. Therefore, we propose a *branch and price* framework, which combines *branch and bound* and *column generation*.

5.2 Branch and Price Framework

Before we introduce our branch and price framework, the following lemma shows that the exponentially large number of binary variables $\mathbf{x}$ in IP (3) can be relaxed without sacrificing optimality (note that $\mathbf{B}$ remains to be binary). This observation will be useful to significantly reduce the size of the branch and bound tree.

LEMMA 3. *The formulation* (3) *is equivalent to its relaxed formulation where* $\mathbf{x}$ *is continuous.*[1]

Figure 2 shows the flow of the branch and price framework. The left part of the figure shows the classic branch and bound tree of solving IP (3) (with $\mathbf{x}$ being relaxed), where the root node in the tree corresponds to the IP (3) and it keeps an *upper bound* (**UB**) on its optimal objective, which can be the objective value of any feasible solution of IP (3). For each created node (an integer program), a *lower bound* (**LB**) is obtained by further relaxing variable $\mathbf{B}$. We refer to the fully relaxed formulation LP relaxation, and denote by $\tilde{\mathbf{B}}^*$ its optimal solution. Two basic operators in branch and bound are *pruning* and *branching*. A node is pruned once its **LB** is not less than **UB** or $\tilde{\mathbf{B}}^*$ is integral. Otherwise, the branching operator will be conducted on a fractional variable B_{ij} in $\tilde{\mathbf{B}}^*$, and two child nodes will be created, one by fixing B_{ij} to 0 and the other with $B_{ij} = 1$. Once a node happens to obtain an **LB** with $\tilde{\mathbf{B}}^*$ being integral, the **UB** of root node will be updated as **UB** $= \min\{\mathbf{LB}, \mathbf{UB}\}$. The method terminates when all leaf nodes are pruned, and the final **UB** of root node will be equal to the optimum of IP (3).

Since the LP relaxation of each node in the branch and bound tree has an exponential number of variables, we use column generation to iteratively compute **LB** and $\tilde{\mathbf{B}}^*$ as illustrated by the right part of the Figure 2. Column generation begins by a master LP with a small subset of variables, and solves the slave problem to add new column(s) or variable(s) with negative reduced cost(s) to the master LP, then

[1]Please see online Appendix A for the proof of LEMMA 3 available at: `http://www.ntu.edu.sg/home/boan/papers/AAMAS16_Coalition_Appendix.pdf`

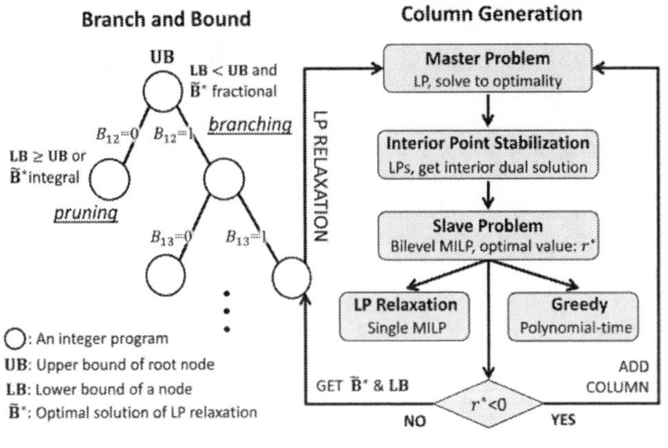

Figure 2: Branch and Price Framework.

resolves the master LP, repeating until no such column(s) exists. The column generation approach terminates with the optimal relaxed solution $\tilde{\mathbf{B}}^*$.

The central challenge and novelty of any column generation approach is how to efficiently compute which columns to add, and to guarantee that when this computation adds no new columns, the solution is optimal. The issues involved in adapting a column generation method to our setting are sufficiently non-trivial as to warrant a separate section.

6. COLUMN GENERATION

The LP relaxation at each node in Figure 2 is decomposed into *master* and *slave* problems for column generation. The former solves for the relaxed defender strategy $\tilde{\mathbf{B}}$, given a restricted set of coalitions $\mathcal{C}' \subset \mathcal{C}$. The objective for the slave is updated based on the solution of the master, and the slave is solved to identify the best new coalition to be added to the $\mathcal{C}'$ of the master problem, as measured by *reduced cost* (explained later). If no new column can improve the solution the algorithm terminates with an optimal solution.

6.1 Master Problem

The master problem (4) starts with a small set of coalitions $\mathcal{C}'$ and solves for the optimal relaxed defender strategy $\tilde{\mathbf{B}}^*$. Note that Eqs.(4a)-(4c) have ensured $\mathbf{x} \leq \mathbf{1}$ and $\tilde{\mathbf{B}} \leq \mathbf{1}$.

$$\min_{\mathbf{x}, \tilde{\mathbf{B}}} \quad \sum_{C_k \in \mathcal{C}'} v_k x_k + \sum_{(i,j) \in E} \tilde{B}_{ij} \lambda_{ij} \qquad (4a)$$

$$\text{s.t.} \quad \sum_{C_k \in \mathcal{C}'} \alpha_{ki} x_k = 1 \qquad i \in N \qquad (4b)$$

$$\sum_{C_k \in \mathcal{C}'} \alpha_{ki}\alpha_{kj} x_k \geq 1 - \tilde{B}_{ij} \quad (i,j) \in E \quad (4c)$$

$$\mathbf{x} \geq \mathbf{0}, \tilde{\mathbf{B}} \geq \mathbf{0} \qquad (4d)$$

Let $\mathbf{f}$ and $\mathbf{g}$ be dual variables of master constraints (4b) and (4c) respectively. After the master problem is solved, the optimal dual solution $(\mathbf{f}^*, \mathbf{g}^*)$ is computed and passed to the slave problem for finding the column (coalition) to add to the current $\mathcal{C}'$, as we will discuss later.

Interior Point Stabilization. Before the slave problem is introduced, it is necessary to understand that the optimal dual solution $(\mathbf{f}^*, \mathbf{g}^*)$ plays a critical role in generating a good column. Since the standard technique computes an optimal dual solution, which is an extreme point of the optimal dual polyhedron and can be characterized by very large values for some dual variables, an *Interior Point Stabilization* (IPS) method [26] is adopted to compute an optimal dual solution taking values in the center (or at least the interior) of the master problem's optimal dual polyhedron by averaging several extreme points of this polyhedron.

The basic idea of IPS is as follows: once the master problem is solved and the optimal solution $(\mathbf{x}^*, \tilde{\mathbf{B}}^*)$ is obtained, we can depict a polyhedron $\mathcal{D}$ of the dual master problem confined by the complementary slackness conditions [5]. To obtain an extreme point of $\mathcal{D}$, we can simply define a random objective function $\boldsymbol{\mu}^T\mathbf{f} + \boldsymbol{\omega}^T\mathbf{g}$ where $\boldsymbol{\mu}, \boldsymbol{\omega} \sim U(0,1)$, i.e., each element of $\boldsymbol{\mu}$ and $\boldsymbol{\omega}$ is uniformly distributed between 0 and 1, and solve the corresponding LP: $(\mathcal{D}^{\boldsymbol{\mu},\boldsymbol{\omega}}) = \min_{(\mathbf{f},\mathbf{g})\in\mathcal{D}} \boldsymbol{\mu}^T\mathbf{f} + \boldsymbol{\omega}^T\mathbf{g}$. After solving several instances of $(\mathcal{D}^{\boldsymbol{\mu},\boldsymbol{\omega}})$ with multiple random objective coefficients $(\boldsymbol{\mu}, \boldsymbol{\omega})$, we can get some extreme points of $\mathcal{D}$. Taking the average of these extreme points provides an interior point of $\mathcal{D}$ that gives much more centered dual values. For the ease of reading, we provide the details of IPS in online Appendix B[1].

6.2 Slave Problem

The slave problem finds the best column (i.e., coalition) to add to the current coalitions in $\mathcal{C}'$. This is done using *reduced cost*, which captures the total change in the defender's utility if a candidate coalition is added to $\mathcal{C}'$. The candidate coalition with minimum reduced cost improves the defender's utility most [5]. The reduced cost r_k of coalition C_k, associated with variable x_k, is given in Eq.(5), where the dual solution $(\mathbf{f}^*, \mathbf{g}^*)$ measures the influence of the associated constraint on the objective and can be calculated using standard techniques or the IPS method.

$$r_k = v_k - \sum_{i\in N} \alpha_{ki} f_i^* - \sum_{(i,j)\in E} \alpha_{ki}\alpha_{kj} g_{ij}^* \qquad (5)$$

The slave problem then boils down to solving $\min_k r_k$ (i.e., minimizing reduced cost). Clearly, if we were to simply iterate through all coalitions k (of which there are an exponential number), nothing would be gained by column generation. We then exploit the structure of this problem by first formulating the reduced cost minimization problem as a *bilevel mixed-integer linear program* (BMILP) (6), where $(\mathbf{f}^*, \mathbf{g}^*)$ is the optimal dual solution of the master problem (4). What makes this problem bilevel is the fact that, in minimizing reduced cost, we must also compute the value of an associated coalition, since we have avoided precomputing all coalitions' values with branch and price.

In the BMILP (6), the coalition C is represented by binary variable $\boldsymbol{\alpha}$ such that $\alpha_i = 1$ if $i \in C$ and $\alpha_i = 0$ otherwise. The upper level constraints ensure that the coalition C induced a connected subgraph, i.e., $C \in \mathcal{C}$, while the lower level program computes the coalition value $v(C)$.

Eq.(6b) ensures that $\xi_{ij} = \alpha_i\alpha_j$ for edge $(i,j) \in E$. Eqs.(6c)–(6f) enforce $\boldsymbol{\alpha}$ to induce a connected subgraph of G using flow balance techniques [28]: According to constraints (6c) and (6d), $w_i = 1$ if and only if i is the smallest index such that $\alpha_i = 1$, which will be set as the starting point of the flows $\mathbf{h}^+$ and $\mathbf{h}^-$; h_{lij}^+ denotes the amount of flow from starting point to ending point l, such that passes through edge (i,j) in positive direction $i \to j$, while h_{lij}^- in negative direction $j \to i$; Eq.(6f) restricts the flow to pass through only edges that are in the subgraph induced by C, i.e., (i,j) with $\xi_{ij} = 1$; Eq.(6e) is the flow balance constraint with $\mathcal{N}(i)$ denoting the set of vertices connected with i, making sure there exists a path, in subgraph induced by C, from starting point $i : w_i = 1$ to any $l \in C$ $(\alpha_l = 1)$. Therefore the subgraph induced by C is restricted to be connected.

The lower level program (6g) computes the coalition's value $v(C)$ where Eq.(6h) restricts C to have enough skill capacities to conduct the attacking plan $\mathbf{a}$ according to Eq.(1).

$$\min_{\substack{\boldsymbol{\alpha},\boldsymbol{\xi},\mathbf{w}\\ \mathbf{h}^+,\mathbf{h}^-}} \quad \sum_{t\in T} p_t a_t - \mathbf{f}^{*\mathbf{T}}\boldsymbol{\alpha} - \mathbf{g}^{*\mathbf{T}}\boldsymbol{\xi} \qquad (6a)$$

$$\text{s.t.} \quad \xi_{ij} \le \alpha_i, \xi_{ij} \le \alpha_j,$$

$$\xi_{ij} \ge \alpha_i + \alpha_j - 1 \quad \forall (i,j) \in E \qquad (6b)$$

$$w_i \le \alpha_i,$$

$$w_i \le 1 - \alpha_j \quad \forall i,j \in N : j < i \qquad (6c)$$

$$\sum_{i\in N} w_i = 1 \qquad (6d)$$

$$\sum_{j\in\mathcal{N}(i)} h_{lij}^+ - \sum_{j\in\mathcal{N}(i)} h_{lij}^- \ge$$

$$w_i - (1 - \alpha_l), \quad \forall i,l \in N : i \ne l \qquad (6e)$$

$$h_{lij}^+ \le \xi_{ij},$$

$$h_{lij}^- \le \xi_{ij}, \quad \forall (i,j) \in E, l \in N \qquad (6f)$$

$$\max_{\mathbf{a}} \quad \sum_{t\in T} p_t a_t \qquad (6g)$$

$$\text{s.t.} \quad \sum_{t\in T} \beta_{ts} a_t \le \sum_{i\in N} \alpha_i \gamma_{is} m_{is} \quad s \in S \qquad (6h)$$

$$\boldsymbol{\alpha} \in \{0,1\}^{|N|}, \boldsymbol{\xi} \in [0,1]^{|E|}, \mathbf{a} \in \mathbb{N}^{|T|}$$

$$\mathbf{h}^+ \ge \mathbf{0}, \mathbf{h}^- \ge \mathbf{0}, \mathbf{w} \ge \mathbf{0}. \qquad (6i)$$

The key challenge of the BMILP is that the inner maximization program described in (6g) has integer variables. If we were to relax the integrality constraint, we could reformulate the bilevel program into a single mixed integer linear program, as we describe next.

Linear Relaxation Approximation. To reformulate the BMILP to an MILP, we first relax the integer program (6g) of computing the coalition's value in the lower level, such that the decision variable $\mathbf{a} \in \mathbb{N}^{|T|}$ is relaxed to $\tilde{\mathbf{a}} \ge \mathbf{0}$. For this relaxed linear program (RLP), let $\mathbf{u}$ be the dual variable associated with constraint (6h). A pair of feasible solutions $\tilde{\mathbf{a}}$ and $\mathbf{u}$ are optimal for the primal and dual RLPs if and only if the following *complementary slackness conditions* are satisfied [5]:

$$\Big(\sum_{s\in S} \beta_{ts} u_s - p_t\Big) \cdot \tilde{a}_t = 0 \quad \forall t \in T \qquad (7a)$$

$$\Big(\sum_{i\in N} \alpha_i \gamma_{is} m_{is} - \sum_{t\in T} \beta_{ts} \tilde{a}_t\Big) \cdot u_s = 0 \quad \forall s \in S \qquad (7b)$$

Therefore, the RLP is equivalent with a set of constraints consisting of the primal and dual constraints restricting the feasibility of $\tilde{\mathbf{a}}$ and $\mathbf{u}$ and the complementary slackness conditions ensuring optimality, and the relaxed BMILP is reformulated as an MILP (8), with Eq.(8c) corresponding to the dual constraint of the RLP, and Eqs.(8d)–(8e) equivalent with the complementary slackness conditions (7). Our next results show that the solution quality of the linear relaxation approximation and, consequently, the resulting branch and price framework, provably achieves a competitive ratio which only depends on the number of skills $|S|$ (which we assume to be constant).

$$\min_{\substack{\boldsymbol{\alpha},\boldsymbol{\xi},\mathbf{w},\mathbf{u},\boldsymbol{\phi}\\ \mathbf{h}^+,\mathbf{h}^-,\tilde{\mathbf{a}},\boldsymbol{\varphi}}} \quad \sum_{t\in T} p_t \tilde{a}_t - \mathbf{f}^{*\mathbf{T}}\boldsymbol{\alpha} - \mathbf{g}^{*\mathbf{T}}\boldsymbol{\xi} \qquad (8a)$$

$$
\begin{aligned}
\text{s.t.}\quad & \text{Eqs.(6b)–(6f), (6h)–(6i)} && \text{(8b)}\\
& \sum\nolimits_{s \in S} \beta_{ts} u_s \geq p_t, \quad \forall t \in T && \text{(8c)}\\
& \sum\nolimits_{i \in N} \alpha_i \gamma_{is} m_{is} - \sum\nolimits_{t \in T} \beta_{ts} \tilde{a}_t \leq M(1-\phi_s),\\
& u_s \leq M\phi_s \quad \forall s \in S && \text{(8d)}\\
& \sum\nolimits_{s \in S} \beta_{ts} u_s - p_t \leq M(1-\varphi_t),\\
& \tilde{a}_t \leq M\varphi_t \quad \forall t \in T && \text{(8e)}\\
& \tilde{\mathbf{a}} \geq \mathbf{0}, \mathbf{u} \geq \mathbf{0}\\
& \phi \in \{0,1\}^{|S|}, \varphi \in \{0,1\}^{|T|}. && \text{(8f)}
\end{aligned}
$$

LEMMA 4. *The coalition value $\tilde{v}(C)$ computed by LP relaxation of IP* (6g) *is bounded by $\tilde{v}(C) \leq (1+|S|)v(C)$.*

PROOF. We first prove the following fact: For the LP relaxation of IP (6g), if the optimal solution $\tilde{\mathbf{a}}^*$ has a fractional value $\tilde{a}_t^* > 0$ for some target type t, then $v(C) \geq p_t$. The idea is that since the coalition has integer capacities for all skills, if $\tilde{a}_t^* > 0$, the coalition's capacity for any skill $s \in S(t)$, which is necessary for attacking target of type t, should be larger than 0, i.e., at least 1. Therefore, the coalition can at least attack one target of type t and $v(C) \geq p_t$.

With the above fact, there are two cases to take into consideration for proving this LEMMA.

Case 1: $v(C) = 0$. In this case, for any target type $t \in T$, there must exist (at least) a necessary skill $s^t \in S(t)$ such that C's capacity of s^t (i.e., $\sum_{i \in N} \alpha_i \gamma_{is} m_{is}$) is 0. For LP relaxation of IP (6g), any fractional solution $\tilde{a}$ with $\tilde{a}_t > 0$ is infeasible for violating the skill capacity constraint (6h) of skill s^t: $\sum_{t \in T} \beta_{ts^t} \tilde{a}_t \leq 0$. Thus $\tilde{v}(C) = v(C) = 0$.

Case 2: $v(C) > 0$. Let $\mathbf{a}^*$ be the optimal integer solution for IP (6g), and $\tilde{\mathbf{a}}^*$ be the optimal fractional integer solution for LP relaxation of IP (6g). According to the property of multidimensional knapsack problem [25], $\tilde{\mathbf{a}}^*$ can take fractional values in at most $|S|$ coordinates. Therefore, suppose p_{max} be the largest value among all target types t with $\tilde{a}_t^*$ fractional, we have: $\tilde{v}(C) = v(\tilde{\mathbf{a}}^*) = v(\lfloor \tilde{\mathbf{a}}^* \rfloor) + v(\tilde{\mathbf{a}}^{\mathbf{f}}) \leq v(\mathbf{a}^*) + |S| p_{max}$, where $\tilde{\mathbf{a}}^{\mathbf{f}} = \tilde{\mathbf{a}}^* - \lfloor \tilde{\mathbf{a}}^* \rfloor$ is the residual part of $\tilde{\mathbf{a}}^*$ after rounding. Since $v(C) = v(\mathbf{a}^*) \geq p_{max}$ according to the fact proved before, we have: $\tilde{v}(C) \leq (1+|S|)v(C)$.

To this end, we conclude that $\tilde{v}(C) \leq (1+|S|)v(C)$. □

THEOREM 3. *The branch and price approach, in which the slave problem of column generation is solved by the linear relaxation approximation, can obtain a defender strategy $\mathbf{B}'$ such that $U_d(\mathbf{B}') \geq (1+|S|)U_d(\mathbf{B}^*)$. Note that $U_d(\mathbf{B}) \leq 0$.*

PROOF. The branch and price approach, in which the slave problem of column generation is solved by linear relaxation approximation, can obtain the optimal solution $\mathbf{B}'$ for the following revised program of IP (3) in which $\tilde{v}_k$ is the value of C_k computed by LP relaxation of IP (6g):

$$
\begin{aligned}
\min_{\mathbf{x},\mathbf{B}}\quad & \sum\nolimits_{C_k \in \mathcal{C}} \tilde{v}_k x_k + \sum\nolimits_{(i,j) \in E} B_{ij} \lambda_{ij} && \text{(9a)}\\
\text{s.t.}\quad & \text{Eqs. (3b)–(3d)} && \text{(9b)}
\end{aligned}
$$

Since $\mathbf{B}'$ is optimal for IP (9), we have:

$$
\begin{aligned}
-U_d(\mathbf{B}') &= \sum\nolimits_{C \in CS^*(\mathbf{B}')} v(C) + \sum\nolimits_{(i,j) \in E} B'_{ij} \lambda_{ij}\\
&\leq \sum\nolimits_{C \in CS^*(\mathbf{B}')} \tilde{v}(C) + \sum\nolimits_{(i,j) \in E} B'_{ij} \lambda_{ij}\\
&\leq \sum\nolimits_{C \in CS^*(\mathbf{B}^*)} \tilde{v}(C) + \sum\nolimits_{(i,j) \in E} B^*_{ij} \lambda_{ij}\\
&\leq (1+|S|)\Big(\sum\nolimits_{C \in CS^*(\mathbf{B}^*)} v(C) + \sum\nolimits_{(i,j) \in E} B^*_{ij} \lambda_{ij}\Big).
\end{aligned}
$$

Therefore, we have $U_d(\mathbf{B}') \geq (1+|S|)U_d(\mathbf{B}^*)$. □

Greedy Approximation. Although the MILP of linear relaxation approximation can obtain an approximately-optimal coalition to add to $\mathcal{C}'$ of master problem, it is still relatively slow. Observe, however, that in each iteration of column generation we actually need not find a minimal reduced cost; rather, any reduced cost that improves solution quality would suffice. Consequently, a fast heuristic approach for generating columns would be satisfactory in most iterations, except when the heuristic is unable to find a solution improving column, at which point we can fall back on the MILP. To this end, we propose a Greedy with Multi-Start (GMS) heuristic (see Algorithm 1). This heuristic is fast, and has an important advantage of enabling generation of multiple coalitions in a single iteration of the column generation algorithm (hence, the name multi-start), significantly reducing the number of column generation iterations.

Algorithm 1: Greedy with Multi-Start (GMS)

Input: optimal dual solution $(\mathbf{f}^*, \mathbf{g}^*)$ of master problem, reduced cost function $r(C)$ defined in Eq.(5)
Output: a set of coalitions with negative reduced costs

```
C_GMS = ∅;
for i ∈ N do
    C = {i}, continue = true;
    while continue do
        î = arg min_{i∈N\C} r(C ∪ {i}) − r(C);
        if r(C ∪ {î}) − r(C) < 0 then C ← C ∪ {î};
        else continue = false;
    if r(C) < 0 then C_GMS ← C_GMS ∪ {C};
return C_GMS;
```

7. EXPERIMENTAL EVALUATION

We demonstrate the effectiveness of our algorithmic framework through extensive numerical evaluations. We use the CPLEX (version 12.6) to solve all linear programs. All computations were performed on a 64-bit PC with 16 GB RAM and a quad-core 3.4 GHz processor. All values are averaged over 40 instances unless otherwise specified. All scale-free graphs are generated by standard Barabási-Albert model [3] widely used for simulating networks with realistic topological properties, denoted by $BA(d)$, in which d represents the average node degree. All random graphs are generated by standard Erdős-Rényi model denoted by $ER(p)$ where p represents the probability of existence of an edge between any pair of nodes [9]. According to the different approaches adopted for the slave problem, the abbreviations of different branch and price algorithms are as follows: LR for *Linear Relaxation Approximation*, GLR for the combination of the GMS with LR such that LR is called only when GMS returns empty set; The optimal dual solution of the master problem is generated through *Interior Point Stabilization* (IPS) for IGMS, ILR, and IGLR. IP (3) is represented by EXACT. Our benchmark is a heuristic algorithm *Genetic Algorithm* (GA), and for the ease of reading, we put the details of GA in online Appendix C[1]. By default, the instances are parameterized as follows: $|T| = 10$ and $|S| = 20$, the necessary

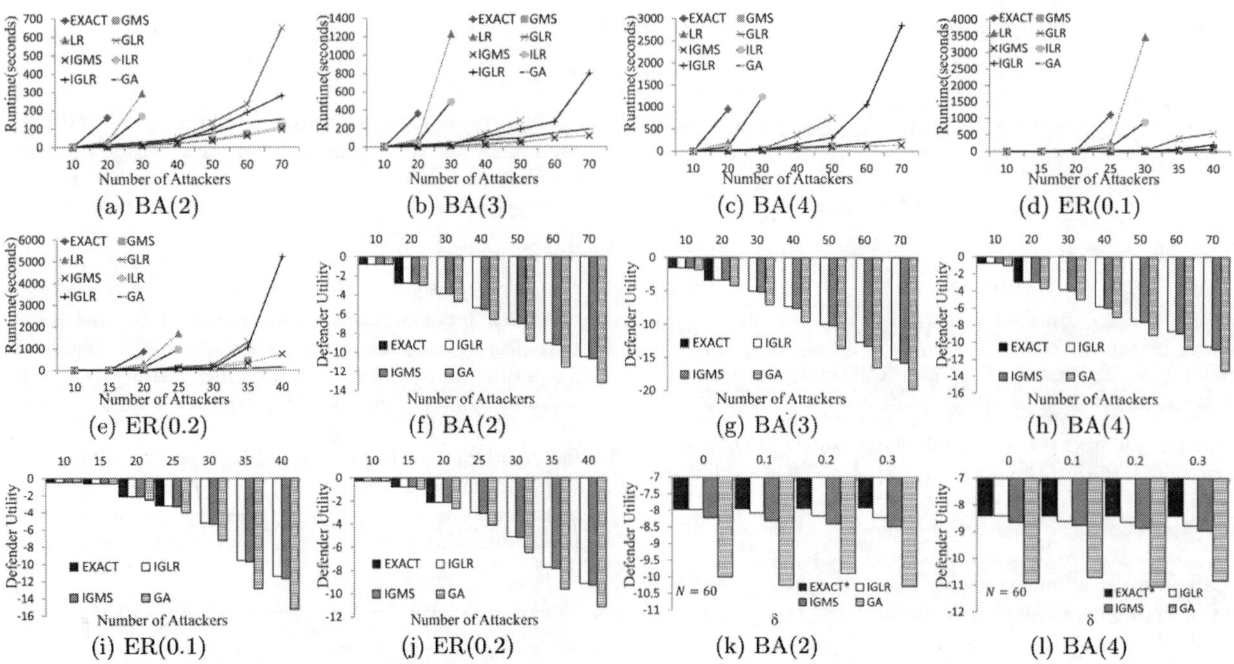

Figure 3: Scalability: (a)–(e); Optimality: (f)–(j); Robustness: (k)–(l).

skills for each target type and the ones owned by each attacker drawn randomly from S, $m_{is} \sim \{1, 2, 3, 4, 5\}$; $p_t \sim [0, 1.0]$ and $\lambda_{ij} \sim [0, r]$ where $r \in [0, 1]$ is chosen randomly.

7.1 Scalability and Optimality

Runtime. We test different algorithms on 5 types of networks, and the results are depicted in Figures 3(a)–3(e), from which we can observe the significant efficiency improvement provided by the branch and price framework. The IPS procedure and the GMS approach are shown to reduce the number of iterations of column generation drastically as they further improve the branch and price framework to scale up to realistic-sized problems. For example, Figure 1 contains 76 groups and the average degree is 3.4, which is well within the scalability of IGLR and IGMS.

Defender Utility. We compare the defender utility of IGLR and IGMS, with EXACT and GA as benchmarks. The results are illustrated in Figures 3(f)–3(j), from which we can see that IGLR can achieve an almost optimal solution which outperforms GA significantly, in accordance with the theoretical analysis of Theorem 3. The solutions obtained by IGMS, which also outperform GA, are near-optimal especially for networks with higher connectivity, such as large-scale networks of type ER(0.1) and ER(0.2). A tradeoff between runtime and solution quality is observed for IGMS and IGLR, as IGMS shows the better scalability while IGLR obtains the solution with higher quality, however, both of them outperform the alternatives significantly.

7.2 Robustness

In the real world, the defender's estimation of target value p_t may not be perfect from attackers' perspective. Therefore, we analyze the performance of our algorithmic framework under the existence of noise of p_t. Let $\bar{p}_t$ be the defender's estimation of p_t while p_t is drawn uniformly within $\bar{p}_t \cdot [1 - \delta, 1 + \delta]$. We compare the defender utility of IGLR and IGMS under different degrees of uncertainty, with the near-optimal solution of IGLR, denoted by EXACT* (IP (3) cannot scale to $N = 60$), and heuristic solution of GA as comparison. The results are shown in Figures 3(k)–3(l), from which a decreasing efficiency is observed for IGLR and IGMS when δ increases. However, IGLR and IGMS solutions still outperform GA significantly under the existence of uncertainty of p_t, and IGLR can obtain an almost optimal solution even when $\delta = 0.3$, which shows the strong robustness of our algorithmic framework.

8. CONCLUSION

For the first time, this paper studies the problem of blocking attacker coalition through efficient allocation of security resources. This paper provides the following key contributions: 1) We formally define and model coalitional security games. 2) We prove the MAX SNP-hardness of defender's decision-making problem and NP-hardness of attackers' decision-making problem. 3) To address the MAX SNP-hardness, we propose an exact integer program and provide a branch and price algorithm, a linear relaxation based column generation with a constant factor approximation bound, an interior point stabilization procedure, and a greedy method to further improve the scalability. 4) Experiments demonstrate that our methods can scale up to realistic-sized instances and achieve near-optimal performance.

Acknowledgments

This research is supported by the NSF (CNS-1238959), ONR (N00014-15-1-2621), AFRL (FA8750-14-2-0180) and the National Research Foundation, Prime Minister's Office, Singapore under its IDM Futures Funding Initiative and administered by the Interactive and Digital Media Programme Office.

REFERENCES

[1] V. Asal and R. K. Rethemeyer. The nature of the beast: Terrorist organizational characteristics and organizational lethality. *Journal of Politics*, 70(2):437–449, 2008.

[2] Y. Bachrach and J. S. Rosenschein. Coalitional skill games. In *Proceedings of the 7th International Joint Conference on Autonomous Agents and Multiagent Systems (AAMAS)*, pages 1023–1030, 2008.

[3] A.-L. Barabási and R. Albert. Emergence of scaling in random networks. *Science*, 286(5439):509–512, 1999.

[4] J. Bennett. Israeli killed as his commandos demolish west bank house. *The New York Times*, 2002.

[5] D. Bertsimas and J. N. Tsitsiklis. *Introduction to Linear Optimization*. Athena Scientific, 1997.

[6] G. W. Bush. *National strategy for combating terrorism*. Wordclay, 2009.

[7] G. Chalkiadakis, E. Elkind, and M. Wooldridge. Computational aspects of cooperative game theory. *Synthesis Lectures on Artificial Intelligence and Machine Learning*, 5(6):1–168, 2011.

[8] E. Dahlhaus, D. S. Johnson, C. H. Papadimitriou, P. D. Seymour, and M. Yannakakis. The complexity of multiterminal cuts. *The SIAM Journal on Computing*, 23(4):864–894, 1994.

[9] P. Erdős and A. Rényi. On random graphs I. *Publ. Math. Debrecen*, 6:290–297, 1959.

[10] J. Gan, B. An, and Y. Vorobeychik. Security games with protection externalities. In *Proceedings of the 29th AAAI Conference on Artificial Intelligence (AAAI)*, pages 914–920, 2015.

[11] M. Jain, B. An, and M. Tambe. An overview of recent application trends at the aamas conference: Security, sustainability and safety. *AI Magazine*, 33(3):14, 2012.

[12] P. Klerks. The network paradigm applied to criminal organizations: Theoretical nitpicking or a relevant doctrine for investigators? Recent developments in the netherlands. *Connections*, 24(3):53–65, 2001.

[13] V. Krebs. Uncloaking terrorist networks. *First Monday*, 7(4), 2002.

[14] K. A. Kronstadt. Terrorist attacks in Mumbai, India, and implications for US interests. *Congressional Research Service*, 2008.

[15] J. Letchford and V. Conitzer. Solving security games on graphs via marginal probabilities. In *Proceedings of the 27th AAAI Conference on Artificial Intelligence (AAAI)*, pages 591–597, 2013.

[16] M. Levitt. Untangling the terror web: Identifying and counteracting the phenomenon of crossover between terrorist groups. *SAIS Review*, 24(1):33–48, 2004.

[17] R. Lindelauf, H. Hamers, and B. Husslage. Cooperative game theoretic centrality analysis of terrorist networks: The cases of Jemaah Islamiyah and Al Qaeda. *European Journal of Operational Research*, 229(1):230–238, 2013.

[18] T. P. Michalak, T. Rahwan, N. R. Jennings, P. L. Szczepański, O. Skibski, R. Narayanam, and M. J. Wooldridge. Computational analysis of connectivity games with applications to the investigation of terrorist networks. In *Proceedings of the 23rd International Joint Conference on Artificial Intelligence (IJCAI)*, pages 293–301, 2013.

[19] A. Nekrassov. Chechen attack: 'terrorists get weapons from abroad, linked to mideast groups'. *Russia Today*, 2014.

[20] C. Papadimitriou and M. Yannakakis. Optimization, approximation, and complexity classes. In *Proceedings of the 20th Annual ACM Symposium on Theory of Computing (ACM STOC)*, pages 229–234, 1988.

[21] M. B. Peterson. *Applications in Criminal Analysis: A Sourcebook*. Greenwood Press Westport, 1994.

[22] B. J. Phillips. *How Terrorist Organizations Survive: Cooperation and Competition in Terrorist Group Networks*. PhD thesis, University of Pittsburgh, 2012.

[23] J. S. Pistole. Identifying, Tracking and Dismantling the Financial Structure of Terrorist Organizations. 2003.

[24] C. L. Powell. Remarks to the United Nations Security Council, February 5, 2003.

[25] D. Pritchard. An LP with integrality gap $1+\epsilon$ for multidimensional knapsack. *arXiv preprint arXiv:1005.3324*, 2010.

[26] L. Rousseau, M. Gendreau, and D. Feillet. Interior point stabilization for column generation. *Operations Research Letters*, 35(5):660–668, 2007.

[27] T. Shanker and E. Schmitt. Three terrorist groups in Africa pose threat to US, American commander says. *The New York Times*, 2011.

[28] S. Shen, J. C. Smith, and R. Goli. Exact interdiction models and algorithms for disconnecting networks via node deletions. *Discrete Optimization*, 9(3):172–188, 2012.

[29] M. K. Sparrow. The application of network analysis to criminal intelligence: An assessment of the prospects. *Social networks*, 13(3):251–274, 1991.

[30] M. Tambe. *Security and Game Theory: Algorithms, Deployed Systems, Lessons Learned*. Cambridge University Press, 2011.

[31] Y. Vorobeychik, B. An, M. Tambe, and S. P. Singh. Computing solutions in infinite-horizon discounted adversarial patrolling games. In *Proceedings of the 24th International Conference on Automated Planning and Scheduling (ICAPS)*, pages 314–322, 2014.

[32] Z. Wang, Y. Yin, and B. An. Computing optimal monitoring strategy for detecting terrorist plots. In *Proceedings of the 30th AAAI Conference on Artificial Intelligence (AAAI)*, 2016.

[33] Y. Yin, B. An, and M. Jain. Game-theoretic resource allocation for protecting large public events. In *Proceedings of the 28th Conference on Artificial Intelligence (AAAI)*, pages 826–834, 2014.

[34] Y. Yin, H. Xu, J. Gan, B. An, and A. X. Jiang. Computing optimal mixed strategies for security games with dynamic payoffs. In *Proceedings of the 24th International Joint Conference on Artificial Intelligence (IJCAI)*, pages 681–688, 2015.

[35] M. Zhao, B. An, and C. Kiekintveld. Optimizing personalized email filtering thresholds to mitigate sequential spear phishing attacks. In *Proceedings of the 30th AAAI Conference on Artificial Intelligence (AAAI)*, 2016.

Attachment Centrality: An Axiomatic Approach to Connectivity in Networks

Oskar Skibski
University of Warsaw
o.skibski@mimuw.edu.pl

Talal Rahwan
Masdar Institute
trahwan@gmail.com

Tomasz P. Michalak
University of Oxford
University of Warsaw
tpm@mimuw.edu.pl

Makoto Yokoo
Kyushu University
yokoo@inf.kyushu-u.ac.jp

ABSTRACT

Centrality indices aim to quantify the importance of nodes or edges in a network. A number of new centrality indices have recently been proposed to try and capture the role of nodes in connecting the network. While these indices seem to deliver new insights, to date not enough is known about their theoretical properties. To address this issue, we propose an axiomatic approach. Specifically, we prove that there exists a unique centrality index satisfying some intuitive properties related to network connectivity. This new index, which we call *Attachment Centrality*, is equivalent to the Myerson value of a particular graph-restricted coalitional game. Building upon our theoretical analysis, we show that our Attachment Centrality has certain computational properties that are more attractive than the Myerson value for an arbitrary game.

General Terms

Measurement, Theory

Keywords

network centrality; axiomatization

1. INTRODUCTION

In many social networks, certain nodes play more important roles than others. For example, popular individuals with frequent social contacts are more likely to spread a disease in the event of an epidemic [8]; airport hubs such as Heathrow or Schiphol concentrate intercontinental passenger traffic [1]; and certain parts of the brain's neural network may be indispensable for breathing or to perform other vital activities [11]. Consequently, the concept of *centrality index*, which aims at identifying the key nodes in the network, has been extensively studied in the literature [12, 7]. Arguably, the most well-known such indices are: *Degree*, *Closeness*, and *Betweenness* centralities [9]. In particular, Degree Centrality quantifies the power of a node by the number of its incident edges. In contrast, Closeness Centrality promotes nodes that are close to all other nodes in the network. Betweenness Centrality counts the shortest paths between any two nodes in the network, and ranks nodes according to the number of the shortest paths they belong to.

Appears in: *Proceedings of the 15th International Conference on Autonomous Agents and Multiagent Systems (AAMAS 2016), J. Thangarajah, K. Tuyls, C. Jonker, S. Marsella (eds.), May 9–13, 2016, Singapore.*

More recently, a number of new centrality indices have been proposed in an attempt to reflect the following fundamental property of nodes: *the role they each play in connecting the network* [10, 3, 4]. Typically, such measures are built upon the well-known coalitional-game model of Myerson [16], where cooperation is restricted to *connected coalitions* (i.e., connected subgraphs of the network). Within this general framework, different centrality indices are obtained by manipulating the function that assigns the payoff from cooperation in each connected coalition.

Unfortunately, although these recent indices offered new insight, they were only evaluated empirically. The lack of a theoretical underpinning not only makes it difficult to choose among them, but also hinders the development of efficient algorihtms to compute them, especially given the inherent computational difficulty of Myerson's model [22].

To address this issue, we propose an axiomatic approach built around five basic requirements. The first two, namely (1) *Locality* and (2) *Normalization*, seem to be reasonable requirements for any centrality index (indeed, all three standard centrality indices satisfy them). Other requirements that we focus on are (3) *Monotonicity* and (4) *Gain-loss*—two somewhat-opposing views of how adding an edge affects other nodes (i.e., nodes that are not part of the edge). In a nutshell, when an edge is added, Monotonicity requires that the indices of other nodes *do not decrease*, whereas Gain-loss implies that they *do not increase*. More precisely, Gain-loss requires that the gain of a node always results in the loss of another. The final requirement is (5) *Fairness*, requiring that the addition of an edge equally affects the two nodes connected by it. Arguably, this requirement seems reasonable when an edge is considered to be equally owned by both nodes. That is to say, both nodes have an equal say in whether the edge is formed or disbanded (e.g., both sides of a relationship must consent to, and can break, the relation). From this point of view, it seems "fair" that both nodes equally benefit from their edge, since they both equally own it.[1]

Building upon these axioms, we prove that Degree Centrality is the unique index satisfying Normalization, Locality, Fairness and Monotonicity. Furthermore, we prove that replacing Monotonicity with Gain-loss leads to yet another unique index, which we call: *Attachment Centrality*; this is the first axiomatized centrality index focusing on connectivity in the literature. Finally, to compute our index, we propose a dedicated algorithm and test it on a relatively large, real-life social network.

[1]Of course one can think of many alternative ways to interpret "fairness". We do not argue that ours is necessarily *the best way*, but rather that it seems to be *a reasonable way*.

2. PRELIMINARIES

Since our work falls at the interface of graph theory and coalitional game theory, this section provides the necessary background and notation from both sides.

Graph theory: A graph, or a network, is a pair, $G = (V, E)$, where V is the set of $n = |V|$ nodes, and E is the set of edges. We sometimes write $|G|$ instead of $|V|$ to denote the number of nodes in G. An edge $\{v, u\} \in E$ is said to be *incident* to nodes v and u. The degree of a node v, denoted by $degree_G(v)$, is the number of edges incident to v, i.e.:

$$degree_G(v) = \big|\{\{v, u\} \in E : u \in V\}\big|.$$

When there is no risk of confusion, we will often omit the G from the notation, and simply write $degree(v)$ instead of $degree_G(v)$. Nodes $u, v \in V$ are said to be *neighbors* if they are connected by an edge. If $degree(v) = 0$, we say that v is *isolated*.

A path, $p = (v_1, \ldots, v_k)$, is a sequence of nodes in which every two consecutive nodes are connected by an edge, i.e., $\{v_i, v_{i+1}\} \in E$, $\forall i \in \{1, \ldots, k-1\}$. The length of a path is the number of edges in it (i.e., the number of nodes in it minus 1). We write $v \in p$ if v is one of the nodes in p. The *distance* between any two nodes, $v, u \in V$, is denoted by $dist(v, u)$, and is defined as the length of a shortest path between them. If there exists no path between u and v, we assume that $dist(v, u) = \infty$.

Next, we introduce the concept of a *minimal path*. In particular, a path, p, between v and u is said to be *minimal* if there exists no shorter path between v and u that can be obtained by removing nodes from p (see Figure 1 for an example). The set of all *shortest* paths between v and u is denoted by $\Pi_s(v, u)$, and the set of all *minimal* paths between v and u is denoted by $\Pi_m(v, u)$. Note that every *shortest* path between u and v is a *minimal* path between u and v, i.e., $\Pi_s(v, u) \subseteq \Pi_m(v, u)$.

Nodes $v, u \in V$ are said to be *connected* if there exists a path between them. A graph G is said to be connected if every two nodes in it are connected. For any subset of nodes, $S \subseteq V$, the *subgraph induced by* S is denoted by $G[S]$ and is defined as a graph whose nodes are S and whose edges are those in G that connect some node in S with some other node in S. Formally:

$$G[S] = (S, \{\{v, u\} \in E : v, u \in S\}).$$

Any subset of nodes, $S \subseteq V$, is said to be connected if the subgraph induced by S is connected. If G is not connected, we denote by $K(G)$ the partition of V into disjoint sets of nodes that each induce a *maximal connected subgraph* in G.

The set of all possible graphs with nodes V is denoted by $\mathcal{G}^V$. Two special graphs are *cliques* and *stars*. Specifically, a graph is a *clique* if every two nodes in it are connected by an edge:

$$(V, \{\{v, u\} : v, u \in V\}).$$

On the other hand, a graph is a *star* if there exists a node v (called the *center* of the star) such that every node $u \in V \backslash \{v\}$ is connected to v and not connected to any other node. That is:

$$(V, \{\{v, u\} : u \in V \setminus \{v\}\}).$$

Centrality indices: A *centrality index*, $F : \mathcal{G}^V \to \mathbb{R}^V$, is a function that assigns to every node a number reflecting its importance. Typically, the higher this number, the more *important* or *central* the node. Arguably, the most well-known centrality indices are the following (we will refer to them *the standard centrality indices*):

- *Degree Centrality* (D_v) is simply the degree of a node, i.e.,

$$D_v(G) = degree_G(v);$$

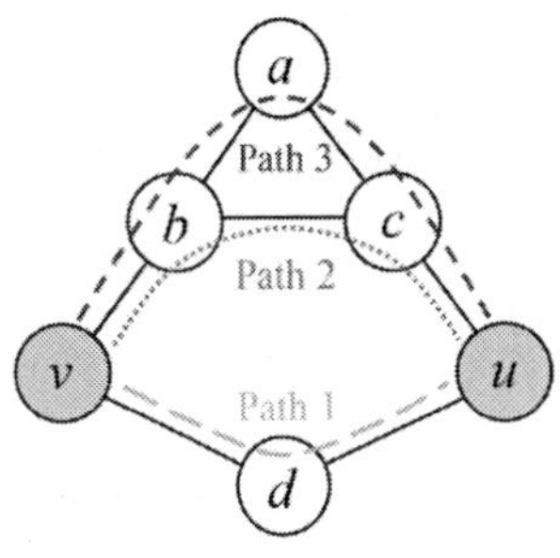

Figure 1: Out of all three paths between v and u, only Path 1 and Path 2 are *minimal* paths. Furthermore, out of those two minimal paths, only Path 1 is a *shortest* path between v and u.

- *Closeness Centrality* (C_v) is the sum of of the inverses of distances to other nodes (under the assumption that $\frac{1}{\infty} = 0$):[2]

$$C_v(G) = \sum_{u \in V \backslash \{v\}} \frac{1}{dist(v, u)};$$

- *Betweenness Centrality* (B_v) is the average percentage of shortest paths between any two other nodes that goes through the node under consideration. More formally, if we denote by $K_v(G)$ the connected component containing v in G, then:

$$B_v(G) = \frac{1}{\binom{|K_v(G)|-1}{2}} \sum_{\substack{s,t \in K_v(G) \\ s \neq v \neq t}} \frac{|\{p \in \Pi_s(s,t) : v \in p\}|}{|\Pi_s(s,t)|}.$$

Note that the above formula of Betweenness Centrality is normalized to ensure that it yields the same range of values as Degree and Closeness centralities, i.e., $[0, n-1]$.

Coalitional game theory: A *game* is a pair (N, f), where N is the set of *players* and $f : 2^N \to \mathbb{R}$ is the *characteristic function*, which assigns a real number to each subset of players (with the only assumption being that $f(\emptyset) = 0$). Any subset of players, $S \subseteq N$, is called a *coalition*, and $f(S)$ is called *the value of coalition* S. In contrast, "*a value of a game*" is a function that assigns a *payoff* to each player $v \in N$, i.e., $\varphi : (2^N \to \mathbb{R}) \to \mathbb{R}^N$. This payoff traditionally represents v's share out of the value of the *grand coalition*, i.e., the coalition of all players. Alternatively, the payoff of v can be interpreted as an assessment of the importance of v in the game. Thus, a *value* of a game plays the same role as a *centrality index* of a network; the former ranks players whereas the latter ranks nodes.

Shapley [21] was the first to propose an axiomatic approach to the problem of payoff division. In particular, Shapley proved that there exists a unique "value" satisfying some intuitive and desirable properties (also known as "*axioms*"). This value—now known as *the Shapley value*—is denoted for player v by $SV_v(f)$, defined as:

$$SV_v(f) = \sum_{S \subseteq N \backslash \{v\}} \beta(S, N)\big(f(S \cup \{v\}) - f(S)\big), \quad (1)$$

where $\beta(S, N) = |S|!(|N| - |S| - 1)!/|N|!$. Here, the expression $f(S \cup \{v\}) - f(S)$ is known as the *marginal contribution* of player v to coalition S; it is the difference that v makes when joining S.

Myerson [16] considered a model under which the cooperation of players is restricted by a communication graph, G. Specifically in this model, only connected coalitions, i.e., coalitions in which all players can communicate (either directly or indirectly through

[2]In the classical definition [20], the summation sign is in the denominator. However, we consider the well-respected version for graphs which do not have to be strongly connected [5].

intermediaries) can generate value added from cooperation. As for any disconnected coalition, its value equals the sum of the values of its connected components. As such, Myerson's model is defined by a graph, G, and a function, f, that specifies the value of every connected subgraph of G. Over the past decades, this became widely accepted as the canonical model of restricted cooperation. Myerson also proposed a value—now known as *the Myerson value*—which is denoted for player i by $MV_i(f, G)$; this value is simply the Shapley value of the *restricted game* $(N, f/G)$ whose characteristic function is defined as follows:

$$f/G(S) = \sum_{C \in K(G[S])} f(C), \quad \text{for every } S \subseteq N. \tag{2}$$

To put it differently, we have:

$$MV_v(f, G) = SV_v(f/G). \tag{3}$$

3. ATTACHMENT CENTRALITY

Our aim in this section is to define a new centrality index that reflects connectivity, by following an "axiomatic approach". That is, we want to identify a set of requirements, and then prove that there exists exactly one possible centrality index that satisfies all of those requirements, or "*axioms*". This way, the axioms would serve as a theoretical foundation for the centrality index that they uniquely define. Ideally, those axioms should be as intuitive and desirable as possible, to justify the use of the resulting index. In reality, however, any such set of axioms would probably be more suitable and intuitive for some settings, and less so for others. Still, identifying such a set of axioms would serve as a important step towards better understanding how centrality can be tailored to reflect or capture connectivity.

To this end, we propose five requirements, namely *Locality*, *Normalization*, *Fairness*, *Monotonicity*, and *Gain-loss*. Starting with Locality, this requirement is defined as follows, where $K_v(G)$ is the connected component containing v in G.

Locality: *For every graph $G = (V, E)$ and every node $v \in V$, the centrality of v depends solely on $G[K_v(G)]$. That is,*

$$F_v(G) = F_v(G[K_v(G)]).$$

As centrality indices are typically defined for connected graphs, the Locality requirement can be interpreted as a natural extension to disconnected graphs. Note that all four standard indices satisfy this requirement.

As for *Normalization*, it is inspired by the observation that Degree, Closeness, and normalized Betweenness all return a *minimum* value of 0, and a *maximum* value of $n-1$. Moreover, they are all *minimized* when the node is isolated, and *maximized* when the node is the center of a star. Normalization generalizes this observation.

Normalization: *For every $G = (V, E)$ and $v \in V$, we have:*

- $F_v(G) \in [0, n-1]$;
- $F_v(G) = 0$ *when v is isolated in G;*
- $F_v(G) = n-1$ *when G is a star, center of which is v.*

The remaining three requirements are concerned with the impact of adding an edge; *Fairness* focuses on how this addition affects both ends of the edge, whereas *Monotonicity* and *Gain-loss* focus on how this addition affects every node other than the two ends of the edge. Next, we explain each requirement in more detail.

Fairness: *For every $G = (V, E)$ and every $v, u \in V$, adding the edge $e = \{u, v\}$ affects the centrality of u and v equally:*

$$F_v((V, E\cup\{e\})) - F_v((V, E)) = F_u((V, E\cup\{e\}) - F_u((V, E))$$

This notion of Fairness was first proposed by Myerson [16]. Arguably, this seems to be a reasonable requirement when the two ends of the edge are considered to be equally responsible for it. This is perhaps more evident in settings where the formation of an edge requires the consent of both ends, and where the edge can be broken at any time by either end, such as friendship relationships for example. Interestingly, Closeness and Betweenness centralities do not satisfy the Fairness requirement. As mentioned earlier, this requirement is clearly not the only possible interpretation of a "fair" centrality index. However, we choose to call it "Fairness" because, at least in some settings, it seems to be reasonably fair.

Moving on to the final two requirements, namely *Monotonicity* and *Gain-loss*; these reflect somewhat-opposing views of how adding an edge affects the indices of the remaining nodes. In a nutshell, *Monotonicity* requires that these indices *do not decrease*, whereas *Gain-loss* implies that they *do not increase*. Next is a formal definition of the two requirements, followed by a discussion of the intuition behind each.

Monotonicity: *For every graph, $G = (V, E)$, adding an edge to E does not decrease the index of any node in V. That is, for every $v, u, w \in V$:*

$$F_v((V, E \cup \{u, w\})) \geq F_v((V, E)).$$

Gain-loss: *For every connected graph, $G = (V, E)$, and every pair of nodes, $u, w \in V$, adding the edge $\{u, w\}$ to E does not affect the sum of indices, i.e.:*

$$\sum_{v \in N} F_v((V, E \cup \{\{u, w\}\})) = \sum_{v \in N} F_v((V, E)).$$

Arguably, from the connectivity point of view, Gain-loss makes more sense compared to Monotonicity. To see why this is this case, consider a situation in which the removal of a node, v, breaks a connected graph, G, into two components, G_1 and G_2. Here, v obviously plays an important role in terms of connectivity, since its presence is necessary to connect G_1 with G_2. Now suppose that the edge $\{u, w\}$ was added to G, where u belongs to G_1 and w belongs to G_2. With this addition, it seems reasonable to claim that the role played by u and w grows more important, whereas the role played by v diminishes, since its presence is no longer necessary to connect G_1 with G_2. From this perspective, the Gain-loss requirement seems reasonable, whereas Monotonicity seems rather unintuitive, since it assumes that the connectivity role of v remains unchanged, or even grows more important, after the addition of $\{u, w\}$.

Note that the Gain-loss requirement only deals with the addition of an edge to an already-connected graph. As for disconnected graphs, if we add an edge that connects some of its components, then the Gain-loss requirement places no assumptions or restriction on how this would affect the centrality of nodes across the graph.

Having described the necessary five requirements, we are now ready to introduce one of our main results.

THEOREM 1. *There exists a unique centrality index that satisfies Locality, Normalization, Fairness, and Monotonicity; this index is Degree Centrality.*

PROOF. We begin by showing that Degree Centrality satisfies the four requirements listed in the statement of the theorem. To this end, for any graph, $G = (V, E)$, and any node, $v \in V$:

- *degree*(v) depends solely on the connected component containing v in G, meaning that Locality is met;
- *degree*$(v) = 0$ when v is isolated, and *degree*$(v) = n-1$ when G is a star center of which is v. It also holds that: $0 \leq$ *degree*$(v) \leq n-1$. Thus, Normalization is met;

- $degree(v)$ does not decrease by adding an edge $\{u, w\}$ for some $u, w \in V \setminus \{v\}$, meaning that Monotonicity is met;
- Adding an edge, $\{v, u\}$ for any $u \in V \setminus \{v\}$ increases the degree of both u and v by 1. Therefore, Fairness is met.

It remains to prove that Degree Centrality is the only possible centrality index satisfying the above four requirements. To put it differently, assuming that F is a centrality index satisfying those requirements, it remains to prove that $F_v(G) = D_v(G)$ for any graph $G = (V, E)$ and any node $v \in V$. We will do so by first proving that $F_v(G) \geq D_v(G)$ and then proving that $F_v(G) \leq D_v(G)$.

Step 1: In this step, we will prove that:

$$F_v(G) \geq D_v(G), \quad \forall v \in V. \tag{4}$$

Let us fix a node, $v \in V$, and remove all the edges from G except those connecting v to its neighbors. In so doing, we obtain a new graph, G', such that $K_v(G')$ forms a star center of which is v, and: $|K_v(G')| = D_v(G) + 1$. Since v is the center of the star $G'(v)$, then based on Normalization: $F_v(G'[K_v(G')]) = |K_v(G')| - 1$. Next, we know from Locality that: $F_v(G') = F_v(G'[K_v(G')])$. Finally, we know from Monotonicity that: $F_v(G) \geq F_v(G')$ which concludes the proof of correctness of (4).

Step 2: In this step, we will prove that:

$$F_v(G) \leq D_v(G), \quad \forall v \in V. \tag{5}$$

To this end, for any set of nodes, V, and any $v \in V$, let $\mathcal{G}_v^\dagger(G)$ denote the set of all possible graphs whose set of nodes is V, and whose set of edges, E, includes every pair in $V \setminus \{v\}$, meaning that all nodes in $V \setminus \{v\}$ form a clique. We will prove that the following holds for all $G \in \mathcal{G}_v^\dagger(G)$:

$$F_v(G) = D_v(G). \tag{6}$$

We will prove this by induction over the degree of v. Specifically, for any graph, $G \in \mathcal{G}_v^\dagger(G)$, if $degree_G(v) = 0$ then v is isolated, implying that (6) holds based on Normalization. Now, assuming that (6) holds for all $G \in \mathcal{G}_v^\dagger(G) : degree_G(v) \leq d$ for some positive integer $d < n - 1$, we will prove that (6) also holds for every graph $G \in \mathcal{G}_v^\dagger(G) : degree_G(v) = d + 1$. Let G' be one such graph, i.e., a graph in $\mathcal{G}_v^\dagger(G)$ such that the degree of v in G' equals $d + 1$. Furthermore, let $u \in V$ be a neighbor of v in G'. Then, if we remove the edge $\{u, v\}$ from G', we obtain a new graph, $G'' \in \mathcal{G}_v^\dagger(G)$, in which the degree of v equals d. This means that $F_v(G'') = D_v(G'')$ based on the aforementioned assumption. Now observe that:

- $D_u(G') = n-1$. This is because u is connected to v in G' (since u and v are neighbors) and connected to every other node in G' (since $V \setminus \{v\}$ forms a clique). Thus, based on Normalization and (4), it holds that: $F_u(G') = n - 1$;
- $D_u(G'') = n - 2$. This is because $D_u(G') = n - 1$, and G'' is identical to G' except that u and v are no longer neighbors. Thus, from Normalization and (4): $n - 2 \leq F_u(G'') \leq n - 1$.

The above two observations imply that, with the addition of $\{v, u\}$ to G'', the centrality of u increases by *at most* 1. That is,

$$F_u(G') - F_u(G'') \leq 1. \tag{7}$$

Now let us turn our attention back to node v. So far, we know that $F_v(G'') = D_v(G'')$ and that $D_v(G') = D_v(G'') + 1$. We also know from (4) that $F_v(G') \geq D_v(G')$. Thus:

$$F_v(G') - F_v(G'') \geq 1. \tag{8}$$

Based on (7) and (8), as well as the Fairness requirement, we conclude that: $F_v(G') - F_v(G'') = 1$, implying that $F_v(G') = D_v(G')$. This concludes our proof of the correctness of (6).

Let us now move back to our original goal in **Step 2**—proving the correctness of (5). Here, we have two possibilities:

- If $V \setminus \{v\}$ happened to form a clique in G, then we know from (6) that $F_v(G) = D_v(G)$, implying that (5) holds;
- If $V \setminus \{v\}$ did not form a clique in G, then we can add every missing edge between pairs of nodes in $V \setminus \{v\}$. In so doing, we end up with a new graph, G^*, in which $V \setminus \{v\}$ forms a clique. Thus, based on (6), we have:

$$F_v(G^*) = D_v(G^*). \tag{9}$$

Furthermore, based on Monotonicity, we know that:

$$F_v(G) \leq F_v(G^*). \tag{10}$$

Finally, since none of the added edges involved v:

$$D_v(G^*) = D_v(G). \tag{11}$$

Taken together, (9), (10) and (11) imply that (5) holds.

Thus, we have proved that (5) always holds, which is what we want to show in **Step 2**. This concludes our proof of Theorem 1. □

Next, we will introduce our *Attachment Centrality*, and then prove that it is the unique index satisfying Locality, Normalization, Fairness and Gain-Loss.

Definition 1. ***Attachment Centrality*** *is the centrality index defined for every graph, $G = (V, E)$, and every node, $v \in V$, as:*

$$A_v(G) = \sum_{S \subseteq V \setminus \{v\}} 2\beta(S, V)(|K(G[S])| - |K(G[S \cup \{v\}])| + 1), \tag{12}$$

where $\beta(S, V) = |S|!(|V| - |S| - 1)!/|V|!$, and $K(G[S])$ denotes the partition of S into disjoint sets of nodes that each induce a maximal connected subgraph in $G[S]$.

In the above definition, for any $S \subseteq V$ (connected or otherwise), the expression $|K(G[S])| - |K(G[S \cup \{v\}])| + 1$ equals the number of components in $G[S]$ that node v connects.

The intuition behind the Attachment Centrality is as follows. If we were to remove nodes from the graph one by one in a random order, then the Attachment Centrality of $v \in V$ would be the expected number of components created from the removal of v, multiplied by 2 for normalization purposes.

By comparing the definition of the Attachment Centrality with Equation (1)—the definition of the Shapley value—we find that:

$$A_v(G) = SV_v(f_G^*), \tag{13}$$

where

$$f_G^*(S) = 2(|S| - |K(G[S])|). \tag{14}$$

To put it in words, the Attachment Centrality is equivalent to the Shapley value of the game (V, f_G^*). Importantly, if we now write $f_G^*(S)$ differently as follows:

$$f_G^*(S) = \sum_{C \in K(G[S])} 2(|C| - 1),$$

we obtain an equation similar to (2)—the equation defining f/G—except that $f(C)$ is now replaced with $2(|C| - 1)$. This observation, together with (3) and (13), imply that:

$$A_v(G) = MV_v(f^*, G), \tag{15}$$

where f^* is computed for every connected coalition, S, as:

$$f^*(S) = 2(|S| - 1). \tag{16}$$

To put it in words, the Attachment Centrality is equivalent to the Myerson value under the model of restricted cooperation defined by the communication graph G and the evaluation function f^*.

THEOREM 2. *There exists a unique centrality index that satisfies Locality, Normalization, Fairness, and Gain-loss; this index is the Attachment Centrality.*

PROOF. We begin by recalling a crucial result of Myerson [16], who proved that for an arbitrary game (V, f), there exists a unique function $\varphi : \mathcal{G}^V \to \mathbb{R}^V$ satisfying the following two properties: (1) *Fairness*—defined exactly as in our paper—and (2) *Component Efficiency*—a property defined for game (V, f) as follows:

Component Efficiency (for game (V, f)***):*** *For every graph, G, and every connected component $C \in K(G)$ of a graph:*

$$\sum_{v \in C} \varphi_v(G) = f(C).$$

Myerson proved that this unique function is actually the Myerson value under the model of restricted cooperation defined by the communication graph G and the evaluation function f.

Having recalled this result of Myerson, we are now ready to prove that the Attachment Centrality satisfies all four requirements listed in the statement of Theorem 2. In particular, Myerson's result, as well as (15) and (16), imply that the Attachment Centrality satisfies Fairness, and that for every graph G and every connected component $C \in K(G)$ we have:

$$\sum_{v \in C} A_v(G) = 2(|C| - 1). \tag{17}$$

This implies that adding an edge between two nodes in a connected component $C \in K(G)$ does not affect the sum of the Attachment Centrality of every node in that component. This, in turn, implies that the Attachment Centrality satisfies the Gain-loss requirement.

Moving on to Normalization; we need to show that the Attachment Centrality satisfies the three conditions outlined in the definition of Normalization. To this end, for every $v \in V$:

- If v is isolated in G, then v forms a connected component by itself, and (17) implies that $A_v(G) = 0$.
- If G is a star center of which is v, then we need to show that $A_v(G) = n - 1$. To this end, for every $S \subseteq V \setminus \{v\}$, the induced subgraph $G[S]$ consist of $|S|$ connected components, whereas the subgraph $G[S \cup \{v\}]$ consists of a single connected component. Thus,

  $$|K(G[S])| - |K(G[S \cup \{v\}])| + 1 = |S|.$$

  This fact, together with (12), imply that:

  $$A_v(G) = \sum_{S \subseteq V \setminus \{v\}} 2\beta(S, V)|S| = \sum_{s=0}^{n-1} \frac{2s}{n} = \sum_{s=0}^{n-1} = n - 1. \tag{18}$$

- Finally, we need to prove that $A_v(G) \in [0, n-1]$. Note that the expression $|K(G[S])| - |K(G[S \cup \{v\}])| + 1$ is always between 0 and $|S|$ (simply because the number of components in $G[S]$ that are connected by v is between 0 and $|S|$). Furthermore, if this expression equals $|S|$ then $A_v(G) = n - 1$; see (18). In contrast, if this expression equals 0, then $A_v(G) = 0$. This implies that $A_v(G) \in [0, n - 1]$.

The above three points imply that the Attachment Centrality satisfies the Normalization requirement.

Next, we prove that the Attachment Centrality satisfies Locality. In other words, given a graph, $G = (V, E)$, and a node, $v \in V$, we prove that $A_v(G) = A_v(G[K_v(G)])$, where $K_v(G)$ is the connected component containing v in G. To this end, let us denote by $mc_v^*(S)$ the marginal contribution of v to S in the (V, f_G^*), i.e.,

$$mc_v^*(S) = 2(|K(G[S])| - |K(G[S \cup \{v\}])| + 1).$$

Observe that $mc_v^*(S)$ is basically the number of components from S that node v connects, multiplied by 2. This number is not influenced by any of the nodes lying outside $K_v(G)$—the connected component containing v in G. Thus, for every $S \subseteq V \setminus \{v\}$: $mc_v^*(S) = mc_v^*(S \cap K_v(G))$. Next, we rewrite (12) as follows:

$$A_v(G) = \sum_{P \subseteq V \setminus K_v(G)} \sum_{S \subseteq K_v(G) \setminus \{v\}} \beta(S \cup P, V) mc_v^*(S).$$

Simple calculations show that for every $S \subseteq K_v(G)$ we have:

$$\sum_{P \subseteq V \setminus K_v(G)} \beta(S \cup P, V) = \beta(S, K_v(G)).$$

Thus, $A_v(G) = A_v(G[K_v(G)])$, i.e., the Attachment Centrality satisfies Locality.

It remains to prove that the Attachment Centrality is the only possible centrality index satisfying all four requirements listed in Theorem 2. To put it differently, given a centrality index, F, that satisfies those requirements, it remains to prove that $F_v(G) = A_v(G)$ for any graph $G = (V, E)$ and any node $v \in V$. We will do so by showing that the sum of the F index of every node belonging to the same connected component S equals: $f^*(S) = 2(|S| - 1)$. In so doing, we show that F satisfies *Component Efficiency* for game (V, f^*). Since F also satisfies *Fairness*, then based on Myerson's result, this index is unique.

Let $G = (V, E)$ be a star with node v being the center, and let u be an arbitrary node in $V \setminus \{v\}$. Normalization implies that:

$$F_v(G) = n - 1.$$

Next, we show that $F_u(G) = 1$. To this end, consider the graph $G' = (V, E \setminus \{\{v, u\}\})$ obtained from G by removing the edge $\{v, u\}$. Since u is now isolated in G', Normalization implies that:

$$F_u(G') = 0,$$

and from Locality, we know that:

$$F_v(G') = F_v(G'[V \setminus \{u\}]) = n - 2.$$

Now since the Fairness requirement implies that the removal of $\{v, u\}$ affects the centrality indices of both v and u equally, then:

$$F_u(G) = F_u(G') + (F_v(G) - F_v(G')) = 1.$$

As node u was chosen arbitrarily from the set $V \setminus \{v\}$, we conclude that every node other than the center of the star has a centrality index of 1. Thus, the sum of indices in a star equals $2(n - 1)$. As every connected graph can be obtained from a star by adding and/or removing edges, the Gain-loss requirement implies that the sum of indices in any connected graph with n nodes equals $2(n - 1)$. Finally, Locality implies that the sum of indices in any connected component S equals $2(|S| - 1)$. □

Note that Theorems 1 and 2 imply that there exist no value that satisfies all five axioms: Locality, Normalization, Fairness, Monotonicity, and Gain-loss.

4. PROPERTIES

In this section, we discuss some key properties of Attachment Centrality, and show that it is closely related to the notion of *minimal paths* between nodes. The following theorem constitutes the cornerstone of our analysis.

THEOREM 3. *Adding an edge $\{v, u\}$ to a graph G affects only the Attachment Centrality of nodes lying on a minimal path between v and u.*

PROOF. Recall that the value of a coalition, S, in the game (V, f_G^*) depends solely on the number of the nodes in S and the number of connected components in S (see Equation (14)). Now, let $G = (V, E)$ be an arbitrary, incomplete graph, and let $v, u \in V$ be two nodes such that $\{v, u\} \notin E$. Finally, let G' be the graph that results from adding $\{v, u\}$ to G, i.e., $G' = (V, E \cup \{\{v, u\}\})$. Next, we analyse how the marginal contribution of some node $w \in V \setminus \{v, u\}$ to a coalition S differs between G and G':

- Suppose that $\{v, u\} \not\subseteq S$, or that $\{v, u\} \subseteq S$ and both v and u belong to the same component in $G[S]$. Either way, edge $\{v, u\}$ does not affect the value of S and $S \cup \{w\}$: $f_G^*(S) = f_{G'}^*(S)$ and $f_G^*(S \cup \{w\}) = f_{G'}^*(S \cup \{w\})$. So, the marginal contribution of w in G is the same as in G';
- On the other hand, suppose that $\{v, u\} \subseteq S$ and that v and u belong to different component in $G[S]$, namely C_v and C_u. In this case, we have two possibilities: Either w is connected to both C_v and C_u or not. If it is not connected to both, then:

$$f_{G'}^*(S \cup \{w\}) - f_{G'}^*(S) = (f_G^*(S \cup \{w\}) + 2) - (f_G^*(S) + 2)$$
$$= f_G^*(S \cup \{w\}) - f_G^*(S),$$

  meaning that the marginal contribution of w in G is the same as in G'. In contrast, if w was connected to both C_v and C_u, then w would unite the two in $G[S \cup \{w\}]$ but not in $G'[S \cup \{w\}]$, because in G' the nodes in S are sufficient to unite the two components; they no longer need w to do that.

To summarize, we have shown that the marginal contribution of w in G can be different than in G' only when all of the following three conditions are met: (1) $\{v, u\} \subseteq S$; (2) v and u belong to different components in $G[S]$; (3) w is connected to both C_v and C_u. Importantly, however, if those three conditions are met, then w must be on some minimal path between v and u. To see why this is case, consider a minimal path p_1 between v and w in C_v, and another minimal path p_2 between u and w in C_u. Since C_v and C_u are not connected in G, merging p_1 and p_2 results in a minimal path between v and u that goes through w.

So far, we have shown that the marginal contribution of w in G can be different than in G' only when w is on some minimal path between v and u. Finally, from (1) and (13), we know that the Attachment Centrality of w is a weighted average of the marginal contributions of w in the game (V, f_G^*). Thus, by adding $\{v, u\}$, the Attachment Centrality of w may change only when w is on some minimal path between v and u. This concludes the proof. □

The above theorem leads to a series of corollaries that provide additional insights on how the Attachment Centrality measures the role of a node in connecting the network. We divide our analysis into two parts: the first focuses on nodes with high connectivity (such as *cut vertices*), whereas the second part focuses on nodes with low connectivity (such as leafs).

High connectivity: Given a *cut vertex*, $v \in V$ (i.e., a node that connects disjoint parts of the graph), we will show that the Attachment centralities of the nodes in each part are not influenced by the other parts. This, in turn, implies that the Attachment Centrality of v is simply the sum of its Attachment Centrality computed for each part separately.

THEOREM 4. *Let G be a connected graph, and let v be a node removal of which breaks G into k disjoint components consisting of the following sets of nodes: $C_1, \dots, C_k$. Then,*

$$A_v(G) = \sum_{i \in \{1,\dots,k\}} A_v(G[C_i \cup \{v\}]).$$

Furthermore, for every $i \in \{1, \dots, k\}$, and every $u \in C_i$:

$$A_u(G) = A_u(G[C_i \cup \{v\}]).$$

PROOF. First, let us focus on an arbitrary node $u \in C_i$ for some $i \in \{1, \dots, k\}$. Now let us remove from G an edge $\{w, w'\} \in E$ such that $w, w' \in C_j \cup \{v\}$ for some $j \neq i$. Note that a minimal path between w and w' cannot contain nodes from C_i. Based on this, Theorem 3 implies that the removal of $\{w, w'\}$ from G does not affect the Attachment Centrality of node u. By removing every such edge one by one, we eventually end up removing from G every edge outside $G[C_i \cup \{v\}]$ without affecting the Attachment Centrality of node u. Based on this, as well as Locality, we have that $A_u(G) = A_u(G[C_i \cup \{v\}])$.

Now, let us turn our attention to node v, and let us start by computing the Attachment centrality of v in each of the following subgraphs separately: $G[C_i \cup \{v\}] : i \in \{1, 2, \dots, k\}$; we find that:

$$A_v(G[C_i \cup \{v\}]) = 2|C_i| - \sum_{u \in C_i} A_u(G[C_i \cup \{v\}]).$$

Since we already proved that $A_u(G[C_i \cup \{v\}]) = A_u(G)$ for every $u \in C_i$, we get:

$$\sum_{i \in \{1,\dots,k\}} A_v(G[C_i \cup \{v\}]) = 2(|C| - 1) - \sum_{u \in C \setminus \{v\}} A_u(G) = A_v(G)$$

which concludes the proof. □

The next corollary concerns bridges, i.e., edges the removal of which increases the number of connected components in the graph. The corollary follows from Theorem 4 and it is based on the observation that both ends of a bridge are cut vertices.

COROLLARY 1. *Removing a bridge decreases the Attachment Centrality of both its ends by 1, and does not affect the Attachment Centrality of other nodes.*

Interestingly, according to the above corollary, the connectivity role played by a bridge is attributed solely to is two ends. Furthermore, the fact that a node v is an end of a bridge does not influence in any way the Attachment centralities of the nodes connecting v to the rest of the network.

Whereas Corollary 1 focuses on *edges* whose removal increases the number of connected components, Theorem 5 focuses on *cliques* whose removal increases the number of connected components (such cliques are known as *cut cliques*).

THEOREM 5. *Let G be a connected graph. If a set of nodes $K \subseteq G$ forms a clique in G, and the removal of K breaks G into k disjoint components consisting of the sets of nodes: $C_1, \dots, C_k$, then for every $v \in K$:*

$$A_v(G) = \sum_{i \in \{1,\dots,k\}} A_v(G[C_i \cup K]) - (k-1)A_v(G[K]).$$

Furthermore, for every $i \in \{1, \dots, k\}$ and every $u \in C_i$:

$$A_u(G) = A_u(G[C_i \cup K]). \tag{19}$$

PROOF. First, let us focus on an arbitrary node $u \in C_i$ for some $i \in \{1, \dots, k\}$. Analogously to the proof of Theorem 4, we argue that any edge between two nodes in $C_j \cup K$ for some $j \neq i$ does not affect the Attachment Centrality of u. This, in turn, implies the correctness of (19).

Now let us turn our attention to an arbitrary node $v \in K$, and let us analyse the marginal contribution of this node to an arbitrary coalition $S \subseteq V \setminus \{v\}$. Without loss of generality, let $K(G[S]) = \{C_1, \dots, C_l\}$ be the components of S, and assume that v is connected to the first m components, where $1 \leq m \leq l$. Following the definition of f^*_G (i.e., Equation (14)) the marginal contribution of v to S equals $2m$. Every connected component C_i for $i \leq m$ either contains all elements $K \cap S$ or is a subset C_j for some j. Thus, whenever S contains at least one element of K, then node v gets 2 for this component k times instead of 1. S contains at least one element of K with the probability $1 - \frac{1}{|K|}$. With the same probability node v has non-zero (and equal 2) marginal contribution in a clique of nodes K. This concludes the proof. □

Low connectivity: This part focuses on nodes with almost no connectivity role. The first corollary concerns *leafs*.

COROLLARY 2. *The Attachment Centrality of a leaf equals* 1. *Furthermore, removing a leaf decreases the Attachment Centrality of its neighbor by 1, and does not affect the Attachment Centrality of any other node in the graph.*

PROOF. Let v be a leaf, and let u be its only neighbor. Furthermore, let $S \subseteq V$ be the set of nodes comprising the component that contains both v and u. The presence of the edge $\{v, u\}$ increases the "*profit*" of $S \cup \{v\}$ by 2, since $f^*(S \cup \{v\}) - f^*(S) - f^*(v) = 2(|S|) - 2(|S| - 1) - 0 = 2$. Furthermore, since we know from the proof of Theorem 2 that the Attachment Centrality satisfies the *Component Efficiency* requirement, we know that the profit of 2 must be divided wholly among the nodes of the graph. However, according to Theorem 3, the edge $\{v, u\}$ only affects the Attachment Centrality of nodes lying on a minimal path between v and u, and since v is a leaf, the edge $\{v, u\}$ only affects the Attachment Centrality of v and u. In other words, the profit must be divided *wholly* between v and u. Finally, according to Fairness, this profit must be divided *equally* between v and u. This implies the correctness of the theorem and concludes the proof. □

So far, we discussed a type of nodes that plays a relatively-small connectivity role, namely a leaf. The following theorem focuses on yet another such type—a node whose set of neighbors forms a clique. The reason such a node, v, plays a relatively-small connectivity role is that v does not appear on any minimal path between any two nodes $u, w \in V \setminus \{v\}$.

THEOREM 6. *Given a node, v, whose set of neighbors, K, forms a clique, the Attachment Centrality of v equals $\frac{2|K|}{|K|+1}$. Furthermore, removing v decreases the Attachment Centrality of each of its neighbors by $\frac{2}{|K|(|K|+1)}$, and does not affect the Attachment Centrality of any other node in the graph.*

PROOF. Let $G = (V, E)$ be a graph in which a node, $v \in V$, has a set of neighbors, K, that forms a clique. It suffices to prove:

$$A_u(G) = \begin{cases} \frac{2|K|}{|K|+1} & \text{if } u = v, \\ A_u(G[V \setminus \{v\}]) + \frac{2}{|K|(|K|+1)} & \text{if } u \in K, \\ A_u(G[V \setminus \{v\}]) & \text{otherwise.} \end{cases}$$

Node v has non-zero marginal contribution to coalition S, equal 2, if and only if S contains at least one of its neighbors. Based on the permutation interpretation of the Shapley value, this happens with the probability $\frac{|K|}{|K|+1} \to 1$. All his neighbors benefit in a marginal contribution from v (have a greater marginal contribution to coalition with v, than without him) only if S does not contain any other neighbor. Such marginal contribution happens with the probability $\frac{1}{|K|(|K|+1)}$. Since other nodes do not appear on the minimal path between v and his neighbors in G', all edges of v can be removed without the change in their value. □

5. ALGORITHM AND APPLICATION

As an application, we focus on the identification of key terrorists in covert organisations. In particular, we analyse of the terrorist network responsible for the 2004 attacks on Madrid trains. The reasons behind our choice of the application and the network are twofold. Firstly, it has been recently argued that connectivity plays a crucial role in identifying the key members of terrorist networks [13, 15]. Secondly, the Madrid network is relatively big and, thus far, has never been analysed with a centrality index of this kind.

The *Madrid network* consists of 70 nodes and 243 edges. The size of the network makes it impractical to compute the existing connectivity-based centrality indices. In more detail, the computation involves enumerating all induced connected subgraphs of the network. Unfortunately, even the state-of-the-art algorithm for this purpose [22] takes over 100 seconds to compute the Myerson value for sparse network with only 36 nodes. Furthermore, the running time grows exponentially with the size of the network; every additional node nearly doubles it. To address this challenge, we use techniques introduced in the previous section to narrow down the set of nodes for which the Myerson value has to be calculated.

The original Madrid network [18] contains 6 isolated nodes. From Normalization, we know that the Attachment Centrality of each of these nodes is 0. We also know from Locality that those 6 nodes can be removed without affecting the Attachment Centrality of others. Furthermore, we observe that the Madrid network contains 8 leaf nodes. From Corollary 2, we know that every such node has an Attachment Centrality of 1, and can easily be removed from the network (since the corollary specifies the impact of this removal). Moreover, from Theorem 6 we know that every node whose set of neighbors, K, forms a clique has an Attachment Centrality of $\frac{2|K|}{|K|+1}$, and can easily be removed from the network (since the theorem specifies the impact of this removal on the Attachment Centrality of other nodes). Note that removing nodes results in a chain reaction, meaning that the above rules can be applied repeatedly (e.g., by removing a leaf, some other node might become a leaf, which can then be removed, and so on).

Our algorithm carries out the above process systematically, by finding the *cut-clique decomposition* of a graph. In a nutshell, the cut-clique decomposition of a graph G is a binary tree in which every node t is labeled with a subset $S \subseteq V$. If subgraph $G[S]$ has a cut-clique, then for a (possibly one of many) cut-clique K both his children are labeled according to the decomposition of $G[S]$ using K. Specifically, children l and r are labeled with two subsets $L, R \subseteq S$ such that $L \cap R = K$, and there exists no edge between $L \setminus K$ and $R \setminus K$. Theorem 5 allows for considering those subgraphs independently. By using the algorithm proposed by Tarjan [23], which utilizes the *simple elimination ordering* [19], we know that only one child can be further decomposed. This simplifies our algorithm (see Algorithm 1 for the pseudocode).

The results of our analysis are summarized in Table 1. As can be seen, the Attachment Centrality significantly differs from the standard centrality indices. For instance, let us consider two nodes with the highest number of edges – 1 and 3 – which are positioned

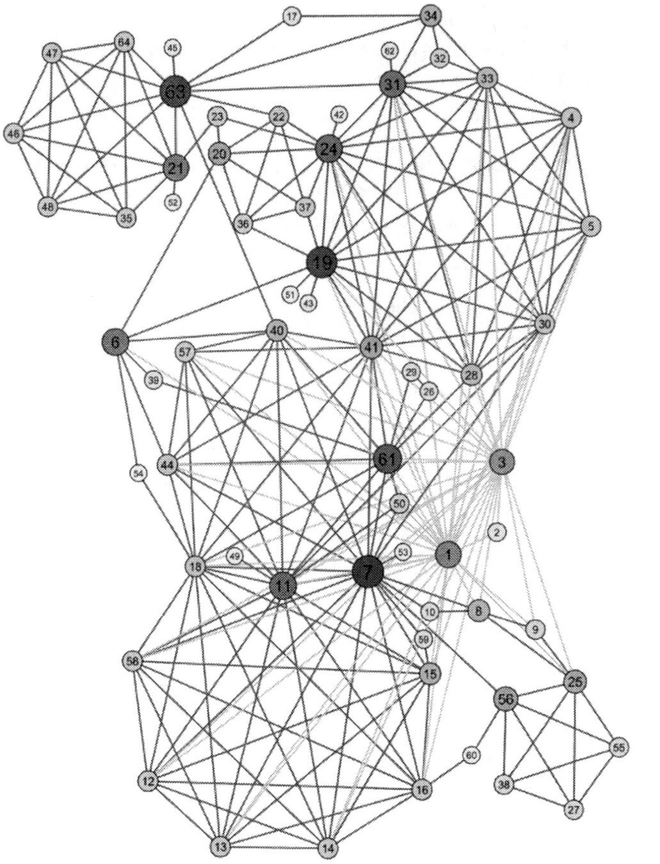

Figure 2: *Madrid network.* The node size reflects the Attachment Centrality (the larger the node the greater its centrality). To highlight the differences even further, the node color is set to reflect the node size (the larger the node the darker the color).

top by Degree and Closeness Centralities. Interestingly, Betweenness Centrality also gives them very high (the second and the third) positions while Attachment Centrality ranks node 1 as the tenth and node 3 even lower. Such a substantial difference between Betweenness and Attachment centralities is quite surprising, given that nodes that connect different parts of the network are more likely to belong to shortest paths than other nodes. However, nodes 1 and 3 have so many neighbors that they are very often parts of the shortest paths in the network, more often than nodes important from the connectivity perspective.

The running time of our algorithm depends on the topology of the graph. In the case of the Madrid network, the largest subgraph for which the Myerson value had to be calculated in line (11) was a subgraph consisting of 26 nodes. The running time on the entire network was 15.01 seconds on a standard desktop PC.

Our analysis revealed a previously unknown aspect of the Madrid network. In particular, we identified several overlapping parts of the network that are almost fully connected, i.e., each part is almost a clique, except for very few missing edges. This new insight confirms the existing belief, that *terrorist networks consist of rather sparsely-connected, highly-dense parts* [24].

6. RELATED WORK

A number of game-theoretic centrality indices have been recently proposed in the literature. In particular, Suri and Narahari [17] proposed an extension of degree centrality defined as the Shapley value of the game $f(S) = |\bigcup_{v \in S} neighbors(v)|$. Michalak et al.

Algorithm 1: Algorithm for the Attachment Centrality

Input: Graph $G = (V, E)$
Output: Attachment Centrality A_v for every $v \in V$

1 *find the simple elimination ordering* π*;*
2 *create a cut-clique decomposition* T *of graph* G *from* π*;*
3 $f \leftarrow$ *function defined as* $f(C) = 2(|C| - 1)$;
4 $t \leftarrow$ *root of* T*;*
5 **while** t *has children* **do**
6 $\quad (l, r) \leftarrow$ *children of* t *(left one without children);*
7 $\quad (L, R) \leftarrow$ *labels of* l, r*;*
8 $\quad K \leftarrow L \cap R$;
9 $\quad$ **foreach** $v \in L$ **do**
10 $\quad\quad$ *calculate* $MV_v(f, G[L])$*;*
11 $\quad\quad A_v \leftarrow A_v + MV_v(f, G[L])$;
12 $\quad\quad$ **if** $v \in K$ **then** $A_v \leftarrow A_v - 2 + \frac{2}{|K|}$;
13 $\quad t \leftarrow r$;
14 **return** A_v *for every* $v \in V$*;*

Rank	A_v		B_v	C_v	D_v
1st	7	(Imad Eddin Barakat)	63	1	1
2nd	63	(Semaan Gaby Eid)	1	3	3
3rd	19	(Abderrahim Zbakh)	3	41	7
4th	61	(Mohamed El Egipcio)	40	7	11
5th	24	(Naima Oulad Akcha)	7	31	41
6th	11	(Amer Azizi)	31	40	18
7th	6	(Mohamed Chedadi)	24	24	24

Table 1: The seven highest ranked nodes in the Madrid network, according to different centrality indices.

[14] considered a number of generalizations of this game. All these measures do not satisfy Fairness and Normalization. Also, if we consider their normalized version then they do not satisfy Locality.

To expose the connectivity role of a node, several authors proposed indices that are based on the Myerson value. Skibski et al. [22] considered several characteristic functions (e.g., $f(S) = |S|^2$ or $f(S)$ = number of edges in $G[S]$) combined with the graph-restrictions from Myerson's model. Depending on the function used, the resulting centrality measures do not satisfy Normalization nor Fairness (note that when the function f used in the Myerson value is based on the graph, Fairness may be violated).

A slightly different model (compared to Myerson's) was proposed by Amer and Gimenez [2], whereby the centrality of a node is the Shapley value of the following function: $f(S) = 1$ if $G[S]$ is connected and $f(S) = 0$ otherwise. This was later expanded by Lindelauf et al. [13] to an arbitrary $f(S)$ when $G[S]$ is connected. The resulting centrality measure does not satisfy Locality, since all centrality indices equal zero in a network with two disjoint parts.

7. CONCLUSIONS

While there were some attempts in the literature to provide theoretical foundations to the standard centrality indices [20, 12, 6], our analysis is the first in the literature that proposes an axiomatization of an index focusing on connectivity.

Acknowledgements: Oskar Skibski and Makoto Yokoo were supported by JSPS KAKENHI Grant (24220003). Tomasz Michalak were supported by the European Research Council under Advanced Grant 291528 ("RACE"). This work was also supported the Polish National Science Center grant DEC-2013/09/D/ST6/03920.

REFERENCES

[1] N. Adler and B. Golany. Evaluation of deregulated airline networks using data envelopment analysis combined with principal component analysis with an application to Western Europe. *European Journal of Operational Research*, 132(2):260 – 273, 2001.

[2] R. Amer and J. M. Giménez. A connectivity game for graphs. *Mathematical Methods of Operations Research*, 60(3):453–470, 2004.

[3] R. Amer, J. M. Giménez, and A. Magaña. Accessibility in oriented networks. *European Journal of Operational Research*, 180(2):700 – 712, 2007.

[4] J. Belau. Consequences of connection failure - centrality and the importance for cohesion. In *Public Choice Society*, 2014.

[5] P. Boldi and S. Vigna. Axioms for centrality. *Internet Mathematics*, 10(3-4):222–262, 2014.

[6] S. P. Borgatti and M. Everett. A graph-theoretic framework for classifying centrality measures. *Social Networks*, 28(4):466–484, 2006.

[7] U. Brandes and T. Erlebach. *Network Analysis: Methodological Foundations*. Springer-Verlag, 2005.

[8] Z. Dezső and A.-L. Barabási. Halting viruses in scale-free networks. *Physical Review E*, 65:055103, 2002.

[9] L. Freeman. Centrality in social networks: Conceptual clarification. *Social Networks*, 1(3):215–239, 1979.

[10] D. Gomez, E. González-Arangüena, C. Manuel, G. Owen, M. del Pozo, and J. Tejada. Centrality and power in social networks: a game theoretic approach. *Mathematical Social Sciences*, 46(1):27–54, 2003.

[11] A. Keinan, C. C. Hilgetag, I. Meilijson, and E. Ruppin. Casual localization of neural function: the Shapley value method. *Neurocomputing*, 58-60(0):215–222, 2004.

[12] D. Koschützki, K. Lehmann, L. Peeters, S. Richter, D. Tenfelde-Podehl, and O. Zlotowski. *Centrality indices. Network analysis*, volume 3418 of *Lecture Notes in Computer Science*, pages 16–61. Springer, 2005.

[13] R. Lindelauf, H. Hamers, and B. Husslage. Cooperative game theoretic centrality analysis of terrorist networks: The cases of Jemaah Islamiyah and Al Qaeda. *European Journal of Operational Research*, 229(1):230 – 238, 2013.

[14] P. T. Michalak, K. V. Aaditha, P. L. Szczepański, B. Ravindran, and N. R. Jennings. Efficient computation of the Shapley value for game-theoretic network centrality. *Journal of Artificial Intelligence Research*, 46:607–650, 2013.

[15] T. P. Michalak, T. Rahwan, P. L. Szczepański, O. Skibski, R. Narayanam, M. J. Wooldridge, and N. R. Jennings. Computational analysis of connectivity games with applications to the investigation of terrorist networks. In *IJCAI*, pages 293–301. AAAI Press, 2013.

[16] R. B. Myerson. Graphs and cooperation in games. *Mathematics of Operations Research*, 2(3):225–229, 1977.

[17] N. Ramasuri and Y. Narahari. Determining the top-k nodes in social networks using the Shapley value. In *AAMAS*, pages 1509–1512, 2008.

[18] J. A. Rodríguez. The March 11 th terrorist network: In its weakness lies its strength. *PhD Thesis*, 2005.

[19] D. J. Rose, R. E. Tarjan, and G. S. Lueker. Algorithmic aspects of vertex elimination on graphs. *SIAM Journal on computing*, 5(2):266–283, 1976.

[20] G. Sabidussi. The centrality index of a graph. *Psychometrika*, 31(4):581–603, 1966.

[21] L. Shapley. A value for n-person games. In H. Kuhn and A. Tucker, editors, *Contributions to the Theory of Games, volume II*, pages 307–317. Princeton University Press, 1953.

[22] O. Skibski, T. P. Michalak, T. Rahwan, and M. Wooldridge. Algorithms for the Shapley and Myerson values in graph-restricted games. In *AAMAS*, pages 197–204, 2014.

[23] R. E. Tarjan. Decomposition by clique separators. *Discrete mathematics*, 55(2):221–232, 1985.

[24] M. Tsvetovat and K. M. Carley. Generation of realistic social network datasets for testing of analysis and simulation tools. Technical report, DTIC Document, 2005.

k-Coalitional Cooperative Games

Oskar Skibski
University of Warsaw
o.skibski@mimuw.edu.pl

Szymon Matejczyk
Polish Academy of Sciences
s.matejczyk@phd.ipipan.waw.pl

Tomasz P. Michalak
University of Oxford
University of Warsaw
tpm@mimuw.edu.pl

Michael Wooldridge
University of Oxford
mjw@cs.ox.ac.uk

Makoto Yokoo
Kyushu University
yokoo@inf.kyushu-u.ac.jp

ABSTRACT

In most previous models of coalition structure generation, it is assumed that agents may partition themselves into any coalition structure. In practice, however, there may be physical and organizational constraints that limit the number of co-existing coalitions. In this paper, we introduce k-coalitional games: a type of partition function game especially designed to model such situations. We propose an extension of the Shapley value for these games, and study its axiomatic and computational properties. In particular, we show that, under some conditions, it can be computed in polynomial time given two existing representations of coalitional games with externalities. Finally, we use k-coalitional games to analyse the relative importance of geographical locations in the game of Diplomacy.

1. INTRODUCTION

Coalitional games have been widely studied in both the game theory and computer science literature [2, 15]. One of the most important problems in coalitional games is that of *coalition structure formation*: partitioning a group of agents into disjoint teams, typically with the goal of maximising some social welfare measure. In most studies of coalition structure generation, it is assumed that *all cooperative arrangements are feasible*, and in particular, that agents may be partitioned into *any* coalition structure. In characteristic function games – the most-studied model of cooperative games – it is further assumed that no coalition influences the value of any other co-existing coalition. This latter assumption is dropped in the more general model of partition function games [32], where the value of any coalition may be subject to *externalities* and, therefore, depend on co-existing coalitions.

Despite the popularity of the above models, it has long been recognized that many potential applications of coalitional games impose restrictions of various kinds on the coalitions and coalition structures that may be formed. This consideration gave rise to formalisms such as graph-restricted games [20], which have been studied by various authors in artificial intelligence (Meir et al. [17], Voice et al. [34], Skibski et al. [28]). Another model was proposed by Rahwan et al. [23], where restrictions on feasible coalitions are defined by logical constraints, while Meir et al. [17] consider games with coalitions of restricted size.

A common feature of all the above models is that they focus on restricting only feasible *coalitions*, rather than *coalition structures*, which are restricted only indirectly, (*i.e.*, by the fact that they cannot contain infeasible coalitions). However, one can see many physical and organizational restrictions that place constraints on feasible coalition structures rather than coalitions. For instance, during the Cold War, any country in Europe belonged either to NATO or the Warsaw Pact, or else remained neutral. Thus, if we consider all neutral countries as a coalition, then any feasible coalition structure would have at most three coalitions. Similar restrictions are likely to occur in a multi-agent system, where, due to cost considerations, only a few agents may be sophisticated enough to play the role of coalition coordinators/leaders (see the work by Coviello and Franceschetti [3] for an analysis of the problem of assigning followers to leaders). Thus, any coalition is feasible, but no coalition structure may contain more coalitions than there are leaders in the system. The only model that we are aware of in which restrictions are placed on the *number* of coalitions in a coalition structure is due to Sless et al. [31], who consider symmetric, additively separable hedonic games over a network with the assumption that any coalition structure should contain *exactly* k coalitions. Furthermore, an implicit assumption that limits the number of coalitions in a coalition structure can be found in the literature on well-known assignment games [25, 21, 13], where, for instance, m workers are hired by n companies [9]. All these models, however, focus on some very specific forms of the characteristic function and no more general transferable-utility model has been developed so far.

Against this background, we introduce *k-coalitional cooperative games* – a subclass of partition function games that are intended to model environments with the characteristics described above. In particular, we assume that any coalition may form, but the number of coalitions in any coalition structure is *limited* by a constant, k. For these new games, we develop a dedicated extension of the Shapley value [24] – a fundamental solution concept for coalitional games. We present two axiom systems that uniquely define the new value. Furthermore, we analyse the computational properties of the new value and show that it can be computed in polynomial time if a game is represented by Partition Decision Trees [29]. Finally, we use our approach to analyse the importance of geographical locations in the well-known board game of Diplomacy.

2. PRELIMINARY DEFINITIONS

Let $N = \{1, 2, \dots, n\}$ be a finite set of agents with $|N| = n$. A *coalition*, S, is any non-empty subset of N. A game without externalities (i.e., in characteristic function form) is given by a function $\hat{v}$ that associates a real number with every coalition of agents: $\hat{v} : 2^N \to \mathbb{R}$, with the assumption $\hat{v}(\emptyset) = 0$. Formally, a game is a pair $(N, \hat{v})$, but we frequently just write $\hat{v}$. We denote the set of all games without externalities by $\mathcal{CG}$.

Appears in: *Proceedings of the 15th International Conference on Autonomous Agents and Multiagent Systems (AAMAS 2016), J. Thangarajah, K. Tuyls, C. Jonker, S. Marsella (eds.), May 9–13, 2016, Singapore.*

In a game with externalities, the value of a coalition depends not just on the members of the coalition, but also on co-existing coalitions. A *partition* of N (also known as a *coalition structure*) is a set of disjoint coalitions that collectively cover N. A pair (S, P), where P is a partition and $S \in P$, is called an *embedded coalition*. The set of all partitions is denoted by $\mathcal{P}$, and all embedded coalitions by $\mathcal{EC}$. Now, in a *game with externalities* (in partition function form) (N, v), the function v associates a real number with every embedded coalition in every partition, *i.e.*, $v : \mathcal{EC} \to \mathbb{R}$ (with $v(\emptyset, P) = 0$ for every partition $P \in \mathcal{P}$). We denote the set of all games with externalities by $\mathcal{PG}$.

We use a shorthand notation for set subtraction and set union operations: $N_{-S} = N \setminus S$ and $S_{+\{i\}} = S \cup \{i\}$. Often, we omit brackets and write S_{+i}. We denote the partition obtained by the transfer of agent i to coalition T in partition P as:

$$\tau_i^T(P) = P \setminus \{P(i), T\} \cup \{P(i)_{-i}, T_{+i}\},$$

where $P(i)$ denotes i's coalition in P. For function $f : N \to X$ and subset $S \subseteq N$ we define $f(S) = \{f(i) \mid i \in S\}$, and, in the same manner, for a set of sets $P = \{S_1, \ldots, S_m\}$, we have $f(\{S_1, \ldots, S_m\}) = \{f(S_1), \ldots, f(S_m)\}$. Also, $f^{-1} : X \to 2^N$ is an inverse function, *i.e.*, $f^{-1}(x) = \{i \in N \mid f(i) = x\}$ for $x \in X$. In particular, combining the above definitions, $f^{-1}(X)$ forms a partition of N.

The Shapley value: A *value* of a game is a vector that divides among agents the payoff of the grand coalition, N. The value of agent i in game v will be denoted $\varphi_i(v)$. In his seminal work, Shapley [24] proved that there exists a unique division scheme in games without externalities that satisfies the following four axioms:

- *Efficiency* (the entire payoff of the grand coalition is distributed): $\sum_{i \in N} \varphi_i(\hat{v}) = \hat{v}(N)$ for every $\hat{v} \in \mathcal{CG}$;
- *Symmetry* (payoffs do not depend on the agents' names): $\varphi_i(f(\hat{v})) = \varphi_{f(i)}(\hat{v})$ for every $\hat{v} \in \mathcal{CG}$ and $f : N \to N$;
- *Additivity* (the sum of payoffs in two separate games equals the payoff in the combined game): $\varphi(\hat{v}_1 + \hat{v}_2) = \varphi(\hat{v}_1) + \varphi(\hat{v}_2)$ for all $\hat{v}_1, \hat{v}_2 \in \mathcal{CG}$;
- *Null-player Axiom* (agents that make no contribution to any coalition receive nothing): if $\hat{v}(S) - \hat{v}(S \setminus \{i\}) = 0$ for every $S \subseteq N, i \in S$, then $\varphi_i(\hat{v}) = 0$, for every $\hat{v} \in \mathcal{CG}$;

Here, games $f(\hat{v})$ (for bijection f) and $\hat{v}_1 + \hat{v}_2$ are defined as follows: $f(\hat{v})(S) = \hat{v}(f(S))$, and $(\hat{v}_1 + \hat{v}_2)(S) = \hat{v}_1(S) + \hat{v}_2(S)$. This unique solution is known as *the Shapley value*:

$$SV_i(\hat{v}) = \sum_{S \subseteq N, i \notin S} \beta(S, N) \cdot (\hat{v}(S \cup \{i\}) - \hat{v}(S)). \quad (1)$$

where $\beta(S, N) = (|S|!(|N| - |S| - 1)!)/(|N|!)$. As an intuition, Shapley provided the following process that leads to his value. Assume that the agents enter the game in a random order with an aim to form the grand coalition. As agent i enters, he receives a payoff that equals his marginal contribution to the group of agents that she joins: $[mc_i(v)](S) = \hat{v}(S) - \hat{v}(S \setminus \{i\})$. The Shapley value is the expected value of agents' contributions over all possible orders.

To formalize this description, we need additional notation. A set of all permutations (orders) of N is denoted by Π. For a given permutation π, the set of agents that appear in π before i is denoted A_i^π, and after Z_i^π. If we include i in these sets, we write A_{i+}^π and Z_{i+}^π. Now, the Shapley value is given by the following formula:

$$SV_i(\hat{v}) = \frac{1}{|N|!} \sum_{\pi \in \Pi} \hat{v}(A_{i+}^\pi) - \hat{v}(A_i^\pi).$$

Extended Shapley values: Translating Shapley's axioms to games with externalities is problematic. While Efficiency, Symmetry, and Additivity can be easily adapted, the Null-player Axiom poses a problem – how should the contribution of an agent to an embedded coalition be defined? In games without externalities, this is the difference between the value of a coalition with and without an agent. But in games with externalities, when agent leaves coalition $S \cup \{i\}$ in partition $\{S \cup \{i\}, T_1, \ldots, T_k\}$, the effect of his move depends on what other coalition he joins, as the value of S when i joins T_1 may differ than the one when i joins T_2. A change associated with the transfer of agent i from coalition $S \cup \{i\}$ that results in partition P is denoted by

$$[emc_i(v)](S, P) = v(S_{+i}, \tau_i^S(P)) - v(S, P),$$

and called the *elementary marginal contribution*.

In the standard, most strict definition of a null-player, we assume that *every* transfer does not change the value of a coalition, *i.e.*, every elementary marginal contributions has value zero:

- *Null-player Axiom (for $\mathcal{PG}$)*: if $[emc_i(v)](S, P) = 0$ for every $(S, P) \in \mathcal{EC}, i \notin S$, then $\varphi_i(v) = 0$, for every $v \in \mathcal{PG}$;

Unfortunately, the (Strict) Null-player Axiom combined with the three other axioms (the so called *standard translation*) is too weak to imply uniqueness. To overcome this problem, a number of singular extensions and two more general approaches were proposed. In the first, (proposed by Macho-Stadler et al. [14] and called the *average approach*), the unique value of each coalition is calculated as a weighted average of its values in various partitions. Then, the Shapley value is applied to the resulting game without externalities:

$$\varphi_i(v) = SV_i(\hat{v}), \text{ where } \hat{v}(S) = \textstyle\sum_{(S,P)} a(S, P) v(S, P), \quad (2)$$

for some weights a.

In the *marginality approach*, used by a number of researchers the marginal contribution of an agent i is defined as a weighted average over elementary marginal contributions associated with leaving a given embedded coalition (S, P). Specifically, $[mc_i(v)](S, P)$ is defined as

$$\sum_{T \in P \setminus S \cup \{\emptyset\}} \alpha_i(S_{-i}, \tau_i^T(P)) \cdot [emc_i(v)](S_{-i}, \tau_i^T(P)), \quad (3)$$

for some weights α. Here, the empty set in the sum corresponds to the creation of a new coalition. Now, agent i is an α-null-player if all his marginal contributions equal zero:

- *α-Null-player Axiom (for $\mathcal{PG}$)*: if $[mc_i(v)](S, P) = 0$ for every $(S, P) \in \mathcal{EC}, i \in S$, then $\varphi_i(v) = 0$, for every $v \in \mathcal{PG}$;

Skibski et al. [30] proved that for every α, Efficiency, Symmetry, Additivity, and the α-Null-player Axiom implies a unique value.

3. K-COALITIONAL GAMES

In this section, we formally define k-coalitional games. Let $\mathbf{K} = \{1, 2, \ldots, k\}$, where $k \leq |N|$. The *size*, $|P|$, of a partition P is simply the number of coalitions it contains. We denote the set of all partitions of size at most k by $\mathcal{P}_k$, and the set of all coalitions embedded in them by $\mathcal{EC}_k$. Now, a *k-coalitional game* is a pair (N, v), where v is a value function $v : \mathcal{EC}_k \to \mathbb{R}$ that associates a real number with every element of $\mathcal{EC}_k$. We denote the set of all k-coalitional games by $\mathcal{PG}_k$.

Let us now consider whether the existing extensions of the Shapley value to games with externalities could be applied to k-coalitional games.[1] Of course, as long as the domains are differ-

[1]Note also that there exist extensions of the Shapley value to games with restricted space of coalitions (see, e.g., [4]) but not restricted space of coalition structures.

ent (i.e., $\mathcal{EC}_k$ vs. $\mathcal{EC}$) the answer is no. Next, consider the following procedure. Let $v^\star$ be a partition-function form game created from $v \in \mathcal{PG}_k$ by assigning zero values to all coalitions embedded in partitions with more than k coalitions: $v^\star(S,P) = v(S,P)$ if $|P| \leq k$ and $v^\star(S,P) = 0$, otherwise. Now, mathematically, every value for partition-function form games can be computed. While at first such an indirect procedure seems appealing, it does not satisfy the Null-player Axiom translated (in a standard way) to k-coalitional games:

- *$\mathcal{EC}_k$-restricted Null-player Axiom* (agents with no effect on the value of any coalition should get nothing): if $[emc_i(v)](S,P) = 0$ for every embedded coalition $(S,P) \in \mathcal{EC}_k$ such that $i \notin S$, then $\varphi_i(v) = 0$, for every $v \in \mathcal{PG}_k$.

In particular, an agent who in game $v \in \mathcal{PG}_k$ does not affect any coalition value (with all elementary marginal contributions zero) may affect it in $v^\star$ by forming a $k+1$'th coalition. Hence, existing solutions for games with externalities – even those satisfying the standard Null-player Axiom – would assign non-zero payoff to such an agent and violate the $\mathcal{EC}_k$-restricted Null-player Axiom:[2]

PROPOSITION 1. *Values proposed by Bolger [1], Pham Do and Norde [22], Hu and Yang [6], Macho-Stadler et al. [14] and Myerson [19] violate the $\mathcal{EC}_k$-restricted Null-player Axiom.*

PROOF. Let $(S,P) \in \mathcal{EC}_k$ be an embedded coalition such that $i \in S$ and $|P| = k$. We define $v \in \mathcal{PG}_k$ as follows: $v(S,P) = 1 = v(S_{-i}, \tau_i^T(P))$ for every $T \in P$, and $v(S',P') = 0$, otherwise. Thus, agent i is a null-player in v. Consider an extension $v^\star$ of game v to general games with externalities. Now, $[emc_i(v)](S_{-i}, \tau_i^\emptyset(P)) = 1$. As the Hu and Yang, Macho-Stadler et al. and the Myerson value take $[emc_i(v)](S_{-i}, \tau_i^\emptyset(P))$ into account, player i will have non-zero payoff. Regarding Pham Do and Norde, the same argument applies if and only if $P \setminus S$ is the set of singletons. □

Given this result, in the next section, we propose a dedicated extension of the Shapley value to k-coalitional games.

4. K-COALITIONAL SHAPLEY VALUE

We begin by formulating a process similar to the one proposed by Shapley [24], which yields the value in expectation. To this end, assume that agents leave (rather than enter) the grand coalition in a random order through one of the $k-1$ exits/doors. We assume that agents that left through the same exit form a coalition; thus, all agents are partitioned according to their selected exits. As agent i leaves, he chooses each exit with the same probability (*i.e.*, $\frac{1}{k-1}$) and receives a payoff that equals his (elementary) marginal contribution to the group of agents that he left. More formally, assuming the agents in S have not yet left, other agents are partitioned into $P \setminus S$, and that i chose the same exit as coalition T, i's elementary marginal contribution equals $v(S,P) - v(S_{-i}, \tau_i^T(P))$. Now, the *$k$-coalitional Shapley value* is the expected outcome of the agent's elementary marginal contributions over all orders. Formally, this value is a function $\varphi^k : \mathcal{PG}_k \to \mathbb{R}^N$:

$$\varphi_i^k(v) = \sum_{\pi \in \Pi} \sum_{f : A_{i+}^\pi \to \mathbf{K}_{-1}} \frac{[emc_i(v)](Z_i^\pi, Z_i^\pi \cup f^{-1}(\mathbf{K}_{-1}))}{|N|!(k-1)^{|A_i^\pi|}} \quad (4)$$

EXAMPLE 1. *Let $N = \{1,2,3\}$ be the set of agents and consider the following 2-coalitional game:*

$$v(N,\{N\}) = 4, v(S,\{S, N \setminus S\}) = |S| \text{ for every } S \subsetneq N.$$

Note that the value $v(\{1\},\{\{1\},\{2\},\{3\}\})$ is not specified, as in a 2-coalitional game 3 coalitions cannot coexist. Consider a permutation $(1,2,3)$. Since there is only one exit, as agents leave the grand coalition, they obtain marginal contributions $2,1,1$. Now, 2-coalitional Shapley value is an average over all possible permutations.

We now propose two axiomatizations of the k-coalitional Shapley value: one that follows the marginality approach (i.e., with an α-Null-player Axiom, see Preliminaries) and one with the standard translation.

Axiomatization with the α-Null-player Axiom: We begin our analysis by deriving a more concise version of formula (4).

LEMMA 1. *The k-coalitional Shapley value satisfies:*

$$\varphi_i^k(v) = \sum_{(S,P) \in \mathcal{EC}_k, i \notin S} \beta(S,N) p(P \setminus S) [emc_i(v)](S,P), \quad (5)$$

where $p(P \setminus S) = \frac{(k-1)!}{(k-|P|)! \cdot (k-1)^{|N|-|S|}}$.

PROOF. Let us calculate the probability of a given transfer that corresponds to elementary marginal contribution $[emc_i(v)](S,P)$. Firstly, exactly agents from S must have not left. Thus, in a permutation, i has to be exactly before the agents from S and after the agents from $N \setminus (S \cup \{i\})$. This happens with the probability $\frac{(|S|)!(|N|-|S|-1)!}{|N|!} = \beta(S,N)$. Secondly, the exit of agent i should lead to partition P. Thus, the first agents (in the permutation) from each coalition in $P \setminus S$ can choose arbitrary – but different – exits (they have exactly $(k-1) \cdots (k-|P|+1)$ such choices). Then, each of the remaining agents must choose exactly the same exit as the first one from his coalition. □

COROLLARY 1. *The k-coalitional Shapley value can be obtained using formula (2) with weights $a(S,P) = p(P \setminus S)$ for $|P| \leq k$, and $a(S,P) = 0$, otherwise.*

Note that for a given S these weights are equal for all partitions P with the same number of coalitions. This property is violated by the well-known value proposed by Macho-Stadler et al. [14].

Let us formalize the notion of the marginal contribution in our value. Assume that $i \in S \in P$. Based on the process described above, the probability that agent i will join any coalition $T \in P$ equals $1/(k-1)$. Thus, the chance of creating a new coalition equals $(k-|P|)/(k-1)$. This leads to the following theorem and first axiomatization of our value.

THEOREM 1. *The k-coalitional Shapley value can be obtained using the marginality approach (Formula (3)) with weights*

$$a_i^k(S,P) = \begin{cases} 1/(k-1) & \text{if } P(i) \neq \{i\}, \\ (k-|P|)/(k-1) & \text{otherwise.} \end{cases}$$

Thus, it is the only value that satisfies Efficiency, Symmetry, Additivity, and the α^k-Null-player Axiom.

PROOF. First, we show that the k-coalitional Shapley value satisfies all four axioms. To argue that Efficiency is satisfied, consider Formula (4). Let us fix permutation $\pi \in \Pi$ and function f. Considering the sum of elementary marginal contributions: $\sum_{i \in N} [emc_i(v)](Z_i^\pi, Z_i^\pi \cup f^{-1}(\mathbf{K}_{-1}))$ we see that it sums up to $v(N,\{N,\emptyset\})$ (as the grand coalition, N, dissolves sequentially to the empty coalition, $\emptyset$, with zero value). Satisfying Additivity and Symmetry can be easily seen, as based on formula (4) $\phi(v_1+v_2) = \phi(v_1) + \phi(v_2)$, and permuting the players names in game will result in the corresponding permutation of payoffs. The fact, that the

[2]The only exception is the McQuillin value [16] which is the special case ($k=2$) of our dedicated extension.

value satisfies the α^k-Null-player Axiom follows from Lemma 1. To see this, note that if $i \notin S$, then $v(S,P)$ appears in the formula only once. On the other hand, if $i \in S$, then $v(S,P)$ appears once for each possible transfer of i from S outside with weight $(|S|-1)!(|N|-|S|)!/|N|!$ times $(k-1)!/((k-|P|)!(k-1)^{|N|-|S|+1})$ for transfers to existing coalitions, and with weight $k-|P|$ replaced by $k-|P|+1$ for a transfer to a new coalition. The proper reformulation leads to the following formula:

$$\varphi_i^k(v) = \sum_{\substack{(S,P)\in\mathcal{EC} \\ i\in S}} \frac{(|S|-1)!(|N|-|S|)!}{|N|!} p(P\setminus S)[mc_i^k(v)](S,P),$$

which proves that if all marginal contributions of player i equal zero, then he gets zero payoff.

The proof of uniqueness follows from [30, Theorem 1] that states Efficiency, Symmetry, Additivity and α-Null-player Axiom imply a unique value for every α. □

In this axiomatization we used a notion of α^k-null-player, where each player that had the sums in Formula (3) equal zero is called a null-player. Our second axiomatization will use only the direct translation of the standard Null-player Axiom to k-coalitional games (see section 'k-Coalitional Games').

Axiomatization with the standard Null-player Axiom: Interestingly, the probability of a transfer to an existing coalition is always the same, regardless of coalition joined/left, and even the size of the partition. We will use this observation to provide our alternative axiomatization. Apart of two special cases, where joining an existing coalition has weight zero or one (proposed by Pham Do and Norde [22] and Skibski [27], respectively), the k-coalitional Shapley value is the first value with this property proposed in the literature.

As already mentioned, the standard translation of the Null-player Axiom is too weak to imply uniqueness. Hence, we obtain uniqueness by introducing two additional axioms – *Sensitivity* and *Fixed Impact*. The former one analyses how increasing the value of one specific coalition influences the agents. The latter one is a very basic condition – we require that increasing the value of a coalition has at least a slight effect on the payoffs of its members.

- *$\mathcal{EC}_k$-restricted Sensitivity* (the value of all coalitions of an agent affects his payoffs): if $v(S,P) \neq v'(S,P)$ for some $(S,P) \in \mathcal{EC}_k$ with $i \in S$, and $v(S',P') = v(S',P')$ for $(S',P') \neq (S,P)$, then $\varphi_i(v) \neq \varphi_i(v')$, for every $v, v' \in \mathcal{PG}_k$.

Note that assuming that the increase of a value of a coalition increases the payoffs of members would lead to the strict version of coalitional monotonicity proposed by Young [35]. The above condition is, however, weaker, and hence more general.

Let us consider how the values of coalitions without player i affect his payoff. To this end, first consider a game without externalities. Now, an increase of the value of both coalitions $S \cup \{i\}$ and S does not change the vector of marginal contributions of agent i, and does not affect his payoff. In games with externalities, we argue that there should exist a constant c such that increase of (S,P) with $i \notin S$ by the value ω is balanced by an increase of $(S_{+i}, \tau_i^S(P))$ by $\omega \cdot c$.

- *$\mathcal{EC}_k$-restricted Fixed Impact* (values of coalitions without an agent affect him similarly to values of coalitions with him): there exists a constant c such that if $v'(S,P) = \omega + v(S,P)$, $v'(S_{+i}, \tau_i^S(P)) = \omega \cdot c + v(S_{+i}, \tau_i^S(P))$ for some $(S,P) \in \mathcal{EC}_k$ such that $\{i\} \notin P$ and $v'(S',P') = v(S',P')$ otherwise, then $\varphi_i(v) = \varphi_i(v')$.

Finally, we show that both new axioms coupled with the standard translation of the original Shapley axioms imply uniqueness.

THEOREM 2. *The k-coalitional Shapley value is the only value that satisfies Efficiency, Symmetry, Additivity, the $\mathcal{EC}_k$-restricted Null-player Axiom, $\mathcal{EC}_k$-restricted Sensitivity, and $\mathcal{EC}_k$-restricted Fixed Impact.*

PROOF. Theorem 1 implies that our value satisfies standard axioms – Efficiency, Symmetry, Additivity and the $\mathcal{EC}_k$-restricted Null-player Axiom. Furthermore, Lemma 1 implies that it satisfies $\mathcal{EC}_k$-restricted Sensitivity, i.e., the change in the value of a embedded coalition, (S,P), affects the corresponding elementary marginal contribution $[emc_i(v)](S,P)$ or $[emc_i(v)](S_{+i}, \tau_i^S(P))$ if $i \notin S$ which a has non-zero weight in Formula 5. $\mathcal{EC}_k$-restricted Fixed Impact is also satisfied based on the same formula for $c = \frac{1}{k-1}$.

Let us now prove uniqueness. Let φ be the value which satisfies all six axioms. An *elementary game* $e^{(S,P)}$ is a game in which only embedded coalition (S,P) has value 1, and is the only coalition with a non-zero value:

$$e^{(S,P)}(S',P') = \begin{cases} 1 & \text{if } (S',P') = (S,P), \\ 0 & \text{otherwise.} \end{cases}$$

From Additivity, we know that

$$\varphi_i(v) = \sum_{(S,P)\in\mathcal{EC}_k} \varphi_i(e^{(S,P)}).$$

Consider $\mathcal{EC}_k$-restricted Sensitivity and $\mathcal{EC}_k$-restricted Fixed Impact. $\mathcal{EC}_k$-restricted Sensitivity implies that in the formula for φ_i every embedded coalition counts:

$$\varphi_i(e^{(S,P)}) \neq 0. \quad \text{for every } (S,P) \in \mathcal{EC}_k. \tag{6}$$

Furthermore, $\mathcal{EC}_k$-restricted Fixed Impact implies that there exist a constant c such that

$$c \cdot \varphi_i(e^{(S,P)}) + \varphi_i(e^{(S_{-i}, \tau_i^T(P))}) = 0 \tag{7}$$

for every $(S,P) \in \mathcal{EC}_k$ such that $i \in S$, and for every $T \in P \setminus \{S\}$. Consider an arbitrary embedded coalition (S,P) such that $i \in S$ and $|P| = k$. Note that player i is a null-player in the following game:

$$e^{(S,P)} + \sum_{T\in P\setminus\{S\}} e^{(S_{-i}, \tau_i^T(P))}.$$

$T = \emptyset$ is not included in the sum, as $(S_{-i}, \tau_i^{\emptyset}(P)) \notin \mathcal{EC}_k$. Thus, $\mathcal{EC}_k$-restricted Null-player Axiom implies that

$$\varphi_i(e^{(S,P)}) = -\sum_{T\in P\setminus\{S\}} \varphi_i(e^{(S_{-i}, \tau_i^T(P))}).$$

This fact combined with (7) implies that

$$\varphi_i(e^{(S,P)}) = c \cdot |P \setminus \{S\}| \cdot \varphi_i(e^{(S,P)}).$$

Finally, Formula (6) implies $c = \frac{1}{k-1}$. □

From the set of all extensions of the Shapley value to games with externalities only one – the McQuillin value [16] – can be applied to our restricted setting. We characterize it using the average approach: let us define the game without externalities as follows: $\hat{v}^{McQ}(S) = v(S, \{S, N \setminus S\})$. The McQuillin value is the Shapley value for this game: $\varphi_i^{McQ}(v) = SV_i(\hat{v}^{McQ})$. We show below that McQuillin's value is a special case of the k-coalitional Shapley value.

PROPOSITION 2. *The McQuillin value is the 2-coalitional Shapley value.*

PROOF. Consider the k-coalitional Shapley value with $k = 2$. As we recall the interpretation of our process, we see there is only one exit and all agents leaving coalition S form one group – $N \setminus S$. Thus, the marginal contribution for every permutation coincides with the marginal contributions in the game $\hat{v}^{McQ}$; hence, both values are equal. □

k-coalitional Shapley value, although proposed for a restricted environments, can be directly applied also for an arbitrary game with externalities. It is easy to verify that the value is uniquely characterize by both axiomatization also in this environment. In the same manner, k-coalitional Shapley value can be applied to m-coalitional games with $m > k$. However, as it ignores values of coalitions embedded in partition bigger than k, it will not satisfy $\mathcal{EC}_m$-restricted Sensitivity. Finally, for n players, the n-coalitional Shapley value is uniquely characterized by non-restricted (as they are restricted to all embedded coalitions: $\mathcal{EC}_n = \mathcal{EC}$) versions of the axioms.

COROLLARY 2. *n-coalitional Shapley value is the only value that satisfies Efficiency, Symmetry, Additivity, Null-player Axiom, Sensitivity, and Fixed Impact.*

We note that only for $n = 2$ this value coincides with an existing one, i.e., with the already mentioned McQuillin's value.

5. COMPUTATIONS UNDER SPECIFIC REPRESENTATIONS

In this section, we discuss the complexity of calculating the k-coalititional Shapley value based on two representations proposed for games with externalities – *Embedded MC-Nets* [18] and *Partition Decision Trees* [29]. As we will prove, there exists an interesting connection between computing the k-coalitional Shapley value and the problem of *k-colorings in a graph.*

We start with a property of the k-coalitional Shapley value that is crucial from a computational perspective.

LEMMA 2. *The k-coalitional Shapley value satisfies the* Strong Null-player Axiom*: if an agent is a null-player (in a strict sense), then he has no impact on the payoffs of others,* i.e., *he can be removed from the game.*

PROOF. Let player j be a null-player. For an embedded coalition (S, P) such that $j \in S$, consider the game $\tilde{v}^{(S,P)}$ defined as:

$$\tilde{v}^{(S,P)} = e^{(S,P)} + \sum_{T \in P \setminus \{S\} \cup \{\emptyset\}} e^{(S_{-j}, \tau_j^T(P))}.$$

See proof of Theorem 2 for a definition of elementary game $e^{(S,P)}$. We can easily check that agent j is a null-player in $\tilde{v}^{(S,P)}$, and the collection of games $\langle \tilde{v}^{(S,P)} \rangle_{(S,P) \in \mathcal{EC}, j \in S}$ forms a basis for games where agent j is a null-player. Now, the game $\tilde{v}^{(S,P)}$ with agent j removed simplifies to the elementary game $e^{(S_{-j}, P_{-j})}$ where only coalition (S_{-j}, P_{-j}) has a non-zero value which is 1 (P_{-j} is a partition of players over $N \setminus \{j\}$). Thus, it is enough to show that $\varphi_i(N, \tilde{v}^{(S,P)}) = \varphi_i(N_{-j}, e^{(S_{-j}, P_{-j})})$ holds for every $i \in N \setminus \{j\}$.

Assume that $i \notin S$. From Lemma 1 we have:

$$\varphi_i^k(\tilde{v}^{(S,P)}) = \frac{|S|!(|N| - |S| - 1)!}{|N|!} p(P \setminus S) +$$

$$+ \sum_{T \in P \setminus \{S\} \cup \{\emptyset\}} \frac{(|S| - 1)!(|N| - |S|)!}{|N|!} p(\tau_j^T(P) \setminus S_{-j}),$$

for $p(P \setminus S) = \frac{(k-1)!}{(k-|P|)! \cdot (k-1)^{|N|-|S|}}$. Simple calculations give:

$$\sum_{T \in P \setminus \{S\} \cup \{\emptyset\}} p(\tau_j^T(P) \setminus S_{-j}) =$$

$$= \frac{(k-1)!}{(k - |P|)! \cdot (k-1)^{|N|-|S|+1}} ((|P| - 1) + (k - |P|)),$$

which equals $p(P \setminus S)$. Thus,

$$\varphi_i^k(\tilde{v}^{(S,P)}) =$$

$$= p(P \setminus S) \left(\frac{(|S|-1)!(|N|-|S|)!}{|N|!} + \frac{|S|!(|N|-|S|-1)!}{|N|!} \right)$$

$$= p(P \setminus S) \frac{(|S|-1)!(|N|-|S|-1)!}{(|N|-1)!} = \varphi_i^k(e^{(S_{-j}, P_{-j})}).$$

As payoffs of all agents not in S remain the same after removing player j, then based on efficiency and symmetry, the payoffs of agents from S also do not change. □

The importance of this lemma comes from the fact that most representations (the aim of which is to provide a concise description of the game) usually focus on modelling relationships between subsets of agents. Following Lemma 2, when calculating the value, we can limit ourselves to agents that matter for a given relationship.

The first representation that we discuss, *Embedded MC-Nets*, is an extension of the MC-Nets representation [7]. The basic building block of the original MC-Nets is a boolean expression over N of the form: $p_1 \wedge p_2 \wedge \ldots \wedge p_k \wedge \neg n_1 \wedge \neg n_2 \wedge \ldots \wedge \neg n_l$, with $p_1, p_2, \ldots p_k \in N$ being positive literals, and $n_1, n_2, \ldots, n_l \in N$ being negative literals. Coalition S satisfies a given boolean expression if it contains all agents corresponding to positive literals, and does not contain any agent corresponding to a negative literal.

Now, a single rule of Embedded MC-Nets is of the form:

$$\alpha \mid \beta_1, \beta_2, \ldots, \beta_m \to w,$$

where $w \in \mathbb{R}$, and $\alpha, \beta_1, \beta_2, \ldots, \beta_m$ are the standard MC-Nets boolean expressions. An embedded coalition (S, P) satisfies the entire rule if S satisfies α and, for every β_i, there exists a coalition $T \in P$ such that T satisfies β_i. We assume also that agents that appear in a negative part of the rules appear also somewhere in the positive ones.

THEOREM 3. *Calculating the k-coalitional Shapley value from a single Embedded MC-Nets rule is equivalent to the problem of counting $(k-1)$-colorings of a graph. Thus, it is #P-complete.*

PROOF. First, we assume that: α does not contain negative literals (each can be added as a separate boolean expression on the right-hand side), sets of positive literals in all boolean expressions $\alpha, \beta_1, \ldots, \beta_m$ do not overlap (if they do, they can be combined, or if not – for example if one of these expressions is α – the rule is self-contradictory), and that each expression is not contrary. Now, based on the Strong Null-player Axiom (Lemma 2), we assume that the game only consists of agents that appear in the rule – N. Thus, the only coalition with a non-zero value in the game described using this rule is a coalition formed by agents from positive literals from α. We will denote it by S. The value, however, is non-zero only in partitions that satisfy boolean expressions from the right-hand side.

Thus, our goal is to compute the sum of weights of all such partitions. Recall that the weight of a partition is the number of functions $f : P \setminus S \to \mathbf{K}_{-1}$ such that $f^{-1}(\mathbf{K}_{-1}) = P \setminus S$ divided by $(k-1)^{|N|-|S|}$ (and using the process interpretation, the number of ways agents can leave the grand coalition and form partition

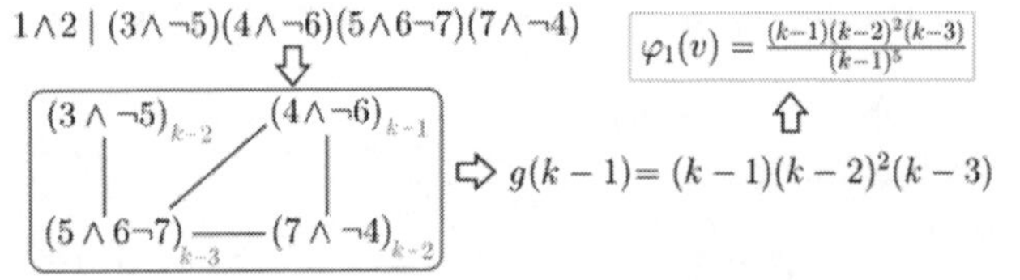

Figure 1: Computing the k-coalitional Shapley value based on an Embedded MC-Nets rule using k-coloring. Here, $g(k)$ is a chromatic polynomial.

$P \setminus S$ outside using k exits). To achieve our goal, consider a graph with m nodes that corresponds to boolean expressions $\beta_1, \ldots, \beta_m$. Now, two expressions are connected if there exists a negative literal in one of them, with agent from the other one. Thus, an edge means that these expressions cannot be merged. Now, each $(k-1)$-coloring of this graph (assigning colors from set $\{1, 2, \ldots, k-1\}$ in such a way that connected nodes have different colors) corresponds to one partition of agents that satisfies the boolean expressions, *i.e.*, one function f that meets the above criteria and the number of colorings divided by $(k-1)^{|N|-|S|}$ is equal to the sum of weights of partitions. □

The intuition behind the above proof is depicted in Figure 1. Rule $(3\wedge\neg 5)(4\wedge\neg 6)(5\wedge 6\wedge\neg 7)(7\wedge\neg 4)$ can be represented by the graph (see the frame) in which every node corresponds to one boolean expression. For this graph, we calculate the chromatic polynomial for $k-1$, i.e., the number of $k-1$-colorings. This value, as argued in the proof, is equal to the k-coalitional Shapley value of player 1.

Although the above result shows that computing our value is hard in general, the relation to k-coloring shows that whenever rules can be modelled by a graph for which counting the number of k-colorings is simple, we have a polynomial algorithm for our problem. We state the two following corollaries.

COROLLARY 3. *The 2-coalitional and 3-coalitional Shapley values can be calculated in polynomial time under the Embedded MC-Nets representation.*

This result comes from trivial algorithms that count k-colorings for $k = 1, 2$.[3] Another result comes from the restriction of the Embedded MC-Nets.

COROLLARY 4. *The k-coalitional Shapley value can be calculated in polynomial time under the Embedded MC-Nets representation restricted to rules without negative literals.*

Note that, without negative literals, the graph that represents restrictions in connecting formulas does not have edges. Another example of the application of Theorem 3 is Corollary 5.

With Partition Decision Trees [29], a game is represented as a set of rooted directed trees, called a *PDT rule*. Each PDT rule is a tree (V, E), with root x and two label functions f_V and f_E – non-leaf nodes are labelled with agents' names, leaf nodes are labelled with payoff vectors, and edges are labelled with numbers that correspond to coalitions. Thus, one path defines a partition of agents and their value. Conciseness of this representation comes from two features. Firstly, not all agents have to appear on a path. Secondly, trees are additive (the value of embedded coalition is the sum of values of this coalition in every tree), thus separate concise rules can be independently described.

[3] For $k = 1$ there exists (only one) k-coloring if a graph have no edges. For $k = 2$, each connected component has two k-colorings if it is bipartite (otherwise, zero k-colorings exists for the whole graph).

COROLLARY 5. *The k-coalitional Shapley value can be calculated from Partition Decision Trees in polynomial time.*

PROOF. Each path of the Partition Decision Trees can be translated into a set of Embedded MC-Nets rules. In such rules, boolean expressions cannot be merged and the graph of restrictions is a clique. As for cliques, the chromatic polynomial (and the number of colorings) is known; hence, based on Theorem 3, we get a polynomial algorithm. □

6. DIPLOMACY AND THE GEOSTRATEGIC IMPORTANCE OF EUROPEAN REGIONS

Diplomacy is a popular board game, created in the 1950s, that was inspired by national rivalries at the outset of World War I [26]. Diplomacy not only achieved enormous success among the general public, but was also played by politicians and diplomats, such as John F. Kennedy and Henry Kissinger. Aspects of the game have proved to be of interest both for game theorists [33] and computer scientists [12, 8, 10]. In this section, we will show how the concepts and techniques developed in this paper may be used to analyse the relative importance of provinces in Diplomacy.

The Diplomacy board is an approximate map of Europe, divided into 75 provinces, with seven players corresponding to empires that existed before WWI. Each player initially controls a few provinces and with his/her armies tries to expand this territory, with the aim of dominating the continent. Conflicting interests lead to battles for contested provinces.

The *attack/defence rules* are as follows: a player that attacks a province wins a battle if his/her attack is stronger than the defence forces and stronger than any other simultaneous attack by other parties. The strength of an attack is measured by the number of armies that attack the province from adjacent provinces. Similarly, the strength of the defence is the number of armies that support the province from the adjacent provinces, plus one if there is an army already in the province.

One particularly interesting feature of the game is that the 75 provinces preserve the geographic advantages of particular locations. Hence, a natural question arises as to the relative importance of each of the provinces, given its strategic position on the map of Europe: Should a player try to position her army in more central provinces, from which it is possible to attack many neighbours but, as such, which are more exposed to enemy attacks? Or is it better to focus on more peripheral provinces, with fewer neighbours?

In what follows, we show that, *under certain simplifying assumptions, it is possible to construct value function that corresponds to the aforementioned attack/defence rules in the game of Diplomacy. Moreover, we show that this value function admits a polynomial algorithm for the k-coalitional Shapley value.* In other words, we develop a scalable method of measuring relative importance of provinces in the context of attack/defence rules. To this end, we model the Diplomacy game board as a graph $G = (V, E)$ in which nodes V represent provinces and edges E connect neighbouring provinces. Next, we construct a k-coalitional game on this graph. In particular, we assume that each province/node is a player in a cooperative game in which at most 7 coalitions can be created. Each such coalition should be interpreted as the territory controlled by a single empire.

Before proceeding with the definition of the value function, let us introduce the following notation. We will denote by $M(i)$ the set of neighbors of node $i \in V$, and by $M_+(i) = M(i) \cup \{i\}$ – the set of neighbors including node i. We define the *strength of the attack* of nodes $S \subseteq V$ on node i as the number of i's neighbors

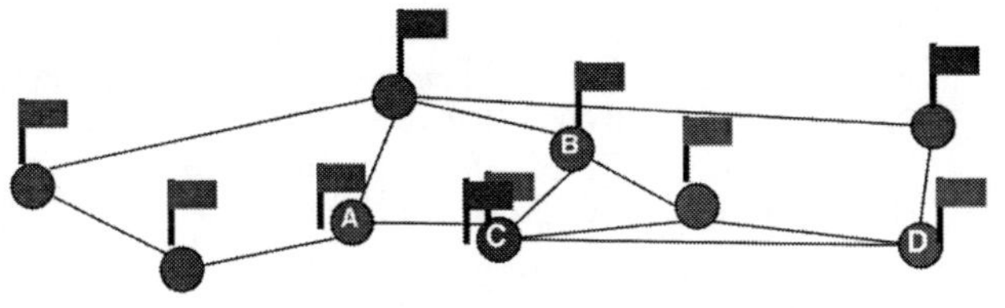

Figure 2: A sample network. Each color denotes a different coalition and flags denote the strongest attackers' colors. Here, node A has 3 red neighbors, so it is counted to the red coalition valuation. Node B has 2 red neighbors, only 1 green, and it is blue itself; hence, B is also captured by the red. Node C has 2 neighbors blue and 2 green. Thus, it has both green and blue flags. Node D is green and has 1 green neighbor, while all the opponents have attack strength of 1; hence, D has a green flag. We have $\nu(red)=4$, $\nu(blue)=3$, $\nu(green)=3$.

(including i) in S: $\text{infl}_i(S) = |M_+(i) \cap S|$. Furthermore, denoting by P a partition of nodes V, let the *strongest attackers* on node i, denoted $\max \text{infl}_i(P)$, be the coalitions in P that have highest attack strength on i. Formally:

$$\max \text{infl}_i(P) = \{S \in P \mid \text{infl}_i(S) = max_{T \in P}\, \text{infl}_i(T)\}.$$

We are ready now to formally define a k-coalitional cooperative game over graph $G = (V, E)$, where $k = 7$, G corresponds to the board of the Diplomacy game, and where the value function corresponds to the attack/defence rules in this game. In particular, let $(G, \nu) \in \mathcal{PG}_k$ with $\nu : \mathcal{EC}_k \to \mathbb{R}$ be defined as:

$$\nu(S, P) = |\{i \in V \mid S \in \max \text{infl}_i(P)\}|.$$

In words, the value of a coalition in our game is the sum of *elements* gained from attacking adjacent provinces: coalition S captures node j only if S is one of its strongest attackers (see Figure 2 for an example). We call (G, ν) the *Network Control Game*. We can also rewrite it as:

$$\nu(S, P) = \textstyle\sum_{j \in V} \mathbb{1}(S \in \max \text{infl}_j(P)),$$

where $\mathbb{1}(\sigma)$ denotes a function that takes values one 1 if the condition σ is satisfied, and 0 otherwise. We will call expression $\mathbb{1}(S \in \max \text{infl}_j(P))$ *j's component of value of S in P.*

Note that our value function assumes the following simplification of Diplomacy attack/defence rules: we do not differentiate between sea and land provinces, we ignore the fact that some provinces are supply centers, and we assume that any configuration of provinces that belong to a single player is feasible.[4]

The key computational result of this section is that the k-coalitional Shapley value for the above game can be computed in polynomial time. To this end, let us focus on the marginal contribution of an arbitrary node. In particular, node i, by leaving coalition S, can decrease its value by changing the value of any of the components from 1 to 0. Because the attack is only local, i can only affect either his own component or any of his neighbors. Moreover, node i can decrease j's component only if coalition $S \not\ni j$ was the strongest attacker on j. If this holds, there are two ways i can decrease the component of node $j \in M_+(i)$:

(a) if there is another coalition that has the same attack strength as S, j's value will be decreased independently of the coalition that i moves to,

(b) if there is no coalition that has the same attack strength on j as S, but there is another coalition T that has attack strength smaller by 1, then i will decrease value of S if and only if he moves to T.

We formalize this observation in the following proposition.

PROPOSITION 3. *Let (G, ν) be the Network Control Game. An elementary marginal contribution $[emc_i(v)](S, P)$ (i.e., the effect that node i has on the value of coalition S if he moves to S in partition P) can be decomposed as follows:*

$$[emc_i(\nu)](S, P) = \nu(S_{+i}, \tau_i^S(P)) - \nu(S, P) =$$
$$= \sum_{j \in M_+(i)} \mathbb{1}(S_{+i} \in \max \text{infl}_j(\tau_i^S(P))) - \mathbb{1}(S \in \max \text{infl}_j(P)).$$

Now, we have the following theorem:

THEOREM 4. *The k-coalitional Shapley value of the Network Control Game can be computed in polynomial time assuming that k is constant.*

PROOF. The proof is based on the following lemma.

LEMMA 3. *Assume we have n numbered items and k colors, and we color each item with a single color. Let's denote $\kappa_k^d(n)$ the number of colorings such that each of the colors is used at most d times. Then, assuming that k is constant, $\kappa_k^d(n)$ can be computed in polynomial time.*

PROOF. First, observe that $\kappa_k^d(n) = 0$ if $n > k \cdot d$. Otherwise, we use exponential generating functions to count the colorings. In this approach, we consider a power series $K(x) = \sum_{i>0} \kappa_k^d(i) \frac{x^i}{i!}$ and using analytical transformation resolve its n-th coefficient.

For $k = 1$, there is only one coloring for each n if $n \leq d$; hence, the corresponding exponential generating function is $\sum_{i=0}^d \frac{x^i}{i!}$. Multiplying this function k times (*i.e.*, taking the convolution of the sequence) and expanding using multinomial theorem, we get:

$$K(x) = \left(\sum_{i=0}^{d} \frac{x^i}{i!}\right)^k = \sum_{a_0 + \ldots + a_d = k} \binom{k}{a_0, \ldots, a_d} \prod_{i=0}^{d} \left(\frac{x^i}{i!}\right)^{a_i}.$$

We can now extract $(\frac{x^n}{n!}) \Leftrightarrow \sum(i \cdot a_i) = n$ coefficient, that is:

$$n! \sum \binom{k}{a_0, \ldots, a_d} \prod_{i=0}^{d} \left(\frac{1}{i!}\right)^{a_i},$$

where we sum over all non-negative integers $a_0, \ldots, a_d$ such that $\sum_{i=0}^d a_i = k$ and $\sum_{i=0}^d i \cdot a_i = n$. To the best of our knowledge this is not computable in polynomial time in general case, as there is an exponential number of all partitions $(a_0, \ldots, a_d)$ of k. However, for constant (or small) k, this can be done efficiently. □

We use the interpretation of the process formalized in Formula (4) to compute the k-coalitional Shapley value. Recall, that according to this interpretation, this value equals to the change in the value of the grand coalition caused by player i in the process of players leaving the grand coalition in a random order and randomly dividing themselves into partition of $k-1$ coalitions. Let π be a permutation and P a partition. We will denote by $P(i, \pi)$ a partition formed before player i leaves, assuming preceding players are partitioned according to P, *i.e.*, $P(i, \pi) = \{S \setminus Z_{i+}^\pi \mid S \in P\} \cup \{Z_{i+}^\pi\}$. Now, to facilitate calculation of the expected value, we define the

[4]We believe that to some extent all such assumptions could be waived, without compromising polynomial complexity of the algorithm. This extension, however, is left for future work.

following events in the space $\Omega = \Pi \times \bigcup_{m \in \mathbf{K}} \mathcal{P}_m$ (*i.e.*, space of all permutations of nodes and all possible partitions) that corresponds to attack strength of player i on player j, and, in particular, cases (a) and (b) from the analysis of marginal contribution.

(a) $\mathrm{CA}^i_j(\pi, P) = ((Z^\pi_{i+}) \in \max \mathrm{infl}_j(P(i,\pi))) \wedge (\exists_{S \in P(i,\pi)} : S \neq Z^\pi_{i+} \wedge \mathrm{infl}_j(S) = \mathrm{infl}_j(Z^\pi_{i+}))$ means that the nodes that follow i in π and i itself are a strongest attacker on node j and there is another coalition with the same attack strength on node j as Z^π_{i+};

(b) $\mathrm{CB}^i_j(\pi, P) = ((Z^\pi_{i+}) \in \max \mathrm{infl}_j(P(i,\pi))) \wedge (\mathrm{infl}_j(P(i) \setminus Z^\pi_i)) + 1 = \mathrm{infl}_j(Z^\pi_{i+})) \wedge \neg \mathrm{CA}^i_j(\pi, P)$ means that the nodes that follow i in π and i itself are a strongest attacker on node j and there is no other coalition with the same attack strength on node j, but the coalition that i leaves to (coalition of i in P without nodes that succeed i) has attack strength smaller only by one.

Combining Proposition 3 with formula for k-coalitional Shapley value (Formula (4)), we have:

$$\varphi^k_i(v) = \sum_{j \in M_+(i)} \mathrm{prob}(\mathrm{CA}^i_j(\pi, P)) + \mathrm{prob}(\mathrm{CB}^i_j(\pi, P)).$$

Here we used additivity of the expected value and the fact that events $\mathrm{CA}^i_j(\pi, P)$ and $\mathrm{CB}^i_j(\pi, P)$ are disjoint.

Let us compute $|\,\mathrm{CA}^i_j(\pi, P)|$. This event means that Z^π_{i+} is one of the strongest attackers of node j, but $Z^\pi_{i+} \setminus \{i\}$ is not (independently of the coalition i joins). First, we observe that only nodes that are j's neighbors matter (let $n = |M_+(j)|$ be the number of them). Among them: (i) the order and partition of nodes succeeding i in π does not matter; (ii) among nodes proceeding i in π there is a coalition S such that $\mathrm{infl}_j(S) = \mathrm{infl}_j(Z^\pi_{i+})$ and there is no stronger attacker on j. We sum over the number of j's neighbors before i in π, denoted by l. From (i) we get $(n-l-1)!(k-1)^{n-l}$ and from (ii) and Lemma 3 $\kappa^{n-l+1}_{k-1}(l) - \kappa^{n-l}_{k-1}(l)$, thus:

$$|\,\mathrm{CA}^i_j(\pi, P)| = \sum_{l=0}^{n-1} (n-l-1)!(k-1)^{n-l} (\kappa^{n-l+1}_{k-1}(l) - \kappa^{n-l}_{k-1}(l)).$$

Similarly to the case of $\mathrm{CA}^i_j(\pi, P)$ we compute $|\,\mathrm{CB}^i_j(\pi, P)|$ (combinatorial details are omitted):

$$|\,\mathrm{CB}^i_j(\pi, P)| = \sum_{l=0}^{n-1} (n-l-1)!(k-1)^{n-l} \frac{l!}{(l-(n-l-1))!} \kappa^{n-l-1}_{k-2}(l-(n-l-1)).$$

At the end, we divide cardinalities of both events by $|\Omega| = n! \cdot (k-1)^n$ (all permutations and all divisions of $M_+(j)$ into $k-1$ coalitions) to obtain the required probabilities. Thus,

$$\varphi^k_i(v) = \sum_{j \in M_+(i)} \frac{|\,\mathrm{CA}^i_j(\pi, P)| + |\,\mathrm{CB}^i_j(\pi, P)|}{|M_+(j)|! \cdot (k-1)^{|M_+(j)|}}, \quad (8)$$

which concludes the proof. □

Let us now compute the k-coalitional Shapley Value for the board of Diplomacy using the above formula. The results are presented in Table 1 and illustrated in Figure 3. They have the following interpretation in the Diplomacy context: *if we add the top province to our empire then, on average, the probability of launching a successful attack by our armies will increase most (assuming the simplified attack/defence rules).* According to the k-coalitional Shapley value, we observe that the worst provinces are either peripheral and poorly connected (Portugal, Skagerrak, Barents Sea) or central on the map and very well connected (Ruhr, Budapest, Berlin). The top provinces, on the other hand, are those that are not central on the map but that are adjacent to more central provinces (Smyrna, Norway, St. Petersburg) and large sea provinces. Interestingly, these results are consistent with the widespread belief that Turkey and Russia have best geostrategic positions [5]. However, according to the same source, England is also believed to have the best position) but it is no identified as such by our method.

Worst Provinces	k-SV	Best Provinces	k-SV
Portugal	0.002	Smyrna	0.311
Skagerrak	0.005	Norway	0.294
Barents Sea	0.005	St. Petersbourg	0.265
Helgoland Bight	0.013	Norwegian Sea	0.262
Ruhr	0.014	Armenia	0.256
Budapest	0.014	W. Mediterranean	0.246
Berlin	0.014	M.-Atlantic Ocean	0.233

Table 1: The best and the worst provinces.

Figure 3: The Diplomacy board. Green provinces are the best according to k-coalitional Shapley value (dark green – top 3). Red provinces are the worst (dark red – top 3).

We emphasise that, our results do not represent a definite statement on which provinces are the most important in Diplomacy: Firstly, we made simplifying assumptions in the definition of the value function. Secondly, because the rules of Diplomacy are complex, the final results does not depend only on the map and attack/defence rules, but on various factors such as the players' level of experience or negotitation skills. Nevertheless, we believe our analysis provides useful strategic insights into the game.

7. CONCLUSIONS

In this paper, we introduced k-coalitional cooperative games – a class of cooperative games designed for settings where no more than k coalitions can co-exist. We proposed a natural extension of the Shapley value to these games and studied its computational properties. Finally, we applied our techniques to analyse the board game Diplomacy. To the best of our knowledge our work is the first study of network properties based on a cooperative games with externalities. In future work, we are keen to study other solution concepts, such as the core for games with externalities [11].

Acknowledgements: Oskar Skibski and Makoto Yokoo were supported by JSPS KAKENHI Grant (24220003). Tomasz Michalak and Michael Wooldridge were supported by the European Research Council under Advanced Grant 291528 ("RACE"). This work was also supported by the Polish National Science Center grant DEC-2013/09/D/ST6/03920.

REFERENCES

[1] E. M. Bolger. A set of axioms for a value for partition function games. *International Journal of Game Theory*, 18(1):37–44, 1989.

[2] G. Chalkiadakis, E. Elkind, and M. Wooldridge. Computational aspects of cooperative game theory. *Synthesis Lectures on Artificial Intelligence and Machine Learning*, 5(6):1–168, 2011.

[3] L. Coviello and M. Franceschetti. Distributed team formation in multi-agent systems: Stability and approximation. In *Decision and Control*, pages 2755–2760, 2012.

[4] J. Derks and H. Peters. A Shapley value for games with restricted coalitions. *International Journal of Game Theory*, 21(4):351–360, 1993.

[5] K. J. Hagan. Global geostrategy: Mackinder and the defence of the west (review). *The Journal of Military History*, 70(2):521–523, 2006.

[6] C.-C. Hu and Y.-Y. Yang. An axiomatic characterization of a value for games in partition function form. *SERIEs*, 1(4):475–487, 2010.

[7] S. Ieong and Y. Shoham. Marginal contribution nets: A complact representation scheme for coalitional games. In *ACM EC*, pages 170–179, 2006.

[8] S. J. Johansson. On using multi-agent systems in playing board games. In *AAMAS*, pages 569–576, 2006.

[9] A. S. Kelso Jr and V. P. Crawford. Job matching, coalition formation, and gross substitutes. *Econometrica*, pages 1483–1504, 1982.

[10] M. Kemmerling, N. Ackermann, and M. Preuss. Nested look-ahead evolutionary algorithm based planning for a believable diplomacy bot. In *Applications of Evolutionary Computation*, pages 83–92. Springer, 2011.

[11] L. Koczy. A recursive core for partition function form games. *Theory and Decision*, 63(1):41–51, 2007.

[12] S. Kraus and D. Lehmann. Designing and building a negotiating automated agent. *Computational Intelligence*, 11(1):132–171, 1995.

[13] T. Lu and C. E. Boutilier. Matching models for preference-sensitive group purchasing. In *ACM EC*, pages 723–740, 2012.

[14] I. Macho-Stadler, D. Perez-Castrillo, and D. Wettstein. Sharing the surplus: An extension of the Shapley value for environments with externalities. *Journal of Economic Theory*, 135(1):339–356, 2007.

[15] M. Maschler, E. Solan, and S. Zamir. *Game Theory*. Cambridge University Press, 2013.

[16] B. McQuillin. The extended and generalized Shapley value: Simultaneous consideration of coalitional externalities and coalitional structure. *Journal of Economic Theory*, 144(2):696–721, 2009.

[17] R. Meir, J. S. Rosenschein, and E. Malizia. Subsidies, stability, and restricted cooperation in coalitional games. In *IJCAI*, pages 301–306, 2011.

[18] T. P. Michalak, D. Marciniak, M. Szamotulski, T. Rahwan, M. Wooldridge, P. McBurney, and N. R. Jennings. A logic-based representation for coalitional games with externalities. In *AAMAS*, pages 125–132, 2010.

[19] R. Myerson. Conference structures and fair allocation rules. *International Journal of Game Theory*, 9:169–82, 1980.

[20] R. B. Myerson. Graphs and cooperation in games. *Mathematics of Operations Research*, 2(3):225–229, 1977.

[21] M. Núñez and C. Rafels. Characterization of the extreme core allocations of the assignment game. *Games and Economic Behavior*, 44(2):311–331, 2003.

[22] K. H. Pham Do and H. Norde. The Shapley value for partition function form games. *International Game Theory Review*, 9(02):353–360, 2007.

[23] T. Rahwan, T. P. Michalak, E. Elkind, P. Faliszewski, and J. Sroka. Constrained coalition formation. In *AAAI*, pages 719–725, 2011.

[24] L. S. Shapley. A value for n-person games. In H. Kuhn and A. Tucker, editors, *Contributions to the Theory of Games, volume II*, pages 307–317. Princeton University Press, 1953.

[25] L. S. Shapley and M. Shubik. The assignment game I: The core. *International Journal of Game Theory*, 1(1):111–130, 1971.

[26] R. Sharp. *The Game of Diplomacy*. A. Barker, 1978.

[27] O. Skibski. Steady marginality: A uniform approach to Shapley value for games with externalities. In *SAGT*, volume 6982 of *LNCS*, pages 130–142. Springer, 2011.

[28] O. Skibski, T. P. Michalak, T. Rahwan, and M. Wooldridge. Algorithms for the Shapley and Myerson values in graph-restricted games. In *AAMAS*, pages 197–204, 2014.

[29] O. Skibski, T. P. Michalak, Y. Sakurai, M. Wooldridge, and M. Yokoo. A graphical representation for games in partition function form. In *AAAI*, pages 1036–1042, 2015.

[30] O. Skibski, T. P. Michalak, and M. Wooldridge. Marginality approach to Shapley value in games with externalities. Technical Report 13-08 Department of Computer Science, University of Oxford, 2013.

[31] L. Sless, N. Hazon, S. Kraus, and M. Wooldridge. Forming coalitions and facilitating relationships for completing tasks in social networks. In *AAMAS*, pages 261–268, 2014.

[32] R. Thrall and W. Lucas. N-person games in partition function form. *Naval Research Logistics Quarterly*, 10:281–298, 1963.

[33] G. J. Tocchet. The 'games' war theorists play. Technical report, DTIC Document, 1997.

[34] T. Voice, S. D. Ramchurn, and N. R. Jennings. On coalition formation with sparse synergies. In *AAMAS*, pages 223–230, 2012.

[35] P. Young. Monotonic solutions of cooperative games. *International Journal of Game Theory*, 14(2):65–72, 1985.

An Empirical Study on Computing Equilibria in Polymatrix Games

Argyrios Deligkas
University of Liverpool, UK

John Fearnley
University of Liverpool, UK

Tobenna Peter Igwe
University of Liverpool, UK

Rahul Savani
University of Liverpool, UK

ABSTRACT

The Nash equilibrium is an important benchmark for behaviour in systems of strategic autonomous agents. Polymatrix games are a succinct and expressive representation of multiplayer games that model pairwise interactions between players. The empirical performance of algorithms to solve these games has received little attention, despite their wide-ranging applications. In this paper we carry out a comprehensive empirical study of two prominent algorithms for computing a sample equilibrium in these games, Lemke's algorithm that computes an exact equilibrium, and a gradient descent method that computes an approximate equilibrium. Our study covers games arising from a number of interesting applications. We find that Lemke's algorithm can compute exact equilibria in relatively large games in a reasonable amount of time. If we are willing to accept (high-quality) approximate equilibria, then we can deal with much larger games using the descent method. We also report on which games are most challenging for each of the algorithms.

General Terms

Algorithms, Economics

Keywords

Game Theory; Nash Equilibrium; Approximate Equilibria; Polymatrix Games; Auctions; Bayesian Two-Player Games; Lemke's Algorithm; Gradient Descent

1. INTRODUCTION

In multiagent systems it is often the case that autonomous agents interact with each other, but do not necessarily have the same objectives or goals. This situation can be described as a game played between the agents, and the tools from game theory can be used to analyse the possible outcomes. In particular, the concept of a Nash equilibrium [37] describes a stable situation in which no agent can increase its reward by changing its behaviour. Therefore, to gain insight into the possible behaviours that a system of rational agents will produce, one can compute the Nash equilibria of the game that is played between the agents.

Appears in: *Proceedings of the 15th International Conference on Autonomous Agents and Multiagent Systems (AAMAS 2016), J. Thangarajah, K. Tuyls, C. Jonker, S. Marsella (eds.), May 9–13, 2016, Singapore.*

Games are often represented in *strategic-form*, where for each possible combination of strategy choices, a numerical payoff is specified for each of the players. However, the size of this representation grows *exponentially* in the number of players. For example, for a game with n players who can each choose between 2 strategies, $n \cdot 2^n$ payoffs must be specified. Hence, the strategic-form is typically unsuitable for the types of games that arise from multiagent systems.

Many realistic scenarios do not need the flexibility that strategic-form games provide. In particular, it is often the case that only the *pairwise* interactions between players are important. In this paper we study *polymatrix games* which model this. In these games the interaction between the players is specified as a graph. Each player plays an independent two-player game against each other player that he is connected to, and the same strategy must be played in all of his games. A player's payoff is then the sum of the payoffs from each of the games. Crucially, the representations of these games grow *quadratically* in the number of players, which makes them more suitable for representing the large multiagent systems that arise from real-world scenarios.

While there has been a large amount of theoretical work on polymatrix games [14, 15, 17, 24, 26, 28], the practical aspects of computing equilibria in polymatrix games have yet to be studied. In this paper, we provide an empirical study of two prominent methods for computing equilibria in these games. Firstly, we study *Lemke's algorithm*. The Lemke-Howson algorithm is a famous algorithm for finding Nash equilibria in bimatrix games [35], and Lemke's algorithm is a more general technique for solving *linear complementarity problems* (LCPs). Miller and Zucker [36] have shown that the problem of finding a Nash equilibrium in a polymatrix game can be reduced to the problem of solving an LCP that can then be tackled by Lemke's algorithm.

Secondly, we study a method for finding *approximate* equilibria in polymatrix games. In contrast to a Nash equilibrium, where no player has an incentive to deviate, an approximate equilibrium allows the players to have a positive, but small, incentive to deviate from their current strategies. Approximate equilibria have received a large amount of interest in theoretical work [9, 11, 18, 22, 30, 45], because the problem of finding an exact Nash equilibrium in a polymatrix game, even for only two players, is known to be PPAD-complete (which implies that there is unlikely to be a polynomial-time algorithm for this problem). From a practical point of view, it is reasonable to use sufficiently accurate approximate equilibria to study real-world systems, because often there is a non-negative cost to changing strategy, which could deter an agent from deviating even if doing so would lead to a small increase in payoff. Also, if the game is derived from real data, then any uncertainty in the actual payoffs of the underlying situation means that agents may be perfectly happy in the real world, even if the game model says that they can gain a small amount through deviation.

We study a recently proposed gradient descent-like algorithm for finding approximate equilibria in polymatrix games [22], which is the only known approximation technique for (general) polymatrix games. It generalizes the algorithm of Tsaknakis and Spirakis (TS) for bimatrix games [45]. A recent study found that the TS algorithm typically finds high-quality approximate equilibria in practice [25], much better that its theoretical worst-case performance.

Our contribution. We provide a thorough empirical study of finding exact and approximate Nash equilibria in polymatrix games. We develop an extensive library of game classes that cover a number of applications of polymatrix games including cooperation games, strictly competitive games, and group-wise zero-sum games. We also study *Bayesian two-player games*, which can be modelled as polymatrix games. In particular, we focus on various forms of *Bayesian auctions* (e.g., item bidding combinatorial auctions) and Bayesian variants of Colonel Blotto games, which have applications to task allocation and resource allocation problems between agents [44]. All of our algorithm implementations and game generators are open source and publicly available[1], so that any new algorithms developed for polymatrix games can be tested against our test suite.

We study Lemke's algorithm and the descent method on all of the problems that we consider. In total we applied Lemke's algorithm to 188,000 instances using 26 months of CPU time, while we applied descent to 213,000 instances using 2.7 months of CPU time. We found that Lemke's algorithm can compute exact equilibria in relatively large games in a reasonable amount of time, though the descent method is much more scalable and can be used to compute approximate equilibria for instances that are an order of magnitude bigger. Moreover, in contrast to its theoretical worst-case performance guarantee, the descent method typically finds very high quality approximate equilibria.

Related work. The problem of equilibrium computation has received much attention from the theoretical point of view. Firstly, it was proven that computing an exact Nash equilibrium is PPAD-complete [14, 17], even for games with only two players. While the class NP captures decision problems, the complexity class PPAD captures problems where it is *known* that a solution exists. It is assumed that it is unlikely that there exists a polynomial time algorithm for PPAD-complete problems. For this reason a line of work that studies approximate notions of Nash equilibria has arisen [9, 11, 18, 30, 45]. Specifically for polymatrix games, there is the recent descent procedure studied in this paper [22], and a recent QPTAS for polymatrix games on trees [6].

There are empirical studies on equilibrium computation both for exact equilibria [4, 5, 25, 40, 43] and approximate equilibria [25], but none of them focused on polymatrix games. Instead, these studies mainly focused on games created by GAMUT [38], the most famous suite of game generators. GAMUT has a generator for some simple polymatrix games, but it converts them to strategic-form games which blows up the representation exponentially.

Polymatrix games have received a lot of attention recently. Computing a Nash equilibrium in a polymatrix game is PPAD-hard even when all the bimatrix games are either zero-sum or coordination games [12]. Recently, it was proven that there is a constant $\epsilon > 0$ such that it is PPAD-hard to compute an ϵ-Nash equilibrium of a polymatrix game [42]. Govindan and Wilson proposed a (non-polynomial-time) algorithm for computing equilibria of an n-player strategic-form game, by approximating the game with a sequence of polymatrix games [28]. Later, they presented a (non-polynomial) reduction that reduces n-player games to polymatrix games while preserving approximate Nash equilibria [29].

Many papers have derived bounds on the Price of Anarchy [8, 27, 41] in item bidding auctions [16]. Only recently Cai and Papadimitriou [13] and Dobzinski, Fu and Kleinberg [23] studied the question of the complexity of the equilibrium computation problem in this setting. Blotto games are a basic model of resource allocation, and have therefore been studied in the agents community [2, 39]. There have also been several papers that study Blotto games with incomplete information as well, see for example [1, 33].

Polymatrix games are examples of *graphical games*, which are succinct representations of games where interactions between players are encoded in a graph. A related succinct representation is that of Action Graph Games (AGGs); introduced by Bhat and Leyton-Brown, AGGs capture local dependencies as in graphical games, and partial indifference to other agents' identities as in anonymous games [7, 20, 32].

2. PRELIMINARIES

Bimatrix games. A bimatrix game is a pair (R, C) of two $n \times n$ matrices: R gives payoffs for the *row* player, and C gives the payoffs for the *column* player. Each player has n *pure* strategies. To play the game, both players simultaneously select a pure strategy: the row player selects a row i, and the column player selects a column j. The row player then receives $R_{i,j}$, and the column player $C_{i,j}$.

A *mixed strategy* is a probability distribution over $[n]$. We denote a row player mixed strategy as a vector $\mathbf{x}$ of length n, such that $\mathbf{x}_i$ is the probability assigned to row i. Mixed strategies of the column player are defined symmetrically. If $\mathbf{x}$ and $\mathbf{y}$ are mixed strategies for the row and the column player, respectively, then the expected payoff for the row player under the strategy profile $(\mathbf{x}, \mathbf{y})$ is given by $\mathbf{x}^T R\mathbf{y}$ and for the column player by $\mathbf{x}^T C\mathbf{y}$.

Polymatrix games. An n-player polymatrix game is defined by an n-vertex graph. Each vertex represents a player. Each edge e corresponds to a bimatrix game that will be played by the players that e connects. Hence, a player with degree d plays d bimatrix games. More precisely, each player picks a strategy x_i and plays that strategy in *all* of the bimatrix games that he is involved in. His expected payoff is given by the sum of the expected payoffs that he obtains over all the bimatrix games that he participates in. We use $\mathbf{x} = (x_1, \ldots, x_n)$ to denote a strategy profile of an n-player game, where x_i denotes the mixed strategy of player $i \in [n]$.

Solution concepts. The standard solution concept for strategic-form games is the *Nash equilibrium* (NE). A relaxed version of this concept is the approximate NE, or ϵ-NE. Intuitively, a strategy profile is an ϵ-NE in an n-player game,

[1] `http://polymatrix-games.github.io/`

if no player can increase his utility more than ϵ by unilaterally changing his strategy. To put it formally, let $\mathbf{x}$ denote a strategy profile for the players and let $u_i(z, \mathbf{x}_{-i})$ denote the utility of player i when he plays the strategy z and the rest of the players play according to $\mathbf{x}$. We say that $\mathbf{x}$ is an ϵ-NE if for every player i it holds that $u_i(x_i, \mathbf{x}_{-i}) \geq u_i(z, \mathbf{x}_{-i}) - \epsilon$ for all possible z. If $\epsilon = 0$, we have an exact Nash equilibrium.

3. ALGORITHMS

Lemke's algorithm is a complementary pivoting algorithm for the Linear Complementarity Problem (LCP) [34]. Miller and Zucker have shown that finding a Nash equilibrium in a polymatrix game can be reduced in polynomial time to a Lemke-solvable LCP [36]. So, we first turn the polymatrix game into an LCP, and then apply Lemke's algorithm. We shall refer to this algorithm as LEMKE.

One drawback is that the reduction assumes a complete interaction graph even if the actual interaction graph is not complete (by padding with all-zero payoff bimatrix games). Hence, for sparse polymatrix games the reduction introduces a significant blowup, which affects the performance of the algorithm. To make this blowup clear, in our results we report the number of payoffs in the original polymatrix game and the number of matrix entries in the resulting LCP.

Descent is a gradient descent-like algorithm proposed in [22]. It tries to minimize the *regret* that a player suffers, which is the difference between the best-response utility and the actual utility he gets. The algorithm starts from an arbitrary strategy profile $\mathbf{x}$ and in each iteration it computes a new profile in which the maximum regret (over the players) has been reduced. The algorithm takes a parameter δ that controls how accurate the resulting approximate Nash equilibrium is. The theoretical results state that the algorithm finds a $(0.5 + \delta)$-NE after $O(\delta^{-2})$ iterations (for a fixed size game). We test the cases where δ is either 0.1 or 0.001, and we provide full results for both cases. We shall refer to this algorithm as DESCENT in our results.

For the strategy profile $\mathbf{x}$, the algorithm first computes a direction vector $(\mathbf{x}' - \mathbf{x})$, and then moves a certain distance in that direction. In other words, the algorithm moves to a new strategy profile $\mathbf{x} + \alpha(\mathbf{x}' - \mathbf{x})$, where α is some constant in the range $(0, 1]$. The theoretical analysis in [22] uses $\alpha = \frac{\delta}{\delta+2}$ in the proof of polynomial-time convergence. In practice we found that using larger step sizes greatly improves the running time. Hence, we adopt a *line search* technique, which we adapt from the two-player setting [46]. It checks a number of equally spaced values for α in $[0, 1]$, and selects the best improvement that is found. We also include $\alpha = \frac{\delta}{\delta+2}$ as an extra value in this check, so that the theoretical worst-case running time is unchanged. In our results, we check 201 different points for α in each iteration. For a justification of the reasonableness of this choice, see Appendix A in the full version of this paper [21].

4. GAME CLASSES

Bayesian Auctions

Combinatorial auctions. In a combinatorial auction, m items are auctioned to n bidders. Each bidder has a valuation function that assigns a non-negative real number to every subset of the items. Notice that in this setting, in general, the size required to represent the valuation function is exponential in m. In combinatorial auctions with *item bidding*, each player bids for every item separately and all the items are auctioned simultaneously. A bidder wins an item if he submitted the highest bid for that item. The bidders pay according to a predefined payment rule. We study three popular payment rules. In a *first price* auction the winner of an item has to pay his bid for that item, in a *second price* auction the winner of an item has to pay the second highest bid submitted for the item, and in an *all pay* auction every bidder has to pay his bid *irrespective* of whether he won the item or not. If more than one bidder has the highest bid for some item, we resolve this tie according to a predefined publicly known rule. We study two tie-breaking rules: either we always favor one of the players, or we choose the winner for each item independently uniformly at random.

We say that a combinatorial auction allows *overbidding* if a bidder is allowed to make a bid for a item greater than his value for it. A common assumption in the literature is that overbidding is not allowed, since allowing overbidding leads to the existence of trivial equilibria. Therefore, in our experiments we do not allow overbidding.

In a *Bayesian* combinatorial auction the valuation function for every player is chosen according to a commonly known joint probability distribution, which in this paper is always discrete. The different valuation functions that may be drawn for a player are known as his *types*.

Item bidding auctions. We create two-bidder Bayesian item bidding combinatorial auctions with 2 to 4 items for sale and 2 to 5 different types per player. Each player's type (valuation function) is chosen uniformly at random. We study several well known valuation functions:

- *Additive*: the value of each bundle of items is the sum of the values of the items contained in the bundle.
- *Budget additive*: the value of each bundle is the minimum of a budget parameter and the sum of the values of the items contained in the bundle.
- *Single minded*: each bidder has positive value for a specific bundle of items (and the same value for any other bundle of items containing that bundle) and zero otherwise.
- *Unit demand*: the value of each bundle is the maximum value the bidder has for any single item contained in the bundle.
- *AND-OR*: the first bidder has positive value only for the grand bundle of items and zero otherwise, while the second one has a unit demand valuation.

To create the valuations, we set a maximum value $M \in \mathbb{N}$ that a player can have for any item, and a minimum value $m \in \mathbb{N}$ such that in every valuation there must be an item with a value of at least m. Bids are restricted to $\mathbb{N}$, so M and m define the number of pure strategies a player has, and consequently the size of the game. For a player with a single-minded valuation function, we choose a random subset of items and a random value for that subset in the range $[m, M]$. For additive and unit demand valuations, we randomly select a value for each item from the set of allowed valuations. The same procedure is extended for budget additive bidders: first we draw values for items as for additive bidders; then we draw the budget as a random integer in $[M, N]$ where N is the sum of the values for the items.

Multi-unit auctions. In these auctions all the items being sold are identical. When there are n items for sale, a valuation is given by an n-tuple $(v_1, \ldots, v_n)$, where v_j represents the player's marginal value for receiving a j-th copy of the item. Hence, the valuation for a bidder when he wins k items is the sum of the values v_1 up to v_k.

Again we study the three most common payment rules: the first price rule, a.k.a. the *discriminatory auction*, where a player that won k items has to pay the sum of his k highest bids; the second price rule, a.k.a. the *uniform-price auction*, where the price for every item is the market-clearing price, i.e., the highest losing bid; and the all-pay rule, where a player has to pay the sum of his bids.

We consider two well known valuation functions: additive, where $v_j = v_1$ for all $j > 1$, and submodular, where $v_j \geq v_{j+1}$ for all $j \in [n-1]$. We create games with 2 to 4 items and 2 to 5 different types per player. The sampling of non-additive sub-modular valuation functions is not described here; we refer the reader to the source code for further details[2].

Other Bayesian Two-player Games

A two-player Bayesian game is played between a row player and a column player. Each player has a set of possible types, and at the start of the game, each player is assigned a type according to a publicly known joint probability distribution. Each player learns his type, but not the type of the other player. Rosenthal and Howson showed that the problem of finding an exact equilibrium in a two-player Bayesian game can be reduced to finding an exact equilibrium in a polymatrix game [31], and this was extended to approximate equilibria in [22]. The underlying graph in the resulting polymatrix game is a complete bipartite graph where the vertices of each side represent the types of a player. More specifically, if the row player has n types and the column player has m types, the corresponding polymatrix game has $n + m$ vertices and the payoff matrix for edge (uv) corresponds to the payoff matrix of the Bayesian game where the row player has type u and the column player has type v. We study the following Bayesian two-player games.

Colonel Blotto games. In Colonel Blotto games, each player has a number of soldiers m_1, m_2 that are simultaneously assigned to n hills. Each player has a value for each hill that he receives if he assigns strictly more soldiers to the hill than his opponent and any ties are resolved by choosing a winner uniformly at random. The value that a player has for a hill is generated independently uniformly at random and the payoff a player gets under a strategy profile is given by the sum of the value of the hills won by that player. We consider games with 3 and 4 hills and 3 to 15 soldiers per player. We study two different Bayesian parameters: the valuations of the players over the hills and the number of soldiers that each player has. In the game we looked at, only one of these two parameters was used (i.e., for the other there was complete information). For both cases we study games with 2 to 4 types per player. When the types correspond to different valuations for hills, for every type, the valuations for each hill were drawn from independent uniform distributions on $[0, 1]$. When the types correspond to the number of soldiers, we drew independently from $\{3, \ldots, 15\}$ for each player and each type.

[2]`http://polymatrix-games.github.io/`

Adjusted Winner games. The adjusted winner procedure fractionally allocates a set of n divisible items to two players [10]. Under the procedure, $n-1$ items stay whole and at most one is split between the players. Each player has a non-negative value for each item, and these values sum to 1. Both players have additive valuations over bundles of items. For a split item that a player has value v for, if the player receives $w \in [0, 1]$ of the item, he gets gets $w \cdot v$ value from this part of the item.

The players simultaneously assign m points to the items. Suppose player 1 assigns α_i points for the items $i = 1, \ldots, n$ with $\sum_i \alpha_i = m$, and similarly player 2's assignment is $(\beta_1, \ldots, \beta_n)$. The procedure starts with an initial allocation in which each item goes to one of the players that assigned most points to it. If the players get equal utilities it stops. Otherwise it next determines which player gets higher utility under this allocation, say player 1. Next it finds the item i that is currently allocated to player 1 and has the smallest ratio α_i/β_i. If possible it splits this item in a such a way as to equalize the total utilities of the two players, or, if not, completely reallocates this item to player 2, and repeats this step until the utilities of the two players are equalized. Thus, at most one item is actually split.

We create Bayesian games where the players' types are different valuations for the items. We study the cases of 2 to 4 items and between 3 and 15 points for the players to assign. Independently for every type, the valuations for each item were drawn from independent uniform distributions on $[0, 1]$, and then normalized to sum up to 1.

Multi-player Polymatrix Games

We study several types of game. For each, we study a range of underlying graphs: complete graphs, cycles, stars, and grid graphs. In each case the entries of the payoff matrices are drawn from independent uniform distributions on $[0, 1]$.

Net coordination games. In these games, every edge e corresponds to a coordination bimatrix game (A_e, A_e). These games posses a pure NE, which is PLS-complete to compute. The complexity of finding a (possibly non-pure) exact equilibrium is in PLS $\cap$ PPAD [12].

Coordination/zero-sum games. Here each edge is either a coordination or zero-sum game, i.e., on edge e the bimatrix game is (A_e, A_e), or $(A_e, -A_e)$. These games are PPAD-complete [12] to solve. We create games having a proportion p of coordination games for $p \in \{0, 0.25, 0.5, 0.75, 1\}$. We study how p affects the running time of the algorithms.

Group-wise zero-sum games. The players are partitioned into groups so that the edges going between groups are zero-sum while those within the same group are coordination games. In other words, players inside a group are "friends" who want to coordinate their actions, while players in different groups are competitors. These games are PPAD-complete [12] to solve even with 3 groups. We create games with 2 and 5 groups, all played on complete graphs. In every case, each group is approximately the same size, and each player is assigned to a group at random.

Strictly competitive games. A bimatrix game is strictly competitive if for every pair of mixed strategy profiles s and s' we have that: if the payoff of one player is better in s than in s', then the payoff of the other player is worse in

s than in s'. We study polymatrix games with strictly competitive games on the edges, which are PPAD-complete [12].

Weighted cooperation games. The unweighted version of these games was introduced in [3]. Each player chooses a colour from a set of available colours. The payoff of a player is the number of neighbours who choose the same colour. These games have a pure NE that can be computed in polynomial time. We study the more general case where each edge has a positive weight. The complexity for the weighted case is unknown [19]. We create games where all players have the same number of available colors k, where k is in $\{15, \ldots, 45\}$. For every player, his available colors are chosen uniformly at random from all k-sized subsets from a universe of colors of size either $2k$ or $5k$.

5. EXPERIMENTAL SETUP

The algorithms and game generators were implemented in C. The CPLEX library was used for solving LPs in the implementation of DESCENT. Our implementation of LEMKE uses integer pivoting in exact arithmetic using the GMP library; we were unable to produce a numerically stable floating point implementation (generally our attempts would start to fail on LCP instances of dimension 60). All experiments had a time-out of 10 minutes. In our results, the average runtime of the algorithms, as well as the approximation guarantee found, include the instances which timed out. The experiments used a cluster of 8 machines with Intel Core i7-2600 CPU's clocked at 3.40GHz and 16GB of memory, running Scientific Linux 6.6 with kernel version 2.6.32.

6. RESULTS

We ran both LEMKE and DESCENT on all of our input instances. Table 1 shows the results for auctions, Table 2 shows the results for other Bayesian two-player games, and Table 5 shows the results for multi-player polymatrix games. While we tested games of many different sizes, for the purposes of exposition, the tables display the largest instances that LEMKE can solve without timing out.

One general feature of our results is that DESCENT is much faster than LEMKE. To illustrate this, Figure 1 shows the performance of the two algorithms on the three types of additive item-bidding auctions included in the study. It can be seen that on the hard instances (first price and all pay), LEMKE starts to struggle when there are around 5 million payoffs in the game, whereas even the slower and more accurate of the two DESCENT variants ($\delta = 0.001$) can handle games with 30 million payoffs in under a minute. Indeed, a runtime regression for Bayesian Blotto games found that LEMKE has roughly quadratic running time (with an R^2 of 0.75 for the regression), while DESCENT has roughly linear running time (with R^2s of 0.88 and 0.96 for the δ values of 0.1 and 0.001 respectively).

However, good runtime performance for DESCENT would be of limited value if it only found poor quality approximate equilibria. Fortunately, our results show that this is not the case. In almost all experiments DESCENT found high quality approximate equilibria. The variant with $\delta = 0.1$ typically found an ϵ-NE with $\epsilon \leq 0.05$, while the variant with $\delta = 0.001$ typically found an ϵ-NE with $\epsilon \leq 0.002$.

Figure 2 shows a box and whisker plot for the quality of approximate equilibrium found by accurate DESCENT variant. It can be seen that even the worst performance of the algorithm is relatively good for several classes of game. The overall worst approximate equilibrium was a 0.1065-NE that was found on a weighted cooperation game. While this is far larger than the average performance, it is still much better than best-known theoretical upper bound of 0.5.

We now make more detailed observations about the specific classes of games that we tested. For auctions, one interesting observation is that on certain classes of auctions LEMKE will often find a pure Nash equilibrium. This is shown in the "% Pure column" of Table 1. This phenomenon is particularly prevalent for second-price auctions, where in some cases we found that LEMKE always finds a pure, and in these cases it does so in a very small amount of time.

We also found that the tie-breaking rule used in the auction can have a huge impact on the time that LEMKE takes to find an exact equilibrium. Table 3 shows the performance of the algorithm on otherwise identical auctions with different tie-breaking rules. It can be seen that resolving ties deterministically makes the game much easier to solve than resolving ties randomly.

Finally, we discuss the results in Table 4 for DESCENT with and without line search. It can be seen that, without line search, the DESCENT algorithm with $\delta = 0.001$ is often slower than LEMKE, and that using line search greatly speeds it up (and so in our other results we always used line search). Interestingly, the line-search variant of the algorithm also finds better quality approximate equilibria; it would be interesting to understand why.

7. CONCLUSIONS

In this paper we extensively studied the performance of two algorithms for computing a sample equilibria of polymatrix games. Both algorithms produce good results for most of the test instances, even though many were drawn from theoretically hard classes. More specifically, we saw that combinatorial auctions with two bidders are relatively easy to solve. This raises the natural question whether we can derive efficient algorithms for auctions with two, or a constant number of players. Furthermore, we saw that tie resolution significantly affects the difficulty of the auctions (see [13] for a discussion of this issue in a theoretical context).

In all of our experiments DESCENT produced ϵ-NE far better than the (best-known) 0.5 theoretical worst-case guarantee, which is not known to be tight. So it would be interesting to understand if this good performance is due to the nature of the games we studied or if there is a better theoretical analysis. In [25], a genetic algorithm was used to construct a bimatrix game for which the Tsaknakis and Spirakis (TS) algorithm computes an 0.3393-NE, which shows the analysis of the TS algorithm is essentially tight. Since bimatrix games are a special case of polymatrix games, this gives a lower bound of 0.03393 for the best-possible approximation guarantee for DESCENT in polymatrix games. Can a better lower bound, closer to the 0.5 upper bound, be found? We believe that it should be easier to construct a bad game for the DESCENT algorithm compared to the TS algorithm, because DESCENT computes a single strategy profile, whereas TS computes three profiles (one by descent, and then two further profiles are derived from that one) and then chooses the best one.

Acknowledgements. The last author is supported by EPSRC grant EP/L011018/1.

Games				Lemke			Descent 0.1 LS		Descent 0.001 LS	
	Valuation	Avg. Size	Auc	Time	% Timeout	% Pure	Time	ϵ	Time	ϵ
Itembidding	Additive	623990	FP	35.005	0.0	0.0	0.200	1.133e-02	1.287	2.630e-04
			SP	0.764	0.0	100.0	0.233	7.103e-03	0.232	2.312e-05
			AP	214.049	12.0	0.0	0.289	6.163e-03	1.610	1.943e-04
	Unit	650417	FP	46.351	0.0	34.0	0.199	6.249e-02	3.336	3.063e-02
			SP	203.107	19.0	58.0	0.459	1.442e-02	1.831	2.647e-04
			AP	14.709	0.0	21.0	0.168	4.182e-02	2.757	1.113e-02
	AndOr	519055	FP	280.322	23.0	0.0	0.194	1.927e-02	1.732	1.594e-04
			SP	1.269	0.0	100.0	0.279	7.026e-03	0.595	1.019e-04
			AP	166.011	9.1	0.0	0.171	8.662e-03	1.328	2.842e-04
	Budget	647583	FP	100.444	5.0	3.16	0.206	3.055e-02	2.003	4.064e-03
			SP	9.438	1.0	84.85	0.348	2.543e-02	0.915	2.186e-04
			AP	248.739	24.0	0.0	0.271	1.990e-02	2.199	2.233e-03
	SingleMinded	606511	FP	82.166	7.37	5.0	0.139	2.775e-02	1.551	1.822e-03
			SP	110.341	17.0	48.19	0.475	1.045e-02	1.359	1.669e-04
			AP	59.942	3.0	1.0	0.162	1.856e-02	1.544	1.038e-03
Multiunit	Additive	836465	D	9.504	0.0	30.0	0.295	1.452e-02	1.481	4.411e-04
			U	0.954	0.0	100.0	0.380	1.321e-02	1.870	3.579e-04
			AP	512.564	64.0	0.0	0.417	4.080e-03	2.182	3.170e-04
	SubModular	878491	D	29.054	0.0	5.0	0.270	1.326e-02	1.954	3.209e-04
			U	5.818	0.0	83.0	0.272	2.636e-02	1.741	8.645e-04
			AP	210.290	12.0	0.0	0.323	1.115e-02	2.192	3.273e-04

Table 1: Results for item bidding and multi-unit auctions with 3 items and 3 types per player. Ties are broken by favouring the second player for item bidding, and by allocating the item uniformly at random in the multi-unit case. For Lemke, we report the average running time, the percentage of instances that exceeded our timeout of 10 minutes, and the percentage of instances for which the algorithm finds a pure equilibrium. For Descent, we report the average running time and the approximation quality of the approximate equilibrium that was found.

Games			Lemke		Descent 0.1 LS		Descent 0.001 LS		
Game	# Types	# Points/Troops	Time	% Timeout	Time	ϵ	Time	ϵ	% Timeout
AdjWinner	30	5	281.407	21.0	0.939	4.450e-02	3.065	7.469e-03	0.0
AdjWinner	3	60	233.963	10.0	138.584	2.683e-02	220.254	1.827e-03	10.0
Blotto	3	8	71.814	0.0	0.032	9.181e-03	0.480	5.281e-04	0.0
Blotto	3	10	382.497	23.0	0.063	8.859e-03	0.845	5.408e-04	0.0
Blotto	3	12	573.663	91.0	0.118	8.590e-03	1.392	6.268e-04	0.0

Table 2: Results for Adjusted Winner and Blotto games. The two rows for Adjusted Winner show similar running times but actually correspond to very different input sizes, with the second row corresponding to much larger games. The underlying reason is that the number of players in the polymatrix game (i.e., number of types) affects the running time much more that the number of actions (i.e., number of items/troops). Also see Appendix B in the full version of this paper [21].

Auc	Player 1		Random	
	Time	% Timeout	Time	% Timeout
FP	63.411	0.0	408.223	43.0
SP	3.663	0.0	39.727	3.0
AP	100.949	4.0	248.665	19.0

Table 3: Results for Lemke showing the impact of the tie-breaking rule. We report on first price (FP), second price (SP) and all-pay (AP) auctions with budget additive valuations, 3 items, and 5 types per player. In the first two columns, all tied items are allocated to player 1, while in the last two, tied items are allocated uniformly at random.

	Lemke	Descent 0.001		Descent LS 0.001	
	Time	Time	ϵ	Time	ϵ
FP	229.4	508.0	5.4e-03	4.894	6.768e-04
SP	1.6	470.8	3.7e-03	0.491	1.013e-05
AP	547.3	496.0	6.5e-03	5.551	3.283e-04

Table 4: Results showing the impact of line search for Descent. We report results for first price (FP), second price (SP), and all-pay (AP) auctions for additive bidders. Lemke timed out on 13% and 44.5% of FP and AP auctions respectively, while Descent without line search times out on 61.5%, 56 % and 94% of instances on the respective auctions.

Games					LEMKE		DESCENT 0.1 LS		DESCENT 0.001 LS		
Game	Graph	# Payoff	LCP	p	Time	% T	Time	ϵ	Time	ϵ	% T
Coord-Zero	Complete	26010	32400	0	1.270	0.0	0.034	2.103e-02	0.760	9.951e-04	0.0
				0.25	63.407	4.0	0.033	2.115e-02	0.748	1.026e-03	0.0
				0.5	337.443	45.0	0.034	1.859e-02	0.750	1.070e-03	0.0
				0.75	522.207	74.0	0.033	1.604e-02	0.725	1.076e-03	0.0
				1	116.354	0.0	0.034	4.844e-03	0.598	5.087e-04	0.0
	Cycle	25920	136900	0	18.430	2.0	0.103	3.352e-02	3.612	1.093e-03	0.0
				0.25	184.451	21.0	0.103	3.157e-02	3.534	1.167e-03	0.0
				0.5	412.947	55.0	0.105	2.859e-02	3.430	1.136e-03	0.0
				0.75	593.414	96.0	0.103	2.626e-02	3.206	1.121e-03	0.0
				1	600.097	100.0	0.107	1.906e-02	2.712	6.557e-04	0.0
	Grid	26136	93636	0	35.447	3.0	0.072	3.143e-02	2.257	1.023e-03	0.0
				0.25	260.455	35.0	0.069	3.239e-02	2.233	1.137e-03	0.0
				0.5	451.699	61.0	0.072	2.955e-02	2.254	1.170e-03	0.0
				0.75	552.286	82.0	0.072	2.786e-02	2.106	1.186e-03	0.0
				1	599.349	99.0	0.070	2.159e-02	1.802	6.489e-04	0.0
	Tree	25992	152100	0	0.276	0.0	0.060	1.012e-02	0.818	1.175e-03	0.0
				0.25	0.542	0.0	0.062	1.997e-02	0.806	1.220e-03	0.0
				0.5	73.443	5.0	0.062	2.139e-02	0.814	1.246e-03	0.0
				0.75	165.418	4.0	0.061	2.150e-02	0.796	1.084e-03	0.0
				1	162.420	0.0	0.063	1.469e-03	0.778	7.686e-04	0.0
Group Zero	Complete	20250	25600	2	368.032	36.0	0.025	1.976e-02	0.564	1.093e-03	0.0
				3	495.919	66.0	0.025	1.762e-02	0.550	1.129e-03	0.0
				5	435.207	29.0	0.025	1.308e-02	0.525	9.926e-04	0.0
		26010	32400	2	438.650	59.0	0.034	1.855e-02	0.760	1.068e-03	0.0
				3	576.439	91.0	0.034	1.583e-02	0.731	1.120e-03	0.0
				5	582.924	88.0	0.033	1.186e-02	0.677	9.738e-04	0.0
		36000	44100	2	545.997	84.0	0.052	1.564e-02	1.073	1.049e-03	0.0
				3	598.616	99.0	0.051	1.396e-02	1.037	1.110e-03	0.0
				5	600.088	100.0	0.051	1.101e-02	0.969	9.721e-04	0.0
Strict	Complete	20250	25600	5	356.009	17.0	0.024	1.878e-02	0.552	1.054e-03	0.0
	Cycle	20480	108900	5	580.891	85.0	0.087	1.729e-02	2.102	1.068e-03	0.0
	Grid	20184	72900	5	551.795	77.0	0.066	1.612e-02	1.428	1.108e-03	0.0
	Tree	20808	122500	5	79.560	0.0	0.048	2.571e-03	0.664	8.111e-04	0.0
Weighted Cooperation	Complete	995000	1440000	2	194.233	8.0	8.455	1.446e-02	86.116	9.603e-04	0.0
				3	410.118	38.0	6.551	1.909e-02	73.485	1.047e-03	0.0
				5	552.583	81.0	4.957	2.585e-02	64.676	1.130e-03	0.0
	Cycle	17500	4410000	2	103.403	0.0	0.227	1.334e-01	577.984	3.094e-02	73.0
				3	90.062	0.0	0.172	1.412e-01	529.581	4.199e-02	48.0
				5	78.883	0.0	0.156	1.427e-01	438.707	3.950e-02	28.0
	Grid	27200	3006756	2	116.157	0.0	0.864	8.298e-02	275.839	5.461e-03	1.0
				3	81.933	0.0	0.464	1.110e-01	480.608	1.368e-02	15.0
				5	58.054	0.0	0.131	1.384e-01	358.662	3.028e-02	2.0
	Tree	24950	9000000	2	240.215	0.0	0.750	0.000e+00	2.768	3.253e-04	0.0
				3	220.510	0.0	0.709	0.000e+00	2.533	1.194e-04	0.0
				5	204.919	0.0	0.653	0.000e+00	2.345	8.947e-05	0.0

Table 5: Results for multi-player (non-Bayesian) polymatrix games. The underlying graphs are complete graphs, cycles, grids and star graphs. $\%T$ is the proportion of the timed out instances. On Cooperation-Zerosum games, the value of p represents the proportion of games which are coordination games, for group zero-sum games, it represents the number of groups, and for weighted cooperation games, it represents the multiplier dictating the total number of colours available, i.e. if there are k colours per player, then there are $k \cdot p$ total colours available.

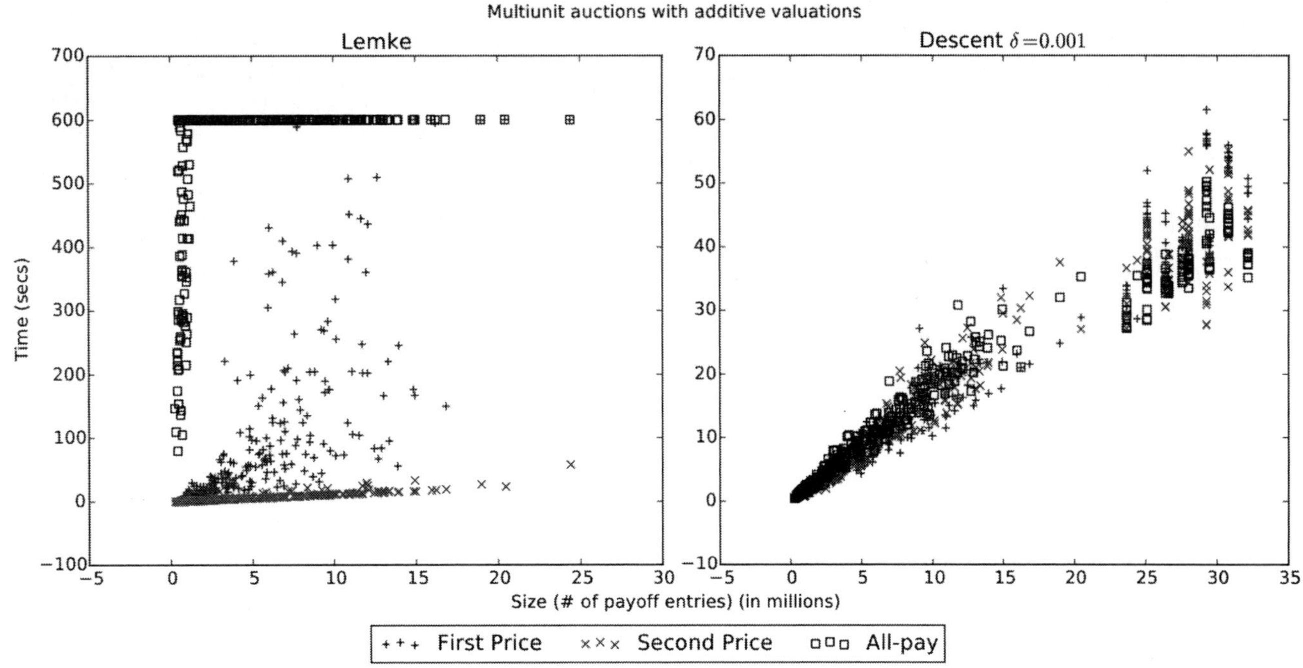

Figure 1: Plots showing the performance of the algorithms on multi-unit auctions with first price, second price, and all-pay payment rules. The left plot shows the performance of LEMKE's algorithm. It can clearly be seen that the allocation rule impacts the performance of the algorithm. The right chart right shows the performance of DESCENT with $\delta = 0.001$. The y-axis scales on the two charts are not equal: DESCENT is much faster than LEMKE.

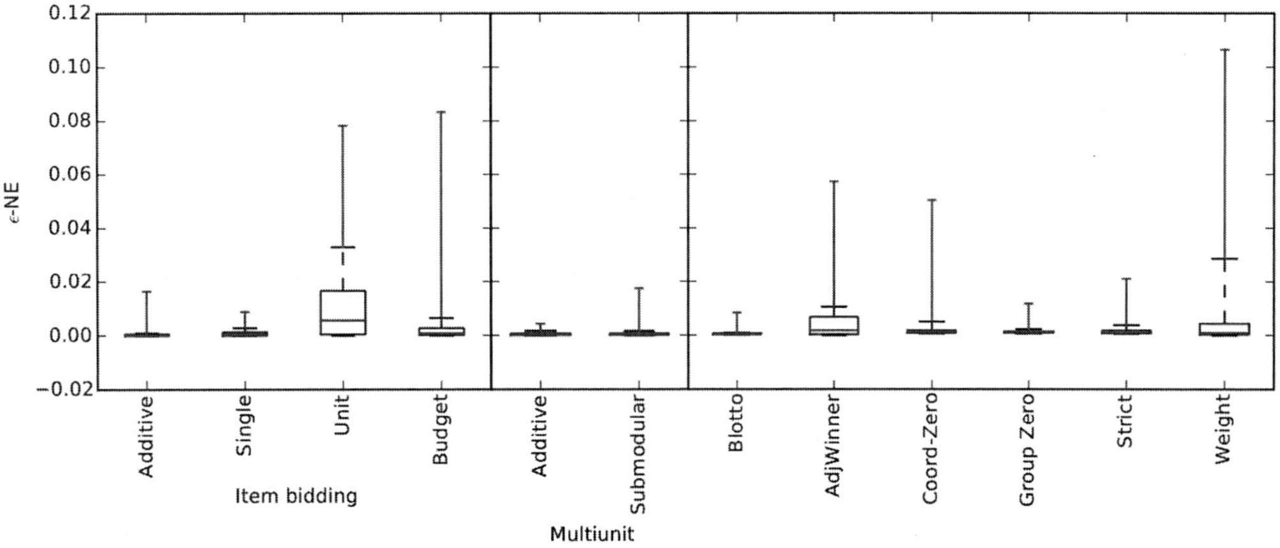

Figure 2: Box and whisker plots showing the approximation quality of the approximate equilibria found by DESCENT with $\delta = 0.001$. The results show that DESCENT almost always finds a high quality approximate equilibrium. It can be seen that on many classes of games, even the worst approximation quality over all test cases is very good.

REFERENCES

[1] T. Adamo and A. Matros. A Blotto game with incomplete information. *Economics Letters*, 105(1):100 - 102, 2009.

[2] A. Ahmadi, M. Hajiaghayi, B. Lucier, H. Mahini, and S. Seddighin. From duels to battlefields: Computing equilibria of Blotto and other games. In *Proc. of AAAI*, 2016.

[3] K. R. Apt, M. Rahn, G. Schäfer, and S. Simon. Coordination games on graphs. *CoRR*, abs/1501.07388, 2015.

[4] C. Audet, S. Belhaiza, and P. Hansen. Enumeration of all the extreme equilibria in game theory: Bimatrix and polymatrix games. *Journal of Optimization Theory and Applications*, 129(3):349–372, 2006.

[5] D. Avis, G. Rosenberg, R. Savani, and B. von Stengel. Enumeration of Nash equilibria for two-player games. *Economic Theory*, 42(1):9–37, 2010.

[6] S. Barman, K. Ligett, and G. Piliouras. Approximating nash equilibria in tree polymatrix games. In *Proc. of SAGT*, pages 285–296, 2015.

[7] N. A. R. Bhat and K. Leyton-Brown. Computing Nash equilibria of action-graph games. In *Proc. of UAI*, pages 35–42, 2004.

[8] K. Bhawalkar and T. Roughgarden. Welfare guarantees for combinatorial auctions with item bidding. In *Proc. of SODA*, pages 700–709, 2011.

[9] H. Bosse, J. Byrka, and E. Markakis. New algorithms for approximate Nash equilibria in bimatrix games. *Theoretical Computer Science*, 411(1):164–173, 2010.

[10] S. J. Brams. Fair division. In *Computational Complexity*, pages 1073–1080. Springer, 2012.

[11] P. Briest, P. W. Goldberg, and H. Röglin. Approximate equilibria in games with few players. *CoRR*, abs/0804.4524, 2008.

[12] Y. Cai and C. Daskalakis. On minmax theorems for multiplayer games. In *Proc. of SODA*, pages 217–234, 2011.

[13] Y. Cai and C. H. Papadimitriou. Simultaneous bayesian auctions and computational complexity. In *Proc. of EC*, pages 895–910, 2014.

[14] X. Chen, X. Deng, and S.-H. Teng. Settling the complexity of computing two-player Nash equilibria. *Journal of the ACM*, 56(3):14:1–14:57, 2009.

[15] X. Chen, D. Paparas, and M. Yannakakis. The complexity of non-monotone markets. In *Proc. of STOC*, pages 181–190, 2013.

[16] G. Christodoulou, A. Kovács, and M. Schapira. Bayesian combinatorial auctions. In *Proc. of ICALP*, pages 820–832, 2008.

[17] C. Daskalakis, P. W. Goldberg, and C. H. Papadimitriou. The complexity of computing a Nash equilibrium. *SIAM Journal on Computing*, 39(1):195–259, 2009.

[18] C. Daskalakis, A. Mehta, and C. H. Papadimitriou. A note on approximate Nash equilibria. *Theoretical Computer Science*, 410(17):1581–1588, 2009.

[19] C. Daskalakis and C. H. Papadimitriou. Continuous local search. In *Proc. of SODA*, pages 790–804, 2011.

[20] C. Daskalakis, G. Schoenebeck, G. Valiant, and P. Valiant. On the complexity of Nash equilibria of action-graph games. In *Proc. of SODA*, pages 710–719, 2009.

[21] A. Deligkas, J. Fearnley, T. P. Igwe, and R. Savani. An Empirical Study on Computing Equilibria in Polymatrix Games. *CoRR*, abs/1602.06865, 2016.

[22] A. Deligkas, J. Fearnley, R. Savani, and P. Spirakis. Computing approximate Nash equilibria in polymatrix games. *Algorithmica*, pages 1–28, 2015.

[23] S. Dobzinski, H. Fu, and R. D. Kleinberg. On the complexity of computing an equilibrium in combinatorial auctions. In *Proc. of SODA*, pages 110–122, 2015.

[24] K. Etessami and M. Yannakakis. On the complexity of Nash equilibria and other fixed points. *SIAM J. Comput.*, 39(6):2531–2597, 2010.

[25] J. Fearnley, T. P. Igwe, and R. Savani. An empirical study of finding approximate equilibria in bimatrix games. In *Proc. of SEA*, pages 339–351, 2015.

[26] U. Feige and I. Talgam-Cohen. A direct reduction from k-player to 2-player approximate Nash equilibrium. In *Proc. of SAGT*, pages 138–149, 2010.

[27] M. Feldman, H. Fu, N. Gravin, and B. Lucier. Simultaneous auctions are (almost) efficient. In *Proc. of STOC*, pages 201–210, 2013.

[28] S. Govindan and R. Wilson. Computing Nash equilibria by iterated polymatrix approximation. *Journal of Economic Dynamics and Control*, 28(7):1229–1241, 2004.

[29] S. Govindan and R. Wilson. A decomposition algorithm for n-player games. *Economic Theory*, 42(1):97–117, 2010.

[30] S. Hémon and M. Santha. Approximate Nash equilibria for multi-player games. In *Proc. of SAGT*, pages 267–278, 2008.

[31] J. Howson, Joseph T. and R. W. Rosenthal. Bayesian equilibria of finite two-person games with incomplete information. *Management Science*, 21(3):pp. 313–315, 1974.

[32] A. X. Jiang, K. Leyton-Brown, and N. A. R. Bhat. Action-graph games. *Games and Economic Behavior*, 71(1):141–173, 2011.

[33] D. Kovenock and B. Roberson. A Blotto game with multi-dimensional incomplete information. *Economics Letters*, 113(3):273 - 275, 2011.

[34] C. E. Lemke. Bimatrix equilibrium points and mathematical programming. *Management Science*, 11(7):pp. 681–689, 1965.

[35] C. E. Lemke and J. Howson, J. T. Equilibrium points of bimatrix games. *Journal of the Society for Industrial and Applied Mathematics*, 12(2):pp. 413–423, 1964.

[36] D. A. Miller and S. W. Zucker. Copositive-plus lemke algorithm solves polymatrix games. *Operations Research Letters*, 10(5):285 - 290, 1991.

[37] J. Nash. Non-cooperative games. *The Annals of Mathematics*, 54(2):286–295, 1951.

[38] E. Nudelman, J. Wortman, Y. Shoham, and K. Leyton-Brown. Run the gamut: A comprehensive approach to evaluating game-theoretic algorithms. In *Proc. of AAMAS*, pages 880–887, 2004.

[39] G. Polevoy, S. Trajanovski, and M. de Weerdt. Nash

equilibria in shared effort games. In *Proc. of AAMAS*, pages 861–868, 2014.

[40] R. Porter, E. Nudelman, and Y. Shoham. Simple search methods for finding a Nash equilibrium. In *Proc. of AAAI*, pages 664–669, 2004.

[41] T. Roughgarden. The price of anarchy in games of incomplete information. In *Proc. of EC*, pages 862–879, 2012.

[42] A. Rubinstein. Inapproximability of Nash equilibrium. In *Proc. of STOC*, pages 409–418, 2015.

[43] T. Sandholm, A. Gilpin, and V. Conitzer. Mixed-integer programming methods for finding Nash equilibria. In *Proc. of AAAI*, pages 495–501, 2005.

[44] Y. Shoham and K. Leyton-Brown. Protocols for multiagent resource allocation: Auctions. In *Multiagent Systems*, pages 315–366. Cambridge University Press, 2008. Cambridge Books Online.

[45] H. Tsaknakis and P. G. Spirakis. An optimization approach for approximate Nash equilibria. *Internet Mathematics*, 5(4):365–382, 2008.

[46] H. Tsaknakis, P. G. Spirakis, and D. Kanoulas. Performance evaluation of a descent algorithm for bi-matrix games. In *Proc. of WINE*, pages 222–230, 2008.

Using Abstractions to Solve Opportunistic Crime Security Games at Scale

Chao Zhang, Victor Bucarey*, Ayan Mukhopadhyay†, Arunesh Sinha, Yundi Qian, Yevgeniy Vorobeychik†, Milind Tambe
University of Southern California, Los Angeles, CA, 90089, USA
*Universidad de Chile,Santiago, Region Metropolitana, Chile
†Vanderbilt University, Nashville, TN 37235, USA
{zhan661, aruneshs, yundi.qian, tambe}@usc.edu, *vbucarey@ing.uchile.cl,
†{ayanmukg, eug.vorobey}@gmail.com

ABSTRACT

In this paper, we aim to deter urban crime by recommending optimal police patrol strategies against *opportunistic criminals* in large scale urban problems. While previous work has tried to learn criminals' behavior from real world data and generate patrol strategies against opportunistic crimes, it cannot scale up to large-scale urban problems. Our first contribution is a game abstraction framework that can handle opportunistic crimes in large-scale urban areas. In this game abstraction framework, we model the interaction between officers and opportunistic criminals as a game with discrete targets. By merging similar targets, we obtain an abstract game with fewer total targets. We use real world data to learn and plan against opportunistic criminals in this abstract game, and then propagate the results of this abstract game back to the original game. Our second contribution is the layer-generating algorithm used to merge targets as described in the framework above. This algorithm applies a mixed integer linear program (MILP) to merge similar and geographically neighboring targets in the large scale problem. As our third contribution, we propose a planning algorithm that recommends a mixed strategy against opportunistic criminals. Finally, our fourth contribution is a heuristic propagation model to handle the problem of limited data we occasionally encounter in large-scale problems. As part of our collaboration with local police departments, we apply our model in two large scale urban problems: a university campus and a city. Our approach provides high prediction accuracy in the real datasets; furthermore, we project significant crime rate reduction using our planning strategy compared to current police strategy.

Categories and Subject Descriptors

I.2.11 [**Artificial Intelligence**]: Distributed Artificial Intelligence

General Terms

Security, Human Factors

Keywords

Security Games; Abstraction; Machine Learning

Appears in: *Proceedings of the 15th International Conference on Autonomous Agents and Multiagent Systems (AAMAS 2016), J. Thangarajah, K. Tuyls, C. Jonker, S. Marsella (eds.), May 9–13, 2016, Singapore.*

1. INTRODUCTION

Managing urban crime has always posed a significant challenge for modern society. Distinct from elaborately planned terrorists attacks, urban crimes are usually committed by *opportunistic criminals* who are less careful in planning the attack and more flexible in executing such plans [25]. Almost universally, preventive police patrolling is used with the goal of deterring these crimes. At the same time, opportunistic criminals observe the police deployment and react opportunistically . Therefore, it is very important to deploy the police resources strategically against informed criminals.

Previous work has tackled the problem of allocating police resources against opportunistic criminals. There are two approaches to recommend patrol strategies. The first approach is security games, such as Stackelberg Security Games [26] and Opportunistic Security Games [27], where the interaction between police officers and opportunistic criminals is modeled as a leader-follower game. Security games contain various extensions to handle different real world scenarios, but the models of adversary behavior are based on expert hypotheses, and lack detail as they are not learned from real-world data for defender's strategy and adversary's reaction. The second approach uses larger amounts of data, such as the patrol allocation history and corresponding crime report, to learn a richer Dynamic Bayesian Network (DBN) model [28] of the interaction between the police officers and opportunistic criminals. The optimal patrol strategy is generated using the learned parameters of the DBN. While this approach predicts criminals' behavior with high accuracy for the problem in which the number of target areas is small, it has three shortcomings: i) it cannot scale up to problems with a large number of targets; ii) the algorithm performs poorly in situations where the defender's patrol data is limited; iii) the planning algorithm only searches for a pure patrol strategy, which quickly converges to a predictable pattern that can be easily exploited by criminals.

In this paper, we focus on the problem of generating effective patrol strategies against opportunistic criminals in large scale urban settings In order to utilize the superior performance of DBN as compared to other models given ample data, we propose a novel abstraction framework. This abstraction framework is our *first contribution*. In this framework we merge the targets with similar properties and extract a problem with a small number of targets. We call this new problem the *abstract layer* and the original problem the *original layer*. We first learn in the abstract layer using the DBN approach [28] and generate the optimal patrol strategy, then we propagate the learned parameters to the original layer and use the resource allocation in the abstract layer to generate a detailed strategy in the original layer. By solving the problem hierarchically through multiple abstractions, we can generate the optimal strategy for the original scenario.

Our *second contribution* is a layer generating algorithm, for which (i) we model it as a districting problem and propose a MILP in order to merge targets in the original problem into geographically compact and contiguous *aggregated targets* keeping the similarity (defined later) within them as homogeneous as possible; (ii) we develop a heuristic to solve this problem in large scale instances; (iii) we propose two approaches to find the optimal aggregated targets. Our *third contribution* is a planning algorithm that generates an optimal mixed strategy against opportunistic criminals. We consider a mixed strategy because (i) it broadens the scope of the defender's strategies; (ii) previous pure strategies depended on the model getting updated periodically; as mentioned earlier, the model usually converged to a single pure strategy that is easy to exploit.

When the defender's patrol data is limited or even missing in the original layer, the learning approach in [28] overfits the data. Therefore, in order to solve this problem, we propose our *fourth contribution* which is a heuristic model to propagate important features from the abstract layer to the original layer. We use models from behavioral game theory, such as Quantal Response, to extract these features. In particular, we first approximate the learned DBN parameters in the abstract layer using behavioral parameters. Then the behavioral parameters are propagated to the original layer.

Finally, we evaluate our abstract game in two scenarios: the University of Southern California (USC) campus [28] and Nashville, TN. We obtain data in USC from [28]. Data in Nashville, TN is obtained as part of the collaboration with the local police department.

2. RELATED WORK

There are five threads of research that are related to our problem. The first line of work we compare with is game theoretic models, such as Stackelberg Security Games (SSG) [26], Opportunistic Security Games (OSG) [27], Patrolling security games (PSG) [5] and Pursuit Evasion Games (PEG) [17]. The interaction between police and criminals is modeled as a Security Game. While SSG is successfully applied in security domains to generate randomized patrol strategies., e.g., in counter-terrorism and fare evasion checks on trains [18], it *assumes* that attackers are perfectly rational. A lot of recent research has focused on attackers with bounded rationality. An example of such work is Opportunistic Security Games (OSG) [27]. In OSGs, attackers are opportunistic criminals who are boundedly rational in planning the attacks but more flexible in executing the plan. An optimal patrol strategy against such opportunistic adversaries is generated in OSGs. Recent work in leader-follower games, PSG, also has made progress in generating patrol strategies against adversaries in arbitrary topology [4]. Different types of adversaries in this game are considered in [6] while different security resources are considered in [3]. Another example of a game theoretic model is PEG, which models a pursuer attempting to catch an evader [17]. In PEG, the evader is trying to avoid capture and the pursuer is trying to capture the evader. However, as stated before, the adversary models in these games are hypothesized based on expert input and not detailed models — detailed in locations and time — learned from large amounts of real-world data that leads to the scale-up challenges addressed in our work.

The second area of work we compare with is data mining and machine learning in the criminology domain. Recent research uses real world crime data to analyze criminal behavior and recommend patrol strategies for police. In [10], the author summarizes the general framework in this domain. In [21], crime detection and crime pattern clustering is achieved through data mining; in [12], machine learning is used for criminal career analysis. However, in this area of research, only crime data is considered. It does not explicitly model and learn the interaction between police and these criminals from real world data; and nor does this work focus on planning police mixed strategies.

The third area of work we compare with is machine learning in game theory. In [28], the interaction between a criminal and the defender is modeled as a Dynamic Bayesian Network (DBN). Crime and patrol data are used to learn such interaction in this DBN and the defender's optimal strategy is generated. Unfortunately, this approach only works in small scale problems. When the number of targets increases, the time complexity and the number of unknown variables increase dramatically; we show in Section 6, that this approach fails to run when the number of targets increases beyond 20. In [8], the payoffs of attackers in SSGs are learned from their responses against the defender's strategy. However, in this approach, the goal is to show defender strategies that enable fast learning of the adversary's payoff instead of learning these models from existing detailed data of defender-adversary interactions. Another example of such work is Green Security Games (GSG)[13, 22], where poaching data may be used to learn a model of poachers' boundedly rational decision making; as noted in our earlier paper[28], our work complements theirs, and applying abstraction hierarchies introduced in this paper in GSGs remains an interesting issue for future work.

The last thread of recent research we compare with is the abstract game that is widely used in large incomplete information games such as Texas Hold'em [14, 16]. There are a number of different approaches including both lossless abstractions [15] and lossy abstractions [23]. In [11] and [1], sub-games are generated to calculate the Nash equilibrium in a normal form games. Abstractions have also been brought into security games. In [2], abstraction is used to design scalable algorithms in PSGs. However, these works focus on clustering similar actions, strategies or states to formulate a simpler game. In our situation, we are physically merging the similar targets to generate simpler games. The criteria of merging targets is different from that of merging actions, strategies or states. Our differing criteria and approach for merging targets, different means of propagating results of our abstractions, and our learning from real-world crime data set our work apart from this work.

3. PROBLEM STATEMENT

TARGET	Case	Type	Date	Time
T2	C1	Theft	4/3/2012	8:00
T9	C2	Traffic	4/3/2012	9:30
T3	C3	Property	4/3/2012	12:00
T5	C4	Theft	4/3/2012	13:13
T6	C5	Service	4/3/2012	15:32
T1	C6	Domestic	4/3/2012	17:00

Figure 1: Sample Crime Report

TARGET	Officer Info	
T1	P1	Mike
T2	P2	Peter
T3	P3	William
T4	P4	Ben
T5	P5	Jack
T6	P6	Lucy

Figure 2: Sample Schedule

In this paper, we focus on limiting opportunistic crimes in large scale urban areas. Such large scale areas are usually divided into N targets by the defenders. At the same time, defenders divide the time into patrol shifts. T denotes the total number of shifts. At the beginning of each patrol shift, the defender assigns each available patrol officer to a target and the officer patrols this target in this shift. The criminals observe the defender's allocation and seek crime opportunities by deciding the target to visit. In order to learn the criminal's opportunistic reaction to the defender's allocation, two categories of data are required for T shifts. The first is about crime activity which contain crime details. Figure 1 shows a snapshot of this kind of data in a campus region. In this paper, we only consider the time and location information of crimes, ignoring the difference among different types of crimes. Therefore, we can summarize the crime report into a table like Table 1. In this table, columns represents the index of each target while rows represents total number of shifts, 1...T. Each element in the table represents the number of crimes at the corresponding target in that shift. $N \times T$ data points are recorded in the table.

Shift	1	2	3	...	N
1	1	1	2	...	2
2	1	1	1	...	1
3	2	1	1	...	1

Table 1: Crime data

The second category is the patrol allocation schedule at these shifts. The snapshot of such data is shown in Figure 2. We ignore the individual difference between officers and assume that the officers are homogeneous and have the same effect on criminals' behavior. Therefore, only the number of officers at each target and shift affects criminals' behavior and we can summarize the patrol data in the similar manner as crime reports, which is shown in Table 2.

Shift	1	2	3	...	N
1	2	1	1	...	1
2	1	1	2	...	2
3	2	1	1	...	1

Table 2: Patrol data

Given the available data for crime and patrol officers, our goal is to recommend efficient patrol strategies to prevent opportunistic crimes in problems with a large number of targets. To begin with, we learn criminals' behavior from data and apply the abstract game framework to hierarchically learn the criminal's behavior. Next, we propose a planning algorithm that generates the mixed strategy that optimizes the defender's utility against the learned behavior of criminals.

4. ABSTRACT GAME

Even though previous approaches [28] deal with opportunistic crimes, they cannot directly be applied to large scale problems. There are two reasons. First, over-fitting is inevitable in the learning process of large scale problems. The number of unknown variables in the learning process is $O(N^2)$ while the number of data points is $O(N \times T)$ [28]. When N increases, the number of variables gets close to the number of data points and causes over-fitting. The second reason is the runtime. The complexity of previous approaches is at least $O(N^{C+1}T)$ where C is the largest value that any variable in the model of [28] can take and it grows quickly with N. In fact, our experiments shows that the algorithm does not converge in one day even with $N = 25$. Therefore, we propose the abstract game framework to deal with opportunistic crimes in large scale urban areas.

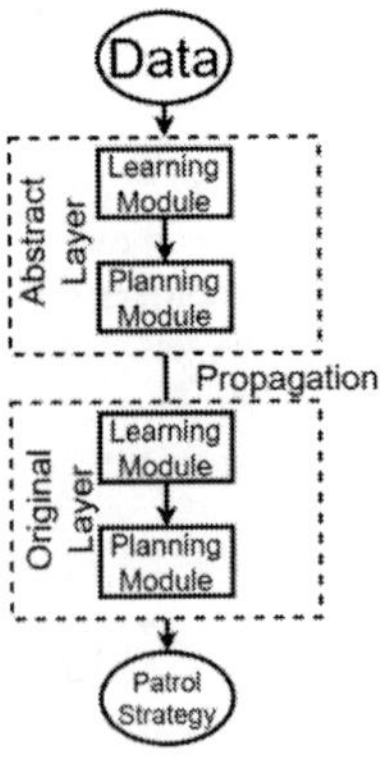

Figure 3: Game Abstraction

The idea of abstracting the most essential properties of a complex real problem to form a simple approximate problem has been widely used in the poker game domain [14]. Using such an abstraction the problem can be solved hierarchically and a useful approximation of an optimal strategy for the real problem is provided. In this paper, we use the concept of abstraction to transform the large scale urban area problem into a smaller abstract problem and solve it hierarchically. Figure 3 illustrates the four steps in our game abstraction framework. First, we need to generate the *abstract layer* from the *original layer* (Section 4.1). Targets that have similar properties are merged together into *aggregated targets*. The set of aggregated targets is called the *abstract layer* while the set of original targets is called the *original layer*. Currently we only consider two layers: the original layer and the abstract layer. If the problem in the abstract layer is still too large to solve, we need to do further abstraction, which we will discuss in Section 4.5. After we obtain the abstract layer, the second step is to learn the criminal's behavior and generate an optimal patrol strategy in the abstract layer (Section 4.2). The third step is to propagate information, such as criminal behavior features, from the abstract layer to the original layer (Section 4.3). Finally, we use the information from the abstract layer and data in the original layer to learn the criminal's behavior and generate an optimal patrol strategy in the original layer (Section 4.4).

4.1 Layer Generating Algorithm

We model the layer generation as a Districting Problem [19, 9]. The districting problem is the well known problem of dividing a geographical region into balanced subregions with the notion of balance differing for different applications. For example, police districting problems focus on workload equality [9]. Our layer generation is a districting problem that group targets in the original layer into *aggregated targets* in the abstract layer. However, distinct from the classic Districting problem where the resources are balanced among different *aggregated targets*, in our problem, we try to maximize the similarity of the targets inside the same *aggregated target*. We do so by modeling the similarity of targets within each aggregated target and use this similarity measure as one of the criteria in the optimization formulation of our problem.

When generating the aggregated targets, there are three principles to follow. First, the aggregated targets should follow the geometric constraints in the districting problem such as contiguity, compactness and environmental constraints. Contiguity means that every target is geographically connected; compactness means that all targets in an aggregated target should be close together; and environmental constraints are the constraints for defender's patrol convenience. For example, if two neighboring targets are divided by a highway, they should not be merged together. Second, the dissimilarity within the aggregated targets should be minimized. We consider two properties of target i, the number of crimes per shift with the defender's presence c_1^i and the number without the defender's presence c_0^i. For target i and target j, we define the Dissimilarity distance function as $Dis_{ij} = |c_1^i - c_1^j| + |c_0^i - c_0^j|$.

Third, the algorithm should consider the scalability constraint for learning algorithm. Let N denote the number of targets in the original layer and n denote the largest scale of problem that the learning and planning algorithms can scale up to. Then there can be no more than n targets inside each *aggregated target* and no more than n *aggregated targets* in the abstract layer. Therefore, $N \leq n^2$ in the original layer. When $N > n^2$, we need multiple layer abstraction that will be introduced later. As we prove next in Lemma 1, the more the aggregated targets are in the abstract layer, the less information is lost during the abstraction. Hence, we would want to have as many targets as possible in the abstract layer. Thus, we set n aggregated targets in the abstract layer.

Let $I = \{1, \ldots, N\}$ be a set of targets in the original layer. A partition of size K of this set I is a collection of sets $\{I_k\}_{k=1}^K$ such that $I_k \neq \emptyset$ for all $k \in \{1, \ldots, K\}$, $I_k \cap I_l = \emptyset$ for all $k, l \in \{1, \ldots, K\}, k \neq l$ and $\bigcup_{k=1}^K I_k = I$. $\{I_k\}_{k=1}^K$ is the set of the aggregated targets in the abstract layer. Let $\mathcal{P}_K(I)$ denote the set of all partitions of I of size K. Given $I_k \subset I$ we define its inner Dissimilarity as $Dis(I_k) = \sum_{i,j \in I_k} Dis_{ij} = \sum_{i,j \in I_k} |c_1^i - c_1^j| + |c_0^i - c_0^j|$. Also we define its Inertia as $In(I_k) = \min_j \sum_{i \in I_k} d_{ij}$, with d_{ij} denoting the physical distance between the geometric centers of targets i, j. In our districting process we want to find a partition which achieves both low inner Dissimilarity and Inertia over all elements of the partition. Given $\alpha > 0$ as a normalization parameter, we define the information loss function $L_I(K)$ as the lowest cost with a partition of size K, mathematically $L_I(K) = \min_{\{I_k\}_{k=1}^K \in \mathcal{P}_K(I)} \sum_{k=1}^K \alpha In(I_k) + Dis(I_k)$.

LEMMA 1. *The information loss decreases with K, that is $L_I(K+1) \leq L_I(K)$.*

The proof of Lemma 1 is in the appendix (`http://bit.ly/1ND81iH`). Based on these three principles, we propose a mixed integer linear program (MILP) to solve the districting problem. We apply an extension of the capacitated K-median problem with $K = n$. While the capacitated K-median problem [24] satisfies the scalability constraint by setting a maximum capacity for each aggregated target, it cannot handle the geometric constraints such as contiguity. A counterexample is shown in the appendix. In this paper, we handle the geometric constraints by considering the inertia of each aggregated target as part of the information loss function.

$$
\begin{aligned}
\min_{x,y,z} \quad & \alpha \textstyle\sum_{i,j} d_{ij} y_{ij} + \sum_{ik} z_{ik} & \\
s.t. \quad & \textstyle\sum_j y_{ij} = 1 & \forall i \in I \\
& y_{ij} \leq x_j & \forall i, j \in I \\
& \textstyle\sum_j x_j = n & \\
& \textstyle\sum_j y_{ij} \leq n & \forall j \in I \quad (1) \\
& z_{ik} \geq Dis_{ik}(y_{ij} + y_{kj} - 1) & \forall i, k, j \in I \\
& z_{ik} \geq 0 & \forall i, k \in I \\
& y_{ij} + y_{kj} \leq 1 & \forall j \in I \\
& y_{ij}, x_j \in \{0, 1\} & \forall i, j \in I
\end{aligned}
$$

x_j is a binary variable. It is 1 if the target j is the center of an aggregated target and 0 otherwise. The variable y_{ij} takes the value 1 when the target i is allocated to the aggregated target centered in j and 0 otherwise. The variable z_{ik} is a continuous non-negative variable that takes the value Dis_{ik} when target i and target k are allocated to the same aggregated target, otherwise z_{ik} is 0. The objective function is the weighted sum of inertia and dissimilarity. α represents the trade-off between geometric shape and the similarity within each aggregated target.

The first set of constraints ensures that every target is allocated to an aggregated target. The second set of constraints ensures that the center of an aggregated target belongs to this aggregated target. The third expression states that there are n aggregated targets. The fourth set of inequalities ensures the size of every aggregated target to be no greater than n. The fifth and sixth constraint ensures that z_{ik} will take the value Dis_{ik} when target i and target k are allocated to the same aggregated target, otherwise z_{ik} will be 0. The seventh constraint is an example of environmental constraints that target i and target k cannot be in the same aggregated target.

Directly solving this MILP is NP-hard [20]. Therefore we use the heuristic constraint generation algorithm (Algorithm 1) to approximately solve the problem. The algorithm has two phases: first, the location problem is solved as a K-median problem. In the second phase, we use the constraint generation technique [7] to solve the optimization problem. The iterative constraint generation algorithm is shown as the for loop (line 2-9). To start with, all the constraints $z_{ik} \geq Dis_{ik}(y_{ij} + y_{kj} - 1)$ for i, j, k are removed completely (denoted by the empty set $Cuts$ in line 1), and then in each iteration of the for loop the MILP is solved (line 3) and then we check whether any of the left out constraints are violated (line 4, 5). If yes, then the most violated constraint is added to $Cuts$ or else the loop stops. The maximum number of iterations is limited by MAX_IT. Constraint generation guarantees an optimal solution given large enough MAX_IT.

Algorithm 1 Constraint Generation Algorithm (I, K)

1: Center ← Location_Problem(I, K); Cuts=∅
2: **for** $i = 1, \cdots, MAX\_IT$ **do**
3: $\quad y^*, z^* \leftarrow$ Allocation_Phase(Center, Cuts)
4: $\quad i^*, j^*, k^* = \text{argmin}_{i,j,k}\, z^*_{ik} - Dis_{ik}(y_{ij} + y_{kj} - 1)$
5: $\quad$ **if** $(z^*_{i^*k^*} - Dis_{i^*k^*}(y_{i^*j^*} + y_{k^*j^*} - 1)) \geq 0$ **then**
6: $\quad\quad$ break
7: $\quad$ **else**
8: $\quad\quad$ Cuts ← Cuts ∪ $\{z_{i^*k^*} \geq Dis_{i^*k^*}(y_{i^*j^*} + y_{k^*j^*} - 1)\}$
9: $\quad$ **end if**
10: **end for**
11: **return** $\{y^*\}$, objective_function

4.2 Abstract Layer

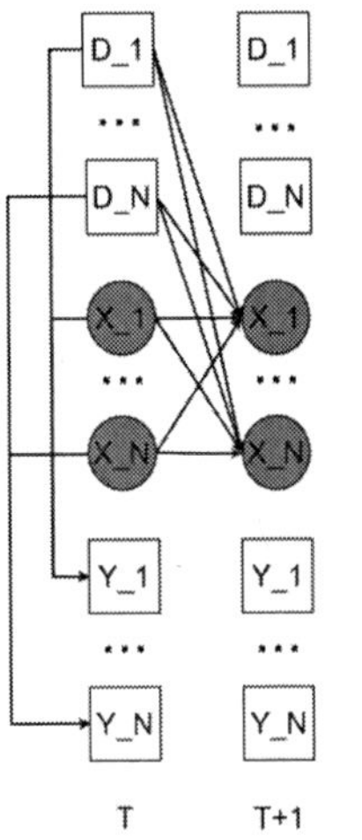

Figure 4: DBN framework

Learning Algorithms: As noted earlier, having generated the abstract layer, the next step is learn the adversary model at the abstract layer. As stated before, the Dynamic Bayes Network (DBN) learning algorithm presented in [28] could not be used in the original layer due to scaling difficulties; however, with a sufficiently small number of targets in the abstract layer, we can now use it. To illustrate its operation, we reproduce the operation with N targets as shown in Figure 4. Three types of variables are considered in the DBN: squares in the top represent the number of defenders at aggregated target i during shift t, $D_{i,t}$, squares in the bottom represent the number of crimes at aggregated target i during shift t, $Y_{i,t}$, while circles represents the number of criminals at aggregated target i during shift t, $X_{i,t}$. As shown in Figure 4, there are two transitions in the DBN: the criminal's transition from shift t to $t+1$, which is modeled as the transition probability and the crime transition at shift t, which is modeled as the crime output probability. Mathematically, a transition probability is defined as $P(X_{i,t+1}|D_{1,t}, ..., D_{N,t}, X_{1,t}, ..., X_{N,t})$ and the crime output probability is defined as $P(Y_{i,t}|D_{1,t}, ..., D_{N,t}, X_{1,t}, ..., X_{N,t})$. This model uses two matrices to represent the transition probabilities, the movement matrix A which consists of all the criminal's transition probability $P(X_{i,t+1}|D_{1,t}, ..., D_{N,t}, X_{1,t}, ..., X_{N,t})$ and the crime matrix B which consists of all the crime output probability $P(Y_{i,t}|D_{1,t}, ..., D_{N,t}, X_{1,t}, ..., X_{N,t})$. A and B contains $C^N \times C^N \times C^N$ unknown parameters.

Given available data about $D_{i,t}$ (patrol schedule), $Y_{i,t}$ (crime report), this model applies the Expectation Maximization algorithm to learn A and B while estimating $X_{i,t}$. The detail of this learning model is present in [28]. The novelty in this paper is propagating adversary behavior parameters (A and B) from the abstract layer to the original layer, which we discuss in Section 4.3; but we do that, we discuss planning in the abstract layer.

Planning Algorithms: In this paper, we focus on planning with mixed strategies for the defender rather than the pure strategy plans from previous work [28]. This change in focus is based on two key reasons. First, this change essentially broadens the scope of the defender's strategies; if pure strategies are superior our new algorithm will settle on those (but it tends to result in mixed strategies). Second, previous work [28] on planning with pure strategies depended on repeatedly cycling through the following steps: planning multiple shifts of police allocation for a finite horizon, followed by updating of the model with data. This approach critically depended on the model getting updated periodically in deployment. Such periodic updating was not always easy to ensure. Thus, within any one cycle, the algorithm in [28] led to a single pure strategy (single police allocation) being repeated over the finite horizon in real-world tests as it tried to act based on the model learned from past data; such repetition was due to a lack of updating of the criminal model with data, and in the real-world, the criminals would be able to exploit such repetition. Instead, here we plan for a mixed strategy. We assume that the model updates may not occur frequently and as a result we plan for a steady state.

We model the planning procedure as an optimization problem where our objective is to maximize the defender's utility per shift. After the defenders' (mixed) strategy is deployed for a long time, criminals receive perfect information of the strategy and their (probabilistic) reaction will not change over time. As a result, the criminals' distribution becomes stationary and this is called criminals' stationary state. In our case, ergodicity guarantees unique stationary state (see appendix). Our planning algorithm assumes criminals' stationary state when maximizing the defender's utility. We define defender's utility as the negation of the number of crimes. Therefore, the objective is to minimize the number of crimes that happen per shift in the stationary state. Let's define $I = \{i\}$ as the set of aggregated targets, D as the total number of defenders that are available for allocation; $d_I = \{d_i\}$ as the set of defender's allocation at target set I, $x_I = \{x_i\}$ as the set of criminal's stationary distribution at target set I with respect to defender's strategy d_I and $y_I = \{y_i\}$ as the set of expected number of crimes at target I. Note that C is the largest value that the variables D_i, X_i and Y_i can take. The optimization problem can be formed as follows:

$$\begin{aligned} \underset{d_I}{\text{minimize}} \quad & \textstyle\sum_{i \in I} y_i \\ \text{subject to} \quad & 0 \leq x_i \leq C, \; i \in I, \\ & 0 \leq d_i \leq C, \; i \in I, \\ & \textstyle\sum_{i \in I} d_i \leq D, \\ & y_i = \textstyle\sum_{Y_{i,t}} Y_{i,t} \cdot \\ & P(Y_{i,t} | d_1, ..., d_N, x_1, ..., x_N), \; i \in I, \\ & x_i = \textstyle\sum_{X_{i,t+1}} X_{i,t+1} \cdot \\ & P(X_{i,t+1} | d_1, ..., d_N, x_1, ..., x_N), \; i \in I. \end{aligned} \tag{2}$$

In this optimization problem, we are trying to minimize the total number of crimes occurring in one shift while satisfying five sets of constraints. The first two constraints ensure the defender and criminal's distribution are non-negative and no more than an upper bound C. The third constraint represents the constraint that the number of deployed defender resources cannot be more than the available defender resources. The fourth constraint is the crime constraint. It sets y_i to be the expected number of crime at target i. The last constraint is the stationary constraint, which means that the criminals' distribution is not changing from shift to shift with respect to the patrol strategy d_I. The transitions are calculated by movement matrix A and crime matrix B. The details of the crime and stationary constraint are shown in the appendix.

4.3 Propagation of learned criminal model

In the previous section, we generate the patrol allocation for the aggregated targets in the abstract layer. In order to provide patrolling instructions for the original layer, we propagate the learned criminal model in the abstract layer to the original layer. We need to address two cases: when there is no detailed patrol data and when there is. In particular, we have found that some police departments record the location of police patrols in detail at the level of targets in the original layer, but many others specifically only keep approximate information and do not record details (even if they record all crime locations in detail); thus leading to the two cases. We start by describing the case with sufficient patrol data in the original layer.

Direct learning (sufficient data): When there is detailed patrol data in the original layer and nothing is approximated away, we know the numbers of police at each target in the original layer at each shift. Then, we can directly learn A and B in this DBN. The learning algorithm is same as that applied in the abstract layer. The data used in the algorithm is the crime report and patrol schedule inside each *aggregated target*. While we directly learn A and B, computation of the patrol strategy at the abstract layer affects the patrol strategy in the detailed layer as discussed in Section 4.4.

Parameter Propagation (limited data): If the patrol data in the original layer is limited, the DBN model that we learned in the original layer will be inaccurate if we still apply the same learning algorithm as the abstract layer to learn matrices A and B. One remedy is to provide addition criminal information to the original layer from the abstract layer to help the process of learning criminal model in the original layer. However, in the abstract layer, movement matrix A and crime matrix B represent the criminal's behavior in aggregated targets. It cannot directly describe the criminal's behavior in the targets in the original layer. Therefore, we propose a human behavior based model of extracting behavior parameters from A and B in the abstract layer. Then we set these behavior parameters of an aggregated target as the behavior parameters for the targets contained within this aggregated target in the original layer.

Parameter extraction: We introduce the process of using a human behavior model to extract the behavior parameters from A and B. The basic assumption of a human behavior model is that the criminal follows certain patterns when moving from shift to shift. Specifically, the criminals follow the movement by the well established Quantal Response (QR). In the learning algorithm [28], one simplification made was breaking down the criminals' transition probabilities into marginal probability $P(X_{j,t+1}|D_{i,t}, X_{i,t})$ which represents the movement of a criminal from target i to target j. Based on the Quantal Response model, we approximate this movement using the following equation: $P(X_{j,t+1} = 1) = \frac{e^{Att_j}}{\sum_{n \in N} e^{Att_n}}$ where Att_n is the attractiveness property of target n. In the DBN, the movement depends not only on the attractiveness, but also on the allocation of defenders and criminals at previous shift. Therefore, we formulate $\hat{P}(X_{j,t+1} = 1|D_{i,t}, X_{i,t})$ as ($\lambda_i, \mu_i \geq 0$):

$$\begin{cases} \frac{e^{Att_j}}{\sum_{n \in N} e^{Att_n}} \cdot e^{\lambda_i X_{i,t} + \mu_i D_{i,t}}, & \text{if } i \neq j \\ \frac{e^{Att_j}}{\sum_{n \in N} e^{Att_n}} \cdot e^{\lambda_i X_{i,t} - \mu_i D_{i,t}}, & \text{otherwise} \end{cases} \tag{3}$$

The reason for the above effect of defender is that the defender at target i disperses criminals to other targets. However, λ, μ and Att are not known and we need to learn them from data. Our approach to compute λ, μ and Att is to find their values that minimize the L_1 distance between $\hat{P}(X_{j,t+1} = 1|D_{i,t}, X_{i,t})$ and the learned marginal probability $P(X_{j,t+1} = 1|D_{i,t}, X_{i,t})$. We can formulate this problem as the following optimization:

$$\min_{Att,\lambda,\mu} \sum_{i,j,D_{i,t},X_{i,t}} \quad ||P(X_{j,t+1} = 1|D_{i,t}, X_{i,t}) - \hat{P}(X_{j,t+1} = 1|D_{i,t}, X_{i,t})||$$
$$\text{subject to} \quad \mu_i \geq 0, \lambda_i \geq 0, i = 1, ..., N$$

The constraints represent the positive effect of number of criminals on the transition probability and more defenders lead to faster dispersion of criminals. λ, μ and Att are the behavior parameters that we propagate to original layer.

Since λ and μ represent the influence of the number of criminals and number of defenders on the criminals' movement in the aggregated target, it is reasonable to assume that the criminals' movement in the targets that belong to the aggregated target inherit these parameters. In other words, this means that the influence of the number of criminals and defenders is the same within the aggregated target. At the same time, Att measures the availability of the crime opportunities. Therefore, within one aggregated target, the attractiveness is distributed among the targets proportional to the total number of crimes in each target. For example, if the attractiveness of an aggregated target I (made up of I_1 and I_2) is 0.6, the total number of crimes at target I_1 is 80 while that at target I_2 is 40, then the attractiveness of A_1 is 0.4 while that of A_2 is 0.2. λ, μ and Att for each target are the behavior parameters that will be used in crime and stationary constraints in the planning algorithm.

4.4 Computing Strategy in the Original Layer

In the previous section, we generated the adversary behavior parameters in the original layer. In order to provide patrolling instructions for the original layer, we utilize the strategy in the abstract layer to assign resources in the original layer. Then, combined with the propagated adversary behavior parameters we generate the strategy at the original layer.

Resource Allocation: In the abstract layer, the optimal strategy recommends the number of resources allocated to each *aggregated target*. We use this recommendation as a constraint on the number of resources in planning within the *aggregated targets* at the original layer. For example, the abstract layer may provide 0.8 as the allocation to an aggregated target say X; then we plan patrols in X in the original layer using 0.8 as the total number of resources.

Next, in the original layer, we treat each *aggregated target* in the abstract layer as an independent DBN as shown in Figure 4. The same algorithm for generating a mixed strategy in the abstract layer can be applied in each of the independent DBNs. The optimization problem is the same as Equation 2. D is the total number of resources allocated to these aggregated targets (e.g., 0.8 to target X).

In addition, the formulations of crime and stationary constraints required in the computation of the mixed strategy are different for the scenario with sufficient and limited data. For the scenario with sufficient data these constraints are formulated using the parameters A and B of the DBN that is learned in this original layer. For the scenario with limited data the propagated values of λ, μ and Att are used to estimate the the A and B parameters for the DBN representation of the adversary behavior in the original layer. The estimation is the inversion of parameter extraction, and it happens in the original layer. For example, we use Equation 3 to estimate the parameters using λ, μ and Att. The details are presented in the appendix. Then, these reconstructed A and B are used to formulate the crime and stationary constraints.

4.5 Extended Abstract Game

When $n^2 < N$, we can use two layers of abstraction to solve the problem. However, when the real problem has $N > n^2$ targets, even two layered abstraction does not suffice since there must be a layer in the game with more than n targets. Therefore, we propose the multiple layer framework to handle problems with an arbitrarily large number of targets. This framework is an extension of the two layer abstract game. We apply an iterative four step process. As a first step, we need to decide the number of layers as well as the districting of targets for each of the layers. Considering the scalability constraints (recall that there cannot be more than n targets within each aggregated target), the number of layers is $M = \lfloor \log_n N \rfloor + 1$. We denote the original layer as Layer 1 and the layer directly generated from Layer m as layer $m + 1$. In this notation, the topmost abstract layer is Layer M. The second step is learning criminals behavior in the top layer. The third step is to generate a patrol strategy at this layer. The fourth step is to propagate parameters to the next layer. We keep executing steps two to four for each layer until we reach the original layer. At each layer, we decide whether to do parameter propagation based on the availability of the patrol data. If we have sufficient patrol data at layer m, we do direct learning at layer m. Otherwise, we do parameter propagation from layer $m + 1$ to layer m.

We propose three different layer generation algorithms. The first algorithm is the direct algorithm. For example, if $N = 50$ and $n = 5$. Then, there should be $M = 3$ layers. For layer 1, there will be 50 targets. For layer 2, the number of targets could be any integer between 10 to 25. For layer 3, the number of targets can be 2 to 5. The direct learning tries all the combinations of three layers and runs the MILP for each combination to generate the optimal segmentation. It calls the MILP in Section 4.1 for $O(N^M \cdot M)$ times; the second algorithm is a dynamic programming approach that ensures the solution is globally optimal. The MILP is called $O(N^2 \cdot M)$ times; the third algorithm is the greedy algorithm that sets the number of targets to be maximum, which for the mth layer is n^{M+1-m}. The number of calls is M while the solution is not necessarily optimal. Details are in the appendix.

5. REAL WORLD VALIDATION

Figure 5: Campus map 1

Figure 6: Campus map 2

We use two sets of real world data to validate the game abstraction framework. In the first case we use the data from the University of Southern California (USC) campus that is provided by [28]. We thank the authors for providing three years (2012-2014) of crime report and patrol schedule from the USC campus. The number of total crime events is on the order of 10^2. [28] reports that the campus patrol area (USC campus and its surroundings) is divided into five patrol areas, which are shown in Fig 5. In order to make the patrols more efficient, the police officers wish to further divide the whole campus into 25 patrol areas and get patrol recommendations on these 25 patrol areas. There are two tasks for us, (a) starting from city blocks (there are 298 city blocks and they form the basis of the USC map), create 25 separate "targets", as in our layer generation problem; (b) generate an optimal patrol strategy for these 25 targets. The creation of 25 targets is also a districting problem and the technique in Section 4.1 can be directly applied. The 25 targets generated by the districting algorithm is shown in Figure 6.

We treat these 25 targets as the original layer. n is set to be 5 as the runtime of learning and planning algorithm with $n = 5$ is reasonably small. So then we use two layer game abstraction to solve this problem with 25 targets. The abstract layer is the five patrol areas in Fig 5. This is because of the center area (the darkest area) is the campus itself and is separated from its environment by fences and gates. These environmental constraints cause our layer generation to automatically create the area into 5 targets as shown in Figure 5. Additionally, police only record their presence in the five areas, and thus, we do not have detailed police presence data; as a result, we use our behavior learning to propagate parameters from the abstract layer to the original layer.

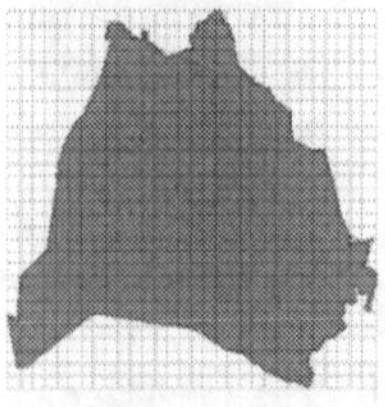

Figure 7: City map

In the second case, we use data about crime and detailed police patrol locations in Nashville, TN, USA. The data covers a total area of 526 sq. miles. Only burglaries (burglary/breaking and entering) have been considered for the analysis. Burglary is the chosen crime type as it is a major portion of all property crimes and is well distributed throughout the county. Data for 10 months in 2009 is used. The number of total crime events is on the order of 10^3. Observations that lacked coordinates were geocoded from their addresses. Police presence is calculated from GPS dispatches made by police patrol vehicles. Each dispatch consists of a unique vehicle identifier, a timestamp and the exact location of the vehicle at that point in time. We divide the whole city into $N = 900$ targets as shown in Figure 7. Since n is 5, the number of layers we need is $M = \lfloor \log_5 900 \rfloor + 1 = 5$. We use the multiple layer abstraction framework to solve this problem.

6. EXPERIMENTAL RESULTS

Experiment setup. We use MATLAB to solve our optimization problems. There are two threads of experiments, one on the USC campus problem and the other on Nashville, TN problem. To avoid leaking confidential information of police departments, all crime numbers shown in the results are normalized. The experiments were run on a machine with 2.4 GHz and 16 GB RAM.

Game Abstraction Framework: Our first experiment is on comparing the performance of our game abstraction framework with the DBN framework proposed in [28] for large scale problems. Since the DBN framework cannot even scale to problems with 25 targets, in this experiment we run on problems with subsets containing N targets ($5 \leq N < 25$) out of these 25 targets in the USC campus. As shown in Figure 8, we compare the runtime of these two frameworks. The x-axis in Fig. 8 is the number of targets N in the problem. For each N, we try ten different subsets and the average runtime is reported. The y-axis indicates the runtime in seconds. The cut-off time is 3600s. As can be seen in Figure 8, the runtime of the DBN framework grows exponentially with the scale of the problem and cannot finish in an hour when $N = 20$. At the same time, the runtime of the game abstraction framework grows linearly with the scale of the problem. It takes less than 5 minutes to solve the problems with $N = 20$. This indicates that the DBN framework fails to scale up to large scale problems while the game abstraction framework can handle many more targets.

In Figure 9 we compare the *prediction accuracy* of these two different frameworks. We divide the 36 months' data sets into two parts, the first 35 months' data is used for learning while we predict the crime distribution for the last month and compare it with the real crime data in that month. For every target and every shift, we measure the *prediction accuracy* as the predicted probability of the number of crimes reported in the data for that target and shift. For example, for target i and shift t, our prediction is that there is 30% probability that no crime occurs and 70% that one crime occurs while in the data there is one crime at target i in shift t. Then, the prediction accuracy for target i for shift t is 0.7. The reported accuracy is the average accuracy over all targets and all shifts over all ten different subsets. The higher the accuracy, the better our prediction. As can be seen in Figure 9, the game abstraction framework achieves similar prediction accuracy compared to the DBN algorithms given any number of targets in the problem. This indicates that even through information may be lost during the abstraction, the game abstraction framework captures important features of the criminal and performs as well as the exact DBN framework while running 100 of times faster.

Layer Generation Algorithm: Next, we use the data from the city to evaluate the performance of our layer generation algorithms. Again, we run the layer generation algorithms on problems with subsets containing N targets ($N \leq 900$) out of the 900 targets in the city map. For each N, we try ten different subsets and report the average value except when $N = 900$ for which only one subset is possible. Figure 10 compares the runtime of different layer generation algorithms in log format. Three different algorithms are compared, the direct algorithm (Direct) that traverses all possible layer combinations; the dynamic programming algorithm (DP) and the greedy algorithm (Greedy). The x-axis in Fig. 10 is the number of targets N. For $N = 25$, two layers are needed; for $N = 50$, three layers are needed; for $N = 200$, four layers are needed and for $N = 900$, five layers are needed. The y-axis is the runtime of different algorithms in seconds. The cut-off time is set at 36000s. When $N = 25$, the runtime of these three algorithms are the same because the layer generation is unique. The number of targets in layer 2 is 5. When $N = 50$, the runtime of the direct algorithm is the same as that of the DP algorithm while the runtime of the greedy algorithm is significantly lower. When $N = 200$, the direct algorithm cannot finish in 10 hours; the DP algorithm takes around five hours while greedy algorithm finishes in less than 10 minutes. When $N = 900$, both direct learning and DP are cut off while the runtime for greedy is less than 15 minutes. This validates our theoretical result that the runtime of direct algorithm grows exponentially with the scale of the problem, that of DP grows polynomially and that of greedy algorithm grows linearly with the number of layers. Since both direct and DP algorithm cannot scale up to the problem with $N = 900$, we use the greedy algorithm as the layer generation algorithm in the city problem.

In Figure 11, we compare the information loss of different layer generation algorithms. The information loss is defined as the objective in Equation 1. As can be seen in Fig. 11, the information loss of DP is the same as that of direct learning in any situations. This is because DP ensures a globally optimal solution. At the same time, the information loss of the greedy algorithm is higher than that of the DP algorithm but no more than 15% higher. This indicates that while greedy algorithm cannot ensure global optimal information loss, it can reach a good approximation in reasonable runtime.

Learning: Third, we evaluate the performance of our learning algorithm. Game abstraction is used for both problems and we evaluate the predictions in the original layer. The result shown in Figure 12 and Figure 13 compares the prediction accuracy of different algorithms in USC campus and the city problem respectively. Three different algorithms are compared: (1) the Random approach, in which the probabilities of each situation are the same (Random), (2) game abstraction with direct learning for both the abstract and original layer (DL) and (3) game abstraction with parameter propagation in the original layer (PP). We divide the whole data sets

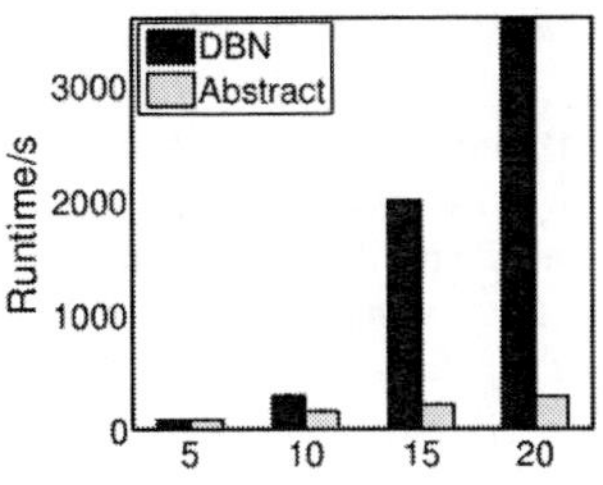

Figure 8: Runtime

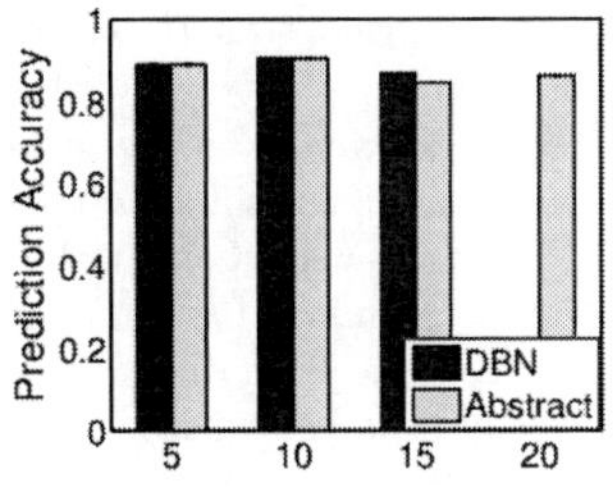

Figure 9: Accuracy

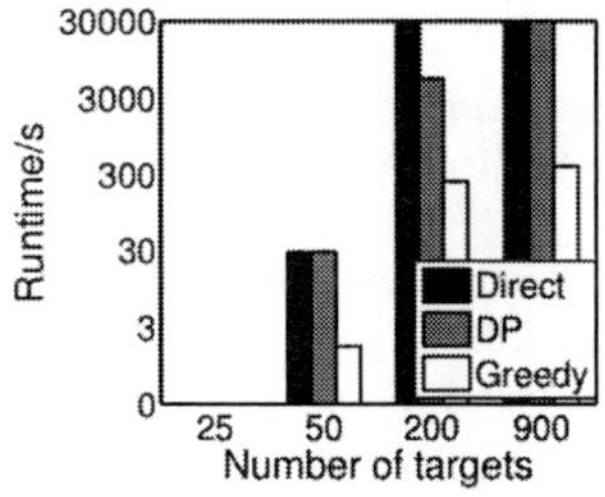

Figure 10: Runtime

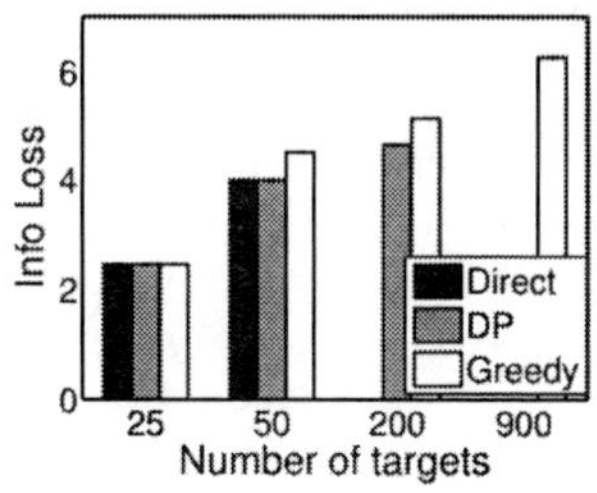

Figure 11: Information Loss

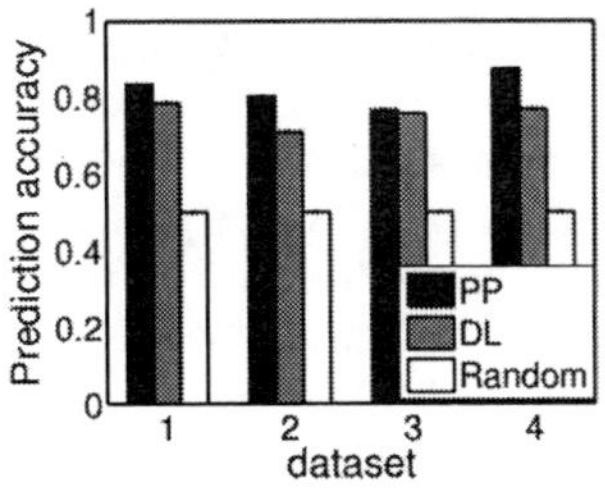

Figure 12: Accuracy (USC)

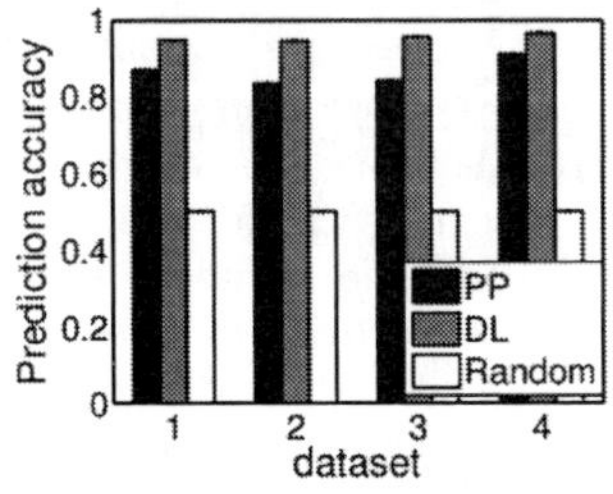

Figure 13: Accuracy (city)

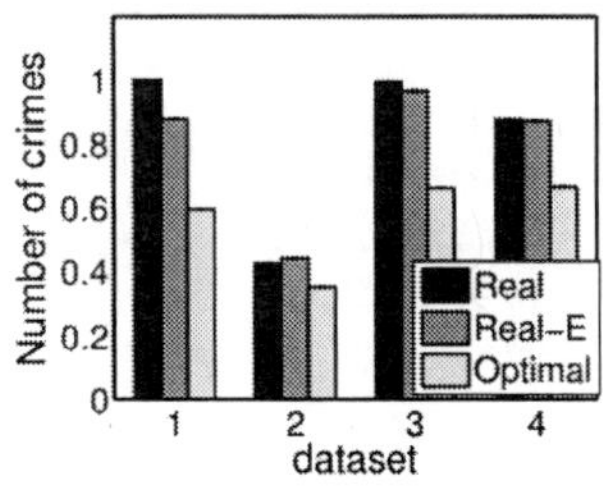

Figure 14: Plan (USC)

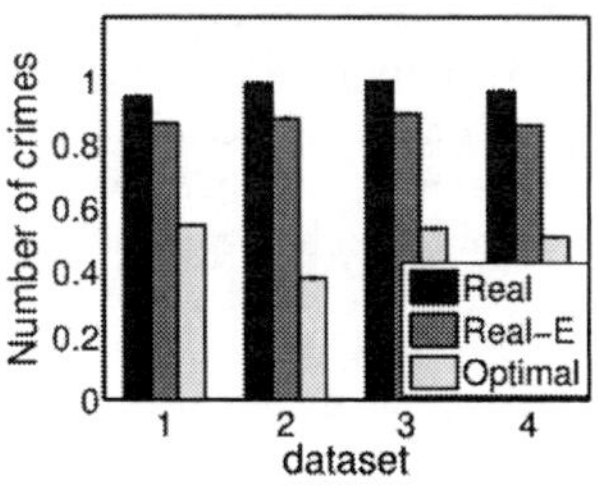

Figure 15: Plan (city)

into four equal parts. For each part, the first 90% of data is used for training while we test on the last 10% of data. The x-axis in Fig. 12 and 13 is the index of the part of data that we evaluate on. y-axis indicates the prediction accuracy on the test set. As can be seen in both figures, the accuracy of both game abstraction based approaches are higher than that of the baseline random algorithm in all the test sets. This indicates that game abstraction models help improve the prediction in large scale problems. In addition, parameter propagation at the original layer outperforms direct learning at this layer in the USC problem in Figure 12. Direct learning outperforms parameter propagation in Nashville problem in Figure 13. This is because the patrol data at the original layer in USC is limited. That is, only the aggregate number of police resources over several targets is available while the resources at each target remain unknown. Parameter propagation is better at handling limited patrol data. However, the patrol data is adequate in the city problem and direct learning is a better fit in such situations. Therefore, in the planning section, we use parameter propagation as the learning algorithm in the USC and direct learning as the learning algorithm in Nashville.

Planning: Next, we evaluate the performance of our planning algorithm in both the problems. Figure 14 and 15 compare strategies generated using the game abstraction framework with the actual deployed allocation strategy generated by the domain experts. Three different scenarios are compared: the real number of crimes, shown as Real; the expected number of crimes with manually generated strategies and learned adversary model with game abstraction, shown as Real-E and the expected number of crimes with the optimal strategy computed using game abstraction, shown as Optimal. As shown in Figure 14 and 15, the expected number of crime with manually generated strategy is close to the real number of crimes, which indicates game abstraction model captures the feature of criminals and provide good estimation of the real number of crimes. In addition, strategy generated using the game abstraction is projected to outperform the manually generated strategy significantly. This shows the effectiveness of our proposed patrol strategy as compared to the current patrol strategy.

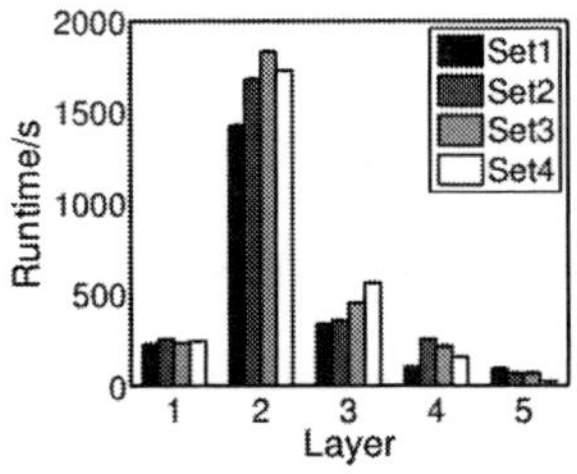

Figure 16: Runtime

Runtime: Finally, we break down the total runtime of the game abstraction framework in the city problem layer by layer and show it in Figure 16. The x-axis is the index of the layer, which goes from the original layer (Layer 1) to the top layer (Layer 5). The y-axis is the total runtime of the propagation, learning and planning algorithm in that layer. As can be seen, the runtime increases as the layer index decreases except for Layer 1. This is because in greedy layer generation, for the fifth layer the number of targets is 5, and for the fourth layer it is 5^2, for third layer it is 5^3, for the second layer it is 5^4 but for the first layer it is only 900. Therefore, the number of targets within each *aggregated target* in layer two is less than $3 < n = 5$. Therefore, the runtime in layer 1 is faster. However, the total runtime of the whole process is less than an hour in each data set. Therefore, the game abstraction framework can be extended to large scale problems with reasonable runtime performance.

7. CONCLUSIONS

This paper introduces a novel game abstraction framework to learn and plan against opportunistic criminals in large-scale urban areas. First, we model the layer-generating process as a districting problem and propose a MILP based technique to solve the problem. Next, we propose a planning algorithm that outputs randomized strategies. Finally, we use a heuristic propagation model to handle the problem with limited data. Experiments with real data in two urban settings shows that our framework can handle large scale urban problems that previous state-of-the-art techniques fail to scale up to. Further, our approach provides high crime prediction accuracy and the strategy generated from our framework is projected to significantly reduce crime compared to current police strategy.

8. ACKNOWLEDGEMENT

This research is supported by MURI grant W911NF-11-1-0332 and Vanderbilt University Discovery grant.

REFERENCES

[1] A. Basak and C. Kiekintveld. Abstraction using analysis of subgames. In *IJCAI Workshop on Algorithmic Game Theory*, 2015.

[2] N. Basilico and N. Gatti. Automated abstractions for patrolling security games. In *AAAI*, 2011.

[3] N. Basilico and N. Gatti. Strategic guard placement for optimal response toalarms in security games. In *Proceedings of the 2014 international conference on Autonomous agents and multi-agent systems*, pages 1481–1482. International Foundation for Autonomous Agents and Multiagent Systems, 2014.

[4] N. Basilico, N. Gatti, and F. Amigoni. Leader-follower strategies for robotic patrolling in environments with arbitrary topologies. In *Proceedings of The 8th International Conference on Autonomous Agents and Multiagent Systems-Volume 1*, pages 57–64. International Foundation for Autonomous Agents and Multiagent Systems, 2009.

[5] N. Basilico, N. Gatti, and F. Amigoni. Patrolling security games: Definition and algorithms for solving large instances with single patroller and single intruder. *Artificial Intelligence*, 184:78–123, 2012.

[6] N. Basilico, N. Gatti, T. Rossi, S. Ceppi, and F. Amigoni. Extending algorithms for mobile robot patrolling in the presence of adversaries to more realistic settings. In *Proceedings of the 2009 IEEE/WIC/ACM International Joint Conference on Web Intelligence and Intelligent Agent Technology-Volume 02*, pages 557–564. IEEE Computer Society, 2009.

[7] D. Bertsimas and J. N. Tsitsiklis. *Introduction to linear optimization*, volume 6. Athena Scientific Belmont, MA, 1997.

[8] A. Blum, N. Haghtalab, and A. D. Procaccia. Learning optimal commitment to overcome insecurity. In *Advances in Neural Information Processing Systems*, pages 1826–1834, 2014.

[9] V. Bucarey, F. Ordóñez, and E. Bassaletti. Shape and balance in police districting. In *Applications of Location Analysis*, pages 329–347. Springer, 2015.

[10] H. Chen, W. Chung, J. J. Xu, G. Wang, Y. Qin, and M. Chau. Crime data mining: a general framework and some examples. *Computer*, 37(4):50–56, 2004.

[11] V. Conitzer and T. Sandholm. A technique for reducing normal-form games to compute a nash equilibrium. In *Proceedings of the fifth international joint conference on Autonomous agents and multiagent systems*, pages 537–544. ACM, 2006.

[12] J. S. De Bruin, T. K. Cocx, W. Kosters, J. F. Laros, J. N. Kok, et al. Data mining approaches to criminal career analysis. In *Data Mining, 2006. ICDM'06. Sixth International Conference on*, pages 171–177. IEEE, 2006.

[13] F. Fang, P. Stone, and M. Tambe. When security games go green: Designing defender strategies to prevent poaching and illegal fishing. In *International Joint Conference on Artificial Intelligence (IJCAI)*, 2015.

[14] A. Gilpin and T. Sandholm. Better automated abstraction techniques for imperfect information games, with application to texas hold'em poker. In *Proceedings of the 6th international joint conference on Autonomous agents and multiagent systems*, page 192. ACM, 2007.

[15] A. Gilpin and T. Sandholm. Lossless abstraction of imperfect information games. *Journal of the ACM (JACM)*, 54(5):25, 2007.

[16] A. Gilpin, T. Sandholm, and T. B. Sørensen. A heads-up no-limit texas hold'em poker player: discretized betting models and automatically generated equilibrium-finding programs. In *Proceedings of the 7th international joint conference on Autonomous agents and multiagent systems-Volume 2*, pages 911–918. International Foundation for Autonomous Agents and Multiagent Systems, 2008.

[17] J. P. Hespanha, M. Prandini, and S. Sastry. Probabilistic pursuit-evasion games: A one-step nash approach. In *Decision and Control, 2000. Proceedings of the 39th IEEE Conference on*, volume 3, pages 2272–2277. IEEE, 2000.

[18] A. X. Jiang, Z. Yin, C. Zhang, M. Tambe, and S. Kraus. Game-theoretic randomization for security patrolling with dynamic execution uncertainty. In *Proceedings of the 2013 international conference on Autonomous agents and multi-agent systems*, pages 207–214. International Foundation for Autonomous Agents and Multiagent Systems, 2013.

[19] J. Kalcsics, S. Nickel, and M. Schröder. Towards a unified territorial design approachâĂŤapplications, algorithms and gis integration. *Top*, 13(1):1–56, 2005.

[20] O. Kariv and S. L. Hakimi. An algorithmic approach to network location problems. ii: The p-medians. *SIAM Journal on Applied Mathematics*, 37(3):539–560, 1979.

[21] S. V. Nath. Crime pattern detection using data mining. In *Web Intelligence and Intelligent Agent Technology Workshops, 2006. WI-IAT 2006 Workshops. 2006 IEEE/WIC/ACM International Conference on*, pages 41–44. IEEE, 2006.

[22] T. H. Nguyen, F. M. Delle Fave, D. Kar, A. S. Lakshminarayanan, A. Yadav, M. Tambe, et al. Making the most of our regrets: Regret-based solutions to handle payoff uncertainty and elicitation in green security games. In *Decision and Game Theory for Security*, pages 170–191. Springer, 2015.

[23] T. Sandholm and S. Singh. Lossy stochastic game abstraction with bounds. In *Proceedings of the 13th ACM Conference on Electronic Commerce*, pages 880–897. ACM, 2012.

[24] H. D. Sherali and F. L. Nordai. Np-hard, capacitated, balanced p-median problems on a chain graph with a continuum of link demands. *Mathematics of Operations Research*, 13(1):32–49, 1988.

[25] M. B. Short, M. R. D'ORSOGNA, V. B. Pasour, G. E. Tita, P. J. Brantingham, A. L. Bertozzi, and L. B. Chayes. A statistical model of criminal behavior. *Mathematical Models and Methods in Applied Sciences*, 18(supp01):1249–1267, 2008.

[26] M. Tambe. *Security and game theory: algorithms, deployed systems, lessons learned*. Cambridge University Press, 2011.

[27] C. Zhang, A. X. Jiang, M. B. Short, P. J. Brantingham, and M. Tambe. Defending against opportunistic criminals: New game-theoretic frameworks and algorithms. In *Decision and Game Theory for Security*, pages 3–22. Springer, 2014.

[28] C. Zhang, A. Sinha, and M. Tambe. Keeping pace with criminals: Designing patrol allocation against adaptive opportunistic criminals. In *AAMAS 2015*.

Simplifying Urban Network Security Games with Cut-Based Graph Contraction

Hiroaki Iwashita[1], Kotaro Ohori[1], Hirokazu Anai[1], and Atsushi Iwasaki[2]
[1]Fujitsu Laboratories Ltd., Kawasaki 211-8588, Japan
{iwashita.hiroak,ohori.kotaro,anai}@jp.fujitsu.com
[2]University of Electro-Communications, Tokyo 182-8585, Japan
iwasaki@is.uec.ac.jp

ABSTRACT

The scalability of the algorithm for solving urban network security games, which is an important challenge concerning security game problems, was improved. State-of-the-art solvers have been scaled up to handle real-world networks with tens of thousands of edges; however, it can take days or more when the inputs are varied. Since they do not essentially overcome exponential growth of the strategy space with increasing graph size, an approach, which can be combined with previous ones, is proposed. In particular, a practical approach of simplifying the graphs so that they can be handled within a realistic time is devised and tested. The key idea behind this approach is to restrict the defender's pure strategies to potential ones before calculating an equilibrium solution. The restriction can be tightened for faster computation and loosened for better solution. The following three techniques for computing an optimal solution to the restricted game are proposed and evaluated: (i) contraction of the network based on the restriction, (ii) compact formulation of the optimization problem using weighted edges in place of multiple edges, and (iii) efficient solution using a mixed-integer quadratic programming oracle. They can naturally cope with an extension of the game to one taking width of the roads into account. Furthermore, a heuristic algorithm of finding effective restriction of the game is also proposed.

Keywords

Game Theory; Optimization; Security; Graph Contraction

1. INTRODUCTION

With the deteriorating security situation around the world, effective safety policies are required to prevent terrorism and drug dealing. However, all possible security checkpoints cannot be covered at every moment because resources are limited. Over recent years, to plan effective resource allocation strategies for patrolling and inspection, game-theoretic approaches have been applied. Security games modeled as Stackelberg games [18] have provided various applications in real-world domains, for example, at LA International Airport [12], the US Federal Air Marshals Service [16], and the US Coast Guard [14, 4].

As one of the important types of game, a security game for urban networks models an attacker and a defender who take decisions on a network consisting of nodes and edges. The defender's strategies represent allocations of their limited resources to edges of the network, while the attacker's strategies represent paths from any source node to any target node. In this study, improving the scalability of the algorithms, which an important challenge concerning security games [15], is focused on. In particular, the strategy spaces for the defender and the attacker increase exponentially with the number of security resources and the size of the network, respectively.

Developed for simple security games in which targets are directly defended or attacked on the basis of pure strategies of each player, a compact security-game model [9] improved the scalability of those games by several orders of magnitude. Instead of enumerating the defender strategies as k-combinations from n targets, this model introduces a "coverage vector" representing the probability that each target is covered. The feasible space of coverage vectors is characterized simply by the sum of its elements being not more than the number of defender resources. A counterpart of that model for urban network security games has not been invented yet; in particular, a coverage vector cannot be defined easily because a defender's pure strategy covers targets indirectly by blocking a huge number of attacker's pure strategies aimed at the target, which is discrete and complicated relation.

Scaling up urban-network security games to handle realistic problem sizes has been attempted in several studies. RANGER [17] obtains an approximate solution for the defender by optimizing marginal probability of selecting individual edges without considering how to combine multiple edges. RUGGED [7] and SNARES [6] are based on a double-oracle approach [10], which does not enumerate all pure strategies for either of the attacker and the defender. SNARES has successfully computed an optimal strategy for the road network of Mumbai comprising 9,503 nodes and 20,416 edges.

However, the above-mentioned algorithms cannot always be applied to real problems without any conditions; that is, the runtime of an algorithm varies significantly with changing conditions such as numbers of targets and resources [8]. In our experience, computation time to obtain a solution increases dramatically as the number of targets and/or resources is increased. Moreover, it was experimentally shown that varying minor conditions (such as source and target placement) significantly affected the runtime of every run.

In light of the above-described issues, a robust method for obtaining effective defender strategies for large-scale networks is proposed and evaluated. After the problem is defined and related works are introduced in Section 2, the key idea behind the proposed method, namely, reducing the problem by contracting the graph, is presented in Section 3. Techniques for efficiently solving the reduced problems, including a column-generation method using a mixed-integer quadratic programming oracle, are shown in Section 4. A heuris-

Appears in: *Proceedings of the 15th International Conference on Autonomous Agents and Multiagent Systems (AAMAS 2016), J. Thangarajah, K. Tuyls, C. Jonker, S. Marsella (eds.), May 9–13, 2016, Singapore.*

tic algorithm utilizing the proposed method, which incrementally adds candidate edges and improves the solution, is introduced in Section 5. Experimental results in Section 6 show the high quality of the determined solutions as well as the robustness of the proposed method.

2. URBAN NETWORK SECURITY GAMES

Urban network security games [17] are zero-sum games with two players: a defender and an attacker. They are defined by 6-tuple $\mathscr{G} = (V, E, S, T, U, k)$, where $G = (V, E)$ is a graph describing a road network, $S \subset V$ is a set of source nodes, $T \subset V$ is a set of target nodes, $U : V \to \mathbb{R}_{\geq 0}$ is a payoff function (value of each node) satisfying $U(v) \neq 0$ if and only if $v \in T$, and k is the number of security resources.

The defender selects at most k edges from E and allocates the resources to them. The attacker moves along E from any one of the sources, $s \in S$, to any one of the targets, $t \in T$. It is assumed that only one target can be attacked at a time; no targets but the last one (t) can be attacked even when there are multiple targets along the attacker path. If one or more defender resources are located on the path, the attack fails and both players get nothing; otherwise the defender and the attacker gain $-U(t)$ and $U(t)$ respectively.

The objective of the game is to find an optimal mixed strategy for the defender, namely, the most-effective plan for allocating the security resources, in terms of minimizing the maximum expected damage. Since the game is a zero-sum game, its optimal solution is a Nash equilibrium as well as a strong Stackelberg equilibrium [20].

Urban network security games can be formulated as follows. Let D be a set of all defender allocations and A be a set of all attacker paths. The defender's mixed strategy is denoted as $\mathbf{x} : D \to [0, 1]$, and expected damage is denoted as z. A successful attacker path ($a \in A$) causes damage $U(t(a))$, where $t(a)$ represents the target of a. The probability that attacker path $a \in A$ becomes successful against defender allocation $d \in D$ is denoted as $P(d, a)$, which, in this problem setting, is either 0 or 1. An urban network security game is formulated as the following minimax linear programming (LP) problem:

$$\min_{\mathbf{x}, z} \quad z \tag{1}$$

$$\text{s.t.} \quad z \geq U(t(a)) \sum_{d \in D} P(d, a)\mathbf{x}(d), \quad \forall a \in A \tag{2}$$

$$\sum_{d \in D} \mathbf{x}(d) = 1 \tag{3}$$

$$0 \leq \mathbf{x}(d) \leq 1, \quad \forall d \in D. \tag{4}$$

Solving formulas (1)–(4) gives defender's optimal mixed strategy and expected damage corresponding to it. Moreover, the solution to its dual LP problem provides attacker's optimal mixed strategy, $\mathbf{y} : A \to [0, 1]$. This simple formulation, however, cannot be applied directly to real-world problems because $|D|$ and $|A|$ increase exponentially with problem size.

2.1 Min-Cut Method

If the number of resources, k, is sufficient, the defender can protect all targets perfectly by allocating them to all minimum cut-sets separating the targets from the sources. Even in the cases that the size of a min-cut is larger than k, it is known that the defender's optimal strategy is to allocate resources to k edges randomly chosen from the cut-set if only one target exists or all targets have the same value [19].

The min-cut method reduces complexity of the problem to polynomial time of finding a minimum s-t cut [2, 1]. However, it does not generally provide a good strategy in the case that the targets' payoff values are not uniform.

2.2 Double-Oracle Method

To solve the minimax LP problem, RUGGED [7] uses a *double-oracle* method [10], which is a kind of constraint and column generation algorithm for solving linear programming problems. It reaches an optimal solution asymptotically by adding pure strategies one by one instead of computing the solution after enumerating all pure strategies.

Algorithm 1: Double-oracle method

```
1 Initialize D by arbitrary defender allocations
2 Initialize A by arbitrary attacker paths
3 repeat
4     Solve the minimax LP problem of equations (1)–(4), and
      let x and y be mixed strategies of the defender and the
      attacker over D and A, respectively
5     Find defender's best response to y and add it to D
6     Find attacker's best response to x and add it to A
7 until convergence
8 return x
```

The double-oracle method is outlined in Algorithm 1. The best-response oracles in lines 5 and 6 are formulated as mixed-integer linear programming problems, which often dominate computation time in RUGGED.

Instead of using the best-response oracles every time, SNARES uses fast heuristic algorithms whenever they give a better response. A method called *mincut-fanout* is used to improve the initial members of D and A. Mincut-fanout first constructs a min-cut that separates the target with the highest value from the sources; it then initializes D by defender allocations, such that each allocation covers k edges in the cut-set, and A by the attacker's best responses to them.

3. PROBLEM REDUCTION

Although the double-oracle method definitely improves the scalability of the solvers, it does not essentially overcome exponential growth of the strategy space with the increasing problem size. In other words, problem reduction can exponentially improve performance of the state-of-the-art solvers.

Generally, a set of defender's pure strategies appearing in an optimal mixed strategy is a fraction of the huge entire space. For example, only edges in $C = \{e_1, e_2, e_3, e_4, e_5, e_6, e_7\}$ are used in an optimal solution to the problem shown in Figure 1(a). If $C \subset E$ is determined in advance by some other algorithm or suggested by a security expert, it becomes possible to reduce the problem.

EXAMPLE 1. *To reduce $G = (V, E)$ in Figure 1(a), unused edges $e \in E \setminus C$ are contracted, and the problem is reduced to a compact one defined on $G_C = (V_C, E_C)$, as illustrated in Figure 1(b). Furthermore, multiple edges in the graph are replaced with a single edge with the capacity to make a more-compact problem on $\hat{G}_C = (\hat{V}_C, \hat{E}_C)$, as shown in Figure 1(c). In later sections, it is shown that optimal solutions computed on both G_C and $\hat{G}_C$ are also optimal on G under the restriction that the defender allocates resources to only C. In this example, C is not the only one best set of candidate edges. If $C' = \{e_2, e_3, e_4, e_5, e_6, e_7, e_8\}$ instead of C is selected, another solution with the same quality is obtained because G_C and $G_{C'}$ are isomorphic.*

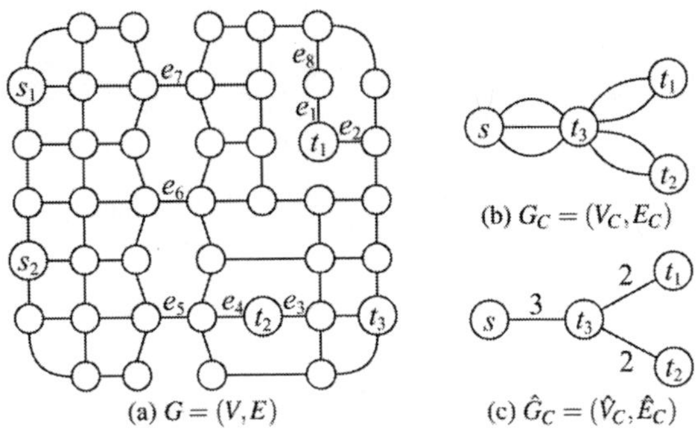

Figure 1: An example of reduction.

Algorithm 2 is a possible manual procedure for finding realistic solutions to large problems. Although quality of the solution depends on the choice of C, the computed security level for the reduced problem is guaranteed also for the original one. Security agencies can therefore determine if the solution is acceptable.

Algorithm 2: Manual task of security scheduling

Determine an initial set of candidate edges C
loop
  Reduce and solve the problem based on C
  if *the problem cannot be solved* **then**
    Shrink C
  else if *the security level is not sufficient* **then**
    Extend C or increase the number of defender resources
  else return

3.1 Contracting Unused Edges

An urban network security game with a restriction on the defender's pure strategies is considered as follows. Here, $C \subset E$ is a set of candidate edges to which the defender can allocate resources. A contracted graph, $G_C = (V_C, E_C)$, is made from an original graph, $G = (V, E)$, by *edge contraction* for all $e \in E \setminus C$, where edge contraction of e is an operation in graph theory that removes e from a graph and merges its two incident nodes. When the correspondence of those nodes is represented by $\varphi_C : V \to V_C$, the original game, $\mathcal{G} = (V, E, S, T, U, k)$, is reduced to $\mathcal{G}_C = (V_C, E_C, S_C, T_C, U_C, k)$ where

$$S_C = \{\varphi_C(s) \mid s \in S\},$$
$$T_C = \{\varphi_C(t) \mid t \in T\},$$
$$U_C(v') = \max\{U(v) \mid \varphi_C(v) = v',\ v \in V\}.$$

Additional two functions are defined for later use. First, $\widetilde{\varphi}_C : V_C \to V$ is the function that maps $v' \in V_C$ to a set of the most valuable nodes in V represented by v', that is,

$$\widetilde{\varphi}_C(v') = \operatorname*{arg\,max}_{v \in V}\{U(v) \mid \varphi_C(v) = v'\}.$$

Secondly, $\widetilde{\psi}_{E_C,E} : E_C \to C$ maps an edge in the contracted graph to the one in the original graph.

LEMMA 1. *When $e_1 \in E$ and $C = E \setminus \{e_1\}$, $\widetilde{\psi}_{E_C,E}$ maps the defender's optimal mixed strategy for $\mathcal{G}_C$ to the one for $\mathcal{G}$ that has the same quality and is optimal under the restriction that the defender allocates resources only to C.*

PROOF. Any defender allocation, $d' \subseteq E_C$, can be simply mapped to $d = \{\widetilde{\psi}_{E_C,E}(e') \mid e' \in d'\}$. Attacker path $a' \subseteq E_C$ to target $t' \in T_C$ can be mapped to $a = \{\widetilde{\psi}_{E_C,E}(e') \mid e' \in a'\}$ if it forms a path to $\widetilde{\varphi}_C(t')$; otherwise, it can be mapped to $a \cup \{e_1\}$, which forms a path to $\widetilde{\varphi}_C(t')$. These mappings do not change the equilibrium between both player's mixed strategy and the best responses against them. Therefore, quality and optimality do not change. □

THEOREM 1. *For all $C \subseteq E$, $\widetilde{\psi}_{E_C,E}$ maps the defender's optimal mixed strategy for $\mathcal{G}_C$ to the one for $\mathcal{G}$ that has the same quality and is optimal under the restriction that the defender allocates resources only to C.*

PROOF. Let $C_0 = C$ and $C_i = C_{i-1} + \{e_i\}$ for $i = 1, \ldots, m$ where $E \setminus C = \{e_1, \ldots, e_m\}$. From Lemma 1, $\widetilde{\psi}_{E_C,E_{C_1}}$ maps the defender's optimal mixed strategy for $\mathcal{G}_C$ to the one for $\mathcal{G}_{C_1}$. If $\widetilde{\psi}_{E_C,E_{C_i}}$ maps the defender's optimal mixed strategy for $\mathcal{G}_C$ to the one for $\mathcal{G}_{C_i}$, it can be mapped over again by $\widetilde{\psi}_{E_{C_i},E_{C_{i+1}}}$ to the one for $\mathcal{G}_{C_{i+1}}$. By using induction, $\widetilde{\psi}_{E_C,E_{C_m}} = \widetilde{\psi}_{E_C,E}$ maps the defender's optimal mixed strategy for $\mathcal{G}_C$ to the one for $\mathcal{G}_E = \mathcal{G}$. □

The following statements give guidelines for selecting the set of candidate edges.

THEOREM 2. *The defender's mixed strategies for G computed with two different set of candidate edges, C and C', have the same quality if G_C and $G_{C'}$ are isomorphic in consideration of node labels of sources, targets, and payoff values.*

PROOF. Apparently, $\mathcal{G}_C$ and $\mathcal{G}_{C'}$ yield the defender's optimal mixed strategies on G_C and $G_{C'}$ respectively that have the same expected utilities. According to Theorem 1, both strategies can be mapped to the ones on G while the same quality is maintained. □

THEOREM 3. *The set of candidate edges that achieves the defender's mixed strategy with the best possible quality can be composed of cut-sets separating one or more targets from all sources.*

PROOF. Let C be a set of candidate edges achieving the defender's mixed strategy with the best possible quality. If self-loop edges are included in E_C, they can be excluded from C without loss of solution quality because they are useless for attacker paths and thus for defender allocation. If non-target node $v' \in V_C \setminus T_C$ has edges only to single node $u' \in V_C$, no edges between u' and v' are used by either player and can be excluded from C without loss of solution quality. Edges between two sources in S_C can also be excluded from C safely. Consequently, all remaining candidate edges are covered by a collection of cut-sets separating one or more targets from all sources. □

3.2 Unifying Multiple Edges

While the reduced problem can be solved as is in the same way as the original one, more compact problem can be formulated by adapting the proposed model. Contraction of many edges often produces multiple edges, which are two or more edges that are incident to the same two nodes. An optimal strategy of the defender should use those edges uniformly (since they are topologically equivalent). Each pair of nodes connected by m edges do not need to be distinguished, and they can be simplified as a single edge (e) with capacity $w_e = m$, as illustrated in Figure 1. In the example, six attacker paths from s to t_1 on G_C are reduced to only one on $\hat{G}_C$. This conversion effectively suppresses combinatorial explosion of the strategy space.

A graph with multiple edges, $G = (V, E)$, is reduced to a more compact weighted graph without multiple edges, $\hat{G} = (\hat{V}, \hat{E})$, in which each edge, $e \in \hat{E}$, has capacity w_e. The game is reduced to $\hat{\mathscr{G}} = (\hat{V}, \hat{E}, \hat{S}, \hat{T}, \hat{U}, k)$ where $\hat{S} \subset \hat{V}$ is a set of source nodes, $\hat{T} \subset \hat{V}$ is a set of target nodes, and $\hat{U} : \hat{V} \to \mathbb{R}_{\geq 0}$ is a payoff function.

Let $d_e \in \{0, \ldots, w_e\}$ denote the number of resources on edge e in defender allocation d. When the defender and the attacker play d and a respectively on $\hat{G}$, the attack succeeds at probability $P(d,a) = \prod_{e \in a}(1 - d_e/w_e)$. Therefore, this game is formulated as the following minimax LP problem:

$$\min_{\hat{\mathbf{x}}, z} \quad z \tag{5}$$

$$\text{s.t.} \quad z \geq \hat{U}(t(a)) \sum_{d \in \hat{D}} \prod_{e \in a} \left(1 - \frac{d_e}{w_e}\right) \hat{\mathbf{x}}(d), \ \forall a \in \hat{A} \tag{6}$$

$$\sum_{d \in \hat{D}} \hat{\mathbf{x}}(d) = 1 \tag{7}$$

$$0 \leq \hat{\mathbf{x}}(d) \leq 1, \quad \forall d \in \hat{D}, \tag{8}$$

where $\hat{D}$ and $\hat{A}$ are all defender allocations and all attacker paths on $\hat{G}$ respectively, $\hat{\mathbf{x}} : \hat{D} \to [0,1]$ is the defender's mixed strategy, z is an expectation of the damage, and $\hat{U}(t(a))$ is the amount of damage when attacker path $a \in \hat{A}$ succeeds.

In fact, this formulation is usable independently of graph contraction. It is a natural extension of urban network security games that edge e is assumed to have capacity w_e, where w_e resources are required to block e.

4. SOLUTION TECHNIQUES

If multiple edges are not unified, the problem after reduction can be still formulated as (1)–(4); conventional techniques are applicable to it as they are. This section presents the solution techniques that can be applied to the problem (5)–(8). Without these techniques, all pure strategies, $\hat{D}$ and $\hat{A}$, must be enumerated beforehand.[1]

4.1 Selecting Pure Strategies

To reduce the cost for solving the minimax LP, the strategy spaces are restricted without sacrificing quality of solutions. First, the defender's strategies that do not affect the quality are identified.

Let $R_e = \{0, \ldots, w_e\}$ and $R_e^- = R_e \setminus \{0, w_e\}$. Edge e is *partially blocked* by defender allocation d when $d_e \in R_e^-$. The following theorem guarantees that even if every defender allocation that partially blocks two or more edges is ignored, a mixed strategy for the defender that yields the optimal expected utility still exists.

THEOREM 4. *At least one optimal mixed strategy for the defender includes no defender allocation by which two or more edges are partially blocked.*

PROOF. Let us assume that defender allocation $\check{d}$ partially blocks edges i and j in an optimal mixed strategy $\hat{\mathbf{x}}$, that is, $1 \leq \check{d}_i \leq w_i - 1$ and $1 \leq \check{d}_j \leq w_j - 1$. New defender allocations $\grave{d}$ and $\acute{d}$ are made by moving as many resources as possible from j to i and i to j respectively:

$$\grave{d}_e = \begin{cases} \check{d}_e + \alpha & \text{if } e = i \\ \check{d}_e - \alpha & \text{if } e = j \\ \check{d}_e & \text{otherwise}, \end{cases} \qquad \acute{d}_e = \begin{cases} \check{d}_e - \beta & \text{if } e = i \\ \check{d}_e + \beta & \text{if } e = j \\ \check{d}_e & \text{otherwise}, \end{cases}$$

$$\alpha = \min(w_i - \check{d}_i, \check{d}_j), \qquad \beta = \min(\check{d}_i, w_j - \check{d}_j),$$

where α and β are the largest possible numbers of moved resources. Note that at most either i or j is partially blocked after the move. A new mixed strategy is defined as:

$$\hat{\mathbf{x}}'(d) = \begin{cases} 0 & \text{if } d = \check{d} \\ \hat{\mathbf{x}}(d) + \frac{\beta}{\alpha+\beta}\hat{\mathbf{x}}(\check{d}) & \text{if } d = \grave{d} \\ \hat{\mathbf{x}}(d) + \frac{\alpha}{\alpha+\beta}\hat{\mathbf{x}}(\check{d}) & \text{if } d = \acute{d} \\ \hat{\mathbf{x}}(d) & \text{otherwise}. \end{cases}$$

The difference of blocking probability of i between $\hat{\mathbf{x}}$ and $\hat{\mathbf{x}}'$ is:

$$\begin{aligned} &\sum_{d \in \hat{D}} \frac{d_i}{w_i}(\hat{\mathbf{x}}'(d) - \hat{\mathbf{x}}(d)) \\ &= -\frac{\check{d}_i}{w_i}\hat{\mathbf{x}}(\check{d}) + \frac{\grave{d}_i}{w_i} \cdot \frac{\beta}{\alpha+\beta}\hat{\mathbf{x}}(\check{d}) + \frac{\acute{d}_i}{w_i} \cdot \frac{\alpha}{\alpha+\beta}\hat{\mathbf{x}}(\check{d}) \\ &= -\frac{\check{d}_i}{w_i}\hat{\mathbf{x}}(\check{d}) + \frac{\check{d}_i + \alpha}{w_i} \cdot \frac{\beta}{\alpha+\beta}\hat{\mathbf{x}}(\check{d}) + \frac{\check{d}_i - \beta}{w_i} \cdot \frac{\alpha}{\alpha+\beta}\hat{\mathbf{x}}(\check{d}) \\ &= 0. \end{aligned}$$

It follows that the probability of blocking i remains unchanged by replacing $\hat{\mathbf{x}}$ with $\hat{\mathbf{x}}'$. Similarly, the probability of blocking j also remains. Therefore, $\hat{\mathbf{x}}'$ is also optimal. By repeating the above modification, it is possible to find an optimal mixed strategy including no defender allocation by which two or more edges are partially blocked. □

Secondly, the way to reduce the attacker's strategy space is rather simple. It can be done by excluding any path passing over target t and attacking t' such that $\hat{U}(t) \leq \hat{U}(t')$. Such a path is worse than its prefix attacking t and is not required by the attacker's optimal strategy. In Figure 1(c), the valid attacker paths are s–t_3 and s–t_3–t_1 if $\hat{U}(t_2) \leq \hat{U}(t_3) < \hat{U}(t_1)$.

4.2 Column Generation

To avoid an explosion of the number of defender's pure strategies to be considered in the case of the minimax LP problem (5)–(8), Algorithm 3, which is a column generation technique using defender's best-response oracle, is introduced.

Algorithm 3: Single-oracle column generation

Initialize D by arbitrary defender allocation
Initialize A by all attacker paths
repeat
  Solve the minimax LP problem (5)–(8), and let $\hat{\mathbf{x}}$ and $\hat{\mathbf{y}}$ be mixed strategies of the defender and the attacker using D and A, respectively
  Find defender's best response to $\hat{\mathbf{y}}$ and add it to D
until *convergence*
return $\hat{\mathbf{x}}$

The oracle finds one of the best defender allocations, d, against the attacker's mixed strategy, $\hat{\mathbf{y}}$. It is formulated as a mixed-integer nonlinear programming (MINLP) problem:

$$\min_{d} \quad \sum_{a \in \hat{A}} \hat{U}(t(a))\hat{\mathbf{y}}(a) \prod_{e \in a}\left(1 - \frac{d_e}{w_e}\right) \tag{9}$$

$$\text{s.t.} \quad \sum_{e \in \hat{E}} d_e \leq k \tag{10}$$

$$d_e \in R_e, \quad \forall e \in \hat{E}. \tag{11}$$

Unfortunately, MINLP introduces a further level of difficulty and can not be accepted directly by many generic optimization solvers.

[1] Actually, it is possible to some extent because the problem reduction drastically compresses the strategy spaces.

It is thus transformed into a mixed-integer quadratic programming (MIQP) problem, which is much easier to solve quickly by state-of-the-art optimization solvers. Let $\lambda(e,r) \in \{0,1\}$ be a variable representing that the number of resources allocated on edge e is r ($d_e = r$). According to Theorem 4, it can be assumed that at most one pair (e,r) of $e \in a$ and $r \in R_e^-$ for each $a \in \hat{A}$ satisfies $\lambda(e,r) = 1$. Equations (9)–(11) are rewritten as follows:

$$\min_{\lambda,\omega} \quad \sum_{a\in\hat{A}} \hat{U}(t(a))\hat{\mathbf{y}}(a)\left(1-\sum_{e\in a}\sum_{r\in R_e^-}\frac{r}{w_e}\lambda(e,r)\right)(1-\omega(a)) \tag{12}$$

$$\text{s.t.} \quad \sum_{e\in\hat{E}}\sum_{r\in R_e} r\lambda(e,r) \le k \tag{13}$$

$$\sum_{e\in\hat{E}}\sum_{r\in R_e^-} \lambda(e,r) \le 1 \tag{14}$$

$$\sum_{r\in R_e} \lambda(e,r) \le 1, \quad \forall e \in \hat{E} \tag{15}$$

$$\omega(a) \le \sum_{e\in a} \lambda(e,w_e), \quad \forall a \in \hat{A} \tag{16}$$

$$\lambda(e,r) \in \{0,1\}, \ \forall e \in \hat{E}, \ \forall r \in R_e \tag{17}$$

$$\omega(a) \in [0,1], \quad \forall a \in \hat{A}. \tag{18}$$

Equation (13) indicates that the total number of allocated resources does not exceed k. Equations (14) and (15) constrain no two edges to be partially blocked. Equation (16) defines the relation between ω and λ; that is, $\omega(a) = 1$ if attacker path a is completely blocked by the defender at some edge $e \in a$; otherwise, $\omega(a) = 0$.

The attacker's best response oracle is not provided here; the all members of $\hat{A}$ is enumerated in advance and $\hat{D}$ only is generated incrementally. As for the proposed method, it is empirically confirmed that the number of valid attacker paths does not increase explosively.

5. HEURISTIC ALGORITHM

Algorithm 2 is replaced by introducing an automatic method for selecting appropriate candidate edges for defender allocations. The min-cut method for single-target problems [19] and mincut-fanout in SNARES [6] imply that min-cuts are strongly associated with defender strategies. A min-cut separating a subset of targets, $T' \subseteq T$, from a set of all sources, S, gives the best set of edges for uniformly enhancing the security of targets in T'. The idea proposed here, called "min-cut arrangement," is to combine multiple such S-T' min-cuts.

A naive implementation of min-cut arrangement would be one that tries to use all $2^{|T|}-1$ nonempty subsets of T as T'. It will surely find the best solution among min-cut-arrangement-based algorithms; however, it is not practical in terms of computational complexity when $|T|$ is large.

Algorithm 4: MiCANS(V,E,S,T,U,k)

```
1 C^0 ← ∅,  T^1 ← argmax_t U(t),  i ← 1
2 loop
3 |   C^i ← C^{i-1} ∪ FindCandidateEdges(V,E,S,T^i)
4 |   if C^i = C^{i-1} then return x̂^{i-1}
5 |   (x̂^i, ŷ^i) = ReduceAndSolve(V,E,S,T,U,k,C^i)
6 |   T^{i+1} ← {v | v ∈ φ̃_{C^i}(t(a)), ŷ^i(a) > 0}
7 |_  i ← i+1
```

Algorithm 4, called MiCANS, is based on min-cut arrangement that aims for both runtime and quality. C^i and T^i represent a set of candidate edges and a set of *critical targets* in the i-th iteration, respectively. Critical targets are the ones that will suffer the highest expectation of damage for the current equilibrium solution. Initially, it is assumed that no target is protected; thus T^1 is a set of the most valuable targets (line 1). Subsequent sets of critical targets are found by extracting targets with non-zero attack probability from $\hat{\mathbf{y}}^i$ and mapping them back to the original graph (line 6).

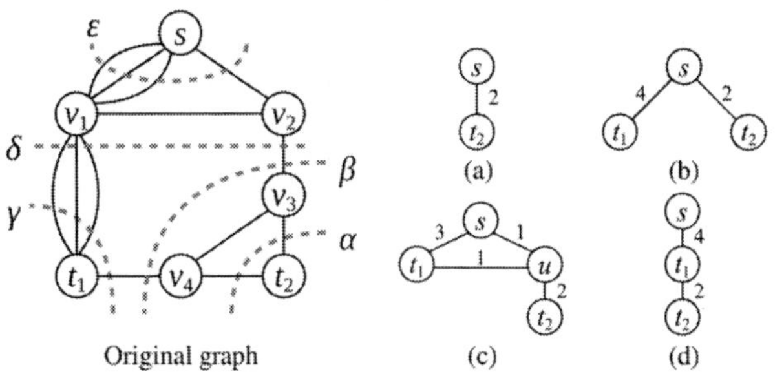

Figure 2: An example of execution.

FindCandidateEdges(V,E,S,T^i) returns a set of edges by computing a min-cut separating T^i from S. When multiple S-T^i min-cuts exist, some heuristics for selecting one or more of them must be devised. One of the simplest heuristics is to choose the min-cut that minimizes the size of the node group containing T^i.

ReduceAndSolve(V,E,S,T,U,k,C^i) stands for the method described in Section 3 and Section 4, which contracts all unused edges, $e \in E \setminus C^i$, of $G = (V,E)$, unifies every bundle of multiple edges into a weighted edge, and solves the minimax LP problem with column generation. The graph is refined in each iteration by adding minimum cut-set separating critical targets. It is repeated until the candidate edges stop growing.

The MiCANS algorithm can be interpreted as a kind of (incomplete) column generation at higher level of abstraction for solving the minimax LP (1)–(4). The defender's strategy space, D, is expanded indirectly by adding candidate edges to E'. Ideally, they should be chosen in such a way that no other choices reduce expected damage if they do not. Although the min-cut edges are efficient candidates for improving the solution, they do not always satisfy such a property; that is, this algorithm does not guarantee that it always converges to an optimal solution.

EXAMPLE 2. *Figure 2 shows an example of execution, in which s is the source, t_1 and t_2 are the targets with values 1 and 2, respectively, and the number of resources is 2. The first critical target set is $T^1 = \{t_2\}$. Two min-cuts separate t_2 from s: α and β. In either case that $C^1 = \alpha$ or $C^1 = \beta$, the first reduced graph is (a), t_2 is completely guarded by two defender resources in the first iteration, expected damage of t_2 changes to zero, and therefore $T^2 = \{t_1\}$. At the second iteration, three min-cuts, γ, δ, and ε, exist between s and t_1. If $C^2 = \alpha \cup \gamma$ is chosen, the reduced graph is (b). As the optimal mixed strategy for the defender balances expected damage of attacks on t_1 and t_2 to 4/5, both targets become critical: $T^3 = \{t_1, t_2\}$. The third reduced graph is (c) and the expected damage is reduced to 2/3, which is the optimal value. The algorithm terminates because $\{t_1, t_2\}$ is critical again. If $C^2 = \beta \cup \varepsilon$ is chosen at the second iteration, reduced graph (d) is obtained, and it yields another solution with the same expected damage, 2/3, even though (c) and (d) are topologically different. Optimal solutions are also obtained from other combinations of min-cuts.*

EXAMPLE 3. *An optimal solution cannot be obtained from the graph in Figure 2(d) if the number of resources is 3. When the de-*

fender completely blocks edge $\{t_1, t_2\}$, the remaining resource must be allocated to edge $\{s, t_1\}$. The security of t_1 is strengthened by blocking one-quarter of attacks. On the other hand, an optimal solution is obtained from the graph in Figure 2(c), in which resource allocation on $\{s, u\}$ and $\{t_1, u\}$ completely protects t_2 and one more resource on $\{s, t_1\}$ blocks one-third of attacks on t_1. In fact, for an optimal solution, it is necessary to choose two out of β, γ, and δ.

Under the assumption that the min-cut that minimizes the size of the target-side is always chosen, MiCANS overlays the cut-sets that do not cross each other. In that case, the size of the reduced graph increases by one after each iteration. The number of iterations in MiCANS, as well as the final size of the reduced graph, becomes linear in relation to the number of targets with different values, namely, $O(|T|)$. In a large problem in which the reduced graph becomes small enough in comparison with the original graph, $G = (V, E)$, min-cut computation dominates the running time. It takes polynomial time with respect to the size of G, namely, $O(|V| \cdot |E|^2)$. Consequently, the total cost of MiCANS under this assumption is $O(|T| \cdot |V| \cdot |E|^2)$.

6. EXPERIMENTAL RESULTS

We have implemented MiCANS and SNARES in Python with the NetworkX graph library [13] and the Gurobi mathematical programming solver. Experiments were performed on a machine with 2.9 GHz CPU and 10 GB memory. The following three types of network models were used:

1. A random road network model called GRE (grid model with random edges) [11], which is a planar connected graph made of a $l \times w$ square grid of nodes. Horizontal/vertical edges between neighbors are controlled by probability p, and diagonal ones by q. It is reported that the values of p spread in $[0.3, 0.9]$ and q in $[0.1, 0.7]$ in models that best match the road networks of Europe. Sources were fixed to w nodes at the bottom end, while the target nodes were selected randomly.

2. Random geometric graphs, which have also been shown to mimic some properties of real road networks [3] and were used to evaluate SNARES. n nodes are distributed uniformly at random in a unit square, and node pairs with a distance not more than a given threshold, d, are connected by edges. Source and target nodes were selected randomly.

3. Real road network data collected in Mumbai, made of 21,132 nodes and 33,603 edges. It was extracted from a rectangle area of latitude 18.84 to 19.36° and longitude 72.75 to 73.16° of Open Street Map [5]. Source and target nodes were selected randomly.

6.1 Effectiveness of Graph Reduction

400 random instances of the GRE were generated; their horizontal and vertical sizes were chosen randomly from $\{10, \ldots, 300\}$, p from $[0.3, 0.9]$, and q from $[0.1, 0.7]$.

Figure 3(a) shows the relation between numbers of nodes and edges of the final reduced graph made by min-cut arrangement. It is confirmed that the numbers of nodes and edges are about the same in every reduced graph; that is, reduced graphs are generally sparse. That is the reason why the number of attacker paths does not explode in reduced graphs. The actual number of attacker paths enumerated on every reduced graph is less than 200 in these examples.

The comparison between original graphs and reduced ones in Figure 3(b) show that the numbers of edges are reduced by several orders of magnitude. It should be further emphasized that no direct correlation was found between them.

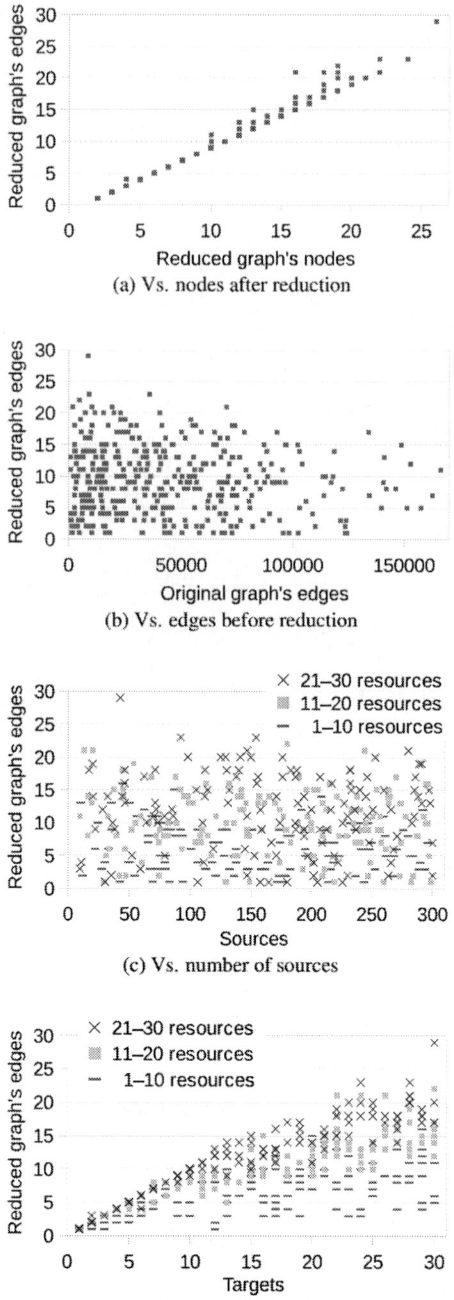

(a) Vs. nodes after reduction
(b) Vs. edges before reduction
(c) Vs. number of sources
(d) Vs. number of targets

Figure 3: Number of edges after reduction.

Figure 3(c) and Figure 3(d) shows that the size of reduced graph is strongly related to the number of targets, but not to sources. The number of edges in each reduced graph becomes likely to proportion to the number of targets when sufficient resources are available with respect to the number of targets.

6.2 Comparison with SNARES

For the GRE graphs, central parameter values are chosen as 10×10 nodes, $(p, q) = (0.6, 0.4)$, 3 targets, and 3 resources. Figure 4 presents runtime in seconds when varying (a) number of nodes,

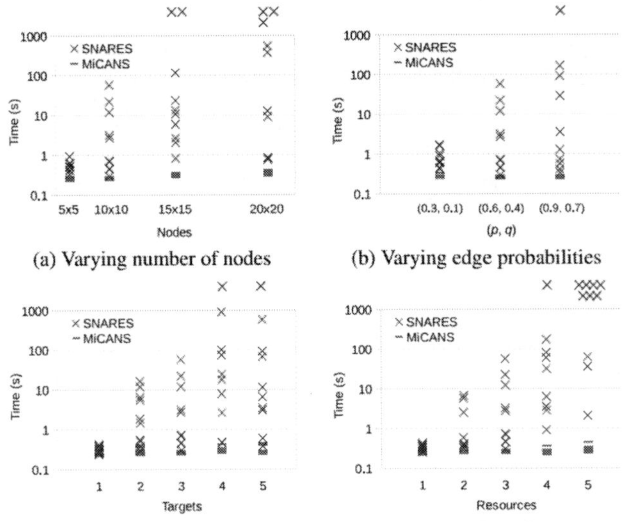

(a) Varying number of nodes (b) Varying edge probabilities

(c) Varying number of targets (d) Varying number of resources

Figure 4: Runtime for small GRE graphs.

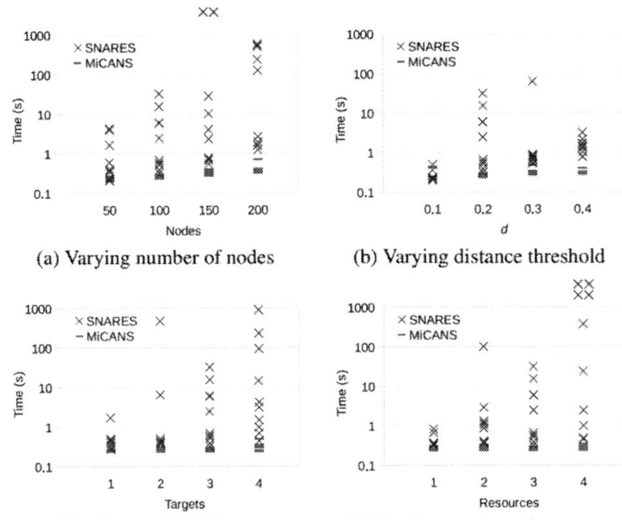

(a) Varying number of nodes (b) Varying distance threshold

(c) Varying number of targets (d) Varying number of resources

Figure 5: Runtime for random geometric graphs.

(b) edge probabilities, (c) number of targets, and (d) number of resources. For each parameter setting, 10 graph instances were generated with different random seeds. The marks on the top margin of the figures indicate the number of runs (of SNARES) that did not finish within 1,000 seconds. All the results show that execution time of SNARES varies significantly, while MiCANS is very robust, and all runs are finished within a second.

Figure 5 presents runtime in seconds for random geometric graphs, where central parameter values were selected as 100 nodes, $d = 0.2$, 3 sources, 3 targets, and 3 resources. The same trends as the GRE graphs can be found in these graphs.

For the problem settings of the Mumbai road network in [6], where the number of resources is 1, 5, 10, or 15, the number of targets is 4 or 8, and the number of sources is fixed to 3, every run of MiCANS took 10 to 30 seconds, including 10 seconds of data reading. SNARES often did not end overnight when the number of resources was set to 5.

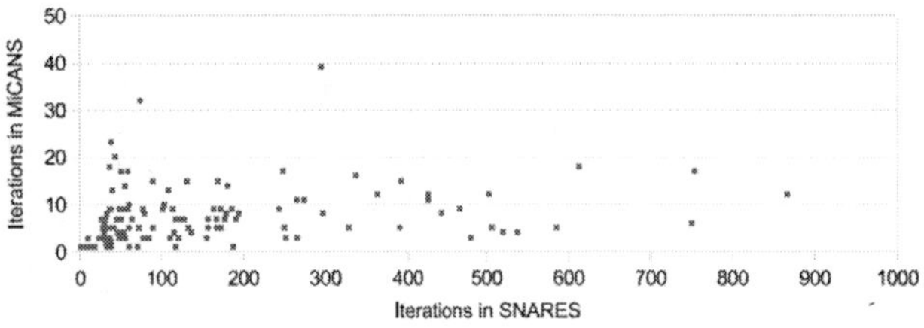

Figure 6: Total number of inner iterations for GRE graphs.

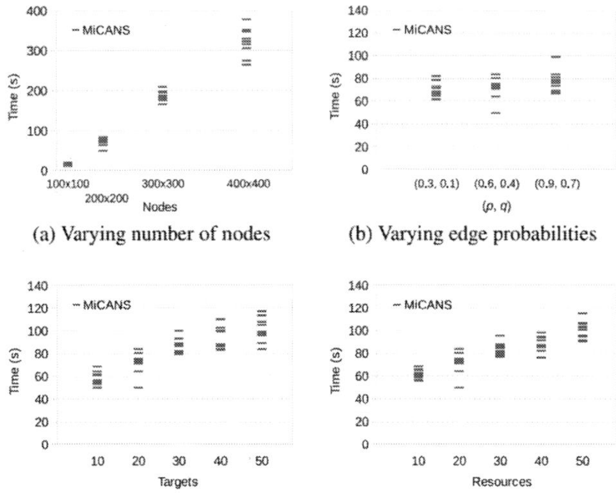

(a) Varying number of nodes (b) Varying edge probabilities

(c) Varying number of targets (d) Varying number of resources

Figure 7: Runtime for large GRE graphs.

Numbers of inner iterations (number of runs of minimax optimizations) for the algorithms are compared in Figure 6. This comparison also shows a significant reduction of iterations by MiCANS and no clear correlation between difficulties concerning the original problem and the reduced one.

Expected payoff values were also compared for the problems that were solved by both SNARES and MiCANS in these experiments (154 GRE graph problems, 154 random geometric graph problems, and 124 Mumbai road network problems). The comparison confirmed that they are always the same; it thus follows that MiCANS successfully found the optimal solutions for these problems.

6.3 Scalability

Scalability of MiCANS was evaluated by using more-difficult problems, which our implementation of SNARES could not solve. It was performed using 10 random instances for each parameter setting. Note that y-axis is changed from a logarithmic scale to a linear scale.

Figure 7 presents runtime in seconds for larger GRE graphs, where central parameter values were selected as 200×200 nodes, $(p,q) = (0.6, 0.4)$, 20 targets, and 20 resources. It shows that the algorithm is still stable for large problems. When the original graph size is very large (e.g. $>$100k nodes), runtime is dominated by mincut computation. These results are similar to those for large random geometric graphs.

Figure 8(a) presents runtime in seconds for the Mumbai road network when the number of targets was varied from 10 to 40 and both numbers of sources and resources were fixed to 20. Figure 8(b) presents runtime in seconds when the number of resources was var-

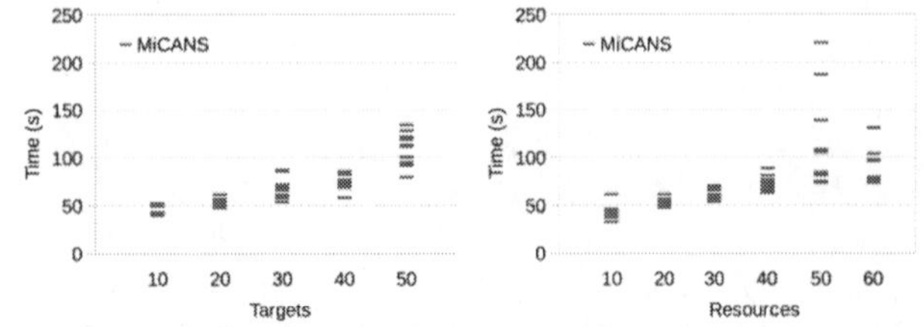

(a) Varying number of targets (b) Varying number of resources

Figure 8: Runtime for Mumbai road network.

Table 1: Solution quality

(a) GRE graphs

	Optimal solutions	Worst case	Time (sec.)
MiCANS	7342/7412 (99.056%)	+12.92%	433.7
AllComb	7409/7412 (99.960%)	+0.08%	4008.0

(b) Random geometric graphs

	Optimal solutions	Worst case	Time (sec.)
MiCANS	7364/7375 (99.851%)	+4.18%	246.7
AllComb	7375/7375 (100.00%)	+0.00%	1836.4

(c) Random graphs

	Optimal solutions	Worst case	Time (sec.)
MiCANS	8280/8295 (99.819%)	+7.11%	313.1
AllComb	8292/8295 (99.964%)	+0.75%	1904.9

ied from 10 to 60 and both numbers of sources and targets were fixed to 20.

Overall, the results for large random geometric graphs, large GRE graphs, and the Mumbai graph are similar. The performance of MiCANS depends on size of the original graph, number of targets, and number of resources. When the original graph size is very large (e.g., $|E| > 100$k), computation time is dominated by min-cut computation. All results show gradual growth in computational cost with respect to size of the problems.

6.4 Solution Quality

Huge number of random tests were performed to evaluate quality of solutions. The number of optimal solutions, the worst-case quality, and the total time for solving all problems are shown in Table 1. For the GRE graphs, horizontal and vertical sizes were chosen randomly from $\{3,\ldots,10\}$, p and q from $[0,1]$, and the numbers of targets and resources from$\{1,\ldots,5\}$. For random geometric graphs, the number of nodes was chosen randomly from $\{10,\ldots,100\}$, d from $[0.1,0.4]$, and the numbers of targets and resources from$\{1,\ldots,5\}$. The number of sources was fixed to 3. Additional tests on random graphs were also performed. 10,000 random instances for each graph types were generated, and the solutions of MiCANS and AllComb were compared with the optimal solutions computed by SNARES, except for the instances that are trivial (perfectly defensible) or unsolvable by SNARES. AllComb enumerates all combinations of targets and selects two min-cuts maximizing and minimizing the size of the node group containing the targets for each combination. MiCANS did not find an optimal solution on rare occasions, and it produced trade-offs between quality and speed.

Figure 9 shows one of the rare cases where both MiCANS and AllComb did not find an optimal solution. The candidate edges selected by MiCANS were $\alpha \cup \beta \cup \gamma$ (expected damage = 35.804); while $\alpha \cup \beta \cup \delta$ were selected by SNARES (expected damage = 35.774). Contrary to expectations, a non-minimum cut, δ, must be selected. δ shares more edges with α and β than γ does, which seems important in this subtle balance of conditions.

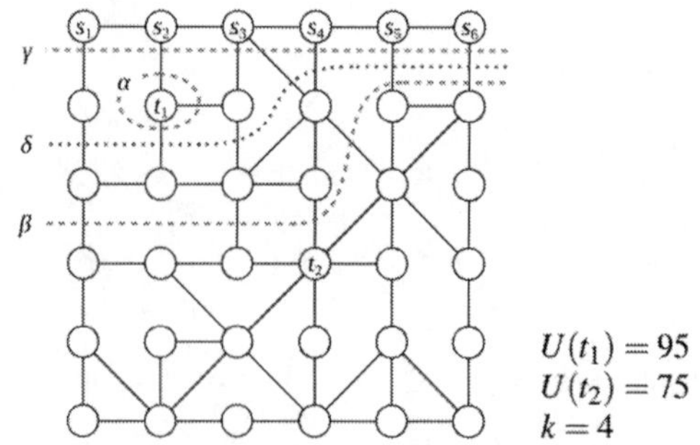

Figure 9: An example of non-optimal solution.

6.5 Warm-Starting SNARES

For some situations in which it is mandatory to guarantee optimality of the solution, MiCANS should still be useful for generating initial sets of the pure strategies for SNARES, which originally used mincut-fanout. Defender allocations on the reduced graph computed by MiCANS can be mapped directly to the original graph. Attacker paths on the reduced graph, however, cannot be restored easily; therefore, we used the shortest paths from the source to the critical targets. They are not optimal and will limit the effectiveness of warm-starting even though defender allocations are optimal. Our preliminary experiments of replacing mincut-fanout with this warm-starting method on small GRE and random geometric graphs showed that computation speed of SNARES is increased five times on average.

7. CONCLUSIONS

A practical approach of simplifying massive urban network security games so that they can be solved within a realistic time was proposed and evaluated. The key idea underpinning this approach is to restrict the defender's pure strategies to potential ones before calculating an equilibrium solution. This restriction can be tightened for faster computation and loosened for better solutions. Output of the proposed method always gives a feasible mixed strategy, which shows an upper bound of the expected damage.

Efficient techniques to solve the problems by using weighted edges to suppress combinatorial explosion of the strategy space were also proposed. These techniques can naturally cope with an extension of the game to one taking width of roads into account, where multiple resources are required for defense.

The weighted edges, however, introduced further level of difficulty in the defender's best-response oracle. It was resolved by identifying the defender's pure strategies that are not essential for optimal solutions and then converting the oracle to an easier problem.

Furthermore, an algorithm called MiCANS, which automatically reduces the original graph to a very small one by abstracting edges that are not essential for the defender's optimal strategy, was proposed. It is shown empirically that MiCANS sometimes fails to find optimal solutions, while the quality of its result is close to the optimal one, even if it is not optimal. Immediate future work will be focused on finding a good bound of the solution quality.

Acknowledgments

This research was partially supported by KAKENHI 26280081.

REFERENCES

[1] T. H. Cormen, C. E. Leiserson, R. L. Rivest, and C. Stein. *Introduction to Algorithms, Third Edition*. MIT press, 2009.

[2] J. Edmonds and R. M. Karp. Theoretical improvements in algorithmic efficiency for network flow problems. *Journal of the ACM (JACM)*, 19(2):248–264, 1972.

[3] D. Eppstein and M. T. Goodrich. Studying (non-planar) road networks through an algorithmic lens. In *Proceedings of the 16th ACM SIGSPATIAL International Conference on Advances in Geographic Information Systems*, GIS '08, pages 16:1–16:10, 2008.

[4] F. Fang, A. X. Jiang, and M. Tambe. Optimal patrol strategy for protecting moving targets with multiple mobile resources. In *International Conference on Autonomous Agents and Multiagent Systems (AAMAS)*, pages 957–964, 2013.

[5] M. Haklay and P. Weber. Openstreetmap: User-generated street maps. *Pervasive Computing, IEEE*, 7(4):12–18, 2008.

[6] M. Jain, V. Conitzer, and M. Tambe. Security scheduling for real-world networks. In *International Conference on Autonomous Agents and Multiagent Systems (AAMAS)*, pages 215–222, 2013.

[7] M. Jain, D. Korzhyk, O. Vaněk, V. Conitzer, M. Pěchouček, and M. Tambe. A double oracle algorithm for zero-sum security games on graphs. In *International Conference on Autonomous Agents and Multiagent Systems (AAMAS)*, pages 327–334, 2011.

[8] M. Jain, K. Leyton-Brown, and M. Tambe. The deployment-to-saturation ratio in security games. In *Conference on Artificial Intelligence (AAAI)*, pages 1362–1370, 2012.

[9] C. Kiekintveld, M. Jain, J. Tsai, J. Pita, F. Ordóñez, and M. Tambe. Computing optimal randomized resource allocations for massive security games. In *International Conference on Autonomous Agents and Multiagent Systems (AAMAS)*, pages 689–696, 2009.

[10] H. B. McMahan, G. J. Gordon, and A. Blum. Planning in the presence of cost functions controlled by an adversary. In *International Conference on Machine Learning*, pages 536–543, 2003.

[11] W. Peng, G. Dong, K. Yang, and J. Su. A random road network model and its effects on topological characteristics of mobile delay-tolerant networks. *IEEE Transactions on Mobile Computing*, 13(12):2706–2718, 2014.

[12] J. Pita, M. Jain, J. Marecki, F. Ordóñez, C. Portway, M. Tambe, C. Western, P. Paruchuri, and S. Kraus. Deployed armor protection: the application of a game theoretic model for security at the los angeles international airport. In *International Conference on Autonomous Agents and Multiagent Systems (AAMAS)*, pages 125–132, 2008.

[13] D. A. Schult and P. Swart. Exploring network structure, dynamics, and function using networkx. In *Proceedings of the 7th Python in Science Conferences (SciPy 2008)*, volume 2008, pages 11–16, 2008.

[14] E. Shieh, B. An, R. Yang, M. Tambe, C. Baldwin, J. DiRenzo, B. Maule, and G. Meyer. Protect: A deployed game theoretic system to protect the ports of the united states. In *International Conference on Autonomous Agents and Multiagent Systems (AAMAS)*, pages 13–20, 2012.

[15] M. Tambe, A. X. Jiang, B. An, and M. Jain. Computational game theory for security: Progress and challenges. In *AAAI Spring Symposium on Applied Computational Game Theory*, 2014.

[16] J. Tsai, S. Rathi, C. Kiekintveld, F. Ordonez, and M. Tambe. Iris-a tool for strategic security allocation in transportation networks. In *International Conference on Autonomous Agents and Multiagent Systems (AAMAS)*, 2009.

[17] J. Tsai, Z. Yin, J.-y. Kwak, D. Kempe, C. Kiekintveld, and M. Tambe. Urban security: Game-theoretic resource allocation in networked physical domains. In *Conference on Artificial Intelligence (AAAI)*, pages 881–886, 2010.

[18] H. Von Stackelberg. *Marktform und Gleichgewicht*. J. Springer, 1934.

[19] A. Washburn and K. Wood. Two-person zero-sum games for network interdiction. *Operations Research*, 43(2):243–251, 1995.

[20] Z. Yin, D. Korzhyk, C. Kiekintveld, V. Conitzer, and M. Tambe. Stackelberg vs. Nash in security games: Interchangeability, equivalence, and uniqueness. In *International Conference on Autonomous Agents and Multiagent Systems (AAMAS)*, pages 1139–1146, 2010.

Learning Adversary Behavior in Security Games: A PAC Model Perspective

Arunesh Sinha, Debarun Kar, Milind Tambe
University of Southern California
{aruneshs, dkar, tambe}@usc.edu

ABSTRACT

Recent applications of Stackelberg Security Games (SSG), from wildlife crime to urban crime, have employed machine learning tools to learn and predict adversary behavior using available data about defender-adversary interactions. Given these recent developments, this paper commits to an approach of directly learning the response function of the adversary. Using the PAC model, this paper lays a firm theoretical foundation for learning in SSGs and provides utility guarantees when the learned adversary model is used to plan the defender's strategy. The paper also aims to answer practical questions such as how much more data is needed to improve an adversary model's accuracy. Additionally, we explain a recently observed phenomenon that prediction accuracy of learned adversary behavior is not enough to discover the utility maximizing defender strategy. We provide four main contributions: (1) a PAC model of learning adversary response functions in SSGs; (2) PAC-model analysis of the learning of key, existing bounded rationality models in SSGs; (3) an entirely new approach to adversary modeling based on a non-parametric class of response functions with PAC-model analysis and (4) identification of conditions under which computing the best defender strategy against the learned adversary behavior is indeed the optimal strategy. Finally, we conduct experiments with real-world data from a national park in Uganda, showing the benefit of our new adversary modeling approach and verification of our PAC model predictions.

1. INTRODUCTION

Stackelberg Security Games (SSGs) are arguably the best example of the application of the Stackelberg game model in the real world. Indeed, numerous successful deployed applications [30] (LAX airport, US air marshal) and extensive research on related topics [5, 18, 6, 7] provide evidence about the generality of the SSG framework. More recently, new application domains of SSGs, from wildlife crime to urban crime, are accompanied by significant amounts of past data of recorded defender strategies and adversary reactions. This has enabled the learning of adversary behavior from such data [36, 35]. Also, analysis of these datasets and human subject experiment studies [26] have revealed that modeling bounded rationality of the adversary enables the defender to further optimize her allocation of limited security resources. Thus, learning the adversary's bounded rational behavior and computing defender strategy based on the learned model has become an important area of research in SSGs.

However, without a theoretical foundation for this learning and strategic planning problem, many issues that arise in practice cannot be explained or addressed. For example, it has been recently observed that in spite of good prediction accuracy of the learned models of adversary behavior, the performance of the defender strategy that is computed against this learned adversary model is poor [12]. A formal study could also answer several other important questions that arise in practice, for example, (1) How many samples would be required to learn a "reasonable" model of adversary behavior in a given SSG? (2) What utility bound can be provided when deploying the best defender strategy that is computed against the learned adversary model?

Motivated by the learning of adversary behavior from data in recent applications [13, 36], we adopt the framework in which the defender first learns the *response function* of the adversary (adversary behavior) and then optimizes against the learned response. This paper is the first theoretical study of the adversary bounded rational behavior learning problem and the optimality guarantees (utility bounds) when computing the best defender strategies against such learned behaviors[1]. Indeed, unlike past theoretical work on learning in SSGs (see related work) where reasoning about adversary response happens through payoff and rationality, we treat the response of the bounded rational adversary as the object to be learned.

Our *first contribution* is using the Probably Approximately Correct (PAC) model [16, 2] to analyze the learning problem at hand. A PAC analysis yields sample complexity, i.e., the number of samples required to achieve a given level of learning guarantee. Hence, the PAC analysis allows us to address the question of required quantity of samples raised earlier. While PAC analysis is fairly standard for classifiers and real valued functions (i.e., regression) it is not an out-of-the-box approach. In particular, PAC-model analysis of SSGs brings to the table significant new challenges. To begin with, given that we are learning adversary response functions, we must deal with the output being a probability distribution over the adversary's actions, i.e., these response functions are vector-valued. We appeal to the framework of Haussler [14] to study the PAC learnability of *vector-valued* response functions. For SSGs, we first pose the learning problem in terms of maximizing the likelihood of seeing the attack data, but without restricting the formulation to any particular class of response functions. This general PAC framework for learning adversary behavior in SSGs enables the rest of the analysis in this paper.

Our *second contribution* is an analysis of the Subjective Utility Quantal Response (SUQR) model of bounded rationality adver-

[1]Our theory results apply to Stackelberg games also. See Appendix.

Appears in: *Proceedings of the 15th International Conference on Autonomous Agents and Multiagent Systems (AAMAS 2016), J. Thangarajah, K. Tuyls, C. Jonker, S. Marsella (eds.), May 9–13, 2016, Singapore.*

sary behavior used in SSGs, which posits a class of parametrized response functions with a given number of parameters (and corresponding features). SUQR is the best known model of bounded rationality in SSGs, resulting in multiple deployed applications [13, 11]. In analyzing SUQR, we advance the state-of-the-art in the mathematical techniques involved in PAC analysis of vector-valued function spaces. In particular, we provide a technique to obtain sharper sample complexity for SUQR than simply directly applying Haussler's original techniques. We decompose the given SUQR function space into two (or more) parts, performing PAC analysis of each part and finally combining the results to obtain the sample complexity result (which scales as $T \log T$ with T targets) for SUQR (see details in Section 5).

Our *third contribution* includes an entirely new behavioral model specified by the *non-parametric Lipschitz* (NPL) class of response functions for SSGs, where the only restriction on NPL functions is Lipschitzness. The NPL approach makes very few assumptions about the response function, enabling the learning of a multitude of behaviors albeit at the cost of higher sample complexity. As NPL has never been explored in learning bounded rationality models in SSGs, we provide a *novel learning technique* for NPL. We also compute the sample complexity for NPL. Further, we observe in our experiments that the power to capture a large variety of behaviors enables NPL to perform better than SUQR with the real-world data from Queen Elizabeth National Park (QENP) in Uganda.

Our *fourth contribution* is to convert the PAC learning guarantee into a bound on the utility derived by the defender when planning her strategy based on the learned adversary behavior model. In the process, we make explicit the assumptions required from the dataset of adversary's attacks in response to deployed defender mixed strategies in order to discover the optimal (w.r.t. utility) defender strategy. These assumptions help explain a puzzling phenomenon observed in recent literature on learning in SSGs [12]—in particular that learned adversary behaviors provide good prediction accuracy, but the best defender strategy computed against such learned behavior may not perform well in practice. We explain this as a mismatch between the adversary model guarantee required for computing the best defender strategy and the guarantee provided by the (PAC based) learning methods. The key is that the dataset for learning must not simply record a large number of attacks against few defender strategies but rather contain the attacker's response against a variety of defender mixed strategies. We discuss the details of our assumptions and its implications for the strategic choice of defender's actions in Section 7.

We also conduct experiments with real-world poaching data from the QENP in Uganda (obtained from [25]) and data collected from human subject experiments. The experimental results support our theoretical conclusions about the number of samples required for different learning techniques. Showing the value of our new NPL approach, the NPL approach outperforms all existing approaches in predicting the poaching activity in QENP. Finally, our work opens up a number of exciting research directions, such as studying learning of behavioral models in active learning setting and real-world application of non-parametric models. [2]

2. RELATED WORK

Learning and planning in SSGs with rational adversaries has been studied in two recent papers [8, 3], and in Stackelberg games by Letchford et al. [20] and Marecki et al. [22]. All these papers study the learning problem under an active learning framework, where the defender can choose the strategy to deploy within the learning process. Also, all these papers study the setting with perfectly rational adversaries. Our work differs as we study bounded rational adversaries in a passive learning scenario (i.e., with given data) and once the model is learned we analyze the guarantees of planning against the learned model. Also, our focus on SSGs differentiates us from recent work on PAC learnability in co-operative games [4], in which the authors study PAC learnability of the value function of coalitions with perfectly rational players. Also, our work is orthogonal to adversarial learning [33], which studies game theoretic models of an adversary attacking a learning algorithm.

PAC learning model has a very rich and extensive body of work [2]. The PAC model provides a theoretical underpinning for most standard machine learning techniques. We use the PAC framework of Haussler [14]. For the parametric case, we derive sharp sample complexity bounds based on covering numbers using our techniques rather than bounding it using the standard technique of pseudo-dimension [28] or fat shattering dimension [2]. For the NPL case we use results from [32] along with our technique of bounding the mixed strategy space of the defender; these results [32] have also been used in the study of Lipschitz classifiers [21] but we differ as our hypothesis functions are real vector-valued.

3. SSG PRELIMINARIES

This section introduces the background and preliminary notations for SSGs. A summary of notations used in this paper is presented in Table 1. An SSG is a two player Stackelberg game between a defender (leader) and an adversary (follower) [27]. The defender wishes to protect T targets with a limited number of security resources K ($K << T$). For ease of presentation, we restrict ourselves to the scenario with no scheduling constraints (see Korzhyk et al. [18]). The defender's pure strategy is to allocate each resource to a target. A defender's mixed-strategy $\tilde{x}$ ($\forall j \in \mathcal{P}.\ \tilde{x}_j \in [0,1], \sum_{j=1}^{\mathcal{P}} \tilde{x}_j = 1$) is then defined as a probability distribution over the set of all possible pure strategies $\mathcal{P}$. An equivalent description (see Korzhyk et al. [18]) of these mixed strategies are coverage probabilities over the set of targets: x ($\forall i \in T.\ x_i \in [0,1], \sum_{i=1}^{T} x_i \leq K$). We refer to this latter description as the mixed strategy of the defender.

A pure strategy of the adversary is defined as attacking a single target. The adversary's mixed strategy is then a categorical distribution over the set of targets. Thus, it can be expressed as parameters q_i ($i \in T$) of a categorical distribution such that $0 \leq q_i \leq 1$ and $\sum_i q_i = 1$. The adversary's response to the defender's mixed strategy is given by a function $q : X \to Q$, where Q is the space of all mixed strategies of the adversary. The matrix U specifies the payoffs of the defender, and her expected utility is $x^T U q(x)$ when she plays a mixed strategy $x \in X$.

Bounded Rationality Models: We discuss the SUQR model and its representation for the analysis in this paper below. Building on prior work on quantal response [24], SUQR [26] states that given n actions, a human player plays action i with probability $q_i \propto e^{w \cdot v}$, where v denotes a vector of feature values for choice i and w denotes the weight parameters for these features. The model is equivalent to conditional logistic regression [23]. The features are specific to the domain, e.g., in case of SSG applications, the set of features include the coverage probability x_i, the reward R_i and penalty P_i of target i. Since, other than the coverage x, remaining features are fixed for each target in real world data, we assume a target-specific feature c_i (which may be a linear combination of re-

[2]Due to lack of space, most proofs are in the online Appendix: `http://teamcore.usc.edu/papers/2016/PAC.Appendix.pdf`

Notation	Meaning
T, K	Number of targets, defender resources
$d_{l_p}(o, o')$	l_p distance between points o, o'
$\bar{d}_{l_p}(o, o')$	Average l_p distance: $= d_{l_p}(o, o')/n$
X	Instance space (defender mixed strategies)
Y	Outcome space (attacked target)
A	Decision space
$h \in \mathcal{H}$	$h : X \rightarrow A$ is the hypothesis function
$\mathcal{N}(\epsilon, \mathcal{H}, d)$	ϵ-cover of set $\mathcal{H}$ using distance d
$\mathcal{C}(\epsilon, \mathcal{H}, d)$	capacity of $\mathcal{H}$ using distance d
$r_h(p), \hat{r}_h(\vec{z})$	true risk, empirical risk of hypothesis h
$d_{L^1(P,d)}(f, g)$	L_1 distance between functions f, g
$q^p(x)$	parameters of true attack distribution
$q^h(x)$	parameters of attack distr. predicted by h

Table 1: Notations

wards and penalties) and analyze the following *generalized*[3] form of SUQR with parameters w_1 and c_i's: $q_i(x) \propto e^{w_1 x_i + c_i}$. As $\sum_{i=1}^{T} q_i(x) = 1$, we have:

$$q_i(x) = \frac{e^{w_1 x_i + c_i}}{\sum_{j=1}^{T} e^{w_1 x_j + c_j}}.$$

Equivalent Alternate Representation: For ease of mathematical proofs, using standard techniques in logistic regression, we take $q_T \propto e^0$, and hence, $q_i \propto e^{w_1(x_i - x_T) + (c_i - c_T)}$. To shorten notation, let $c_{iT} = c_i - c_T$, $x_{iT} = x_i - x_T$. By multiplying the numerator and denominator by $e^{w_1 x_T + c_T}$, it can be verified that $q_i(x) = \frac{e^{w_1 x_{iT} + c_{iT}}}{e^0 + \sum_{j=1}^{T-1} e^{w_1 x_{jT} + c_{jT}}} = \frac{e^{w_1 x_i + c_i}}{\sum_{j=1}^{T} e^{w_1 x_j + c_j}}$.

4. LEARNING FRAMEWORK FOR SSG

First, we introduce some notations: given two n-dimensional points o and o', the l_p distance d_{l_p} between the two points is: $d_{l_p}(o, o') = ||o - o'||_p = (\sum_{i=1}^{n} |o_i - o'_i|^p)^{1/p}$. In particular, $d_{l_\infty}(o, o') = ||o - o'||_\infty = \max_i |o_i - o'_i|$. Also, $\bar{d}_{l_p} = d_{l_p}/n$. KL denotes the Kullback-Leibler divergence [19].

We use the learning framework of Haussler [14], which includes an *instance space* X and *outcome space* Y. In our context, X is same as the space of defender mixed strategies $x \in X$. *Outcome space* Y is defined as the space of all possible categorical choices over a set of T targets (i.e., choice of target to attack) for the adversary. Let t_i denote the attacker's choice to attack the ith target. More formally $\mathrm{t}_i = \langle \mathrm{t}_i^1, \ldots, \mathrm{t}_i^T \rangle$, where $\mathrm{t}_i^j = 1$ for $j = i$ and otherwise 0. Thus, $Y = \{\mathrm{t}_1, \ldots, \mathrm{t}_T\}$. We will use y to denote any general element of Y. To give an example, given three targets T_1, T_2 and T_3, $Y = \{\mathrm{t}_1, \mathrm{t}_2, \mathrm{t}_3\} = \{\langle 1,0,0\rangle, \langle 0,1,0\rangle, \langle 0,0,1\rangle\}$, where t_1 denotes $\langle 1,0,0\rangle$, i.e., it denotes that T_1 was attacked while T_2 and T_3 were not attacked, and so on. The training data are samples drawn from $Z = X \times Y$ using an unknown probability distribution, say given by density $p(x, y)$. Each training data point (x, y) denotes the adversary's response $y \in Y$ (e.g., t1 or attack on target 1) to a particular defender mixed strategy $x \in X$. The density p also determines the true attacker behavior $q^p(x)$ which stands for the conditional probabilities of the attacker attacking a target given x so that $q^p(x) = \langle q_1^p(x), \ldots, q_T^p(x)\rangle$, where $q_i^p(x) = p(\mathrm{t}_i|x)$.

Haussler [14] also defines a *decision space* A, a *space of hypothesis* (functions) $\mathcal{H}$ with elements $h : X \rightarrow A$ and a *loss function* $l : Y \times A \rightarrow \mathbb{R}$. The hypothesis h outputs values in A that enables computing (probabilistic) predictions of the actual outcome. The loss function l captures the loss when the real outcome is $y \in Y$ and the prediction of possible outcomes happens using $a \in A$.

Example 1: Generalized SUQR For the parametric representation of generalized SUQR in the previous section and considering our 3-target example above, $\mathcal{H}$ contains vector valued functions with $(T - 1) = 2$ components that form the exponents of the numerator of prediction probabilities q_1 and q_2. $\mathcal{H}$ contains two components, since the third component q_3 is proportional to e^0 as discussed above. That is, $\mathcal{H}$ contains functions of the form: $\langle w_1(x_1 - x_3) + c_{13}, w_1(x_2 - x_3) + c_{23}\rangle$; $\forall x \in X$. Also, A is the range of the functions in $\mathcal{H}$, i.e., $A \subset \mathbb{R}^2$. Then, given $h(x) = \langle a_1, a_2\rangle$, the prediction probabilities $q_1^h(x), q_2^h(x), q_3^h(x)$ are given by $q_i^h(x) = \frac{e^{a_i}}{1 + e^{a_1} + e^{a_2}}$ (assume $a_3 = 0$).

PAC learnability: The learning algorithm aims to learn a $h \in \mathcal{H}$ that minimizes the *true risk* of using the hypothesis h. The *true risk* $r_h(p)$ of a particular hypothesis (predictor) h, given density function $p(x, y)$ over $Z = X \times Y$, is the expected loss of predicting $h(x)$ when the true outcome is y:

$$r_h(p) = \int p(x, y) l(y, h(x))\, dx\, dy$$

Of course, as p is unknown the true risk cannot be computed. However, given (enough) samples from p, the true risk can be estimated by the *empirical risk*. The *empirical risk* $\hat{r}_h(\vec{z})$, where $\vec{z}$ is a sequence of m training samples from Z, is defined as: $\hat{r}_h(\vec{z}) = 1/m \sum_{i=1}^{m} l(y_i, h(x_i))$. Let h^* be the hypothesis that minimizes the true risk, i.e., $r_{h^*}(p) = \inf\{r_h(p) \mid h \in \mathcal{H}\}$ and let $\hat{h}^*$ be the hypothesis that minimizes the empirical risk, i.e., $\hat{r}_{\hat{h}^*}(\vec{z}) = \inf\{\hat{r}_h(\vec{z}) \mid h \in \mathcal{H}\}$. The following is the well-known PAC learning result [2] for any *empirical risk minimizing* (ERM) algorithm $\mathcal{A}$ yielding hypothesis $\mathcal{A}(\vec{z})$:

$$\begin{aligned} &\text{If } Pr(\forall h \in \mathcal{H}. |\hat{r}_h(\vec{z}) - r_h(p)| < \alpha/3) > 1 - \delta/2 \\ &\text{and } Pr(|\hat{r}_{\mathcal{A}(\vec{z})}(\vec{z}) - \hat{r}_{\hat{h}^*}(\vec{z})| < \alpha/3) > 1 - \delta/2 \\ &\text{then } Pr(|r_{\mathcal{A}(\vec{z})}(p) - r_{h^*}(p)| < \alpha) > 1 - \delta \end{aligned}$$

The final result states that output hypothesis $\mathcal{A}(\vec{z})$ has true risk α-close to the lowest true risk in $\mathcal{H}$ attained by h^* with high probability $1 - \delta$ over the choice of training samples. The first pre-condition states that it must be the case that for all $h \in \mathcal{H}$ the difference between empirical risk and true risk is $\frac{\alpha}{3}$-close with high probability $1 - \frac{\delta}{2}$. The second pre-condition states that the output $\mathcal{A}(\vec{z})$ of the ERM algorithm $\mathcal{A}$ should have empirical risk $\frac{\alpha}{3}$-close to the lowest empirical risk of $\hat{h}^*$ with high probability $1 - \frac{\delta}{2}$. A hypothesis class $\mathcal{H}$ is called (α, δ)-PAC learnable if there exists an ERM algorithm $\mathcal{A}$ such that $\mathcal{H}$ and $\mathcal{A}$ satisfy the two pre-conditions. In this work, our empirical risk minimizing algorithms find $\hat{h}^*$ exactly (upto precision of convex solvers, see Section 6), thus, satisfying the second pre-condition; hence, we will focus more on the first pre-condition. As the empirical risk estimate gets better with increasing samples, a minimum number of samples are required to ensure that the first pre-condition holds (see Theorem 1). Hence we can relate (α, δ)-PAC learnability to the number of samples.

Modeling security games: Having given an example for generalized SUQR, we systematically model learning of adversary behavior in SSGs using the PAC framework for any hypothesis class $\mathcal{H}$. We assume certain properties of functions $h \in \mathcal{H}$ that we present below. First, the vector valued function $h \in \mathcal{H}$ takes the form

$$h(x) = \langle h_1(x), \ldots, h_{T-1}(x)\rangle.$$

Thus, A is the product space $A_1 \times \ldots, A_{T-1}$. Each $h_i(x)$ is assumed to take values between $[-\frac{M}{2}, \frac{M}{2}]$, where $M >> 1$,

[3]This general form is harder to analyze than the *standard* SUQR form in which the exponent function (function of x_i, R_i, P_i) for all q_i is same: $w_1 x_i + w_2 R_i + w_3 P_i$. For completeness, we derive the results for the standard SUQR form in the Appendix.

which implies $A_i = [-\frac{M}{2}, \frac{M}{2}]$. The prediction probabilities induced by any h is $q^h(x) = \langle q_1^h(x), \ldots, q_T^h(x)\rangle$, where $q_i^h(x) = \frac{e^{h_i(x)}}{1+\sum_i e^{h_i(x)}}$ (assume $h_T(x) = 0$). Next, we specify two classes of functions that we analyze in later sections. We choose these two functions classes because (1) the first function class represents the widely used SUQR model in literature [26, 35] and (2) the second function class is very flexible as it capture a wide range of functions and only imposes minimal Lipschitzness constraints to ensure that the functions are well behaved (e.g., continuous).

Parametric $\mathcal{H}$: In this approach we model generalized SUQR. Generalizing from Example 1, the functions $h \in \mathcal{H}$ take a parametric form where each component function is $h_i(x) = w_1 x_{iT} + c_{iT}$.

Non-parametric Lipschitz (NPL) $\mathcal{H}$: Here, the only restriction we impose on functions $h \in \mathcal{H}$ is that each component function h_i is L-Lipschitz where $L \leq \hat{K}$, for given and fixed constant $\hat{K}$. We show later (Lemma 7) that this implies that q^h is Lipschitz also.

Next, given the stochastic nature of the adversary's attacks, we use a loss function (same for parametric and NPL) such that minimizing the empirical risk is equivalent to maximizing the likelihood of seeing the attack data. The loss function $l : Y \times A \to \mathbb{R}$ for actual outcome t_i is defined as:

$$l(\mathrm{t}_i, a) = -\log \frac{e^{a_i}}{1 + \sum_{j=1}^{T-1} e^{a_j}} \qquad (1)$$

It can be readily inferred that minimizing the empirical risk (recall $\hat{r}_h(\vec{z}) = 1/m \sum_{i=1}^{m} l(y_i, h(x_i)))$ is equivalent to maximizing the log likelihood of the training data.

5. SAMPLE COMPLEXITY

In this section we derive the sample complexity for the parametric and NPL case, which provides an indication about the amount of data required to learn the adversary behavior. First, we present a general result about sample complexity bounds for any $\mathcal{H}$, given our loss l. This result relies on sample complexity results in [14]. The bound depends on the capacity $\mathcal{C}$ of $\mathcal{H}$, which we define after the theorem. The bound also assumes an ERM algorithm which we present for our models in Section 6.

THEOREM 1. *Assume that the hypothesis space $\mathcal{H}$ is permissible*[4]. *Let the data be generated by m independent draws from $X \times Y$ according to p. Then, assuming existence of an ERM algorithm and given our loss l defined in Eq. 1, the least m required to ensure (α, δ)-PAC learnability is (recall $\bar{d}_{l_1}$ is average l_1 distance)*

$$\frac{576M^2}{\alpha^2}\Big(\log\frac{1}{\delta} + \log\big(8\mathcal{C}(\frac{\alpha}{96T}, \mathcal{H}, \bar{d}_{l_1})\big)\Big)$$

PROOF SKETCH. Haussler [14] present a result of the above form using a general distance metric defined on the space A for any loss function l: $\rho(a,b) = \max_{y \in Y}|l(y,a) - l(y,b)|$. The main effort in this proof is relating ρ to $\bar{d}_{l_1}$ for our choice of the loss function l given by Equation 1. We are able to show that $\rho(a,b) \leq 2T\bar{d}_{l_1}(a,b)$. Our result then follows from this relation. □

The above sample complexity result is stated in terms of the capacity $\mathcal{C}(\alpha/96T, \mathcal{H}, \bar{d}_{l_1})$. Thus, in order to obtain the sample complexity of the generalized SUQR and NPL function spaces we need to compute the capacity of these function spaces. Therefore, in the rest of this section we will focus on computing capacity $\mathcal{C}(\alpha/96T, \mathcal{H}, \bar{d}_{l_1})$ for both the generalized SUQR and NPL hypothesis space. First, we need to define capacity $\mathcal{C}$ of functions spaces, for which we start by defining the covering number $\mathcal{N}$ of function spaces. Let d be a pseudo metric for the set $\mathcal{H}$. For any $\epsilon > 0$, an ϵ-cover for $\mathcal{H}$ is a finite set $\mathcal{F} \subseteq \mathcal{H}$ such that for any $h \in \mathcal{H}$ there is a $f \in \mathcal{F}$ with $d(f,h) \leq \epsilon$, i.e., any element in $\mathcal{H}$ is at least ϵ-close to some element of the cover $\mathcal{F}$. The *covering number* $\mathcal{N}(\epsilon, \mathcal{H}, d)$ denotes the size of the smallest ϵ-cover for set $\mathcal{H}$ (for the pseudo metric d). We now proceed to define a pseudo metric $d_{L^1(P,d)}$ on $\mathcal{H}$ with respect to any probability measure P on X and any given pseudo-metric d on A. This pseudo-metric is the expected (over P) distance (with d) between the output of f and g.

$$d_{L^1(P,d)}(f,g) = \int_X d(f(x), g(x))\, dP(x) \quad \forall f, g \in \mathcal{H}$$

Then, $\mathcal{N}(\epsilon, \mathcal{H}, d_{L^1(P,d)})$ is the covering number for $\mathcal{H}$ for the pseudo metric $d_{L^1(P,d)}$. However, to be more general, the capacity of function spaces provides a "distribution-free" notion of covering number. The *capacity* $\mathcal{C}(\epsilon, \mathcal{H}, d)$ is:

$$\mathcal{C}(\epsilon, \mathcal{H}, d) = \sup_P \{\mathcal{N}(\epsilon, \mathcal{H}, d_{L^1(P,d)})\}$$

Capacity of vector valued function: The function spaces (both parametric and NPL) we consider are vector valued. Haussler [14] provides an useful technique to bound the capacity for vector valued function space $\mathcal{H}$ in terms of the capacity of each of the component real valued function space. Given k functions spaces $\mathcal{H}_1, \ldots, \mathcal{H}_k$ with functions from X to A_i, he define the *free product* function space $\times_i \mathcal{H}_i$ with functions from X to $A = A_1 \times \ldots A_k$ as $\times_i \mathcal{H}_i = \{\langle h_1, \ldots, h_k\rangle \mid h_i \in \mathcal{H}_i\}$, where $\langle h_1, \ldots, h_k\rangle(x) = \langle h_1(x), \ldots, h_k(x)\rangle$. He shows that:

$$\mathcal{C}(\epsilon, \times_i \mathcal{H}_i, \bar{d}_{l_1}) < \prod_{i=1}^{k} \mathcal{C}(\epsilon, \mathcal{H}_i, d_{l_1}) \qquad (2)$$

Unfortunately, a straightforward application of the above result does not give as tight bounds for capacity in the parametric case as the novel direct sum decomposition of function spaces approach we use in the sub-section. Even for the NPL case where the above result is used we still need to compute $\mathcal{C}(\epsilon, \mathcal{H}_i, d_{l_1})$ for each component function space $\mathcal{H}_i$.

5.1 Parametric case: Generalized SUQR

Recall that the hypothesis function h has $T-1$ component functions $w_1 x_{iT} + c_{iT}$. However, the same weight w_1 in all component functions implies that $\mathcal{H}$ is not a free product of component function spaces, hence we cannot use Equation 2 directly. However, if we consider the space of functions, say $\mathcal{H}'$, in which the ith component function space $\mathcal{H}'_i$ is given by $w_i x_{iT} + c_{iT}$ (note w_i can be different for each i) then we can use Equation 2 to bound $\mathcal{C}(\epsilon, \mathcal{H}', \bar{d}_{l_1})$. Also, the fact that $\mathcal{H} \subset \mathcal{H}'$ allows upper bounding $\mathcal{C}(\epsilon, \mathcal{H}, \bar{d}_{l_1})$ by $\mathcal{C}(\epsilon, \mathcal{H}', \bar{d}_{l_1})$. But, this approach results in a weaker $T\log(\frac{T}{\alpha}\log\frac{T}{\alpha})$ bound (detailed derivation using this approach is in Appendix) than the technique we use below. We obtain a $T\log(\frac{T}{\alpha})$ result below in Theorem 2.

We propose a *novel approach that decomposes $\mathcal{H}$ into a direct sum of two functions spaces* (defined below), each of which capture the simpler functions $w_1 x_{iT}$ and c_{iT} respectively. We provide a general result about such decomposition which allows us to bound $\mathcal{C}(\epsilon, \mathcal{H}, \bar{d}_{l_1})$. We start with the following definition.

DEFINITION 1. *Direct-sum semi-free product of function spaces $\mathcal{G} \subset \times_i \mathcal{G}_i$ and $\times_i \mathcal{F}_i$ is defined as $\mathcal{G} \oplus \times_i \mathcal{F}_i = \{\langle g_1 + f_1, \ldots, g_{T-1} + f_{T-1}\rangle \mid \langle g_1, \ldots, g_{T-1}\rangle \in \mathcal{G}, \langle f_1, \ldots, f_{T-1}\rangle \in \times_i \mathcal{F}_i\}$.*

[4]As noted in Haussler: "This is a measurability condition defined in Pollard (1984) which need not concern us in practice."

Applying the above definition for our case, $\mathcal{G}_i$ contains functions of the form wx_{iT} (w taking different values for different $g_i \in \mathcal{G}_i$). A function $\langle g_1, \ldots, g_{T-1}\rangle \in \times_i \mathcal{G}_i$ can have different weights for each component g_i, and thus we consider the subset $\mathcal{G} = \{\langle g_1, \ldots, g_{T-1}\rangle \mid \langle g_1, \ldots, g_{T-1}\rangle \in \times_i \mathcal{G}_i$, same coefficient w for all $g_i\}$. $\mathcal{F}_i$ contains constant valued functions of the form c_{iT} (c_{iT} different for different functions $f_i \in \mathcal{F}_i$). Then, $\mathcal{H} = \mathcal{G} \oplus \times_i \mathcal{F}_i$. Next, we prove a general result about direct-sum semi-free products:

LEMMA 1. *If $\mathcal{H}$ is the direct-sum semi-free product $\mathcal{G} \oplus \times_i \mathcal{F}_i$*

$$\mathcal{C}(\epsilon, \mathcal{H}, \bar{d_{l_1}}) < \mathcal{C}(\epsilon/2, \mathcal{G}, \bar{d_{l_1}}) \prod_{i=1}^{T-1} \mathcal{C}(\epsilon/2, \mathcal{F}_i, d_{l_1})$$

PROOF. Fix any probability distribution over X, say P. For brevity, we write k instead of $T-1$. Consider an $\epsilon/2$-cover U_i for each $\mathcal{F}_i$; also let V be an $\epsilon/2$-cover for $\mathcal{G}$. We claim that $V \oplus \times_i U_i$ is an ϵ-cover for $\mathcal{G} \oplus \times_i \mathcal{F}_i$. Take any function $h = \langle g_1 + f_1, \ldots g_k + f_k\rangle$. Find functions $f'_i \in U_i$ such that $d_{L^1(P,d_{l_1})}(f_i, f'_i) < \epsilon/2$. Similarly, find function $g' = \langle g'_1, \ldots g'_k\rangle \in V$ such that $d_{L^1(P,\bar{d_{l_1}})}(g, g') < \epsilon/2$ where $g = \langle g_1, \ldots g_k\rangle$. Let $h' = \langle g'_1 + f'_1, \ldots g'_k + f'_k\rangle$. Then,

$$\begin{aligned}
& d_{L^1(P,\bar{d_{l_1}})}(h, h') \\
&= \int_X \frac{1}{k}\sum_{i=1}^{k} d_{l_1}(g_i(x) + f_i(x), g'_i(x) + f'_i(x))\, dP(x) \\
&\leq \int_X \frac{1}{k}\sum_{i=1}^{k} d_{l_1}(g_i(x), g'_i(x)) + d_{l_1}(f_i(x), f'_i(x))\, dP(x) \\
&= d_{L^1(P,\bar{d_{l_1}})}(g, g') + \frac{1}{k}\sum_{i=1}^{k} d_{L^1(P,d_{l_1})}(f_i, f'_i) \\
&< \epsilon/2 + \epsilon/2 = \epsilon
\end{aligned}$$

Thus, the size of ϵ-cover for $\mathcal{G} \oplus \times_i \mathcal{F}_i$ is bounded by $|V|\prod_i |U_i|$.

$$\begin{aligned}
\mathcal{N}(\epsilon, \mathcal{G} \oplus \times_i \mathcal{F}_i, d_{L^1(P,\bar{d_{l_1}})}) &< |V|\textstyle\prod_i |U_i| \\
&= \mathcal{N}(\epsilon/2, \mathcal{G}, d_{L^1(P,\bar{d_{l_1}})}) \textstyle\prod_{i=1}^{k} \mathcal{N}(\epsilon/2, \mathcal{F}_i, d_{L^1(P,d_{l_1})})
\end{aligned}$$

Taking sup over probability distribution P on both sides of the above inequality we get our desired result about capacity. □

Next, we need to bound the capacity of $\mathcal{G}$ and $\mathcal{F}_i$ for our case. We assume the range of all these functions (g_i, f_i) to be $[-\frac{M}{4}, \frac{M}{4}]$ (so that their sum h_i lies in $[-\frac{M}{2}, \frac{M}{2}]$). We can obtain sharp bounds on the capacities of $\mathcal{G}$ and $\mathcal{F}_i$ decomposed from $\mathcal{H}$ in order to obtain sharp bounds on the overall capacity.

LEMMA 2. $\mathcal{C}(\epsilon, \mathcal{G}, \bar{d_{l_1}}) \leq M/4\epsilon$ *and* $\mathcal{C}(\epsilon, \mathcal{F}_i, d_{l_1}) \leq M/4\epsilon$.

PROOF SKETCH. Note that $x_{iT} = x_i - x_T$ lies between $[-1, 1]$. Then, for any two $g, g' \in \mathcal{G}$ we can prove following result: $d_{L^1(P,\bar{d_{l_1}})}(g, g') \leq |(w - w')|$ (details in Appendix). Also, note that since the range of any $g = w(x_i - x_T)$ is $[-\frac{M}{4}, \frac{M}{4}]$ and given $x_i - x_T$ lies between $[-1, 1]$, we can claim that w lies between $[-\frac{M}{4}, \frac{M}{4}]$. Thus, as the distance between functions is bounded by the difference in weights, it is enough to divide the $M/2$ range of the weights into intervals of size 2ϵ and consider functions at the boundaries. Hence the ϵ-cover has at most $M/4\epsilon$ functions.

The proof for constant valued functions $\mathcal{F}_i$ is similar, since the distance between two functions in this space is the absolute difference in the constants, which lie in $[-\frac{M}{4}, \frac{M}{4}]$. □

Then, plugging the result of Lemma 2 (substituting $\epsilon/2$ for ϵ) into Lemma 1 we obtain $\mathcal{C}(\epsilon, \mathcal{H}, \bar{d_{l_1}}) < (M/2\epsilon)^T$. Having bounded $\mathcal{C}(\epsilon, \mathcal{H}, \bar{d_{l_1}})$, we use Theorem 1 to obtain:

THEOREM 2. *The generalized SUQR parametric hypothesis class $\mathcal{H}$ is (α, δ)-PAC learnable with sample complexity*[5]

$$O\Big(\big(\frac{1}{\alpha^2}\big)\big(\log(\frac{1}{\delta}) + T\log(\frac{T}{\alpha})\big)\Big)$$

The above result shows a modest $T\log T$ growth of sample complexity with increasing targets, suggesting the parametric approach can avoid overfitting limited data with increasing number of targets; however, the simplicity of the functions captured by this approach (compared to NPL) results in lower accuracy with increasing data, as shown later in our experiments on real-world data.

5.2 Non-Parametric Lipschitz case

Recall that $\mathcal{H}$ for the NPL case is defined such that each component function h_i is L-Lipschitz where $L \leq \hat{K}$. Consider the functions spaces $\mathcal{H}_i$ consisting of real valued L-Lipschitz functions where $L \leq \hat{K}$. Then, $\mathcal{H} = \times_i \mathcal{H}_i$. Then, using Equation 2: $\mathcal{C}(\epsilon, \mathcal{H}, \bar{d_{l_1}}) \leq \prod_{i=1}^{T-1} \mathcal{C}(\epsilon, \mathcal{H}_i, d_{l_1})$.

Next, our task is to bound $\mathcal{C}(\epsilon, \mathcal{H}_i, d_{l_1})$. Consider the sup-distance metric between real valued functions: $d_{l_\infty}(h_i, h'_i) = \sup_X |h_i(x) - h'_i(x)|$ for $h_i, h'_i \in \mathcal{H}_i$. Note that d_{l_∞} is independent of any probability distribution P, and for all functions h_i, h'_i and any P, $d_{L^1(P,d_{l_1})}(h_i, h'_i) \leq d_{l_\infty}(h_i, h'_i)$. Thus, we can infer [14] that for all P, $\mathcal{N}(\epsilon, \mathcal{H}_i, d_{L^1(P,d_{l_1})}) \leq \mathcal{N}(\epsilon, \mathcal{H}_i, d_{l_\infty})$ and then taking sup over P (recall $\mathcal{C}(\epsilon, \mathcal{H}_i, d_{l_1}) = \sup_P \{\mathcal{N}(\epsilon, \mathcal{H}_i, d_{L^1(P,d_{l_1})})\}$) we get

$$\mathcal{C}(\epsilon, \mathcal{H}_i, d_{l_1}) \leq \mathcal{N}(\epsilon, \mathcal{H}_i, d_{l_\infty}) \tag{3}$$

We bound $\mathcal{N}(\epsilon, \mathcal{H}_i, d_{l_\infty})$ in terms of covering number for X (recall $X = \{x \mid x \in [0,1]^T, \sum_i x_i \leq K\}$) using results from [32].

LEMMA 3. $\mathcal{N}(\epsilon, \mathcal{H}_i, d_{l_\infty}) \leq \Big(2\Big\lceil\frac{M}{\epsilon}\Big\rceil + 1\Big) \cdot 2^{\mathcal{N}(\frac{\epsilon}{2\hat{K}}, X, d_{l_\infty})}$

To use the above result, we still need to bound $\mathcal{N}(\epsilon, X, d_{l_\infty})$. We do so by combining two remarkable results about Eulerian number $\langle{T \atop k}\rangle$ [17] (k has to be integral).

- Laplace [10] [29] discovered that the volume of $X_k = \{x | x \in [0,1]^T, k-1 \leq \sum_i x_i \leq k\}$ is $\langle{T \atop k}\rangle/T!$. Thus, if $X_K = \cup_{k=1}^{K} X_k$, then $vol(X_K) = \sum_{k=1}^{K} vol(X_k) = \sum_{k=1}^{K} \langle{T \atop k}\rangle/T!$.
- Also, it is known [31] that $\langle{T \atop k}\rangle/T! = F_T(k) - F_T(k-1)$, where $F_T(x)$ is the CDF of the probability distribution of $S_T = U_1 + \ldots + U_T$ and each U_i is a uniform random variable on $[0, 1)$.

Combining these results, $vol(X_{K+1}) = F_T(K+1)$. The volume of a l_∞ ball of radius ϵ (l_∞ ball is a hypercube) is $(2\epsilon)^T$ [34]. Then, the number of balls that fit tightly (aligned with the axes) and completely inside X_{K+1} is bounded by $F_T(K+1)/(2\epsilon)^T$. Since $\epsilon << 1$, these balls cover $X_K = X$ completely and the tight packing ensures that the center of the balls forms an ϵ-cover for X. Then, bounding $F_T(K+1)$ using Bernstein's inequality about concentration of random variables we get:

LEMMA 4. *For $K + 1 \leq 0.5T$ (recall $K << T$)*

$$\mathcal{N}(\epsilon, X, d_{l_\infty}) \leq e^{\frac{-3T(0.5-(K+1)/T)^2}{1-(K+1)/T}}/(2\epsilon)^T$$

Plugging the above result into Lemma 3 and then using that in Equation 3, we bound $\mathcal{C}(\epsilon, \mathcal{H}_i, d_{l_1})$. Finally, Equation 2 gives a bound on $\mathcal{C}(\epsilon, \mathcal{H}, \bar{d_{l_1}})$ that we use in Theorem 1 to obtain

[5]In the Appendix, we show that for standard SUQR (simpler than our generalized SUQR) the sample size is $O\big(\frac{1}{\alpha^2}(\log\frac{1}{\delta} + \log\frac{T}{\alpha})\big)$

THEOREM 3. *The non-parametric hypothesis class $\mathcal{H}$ is a (α, δ)-PAC learnable with sample complexity*

$$O\Big(\big(\frac{1}{\alpha^2}\big)\big(\log(\frac{1}{\delta}) + (\frac{T^{T+1}}{\alpha^T})\big)\Big)$$

The above result shows that the sample complexity for NPL grows fast with T suggesting that NPL may not be the right approach to use when the number of targets is large.

6. LEARNING ALGORITHM

As stated earlier, our loss function was designed so that the learning algorithm (empirical risk minimizer in PAC framework) was the same as maximizing log likelihood of data. Indeed, for SUQR, the standard MLE approach can be used to learn the parameters (weights) and has been used in literature [26]. However, for NPL, which has no parameters, maximizing likelihood only provides $h(x)$ for those mixed strategies x that are in the training data.

Hence we present a *novel two step learning algorithm for the NPL case*. In the first step, we estimate the most likely value for $h_i(x)$ (for each i) for each x in the training data, ensuring that for any pair x, x' in the training data, $|h_i(x) - h_i(x')| \leq \hat{K}||x - x'||_1$. In the second step, we construct the function h_i with the least Lipschitz constant subject to the constraint that h_i takes the values for the training data output by the first step.

More formally, assume the training data has s unique values for x in the training set and let these values be $x^1, \ldots, x^s$. Further, let there be n_j distinct data points against x^j, i.e., n_j attacks against mixed strategy x^j. Denote by $n_{j,i}$ the number of attacks at each target i when x^j was used. Let h_{ij} be the variable that stands for the estimate of value $h_i(x^j)$; $i \in \{1, \ldots, T\}, j \in \{1, \ldots, s\}$. Fix $h_{Tj} = 0$ for all j. Then, probability of attack on target i against mixed strategy x^j is given by $q_{ij} = \frac{e^{h_{ij}}}{\sum_i e^{h_{ij}}}$. Thus, the log likelihood of the training data is $\sum_{j=1}^{s}\sum_{i=1}^{T} n_{j,i}\log q_{ij}$. Let $Lip(\hat{K})$ denote the set of L-Lipschitz functions with $L \leq \hat{K}$. Using our assumption that $h_i \in Lip(\hat{K})$, the following optimization problem provides the most likely h_{ij} :

$$\begin{aligned} \max_{h_{ij}} \quad & \sum_{j=1}^{s}\sum_{i=1}^{T} n_{j,i}\log\frac{e^{h_{ij}}}{\sum_i e^{h_{ij}}} \\ \text{subject to} \quad & \forall i, j, j',\ |h_{ij} - h_{ij'}| \leq \hat{K}||x^j - x^{j'}||_1 \\ & \forall i, j,\ -M/2 \leq h_{ij} \leq M/2 \end{aligned}$$

Given solution h^*_{ij} to the above problem, we wish to construct the solution h_i such that its Lipschitz constant (given by K_{h_i}) is the lowest possible subject to h_i taking the value h^*_{ij} for x^j. Such a construction provides the most smoothly varying solution given the training data, i.e., we do not assume any more sharp changes in the adversary response than what the training data provides.

$$\min_{h_i \in Lip(\hat{K})} \ K_{h_i} \ \text{ subject to } \forall i, j.\ h_i(x^j) = h^*_{ij} \quad \text{(MinLip)}$$

The above optimization is impractical to solve computationally as uncountably many constraints are required to relate K_{h_i} to h_i. Fortunately, we obtain an analytical solution:

LEMMA 5. *The following is a solution for problem* MinLip

$$h_i(x) = \min_j\{h^*_{ij} + K^*_i||x - x^j||_1\}$$

where $K^*_i = \max_{j,j':j\neq j'} \frac{|h^*_{ij} - h^*_{ij'}|}{||x^j - x^{j'}||_1}$

PROOF SKETCH. Observe that due to the definition of K^* any solution to MinLip will have Lipschitz constant $\geq K^*$. Thus, it suffices to show that the Lipschitz constant of h_i is K^*, to prove that h_i is a solution of MinLip, which we show in the Appendix. □

Note that for any point x^j is the training data we have $h_i(x^j) = h^*_{ij}$. Then the value of $h_i(x)$ for a x not in the training set and close to x^j is quite likely be the $h_i(x^j)$ plus the scaled distance $K^*_i||x - x^j||_1$ showing the value of x is influenced by nearby training points.

7. UTILITY BOUNDS

Next, we bound the difference between the optimal utility and the utility derived from planning using the learned h. The utility bound is same for the parametric and NPL case. Recall that the defender receives the utility $xUq^p(x)$ when playing strategy x. We need to bound the difference between the true distribution $q^p(x)$ and the predicted distribution $q^h(x)$ of attacks in order to start analyzing bounds on utility. Thus, we transform the PAC learning guarantee about the risk of output h to a bound on $||q^p(x) - q^h(x)||_1$. As the PAC guarantee only bounds the risk between predicted h and the best hypothesis h^* in $\mathcal{H}$, in order to relate the true distribution q^p and predicted distribution q^h, the lemma below assumes a bounded KL divergence between the distribution of the best hypothesis q^{h^*} and the true distribution q^p.

LEMMA 6. *Assume $E[KL(q^p(x) \ || \ q^{h^*}(x))] \leq \epsilon^*$. Given an ERM $\mathcal{A}$ with output $h = \mathcal{A}(\vec{z})$ and guarantee $Pr(|r_h(p) - r_{h^*}(p)| < \alpha) > 1 - \delta$, with prob. $\geq 1 - \delta$ over training samples $\vec{z}$ we have*

$$Pr(||q^p(x) - q^h(x)||_1 \leq \sqrt{2}\Delta) \geq 1 - \Delta$$

where $\Delta = (\alpha + \epsilon^*)^{1/3}$ and x is sampled using density p.

Utility bound: Next, we provide an utility bound, given the above guarantee about learned h. Let the optimal strategy computed using the learned adversary model h be $\tilde{x}$, i.e., $\tilde{x}^T Uq^h(\tilde{x}) \geq x'^T Uq^h(x')$ for all x'. Let the true optimal defender mixed strategy be x^* (optimal w.r.t. true attack distribution $q^p(x)$), so that the maximum defender utility is $x^{*T}Uq^p(x^*)$. Let $B(x, \epsilon)$ denote the l_1 ball of radius ϵ around x. We make the following assumptions:

1. h_i is $\hat{K}$-Lipschitz $\forall i$ and q^p is K-Lipschitz in l_1 norm.
2. $\exists$ small ϵ such that $Pr(x \in B(x^*, \epsilon)) > \Delta$ over choice of x using p.
3. $\exists$ small ϵ such that $Pr(x \in B(\tilde{x}, \epsilon)) > \Delta$ over choice of x using p.

While the first assumption is mild, the last two assumptions for small ϵ mean that the points x^* and $\tilde{x}$ must not lie in low density regions of the distribution p used to sample the data points. In other words, there should be many defender mixed strategies in the data of defender-adversary interaction that lie near x^* and $\tilde{x}$. We discuss the assumptions in details after the technical results below. Given these assumptions, we need Lemma 7 that relates assumption (1) to Lipschitzness of q^h in order to obtain the utility bound.

LEMMA 7. *If h_i is $\hat{K}$-Lipschitz then $\forall x, x' \in X$. $||q^h(x) - q^h(x')||_1 \leq 3\hat{K}||x - x'||_1$, i.e., $q^h(x)$ is $3\hat{K}$-Lipschitz.*

Then, we can prove the following:

THEOREM 4. *Given above assumptions and the results of Lemma 6 and 7, with prob. $\geq 1 - \delta$ over the training samples the expected utility $\tilde{x}^T Uq^h(\tilde{x})$ for the learned h is at least*

$$x^{*T}Uq^p(x^*) - (K+1)\epsilon - 2\sqrt{2}\Delta - 6\hat{K}\epsilon$$

Discussion of assumptions: A puzzling phenomenon observed in recent work on learning in SSGs is that good prediction accuracy of the learned adversary behavior is not a reliable indicator of the defender's performance in practice [12]. The additional assumptions, over and above the PAC learning guarantee, that are made to bound the utility deviation from the optimal utility point towards the possibility of such occurrences. Recall that the second assumption requires the existence of many defender mixed strategies in the dataset near the utility optimal strategy x^*. Of course x^* is not known apriori, hence in order to guarantee utility close to the highest possible utility the dataset must contain defender mixed strategies from all regions of the mixed strategy space; or at-least if it is known that some regions of the mixed strategies dominate other parts in terms of utility then it is enough to have mixed strategies from these regions. Thus, following our assumption, better utility can be achieved by collecting attack data against a variety of mixed strategies rather than many attacks against few mixed strategies.

Going further, we illustrate with a somewhat extreme example where violating our assumptions can lead to this undesirable phenomenon. Consider the extreme example where probability distribution p (recall data points are sampled using p) puts all probability mass on x_0, where the the utility for x_0 is much lower than x^*. Hence, the dataset will contain only one defender mixed strategy x_0 (with many attacks against it). Due to Lipschitzness (assumption 1), the large utility difference between x_0 and x^* implies that x_0 is not close to x^* which in turn violates assumption 2. This example provides a very good PAC guarantee since there is no requirement for the learning algorithm to predict accurately for any other mixed strategies (which occur with zero probability) in order to have good prediction accuracy. The learning technique needs to predict well only for x_0 to achieve a low α, δ. As a result the defender strategy computed against the learned adversary model may not be utility maximizing because of the poor predictions for all defender mixed strategies other than the low utility yielding x_0. More generally, good prediction accuracy can be achieved by good predictions only for the mixed strategies that occur with high probability.

Indeed, in general, the prediction accuracy in the PAC model (and any applied machine learning approach) is not a reliable indicator of good prediction over the entire space of defender mixed strategies unless, following our assumption 2, the dataset has attacks against strategies from all parts of the mixed strategy space. However, in past work [1, 9] researchers have focused on gathering a lot of attack data but on limited number of defender strategies. Our analysis provides a principled explanation of the issues that arise from composing the machine learning module with the defender strategy optimization module in the learning and planning framework used for SSGs. Further, we believe that our analysis provides guidance to overcome these issues and discover the defender's utility maximizing strategy.

8. EXPERIMENTAL RESULTS

We show experimental results on two datasets: (i) real-world poaching data from QENP [25]; (ii) data from human subjects experiments on Amazon Mechanical Turk (AMT) [15], to estimate prediction errors and the amount of data required to reduce the error for both the parametric and NPL learning settings. Also, we compare the NPL approach with both the standard as well as the generalized SUQR approach and show that: (i) the NPL approach, while computationally slow, outperforms the standard SUQR model for Uganda data; and (ii) the performance of generalized SUQR is in between NPL and standard SUQR.

For each dataset, we conduct four experiments with 25%, 50%, 75% and 100% of the original data. We create 100 train-test splits

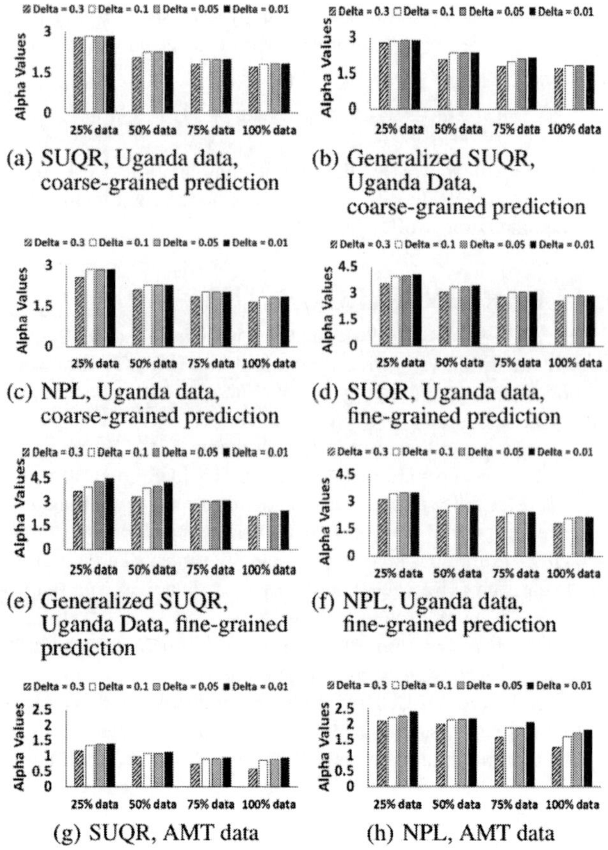

(a) SUQR, Uganda data, coarse-grained prediction
(b) Generalized SUQR, Uganda Data, coarse-grained prediction
(c) NPL, Uganda data, coarse-grained prediction
(d) SUQR, Uganda data, fine-grained prediction
(e) Generalized SUQR, Uganda Data, fine-grained prediction
(f) NPL, Uganda data, fine-grained prediction
(g) SUQR, AMT data
(h) NPL, AMT data

Figure 1: Results on Uganda and AMT datasets for both the parametric and NPL learning settings.

in each of the four experiments per dataset. For each train-test split we compute the average prediction error α (average difference between the log-likelihoods of the attacks in the test data using predicted and actual attack probabilities). We report the α value at the $1 - \delta$ percentile of the 100 α values, e.g., reported $\alpha = 2.09$ for $\delta = 0.1$ means that 90 of the 100 test splits have $\alpha < 2.09$.

8.1 Real-World Poaching data

We first present results of our experiments with real-world poaching data. The dataset obtained contained information about features such as ranger patrols and animal densities, which are used as features in our SUQR model, and the poachers' attacks, with 40,611 total observations recorded by rangers at various locations in the park. The park area was discretized into 2423 grid cells, with each grid cell corresponding to a 1km^2 area within the park. After discretization, each observation fell within one of 2423 target cells and the animal densities and the number of poaching attacks within each target cell were then aggregated. The dataset contained 655 poachers' attacks in response to the defender's strategy for 2012 at QENP. Although the data is reliable because the rangers recorded the latitudes and longitudes of the location for each observation using a GPS device, it is important to note that this data set is extremely noisy because of: (i) Missing observations: all the poaching events are not recorded because the limited number of rangers cannot patrol all the areas in this park all the time; (ii) Uncertain feature values: the animal density feature is also based on incomplete observations of animals; (iii) Uncertain defender strategy: the actual defender mixed strategy is unknown; we estimate the mixed strategies based on the provided patrol data.

In this paper, we provide two types of prediction in our experiments: (i) fine-grained and (ii) coarse-grained. First, to provide a baseline for our error measures, we use the same coarse-grained prediction approach as reported by Nguyen et al. [25], in which the authors only predict whether a target will be attacked or not. The results for coarse-grained predictions with our performance metric (α values for different δ) are shown in Figs. 1(a), 1(b) and 1(c). Next, in the fine-grained prediction approach we predict the *actual* number of attacks on each target in our test set; these results are shown in Figs. 1(d), 1(e) and 1(f). In [25], the authors used a particular metric for prediction performance called the area under the ROC curve (AUC), which we will discuss later in the section.

From our fine-grained and coarse-grained prediction approaches, we make several important observations. First, we observe that α decreases with increasing sample size at a rate proportional to $\frac{1}{\sqrt{m}}$, where m is the number of samples. For example, in Fig. 1(a), the α values corresponding to $\delta = 0.01$ (black bar) for the 25%, 50%, 75% and 100% data are 2.81, 2.38, 2.18 and 1.8 respectively, which fits $\frac{1}{\sqrt{m}}$ with a goodness-of-fit, i.e., r^2=0.97. This observation supports the relationship between α and m shown in Theorem 3 and can be used to approximately infer the number of samples required to reduce the prediction error to a certain value. For example, assuming we collect same number of samples (=655) per year, to reduce α from 1.8 to 1.64, we would require two more years of data. Note here that α is in log-scale and hence the decrease is significant. It is also worth noting here that, for a random classifier, we observe a value of $\alpha = 6.3$ for $\delta = 0.01$ while performing coarse grained predictions with 25% data. This is more than $\alpha = 2.81$ for $\delta = 0.01$ obtained for our standardized SUQR model while performing coarse grained predictions with 25% data. As α is in the log-scale, the increase in error is actually more than two-fold.

Our second observation is that α values for fine-grained predictions (e.g., 2.9 for $\delta = 0.01$ and 100% data for the standardized SUQR model in Fig. 1(d)) are understandably higher than the corresponding values for coarse-grained predictions (1.8 for $\delta = 0.01$ and 100% data for SUQR in Fig. 1(a)) because in the fine-grained case we predict the exact number of attacks.

Third, we observe that the performance of the generalized SUQR model (e.g., 2.47 for $\delta = 0.01$ and 100% data in Fig. 1(e)) is better in most cases than that of the standardized SUQR approach (2.9 for $\delta = 0.01$ and 100% data in Fig. 1(d)), but worse than the NPL approach (2.15 for $\delta = 0.01$ and 100% data in Fig. 1(f)).

Finally, we observe that our NPL model performs better than its parametric counterparts in predicting future poaching attacks for the fine-grained case (see example in previous paragraph), indicating that the true adversary behavior model may indeed be more complicated than what can be captured by SUQR.

Relation to previous work: In earlier work, Nguyen et al. [25] uses the area under curve (of a ROC curve) metric to demonstrate the performance of their approaches. The AUC value of 0.73 reported in their paper is an alternate view of our α, δ metric for the coarse grained prediction approach. While there has been alternate analysis in terms of measuring prediction performances with the AUC metric in earlier papers, in our paper we have shown new trends and insights with the α, δ metric through analysis from the PAC model perspective, which is missing in earlier work. We show: (i) sample complexity results and the relationship between increasing number of samples and the reduction in prediction error for each of our models; (ii) the differences in errors while learning a vector valued response function (fine-grained prediction) as opposed to classifying targets as attacked or not (coarse-grained prediction); and (iii) comparison of the performance of our new NPL model with other parametric approaches in terms of both fine-grained and coarse-grained predictions and its effectiveness on real-world poaching data which was not shown in previous work.

Uganda Parametric	Uganda NPL	AMT Parametric	AMT NPL
0.7188	121.24	0.91	123.4

Table 2: Runtime results (in secs.) for one train-test split

8.2 AMT Data

Here we show fine-grained prediction results on real-world AMT data obtained from [15] to demonstrate the performance of both our approaches on somewhat cleaner data. This dataset is cleaner than the Uganda data because: (i) all attacks are observed, and (ii) animal densities and deployed defender strategies are known. The dataset consisted of 16 unique mixed strategies. There were an average of 40 attack data points per mixed strategy. Each attack had been conducted by an unique individual recruited on AMT. We used attack data corresponding to 11 randomly chosen mixed strategies for training and data for the remaining mixed strategies for testing. Results are shown in Figs. 1(g) and 1(h). We observe that: (i) α values in this case are lower as compared to the Uganda data as the AMT data is cleaner; and (ii) the NPL model's performance on this dataset is poor as compared to SUQR due to, (a) low number of samples in AMT data, and (b) real-world poacher behavior may be more complicated than that of AMT participants and hence SUQR in this case was able to better capture AMT participants' behavior with limited number of samples.[6]

Runtime: While running on Matlab R2015a on an Intel Core i7-5500 CPU@2.40Ghz, 8GB RAM machine with a 64-bit Windows 10, on average, the NPL computation takes longer than the parametric setting, as shown in Table 2.

9. CONCLUSION

Over the last couple of years, a lot of work has used learning methods to learn bounded rationality adversary behavioral models, but there has been no formal study of the learning process and its implication on the defender's performance. The lack of formal analysis also means that many practical questions go unanswered. We have advanced the state of the art in learning of adversary behaviors in SSGs, in terms of their analysis and implications of such learned behaviors on defender's performance.

While we used the PAC framework, it is not an out of the box approach. We needed to come up with innovative techniques to obtain sharp bounds for our case. Furthermore, we also provide a new non-parametric approach which showed promising results with real-world data. Finally, we provided a principled explanation of why prediction accuracy is not enough to guarantee good defender performance by revealing that the PAC learning guarantee is not the guarantee required for discovering the optimal defender strategy. Finally, we hope this work leads to more theoretical work in learning of adversary models and the use of non-parametric models in the real world.

10. ACKNOWLEDGMENT

This research is supported by MURI grant W911NF-11-1-0332. We wish to acknowledge the authors of [25], specifically Andrew Plumptre, for providing us with the Uganda data.

[6]In the Appendix we show that, on simulated data, α does indeed approach zero and NPL outperforms SUQR with enough samples.

REFERENCES

[1] Y. D. Abbasi, M. Short, A. Sinha, N. Sintov, C. Zhang, and M. Tambe. Human adversaries in opportunistic crime security games: Evaluating competing bounded rationality models. In *Conference on Advances in Cognitive Systems*, 2015.

[2] M. Anthony and P. L. Bartlett. *Neural Network Learning: Theoretical Foundations*. Cambridge University Press, New York, NY, USA, 1st edition, 2009.

[3] M.-F. Balcan, A. Blum, N. Haghtalab, and A. D. Procaccia. Commitment without regrets: Online learning in stackelberg security games. In *Proceedings of the Sixteenth ACM Conference on Economics and Computation*, EC '15, 2015.

[4] M.-F. Balcan, A. D. Procaccia, and Y. Zick. Learning cooperative games. In *Proceedings of the International Joint Conference on Artificial Intelligence*, IJCAI '15, 2015.

[5] N. Basilico, N. Gatti, and F. Amigoni. Leader-follower strategies for robotic patrolling in environments with arbitrary topologies. In *Proceedings of The 8th International Conference on Autonomous Agents and Multiagent Systems-Volume 1*, pages 57–64. International Foundation for Autonomous Agents and Multiagent Systems, 2009.

[6] J. Blocki, N. Christin, A. Datta, A. Procaccia, and A. Sinha. Audit games. In *Proceedings of the 23rd international joint conference on Artificial Intelligence (IJCAI'13)*, 2013.

[7] J. Blocki, N. Christin, A. Datta, A. Procaccia, and A. Sinha. Audit games with multiple defender resources. In *Proceedings of the 29th AAAI conference on Artificial Intelligence (AAAI'15)*, 2015.

[8] A. Blum, N. Haghtalab, and A. D. Procaccia. Learning optimal commitment to overcome insecurity. In *Advances in Neural Information Processing Systems*, pages 1826–1834, 2014.

[9] J. Cui and R. S. John. Empirical comparisons of descriptive multi-objective adversary models in stackelberg security games. In *Decision and Game Theory for Security*, pages 309–318. Springer, 2014.

[10] M. de Laplace. Oeuvres complètes. *Oeuvres complètes*, 7:257, 1886.

[11] F. Fang, T. H. Nguyen, B. An, M. Tambe, R. Pickles, W. Y. Lam, and G. R. Clements. Towards addressing challenges in green security games in the wild (extended abstract). In *Workshop of Behavioral, Economic and Computational Intelligence for Security (BECIS) held at IJCAI*, 2015.

[12] B. Ford, T. Nguyen, M. Tambe, N. Sintov, and F. D. Fave. Beware the soothsayer: From attack prediction accuracy to predictive reliability in security games. In *Conference on Decision and Game Theory for Security*, 2015.

[13] W. Haskell, D. Kar, F. Fang, M. Tambe, S. Cheung, and L. E. Denicola. Robust protection of fisheries with compass. In *Innovative Applications of Artificial Intelligence (IAAI)*, 2014.

[14] D. Haussler. Decision theoretic generalizations of the pac model for neural net and other learning applications. *Inf. Comput.*, 100(1):78–150, Sept. 1992.

[15] D. Kar, F. Fang, F. D. Fave, N. Sintov, and M. Tambe. A Game of Thrones: When human behavior models compete in repeated stackelberg security games. In *International Conference on Autonomous Agents and Multiagent Systems (AAMAS)*, 2015.

[16] M. J. Kearns and U. V. Vazirani. *An introduction to computational learning theory*. MIT press, 1994.

[17] D. E. Knuth. *The art of computer programming: sorting and searching*, volume 3. Pearson Education, 1998.

[18] D. Korzhyk, V. Conitzer, and R. Parr. Complexity of computing optimal stackelberg strategies in security resource allocation games. In *In Proceedings of the National Conference on Artificial Intelligence (AAAI)*, pages 805–810, 2010.

[19] S. Kullback. *Information Theory and Statistics*. John Wiley and Sons, 1959.

[20] J. Letchford, V. Conitzer, and K. Munagala. Learning and approximating the optimal strategy to commit to. In *Algorithmic Game Theory*, pages 250–262. Springer, 2009.

[21] U. v. Luxburg and O. Bousquet. Distance–based classification with lipschitz functions. *The Journal of Machine Learning Research*, 5:669–695, 2004.

[22] J. Marecki, G. Tesauro, and R. Segal. Playing repeated stackelberg games with unknown opponents. In *Proceedings of the 11th International Conference on Autonomous Agents and Multiagent Systems-Volume 2*, pages 821–828, 2012.

[23] D. McFadden. Conditional logit analysis of qualitative choice behavior. *Frontiers in Econometrics*, pages 105–142, 1973.

[24] D. McFadden. Quantal choice analysis: A survey. *Annals of Economic and Social Measurement*, 5(4):363–390, 1976.

[25] T. H. Nguyen, F. M. D. Fave, D. Kar, A. S. Lakshminarayanan, A. Yadav, M. Tambe, N. Agmon, A. J. Plumptre, M. Driciru, F. Wanyama, and A. Rwetsiba. Making the most of our regrets: Regret-based solutions to handle payoff uncertainty and elicitation in green security games. In *Conference on Decision and Game Theory for Security*, 2015.

[26] T. H. Nguyen, R. Yang, A. Azaria, S. Kraus, and M. Tambe. Analyzing the effectiveness of adversary modeling in security games. In *Conf. on Artificial Intelligence (AAAI)*, 2013.

[27] P. Paruchuri, J. P. Pearce, J. Marecki, M. Tambe, F. Ordonez, and S. Kraus. Playing games for security: An efficient exact algorithm for solving bayesian stackelberg games. In *Proceedings of the 7th International Joint Conference on Autonomous Agents and Multiagent Systems - Volume 2*, AAMAS, pages 895–902, 2008.

[28] D. Pollard. *Convergence of stochastic processes*. David Pollard, 1984.

[29] R. Stanley. Eulerian partitions of a unit hypercube. *Higher Combinatorics (M. Aigner, ed.), Reidel, Dordrecht/Boston*, 49, 1977.

[30] M. Tambe. *Security and Game Theory: Algorithms, Deployed Systems, Lessons Learned*. Cambridge University Press, New York, NY, USA, 1st edition, 2011.

[31] S. Tanny. A probabilistic interpretation of eulerian numbers. *Duke Mathematical Journal*, 40(4):717–722, 1973.

[32] V. Tikhomirov and A. Kolmogorov. ε-entropy and ε-capacity of sets in functional spaces. In *Selected Works of AN Kolmogorov*, pages 86–170. Springer, 1993.

[33] Y. Vorobeychik and B. Li. Optimal randomized classification in adversarial settings. In *Proceedings of the 2014 international conference on Autonomous agents and multi-agent systems*, pages 485–492. International Foundation for Autonomous Agents and Multiagent Systems, 2014.

[34] X. Wang. Volumes of generalized unit balls. *Mathematics Magazine*, pages 390–395, 2005.

[35] R. Yang, B. Ford, M. Tambe, and A. Lemieux. Adaptive resource allocation for wildlife protection against illegal poachers. In *Proceedings of the 2014 International Conference on Autonomous Agents and Multi-agent Systems*, AAMAS '14, 2014.

[36] C. Zhang, A. Sinha, and M. Tambe. Keeping pace with criminals: Designing patrol allocation against adaptive opportunistic criminals. In *International Conference on Autonomous Agents and Multiagent Systems (AAMAS 2015)*, 2015.

Average Controllability Measures for Solitaire Games*

Marco Faella
Dept. of Electrical Engineering and Information Technologies
University of Naples "Federico II", Italy
m.faella@unina.it

ABSTRACT

We discuss several ways to measure the extent to which a player can exert control over a one-player game, relating them to the existing literature on the "skill vs chance" dichotomy. We focus on measures that depend only on the rules of the games, and not on how people actually play them. After presenting a set of desirable properties, we show that two statistical measures of effect size satisfy them and we estimate the value of such measures on several well-known games.

Keywords

Markov decision processes, solitaire games, skill vs luck

1. INTRODUCTION

Many games played by people feature a combination of determinism and chance. Most card games involve an initial shuffling, board games resort to dice, and electronic games employ pseudo-random number generators.

There is no established way to measure the amount of chance involved in a game, besides some isolated efforts that will be discussed in Section 4. By measuring the amount of chance, we mean assign a real number between 0 and 1 to every game, in such a way that a purely deterministic game, such as Chess, receives value 1, and a purely random game, such as a lottery, receives value 0. In the spirit of our discipline, we are interested in measures that can be automatically computed, or at least approximated to an arbitrary precision. Hence, the candidate measures may depend only on the rules of the game, and not on how people actually play it. This property has the additional advantage that the measures we consider can also be evaluated on games that are not (yet) played by people, perhaps because they are still being designed.

The motivation that drives most of the literature on this subject comes from gambling laws. Many countries distinguish games of chance from games of skill and apply different regulations to each class. Such laws make no attempt to formally define these two classes, leaving this task to judges, who may very well hold different opinions on the subject. In fact, in at least one well-documented case, different courts have expressed contrasting rulings on the game of electronic draw poker (a.k.a. video poker) [13], which is one of the games we examine in Section 7. Our investigation may clearly contribute to these applications, by providing an objective and *a-priori* means to quantify the amount of chance in a game.

Measures of chance can also help players make informed decisions on which games to play according to their tastes, and enable game designers to tune their games for their audience and facilitate innovative game designs. In the words of game designer Soren Johnson [12]: "The appropriate role of chance in a game is ultimately a subjective question, and giving players the ability to adjust the knobs [...] can open up the game to a larger audience with a greater variety of tastes."

Last but not least, we believe that the problem is interesting for its own sake, because it bears connections with different disciplines, ranging from learning theory to psychology. In this paper, we focus on *solitaire games*. Common solitaire games include video poker, Black Jack [1], Minesweeper, etc. Such games can be modeled as finite-state discrete-time Markov Decision Processes (MDPs). We can then rephrase our original problem as a discussion of measures of *controllability* for MDPs. To the best of our knowledge, the only related work focused on MDPs is [21]. There, the authors look for metrics on MDPs that may help choose the best learning algorithm for a planning problem. They propose several metrics and experimentally evaluate their ability to predict the performance of different learning algorithms. The intuition behind their proposals is similar to ours: measure the degree of controllability of the model. However, the purpose and methodology is very different, leading to a number of metrics that have a "local" flavor, in the sense that they are easy to compute based on the information which is available in a state. It is possible that our investigation may prove useful in that domain, although the metrics we propose are likely to be much more computationally demanding than theirs.

An entirely different domain where similar concerns are routinely addressed is in *effect-size statistics*. In many social and life sciences, investigators try to measure the influence of some controllable (or at least measurable) variable on the outcome of a complex process [18]. This is the familiar

*This work was supported by the European Union 7th Framework Program project 600958-SHERPA.

Appears in: *Proceedings of the 15th International Conference on Autonomous Agents and Multiagent Systems (AAMAS 2016), J. Thangarajah, K. Tuyls, C. Jonker, S. Marsella (eds.), May 9–13, 2016, Singapore.*

[1] In Black Jack, the dealer follows a deterministic strategy, so a game between a single player and the dealer is effectively a solitaire.

scenario in which a control group is compared with one or more treatment groups, to evaluate the effect of a drug, a procedure, or some intrinsic attribute of the subjects. The same methodology also applies to Computer Science, when one wants to accurately characterize the influence of some feature of the input on the performance of an algorithm [3]. In most cases, the complex process which transforms inputs into an outcome is treated as a black-box, and statistics is used to analyze the relation between inputs and outputs.

Analogously, the outcome of a solitaire game is influenced by some controllable input (the player's moves) and a random device. Contrary to the complex systems of Biology, Medicine, and Psychology, the process that combines controllable inputs and random events is exactly known, being determined by the rules of the game. On the other hand, the state-space of a real game can be so large that statistical techniques remain the only applicable analysis tool. Effect-size statistics constitute the standard toolbox for analyzing these scenarios. Many different effect-size measures can be found in the literature [9], some of which will be presented in Section 5, and used in Section 6 as measures of average controllability for solitaire games.

The reason for targeting *average* controllability, rather than minimum or maximum controllability, stems from the observation that the first may more accurately approximate the behavior of a population of players of various skill levels. After all, min, average, and max are the three canonical points in the spectrum of rationality, with bounded rationality and actual human players arguably positioned somewhere between the second and the third point.

Summarizing, after the preliminary notions of Section 2, **our contribution** is organized in four sections, followed by some conclusions. In Section 3, we present a small set of axioms that we deem desirable for a measure of controllability. In fact, the property we are trying to measure appears so nebulous that little to no consensus has been reached by the scientific community on its interpretation. Hence, we believe that it is useful to start by enumerating some axioms that focus our investigation and ease the comparison with the related literature. Such comparison is indeed the topic of Section 4, which reviews previous proposals of controllability measures, putting them in the context of solitaire games and analysing them from a computational point of view. We conclude that previous measures are not suitable to our aims, and therefore devote Sections 5 and 6 to outline our proposal, which is based on the effect-size measures "percentage of variance explained" and "percentage of absolute deviation explained". We show that such measures satisfy a basic set of axioms but violate a stronger version of one of the axioms. Then, we prove that these measures define two different orders between games.

In Section 7, we employ a purpose-built game simulation framework to estimate the value of each measure on randomized versions of Tic-tac-toe and simplified variants of Minesweeper, Video Poker, and Black Jack. Moreover, we include in the comparison an individual sport, archery, for which we obtained experimental data from an external source.

2. DEFINITIONS

We represent a solitaire game by a finite-state discrete-time MDP with partial information and a reachability objective.

Definition 1. A *Markov decision process with partial information (PIMDP)* is a tuple $P = (S, s_0, I, A, \Gamma, \delta)$, where S is a finite set of states, $s_0 \in S$ is the initial state, I is a partition of S into information sets, A is a finite set of actions, $\Gamma : I \to 2^A$ gives the set of active actions for each information set, and $\delta : S \times A \times S \to [0,1]$ is the transition function, assigning to each triple (s, a, s') the probability that the process moves from s to s' when action a is selected. Denote by $[s]$ the information set containing s, for all $s \in S$ and $a \in \Gamma([s])$, it holds $\sum_{s' \in S} \delta(s, a, s') = 1$.

PIMDPs are a special case of partially observable MDPs [7] and are similar to the game theoretic notion of extensive game with imperfect information [19]. In particular, states belonging to the same information set are indistinguishable to the player, so that he is forced to take the same action in all of them.

A *path* in P is a finite sequence of states $s_0 s_1 \dots s_n$, such that for all $i = 0, 1, \dots, n-1$ there exists $a \in \Gamma([s_i])$ such that $\delta(s_i, a, s_{i+1}) > 0$. A path is *maximal* if it is not a proper prefix of another path (because its last state has no active actions). For our purposes, it suffices to consider *acyclic* PIMDPs, i.e., PIMDPs having no path with repeated states. Notice that, in order for the process to be acyclic, some states must have no active actions (sink states).

A (memoryless and deterministic) *strategy* is a function $\sigma : I \to A$ such that $\sigma(\mathcal{I}) \in \Gamma(\mathcal{I})$ for all $\mathcal{I} \in I$. A path $s_0 s_1 \dots s_n$ is *consistent* with the strategy σ if for all $i = 0, 1, \dots, n$, it holds that $\delta(s_i, \sigma(s_i), s_{i+1}) > 0$. We denote by $runs(\sigma)$ the set of all maximal paths consistent with σ. As we are assuming that the process is acyclic, each strategy induces a finite set of maximal paths and a discrete probability space over it in the usual way (see [7] for details). We denote by p_σ the probability measure induced by σ. If two strategies give rise to the same probability space, we consider them equivalent. So, when talking about the set of all strategies in a PIMDP, we implicitly refer to the quotient w.r.t. such equivalence.

Definition 2. A *solitaire game* G is a pair (P, T) where P is an acyclic PIMDP and $T \subseteq S$ is a non-empty set of target states.

Given a solitaire game (P, T), assume w.l.o.g. that states in T are sinks, and let val be the function assigning 1 to the paths ending in T, and 0 to all other paths. We denote by E_σ the probability of reaching T under strategy σ. Notice that E_σ is also the expected value of the random variable assigning value $val(r)$ to each run $r \in runs(\sigma)$, under the probability space induced by σ. So, we also call it the *expected value* of σ.

3. DESIRED QUALITIES OF A MEASURE

In this section, we discuss a number of desired properties for a controllability measure for solitaire games, having in mind the applications mentioned in the Introduction. First of all, we choose to restrict to games that can be put in the form of a PIMDP.

Axiom 0. The measure can only depend on the rules of the game, as formalized by Definition 2.

Although Axiom 0 sounds perfectly natural in a computational context, it sets us apart from the previous research on the topic (see Section 4), so let us remark once more its benefits. Axiom 0 makes sure that the measure can be applied to any game that can be put in the form of Definition 2, allowing us to evaluate hypothetical games, or a proposed variant to a real-world game, and ascertain whether it would increase or decrease the randomness of the game.

We say that a game is *chance-less* if there is a single destination for each action, i.e., for all $s \in S$ and $a \in \Gamma([s])$ there exists a unique s' such that $\delta(s,a,s') > 0$. Dually, a game is *skill-less* if there is a single active action from each information set: for all $\mathcal{I} \in I$ it holds that $|\Gamma(\mathcal{I})| = 1$. A skill-less game has a single strategy. Intuitively, all chance-less (resp., skill-less) games should have controllability measure 1 (resp., 0). However, some degenerate games are chance-less and skill-less at the same time, giving rise to a single maximal path. What should be their measure? We stipulate that it should be 0, as our primary objective is to measure to what extent the moves of the player decrease the uncertainty in the outcome. If a game has no uncertainty to begin with, no control can be exerted by the player.

Axiom 1. For all chance-less games G, we have $m(G) = 1$, provided that there are at least two runs r_1, r_2 in the game, with $val(r_1) \neq val(r_2)$.

Axiom 2. For all skill-less games G, we have $m(G) = 0$.

Axioms 1 and 2 are entirely uncontroversial and can be found in all previous works on the subject.

Next, we introduce an axiom which provides a canonical game for each possible value of the measure. The family of games $B_p(G_0, G_1)$ is depicted in Figure 1(c) and accepts as parameters a probability $p \in [0,1]$ and two other games G_0 and G_1. Games *Rand* and *Ctrl* are shown in Figures 1(b) and 1(a), respectively.

Axiom 3. For all $p \in [0,1]$, we have $m\big(B_p(\mathit{Rand}, \mathit{Ctrl})\big) = p$.

Axiom 3 fixes the value of the measure for the family of games that are simple mixtures of a specific game of measure 0 and a specific game of measure 1. It is tempting to replace it with one of the following increasingly stronger versions. In the first version, games *Rand* and *Ctrl* are replaced by arbitrary games having measure 0 and 1, respectively.

Axiom 3'. For all $p \in [0,1]$, let G_0 and G_1 be arbitrary games such that $m(G_0) = 0$ and $m(G_1) = 1$. Then, we have $m\big(B_p(G_0, G_1)\big) = p$.

Notice that Axiom 3' introduces a discontinuity in the measure, in the sense that we can exhibit a sequence of games having measure $\frac{1}{2}$, converging to a game that has measure 1 due to Axiom 1. For $i > 0$, the i-th game in the sequence is $B_{1/2}(H_i, \mathit{Ctrl})$, where H_i is a skill-less game in which the target T is reached with probability $\frac{1}{2^i}$. In itself, this discontinuity should not be a reason to discard Axiom 3'. After all, even in a simple Markov chain (with loops), the probability of eventually reaching a given state is discontinuous w.r.t. the one-step transition probabilities. In the next section, we show that two classical effect size measures recalled in Section 5 satisfy Axiom 3 but not Axiom 3'.

In another, even stronger version of Axiom 3, games G_0 and G_1 are entirely arbitrary.

Axiom 3". For all $p \in [0,1]$, let G_0 and G_1 be arbitrary games. Then, we have

$$m\big(B_p(G_0, G_1)\big) = p \cdot m(G_1) + (1-p)m(G_0).$$

We now show that Axiom 3" is too strong for our intents. Consider the game $B_{1/2}(G_0, G_1)$ where $G_0 = G_1 = \mathit{Ctrl}$. After an initial random move, the player is in total control and can choose between winning and losing. Axiom 3" prescribes measure 1 for this game, because the sub-games G_0 and G_1 are entirely controlled by the player and hence have measure 1 due to Axiom 1. On the other hand, if we identify (types of) players with strategies, this game has four different strategies, depending on the choice of the player in the two sub-games. If the player chooses to win when in G_0 and lose in G_1 (or vice versa), then the outcome is entirely decided by the initial random move. In other words, 2 out of 4 strategies effectively exert no control on the game. For this reason, we reject Axiom 3".

The decision to consider all possible strategies in the game stems from our objective of defining *average* controllability measures. In so doing, we violate the classical principle of Independence of Irrelevant Alternatives. Indeed, we assume that players, due to their bounded rationality, may fail to recognize that the two sub-games G_0 and G_1 are identical, and hence may behave differently in the two sub-games. A similar tension between bounded rationality and the classic tenets of decision theory is noted by Dagsvik [4].

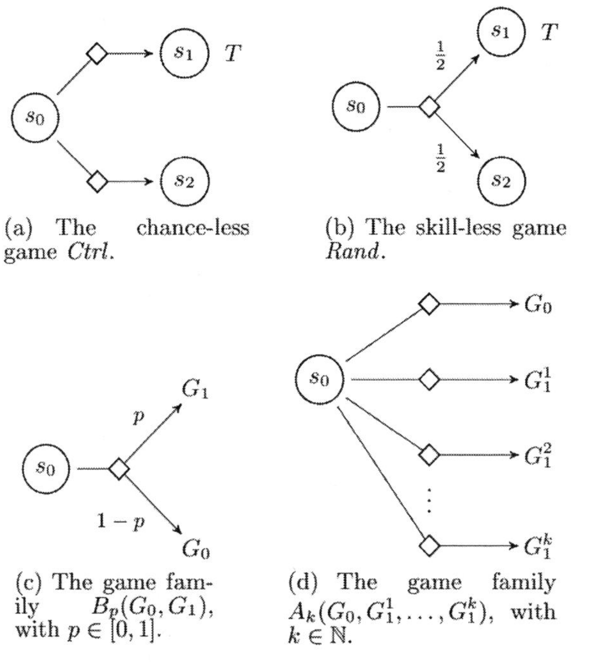

(a) The chance-less game *Ctrl*.

(b) The skill-less game *Rand*.

(c) The game family $B_p(G_0, G_1)$, with $p \in [0,1]$.

(d) The game family $A_k(G_0, G_1^1, \ldots, G_1^k)$, with $k \in \mathbb{N}$.

Figure 1: Significant games. States are circles and actions are diamonds.

A simple measure that satisfies Axioms 0-3 as well as Axiom 3' is the difference between the expected value of the optimal strategy and the expected value of the worst strategy. However, we believe that this measure is too crude to be useful to our inteded applications. In particular, consider two games G', G'' with a thousand strategies each. In G', 999 strategies have expected value $1/2$, which denotes no control on the game outcome, and one strategy has expected value 1. In G'', the opposite happens: 999 strategies win with certainty and one strategy has expected value $1/2$. The measure described above assigns the same measure $1/2$ to both games, whereas we would like $m(G'') > m(G')$. We therefore introduce the following axiom, based on the family of games A_k in Figure 1(d):

Axiom 4. For all $k > j > 0$, we have $m(A_k(\mathit{Rand}, \mathit{Ctrl}, \ldots, \mathit{Ctrl})) > m(A_j(\mathit{Rand}, \mathit{Ctrl}, \ldots, \mathit{Ctrl}))$.

Axiom 4 states that adding more alternatives for the player that lead to completely controllable games raises the value of the measure (even if other controllable alternatives are already available). Essentially, Axiom 4 implies that we are looking for an *average* measure of controllability, rather than the maximum amount of control that a player can exercise. Similarly to Axiom 3, we also consider a stronger version of Axiom 4, which employs generic games with prescribed measures instead of the two canonical games *Rand* and *Ctrl*.

Axiom 4'. For all $k > j > 0$, let $G_0, G_1^1, \ldots, G_1^k$ be games such that $m(G_0) = 0$, there is at least one strategy σ in G_0 s.t. $E_\sigma \in (0,1)$, and $m(G_1^i) = 1$ for all $i = 1, 2, \ldots, k$. Then, we have $m(A_k(G_0, G_1^1, \ldots, G_1^k)) > m(A_j(G_0, G_1^1, \ldots, G_1^j))$.

The second constraint on G_0 ensures that there is some uncertainty if the player chooses that game.

In the next section, we review, in the light of these axioms, the main proposals that have been made in the literature.

4. PREVIOUS APPROACHES

In the literature, the issues we are considering here are often discussed under the "skill vs luck" dichotomy [17]. We believe that such terminology is somewhat misleading, because it may contribute to confounding two different and largely independent issues: the amount of randomness in the rules of a game (the "chance" element) and the difficulty of a game for a human player (the "skill" element). Consider Tic-Tac-Toe and Chess: the rules of both games involve no randomness, but nobody would say that they require the same amount of skill to be played well. Our Axiom 1, shared by similar works in the literature, makes it clear that we are interested in the amount of randomness and not in the difficulty of winning the game. Which (combination) of these two issues should be of interest to the legislator is up for debate and we are in no position to contribute. Here, we focus on measuring the amount of randomness in the rules of a game, and we call *controllability* the lack thereof.

Borm and van der Genugten [2], with later contributions by Dreef [5, 6], seem to be the first to formally define a measure of controllability for games, coming from an Economic background, with gambling laws as the reference application. They subscribe to our Axioms 1 and 2 and propose the following measure:

$$m_1(G) = \frac{\text{learning effect}}{\text{learning effect} + \text{random effect}}.$$

Roughly speaking, the learning effect quantifies the difference between the performance of an expert player and that of a beginner, while the random effect quantifies the advantage given by knowing in advance the realization of the random effects in the game.

The authors then clarify the above definition by semi-formally defining the following three types of players: *(i)* the *optimal* player, who plays the strategy with the highest expected payoff, or, in our setting, the highest probability of reaching the target T; *(ii)* the *fictive* player, who plays optimally and moreover knows in advance the realization of the random events that will occur during play; *(iii)* the *beginner* player, who "has only just familiarized himself with the rules of the game" [5].

Call E_{opt}, E_{fic}, and E_{beg} the expected payoff of the three player categories outlined above, Dreef et al. define the learning effect as $E_{\text{opt}} - E_{\text{beg}}$ and the random effect as $E_{\text{fic}} - E_{\text{opt}}$, leading to the following expression for m_1:

$$m_1(G) = \frac{E_{\text{opt}} - E_{\text{beg}}}{(E_{\text{opt}} - E_{\text{beg}}) + (E_{\text{fic}} - E_{\text{opt}})} = \frac{E_{\text{opt}} - E_{\text{beg}}}{E_{\text{fic}} - E_{\text{beg}}}.$$

Even in the context of the original paper, the authors struggle to define the meaning of the beginner player, discussing three possible ways to ascertain his behavior: *(a)* by postulating that she chooses uniformly at random among the available moves; *(b)* by statistically analyzing the actual behavior of people playing the game; *(c)* by assigning the task to a "gambling expert". In their analysis of *minipoker*, Dreef et al. employ option *(c)*, i.e., they devise an ad-hoc strategy that is deemed appropriate for a beginner. On the other hand, only option (a) satisfies our Axiom 0 and is suitable for a fair comparison between different games.

Regardless of the interpretation chosen for the beginner player, the biggest problem with measure m_1 is that it violates Axiom 3. Indeed, in the game family B_p, knowing in advance the result of the random moves gives *no* advantage to the player. Precisely, for game $B_p(\mathit{Rand}, \mathit{Ctrl})$ we have that $E_{\text{opt}} = E_{\text{fic}} = \frac{p+1}{2}$, and therefore $m_1(B_p(\mathit{Rand}, \mathit{Ctrl})) = 1$ for all $p \in [0, 1]$. This critique to measure m_1 was already raised by Heubeck [10].

On the other hand, if we adopt interpretation (a) for "beginner" (i.e., "uniformly random"), the simple expression $m_2(G) = 2(E_{\text{opt}} - E_{\text{beg}})$, which is twice the "learning effect", gives the desired value p for the game $B_p(\mathit{Rand}, \mathit{Ctrl})$, thus satisfying Axiom 3. However, it is easy to see that m_2 violates Axiom 1. Indeed, let G be a chance-less game with three strategies, two of which lead to the target T. We have $m_2(G) = 2/3$ rather than the prescribed value of 1.

It should be noted that Dreef et al. [5] mention in their conclusions that an alternative approach could be based on the analysis of variance, which is one of the central tenets of the present paper.

In a recent column [22], Wyner presents a critique of Deer et al. and advances his own proposal, accompanied by a set of (semi-formal) axioms he deems desirable. The first two axioms unsurprisingly coincide with our Axioms 1 and 2. We quote the remaining four axioms, slightly adapting them to our notation:

Axiom III. If G^N is the convolution of N rounds of game G, then $\lim_{N\to\infty} m(G^N) = 1$ provided that $m(G) > 0$.

The paper does not define "convolution", but we can surmise it means playing the game multiple times and somehow combine the obtained payoffs. The intended meaning of the axiom is that if a game involves a non-zero amount of skill, in the long-run its outcome will depend entirely on skill. The axiom makes sense for 2-player games: in the long run, chance elements should even out and the different skill (or, in more neutral terms, different strategies) of the two players is what really counts towards establishing a winner. In fact, a similar principle was used in recent work on online multi-player poker [20].

However, applying this axiom to controllability of solitaires appears problematic. In a game with non-zero controllability, the moves of the player have *some* influence on the distribution of outcomes. On the other hand, having perfect control (measure 1) means that there is no randomness in the game and the game outcome is directly determined by the player's moves. If a game with non-zero controllability measure is repeated at will, there is no reason to believe that the outcome has no randomness left.

Axiom IV. The measure should depend on the distribution of skill levels of the population of players.

Although perhaps motivated in a context which is strictly focused on legal applications, this axiom goes squarely against our Axiom 0 and the idea of achieving a fair comparison between different games.

The following axiom is a weaker form of our Axiom 3. In fact, the game family B_p from Figure 1(c) is a straightforward generalization of the *balanced mixture game* of Wyner, which coincides with $B_{1/2}$.

Axiom V. It holds $m\big(B_{1/2}(\mathit{Rand}, \mathit{Ctrl})\big) = \frac{1}{2}$.

The final axiom refers to the fact that several juristictions define games of skill as those games where skill plays a preponderant role, leading to the so-called *preponderance test.* Axiom VI suggests to set the threshold at $1/2$. We briefly comment on this axiom in Section 7, after we present our experimental evaluations.

Axiom VI. Any game G for which $m(G) < \frac{1}{2}$ fails the preponderance test.

After presenting these axioms, Wyner introduces his proposal for a measure of skill in multi-player games. Roughly speaking, he postulates the possibility to quantify the skill level of a player. Then, for two skill levels $k > j$, a match between two players is termed *(j,k)-reversible* if its outcome is reversed when the skill level of the losing player changes from j to k (and the random events somehow remain fixed). The proposed measure is the probability that a match is reversible "when averaged over players of random talent against experts" [22]. Clearly, such semi-formal definition is hard to fit into the current framework, particularly due to our Axiom 0 and the presence of a single player.

Heubeck [11] discusses measures similar to the percentage of absolute deviation explained for games of a special form, in which a completely controllable phase is followed by a completely random choice of payoff.

Finally, a significant amount of attention has been devoted to the balance between skill and chance in (multi-player) Poker [16, 20]. Exploiting the wealth of data currently available on online poker, these works take an empirical approach and estimate the correlation between past and future performance of human players.

5. EFFECT-SIZE MEASURES

We recall the basic definitions pertaining the family of effect-size measures called "percentage of variance explained", commonly associated to the statistical framework ANOVA (analysis of variance) [8]. These measures aim at attributing the spread in the outcomes to two different sources: the strategy giving rise to each outcome and the variation within a single strategy. To compute such a measure, one summarizes each strategy σ by its expected value E_σ; then, one quantifies the spread of such averages and divides it by the total spread, where "spread" can be interpreted in different ways.

Given a set of strategies $\sigma_1, \dots, \sigma_n$, let $\overline{E}$ be the arithmetic mean of $E_{\sigma_1}, \dots, E_{\sigma_n}$, i.e., $\overline{E} = \frac{1}{n}\sum_{i=1}^n E_{\sigma_i}$. We obtain the first measure by interpreting "spread" as variance, leading to the notions of *variance between strategies* $\mathit{Var}_{\text{btw}}$ and *total variance* $\mathit{Var}_{\text{tot}}$:

$$\mathit{Var}_{\text{btw}} = \frac{1}{n}\sum_{i=1}^{n}(E_{\sigma_i} - \overline{E})^2$$

$$\mathit{Var}_{\text{tot}} = \frac{1}{n}\sum_{i=1}^{n}\sum_{r\in \mathit{runs}(\sigma_i)} (\mathit{val}(r) - \overline{E})^2 \cdot p_{\sigma_i}(r).$$

The classical effect size measure η^2, called *percentage of variance explained* is the ratio of the above two statistics:

$$\begin{aligned}\eta^2 = \frac{\mathit{Var}_{\text{btw}}}{\mathit{Var}_{\text{tot}}} &= \frac{\sum_{i=1}^n (E_{\sigma_i} - \overline{E})^2}{\sum_{i=1}^n \sum_{r\in \mathit{runs}(\sigma_i)} (\mathit{val}(r) - \overline{E})^2 \cdot p_{\sigma_i}(r)} \\ &= \frac{\sum_{i=1}^n \left(E_{\sigma_i}^2 + \overline{E}^2 - 2\overline{E}E_{\sigma_i}\right)}{\sum_{i=1}^n \left(E_{\sigma_i} + \overline{E}^2 - 2\overline{E}E_{\sigma_i}\right)} \\ &= \frac{\sum_{i=1}^n E_{\sigma_i}^2 + n\overline{E}^2 - 2\overline{E}\sum_{i=1}^n E_{\sigma_i}}{\sum_{i=1}^n E_{\sigma_i} + n\overline{E}^2 - 2\overline{E}\sum_{i=1}^n E_{\sigma_i}} \\ &= \frac{\sum_{i=1}^n E_{\sigma_i}^2 - n\overline{E}^2}{n(\overline{E} - \overline{E}^2)}.\end{aligned}$$

The value of η^2 is undefined when both its numerator and its denominator are zero, which in our setting happens if and only if $\overline{E} \in \{0,1\}$. Since this corresponds to games whose outcome is independent from the player strategy, in this case we set the value of η^2 to 0. We will also be interested in the square root of η^2, naturally denoted by η, which can be interpreted as the percentage of standard deviation which is explained by the choice of a strategy: $\eta = \sqrt{\eta^2} = \frac{\sqrt{\mathit{Var}_{\text{btw}}}}{\sqrt{\mathit{Var}_{\text{tot}}}}$.

If instead "spread" is interpreted as absolute deviation, we obtain the following definitions of *absolute deviation between strategies* and *total absolute deviation*.

$$\mathit{AD}_{\text{btw}} = \frac{1}{n}\sum_{i=1}^{n}|E_{\sigma_i} - \overline{E}|$$

$$\mathit{AD}_{\text{tot}} = \frac{1}{n}\sum_{i=1}^{n}\sum_{r\in \mathit{runs}(\sigma_i)} |\mathit{val}(r) - \overline{E}| \cdot p_{\sigma_i}(r).$$

Based on the above, the *percentage of absolute deviation explained* γ can be defined as follows:

$$\begin{aligned}\gamma = \frac{\mathit{AD}_{\text{btw}}}{\mathit{AD}_{\text{tot}}} &= \frac{\sum_{i=1}^n |E_{\sigma_i} - \overline{E}|}{\sum_{i=1}^n \sum_{r\in \mathit{runs}(\sigma_i)} |\mathit{val}(r) - \overline{E}| \cdot p_{\sigma_i}(r)} \\ &= \frac{\sum_{i=1}^n |E_{\sigma_i} - \overline{E}|}{2n(\overline{E} - \overline{E}^2)}.\end{aligned}$$

As before, we set $\gamma = 0$ whenever $\mathit{AD}_{\text{btw}} = \mathit{AD}_{\text{tot}} = 0$, which happens iff $\overline{E} \in \{0,1\}$.

6. CONTROLLABILITY MEASURES

In this section, we show that the two effect size measures η and γ satisfy the basic axioms of Section 3, but fail to satisfy the stronger Axiom 3'.

By an abuse of notation, for a game G we write $\eta(G)$ and $\gamma(G)$ to signify $\eta(E_{\sigma_1}, \ldots, E_{\sigma_n})$ and $\gamma(E_{\sigma_1}, \ldots, E_{\sigma_n})$, where $\sigma_1, \ldots, \sigma_n$ are all the strategies in G, modulo equivalence.

First, we characterize the cases in which the two measures have value 1.

PROPOSITION 1. *Let $E_1, \ldots, E_n \in [0,1]$, and $\overline{E}$ be their arithmetic average. The following are equivalent:*

1. $\eta(E_1, \ldots, E_n) = 1$;
2. $\gamma(E_1, \ldots, E_n) = 1$;
3. $E_i \in \{0,1\}$ *for all* $i = 1, \ldots, n$, *and* $\overline{E} \in (0,1)$.

PROOF . [(1)↔(3)]. It holds that

$$\begin{aligned}\eta = 1 &\Leftrightarrow \textstyle\sum_i E_i^2 - n\overline{E}^2 = n\overline{E} - n\overline{E}^2 \\ &\Leftrightarrow \textstyle\sum_i E_i^2 = n\overline{E} \\ &\Leftrightarrow \textstyle\sum_i E_i^2 = \sum_i E_i. \qquad (*)\end{aligned}$$

As $E_i \in [0,1]$, it follows that $E_i^2 \leq E_i$. By (*), we have that $E_i^2 = E_i$ for all i. Since $E_i^2 = E_i$ iff $E_i \in \{0,1\}$, we obtain the thesis.

[(2)↔(3)]. Let $S = \sum_i E_i = n\overline{E}$ and let I^+ (resp., I^-) be the set of indices $i \in \{1, \ldots, n\}$ such that $E_i \geq \overline{E}$ (resp., $E_i < \overline{E}$). Assuming that $\gamma = 1$, by definition we have that $\overline{E} \in (0,1)$. Moreover,

$$\begin{aligned}\textstyle\sum_{i\in I^+}(E_i - \overline{E}) + \sum_{i\in I^-}(\overline{E} - E_i) &= 2n\overline{E}(1-\overline{E}); \\ \sum_{i\in I^+} E_i - |I^+|\cdot\overline{E} + |I^-|\cdot\overline{E} - \sum_{i\in I^-} E_i &= 2S(1-\overline{E}); \\ \frac{\sum_{i\in I^+} E_i}{S} - \frac{\sum_{i\in I^-} E_i}{S} + \frac{|I^-|}{n} - \frac{|I^+|}{n} &= 2(1-\overline{E}); \\ 1 - 2\frac{\sum_{i\in I^-} E_i}{S} + 1 - 2\frac{|I^+|}{n} &= 2 - 2\overline{E}; \\ \frac{|I^+|}{n} + \frac{\sum_{i\in I^-} E_i}{S} &= \overline{E}; \\ |I^+| + \frac{\sum_{i\in I^-} E_i}{\overline{E}} &= \sum_{i\in I^+} E_i + \sum_{i\in I^-} E_i.\end{aligned}$$

Now, write the last equation as $a + b = c + d$, it is easy to see that $a \geq c$ and $b \geq d$. Hence, it holds $a = c$ and $b = d$, which implies (3).

Conversely, assume that (3) holds. We have that $\overline{E} = \frac{|I^+|}{n}$ and hence

$$\begin{aligned}\gamma &= \frac{\sum_{i\in I^+}(1-\overline{E}) + \sum_{i\in I^-}\overline{E}}{2n(\overline{E} - \overline{E}^2)} \\ &= \frac{|I^+| - |I^+|\cdot\overline{E} + |I^-|\cdot\overline{E}}{2n(\overline{E} - \overline{E}^2)} \\ &= \frac{|I^+| - |I^+|\cdot\frac{|I^+|}{n} + (n - |I^+|)\cdot\frac{|I^+|}{n}}{2n(\frac{|I^+|}{n} - \frac{|I^+|^2}{n^2})} \\ &= \frac{2|I^+| - 2\frac{|I^+|^2}{n}}{2|I^+| - 2\frac{|I^+|^2}{n}} = 1.\end{aligned}$$

□

PROPOSITION 2. *Measure η satisfies Axioms 0, 1, 2, 3, and 4'.*

PROOF. Axiom 1 is an immediate consequence of Prop. 1 whereas Axiom 2 follows from the definition of η. Axiom 3 can be verified by simple calculations. As for Axiom 4', let $G_0, G_1^1, G_1^2, \ldots, G_1^k$ be games such that $\eta(G_0) = 0$ and $\eta(G_1^i) = 1$ for all $i = 1, \ldots, k$. We prove that $\eta(A_k(G_0, G_1^1, \ldots, G_1^k)) > \eta(A_{k-1}(G_0, G_1^1, \ldots, G_1^{k-1}))$. By Prop. 1, all strategies in G_1^k have expected value 0 or 1. Hence, it is sufficient to prove that for all $E_1, \ldots, E_n \in [0,1]$, *(i)* $\eta(E_1, \ldots, E_n, 0) > \eta(E_1, \ldots, E_n)$ and *(ii)* $\eta(E_1, \ldots, E_n, 1) > \eta(E_1, \ldots, E_n)$. The thesis then follows by an induction on the number of strategies in the sub-game G_1^k.

We develop the proof for (i), as the one for (ii) is similar. For technical convenience, we prove the result for η^2, as the thesis for η follows as a consequence. Let $\overline{E}$ (resp., S) be the arithmetic average (resp., the sum) of $(E_1, \ldots, E_n)$ and let $\overline{E}'$ be the arithmetic average of $(E_1, \ldots, E_n, 0)$.

$$\begin{aligned}&\eta^2(E_1, \ldots, E_n, 0) - \eta^2(E_1, \ldots, E_n) = \\ &\frac{\sum_i E_i^2 - (n+1)\overline{E}'^2}{(n+1)\overline{E}'(1-\overline{E}')} - \frac{\sum_i E_i^2 - n\overline{E}^2}{n\overline{E}(1-\overline{E})} = \\ &\frac{(1-\overline{E})(\sum_i E_i^2 - \frac{S^2}{n+1}) - (1-\overline{E}')(\sum_i E_i^2 - \frac{S^2}{n})}{S(1-\overline{E}')(1-\overline{E})}.\end{aligned}$$

Since the denominator is clearly non-negative, we can focus on the sign of the numerator.

$$\begin{aligned}&(1-\overline{E})(\textstyle\sum_i E_i^2 - \frac{S^2}{n+1}) - (1-\overline{E}')(\sum_i E_i^2 - \frac{S^2}{n}) = \\ &\textstyle\sum_i E_i^2 - \frac{S^2}{n+1} - \overline{E}\sum_i E_i^2 + \frac{S^3}{n(n+1)} \\ &\quad - \textstyle\sum_i E_i^2 + \frac{S^2}{n} + \overline{E}'\sum_i E_i^2 - \frac{S^3}{n(n+1)} = \\ &S^2\Big(\frac{1}{n} - \frac{1}{n+1}\Big) - S\textstyle\sum_i E_i^2\Big(\frac{1}{n} - \frac{1}{n+1}\Big) = \\ &S(S - \textstyle\sum_i E_i^2)\Big(\frac{1}{n} - \frac{1}{n+1}\Big).\end{aligned}$$

Under the assumptions of Axiom 4', all three terms of the last expression are strictly positive, which proves our thesis. □

PROPOSITION 3. *Measure γ satisfies Axioms 0, 1, 2, 3, and 4.*

PROOF. Axiom 1 is an immediate consequence of Prop. 1 whereas Axiom 2 follows from the definition of γ. Axioms 3 and 4 can be verified by simple calculations. In particular, $\gamma(A_k(\mathit{Rand}, \mathit{Ctrl}, \ldots, \mathit{Ctrl})) = \frac{2k}{k+1}$, which is strictly increasing in k, for $k \geq 1$. □

PROPOSITION 4. *Measures η and γ violate Axiom 3'.*

PROOF. Consider the game $G_\varepsilon = B_{1/2}(H_\varepsilon, \mathit{Ctrl})$, where H_ε is a skill-less game whose only strategy has expected value $\varepsilon \in [0,1]$. Axiom 3' prescribes the measure of G to be $\frac{1}{2}$, for all $\varepsilon \in [0,1]$. On the other hand, simple calculations show that $\eta(G_\varepsilon) = (3 + 4\varepsilon - 4\varepsilon^2)^{-\frac{1}{2}}$ and $\gamma(G_\varepsilon) = (\frac{3}{2} + 2\varepsilon - 2\varepsilon^2)^{-1}$, which are both different from $\frac{1}{2}$ when $\varepsilon \neq \frac{1}{2}$. □

Since our measures span a conventional range from 0 to 1, we are not primarily interested in the actual value assigned to a given game, but rather in the weak order induced on games by the measure. A measure m induces the order $\leq_m$ in the following way: $G_1 \leq_m G_2$ iff $m(G_1) \leq m(G_2)$. Such order is weak because there may be games with the same measure, that end up being equivalent for the corresponding order. Two measures are called *co-monotonic* if they induce the same order. A simple example shows that the two measures we are considering are *not* co-monotonic.

PROPOSITION 5. *Measures η and γ are not co-monotonic.*

PROOF. Consider two games G_1, G_2, with 3 strategies each. The expected values of the strategies and the approximate value of all measures are reported in the following table.

game	E_a	E_b	E_c	η	γ
G_1	0	0.2	0.4	0.41	0.417
G_2	0	0.31	0.31	0.36	0.420

Moving from G_1 to G_2, γ increases while η decreases, thus proving the thesis. □

The next section contains more extreme examples of non-co-monotonicity, such as those arising in the analysis of the game Minesweeper.

7. EXPERIMENTAL EVALUATION

To develop an intuitive understanding of our measures, we set up a game simulation framework and implemented various well-known games in it. The main results are presented in Figure 2.

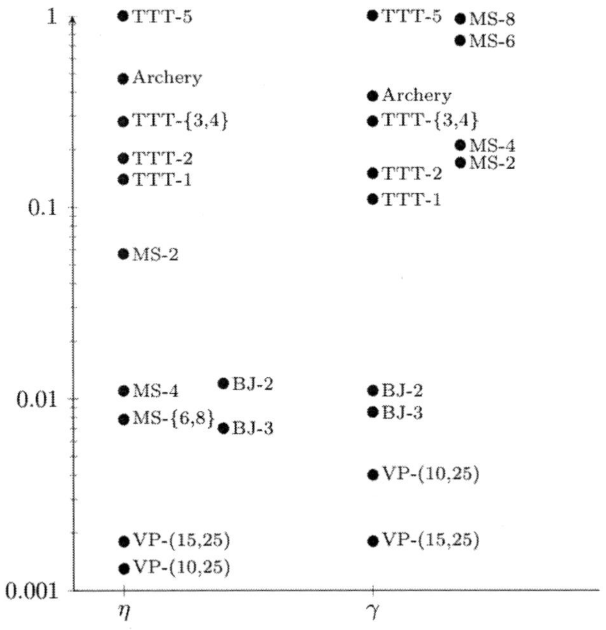

Figure 2: The amount of controllability in games Tic-tac-toe (TTT), Black Jack (BJ), Video Poker (VP), Minesweeper (MS), and an instance of archery, according to measures η and γ. See Section 7 for details.

Estimating the measures. The measures we consider are all based on the expected values of all possible deterministic memoryless strategies in the game. Since the state space of most of the games we consider in this section is extremely large, two levels of sampling were necessary: first, it is not possible to evaluate all strategies; second, it is not even possible to evaluate all possible paths of a single strategy. Both levels were adressed by uniform random sampling. As a rule of thumb, we chose the sizes of the samples in such a way that approximately one hour of computation is devoted to each game, on an Intel Core i5, 3.3Ghz and with a sequential implementation.

The game Tic-tac-toe is an exception, as it allows less than a thousand different strategies and 400 paths for each strategy. Hence, it was possible to analyze it exhaustively. For the other games, the sampling introduces estimation errors whose precise characterization goes beyond the scope of this paper. Indeed, our purpose is to explore and compare different notions of controllability, and the accuracy achieved by the experiments is sufficient to clearly distinguish how different measures evaluate different games.

We now briefly present the games that we have evaluated and discuss the corresponding experimental results. Since our framework is tailored to solitaire games with a Boolean outcome, most games have been modified to fit these constraints.

Tic-tac-toe. Tic-tac-toe is a well-known children game, played on a 3x3 board by two players. We derive 5 different solitaire versions of this game, by fixing the strategy of Player 2 in one of the following ways:

1. Put the token uniformly at random (in one of the available cells).
2. If there is a move that leads to immediate victory of Player 2, play that move, otherwise play uniformly at random.
3. If there is a move that prevents immediate victory of Player 1, play that move, otherwise play uniformly at random.
4. Avoid an immediate loss, or else try to obtain an immediate victory, or else play uniformly at random.
5. Put the token in the first available cell (deterministic strategy).

Moreover, a tie is considered a victory for Player 2. In Figure 2, we refer to Tic-tac-toe with strategy i (for $i = 1, \ldots, 5$) as "TTT-i".

Video Poker. Video poker is a very common solitaire casino game, similar to a slot machine, but based on the basic rules of poker. In our version, at each round the player pays a fixed bet of 1 dollar and is dealt 5 cards from a shuffled deck of 52 cards. Then, he can choose which cards to keep and which to change. Once the discarded cards have been redealt from the same deck, a payoff table associates payments to combinations of cards. If the player has a positive balance, another round is played with a newly shuffled deck of cards. To obtain a Boolean game, we fix two parameters: n is the initial balance in dollars, and k is the number of rounds. The player starts with an initial balance of n dollars and wins if he keeps a positive balance for k rounds. In Figure 2, we refer to the parameterized game as "VP-(n,k)".

Black Jack. Black Jack is a game usually played by several players against a dealer, with no direct interaction between players (except for card counting purposes). The rules of the game can easily be found online. In our simplified version, the player initially pays a fixed bet of 2 dollars and wins back the bet if he scores higher than the dealer (but less than 21) and 3 dollars if he wins with Black Jack (21). Then, if the player has a positive balance, another round is played using the same stack of cards. Hence, contrary to video poker, in the rounds after the first one the player can use a card counting strategy to improve his odds. The player wins if she keeps a positive balance for k rounds, where k is a parameter. In Figure 2, we refer to this game as "BJ-k".

Minesweeper. Our version of Minesweeper is played on a 5x5 grid, on which n mines are randomly positioned at the beginning of each play. The player, who begins with no information on the position of the mines, in each round selects a cell and is told how many mines are located in the 8 adjacent cells. The game continues until either the player chooses a cell containing a mine or all empty cells have been uncovered. In Figure 2, we refer to the game with n mines as "MS-n".

It is intuitively clear that it is very hard to win at Minesweeper by playing at random. Hence, random strategies have very small expected values, while comparatively few strategies have significant chances to win [2].

Archery. We include in the comparison an individual (i.e., solitaire) sport, as an example of human activity that is unanimously considered skill-driven. Archery fits well this role, also because its outcomes are precisely quantifiable with a fine grain, if one is able to measure the distance of each single shot from the center of the target. This is precisely what was done in a recent paper by Kolayiş et al. [15], whose purpose was to statistically characterize the typical spatial distribution of arrows. To this aim, 18 athletes were asked to throw up to 12 arrows each, and the position of each arrow from the target center was measured using digital videography. For evaluating this "game", we consider each athlete as a strategy and the distance of each arrow from the target center as an outcome of that strategy. To turn outcomes into Boolean values, we consider each shot a "win" if it is closer to the center of the target than the average shot. We can then apply our measures to the data because they depend only on the expected values of each strategy.

7.1 Discussion

Figure 2 displays a selection of our experimental results, on the same logarithmic scale. But for a few exceptions, both measures agree on the order in which different games should be put according to player controllability.

In the case of Tic-tac-toe, both measures confirm the intuition that the 5 variants exhibit a decreasing amount of randomness, with variant 1 being the most random. In particular, both measures assign value 1 to version 5 of the game, which is entirely deterministic. All Tic-tac-toe variants are significantly more controllable than the two card games we examine.

In particular, a short game of Black Jack achieves approximately 1% controllability according to both measures, while Video Poker scores even lower.

In analyzing Minesweeper, the measures exhibit a rather extreme case of non-co-monotonicity. Indeed, when increasing the number of mines, η approaches a positive value around $7 \cdot 10^{-3}$, whereas γ approaches 1. We conjecture that this contrast is tied to the extremely low average probability of winning in this game (with 6 mines, the probability of winning by playing at random is about $1.6 \cdot 10^{-5}$).

As expected, archery sits near the top of our ranking, achieving measures $\eta = 0.47$ and $\gamma = 0.38$. With respect to the "preponderance test" mentioned in Section 4, we observe that setting the threshold between games of skill and games of chance at $\frac{1}{2}$ would put even archery in the first class, albeit by a thin margin [3].

8. CONCLUSIONS

The balance between skill and luck in games is a topic of interest for players, game designers, lawmakers, and entrepreneurs in the gambling business. In this paper, we put forward a formal framework to evaluate such balance on 1-player games, general enough to embrace a wide variety of games, both existing and yet-to-come. As a consequence, it is the first time, to the best of our knowledge, that common games ranging from Tic-tac-toe to Black Jack have been compared automatically and on equal footing.

The theoretical and experimental results also show the limits of this preliminary investigation. Both Proposition 5 and the experiments suggest that the proposed axioms are compatible with widely differing weak orders. Hence, it may be desirable to strengthen them to approach a full axiomatic characterization of a single notion of controllability. For instance, all our axioms and measures are symmetrical w.r.t. winning and losing. Breaking this symmetry may lead to measures that are closer in spirit to the common understanding of what constitutes "control" in a game.

Finally, a natural development would be to extend the present investigation to multi-player games. However, that setting poses radically different challenges, starting from the fact that different players may have different control capabilities on the game, as the game needs not be symmetric w.r.t. the players.

Acknowledgments

Clara Pappalardo and Ugo Pugliese originally brought the topic of this paper to the attention of the author. Christos Stergiou took part in preliminary discussions and contributed to the experimental setup described in Section 7. The evaluation of archery was made possible by the kind cooperation of Ipek Kolayiş and her co-authors [15], who agreed to share the data concerning their experiment.

REFERENCES

[1] D. Becerra. Algorithmic approaches to playing Minesweeper, 2015. Bachelor's thesis, Harvard College.

[2] P. Borm and B. van der Genugten. On a relative measure of skill for games with chance elements.

[2] Becerra [1] reports an optimal expected value of at least 0.91 for a board of 9x9 with 10 mines.

[3] Our observations about archery apply to a specific set of data which does not necessarily represent a random sample of athletes.

Trabajos de Investigaciòn Operativa (Top), 9(1):91–114, 2001.

[3] P. Cohen. *Empirical Methods for Artificial Intelligence*. MIT Press, Cambridge, MA, USA, 1995.

[4] J. K. Dagsvik. Choice under Uncertainty and Bounded Rationality. Discussion Papers 409, Statistics Norway, Research Department, Mar. 2005.

[5] M. Dreef, P. Borm, and B. van der Genugten. Measuring skill in games: several approaches discussed. *Mathematical Methods of Operations Research*, 59(3):375–391, 2004.

[6] M. Dreef, P. Borm, and B. van der Genugten. A new relative skill measure for games with chance elements. *Managerial and Decision Economics*, 25(5):255–264, 2004.

[7] E. Feinberg and A. Shwartz, editors. *Handbook of Markov Decision Processes: Methods and Applications*. Springer, 2002.

[8] G. Gamst, L. Meyers, and A. Guarino. *Analysis of Variance Designs*. Cambridge University Press, 2008.

[9] L. Hedhes and I. Olkin. *Statistical Methods for Meta-Analysis*. Academic Press, 1985.

[10] S. Heubeck. Measuring skill in games: a critical review of methodologies. *Gaming Law Review and Economics*, 12(3):231–238, 2008.

[11] S. Heubeck. Measuring skill in games: Evaluating legality. *Review of Law and Economics*, 4(1):25–34, 2008.

[12] S. Johnson. Playing the odds. In C. Steinkuehler, K. Squire, and S. Barab, editors, *Games, Learning, and Society*. Cambridge Univ. Press, 2012.

[13] J. Kadane. *Statistics in the law*. Oxford Univ. Press, 2008.

[14] R. Kaye. Minesweeper is NP-complete. *The Mathematical Intelligencer*, 22(2):9–15, 2000.

[15] I. Kolayiş, M. Çilli, H. Ertan, and J. Knicker. Assessment of target performance in archery. *Procedia - Social and Behavioral Sciences*, 152:451 – 456, 2014. ERPA International Congress on Education, Istanbul, Turkey.

[16] S. Levitt and T. Miles. The role of skill versus luck in poker evidence from the world series of poker. *Journal of Sports Economics*, 15(1):31–44, 2014.

[17] J. McCrory. Video poker and the skill versus chance debate. *Gaming Law Review*, 6(3):223–227, 2002.

[18] S. Olejnik and J. Algina. Measures of effect size for comparative studies: Applications, interpretations, and limitations. *Contemporary Educational Psychology*, 25(3):241 – 286, 2000.

[19] M. Osborne and A. Rubinstein. *A Course in Game Theory*. MIT Press, 1994.

[20] R. Potter van Loon, M. van den Assem, and D. van Dolder. Beyond chance? The persistence of performance in online poker. *PLoS ONE*, 10(3):e0115479, 2015.

[21] B. Ratitch and D. Precup. Characterizing Markov decision processes. In *Proceedings of the 13th European Conference on Machine Learning*, ECML '02, pages 391–404, London, UK, UK, 2002. Springer-Verlag.

[22] A. Wyner. Can the skill level of a game of chance be measured? *Chance*, 25(3):50–53, 2012.

Local Fairness in Hedonic Games via Individual Threshold Coalitions

Nhan-Tam Nguyen
Institut für Informatik
Heinrich-Heine-Universität Düsseldorf
Düsseldorf, Germany
nguyen@cs.uni-duesseldorf.de

Jörg Rothe
Institut für Informatik
Heinrich-Heine-Universität Düsseldorf
Düsseldorf, Germany
rothe@cs.uni-duesseldorf.de

ABSTRACT

Hedonic games are coalition formation games where players only specify preferences over coalitions they are part of. We introduce and systematically study local fairness notions in hedonic games by suitably adapting fairness notions from fair division. In particular, we introduce three notions that assign to each player a threshold coalition that only depends on the player's individual preferences. A coalition structure (i.e., a partition of the players into coalitions) is considered locally fair if all players' coalitions in this structure are each at least as good as their threshold coalitions. We relate our notions to previously studied concepts and show that our fairness notions form a proper hierarchy. We also study the computational aspects of finding threshold coalitions and of deciding whether fair coalition structures exist in additively separable hedonic games. At last, we investigate the price of fairness.

Keywords

Coalition formation; hedonic games; fairness; game theory

1. INTRODUCTION

Coalition formation plays a crucial role in multiagent systems when agents have to cooperate. A commonly studied model of coalition formation is the model of hedonic game. These are coalition formation games with nontransferable utility, which were first studied by Drèze and Greenberg [21] and later on by Banerjee et al. [8] and Bogomolnaia and Jackson [11]. A key feature of hedonic games is that the players' preferences depend only on coalitions they are part of. Since players specify their preferences over an exponential-size domain (in the number of players), various compact representations have been proposed, which either are fully expressive but may still have an exponential size in the worst case or restrict the preference domain [7, 24, 11, 20, 3, 30, 17]. Most of these studies are concerned with stability issues. Intuitively, they capture incentives of (groups of) players to deviate by joining a different coalition so as to increase their individual utility values. Thus stability-related questions address a decentralized aspect of hedonic games.

A more recent approach to hedonic games is welfare maximization [14, 4, 5]. This idea is different because welfare maximization usually presupposes a central authority guiding the maximization process by eliciting preferences and suggesting or enforcing an optimal solution. This enforcement may be necessary because the optimality of a solution is determined by a global criterion, such as utilitarian or egalitarian social welfare, and may affect some players' utility values negatively compared with the status quo.

In this paper we will focus on the concept of local fairness. Fairness is an important aspect besides stability and efficiency (see the related work section and, e.g., [19] for a discussion of fairness in multiagent systems and [12, 31] for fair division of indivisible goods). The only work that we are aware of considering fairness in hedonic games is due to Bogomolnaia and Jackson [11], Aziz et al. [4], Wright and Vorobeychik [38], and Peters [34, 35]. Fairness is related to both centralized approaches and stability issues. On the one hand, the center may want to ensure a certain utility level for each player. This goal can be achieved by a global fairness condition. However, fairness does not per se presuppose the existence of a center. On the other hand, players may not consider their current coalition fair, given their individual preferences. While we agree with Bogomolnaia and Jackson [11] that stability has a " 'restricted fairness' flavor," we add that one can also take the complementary view that lack of fairness can be a major cause of instability.

To make this more concrete, consider a situation where all players except a single player in some coalition consider this coalition their favorite one, yet for that single player this coalition is actually only marginally better than being alone. However, because everyone else prefers this coalition and thus is much better off than that player, she rejects this coalition. This can be considered an unfair situation and is comparable to an ultimatum game situation, where the proposal is very imbalanced and the second player (responder) rejects the proposal because it is below her fair share (see, again, [19]). Note that we would have to contrast the single player's utility to the other players' utility values in order to explain the predicament. This approach of balanced utility values and inequality reduction requires either a center that knows all players' utility values or that players look at coalitions (and even other players' well-being) outside of their own. To some extent, however, this is at odds with the idea of hedonic game because players in such games should only be interested in their own coalition.

The traditional fairness notion of envy-freeness requires players to inspect other coalitions. If there is a large number of coalitions, that is something we would like to avoid. Therefore, we propose and study notions of *local* fairness—restricted fairness notions with the additional constraint that players only compare their current coalition to some bound that *solely* depends on their individual preferences.[1] We feel that this is in the general spirit of the decentralized aspect of hedonic games.

Appears in: *Proceedings of the 15th International Conference on Autonomous Agents and Multiagent Systems (AAMAS 2016), J. Thangarajah, K. Tuyls, S. Marsella, C. Jonker (eds.), May 9–13, 2016, Singapore.*

[1] In case of envy-freeness the bound would also depend on the whole coalition structure.

Contribution: In order to achieve this goal of local fairness criteria, we introduce new fairness notions for hedonic games that are inspired by ideas from the field of fair division of indivisible goods. Our main contributions are the following:

1. We introduce the idea of local fairness and three specific such fairness notions in hedonic games. We show that these concepts form a (strict) hierarchy and relate them to previously studied concepts. Surprisingly, the hierarchy strikingly differs from the scale proposed by Bouveret and Lemaître [13] in the context of fair division of indivisible goods.

2. We systematically study the complexity of finding "threshold coalitions" and of determining whether a fair coalition structure exists in an additively separable hedonic game. We also find that two of our notions coincide in such games.

3. We initiate the study of price of fairness in hedonic games. In addition, we strengthen a result by Brânzei and Larson [14] on coalition structures maximizing social welfare in symmetric additively separable hedonic games.

Related Work: Surveys and book chapters on hedonic games are, for example, due to Aziz and Savani [6], Elkind and Rothe [23], and Hajdukova [26]. Bogomolnaia and Jackson [11] already mention envy-freeness in their work, but they focus on studying stability notions. Aziz et al. [4] study the complexity of determining the existence of stable coalition structures in additively separable hedonic games. They also consider the welfare maximization approach and the notion of envy-freeness. The work by Wright and Vorobeychik [38] is related to ours. They study hedonic games under the perspective of mechanism design and propose mechanisms for solving the team formation problem. A key difference is that they consider additively separable hedonic games with nonnegative values only. Since in this case the grand coalition is most preferred by every player, Wright and Vorobeychik introduce cardinality constraints on feasible coalition sizes. They also consider *envy bounded by a single teammate*, which for the aforementioned reasons is not suitable for our goals. In addition, they introduce the *maximin share guarantee for team formation*, which is based on the idea of replacing players. This, however, leads to a provably different notion than ours (see Theorem 6). More recently introduced stability notions include *strong Nash stability*, proposed by Karakaya [28], and *strictly strong Nash stability*, due to Aziz and Brandl [2]. Brânzei and Larson [14] study social welfare maximization and core stability in additively separable hedonic games. Moreover, they consider the so-called stability gap. Bilo et al. [9, 10] study similar notions in fractional hedonic games.

Pareto optimality can be considered a notion of stability [32] as well. Elkind et al. [22] investigate the price of Pareto optimality in various representations of hedonic games. Peters and Elkind [36] give conditions on when certain classes of hedonic games admit intractable problems regarding the existence of stable coalition structures. Peters [35] considers restrictions of hedonic games that admit fast algorithms and he models allocating indivisible goods as hedonic game.

Fair division of indivisible goods and hedonic games are closely related because both fields deal with partitions of sets. In fair division, a set of goods needs to be partitioned into n subsets, where n is the number of agents. Usually, it is assumed that goods cannot be shared. This is a departure point from hedonic games because the number of coalitions in a partition is only bounded above by n. The no-externality assumption, however, is prevalent (or even defining) in both fields where an agent's utility depends only on the subset of goods that they receive (fair division) or the coalition that they are part of (hedonic games).

Surveys and book chapters on fair division are due, for example, to Chevaleyre et al. [18], Nguyen et al. [33], Lang and Rothe [31], and Bouveret et al. [12]. Inspired by the cut-and-choose protocol from cake cutting, Budish [15] introduced the max-min fair-share criterion. Since then, it has been studied by Procaccia and Wang [37], Kurokawa et al. [29], Amanatidis et al. [1], and Heinen et al. [27]. Bouveret and Lemaître [13] introduce min-max fair share and propose a scale of even more demanding fairness criteria. Caragiannis et al. [16] study the price of fairness in fair division.

Organization of the Paper: In Section 2, we formally define hedonic games and relevant notions of stability. In Section 3, we introduce our notions of fairness and relate them to other stability, fairness, and optimality concepts. In Section 4, we study our notions in additively separable hedonic games under computational aspects. The price of fairness is considered in Section 5, followed by a discussion of our findings and the conclusions in Section 6.

2. PRELIMINARIES

We denote by $N = \{1,\dots,n\}$ the set of *players*. A *coalition* is a subset of N and a *coalition structure* π is a partition of N. The set of all coalition structures over N is $\Pi(N)$. We denote by $\pi(i)$ the unique coalition with player i in coalition structure π and by $\mathcal{N}_i = \{C \subseteq N \mid i \in C\}$ all coalitions that player i is part of. Every player i has a weak and complete preference order $\succeq_i$ over $\mathcal{N}_i$. For $A, B \in \mathcal{N}_i$, we write $A \succeq_i B$ if player i *weakly prefers* coalition A to B; we write $A \succ_i B$ if player i *(strictly) prefers* coalition A to B, i.e., $A \succeq_i B$ but not $B \succeq_i A$; and we write $A \sim_i B$ if $A \succeq_i B$ and $B \succeq_i A$ (i.e., i is indifferent between A and B). Let $\succeq$ be the collection of all $\succeq_i$, $i \in N$. A *hedonic game* is a pair $(N, \succeq)$. It is an *additively separable hedonic game* (ASHG) if for every $i \in N$, there is a valuation function $v_i : N \to \mathbb{Q}$ such that $\sum_{j\in A} v_i(j) \geq \sum_{j\in B} v_i(j) \iff A \succeq_i B$. We write (N, v) for an additively separable hedonic game, where v is the collection of all v_i, $i \in N$. We assume normalization of the valuation functions, that is, $v_i(i) = 0$. We overload the notation to mean $v_i(A) = \sum_{j\in A} v_i(j)$ for each coalition $A \in \mathcal{N}_i$.

Now we define previously studied notions of stability that are relevant for this work. We distinguish, as is common, between group deviations, individual deviations, and other notions.

We consider the following notions of group deviations:

(1) A nonempty coalition $C \subseteq N$ *blocks* a coalition structure π if every $i \in C$ prefers C to $\pi(i)$. A coalition structure π is *core-stable* (CS) if no coalition blocks π.

(2) A coalition $C \subseteq N$ *weakly blocks* a coalition structure π if every $i \in C$ weakly prefers C to $\pi(i)$ and there is some $j \in C$ that prefers C to $\pi(j)$. A coalition structure π is *strictly core-stable* (SCS) if no coalition weakly blocks π.

(3) Given a coalition $H \subseteq N$, coalition structure π' is *reachable from coalition structure $\pi \neq \pi'$ by coalition H* if for all $i, j \in N \setminus H$, we have $\pi(i) = \pi(j) \iff \pi'(i) = \pi'(j)$. A nonempty coalition $H \subseteq N$ *weakly Nash-blocks* coalition structure π if there exists some coalition structure π' that is reachable from π by coalition H such that every $i \in H$ weakly prefers $\pi'(i)$ to $\pi(i)$ and there is some $j \in H$ that prefers $\pi'(j)$ to $\pi(j)$. We say π is *strictly strong Nash-stable* (SSNS) if there is no coalition that weakly Nash-blocks π.

As to individual deviations, we need the following definitions:

(1) A coalition structure π is *Nash-stable* (NS) if every $i \in N$ weakly prefers $\pi(i)$ to $C \cup \{i\}$ for every $C \in \pi \cup \{\emptyset\}$.

(2) A coalition structure π is *contractually individually stable* (CIS) if for every $i \in N$, the existence of a coalition $C \in \pi \cup \{\emptyset\}$ with

$C \cup \{i\} \succ_i \pi(i)$ implies that there exists some $j \in C$ such that $C \succ_j C \cup \{i\}$ or there exists some $k \in \pi(i)$ such that $\pi(k) \succ_k \pi(k) \setminus \{i\}$.

Of the remaining notions we need the following:

(1) A coalition structure π is *perfect* if every $i \in N$ weakly prefers $\pi(i)$ to C for every $C \in \mathscr{N}_i$. We refer to this property by PERFECT.

(2) A coalition structure π' *Pareto-dominates* coalition structure π if every $i \in N$ weakly prefers $\pi'(i)$ to $\pi(i)$ and there is some $j \in N$ that prefers $\pi'(j)$ to $\pi(j)$. A coalition structure π is *Pareto-optimal* (PO) if no coalition structure Pareto-dominates it.

(3) A coalition structure π is *envy-free by replacement* (EF-R) if $\pi(i) \succeq_i (\pi(j) \setminus \{j\}) \cup \{i\}$ for every $i, j \in N$.

(4) A coalition $C \in \mathscr{N}_i$ is acceptable for $i \in N$ if $C \succeq_i \{i\}$. A coalition structure π is *individually rational* (IR) if $\pi(i)$ is acceptable for every $i \in N$.

The following notions are defined only for ASHGs (N,v): A coalition structure $\pi \in \Pi(N)$ maximizes

(1) *utilitarian social welfare* (USW) if for every $\pi' \in \Pi(N)$, $\sum_{i\in N} v_i(\pi(i)) \geq \sum_{i\in N} v_i(\pi'(i))$;

(2) *egalitarian social welfare* (ESW) if for every $\pi' \in \Pi(N)$, $\min_{i\in N} v_i(\pi(i)) \geq \min_{i\in N} v_i(\pi'(i))$.

For the last two definitions we make the common assumption (see, for example, [4, 14]) in coalition formation that values are interpersonally comparable.

We also say that a coalition structure π *satisfies some notion X* if π is X or maximizes X.

Figure 1 shows the relationships between these notions. We refer to the surveys, book chapters, and papers mentioned in the related work section for more explanations of these definitions and their interrelations. The notions are chosen such that our separation results in the next section also apply to intermediate notions such as *contractual strict core stability* and *individual stability*.

3. FAIRNESS IN HEDONIC GAMES

We now introduce our fairness criteria, starting with the weakest one. Individual rationality is the most basic notion of stability. It is also the weakest fairness criterion. Similarly to the example in the introduction, a player who is in a coalition not acceptable to her is exploited by the other players in that coalition if this coalition is acceptable to them. In other words, this player has to be in a disliked coalition just for other players to benefit. In this case, a coalition structure consisting of singletons is more preferable for this player. Lowering the bound of acceptable coalitions would make the situation even worse. Note that individual rationality and perfectness are examples of local fairness criteria that only propose a threshold coalition a player has to be part of. In a sense, we look for criteria situated between these two notions. Because all fairness criteria have to satisfy individual rationality necessarily, we consider such fairness criteria only. Following the definition of envy-freeness by replacement [11], it is not immediately clear which players to replace in the criteria that we will propose and how to motivate this. Therefore, we will focus on definitions that are based on players *joining* coalitions (without replacing any players). This is also another reason for why we do not consider the well-known fairness notion of envy-freeness (based on joining) because it coincides with Nash stability. Similarly, the maximin share guarantee for team formation by Wright and Vorobeychik [38] is defined in terms of replacing a player (and, therefore, is different from max-min fairness considered here).

3.1 Min-Max Fairness

Before we formally define the min-max threshold, we illustrate it with the following situation: A player is arriving late and all other players have already formed a coalition structure without her (where the specific form of the coalition structure is irrelevant for this argument). Because the player could not participate in the coalition formation process, the player is allowed to join any coalition. Clearly, this player joins her most preferred coalition. This describes a fairness criterion because someone who was neglected should be allowed to adapt to the situation in the best possible way.

Definition 1. The *min-max threshold* of $i \in N$ is defined as

$$\text{MinMax}_i = \min_{\pi \in \Pi(N\setminus\{i\})} \max_{C \in \pi \cup \{\emptyset\}} C \cup \{i\},$$

where minimization and maximization are with respect to $\succeq_i$. A coalition structure π satisfies *min-max fairness* (MIN-MAX) if

$$\pi(i) \succeq_i \text{MinMax}_i$$

for every $i \in N$.

This notion is the hedonic-games variant of min-max fair share, originally proposed by Bouveret and Lemaître [13] in fair division. We relate min-max fairness to previously known notions of stability. By definition, min-max fairness satisfies individual rationality. Clearly, since USW is not IR, it cannot satisfy min-max fairness. Similarly, EF-R, PO, and CIS cannot imply min-max fairness. Later (in Section 3.3 on max-min fairness) we will see that min-max fairness is independent of most stability notions in the sense that it does not imply them. Now, we check which stability notions except for perfectness imply min-max fairness.

PROPOSITION 1. *A strictly core-stable coalition structure does not necessarily satisfy min-max fairness.*

PROOF. Consider Example 2 in [11]:

$$\{1,2\} \succ_1 \{1\} \succ_1 \{1,2,3\} \succ_1 \{1,3\},$$
$$\{1,2\} \succ_2 \{2\} \succ_2 \{1,2,3\} \succ_2 \{2,3\},$$
$$\{1,2,3\} \succ_3 \{2,3\} \succ_3 \{1,3\} \succ_3 \{3\}.$$

We compute each player's min-max threshold coalition. Player 1 considers coalition structures $\pi = \{\{2\},\{3\}\}$ and $\pi' = \{\{2,3\}\}$. The best acceptable coalition for player 1 with respect to π is $\{1,2\}$ and with respect to π' it is $\{1\}$. Thus $\text{MinMax}_1 = \{1\}$. Analogously, $\text{MinMax}_2 = \{2\}$ and $\text{MinMax}_3 = \{2,3\}$.

Overall, coalition structure $\{\{1,2\},\{3\}\}$ is SCS but does not satisfy min-max fairness. □

COROLLARY 1. *An individually rational or core-stable coalition structure does not necessarily satisfy min-max fairness.*

On the other hand, Nash stability does imply min-max fairness.

THEOREM 1. *Every Nash-stable coalition structure satisfies min-max fairness.*

PROOF. Let π be a Nash-stable coalition structure and $i \in N$. Then $\pi(i) \succeq_i C \cup \{i\}$ for every $C \in \pi \cup \{\emptyset\}$. Since MinMax_i is a best coalition in a *worst* coalition structure for i, $\pi(i) \succeq_i \text{MinMax}_i$. □

The following example shows that min-max fair coalition structures do not always exist (which is to be expected from any reasonable notion of fairness; envy-freeness is a classic fairness condition in fair division of indivisible goods, but in conjunction with completeness or Pareto optimality such partitions do not always exist either). This also shows that coalition structures that maximize egalitarian social welfare do not necessarily satisfy min-max fairness.

Example 1. Consider the following additively separable hedonic game, defined via the values $v_i(j)$:

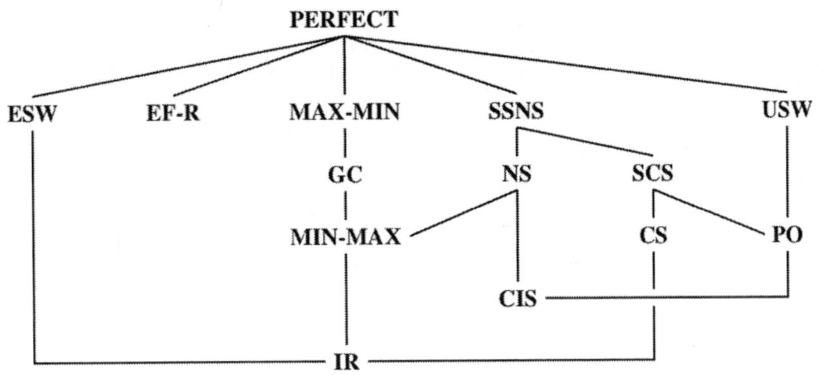

Figure 1: Relations between notions. A line from notion A to a lower notion B means that every coalition structure that is A is also B. For example, every strictly core-stable (SCS) coalition structure is core-stable (CS) and Pareto-optimal (PO).

i \ j	1	2	3
1	0	−10	15
2	−100	0	20
3	10	20	0

The individual min-max thresholds are $\text{MinMax}_1 = 5$, $\text{MinMax}_2 = 0$, and $\text{MinMax}_3 = 20$. Therefore, player 1 has to be in coalition $\{1,3\}$ or $\{1,2,3\}$, player 2 in $\{2\}$ or $\{2,3\}$, and player 3 in $\{2,3\}$ or $\{1,2,3\}$. Hence, there is no min-max fair coalition structure.

Conversely, consider the following hedonic game:

$$\{1,2\} \succ_1 \{1\} \succ_1 \{1,2,3\} \succ_1 \{1,3\},$$
$$\{1,2,3\} \succ_2 \{2,3\} \succ_2 \{1,2\} \succ_2 \{2\},$$
$$\{1,2,3\} \succ_3 \{2,3\} \succ_3 \{1,3\} \succ_3 \{3\}.$$

The players' min-max threshold coalitions are $\text{MinMax}_1 = \{1\}$, $\text{MinMax}_2 = \{2,3\}$, and $\text{MinMax}_3 = \{2,3\}$. Thus $\{\{1\},\{2,3\}\}$ satisfies min-max fairness but not grand-coalition fairness. □

It follows that a coalition structure that satisfies USW, ESW, EF-R, PO, or CIS does not necessarily satisfy grand-coalition fairness (otherwise it would satisfy min-max fairness). Later we will see that grand-coalition fairness is independent of all other considered notions except for perfectness. For now we show that these notions do not imply grand-coalition fairness.

3.2 Grand-Coalition Fairness

Bogomolnaia and Jackson [11] proposed the grand coalition as a notion of fairness. We recover their idea in the context of local fairness. It can be seen as a special variant of proportionality in the setting of hedonic games.

Definition 2. The *grand-coalition threshold* of $i \in N$ is defined as

$$\text{GC}_i = \max\{\{i\}, N\},$$

where we maximize with respect to $\succeq_i$. A coalition structure satisfies *grand-coalition fairness* (GC) if

$$\pi(i) \succeq_i \text{GC}_i$$

for every $i \in N$.

Grand-coalition fairness is a notion of fairness because the grand coalition can be interpreted as an average: Every player has to face both her friends and her enemies. Note that a proportionality threshold is typically defined as the ratio of the valuation for the whole to the number of players. Since players "share" their coalitions, it is not clear which number the valuation of the whole should be compared to. Comparing to the number of coalitions in a coalition structure, however, violates our locality requirement: thresholds that should only depend on a player's own preference.

First, we show that grand-coalition fairness is strictly stronger than min-max fairness.

THEOREM 2. *Every grand-coalition fair coalition structure satisfies min-max fairness, yet a min-max fair coalition structure does not necessarily satisfy grand-coalition fairness.*

PROOF. Let $i \in N$. Every coalition structure serves as an upper bound of MinMax_i. Consider the coalition structure $\{N\}$. Then $\max\{\{i\},N\} \succeq_i \text{MinMax}_i$.

PROPOSITION 2. *A strictly strong Nash-stable coalition structure does not necessarily satisfy grand-coalition fairness.*

PROOF. Consider the following hedonic game:

$$\{1,2\} \succ_1 \{1,3\} \succ_1 \{1\} \succ_1 \{1,2,3\},$$
$$\{1,2,3\} \succ_2 \{1,2\} \succ_2 \{2,3\} \succ_2 \{2\},$$
$$\{2,3\} \succ_3 \{3\} \succ_3 \{1,2,3\} \succ_3 \{1,3\}.$$

Coalition structure $\{\{1,2\},\{3\}\}$ is SSNS but is not grand-coalition fair. □

COROLLARY 2. *An individually rational, Nash-stable, core-stable, or strictly core-stable coalition structure does not necessarily satisfy grand-coalition fairness.*

3.3 Max-Min Fairness

We motivate the next fairness notion with the following situation: Suppose some player is allowed to partition all players excluding herself but does not know which coalition she will be part of in the end. Since she had the right to choose a partition, she has to live with all possible consequences. In other words, she could end up in any of these coalitions, even the worst. Therefore, a player would partition all remaining players so that the worst coalition among them is as good as possible for her.

Definition 3. The *max-min threshold* of $i \in N$ is defined as

$$\text{MaxMin}_i = \max_{\pi \in \Pi(N \setminus \{i\})} \max\{\{i\}, \min_{C \in \pi} C \cup \{i\}\},$$

where maximization and minimization are with respect to $\succeq_i$. A coalition structure π satisfies *max-min fairness* (MAX-MIN) if

$$\pi(i) \succeq_i \text{MaxMin}_i$$

for every $i \in N$.

Note that we cannot include the acceptability constraint into the minimization because then the definition would be weaker than IR. Max-min fairness is the hedonic-games variant of max-min fair share due to Budish [15]. We show that max-min fairness is strictly stronger than grand-coalition fairness.

THEOREM 3. *Every max-min fair coalition structure satisfies grand-coalition fairness, yet a grand-coalition fair coalition structure does not necessarily satisfy max-min fairness.*

PROOF. Let $i \in N$. The coalition structure π consisting of the grand coalition without i is the one where $\max_{C \in \pi \cup \{\emptyset\}} C \cup \{i\}$ and $\max\{\{i\}, \min_{C \in \pi} C \cup \{i\}\}$ become equal. Since every coalition structure gives a lower bound for MaxMin_i and an upper bound for MinMax_i, we have

$$\text{MaxMin}_i \succeq_i \text{GC}_i \succeq_i \text{MinMax}_i.$$

Conversely, consider the following hedonic game:

$$\{1,2\} \succ_1 \{1,3\} \succ_1 \{1,2,3\} \succ_1 \{1\},$$
$$\{1,2,3\} \succ_2 \{1,2\} \succ_2 \{1,3\} \succ_2 \{2\},$$
$$\{2,3\} \succ_3 \{1,2,3\} \succ_3 \{3\} \succ_3 \{1,3\}.$$

Coalition structure $\{\{1,2,3\}\}$ satisfies grand-coalition fairness but not max-min fairness because player 1's max-min threshold coalition is $\{1,3\}$. □

Theorems 2 and 3 give additional motivation of grand-coalition fairness: It is strictly between max-min and min-max fairness. It follows that a USW, ESW, EF-R, PO, or CIS coalition structure does not necessarily satisfy max-min fairness.

Max-min fairness is independent of all other considered notions except for perfectness.

PROPOSITION 3. *A max-min fair coalition structure does not necessarily satisfy contractually individual stability or core stability.*

PROOF. Consider the following hedonic game:

$$\{1,2\} \succ_1 \{1\} \succ_1 \{1,3\} \succ_1 \{1,2,3\},$$
$$\{1,2\} \succ_2 \{2\} \succ_2 \{2,3\} \succ_2 \{1,2,3\},$$
$$\{1,3\} \succ_3 \{3\} \succ_3 \{2,3\} \succ_3 \{1,2,3\}.$$

The max-min threshold coalitions are $\text{MaxMin}_i = \{i\}$, $i \in \{1,2,3\}$. Thus coalition structure $\{\{1\},\{2\},\{3\}\}$ satisfies max-min fairness but neither CIS nor CS. □

COROLLARY 3.
1. *A grand-coalition fair or min-max fair coalition structure does not necessarily satisfy contractually individual stability or core stability.*
2. *A max-min fair, grand-coalition fair, or min-max fair coalition structure does not necessarily satisfy Nash stability, Pareto optimality, strictly strong Nash stability, strict core stability, utilitarian social welfare, or perfectness.*

PROPOSITION 4. *A max-min fair coalition structure does not necessarily satisfy envy-freeness by replacement or egalitarian social welfare.*

PROOF. For EF-R, consider the following hedonic game:

$$\{1,2\} \succ_1 \{1\} \succ_1 \{1,2,3\} \succ_1 \{1,3\},$$
$$\{1,2\} \succ_2 \{2\} \succ_2 \{1,2,3\} \succ_2 \{2,3\},$$
$$\{2,3\} \succ_3 \{3\} \succ_3 \{1,2,3\} \succ_3 \{1,3\}.$$

Coalition structure $\{\{1,2\},\{3\}\}$ satisfies max-min fairness but is not envy-free by replacement.

For ESW, consider the following additively separable hedonic game, defined via the values $v_i(j)$:

$i \backslash j$	1	2	3	4
1	0	10	−20	0
2	10	0	−20	0
3	−10	−10	0	10
4	−10	−10	10	0

Coalition structure $\{\{1,2\},\{3\},\{4\}\}$ satisfies max-min fairness but does not maximize egalitarian social welfare (coalition structure $\{\{1,2\},\{3,4\}\}$ has a higher egalitarian social welfare). □

COROLLARY 4. *A grand-coalition fair or min-max fair coalition structure does not necessarily satisfy envy-freeness by replacement or egalitarian social welfare.*

From Proposition 2 we have the following corollary.

COROLLARY 5. *An individually rational, Nash-stable, core-stable, strictly strong Nash-stable, or strictly core-stable coalition structure does not necessarily satisfy max-min fairness.*

See Figure 1 for a summary of the results of this section.

4. LOCAL FAIRNESS IN ASHGS

In this section we study the existence of fair coalition structures, the complexity of computing fairness thresholds and of deciding whether a hedonic game admits a fair coalition structure. Since additively separable hedonic games are a well-studied (see [6] and the references therein) class of hedonic games, we will focus on this class. In addition, it will be easier to compare our complexity results to some results in fair division with additive utility functions. We begin with min-max fairness.

4.1 Min-Max Fairness

We start by computing min-max fairness thresholds. Since we have valuation functions in ASHGs, we can compare to the *value* of threshold coalitions. In particular, we consider the decision problem MIN-MAX-THRESHOLD: Given a set N of players, a player i's valuation function v, and a rational number k, does it hold that $\text{MinMax}_i \geq k$?

By considering coalition structures consisting of either the grand coalition or only of singletons, we have the following observations that show that MIN-MAX-THRESHOLD is easy to solve for certain restricted valuation functions.

OBSERVATION 1. *If $v_i(N) \leq 0$, then* $\text{MinMax}_i = 0$.

OBSERVATION 2. *If $v_i(j) \geq 0$ for every $j \in N$, then* $\text{MinMax}_i = \max_{j \in N} v(j)$.

For general valuation functions, however, we have this result:

THEOREM 4. MIN-MAX-THRESHOLD *is* coNP*-complete.*

PROOF. We consider the complementary problem, which for the same input asks whether $\text{MinMax}_i < k$ holds. Membership of this problem in NP follows from guessing a coalition structure π and comparing the maximum value of a coalition in π to k.

To show NP-hardness, we reduce from a restricted variant of PARTITION that contains no input numbers of value 1. This problem can be shown to be NP-hard by reducing from the original PARTITION problem and multiplying all values by 2.

The reduction works as follows. Let $b_1, \dots, b_n \in \mathbb{N}$ be a restricted PARTITION instance. We consider valuation function v_i defined as follows: $v_i(j) = b_j$ and $v_i(n+1) = v_i(n+2) = -(L-1)$, where $\sum_{j=1}^{n} b_j = 2L$. Thus $N = \{1, \dots, n, i, n+1, n+2\}$ with i different from $1, \dots, n, n+1, n+2$. In addition, we set the bound k to 2.

We show that there is a partition if and only if $\text{MinMax}_i < k$.

From left to right: Suppose (A, B) is a partition of the numbers $b_1, \dots, b_n$. Consider the coalition structure $\pi = \{A \cup \{n+1\}, B \cup \{n+2\}\}$. We have $\max_{C \in \pi \cup \{\emptyset\}} v_i(C \cup \{i\}) = \max\{1, 1, 0\} = 1$. Therefore, $\text{MinMax}_i \leq 1 < 2 = k$.

From right to left: Suppose for every partition (A, B) we have $\sum_{j \in A} b_j > L$ or $\sum_{j \in B} b_j > L$. Note that for the grand coalition we have $\max_{C \in \{N \setminus \{i\}\} \cup \{\emptyset\}} v_i(C \cup \{i\}) = \max\{2L - 2(L-1), 0\} = 2$.

For every coalition structure consisting of two nonempty coalitions A', B' with $A' \cup B' = N \setminus \{i, n+1, n+2\}$, we have, without loss of generality, $v_i(A' \cup \{i\}) \geq L+1$ and $v_i(B' \cup \{i\}) \leq L-1$. Adding players $n+1$ and $n+2$ to A' would give a maximum of at least 2 because B' is nonempty and $b_j \geq 2$ by assumption. Adding both players to B' would give a maximum of at least $L+1$. Since the partition instance has at least two numbers of value 2, $L \geq 2$. Assigning these players to separate coalitions we have $v_i(A' \cup \{i\} \cup \{n+1\}) \geq L+1-L+1 = 2$. Thus the maximum is at least 2.

For all coalition structures consisting of $\ell > 2$ nonempty coalitions, we have that the maximum value is at least 2 because all numbers of the partition instance are at least 2 and there are only two players with a negative value. Thus there is always a coalition that is valued at least 2.

Since all coalition structures have a coalition which is valued at least 2, we have $\text{MinMax}_i \geq 2 = k$. □

Coming now to the question of existence of fair coalition structures, we first define the decision problem that we study. The input of the problem MIN-MAX-EXIST consists of an additively separable hedonic game. The question is whether a min-max fair coalition structure exists. We start with a simple observation.

OBSERVATION 3. *If $v_i(j) \geq 0$ for every $i, j \in N$, then $\{N\}$ satisfies min-max fairness, i.e., min-max fair coalition structures always exist.*

We say an additively separable hedonic game is *symmetric* if $v_i(j) = v_j(i)$ for every $i, j \in N$. Since there always exist Nash-stable coalition structures in symmetric ASHGs [11], we have

COROLLARY 6. *Symmetric ASHGs always admit min-max fair coalition structures.*

For general additively separable hedonic games, we have NP-hardness as a lower bound and membership in Σ_2^p (the second level of the polynomial hierarchy) as an upper bound. We use a modified version of the game in Example 1 as a gadget.

THEOREM 5. MIN-MAX-EXIST *is NP-hard and in Σ_2^p.*

PROOF. We reduce from MONOTONE-ONE-IN-THREE-3SAT (see, e.g., the comment of Garey and Johnson [25, p. 259], on ONE-IN-THREE-3SAT): Given a boolean formula φ that contains only clauses with three positive literals, does there exist a satisfying assignment such that each clause has exactly one true literal?

Now we describe the reduction. Let $\ell_1, \dots, \ell_n$ be the variables, $C_1, \dots, C_m$ the clauses of φ, and r_i the number of distinct clauses ℓ_i appears in. For every variable ℓ_i that appears in some clause, we introduce three *variable players*, a_i, b_i, and c_i, and for every clause C_k, we add three *clause players*, D_k, E_k, and F_k.

The valuation functions are defined as follows:

Variable players of type 1, a_i, $1 \leq i \leq n$, value every other variable player except for b_i and c_i with $-3m-1$. They value b_i with $3r_i$, c_i with 0, all clause players D_k, E_k, and F_k for which $\ell_i \in C_k$ with -1, and all remaining players with 0. Variable players of type 2, b_i, $1 \leq i \leq n$, value c_i with $3r_i$, all clause players D_k, E_k, and F_k for which $\ell_i \in C_k$ with 1, and all remaining players with 0. Variable players of type 3, c_i, $1 \leq i \leq n$, value every clause player with -1 and all remaining players with 0.

Clause players of type 1, D_k, $1 \leq k \leq m$, value E_k with -10, F_k with 15, and all remaining players with 0. Clause players of type 2, E_k, $1 \leq k \leq m$, value D_k with -20, F_k with 21, all a_i for which $\ell_i \in C_k$ with 20, and all remaining players with 0. Clause players of type 3, F_k, $1 \leq k \leq m$, value D_k with 10, E_k with 20, and all remaining players with 0.

We compute the min-max thresholds before showing the required equivalence. The min-max threshold of type-1 variable players a_i is 0, of type-2 variable players b_i is $3r_i$, of type-3 variable players c_i is 0, of type-1 clause players D_k is 5, of type-2 clause players E_k is 20 (consider the coalition structure where D_k and F_k are together and all remaining players are in single coalitions), and of type-3 clause players F_k is 20. We show that the given formula is satisfied by an assignment with exactly one true literal per clause if and only if there is a coalition structure satisfying min-max fairness.

From left to right: Suppose there is a satisfying assignment τ with the above property. Denote by $\ell_1, \dots, \ell_o$ all variables which are true under τ and by $\ell_{o+1}, \dots, \ell_n$ all remaining variables. Denote by $T(\ell_i)$ the set of clauses that become true under τ via ℓ_i and let $\mathscr{C}(\ell_i) = \{D_k, E_k, F_k \mid C_k \in T(\ell_i)\}$. Consider the following coalition structure: $\pi = \{\mathscr{C}(\ell_1) \cup \{a_1, b_1\}, \{c_1\}, \dots, \mathscr{C}(\ell_o) \cup \{a_o, b_o\}, \{c_o\}, \{a_{o+1}, b_{o+1}, c_{o+1}\}, \dots, \{a_n, b_n, c_n\}\}$. In words, for each clause satisfied by some literal, we put into one coalition the corresponding type-1 and type-2 variable players and all three corresponding clause players. In this case, the corresponding type-3 variable player stays alone. If a variable satisfies no clause, then the corresponding variable players are in a coalition that only consists of them. Since each clause is satisfied by exactly one literal, no player is in multiple coalitions simultaneously.

We compute every player's value. Type-1 clause players D_k are in the same coalition as E_k and F_k. Therefore, they have a value of 5. Similarly, type-3 clause players F_k have a value of 30. For variables ℓ_i that are true under τ, since type-1 variable players a_i never share coalitions with other variable players except for b_i and all clause players corresponding to clauses that contain ℓ_i, these a_i have a value of $-3r_i + 3r_i = 0$. For the same reason, type-2 variable players b_i have a value of $3r_i$ and type-2 clause players E_k have a value of $-20 + 21 + 20 = 21$. Type-3 variable players c_i are alone and, hence, have value 0. For variables ℓ_j that are false under τ, the coalition consisting of all variable players corresponding to such a variable gives the corresponding type-1 and type-2 variable players, a_j and b_j, a value of $3r_j$ and the corresponding type-3 variable player c_j a value of 0. Overall, every player achieves her min-max threshold, so coalition structure π satisfies min-max fairness.

From right to left: Suppose there is some coalition structure π satisfying min-max fairness. Let F_k be the type-3 clause player for some clause C_k. Since $v_{F_k}(\pi(F_k)) \geq 20$, $E_k \in \pi(F_k)$. Because $F_k \in$

$\pi(F_k)$ and $v_{D_k}(\pi(D_k)) \geq 5$, $D_k \in \pi(F_k)$. Thus $\{D_k, E_k, F_k\} \subseteq \pi(F_k)$. Because $v_{E_k}(\pi(F_k)) \geq 20$, some variable player a_i corresponding to a literal occurring in clause C_k has to be in $\pi(F_k)$; otherwise, $v_{E_k}(\pi(F_k)) = 1$. If variable players different from b_i or c_i are in $\pi(F_k)$, no such variable player can satisfy the min-max threshold. Since variable player a_i joins $\{D_k, E_k, F_k\}$, $b_i \in \pi(F_k)$. Because $v_{b_i}(\pi(F_k)) \geq 3r_i$, all clause players that are valued positively by b_i are in $\pi(F_k)$. Otherwise, $c_i \in \pi(F_k)$, but then $u_{c_i}(\pi(F_k)) < 0$ because clause players are in $\pi(F_k)$. If clause players that are valued 0 by a_i are in the same coalition, other variable players have to be in that coalition as well, but then min-max fairness is not satisfied. Therefore, every $\pi(F_k)$ contains exactly one a_i. Then we can construct a satisfying assignment with the one-in-three property by making all variables ℓ_i true where a_i is in a coalition with clause players. □

4.2 Grand-Coalition & Max-Min Fairness

In this section, we can consider grand-coalition and max-min fairness at the same time because of the following result:

THEOREM 6. *In additively separable hedonic games, for every $i \in N$ we have*

$$\text{MaxMin}_i = \text{GC}_i.$$

PROOF. It remains to show $\max\{0, v_i(N)\} = \text{GC}_i \geq \text{MaxMin}_i$ because of Theorem 3.

If $v_i(N) < 0$, suppose there is some π such that $\min_{C \in \pi} v_i(C \cup \{i\}) > 0$. Then $v_i(C \cup \{i\}) > 0$ for every coalition $C \in \pi$. This, however, implies $v_i(N) = \sum_{C \in \pi} v_i(C \cup \{i\}) > 0$.

If $v_i(N) \geq 0$, suppose there is some π such that $\min_{C \in \pi} v_i(C \cup \{i\}) > v_i(N)$. Then $v_i(C \cup \{i\}) > v_i(N)$ for every coalition $C \in \pi$, which would imply $v_i(N) = \sum_{C \in \pi} v_i(C \cup \{i\}) > v_i(N)$. □

Define the threshold and existence problems for grand-coalition and max-min fairness analogously to MIN-MAX-THRESHOLD and MIN-MAX-EXIST. Since computing the value of the grand coalition is easy in additively separable hedonic games, we have

COROLLARY 7. MAX-MIN-THRESHOLD *and* GRAND-COALITION-THRESHOLD *are in* P.

However, checking whether there exists a grand-coalition fair or max-min fair coalition structure is hard.

THEOREM 7. *The problems* GRAND-COALITION-EXIST *and* MAX-MIN-EXIST *are* NP*-complete.*

PROOF. Membership in NP follows from guessing and checking. Checking works in polynomial time because of Corollary 7. We reduce from PARTITION. Let $b_1, \ldots, b_n$ be a PARTITION instance with $\sum_{i=1}^{n} b_i = 2L$.

We construct the following additively separable hedonic game: $N = \{1, \ldots, n, n+1, n+2, n+3, n+4, n+5\}$ with $v_{n+1}(n+2) = -1$, $v_{n+2}(n+1) = -1$, $v_{n+3}(n+1) = v_{n+3}(n+2) = v_{n+4}(n+1) = v_{n+4}(n+2) = L$, $v_{n+3}(i) = v_{n+4}(i) = -b_i$, $v_i(n+3) = v_i(n+4) = 1$, $v_i(n+5) = -1$ for every i, $1 \leq i \leq n$. All other values are 0. The threshold is 1 for player i, $1 \leq i \leq n$, and 0 for the remaining players. We show that there is a partition if and only if there is a coalition structure satisfying grand-coalition (and thus, equivalently in ASHGs, max-min) fairness.

From left to right: Suppose (A, B) is a partition. Then the coalition structure $\{\{n+1, n+3\} \cup A, \{n+2, n+4\} \cup B, \{n+5\}\}$ satisfies grand-coalition fairness: Player $n+1$ is not with player $n+2$. Players $n+3$ and $n+4$ receive 0 value. Each i, $1 \leq i \leq n$, gets a value of 1. Player $n+5$ gets 0.

From right to left: Suppose π satisfies grand-coalition fairness. Then players $n+1$ and $n+2$ are not in the same coalition. Since each i, $1 \leq i \leq n$, needs to get at least a value of 1, every such player is with players $n+3$ or $n+4$. Let C_k contain all i, $1 \leq i \leq n$, that are with player $n+k$, $k \in \{3,4\}$. Then $C_3 \cap C_4 = \emptyset$; otherwise, $n+3$ and $n+4$ are in the same coalition with nonnegative values, which means that $n+1$ and $n+2$ are in the same coalition as well. We also have $C_3 \neq \emptyset$ (otherwise, all i, $1 \leq i \leq n$, are in C_4: $v_{n+4}(\pi(n+4)) \leq -2L + L < 0$). Since $v_{n+3}(\pi(n+3)) \geq 0$, and players $n+1$ and $n+2$ are the only players valued positively by $n+3$, players $n+1$ or $n+2$ are in $\pi(n+3)$. Both of them cannot be in $\pi(n+3)$ because then player $n+4$ would have a negative value. Therefore, $L \geq \sum_{i \in C_k} b_i$, $k \in \{3,4\}$. Since $\sum_{i \in C_3} b_i + \sum_{i \in C_4} b_j = 2L$, we have $\sum_{i \in C_3} b_i = L = \sum_{i \in C_4} b_j$. □

5. PRICE OF FAIRNESS

Now we study the price of fairness in additively separable hedonic games. Informally, the price of fairness captures the loss in social welfare of a worst (best) coalition structure that satisfies some fairness criterion. We denote by $\text{SW}_G(\pi)$ the utilitarian social welfare of coalition structure π in an additively separable hedonic game $G = (N, v)$, that is, $\text{SW}_G(\pi) = \sum_{i \in N} v_i(\pi(i))$. We omit G when it is clear from the context.

Definition 4. Let $G = (N, v)$ be an additively separable hedonic game and let π^* denote a coalition structure maximizing utilitarian social welfare. Define the *maximum price of min-max fairness* by

$$\text{Max-PoMMF}(G) = \max_{\pi \in \Pi(N), \pi \text{ is min-max fair}} \frac{\text{SW}(\pi^*)}{\text{SW}(\pi)}$$

if there is some min-max fair $\pi \in \Pi(N)$ and $\text{SW}(\pi) > 0$ for all min-max fair $\pi \in \Pi(N)$; by $\text{Max-PoMMF}(G) = 1$ if $\text{SW}(\pi^*) = 0$ and $\text{SW}(\pi) = 0$ for some min-max fair $\pi \in \Pi(N)$; and by setting $\text{Max-PoMMF}(G) = +\infty$ otherwise.

Define the *minimum price of min-max fairness* (Min-PoMMF) analogously.

Note that we have $\text{SW}(\pi^*) \geq 0$ and $\text{SW}(\pi) \geq 0$, where π^* maximizes utilitarian social welfare and π is min-max fair.

Because the grand coalition maximizes utilitarian welfare under nonnegative valuation functions, the minimum and maximum price of grand-coalition fairness is one. Since this bound is not really informative, we now make some suitable assumptions to strengthen our results. Elkind et al. [22] argue that these notions are only sensible if the set of coalition structures that we consider is large enough. Because of that we only consider min-max fairness, the weakest fairness notion, in order to constrain the set of feasible coalition structures as least as possible. In addition, Elkind et al. [22] focus on Pareto optimality because such coalition structures always exist. Similarly, we restrict our study to symmetric additively separable hedonic games so as to guarantee the existence of min-max fair coalition structures.

Unfortunately, the maximum price of min-max fairness is not bounded by a constant value even for nonnegative valuation functions.

THEOREM 8. *Let $G = (N, v)$ be a symmetric ASHG of n players with $v_i(j) \geq 0$ for every $i, j \in N$. Then*

$$\text{Max-PoMMF}(G) \leq n - 1.$$

In addition, this bound is tight.

PROOF. If $\text{SW}(\pi^*) = 0$, then $\text{Max-PoMMF}(G) = 1$. Otherwise, there are $i, j \in N$, $i \neq j$, such that $v_i(j) > 0$. We can upper-bound

$SW(\pi^*)$ by $\sum_{i \in N} v_i(N)$. By Observation 2, we can lower-bound the value of every player i by $\max_{j \in N} v_i(j)$. Thus

$$\begin{aligned}
\text{Max-PoMMF}(G) &\leq \frac{\sum_{i \in N} v_i(N)}{\sum_{i \in N} \max_{j \in N} v_i(j)} \\
&\leq \frac{\sum_{i \in N}(n-1)\max_{j \in N} v_i(j)}{\sum_{i \in N} \max_{j \in N} v_i(j)} \\
&= n-1.
\end{aligned}$$

To see that this bound is tight, consider a game with n players, n even. Every player values every other player with $a > 0$. Thus the min-max threshold of every player is a. Therefore, the coalition structure that consists of $n/2$ pairs satisfies min-max fairness and has minimum utilitarian social welfare of na among all min-max fair coalition structures. The coalition structure consisting of the grand coalition that maximizes utilitarian social welfare, however, has a utilitarian social welfare of $n(n-1)a$. □

To obtain a meaningful bound in the above result, we need the existence of a min-max fair coalition structure, which is guaranteed in symmetric ASHGs. We need the following result before we can turn to Min-PoMMF.

THEOREM 9. *Let $G = (N, v)$ be a symmetric ASHG. Then every coalition structure π that maximizes utilitarian social welfare satisfies min-max fairness.*

PROOF. Suppose, for the sake of contradiction, that there is some $i \in N$ with $v_i(\pi(i)) < \text{MinMax}_i$. By a result of Brânzei and Larson [14], we know that every coalition structure maximizing utilitarian social welfare satisfies individual rationality. On the other hand, considering π with respect to MinMax, we have

$$0 \leq v_i(\pi(i)) < \text{MinMax}_i \leq \max_{C_j \in \pi} v_i(C_j \cup \{i\}). \tag{1}$$

Because of the strict inequality $\pi(i) \neq C_\ell$, where C_ℓ is a maximizer of $\max_{C_j \in \pi} v_i(C_j \cup \{i\})$, we have $v_i(\pi(i)) < v_i(C_\ell \cup \{i\})$. Since π is a maximizer of utilitarian social welfare, the social welfare of π should not be lower than the coalition structure where i joins C_ℓ:

$$\sum_{k \in \pi(i)} v_k(\pi(i)) + \sum_{k \in C_\ell} v_k(C_\ell) \geq$$
$$\sum_{k \in \pi(i),\, k \neq i} v_k(\pi(i) \setminus \{i\}) + \sum_{k \in C_\ell} v_k(C_\ell) + 2v_i(C_\ell \cup \{i\}).$$

Using symmetry, this is equivalent to the contradiction

$$v_i(\pi(i)) \geq v_i(C_\ell \cup \{i\}),$$

which completes the proof. □

Since min-max fairness is strictly stronger than individual rationality, Theorem 9 strengthens the result by Brânzei and Larson [14] that we used in the proof. Note that the above theorem also implies that we have an alternative proof of Corollary 6 (that every symmetric additively separable hedonic game admits a min-max fair coalition structure) that does not depend on the guaranteed existence of Nash-stable coalition structures but on the guaranteed existence of coalition structures maximizing utilitarian social welfare. From Theorem 9 we immediately have the following corollary.

COROLLARY 8. *Let G be a symmetric ASHG. Then*

$$\text{Min-PoMMF}(G) = 1.$$

6. DISCUSSION & CONCLUSION

We have introduced three new notions of fairness in hedonic games and studied the connection with previously studied notions. Our notions themselves form a strict hierarchy: Every max-min fair coalition structure is grand-coalition fair (but not vice versa), and every grand-coalition fair coalition structure is min-max fair (but not vice versa). Although our fairness criteria are inspired from the field of fair division, our results are very different. Bouveret and Lemaître's scale of fairness criteria for additive utility functions [13] says that an envy-free partition of goods satisfies min-max fair share, which in turn implies proportionality, which in turn implies max-min fair share. So our strongest notion of fairness is the weakest notion in fair division of indivisible goods (according to this scale). In addition, in additively separable hedonic games, we have seen that grand-coalition fairness and max-min fairness coincide. This is not the case in fair division (if one equates grand-coalition fairness with proportionality). Also note that Nash stability (or, equivalently, a definition of envy-freeness based on joining) implies min-max fairness but none of the stronger notions. In the setting of indivisible goods, envy-freeness even implies min-max fair share. So it is one of the strongest notions there. We consider these results surprising, as the intution from fair division of indivisible goods is no longer valid in this different context. The main reasons are the already mentioned difference between the number of allowed subsets of a partition and that players can "share" coalitions. This missing intuition is also a reason of why we have checked in detail whether any known stability notions imply one of our fairness notions.

Then we have studied the complexity of computing threshold coalitions and deciding whether an additively separable hedonic game admits a fair coalition structure. Although nearly all of these problems are intractable, our fairness criteria still have some meaning. They give additional motivation to notions of stability, such as Nash stability. Moreover, in a decentralized setting the hardness of a problem can be "distributed" (of course, the intractability cannot disappear). Giving players a yardstick for fairness that only depends on their own preferences reduces the amount of communication that is necessary to check whether a coalition structure is fair. Our complexity results are also comparable to the results by Bouveret and Lemaître [13] and Heinen et al. [27] with the exception that no lower bound is known for deciding whether a max-min fair-share allocation exists, whereas in ASHGs we know that the corresponding problem is NP-complete. Also note that with min-max fairness we have found a notion that is strictly stronger than individual rationality, but is still satisfied by every coalition structure maximizing utilitarian social welfare in symmetric additively separable hedonic games. At last, we have initiated the study of price of fairness in hedonic games. Our results here are unsatisfactory in the sense that either the price is unbounded or not very informative.

Therefore, we consider finding suitable restrictions to players' valuation functions such that the maximum price of min-max fairness is bounded by a nontrivial constant an interesting research question for the future. Interesting future work would also be identifying (other) sufficient conditions that imply the existence of a fair coalition structure, determining the complexity of searching for a min-max fair coalition structure in symmetric additively separable hedonic games, and showing Σ_2^p-hardness of MIN-MAX-EXIST.

Acknowledgments

We thank the anonymous reviewers for their helpful comments. This work was supported in part by DFG grant RO-1202/14-2.

REFERENCES

[1] G. Amanatidis, E. Markakis, A. Nikzad, and A. Saberi. Approximation algorithms for computing maximin share allocations. In *Proceedings of the 42nd International Colloquium on Automata, Languages, and Programming*, pages 39–51. Springer-Verlag *Lecture Notes in Computer Science #9134*, July 2015.

[2] H. Aziz and F. Brandl. Existence of stability in hedonic coalition formation games. In *Proceedings of the 11th International Joint Conference on Autonomous Agents and Multiagent Systems*, pages 763–770. IFAAMAS, June 2012.

[3] H. Aziz, F. Brandt, and P. Harrenstein. Fractional hedonic games. In *Proceedings of the 13th International Joint Conference on Autonomous Agents and Multiagent Systems*, pages 5–12. IFAAMAS, May 2014.

[4] H. Aziz, F. Brandt, and H. Seedig. Computing desirable partitions in additively separable hedonic games. *Artificial Intelligence*, 195:316–334, 2013.

[5] H. Aziz, S. Gaspers, J. Gudmundsson, J. Mestre, and H. Täubig. Welfare maximization in fractional hedonic games. In *Proceedings of the 24th International Joint Conference on Artificial Intelligence*, pages 461–467. AAAI Press/IJCAI, July 2015.

[6] H. Aziz and R. Savani. Hedonic games. In F. Brandt, V. Conitzer, U. Endriss, J. Lang, and A. Procaccia, editors, *Handbook of Computational Social Choice*, chapter 15. Cambridge University Press, 2016. To appear.

[7] C. Ballester. NP-completeness in hedonic games. *Games and Economic Behavior*, 49(1):1–30, 2004.

[8] S. Banerjee, H. Konishi, and T. Sönmez. Core in a simple coalition formation game. *Social Choice and Welfare*, 18(1):135–153, 2001.

[9] V. Bilò, A. Fanelli, M. Flammini, G. Monaco, and L. Moscardelli. Nash stability in fractional hedonic games. In *Proceedings of the 10th International Workshop on Internet & Network Economics*, pages 486–491. Springer-Verlag *Lecture Notes in Computer Science #8877*, Dec. 2014.

[10] V. Bilò, A. Fanelli, M. Flammini, G. Monaco, and L. Moscardelli. On the price of stability of fractional hedonic games. In *Proceedings of the 14th International Joint Conference on Autonomous Agents and Multiagent Systems*, pages 1239–1247. IFAAMAS, May 2015.

[11] A. Bogomolnaia and M. Jackson. The stability of hedonic coalition structures. *Games and Economic Behavior*, 38(2):201–230, 2002.

[12] S. Bouveret, Y. Chevaleyre, and N. Maudet. Fair allocation of indivisible goods. In F. Brandt, V. Conitzer, U. Endriss, J. Lang, and A. Procaccia, editors, *Handbook of Computational Social Choice*, chapter 12. Cambridge University Press, 2016. To appear.

[13] S. Bouveret and M. Lemaître. Characterizing conflicts in fair division of indivisible goods using a scale of criteria. *Journal of Autonomous Agents and Multi-Agent Systems*. To appear. A preliminary version appeared in the proceedings of AAMAS-2014.

[14] S. Brânzei and K. Larson. Coalitional affinity games and the stability gap. In *Proceedings of the 21st International Joint Conference on Artificial Intelligence*, pages 79–84. AAAI Press/IJCAI, 2009.

[15] E. Budish. The combinatorial assignment problem: Approximate competitive equilibrium from equal incomes. *Journal of Political Economy*, 119(6):1061–1103, 2011.

[16] I. Caragiannis, C. Kaklamanis, P. Kanellopoulos, and M. Kyropoulou. The efficiency of fair division. *Theory of Computing Systems*, 50(4):589–610, 2012.

[17] K. Cechlárová and A. Romero-Medina. Stability in coalition formation games. *International Journal of Game Theory*, 29(4):487–494, 2001.

[18] Y. Chevaleyre, P. Dunne, U. Endriss, J. Lang, M. Lemaître, N. Maudet, J. Padget, S. Phelps, J. Rodríguez-Aguilar, and P. Sousa. Issues in multiagent resource allocation. *Informatica*, 30(1):3–31, 2006.

[19] S. de Jong, K. Tuyls, and K. Verbeeck. Fairness in multi-agent systems. *The Knowledge Engineering Review*, 23(2):153–180, 2008.

[20] D. Dimitrov, P. Borm, R. Hendrickx, and S. Sung. Simple priorities and core stability in hedonic games. *Social Choice and Welfare*, 26(2):421–433, 2006.

[21] J. Drèze and J. Greenberg. Hedonic coalitions: Optimality and stability. *Econometrica*, 48(4):987–1003, 1980.

[22] E. Elkind, A. Fanelli, and M. Flammini. Price of Pareto optimality in hedonic games. In *Proceedings of the 30th AAAI Conference on Artificial Intelligence*. AAAI Press, Feb. 2016. To appear.

[23] E. Elkind and J. Rothe. Cooperative game theory. In J. Rothe, editor, *Economics and Computation. An Introduction to Algorithmic Game Theory, Computational Social Choice, and Fair Division*, chapter 3, pages 135–193. Springer-Verlag, 2015.

[24] E. Elkind and M. Wooldridge. Hedonic coalition nets. In *Proceedings of the 8th International Joint Conference on Autonomous Agents and Multiagent Systems*, pages 417–424. IFAAMAS, May 2009.

[25] M. Garey and D. Johnson. *Computers and Intractability: A Guide to the Theory of NP-Completeness*. W. H. Freeman and Company, 1979.

[26] J. Hajduková. Coalition formation games: A survey. *International Game Theory Review*, 8(4):613–641, 2006.

[27] T. Heinen, N. Nguyen, and J. Rothe. Fairness and rank-weighted utilitarianism in resource allocation. In *Proceedings of the 4th International Conference on Algorithmic Decision Theory*, pages 521–536. Springer-Verlag *Lecture Notes in Artificial Intelligence #9346*, Sept. 2015.

[28] M. Karakaya. Hedonic coalition formation games: A new stability notion. *Mathematical Social Sciences*, 61(3):157–165, 2011.

[29] D. Kurokawa, A. Procaccia, and J. Wang. When can the maximin share guarantee be guaranteed? In *Proceedings of the 30th AAAI Conference on Artificial Intelligence*. AAAI Press, Feb. 2016. To appear.

[30] J. Lang, A. Rey, J. Rothe, H. Schadrack, and L. Schend. Representing and solving hedonic games with ordinal preferences and thresholds. In *Proceedings of the 14th International Joint Conference on Autonomous Agents and Multiagent Systems*, pages 1229–1238. IFAAMAS, May 2015.

[31] J. Lang and J. Rothe. Fair division of indivisible goods. In J. Rothe, editor, *Economics and Computation. An Introduction to Algorithmic Game Theory, Computational*

Social Choice, and Fair Division, chapter 8, pages 493–550. Springer-Verlag, 2015.

[32] T. Morrill. The roommates problem revisited. *Journal of Economic Theory*, 145(5):1739–1756, 2010.

[33] T. Nguyen, M. Roos, and J. Rothe. A survey of approximability and inapproximability results for social welfare optimization in multiagent resource allocation. *Annals of Mathematics and Artificial Intelligence*, 68(1–3):65–90, 2013.

[34] D. Peters. Complexity of hedonic games with dichotomous preferences. In *Proceedings of the 30th AAAI Conference on Artificial Intelligence*. AAAI Press, Feb. 2016. To appear.

[35] D. Peters. Graphical hedonic games of bounded treewidth. In *Proceedings of the 30th AAAI Conference on Artificial Intelligence*. AAAI Press, Feb. 2016. To appear.

[36] D. Peters and E. Elkind. Simple causes of complexity in hedonic games. In *Proceedings of the 24th International Joint Conference on Artificial Intelligence*, pages 617–623. AAAI Press/IJCAI, July 2015.

[37] A. Procaccia and J. Wang. Fair enough: Guaranteeing approximate maximin shares. In *Proceedings of the 15th ACM Conference on Economics and Computation*, pages 675–692. ACM Press, 2014.

[38] M. Wright and Y. Vorobeychik. Mechanism design for team formation. In *Proceedings of the 29th AAAI Conference on Artificial Intelligence*, pages 1050–1056. AAAI Press, Jan. 2015.

Hedonic Games with Graph-restricted Communication

Ayumi Igarashi
University of Oxford
Oxford, United Kingdom
ayumi.igarashi@cs.ox.ac.uk

Edith Elkind
University of Oxford
Oxford, United Kingdom
elkind@cs.ox.ac.uk

ABSTRACT

We study hedonic coalition formation games in which cooperation among the players is restricted by a graph structure: a subset of players can form a coalition if and only if they are connected in the given graph. We investigate the complexity of finding stable outcomes in such games, for several notions of stability. In particular, we provide an efficient algorithm that finds an individually stable partition for an arbitrary hedonic game on an acyclic graph. We also introduce a new stability concept—in-neighbor stability—which is tailored for our setting. We show that the problem of finding an in-neighbor stable outcome admits a polynomial-time algorithm if the underlying graph is a path, but is NP-hard for arbitrary trees even for additively separable hedonic games; for symmetric additively separable games we obtain a PLS-hardness result.

General Terms

Algorithms, Economics, Theory

Keywords

Hedonic games, coalition formation, communication structure, trees

1. INTRODUCTION

In human and multiagent societies, agents often need to form coalitions in order to achieve their goals. The coalition formation process is guided by agents' beliefs about the performance of each potential coalition. Many important aspects of coalition formation can be studied using the formalism of *hedonic games* [3, 6]. In these games, each agent has preferences over all coalitions that she can be a part of, and an outcome is a partition of agents into coalitions. An important consideration in this context is *coalitional stability*: an outcome should be resistant to individual/group deviations, with different types of deviations giving rise to different notions of stability (such as core stability, individual stability, Nash stability, etc.; see the recent survey of Aziz and Savani [2] for an overview).

The standard model of hedonic games does not impose any restrictions on which coalitions may form. However, in reality we often encounter constraints on coalition formation. Consider, for instance, an international network of natural gas pipelines. It seems unlikely that two cities disconnected in the network would be able to coordinate a trading agreement without any help from intermediaries. Such restrictions on communication structure can be naturally described by undirected graphs, by identifying agents with nodes, communication links with edges, and feasible coalitions with connected subgraphs. In the context of cooperative transferable utility games this model was proposed in the seminal paper of Myerson [19], and has received a considerable amount of attention since then. In contrast, very little is known about hedonic games with graph-restricted communication, though some existing results for general non-transferable utility games have implications for this setting. In particular, the famous result of Demange [9] concerning stability in cooperative games on trees extends to non-transferable utility games, and implies that every hedonic game whose communication structure is acyclic admits a core stable partition (we discuss this result in more detail in Section 5). However, no attempt has been made to obtain similar results for other hedonic games solution concepts, or to explore algorithmic implications of constraints on the communication structure (such as acyclicity or having a small number of connected subgraphs) for computing the core and other solutions. The goal of this paper is to make the first step towards filling this gap.

Our contribution Inspired by Demange's work, we focus on hedonic games on acyclic graphs. We consider several well-studied notions of stability for hedonic games, such as individual stability, Nash stability, core stability and strict core stability (see Section 2 for definitions), and ask two questions: (1) does acyclicity of the communication structure guarantee the existence of a stable outcome? (2) does it lead to an efficient algorithm for computing a stable outcome, and if not, are there additional constraints on the communication structure that can be used to obtain such as algorithm? We remark that, in general, to represent the preferences of a player in an n-player hedonic game, we need to specify $2^{n-1}(2^{n-1}-1)/2$ values, which may be problematic if we are interested in algorithms whose running time is polynomial in n. We consider two approaches to circumvent this difficulty: (a) working in the oracle model, where an algorithm may submit a query of the form (i, X, Y) where X and Y are two coalitions that both contain i, and learn in unit time whether i prefers X to Y, Y to X or is indifferent between them; (b) considering specific succinct representations of hedonic games, such as additively separable hedonic games [6], which can be described using $n(n-1)$ numbers.

We observe that Demange's algorithm for the core runs in time that is polynomial in the number of connected subtrees of the underlying graph G (in the oracle model), and use similar ideas to obtain an algorithm for finding an outcome that is both core stable and individually stable as well as an algorithm for finding a Nash stable outcome (if it exists). The running time of these algorithms can be bounded in the same way; in particular, they run in polynomial time when G is a path. However, we show that when G is a star,

Appears in: *Proceedings of the 15th International Conference on Autonomous Agents and Multiagent Systems (AAMAS 2016), J. Thangarajah, K. Tuyls, C. Jonker, S. Marsella (eds.), May 9–13, 2016, Singapore.*

finding a core stable, strictly core stable or Nash stable outcome is NP-hard, even if we restrict ourselves to very simple subclasses of additively separable hedonic games. For symmetric additively separable hedonic games, we show that the PLS-hardness result for Nash stability [13] holds even if G is a star.

In contrast, acyclicity turns out to be sufficient for individual stability: we show that every hedonic game on an acyclic graph admits an individually stable partition, and, moreover, such a partition can be computed in time polynomial in the number of players (in the oracle model). We believe that this result is remarkable, since in the absence of communication constraints finding an individually stable outcome is hard even for (symmetric) additively separable hedonic games [22, 13], and finding a Nash stable outcome in such games remains hard even for games on stars (Section 6).

Another contribution of our paper is a new stability concept that is tailored specifically to hedonic games on graphs, and captures the intuition that, to join a group, a player should be approved by the members of the group who know him. The resulting solution concept, which we call *in-neighbor stability*, lies between Nash stability and individual stability. However, we show that from the algorithmic perspective it behaves similarly to Nash stability; in particular, finding an in-neighbor stable outcome is NP-hard for additively separable hedonic games on stars and PLS-hard for symmetric additively separable hedonic games on stars. Our computational complexity results are summarized in Table 1.

Related work Sung and Dimitrov [22] were the first to consider complexity issues in additively separable hedonic games (ASHGs); they prove that it is NP-hard to determine if a game admits a core stable, strict core stable, individually stable, or Nash sable outcome (see also [20]). Aziz et al. [1] extend the first two or these results to symmetric additively separable hedonic games (SASHGs). While SASHGs always admit a Nash stable or individually stable partition [6, 7], finding one may still be difficult: Gairing and Savani [13] prove that finding such partitions is PLS-hard (PLS-hardness is a complexity class for total search problems, see [21]). The running time of some of our algorithms is polynomial in the number of connected coalitions; see the recent work of Elkind [12] for a characterization of graph families for which this quantity is polynomial in the number of nodes. Some papers [4, 5] use the phrase "hedonic game on a tree" to refer to a hedonic game where each player i has a value $v_i(j)$ for every other player j, and pairs $\{i, j\}$ such that $v_i(j) \neq 0$ or $v_j(i) \neq 0$ form a tree; the preference relation of player i is computed based on the values $v_i(j)$: the value of a coalition S, $i \in S$, could be $\sum_{j\in S\setminus\{i\}} v_i(j)$ (this corresponds to ASHGs) or $\frac{1}{|S|}\sum_{j\in S\setminus\{i\}} v_i(j)$ (such games are known as *fractional hedonic games*). This framework is different from ours: we allow preferences that are not derived from values assigned to individual players, and in the additively separable case we allow non-adjacent players to have a non-zero value for each other.

Notes and Comments. An extended version with full proofs is available on arXiv [16].

2. PRELIMINARIES

We start by introducing basic notation and definitions of hedonic games and graph theory.

Hedonic games A *hedonic game* is a pair $(N, (\succeq_i)_{i\in N})$ where N is a finite set of players and each $\succeq_i$ is a complete and transitive preference relation over the nonempty subsets of N including player i. The subsets of N are referred to as *coalitions*. We let $\mathcal{N}_i$ denote the collection of all coalitions containing i. We call a coalition $X \subseteq N$ *individually rational* if $X \succeq_i \{i\}$ for all $i \in X$. Let $\succ_i$ denote the strict preference derived from $\succeq_i$, i.e., $X \succ_i Y$ if $X \succeq_i Y$, but $Y \not\succeq_i X$. Similarly, let $\sim_i$ denote the indifference relation induced by $\succeq_i$, i.e., $X \sim_i Y$ if $X \succeq_i Y$ and $Y \succeq_i X$.

An important subclass of hedonic games is *additively separable games*. These games model situations where each player has a specific value for every other player, and ranks coalitions according to the total value of their members [6]. Formally, a preference profile $(\succeq_i)_{i\in N}$ is said to be *additively separable* if there exists a utility matrix $U : N \times N \to \mathbb{R}$ such that for each $i \in N$ and each $X, Y \in \mathcal{N}_i$ we have $X \succeq_i Y$ if and only if $\sum_{j\in X} U(i, j) \geq \sum_{j\in Y} U(i, j)$ [6]. Without loss of generality, we will assume that $U(i, i) = 0$ for each $i \in N$. An additively separable preference is said to be *symmetric* if the utility matrix $U : N \times N \to \mathbb{R}$ is symmetric, i.e., $U(i, j) = U(j, i)$ for all $i, j \in N$. Dimitrov et al. [10] studied a subclass of additively separable preferences, which they called *enemy-oriented preferences*. Under these preferences each player considers every other player to be either a friend or an enemy, and has strong aversion towards her enemies: $U(i, j) \in \{1, -|N|\}$ for each $i, j \in N$ with $i \neq j$.

An *outcome* of a hedonic game is a partition of players into disjoint coalitions. Given a partition π of N and a player $i \in N$, let $\pi(i)$ denote the unique coalition in π that contains i. The first stability concept we will introduce is *individual rationality*, which is often considered to be a minimum requirement that solutions should satisfy. A partition π of N is said to be *individually rational* if all players weakly prefer their own coalitions to staying alone, i.e., $\pi(i) \succeq_i \{i\}$ for all $i \in N$.

The *core* is one of the most studied solution concepts in hedonic games [11, 3, 6]. A coalition $X \subseteq N$ *strongly blocks* a partition π of N if $X \succ_i \pi(i)$ for all $i \in X$; it *weakly blocks* π if $X \succeq_i \pi(i)$ for all $i \in X$ and $X \succ_j \pi(j)$ for some $j \in X$. A partition π of N is said to be *core stable* (CR) if no coalition $X \subseteq N$ strongly blocks π; it is said to be *strictly core stable* (SCR) if no coalition $X \subseteq N$ weakly blocks π.

We will also consider stability notions that capture resistance to deviations by individual players. Consider a player $i \in N$ and a pair of coalitions $X \notin \mathcal{N}_i$, $Y \in \mathcal{N}_i$. A player i *wants to deviate* from Y to X if $X \cup \{i\} \succ_i Y$. A player $j \in X$ *accepts* a deviation of i to X if $X \cup \{i\} \succeq_j X$. A deviation of i from Y to X is

- an *NS-deviation* if i wants to deviate from Y to X.
- an *IS-deviation* if it is an NS-deviation and all players in X accept it.

A partition π is called *Nash stable (NS)* (respectively, *individually stable (IS)*) if no player $i \in N$ has an NS-deviation (respectively, an IS-deviation) from $\pi(i)$ to another coalition $X \in \pi$ or to $\emptyset$.

We have the following containment relations among these classes of outcomes: SCR $\subseteq$ CR, SCR $\subseteq$ IS, NS $\subseteq$ IS. However, a core stable outcome need not be individually stable, and an individually stable outcome may fail to be in the core.

Graphs and digraphs An *undirected graph*, or simply a *graph*, is a pair (N, L), where N is a finite set of *nodes* and $L \subseteq N \times N$ is a collection of *edges* between nodes. In this paper, we only consider graphs without self-loops and parallel edges. Given a set of nodes X, the *subgraph of* (N, L) *induced by* X is the graph (X, L_X), where $L_X = \{\{i, j\} \in L \mid i, j \in X\}$.

For a graph (N, L), a sequence of distinct nodes $(i_1, i_2, \ldots, i_k)$, $k \geq 2$, is called a *path* in L if $\{i_h, i_{h+1}\} \in L$ for $h = 1, 2, \ldots, k-1$. A path $(i_1, i_2, \ldots, i_k)$, $k \geq 3$, is said to be a *cycle* in L if $\{i_k, i_1\} \in L$. A graph (N, L) is said to be a *forest* if it contains no cycles. A subset $X \subseteq N$ is said to be *connected in* (N, L) if for every pair of distinct nodes $i, j \in X$ there is a path between i and j in L_X. The collection of all connected subsets of N in (N, L) is denoted by $\mathcal{F}_L$; also, we write $\mathcal{F}_L(i) = \mathcal{F}_L \cap \mathcal{N}_i$. By convention,

	Acyclic graphs		Stars			Paths
	Arbitrary	Additive	Additive	S-additive	S-enemy	Arbitrary
SCR	-	NP-h	NP-h	NP-h (Th.12)	NP-h* (Th.11)	?
CR	-	NP-h*	NP-h*	NP-h*	NP-h* (Th.10)	P ([9])
NS	-	NP-c	NP-c (Th.16)	PLS-c (Th.19)	P (Prop.20)	P (Th.13)
INS	-	NP-c	NP-c (Th.15)	PLS-c (Th.18)	P	P (Th.13)
IR-INS	-	NP-c ([16])	P (Prop.17)	P	P	P (Th.13)
IS	P (Th.1)	P	P	P	P	P

Table 1: Complexity of computing stable outcomes for hedonic games on acyclic graphs. The top row corresponds to restrictions on graphs; the second row from the top indicates restrictions on preference profiles. The positive results for unrestricted preferences are in the oracle model. To avoid dealing with representation issues, when a problem is NP-hard for additively separable games on trees, we do not consider its complexity for unrestricted preferences (indicated by '-'). The hardness result marked with * holds with respect to Turing reductions. When no reference is given, the result follows trivially from other results in the table. The results for paths hold for all trees with n nodes and $\text{poly}(n)$ connected subtrees.

we assume that $\emptyset \notin \mathcal{F}_L$. A forest (N, L) is said to be a *tree* if N is connected in (N, L). A tree (N, L) is called a *star* if there exists a central node $s \in N$ such that $L = \{\{s, j\} \mid j \in N \setminus \{s\}\}$. A subset $X \subseteq N$ of a graph (N, L) is said to be a *clique* if for every pair of distinct nodes $i, j \in X$ we have $\{i, j\} \in L$.

A *directed graph*, or a *digraph*, is a pair (N, A) where N is a finite set of nodes and A is a family of ordered pairs of nodes from N. The elements of A are called the *arcs*. A sequence of distinct nodes $(i_1, i_2, \dots, i_k)$, $k \geq 2$, is called a *directed path* in A if $(i_h, i_{h+1}) \in A$ for $h = 1, 2, \dots, k-1$. Given a digraph (N, A), let $L(A) = \{\{i, j\} \mid (i, j) \in A\}$: the graph $(N, L(A))$ is the *undirected version* of (N, A). A digraph (N, A) is said to be a *rooted tree* if $(N, L(A))$ is a tree and each node has at most one arc entering it. A rooted tree has exactly one node that no arc enters, called the *root*, and there exists a unique directed path from the root to every node of N.

Let (N, A) be a rooted tree. We say that a node $j \in N$ is a *parent* of i in A if $(j, i) \in A$. We denote by $\text{pr}(i, A)$ the unique parent of i in A. A node $j \in N$ is called a *successor* of i in A if there exists a directed path from i to j in A. We write

$$\text{succ}(i, A) = \{i\} \cup \{j \in N \mid j \text{ is a successor of } i \text{ in } A\}.$$

A node $i \in N$ is called a *child* of $X \subseteq N$ in A if $i \notin X$ and $\text{pr}(i, A) \in X$. We write

$$\text{ch}(X, A) = \{i \in N \mid i \notin X \text{ and } \text{pr}(i, A) \in X\}.$$

The *height* of a node $i \in N$ of (N, A) is defined inductively: $\text{height}(i, A) = 0$ if $\text{succ}(i, A) = \{i\}$ and $\text{height}(i, A) = 1 + \max_{j \in \text{ch}(\{i\}, A)} \text{height}(j, A)$ otherwise.

3. OUR MODEL

The goal of this paper is to study hedonic games where agent communication is constrained by a graph.

DEFINITION 1. *A* hedonic game with graph structure, *or a* hedonic graph game, *is a triple $(N, (\succeq_i)_{i \in N}, L)$ where $(N, (\succeq_i)_{i \in N})$ is a hedonic game, and $L \subseteq \{\{i, j\} \mid i \neq j, i, j \in N\}$ is the set of communication links between players. A coalition $X \subseteq N$ is said to be* feasible *if it is connected in (N, L).*

If (N, L) is a clique, a hedonic graph game $(N, (\succeq_i)_{i \in N}, L)$ is equivalent to the ordinary hedonic game $(N, (\succeq_i)_{i \in N})$.

A partition π of N is said to be *feasible* if $\pi \subseteq \mathcal{F}_L$. An *outcome* of a hedonic graph game is a feasible partition. The standard definitions of stability concepts (see Section 2) can be adapted to hedonic graph games in a straightforward manner. Specifically, we say that a coalitional deviation is *feasible* if the deviating coalition itself is feasible; an individual deviation where player i joins a coalition X is *feasible* if $X \cup \{i\}$ is feasible. Now, we modify the definitions in Section 2 by only requiring stability against feasible deviations.

We use the notation (N, U, L) to denote an additively separable graph game with utility matrix $U : N \times N \to \mathbb{R}$.

EXAMPLE 1. Consider the coalition formation problem in a parliament consisting of three parties: left-wing (ℓ), centrist (c), and right-wing (r). Then ℓ and r cannot form a coalition without c. We describe this scenario as an additively separable graph game (N, U, L) where $N = \{\ell, \mathsf{c}, \mathsf{r}\}$, $L = \{\{\ell, \mathsf{c}\}, \{\mathsf{c}, \mathsf{r}\}\}$, and the utility matrix U is given by

$$U(\ell, \mathsf{c}) = 1, U(\ell, \mathsf{r}) = -2, U(\mathsf{c}, \ell) = 2,$$
$$U(\mathsf{c}, \mathsf{r}) = 0, U(\mathsf{r}, \mathsf{c}) = 2, U(\mathsf{r}, \ell) = 0.$$

The resulting preference profile is as follows:

$$\ell : \{\ell, \mathsf{c}\} \succ_\ell \{\ell\} \succ_\ell \{\ell, \mathsf{c}, \mathsf{r}\} \succ_\ell \{\ell, \mathsf{r}\}$$
$$\mathsf{c} : \{\ell, \mathsf{c}, \mathsf{r}\} \sim_\mathsf{c} \{\ell, \mathsf{c}\} \succ_\mathsf{c} \{\mathsf{c}, \mathsf{r}\} \sim_\mathsf{c} \{\mathsf{c}\}$$
$$\mathsf{r} : \{\ell, \mathsf{c}, \mathsf{r}\} \sim_\mathsf{r} \{\mathsf{c}, \mathsf{r}\} \succ_\mathsf{r} \{\ell, \mathsf{r}\} \sim_\mathsf{r} \{\mathsf{r}\}$$

The individually rational feasible partitions of this game are $\pi_1 = \{\{\ell, \mathsf{c}\}, \{\mathsf{r}\}\}$, $\pi_2 = \{\{\ell\}, \{\mathsf{c}, \mathsf{r}\}\}$, and $\pi_3 = \{\{\ell\}, \{\mathsf{c}\}, \{\mathsf{r}\}\}$. The partition π_1 is both core stable and individually stable. However, there is no Nash stable partition in this game: in π_1, player r wants to join $\{\ell, \mathsf{c}\}$, while in π_2 and π_3, player c wants to join $\{\ell\}$.

4. INDIVIDUAL STABILITY

The main contributions of this section are (1) an efficient algorithm for finding an individually stable feasible partition in a hedonic graph game whose underlying graph is a forest; (2) a proof that in the presence of cycles the existence of an IS feasible partition is not guaranteed.

THEOREM 1. *Suppose that we are given oracle access to the preference relations $\succeq_i$ of all players in a hedonic graph game $\mathcal{G} = (N, (\succeq_i)_{i \in N}, L)$, where (N, L) is a forest. Then we can find an individually stable feasible outcome of $\mathcal{G}$ in time polynomial in $|N|$.*

PROOF. We first give an informal description of our algorithm, followed by pseudocode. If the input graph (N, L) is a forest, we can process each of its connected components separately, so we can assume that (N, L) is a tree. We choose an arbitrary node r to be the root; this transforms (N, L) into a rooted tree (N, A^r)

with root r and determines a hierarchy of players. For each player i, from the bottom player to the top of the hierarchy, we compute a tentative partitioning of the subtree rooted at i. To this end, among all coalitions that i's children belong to, we identify those whose members would be willing to let i join them. Then we let i choose between his most preferred option among all such coalitions and the singleton $\{i\}$. We then check if any of the successors of i who are adjacent to i's coalition want to join it; we let them do so if they are approved by the current coalition members.

For a family of subsets $\mathcal{P} \subseteq \mathcal{N}_i$, we set

$$\max_i \mathcal{P} = \{\, X \in \mathcal{P} \mid X \succeq_i Y \text{ for all } Y \in \mathcal{P} \,\}.$$

Given a pair of nonempty subsets $X, Y \subseteq N$, we write $X \overset{m}{\succeq} Y$ if $X \cap Y \neq \emptyset$ and $X \succeq_i Y$ for all $i \in X \cap Y$.

Algorithm 1 Finding IS partitions

Input: tree (N, L), $r \in N$, oracles for $\succeq_i$, $i \in N$.
Output: $\pi^{(r)}$.

1: make a rooted tree (N, A^r) with root r by orienting all the edges in L.
2: initialize $\mathrm{B}(i) \leftarrow \emptyset$ and $\pi^{(i)} \leftarrow \emptyset$ for each $i \in N$.
3: **for** $t = 0, \ldots, \mathrm{height}(r, A^r)$ **do**
4: **for** $i \in N$ with $\mathrm{height}(i, A^r) = t$ **do**
5: $C(i) = \{\, k \in \mathrm{ch}(\{i\}, A^r) \mid \mathrm{B}(k) \cup \{i\} \overset{m}{\succeq} \mathrm{B}(k) \,\}$.
6: choose $\mathrm{B}(i) \in \max_i(\{\{i\}\} \cup \{\, \mathrm{B}(k) \cup \{i\} \mid k \in C(i) \,\})$.
7: **while** there exists $j \in \mathrm{ch}(\mathrm{B}(i), A^r)$ such that $\mathrm{B}(i) \cup \{j\} \succ_j \mathrm{B}(j)$ and $\mathrm{B}(i) \cup \{j\} \overset{m}{\succeq} \mathrm{B}(i)$ **do**
8: $\mathrm{B}(i) \leftarrow \mathrm{B}(i) \cup \{j\}$
9: **end while**
10: $\pi^{(i)} \leftarrow \{\mathrm{B}(i)\} \cup \{\, \pi^{(k)} \mid k \in \mathrm{ch}(\mathrm{B}(i), A^r) \,\}$
11: **end for**
12: **end for**

We will now argue that Algorithm 1 correctly identifies an individually stable partition. Our argument is based on two lemmas.

LEMMA 2. *For every $i \in N$ and every $k \in ch(\{i\}, A^r)$, if $\mathrm{B}(k) \cup \{i\} \overset{m}{\succeq} \mathrm{B}(k)$, then $\mathrm{B}(i) \succeq_i \mathrm{B}(k) \cup \{i\}$.*

Lemma 2 follows immediately from the choice of $\mathrm{B}(i)$ in Line 6 and the stopping criterion of the **while** loop in lines 7–9.

LEMMA 3. *For each $i \in N$, $j \in succ(i, A^r)$ and all $X \in \pi^{(i)} \cup \{\emptyset\}$ there is no IS feasible deviation of j from $\pi^{(i)}(j)$ to X.*

PROOF. We use induction on $\mathrm{height}(i, A^r)$. For $\mathrm{height}(i, A^r) = 0$ our assertion is trivial. Suppose that it holds for all $j \in N$ with $\mathrm{height}(j, A^r) \leq t - 1$, and consider $i \in N$ with $\mathrm{height}(i, A^r) = t$. Assume towards a contradiction that there exists an IS feasible deviation of $j \in \mathrm{succ}(i, A^r)$ from $\pi^{(i)}(j)$ to $X \in \pi^{(i)} \cup \{\emptyset\}$, i.e., $X \cup \{j\}$ is connected, and

$$X \cup \{j\} \succ_j \pi^{(i)}(j), \text{ and} \tag{1}$$

$$X \cup \{j\} \overset{m}{\succeq} X. \tag{2}$$

By construction, $\pi^{(i)}$ is individually rational, so $X \neq \emptyset$. If $j \notin \mathrm{B}(i)$ and $X \neq \mathrm{B}(i)$, this would contradict the induction hypothesis. Moreover, by the stopping criteria in Line 7, it cannot be the case that $j \notin \mathrm{B}(i)$ and $X = \mathrm{B}(i)$. Thus, $j \in \mathrm{B}(i)$ and $X = \mathrm{B}(k)$ for some $k \in \mathrm{ch}(\{j\}, A^r)$. If $j = i$, Lemma 2 and (2) imply that $\pi^{(i)}(i) = \mathrm{B}(i) \succeq_i \mathrm{B}(k) \cup \{i\}$, contradicting (1). Thus, $j \neq i$.

Suppose that player j joins the coalition $\mathrm{B}(i)$ when $\mathrm{B}(i)$ is initialized in Line 6. Then, $j \in \mathrm{B}(k^*)$ for some $k^* \in \mathrm{ch}(\{i\}, A^r)$. It follows that $\mathrm{B}(k) \in \pi^{(k^*)}$, since $k \notin \mathrm{B}(k^*)$ and $k \in \mathrm{ch}(\{j\}, A^r)$. Further, the second stopping criterion of the **while** loop in Line 7 ensures that j's utility does not decrease during the execution of Algorithm 1. Thus, $\mathrm{B}(i) \succeq_j \mathrm{B}(k^*)$. Combining this with (1) and (2) yields

$$\mathrm{B}(k) \cup \{j\} \succ_j \pi^{(i)}(j) = \mathrm{B}(i) \succeq_j \mathrm{B}(k^*) = \pi^{(k^*)}(j),$$

and $\mathrm{B}(k) \cup \{j\} \overset{m}{\succeq} \mathrm{B}(k)$. It follows that $\pi^{(k^*)}$ admits an IS feasible deviation of j from $\pi^{(k^*)}(j)$ to $\mathrm{B}(k) \in \pi^{(k^*)}$. This contradicts the induction hypothesis.

On the other hand, suppose that player j joins $\mathrm{B}(i)$ during the **while** loop in Lines 7–9. Then at that point player j is made better off by leaving $\mathrm{B}(j)$ and joining $\mathrm{B}(i)$. From then on, she vetoes all candidates whose presence would make her worse off. Hence, $\mathrm{B}(i) \succ_j \mathrm{B}(j)$. However, (2) and Lemma 2 imply that $\mathrm{B}(j) \succeq_j \mathrm{B}(k) \cup \{j\}$. Thus, $\mathrm{B}(i) \succ_j \mathrm{B}(k) \cup \{j\}$, contradicting (1). □

The partition $\pi^{(r)}$ is feasible by construction, so applying Lemma 3 with $i = r$ implies that $\pi^{(r)}$ is an individually stable feasible partition of N.

It remains to analyze the running time of Algorithm 1. Consider the execution of the algorithm for a fixed player i. Let $c = |\mathrm{ch}(\{i\}, A^r)|$, $s = |\mathrm{succ}(i, A^r)|$. Line 5 requires at most s oracle queries: no successor of i is queried more than once. Line 6 requires c oracle queries. Moreover, at each iteration of the **while** loop in lines 7–9 at least one player joins $\mathrm{B}(i)$, so there are at most s iterations, in each iteration we consider at most s candidates, and for each candidate we perform at most s queries. Summing over all players, we conclude that the number or oracle queries is bounded by $O(|N|^4)$. This completes the proof of the theorem. □

Theorem 1 provides a constructive proof that every hedonic graph game whose underlying graph (N, L) is a forest admits an individually stable feasible partition. In contrast, if (N, L) contains a cycle, the players' preferences can always be chosen so that no individually stable feasible partition exists.

PROPOSITION 4. *Suppose that the graph (N, L) contains a cycle $C = \{i_1, i_2, \ldots, i_k\}$ with $k \geq 3$, $\{i_h, i_{h+1}\} \in L$ for $h = 1, 2, \ldots, k$, where $i_{k+1} := i_1$. Then, we can choose preference relations $(\succeq_i)_{i \in N}$ so that the set of IS feasible partitions of the game $(N, (\succeq_i)_{i \in N}, L)$ is empty.*

PROOF. Let d be the smallest natural number that does not divide k. For each $i_h \in C$, define

$$\mathcal{C}(i_h) = \{\, X \in \mathcal{F}_L(i_h) \mid X \subseteq C, |X| \leq d \,\}.$$

Notice that $d \geq 2$, and hence $\{i_h\}, \{i_h, i_{h+1}\} \in \mathcal{C}(i_h)$. Define a graph game $(N, (\succeq_i)_{i \in N}, L)$ so that for each $i_h \in C$ we have

1. $X \succ_{i_h} Y$ for all $X, Y \in \mathcal{C}(i_h)$ such that $i_{h+1} \in X \setminus Y$,
2. $X \sim_{i_h} Y$ for all $X, Y \in \mathcal{C}(i_h)$ such that $i_{h+1} \in X \cap Y$,
3. $X \sim_{i_h} Y$ for all $X, Y \in \mathcal{C}(i_h)$ such that $i_{h+1} \notin X \cup Y$,
4. $X \succ_{i_h} Y$ for all $X \in \mathcal{C}(i_h), Y \notin \mathcal{C}(i_h)$.

Let π be an arbitrary individually rational feasible partition of N. By individual rationality, $\pi(i) \in \mathcal{C}(i)$ for every $i \in C$. Since d does not divide k, there exists $Y \in \pi$ such that $|Y| \leq d - 1$ and $Y \subseteq C$. Let $Y = \{i_{h+1}, i_{h+2}, \ldots, i_m\}$. Then we have $\{i_h\} \cup Y \succ_{i_h} \pi(i_h)$, and $\{i_h\} \cup Y \sim_{i_j} Y$ for all $i_j \in Y$. Thus, π is not individually stable. □

We summarize our results for individually stable feasible partitions in the following corollary.

COROLLARY 5. *For the class of hedonic graph games, the following statements are equivalent.*

(*i*) *(N, L) is a forest.*

(*ii*) *For every hedonic graph game $(N, (\succeq_i)_{i\in N}, L)$ there exists an individually stable feasible partition of N.*

5. CORE STABILITY

As mentioned in Section 1, classic results by Le Breton et al. [18] and Demange [8, 9] for non-transferable utility games imply an analogue of Corollary 5 for core stable partitions.

THEOREM 6 ([18, 8, 9]). *For the class of hedonic games with graph structure, the following statements are equivalent.*

(*i*) *(N, L) is a forest.*

(*ii*) *For every hedonic graph game $(N, (\succeq_i)_{i\in N}, L)$ there exists a core stable feasible partition of N.*

We will now show that these two results can be combined, in the following sense: if (N, L) is acyclic, then every hedonic game on (N, L) admits a feasible partition that belongs to the core and is individually stable; moreover, the converse is also true.

THEOREM 7. *For the class of hedonic games with graph structure, the following statements are equivalent.*

(i) *(N, L) is a forest.*

(ii) *For every hedonic graph game $(N, (\succeq_i)_{i\in N}, L)$, there exists a feasible partition of N that belongs to the core and is individually stable.*

PROOF. The direction (ii) $\Rightarrow$ (i) immediately follows from Theorem 6. We will prove (i) $\Rightarrow$ (ii). Recall that a preference relation $\succeq_1$ on a set X is a *refinement* of a preference relation $\succeq_2$ on X if for every $a, b \in X$ it holds that $a \succ_2 b$ implies $a \succ_1 b$.

Suppose that (N, L) is a forest. For each $i \in N$, let $>_i$ be a refinement of $\succeq_i$ that satisfies $X >_i Y$ whenever $X \sim_i Y$ and $Y \subsetneq X$. By Theorem 6, the game $(N, (>_i)_{i\in N}, L)$ admits a core stable feasible partition π. By construction, π is core stable in the original game $(N, (\succeq_i)_{i\in N}, L)$ as well. We will now argue that it is also individually stable. Assume towards a contradiction that there exists an IS feasible deviation of some player $i \in N$ from $\pi(i)$ to $X \in \pi \cup \{\emptyset\}$. That is, $X \cup \{i\} \in \mathcal{F}_L$, $X \cup \{i\} \succ_i \pi(i)$, and $X \cup \{i\} \succeq_j X$ for each $j \in X$. By construction of $(>_i)_{i\in N}$, this implies that $X \cup \{i\} >_i \pi(i)$ and $X \cup \{i\} >_j X$ for each $j \in X$. This contradicts the fact that π is a core stable partition of the game $(N, (>_i)_{i\in N}, L)$. □

5.1 Computational complexity of CR

Demange's proof that every hedonic graph game on an acyclic graph admits a core stable outcome is constructive: her paper [9] provides an algorithm to find a core stable partition. This algorithm is similar in flavor to Algorithm 1: it processes the players starting from the leaves and moving towards the root, calculates the "guarantee level" of each player, and then partitions the players into disjoint groups in such a way that the final outcome satisfies their "guarantee levels"; this is shown to ensure core stability. While Demange does not analyze the running time of her algorithm, it can be verified that it runs in time polynomial in the number of connected subsets of the underlying graph. Thus, in particular, Demange's algorithm runs in polynomial time if this graph is a path.

THEOREM 8 (IMPLICIT IN [9]). *Suppose that we are given oracle access to the preference relations $\succeq_i$ of all players in a hedonic graph game $\mathcal{G} = (N, (\succeq_i)_{i\in N}, L)$, where (N, L) is a forest. Then we can find a core stable feasible outcome of $\mathcal{G}$ in time polynomial in the number of connected subsets of (N, L).*

Combining Demange's algorithm with the construction in the proof of Theorem 7, we obtain an algorithm that has the same worst-case running time as Demange's algorithm and outputs a feasible partition that belongs to the core and is individually stable.

COROLLARY 9. *Suppose that we are given oracle access to the preference relations $\succeq_i$ of all players in a hedonic graph game $\mathcal{G} = (N, (\succeq_i)_{i\in N}, L)$, where (N, L) is a forest. Then we can find a feasible outcome of $\mathcal{G}$ that belongs to the core and is individually stable in time polynomial in the number of connected subsets of (N, L).*

However, if the number of connected subsets of (N, L) is superpolynomial in $|N|$, so is the running time of Demange's algorithm, because for each player i this algorithm considers all feasible coalitions containing i. Now, for many n-node trees the number of connected subtrees is superpolynomial in n: for instance, this is the case for every tree with $\omega(\log n)$ leaves, simply because we can delete any subset of leaves and still obtain a connected graph. Therefore, it is natural to ask if checking all feasible coalitions is indeed necessary. Note that when the goal is to find an individually stable partition, the answer to this question is "no": Algorithm 1 only considers some of the feasible coalitions, yet is capable of finding an individually stable feasible outcome. In contrast, for the core it seems unlikely that one can obtain a substantial improvement over the running time of Demange's algorithm: our next theorem shows that finding a core stable feasible partition of an additively separable hedonic graph game is NP-hard even if the underlying graph is a star and even if the input game is a symmetric enemy-oriented game.

THEOREM 10. *If one can find a core stable feasible partition in a symmetric enemy-oriented graph game whose underlying graph is a star in time polynomial in the number of players then* P = NP.

PROOF. We provide a reduction from the NP-complete CLIQUE problem [15]. An instance of CLIQUE is a pair (G, t), where G is an undirected graph and t is a positive integer. It is a "yes"-instance if G contains a clique of size at least t and a "no"-instance otherwise. We will show how a polynomial-time algorithm for our problem can be used to decide CLIQUE in polynomial time.

Given an instance (G, t) of CLIQUE, where $G = (V, E)$, we construct a symmetric enemy-oriented graph game as follows. We let $N = V \cup \{s\}$ and $L = \{\{s, v\} \mid v \in V\}$. We will now describe the (symmetric) matrix U. Briefly, player s likes all other players and two players in V like each other if and only if they are connected by an edge of G. Formally, we set $U(s, v) = 1$ for each $v \in V$ and for each $u, v \in V$ we set $U(u, v) = 1$ if $\{u, v\} \in E$ and $U(u, v) = -|V| - 1$ otherwise.

Let π be an individually rational feasible partition of this game. Note that all players in $N \setminus \pi(s)$ form singleton coalitions in π, and $\pi(s) \setminus \{s\}$ is a clique in G. We will now argue that π is core stable if and only if $\pi(s) \setminus \{s\}$ is a maximum-size clique in G.

Indeed, if C is a maximum-size clique in G and $|\pi(s) \setminus \{s\}| < |C|$, every player in $C \cup \{s\}$ strictly prefers $C \cup \{s\}$ to its current coalition. Conversely, suppose that $\pi(s) \setminus \{s\}$ is a maximum-size clique, yet coalition X strictly blocks π. Then it has to be the case that $s \in X$, and hence $|X| > |\pi(s)|$; but this means that $X \setminus \{s\}$

is not a clique, and therefore players in $X \setminus \{s\}$ prefer π to X, a contradiction.

It follows that, by looking at a core stable feasible outcome π, we can decide whether G contains a clique of size at least t. $\square$

Dimitrov et al. [10] show that finding a core outcome in symmetric enemy-oriented games is NP-hard; however, in their model there is no constraint on communication among the players, i.e., their result is for the case where (N, L) is a clique, whereas our result holds even if (N, L) is a star.

5.2 Computational complexity of SCR

Unlike core stable outcomes, strictly core stable outcomes need not exist even in symmetric enemy-oriented games on stars. Consider, for instance, a variant of our parliamentary coalition formation example (Example 1) where the centrist party (c) is equally happy to collaborate with the left-wing party (ℓ) or the right-wing party (r), but the left-wing party and the right-wing party hate each other. This setting can be captured by a symmetric enemy-oriented graph game whose underlying graph is a path, and whose core stable feasible partitions are $\pi_1 = \{\{\ell, \mathsf{c}\}, \{\mathsf{r}\}\}$ and $\pi_2 = \{\{\ell\}, \{\mathsf{c}, \mathsf{r}\}\}$. However, neither π_1 nor π_2 is in the strict core: π_1 is weakly blocked by $\{\mathsf{c}, \mathsf{r}\}$ and π_2 is weakly blocked by $\{\ell, \mathsf{c}\}$.

Our next theorem shows that checking whether a given symmetric enemy-oriented hedonic graph game admits a feasible outcome in the strict core is NP-hard with respect to Turing reductions, even if the underlying graph is a star.

THEOREM 11. *If there exists a polynomial-time algorithm that, given a symmetric enemy-oriented graph game whose underlying graph is a star, decides whether this game has a strictly core stable feasible partition then* P = NP.

PROOF SKETCH. We define UNIQUE CLIQUE as the decision problem of determining whether a graph has a unique maximum-size clique. That is, let s be the size of a maximum clique in G; G is a "yes"-instance of UNIQUE CLIQUE if it contains exactly one clique of size s and a "no"-instance otherwise. CLIQUE admits a Turing reduction to UNIQUE CLIQUE. Specifically, given an instance (G, t) of CLIQUE where $G = (V, E)$, we construct $|V|$ instances of UNIQUE CLIQUE as follows. For each $s = 1, \dots, |V|$, let C_s be a set of size s with $V \cap C_s = \emptyset$, and let $H_s = (V \cup C_s, E_s)$, where $\{u, v\} \in E_s$ if and only if $u, v \in C_s$, or $u, v \in V$ and $\{u, v\} \in E$. Note that the maximum clique size in G is r if and only if H_r is a "no"-instance of UNIQUE CLIQUE, but H_s is a "yes"-instance of UNIQUE CLIQUE for $r = s+1, \dots, |V|$. Hence, a polynomial-time algorithm for UNIQUE CLIQUE can be used to decide CLIQUE in polynomial time.

We will now argue that UNIQUE CLIQUE can be reduced to our problem. Given an undirected graph $G = (V, E)$, we construct the same symmetric enemy-oriented graph game (N, U, L) as in the proof of Theorem 10. Then, one can readily see that the G is a "yes"-instance of UNIQUE CLIQUE if and only if (N, U, L) has a feasible outcome that is strictly core stable. $\square$

For the broader class of symmetric additively separable hedonic graph games on stars, we obtain an NP-hardness result under the more standard notion of a many-one reduction (for games on cliques, this follows from the results of Aziz et al. [1]).

THEOREM 12. *Given a symmetric additively separable hedonic graph game whose underlying graph is a star, it is* NP*-hard to determine whether it has a strictly core stable feasible partition.*

PROOF SKETCH. Again, we provide a reduction from CLIQUE. Given an undirected graph $G = (V, E)$ and a positive integer

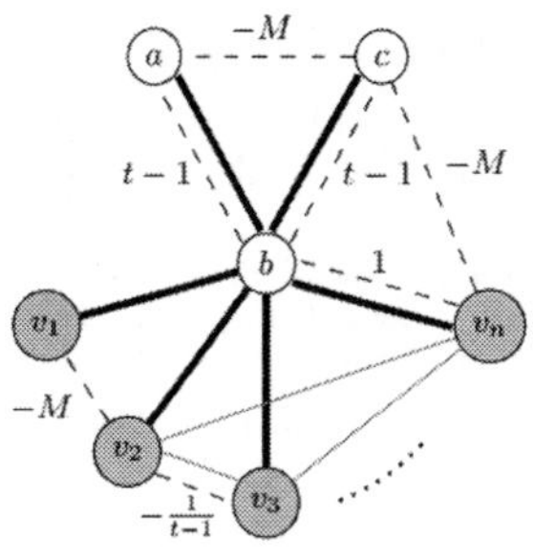

Figure 1: Graph used in the proof of Theorem 12. Thick black lines represent communication links between players, whereas gray lines stand for edges of the given instance G. Values on dashed lines are utilities of players.

$t \geq 2$, we construct a symmetric additively separable graph game (N, U, L) where $N = \{a, b, c\} \cup V$, $L = \{\{a, b\}, \{b, c\}\} \cup \{\{b, v\} \mid v \in V\}$. Let $M = |N| + 1$. The utility matrix $U : N \times N \to \mathbb{R}$ is given as follows (see Figure 1):

$$U(a, b) = U(c, b) = t - 1, U(a, c) = -M,$$
$$U(a, v) = U(c, v) = -M, U(b, v) = 1 \text{ for each } v \in V,$$
$$U(u, v) = -1/(t-1) \text{ if } \{u, v\} \in E$$
$$\text{and } U(u, v) = -M \text{ otherwise, for all } u, v \in V.$$

Suppose that G contains a clique C of size t. Then, the partition $\pi = \{\{a\}, \{c\}, C \cup \{b\}\} \cup \{\{v\} \mid v \in V \setminus C\}$ can be shown to be strictly core stable. Conversely, if there exists a strictly core stable feasible partition π of N, $\pi(b) \setminus \{b\}$ forms a clique of size at least t in G. $\square$

6. IN-NEIGHBOR STABILITY

In many real-life situations, when people move from one group to another, they need approvals from their contacts in the new group. Suppose, for instance, that Alice is an early-career researcher applying for academic positions in universities: her application is unlikely to be accepted if it is rejected by her prospective mentors (even if Alice expects to collaborate with several other faculty members as well).

Motivated by these considerations, we will now describe a new notion of stability, which is specific to hedonic graph games.

DEFINITION 2. *Given a hedonic graph game $(N, (\succeq_i)_{i \in N}, L)$, we say that j is a* neighbor *of i if $\{i, j\} \in L$. A feasible deviation of a player i to $X \notin \mathcal{N}_i$ is called*

- in-neighbor feasible *if it is NS feasible and accepted by all of i's neighbors in X.*
- IR-in-neighbor feasible *if it is in-neighbor feasible and for all $j \in X$ it holds that $X \cup \{i\} \succeq_j \{j\}$.*

A feasible partition π is called in-neighbor stable (INS) *(respectively,* IR in-neighbor stable (IR-INS)*) if no player i has an in-neighbor feasible deviation (respectively, an IR-in-neighbor feasible deviation) from $\pi(i)$ to a coalition $X \in \pi \cup \{\emptyset\}$.*

Note that every INS partition is IR-INS, and each IR-INS partition is individually stable. However, the converse may not be true: partition π_1 in Example 1 is individually stable, but admits an in-neighbor feasible deviation. Indeed, all IR partitions in that example are not in-neighbor stable, so the existence of in-neighbor stable outcomes is not guaranteed, even in additively separable games on paths. Note however, that π_1 is IR-in-neighbor stable.

6.1 Computational complexity of INS

We will now present an algorithm to determine the existence of NS, INS and IR-INS outcomes for games on arbitrary acyclic graphs.

THEOREM 13. *Suppose that we are given oracle access to the preference relations $\succeq_i$ of all players in a hedonic graph game $\mathcal{G} = (N, (\succeq_i)_{i \in N}, L)$, where (N, L) is a forest. Then we can decide whether $\mathcal{G}$ admits a Nash stable, in-neighbor stable or IR-in-neighbor stable feasible outcome (and find one if it exists) in time polynomial in the number of connected subsets of (N, L).*

PROOF. Our algorithm is similar to Demange's algorithm for the core [9]. Again, we assume that (N, L) is a tree. Given a hedonic graph game $(N, (\succeq_i)_{i \in N}, L)$, we make a rooted tree (N, A^r) by orienting edges in L. Then, for each player $i \in N$ and each $X \subseteq \text{succ}(i, A^r)$ with $X \in \mathcal{F}_L(i)$, we determine whether there exists a stable partition π of $\text{succ}(i, A^r)$ with $X \in \pi$. We set $f(X) = 1$ if such a partition exists, and set $f(X) = 0$ otherwise. To this end, for each $j \in \text{ch}(X, A^r)$ we try to find a coalition $X_j \in \mathcal{F}_L(j)$, $X_j \subseteq \text{succ}(j, A^r)$ such that no player wants to move across the "border" between X and $\text{ch}(X, A^r)$ under the given stability requirement. A stable solution exists if and only if $f(X) = 1$ for some coalition $X \in \mathcal{F}_L(r)$. Algorithm 2 describes in detail how $f(X)$ is computed.

Algorithm 2 Determining the existence of α feasible partitions, where $\alpha \in$ {NS, INS, IR-INS}

Input: tree (N, L), $r \in N$, oracles for $\succeq_i$, $i \in N$.
Output: $f : \mathcal{F}_L \to \{0, 1\}$.

1: make a rooted tree (N, A^r) with root r by orienting all the edges in L.
2: initialize $f(X) \leftarrow 1$ for $X \in \mathcal{F}_L$.
3: **for** $t = 0, \ldots, \text{height}(r, A^r)$ **do**
4:   **for** $i \in N$ with $\text{height}(i, A^r) = t$ **do**
5:     **for** $X \in \mathcal{F}_L(i)$ such that $X \subseteq \text{succ}(i, A^r)$ **do**
6:       **if** X is not individually rational **then**
7:         $f(X) \leftarrow 0$
8:       **else**
9:         **for** $j \in \text{ch}(X, A^r)$ **do**
10:           **if** for each $X_j \in \mathcal{F}_L(j)$ such that $X_j \subseteq \text{succ}(j, A^r)$ and $f(X_j) = 1$ the deviation of j from X_j to X or the deviation of $\text{pr}(j, A^r)$ from X to X_j is α feasible **then**
11:             $f(X) \leftarrow 0$
12:           **end if**
13:         **end for**
14:       **end if**
15:     **end for**
16:   **end for**
17: **end for**

LEMMA 14. *For each $\alpha \in$ {NS, INS, IR-INS}, each $i \in N$ and each $X \in \mathcal{F}_L(i)$ such that $X \subseteq \text{succ}(i, A^r)$ we have $f(X) = 1$ if and only if there exists an α feasible partition π of $\text{succ}(i, A^r)$ such that $X \in \pi$.*

PROOF. The proof is by induction on $\text{height}(i, A^r)$. The claim is immediate when $\text{height}(i, A^r) = 0$. Suppose that it holds for all $j \in N$ with $\text{height}(j, A^r) \leq t - 1$, and consider a player i with $\text{height}(i, A^r) = t$. Consider an arbitrary $X \in \mathcal{F}_L(i)$ such that $X \subseteq \text{succ}(i, A^r)$.

Suppose first that $f(X) = 1$. Line 6 ensures that X is individually rational. Hence, if $X = \text{succ}(i, A^r)$, then X is an α feasible partition of $\text{succ}(i, A^r)$. Now, suppose that $X \neq \text{succ}(i, A^r)$, i.e., $\text{ch}(X, A^r) \neq \emptyset$. Since $f(X) = 1$, Line 10 ensures that for each $j \in \text{ch}(X, A^r)$ there exists a coalition $X_j \in \mathcal{F}_L(j)$ such that $X_j \subseteq \text{succ}(j, A^r)$, $f(X_j) = 1$ and neither the deviation of j from X_j to X nor the deviation of $\text{pr}(j, A^r)$ from X to X_j is α feasible. By the induction hypothesis, for each $j \in \text{ch}(X, A^r)$ there exists an α feasible partition of $\text{succ}(j, A^r)$ that contains X_j; combining these partitions with X, we obtain an α feasible partition of $\text{succ}(i, A^r)$ that contains X.

Conversely, if $f(X) = 0$, then X is not individually rational, or the condition of the **if** statement in Line 10 is satisfied. In either case, there is no α feasible partition of $\text{succ}(i, A^r)$ containing X. □

Lemma 14 immediately implies that the input game admits an α feasible partition for $\alpha \in$ {NS, INS, IR-INS} if and only if $f(X) = 1$ for some $X \in \mathcal{F}_L(r)$. If this is the case, an α feasible partition can be found using standard dynamic programming techniques.

It remains to analyze the running time of our algorithm. Let $n = |N|$, $s = |\mathcal{F}_L|$. Algorithm 2 considers each coalition $X \in \mathcal{F}_L$ exactly once. To check that it is individually rational, it makes at most n oracle calls. Further, X has at most n children. For each child j, the algorithm considers at most s candidate coalitions X_j. To check the conditions in Line 10 for a given X_j, we need at most two oracle calls in case of Nash stability and in-neighbor stability and at most n calls in case of IR-in-neighbor stability. We conclude that our algorithm performs at most $O(n^2 s^2)$ oracle calls. □

The following result shows that we should not hope to obtain a polynomial-time algorithm for finding in-neighbor stable outcomes, even for additively separable hedonic graph games on stars.

THEOREM 15. *Given an additively separable hedonic graph game whose underlying graph is a star, it is* NP*-complete to determine whether it has an in-neighbor stable feasible partition.*

PROOF SKETCH. In-neighbor stability can be verified in polynomial time, so our problem is is NP. To prove NP-hardness, we reduce from CLIQUE. Given an undirected graph $G = (V, E)$ and a positive integer t, we construct an additively separable hedonic graph game (N, U, L) as follows. We set $N = V \cup \{a, b, c\}$, and use the same graph (N, L) as in the proof of Theorem 12 (see Figure 1).

Let $M = |N| + 1$. We define the utility matrix $U : N \times N \to \mathbb{R}$ as follows.

$$U(a, b) = 1, U(a, c) = -2, U(b, a) = t,$$
$$U(b, c) = 0, U(c, a) = 0, U(c, b) = 2,$$
$$U(a, v) = U(c, v) = U(v, a) = U(v, c) = -M \text{ for each } v \in V,$$
$$U(b, v) = 1, U(v, b) = 0 \text{ for each } v \in V,$$
$$U(u, v) = 0 \text{ if } \{u, v\} \in E$$

and $U(u, v) = -M$ otherwise, for all $u, v \in V$.

As in the proof of Theorem 12, one can verify that G contains a clique of size t if and only if the game admits an in-neighbor stable feasible partition. We omit the details due to space constraints. □

A similar reduction shows that it is hard to find a Nash stable outcome.

THEOREM 16. *Given an additively separable hedonic graph game whose underlying graph is a star, it is* NP*-complete to determine whether it has a Nash stable feasible partition.*

In contrast, for any hedonic game on a star, we can construct an IR-in-neighbor stable partition efficiently.

PROPOSITION 17. *Every hedonic graph game $(N, (\succeq_i)_{i \in N}, L)$ where (N, L) is a star has an IR-in-neighbor stable partition, and given oracle access to the players' preference relations, such a partition can be found using $O(|N|^3)$ oracle calls.*

PROOF. If the central node strictly prefers being on her own, rather than being in any coalition of size two, a partition with all singletons is IR-in-neighbor stable. Otherwise, choose a favorite two-player coalition of the center, and keep adding players to this coalition one by one if this deviation is IR-in-neighbor feasible. When no player can be added, the resulting partition is IR-in-neighbor stable, since the utility of the central node does not decrease during the execution, and there is no player who can IR-in-neighbor deviate to the coalition of the center. The bound on the running time is immediate. □

6.2 Computational complexity of INS: Symmetric additively separable games

The proof of Theorem 16 is based on the the construction in the proof of Theorem 15, which uses an additively separable hedonic game that is not symmetric. Indeed, Bogomolnaia and Jackson [6] observe that in symmetric additively separable hedonic games, any NS deviation strictly increases the sum of all players' utilities $\sum_{i \in N} \sum_{j \in \pi(i)} U(i, j)$. This implies that for this class of games a sequence of NS deviations converges to a Nash stable outcome. Thereby, the set of Nash stable outcomes (and hence also INS, IR-INS, and IS outcomes) is always non-empty. However, the number of deviations needed to reach a Nash stable outcome may be exponential in the number of players, so it remains unclear if a Nash stable outcome can be computed efficiently.

The complexity class that appears to be useful for capturing the complexity of this problem is PLS (Polynomial Local Search) [17]. A problem in PLS consists of a finite set of candidate solutions, each of which has associated neighborhood and cost. It is specified by three polynomial-time algorithms. The first algorithm computes an initial candidate solution (e.g. the all-singleton partition). The second algorithm returns the cost of each candidate solution (e.g. the social welfare of a partition). Finally, the third algorithm tests whether a given candidate solution is optimal in its neighborhood, and if not, finds a solution with better cost (e.g. an improved partition after a profitable deviation). Given two PLS problems A and B, we say that A is *PLS-reducible* to B if there exist polynomial time computable functions f and g such that f maps instances of A to B and g maps the local optima of B to local optima of A.

Gairing and Savani show that search problems related to NS and IS for symmetric additively separable games are PLS-complete [13, 14]. However, if one were to interpret the hedonic game in their reduction as a graph game, the underlying graph would necessarily contain cycles. In what follows, we will show that computing in-neighbor stable outcomes for symmetric additively separable games is PLS-complete even when the graph (N, L) is a star.

THEOREM 18. *Given a symmetric additively separable hedonic graph game whose underlying graph is a star, it is* PLS*-complete to find an in-neighbor stable feasible partition.*

PROOF SKETCH. With symmetric additively separable preferences, we are able to test local optimality of a partition and, if it is not optimal, find an improving move in polynomial time. Hence, our problem is clearly in PLS. To prove PLS-hardness, we provide a reduction from LOCAL MAX-CUT, which is known to be PLS-complete [21]. Recall that an instance of LOCAL MAX-CUT is given by a weighted graph $G = (V, E, w)$, where $w : V \times V \to \mathbb{N}$ is the weight function with the convention that $w(u, v) = 0$ for each $\{u, v\} \notin E$. A *cut* is a partition of V into two parts S and $V \setminus S$; its *weight* is given by $\sum_{u \in S, v \in V \setminus S} w(u, v)$. The neighborhood of a cut $(S, V \setminus S)$ is defined as the set of all cuts that can be obtained by moving one node from S to $V \setminus S$ or vice versa; the goal is to find a cut that has the maximum weight in its neighborhood.

Given an instance (V, E, w) of LOCAL MAX-CUT, we set $N = V \cup \{s\}$, $L = \{\, \{s, v\} \mid v \in V \,\}$ and construct a symmetric additively separable graph game (N, U, L) with the utility matrix $U : N \times N \to \mathbb{R}$ defined as follows. We set $U(u, s) = \sum_{v \in V} w(u, v)$ for each $u \in V$. For every pair of distinct nodes $u, v \in V$, we define $U(u, v) = -2w(u, v)$ if $\{u, v\} \in E$ and $U(u, v) = 0$ otherwise. Note that every $u \in V$ will be in a coalition with s or on her own in any feasible partition. Moreover, player s will accept all in-neighbor feasible deviations since her utility for every other player is non-negative.

Let π be an in-neighbor stable feasible partition of N. Let $V_1 = \{\, u \in V \mid u \in \pi(s) \,\}$ and $V_2 = V \setminus V_1$. Each player $u \in V_1$ has non-negative utility $U(u, s) + \sum_{v \in V_1} U(u, v)$ by individual rationality. Hence, $\sum_{v \in V_1} w(u, v) \le \sum_{v \in V_2} w(u, v)$ for every $u \in V_1$. On the other hand, no player $u \in V_2$ wants to deviate to $\pi(s)$: by a similar calculation, $\sum_{v \in V_1} w(u, v) \ge \sum_{v \in V_2} w(u, v)$ for every $u \in V_2$. Thus, (V_1, V_2) is a local max-cut of G. □

The construction in the proof of Theorem 18 can also be used to show PLS-completeness of finding a Nash stable partition in this class of games.

THEOREM 19. *Given a symmetric additively separable hedonic graph game whose underlying graph is a star, it is* PLS*-complete to find a Nash stable feasible partition.*

However, we cannot extend Theorem 19 to enemy-oriented games.

PROPOSITION 20. *A Nash stable feasible outcome of a symmetric enemy-oriented game on a star can be computed in polynomial time.*

PROOF. We initialize coalition X to the center of the star; as long as there is a player that likes (and is liked by) all current members of X, we add him to X. Eventually, no player can be added to X. At this point, $\{X\} \cup \{\{i\} \mid i \in N \setminus X\}$ is a Nash stable feasible partition: no player outside of X wants to deviate to X, and no player in X wants to leave. □

7. CONCLUSIONS AND FUTURE WORK

We have explored the existence and computational complexity of stable partitions in hedonic games on acyclic graphs. We obtained a number of algorithmic results in the general oracle-based framework, thereby showing that acyclicity of the communication network has important implications for stability. It remains unknown whether a strictly core stable partition for a hedonic game on a tree can be computed in time polynomial in the number of connected coalitions; we leave this problem as a direction for future work. It would also be interesting to see if our algorithms can be extended to graphs that are "almost" acyclic, and, more broadly, if there are constraints on the communication structure other than acyclicity that lead to existence/tractability results for common hedonic games stability concepts.

Acknowledgements

We would like to thank the reviewers for their very useful comments. The first author acknowledges financial support from Funai Foundation for Information Technology.

REFERENCES

[1] H. Aziz, F. Brandt, and H. G. Seedig. Computing desirable partitions in additively separable hedonic games. *Artificial Intelligence*, 195:316–334, feb 2013.

[2] H. Aziz and R. Savani. Hedonic games. In F. Brandt, V. Conitzer, U. Endriss, J. Lang, and A. Procaccia, editors, *Handbook of Computational Social Choice*. Cambridge University Press, 2015.

[3] S. Banerjee, H. Konishi, and T. Sönmez. Core in a simple coalition formation game. *Social Choice and Welfare*, 18(1):135–153, 2001.

[4] V. Bilò, A. Fanelli, M. Flammini, G. Monaco, and L. Moscardelli. Nash stability in fractional hedonic games. In *WINE'14*, pages 486–491, 2014.

[5] V. Bilò, A. Fanelli, M. Flammini, G. Monaco, and L. Moscardelli. On the price of stability of fractional hedonic games. In *AAMAS'15*, pages 1239–1247, 2015.

[6] A. Bogomolnaia and M. O. Jackson. The stability of hedonic coalition structures. *Games and Economic Behavior*, 38(2):201–230, 2002.

[7] N. Burani and W. Zwicker. Coalition formation games with separable preferences. *Mathematical Social Sciences*, 45(1):27–52, 2003.

[8] G. Demange. Intermediate preferences and stable coalition structures. *Journal of Mathematical Economics*, 23(1):45–58, 1994.

[9] G. Demange. On group stability in hierarchies and networks. *Journal of Political Economy*, 112(4):754–778, 2004.

[10] D. Dimitrov, P. Borm, R. Hendrickx, and S. C. Sung. Simple priorities and core stability in hedonic games. *Social Choice and Welfare*, 26(2):421–433, 2006.

[11] J. H. Drèze and J. Greenberg. Hedonic Coalitions: Optimality and Stability. *Econometrica*, 48(4):987–1003, 1980.

[12] E. Elkind. Coalitional games on sparse social networks. In T. Liu, Q. Qi, and Y. Ye, editors, *WINE'14*, volume 8877 of *Lecture Notes in Computer Science*, pages 308–321. Springer, 2014.

[13] M. Gairing and R. Savani. Computing stable outcomes in hedonic games. In S. Kontogiannis, E. Koutsoupias, and P. Spirakis, editors, *SAGT'10*, volume 6386 of *Lecture Notes in Computer Science*, pages 174–185. Springer Berlin Heidelberg, 2010.

[14] M. Gairing and R. Savani. Computing stable outcomes in hedonic games with voting-based deviations. In *AAMAS'11*, pages 559–566, 2011.

[15] M. Garey and D. Johnson. *Computers and Intractability: A Guide to the Theory of NP-Completeness*. W. H. Freeman and Company, 1979.

[16] A. Igarashi and E. Elkind. Hedonic games with graph-restricted communication. arxiv:1602.05342 [cs.GT], 2016.

[17] D. S. Johnson and C. H. Papadimitriou. How easy is local search? *Journal of Computer and System Sciences*, 37:79–100, 1988.

[18] M. Le Breton, G. Owen, and S. Weber. Strongly balanced cooperative games. *International Journal of Game Theory*, 20(4):419–427, 1992.

[19] R. B. Myerson. Graphs and cooperation in games. *Mathematics of Operations Research*, 2(3):225–229, 1977.

[20] D. Peters and E. Elkind. Simple causes of complexity in hedonic games. In *IJCAI'15*, pages 617–623, 2015.

[21] A. A. Schäffer and M. Yannakakis. Simple local search problems that are hard to solve. *SIAM Journal on Computing*, 20(1):56–87, 1991.

[22] S.-C. Sung and D. Dimitrov. Computational complexity in additive hedonic games. *European Journal of Operational Research*, 203(3):635–639, jun 2010.

Altruistic Hedonic Games

Nhan-Tam Nguyen, Anja Rey, Lisa Rey, Jörg Rothe, and Lena Schend
Heinrich-Heine-Universität Düsseldorf
40225 Düsseldorf, Germany
{ nguyen, rey, lrey, rothe, schend }@cs.uni-duesseldorf.de

ABSTRACT

Hedonic games are coalition formation games in which players have preferences over the coalitions they can join. All models of representing hedonic games studied so far are based upon selfish players only. Among the known ways of representing hedonic games compactly, we focus on friend-oriented hedonic games and propose a novel model for them that takes into account not only a player's own preferences but also her friends' preferences under three degrees of altruism. We study both the axiomatic properties of these games and the computational complexity of problems related to various stability concepts.

Keywords

Hedonic games; coalition formation; stability; altruism

1. INTRODUCTION

Hedonic games, proposed by Drèze and Greenberg [17] and later formally modelled by Bogomolnaia and Jackson [10] and Banerjee et al. [8], are coalition formation games in which players have preferences over coalitions (subsets of players) they can be part of. In the context of decentralized coalition formation, several stability concepts and representations have been studied from an axiomatic and a computational complexity point of view; see Woeginger's survey [33] on this topic and the book chapters by Aziz and Savani [6] and Elkind and Rothe [18] for an overview.

Dimitrov et al. [16] proposed a model that allows for compact representation of hedonic games, namely, the friend-and-enemy encoding of the players' preferences, where each player divides the set of players into friends and enemies. Based on such a network of friends, they suggest two models of preference extensions: appreciation of friends and aversion to enemies. In *friend-oriented hedonic games*, a coalition A is preferred to another coalition B if A contains either more friends than B or the same number of friends as B but fewer enemies than B. This setting corresponds to a network of players represented as a graph. Since we study symmetric friendship relations for stability reasons, this graph is undirected. For example, suppose there are four players, 1, 2, 3, and 4, and let 1 be friends with 2 but neither with 3 nor with 4, while 2 and 3 are friends with each other but not with 4. The corresponding network is displayed in Figure 1.

$$1 — 2 — 3 \qquad 4$$

Figure 1: Example of a network of friends

Now, in the friend-oriented extension model player 2 prefers teaming up with 1 and 3 to forming a coalition with 1 and 4. Player 1, on the other hand, is indifferent between coalitions $\{1,2,3\}$ and $\{1,2,4\}$. Intuitively, however, 1 would have an advantage from being in a coalition with 2 and 3, since 2 and 3—being friends—can be expected to cooperate better than 2 and 4. Also, 1 can be expected to care about her friend 2's interests and thus might prefer a coalition in which 2 is satisfied ($\{1,2,3\}$) to one in which 2 is less satisfied ($\{1,2,4\}$). In order to model these kinds of preferences we will introduce several degrees of altruism, starting from friend-oriented hedonic games. Taking friends' preferences into account does not contradict the idea of hedonic games: In hedonic games player i's utility function depends only on the coalitions that contain i. Since player i is also interested in her friends' satisfaction (with varying degrees), we incorporate this notion into player i's utility function. Note that player i's utility is still a function of the coalitions containing her, which in addition takes her friends' preferences that are in the *same* coalition as player i into account.

Our Contribution and Related Work: Focusing on the friend-oriented encoding of preferences and taking the idea of players caring about their friends' preferences into account, we propose hedonic games with altruistic influences. In particular, we define three degrees of altruism, from being selfish first, over aggregating opinions of a player and her friends equally, to altruistically letting one's friends decide first. The latter is the most altruistic case, as we assume that from a player's perspective only friends can be consulted, while agents further away (such as a friend's friend that is one's enemy) cannot be communicated with or cannot be trusted. In a social network, for example, the whole set of players other than friends might not even be known. The proposed games are compactly representable but not fully expressive. However, they can express other hedonic games than those representable by popular compact representations in the literature. We study both the axiomatic properties of these games and the computational complexity of problems related to common stability concepts.

From a *noncooperative* game-theoretic point of view, the interests of not only selfish, but altruistic agents have been modelled and studied by, for example, Hoefer and Skopalik [24], Chen et al. [14], Apt and Schäfer [2], and Rahn and Schäfer [30]. Salehi-Abari and Boutilier [31] study social choice with empathetic preferences. Their local empathetic model is related to our model. Altruism has also been studied in (experimental) economics [27]. Brânzei and Larson [12] study social distance games: In contrast to degrees of altruism as proposed here, a player's opinion on her friends (players of distance one) has the highest weight while her opinion on play-

Appears in: *Proceedings of the 15th International Conference on Autonomous Agents and Multiagent Systems (AAMAS 2016), J. Thangarajah, K. Tuyls, C. Jonker, S. Marsella (eds.), May 9–13, 2016, Singapore.*

ers farther away counts less. This is similar (but not equivalent) to our selfish-first model to be defined in Section 3.2.

Furthermore, the study of other agents' influence on opinions has gained increasing interest in collective decision making [22, 23]. In the context of voting scenarios, preference extensions and their properties have been studied by Endriss [20]. An overview of axiomatic properties of preference orders can be found, e.g., in the book chapters by Barberà et al. [9] and Lang and Rothe [26]. The work by Darmann et al. [15] combines aspects of voting theory and the theory of coalition formation games: They define a model for selection scenarios for a number of group activities that can also be represented by hedonic games and they study the complexity of stability concepts in this model. Aziz et al. [5] provide a survey of known results for additively separable hedonic games; in particular, two impressive complexity results—NP^{NP}-completeness for the existence of (strictly) core-stable coalition structures—are due to Woeginger [34] and Peters [28]. The concept of Pareto optimality has been studied by Aziz et al. [3] for a number of encodings of hedonic games, while recent work of Brandl et al. [11] is concerned with the complexity of various stability concepts in fractional hedonic games [4]. Lang et al. [25] introduce a new type of hedonic game where agents rank their friends and their enemies (and may, in addition, feel "neutral" about some other players), and these preferences over players are extended to preferences over coalitions.

2. PRELIMINARIES

A *hedonic game* is a pair $(N,\succeq)$, where $N=\{1,\dots,n\}$ is a set of players and $\succeq\ =(\succeq_1,\dots,\succeq_n)$ is a list of the players' preferences. For $i\in N$, let $\mathcal{N}^i=\{C\subseteq N \mid i\in C\}$ denote the set of coalitions containing i. Player i's preference relation $\succeq_i\ \in\mathcal{N}^i\times\mathcal{N}^i$ induces a complete, weak preference order over $\mathcal{N}^i$. For $A,B\in\mathcal{N}^i$, we say that player i *weakly prefers A to B* if $A\succeq_i B$, that *i prefers A to B* ($A\succ_i B$) if $A\succeq_i B$ but not $B\succeq_i A$, and that i is *indifferent between A and B* ($A\sim_i B$) if $A\succeq_i B$ and $B\succeq_i A$. We call $C\in\mathcal{N}^i$ *acceptable for player i* if $C\succeq_i\{i\}$. A *coalition structure* is a partition $\Gamma=\{C_1,\dots,C_k\}$ of the players into k coalitions $C_1,\dots,C_k\subseteq N$ (i.e., $\bigcup_{r=1}^k C_r=N$ and $C_r\cap C_s=\emptyset$ for all r and s, $1\leq r\neq s\leq k$). The unique coalition in Γ containing player $i\in N$ is denoted by $\Gamma(i)$.

In order to avoid exponentially large preference orders in the number of players, a common way to represent players' preferences is to consider a network of friends [16]. Each player $i\in N$ has a set of friends $F_i\subseteq N\setminus\{i\}$ and a set of enemies $E_i=N\setminus(F_i\cup\{i\})$. Visually, let the players in $N=\{1,\dots,n\}$ be represented by the vertices in a graph $G=(N,H)$, and let a directed edge $(i,j)\in H$ denote that j is i's friend, that is, the open neighborhood of i represents the set of i's friends $F_i=\{j \mid (i,j)\in H\}$. Since in the context of stability it is reasonable to consider symmetric friendship relations [33], we will focus on undirected graphs representing networks of friends. In the *friend-oriented* preference extension [16] more friends are preferred to fewer friends, and in case of an equal number of friends, fewer enemies are preferred. Formally, define

$$A\succeq_i^F B \iff |A\cap F_i|>|B\cap F_i| \text{ or } \quad (1)$$
$$(|A\cap F_i|=|B\cap F_i| \text{ and } |A\cap E_i|\leq|B\cap E_i|).$$

Note that friend-oriented preferences can be represented additively, by assigning a value of $n=|N|$ to each friend and a value of -1 to each enemy [16]: For any player $i\in N$ and for any coalition $A\in\mathcal{N}^i$, define the *value of a coalition* by

$$v_i(A)=n|A\cap F_i|-|A\cap E_i|.$$

Then, for $A,B\in\mathcal{N}^i$, we have $A\succeq_i^F B \iff v_i(A)\geq v_i(B)$.

Relatedly, other representations and their preference extensions are enemy-oriented preferences [16], additively separable [32] and fractional hedonic games [4], and singleton encodings [13] (which each are compactly representable but not fully expressive or complete), individually rational encodings [7], and hedonic coalition nets [19] (which are fully expressive but not compact in the sense of polynomial-size representation). See Section 4 for a discussion of how our models differ from representations known from the literature.

2.1 Properties of Preference Extensions

Below we give a selection of properties of preference extensions inspired by various related topics such as voting theory and resource allocation. Let $N=\{1,\dots,n\}$ be a set of players and F_i and E_i the sets of player i's friends and enemies, respectively. Let $G=(N,H)$ be the corresponding network of friends. Consider player i's preference relation $\succeq_i$ on $\mathcal{N}^i$. We say $\succeq_i$ is *reflexive* if $A\succeq_i A$ for each coalition $A\in\mathcal{N}^i$; $\succeq_i$ is *transitive* if for any three coalitions $A,B,C\in\mathcal{N}^i$, $A\succeq_i B$ and $B\succeq_i C$ implies $A\succeq_i C$; $\succeq_i$ is *polynomial-time computable* if for a given player i and two given coalitions $A,B\in\mathcal{N}^i$, it can be decided in polynomial time whether or not $A\succeq_i B$; and $\succeq_i$ is *anonymous* if renaming the players in N does not change $\succeq_i$. Clearly, the first three properties are necessary to have efficiently computable and rational preferences, and anonymity means that only the structure of the friendship network is important. We further define the following properties.

Weak Friend-Orientedness: If coalition A is acceptable for i, then $A\cup\{f\}$ is also acceptable for i, where $f\in F_i\setminus A$.

Favoring Friends: If $x\in F_i$ and $y\in E_i$ then $\{x,i\}\succ_i\{y,i\}$.

Indifference between Friends: If $x,y\in F_i$ then $\{x,i\}\sim_i\{y,i\}$.

Indifference between Enemies: If $x,y\in E_i$ then $\{x,i\}\sim_i\{y,i\}$.

Note that these four properties hold for friend-oriented preferences, see the work of Alcantud and Arlegi [1].

Sovereignty of Players: For a fixed player i and each $C\in\mathcal{N}^i$, there exists a network of friends such that C ends up as i's most preferred coalition.

Monotonicity: Let $j\neq i$ be a player with $j\in E_i$ and $A,B\in\mathcal{N}^i$, and $\succeq_i'$ be the preference relation resulting from $\succeq_i$ when j turns from being i's enemy to being i's friend (all else being equal). We call $\succeq_i$ *type-I-monotonic* if it holds that (1) if $A\succ_i B$, $j\in A\cap B$, and $A\succeq_j^F B$, then $A\succ_i' B$, and (2) if $A\sim_i B$, $j\in A\cap B$, and $A\succeq_j^F B$, then $A\succeq_i' B$. We call $\succeq_i$ *type-II-monotonic* if it holds that (1) if $A\succ_i B$ and $j\in A\setminus B$, then $A\succ_i' B$, and (2) if $A\sim_i B$ and $j\in A\setminus B$, then $A\succeq_i' B$.
Type-I-monotonicity ensures i's preference of A over B not to become worse if an enemy j who is contained in both coalitions, turns into i's friend, while j is weakly preferring A to B. Type-II-monotonicity, on the other hand, requires that j is only in A (hence has no opinion on B), but still i's preference of A over B should not become worse.

Symmetry: Let j and k be two distinct players with $j\neq i\neq k$. We say that $\succeq_i$ is *symmetric* if it holds that if swapping the positions of j and k in G is an automorphism then $(\forall C\in\mathcal{N}^i\setminus(\mathcal{N}^j\cup\mathcal{N}^k))\ [C\cup\{j\}\sim_i C\cup\{k\}]$.

Local Friend Dependence: The preference order $\succeq_i$ can depend on the sets of friends $F_1,\dots,F_n$. Let $A,B\in\mathcal{N}^i$. We say that comparison (A,B) is

- *friend-dependent in* $\succeq_i$ if (1) $A\succeq_i B$ is true (false) and (2) can be made false (true) by changing the set of friends of some players (except for i);
- *locally friend-dependent in* $\succeq_i$ if (1) $A\succeq_i B$ is true (false), (2) can be made false (true) by changing the set of friends

of some players that are in A or B and are i's friends, and (3) changing the set of friends of all other players in $N \setminus (\{i\} \cup (F_i \cap (A \cup B))$ does not affect the status of the comparison.

We say $\succeq_i$ is *locally friend-dependent* if (1) there are $A, B \in \mathcal{N}^i$ such that (A, B) is friend-dependent in $\succeq_i$ and (2) every (A', B') that is friend-dependent in $\succeq_i$ is locally friend-dependent in $\succeq_i$.

This property says that an agent's preference over some coalition can change if the set of a friend's friends changes. This friend also has to be a member of a coalition that is under consideration. Thus local friend dependence is a crucial property that tries to capture the essence of the proposed approach to altruism in hedonic games.

Friend-Oriented Unanimity: Let $A, B \in \mathcal{N}^i$ with $A \cap F_i = B \cap F_i$. We say that $\succeq_i$ is *friend-orientedly unanimous* if $A \succ_j^F B$ for each $j \in (F_i \cup \{i\}) \cap A$ implies that $A \succ_i B$.

Note that the definition of friend-oriented unanimity covers all cases where the same subset of friends is consulted who all have a unanimous opinion in terms of friend-oriented preferences, in particular the case considering all friends' opinions: $F_i \subseteq A \cap B$.

2.2 Stability Concepts

The following stability concepts are commonly studied in hedonic games.

Definition 1. *Let $(N, \succeq)$ be a hedonic game and Γ be a coalition structure. A coalition $C \subseteq N$* blocks *Γ if for each $i \in C$ it holds that $C \succ_i \Gamma(i)$. If there is at least one $i \in C$ with $C \succ_i \Gamma(i)$ while $C \succeq_j \Gamma(j)$ holds for the other players $j \neq i$ in C, we call C* weakly blocking. *A coalition structure Γ is said to be*

1. individually rational *if for all $i \in N$, $\Gamma(i)$ is acceptable;*
2. Nash-stable *if for all $i \in N$ and for each $C \in \Gamma \cup \{\emptyset\}$ with $\Gamma(i) \neq C$, it holds that $\Gamma(i) \succeq_i C \cup \{i\}$;*
3. individually stable *if for all $i \in N$ and for each $C \in \Gamma \cup \{\emptyset\}$, it either holds that $\Gamma(i) \succeq_i C \cup \{i\}$ or there is a player $j \in C$ with $C \succ_j C \cup \{i\}$;*
4. contractually individually stable *if for all $i \in N$ and for each $C \in \Gamma \cup \{\emptyset\}$, it either holds that $\Gamma(i) \succeq_i C \cup \{i\}$, or there is a player $j \in C$ with $C \succ_j C \cup \{i\}$, or there is a player $k \in \Gamma(i)$ with $i \neq k$ and $\Gamma(i) \succ_k \Gamma(i) \setminus \{i\}$;*
5. strictly popular *if it beats every other coalition structure $\Gamma' \neq \Gamma$ in pairwise comparison, that is, if $|\{i \in N \mid \Gamma(i) \succ_i \Gamma'(i)\}| > |\{i \in N \mid \Gamma'(i) \succ_i \Gamma(i)\}|$;*
6. (strictly) core-stable *if there is no (weakly) blocking coalition;*
7. perfect *if for all $i \in N$ and for all $C \in \mathcal{N}^i$, it holds that $\Gamma(i) \succeq_i C$.*

3. ALTRUISTIC HEDONIC GAMES

In this section, we introduce our new model that refines friend-oriented hedonic games by taking altruistic influences into account. In this model, each player still wants to be with as many friends and as few enemies as possible, but in addition she wants her friends to be as satisfied as possible.

3.1 Naïve Approach

A first attempt to formalize this idea (that will turn out to fail) is the following. Consider the scenario where $i \in N$ has a friend-oriented preference extension (according to Equivalence (1)) except that, whenever the number of friends in A and B is the same and so is the number of enemies in A and B (i.e., $A \sim_i^F B$), i now prefers A to B if more of i's friends that are contained in A and B prefer A to B than B to A (according to Equivalence (1)). Formally:

$$\begin{aligned} A \succeq_i^{NA} B \iff & |A \cap F_i| > |B \cap F_i| \text{ or} \\ & (|A \cap F_i| = |B \cap F_i| \text{ and } |A \cap E_i| < |B \cap E_i|) \text{ or} \\ & (|A \cap F_i| = |B \cap F_i| \text{ and } |A \cap E_i| = |B \cap E_i| \text{ and} \\ & |\{j \in A \cap B \cap F_i \mid A \succ_j^F B\}| \geq \\ & |\{j \in A \cap B \cap F_i \mid B \succ_j^F A\}|). \end{aligned} \quad (2)$$

Intuitively, according to (2), a player is selfish first, but as soon as she is indifferent between two coalitions in the sense of (1), she cares about her friends' preferences. A major disadvantage of this definition, however, is that *irrational* preference orders can arise, i.e., preference orders that are not transitive in general: Consider, e.g., the hedonic game $(N, \succeq^{NA})$ with $N = \{1,2,3,4,5,6,7\}$ and the network of friends shown in Figure 2a. For coalitions $A = \{1,2,3,5\}$, $B = \{1,2,4,7\}$, and $C = \{1,3,4,6\}$, it holds that $A \succ_1^{NA} B$ and $B \succ_1^{NA} C$, yet $C \succ_1^{NA} A$, violating transitivity.

(a) Used, e.g., in the proof of Proposition 7

(b) Illustrating distinct degrees of altruism in Example 1

Figure 2: Two networks of friends representing hedonic games

In order to ensure transitivity, we have to add an extra condition to Equivalence (2). One idea would be to demand indifference between all coalitions that are involved in a $\succ_i^{NA}$-cycle by (2). This, however, can lead to a comparison of all coalitions containing a player, so determining a relation between two coalitions might comprise an exponential number of steps in the number of players. Then it would have been easier to give an arbitrary preference order as an input in the first place. Another idea would be to include the preferences of all friends, not only of those contained in the considered coalitions, but this would contradict the concept of hedonic game. In the following, we take a different approach.

3.2 Modelling Altruistic Influences

Given the failure of extending friend-oriented preferences by breaking ties with "majority voting," we consider the following model instead: Player $i \in N$ prefers coalition A over B if the average value of i's friends in A is larger than the average value of i's friends in B. In more detail, using the friend-oriented encoding, we obtain a friend j's opinion on a coalition containing both player i and j, which can have an influence on i's preference relation in the following ways. Since we consider friends to be equally important and focus on the average valuation, assigning a weight to player i's own contribution in comparison to her friends' influence on her preference, we will distinguish between three *degrees of altruism*: A player may (a) be selfish first and ask her friends only in case of indifference, (b) treat her friends and herself equally, or (c) be truly altruistic by asking her friends first and deciding herself only in case of indifference. Next to the definition we will show that the preferences capture the intuitive ideas behind them. For $i \in N$ and $A \in \mathcal{N}^i$, let

$$\mathrm{avg}_i^F(A) = \sum_{a \in A \cap F_i} \frac{v_a(A)}{|A \cap F_i|}.$$

In each of the three cases below, a player's *utility* u_i of a coalition is used as a measure of comparison combining the values v_i and v_j for $j \in F_i$. Note that $u_i = v_i$ under friend-oriented extensions.

(a) Selfish First: A player initially decides upon her preference over two coalitions friend-orientedly (i.e., according to (1)) and, if and only if she is indifferent between them, she asks her friends for a vote. For $M \geq n^5$, we define:

$$A \succeq_i^{SF} B \iff M(n|A\cap F_i| - |A\cap E_i|) + \sum_{a\in A\cap F_i} \frac{n|A\cap F_a| - |A\cap E_a|}{|A\cap F_i|} \geq M(n|B\cap F_i| - |B\cap E_i|) + \sum_{b\in B\cap F_i} \frac{n|B\cap F_b| - |B\cap E_b|}{|B\cap F_i|}. \tag{3}$$

THEOREM 1. *For $M \geq n^5$, $v_i(A) > v_i(B)$ implies $A \succ_i^{SF} B$.*

PROOF. The claim clearly holds for $\mathrm{avg}_i^F(A) \geq \mathrm{avg}_i^F(B)$. For $\mathrm{avg}_i^F(A) < \mathrm{avg}_i^F(B)$, it holds if and only if $M > \frac{\mathrm{avg}_i^F(B) - \mathrm{avg}_i^F(A)}{v_i(A) - v_i(B)}$. The numerator is upper-bounded by $\frac{n|B\cap F_i|\cdot|B|}{|B\cap F_i|} + \frac{|A\cap F_i|\cdot|A|}{|A\cap F_i|} \leq n^2 + n$. Since $v_i(A)$ and $v_i(B)$ are integral, $v_i(A) - v_i(B) \geq 1$. Thus $M > n^2 + n$ suffices. □

(b) Equal Treatment: A player and her friends "vote" friend-orientedly at the same time, equally taking part in the decision:

$$A \succeq_i^{EQ} B \iff \sum_{a\in A\cap(F_i\cup\{i\})} \frac{n|A\cap F_a| - |A\cap E_a|}{|A\cap(F_i\cup\{i\})|} \geq \sum_{b\in B\cap(F_i\cup\{i\})} \frac{n|B\cap F_b| - |B\cap E_b|}{|B\cap(F_i\cup\{i\})|}. \tag{4}$$

(c) Altruistic Treatment: A player first asks her friends for their opinion on a coalition they are contained in and adopts their average opinion; if and only if the consensus is indifference, the player decides for herself. For $M \geq n^5$, we define:

$$A \succeq_i^{AL} B \iff n|A\cap F_i| - |A\cap E_i| + M\sum_{a\in A\cap F_i} \frac{n|A\cap F_a| - |A\cap E_a|}{|A\cap F_i|} \geq n|B\cap F_i| - |B\cap E_i| + M\sum_{b\in B\cap F_i} \frac{n|B\cap F_b| - |B\cap E_b|}{|B\cap F_i|}. \tag{5}$$

THEOREM 2. *For $M \geq n^5$, $\mathrm{avg}_i^F(A) > \mathrm{avg}_i^F(B)$ implies $A \succ_i^{AL} B$.*

PROOF. The claim clearly holds for $v_i(A) \geq v_i(B)$. For $v_i(A) < v_i(B)$, the claim holds if and only if $M > \frac{v_i(B) - v_i(A)}{\mathrm{avg}_i^F(A) - \mathrm{avg}_i^F(B)}$. The numerator is upper-bounded by $n^2 + n$. Note that $v_i(A) < v_i(B)$ implies $|A\cap F_i| \leq |B\cap F_i|$. We distinguish three cases.

1. If $\mathrm{avg}_i^F(A)|A\cap F_i| > \mathrm{avg}_i^F(B)|B\cap F_i|$, then by the integrality of v, we have $\mathrm{avg}_i^F(A)|A\cap F_i| - \mathrm{avg}_i^F(B)|B\cap F_i| \geq 1$. Thus $\mathrm{avg}_i^F(A) - \mathrm{avg}_i^F(B) \geq \frac{\mathrm{avg}_i^F(A)|A\cap F_i| - \mathrm{avg}_i^F(B)|B\cap F_i|}{|A\cap F_i|} \geq \frac{1}{n}$, as $\mathrm{avg}_i^F(X)$ is always positive if X contains a friend of i and $|A\cap F_i| \leq |B\cap F_i|$.
2. If $\mathrm{avg}_i^F(A)|A\cap F_i| = \mathrm{avg}_i^F(B)|B\cap F_i|$, then we have $\sum_{a\in A\cap F_i} v_a(A)\left(\frac{1}{|A\cap F_i|} - \frac{1}{|B\cap F_i|}\right) \geq |A\cap F_i|\left(\frac{1}{|A\cap F_i|} - \frac{1}{|B\cap F_i|}\right)$. This is equal to $1 - \frac{|A\cap F_i|}{|B\cap F_i|}$, which is lower-bounded by $\frac{1}{n}$: Suppose that the lower bound does not hold. Then $n(|B\cap F_i| - |A\cap F_i|) < |B\cap F_i|$. Hence, we have the contradiction $n < |B\cap F_i|$.
3. If $\mathrm{avg}_i^F(A)|A\cap F_i| < \mathrm{avg}_i^F(B)|B\cap F_i|$, then $|B\cap F_i| > |A\cap F_i|$. Suppose that $\mathrm{avg}_i^F(A) - \mathrm{avg}_i^F(B) < \frac{1}{n^2}$. Since by the premise we have $|B\cap F_i| \sum_{a\in A\cap F_i} v_a(A) - |A\cap F_i| \sum_{b\in B\cap F_i} v_b(B) \geq 1$, this is equivalent to $n^2 < \frac{|A\cap F_i|\cdot|B\cap F_i|}{|B\cap F_i| \sum_{a\in A\cap F_i} v_a(A) - |A\cap F_i| \sum_{b\in B\cap F_i} v_b(B)}$. The right-hand side is upper-bounded by $n^2 - n$, implying the contradiction $n^2 < n^2 - n$.

Overall, $M > n^4 + n^3$ suffices in all three cases. □

For consistency we choose $M \geq n^5$. In all three cases in the proof of Theorem 2, normalization by the number of i's friends in a coalition prevents a "tyranny of the many" (otherwise, large coalitions would be preferred merely by the fact that the total number of friends is larger). The following example represents the different approaches to altruism in hedonic games.

EXAMPLE 1. *Consider the game with five players $N = \{1,2,3,4,5\}$ and the network in Figure 2b. Table 1 gives an overview of the relevant values and average values needed to determine player 1's utilities for different acceptable coalitions depending on the degree of altruism. A dash indicates that a value does not exist.*

C	$\{1,2,3\}$	$\{1,2,3,4\}$	$\{1,2,3,5\}$	N	$\{1,2\}$	$\{1,3\}$	$\{1,2,4\}$	$\{1,2,5\}$	$\{1,3,4\}$
$v_1(C)$	10	9	9	8	5	5	4	4	4
$v_2(C)$	4	3	9	8	5	–	4	10	–
$v_3(C)$	4	9	3	8	–	5	–	–	10
$\mathrm{avg}_1^F(C)$	4	6	6	8	5	5	4	10	10
EQ: $u_1(C)$	6	7	7	8	5	5	4	7	7

Table 1: Values and average values of the players in Example 1

All four weak preference orders are different. Under the friend-oriented preference extension (1), player 1's weak preference order is given in the first line according to the values of v_1. For the selfish-first *extension (3), the order remains the same; however, indifferences are dissolved, as is the case here with $\{1,2,5\} \succ_1^{SF} \{1,2,4\}$ by Theorem 1. Under the* equal-treatment *extension (4), the grand coalition is the most preferred one; intuitively, because all friends have a large number of friends at the same time. Finally, under the most altruistic extension (5), player 1's friends consider $\{1,2,5\}$ and $\{1,3,4\}$ the best coalition. As they agree on that, player 1 altruistically adopts this opinion by Theorem 2.*

A player's utility of a coalition can also be deduced from the corresponding network of friends itself.

PROPOSITION 3. *Let G be a network of friends, i a player, and $C \in \mathcal{N}^i$ a coalition. Let λ be the number of edges $\{i,j\}$ where $j \in C$, i.e., $\lambda = |F_i \cap C|$. Let μ be the number of edges between i's friends in C, i.e., $\mu = |\{\{j,k\} \mid j,k \in F_i \cap C\}|$, and let ν denote the number of edges between i's friends in C and those friends of j in C who are i's enemies, i.e., $\nu = |\{\{j,k\} \mid j \in F_i \cap C,\ k \in F_j \cap C,\ k \notin F_i\}|$. Then i's utility of C under selfish-first preferences is*

$$M\cdot\lambda(n+1) + M + n + 2 - (M+1)|C| + \frac{(n+1)(2\mu+\nu)}{\lambda};$$

under equal-treatment preferences it is

$$\frac{(2\lambda+2\mu+\nu)(n+1)}{\lambda+1} - |C| + 1;$$

and under altruistic-treatment preferences it is

$$M(n+2) + \lambda(n+1) + 1 - (M+1)|C| + \frac{M(n+1)(2\mu+\nu)}{\lambda}.$$

The proof of Proposition 3 is omitted due to limitation of space.

4. PROPERTIES OF HEDONIC GAMES WITH ALTRUISTIC INFLUENCES

In this section, we show which of the desirable properties from Section 2.1 are satisfied by our model. First, however, we start with a discussion of expressiveness, focusing on model (4):

First, as the original definition of friend-oriented preferences is recovered for coalitions that only consist of enemies, our models are not fully expressive. This follows from indifference between friends and enemies, respectively.

Second, we show that the expressiveness of model (4) is incomparable to (additively) separable hedonic games, fractional hedonic games, hedonic games with $\mathcal{B}$- or $\mathcal{W}$-preferences, and B- and W-hedonic games (see, for example, the book chapter by Aziz and Savani [6] for the definitions of these representations of hedonic games). In all of the above models two players' preference orders are independent but in our model they might depend on each other. Players are independent in choosing friends; however, the induced preferences depend crucially on friends' relations to other players. In other words, a player's preference is constrained by her friends' preferences. Hence, there is a tradeoff between the expressiveness of preferences and the expressiveness of profiles.

Third, model (4) can express preferences that are not separable: Consider a game with players $N = \{i,a,b,j\}$ and $F_i = \{a,b,j\}$, $F_a = \{i,b\}, F_b = \{i,a\}, F_j = \{i\}$. Denote the left-hand side of the inequality in (4) by $u_i^*(A) = \sum_{a' \in A \cap (F_i \cup \{i\})} \frac{n|A \cap F_{a'}| - |A \cap E_{a'}|}{|A \cap (F_i \cup \{i\})|}$. Then $u_i^*(\{i,a,b\}) = 2n$ and $u_i^*(\{i,a,b,j\}) = 2n-1$. Thus $\{i,a,b\} \succ_i^{EQ} \{i,a,b,j\}$ but $\{i,j\} \succ_i^{EQ} \{i\}$, because j is a friend. However, additively separable preferences can express strict preferences over coalitions with a single friend, which is not possible in model (4) because of indifference between friends. Similarly, fractional preferences can express strict preferences over pairs. In addition, they can express nonseparable relations by losing the ability to express indifference between pairs. $\mathcal{B}$- and $\mathcal{W}$-preferences can express indifference between pairs but this constraints the preferences over larger coalitions. In this case, however, depending on the network of friends, model (4) can express every possible relation between some specific coalitions. For B- and W-hedonic games, there is a simple example with two coalitions of size two only one of which is acceptable, where the implied relation over the coalition with both players does not hold under model (4).

Overall, neither is model (4) more expressive than any of the other considered models nor the other way around. Similar examples also exist for the other two models. It is not hard to see that all three degrees of altruism are locally friend-dependent, because (except for player i's own preference) only her friends in the current coalition affect its value. Note that this is a crucial property that distinguishes our model from previous work. We omit the proof of Proposition 4.

PROPOSITION 4. *Under all three degrees of altruism* (3)–(5), *the following properties are satisfied: reflexivity, transitivity, polynomial-time computability, as well as anonymity.*

THEOREM 5. *Under all three degrees of altruism* (3)–(5), *weak friend-orientedness, favoring friends, indifference between friends, indifference between enemies, sovereignty of players, symmetry, and friend-oriented unanimity are satisfied.*

PROOF. We show these properties only for equal treatment (4).

Weak friend-orientedness: Suppose that A is acceptable for $i \in A$, that is, we have $A \succeq_i^{EQ} \{i\}$, which is equivalent to the inequality

$$\sum_{a \in A \cap (F_i \cup \{i\})} \frac{v_a(A)}{|A \cap (F_i \cup \{i\})|} \geq \frac{v_i(\{i\})}{|\{i\} \cap (F_i \cup \{i\})|} = 0.$$

$A \cup \{f\} \succeq_i^{EQ} \{i\}$ if and only if $\sum_{a \in (A \cup \{f\}) \cap (F_i \cup \{i\})} v_a(A \cup \{f\}) \geq 0$. The left-hand side of this inequality equals

$$\sum_{a \in A \cap (F_i \cup \{i\})} v_a(A) + \sum_{a \in A \cap (F_i \cup \{i\})} v_a(\{f\}) + v_f(A \cup \{f\}). \tag{6}$$

The second sum and $v_f(A \cup \{f\})$ are greater than zero because i is f's friend (and vice versa) and there are at most $n-1$ enemies for f. Thus, in total, we have that (6) is nonnegative and, therefore, $A \cup \{f\}$ is acceptable for i as well.

Favoring friends: This property holds due to the fact that

$$\sum_{a \in \{x,i\} \cap (F_i \cup \{i\})} \frac{n|\{x,i\} \cap F_a| - |\{x,i\} \cap E_a|}{|\{x,i\} \cap (F_i \cup \{i\})|} = \frac{v_x(\{x,i\})}{|\{x,i\} \cap (F_i \cup \{i\})|} +$$

$$\frac{v_i(\{x,i\})}{|\{x,i\} \cap (F_i \cup \{i\})|} = n \geq -1 = \sum_{b \in \{y,i\} \cap (F_i \cup \{i\})} \frac{v_b(\{y,i\})}{|\{y,i\} \cap (F_i \cup \{i\})|}.$$

Indifference between friends: Let $x, y \in F_i$. As their names can be swapped, the sum for both friends is n and, therefore, we have both $\{x,i\} \succeq_i^{EQ} \{y,i\}$ and $\{y,i\} \succeq_i^{EQ} \{x,i\}$.

Indifference between enemies: Analogously to the indifference between friends, both sums equal -1.

Sovereignty of players: We construct the network G such that for all pairs of players $x, y \in C$, $x \neq y$, there is an edge $\{x,y\}$ in G, while there are no other edges in G.

Symmetry: Suppose that swapping the positions of j and k in G is an automorphism. If j is a friend of a player i, so is k. The same holds for enemies. Therefore, the sum over all players in $(C \cup \{j\}) \cap (F_i \cup \{i\})$ equals the sum over all players in $(C \cup \{k\}) \cap (F_i \cup \{i\})$ if j (and k) are not in F_i. If j (and, therefore, k) are i's friends, the additional summands equal each other, as j is neither in F_j nor in E_j and as k is neither in F_k nor in E_k.

Friend-oriented unanimity: As $A \cap F_i = B \cap F_i$ and both $A, B \in \mathcal{N}^i$, we have $|A \cap (F_i \cup \{i\})| = |B \cap (F_i \cup \{i\})|$. Thus it suffices to show that $\sum_{a \in A \cap (F_i \cup \{i\})} v_a(A) > \sum_{a \in A \cap (F_i \cup \{i\})} v_a(B)$. According to the friend-oriented model, we subdivide the sum on the left-hand side above as follows:

$$\sum_{a \in A \cap (F_i \cup \{i\})} v_a(A) = \sum_{a_1 \in A \cap (F_i \cup \{i\})} v_{a_1}(A) + \sum_{a_2 \in A \cap (F_i \cup \{i\})} v_{a_2}(A),$$

where a_1 are those $a \in A \cap (F_i \cup \{i\})$ for which $|A \cap F_a| > |B \cap F_a|$, and a_2 are those $a \in A \cap (F_i \cup \{i\})$ for which $|A \cap F_a| = |B \cap F_a|$ and $|A \cap E_a| < |B \cap E_a|$.

Considering a_1, we note that $v_{a_1}(A) > v_{a_1}(B)$, as even for $|A \cap F_{a_1}| = |B \cap F_{a_1}| + 1$ and $|A \cap E_{a_1}| = n-1$ and $|B \cap E_{a_1}| = 0$, we have $n(|B \cap F_{a_1}| + 1) - (n-1) > n|B \cap F_{a_1}|$. For a_2, we see that $n|A \cap F_{a_2}| - |A \cap E_{a_2}| = n|B \cap F_{a_2}| - |A \cap E_{a_2}| > n|B \cap F_{a_2}| - |B \cap E_{a_2}|$. Thus $A \succ_i^{EQ} B$, showing friend-oriented unanimity.

This proves (4); the proof for (3) and (5) is similar. □

Regarding the property of symmetry, note that whenever two interchangeable players have a distance of at most two, then the statement $(\forall C \in \mathcal{N}^i \setminus (\mathcal{N}^j \cup \mathcal{N}^k))\ [C \cup \{j\} \sim_i C \cup \{k\}]$ implies that swapping i and j in G is an automorphism.

THEOREM 6. *Selfish-first preferences* (3) *are type-I-monotonic and type-II-monotonic.*

PROOF. Let $i \in N$, $A, B \in \mathcal{N}^i$, and $j \in E_i$. We denote with $\widehat{\succeq_i^{SF}}$ the preference of i resulting from $\succeq_i^{SF}$ when j is moved from E_i to F_i and i is moved from E_j to F_j (all else being equal), and we denote the new friend sets of i and j with $F_i' = F_i \cup \{j\}$ and $F_j' = F_j \cup \{i\}$. Recall that $A \succeq_j^{SF} B$ means that (i) if $A \sim_j^{SF} B$ then $A \sim_j^{F} B$ has to hold and $\mathrm{avg}_j^F(A) = \mathrm{avg}_j^F(B)$ (where $\mathrm{avg}_j^F(A) = \sum_{a \in A\cap F_j} \frac{v_a(A)}{|A\cap F_j|}$), and (ii) if $A \succ_j^{SF} B$ then either (a) $A \sim_j^F B$ and $\mathrm{avg}_j^F(A) > \mathrm{avg}_j^F(B)$, or (b) $A \succ_j^F B$. Suppose $A \sim_i^{SF} B$. Then we have that $A \sim_i^F B$ and

$$\mathrm{avg}_i^F(A) = \mathrm{avg}_i^F(B). \tag{7}$$

Since $j \in A\cap B$, $A \widehat{\sim_i^{SF}} B$, so we have to compare $\sum_{a\in A\cap F_i'} \frac{v_a(A)}{|A\cap F_i|+1}$ and $\sum_{b\in B\cap F_i'} \frac{v_b(B)}{|B\cap F_i|+1}$, the former being equal to

$$\underbrace{\frac{|A\cap F_i|}{|A\cap F_i|+1}}_{\text{(part 1)}} \left(\underbrace{\frac{n|A\cap F_j|+n-|A\cap E_j|+1}{|A\cap F_i|}}_{\text{(part 2)}} + \underbrace{\mathrm{avg}_i^F(A)}_{\text{(part 3)}} \right) \tag{8}$$

and the latter being equal to

$$\underbrace{\frac{|B\cap F_i|}{|B\cap F_i|+1}}_{\text{(part 4)}} \left(\underbrace{\frac{n|B\cap F_j|+n-|B\cap E_j|+1}{|B\cap F_i|}}_{\text{(part 5)}} + \underbrace{\mathrm{avg}_i^F(B)}_{\text{(part 6)}} \right). \tag{9}$$

We know from $A \sim_i^F B$ that (part 1) = (part 4), we know from (7) that (part 3) = (part 6), and we know that the denominators in (part 2) and (part 5) are equal. So calculating (part 2) − (part 5) leads to

$$n|A\cap F_j| - |A\cap E_j| - (n|B\cap F_j| - |B\cap E_j|) \begin{cases} = 0 & \text{if } A \sim_j^F B, \\ \geq 0 & \text{if } A \succeq_j^F B. \end{cases}$$

In total, we have (8) $\geq$ (9) if $A \succeq_j^F B$, thus $A \widehat{\succeq_i^{SF}} B$.

Assume now that $A \succ_i^{SF} B$. If $A \succ_i^F B$, nothing changes by making j a friend of i. If $A \sim_i^F B$, then it has to hold that

$$\sum_{a\in A\cap F_i} \frac{v_a(A)}{|A\cap F_i|} > \sum_{b\in B\cap F_i} \frac{v_b(B)}{|B\cap F_i|}. \tag{10}$$

By making j a friend of a, the relation $A \sim_i^F B$ is not changed. So, analogously to the first part, we have to compare the sums in (8) and (9). By $A \sim_i^F B$, we know that (part 1) = (part 4) and from (10) we know that (part 3) > (part 6). By the same argument as above, we know that (part 2) $\geq$ (part 5) if $A \succeq_j^F B$, and, in total, we have that $A \widehat{\succ_i^{SF}} B$.

It remains to prove type-II monotonicity. In this case, we have $j \in A \setminus B$. Suppose $A \sim_i^{SF} B$. This implies that $A\cap F_i = B \cap F_i$. Since j is not contained in B, we have that $|A\cap F_i'| > |B\cap F_i'|$, which gives $A \widehat{\succ_i^{SF}} B$. Assume now that $A \succ_i^{SF} B$. There are two cases. First, if $A \sim_i^F B$, then $A \widehat{\succ_i^{SF}} B$ follows by the same argumentation as above. Second, if $A \succ_i^F B$, then adding a further friend to A who is not contained in B does not change this relation. Thus $A \widehat{\succ_i^{SF}} B$. □

PROPOSITION 7. *Equal-treatment preferences* (4) *and altruistic-treatment preferences* (5) *are not type-II-monotonic.*

PROOF. Let $\mathcal{G}_1$ be a game with the network of friends shown in Figure 2a. We see that $7 \notin F_1$ and $A \sim_1^{EQ} B$ for $A = \{1,2,3,7\}$ and $B = \{1,3,4,5\}$. Making 7 a friend of 1 leads to $\mathcal{G}_1'$ with the network of friends shown in Figure 3a, and in $\mathcal{G}_1'$ we have that $B \succ_1^{EQ} A$, violating type-II monotonicity. With an analogous argumentation for the games $\mathcal{G}_2$ and $\mathcal{G}_2'$ (illustrated in Figure 3b and 3c), altruistic-treatment preferences are not type-II-monotonic. □

Note that the above result is a desirable outcome since this behavior exactly captures the intuition behind the definition of the equal treatment and the altruistic treatment.

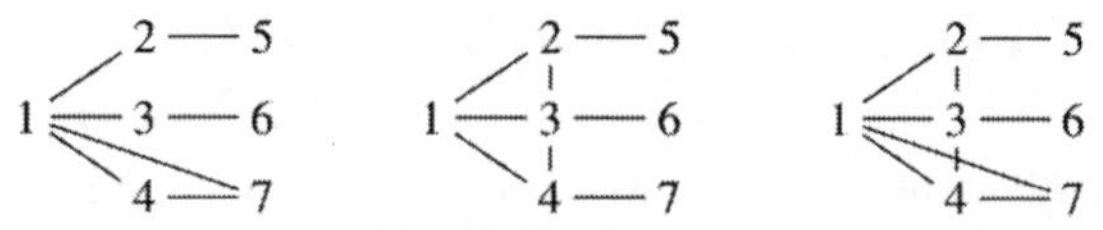

(a) Network of $\mathcal{G}_1'$ (b) Network of $\mathcal{G}_2$ (c) Network of $\mathcal{G}_2'$

Figure 3: Network of friends in the proof of Proposition 7

Based on a similar line of thought we note the following: In addition to the axiomatic properties in Section 2.1, one could consider notions of independence (see, e.g., [1] for a characterization of friend-oriented preferences using an independence axiom). Classic independence axioms say that a relation between two coalitions, A and B, continues to hold even if a new (and the same) player is introduced to both coalitions. However, independence axioms of this type are not desirable in our model because the new player can be valued very differently in both coalitions. This would be the case, for example, if the new player were an enemy to most of i's friends in A but were loved by most of i's friends in B. Similarly, $\mathcal{B}$- and $\mathcal{W}$-preferences [13] are natural extensions from singleton encodings that are not independent.

5. STABILITY

In this section, we study several common stability concepts in our model. Questions of interest are how hard it is to verify whether a given coalition structure satisfies a certain concept in a given hedonic game and whether stable coalition structures for certain concepts always exist. If, for some concept, such a coalition structure does not always exist, we are also interested in the computational complexity of deciding whether or not some such coalition structure exists in a given hedonic game. Recently, Peters and Elkind [29] established metatheorems that help proving NP-hardness results for stability concepts in hedonic games. However, their results do not seem to be immediately applicable.

OBSERVATION 8. *Under all three degrees of altruism* (3)–(5), *a coalition structure* Γ *is individually rational if and only if for each* $i \in N$, $\Gamma(i) \cap F_i \neq \emptyset$ *or* $\Gamma(i) = \{i\}$.

PROPOSITION 9. *For all three degrees of altruism* (3)–(5), *it can be tested in polynomial time whether a given coalition structure in a given game is Nash-stable, individually stable, or contractually individually stable.*

PROOF. Let Γ be a coalition structure. We need to check if for each player $i \in N$ and for each existing coalition C in Γ or for $C = \emptyset$, i prefers $\Gamma(i)$ to being added to C. For n players, there are at most $n+1$ such coalitions, and the preference relation can be verified in polynomial time by Proposition 4. Similar arguments apply to individual and contractually individual stability. □

LEMMA 10. *For all three degrees of altruism the following hold:*

1. For each player i, *each* $j \in F_i$ *assigns a positive value to any coalition* $C \in \mathcal{N}^i \cap \mathcal{N}^j$.

2. If a player has at least one friend, her favorite coalition contains at least one friend.

PROOF. 1. For symmetric friendship relationships, a friend always has at least one friend in a coalition she is asked to evaluate. Therefore, if a valuation of a friend is considered to influence a preference, it is always positive.

2. Suppose that a coalition contains player i and none of her friends. Then the overall value is at most zero.

This completes the proof. □

THEOREM 11. *For all three degrees of altruism* (3)–(5), *there always exist Nash-stable, individually stable, and contractually individually stable coalition structures.*

PROOF. Let $E = \{i \in N \mid F_i = \emptyset\}$ and rename its members by $E = \{e_1, \dots, e_k\}$. The coalition structure $\{\{e_1\}, \dots, \{e_k\}, N \setminus E\}$ is Nash-stable: For each $i \in E$, $v_i(N \setminus E) < 0$, since there are no friends to be evaluated positively nor to be asked for their valuation, i would rather stay alone. For each $i \notin E$, $v_i(N \setminus E) > 0$, since there is at least one friend who leads to a positive value and i herself contributes a positive value by Lemma 10.1, i would rather like to stay in $N \setminus E$ than to move alone to the empty coalition.

Nash stability implies individual stability, which in turn implies contractually individual stability. □

On the other hand, for all three degrees of altruism, there exists a game such that no coalition structure is strictly popular.

EXAMPLE 2. *Consider the game from Example 1 and the coalition structures* $\Gamma_1 = \{\{1,2,5\},\{3,4\}\}$, $\Gamma_2 = \{\{1,3,4\},\{2,5\}\}$, $\Gamma_3 = \{\{1,2,3,4\},\{5\}\}$, $\Gamma_4 = \{\{1,2,3,5\},\{4\}\}$, *and* $\Gamma_5 = \{N\}$.

1. Under selfish-first preferences (3), Γ_1 *and* Γ_2 *are more popular than all other coalition structures, but are in a tie.*

2. Under equal-treatment preferences (4), *even three coalition structures are in a tie:* Γ_3, Γ_4, *and* Γ_5.

3. Under altruistic-treatment preferences (5), Γ_2 *is more popular than* Γ_3, *which in turn is more popular than* Γ_5. Γ_5 *and* Γ_2 *are in a tie. Further,* Γ_1 *is more popular than* Γ_4*; the two coalition structures behave analogously to* Γ_2 *and* Γ_3, *respectively, due to symmetries. There is no other coalition structure that is not beaten by any of the above-mentioned coalition structures. Hence, no coalition structure is strictly popular.*

We now turn to the complexity of the verification and the existence problem for strict popularity in selfish-first hedonic games.

THEOREM 12. *Under selfish-first preferences* (3), *the problem of whether a given coalition structure in a given game is strictly popular is* coNP-*complete and the problem of whether there exists a strictly popular coalition structure in a given game is* coNP-*hard.*

PROOF. The first problem belongs to coNP, since the complementary problem can be decided by nondeterministically choosing another coalition structure and verifying whether a larger number of players prefer the latter to the former than the other way around. Verification can be done in polynomial time by Proposition 4. We show coNP-hardness by means of a polynomial-time many-one reduction from EXACT COVER BY 3-SETS (XC_3) to the complement of the first problem. An XC_3 instance consists of a set $B = \{1, \dots, 3k\}$ and a family $\mathscr{S} = \{S_1, \dots, S_m\}$ of subsets $S_i \subseteq B$ with $|S_i| = 3$, for each i, $1 \le i \le m$, and the question is whether there exists an exact cover for B in $\mathscr{S}$, i.e., a subfamily $\mathscr{S}' \subseteq \mathscr{S}$ such that each element of B occurs in exactly one set in $\mathscr{S}'$. We may assume that each $b \in B$ occurs at most three times in the sets of $\mathscr{S}$ (see [21]). The following construction is inspired by methods used by Sung and Dimitrov [32], which will be adapted in a nontrivial way, though. Given an XC_3 instance $(B, \mathscr{S})$, we consider the set of players $N = \{\beta_b \mid b \in B\} \cup \{\zeta_{S,\ell} \mid S \in \mathscr{S}, 1 \le \ell \le 3k\} \cup \{\eta_{S,j} \mid S \in \mathscr{S}, 1 \le j \le 3k+3\}$. The network of friends, as displayed in Figure 4, is the following: All players in $\{\beta_b \mid b \in B\}$ are friends with each other; β_b and $\zeta_{S,\ell}$ are each others' friends if $b \in S$, for each $S \in \mathscr{S}$, $1 \le \ell \le 3k$; for each $S \in \mathscr{S}$, all players in $Q_S = \{\zeta_{S,\ell}, \eta_{S,j} \mid 1 \le \ell \le 3k, 1 \le j \le 3k+3\}$ are each others' friends; and there are no other friendship relations.

Define the coalition structure $\Gamma = \{\{\beta_1, \dots, \beta_{3k}\}, Q_{S_1}, \dots, Q_{S_m}\}$. We show that Γ is strictly popular if and only if there exists no exact cover for B in $\mathscr{S}$.

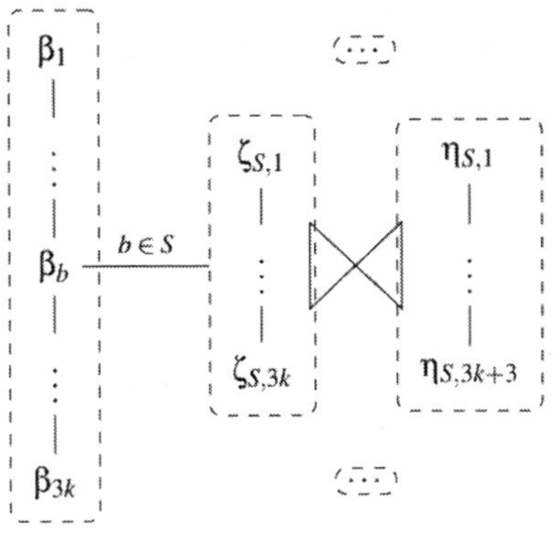

Figure 4: Network of friends in the proof of Theorem 12

Only if: Assume there exists an exact cover $\mathscr{S}' \subseteq \mathscr{S}$ such that $\bigcup_{S \in \mathscr{S}'} S = B$ and $|\mathscr{S}'| = k$. Then, for the coalition structure $\Delta = \{\{\beta_b \mid b \in S\} \cup Q_S \mid S \in \mathscr{S}'\} \cup \{Q_S \mid S \in \mathscr{S} \setminus \mathscr{S}'\}$, it holds that $|\{i \mid \Delta(i) \succ_i^{SF} \Gamma(i)\}| = 3k + k \cdot 3k = k(3k+3) = |\{j \mid \Gamma(j) \succ_j^{SF} \Delta(j)\}|$. Hence, Γ cannot be strictly popular.

If: If, on the other hand, Γ is not strictly popular, there exists some coalition structure Δ that is preferred to Γ by at least as many players as the number of those players preferring Γ to Δ. This is only possible if such a Δ implies the existence of an exact cover for B. Note that while eliminating all other possibilities, the friends' influences on a player $\zeta_{S,\ell}$ would be employed in favor of a clique Q_S in comparison to other coalitions that $\zeta_{S,\ell}$ may be indifferent between from a selfish-first point of view.

For the second problem, consider the same reduction as above, except that Γ is not given. If, on the one hand, there is no exact cover for B in $\mathscr{S}$, a strictly popular coalition structure exists, namely, Γ as considered above. If, on the other hand, there is an exact cover for B in $\mathscr{S}$, note that Γ beats every other coalition structure in pairwise comparison, but is in a tie in comparison to Δ as defined above. Therefore, Γ as well as any other coalition structure cannot be strictly popular. □

Theorem 13 is inspired by a result of Dimitrov et al. [16].

THEOREM 13. *In games with selfish-first preferences* (3), *there always exists a (strictly) core-stable coalition structure.*

PROOF. For a given game with the player set N and selfish-first preferences, we assume that the corresponding network of friends consists of k connected components. We show that the coalition structure $\Gamma = \{\Gamma_1, \Gamma_2, \dots, \Gamma_k\}$ consisting of these k components is (strictly) core-stable. We know that the players from different coalitions in Γ are not friends: Each $i \in N$ has all of her friends in $\Gamma(i)$. Clearly, a (weakly) blocking coalition C cannot contain players from different Γ_ℓ, for $1 \le \ell \le k$, as each of these players would prefer their assigned coalition because it either contains more friends than C or, if all friends are also in C, less enemies.

This allows us to argue for the special case of a network consisting of only one connected component and we show that the coalition structure $\Gamma = \{N\}$ is (strictly) core-stable. For a contradiction, we assume that there exists a blocking coalition $C \subset N$. So, for every $j \in C$ we have that $C \succ_j^{SF} N$, which implies that either (a) $C \succ_j^F N$ or (b) $C \sim_j^F N$ and $\text{avg}_i^F(C) > \text{avg}_i^F(N)$.

All of j's friends are contained in N, so the first case can only occur if C contains all of j's friends and a proper subset of j's enemies. The same has to hold for each $i \in F_j \subseteq C$, and for each of i's friends, as well. This can be continued following the paths through the network of friends, and since we assume that the network is connected, we obtain that $C = \bigcup_{i \in N} F_i = N$. In the second case, $C \sim_j^F N$ implies that $v_j(C) = v_j(N)$, thus $C = N$.

Overall, there is no blocking coalition. The same argumentation also holds for a weakly blocking coalition: At least one $j \in C$ has to prefer C to N while we need $C \succeq_i^{SF} N$ to hold for the remaining $i \in C$. The latter also implies that for each $i \in C$, the set of friends has to be in C, leading to $C = N$ as above. □

Under selfish-first preferences, it is easy to figure out whether there exists a perfect coalition structure: This is the case if and only if each connected component is a clique.

LEMMA 14. *Let C be player i's most preferred coalition in a game with equal-treatment preferences* (4). *If a friend j is in $F_i \cap C$, then $F_j \setminus F_i \subseteq C$.*

PROOF. If i has at least one friend, the value of C is positive by Lemma 10.1. Assume that there is a $k \in F_j \setminus F_i$ with $k \notin C$. Then

$$\frac{\sum_{a \in (F_i \cup \{i\}) \cap (C \cup \{k\})} v_a(C \cup \{k\})}{|(F_i \cup \{i\}) \cap (C \cup \{k\})|} - \frac{\sum_{a \in C \cap (F_i \cup \{i\})} v_a(C)}{|(F_i \cup \{i\}) \cap C|}$$

$$= \frac{\sum_{a \in C \cap (F_i \cup \{i\})} (v_a(C \cup \{k\}) - v_a(C))}{|F_i \cap C| + 1}$$

$$= \frac{\sum_{a \in C \cap (F_i \cup \{i\}) \cap F_k} (n) - \sum_{a \in C \cap (F_i \cup \{i\}) \setminus F_k} (1)}{|F_i \cap C| + 1} \geq \frac{n - (n-2)}{|F_i \cap C| + 1} > 0.$$

Thus $C \cup \{k\} \succ_i^{EQ} C$, since i asks the same number of friends and the value of $C \cup \{k\}$ increases by n for at least one player and decreases by 1 for at most $n-2$ players. □

PROPOSITION 15. *Whenever a perfect coalition structure exists under equal-treatment preferences* (4), *it is unique and consists of all connected components.*

PROOF. Let C be a coalition in a perfect coalition structure. Due to Lemma 10.2, C is connected. Suppose C is a proper subset of a connected component. Then there exists an edge $\{k, \ell\}$ with $k \in C$ and $\ell \notin C$. By Lemma 10.2, there exists another friend j of k's in C.

Case 1: Assume that there exists a player j with $\ell \notin F_j$. Then, by Lemma 14, this is a contradiction to C being j's favorite coalition, because $C \cup \{\ell\} \succ_j^{EQ} C$.

Case 2: For each $j \in F_k \cap C$, it holds that $\ell \in F_j$ (and $j \in F_\ell$ by symmetry). (a) Assume that there exists another $x \in C$ with $\ell \notin F_x$. By Lemma 10.2, there exists a $j \in F_k$ with $x \in F_j$ (and $j \in F_x$). Again, with $\ell \in F_j$ this is a contradition to C being x's most preferred coalition by Lemma 14. (b) Finally, for each $x \in C$, $\ell \in F_x$. This implies that $v_\ell(C \cup \{\ell\}) = n \cdot |C| - 0$. Thus, comparing coalitions $C \cup \{\ell\}$ and C from k's point of view, and letting λ denote $|F_k \cap C|$, we obtain:

$$\frac{v_k(C \cup \{\ell\}) + \sum_{j \in F_k \cap C} v_j(C \cup \{\ell\}) + v_\ell(C \cup \{\ell\})}{1 + \lambda + 1} - \frac{v_k(C) + \sum_{j \in F_k \cap C} v_j(C)}{1 + \lambda}$$

$$\geq \frac{n + |E_k \cap C| + \lambda(1+\lambda)n - \lambda|C|n + (1+\lambda)(n \cdot |C|)}{(2+\lambda)(1+\lambda)}$$

$$= \frac{n + |E_k \cap C| + \lambda(1+\lambda)n + n \cdot |C|}{(2+\lambda)(1+\lambda)} > 0.$$

Therefore, $C \cup \{\ell\} \succ_k^{EQ} C$, which means that C has to be the whole connected component. This completes the proof. □

COROLLARY 16. *If there exists a perfect coalition structure under equal treatment* (4), *all connected components have a diameter of at most two.*

There do exist networks with a diameter of at most two that do not allow a perfect coalition structure, e.g., stars (i.e., one central vertex connected to a number of leaves).

PROPOSITION 17. *Under equal treatment* (4), *trees with at least three vertices do not allow a perfect coalition structure.*

PROOF. Note that trees with diameter two are stars. Let i be the central player and j a leaf. It holds that $N \setminus \{j\} \succ_i^{EQ} N$ such that $\{N\}$ is not perfect, which in turn implies that there cannot be a perfect coalition structure by Proposition 15. □

6. CONCLUSIONS AND FUTURE WORK

We have introduced and studied hedonic games with altruistic influences where the agents' utility functions depend on their friends' preferences. Axiomatically, we have defined desirable properties and have shown that these are satisfied by our model, depending on the degree of altruism. When tailored to other well-studied preference models, such as friend-oriented, enemy-oriented, additively separable, and $\mathcal{B}$- and $\mathcal{W}$-preferences, we note that all of these five extension principles fulfill the introduced properties of anonymity, symmetry, and type-II-monotonicity, while only the former three satisfy independence.

In terms of stability, hedonic games with altruistic influences always admit, e.g., Nash-stable coalition structures. However, both the verification and the existence problems of strictly popular coalition structures are computationally intractable.

We consider it important future work to completely characterize when certain properties hold or stable coalition structures exist (e.g., to characterize when the grand coalition is perfect). Also, it might be useful to extend the model and normalize by the size of the coalition to consider only relative contributions of friend-of-a-friend relationships. This can be compared to a friend-oriented restriction of a fractional hedonic game [4]. For example, one could define

$$A \succeq_i^{EQ_f} B \iff \sum_{a \in A \cap (F_i \cup \{i\})} \frac{n|A \cap F_a| - |A \cap E_a|}{|A| \cdot |A \cap (F_i \cup \{i\})|} \geq \sum_{b \in B \cap (F_i \cup \{i\})} \frac{n|B \cap F_b| - |B \cap E_b|}{|B| \cdot |B \cap (F_i \cup \{i\})|}. \tag{11}$$

This definition clearly extends to the altruistic case. For the selfish-first case, the normalization is without effect. Hence, the fractional variant is equivalent to the selfish-first case we have considered.

In addition, we propose considering restrictions of the input such as constraining networks to special graph classes (such as interval graphs, where the width of an interval represents an agent's "tolerance"), studying problems of strategic influence (e.g., misreporting preferences to friends, pretending to be a friend while one in fact is an enemy, asserting control over the game as a whole). The model can be extended in multiple ways. To model more realistic situations, it would be suitable to allow for different degrees of altruism for distinct players and other representations of preferences and aggregators. So far, a player takes only her friends' preferences into consideration, that is, a player tries to satisfy her friends with respect to their preferences. Since players derive utility based on their own preferences and their friends' preferences, an interesting model would be to consider players that try to maximize their friends utilities (see, e.g., [31]). In a similar vein, the model can be extended to edge-weighted graphs, where the influence of a friend (or of a friend's friend) diminishes with the distance as in, e.g., social distance games [12].

Acknowledgements

We thank the reviewers for their helpful comments and suggestions. This work was supported in part by DFG grant RO-1202/14-2.

REFERENCES

[1] J. Alcantud and R. Arlegi. An axiomatic analysis of ranking sets under simple categorization. *SERIEs*, 3(1–2):227–245, 2012.

[2] K. Apt and G. Schäfer. Selfishness level of strategic games. In *Proc. SAGT'12*, pages 13–24. Springer-Verlag *LNCS #7615*, 2012.

[3] H. Aziz, F. Brandt, and P. Harrenstein. Pareto optimality in coalition formation. *Games and Economic Behavior*, 82:562–581, 2013.

[4] H. Aziz, F. Brandt, and P. Harrenstein. Fractional hedonic games. In *Proc. AAMAS'14*, pages 5–12. IFAAMAS, 2014.

[5] H. Aziz, F. Brandt, and H. Seedig. Computing desirable partitions in additively separable hedonic games. *Artificial Intelligence*, 195:316–334, 2013.

[6] H. Aziz and R. Savani. Hedonic games. In F. Brandt, V. Conitzer, U. Endriss, J. Lang, and A. Procaccia, editors, *Handbook of Computational Social Choice*, chapter 15. Cambridge University Press, 2016. To appear.

[7] C. Ballester. NP-completeness in hedonic games. *Games and Economic Behavior*, 49(1):1–30, 2004.

[8] S. Banerjee, H. Konishi, and T. Sönmez. Core in a simple coalition formation game. *Social Choice and Welfare*, 18(1):135–153, 2001.

[9] S. Barberà, W. Bossert, and P. Pattanaik. Ranking sets of objects. In S. Barberà, P. Hammond, and C. Seidl, editors, *Handbook of Utility Theory*, volume 2: Extensions, chapter 17, pages 893–977. Kluwer Academic Publishers, 2004.

[10] A. Bogomolnaia and M. Jackson. The stability of hedonic coalition structures. *Games and Economic Behavior*, 38(2):201–230, 2002.

[11] F. Brandl, F. Brandt, and M. Strobel. Fractional hedonic games: Individual and group stability. In *Proc. AAMAS'15*, pages 1219–1227. IFAAMAS, 2015.

[12] S. Brânzei and K. Larson. Social Distance Games. *Proc. IJCAI'11*, pages 91–96, AAAI Press/IJCAI, 2011.

[13] K. Cechlárová and A. Romero-Medina. Stability in coalition formation games. *International Journal of Game Theory*, 29(4):487–494, 2001.

[14] P. Chen, D. de Keijzer, D. Kempe, and G. Schäfer. The robust price of anarchy of altruistic games. In *Proc. WINE'11*, pages 383–390. Springer-Verlag *LNCS #7090*, 2011.

[15] A. Darmann, E. Elkind, S. Kurz, J. Lang, J. Schauer, and G. Woeginger. Group activity selection problem. In *Proc. WINE'12*, pages 156–169. Springer Verlag *LNCS #7695*, 2012.

[16] D. Dimitrov, P. Borm, R. Hendrickx, and S. Sung. Simple priorities and core stability in hedonic games. *Social Choice and Welfare*, 26(2):421–433, 2006.

[17] J. Drèze and J. Greenberg. Hedonic coalitions: Optimality and stability. *Econometrica*, 48(4):987–1003, 1980.

[18] E. Elkind and J. Rothe. Cooperative game theory. In J. Rothe, editor, *Economics and Computation. An Introduction to Algorithmic Game Theory, Computational Social Choice, and Fair Division*, chapter 3, pages 135–193. Springer-Verlag, 2015.

[19] E. Elkind and M. Wooldridge. Hedonic coalition nets. In *Proc. AAMAS'09*, pages 417–424. IFAAMAS, 2009.

[20] U. Endriss. Sincerity and manipulation under approval voting. *Theory and Decision*, 74(3):335–355, 2013.

[21] M. Garey and D. Johnson. *Computers and Intractability: A Guide to the Theory of NP-Completeness*. W. H. Freeman and Company, 1979.

[22] S. Ghosh and F. Velázquez-Quesada. Agreeing to agree: Reaching unanimity via preference dynamics based on reliable agents. In *Proc. AAMAS'15*, pages 1491–1499. IFAAMAS, 2015.

[23] U. Grandi, E. Lorini, and L. Perrussel. Propositional opinion diffusion. In *Proc. AAMAS'15*, pages 989–997. IFAAMAS, 2015.

[24] M. Hoefer and A. Skopalik. Altruism in atomic congestion games. In *Proc. ESA'09*, pages 179–189. Springer-Verlag *LNCS #5757*, 2009.

[25] J. Lang, A. Rey, J. Rothe, H. Schadrack, and L. Schend. Representing and solving hedonic games with ordinal preferences and thresholds. In *Proc. AAMAS'15*, pages 1229–1238. IFAAMAS, 2015.

[26] J. Lang and J. Rothe. Fair division of indivisible goods. In J. Rothe, editor, *Economics and Computation. An Introduction to Algorithmic Game Theory, Computational Social Choice, and Fair Division*, chapter 8, pages 493–550. Springer-Verlag, 2015.

[27] D. Levine. Modeling altruism and spitefulness in experiments. *Review of Economic Dynamics*, 1(3):593–662, 1998.

[28] D. Peters. Σ_2^p-complete problems on hedonic games. Technical Report arXiv:1509.02333v1[cs.GT], Computing Research Repository (CoRR), Sept. 2015.

[29] D. Peters and E. Elkind. Simple causes of complexity in hedonic games. In *Proc. IJCAI'15*, pages 617–623. AAAI Press/IJCAI, 2015.

[30] M. Rahn and G. Schäfer. Bounding the inefficiency of altruism through social contribution games. In *Proc. WINE'13*, pages 391–404. Springer-Verlag *LNCS #8289*, 2013.

[31] A. Salehi-Abari and C. Boutilier. Empathetic social choice on social networks. In *Proc. AAMAS'14*, pages 693–700. IFAAMAS, 2014.

[32] S. Sung and D. Dimitrov. Computational complexity in additive hedonic games. *European Journal of Operational Research*, 203(3):635–639, 2010.

[33] G. Woeginger. Core stability in hedonic coalition formation. In *Proc. SOFSEM'13*, pages 33–50. Springer-Verlag *LNCS #7741*, 2013.

[34] G. Woeginger. A hardness result for core stability in additive hedonic games. *Mathematical Social Sciences*, 65(2):101–104, 2013.

On the Interplay between Games, Argumentation and Dialogues

Xiuyi Fan
Nanyang Technological University, Singapore
xyfan@ntu.edu.sg

Francesca Toni
Imperial College London, United Kingdom
ft@imperial.ac.uk

ABSTRACT

Game theory, argumentation and dialogues all address problems concerning inter-agent interaction, but from different perspectives. In this paper, we contribute to the study of the interplay between these fields. In particular, we show that by mapping games in normal form into structured argumentation, computing *dominant solutions* and *Nash equilibria* is equivalent to computing *admissible sets of arguments*. Moreover, when agents lack complete information, computing dominant solutions/Nash equilibria is equivalent to constructing *successful (argumentation-based) dialogues*. Finally, we study agents' behaviour in these dialogues in reverse game-theoretic terms and show that, using specific notions of utility, agents engaged in (argumentation-based) dialogues are guaranteed to be *truthful and disclose relevant information*, and thus can converge to dominant solutions/Nash equilibria of the original games even under incomplete information.

Categories and Subject Descriptors

I.2.11 [**Artificial Intelligence**]: Distributed Artificial Intelligence-multiagent systems, coherence and coordination

Keywords

Argumentation; Dialogues; Games

1. INTRODUCTION

Argumentation (see [3, 4, 37, 28] for overviews) provides means to reason with incomplete and inconsistent information, e.g. when this is held by collaborative or competing agents. Argumentation-based dialogues (e.g. see [2, 31, 32, 30, 6, 26, 39, 21]) study dialectical interactions amongst agents. Game theory (see e.g. [42] for an overview) studies agents' strategic behaviour. The interplay between these three fields brings interesting research opportunities, including addressing the following questions:

- **Q1:** Could argumentation be used to solve game-theoretic problems? If so, what are suitable representations, semantics and interaction models?
- **Q2:** Could game theory be used to analyse agents' behaviour in argumentation? If so, how to formulate behaviour and how to ensure "good" behaviour?

Appears in: *Proceedings of the 15th International Conference on Autonomous Agents and Multiagent Systems (AAMAS 2016), J. Thangarajah, K. Tuyls, C. Jonker, S. Marsella (eds.), May 9–13, 2016, Singapore.*

Both questions have been partially looked at before, for example, [9] studied how the stable marriage problem can be modelled using abstract argumentation (AA); [36, 34, 29] discussed conditions under which direct mechanisms based on grounded and preferred semantics for AA [9] are strategy-proof; [16, 25] analysed the computational complexity of behaving strategically in argumentation dialogues. We look at these questions in the context of *Assumption-based Argumentation (ABA)*, a form of structured argumentation (see [10, 41] for overviews). ABA is an instance of AA [11] and it admits AA as an instance [40]. ABA is well-studied with readily usable results, including a dialectical counterpart (referred to as *ABA dialogues* [15]) and soundness results connecting argumentation and dialogues [15]. ABA affords a finer level of granularity than AA, allowing, in particular, multiple agents to construct arguments jointly in dialogues, while assessing their acceptability as in AA. At the same time, ABA is an instance of other structured argumentation frameworks (such as ASPIC+ [27]) with just enough constructs to support our analysis in this paper (for example, preferences over rules, accommodated in ASPIC+ but not directly in ABA, are not required in our analysis).

For both **Q1** and **Q2**, we consider two agents α and β, such that:

1. each agent $x \in \{\alpha, \beta\}$ has a set of *strategies* Σ_x; strategies are *public*, namely each agent is aware of the set of strategies of the other;
2. each agent x is equipped with a *payoff function* π_x, namely a mapping from pairs of strategies to real numbers such that, for $(\sigma_\alpha, \sigma_\beta) \in \Sigma_\alpha \times \Sigma_\beta$, $\pi_x(\sigma_\alpha, \sigma_\beta)$ denotes the payoff value of $(\sigma_\alpha, \sigma_\beta)$ for x; the payoff functions are *private*, namely each agent is only aware of its own payoff function;
3. a *game* between α, β is a tuple $\langle \Sigma_\alpha, \Sigma_\beta, \pi_\alpha, \pi_\beta \rangle$.

We study two well-known solution concepts for these types of games: dominant solutions and Nash equilibria. A pair of strategies $(\sigma^\star_\alpha, \sigma^\star_\beta)$ is a *dominant solution* iff for all pairs of strategies $(\sigma_\alpha, \sigma_\beta)$ it holds that

$$\pi_\alpha(\sigma^\star_\alpha, \sigma^\star_\beta) \geq \pi_\alpha(\sigma_\alpha, \sigma_\beta) \text{ and } \pi_\beta(\sigma^\star_\alpha, \sigma^\star_\beta) \geq \pi_\beta(\sigma_\alpha, \sigma_\beta).$$

Also, $(\sigma^\star_\alpha, \sigma^\star_\beta)$ is a *Nash equilibrium* iff for all $(\sigma_\alpha, \sigma_\beta)$ it holds that

$$\pi_\alpha(\sigma^\star_\alpha, \sigma^\star_\beta) \geq \pi_\alpha(\sigma_\alpha, \sigma^\star_\beta) \text{ and } \pi_\beta(\sigma^\star_\alpha, \sigma^\star_\beta) \geq \pi_\beta(\sigma^\star_\alpha, \sigma_\beta).$$

In words, dominant solutions are strategy pairs which give the highest payoffs to both agents, whereas Nash equilibria are such that given the strategy adopted by the other agent, neither agent could do strictly better by adopting another strategy.

We illustrate games and solution concepts with a simple example, used throughout the paper.

		Wife (β)	
		r	**w**
Husband (α)	**m**	2,1	0,0
	f	0,0	1,2

Table 1: Dinner Party Game payoff matrix.

EXAMPLE 1.1. *(**Dinner Party Game**) Two agents ("husband" and "wife") want to organise a dinner party. They decide to split tasks: the husband will buy either meat (m) or fish (f) for the main course; the wife will buy either red wine (r) or white wine (w) as accompanying beverage. The husband (α) has strategies $\Sigma_\alpha = \{m, f\}$; the wife (β) has strategies $\Sigma_\beta = \{r, w\}$. The payoffs are given in Table 1, e.g. $\pi_\alpha(m, r) = 2, \pi_\beta(m, r) = 1$. Both (m, r) and (f, w) are Nash equilibria; there is no dominant solution for this game.*

Since we are assuming that payoffs are private (and thus agents have incomplete information), dominant solutions/Nash equilibria cannot be computed without some information exchange. In our model, agents use dialogues to support this exchange. As an illustration, for Example 1.1, agents can identify the Nash equilibrium (m, r) using the following dialogue (expressed in natural language here and formalised as an ABA dialogue later in Example 4.1):

Husband: meat and red wine make a good combination.
Husband: I assume you are OK with this choice.
Husband: Please let me know if you disagree.
Wife: It is not good if you prefer fish and red wine.
Husband: No, I don't.
Husband: And you don't prefer meat and white wine either?
Wife: No, I don't.

In this dialogue, the agents jointly identify a good combination of food and wine (a Nash equilibrium) by sharing (and disclosing) information, but no more than strictly necessary (e.g. the wife does not disclose her payoff for (m, r) or for any other strategy pair).

In this paper, we address **Q1** by using ABA dialogues to compute, in a distributed manner, dominant solutions and Nash equilibria for the kinds of games we consider (Section 4), based upon ABA formulations of games such that the solution concepts correspond to admissibility of arguments (Section 3). Moreover, we address **Q2** by modelling ABA dialogues themselves as games and studying dialectical strategies as agents' game strategies (Section 5). To ensure truthfulness and disclosure of relevant information from agents, we use reverse game theory (also known as mechanism design, see e.g. [19]) and define specific notions of utility to ensure truthfulness and disclosure in dialogue sequences (Section 6). As a result, we prove that agents engaged in ABA dialogues can converge to dominant solutions/Nash equilibria of the original games even under incomplete information.

2. BACKGROUND

Assumption-based Argumentation (ABA) *frameworks* [41] are tuples $\langle \mathcal{L}, \mathcal{R}, \mathcal{A}, \mathcal{C} \rangle$ where

- $\langle \mathcal{L}, \mathcal{R} \rangle$ is a deductive system, with $\mathcal{L}$ the *language* and $\mathcal{R}$ a set of *rules* of the form $s_0 \leftarrow s_1, \ldots, s_m (m \geq 0, s_i \in \mathcal{L})$;
- $\mathcal{A} \subseteq \mathcal{L}$ is a (non-empty) set, whose elements are *assumptions*;
- $\mathcal{C}$ is a total mapping from $\mathcal{A}$ into $2^{\mathcal{L}} - \{\{\}\}$, where each $s \in \mathcal{C}(a)$ is a *contrary* of a, for $a \in \mathcal{A}$.

Given a rule $\rho = s_0 \leftarrow s_1, \ldots, s_m$, s_0 is referred to as the *head* (denoted $Head(\rho) = s_0$) and $s_1, \ldots, s_m$ as the *body* (denoted $Body(\rho) = \{s_1, \ldots, s_m\}$). All ABA frameworks in this paper are *flat*, namely such that no assumption is the head of a rule.

In ABA, *arguments* are deductions of claims using rules and supported by sets of assumptions, and *attacks* are directed at the assumptions in the support of arguments. Following [10]:

- *an argument for (claim) $s \in \mathcal{L}$ supported by $A \subseteq \mathcal{A}$* (denoted $A \vdash s$) is a finite tree with nodes labelled by sentences in $\mathcal{L}$ or by τ[1], the root labelled by s, leaves either τ or assumptions in A, and non-leaves s' with, as children, the elements of the body of some rule ρ with head s' (we say that ρ is *in* $A \vdash s$);
- *an argument* $A_1 \vdash s_1$ attacks an argument $A_2 \vdash s_2$ iff s_1 is a contrary of some assumption in A_2.

A *set of arguments Δ is admissible* iff Δ is *conflict-free* (i.e. no argument in Δ attacks any argument in Δ) and all arguments attacking some argument in Δ are counter attacked by arguments in Δ; an *argument is admissible* iff it belongs to an admissible set of arguments; a *sentence is admissible* iff it is the claim of an admissible argument.

Two ABA frameworks can be "merged" to form a single *joint framework* [13]: given $AF = \langle \mathcal{L}, \mathcal{R}, \mathcal{A}, \mathcal{C} \rangle$, $AF' = \langle \mathcal{L}, \mathcal{R}', \mathcal{A}', \mathcal{C}' \rangle$, the joint framework (of AF and AF') is $AF_J = \langle \mathcal{L}, \mathcal{R} \cup \mathcal{R}', \mathcal{A} \cup \mathcal{A}', \mathcal{C}_J \rangle$, with $\mathcal{C}_J(a) = \mathcal{C}(a) \cup \mathcal{C}'(a)$, for all $a \in \mathcal{A} \cup \mathcal{A}'$.

ABA-dialogues [12, 15] are conducted between two agents, say α and β, that can be thought of as being equipped with ABA frameworks $\langle \mathcal{L}, \mathcal{R}_\alpha, \mathcal{A}_\alpha, \mathcal{C}_\alpha \rangle$ and $\langle \mathcal{L}, \mathcal{R}_\beta, \mathcal{A}_\beta, \mathcal{C}_\beta \rangle$ respectively, sharing a common language $\mathcal{L}$. An ABA-dialogue is made of *utterances* (from agent $x \in \{\alpha, \beta\}$) of the form $\langle x, y, T, C, ID \rangle$ (for $y \in \{\alpha, \beta\}, x \neq y$) where: C (the *content*) is one of: $claim(s)$ for some $s \in \mathcal{L}$, $rl(s_0 \leftarrow s_1, \ldots, s_m)$ for some $s_0, \ldots, s_m \in \mathcal{L}$, $asm(a)$ for some $a \in \mathcal{L}$, $ctr(a, s)$ for some $a, s \in \mathcal{L}$, a *pass* sentence $\pi \notin \mathcal{L}$; $ID \in \mathbb{N}$ (the *identifier*); $T \in \mathbb{N} \cup \{0\}$ (the *target*) such that $T < ID$. In the remainder, $\mathcal{U}^x$ will denote the set of all possible utterances from agent x.

A *dialogue $\mathcal{D}^x_y(\chi)$ (between x and y, $x, y \in \{\alpha, \beta\}$, $x \neq y$, for $\chi \in \mathcal{L}$)*, is a sequence $\langle u_1, \ldots, u_n \rangle$, $n \geq 0$, where each u_l, $l = 1, \ldots, n$, is an utterance, and: $u_1 = \langle x, y, \_, \_, \_ \rangle$;[2] the content of u_l is $claim(\chi)$ iff $l = 1$; the target of pass and claim utterances is 0; the target of regular utterances is not 0; the identifier of an utterance represents the position of the utterance in a dialogue, and the target of a non-pass, non-claim utterance is the identifier of some earlier utterance.

The *framework drawn from dialogue* $\delta = \langle u_1, \ldots, u_n \rangle$ is $F_\delta = \langle \mathcal{L}, \mathcal{R}_\delta, \mathcal{A}_\delta, \mathcal{C}_\delta \rangle$ where

- $\mathcal{R}_\delta = \{\rho | rl(\rho)$ is the content of some u_i in $\delta\}$;
- $\mathcal{A}_\delta = \{a | asm(a)$ is the content of some u_i in $\delta\}$;
- $\mathcal{C}_\delta(a) = \{s | ctr(a, s)$ is the content of some u_i in $\delta\}$.

Restrictions can be imposed on dialogues so that they fulfil desirable properties, and in particular that P1) the framework drawn from them is a flat ABA framework , and P2) utterances are related to their target utterances, where $u_j = \langle \_, \_, T, C_j, \_ \rangle$ is *related to* $u_i = \langle \_, \_, \_, C_i, ID \rangle$ iff $T = ID$ and one of the following holds:

- $C_j = rl(\rho_j)$, $Head(\rho_j) = s$ and either $C_i = rl(\rho_i)$ with $s \in Body(\rho_i)$, or $C_i = ctr(\_, s)$, or $C_i = claim(s)$;
- $C_j = asm(a)$ and either $C_i = rl(\rho)$ with $a \in Body(\rho)$, or $C_i = ctr(\_, a)$, or $C_i = claim(a)$;
- $C_j = ctr(a, \_)$ and $C_i = asm(a)$.

Properties P1) and P2) above can be enforced using *legal-move functions*, which are mappings from dialogues to sets of utterances such that there is no repeated utterance to the same target in a dialogue *compatible* with a legal-move function. We assume that dialogues compatible with legal-move functions defined later in the paper also satisfy both P1 and P2.

ABA dialogues can be used to check admissibility of claims: an ABA dialogue is deemed *successful* iff its claim is admissible

[1] $\tau \notin \mathcal{L}$ represents "true" and stands for the empty body of rules.
[2] Throughout, _ stands for an anonymous variable as in Prolog.

in the ABA framework drawn from the dialogue [15].[3] *Strategy-move* functions [13] can be used to model agents' behaviour, towards fulfillment of their aims, in ABA dialogues. A strategy-move function for agent x is a mapping ϕ from dialogues and legal-move functions to $\mathcal{U}^x$ such that $\phi(\delta, \lambda) \subseteq \lambda(\delta)$. Given a dialogue $\delta = \langle u_1, \dots, u_n \rangle$ between agents x, y compatible with a legal-move function λ and a strategy-move function ϕ for x, if for all utterances u_m made by x, $u_m \in \phi(\langle u_1, \dots, u_{m-1} \rangle, \lambda)$, then x *uses* ϕ in δ. If x and y both use ϕ, then δ is *constructed with* ϕ. The strategy-move function we use in this work is the *thorough strategy-move* function, ϕ_h. Informally, a dialogue constructed with ϕ_h contains all information that is relevant to the claim from both agents. Dialogues constructed with ϕ_h have the desirable property that admissible arguments obtained in the dialogue are admissible in the joint ABA framework of the two agents, see Theorem 1 in [13]. It is important to note that the thorough strategy-move function does not force agents to utter all knowledge but only information relevant to the claim.

Mechanism Design (e.g. see [19]) provides an abstraction of distributed problem solving amongst self-interested agents interacting with each other. In the language of mechanism design, agents are characterised by *types*, which are abstractions of their internal, private beliefs. Given two agents, α, β, the space of possible types for agent $x \in \{\alpha, \beta\}$ is denoted by Θ_x and its type is $\theta_x \in \Theta_x$. Moreover, $\Theta = \Theta_\alpha \times \Theta_\beta$.

Inter-agent interactions have a number of potential *outcomes* $\mathcal{O}$. A given *social choice function* $f : \Theta \to \mathcal{O}$ characterises what can be deemed to be a *socially* optimal outcome of the interaction. Agents' self-interest is expressed in terms of (private) *utility functions* $v_x : \mathcal{O} \times \Theta_x \to \mathbb{R}$. A_x is the set of possible actions of agent x and $A = A_\alpha \times A_\beta$. The decision for agent x of which action to perform is given by a *strategy*[4]. Let S_x denote the space of possible strategies for agent x, $S = S_\alpha \times S_\beta$. Then a strategy $s_x \in S_x$ is a function $s_x : \Theta_x \times A \to A_x$.

Finally, a *mechanism* $\mathcal{M} = (A, g)$ consists of the action space A and an *outcome function* $g : S \to \mathcal{O}$, where $g(s)$ is the outcome implemented by $\mathcal{M}$ for strategy $s = (s_\alpha, s_\beta)$.

A social choice function specifies the desired goal of an interaction, whereas a mechanism is a means of characterising the agents' behaviour in the interaction. Several characterisations of strategies have been provided as ways to predict how (rational) agents will behave in a mechanism. In particular, a strategy s_x is *dominant* (for x) if it maximises the agent's utility irrespectively of the other agent's strategy. For a mechanism $\mathcal{M} = (A, g)$ and a social choice function f, $\mathcal{M}$ *implements* f iff $g(s) = f(\theta)$, where s is a dominant strategy.

3. GAME SOLUTIONS IN ABA

As a general purpose framework, ABA can be used to represent knowledge in many applications [41]. Here, we give ABA representations of games of the kind presented in Section 1 and show a correspondence between admissible sentences in these frameworks and dominant solutions / Nash equilibria for the games.

Firstly, we specify the languages underlying the ABA frameworks we will use.

DEFINITION 3.1. *Given a game* $\langle \Sigma_\alpha, \Sigma_\beta, \pi_\alpha, \pi_\beta \rangle$, *the* Dominant/Nash languages *are (respectively):*

- $\mathcal{L}_D = \{d(\sigma_\alpha, \sigma_\beta), nD(\sigma_\alpha, \sigma_\beta), vA(\sigma_\alpha, \sigma_\beta) > vA(\sigma'_\alpha, \sigma'_\beta), vB(\sigma_\alpha, \sigma_\beta) > vB(\sigma'_\alpha, \sigma'_\beta) | \sigma_\alpha, \sigma'_\alpha \in \Sigma_\alpha, \sigma_\beta, \sigma'_\beta \in \Sigma_\beta\}$;
- $\mathcal{L}_N = \{n(\sigma_\alpha, \sigma_\beta), nN(\sigma_\alpha, \sigma_\beta), vA(\sigma_\alpha, \sigma_\beta) > vA(\sigma'_\alpha, \sigma'_\beta), vB(\sigma_\alpha, \sigma_\beta) > vB(\sigma'_\alpha, \sigma'_\beta) | \sigma_\alpha, \sigma'_\alpha \in \Sigma_\alpha, \sigma_\beta, \sigma'_\beta \in \Sigma_\beta\}$.

Intuitively, the sentences in $\mathcal{L}_D$/$\mathcal{L}_N$ can be read as follows: $d(\sigma_\alpha, \sigma_\beta)/n(\sigma_\alpha, \sigma_\beta)$ stands for "$(\sigma_\alpha, \sigma_\beta)$ is a dominant solution/ Nash equilibrium" (respectively); $nD(\sigma_\alpha, \sigma_\beta)/nN(\sigma_\alpha, \sigma_\beta)$ stands for "$(\sigma_\alpha, \sigma_\beta)$ is *not* a dominant solution /Nash equilibrium" (respectively); $vA(\sigma_\alpha, \sigma_\beta) > vA(\sigma'_\alpha, \sigma'_\beta)$ represents that, for agent α, the payoff value of $(\sigma_\alpha, \sigma_\beta)$ is higher than the payoff value of $(\sigma'_\alpha, \sigma'_\beta)$; $vB(\sigma_\alpha, \sigma_\beta) > vB(\sigma'_\alpha, \sigma'_\beta)$ can be read similarly for agent β.

Preferences between strategy pairs (namely sentences of the form $vA(\sigma_\alpha, \sigma_\beta) > vA(\sigma'_\alpha, \sigma'_\beta)$) are heads of *preference rules*, determined by the agents' private payoff functions, as follows:

DEFINITION 3.2. *Given a game* $\langle \Sigma_\alpha, \Sigma_\beta, \pi_\alpha, \pi_\beta \rangle$, *the* preference rules $\mathcal{R}^p_\alpha$, *for* α, *and* $\mathcal{R}^p_\beta$, *for* β, *are:*

$$\mathcal{R}^p_\alpha = \{vA(\sigma_\alpha, \sigma_\beta) > vA(\sigma'_\alpha, \sigma'_\beta) \leftarrow | \sigma_\alpha, \sigma'_\alpha \in \Sigma_\alpha, \sigma_\beta, \sigma'_\beta \in \Sigma_\beta, \pi_\alpha(\sigma_\alpha, \sigma_\beta) > \pi_\alpha(\sigma'_\alpha, \sigma'_\beta)\};$$
$$\mathcal{R}^p_\beta = \{vB(\sigma_\alpha, \sigma_\beta) > vB(\sigma'_\alpha, \sigma'_\beta) \leftarrow | \sigma_\alpha, \sigma'_\alpha \in \Sigma_\alpha, \sigma_\beta, \sigma'_\beta \in \Sigma_\beta, \pi_\beta(\sigma_\alpha, \sigma_\beta) > \pi_\beta(\sigma'_\alpha, \sigma'_\beta)\}.$$

EXAMPLE 3.1. *(Example 1.1 cont.) For the husband,* $\mathcal{R}^p_\alpha$ *is:*

$$\{vA(m,r) > vA(m,w) \leftarrow, \quad vA(m,r) > vA(f,r) \leftarrow, \quad vA(m,r) > vA(f,w) \leftarrow, \quad vA(f,w) > vA(f,r) \leftarrow, \quad vA(f,w) > vA(m,w) \leftarrow\}.$$

For the wife, $\mathcal{R}^p_\beta$ *is:*

$$\{vB(m,r) > vB(m,w) \leftarrow, \quad vB(m,r) > vA(f,r) \leftarrow, \quad vB(f,w) > vB(f,r) \leftarrow, \quad vB(f,w) > vA(m,w) \leftarrow, \quad vB(f,w) > vB(m,r) \leftarrow\}.$$

We then define ABA frameworks for capturing dominant solutions.

DEFINITION 3.3. *Given a game* $\langle \Sigma_\alpha, \Sigma_\beta, \pi_\alpha, \pi_\beta \rangle$, *the* Dominant ABA framework $\langle \mathcal{L}_D, \mathcal{R}_D, \mathcal{A}_D, \mathcal{C}_D \rangle$ *has:*

- $\mathcal{R}_D$ *consisting of* $\mathcal{R}^p_\alpha \cup \mathcal{R}^p_\beta$ *together with:*[5]
  $nD(\sigma_\alpha, \sigma_\beta) \leftarrow vA(\_, \_) > vA(\sigma_\alpha, \sigma_\beta)$,
  $nD(\sigma_\alpha, \sigma_\beta) \leftarrow vB(\_, \_) > vB(\sigma_\alpha, \sigma_\beta)$;
- $\mathcal{A}_D = \{d(\sigma_\alpha, \sigma_\beta) | \sigma_\alpha \in \Sigma_\alpha, \sigma_\beta \in \Sigma_\beta\}$;
- *for each* $d(\sigma_\alpha, \sigma_\beta) \in \mathcal{A}_D$, $\mathcal{C}_D(d(\sigma_\alpha, \sigma_\beta)) = \{nD(\sigma_\alpha, \sigma_\beta)\}$.

Note that Dominant ABA frameworks are flat (see Section 2).

The intuition of this definition is the following. Each strategy pair can be *assumed* to be a dominant solution (in that $d(\sigma_\alpha, \sigma_\beta) \in \mathcal{A}_D$ for each $(\sigma_\alpha, \sigma_\beta)$). A pair $(\sigma_\alpha, \sigma_\beta)$ can be deemed to be not dominant iff there is another pair $(\sigma'_\alpha, \sigma'_\beta)$ such that either $\pi_\alpha(\sigma'_\alpha, \sigma'_\beta) > \pi_\alpha(\sigma_\alpha, \sigma_\beta)$ or $\pi_\beta(\sigma'_\alpha, \sigma'_\beta) > \pi_\beta(\sigma_\alpha, \sigma_\beta)$, described by the the definition of contrary and by the two rule schemata in Definition 3.3, respectively (by instantiating $vA(\_, \_)$, $vB(\_, \_)$ to $vA(\sigma'_\alpha, \sigma'_\beta)$, $vB(\sigma'_\alpha, \sigma'_\beta)$, respectively).

Admissible sentences in Dominant ABA frameworks correspond to dominant solutions, as follows.

THEOREM 3.1. *Given a game* $\langle \Sigma_\alpha, \Sigma_\beta, \pi_\alpha, \pi_\beta \rangle$, *a strategy pair* $(\sigma^\star_\alpha, \sigma^\star_\beta)$ *is a dominant solution iff* $d(\sigma^\star_\alpha, \sigma^\star_\beta)$ *is admissible in the Dominant ABA framework.*

[3]ABA dialogues for the grounded and ideal semantics have also been defined in [15], but we only need admissiblity in this work.

[4]In Section 1, including Example 1.1, strategies are considered as actions directly, for ease of presentation.

[5]For brevity, here and in the remainder of the paper, we use *schemata* with variables $(\sigma_\alpha, \sigma_\beta)$ and anonymous variables (_) to represent compactly all rules that can be obtained by instantiating the variables over the appropriate domains.

PROOF. ($\Rightarrow$) To show $(\sigma_\alpha^\star, \sigma_\beta^\star)$ is a dominant solution is to show for all other strategy pairs $(\sigma_\alpha, \sigma_\beta)$, $\pi_\alpha(\sigma_\alpha^\star, \sigma_\beta^\star) \geq \pi_\alpha(\sigma_\alpha, \sigma_\beta)$ and $\pi_\beta(\sigma_\alpha^\star, \sigma_\beta^\star) \geq \pi_\beta(\sigma_\alpha, \sigma_\beta)$. Suppose otherwise, namely there is $(\sigma'_\alpha, \sigma'_\beta)$ such that $\pi_\alpha(\sigma'_\alpha, \sigma'_\beta) > \pi_\alpha(\sigma_\alpha^\star, \sigma_\beta^\star)$. Thus, by Definition 3.2, $vA(\sigma'_\alpha, \sigma'_\beta) > vA(\sigma_\alpha^\star, \sigma_\beta^\star) \leftarrow \in \mathcal{R}_\alpha^p$. Given the rule $nD(\sigma_\alpha, \sigma_\beta) \leftarrow vA(\sigma'_\alpha, \sigma'_\beta) > vA(\sigma_\alpha, \sigma_\beta)$ in the Dominant ABA framework, let $\sigma_\alpha = \sigma_\alpha^\star$ and $\sigma_\beta = \sigma_\beta^\star$; then argument $\{\} \vdash nD(\sigma_\alpha^\star, \sigma_\beta^\star)$ attacks $\{d(\sigma_\alpha^\star, \sigma_\beta^\star)\} \vdash d(\sigma_\alpha^\star, \sigma_\beta^\star) = A$. Therefore A is not admissible, so $d(\sigma_\alpha^\star, \sigma_\beta^\star)$ is not admissible either. Contradiction.

($\Leftarrow$) To show $d(\sigma_\alpha^\star, \sigma_\beta^\star)$ is admissible is to show that there is a set of argument Δ such that $\{d(\sigma_\alpha^\star, \sigma_\beta^\star)\} \vdash d(\sigma_\alpha^\star, \sigma_\beta^\star) = A \in \Delta$ and Δ is conflict-free and counterattacks all attacking arguments. Since $\mathcal{C}(d(\sigma_\alpha^\star, \sigma_\beta^\star)) = \{nD(\sigma_\alpha^\star, \sigma_\beta^\star)\}$, arguments attacking A are of the form $\{\} \vdash nD(\sigma_\alpha^\star, \sigma_\beta^\star)$. Since $(\sigma_\alpha^\star, \sigma_\beta^\star)$ is a dominant solution, there is no $(\sigma'_\alpha, \sigma'_\beta)$ such that $\pi_\alpha(\sigma'_\alpha, \sigma'_\beta) > \pi_\alpha(\sigma_\alpha^\star, \sigma_\beta^\star)$. Thus $vA(\sigma'_\alpha, \sigma'_\beta) > vA(\sigma_\alpha^\star, \sigma_\beta^\star) \leftarrow \notin \mathcal{R}_\alpha^p$. Therefore $\{\} \vdash nD(\sigma_\alpha^\star, \sigma_\beta^\star)$ is not an argument and $\Delta = \{A\}$ is not attacked. Thus $d(\sigma_\alpha^\star, \sigma_\beta^\star)$ is admissible. □

EXAMPLE 3.2. *(Example 3.1 cont.) There is no dominant solution in this game. Indeed, for any $(\sigma_\alpha^\star, \sigma_\beta^\star)$, $d(\sigma_\alpha^\star, \sigma_\beta^\star)$ is not admissible in the Dominant ABA framework. For instance, for $\sigma_\alpha^\star = m$ and $\sigma_\beta^\star = r$, the argument $\{d(m, r)\} \vdash d(m, r)$ is attacked by the argument $\{\} \vdash nD(m, r)$ (this argument uses the rule $vB(f, w) > vB(m, r) \leftarrow$, and cannot be counter-attacked). Thus, an argumentative reading of the process for sanctioning $d(\sigma_\alpha^\star, \sigma_\beta^\star)$ as non-dominant is:*

1. *$\{d(m, r)\} \vdash d(m, r)$: let us assume that (m, r) is dominant;*
2. *$\{\} \vdash nD(m, r)$ (using $vB(f, w) > vB(m, r) \leftarrow$) attacks the assumption/argument supporting the assumption:[6] (m, r) is not dominant because (f, w) has a higher payoff value than (m, r) for agent β.*

We can also easily define ABA frameworks for capturing Nash Equilibria as follows.

DEFINITION 3.4. *Given a game $\langle \Sigma_\alpha, \Sigma_\beta, \pi_\alpha, \pi_\beta \rangle$, the* Nash ABA framework *$\langle \mathcal{L}_N, \mathcal{R}_N, \mathcal{A}_N, \mathcal{C}_N \rangle$ has:*

- *$\mathcal{R}_N$ consisting of $\mathcal{R}_\alpha^p \cup \mathcal{R}_\beta^p$ together with:*

  $nN(\sigma_\alpha, \sigma_\beta) \leftarrow vA(\_, \sigma_\beta) > vA(\sigma_\alpha, \sigma_\beta)$,

  $nN(\sigma_\alpha, \sigma_\beta) \leftarrow vB(\sigma_\alpha, \_) > vB(\sigma_\alpha, \sigma_\beta)$;
- *$\mathcal{A}_N = \{n(\sigma_\alpha, \sigma_\beta) | \sigma_\alpha \in \Sigma_\alpha, \sigma_\beta \in \Sigma_\beta\}$;*
- *for each $n(\sigma_\alpha, \sigma_\beta) \in \mathcal{A}_N$, $\mathcal{C}_N(n(\sigma_\alpha, \sigma_\beta)) = \{nN(\sigma_\alpha, \sigma_\beta)\}$.*

Note that Nash ABA frameworks are also flat (see Section 2).

The intuition behind this definition is analogous to that behind Definition 3.3, except that upon checking Nash equilibria, one agent's payoff in a strategy pair only needs to be compared to strategy pairs with the other agent playing the same strategy (see the two rule schemata in Definition 3.4).

THEOREM 3.2. *Given a game $\langle \Sigma_\alpha, \Sigma_\beta, \pi_\alpha, \pi_\beta \rangle$, a strategy pair $(\sigma_\alpha, \sigma_\beta)$ is a Nash equilibrium iff $n(\sigma_\alpha, \sigma_\beta)$ is admissible in the Nash ABA framework.*

[6]Note that, in flat ABA frameworks, arguments supporting assumptions necessarily use no rules and are supported by the assumptions themselves.

The proof of Theorem 3.2 is similar to the one of Theorem 3.1.

EXAMPLE 3.3. *(Example 3.1 cont.) The two Nash Equilibria are: (m, r) and (f, w); indeed, both $n(m, r)$ and $n(f, w)$ are admissible in the Nash ABA framework. For instance, again for $\sigma_\alpha^\star = m$ and $\sigma_\beta^\star = r$, we can see that the argument $\{n(m, r)\} \vdash n(m, r)$ is not attacked by any argument as there is no rule with head $vA(f, r) > vA(m, r)$ or $vB(m, w) > vB(m, r)$. Argumentatively, (m, r) is a Nash Equilibrium since α does not think (f, r) has a higher payoff value than (m, r) and β does not think (m, w) has a higher payoff value than (m, r).*

Note that as we can see that both Dominant ABA frameworks and Nash ABA frameworks are identical except for some rules, we could use a unified framework by taking the "union" of the two. We leave them seperate in this work for clarity.

4. GAME SOLUTIONS VIA ABA DIALOGUES

In addition to computing solutions with complete information statically, dominant solutions and Nash equilibria can be computed dynamically, with only partial information held by each agent, through ABA dialogues. More specifically, each agent is only aware of its own *half* of the overall payoff matrix and the corresponding preference rules; however, both agents hold the rules for computing solutions (represented in the shared schemata, assumptions and contraries in Definitions 3.3 and 3.4, respectively).

In the remainder of the paper, unless specified otherwise, we assume as given a game $\langle \Sigma_\alpha, \Sigma_\beta, \pi_\alpha, \pi_\beta \rangle$ and corresponding Dominant / Nash ABA framework $\langle \mathcal{L}_X, \mathcal{R}_X, \mathcal{A}_X, \mathcal{C}_X \rangle$ (for $X = D$ / N respectively). Then, the ABA frameworks held by α and β will be denoted by $\alpha = \langle \mathcal{L}_X, \mathcal{R}_\alpha, \mathcal{A}_\alpha, \mathcal{C}_\alpha \rangle$ and $\beta = \langle \mathcal{L}_X, \mathcal{R}_\beta, \mathcal{A}_\beta, \mathcal{C}_\beta \rangle$, such that:

- $\mathcal{R}_\alpha = \mathcal{R}_X \setminus \mathcal{R}_\beta^p$; • $\mathcal{R}_\beta = \mathcal{R}_X \setminus \mathcal{R}_\alpha^p$;
- $\mathcal{A}_\alpha = \mathcal{A}_\beta = \mathcal{A}_X$; • $\mathcal{C}_\alpha(a) = \mathcal{C}_\beta(a) = \mathcal{C}_X(a)$, for all $a \in \mathcal{A}_X$.

Thus, the ABA framework held by an agent contains exactly the same information as the available strategies and (private) payoff function, as well as information as to which notion of solution the agents are striving towards.

Through ABA dialogues, while exchanging relevant information, agents can identify solutions even if they hold only incomplete information. *Dominant / Nash dialogues* for computing dominant solutions and Nash Equilibria use specific legal-move functions:

DEFINITION 4.1. *The* Dominant Legal-move *function λ_d is such that given a dialogue δ, each utterance $u \in \lambda_d(\delta)$ has content in one of the following forms (for some $\sigma_\alpha, \sigma'_\alpha \in \Sigma_\alpha, \sigma_\beta, \sigma'_\beta \in \Sigma_\beta$):*

- *$claim(d(\sigma_\alpha, \sigma_\beta))$,*
- *$asm(d(\sigma_\alpha, \sigma_\beta))$,* • *$ctr(d(\sigma_\alpha, \sigma_\beta), nD(\sigma_\alpha, \sigma_\beta))$,*
- *$rl(nD(\sigma_\alpha, \sigma_\beta) \leftarrow vA(\sigma'_\alpha, \sigma'_\beta) > vA(\sigma_\alpha, \sigma_\beta))$,*
- *$rl(nD(\sigma_\alpha, \sigma_\beta) \leftarrow vB(\sigma'_\alpha, \sigma'_\beta) > vB(\sigma_\alpha, \sigma_\beta))$,*
- *$rl(vA(\sigma'_\alpha, \sigma'_\beta) > vA(\sigma_\alpha, \sigma_\beta) \leftarrow)$,*
- *$rl(vB(\sigma'_\alpha, \sigma'_\beta) > vB(\sigma_\alpha, \sigma_\beta) \leftarrow)$.*

The Nash Legal-move *function λ_n is defined as λ_d with*

- *$d(\sigma_\alpha, \sigma_\beta)$ replaced by $n(\sigma_\alpha, \sigma_\beta)$;*
- *$nD(\sigma_\alpha, \sigma_\beta)$ replaced by $nN(\sigma_\alpha, \sigma_\beta)$;*
- *the two rule schemata with heads $nD(\sigma_\alpha, \sigma_\beta)$ replaced by their counterparts in the Nash ABA framework with heads $nN(\sigma_\alpha, \sigma_\beta)$.*

A dialogue δ is a Dominant / Nash dialogue *iff δ is compatible with λ_d / λ_n, respectively. The strategy pair in the claim of δ is called the* claim pair.

Definition 4.1 gives the dialectical counterpart of Definitions 3.3 and 3.4. It specifies the allowed utterances for agents in Dominant /

Nash dialogues. However, it does not force agents to disclose their private preferences. In particular, the last two rules in the definition of λ_d may not be preference rules in the ABA framework of the utterer (in other words, they may be lies). As seen in Section 2, the thorough strategy-move function ϕ_h can be used to dictate agents to be *honest*, by disclosing all relevant information they hold.

THEOREM 4.1. *For any Dominant / Nash dialogue δ with claim pair $(\sigma^\star_\alpha, \sigma^\star_\beta)$ constructed with ϕ_h, δ is successful iff $(\sigma^\star_\alpha, \sigma^\star_\beta)$ is a dominant solution / Nash equilibrium.*

PROOF. Follows from Theorems 3.1 and 3.2, and Theorem 1 in [13]. □

Note that Theorem 4.1 sanctions both directions of the "equivalence" between dialogues and games.

EXAMPLE 4.1. *(Example 3.3 cont.) We illustrate the Nash dialogue $\mathcal{D}^\alpha_\beta(n(m,r))$ being successful as follows:*

$\langle \alpha, \beta, 0, claim(n(m,r)), 1 \rangle$
$\langle \alpha, \beta, 1, asm(n(m,r)), 2 \rangle$
$\langle \alpha, \beta, 2, ctr(n(m,r), nN(m,r)), 3 \rangle$
$\langle \beta, \alpha, 3, rl(nN(m,r) \leftarrow vA(f,r) > vA(m,r)), 4 \rangle$
$\langle \alpha, \beta, 0, \pi, 5 \rangle$
$\langle \alpha, \beta, 3, rl(nN(m,r) \leftarrow vB(m,w) > vB(m,r)), 6 \rangle$
$\langle \beta, \alpha, 0, \pi, 7 \rangle$

This is a Nash dialogue as it is compatible with the Nash legal-move function given in Definition 4.1. A natural language reading of this dialogue is given in Section 1. In utterances 1-3, α assumes (m,r) being a Nash equilibrium with contrary $nN(m,r)$. β utters the two rules for $nN(m,r)$ in utterances 4, 5. Since α does not prefer (f,r) to (m,r) nor β prefers (m,w) to (m,r), no more utterances are made. Thus, jointly the agents verify that (m,r) is a Nash equilibrium. Overall, the only argument they generate and exchange (implicitly) is $\{n(m,r)\} \vdash n(m,r)$ (this is the only argument in the ABA framework drawn from the dialogue). Since there is no attack against this argument (in the ABA framework drawn from the dialogue), the claim is admissible and the dialogue is successful.

Example 4.1 also illustrates a difference between using structured rather than abstract argumentation (AA) as the argumentation framework underlying interactions between agents (in general and in the context of determining game solutions). From an AA view point, the dialogue in Example 4.1 solely introduces an argument (for (m,r) being a Nash equilibrium). The dialogue also attempts to generate attacks against this argument (one attempt is given by utterances 3 and 4, another by utterances 3 and 6). The attempts allow to share additional information (as to the absence of preferences in this case). This may be useful, for example, when agents have only partial information about the world before engaging in a dialogue, and may benefit from information from the other agents to even determine their payoff functions. We leave this extension to our current, standard game model as future work.

The following example further illustrates how ABA dialogues support the sharing of information, but in the case of non-successful Dominant dialogues.

EXAMPLE 4.2. *(Example 3.2 cont.) The following Dominant dialogue $\mathcal{D}^\alpha_\beta(d(m,r))$, attempting to determine whether $d(m,r)$ is a dominant solution, is not successful:*

$\langle \alpha, \beta, 0, claim(d(m,r)), 1 \rangle$
$\langle \alpha, \beta, 1, asm(d(m,r)), 2 \rangle$
$\langle \alpha, \beta, 2, ctr(d(m,r), nD(m,r)), 3 \rangle$
$\langle \beta, \alpha, 3, rl(nD(m,r) \leftarrow vA(m,w) > vA(m,r)), 4 \rangle$
$\langle \alpha, \beta, 3, rl(nD(m,r) \leftarrow vA(f,r) > vA(m,r)), 5 \rangle$
$\langle \alpha, \beta, 3, rl(nD(m,r) \leftarrow vA(f,w) > vA(m,r)), 6 \rangle$
$\langle \alpha, \beta, 3, rl(nD(m,r) \leftarrow vB(m,w) > vB(m,r)), 7 \rangle$
$\langle \alpha, \beta, 3, rl(nD(m,r) \leftarrow vB(f,r) > vB(m,r)), 8 \rangle$
$\langle \alpha, \beta, 3, rl(nD(m,r) \leftarrow vB(f,w) > vB(m,r)), 9 \rangle$
$\langle \beta, \alpha, 9, rl(vB(f,w) > vB(m,r) \leftarrow), 10 \rangle$
$\langle \alpha, \beta, 0, \pi, 11 \rangle$
$\langle \beta, \alpha, 0, \pi, 12 \rangle$

This is a Dominant dialogue as it is compatible with the Dominant legal-move function of Definition 4.1. It constructs two arguments: $\{d(m,r)\} \vdash d(m,r)$ and $\{\} \vdash nD(m,r)$; the latter attacks the former. Therefore, the claim $d(m,r)$ is not admissible (in the ABA framework drawn from the dialogue) and the dialogue is not successful. Nonetheless, after the dialogue the agents share information of the preference by β of (f,w) over (m,r) (although not the utility of either for β). Whether this is an actual preference of β depends on whether β has been truthfully honest in the dialogue. This is the topic of the next section.

5. DIALECTICAL STRATEGIES FOR ABA DIALOGUES

The dialogue in Example 4.1 is constructed with ϕ_h (see Section 2). However, if we consider agents being self interested, we need to ask:

> *What are the conditions for agents to be honest in dialogues?*

We pose this question in a game theoretic setting and analyse agent behaviours in dialogues understood as games themselves. Thus, we introduce a *meta-level dialectical game* on top of the original *underlying game* (e.g. the Dinner party game in Example 1.1). Note that although both agents carry information from the underlying game into the meta-level game, they do not necessarily carry the payoffs. Indeed, *designing* appropriate utilities for the meta-level game is needed to ensure good behaviour (truthfulness and disclosure) from agents.

We formulate (reverse) game-theoretic notions for dialogues as follows. We first define the types of agents as their strategies and payoffs in the underlying game, represented within their (Dominant or Nash) ABA frameworks.

DEFINITION 5.1. *The* types *of agents α and β are $\theta_\alpha = \alpha$ and $\theta_\beta = \beta$, respectively.*

In ABA dialogues, agents put forward claims, rules, assumptions and contraries. We hence view sequences of utterances as agents' actions in the meta-level dialectical game and define strategies in the meta-level dialectical game as functions determining utterances in dialogues (that can be equated with strategy-move functions, as we shall see). Formally:

DEFINITION 5.2. *The* action space *for agent $x \in \{\alpha, \beta\}$ is $2^{\mathcal{U}^x}$.*

DEFINITION 5.3. *A* strategy *for agent $x \in \{\alpha, \beta\}$ (in the meta-level dialectical game) is a function s^δ_x, for some dialogue δ, such that $s^\delta_x(\theta_x, \delta) = \{u | u = \langle x, \_, \_, \_, \_ \rangle \in \delta\}$.*

Since s^δ_x returns the set of utterances made by x in δ, which is determined by the strategy-move function ϕ used by x, we can equate strategies in the meta-level dialectical game with strategy-move functions. If δ is constructed with ϕ_h, then s^δ_x is called the *honest strategy* (in the meta-level dialectical game).

Since a dialogue can either be successful or not, we let the meta-level outcome depend on the dialogue outcome such that if the dialogue is successful, then the outcome is the claim pair; otherwise, the outcome is the empty set, formally:

DEFINITION 5.4. *Given a dialogue* $\delta = \mathcal{D}^x_y(X(\sigma^\star_\alpha, \sigma^\star_\beta)), x, y \in \{\alpha, \beta\}, x \neq y, X \in \{d, n\}$, *the* outcome function $g(\delta)$ *is such that:*

$$g(\delta) = \begin{cases} (\sigma^\star_\alpha, \sigma^\star_\beta) & \text{if } \delta \text{ is successful,} \\ \{\} & \text{otherwise.} \end{cases}$$

Note that success of a dialogue amounts to admissibility of its claim in the ABA framework *drawn from the dialogue* (see Section 2). Thus, if the agents are not truthful within the dialogue, the claim pair may not be a dominant solution/Nash equilibrium.

To define the utility function, we first define the *honesty reward*, a means to encourage agents' truthfulness. Inspired by Vickrey auctions[23], in Dominant dialogues, the honesty reward for each agent is set to the second highest payoff of the underlying game; in Nash dialogues, the honesty reward is the second highest payoff *given the other agent's behaviour* in the underlying game. Formally:

DEFINITION 5.5. *The* honesty reward $\mathcal{W}_x \in \mathbb{R}$ *(for* $x \in \{\alpha, \beta\}$*) is given as follows:*

- *For Dominant dialogues, let* $\langle v^1_x, v^2_x, \ldots \rangle$ *be the list of of payoffs of agent* x *such that* $v^1_x > v^2_x > \ldots$*; then* $\mathcal{W}_x = v^2_x$*;*
- *For Nash dialogues, let* $(\sigma^\star_\alpha, \sigma^\star_\beta)$ *be the claim pair, and*
  - *let* $\langle v^1_\alpha, v^2_\alpha, \ldots \rangle$ *be the list of payoffs of* α *when* β *plays* $\sigma^\star_\beta$ *in the underlying game, such that* $v^1_\alpha > v^2_\alpha > \ldots$*; then* $\mathcal{W}_\alpha = v^2_\alpha$*;*
  - *let* $\langle v^1_\beta, v^2_\beta, \ldots \rangle$ *be the list of payoffs of* β *when* α *plays* $\sigma^\star_\alpha$ *in the underlying game, such that* $v^1_\beta > v^2_\beta > \ldots$*; then* $\mathcal{W}_\beta = v^2_\beta$*.*

An agent's utility is defined so that the agent either gets its payoff in the underlying game (when the dialogue is successful) or its honesty reward (otherwise):

DEFINITION 5.6. *The* utility of agent $x \in \{\alpha, \beta\}$ in dialogue δ *is* v_x *such that:*

$$v_x = \begin{cases} \pi_x(\sigma^\star_\alpha, \sigma^\star_\beta) & \text{if } g(\delta) = (\sigma^\star_\alpha, \sigma^\star_\beta), \\ \mathcal{W}_x & \text{otherwise.} \end{cases}$$

Generally speaking, the honesty reward is set to ensure that being truthful yields a higher utility than being dishonest for both agents while participating in Dominant / Nash dialogues. Indeed, with utilities defined as such, we show that truthfully disclosing all relevant information is the best option for both agents. Formally:

THEOREM 5.1. *Given a Dominant / Nash dialogue* δ*, the honest strategy* s^δ_x *is dominant (for agent* x*).*

PROOF. (Sketch.) We show the case for Dominant dialogues- The other case, Nash dialogues, is similar. To show that s^δ_x is a dominant strategy is to show that being thorough gives the highest utility. There are four possible cases in total. (Below, we say that a strategy pair is *dominant* for x if it gives the highest payoff to x.[7])

C1: $(\sigma^\star_\alpha,\sigma^\star_\beta)$ is dominant for both agents;
C2: $(\sigma^\star_\alpha,\sigma^\star_\beta)$ is dominant for β, but not α;
C3: $(\sigma^\star_\alpha,\sigma^\star_\beta)$ is dominant for α, but not β;
C4: $(\sigma^\star_\alpha,\sigma^\star_\beta)$ is not dominant for either α or β.

[7]Note that *dominant* is overloaded in this paper. A pair of strategies can be a dominant solution as defined in Section 1; a single strategy can be dominant as defined at the end of Section 2; and a pair of strategies can be dominant for a single agent as used here.

C1		β	
		H	**D**
α	**H**	$(\sigma^\star_\alpha,\sigma^\star_\beta)$	{}
	D	{}	{}

C2		β	
		H	**D**
α	**H**	{}	{}
	D	$(\sigma^\star_\alpha,\sigma^\star_\beta)$	{}

C3		β	
		H	**D**
α	**H**	{}	$(\sigma^\star_\alpha,\sigma^\star_\beta)$
	D	{}	{}

C4		β	
		H	**D**
α	**H**	{}	{}
	D	{}	$(\sigma^\star_\alpha,\sigma^\star_\beta)$

Table 2: Four possible Cases C1 - C4.

Agents can either be *honest* (**H**) or *dishonest* (**D**). Dialogues can either return its claim pair (if it is successful) or the empty set (otherwise). The dialectical interaction can be viewed as games summarised in Table 2.

C1: In this case, $(\sigma^\star_\alpha, \sigma^\star_\beta)$ is a dominant solution, honesty from both agents ensures a successful dialogue (Theorem 4.1), giving the top left cell (**H, H**). Thus, by Definition 5.6, honesty from both agents gives the highest possible utility, $\pi_x(\sigma^\star_\alpha, \sigma^\star_\beta)$ for $x \in \{\alpha, \beta\}$. Moreover, regardless what the other agent does, being honest yields no less utility.

C2: We first explain how this table is computed.

Since $(\sigma^\star_\alpha, \sigma^\star_\beta)$ is not dominant for α, there is some strategy pair $(\sigma_\alpha, \sigma_\beta)$ such that $\pi_\alpha(\sigma_\alpha, \sigma_\beta) > \pi_\alpha(\sigma^\star_\alpha, \sigma^\star_\beta)$, which gives $vA(\sigma_\alpha, \sigma_\beta) > vA(\sigma^\star_\alpha, \sigma^\star_\beta) \leftarrow$ in $\mathcal{R}^p_\alpha$ (Definition 3.2). Thus, as long as α is honest, by uttering this rule in δ, δ will be unsuccessful and return $\{\}$ (the top row in the C2 table).

If α is dishonest, i.e. α hides this rule in δ, while β is being honest (resulting in the cell (**H, D**)), since $(\sigma^\star_\alpha, \sigma^\star_\beta)$ is dominant for β, β has no rule to attack $d(\sigma^\star_\alpha, \sigma^\star_\beta)$, thus δ will be successful and the outcome of δ is the claim pair $(\sigma^\star_\alpha, \sigma^\star_\beta)$ (lower left cell in the C2 table).

If both α and β are dishonest (**D, D**), β lies about having $(\sigma_\alpha, \sigma_\beta)$ such that $vB(\sigma_\alpha, \sigma_\beta) > vB(\sigma^\star_\alpha, \sigma^\star_\beta) \leftarrow$ is uttered in δ and δ is unsuccessful and returns $\{\}$ (lower right cell in the C2 table).

With the C2 table constructed as such, we observe that α should choose to be honest (i.e. choose to be in the top row) to receive $\mathcal{W}_\alpha$ as, by Definition 5.5, $\mathcal{W}_\alpha \geq \pi_\alpha(\sigma^\star_\alpha, \sigma^\star_\beta)$ (since $(\sigma^\star_\alpha, \sigma^\star_\beta)$ is not dominant for α). β should also choose to be honest as β either receives $\mathcal{W}_\beta$ (when α is honest, resulting in (**H, H**)) or $\pi_\beta(\sigma^\star_\alpha, \sigma^\star_\beta)$ (when α lies, resulting in (**D, H**)). Since $(\sigma^\star_\alpha, \sigma^\star_\beta)$ is dominant for β, $\pi_\beta(\sigma^\star_\alpha, \sigma^\star_\beta) > \mathcal{W}_\beta$. Thus, being honest is also dominant for β.

C3: This case is case **C2** with the two agents swapped.

C4: Honesty gives both agents $\mathcal{W}_x$, otherwise each receives either $\pi_x(\sigma^\star_\alpha, \sigma^\star_\beta)$ or $\mathcal{W}_x$, $x \in \{\alpha, \beta\}$. Since $(\sigma^\star_\alpha, \sigma^\star_\beta)$ is not dominant for the agents, by Definition 5.5, $\mathcal{W}_x \geq \pi_x(\sigma^\star_\alpha, \sigma^\star_\beta)$.

In all cases, the honest strategy dominates. □

We observe that the honesty reward as defined in Definition 5.5 gives enough incentive to both agents to be honest so hiding information or inserting false information does not bring higher utility to either of the two. Moreover, from the proof of Theorem 5.1, we observe that the setting for the honesty reward is very crucial to this result. Indeed, the following lemma holds.

LEMMA 5.1. *Given a Dominant / Nash dialogue* δ*, the honest strategy* s^δ_x *is not dominant (for agent* x*) if the honesty reward* $\mathcal{W}_x$ *is such that* $\mathcal{W}_x < v^2_x$*, for* v^2_x *as in Definition 5.5.*

PROOF. (Sketch.) Again, we only show the Dominant case as the Nash case is similiar. As in the proof of Theorem 5.1, we need to consider four possible cases C1-C4. The outcomes remain the same as in Table 2. In the case of C2, suppose that $\pi_\alpha(\sigma^\star_\alpha, \sigma^\star_\beta) =$

v_α^2. If $\mathcal{W}_x < v_x^2$, then α is better off being dishonest and hiding the rule $vA(\sigma_\alpha, \sigma_\beta) > vA(\sigma^\star_\alpha, \sigma^\star_\beta) \leftarrow$ to make δ successful. By doing so, α could receive v_α^2 (if β is honest), which is better than $\mathcal{W}_\alpha$, which is the utility of α while being honest (δ would not be successful when α is honest). Thus, the honest strategy s_x^δ is not dominant. □

6. DIALOGUE SEQUENCES FOR FINDING SOLUTIONS

A single Dominant / Nash dialogue only tests if a single strategy pair is a dominant solution or a Nash equilibrium. To identify all dominant solutions / Nash equilibria, multiple dialogues are needed. We define *dialogue sequences* as follows.

DEFINITION 6.1. *A (dialogue) sequence S between α, β is a set of dialogues $S = \{\mathcal{D}^{y_1}_{x_1}(\chi_1), \ldots, \mathcal{D}^{y_n}_{x_n}(\chi_n)\}$ such that $n > 0$ and for all $i, j = 1, \ldots, n$, $x_i, y_i \in \{\alpha, \beta\}, x_i \neq y_i$ and if $i \neq j$ then $\chi_i \neq \chi_j$.*

A sequence is a dominant / Nash *sequence iff (1) all dialogues in the sequence are Dominant / Nash dialogues (respectively); (2) for all $\sigma_\alpha \in \Sigma_\alpha$ and $\sigma_\beta \in \Sigma_\beta$, $(\sigma_\alpha, \sigma_\beta)$ is the claim pair for some dialogue in the sequence; and (3) all claims of dialogues in the sequences are claim pairs $(\sigma_\alpha, \sigma_\beta)$, for $\sigma_\alpha \in \Sigma_\alpha$ and $\sigma_\beta \in \Sigma_\beta$.*

Here, we only consider Dominant or Nash sequences.

We do not repeat the definition for action space but assume the one given in Definition 5.2 remains unchanged for sequences.

Similarly to Definition 5.3, we define *sequence strategies* as returning utterances in (all dialogues in) the sequence. Note that this setting also effectively equates sequence strategies with strategy-move functions used in dialogues in the sequence.

DEFINITION 6.2. *For any sequence $S = \{\delta_1, \ldots, \delta_n\}$ between α and β, the* sequence strategy *s_x^S for $x \in \{\alpha, \beta\}$ is such that $s_x^S(\theta_x, S) = \{u | u = \langle x, \_, \_, \_, \_\rangle \in \delta_i, 1 \leq i \leq n\}$.*

We refer to a sequence strategy s_x^S as *honest* iff the strategy-move function used by x in its dialogues is ϕ_h.

The outcome function g wrt a sequence is as follows.

DEFINITION 6.3. *Given a sequence S, the* outcome function *g_X, for $X = D/N$, is such that $g_X(S) = \{(\sigma^\star_\alpha, \sigma^\star_\beta) | Y(\sigma^\star_\alpha, \sigma^\star_\beta)$ is the topic of $\delta \in S$, for $Y = d/n$, respectively, and δ is successful$\}$.*

We continue to use the utility setting for single dialogues given in Definition 5.6 and let the utility of a sequence be the sum of the utilities of dialogues in the sequence, defined as follows.

DEFINITION 6.4. *The* utility *of agent $x \in \{\alpha, \beta\}$ in sequence $S = \{\delta_1, \ldots, \delta_n\}$ is $sv_x = \sum_{i=1}^n v_x^i$, where, for $i = 1 \ldots n$, v_x^i is the utility of x in δ_i, as in Definition 5.6.*

As a corollary to Theorem 5.1, the following holds.

COROLLARY 6.1. *Given a Dominant / Nash sequence S, the honest sequence strategy s_x^S is dominant (for agent x).*

We define the Dominant / Nash social choices as follows.

DEFINITION 6.5. *The* Dominant social choice *function is defined as*

$$f_d(\theta_\alpha, \theta_\beta) = \{(\sigma^\star_\alpha, \sigma^\star_\beta) | (\sigma^\star_\alpha, \sigma^\star_\beta) \text{ is a dominant solution, for } \sigma^\star_\alpha \in \Sigma_\alpha, \sigma^\star_\beta \in \Sigma_\beta\}.$$

The Nash social choice *function is defined as*

$$f_n(\theta_\alpha, \theta_\beta) = \{(\sigma^\star_\alpha, \sigma^\star_\beta) | (\sigma^\star_\alpha, \sigma^\star_\beta) \text{ is a Nash equilibrium, for } \sigma^\star_\alpha \in \Sigma_\alpha, \sigma^\star_\beta \in \Sigma_\beta\}.$$

Namely, the Dominant / Nash social choice function returns all dominant solutions / Nash equilibria (respectively) in the underlying game. The following theorem holds.

THEOREM 6.1. *The mechanism $\mathcal{M} = (A, g_X)$, where A is the action space, as given in Definition 5.2, and g_X is the outcome function, as given in Definition 6.3, with $X = D/N$,* implements *the social choice function f_d / f_n (respectively).*

PROOF. (Sketch.) This is to show that both agents reveal their true types in dialogue sequences. Since Corollary 6.1 shows that being honest is the dominant strategy, this holds. □

The following example illustrates the use of Nash sequences as a mechanism implementing the Nash social choice function.

EXAMPLE 6.1. *(Example 4.1 cont.) To find all Nash equilibria in the game of Example 1.1, four Nash dialogues, forming a Nash sequence, are conducted with claims $n(m, r)$, $n(m, w)$, $n(f, r)$ and $n(f, w)$, respectively (with both agents use the honest sequence strategy). Example 4.1 gives one of the four dialogues. Dialogues $\mathcal{D}^\alpha_\beta(n(m, w))$ and $\mathcal{D}^\alpha_\beta(n(f, w))$ are as follows:*

$\langle \alpha, \beta, 0, claim(n(m, w)), 1\rangle$
$\langle \alpha, \beta, 1, asm(n(m, w)), 2\rangle$
$\langle \alpha, \beta, 2, ctr(n(m, w), nN(m, w)), 3\rangle$
$\langle \beta, \alpha, 3, rl(nN(m, w) \leftarrow vA(f, w) > vA(f, w)), 4\rangle$
$\langle \alpha, \beta, 4, rl(vA(f, w) > vA(m, w) \leftarrow), 5\rangle$
$\langle \alpha, \beta, 3, rl(nN(m, w) \leftarrow vB(m, r) > vB(m, w)), 6\rangle$
$\langle \beta, \alpha, 6, rl(vB(m, r) > vB(m, w) \leftarrow), 7\rangle$
$\langle \beta, \alpha, 0, \pi, 8\rangle$
$\langle \alpha, \beta, 0, \pi, 9\rangle$

$\langle \alpha, \beta, 0, claim(n(f, w)), 1\rangle$
$\langle \alpha, \beta, 1, asm(n(f, w)), 2\rangle$
$\langle \alpha, \beta, 2, ctr(n(f, w), nN(f, w)), 3\rangle$
$\langle \beta, \alpha, 3, rl(nN(f, w) \leftarrow vA(m, w) > vA(f, w)), 4\rangle$
$\langle \alpha, \beta, 0, \pi, 5\rangle$
$\langle \alpha, \beta, 3, rl(nN(f, w) \leftarrow vB(f, r) > vB(f, w)), 6\rangle$
$\langle \beta, \alpha, 0, \pi, 7\rangle$

Clearly, $\mathcal{D}^\alpha_\beta(n(m, w))$ is not successful, whereas $\mathcal{D}^\alpha_\beta(n(f, w))$ is. It is also easy to see that $\mathcal{D}^\alpha_\beta(n(f, r))$ cannot be successful. Thus, the outcome of this sequence is $\{(m, r), (f, w)\}$, which is the same as the output of the Nash social choice function.

The notions we have introduced in Sections 5 and 6 are summarised in Table 3.

7. RELATED WORKS

Dung's seminal work [9] introduces AA frameworks and studies, as an illustration of the use of AA, modelling n-person games and stable marriage problems with AA. The first half of this paper (sections 3 and 4) continues this spirit, yet instead of modelling a single type of game, we give an ABA modelling for any game in normal form.

[36] and [29] have introduced Argumentation Mechanism Design. Their works give conditions on argumentation framework structures that ensure truthfulness of agents. Instead of putting restrictions on argumentation frameworks, we look at utility settings for enforcing truthfulness. Furthermore, [36] and [29] used the AA framework whereas our work is based on ABA and ABA dialogues.

[35] present examples of logical mechanism design. The main point of their work is to demonstrate introducing mechanism design as a tool in the design of logical inference procedures, whereas our paper focuses on directly applying mechanism design in ABA dialogues.

Mechanism Design Concepts	$(x \in \{\alpha, \beta\})$	Argumentation Dialogues	Dialogue Sequences
Type space (of agent x)	Θ_x	$\Sigma_x, \pi_x, \langle \mathcal{L}, \mathcal{R}_x, \mathcal{A}_x, \mathcal{C}_x \rangle$ (Defn 5.1)	*as in dialogues*
Outcomes	$\mathcal{O}$	$(\sigma^\star_\alpha, \sigma^\star_\beta)$ or $\{\}$ (Defn 5.4)	$\{(\sigma^1_\alpha, \sigma^1_\beta), (\sigma^2_\alpha, \sigma^2_\beta), \ldots\}$ (Defn 6.3)
Utility function (for agent x)	$v_x : \mathcal{O} \times \theta_x \to \mathbb{R}$	$\pi_x(\sigma^\star_\alpha, \sigma^\star_\beta)$ or $\mathcal{W}_x$ (Defn 5.6)	$sv_x = \sum v^i_x$ (Defn 6.4)
Action space	$A = A_\alpha \times A_\beta$	$2^{\mathcal{U}^\alpha} \times 2^{\mathcal{U}^\beta}$ (Defn 5.2)	*as in dialogues*
Strategy (of agent x)	$s_x : \Theta_x \times A \to A_x$	s^δ_x (Defn 5.3)	s^S_x (Defn 6.2)
Social choice function	$f : \Theta_\alpha \times \Theta_\beta \to \mathcal{O}$	-	f_d & f_n (Defn 6.5)

Table 3: Dialogues and dialogue sequences as mechanisms

[14] present a work on applying mechanism design in persuasion dialogues. Ours work models generic games with ABA and uses a different set of utility settings to ensure truthfulness of agents.

[20] present a work on designing mechanisms for agents in persuasion and conflict resolution dialogues with the DC system [24]. They are concerned with analysing existing dialogues with game theoretic notions whereas we have studied the interplay between dialogues and games in both directions.

[7] also use the Mackenzie dialogue system to study game strategies. The difference is that they aim at implementing dialogue protocols with game theoretic notions whereas ours is about enforcing good agents' behaviours. Argumentation and dialogue settings used in these two works are also different.

[1] present a work on studying agent strategies in persuasion dialogues. Their approach derives dialogue strategies from predefined agent profiles, e.g. *agreeable* agents that accept everything, *argumentative* agents that challenge everything, etc, but without linking dialogue results with agents' internal beliefs.

Argumentation dialogues have been studied by various researchers (e.g, see [26, 32, 5]). The dialogue model used here uses elements from the model presented in [12] and [15]. They focus on presenting the dialogue model rather than being concerned with games.

[22] present a study on collaborative agent behaviours for resource sharing with a game theoretic approach with specific constraints. It is not linked to argumentation or dialogues.

[33] extends AA to a Game-based Argumentation Framework to model agents with private knowledge engaging in sequences of argumentation dialogues, where each dialogue is associated with payoffs. That work does not formally study the relations between extensive games and argumentation dialogues as it does not model game-theoretic solution concepts with argumentation notions.

[38] investigate how to determine optimal strategies in argumentation dialogues. The authors model dialogues as extensive games with perfect information. They present computation of agents' utilities in games with different dialogue strategies. [16] use an example in [38] on modelling a legal argumentation dialogue with an extensive game. It also observes that argumentation dialogues are games of incomplete information, i.e. agents types, actions and payoffs may be private. They have not studied ensuring agents' good behaviour with games.

[18] introduce a persuasion game in which two arguers exchange arguments for the purpose of persuading an audience witnessing the argument. They study the problem in the case where there is uncertainty on audience types. Although they introduce game-theoretic elements, such as agents' payoffs, their work does not focus on modelling dialogues as games.

[17] and [25] study the computational complexity of "strategic argumentation". In both works, the authors consider argumentation dialogues not unlike ours. [17] have shown that the problem of identifying most suitable utterances in dialogues is NP-complete. They have used two argumentation formalisms, argumentation logic and agent logic, both structured argumentation formalisms, in their work. Their dialogue model also supports information exchange in the level of sub-argument, i.e. literals and rules. [25] have shown several additional complexity results with strategic argumentation. Both works focus on complexity rather than agent behaviours in the context of games.

[5] present a study on dialogue systems that support deliberation dialogues. Their underlying argumentation framework is the *instantiated value-based argumentation framework*. Their dialogue model and results are concerned with agents with preferences. Their system relies upon agents estimating their counterparts' preferences and does not study strategies with mechanism design.

8. CONCLUSION AND FUTURE WORK

We have shown how argumentation in the form of ABA can be used to solve game theory problems, both statically and distributedly via dialogues. We have built a correspondence between dominant solutions, Nash equilibria, admissible arguments, and successful dialogues. We have also studied agents' strategic behaviours in dialogues with (reverse) game-theoretic notions. Finally, we have shown that, with specific utility settings, truthfulness of and disclosure by agents can be ensured. The approach taken in the paper consists of different "layers": a bottom layer (the game to be simulated, that we refer to as the underlying game), a middle layer (the ABA framework and the dialogue sharing parts of the framework), and a top-layer (a meta-level game, on top of the first two layers, that has as a dominant solution a truthful dialogue).

This work opens many questions for future work. We have focused on dominance and Nash equilibria as solution concepts in the underlying games. Could other concepts, such as Pareto Optimality, be usefully computed via argumentation? We have considered pure strategies, what about mixed strategies in games? Could they be computed with argumentation? Also, we have considered (underlying) games in normal form. Could games in extensive form of incomplete information be represented in ABA and ABA dialogues? We have treated the meta-level dialogical game as a normal form game too, could this be interpreted instead as a game in extensive form? Results presented in this work rely upon assigning the honesty reward $\mathcal{W}$ to agents. How should $\mathcal{W}$ be estimated in general? Lemma 5.1 shows that no lower $\mathcal{W}$ could work for the given utility setting. Is there any other way of ensuring honesty under different utility settings? Is there any relation between our honesty reward and Vickrey auctions [23], in which the winner pays the second-highest bid? Finally, it would be interesting to study the computational complexity of our approach, making use of existing results for ABA [8] and instantiating our approach within practical MAS applications of games.

Acknowledgements

This research was supported by the EPSRC TRaDAr project *Transparent Rational Decisions by Argumentation*: EP/J020915/1 and by the National Research Foundation Singapore under its Interactive Digital Media (IDM) Strategic Research Programme.

REFERENCES

[1] L. Amgoud and S. Parsons. An argumentation framework for merging conflicting knowledge bases. In *JELIA Proc.*, pages 27–37, London, UK, 2002. Springer.

[2] L. Amgoud, S. Parsons, and N. Maudet. Modelling dialogues using argumentation. In *ICMAS Proc.*, pages 31–38, Boston, MA, 2000. IEEE Press.

[3] T. J. M. Bench-Capon and P. E. Dunne. Argumentation in artificial intelligence. *Artificial Intelligence*, 171(10-15):619–641, 2007.

[4] P. Besnard and A. Hunter. *Elements of Argumentation*. The MIT Press, 2008.

[5] E. Black and K. Atkinson. Choosing persuasive arguments for action. In *The 10th International Conference on Autonomous Agents and Multiagent Systems*, 2011.

[6] E. Black and A. Hunter. An inquiry dialogue system. *JAAMAS*, 19:173–209, 2009.

[7] G. Boella, J. Gerbrandy, and J. Hulstijn. A flexible mechanism for dialogue design. In *Proceedings of the 11th conference on Theoretical aspects of rationality and knowledge*, pages 160–168, 2007.

[8] Y. Dimopoulos, B. Nebel, and F. Toni. On the computational complexity of assumption-based argumentation for default reasoning. *Artificial Intelligence*, 141:57–78, 2002.

[9] P. Dung. On the acceptability of arguments and its fundamental role in nonmonotonic reasoning, logic programming and n-person games. *AIJ*, 77(2):321–357, 1995.

[10] P. Dung, R. Kowalski, and F. Toni. Assumption-based argumentation. In *Argumentation in Artificial Intelligence*, pages 199–218. Springer, 2009.

[11] P. Dung, P. Mancarella, and F. Toni. Computing ideal sceptical argumentation. *AIJ*, 171(10–15):642–674, 2007.

[12] X. Fan and F. Toni. Assumption-based argumentation dialogues. In *Proc. IJCAI*, 2011.

[13] X. Fan and F. Toni. Agent Strategies for ABA-based Information-seeking and Inquiry Dialogues. In *Proc. ECAI*, 2012.

[14] X. Fan and F. Toni. Mechanism design for argumentation-based persuasion. In *Proc. COMMA*. IOS Press, 2012.

[15] X. Fan and F. Toni. A general framework for sound assumption-based argumentation dialogues. *Artificial Intelligence*, 216:20–54, 2014.

[16] G. Governatori, F. Olivieri, A. Rotolo, S. Scannapieco, and G. Sartor. Two faces of strategic argumentation in the law. In *JURIX proc.*, pages 81–90, 2014.

[17] G. Governatori, F. Olivieri, S. Scannapieco, A. Rotolo, and M. Cristani. Strategic argumentation is np-complete. In *Proc. ECAI*, pages 399–404, 2014.

[18] D. Grossi and W. van der Hoek. Audience-based uncertainty in abstract argument games. In *IJCAI Proc.*, 2013.

[19] M. Jackson. Mechanism theory. In U. Derigs, editor, *Optimization and Operations Research*. EOLSS Publishers, Oxford UK, 2003.

[20] M. Kacprzak, M. Dziubinski, and K. Budzynska. Strategies in dialogues: A game-theoretic approach. In *Proc. COMMA*, pages 333–344. IOS Press, 2014.

[21] E. Kok, J.-J. Meyer, H. Prakken, and G. Vreeswijk. Testing the benfits of structured argumentation in multi-agent deliberation dialogues. In *ArgMAS Proc.*, 2012.

[22] S. Kraus and O. Schechter. Strategic-negotiation for sharing a resource between two agents. *Computational Intelligence*, 19:2003, 2003.

[23] V. Krishna. *Auction Theory*. Academic Press, 2002.

[24] J. Mackenzie. Question begging in noncumulative systems. *Journal of Philosophical Logic*, 1(8), 1979.

[25] M. Maher. Complexity of exploiting privacy violations in strategic argumentation. In *PRICAI Proc.*, pages 523–535. Springer International Publishing, 2014.

[26] P. McBurney and S. Parsons. Dialogue games for agent argumentation. In *Argumentation in Artificial Intelligence*, pages 261–280. Springer, 2009.

[27] S. Modgil and H. Prakken. The *ASPIC*$^+$ framework for structured argumentation: a tutorial. *Argument & Computation*, 5(1):31–62, 2014.

[28] S. Modgil, F. Toni, F. Bex, I. Bratko, C. Chesñevar, W. Dvořák, M. Falappa, X. Fan, S. Gaggl, A. García, M. González, T. Gordon, J. Leite, M. Možina, C. Reed, G. Simari, S. Szeider, P. Torroni, and S. Woltran. The added value of argumentation. In *Agreement Technologies*, volume 8, pages 357–403. Springer, 2013.

[29] S. Pan, K. Larson, and I. Rahwan. Argumentation mechanism design for preferred semantics. In *COMMA*, pages 403–414. IOS Press, 2010.

[30] S. Parsons, P. McBurney, E. Sklar, and M. Wooldridge. On the relevance of utterances in formal inter-agent dialogues. In *Proc. AAMAS*, pages 47–62, 2007.

[31] S. Parsons, M. Wooldridge, and L. Amgoud. Properties and complexity of some formal inter-agent dialogues. *Journal of Logic and Computation*, 13:347–376, 2003.

[32] H. Prakken. Formal systems for persuasion dialogue. *Knowledge Engineering Review*, 21(2):163–188, 2006.

[33] A. D. Procaccia and J. S. Rosenschein. Extensive-form argumentation games. In *EUMAS Proc.*, pages 312–322, 2005.

[34] I. Rahwan and K. Larson. Argumentation and game theory. In *Argumentation in Artificial Intelligence*, pages 321–339. Springer, 2009.

[35] I. Rahwan and K. Larson. Logical mechanism design. *Knowledge Engineering Review*, 26(1):61–69, 2011.

[36] I. Rahwan, K. Larson, and F. A. Tohmé. A characterisation of strategy-proofness for grounded argumentation semantics. In *Proc. IJCAI*, pages 251–256, 2009.

[37] I. Rahwan and G. R. Simari. *Argumentation in Artificial Intelligence*. Springer, 2009.

[38] R. Riveret, H. Prakken, A. Rotolo, and G. Sartor. Heuristics in argumentation: A game theory investigation. In *COMMA Proc.*, pages 324–335, 2008.

[39] P. Thang, P. Dung, and N. Hung. Towards argument-based foundation for sceptical and credulous dialogue games. In *Proc. COMMA*, pages 398–409. IOS Press, 2012.

[40] F. Toni. Reasoning on the web with assumption-based argumentation. In *Reasoning Web. Semantic Technologies for Advanced Query Answering*, volume 7487, pages 370–386. Springer, 2012.

[41] F. Toni. A tutorial on assumption-based argumentation. *Argument & Computation, Special Issue: Tutorials on Structured Argumentation*, 5(1):89–117, 2014.

[42] J. N. Webb. *Game Theory*. Springer, 2007.

Online Non-Preemptive Story Scheduling in Web Advertising

Tie-Yan Liu
Microsoft Research
Beijing, China
tyliu@microsoft.com

Weidong Ma
Microsoft Research
Beijing, China
weima@microsoft.com

Tao Qin
Microsoft Research
Beijing, China
taoqin@microsoft.com

Pingzhong Tang
Tsinghua University
Beijing, China
kenshinping@gmail.com

Guang Yang
Tsinghua University &
Institute of Computing
Technology, CAS
Beijing, China
guang.research@gmail.com

Bo Zheng
Tsinghua University
Beijing, China
zhengb06science@gmail.com

ABSTRACT

This paper is concerned with online story scheduling, motivated by storyboarding in online advertising. In storyboarding, triggered by the browsing history of a user, advertisers arrive online and wish to present a sequence of ads (stories) on the website. The user ceases to browse with probability $1-\beta$ at each time step. Once the user finishes watching an ad, the advertiser derives a reward. The goal of the website is to determine a schedule that maximizes the expected total reward. This problem was first introduced by Dasgupta et al.(SODA'09) [7], and then improved by Alberts and Passen (ICALP'13) [4]. In this paper, we abandon the preemptive assumption in [7] and [4], and consider a more realistic setting: online non-preemptive story scheduling, i.e., a running job (correspond to advertiser' story) *cannot* be preempted even if another job leads to a higher reward.

Specifically, we study the setting where only 1-lengthed and k-lengthed ads are allowed. We first present a greedy algorithm which achieves a competitive ratio of β^{k-1}, and prove that this ratio is optimal for deterministic algorithms. Then, we propose a randomized algorithm with a competitive ratio of $\frac{1}{k+1}$ for general β, and then show that no randomized algorithm can achieve a competitive ratio better than $(1+\frac{(1-\beta^{k-1})^k}{(1-\beta^k)^{k-1}})^{-1}$.

1. INTRODUCTION

Online advertising [11, 13, 14, 22] is very popular in numerous industry sectors. It has even become the major source of revenue for several distinguished Internet companies [6]. As an advanced form of online ads, storyboarding was first launched in New York Times Digital [24] and has been gaining increasing attention recently.

Storyboarding is also referred to as sequence advertising or surround sessions [24]. In storyboarding, triggered by user's browsing history in a website, advertisers arrive online and wish to present a sequence of ads to the user. From one time to another, there is only one selected advertiser who owns the right to use a sequence of consecutive pages for advertising purpose. To convey his/her message, the advertiser can use these pages to create a story line of a given product.

The algorithmic approach to achieve storyboarding is referred to as story scheduling, which was first introduced by Dasgupta et al.(SODA'09) [7]. In their setting, stories (jobs) arrive online, and value is obtained for each scheduled unit. Jobs can be preempted, however, no further value can be derived from the remaining unscheduled units. Online algorithms were proposed in [7] and [4] for story scheduling, whose total rewards are competitive against that of the optimal offline scheduler with the knowledge of all jobs.

Different from the setting in [7] and [4], in this paper, we consider the more realistic non-preemption setting. The preemptive setting is not realistic for several reasons. First, user experience is bad if an ad (e.g., a video ad) is interrupted while it is being watched by a user. Second, it is troublesome to evaluate the reward of an interrupted ad, and thus is difficult for the website to charge fees for the advertiser. In our setting, once a job is scheduled, other arriving jobs must wait until that job is completed. No job (even with much higher value) can preempt an on-going job. For this new setting, we design two effective scheduling algorithms and conduct competitive analysis on them.

1.1 Model and Problem Formulation

Time is discretized throughout this paper. Consider a user who starts visiting a website at time $t=0$. At each time step, the user continues surfing with probability β, where $0<\beta<1$, and stops surfing with probability $1-\beta$. Jobs (stories) arrive online, and each job i is characterized by a vector $\langle a_i, l_i, v_i\rangle$, where a_i is the arrival time of the job, l_i is the length of the job (i.e., the length of story the advertiser would like to display), and v_i is the per-unit value[1] of the job. Note that the user may cease with probability $1-\beta$ at each step, so the real (expected) reward should be discounted by the show time of the job. For example, a job with length

Appears in: *Proceedings of the 15th International Conference on Autonomous Agents and Multiagent Systems (AAMAS 2016), J. Thangarajah, K. Tuyls, C. Jonker, S. Marsella (eds.), May 9–13, 2016, Singapore.*

[1] In this paper, we do not restrict the range of per-unit value, i.e., the per-unit value of a job can be arbitrary large.

2 will get expected reward of $v_i + v_i\beta$ if shown at time 0 and of $v_i\beta^2 + v_i\beta^3$ if at time 2. As a result, the expected reward of a job that is scheduled at time t can be written as $v_i \sum_{j=t}^{t+l_i-1} \beta^j = v_i \cdot \beta^t \cdot \frac{1-\beta^{l_i}}{1-\beta}$.

In practice, many websites impose certain constraints on the lengths of the stories. In this paper, we assume the website allows either 1-lengthed ad or k-lengthed ($k \geq 2$) ad, for simplicity and without loss of much generality. Actually, we can regard the 1-lengthed ad as a single shot ad, and the k-lengthed ad as a storyline of ads (or ad sequence) [14].

We study the *no-deadline* model, i.e., a job i can be scheduled at any time after its arrival (the time horizon is infinite). For a certain job scenario $\mathcal{S}$, a schedule $\mathcal{A}$ specifies which job to execute at each time $t \geq 0$. Note that preemption of jobs is not allowed. Therefore, the expected reward $R_{\mathcal{A}}(\mathcal{S})$ can be written $\sum_{t=0}^{\infty} \beta^t \cdot v(t)$, where $v(t)$ is the per-unit value of the job scheduled at time t. The goal of our algorithm design is to maximize the expected reward.

Similar to [7], we use competitive ratio [19] to evaluate the performance of an online scheduling algorithm. We say that an algorithm (scheduler) $\mathcal{A}$ is c-competitive (has a competitive ratio of c), if $R_{\mathcal{A}}(\mathcal{S}) \geq c \cdot R_{opt}(\mathcal{S})$ holds for any scenario $\mathcal{S}$, where $0 < c \leq 1$ and *opt* is the optimal offline schedule which has full information about all the future jobs of scenario $\mathcal{S}$.

1.2 Our Work

For deterministic algorithms, we observe that the best competitive ratio one can hope is β^{k-1}. We design a greedy algorithm $\mathcal{A}_1$ (higher per-unit value first) in Section 3 and prove that it achieves this optimal ratio (see Theorem 1).

Note that although the greedy algorithm is natural, it remains a great challenge to analyze its competitive ratio. The challenge comes from several aspects:

(1) Delayed Effect: It is possible that the scheduling time of a job under the greedy algorithm be much later[2] than that under the optimal algorithm. See Example 1 for some intuitive sense . Therefore, there does not exist such a simple "mapping", by which the optimal value obtained from any time unit can be "mapped" to either the same time unit or one of the next $k-1$ ones under the greedy algorithm.

EXAMPLE 1. *When a high-value job a_2 arrives, there is a low-value long job a_1 being scheduled. According to the non-preemption rule, job a_2 has to wait until a_1 is completed. Note that just after the time that a_1 is completed, jobs (denote as set C_1) with higher values (higher than that of a_2) might arrive one by one. Thus, under the greedy algorithm, a_2 would be delayed again and again. However, under the optimal offline algorithm, it is possible that a_2 is scheduled at the time it just arrives, as the optimal offline algorithm is clairvoyant to schedule the low-value long job a_1 somewhere else.*

(2) Nested Effect: The delayed effect may be nested. Take the job set C_1 mentioned above for example. It is possible that there is a job in C_1 encountering a similar situation as a_2. Formally, $a_{j+1} \in C_1$ has higher value than $a_j \in C_1$, but a_{j+1} arrives later than a_j. Then a_{j+1} may be delayed by a_j. Right after a_j is completed, jobs (denoted by C_2, where $C_2 \subset C_1$) with higher values (than a_{j+1}) could arrive one by one. Thus, the greedy algorithm would delay a_2 further, until all jobs in C_2 are accomplished. However, since the time horizon is infinite and the value of each job is unbounded, the adversary is able to design an unlimited number of such nesting. Clearly, the worst-case analysis would become significantly involved and hard to follow when the nesting is very deep.

(3) Chain Effect: Due to non-preemption rule, a job has to wait until the current job is completed. So a low-value long job may delay a high-value job. The chain effect happens when the delayed high-value job itself is a long job, so this long job may delay a subsequent higher-value job. Formally, let $a_1, \ldots, a_n$ be long jobs, such that for every $j = 1, \ldots, n-1$, a_j arrives just before a_{j+1} but the value of a_{j+1} is greater than that of a_j. As the time horizon is infinite and the value of a job is not upper bounded, this may cause a lot of delay and utility loss as beta goes down. It is not easy to estimate the accumulated delay cost compared with the optimal offline algorithm, let alone the chain effect may be deeply entwined with the nested effect.

Given this situation, a carefully designed competitive analysis is needed. Actually, we obtain a stronger result as we use the offline optimal preemptive allocation as the benchmark, which has a larger expected reward than the non-preemptive optimal allocation, and show the greedy algorithm can be β^{k-1} competitive regards to this benchmark.

We first introduce Lemma 2, which is universally applicable in the discounted time horizon scheduling. In brief, Lemma 2 presents a new algorithm $\mathcal{A}_d$, which is the same as Greedy Algorithm $\mathcal{A}_1$ except that it has to schedule jobs from time $k-1$ on. Lemma 2 says that the expected reward obtained by $\mathcal{A}_d$ is at least β^{k-1} times that obtained by $\mathcal{A}_1$.

At first sight, Lemma 2 may be misunderstood as trivial, because a careless thought may arise: *$\mathcal{A}_d$ schedules jobs in the same order as $\mathcal{A}_1$, except for that all jobs are scheduled $k-1$ time units later.*

This thought misses the important restriction that $\mathcal{A}_d$ itself is a greedy algorithm. For example, a short job 1 arrives at time 0 and a long job 2 (with higher per-unit value than job 1) arrives at time 1. Clearly, $\mathcal{A}_1$ will schedule job 1 at time 0 and schedule job 2 at time 1. Note that $\mathcal{A}_d$ will schedule job 2 at time $k-1$ and schedule job 1 at time unit $2k-1$, rather than *schedule job* 1 *at time* $k-1$ *and schedule job* 2 *at time* k. So, the order of scheduling jobs in $\mathcal{A}_d$ can be very different from that in $\mathcal{A}_1$. Therefore, the β^{k-1} approximation can not be derived directly. In fact, the proof is technical and involved.

Lemma 2 works as a useful tool to prove Theorem 1.

Then we prove the β^{k-1} upper bound for the competitive ratio of any online deterministic algorithm (see Theorem 2). In this way, we can come to the conclusion that the greedy algorithm is an optimal deterministic algorithm.

We then consider randomized algorithms. The motivation is that the deterministic greedy algorithm may perform poorly when β is extremely small or k is extremely large. To handle this issue, we design a randomized algorithm $\mathcal{A}_2$ in Section 4 and prove its competitive ratio to be $\frac{1}{k+1}$ (see Theorem 3). The key idea behind $\mathcal{A}_2$ is to ensure that each job has the chance of exactly $\frac{1}{k+1}$ to be scheduled at a unique time t, which estimates the earliest time of scheduling this job under *opt*.

[2]Later than $k-1$ time units.

We further derive an upper bound on the competitive ratio for any online randomized algorithms (see Theorem 4), which is $(1+\frac{(1-\beta^{k-1})^k}{(1-\beta^k)^{k-1}})^{-1}$, through classical adversary analysis. Note that we allow the adversary to use randomized strategy.[3]

The rest of this paper is organized as follows. In Section 2, we introduce several related works. In Section 3, we present the greedy algorithm and an upper bound for all deterministic algorithms. Our randomized algorithm and the upper bound for randomized algorithms are given in Section 4 and Section 5, respectively. Finally, we conclude our paper in Section 6.

2. RELATED WORK

Motivated by applications in web advertising, several variants and generalizations of online advertising have been studied recently [1, 2, 3, 11, 13, 14, 22]. As far as we know, storyboarding as an important form of advertising has only been studied by [4, 7]. Dasgupta et al. [7] give a deterministic $\frac{1}{7}$-competitive algorithm for the storyboarding problem, and show that no deterministic online algorithm can achieve a competitive ratio better than $\frac{1}{2}$, for general β. Alberts and Passen [4] improve the results by giving a $\frac{1}{1+\phi}$-competitive algorithm, where $\phi = (1+\sqrt{5})/2$ is the Golden Ratio. The main difference between their work and ours is that they consider a preemptive setting.

There is a long research line regarding of online scheduling problems (see [18, 21, 28] for a survey). However, the traditional scheduling problem does not consider a discount time horizon and usually specify a deadline for each job, which is the main difference from our work. Zhang et al. [29] study a model in which the job value discounts with the delay: the duration between its arrival time and schedule time. This model is most close to ours, but not identical, because in our model the value of every job discounts with the absolute time, regardless of what time the job arrives.

There is also a rich literature which is concerned with non-preemptive scheduling [20, 15, 16, 9, 8, 10]. In these works, all jobs have deadlines and the job values are not discounted with the time. By assuming the so called *proportional values* (i.e., the value of each job is proportional to the length), in [15], a tight upper and lower bound of 2 are given for the deterministic competitiveness when all jobs have equal lengths, and a $6(\lfloor\log_2 \kappa\rfloor + 1)$-competitive randomized algorithm is provided when jobs' values are restricted in $[1, k]$, matching the $\Omega(\log k)$ lower bound [20] within a constant factor.

Recently, the online scheduling problem has attracted the attention of computational economics community, and many results are obtained from a viewpoint of mechanism design [5, 12, 17, 19, 23, 25, 27]. These models differ from ours in multiple ways, most notably in not having a discounted time horizon.

3. DETERMINISTIC ALGORITHM

The main challenge of designing online algorithms for the non-preemptive scheduling problem is the competition of a current low-value job and a possible future high-value job: As the online algorithm has no information about future jobs, when it is executing a long job (with length k), it is possible that a job with much higher value arrives. Thus the more valuable job has to be delayed and incurs a loss. The loss may be extremely large when the value of a job is not upper bounded.

In this section we propose a greedy algorithm and analyze its competitive ratio. We prove that the algorithm is an optimal deterministic algorithm in terms of competitive ratio by charactering an upper bound on the competitive ratio of any deterministic algorithm.

3.1 The Greedy Algorithm

The greedy algorithm is described in Algorithm 1. Here, a time point t is called *available* if no job is being processed at t.

Algorithm 1 The Greedy Algorithm $\mathcal{A}_1$

```
for each available time t ≥ 0 do
    Schedule the job with the highest per-unit value.
end for
```

From now on, we will prove the competitive ratio of $\mathcal{A}_1$, which is shown in Theorem 1.

THEOREM 1. *The greedy algorithm $\mathcal{A}_1$ has a competitive ratio of β^{k-1}.*

As aforementioned, let *opt* denote the optimal offline scheduling when the full information of future jobs is known in advance. Furthermore, let *opt** denote the optimal offline scheduling when the full information of future jobs is known in advance and preemption is allowed. Obviously, *opt** always leads to a reward no less than *opt*. To analyze the competitive ratio of $\mathcal{A}_1$, in principle, we need to compare with *opt*. Here, instead of comparing with *opt* directly, we achieve a slightly stronger result since we compare with a stronger benchmark *opt**. In the proof, we will show that $\mathcal{A}_1$ obtains a competitive ratio of at least β^{k-1} even if the benchmark is *opt** instead of *opt*.

To make the proof more readable, we introduce the following lemma.

LEMMA 2. *For any job set $\mathcal{S}$, suppose w.l.o.g. that the earliest arrival time of jobs in $\mathcal{S}$ is 0. We define a new algorithm $\mathcal{A}_d$ which is the same as Greedy Algorithm $\mathcal{A}_1$ except that it has to schedule the jobs from time $k-1$ on. We claim that the expected reward obtained by $\mathcal{A}_d$ is at least β^{k-1} times that obtained by $\mathcal{A}_1$.*

PROOF. We use induction to prove this lemma. If there is only one job, the theorem holds trivially. Now we only need to prove the case of n jobs given that the theorem holds for less than n jobs. First, we introduce the definition of *conformity*.

DEFINITION 1. *We say a job sequence scheduled by $\mathcal{A}_d$ during the period $[t_1+k-1, t_2+k-1]$ is in* conformity *with the job sequence scheduled by $\mathcal{A}_1$ during the period $[t_1, t_2]$, if the job scheduled by $\mathcal{A}_d$ at time $t+k-1$ is the same as the job scheduled by $\mathcal{A}_1$ at time t, for any time $t \in [t_1, t_2]$.*

If the job sequence scheduled by $\mathcal{A}_d$ is in conformity with $\mathcal{A}_1$ all the time, then the reward obtained by $\mathcal{A}_d$ is β^{k-1}

[3]There is still a gap between the competitive ratio of $\mathcal{A}_2$ and the upper bound, since $(1+\frac{(1-\beta^{k-1})^k}{(1-\beta^k)^{k-1}})^{-1}$ is always greater than $\frac{1}{2}$ when $k \geq 2$ and $0 < \beta < 1$.

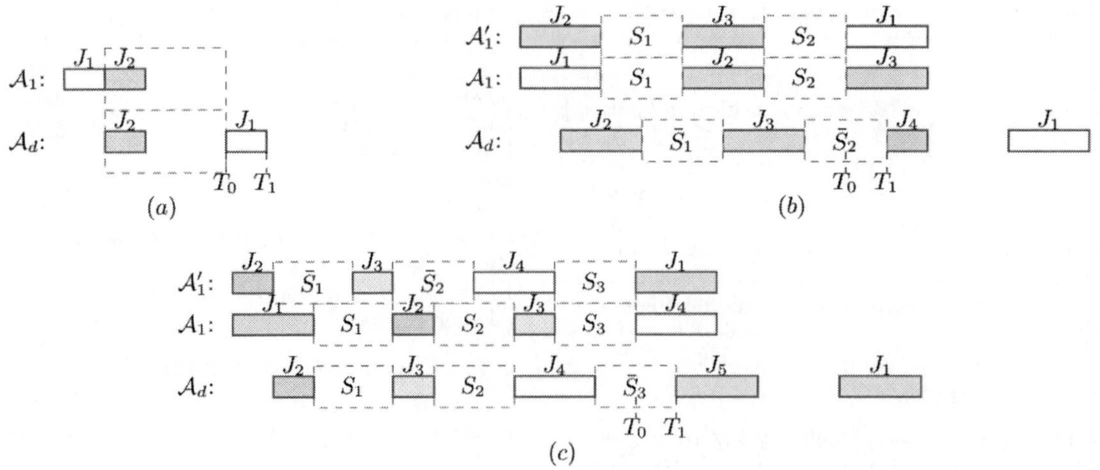

Figure 1: Compare the scheduling under $\mathcal{A}_1$ and $\mathcal{A}_d$

times that obtained by $\mathcal{A}_1$, clearly. Therefore, it suffices to compare the sequences at the time when unconformity occurs. There are three possible cases that may happen, as shown in Figure 1. For a job J_i scheduled by $\mathcal{A}_1$ (resp. $\mathcal{A}_d$), we denote its starting time as s_i (resp. s_i^d) and its finishing time as f_i (resp. f_i^d).

(a) Fig 1 (a) describes such a case: when the unconformity occurs, $\mathcal{A}_1$ has just finished a short job J_1. At this time (i.e., time f_1), $\mathcal{A}_d$ schedules a job J_2 instead of J_1.[4] In fact, J_2 is the job with highest per-unit value at that time, so it is also scheduled by $\mathcal{A}_1$ at the same time. We claim that, before the time $\mathcal{A}_d$ schedules J_1, the sequences (in the dashed boxes) under $\mathcal{A}_1$ and $\mathcal{A}_d$ must be identical. In particular, these are the jobs with higher per-unit value than J_1 and arrival time earlier than $T_0 = s_1^d$. Obviously, the reward obtained by $\mathcal{A}_d$ before $T_1 = f_1^d$ is at least β ($\geq \beta^{k-1}$) times that obtained by $\mathcal{A}_1$ before T_0. Thus the problem is reduced to analyze the remaining part of $\mathcal{A}_d$ from T_1 on (comparing with $\mathcal{A}_1$ from T_0 on), which is already covered by the induction hypothesis.

(b) Fig 1 (b) describes such a case: when the unconformity occurs, $\mathcal{A}_1$ schedules a long job J_1, but $\mathcal{A}_d$ schedules another long job J_2 instead. It is obvious that J_2 must have a higher per-unit value than J_1. Therefore, $s_2 \leq s_1^d - 1$. Now, we consider the job scheduled by $\mathcal{A}_d$ at time $f_2 - 1$. There are three cases: (1) it is just the job J_1; (2) it is a short job; (3) it is a long job other than J_1. For simplicity, we combine these cases in the example in Figure 1 (b). In this example, a long job J_3 is scheduled by $\mathcal{A}_d$ at time $f_2 - 1$. Then similarly, we have $s_3 \leq s_1^d - 1$ and continue to discuss the job scheduled by $\mathcal{A}_d$ at time $f_3 - 1$. In this example, a short job J_4 is scheduled by $\mathcal{A}_d$ at time $f_3 - 1$. We now consider a subsidiary allocation[5] $\mathcal{A}'_1$ which is the same as $\mathcal{A}_1$ except the allocation of J_1, J_2, J_3 (see the figure). Since the per-unit value of J_1 is less than J_2 and J_3, the reward of $\mathcal{A}'_1$ is greater than that of $\mathcal{A}_1$. By comparing $\mathcal{A}_d$ with $\mathcal{A}_1$, we notice that S and $\bar{S}_1$ share the same constitution. That is, the same set of jobs, though the orders may differ. Therefore, using the induction hypothesis, $\bar{S}_1$ has reward at least β^{k-1} times that of S_1. Thus, the reward of $\mathcal{A}_d$ before time $T_1 = f_3 - 1$ is at least β^{k-1} times that of $\mathcal{A}'_1$ before $T_0 = s_3$. The remaining part of this problem (the subsequence of $\mathcal{A}_d$ from T_1 on) reduces to case (c).

(c) Fig 1 (c) describes such a case: $\mathcal{A}_d$ schedules a short job J_2 instead of J_1 when the unconformity occurs. Similar to our argument for case (b), we discuss the behavior of $\mathcal{A}_d$ at s_2 and so forth. As depicted in the figure, a short job J_3 is scheduled at s_2, and a long job J_4 is scheduled at s_3. Through the subsidiary allocation $\mathcal{A}'_1$, which differs from $\mathcal{A}_1$ in the allocations of J_1, J_2, J_3, J_4 (see the figure), we will get: on the one hand, the reward of $\mathcal{A}'_1$ is greater than $\mathcal{A}_1$; on the other hand, the reward of $\mathcal{A}_d$ before $T_1 = f_4 - 1$ is at least β^{k-1} times the reward of $\mathcal{A}'_1$ before $T_0 = s_4$. It remains to discuss the sequence scheduled by $\mathcal{A}_d$ starting from T_1. This can be reduced to case (c) if J_5 is a short job, to case (b) if J_5 is a long job other than J_1, and to the induction hypothesis if it is job J_1.

□

[4]In fact, it does not matter whether J_1 is a short job or a long job. Without loss of generality, we depict it as a short one in the figure.

[5]Note, $\mathcal{A}'_1$ is not a legal scheduling of jobs, since J_2 has not arrived at time 0 and hence cannot be scheduled there.

3.2 Proof of Theorem 1

In this subsection, we apply Lemma 2 to prove the competitive ratio of $\mathcal{A}_1$. To make it easier to follow the technique, we first prove the special case, i.e., $k = 2$. The proof for general k is similar, and we will introduce it afterwards.

PROOF. Consider the job sequence arranged by *opt**. If there does not exist preemption-resume, then $\mathcal{A}_1$ must arrange the same sequence as *opt** does, and the ratio is 1 obviously. So in the following, we assume there exists preemption-resume. We denote the first preempted long job as job a, and its two segments as a_1 and a_2 (refer to Fig 2 (a)). Clearly, a_1 and a_2 are both of length 1 and a_1 is scheduled earlier than a_2. Fig 2 (a) depicts a part of job sequence under *opt**,

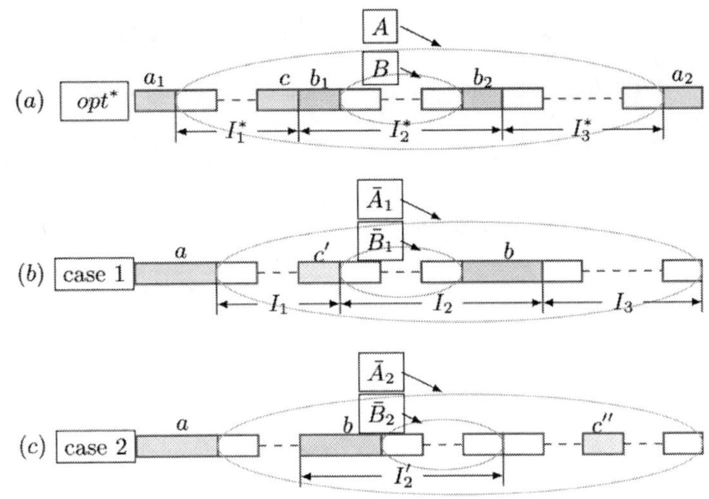

Figure 2: Compare the scheduling under *opt and Greedy Algorithm**

which includes a_1, A and a_2. Here, we use A to represent the job sequence scheduled between a_1 and a_2. First, we give a useful observation below.

OBSERVATION 1. *Each time unit between a_1 and a_2 are occupied and every job scheduled between a_1 and a_2 has a higher per-unit value than job a.*

Fig 2 (b) and Fig 2 (c) depict two possible sequences under $\mathcal{A}_1$, and in these two cases we denote the job sequence after a as $\bar{A}_1$ and $\bar{A}_2$ respectively. By taking Observation 1 into consideration, we have another two observations as follows.

OBSERVATION 2. *The constitutions of A, $\bar{A}_1$ and $\bar{A}_2$ are the same, i.e., they include the same jobs.*

OBSERVATION 3. *There may exist jobs whose preemption and resume both occur between a_1 and a_2 (or occur after a_2), but cannot exist such situation: preemption occurs between a_1 and a_2, but resume occurs after a_2.*

Observation 2 and Observation 3 are non-negligible, since then we can focus on sequence $\langle a_1, A, a_2\rangle$ without loss of generality.

We look into the job sequence A. If there does not exist preemption-resume in A, then the jobs in A are scheduled greedily under *opt**. Because $\mathcal{A}_1$ has to schedule the jobs in A after completing a, which leads to one time-unit delay, we can apply Lemma 2 here, and derive our desired result directly.

Otherwise, if there exists preemption-resume in A, then we denote the first preempted long job as b, and its two segments b_1 and b_2 respectively. We may have two possible cases:

(1) Job b is scheduled at the time that b_2 is scheduled by *opt**, please refer to Fig 2 (b). Actually, $\bar{B}_1$ is identical to B in this case. Fig 2 (a) shows that the job sequence of A is divided into three parts: I_1^*, I_2^* and I_3^*. Fig 2 (b) shows that the job sequence of $\bar{A}_1$ is also divided into three parts I_1, I_2 and I_3. Then applying Lemma 2 to I_1, I_2 and I_3 respectively, we can get that the reward obtained by $\mathcal{A}_1$ during I_1, I_2 or I_3 is at least β times of that obtained by *opt** during I_1^*, I_2^* or I_3^* respectively. So in this case the sequence in $\mathcal{A}_1$ must have reward at least β times of that in *opt**.

(2) Job b is scheduled at the time that b_1 is scheduled by *opt**, please refer to Fig 2 (c). Clearly, job sequence I_2' is in accord with I_2^*, and we will discuss them later. We first consider the remaining parts in A and $\bar{A}_2$, and denote them as $A - I_2^*$ and $\bar{A}_2 - I_2'$ respectively. We can apply Lemma 2 to job sequence $\bar{A}_2 - I_2'$, and derive that the reward obtained by $\mathcal{A}_1$ during $\bar{A}_2 - I_2'$ is at least β times of that obtained by *opt** during $A - I_2^*$. We now turn to discuss I_2' and I_2^*. Since jobs in sequence $\bar{B}_2$ are "delayed" compared to the jobs in sequence B, we reduce to analyze the job sequence B, and the analysis is the same as that of A.

Then, we can apply reduction until the proof is completed.

As for the case of general k, the proof is similar. We can still refer to Fig 2, though some notations in Fig 2 have different meanings now: a_1 (resp. b_1) and a_2 (resp. b_2) denote the first and last segments of job a (resp. b) in *opt**. Different from the case of $k = 2$, when $k > 2$, a_1 (resp. b_1) and a_2 (resp. b_2) can be integers other than 1, and A (resp. B) can include other segments of a (resp. b). We denote the segments of a (resp. b) in A (resp. B) as A' (resp. A'), and denote $\bar{A} = A - A'$ (resp. $\bar{B} = B - B'$). Clearly, all jobs in $\bar{A}$ (resp. $\bar{B}$) have higher per-unit value than a (resp. b).

If there does not exist any preemption-resume in A, then the jobs in A are scheduled greedily under *opt**. Since $\mathcal{A}_1$ has to schedule the jobs in A after completing a, which induces $|a| - |a_1|$ time units (less than $k - 1$) delay, we can apply Lemma 2 here and derive our desired result directly.

If there does exist preemption-resumes in A, then we discuss the time that b is scheduled under $\mathcal{A}_1$. Case 1 denotes the case in which job b is scheduled after the jobs in B, and case 2 denotes the case in which job b is scheduled before the jobs in B. Refer to Fig 2 (b) and Fig 2 (c) respectively.

OBSERVATION 4. *In both case 1 and case 2, the jobs scheduled in I_3^* under opt* must be scheduled after job b under $\mathcal{A}_1$.*

In Fig 2 (b), I_1 contains part (all) of the jobs which are scheduled in I_1^* under *opt**, $\bar{B}_1$ contains all the jobs in $\bar{B}$

and part of jobs scheduled in I_1^*, and I_3 contains all the jobs scheduled in I_3^* and part of jobs scheduled in I_1^*.

In Fig 2 (c), $\bar{B}_2$ only contains all the jobs in $\bar{B}$, as all jobs in $\bar{B}$ (thus $\bar{B}_2$) have higher per-unit values than job b.

We now discuss the reward obtained by $\mathcal{A}_1$ under the above two cases.

(1) In case 1, we construct a subsidiary allocation, in which, "all" the jobs in I_1^* (resp. $\bar{B}$ and I_3^*) are scheduled greedily in I_1 (resp. $\bar{B}_1$ and I_3). On one hand, similar to the $k=2$ case, we can get that the reward obtained by the subsidiary allocation during I_1, I_2 or I_3 is at least β^{k-1} times of that obtained by opt^* during I_1^*, I_2^* or I_3^* respectively. On the other hand, the reward of $\mathcal{A}_1$ must be no less than that of the subsidiary allocation, due to the greedy property. In fact, the time b scheduled under $\mathcal{A}_1$ might be no later than that under the subsidiary allocation. Therefore, in this case the sequence in $\mathcal{A}_1$ must have reward at least β^{k-1} times of that in opt^*.

(2) In case 2, similar to the $k=2$ case, we first consider $A - I_2^*$ and $\bar{A}_2 - I_2'$. We can apply Lemma 2 to job sequence $\bar{A}_2 - I_2'$, and derive that the reward obtained by $\mathcal{A}_1$ during $\bar{A}_2 - I_2'$ is at least β^{k-1} times of that obtained by opt^* during $A - I_2^*$. We then discuss I_2' and I_2^*. It is easy to know that jobs in sequence $\bar{B}_2$ are delayed (no more than $k-1$ time units) compared to the jobs in sequence B. We reduce to analyze the job sequence B, and the analysis is the same as that of A.

Similarly, we apply reduction until the proof is completed. □

3.3 Upper Bound for the Deterministic Algorithms

One may wonder whether there exists a deterministic algorithm which can achieve a competitive ratio better than β^{k-1}. The following theorem gives a negative answer, and thus bounds the power of deterministic algorithms.

THEOREM 2. *No deterministic algorithm can achieve a competitive ratio better than* β^{k-1}.

PROOF. We use an adversary argument. Consider the following scenario: at time 0, a long job (with length k) with per-unit value v_a (thus total value $v_a' = v_a \cdot \frac{1-\beta^k}{1-\beta}$) arrives. If a deterministic algorithm $\mathcal{A}$ was to schedule it at time t, then the adversary would release a dominant short job with per-unit value v_b (v_b is sufficiently large) at time $t+1$. In such case, $\mathcal{A}$ obtains a reward $\beta^t \cdot (v_a' + \beta^k \cdot v_b)$, while the optimal offline algorithm can obtain $\beta^t \cdot (\beta \cdot v_b + \beta^2 \cdot v_a')$. Therefore, the competitive ratio is at best $\frac{\beta^t \cdot (v_a' + \beta^k \cdot v_b)}{\beta^t \cdot (\beta \cdot v_b + \beta^2 \cdot v_a')} \to \beta^{k-1}$, when $\frac{v_b}{v_a'} \to \infty$. □

In this way, we come to the conclusion that the greedy algorithm is among the optimal deterministic algorithms.

4. A $\frac{1}{K+1}$-COMPETITIVE RANDOMIZED ALGORITHM

In the previous section, we study the performance of deterministic algorithms. Although the performance of greedy algorithm matches the upper bound for any deterministic algorithms, it may perform poorly when β is extremely small or k is extremely large. Therefore, in the following two sections, we focus on randomized algorithms, and consider whether randomization will help improve the performance of algorithms. We introduce a randomized algorithm which can ensure a competitive ratio of $\frac{1}{k+1}$ in this section.

The algorithm $\mathcal{A}_2$ is described in Algorithm 2. In $\mathcal{A}_2$, $\mu(\cdot)$ is an indicator function: if input is a non-zero set, then $\mu(\cdot) = 1$, otherwise $\mu(\cdot) = 0$.

$\mathcal{A}_2$ operates as follows: for each available time[6] t, $\mathcal{A}_2$ selects a long job l^* with highest per-unit value (Line 2) and schedules it at t according to a well-defined probability (Line 6). If there exist other long jobs, we delay them to time $t+k$ as if their arrival time was $t+k$ (Line 3). This process is based on the fact that in *opt* the reasonable earliest scheduling time of these jobs is not earlier than $t+k$, since job l^* has higher per-unit value than them. If there exist short jobs, we denote the one with highest per-unit value as s^* (Line 2), and delay the others to time $t+1$ as if their arrival time was $t+1$ (Line 3).

Intuitively, the probability of scheduling l^* at time t depends on how many long jobs arrive before t whose execution may interfere with the execution of l^* at t. In precise, we only need to check the $k-1$ time points: $\{t-k+1, \ldots, t-2, t-1\}$. Taking the interference into consideration, we intend to ensure the scheduling of l^* at time t with probability $\frac{1}{k+1}$ finally.

Algorithm 2 The Randomized Algorithm $\mathcal{A}_2$

1: **for** each time $t \geq 0$ **do**
2: Denote the set of long (resp. short) jobs arriving at t as $L(t)$ (resp. $S(t)$), the job with highest per-unit value in $L(t)$ (resp. $S(t)$) as l^* (resp. s^*).
3: Delay all jobs in $L(t) \setminus l^*$ (resp. $S(t) \setminus s^*$) to the time $t+k$ (resp. $t+1$), as if their arrival time was $t+k$ (resp. $t+1$).
4: **if** time t is available **then**
5: **if** $L(t) \neq \emptyset$ **then**
6: Schedule the job l^* with probability
$$\sigma(t) = \frac{1}{k+1-\sum_{i=1}^{k-1} \mu(L(t-i))}.$$
7: **if** job l^* is scheduled after randomization **then**
8: Throw away job s^*, if any.
9: **else**
10: Schedule job s^*, if any.
11: Throw away job l^*.
12: **end if**
13: **else**
14: Schedule job s^*, if any.
15: **end if**
16: **else**
17: Throw away job l^* and job s^*, if any.
18: **end if**
19: **end for**

After randomization, there exist two cases:

- If l^* is scheduled, throw away the short job with highest per-unit value (s^*) (Line 8).
- If l^* is not scheduled, throw away l^* (Line 11) and

[6]A time point t is *available* if there is no job processed at t.

"plug in" the short job with highest per-unit value (i.e., s^*) if any (Line 10).

If there does not exist any long job at time t, $\mathcal{A}_2$ schedules the short job with highest per-unit value (i.e., s^*, if any) directly (Line 14).

Note that for the unavailable time, i.e., some long job is under process, the possible job l^* and s^* at that time (the definitions are the same as above) should also be thrown away (Line 17).

In Figure 3, we use an example to illustrate the operation of algorithm $\mathcal{A}_2$.

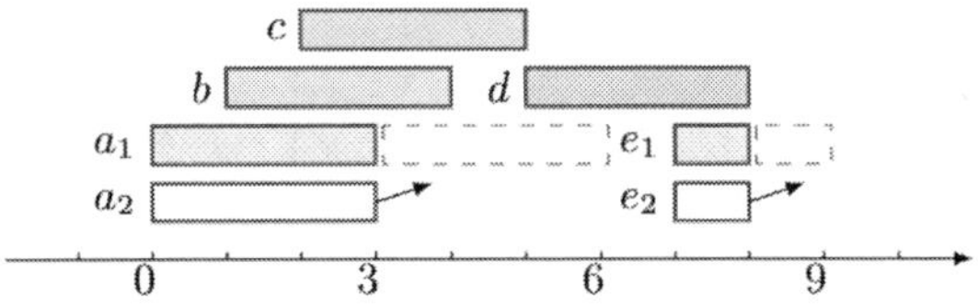

Figure 3: An example of the processing of $\mathcal{A}_2$

EXAMPLE 3. *In this $k = 3$ example, we have two long jobs (a_1 and a_2) which arrive at time 0, and job a_1 has a higher per-unit value than a_2 does. So at the time 0, our algorithm delays a_2 to time 3 and schedules job a_1 with probability $\frac{1}{4}$. If a_1 is finally scheduled at time 0, then job b and job c will be thrown away at time 1 and 2 respectively. Otherwise, the algorithm throws a_1 and schedules job b with probability $\frac{1}{3}$ at time 1. Note that the final probability that job b would be scheduled is $(1 - \frac{1}{4}) \cdot \frac{1}{3} = \frac{1}{4}$.*

In the same way, if job c (or job a_2) had not been thrown away before, then it would be considered to be scheduled with probability $\frac{1}{2}$. The reason is: for job c, there were two jobs (a_1 and b) which might interfere with it; for job a_2 (remember we regard the arrival time of a_2 as time 3), there were also two job (b and c) which might interfere with it. Therefore, we get the desired final probability $\frac{1}{4}$ that job c or job a_2 would be scheduled ($(1 - 2 \cdot \frac{1}{4}) \cdot \frac{1}{2} = \frac{1}{4}$).

As for job d, because there would be only one job (a_2) that might interfere with it, if it had not been thrown away, it would be considered to be scheduled with probability $\frac{1}{3}$, thus, we get the desire final probability $\frac{1}{4}$.

The situation for short jobs (e_1 and e_2) is relatively simple. As e_1 has a higher per-unit value than e_2, e_2 is delayed one time unit afterwards anyway. If job d is scheduled finally, e_1 will be thrown away, otherwise, e_1 will be scheduled.

THEOREM 3. *Algorithm $\mathcal{A}_2$ achieves a competitive ratio of $\frac{1}{k+1}$, for general β.*

PROOF. The proof idea is rooted in the process of this algorithm. Actually, according to the rule of $\mathcal{A}_2$, every long job has the chance of $\frac{1}{k+1}$ to be scheduled at some time t. It is worth mentioning that t is the earliest possible time this job would be scheduled under *opt*.

We now explain how $\frac{1}{k+1}$ comes out. As for the first arrived long job, the algorithm will schedule it with probability $\frac{1}{k+1}$ clearly. By induction, if we assign $\sigma(t)$ as the probability to schedule for a long job at time t, then in consideration of the interference from possible earlier scheduled jobs, the final probability to schedule this job should be

$$
\begin{aligned}
&(1 - \frac{1}{k+1} \cdot \sum_{i=1}^{k-1} \mu(L(t-i))) \cdot \sigma(t) \\
=&\frac{1 - \frac{1}{k+1} \cdot \sum_{i=1}^{k-1} \mu(L(t-i))}{k+1-\sum_{i=1}^{k-1} \mu(L(t-i))} \\
=&\frac{1}{k+1}.
\end{aligned} \tag{1}
$$

As for the short job that arrives at t, the the final probability to schedule is at least

$$1 - \frac{1}{k+1} \cdot \sum_{i=0}^{k-1} \mu(L(t-i)) \geq \frac{1}{k+1}. \tag{2}$$

Since every job has at least $\frac{1}{k+1}$ chance to schedule at some time t which is no later than its earliest possible scheduled time under *opt*. Therefore, the competitive ratio obtained by $\mathcal{A}_2$ is at least $\frac{1}{k+1}$. □

The following table shows the threshold β^* for several typical value of k. That is, given a fixed k, the randomized algorithm $\mathcal{A}_2$ performs better than the deterministic algorithm $\mathcal{A}_1$ when $\beta < \beta^*$.

k	2	3	4	5	10	general k
β^*	1/3	1/2	0.58	0.64	0.77	$(k+1)^{\frac{-1}{k-1}}$

5. BOUNDING THE POWER OF RANDOMIZATION

In this section, we characterize the boundary of our research and give an upper bound on the competitive ratios of any randomized algorithms. Formally, we have the following theorem.

THEOREM 4. *No randomized algorithm can achieve a competitive ratio better than $(1 + \frac{(1-\beta^{k-1})^k}{(1-\beta^k)^{k-1}})^{-1}$.*

PROOF. Let us take the $k = 3$ case for example, and the proof for general k is essentially the same. We will use an adversary argument and show that under some scenarios, no algorithm can achieve a ratio better than $(1 + \frac{(1-\beta^{k-1})^k}{(1-\beta^k)^{k-1}})^{-1}$.

The adversary will release at most two jobs: a long job l (with length 3) and a short *dominant* job s (with length 1 and much larger per-unit value than l).

At time 0, the long job l is released. For an arbitrary randomized algorithm $\mathcal{A}$, we can use a vector $\langle x_1, x_2, x_3, x_4 \rangle$ to represent the probability that $\mathcal{A}$ starts to schedule l at each time point. Formally, x_1, x_2 and x_3 represent the probability that $\mathcal{A}$ intends to schedule the job at time 0, 1 and 2 respectively, and x_4 is the probability to schedule the job at or later than time 3. Clearly, we have $x_1 + x_2 + x_3 + x_4 = 1$.

Given $\mathcal{A}$, we construct the following possible adversarial behaviors:

(1) No other job is released any more. Then, $\mathcal{A}$ obtains an (expected) reward no greater than $(x_1 + \beta \cdot x_2 + \beta^2 \cdot x_3 + \beta^3 \cdot x_4) \cdot v_l$, while the *opt* can obtain a reward v_l. So the competitive ratio is no greater than $x_1 + \beta \cdot x_2 + \beta^2 \cdot x_3 + \beta^3 \cdot x_4$.

(2) The short dominant job s is released at time 2. Then, $\mathcal{A}$ obtains a competitive ratio of no greater than $\beta \cdot x_1 + \beta^2 \cdot x_2 + x_3 + x_4$.

(3) The short dominant job s is released at time 1. Then, $\mathcal{A}$ obtains a competitive ratio of no greater than $\beta^2 \cdot x_1 + x_2 + x_3 + x_4$.

Suppose the adversary also uses a randomized strategy $\langle y_1, y_2, y_3 \rangle$, i.e., the adversary chooses the i-th adversarial behavior (mentioned above) with probability y_i, $i = 1, 2, 3$, and $y_1 + y_2 + y_3 = 1$. In order to find an upper bound, we come to a min max problem, which is formulated as follows.

$$\min_{y_1,y_2,y_3} \max_{x_1,x_2,x_3,x_4} \begin{pmatrix} y_1 & y_2 & y_3 \end{pmatrix} \begin{pmatrix} 1 & \beta & \beta^2 & \beta^3 \\ \beta & \beta^2 & 1 & 1 \\ \beta^2 & 1 & 1 & 1 \end{pmatrix} \begin{pmatrix} x_1 \\ x_2 \\ x_3 \\ x_4 \end{pmatrix}.$$

Notice that the coefficients of x_4 is dominated by that of x_3, thus $x_4 = 0$ is a dominant strategy for $\mathcal{A}$. Therefore, the min max problem can be simplified to the following style:

$$\min_{y_1,y_2,y_3} \max_{x_1,x_2,x_3} \begin{pmatrix} y_1 & y_2 & y_3 \end{pmatrix} \begin{pmatrix} 1 & \beta & \beta^2 \\ \beta & \beta^2 & 1 \\ \beta^2 & 1 & 1 \end{pmatrix} \begin{pmatrix} x_1 \\ x_2 \\ x_3 \end{pmatrix}.$$

It is interesting that the matrix is a Toeplitz matrix, and we find that the min max problem is not difficult to solve based on the following observation:

OBSERVATION 5. *As the adversary choose his strategy after algorithm $\mathcal{A}$ does, the best strategy for $\mathcal{A}$ is to offer a menu with identical items.*

That is, elements in the following vector must be the same.

$$\begin{pmatrix} 1 & \beta & \beta^2 \\ \beta & \beta^2 & 1 \\ \beta^2 & 1 & 1 \end{pmatrix} \begin{pmatrix} x_1 \\ x_2 \\ x_3 \end{pmatrix} = \begin{pmatrix} x_1 + \beta \cdot x_2 + \beta^2 \cdot x_3 \\ \beta \cdot x_1 + \beta^2 \cdot x_2 + x_3 \\ \beta^2 \cdot x_1 + x_2 + x_3 \end{pmatrix}.$$

Together with the constraint $x_1 + x_2 + x_3 = 1$, we can solve x_1, x_2 and x_3, and the upper bound is exactly the result of the min max problem.

For a general k, the proof idea is similar: At time 0, a long job (with length k) is released. Each algorithm $\mathcal{A}$ is associated with a probability vector $\langle x_1, x_2, \ldots, x_k, x_{k+1} \rangle$ (x_{k+1} will be proved to be 0). We then construct k adversarial behaviors, and in fact the adversary can randomly choose such behaviors. Therefore, we come to solve a min max problem:

$$\min_{\vec{y}} \max_{\vec{x}} \vec{y}\, T\, \vec{x}', \tag{3}$$

where $\vec{x} = \langle x_1, \ldots, x_k \rangle$, $\vec{y} = \langle y_1, \ldots, y_k \rangle$ and T is the Toeplitz matrix as follows:

$$\begin{pmatrix} 1 & \cdots & \cdots & \beta^{k-1} \\ \beta & \cdots & \beta^{k-1} & 1 \\ \vdots & \vdots & \vdots & \vdots \\ \beta^{k-1} & \cdots & 1 & 1 \end{pmatrix}. \tag{4}$$

By the similar analysis, we can construct equations and obtain the upper bound $(1 + \frac{(1-\beta^{k-1})^k}{(1-\beta^k)^{k-1}})^{-1}$. □

By observing the form of $(1 + \frac{(1-\beta^{k-1})^k}{(1-\beta^k)^{k-1}})^{-1}$, we know the upper bound is increasing with β and decreasing with k. Moreover, the upper bound is always greater than $\frac{1}{2}$ when $k \geq 2$ and $0 < \beta < 1$. There is still a gap between the competitive ratio of $\mathcal{A}_2$ and the upper bound.

6. CONCLUSIONS

In this paper, we studied the online non-preemptive story scheduling problem in web advertising. This new scheduling problem is different from those classic problems studied in the 90's (see [26] for an overview) because of the motivation of online advertising. The key factors which constitute the new problem are (1) discounted time horizon, (2) no deadline, and (3) no preemption. We designed both deterministic and randomized algorithms and proved they all have good performance (in terms of expected reward) through competitive analysis. We also showed upper bounds of competitive ratio for any deterministic and randomized algorithms.

There are multiple aspects to study in the future.

- It remains to close the gap between the upper bound and lower bound for randomized algorithms in our setting. Our hypothesis is that the tight bound is $\frac{\sum_{i=0}^{k-1} \beta^i}{k}$.
- Although the setting of two possible lengths seems to be restrictive, it has already posed great challenge for the competitive analysis of the simplest Greedy algorithm. Our work is the first step towards a general setting, in which job lengths can be any integer in $\{1, 2, \ldots, k\}$. We plan to study this generalization.
- We assumed that a website has no information about future jobs and focused on worst-case analysis in this work. When the website accumulates more and more data as time goes on, it can get some distribution information about future jobs and thus it is interesting to design better algorithms leveraging the distribution information.
- We did not consider advertisers' strategic behaviors, e.g., they may misreport their stories. Taking the strategic behaviors into consideration, this problem can be explored from the perspective of mechanism design.

7. ACKNOWLEDGEMENTS

This work was supported by the National Basic Research Program of China Grant 2011CBA00300, 2011CBA00301, the Natural Science Foundation of China Grant 61033001, 61361136003, 61303077, 61561146398, 61170062, 61222202, 61433014, a Tsinghua Initiative Scientific Research Grant and a China Youth 1000-talent program.

REFERENCES

[1] G. Aggarwal, Y. Cai, A. Mehta, and G. Pierrakos. Biobjective online bipartite matching. In *Web and Internet Economics*, pages 218–231. Springer, 2014.

[2] S. Alaei, E. Arcaute, S. Khuller, W. Ma, A. Malekian, and J. Tomlin. Online allocation of display advertisements subject to advanced sales contracts. In *Proceedings of the third international workshop on data mining and audience intelligence for advertising*, pages 69–77. ACM, 2009.

[3] S. Alaei, M. Hajiaghayi, and V. Liaghat. Online prophet-inequality matching with applications to ad allocation. In *Proceedings of the 13th ACM Conference on Electronic Commerce*, pages 18–35. ACM, 2012.

[4] S. Albers and A. Passen. New online algorithms for story scheduling in web advertising. In *Automata, Languages, and Programming*, pages 446–458. Springer, 2013.

[5] G. Christodoulou, E. Koutsoupias, and A. Vidali. A lower bound for scheduling mechanisms. *Algorithmica*, 55(4):729–740, 2009.

[6] P. W. H. Coopers. *IAB internet advertising revenue report*. Coopers, Price Water House, 2014.

[7] A. Dasgupta, A. Ghosh, H. Nazerzadeh, and P. Raghavan. Online story scheduling in web advertising. In *Proceedings of the twentieth Annual ACM-SIAM Symposium on Discrete Algorithms*, pages 1275–1284. Society for Industrial and Applied Mathematics, 2009.

[8] J. Ding, T. Ebenlendr, J. Sgall, and G. Zhang. Online scheduling of equal-length jobs on parallel machines. In *Proceedings of the 15th annual European conference on Algorithms*, pages 427–438. Springer-Verlag, 2007.

[9] J. Ding and G. Zhang. Online scheduling with hard deadlines on parallel machines. In *Algorithmic Aspects in Information and Management*, pages 32–42. Springer, 2006.

[10] T. Ebenlendr and J. Sgall. A lower bound for scheduling of unit jobs with immediate decision on parallel machines. In *Approximation and Online Algorithms*, pages 43–52. Springer-Verlag, 2009.

[11] J. Feldman, N. Korula, V. Mirrokni, S. Muthukrishnan, and M. Pál. Online ad assignment with free disposal. In *Internet and network economics*, pages 374–385. Springer, 2009.

[12] E. J. Friedman and D. C. Parkes. Pricing wifi at starbucks: issues in online mechanism design. In *Proceedings of the 4th ACM conference on Electronic commerce*, pages 240–241. ACM, 2003.

[13] A. Ghosh and A. Sayedi. Expressive auctions for externalities in online advertising. In *Proceedings of the 19th international conference on World wide web*, pages 371–380. ACM, 2010.

[14] G. Goel, M. Hajiaghayi, and M. R. Khani. Randomized revenue monotone mechanisms for online advertising. In *Web and Internet Economics*, pages 324–337. Springer, 2014.

[15] S. A. Goldman, J. Parwatikar, and S. Suri. Online scheduling with hard deadlines. *Journal of Algorithms*, 34(2):370–389, 2000.

[16] M. H. Goldwasser. Patience is a virtue: The effect of slack on competitiveness for admission control. *Journal of Scheduling*, 6(2):183–211, 2003.

[17] M. Hajiaghayi, R. Kleinberg, M. Mahdian, and D. C. Parkes. Online auctions with re-usable goods. In *Proceedings of the 6th ACM conference on Electronic commerce*, pages 165–174. ACM, 2005.

[18] A. W. Kolen, J. K. Lenstra, C. H. Papadimitriou, and F. C. Spieksma. Interval scheduling: A survey. *Naval Research Logistics (NRL)*, 54(5):530–543, 2007.

[19] R. Lavi and N. Nisan. Competitive analysis of incentive compatible on-line auctions. In *Proceedings of the 2nd ACM conference on Electronic commerce*, pages 233–241. ACM, 2000.

[20] R. Lipton. Online interval scheduling. In *Proceedings of the fifth annual ACM-SIAM symposium on Discrete Algorithms*, pages 302–311. Society for Industrial and Applied Mathematics, 1994.

[21] A. Mäcker, M. Malatyali, F. Meyer auf der Heide, and S. Riechers. Non-preemptive scheduling on machines with setup times. In *Proceedings of the 13th International Symposium on Algorithms and Data Structures (WADS)*, LNCS. Springer, 2015.

[22] A. Mehta, A. Saberi, U. Vazirani, and V. Vazirani. Adwords and generalized online matching. *Journal of the ACM (JACM)*, 54(5):22, 2007.

[23] N. Nisan and A. Ronen. Algorithmic mechanism design. In *Proceedings of the thirty-first annual ACM symposium on Theory of computing*, pages 129–140. ACM, 1999.

[24] N.Y.Times. What is surround sessions?, 2002.

[25] D. C. Parkes. Online mechanisms. *Algorithmic Game Theory, ed. N. Nisan, T. Roughgarden, E. Tardos, and V. Vazirani, Cambridge University Press*, pages 411–439, 2007.

[26] M. L. Pinedo. *Scheduling: theory, algorithms, and systems*. Springer Science & Business Media, 2012.

[27] R. Porter. Mechanism design for online real-time scheduling. In *Proceedings of the 5th ACM conference on Electronic commerce*, pages 61–70. ACM, 2004.

[28] K. Pruhs, J. Sgall, and E. Torng. Online scheduling. *Handbook of scheduling: algorithms, models, and performance analysis*, pages 15–1, 2004.

[29] H. Zhang, B. Li, H. Jiang, F. Liu, A. V. Vasilakos, and J. Liu. A framework for truthful online auctions in cloud computing with heterogeneous user demands. In *Proceedings of INFOCOM*, pages 1510–1518. IEEE, 2013.

Provision-After-Wait with Common Preferences

Hau Chan
Department of Computer Science
Trinity University
San Antonio, TX 78212
hchan@trinity.edu

Jing Chen
Department of Computer Science
Stony Brook University
Stony Brook, NY 11794
jingchen@cs.stonybrook.edu

ABSTRACT

We study the Provision-after-Wait problem in healthcare introduced by Braverman, Chen, and Kannan (2016). In this setting, patients seek a medical procedure, and the procedure can be performed by different hospitals of different costs. Each patient has a value for each hospital, and a budget-constrained government/planner pays for the medical expenses of the patients. The planner's goal is to find an optimal stable assignment that is envy-free and maximizes the social welfare while keeping the expenses within the budget.

In this work, we focus on the settings where the patients have a common preference of the hospitals. We show that computing the optimal stable assignment for maximizing social welfare is NP-hard. Furthermore, we construct a fully polynomial-time approximation scheme (FPTAS) that runs in time $O((n+m)n^3m/\epsilon)$, where m and n are the number of hospitals and patients, respectively. In order to develop the FPTAS, we have defined and studied a new problem, ordered Knapsack.

We also consider the setting where the planner uses lottery as a rationing tool. For a large sub-class of our settings, we show the conditions under which the optimal lottery scheme has a simple structure and generates more social welfare than the optimal stable assignment. Moreover, such optimal lottery scheme can be computed by a linear program.

Keywords

budget, NP-hardness, approximation, FPTAS, waiting, lottery, envy-free, assignment, matching

1. INTRODUCTION

We study the Provision-after-Wait problem in healthcare [5], which considers the interaction among the patients, the hospitals, and a planner. Each patient seeks a medical service, such as X-ray or MRI, and has different values for different hospitals. Each hospital has a cost for serving one patient, which must be paid. Yet, the patients do not pay for the service and, instead, the planner pays for all of them. However, the planner has a budget and might not be able to afford the costs incurred by all patients going to their most preferred hospitals. Thus, the planner decides how to distribute his budget among the hospitals and, thus, how many patients he can afford each hospital to serve (in one budget period, say a month or a year). Patients choose their favorite hospitals and, if a hospital is over-demanded, then naturally a line will form and a waiting-time is specified at that hospital: the amount of time each patient has to wait before getting served there. Given the waiting times, a patient selects the hospital that maximizes his utility, which is his value minus the waiting time. De facto, *the planner uses waiting times as a rationing tool* and sets the hospitals' waiting times such that when the patients pick their utility-maximizing hospitals, the social welfare is maximized while the total cost is within the budget. In other words, the planner wants to produce a *stable* assignment: where each patient has non-negative utility and gets the hospital that maximizes his utility (thus a stable assignment is automatically envy-free).

Even when each patient is "narcissistic" and only has positive value for a single distinct hospital, the problem of computing the optimal budget feasible social welfare is already NP-hard [5]. Beyond this, little is known about computing the optimal social welfare when the patients' preferences are structured. In this paper, we consider the setting where the patients have a *common preference* of the hospitals: that is, the patients have the same ranking over the hospitals and perceive the hospitals based on the same quality measurement. This type of preferences is considered in position auctions [3, 21] where the patients in our setting correspond to the advertisers there, the hospitals correspond to the slots, and all advisers know the click-through rates of all slots. Similarly, in our setting, the patients know a ranking and quantitative measurements of the hospitals (i.e., based on ranking and reviews from U.S. News Best Hospitals 2015-16[1] or Centers for Medicare and Medicaid Services[2] of the US government).

1.1 Our Results

In the common-preference setting, each patient has a value for receiving the medical service and each hospital has a quality factor that is publicly known. The value of a patient for a hospital is the product of the two: that is, a consumer's value for a provider is proportional to the provider's quality. This is typical in position auctions [3, 21] where quality means view-through or click-through rate, or in scenarios where quality means the probability of obtaining the same

[1] http://health.usnews.com/best-hospitals
[2] http://www.cms.gov/

Appears in: *Proceedings of the 15th International Conference on Autonomous Agents and Multiagent Systems (AAMAS 2016), J. Thangarajah, K. Tuyls, C. Jonker, S. Marsella (eds.), May 9–13, 2016, Singapore.*

resource [13, 15, 16]. In the Provision-after-Wait problem, a hospital's quality can be considered as a scale-down from a perfect hospital: the "star ratings" on the Internet for hospitals are illustrative examples for such measurements.

Our model and results for waiting times are formally presented in Sections 2 and 3, and those for lotteries are in Section 4. Below we summarize our main results. Due to lack of space, most of the proofs are provided in the full version of the paper [9].

Optimal Stable Assignments.

For computing an optimal stable assignment of the Provision-after-Wait problem with common preference, we have the following two theorems.

THEOREM 1 (restated). *It is NP-hard to compute an optimal stable assignment.*

THEOREM 2 (restated). *There exists a fully polynomial-time approximation scheme (FPTAS) for the optimal stable assignment problem which, given any $\epsilon > 0$, runs in time $O((n+m)n^3m/\epsilon)$, where n and m are respectively the number of patients and hospitals.*

To construct the desired FPTAS we introduce another problem, *ordered Knapsack*. Roughly speaking, this is a bounded Knapsack problem where the items' values are affected by the order in which the items are packed into the knapsack. We construct an FPTAS for this problem and show how to use it to approximate the optimal stable assignment. We believe that the ordered Knapsack problem itself is of independent interest and is worth further study. Detailed discussions on Theorems 1 and 2 are in Sections 3.1 and 3.2, respectively. These results provide us a relatively complete understanding about the computation problem in our setting.

Moreover, it is worth pointing out that, our results are robust against small perturbations of the patients' valuations that may destroy the common-preference property: they remain true as long as the perturbed valuations keep a desired "ordering" among the patients. A more detailed discussion about this issue is in the full version.

Optimal Lottery Assignments.

In this part, we consider the patients as a continuous population instead of a discrete set, so that the solutions have a clean formula. Indeed, in the healthcare literature it is often assumed that there is a continuous population of patients, since in reality the number of patients is usually huge. By discretizing the patient space, similar results can be obtained for discrete settings.

Consider the patients as a continuous population represented by the interval $[0, 1]$. Their values for the medical service can be specified by a function v mapping each patient $x \in [0, 1]$ to a non-negative real, such that the value of patient x at a hospital is $v(x)$ times the hospital's quality. The function v is called the patients' *valuation profile*.[3] We assume v to be increasing, which is without loss of generality, since we can reorder and rename the patients: we can also do this in the discrete case, so that the value of patient 1 is smaller than that of patient 2, etc. Moreover, some regularity assumptions about v are typically used to ease the discussion, such as piece-wise continuity (see Section 4).

A lottery scheme is essentially a menu of randomized (hospital, waiting time) pairs for the patients to choose from, where the waiting times may or may not be non-zero. It is somewhat surprising that, given the extremely rich structures of the possible lottery schemes, for a large class of Provision-after-Wait problems, the optimal lottery scheme has a very simple form: that is, there is a single distribution from which all patients' hospitals are drawn, and no waiting time is imposed. We call such a lottery scheme a *randomized assignment*, and we have the following.

THEOREM 4 (restated). *For any $v(x)$ such that $(1-x)v'(x)$ is non-increasing, the optimal randomized assignment is optimal among all lottery schemes, including those with waiting times.*

In Section 4.1 we show that the optimal randomized assignment can be solved by a linear program, so does the optimal lottery scheme whenever the condition in Theorem 4 holds. In particular, the condition holds when $v(x)$ is *concave*, and for many other cases where it is neither concave nor convex, but does not increase "too fast". When the condition holds, the ratio between the social welfare of the optimal randomized assignment and that of the optimal stable assignment can be arbitrarily large. This condition is tight in the sense that, when it does not hold, there are cases where optimal stable assignments generate more social welfare: we provide examples in the full version.

Moreover, it is worth pointing out that, given a randomized assignment, we do not need to sample the patients' hospitals independently: our result holds as long as the marginal distribution for each patient is as specified by the assignment. Thus the optimal randomized assignment can be implemented so that the budget constraint is satisfied with probability 1 (see Section 4.2).

Interestingly, the condition in Theorem 4 has a very natural interpretation from another aspect. If we consider a single patient whose "type" x is drawn uniformly at random from $[0, 1]$ and set his value to $v(x)$, then the condition in Theorem 4 holds if and only if the distribution of the resulting value has *monotone hazard rate* (MHR). This immediately connects our result with lottery pricing schemes [10] with a single buyer and multiple items, where optimal pricing schemes are studied when the distributions of the buyer's values have MHR. Indeed, besides being succinct, one benefit of consider a continuous population of patients is that it lets us see clearly the connection between our condition and MHR, which is typically studied for continuous distributions.

We further generalize our result to settings where the patients do not perceive the hospitals based on the same quality measurement but still have the same ranking for them. Here the randomized assignment may not be optimal among all lottery schemes, but we have the following.

THEOREM 5 (restated). *Under similar conditions as in Theorem 4, the optimal randomized assignment is better than the optimal stable assignment.*

Theorem 5 is formalized in Section 4.3. Moreover, when the conditions do not hold there are cases where optimal stable assignments do better.

In conclusion, we have studied the computation and the structure of the optimal Provision-after-Wait schemes when

[3] We do not call v the valuation *function* because it applies to all patients, in which sense it corresponds to a valuation profile in the discrete case.

waiting times and lotteries are used as rationing tools. Our results suggest that neither rationing tool is absolutely better than the other in terms of generating social welfare, and we have identified conditions that enable the comparison of their performances. A planner should choose an appropriate tool based on the patients' valuations as specified by Theorems 4 and 5. Our results then allow the planner to compute/approximate the optimal allocations efficiently.

1.2 Related Work

The Provision-after-Wait problem was introduced in [5]. Since the authors allow arbitrary values of the patients for the hospitals, the NP-hardness for computing the optimal equilibrium there is much easier to show than ours. Also, in [5] the authors study optimal lotteries when there are two hospitals. Since we allow any number of hospitals, our results on optimal lotteries and randomized allocations are more general.

In unit-demand pricing schemes, n items are to be sold to m buyers and each buyer only wants one of them. This is similar to our case: each patient needs to be assigned to one hospital. Envy-freeness is a widely adopted solution concept there, but the goal of pricing schemes is to maximize revenue. In [13, 16], the authors study pricing problems where the buyers' valuations are similar to ours, and they characterize the optimal envy-free solutions for generating revenue [13, 16] and total value [13]. Their characterizations are analogous to ours, but their goals are different and they do not further study the computation complexity of the optimal solutions. While most works on pricing schemes study deterministic optimal item-pricing [6, 10, 12, 14, 16], a few consider lotteries [7, 11, 19, 20] and show that they can generate more revenue than deterministic item-pricing in various cases. However, the structures of optimal lottery pricing schemes are far from being well understood.

Finally, one key difference we see between the Provision-after-Wait model and the model of [17], a classic study about matching, is that, in [17] there is only one "currency", the salary (in particular, gross product is measured in the same unit as salary); while in our model there are two "currencies", money and time, and they are not exchangeable since patients do not care about money paid to the hospital.

2. THE MODEL

In the Provision-after-Wait problem [5], there are n *patients*, indexed by $[n] = \{1, 2, ..., n\}$, and m *hospitals*, indexed by $[m] = \{1, 2, ..., m\}$. Each patient wants a single medical service, which can be provided by any one of the hospitals. For each hospital $j \in [m]$, there is a *cost* $c_j \in \mathbb{Z}^+$ for serving one patient.[4] Moreover, each patient $i \in [n]$ has a value $v_{ij} \in \mathbb{Z}^+$ for receiving the service in hospital $j \in [m]$. As mentioned earlier, the patients do not pay for the service. Instead, the *planner* (e.g., government) pays for everybody's service through some funding program (e.g., the Patient Protection and Affordable Care Act in United States—that is, Obamacare). The planner has a *budget* $B \in \mathbb{Z}^+$ that limits the total amount that he can spend. To ensure the planner does not spend more than the budget (and while ensuring free-choice of the patients), the planner determines the *waiting time* w_j for each hospital $j \in [m]$.The planner's goal is to produce a solution that maximizes *social welfare*.

It is worth pointing out that, although in the model it is the planner who decides the waiting times, it has been shown in [5] that waiting times derive endogenously from the budget constraint and the dynamics between patients and hospitals: the planner only needs to decide each hospital's supply given the budget, and the demand and supply together determine waiting times and social welfare. If a hospital is over-demanded and there is no budget to increase its supply, then its waiting time increases in the dynamics.

Solution Concept.

A solution to the Provision-after-Wait problem is called an *assignment*. An assignment A consists of an *assignment function* $a : [n] \to [m]$ and a *waiting vector* $w = (w_1, \ldots, w_m)$ where $w_j \geq 0$ for each $j \in [m]$: $a(i)$ is the hospital to whom patient i is assigned and w_j is the waiting time for any patient assigned to hospital j. The total *cost* of A is $C(A) = \sum_{i \in [n]} c_{a(i)}$. The planner has a *budget* $B \geq 0$, and A is *budget-feasible* if $C(A) \leq B$. Given A, each patient i's *utility* is $v_{ia(i)} - w_{a(i)}$,[5] and the *social welfare* of A is $SW(A) = \sum_{i \in [n]} v_{ia(i)} - w_{a(i)}$.

An assignment A is *stable* if for any patient i, (1) $v_{ia(i)} - w_{a(i)} \geq 0$ and (2) for any hospital j, $v_{ia(i)} - w_{a(i)} \geq v_{ij} - w_j$. Notice that we could have allowed different patients to have different waiting times at the same hospital. However, an assignment is *envy-free* if for any patients i and i', $v_{ia(i)} - w_{a(i)} \geq v_{ia(i')} - w_{a(i')}$. Thus envy-freeness automatically implies that patients assigned to the same hospital have the same waiting time, and our model is without any loss of generality. We are interested in mechanisms that, given the patients' values, output assignments that are stable and budget-feasible, and maximize the social welfare.

DEFINITION 1. *A stable assignment A is* optimal *if $A \in \mathrm{argmax}_{A' \text{ is stable and budget-feasible}} SW(A')$.*

Without loss of generality we assume $nc_{max} > B$ and $nc_{min} \leq B$, where c_{max} and c_{min} are the maximum and the minimum costs of the hospitals, respectively. Moreover, it is often useful to consider optimal stable assignments with respect to a particular assignment function, as follows.

DEFINITION 2. *For any assignment function a, a stable assignment $A = (a, w)$ is* optimal *with respect to a if $A \in \mathrm{argmax}_{A'=(a,w') \text{ and } A' \text{ is stable}} SW(A')$.*

Note that budget-feasibility is not required in Definition 2: the cost of all such assignments is solely decided by a, thus either all of them are budget-feasible or none is.

Common Preference.

In the general Provision-after-Wait problem, the patients' values for the hospitals can be arbitrary. For the special class of "narcissistic" valuations where each patient $i \in [n]$

[4]That is, one hospital provides the same service to all patients, while different hospitals may provide different services. For example, one "hospital" may actually represent X-ray services and another one may represent MRI services.

[5]Utilities are quasi-linear in waiting time because we measure patients' valuations as "willingness to wait", in parallel with "willingness to pay" in auctions, where utilities are quasi-linear in price. The planner doesn't need to intentionally delay care to preserve fairness: as mentioned previously, the desired waiting times will appear endogenously from the dynamics between hospitals and patients.

has a value $v_{ij} > 0$ for $j = i$ and $v_{ij} = 0$ for all $j \neq i$, the problem of computing an optimal stable assignment is already NP-hard [5]. Beyond this result, little is known for the computational complexity of the problem.

Here, we consider a different class of valuations where the patients have a *common preference* over the hospitals. In particular, for each hospital $j \in [m]$, there is a quality factor $q_j \in \mathbb{Z}^+$ that is publicly known. Without loss of generality, we can rename the hospitals such that $q_1 \geq q_2 \geq ... \geq q_m$. For each patient $i \in [n]$, there is a value $v_i \in \mathbb{Z}^+$ specifies i's happiness for getting the medical service. For each patient $i \in [n]$ and hospital $j \in [m]$, i's value for hospital j is $v_{ij} = v_i q_j$. Thus, $v_{i1} \geq v_{i2} \geq ... \geq v_{im}$ for all patients $i \in [n]$. The setting where a consumer's value for a provider is proportional to its value and the provider's quality has been explored in other context under different economic incentive settings [2, 13, 15, 16, 21]. We will consider this type of valuations throughout the paper and we will explicitly represent the value v_{ij} as $v_i q_j$ for clarity.

3. OPTIMAL STABLE ASSIGNMENTS

In this section, we show that (1) computing an optimal stable assignment is NP-hard; and (2) there is a fully polynomial time approximation scheme (FPTAS) that returns an assignment with social welfare ϵ-close to the optimum.

3.1 Finding Optimal Stable Assignments

In this and next sections, without loss of generality we rename the patients and the hospitals so that

$$v_1 \geq v_2 \geq \cdots \geq v_n \quad \text{and} \quad q_1 \geq q_2 \geq \cdots \geq q_m. \qquad (1)$$

THEOREM 1. *It is NP-hard to compute an optimal stable assignment.*

To prove Theorem 1, we first characterize the social welfare of optimal stable assignments. Our approach is similar to that in [13, 16], but the formulas are different. Indeed, their goals were to maximize the total payment and/or the total value in the context of revenue maximization. In particular, our Definition 4 and Lemma 3 are equivalent to Lemma 2.1 in [13], but the remaining parts are new. In this section, we only state our key lemmas and we refer the readers to the full version [9] for a detailed analysis.

DEFINITION 3. *An assignment function a is* ordered *if $a(1) \leq a(2) \leq \cdots \leq a(n)$.*

Lemma 1 shows that it is sufficient to consider stable assignments $A = (a, w)$ with a ordered.

LEMMA 1. *Given any stable assignment $A = (a, w)$, in polynomial time it can be modified so that: a beomes ordered, A is still stable, and the total cost and the utility of each patient remain the same.*

Therefore, for any stable assignment $A = (a, w)$ with a ordered, we can deduce that $q_{a(1)} \geq q_{a(2)} \geq \cdots \geq q_{a(n)}$ and $w_{a(1)} \geq w_{a(2)} \geq \cdots \geq w_{a(n)}$. In other words, patients with higher values are assigned to hospitals with higher quality, and hospitals with higher quality have higher waiting times than those with lower quality: indeed, if hospital i has higher quality than hospital j, but lower waiting time, then patients assigned to j want to deviate to i, since it gives them higher utilities.

DEFINITION 4. *For any ordered assignment function a, an assignment $A = (a, w)$ is* tight *at a if for any $i < n$*

$$w_{a(n)} = 0 \text{ and } w_{a(i)} = (q_{a(i)} - q_{a(i+1)})v_{i+1} + w_{a(i+1)}.$$

Notice that, by the inequality on $q_{a(i)}$'s, the $w_{a(i)}$'s in Definition 4 are all non-negative. Also notice that, being tight at a implies that for any $i < n$, $v_{i+1}q_{a(i+1)} - w_{a(i+1)} = v_{i+1}q_{a(i)} - w_{a(i)}$. That is, patient $i+1$ is indifferent between his utility at $a(i+1)$ and that at $a(i)$.

The following lemmas show that we only need to consider assignment A that is tight at a.

LEMMA 2. *For any ordered assignment function a, let $A = (a, w)$ be an assignment such that A is tight at a and $w_j = v_1 q_1$ for any $j \notin a(\{1, \ldots, n\})$. Then A is stable.*

LEMMA 3. *For any ordered assignment function a and any stable assignment $A = (a, w)$, A is optimal with respect to a if and only if it is tight at a.*

The following lemma shows that the social welfare of any stable assignment optimal with respect to a can be explicitly calculated from the patients' values and the hospitals' qualities.

LEMMA 4. *For any ordered assignment function a and any stable assignment $A = (a, w)$ optimal with respect to a, $SW(A) = \sum_{i<n} i \cdot q_{a(i)} \cdot (v_i - v_{i+1}) + n \cdot q_{a(n)} \cdot v_n$.*

Given the above lemmas, we now present the proof of Theorem 1.

PROOF OF THEOREM 1. Consider the decision version of the Provision-after-Wait problem: $DPaW = \{(q_1, \ldots, q_m, c_1, \ldots, c_m, v_1, \ldots, v_n, B, V)$: there exists a stable budget feasible assignment A such that $SW(A) \geq V\}$.

It is clear that if one can find an optimal stable assignment for every instance of the Provision-after-Wait problem then one can decide $DPaW$. We shall show that $DPaW$ is NP-complete by a reduction from the Subset-Sum problem: $SubsetSum = \{(s_1, \ldots, s_n, T)$: there exists $S \subseteq [n]$ such that $\sum_{i \in S} s_i = T\}$. Given an instance $\alpha = (s_1, \ldots, s_n, T)$ of $SubsetSum$, we assume without loss of generality that $s_1 \geq s_2 \geq \cdots \geq s_n$, and construct an instance $\gamma = (q_1, \ldots, q_m, c_1, \ldots, c_m, v_1, \ldots, v_n, B, V)$ of $DPaW$ as follows. Notice that we use the same symbol for both a variable and its binary representation, and the 1st bit refers to the rightmost bit.

- There are $m = 2n$ hospitals and n patients.
- For each $i \in [n]$, $q_i = c_i = s_i \cdot 2^{n(\lceil \log n \rceil + 1)} + 2^{(n-i)(\lceil \log n \rceil + 1)}$: q_i and c_i are obtained by appending $n(\lceil \log n \rceil + 1)$ bits of 0's to the right of the binary representation of s_i, and then setting the $(n-i)(\lceil \log n \rceil + 1) + 1$st bit to 1.
- For each $i \in [n]$, $q_{n+i} = c_{n+i} = 2^{(n-i)(\lceil \log n \rceil + 1)}$. That is, q_{n+i} and c_{n+i} consist of one bit of 1 followed by $(n-i)(\lceil \log n \rceil + 1)$ bits of 0's. Notice that the unique bit of 1 in q_{n+i} and c_{n+i} is aligned with the unique bit of 1 after s_i in q_i and c_i.
- $B = V = T \cdot 2^{n(\lceil \log n \rceil + 1)} + \sum_{i \in [n]} 2^{(n-i)(\lceil \log n \rceil + 1)}$. That is, B and V are obtained by appending $n(\lceil \log n \rceil + 1)$ bits of 0's to the right of the binary representation of T, and then set the $(n-i)(\lceil \log n \rceil + 1) + 1$st bit to 1 for each $i \in [n]$.

- For each $i \in [n]$, $v_i = \sum_{k=i}^{n} \frac{1}{k}$.

It is easy to see that the construction takes polynomial time and that γ satisfies Inequality 1. We have the following two lemmas.

LEMMA 5. *$\gamma \in DPaW \Rightarrow \alpha \in SubsetSum$.*

PROOF. Let $A = (a, w)$ be an optimal stable assignment of γ. By definition, A is optimal with respect to a. By Lemma 1 we assume without loss of generality that a is ordered. Thus by Lemma 4 we have $SW(A) = \sum_{i<n} i \cdot q_{a(i)} \cdot (v_i - v_{i+1}) + n \cdot q_{a(n)} \cdot v_n = \sum_{i<n} i \cdot q_{a(i)} \cdot \frac{1}{i} + n \cdot q_{a(n)} \cdot \frac{1}{n} = \sum_{i\in[n]} q_{a(i)}$. Since $q_j = c_j$ for any $j \in [m]$ and since A is budget feasible, $SW(A) = \sum_{i\in[n]} c_{a(i)} = C(A) \leq B = V$. Since $\gamma \in DPaW$, we have $SW(A) \geq V$ and thus $SW(A) = V$. In particular, for any $j \in [n]$, $SW(A)$ has a 1 at the $(n-j)(\lceil \log n \rceil + 1) + 1$st bit preceded by $\lceil \log n \rceil$ bits of 0's. We now show that for any $j \in [n]$,

$$|\{i \in [n] : a(i) \in \{j, n+j\}\}| = 1, \tag{2}$$

that is, there is exactly one patient assigned to either hospital j or hospital $n+j$.

To see why Equation 2 is true, notice that for any $k \in [n]$ there are $\lceil \log n \rceil$ bits of 0's between the $(n-k+1)(\lceil \log n \rceil + 1) + 1$st bit and the $(n-k)(\lceil \log n \rceil + 1) + 1$st bit in the binary representation of any q_j. Since there are n patients, there is no carry to the $(n-k+1)(\lceil \log n \rceil + 1) + 1$st bit when computing $SW(A)$. Further notice that the only hospitals whose qualities contribute a 1 to the $(n-j)(\lceil \log n \rceil + 1) + 1$st bit of $SW(A)$ are hospitals j and $n+j$.

If more than one patients are assigned to either j or $n+j$, then the $\lceil \log n \rceil$ bits preceding the $(n-j)(\lceil \log n \rceil + 1) + 1$st bit of $SW(A)$ cannot be all 0's, and $SW(A) \neq V$. If no patient is assigned to either j or $n+j$, then the $(n-j)(\lceil \log n \rceil + 1) + 1$st bit of $SW(A)$ cannot be a 1, and again $SW(A) \neq V$. Thus there must be exactly one patient assigned to either hospital j or hospital $n+j$, and Equation 2 holds.

By Equation 2, the two sets $S = \{j \in [n] : j \in a(\{1, \ldots, n\})\}$ and $S' = \{j \in [n] : n+j \in a(\{1, \ldots, n\})\}$ form a partition of $[n]$, and $SW(A) = \sum_{i\in[n]} q_{a(i)} = \sum_{j\in S} q_j + \sum_{j\in S'} q_{n+j} = \sum_{j\in S} s_j \cdot 2^{n(\lceil \log n \rceil+1)} + \sum_{j\in[n]} 2^{(n-j)(\lceil \log n \rceil+1)}$. Since $SW(A) = V = T \cdot 2^{n(\lceil \log n \rceil+1)} + \sum_{i\in[n]} 2^{(n-i)(\lceil \log n \rceil+1)}$, we have $\sum_{j\in S} s_j = T$. Thus $\alpha \in SubsetSum$ and Lemma 5 holds. □

LEMMA 6. *$\alpha \in SubsetSum \Rightarrow \gamma \in DPaW$.*

PROOF. Since $\alpha \in SubsetSum$, there exists $S \subseteq [n]$ such that $\sum_{i\in S} s_i = T$. Let $k = |S|$ and $S = \{j_1, \ldots, j_k\}$, with $j_1 \leq j_2 \leq \cdots \leq j_k$. Further, let $S' = [n] \backslash S = \{j_{k+1}, \ldots, j_n\}$, with $j_{k+1} \leq j_{k+2} \leq \cdots \leq j_n$. We construct an assignment $A = (a, w)$ as follows.

- $a(i) = j_i$ for any $i \leq k$, and $a(i) = n + j_i$ for any $i \geq k+1$.
- $w_{a(n)} = 0$, $w_{a(i)} = (q_{a(i)} - q_{a(i+1)})v_{i+1} + w_{a(i+1)}$ for any $i < n$, and $w_j = v_1 q_1$ for any $j \notin a(\{1, \ldots, n\})$.

Notice that $a(1) \leq a(2) \leq \cdots \leq a(n) = n + j_n \leq m$. Thus a is a well defined function from $[n]$ to $[m]$ and is ordered. Also notice that A is tight at a.

The cost of A is $C(A) = \sum_{i\in[n]} c_{a(i)} = \sum_{i\leq k} c_{j_i} + \sum_{i\geq k+1} c_{n+j_i} = T \cdot 2^{n(\lceil \log n \rceil+1)} + \sum_{j\in[n]} 2^{(n-j)(\lceil \log n \rceil+1)} = B$. Thus A is budget feasible.

Since A is tight at a, by Lemma 2, A is stable. By Lemma 3, A is optimal with respect to a. Thus $SW(A) = \sum_{i=1}^{n-1} i \cdot q_{a(i)} \cdot (v_i - v_{i+1}) + n \cdot q_{a(n)} \cdot v_n = \sum_{i=1}^{n-1} i \cdot q_{a(i)} \cdot \frac{1}{i} + n \cdot q_{a(n)} \cdot \frac{1}{n} = \sum_{i\in[n]} q_{a(i)} = \sum_{i\in[n]} c_{a(i)} = C(A) = B = V$. Therefore A is a stable budget feasible assignment with $SW(A) \geq V$. Accordingly, $\gamma \in DPaW$ and Lemma 6 holds. □

By Lemmas 5 and 6, $\alpha \in SubsetSum$ if and only if $\gamma \in DPaW$. Thus, $DPaW$ is NP-complete and Theorem 1 holds.

3.2 An FPTAS for Optimal Stable Assignments

Next, we show that there is an efficient algorithm that produces a stable assignment with social welfare arbitrarily close to the optimum. Letting A^{opt} be an optimal stable assignment, we have the following.

THEOREM 2. *There exists an algorithm for the Provision-after-Wait problem such that, given any $\epsilon > 0$, it runs in time $O((n+m)n^3 m/\epsilon)$ and outputs a stable budget feasible assignment $A = (a, w)$ such that $SW(A) \geq (1-\epsilon)SW(A^{opt})$.*

The complete proof of Theorem 2 is in the full version of the paper [9]. Below, we describe the general ideas. Notice that by Lemma 4, for any ordered assignment function a we can define the *social welfare of a*, $SW(a)$, to be the social welfare of stable assignments optimal with respect to a. That is, $SW(a) = \sum_{i<n} i \cdot q_{a(i)} \cdot (v_i - v_{i+1}) + n \cdot q_{a(n)} \cdot v_n$. An assignment function a is *budget feasible* if $C(a) = \sum_{i\in[n]} c_{a(i)} \leq B$.

DEFINITION 5. *An ordered assignment function a is* optimal *if* $a \in \underset{a' \text{is ordered and budget feasible}}{\operatorname{argmax}} SW(a')$.

Given an ordered assignment function a, by Lemmas 2 and 3, we can construct, in time $O(m+n)$, a stable assignment A optimal with respect to a: that is, the assignment defined in Lemma 2. If a is optimal, then A is an optimal stable assignment. Thus, to prove Theorem 2 it suffices to approximate the optimal ordered assignment function.

Notice that if there exists a hospital j such that $c_j < c_{j+1}$, then for any ordered assignment function a and for all patients assigned to hospital $j+1$, by reassigning them to j we get another ordered assignment a' such that $C(a') \leq C(a)$ and $SW(a') \geq SW(a)$. Accordingly, we can further focus on ordered assignment functions that do not assign any patient to $j+1$. That is, we can assume without loss of generality that $c_1 \geq c_2 \geq \cdots \geq c_m$. Below we define a more general problem and construct an FPTAS for it, which will give us an FPTAS for the optimal ordered assignment function.

3.3 The Ordered Knapsack Problem

DEFINITION 6. *The* ordered Knapsack *problem has m items, n players, and a budget B. Each item j has n copies, with cost c_j each. Each player i has value u_{ij} for item j. We have $c_1 \geq c_2 \geq \cdots \geq c_m$, $u_{i1} \geq u_{i2} \geq \cdots \geq u_{im}$ for each $i \in [n]$, and $nc_m \leq B < nc_1$. An* assignment *is a function $a : [n] \to [m]$ such that $a(1) \leq a(2) \leq \cdots \leq a(n)$. The* social welfare *of a is $SW(a) = \sum_{i\in[n]} u_{ia(i)}$, and the* cost *is $C(a) = \sum_{i\in[n]} c_{a(i)}$. The goal is to find an assignment with cost no larger than B and the maximum social welfare.*

Intuitively, the ordered-Knapsack problem has a knapsack where the order of the items packed in it affects their values —the "players" can be considered as ordered slots in the knapsack.[6] We can reduce the problem of the optimal ordered assignment function to the ordered Knapsack problem by taking, for any $j \in [m]$, $u_{ij} = iq_j(v_i - v_{i+1})$ for any $i < n$ and $u_{nj} = nq_jv_n$. Any assignment of the resulting ordered Knapsack problem is an ordered assignment function of the original Provision-after-Wait problem, with the same cost and the same social welfare. Thus, letting a^{opt} be the optimal assignment for the ordered Knapsack problem, to prove Theorem 2 it suffices to construct an FPTAS for a^{opt}.

THEOREM 3. *There exists an algorithm for the ordered Knapsack problem such that, given any $\epsilon > 0$, it runs in time $O((n+m)n^3m/\epsilon)$ and outputs an assignment a with $C(a) \le B$ and $SW(a) \ge (1-\epsilon)SW(a^{opt})$.*

PROOF OF THEOREM 3 (SKETCH). We first construct a dynamic program that computes the optimal assignment in pseudo-polynomial time, and then run it on properly scaled inputs to get the desired FPTAS. We refer the readers to the full version of the paper [9] for the complete proof, and here we only provide the objective function for our dynamic program. (We are abusing the notation C a bit, but it always represents the cost that we want to measure.)

For any assignment a and player i, let $SW(a,i) = \sum_{i'=i}^{n} u_{i'a(i')}$ be the contribution of players $i,\dots,n$ to $SW(a)$. For any $i \in [n]$, $j \in [m]$, and $s \in \{0,1,\dots,nV\}$, we are interested in the *minimum cost*, denoted by $C(i)(j)(s)$, needed for players $i,\dots,n$ to make contribution s to the social welfare, when player i is assigned to item j. More precisely, let $SW(i,j) = \sum_{i'=i}^{n} u_{i'j}$ be the contribution of players $i,\dots,n$ when they are all assigned to j. If $SW(i,j) \ge s$ then $C(i)(j)(s) = c_j + \min_{a: j=a(i)\le\cdots\le a(n), SW(a,i)\ge s} \sum_{i'>i} c_{a(i')}$, and $C(i)(j)(s) = +\infty$ otherwise. Notice that $C(i)(j)(s) = +\infty$ means it is impossible for players $i,\dots,n$ to make contribution s to the social welfare even if all of them are assigned to j, and thus impossible to make such contribution at j and items after j. In practice, $+\infty$ can be replaced by $B+1$ (or any number larger than B and of polynomial length). Moreover, we observe that (a) for any optimal assignment a, $SW(a) = \max\{s : \min_{j\in[m]} C(1)(j)(s) \le B\}$; and (b) $C(n)(j)(s) = c_j$ for any $j \in [m]$ and $s \le u_{nj}$, $C(i)(j)(0) = c_j + (n-i)c_m$ for any $i < n$ and $j \in [m]$, and for any $i < n$, $j \in [m]$ and $0 < s \le SW(i,j)$,

$$C(i)(j)(s) = c_j + \min_{j' \ge j} C(i+1)(j')(\max\{s - u_{ij}, 0\}).$$

Finally, $C(i)(j)(s) = +\infty$ in all other cases. The dynamic program thus computes the function C and the optimal assignment a. □

[6]Such a scenario widely exists in real life. For example, in school choices the order may represent the priority of being admitted to different schools. Indeed, priority list has been widely studied in the Economics literature (see, e.g., [4, 1, 8]). But the model and the concerns there are different from ours, e.g., the optimization goal is usually not utilitarian, and there is no budget constraints. Thus we do not elaborate on this line of research. Also notice that the ordered Knapsack problem is quite different from the partially ordered Knapsack problem studied in [18]. In the latter each item has a fixed value and the outcome is a set instead of a function from players to items.

REMARK 1. *In fact, we can construct a pseudo-polynomial time dynamic program directly for the Provision-after-Wait problem. Then one may try to scale down the hospitals' qualities q_j and patients' values v_i separately and apply the dynamic program on the scaled inputs. However, when scaling everything back, the errors in the social welfare will accumulate multiplicatively, due to the terms $iq_{a(i)}(v_i - v_{i+1})$. Thus the desired approximation ratio cannot be guaranteed. The idea is to scale down each $iq_j(v_i - v_{i+1})$ as a whole, but the resulted parameters may not lead to a well defined Provision-after-Wait problem with qualities and values—that is where the ordered Knapsack problem comes into play.*

4. ASSIGNMENTS USING LOTTERIES

If no randomness is allowed, the optimal stable assignment is our best rationing tool. However, if the planner can ask the patients to enter lotteries, the space of possible mechanisms becomes much larger and better social welfare can be obtained. In this section, we first characterize the structure of the optimal lotteries for a large sub-class of the Provision-after-Wait problem. Furthermore, for a class of valuations more general than what we currently consider, we characterize the conditions under which a particular lottery achieves more social welfare than the optimal stable assignment.

Although our results apply to the discrete case of n patients, they are more succinct to state for a continuous population of patients. Thus, we let the patients be indexed by the interval $[0,1]$, and use the valuation function $v(x)$ to specify the value of each patient x. We assume $v(x)$ is strictly increasing and twice differentiable, so that the integrations and differentiations used below are always well defined.[7] Also, by shifting down all patients' values by $v(0)$, we assume without loss of generality that $v(0) = 0$.

DEFINITION 7. *A* lottery λ *for the Provision-after-Wait problem is a tuple of non-negative reals, $\lambda = (p_1,\dots,p_m,w)$, s.t. $\sum_{j\in[m]} p_j \le 1$. A* lottery scheme L *is a set of lotteries, s.t. there exists $\lambda = (p_1,\dots,p_m,w) \in L$ with $w = 0$.*

A patient taking lottery λ will wait for time w and then be assigned to each hospital j with probability p_j. Patient x's *(expected) utility* under λ is $u(x,\lambda) = (\sum_{j\in[m]} p_jq_jv(x)) - w$.[8] Given L, each patient chooses a lottery to maximize his own utility. That is, denoting by $\lambda^L(x) = (p_1^L(x),\dots,p_m^L(x), w^L(x)) \in L$ the choice of patient x, we have that for any $\lambda \in L$,

$$u(x,\lambda^L(x)) \ge u(x,\lambda). \tag{3}$$

The definition of a lottery scheme ensures $u(x,\lambda^L(x)) \ge 0$ for any x, and $u(0,\lambda^L(0)) = 0$.

[7]Our approach works as long as $v(x)$ is non-decreasing (which is without loss of generality since we can reorder and rename the patients) and piecewise twice differentiable. But in this more general setting the analysis is unnecessarily complicated without bringing in interesting views. Thus we stick to our current setting so as to highlight the key ideas. Moreover, following Inequality 1, we could have assumed $v(x)$ is decreasing. But assuming $v(x)$ to be increasing will make the statements and the analysis more succinct.

[8]If $\sum_j p_j < 1$ then with probability $1 - \sum_j p_j$ the patient waits for time w but does not get any resource. If each patient has to be served, then we just need to require $\sum_j p_j = 1$ in the definitions and our results still hold.

Since for any two lotteries $\lambda_1, \lambda_2 \in L$, any convex combination $\alpha\lambda_1 + (1-\alpha)\lambda_2$ can be realized by a patient choosing λ_1 with probability α and λ_2 with probability $1-\alpha$, without loss of generality we assume that L is convex. Accordingly, the patients' choices are on the boundary of L.

Since the patients are infinitesimal, each hospital j's cost c_j denotes the cost for serving 1 unit of the population at j, and the *(expected) cost* of L is $C(L) = \int_0^1 \sum_{j\in[m]} p_j^L(x)c_j dx$. L is *budget feasible* if $C(L) \leq B$. The *(expected) social welfare* of L is $SW(L) = \int_0^1 u(x, \lambda^L(x))dx$. We denote by L^{opt} the *optimal lottery scheme*:

$$L^{opt} \in \underset{L \text{ is budget feasible}}{\text{argmax}} \quad SW(L).$$

For each $x \in [0,1]$, we denote by $\lambda^{opt}(x) = (p_1^{opt}(x), \ldots, p_m^{opt}(x), w^{opt}(x))$ the choice of patient x under L^{opt}.

A stable assignment $A = (a, w)$ is defined as before, except a is now a function on $[0,1]$. It is easy to see that A is equivalent to a lottery scheme L which is the convex hull of a set of lotteries $\{\lambda_1, \ldots, \lambda_m\}$: for each $j \in [m]$, $\lambda_j = (p_1, \ldots, p_m, w_j)$, $p_j = 1$ and $p_{j'} = 0$ for any $j' \neq j$. Given L, each patient x chooses $\lambda_{a(x)}$, which corresponds to being assigned to $a(x)$ with probability 1 after waiting $w_{a(x)}$. Thus we have $SW(L^{opt}) \geq SW(A^{opt})$, where A^{opt} is the optimal stable assignment.

Besides stable assignments, another class of lottery schemes is of particular interest: those with waiting time 0. Such a lottery scheme L reduces to a single lottery $(p_1, \ldots, p_m, 0)$ whose expected quality $\sum_{j\in[m]} p_j q_j$ is the maximum in L, since this lottery maximizes all patients' utilities over L. We call a lottery scheme of this form a *randomized assignment*, formally defined below.

DEFINITION 8. *A randomized assignment R is a tuple of non-negative reals, $R = (p_1, \ldots, p_m)$, s.t. $\sum_{j\in[m]} p_j \leq 1$.*

According to R, each patient is assigned to each hospital j with probability p_j and waiting time 0. The expected social welfare of R is $SW(R) = \int_0^1 \sum_{j\in[m]} p_j q_j v(x)dx$, and the expected cost is $C(R) = \sum_{j\in[m]} p_j c_j$. We denote by R^{opt} the *optimal randomized assignment*, that is, $R^{opt} \in \text{argmax}_{R \text{ is budget feasible}} SW(R)$. As a randomized assignment is a special lottery scheme, $SW(L^{opt}) \geq SW(R^{opt})$.

Notice that a lottery scheme is "stable in expectation", since a patient chooses a lottery that maximizes his expected utility. This is also true for a randomized assignment, since there is only one lottery to choose from. But a lottery scheme may not be "ex-post stable": the realized assignment may not maximize a patient's utility among all hospitals.

4.1 Optimal Lottery Schemes

The structure of the optimal lottery scheme is hard to characterize in general, but as we show in the following theorem, for a large sub-class of the problem, the optimal randomized assignment is optimal among all lottery schemes.

THEOREM 4. *For any $v(x)$ such that $(1-x)v'(x)$ is non-increasing, $SW(R^{opt}) = SW(L^{opt})$.*

PROOF OF THEOREM 4 (SKETCH). To show Theorem 4, we rely on the facts (as shown in the full version [9]) that (a) for any lottery scheme L, the function $\sum_{j\in[m]} p_j^L(x)q_j$ is non-decreasing, and (b) for any lottery scheme L and any patient $x \in [0,1]$, $u(x, \lambda^L(x)) = \int_0^{v(x)} \sum_{j\in[m]} q_j p_j^L(\hat{v})d\hat{v}$.

Since $SW(L^{opt}) \geq SW(R^{opt})$ by definition, we only need to show that $SW(R^{opt}) \geq SW(L^{opt})$. To show this, we first define, for any budget feasible lottery scheme L, $R = (p_1, \ldots, p_m)$ to be the randomized assignment where for any $j \in [m]$, $p_j = \int_0^1 p_j^L(x)dx$. That is, each p_j is the average of $p_j^L(x)$ over $[0,1]$. Letting $L = L^{opt}$, (a) and (b) imply $SW(R) \geq SW(L^{opt})$. Thus $SW(R^{opt}) \geq SW(L^{opt})$. □

The following shows that the class of valuation functions satisfying Theorem 4 is very broad: in particular it includes all concave valuation functions.

COROLLARY 1. *For any concave valuation function $v(x)$, $SW(R^{opt}) = SW(L^{opt})$.*

PROOF. Letting $g(x) = (1-x)v'(x)$, we have $g'(x) = -v'(x) + (1-x)v''(x)$. Since $v(x)$ is concave, $v''(x) \leq 0$. Since $v'(x) > 0$ and $x \in [0,1]$, we have $g'(x) \leq 0$. Thus $g(x)$ is non-increasing. □

Clearly, Theorem 4 applies to many other valuation functions that are not concave. For example, letting $v(x) = e^x - 1$, we have $(1-x)v'(x) = (1-x)e^x$, which is non-increasing on $[0,1]$. Thus the optimal randomized assignment is optimal among all lottery schemes in this case.

Theorem 4 in Terms of Monotone Hazard Rate.

Interestingly, the condition in Theorem 4 has a very natural interpretation from another viewpoint. Consider an assignment problem where there is a single patient and multiple hospitals. The planner's budget is lower than the cost of the patient's favorite hospital, thus he cannot simply be assigned there with probability 1. There is a distribution D from which the patient's value is drawn: his *type* is uniformly distributed over $[0,1]$ and his value at type x is $v(x)$. Letting $y = v(x)$, it is easy to see that for any value v_0 and $x_0 = v^{-1}(v_0)$, the cumulative distribution function is $F(v_0) = \Pr[y \leq v_0] = \Pr[v^{-1}(y) \leq x_0] = x_0 = v^{-1}(v_0)$, and the probability density function is $f(v_0) = F'(v_0) = \frac{1}{v'(x_0)}$. Accordingly, $(1-x_0)v'(x_0) = \frac{1-F(v_0)}{f(v_0)} = \frac{1}{h(v_0)}$, where $h(v) \triangleq \frac{f(v)}{1-F(v)}$ is the *hazard rate* of D. Recall that a distribution has *monotone hazard rate* (MHR) if h is non-decreasing. Thus $(1-x)v'(x)$ is non-increasing *if and only if* D has MHR, and we immediately have the following.

COROLLARY 2. *For any value distribution D that has MHR, $SW(R^{opt}) = SW(L^{opt})$.*

4.2 Important Properties of the Optimal Randomized Assignment

In this subsection, we further discuss several interesting properties of the optimal randomized assignment.

Computability.

In general Provision-after-Wait problems, there may not be an efficient algorithm for finding an optimal lottery scheme. But the optimal randomized assignment is always defined by the following linear program.

$$\begin{aligned}
\max_{p_1,\ldots,p_m} \quad & \sum_{j\in[m]} p_j q_j \int_0^1 v(x)dx \\
\text{s.t.} \quad & p_j \geq 0 \ \forall j \in [m], \\
& \sum_{j\in[m]} p_j \leq 1, \\
& \sum_{j\in[m]} p_j c_j \leq B.
\end{aligned}$$

Since the integral $\int_0^1 v(x)dx$ is a constant in the linear program, the linear program can be solved in polynomial time. Of course, we need the value of $\int_0^1 v(x)dx$ so as to compute $SW(R^{opt})$. If $\int_0^1 v(x)dx$ has a closed form and can be computed in polynomial time, then $SW(R^{opt})$ can be computed in polynomial time. Otherwise, by computing $\int_0^1 v(x)dx$ numerically, $SW(R^{opt})$ can also be computed numerically.

Ex-post Budget feasibility.

A lottery scheme in general only satisfies the budget constraint in expectation, and it is possible that under some realization of the lotteries the total cost is much higher than the budget. Yet, given a randomized assignment $R = (p_1, \ldots, p_m)$, the planner can first choose an ordering of the patients uniformly at random, and then assign the first p_1 *fraction* of them to hospital 1, the next p_2 fraction to hospital 2, and so on. By doing so, each patient is assigned to the hospitals according to the correct distribution $(p_1, \ldots, p_m)$, thus the expected social welfare equals $SW(R)$. While in any realized assignment the total cost is $\sum_{j\in[m]} p_j c_j$, exactly the expected cost of the randomized assignment, and thus the budget constraint is satisfied with probability 1.[9]

Advantage in Generating Social Welfare.

When Theorem 4 applies, not only the social welfare of the optimal randomized assignment is no less that of the optimal stable assignment, but the ratio between them can be arbitrarily large, since in the latter a lot of social welfare may be burnt by letting the patients wait. As an example, consider the case where $v(x) = v_0$ is a positive constant, $q_1 = \epsilon \ll 1$, $1 \ll q_2 < \cdots < q_m$, $B \gg 1$, $c_1 = 1$, $c_2 = \cdots = c_m = \frac{B-\epsilon}{1-\epsilon}$. It is easy to see that one particular optimal stable assignment is to assign all patients to hospital 1 with waiting time 0, where the social welfare is $q_1 \int_0^1 v(x)dx = \epsilon v_0$ (assigning some patients to better hospitals won't help, since all patients must have the same utility anyway). While there is a randomized assignment that assigns each patient to hospital m with probability $1-\epsilon$ and to hospital 1 with probability ϵ, resulting in total cost $(1-\epsilon)c_m + \epsilon c_1 = B$ and social welfare $((1-\epsilon)q_m + \epsilon q_1)\int_0^1 v(x)dx = ((1-\epsilon)q_m + \epsilon^2)v_0 \geq (1-\epsilon)v_0 \gg \epsilon v_0$. To make $v(x)$ strictly increasing, just take $v(x) = \alpha x$ with some arbitrarily small $\alpha > 0$: the analysis is essentially the same as when $v(x)$ is a constant.

4.3 Randomized v.s. Stable Assignments

Finally, we extend our approach to settings where the patients' values are not proportional to the hospitals' qualities, but there are still orders among the hospitals and the patients. More precisely, for each $j \in [m]$, let function $v_j(x)$ be the value that patient $x \in [0,1]$ receives when assigned to hospital j. Again by shifting each function $v_j(x)$ down by $v_j(0)$, we assume without loss of generality that $v_j(0) = 0$ for each j. We consider the cases where each $v_j(x)$ is strictly increasing and $v_1(x) \leq v_2(x) \leq \cdots \leq v_m(x)$ for each x.

As will become clear in the analysis, the key factors affecting the social welfare are not the patients' values, but the *differences* among each patient's values at different hospitals. Accordingly, for each $j \in [m]$, letting $f_j(x)$ be a function on $[0,1]$ that is strictly increasing, twice differentiable and $f_j(0) = 0$,[10] we consider the patients' values such that $v_j(x) = \sum_{k=1}^{j} f_k(x)$ for any $x \in [0,1]$. Notice this setting includes that of Section 4.1 as a special case: after renaming the hospitals s.t. $q_1 \leq q_2 \leq \cdots \leq q_m$, take $f_1(x) = q_1 v(x)$ and $f_j(x) = (q_j - q_{j-1})v(x)\ \forall j > 1$.

In this more general setting, it is unclear how to compare the optimal lottery scheme and the optimal randomized assignment, but we have the following.

THEOREM 5. *If $(1-x)f_j'(x)$ is non-increasing for every $j \in [m]$, then $SW(R^{opt}) \geq SW(A^{opt})$.*

PROOF OF THEOREM 5 (SKETCH). The proof uses related but different ideas from those for Theorem 4. We only present a key claim here.

CLAIM 1. *For any stable assignment $A = (a, w)$, there exists $x_0, \cdots, x_m$ with $0 = x_0 \leq x_1 \leq x_2 \leq \cdots \leq x_{m-1} \leq x_m = 1$, s.t. for any $j \in [m]$ and $x \in (x_{j-1}, x_j)$, $a(x) = j$.*

Moreover, if A is optimal with respect to a, then $w_1 = 0$ and for any $j > 1$, $w_j = v_j(x_{j-1}) - v_{j-1}(x_{j-1}) + w_{j-1} = f_j(x_{j-1}) + w_{j-1} = \cdots = \sum_{k=1}^{j} f_k(x_{k-1})$.

Let $A = (a, w)$ be a stable assignment that is budget feasible and optimal with respect to a, and $x_0, \ldots, x_m$ as specified in Claim 1. Defining the randomized assignment $R = (p_1, \ldots, p_m)$ where $p_j = x_j - x_{j-1}$ for each $j \in [m]$ and comparing $SW(R)$ and $SW(A)$ will prove our theorem. □

COROLLARY 3. *If $f_j(x)$ is concave for every $j \in [m]$, then $SW(R^{opt}) \geq SW(A^{opt})$.*

Again, R^{opt} can be computed by a linear program, and when the conditions in Theorem 5 hold the ratio between $SW(R^{opt})$ and $SW(A^{opt})$ can be arbitrarily large. When the conditions do not hold, the relation between randomized assignments and stable assignments depend on the budget and the hospitals' costs, as shown in the full version [9]. As a future direction, it would be interesting to not only characterize the conditions under which the optimal stable assignment does better, but also quantify the ratio or difference between the social welfare of the two. Moreover, it is easy to see the FPTAS in Section 3.2 can be generalized to the setting of Section 4.3 with discrete patients. Finally, the conditions in Theorem 5 can also be interpreted in terms of MHR in the corresponding single-player Bayesian assignment problem.

Acknowledgments

We thank several anonymous reviewers for their comments.

[9]How to implement lotteries so that the desired constraints are satisfied ex-post is an important research topic in the Economics literature, see, e.g., [8].

[10]Again, our approach works as long as each $f_j(x)$ is non-decreasing and piecewise differentiable.

REFERENCES

[1] A. Abdulkadiroğlu, P. A. Pathak, and A. E. Roth. The New York City High School Match. *American Economic Review*, 95(2):364–367, May 2005.

[2] S. Alaei, A. Malekian, and A. Srinivasan. On random sampling auctions for digital goods. *ACM Trans. Econ. Comput.*, 2(3):11:1–11:19, July 2014.

[3] S. Athey and G. Ellison. Position Auctions with Consumer Search. NBER Working Papers 15253, National Bureau of Economic Research, Inc, Aug. 2009.

[4] A. Bogomolnaia and H. Moulin. A New Solution to the Random Assignment Problem. *Journal of Economic Theory*, 100(2):295–328, October 2001.

[5] M. Braverman, J. Chen, and S. Kannan. Optimal provision-after-wait in healthcare. *Mathematics of Operations Research*, 41(1):352–376, 2016.

[6] P. Briest. Uniform budgets and the envy-free pricing problem. In *Proceedings of the 35th International Colloquium on Automata, Languages and Programming, Part I*, ICALP '08, pages 808–819, Berlin, Heidelberg, 2008. Springer-Verlag.

[7] P. Briest, S. Chawla, R. Kleinberg, and S. M. Weinberg. Pricing randomized allocations. In *Proceedings of the Twenty-first Annual ACM-SIAM Symposium on Discrete Algorithms*, SODA '10, pages 585–597, Philadelphia, PA, USA, 2010. Society for Industrial and Applied Mathematics.

[8] E. Budish, Y.-K. Che, F. Kojima, and P. Milgrom. Designing random allocation mechanisms: Theory and applications. *American Economic Review*, 103(2):585–623, 2013.

[9] H. Chan and J. Chen. Provision-after-wait with common preferences, full version. `http://www.cs.stonybrook.edu/~jingchen/`, 2016.

[10] S. Chawla, J. D. Hartline, and R. Kleinberg. Algorithmic pricing via virtual valuations. In *Proceedings of the 8th ACM Conference on Electronic Commerce*, EC '07, pages 243–251, New York, NY, USA, 2007. ACM.

[11] S. Chawla, D. L. Malec, and B. Sivan. The power of randomness in Bayesian optimal mechanism design. In *Proceedings of the 11th ACM Conference on Electronic Commerce*, EC '10, pages 149–158, New York, NY, USA, 2010. ACM.

[12] X. Chen, I. Diakonikolas, D. Paparas, X. Sun, and M. Yannakakis. The complexity of optimal multidimensional pricing. In *Proceedings of the Twenty-Fifth Annual ACM-SIAM Symposium on Discrete Algorithms*, SODA '14, pages 1319–1328. SIAM, 2014.

[13] N. R. Devanur, B. Q. Ha, and J. D. Hartline. Prior-free auctions for budgeted agents. In *Proceedings of the Fourteenth ACM Conference on Electronic Commerce*, EC '13, pages 287–304, New York, NY, USA, 2013. ACM.

[14] V. Guruswami, J. D. Hartline, A. R. Karlin, D. Kempe, C. Kenyon, and F. McSherry. On profit-maximizing envy-free pricing. In *Proceedings of the Sixteenth Annual ACM-SIAM Symposium on Discrete Algorithms*, SODA '05, pages 1164–1173, Philadelphia, PA, USA, 2005. Society for Industrial and Applied Mathematics.

[15] B. Q. Ha and J. D. Hartline. Mechanism design via consensus estimates, cross checking, and profit extraction. *ACM Trans. Econ. Comput.*, 1(2):8:1–8:15, May 2013.

[16] J. Hartline and Q. Yan. Envy, truth, and profit. In *Proceedings of the 12th ACM Conference on Electronic Commerce*, EC '11, pages 243–252, New York, NY, USA, 2011. ACM.

[17] A. S. Kelso and V. P. Crawford. Job Matching, Coalition Formation, and Gross Substitutes. *Econometrica*, 50(6):1483–1504, November 1982.

[18] S. G. Kolliopoulos and G. Steiner. Partially ordered knapsack and applications to scheduling. *Discrete Appl. Math.*, 155(8):889–897, Apr. 2007.

[19] A. M. Manelli and D. R. Vincent. Bundling as an optimal selling mechanism for a multiple-good monopolist. *Journal of Economic Theory*, 127(1):1–35, March 2006.

[20] J. Thanassoulis. Haggling over substitutes. *Journal of Economic Theory*, 117(2):217–245, August 2004.

[21] H. R. Varian. Position auctions. *International Journal of Industrial Organization*, 25(6):1163–1178, December 2007.

Arguing about Voting Rules

Olivier Cailloux
Université Paris-Dauphine
PSL Research University
CNRS, UMR 7243, LAMSADE
75016 Paris, France
olivier.cailloux@dauphine.fr

Ulle Endriss
Institute for Logic, Language and Computation
University of Amsterdam
P.O. Box 94242
1090 GE Amsterdam, The Netherlands
ulle.endriss@uva.nl

ABSTRACT

When the members of a group have to make a decision, they can use a voting rule to aggregate their preferences. But which rule to use is a difficult question. Different rules have different properties, and social choice theorists have found arguments for and against most of them. These arguments are aimed at the expert reader, used to mathematical formalism. We propose a logic-based language to instantiate such arguments in concrete terms in order to help people understand the strengths and weaknesses of different voting rules. Our approach allows us to automatically derive a justification for a given election outcome or to support a group in arguing over which voting rule to use. We exemplify our approach with an in-depth study of the Borda rule.

Keywords

Social Choice Theory; Argumentation; Decision Support

1. INTRODUCTION

When the members of a committee need to make a decision, they can use a *voting rule* to aggregate their individual preferences over the available alternatives to arrive at a suitable collective choice. The normative and mathematical analysis of such voting rules is part of *social choice theory* [1], and their algorithmic properties are studied in *computational social choice* [6]. The significant interest amongst AI researchers in social choice theory in recent years, initially sparked by the relevance of the theory to AI applications in areas such as recommender systems, multiagent systems, and search technologies, has opened up several entirely new perspectives on the old problem of voting and has led to novel synergies with a variety of fields in AI and computer science, such as algorithms, knowledge representation, and machine learning. In this paper, we propose to explore a new such synergy and show how to fruitfully apply ideas from automated reasoning and principles of argumentation as studied in AI to a new kind of problem in voting.

There are many different voting rules: *Plurality, Veto, Borda, Copeland, Approval*, and so forth [18]. Each of them satisfies certain appealing properties, but none is perfect. Multiple arguments in favour and against different rules have been put forward in the literature, starting with the famous dispute between Condorcet and Borda in the 18th century [13]. However, these arguments are dispersed in the specialised literature and are often developed in a highly formal and abstract manner. It therefore is difficult, if not impossible, for an untrained individual to understand them. This means that the members of our committee can hardly have an informed discussion about which voting rule to use. We would like to enable such discussions, by making arguments regarding voting rules understandable to non-experts and by providing tools for generating and applying those arguments in concrete situations.

In this paper, we make two contributions towards this long-term goal of enabling informed argumentation about voting rules between non-expert users. First, we develop a general framework for modelling arguments for and against specific outcomes of a voting rule, given a concrete election instance. This framework allows us to represent many important arguments, either new or taken from the literature, and either highly specific or in the general and abstract form of *axioms* encoding high-level properties. Because the framework instantiates these arguments on concrete examples, it does not require the audience to understand the axioms in their full generality. Nevertheless, an argument in our framework can still be general in the sense of being applicable to any concrete election instance. Importantly, our framework is not tailored to defend a specific rule: it permits the use of arguments in favour of different voting rules. As a second contribution, we instantiate our framework by providing an algorithm for generating arguments justifying the outcome recommended by the *Borda rule* for any given election. The technique we use builds on the axiomatisation of that rule developed by Young [21].

Example 1. To illustrate what we ultimately aim for, consider an election with three alternatives, $\{a, b, c\}$, and three voters. Voters v_1 and v_2 both prefer a to b to c, while voter v_3 preferes c to b to a. The situation is summarised in Figure 1 in the form of preference profile $\boldsymbol{R}$. Which alternative wins this election depends on the voting rule used. The Veto rule, for instance, recommends electing the alternative that is ranked at the bottom least often, i.e., it would elect alternative b. The Borda rule, on the other hand, awards 2 points every time an alternative is ranked first, 1 point every time it is ranked second, and 0 points every time it is ranked last, i.e., under the Borda rule alternative a would win (with $2+2+0$ points against $1+1+1$ for b and $0+0+2$ for c). So which alternative is the "right" winner? What we envision is a system that would be able to automatically generate an

Appears in: *Proceedings of the 15th International Conference on Autonomous Agents and Multiagent Systems (AAMAS 2016), J. Thangarajah, K. Tuyls, C. Jonker, S. Marsella (eds.), May 9–13, 2016, Singapore.*

$$R = \begin{array}{ccc} v_1 & v_2 & v_3 \\ a & a & c \\ b & b & b \\ c & c & a \end{array}, \quad R_1 = \begin{array}{c} v_1 \\ a \\ b \\ c \end{array}, \quad R_2 = \begin{array}{cc} v_2 & v_3 \\ a & c \\ b & b \\ c & a \end{array}.$$

Figure 1: The profiles used in the introductory example. Each column represents the preference ordering of one voter.

easy-to-understand sequence of arguments for justifying, for instance, that alternative a is the deserving winner. Such a system might initiate the following dialogue.

System: Consider election $\boldsymbol{R}_1$, involving only voter v_1 (see also Figure 1). Do you agree that a, enjoying unanimous support, should win this election?

User: Yes, of course.

System: Now consider election $\boldsymbol{R}_2$, involving only voters v_2 and v_3. Do you agree that, for symmetry reasons, the outcome should be a three-way tie?

User: Yes, that sounds reasonable.

System: Observe that when we combine $\boldsymbol{R}_1$ and $\boldsymbol{R}_2$, we obtain our election of interest, namely $\boldsymbol{R}$. Do you agree that in this combined election, as there was a three-way tie in $\boldsymbol{R}_2$, $\boldsymbol{R}_1$ should be used to decide the winner?

User: Yes, I do.

System: To summarise, you agree that a should win for $\boldsymbol{R}$.

The reader familiar with the axiomatic method in social choice theory may recognise some of the standard axioms satisfied by the Borda rule at the core of two of these arguments (namely Pareto dominance and reinforcement). We will formally introduce these axioms in Section 2. If the user disagrees with one of the steps, the system might try another strategy of arguing in favour of a. Alternatively, we might also ask our system to generate a sequence of arguments to justify that b should win. △

In this paper, we do not address the rendering of such arguments in natural language. Rather, we address the challenge of automatically generating the arguments themselves, expressed in a simple logic-based language. Our framework offers a general solution to the problem of representing such arguments to justify any given outcome for any given election. Of course, a given user will only find some of the arguments that can be represented in principle convincing in practice. For any "natural" voting rule, one should expect that there will be (by virtue of its naturalness) a convincing set of arguments that can be used to justify the outcomes recommend by that rule. The challenge then is to automatically generate a concrete sequence of such arguments for a given outcome to be justified. We provide a solution to this algorithmic problem for the case of the Borda rule.

The remainder of this paper is organised as follows. Section 2 introduces a logic for specifying reasonableness criteria (i.e., axioms) for voting rules. We prove the logic to be complete and demonstrate how it can be used to justify an election outcome. In Section 3 we provide an algorithm for justifying outcomes returned by the Borda rule for arbitrary elections. While our main technical contributions concern the challenge of justifying a given election outcome, in Section 4 we briefly explore other further applications of our approach to richer forms of argumentation about voting rules. Section 5 concludes with a discussion of related work.

2. GENERAL FRAMEWORK

In this section we introduce a formal model of voting rules for variable electorates, we show how to describe such rules and their properties in a simple logical language, and we then use this language to develop a framework for reasoning and arguing about voting rules.

2.1 Voting Rules

We begin by introducing what is essentially the standard formal model of voting familiar from social choice theory [9, 18], with varying sets of voters.

Let $\mathcal{A}$, with $m = |\mathcal{A}|$, be the finite set of *alternatives*. Let $\mathcal{P}_\emptyset(\mathcal{A})$ denote the powerset of $\mathcal{A}$, excluding the empty set. We use the letters $A \subseteq \mathcal{A}$ and $\alpha \subseteq \mathcal{P}_\emptyset(\mathcal{A})$ to designate subsets of alternatives and sets of subsets of alternatives, respectively. We model *preferences* as (strict) linear orders (transitive, irreflexive, and connected binary relations) over $\mathcal{A}$. Let $\mathcal{N}$ be the infinite universe of potential *voters*. A *profile* $\boldsymbol{R}$ is a mapping from a finite subset of voters $N_{\boldsymbol{R}} \subseteq \mathcal{N}$ to linear orders over $\mathcal{A}$. For technical reasons, we allow $N_{\boldsymbol{R}}$ to be empty, in which case we call $\boldsymbol{R}$ the *null profile*. Let $\mathcal{R}$ denote the set of all non-null profiles. A *voting rule* f maps each non-null profile $\boldsymbol{R}$ to a non-empty subset of $\mathcal{A}$, the set of (tied) election winners for the profile in question.

Given a profile $\boldsymbol{R}$, let $\overline{\boldsymbol{R}}$ be the profile consisting of the reverses of the linear orders found in $\boldsymbol{R}$. For two profiles $\boldsymbol{R}_1$ and $\boldsymbol{R}_2$ defined over disjoint sets of voters, we define their *sum* $\boldsymbol{R}_1 \oplus \boldsymbol{R}_2$ as the profile $\boldsymbol{R}_1 \cup \boldsymbol{R}_2$. (Note that the union of two functions, considered as sets of input-output pairs, defined over disjoint domains, is itself a well-defined function.) In this paper, we will only use addition of profiles in contexts where the identities of the voters do not matter. Therefore, we also define addition over profiles that are not defined over disjoint sets of voters, the addition then being preceded by an arbitrary renaming of the voters of the second profile. Formally, given two profiles $\boldsymbol{R}_1, \boldsymbol{R}_2$ with $N_{\boldsymbol{R}_1} \cap N_{\boldsymbol{R}_2} \neq \emptyset$, define s as an arbitrary injection mapping every voter $i \in N_{\boldsymbol{R}_2}$ to a voter $s(i) \in \mathcal{N} \setminus N_{\boldsymbol{R}_1}$; define $t(\boldsymbol{R})$ as the profile $\{ (s(i), P) \mid (i, P) \in \boldsymbol{R} \}$; and define $\boldsymbol{R}_1 \oplus \boldsymbol{R}_2 = \boldsymbol{R}_1 \cup t(\boldsymbol{R}_2)$. E.g., for $\boldsymbol{R} = \{ (i, (a, b)) \}$, $\boldsymbol{R} \oplus \boldsymbol{R}$ is $\{ (i, (a, b)), (i', (a, b)) \}$, with $i' \neq i$ an arbitrary voter. A profile $\boldsymbol{R}$ may be multiplied by a natural number $k \in \mathbb{N}$, defined in the natural way as repeated addition with copies of itself and denoted by $k\boldsymbol{R}$. Multiplying a profile by zero yields the null profile. Throughout this paper, natural numbers are taken to include zero.

2.2 Logical Language and Axioms

To formally describe voting rules we will make use of the language of propositional logic over the set of atomic propositions $\{ p_{\boldsymbol{R},A} \mid \boldsymbol{R} \in \mathcal{R}, \emptyset \subset A \subseteq \mathcal{A} \}$. This set includes one atom for every possible non-null profile $\boldsymbol{R}$ and every possible non-empty subset A of alternatives. The language $\mathcal{L}$ is the set of all formulæ that can be formed using these atoms and the propositional connectives $\neg, \wedge, \vee$, and $\rightarrow$ as well as the special propositions $\top$ and $\bot$, in the usual manner [19]. A *literal* is an atom or its negation; a *clause* is a disjunction of literals.

The semantics of $\mathcal{L}$ is defined as follows. Given a voting rule f, the *model* v_f assigns the value T (*true*) to the atom

$p_{\boldsymbol{R},A}$ if $f(\boldsymbol{R}) = A$ and the value F (*false*) otherwise. That is, $p_{\boldsymbol{R},A}$ is true if f chooses A as the set of winners whenever the voters vote as in profile $\boldsymbol{R}$. The definition of v_f extends to the whole set of formulæ using the usual semantics of propositional logic. We say that v_f *satisfies* a set of formulæ *iff* it assigns the value T to every formula in the set.

To make the semantics of the atoms explicit in the language, we from now on write $[\boldsymbol{R} \mapsto A]$ instead of $p_{\boldsymbol{R},A}$. We also write $[\boldsymbol{R} \overset{\in}{\mapsto} \alpha]$, for any non-empty $\alpha \subseteq \mathcal{P}_\emptyset(\mathcal{A})$, as a shorthand for $\bigvee_{A \in \alpha} [\boldsymbol{R} \mapsto A]$. We will refer to such clauses involving only one profile, i.e., formulæ specifying the possible sets of winners for a given profile, as *uni-profile clauses.*

We can express familiar as well as new axioms of social choice theory in our language. We call any such rendering of an axiom in $\mathcal{L}$ an $\mathcal{L}$*-axiom.* Formally, an $\mathcal{L}$-axiom is simply a set of formulæ. Here are some examples for $\mathcal{L}$-axioms.

Dom *Dominance* postulates that a Pareto-dominated alternative (i.e., an alternative to which some other alternative is preferred by every voter) should not win. The formulæ are, for each $\boldsymbol{R} \in \mathcal{R}$, $[\boldsymbol{R} \overset{\in}{\mapsto} \mathcal{P}_\emptyset(U_{\boldsymbol{R}})]$, where $U_{\boldsymbol{R}}$ is the set of alternatives that are not Pareto-dominated in $\boldsymbol{R}$.

Anon *Anonymity* asks for symmetry w.r.t. voters: for all $\boldsymbol{R} \in \mathcal{R}$, $\emptyset \subset A \subseteq \mathcal{A}$, $N' \subseteq \mathcal{N}$, bijections $\sigma : N' \to N_{\boldsymbol{R}}$, anonymity requires $[\boldsymbol{R} \mapsto A] \to [(\boldsymbol{R} \circ \sigma) \mapsto A]$.

Cond This axiom says that, if there is a *Condorcet winner* (an alternative beating all other alternatives in one-on-one majority contests), then it should be the sole winner: thus, for each profile $\boldsymbol{R}$ with Condorcet winner a, it requires $[\boldsymbol{R} \mapsto \{a\}]$.

Reinf *Reinforcement* requires that, when joining two profiles for which the winning sets have a non-empty intersection, the resulting profile must have that intersection as the only winners: for each $\boldsymbol{R}_1, \boldsymbol{R}_2, N_{\boldsymbol{R}_1} \cap N_{\boldsymbol{R}_2} = \emptyset, A_1 \cap A_2 \neq \emptyset$, reinforcement imposes the formula $([\boldsymbol{R}_1 \mapsto A_1] \wedge [\boldsymbol{R}_2 \mapsto A_2]) \to [\boldsymbol{R}_1 \oplus \boldsymbol{R}_2 \mapsto A_1 \cap A_2]$.

SymCanc *Symmetric cancellation* says that, when a profile consists of a linear order and its inverse, then the only reasonable outcome is the full set of alternatives: for each such profile $\boldsymbol{R}$, this axiom thus requires $[\boldsymbol{R} \mapsto \mathcal{A}]$.

Reinforcement, also known as *consistency* in the literature, was introduced by Young [21]. Like dominance and the Condorcet principle, it is one of the classical axioms considered in social choice theory [9]. SymCanc is an *ad hoc*, but intuitively appealing, axiom we will use in Example 2.

An $\mathcal{L}$-axiom may also be limited to capturing what an adequate behaviour is on a few specific cases, or even just a single specific case. As an example, let us inspect the argument put forward by Fishburn [8, p. 544] against the Condorcet principle. Consider the profile $\boldsymbol{R}_F$ shown in Figure 2, involving 9 alternatives and 101 voters.[1] Observe that w is the Condorcet winner, as it is preferred to any other alternative by 51 out of 101 voters. Yet, it is intuitively appealing to postulate that alternative a is in fact a more deserving winner of this election. This may be seen by looking at the numbers of times alternatives a and w obtain a given rank (also displayed in Figure 2).

[1]Fishburn explains his argument without giving a fully worked out example. The profile used here is taken from `http://rangevoting.org/FishburnAntiC.html`.

	number of voters					
	31	19	10	10	10	21
1	a	a	f	g	h	h
2	b	b	w	w	w	g
3	c	c	a	a	a	f
4	d	d	h	h	f	w
5	e	e	g	f	g	a
6	w	f	e	e	e	e
7	g	g	d	d	d	d
8	h	h	c	c	c	c
9	f	w	b	b	b	b

	w	a
1	0	50
2	30	0
3	0	30
4	21	0
5	0	21
6	31	0
7	0	0
8	0	0
9	19	0

Figure 2: The profile Fishburn uses to argue against the Condorcet property; and the number of voters placing alternative w or a at a given rank.

FvsC The *Fishburn-versus-Condorcet* $\mathcal{L}$*-axiom* is defined as the formula $[\boldsymbol{R}_F \mapsto \{a\}]$.

2.3 Reasoning about Voting Rules

Now that we have a logical language for describing the outcomes of a voting rule for different profiles in place, we want to be able to reason about statements in this language. To this end, we first fix some additional terminology regarding the relationship between $\mathcal{L}$-axioms and voting rules.

Definition 1. An $\mathcal{L}$*-axiomatisation* is a set of $\mathcal{L}$-axioms. A voting rule f *conforms* to the $\mathcal{L}$-axiomatisation J iff v_f satisfies all $\mathcal{L}$-axioms j in J. An $\mathcal{L}$-axiomatisation J is *consistent* iff some voting rule conforms to it. J *characterises* f iff f is the only voting rule conforming to it.

Given a set of assumptions of what makes a good voting rule, expressed in the form of an $\mathcal{L}$-axiomatisation, we want to be able to decide whether a given claim about a given set of alternatives being the deserving winners for a given profile logically follows from those assumptions. In other words, we want to be able to justify election outcomes in terms of a given $\mathcal{L}$-axiomatisation. The next definition fixes the semantics of what it means for such a claim to be valid.

Definition 2. Consider an $\mathcal{L}$-axiomatisation J and a formula φ in our language. We say that φ is a *valid claim* given J iff $v_f(\varphi) = \mathtt{T}$ for all voting rules f conforming to J.

We use the term 'claim' instead of 'formula' when we want to emphasise that a formula is used to make a point about specific voting rules. As our proposal is aimed at making arguments as easy to understand as possible, we suggest to restrict claims to uni-profile clauses, which have an easily interpretable meaning. Our results are general however. Note that if J is inconsistent, then all claims are vacuously valid.

We can now define a formal proof system to allow us to establish whether a given claim is valid. Let us first define κ, representing our domain knowledge. It is the set of all formulæ of the form $[\boldsymbol{R} \mapsto A_1] \wedge [\boldsymbol{R} \mapsto A_2] \to \bot$, for all profiles $\boldsymbol{R}$ and $\emptyset \subset A_1 \neq A_2 \subseteq \mathcal{A}$ (saying that a voting rule f cannot select more than one set of winners), plus all formulæ of the form $[\boldsymbol{R} \overset{\in}{\mapsto} \mathcal{P}_\emptyset(\mathcal{A})]$ (saying that f must select at least one set of winners). Thus, κ encodes the requirement of f being a function. We now define a proof of a claim φ grounded

$$\boldsymbol{R} = \begin{matrix} a & b & a & c \\ b & c & b & b \\ c & a & c & a \end{matrix}, \quad \boldsymbol{R}_D = \begin{matrix} a & b \\ b & c \\ c & a \end{matrix}, \quad \boldsymbol{R}_S = \begin{matrix} a & c \\ b & b \\ c & a \end{matrix}.$$

Figure 3: The profiles used in Example 2. Each column represents the preference ordering of one voter.

in J as a demonstration that φ can be inferred from J and κ, i.e., that $(\bigcup J) \cup \kappa \vdash \varphi$. Natural deduction [19], which is widely regarded as producing proofs of good readability, is particularly suited to this purpose, but any other system that is sound and complete for propositional logic could be used as well.

Definition 3. A *proof* of claim φ grounded in $\mathcal{L}$-axiomatisation J is a natural deduction proof for $(\bigcup J) \cup \kappa \vdash \varphi$.

For the purposes of presenting examples, in this paper, we will take certain shortcuts and omit the detailed derivation of simple facts about propositional logic. We will justify such steps as being inferred 'by propositional reasoning' (PR), together with a reference to the premises used. What is important in view of our ultimate goal of justifying election outcomes to users is that any such propositional reasoning step can be decomposed into a sequence of basic steps in a natural deduction proof, which can then be translated into an argument in natural language that can be explained to a non-expert user [2, 14, 20].

Example 2. We prove below, on the basis of $\mathcal{L}$-axioms Dom, SymCanc, and Reinf defined earlier, that the profile $\boldsymbol{R}$ of Figure 3 must have as winners either $\{a\}$, $\{b\}$, or $\{a,b\}$, i.e., that c should not win. Each line consists of a formula we have shown to be true, followed by the justification for that proof step. The profiles $\boldsymbol{R}_D$ and $\boldsymbol{R}_S$ are also defined in Figure 3. Note that $\boldsymbol{R} = \boldsymbol{R}_D \oplus \boldsymbol{R}_S$.

1. $[\boldsymbol{R}_D \overset{\in}{\mapsto} \{\{a\},\{b\},\{a,b\}\}]$ (Dom)
2. $[\boldsymbol{R}_S \mapsto \{a,b,c\}]$ (SymCanc)
3. $([\boldsymbol{R}_D \mapsto \{a\}] \wedge [\boldsymbol{R}_S \mapsto \{a,b,c\}]) \to [\boldsymbol{R} \mapsto \{a\}]$ (Reinf)
4. $([\boldsymbol{R}_D \mapsto \{b\}] \wedge [\boldsymbol{R}_S \mapsto \{a,b,c\}]) \to [\boldsymbol{R} \mapsto \{b\}]$ (Reinf)
5. $([\boldsymbol{R}_D \mapsto \{a,b\}] \wedge [\boldsymbol{R}_S \mapsto \{a,b,c\}]) \to [\boldsymbol{R} \mapsto \{a,b\}]$ (Reinf)
6. $[\boldsymbol{R}_D \mapsto \{a\}] \to [\boldsymbol{R} \mapsto \{a\}]$ (PR from 2 & 3)
7. $[\boldsymbol{R}_D \mapsto \{b\}] \to [\boldsymbol{R} \mapsto \{b\}]$ (PR from 2 & 4)
8. $[\boldsymbol{R}_D \mapsto \{a,b\}] \to [\boldsymbol{R} \mapsto \{a,b\}]$ (PR from 2 & 5)
9. $[\boldsymbol{R}_D \mapsto \{a\}] \vee [\boldsymbol{R}_D \mapsto \{b\}] \vee [\boldsymbol{R}_D \mapsto \{a,b\}]$ (rewrite 1)
10. $[\boldsymbol{R} \mapsto \{a\}] \vee [\boldsymbol{R} \mapsto \{b\}] \vee [\boldsymbol{R} \mapsto \{a,b\}]$ (PR from 6–9)
11. $[\boldsymbol{R} \overset{\in}{\mapsto} \{\{a\},\{b\},\{a,b\}\}]$ (rewrite 10)

Each of these steps is simple enough to be rendered in natural language, so as to be presented to a non-expert user, just as in Example 1. For instance, steps 2 and 3 directly correspond to steps also present in Example 1, while step 6 might be explained by pointing out that when two premises imply a conclusion, then that conclusion is implied by the first premise alone once we have established that the second premise is in fact true. △

Remark 1. It is important to understand that two $\mathcal{L}$-axioms may be equivalent, logically speaking, while leading to proofs that differ in terms of how easy or difficult they are to understand for a human reader. In our proposal, it is important to choose $\mathcal{L}$-axioms not only according to what they entail (their logical power), but also according to the ease of understanding them. This is similar to the general goal of axiomatising a function: we search for axioms that have, as much as possible, an intuitive content. In our case, however, an $\mathcal{L}$-axiomatisation is good if it strikes an appropriate balance between the lengths of proofs it produces and the intuitiveness of the concrete instantiations of the $\mathcal{L}$-axioms it contains. As an illustration, Reinf could be changed in order to shorten the proof of Example 2. A modified Reinf would say, for example, that a profile associated with a set of possible sets of winners, when added to a profile that has the full set $\mathcal{A}$ as the winners, must still be associated with the same set of possible sets of winners. This axiom would yield, in a single step, that $[\boldsymbol{R}_D \overset{\in}{\mapsto} \{\{a\},\{b\},\{a,b\}\}] \wedge [\boldsymbol{R}_S \mapsto \{a,b,c\}]) \to [\boldsymbol{R} \overset{\in}{\mapsto} \{\{a\},\{b\},\{a,b\}\}]$.

We now want to show that, with our definition of proofs, we can prove only and all claims that indeed are valid.

Theorem 1 (Completeness). *For any $\mathcal{L}$-axiomatisation J and any claim φ, there exists a proof of φ grounded in J iff φ is valid given J.*

Proof. The theorem follows from the (soundness and) completeness of natural deduction for classical propositional logic [19], together with the fact that there exists a bijection between voting rules conforming to J and models satisfying J and κ. Indeed, for each f conforming to J, the corresponding model v_f satisfies J and κ. Now take any v satisfying J and κ. As the model satisfies κ, we can define a rule f from that model, taking $f(\boldsymbol{R}) = A$ when the model says $[\boldsymbol{R} \mapsto A]$ is true. Because $v = v_f$, f conforms to J. □

Thus, while our logical language permits us to speak about voting rules by making arbitrary claims about the possible sets of winners for a given profile, we now have a proof system in place for deriving any valid such claim from a given axiomatisation provided in the same language. The renderings of the axioms themselves may be long and unwieldy (e.g., Dom explicitly lists all undominated alternatives for every profile), but the concrete proofs produced nevertheless can be expected to be relatively simple and human-readable (as seen in Example 2). Finding the right concrete profiles (e.g., $\boldsymbol{R}_D$ and $\boldsymbol{R}_S$ in Example 2) to use in a proof may be hard, but reading an existing proof is easy. In Section 3 we will address this challenge of actually producing proofs.

3. JUSTIFYING BORDA OUTCOMES

The *Borda rule* is one of the most important voting rules in the literature [18]. Under this rule, an alternative a earns as many points from a given voter as that voter ranks other alternatives below a. The Borda score of an alternative is the sum of points it earns in this manner; the alternatives with the highest Borda score win. For our purposes, it will be convenient to use the following alternative definition.

Definition 4. Given a profile, the *beta score* of an alternative is the sum of the numbers of alternatives it beats in each linear order, minus the sum of the numbers of alternatives it is beaten by in each linear order. Under the *Borda rule* f_B the alternatives with the highest beta score win.

Remark 2. Observe that Borda scores and beta scores define the same rule. Indeed, let n be the number of voters and recall that m is the number of alternatives. The beta score, for a given voter, is $b-(m-1-b)=2b-(m-1)$, where b is the Borda score of that same voter. Thus, the total beta score of an alternative is twice its total Borda score minus $n(m-1)$.

In this section we want to use our logic to justify a given outcome of Borda. That is, starting from any profile $\boldsymbol{R}^*$, we want to be able to give a proof, grounded in $\mathcal{L}$-axioms that are as appealing as possible, for the claim that the only "reasonable" winners must be the ones Borda picks (provided the reader of the argument finds these instantiations of axioms indeed reasonable). We will thus, first, present an $\mathcal{L}$-axiomatisation of Borda and, second, provide an algorithm that, given any $\boldsymbol{R}^*$, builds a proof for $[\boldsymbol{R}^* \mapsto f_B(\boldsymbol{R}^*)]$.

3.1 Borda $\mathcal{L}$-Axiomatisation

To present the $\mathcal{L}$-axiomatisation that we will use to argue in favour of Borda, we require a few definitions. Fix an arbitrary linear order $\succ$ on $\mathcal{A}$. (We will use the alphabetic ordering in our illustrative examples.)

Definition 5. The *elementary profile* $\boldsymbol{R}_e^A$, $\emptyset \subset A \subseteq \mathcal{A}$, has two voters and is defined as follows. Let $k = \succ|_A$ be the restriction of $\succ$ on A and let $\ell = \succ|_{\mathcal{A}\setminus A}$. The first voter has the linear order defined by k then ℓ; the second has $\overline{k}$ then $\overline{\ell}$.

Example 3. The elementary profile $\boldsymbol{R}_e^{\{a,b\}}$ corresponding to $A = \{a,b\}$, with $\mathcal{A} = \{a,b,c,d\}$, is composed of the linear orders (a,b,c,d) and (b,a,d,c). △

Let us call a bijection S on $\mathcal{A}$ an *m-cycle* if $(\mathcal{A}, S)$ is a strongly connected graph, thus, if S represents a cycle that visits each alternative in $\mathcal{A}$ exactly once. It is formally defined as a set of pairs of alternatives, but we will denote such a cycle using a tuple of alternatives, where the first and last alternatives are equal, and all other alternatives appear exactly once. For example, $\langle a,c,b,d,a\rangle$ denotes the m-cycle $\{(a,c),(c,b),(b,d),(d,a)\}$ in $\{a,b,c,d\}$. This cycle can also be represented as $\langle b,d,a,c,b\rangle$. We say that a cycle in $\mathcal{A}$ *generates* $m = |\mathcal{A}|$ linear orders on $\mathcal{A}$, in the natural way. For example, $\langle a,c,b,a\rangle$ generates (a,c,b), (c,b,a), and (b,a,c). We write linear orders with regular parentheses $(\cdots)$ to distinguish them from cycles $\langle\cdots\rangle$. Conversely, observe that a linear order involving all alternatives in $\mathcal{A}$ is generated by exactly one m-cycle.

Definition 6. The *cyclic profile* $\boldsymbol{R}_c^S$, with S an m-cycle, is the profile composed of all m linear orders generated by S.

Example 4. The cyclic profile $\boldsymbol{R}_c^{\langle a,b,c,d,a\rangle}$ corresponding to $S = \langle a,b,c,d,a\rangle$ with $\mathcal{A} = \{a,b,c,d\}$ has the preference orders (a,b,c,d), (b,c,d,a), (c,d,a,b) and (d,a,b,c). △

A *delta vector* δ is a mapping from $\succ$ to the rationals: such a vector has $\binom{m}{2}$ coordinates, each mapping a pair of alternatives to a rational number. For every pair of alternatives $(a,b) \in \succ$, define $\delta_{ba} = -\delta_{ab}$ (slightly abusing notation). The set of delta vectors, denoted by $\boxed{\delta}$, together with addition and multiplication by a rational defined in the natural way, is a vector space.

Definition 7. For any profile $\boldsymbol{R}$, the *delta vector* $\delta^{\boldsymbol{R}}$ maps every $(a,b) \in \succ$ to the signed number of victories of a against b, i.e., $\delta_{ab}^{\boldsymbol{R}}$ is the number of voters who prefer a to b minus the number of voters who prefer b to a.

Thus, $\delta^{\boldsymbol{R}}$ represents the *weighted majority graph* of $\boldsymbol{R}$.

We say that two profiles $\boldsymbol{R}$ and $\boldsymbol{R}'$ *cancel* when $\delta^{\overline{\boldsymbol{R}}} = \delta^{\boldsymbol{R}'}$, thus when $\overline{\boldsymbol{R}}$ and $\boldsymbol{R}'$ have the same weighted majority graph, or equivalently, observing that $\delta^{\overline{\boldsymbol{R}}} = -\delta^{\boldsymbol{R}}$, when $\delta^{\boldsymbol{R}\oplus\boldsymbol{R}'} = \boldsymbol{0}$, where $\boldsymbol{0}$ is the zero vector.

Below is the $\mathcal{L}$-axiomatisation that we use for the Borda rule. The fact that it is a *correct* axiomatisation of the Borda rule will follow from Theorem 2 below. As discussed below, in Section 3.4, our axiomatisation is very similar but not identical to the axiomatisation given by Young [21].

Elem For any elementary profile $\boldsymbol{R}_e^A$, the only reasonable set of winners is A: for all $\emptyset \subset A \subseteq \mathcal{A}$, $[\boldsymbol{R}_e^A \mapsto A]$.

Cycl For any cyclic profile $\boldsymbol{R}_c^S$, the only reasonable set of winners is $\mathcal{A}$: for all m-cycles S, $[\boldsymbol{R}_c^S \mapsto \mathcal{A}]$.

Canc If all pairs of alternatives (a,b) are such that a is preferred to b as many times as b is to a, then the set of winners must be $\mathcal{A}$: for all $\boldsymbol{R}$ such that $\delta_{ab}^{\boldsymbol{R}} = 0$ for all $(a,b) \in \succ$, $[\boldsymbol{R} \mapsto \mathcal{A}]$.

Reinf Reinforcement, as defined earlier (cf. Section 2.2).

Reinf-sub Subtracting a profile with a full winner-set does not change the outcome. For all $\boldsymbol{R}, \boldsymbol{R}', \emptyset \subset A \subseteq \mathcal{A}$: $([\boldsymbol{R} \oplus \boldsymbol{R}' \mapsto A] \wedge [\boldsymbol{R}' \mapsto \mathcal{A}]) \rightarrow [\boldsymbol{R} \mapsto A]$.

Simp If a profile consists of a repetition of the same sub-profile, then the sub-profile must have the same winners (i.e., we can simplify): for all $\boldsymbol{R}$, $2 \leq k \in \mathbb{N}$, $\emptyset \subset A \subseteq \mathcal{A}$, $[k\boldsymbol{R} \mapsto A] \rightarrow [\boldsymbol{R} \mapsto A]$.

We denote our $\mathcal{L}$-axiomatisation by J_B, the set of all six sets of formulæ just defined.

Remark 3. Observe that Simp and Reinf-sub logically follow from Reinf, i.e., they are in fact not required for the characterisation itself. We introduce them nevertheless, as explained in Remark 1, because they can shorten proofs, and because we assume they will appear sufficiently intuitive to the reader of such proofs to be used without requiring separate justification themselves.

3.2 An Example

Consider the set of alternatives $\mathcal{A} = \{a,b,c,d\}$ and a profile $\boldsymbol{R}^*$ composed of the two preference orders (a,b,d,c) and (c,b,a,d). Observe that Borda selects $\{a,b\}$ as winners for this profile. We will now build a proof grounded in J_B of the claim $[\boldsymbol{R}^* \mapsto \{a,b\}]$.

The proof consists of two parts. First (steps 1–8 in this example), we define a profile $\boldsymbol{R}'$ that is the sum of several profiles for which the winners are uncontroversial, either because of Elem or because of Cycl, and use this to argue that our Borda winners should win for $\boldsymbol{R}'$. For our example, let $\boldsymbol{R}_E = \boldsymbol{R}_e^{\{a,b\}} \oplus 2\boldsymbol{R}_e^{\{a,b,c\}}$, $\boldsymbol{R}_C = \boldsymbol{R}_c^{\langle a,d,c,b,a\rangle} \oplus \boldsymbol{R}_c^{\langle a,b,d,c,a\rangle}$, and $\boldsymbol{R}' = \boldsymbol{R}_E \oplus \boldsymbol{R}_C$. Second (steps 9–16 in this example), we argue that $\boldsymbol{R}'$ must have the same winners as $\boldsymbol{R}^*$. This works, because we also chose $\boldsymbol{R}'$ in such a way that it has the same weighted majority graph as some multiple of $\boldsymbol{R}^*$. Indeed, step 12 uses the fact that $\overline{4\boldsymbol{R}^*}$ and $\boldsymbol{R}'$ cancel (this can be verified manually by counting the number of wins for each pair of alternatives). Step 9 is valid, as any profile cancels with its inverse.

1. $[\boldsymbol{R}_e^{\{a,b\}} \mapsto \{a, b\}]$ (Elem)
2. $[\boldsymbol{R}_e^{\{a,b,c\}} \mapsto \{a, b, c\}]$ (Elem)
3. $[\boldsymbol{R}_c^{\langle a,d,c,b,a\rangle} \mapsto \mathcal{A}]$ (Cycl)
4. $[\boldsymbol{R}_c^{\langle a,b,d,c,a\rangle} \mapsto \mathcal{A}]$ (Cycl)
5. $((1) \wedge (2)) \to [\boldsymbol{R}_E \mapsto \{a, b\}]$ (Reinf)
6. $((3) \wedge (4)) \to [\boldsymbol{R}_C \mapsto \mathcal{A}]$ (Reinf)
7. $([\boldsymbol{R}_E \mapsto \{a, b\}] \wedge [\boldsymbol{R}_C \mapsto \mathcal{A}]) \to [\boldsymbol{R}' \mapsto \{a, b\}]$ (Reinf)
8. $[\boldsymbol{R}' \mapsto \{a, b\}]$ (PR from 5–7)
9. $[4\boldsymbol{R}^* \oplus \overline{4\boldsymbol{R}^*} \mapsto \mathcal{A}]$ (Canc)
10. $([4\boldsymbol{R}^* \oplus \overline{4\boldsymbol{R}^*} \mapsto \mathcal{A}] \wedge [\boldsymbol{R}' \mapsto \{a, b\}]) \to [4\boldsymbol{R}^* \oplus \overline{4\boldsymbol{R}^*} \oplus \boldsymbol{R}' \mapsto \{a, b\}]$ (Reinf)
11. $[4\boldsymbol{R}^* \oplus \overline{4\boldsymbol{R}^*} \oplus \boldsymbol{R}' \mapsto \{a, b\}]$ (PR from 8–10)
12. $[\overline{4\boldsymbol{R}^*} \oplus \boldsymbol{R}' \mapsto \mathcal{A}]$ (Canc)
13. $([4\boldsymbol{R}^* \oplus \overline{4\boldsymbol{R}^*} \oplus \boldsymbol{R}' \mapsto \{a, b\}] \wedge [\overline{4\boldsymbol{R}^*} \oplus \boldsymbol{R}' \mapsto \mathcal{A}]) \to [4\boldsymbol{R}^* \mapsto \{a, b\}]$ (Reinf-sub)
14. $[4\boldsymbol{R}^* \mapsto \{a, b\}]$ (PR from 11–13)
15. $[4\boldsymbol{R}^* \mapsto \{a, b\}] \to [\boldsymbol{R}^* \mapsto \{a, b\}]$ (Simp)
16. $[\boldsymbol{R}^* \mapsto \{a, b\}]$ (PR from 14 & 15)

Simplifications are possible. For instance, step 8 could be presented to a user as following directly from steps 1–4, together with Reinf and basic propositional reasoning.

3.3 The General Algorithm

We now define an algorithm, *Borda-expl*, which, given any profile $\boldsymbol{R}^*$, builds a proof grounded in J_B of the claim $[\boldsymbol{R}^* \mapsto f_B(\boldsymbol{R}^*)]$, i.e., a justification for the Borda outcome. Our proofs all have the same structure as in the example above; only the concrete profiles used along the way differ. We show how to compute a natural number r, a profile $\boldsymbol{R}_E$ that is the sum of several elementary profiles, and a profile $\boldsymbol{R}_C$ that is the sum of several cyclic profiles such that, for $\boldsymbol{R}' = r\boldsymbol{R}_E \oplus \boldsymbol{R}_C$, (*i*) the winners for $\boldsymbol{R}'$ are $f_B(\boldsymbol{R}^*)$, and (*ii*) $rm\boldsymbol{R}^*$ and $\boldsymbol{R}'$ have the same weighted majority graph.

First, let us define $\boldsymbol{R}_E$. Define a beta vector as a vector mapping alternatives from $\mathcal{A}$ to rationals, with the condition that it sums to zero. The set of beta vectors, denoted by $\boxed{\beta}$, together with addition and multiplication by a rational defined in the natural way, is a vector space. We write $\beta^{\boldsymbol{R}} = \langle \beta_a^{\boldsymbol{R}}, a \in \mathcal{A} \rangle$ for the beta vector corresponding to a profile $\boldsymbol{R}$, where $\beta_a^{\boldsymbol{R}}$ denotes the beta score of a in $\boldsymbol{R}$. Name alternatives $a_1, a_2, \ldots, a_m$ by decreasing beta score in $\boldsymbol{R}^*$, thus $\beta_{a_1}^{\boldsymbol{R}^*} \geq \beta_{a_2}^{\boldsymbol{R}^*} \geq \ldots \geq \beta_{a_m}^{\boldsymbol{R}^*}$. Define $\boldsymbol{R}_E = \bigoplus_{i=1}^{m-1} \frac{\beta_{a_i}^{\boldsymbol{R}^*} - \beta_{a_{i+1}}^{\boldsymbol{R}^*}}{2} \boldsymbol{R}_e^{\{a_1,\ldots,a_i\}}$.

Remark 4. This definition of $\boldsymbol{R}_E$ is legal as the coefficients are natural numbers: $(\beta_{a_i}^{\boldsymbol{R}^*} - \beta_{a_{i+1}}^{\boldsymbol{R}^*})$ is even because, depending on m, either all beta scores are even, or all are odd (as may be seen by revisiting Remark 2).

We can now show that $\boldsymbol{R}_E$ has the same beta scores as $m\boldsymbol{R}^*$, which is equivalent to a result due to Young [21].

Lemma 1 (Young, 1974). *With the above definitions, for each $a \in \mathcal{A}$: $\beta_a^{\boldsymbol{R}_E} = \beta_a^{m\boldsymbol{R}^*}$.*

Proof. First observe that $\forall \emptyset \subset A \subseteq \mathcal{A}$, $\beta_a^{\boldsymbol{R}_e^A}$ equals $2(m - |A|)$ if $a \in A$ and $-2|A|$ if $a \notin A$. Write β_a instead of $\beta_a^{\boldsymbol{R}^*}$. Now $\beta_{a_i}^{\boldsymbol{R}_E} = \sum_{j=1}^{i-1} \frac{\beta_{a_j} - \beta_{a_{j+1}}}{2}(-2j) + \sum_{j=i}^{m-1} \frac{\beta_{a_j} - \beta_{a_{j+1}}}{2} 2(m - j) = \sum_{j=1}^{m-1}(\beta_{a_j} - \beta_{a_{j+1}})(-j) + \sum_{j=i}^{m-1}(\beta_{a_j} - \beta_{a_{j+1}})m = (\sum_{j=1}^{m-1} -\beta_{a_j}) + (m-1)\beta_{a_m} + m\beta_{a_i} - m\beta_{a_m} = (\sum_{j=1}^{m} -\beta_{a_j}) + m\beta_{a_i}$. The claim now follows from $\sum_{a \in \mathcal{A}} \beta_a = 0$. □

Thus, $\boldsymbol{R}_E$ and $m\boldsymbol{R}^*$ have the same Borda winners.[2] We now have to define $\boldsymbol{R}'$. Recall that we want $\boldsymbol{R}'$ and $rm\boldsymbol{R}^*$ to have equal weighted majority graphs for some r. Thus, our objective is to obtain $\delta^{\boldsymbol{R}'} = \delta^{rm\boldsymbol{R}^*}$. Assume we can find a set of m-cycles $\mathcal{S}$ and rationals $\langle q_S, S \in \mathcal{S} \rangle$ that solve the linear system of equations $\delta^{m\boldsymbol{R}^*} = \delta^{\boldsymbol{R}_E} + \sum_{S \in \mathcal{S}} q_S \delta^{\boldsymbol{R}_c^S}$. (We will shortly define $\mathcal{S}$ and prove that this system always admits a solution.) Because $\delta^{\boldsymbol{R}_c^S} = -\delta^{\boldsymbol{R}_c^{-S}}$, where $-S$ denotes the inverse cycle of S, we can then choose coefficients q_S that are all non-negative. Then, it remains only to define r as the smallest strictly positive integer such that $\{ rq_S, S \in \mathcal{S} \}$ are all natural numbers, and to define $\boldsymbol{R}_C = \bigoplus_S rq_S \boldsymbol{R}_c^S$. Indeed, $\boldsymbol{R}' = r\boldsymbol{R}_E \oplus \boldsymbol{R}_C$ then has the same winners as $\boldsymbol{R}_E$ (hence, the same as $\boldsymbol{R}^*$), and $\delta^{rm\boldsymbol{R}^*} = \delta^{\boldsymbol{R}'}$. (The comment made in Footnote 2 applies here as well.)

It remains to show that the system above can be solved. Indeed, even considering all $(m-1)!$ m-cycles as the set $\mathcal{S}$, the claim that such a system can always be solved requires a proof. Furthermore, our proof permits to use a quadratic—instead of a factorial—number of unknowns, as we define precisely which cycles $\mathcal{S}$ must contain.

Lemma 2. *There exists a set of m-cycles $\mathcal{S}$ such that, for any two profiles $\boldsymbol{R}^*, \boldsymbol{R}_E$ satisfying $\beta^{m\boldsymbol{R}^*} = \beta^{\boldsymbol{R}_E}$, there exist rationals q_S with $\sum_{S \in \mathcal{S}} q_S \delta^{\boldsymbol{R}_c^S} = \delta^{m\boldsymbol{R}^*} - \delta^{\boldsymbol{R}_E}$.*

In order to prove Lemma 2, we will first define a beta transformation $\hat{\beta}$, a linear transformation from $\boxed{\delta}$ to $\boxed{\beta}$. We will then show that $\delta^{m\boldsymbol{R}^*} - \delta^{\boldsymbol{R}_E}$ belongs to its kernel $\mathcal{K}(\hat{\beta})$ (Lemma 3). Next, we will define $\mathcal{S}$ and show that we can find rationals q_S with $\sum_{S \in \mathcal{S}} q_S \delta^{\boldsymbol{R}_c^S} = \delta$, for any delta vector $\delta \in \mathcal{K}(\hat{\beta})$. Equivalently, defining $\rho = \left\{ \delta^{\boldsymbol{R}_c^S}, S \in \mathcal{S} \right\}$, we will show that ρ spans $\mathcal{K}(\hat{\beta})$ (Lemma 4). In order to do this, observing that $\rho \subseteq \mathcal{K}(\hat{\beta})$, we will show that $\dim \mathcal{K}(\hat{\beta}) = \dim \rho$, or equivalently, that ρ has $\dim \mathcal{K}(\hat{\beta})$ independent vectors.

Define the beta transformation $\hat{\beta}(\delta)$ of a delta vector δ as the following beta vector: $\hat{\beta}(\delta)_a = \sum_{b \in \mathcal{A} \setminus \{a\}} \delta_{ab}$. Let $\mathcal{K}(\hat{\beta})$ denote the kernel of the beta transformation, the vector space of vectors δ such that $\hat{\beta}(\delta) = \boldsymbol{0}$. Because $\hat{\beta}$ is a surjective linear transformation from $\boxed{\delta}$ of dimension $\binom{m}{2}$ to $\boxed{\beta}$ of dimension $m-1$, $\dim \mathcal{K}(\hat{\beta}) = \binom{m}{2} - (m-1)$.

Lemma 3 (Young, 1974). *For any two profiles $\boldsymbol{R}^*, \boldsymbol{R}_E$ satisfying $\beta^{m\boldsymbol{R}^*} = \beta^{\boldsymbol{R}_E}$, $\delta^{m\boldsymbol{R}^*} - \delta^{\boldsymbol{R}_E} \in \mathcal{K}(\hat{\beta})$.*

Proof. Because $\hat{\beta}$ is linear and for any $\boldsymbol{R}$, $\beta^{\boldsymbol{R}} = \hat{\beta}(\delta^{\boldsymbol{R}})$, we get $\hat{\beta}(\delta^{m\boldsymbol{R}^*} - \delta^{\boldsymbol{R}_E}) = \beta^{m\boldsymbol{R}^*} - \beta^{\boldsymbol{R}_E}$. By the hypothesis of this lemma, this equals zero. Thus, $\delta^{m\boldsymbol{R}^*} - \delta^{\boldsymbol{R}_E} \in \mathcal{K}(\hat{\beta})$. □

---

[2]If $\boldsymbol{R}_E$ or $\boldsymbol{R}_C$ are null profiles, then the Borda winners for these profiles are undefined. We describe here our algorithm assuming these profiles to be non-null. The reader will easily find out which modifications are required in those simpler cases.

$\mathcal{S}$	S^{ab}	S^{ac}	S^{bc}
	$\langle a,$	$\langle b,$	$\langle b,$
	$b,$	$a,$	$c,$
	$c,$	$c,$	$a,$
	$d,$	$d,$	$d,$
	$a\rangle$	$b\rangle$	$b\rangle$

T	ab	ac	ad	bc	bd	cd
ab	1	0	−1	0	1	0
ac	0	1	−1	0	0	1
bc	0	0	0	1	−1	1

M	$\delta \boldsymbol{R}_c^{S^{ab}}$	$\delta \boldsymbol{R}_c^{S^{ac}}$	$\delta \boldsymbol{R}_c^{S^{bc}}$
ab	2	−2	0
ac	0	2	−2
ad	−2	0	2
bc	2	0	2
bd	0	−2	−2
cd	2	2	0

TM	k^{ab}	k^{ac}	k^{bc}
ab	4	−4	−4
ac	4	4	−4
bc	4	4	4

Figure 4: Illustrations for Lemma 2, with $\mathcal{A} = \{a, b, c, d\}$. The set $\mathcal{S}$ (up, right) defines the delta vectors in ρ forming the columns of the matrix M (middle, right), which get transformed by T (middle, left), obtaining $T\delta^{\boldsymbol{R}_c^{S^{tu}}} = k^{tu}$.

LEMMA 4. *There exists a set of m-cycles $\mathcal{S}$ such that $\rho = \{\delta^{\boldsymbol{R}_c^S}, S \in \mathcal{S}\}$ spans $\mathcal{K}(\hat{\beta})$.*

PROOF. Let z denote the least alternative in $\succ$. For $(t, u) \in \succ|_{\mathcal{A}\setminus\{z\}}$, define S^{tu} as the m-cycle constituted by all alternatives that are in between t and u in $\succ$ (in the order they come in $\succ$), followed by t, followed by u, followed by all alternatives that come after u in $\succ$ except z (in the order they come in $\succ$), followed by all alternatives that come before t (in the reverse order of the order they come in $\succ$), followed by z. Let $\mathcal{S}$ be the set of m-cycles $\{S^{tu}, (t, u) \in \succ|_{\mathcal{A}\setminus\{z\}}\}$ (Figure 4, top right).

Let ρ denote the set of vectors $\{\delta^{\boldsymbol{R}_c^S}, S \in \mathcal{S}\}$ (Figure 4, middle right). Let us show that ρ spans $\mathcal{K}(\hat{\beta})$. We leave it to the reader to check that $\rho \subseteq \mathcal{K}(\hat{\beta})$. It remains to show that ρ is constituted of $\binom{m}{2} - (m-1) = \binom{m-1}{2}$ independent vectors. We do so by transforming each of the $\binom{m-1}{2}$ vectors in ρ using linear combinations of their coordinates. Their independence will then be visible from their simple format. This is equivalent to defining a linear transform T, defining a matrix M constituted by the vectors $\delta \in \rho$ as column vectors, and showing that TM is non-singular.

Let us transform $\delta^{tu} = \delta^{\boldsymbol{R}_c^{S^{tu}}} \in \rho$ into a new vector k^{tu}, of size $\binom{m-1}{2}$, with coordinates indexed using the pairs in $\succ|_{\mathcal{A}\setminus\{z\}}$. For each pair $(v, w) \in \succ|_{\mathcal{A}\setminus\{z\}}$, define $k^{tu}_{vw} = -\delta^{tu}_{vz} + \delta^{tu}_{vw} + \delta^{tu}_{wz}$. Equivalently, define a $\binom{m-1}{2} \times \binom{m}{2}$ matrix T whose line T_{vw}, $vw \in \succ|_{\mathcal{A}\setminus\{z\}}$, is defined as $T^{vz}_{vw} = -1$, $T^{vw}_{vw} = T^{wz}_{vw} = 1$, the rest of the line being zero (Figure 4, middle left). This yields $T_{vw}\delta^{tu} = k^{tu}_{vw}$.

$$
\boldsymbol{R}_c^{\langle a,b,c,y,d,e,x,a\rangle} = \begin{matrix} a & b & c & y & d & e & x \\ b & c & y & d & e & x & a \\ c & y & d & e & x & a & b \\ y & d & e & x & a & b & c \\ d & e & x & a & b & c & y \\ e & x & a & b & c & y & d \\ x & a & b & c & y & d & e \end{matrix} .
$$

Figure 5: Illustration of the computation of the delta score corresponding to an m-cycle, here with $d = 4$ the distance between x and y in the cycle.

Observe that $\delta^{tu}_{xy} = m - 2d_{xy}$ for any $xy \in \succ|_{\mathcal{A}\setminus\{z\}}$, where d_{xy} is the number of alternatives in between x and y in the cycle S^{tu}, counting y but not x. To see this, recall δ^{tu}_{xy} is the signed number of victories of x against y in the profile $\boldsymbol{R}_c^{S^{tu}}$, composed of all preference orders obtained by starting the cycle S^{tu} at different positions. Assume the distance between x and y is d in S^{tu}. See Figure 5. Consider first the preference order starting with the $(d-1)$ alternatives in between x and y, then y, then the remaining $m-d$ alternatives in $\mathcal{A}$ ending with x. In this preference order, y is better than x, and this will be the case for the preference orders of the first d voters where we gradually shift (cyclically) y towards the first position in the ranking. The next shift will make y beaten by x, and it will remain so for the rest of the voters. Thus, x has won $m-d$ times and y has won d times.

We obtain $k^{tu}_{vw} = 3m - 2(d_{zv} + d_{vw} + d_{wz})$. Now only two cases need to be distinguished, thanks to the order of the alternatives in the cycle S^{tu} compared to the ordering $\succ$. Consider as an example $\succ = (a, b, c, t, d, e, f, u, g, h, z)$, $S^{tu} = \langle d, e, f, t, u, g, h, c, b, a, z, d\rangle$. (The reasoning which follows is general though.) Because (t, u) and (v, w) are taken in $\succ|_{\mathcal{A}\setminus\{z\}}$, we know that in $\succ$, t comes before u and v comes before w, and all are different from z. Consider any $v \in \mathcal{A}\setminus\{z\}$. Assume $t \succ v$. Then, w being in between v and z in $\succ$ implies that w is in between v and z in S^{tu}. Similarly, w is in between v and z in S^{tu} whenever $(t = v \wedge u = w)$ or $(t = v \wedge u \succ w)$. It is easy to check that in all other cases, v is in between w and z in S^{tu}. Finally, observe that $d_{zv} + d_{vw} + d_{wz}$ equals m when w is in between v and z in S^{tu} and equals $2m$ otherwise.

We conclude that $k^{tu}_{vw} = m$ whenever $t \succ v \vee (t = v \wedge u = w) \vee (t = v \wedge u \succ w)$, and $k^{tu}_{vw} = -m$ in the remaining cases. Hence, TM (Figure 4, bottom) has its entries on the diagonal and below equal to m and the rest equal to $-m$, which shows it is nonsingular, or equivalently, that $\{k^{tu}, tu \in \succ|_{\mathcal{A}\setminus\{z\}}\}$ is a set of $\binom{m-1}{2}$ independent vectors. □

Once suitable values for r, $\boldsymbol{R}_E$ and $\boldsymbol{R}_C$ have been found, it suffices to present a proof following the structure presented in Section 3.2 (or simple modifications thereof, in case some of the profiles found are null profiles). This terminates the proof of correctness of our Borda-expl algorithm.

THEOREM 2 (BORDA JUSTIFICATION). *For any given profile,* Borda-expl *computes a proof justifying the outcome of the Borda rule in terms of the $\mathcal{L}$-axiomatisation J_B.*

PROOF. This is a consequence of Lemma 2, which itself follows from Lemma 3 and Lemma 4. □

3.4 Comparison with Young's Axiomatisation

This instantiation of our framework is based on the axiomatisation of the Borda rule given by Young [21]. Young used the axioms of *neutrality, faithfulness, cancellation,* and *reinforcement.* We chose a slightly different set of axioms to make the argument more concrete and the proofs built by our algorithm shorter. In particular, we included elementary and cyclic profiles in the axioms themselves (rather than make them follow from the axioms of Young).

Young's work also inspired our approach to proving correctness of our algorithm. Lemmas 1 and 3, the idea of using the spaces $\boxed{\delta}$, $\boxed{\beta}$ and the transformation $\widehat{\beta}$ are due to him. The novelty in our approach is that our vectors can be defined from a restricted set of cyclic profiles, whereas Young uses a more general construction. Thus, the results specific to the space of cyclic profiles (the construction and exploitation of $\mathcal{S}$ as done in Lemma 4) are new.

4. BEYOND OUTCOME JUSTIFICATION

In this section we briefly explore additional opportunities for putting our general framework to use and sketch how it may be applied to argue about voting rules in other ways that simply justifying a given outcome.

4.1 Types of Arguments

Proofs of claims may be used in various ways to argue in favour of one voting rule or to attack another rule. There are clear links with argumentation theory [3], which could be further developed to arrive at a fully fledged framework for arguing about voting rules. Here we only define a few categories of arguments we can create in our framework. In the context of a voting rule f, a proof for a claim $[\boldsymbol{R} \overset{\in}{\mapsto} \alpha]$, saying that in profile $\boldsymbol{R}$ the set of winners should be selected from α, can constitute different types of arguments:

- a *partial justification* for f when $f(\boldsymbol{R}) \in \alpha$;
- a *full justification* for f on $\boldsymbol{R}$ when $\alpha = \{ f(\boldsymbol{R}) \}$;
- an *attack* against f when $f(\boldsymbol{R}) \notin \alpha$.

An argument may belong to more than one of these categories, e.g., it may simultaneously be a justification for some rule and an attack against some other rules.

An argument can also attack an $\mathcal{L}$-axiomatisation instead of a specific voting rule. A system using an $\mathcal{L}$-axiomatisation J could establish that J' is incompatible with J (meaning that voting rules conforming to J necessarily give different results in some cases from rules conforming to J') and, assuming that the user will favour J over J' when realising that they are incompatible, could thus argue by simply giving an example illustrating the incompatibility. It is then up to that system to choose its example as wisely as possible. Formally, an attack against J' by J consists of two proofs, one of $[\boldsymbol{R} \overset{\in}{\mapsto} \alpha]$ grounded in J and one of $[\boldsymbol{R} \overset{\in}{\mapsto} \alpha']$ grounded in J', for some profile $\boldsymbol{R}$ and some sets α and α' with $\alpha \cap \alpha' = \emptyset$. An attack against J' is also an attack against any rule f' conforming to J'.

4.2 Attacking and Defending Borda

As an illustration, we present here, first, an argument that could be given against Borda, namely, that it does not satisfy the Condorcet property. We then also show how to defend Borda against this argument by producing a counter-argument to the Condorcet argument.

Consider $J_C = \{ \textsc{Cond} \}$, including only the $\mathcal{L}$-axiom saying that, if there is a Condorcet winner, it must be returned as the sole winner. Now take any profile with a Condorcet winner where Borda does not select that Condorcet winner. For example, take $\mathcal{A} = \{ a, b, c \}$ and $\boldsymbol{R}$ defined as follows:

$$\boldsymbol{R} = \begin{matrix} b & b & a & a & a \\ c & c & b & b & b \\ a & a & c & c & c \end{matrix}.$$

Although a is the Condorcet winner, Borda shamelessly selects $\{ b \}$. Thus, an attack against Borda can be built by putting forward the claim $[\boldsymbol{R} \mapsto \{ a \}]$ and its (trivial) proof grounded in J_C, whilst observing that this contradicts Borda's choice.

As a defence, a system arguing for Borda may give a justification for choosing $\{ b \}$ using its own $\mathcal{L}$-axiomatisation, by giving an argument for $[\boldsymbol{R} \mapsto \{ b \}]$ grounded in J_B as computed by Borda-expl. But this is unlikely to be convincing: such an attack rather calls for a more specific response. The system could also counter-attack by saying that we do not want to follow Condorcet in general, by using Fishburn's argument. Define J'_B as the set of $\mathcal{L}$-axioms for Borda described above, together with FvsC, the Fishburn-versus-Condorcet $\mathcal{L}$-axiom (see Section 2.2). An attack against J_C can now be produced by giving a proof grounded in J'_B for $[\boldsymbol{R}_F \mapsto \{ a \}]$, together with a proof grounded in J_C for $[\boldsymbol{R}_F \mapsto \{ w \}]$. This shows the incompatibility between these two $\mathcal{L}$-axiomatisations.

5. CONCLUSION AND RELATED WORK

We have developed a general logic-based framework for representing arguments in favour of or against specific election outcomes. While these arguments can be based on general axioms familiar from social choice theory, when actually used, they apply to concrete instances of elections, thereby making them understandable to non-experts. We have also devised a practical algorithm for generating the arguments required to justify the election outcome selected by the Borda rule, for any given profile of preferences.

Related work has aimed at explaining or justifying recommendations [4, 10, 11, 12] or outcomes of elections [15, 16]. However, these approaches are all based on specific ways of justifying decisions and propose no general framework capable of integrating different kinds of arguments, including in particular counter-arguments against their own claims.

Our work is also related to existing work on logic and automated reasoning for social choice theory [5, 7, 17], aimed at automatically deriving theorems in social choice theory. However, to date work in that literature has not attempted to tackle the problem of justifying election outcomes.

Acknowledgments

Part of this work was carried out while the first author was employed at the ILLC, University of Amsterdam, and then at the Université de technologie de Compiègne, France. It was supported by the Dutch Government through an NWO Free Competition Grant (No. 612.001.015), and funded in the framework of the Labex MS2T supported by the French Government through the programme "Investments for the future" managed by the National Agency for Research (Reference ANR-11-IDEX-0004-02), respectively.

References

[1] K. J. Arrow, A. K. Sen, and K. Suzumura, editors. *Handbook of Social Choice and Welfare*, volume 1. North-Holland, 2002.

[2] Y. Bertot and L. Théry. A generic approach to building user interfaces for theorem provers. *Journal of Symbolic Computation*, 25(2):161–194, 1998.

[3] P. Besnard and A. Hunter. *Elements of Argumentation*. MIT Press, 2008.

[4] D. Bouyssou and M. Pirlot. Conjoint measurement tools for MCDM. In J. Figueira, S. Greco, and M. Ehrgott, editors, *Multiple Criteria Decision Analysis: State of the Art Surveys*, pages 73–132. Springer-Verlag, 2005.

[5] F. Brandt and C. Geist. Finding strategyproof social choice functions via SAT solving. In *Proc. 13th International Conference on Autonomous Agents and Multiagent Systems (AAMAS-2014)*, pages 1193–1200, 2014.

[6] F. Brandt, V. Conitzer, and U. Endriss. Computational social choice. In G. Weiss, editor, *Multiagent Systems*, pages 213–283. MIT Press, 2013.

[7] U. Endriss. Logic and social choice theory. In A. Gupta and J. van Benthem, editors, *Logic and Philosophy Today*, volume 2, pages 333–377. College Publications, 2011.

[8] P. C. Fishburn. Paradoxes of voting. *The American Political Science Review*, 68(2):537–546, 1974.

[9] W. Gaertner. *A Primer in Social Choice Theory*. LSE Perspectives in Economic Analysis. Oxford University Press, 2006.

[10] R. L. Keeney and H. Raiffa. *Decisions with Multiple Objectives: Preferences and Value Tradeoffs*. Cambridge University Press, 2nd edition, 1993.

[11] C. Labreuche. A general framework for explaining the results of a multi-attribute preference model. *Artificial Intelligence*, 175(7–8):1410–1448, 2011.

[12] C. Labreuche, N. Maudet, V. Mousseau, and W. Ouerdane. Explanation of the robust additive preference model by even swap sequences. In *Proc. 6th Multidisciplinary Workshop on Advances in Preference Handling*, pages 21–26, 2012.

[13] I. McLean and A. B. Urken. *Classics of Social Choice*. University of Michigan Press, 1995.

[14] A. Ranta. Translating between language and logic: What is easy and what is difficult. In N. Bjørner and V. Sofronie-Stokkermans, editors, *Proc. 23rd International Conference on Automated Deduction (CADE-2011)*, pages 5–25. Springer-Verlag, 2011.

[15] D. G. Saari. Explaining all three-alternative voting outcomes. *Journal of Economic Theory*, 87(2): 313–355, 1999.

[16] D. G. Saari. *Decisions and Elections: Explaining the Unexpected*. Cambridge University Press, 2001.

[17] P. Tang and F. Lin. Computer-aided proofs of Arrow's and other impossibility theorems. *Artificial Intelligence*, 173(11):1041–1053, 2009.

[18] A. D. Taylor. *Social Choice and the Mathematics of Manipulation*. Cambridge University Press, 2005.

[19] D. van Dalen. *Logic and Structure*. Springer-Verlag, 5th edition, 2013.

[20] M. Wenzel. Isar: A generic interpretative approach to readable formal proof documents. In *Proc. 12th International Conference on Theorem Proving in Higher Order Logics (TPHOLs-1999)*, pages 167–183. Springer-Verlag, 1999.

[21] H. P. Young. An axiomatization of Borda's rule. *Journal of Economic Theory*, 9(1):43–52, 1974.

Achieving Fully Proportional Representation by Clustering Voters

Piotr Faliszewski
AGH University
Krakow, Poland
faliszew@agh.edu.pl

Arkadii Slinko
University of Auckland
Auckland, New Zealand
a.slinko@auckland.ac.nz

Kolja Stahl
TU Berlin, Germany
kstahl@mailbox.tu-berlin.de

Nimrod Talmon*
Weizmann Institute of Science
Rehovot, Israel
nimrodtalmon77@gmail.com

ABSTRACT

Both the Chamberlin–Courant and Monroe rules are voting rules solving the problem of so-called fully proportional representation: they select committees whose members represent the voters so that voters' satisfaction with their assigned representatives is maximized. These rules suffer from a common disadvantage, being that it is computationally intractable to compute the winning committee exactly. As both of these rules, explicitly or implicitly, partition voters, they can be seen as clustering the voters so that the voters in each group share the same representative. This suggests studying approximation algorithms for these voting rules by means of cluster analysis, which is the subject of this paper. We develop several algorithms based on clustering the voters and analyze their performance experimentally.

General Terms

Algorithms, Experimentation

Keywords

multiwinner elections, clustering, voting

1. INTRODUCTION

We study the problem of winner determination under the Chamberlin–Courant [4] and Monroe [13] multiwinner rules. These remarkable rules achieve two goals simultaneously: they select a representative committee, thus solving the problem of proportional representation of voters in an indirect democracy, and also assign a representative to each voter, securing the accountability of elected representatives to the electorate. These two rules are among the very few known rules that achieve both these goals[1] but, unfortunately, computing the winners for both Chamberlin–Courant and Monroe rules is NP-hard [2, 9, 15]. A number of algorithms for this problem has been developed. Some of them are exact, computing winners in polynomial time in restricted domains [2, 19, 22], some are fixed-parameter tractable [2] and hence computing winners efficiently when certain parameters are small, and some are fast approximation algorithms that work on the universal domain [2, 9, 18, 14, 16]. Here we focus on the approximation approach and show that by using randomization and some ideas from cluster analysis, we can design algorithms that perform noticeably better than some of the algorithms known from the literature. We evaluate our algorithms experimentally.

The Chamberlin–Courant and Monroe rules operate as follows. We are given a set C of candidates, a set V of voters, and a number k, which is the size of the committee to be elected. Each voter ranks the candidates from the most to the least desirable one, and the goal is to pick a size-k committee of candidates that, in some sense, represents the voters in the best possible way. A convenient way of thinking about the setting is that we must elect a parliament of predetermined size k to act on behalf of the voters.

To measure the quality of the assignment, there is a universal satisfaction function γ, such that for each number i, $\gamma(i)$ quantifies the satisfaction of a voter from being represented by a candidate that this voter ranks as its ith best.[2] The Monroe and Chamberlin–Courant rules match each voter to her[3] representative so that: (a) There are at most k candidates that represent the voters (these are the winners of the election; that is, the parliament members), and (b) the sum of the satisfactions of the voters from their representatives is as high as possible. Under the Monroe rule, we additionally require that every selected candidate represents the same number of voters (plus or minus one, due to divisibility issues). Under Chamberlin-Courant the 'one man, one vote' principle is solved differently: in the elected

*Main work was done while affiliated with TU Berlin.

[1]A common practice of splitting the electorate into electoral districts and using a single-winner voting rule in each district can solve the second problem but not the first. Single transferable vote, STV, can be seen as another example of a rule that achieves proportional representation but not accountability.

[2]The most typical satisfaction function, used in the original definitions of Monroe and Chamberlin–Courant, is the Borda score, which for m alternatives is $\gamma_{\mathrm{Borda}}(i) = m - i$.

[3]For clarity, we refer to the voters as females and to the candidates as males.

Appears in: *Proceedings of the 15th International Conference on Autonomous Agents and Multiagent Systems (AAMAS 2016), J. Thangarajah, K. Tuyls, C. Jonker, S. Marsella (eds.), May 9–13, 2016, Singapore.*

assembly a representative is given a weight proportional to the number of voters he represents.

The Monroe and Chamberlin–Courant rules have a number of applications beyond selecting representative bodies in indirect democracies (such as parliaments, university senates, etc.), that include various business planning tasks and public decision making problems [6, 9, 10, 17]. For example, one can imagine a company that needs to pick k products that it would offer to its customers (e.g., because it is too expensive to manufacture more than k different types of products). The company could perform market analysis to find out how customers rank possible products, and then use the Chamberlin–Courant rule to compute which k of them would ensure the customers' highest satisfaction (under the assumption that each customer buys only one product, the one that he or she likes best).

Due to the NP-hardness of computing the winners under the Monroe and the Chamberlin–Courant rules, it is usually difficult to use these rules directly. Thus, using approximation algorithms in many circumstances is inevitable. There are two main ways of doing so:

Direct approach. In this case, we use an approximation algorithm for either the Monroe or Chamberlin–Courant rule as a replacement for the rule itself. This is approach is suitable for business-related settings and recommendation systems. In these settings the input data is, typically, already distorted and the additional distortion introduced by using an approximation algorithm is inconsequential. On the other hand, this approach is more controversial in the case of political elections. If one were to use an approximation algorithm as a voting rule, one would have to, for example, argue that it has desirable axiomatic properties (interestingly, Elkind et al. [6] have shown that this is the case for one of the approximation algorithms for the Monroe rule; earlier, Caragiannis et al [3] have shown an approximation algorithm for Dodgson's rule that has better axiomatic properties than the rule itself).

Indirect approach. This approach is suitable in the political elections setting. The election organizers announce that the election is to be held using, say, Monroe's rule with a given satisfaction function. Afterwards, they collect the votes, and make the raw election data available to the society. In a given amount of time, everyone is allowed to submit an election outcome (that is, an assignment of the representatives to the voters). The electoral committee also makes its own calculation. The assignment that leads to the highest total satisfaction is implemented. This approach can be taken in high-stake elections, e.g., in parliamentary elections, where one can expect the interested parties to invest significant effort into obtaining the best—the highest scoring—assignment (naturally, one should expect different parties to try to obtain the highest number of seats for themselves, but since at least two parties would be competing, the result should be fair).

Whatever the approach, it is important to have efficient approximation algorithms for our rules. Luckily, in both cases it is perfectly natural for the algorithms to be randomized. Randomization is noncontroversial in the direct approach due to the fact that, typically, the input data is distorted anyway (e.g, is based on the market analysis, which itself is noisy), and in the indirect approach it does not matter how one obtains the committee as long as its total satisfaction is good.

Our contribution. Currently, the best approximation algorithms for the Monroe and Chamberlin–Courant rules (in terms of the guaranteed approximation ratio) are due to Skowron et al. [18]. Another, very practical, approximation algorithm (for the Chamberlin–Courant rule only) is due to Lu and Boutilier [9]. In this paper we provide heuristic means of improving the outcomes of these algorithms and we show, through appropriate experiments, that our techniques indeed lead to substantial improvements.

Our main idea is to treat the problem of computing the winning committee as a clustering problem. Consider a situation where we are given a specific committee of size k. For both the Monroe and the Chamberlin–Courant rules, it is possible to compute the optimal assignment of the voters to the candidates in this committee efficiently [2]. This assignment partitions the voters into natural clusters (each cluster contains the voters represented by the same candidate).

On the other hand, given a partition, the optimal way to select a committee of representatives would be to assign to voters of each part the Borda winner of the subelection conducted in that part. We can now put both considerations together in the following algorithm. Starting from a certain initial partition and initial assignment, we can reassign representatives optimally, then calculate the Borda winners in each part of the new partition and form the committee and the assignment for the next iteration. Each step increases the total satisfaction of the voters and we repeat this process until we reach a fixed-point, where the representative of each cluster is its local winner. It is easy to see that this procedure is an incarnation of the standard iterative clustering algorithm [5, 8] (in a certain way, our idea also resembles cluster sampling; see, e.g., the textbook of Thompson [20]).

It is quite intuitive that the quality of the committee output by the above procedure depends strongly on the quality of the initial committee, and there are several ways in which to choose it. One can, for example, select the candidates at random, or use the output of an approximation algorithm, e.g., that of Lu and Boutilier [9] or Skowron et al. [18]. Neither of these approaches appears to be perfect, though, since both quickly lead to finding local optima that the algorithm cannot escape (in the former case, this is due to starting from a random committee that, possibly, cannot be improved well in our iterative fashion; in the latter case, because the starting committee is *too good*). Yet, we find that combining both these strategies gives very good results.

We evaluate our clustering algorithm on a number of elections that we obtain using the Polya-Eggenberger urn model [1]. It turns out that the results of our best algorithm, on the average, are noticeably better than those obtained using approximation algorithms known from the literature.

2. PRELIMINARIES

An election E is a pair (C, V), where $C = \{c_1, \ldots, c_m\}$ is a set of candidates and $V = (v_1, \ldots, v_n)$ is the collection of voters. Each voter v_i has a total order $\succ_{v_i}$ over C, referred to as her preference order. We write $\mathrm{rank}_v(c)$ to denote the position of candidate c in v's preference order (e.g., if v ranks c on the top position, then $\mathrm{rank}_v(c) = 1$).

A multiwinner voting rule $\mathcal{R}$ is a function that, given an election $E = (C, V)$ and an integer k, $k \leq |C|$, returns a set $\mathcal{R}(E, k)$ of size-k winning committees; each committee in the set ties as a winner of the election. Below we describe the Monroe [13] and Chamberlin–Couarant rules [4].

Assignment functions. Consider an election $E = (C, V)$ with $V = (v_1, \ldots, v_n)$, and let k be the size of the committee to be elected. A k-CC-assignment function for this election is a function $\Phi\colon V \to C$ such that $|\Phi(V)| = |\{\Phi(v_i) \mid v_i \in V\}| \leq k$. Intuitively, we say that the candidate $\Phi(v_i)$ is the representative of voter v_i, and we say that candidate c represents voters from the set $\Phi^{-1}(c) = \{v_i \in V \mid \Phi(v_i) = c\}$. A k-Monroe-assignment function is a k-CC-assignment function that additionally satisfies the following condition: For each candidate c that represents a nonempty set of voters, it holds that $\lfloor \frac{n}{k} \rfloor \leq |\Phi^{-1}(c)| \leq \lceil \frac{n}{k} \rceil$.

Satisfaction function. Consider an election $E = (C, V)$ with the candidate set $C = \{c_1, \ldots, c_m\}$. We say that the function $\gamma\colon \{1, \ldots, m\} \to \mathbb{N}$ is a satisfaction function if it is nonincreasing. Intuitively, $\gamma(i)$ is the measure of satisfaction that a voter gets from being represented by the candidate that she ranks as her i'th best. The classical versions of the Chamberlin-Courant and Monroe rules use the Borda satisfaction function $\gamma_{\mathrm{Borda}}(i) = m - i$.

Monroe and Chamberlin–Courant rules. Consider an election $E = (C, V)$, the size of the committee k, and a satisfaction function γ. Let Φ be a k-CC-assignment function for E. We define the total satisfaction of the voters with Φ to be:

$$\Gamma(\Phi) = \textstyle\sum_{v \in V} \gamma(\mathrm{rank}_v(\Phi(v))).$$

The Chamberlin–Courant rule for γ, denoted γ-CC, outputs all size-k committees W for which there exists a k-CC-assignment function Φ such that: (a) $\Gamma(\Phi)$ has maximum value, and (b) $\Phi(V) \subseteq W$.[4] The Monroe rule for γ, denoted γ-Monroe, is defined in the same way, but with the exception that we consider k-Monroe-assignment functions only.

It is well-known that computing even a single winning committee under either Monroe or Chamberlin–Courant rules is NP-hard [9, 15] and hard in the parameterized sense [2]. Nonetheless, given a set of k candidates, it is possible to efficiently compute an optimal k-CC-assignment function and an optimal k-Monroe-assignment function that uses these candidates as representatives. For the case of γ-CC, this is obvious (by simply picking, for each voter, the candidate from the given set of k candidates which she prefer the best) and for Monroe there is a network-flow-based algorithm which is due to Betzler et al. [2]; later, we will refer to this algorithm as the BSU-algorithm.

We use variants of these algorithms that also work for partial committees, that is, for sets of *up to* k candidates. In the case of γ-CC rules, this is trivial (for each $k' \leq k$, every k'-CC-assignment function is also a k-CC-assignment function). For the case of γ-Monroe rules, the situation is a bit more complicated because each candidate can represent at most $\lceil \frac{n}{k} \rceil$ voters. So, when we consider partial committees for γ-Monroe, we also consider partial k-Monroe-assignment functions. A partial k-Monroe-assignment function is a regular k-Monroe-assignment functions that can assign the *null* candidate $\bot$ to some voters. There is no constraint on the number of voters to whom the null candidate is assigned, and we assume that for each voter v we have $\gamma(\mathrm{rank}_v(\bot)) = 0$.

[4]This last condition, if a bit weird at first sight, takes into account the possibility that while the committee is required to contain k candidates, there can be fewer than k candidates that represent any voters.

Approximation algorithms. Let γ be a satisfaction function and let $\mathcal{R}$ be either the Monroe or Chamberlin–Courant rule for γ. We consider an election $E = (C, V)$ and committee size k. For $\beta \in [0, 1]$, we say that a k-$\mathcal{R}$-assignment function Φ is a β-approximation of $\mathcal{R}(E, k)$, if it holds that $\Gamma(\Phi) \geq \beta \cdot \mathrm{OPT}$, where OPT is the highest possible total voter satisfaction under $\mathcal{R}$ in the election E. We also speak of committees as β-approximations: We say that a committee W is β-approximate for a given election, if the optimal assignment function computed for this committee is β-approximate. A β-approximation algorithm for $\mathcal{R}$ is an algorithm that always outputs a β-approximate committee.

There are several approximation algorithms for Monroe and Chamberlin–Courant rules [9, 16, 14, 18]. We will discuss the two most relevant ones to our work in Section 3.2, where we describe the initialization step of our heuristics.

3. ALGORITHMS

In this section we describe our algorithms. We first describe two of their most important components, the clustering heuristic and the initialization heuristics (which, in fact, can be used on its own, without the clustering step), and then, based on these, we suggest six algorithms.

3.1 Clustering Heuristic

Let $\mathcal{R}$ be either Monroe or CC. We are given an election $E = (C, V)$, a committee size k, and a satisfaction function γ. The goal is to compute a β-approximate solution for $\mathcal{R}$, for as high a value of β as possible.

Our algorithms are inspired by the heuristic algorithms that are commonly employed for k-means clustering [8] and proceed according to the following steps:

1. Obtain an initial committee W_1 (e.g., by random choice, but we will describe more involved scenarios later). Then, using the BSU-algorithm, compute the initial assignment function Φ_1 that uses the candidates from W_1.

2. Keep generating assignment functions Φ_i, for $i = 2, 3, \ldots$, using the following steps, until you generate a function Φ_i that is equal to Φ_{i-1}:

   (a) For each candidate $c \in W_{i-1}$, compute the set of voters $V_c = \Phi_{i-1}^{-1}(c)$.

   (b) For each V_c computed in the previous step, find a candidate c' such that $\sum_{v \in V_c} \gamma(\mathrm{rank}_v(c'))$ is maximal.

   (c) Let W_i be the set of candidates c' computed in the previous step. If $|W_i| \leq k$, add to it $k - |W_i|$ randomly chosen candidates.

   (d) Using the BSU-algorithm, compute the assignment function Φ_i for committee W_i.

3. When the procedure stops for some value $i = t$, output the committee W_t and the assignment function Φ_t.

To get some feeling for how the procedure works, let us consider an example.

EXAMPLE 1. *Consider an election with the set of candidates $\{a, b, c\}$ and the following voters: $v_1: a \succ b \succ c$, $v_2: c \succ b \succ a$, $v_3: c \succ b \succ a$. We use a satisfaction function γ such that $\gamma(1) = 4$, $\gamma(2) = 3$, and $\gamma(3) = 0$. We set the committee size to be $k = 2$. The optimal solution is $\{a, c\}$ and irrespective of which committee our clustering heuristic starts with, after a single iteration it outputs the optimal solution. For example, if it starts with $W_1 = \{b, c\}$, then we have Φ_1 such that $\Phi^{-1}(b) = \{v_1\}$ and $\Phi^{-1}(c) = \{v_2, v_3\}$. The algorithm computes $W_2 = \{a, c\}$ and terminates.*

Let us now discuss some details of the procedure. First, we note that it always terminates. This is so, because in every iteration within Step 2, if we obtain $\Phi_i \neq \Phi_{i-1}$, then it must be the case that $\Gamma(\Phi_i) > \Gamma(\Phi_{i-1})$.[5] In fact, if the satisfaction function is polynomially bounded, then the clustering procedure terminates in polynomial time (in essence, because there are only polynomially many different scores a committee may have, and the score of a committee improves in every step).

PROPOSITION 1. *If the satisfaction function used by $\mathcal{R}$ is polynomially bounded, then the clustering procedure runs in polynomial time.*

Naturally, the clustering heuristic never outputs a solution that is worse than the initial assignment. Also, as we will also see in the experimental evaluation of our heuristics, the choice of the initial committee W_1 is very important and needs to balance two factors. On the one hand, the committee W_1 should be of a relatively high quality, so that the algorithm starts near a very good solution. On the other hand, it should be sufficiently random, to avoid getting stuck in local maxima.

3.2 Initialization Heuristics

Our algorithms for computing the initial assignment are based on the greedy approximation algorithms of Lu and Boutilier [9] and Skowron et al. [18] (specifically, we merge the ideas of Skowron et al.'s Algorithms C and GM, which generalizes the algorithm of Lu and Boutilier). We first present the general skeleton of our initialization algorithm and then describe how to instantiate it to obtain the particular algorithms we are interested in (the algorithms of Lu and Boutilier and Skowron et al. are special cases of these).

We are given an election $E = (C, V)$, a committee size k, and a satisfaction function γ. We also have a parameter d that specifies how many partial committees we keep after each iteration (the idea of keeping several committees is due to Skowron et al. [18]). Our algorithm proceeds as follows:

1. We form the initial set D_0 of partial committees that contains only one partial committee, the empty set.
2. We execute k iterations, in each one we extend each partial committee in D by one candidate. Each iteration is either a *greedy iteration* or a *randomized iteration*, depending on a given criterion (to be specified separately for each of the algorithms which we use). Let i be the number of the iteration to be executed:

   Greedy iteration. For each partial committee W from D_{i-1}, we form all partial committees that result from extending W by a single candidate (not yet in W). We insert all the partial committees that we obtain into set D'_i. For each partial committee in D'_i we compute an optimal assignment Φ (using the BSU-algorithm) and compute its voter satisfaction $\Gamma(\Phi)$. We form the set D_i by picking up to d partial committees from D'_i that have the highest voter satisfactions.

   Randomized iteration. We start by setting D_i to be empty. Then we repeat the following procedure d times: We choose one of the d committees from D_{i-1} uniformly at random and extend it by one of the candidates not in the committee, who is also chosen uniformly at random. We put the resulting partial committee into D_i.
3. Finally, D_k contains up to d committees, each with k candidates. We output the one with the highest voter satisfaction (as computed by the BSU-algorithm).

Based on this general skeleton, we form the following algorithms for the initialization step (we set the parameter d to either be 1—for the simplest settings—or to be 5, since the results of Skowron et al. [18, Fig. 13] suggest that this is a sufficiently large value to obtain the benefit of keeping multiple committees, and, at the same time, is small enough to not affect the running time too much):

G1. This algorithm uses greedy iterations only and $d = 1$. This is exactly the algorithm of Lu and Boutlier [9] for the Chamberlin–Courant family of rules and the GM algorithm of Skowron et al. [18] for the case of the Monroe family of rules. The algorithm guarantees that the committee it outputs is $(1 - \frac{1}{e})$-approximate. (For the case of γ_{Borda}-Monroe, the approximation ratio is guaranteed to be $1 - \frac{k-1}{2(m-1)} - \frac{H_k}{k}$, where m is the number of candidates and H_k is the k'th harmonic number [18]).

G5. This is the same algorithm as G1, except that it uses parameter $d = 5$. Naturally, it provides the same approximation guarantees as G1.

D1. This algorithm combines greedy iterations and randomized ones in the following way. We are given two additional parameters, p and e, such that $0 < p < 1$ and $e \in \mathbb{R}_+$, and at the i'th iteration we make a randomized step with probability $p^{i \cdot e}$ and a greedy step with probability $1 - p^{i \cdot e}$. (The name of the algorithms stands for *decaying probability of a random iteration.*) We set the parameter $d = 1$.

D5. The same as D1, but with $d = 5$.

R(1,5). This algorithm combines the two above algorithms. We run D1 five times to obtain five committees. Then we run D5 five times to obtain another five committees. Out of these ten committees, we output the one with the highest voter satisfaction.

While algorithm R(1,5) may appear somewhat ad hoc, the underlying idea is quite clear. We run algorithms D1 and D5 to explore the space of committees that should be *relatively good*, due to the greedy steps, but are not *too good*, due to the randomized steps. We use both D1 and D5 to obtain some more varied committees. Naturally, in practical situations, one should likely tweak the algorithm in various ways. Perhaps use only D5 and not D1, perhaps use more or fewer iterations, etc. Our point here is not necessarily to show the most effective initialization algorithm, but rather to show

[5] Technically, for this to hold we need to assume that when computing the candidates c', we break ties in favor of the representative c.

the power of combining greedy and randomized steps (indeed, if one were to use our algorithms to compute the result of a political election, as in the indirect approach from the introduction, one would likely try as many various combinations of the parameters of the algorithms as time would permit).

3.3 Putting the Algorithms Together

Altogether, in our experimental section we consider six algorithms. The first three are, simply, the initialization algorithms G1, G5, and R(1,5) that we have described above. The next three, algorithms G1C, G5C, and R(1,5)C, first use the respective initialization algorithm to find a set of committees (we let the algorithms output all the committees they construct, without picking the best one), then we apply the clustering heuristic to each of them, and finally output the committee with the highest voter satisfaction. The algorithms with the clustering step are bound to be better than those without it. It is interesting—and we evaluate it in the next section—how often and to what extent the clustering step improves the solution.

For algorithms R(1,5) and R(1,5)C, we use the following parameters. We set $p = 0.75$ and $e = 1$ (e.g., in the first iteration, D1 has 0.75 probability of executing a randomized step, in the second iteration ≈ 0.56, in the third iteration ≈ 0.42, and so on).

4. EXPERIMENTAL ANALYSIS

We now present our experimental results. We have three main goals. First, we would like to evaluate how well our algorithms perform (that is, how close are the solutions they produce to optimal outcomes). Second, we would like to evaluate how effective is the randomization in algorithms R(1,5) and R(1,5)C, as compared to the other, fully deterministic, algorithms. Third, we would like to evaluate how effective the clustering step is.

4.1 Experimental Setup

We have run our algorithms in a number of experiments. For each experiment we have generated 500 instances of elections (we used the Polya-Eggenberger urn model; see below), each with $m = 100$ candidates and $n = 100$ voters. For each experiment we used three satisfaction functions: γ_{Borda}, γ_{convex}, and $\gamma_{\mathrm{concave}}$.

Function γ_{Borda} is the Borda satisfaction function, i.e., $\gamma_{\mathrm{Borda}}(i) = m - i$, for $i \in [m]$. Functions γ_{convex} and $\gamma_{\mathrm{concave}}$ are certain convex and concave functions (respectively) and are depicted in Figure 1. Formally, they are defined as:

$$\gamma_{\mathrm{concave}}(i) = m\left(\frac{-m+i+1}{m-1}\right)^7 + m \ , \ \gamma_{\mathrm{convex}}(i) = m\left(\frac{m-i-1}{m-1}\right)^7.$$

In most cases we have considered relatively small committees ($k = 3$ and $k = 5$), but we have also considered several much larger committees ($k = 27$ and $k = 47$). For each experiment, we run our six algorithms, and additionally we computed the optimal solution using an ILP solver (see the works of Lu and Boutilier [9] and Skowron et al. [18] for ILP formulations of the winner determination problems).[6]

[6]This is why we chose elections with 100 candidates and 100 voters: They are small enough to compute optimal solutions using ILP, but large enough to have some nontrivial structure.

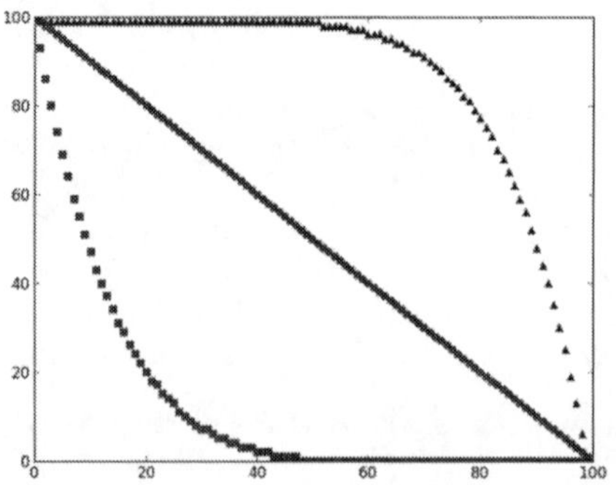

Figure 1: Our satisfaction functions: γ_{convex} (red rectangles; bottom), γ_{Borda} (green circles; center), and $\gamma_{\mathrm{concave}}$ (blue triangles; top).

We generated the elections using the Polya–Eggenberger urn model (see the works of Skowron et al. [18], Berg and Lepelley [1], McCabe-Dansted and Slinko [12], Walsh [21], and Erdelyi et al. [7] for some other examples where this model was used). This model operates as follows: For a candidate set C, we create an urn which initially contains one copy of each of the $|C|!$ possible preference orders over C. To generate a vote, we draw a preference order randomly from the urn and include it in the election. Then we return this order back to the urn, together with $\alpha \cdot |C|!$ additional copies, where α is a parameter of contagion (for $\alpha = 0$ we would get the impartial culture model, where votes are drawn uniformly at random).

The sheer number of experiments that we have run is too large for presenting all the results which we have obtained. Thus, in the discussion below, we present only some representative results (we show results for $k = 3$, $\alpha \in \{0.05, 0.25\}$, for both Monroe and CC, for all our satisfaction functions; we also show three other interesting experiments).

4.2 Discussion of the Results

We present the results of our experiments in Figures 2–16. For each of the plots we indicate the voting rule (Chamberlin–Courant or Monroe), the satisfaction function ($\gamma_{\mathrm{concave}}$, γ_{Borda}, γ_{convex}), the size of the committee (3, 5, 27, 47), and the value of the parameter α for the urn model (0.05 or 0.25). The plots show the distribution of the voter satisfaction achieved by each of our algorithms (averaged over 500 elections generated in each given experiment), scaled so that the optimal satisfaction is 1. The red line (in the middle of each rectangle) indicates the median quality of the obtained solutions. The blue rectangle covers solutions from the 25th to 75th percentile (i.e., it shows the range of the satisfaction values of solutions worse than the best quarter of the obtained solutions, but better than the worst quarter of the solutions). The top and bottom black lines indicate 1.5 times the interquartile range, and smaller blue crosses below and above them indicate outliers.

In each of our plots, each column stands for one of our six algorithms. The number next to G1C (G5C, R(1,5)C) is the number of instances for which G1C (G5C, R(1,5)C) performed better than G1 (G5, R(1,5)). This number shows how frequently the clustering step provides an improvement.

How well do our algorithms perform? All our algorithms achieve very good approximation ratios, though there are noticeable differences in their quality. Typically, G1 performs worst of all (but still, the median result tends to be at least 0.95 of the voter satisfaction in the optimal solution) and R(1,5)C tends to perform best.

How effective are the randomization steps? It is quite evident that introducing the randomization steps has very positive impact on the quality of the generated solutions. If we compare the results for R(1,5) and R(1,5)C to the results for G5 and G5C, respectively, then the randomized algorithms never perform noticeably worse, and often achieve slightly better results (but see the next point).

How effective is the clustering step? It turns out that in most scenarios applying the clustering step improves the solution by, at least, some amount, and in some scenarios it improves it greatly. This is most evident when we compare the results of algorithms R(1,5) and R(1,5)C for the Monroe family of rules. In this case, applying the clustering step often improves (quite significantly, judging by the improvement of the median satisfaction of the voters) the solution in many more than half of the instances. On the other hand, if we compare the results of G1 and G1C, or of G5 and G5C, then the clustering step does help, but on fewer instances and to a lesser extent. This confirms that generating an appropriate initial committee is very important.

Contrasting the figures corresponding to $\alpha = 0.05$ to the figures corresponding to $\alpha = 0.25$, we see that with the increase of the coefficient of contagion (i.e., the homogeneity of the population) the clustering step is becoming noticeably more useful. The reason for this is not exactly clear but, intuitively, with the increase of contagion the clusters in the data become more pronounced, hence the clustering step becomes more useful.

5. SUMMARY

We have considered the problem of computing approximate solutions for the Monroe and Chamberlin–Courant rules via algorithms combining the existing greedy approximation algorithms, randomized steps, and clustering. We have shown that putting these ideas together leads to noticeably more effective algorithms than previously known from the literature. In particular, our results have shown that interleaving greedy steps with randomized steps leads to committees that are very good starting points for the clustering step. Our algorithms can quite easily be modified to satisfy soft constraints such as "try to find as good a committee as possible with as many members of a given party as possible."

For future work, it would be interesting to perform similar experiments as ours on real election data (e.g., from PrefLib [11]). Second, it would be interesting to find a principled way of setting the parameters of our procedures (we relied on ad hoc settings). Third, we are interested in theoretical explanations of why interleaving greedy and random step gives better outcomes than greedy steps alone.

Acknowledgments

We are grateful to the reviewers for their comments. Piotr Faliszewski was supported by NCN grant DEC-2012/06/M/ST1/00358. Arkadii Slinko was supported by the Royal Society of NZ Marsden Fund UOA-254. Kolja Stahl was supported by DFG project PAWS (NI 369/10). Nimrod Talmon was supported by the DFG Research Training Group MDS (GRK 1408).

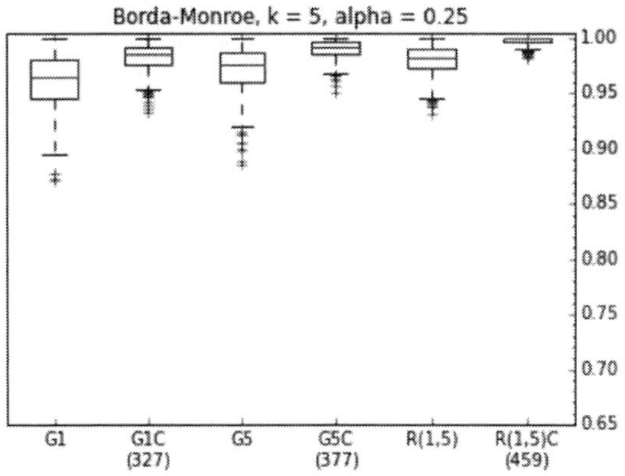

Figure 2: Performance of our algorithms for the Monroe voting rule, committee size = 5, Borda scores, and the urn model with $\alpha = 0.25$.

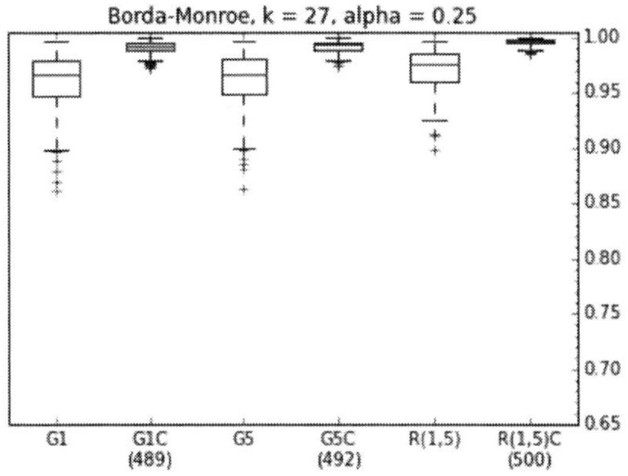

Figure 3: Performance of our algorithms for the Monroe voting rule, committee size = 27, Borda scores, and the urn model with $\alpha = 0.25$.

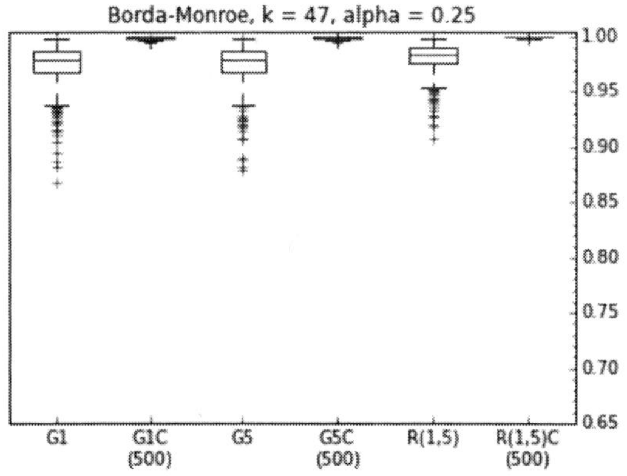

Figure 4: Performance of our algorithms for the Monroe voting rule, committee size = 47, Borda scores, and the urn model with $\alpha = 0.25$.

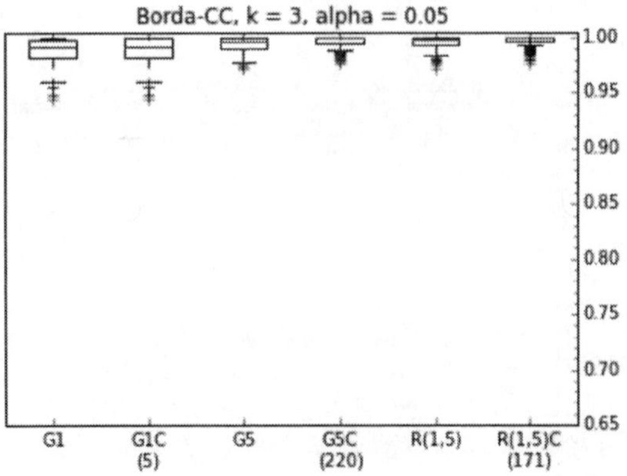

Figure 5: Performance of our algorithms for the Chamberlin–Courant voting rule, committee size = 3, Borda scores, and the urn model with $\alpha = 0.05$.

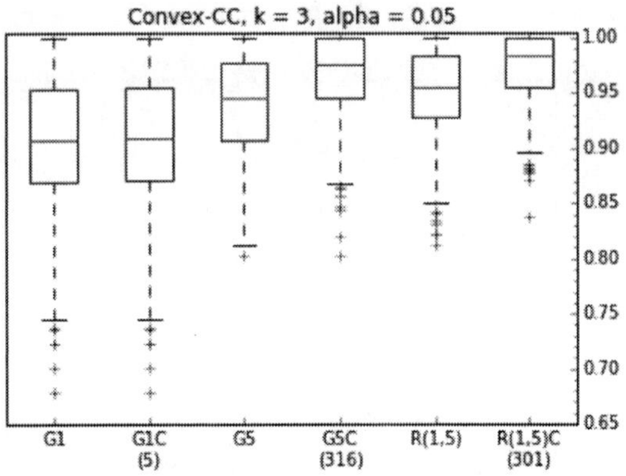

Figure 6: Performance of our algorithms for the Chamberlin–Courant voting rule, committee size = 3, Convex scores, and the urn model with $\alpha = 0.05$.

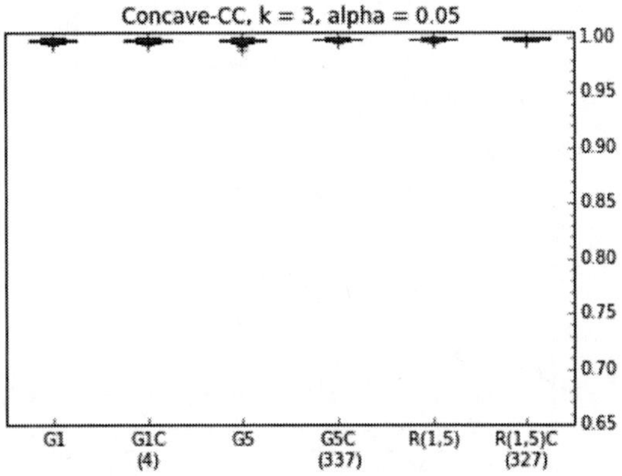

Figure 7: Performance of our algorithms for the Chamberlin–Courant voting rule, committee size = 3, Concave scores, and the urn model with $\alpha = 0.05$.

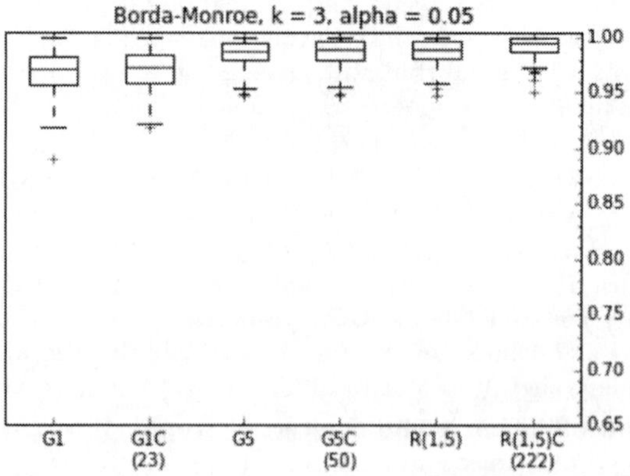

Figure 8: Performance of our algorithms for the Monroe voting rule, committee size = 3, Borda scores, and the urn model with $\alpha = 0.05$.

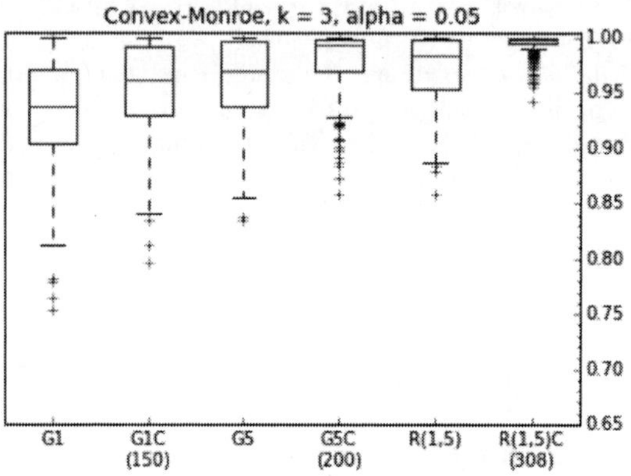

Figure 9: Performance of our algorithms for the Monroe voting rule, committee size = 3, Convex scores, and the urn model with $\alpha = 0.05$.

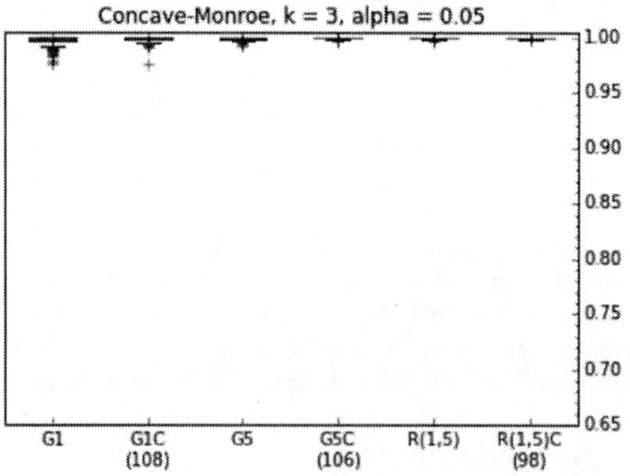

Figure 10: Performance of our algorithms for the Monroe voting rule, committee size = 3, Concave scores, and the urn model with $\alpha = 0.05$.

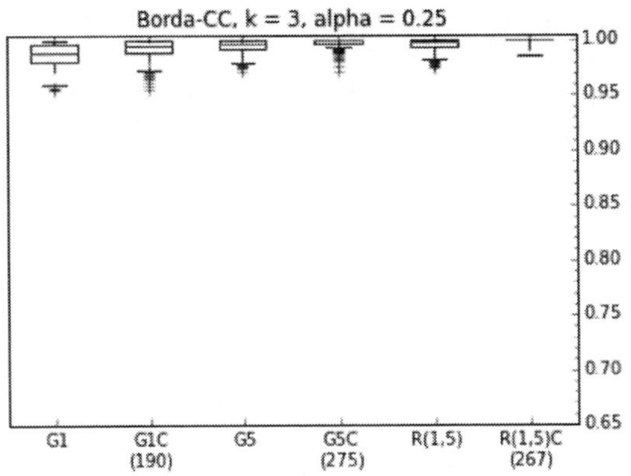

Figure 11: Performance of our algorithms for the Chamberlin–Courant voting rule, committee size = 3, Borda scores, and the urn model with $\alpha = 0.25$.

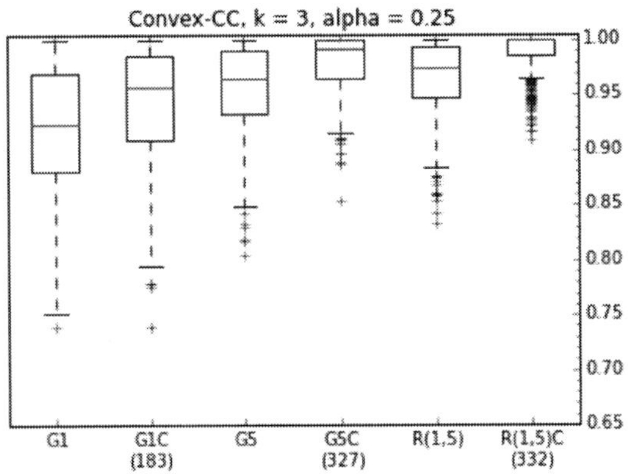

Figure 12: Performance of our algorithms for the Chamberlin–Courant voting rule, committee size = 3, Convex scores, and the urn model with $\alpha = 0.25$.

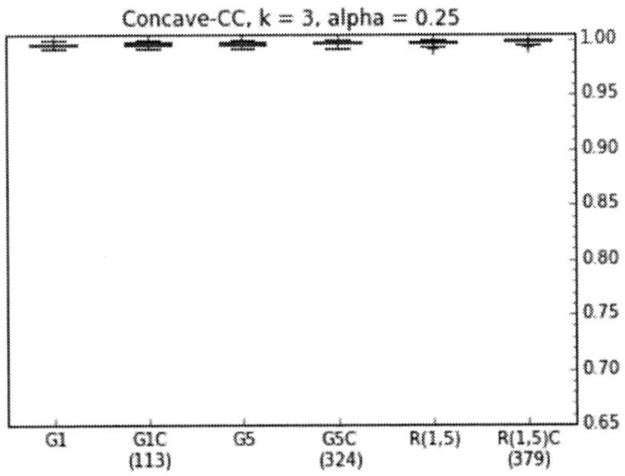

Figure 13: Performance of our algorithms for the Chamberlin–Courant voting rule, committee size = 3, Concave scores, and the urn model with $\alpha = 0.25$.

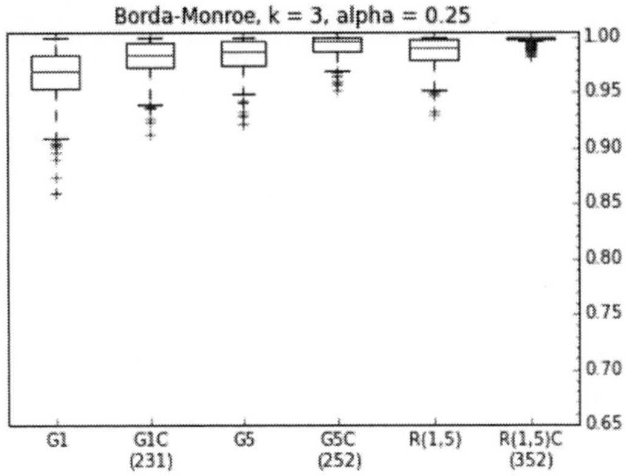

Figure 14: Performance of our algorithms for the Monroe voting rule, committee size = 3, Borda scores, and the urn model with $\alpha = 0.25$.

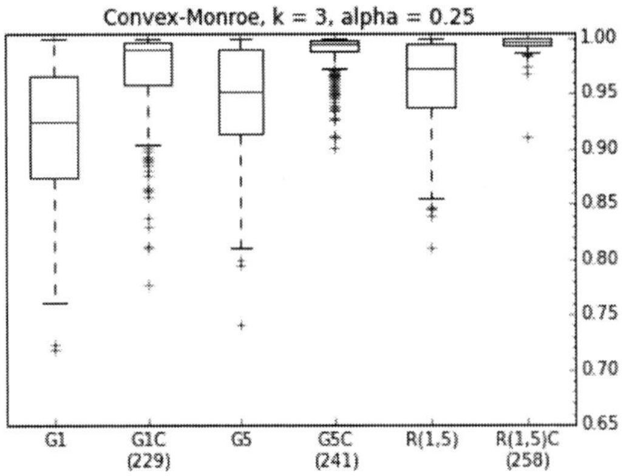

Figure 15: Performance of our algorithms for the Monroe voting rule, committee size = 3, Convex scores, and the urn model with $\alpha = 0.25$.

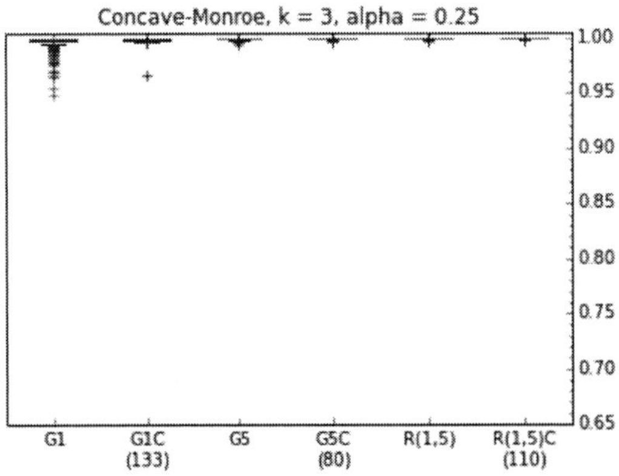

Figure 16: Performance of our algorithms for the Monroe voting rule, committee size = 3, Concave scores, and the urn model with $\alpha = 0.25$.

REFERENCES

[1] S. Berg and D. Lepelley. On Probability Models in Voting Theory. *Statistica Neerlandica*, 48(2):133–146, 1994.

[2] N. Betzler, A. Slinko, and J. Uhlmann. On the computation of fully proportional representation. *Journal of Artificial Intelligence Research*, 47:475–519, 2013.

[3] I. Caragiannis, C. Kaklamanis, N. Karanikolas, and A. Procaccia. Socially desirable approximations for Dodgson's voting rule. In *Proceedings of the 11th ACM Conference on Electronic Commerce*, pages 253–262. ACM Press, June 2010.

[4] B. Chamberlin and P. Courant. Representative deliberations and representative decisions: Proportional representation and the Borda rule. *American Political Science Review*, 77(3):718–733, 1983.

[5] R. O. Duda, P. E. Hart, et al. *Pattern classification and scene analysis*, volume 3. Wiley New York, 1973.

[6] E. Elkind, P. Faliszewski, P. Skowron, and A. Slinko. Properties of multiwinner voting rules. In *Proceedings of the 13th International Conference on Autonomous Agents and Multiagent Systems*, pages 53–60, May 2014.

[7] G. Erdélyi, M. R. Fellows, J. Rothe, and L. Schend. Control complexity in Bucklin and fallback voting: An experimental analysis. *J. Comput. Syst. Sci.*, 81(4):661–670, 2015.

[8] J. A. Hartigan. *Clustering algorithms*. John Wiley & Sons, Inc., 1975.

[9] T. Lu and C. Boutilier. Budgeted social choice: From consensus to personalized decision making. In *Proceedings of the 22nd International Joint Conference on Artificial Intelligence*, pages 280–286, 2011.

[10] T. Lu and C. Boutilier. Value-directed compression of large-scale assignment problems. In *Proceedings of the 29th AAAI Conference on Artificial Intelligecne*, pages 1182–1190, 2015.

[11] N. Mattei and T. Walsh. Preflib: A library for preferences. In *Proceedings of the 3nd International Conference on Algorithmic Decision Theory*, pages 259–270, 2013.

[12] J. C. McCabe-Dansted and A. Slinko. Exploratory analysis of similarities between social choice rules. *Group Decision and Negotiation*, 15(1):77–107, 2006.

[13] B. Monroe. Fully proportional representation. *American Political Science Review*, 89(4):925–940, 1995.

[14] J. Oren and B. Lucier. Online (budgeted) social choice. In *Proceedings of the 28th AAAI Conference on Artificial Intelligecne*, pages 1456–1462, July 2014.

[15] A. Procaccia, J. Rosenschein, and A. Zohar. On the complexity of achieving proportional representation. *Social Choice and Welfare*, 30(3):353–362, 2008.

[16] P. Skowron and P. Faliszewski. Fully proportional representation with approval ballots: Approximating the MaxCover problem with bounded frequencies in FPT time. In *Proceedings of the 29th AAAI Conference on Artificial Intelligecne*, pages 2124–2130, 2015.

[17] P. Skowron, P. Faliszewski, and J. Lang. Finding a collective set of items: From proportional multirepresentation to group recommendation. In *Proceedings of the 29th AAAI Conference on Artificial Intelligecne*, 2015.

[18] P. Skowron, P. Faliszewski, and A. Slinko. Achieving fully proportional representation: Approximability result. *Artificial Intelligence*, 222:67–103, 2015.

[19] P. Skowron, L. Yu, P. Faliszewski, and E. Elkind. The complexity of fully proportional representation for single-crossing electorates. *Theoretical Computer Science*, 569:43–57, 2015.

[20] S. Thompson. *Sampling*. Wiley, 2012.

[21] T. Walsh. Where are the hard manipulation problems? *Journal of Artificial Intelligence Research*, pages 1–29, 2011.

[22] L. Yu, H. Chan, and E. Elkind. Multiwinner elections under preferences that are single-peaked on a tree. In *Proceedings of the 23rd International Joint Conference on Artificial Intelligence*, pages 425–431, 2013.

Algorithms for Destructive Shift Bribery

Andrzej Kaczmarczyk
AGH University
Krakow, Poland
kaczmarczyk.andrzej@gmail.com

Piotr Faliszewski
AGH University
Krakow, Poland
faliszew@agh.edu.pl

ABSTRACT

We study the complexity of DESTRUCTIVE SHIFT BRIBERY. In this problem, we are given an election with a set of candidates and a set of voters (ranking the candidates from best to worst, each), a despised candidate d (typically, one of the current winners), a budget B, and prices for shifting d down in voters' rankings. The goal is to ensure that d is not a winner of the election. We show that this problem is polynomial-time solvable for all scoring protocols (encoded in unary) and the Maximin rule, but is NP-hard for the Copeland rule. This contrasts with the results for the constructive setting (known from the literature), for which the problem is polynomial-time solvable for k-Approval family of rules, but is NP-hard for the Borda, Copeland, and Maximin rules.

Categories and Subject Descriptors

I.2.11 [**Artificial Intelligence**]: Distributed Artificial Intelligence—*Multiagent systems*

Keywords

algorithms, computational complexity, voting, campaign management, bribery

1. INTRODUCTION

We study the complexity of the destructive variant of the SHIFT BRIBERY problem. We consider the family of all (unary encoded) scoring protocols (including the Borda rule and all k-Approval rules), and the Copeland and maximin rules. It turns out that for all of them—except for the Copeland rule—the problem can be solved in polynomial time. This stands in sharp contrast to the constructive case, where the problem is NP-hard [14] (and hard in the parameterized sense [4]) for the Borda, Copeland, and Maximin rules (and is in P for the k-Approval family of rules).

The SHIFT BRIBERY problem was introduced by Elkind et al. [14] to model (a kind of) campaign management problem in elections. The problem is as follows: We are given an election, i.e., a set of candidates and a set of voters that rank the candidates from the most to the least desirable one, a preferred candidate p, a budget B, and the costs for shifting p up in voters' rankings. Our goal is to decide if it is possible to ensure p's victory by shifting p up, without exceeding the budget. In this paper we study a destructive variant of the problem, where the goal is to ensure that a given despised candidate d loses the election, by shifting him or her down in voters' rankings (but, again, each shift comes at a cost and we cannot exceed the given budget).

Studying destructive variants of election problems where the goal is to change the current winner (such as manipulation [8], control [20], and bribery [16, 21, 6, 32]) is a common practice in computational social choice, but our setting is somewhat special. So far, all the destructive variants of the problems were defined by changing the goal from "ensure the victory of the preferred candidate" to "preclude the despised candidate from winning," but the set of available actions remained unaffected e.g. in both the constructive and the destructive problem of control by adding voters, we can add some voters from a given pool of voters and in both the constructive and the destructive bribery problem, we can pay voters to change their votes in some way. In our case, we feel that it is natural to divert from this practice and change the ability of "shifting the distinguished candidate up" to the ability of "shifting the distinguished candidate down". Below we explain why.

If, when defining our destructive problem, we stuck with the "ability to shift up," as in the CONSTRUCTIVE SHIFT BRIBERY problem, we would get the following problem: Ensure that a given despised candidate does not win the election by shifting him or her forward in some of the votes (without exceeding the budget). However, for a monotone voting rule, if a candidate is already winning an election, then shifting him or her forward certainly cannot preclude him or her from winning. This would make our problem interesting only for a relatively small set of nonmonotone rules.[1] Further, the problem certainly would not be modeling what one would intuitively think of as negative, destructive campaigning. Thus, while it certainly would be interesting to study how to exploit nonmonotonicity of rules such as STV and Dodgson to preclude someone from winning, it would not be the most practical way of defining DESTRUCTIVE SHIFT BRIBERY.

Related Work. In recent years, CONSTRUCTIVE SHIFT BRIBERY received quite some attention. The problem was defined by Elkind et al. [14], as a simplified variant of SWAP BRIBERY (which itself received some attention, e.g., in the

Appears in: *Proceedings of the 15th International Conference on Autonomous Agents and Multiagent Systems (AAMAS 2016), J. Thangarajah, K. Tuyls, C. Jonker, S. Marsella (eds.), May 9–13, 2016, Singapore.*

[1] Nonetheless, there are interesting nonmonotone rules, such as the single transferable rule (STV) and the Dodgson rule.

works of Dorn and Schlotter [12], Faliszewski et al. [17], and papers regarding combinatorial domains, such as those of Mattei et al. [23] and Dorn and Krüger [11]; importantly, Shiryaev et al. [31] studied a variant of DESTRUCTIVSWAP BRIBERY and we comment on their work later). Elkind et al. have shown that SHIFT BRIBERY is NP-hard for Borda, Copeland, and Maximin voting rules, but polynomial-time solvable for the k-Approval family of rules. They also gave a 2-approximation algorithm for the case of Borda, that was later generalized to the case of all scoring rules by Elkind and Faliszewski [13]. Chen et al. [4] considered parametrized complexity of CONSTRUCTIVE SHIFT BRIBERY, and have shown a varied set of results (in general, parametrization by the number of positions by which the preferred candidate is shifted tends to lead to FPT algorithms, parametrization by the number of affected voters tends to lead to hardness results, and parametrization by the available budget gives results between these two extremes). Very recently, Bredereck et al. [5] studied the complexity of COMBINATORIAL SHIFT BRIBERY, where a single shift action can affect several voters at a time. The paper is quite related to ours, because it was the first one in which shifting a candidate backward was possible (albeit as a negative side effect, since the authors study the constructive setting).

SHIFT BRIBERY falls into the general group of bribery-related problems, that were first studied by Faliszewski et al. [15] (see also the work of Hazon et al. [19] for a similar problem), and that received significant attention within computational social choice literature (see the survey of Faliszewski and Rothe [18]). Briefly put, in the regular BRIBERY problem, the goal is to ensure that a given candidate is a winner of an election by modifying—in an arbitrary way—up to k votes, where k is part of the input. Many types of bribery problems were already studied, including—in addition to SWAP and SHIFT BRIBERY—SUPPORT BRIBERY [30], EXTENSION BRIBERY [2, 17], and others (e.g., in judgment aggregation [1], and in the setting of voting in combinatorial domains [23, 11, 22]). However, from our point of view the most interesting variant of the problem is DESTRUCTIVE BRIBERY first studied by Faliszewski et al. [16], and then later—independently—by Magrino et al. [21] and Cary [6], and followed by Xia [32] and Dey and Narahari [10], under the name of MARGIN OF VICTORY. The idea behind the MARGIN OF VICTORY problem is that it can be very helpful in validating election results: If it is possible to change the election result by changing (bribing) relatively few votes, then one may suspect that—possibly—the election was tampered with. Bribery problems are also related to lobbying problems [7, 3, 25].

A variant of DESTRUCTIVE SWAP BRIBERY was studied by Shiryaev et al. in their work about robustness of winners [31]. They presented an analysis of the case where every swap has a unit price and a budget, which cannot be exceeded, is given. Authors show that the problem is easy for scoring protocols and the Condorcet rule. This work is very closely related to ours but the definition of the problem is somewhat different (more general types of swaps, but less general price functions).

Our Contribution. We believe that DESTRUCTIVE SHIFT BRIBERY is worth studying for three main reasons. First, it simply is a natural variant of the CONSTRUCTIVE SHIFT BRIBERY problem, which received quite some attention already. Second, it models natural negative campaigning actions, aimed at decreasing the popularity of a given candidate. Third, it serves a similar purpose as the MARGIN OF VICTORY problem [21, 32]: If it is possible to preclude a given candidate from winning through a low-cost destructive shift bribery, then it can be taken as a signal that the election was tampered with, or that some agent performed (possibly) an illegal form of campaigning. Below we summarize the main contributions of this paper:

1. We define the DESTRUCTIVE SHIFT BRIBERY problem and justify why a definition that diverts from the usual way of defining destructive election problems is appropriate in this case.

2. We show that DESTRUCTIVE SHIFT BRIBERY is a significantly easier problem than constructive shift bribery. To this end, we show polynomial time algorithms for destructive shift bribery for k-Approval family of rules, for Borda, and for Maximin.

3. We show that in spite of our easiness results, there still are voting rules for which the problem is computationally hard. We exemplify this by proving NP-hardness for the case of Copeland$^\alpha$ family of rules.

We believe that DESTRUCTIVE SHIFT BRIBERY is an interesting problem and it is worthwhile to study it in detail.

2. PRELIMINARIES

For each positive integer t, by $[t]$ we mean the set $\{1, \dots, t\}$. We assume the reader is familiar with standard notions regarding algorithms and complexity theory, as presented in the textbook of Papadimitriou [29]. Occasionally, we will also use basic knowledge regarding parametrized complexity (see, e.g., the textbooks of Niedermeier [26] and Cygan et al. [9]). Below we present the necessary background regarding elections, and define our problem.

2.1 Elections and Election Rules

An election is a pair $E = (C, V)$, where $C = \{c_1, ..., c_m\}$ is a set of candidates and $V = \{v_1, ..., v_n\}$ is a multiset of voters. Each voter is associated with his or her preference order $\succ_i$, i.e., a strict ranking of the candidates from the best to the worst (according to this voter). For example, we may have election $E = (C, V)$ with $C = \{c_1, c_2, c_3\}$ and $V = \{v_1, v_2\}$, where v_1 has preference order $v_1 : c_1 \succ c_2 \succ c_3$. If c is a candidate and v is a voter, we write $\mathrm{pos}_v(c)$ to denote the position of c in v's ranking (e.g., in the preceding example we would have $\mathrm{pos}_{v_1}(c_1) = 1$). Given an election $E = (C, V)$, by $N_E(c, d)$, where c and d are two candidates, we mean the number of voters who prefer c over d.

An election rule $\mathcal{R}$ is a function that given an election $E = (C, V)$ outputs a set $W \subseteq C$ of tied election winners (typically, we expect to have a single winner, but due to symmetries in the profile, it is necessary to allow for the possibility of ties). We use the unique-winner model, i.e., we require a candidate to be the only member of $\mathcal{R}(E)$ to be considered E's winner (see the works of Obraztsova et al. [27, 28] for various other tie-breaking mechanisms and algorithmic consequences of implementing them; there are situations where the choice of the tie-breaking rule affects the complexity of election-related problems).

We consider the following voting rules (for the description below, we consider election $E = (C, V)$ with m candidates;

for each rule we describe the way it computes candidates' scores, so that the candidates with the highest score are the winners):

Scoring protocols. A scoring protocol is defined through vector $\alpha = (\alpha_1, \dots, \alpha_m)$ of nonincreasing, nonnegative integers. The α-score of a candidate $c \in C$ is defined as $\sum_{v \in V} \alpha_{\mathrm{pos}_v(c)}$. The most popular scoring protocols include the family of k-Approval rules (for each k, k-Approval scoring protocol is defined through vector of k ones followed by zeros) and the Borda rule, defined by vector $(m-1, m-2, \dots, 0)$. 1-Approval is known as the Plurality rule.

Copeland . Let α, $0 \le \alpha \le 1$, be a rational number. The score of a candidate c in Copeland$^\alpha$ election is defined as:

$$|\{d \in C \setminus \{c\} \mid N_E(c,d) > N_E(d,c)\}|$$
$$+\alpha|\{d \in C \setminus \{c\} \mid N_E(c,d) = N_E(d,c)\}|.$$

In other words, candidate c receives one point for each candidate that he or she defeats in their head-to-head contest (i.e., to which c is preferred by a majority of voters) and α points for each candidate with whom c ties their head-to-head contest.

Maximin. The Maximin score of candidate c is defined as $\min_{d \in C \setminus \{c\}} N_E(c,d)$.

We write $\mathrm{score}_E(c)$ to denote the score of candidate c in election E (the election rule will be clear from the context).

2.2 Destructive Shift Bribery

The DESTRUCTIVE SHIFT BRIBERY problem for a given election rule $\mathcal{R}$ is defined as follows. We are given an election $E = (C, V)$, a despised candidate $d \in C$ (typically, the current election winner), budget B (a nonnegative integer), and the prices for shifting d backward for each of the voters (see below). The goal is to ensure, by shifting d backward, that he or she is not the unique $\mathcal{R}$-winner of the resulting election (without exceeding the budget).

We model the "prices for shifting d backward" as destructive shift-bribery price functions. Let us fix an election $E = (C, V)$, with $C = \{c_1, ..., c_m\}$, $V = \{v_1, ..., v_n\}$, and let the despised candidate be d. Let v be some voter and let $j = \mathrm{pos}_v(d)$. Function $\rho\colon \mathbb{N} \to \mathbb{N} \cup \{+\infty\}$ is a destructive shift-bribery price function for voter v if it satisfies the following conditions:

1. $\rho(0) = 0$,
2. for each two i, i', $i < i' \le m - j$, it holds that $\rho(i) \le \rho(i')$ for $i < i' \le m - j$, and
3. $\rho(i) = +\infty$ for $i > m - j$

For each i, we interpret the value $\rho(i)$ as the price for shifting d down by i positions on v's preference order. The value $+\infty$ indicates that shifting d below the last position is impossible. We assume that in each instance, the price functions are encoded by simply listing their values for all arguments for which it is not $+\infty$.

Example 1. *Let us consider an instance of* DESTRUCTIVE SHIFT BRIBERY, *for the Borda rule, with the following election:*

$$v_1 : b \succ a \succ c \succ d, \qquad v_2 : d \succ b \succ a \succ c,$$
$$v_3 : d \succ c \succ a \succ b, \qquad v_4 : d \succ a \succ b \succ c.$$

We take d to be the despised candidate, and assume that each voter has the same price function, $\rho(i) = i$. In this election, candidate d wins with 9 points (the second-best candidate, a, has 6 points). However, if we shift d two positions backward in v_4's preference order, then d's score will decrease to 7 and a's score will increase to 7. Thus, d will no longer be the unique winner. Thus, for budget $B = 2$ this would be a "yes"-instance of SHIFT BRIBERY, *whereas for $B = 1$ it would be a "no"-instance.*

3. RESULTS

We now present our main results regarding the DESTRUCTIVE SHIFT BRIBERY problem. We show polynomial-time algorithms for the k-Approval family of rules, the Borda rule, all scoring protocols (provided that they are encoded in unary or that the destructive shift bribery price functions are encoded in unary), and the Maximin rule. For the Copeland$^\alpha$ family of rules, we prove NP-hardness.

3.1 The k-Approval Family of Rules

We start with the k-Approval family of rules. In this case, our algorithm is very simple: If d is the despised candidate then in each vote we should either shift him or her from one of the top k positions (where each candidate receives a single point) to the $(k+1)$'st position (where he or she would receive no points), in effect shifting the candidate previously at the $(k+1)$'st position one place up, or we should not shift d at all. Choosing which action to do for each particular voter is easy via the following greedy/brute-force algorithm.

Theorem 1. *For each $k \in \mathbb{N}$, the* DESTRUCTIVE SHIFT BRIBERY *problem for the k-Approval rule is in* P.

Proof. Let $E = (C, V)$ be the input election with $C = \{c_1, \dots, c_m\}$ and $V = \{v_1, \dots, v_n\}$, let $d \in C$ be the despised candidate, let B be the budget, and let $(\rho_1, \dots, \rho_n)$ be the destructive shift-bribery price functions for the voters. Our algorithm works as follows.

For every candidate $c \in C \setminus \{d\}$, we test if it is possible to guarantee that the score of c is at least as high as that of d, by spending at most B units of budget, as follows:

1. We partition the voters into three groups $V_{d,c}$, V_d, and V' such that: $V_{d,c}$ contains exactly the voters that rank c on the $(k+1)$'st position and that rank d above c, V_d contains the remaining voters that rank d among top k positions, and V' contains the other remaining voters.
2. We guess two numbers, a and b, such that $|V_{d,c}| \le a$ and $|V_d| \le b$.
3. We pick a voters from $V_{d,c}$ for which shifting d to the $(k+1)$'st position is least expensive, and perform the shift. Similarly, we pick b voters from V_d for which shifting d to the $(k+1)$'st position is least expensive and perform the shift.

4. If d is not the unique winner in the resulting election and the total cost of performed shifts is smaller than or equal to budget B, then we accept. Otherwise, we either try a different candidate c or different values of a and b. After trying all possible combinations, we reject.

The algorithm runs in polynomial time. It requires trying at most $O(m)$ different candidates and $O(n^2)$ different values of a and b. All the other parts of the algorithm require polynomial time (in fact, a careful implementation can achieve running time $O(mn^2)$).

A proof of correctness is pretty straightforward. Certainly, it is never beneficial to shift d below position $k+1$. Further, an optimal solution after which some candidate c has at least as high a score as d can consist solely of actions that shift d backward from one of the top k positions to the $(k+1)$'st one, in effect either promoting c to the k'th position (shifts in voter group $V_{d,c}$), or promoting some other candidate (shifts in voter group V_d). We simply guess how many of each type of the shifts to perform and execute the least costly ones. □

The polynomial time algorithm for CONSTRUCTIVE SHIFT BRIBERY, due to Elkind et al. [14], is based on a similar idea.

3.2 The Borda Rule and All Scoring Rules

Let us now consider the Borda rule and then move to the discussion of all scoring rules. For the case of the Borda rule, we also obtain a polynomial-time algorithm, but this time we resort to dynamic programming.

Theorem 2. *The* DESTRUCTIVE SHIFT BRIBERY *problem for the Borda rule is in* P.

Proof. Let $E = (C, V)$ be the input election with $C = \{c_1, \dots, c_m\}$ and $V = \{v_1, \dots, v_n\}$, let $d \in C$ be the despised candidate, let B be the budget, and let $(\rho_1, \dots, \rho_n)$ be the destructive shift-bribery price functions for the voters. As in the case of the proof of Theorem 1, we give an algorithm that first guesses some candidate $c \in C \setminus \{d\}$ and then checks if it is possible to ensure—by shifting d backward without exceeding budget B—that c has at least as high a score as d. The algorithm performing this test is based on dynamic programming. However, before we describe it, we need to introduce some additional notation.

We fix c to be the candidate that we want to have score at least as high as d. For each $j \in [n]$ and each $k \in [m]$, we write $P(j,k)$ to denote the cost of shifting candidate d on v_j's preference order by k positions down (if moving d by k positions is impossible, we have $P(j,k) = \infty$). Further, for each $j \in [n]$ and $k \in [m]$, we set $A(j,k)$ to be 1 if v_j ranks c among first k positions below d, and we set it to be 0 otherwise. Finally, we write s to denote the difference between the scores of d and c, i.e., $s = \text{score}_E(d) - \text{score}_E(c)$ (it must be that $s > 0$; otherwise we could accept immediately since d would not be the unique winner of the election).

For each $j \in [n]$ and each positive integer k, we define $f(j,k)$ to be the smallest cost for shifting d backward in the preference orders of the voters from the set $\{v_1 \dots, v_j\}$, so that, if E' is the resulting election, it holds that:

$$s - (\text{score}_{E'}(d) - \text{score}_{E'}(c)) \geq k.$$

In other words, $f(j,k)$ is the lowest cost of shifting d backward in the preference orders of voters from the set $\{v_1, \dots, v_j\}$ so that the relative score of c with respect to d increases by at least k points. Our goal is to compute $f(n,s)$; if it is at most B then it means that we can ensure that c has at least as high a score as d by spending at most B units of the budget.

Before we give an algorithm for computing the values $f(\cdot,\cdot)$, we make the following observation.

Observation 1. *Shifting candidate d backward by some k positions decreases the score of d by k points and, if d passes c, increases the score of c by one point. In effect, relative to d, c gains, respectively, k or $k+1$ points.*

Now, we can express function f as follows. We have that $f(0,0) = 0$ and for each positive k we have $f(k,0) = \infty$ (for technical reasons, whenever $k < 0$, we take $f(j,k) = 0$). For each $j \in [n]$, we have:

$$f(j,k) = \min_{k' \leq k} f(j-1, k-(k'+A(j,k'))) + P(j,k').$$

To explain the formula, we make the following observations:

1. The minimum is taken over the value k'; k' gives the number of positions by which we shift d backward in vote v_j.

2. When we shift d backward by k' positions, relative to d, candidate c gains $k' + A(j,k')$ points.

3. The cost of this shift is $P(j,k')$.

Based on these observations, we can conclude that the formula is correct. It is clear that based on this formula and standard dynamic programming techniques, we can compute $f(n,s)$ in polynomial time with respect to n and m. This means that we can test in polynomial time, for a given candidate c, if it is possible to ensure that c's score is at least as high as that of d.

Our algorithm for the DESTRUCTIVE SHIFT BRIBERY for Borda simply considers each candidate $c \in C \setminus \{d\}$ and tests if, within budget B, it is possible to ensure that c has at least as high a score as d. If this test succeeds for some c, we accept. Otherwise we reject. □

A careful inspection of the above proof shows that there is not much in it that is specific to the Borda rule (as opposed to other scoring protocols). Indeed, there are only the following two dependencies:

1. The fact that the difference between the scores of candidate d and candidate c (value s) can be bounded by a polynomial of the number of voters and the number of candidates (dynamic programming requires us to store a number of values of the function f that is proportional to s, so it is important that this value is polynomially bounded).

2. The way we compute the increase of the score of c, relative to d, in the recursive formula for $f(j,k)$.

Since it is easy to modify the formula for $f(j,k)$ to work for an arbitrary scoring protocol α, we have the following corollary (the assumption about unary encoding of the input scoring protocol ensures that the first point in the above list of dependencies is not violated).

Corollary 1. *There exists an algorithm that given as input a scoring protocol α (for m candidates) encoded in unary and an instance I of the* DESTRUCTIVE SHIFT BRIBERY *problem (with the same number m of candidates), tests in polynomial time if I is a "yes"-instance for the voting rule defined by the scoring protocol α.*

What can we do if, in fact, our scoring protocol is impractical to encode in unary (e.g., if our scoring protocol is of the form $(2^{m-1}, 2^{m-2}, \dots, 1)$)? In this case, it is easy to show the following result.

Corollary 2. *There exists an algorithm that given as input a scoring protocol α (for m candidates) and an instance I of the* DESTRUCTIVE SHIFT BRIBERY *problem (with the same number m of candidates), with price functions encoded in unary, tests in polynomial time if I is a "yes"-instance for the voting rule defined by the scoring protocol α.*

To prove this result, we use the same argument as before, but now function f has slightly different arguments: $f(j,t)$ is the maximum increase of the score of c, relative to d, that one can achieve by spending at most t units of budget (using such "dual" formulation is standard for bribery problems and was applied, e.g., by Faliszewski et al. [15, Theorem 3.8] in the first paper regarding the complexity of bribery problems).

On the other hand, if the scoring protocol is encoded in binary and the price functions are encoded in binary, and the scoring protocol is part of the input, then the problem is NP-complete. (This follows via a simple reduction from the standard PARTITION problem.)

3.3 The Copeland Rule

Let us now move on to the case of Copeland$^\alpha$ family of rules. We show that irrespective of the choice of α, $0 \le \alpha \le 1$, the DESTRUCTIVE SHIFT BRIBERY problem is NP-complete for Copeland$^\alpha$. We give a reduction from the classic NP-complete problem, EXACT COVER BY 3-SETS (X3C).

Definition 1. *In the* X3C *problem, we are given a set $U = \{u_1, u_2, ..., u_{3k}\}$ and family $S = \{s_1, s_2, \dots, s_n\}$ of three-element subsets of U. We ask if there exists a family S', $S' \subseteq S$, such that $|S'| = k$ and $U = \bigcup_{s_i \in S'} s_i$.*

We use the following notation in the proof below. By putting some subset of U in a preference order (where U is the set from an X3C instance), we mean listing the contents of the set in the order of increasing indices (i.e., if we wrote U in a preference order, it would mean $u_1 \succ u_2 \succ \dots \succ u_{3k}$). In the proof below, we sometimes also list sets other than subsets of U within preference orders; in their case we also mean listing their members in the order of increasing indices.

Theorem 3. *For each (rational) value of α, $0 \le \alpha \le 1$, the* DESTRUCTIVE SHIFT BRIBERY *problem for the Copeland$^\alpha$ rule is* NP*-complete.*

Proof. We can immediately claim that our problem belongs to NP (we can guess in which votes to shift the despised candidate and by how many positions; checking if this ensures that the despised candidate is not the unique winner is an easy, polynomial-time task). It remains to show that the problem is NP-hard.

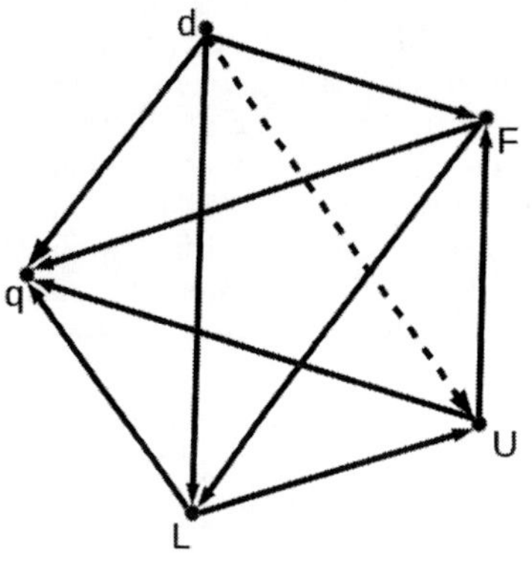

Figure 1: A graph presenting the relations between candidates in the constructed election.

Let us fix a value of α. We give a reduction from the X3C problem. Consider an instance I of X3C with $U = \{u_1, \dots, u_{3k}\}$ and $S = \{s_1, \dots, s_n\}$. We construct an election $E = (C, V)$ as follows. We let the set of candidates be $C = \{d, q\} \cup U \cup F \cup L$, where $F = \{f_1, f_2, ..., f_{3k}\}$, $L = \{l_1, l_2, ..., l_{3k}\}$ are dummy candidates needed for our construction. We introduce the following voters:

1. For each $i \in [n]$, we introduce a single voter, v_i, with preference order $v_i\colon d \succ s_i \succ q \succ U \setminus s_i \succ F \succ L$, and a single voter v_i' whose preference order is the reverse of that of v_i.

2. We additionally introduce $6k + 1$ voters with the following preference orders:

k votes:	$U \succ d \succ F \succ L \succ q$
k votes:	$U \succ d \succ F \succ L \succ q$
k votes:	$d \succ L \succ U \succ F \succ q$
k votes:	$q \succ d \succ L \succ U \succ F$
k votes:	$F \succ L \succ U \succ q \succ d$
k votes:	$d \succ F \succ L \succ U \succ q$
1 vote :	$q \succ d \succ U \succ F \succ L$

We set the budget to be $B = k$, and we set the price functions as follows. For each of the voters $v_1, \dots, v_n$, we use price function ρ such that $\rho(0) = 0$, $\rho(1) = \rho(2) = \rho(3) = 1$, and $\rho(t) = B + 1$ for all $t \ge 4$. For all the other voters, we use price function ρ' such that $\rho'(0) = 0$ and $\rho'(t) = B + 1$ for all $t \ge 1$.

To clarify the relations between the candidates in our election, we provide Figure 1 with the following graph: The vertices correspond to particular candidates or groups of candidates and the edges are pointing from a candidate (or a group of candidates) that is winning the given head-to-head contest to a candidate (or a group of them) that is losing (e.g., an edge from d to F means that d wins his or her head-to-head contests against each member of F). Solid edges represent the results of head-to-head contests that cannot change by applying shifts within given budget.

Figure 1 does not show results of the head-to-head contests between candidates within particular sets. Nonetheless, given the graph, the description of the voters, and the convention regarding putting sets in preference orders (see the paragraph just before the theorem statement), it is straightforward to calculate the scores of all the candidates. We present them in Table 1 (and below explain how it to verify these values easily; note that the number of voters is odd and so the value of α is irrelevant).

We see that d wins with every other candidate and q loses with everyone. For candidates from U, F, and L, the situation is symmetric so let us consider some candidate $u_i \in U$. He or she wins their head-to-head contest with candidate q and all the candidates from L. This gives him or her $3k+1$ points. Moreover, u_i wins with all the candidates $u_j \in U$ such that $j > i$. This give him or her $3k - i$ points. Altogether, the score of u_i is $6k + 1 - i$.

We set up the election in such a way that the only results of head-to-head elections that can change due to shifts (within the budget) are between d and members of U. In Table 2 we summarize the values of function $N_E(\cdot,\cdot)$. The major conclusion from Table 2 is as follows:

$$N(d, u_i) = N(u_i, d) + 1 \qquad (1)$$

Based on the above discussion, we now make a series of observations:

Observation 2. *The only voters in whose preference orders d can be shifted without exceeding the available budget are voters $v_1, \dots, v_n$.*

Observation 3. *Only the candidates from U can have their scores increased as a result of (within budget) shifts, and only d can have its score decreased by such shifts (this is, in particular, due to Equation (1)).*

Observation 4. *We can shift d in the preference orders of at most k voters. Each time, we can shift d below, at most, 3 (distinct) candidates from U. This means that d can be shifted below at most $3k$ distinct candidates from U. (This is due to the value of the budget, the nature of our price functions, and the structure of preferences of the voters $v_1, \dots, v_n$.)*

Observation 5. *The lowest score that candidate d can have after (within budget) shifts is $6k + 1$. This happens if and only if he or she passes each candidate from U at least once.*

Observation 6. *The highest score a candidate from U may have is $6k + 1$. This happens if d is shifted below u_1.*

candidate	score
d	$9k+1$
q	0
$u_i \in U$	$6k+1-i$
$f_i \in F$	$6k+1-i$
$l_i \in L$	$6k+1-i$

Table 1: Table containing scores of all of the candidates in the constructed election.

$N(\cdot,\cdot)$	d	$u_i \in U$
d	–	$n+3k+1$
$u_i \in U$	$n+3k$	–

Table 2: Table presenting values of function N for candidate d and candidates in U.

By combining the above observations, we see that d can stop being the unique winner of our election if and only if there is a sequence of shifts, on the preference orders of the voters $v_1, \dots, v_n$, each moving d by three positions down, such that d passes each member of U. However, this is possible if and only if there is a solution for the input X3C instance. Since the reduction is computable in polynomial time, this completes the proof. □

The above result and proof requires some comments. As a technical remark, the reader may wonder what the role of candidate q is. For the result as we state it, it would be possible to simply remove him or her. However, our construction allows for a simple tweak: If we extended the price functions of voters $v_1, \dots, v_n$ to allow shifting d backward one position more, to pass q, our proof would work for the case where we have to ensure that the resulting election has a unique winner (this is not a requirement in our model, but we find it appealing that the result appears to be immune to various tie-breaking tweaks).

The fact that Destructive Shift Bribery is NP-complete immediately raises the question about its parameterized complexity. While in this paper we, mostly, focus on classic complexity results, the proof of Theorem 3 allows us to make some conclusions. First, instead of reducing from X3C, we could have given a reduction from SetCover (a problem where neither the size of U nor the sizes of the sets in the family S are constrained, and where k—the number of sets one can use in the solution—is an additional part of the input) with only minor modifications. Since SetCover is well-known to be $W[2]$-hard for the parameter k and since our construction uses budget $B = k$, we immediately get that Destructive Shift Bribery for Copeland$^\alpha$ rules is $W[2]$-hard when parameterized by the budget value, or when parameterized by the total number of affected voters (see the work of Chen et al. [4] for a discussion of these parameters; for other parameters considered by Chen et al., such as the number of unit shifts used or the number of voters, our proof does not apply and we would need additional constructions).

Corollary 3. *For each (rational) value of α, $0 \le \alpha \le 1$, the* Destructive Shift Bribery *problem for the Copeland$^\alpha$ rule is $W[2]$-hard for the parametrization by the budged value, and for the parametrization by the number of affected voters.*

3.4 The Maximin Rule

In spite of the hardness results from the previous section, it certainly is not the case that Destructive Shift Bribery is hard for all Condorcet-consistent rules. We now show a polynomial time algorithm for the case of Maximin.

Theorem 4. *The* Destructive Shift Bribery *problem for the Maximin rule is in* P.

Proof. Let $E = (C, V)$ be the input election with $C = \{c_1, \dots, c_m\}$ and $V = \{v_1, \dots, v_n\}$, let $d \in C$ be the despised candidate, let B be the budget, and let $(\rho_1, \dots, \rho_n)$ be the destructive shift-bribery price functions for the voters. Before we give our algorithm for the problem, we first identify a certain property that we can assume our solutions to have.

A solution for our instance of Destructive Shift Bribery can be understood as a vector of n integers,

$(k_1, \ldots, k_n)$, each specifying by how many positions we shift d back on the preference order of the respective voter. So, let $(k_1, \ldots, k_n)$ be some solution for our instance, and let $E' = (C, V')$ be an election that we obtain after, for each $i \in [n]$, we shift d back by k_i positions on v_i's preference order. We denote the voters in V' as $v'_1, \ldots, v'_n$, where for each $i \in [n]$, v'_i corresponds to v_i.

Let $w \in C \setminus \{d\}$ be a Maximin winner of E' (we can assume that $w \neq d$ because $(k_1, \ldots, k_n)$ is a solution for the problem). Also, let t be a candidate such that $\text{score}_{E'}(d) = N_{E'}(d,t)$. That is, t is the candidate that "implements" the score of d in the final election. We claim that we can assume that for every voter v'_i such that $k_i \neq 0$, it holds that either v'_i ranks w just above d, or v'_i ranks t just above d (we refer to solutions where this holds as *tight*). Below we argue why this is the case.

Let us consider some voter v'_i. We consider the following cases:

1. If v'_i ranks d above both w and t, then we modify the solution $(k_1, \ldots, k_n)$ so that $k_i = 0$ (i.e., we undo whatever shift was applied to v_i). The reason is that since d did not pass either w or t, the shift within v_i could not have affected the scores of w and d (due to our choice of t). Thus, even after undoing this shift, w still has at least as high a score as d.

2. If v'_i ranks d below w, or below t, or below both of them, then we decrease k_i so that d either ranks d just below w or just below t (whichever requires decreasing k_i by a smaller value). If this is impossible (e.g., because the relative order of d, t, and w is the same for both v_i and v'_i) then we set $k_i = 0$. The reasoning is the same as in the above step: The introduced change does not affect the scores of d and w.

The changes to the solution described above, when implemented for each of the voters, do not change the scores of d and w, but may lower the cost of the solution. Thus it is correct to assume that whenever there is some solution for our instance, there is also a tight one.

Our algorithm proceeds by first guessing the candidates w and t (from $C \setminus \{d\}$) and then checks if there is a tight solution for them that does not exceed the budget. We use the following notation. For each two candidates c_1, c_2, we write $\mathit{Pref}(c_1, c_2)$ to denote the set of voters (from V) that prefer c_1 over c_2. Let us $Pr(v, c)$ be the cost of shifting candidate d just behind c in v's preference order.

Since we are looking for a tight solution, we focus on voters in the set $\mathit{Pref}(d, w) \cup \mathit{Pref}(d, t) = \{v''_1, \cdots, v''_\ell\}$ (i.e., voters who prefer d to at least one of w and t). For given candidates w, t, $w \neq t$, and integers $j, x, y \in \{0, \ldots, \ell\}$, we define function $f_{w,t}$, so that $f_{w,t}(j, x, y)$ is the lowest cost for shifting d backward in the preference orders of the voters from $\{v''_1, \ldots, v''_j\}$ so that d moves x times below w and y times below t. Given function $f_{w,t}$, we will be able to check for an existence of a tight solution for w and t. Before we describe how to do it, let us argue that we can compute the values of function $f_{w,t}$ in polynomial time. To this end, we use dynamic programming.

First, we note that for each $j, x, y \in \{0, \ldots, \ell\}$, we have $f_{w,t}(j, 0, 0) = 0$ and, if $x > 0$ or $y > 0$, $f_{w,t}(0, x, y) = \infty$ (to indicate the impossibility). For other values of the arguments, we express the value $f_{w,t}(j, x, y)$ recursively as follows. Let us fix some values of $j \in [\ell]$, and $x, y \in \{0, \ldots, \ell\}$. There are three cases to consider:

Case 1: If $v''_j \in \mathit{Pref}(d, w) \setminus \mathit{Pref}(d, t)$, i.e., if v''_j prefers d to w, but not to t, then we have:

$$f_{w,t}(j, x, y) = \min \left\{ \begin{array}{l} f_{w,t}(j-1, x, y), \\ f_{w,t}(j-1, x-1, y) + Pr(w) \end{array} \right\}.$$

To see the correctness of the formula, note that to ensure that d moves x times below w and y times below t for the voters $v''_1, \ldots, v''_j$, we either ensure that this happens already for the voters $v''_1, \ldots, v''_{j-1}$ and leave v''_j intact, or we ensure that d moves $x - 1$ times below w and y times below t for voters $v''_1, \ldots, v''_{j-1}$, and moves once below w in the the preference order of v''_j (from now on we will omit such detailed description, but the general idea for each of the cases is the same).

Case 2: If v''_j is in $\mathit{Pref}(d, t) \setminus \mathit{Pref}(d, w)$, then we have:

$$f_{w,t}(j, x, y) = \min \left\{ \begin{array}{l} f_{w,t}(j-1, x, y), \\ f_{w,t}(j-1, x, y-1) + Pr(t) \end{array} \right\}.$$

Case 3: If v''_j is in $\mathit{Pref}(d, w) \cap \mathit{Pref}(d, t)$ and v''_j prefers d to w and w to t, then we have:

$$f_{w,t}(j, x, y) = \min \left\{ \begin{array}{l} f_{w,t}(j-1, x, y), \\ f_{w,t}(j-1, x-1, y) + Pr(w), \\ f_{w,t}(j-1, x-1, y-1) + Pr(t) \end{array} \right\}.$$

On the other hand, if v''_j prefers d to t and t to w then we have:

$$f_{w,t}(j, x, y) = \min \left\{ \begin{array}{l} f_{w,t}(j-1, x, y), \\ f_{w,t}(j-1, x, y-1) + Pr(t), \\ f_{w,t}(j-1, x-1, y-1) + Pr(w) \end{array} \right\}.$$

Given this discussion, it is clear that using standard dynamic-programming approach it is possible to compute function $f_{w,t}$ in polynomial time.

Finally, using function $f_{w,t}$, we can compute the cost of the cheapest tight solution for candidates w and t. It suffices to try all values $x, y \in \{0, \ldots, \ell\}$. For each such pair it is immediate to compute the score that candidates d and w would have after d shifted x times below w and y times below t. We would accept if the score of w were at least as high as that of d and we had $f_{w,t}(\ell, x, y) \leq B$. We reject if there is no choice of w, t, x, and y that leads to acceptance. (Technically, we should also consider the case where $w = t$. It is straightforward to adapt the description of function $f_{w,t}$ to this case.) This concludes our proof. □

It is interesting to ask what feature of the Maximin rule—as opposed to the Copeland rule—lead to the fact that DESTRUCTIVE SHIFT BRIBERY is polynomial-time solvable. We believe that the reason is that it is safe to focus on a small number of candidates (the candidates w and t). For Copeland elections, on the other hand, one has to keep track of all the candidates that the despised candidate passes, because each such pass could, in effect, decrease the despised candidate's score. (Interestingly, the same is true for the Borda rule—each time the despised candidate passes a candidate, the despised candidate's score decreases. However, in the case of Borda this process is unconditional, whereas in the case of Copeland's rule, the decrease may or may not happen, depending on shifts in other preference orders).

Election rule	Constructive Shift Bribery	Destructive Shift Bribery
Plurality	P	P
k-Approval	P	P
Borda	NP-com.	P
Maximin	NP-com.	P
Copeland$^\alpha$	NP-com.	NP-com.

Table 3: The complexity of Shift Bribery for various election rules. The results for the constructive case are due to Elkind et al. [14] and the results regarding the destructive case are due to this paper.

4. CONCLUSIONS

We have introduced and studied a destructive variant of the SHIFT BRIBERY problem. In our problem, we ask if it is possible to preclude a given candidate from being the winner of an election by shifting this candidate backward in some of the votes (at a given cost, within a given budget), whereas in the constructive variant of the problem one asks if it is possible to ensure a given candidate's victory by shifting him or her forward. Thus, our approach to defining DESTRUCTIVE SHIFT BRIBERY is somewhat nonstandard: Not only we change the goal (from the constructive to the destructive one), but also we modify the set of available actions. We do so, because otherwise our problem would be meaningful only for non-monotone rules and would be quite unnatural (increasing the support for a given candidate to preclude him or her from winning, while possible and indeed occurring in real life, e.g., in STV elections, is quite a tricky, and perhaps controversial, issue).

We have shown that DESTRUCTIVE SHIFT BRIBERY is polynomial-time solvable for the k-Approval family of rules (in effect, including the Plurality rule), the Borda rule, all scoring protocols (as long as either the protocol or the price functions can be assumed to be encoded in unary), and the Maximin rule. On the other hand, we have shown that for each rational value of α, the problem is NP-complete for Copeland$^\alpha$ (and we have drawn initial conclusions regarding the problem's parameterized complexity in this case). We summarize our results in Table 3.

Our work leads to several open questions. First, one could always study more elections rules. Second, at a technical level, it is tempting to study the parameterized complexity of our problem for Copeland in more depth. Third, it would be interesting to perform an empirical test to measure, for example, by how much we need to shift back the election winner to change the result under various assumptions regarding the voters' preference orders (and in real-life elections, such as those collected in PrefLib [24]).

Acknowledgments

We are grateful to AAMAS reviewers for their helpful comments. The authors were supported by the AGH University grant 11.11.230.124 (statutory research).

REFERENCES

[1] D. Baumeister, G. Erdélyi, and J. Rothe. How hard is it to bribe judges? A study of the complexity of bribery in judgement aggregation. In *Proceedings of the 2nd International Conference on Algorithmic Decision Theory*, pages 1–15. Springer-Verlag *Lecture Notes in Computer Science #6992*, Oct. 2011.

[2] D. Baumeister, P. Faliszewski, J. Lang, and J. Rothe. Campaigns for lazy voters: Truncated ballots. In *Proceedings of AAMAS-12*, pages 577–584. International Foundation for Autonomous Agents and Multiagent Systems, June 2012.

[3] D. Binkele-Raible, G. Erdélyi, H. Fernau, J. Goldsmith, N. Mattei, and J. Rothe. The complexity of probabilistic lobbying. *Discrete Optimization*, 11:1–21, 2014.

[4] R. Bredereck, J. Chen, P. Faliszewski, A. Nichterlein, and R. Niedermeier. Prices matter for the parameterized complexity of shift bribery. In *Proceedings of AAAI-14*, pages 1398–1404. AAAI Press, 2014.

[5] R. Bredereck, P. Faliszewski, R. Niedermeier, and N. Talmon. Large-scale election campaigns: Combinatorial shift bribery. In *Proceedings of AAMAS-15*, pages 67–75, 2015.

[6] D. Cary. Estimating the margin of victory for instant-runoff voting. Presented at the 2011 Electronic Voting Technology Workshop/Workshop on Trustworthy Elections, 2011.

[7] R. Christian, M. Fellows, F. Rosamond, and A. Slinko. On complexity of lobbying in multiple referenda. *Review of Economic Design*, 11(3):217–224, 2007.

[8] V. Conitzer, T. Sandholm, and J. Lang. When are elections with few candidates hard to manipulate? *Journal of the ACM*, 54(3):Article 14, 2007.

[9] M. Cygan, F. Fomin, Ł. Kowalik, D. Lokshtanov, D. Marx, M. Pilipczuk, M. Pilipczuk, and S. Saurabh. *Parameterized Algorithms*. Sprigner, 2015.

[10] P. Dey and Y. Narahari. Estimating the margin of victory of an election using sampling. In *Proceedings of the 24th International Joint Conference on Artificial Intelligence*, pages 1120–1126, July 2015.

[11] B. Dorn and D. Krüger. On the hardness of bribery variants in voting with CP-nets. *Annals of Mathematics and Artificial Intelligence*, To appear.

[12] B. Dorn and I. Schlotter. Multivariate complexity analysis of swap bribery. *Algorithmica*, 64(1):126–151, 2012.

[13] E. Elkind and P. Faliszewski. Approximation algorithms for campaign management. In *Proceedings of the 6th International Workshop On Internet And Network Economics*, pages 473–482. Springer-Verlag *Lecture Notes in Computer Science #6484*, Dec. 2010.

[14] E. Elkind, P. Faliszewski, and A. Slinko. Swap bribery. In *Proceedings of the 2nd International Symposium on Algorithmic Game Theory*, pages 299–310. Springer-Verlag *Lecture Notes in Computer Science #5814*, Oct. 2009.

[15] P. Faliszewski, E. Hemaspaandra, and L. Hemaspaandra. How hard is bribery in elections? *Journal of Artificial Intelligence Research*, 35:485–532, 2009.

[16] P. Faliszewski, E. Hemaspaandra, L. Hemaspaandra, and J. Rothe. Llull and Copeland voting computationally resist bribery and constructive

control. *Journal of Artificial Intelligence Research*, 35:275–341, 2009.

[17] P. Faliszewski, Y. Reisch, J. Rothe, and L. Schend. Complexity of manipulation, bribery, and campaign management in Bucklin and fallback voting. *Autonomous Agents and Multiagent Systems*, 29(6):1091–1124, 2015.

[18] P. Faliszewski and J. Rothe. Control and bribery in voting. In F. Brandt, V. Conitzer, U. Endriss, J. Lang, and A. D. Procaccia, editors, *Handbook of Computational Social Choice*, chapter 7. Cambridge University Press, To appear.

[19] N. Hazon, R. Lin, and S. Kraus. How to change a group's collective decision? In *Proceedings of the 23rd International Joint Conference on Artificial Intelligence*, pages 198–205. AAAI Press, 2013.

[20] E. Hemaspaandra, L. Hemaspaandra, and J. Rothe. Anyone but him: The complexity of precluding an alternative. *Artificial Intelligence*, 171(5–6):255–285, 2007.

[21] T. Magrino, R. Rivest, E. Shen, and D. Wagner. Computing the margin of victory in IRV elections. Presented at 2011 Electronic Voting Technology Workshop/Workshop on Trushworthy Elections, Aug. 2011.

[22] A. Maran, N. Maudet, M. Pini, F. Rossi, and K. Venable. A framework for aggregating influenced cp-nets and its resistance to bribery. In *Proceedings of AAAI-13*, pages 668–674. AAAI Press, 2013.

[23] N. Mattei, M. Pini, F. Rossi, and K. Venable. Bribery in voting over combinatorial domains is easy. In *Proceedings of AAMAS-12*, pages 1407–1408. International Foundation for Autonomous Agents and Multiagent Systems, June 2012.

[24] N. Mattei and T. Walsh. Preflib: A library for preferences. In *Proceedings of the 3nd International Conference on Algorithmic Decision Theory*, pages 259–270, 2013.

[25] I. Nehama. Complexity of optimal lobbying in threshold aggregation. In *Proceedings of the 4th International Conference on Algorithmic Decision Theory*, pages 379–395. Springer-Verlag *Lecture Notes in Computer Science #9346*, Sept. 2015.

[26] R. Niedermeier. *Invitation to Fixed-Parameter Algorithms*. Oxford University Press, 2006.

[27] S. Obraztsova and E. Elkind. On the complexity of voting manipulation under randomized tie-breaking. In *Proceedings of the 22nd International Joint Conference on Artificial Intelligence*, pages 319–324, July 2011.

[28] S. Obraztsova, E. Elkind, and N. Hazon. Ties matter: Complexity of voting manipulation revisited. In *Proceedings of AAMAS-11*, pages 71–78, May 2011.

[29] C. Papadimitriou. *Computational Complexity*. Addison-Wesley, 1994.

[30] I. Schlotter, P. Faliszewski, and E. Elkind. Campaign management under approval-driven voting rules. *Algorithmica*, To appear.

[31] D. Shiryaev, L. Yu, and E. Elkind. On elections with robust winners. In *Proceedings of AAMAS-13*, pages 415–422. International Foundation for Autonomous Agents and Multiagent Systems, 2013.

[32] L. Xia. Computing the margin of victory for various voting rules. In *Proceedings of the 13th ACM Conference on Electronic Commerce*, pages 982–999. ACM Press, June 2012.

Optimal Bounds for the No-Show Paradox via SAT Solving

Felix Brandt
TU München
Munich, Germany
brandtf@in.tum.de

Christian Geist
TU München
Munich, Germany
geist@in.tum.de

Dominik Peters
University of Oxford
Oxford, UK
dominik.peters@cs.ox.ac.uk

ABSTRACT

Voting rules allow multiple agents to aggregate their preferences in order to reach joint decisions. Perhaps one of the most important desirable properties in this context is *Condorcet-consistency*, which requires that a voting rule should return an alternative that is preferred to any other alternative by some majority of voters. Another desirable property is *participation*, which requires that no voter should be worse off by joining an electorate. A seminal result in social choice theory by Moulin [28] has shown that Condorcet-consistency and participation are incompatible whenever there are at least 4 alternatives and 25 voters. We leverage SAT solving to obtain an elegant human-readable proof of Moulin's result that requires only 12 voters. Moreover, the SAT solver is able to construct a Condorcet-consistent voting rule that satisfies participation as well as a number of other desirable properties for up to 11 voters, proving the optimality of the above bound. We also obtain tight results for set-valued and probabilistic voting rules, which complement and significantly improve existing theorems.

Keywords

Computer-aided theorem proving; social choice theory; SAT; no-show paradox; participation; Condorcet

1. INTRODUCTION

Whenever a group of autonomous software agents or robots needs to decide on a joint course of action in a fair and satisfactory way, they need to aggregate their preferences. A common way to achieve this is to use voting rules. Voting rules are studied in detail in social choice theory and are coming under increasing scrutiny from computer scientists who are interested in their computational properties or want to utilize them in multiagent systems (see, e.g., [31, 9]).

In social choice theory, voting rules are usually compared using desirable properties (so-called axioms) that they may or may not satisfy. There are a number of well-known impossibility theorems—among which Arrow's impossibility is arguably the most famous—which state that certain axioms are incompatible with each other. These results, which show the non-existence of voting rules that satisfy a given set of axioms, are important because they clearly define the boundary of what can be achieved at all. This applies to the explicitly stated axioms as well as implicit ones such as boundaries on the number of voters or alternatives. For instance, if there are only two alternatives, Arrow's theorem does not apply and there are many voting rules, including majority rule, that satisfy the conditions used in Arrow's theorem. One impossibility that requires unusually high bounds on the number of voters and alternatives is Moulin's *no-show paradox* [28], which states that the axioms of Condorcet-consistency and participation are incompatible whenever there are at least 4 alternatives and 25 voters. Moulin proves that the bound on the number of alternatives is tight by showing that the maximin voting rule (with lexicographic tie-breaking) satisfies the desired properties when there are at most 3 alternatives. The tightness of the more restrictive condition on the number of voters was left open, however. The goal of this paper is to give tight bounds on the number of voters required for Moulin's theorem and related theorems that appear in the literature. To achieve this, we encode these problems as formulas in propositional logic and then use SAT solvers to decide their satisfiability and extract minimal unsatisfiable sets (MUSes) in the case of unsatisfiability. This approach is based on previous work by Tang and Lin [35], Geist and Endriss [20], Brandt and Geist [8], and Brandl et al. [4]. However, it turned out that a straightforward application of this methodology is insufficient to deal with the magnitude of the problems we considered. Several novel techniques were necessary to achieve our results. In particular, we extracted knowledge from computer-generated proofs of weaker statements and then used this information to guide the search for proofs of more general statements.

As mentioned above, Moulin's theorem uses the axioms of Condorcet-consistency and participation. Condorcet-consistency goes back to one of the most influential notions in social choice theory, namely that of a *Condorcet winner*. A Condorcet winner is an alternative that is preferred to any other alternative by a majority of voters. The Marquis de Condorcet, after whom this concept is named, argued that, whenever a Condorcet winner exists, it should be elected [15]. A voting rule satisfying this condition is called *Condorcet-consistent*. Apart from the intuitive appeal of this condition, Condorcet-consistent rules are more robust to changes in the of feasible alternatives and less susceptible to strategic manipulation than other voting rules (such as Borda's rule) (see, e.g., [11, 14]). While the desirability of Condorcet-consistency—as that of any other axiom—

Appears in: *Proceedings of the 15th International Conference on Autonomous Agents and Multiagent Systems (AAMAS 2016), J. Thangarajah, K. Tuyls, C. Jonker, S. Marsella (eds.), May 9–13, 2016, Singapore.*

has been subject to criticism, many scholars agree that it is very appealing—if not indispensable—and a large part of the social choice literature deals exclusively with Condorcet-consistent voting rules (e.g., [17, 25, 9]). *Participation* was first considered by Fishburn and Brams [18] and requires that no voter should be worse off by joining an electorate, or—alternatively—that no voter should benefit by abstaining from an election. The desirability of this axiom in any context with voluntary participation is evident. All the more surprisingly, Fishburn and Brams have shown that single transferable vote (STV), a common voting rule, violates participation and referred to this phenomenon as the *no-show paradox*. Moulin [28], perhaps even more startlingly, proved that no Condorcet-consistent voting rule satisfies participation when there are at least 25 voters.

We leverage SAT solving to obtain an elegant human-readable proof of Moulin's result that requires only 12 voters. While computer-aided solving techniques allow us to tackle difficult combinatorial problems, they usually do not provide additional insight into these problems. Somewhat surprisingly, the computer-aided proofs we found possess a certain kind of symmetry that has not been exploited in previous proofs. Moreover, the SAT solver is able to construct a Condorcet-consistent voting rule that satisfies participation as well as a number of other desirable properties for up to 11 voters, proving the optimality of the above bound. This computer-generated voting rule is compatible with the maximin voting rule in 99.8% of all cases and, in contrast to maximin, only selects alternatives from the top cycle. As a practical consequence of our theorem, strategic abstention need not be a concern for Condorcet-consistent voting rules when there are at most 4 alternatives and 11 voters, for instance when voting in a committee. We also use our techniques to provide optimal bounds for related results about set-valued and probabilistic voting rules [22, 36]. In particular, we give a tight bound of 17 voters for the optimistic preference extension, 14 voters for the pessimistic extension, and 12 voters for the stochastic dominance preference extension. These results are substantial improvements of previous results. For example, the previous statement for the pessimistic extension requires an additional axiom, at least 5 alternatives, and at least 971 voters [22]. Our results are summarized in Table 1.

2. RELATED WORK

The no-show paradox was first observed by Fishburn and Brams [18] for the STV voting rule. Ray [30] and Lepelley and Merlin [26] investigate how frequently this phenomenon occurs in practice. The main theorem addressed in this paper is due to Moulin [28] and requires at least 25 voters. This bound was recently brought down to 21 voters by Kardel [23]. Simplified proofs of Moulin's theorem are given by Schulze [33] and Smith [34]. Holzman [21] and Sanver and Zwicker [32] strengthen Moulin's theorem by weakening Condorcet-consistency and participation, respectively. Jimeno et al. [22] prove variants of Moulin's theorem for set-valued voting rules based on the optimistic and the pessimistic preference extension. Pérez [29] defines a weaker notion of participation in the context of set-valued voting rules and shows that all common Condorcet extensions except the maximin rule and Young's rule violate this property. Pérez notes that "a practical question, which has not been dealt with here, refers to the number of candidates and voters that are necessary to invoke the studied paradoxes" ([29], p. 614).

When assuming that voters have incomplete preferences over sets or lotteries, participation and Condorcet-consistency can be satisfies simultaneously and positive results for common Condorcet-consistent voting rules have been obtained by Brandt [7] and Brandl et al. [4, 5, 6]. Abstention in slightly different contexts than the one studied in this paper recently caught the attention of computer scientists working on voting equilibria and campaigning [16, 1].

The computer-aided techniques in this paper are inspired by Tang and Lin [35], who reduced well-known impossibility results from social choice theory—such as Arrow's theorem—to finite instances, which can then be checked by a SAT solver. This methodology has been extended and applied to new problems by Geist and Endriss [20], Brandt and Geist [8], and Brandl et al. [4]. The results obtained by computer-aided theorem proving have already found attention in the social choice community [12]. More generally, SAT solvers have also proven to be quite effective for other problems in economics. A prominent example is the ongoing work by Fréchette et al. [19] in which SAT solvers are used for the development and execution of the FCC's upcoming reverse spectrum auction. In some respects, our approach also bears some similarities to *automated mechanism design* (see, e.g., [13]), where desirable properties are encoded and mechanisms are computed to fit specific problem instances.

3. PRELIMINARIES

Let A be a set of m alternatives and $\mathcal{N}$ be a set of n voters. Whether no-show paradoxes occur depends on the exact values of m and n. By $\mathcal{E}(\mathcal{N}) := 2^{\mathcal{N}} \setminus \{\emptyset\}$ we denote the set of *electorates*, i.e., non-empty subsets of $\mathcal{N}$. For many of our results, we will take $A = \{\mathtt{a}, \mathtt{b}, \mathtt{c}, \mathtt{d}\}$, and we use the labels $\mathtt{x}, \mathtt{y}$ for arbitrary elements of A.

A *(strict) preference relation* is a complete, antisymmetric, and transitive binary relation on A. The preference relation of voter i is denoted by $\succcurlyeq_i$. The set of all preference relations over A is denoted by $\mathcal{R}$. For brevity, we denote by $\mathtt{abcd}$ the preference relation $\mathtt{a} \succcurlyeq_i \mathtt{b} \succcurlyeq_i \mathtt{c} \succcurlyeq_i \mathtt{d}$, eliding the identity of voter i, and similarly for other preferences.

A *preference profile* R is a function from an electorate $N \in \mathcal{E}(\mathcal{N})$ to the set of preference relations $\mathcal{R}$. The set of all preference profiles is thus given by $\mathcal{R}^{\mathcal{E}(\mathcal{N})}$. For the sake of adding and deleting voters, we define for any preference profile $R \in \mathcal{R}^N$ with $(i, \succcurlyeq_i) \in R$, and $j \in \mathcal{N} \setminus N$, $\succcurlyeq_j \in \mathcal{R}$

$$R - i := R \setminus \{(i, \succcurlyeq_i)\}, \quad R + (j, \succcurlyeq_j) := R \cup \{(j, \succcurlyeq_j)\}.$$

If the identity of the voter is clear or irrelevant we sometimes, in slight abuse of notation, refer to $R - i$ by $R - \succcurlyeq_i$, and write $R + \succcurlyeq_j$ instead of $R + (j, \succcurlyeq_j)$. If k voters with the same preferences $\succcurlyeq_i$ are to be added or removed, we write $R + k \cdot \succcurlyeq_i$ and $R - k \cdot \succcurlyeq_i$, respectively.

The *majority margin* of R is the map $g_R \colon A \times A \to \mathbb{Z}$ with $g_R(\mathtt{x}, \mathtt{y}) = |\{i \in N \mid \mathtt{x} \succcurlyeq_i \mathtt{y}\}| - |\{i \in N \mid \mathtt{y} \succcurlyeq_i \mathtt{x}\}|$. The majority margin can be viewed as the adjacency matrix of a *weighted tournament* T_R. We say that a preference profile R *induces* the weighted tournament T_R.

An alternative $\mathtt{x}$ is called *Condorcet winner* if it wins against any other alternative in a majority contest, i.e., if $g_R(\mathtt{x}, \mathtt{y}) > 0$ for all $\mathtt{y} \in A \setminus \{\mathtt{x}\}$. Conversely, an alternative $\mathtt{x}$ is a *Condorcet loser* if $g_R(\mathtt{x}, \mathtt{y}) < 0$ for all $\mathtt{y} \in A \setminus \{\mathtt{x}\}$.

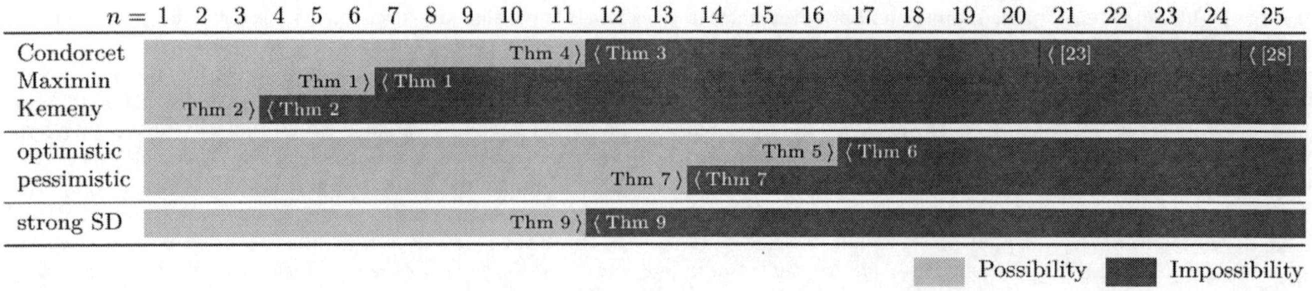

Table 1: Bounds on the number of voters for which Condorcet extensions can satisfy participation. Green cells indicate the existence of a Condorcet extension satisfying participation (for $m = 4$). Red cells indicate that no Condorcet extension satisfies participation (for $m \geqslant 4$).

Our central object of study are *voting rules*, i.e., functions that assigns every preference profile a socially preferred alternative. Thus, a voting rule is a function $f\colon \mathcal{R}^{\mathcal{E}(\mathcal{N})} \to A$.

In this paper, we study voting rules that satisfy *Condorcet-consistency* and *participation.*

DEFINITION 1. *A* Condorcet extension *is a voting rule that selects the Condorcet winner whenever it exists. Thus, f is a Condorcet extension if for every preference profile R that admits a Condorcet winner* $\mathtt{x}$, *we have* $f(R) = \mathtt{x}$. *We say that f is* Condorcet-consistent.

DEFINITION 2. *A voting rule f satisfies* participation *if all voters always weakly prefer voting to not voting, i.e., if $f(R) \succcurlyeq_i f(R-i)$ for all $R \in \mathcal{R}^N$ and $i \in N$ with $N \in \mathcal{E}(\mathcal{N})$.*

Equivalently, participation requires that for all preference profiles R not including voter j, we have $f(R+\succcurlyeq_j) \succcurlyeq_j f(R)$.

4. MAXIMIN AND KEMENY'S RULE

The proofs of both positive and negative results to come were obtained through automated techniques that we describe in Section 5. To become familiar with the kind of arguments produced in this way, we will now study a more restricted setting which is of independent interest.

Specifically, let us consider voting rules that select winners in accordance with the popular *maximin* and *Kemeny* rules. For a preference profile R, an alternative $\mathtt{x}$ is a *maximin winner* if it maximizes $\min_{\mathtt{y}\in A\setminus\{\mathtt{x}\}} g_R(\mathtt{x},\mathtt{y})$; thus, $\mathtt{x}$ never gets defeated too badly in pairwise comparisons. An alternative $\mathtt{x}$ is a *Kemeny winner* if it is ranked first in some *Kemeny ranking.* A Kemeny ranking is a preference relation $\succcurlyeq_K \in \mathcal{R}$ maximizing agreement with voters' individual preferences, i.e., it maximizes the quantity $\sum_{i\in N} |\succcurlyeq_K \cap \succcurlyeq_i|$.

We call a voting rule a *maximin extension* (resp. *Kemeny extension*) if it always selects a maximin winner (resp. Kemeny winner). Since a Condorcet winner, if it exists, is always the unique maximin and Kemeny winner of a preference profile, any such voting rule is also a Condorcet extension. We can now prove an easy version of Moulin's theorem for these more restricted voting rules.

To this end, we first prove a useful lemma allowing us to extend impossibility proofs for 4 alternatives to also apply if there are more than 4 alternatives. Its proof gives a first hint on how Condorcet-consistency and participation interact.

LEMMA 1. *Suppose that f is a Condorcet extension satisfying participation. Let R be a preference profile and $B \subsetneq A$ a set of* bad *alternatives such that each voter ranks every $\mathtt{x} \in B$ below every $\mathtt{y} \in A \setminus B$. Then $f(R) \notin B$.*

PROOF. By induction on the number of voters $|N|$ in R. If R consists of a single voter i, then, since f is a Condorcet extension, $f(R)$ must return i's top choice, which is not bad. If R consists of at least 2 voters, and $i \in N$, then by participation $f(R) \succcurlyeq_i f(R-i)$. If $f(R)$ were bad, then so would be $f(R-i)$, contradicting the inductive hypothesis. □

The following computer-aided proofs, just like the more complicated proofs to follow, can be understood solely by carefully examining the corresponding 'proof diagram'. An arrow such as R —+ abcd⟶ R' indicates that profile R' is obtained from R by adding a voter abcd, and is read as "if one of the bold green alternatives (here ab) is selected at R, then one of them is selected at R'" (by participation). A circled node ⓐ indicates a profile admitting Condorcet winner a, although in the proofs of Theorems 1 and 2, we use it to refer to maximin and Kemeny winners, respectively.

THEOREM 1. *There is no maximin extension that satisfies participation for $m \geqslant 4$ and $n \geqslant 7$. (For $m = 4$ and $n \leqslant 6$, such a maximin extension exists.)*

PROOF. Let f be a maximin extension which satisfies participation. Consider the following 6-voter profile R:

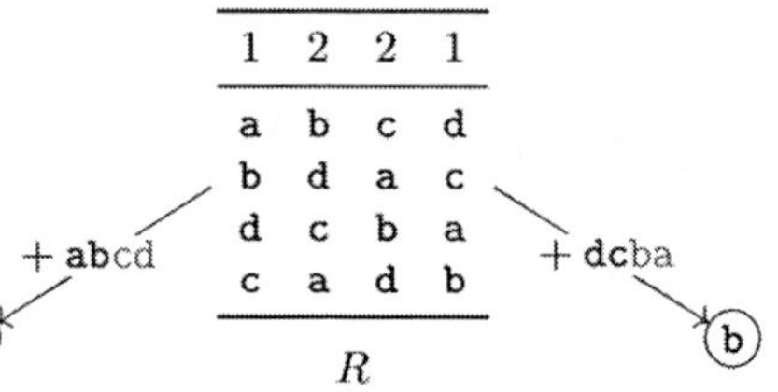

Suppose $f(R) \in \{\mathtt{a},\mathtt{b}\}$. Adding an abcd vote leads to a weighted tournament in which alternative c is the unique maximin winner. But this contradicts participation since the added voter would benefit from abstaining the election.

Symmetrically, if $f(R) \in \{\mathtt{c},\mathtt{d}\}$, then adding a dcba vote leads to a weighted tournament in which b is the maximin winner, again contradicting participation. The symmetry of the argument is due to an automorphism of R, namely the relabelling of alternatives according to abcd ↦ dcba.

If $m > 4$, we add new bad alternatives $\mathtt{x}_1, \mathtt{x}_2, \dots, \mathtt{x}_{m-4}$ to the bottom of R and of the additional voters. By Lemma 1, f chooses from $\{\mathtt{a},\mathtt{b},\mathtt{c},\mathtt{d}\}$ at each step, completing the proof.

The existence result for $n \leqslant 6$ is established by the methods described in Section 5. □

For 3 alternatives, Moulin [28] proved that the voting rule that chooses the lexicographically first maximin winner satisfies participation. Theorem 1 shows that this is not the case for 4 alternatives, even if there are only 7 voters and no matter how we pick among maximin winners.

THEOREM 2. *There is no Kemeny extension that satisfies participation for $m \geqslant 4$ and $n \geqslant 4$. (For $m = 4$ and $n \leqslant 3$, such a Kemeny extension exists.)*

PROOF. Let f be a Kemeny extension which satisfies participation. Consider the following 4-voter profile R:

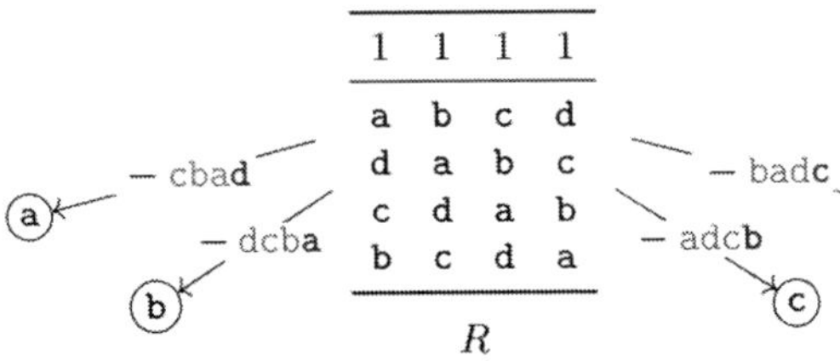

R

Suppose $f(R) = \text{d}$. Then removing cbad from R yields a weighted tournament in which a is the (unique) Kemeny winner, which contradicts participation. Analogously, we can exclude the other three possible outcomes for R by letting a voter abstain, which always leads to a unique Kemeny winner and a contradiction with participation. The arguments are identical because R is completely symmetric in the sense that for any pair of alternatives x and y, there is an automorphism of R that maps x to y.

Just like for Theorem 1, if $m > 4$, we add new bad alternatives $x_1, x_2, \dots, x_{m-4}$ to the bottom of R and of the additional voters. By Lemma 1, f chooses from $\{a, b, c, d\}$ at each step, completing the proof. □

One remarkable and unexpected aspect of the computer-aided proofs above is that their simplicity is due to automorphisms of the underlying preference profiles. Similar automorphisms will also be used in the proofs of the stronger theorems in Sections 6, 7, and 8. We emphasize that these symmetries are not hard-coded into our problem specification and, to the best of our knowledge, have not been exploited in previous proofs of similar statements.

5. METHOD: SAT SOLVING FOR COMPUTER-AIDED PROOFS

The bounds in this paper were obtained with the aid of a computer. In this section, we describe the method that we employed. The main tool in our approach is an encoding of our problems into propositional logic. We then use SAT solvers to decide whether (in a chosen setting) there exists a Condorcet extension satisfying participation. If the answer is yes, the solver returns an explicit such voting rule. If the answer is no, we use a process called *MUS extraction* to find a short certificate of this fact which can be translated into a human-readable proof. By successively proving stronger theorems and using the insights obtained through MUS extraction, we arrived at results as presented in their full generality in this paper.

5.1 SAT Encoding

"For n voters and 4 alternatives, is there a voting rule f that satisfies Condorcet-consistency and participation?"

A natural encoding of this question into propositional logic proceeds like this: Generate all profiles over 4 alternatives with at most n voters. For each such profile R, introduce 4 propositional variables $x_{R,\text{a}}$, $x_{R,\text{b}}$, $x_{R,\text{c}}$, $x_{R,\text{d}}$, where the intended meaning of $x_{R,\text{a}}$ is

$$x_{R,\text{a}} \text{ is set true} \iff f(R) = \text{a}.$$

We then add clauses requiring that for each profile R, $f(R)$ takes *exactly one* value, and we add clauses requiring f to be Condorcet-consistent and satisfy participation.

Sadly, the encoding sketched above is not tractable for the values of n that we are interested in: the number of variables and clauses used grows as $\Theta(24^n)$, because there are $4! = 24$ possible preference relations over 4 alternatives and thus 24^n profiles with n voters. For $n = 7$, this leads to more than 400 billion variables, and for $n = 15$ we exceed 10^{22} variables.

To escape this combinatorial explosion, we will temporarily restrict our attention to *pairwise* voting rules. This means that we assign an outcome alternative $f(T)$ to every weighted tournament T. We then define a voting rule that assigns the outcome $f(T_R)$ to each preference profile R, where T_R is the weighted tournament induced by R.

The number of tournaments induced by profiles with n voters grows much slower than the number of profiles—our computer enumeration suggests a growth of order about 1.5^n. This much more manageable (yet still exponential) growth allows us to consider problem instances up to $n \approx 16$ which turns out to be *just* enough.

Other than referring to (weighted) tournaments instead of profiles, our encoding into logic now proceeds exactly like before. For each tournament T, we introduce the variables $x_{T,\text{a}}$, $x_{T,\text{b}}$, $x_{T,\text{c}}$, $x_{T,\text{d}}$ and define the formulas

$$\text{non-empty}_T := x_{T,\text{a}} \lor x_{T,\text{b}} \lor x_{T,\text{c}} \lor x_{T,\text{d}}$$

$$\text{mutex}_T := \bigwedge_{\text{x} \neq \text{y}} (\neg x_{T,\text{x}} \lor \neg x_{T,\text{y}})$$

With our intended interpretation of the variables $x_{T,\text{x}}$, all models of $\bigwedge_T \text{non-empty}_T \land \text{mutex}_T$ are functions from tournaments into $\{a, b, c, d\}$. (The word mutex abbreviates 'mutual exclusion' and corresponds to the voting rule selecting a unique winner.)

Since we are interested in voting rules that satisfy participation, we also need to encode this property. To this end, let $T = T_R$ be a tournament induced by R and let $\succcurlyeq$ be a preference relation. Define $T + \succcurlyeq \, := T_{R+\succcurlyeq}$. (The tournament $T + \succcurlyeq$ is independent of the choice of R.) We define

$$\text{participation}_{T,\succcurlyeq} := \bigwedge_{\text{x}} \left(x_{T,\text{x}} \to \bigvee_{\text{y} \succcurlyeq \text{x}} x_{T+\succcurlyeq,\text{y}} \right).$$

Requiring f to be Condorcet-consistent is straightforward: if tournament T admits b as the Condorcet winner, we add

$$\text{condorcet}_T := \neg x_{T,\text{a}} \land x_{T,\text{b}} \land \neg x_{T,\text{c}} \land \neg x_{T,\text{d}},$$

and we add similar formulas for each tournament that admits a Condorcet winner. Then the models of the conjunction of all the non-empty, mutex, participation, and condorcet formulas are precisely the pairwise voting rules satisfying Condorcet-consistency and participation.

By adapting the condorcet formulas, we can impose more stringent conditions on f—this is how our results for maximin and Kemeny extensions are obtained. We can also use this to exclude Pareto-dominated alternatives, and to require f to always pick from the top cycle.

For some purposes it will be useful not to include the mutex clauses in our final formula. Models of this formula then correspond to *set-valued* voting rules that satisfy participation interpreted according to the optimistic preference extension. See Section 7 for results in this setting.

5.2 SAT Solving and MUS Extraction

The formulas we have obtained above are all given in *conjunctive normal form* (CNF), and thus can be evaluated without further transformations by any off-the-shelf SAT solver. In order to physically produce a CNF formula as described, we employ a straightforward Python script that performs a breadth-first search to discover all weighted tournaments with up to n voters (see Algorithm 1 for a schematic overview of the program). The script outputs a CNF formula in the standard DIMACS format, and also outputs a file that, for each variable $x_{T,\mathtt{x}}$, records the tournament T and alternative $\mathtt{x}$ it denotes. This is necessary because the DIMACS format uses uninformative variable descriptors (consecutive integers) and memorizing variable meanings allows us to interpret the output of the SAT solver.

Algorithm 1 Generate formula for up to n voters

$T_0 \leftarrow$ {weighted tournament on $\{\mathsf{a},\mathsf{b},\mathsf{c},\mathsf{d}\}$ with all edges having weight 0}.
for $k = 1, \ldots, n$ **do**
  $T_k \leftarrow \emptyset$
  for $T \in T_{k-1}$ **do**
    for $\succcurlyeq \in \mathcal{R}$ **do**
      Calculate $T' := T + \succcurlyeq$
      Add T' to T_k
      Write non-empty$_{T'}$, mutex$_{T'}$, condorcet$_{T'}$
      Write participation$_{T,\succcurlyeq}$

As an example, the output formula for $n = 15$ in DIMACS format has a size of about 7 GB and uses 50 million variables and 2 billion clauses, taking 6.5 hours to write. Plingeling [3], a popular SAT solver that we used for all results in this paper, solves this formula in 50 minutes of wall clock time, half of which is spent parsing the formula.

In case a given instance is satisfiable, the solver returns a satisfying assignment, giving us an existence proof and a concrete example for a voting rule satisfying participation (and any further requirements imposed). In case a given instance in unsatisfiable, we would like to have short certificate of this fact as well. One possibility for this is having the SAT solver output a resolution proof (in DRUP format, say). This yields a machine-checkable proof, but has two major drawbacks: the generated proofs can be uncomfortably large [24], and they do not give human-readable insights about *why* the formula is unsatisfiable.

We handle this problem by computing a *minimal unsatisfiable subset (MUS)* of the unsatisfiable CNF formula. An MUS is a subset of the clauses of the original formula which itself is unsatisfiable, and is minimally so: removing any clause from it yields a satisfiable formula. We used the tools MUSer2 [2] and MARCO [27] to extract MUSes. If an unsatisfiable formula admits a very small MUS, it is often possible to obtain a human-readable proof of unsatisfiability from it [8, 4].

Note that for purposes of extracting human-readable proofs, it is desirable for the MUS to be as small as possible, and also to refer to as few different tournaments as possible. The first issue can be addressed by running the MUS extractor repeatedly, instructing it to order clauses randomly (note that clause sets of different cardinalities can be minimally unsatisfiable with respect to set inclusion); similarly, we can use MARCO to enumerate all MUSes and look for small ones. The second issue can be addressed by computing a *group MUS*: here, we partition the clauses of the CNF formula into *groups*, and we are looking for a minimal set of groups that together are unsatisfiable. In our case, the clauses referring to a given tournament T form a group. In practice, finding a group MUS first and then finding a standard (clause-level) MUS within the group MUS yielded sets of size much smaller than MUSes returned without the intermediate group-step (often by a factor of 10).

To translate an MUS into a human-readable proof, we created another program that visualized the MUS in a convenient form.[1] Indeed, this program outputs the 'proof diagrams' like Figure 1 that appear throughout this paper (though we re-typeset them). We think that interpreting these diagrams is quite natural (and is perhaps even easier than reading a textual translation). More importantly, the automatically produced graphs allowed us to quickly judge the quality of an extracted MUS.

5.3 Incremental Proof Discovery

The SAT encoding described in Section 5.1 only concerns pairwise voting rules, yet none of the (negative) results in this paper require or use this assumption. This is the product of multiple rounds of generating and evaluating SAT formulas, extracting MUSes, and using the insights generated by this as 'educated guesses' to solve more general problems.

Following the process as described so far led to a proof that for 4 alternatives and 12 voters, there is no pairwise Condorcet extension that satisfies participation. That proof used the assumption of pairwiseness, i.e., it assumed that the voting rule returns the same alternative on profiles inducing the same weighted tournament. However, intriguingly, the preference profiles mentioned in the proof did not contain all $4! = 24$ possible preference relations over $\{\mathsf{a},\mathsf{b},\mathsf{c},\mathsf{d}\}$. In fact, it only used 10 of the possible orders. Further, each profile included $R_0 = \{\mathsf{abdc}, \mathsf{bdca}, \mathsf{cabd}, \mathsf{dcab}\}$ as a subprofile. As we argued at the start of Section 5.1, it is intractable to search over the entire space of preference profiles. On the other hand, it is much easier to merely search over all extensions of R_0 that contain at most $n = 12$ voters and only contain copies of the 10 orders previously identified. The SAT formula produced by doing exactly this turned out to be unsatisfiable, and a small MUS extracted from it gave rise to Theorem 3.

The proof of Theorem 6 for 17 voters was obtained by running Algorithm 1 with T_0 initialized to the weighted tournament induced by the initial profile R used in the proof of Theorem 3. Before finding this tournament, we tried various other tournaments as T_0, including ones featuring in Moulin's original proof, and ones occurring at other steps in the proof of Theorem 3, but R turned out to give the best

[1] Roughly, the visualization program proceeds by drawing an edge for every participation$_{T,\succcurlyeq}$ clause that occurs in the MUS, and marks the nodes for which condorcet$_T$ clauses appear in the MUS.

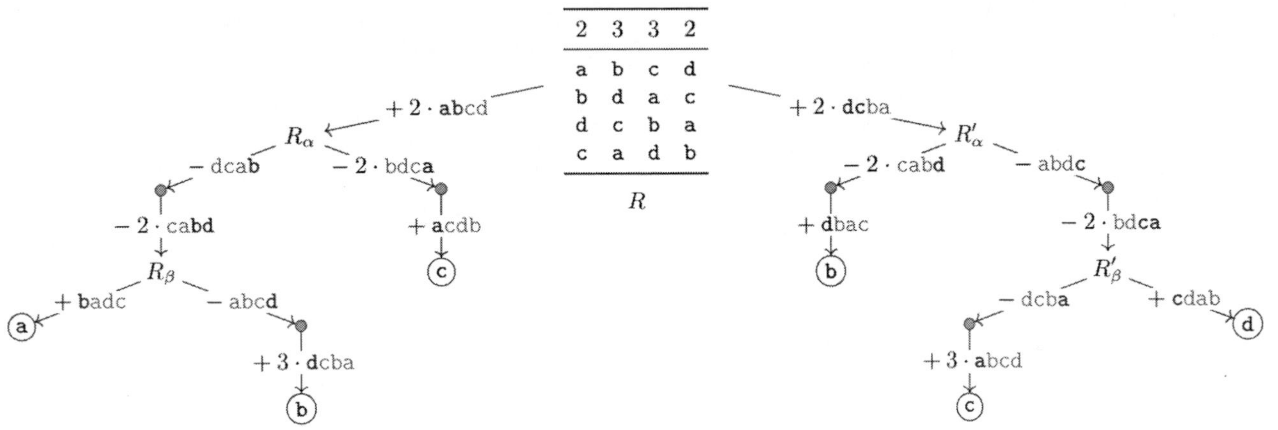

Figure 1: Computer-aided proof of Theorem 3 in graphical form, showing that there is no Condorcet extension that satisfies participation for $m \geqslant 4$ and $n \geqslant 12$. See Section 4 for an explanation of how to read this diagram.

(and indeed a tight) bound, and additionally exhibits a lot of symmetry that was also present in the MUS we extracted.

6. MAIN RESULT

We are now in a position to state and prove our main claim that Condorcet extensions cannot avoid the no-show paradox for 12 or more voters (when there are at least 4 alternatives), and that this result is optimal.

THEOREM 3. *There is no Condorcet extension that satisfies participation for $m \geqslant 4$ and $n \geqslant 12$.*

PROOF. The proof follows the structure depicted in Figure 1. Let R be the preference profile shown there.

Since R remains fixed after relabelling alternatives according to abcd $\mapsto$ dcba, we may assume without loss of generality that $f(R) \in \{\mathtt{a}, \mathtt{b}\}$. (An explicit proof in case $f(R) \in \{\mathtt{c}, \mathtt{d}\}$ is indicated in Figure 1.)

By participation, it follows from $f(R) \in \{\mathtt{a}, \mathtt{b}\}$ that also $f(R_\alpha := R + 2 \cdot \mathtt{abcd}) \in \{\mathtt{a}, \mathtt{b}\}$ since the voters with preferences abcd cannot be worse off by joining the electorate. If $f(R_\alpha) = \mathtt{a}$, again by participation, removing 2 voters with preferences bdca does not change the winning alternative (so $f(R_\alpha - 2 \cdot \mathtt{bdca}) = \mathtt{a}$), and neither does adding acdb, so $f(R_\alpha - 2 \cdot \mathtt{bdca} + \mathtt{acdb}) = \mathtt{a}$, which, however, is in conflict with $R_\alpha - 2 \cdot \mathtt{bdca} + \mathtt{acdb}$ having a Condorcet winner, c.

Thus we must have $f(R_\alpha) = \mathtt{b}$, which implies that $f(R_\alpha - \mathtt{dcab}) = \mathtt{b}$, and thus $f(R_\beta := R_\alpha - \mathtt{dcab} - 2 \cdot \mathtt{cabd}) \in \{\mathtt{b}, \mathtt{d}\}$.

We again proceed by cases: If $f(R_\beta) = \mathtt{b}$, we can add a voter badc to obtain a profile with Condorcet winner a, which contradicts participation. But then, if $f(R_\beta) = \mathtt{d}$, we get that $f(R_\beta - \mathtt{abcd}) = \mathtt{d}$ and, by another application of participation, that $f(R_\beta - \mathtt{abcd} + 3 \cdot \mathtt{dcba}) = \mathtt{d}$ in contrast to the existence of Condorcet winner b, a contradiction.

If $m > 4$, we add bad alternatives $\mathtt{x}_1, \mathtt{x}_2, \ldots, \mathtt{x}_{m-4}$ to the bottom of R and all other voters. By Lemma 1, f chooses from $\{\mathtt{a}, \mathtt{b}, \mathtt{c}, \mathtt{d}\}$ at each step, completing the proof. □

The following result establishes that our bound on the number of voters is tight. A very useful feature of our computer-aided approach is that we can easily add additional requirements for the desired voting rule. Two common requirements for voting rules are that they should only return alternatives that are *Pareto-optimal* and contained in the *top cycle* (also known as the *Smith set*) (see, e.g., [17]).

THEOREM 4. *There is a Condorcet extension f that satisfies participation for $m = 4$ and $n \leqslant 11$. Moreover, f is pairwise, Pareto-optimal, and a refinement of the top cycle.*

The Condorcet extension f is given as a look-up table, which is derived from the output of a SAT solver. The look-up table lists all 1,204,215 weighted tournaments inducible by up to 11 voters and assigns each an output alternative (see Figure 2 for an excerpt). The relevant text file has a size of 28 MB (gzipped 4.5 MB) and is available as part of an arXiv version of this paper [10].

Comparing this voting rule with known voting rules, it turns out that it picks a maximin winner in 99.8% and a Kemeny winner in 98% of all weighted tournaments. Moreover, the rule agrees with the maximin rule with lexicographic tie-breaking on 95% of weighted tournaments. The similarity with the maximin rule is interesting insofar as a well-documented flaw of the maximin rule is that it fails to be a refinement of the top cycle (and may even return Condorcet losers). Our computer-generated rule always picks from the top cycle while it remains very close to the maximin rule.

80% of the considered weighted tournaments admit a Condorcet winner, which uniquely determines the output of the rule; this can be used to reduce the size of the look-up table.

7. SET-VALUED VOTING RULES

A drawback of voting rules, as we defined them so far, is that that the requirement to always return a single winner is in conflict with basic fairness conditions, namely anonymity and neutrality. A large part of the social choice literature therefore deals with set-valued voting rules, where ties are usually assumed to be eventually broken by some tie-breaking mechanism.

A *set-valued voting rule* (sometimes known as a voting *correspondence* or as an *irresolute* voting rule) is a function $F\colon \mathcal{R}^{\mathcal{E}(\mathcal{N})} \to 2^A \setminus \{\emptyset\}$ that assigns each preference profile R a non-empty set of alternatives. The function F is a *(set-valued) Condorcet extension* if for every preference profile R that admits a Condorcet winner x, we have $F(R) = \{\mathtt{x}\}$.

Following the work of Pérez [29] and Jimeno et al. [22], we seek to study the occurrence of the no-show paradox in

```
a,#1,(1,1,1,1,1,1)
a,#1,(1,1,1,1,1,-1)
a,#1,(1,1,1,-1,1,1)
a,#1,(1,1,1,-1,-1,1)
a,#1,(1,1,1,1,-1,-1)
a,#1,(1,1,1,-1,-1,-1)
b,#1,(-1,1,1,1,1,1)
b,#1,(-1,1,1,1,1,-1)
b,#1,(-1,-1,1,1,1,1)
b,#1,(-1,-1,-1,1,1,1)
b,#1,(-1,1,-1,1,1,-1)
b,#1,(-1,-1,-1,1,1,-1)
c,#1,(1,-1,1,-1,1,1)
c,#1,(1,-1,1,-1,-1,1)
a,#11,(9,11,3,9,1,-9)
a,#11,(11,9,3,7,1,-9)
c,#11,(5,-9,-1,-11,-1,7)
c,#11,(5,-9,-1,-11,-1,5)
c,#11,(3,-11,-1,-9,1,7)
c,#11,(3,-11,-3,-9,1,7)
c,#11,(3,-11,-3,-11,-1,7)
b,#11,(-1,3,-5,-3,5,-3)
b,#11,(-3,3,-7,-3,5,-3)
b,#11,(-3,1,-7,-3,5,-3)
c,#11,(-3,1,-5,-5,5,-1)
a,#11,(3,7,11,-3,9,11)
a,#11,(3,7,11,-3,9,9)
a,#11,(3,7,11,-5,9,11)
```

Figure 2: Excerpt of look-up table giving a pairwise Condorcet extension satisfying participation for $n \leqslant 11$ voters (from Theorem 4). Each row lists a weighted tournament as $(g_R(\mathsf{a},\mathsf{b}), g_R(\mathsf{a},\mathsf{c}), g_R(\mathsf{a},\mathsf{d}), g_R(\mathsf{b},\mathsf{c}), g_R(\mathsf{b},\mathsf{d}), g_R(\mathsf{c},\mathsf{d}))$ with a chosen alternative, and with the number of voters inducing the tournament.

this setting. To do so, we need to define appropriate notions of participation, and for this we will need to specify agents' preferences over *sets* of alternatives. Here, we use the *optimistic* and *pessimistic preference extensions.* An optimist prefers sets with better most-preferred alternative, while a pessimist prefers sets with better least-preferred alternative. For example, if $U = \{\mathsf{a},\mathsf{b},\mathsf{d}\}$ and $V = \{\mathsf{b},\mathsf{c}\}$, then an optimist with preferences abcd prefers U to V, while a pessimist prefers V to U. With these notions, we extend the participation property to set-valued voting rules.

DEFINITION 3. *A set-valued voting rule F satisfies* optimistic participation *if* $\max_{\succcurlyeq_i} F(R + \succcurlyeq_i) \succcurlyeq_i \max_{\succcurlyeq_i} F(R)$.
A set-valued voting rule F satisfies pessimistic participation *if* $\min_{\succcurlyeq_i} F(R) \succcurlyeq_i \min_{\succcurlyeq_i} F(R - i)$.

A set-valued voting rule F is called *resolute* if it always selects a single alternative, so that for all R we have $|F(R)| = 1$. A (single-valued) voting rule f is naturally identified with a resolute set-valued voting rule F; if f satisfies participation, then this F satisfies both optimistic and pessimistic participation. Hence, by Theorem 4, there is a (resolute) set-valued Condorcet extension F that satisfies both optimistic and pessimistic participation. However, there might be hope that allowing voting rules to be irresolute also allows for participation to be attainable for more voters, and indeed this is the case.

THEOREM 5. *There is a set-valued Condorcet extension F that satisfies optimistic participation for $m = 4$ and $n \leqslant 16$, and also is Pareto-optimal and a refinement of the top cycle.*

The SAT solver indicates that no such set-valued voting rule is pairwise. Theorem 5 is optimal in the sense that optimistic participation cannot be achieved if we allow for one more voter.

THEOREM 6. *There is no set-valued Condorcet extension that satisfies optimistic participation for $m \geqslant 4$ and $n \geqslant 17$.*

PROOF. Let F be such a function, and consider the following 10-voter profile R:

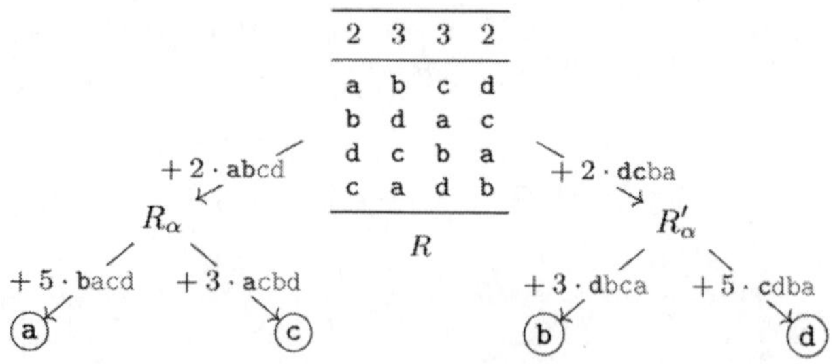

Suppose that either $\mathsf{a} \in F(R)$ or $\mathsf{b} \in F(R)$. (The case of $\mathsf{c} \in F(R)$ or $\mathsf{d} \in F(R)$ is symmetric.) Then let $R_\alpha := R + 2 \cdot \mathsf{abcd}$. By optimistic participation, we then have either $\mathsf{a} \in F(R_\alpha)$ or $\mathsf{b} \in F(R_\alpha)$. If we had $\mathsf{a} \in F(R_\alpha)$, then also $\mathsf{a} \in F(R_\alpha + 3 \cdot \mathsf{acbd})$ but this profile has Condorcet winner c, and if $\mathsf{b} \in F(R_\alpha)$ then also $\mathsf{b} \in F(R_\alpha + 5 \cdot \mathsf{bacd})$ but this profile has Condorcet winner a. This is a contradiction.

This argument extends to more than 4 alternatives by appealing to a set-valued analogue of Lemma 1. □

Inspecting Moulin's original proof [28] shows that it also establishes an impossibility for optimistic participation (for 25 voters). Apparently unaware of this, Jimeno et al. [22] explicitly establish such a result for 27 voters and 5 alternatives. It is worth observing that each step of the proof of Theorem 6 involves *adding* voters to the current profile, and we never remove voters. In light of Definition 3, this is the reason why the proof establishes a result for optimistic participation. If we restrict ourselves to deleting voters, we obtain a result for pessimistic participation.

THEOREM 7. *There is no set-valued Condorcet extension that satisfies pessimistic participation for $m \geqslant 4$ and $n \geqslant 14$. On the other hand, for $m = 4$ and $n \leqslant 13$, there exists such a set-valued voting rule.*

PROOF SKETCH. The proof has a similar structure to the proof of Theorem 3, displayed in Figure 1. The initial profile of this proof is $R + 2 \cdot \mathsf{abcd} + 2 \cdot \mathsf{dcba}$, taking R to be the profile of Figure 1. We further replace proof steps in which voters are added by similar ones where voters are deleted, and invoke pessimistic participation at each such step to obtain a contradiction. □

This result strengthens a result of Jimeno et al. [22], who show that for $m \geqslant 5$ no set-valued Condorcet extension satisfying a property called "weak translation invariance" can also satisfy pessimistic participation. Our proof does not need the extra assumption, already works for $m = 4$ alternatives, and uses just 14 instead of 971 voters.[2]

As previously observed, adding voters in our impossibility proofs corresponds to optimistic participation, while removing voters corresponds to pessimistic participation. In the proof of Theorem 3, we use both operations, which allows for a tighter bound of just 12 voters. In the set-valued setting, we can formulate this result in a slightly stronger way.

[2]The large number of voters is due to several applications of the "weak translation invariance" axiom, each of which adds $5! = 120$ voters to the preference profile under consideration.

THEOREM 8. *There is no set-valued Condorcet extension that satisfies optimistic and pessimistic participation simultaneously for $m \geqslant 4$ and $n \geqslant 12$. On the other hand, for $m = 4$ and $n \leqslant 11$ such a set-valued rule exists (and also is Pareto-optimal and a refinement of the top cycle).*

PROOF. Use the proof of Theorem 3, invoking optimistic participation for edges labelled with the addition of a voter (+), and invoking pessimistic participation for edges labelled with removal of a voter (−). On the other hand, the (single-valued) voting rule of Theorem 4 clearly satisfies both optimistic and pessimistic participation. □

The preference extension combining the optimistic and pessimistic preference extension is also known as the *Egli-Milner extension.*

8. PROBABILISTIC VOTING RULES

A *probabilistic voting rule* (also known as a *social decision scheme*) assigns to each preference profile R a probability distribution (or *lottery*) over A. Thus, a probabilistic voting rule might assign a fair coin flip between a and b as the outcome of an election.

Formally, let $\Delta(A) = \{\mathbf{p} : A \to [0,1] : \sum_{x \in A} \mathbf{p}(x) = 1\}$ be the set of lotteries over A; a lottery $\mathbf{p} \in \Delta(A)$ assigns probability $\mathbf{p}(x)$ to alternative x. A probabilistic voting rule f is a function $f : \mathcal{R}^{\mathcal{E}(\mathcal{N})} \to \Delta(A)$. In this context, we say that f is a *Condorcet extension* if $f(R)$ puts probability 1 on the Condorcet winner of R whenever it exists: if R admits x as the Condorcet winner, then $f(R)(x) = 1$.

As in the set-valued case, we need a notion of comparing outcomes in order to extend the definition of participation. Here, we use the concept of *stochastic dominance (SD).*

DEFINITION 4. *Let $\succcurlyeq \in \mathcal{R}$ be a preference relation over A, and let $\mathbf{p}, \mathbf{q} \in \Delta(A)$ be lotteries. Then $\mathbf{p}$ is (weakly) SD-preferred over $\mathbf{q}$ by $\succcurlyeq$ if for each alternative x, we have*

$$\sum_{y \succcurlyeq x} \mathbf{p}(y) \geqslant \sum_{y \succcurlyeq x} \mathbf{q}(y).$$

In this case, we write $\mathbf{p} \succcurlyeq^{SD} \mathbf{q}$.

For example, the lottery $\frac{2}{3}a + \frac{1}{3}c$ is SD-preferred to the lottery $\frac{1}{3}a + \frac{1}{3}b + \frac{1}{3}c$ by a voter with preferences abcd. A voter with preferences bacd will feel the other way around. The main appeal of stochastic dominance stems from the following equivalence: $\mathbf{p} \succcurlyeq^{SD} \mathbf{q}$ if and only if $\mathbf{p}$ yields at least as much von-Neumann-Morgenstern utility as $\mathbf{q}$ under any utility function that is consistent with the ordinal preferences $\succcurlyeq$. Using this notion of comparing lotteries, we can define participation analogously to the previous settings.

DEFINITION 5. *A probabilistic voting rule f satisfies* strong SD-participation *if $f(R) \succcurlyeq_i^{SD} f(R-i)$ for all $R \in \mathcal{R}^N$ and $i \in N$ with $N \in \mathcal{E}(\mathcal{N})$.*

Any (single-valued) voting rule f can be seen as a probabilistic voting rule that puts probability 1 on its chosen alternative. If f satisfies participation, then this derived probabilistic voting rule is easily seen to satisfy strong SD-participation. Hence Theorem 4 gives us a probabilistic Condorcet extension that satisfies strong SD-participation for $n \leqslant 11$ voters and $m = 4$ alternatives.

We now establish a connection between strong SD-participation and the set-valued notions of participation that we considered in Section 7. This connection will allow us to translate the impossibility results we obtained there to the probabilistic setting. To set up this connection, let us define the *support* of a lottery $\mathbf{p} \in \Delta(A)$ to be $\text{supp}(\mathbf{p}) := \{x \in A : \mathbf{p}(x) > 0\}$.

PROPOSITION 1. *Let f be a probabilistic voting rule satisfying strong SD-participation. Let $F = \text{supp} \circ f$ be the support of f, i.e., $F(R) = \text{supp}(f(R))$ for all profiles R. Then F satisfies both optimistic and pessimistic participation.*

PROOF. We only verify optimistic participation; the pessimistic case is similar. Let R be a preference profile with electorate $N \in \mathcal{E}(\mathcal{N})$, and let $i \in \mathcal{N} \setminus N$ be a voter with preferences $\succcurlyeq_i$. Let $x = \max_{\succcurlyeq_i} F(R)$, and let $U = \{y : y \succcurlyeq_i x\}$. We need to show that $\max_{\succcurlyeq_i} F(R + \succcurlyeq_i) \succcurlyeq_i x$, by finding an alternative $y \in U$ that is in the support of $f(R + \succcurlyeq_i)$.

But since f satisfies strong SD-participation, we have

$$\sum_{y \in U} f(R + \succcurlyeq_i)(y) \geqslant \sum_{y \in U} f(R)(y) > 0,$$

where the strict inequality follows from the definition of the support and of x. Hence some alternative from U is in the support of $f(R + \succcurlyeq_i)$, as required. □

Putting these results together with the impossibility result of Theorem 8, we obtain the following.

THEOREM 9. *There is no probabilistic Condorcet extension that satisfies strong SD-participation for $n \geqslant 12$ and $m \geqslant 4$. On the other hand, for $m = 4$ and $n \leqslant 11$, such a probabilistic voting rule exists.*

Theorem 9 resolves an open problem mentioned by Brandl et al. [5, Sec. 6].

9. CONCLUSIONS AND FUTURE WORK

We have given tight results delineating in which situations no-show paradoxes must occur. As such, our results nicely complement recent advances to satisfy Condorcet-consistency and participation by exploiting uncertainties of the voters about their preferences or about the voting rule's tie-breaking mechanism [4, 5, 6].

Due to unmanageable branching factors when there are 5 alternatives (and hence $5! = 120$ possible preference relations), we were unable to check using our approach whether no-show paradoxes occur with even less voters when the number of alternatives grows. It would be interesting to gain a deeper understanding of the computer-generated Condorcet extension that satisfies participation for up to 11 voters. So far, we only know that it (slightly) differs from all Condorcet extensions that are usually considered in the literature. As a first step, it would be desirable to obtain a representation of this rule that is more concise than a look-up table.

Another interesting topic for future research is to find optimal bounds for a variant of the no-show paradox due to Sanver and Zwicker [32], in which participation is weakened to half-way monotonicity. Their proof requires 702 voters.

Acknowledgments

Christian Geist is supported by Deutsche Forschungsgemeinschaft under grant BR 2312/9-1. Dominik Peters is supported by EPSRC. Part of this work was conducted while Dominik Peters visited TUM, supported by the COST Action IC1205 on Computational Social Choice.

REFERENCES

[1] D. Baumeister, P. Faliszewski, J. Lang, and J. Rothe. Campaigns for lazy voters: truncated ballots. In *Proc. of 11th AAMAS Conference*, pages 577–584. IFAAMAS, 2012.

[2] A. Belov and J. Marques-Silva. MUSer2: An efficient MUS extractor. *Journal on Satisfiability, Boolean Modeling and Computation*, 8:123–128, 2012.

[3] A. Biere. Lingeling, Plingeling and Treengeling entering the SAT competition 2013. In *Proc. of SAT Competition 2013*, pages 51–52, 2013.

[4] F. Brandl, F. Brandt, C. Geist, and J. Hofbauer. Strategic abstention based on preference extensions: Positive results and computer-generated impossibilities. In *Proc. of 24th IJCAI*, pages 18–24. AAAI Press, 2015.

[5] F. Brandl, F. Brandt, and J. Hofbauer. Incentives for participation and abstention in probabilistic social choice. In *Proc. of 14th AAMAS Conference*, pages 1411–1419. IFAAMAS, 2015.

[6] F. Brandl, F. Brandt, and J. Hofbauer. Welfare maximization entices participation. 2015. Working Paper.

[7] F. Brandt. Set-monotonicity implies Kelly-strategyproofness. *Social Choice and Welfare*, 45(4): 793–804, 2015.

[8] F. Brandt and C. Geist. Finding strategyproof social choice functions via SAT solving. *Journal of Artificial Intelligence Research*, 55:565–602, 2016.

[9] F. Brandt, V. Conitzer, U. Endriss, J. Lang, and A. Procaccia, editors. *Handbook of Computational Social Choice*. Cambridge University Press, 2016.

[10] F. Brandt, C. Geist, and D. Peters. Optimal bounds for the no-show paradox via SAT solving. Technical report, http://arxiv.org/abs/1602.08063, 2016.

[11] D. E. Campbell and J. S. Kelly. A strategy-proofness characterization of majority rule. *Economic Theory*, 22(3):557–568, 2003.

[12] S. Chatterjee and A. Sen. Automated reasoning in social choice theory — some remarks. *Mathematics in Computer Science*, 8(1):5–10, 2014.

[13] V. Conitzer and T. Sandholm. Complexity of mechanism design. In *Proc. of 18th UAI Conference*, pages 103–110, 2002.

[14] P. Dasgupta and E. Maskin. On the robustness of majority rule. *Journal of the European Economic Association*, 6(5):949–973, 2008.

[15] M. de Condorcet. *Essai sur l'application de l'analyse à la probabilité des décisions rendues à la pluralité des voix*. Imprimerie Royale, 1785. Facsimile published in 1972 by Chelsea Publishing Company, New York.

[16] Y. Desmedt and E. Elkind. Equilibria of plurality voting with abstentions. In *Proc. of 11th ACM-EC Conference*, pages 347–356. ACM Press, 2010.

[17] P. C. Fishburn. Condorcet social choice functions. *SIAM Journal on Applied Mathematics*, 33(3):469–489, 1977.

[18] P. C. Fishburn and S. J. Brams. Paradoxes of preferential voting. *Mathematics Magazine*, 56(4):207–214, 1983.

[19] A. Fréchette, N. Newman, and K. Leyton-Brown. Solving the station repacking problem. In *Proc. of 30th AAAI Conference*. AAAI Press, 2016.

[20] C. Geist and U. Endriss. Automated search for impossibility theorems in social choice theory: Ranking sets of objects. *Journal of Artificial Intelligence Research*, 40:143–174, 2011.

[21] R. Holzman. To vote or not to vote: What is the quota? *Discrete Applied Mathematics*, 22(2):133–141, 1988.

[22] J. L. Jimeno, J. Pérez, and E. García. An extension of the Moulin No Show Paradox for voting correspondences. *Social Choice and Welfare*, 33(3):343–459, 2009.

[23] K. Kardel. Participation and group-participation in social choice theory. Master's thesis, Technische Universität München, 2014.

[24] B. Konev and A. Lisitsa. A SAT attack on the Erdős discrepancy conjecture. In *Theory and Applications of Satisfiability Testing–SAT 2014*, pages 219–226. Springer, 2014.

[25] J.-F. Laslier. *Tournament Solutions and Majority Voting*. Springer, 1997.

[26] D. Lepelley and V. Merlin. Scoring run-off paradoxes for variable electorates. *Economic Theory*, 17(1):53–80, 2000.

[27] M. H. Liffiton, A. Previti, A. Malik, and J. Marques-Silva. Fast, flexible MUS enumeration. *Constraints*, pages 1–28, 2015.

[28] H. Moulin. Condorcet's principle implies the no show paradox. *Journal of Economic Theory*, 45:53–64, 1988.

[29] J. Pérez. The strong no show paradoxes are a common flaw in Condorcet voting correspondences. *Social Choice and Welfare*, 18(3):601–616, 2001.

[30] D. Ray. On the practical possibility of a 'no show paradox' under the single transferable vote. *Mathematical Social Sciences*, 11(2):183–189, 1986.

[31] J. Rothe, editor. *Economics and Computation: An Introduction to Algorithmic Game Theory, Computational Social Choice, and Fair Division*. Springer, 2015.

[32] M. R. Sanver and W. S. Zwicker. One-way monotonicity as a form of strategy-proofness. *International Journal of Game Theory*, 38(4):553–574, 2009.

[33] M. Schulze. Condorcet and Participation. Election-Methods mailing list. http://lists.electorama.com/pipermail/election-methods-electorama.com/2003-October/011042.html, 2003. (Accessed: 7 Nov 2015).

[34] W. D. Smith. "Participation failure" is forced in Condorcet methods with at least 4 candidates. The Center for Range Voting. http://rangevoting.org/CondPF.html, 2007. (Accessed: 7 Nov 2015).

[35] P. Tang and F. Lin. Computer-aided proofs of Arrow's and other impossibility theorems. *Artificial Intelligence*, 173(11):1041–1053, 2009.

[36] D. R. Woodall. Monotonicity of single-seat preferential election rules. *Discrete Applied Mathematics*, 77 (1):81–98, 1997.

Fault Tolerant Mechanism Design for General Task Allocation*

Dengji Zhao Sarvapali D. Ramchurn Nicholas R. Jennings
Electronics and Computer Science
University of Southampton
Southampton, SO17 1BJ, UK
{dz1a13, sdr, nrj}@ecs.soton.ac.uk

ABSTRACT

We study a general task allocation problem, involving multiple agents that collaboratively accomplish tasks and where agents may fail to successfully complete the tasks assigned to them (known as execution uncertainty). The goal is to choose an allocation that maximises social welfare while taking their execution uncertainty into account (i.e., fault tolerant). To achieve this, we show that the post-execution verification (PEV)-based mechanism presented by Porter et al. (2008) is applicable if and only if agents' valuations are risk-neutral (i.e., the solution is almost universal). We then consider a more advanced setting where an agent's execution uncertainty is not completely predictable by the agent alone but aggregated from all agents' private opinions (known as trust). We show that PEV-based mechanism with trust is still applicable if and only if the trust aggregation is multilinear. Given this characterisation, we further demonstrate how this mechanism can be successfully applied in a real-world setting. Finally, we draw the parallels between our results and the literature of efficient mechanism design with general interdependent valuations.

CCS Concepts

•Theory of computation → Algorithmic mechanism design; •Computing methodologies → Multi-agent systems;

Keywords

Execution uncertainty; interdependent valuations; type verification; trust aggregation

1. INTRODUCTION

We study a general task allocation problem, where multiple agents collaboratively accomplish a set of tasks. However, agents may fail to successfully complete the task(s) allocated to them (known as execution uncertainty). Such task allocation problems arise in many real-world applications such as transportation networks [17], data routing [16], cloud computing [1] and the sharing economy [2]. Execution uncertainty is typically unavoidable in these applications due to unforeseen events and limited resources, especially sharing economy applications such as *Uber* and *Freelancer.com*, where services are mostly provided by individuals with no qualifications or certifications.

In addition to the execution uncertainty underlying the task allocation problem, the completion of a task may also depend on the completion of other tasks, e.g., in *Uber* a rider cannot travel without a driver offering the ride. The completion of the tasks of an allocation gives a (private) value to each agent, and our goal is to choose an allocation of tasks that maximises the total value of all agents, while taking their execution uncertainty into account.

It has been shown that traditional mechanism design (based on Groves mechanisms [5]) is not applicable to settings that involve execution uncertainty [14, 4]. This is because execution uncertainty implies interdependencies between the agents' valuations (e.g., a rider's value for a ride will largely depend on whether the driver will successfully finish the drive). To combat this problem, Porter et al. [14] have proposed a solution based on post-execution verification (PEV), which is broadly aligned with type verification [11]. The key idea behind the PEV-based mechanism is that agents are paid according to their task executions (i.e., whether they complete their tasks or not), rather than what they have reported.

While Porter et al. [14] considered a single task requester setting where one requester has multiple tasks that can be completed by multiple workers, Stein et al. [18] and Conizter and Vidali [4] studied similar settings but considering workers' uncertain task execution time. Moreover, Ramchurn et al. [15] looked at a more complex setting where each agent is a task requester and is also capable of completing some tasks for the others. Apart from considering different settings, all the solutions in these studies are PEV-based. However, these results may not apply to other different problem settings where, for example, agents' valuations may have externalities, e.g., agent A prefers working with B instead of others [7], and an agent may even incur some costs without doing any task, e.g., when a government builds a costly public good [8].

Therefore, in this paper, we study a general task allocation setting where agents' valuations are not constrained (as in previous works). Under this general setting, we characterise the applicability of the PEV-based mechanism. Our

*The authors acknowledge funding from the EPSRC-funded International Centre for Infrastructure Futures (ICIF) (EP/K012347/1).

Appears in: *Proceedings of the 15th International Conference on Autonomous Agents and Multiagent Systems (AAMAS 2016), J. Thangarajah, K. Tuyls, C. Jonker, S. Marsella (eds.), May 9–13, 2016, Singapore.*

contributions advance the state of the art in the following ways:

- We propose a generalisation of the work of Porter et al. [14] and Ramchurn et al. [15]: (1) Both [14] and [15] showed that PEV-based mechanisms are ex-post truthfully implementable in their limited settings, while this paper shows that PEV-based mechanisms are ex-post truthful for all risk-neutral settings (with or without externalities). (2) Ramchurn et al. [15] further showed that PEV-based mechanisms are also ex-post truthful in a trust-based environment with linear trust aggregation, while this paper shows that truthfulness still holds for a much wider class of trust aggregations, namely all multilinear aggregations.

- We also bound the applicability of the PEV-based mechanisms by showing that risk-neutral valuations and multilinear aggregations are also necessary conditions for achieving ex-post truthfulness. This bound has never been shown in any valuation setting before.

- Given the above characterisation, we demonstrate how this mechanism can be successfully applied in the real-world. We consider ridesharing as an example, where people may have very complex preferences for sharing with others (i.e., externalities exist naturally).

- Since our problem setting is essentially an interdependent valuation setting, we also draw the parallels between our results and the literature of efficient mechanism design with interdependent valuations, which further demonstrates the significance of the PEV-based mechanism.

The remainder of the paper is organized as follows. Section 2 presents the general task allocation model. Section 3 introduces the PEV-based mechanism and characterises its applicability. We then extend the characterisation to trust-based environments in Section 4 and show a promising application example in Section 5. Lastly, we compare our results to the literature of efficient design with general interdependent valuations.

2. THE MODEL

We study a task allocation problem where there are n agents denoted by $N = \{1, ..., n\}$ and a finite set of task allocations T[1] (e.g., rides to ride-sharers or packages to delivery trucks). Each allocation $\tau \in T$ is defined by $\tau = (\tau_i)_{i\in N}$, where τ_i is a set of tasks assigned to agent i. Let $\tau_i = \emptyset$ if there is no task assigned to i in τ. For each allocation τ, agent i may fail to successfully complete her tasks τ_i, which is modelled by $p_i^\tau \in [0,1]$, the probability that i will successfully complete her tasks τ_i. Let $p_i = (p_i^\tau)_{\tau\in T}$ be i's **probability of success (PoS)** profile for all allocations T, and $p^\tau = (p_i^\tau)_{i\in N}$ be the PoS profile of all agents for allocation τ.

Note that the completion of one task in an allocation may depend on the completion of the other tasks. Take the delivery example in Figure 1 with two agents 1, 2 delivering one package from S to D. There are two possible task allocations to finish the delivery: τ is collaboratively executed

[1] T is the task allocation outcome space, which may contain all feasible task allocations (with or without redundancy) that agents can execute. The precise definition depends on the applications.

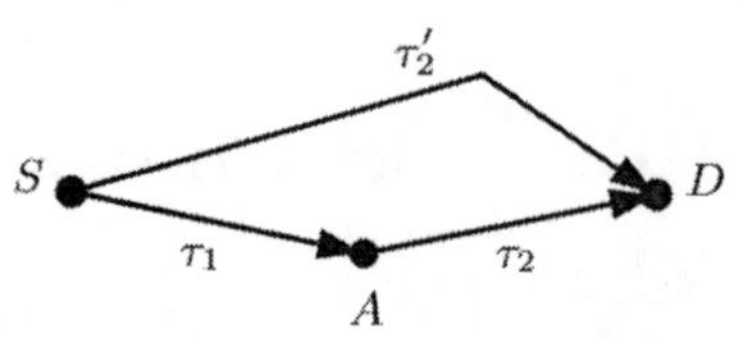

Allocations: $\tau = (\tau_1 = \{S \to A\}, \tau_2 = \{A \to D\})$
$\tau' = (\tau_1' = \emptyset, \tau_2' = \{S \to D\})$

Figure 1: Package delivery from S to D with two agents 1, 2

agent	allocation	p_i	v_i
1	τ	$p_1^\tau = 0$	$v_1(\tau, p^\tau) = 0$
	τ'	$p_1^{\tau'} = 0$	$v_1(\tau', p^{\tau'}) = 0$
2	τ	$p_2^\tau = 1$	$v_2(\tau, p^\tau) = p_1^\tau \times p_2^\tau$
	τ'	$p_2^{\tau'} = 0.5$	$v_2(\tau', p^{\tau'}) = p_2^{\tau'}$

Table 1: A valuation setting for the exmaple in Figure 1

by agents 1 and 2, while τ' is done by agent 2 alone. It is clear that task τ_2 depends on τ_1. However, p_2^τ only indicates 2's PoS for τ_2, assuming that 1 will successfully complete τ_1. That is, p_i^τ does not include task dependencies and it only specifies i's probability to successfully complete τ_i, if τ_i is ready for i to execute.

For each allocation $\tau \in T$, the completion of τ brings each agent i a value (either positive or negative), which combines costs and benefits. For example, offering a ride to someone in ridesharing may incur a detour cost to the driver, but it may also bring both the driver and the rider a valuable journey. Considering the execution uncertainty, agent i's valuation is modelled by a function $v_i : T \times [0,1]^N \to \mathbb{R}$, which assigns a value to each allocation τ, for each PoS profile $p^\tau = (p_i^\tau)_{i\in N}$.

For each agent i, we assume that v_i and p_i are privately observed by i, known as i's **type** and denoted by $\theta_i = (v_i, p_i)$. Let $\theta = (\theta_i)_{i\in N}$ be the type profile of all agents, θ_{-i} be the type profile of all agents except i, and $\theta = (\theta_i, \theta_{-i})$. Let Θ_i be i's type space, $\Theta = (\Theta_i)_{i\in N}$ and $\Theta_{-i} = (\Theta_j)_{j\neq i\in N}$.

Given the above setting, our goal is to choose one task allocation from T that maximises all agents' valuations, i.e., a socially optimal allocation. This can be achieved (according to the revelation principle [10]) by designing a mechanism that directly asks all agents to report their types and then chooses an allocation maximising their valuations. However, agents may not report their types truthfully. Therefore, we need to incentivize them to reveal their true types, which is normally achieved by choosing a specific allocation of tasks and an associated monetary transfer to each agent. The direct revelation **allocation mechanism** is defined by a task **allocation choice** function $\pi : \Theta \to T$ and a **payment** function $x = (x_1, ..., x_n)$ where $x_i : \Theta \to \mathbb{R}$ is the payment function for agent i.

2.1 Solution Concepts

The goal of the allocation mechanism is to choose a task allocation that maximises the valuation of all agents, i.e., the social welfare. Since the agents' types are privately observed by the agents, the mechanism is only able to maximise social welfare if it can receive their true types. Therefore, the mechanism needs to incentivise all agents to report their types truthfully. Moreover, agents should not lose when they participate in the task allocation mechanism, i.e., they are not forced to join the allocation. In the following, we formally define these concepts.

We say an allocation choice π is efficient if it always chooses an allocation that maximises the expected social welfare for all type report profiles.

DEFINITION 1. *Allocation choice π is **efficient** if and only if for all $\theta \in \Theta$, for all $\tau' \in T$, let $\tau = \pi(\theta)$, we have:*

$$\sum_{i \in N} v_i(\tau, p^\tau) \geq \sum_{i \in N} v_i(\tau', p^{\tau'})$$

where $p^\tau = (p_i^\tau)_{i \in N}$, and $p^{\tau'} = (p_i^{\tau'})_{i \in N}$.

Note that the expected social welfare calculated by π is based on the agents' reported types, which are not necessarily their true types. However, agents' actual/realized valuation for an allocation only depends on their true types.

Given the agents' true type profile θ, their reported type profile $\hat{\theta}$ and the allocation mechanism (π, x), agent i's expected **utility** is quasilinear and defined as:

$$u_i(\theta_i, \pi(\hat{\theta}), x_i(\hat{\theta}), p^{\pi(\hat{\theta})}) = v_i(\pi(\hat{\theta}), p^{\pi(\hat{\theta})}) - x_i(\hat{\theta}),$$

where $p^{\pi(\hat{\theta})} = (p_i^{\pi(\hat{\theta})})_{i \in N}$ is agents' true PoS profile for task $\pi(\hat{\theta})$ and $\hat{p}^{\pi(\hat{\theta})} = (\hat{p}_i^{\pi(\hat{\theta})})_{i \in N}$ is what they have reported.

DEFINITION 2. *Mechanism (π, x) is **individually rational** if for all $i \in N$, for all $\theta \in \Theta$, for all $\hat{\theta}_{-i} \in \Theta_{-i}$, $u_i(\theta_i, \pi(\theta_i, \hat{\theta}_{-i}), x_i(\theta_i, \hat{\theta}_{-i}), p^{\pi(\theta_i, \hat{\theta}_{-i})}) \geq 0$.*

That is, an agent never receives a negative expected utility in an individually rational mechanism if she reports truthfully, no matter what others report.

Furthermore, we say the mechanism is **truthful** (aka *dominant-strategy incentive-compatible*) if it always maximises an agent's expected utility if she reports her type truthfully no matter what the others report, i.e., reporting type truthfully is a dominant strategy. It has been shown that truthful and efficient mechanism is impossible to achieve in a special settings of the model [14]. Instead we focus on a weaker solution concept (but still very valid) called *ex-post truthful*, which requires that reporting truthfully maximises an agent's expected utility, if everyone else also reports truthfully (i.e., reporting truthfully is an ex-post equilibrium).

DEFINITION 3. *Mechanism (π, x) is **ex-post truthful** if and only if for all $i \in N$, for all $\theta \in \Theta$, for all $\hat{\theta}_i \in \Theta_i$, we have $u_i(\theta_i, \pi(\theta_i, \theta_{-i}), x_i(\theta_i, \theta_{-i}), p^{\pi(\theta_i, \theta_{-i})}) \geq$ $u_i(\theta_i, \pi(\hat{\theta}_i, \theta_{-i}), x_i(\hat{\theta}_i, \theta_{-i}), p^{\pi(\hat{\theta}_i, \theta_{-i})})$.*

2.2 Failure of the Groves Mechanism

The Groves mechanism is a well-known class of mechanisms that are efficient and truthful in many domains [5]. However, they are not directly applicable in our domain due to the interdependent valuations created by the execution uncertainty. As we will see later, a simply variation of the Groves mechanism can solve the problem. In the following, we briefly introduce the Groves mechanism and show why it cannot be directly applied.

Given agents' type report profile θ, Groves mechanisms compute an efficient allocation $\pi^*(\theta)$ (π^* denotes the efficient allocation choice function) and charge each agent i

$$x_i^{Groves}(\theta) = h_i(\theta_{-i}) - V_{-i}(\theta, \pi^*) \quad (1)$$

where

- h_i is a function that only depends on θ_{-i},
- $V_{-i}(\theta, \pi^*) = \sum_{j \neq i} v_j(\pi^*(\theta), p^{\pi^*(\theta)})$ is the social welfare for all agents, excluding i, under the efficient allocation $\pi^*(\theta)$.

Since h_i is independent of i's report, we can set $h_i(\theta_{-i}) = 0$, and then each agent's utility is $v_i(\pi^*(\theta)) + V_{-i}(\theta, \pi^*)$, which is the social welfare of the efficient allocation. The following example shows that the Groves mechanism is not directly applicable in our task allocation setting.

Take the example from Figure 1 with the setting from Table 1. If both 1 and 2 report truthfully, the efficient allocation is τ' with social welfare 0.5 (which is also their utility if $h_i(\theta_{-i}) = 0$). Now if 1 misreported $\hat{p}_1^\tau > 0.5$, then the efficient allocation will be τ with social welfare $\hat{p}_1^\tau > 0.5$, i.e., 1 can misreport to receive a higher utility.

3. APPLICABILITY OF PEV-BASED MECHANISMS

As shown in the last section, the Groves mechanisms are not directly applicable due to the interdependency of agents' valuations created by their probability of success (PoS). The other reason is that the Groves payment is calculated from agents' reported PoS rather than their realized/true PoS.

The fact is that we can partially verify their reported PoS by delaying their payments until they have executed their tasks (post-execution verification). In line with this, Porter et al. [14] have proposed a variation of the Groves mechanism which pays an agent according to their actual task completion, rather than what they have reported. More specifically, we define two payments for each agent: a reward for successful completion and a penalty for non-completion. Let us call this mechanism *PEV-based mechanism*.

Porter et al. [14] have considered a simple setting where there is one requester who has one or multiple tasks to be allocated to multiple workers each of whom have a fixed cost to attempt each task. Later, Ramchurn et al. [15] extended Porter et al.'s model to a multiple-requester setting (a combinatorial task exchange) and especially considered trust information which will be further studied later in this paper. Our setting generalises both models and allows any types of valuations and allocations. In what follows, we formally define the PEV-based mechanism and analyse its applicability in our general domain.

Given the agents' true type profile θ and their reports $\hat{\theta}$, let p_{-i}^τ be the true PoS profile of all agents except i for task τ, $p^\tau = (p_i^\tau, p_{-i}^\tau)$, and $\hat{p}_{-i}^\tau, \hat{p}^\tau$ be the corresponding reported, PEV-based payment x^{PEV} for each agent i is defined as:

$$x_i^{PEV}(\hat{\theta}) = \begin{cases} h_i(\hat{\theta}_{-i}) - V_{-i}^1(\hat{\theta}, \pi^*) & \text{if } i \text{ succeeded,} \\ h_i(\hat{\theta}_{-i}) - V_{-i}^0(\hat{\theta}, \pi^*) & \text{if } i \text{ failed.} \end{cases} \quad (2)$$

where

- $h_i(\hat{\theta}_{-i}) = \sum_{j \in N \setminus \{i\}} \hat{v}_j(\pi^*(\hat{\theta}_{-i}), (0, \hat{p}_{-i}^{\pi^*(\hat{\theta}_{-i})}))$ is the maximum expected social welfare that the other agents can achieve without i's participation,
- $V_{-i}^1(\hat{\theta}, \pi^*) = \sum_{j \in N \setminus \{i\}} \hat{v}_j(\pi^*(\hat{\theta}), (1, p_{-i}^{\pi^*(\hat{\theta})}))$ is the realized expected social welfare of all agents except i under the efficient allocation $\pi^*(\hat{\theta})$ when $p_i^{\pi^*(\hat{\theta})} = 1$, i.e., i

succeeded. $V^0_{-i}(\hat{\theta}, \pi^*) = \sum_{j \in N\setminus\{i\}} \hat{v}_j(\pi^*(\hat{\theta}), (0, p_{-i}^{\pi^*(\hat{\theta})}))$ is the corresponding social welfare when $p_i^{\pi^*(\hat{\theta})} = 0$.

Note that $h_i(\hat{\theta}_{-i})$ is calculated according to what agents have reported, while $V^1_{-i}(\hat{\theta}, \pi^*), V^0_{-i}(\hat{\theta}, \pi^*)$ are based on the realization of their task completion, which is actually their true PoS as we used in the calculation. x_i^{PEV} pays/rewards agent i the social welfare increased by i if she completed her tasks, otherwise penalizes her the social welfare loss due to her failure.

Porter et al. [14] have shown that the mechanism (π^*, x^{PEV}) is ex-post truthful and individually rational if the dependencies between tasks are non-cyclical. In Theorem 1, we show that (π^*, x^{PEV}) is ex-post truthful in general if agents' valuations satisfy a multilinearity condition (Definition 4), which generalizes the non-cyclical task dependencies condition applied in [14].

DEFINITION 4. *Valuation v_i of i is **multilinear in PoS** if for all type profiles $\theta \in \Theta$, for all allocations $\tau \in T$, for all $j \in N$, $v_i(\tau, p^\tau) = p_j^\tau \times v_i(\tau, (1, p_{-j}^\tau)) + (1 - p_j^\tau) \times v_i(\tau, (0, p_{-j}^\tau))$.*

Intuitively, v_i is multilinear in PoS if all its variables but p_j^τ are held constant, v_i is a linear function of p_j^τ, which also means that agent i is risk-neutral (with respect to j's execution uncertainty). However, multilinearity in PoS does not indicate that v_i has to be a linear form of $v_i(\tau, p^\tau) = b + a_1 p_1^\tau + ... + a_n p_n^\tau$, where b, a_i are constant (see Table 1 for example).

3.1 Multilinearity in PoS is Sufficient for Truthfulness

THEOREM 1. *Mechanism (π^*, x^{PEV}) is ex-post truthful if for all $i \in N$, v_i is multilinear in PoS.*

PROOF. According to the characterization of truthful mechanisms given by Proposition 9.27 from [13], we need to prove that for all $i \in N$, for all $\theta \in \Theta$:

1. $x_i^{PEV}(\theta)$ does not depend on i's report, but only on the task allocation alternatives;

2. i's utility is maximized by reporting θ_i truthfully if the others report θ_{-i} truthfully.

From the definition of x_i^{PEV} in (2), we can see that given the allocation $\pi^*(\theta)$, agent i cannot change $V^1_{-i}(\theta, \pi^*)$ and $V^0_{-i}(\theta, \pi^*)$ without changing the allocation $\pi^*(\theta)$. Therefore, x_i^{PEV} does not depend on i's report, but only on the task allocation outcome $\pi^*(\theta)$.

In what follows, we show that for each agent i, if the others report types truthfully, then i's utility is maximized by reporting her type truthfully.

Given an agent i' of type θ_i and the others' true type profile θ_{-i}, assume that i reported $\hat{\theta}_i \neq \theta_i$. For the allocation $\tau = \pi^*(\hat{\theta}_i, \theta_{-i})$, according to x_i^{PEV}, when i finally completes her tasks, i's utility is $u_i^1 = v_i(\tau, (1, p_{-i}^\tau)) - h_i(\theta_{-i}) + V^1_{-i}((\hat{\theta}_i, \theta_{-i}), \pi^*)$ and her utility if she fails is $u_i^0 = v_i(\tau, (0, p_{-i}^\tau)) - h_i(\theta_{-i}) + V^0_{-i}((\hat{\theta}_i, \theta_{-i}), \pi^*)$. Note that i's expected valuation depends on her true valuation v_i and all agents' true PoS. Therefore, i's expected utility is:

$$p_i^\tau \times u_i^1 + (1 - p_i^\tau) \times u_i^0 =$$
$$p_i^\tau \times v_i(\tau, (1, p_{-i}^\tau)) \quad (3)$$
$$+ (1 - p_i^\tau) \times v_i(\tau, (0, p_{-i}^\tau)) \quad (4)$$
$$+ p_i^\tau \sum_{j \in N\setminus\{i\}} v_j(\tau, (1, p_{-i}^\tau)) \quad (5)$$
$$+ (1 - p_i^\tau) \sum_{j \in N\setminus\{i\}} v_j(\tau, (0, p_{-i}^\tau)) \quad (6)$$
$$- h_i(\theta_{-i}).$$

Since all valuations are multilinear in PoS, the sum of (3) and (4) is equal to $v_i(\tau, p^\tau)$, and the sum of (5) and (6) is $\sum_{j \in N\setminus\{i\}} v_j(\tau, p^\tau)$. Thus, the sum of (3), (4), (5) and (6) is the social welfare under allocation $\pi^*(\hat{\theta}_i, \theta_{-i})$. The social welfare is maximized when i reports truthfully because π^* maximizes social welfare (note that this is not the case when θ_{-i} is not truthfully reported). Moreover, $h_i(\theta_{-i})$ is independent of i's report and is the maximum social welfare that the others can achieve without i. Therefore, by reporting θ_i truthfully, i's utility is maximized. □

Theorem 1 shows that multilinearity in PoS is sufficient to truthfully implement (π^*, x^{PEV}) in an ex-post equilibrium (ex-post truthful), but not in dominant strategies (truthful). It has been shown in similar settings that ex-post truthfulness is the best we can achieve here [14, 15, 18, 4].

3.2 Multilinearity in PoS is also Necessary

In the above we showed that multilinearity in PoS is sufficient for (π^*, x^{PEV}) to be ex-post truthful. Here we show that the multilinearity is also necessary.

THEOREM 2. *If (π^*, x^{PEV}) is ex-post truthful for all type profiles $\theta \in \Theta$, then for all $i \in N$, v_i is multilinear in PoS.*

PROOF. By contradiction, assume that v_i of agent of type θ_i is not multilinear in PoS, i.e., there exist a θ_{-i}, an allocation $\tau \in T$, and a $j \in N$ (without loss of generality, assume that $j \neq i$) such that:

$$v_i(\tau, p^\tau) \neq p_j^\tau \times v_i(\tau, (1, p_{-j}^\tau)) + (1 - p_j^\tau) \times v_i(\tau, (0, p_{-j}^\tau)) \quad (7)$$

Under the efficient allocation choice function π^*, it is not hard to find a type profile $\hat{\theta}_{-i}$ such that $\pi^*(\theta_i, \hat{\theta}_{-i}) = \tau$ and the PoS profile is the same between θ_{-i} and $\hat{\theta}_{-i}$. We can choose $\hat{\theta}_{-i}$ by setting $\hat{v}_j(\tau, p^\tau)$ to a sufficiently large value for each $j \neq i$.

Applying (π^*, x^{PEV}) on profile $(\theta_i, \hat{\theta}_{-i})$, when j finally successfully completes her tasks τ_j, her utility is $u_j^1 = \hat{v}_j(\tau, (1, p_{-j}^\tau)) - h_j((\theta_i, \hat{\theta}_{-i})_{-j}) + V^1_{-j}((\theta_i, \hat{\theta}_{-i}), \pi^*)$ and her utility if she fails is $u_j^0 = \hat{v}_j(\tau, (0, p_{-j}^\tau)) - h_j((\theta_i, \hat{\theta}_{-i})_{-j}) + V^0_{-j}((\theta_i, \hat{\theta}_{-i}), \pi^*)$. Thus, j's expected utility is (note that

$\hat{p}_j^\tau = p_j^\tau$):

$$p_j^\tau \times u_j^1 + (1 - p_j^\tau) \times u_j^0 =$$
$$p_j^\tau \times v_i(\tau, (1, p_{-j}^\tau)) \quad (8)$$
$$+ (1 - p_j^\tau) \times v_i(\tau, (0, p_{-j}^\tau)) \quad (9)$$
$$+ p_j^\tau \sum_{k \in N \setminus \{i\}} \hat{v}_k(\tau, (1, p_{-j}^\tau)) \quad (10)$$
$$+ (1 - p_j^\tau) \sum_{k \in N \setminus \{i\}} \hat{v}_k(\tau, (0, p_{-j}^\tau)) \quad (11)$$
$$- h_j(\theta_{-j}).$$

Given the assumption (7), terms (8) and (9) together can be written as $v_i(\tau, p^\tau) + \delta_i$ where $\delta_i = (8) + (9) - v_i(\tau, p^\tau)$. Similar substitutions can be carried out for all other agents $k \in N \setminus \{i\}$ in terms (10) and (11) regardless of whether v_k is mutlilinear in PoS. After this substitution, j's utility can be written as:

$$p_j \times u_j^1 + (1 - p_j) \times u_j^0 =$$
$$v_i(\tau, p^\tau) + \sum_{k \in N \setminus \{i\}} \hat{v}_k(\tau, p^\tau) \quad (12)$$
$$+ \sum_{k \in N} \delta_k \quad (13)$$
$$- h_j(\theta_{-j}).$$

Now consider a suboptimal allocation $\hat{\tau} \neq \tau$, if $\hat{\tau}$ is chosen by the mechanism, then j's utility can be written as:

$$\hat{u}_j =$$
$$v_i(\hat{\tau}, p^{\hat{\tau}}) + \sum_{k \in N \setminus \{i\}} \hat{v}_k(\hat{\tau}, p^{\hat{\tau}}) \quad (14)$$
$$+ \sum_{k \in N} \hat{\delta}_k \quad (15)$$
$$- h_j(\theta_{-j}).$$

In the above two utility representations, we know that terms (12) > (14) because π^* is efficient, but terms (13) and (15) can be any real numbers.

In what follows, we tune the valuation of j such that the optimal allocation is either τ or $\hat{\tau}$, and in either case j is incentivized to misreport.

In the extreme case where all agents except i's valuations are multilinear in PoS, we have $\delta_k = 0, \hat{\delta}_k = 0$ for all $k \neq i$ in (13) and (15). Therefore, $\sum_{k \in N} \delta_k = \delta_i \neq 0$ and $\sum_{k \in N} \hat{\delta}_k = \hat{\delta}_i$ (possibly $= 0$). It might be the case that $\delta_i = \hat{\delta}_i$, but there must exist a setting where $\delta_i \neq \hat{\delta}_i$, otherwise v_i is multilinear in PoS, because constant δ_i for any PoS does not violate the multilinearity definition.

1. If $\delta_i > \hat{\delta}_i$, we have $(12) + \delta_i > (14) + \hat{\delta}_i$. In this case, we can increase $\hat{v}_j(\hat{\tau}, p^{\hat{\tau}})$ such that $\hat{\tau}$ becomes optimal, i.e., (12) < (14), but $(12) + \delta_i > (14) + \hat{\delta}_i$ still holds. Therefore, if j's true valuation is the one that chooses $\hat{\tau}$ as the optimal allocation, then j would misreport to get allocation τ which gives her a higher utility.

2. If $\delta_i < \hat{\delta}_i$, we can easily modify $\hat{v}_j(\hat{\tau}, p^{\hat{\tau}})$ such that $(12) + \delta_i < (14) + \hat{\delta}_i$ but (12) > (14) still holds. In this case, if j's true valuation again is the one just modified, j would misreport to get allocation $\hat{\tau}$ with a better utility.

In both of the above situations, agent j is incentivized to misreport, which contradicts that (π^*, x^{PEV}) is ex-post truthful. Thus, v_i has to be multilinear in PoS. □

It is worth mentioning that Theorem 2 does not say that given a specific type profile θ, all v_i have to be multilinear in PoS for (π^*, x^{PEV}) to be ex-post truthful. Take the delivery example from Table 1 and change agent 2's valuation for τ to be $v_2(\tau, p^\tau) = (\mathbf{p}_1^\tau)^2 \times p_2^\tau$ which is not multilinear in PoS. It is easy to check that under this change, no agent can gain anything by misreporting if the other agent reports truthfully. However, given each agent i of valuation v_i, to truthfully implement (π^*, x^{PEV}) in an ex-post equilibrium for all possible type profiles of the others, Theorem 2 says that v_i has to be multilinear in PoS, otherwise, there exist settings where some agent is incentivized to misreport.

3.3 Conditions for Achieving Individual Rationality

PEV-based mechanism is individually rational in Porter et al. [14]'s specific setting. However, in the general model we consider here, it may not guarantee this property. For example, there is an allocation where an agent has no task to complete in an allocation, but has a negative valuation for the completion of the tasks assigned to the others (i.e. she is penalised if the others complete their tasks). If that allocation is the optimal allocation and the allocation does not change with or without that agent, then she will get a zero payment therefore a negative utility.

Proposition 1 shows that by restricting agents' valuations to some typical constraint, PEV-based mechanism can be made individually rational. The constraint says if an agent is not involved in a task allocation (i.e., when the tasks assigned to her is empty), she will not be penalised by the completion of the others' tasks.

PROPOSITION 1. *Mechanism (π^*, x^{PEV}) is individually rational if and only if for all $i \in N$, for all $\tau \in T$, if $\tau_i = \emptyset$, then $v_i(\tau, p^\tau) \geq 0$ for any $p^\tau \in [0, 1]^N$.*

PROOF. (If part) For all type profile $\theta \in \Theta$, for all $i \in N$, let $\tau = \pi^*(\theta)$ and $\hat{\tau} = \pi^*(\theta_{-i})$, i's utility is given by $\sum_{k \in N} v_k(\tau, p^\tau) - \sum_{k \in N \setminus \{i\}} v_k(\hat{\tau}, p_{-i}^{\hat{\tau}})$, where the first term is the optimal social welfare with i's participation and the second term is the optimal social welfare without i's participation. It is clear that $\hat{\tau}_i = \emptyset$ as $\hat{\tau}$ is the optimal allocation without i's participation. $\sum_{k \in N \setminus \{i\}} v_k(\hat{\tau}, p_{-i}^{\hat{\tau}}) + v_i(\hat{\tau}, p^{\hat{\tau}})$ is the social welfare for allocation $\hat{\tau}$. Since τ is optimal, we get that $\sum_{k \in N} v_k(\tau, p^\tau) \geq \sum_{k \in N \setminus \{i\}} v_k(\hat{\tau}, p_{-i}^{\hat{\tau}}) + v_i(\hat{\tau}, p^{\hat{\tau}})$. Thus, $\sum_{k \in N} v_k(\tau, p^\tau) - \sum_{k \in N \setminus \{i\}} v_k(\hat{\tau}, p_{-i}^{\hat{\tau}}) \geq v_i(\hat{\tau}, p^{\hat{\tau}}) \geq 0$, i.e. i's utility is non-negative.

(Only if part) If there exist an i of type θ_i, a τ, a $p^\tau \in [0, 1]^N$ such that $\tau_i = \emptyset$ and $v_i(\tau, p^\tau) < 0$. We can always find a profile $\hat{\theta}_{-i}$ s.t. $\hat{p}^\tau = p^\tau$ and $\pi^*(\theta_i, \hat{\theta}_{-i}) = \pi^*(\hat{\theta}_{-i}) = \tau$. It is clear that the payment for i is 0 and her utility is $v_i(\tau, p^\tau) < 0$ (violates individual rationality). □

4. EXTENSION TO TRUST-BASED ENVIRONMENTS

So far, we have assumed that each agent can correctly predict her probability of success (PoS) for each task, but in some environments, an agent's PoS is not perfectly perceived by the agent alone. Instead, multiple other agents may have had prior experiences with a given agent and their experiences can be aggregated to create a more informed measure of the PoS for the given agent. This measure is termed the trust in the agent [15]. Ramchurn et al. have extended Porter et al.'s mechanism to consider agents' trust information and showed that the extension is still truthfully implementable in their settings.

Similarly, our general model can also be extended to handle the trust information by changing singleton p_i^τ to be a vector $p_i^\tau = (p_{i,1}^\tau, ..., p_{i,j}^\tau, ..., p_{i,n}^\tau)$ where $p_{i,j}^\tau$ is the probability that i believes j will complete j's tasks in τ. Agent i's aggregated/true PoS for task τ is given by a function $f_i^\tau : [0,1]^N \to [0,1]$ with input $(p_{1,i}^\tau, ..., p_{n,i}^\tau)$. Given this extension, for any type profile θ, let $\rho_i^\tau = f_i^\tau(p_{1,i}^\tau, ..., p_{n,i}^\tau)$, the social welfare of a task allocation τ is defined as:

$$\sum_{i \in N} v_i(\tau, \rho^\tau) \quad (16)$$

where $\rho^\tau = (\rho_1^\tau, ..., \rho_n^\tau)$.

As shown in [15], the PEV-based mechanism can be extended to handle this trust information by simply updating the efficient allocation choice function π^* with the social welfare calculation given by Equation (16). Let us call the extended mechanism $\mathcal{M}^{trust}$. Ramchurn et al. have demonstrated that $\mathcal{M}^{trust}$ is ex-post truthful in their settings when the PoS aggregation function is the following linear form:

$$f_i^\tau(p_{1,i}^\tau, ..., p_{n,i}^\tau) = \sum_{j \in N} \omega_j \times p_{j,i}^\tau \quad (17)$$

where constant $\omega_j \in [0,1]$ and $\sum_{j \in N} \omega_j = 1$.

Following the results in Theorems 1 and 2, we generalize Ramchurn et al.'s results to characterize all aggregation forms under which $\mathcal{M}^{trust}$ is ex-post truthful.

DEFINITION 5. *A PoS aggregation $f_i = (f_i^\tau)_{\tau \in T}$ is* ***multilinear*** *if for all $j \in N$, for all $\tau \in T$, for all $\theta \in \Theta$, $f_i^\tau(p_{1,i}^\tau, ..., p_{j,i}^\tau, ..., p_{n,i}^\tau) = p_{j,i}^\tau \times f_i^\tau(p_{1,i}^\tau, ..., p_{j-1,i}^\tau, 1, p_{j+1,i}^\tau, ..., p_{n,i}^\tau) + (1 - p_{j,i}^\tau) \times f_i^\tau(p_{1,i}^\tau, ..., p_{j-1,i}^\tau, 0, p_{j+1,i}^\tau, ..., p_{n,i}^\tau)$.*

Definition 5 is similar to the multilinear in PoS definition given by Definition 4. Multilinear aggregations cover the linear form given by Equation (17), but also consist of many non-linear forms such as $\prod_{j \in N} p_{j,i}^\tau$. The following corollary directly follows Theorems 1 and 2. We omit the proof here. The basic idea of the proof is that given a multilinear function, if we substitute another multilinear function (with no shared variables) for one variable of the function, then the new function must be multilinear.

COROLLARY 1. *Trust-based mechanism $\mathcal{M}^{trust}$ is ex-post truthful if and only if for all $i \in N$, v_i is multilinear in PoS, and the PoS aggregation f_i is multilinear.*

For $\mathcal{M}^{trust}$ to be individually rational, the constraint specified in Proposition 1 is still sufficient and necessary, if we change h_{-i} in the payment definition (Equation (2)) to be the optimal social welfare that the others can achieve without i, but assume that i offered the worst trust in the others (see [15] for more details).

5. APPLYING PEV TO RIDESHARING

The literature has studied a few task allocation applications with execution uncertainty such as scheduling computational tasks to computing service providers or computing machines [18, 4]. In this section, we consider a ridesharing application such as *Uber* and *Lyft* in the increasingly important sharing economy, where the valuation setting has not been considered with execution uncertainty yet. The principle of ridesharing is to efficiently utilise the extra seats available in commuters' cars and therefore to reduce the number of cars on the road, travel costs and CO_2 emissions. However, existing ridesharing services such as *Uber* mainly allow professional drivers to share their cars, and these services are essentially not different from taxi services and even pull out more cars on the road (create more congestions).

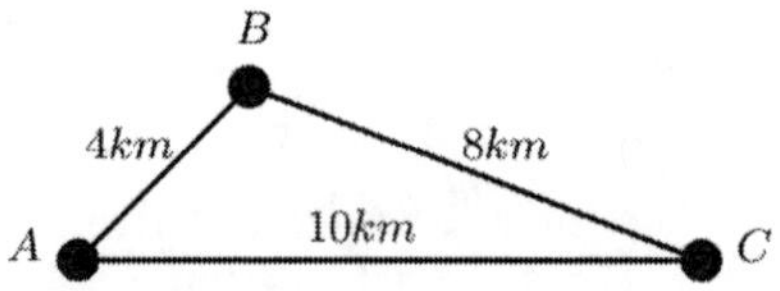

Bob: $(A \to C, drive, cost: 15)$
Tom: $(A \to C, drive, cost: 10)$
Alice: $(B \to C, taxi, cost: 20)$

Allocation space T:
$\tau^1 = (\{Bob\}, \{Tom\}, \{Alice\})$
$\tau^2 = (\{Bob(drive), Tom\}, \{Alice\})$
$\tau^3 = (\{Bob, Tom(drive)\}, \{Alice\})$
$\tau^4 = (\{Bob\}, \{Tom, Alice\})$
$\tau^5 = (\{Bob, Alice\}, \{Tom\})$

Figure 2: Ridesharing example

To incentivise the whole community, not just professional drivers, to efficiently share their cars, it is essential to sufficiently evaluate the quality of the sharing services offered by individuals, and to establish a proper trust mechanism in the community[2]. Execution uncertainty is likely to have a strong impact on service quality. Following the above theoretical results, in what follows, we show how execution uncertainty can be modelled to increase service quality in ridesharing and how trust can be further incorporated.

We consider a ridesharing setting where there are multiple commuters, each of whom has a trip to finish via driving or taking other form of transport. Each commuter's trip is modelled by departure/arrival locations, travel time window, travel costs and etc (see [19] for an example). For the sake of clarity, we consider a simple ridesharing setting given in Figure 2. There are three commuters, Bob, Tom and Alice, who are planning a travel to attend a party at location C. Both Bob and Tom depart from location A and plan to drive with different costs, while Alice departs from location B and plans to take a taxi with a cost of 20 (the costs are based on the shortest route to finish their trips). Assume that they are flexible about their travel time, but all of them have to arrive at location C before the party starts. We further assume that both Bob and Tom have one extra seat in their cars that can be shared to others. We then get the sharing allocation space T presented in Figure 2 (people in one set share(s) a car).

For each task allocation $\tau \in T$, commuter i's probability of success (PoS) p_i^τ is the probability that i will finish the

[2]For example, *Maramoja* provides ridesharing/taxi services in Nairobi and relies on trust metrics to guarantee riders/drivers successful trips.

	v_b	v_t	v_a
τ^1	0	0	0
τ^2	$-\alpha \times p_b \times p_t$	$10 \times p_b \times p_t$	0
τ^3	$(15-\alpha) \times p_b \times p_t$	0	0
τ^4	$-\beta \times p_t \times p_a$	$(-2+\gamma \times p_a) \times p_t$	$20 \times p_a \times p_t$
τ^5	$(-3+\delta \times p_a) \times p_b$	0	$20 \times p_a \times p_b$

Table 2: A valuation setting for the exmaple in Figure 2, where parameters $\alpha, \beta, \gamma, \delta > 0$.

	v_b	v_t	v_a
τ^1	0	0	0
τ^2	$-\alpha$	10	0
τ^3	$15-\alpha$	0	0
τ^4	$-\beta$	$-2+\gamma$	20
τ^5	$-3+\delta$	0	20

Table 3: A valuation setting of Table 2 given $p_b = p_t = p_a = 1$.

trip and attend the party (without sharing). It is natural to assume that a commuter's intention to attend the party is the same among all sharing allocations, and let p_b, p_t and p_a be the PoS of Bob, Tom and Alice respectively.

We define their valuations v_b, v_t, v_a for Bob, Tom and Alice respectively according to Table 2. The basic intuition behind the valuation setting is that if a commuter takes a ride offered by others, then she will save her original trip cost (i.e., her valuation is positive), while if she offers a ride to others, then she will incur a detour cost if there is any (i.e., her valuation is negative). The detour costs for Bob and Tom to offer a ride to Alice are 15×0.2 and 10×0.2 respectively (as they travel 20% more than their shortest trip). In addition, commuters may have externalities. In this example, Bob has a higher preference to offer a ride to Alice than to Tom, and would prefer that Tom and Alice do not travel together (because, e.g., Bob is afraid of that Alice might discuss their joint business ideas with Tom). Bob gets a positive value δ if he shares with Alice, while receives a negative value $-\alpha$ to share with Tom. Bob also gets a negative value $-\beta$ if Tom shares with Alice. Tom also prefers Alice to Bob, but Alice has no preference between Bob and Tom. This valuation setting makes previous work insufficient, because there are externalities and there is no cost for a commuter to not execute her trip.

Without loss of generality, assume that Bob, Tom and Alice are all certain about attending the party, i.e., $p_b = p_t = p_a = 1$. Then, their valuations are simplified to be those in Table 3. Assume that τ^5 is the only efficient allocation and τ^4 is the second best, i.e., $17 + \delta > 18 - \beta + \gamma > 15 - \alpha$. Applying the PEV-based mechanism, the payment for Bob is the following (according to Equation (2)):

$$x_b^{PEV} = \begin{cases} (18+\gamma) - 20 & \text{if Bob attended,} \\ (18+\gamma) - 0 & \text{if Bob didn't attend.} \end{cases}$$

where $18 + \gamma$ is the social welfare that Tom and Alice can achieve without Bob (allocation τ^4), and 20 is the cost that Bob saved for Alice (allocation τ^5) if Bob attended the party (i.e., Bob finished his trip). The payment indicates that Bob will receive a reward $-(\gamma - 2)$ if he attends the party, while he will pay a penalty of $18 + \delta$ if he fails to attend. Thus, Bob's utility is $u_b = ((-3+\delta) - (\gamma - 2)) \times p_b + (0 - (18 + \gamma)) \times (1 - p_b) = \delta - \gamma - 1$. Notice that Bob's utility might be negative because he is unhappy if Tom and Alice share together (see Proposition 1 for more details).

In what follows, we further consider how trust between Bob, Tom and Alice can be incorporated in the above ridesharing allocation. Apart from the probability of success p_b, p_t, p_a they have predicated for themselves, each of them also holds a measure of trust about how likely the others will attend the party (according to their past social experiences with each other). Then each commuter's final probability of attending the party is aggregated from all commuters' predications (see Section 4 for the detailed model). We have assumed that all of them are certain about their own trips, i.e., $p_b = p_t = p_a = 1$. However, Tom and Alice do not trust Bob, i.e., Tom and Alice believe that Bob may not attend the party in the end according to their experiences. If Bob's true probability of attending the party is averaged from all commuters' opinion, then Bob's probability of attending the party is $\hat{p}_b < 1$. Assume the other trust values are all one, i.e., the aggregated PoSs of Tom and Alice are both one. Then the social welfare of allocation τ^5 under trust is $(17+\delta)\hat{p}_b$. If $(17+\delta)\hat{p}_b$ is less than $18 - \beta + \gamma$ (the social welfare of allocation τ^4), Bob will not be allocated to share with Alice, which is different from what we had without considering trust in the above.

It is worth mentioning that in a complex ridesharing setting, a driver may take more than one rider and a rider may transfer between drivers to reach her destination. It is often quite challenging to compute an efficient allocation in a complex setting with many commuters, even without considering execution uncertainty and trust. To tackle this computational challenge, we may limit the allocation space by, for example, limiting the number of people can share in one car (e.g., *UberPool* only considers at most two passengers to share an Uber taxi) and limiting the number of transfers for a rider to get to her destination (e.g., no existing ridesharing service has considered transfer/multi-hop). Searching an optimal allocation under the limited allocation space will be a lot easier and more importantly the truthfulness property still holds [12].

Apart from ridesharing, there are many other sharing economy business models where execution uncertainty is unavoidable. For instance, in the knowledge sharing sector such as *Freelancer.com*, freelancers cannot always guarantee the completion of the tasks assigned to them and therefore rating/trust mechanism has been established to help employers to find the right freelancers for their tasks. In *Freelancer.com*, when an employer posts tasks, many freelancers will bid for the tasks with different completion speeds and costs. Some freelancers have good experiences (e.g., high completion rate and high employer rating) and some do not. Therefore, the employer faces the challenge of finding the best set of freelancers among all the bidders, which fits perfectly to the problem setting of this paper.

6. WHEN PEV IS NOT AVAILABLE

We have characterised and bounded the applicability of the post-execution verification (PEV)-based mechanism and its extension with trust in a general task allocation setting, and have further demonstrated its applicability in the real-world. The key feature of the PEV-based mechanism is that the mechanism can verify whether an agent has successfully completed the tasks assigned to her and pays her accordingly, which is feasible in many task allocation domains.

However, when post-execution verification is not available, the problem that arises requires the design of an efficient mechanism in a general interdependent valuation setting, where the interdependence comes from agents' execution uncertainty. Under a general interdependent valuation setting, Jehiel and Moldovanu [6] have demonstrated the difficulty of designing an efficient and Bayes-Nash truthful[3] mechanism (see also [9, 3]). They have proved a general impossibility and further identified a necessary condition for implementing an efficient and Bayes-Nash truthful mechanism (see Proposition 2). In the rest, we show how to model the task allocation problem as a general interdependent valuation setting and draw the implication of the necessary condition in the task allocation domain.

We first briefly introduce the general interdependent valuation setting based on [6, 3] and then show how to fit the task allocation problem to the general setting. The general interdependent valuation setting is the following:

- There are K social alternatives/outcomes and N agents.
- Each agent i has a (private) type (called *signal*) s_i drawn from a space $S_i \subseteq \mathbb{R}^{K\times N}$ according to a continuous density function $f_i(s_i) > 0$ and f_i is common knowledge. Coordinate $s_{i,j}^k$ of s_i influences the valuation of agent j in alternative k.
- One alternative k will be chosen, and i's valuation for k is defined as:

$$v_i^k(s_{1,i}^k, ..., s_{n,i}^k) = \sum_{j\in N} \alpha_{j,i}^k \times s_{j,i}^k \tag{18}$$

  where parameters $\alpha_{j,i}^k \geq 0$ are common knowledge.

It is evident that the interdependence between agents' valuations is caused by their private signals s_i, which is their probability of success in our task allocation setting.

The task allocation problem can be modelled as the above with the following setup:

- Let $K = T$, for all $k \in K$, $s_{i,j}^k = p_i^k$ for all $j \in N$, where p_i^k (i's PoS for k) is drawn from $[0,1]$ with a density function f[4]. That is, there is only one signal from i for each k, which is i's PoS for k.
- Applying (18), i's valuation for allocation k is a linear function of all PoSs p_j^k for all $j \in N$, and parameter $\alpha_{i,j}^k \geq 0$ represents the value that j will get if i completes her tasks k_i in k.

We can see that the above model can only model a very small portion of our general task allocation, namely the settings in which the tasks between agents are independent (due to the linear form of their valuation functions) and also their valuations become public[5] (because parameters $\alpha_{i,j}^k \geq 0$ are public and not part of their type).

[3] *Bayes-Nash truthful* is weaker than ex-post truthful and it assumes that all agents know the correct probabilistic distribution of each agent's type.

[4] We can set f to be any random distribution, which is not important in our model.

[5] Public valuation does not affect our results because the main challenge in our setting is that their private PoS creates valuation interdependencies.

Even under this limited task allocation setting, Jehiel and Moldovanu [6] have showed that the following condition (Equation (19)) has to hold for implementing an efficient and Bayes-Nash truthful mechanism. We will discuss the implication of the necessary condition in the task allocation setting.

PROPOSITION 2. *[Theorem 4.3 in [6]] If there exists an efficient and Bayes-Nash truthful mechanism, then the following must hold:*

$$\frac{\alpha_{i,i}^{\hat{k}}}{\alpha_{i,i}^{k}} = \frac{\sum_{j\in N}\alpha_{i,j}^{\hat{k}}}{\sum_{j\in N}\alpha_{i,j}^{k}} \tag{19}$$

for all i of type s_i, for all $k \neq \hat{k} \in K$, if $\alpha_{i,i}^k \neq 0$ and there exist $s_{-i} \neq \hat{s}_{-i}$ such that $\pi^*(s_i, s_{-i}) = k$ and $\pi^*(s_i, \hat{s}_{-i}) = \hat{k}$ where π^* is an efficient allocation.

In our model, condition (19) says that the ratio of the values that i gets from the completion of her own tasks in two different allocations $k, \hat{k}$ is equal to the ratio of the values that i brings to all agents including herself. In other words, if i prefers tasks k_i to $\hat{k}_i$, then all agents together also prefer k_i to $\hat{k}_i$ for i.

However, condition (19) is just one necessary condition and we are not aware of any efficient and Bayes-Nash truthful mechanism existing for the general interdependent valuation setting (except for a very simple setting where agents' signals are one-dimensional [6], in which case the efficient and truthful mechanism actually follows the VCG logic).

From the above analysis, we see that without post-execution verification, we can hardly design a truthful mechanism and the necessary condition for designing a truthful mechanism already restricts us to a very small portion of the whole valuation space. With post-execution verification, we are not restricted by the necessary condition (19). Our results showed that the PEV-based mechanism is ex-post truthful in the above general setting without any other condition, because the valuation setting (Equation (18)) is risk-neutral (multilinear in PoS) by definition.

7. CONCLUSIONS

We studied a general task allocation problem where multiple agents collaboratively accomplish a set of tasks, but they may fail to successfully complete tasks assigned to them. To design an efficient task allocation mechanism for this problem, we showed that post-execution verification based mechanism is truthfully implementable, if and only if all agents are risk-neutral with respect to their execution uncertainty. We also showed that trust information between agents can be integrated into the mechanism without violating its properties, if and only if the trust information is aggregated by a multilinear function. It is the first time that this characterisation and bound of the applicability of the post-execution verification based mechanism is studied. We further demonstrated the applicability of the mechanism in the real-world and showed the significance of the post-execution verification in the design. For future work, apart from investigating other interesting applications of the PEV-based mechanism, the results also indicate that we need to search different solutions to handle settings where agents are not risk-neutral (e.g., in ridesharing, a rider may not want to ride with a driver who has high execution uncertainty for important trips).

REFERENCES

[1] M. Armbrust, A. Fox, R. Griffith, A. D. Joseph, R. Katz, A. Konwinski, G. Lee, D. Patterson, A. Rabkin, I. Stoica, and M. Zaharia. A view of cloud computing. *Commun. ACM*, 53(4):50–58, Apr. 2010.

[2] R. Belk. You are what you can access: Sharing and collaborative consumption online. *Journal of Business Research*, 67(8):1595 – 1600, 2014.

[3] T. Börgers. *An introduction to the theory of mechanism design*. 2015.

[4] V. Conitzer and A. Vidali. Mechanism design for scheduling with uncertain execution time. In *Proceedings of the Twenty-Eighth AAAI Conference on Artificial Intelligence*, pages 623–629. AAAI Press, 2014.

[5] T. Groves. Incentives in Teams. *Econometrica*, 41(4):617–31, July 1973.

[6] P. Jehiel and B. Moldovanu. Efficient Design with Interdependent Valuations. *Econometrica*, 69(5):1237–59, September 2001.

[7] P. Jehiel, B. Moldovanu, and E. Stacchetti. Multidimensional Mechanism Design for Auctions with Externalities. *Journal of Economic Theory*, 85(2):258–293, April 1999.

[8] F. Maniquet and Y. Sprumont. Sharing the cost of a public good: An incentive-constrained axiomatic approach. *Games and Economic Behavior*, 68(1):275 – 302, 2010.

[9] P. R. Milgrom and R. J. Weber. A Theory of Auctions and Competitive Bidding. *Econometrica*, 50(5):1089–1122, September 1982.

[10] R. B. Myerson. revelation principle. In S. N. Durlauf and L. E. Blume, editors, *The New Palgrave Dictionary of Economics*. Palgrave Macmillan, Basingstoke, 2008.

[11] N. Nisan and A. Ronen. Algorithmic mechanism design. *Games and Economic Behavior*, 35(1âĂŞ2):166 – 196, 2001.

[12] N. Nisan and A. Ronen. Computationally feasible vcg mechanisms. *J. Artif. Int. Res.*, 29(1):19–47, May 2007.

[13] N. Nisan, T. Roughgarden, Éva Tardos, and V. V. Vazirani. *Algorithmic Game Theory*. Cambridge University Press, 2007.

[14] R. Porter, A. Ronen, Y. Shoham, and M. Tennenholtz. Fault tolerant mechanism design. *Artif. Intell.*, 172(15):1783–1799, Oct. 2008.

[15] S. D. Ramchurn, C. Mezzetti, A. Giovannucci, J. A. Rodriguez-Aguilar, R. K. Dash, and N. R. Jennings. Trust-based mechanisms for robust and efficient task allocation in the presence of execution uncertainty. *J. Artif. Int. Res.*, 35(1):119–159, June 2009.

[16] T. Roughgarden. Routing games. In *Algorithmic Game Theory*. Cambridge University Press, 2007.

[17] T. Sandholm. An implementation of the contract net protocol based on marginal cost calculations. In *Proceedings of the Eleventh National Conference on Artificial Intelligence*, AAAI'93, pages 256–262. AAAI Press, 1993.

[18] S. Stein, E. Gerding, A. Rogers, K. Larson, and N. Jennings. Algorithms and mechanisms for procuring services with uncertain durations using redundancy. *Artificial Intelligence*, 175(14-15):2021–2060, 2011.

[19] D. Zhao, D. Zhang, E. H. Gerding, Y. Sakurai, and M. Yokoo. Incentives in ridesharing with deficit control. In *Proceedings of the 2014 International Conference on Autonomous Agents and Multi-agent Systems*, AAMAS '14, pages 1021–1028. International Foundation for Autonomous Agents and Multiagent Systems, 2014.

False-Name-Proof Recommendations in Social Networks

Markus Brill
Duke University
brill@cs.duke.edu

Vincent Conitzer
Duke University
conitzer@cs.duke.edu

Rupert Freeman
Duke University
rupert@cs.duke.edu

Nisarg Shah
Carnegie Mellon University
nkshah@cs.cmu.edu

ABSTRACT

We study the problem of finding a recommendation for an uninformed user in a social network by weighting and aggregating the opinions offered by the informed users in the network. In social networks, an informed user may try to manipulate the recommendation by performing a false-name manipulation, wherein the user submits multiple opinions through fake accounts. To that end, we impose a *no harm axiom*: false-name manipulations by a user should not reduce the weight of other users in the network. We show that this axiom has deep connections to false-name-proofness. While it is impossible to design a mechanism that is best for every network subject to this axiom, we propose an intuitive mechanism LEGIT^{+}, and show that it is uniquely optimized for small networks. Using real-world datasets, we show that our mechanism performs very well compared to two baseline mechanisms in a number of metrics, even on large networks.

Keywords

Social choice, Recommendation systems, Social networks, False-name-proofness

1. INTRODUCTION

Consider the following problem. An agent wants to receive a recommendation on a specific item—say, a movie the agent has not previously watched. Others have evaluated this item, perhaps by giving it a "thumbs up" or "thumbs down" (0 or 1), or by rating it on a more detailed scale, say, from 0 to 5. We want to give the agent in question an aggregate rating, such as "73% positive" or 2.7. Alternatively, perhaps the question is merely whether to recommend this item to the agent at all, in which case the aggregate outcome must be binary. How should we arrive at this aggregate outcome?

For simplicity, let us assume that we do not have any information about which agents have preferences most similar to the agent in question. In this case, a natural approach is to simply take the average of all the ratings so far. One problem is that if ratings are not binary, this is not strategy-proof: when the current average is 2.7, an agent who feels the item is a 4 may prefer to report 5 to pull the average closer to his evaluation. As is well known in social choice theory, a good alternative is to choose the *median* rating instead: this is in fact group-strategy-proof (when preferences are single-peaked, as is likely to be the case here) [21, 4, 6]. Note that for binary ratings, the median is simply the majority choice.

Appears in: *Proceedings of the 15th International Conference on Autonomous Agents and Multiagent Systems (AAMAS 2016), J. Thangarajah, K. Tuyls, C. Jonker, S. Marsella (eds.), May 9–13, 2016, Singapore.*

The median, however, remains vulnerable to another type of manipulation, commonly known as *false-name manipulation* [36]: an agent can rate the same item many times by opening fake accounts, and move the median closer to his evaluation. Thus, the median is not false-name-proof. In fact, without imposing further structure on the problem, no reasonable rule is false-name-proof [9, 30, 31]. On the other hand, if we assume that agents are organized as the nodes of a (say, undirected) social network, possibilities open up [10]. For example, rather than reporting to the agent the median of all the ratings, we can simply report the median of his friends' ratings. Assuming that the agent will not be duped into befriending fake accounts, this will in fact be false-name-proof.

The downside of this methodology is that, with the exception of very popular items, none or very few of the agent's friends may have rated the item. Consequently, the median-of-friends rule conveys too little information. Could we include the friends of the agent's friends as well? Done naïvely, this may give the friends an incentive to create many fake friends of their own. But more subtly, when a friend does *not* rate the item, we can pretend that his rating was the median of *his* friends' ratings. This does not give the friends an incentive to create fake accounts: all this would do for them is change their own hallucinated ratings, but they can more easily just specify those ratings directly. This median-of-medians approach closely resembles the majority-of-majorities rule from Andersen et al. [2]. Note, however, that this rule ends up double-counting the rating of an agent who is a friend of two of the agent's friends. Can we circumvent this issue? Also, can we retrieve ratings from deeper in the social network?

Our results. In this paper, we focus on a two-step approach. In the first step, we use a *weight-selecting mechanism* to assign weights to the agents offering an opinion/rating, called *voters*, without looking at their opinions (thus, looking only at the network structure). In the second step, we perform a weighted aggregation of the opinions to output a recommendation by only looking at the weights assigned to voters and their opinions. To make the weight-selecting mechanism robust to false-name manipulations, we impose a *no harm axiom*: false-name manipulations by an agent should not reduce the weight of other agents in the network.

We show that with weighted median aggregation, the no harm axiom implies false-name-proofness (Theorem 1) and, under some conditions, is actually equivalent to false-name-proofness (Theorem 2). We thus focus on designing weight-selecting mechanisms subject to this axiom.

We focus on the case where, ideally, we would like to weight the voters uniformly. As explained in detail in Section 2, this is for multiple reasons. While this does not utilize the network structure for inferring the closeness in opinions of two nodes, it clearly outlines how to use the network structure for a distinct purpose — achieving the no harm axiom. Section 6 discusses how our results can be extended to take into account correlation among opinions. Second, weighting the voters equally can indeed be ideal, e.g., when aggregating independent noisy estimates of an underlying objective ground truth (see Section 5), or when the goal is not to find a recommendation but to conduct a fair vote.

Unfortunately, weighting all the voters uniformly violates the no harm axiom. What is the "most uniform" weight vector we can return subject to this axiom? In order to formalize what "more uniform" means, we use the classic leximin criterion that compares weight vectors by their smallest weights (preferring the vector with greater smallest weight), and then breaks ties using the second smallest weights, and so on. We show that a weight-selecting mechanism cannot always return the leximin-optimal weight vector subject to the no harm axiom (Theorem 4). We then present an intuitive mechanism and show that it is uniquely optimized for small networks subject to the no harm axiom (Theorem 5), that is, (informally) if a mechanism outputs a more uniform weight vector than our mechanism does on some network, then there is a *strict subgraph* of the network on which our mechanism outputs a more uniform weight vector.

Using a non-trivial result from graph theory [15], we show that our mechanism can be computed in linear time in the size of the network (Theorem 6). In Section 5, we present experiments with real-world social networks in which our mechanism significantly outperforms two baseline mechanisms in a number of metrics.

Related work. Recommendation systems have been studied extensively in the machine learning literature, see, e.g., [14, 1, 26, 5]. Popular techniques include content-based recommendation [25], where the decision of whether to suggest an item to a target user is made by considering the attributes of the item and the target user's previously expressed preferences; collaborative filtering [13], where the preferences of other users in the network are given, and their similarity with the target user's preferences is learned to find a good recommendation; or, both combined [3]. In contrast, we solely focus on the use of the social network structure to design recommendation mechanisms that are robust to false-name manipulations.

Besides the works cited previously, false-name manipulations have also been studied rigorously in a variety of anonymous environments, such as combinatorial auctions [35, 34, 36, 32, 17], matching [29], and voting [33].

2. MODEL

We are given a *social network* (or simply, a network), which is an undirected simple graph[1] denoted G. The set of nodes and the set of edges of G are denoted $V(G)$ and $E(G)$ (or V and E, when the graph is clear from the context), respectively. For $T \subseteq V$, let G_T denote the subgraph of G induced by T.

Our task is to find a recommendation for a given node $v^* \in V$. This task could arise in a number of contexts: we may want to decide whether to recommend a given movie or restaurant to an individual (in which case, we want a binary recommendation), or we may want to show the rating of the movie or restaurant (in which case, we no longer want a binary recommendation). To aid our decision-making, a set of nodes $S \subseteq V \setminus \{v^*\}$ offer their personal opinion. We call these nodes *voters*, and denote the opinion offered by voter $v \in S$ as r_v. Target node v^* is not a voter itself. As we explain in Section 3, the mechanisms of our interest must discard voters not connected to v^*; thus, for simplicity we assume that G is connected and has at least one voter.

Weight-Selecting Mechanisms: In this paper, we are interested in finding recommendations through a two-step approach: i) using a *weight-selecting mechanism* to assign a weight to each voter in the network only as a function of the network structure G, the subset of voters S, and the target node v^* (thus, *independent* of the voters' opinions), and ii) using a *weighted aggregation function* that takes as input the weights assigned by the weight-selecting mechanism and the voters' opinions, and outputs the final recommendation. Popular choices for the weighted aggregation function include weighted mean and weighted median; Section 3.1 discusses how this choice impacts the overall recommendation system. For the remaining parts of the paper, we are only interested in studying weight-selecting mechanisms and their properties (the first step). For a weight-selecting mechanism — ignorant of the voters' opinions — a problem instance is given by the tuple (G, S, v^*).

Definition 1 (Weight-Selecting Mechanisms). *Given an instance (G, S, v^*), a weight-selecting mechanism outputs a weight vector $\mathbf{w} = (w_v)_{v \in S}$ such that $w_v \geq 0$ for $v \in S$, and $\sum_{v \in S} w_v = 1$.*

Weight-selecting mechanisms are compelling because they allow harmonious aggregation of opinions of various formats, ranging from binary to real-valued opinions.

False-Name Manipulations: In the absence of additional restrictions, one can simply choose the weight-selecting mechanism that returns the most appropriate weight vector for the setting of interest. In this paper, however, we consider an important restriction that stems from game-theoretic considerations: *preventing false-name manipulations*.

Online social networks typically lack a proof of authenticity of nodes, thus allowing users to easily create fake accounts. In this case, a weight-selecting mechanism may inadvertently provide an incentive to a malicious user for creating multiple fake accounts and voting through them in order to gain a higher total weight, and thus a greater influence on the final recommendation. Such manipulations are known as *false-name manipulations* or *sybil attacks*.

In a false-name manipulation, the malicious node in the network can easily create any desired subset of edges among the identities it controls: its own node, and the fake nodes it creates. Altering edges with other real nodes (e.g., creating new edges or deleting existing edges), on the other hand, is often more costly. Given that (arguably) recommendations are not the primary objective in most social networks, we assume that nodes do not alter their edges with other real nodes as part of a false-name manipulation due to lack of sufficient incentive. That said, alterations to edges with real nodes are a powerful form of manipulation, and preventing such manipulations is an interesting theoretical challenge (see Section 6).

Definition 2 (False-Name Manipulations). *In an instance (G, S, v^*), a voter $v \in S$ can perform a false-name manipulation by creating a set of false nodes M, and edges between a subset of pairs of nodes in $M' \times M'$, where $M' = M \cup \{v\}$. Also, v can choose a subset of nodes in M' to act as voters, and their recommendations. The resulting instance is given by (G', S', v^*), where $V(G') = V \cup M$, $S' \cap (V \setminus \{v\}) = S \setminus \{v\}$, and $E(G') \cap (V \times V) = E$.*

A node that has a personal opinion may choose to abstain from voting as part of a manipulation. Such a node would be a voter in the underlying true instance, but not in the manipulated instance observed by the mechanism. We refer to it as an "opinionated node" to avoid confusing it with "voters" in the observed instance. In this

[1]A simple graph has no self-loops and at most one edge between every pair of vertices.

paper, we only focus on false-name manipulations by individual nodes; Section 6 briefly discusses group false-name manipulations.

Optimal Weight Vector: Preventing false-name manipulations may prohibit us from always choosing the most desirable weight vector for the setting at hand. For the purpose of this paper, we assume a setting in which the ideal weight vector has equal weights for all voters, i.e., in the ideal weight vector each voter in S has weight $1/|S|$. This is interesting due to multiple reasons:

- False-name-proof recommendation mechanisms can employ the knowledge of the social network structure in two clearly distinct ways: i) to weight nodes in a way that provides no incentive for false-name manipulations, and ii) to weight nodes to reflect their level of homophily[2] or trust with the target node. Treating the uniform weight vector as the ideal focuses exclusively on the former purpose. This is also the appropriate choice for networks where no prior information about user opinions is available to conclude homophily.
- Our model also applies to the case where the goal is not to find a recommendation for the target node; instead, the target node conducts a vote on the network, and invites its peers to vote. In this case, treating all voters equally is the de facto fairness consideration in the voting literature, often termed "one person, one vote."
- Finally, if the opinions offered by the individuals are not subjective preferences, but rather i.i.d. noisy estimates of an objective ground truth, using equal weights for aggregation provably yields the most accurate (e.g., the least squared error) estimation of the underlying ground truth.

That said, aggregating subjective opinions of nodes into a recommendation by weighting the nodes according to their homophily (closeness of opinion) with the target node is an interesting and widely studied topic. As we discuss in Section 6, our results have interesting implications about designing false-name-proof recommendation mechanisms when a model of homophily is given; in this sense, we also view our paper as a stepping stone for studying this more general setting.

Finally, we impose a mild restriction—*symmetry*—on the weight-selecting mechanism. Informally, this requires the mechanism to assign equal weight at least to the nodes that are "symmetrically placed" in the network with respect to the target node.

Definition 3 (Symmetric Mechanisms). *We call a weight-selecting mechanism* symmetric *if, given an instance (G, S, v^*), it assigns equal weights to voters v_1 and v_2 whenever there exists an automorphism of G (i.e., an isomorphism from G to itself) that fixes v^* and maps v_1 to v_2.*

Unless stated otherwise, throughout the paper we will assume a weight-selecting mechanism to be symmetric.

3. UNIFORM AGGREGATION

In the context of this paper, the ideal weight-selecting mechanism returns the weight vector that has equal weight for all voters. However, this mechanism suffers from a crucial problem. A node that performs a false-name manipulation by creating an arbitrarily large number of fake nodes and voting through them can accrue a weight arbitrarily close to 1, thus becoming a dictator. Crucially, this manipulation also hurts the other nodes in the network by reducing their weights. To design a robust mechanism, we require that this should not be possible.

[2]Homophily is a commonly observed phenomenon where nodes closer in a network are more likely to agree on opinions.

Definition 4 (No Harm Axiom). *We say that a weight-selecting mechanism satisfies the* no harm axiom *if a false-name manipulation by a node does not reduce the weight of any other node in the network. We let $\mathcal{M}^{NH}$ denote the family of symmetric weight-selecting mechanisms satisfying the no harm axiom.*

3.1 No Harm Versus False-Name-Proofness

The standard desideratum in the literature on false-name manipulations is *false-name-proofness*, which requires that even with full information an agent should not be able to find a beneficial false-name manipulation. In our setting, this means a voter should not be able to move the recommendation closer to its opinion through a false-name manipulation even if the voter knows the network G, the set of voters S, their opinions $\mathbf{r}$, and the target node v^*.

The no harm axiom directly implies that a voter cannot gain weight by performing a false-name manipulation. Could the voter, however, increase the weights of other voters with similar opinions, thereby achieving a more favorable recommendation? This of course depends on how the recommendation mechanism uses the weights to aggregate the opinions. We show that for the weighted median aggregation, the no harm axiom implies false-name-proofness.

Theorem 1. *With real-valued opinions and aggregate recommendation, computing the weighted median of the opinions using the weights returned by a weight-selecting mechanism satisfying the no harm axiom is false-name-proof.*

Proof. Let (G, S, v^*) be the true instance for which the weight vector is $\mathbf{w}$ and the recommendation is x. Suppose $v \in S$ performs a false-name manipulation, after which the weight vector becomes $\mathbf{w}'$ and the recommendation becomes x'. If $r_v = x$, then v has nothing to gain. Without loss of generality, let $r_v > x$. Define $T = \{u \in S \mid r_u \leq x\}$. Let $w(T) = \sum_{u \in T} w_u$ and $w'(T) = \sum_{u \in T} w'_u$. Then, by the no harm axiom and the definition of weighted median, we have $w'(T) \geq w(T) \geq 0.5$, which implies $x' \leq x$. Hence, the manipulation is not beneficial to v. ■

Theorem 1 shows that the no harm axiom easily yields false-name-proofness. But at first glance, it may seem too strong if the ultimate goal is false-name-proofness. The following result shows that in a simple setting with binary (0/1) opinions and reasonable weighted aggregation functions (e.g., the weighted average), the no harm axiom is *equivalent* to false-name-proofness.

Theorem 2. *Let the opinions be binary (i.e., in $\{0, 1\}$), and the recommendation be computed using a weighted aggregation function that is strictly monotonically increasing in the total weight of all voters with opinion 1, where the weights are computed using a weight-selecting mechanism M. Then, the recommendation system is false-name-proof if and only if M satisfies the no harm axiom.*

Proof. Suppose M satisfies the no harm axiom. Without loss of generality, consider a voter with opinion 0. If the voter performs a false-name manipulation, none of the real voters with opinion 1 lose weight due to the no harm axiom. Hence, the total weight of all voters with opinion 1 does not decrease after the manipulation. Hence, due to monotonicity of the weighted aggregation function, the recommendation cannot decrease due to the manipulation. That is, no false-name manipulation can be beneficial, implying that the recommendation system is false-name-proof.

Now, suppose that M does not satisfy the no harm axiom. Then, there exists an instance (G, S, v^*), a false-name manipulation by $v \in S$ that results in an instance (G', S', v^*), and a voter $u \in S \setminus \{v\}$ such that under M, voter u receives less weight in

(G', S', v^*) than in (G, S, v^*). Suppose in (G, S, v^*) all voters in $S\backslash\{u\}$ vote for 1, and only u votes for 0. Since the weights sum to 1 and u loses weight after the manipulation, the total weight of voters with opinion 1 increases after the manipulation. Strict monotonicity of the weighted aggregation function implies that the manipulation would bring the recommendation closer to v's true opinion, 1. Hence, the recommendation system is not false-name-proof in this case. ■

3.2 Search for a Robust Mechanism

Our starting point is a compelling mechanism proposed by Andersen et al. [2] for binary (0/1) recommendations. Imagine doing a random walk on the social network graph starting from the node v^*,[3] and terminating the walk as soon as a voter is encountered. Then, their mechanism recommends an opinion such that the walk is more likely to terminate on a node having that opinion than terminating on a node having the alternative opinion. We observe that this mechanism, which we denote RANDOMWALK, can be viewed as a weight-selecting mechanism.

Definition 5 (RANDOMWALK). *Given an instance (G, S, v^*), the weight-selecting mechanism* RANDOMWALK *outputs the weight vector* $\mathbf{w}$ *such that for $v \in S$, w_v is the probability that a random walk starting from v^* encounters v before any other voter.*

Our assumption of G being connected and having at least one voter implies that the weights assigned by RANDOMWALK sum to 1. Also, we assume that the edges of the undirected graph G are essentially bidirectional, that is, a walk can traverse an edge in either direction. Crucially, observe that RANDOMWALK satisfies the no harm axiom: Fix a voter v and a walk that leads the random walk to v. When a voter $v' \neq v$ performs a false-name manipulation, the neighborhoods of nodes on the walk do not change. Hence, the walk still leads the random walk to v with the same probability post-manipulation. As this argument applies to every walk leading the random walk to v in the original graph, the total probability of the random walk terminating on v does not reduce after the manipulation. It is also clear that RANDOMWALK is symmetric.

Theorem 3. RANDOMWALK *is a symmetric weight-selecting mechanism satisfying the no harm axiom.*

Example 1. Let G be the network shown on the right. Here, filled nodes represent voters. It is evident that neither v_1 nor v_2 is fake (i.e., they cannot be artificial nodes created by a single node in the network through a false-name manipulation).

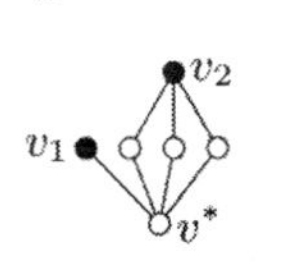

Hence, for uniform aggregation we should weight them equally, if possible. Under RANDOMWALK, voters v_1 and v_2 receive (unequal) weights 2/5 and 3/5, respectively. This can be shown by solving systems of linear equations (see Section 4). Note that these probabilities are not 1/4 and 3/4, respectively, due to walks that go from v^* to one of its three non-voter neighbors and return to v^* a number of times, before finally going to v_1.

Admittedly, Andersen et al. [2] study a slightly different setting than ours. Their ultimate goal, unlike ours, is not to uniformly aggregate the opinions; they want the opinion of a voter to be weighted by the level of "trust" v^* can plausibly have for the voter. Hence, in their setting it makes sense to weight the two voters unequally. In other words, our goal is *not* to evaluate RANDOMWALK in our setting, because RANDOMWALK is not designed to give equal weight to voters in the first place. We use Example 1 simply to demonstrate the need to investigate whether there exists a mechanism satisfying the no harm axiom that can provide more uniform weights.

[3]That is, in each step, move from the current vertex to one of its neighbors chosen uniformly at random.

3.3 An Impossibility Result

As the no harm axiom prohibits always selecting the uniform weight vector (with equal weight for all voters), our goal is to find a weight vector that is *as uniform as possible*. To formalize the notion of "uniformity", we use the classic leximin criterion that compares two weight vectors by their minimum weights (and prefers the one with greater minimum weight), and then breaks ties by comparing their second minimum weights, and so on. For example, according to the leximin criterion, weight vector $(0.3, 0.5, 0.2)$ is better (i.e., more uniform) than weight vector $(0.4, 0.5, 0.1)$, but is no different than weight vector $(0.5, 0.3, 0.2)$. The leximin criterion has been studied extensively in the literature [28, 22, 23], and has been applied successfully in a broad spectrum of domains including constraint programming [7], wireless networks [16], resource allocation [12, 19], cake-cutting [8], and kidney exchange [27].

Definition 6 (Leximin Comparison). *On an instance (G, S, v^*), let weight-selecting mechanisms M and M' return weight vectors* $\mathbf{w}$ *and* $\mathbf{w}'$, *consisting of weights $(w_1, \ldots, w_{|S|})$ and $(w'_1, \ldots, w'_{|S|})$, respectively, sorted in the non-decreasing order. Then, M is* leximin-better *than M' on (G, S, v^*) if there exists $t \in \{1, \ldots, |S|\}$ such that $w_i = w'_i$ for all $i \in \{1, \ldots, t-1\}$ and $w_t > w'_t$.*

Comparing mechanisms across instances, we say that M is leximin-better than M' if M' is not leximin-better than M on any instance, and M is leximin-better than M' on at least one instance.

Definition 7 (Leximin-Optimality). *In a family of weight-selecting mechanisms $\mathcal{C}$, mechanism $M \in \mathcal{C}$ is called leximin-optimal for $\mathcal{C}$ if M is leximin-better than every other mechanism in $\mathcal{C}$.*

We can now cast our search for a good mechanism as a formal question. *Does there exist a mechanism that is leximin-optimal for the family $\mathcal{M}^{NH}$ of symmetric weight-selecting mechanisms satisfying the no harm axiom?* Note that at most one mechanism could satisfy this desideratum. Unfortunately, the next result shows that in our case none meets the bar.

Theorem 4. *No mechanism is leximin-optimal for $\mathcal{M}^{NH}$.*

Proof. Let G_1 and G_2 be the networks shown below.

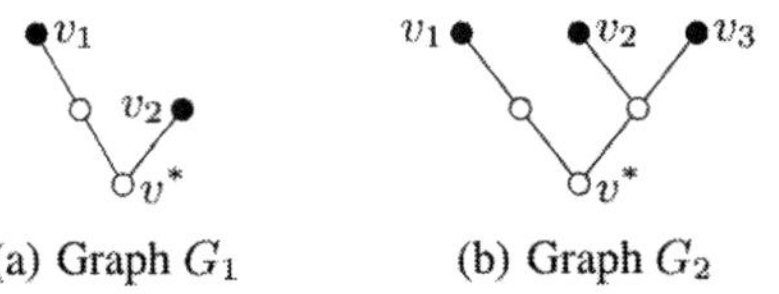

(a) Graph G_1 (b) Graph G_2

Suppose for contradiction that there exists a weight-selecting mechanism $M \in \mathcal{M}^{NH}$ that is leximin-optimal for $\mathcal{M}^{NH}$. It can be shown that there exists a mechanism in $\mathcal{M}^{NH}$ that weights both voters in G_1 equally. While RANDOMWALK does not satisfy this, the reader may check that the mechanism LEGIT$^+$ that we later propose in Section 3.4 does. Leximin-optimality of M now implies that M must assign weight 1/2 to both voters in G_1.

Next, note that G_2 is created when voter v_2 in G_1 performs a false-name manipulation. Thus, the no harm axiom implies that M must still assign a weight of at least 1/2 to v_1 in G_2. As the remaining weight is divided equally among the remaining two voters by symmetry, it follows that the minimum weight in G_2 under M is at most $1/4$. However, it can be checked that the minimum weight in G_2 under RANDOMWALK is $2/7$, which is greater than $1/4$. Hence, RANDOMWALK $\in \mathcal{M}^{\text{NH}}$ is leximin-better than M on G_2, which contradicts leximin-optimality of M for $\mathcal{M}^{\text{NH}}$. ■

3.4 A Possibility Result

Theorem 4 implies that subject to the no harm axiom, a mechanism cannot be the best on every instance. It faces an inevitable trade-off whereby choosing to be better on one instance requires it to be worse on another. Which instances should get more emphasis? In social networks, often very few users make the effort to vote, and this scarcity of information is further exacerbated in smaller networks. Thus, arguably, achieving a uniform weight vector is more important in smaller networks so that every opinion counts. In larger networks, it is often excusable to discard a few opinions in order to achieve robustness. We translate this informal goal of giving more importance to smaller networks into a formal desideratum, *"optimized for small networks"*, which we view as a novel conceptual contribution of the paper as its formulation may be useful in other settings as well.

Definition 8 (Domination). *For weight-selecting mechanisms M and M', we say that M* dominates *M' on network G for target node v^* if M' is not leximin-better than M on (G, S, v^*) for any $S \subseteq V(G) \setminus \{v^*\}$, and M is leximin-better than M' on (G, S, v^*) for some $S \subseteq V(G) \setminus \{v^*\}$.*

Definition 9 (Optimized for Small Networks). *For a family of weight-selecting mechanisms $\mathcal{C}$ and $M \in \mathcal{C}$, we say that M is optimized for small networks within $\mathcal{C}$ if the following holds: If $M' \in \mathcal{C}$ is leximin-better than M on an instance (G, S, v^*), there exists a strict subgraph H of G with $v^* \in V(H)$ such that M dominates M' on H for target node v^*.*

While being optimized for small networks is weaker than (is implied by) leximin-optimality, the bar is still high, as the next observation shows. Its simple proof appears in the full version of the paper.[4]

Proposition 1. *In a family of weight-selecting mechanisms, at most one mechanism is optimized for small networks.*

We now design an intuitive weight-selecting mechanism, and show that it is optimized for small networks within the family $\mathcal{M}^{\text{NH}}$. A key idea behind the mechanism is due to Conitzer et al. [10], who propose a method of identifying *certifiably legitimate nodes* in a network in the presence of false-name manipulations. In their more general setting, this is a tricky problem, but in our setting it boils down to a simple observation: *v could possibly be a fake node created by u if and only if removing u disconnects v from v^*.*

Let $F(u)$, called the *lobe* of u, be the set of all nodes that become disconnected from v^* by removing u. As a convention, $u \notin F(u)$, and $F(v^*)$ is undefined. Now, node v is certifiably legitimate if $v \notin F(u)$ for any $u \in V \setminus \{v^*\}$. In other words, v should remain connected to v^* after removing any single node. Equivalently, it should either be a direct neighbor of v^*, or be 2-vertex-connected to v^*.[5] Suppose we can weight all certifiably legitimate voters equally. The following lemma helps us deal with the remaining voters.

Lemma 1. *A symmetric weight-selecting mechanism satisfying the no harm axiom cannot assign a positive weight to any node in the lobe of a voter.*

Proof. Suppose for contradiction that node $v \in F(u)$ receives weight $\delta > 0$, where u is a voter. Suppose all nodes in the graph (including those in $F(u)$) are real. As the nodes in $F(u)$ are only connected to the remaining network through u, under a false-name manipulation u can create N copies of $F(u)$ that are attached to u in a way identical to how $F(u)$ is attached. The no harm axiom implies that v still receives weight at least δ, and by symmetry, now so does each of its N copies. However, this is infeasible when $N > 1/\delta$ as the weights must sum to 1. ■

ALGORITHM 1: Mechanism LEGIT$^+$

Data: Social network G, set of voters S, central node v^*
Result: Weight vector $\mathbf{w} = (w_v)_{v \in S}$
$\forall u \in V \setminus \{v^*\}, F(u) \leftarrow \{t \in V \setminus \{u\} \mid t \text{ is not connected to } v^* \text{ in } G_{V \setminus \{u\}}\}$;
$L \leftarrow \{v \in V \setminus \{v^*\} \mid (\nexists u \in V \setminus \{v^*\} : v \in F(u)) \wedge (F(v) \cup \{v\}) \cap S \neq \emptyset\}$;
$\forall v \in S, w_v \leftarrow 0$;
for $v \in L$ **do**
  if $v \in S$ **then**
    $w_v \leftarrow 1/|L|$;
  else
    $T \leftarrow F(v) \cup \{v\}$;
    $\mathbf{w}^{\text{rec}} \leftarrow \text{LEGIT}^+(G_T, S \cap T, v)$;
    for $u \in F(v) \cap S$ **do** $w_u \leftarrow w_u^{\text{rec}} \cdot 1/|L|$;
  end
end
return $\mathbf{w} = (w_v)_{v \in S}$;

While Lemma 1 requires us to discard all nodes in the lobe of a voter, it does not prevent us from distributing the weight that a certifiably legitimate non-voter would have received (had it been a voter) to the nodes in its lobe. In fact, such distribution is necessary for the weights to sum to 1 when all voters reside in lobes of other nodes. A natural way is to apply this procedure recursively in each such lobe. This leads to our mechanism, which we call LEGIT$^+$ because it recursively passes legitimacy to nodes. It is presented as Algorithm 1. Crucially, we only recursively apply the mechanism to a lobe if it has a voter. Note that our mechanism assigns a positive weight to the maximal set of nodes subject to Lemma 1. This leads us to the next result.

Lemma 2. *If a node receives zero weight under* LEGIT$^+$, *it receives zero weight under all mechanisms in $\mathcal{M}^{\text{NH}}$.*

We are now ready for the main result of this paper.

Theorem 5. LEGIT$^+$ *is optimized for small networks within the family $\mathcal{M}^{\text{NH}}$.*

Proof. We first show that LEGIT$^+ \in \mathcal{M}^{\text{NH}}$. When an opinionated node v (a voter in the true instance) performs a false-name manipulation, LEGIT$^+$ either keeps the weights of all original voters invariant (if v remains a voter after the manipulation), or distributes the weight of v among the voters in its lobe (if v does not vote after the manipulation). As the real nodes in the lobe of v previously had zero weight, in both cases no real voter other than v loses weight due to the manipulation. Also, LEGIT$^+$ is symmetric by definition.

Before proving that LEGIT$^+$ is optimized for small networks within $\mathcal{M}^{\text{NH}}$, we need to prove a special structure of the lobes.

[4]Available at `http://www.cs.duke.edu/~conitzer/`.

[5]Using Menger's theorem [20], being 2-vertex-connected to v^* is equivalent to having two vertex-disjoint paths to v^*.

Lemma 3. *For two distinct nodes v_1 and v_2, we have i) $v_1 \in F(v_2)$ implies $F(v_1) \subseteq F(v_2)$, ii) $\emptyset \neq F(v_1) \subseteq F(v_2)$ implies $v_1 \in F(v_2)$, and iii) $F(v_1) \cap F(v_2) \in \{\emptyset, F(v_1), F(v_2)\}$.*

Proof. For part i), $v_1 \in F(v_2)$ implies that all paths from v^* to v_1 pass through v_2. For any $t \in F(v_1)$, all paths from v^* to t must pass through v_1. But since the path segment from v^* to v_1 must involve v_2, it follows that all paths from v^* to t involve v_2 as well. Hence, $t \in F(v_2)$ for all $t \in F(v_1)$, i.e., $F(v_1) \subseteq F(v_2)$.

For part ii), since $F(v_1) \neq \emptyset$, there exists a direct neighbor of v_1 in $F(v_1)$.[6] Call it t. Then, we have $t \in F(v_2)$. However, after removal of v_2, t and v_1 should belong to the same connected component, and t and v^* belong to different connected components. Hence, removal of v_2 also disconnects v_1 from v^*. Thus, $v_1 \in F(v_2)$, as required.

For part iii), if $F(v_1) \cap F(v_2) = \emptyset$, we are done. Else, let $v \in F(v_1) \cap F(v_2)$. Then, every path from v^* to v must include both v_1 and v_2. Choose an arbitrary path, and without loss of generality, let it be composed of path P_1 from v^* to v_1, path P_2 from v_1 to v_2, and path P_3 from v_2 to v. If there exists a path from v^* to v_2 that does not include v_1, then combining that with P_3 would give us a path from v^* to v that does not include v_1, which is a contradiction. Hence, there exists no path from v^* to v_2 that does not include v_1, i.e., $v_2 \in F(v_1)$. By part i), it implies $F(v_2) \subseteq F(v_1)$, i.e., $F(v_1) \cap F(v_2) = F(v_2)$, as required. ■ (Proof of Lemma 3)

We now prove a seemingly weaker guarantee, but later show that it is sufficient for our purpose.

Lemma 4. *For a mechanism $M \in \mathcal{M}^{NH}$, if M is leximin-better than* LEGIT$^+$ *on an instance (G, S, v^*), then* LEGIT$^+$ *is leximin-better than M on an instance (H, T, v^*), where H is a strict subgraph of G, and $T \subseteq V(H) \setminus \{v^*\}$.*

Proof. Consider the instance (G, S, v^*). Since M returns a different weight vector than LEGIT$^+$ on this instance, there must exist a vertex u_1 such that its weight under M (denoted $w^M_{u_1}$) is less than its weight under LEGIT$^+$ (denoted $w^L_{u_1}$). Consider the *maximal chain* $u_1, u_2, \ldots, u_k$ such that $u_i \in F(u_{i+1})$ for $i \in \{1, \ldots, k-1\}$. From part (i) of Lemma 3, we immediately have $F(u_i) \subseteq F(u_{i+1})$ for $i \in \{1, \ldots, k-1\}$. Let $U = \{u_1, \ldots, u_k\}$. Next, we show a technical condition.

$$\text{For } v \notin U, u_1 \notin F(v). \qquad (*)$$

This is intuitively clear: Because lobes are either contained in one another or completely disjoint (by Lemma 3), if $u_1 \in F(v)$, then either $F(v)$ contains even the outermost lobe $F(u_k)$, or there exists an $i \in \{2, \ldots, k\}$ such that $F(u_{i-1}) \subset F(v) \subset F(u_i)$. In that case, we should be able to extend the maximal chain, which is a contradiction. Proving this formally is a bit tricky.

In order to prove (*), suppose for contradiction that $u_1 \in F(v)$. First, since v alone could create a chain of length 2, we have $k \geq 2$. Hence, $u_1 \in F(u_k) \neq \emptyset$. Now, due to part (i) of Lemma 3, $u_1 \in F(v)$ implies $F(u_1) \subseteq F(v)$. Choose i to be the largest integer such that $F(u_i) \subseteq F(v)$. If $i = k$, then $F(u_k) \neq \emptyset$ and $F(u_k) \subseteq F(v)$ implies $u_k \in F(v)$ by part (ii) of Lemma 3. This means we could have extended the chain by adding $u_{k+1} = v$, which is a contradiction. Hence, $i < k$. We first show that $u_i \in F(v)$. If $i = 1$, this is assumed, and if $i \geq 2$, it follows from $F(u_i) \subseteq F(v)$, $F(u_i) \neq \emptyset$, and part (ii) of Lemma 3. Next, we show that $v \in F(u_{i+1})$. Note that $u_1 \in F(v) \cap F(u_{i+1})$. Hence, the intersection is not empty. Further, $F(u_{i+1}) \not\subseteq F(v)$. Hence, by part (iii) of Lemma 3, we have $F(v) \subseteq F(u_{i+1})$. Further, $u_1 \in F(v)$. Hence, $F(v) \neq \emptyset$. Thus, by part (ii) of Lemma 3, we have $v \in F(u_{i+1})$. Thus, we have proved that $u_i \in F(v)$ and $v \in F(u_{i+1})$, which is a contradiction because it means we could have extended the chain by inserting v between u_i and u_{i+1}. Thus, for $v \notin U$, $u_1 \notin F(v)$.This completes the proof of (*).

Next, we perform a sequence of operations to transform the instance. In each step, we find an arbitrary node $v \notin U$ such that $F(v) \neq \emptyset$. By (*), $u_1 \notin F(v)$. We remove the vertices in the lobe $F(v)$, and make v a voter (if that was not already the case). Note that this operation is the reverse of a false-name manipulation by v. Hence, by the no harm axiom, the weight of u_1 under M should *not increase* during this operation. On the other hand, it is easy to check that the weight of u_1 stays invariant under LEGIT$^+$ during this operation. Hence, even in the resulting instance, the weight of u_1 under M is less than its weight under LEGIT$^+$.

We continue these operations until we cannot find a node $v \notin U$ such that $F(v) \neq \emptyset$. Let the final instance be denoted (H, T, v^*). In the instance (H, T, v^*), suppose LEGIT$^+$ assigns zero weight to l voters. Then, by Lemma 2, M must also assign zero weight to at least l voters. Also, under LEGIT$^+$ the $(l+1)^{st}$ smallest weight is the weight of u_1, which is $w^L_{u_1}$, since u_1 is contained in every non-empty lobe that remains in H. In contrast, under M the $(l+1)^{st}$ smallest weight is at most the weight of u_1, which is at most $w^M_{u_1} < w^L_{u_1}$. Hence, LEGIT$^+$ is leximin-better than M on (H, T, v^*). By our construction, H is already a subgraph of G. To see why it is a strict subgraph of G, recall that M was leximin-better than LEGIT$^+$ on the original instance (G, S, v^*). Hence, we must have made at least one "reverse false-name manipulation" operation, which must have resulted in a strictly smaller subgraph. ■ (Proof of Lemma 4)

Finally, to prove that LEGIT$^+$ is optimized for small networks in $\mathcal{M}^{NH}$, consider a different mechanism $M \in \mathcal{M}^{NH}$, and suppose M is leximin-better than LEGIT$^+$ on an instance (G, S, v^*). Then, by Lemma 4 there exists an instance (H, T, v^*) on which LEGIT$^+$ is leximin-better than M and where H is a strict subgraph of G. Among all such instances, choose one with the smallest number of nodes in H. We show that LEGIT$^+$ dominates M on network H for target node v^*. To see this, take a subset of voters $Q \subseteq V(H) \setminus \{v^*\}$. If M is leximin-better than LEGIT$^+$ on (H, Q, v^*), then by Lemma 4 there exists another instance (H', Q', v^*) on which LEGIT$^+$ is leximin-better than M and where H' is a strict subgraph of H (and therefore, of G). However, this violates the minimality of the number of nodes in H in our choice of the instance (H, T, v^*). Hence, M must not be leximin-better than LEGIT$^+$ on (H, Q, v^*), as required. ■ (Proof of Theorem 5)

4. COMPUTATIONAL COMPLEXITY

Let us begin with RANDOMWALK. Andersen et al. [2] show that aggregating binary recommendations under RANDOMWALK amounts to solving a single system of linear equations $Ax = b$, where the LHS matrix A is $n \times n$ ($n = |V|$ is the number of nodes) and the RHS vector b is $n \times 1$. Solving this system can take, even with recent exact solvers, $O(|V|^{1.5} \cdot (|V| + |E|))$ time [11]. Implementing RANDOMWALK as a weight-selecting mechanism is computationally even more difficult. We need to solve one system of linear equations for each voter, which can take $O(|V|^{2.5} \cdot (|V| + |E|))$ time [11].

Let us now consider LEGIT$^+$. Arguably, it is harder to describe than RANDOMWALK, and Algorithm 1 is more intricate than simply solving a collection of linear systems. More specifically, in the first step of Algorithm 1 simply computing $F(u)$ for every node u

[6] This is because we assume the original graph to be connected.

would naïvely take $O(|V|\cdot(|V|+|E|))$ time. Surprisingly, we show that there exists a more efficient implementation that computes the weights under LEGIT$^+$ in merely $O(|V|+|E|)$ (linear) time. This implementation uses as a subroutine the remarkable linear time algorithm by Hopcroft and Tarjan [15] for finding biconnected components in a graph. A *biconnected component* (or a *block*) is a maximal 2-vertex-connected subgraph. Nodes that belong to multiple blocks (i.e., whose removal disconnects the graph) are called *cut vertices* or *articulation points*. A connected graph G decomposes into a *block-cut tree* T whose vertices are the blocks and the articulation points of G, and a block B and an articulation point u are connected if $u \in B$.

Let A denote the set of articulation points of G, and $\mathcal{B}_u$ denote the set of blocks of G containing u. First, u has a non-empty lobe $F(u)$ if and only if $u \in A$. Next, if $u \in A$, the lobe $F(u)$ can be computed as follows. Remove the vertex of T representing u, which disconnects T into connected components, one of which contains all blocks containing v^*. The set of nodes in the blocks contained in every other connected component of the tree (except u itself) constitute $F(u)$. This key observation leads us to the linear time implementation of LEGIT$^+$ presented as Algorithm 2. The proof of its correctness and running time analysis appear in the full version of the paper.

Theorem 6. *Weights under mechanism* LEGIT$^+$ *can be computed in* $O(|V|+|E|)$ *time.*

ALGORITHM 2: LEGIT$^+$ in linear time

Data: Social network G, set of voters $S \subseteq V(G) \setminus \{v^*\}$,
central node $v^* \in V(G)$
Result: Weight vector $\mathbf{w} = (w_v)_{v \in S}$

$\mathcal{B} \leftarrow$ set of biconnected components of G;
$A \leftarrow$ set of articulation points of G;
$\forall u \in V, \mathcal{B}_u \leftarrow \{B \in \mathcal{B} \mid u \in B\}$;
/* $\mathcal{B}$, A, and $\{\mathcal{B}_u\}_{u\in V}$ are computed using the linear time algorithm from [15] */
$\forall u \in A \setminus S$, $VL_u \leftarrow$ false;
$\forall u \in S, w_u \leftarrow 0$;
voting_lobes($v^*, \emptyset$);
weight_helper($v^*, 1, \emptyset$);
return $\mathbf{w} = (w_u)_{u \in S}$;

Procedure voting_lobes (v, B^*)
  $b \leftarrow$ false;
  for $B \in \mathcal{B}_v \setminus B^*$ **do**
    for $u \in B \setminus \{v\}$ **do**
      if $u \in S$ **then**
        $b \leftarrow$ true;
      else if $u \in A$ **then**
        $VL_u \leftarrow$ voting_lobes($u, \{B\}$);
        if VL_u **then** $b \leftarrow$ true;
      end
    end
  end
  return b;

Procedure weight_helper (v, T, B^*)
  $L \leftarrow \{u \in V \mid (u \in B \in \mathcal{B}_v \setminus B^*) \wedge (u \in S \vee (u \in A \wedge VL_u))\}$;
  $N \leftarrow |L|$;
  for $u \in L$ **do**
    if $u \in S$ **then**
      $w_u = T/N$;
    else if $u \in A$ **then**
      weight_helper($u, T/N, \{B\}$);
    end
  end

5. EXPERIMENTS

We compare LEGIT$^+$ with two baseline mechanisms: LEGIT and RANDOMWALK. We define weight-selecting mechanism LEGIT as the simpler version of LEGIT$^+$ that assigns equal weight to all certifiably legitimate voters, but does *not* apply the procedure recursively within the lobes of certifiably legitimate non-voters. Thus, comparison with LEGIT indicates the gain from recursively applying LEGIT$^+$ within the lobes of certifiably legitimate non-voters. We note that LEGIT$^+$ is expected to (though theoretically not guaranteed to) outperform RANDOMWALK, because RANDOMWALK is not designed to assign uniform weights.

We perform experiments using 16 real-world social networks from the KONECT project [18]. The number of nodes and edges in these networks vary from 23 to 26,475, and from 78 to 146,385, respectively.[7] For each network G, we sample the target node v^* uniformly at random. For each pair (G, v^*), we determine the set of voters by making each node in the network a voter independently with probability p_{vote}. We use both low values (from 0.01 to 0.09 in increments of 0.02) and high values (from 0.1 to 0.9 in increments of 0.2) of p_{vote}, representative of varying levels of voter engagement. For each network and each of 10 values of p_{vote}, we choose 100 random target nodes, and for each target node, choose 100 random subsets of voters. In the results presented below, we compare LEGIT$^+$ with LEGIT and RANDOMWALK across the simulations for each network. To solve the linear system in RANDOMWALK, we use Matlab's mldivide operator, and to find the biconnected components in LEGIT$^+$, we use the MatlabBGL library [8].

Figure 1(c) shows a log-log plot of the running time of all three mechanisms (LEGIT$^+$ as magenta diamonds, LEGIT as red circles, and RANDOMWALK as blue stars) as a function of the number of nodes in the network. The experiments were performed on a dual-core machine with 3.10 GHz processors and 8 GB RAM. While LEGIT is trivially faster than LEGIT$^+$ (as it requires a strictly less number of operations), the difference is not significant. On the other hand, while RANDOMWALK is slightly faster than LEGIT$^+$ on smaller networks, LEGIT$^+$ is significantly faster on networks with more than 200 nodes. This is consistent with our result from Section 4 that the worst-case complexity is significantly lower for LEGIT$^+$ than for RANDOMWALK (linear versus super-quadratic). Across the entire experiment, LEGIT$^+$ ran about 13 times faster than RANDOMWALK, and only about 3 times slower than LEGIT.

In the remaining figures, we only plot two lines: one that compares LEGIT$^+$ with LEGIT (with red circles), and one that compares LEGIT$^+$ with RANDOMWALK (with blue stars).

Our next goal is to determine which mechanism outputs a more uniform weight vector. Lacking an objective definition of uniformity, we use three metrics: i) leximin comparison as used in our theoretical results in Section 3, ii) the percentage of voters discarded, i.e., assigned zero weight to (the lower, the better), iii) the (L^2-)distance from the uniform weight vector, which is equal to the variance of the weight vector (the lower, the better).

Figure 1(d) shows that LEGIT$^+$ is leximin-better than both

[7] Running experiments on the larger datasets was infeasible due to the prohibitive running time of RANDOMWALK.

[8] `https://www.cs.purdue.edu/homes/dgleich/packages/matlab_bgl/`

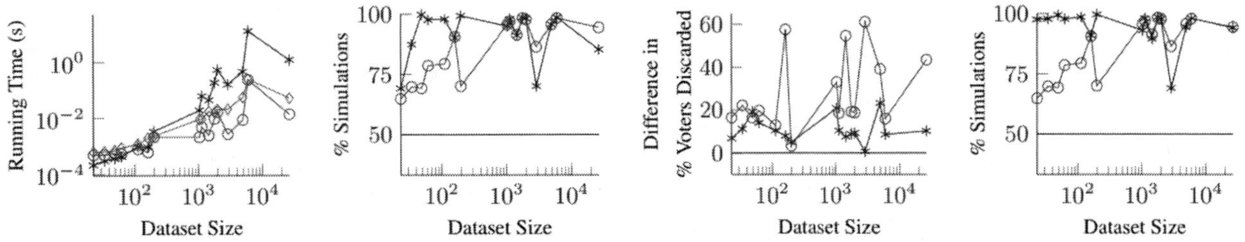

(c) Running Time (d) Leximin Comparison (e) Diff. in % Voters Discarded (f) Comparing Variance

Figure 1: Comparison of LEGIT$^+$ with RANDOMWALK on real-world social networks

LEGIT and RANDOMWALK in more than 50% simulations in each network. In fact, it is leximin-better than LEGIT (resp. RANDOMWALK) in more than 75% (resp. 85%) simulations in all but one (resp. two) networks. Superior empirical performance in such large networks nicely complements our theoretical result (Theorem 5), which indicates that LEGIT$^+$ should be superior in small networks in general.

Next, while Lemma 2 ensures that LEGIT$^+$ discards the smallest subset of voters subject to the no harm axiom, Figure 1(e) shows that LEGIT and RANDOMWALK can discard up to 60% and 20% more voters, respectively, than LEGIT$^+$ (about 30% and 10%, respectively, on average across networks).

Finally, comparing variance of the returned weight vector, Figure 1(f) shows that LEGIT$^+$ performs better than both LEGIT and RANDOMWALK in more than 50% simulations in each network. Further, it outperforms LEGIT in at least 69% simulations in all but one network, and RANDOMWALK in at least 89% simulations in all but one network.

So far we have focused on the setting where the opinions of voters are subjective, and the goal is to find a weight vector as close to uniform as possible. We now present empirical results for a slightly different setting in which there exists a binary (0/1) ground truth, and the goal is to pinpoint it by aggregating binary opinions of voters, each of which is "correct" with probability $p_{\text{acc}} > 0.5$. The accuracy of a weight-selecting mechanism on an instance (G, S, v^*) is the probability that the mechanism assigns higher total weight to voters with the correct opinion than to voters with the incorrect opinion. While we do not have theoretical results for this setting, we can evaluate the mechanisms empirically. For p_{acc}, we use both low values (0.51 to 0.59 in increments of 0.02) and high values (0.6 to 0.9 in increments of 0.1).

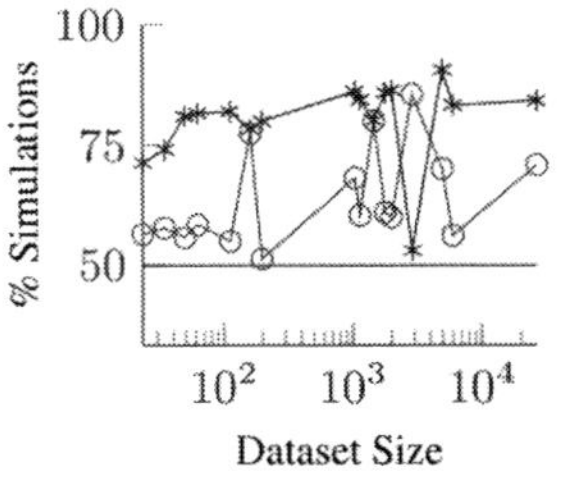

Figure 2: Accuracy

Figure 2 shows that LEGIT$^+$ achieves better accuracy than both LEGIT and RANDOMWALK in more than 50% simulations in each network. Also, note that LEGIT$^+$ achieves better accuracy than RANDOMWALK in at least 70% simulations in all but one network.

6. DISCUSSION

Recall the median-of-medians rule from the introduction: the recommendation is the median of the opinions of the target agent's friends, and for a friend who does not provide an opinion, we construct one by taking the median of *his* friends' opinions, and so on. In conjunction with the weighted median aggregation rule (as in Theorem 1), LEGIT$^+$ can be seen as a similar rule, "median-of-medians for legitimate nodes": instead of taking the median of friends' opinions, take the median of the opinions of (certifiably) legitimate nodes, and for such nodes that do not provide an opinion, construct one recursively from opinions in their lobes.

We uniquely characterize LEGIT$^+$ within the family of symmetric weight-selecting mechanisms satisfying the no harm axiom. We show this axiom to be closely related, but in the general setting incomparable, to false-name-proofness. The no harm axiom is only defined for weight-selecting mechanisms. It remains to be seen whether we can pinpoint an overall recommendation mechanism that uses LEGIT$^+$ (e.g., median-of-median for legitimate nodes) within the more general family of false-name-proof mechanisms.

Importantly, in this paper we consider the uniform weight vector as idealistic. In the context of aggregating subjective opinions into a personal recommendation for the target node, this only makes sense in the absence of knowledge of correlation among user preferences (e.g., homophily of opinions). However, note that Lemma 1 provides a necessary condition for satisfying the no harm axiom — in the form of having to assign zero weight to specific nodes — *even in the presence of homophily*. Given a model of homophily, we must start by assigning zero weight to such nodes. Weighting the remaining nodes to maximally align the recommendation with the target node's preference is still a difficult problem. Fortunately, it can be shown that choosing the remaining weights as a function of the vertex-connectivity of a node to the target node is sufficient to guarantee the no harm axiom. However, this approach is likely to be suboptimal. An immediate next step is to design better ways of incorporating homophily subject to the no harm axiom.

An interesting direction for future research is to study stronger manipulations. For example, LEGIT$^+$ does not prevent group false-name manipulations or manipulations where nodes may delete their existing edges with other real nodes. Can we effectively prevent them? While RANDOMWALK is group false-name-proof, it can be shown that it is not optimized for small networks among symmetric group false-name-proof mechanisms. Does there exist such a mechanism (recall that there can be at most one)?

False-name manipulations are an increasingly serious concern in social networks, especially with the effortless accessibility and increasing popularity of automated tools for creating fake accounts [24]. Given the difficulty of distinguishing fake accounts from real ones, we believe that the study of false-name-proofness is the key to building the next generation of reliable recommendation systems.

Acknowledgments

We are thankful for support from NSF under awards IIS-1527434, IIS-0953756, CCF-1101659, and CCF-1337215, ARO under grants W911NF-12-1-0550 and W911NF-11-1-0332, ERC under StG 639945 (ACCORD), a Guggenheim Fellowship, and a Feodor Lynen research fellowship of the Alexander von Humboldt Foundation. This work was done in part while Conitzer was visiting the Simons Institute for the Theory of Computing.

REFERENCES

[1] G. Adomavicius and A. Tuzhilin. Toward the next generation of recommender systems: A survey of the state-of-the-art and possible extensions. *IEEE Transactions on Knowledge and Data Engineering*, 17(6):734–749, 2005.

[2] R. Andersen, C. Borgs, J. Chayes, U. Feige, A. Flaxman, A. Kalai, V. Mirrokni, and M. Tennenholtz. Trust-based recommendation systems: an axiomatic approach. In *Proceedings of the 17th International World Wide Web Conference (WWW)*, pages 199–208, 2008.

[3] M. Balabanović and Y. Shoham. Fab: content-based, collaborative recommendation. *Communications of the ACM*, 40(3):66–72, 1997.

[4] S. Barbera, H. Sonnenschein, and L. Zhou. Voting by committees. *Econometrica*, pages 595–609, 1991.

[5] J. Bennett and S. Lanning. The Netflix prize. In *Proceedings of KDD cup and workshop*, page 35, 2007.

[6] K. Border and J. Jordan. Straightforward elections, unanimity and phantom voters. *Review of Economic Studies*, 50:153–170, 1983.

[7] S. Bouveret and M. Lemaître. Computing leximin-optimal solutions in constraint networks. *Artificial Intelligence*, 173(2):343–364, 2009.

[8] Y. Chen, J. K. Lai, D. C. Parkes, and A. D. Procaccia. Truth, justice, and cake cutting. *Games and Economic Behavior*, 77:284–297, 2013.

[9] V. Conitzer. Anonymity-proof voting rules. In *Proceedings of the 4th International Workshop on Internet and Network Economics (WINE)*, pages 295–306, 2008.

[10] V. Conitzer, N. Immorlica, J. Letchford, K. Munagala, and L. Wagman. False-name-proofness in social networks. In *Proceedings of the 6th International Workshop on Internet and Network Economics (WINE)*, pages 209–221, 2010.

[11] W. Eberly, M. Giesbrecht, P. Giorgi, A. Storjohann, and G. Villard. Solving sparse rational linear systems. In *Proceedings of the 2006 International Symposium on Symbolic and Algebraic Computation (ISSAC)*, pages 63–70. ACM, 2006.

[12] A. Ghodsi, M. Zaharia, B. Hindman, A. Konwinski, S. Shenker, and I. Stoica. Dominant resource fairness: Fair allocation of multiple resource types. In *Proceedings of the 8th USENIX Conference on Networked Systems Design and Implementation (NSDI)*, pages 24–37, 2011.

[13] J. Golbeck. *Generating predictive movie recommendations from trust in social networks*. Springer, 2006.

[14] J. He and W. W. Chu. *A social network-based recommender system (SNRS)*. Springer, 2010.

[15] J. Hopcroft and R. Tarjan. Algorithm 447: Efficient algorithms for graph manipulation. *Communications of the ACM*, 16(6):372–378, 1973.

[16] X. L. Huang and B. Bensaou. On max-min fairness and scheduling in wireless ad-hoc networks: analytical framework and implementation. In *Proceedings of the 2nd ACM International Symposium on Mobile Ad Hoc Networking & Computing (MobiHoc)*, pages 221–231, 2001.

[17] A. Iwasaki, V. Conitzer, Y. Omori, Y. Sakurai, T. Todo, M. Guo, and M. Yokoo. Worst-case efficiency ratio in false-name-proof combinatorial auction mechanisms. In *Proceedings of the 9th International Conference on Autonomous Agents and Multi-Agent Systems (AAMAS)*, pages 633–640, 2010.

[18] J. Kunegis. KONECT - The Koblenz network collection. In *Proceedings of the Int. Web Observatory Workshop*, 2013.

[19] D. Kurokawa, A. D. Procaccia, and N. Shah. Leximin allocations in the real world. In *Proceedings of the 16th ACM Conference on Economics and Computation (EC)*, pages 345–362, 2015.

[20] K. Menger. Zur allgemeinen Kurventheorie. *Fundamenta Mathematicae*, 1(10):96–115, 1927.

[21] H. Moulin. On strategy-proofness and single-peakedness. *Public Choice*, 35:437–455, 1980.

[22] H. Moulin. *Axioms of cooperative decision making*. Cambridge University Press, 1991.

[23] H. Moulin. *Fair Division and Collective Welfare*. MIT Press, 2003.

[24] A. Pathak. *An analysis of various tools, methods and systems to generate fake accounts for social media*. PhD thesis, Northeastern University Boston, 2014.

[25] M. Pazzani and D. Billsus. Content-based recommendation systems. *The Adaptive Web*, pages 325–341, 2007.

[26] F. Ricci, L. Rokach, and B. Shapira. *Introduction to recommender systems handbook*. Springer, 2011.

[27] A. E. Roth, T. Sönmez, and M. U. Ünver. Pairwise kidney exchange. *Journal of Economic Theory*, 125:151–188, 2005.

[28] A. Sen. *Collective Choice and Social Welfare*. North-Holland, 1970.

[29] T. Todo and V. Conitzer. False-name-proof matching. In *Proceedings of the 12th International Conference on Autonomous Agents and Multi-Agent Systems (AAMAS)*, pages 311–318, 2013.

[30] T. Todo, A. Iwasaki, and M. Yokoo. False-name-proofness in facility location problem on the real line. In *Proceedings of the 6th International Workshop on Internet and Network Economics (WINE)*, pages 559–562, 2010.

[31] T. Todo, A. Iwasaki, and M. Yokoo. False-name-proof mechanism design without money. In *Proceedings of the 10th International Conference on Autonomous Agents and Multi-Agent Systems (AAMAS)*, pages 651–658, 2011.

[32] T. Todo, A. Iwasaki, M. Yokoo, and Y. Sakurai. Characterizing false-name-proof allocation rules in combinatorial auctions. In *Proceedings of the 8th International Conference on Autonomous Agents and Multi-Agent Systems (AAMAS)*, pages 265–272, 2009.

[33] L. Wagman and V. Conitzer. Optimal false-name-proof voting rules with costly voting. In *Proceedings of the 23rd AAAI Conference on Artificial Intelligence (AAAI)*, pages 190–195, 2008.

[34] M. Yokoo. Characterization of strategy/false-name proof combinatorial auction protocols: Price-oriented, rationing-free protocol. In *Proceedings of the 18th International Joint Conference on Artificial Intelligence (IJCAI)*, pages 733–739, 2003.

[35] M. Yokoo, Y. Sakurai, and S. Matsubara. Robust combinatorial auction protocol against false-name bids. *Artificial Intelligence*, 130(2):167–181, 2001.

[36] M. Yokoo, Y. Sakurai, and S. Matsubara. The effect of false-name bids in combinatorial auctions: New fraud in internet auctions. *Games and Economic Behavior*, 46(1):174–188, 2004.

Parameterized Complexity of Winner Determination in Minimax Committee Elections

Hong Liu*
School of Computer Science and Technology, Shandong University
1500 Shunhua Road, Jinan 250101, P.R. China
hong-liu@sdu.edu.cn

Jiong Guo†
School of Computer Science and Technology, Shandong University
1500 Shunhua Road, Jinan 250101, P.R. China
jguo@sdu.edu.cn

ABSTRACT

Recently, the winner determination problem of minimax approval committee (or referenda) elections has been extensively studied. In particular, Misra et al. [AAMAS 2015] investigated its parameterized complexity with respect to various parameters. Among others, they showed that this problem is FPT with the Hamming distance upper-bound as parameter. Following the suggestion of Baumeister and Dennisen [AAMAS 2015], we consider minimax committee election rules for trichotomous votes, linear orders, and partial orders. Complementing the classical complexity results for these rules by Baumeister et al. [ADT 2015], we show that the winner determination problem on trichotomous votes admits similar parameterized complexity behavior as on dichotomous votes. To this end, we fix a flaw in the parameterized algorithm given by Misra et al. [AAMAS 2015], which uses the Hamming distance upper-bound as parameter. Moreover, we prove that on both linear and partial orders, it is W[2]-hard to determine the winners with respect to the size of the committee. Even with both the size of the committee and the number of votes as parameters, this problem remains fixed-parameter intractable; here, it becomes W[1]-hard. We also present FPT algorithms for both linear and partial orders with the distance upper-bound as parameter. Finally, we show that in several special settings, the winner determination problem of a minimax approval committee election is polynomial-time solvable. These special settings have been considered for similar voting problems.

Keywords

Computational Social Choice; Fixed-Parameter Tractability; Minimax Committee Election

1. INTRODUCTION

The problem of aggregating the preferences of different agents occurs in diverse situations and plays a fundamental role in artificial intelligence and social choice [9, 12]. Here, agents (voters) express their preferences over candidates and a voting rule is employed to determine which candidate wins. While the most studied setting is the single-winner case, voting can also be used to elect a fixed-size set of winners, a so-called committee. Real-world examples include parliamentary elections, selecting committees, understanding heredity and signals in DNA, and recommendation systems (see [3] and the references therein). Recently, we witness an increasing interest in the study of the axiomatic and algorithmic aspects of committee elections [1, 2, 3, 6, 11, 15, 20, 23, 22, 26]

Approval voting. A widely used rule for committee election is the approval voting (AV) approach, where the voters decide for each candidate, whether they approve or disapprove of this candidate. Such votes are called *approval votes.* The winning committee consists of the k candidates with the most approvals. Brams et al. [8] suggested a distance-based variant of AV, called minimax approval voting, which selects a set of k candidates that minimize the maximum Hamming distance from the given votes. Another popular distance-based AV variant is the minisum approval voting, whose optimization goal is to minimize the total Hamming distance of the committee to all given votes. Amanatidis et al. [1] introduced a so-called ordered weighted averaging operator to the distance-based AV approach, generalizing both minimax and minisum approval rules. Other variants of AV include proportional approval voting, reweighted approval voting, and satisfaction approval voting (see [3] for more details).

Extensions of minimax and minisum AV. In 2015, Baumeister and Dennisen [5] extended the minimax and minisum approaches to other forms of votes such as trichotomous votes, linear orders, and partial orders. A voting with trichotomous votes allows the voters in addition to approval and disapproval to abstain for a candidate [18], which could be of particular interest in the multiple referenda elections.[1] A trichotomous vote can be represented as a vector over the candidates, where 1 and -1 stand for approval and disapproval of candidates, and 0 stands for abstention. The committee is then a vector with entries from 1 and -1. Baumeister and Dennisen proposed a modified Hamming distance to measure the distance between the committee and the votes. In the case of linear orders, every voter's preference is represented as a total, transitive and asymmetric binary relation of the candidates and the rank-sum distance is used

*Partially supported by Natural Science Foundation of Shandong Province, China (No. ZR2013FM030)

†Partially supported by the Taishan project of Shandong, China

Appears in: *Proceedings of the 15th International Conference on Autonomous Agents and Multiagent Systems (AAMAS 2016), J. Thangarajah, K. Tuyls, C. Jonker, S. Marsella (eds.), May 9–13, 2016, Singapore.*

[1]Multiple referenda elections seek for a collective decision over several binary propositions and thus, share similar properties with committee elections.

to select the winning committee. Partial orders are also transitive and asymmetric, but not necessarily total. The dissatisfaction of the voters with a committee is measured by a generalized Kemeny distance. See the preliminaries for the definitions of the votes and distance functions. Baumeister et al. [6] proved that concerning the classical complexity, the minimax and minisum winner determination problems admit the same behavior for all three forms of votes. That is, as in the case of approval votes, the minisum version is polynomial-time solvable and the minimax version is NP-hard for all three forms of votes.[2]

Parameterized Complexity. We focus on the parameterized complexity of the above three extensions of the minimax approval voting. Parameterized complexity allows to give a more refined analysis of computational problems and in particular, can provide a deep exploration of the connection between the problem complexity and various problem-specific parameters [14]. In the last years, parameterized complexity analysis has been applied to diverse problems from computational social choice, including winner determination, control, and bribery [7, 10]. Misra et al. [24] initialized the study of parameterized complexity of the minimax approval voting. They showed, among others, that the winner determination problem of minimax approval voting is fixed-parameter tractable with respect to the Hamming distance upper-bound, the number of candidates, or the number of candidates, while it becomes fixed-parameter intractable (W[2]-hard) with respect to the size of the committee.

Our results. As in [24], we also consider four parameters: the number n of votes, the number m of candidates, the size k of committee, and the distance upper-bound d.

Our main findings is that, in contrast to the classical complexity, the winner determination problem admits different parameterized complexity behavior for the considered vote forms. First, compared to the case with approval votes, the introduction of trichotomous votes essentially has no impact on the parameterized complexity with respect to all four parameters. Hereby, we identify and fix a flaw in the algorithm by Misra et al. for the case of approval votes with d as parameter. Moreover, we propose two parameterized algorithms for the linear and partial orders cases with d as parameter, which are based on completely different idea than the one for the approval and trichotomous votes cases and need much more algorithmic effort. However, the resulting running times are comparable with the ones for the approval and trichotomous votes cases. In particular, we show that with the linear and partial orders, the winner determination problem becomes fixed-parameter intractable, i.e., W[1]-hard, even with both k and n as parameters, in contrast to the FPT-result with the same parameterization for the approval and trichotomous votes cases. Finally, we present polynomial time algorithms for two special cases of the maximin approval voting with approval votes. These two special cases have been studied for similar voting problems [16, 17].

2. PRELIMINARIES

In this section, we introduce the definitions and notations used in this paper. An *election* is a pair (C, V), where $C = \{c_1, \ldots, c_m\}$ is a set of candidates (or alternatives) and $V = \{v_1, \ldots, v_n\}$ is an ordered list of voters. Each voter's preference among the candidates in C is expressed through the vote he casts. We also use V to denote the list of votes that the voters in V cast. We will refer to the list V as a *preference profile*, and denote the number of voters in V by n, and the number of candidates in C by m. A committee election is a triple (C, V, k), where k is the size of the committee. A *committee election system* is a mapping that takes as input an committee election (C, V, k), and outputs a size-k subset K of C, i.e., the *committee*.

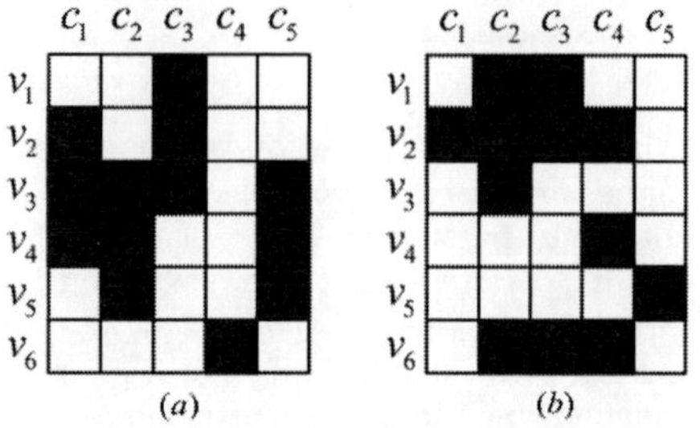

Figure 1: Voter Interval and Candidate Interval. A black cell stands for a "1", and a white cell stands for a "0".

As in [6], we consider four different forms of votes:

Approval votes. An approval vote v on C is a subset of C. While the corresponding voter approves of the candidates in v, he disapproves of the candidates in $C \backslash v$. For a fixed order of the candidates in C, each vote v can also be represented as a $\{0, 1\}^m$ vector, where a 1 stands for approval and a 0 for disapproval of the corresponding candidate. We use $v[i]$ to denote the ith entry of v. We call the number of 1's in an approval vote v as its weight. For the same order of the candidates in C, a committee K can also be represented by a $\{0, 1\}^m$ vector with weight k.

The distance for an approval vote v with a committee K is defined as $HD(K, v) = \sum_{1 \leq i \leq m} |K[i] - v[i]| = |K \oplus v|$, that is, the Hamming distance between K and v, where $K \oplus v$ is the symmetric difference of K and v.

Given an election (C, V), we say that V satisfies the *voter interval* (VI) property if the votes in V can be ordered such that for every candidate $c \in C$ the voters that approve of c form an interval of that ordering [16]. See Figure 1(a) for an example. We say that V satisfies the *candidate interval* (CI) property if the candidates in C can be ordered such that for every voter $v \in V$ the candidates that v approves of form an interval of that ordering [17]. See Figure 1(b) for an example.

Trichotomous votes. A trichotomous vote on C is a partition of C into three disjoint subsets C_1, C_0 and C_{-1}. The corresponding voter approves of the candidates in C_1, disapproves of the candidates in C_{-1}, and abstains for the candidates in C_0. For a fixed order of the candidates in C, each vote can also be represented as a $\{-1, 0, 1\}^m$ vector, where 1 stands for approval, -1 for disapproval and 0 for abstention. Given a trichotomous vote v and a candidate c, we will denote the opinion of v on c, i.e., 1, 0, or -1, by $value(v, c)$. We call the number of 1's in a trichotomous vote v as its weight, and denote it by $|v|$. For the same order, a committee K can be represented by a $\{1, -1\}^m$ vector with weight k.

[2]In [6], the complexity of the minimax version with linear orders was left open. According to [4], this problem is NP-hard as well.

The distance between two trichotomous votes u, v is defined as $d_T(u,v) = \sum_{1\le i\le m} |u[i] - v[i]|$. The distance between a trichotomous vote v and a committee K is defined as $\delta(K,v) = d_T(K,v)$.

Linear orders. A linear order is a total, transitive, and asymmetric binary relation over C. We denote the vote of voter v by $\succ_v$, where $c \succ_v d$ means that v prefers candidate c to candidate d. When the identity of the voter is clear from the context, we omit the subscript and write $\succ$ instead of $\succ_v$.

In this case, the distance for a vote v with a committee K is defined as the normalized sum of ranks of the committee members in vote v, i.e., $RS(K,v) = \sum_{c\in K} pos(c,v) - \frac{k(k+1)}{2}$, where $pos(c,v)$ denotes the position of candidate c in vote v. For convenience, we can also express the distance in another way. Given a committee K, let $npos(c,v)$ denote the "normalized" position of candidate c in vote v, i.e., the number of candidates that procede c in v but are not in K, or formally, $npos(c,v) = |\{c' | c' \in C \setminus K, c' \succ c\}|$. Then, $RS(K,v) = \sum_{c\in K} npos(c,v)$.

Partial orders. A partial order is a transitive and asymmetric, but not necessarily total binary relation over C. We denote the vote of voter v also by $\succ_v$, where $c \succ_v d$ means that v prefers candidate c to candidate d. If the relation between c and d is unknown (or uncomparable), then we write $c \sim_v d$.

In this case, Baumeister and Dennisen [5] introduced a so-called "generalized Kemeny distance" between a committee K and a vote v: $Dist(K,v) = \sum_{a,b\in C} d_{K,v}(a,b)$, where $d_{K,v}(a,b)$ is the distance between K and v regarding two candidates a and b defined as:

$$d_{K,v}(a,b) = \begin{cases} 1 & \text{if } a \sim_v b \wedge ((a \in K \wedge b \notin K) \vee (a \notin K \wedge b \in K)), \\ 2 & \text{if } (a \in K \wedge b \notin K \wedge b \succ_v a) \vee \\ & \quad (a \notin K \wedge b \in K \wedge a \succ_v b), \\ 0 & \text{otherwise.} \end{cases}$$

We now define the social choice problem that is central to this work.

DEFINITION 1. [*Δ-Minimax-Voting*] *Given a list of votes $V = \{v_1, \dots, v_n\}$ over a set of candidates $C = \{c_1, \dots, c_m\}$, and two non-negative integers d and k, find a size-k subset K of C (committee) with $\max_{i=1,\dots,n} \Delta(K, v_i) \le d$, where $\Delta \in \{HD, \delta, RS, Dist\}$ stands for the distance function for approval votes, trichotomous votes, linear orders or partial orders, respectively.*

Note that there might be more than one committee satisfying the distance upper-bound. For Δ-Minimax-Voting, it suffices to find one of them.

Finally, we briefly introduce the relevant notions of parameterized complexity theory [13, 19, 25]. A parameterized decision problem is a language $\mathcal{L} \subseteq \Sigma^* \times \mathrm{N}$. $\mathcal{L}$ is *fixed-parameter tractable* (or in the class FPT) if for each (x,k) in $\Sigma^* \times \mathrm{N}$, there exists an algorithm determining whether (x,k) is in $\mathcal{L}$ with running time $O(f(k)\cdot|x|^c)$, where f is some computable function, c is a constant, and k is the parameter. If no such algorithm exists for $\mathcal{L}$, $\mathcal{L}$ is called *fixed-parameter intractable.*

Given two parameterized problems $\mathcal{L}$ and $\mathcal{L}'$ (both encoded over $\Sigma^* \times \mathrm{N}$), we say $\mathcal{L}$ is *FPT-reducible* to $\mathcal{L}'$ if there is an algorithm that can map a given instance (x,k) of $\mathcal{L}$ to an instance (x',k') of $\mathcal{L}'$ in time $O(f(k)\cdot|x|^c)$, where $k' \le g(k)$, and f and g are computable functions, such that (x,k) is a yes-instance of $\mathcal{L}$ if and only if (x',k') is a yes-instance of $\mathcal{L}'$. Parameterized reductions are used to prove hardness of problems in the sense of parameterized complexity. The basic class of fixed-parameter intractable problems is W[1]. A parameterized problem $\mathcal{L}$ is said to be *$W[t]$-hard* for $t \ge 1$ if all the problems in $W[t]$ are FPT-reducible to $\mathcal{L}$.

The following table gives a summary of the parameterized complexity of the winner determination problem in the minimax committee elections for the above four forms of votes.

Table 1: Summary of parameterized complexity results for Δ-Minimax-Voting, where $\Delta \in \{HD, \delta, RS, Dist\}$ stands for the distance function for approval votes, trichotomous votes, linear orders or partial orders, respectively. The results with m as parameter are trivial. New results of this paper are in boldface. W[1]-h. (or W[2]-h.) stands for W[1]-hard (or W[2]-hard).

	HD	δ	RS	Dist
k	W[2]-h. [24]	W[2]-h. [24]	**W[2]-h.**	**W[2]-h.**
d	FPT [24]	**FPT**	**FPT**	**FPT**
n	FPT [24]	**FPT**	**W[1]-h.**	**W[1]-h.**
m	FPT	FPT	FPT	FPT
k, n	FPT [24]	**FPT**	**W[1]-h.**	**W[1]-h.**

3. PARAMETERIZED COMPLEXITIES

3.1 δ-Minimax-Voting

3.1.1 *Parameter d: FPT*

We show here that δ-Minimax-Voting is fixed-parameter tractable with respect to the parameter d, by extending the algorithm by Misra et al. [24] for HD-Minimax-Voting.

The algorithm by Misra et al. starts with constructing a candidate committee. To do this, it modifies an arbitrary given vote v. If v has exactly k 1's, then v is used as the candidate committee; if v has more than k 1's, the algorithm changes arbitrarily $|v| - k$ 1's to 0's. In the case of less than k 1's, $k - |v|$ 0's are changed to 1's. Let K denote the resulting vote. Then if there is a vote $v \in V$ with $HD(K,v) > 2d$, the algorithm outputs NOT FOUND; if there is no vote with $HD(K,v) > d$, then K is output as solution. Otherwise, there exists at least one vote $v \in V$ that satisfies $d < HD(K,v) \le 2d$. For an arbitrary such vote, a search tree approach is applied. We note that this algorithm contains a flaw by giving a counterexample: $d = 3$, $k = 2$, $|C| = 8$, and $V = \{v_1 := 11111000, v_2 := 00011111\}$. If the algorithm uses v_1 to construct K and changes the last three 1's to 0's, then we have $K = 11000000$ and $HD(K,v_2) > 2d$. This means that the algorithm reports NOT FOUND. However, it is not hard to check that there exists a unique solution 00011000 for the given instance. The problem of the algorithm lies in the newly constructed candidate committee K. Even if the distance between any pair of votes in the original V is at most $2d$, the distance between K and some vote in V may be greater than $2d$. Thus, the algorithm by Misra et al. cannot always return the right answer.

By extending the upper-bound in the first if-condition from $2d$ to $3d$ and incorporating new idea dealing with trichotomous votes, we derive an algorithm for δ-Minimax-Voting running in $O^*(d^d)$ time[3].

THEOREM 1. *δ-Minimax-Voting can be solved in $O^*(d^d)$ time with the distance upper-bound d as parameter and thus, is fixed-parameter tractable.*

3.1.2 Parameter n: FPT

THEOREM 2. *With n as parameter, δ-Minimax-Voting is fixed-parameter tractable.*

PROOF. We describe an integer linear program (ILP) with at most $2\cdot 3^n$ variables that solves δ-Minimax-Voting. Fixed-parameter tractability then follows from the result that ILP is fixed-parameter tractable with the number of variables as parameter [21].

Consider the list of votes as an $n \times m$ matrix. Then each of the m columns of this matrix is an element in $\{1, 0, -1\}^n$. Thus, there are at most 3^n different *column types*. Based on this observation, we can get an instance of ILP that is equivalent to the δ-Minimax-Voting instance. Let T denote the set of all column types, and for each type $t \in T$, let n_t denote the number of columns in the input of type t. Also, let $\varphi_{t,i} \in \{1, 0, -1\}$ denote the letter (or value) at position i in a given column type t.

The instance of ILP is defined over a set of $|\{1,-1\}|\cdot|T| \leq 2 \cdot 3^n$ variables, one variable $x_{t,\varphi}$ for each $t \in T$ and $\varphi \in \{1, -1\}$. The variable $x_{t,\varphi}$ contains the number of columns of type t whose corresponding positions of the solution vector will be set to the value φ. The ILP instance then consists of the following constraints:

$$\sum_{t\in T}\sum_{\varphi\in\{1,-1\}} |\varphi - \varphi_{t,i}| \cdot x_{t,\varphi} \leq d \qquad \forall 1 \leq i \leq n$$

$$\sum_{\varphi\in\{1,-1\}} x_{t,\varphi} = n_t \qquad \forall t \in T$$

$$\sum_{t\in T} x_{t,1} = k$$

$$x_{t,\varphi} \in \{0, 1, 2, \dots\} \qquad \forall t \in T, \forall \varphi \in \{1, -1\}$$

Let K denote a vector formed from a feasible solution to the above ILP. The i-th constraint of the first type ensures that $d_T(K, v_i) \leq d$ for vote v_i. It is not difficult to verify that the above ILP has a feasible solution if and only if the δ-Minimax-Voting instance has a solution. □

3.2 RS-Minimax-Voting

3.2.1 Parameter k: W[2]-Hard

The W[2]-hardness result is proved by a reduction from the W[2]-complete problem Dominating Set [13]. Given a graph $\mathcal{G} = (\mathcal{V}, \mathcal{E})$, with $\mathcal{V} = \{v_1, v_2, \cdots, v_n\}$, the *closed neighborhood* of a vertex $v_i \in \mathcal{V}$ is defined to be $\{v_j | \{v_i, v_j\} \in \mathcal{E}\} \cup \{v_i\}$, denoted by $\mathbb{N}[v_i]$. A subset $\mathcal{V}' \subseteq \mathcal{V}$, where $\mathcal{V}' = \{v'_1, v'_2, \cdots, v'_{k'}\}$, is called a *size-$k'$ dominating set* of $\mathcal{G}$ if and only if every vertex $v \in \mathcal{V}$ is adjacent to at least one vertex in $\mathcal{V}'$, i.e., v is in at least one of the closed neighborhoods $\mathbb{N}[v'_1], \dots, \mathbb{N}[v'_{k'}]$. Dominating Set asks for a size-k' dominating set.

[3]In the O^* notation we omit the polynomial terms, so that $O^*(f(d))$ stands for $O(f(d)p(n))$ for some polynomial p.

THEOREM 3. *RS-Minimax-Voting is W[2]-hard with respect to the parameter k.*

PROOF. Given a DOMINATING SET instance $(\mathcal{G} = (\mathcal{V}, \mathcal{E}), k')$, where $\mathcal{V} = \{v_1, \dots, v_n\}$, we construct a RS-MINIMAX-VOTING instance (A, P, d, k) as follows:

Let $k = k'$ and $d = (\alpha + 2n)(k-1) + n$, where $\alpha = n(k-1)+1$. With every $v_i \in \mathcal{V}$, we associate a candidate c_i. Denote by C the set $\{c_1, \dots, c_n\}$. Additionally, for each $v_i \in \mathcal{V}$, we introduce three sets of dummy candidates, $X_i = \{x_{i1}, \dots, x_{in}\}$, $Y_i = \{y_{i1}, \dots, y_{i\alpha}\}$, and $Z_i = \{z_{i1}, \dots, z_{i\beta}\}$, where $\beta = k(\alpha + 2n)$. Thus, $A = C \cup X_1 \cup \dots \cup X_n \cup Y_1 \cup \dots \cup Y_n \cup Z_1 \cup \dots \cup Z_n$. For every vertex $v_i \in \mathcal{V}$, we have a corresponding vote v_i. The set of candidates corresponding to the vertices in $\mathbb{N}[v_i]$ is denoted by $\mathbb{C}[c_i]$, i.e., $\mathbb{C}[c_i] = \{c_j | v_j \in \mathbb{N}[v_i]\}$. For every v_i, we arbitrarily select $n - |\mathbb{C}[c_i]|$ elements from X_i and put them in a set denoted by X'_i. The vote v_i is set as follows:

$$\mathbb{C}[c_i] \succ X'_i \succ Y_i \succ C \setminus \mathbb{C}[c_i] \succ X_i \setminus X'_i \succ Z_i \succ \bigcup_{j\in[n],j\neq i} X_j \succ \bigcup_{j\in[n],j\neq i} Y_j \succ \bigcup_{j\in[n],j\neq i} Z_j,$$

where $R \succ S$ for two sets of candidates R and S means that $\forall a \in R$ and $b \in S$, we have $a \succ b$ but the ordering of R (or S) can be arbitrary.

In the following, we show that the Dominating Set instance has a size-k dominating set if and only if there is a size-k subset K of A such that $\max_{i=1,\dots,n} RS(K, v_i) \leq d$.

$\Rightarrow$: Suppose that there exists a dominating set $\mathcal{V}' = \{v'_1, \dots, v'_k\}$ in $\mathcal{G}$. Denote by K the set of candidates $c'_1, \dots, c'_k$ in C that correspond to the vertices in $\mathcal{V}'$. For each $v_i \in P$, at least one candidate $c'_i \in K$ $(1 \leq i \leq k)$ is in $\mathbb{C}[c_i]$ and $npos(c'_i, v_i) < n$. On the other hand, we have $|K \cap (C \setminus \mathbb{C}[c_i])| \leq k-1$ and, for each candidate in $K \cap (C \setminus \mathbb{C}[c_i])$, its "normalized" position in v_i is less than $\alpha + 2n$. It is easy to see that $RS(K, v_i) < n + (\alpha + 2n)(k-1) = d$. Thus, $\max_{i=1,\dots,n} RS(K, v_i) \leq d$.

$\Leftarrow$: Now suppose there is a size-k subset $K = \{c'_1, \dots, c'_k\}$ of A such that $\max_{i=1,\dots,n} RS(K, v_i) \leq d$. Denote by $\mathcal{V}'$ the set of vertices $v'_1, \dots, v'_k$ in $\mathcal{V}$ that correspond to the candidates in K.

First, we claim that, in each vote v_i, none of the candidates in K appears after Z_i. If this is not true, there is a candidate $c \in K$ that lies after Z_i in vote v_i. Then, $npos(c, v_i) \geq |C| + |X_i| + |Y_i| + |Z_i| - \frac{k(k-1)}{2} = 2n + \alpha + k(\alpha + 2n) - \frac{k(k-1)}{2} > (\alpha + 2n)(k-1) + n = d$, which implies that $RS(K, v_i) > d$. The above claim implies that, in any vote v_i, none of the candidates in K appears in X_i, Y_i, or Z_i. Thus, all elements of K are from C. Next, we show that, in each vote v_i, at least one of the candidates in K appears in $\mathbb{C}[c_i]$. If this is not true, then there is a vote v_i such that all the candidates in K appear in $C \setminus \mathbb{C}[c_i]$. Then, $npos(K, v_i) \geq (n + \alpha)k > (\alpha + 2n)(k-1) + n = d$, a contradiction. The above claim implies that the vertex corresponding to candidate c_i must be adjacent to at least one of the vertices that correspond to the candidates in K. In other words, every vertex $v_i \in \mathcal{V}$ must be in at least one of the closed neighborhoods $\mathbb{N}[v'_1], \dots, \mathbb{N}[v'_k]$. By definition, set $\mathcal{V}'$ forms a dominating set of graph $\mathcal{G}$. □

3.2.2 Parameter d: FPT

THEOREM 4. *RS-Minimax-Voting can be solved in $O^*(4^d)$*

time and thus is fixed-parameter tractable with respect to the parameter d.

PROOF. Let v_i be an arbitrary vote in V. Note that all candidates $c \in C$ with $pos(c, v_i) > k + d$ cannot be in K, since otherwise, $npos(c, v_i)$ would be greater than d, which implies that $RS(K, v_i) > d$. In the following, we distinguish two cases:

$k \leq d$: In this case, we check for every size-k subset K of the first $k + d$ candidates in vote v_i whether it satisfies $\max_{j=1,\ldots,n} RS(K, v_j) \leq d$. The time complexity is $O^*\left(\binom{d+k}{k}\right) = O^*\left(\binom{d+k}{d}\right) = O^*\left(\binom{2d}{d}\right) = O^*\left(4^d\right)$.

$k > d$: We claim that the first $k - d$ candidates in vote v_i must be in K. For the purpose of contradiction, suppose that at least one of the first $k - d$ candidates in v_i is not in K. Then at least $k - (k - d - 1) = d + 1$ candidates, whose positions are greater than $k - d$, must be in K. This would imply that $RS(K, v_i) > d$. Based on the above claim, all possible solutions have to contain the first $k - d$ candidates in v_i and $k - (k - d) = d$ candidates from the candidates whose positions in vote v_i are greater than $k - d$ and at most $k + d$. The brute-force approach leads to a time complexity of $O^*\left(\binom{2d}{d}\right) \leq O^*\left(4^d\right)$. □

3.2.3 Parameters k and n: W[1]-hard

THEOREM 5. *RS-Minimax-Voting is W[1]-hard with respect to the parameters k and n.*

PROOF. We reduce from the Multi-Colored Clique (MCC) problem, which, given an undirected graph $\mathcal{G} = (\mathcal{V}, \mathcal{E})$ and an integer $k' \geq 0$, where $\mathcal{V}$ can be partitioned into k' subsets and all edges in $\mathcal{E}$ are between different subsets, asks for a clique which contains exactly one vertex from each of the subsets. MCC is known to be W[1]-hard with respect to k', even if all subsets have the same cardinality n [14]. Moreover, it is not hard to prove the following claim:

Claim. MCC remains W[1]-hard with k' as parameter even if

1. all subsets have the same cardinality n.
2. there exists a non-constant integer D, such that for each two subsets S_1 and S_2 and each vertex $v \in S_1$, it holds that $|\mathbb{N}(v) \cap S_2| = D$, where $\mathbb{N}(v)$ is the *neighborhood* of vertex v, i.e., $\mathbb{N}(v) = \{v_i | \{v, v_i\} \in \mathcal{E}\}$.

The basic idea of the reduction is to construct $(k'-1) \cdot D + 1$ candidates for every vertex, one for the vertex itself and one for each of its neighbors. Then, we construct for each of the k' subsets $A \subset \mathcal{V}$ a vote, denoted by v_A, with the candidates that represent the vertices from this subset being in the first n positions. The distance d is set properly to make sure that at least one of these n candidates needs to be in the committee, encoding that at least one vertex from this subset has to be in the clique. Moreover, we construct $3(k' - 1)$ votes for each subset A, three votes for each subset B with $A \neq B$. In the first vote $v^1_{A,B}$ for B, the candidates which represent the B-neighbors of the vertices in A are placed in the first $n \cdot D$ positions. The distance d guarantees that at least one of these $n \cdot D$ candidates has to be in the committee. Further, the other two votes $v^2_{A,B}$ and $v^3_{A,B}$ guarantee that the candidate selected due to v_A and the candidate selected due to $v^1_{A,B}$ correspond to the same vertex in A. Finally, we construct four votes to check the adjacency of the vertices correpsonding to the candidates which have been selected due to v_A and v_B respectively. In the following we present the details of the reduction.

We also use a_i to denote the vertex candidate representing the vertex $a_i \in A$. Further the neighbor candidate representing the neighbor $b_j \in B$ of a_i is denoted as $a_i^{b_j}$. Let C' be the set of candidates constructed for the vertices in $\mathcal{V}$. Then, $|C'| = k' \cdot n \cdot (D(k' - 1) + 1)$. We set the size k of the committee equal to k'^2. The first subset of votes contains k votes, one for each vertex subset. For instance, the vote v_A for A has $a_1 \succ a_2 \succ, \ldots, \succ a_n$ in the first n positions. Between these n candidates and other candidates in C' there are $x := (k'^2 - 1)(|C'| - n) + D$ many "dummy" candidates; they are ordered arbitrarily. Let d denote the distance upper-bound, which will be set in the following. Each dummy candidate can be in the first d positions of only one vote and thus, can never be in a committe with distance at most d to the votes. The remaining candidates in C' are placed directly after the dummy candidates, with an arbitrary order among them. By setting the distance upper-bound d equal to $(k'^2 - 1)(|C'| + x) + n + D$, we observe that if none of the first n candidates in C' is added to the committee, then the distance between v_A and the resulting committee is at least $k'^2(x + n)$ which is clearly greater than d. Thus, at least one candidates from $a_1, \ldots, a_n$ has to be in the committee.

Next, we present the three votes $v^1_{A,B}$, $v^2_{A,B}$, and $v^3_{A,B}$. In the first $n \cdot D$ positions of $v^1_{A,B}$, we have $a_1^{b_{j1}} \succ \ldots \succ a_1^{b_{jD}} \succ a_2^{b_{l1}} \succ \ldots \succ a_n^{b_{sD}}$, where the first D candidates represent the neighbors of a_1 in B, the next D candidates the neighbors of a_2, and so on. After them, there are $y = x - (nD - n - D)/(k'^2 - 1)$ many dummy candidates, and the order among these dummy candidates is arbitrary. Without loss of generality, we may assume here $nD - n - D$ can be divided by $k'^2 - 1$. The remaining candidates from C' are placed after the dummy candidates with an arbitrary order. By the same argrument as for v_A, at least one candidate in the first $n \cdot D$ positions has to be in the committee. Since we have $k' - 1$ such v^1-votes for every vertex subset and these $k' - 1$ v^1-votes have distinct candidates in their first $n \cdot D$ positions, all feasible committees contain exactly one candidate in the first $n \cdot D$ positions of each v^1-vote. That is, for each of the k' vertex subsets $A \subseteq \mathcal{V}$, a feasible committee contains exactly one vertex candidate a_i which corresponds to a vertex in A and exactly one neighbor candidate $a_j^{b_l}$ with $b_l \in B$ for every other subset $B \neq A$.

The votes $v^2_{A,B}$ and $v^3_{A,B}$ are constructed to force $i = j$. Both votes $v^2_{A,B}$ and $v^3_{A,B}$ put the candidates in $C' \setminus (\{a_1, a_2, \ldots, a_n\} \cup \{a_i^{b_j} | a_i \in A\})$ in the first $|C'| - nD - n$ positions. Then, the next $z = ((k'^2 - 2)|C'| + (k'^2 - 1)x)/n + D + 2$ positions of $v^2_{A,B}$ are occupied by dummy candidates, followed by a_1, and then, again z many dummy candidates, followed by a_2, till a_n is placed in the $(|C'| - nD + n \cdot z)$-th position. After a_n, we have again z many dummy candidates followed by the D neighbor candidates of a_n, which correspond to the B-neigbhors of a_n; the order among these neighbor candidates is arbitrary. After these neighbor candidates, we have again z many dummy candidates and then the neighbor candidates of a_{n-1}. The last neighbor candidate of a_1 is in the $(|C'| + 2n \cdot z)$-th position. The vote $v^3_{A,B}$ has almost the same construction as $v^2_{A,B}$ with the only exception that the order of the vertex candidetes of A is reversed, that is, a_n appears as the first vertex candidate, then a_{n-1}, and so on; the appearance order of the neighbor candidates is also reversed, first the neighbor candidates of a_1, then the ones of a_2, and the last one being a neighbor candidate of a_n. With these two votes, we can guarantee that if a vertex candidate a_i is added to committee due to the vote v_A, then the vote $v^1_{A,B}$ must add one neighbor candidate of a_i to the committee. By doing so, we have a committee with a distance of less than $|C'| - (D+1)n + n \cdot z + D = d$ to both $v^2_{A,B}$ and $v^3_{A,B}$. If the chosen neighbor candidate is not of a_i, then at least one of $v^2_{A,B}$ and $v^3_{A,B}$ has a distance of more than $(n+1) \cdot z > d$ to the committee.

Finally, we have for each vertex subset $2(k'-1)$ votes to check the adajency between the vertex candidate of this subset and other chosen vertex candidates, two votes for each other subset. For instance, we have the following two votes for $A \subseteq \mathcal{V}$ to check whether the vertex candidate added to the committee due to v_A is adjacent with the vertex candidate of B. These two votes are very similar to $v^2_{A,B}$ and $v^3_{A,B}$. Both have the candidates in $C' \setminus (\{a_1, a_2, \ldots, a_n\} \cup \{b_j^{a_i} | a_i \in A\})$ at the beginning. Then, both have the a_i's blocks, each consisting of dummy candidates and one vertex candidate at the end, but one in the ascending order of the indices and the other in the descending order. The difference lies in the blocks of neighbor candidates. Here, for a vertex candidate a_i, the corresponding block contains instead of the neighbor candidates $a_i^{b_l}$'s but the neighbor candidates of b_l, that is, $b_l^{a_i}$'s. Again, the blocks appear in one vote in ascending order of the indices of a_i's, and the orther in descending order. By the same argument, if a_i is in the committee, then at least one of $b_l^{a_i}$'s has to be in the committee, which means the corresponding vertices are adjecent. Since this is true for every pair of subsets, a committee of size k with distance at most d to all votes can be directly transformed to a clique of size k' in the original graph. Moreover, the number of votes and the size of the committee depend only on k', which completes the theorem. □

3.3 Dist-Minimax-Voting

Since Dist-Minimax-Voting is a generalized version of RS-Minimax-Voting, one can easily conclude that this problem is W[2]-hard with the committee size k as parameter and W[1]-hard with both k and the number n of votes as parameters. It remains to prove that the parameterization of the distance upper-bound leads to an FPT-result.

THEOREM 6. *With the distance upper-bound d as parameter, Dist-Minimax-Voting is fixed-parameter tractable.*

PROOF. We distinguish two cases $d < k$ and $d \geq k$. If $d \geq k$, then we consider an arbitrary vote v and apply a depth-bounded search tree approach to enumerate all possible committees which have distance at most d to v. These feasible committees can then be checked against all other votes with the same time bound. The depth of the search tree is bounded by $k+d$ and thus, its size by $2^{k+d} < 4^d$. During the branching process, we maintain three sets K, U, and N and initialize K and N as empty sets and $U = C$. The set K contains the candidates which should be added to the committee, the set N the candidates not to add to the committee, while the candidates in U are still undecided. The branching is terminated, if $U = \emptyset$, $d < 0$, or $k = 0$.

At a node of the search tree, we compute the set $S = \{a \in U | \nexists b \in U \text{ with } b \succ_v a\}$ and consider an arbitrary candidate $a \in S$. Note that $U \neq \emptyset$ implies $S \neq \emptyset$. We branch into two subcases: 1) $N := N \cup \{a\}$ and $d := d - k$; 2) If $k > 0$, then add a to K and set $k := k - 1$. Moreover, for each candidate $b \in N$ with $b \succ_v a$ decrease d by one;. If at one leaf, we have $k \geq 0$ and $d \geq 0$, then output K as solution.

The branching is clearly complete. In the first subcase, a is not added to the committee. Then, by the definition of S, we have $a \succ_v b$ or $a \sim_v b$ for each candidate b which will be added to K. Therefore, it is safe to decrease parameter d by k. If we add a to the committee, the parameter k should be decreased by one. Further, since for the candidates $b \in N$ with $b \succ_v a$ we only decreased the parameter d by one at the node dealing with b, we need to decrease d by one. Thus, the search tree algorithm is correct. Since in one subcase we decrease k by one and in the other d is decreased by at least one, the total running time is then bounded by $O^*(2^{k+d}) = O^*(4^d)$. This completes the proof for $k < d$.

Concerning the case $k > d$, we again apply a search tree approach to enumerate all feasible committees for a fixed vote v. Note that in each step of the branching, the parameter d is also decreased accordingly. The branching is terminated once $k < 0$ or $d < 0$. First we compute $S_0 := \{a \in C \mid \nexists b \text{ with } b \succ_v a\}$ and then for $i > 0$, $S_i := \{a \in (C \setminus \bigcup_{j<i} S_j) \mid \exists b \in S_{i-1} \text{ with } b \sim_v a\}$. Let l be the maximal index with $S_l \neq \emptyset$ and set $S_{l+1} = C \setminus \bigcup_{i \leq l} S_i$. We need the following claim to prove the correctness of our algorithm.

Claim. For all subsets S_i and S_j, if $j \geq i+2$, then we have $a \succ_v b$ for all $a \in S_i$ and $b \in S_j$.

Proof of claim: We prove this claim by contradiction. If $a \succ_v b$ is not true, then by the definition of S_i, we have $b \succ_v a$. Clearly, $a \notin S_0$. Then, there exists a candidate $a_1 \in S_{i-1}$ with $a_1 \sim_v a$. Since $b \notin S_i$, we have either $b \succ_v a_1$ or $a_1 \succ_v b$. Since $a_1 \succ_v b$ would imply $a_1 \succ_v a$ by transitivity of the linear order, we have $b \succ_v a_1$. This argument can then be applied to a candidate in S_{i-2}, which leads to the conclusion that there is a candidate c in S_0 with $b \succ_v c$, contradicting to the definition of S_0. This completes the proof of the claim. □

Clearly, for each feasible committee K, there exists a minimal index i with $S_i \setminus K \neq \emptyset$. Moreover, we can observe that $i \geq 1$: Suppose there is a size-k committee K with $S_0 \setminus K \neq \emptyset$. Let a be a candidate in $S_0 \setminus K$. Then, for each candidate $b \in K$ we have then $a \succ_v b$ or $a \sim_v b$, due to the definition of S_0. The distance between K and v is then at least $k > d$. Therefore, we iterate from $i = 1$ to $i = l+1$ and assume that $N := S_i \setminus K \neq \emptyset$ and $S_j \subseteq K$ for all $j < i$. The set K is initialized as $\bigcup_{j<i} S_j$, while the set N, the set of the candidates not to be added to K, is initialized as empty.

If $|S_i| \leq d$, then we branch on every subset X of S_i and assume X is not in K. This branch adds $S_i \setminus X$ to K, X to N, and decreases d by $2 \cdot |\{(a,b) \mid a \in X \text{ and } b \in K \text{ with } a \succ_v b\}| + |\{(a,b) \mid a \in X \text{ and } b \in K \text{ with } a \sim_v b\}|$. Since for every candidate $a \in S_i$ there is a candidate $b \in S_{i-1} \subseteq K$ with $a \sim_v b$, this branching leads to a $|S_i|$-bit branching vector with all entries being at least one.

If $|S_i| > d$, then we first consider the subset $S_i^0 := \{a \in S_i \mid \nexists b \in S_i \text{ with } a \succ_v b\}$. If $|S_i^0| > d$, then we can conclude that there is no feasible committee K with $S_i \setminus K \neq \emptyset$: None of the candidates in S_i^0 can be in $S_i \setminus K$, since for each candidate $a \in S_i$ there is a candidate $b \in S_{i-1} \subseteq K$ with $b \sim_v a$ and for every two candidates $a, b \in S_i^0$, we have $a \sim_v b$. If $S_i^0 \subseteq K$, then by $|S_i^0| > d$, no candidate of S_i can be in $S_i \setminus K$ due to the definition of S_i^0. Next, we compute the set $S_i^1 := \{a \in (S_i \setminus S_i^0) | \nexists b \in S_i \setminus S_i^0 \text{ with } a \succ_v b\}$. By transitivity of the linear order and the facts that $|S_i^0| \leq d$ and $|S_i| > d$, $S_i^1 \neq \emptyset$. If $|S_i^0 \cup S_i^1| > d$, then $(S_i^0 \cup S_i^1) \setminus K \neq \emptyset$, since each candidate a in $S_i \setminus K$ has $a \succ_v b$ or $a \sim_v b$ with each $b \in (S_i^1 \cup S_i^0)$ and thus, $(S_i^0 \cup S_i^1) \setminus K = \emptyset$ would result in that the distance between K and v exceeds d. With the same argument, we can conclude that for all j's, if $|\bigcup_{l \leq j} S_i^l| > d$, then $(\bigcup_{l \leq j} S_i^l) \setminus K \neq \emptyset$. Let j be the minimal index with $|\bigcup_{l \leq j} S_i^l| > d$. Since $|S_i| > d$, such an index j must exist. Thus, $(\bigcup_{l \leq j-1} S_i^l) \setminus K \neq \emptyset$ or $S_i^j \setminus K \neq \emptyset$. By the same argument as for S_i^0, if $(\bigcup_{l \leq j-1} S_i^l) \setminus K = \emptyset$, then $|S_i^j| \leq d$. We apply here a branching into at most $2k$ subcases: If $|S_i^j| > d$, then branch into at most $2d$ subcases; each adds one candidate a in $\bigcup_{l \leq j-1} S_i^l$ to N and decreases d by $2 \cdot |\{b \in K \mid a \succ_v b\}| + |\{b \in K \mid a \sim_v b\}|$. If $|S_i^j| \leq d$, then branch into at most d subcases; each adds one candidate a in $\bigcup_{l \leq j} S_i^l$ to N and decreases d accordingly. Again, since for every candidate $a \in S_i$ there is a candidate $b \in S_{i-1} \subseteq K$ with $a \sim_v b$, this branching leads to a branching vector better than the vector with $2d$ 1-entries.

After all candidates in S_i have been added to either K or N, we recompute the partition of the remaining candidates. While setting $S_0 := K$, we recompute $S_1 := \{a \in C \setminus (K \cup N) \mid \exists b \in S_0 \text{ with } b \sim_v a\}$. Observe that all candidates a in S_1 have $b \succ_v a$ or $b \sim_v a$ with all candidates $b \in N$. Therefore, adding a candidate $a \in S_1$ to K will decrease d by at least one. Be the definition of S_1, adding a to N decreases d by at least one too. This leads to a $(1,1)$-branching. We can then repeat this branching till $S_1 = \emptyset$. Note that every time we add a candidate to N or K we recompute S_1.

At this point, we have that all candidates a in $C \setminus (K \cup N)$ satisfy $b \succ_v a$ or $b \sim_v a$ for all $b \in N \cup K$. If $|K| < k$ we have to add some of the remaining candidates to K. We now further partition these remaining candidates into subsets: $S_0 := \{a \in C \setminus (K \cup N) \mid \nexists b \in C \setminus (K \cup N) \text{ with } b \succ_v a\}$ and for $j > 0$, $S_j := \{a \in C' \setminus (N \cup \bigcup_{l<j} S_l) \mid \nexists b \in (N \cup \bigcup_{l<j} S_l) \text{ with } b \succ_v a\}$. Note that none of the vertices in S_j with $j \geq d$ can be added to K without violating the distance upper-bound d. Moreover, consider a S_j with $j < d$. If $|S_j| > d$, then none of the candidates in $\bigcup_{l \geq j} S_l$ can be added to K. Therefore, we have at most d^2 possible candidates to add to K. Since all candidates a in $C \setminus (K \cup N)$ satisfy $b \succ_v a$ or $b \sim_v a$ for all $b \in N$, we can add at most d candidates to K. Thus, we have at most $\binom{d^2}{d}$ possibilities.

Altogether, we have at most $m \cdot \binom{d^2}{d}$ many possible committees which have distance at most d to the vote v. All these committees can be enumerated in $O^*(\binom{d^2}{d})$ time. To verify whether a committee has distance at most d to all other votes can be done in polynomial time, which completes the proof. □

4. SPECIAL CASES OF HD-MINIMAX -VOTING

4.1 V satisfies VI

We present a polynomial-time algorithm (Algorithm 1) to solve HD-Minimax-Voting for the special case that the input V satisfies VI.

Our algorithm adopts a greedy strategy. Starting with an empty partial committee, it gradually expands the partial committee by processing the votes, one by one, following the VI order of the votes. In each step, it adds some candidates to the partial committee, without violating the distance upper-bound between the current vote and the partial committee. When doing this, the algorithm greedily selects such new candidates that are included in as many as possible votes that have not been processed so far. The algorithm stops, if either the distance between the current vote and the current partial committee exceeds the upper-bound, or the partial committee has k candidates.

THEOREM 7. *Given a HD-Minimax-Voting instance (C, V, k, d), if V satisfies VI, then Algorithm 1 can find a solution in $O(nm \log m)$ time.*

Algorithm 1: Algorithm for HD-Minimax-Voting in case that V satisfies VI.

```
Input : List of votes V = {v_1, ..., v_n} over candidate
        set C = {c_1, ..., c_m}, an order of the votes
        v_1 ⊑ ··· ⊑ v_n with respect to which V
        satisfies VI, integers d and k.
Output: A committee K with
        max_{i=1,...,n} HD(K, v_i) ≤ d if it exists, and
        NOT FOUND otherwise.
K ← ∅;
for i ← 1 to n do
    X ← v_i \ K;
    if |K ⊕ v_i| + k − |K| > d then
        r ← ⌈(|K ⊕ v_i| + k − |K| − d) / 2⌉;
        if r > k − |K| or r > |X| then
            return NOT FOUND
        Sort the candidates c ∈ X in the non-increasing
          order of the number of votes that contain c
          and are after v_i in the order v_1 ⊑ ··· ⊑ v_n;
        Add the first r elements in the sorted X to K;
if k > |K| then
    Add arbitrary k − |K| candidates from C \ K to K;
return K;
```

4.2 V satisfies CI

We present a polynomial-time algorithm (Algorithm 2) to solve HD-Minimax-Voting for the special case that the input V satisfies CI.

Since V satisfies CI, each vote occupies a consecutive block of the given CI order of the candidates. For a vote $v \in V$, we call the first and last candidates of the block its *head* and *tail*, respectively. Our algorithm first sorts the votes in V according to the ascending order of the positions of their heads. If two votes have the same head position, then the vote with smaller weight lies in front of the other. Algorithm 2 adopts a similar greedy strategy as Algorithm 1. The main difference lies in how they select new candidates to modify the current partial committee.

THEOREM 8. *Given a HD-Minimax-Voting instance*

(C, V, k, d), *if V satisfies CI, then Algorithm 2 can find a solution in time $O(nm \log m)$.*

Algorithm 2: Algorithm for δ-Minimax-Voting in case that V satisfies CI.

Input : List of votes $V = \{v_1, \ldots, v_n\}$ over candidate set $C = \{c_1, \ldots, c_m\}$, an order of the candidates $c_1 \lhd \cdots \lhd c_m$ with respect to which V satisfies CI, integers d and k.

Output: A committee K with $\max_{i=1,\ldots,n} HD(K, v_i) \leq d$ if it exists, and NOT FOUND otherwise.

$V' \leftarrow V$, $V \leftarrow$ empty list, $V'' \leftarrow$ empty list;
for $i \leftarrow 1$ **to** m **do**
    if V' *is not empty* **then**
        $V'' \leftarrow$ all votes in V' that contain c_i;
        $V' \leftarrow V' \setminus V''$;
    if V'' *is not empty* **then**
        Sort the votes in V'' in the non-decreasing order of their weights;
        Add V'' at the end of V;
$K \leftarrow \emptyset$;
for $i \leftarrow 1$ **to** n **do**
    $X \leftarrow v_i \setminus K$;
    if $|K \oplus v_i| + k - |K| > d$ **then**
        $r \leftarrow \left\lceil \frac{|K \oplus v_i| + k - |K| - d}{2} \right\rceil$;
        if $r > k - |K|$ *or* $r > |X|$ **then**
            return NOT FOUND
        $Y \leftarrow$ all candidates in K which lie after the tail of v_i in the order $c_1 \lhd \cdots \lhd c_m$;
        Remove from K $\min\{r, |Y|\}$ many candidates that have the minimal indices in the order $c_1 \lhd \cdots \lhd c_m$;
        Add into K such r elements in X that have the maximal indices in the order $c_1 \lhd \cdots \lhd c_m$;
if $k > |K|$ **then**
    Add arbitrary $k - |K|$ candidates from $C \setminus K$ to K;
return K;

5. FUTURE RESEARCH DIRECTION

Amanatidis et al. [1] proposed a mixture of the minisum and minimax versions of approval voting, where an ordered weighted averaging operator balances the total distance of the committee to all votes and its maximal distance to individuals. They proved that for most relevant cases, the winner determination problem under the mixture model turns out to be NP-hard. It would be interesting to explore its parameterized complexity with respect to the parameters considered in this paper.

Aziz et al. [3] studied the complexity of several variants of the approval voting rule and among others, they proved that the winner determination problem for the proportional approval voting is fixed-parameter intractable with respect to the size of committee. The parameterized complexity of this problem with respect to other parameters and of other variants remains unexplored, a promising research direction.

Acknowledgments

We are grateful to the anonymous reviewers of AAMAS'2016, whose comments greatly improve the readability of this paper.

REFERENCES

[1] G. Amanatidis, N. Barrot, J. Lang, E. Markakis, and B. Ries. Multiple referenda and multiwinner elections using hamming distances: Complexity and manipulability. In *Proceedings of the International Conference on Autonomous Agents and Multiagent Systems (AAMAS'15)*, pages 715–723, 2015.

[2] H. Aziz, M. Brill, V. Conitzer, E. Elkind, R. Freeman, and T. Walsh. Justified representation in approval-based committee voting. In *Proceedings of the 29th AAAI Conference on Artificial Intelligence (AAAI'15)*, 2015.

[3] H. Aziz, S. Gaspers, J. Gudmundsson, S. Mackenzie, N. Mattei, and T. Walsh. Computational aspects of multi-winner approval voting. In *Proceedings of the International Conference on Autonomous Agents and Multiagent Systems (AAMAS'15)*, pages 107–115, 2015.

[4] D. Baumeister. Personal communication, 2015.

[5] D. Baumeister and S. Dennisen. Voter dissatisfaction in committee elections. In *Proceedings of the International Conference on Autonomous Agents and Multiagent Systems (AAMAS'15)*, pages 1707–1708, 2015.

[6] D. Baumeister, S. Dennisen, and L. Rey. Winner determination and manipulation in minisum and minimax committee elections. In *Proceedings of the 4th International Conference on Algorithmic Decision Theory (ADT'15)*, volume 9346 of *LNCS*, pages 469–485. Springer, 2015.

[7] N. Betzler, R. Bredereck, J. Chen, and R. Niedermeier. Studies in computational aspects of voting - A parameterized complexity perspective. In *The Multivariate Algorithmic Revolution and Beyond - Essays Dedicated to Michael R. Fellows on the Occasion of His 60th Birthday*, volume 7370 of *Lecture Notes in Computer Science*, pages 318–363. Springer, 2012.

[8] S. J. Brams, D. M. Kilgour, and M. R. Sanver. A minimax procedure for electing committees. *Public Choice*, 132:401–420, 2007.

[9] F. Brandt, V. Conitzer, U. Endriss, J. Lang, and A. Procaccia, editors. *Handbook of Computational Social Choice*. Cambridge University Press, 2016.

[10] R. Bredereck, J. Chen, P. Faliszewski, J. Guo, R. Niedermeier, and G. J. Woeginger. Parameterized algorithmics for computational social choice: Nine research challenges. *Tsinghua Science and Technology*, 19(4):358–373, 2014.

[11] I. Caragiannis, D. Kalaitzis, and E. Markakis. Approximation algorithms and mechanism design for minimax approval voting. In *Proceedings of the 24th AAAI Conference on Artificial Intelligence (AAAI'10)*, 2010.

[12] V. Conitzer. Making decisions based on the preferences of multiple agents. *Commun. ACM*, 53(3):84–94, 2010.

[13] R. G. Downey and M. R. Fellows. *Parameterized complexity.* Springer, 1999.

[14] R. G. Downey and M. R. Fellows. *Fundamentals of Parameterized Complexity.* Springer, 2013.

[15] E. Elkind, P. Faliszewski, P. Skowron, and A. Slinko. Properties of multiwinner voting rules. In *Proceedings of International conference on Autonomous Agents and Multi-Agent Systems (AAMAS'14)*, pages 53–60, 2014.

[16] E. Elkind and M. Lackner. Structure in dichotomous preferences. In *Proceedings of the 24th International Conference on Artificial Intelligence (IJCAI'15)*, pages 2019–2025, 2015.

[17] P. Faliszewski, E. Hemaspaandra, L. A. Hemaspaandra, and J. Rothe. The shield that never was: Societies with single-peaked preferences are more open to manipulation and control. *Information and Computation*, 209(2):89–107, 2011.

[18] D. Felsenthal. On combining approval with disapproval voting. *Behavioral Science*, 34:53–60, 1989.

[19] J. Flum and M. Grohe. *Parameterized complexity theory.* Springer, 2006.

[20] R. LeGrand, E. Markakis, and A. Mehta. Some results on approximating the minimax solution in approval voting. In *Proceedings of the International Joint Conference on Autonomous Agents and Multiagent Systems (AAMAS'07)*, 2007.

[21] H. W. Lenstra. Integer programming with a fixed number of variables. *Mathematics of operations research*, 8(4):538–548, 1983.

[22] R. Meir, A. D. Procaccia, and J. S. Rosenschein. A broader picture of the complexity of strategic behavior in multi-winner elections. In *Proceedings of the 7th International Joint Conference on Autonomous Agents and Multiagent Systems (AAMAS'08)*, pages 991–998, 2008.

[23] R. Meir, A. D. Procaccia, J. S. Rosenschein, and A. Zohar. Complexity of strategic behavior in multi-winner elections. *Journal of Artificial Intelligence Research*, 33:149–178, 2008.

[24] N. Misra, A. Nabeel, and H. Singh. On the parameterized complexity of minimax approval voting. In *Proceedings of the International Conference on Autonomous Agents and Multiagent Systems (AAMAS'15)*, pages 97–105, 2015.

[25] R. Niedermeier. *Invitation to fixed-parameter algorithms.* Oxford University Press, 2006.

[26] S. Obraztsova, Y. Zick, and E. Elkind. On manipulation in multi-winner elections based on scoring rules. In *Proceedings of International conference on Autonomous Agents and Multi-Agent Systems (AAMAS'13)*, pages 359–366, 2013.

Rationalisation of Profiles of Abstract Argumentation Frameworks

Stéphane Airiau
LAMSADE, Univ. Paris-Dauphine
stephane.airiau@dauphine.fr

Elise Bonzon
LIPADE, Univ. Paris Descartes
elise.bonzon@parisdescartes.fr

Ulle Endriss
ILLC, University of Amsterdam
ulle.endriss@uva.nl

Nicolas Maudet
LIP6, Univ. Pierre et Marie Curie
nicolas.maudet@lip6.fr

Julien Rossit
LIPADE, Univ. Paris Descartes
julien.rossit@parisdescartes.fr

ABSTRACT

Different agents may have different points of view. This can be modelled using different abstract argumentation frameworks, each consisting of a set of arguments and a binary attack-relation between them. A question arising in this context is whether the diversity of views observed in such a profile of argumentation frameworks is consistent with the assumption that every individual argumentation framework is induced by a combination of, first, some basic factual attack-relation between the arguments and, second, the personal preferences of the agent concerned. We treat this question of *rationalisability* of a profile as an algorithmic problem and identify tractable and intractable cases. This is useful for understanding what types of profiles can reasonably be expected to come up in a multiagent system.

Keywords

Argumentation; Social Choice Theory

1. INTRODUCTION

The model of abstract argumentation introduced by Dung [12] is at the root of a vast amount of work in artificial intelligence and multiagent systems. In a nutshell, this model abstracts away from the content of an argument, and thus sees argumentation frameworks as directed graphs, where the nodes are arguments and the edges are attacks between arguments—in the sense that one argument undercuts or contradicts another argument. Different semantics provide principled approaches to selecting sets of arguments that can be viewed as coherent when taken together. The simplicity and generality of this framework, as well as its links with nonmonotonic reasoning, have stimulated a number of directions of research, e.g., at the level of the definition of the semantics, of their computation, of the expressivity of such frameworks, or regarding their application in a multiagent system.

In recent years, a number of authors have addressed the problem of aggregating several argumentation frameworks, each associated with the stance taken by a different individual agent, into a single collective argumentation framework that would appropriately represent the views of the group as a whole. Examples include the contributions of Coste-Marquis et al. [11], Tohmé et al. [27], Bodanza and Auday [8], and Dunne et al. [14]. Aggregating argumentation frameworks is a form of graph aggregation [15]: We are given a profile of attack-relations, one for each agent, and are asked to compute a suitable compromise attack-relation. This is an interesting and fruitful line of research, bringing together concerns in abstract argumentation with the methodology of social choice theory,[1] but it raises one important question: For a given profile of argumentation frameworks, is it in fact conceivable that that profile would manifest itself? Intuitively speaking, it will often seem more natural to encounter a profile with similar individual attack-relations rather than one with attack-relations that differ radically. How do we explain the differences in perspective of the individual agents for a given profile?

The point that the attack-relation should not be viewed as absolute and objective, but may very well depend on the individual circumstances of the agent considering the arguments in question, has been made before by multiple authors [2, 4, 9, 17, 16]. In fact, it is central to the study of argumentation, as also suggested by Modgil [22], who noted that abstract argumentation frameworks "should more properly be viewed as modelling human reasoning and debate, rather than as abstractions of underlying theories in some formal logic." A widespread explanation for such diversity of views is that agents have different preferences regarding the arguments at hand. For instance, arguments may come from different sources, which agents may trust more or less. Or arguments may be attached to different values, which agents may prioritise differently. This perspective still assumes an underlying ground truth, which however may be interpreted differently, depending on the agents. The same position is also taken by Searle [26]:

> "Assume universally valid and accepted standards of rationality, assume perfectly rational agents operating with perfect information, and

[1] The approach sketched here must be clearly distinguished from a second approach combining abstract argumentation and social choice theory found in the literature, which addresses the question of how to aggregate different extensions (or labellings) for a common argumentation framework. This is the approach of, amongst others, Caminada and Pigozzi [10] as well as Rahwan and Tohmé [24]. Bodanza and Auday [8] compare the two approaches explicitly.

Appears in: *Proceedings of the 15th International Conference on Autonomous Agents and Multiagent Systems (AAMAS 2016), J. Thangarajah, K. Tuyls, C. Jonker, S. Marsella (eds.), May 9–13, 2016, Singapore.*

> you will find that rational disagreement will still occur; because, for example, the rational agents are likely to have different and inconsistent values and interests, each of which may be rationally acceptable." (page *xv*)

In the literature on abstract argumentation, frameworks for modelling this phenomenon have been proposed by several authors, including Amgoud and Cayrol [1] and Bench-Capon [6]. Here we adopt a preference-based approach, in the *value-based* variant originally due to Bench-Capon [6]. In his model, whether argument A ultimately defeats argument B does not only depend on whether A attacks B in an objective sense, but also on how we rank the importance of the social or moral values attached to A and B: If we rank the value associated with B strictly above that associated with A, we may choose to ignore any attacks of A on B.

At the technical level, we thus ask the following question: Given a profile of argumentation frameworks $(AF_1, \ldots, AF_n)$, one for each agent, can this profile be explained in terms of a single master argumentation framework, an association of arguments with values, and a profile of preference orders over values $(\succcurlyeq_1, \ldots, \succcurlyeq_n)$, one for each agent? Or, as we shall put it: Can the profile of argumentation frameworks observed be *rationalised*? To be able to answer this question in the affirmative, for every agent i, we require AF_i to be exactly the argumentation framework we obtain when the master argumentation framework with its associated values is reduced using the preference order $\succcurlyeq_i$.

Of course, alternative justifications can be given for the fact that individual argumentation frameworks may differ, not just the preference-based explanation adopted here. In particular, agents may interpret arguments differently, especially when they are incomplete [7]. Also, while we adopt Bench-Capon [6]'s value-based approach as the technical foundation on the basis of which to construct our framework and for which to prove our results, there are alternative models of preference-based argumentation, for instance relying on meta-level argumentation [21]. We do not wish to commit to one specific view on the complex question of how to best model preferences in argumentation (see the work of Amgoud and Vesic [3] for an example of a contribution to this debate). Indeed, we believe that our general point is relevant beyond such specific modelling choices, and we see our contribution to be first and foremost as a methodological one. The same type of investigation could be undertaken for other models as well.[2] In a sense, this multiplicity of models is precisely what makes our contribution useful: by providing a collection of results that allow to check whether a profile can be rationalised on such grounds, we provide evidence for guiding the modelling process. The good news is that in many—albeit not all—cases verification of rationalisability can be performed efficiently, even when the assignment of values to arguments is not known beforehand.

The remainder of this paper is organised as follows. Section 2 presents the relevant background regarding value-based argumentation. Section 3 formally introduces the problem of rationalising a given profile of argumentation frameworks provided by a set of agents, and presents the different types of constraints on solutions we will consider. Section 4 analyses the single-agent case in detail, while Section 5 investigates the multiagent case. Finally, Section 6 discusses a number of application scenarios for our approach and Section 7 concludes with a review of open questions and possible directions for future work.

2. NOTATION AND TERMINOLOGY

Following Dung [12], below we define an *argumentation framework* (AF) as a binary attack-relation declared over a set of arguments. We will restrict ourselves to scenarios for which the set of available arguments is finite.

Definition 1 (AF). *An argumentation framework is a pair $AF = \langle Arg, \rightharpoonup \rangle$, where Arg is a finite set of arguments and $\rightharpoonup$, the attack-relation, is an irreflexive binary relation defined on Arg.*

If $A \rightharpoonup B$ holds for $A, B \in Arg$, then we say that A *attacks* B.

Example 1. *Pollution in the big cities is becoming a major health problem. City councils are facing the question of possibly banning polluting vehicles, and specifically diesel cars, from the inner centres of such cities. A city council might be entertaining the following arguments:*

- (A) *Diesel cars should be banned from in the inner city centre in order to decrease pollution.*
- (B) *Artisans, who deserve special protection by the city council, cannot change their vehicles, as that would be too expensive for them.*
- (C) *The city can offer financial assistance to artisans.*
- (D) *There are few alternatives: autonomy of electric cars is poor, as there are not enough charging stations around.*
- (E) *The city can set up more charging stations.*
- (F) *In times of financial crisis, the city should not commit to spending additional money.*
- (G) *Health and climate change issues are important, so the city has to spend what is needed to tackle pollution.*

The following graph shows the AF generated by these arguments and a natural attack-relation $\rightharpoonup$ between them:

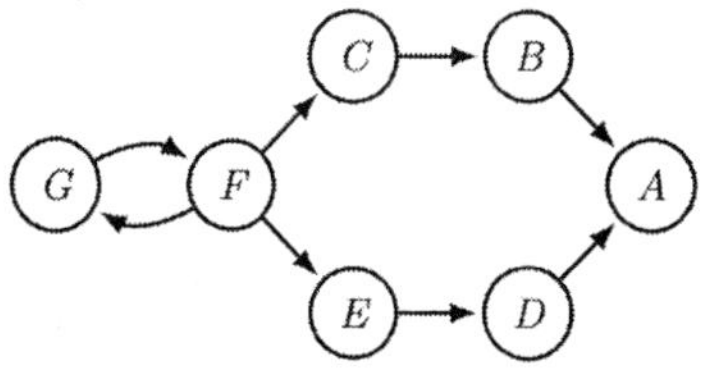

Observe that for this AF it is ambiguous whether or not we should accept argument A and ban diesel cars: Accepting either $\{A, C, E, G\}$ or $\{B, D, F\}$ is intuitively admissible.

Recall that a *preorder* is a binary relation that is reflexive and transitive, and a *weak order* in addition is also complete [25]. We use preorders and weak orders to model *preferences*. Using a preorder means allowing for strict preferences, indifferences, and incomparabilities, while using a weak order excludes the possibility of two items being incomparable. We will use the terms 'preference order' and 'preorder' synonymously, i.e., a 'complete preference order' refers to a weak order. The strict part of a preference order $\succcurlyeq$ is denoted as $\succ$ and its indifference part as $\sim$.

[2] While some preference-based approaches are special cases of the one used here—e.g., in the work of Amgoud and Cayrol [1] each argument is mapped to a different value—others would require extensions, e.g., allowing several values per argument as in the work of Kaci and van der Torre [19].

Following Bench-Capon [6], we define an *audience-specific value-based argumentation framework* (AVAF) as an AF equipped with a function associating each argument with the social or moral value it advances, combined with a preference order declared over those values. While the mapping from arguments to values is fixed, the preferences over values are those of a particular agent (the "audience").

Definition 2 (AVAF). *An audience-specific value-based argumentation framework is defined as a 5-tuple* $\langle Arg, \rightharpoonup, Val, val, \succcurlyeq\rangle$, *where* $\langle Arg, \rightharpoonup\rangle$ *is an argumentation framework,* Val *is a finite set of values,* $val : Arg \to Val$ *is a mapping from arguments to values, and* $\succcurlyeq$ *is the audience's preference order on* Val.

We call $\langle Val, val\rangle$ the AVAF's *value-labelling*. Let $=_{val}$ be the equivalence relation on arguments induced by val: $A =_{val} B$ if and only if $val(A) = val(B)$.

Now suppose an agent is presented with an AF and a value-labelling. In Bench-Capon's model [6], this agent will uphold a proposed attack $A \rightharpoonup B$ and therefore accept that A *defeats* B, unless she strictly prefers the value associated with B to the value associated with the attacker A.

Definition 3 (Defeated Arguments). *Given an AVAF* $\langle Arg, \rightharpoonup, Val, val, \succcurlyeq\rangle$, *we say that argument* $A \in Arg$ *defeats argument* $B \in Arg$, *denoted* $A \rightleftharpoons B$, *if and only if* $A \rightharpoonup B$ *but not* $val(B) \succ val(A)$.

We call $\rightleftharpoons$ the defeat-relation *induced* by the AVAF. Note that saying '$val(B) \succ val(A)$ is not the case' is the same as saying '$val(A) \succcurlyeq val(B)$ is the case' only when the preference order $\succcurlyeq$ is complete.

Note that for any given AVAF $\langle Arg, \rightharpoonup, Val, val, \succcurlyeq\rangle$ the induced defeat-relation $\rightleftharpoons$ is, just like an attack-relation $\rightharpoonup$, an irreflexive binary relation on Arg. That is, we can (and will) think of $\langle Arg, \rightleftharpoons\rangle$ as just another AF.

Example 1 (continued). *Recall our earlier example about the arguments pondered by our city council. We can associate the arguments presented in this example with four types of values. Arguments A and G concern environmental responsibility* (`env`), *B and C are about social fairness* (`soc`), *F promotes economic viability* (`econ`), *and D and E pertain to infrastructure efficiency* (`infra`). *We thus have that* $Val = \{\texttt{env}, \texttt{soc}, \texttt{econ}, \texttt{infra}\}$, *as well as that* $val(A) = val(G) = \texttt{env}$, $val(B) = val(C) = \texttt{soc}$, $val(F) = \texttt{econ}$, *and* $val(D) = val(E) = \texttt{infra}$.

Let us now assume that a particular councillor wants to promote the values of environmental responsibility and infrastructure efficiency over the other two values. So her preferences might be given by the following weak order:

$$\texttt{env} \sim \texttt{infra} \succ \texttt{soc} \sim \texttt{econ}$$

This induces a defeat-relation $\rightleftharpoons$ *for our councillor that corresponds to the following graph:*

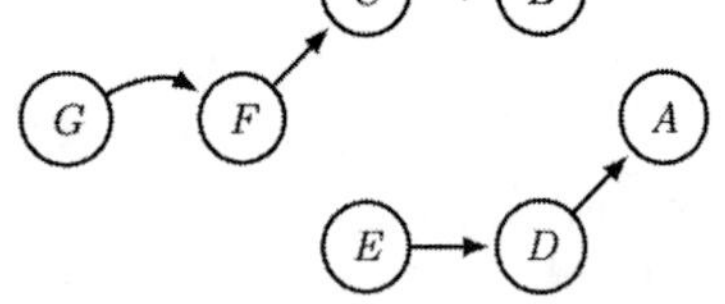

That is, three attacks have been removed. For this new AF it is unambiguously clear that argument A should be accepted (the only argument attacking A is itself attacked by an argument without any remaining attackers), and thus that diesel cars should be banned from the city centre.

In the sequel, we use standard set-theoretical operations (e.g., $\cap$, $\subseteq$) on binary relations (understood as sets of pairs). Furthermore, $R^{-1} = \{(x, y) \mid yRx\}$ is the inverse of a binary relation, R^+ its transitive closure, and R^* its reflexive-transitive closure. $R \circ R'$ is the composition of R and R'. We also define $R^+_{val} := (R \cup =_{val})^* \circ R \circ (R \cup =_{val})^*$, which is like the usual transitive closure, except that we can move to arguments with the same value, even if not connected by R.

3. THE RATIONALISABILITY PROBLEM

Let $\mathcal{N} = \{1, \dots, n\}$ be a finite set of *agents* (or *audiences*). Suppose each of these agents supplies us with an AF, not necessarily over the same set of arguments.[3] We call this a *profile* of AF's. Then we may ask whether the observed profile can be *rationalised* (explained) in terms of a common master AF and a common value-labelling, together with a profile of preference orders, one for each agent. As we think of each AF in the profile as the result of having imposed the relevant agent's preferences, we write individual AF's as $\langle Arg_i, \rightleftharpoons_i\rangle$ (rather than as $\langle Arg_i, \rightharpoonup_i\rangle$). Here, Arg_i is the set of arguments agent i is *aware* of and $\rightleftharpoons_i$ is the defeat-relation on Arg_i adopted by i. A profile of such AF's is denoted as $\boldsymbol{AF} = (\langle Arg_1, \rightleftharpoons_1\rangle, \dots, \langle Arg_n, \rightleftharpoons_n\rangle)$. Let $Arg := Arg_1 \cup \dots \cup Arg_n$ denote the set of all arguments.

We now define the *rationalisability problem* as the problem of deciding whether a given profile can be rationalised in this sense.[4] In fact, we define an entire family of rationalisability problems, parameterised by a set of *constraints* imposed on the solutions admitted (concrete examples are given below).

Definition 4 (Rationalisability). *A profile of AF's* $\boldsymbol{AF} = (\langle Arg_1, \rightleftharpoons_1\rangle, \dots, \langle Arg_n, \rightleftharpoons_n\rangle)$ *is called rationalisable under a given set of constraints, if there exist an attack-relation* $\rightharpoonup$ *on* $Arg = Arg_1 \cup \dots \cup Arg_n$, *a set of values* Val *with a mapping* $val : Arg \to Val$, *and a profile* $(\succcurlyeq_1, \dots, \succcurlyeq_n)$ *of preference orders on* Val, *all meeting said constraints, such that, for all agents* $i \in \mathcal{N}$ *and all arguments* $A, B \in Arg_i$, *it is the case that* $A \rightleftharpoons_i B$ *if and only if* $A \rightharpoonup B$ *but not* $val(B) \succ_i val(A)$.

We will refer to $\langle Arg, \rightharpoonup\rangle$ as the *master AF*, and consequently to $\rightharpoonup$ as the *master attack-relation*.

In this paper, we will consider the following types of constraints (but others may be of interest as well):

- the master attack-relation $\rightharpoonup$ may be fixed,
- the value-labelling $\langle Val, val\rangle$ may be fixed,
- the number of values may be bounded from above,
- the preference orders may be required to be complete.

[3] A common assumption in the literature on the aggregation of AF's is that every individual agent reports an AF over the exact *same set of arguments* [8, 14, 27]. Here, we instead follow Coste-Marquis et al. [11], who have argued that allowing for differences in the individual sets of arguments is more realistic. Note that the case of a single shared set of arguments is covered by our model as a special case.

[4] A different problem of rationalisability has recently been proposed by Dunne et al. [13]: If you observe a set of subsets of arguments, can it possibly correspond, for a given semantics, to different extensions of *some* single AF?

With these definitions in place, we may now ask: For a given set of constraints, can we characterise the class of all profiles of AF's that can be rationalised? And can we check efficiently whether a given profile is rationalisable?

4. THE SINGLE-AGENT CASE

We first consider the single-agent case of the rationalisability problem. This is not only useful for gaining an understanding of the multiagent case, but is also interesting in its own right. For example, it may be the case that there is some 'ground truth' available and we know what the correct attack-relation is (e.g., due to the logical structure of the arguments), but that a specific agent is still reporting a different AF. Can this subjective AF be explained in terms of the value-based model? That is, is this framework compatible with what we know to be the ground truth?

EXAMPLE 2. *Consider a scenario with three arguments, $Arg = \{A, B, C\}$, with a fixed master attack-relation $\rightharpoonup$ such that $A \rightharpoonup B$, $B \rightharpoonup C$, and $A \rightharpoonup C$. Suppose we observe a single agent who only declares $A \rightleftharpoons B$ and $B \rightleftharpoons C$. Can we rationalise this omission of the attack of A on C? Clearly, rationalisation requires A and C to be labelled with distinct values, say v_A and v_C, and our agent must prefer v_C to v_A for $A \rightharpoonup C$ to get cancelled. Are two values enough? The answer is no: If we reuse, say, value v_A to also label argument B, then $B \rightharpoonup C$ would get cancelled as well. Similarly, if we reuse v_C for B, then $A \rightharpoonup B$ would get cancelled. Thus, we need a third value v_B. Now there is a rationalisation, with the agent's preference order ranking v_C above v_A, and v_B being incomparable to the other two values. Observe that, even with three values, rationalisation is impossible if we require the preference order to be complete, i.e., if we require it to not leave any two values incomparable.*

In the single-agent case, we are given an AF $\langle Arg, \rightleftharpoons\rangle$. A solution consists of an AVAF $\langle Arg, \rightharpoonup, Val, val, \succcurlyeq\rangle$, over the same set of arguments Arg, that induces $\rightleftharpoons$. We consider this problem for several types of constraints on solutions.

FACT 1 (NO CONSTRAINTS). *In the absence of constraints, every single AF is rationalisable.*

PROOF. Given the AF $\langle Arg, \rightleftharpoons\rangle$ to be rationalised, let $(\rightharpoonup) := (\rightleftharpoons)$, choose the value-labelling $\langle Val, val\rangle$ arbitrarily, and let $(\succcurlyeq) := Val \times Val$ (meaning that our agent is indifferent between any two values). Then it is easy to check that $\rightleftharpoons$ is induced by the AVAF $\langle Arg, \rightharpoonup, Val, val, \succcurlyeq\rangle$. □

Our proof shows that the same result also applies to rationalisation under any set of constraints referring only to *Val* and *val*. It also continues to apply if we require the preference order to be complete. The main insight here is that any natural instance of the single-agent problem that is nontrivial will involve a constraint on the master attack-relation. Therefore, for the remainder of this section, we only consider rationalisability problems with a given fixed master attack-relation.

PROPOSITION 2 (FIXED ATTACK-RELATION). *A single AF $\langle Arg, \rightleftharpoons\rangle$ is rationalisable by an AVAF with a given fixed master attack-relation $\rightharpoonup$ if and only if all of the following are the case:*

(*i*) $(\rightleftharpoons) \subseteq (\rightharpoonup)$;

(*ii*) $(\rightharpoonup \setminus \rightleftharpoons)$ *is acyclic;*

(*iii*) $(\rightleftharpoons) \cap (\rightharpoonup \setminus \rightleftharpoons)^+ = \varnothing$.

PROOF SKETCH. In this setting, there are no constraints on $\langle Val, val\rangle$. The first important insight then is that having more available values means more flexibility: we can rationalise if and only if we can rationalise by labelling every argument with a distinct value. Thus, we may think of the arguments *themselves* as representing values: w.l.o.g., assume that $Val = Arg$ and that *val* is the identity function. Hence, we can think of $\succcurlyeq$ as operating directly on arguments and need not consider values any longer.

Condition (*i*) is required, as our agent can never add (but only remove) edges. Let $R := (\rightharpoonup \setminus \rightleftharpoons)$ denote the set of edges to be removed. We must have $R^{-1} \subseteq (\succ)$ to ensure that the agent's preference order does indeed remove all of these edges. The second important insight now is that it is never beneficial to add more pairs to the preference order than we are absolutely forced to. That is, we should choose $\succ$ as small as possible, namely as the transitive closure of R^{-1}. We then still need to check two things. First, we need to check that $(R^{-1})^+$ is the strict part of some preorder, i.e., that it is transitive and irreflexive. This is equivalent to condition (*ii*), to R being acyclic. Second, we need to check that we are not removing any edges that should in fact stay, i.e., we need to make sure that $(\rightleftharpoons) \cap R^+ = \varnothing$, which is condition (*iii*). □

All three conditions can be checked in polynomial time, so we obtain a tractability result:

COROLLARY 3 (FIXED ATTACK-RELATION). *Whether a single AF is rationalisable by an AVAF with a given fixed master attack-relation can be decided in polynomial time.*

Note that our proof of Proposition 2 shows that requiring the preference order to be strict (i.e., not allowing any indifferences) does not affect rationalisability. On the other hand, our proof does not apply in case the preference order is required to be complete (this case will instead be covered by Proposition 6 below).

As discussed, a crucial ingredient of Proposition 2 and its proof was the fact that there were no constraints on the value-labelling. We now investigate what happens when we add such constraints, and first consider the most extreme case where the full value-labelling is fixed from the outset. This is a natural scenario to consider in those cases in which we are willing to assume that the question of which value a given argument relates to is a matter that can be settled in an objective manner.

PROPOSITION 4 (FIXED VALUE-LABELLING). *A single AF $\langle Arg, \rightleftharpoons\rangle$ is rationalisable by an AVAF with a given fixed master attack-relation $\rightharpoonup$ and a given fixed value-labelling $\langle Val, val\rangle$ if and only if all of the following are the case:*

(*i*) $(\rightleftharpoons) \subseteq (\rightharpoonup)$;

(*ii*) *the relation* $\bigcup_{A(\rightharpoonup \setminus \rightleftharpoons)B}\{(val(A), val(B))\}$ *is acyclic;*

(*iii*) $(\rightleftharpoons) \cap (\rightharpoonup \setminus \rightleftharpoons)^+_{val} = \varnothing$.

PROOF SKETCH. As for Proposition 2, condition (*i*) reflects that our agent cannot add new edges. The crucial difference to the scenario of Proposition 2 is that now we cannot remove edges between arguments that are labelled with the same value. Let $R := (\rightharpoonup \setminus \rightleftharpoons)$ be the set of edges we need to remove. At the level of the values, this induces the relation $\bigcup_{(A,B)\in R}\{(val(A), val(B))\}$ mentioned in condition (*ii*). As before, the best we can do is to choose as small a preference order as possible, so we should use the transitive closure of the inverse of that relation on values. Condition (*ii*) then amounts to checking that this is indeed a well-formed preference order. Note that acyclicity implies irreflexivity, so we are correctly checking that we are not trying to remove an edge between two arguments labelled with the same value. Finally, we need to check that we are not removing any edges that should stay. This is taken care of by condition (*iii*). To see this, note that R^+_{val} is the set of edges getting removed. □

Also this characterisation immediately provides us with a polynomial algorithm. Thus, we obtain the following result.

COROLLARY 5 (FIXED VALUE-LABELLING). *Whether a single AF is rationalisable by an AVAF with a given fixed master attack-relation and a given fixed value-labelling can be decided in polynomial time.*

The final single-agent scenario we want to consider here is one where we are not given the full value-labelling but merely an upper bound on the number of values that may be used for rationalisation.[5] This scenario comes about when there is no unique objective mapping from arguments to values and we are looking for a "simple" explanation for an observed defeat-relation only involving a limited number of different values. From an algorithmic point of view, this is the most demanding problem considered so far. Still, at least for the case of complete preferences, also for this problem we are able to establish the existence of a polynomial algorithm, as the following result shows.

PROPOSITION 6 (BOUND ON VALUES). *Whether a single AF is rationalisable by an AVAF with a given fixed master attack-relation, a given upper bound on the number of values, and a complete preference order can be decided in polynomial time.*

PROOF. We are going to show how to translate our problem into an integer program with at most two variables per inequality. Deciding feasibility of such programs is known to be polynomial [18].

Let $\langle Arg, \rightharpoonup\rangle$ be the AF, $\rightharpoonup$ the master attack-relation, and k (with $k \leqslant |Arg|$) the upper bound on the number of values. Observe that, if rationalisation is possible with fewer than k values, then it certainly is possible with exactly k values. As the rationalising preference order is required to be complete, w.l.o.g., we may assume that $Val = \{1, \ldots, k\}$ and that $\succcurlyeq$ is the usual relation $\geqslant$ defined over the natural numbers. Clearly, if $(\rightleftharpoons) \not\subseteq (\rightharpoonup)$, then rationalisation is impossible. So, from now on, assume that $(\rightleftharpoons) \subseteq (\rightharpoonup)$.

For every argument $A \in Arg$, introduce an integer variable x_A. We use inequalities of the form $1 \leqslant x_A$ and $x_A \leqslant k$ to ensure that each such variable must take a value from Val. Thus, these variables encode val. We have to be able to model two types of constraints. First, if $A \rightharpoonup B$ but not $A \rightleftharpoons B$, then we must ensure that the value of B is strictly preferred to the value of A: $x_A + 1 \leqslant x_B$. Second, if $A \rightleftharpoons B$ (and thus, by our assumption, also $A \rightharpoonup B$), then we must ensure that the value of B is *not* strictly preferred to the value of A: because of completeness, this can be written as $x_B \leqslant x_A$. The integer program thus constructed is feasible if and only if rationalisation is possible. □

[5]Thus, this scenario requires solving the decision problem corresponding to the optimisation problem of computing the minimal number of values needed for rationalisation.

Let us reiterate that our proof makes use of the condition that the rationalising preference order should be complete. Without it, we would not be able to map requirements of the form $val(B) \not\succ val(A)$ into linear constraints. Assuming completeness of the preference order (i.e., excluding the possibility of an agent not being able to compare the importance of two given values) is sometimes reasonable, but certainly not always. Whether single-agent rationalisability for a bounded number of values remains polynomial for possibly incomplete preferences is an open question.

5. THE MULTIAGENT CASE

We now turn to the multiagent case. In presenting our results for each type of constraint considered, we will specifically focus on the extent to which the (positive) results obtained for the single-agent case carry over to this more general scenario. To get started, recall that we have seen that in the absence of constraints, *every* single AF can be rationalised (Fact 1). The following example shows that this result does not generalise to profiles with (at least) two AF's.

EXAMPLE 3. *Consider a profile of two AF's over a common set of three arguments. Suppose $A \rightleftharpoons_1 B$, $B \rightleftharpoons_1 C$, and $C \rightleftharpoons_1 A$, while $(\rightleftharpoons_2) = \varnothing$. Any value-labelled AF and preference profile that could possibly rationalise this profile would have to have an attack-relation $\rightharpoonup$ that includes, at least, the attacks $A \rightharpoonup B$, $B \rightharpoonup C$, and $C \rightharpoonup A$, as otherwise these edges could not have occurred in the first AF. But this means that the second preference order, to be able to cancel these attacks, must at least include the comparisons $val(B) \succ_2 val(A)$, $val(C) \succ_2 val(B)$, and $val(A) \succ_2 val(C)$. But then $\succ_2$ is not acyclic. Thus, this profile cannot be rationalised, even in the absence of any kind of constraint.*

Under what circumstances can we decompose a given multiagent rationalisability problem into a set of n single-agent rationalisability problems that can be solved independently of each other? For the scenarios covered by Propositions 2 and 4 this is easily seen to be possible:

- If the only constraint is that the master attack-relation is fixed, then every agent's rationalisability problem can be solved independently.
- If the only constraints are that master attack-relation and value-labelling are fixed, then every agent's rationalisability problem can also be solved independently.

But what if the master attack-relation is not given? Consider profile $\boldsymbol{AF} = (\langle Arg_1, \rightleftharpoons_1\rangle, \ldots, \langle Arg_n, \rightleftharpoons_n\rangle)$. Any rationalisation of $\boldsymbol{AF}$ must involve a master attack-relation $\rightharpoonup$ with $(\rightharpoonup) \supseteq (\rightleftharpoons_1) \cup \cdots \cup (\rightleftharpoons_n)$, because no agent can create an edge not already included in $\rightharpoonup$. Any additional edges in $\rightharpoonup$ will make rationalisation only harder, if they make a difference at all. Thus, rationalisation is possible at all if and only if rationalisation is possible with the fixed master attack-relation $(\rightharpoonup) := (\rightleftharpoons_1) \cup \cdots \cup (\rightleftharpoons_n)$.

Given these insights, together with Corollaries 3 and 5, we obtain the following result:

PROPOSITION 7 (DECOMPOSABLE CASES). *Whether a profile of AF's is rationalisable can be decided in polynomial time by solving the problem independently for each agent, in at least the following cases:*

(*a*) *No constraints are given.*

(*b*) *Only the master attack-relation is fixed.*

(*c*) *Only the value-labelling is fixed.*

(*d*) *Master attack-relation and value-labelling are fixed.*

Thus, of all the constraints we have considered here, only the one specifying an upper bound on the number of values actually leads to a "genuine" multiagent rationalisation problem. Let us now consider this problem in some detail.

For the remainder of the paper, we will always assume that a fixed master attack-relation $\rightharpoonup$ is part of the constraints considered. By our reasoning above, any tractability result obtained under this assumption immediately extends to the case where no master attack-relation is specified.

Our first result on multiagent rationalisation with a bound on the number of values to be used is negative: In the most general case this problem is intractable.

PROPOSITION 8 (GENERAL CASE). *Deciding whether a profile of AF's is rationalisable by an AVAF with a given fixed master attack-relation and a given upper bound (of at least 3) on the number of values is an NP-complete problem.*

PROOF. NP-membership is immediate. To prove NP-hardness we provide a reduction from GRAPH COLOURING, which is known to be NP-hard [20]. Recall that in GRAPH COLOURING we are given an undirected graph $G = (V, E)$ and ask whether it is possible to colour the vertices V using at most $k \geqslant 3$ colours such that no two vertices with the same colour are linked by an edge in E.

So take any instance of GRAPH COLOURING with graph $G = (V, E)$ and bound k. Let $m := |V|$. We build an instance of our rationalisation problem for m arguments, $n := \binom{m}{2}$ agents, and a bound of k on the number of values as follows. First, let $Arg := V$ be the full set of arguments, and let the master attack-relation $\rightharpoonup$ be an arbitrary orientation of G. Second, for every pair $A \neq B \in Arg$ we create exactly one agent i, with $Arg_i = \{A, B\}$ and an empty defeat-relation $(\rightleftharpoons_i) = \emptyset$. (That is, there indeed are $\binom{m}{2}$ agents.) Now consider any edge (A, B) in G. As either $A \rightharpoonup B$ or $B \rightharpoonup A$, but neither $A \rightleftharpoons_i B$ nor $B \rightleftharpoons_i A$, the corresponding agent i must strictly rank $val(A)$ and $val(B)$, i.e., they must be different. As this is so for all edges in G and all agents, any two arguments linked in G must get labelled with distinct values. Hence, G is k-colourable if and only if the profile of AF's we constructed can be rationalised using at most k values. □

This is bad news. But are there special cases where rationalisability is tractable after all? Observe that our proof heavily relied on the fact that different agents may be aware of different sets of arguments. This often is a reasonable assumption [11], but the special case where all agents consider the exact same set of arguments certainly is also of interest. Whether rationalisability for a given bound on the number of values remains intractable for this domain restriction is an open question. Furthermore, note that GRAPH COLOURING is *not* NP-hard for $k = 2$ colours, so our proof of intractability does not cover the case of exactly two values. Whether Proposition 8 can be strengthened to a bound of 2 is yet another interesting open question.

Recall that in case there is no bound on the number of values (or, equivalently, if $k = |Arg|$), we already know that rationalisation is tractable (as this follows from Proposition 7). Our final result shows that the problem remains tractable when the bound k is "large"—in the sense of only reducing the number of allowed values by a constant d (relative to the maximum $k = |Arg|$).

PROPOSITION 9 (LARGE BOUND ON VALUES). *Let $d \in \mathbb{N}$ be an arbitrary constant. Whether $\boldsymbol{AF} = (\langle Arg_1, \rightleftharpoons_1\rangle, \ldots, \langle Arg_n, \rightleftharpoons_n\rangle)$ is rationalisable by an AVAF with a given fixed master attack-relation and at most $k := |Arg_1 \cup \cdots \cup Arg_n| - d$ values can be decided in polynomial time.*

PROOF. Let $m := |Arg_1 \cup \cdots \cup Arg_n|$. There are $p := \binom{\binom{m}{2}}{d}$ ways of selecting d pairs from amongst all pairs of distinct arguments. This number is exponential only in d (not in m). Thus, as d is constant, p is polynomial. Note that p is a (generous) upper bound on the number of ways we can divide the m arguments into $k = m - d$ clusters: For any desired division into k clusters, there exists a choice of d pairs such that we obtain that clustering by merging exactly those pairs.

Note that it is not important *which* value is used to label a given argument: if rationalisation is possible at all, it remains possible after any given permutation of the values. The class of all clusterings with k clusters thus represents all relevant value-labellings with k values. Also note that, if rationalisation is possible with fewer than k values, then it certainly is possible with exactly k values. So we only need to check labellings with exactly k values.

To summarise, we have shown that our original rationalisation problem can be reduced to polynomially many (namely, p) new rationalisation problems, each for the same fixed master attack-relation and its own fixed value-labelling. But each of these individual problems is polynomial by Proposition 7 (item d), so we are done. □

6. APPLICATION SCENARIOS

There are a number of different application scenarios where dealing with questions of rationalisability will be valuable. In this section, we list and illustrate some of them.

First, given the growing interest in the abstract argumentation research community in questions of aggregation of AF's [8, 11, 14, 27], it is important to have a clear understanding for what types of scenarios the question of aggregation is in fact relevant. Our notion of rationalisability provides a suitable definition for this purpose. It allows for a systematic scan of the different examples used in the literature—not to dismiss those failing the test, but to point out that one must be careful with the interpretation used. For instance, let us see whether the example given by Coste-Marquis et al. [11, Example 7] passes the test. We are given $AF_1 = \langle\{A, B, E, F\}, \{(A, B), (B, A), (E, F)\}\rangle$, $AF_2 = \langle\{B, C, D, E, F\}, \{(B, C), (C, D), (F, E)\}\rangle$, and $AF_3 = \langle\{E, F\}, \{(E, F)\}\rangle$. It indeed does pass the test. This profile is rationalisable using as master attack-relation the union of the individual relations. But how many values are required to rationalise it? We see that it is sufficient to set $val(E) \neq val(F)$, while A, B, C, D can take the same value, either that of E or that of F. Thus, two values suffice.

Second, in applications where multiple AF's need to be aggregated, we may use the notion of rationalisability to choose between alternative aggregation techniques, depending on the result of the rationalisability test. For example, if a profile turns out to be rationalisable for a given preference model (e.g., for complete preference orders), we may reasonably assume that this model is a good abstraction of reality and aggregate the AF's by aggregating the inferred preferences (which is a much better studied problem than that of aggregating AF's). For instance, we may use the well-known Kemeny rule to aggregate the preferences, and then apply the collective preference order obtained to the master attack-relation inferred. But when rationalisation fails, this approach does not make sense, and we should look for a different method of aggregation. In that case, there is a more substantial disagreement: maybe the model of preferences has to be changed, maybe the agents differ on the assignment of values to arguments, or maybe the agents interpret the arguments differently. Importantly, failure of rationalisation can also provide hints as to where disagreement occurs.

Third, value-based argumentation systems are used in practice as a modelling tool for online debating platforms [23]. In this context, AF's are (typically) not obtained via a one-shot process, but rather retrieved interactively. Our approach could be used to detect inconsistencies as they occur, and thus to trigger clarification questions on the fly. Suppose, for instance, the following sequence occurs:

- Agent 1: A defeats B.
- Agent 2: B defeats A.
- Agent 3: There is no defeat between A and B.

At this stage it is clear that this collection of AF's cannot be rationalised. A clarification is required to identify the mismatch. For example, the system could ask agent 3 whether she really believes there is no attack between A and B.

Finally, it is interesting to note that our methodology can also be fruitfully combined with other approaches. Specifically, in many contexts, the input information provided is not directly an AF, but rather a set of acceptable arguments (i.e., an extension). This is the case, in particular, when the objective is to analyse *a posteriori* whether a given decision can be explained. A recent example of this kind is the study of a participatory decision setting involving an environmental project in Québec reported on by Tremblay and Abi-Zeid [28]. In their case analysis, they extracted seven values and attached them to arguments. They then enumerated all possible AVAF's, getting an overwhelming number of such frameworks, to test whether and how often the decision recommended by a given framework coincides with the decision actually observed in practice. Interestingly, by combining our technique and an approach for inferring AF's from target extensions [5, 13], a different methodology could be used instead: For a set of observed acceptable arguments, we may first apply such a technique to obtain candidate rationalisable AF's, and then apply our rationalisation method to check whether the AF is rationalisable for some values, against the ground truth built by extraction.

Suppose, for instance, that, regarding three arguments $\{A, B, C\}$ and using one of Dung's semantics, agent 1 reports extension $\{A\}$, agent 2 reports $\{A, C\}$, and agent 3 reports $\{A, B\}$. Realising these extensions—starting from an empty AF and considering a single defeat relation amongst arguments for simplicity—it must be the case that $A \rightharpoonup_1 B$ and $A \rightharpoonup_1 C$, while the relation between B and C is either (1-*i*) $B \rightharpoonup_1 C$, (1-*ii*) $C \rightharpoonup_1 B$, or (1-*iii*) no defeat between B and C. Now, for agent 2, there must be no defeat between A and C, leaving five possible cases: (2-*i*) $A \rightharpoonup_2 B$ and $C \rightharpoonup_2 B$, (2-*ii*) $A \rightharpoonup_2 B$ and $B \rightharpoonup_2 C$, (2-*iii*) $C \rightharpoonup_2 B$ and $B \rightharpoonup_2 A$, (2-*iv*) $A \rightharpoonup_2 B$, or (2-*v*) $C \rightharpoonup_2 B$. Finally, for agent 3, we have no defeat relation between A and B, and thus either (3-*i*) $A \rightharpoonup_3 C$ and $B \rightharpoonup_3 C$, (3-*ii*) $B \rightharpoonup_3 C$ and $C \rightharpoonup_3 A$, (3-*iii*) $A \rightharpoonup_3 C$ and $C \rightharpoonup_3 B$, (3-*iv*) $A \rightharpoonup_3 C$, or (3-*v*) $B \rightharpoonup_3 C$. But now, in terms of rationalisation, we see that some combinations are impossible, such as for instance (1-*iii*, 2-*ii*, 3-*iii*). To see this, note that the master attack-relation would have to contain both $B \rightharpoonup C$ (for agent 2) and $C \rightharpoonup B$ (for agent 3). But then agent 1 would have to have one of these attack relations in her system, as she cannot both strictly prefer the value of B to that of C and *vice versa*. While this does not allow us to uniquely define a collection of AF's, this method can nevertheless guide the search for AF's compatible with the extensions observed.

7. CONCLUSION

We have introduced the concept of *rationalisability* of a profile of abstract argumentation frameworks, proposed a specific instantiation of the general idea in terms of social values associated with the arguments and preferences over those values held by the agents, and studied the resulting decision problem from an algorithmic point of view, for several types of constraints on admissible solutions. We have been able to show that the single-agent rationalisability problem is tractable for all the constraints considered. These positive results extend to the multiagent case for several types of constraints. However, in the presence of a constraint limiting the number of values we may use, the most general variant of the multiagent problem is NP-complete.[6]

While our technical results offer a good initial overview of the landscape of rationalisability, our work also pinpoints a number of interesting open questions. These include the complexity of single-agent rationalisability with a limited number of values for incomplete preferences, as well as the identification of further tractable cases of the multiagent rationalisability problem with a limited number of values.

Besides addressing these questions, future work should also investigate alternative instantiations of the general idea of rationalisability expounded here. For instance, as mentioned already in the introduction, the model of Bench-Capon [6] is but one approach to modelling the emergence of different individual argumentation frameworks. Defining the rationalisability problem for competing approaches is likely to be fruitful as well. Another idea, still within the value-based framework, is to treat the fact that agents may be aware of different sets of arguments somewhat differently. In this paper, we have projected the master attack-relation onto each individual argument set before rationalisation. Alternatively, one could ask whether there exists a *possible completion* of an agent's individual defeat-relation for the full set of arguments induced by her preferences.

Acknowledgments. This work has been partly supported by COST Action IC1205 on Computational Social Choice as well as project AMANDE ANR-13-BS02-0004 of the French National Research Agency.

[6]Recall that we have assumed attack relations to be irreflexive. The complexity of the rationalisability problem is not affected by this assumption. As no assignment of values and choice of preference orders can ever cancel out a self-attack, all you need to do on top of checking our existing conditions is checking that all agents agree on all self-attacks.

REFERENCES

[1] L. Amgoud and C. Cayrol. A reasoning model based on the production of acceptable arguments. *Annals of Mathematics and Artificial Intelligence*, 34:197–216, 2002.

[2] L. Amgoud, Y. Dimopoulos, and P. Moraitis. Making decisions through preference-based argumentation. In *Proceedings of the 11th International Conference on Principles of Knowledge Representation and Reasoning (KR-2008)*, 2008.

[3] L. Amgoud and S. Vesic. A new approach for preference-based argumentation frameworks. *Annals of Mathematics and Artifcial Intelligence*, 63(2):149–183, 2011.

[4] R. Baumann. What does it take to enforce an argument? Minimal change in abstract argumentation. In *Proceedings of the 20th European Conference on Artificial Intelligence (ECAI-2012)*. IOS Press, 2012.

[5] R. Baumann and G. Brewka. Expanding argumentation frameworks: Enforcing and monotonicity results. In *Proceedings of the 3rd International Conference on Computational Models of Argument (COMMA-2010)*. IOS Press, 2010.

[6] T. J. M. Bench-Capon. Persuasion in practical argument using value-based argumentation frameworks. *Journal of Logic and Computation*, 13(3):429–448, 2003.

[7] E. Black and A. Hunter. A relevance-theoretic framework for constructing and deconstructing enthymemes. *Journal of Logic and Computation*, 22(1):55–78, 2012.

[8] G. A. Bodanza and M. R. Auday. Social argument justification: Some mechanisms and conditions for their coincidence. In *Proceedings of the 10th European Conference on Symbolic and Quantitative Approaches to Reasoning with Uncertainty (ECSQARU-2009)*. Springer-Verlag, 2009.

[9] R. Booth, S. Kaci, and T. Rienstra. Property-based preferences in abstract argumentation. In *Proceedings of the 3rd International Conference on Algorithmic Decision Theory (ADT-2013)*. Springer-Verlag, 2013.

[10] M. Caminada and G. Pigozzi. On judgment aggregation in abstract argumentation. *Journal of Autonomous Agents and Multiagent Systems*, 22(1):64–102, 2011.

[11] S. Coste-Marquis, C. Devred, S. Konieczny, M.-C. Lagasquie-Schiex, and P. Marquis. On the merging of Dung's argumentation systems. *Artificial Intelligence*, 171(10–15):730–753, 2007.

[12] P. M. Dung. On the acceptability of arguments and its fundamental role in nonmonotonic reasoning, logic programming and n-person games. *Artificial Intelligence*, 77(2):321–358, 1995.

[13] P. E. Dunne, W. Dvorák, T. Linsbichler, and S. Woltran. Characteristics of multiple viewpoints in abstract argumentation. In *Proceedings of the 14th International Conference on Principles of Knowledge Representation and Reasoning (KR-2014)*, 2014.

[14] P. E. Dunne, P. Marquis, and M. Wooldridge. Argument aggregation: Basic axioms and complexity results. In *Proceedings of the 4th International Conference on Computational Models of Argument (COMMA-2012)*. IOS Press, 2012.

[15] U. Endriss and U. Grandi. Collective rationality in graph aggregation. In *Proceedings of the 21st European Conference on Artificial Intelligence (ECAI-2014)*. IOS Press, 2014.

[16] S. Gabbriellini and P. Torroni. Arguments in social networks. In *Proceedings of the 12th International Conference on Autonomous Agents and Multiagent Systems (AAMAS-2013)*. IFAAMAS, 2013.

[17] D. Grossi and W. van der Hoek. Audience-based uncertainty in abstract argument games. In *Proceedings of the 23rd International Joint Conference on Artificial Intelligence (IJCAI-2013)*, 2013.

[18] D. S. Hochbaum and J. Naor. Simple and fast algorithms for linear and integer programs with two variables per inequality. *SIAM Journal on Computing*, 23(6):1179–1192, 1994.

[19] S. Kaci and L. van der Torre. Preference-based argumentation: Arguments supporting multiple values. *International Journal of Approximate Reasoning*, 48(3):730–751, 2008.

[20] R. M. Karp. Reducibility among combinatorial problems. In *Proceedings of a Symposium on the Complexity of Computer Computations*. Plenum Press, 1972.

[21] S. Modgil. Reasoning about preferences in argumentation frameworks. *Artificial Intelligence*, 173(9):901–934, 2009.

[22] S. Modgil. Revisiting abstract argumentation frameworks. In *Proceedings of the 2nd International Workshop on Theory and Applications of Formal Argumentation (TAFA-2013)*. Springer-Verlag, 2014.

[23] S. Pulfrey-Taylor, E. Henthorn, K. Atkinson, A. Wyner, and T. J. M. Bench-Capon. Populating an online consultation tool. In *Proceedings of the 24th Annual Conference on Legal Knowledge and Information Systems (JURIX-2011)*. IOS Press, 2011.

[24] I. Rahwan and F. A. Tohmé. Collective argument evaluation as judgement aggregation. In *Proceedings of the 9th International Conference on Autonomous Agents and Multiagent Systems (AAMAS-2010)*. IFAAMAS, 2010.

[25] F. S. Roberts. *Measurement Theory*. Addison-Wesley, 1979.

[26] J. R. Searle. *Rationality in Action*. MIT Press, 2001.

[27] F. A. Tohmé, G. A. Bodanza, and G. R. Simari. Aggregation of attack relations: A social-choice theoretical analysis of defeasibility criteria. In *Proceedings of the 5th International Symposium on Foundations of Information and Knowledge Systems (FoIKS-2008)*. Springer-Verlag, 2008.

[28] J. Tremblay and I. Abi-Zeid. Value-based argumentation for policy decision analysis: Methodology and an exploratory case study of a hydroelectric project in Québec. *Annals of Operations Research*, 236(1):233–253, 2016.

On the Computational Hardness of Manipulating Pairwise Voting Rules

Rohit Vaish
Indian Institute of Science
India
rohit.vaish@csa.iisc.ernet.in

Neeldhara Misra
IIT Gandhinagar
India
mail@neeldhara.com

Shivani Agarwal
Indian Institute of Science
India
shivani@csa.iisc.ernet.in

Avrim Blum
Carnegie Mellon University
USA
avrim@cs.cmu.edu

ABSTRACT

Standard voting rules usually assume that the preferences of voters are provided in the form of complete rankings over a fixed set of alternatives. This assumption does not hold in applications like recommendation systems where the set of alternatives is extremely large and only partial preferences can be elicited. In this paper, we study the problem of strategic manipulation of voting rules that aggregate voter preferences provided in the form of pairwise comparisons between alternatives. Our contributions are twofold: first, we show that any onto pairwise voting rule is manipulable in principle. Next, we analyze how the computational complexity of manipulation of such rules varies with the structure of the graph induced by the pairs of alternatives that the manipulator is allowed to vote over and the type of the preference relation. Building on natural connections between the pairwise manipulation and sports elimination problems (including a mixed-elimination variant that we introduce in this paper), we show that manipulating pairwise voting rules can be computationally hard even in the single-manipulator setting, a setting where most standard voting rules are known to be easy to manipulate.

General Terms

Algorithms, Economics, Theory

Keywords

Social Choice Theory; Voting; Manipulation; Pairwise Preferences

1. INTRODUCTION

A central result in social choice theory [1] is the Gibbard-Satterthwaite theorem [2, 3] which states that any non-dictatorial voting rule over at least three candidates under which each candidate has some chance of winning is susceptible to strategic voting i.e. is *manipulable*. Given the impossibility suggested by this theorem, there has been substantial work concerning a finer analysis of the situation and finding possible workarounds. A prominent example of this is the seminal work of Bartholdi, Tovey and Trick [4] who proposed the possibility of using computational hardness as a barrier against manipulation of voting rules. They argue that although opportunities for manipulation always exist in principle, there might not exist any efficient general purpose algorithm for finding them in practice.

Since then, a considerable body of work has developed around the computational study of manipulation (see [5] for a survey on this topic). Much of this work models voter preferences as *complete rankings* over a fixed set of alternatives (or candidates). While this is a reasonable choice for certain situations, many large-scale settings prevalent today (like recommendation systems) involve extremely large candidate sets (such as movies, products, webpages etc.). It is therefore unreasonable, and often impractical, to elicit preferences from users in the form of complete rankings of these alternatives. For these settings, it is decidedly more natural to aggregate *partial* user preferences to arrive at an outcome (e.g. top-k preferences [6, 7], partial orders [8] etc.). Similarly, some situations call for relaxing the requirement of *transitivity* among the preferences. Indeed, when alternatives are compared using not one but multiple quality parameters, it is natural to permit possibly cyclic preferences [9].

In this work, we consider the model of *pairwise preferences*, where every vote is simply a collection of pairwise comparisons between alternatives with no constraints other than anti-symmetry (i.e. $A \succ B \Rightarrow B \not\succ A$). The preferences provided by voters in this setting can be *incomplete* (i.e. not all pairs of candidates are compared by a voter) and can contain *cycles* ($A \succ B, B \succ C, C \succ A$). Thus, all the situations described above are subsumed by this model. This is a simple model that offers substantial generality, and as a result there has been growing interest in designing preference aggregation algorithms that elicit pairwise preferences from the users [10, 11, 12, 13, 14]. Although these studies explore the statistical properties of aggregation algorithms for pairwise preferences, the question of whether these algorithms (or *pairwise voting rules*) are resistant to strategic user behavior remains to be answered. The focus of the present work is to address these questions from both axiomatic and computational perspectives.

Appears in: *Proceedings of the 15th International Conference on Autonomous Agents and Multiagent Systems (AAMAS 2016), J. Thangarajah, K. Tuyls, C. Jonker, S. Marsella (eds.), May 9–13, 2016, Singapore.*

<table>
<tr><td colspan="2"></td><td colspan="4"><code>pref-type</code></td></tr>
<tr><td colspan="2"></td><td>strict + acyclic</td><td>acyclic</td><td>strict</td><td>unrestricted</td></tr>
<tr><td rowspan="4">$\mathcal{A}$</td><td>tree/ max deg=2</td><td colspan="4">P</td></tr>
<tr><td>complete</td><td rowspan="3">P</td><td colspan="3" rowspan="3">NP-complete</td></tr>
<tr><td>bipartite</td></tr>
<tr><td>general</td></tr>
</table>

Table 1: *The complexity of* pBorda-MANIPULATION *under the conditions specified by the corresponding action space $\mathcal{A}$ and type of preference relation* `pref-type` *(refer Definition 2.1 in Section 2).*

Contributions

Our contributions can be summarized as follows:

1. We show that any pairwise voting rule that is onto (i.e. under which each candidate has some chance of winning) must be manipulable (Theorem 3.1).

2. Given the above impossibility, we study settings under which computational difficulty acts as a worst-case barrier against manipulation (Sections 3.2 and 3.3) Specifically, we study the problem of manipulation of pairwise voting rules along the following two dimensions: (i) the *structure of the graph* induced by the set of candidate pairs that the manipulator is allowed to vote over (e.g. tree, bipartite, complete) and (ii) the *type of preference relation* (e.g. strict, acyclic). Our analysis is focused on the *pairwise Borda* (pBorda) rule and the Copeland$^\alpha$ family of voting rules. Tables 1 to 4 summarize our results for these rules. The essence of our results is that *the structure of the induced graph and the type of revealed preferences (and the parameter α in case of* Copeland$^\alpha$*) can shape the complexity landscape in important ways.* We remark that while the manipulation problem in the context of rankings is polynomially solvable for most voting rules [4], we already encounter hardness results in the setting of pairwise comparisons with one manipulator for the relatively simple pBorda and Copeland$^\alpha$ rules, which we consider an important contrast[1].

Organization of this paper.

After setting the requisite notation and definitions in Section 2, we describe the main ideas and proof techniques involved in the axiomatic (Section 3.1) and classical complexity-theoretic results for pairwise Borda (Section 3.2) and Copeland$^\alpha$ (Section 3.3) rules. A survey of the related literature is provided in Section 4. We conclude by identifying further implications of our results and directions for future research in Section 5. Due to space constraints, we defer the detailed proofs of all the results presented here to the full version of the paper.

[1]Even in the context of rankings, however, voting rules like the second-order Copeland rule [4] and many elimination-style rules [15, 16, 17, 18] are known to be computationally resistant to manipulation by a single voter.

<table>
<tr><td colspan="2"></td><td colspan="4"><code>pref-type</code></td></tr>
<tr><td colspan="2"></td><td>strict + acyclic</td><td>acyclic</td><td>strict</td><td>unrestricted</td></tr>
<tr><td rowspan="4">$\mathcal{A}$</td><td>tree/ max deg=2</td><td colspan="4" rowspan="4">P</td></tr>
<tr><td>complete</td></tr>
<tr><td>bipartite</td></tr>
<tr><td>general</td></tr>
</table>

Table 2: *The complexity of* Copeland^0-MANIPULATION *and* Copeland^1-MANIPULATION.

<table>
<tr><td colspan="2"></td><td colspan="4"><code>pref-type</code></td></tr>
<tr><td colspan="2"></td><td>strict + acyclic</td><td>acyclic</td><td>strict</td><td>unrstd.</td></tr>
<tr><td rowspan="4">$\mathcal{A}$</td><td>tree/ max deg=2</td><td colspan="4">P</td></tr>
<tr><td>complete</td><td colspan="2" rowspan="3">P</td><td rowspan="3">NP-complete</td><td rowspan="3">P</td></tr>
<tr><td>bipartite</td></tr>
<tr><td>general</td></tr>
</table>

Table 3: *The complexity of* Copeland$^{0.5}$-MANIPULATION.

<table>
<tr><td colspan="2"></td><td colspan="4"><code>pref-type</code></td></tr>
<tr><td colspan="2"></td><td>strict + acyclic</td><td>acyclic</td><td>strict</td><td>unrestricted</td></tr>
<tr><td rowspan="4">$\mathcal{A}$</td><td>tree/ max deg=2</td><td colspan="4">P</td></tr>
<tr><td>complete</td><td rowspan="3">P</td><td colspan="3" rowspan="3">NP-complete</td></tr>
<tr><td>bipartite</td></tr>
<tr><td>general</td></tr>
</table>

Table 4: *The complexity of* Copeland$^\alpha$-MANIPULATION *for $\alpha \in \mathbb{Q} \cap (0,1) \setminus \{0.5\}$.*

2. PRELIMINARIES

Let $[n] = \{1, 2, \dots, n\}$ denote the set of *candidates* and $\mathcal{U} = \{u_1, u_2, \dots, u_m\}$ denote the set of *voters* in an election.

Pairwise preferences and pairwise voting rules.

Let $\succ_u \subseteq [n] \times [n]$ denote the binary relation indicating the preferences of voter u, so that $i \succ_u j$ indicates that voter u prefers candidate i over candidate j. For each pair of candidates i, j and each voter u, we can have exactly one of $i \succ_u j$, $j \succ_u i$ or neither (i.e. voter u *skips* the comparison between i and j). We let $\mathcal{R}$ denote the set of all such anti-symmetric and irreflexive binary relations on $[n]$; and let $\Pi = (\succ_{u_1}, \succ_{u_2}, \cdots, \succ_{u_m}) \in \mathcal{R}^m$ denote the *pairwise preference profile* of the voters.

A *pairwise voting rule* r maps a pairwise preference profile $\Pi \in \cup_{k=1}^{\infty} \mathcal{R}^k$ to a unique candidate $r(\Pi) \in [n]$. Given a preference profile $\Pi \in \mathcal{R}^m$ and a pair of candidates i, j, let $m_{ij}(\Pi)$ denote the number of voters who strictly prefer candidate i over candidate j, i.e. $m_{ij}(\Pi) = \sum_{k=1}^{m} \mathbf{1}(i \succ_{u_k} j)$ where $\mathbf{1}(.)$ is the indicator function. A *score-based pairwise voting rule* is any pairwise voting rule r for which there exists a (natural) scoring function $\mathbf{s} : \cup_{k=1}^{\infty} \mathcal{R}^k \to \mathbb{R}^n$ such that $r(\Pi)$ is the highest-scoring candidate according to $\mathbf{s}(\Pi)$ under some fixed tie-breaking rule. That is, $r(\Pi) = T(\arg\max_i s_i(\Pi))$ for some tie-breaking rule $T : 2^{[n]} \setminus \{\emptyset\} \to [n]$ satisfying $T(S) \in S$ for

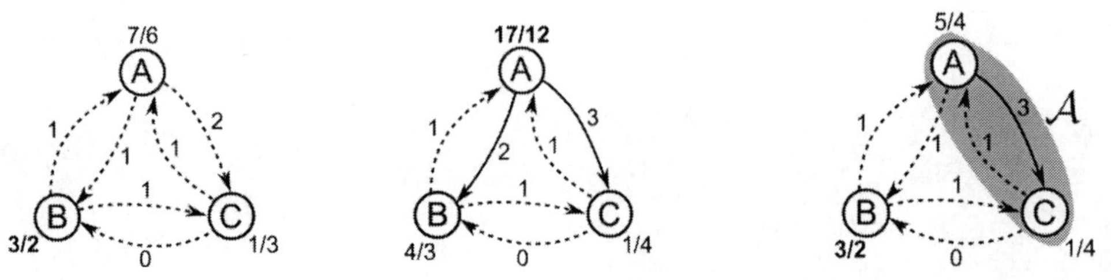

(a) *Before manipulation* **(b)** *After manipulation* **(c)** *After restricted manipulation*

Figure 1: *An illustration of the election instance in Example 2.1. (a) Each vertex of the multigraph represents a candidate and each dashed edge represents the number of voters with that preference (e.g. two voters prefer A≻C). (b) The pairwise comparisons made by the manipulator are represented by solid edges and the* pBorda *score of the winning candidate is indicated in boldface. (c) The restricted action space of the manipulator ($\mathcal{A} = \{(A, C)\}$) is shaded in grey.*

all non-empty $S \subseteq [n]$. Some examples of score-based pairwise voting rules are as follows:

(i) *Pairwise Borda Rule* (pBorda) [14]: The pBorda score of candidate i under preference profile Π is given by[2]:

$$s_i^{\text{pBorda}}(\Pi) = \sum_{j=1}^{n} \frac{m_{ij}(\Pi)}{m_{ij}(\Pi) + m_{ji}(\Pi)}.$$

(ii) *Copeland$^\alpha$ Rule* [19]: The Copeland$^\alpha$score ($\alpha \in [0, 1]$) of candidate i under preference profile Π is given by:

$$s_i^{\text{Copeland}^\alpha}(\Pi) = \sum_{j=1}^{n} \mathbf{1}\big(m_{ij}(\Pi) > m_{ji}(\Pi)\big) + \alpha \cdot \mathbf{1}\big(m_{ij}(\Pi) = m_{ji}(\Pi)\big).$$

Manipulation of pairwise voting rules.

We focus on manipulation by a single strategic voter (the *manipulator*) who has *complete information* about the votes of all other voters (the *non-manipulators*). Formally, a pairwise voting rule r is said to be *manipulable* if there exists a pair of profiles $\Pi = (\succ_{u_1}, \succ_{u_2}, \ldots, \succ_{u_m}), \Pi' = (\succ_{u_1}, \succ_{u_2}, \ldots, \succ_{u_{m-1}}, \succ'_{u_m}) \in \mathcal{R}^m$ differing only in the preference of voter u_m such that $r(\Pi') \succ_{u_m} r(\Pi)$. That is, the manipulator u_m strictly prefers the new outcome over the old one. The corresponding computational problem, referred to as r-MANIPULATION, is defined as follows:

DEFINITION 2.1. r-MANIPULATION

Instance: *A tuple* $\langle \Pi, i^*, \mathcal{A}, \texttt{pref-type} \rangle$ *where* $\Pi \in \mathcal{R}^{m-1}$ *is the preference profile of the non-manipulators* $(u_1, u_2, \ldots, u_{m-1})$*,* $i^* \in [n]$ *is the distinguished candidate,* $\mathcal{A} \subseteq \binom{[n]}{2}$ *is the set of pairwise comparisons that the manipulator is allowed to make and* `pref-type` $\in$ {strict+acyclic, strict, acyclic, unrestricted} *is the preference constraint with respect to* $\mathcal{A}$*.*

Question: *Does there exist a vote* $\succ_{u_m}$ *over* $\mathcal{A}$ *satisfying* `pref-type` *such that* $r((\Pi, \succ_{u_m})) = i^*$*?*

Here $\mathcal{A} \subseteq \binom{[n]}{2}$ denotes the *action space* of the manipulator i.e. the pairs of candidates that the manipulator is allowed to vote over. Alternately, no pair of candidates outside $\mathcal{A}$ can be compared by the manipulator. Given $\mathcal{A}$, we say that a vote $\succ_u$ by a voter u over $\mathcal{A}$ has a *strict* preference type (i.e. `pref-type` = strict) if for all candidate pairs $\{i, j\} \in \mathcal{A}$, either $i \succ_u j$ or $j \succ_u i$ (i.e. voter u is not allowed to skip comparisons). Similarly, a vote satisfying `pref-type` = acyclic is not allowed to contain directed cycles (i.e. $1 \succ_u 2, 2 \succ_u 3, 3 \succ_u 1$ is forbidden etc.). A vote with `pref-type` = strict+acyclic is required to simultaneously satisfy the strictness and acyclicity constraints while `pref-type` = unrestricted imposes none of these restrictions.

We will refer to the instantiation of r-MANIPULATION for pBorda rule (resp. Copeland$^\alpha$) as pBorda-MANIPULATION (resp. Copeland$^\alpha$-MANIPULATION). Example 2.1 illustrates the role of the space $\mathcal{A}$ in the manipulation problem.

EXAMPLE 2.1 (THE ROLE OF ACTION SPACE $\mathcal{A}$). *Consider the election setting shown in Figure 1a, where the* pBorda *scores of the candidates A, B & C respectively are 7/6, 3/2 & 1/3 and B is the* pBorda *winner. Suppose we now add the manipulator* u_4 *to this election whose favorite candidate is A. Observe that if the manipulator casts the vote* $\{(A \succ B), (A \succ C)\}$ *(see Figure 1b), the new* pBorda *scores for A, B & C will be 17/12, 4/3 & 1/4 respectively and A becomes the winner. Thus, the answer to* pBorda-MANIPULATION *for this election instance is YES when* $\mathcal{A} = \{(A, B), (A, C)\}$ *or* $\mathcal{A} = \{(A, B), (A, C), (B, C)\}$ *and* `pref-type` = unrestricted. *However, if the manipulator is only allowed to compare the candidates A and C, then despite voting in favor of A, the manipulator cannot make A win (Figure 1c). Therefore, the answer to* pBorda-MANIPULATION *is NO when* $\mathcal{A} = \{(A, C)\}$*. It is easy to see that the above observations also hold for* `pref-type` $\in$ {strict, acyclic, strict+acyclic}.

Excess scores.

The excess score of a candidate i is the amount by which the score of i exceeds the score of the distinguished candidate i^* in a given election. For instance, in Figure 1c, the excess pBorda scores of candidates B and C (with respect to distinguished candidate A) are $1/4$ and -1 respectively. Hence, r-MANIPULATION for a score-based voting rule r can be restated as finding a vote for the manipulator such that the final excess scores of all candidates are zero or less.

Elimination problem in sports.

The elimination problem [20] asks whether a team i^* can still win a sports competition, given the current scores and set of remaining games. As we will see, this problem turns out to be intimately connected to r-MANIPULATION.

[2]where we adopt the convention $0/0 = 0$.

Formally, let $[N] = \{1, 2, \ldots, N\}$ be the set of N teams and let $s_i \in \mathbb{R}$ denote the current score of team $i \in [N]$. Let $\mathcal{G} \subseteq \binom{[N]}{2}$ denote the set of remaining games between pairs of teams . A *scoring system* S determines the points awarded to each team in a pairwise game based on the outcome of the game (e.g. *home win, draw* or *away win*).

DEFINITION 2.2. SCORING SYSTEM: *A scoring system S is a tuple of ordered pairs of rational numbers $[(\alpha_1, \beta_1), (\alpha_2, \beta_2), \cdots, (\alpha_t, \beta_t)]$ where the subscript $1, 2, \cdots, t$ corresponds to the outcome of a game and the first and second entries of each pair (denoted by α and β) correspond to the points awarded respectively to the home and away team under that outcome. For example, the well-known European football scoring system, where $S_1 = [(3,0),(1,1),(0,3)]$ and $t = 3$, awards 3 points for win, 1 point for draw and 0 for loss, regardless of home-away distinction. Similarly, $S_2 = [(3,0),(1,2),(0,3)]$ awards an extra point to the away team under a draw outcome. Finally, $S_3 = [(3,0),(0,3)]$ allows only win-loss outcomes and the winner gets 3 points.*

Given the current scores $\mathbf{s}$ and the set of games to be played between the teams $\mathcal{G}$, S-ELIMINATION asks the question *"can team i^* still win?"* [21]

DEFINITION 2.3. S-ELIMINATION

> ***Instance:*** *A tuple $\langle \mathbf{s}, i^*, \mathcal{G} \rangle$ where $\mathbf{s} = (s_1, s_2, \ldots, s_N)^T$ is the vector of current scores of the N teams, $i^* \in [N]$ is the distinguished team and $\mathcal{G} \subseteq \binom{[N]}{2}$ is the set of remaining games between the teams.*
>
> ***Question:*** *Does there exist an assignment of outcomes for the games in $\mathcal{G}$ such that i^* ends up with the (joint) highest total score among all teams under the scoring system S ?*

A comprehensive characterization of the computational difficulty of this question was provided by Kern and Paulusma [21] in terms of the nature of scoring system S used to award points to the teams.

THEOREM 2.1 (KERN AND PAULUSMA [21]). *Let S be a scoring system satisfying[3] $\alpha_1 > \cdots > \alpha_{t-1} = 1 > \alpha_t = 0$ and $0 = \beta_1 < 1 \leq \beta_2 < \cdots < \beta_t$. Then S-ELIMINATION is polynomially solvable if $S = \{(t-1-i, i) : 0 \leq i \leq t-1\}$ for some $t \in \mathbb{N}$. In all other cases, the problem is NP-complete.*

3-dimensional Matching [22].

DEFINITION 2.4. 3-D MATCHING

> ***Instance:*** *A tuple $\langle W, X, Y, R \rangle$ where W, X, Y are disjoint sets each of size q and $R \subseteq W \times X \times Y$ is a set of triples such that each $w \in W$ (similarly $x \in X$ and $y \in Y$) features in exactly two triples.*
>
> ***Question:*** *Does there exist a subset $R' \subseteq R$ such that R' covers $W \cup X \cup Y$ exactly i.e. each $w \in W$(similarly $x \in X, y \in Y$) is present in exactly one triple in R'?*

3-D MATCHING remains NP-complete even when each element of W, X, Y occurs in exactly two triples in R [23].

[3]This is without loss of generality, since any given instance of S-ELIMINATION can be transformed into an equivalent instance where the scoring system satisfies these conditions by the normalization procedure described in [21].

3. OUR RESULTS AND TECHNIQUES

3.1 Axiomatic result

In its standard form, the Gibbard-Satterthwaite theorem [2, 3] requires voter preferences over the set of candidates to be complete, transitive and unrestricted (i.e. voters are allowed to pick any possible ranking). Several follow-up works have studied generalizations of this result to settings such as (i) minimally rich subsets of the domain of rankings [24, 25, 26, 27], (ii) incomplete preferences such as partial orders or top-k choices [7, 8], (iii) voting rules with multiple winners [28, 8], etc. Our axiomatic result can be seen as belonging to this line of research where we simultaneously relax the assumptions of transitivity and completeness.

Specifically, we show that the inevitability of strategic voting extends to the more general domain of pairwise preferences. We might expect this intuitively – indeed, if r is a non-manipulable pairwise voting rule, then the projection of r to the domain of rankings will also be non-manipulable. However, the projection of a "non-dictatorial" pairwise voting rule r to the domain of rankings might still turn out to be dictatorial, making the desired contradiction elusive.

THEOREM 3.1 (AXIOMATIC RESULT). *If there are at least three candidates and at least two voters, then any pairwise voting rule that is onto must also be manipulable.*

PROOF. Let us assume that the voting rule r is onto. Consider a preference profile Π_1 where all votes are identical directed cycles of the form $n \succ n-1$, $n-1 \succ n-2$, $\cdots$, $2 \succ 1$, $1 \succ n$. We require $n \geq 3$ for this to be well defined. Let $r(\Pi_1) = 1$. Starting from voter u_1, sequentially modify the votes of all voters $u_1, u_2, \ldots, u_m$ such that in each vote, 2 beats all other candidates and 1 beats everyone except for 2. At each stage of this modification process, 1 must remain the election winner (if 2 wins at any stage, then the swing voter has an incentive to switch to the new vote; if some other candidate $i \neq 1, 2$ wins, then the swing voter can switch back to the old vote). Call this new profile Π_2. Hence $r(\Pi_2) = 1$. Ontoness of r implies that there exists a preference profile Π such that $r(\Pi) = 2$. Without loss of generality, Π can be transformed into a profile Π_3 where 2 beats everyone in each vote and continues to be the winner, i.e. $r(\Pi_3) = 2$. Starting from Π_3, sequentially modify the votes to transform it into Π_2. At some point during this process 2 must lose, providing the desired manipulation. □

3.2 Complexity of manipulating pairwise Borda

We build a comprehensive landscape of the computational complexity of pBorda-MANIPULATION for various combinations of possibilities that arise along the two dimensions mentioned earlier, namely (i) the structure of the *action space* ($\mathcal{A}$ = tree, bipartite, complete graph etc.) and (ii) the *preference type* (`pref-type` = strict, acyclic etc.). Our results show that the manipulation problem turns out to be easy (i.e. polynomial time) whenever the graph structure is *simple enough* (e.g. tree/max degree=2), regardless of the preference type. However, for more complex structures like bipartite/complete graphs, requiring either strictness or acyclicity (but not both) can lead to computational hardness (i.e. NP-hardness). Our results for pBorda-MANIPULATION are summarized in Table 1 and stated as Theorems 3.2 to 3.5.

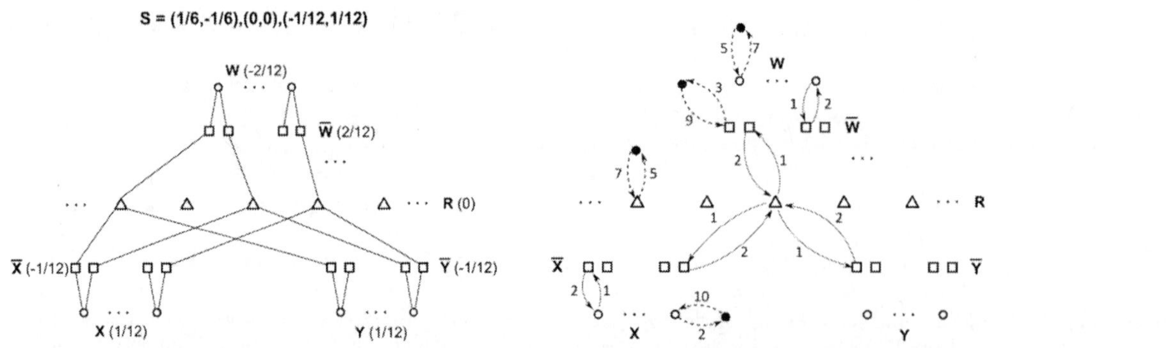

(a) *Sports instance* (b) *Election instance*

Figure 2: *Figure (a) on the left shows the graph structure of the reduced* S-ELIMINATION *instance in [21] with the scores of the teams listed inside parentheses. Figure (b) on the right shows the graph structure of the corresponding* pBorda-MANIPULATION *instance. The solid circles in figure (b) correspond to the dummy candidates and the dashed/solid edges represent the votes of the non-manipulators for comparisons involving/not involving a dummy candidate.*

THEOREM 3.2. pBorda-MANIPULATION *is polynomially solvable in the following cases: (a) for any choice of* `pref-type` *when* $\mathcal{A}$ *is a* tree *and (b) for any choice of* $\mathcal{A}$ *when* `pref-type` = strict+acyclic.

PROOF. *(Sketch.)* Part (a) above is shown by a bottom-up greedy algorithm that starts at the leaves of the tree and forces an option for the manipulator without loss of generality. For example, if a leaf has a positive excess score, then it must lose against its parent (and if this is not enough, then it is legitimate to abort). Similarly, if a leaf has negative excess, then it might as well win the pairwise comparison with its parent whenever the score transfer is feasible.

Part (b) is shown by a greedy approach similar to the one used in the classical setting of rankings [4]. At each step, the algorithm checks whether some vertex can be made a *source* vertex for the remaining graph (i.e. all its incident edges are oriented as outgoing). If yes, the algorithm updates the excess scores for all vertices and proceeds with the remaining (smaller) graph; otherwise, the algorithm outputs No. □

REMARK 3.1. *The proofs for both parts (a) and (b) of Theorem 3.2 rely only on a locality property of score-based pairwise voting rules — which is that adding a pairwise comparison between a pair of candidates only affects the scores of the two candidates involved. For this reason, other score-based pairwise voting rules with this locality property (e.g.* Copeland$^\alpha$*) also admit polynomial time manipulation algorithms in the settings described above (refer Tables 2 to 4).*

THEOREM 3.3. pBorda-MANIPULATION *is* NP-complete *for* $\mathcal{A} \in$ {bipartite, general graph} *and* `pref-type` $\in$ {acyclic, unrestricted}.

PROOF. We reduce from the instance of S-ELIMINATION with $S = [(1/6, -1/6), (0,0), (-1/12, 1/12)]$ that was used by Kern and Paulusma [21] in their NP-hardness proof [4]. Specifically, the instance consists of seven groups of teams comprising $[N]$, namely $W, \bar{W}, R, \bar{X}, \bar{Y}, X$ and Y, represented as circles, squares and triangles in Figure 2a. The current scores of all teams in each group are listed inside parentheses. Also as shown, each team in the groups W, X, Y has two remaining games against teams in $\bar{W}, \bar{X}, \bar{Y}$ resp., while each team in the group R has three remaining games - one apiece against teams in $\bar{W}, \bar{X}, \bar{Y}$. The distinguished team i^* (not shown in the figure) has no remaining games and has an initial score of 0. Finally, for any game in $\mathcal{G}$ the team from the groups $\bar{W}, \bar{X}, \bar{Y}$ should be considered the *away* team.

The reduced election instance (Figure 2b) is constructed as follows: the set of candidates $[n]$ consists of (i) a candidate i for each team $i \in [N]$ (including a candidate i^* for the team i^*) and (ii) the dummy candidates $N+1, \dots, N+\ell$ (shown as solid circles) where $\ell \leq N$ i.e. at most one per team (hence $n = N + \ell$). The action space $\mathcal{A}$ of the manipulator corresponds to the set of remaining games $\mathcal{G}$. The votes of non-manipulators (twelve in total — $u_1, \dots, u_{12}$) are set up as follows: (i) *votes between candidate pairs* (i,j) *in* $\mathcal{A}$: for each game $(i,j) \in \mathcal{G}$ where i is the home team and j is the away team, the votes between the corresponding candidate pair $(i,j) \in \mathcal{A}$ are set up in a 1:2 configuration[5]; (ii) *votes involving dummy candidates*: for each candidate corresponding to a team in the groups $W, \bar{W}, R, X$ or Y, we add a dummy candidate and set the votes between them in the configurations 7:5, 3:9, 5:7, 2:10 or 2:10 respectively (see Figure 2b); and (iii) *votes involving the distinguished candidate* i^*: the pairs $(i^*, N+1)$ and $(i^*, N+2)$ are set up in the configurations 1:0 and 5:7 respectively.

It is easy to check that the excess scores of the candidates match the excess scores of the corresponding teams in the sports instance. Besides, for each candidate pair in $\mathcal{A}$ (set-up in a 1:2 configuration), the pBorda scores of the pair can change by $(1/6, -1/6)$,$(0,0)$ or $(-1/12, 1/12)$ depending on how the manipulator votes, which is exactly the scoring system S in original sports instance. The equivalence of the two solutions is now straightforward.

Note that the graph $\mathcal{G}$ in the original sports instance (Figure 2a) is *bipartite*. Besides, any valid orientation of the remaining games in that construction turns out to be

[4]The proof in [21] was actually presented for S-ELIMINATION with $S = [(3,0), (1,2), (0,3)]$, which can be reduced to our problem using the following normalization scheme: start by awarding, for each remaining game in $\mathcal{G}$, 1 and 2 points respectively to each home and away team *in advance*, followed by scaling down all score values by 12.

[5]A *vote configuration* of 1:2 between a pair of candidates (i,j) means that one voter (say u_1) votes $i \succ_{u_1} j$ while two other voters (say u_2, u_3) vote $j \succ_{u_2} i$ and $j \succ_{u_3} i$.

acyclic. As a consequence, pBorda-MANIPULATION remains NP-complete when $\mathcal{A}$ = bipartite graph and **pref-type** = acyclic. The implications for $\mathcal{A}$ = general graph and **pref-type** = unrestricted follow. □

REMARK 3.2. *Since the above reduction requires at most* 12 *non-manipulators,* pBorda-MANIPULATION *is NP-complete* even with $\mathcal{O}(1)$ non-manipulators.

Our next result (Theorem 3.4) shows that pBorda-MANIPULATION is NP-complete when the manipulator is not allowed to skip any pairwise comparison in $\mathcal{A}$ (i.e. **pref-type** = strict). Our proof consists of two parts: first, we introduce a generalization of S-ELIMINATION (which we call MIXED-ELIMINATION) and show that the problem is NP-complete via reduction from 3-D MATCHING (Lemma 3.1). Next, we show that MIXED-ELIMINATION reduces to pBorda-MANIPULATION when **pref-type** = strict. We start by describing the problem of MIXED-ELIMINATION.

MIXED-ELIMINATION generalizes S-ELIMINATION to competitions where different games can be played under different scoring systems. That is, instead of a single scoring system S as in S-ELIMINATION, MIXED-ELIMINATION consists of k different scoring systems $S_1, S_2, \ldots, S_k$ and an assignment function η which maps each game in $\mathcal{G}$ to exactly one of these scoring systems i.e. $\eta(\mathcal{G}) \in [k]^{|\mathcal{G}|}$. As before, the question of interest is: *can team i^* still win?*

DEFINITION 3.1. MIXED-ELIMINATION($S_1, S_2, \ldots, S_k$)

Instance: *A tuple $\langle \mathbf{s}, i^*, \mathcal{G}, \eta \rangle$ where $\mathbf{s} = (s_1, s_2, \ldots, s_N)^T$ is the vector of current scores of the N teams, $i^* \in [N]$ is the distinguished team, $\mathcal{G} \subseteq \binom{[N]}{2}$ is the set of remaining games between the teams and η is a function that assigns a scoring system from $\{S_1, S_2, \ldots, S_k\}$ to each game in $\mathcal{G}$.*

Question: *Does there exist an assignment of outcomes for the games in $\mathcal{G}$ which when scored according to the scoring systems chosen by η make i^* the team with the (joint) highest score?*

Our proof of Theorem 3.4 focuses on MIXED-ELIMINATION(S_1, S_2) where $S_1 = [(10, -10), (-5, 5)]$ and $S_2 = [(8, -8), (-2, 2)]$. Thus, each remaining game is scored according to either S_1 or S_2 and no game can end in a draw. We already know from Theorem 2.1 that the *pure* elimination problems with either of these scoring systems (i.e. S_1-ELIMINATION or S_2-ELIMINATION) admit polynomial time algorithms[6]. As we show below, however, the *mixed* elimination problem with these two scoring systems together is computationally hard.

LEMMA 3.1. MIXED-ELIMINATION(S_1, S_2) *with* $S_1 = [(10, -10), (-5, 5)]$ *and* $S_2 = [(8, -8), (-2, 2)]$ *is* NP-complete *when the set of remaining games $\mathcal{G}$ induces a bipartite graph.*

PROOF. We reduce from a variant of 3-D MATCHING where each element of the sets W, X, Y occurs in exactly two triples in R [23] (refer Definition 2.4). Our proof follows the template of a similar proof in [21] where a reduction from the standard 3-D MATCHING problem is used to show hardness of S-ELIMINATION. The main idea of the proof in [21] is to treat the nodes in the *matching graph* of the given 3-D MATCHING instance (see Figure 3) as teams and the edges as the set of remaining games between teams. We use this idea to set up a sports instance where the games in the upper half of the matching graph are scored according to $S_1 = [(10, -10), (-5, 5)]$ and those in lower half according to $S_2 = [(8, -8), (-2, 2)]$, shown as solid and dashed edges in Figure 3.

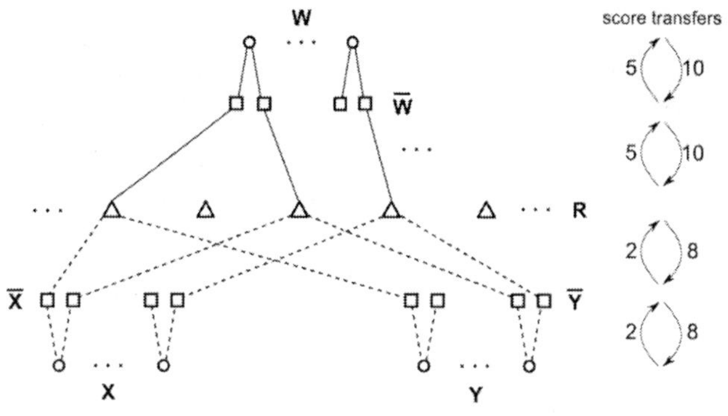

Figure 3: *This figure shows the matching graph for a given* 3-D MATCHING *instance (left) and score transfers between teams at each level (right). The base sets W, X, Y and the set of triples R are represented as circles and triangles respectively. Each element of the set W (resp. X, Y) is connected to two elements of the set $\bar{W}$ (resp. $\bar{X}, \bar{Y}$) (shown as square nodes) representing the two occurrences of this element in R.*

Formally, given an instance $\langle W, X, Y, R \rangle$ of 3-D MATCHING, we construct an instance $\langle \mathbf{s}, i^*, \mathcal{G}, \eta \rangle$ of MIXED-ELIMINATION(S_1, S_2) as follows: (i) the *set of teams* $[N]$ is the union of the sets $W, X, Y, \bar{W}, \bar{X}, \bar{Y}, R$ (i.e. one team per element) along with the distinguished team i^*; (ii) the *set of remaining games* $\mathcal{G}$ is precisely the set of all solid and dashed edges in the matching graph; (iii) the *assignment function* η is such that all games involving teams from $\bar{W}$ are scored according to S_1, while all other games in $\mathcal{G}$ are scored according to S_2. Furthermore, for any game, a team *higher up* in the matching graph should be considered the *away* team; and (iv) the *current score* of the team i^* is fixed at 0 without loss of generality. The excess scores of all teams in the sets $W, \bar{W}, R, \bar{X}, \bar{Y}, X$ and Y are respectively $0, -1, 0, -1, -1, -7$ and -7. We now show the equivalence of the two instances.

($\Rightarrow$) Suppose there exists a 3-dimensional matching $R' \subseteq R$. Then a winning assignment can be constructed as follows: (i) each team $r = (w, x, y)$ in the matching set (i.e. $r \in R'$) beats the team $\bar{w} \in \bar{W}$ corresponding to the element w, and loses to the teams $\bar{x} \in \bar{X}$ and $\bar{y} \in \bar{X}$ corresponding to the element x (and y); (ii) each $r \in R \setminus R'$ does the exact opposite by losing to the team above it and beating the teams below it in the matching graph and (iii) if a team $\bar{w} \in \bar{W}$ loses the game against the team in R, then it wins its only other remaining game against w and vice versa. Similarly for teams in $\bar{X}$ and $\bar{Y}$. It can now be easily checked that the above assignment of outcomes is a winning one for team i^*.

[6]This is because any instance of S-ELIMINATION with $S = S_1$ can be transformed into an equivalent (efficiently solvable) instance of S-ELIMINATION with $S = [(1, 0), (0, 1)]$ by first, awarding *in advance* -5 and -10 points respectively to each home and away team for each remaining game in $\mathcal{G}$; followed by scaling down all team scores by 15. Similarly for $S = S_2$.

($\Leftarrow$) Now suppose there exists an assignment of the remaining games that makes team i^* win. Without loss of generality, each team in R under such an assignment either wins its game against the team in $\bar{W}$ (in which case it loses against teams in $\bar{X}$ and $\bar{Y}$) or loses against the team in $\bar{W}$ (in which case it wins against the teams in $\bar{X}$ and $\bar{Y}$). The set of teams in R that win against teams in $\bar{W}$ can now be shown to constitute a valid 3-dimensional matching.

Finally, observe that the graph $\mathcal{G}$ in the reduced instance is bipartite. This proves Lemma 3.1. □

THEOREM 3.4. pBorda-MANIPULATION *is* NP-complete *for* $\mathcal{A} \in$ {bipartite, general graph} *and* `pref-type` = strict.

PROOF. *(Sketch.)* Our proof uses a reduction from MIXED-ELIMINATION(S_1, S_2) with $S_1 = [(10,-10),(-5,5)]$ and $S_2 = [(8,-8),(-2,2)]$, which was shown to be NP-complete in Lemma 3.1 even when the graph induced by the set of remaining games is bipartite. Just like in the proof of Theorem 3.3, we match teams with candidates and the set of remaining games with the action space of the manipulator. Furthermore, if a game between two teams is scored according to S_1 (respectively S_2), then the votes of non-manipulators between the corresponding candidates are set up in a 1:2 (respectively 1:4) configuration. The win-loss-only condition translates to `pref-type` = strict. □

REMARK 3.3. *It is worth pointing out that when* `pref-type`=strict, *we cannot show hardness for* pBorda-MANIPULATION *by reduction from* S-ELIMINATION. *The reason is that for a scoring system S to correspond to the changes in* pBorda *scores due to the manipulator's vote, it must be of the form* $[(\alpha,-\alpha),(0,0),(-\beta,\beta)]$, *where* $\alpha, \beta \in \mathbb{N}$. *When skipping a comparison is not allowed (as is the case with* `pref-type`=strict*), the required form becomes* $S = [(\alpha,-\alpha),(-\beta,\beta)]$, *which can in turn be reduced (via translation and scaling) to the trivial* $[(0,0)]$ *system. This motivates the need to consider instances with more than one scoring system, as in* MIXED-ELIMINATION.

THEOREM 3.5. pBorda-MANIPULATION *is* NP-complete *for* $\mathcal{A}$ = complete graph *and* `pref-type` $\in$ {strict, acyclic, unrestricted}.

PROOF. *(Sketch.)* For any fixed choice of `pref-type`, we reduce from the corresponding pBorda-MANIPULATION problem with $\mathcal{A}$ = general graph, which was shown to be NP-complete in Theorems 3.3 and 3.4. The set of candidates in the original and the reduced instances are identical. The votes of non-manipulators between candidate pairs within $\mathcal{A}$ in the original instance are also identical to the votes between corresponding candidate pairs in the reduced instance. For candidate pairs outside $\mathcal{A}$ in the original instance that are set up in $a:b$ configuration, the corresponding candidate pairs in the reduced instance are set up in $aK:bK$ configuration, where K is sufficiently large (yet polynomial in n, m). 'Scaling up' votes in this manner not only preserves the exact pBorda scores (and therefore the excess scores) of the candidates in the reduced instance, but it also forces the manipulator to effectively work with candidate pairs corresponding to the action space A of the original instance. This is because a large number of non-manipulators' votes between a pair of candidates nullifies the change in pBorda scores brought about by the manipulator's vote. □

3.3 Complexity of manipulating Copeland$^\alpha$

Our results for the complexity of Copeland$^\alpha$-MANIPULATION are summarized in Tables 2 to 4 and are stated as Theorems 3.6 to 3.8.

The family of Copeland$^\alpha$ voting rules (parameterized by α) was first studied by Faliszewski et al. [19] in the context of manipulation by a coalition of two voters (recall from Remark 3.1 that manipulation by a single voter is polynomial time). Together with [29], these papers showed that Copeland$^\alpha$-MANIPULATION with two manipulators is NP-complete for all $\alpha \in \mathbb{Q} \cap [0,1] \setminus \{0.5\}$ when $\mathcal{A}$ = complete graph and `pref-type` = strict+acyclic (i.e. when votes are complete rankings). However, when votes are allowed to be *tournaments* (i.e. $\mathcal{A}$ = complete graph, `pref-type` = strict), Copeland$^\alpha$-MANIPULATION was shown to admit a polynomial time algorithm for $\alpha \in \{0,1\}$ for any given number ($k \geq 1$) of manipulators[7] [29] . This algorithm can be easily modified to work for any general graph $\mathcal{A}$. Our first result in this section (Theorem 3.6) generalizes the tractability of Copeland$^\alpha$-MANIPULATION for $\alpha \in \{0,1\}$ to any choice of $\mathcal{A}$ when `pref-type` $\in$ {strict, acyclic, unrestricted} (Table 2). We also show that Copeland$^{0.5}$-MANIPULATION is efficiently solvable for any choice of $\mathcal{A}$ when `pref-type` $\in$ {acyclic, unrestricted} (Table 3).

THEOREM 3.6. Copeland$^\alpha$-MANIPULATION *is polynomially solvable in the following cases: (a) for* $\alpha \in \{0,1\}$ *for any choice of* $\mathcal{A}$ *when* `pref-type` $\in$ {strict, acyclic, unrestricted} *and (b) for* $\alpha = 0.5$ *for any choice of* $\mathcal{A}$ *when* `pref-type` $\in$ {acyclic, unrestricted}.

PROOF. *(Sketch.)* Since the manipulator cannot affect the Copeland outcomes for pairwise contests between candidate pairs (i,j) with $|m_{ij} - m_{ji}| > 1$, we assume without loss of generality that the manipulator either *skips* such comparisons (if `pref-type` $\in$ {acyclic, unrestricted}) or provides *arbitrary preferences* over them (if `pref-type` = strict). Hence, for the rest of the proof, we will only consider the pairs (i,j) where $|m_{ij} - m_{ji}| \leq 1$.

Part (a): We start with Copeland^0-MANIPULATION. Here, the manipulator prefers to have as many *ties* between pairs of non-distinguished candidates as possible. Thus, when `pref-type` = unrestricted, the manipulator votes $j \succ i$ whenever $m_{ij} = m_{ji} + 1$ and skips the comparison otherwise.

When `pref-type` = strict, the manipulator can no more skip the comparisons with $m_{ij} = m_{ji}$. For such pairs, the Copeland scores of candidates (i,j) can change by $(+1,0)$ or $(0,+1)$ for the vote $i \succ j$ or $j \succ i$ of the manipulator. This subproblem is identical to S-ELIMINATION with $S = [(1,0),(0,1)]$, which is efficiently solvable (Theorem 2.1).

Finally, when `pref-type` = acyclic, the manipulator once again votes $j \succ i$ whenever $m_{ij} = m_{ji} + 1$ and skips the comparison otherwise. Such a vote suffices if already acyclic.

[7]Theorem 5.2 in [29] states that Copeland$^{0.5}$-MANIPULATION (given $k \geq 1$ manipulators) is also in P when $\mathcal{A}$ = complete graph and `pref-type` = strict. The proof refers to a related problem called *microbribery* of Copeland$^\alpha$ elections, which was shown to be tractable only for $\alpha \in \{0,1\}$ but not for $\alpha = 0.5$ [30]. We fix this by showing that Copeland$^{0.5}$-MANIPULATION is in fact NP-complete when $\mathcal{A} \in$ {bipartite, complete graph} and `pref-type` = strict (Theorem 3.8), implying the same for the corresponding microbribery problem (of which the manipulation problem is a special case).

Otherwise, we claim that it suffices to run the greedy algorithm from Theorem 3.2 over the action space $\mathcal{A}$ restricted to the pairs with $m_{ij} = m_{ji} + 1$ (and skip all other comparisons). Indeed, notice that the Copeland scores of such pairs (i, j) can change by $(0, 0)$, $(0, 0)$ or $(-1, 0)$ for the comparisons $i \succ j$, skip or $j \succ i$ respectively. Any valid vote that skips such a comparison can therefore be replaced by a vote that makes a strict comparison instead. Thus, the restriction of any valid vote to such pairs has `pref-type` = strict+acyclic for which the greedy algorithm from Theorem 3.2 suffices.

Now consider Copeland^1-MANIPULATION. Here, the manipulator tries to *avoid ties* between non-distinguished candidates by mimicing the majority vote for pairs (i, j) where $m_{ij} = m_{ji} + 1$ and either skipping (if `pref-type` = unrestricted) or using the same S-ELIMINATION routine as above for the remaining pairs (if `pref-type` = strict). The case of `pref-type` = acyclic is also handled similarly.

Part (b): For Copeland$^{0.5}$-MANIPULATION and `pref-type` = unrestricted, the Copeland scores of a pair (i, j) with $m_{ij} = m_{ji} + 1$ can change by $(0, 0)$, $(0, 0)$ or $(-0.5, +0.5)$ for the comparisons $i \succ j$, skip or $j \succ i$ respectively. Similarly, for a pair (i, j) with $m_{ij} = m_{ji}$, the change can be $(+0.5, -0.5)$, $(0, 0)$ or $(-0.5, +0.5)$ respectively. Using the normalization scheme suggested in [21], this problem can be shown to be an instance of MIXED-ELIMINATION(S_1, S_2) with $S_1 = [(1, 0), (0, 1)]$ and $S_2 = [(2, 0), (1, 1), (0, 2)]$, which is efficiently solvable using the maximum flow formulation of [21].

When `pref-type` = acyclic, the vote constructed above suffices if already acyclic. Otherwise, any directed cycle can be completely replaced by an equivalent undirected cycle (i.e. skip votes). This is because an incoming and an outgoing edge for a vertex together amount to a simultaneous decrease and increase of 0.5, which is the same as 'no change in score' due to the undirected edges. □

Our next result shows that Copeland$^\alpha$-MANIPULATION is NP-complete for all $\alpha \in \mathbb{Q} \cap (0, 1) \setminus \{0.5\}$ when $\mathcal{A} \in$ {bipartite, complete graph} and `pref-type` $\in$ {acyclic, unrestricted} (Table 4). The reduction is from S-ELIMINATION with $S = [(1/\alpha, 0), (1, 1), (0, 1/\alpha)]$ which is NP-complete for all scoring systems except for $\alpha = 0.5$ (Theorem 2.1). We omit the proof due to space constraints and note that it closely follows the proof of Theorem 3.3.

THEOREM 3.7. Copeland$^\alpha$-MANIPULATION *is* NP-complete *for all* $\alpha \in \mathbb{Q} \cap (0, 1) \setminus \{0.5\}$ *when* $\mathcal{A} \in$ {bipartite, complete graph} *and* `pref-type` $\in$ {acyclic, unrestricted}.

Our final result shows that Copeland$^\alpha$-MANIPULATION is NP-complete for all $\alpha \in \mathbb{Q} \cap (0, 1)$ when the manipulator is required to provide strict preferences over a bipartite/complete graph. The reduction is from MIXED-ELIMINATION(S_1, S_2) with $S_1 = [(1, 0), (0, 1)]$ and $S_2 = [(1 - \alpha, 0), (0, \alpha)]$, which in turn can be shown to be NP-complete for all $\alpha \in \mathbb{Q} \cap (0, 1)$ via reduction from 3-D MATCHING following the template outlined in the proof of Theorem 3.4. We omit the proof due to space constraints.

THEOREM 3.8. Copeland$^\alpha$-MANIPULATION *is* NP-complete *for all* $\alpha \in \mathbb{Q} \cap (0, 1)$ *when* $\mathcal{A} \in$ {bipartite, complete graph} *and* `pref-type` = strict.

4. RELATED WORK

Manipulation under partial preferences: A number of recent studies have looked at the problem of manipulation of voting rules where voters provide partial preferences in the form of top-k choices or rankings with ties [31, 32, 33, 34]. However, most voting rules used in these studies crucially depend on the *position* of a candidate in each vote, making it difficult to generalize them to the pairwise setting. An exception is the Copeland$^\alpha$ family of rules, for which the coalitional manipulation problem has been studied in the context of weighted votes. Even here, a direct comparison with our setting is not possible because these papers study a more general problem than ours (namely, coalitional manipulation with weighted votes) over a strict subdomain of pairwise preferences (namely, partial rankings).

Possible and Necessary Winners: By far, the most common approach for dealing with incomplete preferences in the computational social choice literature is via *possible* and *necessary winners* [35, 36, 37, 38, 39, 40, 41]. A *possible* (respectively *necessary*) winner for an incomplete preference profile is a candidate chosen by the voting rule for at least one (respectively all) completion(s) of the partial votes. The notion of a completion (or extension) is crucial to these studies because the voting rules considered by them are well-defined only when either all votes are provided as complete rankings or when all pairs of candidates have been compared by each voter. Pairwise voting rules, on the other hand, deal with incomplete preferences *directly* without the need for extending each incomplete vote.

5. CONCLUDING REMARKS

We studied the problem of manipulation of voting rules in the model of pairwise preferences and showed results of both axiomatic and computational flavor. In particular, we provided a complete understanding of how the computational complexity of manipulating pairwise Borda (pBorda) rule and Copeland$^\alpha$ family of voting rules is influenced by the action space of the manipulator and the type of preference relation, up to the point of distinguishing the polynomial time cases from the NP-complete ones.

The most natural direction for future research would be to understand the complexity of manipulation in the pairwise preference model for other voting rules like PageRank [42], HodgeRank [11], Ranked Pairs, Schulze's rule [43] etc. An ambitious question in this context would be a complete classification of the complexity of manipulation (by a single voter) in the space of voting rules on pairwise preferences.

6. ACKNOWLEDGEMENTS

The authors thank the anonymous reviewers for their helpful comments. This work was supported in part by an Indo-US Joint Center grant (SA,AB), a DST INSPIRE Faculty grant [IFA12-ENG-31] (NM), DST Ramanujan Fellowship (SA), and NSF grant CCF-1525971 (AB). Part of this work was done when RV was visiting Carnegie Mellon University as part of a student visit under the Indo-US Joint Center for Advanced Research in Machine Learning, Game Theory and Optimization supported by the Indo-US Science and Technology Forum. RV also thanks Google and Microsoft Research for travel grants to present this work at AAMAS 2016.

REFERENCES

[1] Kenneth J Arrow, Amartya Sen, and Kotaro Suzumura. *Handbook of Social Choice & Welfare*, volume 2. Elsevier, 2010.

[2] A. Gibbard. Manipulation of Voting Schemes: a General Result. *Econometrica: Journal of the Econometric Society*, pages 587–601, 1973.

[3] M.A. Satterthwaite. Strategy-proofness and Arrow's Conditions: Existence and Correspondence Theorems for Voting Procedures and Social Welfare Functions. *Journal of Economic Theory (JET)*, 10(2):187–217, 1975.

[4] John J. Bartholdi III, Craig A. Tovey, and Michael A. Trick. The computational difficulty of manipulating an election. *Social Choice and Welfare*, 6(3):227–241, 1989.

[5] Piotr Faliszewski and Ariel D. Procaccia. AI's war on manipulation: Are we winning? *AI MAGAZINE*, 31(4):53–64, 2010.

[6] Nir Ailon. Aggregation of partial rankings, p-ratings and top-m lists. *Algorithmica*, 57(2):284–300, 2010.

[7] Alexander Reffgen. Generalizing the Gibbard–Satterthwaite theorem: partial preferences, the degree of manipulation, and multi-valuedness. *Social Choice and Welfare*, 37(1):39–59, 2011.

[8] Maria Silvia Pini, Francesca Rossi, Kristen Brent Venable, and Toby Walsh. Aggregating Partially Ordered Preferences. *Journal of Logic and Computation*, 19(3):475–502, June 2009.

[9] Edith Elkind and Nisarg Shah. Electing the Most Probable Without Eliminating the Irrational: Voting Over Intransitive Domains. In Nevin L. Zhang and Jin Tian, editors, *UAI*, pages 182–191. AUAI Press, 2014.

[10] Nir Ailon. An Active Learning Algorithm for Ranking from Pairwise Preferences with an Almost Optimal Query Complexity. *Journal of Machine Learning Research*, 13(1):137–164, January 2012.

[11] Xiaoye Jiang, Lek-Heng Lim, Yuan Yao, and Yinyu Ye. Statistical ranking and combinatorial Hodge theory. *Mathematical Programming*, 127(1):203–244, March 2011.

[12] Sahand Negahban, Sewoong Oh, and Devavrat Shah. Iterative ranking from pair-wise comparisons. In *Advances in Neural Information Processing Systems*, pages 2474–2482, 2012.

[13] Xi Chen, Paul N Bennett, Kevyn Collins-Thompson, and Eric Horvitz. Pairwise ranking aggregation in a crowdsourced setting. In *Proceedings of the sixth ACM International Conference on Web Search and Data Mining*, pages 193–202. ACM, 2013.

[14] Arun Rajkumar and Shivani Agarwal. A statistical convergence perspective of algorithms for rank aggregation from pairwise data. In *Proceedings of the 31st International Conference on Machine Learning*, pages 118–126, 2014.

[15] John J Bartholdi III and James B Orlin. Single transferable vote resists strategic voting. *Social Choice and Welfare*, 8(4):341–354, 1991.

[16] Lirong Xia, Michael Zuckerman, Ariel D Procaccia, Vincent Conitzer, and Jeffrey S Rosenschein. Complexity of Unweighted Coalitional Manipulation under Some Common Voting Rules. In *IJCAI*, volume 9, pages 348–352. Citeseer, 2009.

[17] Jessica Davies, Nina Narodytska, and Toby Walsh. Eliminating the Weakest Link: Making Manipulation Intractable? In *Proceedings of the 26th AAAI Conference on Artificial Intelligence*, pages 1333–1339. AAAI Press, 2012.

[18] Jessica Davies, George Katsirelos, Nina Narodytska, Toby Walsh, and Lirong Xia. Complexity of and algorithms for the manipulation of Borda, Nanson's and Baldwin's voting rules. *Artificial Intelligence*, 217:20–42, 2014.

[19] Piotr Faliszewski, Edith Hemaspaandra, and Henning Schnoor. Copeland voting: Ties matter. In *Proceedings of the 7th International Joint Conference on Autonomous Agents and Multiagent Systems-Volume 2*, pages 983–990. International Foundation for Autonomous Agents and Multiagent Systems, 2008.

[20] Benjamin L Schwartz. Possible winners in partially completed tournaments. *SIAM Review*, 8(3):302–308, 1966.

[21] Walter Kern and Daniël Paulusma. The Computational Complexity of the Elimination Problem in Generalized Sports Competitions. *Discrete Optimization*, 1(2):205–214, November 2004.

[22] Michael R. Garey and David S. Johnson. *Computers and Intractability: A Guide to the Theory of NP-Completeness*. W. H. Freeman & Co., New York, NY, USA, 1979.

[23] Miroslav Chlebík and Janka Chlebíková. Approximation Hardness for Small Occurrence Instances of NP-hard Problems. In *Algorithms and Complexity*, pages 152–164. Springer, 2003.

[24] Arunava Sen. Another direct proof of the Gibbard–Satterthwaite theorem. *Economics Letters*, 70(3):381–385, 2001.

[25] Navin Aswal, Shurojit Chatterji, and Arunava Sen. Dictatorial domains. *Economic Theory*, 22(1):45–62, 2003.

[26] Shin Sato. Circular domains. *Review of Economic Design*, 14(3-4):331–342, 2010.

[27] Anup Pramanik. Further results on dictatorial domains. *Social Choice and Welfare*, 45(2):379–398, 2015.

[28] John Duggan and Thomas Schwartz. Strategic manipulability without resoluteness or shared beliefs: Gibbard-Satterthwaite generalized. *Social Choice and Welfare*, 17(1):85–93, 2000.

[29] Piotr Faliszewski, Edith Hemaspaandra, and Henning Schnoor. Manipulation of Copeland Elections. In *Proceedings of the 9th International Conference on Autonomous Agents and Multiagent Systems: volume 1-Volume 1*, pages 367–374. International Foundation for Autonomous Agents and Multiagent Systems, 2010.

[30] Piotr Faliszewski, Edith Hemaspaandra, Lane A Hemaspaandra, and Jörg Rothe. Llull and Copeland voting computationally resist bribery and constructive control. *Journal of Artificial Intelligence Research*, pages 275–341, 2009.

[31] Nina Narodytska and Toby Walsh. The Computational Impact of Partial Votes on Strategic Voting. In

Proceedings of the 21st European Conference on Artificial Intelligence (ECAI), pages 657–662, 2014.

[32] Zack Fitzsimmons and Edith Hemaspaandra. Complexity of Manipulative Actions When Voting with Ties. In *Algorithmic Decision Theory*, pages 103–119. Springer, 2015.

[33] Vijay Menon and Kate Larson. Complexity of Manipulation in Elections with Top-truncated Ballots. *arXiv preprint arXiv:1505.05900*, 2015.

[34] Vijay Menon and Kate Larson. Reinstating Combinatorial Protections for Manipulation and Bribery in Single-Peaked and Nearly Single-Peaked Electorates. In *AAAI*, 2016.

[35] Kathrin Konczak and Jérôme Lang. Voting procedures with incomplete preferences. In *Proc. IJCAI-05 Multidisciplinary Workshop on Advances in Preference Handling*, volume 20, 2005.

[36] Toby Walsh. Uncertainty in Preference Elicitation and Aggregation. In *AAAI*, volume 7, pages 3–8, 2007.

[37] Nadja Betzler and Britta Dorn. Towards a dichotomy for the possible winner problem in elections based on scoring rules. *Journal of Computer and System Sciences*, 76(8):812–836, 2010.

[38] M. S. Pini, F. Rossi, K. B. Venable, and T. Walsh. Incompleteness and incomparability in preference aggregation: Complexity results. *Artificial Intelligence*, 175(7–8):1272–1289, May 2011.

[39] Dorothea Baumeister and Jörg Rothe. Taking the final step to a full dichotomy of the possible winner problem in pure scoring rules. *Information Processing Letters*, 112(5):186–190, February 2012.

[40] Serge Gaspers, Victor Naroditskiy, Nina Narodytska, and Toby Walsh. Possible and Necessary Winner Problem in Social Polls. In *Proceedings of the 2014 International Conference on Autonomous Agents and Multi-agent Systems*, pages 613–620. International Foundation for Autonomous Agents and Multiagent Systems, 2014.

[41] Lirong Xia and Vincent Conitzer. Determining Possible and Necessary Winners under Common Voting Rules Given Partial Orders. *Journal of Artificial Intelligence Research*, pages 25–67, 2011.

[42] Sergey Brin and Lawrence Page. Reprint of: The anatomy of a large-scale hypertextual web search engine. *Computer networks*, 56(18):3825–3833, 2012.

[43] David C Parkes and Lirong Xia. A complexity-of-strategic-behavior comparison between Schulze's rule and ranked pairs. In *Proceedings of the 26th AAAI Conference on Artificial Intelligence (AAAI'12)*. American Association for Artificial Intelligence, 2012.

The Echo Chamber: Strategic Voting and Homophily in Social Networks

Alan Tsang
Cheriton School of Computer Science
University of Waterloo
Waterloo, Ontario, Canada
akhtsang@uwaterloo.ca

Kate Larson
Cheriton School of Computer Science
University of Waterloo
Waterloo, Ontario, Canada
klarson@uwaterloo.ca

ABSTRACT

We propose a model where voters are embedded in a social network. Each voter observes the ballots of her neighbors in the network, from which she infers the likely outcome of the election. Each voter may then revise her vote strategically, to maximize her expected utility. Our work focuses on plurality voting, where strategic voting is a major concern. We show that in practice, strategization increases with voter knowledge, yet can improve the social welfare for the population. Real world social networks exhibit a property called homophily; sometimes called "The Echo Chamber Effect", which is the tendency for friends to have similar ideologies. We find that homophily dampens the benefits of strategization, and correspondingly, lowers the frequency of its occurrence. This effect may contribute to the low number of strategic voters observed in real world elections. Additionally, strategization may lead to the elimination of less popular candidates, as voters revise their votes to less preferred but more hopeful candidates. This phenomenon is known as Duverger's Law in political science, and we show that it does not hold in certain network structures.

Categories and Subject Descriptors

I.2.11 [**Artificial Intelligence**]: Distributed Artificial Intelligence—*Multiagent Systems*; J.4 [**Computer Applications**]: Social and Behavioral Sciences—*Sociology*

General Terms

Economics,Experimentation

Keywords

Behavioral game theory, Social choice theory, Social simulation, Emergent behavior, Iterative voting

1. INTRODUCTION

The last decade has seen tremendous growth in the popularity of social networks in both popular media and research communities. These networks represent a complex web of interactions between both individuals and institutions. They capture relationships and social structures that define communities both niche and vast. The relationships within these communities hold the key to how information flows within the network, and ultimately, how individuals' actions may be influenced by each other and by the institutions whom they respect.

Voting is a method of social choice where a community elicits the personal preferences of individuals to conduct collective decision making. A major concern in voting systems is manipulation via strategic voting. This happens when voters benefit from casting a ballot that does not reflect their true preferences; while this may be beneficial for the voter, it misinforms the community on the needs of its constituents. In order for voters to manipulate successfully, they must have some knowledge regarding the outcome of the election. One reasonable model is to view the election as a series of rounds, where voters put forth tentative ballots that may be continually revised; this is called Iterative Voting, which assumes voters have complete information on the ballots of all other voters [17]. In a social network, however, voters are restricted to observing only the actions of their neighbors. Each voter must form a model of the likely outcome of the election based on this incomplete information, and use this model to inform their actions. This assumption may appear unrealistic at first glance. Since, after all, one does not simply make decisions based on a sampling of opinions from Facebook friends. However, our use of the term social network extends beyond relationships in online social media platforms, and also include experts and associates, media outlets, and any other source of opinion and information that may contribute to the decision making process.

Real world social networks exhibit a number of interesting properties that may impact the strategic behavior of its voters, and should be considered in any realistic model. Of particular interest to our voting model is a property called *homophily*: the tendency for people to connect and socialize with those sharing similar characteristics, beliefs and values. This concept dates as far back as Plato, who wrote in *Phaedrus* that "similarity begets friendship". In their seminal work, McPherson, Smith-Lovin and Cook offer a survey of evidence that adults, in particular, preferentially associate with those of similar political persuasions [15]. This effect is not only limited to individuals. Hargittai, Gallo and Kane examined the link relationships between sites of top conservative and liberal bloggers discussing political issues, and found homophily to be prevalent; i.e. sites were much more likely to discuss and reference each other when they shared political views. Even more importantly, upon examining the context of links between conservative and liberal blogs, they found that fully half of them were embedded with "straw-man" arguments that reinforced the political position of the author by distorting the opposition's position [12]. This is especially relevant

Appears in: *Proceedings of the 15th International Conference on Autonomous Agents and Multiagent Systems (AAMAS 2016), J. Thangarajah, K. Tuyls, C. Jonker, S. Marsella (eds.), May 9–13, 2016, Singapore.*

to our model because voters derive information about the election from their neighbors in the social network. A homophily of opinions can lead to the so called *Echo Chamber Effect*, where a voter is surrounded by associates that share similar beliefs, reinforcing its validity regardless of its merit.

In this paper, we present a behavioral model of voters embedded in a social network. Voting occurs in successive rounds during which voters may alter their ballots. Voters can observe only the ballots of their friends in the social network. Each voter assumes her friends are representative of the wider population, and will vote strategically to maximize her own expected utility. We explore the behavior of this model on a variety of random graph networks, including ones that exhibit homophily. We focus on using plurality as our voting system. While strategization is a major concern in plurality, we find that it improves the social welfare compared to truthful voting. We also find evidence of the Echo Chamber Effect in our data: interestingly, it lowers social welfare by decreasing the amount of strategization that occurs. This may explain the relatively low percentage of voters that strategize in many real world elections (for example, in [3] and [11]). Finally, while our model converges quickly in practice, we show a counterexample where voters never converge to a stable state.

2. MODEL

Let $V = \{1, 2, \ldots n\}$ represent our set of voters. They are embedded in a social network, represented as a simple, directed graph $G = (V, E)$. We adopt the convention that a directed edge $(i, j) \in E$ denotes that voter i observes voter j and as such, j's actions may influence i. An edge may represent communication between friends, a leader's influence on followers, or patronage of media and news platforms. Let $\mathcal{N}(i)$ denote the set of voters observed by i; i.e. $\mathcal{N}(i)$ is the out-neighbors of i.

Let $C = \{c_1, c_2, \ldots c_m\}$ represent the set of available candidates. Let $\mathcal{F}$ be the voting function used to aggregate those ballots to choose a single winner; it may or may not be deterministic. The choice of $\mathcal{F}$ will define a set of valid ballots that can be submitted by voters; let us denote this set as $\mathcal{B}$.

The voting process proceeds in rounds. In round t, each voter $i \in V$ submits a ballot $b_i^{(t)} \in \mathcal{B}$. The voter formulates this ballot as a response $R_i : \mathcal{B}^{|\mathcal{N}(i)|} \to \mathcal{B}$ based on her observations of her friends – i.e. the previous ballots of her out-neighbors. These rounds may represent a series of preliminary polls leading up to the final election. We assume all voters begin with the truthful ballot.[1] Voting continues until no agents choose to revise their ballots, whereupon the winner is decided by the voting function $\mathcal{F}$. When no voters wish to deviate from their current ballot, the system has converged to an equilibrium. If it reaches this state, we say the system is stable.

2.1 Model of Voters

Models of voters in multiagent systems literature are divided between those utilizing ordinal preferences (where only the ordering of outcomes matter) and cardinal preferences (where outcomes are associated with utility values).[2] While each model has its own merits, we choose the latter model because our voters infer and weight the probabilities of the different outcomes, and act rationally to maximize expected utility.

Formally, voters derive utility based on the candidate that is elected by $\mathcal{F}$. Each candidate $c_i \in C$ advocates a position $p(c_i)$ in some domain $\mathcal{D}$ that is common knowledge. Each voter i favors a position $p_i \in \mathcal{D}$ known only to herself. If $\hat{c}$ is the winning candidate elected by $\mathcal{F}$, then a utility function $u_i(p_i, p(\hat{c})) : \mathcal{D} \times \mathcal{D} \to \mathbb{R}$ determines the value of this outcome.

For the purpose of this paper, $\mathcal{D}$ are the integers from 0 to 100 (inclusive), and preferences are single-peaked. This allows us to benchmark our result to previous work (e.g. [7, 8]); this one dimensional scale is also commonly used in political science literature to represent the left-right political spectrum [2, 13]. We assume the utility a voter derives from the outcome decreases with the square of the distance between her favored position p_i and the winner's advocated position $\hat{p}$:

$$u_i(p_i, \hat{p}) = -|p_i - \hat{p}|^2.$$

For brevity, we write u_i to imply $u_i(p_i, \hat{p})$ where the position of the candidate c_i and the position favored by the agent is clear from the context. Throughout this paper, we will refer to the social welfare of the elected outcome. If $\hat{p}$ is the position of the elected candidate, the social welfare $SW(V)$ is the sum of the utilities for all voters for that outcome:

$$SW(V) = \sum_i u_i(p_i, \hat{p}).$$

2.2 Response Model

Each voter assumes her friends are representative of the wider population. If a ballot b is observed in a fraction f of her friends, then she assumes any voter within the network will submit ballot b with probability f.

We formally specify the response model for plurality voting for simplicity, but it can be adapted to any voting system with finite $|\mathcal{B}|$. This means each ballot is an individual candidate, and $\mathcal{B} = C$. Let $(s_1, s_2, \ldots s_m)$ represent the number of voters in $\mathcal{N}(i)$ voting for candidates $(c_1, c_2, \ldots c_m)$. Voter i will then assume each voter (other than herself) in the network will support candidate c_x with probability $\frac{s_x+1}{S}$, where S is a normalizing constant to make the probabilities sum to 1. The +1 is a Laplace smoothing, and is necessary to ensure that all ballots remain possible. This means the ballots from the rest of the electorate follow a multinomial distribution with support $\mathbf{s} = (\frac{s_1+1}{S}, \frac{s_2+1}{S}, \ldots \frac{s_m+1}{S})$, $S = |\mathcal{N}(i)| + m$.

We can calculate the probability of any outcome of the election by using the multinomial distribution. Let the vector $\mathbf{b} = (b_1, b_2, \ldots b_m)$ denote the outcome where the remaining $n-1$ voters in the network contribute b_i ballots supporting candidate c_i. The probability of this outcome is calculated as follows:

$$Pr(\mathbf{b}; n-1; \mathbf{s}) = \frac{(n-1)!}{b_1! b_2! \ldots b_m!} \frac{\prod_{i=1}^{m} (s_i + 1)^{b_i}}{S^{n-1}}$$

With complete information, a rational voter only profits from casting a ballot when it is pivotal. With incomplete information, however, our voter must calculate the probability of each winning tie, and cast a ballot that, in expectation, will break ties to maximize her utility. For simplicity, we assume that winning ties between 3 or more candidates are such remote possibilities that they functionally have probability zero. Then, let $T(y, x)$ be the probability of a winning tie between candidates x and y, calculated by enumerating all possible such ties and summing their probabilities. Additionally, we also consider all near-ties, where the addition of one vote to candidate x will cause a winning tie with y; let $\widetilde{T}(y, x)$ be the probability of this outcome.

[1] Or *a* truthful ballot, depending on the voting system

[2] Cardinal utility models are used commonly in the literature, for example in Random Utility Theory [1].

Finally, voter i revises her ballot to support the candidate x with the maximal marginal gain in expected utility $\mathcal{C}_x$, calculated below. If a voter observes no other ballots (i.e. $\mathcal{N}(i) = \emptyset$), her ballot remains fixed.

We consider two tie-breaking rules: probabilistic and lexicographic tie-breaking. Below is a modification of prospective ratings introduced by Myerson and Weber [18], for unbiased probabilistic tie-breaking and risk-neutral voters:

$$\mathcal{C}_x = \sum_{y=1}^{m} \left(\tfrac{1}{2}T(y,x)(u_x - u_y) + \tfrac{1}{2}\widetilde{T}(y,x)(u_x - u_y) \right)$$

An analogous modification exists for lexicographic tie-breaking, where $\mathbf{1}_{x<y}$ is an indicator variable with $\mathbf{1}_{x<y} = 1$ when x lexicographically precedes y, and 0 otherwise:

$$\mathcal{C}_x = \sum_{y=1}^{m} \left(\mathbf{1}_{x>y}T(y,x)(u_x - u_y) + \mathbf{1}_{x<y}\widetilde{T}(y,x)(u_x - u_y) \right)$$

2.3 Sequential vs Simultaneous Updates

We consider two methods for scheduling when opinion updates take place: sequential and simultaneous. In sequential updates, voters are updated one at a time in a fixed order in each round, and they observe the most up-to-date ballots of their neighbors (which may be updated earlier in the current round, or in the previous round). In contrast, in simultaneous updates, all voters respond simultaneously to observed ballots from the previous round.

2.4 Graph Models

We will study the behavior of strategic voters within randomly generated networks. Two important structural characteristics of real world social networks are that they are *small-world* and *scale-free*.

In small-world networks, the average distance between any two vertices in the graph grows as a logarithm of the number of vertices. We expect information to travel quickly through small-world networks, which may have an effect on the aggregate strategic behavior of the population.

Real world networks are often scale-free, which means they are comprised of a handful of highly-connected hubs and many sparsely connected vertices. Highly-connected hubs may represent popular public figures or mass media outlets. In strategic voting, they may wield considerable influence within the network.

We consider 4 graph models in our paper: the Erdös-Renyi (ER) and the Barabási-Albert (BA) random graph models, as well as modifications of these models to incorporate homophily.

Erdös-Renyi is a random graph model that incorporates minimal assumptions. Given density parameter pr, a directed edge connects any vertices i and j with probability pr. Edge (i, j) is added with probability independent of the addition of (j, i). Erdös-Renyi random graphs are small-world, but not scale-free.

We modify the Erdös-Renyi model to incorporate homophily (hER) by multiplying the probability of adding edge (i, j) by the homophily factor $h = 1 - |p_i - p_j|/100$. Two voters having the same private position have the largest probability of being connected, while voters having diverging positions are decreasingly likely to be connected. Note that the edge density of the resulting graph is decreased as a result of this change.

Barabási-Albert is a preferential attachment model that generates scale-free networks. These networks have many properties similar to human generated social networks. Given attachment parameter d, each new vertex is added to the graph connected to d existing vertices. These vertices are selected randomly, with probability proportional to the out-degree of the vertex. In this model, when a new vertex i is connected to j, we add *both* the edges (i, j) and (j, i) to E. This ensures information has the opportunity to flow throughout the network. Barabási-Albert random graphs are both small-world and scale-free.

We incorporate homophily into the Barabási-Albert model (hBA) by multiplying the likelihood of an existing vertex by the same homophily factor h described above. Note that the edge density of the resulting graph is *unchanged*.

Figure 1 shows an undirected example from each (non-homophilic) random graph model. Both graphs have 40 vertices and are parameterized so that each node has average degree 3.

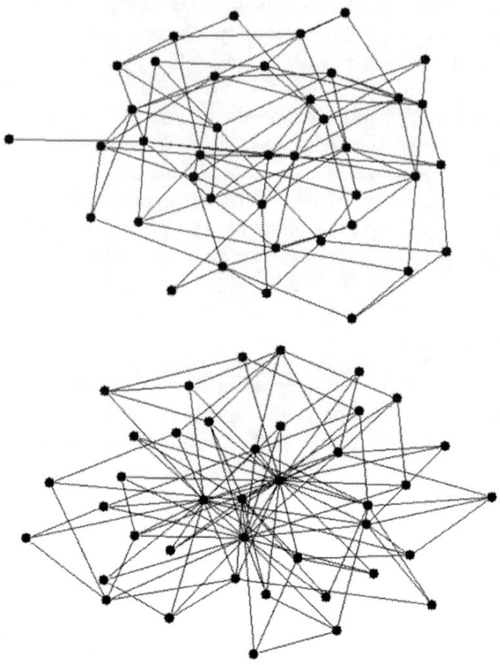

Figure 1: ***Example of an ER random graph (top) and a BA random graph (bottom).***

3. EXPERIMENTAL DESIGN

Our investigation will focus only on the plurality voting rule. We first investigate the effects of the two tie-breaking schemes and update methods. As with Clough's investigation [7], we initialize a population of 169 voters in the baseline graph models: ER and BA. For tractability, we limit ourselves to 3- and 4-candidate scenarios. The positions of candidates and voters are drawn independently, uniformly at random from the interval [0,100]. The parameters of the graph models are chosen so that the resulting conditions have average out-degree approximately 8, 12, 16, 20, 24, and 28.

In our second set of experiments, we investigate the effects of graph structure and homophily on the behavior of voters and the social welfare of the selected outcome. We focus the experiment on sequential updates and lexicographic tie-breaking, but extend the conditions to include all four graph models. Once again, parameters are chosen to produce the same set of average out-degrees. Note that the density parameter pr of hER graphs must be doubled to ensure sufficient edge density.

The simulation is written in the D programming language, and compiled using using DMD32 D Compiler v2.067.1 on a 64-bit Windows 7 machine. We limit each election to a maximum of 25

Update/Tie	% Strat	Updates	Avg PoH	Avg PoS
Erdös-Renyi Random Graph				
seq / lex	0.268	57.9	1.2312	1.0795
seq / prob	0.267	57.2	1.2287	1.0776
sim / lex	0.277	78.6	1.2523	1.0689
Barabási-Albert Random Graph				
seq / lex	0.243	44.9	1.2128	1.0866
seq / prob	0.235	43.3	1.2133	1.1002
sim / lex	0.252	68.6	1.2149	1.0885

Table 1: ***Effects of update and tie-breaking methods (ER and BA graphs with m=4). The metrics measured are the percentage of agents casting strategic ballots, the number of updates before convergence, the Price of Honesty and the Price of Stability.***

rounds, though this limit is never reached. Each data point in the first set of experiments is the average of 400 replications; each data point in the second set is the average of 800 replications.

4. RESULTS

We define several metrics measured across our experiments. The **Price of Honesty** (PoH) is defined as the ratio of social welfare of the truthful outcome to that of the strategic outcome.[3] Since both utility values are negative, the larger the PoH, the more costly the truthful outcome is, relative to the strategic outcome. Likewise, we define the **Price of Stability** (PoS) is the ratio of social welfare of the strategic outcome to that of the optimal outcome.[4] We also measure the percentage of voters that engage in strategic play – i.e. the fraction of voters who converge to a ballot that is not truthful – as well as the average number of updates required to reach stability.

Table 1 summarizes these four metrics measured on ER and BA graphs ($m = 4$). Within each graph type, there is little change in the amount of strategization, PoH nor PoS across the three conditions. Despite reaching a similar amount of strategization, simultaneous updates requires a larger number of updates to reach stability. By comparison, the differences between strategization, PoH and PoS is much larger between the two graph types. The same pattern appears in each of the other conditions. We conclude that neither the update methods nor tie-breaking mechanism has a significant impact on the behavior of the voters or the result of the voting process.

Next, we move to the second series of experiments, and the central findings of the paper. We compare the four aforementioned metrics across the four graph models. Strategization is a major concern in elections using the plurality system. However, we show in our experiments that it actually improves the overall social welfare of the elected outcome. Throughout our experiment (> 4800 total trials), we found consistently that the average PoH for each condition is greater than 1; that is, in expectation, the candidate selected by strategic voting achieves a higher social welfare than that selected by truthful voting.

As one might expect, the amount of strategic play increases as voters gain access to more information as connectivity increases (see Figure 2). However, this gain is asymptotic and the ceiling of strategic play is reached relatively quickly. Interestingly, the ceiling is lower in graphs with homophily than than those without. The rate at which strategic play increases (with edge density) is dependent on the graph type, with ER graphs reaching saturation more quickly than BA graphs.

Figure 3 shows the Price of Honesty and the Price of Stability under the different graph models.[5] We include only $m = 4$ plots, but the same qualitative trends occur for $m = 3$. Here we see a possible explanation for the lower strategic ceiling observed in homophilic graphs: it is simply less profitable. The PoH is consistently lower than PoS in these graphs, though they begin to converge at higher edge densities. That is, in these graphs, the social welfare of the strategic outcome is closer to that of the truthful outcome than the optimal outcome.

As strategization occurs in plurality elections, voters begin to abandon less promising candidates for the likely winners, even if they are less preferable. The net result of this behavior is that a multi-party system using the plurality rule will eventually devolve into a race between the two front running candidates. This tendency of plurality favoring 2-party systems is observable in electoral systems around the world, and is known in political science as Duverger's Law [10].[6]

The consistency of Duverger's Law is measured by the SF Ratio: the ratio of support for the third and second place candidates [9].[7] Complete agreement with Duverger's Law would mean no voters will "waste" their votes on lower ranking candidates, and will only cast their ballots in favor of the two leading candidates. This would be reflected by an SR Ratio of 0. Figure 4 shows the distribution of SF Ratios under different graph models, at the condition with the lowest edge density conditions (average out-degree 8). Duverger's Law would predict that the distribution of SF Ratios be concentrated as a sharp peak near 0. In both 3- and 4- candidate elections, there is little agreement to Duverger's Law in most graphs, with fewer than 50% of the instances exhibiting an SR Ratio of less than 0.1 (i.e. the third place candidate enjoy less than 10% of the support of the second place candidate). If hER graphs are excluded, at least 50% account for those instances with SF Ratio of at least 0.2. It is interesting to note that in both 3- and 4- candidate elections, hER graphs standout as showing the most agreement to Duverger's Law. Notably, the dominant feature of these graphs is homophily, suggesting it helps voters enact Duverger's Law, even when little information is available to an individual voter.

Figure 5 is a histogram showing the distributions of SF Ratios for ER and hER models, for the three lowest connectivity settings. The bars in blue represents the same data as presented in Figure 4, which is gathered at the lowest connectivity setting (with average out-degree 8). The orange bars shows the distribution of SF Ratios in graphs with average out-degree 12. Here, it is clear that the distribution peaks at 0, and Duverger's Law is rapidly being restored due to an increase of information available to individual voters. In approximately 65% of the hER instances, the SF Ratio is below 0.1; in the ER graphs, the percentage increases to 80%. The trend continues as we increase the connectivity, as shown in the average out-degree 16 condition (shown as gray bars).

[3]There are various names given for this metric: for example, "improvement in social welfare over truthful" in [16], and "dynamic price of anarchy" in [4]

[4]Since the voter response is deterministic, we may view the outcome of the strategic voting process as unique, and this definition parallels the usual definition of Price of Stability or Price of Anarchy. If viewed as an online algorithm, this measure is analogous to the competitive ratio.

[5]Mann-Whitney $U < 303,000$, $n_1 = n_2 = 800$, $P < 0.01$, one-tailed, for all conditions in Figure 3, with two exceptions: ER (avg out-degree 8), and BA (avg out-degree 12). We obtain similar results of statistical significance on $m = 3$ conditions.

[6]Canada and India are notable exceptions to this rule.

[7]The term SF Ratio refers to the second and first runner-up candidates.

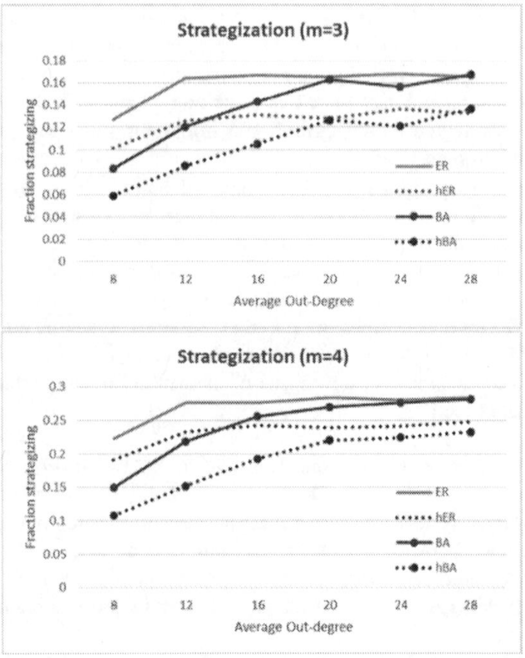

Figure 2: ***Fraction of agents strategizing (3- and 4-candidates). Note the different scales in the vertical axis.***

5. CONVERGENCE

In our empirical simulation, all trials converge to stability, and do so quickly. It is natural to ask whether the response model is guaranteed to reach an equilibrium in either the sequential or the simultaneous settings. Figure 6 sketches an undirected social network with preferences such that the voter responses result in a cycling of ballots. In this network, there are three candidates, denoted A, B, and C. The vertices of the graph are divided into four groups, labelled V_1, V_2, A and B. A and B are cliques on n' vertices; all voters in A have candidate A as their top preference, and correspondingly with B, for candidate B. V_1 contains n' vertices; each has preference $A \succ B \succ C$, and is connected to every vertex in B and V_2, but not to each other. Similarly, V_2 contains n' vertices; each has preference $C \succ A \succ B$, and is connected to every vertex in A and V_1, but not to each other. n' may be some large number, such as 10.

It is easy to see that there exist positions for the candidates such that none of the vertices in A or B will change their ballots. Each sees strong support for her favorite candidate, which ensures the most likely winning ties will involve that candidate.

Let us consider the sequential update process that updates the vertices of V_1 before V_2. Each agent votes truthfully in the first round. In the second round, each vertex in V_1 sees n' supporters for B and C, and infers that the outcome will be a likely tie between those two candidates; each vertex switches support to their second-choice B. Each vertex in V_2 then observes a tie between A and B, and also switches to their second-choice: A. One can then verify that these fickle changes are reversed in the third round, with all voters in V_1 and V_2 reverting back to their truthful choices; thus, the cycle perpetuates.[8]

[8]A number of positions for our candidates and voter blocs will produce this behavior. For example, consider candidates A, B, and C having positions 10, 9, 12 respectively. Let blocs B and V_1 prefer position 10 (therefore prefers candidates $A \succ B \succ C$), and A and V_2 prefer position 12 (prefers candidates $C \succ A \succ B$).

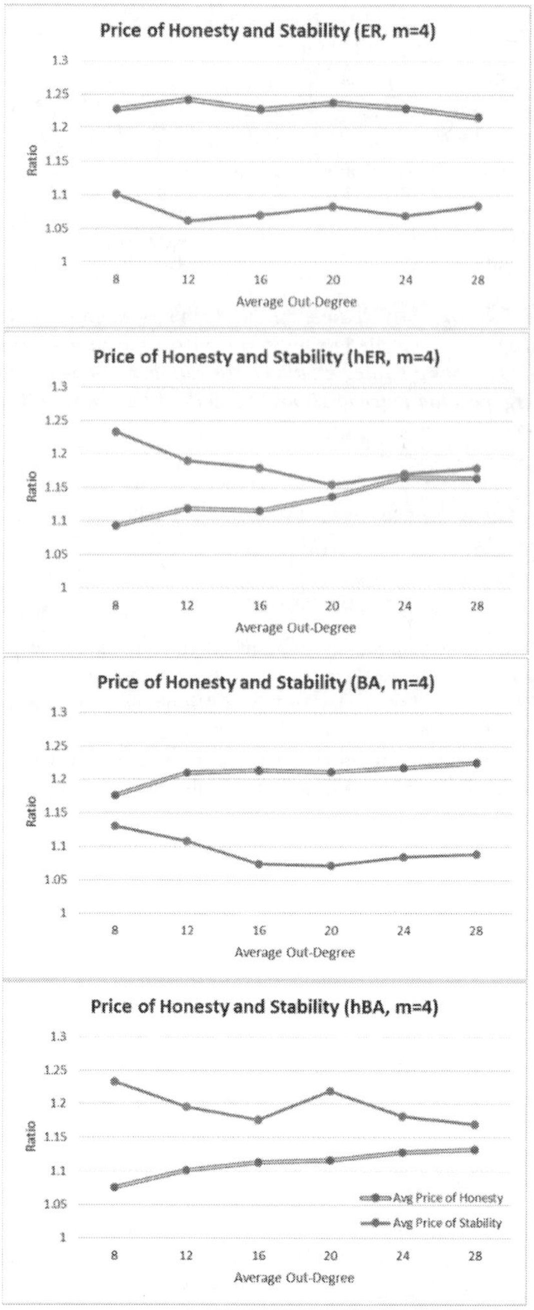

Figure 3: ***Price of Honesty and Stability.***

The same counterexample works for the simultaneous update process, with V_1 and V_2 changing in alternate rounds.

Contrast this result with convergence results in the related model of Iterative Voting. By comparison, Iterative Voting occurs in the absence of a social network, where all ballots are common knowledge. Voters iteratively revise their ballots only if it alters the outcome to their benefit. Meir et al. showed that Iterative Voting converges under plurality when voters respond one-at-a-time, but not when they update simultaneously. [17] Lev and Rosenschein demonstrated a similar result for veto, and showed that there is no guarantee of convergence in other scoring rules. [14]

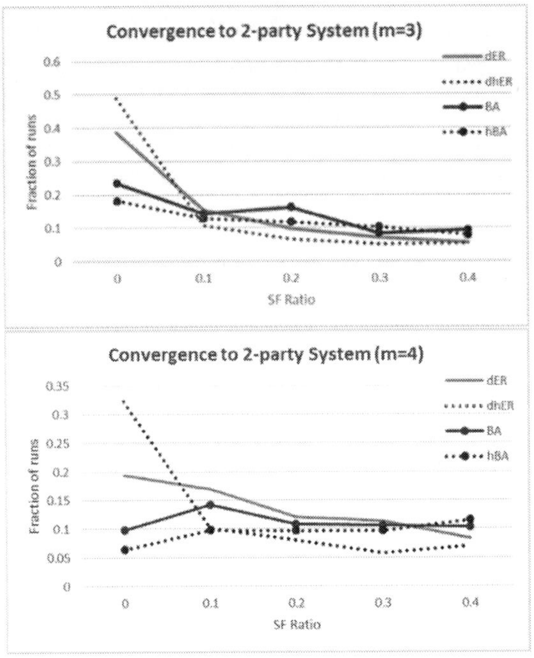

Figure 4: ***Degree of convergence to a 2-candidate system, measured as the SF ratio (3- and 4-candidates). Note the different scales in the vertical axis.***

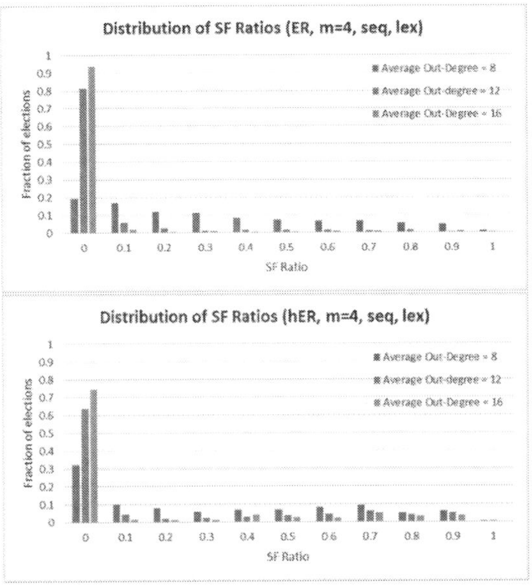

Figure 5: ***Distribution of SF Ratios show the degree with which results from each graph model conform to Duverger's Law.***

6. DISCUSSION

While we have obtained empirical results for our model, the question remains as to how well it generalizes to real world scenarios. As was alluded to in the Introduction, the social network we depict with our model is a general social network. The neighbors in the network describe not merely "Facebook friends", but include all sources of information that may be considered by a voter in deciding on her ballot. This may include close friends, trusted confidants and knowledgeable associates, but will also news feeds, political blogs, and subscriptions to any number of popular media outlets. Such institutions acts as highly-connected nodes in the social network, much like hubs in Barabási-Albert random graphs. Further, as is shown in Hargittai, Gallo and Kane [12], even such social institutions are not immune to the same homophily exhibited in people.

The successive rounds of voter revision in our model represents the preliminary period preceding an election where voters may discuss and revise their opinions. In the real world, this is often accompanied by a series of preliminary polls leading up to the main election. These polls can be a major factor in strategic voting. Such polls are comprised of (tentative) ballots sampled from a random subset of the population. This is exactly the relationship captured by the (non-homophilic) Erdös-Renyi random graphs, where each voter may view the ballots of a number of other voters sampled uniformly, independently at random from the population.

With homophily being such an intrinsic property of real world networks, it is interesting to note that the graph depicted in Figure 6 shows a very low degree of homophily (for vertices in V_1 and V_2). This lack of homophily is necessary for the counterexample to function. Voters that are connected to likeminded voters are less likely to change their votes away from their truthful ballot. They observe many other voters declaring the same ballot, and therefore their favorite candidate is very likely to participate in winning ties. In fact, a careful analysis of the graph structure of Figure 6 reveals what is needed to cause a faithful voter to vote strategically: they view their own position as hopeless, and must be convinced to "pitch in" to resolve a close race between two less-favored candidates. This is in agreement with observations of political elections, such as the empirical study conducted in Cain [5].

This observation may give insights as to why there is less strategic voting in the presence of homophily, and also why the strategic outcome is (comparatively) less profitable. When voters are surrounded with those of similar opinions, it creates an Echo Chamber Effect where they view their own position as being more widely supported than it is. It causes them to be further entrenched in their current position, and they require a larger amount of conflicting evidence to change their minds. The effect causes a voter to have a harder time discerning whether their own position is in the minority, and prevents them from shifting to a more strategic choice. This, as it turns out, has a net negative effect on the social welfare of the elected outcome. Moreover, this effect may explain the relatively small number of strategic voters observed in real world elections (for example, in [3] and [11]): it is not that few voters are strategic, it may be that many voters fail to recognize the strategic opportunity due to their Echo Chamber.

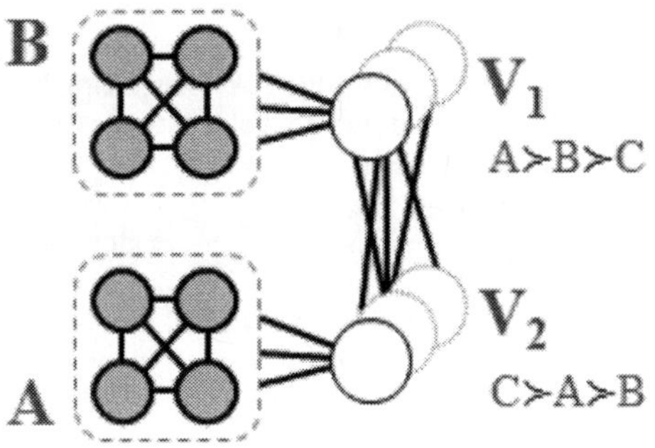

Figure 6: ***Voters need not converge to stability.***

7. RELATED WORKS

A cornerstone of our model is the Knowledge Graph model [6]. In their paper, the authors propose a general framework for limiting voting knowledge, restricting each voters' observations to their neighbors in the knowledge graph. However, they do not define any response behavior for individual voters, nor explore the aggregate behavior of the population.

The behavioral nature of our voter model can be attributed to Myerson and Weber [18]. In this paper, the authors propose the concept of a Voting Equilibrium, a refinement of the Nash Equilibrium. Motivated by the process of political elections, they consider that strategic voters may reason on the result of a preliminary poll by considering the tie-probabilities between the various candidates. Then, if strategic voting produces results consistent with the original poll, we are said to be at a Voting Equilibrium.

Clough presented an early political science exploration of strategic voting in social networks [7, 8]. However, the network she uses is a simple 13×13 grid-based undirected graph on 169 nodes, which is neither small-world nor scale-free. Each voter responds by considering only tie-probabilities, while our model considers all pivotal cases under different tie-breaking rules. Her work focuses solely on investigating Duverger's Law. Her finds parallel ours: SF Ratios drop dramatically when going from 28 to 8 neighbors. Unfortunately, her model does not offer any finer levels of granularity for investigating this behavior.

A more recent line of inquiry inspired by Myerson and Weber is Iterative Voting [17]. As has been mentioned several times already, Iterative Voting proceeds in rounds. In each round, voters best respond to the previous ballots, either simultaneously or sequentially. Voters have complete information on all ballots, and revise their ballots only when it will change the outcome. Unlike our model, Iterative Voting is guaranteed to converge from a truthful state under plurality and veto [17, 14]. Whereas the update method and the tie-breaking rule were important to their results, we find that our model is robust against changes in these criteria. Branzei et al. have also investigated social welfare of iterative voting under different voting systems (Plurality, Veto and Borda) [4]. They define the Dynamic Price of Anarchy (DPoA) to be the worst case ratio between the social welfare of the winner elected under truthful voting versus strategic voting. This is similar to our definition for Price of Honesty. Since their model does not operate under a social network, they are able to compute analytical bounds for DPoA under different voting rules. Similar to us, they show that strategic voting improves the elected outcome under Plurality.

Iterative voting has been applied to social networks only very recently in Sina et al. [20], which focuses on manipulation by a chair under plurality voting. Our model differs from Sina et al.'s in that our voters individually infer the likely outcomes of the election based on their limited information, and always act upon this information (to maximize their expected utility based on tie-probabilities). By contrast, in the Iterative Voting model applied by Sina et al., agents only choose to revise their vote when they observe an exact pivotal condition in their neighborhood.

Reijngoud and Endriss have also modeled how voters might respond to information from a series of polls [19]. In their paper, they consider different mechanisms (poll information functions, or PIFs) for summarizing the information present in the current ballot profile. They analyze the susceptibility and immunity to manipulation of different voting rules and PIFs. They also propose models for strategic agents with ordinal preferences, and analyze the performance of different voting rules in the presence of these agents.

8. CONCLUSION AND FUTURE WORK

In this paper, we proposed a model of strategic voting on social networks, based on a natural assumption on the part of voters that their friends are representative of the population. We show that strategization leads to improved social welfare of the elected outcome in all conditions. Network structure has an effect on the social welfare of the elected outcome. However, as edge density increases, the amount of information available to each voter also increases, and the number of strategic voters quickly saturate at a ceiling. The ceiling is independent of graph structure, but highly dependent on homophily.

It is this network homophily that causes the Echo Chamber Effect. This may offer insight on why a relatively low number of voters are strategic in real world elections. When surrounded by others with similar opinions, voters do not see an opportunity or even a need to strategize, even when their position holds little merit. This ends up hurting social welfare of the elected result.

As Figure 6 demonstrates, our model is not guaranteed to converge to stability. However, stability is reached relatively quickly in practice. In our simulations, no instances used more than 10 rounds to reach stability. It is unclear why this is the case, and may be a direction for future work. Are such cyclic instances rare? Under what conditions can we guarantee stability? Are such conditions natural to human networks?

Another natural question to ask is, how susceptible to manipulation are voters on a social network? Will voter strategization hinder or amplify the effects of manipulations? If candidates have knowledge of the social network, what strategies may they take to improve their own odds?

Finally, it would be interesting to extend this framework to other, more interesting voting systems. Duverger's Law applies only to plurality, so we expect to see less convergence to 2-party systems when using other voting rules. What effects will this have on strategization and social welfare? Tie-probability modeling for other systems remains an exciting open question.

REFERENCES

[1] H. Azari, D. Parks, and L. Xia. Random utility theory for social choice. In *Advances in Neural Information Processing Systems*, pages 126–134, 2012.

[2] D. Black. On the rationale of group decision-making. *The Journal of Political Economy*, pages 23–34, 1948.

[3] A. Blais. Why is there so little strategic voting in Canadian plurality rule elections? *Political Studies*, 50(3):445–454, 2002.

[4] S. Brânzei, I. Caragiannis, J. Morgenstern, and A. Procaccia. How bad is selfish voting? In *Twenty-Seventh AAAI Conference on Artificial Intelligence*, 2013.

[5] B. E. Cain. Strategic voting in Britain. *American Journal of Political Science*, pages 639–655, 1978.

[6] S. Chopra, E. Pacuit, and R. Parikh. Knowledge-theoretic properties of strategic voting. In *Logics in Artificial Intelligence*, pages 18–30. Springer, 2004.

[7] E. Clough. Strategic voting under conditions of uncertainty: A re-evaluation of Duverger's law. *British Journal of Political Science*, 37(02):313–332, 2007.

[8] E. Clough. Talking locally and voting globally Duverger's law and homogeneous discussion networks. *Political Research Quarterly*, 60(3):531–540, 2007.

[9] G. W. Cox. *Making votes count: Strategic coordination in the world's electoral systems*, volume 7. Cambridge Univ Press, 1997.

[10] M. Duverger. Factors in a two-party and multiparty system. *Party Politics and Pressure Groups*, pages 23–32, 1972.

[11] D. S. Felsenthal and A. Brichta. Sincere and strategic voters: An Israeli study. *Political Behavior*, 7(4):311–324, 1985.

[12] E. Hargittai, J. Gallo, and M. Kane. Cross-ideological discussions among conservative and liberal bloggers. *Public Choice*, 134(1-2):67–86, 2008.

[13] M. J. Hinich and M. C. Munger. *Analytical politics*. Cambridge University Press, 1997.

[14] O. Lev and J. S. Rosenschein. Convergence of iterative voting. In *Proceedings of the 11th International Conference on Autonomous Agents and Multiagent Systems-Volume 2*, pages 611–618. International Foundation for Autonomous Agents and Multiagent Systems, 2012.

[15] M. McPherson, L. Smith-Lovin, and J. M. Cook. Birds of a feather: Homophily in social networks. *Annual Review of Sociology*, pages 415–444, 2001.

[16] R. Meir, O. Lev, and J. S. Rosenschein. A local-dominance theory of voting equilibria. In *Proceedings of the 15th ACM Conference on Economics and Computation*, pages 313–330. ACM, 2014.

[17] R. Meir, M. Polukarov, J. S. Rosenschein, and N. R. Jennings. Convergence to equilibria in plurality voting. In *Proc. of 24th Conference on Artificial Intelligence (AAAI-10)*, pages 823–828, 2010.

[18] R. B. Myerson and R. J. Weber. A theory of voting equilibria. *American Political Science Review*, 87(01):102–114, 1993.

[19] A. Reijngoud and U. Endriss. Voter response to iterated poll information. In *Proceedings of the 11th International Conference on Autonomous Agents and Multiagent Systems-Volume 2*, pages 635–644. International Foundation for Autonomous Agents and Multiagent Systems, 2012.

[20] S. Sina, N. Hazon, A. Hassidim, and S. Kraus. Adapting the social network to affect elections. In *Proceedings of the 14th International Conference on Autonomous Agents and Multiagent Systems*, pages 705–713. International Foundation for Autonomous Agents and Multiagent Systems, 2015.

Recovering Social Networks by Observing Votes

Benjamin Fish
Mathematics, Statistics, & Computer Science
University of Illinois at Chicago,
Chicago, IL 60607
bfish3@uic.edu

Yi Huang
Mathematics, Statistics, & Computer Science
University of Illinois at Chicago,
Chicago, IL 60607
yhuang89@uic.edu

Lev Reyzin
Mathematics, Statistics, & Computer Science
University of Illinois at Chicago,
Chicago, IL 60607
lreyzin@math.uic.edu

ABSTRACT

We investigate how to reconstruct social networks from voting data. In particular, given a voting model that considers social network structure, we aim to find the network that best explains the agents' votes. We study two plausible voting models, one edge-centric and the other vertex-centric.

For these models, we give algorithms and lower bounds, characterizing cases where network recovery is possible and where it is computationally difficult. We also test our algorithms on United States Senate data.

Despite the similarity of the two models, we show that their respective network recovery problems differ in complexity and involve distinct algorithmic challenges. Moreover, the networks produced when working under these models can also differ significantly. These results indicate that great care should be exercised when choosing a voting model for network recovery tasks.

1. INTRODUCTION

One approach to investigating voting data assumes that agents' votes are independent of one another, conditioned on some underlying (sometimes probabilistic) model of ground truth. This is usually an unrealistic assumption, leading to a more recent line of inquiry which asks how the social network structure of the voters affects the relationship between votes. Each agent in a social network expresses a position (votes for or against a bill, prefers one brand over another, etc.) that is influenced by their social connections. In this view, it is possible to detect the organization and evolution of voting communities by looking at the social network structure. The literature on congressional and political voting networks focuses on detecting community structure, partisanship, and evolutionary dynamics [1, 9, 11, 15, 20, 21], while the literature on idea propagation investigates how to best maximize the spread of ideas through a population [3, 10].

However, it is often not necessarily clear how to build this social network graph. For example, Macon et al. give a few different variants on how to define the social network of the voters of the United Nations [11]. In this approach, different graphs may reveal different aspects of the social network structure.

This corresponds neatly with a typical view in social choice theory that votes are manifestations of subjective preferences. At the other extreme, a voter votes according to a noisy estimate of the ground-truth qualities of the possible choices on which he or she is voting. While both are over-simplified extremes, it is useful to consider the extremes in order to investigate their consequences [4].

In this paper, as in previous work, we assume there is a fixed probabilistic model which is used to determine the relationship between initial preferences for the possible choices and how each individual ends up voting for those choices. This probabilistic model takes into account the social network structure in which the voters are embedded.

In this approach, it is typically assumed that the social network of the voters is known. The goal is then to find the correct choice from votes, as tackled by Conitzer and then others [4, 16, 19]. This can be made more difficult depending on the structure of a social network, which may enforce the wrong choice by aggregating individual opinions over dense subgraphs, leading voters with low degree to possibly change their mind to the majority view of the subgraph.

In practice, the social network is usually not known and it is not necessarily clear how to infer the graph. In this paper, we tackle the problem of inferring the social network from the votes alone. We discuss two similar but distinct voting models in the vein of Conitzer [4], and show how to recover the graph given the votes under these voting models and under several notions of what it means to recover the graph. We show that your ability to learn the graph from the votes is highly dependent on the underlying voting model - in some settings, it is computationally hard to do so but not in others. Moreover, we demonstrate that the resulting learned graphs can differ significantly depending on which underlying voting model is assumed.

2. MODELS AND RESULTS

We give results for two similar models: an edge-centric model, which Conitzer calls the *independent conversation model* [4], and a vertex-centric model, introduced in this paper, which we will call the *common neighbor model*.

Similar to some existing models, the common neighbor model is, for instance, equivalent to the "deterministic binary majority process" run for one step (where the initial assignment is random). This process was examined by Goles and Olivos [6] and related work, e.g. by Frischknecht et al. [5], and it has been used in the press to illustrate the disproportionate influence of certain voters [17]. The models we consider herein also resemble settings in multiple previous works, e.g. by Grabisch and Rusinowska [7], Grandi et al. [8], and Schwind et al. [18].

In both of our models, there is an unknown simple undirected graph G on n vertices. Each vertex is an agent, who can vote "-1" or "1". Both models describe how each agent votes in one round of voting. We consider m rounds of voting and in each round every

Appears in: *Proceedings of the 15th International Conference on Autonomous Agents and Multiagent Systems (AAMAS 2016), J. Thangarajah, K. Tuyls, C. Jonker, S. Marsella (eds.), May 9–13, 2016, Singapore.*

vertex votes, leading to a sequence of vote sets $V^{[m]} = V_1, \ldots, V_m$, where each V_i is the set of votes from all voters. The problem is to recover G from $V^{[m]}$.

First, we define the independent conversation model, a two-step process where edges represent conversations between voting agents, and each agent votes according to the majority outcome of his conversations.

DEFINITION 1 **(INDEPENDENT CONVERSATION MODEL).** *First, each edge flips a coin i.i.d. that with probability p is 1 and with probability $(1-p)$ is -1. Then each vertex votes according to the majority of its adjacent edges' preferences. If there is a tie, then it is broken in favor of voting 1 with probability q and -1 with probability $1-q$.*

This process is depicted for a particular graph in Figure 1. Note that the set of votes V_i only includes the final votes, not the initial preferences.

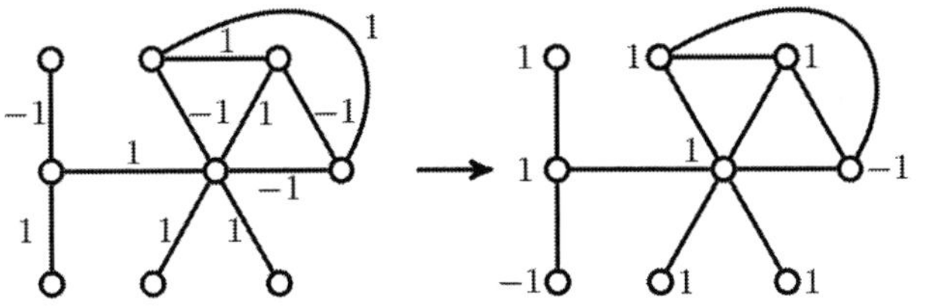

Figure 1: Left: the outcome of pairwise "conversations" between connected neighbors. Right: the resulting votes. For simplicity, the edge probabilities are not depicted.

The common neighbor model is similar, except here the initial preferences are on the vertices, not the edges:

DEFINITION 2 **(COMMON NEIGHBOR MODEL).** *Each vertex initially flips a coin i.i.d. that with probability p is 1 and with probability $1-p$ is -1. Then each vertex votes 1 if more adjacent vertices' initial preferences were 1 then -1 and vice versa. If there is a tie, then it is broken in favor of voting 1 with some probability q and -1 with probability $1-q$.*

This process is illustrated in Figure 2.

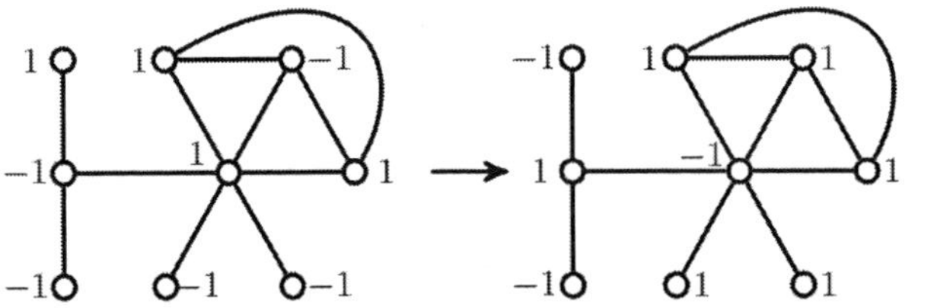

Figure 2: Left: the initial preferences of the nodes. Right: the resulting votes. For simplicity, the preference probabilities are not depicted.

It is straightforward to see how they are different. In the independent conversation model, two vertices' votes are independent of each other if and only if they do not share an edge, while in the common neighbor model, they are independent if and only if they have no common neighbors.

Our main contribution consists of algorithms to recover the hidden graph G from the votes, lower bounds, and experiments for both models.

Our results span a few different notions of what it means to recover the unknown graph. First, we ask whether there exists a polynomial-time algorithm that succeeds with high probability (given only a polynomial number of votes in the number of voters) in finding the unknown graph G when the votes were drawn from G. The algorithm must take time polynomial in both the number of votes given as input and the number of vertices. We refer to this as *exact learning*. We show the following:

RESULT 1. *In the independent conversation model, there is a polynomial-time algorithm that exactly learns the unknown graph when $p = 1/2$ (with high probability). Moreover, for constant $p \neq 1/2$, an exponential number of votes are required to exactly learn the graph. (See **Observation 1** and **Theorem 2**.)*

Our algorithm is a statistical test for edges between pairs of vertices by calculating sample covariances of their votes, which here measures how likely it is that two voters vote the same way. This is very similar to how voting networks are often constructed in the literature [2, 11, 20]. This result can then be seen as a formal motivation for why this type of method should be used.

RESULT 2. *In the common neighbor model, no algorithm can exactly recover the unknown graph. (See **Observation 8**.)*

The above two results motivate us to consider other notions of what it means to recover the graph because the graph is generally not recoverable efficiently here. Moreover, in a setting where there is not necessarily a ground-truth graph from which the votes were drawn, we are still interested in finding a graph that explains the votes.

We make this precise by asking for the maximum likelihood estimator (MLE) graph, that graph that maximizes the probability of the observed votes over the distribution of votes induced by a fixed voting model. As is standard for the maximum likelihood estimator, we assume that the prior over graphs is uniform. We refer to this as *maximum likelihood learning*. Under this model of learning, votes do not necessarily need to come from any particular hidden graph. Nevertheless, the goal is to produce the MLE graph under a voting model for a set of input votes regardless of where the votes came from.

RESULT 3. *In the independent conversation model, there is a polynomial-time bounded-probability random reduction from a #P-complete problem to finding the likelihood of the MLE graph. However, if enough votes are drawn from a hidden graph G when $p = 1/2$, there is a polynomial-time algorithm that finds the MLE graph on the votes with high probability. (See **Theorem 5** and **Theorem 7**.)*

This lower bound is an indication that computing the likelihood of the MLE graph is difficult, since if there were an efficient algorithm to compute this quantity then there would be an efficient algorithm to solve a #P-complete problem that succeeds with high probability.

On the other hand, merely trying to find the MLE graph is possible, at least if there is enough votes given as input (specifically, for n voters, order n^4 votes suffices).

In the common neighbor model, we investigate a third approach to finding a graph that explains the votes. Given that we recover graphs in the independent conversation model using covariances between votes, it is natural to ask whether it is possible to find a graph whose expected covariances are close to the observed covariances in the common neighbor model. We show that even if you were to know the expected covariances exactly, it would still be computationally difficult to find such a graph.

RESULT 4. *For the common neighbor model, finding a graph with given expected covariances between votes is at least as hard as recovering an adjacency matrix from its square. Moreover, a generalization of this problem, namely the generalized squared adjacency problem, is NP-hard. (See **Observation 9** and **Theorem 11**.)*

The squared adjacency problem and its generalized version are defined as follows:

DEFINITION 3. *The input for the squared adjacency matrix problem is a matrix B, and the decision problem asks if there is an adjacency matrix A of a simple graph such that $A^2 = B$.*

DEFINITION 4. *The input for the generalized squared adjacency problem is a collection of n^2 sets S_{ij}, and the decision problem asks if there is a simple graph whose adjacency matrix is A such that $A_{ij}^2 \in S_{ij}$ for each entry A_{ij}^2 of A^2.*

To the best of our knowledge, the squared adjacency matrix problem is not known to be NP-hard nor is it known to be in P. It is a difficult open problem in its own right, and other versions of it have been proven NP-hard [12]. It is equivalent to the special case of the generalized version where the set sizes are exactly one.

3. THE INDEPENDENT CONVERSATION MODEL

In this section, we show when there is a algorithm to recover the hidden graph. We will also show that it is hard to find the likelihood of the maximum likelihood graph for an input sequence of votes. Before we present those two results, we start with the following observation:

OBSERVATION 1. *For constant $p \neq 1/2$, under the independent conversation model, it takes exponentially many votes to distinguish with high probability between the complete graph and the complete graph minus an edge.*

This follows directly from the fact that in both the complete graph and the complete graph minus an edge, if $p \neq 1/2$, with exponentially high probability every voter will vote 1. Our only hope is that it becomes possible to recover the graph G when $p = 1/2$, which we show to be the case.

3.1 An algorithm for $p = 1/2$

In this section, we prove the following:

THEOREM 2. *Let $p = q = 1/2$. For any graph G on n vertices and $\delta > 0$, if $m = \Omega\left(n^2\left(\ln n + \ln \frac{1}{\delta}\right)\right)$ votes are drawn from G under the independent conversation model, there is a polynomial-time algorithm that will recover G with probability at least $1 - \delta$.*[1]

Let $X_u \in \{1, -1\}$ be the random variable representing the outputted vote of vertex u, so $X_u = 1$ if u votes 1 and -1 otherwise. Now consider two vertices u and v. The votes of u and v are independent if and only if (u, v) is not an edge. This yields a natural approach to determining if (u, v) is an edge of G: measure the sample covariance between the votes of u and v and if this covariance is sufficiently far away from zero, there must be an edge.

To formalize this, we need to calculate the covariance between X_u and X_v if there is an edge between them:

[1]This result actually remains true for arbitrary values of q, but we restrict the Theorem to $q = 1/2$ to simplify the proof in this version.

LEMMA 3. *For any edge (u, v) of G, let d_u and d_v be the degrees of u and v. For convenience, let $\rho = (1 - 2p)q + p$. Then $Cov\,(X_u, X_v)$ is*

$$\begin{cases} 4\rho^2 \binom{d_u-1}{\frac{d_u-2}{2}} \binom{d_v-1}{\frac{d_v-2}{2}} (p(1-p))^{\frac{d_u+d_v-2}{2}}, & \text{even } d_u, d_v \\ 4\rho \binom{d_u-1}{\frac{d_u-2}{2}} \binom{d_v-1}{\frac{d_v-1}{2}} (p(1-p))^{\frac{d_u+d_v-1}{2}}, & \text{even } d_u, \text{ odd } d_v \\ 4\rho \binom{d_u-1}{\frac{d_u-1}{2}} \binom{d_v-1}{\frac{d_v-2}{2}} (p(1-p))^{\frac{d_u+d_v-1}{2}}, & \text{odd } d_u, \text{ even } d_v \\ 4 \binom{d_u-1}{\frac{d_u-1}{2}} \binom{d_v-1}{\frac{d_v-1}{2}} (p(1-p))^{\frac{d_u+d_v}{2}}, & \text{odd } d_u, d_v. \end{cases}$$

PROOF. Consider an edge $(u, v) \in E(G)$. Since u and v vote independently given the vote of the edge (u, v), we will write the probability that each of these vertices vote 1 given the edge vote.

Namely, call $P_u^1 = \mathbb{P}\left(X_u = 1 | \text{edge } (u, v) \text{ votes } 1\right)$ and $P_u^{-1} = \mathbb{P}\left(X_u = 1 | \text{edge } (u, v) \text{ votes -}1\right)$ and similarly P_v^1, P_v^{-1} the analogous probabilities for v.

We can write the covariance in terms of these four probabilities: $Cov\,(X_u, X_v) = 4p(1-p)(P_u^1 - P_u^{-1})(P_v^1 - P_v^{-1})$.

To show this, it suffices to write the covariance as a function of the joint probabilities $P(X_u = 1, X_v = 1)$, etc., and then write each joint probability as a function of the probabilities that a vertex votes 1 given that how the adjacent edge votes. For example, by conditioning on the vote of edge (u, v),

$$P(X_u = X_v = 1) = pP_u^1 P_v^1 + (1-p)P_u^{-1}P_v^{-1}.$$

The others are similar.

To complete the proof, all we need are formulae for P_u^1 and P_u^{-1} (P_v^1 and P_v^{-1} are calculated analogously). This is done by choosing edges to form the majority vote of u's neighborhood.

Recall $d(u) - 1$ and $d(v) - 1$ are the degrees of u and v, respectively, minus 1 (in order to discount the edge (u, v)). We then have

$$P_u^1 = \begin{cases} \sum_{i=0}^{\frac{d(u)-2}{2}} \binom{d(u)-1}{i} (1-p)^i p^{d(u)-1-i} & \text{even } d(u) \\ + q\binom{d(u)-1}{\frac{d(u)}{2}} (1-p)^{\frac{d(u)}{2}} p^{\frac{d(u)-2}{2}}, & \\ \sum_{i=0}^{\frac{d(u)-1}{2}} \binom{d(u)-1}{i} (1-p)^i p^{d(u)-1-i}, & \text{odd } d(u). \end{cases}$$

and

$$P_u^{-1} = \begin{cases} \sum_{i=0}^{\frac{d(u)-4}{2}} \binom{d(u)-1}{i} (1-p)^i p^{d(u)-1-i} & \text{even } d(u) \\ + q\binom{d(u)-1}{\frac{d(u)-2}{2}} (1-p)^{\frac{d(u)-2}{2}} p^{\frac{d(u)}{2}}, & \\ \sum_{i=0}^{\frac{d(u)-3}{2}} \binom{d(u)-1}{i} (1-p)^i p^{d(u)-1-i}, & \text{odd } d(u), \end{cases}$$

The statement of the lemma then follows. □

In the case where $p = 1/2$, the covariance will be sufficiently large; namely that it will be $\Omega(1/n)$, where n is the number of vertices of G:

COROLLARY 4. *When $p = 1/2$ and (u, v) is an edge of G,*

$$Cov\,(X_u, X_v) \geq \frac{1}{2\pi} \frac{1}{\sqrt{d_u d_v}} \geq \frac{1}{2\pi n}.$$

PROOF. We simplify the formula for the covariance derived in Lemma 3 by giving lower bounds for the central binomial coefficients, from which the result immediately follows: For any positive integer k, the central binomial coefficient(s) satisfy

$$\binom{k}{\lceil \frac{k-1}{2} \rceil} \geq \frac{2^k}{\sqrt{\pi k}}.$$

These lower bounds follow from Sterling's approximation $k! = \sqrt{2\pi k}\left(\frac{k}{e}\right)^k\left(1 + O\left(\frac{1}{k}\right)\right)$. □

Note this lower bound was only polynomial in $1/n$ because $p = 1/2$; otherwise, the exponential term $(p(1-p))^n$, for p constant, ensures that the covariance goes to 0 exponentially quickly in n.

We are now ready to prove Theorem 2, which uses the Hoeffding bound to establish that the sample covariance converges quickly enough to its expectation, which if there is an edge is given in Lemma 3 and if there is no edge is just 0.

PROOF OF THEOREM 2. Recall that in the independent conversation model, we are given m votes $X_{u,i} \overset{i.i.d.}{\sim} X_u$ for $i = 1, \ldots, m$ and all u in G, where X_u is the $\{-1, 1\}$-valued random variable found by taking the majority vote of the initial votes of u's neighborhood.

For $p = q = 1/2$, $\mathbb{E}(X_u) = 0$ for each vertex u, which means that $Cov(X_v, X_u) = \mathbb{E}(X_u X_v)$. This means that the sample covariance between u and v is

$$C^m_{u,v} = \frac{1}{m}\sum_i^m X_{u,i}X_{v,i}.$$

The algorithm to recover G from the m votes is straightforward: For each pair of vertices u, v, calculate the sample covariance $C^m_{u,v}$. If $C^m_{u,v} > \frac{1}{4\pi n}$, then the algorithm claims there is an edge between u and v, and otherwise, the algorithm claims there is no such edge. We call this the *covariance test*. It suffices to show that the probability that the covariance test is wrong is low. Using Corollary 4, we get for edge (u, v),

$$\mathbb{P}\left(C^m_{u,v} < \frac{1}{4\pi n}\right) \le \mathbb{P}\left(C^m_{u,v} - \mathbb{E}\left(C^m_{u,v}\right) < -\frac{1}{4\pi n}\right),$$

and for $(u, v) \notin E(G)$,

$$\mathbb{P}\left(C^m_{u,v} > \frac{1}{4\pi n}\right) = \mathbb{P}\left(C^m_{u,v} - \mathbb{E}\left(C^m_{u,v}\right) > \frac{1}{4\pi n}\right).$$

By the Hoeffding bound each of these two terms is bounded above by $e^{-\frac{cm}{n^2\pi^2}}$ for some constant c.

Let G' be the network inferred by the above algorithm. Then the probability that G' is not G is no more than

$$\sum_{u,v\in E}\mathbb{P}\left(C^m_{u,v} < \frac{1}{4\pi n}\right) + \sum_{u,v\notin E}\mathbb{P}\left(C^m_{u,v} > \frac{1}{4\pi n}\right),$$

which is bounded from above by $\binom{n}{2}e^{-\frac{cm}{n^2\pi^2}}$.

Hence, for any $\delta > 0$, setting $m = \Omega\left(n^2\left(\ln n + \ln\frac{1}{\delta}\right)\right)$ suffices so that $\binom{n}{2}e^{-\frac{cm}{n^2\pi^2}} < \delta$. $\square$

3.2 Moving from exact learning to maximum likelihood learning

In the previous section, we showed that exact learning is possible when $p = q = 1/2$. We now show that it is possible to not only exactly learn the graph, but also find the maximum likelihood graph for the votes when $p = q = 1/2$, assuming we are given enough data. Recall the maximum likelihood graph (which we will also refer to as the MLE graph) is the graph that maximizes the probability of the observed votes over the distribution of votes.

THEOREM 5. *Let $p = q = 1/2$. For any graph G on n vertices and $\delta > 0$, if $m = \Omega\left(n^2\left(n^2 + \ln\frac{1}{\delta}\right)\right)$ votes are drawn from G under the independent conversation model, there is a polynomial-time algorithm that will find the maximum likelihood graph on the drawn votes with probability at least $1 - \delta$.*

In other words, if the votes really do come from a hidden graph and we are given order n^4 votes, we can find the maximum likelihood graph. Specifically, what we show is that if you are given this many votes from a hidden graph, then the MLE graph *is* the hidden graph with high probability. The proof of Theorem 5 then follows from applying Theorem 2, i.e. using the covariance test to find the hidden graph, which is the MLE graph. This moves a statement about exact learning to a statement about maximum likelihood learning.

We now prove (Lemma 6) that the MLE graph is the hidden graph for a sufficiently large set of votes drawn from a hidden graph. Indeed, we show something stronger: the hidden graph will be more likely (under this model) than any other graph by an arbitrarily large factor α (where the number of votes given as input needs to increase logarithmically in α). This stronger result will also be needed for the proof of Theorem 7.

The statement of this will need some notation: For any graph G on n vertices, let $\mathcal{V}_G$ be the distribution over a set of n votes induced by G under the independent conversation model for $p = q = 1/2$. For convenience we will denote the m-product distribution $\mathcal{V}_G \times \ldots \times \mathcal{V}_G$ as $\mathcal{V}_G^{[m]}$. That is, for any vote $V \in \{-1, 1\}^n$, $\mathbb{P}_{\mathcal{V}_G}(V) = \mathbb{P}(V|G)$ is the probability mass of V under $\mathcal{V}_G$. Similarly, for a sequence of votes $V^{[m]}$, $\mathbb{P}_{\mathcal{V}_G^{[m]}}\left(V^{[m]}\right) = \mathbb{P}\left(V^{[m]}|G\right)$ is the probability mass of $V^{[m]}$ under $\mathcal{V}_G^{[m]}$.

LEMMA 6. *For $\delta > 0$, $\alpha > 1$,*

$$\mathbb{P}_{V^{[m]}\sim\mathcal{V}_G^{[m]}}\left(\mathbb{P}\left(V^{[m]}|G\right) \le \alpha \max_{G'\neq G}\mathbb{P}\left(V^{[m]}|G'\right)\right) < \delta$$

for $m = \Omega\left(n^2\left(n^2 + \ln\frac{1}{\delta} + \ln\alpha\right)\right)$.

PROOF. Fix $\alpha > 1$ and denote by E the event that

$$\frac{\max_{G'\neq G}\mathbb{P}(V^{[m]}|G')}{\mathbb{P}(V^{[m]}|G)} \ge \frac{1}{\alpha}.$$

(If $\mathbb{P}(V^{[m]}|G) = 0$, then this event occurs, so we can safely assume the converse.) The idea of this proof is that we will show the probability of E happening is small by conditioning on what the vote sequence $V^{[m]}$ looks like when drawn from G. Specifically, in the proof of Theorem 2, we show that the covariance test would have successfully found G with high probability, so we condition on this happening.

Fix a graph $G' \neq G$. We will want to show that the probability that $V^{[m]}$ is pulled from G' (instead of G) is sufficiently small. The covariance test failed if $V^{[m]}$ were pulled from G': the covariance test returned G on $V^{[m]}$ instead of G'. And again, the probability that the covariance test failed is low, as showed in the proof of Theorem 2, so the probability that $V^{[m]}$ is pulled from G' must be small.

We denote the set of vote sequences for which the covariance test returns G by Φ_G. Using this notation, we condition on $V^{[m]}$ being in Φ_G or not and then get an immediate upper bound:

$$\mathbb{P}_{\mathcal{V}_G^{[m]}}(E) \le \mathbb{P}_{\mathcal{V}_G^{[m]}}\left(E|V^{[m]} \in \Phi_G\right) + \mathbb{P}_{\mathcal{V}_G^{[m]}}\left(V^{[m]} \notin \Phi_G\right).$$

We then bound each of these two terms. The probability that the covariance test failed on $V^{[m]}$ is small: By inspecting the proof of Theorem 2, we have that for some constant c,

$$\mathbb{P}_{\mathcal{V}_G^{[m]}}\left(V^{[m]} \notin \Phi_G\right) \le \binom{n}{2}e^{-\frac{cm}{n^2\pi^2}}. \quad (1)$$

Otherwise, the covariance test succeeded and we condition on $V^{[m]} \in \Phi_G$. We now show that

$$\mathbb{P}_{\mathcal{V}_G^{[m]}}\left(E|V^{[m]} \in \Phi_G\right) \le \alpha\left(2^{\binom{n}{2}} - 1\right)\binom{n}{2}e^{-\frac{cm}{n^2\pi^2}}. \quad (2)$$

Markov's inequality gives

$$\mathbb{P}_{\mathcal{V}_G^{[m]}}\left(\frac{\max_{G'\neq G}\mathbb{P}(V^{[m]}|G')}{\mathbb{P}(V^{[m]}|G)} \geq \frac{1}{\alpha}\middle| V^{[m]}\in\Phi_G\right) \leq \alpha\cdot\mathbb{E}_{\mathcal{V}_G^{[m]}}\left(\frac{\max_{G'\neq G}\mathbb{P}(V^{[m]}|G')}{\mathbb{P}(V^{[m]}|G)}\middle| V^{[m]}\in\Phi_G\right).$$

It is then enough to expand this expected value using the definition to get that

$$\mathbb{P}_{\mathcal{V}_G^{[m]}}\left(E|V^{[m]}\in\Phi_G\right)\leq\alpha\sum_{V^{[m]}\in\Phi_G}\max_{G'\neq G}\mathbb{P}\left(V^{[m]}|G'\right).$$

Now we group the terms of the sum by which graph $G'\neq G$ maximizes the probability $\mathbb{P}\left(V^{[m]}|G'\right)$. There may be many terms in the sum that any one graph G' maximizes, but certainly each vote sequence associated with each term is in Φ_G. There are of course $2^{\binom{n}{2}}-1$ such graphs, so

$$\sum_{V^{[m]}\in\Phi_G}\max_{G'\neq G}\mathbb{P}\left(V^{[m]}|G'\right)\leq\sum_{G':G'\neq G}\sum_{V^{[m]}\in\Phi_G}\mathbb{P}\left(V^{[m]}|G'\right) = \left(2^{\binom{n}{2}}-1\right)\mathbb{P}\left(V^{[m]}\in\Phi_G|G'\right).$$

If $V^{[m]}$ were in Φ_G but $V^{[m]}$ was pulled from G', then the covariance test has failed at returning G'. So

$$\mathbb{P}\left(V^{[m]}\in\Phi_G|G'\right)\leq\binom{n}{2}e^{-\frac{cm}{n^2\pi^2}},$$

implying Equation 2. Combining Equations 1 and 2, we get

$$\mathbb{P}_{\mathcal{V}_G^{[m]}}(E)\leq\alpha 2^{\binom{n}{2}}\binom{n}{2}e^{-\frac{cm}{n^2\pi^2}}.$$

For $\mathbb{P}_{\mathcal{V}_G^{[m]}}(E)$ to be upper-bounded by $\delta>0$, it suffices to set $m=\Omega\left(n^2\left(n^2+\ln\frac{1}{\delta}+\ln\alpha\right)\right)$. □

3.3 Hardness of computing the MLE

As we have seen, when $p=q=1/2$, distinguishing between graphs can be done in polynomial time. This might give hope that, in this case, computing the likelihood of the MLE graph, given a set of votes, may be easy. That is, given a graph G which is the maximum likelihood graph for a set of input votes $V^{[m]}$ over G, we wish to compute $\mathbb{P}(V^{[m]}|G)$. Alas, we give hardness results indicating this is not easy to do.

We reduce from Conitzer's problem of computing $\mathbb{P}(V^*|G)$, where V^* is a vote produced by a given graph G [4].[2] He shows that this is problem is #P-hard by reducing from counting the number of perfect matchings in a bipartite graph. Surprisingly, our proof of this hardness result uses the easiness of finding the MLE graph in polynomial time in the case when $p=q=1/2$. Namely, we use Lemma 6 to be able to say when the input G is the maximum likelihood graph for a set of votes $V^{[m]}$, which in turn says when the oracle will successfully compute $\mathbb{P}(V^{[m]}|G)$. Formally, we prove the following theorem:

THEOREM 7. *There is a randomized polynomial-time oracle reduction from computing the MLE of the maximum likelihood graph from a sequence of votes with high probability to counting the number of perfect matchings in a balanced bipartite graph.*

[2]While the problem Conitzer considers is slightly different than computing $\mathbb{P}(V^*|G)$, in the case where $p=1/2$, his problem reduces to computing $\mathbb{P}(V^*|G)$.

PROOF SKETCH. It suffices to consider the case where $p=q=1/2$. Instead of directly reducing from the #P-hard problem of counting the number of perfect matchings in a balanced bipartite graph, we reduce from the #P-hard problem of computing $\mathbb{P}(V^*|G)$ given a graph G and vote V^* on n voters under the independent conversation model.

The idea of the proof is going to be to build a sequence of votes $V^{[m]}$ whose MLE we know to be the input G, and then compute

$$\mathbb{P}(V^*|G)=\frac{\mathbb{P}(V^{[m]},V^*|G)}{\mathbb{P}(V^{[m]}|G)}.$$

Our oracle will give us the values of the right-hand side. This approach will work if $\mathbb{P}(V^*|G)\neq 0$.

So we first test for the case if $\mathbb{P}(V^*|G)=0$. Conitzer provides a way to do this for a similar problem when the vertices of the graph have all odd degree: his reduction is from the maximum weighted b-matching problem, which we can adapt to the so-called "c-capacitated" version that we need [4, 14].

Else, $P(V^*|G)\neq 0$. We draw a sequence of votes $V^{[m]}\overset{i.i.d.}{\sim}\mathcal{V}_G\times\ldots\times\mathcal{V}_G$. Lemma 6 immediately implies that G will be the MLE for $V^{[m]}$ with failure probability less than $\delta/2$ when $m=\Omega(n^2(n^2+\ln\frac{2}{\delta}))$. In other words, with just $\Omega(n^4)$ votes we will successfully query the oracle for $\mathbb{P}(V^{[m]}|G)$ with high probability.

It suffices to ensure that with high probability we will also successfully query the oracle for the $m+1$-length sequence $V^{[m]},V^*$. Recall that since $\mathbb{P}(V^*|G)$ is the sum, over all satisfying edge votes, of the quantity $\left(\frac{1}{2}\right)^{|E(G)|}$, where $E(G)$ is the edge set of G and $p=1/2$. There must be at least one satisfying edge-vote assignment since $\mathbb{P}(V^*|G)\neq 0$, so $\mathbb{P}(V^*|G)\geq\left(\frac{1}{2}\right)^{|E(G)|}$. In addition, again by Lemma 6, for any $G'\neq G, \frac{\mathbb{P}(V^{[m]}|G)}{\mathbb{P}(V^{[m]}|G')}>\alpha$ with failure probability no more than $\delta/2$ when $m=\Omega(n^2(n^2+\ln\frac{2}{\delta}+\ln\alpha))$. Then for any $G'\neq G$,

$$\mathbb{P}(V^{[m]},V^*|G')<\left(\frac{1}{\alpha}\mathbb{P}(V^{[m]}|G)\right)\left(2^{|E(G)|}\mathbb{P}(V^*|G)\right) = \frac{2^{|E(G)|}}{\alpha}\mathbb{P}(V^{[m]},V^*|G).$$

Setting $\alpha=\Omega(e^{n^2})$ suffices to ensure that $\alpha>2^{|E(G)|}$. Thus setting

$$m=\Omega(n^2(n^2+\ln\frac{2}{\delta}+\ln\alpha))$$

as above for this setting of α, a query to the oracle for $\mathbb{P}(V^{[m]},V^*|G)$ will fail with probability less than $\delta/2$. Setting δ to be, say, $\Theta(\frac{1}{2^n})$, yields that $m=\Omega(n^4)$. The oracle reduction, once it tests for the existence of at least one valid edge vote, simply consists of drawing m votes from G and then querying the oracle for $\mathbb{P}(V^{[m]},V^*|G)$ and $\mathbb{P}(V^{[m]}|G)$. The reduction then succeeds with probability at least $1-\delta$. □

4. THE COMMON NEIGHBOR MODEL

We now turn our attention to the common neighbor model. Again, we ask if it is possible to recover G by seeing only polynomially many votes. In general, it is not possible to recover G at all, let alone with only polynomially many votes:

OBSERVATION 8. *Under the common neighbor model, no algorithm can distinguish between two different perfect matchings.*

If G is a matching between the vertices, each vertex will vote how its neighbor votes, meaning that each vertex votes i.i.d. with probability p regardless. Thus there is no way to distinguish between different matchings.

4.1 Recovering A^2 from covariances

Given the impossibility of recovering the graph, we relax the problem to the following: Find a graph that is likely to produce the given votes in the sense that the expected covariances of this graph should be as close as possible (under some norm) to the covariances of the observed votes. This problem is motivated by the algorithm for the independent conversation model which finds a graph whose expected covariances match the measured covariances.

Yet even if we were to know the *expected* covariances of the input votes, finding a graph whose expected covariances are close to those input covariances remains challenging:

OBSERVATION 9. *For the common neighbor model, finding a graph with given expected vote covariances is at least as hard as recovering an adjacency matrix from its square.*

To prove this observation, it suffices to show that the expected covariances are a function solely of the entries of A^2. Then recovering A from A^2 consists of using the entries of A^2 to compute the expected covariances, at which point the adjacency matrix of a graph with those covariances will be exactly A. The i, jth entry of A^2 is the number of length-two paths between i and j, so it is enough to write the covariances of a graph in terms of the following: For $\Gamma(v)$ the neighborhood of a vertex v, denote $d_{uv} = |\Gamma(v) \cap \Gamma(u)|$, $d_u = |\Gamma(u) \setminus (\Gamma(v) \cap \Gamma(u))|$, and d_v analogously. The covariances are a function of d_u, d_v, and d_{uv}. For the sake of simplicity we will assume that $|\Gamma(u)|$ and $|\Gamma(v)|$ are odd, but it is straightforward to modify the formula given below in the cases when they are not.

LEMMA 10. *Assume $|\Gamma(u)|$ and $|\Gamma(v)|$ are odd. For $p = 1/2$,*

$$Cov(X_u, X_v) = \frac{1}{2^{d_{uv}-2}} \left(\sum_{k=0}^{d_{uv}} \binom{d_{uv}}{k} P_{u,v}(k) P_{v,u}(k) \right) - 1,$$

where, for $\theta_{u,v} = (d_{uv} + d_u + 1)/2 - k$,

$$P_{u,v}(k) = \begin{cases} \frac{1}{2^{d_u}} \sum_{i=\theta_{u,v}}^{d_u} \binom{d_u}{i} & \text{if } 0 \le \theta_{u,v} \le d_u \\ 0 & \text{if } \theta_{u,v} > d_u \\ 1 & \text{if } \theta_{u,v} \le 0. \end{cases}$$

PROOF. Let X_u represent vertex u's vote. When $p = 1/2$, $E[X_u] = 0$, and $P(X_u = X_v = 1) = P(X_u = X_v = 0)$, so the covariance $Cov(X_u, X_v)$ is

$$E[X_u X_v] = 2P(X_u = X_v) - 1 = 4P(X_u = X_v = 1) - 1.$$

To determine $P(X_u = X_v = 1)$, we condition on the number of common neighbors that voted 1:

Assuming some k common neighbors vote 1, in order for u to vote 1, u needs an additional $\frac{d_{uv}+d_u+1}{2} - k$ neighbors to vote 1. If k is already at least $\frac{d_{uv}+d_u+1}{2}$, then the probability of voting 1 is already 1; on the other hand if there aren't enough remaining vertices to vote 1, then the probability is 0. This yields $P_{u,v}(k)$ as the probability that u votes 1 given that k common neighbors of u and v voted 1.

Now we can write $P(X_u = X_v = 1)$ as

$$\sum_{k=0}^{d_{uv}} \binom{d_{uv}}{k} p^k (1-p)^{d_{uv}-k} P_{u,v}(k) P_{v,u}(k),$$

completing the proof. □

When recovering a graph from a sequence of input votes, we are not even given the expected covariances of the input votes. Instead we can calculate the measured covariances, from which we can determine A^2. At this point, we have a function inversion problem on our hands: We can find A^2 merely by recovering these d_{uv}'s and d_u's from the covariances, but given that the formula given in Lemma 10 is not closed, this is not trivial. Since there are only polynomially many possible values for d_{uv} and d_u, we can simply try all values to find the covariance closest to the observed value. However, there may be covariances that are exponentially close to each other, making it impossible to distinguish between these values for given d_{uv}, d_u. In this case the values recovered for the entries of A^2 may not be unique, which in the worst case leads to the generalized squared adjacency problem. Even in the case when we recover unique values, it still reduces to the squared adjacency problem.

While the squared adjacency problem is open, we show the following:

THEOREM 11. *The generalized squared adjacency problem is* NP-*hard.*

PROOF. The reduction is from CLIQUE, which asks if there is a clique of size k on the input graph. Given a graph $G = (V, E)$ and an integer k, we construct a set system $\{S_{ij}\}$ with $(n+1)^2$ sets, where $n = |V|$. We then show that G has a clique of size k if and only if there is a graph $G' = (V \cup \{v\}, E')$ such that the i, jth entry of $A(G')^2$ is in $S_{i,j}$, where $A(G')$ is the adjacency matrix of G'. The $(n+1)^2$-sized set system $\{S_{i,j}\}$ is defined as follows:

$$S_{ij} = \begin{cases} \{0,1\} & \text{if } i \ne j \text{ and } i, j \ne v \text{ and } (i,j) \in E(G) \\ \{0\} & \text{if } i \ne j \text{ and } i, j \ne v \text{ and } (i,j) \notin E(G) \\ \{0\} & \text{if } i = v \text{ and } j \ne v \\ \{0\} & \text{if } j = v \text{ and } i \ne v \\ \{k\} & \text{if } i = j = v \\ \{0,1\} & \text{if } i = j \text{ and } i, j \ne v \end{cases}$$

Assume there is a clique of size k in G. Then G' is defined as follows: Denote the vertex set of the clique in G by C. G' will have an edge between v and all members of C, and no other edges. It is straightforward to check that the i, jth entry of $A(G')^2$ is in S_{ij} by noting that the diagonal entries of $A(G')^2$ are the vertices' degrees and the off-diagonal entries counts the number of common neighbors.

In the other direction, assume there is such a graph G' whose squared adjacency matrix satisfies the constraints imposed by the set system $\{S_{i,j}\}$. In this case, the clique of size k in G will be exactly the neighborhood of v in G' (not including v itself). Call $N(v)$ the neighborhood of v in G'. Note the degree of v in G' must be k, by definition of S_{vv}, i.e. $|N(v)| = k$. Consider a distinct pair of vertices i, j in $N(v)$. The vertices i and j have at least one common neighbor in G', namely v, because both are in $N(v)$, meaning that $A(G')^2_{ij} \ge 1$. But if (i, j) is not an edge in G then $S_{ij} = \{0\}$ by the definition of S_{ij}, a contradiction, forcing $N(v)$ to be a clique as required. □

4.2 A heuristic approach

Unlike in the independent conversation model, we have no efficient algorithm for producing the social network under the common neighbor model. Hence, we employ a heuristic to find a graph that satisfies or comes close to satisfying the constraints imposed on it by the measured covariances.

Because of the computational hardness of this problem, we propose a heuristic approach to learn networks under the common neighbor model. This heuristic will be used in our experimental results in Section 5. Our heuristic, Algorithm 1, finds those pairs of

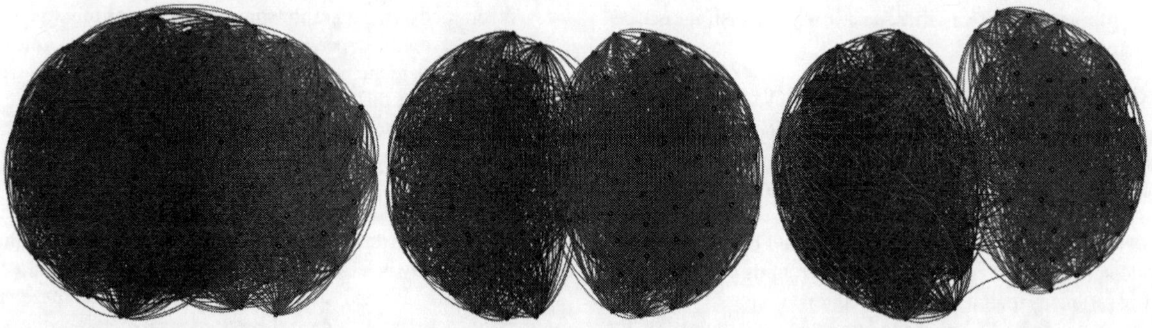

(a) 101st Congress (1989-1990) (b) 106th Congress (1999-2000) (c) 113th Congress (2013-2014)

Figure 3: Graphs of the US Senate for three congressional terms under the independent conversation model. Democrats are colored blue, Republicans are red, and Independents are green.

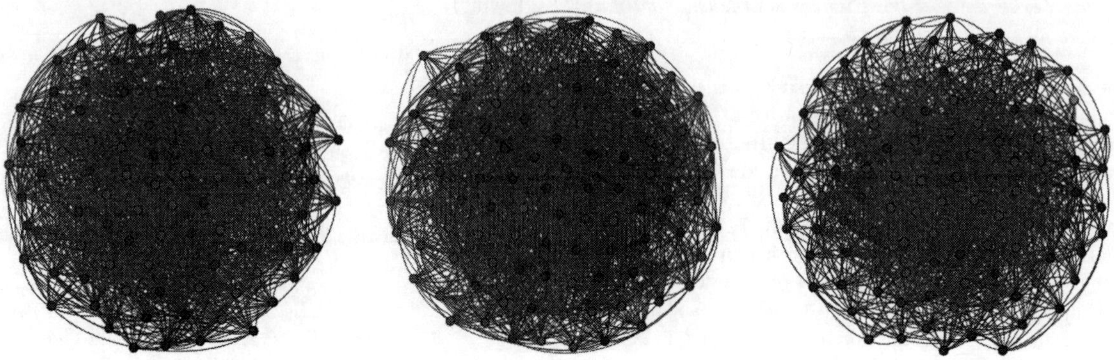

(a) 101st Congress (1989-1990) (b) 106th Congress (1999-2000) (c) 113th Congress (2013-2014)

Figure 4: Graphs of the US Senate for three congressional terms under the common neighbor model. Democrats are colored blue, Republicans are in red, and Independents are in green.

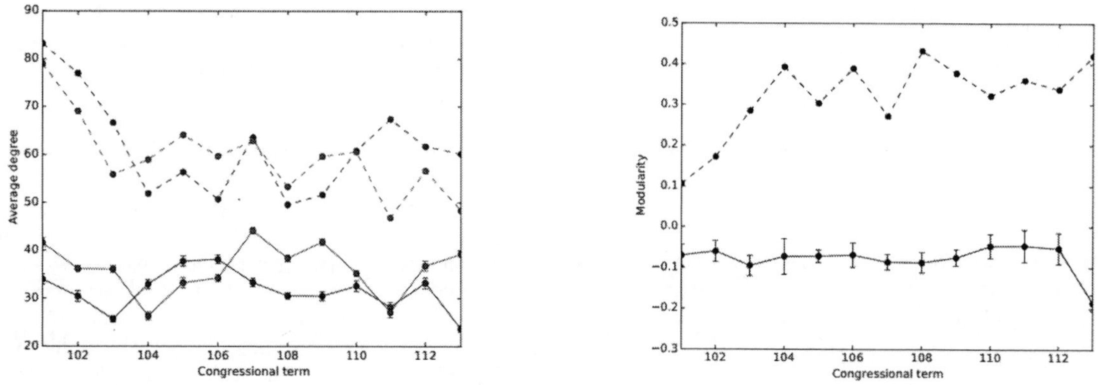

(a) Average degree. The blue and red lines are the average degree of the Democrats and the Republicans, respectively.

(b) Modularity between Democrats and Republicans. (Independents are included with the party with which they caucus.)

Figure 5: Data for the 101st-113th Congress. Dashed and solid lines are statistics for the independent conversation model and common neighbor model, respectively. Error bars represent one standard deviation, over 20 trials.

vertices whose current expected covariance (assuming $p = 1/2$) is farthest away from the measured covariance and modifies the graph to decrease that gap.

The local changes we want to make clearly cannot just consist of adding/removing single edges: Say the covariance between a given pair of vertices needs to go up and those vertices' neighborhoods are currently empty. The only way to increase the covariance is to add at least two edges: (i, v) and (v, j) for some other vertex v. The natural compromise is then to add or remove the minimal number of edges (either one or two) to change the covariance, as seen in Algorithm 2.

5. EXPERIMENTAL RESULTS

In this section, we test our algorithms on United States Senate roll call votes. We examine each two-year congressional session as

Algorithm 1 Common neighbor heuristic

Input: $\{\hat{c}_{ij}\}$, measured covariances between voters i and j, and T, the number of iterations to run.
  $G \sim \mathcal{G}(n, 1/2)$, $G_{best} := \emptyset$
  $\{c_{ij}\} := \{\sigma(i,j)\}$ # calculate expected covariances
  for 0 to T **do**
    $i, j := \text{argmax}_{i,j}|c_{ij} - \hat{c}_{i,j}|$
    $G :=$ Modify$G(G, i, j, \hat{c}_{ij}, c_{ij})$
    $\{c_{ij}\} := \{\sigma(i,j)\}$ # update the expected covariances
    if $\sum_{i,j} c_{ij} - \hat{c}_{ij}$ is smallest so far **then** $G_{best} := G$
  end for
  return G_{best}

Algorithm 2 Modify$G$

Input: Graph G; vertices i, j; $\hat{c}_{ij}$, c_{ij} the measured and expected covariances between i and j.
  $unconnected := V(G) \setminus (\Gamma(i) \cup \Gamma(j) \cup \{i, j\})$
  $cn := \Gamma(i) \cap \Gamma(j)$
  if $c_{ij} - \hat{c}_{ij} > 0$ **then**
    randomize among whichever of these are available:
    1: x := random(i, j), y := random(*unconnected*)
      add edge (x, y) to G
    2: x := random(i, j), y := random(*cn*).
      delete edge (x, y) from G
    3: y := random(*cn*)
      delete edges (i, y) and (j, y) from G
  else if $c_{ij} - \hat{c}_{ij} < 0$ **then**
    randomize among whichever of these are available:
    1: y := random(*unconnected*)
      add edges (i, y) and (j, y) to G
    2: y := random($\Gamma(i) \setminus cn$)
      add (i, y) or delete (j, y) from G randomly
    3: y := random($\Gamma(j) \setminus cn$)
      add (j, y) or delete (i, y) from G randomly
  end if
  return G
  # where random(.) selects an element of its input u.a.r.

one voting network. Each Senate member is an agent who either votes for the bill in question, against, or does not vote (either because the senator served only part of the term or because the senator just didn't vote on the bill), yielding votes from the set $\{-1, 0, 1\}$.

Obviously, our models are simplifications — they don't take into account evolution of opinion, nor do they take into account the possibility of anti-correlated voters. Even assuming that either model is representative, when presented real data, the parameter p is not given, as is assumed above. The algorithms we present assume that $p = 1/2$, which is not necessarily the case. Finally, we are given a fixed amount of data, independent of the number of voters.

Despite these limitations, for the independent conversation model, our covariance test, which forms the basis for Theorem 2, results in intuitive behavior. Note that while our model assumes binary votes, our covariance test is general enough to handle such votes — covariance is calculated between the $\{-1, 0, 1\}$-valued votes and the threshold remains the same as in the original covariance test.[3] Examples of the results from this covariance test on the US Senate are shown in Figure 3. Given the highly structured nature of these graphs, it is possible to recover senators' places on the left/right political spectrum, but since this is not the focus of this paper, we do not go into any further detail here.

For the common neighbor model, we use Algorithm 1. Examples of results of this heuristic run on US Senate data are shown in Figure 4. Graphs under this model appear to be very different from those found using the covariance test under the independent conversation model.

To demonstrate these marked differences, in Figure 5 we give modularity values and average degrees of Democrats and Republicans under both models for the period 1989-2014 (corresponding to the 101st through 113th Congresses). Modularity is a standard measure of the amount of division between communities [13]. Both average degree and modularity are much higher under the independent conversation model (dashed lines in Figure 5) than under the common neighbor model (solid lines). Since the heuristic is randomized, we average these statistics over twenty graphs, each of which is an independent run of the heuristic with 100,000 rounds.

6. CONCLUSION

In this paper we derive algorithms and lower bounds for recovering graphs from their vertices' votes under two distinct models. We also present experiments on the U.S. Senate voting network. In the independent conversation model, we show when the graph is recoverable using only a polynomial number of votes. However, if we want to instead take a maximum likelihood approach to recovering graphs, then the task becomes computationally hard.

The common neighbor model, on the other hand, leads to significantly different results. Not only is it impossible to recover the graph using only polynomially many votes, finding a graph whose votes' covariances are close to the observed covariances leads to having to solve a hard problem (the generalized squared adjacency problem).

This implies that these models really are very different from each other, despite their very similar definitions. This is strong evidence that much care needs to be taken when choosing voting models for network inference. Experiments on U.S. Senate roll call data support this conclusion.

7. ACKNOWLEDGEMENTS

This research was funded in part by Army Research Office grant #66497-NS under the Young Investigator Program. We thank Vincent Conitzer, Jeremy Kun, Madhu Sudan, and Avi Wigderson for helpful discussions.

[3]We do, however, use the unbiased sample covariance instead of the biased sample covariance, as the assumption that $p = 1/2$ no longer necessarily holds, despite the analysis of the algorithm assuming it.

REFERENCES

[1] A. Amelio and C. Pizzuti. Analyzing voting behavior in Italian Parliament: Group cohesion and evolution. In *IEEE/ACM International Conference on Advances in Social Networks Analysis and Mining (ASONAM), 2012*, pages 140–146. IEEE, 2012.

[2] C. Andris, D. Lee, M. J. Hamilton, M. Martino, C. E. Gunning, and J. A. Selden. The rise of partisanship and super-cooperators in the US House of Representatives. *PLoS ONE*, 10(4), 2015.

[3] W. Chen, L. V. Lakshmanan, and C. Castillo. Information and influence propagation in social networks. *Synthesis Lectures on Data Management*, 5(4):1–177, 2013.

[4] V. Conitzer. The maximum likelihood approach to voting on social networks. In *Communication, Control, and Computing (Allerton), 2013 51st Annual Allerton Conference on*, pages 1482–1487. IEEE, 2013.

[5] S. Frischknecht, B. Keller, and R. Wattenhofer. Convergence in (social) influence networks. In *Distributed Computing*, pages 433–446. Springer, 2013.

[6] E. Goles and J. Olivos. Periodic behaviour of generalized threshold functions. *Discrete Mathematics*, 30(2):187–189, 1980.

[7] M. Grabisch and A. Rusinowska. A model of influence in a social network. *Theory and Decision*, 69(1):69–96, 2008.

[8] U. Grandi, E. Lorini, and L. Perrussel. Propositional opinion diffusion. In *Proceedings of the 2015 International Conference on Autonomous Agents and Multiagent Systems, AAMAS 2015, Istanbul, Turkey, May 4-8, 2015*, pages 989–997, 2015.

[9] A. Jakulin, W. Buntine, T. M. La Pira, and H. Brasher. Analyzing the US Senate in 2003: Similarities, clusters, and blocs. *Political Analysis*, 17(3):291–310, 2009.

[10] D. Kempe, J. Kleinberg, and É. Tardos. Maximizing the spread of influence through a social network. *Theory of Computing*, 11(4):105–147, 2015.

[11] K. T. Macon, P. J. Mucha, and M. A. Porter. Community structure in the united nations general assembly. *Physica A: Statistical Mechanics and its Applications*, 391(1):343–361, 2012.

[12] R. Motwani and M. Sudan. Computing roots of graphs is hard. *Discrete Applied Mathematics*, 54(1):81–88, 1994.

[13] M. E. Newman and M. Girvan. Finding and evaluating community structure in networks. *Physical Review E*, 69(2):026113, 2004.

[14] M. Penn and M. Tennenholtz. On multi-object auctions and matching theory: Algorithmic aspects. In *Graph Theory, Combinatorics and Algorithms*, pages 173–188. Springer, 2005.

[15] M. A. Porter, P. J. Mucha, M. E. Newman, and A. J. Friend. Community structure in the United States House of Representatives. *Physica A: Statistical Mechanics and its Applications*, 386(1):414–438, 2007.

[16] A. D. Procaccia, N. Shah, and E. Sodomka. Ranked voting on social networks. In *Proceedings of the Twenty-Fourth International Joint Conference on Artificial Intelligence, IJCAI 2015, Buenos Aires, Argentina, July 25-31, 2015*, pages 2040–2046, 2015.

[17] K. Schaul. A quick puzzle to tell whether you know what people are thinking, October 2015. [The Washington Post; posted online 09-October-2015].

[18] N. Schwind, K. Inoue, G. Bourgne, S. Konieczny, and P. Marquis. Belief revision games. In *Proceedings of the Twenty-Ninth AAAI Conference on Artificial Intelligence, January 25-30, 2015, Austin, Texas, USA.*, pages 1590–1596, 2015.

[19] A. Tsang, J. A. Doucette, and H. Hosseini. Voting with social influence: Using arguments to uncover ground truth. In *Proceedings of the 2015 International Conference on Autonomous Agents and Multiagent Systems, AAMAS 2015, Istanbul, Turkey, May 4-8, 2015*, pages 1841–1842, 2015.

[20] A. S. Waugh, L. Pei, J. H. Fowler, P. J. Mucha, and M. A. Porter. Party polarization in Congress: A network science approach. *arXiv preprint arXiv:0907.3509*, 2009.

[21] Y. Zhang, A. Friend, A. L. Traud, M. A. Porter, J. H. Fowler, and P. J. Mucha. Community structure in Congressional cosponsorship networks. *Physica A: Statistical Mechanics and its Applications*, 387(7):1705–1712, 2008.

Analyzing the Practical Relevance of Voting Paradoxes via Ehrhart Theory, Computer Simulations, and Empirical Data

Felix Brandt
TU München
Munich, Germany
brandtf@in.tum.de

Christian Geist
TU München
Munich, Germany
geist@in.tum.de

Martin Strobel
TU München
Munich, Germany
martin.r.strobel@gmail.com

ABSTRACT

Results from social choice theory are increasingly used to argue about collective decision making in computational multiagent systems. A large part of the social choice literature studies voting paradoxes in which seemingly mild properties are violated by common voting rules. In this paper, we investigate the likelihood of the Condorcet Loser Paradox (CLP) and the Agenda Contraction Paradox (ACP) using Ehrhart theory, computer simulations, and empirical data. We present the first analytical results for the CLP on four alternatives and show that our experimental results, which go well beyond four alternatives, are in almost perfect congruence with the analytical results. It turns out that the CLP—which is often cited as a major flaw of some Condorcet extensions such as Dodgson's rule, Young's rule, and MaxiMin—is of no practical relevance. The ACP, on the other hand, frequently occurs under various distributional assumptions about the voters' preferences. The extent to which it is real threat, however, strongly depends on the voting rule, the underlying distribution of preferences, and, somewhat surprisingly, the parity of the number of voters.

Keywords

Social choice theory; voting; Ehrhart theory

1. INTRODUCTION

Results from social choice theory are increasingly used to argue about collective decision making in computational multiagent systems (see, e.g., [12, 8, 30, 9]). A large part of the social choice literature studies voting paradoxes in which seemingly mild properties are violated by common voting rules. Moreover, there are a number of sweeping impossibilities, which entail that there exists no "optimal" voting rule that avoids all paradoxes. As a consequence, much of the research in social choice theory is concerned with whether a paradox can appear for a given voting rule or not. However, it turns out that some paradoxes—while possible in principle—will almost never occur in practice.

An extreme example of this phenomenon was recently revealed for the voting rule *TEQ*. Due to its unwieldy recursive definition, it was unknown for more than 20 years whether *TEQ* satisfies any of a number of very basic desirable properties. In 2011, Brandt et al. [7] have shown that *TEQ* violates all of these properties. However, their proof is non-constructive and only shows the existence of astronomically large counterexamples requiring about 10^{136} alternatives. While there are smaller computer-generated counterexamples [4], computer experiments have shown that these counterexamples are *extremely* rare and that *TEQ* satisfies the desirable properties for all practical purposes [6]. These findings motivated us to provide analytical, experimental, and empirical justifications for such statements.

In this paper, we study two voting paradoxes. The first is the well-known Condorcet loser paradox (CLP), which occurs when a voting rule selects the Condorcet loser, an alternative that loses against every other alternative in pairwise majority contests. Perhaps surprisingly, this paradox affects some Condorcet extensions, i.e., voting rules that are guaranteed to select an alternative that *wins* against every other alternative in pairwise majority contests. Common affected Condorcet extensions are Dodgson's rule, Young's rule, and MaxiMin [18]. The second paradox, called agenda contraction paradox (ACP), occurs when removing losing alternatives changes the set of winners. There are only few voting rules that do not suffer from this paradox, one of them being the essential set. In fact, all common voting rules that violate the CLP also violate the ACP.

In principle, quantitative results on voting paradoxes can be obtained via three different approaches. The analytical approach uses theoretical models to quantify paradoxes based on certain assumptions about the voters' preferences. Analytical results usually tend to be quite hard to obtain and are limited to simple—and often unrealistic—assumptions. The experimental approach uses computer simulations based on underlying stochastic models of how the preference profiles are distributed. Experimental results have less general validity than analytical results, but can be obtained for arbitrary distributions of preferences. Finally, the empirical approach is based on evaluating real-world data to analyze how frequently paradoxes actually occur or how frequently they would have occurred if certain voting rules had been used for the given preferences. Unfortunately, only very limited real-world data for elections is available.

Our main results are as follows.

Using Ehrhart theory, we compute upper bounds for the CLP as well as the exact probabilities under which the CLP occurs for MaxiMin when there are four alternatives and preferences are distributed according to the Impartial Anonymous Culture (IAC) distribution. This approach also

Appears in: *Proceedings of the 15th International Conference on Autonomous Agents and Multiagent Systems (AAMAS 2016), J. Thangarajah, K. Tuyls, C. Jonker, S. Marsella (eds.), May 9–13, 2016, Singapore.*

yields the exact limit probabilities (for CLP and ACP) when the number of voters goes to infinity. To the best of our knowledge, these are the first analytical results for the CLP on four alternatives (which is the minimal number of alternatives for which the voting rules we consider exhibit the CLP).

For both the CLP and the ACP, we throughly analyze a variety of other settings with more alternatives and other stochastic preference models using computer simulations. For those settings in which the analytical approach is also feasible, our results are in almost perfect congruence with the analytical results. This is strong evidence for the accuracy of our simulation results.

It turns out that the CLP—which is often cited as a major flaw of some Condorcet extensions—is of no practical relevance. The maximum probability under all preference models we studied is 2.2% (for MaxiMin, three voters, four alternatives, and IAC). In more realistic settings, it is much lower. For Dodgson's rule, it never exceeds 0.01%. We did not find any occurrence of the paradox in real-world data, neither in the PrefLib library [25] nor in millions of elections based on data from the Netflix Prize [3].

The ACP, on the other hand, frequently occurs under various distributional assumptions about the voters' preferences. The extent to which it is real threat, however, strongly depends on the voting rule, the underlying distribution of preferences, and the parity of the number of voters. If the number of voters is much larger than the number of alternatives, less discriminating voting rules seem to fare better than more discriminating ones. For example, when there are 1,000 voters and four alternatives, the probability for the ACP under Copeland's rule and IAC is 9% while it occurs with a probability of 33% for Borda's rule. When there are fewer voters, the parity of the number of voters plays a surprisingly strong role. For example, if there are 6 alternatives, the ACP probability for Copeland's rule is 44% for 50 voters, but only 26% for 51 voters. These results are in line with the empirical data we analyzed.

2. RELATED WORK

There is a huge body of research on the quantitive study of voting paradoxes. Gehrlein [19] focusses on the nonexistence of Condorcet winners, arguably the most studied voting paradox. Gehrlein and Lepelley [20], on the other hand, provide an overview of many paradoxes and, in particular, analyze the influence of group coherence. In addition, Gehrlein and Lepelley [20] survey different tools and techniques that have been applied over the years for the quantitive study of voting paradoxes.

The analytical study of voting paradoxes under the assumption of IAC is most effectively done via Ehrhart theory, which goes back to the year 1962 and the French mathematician Eugène Ehrhart [16]. Interestingly, parts of these results have been reinvented (in the context of social choice) by Huang and Chua [22] in 2000, before Ehrhart's original work was independently rediscovered for social choice by Wilson and Pritchard [34] and Lepelley et al. [23] more than forty years later.

Current research on the probability of voting paradoxes under IAC is based on algorithms that build upon Ehrhart's results, such as the algorithm developed by Barvinok [2]. For many years, these approaches were limited to cases with three or fewer alternatives. Recent advances in software tools and mathematical modeling enabled the study of elections with four alternatives. Bruns and Söger [10] and Schürmann [31] provide such results for Condorcet's paradox, the Condorcet efficiency of plurality and the similarity between plurality and plurality with runoff. Schürmann [31] further shows how symmetries in the formulation of the paradoxes can be exploited to facilitate the corresponding computations.

For the CLP (sometimes also referred to as "Borda's paradox") many quantitive results are known [20], which are, however, limited to simple voting rules and scoring rules in particular. These results also include some empirical evidence for the paradox under plurality ([20], p.15) and suggest that it is an unlikely yet possible problem in practice. Interestingly, the CLP for *Condorcet extensions* has—to the best of our knowledge—only been considered by Plassmann and Tideman [28]. However, they restrict their analysis to the three-alternative case and find that the CLP never occurs, which is unsurprising since provably four alternatives are required for the Condorcet extensions they considered.

The ACP appears to have received less attention in the quantitative literature on voting paradoxes. Some limit probabilities for scoring rules were obtained by Gehrlein and Fishburn (see [20], p. 282–284). Fishburn [17] experimentally studied a variant of this paradox called "winner turns loser paradox" for Borda's rule under Impartial Culture. For Condorcet extensions, Plassmann and Tideman [28] considered another variant of the ACP under a spatial model, but again limit their experiments to three alternatives. These few results already seem to indicate that the ACP might occur even under realistic assumptions. However, there are no results for more than three alternatives, Condorcet extensions, and the ACP in its full generality.

The preference models we consider (such as IC, IAC, and the Mallows-ϕ model) have also found widespread acceptance for the experimental analysis of voting rules within the multiagent systems and AI community (see, e.g., [1, 5, 21, 27]).

3. MODELS AND DEFINITIONS

Let A be a set of m alternatives and $N = \{1, \ldots, n\}$ a set of voters. Each voter is equipped with a *(strict) preference relation* $\succ_i$, i.e., a connex,[1] transitive, and asymmetric binary relation on A. We read $x \succ_i y$ as voter i (strictly) preferring alternative x to alternative y.

A *(preference) profile* (or an *election*) is an n-tuple of preference relations and will be denoted by $R := (\succ_1, \ldots, \succ_n)$. We will sometimes consider the restriction of $\succ_i$ to a subset of alternatives $B \subseteq A$, called an *agenda*. Such a restriction will be denoted by $R|_B := (\succ_1|_B, \ldots, \succ_n|_B)$.

3.1 Stochastic Preference Models

In this paper we consider five of the most common stochastic preference models. These models vary in their degree of realism. Impartial culture (IC) and impartial anonymous culture (IAC), for example, are usually considered as rather unrealistic. However, the simplicity of these models enables

[1]A binary relation $\succ_i$ on A is connex if $x \succ_i y \vee y \succ_i x$ for all $x \neq y \in A$. One may alternatively define $\succ_i$ as the irreflexive component of a complete, antisymmetric, and transitive relation $\succcurlyeq_i$.

the use of analytical tools that cannot be applied to the other models. IC and IAC typically yield higher probabilities for paradoxes than other preference models and can therefore be seen as worst-case estimates (see, e.g., [29]). We only give informal definitions here; for more extensive treatments see, e.g., Critchlow et al. [14] and Marden [24].

Impartial culture The most widely-studied distribution is the so-called *impartial culture (IC)*, under which every possible preference relation has the same probability of $\frac{1}{m!}$. Thus, every preference profile is equally likely to occur.

Impartial anonymous culture In contrast to IC the *impartial anonymous culture (IAC)* is not based on the probabilities of individual preferences but on the probabilities of whole profiles. Under IAC one assumes that each possible *anonymous* preference profile on n voters is equally likely to occur. A more formal definition is given in Section 4.1.

Mallows-ϕ model In *Mallows-ϕ model*, the distance to a reference ranking (or ground truth) is measured by means of the Kendall-tau distance[2] and a parameter ϕ is used to indicate the dispersion. The case of $\phi = 1$ means absolute dispersion and coincides with IC, the case $\phi = 0$ corresponds to no dispersion and every voter always picks the "true" ranking. We chose $\phi = 0.8$ to simulate voters with relatively bad estimates, which leads to situations in which paradoxes are more likely to occur.

Pólya-Eggenberger urn model In the Pólya-Eggenberger *urn model*, each possible preference relation is represented by a ball in an urn from which individual preferences are drawn. After each draw, the chosen ball is put back and $\alpha \in \mathbb{N}_0$ new balls of the same kind are added to the urn. While the urn model subsumes both impartial culture ($\alpha = 0$) and impartial anonymous culture ($\alpha = 1$), we set $\alpha = 10$ to obtain a reasonably realistic interdependence of individual preferences.

Spatial model In the *spatial model* alternatives and agents are placed in a multi-dimensional space uniformly at random and the agents' preferences are then determined by the Euclidean distances to the alternatives (closer alternatives are preferred to more distant ones). The spatial model is considered particularly realistic in political science where the dimensions are interpreted as different aspects of the alternatives [32]. We chose the simple case of two dimensions for our analysis.[3]

3.2 Voting Rules

A *voting rule* is a function f that maps a preference profile to a non-empty *set of winners.*

For a preference profile R, let $g_{xy} := |\{i \in N : x \succ_i y\}| - |\{i \in N : y \succ_i x\}|$ denote the *majority margin* of x against y. A very influential concept in social choice is the notion of a Condorcet winner, an alternative that wins against any other alternative in a pairwise majority contest. Alternative x is a *Condorcet winner (CW)* of a profile R if $g_{xy} > 0$ for all $y \in A \setminus \{x\}$. Conversely, alternative x is a *Condorcet loser (CL)* if $g_{yx} > 0$ for all $y \in A \setminus \{x\}$. Neither CWs nor CLs necessarily exist, but whenever they do they are unique. A voting rule f is called a *Condorcet extension* if $f(R) = \{x\}$ whenever x is the CW in R.

In the following paragraphs we briefly introduce the voting rules considered in this paper.

Borda's Rule Under *Borda's rule* each alternative receives from 0 to $|A| - 1$ points from each voter (depending on the position the alternative is ranked in). The alternatives with highest accumulated score win.

MaxiMin The *MaxiMin* rule is only concerned with the highest defeat of each alternative in a pairwise majority contest. It yields all alternatives as winners which have the maximal value of $\min_{y \in A} g_{xy}$.

Young's Rule *Young's rule* yields all alternatives that can be made a CW by removing a minimal number of voters.

Dodgson's Rule *Dodgson's rule* selects all alternatives that can be made a CW by a minimal number of pairwise swaps of adjacent alternatives in the individual preference relations.

Essential Set Consider the symmetric two-player zero-sum game G given by the skew-symmetric matrix with entries g_{xy} for all pairs of alternatives x, y. The *essential set* is the set of all alternatives that are played with positive probability in some mixed Nash equilibrium of G.[4]

Except for Borda's rule, all presented voting rules are in fact Condorcet extensions. While Borda's rule, MaxiMin, and the essential set can be computed efficiently, Young's rule and Dodgson's rule have been shown to be complete for parallel access to NP. The essential set is one of the few voting rules that do suffer from neither the CLP nor the ACP, and is merely included as a reference. For more formal definitions and computational properties of these rules, we refer to Brandt et al. [9].

3.3 Voting Paradoxes

In this paper we focus on two voting paradoxes whose occurrence can be determined given a voting rule f and a preference profile R.

Let f be a voting rule. Formally, a *(voting) paradox* is a characteristic function that maps a preference profile to 0 or 1. In the latter case, we say the paradox *occurs* for voting rule f at profile R.

The *Condorcet Loser Paradox (CLP)* occurs when a voting rule selects the CL as a winner.

DEFINITION 1. *Given a voting rule f the* Condorcet loser paradox CLP_f *is defined as*

$$CLP_f(R) = \begin{cases} 1 & \text{if } f(R) \text{ contains a CL} \\ 0 & \text{otherwise.} \end{cases}$$

The *agenda contraction paradox (ACP)* occurs when reducing the set of alternatives, by eliminating unchosen alternatives, influences the outcome of an election.

DEFINITION 2. *Given a voting rule f the* agenda contraction paradox ACP_f *is a paradox defined as*

$$ACP_f(R) = \begin{cases} 1 & \text{if } f(R|_B) \neq f(R) \text{ for some } B \supseteq f(R) \\ 0 & \text{otherwise.} \end{cases}$$

[2]The Kendall-tau distance counts the number of pairwise disagreements.

[3]In a related study, Brandt and Seedig [5] have found that the number of dimensions does not seem to have a large impact on the results as long as it is at least two.

[4]These mixed equilibria are also known as *maximal lotteries* in probabilistic social choice.

4. QUANTIFYING VOTING PARADOXES

In this section we present the three general approaches for quantifying voting paradoxes: the analytical approach via Ehrhart theory, the experimental approach via computer simulations, and the empirical approach via real-world data.

4.1 Exact Analysis via Ehrhart Theory

Anonymous preference profiles only count the number of voters for each of the $m!$ possible rankings on m alternatives. An anonymous preference profile can hence be viewed as an integer point in a space of $d := m!$ dimensions. Formally, the set $S_{m,n}$ of anonymous preference profiles on m alternatives with n voters can be identified with the set of all integer points $z = (z_1, \ldots, z_{m!}) \in \mathbb{Z}^{m!}$ which satisfy

$$z_i \geq 0 \text{ for all } i \in \{1, \ldots, m!\}, \text{ and } \sum_{i=1}^{m!} z_i = n.$$

Under IAC each anonymous preference profile is assumed to be equally likely to occur. Hence, in order to determine the probability of a paradox *under IAC* it is enough to compute the number of points belonging to preference profiles in which the paradox occurs and compare them to the total number of points in $S_{m,n}$, which is known to be $|S_{m,n}| = \binom{m!+n-1}{m!-1}$.[5]

In this framework, many paradoxes X can be described with the help of linear constraints, i.e., the set of points belonging to the event can be described with the help of (in)equalities, a polytope. For variable n, this approach then describes a *dilated polytope* $P_n = nP := \{n\vec{x} \colon \vec{x} \in P\}$. Hence, we know that the probability of a paradox X_n under IAC is given by:

$$\mathbb{P}(X_n) = \frac{|nP \cap \mathbb{Z}^d|}{|S_{m,n}|}.$$

and we can determine the probability of (many) voting paradoxes under IAC by evaluating the function $L(P, n) := |nP \cap \mathbb{Z}^d|$, which describes the number of integer points inside the dilation nP. This can be done with the help of Ehrhart theory. Ehrhart [16] was the first to show that $L(P, n)$ can be described by special functions, called quasi- or Ehrhart-polynomials. A function $f : \mathbb{Z} \to \mathbb{Q}$ is a *quasi-polynomial* of degree d and period q if there exists a list of q polynomials $f_i \colon \mathbb{Z} \to \mathbb{Q}$ $(0 \leq i < q)$ of degree d such that $f(n) = f_i(n)$ if $n \equiv i \mod q$.

Quasi-polynomials can be determined with the help of computer programs such as LATTE (De Loera et al. [15]) or NORMALIZ (Bruns et al. [11]). Unfortunately, the computation of our quasi-polynomials is computationally very demanding, especially because the dimension of the polytopes grows super-exponentially in the number of alternatives. This limits analytical results under IAC to rather small numbers of alternatives. To the best of our knowledge, NORMALIZ is the only program which is able to compute polytopes corresponding to elections with up to *four* alternatives. And even NORMALIZ is not always able to compute the whole quasi-polynomial, but sometimes we had to resort to computing the leading coefficients only of the polynomial, which fortunately suffices for determining the limit probability of a paradox when the number of voters goes to infinity.

An overview of our analytical findings obtained in this way is provided in Table 1.

Paradox	Voting rule(s)	Result
CLP	Condorcet extensions	upper bound ($\forall n \in \mathbb{N}$)
	MaxiMin	probability ($\forall n \in \mathbb{N}$)
	Tideman's rule	limit prob. ($n \to \infty$)
ACP	MaxiMin	limit prob. ($n \to \infty$)

Table 1: Theoretical results obtained via Ehrhart theory (for four alternatives and under IAC)

Finding a Quasi-polynomial for MaxiMin

As an example for the method just described, we consider the $\text{CLP}_{\text{MaxiMin}}$ in four-alternative elections under IAC, the probabilities of which can be computed from a quasi-polynomial with degree 23 and a period of 5,040.[6]

In order to determine the polynomial, we first need to describe the corresponding polytope with equalities and inequalities. Recall the definition of MaxiMin from Section 3.2:

$$f_{\text{MaxiMin}}(R) := \arg\max_{x \in A} \min_{y \in A} g_{xy}.$$

For $\text{CLP}_{\text{MaxiMin}}(R) = 1$ the CL of R has to have the lowest highest defeat. Formally, there is $x \in A$ such that for all $y \in A \backslash \{x\}$,

$$g_{yx} > 0, \text{ and} \tag{1}$$

$$\max_{z \in A\backslash\{x\}} g_{zx} \leq \max_{z \in A\backslash\{y\}} g_{zy}. \tag{2}$$

Now let $A = \{a, b, c, d\}$ and assume $x = d$. We then have that $g_{ad}, g_{bd}, g_{cd} > 0$, which implies $\max_{z \in A\backslash\{d\}} g_{zd} > 0$. Furthermore,

$$\max_{z \in A\backslash\{y\}} g_{zy} > 0 \text{ for all } y \in \{a, b, c\},$$

from which it follows that either $g_{ab}, g_{bc}, g_{ca} > 0$ or $g_{ba}, g_{cb}, g_{ac} > 0$. In both cases there is a majority cycle between a, b, and c. Due to symmetry we can choose one direction of the cycle arbitrarily and assume $g_{ab}, g_{bc}, g_{ca} > 0$. Then,

$$\max_{z \in A\backslash\{a\}} g_{za} = g_{ca}, \max_{z \in A\backslash\{b\}} g_{zb} = g_{ab}, \text{ and } \max_{x \in A\backslash\{c\}} g_{zc} = g_{ac}.$$

Condition (1) is already represented in the form of linear inequalities. In order to model condition (2) we determine $\max_{z \in A\backslash\{d\}} g_{zd}$ and distinguish cases for the seven possible outcomes. The inequalities for the case $\max_{z \in A\backslash\{d\}} g_{zd} = \{g_{ad}\}$ are

$$g_{ad} - g_{bd} > 0 \quad \text{and} \quad g_{ad} - g_{cd} > 0.$$

[5]For most preference models other than IAC this approach does not work. While for specific combinations of (simple) distributions and voting rules there are some highly tailor-made computations in the literature (cf. Section 2), these have to be redesigned for each individual setting.

[6]In theory, the analysis can be adapted to also cover more complex rules (e.g., Dodgson's and Young's rule, which involve solving an ILP). It is unclear, however, how one would translate their definitions to linear inequalities.

Condition (2) furthermore yields

$$g_{ca} - g_{ad} \geq 0, \qquad g_{ab} - g_{ad} \geq 0, \qquad \text{and} \qquad g_{bc} - g_{ad} \geq 0.$$

Each case belongs to a different polytope and the polytopes are pairwise distinct, so we can compute each quasi-polynomial separately and later combine them to one. To get the final polynomial we have to multiply by eight for the four different possible choices of a CL and the two possible directions of the majority cycle. This then enables us to efficiently evaluate the *exact* probabilities for any number of voters. The results are depicted in Figure 2. The leading coefficient of the quasi-polynomial can also be used to determine the limit probability which is given by

$$\mathbb{P}(\text{CLP}_{\text{MaxiMin}} = 1 \mid m = 4, n \to \infty)$$
$$= 8 \cdot \frac{485052253637930099}{6443662124777472000000} \approx \underline{\underline{0.06\%}}.$$

4.2 Experimental Analysis

As we will see, simulating elections with the help of computers is a viable way of achieving very good approximations for the probabilities we are looking for. It even turns out that the results of our simulations are almost indistinguishable from the theoretical result obtained via Ehrhart theory (with the exception of the limit case, which cannot be realized via simulations).

More specifically, the experimental approach works as follows: a profile source creates random preference profiles according to a specific preference model. The profiles are then used to compute the winner(s) according to a given voting rule and to determine if the paradox occurs. Any such experiment is carried out for each pair of n and m and repeated frequently. In many cases in which we covered a wide range of voters, we did not consider every possible value of n but, more economically, only simulated the values: 1–30, 49–51, 99–101, 199–201, 499–501, 999–1,001.

In contrast to many other studies, we are concerned about the statistical significance of our experimental results. Thus, we also computed 99%-confidence intervals for each data point we generated. To this end, we used the `binofit` function in MATLAB which is based on the standard approach by Clopper and Pearson [13]. It shows that, based on our sampling rate of 10^5 and 10^6, respectively, the 99%-confidence intervals are pleasantly small. Hence, even though they are depicted in all of the figures throughout this paper, sometimes it can be difficult to recognize them.

4.3 Empirical Analysis

The most valuable quantification of voting paradoxes would be their actual frequency in real-world elections. As mentioned before, real-world election data is generally relatively sparse, incomplete, and inaccurate. This makes empirical research on this topic rather difficult. Otherwise, the empirical approach strongly resembles the experimental approach.

For this paper we used two sources of empirical data. First, we used the 314 profiles with strict order preferences from the PrefLib library [25]. Second, we had access to the 54,650 preference profiles over four alternatives without a CW which belong to the roughly 11 million four-alternative elections which Mattei et al. [26] derived from the Netflix Prize data [3]. Non-existence of Condorcet winners is a prerequisite for the paradoxes we study.

5. CONDORCET LOSER PARADOX

In this section we present our findings on the CLP. We conclude that—even though the CLP is possible in principle—it is so unlikely that it cannot be used as a serious argument against any of the Condorcet extensions we considered.

5.1 An Upper Bound

Before analyzing the CLP for concrete voting rules, we discuss an upper bound valid for all Condorcet extensions. For a Condorcet extension to choose the CL a profile obviously has to satisfy two conditions. First, there has to exist a CL in the profile. Second, no CW may exist in the profile. In the case of four-alternative elections—which is the first interesting case—we can compute the quasi-polynomial via Ehrhart theory and hence know the exact probabilities for any number of voters. The derivation and presentation of the quasi-polynomial, which has degree 23 and contains 24 polynomials, is omitted due to space constraints. The resulting probabilities for up to 1 000 voters—and a comparison with the results of an experimental analysis—can be obtained from Figure 1. The value of the limit probability is approximately 8%.

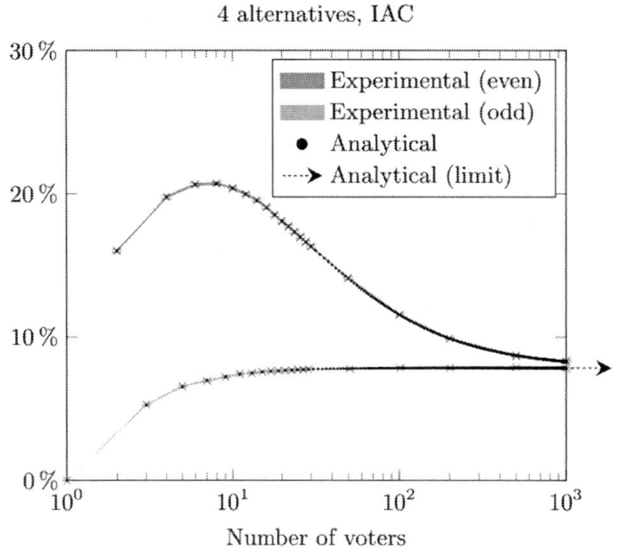

Figure 1: Probability of the event that a Condorcet extension could choose a CL in four-alternative elections under IAC

Especially for small even numbers of voters, where the probability is around 20%, the upper bound is too high to discard the CLP for Condorcet extensions altogether, and even the limit probability of 8% is relatively large. Also, for an increasing number of alternatives this problem does not vanish (for elections with 50 and 51 one voters and up to 100 alternatives the probabilities range between 5% and 25%).[7]

Note that differences between odd and even number of voters were to be expected since even numbers allow for majority ties, which have significant consequences for the paradoxes; this effect decreases for larger electorates. In the

[7]These upper bounds turn out to be relatively independent from the underlying preference distribution (among the models we considered, cf. Section 5.3).

specific case under consideration, the upper bound is generally higher for an even number of voters because the much higher likelihood of not having a CW more than counterbalances the lower likelihood of having a CL.

5.2 Results under IAC

Despite the high upper bounds from the previous section, the picture is quite clear for concrete Condorcet extensions: even under IAC, the risk of the considered Condorcet extensions selecting the CL is very low, as shown in Figure 2 and Figure 3 for four-alternative elections. The highest probability was found for $CLP_{MaxiMin}$ with 2.2% for three voters (CLP_{Young} with about 0.9%). The limit probability of $CLP_{MaxiMin}$, with 0.06% is so low that for sufficiently large electorates it would occur in only one out of 10,000 elections. The same seems to hold for the limit probability for CLP_{Young}. The probability of $CLP_{Dodgson}$ is even significantly lower, with a maximum of about 0.01% in elections with 9,999 voters. We could determine the limit probability of 0.01% only for an approximation of Dodgson's rule by Tideman [33], which seems to be close to that for Dodgson's rule, based on our experimental data.

When increasing the number of alternatives the probabilities drop even further. For elections with more than ten alternatives they reach a negligibly small level of less than 0.005% for all considered rules and in no simulations with twelve or more alternatives we could find any occurrence of the paradox.

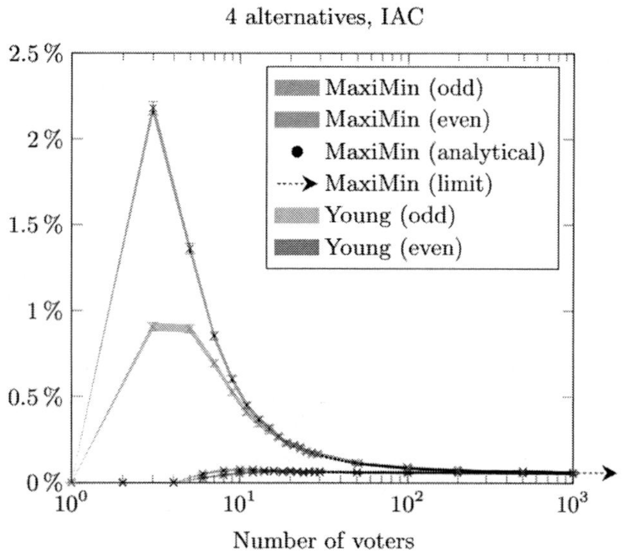

Figure 2: Comparison between CLP probabilities for MaxiMin and Young's rule under IAC in four-alternative elections

5.3 Results under Other Preference Models

Figure 4, as one would expect, shows that under more realistic assumptions the probability of the CLP decreases further in four-alternative elections with 50/51 voters, with the highest probability occurring under the unrealistic assumption of IC and the lowest probability under what may be the most realistic model in many settings, the spatial

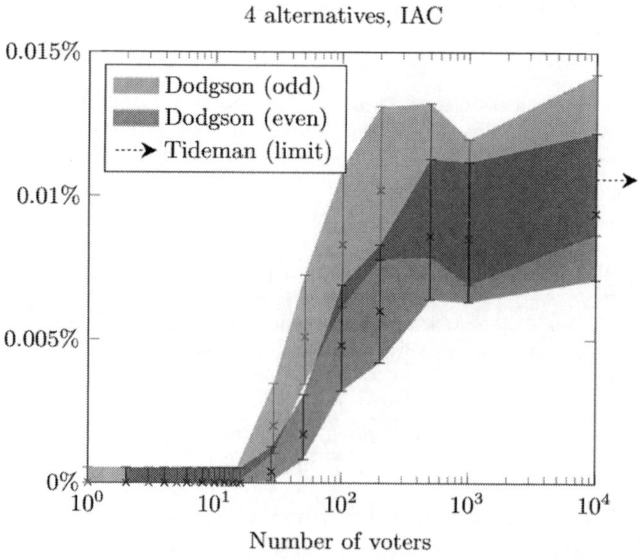

Figure 3: CLP probabilities for Dodgson's rule under IAC in four-alternative elections; the seemingly large confidence intervals are due to the small scale of the graph.

model. In our experiments, Dodgson's rule *never* selected a CL in the spatial model.

Similarly, we could not find any occurrence of the CLP in real-world data, which may be considered the strongest evidence that the CLP virtually never materializes in practice.[8]

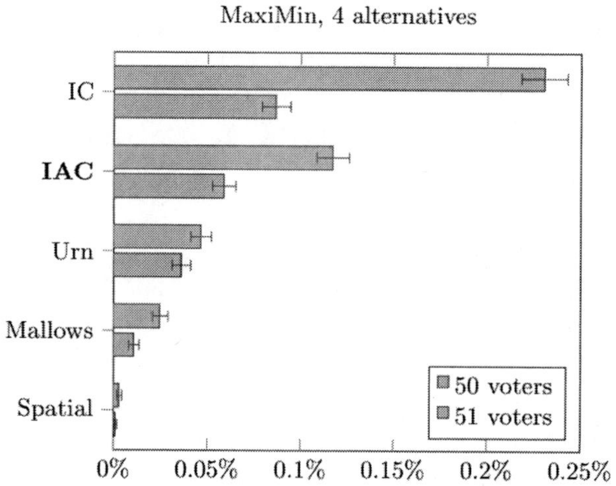

Figure 4: CLP probabilities in four-alternative elections for varying preference models and MaxiMin

[8]We tested 314 preference profiles with strict orders from the PrefLib library as well as the roughly 11 million four-alternative elections which Mattei et al. [26] derived from the Netflix Prize data. While about 54,000 of those elections were susceptible to the CLP, it never occurred under the rules we considered in this paper. In contrast, under plurality it already occurred in twelve out of the 314 PrefLib-instances.

6. AGENDA CONTRACTION PARADOX

Recall that the *agenda contraction paradox (ACP)* occurs when a reduced set of alternatives (created by the unavailability of losing alternatives) influences the outcome of an election. For many cases, it may be considered a generalization of the CLP as the following argument shows. Suppose the CL x is uniquely selected by a voting rule which implements majority rule on two-alternative choice sets. Then restricting A to $\{x, y\}$ for some alternative $y \neq x$ yields the new winner y (since $g_{xy} > 0$).

As we will see, the ACP is much more of a practical problem than the CLP. The picture, however, is not black and white. Whether or not it is a serious threat depends on the voting rule, the underlying preference distribution, and on the parity of the number of voters.

6.1 Varying Voting Rules

The ACP probability strongly varies for different voting rules (see Figure 5). Borda's rule generally exhibits the worst behavior of the rules studied, with probabilities of up to 56%, and with 34% for large electorates with 1,000 voters. In contrast, Copeland's rule is quite robust to the ACP for large electorates (with only about 8% occurrence probability for 1,000 voters).[9]

The reason for this gap between Borda's and Copeland's rule appears to be two-fold: First, Condorcet extensions are safe from this paradox as long as a CW exists; Borda's rule, by contrast, is not. Second, the discriminatory power of voting rules (i.e., their ability to select small winning sets) strongly supports the paradox. As soon as a single majority-dominated alternative is selected, the ACP has to occur. For large numbers of voters, this is in line with Copeland's rule being least discriminating among those evaluated. The essential set is among the most discriminating known voting rules immune to the ACP, but presumably less discriminating than Copeland's rule.

The behavior of MaxiMin is almost identical to that of Young's and Dodgson's rule. Confirming our approximate "limit" results of 1,000 voters, we were able to analytically compute the limit probability for MaxiMin as $\frac{331}{2048} \approx 16\%$. This is in perfect congruence with the (rounded) values for MaxiMin, Young's rule, and Dodgson's rule.

It should also be noted that with fewer than 100 voters, the parity of the number of voters plays a major role. For even numbers, significantly higher probabilities arise (which is particularly true for Copeland's rule, see above). At least part of this can be explained by a reduced probability for CWs in these cases.

For more alternatives (see the right-hand side of Figure 5), the relative behavior remains vastly unchanged with probabilities further increasing to values larger than 40% to 80% (mostly since the likelihood of a CW decreases roughly at the same rate).

6.2 Varying Preference Models

Figure 6 extends the analysis of the previous section by additionally considering preference models beyond IAC. The overall picture regarding the different rules remains the same. For large electorates Copeland's rule outperforms the other rules, whereas Borda's rule performs worst.

Regarding the different preference models, three classes emerge from Figure 6.

First, for Mallows-ϕ we observe probabilities that are vanishing with increased numbers of voters. Under the spatial model this is true as well, with the surprising exception of Borda's rule, for which the picture looks completely different and the probability does not go below 20% in the spatial model. Presumably, this can be explained by Borda's inability to select the CW in this setting, a hypothesis that deserves further study, however. On the contrary, the other rules appear to be benefitting from the fact that the existence of a CW becomes very likely under models with high voter interdependence.

Second, as expected, the assumption of IC serves as an upper bound for all other preference models. The results for IAC are not much lower, fostering the impression that IAC could also be an unrealistic upper bound.

Third, the urn model yields much lower values compared to IAC and IC. The absolute numbers, however, are still beyond acceptable levels (between 4% and 23% for 1,000 voters).

The findings in the empirical data corroborate our experimental findings. In PrefLib the ACP occurs 17 times for Borda, three times for Copeland and exactly once for MaxiMin as well as Young's and Dodgson's rule. In the Netflix data set, where the number of voters is at least 350, Copeland performs much better than the other Condorcet extensions (4,400 compared to 18,470 occurrences for the other Condorcet extensions). Borda's rule virtually always suffers from the ACP on this data set: there are 54,620 instances of ACPs already when considering profiles that do not have a CW (there are 54,650 of such).

7. CONCLUSION

We investigated the likelihood of the CLP and the ACP using Ehrhart theory, computer simulations, and empirical data. The CLP is often cited as a major flaw of some Condorcet extensions such as Dodgson's rule, Young's rule, and MaxiMin. For example, Fishburn regards Condorcet extensions that suffer from the CLP (specifically referring to the three rules mentioned above) as " 'dubious' extensions of the basic Condorcet criterion" ([18], p. 480).[10] While this is intelligible from a theoretical point of view, our results have shown that the CLP is of virtually no practical concern. The ACP, on the other hand, frequently occurs under various distributional assumptions about the voters' preferences. The extent to which it is real threat, however, strongly depends on the voting rule, the underlying distribution of preferences, and, surprisingly, the parity of the number of voters. Our main quantitative results for the worst case are summarized in Table 2. Potential future work includes the analysis of other voting paradoxes (such as monotonicity failures or the no-show paradox) and other rules (such as Nanson's rule or Black's rule).

Acknowledgments

Christian Geist was supported by Deutsche Forschungsgemeinschaft under grant BR 2312/9-1. The authors also thank Nicholas Mattei for providing the Netflix Prize data and Christof Söger for his guidance regarding Normaliz.

[9]For small *even* numbers of voters, Copeland's rule also frequently fails agenda contraction, which is also visible in Figure 6 and explains the seemingly high values in Table 2.

[10]Fishburn [18] actually analyzes violations of "Smith's Condorcet principle", which is weaker than the CLP.

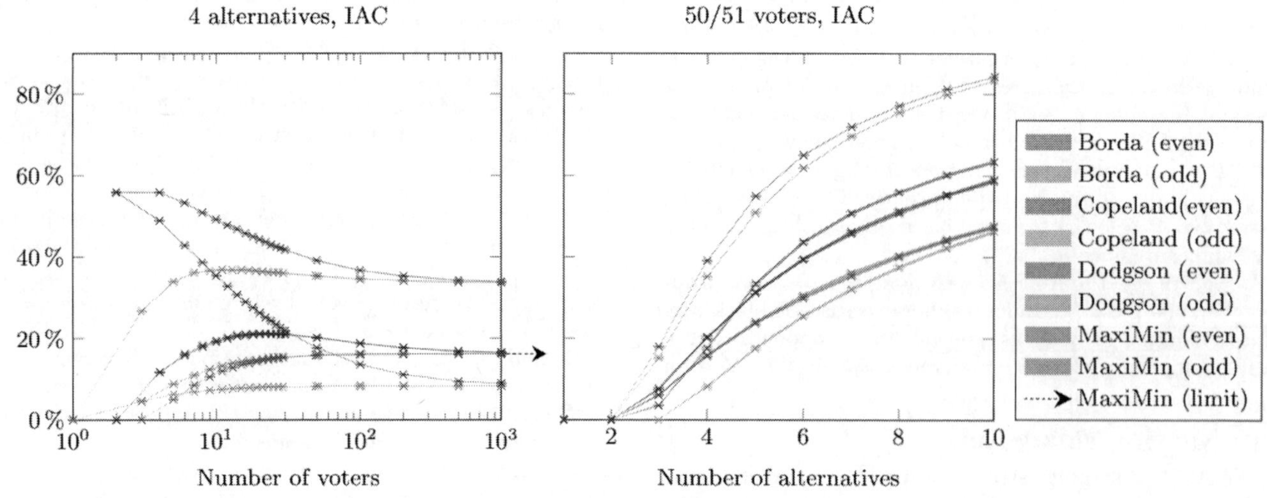

Figure 5: Comparison between ACP probabilities for different voting rules under IAC

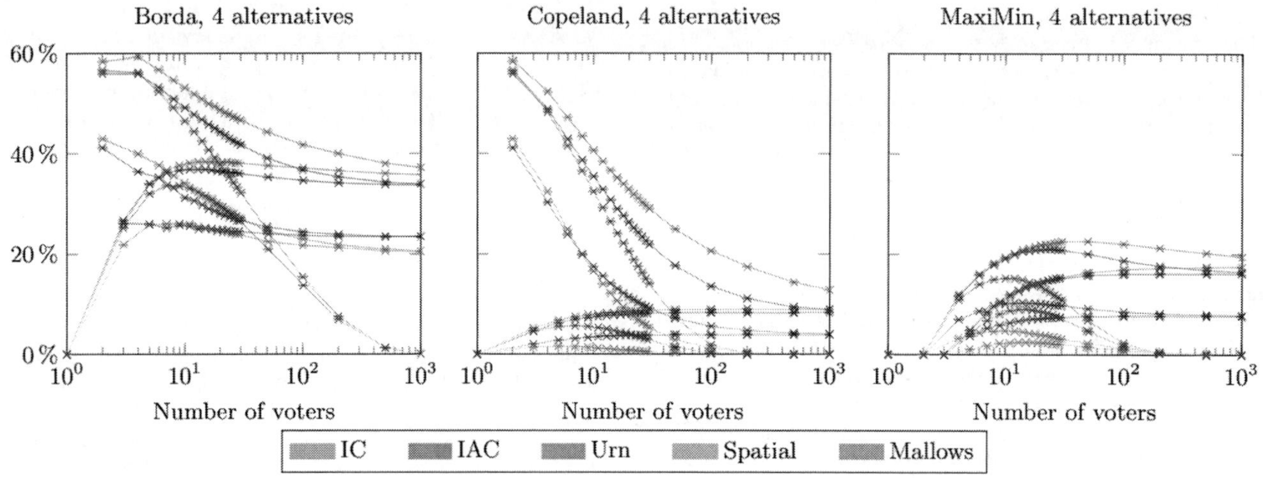

Figure 6: Comparison between $\text{ACP}_{\text{Borda}}$, $\text{ACP}_{\text{MaxiMin}}$ and $\text{ACP}_{\text{Copeland}}$ for varying preference models in four-alternative elections; the values of $\text{ACP}_{\text{Young}}$ and $\text{ACP}_{\text{Dodgson}}$ are omitted since they strongly resemble the ones of $\text{ACP}_{\text{MaxiMin}}$.

Paradox	Condorcet loser paradox (CLP)			Agenda contraction paradox (ACP)		
Model	IAC		IC	IAC		IC
n	$\{1,\ldots,1000\}$	$\{50,51\}$	$\{50,51\}$	$\{1,\ldots,1000\}$	$\{50,51\}$	$\{1,\ldots,1000\}$
m	4	$\{1,\ldots,10\}$	4	4	$\{1,\ldots,10\}$	4
Essential set	0%	0%	0%	0%	0%	0%
Borda	0%	0%	0%	56%	84%	59%
Copeland	0%	0%	0%	56%	63%	58%
Dodgson	0.01%	0.005%	0.005%	21%	59%	23%
Young	1%	0.15%	0.25%	21%	59%	23%
MaxiMin	2.2%	0.15%	0.25%	21%	59%	23%

Table 2: Rounded maximal CLP and ACP probabilities which occurred during our simulations

REFERENCES

[1] H. Aziz, S. Gaspers, N. Mattei, N. Narodytska, and T. Walsh. Ties matter: Complexity of manipulation when tie-breaking with a random vote. In *Proc. of 27th AAAI Conference*, pages 74–80. AAAI Press, 2013.

[2] A. I. Barvinok. A polynomial time algorithm for counting integral points in polyhedra when the dimension is fixed. *Mathematics of Operations Research*, 19(4):769–779, 1994.

[3] J. Bennett and S. Lanning. The Netflix prize. In *Proceedings of KDD Cup and Workshop*, 2007.

[4] F. Brandt and H. G. Seedig. A tournament of order 24 with two disjoint TEQ-retentive sets. Technical report, `http://arxiv.org/abs/1302.5592`, 2013.

[5] F. Brandt and H. G. Seedig. On the discriminative power of tournament solutions. In *Proc. of 1st AAMAS Workshop on Exploring Beyond the Worst Case in Computational Social Choice (EXPLORE)*, 2014.

[6] F. Brandt, F. Fischer, P. Harrenstein, and M. Mair. A computational analysis of the tournament equilibrium set. In *Proc. of 23rd AAAI Conference*, pages 38–43. AAAI Press, 2008.

[7] F. Brandt, M. Chudnovsky, I. Kim, G. Liu, S. Norin, A. Scott, P. Seymour, and S. Thomassé. A counterexample to a conjecture of Schwartz. *Social Choice and Welfare*, 40:739–743, 2013.

[8] F. Brandt, V. Conitzer, and U. Endriss. Computational social choice. In G. Weiß, editor, *Multiagent Systems*, chapter 6, pages 213–283. MIT Press, 2nd edition, 2013.

[9] F. Brandt, V. Conitzer, U. Endriss, J. Lang, and A. Procaccia, editors. *Handbook of Computational Social Choice*. Cambridge University Press, 2016.

[10] W. Bruns and C. Söger. The computation of generalized Ehrhart series in Normaliz. *Journal of Symbolic Computation*, 68(2):75–86, 2015. Effective Methods in Algebraic Geometry.

[11] W. Bruns, B. Ichim, T. Römer, R. Sieg, and C. Söger. Normaliz. Algorithms for rational cones and affine monoids. Available at `https://www.normaliz.uni-osnabrueck.de`.

[12] Y. Chevaleyre, U. Endriss, J. Lang, and N. Maudet. A short introduction to computational social choice. In *Proc. of 33rd Conference on Current Trends in Theory and Practice of Computer Science (SOFSEM)*, volume 4362 of *LNCS*, pages 51–69. Springer, 2007.

[13] C. J. Clopper and E. S. Pearson. The use of confidence or fiducial limits illustrated in the case of the binomial. *Biometrika*, 26(4):404–413, 1934.

[14] D. E. Critchlow, M. A. Fligner, and J. S. Verducci. Probability models on rankings. *Journal of Mathematical Psychology*, 35:294–318, 1991.

[15] J. A. De Loera, R. Hemmecke, J. Tauzer, and R. Yoshida. Effective lattice point counting in rational convex polytopes. *Journal of Symbolic Computation*, 38(4):1273–1302, 2004.

[16] E. Ehrhart. Sur les polyedres rationnels homothetiques á n dimensions. *Compte-Rendus de l'académie des Sciences*, 254(4):616, 1962.

[17] P. C. Fishburn. Paradoxes of voting. *The American Political Science Review*, 68(2):537–546, 1974.

[18] P. C. Fishburn. Condorcet social choice functions. *SIAM Journal on Applied Mathematics*, 33(3):469–489, 1977.

[19] W. V. Gehrlein. *Condorcet's Paradox*. Springer, 2006.

[20] W. V. Gehrlein and D. Lepelley. *Voting paradoxes and group coherence: the Condorcet efficiency of voting rules*. Springer-Verlag, 2010.

[21] J. Goldsmith, J. Lang, N. Mattei, and P. Perny. Voting with rank dependent scoring rules. In *Proc. of 28th AAAI Conference*, pages 698–704. AAAI Press, 2014.

[22] H. C. Huang and V. C. H. Chua. Analytical representation of probabilities under the IAC condition. *Social Choice and Welfare*, 17(1):143–155, 2000.

[23] D. Lepelley, A. Louichi, and H. Smaoui. On Ehrhart polynomials and probability calculations in voting theory. *Social Choice and Welfare*, 30(3):363–383, 2008.

[24] J. I. Marden. *Analyzing and Modeling Rank Data*. Number 64 in Monographs on Statistics and Applied Probability. Chapman & Hall, 1995.

[25] N. Mattei and T. Walsh. PrefLib: A library for preference data. In *Proc. of 3rd ADT*, volume 8176 of *LNCS*, pages 259–270. Springer, 2013.

[26] N. Mattei, J. Forshee, and J. Goldsmith. An empirical study of voting rules and manipulation with large datasets. In *Proc. of 4th COMSOC*, 2012.

[27] J. Oren, Y. Filmus, and C. Boutilier. Efficient vote elicitation under candidate uncertainty. In *Proc. of 23rd IJCAI*, pages 309–316. AAAI Press, 2015.

[28] F. Plassmann and N. Tideman. How frequently do different voting rules encounter voting paradoxes in three-candidate elections? *Social Choice and Welfare*, 42(1):31–75, 2014.

[29] M. Regenwetter, B. Grofman, A. A. J. Marley, and I. M. Tsetlin. *Behavioral Social Choice: Probabilistic Models, Statistical Inference, and Applications*. Cambridge University Press, 2006.

[30] J. Rothe, editor. *Economics and Computation: An Introduction to Algorithmic Game Theory, Computational Social Choice, and Fair Division*. Springer, 2015.

[31] A. Schürmann. Exploiting polyhedral symmetries in social choice. *Social Choice and Welfare*, 40(4):1097–1110, 2013.

[32] N. Tideman and F. Plassmann. Modeling the outcomes of vote-casting in actual elections. In D. S. Felsenthal and M. Machover, editors, *Electoral Systems: Paradoxes, Assumptions, and Procedures*, Studies in Choice and Welfare. Springer, 2012.

[33] T. N. Tideman. Independence of clones as a criterion for voting rules. *Social Choice and Welfare*, 4(3):185–206, 1987.

[34] M. C. Wilson and G. Pritchard. Probability calculations under the IAC hypothesis. *Mathematical Social Sciences*, 54(3):244–256, 2007.

Complexity of Finding Equilibria of Plurality Voting Under Structured Preferences

Edith Elkind
University of Oxford
Oxford, United Kingdom
elkind@cs.ox.ac.uk

Evangelos Markakis
Athens University of Economics and Business
Athens, Greece
markakis@gmail.com

Svetlana Obraztsova
I-CORE, Hebrew University of Jerusalem
Jerusalem, Israel
svetlana.obraztsova@gmail.com

Piotr Skowron
University of Oxford
Oxford, United Kingdom
p.k.skowron@gmail.com

ABSTRACT

We study the complexity of finding pure Nash equilibria in voting games over well-known restricted preference domains, such as the domains of single-peaked and single-crossing preferences. We focus on the Plurality rule, and, following the recent work of Elkind et al. [15], consider three popular tie-breaking rules (lexicographic, random-candidate, and random-voter) and two types of voters' attitude: lazy voters, who prefer to abstain when their vote cannot affect the election outcome, and truth-biased voters, who prefer to vote truthfully in such cases. Elkind et al. [15] have shown that for most of these combinations of tie-breaking rules and voters' attitudes finding a Nash equilibrium is NP-hard; in contrast, we demonstrate that in almost all cases this problem is tractable for preferences that are single-peaked or single-crossing, under mild technical assumptions.

General Terms

Algorithms, Economics, Theory

Keywords

Nash equilibrium; Plurality; algorithms; single-peaked; single-crossing

1. INTRODUCTION

Since the famous Arrow's impossibility theorem [1] and its further consequences pointed out by Gibbard [21] and Satterthwaite [27], we know that virtually every voting rule creates incentives for the voters to act strategically, i.e., to misreport their preferences in order to enforce a more preferable outcome. These results are often viewed as disappointing, since negative consequences of strategic voting may be disastrous [19, 8]. Consequently, in order to understand various voting rules and to make a conscious decision as to which voting rule to use in a given scenario, one needs to study how these rules operate in a strategic environment.

Appears in: *Proceedings of the 15th International Conference on Autonomous Agents and Multiagent Systems (AAMAS 2016), J. Thangarajah, K. Tuyls, C. Jonker, S. Marsella (eds.), May 9–13, 2016, Singapore.*

As first pointed out by Farquharson [20], outcomes of elections with strategic voters can be better understood through analyzing the corresponding voting games, and in particular by describing their Nash equilibria. This line of research has received a considerable amount of attention in the social choice literature, see, e.g., [31, 3, 10]. Consequently, it is important to investigate the computational complexity of finding Nash equilibria in voting games: efficient algorithms for this problem would allow to predict an outcome of a specific election instance or to derive general conclusions by analyzing the structure of equilibria for real data describing voters' preferences [23].

In this paper we focus on equilibria of the Plurality rule, which is one of the most popular tools for making collective decisions. Under Plurality, each voter specifies her most preferred candidate or abstains from voting. If there exists a unique candidate who received the highest number of votes, then she is the winner; otherwise, a tie-breaking rule is used to select the winner from the set of top-scoring candidates. Popular tie-breaking rules include the *lexicographic rule*, where we fix an order over the set of candidates and select the candidate with the lowest rank in this order, the *random candidate rule*, where the winning candidate is selected uniformly at random from the set of top-scorers, and the *random voter rule*, where the ties are resolved according to the preferences of a single voter who is selected uniformly at random (the random voter rule is used to break ties under, e.g., the Schulze method [28]).

Unfortunately, Plurality voting admits highly counterintuitive equilibria: e.g., if there are at least 3 voters, even if all voters have identical rankings, the profile where they all vote for a candidate they rank last is a Nash equilibrium. Therefore, a common approach is to endow voters with secondary preferences over outcomes and study the equilibria of the resulting game. Recent work focused on two types of secondary preferences: *lazy voters*, who prefer to abstain if their vote cannot influence the outcome of elections, and the *truth-biased voters*, who prefer to vote truthfully in such a case; see, e.g., [3, 6, 29, 13, 22, 24, 32]. In particular, Elkind et al. [15], building on the earlier work of Desmedt and Elkind [11] and Obraztsova et al. [26], characterized the Nash equilibria of games that correspond to all six possible combinations of secondary preferences and tie-breaking rules, and showed that for five of them finding Nash equilibria is NP-hard (the only easy combination is lazy voters and lexicographic tie-breaking).

While these intractability results are discouraging, they rely on building complicated preference profiles. Therefore, one may hope that they can be circumvented by imposing additional structural constraints on voters' preferences. In particular, many problems in computational social choice have recently been shown to become easier when the voters' preferences are single-peaked [5] or single-crossing [25]; see, e.g., the work by Faliszewski et al. [18], Brandt et al. [7] and Faliszewski et al. [17] for results on manipulation, control and bribery, and by Betzler et al. [4] and Skowron et al. [30] on committee selection rules.

In this paper, we pursue this direction for the problem of finding Nash equilibria of Plurality voting. Specifically, we consider the five hard combinations of secondary preferences and tie-breaking rules studied by Elkind et al. [15], and, for each of them, investigate the complexity of finding a Nash equilibrium under single-peaked or single-crossing preferences. For almost all of these scenarios, we derive polynomial-time algorithms for our problem, under a mild technical assumption, which we refer to as *tie-consistency*. We view our results as a first step towards designing algorithms for finding Nash equilibria in realistic voting scenarios: while we do not expect typical real-life elections to be single-peaked or single-crossing, it is plausible that they are often not too far from having these properties, for an appropriate notion of distance, and one may be able to develop an efficient procedure for handling such 'almost structured' instances by building on our ideas.

2. PRELIMINARIES

Preferences, utilities, ballots. For each positive integer t, we set $[t] = \{1, \dots, t\}$. Let $N = [n]$ be a set of voters and let $C = \{c_1, \dots c_m\}$ be a set of *candidates*. Each voter $i \in N$ is endowed with a *utility function* $u_i : C \to \mathbb{N}$: for each $c_j \in C$ the quantity $u_i(c_j)$ is the intrinsic utility that i gains when c_j becomes the unique election winner. We assume that each voter assigns different utilities to different candidates. A *utility profile* is a list $\mathbf{u} = (u_1, \dots, u_n)$ of utility functions of all voters. For each $i \in N$, the utility function u_i induces a *preference order* $\succ_i$ over C: we set $c \succ_i c'$ if and only if $u_i(c) > u_i(c')$. A *preference profile* is a list of preference orders of all voters. For each voter $i \in N$, let a_i denote i's most preferred candidate, and let $\mathbf{a} = (a_1, \dots, a_n)$.

Under the Plurality rule each voter submits her *ballot* b_i, which is the name of a single candidate or, if i chooses to abstain, $b_i = \varnothing$. A *ballot profile* $\mathbf{b} = (b_1, \dots, b_n)$ is a list of ballots of all voters. We write $(\mathbf{b}_{-i}, b')$ to denote the profile obtained from $\mathbf{b}$ by replacing the ballot of the i-th voter, b_i, with b'. Let $\mathrm{sc}(c_j, \mathbf{b}) = |\{i \in N \mid b_i = c_j\}|$ denote the *score* of candidate c_j. Let $M(\mathbf{b}) = \max_{c \in C} \mathrm{sc}(c, \mathbf{b})$ be the maximum score of a candidate in the ballot vector $\mathbf{b}$. The *winning set* $W(\mathbf{b}) = \{c \in C \mid \mathrm{sc}(c, \mathbf{b}) = M(\mathbf{b})\}$ is the set of all candidates who received the highest score. The winner is selected from the winning set according to a tie-breaking rule. Additionally, we define the following sets that will be useful in our analysis: $H(\mathbf{b}) = \{c \in C \mid \mathrm{sc}(c, \mathbf{b}) = M(\mathbf{b}) - 1\}$, $H'(\mathbf{b}) = \{c \in C \mid \mathrm{sc}(c, \mathbf{b}) = M(\mathbf{b}) - 2\}$.

Tie-breaking rules. A *lottery* over a candidate set X is a vector $\mathbf{p} = (p_j)_{j \in X}$ with $p_j \geq 0$ for each $j \in X$ and $\sum_{j \in X} p_j = 1$. A *tie-breaking rule* returns a (possibly degenerate) lottery over the winning set. The *expected utility* of a voter $i \in N$ in an election with ballot profile $\mathbf{b}$ and tie-breaking rule R is computed as $\sum_{j \in W(\mathbf{b})} u_i(c_j)p_j$, where $\mathbf{p}$ is the lottery returned by R.

We consider three ways of resolving ties. The *lexicographic rule* R^L outputs the candidate $w \in W(\mathbf{b})$ with the lowest index, i.e., if $W(\mathbf{b}) = \{c_{j_1}, \dots, c_{j_k}\}$, $j_1 < \dots < j_k$, it sets $p_{j_1} = 1$, $p_{j_\ell} = 0$ for $\ell = 2, \dots, k$. The *random candidate rule* R^C returns the lottery $\mathbf{p}$ such that $p_j = 1/|W(\mathbf{b})|$ for each $c_j \in W(\mathbf{b})$. Under the *random voter rule* R^V we ask a random voter to pick her most preferred candidate from $W(\mathbf{b})$. Formally, the random voter rule returns the lottery $\mathbf{p}$ with $p_j = |B(c_j, W(\mathbf{b}))|/n$ for each $c_j \in W(\mathbf{b})$, where $B(c_j, W(\mathbf{b}))$ is the number of voters whose favorite candidate in $W(\mathbf{b})$ is c_j.

Lazy and truth-biased voters. Following Elkind et al. [15] (see also references therein), we consider *lazy* voters, who prefer to abstain when their vote has no effect on the election outcome, and *truth-biased* voters, who prefer to vote truthfully in such a case. These attitudes are formally captured by the formulas defining agents' overall utilities. Let ε be a constant satisfying $0 < \varepsilon < \min\{\frac{1}{m^2}, \frac{1}{n^2}\}$. Let $\mathbf{p}$ be the lottery produced by the tie-breaking rule on the candidate set $W(\mathbf{b})$. We say that a voter $i \in N$ is *lazy* if her utility at $\mathbf{b}$ is given by

$$U_i(\mathbf{b}) = \begin{cases} \sum_{c_j \in W(\mathbf{b})} p_j u_i(c_j) & \text{if } b_i \in C, \\ \sum_{c_j \in W(\mathbf{b})} p_j u_i(c_j) + \varepsilon & \text{if } b_i = \varnothing; \end{cases}$$

we say that she is *truth-biased* if her utility at $\mathbf{b}$ is given by

$$U_i(\mathbf{b}) = \begin{cases} \sum_{c_j \in W(\mathbf{b})} p_j u_i(c_j) & \text{if } b_i \in C \setminus \{a_i\}, \\ \sum_{c_j \in W(\mathbf{b})} p_j u_i(c_j) + \varepsilon & \text{if } b_i = a_i, \\ -\infty & \text{if } b_i = \varnothing. \end{cases}$$

Computational problems. From the above discussion we see that the voting game is determined by three parameters: the voters' attitude (lazy or truth-biased), the tie-breaking rule, and the voters' utility profile. Formally, a voting game is a triple $(\mathcal{S}, R, \mathbf{u})$, where $\mathcal{S} \in \{\mathcal{L}, \mathcal{T}\}$, $R \in \{R^C, R^V, R^L\}$, and $\mathbf{u}$ is the utility profile. The action space of each voter is $C \cup \{\varnothing\}$. A ballot vector $\mathbf{b}$ is a *pure Nash equilibrium (PNE)* of the game $(\mathcal{S}, R, \mathbf{u})$ if for each voter $i \in N$ and each action $b' \in C \cup \{\varnothing\}$ it holds that $U_i(\mathbf{b}) \geq U_i(\mathbf{b}_{-i}, b')$ (where the definition of U_i depends on $\mathcal{S}$ and R, as specified above). We are now ready to define the computational problems we consider.

DEFINITION 1 (EXISTNE, TIENE, SINGLENE). *Fix $\mathcal{S} \in \{\mathcal{L}, \mathcal{T}\}$ and $R \in \{R^C, R^V, R^L\}$. In $(\mathcal{S}, R)$-*EXISTNE *we are given a utility profile $\mathbf{u}$ and ask whether the voting game $(\mathcal{S}, R, \mathbf{u})$ admits a PNE. In $(\mathcal{S}, R)$-*TIENE *and $(\mathcal{S}, R)$-*SINGLENE *we are given a utility profile $\mathbf{u}$ and a distinguished candidate $c_j \in C$; in $(\mathcal{S}, R)$-*TIENE *we ask whether G admits a PNE $\mathbf{b}$ with $|W(\mathbf{b})| > 1$ and $c_j \in W(\mathbf{b})$, and in $(\mathcal{S}, R)$-*SINGLENE *we ask whether G admits a PNE $\mathbf{b}$ with $W(\mathbf{b}) = \{c_j\}$.*

Note that polynomial-time algorithms for SINGLENE and TIENE can be used to solve EXISTNE in polynomial time.

Structured preference domains. We will consider elections that are single-dimensional in the following sense: voters or candidates can be ordered along a single axis so that voters' preferences are consistent with this axis. Formalizing this idea gives rise to single-peaked [5] and single-crossing [25] profiles.

DEFINITION 2. *Let $\lhd$ be a strict linear order over a candidate set C. A preference order $\succ$ over C is* single-peaked *with respect to $\lhd$ if for every triple of distinct candidates $a, b, c \in C$ it holds that if $a \lhd b \lhd c$ then $b \succ c$ or $b \succ a$. A preference profile $(\succ_1, \dots, \succ_n)$ over C is* single-peaked *if there exists a strict linear order $\lhd$ over C such that for every $i = 1, \dots, n$ the preference order $\succ_i$ is single-peaked with respect to $\lhd$.*

DEFINITION 3. *A preference profile $(\succ_1, \dots, \succ_n)$ over a candidate set C is called* single-crossing with respect to a voter order $(i_1, \dots, i_n)$ *if for every pair of candidates $a, b \in C$ such that $a \succ_{i_1} b$ there exists a $p \in \{1, \dots, n\}$ such that $a \succ_{i_k} b$ for all $k \leq p$ and $b \succ_{i_k} a$ for all $k > p$.*

There exist polynomial-time algorithms that detect whether a given preference profile is single-peaked [2, 12, 16] or single-crossing [12, 14, 9], and, if so, find an order of candidates/voters that witnesses this. Therefore, in what follows, when considering single-peaked profiles over a candidate set $\{c_1, \dots, c_m\}$, we assume that they are single-peaked with respect to the candidate order $c_1 \lhd \dots \lhd c_m$, and when considering single-crossing profiles, we assume that they are single-crossing with respect to the voter order $(1, \dots, n)$.

Tie-consistent utilities. If a ballot profile $\mathbf{b}$ results in a tie, a voter i may change her vote to some $c \in W(\mathbf{b}) \setminus \{b_i\}$ to make c the unique election winner. In what follows, we will consider voters who make all such decisions in the same way, i.e., always prefer the lottery over $W(\mathbf{b})$ induced by the tie-breaking rule or always prefer their top candidate in $W(\mathbf{b}) \setminus \{b_i\}$. Formally, we say that a voter i is *tie-loving* if for every set of candidates X, $|X| \geq 3$, she weakly prefers the uniform lottery over X to her second most preferred candidate in X being the unique winner; we say that i is *tie-hating* if for every set of candidates X, $|X| \geq 3$, she weakly prefers her second most preferred candidate in X being the unique winner to the uniform lottery over X. A voter is *tie-consistent* if she is tie-loving or tie-hating. For one of our proofs we need a stronger notion: we say that a voter i is *strongly tie-loving* if for every set of candidates X, $|X| \geq 3$, she weakly prefers any lottery over X that assigns the probability at least $1/m$ to her top candidate in X over her second most preferred candidate in X being the unique winner.

There are many utility functions that ensure tie-consistency. For example, if a voter's utility for a candidate declines quickly with the candidate's position in that voter's preference order, she is likely to be tie-loving. More precisely, we say that a utility function u over a candidate set C, $|C| = m$, is *exponentially decreasing* if for every pair of candidates $c, c' \in C$ it holds that $u(c) > u(c')$ implies $u(c) \geq m \cdot u(c')$. If a voter's utility function u is exponentially decreasing, then she is strongly tie-loving: indeed, if she ranks the candidates in X as $c \succ c' \succ \dots$ then under the lottery over X that assigns probability at least $\frac{1}{m}$ to c her utility is at least $\frac{1}{m}u(c)$ and if c' wins, her utility is $u(c') \leq \frac{1}{m}u(c)$. Conversely, if a voter's utility declines very slowly with the candidate's ranking, she is likely to be tie-hating. For instance, consider a voter whose utility function is given by $u(c_j) = 2^m - 2^j$ for $j \in [m]$. If her second most preferred candidate in a set X, $|X| \geq 3$, is c_k, then her utility from the uniform lottery over X is at most $2^m - \frac{1}{|X|}(2 + 2^k + (|X| - 2)2^{k+1}) < 2^m - 2^k = u(c_k)$. However, if a voter's utility function is linear (i.e., she assigns a utility of $m - i$ to her i-th most preferred candidate) she is neither tie-loving nor tie-hating: if $|C| = 4$ and she ranks the candidates as $a \succ b \succ c \succ d$, she prefers b to the uniform lottery over $\{a, b, d\}$, but she prefers the uniform lottery over $\{a, c, d\}$ to c.

For most of our results, we assume that all voters in the input profile are tie-consistent; note that we allow profiles where tie-loving and tie-hating voters coexist. We need this assumption for technical reasons; while it is clearly restrictive, as argued above, it is satisfied by some interesting utility functions. We believe that (strongly) tie-loving voters are particularly natural: such voters are optimistic about the coin tosses of the tie-breaking rule, and do not want to deny their preferred candidate a chance of winning. Importantly, all hardness results of Elkind et al. [15] hold for voters with exponentially decreasing utilities, so tie-consistency alone does not make our computational problems easy.

3. LAZY VOTERS

Elkind et al. [15] have shown that for lazy voters and lexicographic tie-breaking, all our computational problems are in P, and that $(\mathcal{L}, R)$-SINGLENE is easy even for randomized tie-breaking rules. Therefore, we focus on EXISTNE and TIENE, and on randomized tie-breaking rules.

We say that a candidate set $X = \{c_{\ell_1}, \dots, c_{\ell_k}\}$ with $2 \leq k \leq \min(n/2, m)$ is *balanced with respect to a utility profile* $\mathbf{u}$ if the voters can be split into k groups $N_1, \dots, N_k$ of size n/k each so that for all $j \in [k]$, $i \in N_j$ and $c \in X \setminus \{c_{\ell_j}\}$ we have $c_{\ell_j} \succ_i c$; we say that it is *strongly balanced* if, moreover, $\frac{1}{k}\sum_{c \in X} u_i(c) \geq \max_{c \in X \setminus \{c_{\ell_j}\}} u_i(c)$. Elkind et al. [15] characterize PNE of Plurality voting for lazy voters and randomized tie-breaking.

THEOREM 1 (ELKIND ET AL. [15], THEOREM 2). *Let $\mathbf{u} = (u_1, \dots, u_n)$ be a utility profile over C, $|C| = m$, and let $R \in \{R^C, R^V\}$. Then the game $G = (\mathcal{L}, R, \mathbf{u})$ admits a PNE if and only if one of the following conditions holds:*

1. *all voters rank some candidate $c_j \in C$ first;*
2. *each candidate is ranked first by at most one voter, and $\forall \ell \in N$: $\frac{1}{n}\sum_{i \in N} u_\ell(a_i) \geq \max_{i \in N \setminus \{\ell\}} u_\ell(a_i)$.*
3. *there exists a strongly balanced set of candidates for $\mathbf{u}$.*

Elkind et al. [15] use this characterization to show that $(\mathcal{L}, R)$-EXISTNE and $(\mathcal{L}, R)$-TIENE with $R \in \{R^C, R^V\}$ are NP-hard for general preferences, even if voters' utilities are exponentially decreasing. In contrast, we will now show that for tie-consistent voters these problems become easy if the voters' preferences are single-crossing or single-peaked.

THEOREM 2. *$(\mathcal{L}, R)$-EXISTNE and $(\mathcal{L}, R)$-TIENE with $R \in \{R^C, R^V\}$ admit polynomial-time algorithms if voters are known to be tie-consistent and the preference profile induced by $\mathbf{u}$ is single-crossing with respect to the voter order $(1, \dots, n)$.*

PROOF. We will show that for single-crossing preferences the conditions of Theorem 1 can be verified in polynomial time. Conditions (1) and (2) are straightforward to check. Further, it is easy to check if any of the voters is tie-hating (given that a voter is tie-consistent, we can check if she is tie-hating by checking her utilities for at most two triples of candidates), and if that is the case, no set is strongly balanced. Finally, for tie-loving voters every balanced set is strongly balanced. Hence, in the rest of the proof we will show how to check if $\mathbf{u}$ admits a balanced set of a fixed size $k \in \{2, \ldots, \min(n/2, m)\}$. We assume that k divides n, since otherwise the answer is obviously "no".

We first prove that the voter partition witnessing that X is balanced has to be such that the voters in each group form a block in $(1, \ldots, n)$.

LEMMA 1. *If a voter partition $N_1, N_2, \ldots, N_k$ witnesses that a subset of candidates X is balanced, then the groups of voters can be renumbered so that for each $j \in [k]$ we have $N_j = \{(j-1)k+1, \ldots, jk\}$.*

PROOF. Assume for the sake on contradiction that there exist $c, c' \in X$ and $1 \leq i < i' < i'' \leq n$ such that voters i and i'' prefer c to all other candidates in X, but voter i' prefers c' to all other candidates in X. But then the pair (c, c') violates the condition in Definition 3, a contradiction. □

We will now use Lemma 1 to develop a graph-theoretic algorithm for our problem. Our solution characterizes all size-k winning sets for PNE ballot vectors as paths in a certain graph.

Assume that $N_j = \{(j-1)k+1, \ldots, jk\}$ for $j \in [k]$. We construct a directed graph $\mathcal{G}^k = (\mathcal{V}^k, \mathcal{E}^k)$ as follows. Let

$$\mathcal{V}^k = \{s, t\} \cup \{(j, \ell) \mid j \in [k], c_\ell \in C\}.$$

The set $\mathcal{E}^k$ contains edges $(s, (1, \ell))$ and $((k, \ell), t)$ for each $c_\ell \in C$. Further, for each $j \in [k-1]$ and every $c_\ell, c_r \in C$ there is an edge from (j, ℓ) to $(j+1, r)$ if and only if the last voter in N_j prefers c_ℓ to c_r, but the first voter in N_{j+1} prefers c_r to c_ℓ. This completes the description of $\mathcal{G}^k$.

By construction, every s–t path in $\mathcal{G}^k$ is of the form

$$P = (s, (1, \ell_1), \ldots, (k, \ell_k), t).$$

We claim that for any such path $r \neq j$ implies $\ell_r \neq \ell_j$, i.e., P corresponds to a subset of candidates $X(P) = \{c_{\ell_1}, \ldots, c_{\ell_k}\}$ of size k. Moreover, for every set $X \subseteq C$ of size k there is a path P in $\mathcal{G}^k$ such that $X = X(P)$ if and only if there exists a one-to-one mapping π between $\{N_1, \ldots, N_k\}$ and X such that for each $j \in [k]$ all voters in N_j prefer $\pi(N_j)$ to all other candidates in X.

Indeed, consider a path $P = (s, (1, \ell_1), \ldots, (k, \ell_k), t)$ and a mapping π given by $\pi(N_j) = c_{\ell_j}$ for all $j \in [k]$. We will argue that for each $j \in [k]$ all voters from the set N_j prefer c_{ℓ_j} to c_{ℓ_r} for all $r \in [k] \setminus \{j\}$; this also shows that $\ell_r \neq \ell_j$ whenever $r \neq j$. Indeed, pick an arbitrary $j \in [k]$ and a voter $i \in N_j$. Consider a candidate c_{ℓ_r} with $r < j$. Since $((r, \ell_r), (r+1, \ell_{r+1}))$ is an edge of P, the last voter in N_r prefers c_{ℓ_r} to $c_{\ell_{r+1}}$, but the first voter in N_{r+1} prefers $c_{\ell_{r+1}}$ to c_{ℓ_r}. Since our election is single-crossing, it follows that voter i prefers $c_{\ell_{r+1}}$ to c_{ℓ_r}. As this holds for any $r < j$ and i's preference order is transitive, it follows that i prefers c_{ℓ_j} to c_{ℓ_r} for all $r < j$. The case $r > j$ is analyzed similarly.

Conversely, consider a set $X = \{c_{\ell_1}, \ldots, c_{\ell_k}\}$ and a one-to-one mapping π such that for each $j \in [k]$ all voters from the set N_j prefer $\pi(N_j)$ to all other candidates in X. By renumbering the candidates in X, we can assume that $\pi(N_j) = c_{\ell_j}$ for all $j \in [k]$. We will argue that $(s, (1, \ell_1), \ldots, (k, \ell_k), t)$ is a path in $\mathcal{G}^k$. Indeed, by construction $\mathcal{G}^k$ contains edges $(s, (1, \ell_1))$ and $((k, \ell_k), t)$. Now, consider some $r \in [k-1]$. The voters in N_r prefer c_{ℓ_r} to all other candidates in X. Thus, in particular, the last voter in N_r prefers c_{ℓ_r} to $c_{\ell_{r+1}}$. On the other hand, the voters in N_{r+1} prefer $c_{\ell_{r+1}}$ to all other candidates in X. Thus, in particular, the first voter in N_{r+1} prefers $c_{\ell_{r+1}}$ to c_{ℓ_r}. This means that $\mathcal{G}$ contains the edge $((r, \ell_r), (r+1, \ell_{r+1}))$. As this holds for every $r \in [k-1]$, our claim is proved.

To find a balanced set of candidates of size k, we construct the graph $\mathcal{G}^k$ as described above and check if it has a path from s to t. We output "yes" if this is the case for at least one value of $k \in \{2, \ldots, \min(n/2, m)\}$. For each k, this check can be performed in polynomial time. This completes the proof for $(\mathcal{L}, R)$-ExistNE.

For $(\mathcal{L}, R)$-TieNE, we modify our algorithm as follows. It is straightforward to check if c_p can be in $W(\mathbf{b})$ for some equilibrium ballot vector $\mathbf{b}$ corresponding to condition (2). To see whether c_p is contained in a strongly balanced set, we first verify that all voters are tie-loving. Then, for each $k = 2, \ldots, \min(n/2, m)$ we construct the graph $\mathcal{G}^k$ as described above and, for each $i \in [k]$, check whether $\mathcal{G}^k$ contains an s–t path passing through (i, p). We output "yes" if the answer is positive for some values of k and i. Clearly, this procedure can be implemented in polynomial time. □

THEOREM 3. *$(\mathcal{L}, R)$-ExistNE and $(\mathcal{L}, R)$-TieNE with $R \in \{R^C, R^V\}$ admit polynomial-time algorithms if voters are known to be tie-consistent and the preference profile induced by $\mathbf{u}$ is single-peaked with respect to the candidate order $c_1 \lhd \ldots \lhd c_m$.*

PROOF. Just as in the proof of Theorem 2, it suffices to show how to find a balanced set of candidates of size k, for a value of k that divides n. Fix $k \geq 2$. For each $s \in [k] \setminus \{1\}$, $i \in [m]$, $j \in [m] \setminus [i]$, set $A[s, i, j] = 1$ if there is a set of candidates $Y = \{c_{\ell_1}, c_{\ell_2}, \ldots, c_{\ell_s}\}$ with $\ell_1 < \ell_2 < \ldots < \ell_s$ such that $c_{\ell_{s-1}} = c_i$, $c_{\ell_s} = c_j$, and each candidate in $Y \setminus \{c_j\}$ is preferred to all other candidates in Y by exactly n/k voters; otherwise, set $A[s, i, j] = 0$. Clearly, there exists a balanced set X of size k if and only if $A[k, i, j] = 1$ for some $i, j \in [m]$; indeed, if Y is a set witnessing that $A[k, i, j] = 1$, we can set $X = Y$. We will now show how to compute the quantities $A[s, i, j]$ inductively.

Clearly, we have $A[2, i, j] = 1$ if and only if exactly n/k voters prefer c_i to c_j. For the inductive step, we use the following lemma.

LEMMA 2. *For any $s = 2, \ldots, k$, any $i = 1, \ldots, m$ and any $j = i+1, \ldots, m$ we have $A[s+1, i, j] = 1$ if and only if there exists an $r < i$ such that $A[s, r, i] = 1$ and exactly n/k voters prefer c_i to both c_r and c_j.*

PROOF. If $A[s+1, i, j] = 1$, let $Y = \{c_{\ell_1}, c_{\ell_2}, \ldots, c_{\ell_{s+1}}\}$ be a set that witnesses this, where $c_{\ell_s} = c_i$, $c_{\ell_{s+1}} = c_j$. Let $r = \ell_{s-1}$. By construction exactly n/k voters prefer c_i to all candidates in Y, and, in particular, to c_r and c_j. Further, the set $Y \setminus \{c_j\}$ witnesses that $A[s, r, i] = 1$.

Conversely, suppose that $A[s, r, i] = 1$ for some r such that exactly n/k voters prefer c_i to both c_r and c_j. Let Y' be a set witnessing that $A[s, r, i] = 1$ and set $Y = Y' \cup \{c_j\}$. We need to show that each candidate in Y' is preferred to all candidates in Y by exactly n/k voters. Consider first candidate c_i. There are exactly n/k voters who prefer c_i to c_r and c_j. Since our election is single-peaked and $r < i$, each of these voters prefers c_i to any candidate c_p with $p < r$, and hence to all candidates in Y. Now, consider a candidate $c_p \in Y' \setminus \{c_i\}$. There are exactly n/k voters who prefer c_p to any candidate in Y', and, in particular, to c_i. Since our election is single-peaked and $i < j$, each of these voters has to prefer c_i to c_j, so by transitivity each of these voters prefers c_p to any candidate in Y. This completes the proof. □

Using Lemma 2, we can efficiently compute $A[\ell, i, j]$ for all $s \in [k] \setminus \{1\}$, $i \in [m]$, $j \in [m] \setminus [i]$. We output "yes" if $A[k, i, j] = 1$ for some $i, j \in [m]$. This completes the proof for $(\mathcal{L}, R)$-ExistNE.

We now consider $(\mathcal{L}, R)$-TieNE. As argued in the proof of Theorem 2, it suffices to design an efficient algorithm that, given a value of $k \in \{2, \dots, \min(n/2, m)\}$, checks whether $c_p \in X$ for some set balanced X of size k. To solve this problem, we modify our dynamic program as follows. For each $q \in [p]$, we set $A^q[s, i, j] = 1$ if there exists a set $Y = \{c_{\ell_1}, c_{\ell_2}, \dots, c_{\ell_s}\}$ with $\ell_1 < \ell_2 < \dots < \ell_s$ such that $c_{\ell_{s-1}} = c_i$, $c_{\ell_s} = c_j$, each candidate in $Y \setminus \{c_j\}$ is preferred to all other candidates in Y by exactly n/k voters, and if $q \leq s$ then $\ell_q = p$; otherwise, set $A^q[s, i, j] = 0$. The quantities $A^q[s, i, j]$ can be computed similarly to $A[s, i, j]$. Specifically, for $s < q$ we have $A^q[s, i, j] = A[s, i, j]$, for $s = q$ we have $A^q[s, i, j] = 1$ if $A[s, i, j] = 1$ and $j = p$ and $A^q[s, i, j] = 0$ otherwise, and for $s > q$ we have $A^q[s, i, j] = 1$ if $A^q[s-1, r, i] = 1$ for some $r < i$ and exactly n/k voters prefer c_i to both c_r and c_j, and $A^q[s, i, j] = 0$ otherwise. Now it is easy to see that $c_p \in X$ for some balanced set X of size k if and only if $A^q[k, i, j] = 1$ for some $q \leq p$ and some $i, j \in [m]$. □

4. TRUTH-BIASED VOTERS

We will now consider truth-biased voters. We first present our results for randomized tie-breaking. Again, we build on the work of Elkind et al. [15], who characterize PNE of Plurality voting for this case. Their characterization are presented below (Theorem 4 deals with ties, and Theorem 5 describes equilibria with a unique winner).

Theorem 4 (Elkind et al. [15], Theorem 4). *Let $\mathbf{u} = (u_1, \dots, u_n)$ be a utility profile over C, $|C| = m$, and let $R \in \{R^C, R^V\}$. The game $G = (\mathcal{T}, R, \mathbf{u})$ admits a PNE with a winning set of size at least 2 if and only if one of the following conditions holds:*

1. *each candidate is ranked first by at most one voter, and, moreover, $\frac{1}{n}\sum_{i \in N} u_\ell(a_i) \geq \max_{i \in N \setminus \{\ell\}} u_\ell(a_i)$ for each $\ell \in N$;*
2. *there exists a strongly balanced set of candidates for $\mathbf{u}$.*

Further, if condition (1) holds, then G has the truthful ballot vector $\mathbf{a}$ as a PNE, and if condition (2) holds for some set X, then G has a PNE where each voter votes for her favorite candidate in X. The game G has no other PNE.

Theorem 5 (Elkind et al. [15], Theorems 5 & 6). *Let $\mathbf{u} = (u_1, \dots, u_n)$ be a utility profile over C, let $R \in \{R^C, R^V\}$, and consider a ballot vector $\mathbf{b}$ with $W(\mathbf{b}) = \{c_j\}$ for some $c_j \in C$. If $\mathbf{b} = \mathbf{a}$, then $\mathbf{b}$ is a PNE of the game $G = (\mathcal{T}, R, \mathbf{u})$ if and only if for every $i \in N$ and every $c_k \in H(\mathbf{a}) \setminus \{a_i\}$ it holds that $c_j \succ_i c_k$. On the other hand, if $\mathbf{b} \neq \mathbf{a}$, then $\mathbf{b}$ is a PNE of $G = (\mathcal{T}, R, \mathbf{u})$ if and only if all of the following conditions hold:*

1. *$b_i \in \{a_i, c_j\}$ for all $i \in N$;*
2. *$H(\mathbf{b}) \neq \varnothing$;*
3. *$c_j \succ_i c_k$ for all $i \in N$ and all $c_k \in H(\mathbf{b}) \setminus \{b_i\}$;*
4. *for each candidate $c_\ell \in H'(\mathbf{b})$ each voter $i \in N$ with $b_i = c_j$ prefers c_j to the lottery where a candidate is chosen from $H(\mathbf{b}) \cup \{c_j, c_\ell\}$ according to R.*

Finally, Proposition 1 establishes a useful property of PNE for truth-biased voters.

Proposition 1 (Elkind et al. [15], Proposition 2). *For every $R \in \{R^L, R^C, R^V\}$ and every utility profile $\mathbf{u}$, if a ballot vector $\mathbf{b}$ is a PNE of $(\mathcal{T}, R, \mathbf{u})$ then for every voter $i \in N$ either $b_i = a_i$ or $b_i \in W(\mathbf{b})$.*

Elkind et al. [15] show that ExistNE, TieNE and SingleNE are NP-complete for truth-biased voters and randomized tie-breaking, even if voters' utilities are exponentially decreasing. We will now show that these hardness results disappear when preferences are single-peaked or single-crossing, under an appropriate assumption on the voters' attitude to ties. Interestingly, for TieNE it suffices to assume that voters are tie-consistent, whereas for SingleNE (which is not even concerned with ties!) we need the stronger assumption that all voters are (strongly) tie-loving.

Theorem 6. *$(\mathcal{T}, R)$-TieNE with $R \in \{R^C, R^V\}$ (respectively, $(\mathcal{T}, R^C)$-SingleNE and $(\mathcal{T}, R^V)$-SingleNE) admits a polynomial-time algorithm if all voters are tie-consistent (respectively, tie-loving and strongly tie-loving) and the preference profile induced by $\mathbf{u}$ is single-peaked or single-crossing. $(\mathcal{T}, R)$-ExistNE with $R \in \{R^C, R^V\}$ is in P whenever $(\mathcal{T}, R)$-SingleNE is in P.*

Proof. Theorem 4 is very similar (though not identical) to Theorem 1, so the algorithms described in the proofs of Theorem 2 (for single-crossing preferences) and Theorem 3 (for single-peaked preferences) can be used to solve $(\mathcal{T}, R)$-TieNE for $R \in \{R^C, R^V\}$ in polynomial time when voters are tie-consistent. Thus, from now on we focus on $(\mathcal{T}, R)$-SingleNE.

We first consider single-peaked preferences. Fix $R \in \{R^C, R^V\}$. We will describe an efficient algorithm that, given a utility profile $\mathbf{u}$, a candidate $c_j \in C$ and a score s, decides whether the game $G = (\mathcal{T}, R, \mathbf{u})$ has a PNE $\mathbf{b}$ with $W(\mathbf{b}) = \{c_j\}$ such that $\mathrm{sc}(c_j, \mathbf{b}) = s$ and $a_i \neq b_i$ for some $i \in N$. To solve $(\mathcal{T}, R)$-SingleNE, we check whether the truthful profile $\mathbf{a}$ is a PNE (which is easy), and then run our algorithm for c_p and for all $s \in [n]$.

We will first describe a few key properties of PNE for truth-biased voters. Suppose that $G = (\mathcal{T}, R, \mathbf{u})$ has a PNE $\mathbf{b}$ with $W(\mathbf{b}) = \{c_j\}$ such that $\mathrm{sc}(c_j, \mathbf{b}) = s$ and $a_i \neq b_i$ for some $i \in N$. Then by Theorem 5 $H(\mathbf{b}) = \{c \mid \mathrm{sc}(c, \mathbf{b}) = s-1\} \neq \varnothing$. Further, $\mathrm{sc}(c_j, \mathbf{a}) < s$ by Proposition 1.

Let $X = \{c \mid \mathrm{sc}(c, \mathbf{a}) \geq s\}$, $Y = \{c \mid \mathrm{sc}(c, \mathbf{a}) = s-1\} \setminus \{c_j\}$, $Z = \{c \mid \mathrm{sc}(c, \mathbf{a}) = s-2\} \setminus \{c_j\}$.

Lemma 3. *$\mathrm{sc}(c, \mathbf{b}) \leq s-3$ for all $c \in X$, $\mathrm{sc}(c, \mathbf{b}) \leq s-3$ or $\mathrm{sc}(c, \mathbf{b}) = s-1$ for all $c \in Y$, $\mathrm{sc}(c, \mathbf{b}) \leq s-2$ for all $c \in Z$.*

PROOF. In $\mathbf{b}$ candidate c_j is the unique winner with s points, and, by Proposition 1, all voters that vote non-truthfully vote for him. This implies that $\mathrm{sc}(c, \mathbf{b}) \leq s-2$ for every $c \in Z$. $\mathrm{sc}(c, \mathbf{b}) \leq s-1$ for every $c \in Y$, and $\mathrm{sc}(c, \mathbf{b}) \leq s-1$ for every $c \in X$. Now, if $c \in X$ and $\mathrm{sc}(c, \mathbf{b}) = s-1$, then there exists a voter i with $a_i = c$, $b_i = c_j$. But then $c \in H(\mathbf{b})$ and $c \succ_i c_j$, a contradiction with condition (3) of Theorem 5. Similarly, if $c \in X$ and $\mathrm{sc}(c, \mathbf{b}) = s-2$, then $c \in H'(\mathbf{b})$ and there exists a voter i with $a_i = c$, $b_i = c_j$. If this voter changes her vote back to c, the outcome will be chosen from $H(\mathbf{b}) \cup \{c, c_j\}$ according to R. If $R = R^C$, then i has to choose between the uniform lottery over $H(\mathbf{b}) \cup \{c, c_j\}$ and c_j. Since i is tie-loving, she would choose the lottery, a contradiction with $\mathbf{b}$ being a PNE. Now, suppose that $R = R^V$. In the new ballot vector candidate c would be ranked first by $s-1$ voters, and all other candidates would be ranked first by at most $s-1$ voters, so $n \leq (s-1)m$, and hence under R^V candidate c is selected with probability at least $1/m$. Thus, since i is strongly tie-loving, she would choose the lottery, a contradiction with $\mathbf{b}$ being a PNE. By the same argument, for every $c \in Y$ we have either $\mathrm{sc}(c, \mathbf{b}) = s-1$ or $\mathrm{sc}(c, \mathbf{b}) \leq s-3$. □

The proof of Lemma 3 uses the assumption that voters are (strongly) tie-loving. This lemma implies that $H(\mathbf{b}) \subseteq Y$, $H'(\mathbf{b}) \subseteq Z$. Now, let $C_1 = \{c_1, \dots, c_{j-1}\}$, $C_2 = \{c_{j+1}, \dots, c_m\}$, $Y_1 = Y \cap C_1$, $Y_2 = Y \cap C_2$, $Z_1 = Z \cap C_1$, $Z_2 = Z \cap C_2$, $H_1 = H(\mathbf{b}) \cap C_1$, $H_2 = H(\mathbf{b}) \cap C_2$, $H'_1 = H'(\mathbf{b}) \cap C_1$, $H'_2 = H'(\mathbf{b}) \cap C_2$.

For two candidate sets $A, B \subseteq C$ with $A \subseteq B$, we say that A forms a *prefix* of B if $\ell < r$, $c_\ell, c_r \in B$ and $c_r \in A$ implies $c_\ell \in A$; we say that A forms a *suffix* of B if $\ell < r$, $c_\ell, c_r \in B$ and $c_\ell \in A$ implies $c_r \in A$. The proof of the following lemma again uses the assumption that voters are (strongly) tie-loving.

LEMMA 4. *H_1 forms a prefix of Y_1, H_2 forms a suffix of Y_2, H'_1 forms a prefix of Z_1, and H'_2 forms a suffix of Z_2.*

PROOF. We provide the proof for H_1 and Y_1; other cases are similar (for H'_1 and Z_1 and for H'_2 and Z_2 we need the assumption that voters are (strongly) tie-loving). If $c_r \in H_1$, but $c_\ell \notin H_1$, there exists a voter i with $a_i = c_\ell$, $b_i = c_j$. Since i's preferences are single-peaked with respect to $\lhd$, she ranks c_ℓ first, and $\ell < r < j$, it follows that $c_r \succ_i c_j$; since $c_r \in H(\mathbf{b})$, voter i can profitably deviate to voting c_r, a contradiction. □

We are now ready to describe our algorithm. Given a profile $\mathbf{u}$, a candidate c_j, and a score s, we check that $\mathrm{sc}(c_j, \mathbf{a}) < s$, and reject if this is not the case. We then determine the sets Y_1, Y_2, Z_1, and Z_2. Then, for each $y_1 = 0, \dots, |Y_1|$, $y_2 = 0, \dots, |Y_2|$, $z_1 = 0, \dots, |Z_1|$, $z_2 = 0, \dots, |Z_2|$, we perform the following procedure.

If $y_1 + y_2 = 0$, we discard the 4-tuple (y_1, y_2, z_1, z_2). Otherwise, we let H_1 be the size-y_1 prefix of Y_1, let H_2 be the size-y_2 suffix of Y_2, let H'_1 be the size-z_1 prefix of Z_1, let H'_2 be the size-z_2 suffix of Z_2, and set $H = H_1 \cup H_2$, $H' = H'_1 \cup H'_2$. We then check that for each $i \in N$ we have $c_j \succ_i c_\ell$ for every $c_\ell \in H \setminus \{a_i\}$, and reject if this is not the case. Next, for each $c_r \in X \cup (Y \setminus H) \cup (Z \setminus H')$ we try to select $\mathrm{sc}(c_r, \mathbf{a}) - s + 3$ voters who rank c_r first and, for every candidate $c_\ell \in H'$, prefer c_j to the lottery where a candidate is chosen from $H \cup \{c_j, c_\ell\}$ according to R. We reject if for some c_r there are not enough voters whose preferences satisfy this requirement. Otherwise, let s' be the number of voters picked so far. If $s' > s - \mathrm{sc}(c_j, \mathbf{a})$, we reject, and if $s' < s - \mathrm{sc}(c_j, \mathbf{a})$, we try to pick additional $s - \mathrm{sc}(c_j, \mathbf{a}) - s'$ voters who rank some candidate in $C \setminus (H \cup H' \cup \{c_j\})$ first and, for every candidate $c_\ell \in H'$, prefer c_j to the lottery where a candidate is chosen from $H \cup \{c_j, c_\ell\}$ according to R. If we succeed, we terminate and report success, and otherwise we proceed to the next 4-tuple (y_1, y_2, z_1, z_2).

There are at most m^4 tuples to consider, and for each of them our procedure can be performed in polynomial time. Thus, the running time of our algorithm is polynomial.

It is not hard to see that if we report success, then there exists a non-truthful PNE where c_j wins with s points. Indeed, consider the 4-tuple (y_1, y_2, z_1, z_2) on which the algorithm terminates and the sets H and H' constructed for these values of y_1, y_2, z_1, and z_2, and let S be the set of voters picked in the respective iteration of our algorithm. Set $b_i = c_j$ for $i \in S$, $b_i = a_i$ for $i \notin S$. By construction we have $H(\mathbf{b}) = H \neq \varnothing$, $H'(\mathbf{b}) = H'$, $\mathrm{sc}(c_j, \mathbf{b}) = s$, and $b_i \neq a_i$ for some $i \in N$. Further, our procedure ensures that all conditions of Theorem 5 are satisfied.

Conversely, suppose that there exists a non-truthful PNE $\mathbf{b}$ where c_j wins with s points. Let $H_1 = H(\mathbf{b}) \cap C_1$, $H_2 = H(\mathbf{b}) \cap C_2$, $H'_1 = H'(\mathbf{b}) \cap C_1$, $H'_2 = H'(\mathbf{b}) \cap C_2$, and set $y_1 = |H_1|$, $y_2 = |H_2|$, $z_1 = |H'_1|$, $z_2 = |H'_2|$. Lemmas 3 and 4 imply that, when considering the 4-tuple (y_1, y_2, z_1, z_2), our procedure would report success.

For single-crossing preferences, we can prove an analogue of Lemma 4 for the ordering of the candidates in $A = \{a_i \mid i \in N\}$ induced by the order of the voters, which enables us to use essentially the same algorithm as above; we omit the details. □

It remains to consider truth-biased voters and lexicographic tie-breaking. For general preferences, this setting has been studied in detail by Obraztsova et al. [26], and subsequently Elkind et al. [15] have shown that the computational problems $(\mathcal{T}, R^L)$-EXISTNE, $(\mathcal{T}, R^L)$-TIENE and $(\mathcal{T}, R^L)$-SINGLENE are NP-complete. Our results for this model differ from the results in the rest of the paper: on the one hand, for single-peaked preferences we obtain a polynomial-time algorithm even *without* assuming that voters are tie-consistent, and on the other hand, we have not been able to obtain efficient algorithms for our problems for single-crossing preferences.

THEOREM 7. *$(\mathcal{T}, R^L)$-EXISTNE, $(\mathcal{T}, R^L)$-TIENE and $(\mathcal{T}, R^L)$-SINGLENE admit polynomial-time algorithms if the input profile is single-peaked.*

PROOF SKETCH. We only give a brief sketch of the algorithm for the TIENE problem. Suppose the target winner is candidate c_ℓ. Recall that we want to check if there exists a PNE $\mathbf{b}$ such that $c_\ell \in W(\mathbf{b})$ and $W(\mathbf{b}) > 1$. Starting from the truthful preference profile, the algorithm will try to construct the desirable PNE $\mathbf{b}$ if one exists.

First, we can assume that we seek a PNE where the winner has at least 4 points (we can check in polynomial time if there exists a PNE $\mathbf{b}$ where the score of c_ℓ is at most 3).

The algorithm will iterate through all possible values for the winning score of c_ℓ. Let s be the score we examine in a fixed iteration ($s \geq 4$). The algorithm performs the following steps in each iteration:

Step 1: Building the set of potential threshold candidates. We construct the set S, which consists of all potential threshold candidates with score s (the possible candidates who could tie with c_ℓ at equilibrium). This is essentially the s-eligible threshold set, as defined by Obraztsova et al. [26]. We then examine each candidate from S and check if any of them can be made to be an actual threshold candidate at the equilibrium we are looking for. We start by considering the lowest-indexed candidate. In each subsequent iteration we examine the candidate from S who has the lowest index among the ones we have not examined yet. Let t be the candidate we examine in a given iteration over S. We call t the *main threshold candidate.* Note that the tie-breaking rule should favor c_ℓ over t, since they both have the same score.

Step 2a: Reducing the support of candidates with high enough score. Given the score s and the main threshold candidate t, we will now start blocking other candidates from being winners at the PNE $\mathbf{b}$ that we are trying to construct and also from threatening the stability of $\mathbf{b}$. Given a candidate c, we say that we "block" c when we modify the votes of her supporters one by one so as to vote for c_ℓ , always starting from the votes where c_ℓ is ranked higher in the switched vote than in any other vote with the same top choice (ties are broken arbitrarily). This blocking procedure continues until c has $s-2$ points. We apply this procedure to each candidate who cannot become the winner with a unilateral deviation if he reaches $s-2$ points. We denote by T the set of all s-eligible threshold candidates who are either beaten by t in tie-breaking or have $s-1$ points. We apply the blocking procedure as follows:

- Block all candidates who have more than s points in the truthful ballot vector.
- Block all candidates with exactly s points that are not included in $T \cup \{t\}$.
- Block all candidates who have exactly $s-1$ points, beat c_ℓ in tie-breaking, and are not included in $T \cup \{t\}$.

If $\mathbf{b}'$ is the profile that has been obtained after blocking candidates as above, we refer to a vote as a *modified* vote in $\mathbf{b}'$ if we have already changed it from its initial value at this point in the algorithm.

Step 2b: remaining candidates with $s-1$ points. Given $\mathbf{b}'$, we denote by $D(\mathbf{b}')$ the set of all candidates c in the profile $\mathbf{b}'$ such that

- $\text{sc}(c, \mathbf{a}) = s-1$;
- the tie-breaking rule favors c_ℓ over c and c over t;
- c appears above c_ℓ in at least one modified vote;
- c is not blocked in $\mathbf{b}'$.

We will now block the candidates from $D(\mathbf{b}')$, updating this set at every step until it becomes empty. If after this step the score of c_ℓ is larger than s, the algorithm reports that there is no PNE with t being the threshold candidate. If the score is exactly s, the algorithm returns "yes" and outputs the current ballot vector.

Step 3: gaining additional support for c_ℓ. The challenging case is when the current score of c_ℓ is less than s. In this case, we need to further modify the votes in $\mathbf{b}'$ in favor of c_ℓ so as to make her a winner with score s. This is a more subtle task, for which we need to use the fact that preferences are single-peaked.

Towards this, we define a set of *safe* votes, which are the pool of votes that we will be allowed to change in favor of c_ℓ in the attempt to construct the desired equilibrium $\mathbf{b}$. Let B be the set of candidates that have been blocked so far. We say that a vote is *safe* if its top-ranked candidate is neither c_ℓ nor t and the intersection of the set of candidates above c_ℓ in the vote and $D(\mathbf{a}) \setminus B$ is empty; we denote the set of safe votes by $S(\mathbf{b}')$.

The rest of the algorithm proceeds by trying to find a large enough set of safe votes to change in favor of c_ℓ. This is done by identifying an appropriate pair of candidates in the axis of the single-peaked preferences, one to the left of c_ℓ and one to the right of c_ℓ, say, c_L and c_R, respectively. We then block all the candidates within the interval between c_L and c_R who have not already been blocked. Doing so provides us with a set of safe votes that we can transform in favor of c_ℓ, if this is a "yes"-instance. We omit further details of identifying this appropriate interval from this version. □

	R^L	R^C	R^V
$\mathcal{L}$	any [15]	SP/SC (tc)	SP/SC (tc)
$\mathcal{T}$	SP	SP/SC (tl)	SP/SC (stl)

Table 1: Summary of our results: the cells of the table indicate sufficient conditions for the existence of polynomial-time algorithms for ExistNE. SP stands for 'single-peaked', 'SC' stands for 'single-crossing', tc stands for 'tie-consistent', tl stands for 'tie-loving', stl stands for 'strongly tie-loving'.

5. CONCLUSIONS AND FUTURE WORK

We have shown that for single-peaked/single-crossing preferences PNE of Plurality voting games can be found in polynomial time for almost all scenarios considered by Elkind et al. [15], under the assumption of tie-consistency and its variants; our results are summarized in Table 1. The most obvious open problems suggested by our work are relaxing the assumption of tie-consistency, and extending our results to preferences that are *almost* single-peaked/single-crossing, to capture a broader and more realistic range of social choice scenarios.

From the point of view of social choice theory, single-peaked and single-crossing preferences are considered to be 'good' as they ensure that the majority relation is transitive. Our work, together with the recent work on manipulation, control, bribery and committee selection rules (see references in Section 1) provides a new perspective on these preference domains, by demonstrating that they are also attractive for purely algorithmic reasons (which appear to be unrelated to transitivity of majority preferences).

Acknowledgements. Edith Elkind and Piotr Skowron were supported by ERC-StG 639945. Svetlana Obraztsova was supported by Israeli Science Foundation (ISF) via I-CORE postdoctoral scholarship. This work was partially supported by COST Action IC1205 on Computational Social Choice.

REFERENCES

[1] K. J. Arrow. A difficulty in the concept of social welfare. *Journal of Political Economy*, 58(4):328–346, 1950.

[2] J. Bartholdi and M. Trick. Stable matching with preferences derived from a psychological model. *Operations Research Letters*, 5(4):165–169, 1986.

[3] M. Battaglini. Sequential voting with abstention. *Games and Economic Behavior*, 51:445–463, 2005.

[4] N. Betzler, A. Slinko, and J. Uhlmann. On the computation of fully proportional representation. *Journal of AI Research*, 47:475–519, 2013.

[5] D. Black. *The Theory of Committees and Elections.* Cambridge University Press, 1958.

[6] T. Borgers. Costly voting. *American Economic Review*, 94(1):57–66, 2004.

[7] F. Brandt, M. Brill, E. Hemaspaandra, and L. Hemaspaandra. Bypassing combinatorial protections: Polynomial-time algorithms for single-peaked electorates. *Journal of Artificial Intelligence Research*, 53:439–496, 2015.

[8] S. Brânzei, I. Caragiannis, J. Morgenstern, and A. D. Procaccia. How bad is selfish voting? In *AAAI'13*, pages 138–144, 2013.

[9] R. Bredereck, J. Chen, and G. Woeginger. A characterization of the single-crossing domain. *Social Choice and Welfare*, 41(4):989–998, 2013.

[10] E. Dekel and M. Piccione. Sequential voting procedures in symmetric binary elections. *Journal of Political Economy*, 108(1):34–55, 2000.

[11] Y. Desmedt and E. Elkind. Equilibria of plurality voting with abstentions. In *ACM EC'10*, pages 347–356, 2010.

[12] J. Doignon and J. Falmagne. A polynomial time algorithm for unidimensional unfolding representations. *Journal of Algorithms*, 16(2):218–233, 1994.

[13] B. Dutta and A. Sen. Nash implementation with partially honest individuals. *Games and Economic Behavior*, 74(1):154–169, 2012.

[14] E. Elkind, P. Faliszewski, and A. Slinko. Clone structures in voters' preferences. In *ACM EC'12*, pages 496–513, 2012.

[15] E. Elkind, E. Markakis, S. Obraztsova, and P. Skowron. Equilibria of plurality voting: Lazy and truth-biased voters. In *SAGT'15*, 2015.

[16] B. Escoffier, J. Lang, and M. Öztürk. Single-peaked consistency and its complexity. In *ECAI'08*, pages 366–370, 2008.

[17] P. Faliszewski, E. Hemaspaandra, and L. Hemaspaandra. The complexity of manipulative attacks in nearly single-peaked electorates. *AI Journal*, 207:69–99, 2014.

[18] P. Faliszewski, E. Hemaspaandra, L. Hemaspaandra, and J. Rothe. The shield that never was: Societies with single-peaked preferences are more open to manipulation and control. *Information and Computation*, 209(2):89–107, 2011.

[19] P. Faliszewski and A. Procaccia. AI's war on manipulation: Are we winning? *AI Magazine*, 31(4):52–64, 2010.

[20] R. Farquharson. *Theory of Voting.* Yale University Press, 1969.

[21] A. Gibbard. Manipulation of voting schemes. *Econometrica*, 41(4):587–601, 1973.

[22] M. Lombardi and N. Yoshihara. A full characterization of Nash implementation with strategy space reduction. *Economic Theory*, 54(1):131–151, 2013.

[23] N. Mattei and T. Walsh. PrefLib: A library of preference data. In *ADT'13*, pages 259–270, 2013.

[24] R. Meir, M. Polukarov, J. S. Rosenschein, and N. R. Jennings. Convergence to equilibria of plurality voting. In *AAAI'10*, pages 823–828, 2010.

[25] J. A. Mirrlees. An Exploration in the Theory of Optimum Income Taxation. *Review of Economic Studies*, 38(114):175–208, April 1971.

[26] S. Obraztsova, E. Markakis, and D. R. M. Thompson. Plurality voting with truth-biased agents. In *SAGT'13*, pages 26–37, 2013.

[27] M. Satterthwaite. Strategy-proofness and Arrow's conditions: Existence and correspondence theorems for voting procedures and social welfare functions. *Journal of Economic Theory*, 10(2):187–217, 1975.

[28] M. Schulze. A new monotonic, clone-independent, reversal symmetric, and Condorcet-consistent single-winner election method. *Social Choice and Welfare*, 36(2):267–303, 2011.

[29] F. D. Sinopoli and G. Iannantuoni. On the generic strategic stability of Nash equilibria if voting is costly. *Economic Theory*, 25(2):477–486, 2005.

[30] P. Skowron, L. Yu, P. Faliszewski, and E. Elkind. The complexity of fully proportional representation for single-crossing electorates. *Theoretical Computer Science*, 569:43–57, 2015.

[31] B. Sloth. The theory of voting and equilibria in noncooperative games. *Games and Economic Behavior*, 5(1):152–169, 1993.

[32] D. R. M. Thompson, O. Lev, K. Leyton-Brown, and J. S. Rosenschein. Empirical analysis of plurality election equilibria. In *AAMAS'13*, pages 391–398, 2013.

Optimal Reallocation under Additive and Ordinal Preferences

Haris Aziz
Data61
and UNSW
Sydney, Australia
haris.aziz@nicta.com.au

Péter Biró
Hungarian Academy of Sciences
Budapest, Hungary
biro.peter@krtk.mta.hu

Jérôme Lang
LAMSADE, Université Paris-Dauphine
Paris, France
lang@lamsade.dauphine.fr

Julien Lesca
LAMSADE, Université Paris-Dauphine
Paris, France
julien.lesca@dauphine.fr

Jérôme Monnot
LAMSADE, Université Paris-Dauphine
Paris, France
jerome.monnot@dauphine.fr

ABSTRACT

Reallocating resources to get mutually beneficial outcomes is a fundamental problem in various multi-agent settings. In the first part of the paper we focus on the setting in which agents express additive cardinal utilities over objects. We present computational hardness results as well as polynomial-time algorithms for testing Pareto optimality under different restrictions such as two utility values or lexicographic utilities. In the second part of the paper we assume that agents express only their (ordinal) preferences over single objects, and that their preferences are additively separable. In this setting, we present characterizations and polynomial-time algorithms for possible and necessary Pareto optimality.

General Terms

Economics, Theory and Algorithms

Keywords

Game theory (cooperative and non-cooperative), Social choice theory

1. INTRODUCTION

Reallocation of resources to achieve mutually better outcomes is a central concern in multi-agent settings. A desirable way to achieve 'better' outcomes is to obtain a Pareto improvement in which each agent is at least as happy and at least one agent is strictly happier [1, 5, 28, 30]. Pareto improvements are desirable for two fundamental reasons: they result in strictly more welfare for any reasonable notion of welfare (such as utilitarian or leximin). Secondly, they satisfy the minimal requirement of individual rationality in the sense that no agent is worse off after the trade. If a series of Pareto improvements results in a Pareto optimal outcome, that is even better because there exists no other outcome which each agent weakly prefers and at least one agent strictly prefers.

We consider the setting in which agents are initially endowed with objects and they also have additive preferences for the objects. In the absence of endowments, achieving a Pareto optimal assignment is easy: simply assign every object to the agent who values it the most. On the other hand, in the presence of endowments, finding a Pareto optimal assignment that respects individual rationality is more challenging. The problem is closely related to the problem of testing Pareto optimality of the initial assignment. A certificate of Pareto dominance gives an assignment that respects individual rationality and is a Pareto improvement. In fact, if testing Pareto optimality is NP-hard, then finding an individually rational and Pareto optimal assignment is NP-hard as well. In view of this, we focus on the problem of testing Pareto optimality. In all cases where we are able to test it efficiently, we also present algorithms to compute individually rational and Pareto optimal assignments.

Contributions.

We first relate the problem of computing an individually rational and Pareto optimal assignment to the more basic problem of testing Pareto optimality of a given assignment. We show for unbounded number of agents, testing Pareto optimality is strongly coNP-complete even if the assignment assigns at most two objects per agent.

We then identify some natural tractable cases. In particular, we present a pseudo-polynomial-time algorithm for the problem when the number of agents is constant. We characterize Pareto optimality under lexicographic utilities (i.e., lexicographic preferences) and we show that Pareto optimality can be tested in linear time. For dichotomous preferences in which utilities can take values α or β, we present a characterization of Pareto optimal assignments which also yields a polynomial-time algorithm to test Pareto optimality.

In the ordinal setting, we consider two versions of Pareto optimality: *possible Pareto optimality* and *necessary Pareto optimality*. For both properties, we present characterizations that lead to polynomial-time algorithms for testing the property for a given assignment.

Appears in: *Proceedings of the 15th International Conference on Autonomous Agents and Multiagent Systems (AAMAS 2016), J. Thangarajah, K. Tuyls, C. Jonker, S. Marsella (eds.), May 9–13, 2016, Singapore.*

Related Work.

The setting in which agents express additive cardinal utilities and a welfare maximizing or fair assignment is computed is a very well-studied problem in computer science [2, 10, 11, 13, 19, 18, 23, 26, 27, 31, 32]. Although computing a utilitarian welfare maximizing assignment is easy, the problem of maximizing egalitarian welfare is NP-hard.

Algorithmic aspects of Pareto optimality have received attention in discrete allocation of indivisible goods, randomized allocation of indivisible goods, two-sided matching, and coalition formation under ordinal preferences [1, 5, 8, 21, 28]. Since we are interested in Pareto improvements, our paper is also related to housing markets with endowments and ordinal preferences [4, 22, 25, 33, 34]. Recently, Damamme et al. [17] examined restricted Pareto optimality under ordinal preferences.

de Keijzer et al. [18] study the complexity of deciding whether there exists a Pareto optimal and envy-free assignment when agents have additive utilities. They also showed that testing Pareto optimality under additive utilities is coNP-complete. We show that this result holds even if each agent has two objects.

Cechlárová et al. [16] proved Pareto optimality of an assignment under lexicographic utilities can be tested in polynomial time. In this paper, we present a simple characterization of Pareto optimality under lexicographic utilities that leads to a linear-time algorithm to test Pareto optimality.

Bouveret et al. [14] consider necessary Pareto optimality as Pareto optimality for all completions of the responsive set extension,[1] and present some computational results when necessary Pareto optimality is considered *in conjunction* with other fairness properties. Reallocating resources to improve fairness has also been studied before [20].

2. PRELIMINARIES

We consider the setting in which we have $N = \{1, \ldots, n\}$ a set of agents, $O = \{o_1, \ldots, o_m\}$ a set of objects, and the preference profile $\succsim = (\succsim_1, \ldots, \succsim_n)$ specifies for each agent i her complete, transitive and reflexive preferences $\succsim_i$ over O. Agents may be indifferent among objects. Let $\sim_i$ and $\succ_i$ denote the symmetric and anti-symmetric part of $\succsim_i$, respectively. We denote by $E_i^1, \ldots, E_i^{k_i}$ the k_i equivalence classes of an agent $i \in N$. Those classes partition O into k_i sets of objects such that agent i is indifferent between two objects belonging to the same class, and she strictly prefers an object of E_i^k to an object of E_i^l whenever $k < l$.

Each agent may additionally express a cardinal utility function u_i consistent with $\succsim_i$: $u_i(o) > u_i(o')$ iff $o \succ_i o'$ and $u_i(o) = u_i(o')$ iff $o \sim_i o'$. We will assume that each object is positively valued, i.e, $u_i(o) > 0$ for all $i \in N$ and $o \in O$. The set of all utility functions consistent with $\succsim_i$ is denoted by $\mathfrak{U}(\succsim_i)$. We will denote by $\mathfrak{U}(\succsim)$ the set of all utility profiles $u = (u_1, \ldots, u_n)$ such that $u_i \in \mathfrak{U}(\succsim_i)$ for each $i \in N$. When we consider agents' valuations according to their cardinal utilities, then we will assume additivity, that is $u_i(O') = \sum_{o \in O'} u_i(o)$ for each $i \in N$ and $O' \subseteq O$. An assignment $p = (p(1), \ldots, p(n))$ is a partition of O into n subsets, where $p(i)$ is the bundle assigned to agent i. We denote by $\mathcal{X}$ the set of all possible assignments.

An assignment $p \in \mathcal{X}$ is said to be *individually rational* for an initial endowment $e \in \mathcal{X}$ if $u_i(p(i)) \geq u_i(e(i))$ holds for any agent i. An assignment $p \in \mathcal{X}$ is said to be *Pareto dominated* by another $q \in \mathcal{X}$ if (i) for any agent $i \in N$, $u_i(q(i)) \geq u_i(p(i))$ holds, (ii) for at least one agent $i \in N$, $u_i(q(i)) > u_i(p(i))$ holds. An assignment is *Pareto optimal* iff it is not Pareto dominated by another assignment. Finally, whenever cardinal utilities are considered, the *social welfare* of an assignment p is defined as $SW(p) = \sum_{i \in N} u_i(p(i))$.

[1]Brams et al. [15] used the term *Pareto ensuring* for Pareto optimality for all completions of the responsive set extension.

EXAMPLE 1. *Let $n = 3$, $m = 5$, and the utilities of the agents be represented as follows.*

	o_1	o_2	o_3	o_4	o_5
1	16	8	4	2	1
2	9	3	1	1	3
3	6	1	2	6	2

Since $u_1(o_1) > u_1(o_2)$, we can say that $o_1 \succ_1 o_2$. An example of an assignment is $p = (o_2o_4|o_1|o_3o_5)$ in which $p(1) = \{o_2, o_4\}$, $p(2) = \{o_1\}$, and $p(3) = \{o_3, o_5\}$.

3. ADDITIVE UTILITIES

In this section we assume that each agent expresses a cardinal utility function u_i over O, where $u_i(o) > 0$ for all $i \in N$ and $o \in O$.

3.1 Complexity of testing Pareto optimality

We will consider Pareto optimality and individual rationality with respect to additive utilities. The following lemma shows that the computation of an individually rational and Pareto-improving assignment is at least as hard as the problem of deciding whether a given assignment is Pareto optimal:

LEMMA 1. *If there exists a polynomial-time algorithm to compute a Pareto optimal and individually rational assignment, then there exists a polynomial-time algorithm to test Pareto optimality.*

PROOF. We assume that there is a polynomial-time algorithm A to compute an individually rational and Pareto optimal assignment. Consider an assignment p for which Pareto optimality needs to be tested. We can use A to compute an assignment q which is individually rational for the initial endowment p and Pareto optimal. By individual rationality $u_i(q(i)) \geq u_i(p(i))$ for all $i \in N$. If $u_i(q(i)) = u_i(p(i))$ for all $i \in N$, then p is Pareto optimal simply because q is Pareto optimal. However if there exists $i \in N$ such that $u_i(q(i)) > u_i(p(i))$, it means that p is *not* Pareto optimal. □

A Pareto optimal assignment can be computed trivially by giving each object to the agent who values it the most. Bouveret and Lang [12] proved that a problem concerning coalitional manipulation in sequential allocation is NP-complete (Proposition 6). The result can be reinterpreted as follows.

THEOREM 1. *Testing Pareto optimality of a given assignment is weakly coNP-complete for $n = 2$ and identical preferences.*

COROLLARY 1. *Computing an individually rational and Pareto optimal assignment is weakly NP-hard for $n = 2$.*

One may additionally require the *balanced* property, i.e., each agent gets as many objects as she initially owned. Both the theorem above and the corollary above can be extended to that case easily. If there are an unbounded number of agents, then testing Pareto optimality of a given assignment is strongly coNP-complete [18]. Next, we show that the problem remains strongly coNP-complete even if each agent receives exactly 2 objects.

THEOREM 2. *Testing Pareto optimality of a given assignment is strongly coNP-complete for an unbounded number of agents even if each agent receives exactly 2 objects.*

PROOF. The reduction is done from 2-NUMERICAL MATCHING WITH TARGET SUMS (2NMTS in short). The inputs of 2NMTS is a sequence $a_1, \dots, a_k$ of k positive integers such that $\sum_{i=1}^{k} a_i = k(k+1)$ and $1 \leq a_i \leq 2k-1$ for $i = 1, \dots, k$, and $a_1 \leq a_2 \dots \leq a_k$. We want to decide if there are two permutations π and θ of the integers $\{1, \dots, k\}$ such that $\pi(i) + \theta(i) = a_i$ for $i = 1, \dots, k$. 2NMTS is known to be strongly NP-complete [35].

The reduction from an instance of 2NMTS is as follows. There are $3k+1$ agents $N = L \cup C \cup R \cup \{d\}$ where $L = \{\ell_1, \dots, \ell_k\}$, $R = \{r_1, \dots, r_k\}$ and $C = \{c_1, \dots, c_k\}$ and $6k+2$ objects $O = F \cup G \cup H \cup \{o\}$ where $F = \{f_i^L, f_i^R : i = 1, \dots, k\}$, $G = \{g_i^L, g_i^R : i = 1, \dots, k\} \cup \{g^C\}$, $H = \{h_i^{CL}, h_i^{CR} : i = 1, \dots, k\}$. Let ε be a positive value strictly lower than $1/2$. The following table summarizes the non-zero utilities provided by the different objects, where agt#1 is the agent which receives the object in the initial assignment and $u_{agt\#1}$ is her utility for it, and where agt(s)#2 lists the other agents with non-zero utility for the object and $u_{agt(s)\#2}$ corresponds to their utility for it:

object	agt#1	$u_{\text{agt}\#1}$	agt(s)#2	$u_{\text{agt(s)}\#2}$
h_i^{CL}	c_i	a_i	ℓ_i	$1+\varepsilon$
h_i^{CR}	c_i	$3k$	r_i	$1-\varepsilon$
f_i^L	ℓ_i	1	c_j with $a_j \geq i+1$	i
f_i^R	r_i	1	c_j with $a_j \geq i+1$	$3k+i$
g_i^R	r_i	3	r_{i+1} if $i<k$ d if $i=k$	$3+\varepsilon$ $3+\varepsilon$
g_i^L	ℓ_i	3	ℓ_{i-1} if $i>1$ r_1 if $i=1$	$3-\varepsilon$ $3+\varepsilon$
g^C	d	3	ℓ_k	$3-\varepsilon$
o	d	1		

The initial assignment provides the following utilities to the agents: $u_{c_i}(\{h_i^{CL}, h_i^{CR}\}) = 3k + a_i$, $u_{\ell_i}(\{f_i^L, g_i^L\}) = 4$ and $u_{r_i}(\{f_i^R, g_i^R\}) = 4$ for $i = 1 \dots k$, and $u_d(\{g^C, o\}) = 4$.

Clearly, this instance is constructed within polynomial time and each agent has two items in the initial assignment. We claim that there is a Pareto improvement of the initial assignment iff $\{a_i : i = 1 \dots k\}$ is a yes-instance of 2NMTS.

Assume that there exist π and θ such that $\pi(i) + \theta(i) = a_i$ for $i = 1 \dots k$, i.e., $\{a_i : i = 1 \dots k\}$ is a yes-instance of 2NMTS. Note that this implies for any $i = 1 \dots k$ that

$$\pi(i) + 1 \leq a_i \quad \text{and} \quad \theta(i) + 1 \leq a_i \tag{1}$$

because $\pi(i) \geq 1$ and $\theta(i) \geq 1$. Then consider the following assignment:

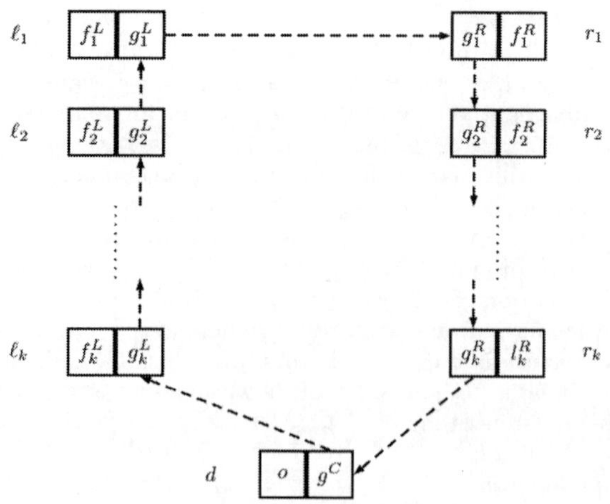

Figure 1: Initial assignment for agents of $L \cup R \cup \{d\}$.

- $\{h_i^{CL}, g_{i+1}^L\}$ (resp. $\{h_k^{CL}, g^C\}$) is assigned to ℓ_i with $i<k$ (resp. to ℓ_k) with utility 4.
- $\{h_i^{CR}, g_{i-1}^R\}$ (resp. $\{h_1^{CR}, g_1^L\}$) is assigned to r_i with $i>1$ (resp. to r_1) with utility 4.
- $\{f_{\pi(i)}^R, f_{\theta(i)}^L\}$ is assigned to c_i. Using (1), the utility of agent c_i is $3k + \pi(i) + \theta(i) = 3k + a_i$.
- $\{o, g_k^R\}$ is assigned to d with utility $4+\varepsilon$.

This allocation is clearly a Pareto improvement of the initial allocation.

Assume now that $\{a_i : i = 1 \dots k\}$ is a no-instance of 2NMTS. By contradiction, assume that there exists a Pareto improvement p of the initial assignment. Note first that any agent should receive in p at least two objects. Indeed there is no object which provides a utility greater than $3+\varepsilon$ to any agent of $L \cup R \cup \{d\}$, and any of those agents receives a utility 4 in the initial assignment. Furthermore, any good f_i^R provides a utility at most $3k+i$ to an agent c_j, which is strictly lower than her utility $3k+a_j$ in the initial assignment because $a_j \geq i+1$ (otherwise c_j would get utility 0 from f_i^R). Since the number of objects is twice the number of agents, we can conclude that p assigns exactly 2 objects to every agent.

Let us focus first on the objects of G. Those objects are the only ones which can provide a utility at least $3-\varepsilon$ to the agents of $L \cup R \cup \{d\}$. All other objects provide a utility at most $1+\varepsilon$ to the agents in $L \cup R \cup \{d\}$. So, to achieve a utility at least 4 for all those agents in $L \cup R \cup \{d\}$, each of them should receive exactly one good from G (with non-zero utility for it) because $|L \cup R \cup \{d\}| = |G| = 2k+1$. Figure 1 illustrates the initial assignment for the agents of $L \cup R \cup \{d\}$. In this figure, a dotted arrow from an object of G means that this object can be reassigned to the pointed agent with a non zero utility. Figure 1 illustrates the fact that the goods of G could be allocated in only two different manners in p to be a Pareto improvement of the initial endowment: either every good of G is assigned to the same agent as in the initial assignment, or every good of G is assigned to the agent pointed by the corresponding arrow in Figure 1.

First, we consider the case where all goods of G are assigned in p exactly as in the initial assignment. To achieve a utility at least 4, every agent r_i should receive the object f_i^R to complete her bundle of two objects. This implies that those objects cannot be assigned to agent c_i, with $i = 1 \dots k$, in order to ensure that they get a utility at least $3k + a_i$. Therefore every agent c_i should receive the object h_i^{CR} with utility $3k$. Furthermore no agent c_i can receive an object f_j^R to complete her bundle of two objects because this object would provide her a utility at most $a_i - 1$. So, every agent c_i should receive the object h_i^{CL}. From this, we conclude that p should be exactly the same assignment as the initial assignment, which contradicts p Pareto-dominates this initial assignment.

From the previous paragraphs, we know that any good of G should be assigned in p to the agent pointed by the corresponding dotted arrow in Figure 1. To achieve a utility at least 4, any agent ℓ_i should receive the good h_i^{CL} to complete her bundle of two objects. If an agent c_i did not receive at least one good f_j^R such that $a_i \geq j + 1$, then the maximal utility achievable by c_i would be $3k + a_i - 1$, which would be strictly lower than her utility in the initial assignment. So, every agent c_i should receive exactly one good f_j^R such that $a_i \geq j + 1$. Therefore no good f_i^R can be assigned to agent r_i. So, to achieve a utility at least 4, any agent r_i should receive the good h_i^{CR} to complete her bundle of two objects. Then the good o should be assigned to agent d to complete her bundle of two goods. Finally it remains to assign to every agent c_i a good f_j^L such that $a_i \geq j + 1$.

Now let us focus on the pair of goods assigned in p to agent c_i with $i = 1 \dots k$. Note that those two objects belong to F. We know that the total amount of utility provided by the goods of F to the agents of C should be exactly equal to $3k^2 + k(k + 1)$. Furthermore any agent c_i should receive a share of at least $3k + a_i$ of this total amount of utility. Since $\sum_{i=1}^{k}(3k + a_i) = 3k^2 + k(k + 1)$, any agent c_i should receive two objects f_j^L and $f_{j'}^R$ such that $u_{c_i}(\{f_j^L, f_{j'}^R\}) = 3k + a_i$. Let π and θ be the two permutations of $\{1, \dots, k\}$ such that for any $i = 1 \dots k$, the objects $f_{\pi(i)}^L$ and $f_{\theta(i)}^R$ are assigned in p to agent c_i. Those two permutations are such that for any $i = 1 \dots k$, $\pi(i) + \theta(i) = a_i$. This leads to a contradiction with $\{a_i : i = 1 \dots k\}$ is a no-instance. □

Note that Theorem 2 is the best possible NP-hardness result that we can obtain according to the number of objects received by each agent because if initially each agent has exactly one object in assignment p, then our problem can be solved in linear-time.

3.2 Complexity of testing Pareto optimality: tractable cases

We now identify conditions under which the problem of computing individually rational and Pareto optimal assignments is polynomial-time solvable.

3.2.1 *Constant number of agents and small weights*

LEMMA 2. *If there is a constant number of agents, then the set of all vectors of utilities that correspond to a feasible assignment can be computed in pseudo-polynomial time.*

PROOF. Consider the following algorithm (by 0^k we denote $0, \dots, 0$ with k occurrences of 0).

Let W be the maximal social welfare that is achievable; then, at any step of the algorithm, the number of vectors in L cannot exceed $(W + 1)^n$. Hence the algorithm runs

```
L ← {(0^n)};
for j = 1 to m do
    L' ← {l + (0^{i-1}, u_i(o_j), 0^{n-i}) | i ∈ N; l ∈ L}
    L ← L'
end for
return L
```

in $O(W^n \cdot n \cdot m)$. Now, $W \leq \sum_{i,j} u_i(o_j)$, and since n is constant, the algorithms runs in pseudopolynomial time.

We can prove by induction on k that a vector of utilities $l = (v_1, \dots, v_n)$ can be achieved by assigning objects $o_1, \dots, o_k$ to the agents if and only if l belongs to L after objects $o_1, \dots, o_k$ have been considered. This is obviously true at the start of the algorithm, when no object at all has been considered. Now, suppose the induction assumption is true for k. If l belongs to L after iteration k, then l' belongs to L after iteration $k+1$ iff l' is obtained from l by adding $u_i(o_k)$ to the utility of some agent i, that is, if $l = (v_1, \dots, v_n)$ can be achieved by assigning objects $o_1, \dots, o_{k+1}$. □

THEOREM 3. *If there is a constant number of agents, then there exists a pseudo-polynomial-time algorithm to compute a Pareto optimal and individually rational assignment.*

PROOF. We apply the algorithm of Lemma 2, but in addition we keep track, for each $l \in L$, of a partial assignment that supports it: every time we add $l + (0^{i-1}, u_i(o_j), 0^{n-i})$ to L', the corresponding partial assignment is obtained from the partial assignment corresponding to l, and then mapping o_j to i. If several partial assignments correspond to the same utility vector, we keep an arbitrary one. At the end, we obtain the list L of all feasible utility vectors, together with, for each of them, one corresponding assignment. For each of them, check whether there is at least one l' in L that Pareto dominates it, which takes at most $O(|L|^2)$, and we recall that L is polynomially large. The assignments that correspond to the remaining vectors are Pareto optimal.[2] □

3.2.2 *Lexicographic Utilities*

We say that utilities are *lexicographic* if for each agent $i \in N$, $u_i(o) > \sum_{o' \prec_i o} u_i(o')$. By $q(i) \succsim_i p(i)$, we will mean $u_i(q(i)) \geq u_i(p(i))$.

In order to test the Pareto optimality of an assignment p, we construct a directed graph $G(p) = (V(p), E(p))$. The set of vertices $V(p)$ contains one vertex per object belonging to O. Furthermore, for any vertex of $V(p)$ associated to an object o, the set of edges $E(p)$ contains one edge (o, o') for any object o' belonging to $O \setminus \{o\}$ such that $o' \succsim_i o$, where i is the agent who receives the good o in p. For example, Figure 2 illustrates such graph for the assignment p provided by Example 2. In Figure 2, dotted edges represent indifferences (when $o' \sim o$) and plain edges represent strict preferences (when $o' \succ o$). It follows from [16] that Pareto optimality of an assignment under lexicographic utilities can be tested in polynomial time. We provide a simple characterization of a Pareto optimal assignment under lexicographic utilities. The characterization we present also provides an interesting connection with the possible Pareto optimality that we consider in the next section.

[2]Note that it is generally not the case that we get *all* Pareto optimal assignments: if there are several assignments corresponding to the same utility vector, then we'll obtain only one.

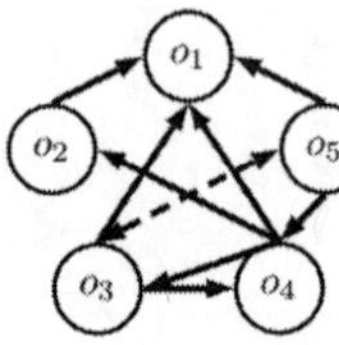

Figure 2: Graph $G(p)$ for assignment p in Example 2.

THEOREM 4. *An assignment p is not Pareto optimal wrt lexicographic utilities iff there exists a cycle in $G(p)$ which contains at least one edge corresponding to a strict preference.*

PROOF. Assume that there exists a cycle C which contains at least one edge corresponding to a strict preference. Then, the exchange of objects along the cycle by agents owning the objects corresponds to a Pareto improvement.

Assume now that p is not Pareto optimal and let q_1 be an assignment which Pareto dominates p. For at least one agent i, $q_1(i) \succ_i p(i)$. So there exist at least one object o_1 in $q_1(i) \setminus p(i)$. Let i_1 be the owner of o_1 in p. Since preferences are lexicographic, in compensation of the loss of o_1, agent i_1 must receive an object o_2 in q_1 which is at least as good as o_1 according to her own preferences. Let i_2 be the owner of o_2 in p and so on. Since O is finite, there must exist k and k' such that the sequence $o_k \rightarrow o_{k+1} \rightarrow \ldots \rightarrow o_{k'}$ forms a cycle, i.e., $o_k = o_{k'}$. If $\nexists l \in [k, k'-1]$ such that $o_{l+1} \succ_{i_l} o_l$ then we consider the assignment q_2 derived from q_1 by reassigning any object o_{l+1}, with $l \in [k, k'-1]$, to agent i_l. It is obvious that this assignment q_2 is at least as good as q_1 for all the agents. So q_2 Pareto dominates p. By following the same reasoning as above, we can state that there exists a sequence of objects $o_k \rightarrow o_{k+1} \rightarrow \ldots \rightarrow o_{k'}$ such that $o_k = o_{k'}$ and for any $l \in [k, k'-1]$, o_{l+1} is assigned to agent i_l in q_2 to compensate the loss of o_l assigned to him in p (obviously with $o_{l+1} \succsim_{i_l} o_l$). Once again if $\nexists l \in [k, k'-1]$ such that $o_{l+1} \succ_{i_l} o_l$ then we consider the assignment q_3 derived from q_2 by reassigning any object o_{l+1}, with $l \in [k, k'-1]$, to agent i_l... Since for any $s > 1$ we have $\sum_{i \in N} |q_{s-1}(i) \cap p(i)| < \sum_{i \in N} |q_s(i) \cap p(i)|$, there must exist a finite value t such that $\exists l \in [k, k'-1]$ such that $o_{l+1} \succ_{i_l} o_l$ for the cycle $o_k \rightarrow o_{k+1} \rightarrow \ldots \rightarrow o_{k'}$ founded in q_t. Indeed otherwise after a finite number of steps t we should have $q_t(i) = p(i)$ for all $i \in N$, which leads to a contradiction with q_t Pareto dominates p. So there exists a cycle $o_k \rightarrow \ldots \rightarrow o_{k'}$ in $G(p)$ with at least one edge corresponding to a strict preference. □

It is clear that the graph $G(p)$ can be constructed in linear time for any assignment p. Furthermore, the search of a cycle containing at least one strict preference edge in $G(p)$ can be computed in linear time by applying a graph traversal algorithm for any strict preference edge in $G(p)$. Therefore testing if a given assignment is Pareto optimal can be done in linear time when utilities are lexicographic.

EXAMPLE 2. *Let $n = 3$, $m = 5$, and the following ordinal information about preferences corresponding to the lexicographic utilities in Example 1 (as a consequence of Theorem 4, ordinal preferences are enough information to check Pareto optimality).*

$$1 : o_1 \succ o_2 \succ o_3 \succ o_4 \succ o_5$$
$$2 : o_1 \succ o_2 \sim o_5 \succ o_3 \sim o_4$$
$$3 : o_1 \sim o_4 \succ o_3 \sim o_5 \succ o_2$$

Let $p = (o_2o_4|o_1|o_3o_5)$ be the initial assignment. The construction of Theorem 4 gives us that it is Pareto dominated by $(o_2o_3|o_1|o_4o_5)$, hence it is not Pareto optimal.

3.2.3 Two utility values

In this section we assume the agents use at most two utility values for the objects. We say that the collection of utility functions $(u_1, \ldots, u_n)$ is *bivalued* if there exist two numbers $\alpha > \beta > 0$ such that for every agent i and every object o, $u_i(o) \in \{\alpha, \beta\}$. (The result would still hold if each agent i has a different pair of values (α_i, β_i), provided that $\frac{\alpha_i}{\beta_i} = \frac{\alpha_j}{\beta_j}$ for all i, j.) This means that for every agent i, the set of objects O is partitioned into two subsets $E_i^1 = \{o \in O, u_i(o) = \alpha\}$ and $E_i^2 = \{o \in O, u_i(o) = \beta\}$ (with possibly $E_i^2 = \emptyset$). Given an assignment q, let $q^+(i) = q(i) \cap E_i^1$, and $q^-(i) = q(i) \cap E_i^2$.

We provide a first requirement for an assignment to Pareto dominate another one:

LEMMA 3. *If an assignment p is Pareto dominated by an assignment q then $|\bigcup_{i \in N} q^+(i)| > |\bigcup_{i \in N} p^+(i)|$.*

PROOF. For contradiction we assume that $|\bigcup_{i \in N} q^+(i)| \leq |\bigcup_{i \in N} p^+(i)|$. In that case $SW(q) = |\bigcup_{i \in N} q^+(i)|\alpha + |\bigcup_{i \in N} q^-(i)|\beta = |\bigcup_{i \in N} q^+(i)|(\alpha - \beta) + |O|\beta \leq |\bigcup_{i \in N} p^+(i)|(\alpha - \beta) + |O|\beta = \alpha|\bigcup_{i \in N} p^+(i)| + \beta|\bigcup_{i \in N} p^-(i)|$. So $SW(p) \geq SW(q)$, which contradicts the assumption that q Pareto dominates p. □

LEMMA 4. *If an assignment p is not Pareto optimal then there exists an assignment q such that (i) $\forall i \in N, |q^+(i)| \geq |p^+(i)|$ and (ii) $\exists j \in N, |q^+(j)| > |p^+(j)|$ and $p^-(j) \neq \emptyset$.*

PROOF. Assume that p is not Pareto optimal. Then there exists an assignment q_* which Pareto dominates p. We claim that we can reassign the objects in q_* in order to obtain an assignment q such that (i) and (ii) hold.

For any agent i we initialize $q(i)$ to $q_*^+(i)$. In order to obtain (i), while there exists $i \in N$ such that $|q^+(i)| < |p^+(i)|$, we choose $o \in p^+(i) \setminus q^+(i)$ and we assign o to agent i in q. Note that o may belong to another agent in q but nevertheless the total number of object assigned in q never decreases. Furthermore, after at most $|\bigcup_{i \in N} p^+(i)|$ steps, condition (i) will hold because an object $\bigcup_{i \in N} p^+(i)$ can be reassigned at most once. Finally, Lemma 3 implies that $|\bigcup_{i \in N} q_*^+(i)| > |\bigcup_{i \in N} p^+(i)|$ and $|\bigcup_{i \in N} q(i)| \geq |\bigcup_{i \in N} q_*^+(i)|$. Therefore $|\bigcup_{i \in N} q(i)| > |\bigcup_{i \in N} p^+(i)|$.

Let $A = \{i \in N \mid p^-(i) \neq \emptyset\}$ and $B = \{i \in N \mid |q(i)| > |p^+(i)|\}$. Note first that $A \neq \emptyset$ because otherwise p would be Pareto optimal. If $A \cap B \neq \emptyset$ then condition (ii) holds. Otherwise, if $\exists i \in A$ and $o \in O \setminus \bigcup_{j \in N} q(j)$ such that $o \in E_i^1$ then assign o to i in q and condition (ii) holds. Otherwise if $\exists i \in A, \exists j \in B$ and $\exists o \in q(j)$ such that $o \in E_i^1$ then reassign object o to i in q and condition (ii) holds (note that (i) remains true).

Finally we show that other cases never occur. Indeed otherwise we would have $A \cap B = \emptyset$ and $\forall i \in A, \forall o \in O \setminus \bigcup_{j \in N} q(j), o \in E_i^2$ and $\forall i \in A, \forall j \in B, \forall o \in q(j), o \in E_i^2$.

This would mean that $|\bigcup_{i \in A} E_i^1| = |\bigcup_{i \in A} p(i) \cap E_i^1|$. Therefore we would have $|\bigcup_{i \in A} q_*(i) \cap E_i^1| \leq |\bigcup_{i \in A} p(i) \cap E_i^1|$. But q_* Pareto dominates p implies $\forall i \in A, u_i(q_*(i)) \geq u_i(p(i))$. Therefore $\sum_{i \in A} |q_*(i) \cap E_i^1|\alpha + |q_*(i) \cap E_i^2|\beta \geq \sum_{i \in A} |p(i) \cap E_i^1|\alpha + |p(i) \cap E_i^2|\beta$ which implies $|q_*(i) \cap E_i^2| \geq |p(i) \cap E_i^2|$. We can now bound the social welfare of q_* by $\sum_{i \in A} |q_*(i) \cap E_i^1|\alpha + \sum_{i \in A} |q_*(i) \cap E_i^2|\beta + |O \setminus \bigcup_{i \in A} q_*(i)|\alpha = \sum_{i \in A}(\beta - \alpha)|q_*(i) \cap E_i^2| + |O|\alpha \leq \sum_{i \in A}(\beta - \alpha)|p(i) \cap E_i^2| + |O|\alpha = \sum_{i \in A} |p(i) \cap E_i^2|\beta + |O \setminus (\bigcup_{i \in A} p(i) \cap E_i^2)|\alpha = \sum_{i \in N} u_i(p(i))$ which is a contradiction with q_* Pareto dominates p. □

Based on the lemma, we obtain the following characterization of Pareto optimality in the bivalued case.

THEOREM 5. *An assignment p is Pareto dominated iff there exists an assignment q such that (i) $\forall i \in N, |q^+(i)| \geq |p^+(i)|$ and (ii) $\exists j \in N, |q^+(j)| > |p^+(j)|$ and $p^-(j) \neq \emptyset$.*

PROOF. One implication has already been proved in Lemma 4. To prove the second implication we assume first that there exists q such that (i) and (ii) holds. Let j be as described as in (ii). For any $i \in N \setminus \{j\}$, let $A_i \subseteq q^+(i)$ such that $|A_i| = |p^+(i)|$. Let $A_j \subseteq q^+(j)$ such that $|A_j| = |p^+(j)|+1$. Let $\bar{A} = O \setminus \bigcup_{i \in N} A_i$. Note that by definition $|\bar{A}| = |\bigcup_{i \in N} p^-(i)| - 1$ because $|\bar{A}| = |O| - |\bigcup_{i \in N} A_i| = \sum_{i \in N} |p(i)| - \sum_{i \in N} |p^+(i)| - 1 = \sum_{i \in N} |p^-(i)| - 1$.

We partition $\bar{A}$ into n subsets $\bar{A}_1, \ldots \bar{A}_n$ such that $\forall i \in N \setminus \{j\}, |\bar{A}_i| = |p^-(i)|$ and $|\bar{A}_j| = |p^-(j)| - 1$. Finally, let q' be the assignment such that $\forall i \in N, q'(i) = A_i \cup \bar{A}_i$. It is clear that $\forall i \in N \setminus \{j\}, u_i(q'(i)) \geq |A_i|\alpha + |\bar{A}_i|\beta = u_i(p(i))$ and $u_j(q'(j)) \geq |A_j|\alpha + |\bar{A}_j|\beta > u_j(p(j))$. So p is Pareto dominated by q'. □

THEOREM 6. *Under bivalued utilities, there exists a polynomial-time algorithm for checking Pareto optimality and finding a Pareto improvement, if any.*

PROOF. According to Theorem 5, a Pareto improvement can be computed by focusing on the assignment of top objects for the agents. We describe an algorithm based on maximum flow problems to obtain such assignment. For any $i \in N$, let $G_i = (V_i, E_i)$ be a directed graph which models the search of a Pareto improvement for agent i as a flow problem. The set of vertices V_i contains one vertex per agent and per object, plus a source s and a sink t. To ease the notation, we do not discriminate between the vertices and the agents or objects that they are representing, therefore, we note $V_i = N \cup O \cup \{s, t\}$.The set of edges E_i and their capacities are constructed as follow:

- For any $l \in N$ and $o \in O$ such that $o \in E_l^1$ there is an edge (l, o) with capacity 1.
- For any $o \in O$ there is an edge (o, t) with capacity 1.
- For any $l \in N \setminus \{i\}$ there is an edge (s, l) with capacity $|p^+(l)|$, and there is an edge (s, i) with capacity $|p^+(i)| + 1$.

It is easy to show that there exists a flow of value $\sum_{l \in N} |p^+(l)| + 1$ iff there exists an assignment such that any agent $l \in N \setminus \{i\}$ receives at least $|p(l) \cap E_l^1|$ top objects and agent i receives $|p^+(l)| + 1$ top objects. So by Theorem 5, there exists a Pareto improvement of p iff there exists $i \in N$ such that $p(i) \cap E_i^2 \neq \emptyset$ and there exists a flow of value $\sum_{l \in N} |p^+(l)| + 1$ in G_i. Therefore finding a Pareto improvement can be performed in polynomial time by solving at most n maximum-flow problems. In each Pareto improvement the number of top objects increases by at least one so there can be at most m Pareto improvements. □

Note that we can also find a Pareto optimal Pareto improvement in polynomial time as well: in each Pareto improvement the number of top objects increases by at least one so there can be at most m Pareto improvements.

EXAMPLE 3. *Let $n = 3$, $m = 6$, $E_1^1 = \{o_1, o_2, o_3\}$, $E_2^1 = \{o_2\}$, $E_3^1 = \{o_1, o_3, o_5, o_6\}$, and $p = (o_1o_4|o_2o_5|o_3o_6)$. G_1 is depicted in Figure 3. The flow of value 5 (boldface) gives the assignment $(o_1o_3|o_2o_4|o_5o_6)$, which Pareto-dominates p.*

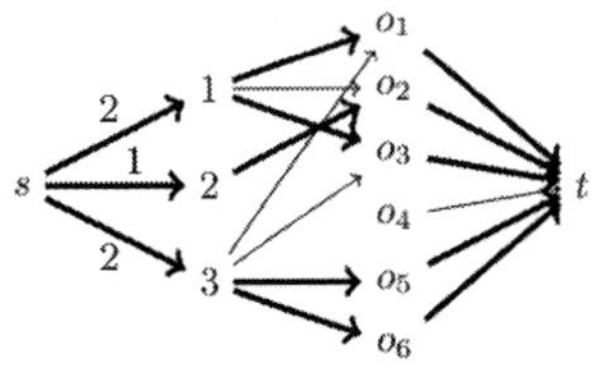

Figure 3: Flow network G_1 in Example 3.

4. ORDINAL PREFERENCES

In this section, we consider the setting in which the agents have additive cardinal utilities but only their ordinal preferences over the objects is known by the central authority. This could be because the elicitation protocol did not ask the agents to communicate their utilities, or simply because they don't know them precisely. In this case, one can still reason whether a given assignment is Pareto optimal with respect to some or all cardinal utilities consistent with the ordinal preferences. An assignment p is *possibly Pareto optimal* with respect to $\succsim$ if there exists $u \in \mathfrak{U}(\succsim)$ such that p is Pareto optimal for u. An assignment is *necessarily Pareto optimal* with respect to $\succsim$ if for any $u \in \mathfrak{U}(\succsim)$ the assignment p is Pareto optimal for u.

4.1 Possible Pareto Optimality

We first note that necessary Pareto optimality implies possible Pareto optimality. Secondly, at least one necessarily Pareto optimal assignment exists in which all the objects are given to one agent. We focus on the problems of testing possible and necessary Pareto optimality.

In order to characterize possible Pareto optimality, we first define *stochastic dominance (SD)* which extends ordinal preferences over objects to preferences over sets of objects (and even over fractional allocations in which agents can get fractions of items). We say that an allocation $q(i)$ *stochastically dominates* an allocation $p(i)$, denoted by $q(i) \succsim_i^{SD} p(i)$, iff $|q(i) \cap \bigcup_{j=1}^k E_i^j| \geq |p(i) \cap \bigcup_{j=1}^k E_i^j|$ for all $k \in \{1, \ldots, k_i\}$. In the case of fractional allocations, $q(i) \cap \bigcup_{j=1}^k E_i^j$ denotes the units of items give to i for items in $\bigcup_{j=1}^k E_i^j$.

The SD relation is equivalent to the *responsive set extension* [9], which also extends preferences over objects to preferences over sets of objects. Formally, for agent $i \in N$, her preferences $\succsim_i$ over O are extended to her preferences $\succsim_i^{RS}$ over 2^O as follows: $q(i) \succsim_i^{RS} p(i)$ iff there exists an injection

f from $p(i)$ to $q(i)$ such that for each $o \in p(i)$, $f(o) \succsim_i o$. Since $\succsim_i^{RS}$ is a partial order, we say a preference R_i is a *completion* of $\succsim_i^{RS}$ if it is a complete and transitive relation over sets of objects that is consistent with $\succsim_i^{RS}$. We say that an assignment is *SD-efficient* if it is Pareto optimal with respect to the SD relation of the agents, and *RS-efficient* if it is Pareto optimal with respect to the RS set extension relation of the agents. Under ordinal preferences, an agent i prefers one allocation $q(i)$ over another $p(i)$ with respect to responsive set extension iff she prefers it with respect to stochastic dominance [14, 7]. Thus, a (discrete) assignment is RS-efficient iff it is SD-efficient. We say that q strictly RS-dominates p if q Pareto dominates p with respect to RS.

THEOREM 7. *An assignment is possibly Pareto optimal iff it is SD-efficient iff it is RS-efficient iff there exists no cycle in $G(p)$ which contains at least one edge corresponding to a strict preference.*

PROOF. By the ordinal welfare theorem, a fractional assignment is possibly Pareto optimal iff it is SD-efficient (among the set of fractional assignments) [3, 6, 29]. Furthermore, a discrete assignment p that is SD-efficient among all discrete assignments is also SD-efficient among all fractional assignments because SD-efficiency of p depends on the non-existence of a cycle with a strict edge in the underlying graph $G(p)$ [3, 24]. Hence, we obtain the equivalences. □

Since the characterization in Theorem 4 also applies to RS-efficiency and possible Pareto optimality, hence possible Pareto optimality can be tested in linear time. The argument in the proof above also showed that possible Pareto optimality is equivalent to Pareto optimality under lexicographic preferences.

We point out that a possibly Pareto optimal assignment may not be a necessarily Pareto optimal assignment.

EXAMPLE 4. *Consider two agents with identical preferences $o_1 \succ o_2 \succ o_3 \succ o_4$. Every assignment is possibly Pareto optimal; however the assignment p in which agent 1 gets $\{o_1, o_4\}$ and 2 gets $\{o_2, o_3\}$ is not necessarily Pareto optimal since it is not Pareto optimal for the following utilities.*

	o_1	o_2	o_3	o_4
1	10	9	8	7
2	10	3	2	1

4.2 Necessary Pareto Optimality

Next we present two characterizations of necessary Pareto optimality. The first highlights that necessary Pareto optimality is identical to the necessary Pareto optimality considered by Bouveret et al. [14].

THEOREM 8. *An assignment is necessarily Pareto optimal iff it is Pareto optimal under all completions of the responsive set extension.*

PROOF. If an assignment is not Pareto optimal under certain additive preferences, it is by definition not Pareto optimal under this particular completion of responsive preferences.

Assume that an assignment p is not Pareto optimal under some completion of the responsive set extension. Then there exists another assignment q in which for all $i \in N$ $q(i) \succsim_i^{RS} p(i)$ or $p(i) \not\succ_i^{RS} q(i)$ and $q(i) \not\succ_i^{RS} p(i)$, and for some $i \in N$, $q(i) \succ_i^{RS} p(i)$ or $p(i) \not\succ_i^{RS} q(i)$ and $q(i) \not\succ_i^{RS} p(i)$. For both the cases, if the allocations are incomparable with respect to responsive set extension, then there exists an object o such that $|q(i) \cap \{o' : o \succsim_i o\}| > |p(i) \cap \{o' : o \succsim_i o\}|$. In that case, consider a utility function u_i in which $u_i(o''') - u_i(o'') \leq \epsilon$ for all $o''', o'' \succsim_i o$ and $u_i(o) > \sum_{o' \prec_i o} u_i(o') + |O|\epsilon$. For u_i, $u_i(q(i)) > u_i(p(i))$. □

For characterizing necessarily Pareto optimal assignments, we define a *one-for-two Pareto improvement swap* as an exchange between two agents i_j and i_k involving objects $o_j^1, o_j^2 \in p(i_j)$ and $o_k \in p(i_k)$ such that $o_k \succ_{i_j} o_j^1 \succsim_{i_j} o_j^2$.

THEOREM 9. *An assignment p is necessarily Pareto optimal iff (i) it is possibly Pareto optimal and (ii) it does not admit a one-for-two Pareto improvement swap.*

PROOF. We first show that if an assignment does not satisfy the two conditions, then it is not necessarily Pareto optimal. Possible Pareto optimality is a requirement for the assignment to be necessarily Pareto optimal. To see that the second condition is also necessary, we have to show that if p admits a one-for-two Pareto improvement swap then p is not necessarily Pareto optimal. This is because the swap could indeed be a Pareto improvement for these two agents with the following utilities: $u_{i_j}(o_k) > 2u_{i_j}(o_j^1)(\geq u_{i_j}(o_j^1) + u_{i_j}(o_j^2))$ and $u_{i_k}(o_k) < u_{i_k}(o_j^1) + u_{i_k}(o_j^2)$. These utilities are compatible with the ordinal preferences of these agents, because of the assumption $o_k \succ_{i_j} o_j^1 \succsim_{i_j} o_j^2$ (and irrespective to the ordinal preferences of i_k).

Conversely, to show that conditions (i) and (ii) are sufficient for the assignment to be necessarily Pareto optimal, suppose for a contradiction that (1) p is not necessarily Pareto optimal and (2) p does not admit a one-for-two Pareto improvement swap. We will then show that there is an assignment that strictly RS-dominates p, implying that p cannot be possibly Pareto optimal.

From (1) and Theorem 8, we have (3) there is another assignment q and a collection of additive utility functions $u = (u_1, \ldots, u_n) \in \mathcal{U}(\succsim)$ such that q Pareto dominates p with respect to u.

Without loss of generality

we may assume that each agent receives a nonempty bundle in p. Regarding **the structure** of p, first we observe that the lack of one-for-two Pareto improvement swaps implies that every agent is assigned to some (or none) of her top objects and possibly to one additional object that she ranks lower. Formally, let $T_p(i)$ denote a set of i's top objects she is assigned to in p, i.e., $T_p(i) = \{o : o \in p(i) \text{ s.t. } \nexists o' \notin p(i), o' \succ_i o\}$. Then $p(i) = T_p(i) \cup w_p(i)$, where $w_p(i)$ is either a single object or the empty set.

We show that $|q(i)| = |p(i)|$ must hold for every agent i. Suppose not, then there is an agent i for which $|q(i)| < |p(i)|$. By the definition of $T_p(i)$ it is straightforward that if $w_p(i) = \emptyset$ then $u_i(p(i)) = u_i(T_p(i)) > u_i(q(i))$, and if $w_p(i) \neq \emptyset$ then $u_i(p(i)) = u_i(T_p(i) \cup w_p(i)) > u_i(T_p(i)) \geq u_i(q(i))$, a contradiction. Furthermore, for every agent i, if $w_p(i) \neq \emptyset$ then for any object $o \in q(i)$ we have $o \succsim_i w_p(i)$. Otherwise, if there was an agent i with $o \in q(i)$ such that $w_p(i) \succ_i o$, then $u_i(T_p(i)) \geq u_i(q(i) \setminus \{o\})$ would imply $u_i(p(i)) = u_i(T_p(i) \cup w_p(i)) > u_i(q(i))$.

Now we construct a so-called **Pareto improvement sequence** with respect to p and q, which consists of a sequence of agents $\{i_1, i_2, \ldots i_k\}$ with possible repetitions and a set of distinct objects $\{o_1, o_2, \ldots, o_m\}$ such that

- $o_1 \in q(i_2) \setminus p(i_2)$, $o_2 \in p(i_2) \setminus q(i_2)$, and $o_1 \succsim_{i_2} o_2$;
- $o_2 \in q(i_3) \setminus p(i_3)$, $o_3 \in p(i_3) \setminus q(i_3)$, and $o_2 \succsim_{i_3} o_3$;
- ...
- $o_m \in q(i_1) \setminus p(i_1)$, $o_1 \in p(i_1) \setminus q(i_1)$, and $o_m \succsim_{i_1} o_1$.

and with strict preference for at least one agent.

The presence of the above Pareto improvement sequence would imply the existence of an assignment q' that RS-dominates p, obtained by letting the agents exchange their objects along the sequence, i.e., with $q'(i) = p(i) \cup \{o_{k-1} : i_k = i, k = 1, \dots, m\} \setminus \{o_k : i_k = i, k = 1, \dots, m\}$. This would contradict our assumption that p is possibly Pareto optimal.

We first define three types of agents, and a **one-to-one mapping** π over some of the objects they are indifferent between in p and q. In the set X we put all the agents with either no $w_p(i)$ or with $w_p(i) \in q(i)$. Each agent i in this set must be indifferent between all objects in $(p(i) \setminus q(i)) \cup (q(i) \setminus p(i))$ (i.e., these object are in a single tie in i's preference list) by the following reasons. $|p(i)| = |q(i)|$ implies $|p(i) \setminus q(i)| = |q(i) \setminus p(i)|$. By the definition of $T_p(i)$ it follows that any object in $p(i) \setminus q(i)$ is weakly preferred to any object in $q(i) \setminus p(i)$ by i. However, from (3) we have $u_i(q(i)) \geq u_i(p(i))$, which implies that $u_i(q(i) \setminus p(i)) \geq u_i(p(i) \setminus q(i))$, which can only happen if i is indifferent between any two objects in $(p(i) \setminus q(i)) \cup (q(i) \setminus p(i))$. Let π be any one-to-one mapping from $q(i) \setminus p(i)$ to $p(i) \setminus q(i)$.

Next, let Y contain every agent i who has object $w_p(i)$ such that there is an object $o \in q(i) \setminus p(i)$ with $o \sim_i w_p(i)$. In this case i must be indifferent between all objects in $(T_p(i) \setminus (q(i) \setminus \{o\})) \cup ((q(i) \setminus \{o\}) \setminus T_p(i))$.

Indeed, $|p(i)| = |q(i)|$ implies $|T_p(i) \setminus (q(i) \setminus \{o\})| = |(q(i) \setminus \{o\}) \setminus T_p(i)|$.

By the definition of $T_p(i)$ any object in $T_p(i) \setminus (q(i) \setminus \{o\})$ is weakly preferred to any object in $(q(i) \setminus \{o\}) \setminus T_p(i)$ by i. On the other hand, $u_i(q(i)) \geq u_i(p(i))$ and $o \sim_i w_p(i)$ implies $u_i((q(i) \setminus \{o\}) \setminus T_p(i)) \geq u_i(T_p(i) \setminus (q(i) \setminus \{o\}))$, leading to the conclusion that i must be indifferent between all objects in $(T_p(i) \setminus (q(i) \setminus \{o\})) \cup ((q(i) \setminus \{o\}) \setminus T_p(i))$. Therefore π can map o to $w_p(i)$ in π and $(q(i) \setminus \{o\}) \setminus T_p(i)$ to $T_p(i) \setminus q(i) \setminus \{o\})$.

Thirdly, let Z contain every agent i with object $w_p(i)$ such that for every $o \in q(i)$, $o \succ_i w_p(i)$. Note that there is at least one agent in Z, the one who gets strictly better off in q, as otherwise, if there was an object $o \in q(i)$ such that $w_p(i) \succsim_i o$, then $u_i(T_p(i)) \geq u_i(q(i) \setminus \{o\})$ would imply $u_i(p(i)) = u_i(T_p(i) \cup w_p(i)) \geq u_i(q(i))$.

Finally, we shall note that if $T_p(i)$ is empty then $|p(i)| = |q(i)| = 1$, so either i is indifferent between $p(i) = w_p(i)$ and $q(i)$, in which case i is in Y with $\pi(q(i)) = p(i)$, or i strictly prefers $q(i)$ to $p(i)$ and then i belongs to Z.

To summarize, so far we have that for any $i \in X \cup Y$ and $o \in q(i) \setminus p(i)$ we associate an object $\pi(o) \in p(i) \setminus q(i)$ such that $o \sim_i \pi(o)$. Furthermore, for any $i \in Z$ and $o \in q(i) \setminus p(i)$ we have that $o \succ_i w_p(i)$.

We build a Pareto improvement sequence as a part of a sequence involving agents $i_1, i_2, \dots$ with corresponding objects $o_1, o_2, \dots$ starting from any $i_1 \in Z$ with $o_1 = w_p(i)$. For every $k \geq 2$, let i_k be the agent who receives o_{k-1} in q. If $i_k \in X \cup Y$ then let $o_k = \pi(o_{k-1})$, and if $i_k \in Z$ then let $o_k = w_p(i)$. We terminate the sequence when an object is first repeated. This repetition must occur at some agent in Z, since for any agent i the objects in $q(i) \setminus p(i)$ are in a one-to-one correspondence with those in $p(i) \setminus q(i)$ with π.

Let the first repeated object belong to, say, $i_s = i_t \in Z$ for indices $1 \leq s < t$. We show that the sequence $i_s, \dots i_{t-1}$ is a Pareto improvement sequence. To see this, let us first consider an agent $i \in X \cup Y$. Whenever i appears in the sequence as $i_k \in \{i_{s+1}, \dots i_t\}$ she receives object $o_{k-1} \in q(i) \setminus p(i)$ and in return she gives away $\pi(o_{k-1}) = o_k \in p(i) \setminus q(i)$, where i is indifferent between o_{k-1} and o_k. Now, let $i \in Z \setminus \{i_t\}$ that appears as $i_l \in \{i_{s+1}, \dots i_t\}$. She receives object $o_{l-1} \in q(i) \setminus p(i)$ and in return she gives away $w_p(i) = o_k \in p(i) \setminus q(i)$, where $o_{l-1} \succ_i w_p(i)$ by the definition of Z. Since i appears in this sequence only once, it is obvious that $u_i(q'(i)) > u_i(p(i))$. Finally, regarding $i = i_s = i_t \in Z$, i receives $o_{t-1} \in q(i) \setminus p(i)$ and she gives away $w_p(i) = o_s \in p(i) \setminus q(i)$, where $o_{t-1} \succ_i w_p(i)$. So we constructed a Pareto improvement sequence, and therefore p is not possibly Pareto optimal, a contradiction. $\square$

In Example 4, p is not necessarily Pareto optimal because it admits a one-for-two Pareto improvement swap: o_2, $o_3 \in p(2)$, $o_1 \in p(1)$ and $o_1 \succ_2 o_2 \succsim_2 o_3$. It also shows that although an assignment may not be necessarily Pareto optimal there may not be any assignment that Pareto dominates it for *all* utilities consistent with the ordinal preferences. The characterization above also gives us a polynomial-time algorithm to test necessary Pareto optimality.

5. CONCLUSIONS

We have studied, from a computational point of view, Pareto optimality in resource allocation under additive utilities and ordinal preferences. Many of our positive algorithmic results come with characterizations of Pareto optimality that improve our understanding of the concept and may be of independent interest. Future work includes identifying other important subdomains in which Pareto optimal and individually rational reallocation can be done in a computationally efficient manner.

Acknowledgements

Haris Aziz is funded by the Australian Government through the Department of Communications and the Australian Research Council through the ICT Centre of Excellence Program. Péter Biró acknowledges support from the Hungarian Academy of Sciences under its Momentum Programme (LD-004/2010), the Hungarian Scientific Research Fund, OTKA, Grant No. K108673, and the János Bolyai Research Scholarship of the Hungarian Academy of Sciences. Jérôme Lang, Julien Lesca and Jérôme Monnot acknowledge support from the ANR project CoCoRICo-CoDec. Part of the work was conducted when Péter Biró visited Paris Dauphine and when Julien Lesca visited Corvinus University of Budapest sponsored by COST Action IC1205 on Computational Social Choice.

REFERENCES

[1] D. J. Abraham, K. Cechlárová, D. Manlove, and K. Mehlhorn. Pareto optimality in house allocation problems. In *Proc. of 16th International Symposium on Algorithms and Computation (ISAAC)*, volume 3341, pages 1163–1175, 2005.

[2] A. Asadpour and A. Saberi. An approximation algorithm for max-min fair allocation of indivisible goods. *SIAM Journal on Computing*, 39(7):2970–2989, 2010.

[3] S. Athanassoglou. Efficiency under a combination of ordinal and cardinal information on preferences. *Journal of Mathematical Economics*, 47(2):180–185, 2011.

[4] H. Aziz and B. de Keijzer. Housing markets with indifferences: a tale of two mechanisms. In *Proc. of 26th AAAI Conference*, pages 1249–1255, 2012.

[5] H. Aziz, F. Brandt, and P. Harrenstein. Pareto optimality in coalition formation. *Games and Economic Behavior*, 82:562–581, 2013.

[6] H. Aziz, F. Brandl, and F. Brandt. Universal dominance and welfare for plausible utility functions. *Journal of Mathematical Economics*, 2015.

[7] H. Aziz, S. Gaspers, S. Mackenzie, and T. Walsh. Fair assignment of indivisible objects under ordinal preferences. *Artificial Intelligence*, 227:71–92, 2015.

[8] H. Aziz, S. Mackenzie, L. Xia, and C. Ye. Ex post efficiency of random assignments. In *Proc. of 14th AAMAS Conference*, pages 1639–1640, 2015.

[9] S. Barberà, W. Bossert, and P. K. Pattanaik. *Ranking sets of objects*. Springer, 2004.

[10] I. Bezáková and V. Dani. Allocating indivisible goods. *SIGecom Exchanges*, 5(3):11–18, 2005.

[11] S. Bouveret and J. Lang. Efficiency and envy-freeness in fair division of indivisible goods: logical representation and complexity. *Journal of Artificial Intelligence Research*, 32(1):525–564, 2008.

[12] S. Bouveret and J. Lang. Manipulating picking sequences. In *Proc. of 21st ECAI*, pages 141–146, 2014.

[13] S. Bouveret and M. Lemaître. Characterizing conflicts in fair division of indivisible goods using a scale of criteria. In *Proc. of 13th AAMAS Conference*, pages 1321–1328, 2014.

[14] S. Bouveret, U. Endriss, and J. Lang. Fair division under ordinal preferences: Computing envy-free allocations of indivisible goods. In *Proc. of 19th ECAI*, pages 387–392, 2010.

[15] S. J. Brams, P. H. Edelman, and P. C. Fishburn. Fair Division Of Indivisible Items. *Theory and Decision*, 55 (2):147–180, 09 2003.

[16] K. Cechlárová, P. Eirinakis, T. Fleiner, D. Magos, D. F. Manlove, I. Mourtos, E. Ocel'áková, and B. Rastegari. Pareto optimal matchings in many-to-many markets with ties. In *Proc. of 8th SAGT*, pages 27–39, 2015.

[17] A. Damamme, A. Beynier, Y. Chevaleyre, and N. Maudet. The power of swap deals in distributed resource allocation. In *Proc. of 14th AAMAS Conference*, pages 625–633, 2015.

[18] B. de Keijzer, S. Bouveret, T. Klos, and Y. Zhang. On the complexity of efficiency and envy-freeness in fair division of indivisible goods with additive preferences. In *Proc. of 1st International Conference on Algorithmic Decision Theory*, pages 98–110, 2009.

[19] S. Demko and T. P. Hill. Equitable distribution of indivisible obejcts. *Mathematical Social Sciences*, 16: 145–158, 1988.

[20] U. Endriss. Reduction of economic inequality in combinatorial domains. In *Proc. of 12th AAMAS Conference*, pages 175–182, 2013.

[21] A. Erdil and H. Ergin. Two-sided matching with indifferences. June 2015.

[22] E. Fujita, J. Lesca, A. Sonoda, T. Todo, and M. Yokoo. A complexity approach for core-selecting exchange with multiple indivisible goods under lexicographic preferences. In *Proc. of 29th AAAI Conference*, pages 907–913, 2015.

[23] D. Golovin. Max-min fair allocation of indivisible goods. Technical Report CMU-CS-05-144, Carnegie Mellon University, 2005.

[24] A.-K. Katta and J. Sethuraman. A solution to the random assignment problem on the full preference domain. *Journal of Economic Theory*, 131(1):231–250, 2006.

[25] H. Konishi, T. Quint, and J. Wako. On the Shapley-Scarf economy: the case of multiple types of indivisible goods. *Journal of Mathematical Economics*, 35(1):1–15, 2001.

[26] J. Lesca and P. Perny. LP solvable models for multiagent fair allocation problems. In *Proc. of 19th ECAI*, pages 393–398, 2010.

[27] R. J. Lipton, E. Markakis, E. Mossel, and A. Saberi. On approximately fair allocations of indivisible goods. In *Proc. of 5th ACM-EC Conference*, pages 125–131, 2004.

[28] D. Manlove. *Algorithmics of Matching Under Preferences*. World Scientific Publishing Company, 2013.

[29] A. McLennan. Ordinal efficiency and the polyhedral separating hyperplane theorem. *Journal of Economic Theory*, 105(2):435–449, 2002.

[30] H. Moulin. *Fair Division and Collective Welfare*. The MIT Press, 2003.

[31] T. T. Nguyen, M. Roos, and J. Rothe. A survey of approximability and inapproximability results for social welfare optimization in multiagent resource allocation. *Annals of Mathematics and Artificial Intelligence*, pages 1–26, 2013.

[32] A. D. Procaccia and J. Wang. Fair enough: Guaranteeing approximate maximin shares. In *Proc. of 15th ACM-EC Conference*, pages 675–692, 2014.

[33] A. Sonoda, T. Todo, H. Sun, and M. Yokoo. Two case studies for trading multiple indivisible goods with indifferences. In *Proc. of 28th AAAI Conference*, pages 791–797, 2014.

[34] T. Todo, H. Sun, and M. Yokoo. Strategyproof exchange with multiple private endowments. In *Proc. of 28th AAAI Conference*, pages 805–811, 2014.

[35] W. Yu, H. Hoogeveen, and J. K. Lenstra. Minimizing makespan in a two-machine flow shop with delays and unit-time operations is np-hard. *Journal of Scheduling*, 7:333–348, 2004.

Group Manipulation in Judgment Aggregation

Sirin Botan
ILLC, University of Amsterdam
botan.sirin@gmail.com

Arianna Novaro
ILLC, University of Amsterdam
arianna.novaro@gmail.com

Ulle Endriss
ILLC, University of Amsterdam
ulle.endriss@uva.nl

ABSTRACT

We introduce the concept of group manipulation into the study of judgment aggregation and investigate the circumstances under which an aggregation rule may be subject to strategic misrepresentation of judgments by a group of agents. Our focus is on neutral aggregation rules, which treat all propositions to be judged symmetrically, and we assume that agents strategise to minimise the number of propositions on which they disagree with the outcome of a rule. We find that strategic manipulation by groups of two agents can be ruled out for the independent and monotonic aggregation rules. This family of rules, which is precisely the family of rules for which manipulation by a single agent can be ruled out, includes the widely used uniform quota rules. When three or more agents may coordinate their manipulation, on the other hand, essentially all attractive rules are susceptible to strategic manipulation. However, we are able to recover the family of independent and monotonic rules as being immune to manipulation, if we add the assumption that the members of a group of manipulating agents fear that the others might opt out of the jointly agreed plan.

Keywords

Collective Decision Making, Social Choice Theory

1. INTRODUCTION

Judgment aggregation [16] is a formal framework for integrating the views of several autonomous agents into a single collective view. Originating in Philosophy and Economics, and inspired by the *doctrinal paradox* observed in Legal Theory [15], it has recently received increased attention in Computer Science and Artificial Intelligence [7], where the related framework of belief revision had been studied for some time already [10, 14]. One reason for this interest is its great potential for applications, e.g., for argumentation in multiagent systems [20] or for crowdsourcing [19].

Agents will sometimes want to manipulate the process of aggregation by misreporting their true judgments. This, the analysis of strategic behaviour, is central to the closely related study of voting and preference aggregation, in both Economics [1] and Computer Science [3], but it has received very little attention in judgment aggregation to date. The reason is that here, unlike for preference aggregation, there is no single most natural way of modelling the incentives of a strategic agent. One concrete proposal for modelling such incentives is due to Dietrich and List [5], who initiated the study of strategic manipulation in judgment aggregation. They proposed a simple manner in which to induce preferences from an agent's judgment set, namely to assume that an agent's preferences only depend on the number of propositions for which their own judgment agrees with that of the rule. This initial contribution on strategic manipulation in judgment aggregation, focussing on axiomatic characterisation results, was later followed up by work on the computational complexity of manipulation by Endriss et al. [8] and Baumeister et al. [2].

All of these contributions have dealt with manipulation by a single agent at a time, rather than with the coordinated manipulation by a group. The same holds for related work on strategic manipulation in belief merging [9]. In this paper, we define a suitable notion of group manipulation for judgment aggregation and characterise the class of rules that are immune to this kind of interference. In doing so, we focus on neutral aggregation rules, i.e., rules that treat all propositions to be judged symmetrically. While our main results are axiomatic and apply to large families of rules that meet certain desirable axiomatic properties (notably neutrality, a closely related property called unbiasedness we introduce here, independence, and monotonicity), we pay special attention to a particularly natural family of concrete aggregation rules often used in practice, namely the *uniform quota rules*, and discuss the impact of our results on these rules in some detail.

The remainder of this paper is organised as follows. In Section 2 we recall relevant concepts from the judgment aggregation literature and fix our notation and terminology. In Section 3 we discuss previous work on strategic manipulation by a single agent and prove a new characterisation result for aggregation rules that are immune to single-agent manipulation. This result then serves as a base line for our work on group manipulation. Our main results can be found in Section 4, where we define the notion of group manipulation and characterise the family of aggregation rules that are immune to it, showing that essentially all reasonable rules are susceptible to this form of manipulation. This is true, in particular, for all (nontrivial) uniform quota rules, even though these rules are known to be single-agent strategyproof. Following this negative result, in Section 5 we consider a variant of our main notion of group manipula-

Appears in: *Proceedings of the 15th International Conference on Autonomous Agents and Multiagent Systems (AAMAS 2016), J. Thangarajah, K. Tuyls, C. Jonker, S. Marsella (eds.), May 9–13, 2016, Singapore.*

tion, under which individual agents may opt out of a coalition of manipulators. We show that under this alternative definition we can obtain more positive results, and that the difference between immunity against single-agent and group manipulation disappears again. Section 6 concludes.

2. PRELIMINARIES

In this section, we introduce the relevant notation and terminology to speak about judgment aggregation (JA). Specifically, we shall work with the standard framework of JA [7, 13, 17], going back to the work of List and Pettit [16]. We also introduce a number of novel concepts we require for our purposes that may be of independent interest, namely the axiom of *unbiasedness* and the notions of *flipping* a formula in a judgment set and of *restricting* an aggregation rule.

2.1 Basic Notation and Terminology

An *agenda* is a finite set of formulas of propositional logic of the form $\Phi = \Phi^+ \cup \{\neg\varphi \mid \varphi \in \Phi^+\}$, such that Φ^+, the *pre-agenda*, only contains formulas that are not negated. We call Φ *atomic* in case Φ^+ only contains atomic propositions.[1] A *judgment set* for Φ is a subset $J \subseteq \Phi$. We call J *complete* if $\varphi \in J$ or $\neg\varphi \in J$ for all $\varphi \in \Phi^+$; we call J *complement-free* if $\varphi \notin J$ or $\neg\varphi \notin J$ for all $\varphi \in \Phi^+$; and we call J *consistent* if it is logically consistent. $\mathcal{J}(\Phi)$ denotes the set of all complete and consistent judgment sets over Φ.

Let $\mathcal{N} = \{1, \dots, n\}$ be a finite set of *agents*. A *profile* $\boldsymbol{J} = (J_1, \dots, J_n)$ is a vector of judgment sets, one for each agent. Agent i is said to *accept* formula $\varphi \in \Phi$ if $\varphi \in J_i$; otherwise she *rejects* φ. We write $N_\varphi^{\boldsymbol{J}} = \{i \in \mathcal{N} \mid \varphi \in J_i\}$ for the *coalition of supporters* of φ in profile $\boldsymbol{J}$, i.e., for the set of agents who accept φ in $\boldsymbol{J}$. We furthermore write $(\boldsymbol{J}_{-i}, J_i')$ for the profile that is like $\boldsymbol{J}$, except that J_i has been replaced by J_i'. We say that profiles $\boldsymbol{J}$ and $\boldsymbol{J}'$ are *C-variants*, for some coalition $C \subseteq \mathcal{N}$, if $J_i = J_i'$ for all $i \in \mathcal{N} \setminus C$. A profile is called *unanimous* if it is of the form $\boldsymbol{J} = (J, \dots, J)$.

For $\varphi \in \Phi^+$, we denote with $J^{\rightleftarrows\varphi}$ the result of *flipping* φ in judgment set J (i.e., of replacing φ by $\neg\varphi$ or $\neg\varphi$ by φ). Analogously, for $S \subseteq \Phi^+$, we denote with $J^{\rightleftarrows S}$ the result of flipping all the formulas in S in judgment set J. For example, $\{p, \neg q, r\}^{\rightleftarrows\{p,q\}} = \{\neg p, q, r\}$. Note that this flipping operation is cardinality-preserving, i.e., we always have $|J| = |J^{\rightleftarrows S}|$, for any J and S. Finally, we use $\boldsymbol{J}^{\rightleftarrows S}$ to denote the result of flipping the formulas in S in all the judgment sets in a given profile $\boldsymbol{J}$.

2.2 Aggregation Rules

An *aggregation rule* is a function $F : \mathcal{J}(\Phi)^n \to 2^\Phi$ that assigns a collective judgment set $F(\boldsymbol{J}) \subseteq \Phi$ to every complete and consistent profile (2^Φ denotes the powerset of Φ). If $\varphi \in F(\boldsymbol{J})$, then that means that the group accepts φ.

An example for an aggregation rule is the (weak) *majority rule*, which accepts a formula if and only if at least half of the agents do. A *uniform quota rule* F_q is an aggregation rule induced by a number $q \in \{0, 1, \dots, n+1\}$ such that:

$$F_q(\boldsymbol{J}) \;=\; \{\varphi \in \Phi \mid \#N_\varphi^{\boldsymbol{J}} \geqslant q\}$$

Thus, we obtain the majority rule for $q = \lceil \frac{n}{2} \rceil$. The *unanimity rule* is the uniform quota rule with quota $q = n$ (requiring all agents to accept a formula for it to get accepted) and the *nomination rule* is the uniform quota rule with $q = 1$ (requiring acceptance by at least one agent).

A *constant rule* is a rule that returns the same fixed judgment set for every possible profile. Two examples for constant rules are the *trivial uniform quota rules* with quotas $q = 0$ and $q = n + 1$, respectively, which always accept or reject all formulas, respectively. The *dictatorship* of agent $i \in \mathcal{N}$ is the rule $F^i : \boldsymbol{J} \mapsto J_i$, returning the judgment set of i, whatever the judgments of the others.

We define the *restriction* of an aggregation rule F to a coalition $C \subseteq \mathcal{N}$ and a subset $\Psi^+ \subseteq \Phi^+$ of the pre-agenda for a given profile $\boldsymbol{J} \in \mathcal{J}(\Phi)^n$ as the following aggregation rule F', defined for the agents in C and the agenda $\Psi := \Psi^+ \cup \{\neg\psi \mid \psi \in \Psi^+\}$. F' receives a profile in $\mathcal{J}(\Psi)^{|C|}$ as input. We then amend this small profile to obtain a large profile in $\mathcal{J}(\Phi)^n$ by fixing the judgment sets of agents not in C as in $\boldsymbol{J}$ and by fixing the judgments of agents in C on agenda formulas not in Ψ also as in $\boldsymbol{J}$. Finally, we compute the output of F for the large profile and return the judgments as far as the agenda formulas in Ψ are concerned as the output of F'.[2] Note that for every C and Ψ^+, there are several restrictions of F (namely one for every $\boldsymbol{J}$).

2.3 Axioms

Any given rule may or may not satisfy a number of normatively desirable properties, usually referred to as *axioms*. Several such axioms will play a role in this paper.

First, F is *independent* if $N_\varphi^{\boldsymbol{J}} = N_\varphi^{\boldsymbol{J}'}$ implies $\varphi \in F(\boldsymbol{J}) \Leftrightarrow \varphi \in F(\boldsymbol{J}')$, i.e., if acceptance of a formula only depends on which agents accept that same formula. Second, F is *monotonic* if $\varphi \in J_i' \setminus J_i$ for some $i \in \mathcal{N}$ implies $\varphi \in F(\boldsymbol{J}) \Rightarrow \varphi \in F(\boldsymbol{J}_{-i}, J_i')$, i.e., if additional support for an accepted formula never causes that formula to be rejected. The following simple result provides a convenient characterisation of rules that are both independent and monotonic.

LEMMA 1. *An aggregation rule F is both independent and monotonic if and only if, for all profiles $\boldsymbol{J}, \boldsymbol{J}' \in \mathcal{J}(\Phi)^n$ and all formulas $\varphi \in \Phi$, it is the case that $N_\varphi^{\boldsymbol{J}} \subseteq N_\varphi^{\boldsymbol{J}'}$ implies $\varphi \in F(\boldsymbol{J}) \Rightarrow \varphi \in F(\boldsymbol{J}')$.*

PROOF. ($\Leftarrow$) Suppose the stated condition holds. Independence follows by observing that $N_\varphi^{\boldsymbol{J}} = N_\varphi^{\boldsymbol{J}'}$ implies both $N_\varphi^{\boldsymbol{J}} \subseteq N_\varphi^{\boldsymbol{J}'}$ and $N_\varphi^{\boldsymbol{J}'} \subseteq N_\varphi^{\boldsymbol{J}}$. Monotonicity follows when we consider two profiles that are $\{i\}$-variants of each other.

($\Rightarrow$) Suppose F is both independent and monotonic. Consider a scenario with $N_\varphi^{\boldsymbol{J}} \subseteq N_\varphi^{\boldsymbol{J}'}$ and $\varphi \in F(\boldsymbol{J})$. We need to show $\varphi \in F(\boldsymbol{J}')$. In case $N_\varphi^{\boldsymbol{J}} = N_\varphi^{\boldsymbol{J}'}$, the claim follows from independence. Otherwise, let $\{i_1, \dots, i_\ell\} = N_\varphi^{\boldsymbol{J}'} \setminus N_\varphi^{\boldsymbol{J}}$, with $\ell > 0$, be the agents who change their mind on φ as we move from $\boldsymbol{J}$ to $\boldsymbol{J}'$. Define a sequence of complete and consistent profiles as follows:

[1]While much of the theoretical literature on JA is concerned with the challenge of preserving complex logical dependencies during aggregation, many practical applications of JA can be accurately modelled using atomic agendas. An example is collective annotation using crowdsourcing [19].

[2]We will make use of such restrictions in two cases. In one case $\Psi^+ = \Phi^+$, and in the other Φ is assumed to be atomic. Thus, restrictions are well-defined in both cases. In the general case, care needs to be taken as not all consistent judgment sets over Ψ will necessarily remain consistent when extended with the fixed choices made for formulas in $\Phi \setminus \Psi$.

$$J^0 := J$$
$$J^k := (J^{k-1}_{-i_k}, J'_{i_k}) \quad \text{for } k \in \{1, \ldots, \ell\}$$

Thus, we start with $\boldsymbol{J}$ and replace the judgment sets of one agent at a time to eventually arrive at $\boldsymbol{J}^\ell = \boldsymbol{J}'$. By monotonicity, $\varphi \in F(\boldsymbol{J}^{k-1}) \Rightarrow \varphi \in F(\boldsymbol{J}^k)$ for all $k \in \{1, \ldots, \ell\}$. Hence, by induction, we get $\varphi \in F(\boldsymbol{J}^\ell) = F(\boldsymbol{J}')$. □

Third, an aggregation rule F is *neutral* if $N^{\boldsymbol{J}}_\varphi = N^{\boldsymbol{J}}_\psi$ implies $\varphi \in F(\boldsymbol{J}) \Leftrightarrow \psi \in F(\boldsymbol{J})$. Thus, a neutral rule treats all propositions symmetrically, in the sense of either accepting all or none of any set of formulas with exactly the same coalition of supporters.

This standard axiom of neutrality, however, does not capture all symmetry requirements that one might reasonably want to impose. Specifically, as two complementary formulas φ and $\neg\varphi$ can never have the same coalition of supporters in a given profile (as accepting both would be inconsistent and as accepting neither would be incomplete), neutrality does not have to say anything about their relative treatment by the aggregation rule. To address this issue, we introduce a new axiom. We call an aggregation rule F *unbiased* if $F(\boldsymbol{J}^{\rightleftarrows S}) = F(\boldsymbol{J})^{\rightleftarrows S}$ for any profile $\boldsymbol{J} \in \mathcal{J}(\Phi)^n$ and set $S \subseteq \Phi^+$ such that also $\boldsymbol{J}^{\rightleftarrows S} \in \mathcal{J}(\Phi)^n$. Thus, unbiasedness of F requires that when we flip the formulas in the input, then the formulas in the output returned by F should flip in the same way. In other words, F is not biased for or against negated formulas.[3]

The following technical lemma will be useful later on.

LEMMA 2. *Let F be an unbiased aggregation rule. Then $|F(\boldsymbol{J})| = |F(\boldsymbol{J}^{\rightleftarrows S})|$ for any profile $\boldsymbol{J} \in \mathcal{J}(\Phi)^n$ and any set $S \subseteq \Phi^+$ such that $\boldsymbol{J}^{\rightleftarrows S} \in \mathcal{J}(\Phi)^n$.*

PROOF. We get $|F(\boldsymbol{J})| = |F(\boldsymbol{J})^{\rightleftarrows S}|$ as $F(\boldsymbol{J})$ is a judgment set, and $|F(\boldsymbol{J})^{\rightleftarrows S}| = |F(\boldsymbol{J}^{\rightleftarrows S})|$ as F is unbiased. □

As is well known, all uniform quota rules are independent, monotonic, and neutral [4].[4] It is easy to check that they also are unbiased, and that the same holds for the dictatorships. Constant rules are independent and monotonic, but (with the exception of the trivial rules that accept all formulas or reject all formulas) they are neither neutral nor unbiased.

3. SINGLE-AGENT MANIPULATION

In this section, we establish a baseline result on strategic manipulation by a single agent and discuss the relationship between our result and a closely related result by Dietrich and List [5]. We begin by fixing a notion of preference over judgment sets, which we will also make use of later on when discussing strategic manipulation by groups of agents.

[3]Our unbiasedness axiom is related to a different axiom by the same name used by Grossi and Pigozzi [13], which itself is a variant of the *acceptance-rejection neutrality* axiom introduced by Dietrich and List [6]. Both of these axioms are considerably stronger than unbiasedness as defined here, because we require the judgments on all non-flipped formulas to be identical in the two profiles, which these authors do not, meaning that they obtain axioms that in spirit are much closer to independence. On the other hand, we allow for more than one formula to get flipped, which they do not, so in that sense our axiom is moderately stronger.

[4]The same is not true for many other practically useful aggregation rules. In particular, many of them, such as the distance-based rules [18], violate independence.

3.1 Preferences

To model the incentives of an agent to engage in strategic manipulation, we need to model her preferences. Following Dietrich and List [5], we will assume that the most preferred judgment set of agent i is always her own truthfully held judgment set J_i and that other judgment sets are ranked in terms of their distance to J_i. The *Hamming distance* between two judgment sets $J, J' \in 2^\Phi$ is defined as the number of formulas on which they disagree:

$$H(J, J') = |J \setminus J'| + |J' \setminus J|$$

For a given profile $\boldsymbol{J} = (J_1, \ldots, J_n)$, each J_i thus induces a weak order $\succcurlyeq^{\boldsymbol{J}}_i$ on judgment sets:

$$J \succcurlyeq^{\boldsymbol{J}}_i J' \quad \Leftrightarrow \quad H(J, J_i) \leqslant H(J', J_i)$$

The strict part $\succ^{\boldsymbol{J}}_i$ of $\succcurlyeq^{\boldsymbol{J}}_i$ is defined in the usual manner, i.e., $J \succ^{\boldsymbol{J}}_i J'$ if and only if $J \succcurlyeq^{\boldsymbol{J}}_i J'$ but not $J' \succcurlyeq^{\boldsymbol{J}}_i J$. All results in this paper apply to this specific type of modelling preferences, sometimes called *Hamming-distance preferences*, even when we do not always state this explicitly.

At the time of writing, this is the only standard model of preferences in the JA literature. On the other hand, it is widely recognised that this model has its limitations and that identifying richer models of preferences constitutes an important future research direction for the field. Hamming-distance preferences belong to the family of *closeness-respecting preferences*, also introduced by Dietrich and List [5], which merely demand that, for two judgment sets in $\mathcal{J}(\Phi)$, J should be (weakly) preferred to J' by agent i if $J_i \cap J \supseteq J_i \cap J'$. Some of the complexity results of Baumeister et al. [2] apply to all preference models in this class.

3.2 Strategyproofness

If agent i strictly prefers the outcome returned by F when she reports J'_i rather than her true judgment set J_i, then she has an incentive to do so, and we say that F is *susceptible* to strategic manipulation. Otherwise, we say that F is *immune* to strategic manipulation, or simply *strategyproof*.

DEFINITION 1. *A rule F is called **strategyproof**, if for all profiles $\boldsymbol{J} \in \mathcal{J}(\Phi)^n$, agents $i \in \mathcal{N}$, and judgment sets $J'_i \in \mathcal{J}(\Phi)$ it is the case that $F(\boldsymbol{J}) \succcurlyeq^{\boldsymbol{J}}_i F(\boldsymbol{J}_{-i}, J'_i)$.*

We will sometimes write 'single-agent strategyproof' rather than just 'strategyproof' to differentiate the property from group-strategyproofness discussed later on. Every aggregation rule F that is independent and monotonic is also single-agent strategyproof. This follows from a result due to Dietrich and List [5], and may also be understood independently of their result: By independence, we can focus on one formula φ at a time. By monotonicity, if an agent wants φ to get accepted, it is in her best interest to accept φ herself (and accordingly, if she wants φ to get rejected).

The following is an immediate corollary to this result, when taken together with the observation that the uniform quota rules are both independent and monotonic, which is also due to Dietrich and List [4].

PROPOSITION 3 (DIETRICH & LIST, 2007). *Every uniform quota rule F_q is single-agent strategyproof.*

Dietrich and List are sometimes misquoted as also having proved that strategyproofness implies independence and monotonicity. In fact, this is not the case, as the following counterexample demonstrates.

EXAMPLE 1. *Consider an aggregation problem with pre-agenda $\Phi^+ = \{p, q\}$ and a rule F for which the outcome only depends on agent 1. F returns $\{p, q\}$ in case agent 1 accepts p, and F returns $\{\neg p, \neg q\}$ in case agent 1 accepts $\neg p$. Thus, F does not take agent 1's judgment on q into account. F is neither independent (because the acceptance of q depends on the acceptance of p) nor monotonic (because agent 1 can switch from rejecting to accepting q, with the result being that the collective switches from accepting to rejecting q). Nevertheless, F is strategyproof: in all four possible situations, agent 1 cannot increase the number of agreements between the outcome and her sincere judgment set by switching to a different judgment set.*

Hence, the set of independent and monotonic rules is a strict subset of the set of single-agent strategyproof rules. What Dietrich and List [5] *did* prove, however, is that an aggregation rule F is independent and monotonic if and only if F is strategyproof for agents with *any* kind of closeness-respecting preferences—rather than just for those with Hamming-distance preferences. For agents with Hamming-distance preferences, so far no characterisation of the class of strategyproof aggregation rules has been known. We provide such a result here that characterises the strategyproof rules *within* the class of neutral-unbiased rules.

THEOREM 4. *A neutral and unbiased aggregation rule F is single-agent strategyproof if and only if it is both independent and monotonic.*

PROOF. As we have seen earlier, the right-to-left direction holds even without the assumptions of neutrality and unbiasedness. It is a direct consequence of the aforementioned result by Dietrich and List [5]. For the other direction, we shall establish the contrapositive. So let F be neutral and unbiased, but not both independent and monotonic. We need to find a profile where F can be manipulated.

By Lemma 1, there is a situation where $N_\varphi^{\boldsymbol{J}} \subseteq N_\varphi^{\boldsymbol{J}'}$ and $\varphi \in F(\boldsymbol{J})$, but $\varphi \notin F(\boldsymbol{J}')$. When moving from $\boldsymbol{J}$ to $\boldsymbol{J}'$, one agent must be the first to trigger this change, so w.l.o.g., we may assume only agent i changed her judgment set between the two, i.e., $\boldsymbol{J}$ and $\boldsymbol{J}'$ are $\{i\}$-variants.

First, consider the special case where i is the only agent in the group (i.e., where $n = 1$). Let $S \subseteq \Phi^+$ be the set of pre-agenda formulas on which J_i and J_i' differ, i.e., $J_i^{\rightleftarrows S} = J_i'$ and thus $\boldsymbol{J}^{\rightleftarrows S} = \boldsymbol{J}'$. Hence, by unbiasedness, $F(\boldsymbol{J}') = F(\boldsymbol{J})^{\rightleftarrows S}$. As $F(\boldsymbol{J})$ and $F(\boldsymbol{J}')$ differ on φ, this means that S must contain φ (or φ', in case φ is of the form $\varphi = \neg\varphi'$). Thus, also J_i and J_i' differ on φ. In other words, this excludes the case of $N_\varphi^{\boldsymbol{J}} = N_\varphi^{\boldsymbol{J}'}$. So we must have $N_\varphi^{\boldsymbol{J}} \subset N_\varphi^{\boldsymbol{J}'}$, meaning that $\varphi \notin J_i$ and $\varphi \in J_i'$. As $n = 1$, for any formula $\psi \in \Phi$, the coalitions of supporters of ψ in the two profiles, $N_\psi^{\boldsymbol{J}}$ and $N_\psi^{\boldsymbol{J}'}$, are either empty or the singleton $\{i\}$. This allows us to apply neutrality in the following way: If agent i agrees on φ and ψ, then also the outcome must agree on φ and ψ. Now partition Φ into four sets: the formulas agent i accepts in both profiles ($J_i \cap J_i'$), the formulas she rejects in both profiles ($\Phi \setminus (J_i \cup J_i')$), the formulas she initially rejects and then accepts ($J_i' \setminus J_i$), and those she initially accepts and then rejects ($J_i \setminus J_i'$). This perspective allows us to fully determine which formulas are either accepted or rejected in each of the two profiles:

	$F(\boldsymbol{J})$	$F(\boldsymbol{J}')$
$J_i \cap J_i'$	**out** (by Lemma 2)	**out** (by neutrality)
$\Phi \setminus (J_i \cup J_i')$	**in** (by neutrality)	**in** (by Lemma 2)
$J_i' \setminus J_i$	**in** (by neutrality)	**out** (by neutrality)
$J_i \setminus J_i'$	**out** (by Lemma 2)	**in** (by Lemma 2)

All table entries that are marked 'by neutrality' follow from neutrality together with what we know about the acceptance/rejection of φ. The remaining four table entries then follow from Lemma 2, according to which $|F(\boldsymbol{J})| = |F(\boldsymbol{J}')|$, because no other option would permit us to preserve the cardinality of the outcome when moving between the two profiles. To see this, observe (i) that $J_i, J_i' \in \mathcal{J}(\Phi)$ entails $|J_i' \setminus J_i| = |J_i \setminus J_i'|$ and that (ii) all formulas coverd by any given table entry must all behave in the same way (again, due to neutrality). In conclusion, we obtain $F(\boldsymbol{J}) = [\Phi \setminus (J_i \cup J_i')] \cup [J_i' \setminus J_i] = \Phi \setminus J_i$ and $F(\boldsymbol{J}') = \Phi \setminus J_i'$. In other words, agent i has a clear incentive to manipulate when in profile $\boldsymbol{J}$ and to report J_i' instead of J_i.

Now suppose $n > 1$. Instead of showing directly that F can be manipulated, we instead show that if F were to be strategyproof, then there would exist another rule F' for single-agent profiles that is neutral, unbiased, not both independent and monotonic, and yet strategyproof. As we have just seen that the latter is not the case, the former cannot be the case either. So suppose F is strategyproof. We construct $F' : \mathcal{J}(\Phi)^1 \to 2^\Phi$ as follows. For any $J \in \mathcal{J}(\Phi)^1$, let $F' : (J) \mapsto F(\boldsymbol{J}_{-i}, J)$. That is, F' is the restriction of F to agent i, with the judgments of the other agents being fixed as in $\boldsymbol{J}$ and $\boldsymbol{J}'$ (recall that $\boldsymbol{J}_{-i} = \boldsymbol{J}'_{-i}$). Neutrality, unbiasedness, and strategyproofness immediately transfer from F to F', for any restriction of this kind. Only for the property of *not* being both independent and monotonic, we need to verify that the characterising property of Lemma 1 really is violated for F' as well. But this is easily seen to be the case: we have $N_\varphi^{(J_i)} \subseteq N_\varphi^{(J_i')}$ and $\varphi \in F'((J_i)) = F(\boldsymbol{J})$ but $\varphi \notin F'((J_i')) = F(\boldsymbol{J}')$. This concludes the proof. □

As an aside, we note that Theorem 4 is not in conflict with the classical Gibbard-Satterthwaite Theorem [12, 21] in voting theory, which—loosely speaking—says that no non-dictatorial voting rule for three or more alternatives can be strategyproof. The reason is that here we are lacking a counterpart for those three alternatives. Rather, in the context of the independence axiom, JA may be seen as a series of elections with two (i.e., fewer than three) alternatives, one for each formula φ in the pre-agenda, with the two alternatives being φ and $\neg\varphi$. To obtain results in JA that resemble the Gibbard-Satterthwaite Theorem one has to focus on aggregation problems with specific agendas to model preferences. Dietrich and List [5] establish a result of this kind.

4. GROUP MANIPULATION

In this section, we generalise the definition of strategyproofness discussed earlier to obtain a definition of group-strategyproofness, requiring that no coalition of agents should ever have an incentive to misreport their judgments. We then characterise the family of (neutral and unbiased) aggregation rules that is group-strategyproof in this sense.

4.1 Definition of the Concept

As we will see, the *size* of the coalition of manipulators is an important parameter in our characterisation of group-strategyproof rules. For instance, a given rule may be subject to manipulation by three agents, but not by one or two agents. We therefore formulate our definition relative to a number k, the maximum number of agents that may form a coalition for the purposes of strategic manipulation.

DEFINITION 2. *An aggregation rule F is called* ***group-strategyproof*** *against coalitions of up to k manipulators, if for all profiles $\boldsymbol{J} \in \mathcal{J}(\Phi)^n$, coalitions $C \subseteq \mathcal{N}$ with $|C| \leqslant k$, and C-variants $\boldsymbol{J}' \in \mathcal{J}(\Phi)^n$ of $\boldsymbol{J}$ it is the case that $F(\boldsymbol{J}) \succcurlyeq_i^J F(\boldsymbol{J}')$ for all agents $i \in C$.*

In the above definition, C is the set of manipulators and the other agents are truthful. $\boldsymbol{J}$ is the truthful profile and $\boldsymbol{J}'$ is the result of the agents in C misreporting their judgments. Intuitively, the definition says that there exists no group of up to k agents who can, in at least one situation, change their judgment sets in such a way that they all (strictly) prefer the new outcome over the old one. Note that for the special case of $k = 1$, we recover Definition 1.

EXAMPLE 2. *Consider the following profile with five agents and the pre-agenda $\Phi^+ = \{\varphi_1, \varphi_2, \varphi_3\}$:*

	φ_1	φ_2	φ_3	$\neg\varphi_1$	$\neg\varphi_2$	$\neg\varphi_3$
Agent 1	×	✓	✓	✓	×	×
Agent 2	✓	×	✓	×	✓	×
Agent 3	✓	✓	×	×	×	✓
Agent 4	×	×	×	✓	✓	✓
Agent 5	×	×	×	✓	✓	✓
Majority	×	×	×	✓	✓	✓

Now suppose the first three agents manipulate by flipping their judgments corresponding to the cells shaded in grey. This will cause every single formula in the majority outcome to flip as well. In the initial profile, for each of the manipulators, the Hamming distance between the outcome and her individual judgment set is 4. After the change, the distance between the new outcome and the old (i.e., truthful) individual judgment set shrinks to 2 for each of them. Hence, the majority rule is not group-strategyproof against three manipulators—at least not in a world with a population of five. Importantly, observe that each manipulator performs a manipulation on one formula (and its complement) that damages her own interests, but this is made up for by the other two performing manipulations that benefit her.

Two families of aggregation rules that are immediately seen to be group-strategyproof, against coalitions of any size, are the dictatorships and the constant rules.

Observe that group-strategyproofness for (up to) k implies group-strategyproofness for (up to) $k-1$. Thus, for positive results we will look for the largest k for which they apply, while for negative results we will look for the smallest such k. If F is group-strategyproof for any coalition size k, we simply say that F is group-strategyproof.

4.2 Manipulation by Two Agents

We first analyse the case of $k = 2$, i.e., the case of up to two agents manipulating, and find that the situation is no worse than for the single-agent case covered by Theorem 4.

THEOREM 5. *A neutral and unbiased aggregation rule F is group-strategyproof against coalitions of up to two manipulators if and only if it is both independent and monotonic.*

PROOF. ($\Rightarrow$) We proceed by contraposition. Suppose F is neutral and unbiased but not both independent and monotonic. Then, by Theorem 4, F is not group-strategyproof even against a single agent (i.e., a coalition of one manipulator). Hence, F certainly is not group-strategyproof for coalitions of *up to* two manipulators.

($\Leftarrow$) Assume F is neutral, unbiased, independent, and monotonic. By Theorem 4, there cannot be a manipulation with a coalition of a single agent. So, w.l.o.g., suppose there are *exactly* two manipulators. Since F is monotonic, the manipulators cannot manipulate on formulas for which their individual judgment sets agree (because their truthful judgments on such formulas are optimal for both of them already). Therefore, any manipulator who changes her individual judgment set to have an effect on the outcome must go against her own preferences in order to benefit the other agent. As preferences are defined in terms of the Hamming distance, each of the two manipulators will have to require the other one to perform *strictly more* such manipulations on individual formulas than she performs herself. But this clearly is a contradiction. □

4.3 Manipulation by More Than Two Agents

To understand the case of arbitrary numbers of manipulators, we first focus on the case of $k = 3$ manipulators. We will require a definition of what it means for an agent to be able to have an effect on a given formula in a given profile.

DEFINITION 3. *Agent $i \in \mathcal{N}$ is called* ***effective*** *on formula $\varphi \in \Phi^+$ in profile $\boldsymbol{J} \in \mathcal{J}(\Phi)^n$ with $J_i^{\rightleftarrows\varphi} \in \mathcal{J}(\Phi)$ if it is the case that both $\varphi \in F(\boldsymbol{J}) \not\Leftrightarrow \varphi \in F(\boldsymbol{J}_{-i}, J_i^{\rightleftarrows\varphi})$ and $\neg\varphi \in F(\boldsymbol{J}) \not\Leftrightarrow \neg\varphi \in F(\boldsymbol{J}_{-i}, J_i^{\rightleftarrows\varphi})$.*

Thus, agent i is effective on φ in $\boldsymbol{J}$, if she can flip her judgment on φ whilst remaining complete and consistent, and if due to that flip the status of both φ and $\neg\varphi$ changes in the outcome. If, for the initial outcome $F(\boldsymbol{J})$, it is the case that exactly one of φ and $\neg\varphi$ is accepted (i.e., if F is complete and complement-free in this instance), then this property is preserved in the changed outcome $F(\boldsymbol{J}_{-i}, J_i^{\rightleftarrows\varphi})$. Otherwise, it continues to be violated.

We now prove a technical lemma that fully characterises the class of group-strategyproof aggregation rules for the special case of three agents (and thus at most three manipulators) and an agenda of three positive formulas (i.e., six formulas overall). We will later use this characterisation as a gadget to characterise rules for arbitrary numbers of agents and arbitrary agendas that are group-strategyproof against up to three manipulators. The first part of the proof of the following lemma amounts to a generalisation of the technique employed in Example 2 to obtain a profile in which a successful manipulation may occur.

LEMMA 6. *Suppose $\mathcal{N} = \{1, 2, 3\}$ and $|\Phi^+| = 3$. Then a neutral and unbiased aggregation rule F is group-strategyproof if and only if it is independent and monotonic and there are no unanimous profile $(J, J, J) \in \mathcal{J}(\Phi)^3$ and bijection $g : \mathcal{N} \to \Phi^+$ such that, for all $i \in \mathcal{N}$, agent i is effective on agenda formula $g(i)$ in profile $(J^{\rightleftarrows g(1)}, J^{\rightleftarrows g(2)}, J^{\rightleftarrows g(3)}) \in \mathcal{J}(\Phi)^3$.*

PROOF. ($\Rightarrow$) We prove the contrapositive. Let F be a neutral and unbiased aggregation rule. First of all, if F is not both independent and monotonic, we know that it is manipulable by a single agent by Theorem 4. Therefore, assume F is independent and monotonic, and suppose that there are a unanimous profile (J, J, J) and a bijection g as described above. Let $\Phi^+ = \{\varphi_1, \varphi_2, \varphi_3\}$. W.l.o.g., as we can rename the formulas, we may assume that $g(i) = \varphi_i$ for all $i \in \mathcal{N}$. Also w.l.o.g., we may assume that $J = \{\varphi_1, \varphi_2, \varphi_3\}$, because for any aggregation problem where a negative formula $\neg\varphi_i$ occurs in J, there exists an equivalent aggregation problem where $\neg\varphi_i$ has been replaced by the positive formula $\top \wedge \neg\varphi_i$ and φ_i by its negation. We now need to show that there exists a profile in which manipulation can occur. This profile is $\boldsymbol{J} = (J^{\rightleftarrows\varphi_1}, J^{\rightleftarrows\varphi_2}, J^{\rightleftarrows\varphi_3})$. Indeed, let $\boldsymbol{J}$ be the truthful profile. Then the result of each agent i manipulating by flipping formula φ_i is profile (J, J, J). As all three agents are effective, all three formulas must have changed status during manipulation. By monotonicity, this change must have occurred "in the right direction", i.e., we have $F(\boldsymbol{J}) = \{\neg\varphi_1, \neg\varphi_2, \neg\varphi_3\}$ and $F(J, J, J) = \{\varphi_1, \varphi_2, \varphi_3\}$.

We can now easily verify that for each agent i the Hamming distance between her truthful judgment set $J^{\rightleftarrows\varphi_i}$, e.g., $\{\neg\varphi_1, \varphi_2, \varphi_3\}$ for agent 1, and the nonmanipulated outcome $\{\neg\varphi_1, \neg\varphi_2, \neg\varphi_3\}$ is higher than the Hamming distance between her truthful judgment set and the manipulated outcome $\{\varphi_1, \varphi_2, \varphi_3\}$, namely $H(J^{\rightleftarrows\varphi_i}, F(\boldsymbol{J})) = 4$ rather than $H(J^{\rightleftarrows\varphi_i}, F(J, J, J)) = 2$. Therefore, F is not group-strategyproof against manipulation by all three agents.

($\Leftarrow$) Let F be an aggregation rule that is neutral, unbiased, independent, and monotonic. Now suppose that for every unanimous profile (J, J, J) and for every bijection g there is some agent i such that i is not effective on formula $g(i)$. This amounts to saying that, for every unanimous profile (J, J, J) and every possible bijection g, there will always be at most two effective agents over the formulas in Φ^+. Hence, it will always be possible to use the reasoning employed in the proof of the right-to-left direction of Theorem 5 to show that F must be group-strategyproof. □

Observe that independence and neutrality of an aggregation rule F together imply that F must be induced by a local rule, a boolean function over subsets of $\mathcal{N}$, that decides for each formula φ in the agenda whether it should be accepted based only on the coalitions of individual agents that accept φ. This observation is useful in that it allows us to fully classify all aggregation rules covered by Lemma 6 as either group-strategyproof or susceptible to strategic manipulation. For three agents and one formula (that may be accepted or rejected), there are $2^{2\cdot 2\cdot 2} = 256$ possible local rules. But only 20 of them are monotonic.[5] We have enumerated these rules using a simple computer program. They consist of 3 *dictatorships* (one for each agent), 2 *constant rules* (always-accept and always-reject), the *nomination rule* (the quota rule with quota 1), the *majority rule* (the quota rule with quota 2), the *unanimity rule* (the quota rule with quota 3), 6 *two-agent rules* (with one dummy agent and the other two using either a nomination or a unanimity rule), and 6 *weighted quota rules* (with one agent having weight 2, two having weight 1, and the quota being either 2 or 3).

Using Lemma 6 it is now easy to check that, for $n = 3$ and $|\Phi^+| = 3$, amongst the neutral, unbiased, independent, and monotonic aggregation rules, the only ones that can be manipulated by the full group are the nomination rule and the unanimity rule. For example, for the nomination rule all three agents are effective for φ in any situation where currently none of them accepts φ. On the other hand, for the majority rule, for instance, it is impossible to find a situation where all three agents are effective for φ whilst currently agreeing on φ (agent 1 is effective only when agents 2 and 3 disagree, and so forth). Thus, we may rewrite Lemma 6 in the following simplified form.

LEMMA 7. *Suppose $n = 3$ and $|\Phi^+| = 3$. Then a neutral and unbiased aggregation rule F is group-strategyproof if and only if it is independent and monotonic, and if it is neither the nomination rule nor the unanimity rule.*

Unfortunately, as Example 2 demonstrates, this very positive result does not generalise to larger numbers of agents. Specifically, although the majority rule is group-strategyproof for three agents, it can be manipulated by three agents when the overall number of agents is five. The reason is that, when we use the majority rule for five agents and keep the judgments of two (sincere) agents fixed, then the resulting rule implicitly defined over the remaining three agents is in fact the nomination rule, which we have seen to be manipulable in a world with only three agents.

For our next result we are going to generalise this idea of a rule for three agents being implicitly defined by a rule for a larger population when we keep the judgments of all but three agents fixed. Note that this result only applies to the case of atomic agendas; the implications of this restriction are discussed at the end of this section.

THEOREM 8. *Suppose the agenda Φ is atomic. Then a neutral and unbiased aggregation rule F is group-strategyproof against coalitions of up to three manipulators if and only if F is independent and monotonic, and if none of the restrictions of F to three agents and three pre-agenda formulas is either the nomination rule or the unanimity rule.*

PROOF. By Theorem 4, amongst the neutral and unbiased aggregation rules, only the independent and monotonic rules can potentially be group-strategyproof. Thus, what the theorem claims on top of this basic insight is that a neutral, unbiased, independent, and monotonic rule F can be manipulated by a coalition of 3 agents *if and only if* there exist a set of 3 agents and a set of 3 formulas in the pre-agenda such that, when we keep everything else fixed (the judgments of the other $n-3$ agents on everything and the judgments of the 3 selected agents on the other agenda formulas), the resulting aggregation rule is either the nomination rule or the unanimity rule. The right-to-left direction of this latter claims is an immediate consequence of Lemma 7: If there is such a restriction that is the nomination or the unanimity rule, then that restricted rule can be manipulated by Lemma 7, and thus F can be manipulated by the very same moves. The left-to-right direction of the same claim is also immediate in case the original aggregation problem has a pre-agenda of 3 formulas only.

So all that remains to be shown is that the focus on 3 pre-agenda formulas at a time is sufficient to catch at least one situation in which manipulation is possible whenever manipulation is possible at all. So suppose that in a world with 3 agents there exists a successful manipulation involving m positive formulas. We need to show that then there also

[5]Readers familiar with coalitional game theory may recognise 20, the third Dedekind number [11], as the number of simple games for three players [22].

exists a manipulation involving only 3 of those formulas.[6] First, w.l.o.g., we may assume that every formula involved in the manipulation changed its acceptance status in the outcome (otherwise, simply not manipulating such a formula does not change the result). Second, w.l.o.g., we may assume that none of the formulas involved in the manipulation was flipped by all 3 agents (because otherwise none of them would have benefitted from getting this formula flipped in the outcome). So every formula involved is flipped by either one or two agents. The agents flipping φ always prefer the sincere outcome for φ, and the ones not flipping φ always prefer the insincere outcome for φ (just as in Example 2). Thus, there are six types of formulas: $(+1, +1, -1)$-formulas are those where the manipulation benefits agents 1 and 2 but harms agent 3; $(+1, -1, -1)$-formulas are those where the manipulation benefits 1 but harms 2 and 3; and so forth. The numbers, $+1$ and -1, indicate the changes to the Hamming distances for the 3 agents caused by the formula in question. When adding up the vectors corresponding to the m formulas we must get a positive number in each of the 3 positions (otherwise the corresponding agent does not benefit from the overall manipulation). It is easy to see that this is only possible if of $(+1, +1, -1)$, $(+1, -1, +1)$, and $(-1, +1, +1)$, i.e., the formulas benefitting two agents and harming only one agent, each shows up at least once. But if the agents only manipulate on the corresponding 3 formulas, they also all benefit, i.e., we have shown that a manipulation involving only 3 positive formulas is feasible. □

We must emphasise that Theorem 8 is a negative result, as it implies that essentially all reasonable (neutral and unbiased) aggregation rules are susceptible to strategic manipulation by groups of agents. To substantiate this claim, let us see what Theorem 8 implies for the large and important family of the the uniform quota rules.

COROLLARY 9. *No uniform quota rule F_q with a quota q satisfying $3 \leqslant q \leqslant n$ or $1 \leqslant q \leqslant n-2$ that is defined on an atomic agenda Φ is group-strategyproof.*

PROOF. All uniform quota rules are neutral, unbiased, independent, and monotonic. Thus, by Theorem 8, to show a failure of group-strategproofness, we must find a restriction of F_q to 3 agents and 3 pre-agenda formulas for which the local rule deciding on the acceptance of each individual formula is either the nomination or the unanimity rule.

First, suppose $3 \leqslant q \leqslant n$. In this case, we can find a restriction of F_q to 3 agents and 3 pre-agenda formulas that is the unanimity rule: simply consider a profile in which $q-3$ sincere agents accept φ and $n-q$ sincere agents reject φ. Then φ will get accepted if and only if the three manipulators unanimously accept φ. Note that, due to our assumptions on q, this construction is well-defined: $q-3 \geqslant 0$, $n-q \geqslant 0$, and $(q-3)+(n-q)+3=n$.

Second, suppose $1 \leqslant q \leqslant n-2$. In this case, we can find a restriction of F_q that is the nomination rule in an analogous manner: consider a profile in which $q-1$ sincere agents accept φ and $n-2-q$ sincere agents reject φ. Then φ will get accepted if and only if at least one of the manipulators accepts it. Also this construction is well-defined: $q-1 \geqslant 0$, $n-2-q \geqslant 0$, and $(q-1)+(n-2-q)+3=n$. □

[6]Because of our assumption that Φ is atomic, we are free to change the judgments for the remaining $m-3$ formulas back to what they were in the sincere judgment sets. This is the only reason for this assumption.

The assumptions on the quota under which Corollary 9 applies are very weak. Observe that $n > 3$ implies that either $3 \leqslant q$ or $q \leqslant n-2$ (or both). Thus, for aggregation problems with $n > 3$ agents, the only uniform quota rules that are group-strategyproof are the trivial rules that either accept or reject all formulas. These are the rules we obtain for $q = 0$ and $q = n+1$, respectively. For the special case of $n = 3$ agents, as we have seen in the discussion following Lemma 6, in addition the majority rule is group-strategyproof. For $n < 3$ agents, all uniform quota rules are group-strategyproof. This follows from Theorem 5.

Theorem 8 is stated for the case of (up to) $k = 3$ manipulators, rather than for arbitrary k. As pointed out in Section 4.1, as it is essentially a negative result (i.e., the contrapositive of the left-to-right direction, giving sufficient conditions for manipulability, is what matters most), this is the strongest possible form of this kind of result. Indeed, as essentially every reasonable neutral rule may be manipulated by coalitions of up to 3 manipulators, it certainly is the case that they also are subject to manipulation by coalitions of up to $k = 4, 5, \ldots$ manipulators.

Finally, Theorem 8 only applies to atomic agendas. We required this restriction to be able to show that any manipulation involving m positive formulas can be reduced to a manipulation involving 3 positive formulas. For an agenda with strong logical dependencies between formulas, more positive results are possible in principle. For example, in the most extreme case, when an agenda consists of tautologies and their negations only (and assuming *unanimity*),[7] strategic manipulation is impossible, because every agent will have the exact same sincere judgment set.[8] However, for any agenda permitting a fair degree of variation in the range of admissible judgment sets, our results suggest that group-strategyproofness is rarely an option. A full analysis of how agenda conditions impact on group-strategyproofness constitutes an important direction for future work.

5. UNSTABLE MANIPULATION

In this section, we propose a variant of the notion of group-strategyproofness defined earlier and show that under this new definition much more positive results are feasible. This alternative definition is inspired by the following example.

EXAMPLE 3. *Recall the scenario discussed in Example 2, where five agents were using the majority rule to decide on three pairs of formulas, and the first three agents had an incentive to manipulate. Below is the profile $\boldsymbol{J}'$ we obtain after they manipulate as indicated before (starting from $\boldsymbol{J}$):*

	φ_1	φ_2	φ_3	$\neg\varphi_1$	$\neg\varphi_2$	$\neg\varphi_3$
Agent 1	✓	✓	✓	×	×	×
Agent 2	✓	✓	✓	×	×	×
Agent 3	✓	✓	✓	×	×	×
Agent 4	×	×	×	✓	✓	✓
Agent 5	×	×	×	✓	✓	✓
Majority	✓	✓	✓	×	×	×

Consider what happens when agent 1 opts out of the joint plan and reverses her manipulation, i.e., when we flip the

[7]The unanimity axiom states that any reasonable aggregation rule should map unanimous profiles $(J, \ldots, J)$ to J.
[8]Recall that individual judgment sets are always complete and consistent, i.e., all agents accept all tautologies.

judgments corresponding to the cells shaded in grey. Then the majority judgment on φ_1 and $\neg\varphi_1$ changes as well. As a result, agent 1 will obtain her most preferred outcome $F(\boldsymbol{J}'_{-1}, J_1) = \{\neg\varphi_1, \varphi_2, \varphi_3\}$, which is equal to her truthful judgment set. So agent 1's preferences in our example are actually $F(\boldsymbol{J'}_{-1}, J_1) \succ_1^J F(\boldsymbol{J'}) \succ_1^J F(\boldsymbol{J})$. Thus, she has an incentive to opt out of the joint plan—and for symmetry reasons, so does every other agent.[9]

This is in contrast with our previous notion of manipulation, where any agreed-upon manipulation is guaranteed to be carried out by all agents in the coalition of manipulators. Now coalitions are *fragile* in the sense that any one agent may opt out of a previously agreed upon manipulation, if doing so is in her own interest.

DEFINITION 4. *An aggregation rule F is called* ***group-strategyproof against fragile coalitions*** *of up to k manipulators, if for all profiles $\boldsymbol{J} \in \mathcal{J}(\Phi)^n$, coalitions $C \subseteq \mathcal{N}$ with $|C| \leqslant k$, and C-variants $\boldsymbol{J'} \in \mathcal{J}(\Phi)^n$ of $\boldsymbol{J}$ with $F(\boldsymbol{J'}) \succ_i^J F(\boldsymbol{J})$ and $F(\boldsymbol{J'}_{-i}, J_i) \neq F(\boldsymbol{J'})$ for all $i \in C$ it is the case that $F(\boldsymbol{J'}_{-i}, J_i) \succ_i^J F(\boldsymbol{J'})$ for some $i \in C$.*

Intuitively, F is group-strategyproof against fragile coalitions if any coalition attempting manipulation is one where every agent in the coalition has an incentive to opt out of the manipulation (i.e., to go back to her truthful judgment set). In the above definition, C is the coalition of manipulators. Condition $F(\boldsymbol{J'}) \succ_i^J F(\boldsymbol{J})$ says that all agents in the coalition benefit from the manipulation and condition $F(\boldsymbol{J'}_{-i}, J_i) \neq F(\boldsymbol{J'})$ says that every member of the coalition is in fact needed to achieve the new outcome. Finally, $F(\boldsymbol{J'}_{-i}, J_i) \succ_i^J F(\boldsymbol{J'})$ says that agent i benefits from opting out once we are in the new profile $\boldsymbol{J'}$.

Our new definition makes manipulation more difficult and thereby immunity against manipulation more likely. Indeed, we are able to fully recover the class of aggregation rules that was shown to be single-agent strategyproof in Theorem 4, but now against coalitions of manipulators of any size, provided those coalitions are fragile.

THEOREM 10. *A neutral and unbiased aggregation rule F is group-strategyproof against fragile coalitions of manipulators if and only if it is independent and monotonic.*

PROOF. ($\Rightarrow$) Observe that F is single-agent strategyproof if and only if it is group-strategyproof against fragile coalitions of size 1 (as no single manipulator would ever want to opt out of its own coalition). Hence, group-strategyproofness against fragile coalitions of manipulators implies standard single-agent strategyproofness. The claim then follows from Theorem 4.

($\Leftarrow$) Let F be independent and monotonic. Consider two C-variants $\boldsymbol{J}, \boldsymbol{J'} \in \mathcal{J}(\Phi)^n$ such that $F(\boldsymbol{J'}) \succ_i^J F(\boldsymbol{J})$ and $F(\boldsymbol{J'}_{-i}, J_i) \neq F(\boldsymbol{J'})$ for all $i \in C$. The latter means that every single agent in C is effective in their manipulation. By independence, we can reason formula-by-formula. By monotonicity, the effect that an agent i has on a formula she is effective for must be against her own true preferences. Thus, if she reverts back to her truthful judgment set, she will necessarily obtain a strictly preferred outcome. □

[9]Also consider what happens if agents 1 and 2 both opt out. Then we end up in a profile with outcome $\{\neg\varphi_1, \neg\varphi_2, \varphi_3\}$, which is the worst possible outcome for agent 3. Thus, if agent 3 is afraid that the others may opt out, she will not agree on a joint manipulation in the first place.

In other words, under the alternative notion of strategyproofness discussed in this section, and when restricting attention to neutral and unbiased aggregation rules, single-agent strategyproofness and group-strategyproofness in fact define the same class of aggregation rules.

6. CONCLUSION

We have introduced the notion of group-strategyproofness into JA and found that it is a considerably more demanding property than ordinary strategyproofness against a single manipulator. For example, we have seen that, while all uniform quota rules are single-agent strategyproof (see Proposition 3), essentially none of them are group-strategyproof (see Corollary 9). Our main result, Theorem 8, shows that, for a neutral and unbiased aggregation rule, single-agent strategyproofness extends to group-strategyproofness only in case the rule is such that it is impossible to obtain either the unanimity rule or the nomination rule by fixing the judgments of all but three agents as well as the judgments of those three agents on all but three (pairs of) formulas. That this condition is highly unlikely to be satisfied is convincingly demonstrated by the aforementioned instantiation of this result to the uniform quota rules.

We have also seen that when the contracts manipulating agents make with each other are not binding, then no coordinated group manipulation is stable. This may be interpreted as offering protection against group manipulation in practice. Other forms of protection are interesting topics for future research. For instance, as we have already indicated, strong logical dependencies in the agenda will reduce opportunities for manipulation, and narrow *domain restrictions* [6] may offer full protection. Another avenue to pursue in this context is to extend existing work on the *complexity of manipulation* [2, 8] to group manipulation.

Our characterisation result for single-agent strategyproofness is of some interest in its own right and clarifies an issue that had remained vague in the literature to date, namely that independence and monotonicity alone are not sufficient to guarantee single-agent strategyproofness when an agent's preferences are induced by the Hamming distance between the outcome and an agent's true judgment set. Our Theorem 4 shows that, within the class of the neutral and unbiased rules, single-agent strategyproofness is fully characterised by independence and monotonicity. When neutrality and unbiasedness are dropped as assumptions, it is known that independence and monotonicity still are sufficient conditions for strategyproofness, but a full characterisation of the strategyproof rules for Hamming-distance preferences remains an open problem.

We have made the common assumption that preferences are induced by the Hamming distance. Our main result is negative, so it also applies to the larger class of closeness-respecting preferences. On the other hand, our positive result on group-strategyproofness against two manipulators does not extend to closeness-respecting preferences more generally, as our proof directly exploits the properties of the Hamming distance. Nevertheless, considering other forms of preferences constitutes an important direction for future work on strategic behaviour in JA, and this includes future work on group-strategyproofness.

Acknowledgments. We would like to thank the anonymous reviewers for the helpful feedback provided.

REFERENCES

[1] K. J. Arrow, A. K. Sen, and K. Suzumura, editors. *Handbook of Social Choice and Welfare*. North-Holland, 2002.

[2] D. Baumeister, G. Erdélyi, O. J. Erdélyi, and J. Rothe. Complexity of manipulation and bribery in judgment aggregation for uniform premise-based quota rules. *Mathematical Social Sciences*, 76:19–30, 2015.

[3] F. Brandt, V. Conitzer, and U. Endriss. Computational social choice. In G. Weiss, editor, *Multiagent Systems*, pages 213–283. MIT Press, 2013.

[4] F. Dietrich and C. List. Judgment aggregation by quota rules: Majority voting generalized. *Journal of Theoretical Politics*, 19(4):391–424, 2007.

[5] F. Dietrich and C. List. Strategy-proof judgment aggregation. *Economics and Philosophy*, 23(3):269–300, 2007.

[6] F. Dietrich and C. List. Majority voting on restricted domains. *Journal of Economic Theory*, 145(2):512–543, 2010.

[7] U. Endriss. Judgment aggregation. In F. Brandt, V. Conitzer, U. Endriss, J. Lang, and A. D. Procaccia, editors, *Handbook of Computational Social Choice*. Cambridge University Press, 2016.

[8] U. Endriss, U. Grandi, and D. Porello. Complexity of judgment aggregation. *Journal of Artificial Intelligence Research (JAIR)*, 45:481–514, 2012.

[9] P. Everaere, S. Konieczny, and P. Marquis. The strategy-proofness landscape of merging. *Journal of Artificial Intelligence Research (JAIR)*, 28(1):49–105, 2007.

[10] P. Everaere, S. Konieczny, and P. Marquis. Belief merging versus judgment aggregation. In *Proceedings of the 14th International Conference on Autonomous Agents and Multiagent Systems (AAMAS-2015)*, 2015.

[11] R. Fidytek, A. W. Mostowski, R. Somla, and A. Szepietowski. Algorithms counting monotone Boolean functions. *Information Processing Letters*, 79(5):203–209, 2001.

[12] A. Gibbard. Manipulation of voting schemes: A general result. *Econometrica*, 41(4):587–601, 1973.

[13] D. Grossi and G. Pigozzi. *Judgment Aggregation: A Primer*. Synthesis Lectures on Artificial Intelligence and Machine Learning. Morgan & Claypool Publishers, 2014.

[14] S. Konieczny and R. Pino Pérez. Merging information under constraints: A logical framework. *Journal of Logic and Computation*, 12(5):773–808, 2002.

[15] L. A. Kornhauser and L. G. Sager. The one and the many: Adjudication in collegial courts. *California Law Review*, 81(1):1–59, 1993.

[16] C. List and P. Pettit. Aggregating sets of judgments: An impossibility result. *Economics and Philosophy*, 18(1):89–110, 2002.

[17] C. List and C. Puppe. Judgment aggregation: A survey. In P. Anand, P. Pattanaik, and C. Puppe, editors, *Handbook of Rational and Social Choice*. Oxford University Press, 2009.

[18] M. K. Miller and D. Osherson. Methods for distance-based judgment aggregation. *Social Choice and Welfare*, 32(4):575–601, 2009.

[19] C. Qing, U. Endriss, R. Fernández, and J. Kruger. Empirical analysis of aggregation methods for collective annotation. In *Proceedings of the 25th International Conference on Computational Linguistics (COLING-2014)*, 2014.

[20] I. Rahwan and F. Tohmé. Collective argument evaluation as judgement aggregation. In *Proceedings of the 9th International Conference on Autonomous Agents and Multiagent Systems (AAMAS-2010)*, 2010.

[21] M. A. Satterthwaite. Strategy-proofness and Arrow's conditions: Existence and correspondence theorems for voting procedures and social welfare functions. *Journal of Economic Theory*, 10(2):187–217, 1975.

[22] A. D. Taylor and W. S. Zwicker. *Simple Games: Desirability Relations, Trading, Pseudoweightings*. Princeton University Press, 1999.

Algorithm Diversity - A Mechanism for Distributive Justice in a Socio-Technical MAS

Vivek Nallur, Eamonn O'Toole, Nicolás Cardozo, Siobhán Clarke
Future Cities, Trinity College Dublin
Dublin, Ireland
{vivek.nallur|otooleea|cardozon|siobhan.clarke}@scss.tcd.ie

ABSTRACT

Socio-technical MAS are an intrinsic part of our daily lives. Domains like energy, transport, etc. are increasingly using technology to allow individual users to adapt to, and even influence the aggregate performance of the system. This raises expectations of fairness and equitability, while being engaged in such MAS. Given the autonomous and decentralized nature of socio-technical MAS, it can be difficult to ensure that each agent gets a fair reward for participating in the system. We introduce the notion of algorithmic diversity as a mechanism for nudging the system, in a decentralized manner, to a more equitable state. We use the minority game as an exemplar of a transportation network in a city, and show how diversity of algorithms results in a fairer reward distribution than any individual algorithm alone.

General Terms

Algorithms; Design

Keywords

Algorithm Diversity; Methodologies for agent-based systems; Engineering Multi-Agent Systems

1. INTRODUCTION

The modern world is filled with self-adaptive socio-technical multi-agent systems (socio-technical MAS). From homes in a Smart Grid environment to commuters using the latest traffic and route updates on their smartphones, the number of multi-agent systems where human beings explicitly utilize device/machine intelligence to make decisions or participate in an aggregate common-pooling of resources, is increasing. In this context, there is a legitimate expectation that such socio-technical MAS ensure an equitable allocation of resources, or reward the participating agents using a fair mechanism. However, by design, socio-technical MAS are decentralized and autonomous in nature. That is, there is no centralized authority that can control the actions of the individual agents, except through indirect mechanisms such as incentives and penalties. This implies that any aggregate property that the MAS exhibits, such as efficiency / fairness (or the lack of it) must result from the actions of the individual agents themselves. The field of computational social choice is particularly interested in the design and analysis of methods that result in choices being made through collective action [9]. Computational social choice is concerned with multiple types of social choices, such as preference aggregation, voting, fair division of resources, coalition formation, judgement aggregation, ranking systems, etc. In this paper, we are concerned with only one aspect of social choice, *viz*, fairness in resource allocation. Typical multi-agent resource allocation strategies concern themselves with *Pareto Efficiency*, which refers to an allocation such that no other allocation would increase the utility of some agents without being worse for the others. Fairness conditions are typically codified as *Envy-Freeness*, where no agent would rather obtain the resource bundle held by another. Human beings, even though aiding or aided by computational devices/agents, perceive equity to be more than simple utility of a resource bundle [37]. Hence, *envy-freeness does not suffice* for a socio-technical MAS. A more nuanced notion of fairness is introduced by the idea of distributive justice, based on the principles of legitimate claims, as elucidated by Rescher [35]. As an example, a route-choice problem through a city (*i.e.*, pick road A or road B to reach a destination) must yield a satisfactory outcome for the agent making a particular choice, *at least some of the time.* This is in contrast to problem formulations, where the only concern is to optimize the traffic flow through that route. This is a familiar situation in many cities, where multiple humans, utilizing commonly known (albeit coarse-grained) information about traffic flows, along with their own private heuristics (*e.g.*, road A is generally clogged from 7:30 - 8:30 am), make route choices to reach their destination. These agents may use additional device/machine intelligence in the form of real-time traffic updates through GPS devices/smartphones, while making their choices. The reward for this choice is determined dynamically, based on the aggregate number of agents that make a particular choice without prior coordination, *i.e.*, the driver that chooses the 'road less travelled' would experience lower congestion. Distributive justice, *in this case*, would be the evenness of the rewards that accumulate to agents, over multiple days. We **hypothesize** that *introducing algorithm diversity can lead to distributive justice, without centralized oversight of the game or the agents.* That is, the presence of algorithm diversity will contribute to a higher degree of evenness of accumulated reward.

Appears in: *Proceedings of the 15th International Conference on Autonomous Agents and Multiagent Systems (AAMAS 2016), J. Thangarajah, K. Tuyls, C. Jonker, S. Marsella (eds.), May 9–13, 2016, Singapore.*

Through the rest of this paper, we first describe what we mean by algorithm diversity (section 2), explain the MAS that we use for experimentation (section 3) and the experimental setup (section 4). Finally, we look at the efficacy of algorithm diversity in ensuring evenness (section 5) and offer some concluding thoughts.

2. ALGORITHM DIVERSITY

By algorithm diversity, we refer to the simultaneous use of multiple algorithms (having the same functional goal), or in the *same running* instance of the system. Algorithm diversity exploits the natural diversity of algorithms that are present in the same domain. For instance, there are a multiplicity of sorting algorithms, compression algorithms, load-balancing algorithms and typically, the informed programmer makes an intelligent choice amongst the various available algorithms based on the particular characteristics of the operating domain. However, in situations where there is a high degree of uncertainty, it has been shown that diversity can lead to a better performance on many parameters [16, 22, 30, 34, 40]. In Ecology, this is referred to as the *Insurance Hypothesis* [42], where a species copes with a changing environment, by exhibiting a diversity of features that may / may not be useful all the time.

However, in all these works of diversification of software systems, there has been no work that actively *measures* the amount of diversity present in a system, and relates this to the performance of the system. This paper introduces a quantification of diversity present in the system, and relates it to system performance, specifically evenness of rewards.

From our definition of algorithmic diversity, it is easy to envisage a system that diversifies its output, based on environmental cues, by switching between multiple algorithms. However, a more interesting case is when for the same input environment, different parts of the system use different algorithms. A MAS is an example of such a system, where multiple agents can potentially use different algorithms to achieve the same goals, for *exactly* the same input environment. This allows us to clearly identify the gains made due to diversification, as opposed to some other modification or environmental change. In this paper, we use the *Minority Game* as an exemplar MAS for algorithm diversification. In doing so, we deviate from the traditional research on the Minority Game, which is focussed on analysis of system dynamics due to a newly introduced strategy.

Measuring Algorithm Diversity.

A diversity index is a quantitative measure of the number of different types and the abundance of those types, in a given dataset. Intuitively, the higher the diversity index, the higher the diversity of the dataset. There are no mechanisms for differentiating amongst algorithms, that can be commonly applied across multiple domains, apart from the *Big-O* complexity calculation. The *Big-O* notation does not, however, yield useful information about the *differentness* of algorithms. There may be two algorithms that have the same *Big-O class*, but are completely different in terms of data-structures. For instance, Quicksort and Heapsort are very different algorithms, but their average case time complexity is the same, $O(nlog(n))$! It also does not help us differentiate between two algorithms that use the same data-structures but return *different outputs*. Our interest in algorithm diversity is due to the potential differences in the functional pathways, and consequently the outputs, for the same given input-sequence. This is so because it is this diversity of outputs that we wish to exploit, as a strategy to deal with dynamic environments. In such cases, the Big-O calculation does not yield any useful insights. Hence, we look to Ecology for inspiration, where the notion of diversity has been discussed extensively [41]. There are many measures of species diversity that are used in ecological literature. One of the most famous ones is the *Shannon Index* (eq. 1). The Shannon Index measures the entropy (or uncertainty) in picking an individual of a particular type, from a dataset. Thus, for instance, if all the agents in a MAS implement exactly the same algorithm, the entropy (or uncertainty) will be zero. The higher the diversity in the population, the higher is the Shannon Index. In eq. 1, R is the number of types in the population, and p is the proportion of individuals in the population with type i.

$$H' = -\sum_{i=1}^{R} p_i \ln p_i \tag{1}$$

The Shannon Index is a measure of both, the *richness of species* (number of different algorithms) and *evenness of species* (abundance of agents implementing an algorithm). We use the Shannon Index[1] to measure how much algorithms differ, in their key parameters. Thus, if a particular initialization parameter (that has an effect on the functional pathway) can take multiple values, the Shannon Index will measure how many such differentiated types exist and how many individuals implement that type, as a proportion of the total population.

3. MINORITY GAME

We use the Minority Game [8] as our exemplar MAS, primarily because it has been well-studied and well-understood. The Minority Game (MG), introduced by Challet and Zhang, consists of an odd number (N) of agents, playing a game in an iterated fashion. At each timestep, each agent chooses from one of two actions (+1 or -1), and the group that is in the minority, wins. Since N is an odd integer, there is guaranteed to be a minority. Winners receive a reward, while losers receive nothing. After each round, all agents are told which action was in the minority. This feedback loop induces the agents to re-evaluate their action for the next iteration. While simple in its conception, this game has been used in many fields like econophysics [5, 7, 43], multi-agent resource allocation [25, 27], emergence of cooperation [13], and heterogeneity [21, 26]. The Minority Game (MG) is intuitively applicable to many domains, such as traffic (the driver that chooses the 'less-travelled' road experiences less congestion), packet traffic in networks, ecologies of foraging animals, etc. The Minority Game has been used, primarily, to investigate the *efficiency* of strategies in the system when individuals have bounded rationality (for an extensive review, see [29]).

3.1 Best Play Strategy

Challet and Zhang also introduced a very simple strategy, called *Best Play* strategy [8], which in spite of being simple, exhibited interesting dynamics at the aggregate level. In this strategy, all players had access to a bounded collective

[1] We also have measurements using the Gini-Simpson Index, but we omit them here due to lack of space

memory (m) of the game, along with a pool of strategies(s). Collective memory is implemented in the form of a history of which action (+1 or -1) was in the minority, at each timestep. Each player drew s strategies randomly from a strategy space, that indicated which action to play next, based on the history of the game. Each player allocated virtual points amongst all its strategies, based on the continually changing history of the game. Strategies that correctly predicted the correct output, regardless of whether they were used or not, received virtual points. Each player, for the next round, used the top-ranking strategy amongst his pool of strategies. Table 1 shows a sample strategy pool used by a player. The size of each strategy depends on m, the memory of the game, while the total number of strategies in the pool depends on the computational power the agent possesses. Table 1 is therefore taken from a game with a memory of size 3, while the agent has a pool size (k) of 4. Typically, each agent in the entire game has the same pool size (k). While it is intuitively obvious, that the greater the pool size, the greater the probability of an agent drawing good strategies, it is impossible for an agent to have a pool size that exhaustively covers every possible strategy, since the strategy space grows hyper-exponentially(2^{2^m}) with increase in m.

Strategy	Output
[+1 -1 +1]	-1
[-1 -1 -1]	-1
[-1 -1 +1]	+1
[+1 +1 +1]	-1

Table 1: Sample Strategy Pool for a Player

3.2 Reinforcement Learning Strategy

We implement a Reinforcement-Learning algorithm, called Roth-Erev [36]. Reinforcement-Learning(RL) is a class of machine-learning algorithms where an agent tries to learn the optimal action to take, in a certain environment, based on a succession of *action-reward* pairs. Given a set of actions (a) that an agent can take, the Roth-Erev learning algorithm performs the following steps:

1. Initialize initial propensities (q) amongst all actions (N)
2. Initialize strength (s) of initial propensities
3. Initialize recency (φ) as the 'forgetting' parameter
4. Initialize epsilon (ε) as the exploration parameter
5. Choose action (a_k) at time (t), based on q
6. Based on reward(r_k) for a_k, update q using the following formula:

$$q_j(t+1) = [1-\varphi]q_j(t) + E_j(\varepsilon, N, k, t)$$

$$E_j(\varepsilon, N, k, t) = \begin{cases} r_k(t)[1-\varepsilon] & \text{if } j = k \\ r_k(t)\frac{\varepsilon}{N-1} & \text{otherwise} \end{cases}$$

7. Probability of choosing action j at time (t) is given by:

$$P_j(t) = \frac{q_j(t)}{\sum_{n=1}^{N}[q_n(t)]}$$

8. Repeat from step 5

3.3 Evolutionary Strategy

Evolutionary algorithms have been used quite successfully in multiple domains [1,11]. As pointed out in [14], evolutionary algorithms are now being compared to human beings, in their ability to solve hard problems. We have implemented an evolutionary algorithm that uses *BestPlay*'s strategy representation as a genome and performs crossover and mutation on it. The strategy is as follows: At every reproduction cycle, the ten most poorly performing agents get rid of their strategies and adopt a combination of strategies from two parents randomly selected from the ten best performing agents. Effectively, two of the ten best performing agents have reproduced to create an offspring that replaces one of the ten worst agents. The offspring mutates the strategies obtained from its parents, by some small mutation probability. This allows the offspring to get better, as well as explore more of the strategy space. The reproduction cycle refers to the rounds after which evolution occurs. A frequency of 20 cycles means that after every 20 rounds of the game, the worst 10 agents discard their strategies and inherit good strategies from 2 of the top 10 agents. These are then mutated according to the agents' own mutation probability.

4. EXPERIMENTAL SETUP

Table 2 shows the constant factors in each experiment. Each minority game was played with a population size of 501 agents, through a simulation time period of 2000 steps. For each variation in the experimental setup, the data is reported as an average of 100 simulations.

Variable	Value
Population Size	501
Simulation Period (rounds)	2000
Repetition of Variation	100

Table 2: Experimental constants

The parameters that were varied were as follows:

1. **Number of Algorithms**: This reflects the effective number of families (or *genera*) of species that are present in the population.

2. **Proportion of population implementing an algorithm**: Depending on the relative number of each specie, the aggregate payoff in the game changes.

3. **Parameters within algorithms that were diversified**: Variation in critical parameters for an algorithm results in effectively creating a new specie, since the functional pathway (and resultant output) begins to change depending on the environment. For each of the three families, the following parameters were diversified within the algorithm:

   (a) Best Play Strategy: k – which is the pool of strategies, a player has(strategies-per-agent).

   (b) Evolutionary Strategy: The mutation probability that allows an agent to explore the strategy space, by mutating known good strategies.

   (c) Reinforcement Learning Strategy: The parameters of *recency* (φ), and *exploration* (ε)

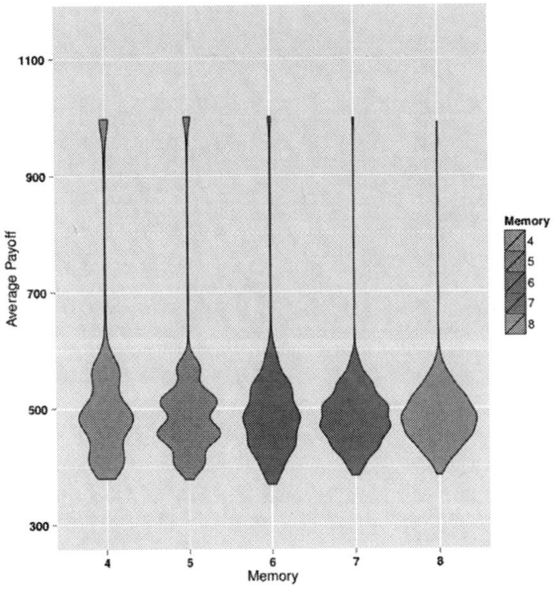

Figure 1: Best-Play strategy with different values of memory

5. RESULTS

We now show the results of diversification of algorithms, on two levels: *(a)* Parameter Diversification, and *(b)* Strategy Diversification[2]. *Parameter Diversification* refers to each agent in the population implementing the same algorithm, however they change their initialization parameters. For instance, agents playing the Evolutionary strategy would draw their mutation probabilites from a gaussian distribution, drawn from the best mean of *Normal Play*. Normal Play refers to a situation, where each agent in the game plays with `exactly` the same algorithm and initialization parameters. *Strategy Diversification* refers to creating a population that has a mix of strategies. The diversity level of the population would differ according to the proportion of agents implementing a particular strategy. First, we show results of all three strategies with Normal Play, since they form the baseline with which the results of diversification are compared. In all cases, the graphs show the distribution of the population achieving a particular level of average payoff. The 'fatter' the graph, the more evenly rewards are distributed, and vice-versa.

5.1 Normal Play — Baseline

In Figure 1, we see the average payoff (y-axis) from the Best-Play strategy, with different levels of memory(x-axis). The average payoff is the average number of times, an agent is able to make the correct choice and be in the minority. The graph shows the distribution of population that was able to secure rewards, during the entire game. The *fatter* the distribution, the fairer the result, since it implies that, on average, most players secured the same amount of payoff. In Figure 1, we see that with a memory of 8, the distribution of payoff is more equitable, since most of the population is concentrated in one area.

[2]All code and results are available at: `https://www.bitbucket.org/viveknallur/aamas2016.git`

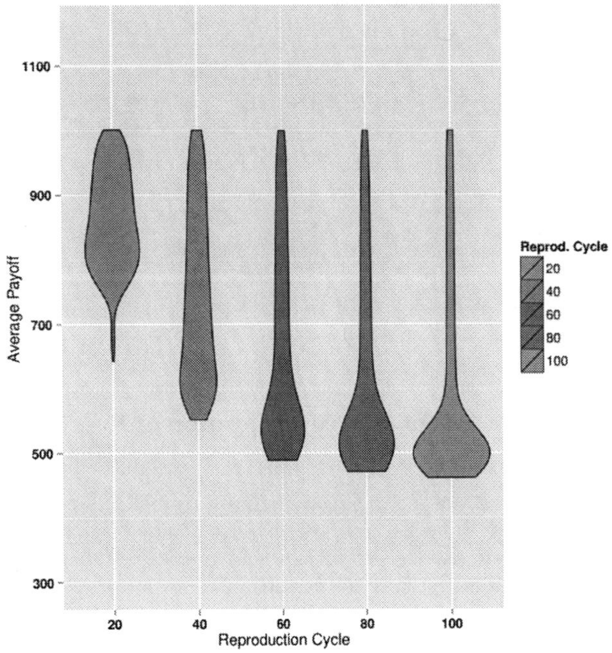

Figure 2: Evolutionary strategy

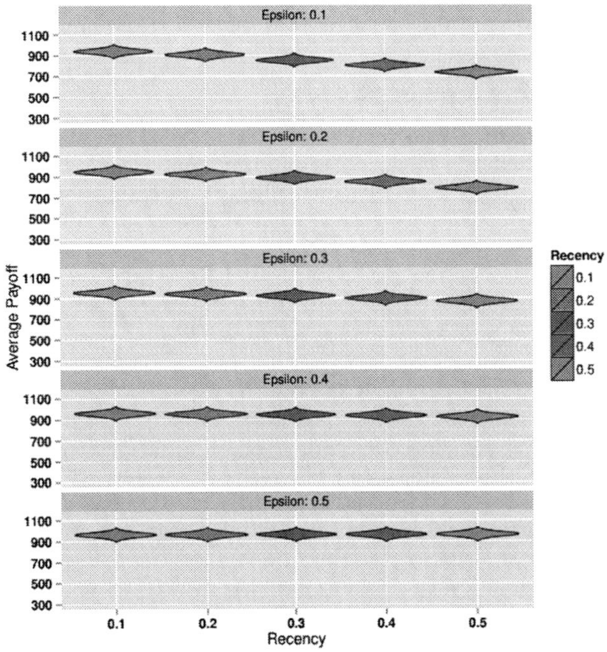

Figure 3: Roth-Erev strategy

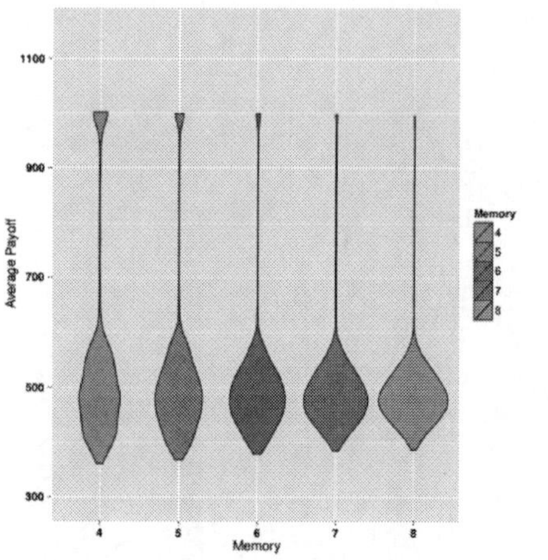

Figure 4: Parameter Diversification of Best Play

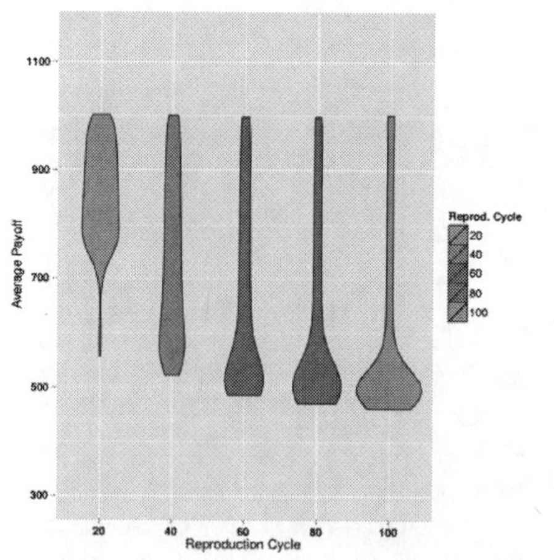

Figure 5: Parameter Diversification of Evolutionary strategy

In Figure 2, we see the average payoff from the Evolutionary strategy. The x-axis shows the frequency of the reproduction cycle, *i.e.*, reproduction and mutation takes place every 20, 40, 60, 80 and 100 rounds. Figure 2 clearly shows that when reproduction and mutation is frequent (every 20 rounds), more of the population earns a higher payoff. That is, most of the population earns a payoff between 700 and 1000, whereas with reproduction cycles of 60 and greater, most of the population earns a lower reward, with a few individuals earning higher payoff.

Figure 3 shows the average payoff when the Roth-Erev strategy is used. Again, the fatter the distribution, the fairer the outcome. Hence, we see that low values of *Recency* (0.1, 0.2) contribute to a fairer distribution of payoff.

In all of these, the diversity of the population is *zero* (0), since there is only one algorithm, and all agents implement exactly the same code.

5.2 Parameter Diversity

Parameter diversity refers to diversity in the initialization parameters of the algorithm being implemented by the agents. That is, for any game, all agents still implement the same code, but some parameter in the algorithm is diversified. The specific parameters being diversified are given in section 4. For the Evolutionary and Roth-Erev strategies, even minute differences within the initialization parameters can cause aggregate average payoff to vary.

Parameter Diversity with Best Play.

In general, there is less parameter diversity with the Best Play strategy, since the parameter being diversified is the number of strategies that player holds. These are drawn from a gaussian distribution with the mean being the size of the history available to agents, and a standard deviation of 1. This leads to there being a low diversity, since many agents end up with the same amount of strategies-per-agent. Figure 4 therefore shows very little difference in distribution of payoffs obtained, as compared to Figure 1.

Parameter Diversity with Evolutionary Strategy.

The evolutionary strategy changes the performance of the agents, depending on the strategies that the 'evolved' child agents get. The evolutionary process allows poorly performing agents to quickly change their strategies to match the best agents. However, this also leads to a homogeneity in the strategies being used by the agents. The parameter that diversifies each agent is the mutation probability that it possesses. This causes agents to mutate their inherited strategies. Figure 5 shows the difference in average payoff, when the reproduction cycle is varied.

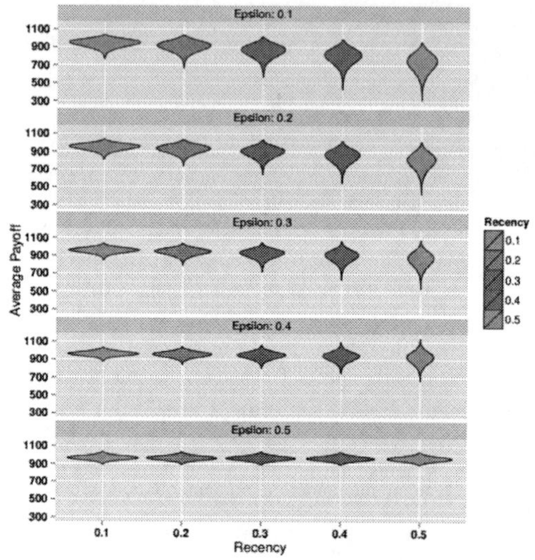

Figure 6: Parameter Diversification of Roth-Erev strategy

Parameter Diversity with Roth-Erev.

Roth-Erev allows for the highest amount of diversification, since there are two parameters (recency and epsilon) that can be changed for each agent. Also, the algorithm is extremely sensitive to the values of these parameters, and each agent's decision-making is affected significantly. Hence, the population as a whole becomes extremely diverse. Figure 6 shows the effect of diversification for mean values of recency and epsilon.

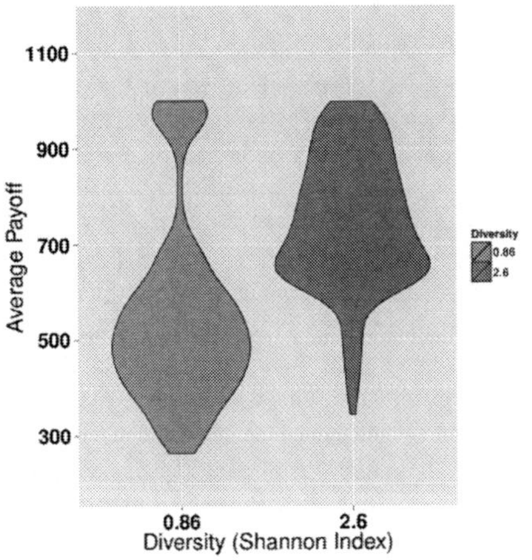

Figure 7: Mix of Best-Play and Evolutionary Strategies

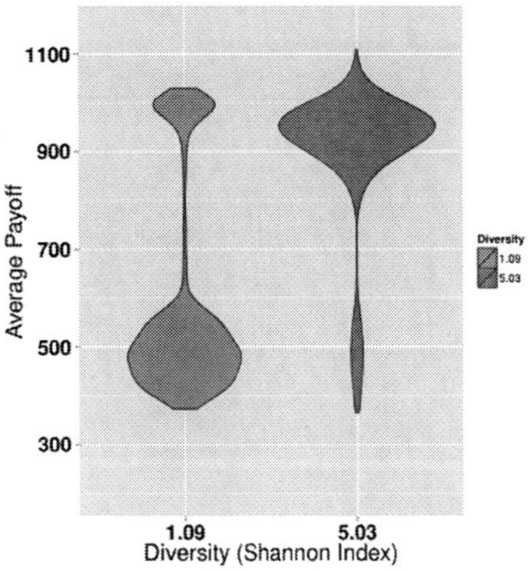

Figure 8: Mix of Best-Play and Roth-Erev Strategies

Both Roth-Erev and the Evolutionary strategy exhibit higher levels of diversity, due to the probabilistic nature of the variable being diversified. In the Evolutionary strategy, the mutation-probability is different for every agent, thereby making each agent into its own separate type. In Roth-Erev, *both* recency and epsilon are diversified, which results in a higher level of diversity. This increase in diversity is reflected in both, the fairness of the average payoff, and the levels of average payoff. That is, for Roth-Erev populations, most of the payoff is at the 800 level, while for the Evolutionary strategy, most of the payoff is around 500.

5.3 Strategy Diversity

We go further and mix agents implementing different strategies into one population. The diversification here takes place on two levels, parameter-diversification (as before), as well as proportion of population implementing a particular strategy. The total population of agents in all scenarios is kept constant, but the proportion of agents playing a particular strategy is varied. This leads to different levels of diversification, for each combination of strategies. Due to lack of space, we show only the population mixes with the *lowest* and *highest* amount of diversity, for each combination of strategies. The x-axis shows the diversity levels (as measured by the Shannon Index) and the y-axis, the distribution of average payoff.

Figure 7 shows the distribution of payoffs when a set of agents playing Best Play, is mixed with a set of agents playing the Evolutionary strategy. Figure 8 shows the distribution of payoffs when a set of agents playing Best Play, is mixed with a set of agents playing the Roth-Erev strategy. Figure 9 shows the distribution of payoffs when a set of agents playing Evolutionary strategy, is mixed with a set of agents playing the Roth-Erev strategy. Figure 10 shows the distribution of payoffs, when all three strategies are combined into one population.

All compared together.

Finally, we overlay the results from Figures 7–10 to illustrate the comparative payoffs at different levels of diversity. Figure 11 clearly shows that higher the diversity level, the fairer the average payoff. Note that the highest level (5.13) was **not** a consequence of mixing all three strategies, but rather by mixing Evolutionary and Roth-Erev strategies (see

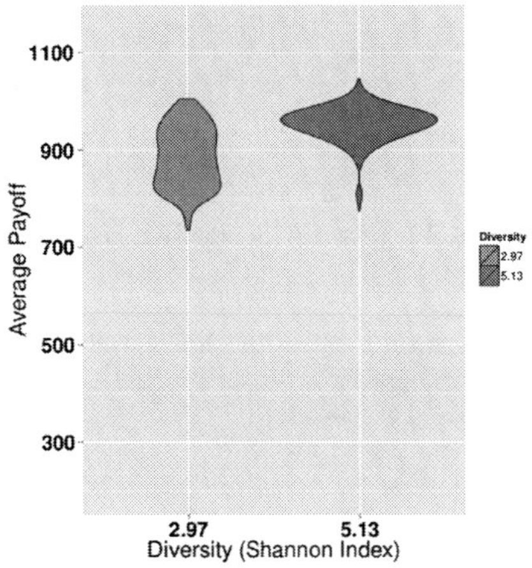

Figure 9: Mix of Evolutionary and Roth-Erev Strategies

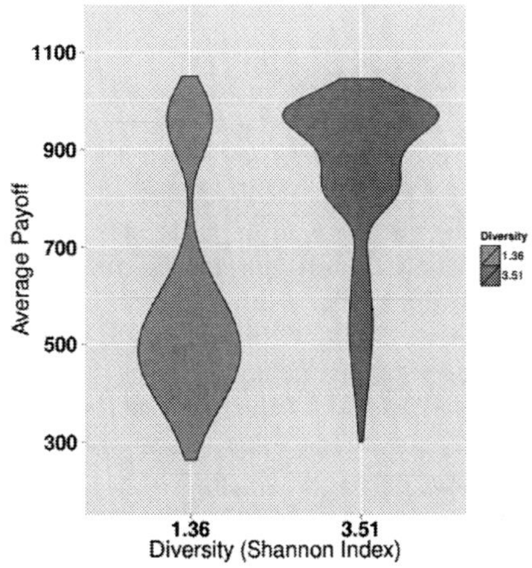

Figure 10: Mix of three strategies

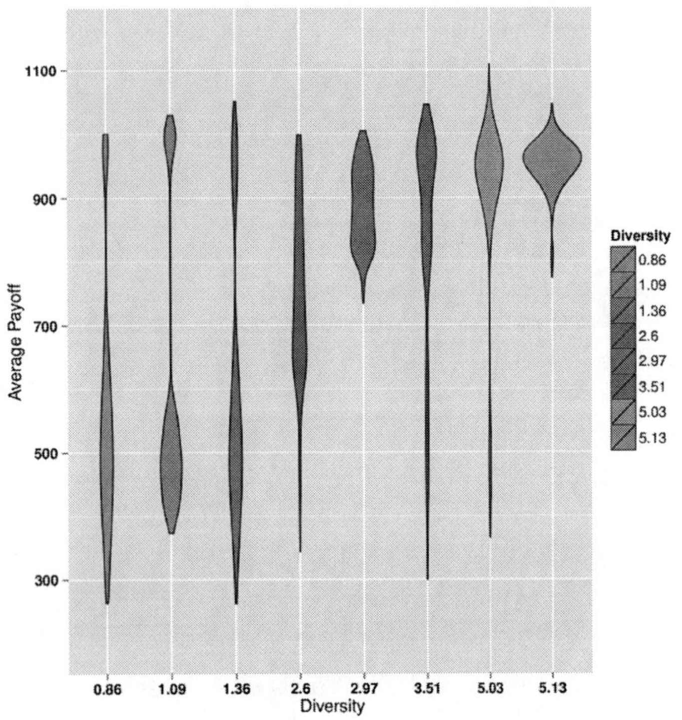

Figure 11: Payoff across all mixes

Fig 9). This confirms our intuition that merely mixing more strategies does not lead to greater diversity and measurement using indices is essential.

Table 3 shows the payoff at the lowest, median and highest agent reward levels, due to the different algorithms used. Notice that the median levels of payoff are the greatest when diversity is greatest ($d = 5.13$). Recall from our hypothesis, that we seek to check whether algorithm diversity leads to distributive justice, without centralized oversight. From Table 3 and the graphs (Figure 11), it is apparent that the hypothesis is true. The *effect of diversity is to push the population, as a whole, towards a more even distribution of rewards, without needing a centralized guiding hand.*

6. RELATED WORK

There has been much work on distributive justice in a sociological and organizational context [10, 12, 24], but most work in multi-agent systems is characterized by *Envy Freeness* [18]. Envy-freeness is simply understood to be an allocation of a resource bundle in such a manner, that for any agent, the utility of its own allocation is greater than any other allocation. However, utility-based models fail to capture the nuances of distributive justice, particularly so in a socio-technical MAS. There has been some work on making multi-agent systems adapt in an organized fashion, obeying certain norms [3, 17, 20, 32, 33]. There has also been a plethora of work on the introduction of diversity in software engineering. *Forrest et al.* [19] were among the first to advocate diversity as a mechanism to prevent attackers from learning internal details of a computer system. Memory obfuscation [4] and instruction-set randomization [23] have been used as an instantiation of the diversification principle, to increase security of computer systems. Efforts have been made at introducing diversity into the source code of systems, in order to reduce the chances of bugs through N-version programming [2], and genetic programming [16]. Other work in security such as creation of moving targets [22], increasing dependability [30] have all advocated diversification as a fundamental idea. Even in other domains, such as machine-learning [28], sensor-networks [34, 38], and fault-tolerant systems [39] diversity has been identified as an idea that improves the robustness of systems, in the presence of uncertainty. The domain of distributed and multi-agent systems [6, 15] have also considered diversity as a critical component in systems with varying degrees of intelligence. However, this is the first work that we are aware of, that **quantifies** the amount of diversity present in a system, and then systematically compares level of diversity with aggregate performance. A closely related agent-based domain, electronic trading markets, have been studied in [31] with an emphasis on auction mechanism design. The focus of that study, however, has been on economic outcomes and game-theoretic methods, without any investigation into diversity as a distinguishing attribute.

7. CONCLUSION

A caveat about measuring algorithm diversity in this manner, is that it requires knowledge of the algorithms and their functional pathways. While this is not ideal from a black-box engineering point of view, nevertheless, we believe that it holds great potential as a technique for achieving certain aggregate properties in a socio-technical MAS. Another potential drawback is the requirement for problem decomposition into individuals and species. This may not be possible in all domains. Algorithm diversity is not a silver bullet for ensuring distributive justice of rewards in a socio-technical MAS. In further work, we would like to work on quantifying diversity in algorithms, even if the problem is not as easily decomposed into agents, such as the minority game. We believe that there are many domains that would benefit from a rigorous mechanism for quantifying diversity in algorithms, and this would allow them to make reasoned tradeoff decisions between diversity, and other system metrics such as performance.

Acknowledgments

This work was partially supported by the EU FET-Project Diversify FP7-ICT-2011-9

REFERENCES

[1] D. Ashlock. *Evolutionary Computation for Modeling and Optimization.* Springer-Verlag New York, 2006.

[2] A. Avizienis. The methodology of n-version programming. *Software fault tolerance*, 3:23–46, 1995.

[3] T. Balke, M. De Vos, and J. Padget. I-abm: combining institutional frameworks and agent-based modelling for the design of enforcement policies. *Artificial Intelligence and Law*, 21(4):371–398, 2013.

[4] S. Bhatkar, D. C. DuVarney, and R. Sekar. Address obfuscation: An efficient approach to combat a board range of memory error exploits. In *12th Conference on USENIX Security Symposium*, 12:105–120, Berkeley, CA, USA, 2003.

Strategy	Lowest Payoff	Median Payoff	Highest Payoff
Pure			
BestPlay	368	483	1001
Evo	460	680	1003
Roth-Erev	666	929	1035
Combination			
Evo-BestPlay (d = 0.86)	263	509	1001
Evo-BestPlay (d = 2.60)	340	733	1002
RothErev-BestPlay (d = 1.09)	371	499	1030
RothErev-BestPlay (d = 5.03)	362	939	1112
Evo-RothErev (d = 2.97)	734	883	1004
Evo-RothErev (d = 5.13)	**774**	**957**	**1046**
BestPlay-Evo-RothErev (d = 1.36)	260	526	1053
BestPlay-Evo-RothErev (d = 3.51)	297	905	1048

Table 3: Various levels of diversity compared to 'pure play' of single strategies

[5] G. Bianconi, T. Galla, M. Marsili, and P. Pin. Effects of Tobin taxes in minority game markets. *Journal of Economic Behavior & Organization*, 70(1-2):231–240, May 2009.

[6] A. Campbell, C. Riggs, and A. Wu. On the impact of variation on self-organizing systems. In *5th Intl. Conf on Self-Adaptive and Self-Organizing Systems*, pages 119–128, Oct 2011.

[7] D. Challet. Inter-pattern speculation: Beyond minority, majority and $-games. *Journal of Economic Dynamics and Control*, 32(1):85–100, Jan. 2008.

[8] D. Challet and Y. Zhang. Emergence of cooperation and organization in an evolutionary game. *Physica A: Statistical Mechanics and its Applications*, 246(34):407 – 418, 1997.

[9] Y. Chevaleyre, U. Endriss, J. Lang, and N. Maudet. A short introduction to computational social choice. volume 4362 of *Lecture Notes in Computer Science*, pages 51–69. Springer Berlin Heidelberg, 2007.

[10] Y. Cohen-Charash and P. E. Spector. The role of justice in organizations: A meta-analysis. *Organizational Behavior and Human Decision Processes*, 86(2):278 – 321, 2001.

[11] K. De Jong. *Evolutionary Computation: A Unified Approach.* MIT Press, 2006.

[12] M. Deutsch. Equity, equality, and need: What determines which value will be used as the basis of distributive justice? *Journal of Social Issues*, 31(3):137–149, 1975.

[13] D. Dhar, V. Sasidevan, and B. K. Chakrabarti. Emergent cooperation amongst competing agents in minority games. *Physica A: Statistical Mechanics and its Applications*, 390(20):3477–3485, Oct. 2011.

[14] A. E. Eiben and J. Smith. From evolutionary computation to the evolution of things. *Nature*, 521:476–482, 2015.

[15] L. Esterle, P. R. Lewis, X. Yao, and B. Rinner. Socio-economic vision graph generation and handover in distributed smart camera networks. *ACM Transactions on Sensor Networks*, 10(2), 2014.

[16] R. Feldt. Generating diverse software versions with genetic programming: an experimental study. *IEE Proceedings-Software*, 145(6):228–236, 1998.

[17] D. Fitoussi and M. Tennenholtz. Choosing social laws for multi-agent systems: Minimality and simplicity. *Artificial Intelligence*, 119(1–2):61–101, 2000.

[18] D. Foley. Resource allocation an the public sector. *Yale economic essays*, 7(1):45–98, 1967.

[19] S. Forrest, A. Somayaji, and D. Ackley. Building diverse computer systems. In *6th Workshop on Hot Topics in Operating Systems.* IEEE Comp Soc, 1997.

[20] T. F. Gordon. *The Pleadings Game: An Artificial Intelligence Model of Procedural Justice.* Springer Netherlands, 1995.

[21] G. W. Greenwood. Deceptive strategies for the evolutionary minority game. In *5th Intl Conf on Computational Intelligence and Games*, pages 25–31, 2009.

[22] Y. Huang and A. K. Ghosh. Introducing diversity and uncertainty to create moving attack surfaces for web services. volume 54, pages 131–151. Springer, 2011.

[23] G. S. Kc, A. D. Keromytis, and V. Prevelakis. Countering code-injection attacks with instruction-set randomization. In *10th ACM conference on Computer and communications security*, pages 272–280. ACM, 2003.

[24] G. Leventhal, J. Karuza, and W. R. Fry. *Beyond fairness: A theory of allocation preferences.* Justice and Social Interaction. Springer, 1980.

[25] Y. Li and R. Savit. Toward a theory of local resource competition: the minority game with private information. *Physica A: Statistical Mechanics and its Applications*, 335(1-2):217–239, Apr. 2004.

[26] B. A. Mello and D. O. Cajueiro. Minority games, diversity, cooperativity and the concept of intelligence. *Physica A: Statistical Mechanics and its Applications*, 387(2-3):557–566, Jan. 2008.

[27] R. Metzler and C. Horn. Evolutionary minority games: the benefits of imitation. *Physica A: Statistical Mechanics and its Applications*, 329(3-4):484–498, Nov. 2003.

[28] L. Minku and X. Yao. Ddd: A new ensemble approach for dealing with concept drift. *Knowledge and Data Engineering, IEEE Transactions on*, 24(4):619–633, April 2012.

[29] E. Moro. The minority game: an introductory guide. In *Advances in Condensed Matter and Statistical Physics*, pages 263–286. Nova Science Publishers, 2003.

[30] A. Nguyen-Tuong, D. Evans, J. Knight, B. Cox, and J. Davidson. Security through redundant data diversity. In *Dependable Systems and Networks With FTCS and DCC*, pages 187–196, 2008.

[31] J. Niu, K. Cai, S. Parsons, E. Gerding, P. McBurney, T. Moyaux, S. Phelps, and D. Shield. Jcat: A platform for the tac market design competition. In *7th International Joint Conference on Autonomous Agents and Multiagent Systems*, pages 1649–1650, 2008.

[32] J. Pitt, D. Busquets, and S. Macbeth. Distributive justice for self-organised common-pool resource management. *ACM Trans. Auton. Adapt. Syst.*, 9(3):14:1–14:39, Oct. 2014.

[33] J. Pitt, D. Ramirez-Cano, M. Draief, and A. Artikis. Interleaving multi-agent systems and social networks for organized adaptation. *Computational and Mathematical Organization Theory*, 17(4):344–378, 2011.

[34] A. Prasath, A. Venuturumilli, A. Ranganathan, and A. Minai. *Sensor Networks: Where Theory Meets Practice*, pages 39–59. Springer Berlin, 2009.

[35] N. Rescher. *Distributive Justice: A Constructive Critique of the Utilitarian Theory of Distribution*. The Bobbs-Merrill Co. Inc., New York, 1966.

[36] A. E. Roth and I. Erev. Learning in extensive-form games: Experimental data and simple dynamic models in the intermediate term. *Games and Economic Behavior*, 8(1):164–212, 1995.

[37] A. E. Roth, V. Prasnikar, M. Okuno-Fujiwara, and S. Zamir. Bargaining and market behavior in jerusalem, ljubljana, pittsburg, and tokyo: An experimental study. *American Economic Review*, 81(5):1068–1095, December 1991.

[38] N. Salazar, J. Rodriguez-Aguilar, and J. Arcos. Self-configuring sensors for uncharted environments. In *4th IEEE Conf. on Self-Adaptive and Self-Organizing Systems*, pages 134–143, Sept 2010.

[39] T. Schnier and X. Yao. Using negative correlation to evolve fault-tolerant circuits. In *5th International Conference on Evolvable Systems: From Biology to Hardware*, volume 2606, pages 35–46. Springer, 2003.

[40] H. Song, A. Elgammal, V. Nallur, F. Chauvel, F. Fleurey, and S. Clarke. On architectural diversity of dynamic adaptive systems. In *37th Intl Conf on Software Engineering: NIER Track*, 2015.

[41] H. Tuomisto. A consistent terminology for quantifying species diversity? yes, it does exist. *Oecologia*, 164(4):853–860, 2010.

[42] S. Yachi and M. Loreau. Biodiversity and ecosystem productivity in a fluctuating environment: the insurance hypothesis. *National Academy of Sciences of the United States of America*, 96(4):1463–1468, 1999.

[43] C. A. Zapart. On entropy, financial markets and minority games. *Physica A: Statistical Mechanics and its Applications*, 388(7):1157–1172, Apr. 2009.

Learning from Demonstration for Shaping through Inverse Reinforcement Learning

Halit Bener Suay
Worcester Polytechnic Institute
benersuay@wpi.edu

Tim Brys
Vrije Universiteit Brussel
timbrys@vub.ac.be

Matthew E. Taylor
Washington State University
taylorm@eecs.wsu.edu

Sonia Chernova
Georgia Institute of Technology
chernova@cc.gatech.edu

ABSTRACT

Model-free episodic reinforcement learning problems define the environment reward with functions that often provide only sparse information throughout the task. Consequently, agents are not given enough feedback about the fitness of their actions until the task ends with success or failure. Previous work addresses this problem with reward shaping. In this paper we introduce a novel approach to improve model-free reinforcement learning agents' performance with a three step approach. Specifically, we collect demonstration data, use the data to recover a linear function using inverse reinforcement learning and we use the recovered function for potential-based reward shaping. Our approach is model-free and scalable to high dimensional domains. To show the scalability of our approach we present two sets of experiments in a two dimensional Maze domain, and the 27 dimensional Mario AI domain. We compare the performance of our algorithm to previously introduced reinforcement learning from demonstration algorithms. Our experiments show that our approach outperforms the state-of-the-art in cumulative reward, learning rate and asymptotic performance.

Keywords

Learning and Adaptation; Reward structures for learning; Learning agent capabilities (agent models, communication, observation)

1. INTRODUCTION

Model-free episodic Reinforcement Learning (RL) problems require agents to explore the state space and iteratively find a solution, which can be costly in terms of learning time. These problems are typically defined by an environment reward that rarely changes throughout the state-space. For example, in the Cart-Pole domain [2, 21], the environment provides a reward of $r_{env} = +1$ after each step of the task until the terminal state, where the reward is $r_{env} = 0$ to emphasize that the cart has failed at balancing the pole. The information provided by the environment is *sparse* as the change in the reward signal is infrequent. The environment lets the agent know about an obstacle or the terminal state without providing much information right until then. On the one hand, it is easy to define a sparse reward function manually and the interpretation of rewards becomes very intuitive for humans. On the other hand, with this type of environment reward agents are not given enough information about how appropriate the chosen actions are throughout the task. A model-free RL agent can benefit immensely from having a *dense* reward function that provides more information about the task.

An extensively explored way to provide denser information is through *shaping* the existing reward function by adding an extra signal, thus providing the agent with a composite reward [14, 6, 4, 8, 25]. Research in reward shaping shows that potential based shaping functions provide a theoretically sound way of incorporating additional, informative reward functions in existing reinforcement learning problems without altering the problem definition [14]. Potential based shaping rewards can improve an agent's learning efficiency by reducing the number of episodes before convergence [14]. To give an example for the Cart-Pole problem, a potential based shaping reward could be the negative of the angular distance of the pole from the center at each step. There are multiple ways to define a shaping reward function. One way is to use a priori knowledge of the domain characteristics, however, doing so requires extensive knowledge of the state space and becomes infeasible as the number of state variables increases. Recent work has shown that shaping reward can also be effectively extracted from an expert's demonstration by computing the similarity between demonstrated states and observed states throughout learning [4].

Expert demonstrations have also been applied in the context of Markov decision processes for inverse reinforcement learning (IRL), that is, for extracting a reward function given observed optimal behavior [15]. In domains where the reward function is *unknown*, IRL algorithms are used with the purpose of obtaining a reward function for optimal control.

In this work we introduce Static IRL Shaping (SIS), and Dynamic IRL Shaping (DIS), two variations of a novel approach in which we combine reward shaping and inverse reinforcement learning. SIS and DIS improve upon previ-

Appears in: *Proceedings of the 15th International Conference on Autonomous Agents and Multiagent Systems (AAMAS 2016), J. Thangarajah, K. Tuyls, C. Jonker, S. Marsella (eds.), May 9–13, 2016, Singapore.*

ous work's use of an expert's demonstrations by capturing the demonstrator's general policy over the state-space for shaping, as opposed to using the observed demonstration samples directly. By using model-free IRL, we encode a demonstrator's task description as a heuristic which *complements* the environment reward function. Our approach consists of three main steps: i) collecting demonstrations, ii) recovering a potential function from demonstrations, and iii) using the recovered potential function for computing shaping rewards in reinforcement learning. Reward functions we recover let us compute a linear potential based shaping reward. It is important to note that, even though we use expert demonstrations in this paper, there is no strict requirement for the demonstrations to be optimal. We use reward shaping as a heuristic, while the agent still receives the information provided by the environment reward. This means that even if demonstrations are suboptimal, the agent will ultimately be able to learn the task. This is due to the guarantees of policy invariance provided by potential-based reward shaping approaches, and that reward shaping that is not potential-based may alter the optimal policy of the problem. Our goal is to show that using a model-free IRL technique, we can extract additional information for summarizing the task for a standard RL agent and the agent can use this information to learn the task faster. To the best of our knowledge, the use of IRL for potential-based shaping reward functions has not been investigated in the literature.

In order to show that our approach is scalable over different number of state variables, we evaluate our approach in two domains: a Maze domain and the Mario AI domain. We compare SIS and DIS with the standard SARSA(λ) and Q(λ)-learning agents, as well as with two previously introduced RL algorithms that leverage demonstration data. Our experiment results show that a) both of our approaches result in significantly (p-values < 0.0001) more cumulative reward in both domains compared to other techniques, b) DIS results in faster learning in both domains and c) both approaches have better asymptotic performance than the human demonstrator.

2. BACKGROUND

Our approach builds on several research areas; we provide a high-level overview of each below.

2.1 Reinforcement Learning

RL is the problem of choosing which actions to take in observed states. We define reinforcement learning using the standard notation of Markov Decision Processes (MDPs) [16, 22]. At every time step the agent observes its state $s \in S$ as a vector of k state variables such that $s = \langle x_1, \ldots, x_k \rangle$. The agent selects an action from the set of available actions A at every time step. An MDP's reward function $R : S \times A \mapsto \mathbb{R}$ and (stochastic) transition function $T : S \times A \mapsto S$ fully describe the system's dynamics. The agent attempts to maximize the long-term reward determined by the reward and transition functions that are initially unknown to the agent.

A learner chooses which action to take in a state via a policy, $\pi : S \mapsto A$. Policy π is modified by the learner over time to improve performance, which is defined as the expected total reward. Instead of learning π directly, model-free RL algorithms instead approximate the action-value function, $Q : S \times A \mapsto \mathbb{R}$, which maps state-action pairs to the expected real-valued return.

2.2 Reward Shaping

Reward shaping, derived from behavioral psychology [20], is a way of incorporating prior knowledge in the learning process. A shaping reward F provides an agent with additional information after each state transition. With shaping rewards, an agent is rewarded for taking appropriate steps toward the goal. This extra reward supplements the environment reward which is typically defined as a sparse function for practical reasons.

The extra reward signal F, defined by agent designers, is added to the environment reward R, defined by problem designers. The agent learns a task using the shaped reward R':

$$R'(s, a, s') = R(s, a, s') + F(s, a, s') \qquad (1)$$

F function usually encodes heuristic knowledge, and is intended to complement the typically less informative signal R. As we mentioned earlier, the agent's goal is defined by the reward function, and by manipulating the reward signal we may risk changing the task. Ng et al. [14] proved that potential-based shaping is a sound way to provide a shaping reward without changing the reinforcement learning problem.

2.3 Inverse Reinforcement Learning

IRL is the problem of learning a reward function using a set of observations from expert demonstrations [15, 1]. Two possible general representations of a task for MDPs are through defining a policy or a reward function. IRL algorithms aim to find a good representation of the demonstrated task by finding the most fitting reward function based on a set of demonstrations. Although there are different solutions for the IRL problem, many of them require the environment model (i.e. the transition function) to be known [17, 26, 11]. Recently Boularias et al. [3] and Klein et al. [10] introduced two different algorithms for model-free IRL. Boularias et al. introduced a sampling based algorithm Relative Entropy Inverse Reinforcement Learning (RE-IRL) that leverages statistical properties of human demonstrations [3]. Klein et al. introduced Cascaded Supervised IRL (CSI) which combines classification with regression in order to generate a reward signal based on human demonstrations [10]. In this work we use RE-IRL due to its simplicity and availability however a comparison of different IRL algorithms for our particular use can be a future investigation topic.

2.4 RL from Demonstration

RL from Demonstration (RLfD) is a learning setting for RL agents where both demonstrations and an environment reward signal are available. Algorithms use different methods to convert demonstrations into a representation that the agent will be able to use as heuristic information and the environment reward is treated as the ground truth for learning. Early work on Reinforcement Learning from Demonstration (RLfD) was presented by Schaal [19], in which the term described a set of approaches that leveraged initial training for learning a policy and a value function from demonstrations, followed by a "trial by trial learning" with RL.

Later, Taylor et al. introduced Human - Agent Transfer (HAT), a transfer learning algorithm that employs rule transfer [23] in order to summarize a set of human demonstrations for bootstrapping a reinforcement learning agent's performance. HAT follows a three step approach: i) A human demonstrator controls the agent and performs the task; ii)

Saved demonstrations are used as the input data for a rule learning algorithm; iii) A RL agent uses the summarized policy to initialize the state-action value function.

Most recently, Brys et al. introduced a new algorithm we refer to as Similarity Based Shaping (SBS) [4]. With the SBS algorithm Brys et al. took a different approach to investigate the use of prior knowledge as a potential-based shaping reward. The SBS algorithm uses human demonstrations as a potential function $\Phi^D(s,a)$ for potential-based shaping. With this approach each demonstrated state-action pair is assumed to be desirable for the agent, and using a similarity metric, the SBS algorithm computes a shaping reward F. During learning, the agent receives a shaped reward signal $R' = R + F$ which is the combination of the environment reward (i.e. ground truth) and the shaping reward. The SBS algorithm uses non-normalized multi-variate Gaussian distributions to compute the similarity between demonstrated states and observed states throughout learning.

HAT and SBS algorithms allow the use of multiple demonstrations, combining observations obtained from these demonstrations in different ways. In practice, the use of multiple demonstrations increases the possibility of recording noisy or sometimes conflicting state-action pairs. If that is the case, using demonstrations directly similar to the SBS algorithm may result in conflicting rewards for the agent. We use IRL because as a method it generalizes over multiple demonstrations. Our novel algorithms improve on the above techniques by leveraging IRL in combination with reward shaping. We compare our results to HAT and SBS.

3. METHODOLOGY

In this section, we present our approach for using a model-free IRL algorithm to obtain a shaping reward and speed up reinforcement learning. Our goal is to incorporate human task demonstration in an intuitive way and incorporate this knowledge in reinforcement learning without changing the task (i.e. the main goal). We aim to reinforce appropriate action selection as soon as an episode starts, much before the agent reaches the terminal state. Each shaping reward signal can be thought of as a *hint* for the agent to make better decisions. To the best of our knowledge, using a potential-based shaping reward function recovered with IRL has not been investigated in the literature. Our method has three main steps:

Collecting Expert Demonstrations: First, we collect observation data from a demonstrator. Each demonstration is a set of sequential observations in time. In this paper our focus is on episodic, simulated environments and we collect the agent's state vector as demonstrations. The demonstrator was an expert teacher, however this is not a requirement for our setup. We assume that the demonstrations are not malicious, that is, the intent of each demonstrated state transition is to perform well on the task. RE-IRL requires trajectories to have equal lengths. To equalize the length of demonstrations we process the demonstration data by repeating the last observation (in our first test domain) or pruning longer demonstrations (in the second test domain). Depending on the task, if demonstrating the goal state carries importance one could prefer to append a repetition of the goal state in the set of demonstrated observations, or otherwise prune the observations. In the end we obtain a set of demonstrations $\mathcal{T}$. The input for the next step (i.e. RE-IRL) is $\mathcal{T}$, where each trajectory $\tau \in \mathcal{T}$ is a set of observations of equal length, $\tau = \{s_1, \ldots, s_l\}$.

Recovering a Linear Function: Once we obtain $\mathcal{T}$, we use RE-IRL and compute the vector of reward feature weights $\mathbf{w}$ to use in $R_{IRL}(s)$. RE-IRL recovers a reward function $R_{IRL}(s,a)$ for the set of demonstrations $\mathcal{T}$ as a linear combination of observed reward features $\mathbf{f} = \langle f_1, \ldots, f_n \rangle$, weighted with $\mathbf{w}$. The output is the vector of feature weights $\mathbf{w} = \langle w_1, \ldots, w_n \rangle$:

$$R_{IRL}(s) = \sum_{i=1}^{n} \omega_i f_i(s) \quad (2)$$

where, f_i is ith reward feature, ω_i is ith feature weight, s is the state vector for the current state of the agent. Each reward feature is computed from the state vector s and the mapping from state variables to reward features is typically domain dependent, defined by agent designers.

In our representation, we only use the state variables to represent the path of the agent and the policy of the demonstrator, hence the potential function is independent of the actions. RE-IRL obtains the weight vector $\mathbf{w}$ by finding a distribution $\mathcal{P}$ that minimizes the KL-Information loss $I(\mathcal{P}, \mathcal{Q})$ over trajectories. KL-Information loss $I(\mathcal{P}, \mathcal{Q})$ is the information lost when the distribution $\mathcal{Q}$ is used to approximate the distribution $\mathcal{P}$ [5]. For this work we are interested in transferring the expert demonstration policy from humans to agents, hence we use the distribution $\mathcal{Q}$ as the distribution of observed expert trajectories in state space. RE-IRL tries to find a vector $\mathbf{w}$ that minimizes the KL-Information loss. With $\mathbf{w}$, during learning, when $\mathbf{f_{observed}} \approx \mathbf{f_{demonstration}}$ feature weights return a higher reward to reinforce the agent's state-action values. For the full derivation of the solution we refer readers to [3]. An explanation of RE-IRL with a pseudo-code for the algorithm is also presented by Muelling et al. [13].

Using The Recovered Function: Last, we compute potential-based shaping rewards that the agent receives during learning. For this step we tested the use of the recovered linear function as a traditional, static potential function and also as a dynamic potential function. To implement potential-based shaping we define the above potential function $\Phi : S \mapsto \mathbb{R}$ over the state space, and define the shaping reward F as the difference between the potential of the new state s' and the old state s:

$$F(s,a,s') = \gamma\Phi(s') - \Phi(s) \quad (3)$$

where $0 \leq \gamma \leq 1$ is the discount factor which describes the present value of future rewards and potentials [22]. The effect of shaping is that the agent's exploration is less random and the agent is biased towards states with high potential. In this work we use inverse reinforcement learning to obtain a linear function $\Phi(s) = R_{IRL}(s)$ from expert teacher demonstrations. We call this approach Static IRL Shaping (SIS). We name the approach *static* since the potential function does not change over time.

The formulation given in Eq.(3) is limited in that the shaping reward is dependent only upon the states encountered by the agent and not its actions. Wiewiora et al. [25] extend the definition of F and Φ to state-action pairs (s,a) as:

$$F(s,a,s',a') = \gamma\Phi(s',a') - \Phi(s,a) \quad (4)$$

This formulation allows more information to be incorporated, as it is not limited to states but uses action choices for computing the shaping reward.

Devlin et al. [6] extended Ng's potential-based reward shaping to dynamic potential-based shaping, allowing the shaping function to change over time:

$$F(s,t,s',t') = \gamma\Phi(s',t') - \Phi(s,t) \tag{5}$$

By changing the shaping function over time, this formulation allows incorporating learning in the shaping function based on agent's experience in order to improve the shaping function. Harutyunyan et al. [8] combine these two extensions into *dynamic shaping* over state-action pairs:

$$F(s,a,t,s',a',t') = \gamma\Phi(s',a',t') - \Phi(s,a,t) \tag{6}$$

Importantly, the above variants of shaping all preserve the guarantees such as policy invariance and consistent Nash Equilibria proven by Ng et al [14], and Devlin and Kudenko [6]. Using dynamic shaping, any expert provided reward function $R^\dagger$ can be transformed into a potential-based shaping function by learning a secondary Q-function $\Phi^\dagger$, which serves as the potential function for shaping. The formulation below defines the dynamic potential-based shaping reward. The secondary value function must be learned on-policy, with a technique such as SARSA [18]:

$$\Phi^\dagger(s,a) \leftarrow \Phi^\dagger(s,a) + \beta\delta^{\Phi^\dagger} \tag{7}$$

Where β is the learning rate, and $\delta^{\Phi^\dagger}$ is defined as the temporal difference (TD) error of the state transition:

$$\delta^{\Phi^\dagger} = r^{\phi^\dagger} + \gamma\Phi^\dagger(s',a') - \Phi^\dagger(s,a) \tag{8}$$

As the secondary Q-function $\Phi^\dagger$ gets updated after each step the shaping function becomes:

$$F = \gamma\Phi^\dagger(s',a') - \Phi^\dagger(s,a) \tag{9}$$

By substitution we obtain:

$$\delta_t^{\Phi^\dagger} = r^{\phi^\dagger} + F \tag{10}$$

By definition, the temporal difference error (i.e. the error between the estimated Q-value and the actual return) goes to 0 at the time of convergence. Thus for $\delta^{\Phi^\dagger} = 0$:

$$r^{\phi^\dagger} + F = 0 \tag{11}$$

And finally at the time of convergence the potential-based shaping function becomes:

$$F(s,a) = R^\dagger(s,a) = -r^{\phi^\dagger} \tag{12}$$

When the secondary value function has converged (i.e. when $\delta^{\Phi^\dagger} = 0$), the main value function $Q(s,a)$ will be supplied with a potential-based reward shaping that is equivalent to the reward function $R^\dagger$. Even before convergence, $\Phi^\dagger$ provides useful information about $R^\dagger$, just like the main Q-function provides information about good policies before converging to an optimal policy. As implied by the last equation above, we learn the secondary Q-function $\Phi^\dagger$ using the negative of the expert defined reward $r^{\phi^\dagger} = -R^\dagger$. In our work, $R^\dagger(s,a,s') = R_{IRL}(s)$ is the reward function we recover using inverse reinforcement learning. We call this approach Dynamic IRL Shaping (DIS), as the potential function changes over time based on the learned, secondary Q-function which uses Equation 2 as its reward input.

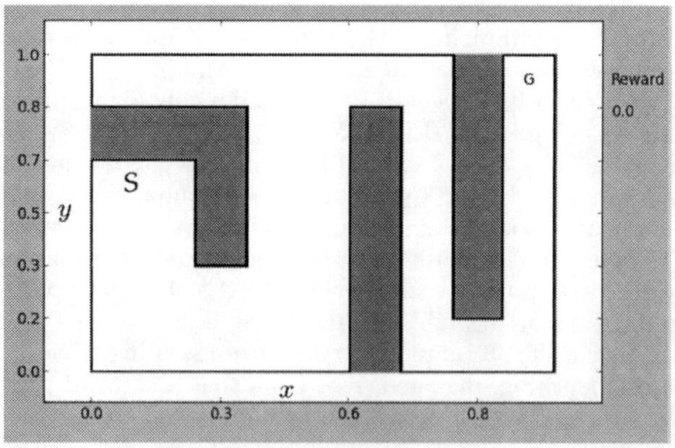

Figure 1: Maze domain. The state-space consists of two continuous variables x, y that define the horizontal and vertical location of the agent in the maze with reference to the lower-left corner. The agent starts from S and its goal is to navigate around the gray walls and reach the goal destination G.

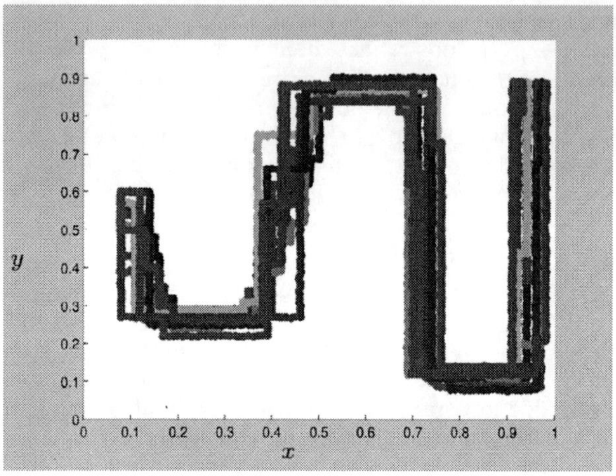

Figure 2: Suboptimal demonstrations in the Maze domain.

4. EXPERIMENTAL VALIDATION

In order to validate our approach we compare the performance of our algorithms against HAT with value-bonus [24] and SBS in two domains: a relatively simple Maze domain, and the Mario AI [9] domain. For both domains, we investigate the initial performance, the asymptotic performance, and the total cumulative reward for evaluation.

In both domains we have 5 agents: a standard RL agent, a SIS agent, a DIS agent, a HAT agent and a SBS agent. For the Maze domain we use SARSA(λ) as the standard learner and the underlying learning algorithm for all other agents. For the Mario AI domain we use Q(λ)-learning as the standard learner and the underlying learning algorithm for all other agents (with the exception of the secondary learner in DIS, which has to be a SARSA learner).

4.1 Maze

The Maze domain shown in Fig.1 is a modified version of the Dyna Maze domain introduced by Sutton and Barto [22]. In this domain the goal of the agent is to start from the position marked with *S*, navigate around the walls shown as

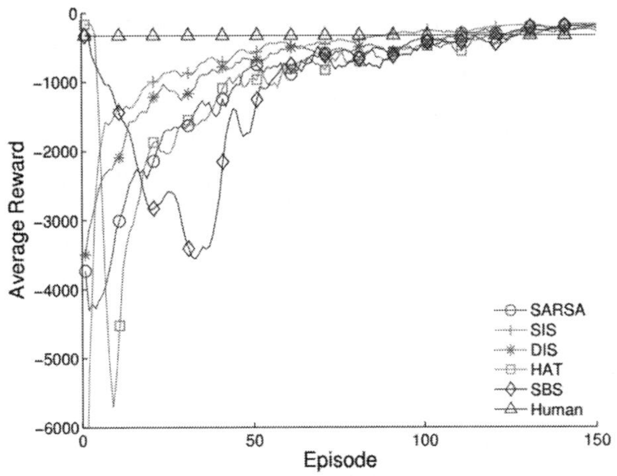

Figure 3: Maze domain experiment results.

Table 1: Average initial (first episode) performance, asymptotic performance, and cumulative reward with standard deviations for all agents in the Maze domain. Maximum values are shown in bold. Higher values are better. SAR: SARSA, HMN: average of the reward human demonstrator received in 10 demonstrations.

Agents	μ_{init}	μ_{asymp}	μ_{cumul}
SAR	-3,730.36	-222.52	-151,525.96
SIS	-7,973.16	**-165.88**	**-93,591.96**
DIS	-3,494.08	-267.88	-113,689.12
HAT	**-164.68**	-222.36	-150,141.28
SBS	-324.04	-185.84	-159,634.52
HMN	-327.5	-327.5	

dark gray cells and reach the goal state marked with G. In our version the state-space consists of two continuous variables $0 \leq x, y < 1.0$. The agent starts at $s = (x : 0.08, y : 0.6)$, and chooses one of four available actions: left, right, up, and down. Step size for each action is 0.02. After each step the agent receives an environment reward of -1. If the agent tries to get outside the domain boundaries in any direction, or hits a wall, it receives an environment reward of -10. The terminal condition is $(x \geq 0.9)$ && $(y \geq 0.9)$ with an environment reward of $+10$. This is an episodic task and each episode starts form the initial state and ends at the goal state (or terminates with failure after 6000 steps).

In order to evaluate our approach we collected 10 suboptimal demonstrations in the Maze domain. The demonstrator was the first author who also designed and implemented the modifications to the original Dyna Maze domain. Fig. 2 shows the suboptimal demonstrations. Features we recorded during demonstrations were the horizontal and vertical location of the agent at each time-step, that is, $s_t(x_t, y_t)$ for each observation s_t. The shortest demonstration took 328 steps to reach the goal and the longest demonstration was 353 steps long ($\mu = 337.5$ and $\sigma = 10.71$ steps). None of the demonstrations had the agent collide with the walls or the borders of the maze. For RE-IRL, we appended the last observation of the shorter demonstrations repeatedly in order to equalize the lengths of the demonstrations. We used the following parameters for our agents: number of tiles = 32,

Table 2: Statistical analysis for the Maze domain results show p-values for two-sample t-tests. SAR stands for SARSA. Columns show the statistical significance of the difference between the initial (first episode) performance, asymptotic (last episode) performance, and cumulative reward (i.e. total reward throughout the trial).* p $\leq$ 0.05, p $\leq$ 0.01,*** p $\leq$ 0.001,**** p $\leq$ 0.0001.**

Agents	Initial	Asymp.	Cumulative
SAR vs SIS	3.8929e-16****	0.051603	1.4592e-44****
SAR vs DIS	0.62928	0.56365	8.3354e-33****
SAR vs HAT	1.5995e-13****	0.99673	0.51621
SAR vs SBS	1.6913e-12****	0.26082	0.022387*
DIS vs HAT	3.4262e-13****	0.56402	1.0199e-22****
DIS vs SIS	9.6501e-18****	0.17313	5.2131e-26****
DIS vs SBS	4.1881e-12****	0.28159	5.4586e-18****
SIS vs HAT	3.0772e-94****	0.060007	4.3662e-32****
SIS vs SBS	2.597e-55****	0.32015	9.6945e-25****
SBS vs HAT	0.062916	0.27499	0.015977*

$\alpha = 0.25/\#tiles$, $\beta = 0.05/\#tiles$, $\gamma = 1.0$, $\lambda = 0.25$, with $\epsilon-$greedy action selection where $\epsilon = 0.02$. Finally, we used a scaling of 100 for all shaping reward signals, except for the HAT agent where the scaling was 10.

Fig. 3 shows the agents' performance in 150 episodes, averaged over 25 trials. The vertical axis shows the agents' performance in terms of total reward received per episode and the horizontal axis shows the number of episodes. Each line shows the performance of a different agent. For comparison we also show human demonstrator's performance averaged over 10 demonstrations. Average initial (first episode), asymptotic (last episode), and cumulative reward are detailed in Table 1.

First, we note that all five algorithms are able to achieve a similar asymptotic performance in this domain, although they reach it at different rates. For example, if we consider the number of episodes each algorithm takes to surpass the performance of the demonstrator, then we see that SARSA(λ), SIS, DIS, HAT and SBS require 110, 90, 115, 135, and 136 episodes, respectively. In summary, SIS learns the task remarkably faster than all other methods.

The performance of the different techniques also varies largely during the learning process. The standard SARSA(λ) agent starts from $-3,730$ and reaches its asymptotic performance after 130 episodes. The SIS approach starts with the worst performance, $-7,973$, however is the fastest to surpass the demonstrator's performance only after 90 episodes. In comparison the DIS approach starts with an initial performance of $-3,494$ and learns the task comparably fast.

The HAT algorithm, initializes the Q-function with the potential function at the very beginning. The first column of Table 1 shows that the initialization results in high performance during first episodes.However later on, as the agent probabilistically explores the state-space its performance degrades over time. It is important to point out that the performance boost gained by amount of initial jump-start is dependent of the demonstration quality and demonstrator's ability. Taylor et al. [24] have investigated the impact of demonstration quality and demonstrator expertise. HAT suffers from a performance loss after about 10 episodes due to the negative step reward. The agent starts with the "good" policy, however receives negative reward at every step and thus starts

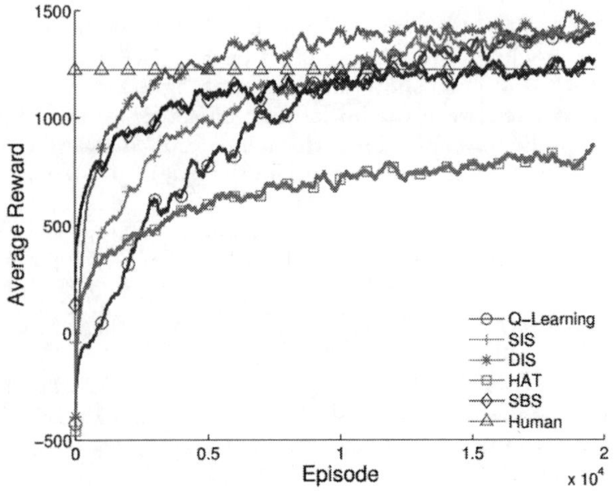

Figure 4: Mario domain experiment results.

to explore beyond the good policy. After exploring different states only to learn that they were "bad" states, the agent recovers and improves its performance to catch-up with the learning speed of the standard SARSA(λ) agent. This finding is in parallel with Taylor et al.'s [24] observations, in the sense that human demonstrations do not hurt the agent's final performance.

Similarly, the SBS approach implements Q-function initialization and starts with a high performance which degrades over time with exploration. After about 136 episodes the SBS agent reaches the demonstrator's performance and soon after converges to its asymptotic performance of -186.

Using the rewards agents collected per trial, we performed two-sample t-tests to evaluate whether the agents' initial performance, asymptotic performance and cumulative reward were significantly different from each other (Table 2, sample size: 25 trials).

The difference in asymptotic performance is not significant as can be obvious from Fig. 3. That being said, we would like to underline that all methods have surpassed human demonstrator's average performance. Especially SIS results in about a 50% increase in asymptotic performance after 150 episodes w.r.t the demonstrator's performance (second column of Table 1).

As for the initial performance data, there wasn't a significant difference between the DIS and the SARSA agents. However, the HAT and the SBS agents performed significantly better than the SARSA agent.

Finally, both the SIS and the DIS agents collected significantly more reward throughout 150 episodes (i.e. cumulative reward) than the SARSA, the HAT and the SBS agents.

In summary, the SIS agent shows the steepest learning curve by converging to a stable policy fastest and collects the highest cumulative reward of approximately -93,000 after 150 episodes. The DIS agent performs comparably good with a better initial performance than SIS, however collects less cumulative reward, approximately -113,000.

4.2 Mario AI

Super Mario Bros is a popular 2-D side-scrolling video game developed by the Nintendo Corporation. In this work we use the publicly available Mario AI version released by Karakovskiy and Togelius [9]. There are many possible representations of the state-space in this domain and here in order to test our approach in a large state-space, we use 27 discrete state-variables. Boolean state variables *jump*, *ground*, and *shoot* define whether Mario is able to jump, is standing on a tile, or is able to shoot fireballs. We use *x-dir* and *y-dir* variables that can take on either one of $\{-1, 0, 1\}$ values to define the direction of the agent's movements. The immediate surrounding of the agent is discretized in 8 grid cells. For each grid cell we have a state variable *close-enemies* defining whether there is a enemy in the matching cell. We also keep track of the grid cells that are one step farther than the immediate cells, and we have 8 boolean variables called *mid-enemies*. We keep four boolean state variables *obstacle* to identify whether the four vertical cells to the immediate right of Mario are occupied by obstacles such as pipes. Finally we have two variables *closest-enemy-x* and *closest-enemy-y* that define the Euclidean distance between the agent and the closest enemy within a 22x22 grid. This state space is inspired by Liao's work [12]. We note that this domain is a relatively high dimensional domain compared to most standard RL benchmarking domains. The main reason of our evaluation in the Mario AI domain is to show that our model-free approach is scalable. The agent can choose one of 12 actions combining one of each options of the following three sets: {left, right, no-action}, {jump, do not jump}, {run, do not run}. The goal of the agent is to maximize the total reward it receives throughout the level. The agent receives a reward of $+10$ for stepping on an enemy, $+58$ for eating a mushroom, $+64$ for eat-

Table 3: Performance metrics for the agents in Mario AI: initial performance, asymptotic performance, cumulative reward (average of 10 trials). Maximum values are shown in bold. Higher values are better.

Agents	μ_{init}	μ_{asymp}	μ_{cumul}
QLR	-424.6	1,410.4155	20,101,973.6
SIS	-43.6	**1,431.5328**	22,341,947.6
DIS	-391.2	1,398.7714	**25,725,731.6**
HAT	-457	867.2241	13,250,664.4
SBS	**129.8**	1,267.8642	22,332,848.2
HMN	1,224	1,224	

Table 4: Statistical analysis for the Mario AI domain results show p-values for two-sample t-tests. QLR stands for Q-Learning. Columns show the statistical significance of the difference between the initial performance, asymptotic (final) performance, and cumulative reward (i.e. total reward throughout the trial).

Agents	Initial	Asymp.	Cumulative
QLR vs SIS	0.018698*	0.99448	0.0010416**
QLR vs DIS	0.65987	0.11448	5.5167e-09****
QLR vs HAT	0.60982	0.71677	9.0692e-12****
QLR vs SBS	0.050229	0.059223	0.00014223***
DIS vs HAT	0.40846	0.23382	1.6551e-18****
DIS vs SIS	0.037257*	0.094503	1.9024e-06****
DIS vs SBS	0.067898	9.1049e-05****	1.9184e-08****
SIS vs HAT	0.012506*	0.70797	4.121e-15****
SIS vs SBS	0.56634	0.040042*	0.98207
SBS vs HAT	0.039996*	0.023199*	4.0285e-21****

ing a fire-flower, +16 for collecting a coin, +24 for finding a hidden block, +1024 for successfully finishing the level, −42 for getting hurt by an enemy (e.g. losing fire-flower), and −512 for dying. The maximum number of steps per episode is limited by the game's timer and the default timeout is 200 seconds. In the context of potential-based reward shaping, recent work by Harutyunyan et al. [7] implements and evaluates their reward shaping framework [8] in Mario AI domain as well.

We used the 10 demonstrations' first 953 observations for RE-IRL, and used the same demonstrations in full length for all other methods. For RE-IRL, the 10th longest demonstration was 953 observations long and we pruned the first nine demonstrations at this length to keep the demonstration length consistent. We used the following parameters for our agents: number of tiles = 32, $\alpha = 0.01/\#tiles$, $beta = 0.05$, $\gamma = 0.9$, $\lambda = 0.5$, with ϵ−greedy action selection where $\epsilon = 0.05$, and $scaling = 1$ for the shaping reward.

We ran 10 trials for all five agents' performance evaluation. The level our agent played in Mario was designed as an episodic task where the agent finishes a level either with success or the level ends with failure with the agent's death, or a timeout of 200 seconds. Every episode, the agent plays a randomly generated level, starting from a randomly selected mode (small, large, fire-mario).

Fig. 4 shows the agents' performance in 20,000 episodes, averaged over 10 trials. The vertical axis shows the average total reward (i.e. points) agents collected during each episode. The horizontal axis shows the number of episodes. Each line shows the performance of an agent. Again, for comparison, we also show the human demonstrator's performance. Table 3 shows the average initial performance, asymptotic performance, and cumulative reward for each agent. On average the demonstrator scored 1224 points in this domain.

Unlike the previous domain not every agent was able to achieve the same asymptotic performance after 20,000. Three agents' asymptotic performance (SIS, DIS, and Q(λ)) is significantly better than the remaining two (HAT and SBS). Again, if we consider the number of episodes each agent takes to surpass the performance of the user, then we see that Q(λ), SIS, DIS, and SBS require 11,000, 10,000, 4,000 and 12,000 episodes respectively. The HAT agent was unable to reach or surpass the demonstrator's performance.

Similar to our previous experiment we observe a great difference in the learning process. With the exception of the SBS agent, most agents start with similar initial performance and negative total reward for their first several hundred episodes. The SBS agent leverages Q-function initialization and starts with a positive initial performance. The initial performance of the SIS agent was significantly better than the standard Q(λ)-learning agent, the DIS agent and the HAT agent. That said, the SIS agent's asymptotic performance was only better compared to the SBS and the HAT agents.

In terms of cumulative reward, the SIS agent performed significantly better than all other agents but the DIS agent. Table 3 shows that the DIS agent has the best overall cumulative reward performance, exceeding a cumulative reward of 25M in 20,000 episodes. The DIS agent also is the fastest to reach to the demonstrator's performance after about 4,000 episodes, reaching the best asymptotic performance after about 8,000 episodes before any of the other methods even reach the level of the demonstrator.

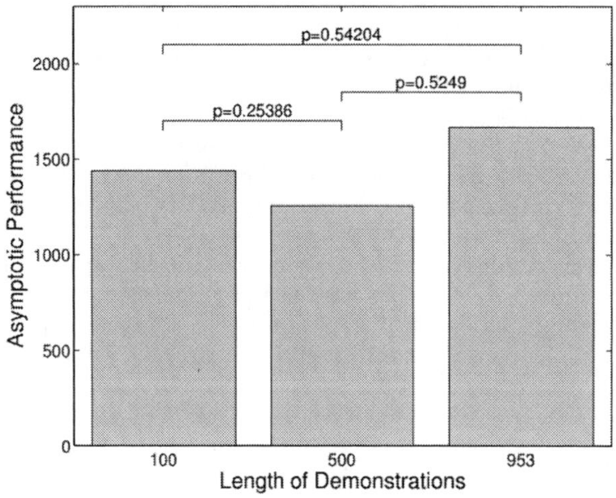

Figure 5: Asymptotic performance of the DIS agent after 20,000 episodes in Mario AI. Here the performance is a function of the length of demonstrations (the number of state-action pairs recorded per demonstration). Each condition has 10 demonstrations. P-values obtained with two-sample *t*-tests between marked conditions for 10 trials. Values for the bar plot are the average of 10 trials.

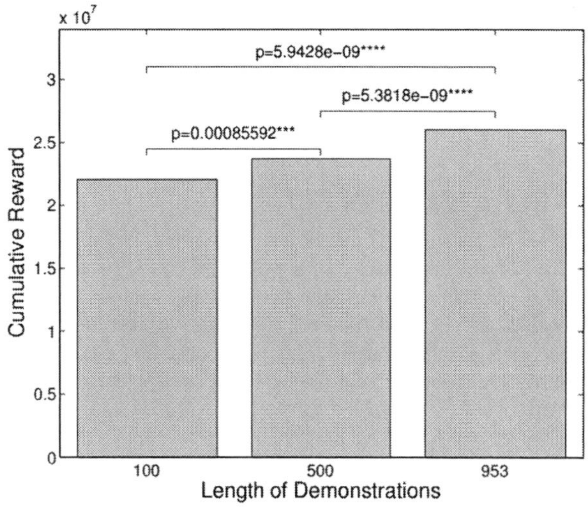

Figure 6: Cumulative reward the DIS agent received during 20,000 episodes in Mario AI. Here the cumulative reward is a function of the length of demonstrations (the number of state-action pairs recorded per demonstration). Each condition has 10 demonstrations. P-values obtained with two-sample *t*-tests between marked conditions for 10 trials.

The SBS algorithm shows quick convergence however its final performance remains limited at about 1,267 points, very close to demonstrator's performance, after 20,000 episodes. This is because SBS takes observed state's similarity with demonstrations and rewards the agent if the agent acts similar to demonstrations. As pointed out by Brys et al. [4] SBS performs better with minimum amount of consistent demonstrations (even with a single demonstration in the case of Cart-Pole domain). Although given enough number of episodes the algorithm is guaranteed to reach the underlying Q(λ)-learning's performance, suboptimal demonstrations affect the speed of learning. Finally, the HAT agent performs slightly better than standard Q(λ)-learning only for the first 250 episodes. This is because it is difficult to summarize the demonstrator's policy based on a limited number of observations. This shows the slight performance boost that policy transfer brings, however for the rest of the trials, HAT agent shows slow improvement resulting in the significantly worst performance after 20,000 episodes.

After an analysis of learning curves and the agents' performance, we also briefly investigated the effect of the length of demonstrations on the asymptotic performance and the cumulative reward. For this set of experiments, we chose the Mario AI domain as it is a harder task and we used the DIS agent as it was the fastest learner with the highest cumulative reward in our previous experiment.

Fig. 5 shows the average asymptotic performance results for 10 trials using 100, 500 and 953 observations for 10 demonstrations. We did *not* find a significant difference between the asymptotic performance data for varying length of demonstrations. We conclude that this is because the DIS agent learns using a secondary Q-function, and even if the demonstrations do not contain enough information, in this case 20,000 episodes were enough for using the environment reward to eventually achieve the same asymptotic performance. However, we did find a significant difference in the cumulative reward of the agents. Fig. 6 shows that as the number of observations per demonstration increase, the cumulative reward significantly increases. The results in Fig. 5 and Fig. 6 imply that the length of demonstrations do affect the learning *speed* without affecting the asymptotic performance of the DIS agent.

5. CONCLUSION

In this paper we introduced a novel, three step approach to use human demonstrations for potential-based reward shaping in reinforcement learning. Specifically, with our method, we collect demonstrations in a domain, we then use the demonstrations to recover a linear function using inverse reinforcement learning, finally we use this recovered function to compute a shaping reward for potential-based shaping in reinforcement learning. Our approach is model-free and scalable. To show the scalability of our approach we ran two sets of experiments in a simple two dimensional continuous Maze domain, and a complex, 27 dimensional Mario domain with discrete state-variables. We compared our algorithm to standard RL and two previously introduced reinforcement learning from demonstration algorithms. Our experiments show that our approach results in a significant increase in cumulative reward collected by the agents. Our agents' asymptotic performance surpasses the human demonstrator's average performance. One of our approaches, Static IRL Shaping results in faster learning with higher cumulative reward in the simpler Maze domain, whereas our second approach, Dynamic IRL Shaping results in faster learning with higher cumulative reward in the more complicated Mario AI domains. One possible explanation for this behavior is that the Maze task was not complex enough to observe the benefits of the secondary policy the DIS algorithm learns. This indicates that in simple domains, learning a reward function by demonstrations can be enough to improve a learner's performance compared to previously introduced transfer learning techniques. It is also likely that the high dimensionality and the state representation of the Mario AI domain makes it difficult for the IRL algorithm to recover a suitable reward function for all sections of the state space. The intuition behind the DIS algorithm is that the secondary policy can generalize over the state space and provide a more informative, adaptive shaping reward signal for the agent. Which may explain why the DIS agent performs better in this domain. Finally we also briefly investigated the effect of the number of observations on learning. We found that our approach learns faster as the demonstrations contain more observations as this results in a more complete representation of the task.

We believe that using demonstrations originating either from a human teacher or another agent, is a promising direction of research for incorporating a priori knowledge in reinforcement learning. For future work, we are investigating the impact of demonstration *quality* on learning and the use of multiple, locally weighted, learned shaping rewards.

Acknowledgments

Halit Bener Suay's work is supported by the Office of Naval Research award N000141410795. Tim Brys is funded by a PhD scholarship of the Research Foundation Flanders (FWO). This research has taken place in part at the Intelligent Robot Learning (IRL) Lab, Washington State University. IRL research is supported in part by grants AFRL FA8750-14-1-0069, AFRL FA8750-14-1-0070, NSF IIS-1149917, NSF IIS-1319412, USDA 2014-67021-22174, and a Google Research Award.

REFERENCES

[1] P. Abbeel and A. Y. Ng. Apprenticeship learning via inverse reinforcement learning. In *Twenty-first international conference on Machine learning - ICML '04*, New York, New York, USA, 2004.

[2] A. Barto, R. Sutton, and C. Anderson. Neuronlike adaptive elements that can solve difficult learning control problems. *Systems, Man and Cybernetics, IEEE Transactions on*, SMC-13(5):834–846, 1983.

[3] A. Boularias, J. Kober, and J. Peters. Relative entropy inverse reinforcement learning. In *Proceedings of the Fourteenth International Conference on Artificial Intelligence and Statistics, AISTATS 2011, Fort Lauderdale, USA, April 11-13, 2011*, pages 182–189, 2011.

[4] T. Brys, A. Harutyunyan, H. B. Suay, S. Chernova, M. E. Taylor, and A. Nowé. Reinforcement learning from demonstration through shaping. In *Proceedings of the International Joint Conference on Artificial Intelligence (IJCAI)*, 2015.

[5] K. P. Burnham and D. R. Anderson. *Model selection and multimodel inference: a practical information-theoretic approach*. Springer, 2002.

[6] S. Devlin and D. Kudenko. Dynamic potential-based reward shaping. In *Proceedings of the 11th International Conference on Autonomous Agents and Multiagent Systems-Volume 1*, pages 433–440. International Foundation for Autonomous Agents and Multiagent Systems, 2012.

[7] A. Harutyunyan, T. Brys, P. Vrancx, and A. Nowé. Shaping mario with human advice. In *Proceedings of the 2015 International Conference on Autonomous Agents and Multiagent Systems*, AAMAS '15, pages 1913–1914, Richland, SC, 2015.

[8] A. Harutyunyan, S. Devlin, P. Vrancx, and A. Nowe. Expressing arbitrary reward functions as potential-based advice. In *AAAI Conference on Artificial Intelligence*, 2015.

[9] S. Karakovskiy and J. Togelius. The mario ai benchmark and competitions. *Computational Intelligence and AI in Games, IEEE Transactions on*, 4(1):55–67, 2012.

[10] E. Klein, B. Piot, M. Geist, and O. Pietquin. *ECML, Prague, Czech Republic, 2013*, A Cascaded Supervised Learning Approach to Inverse Reinforcement Learning, pages 1–16. Springer Berlin Heidelberg, 2013.

[11] S. Levine and V. Koltun. Continuous inverse optimal control with locally optimal examples. In *ICML '12: Proceedings of the 29th International Conference on Machine Learning*, pages 41–48, 2012.

[12] Y. Liao, K. Yi, and Z. Yang. Cs229 final report reinforcement learning to play mario. Technical report, Stanford University, 2012.

[13] K. Muelling, A. Boularias, B. Mohler, B. Schölkopf, and J. Peters. Learning strategies in table tennis using inverse reinforcement learning. *Biological cybernetics*, 108(5):603–19, Oct. 2014.

[14] A. Y. Ng, D. Harada, and S. Russell. Policy invariance under reward transformations: Theory and application to reward shaping. In *In Proceedings of the Sixteenth International Conference on Machine Learning*, pages 278–287. Morgan Kaufmann, 1999.

[15] A. Y. Ng and S. J. Russell. Algorithms for Inverse Reinforcement Learning. In *Proceedings of the Eighteenth International Conference on Machine Learning*, pages 663–670. Morgan Kaufmann Publishers Inc., 2000.

[16] M. L. Puterman. *Markov Decision Processes: Discrete Stochastic Dynamic Programming*. John Wiley & Sons, Inc., 1994.

[17] N. Ratliff, J. Bagnell, and M. Zinkevich. Maximum margin planning. *Proceedings of the 23rd International Conference on Machine Learning*, 2006.

[18] G. A. Rummery and M. Niranjan. On-line q-learning using connectionist systems. Technical report, University of Cambridge, Department of Engineering, 1994.

[19] S. Schaal. Learning from demonstration. In *Advances in Neural Information Processing Systems 9*, pages 1040–1046. MIT Press, 1997.

[20] B. F. Skinner. *The behavior of organisms: An experimental analysis*. Appleton-Century, 1938.

[21] R. S. Sutton. *Temporal Credit Assignment in Reinforcement Learning*. PhD thesis, University of Massachusetts - Amherst, 1984.

[22] R. S. Sutton and A. G. Barto. *Introduction to Reinforcement Learning*. MIT Press, Cambridge, MA, USA, 1998.

[23] M. E. Taylor and P. Stone. Cross-domain transfer for reinforcement learning. In *Proceedings of the 24th international conference on Machine learning*, pages 879–886. ACM, 2007.

[24] M. E. Taylor, H. B. Suay, and S. Chernova. Integrating reinforcement learning with human demonstrations of varying ability. In *The 10th International Conference on Autonomous Agents and Multiagent Systems-Volume 2*, pages 617–624. International Foundation for Autonomous Agents and Multiagent Systems, 2011.

[25] E. Wiewiora, G. W. Cottrell, and C. Elkan. Principled methods for advising reinforcement learning agents. In *Proceedings of the Twentieth International Conference on Machine Learning (ICML)*, pages 792–799, 2003.

[26] B. D. Ziebart, A. L. Maas, J. A. Bagnell, and A. K. Dey. Maximum Entropy Inverse Reinforcement Learning. In *AAAI*, pages 1433–1438, 2008.

PAC Continuous State Online Multitask Reinforcement Learning with Identification

Yao Liu
Peking University
Beijing, PR China
liuyao@pku.edu.cn

Zhanhan Guo
Carnegie Mellon University
Pittsburgh, PA, United States
zguo@cs.cmu.edu

Emma Brunskill
Carnegie Mellon University
Pittsburgh, PA, United States
ebrun@cs.cmu.edu

ABSTRACT

One key feature of a general intelligent autonomous agent is to be able to learn from past experience to improve future performance. In this paper we consider how an agent can leverage prior experience from performing reinforcement learning in order to learn faster in future tasks. We introduce the first, to our knowledge, probably approximately correct (PAC) RL algorithm COMRLI for sequential multi-task learning across a series of continuous-state, discrete-action RL tasks. We assume tasks are sampled from a finite number of clusters of Markov decision processes, and provide a bound on the number of steps on which the algorithm makes a suboptimal decision that is substantially smaller on later tasks. We also provide preliminary evidence to suggest our approach may be useful in practice, by showing encouraging simulation performance in a standard domain where it compares favorably to a state-of-the-art algorithm.

General Terms

Algorithms

1. INTRODUCTION

A key feature of an intelligent, autonomous agent is to be able to learn from past experience to improve future performance. In many applications, including robotics, consumer marketing, and healthcare, such an agent will be performing a series of reinforcement learning (RL) tasks modeled as Markov Decision Processes (MDPs) with a continuous state space and a discrete action space. In this paper we are interested in formally quantifying the amount of experience needed for the agent to learn to make good decisions while learning from past experience in a series of such tasks.

Our work falls into the broader class of transfer, lifelong and multi-task sequential decision making. There has been significant interest in this area for the past two decades, and novel algorithms have been introduced with promising empirical performance. Transfer learning has typically focused on leveraging experience from a single source task to improve performance on a single target task. Lifelong learning typically refers to doing a series of tasks and improving performance on later tasks. Multi-task learning often refers to having experience from a set of distinct tasks, and using that experience to improve performance on a new target task. This can be done in either a batch setting, or an online setting where the new target task is added to the set of source tasks to accelerate performance on later tasks. This final setting is the one we consider in this paper. Note that the topic of curriculum learning, where an agent may choose the order in which to complete tasks, is a very interesting question that is outside the scope of our current work: here we assume that the stochastic environment selects the next task to provide to an agent.

Encouraging recent work has shown substantially improved empirical performance on online multi-task continuous state RL [1, 4]. However, there has been very little theoretical analysis of this setup. Exceptions include work by Lazaric et al. [12] that shows a bound on the estimated value function used by transferring samples from prior tasks, but they consider the batch setting (where one has a set of samples from a target task) and do not handle online exploration/exploitation. Very recent work by Eaton et al. [2] uses a policy search method and provides regret bounds, but the regret bounds are with respect to the best policy in their policy class with additional structural assumptions, rather than the true optimal policy. To our knowledge there has been no work on bounding the amount of experience needed to make good decisions in later continuous-state RL tasks by leveraging prior experience in tasks with the same state and action space, but different dynamics and/or reward models.

In this paper we help to fill this gap by introducing a PAC RL algorithm (Continuous-State Online Multitask RL with Identification a.k.a COMRLI) for online multi-task learning across a series of continuous-state, discrete-action RL tasks with the same state and action spaces. We assume that each task is drawn from a stationary distribution over C MDP clusters: though for simplicity most of our analysis will assume that there is a single MDP within each cluster, our results also extend to when each cluster consists of MDPs with very similar transition and reward models. We prove that the number of steps on which the agent may take a non ϵ-optimal action, known as the sample complexity, will be substantially smaller in later tasks, scaling as a function of C rather than the size (covering number) of the state-action space. Our work builds on recent advances in PAC discrete-state online multi-task RL algorithms [5] and single task PAC continuous-state reinforcement learning [16]. We also provide encouraging, preliminary empirical performance on a standard domain where our algorithm exceeds a state-of-the-art continuous-state multitask RL algorithm.

Appears in: *Proceedings of the 15th International Conference on Autonomous Agents and Multiagent Systems (AAMAS 2016), J. Thangarajah, K. Tuyls, C. Jonker, S. Marsella (eds.), May 9–13, 2016, Singapore.*

Our algorithm proceeds in two stages. In the first stage, our approach learns a good estimate of the optimal Q-function of every given task (in our setting, after a bounded number of tasks, all C tasks will have been encountered with high probability). In the second stage, we leverage this prior information to speed learning in new tasks by using a novel method to quickly identify the new task. Intuitively we leverage a mixing assumption on the underlying MDPs to enable us to eliminate possible MDPs by checking that we can reach different states in a bounded number of steps with high probability. This identification process, paired with assuming that tasks are sampled from a stationary (not adversarial) distribution, enables our overall sample complexity to scale as a function of the number of tasks rather than the size of the state-action space.

2. RELATED WORK

There has been much research on methods for leveraging past experience. One of the simple batch settings focuses on transferring experience from a single source task to a single target task. In many cases only the reward of the task is assumed to differ; this reflected domains where the transition dynamics were the same but the goals were different. Later work relaxed the assumption to also allow the transition dynamics to differ, and even allowed partial sharing of the state space. The multi-task setting has also been explored under similar structural assumptions. These approaches all have been shown to improve performance empirically [17].

However there has been far less work that have theoretical guarantees on performance; without theory there is no guarantee that leveraging past experience would not end up harming future performance (negative transfer). The lack of theory is not surprising considering formal bounds for single task RL performance have only been recently developed [11, 10]. These bounds are called Probability Approximately Correct (PAC), since they bound the number of steps in which an algorithm performs less than near-optimal (sample complexity) with high probability. The early work studied discrete state spaces, but more recent work has also developed PAC bounds for continuous state spaces [16, 6], which we build upon.

Some recent work do have theoretical bounds on transfer, but only focus on the simple batch setting of transferring experience from a single source task to a single target task. They also include other assumptions such as access to a generative model of the source task, a linear approximation of the value function in [12], or a discrete state space in [14]. These approaches do not consider the exploration-exploitation trade-off in the online RL setting.

We focus on the continuous state space, multi-task, lifelong learning setting, in which an infinite sequence of tasks are presented sequentially to the algorithm. There has been recent work in this setting using policy gradient [1, 4], and even theoretical bounds [2]; however they require all tasks to share an underlying structure in their policies. Using policy gradient also restricts the scope of their policy class, which the optimal policy may not be a part of.

Our approach builds on related work for the discrete state, multi-task setting [5]: identifying whether a task is the same as a previous task is much faster than learning from scratch. However we use our novel method to quickly identify the current task in a continuous state space.

3. PROBLEM SETTING

In our continuous multi-task RL setting, we assume tasks are drawn sequentially and iid over a finite set $\mathcal{C}$ of C tasks (we will mention in section 4 how this can be relaxed to C clusters of tasks). Each task is a Markov Decision Process (MDP) that can be described by a tuple $(S, A, T, R, \gamma, H, b_0)$: S is a continuous set of states; A is a discrete set of actions; $T(s'|s,a)$ is the probability of transitioning to state s' from s after executing action a; $R(s,a) \in [0,1]$ is the expected reward from executing action a in state s. The initial state is drawn from b_0. An RL algorithm then executes an action a at every time-step t, after which the MDP returns some reward r_t according to $R(s,a)$, and transitions to a new state according to $T(s'|s,a)$. At every step, the data sample (s_t, a_t, r_t, s_{t+1}) is collected. A task is finished after H steps have passed. The objective of the RL algorithm is to maximize the accumulated discounted rewards i.e. to maximize the value function $V(s) = \mathbb{E}[\sum_{t=1}^{H} \gamma^{t-1} r_t | s_0 = s]$; $\gamma \in [0,1]$ is the discounted factor, which determines the significance of future rewards. The optimal value function is denoted as $V^*(s)$, and $Q(s,a)$ is the optimal state-action value of starting with action a in state s and then following the optimal policy. Q_{max} is the maximium Q-value in a domain and $Q_{max} \leq \frac{1}{1-\gamma}$.

We assume all tasks have the same state-action space $S \times A$, discount factor γ, and task length H; but, the parameters (T, R, b_0) can differ. The overall objective of the algorithm is to maximize the value function $V(s)$ for all tasks.

While we acknowledge that our assumptions are not suitable for all situations, we believe our setting captures a general set of important domains such as user modeling where different groups of users may have similar behavior (see examples from [13] or [15]).

We prove a high probability, polynomial bound on the sample complexity of our algorithm (PAC bound). The sample complexity is the total number of steps on which the expected value of algorithm is less than ϵ-optimal i.e. formally, the number of steps t where $V(s_t) \leq V^*(s_t) - \epsilon$ for all tasks.

4. ALGORITHM

Intuitively, identifying which of C possible tasks a new task is should require much less experience than learning the parameters of a new task from scratch. Once a task's identity is known, we can leverage all prior knowledge about this task, and immediately start using a good policy.

We use the optimal Q-function instead of the model parameters as the evidence to distinguish different tasks; however we still assume that different tasks have different models, so we only cluster tasks that have the same model. As we will discuss later on, the main reason for using Q-functions rather than model parameters like in prior work is due to the continuous state space.

We divide the sequence of tasks into two phases. In phase 1, in each task, we try to explore the whole state space efficiently to learn a good estimate of the optimal Q-function of every task over the entire state space. At the end of phase 1, we cluster the tasks according to the estimated Q-functions. Since tasks are sampled iid from C possible tasks, we can set the length of phase 1 (see Lemma 2) so that, with high probability, all C types are encountered. In phase 2, at the beginning of each task we try to identify which of the C task clusters it belongs to. After identifying it, we run the single

Algorithm 1 Continuous State Online Multitask RL with Identification (COMRLI)

Require: $T_1, \bar{C}, L_Q, \epsilon, \Gamma, H$
  for $t = 1, 2, \ldots T_1$ **do**
    Receive an unknown MDP $M_t \in \mathcal{M}$
    Run algorithm 2 on M_t with (Γ, D)-*known*.
    For all remaining steps until H steps, execute C-PACE algorithm on M_t
    Store all samples as a set $Sample_{M_t}$
  Cluster all tasks into $\widehat{C} \leq \bar{C}$ groups and combine their sample sets.
  for $t = T_1 + 1, \ldots T$ **do**
    Receive unknown MDP $M_t \in \mathcal{M}$
    Run algorithm 3 on M_t
    if M_t is identified **then**
      Combine samples from M_t to the group

task C-PACE algorithm using the all the previous samples collected from all the tasks within that cluster. Phase 2 is used for all subsequent tasks. We will shortly prove that this approach allows us to improve the sample complexity without incurring negative transfer in terms of our theoretical bounds.

4.1 Assumptions and definitions

Before we illustrate details of our algorithm, we need to introduce some assumptions:

1. There exists a distance metric $d[\cdot,\cdot]$ (e.g. Euclidean in our experiments) in which the optimal Q-function $Q_{M_i}(s,a)$ is Lipschitz continuous over (s,a), for any M_i in $\mathcal{C}$.

2. Tasks are sampled from a finite set of C distinct MDPs, and $\bar{C}$ is a known upper bound on C.

3. The optimal Q function for each of the C MDPs must differ in at least one state-action pair, e.g. for any two MDPs M_i and M_j, there must exist at least one (s,a) pair such that $||Q_i(s,a) - Q_j(s,a)||_2 \geq \Gamma > 0$.

4. There is a finite diameter $D(\epsilon)$: any (s,a) pair's neighborhood (radius at most ϵ) is reachable from any other (s,a) pair in at most an expected $D(\epsilon)$ steps.

The first assumption is a smoothness property over the Q-functions for any MDP. Intuitively, this ensures that close-by state-action pairs can only differ by a bounded amount in their Q-values. This is essential for near optimal learning to be efficient: if any two arbitrarily close state-action pairs can differ an arbitrary amount in their value, then it is necessary to visit all state–action pairs in the space to learn a near-optimal policy; this is an impossible task to do in finite time because the state space is infinite and continuous. Note that the Q-funtion is also Lipschitz continuous over the action space if we use proper a metric (e.g. our experiments). This assumption also implies that one could approximate such an MDP using a finite set of states and actions, because near-by states can only differ a finite amount in their resulting state–action values. This assumption was used and resulted in the tabular representation of the Q-function by a prior paper that introduced a PAC RL algorithm for single task continuous-state MDPs[16].

The second assumption describes our multi-task setting. For simplicity, we assume that there are C distinct MDP clusters with only one MDP in each cluster i.e. only C distinct MDPs, and that each task is one of the MDPs. It is straightforward to relax the assumption to the case where each cluster is made up of MDPs with similar dynamics. [1]

The third assumption says that we require tasks that are from distinct MDPs to differ in their optimal Q-values in at least one state–action pair. This is quite mild: if two tasks do not differ in their optimal Q-values in any state–action pair, then they have identical Q-values and optimal policies, and are likely to have the same model parameters.

The fourth assumption is perhaps the strongest, and represents a restriction on the mixing property of the MDPs considered. A similar assumption has been employed in discrete state–action spaces[3, 5, 8]. Intuitively, it ensures that it is possible to go between two regions of state–action space under some policy in a bounded number of steps. This assumption is needed for our algorithm to perform identification of the current task during phase 2. Fortunately there do exist a number of domains which have bounded diameter. For example, many interesting RL domains are episodic. In episodic settings, the diameter can be no more than twice the episode length for any two states that are reachable within one episode from the starting distribution. Also note that in an episodic domain, only the states that are reachable within one episode from the starting state are relevant to the optimal policy and value function.

Our algorithm also depends on the *Q-gap* between distinct optimal Q-functions.

Definition 1. The Q-gap, Γ, is a positive constant that satisfies that for any two MDP clusters[2] M_i, $M_j \in \mathcal{M}$, there exist some state–action pair (s,a) such that $|Q^*_{M_i}(s,a) - Q^*_{M_j}(s,a)| \geq \Gamma$.

Note that according to the third assumption, the *Q-gap* must always be greater than 0. We do assume our algorithm has an estimate of a lower bound on Γ. In many real world domains, we don't know Γ in advance; in this case the lower bound can be set to $\epsilon/2$, since if the Q-functions between two tasks are closer than $\epsilon/2$, the ϵ-optimal policy for one is still an ϵ-optimal policy for the other and the two tasks would be most likely almost identical anyway. However in most cases, Γ would be much larger than ϵ.

Some more definitions used in algorithm are clarified here:

Definition 2. A state-action is known if it has k visited neighbors, which means $L_Q d[(s,a),(s_i,a_i)] \leq \frac{\epsilon(1-\gamma)}{8}$, where $k = O(\frac{1}{\epsilon^2(1-\gamma)^2})$ according to theorem 3.16 in [16]. This kind of knownness is called as ϵ-known. The knownness in phase 1, (Γ, D)-known, is different and will be discussed later.

[1]If we have C clusters of MDPs, where all MDPs in the same cluster have highly similar transition and reward models, then, our results can be extended; our results immediately apply following 3 if MDPs in the i-th cluster (of C clusters), satisfy the following property: for any two MDP M_1, M_2 in cluster i, for any (s,a) pair,

$$|r_{M_1}(s,a) - r_{M_2}(s,a)| < \frac{\epsilon(1-\gamma)}{16}$$

$$\int_S |T_{M_1}(s'|s,a) - T_{M_2}(s'|s,a)| ds' < \frac{\epsilon(1-\gamma)^2}{16}$$

[2]Note that different MDP clusters have distinct Q-functions, given our assumption 3 and lemma 3.

Definition 3. For an MDP $M = < S, A, T, R, \gamma, H, b_0 >$, let K be the set of known state-action pairs. The known MDP $M_K = < K \cup sa_{uk}, T, R, \gamma, H, b_0 >$ is defined as follows. sa_{uk} is an additional s-a pair to denote all the unknown s-a pairs. For state-action pairs in K, $r(s,a) = 0$, and for the sa_{uk} state-action, r$(s,a) = 1$. All the unknown state-action pairs are merged into sa_{uk} and it is an absorbing state-action pair. Transitions to unknown pairs in M are redirected to sa_{uk}, and transitions within K are identical to those defined in the original MDP M.

Definition 4. For a Q-function Q_{M_i}, we use π_{M_i} to denote the greedy policy introduced by Q_{M_i}.

Algorithm 2 Phase 1: Continuous PAC Explore

Require: T_e, L_Q, Γ
Set the neighborhood radius to $\frac{min\{\Gamma/4, 1/24\}}{L_Q}$
while some (s,a) is unknown (see Def.7) **do**
  This is a start of new T_e-step episode.
  Find a T_e-step undiscounted optimistic Q-function Q_{0,T_e} by:
  Initialize: $Q_{T_e,T_e}(s,a) = 0$
  for $t = T_e - 1, \ldots, 0$ **do**
    if (s,a) is known **then**
      Find k-NN of (s,a): $(s_j, a_j, r_j, s_j^{'})_{j=1}^{k}$
      $Q_{t,T_e} = \frac{1}{k}\sum_{j=1}^{k}\left(r_j + \max_a Q_{t+1,T_e}\left(s_j^{'}, a\right) + L_Q d_{ij}\right)$
    else
      $Q_{t,T_e} = (T_e - t)$
  Take greedy policy of $Q_{0,T_e}(s,a)$ for next T_e steps.
  if (s,a) is unknown **then**
    Add (s,a,r,s') to the sample set

4.2 Phase 1

In the first phase, we efficiently explore each task to get a good estimate of their optimal Q-functions. We only need the estimated Q-functions to be (Γ, D) known, which means $O(\Gamma)$ (the precise value is set later in the theory section) within the true Q-function, in order to correctly cluster the tasks. Note that Γ may be much bigger than ϵ so phase 1 may not yet give us an ϵ-optimal policy for the tasks. We extend the PAC-EXPLORE algorithm [8] to continuous spaces while maintaining the same guarantees, and use it to explore (see Algorithm 2). To achieve efficient exploration, we construct a new MDP called *known MDP* (see definition 3). Then we find a T_e-step undiscounted optimistic Q-function on this MDP through value iteration, where the notation Q_{t,T_e} means the T_e-step optimistic function in the tth step. The policy introduced by this Q-function will direct exploration towards the less explored (unknown) state-action pairs. After the Q-function is (Γ, D) known, we then execute C-PACE for remaining steps of the task. The k nearest neighbors are defined by the distance used in the Lipschitz property. Note that the number of tasks in Phase 1 is defined in advance, in order to ensure all underlying C tasks are experienced with high probability.

4.2.1 Clustering and Informative State–action Pairs

At the end of each task in phase 1, we solve the fixed-point equations (equation (1) in [16]) in C-PACE to estimate the optimal Q-function of that task given the data gathered. Our analysis in the next section shows that the distance between the estimated Q-functions and the true optimal Q-functions for each task is no more than $\frac{\Gamma}{4}$. This allows our algorithm to cluster together all tasks whose true optimal Q-function differ by no more than a fixed threshold (defined below). After the clustering completes, all the samples within a cluster are merged to form a single sample set. The algorithm then runs the fixed-point method from C-PACE to estimate the optimal Q-function for each cluster. Note that depending on the amount of experience in the cluster, this estimated function may or may not be ϵ-optimal yet.

Once the algorithm computes an estimated optimal Q-function for each cluster, these functions are used to compute a set of informative state–action pairs.

Definition 5. Given a set of Q-functions, a state-action (s,a) is informative if there exist at least two distinct Q-functions, Q_i and Q_j, such that $|Q_i(s,a) - Q_j(s,a)| \geq \frac{7\Gamma}{8}$.

These informative pairs are the state–action pairs where Q-functions significantly differ, and so distinguish between distinct Q-functions. We will make heavy use of these pairs to identify which cluster new tasks will belong to in phase 2.

Algorithm 3 Phase 2: Continuous Identify

Require: $\Gamma, \epsilon, \bar{C}, H, T_i, n$
Initialize version space: $\mathcal{C} \leftarrow \{1, \ldots, \bar{C}\}$
while $h < H$ **do**
  for $c \in \mathcal{C}$ **do**
    Use algorithm 2 with samples from M_c to find a informative pair (s,a), *s.t.* $\left|Q_{M_i}^{\pi_i}(s,a) - Q_{M_j}^{\pi_j}(s,a)\right| \geq \frac{7\Gamma}{8}$
    if informative pair (s,a) is reached **then**
      Break the loop.
  for $g = \{i, j\}$ **do**
    for $t = 1 \ldots T_i$ **do** (Monte Carlo estimate)
      Run the greedy policy of Q_{M_g}, π_g, for n steps
      $R_{gt} \leftarrow r(s,a) + \sum_{l=1}^{n} \gamma^l r_l, h \leftarrow h + n$
      $\widetilde{D} \leftarrow 1$
      while Haven't returned to (s,a) **do**
        for $c \in \mathcal{C}$ **do**
          Use M_c to create an informative MDP, and try to go back to (s,a) within $12\widetilde{D}\ln\frac{\bar{C}}{\delta}$ steps.
          if get back to (s,a) **then**
            Break the loop.
        $\widetilde{D} \leftarrow 2\widetilde{D}$
    $R_g \leftarrow \frac{1}{T_i}\sum_{t=1}^{T_i} R_{gt}$
    if $\left|R_g - Q_{M_g}(s,a)\right| \geq \frac{\Gamma}{8}$ **then**
      $\mathcal{C} \leftarrow \mathcal{C}\backslash\{g\}$
  if Both i,j haven't been eliminated **then**
    Eliminate the model k with a smaller R_g.
  if Only one group left **then**
    Combine the sample sets and run C-PACE

4.3 Phase 2

After clustering all the tasks from phase 1, we end up with $\widehat{C}$ clusters, each of which consist of a (merged) sample set and an estimated optimal Q-function. In this phase, we try to identify which cluster each new task belongs to, and once we do we can use that cluster's sample set to jumpstart learning – we may even immediately get a near-optimal policy if we have enough data in the cluster's sample set.

Identifying the current task requires some care since we only know that the current task has an optimal Q-function that matches one of the $\widehat{C}$ clusters. Of course, if we compute an approximate Q-function in the current task of sufficient accuracy, that is enough to identify which cluster it belongs to; however by the time we have enough data to achieve that accuracy in computing the Q-function, we will only get a little benefit to leveraging prior samples. This will only reduce the exploration needed to being a function of Γ instead of ϵ, but it will not impact the dependence on the size of the state–action space covering number.

Instead, we will rely on informative pairs for identification. For each task in phase 2, we start with a set of $\widehat{C}$ candidate clusters that the new task potentially belongs to. Then we can use their associated Q-functions to compute the set of informative pairs I; we will need at most one informative pair for every pair of distinct clusters. We then repeatedly visit an informative pair and compute an estimate of its Q-value for the current task. Each informative pair distinguishes between two clusters' Q-functions. Then we will compare the estimate to the two optimal Q-functions to determine which cluster should be eliminated as a candidate. Then we move onto another informative pair to eventually eliminate another candidate. This process is repeated until there is only one candidate left. More details follow.

Given an informative set of pairs, we define an informative MDP for the current task:

Definition 6. For an MDP $M = < S \times A, T, R, \gamma >$, let I be the set of informative state-action pairs. The MDP $M_{inform} = < S \times A \setminus I \cup sa_{inform}, T, R, \gamma >$ is defined in a similar way as known MDP in definition 3, replacing the unknown state-action pairs with informative pairs.

To start, we need to quickly reach an informative pair. The main issue with trying to visit informative pairs quickly is that the identity of the new task is unknown. If we knew the identity, then we could create an M_{inform} based on the associated cluster, and execute the resulting policy. Because of our diameter assumption, this policy will quickly reach the target informative pair. But since we actually don't know the identity of the new task, we need to do something else. What we do is try to use the M_{inform} of every candidate cluster. If we fail to reach the target informative pairs, we just move on and try to use M_{inform} of the next candidate cluster. Since we know that one of candidate cluster is the true cluster, we will eventually use its M_{inform}, and successfully reach the target pair. This will require trying to use the M_{inform} of each candidate cluster at most once. With this process, first we can create M_{inform} for each candidate with all the informative pairs I to try to reach any informative pair. After that, we can create M_{inform} for each candidate with a single target informative pair to try to return to that particular informative pair.

Next, we need to use the informative pair to try to eliminate candidates. Note that an informative (s,a) pair is only guaranteed to be informative for a particular pair of candidates (the pair may actually be informative for more than two candidates, but for simplicity we only consider two). After we reach an informative state-action pair, for example where Q_{M_i} and Q_{M_j} is sufficiently different, we run T_i trajectories of π_{M_i} and π_{M_j} from here (using the previous process to return to the informative pair after each trajectory) for an estimate of this task's Q-value at this pair. This is to test which one of these two Q-functions is different with the current new task's Q-function. Since Q_{M_i} and Q_{M_j} are sufficiently different, we know at least one of them will differ with the current new task's Q-value. If the estimate of the Q-value of the current task is not close to the Q-value computed from its candidate, this candidate will be eliminated. If both policies being tested have estimates that are close enough to what they are supposed to be, we will eliminate the candidate with the smaller computed Q-value. Once we eliminate one or both of these candidates, we pick another informative pair belonging to two other candidates to test. Every informative pair leads to eliminating at least one candidate, so we will eventually result in only one candidate left i.e. a successful identification.

After a successful identification it may immediately result in an ϵ-optimal policy if there are enough samples from the cluster; otherwise the data of the current task is collected and merged with the cluster's data. Later on, after encountering tasks from the same cluster over and over again there will eventually be enough data for an ϵ-optimal policy. Thereafter, every new task will get an ϵ-optimal policy immediately after identification. Since identification does not depend on the covering number of the state-action space, the sample complexity of new tasks will then also no longer depend on the size (covering number) of the state-action space. This is the source of the sample efficiency.

4.4 Motivation for Using Q-functions

In prior work [5], the difference between model parameters (the transition and reward dynamics) is used to distinguish between different tasks and to identify a new task. However complications arise if we try the same approach here due to a continuous state space. The transition function becomes a probability density and is hard to represent. We can parameterize it, but that restricts the structure of the transition function. Alternatively, we can use a nonparametric method such as Gaussian Processes (GPs) like in [7], however that introduces extra computational complexities, as opposed to using a simple table to maintain a Q-function. Also, using a GP results in slower learning for single tasks than using the Q-function based method C-PACE [7]. Our approach of using Q-functions is simpler since the representation is just a table, and this same representation is also used for the policy. The only smoothness assumption is on the Q-function, and not on the model parameters.

Using Q-functions rather than model parameters to cluster also opens a new opportunity. Without assuming that different MDPs have different Q-functions, it may be possible that different MDPs end up having the same Q-function and can be clustered together. However we would no longer be able to identify new tasks quickly. Our identification relies on quickly reaching informative states. Computing these policies to reach informative states requires that the dynamics of the new task resemble the dynamics of the cluster it belongs to. If we allowed different MDPs with the same Q-function to be clustered together, we would no longer be able to guarantee that we can reach an informative state quickly.

5. THEORETICAL GUARANTEES

To start the analysis of the sample complexity, we need some additional assumptions and definitions.

1. Each task has at least $p_{min} > 0$ probability to be drawn in phase 1, and phase 1 has at least $\frac{\ln \bar{C}}{p_{min}\delta}$ tasks.

2. The covering number $\mathcal{N}_{SA}(L_Q, \epsilon)$ is the size of the largest minimal covering set S_c of the state-action space, which means that for any (s, a) there exist k points in S_c, such that for any one of the k points (s_i, a_i): $L_Q d[(s, a), (s_i, a_i)] \leq \epsilon(1-\gamma)$

3. Given an input δ, all tasks in phase 1 and 2 should be executed for more than H_{min} steps, where:

$$H_{min} = O\left(max \left\{ D^2 \ln\left(\frac{\mathcal{N}_{SA}(L_Q, \Gamma)}{\delta} \right), \frac{Q_{max}^2}{\Gamma^2(1-\gamma)^2} \ln\left(\frac{T_1 \mathcal{N}_{SA}(L_Q, \Gamma)}{\delta} \right) \right\} \mathcal{N}_{SA}(L_Q, \Gamma) D \right)$$

The first assumption makes sure we will encounter all distinct tasks in phase 1, and is a common assumption in previous work [5]. The second assumption is to ensure we can sufficiently explore to create good enough estimates of the Q-functions in phase 1. The main PAC bound for our algorithm is described in the theorem below.

THEOREM 1. *For any ϵ and δ, if we run Algorithm 1 for T sequential tasks, each for $H \geq H_{min}$ steps, where H_{min} meets the requirement in the third assumption above. Then the algorithm will select an ϵ-optimal policy on all but at most*

$$O\left(T_1 \max\left\{H_{min}, \min\left\{\zeta_s, H\right\}\right\} + \bar{C}\zeta_s + (T - T_1) \frac{Q_{max}^2 \bar{C}}{\Gamma^2} \ln \frac{\bar{C}}{\delta} \left(\bar{C} D \ln \frac{\bar{C}}{\delta} + \log_\gamma \Gamma\right)\right)$$

steps, with probability $1-\delta$. ζ_s is the sample complexity of a single task C-PACE algorithm, which is at most $O\left(\frac{Q_{max}^2}{\epsilon^2(1-\gamma)^2} \ln\left(\frac{1}{\epsilon(1-\gamma)}\right) \ln\left(\frac{\mathcal{N}_{SA}(L_Q,\epsilon)}{\delta}\right) \mathcal{N}_{SA}(L_Q, \epsilon)\right)$.

T_1 is the number of tasks in phase 1. Before going into the proofs, we are going to examine the improvement in sample complexity of our algorithm over a single-task algorithm.

First, consider the sample complexity of phase 1, which is the first term of the bound. We want to compare H_{min} and ζ_s. If H_{min} is less than or equal to ζ_s, then the single-task complexity ζ_s dominates and we do no worse than the single task case. In most cases, $T_1 < \mathcal{N}_{SA}(L_Q, \Gamma)$, so H_{min} can be simplified to

$$O\left(max \left\{ D^2, \frac{Q_{max}^2}{\Gamma^2(1-\gamma)^2} \right\} \ln\left(\frac{\mathcal{N}_{SA}(L_Q, \Gamma)}{\delta} \right) D \mathcal{N}_{SA}(L_Q, \Gamma) \right)$$

Note that the $\mathcal{N}_{SA}(L_Q, \epsilon)$ term for C-PACE can be much larger than the $\mathcal{N}_{SA}(L_Q, \Gamma)$ term for H_{min} due to Γ being larger than ϵ. If D is at most $O\left(\frac{1}{\epsilon^{\frac{2}{3}}}\right)$ and $\frac{D}{\Gamma^2}$ is at most $O\left(\frac{1}{\epsilon^2}\right)$, then the sample complexity of phase 1 is no more than C-PACE.

Now we compare the total sample complexity of our algorithm with a single-task algorithm. Even in the worst case, the total sample complexity of our algorithm is about

$$\tilde{O}\left((\bar{C} + T_1 D)\zeta_s + (T - T_1) \frac{\bar{C}^2 D Q_{max}^2}{\Gamma^2} \right)$$

Since in most cases $\bar{C} << \mathcal{N}_{SA}$ and $\bar{C} + T_1 D$ is constant as T increases, assuming again that $\frac{D}{\Gamma^2}$ is at most $O\left(\frac{1}{\epsilon^2}\right)$ we can get a notable improvement over single task algorithms whose sample complexity is linear with respect to $\mathcal{N}_{SA}$.

Now we start to prove the theorem. We firstly divide the suboptimal steps of our algorithm into 3 parts, and bound each part. The first part consists of steps in phase 1; the second part consists of steps in phase 2 before identification succeeds; and the third part consists of suboptimal steps after identification succeeds. Besides analyzing the sample complexity, we also need to prove the accuracy of clustering and the correctness of identification. Before that, we introduce some supporting lemmas. Proofs, when omitted, are provided in the supplement.[3]

5.1 Lemmas

PROPOSITION 1. *(lemma 4.5 in [9]) There are at most $k\mathcal{N}_{SA}(L_Q, \Gamma)$ number of visits to unknown state-action pairs in Algorithm 2, where a known state-action pair means it has k visited neighbors within a distance of $\frac{\Gamma(1-\gamma)}{8L_Q}$.*

PROPOSITION 2. *In algorithm 2, denoting exact Bellman operator by B and the upper bound of Q-value by Q_{max}, if*

$$\frac{4Q_{max}^2}{\epsilon^2} \ln\left(\frac{4\mathcal{N}_{SA}(L_Q, \Gamma)}{\delta}\right) \leq k \leq \frac{4\mathcal{N}_{SA}(L_Q, \Gamma)}{\delta}$$

and the radius of the neighborhood is no more than $\frac{\Gamma}{2L_Q}$, then w.p. $1-\delta/2$, for all known (s, a) (Known is defined in proposition 1), we have for any $t < T_e$:

$$|Q_{t,T_e}(s, a) - BQ_{t+1,T_e}(s, a)| \leq \Gamma$$

where T_e is the finite horizon length in algorithm 2.

PROPOSITION 3. *Assume $R \in [0, 1]$. Suppose in Algorithm 2, $|Q_{t,T_e}(s, a) - BQ_{t+1,T_e}(s, a)| \leq \Gamma$, π is a T_e-step greedy policy introduced by Q_{t,T_e}, and Q_{t,T_e}^{π} is the Q value of this policy. Then $\forall$ known (s, a) (Known is defined in proposition 1), $t<T$, $\left|Q_{t,T_e}^{*}(s, a) - Q_{t,T_e}^{\pi}(s, a)\right| \leq 2(T_e - t)\Gamma$, and*

$$\left|V_{t,T_e}^{*}(s) \leq V_{t,T_e}^{\pi}(s)\right| \leq 2(T_e - t)\Gamma$$

Before we introduce the following lemmas, we need to introduce a new concept of knownness, (Γ, D)-known.

Definition 7. A state-action pair is (Γ, D)-known when it has at least

$$max \left\{ D^2 \ln\left(\frac{\mathcal{N}_{SA}(L_Q, \Gamma)}{\delta} \right), \frac{Q_{max}^2}{\Gamma^2(1-\gamma)^2} \ln\left(\frac{T_1 \mathcal{N}_{SA}(L_Q, \Gamma)}{\delta} \right) \right\}$$

visited neighbors within a distance of $\frac{\Gamma(1-\gamma)}{8L_Q}$.

LEMMA 1. *After no more than $O\left(\left(k\mathcal{N}_{SA}(L_Q, \Gamma) + \ln \frac{1}{\delta}\right) D\right)$ steps of Algorithm 2, every state-action pair will have at least k visited neighbors, with probability of $1-\delta$, where $k \geq k_{min} = O\left(D^2 \ln\left(\frac{\mathcal{N}_{SA}(L_Q,\Gamma)}{\delta}\right)\right)$, $k \leq k_{max} = O\left(\frac{\mathcal{N}_{SA}(L_Q,\Gamma)}{\delta}\right)$.*

PROOF. (Sketch) Following the three proposition above, this proof is similar to the proof of Theorem 2 in [8]. The key intuition here is to construct a known MDP and try to achieve an ϵ-optimal policy in this MDP, directing exploration to unknown state-action pairs quickly. □

[3]http://cs.cmu.edu/ ebrun/pac_continuous_multitask_aamas2016.pdf

LEMMA 2. *(lemma 1 in [5]) If* $T_1 \geq \frac{\ln \frac{\bar{C}}{\delta}}{p_{min}}$ *then w.p.* $1-\delta$*, all distinct MDPs will be encountered in phase 1.*

LEMMA 3. *If* M_1 *and* M_2 *are 2 MDPs s.t. for any (s,a),*

$$|r_{M_1}(s,a) - r_{M_2}(s,a)| < \frac{\epsilon(1-\gamma)}{2}$$

$$\int_S |T_{M_1}(s'|s,a) - T_{M_2}(s'|s,a)| \mathrm{d}s' < \frac{\epsilon(1-\gamma)^2}{2}$$

then the optimal Q-functions for M_1 *and* M_2*,* Q_{M_1} *and* Q_{M_2}*, satisfy that for any (s,a) pair*

$$|Q_{M_1}(s,a) - Q_{M_2}(s,a)| < \epsilon$$

This lemma allows us to relax the assumption of C distinct tasks to C fuzzy clusters. It shows if the tasks within a cluster are similar enough, the Q functions would be viewed as the same, in the sense of ϵ-accuracy.

LEMMA 4. *If all tasks in phase 1 are run for at least* H_{min} *steps, with probability* $1-\delta$*, the following holds:*

1. *For all tasks, any state-action pair is* (Γ, D)*-known.*
2. *Tasks in phase 1 will be clustered correctly w.h.p..*
3. *For any cluster, the max-norm distance between the approximate Q-function and the true optimal Q-function for any task in this cluster is at most* $\frac{5\Gamma}{16}$.

LEMMA 5. *Assume every state-action pair is* (Γ, D)*-known. Then given any start state and desired state-action pair, it is possible to visit the desired state-action pair's neighborhood in no more than* $\widetilde{O}(D)$ *steps with high probability.*

PROOF. Firstly, we construct an MDP M_{inform} such that the desired state-action pairs have unit reward and all others have 0 reward. The desired pair is a self-loop and other transition probabilities are inherited from the true MDP dynamics. We know which point is desired, so we can modify the original samples to become samples in the new MDP M_{inform}. Because now every pair is (Γ, D)-known, so we have $O(D^2)$ samples in every state-action's neighborhood in this M_{inform}. Following a similar analysis of lemma 1, we could find a policy who will reach the desired region within $3D$ steps w.p. $\frac{1}{4}$. Then after $3D \log_{\frac{3}{4}} \delta$ steps the policy could reach the desired region with probability of $1-\delta$. □

LEMMA 6. *When we face an unknown task in phase 2, we could reach any desired state-action pair within* $O(\bar{C}D \ln \frac{\bar{C}}{\delta})$ *steps with probability* $1 - \frac{\delta}{\bar{C}}$.

PROOF. First, consider the case where we know the diameter D. The unknown task must be one of the $\bar{C}$ tasks from phase 1. Our algorithm tries to run each policy in $3D \ln \frac{\bar{C}}{\delta}$ steps to the desired state-action pair using the samples from one of the $\bar{C}$ tasks, thus lemma 6 holds with probability $1 - \frac{\bar{C}}{\delta}$. By trying all policies from the $\bar{C}$ tasks, we will encounter the one policy that corresponds to the same task and reach the desired region with high probability.

If we don't know the diameter, we could use the doubling trick to find an upper bound on D without an increase in the sample complexity. First we try the whole process with $\widetilde{D} = 1$. If we fail, we double the $\widetilde{D}$ and begin a new trial. When $\widetilde{D}$ is bigger than the true value of D, the rest of the analysis is the same as when we know the true diameter. □

LEMMA 7. *If* T_i *in algorithm 3 is at least* $O\left(\frac{Q^2_{max}}{\Gamma^2} \ln \frac{\bar{C}}{\delta}\right)$ *and n is at least* $O(\log_\gamma \Gamma)$*, we could compute an approximate Q value of policy* π *over current task* M'*:* $\widehat{Q}^{\pi_i}_{M'}(s,a) = R_i$ *such that for any* (s,a)*,* $\left|\widehat{Q}^{\pi_i}_{M'}(s,a) - Q^{\pi_i}_{M'}(s,a)\right| \leq \frac{\Gamma}{16}$ *with probability* $1 - \frac{\delta}{\bar{C}}$.

PROOF. (Sketch) The key insight to prove this lemma is that R_i is the empirical mean of discounted rewards ignoring the tail rewards, so we could use concentration measures to bound the difference of R_i with $Q^{\pi_i}_{M'}(s,a)$, which implies T_i should be at least $O\left(\frac{Q^2_{max}}{\Gamma^2} \ln \frac{\bar{C}}{\delta}\right)$. □

LEMMA 8. *If both model* M_i *and* M_j *haven't been eliminated by* $\left|R_g - Q_{M_g}(s,a)\right| \geq \frac{\Gamma}{8}$ *in algorithm 3, then the true model would have a greater* R_g *with high probability.*

PROOF. (Sketch) Without loss of generality, we assume M_i is the true model M'. The condition in the lemma implies $\widehat{Q}^{\pi_i}_{M_i}(s,a)$ is very close to $Q^{\pi_i}_{M_i}(s,a)$ and $\widehat{Q}^{\pi_j}_{M_i}(s,a)$ is very close to $Q^{\pi_j}_{M_j}(s,a)$. Note that π_i is a nearly optimal policy and the difference of $Q^{\pi_i}_{M_i}(s,a)$ with $Q^{\pi_j}_{M_j}(s,a)$ is $O(\Gamma)$ according to the Q-gap assumption. So the $\widehat{Q}^{\pi_j}_{M_i}(s,a)$ would be no more than $\widehat{Q}^{\pi_i}_{M_i}(s,a)$, otherwise it would exceed the optimal Q value. □

LEMMA 9. *After* $O\left(\frac{Q^2_{max}}{\Gamma^2}\bar{C} \ln \frac{\bar{C}}{\delta} \left(\bar{C}D \ln \frac{\bar{C}}{\delta} + \log_\gamma \Gamma\right)\right)$ *steps in phase 2, we could correctly identify the new task w.p.* $1-\delta$.

PROOF. (Sketch) This lemma straightforward follows from lemma 6 and 8. □

5.2 Proof of Main Theorem

PROOF. Recall that we divide the sample complexity into 3 parts. We will show the bound of each part to prove the whole sample complexity.

The first part consists of the steps in phase 1. H_{min} is the lower bound of steps we need to run algorithm 2 in phase 1. After we finish the exploration, we can run C-PACE for remaining steps of the episode $(H - H_{min})$. Note that the unknown state-action pairs of algorithm 2 is actually a subset of the unknown state-action pairs in ϵ-known C-PACE (since $\Gamma \geq \epsilon$ so more states are unknown under the threshold of ϵ-known). So we could view algorithm 2 as part of the initial exploration done in C-PACE. The total sample complexity in phase 1 would be no more than $max\{H_{min}, min(\zeta_s, H)\}$.

The second part consists of the identification during phase 2. Following from lemma 9 we need

$$O\left((T - T_1)\frac{Q^2_{max}\bar{C}}{\Gamma^2} \ln \frac{\bar{C}}{\delta} \left(\bar{C}D \ln \frac{\bar{C}}{\delta} + \log_\gamma \Gamma\right)\right)$$

samples in $T - T_1$ tasks in phase 2.

The third part is after the identification in phase 2. If the cluster has gathered enough samples we will get an ϵ-optimal policy immediately. If not, we still need to gather more. But since the samples are gathered across all the tasks in one cluster and the number of clusters is at most $\bar{C}$, this only yields an additional sample complexity of $\bar{C}\zeta_s$. Note that to run the C-PACE algorithm, we set all $\epsilon_s, \epsilon_T, \epsilon_d, \epsilon_K$ in C-PACE to $\frac{\epsilon(1-\gamma)}{8}$ so that we could get an ϵ-optimal policy. □

6. EXPERIMENTS

Though our primary contribution is to prove online multi-task RL enables a lower sample complexity in later continuous-state tasks, we also tested its empirical performance on a popular simulated domain, the spring mass damper system.

This domain is characterized by 3 parameters: the spring constant k, the damping constant d and the mass m. The ranges are: $k \in [1, 10]$ $d \in [0.01, 0.2]$ $m \in [0.5, 5]$, which are mirrored from [1]. The state is parameterized by the position and velocity of the mass, and the action is a horizontal force on the mass. Due to the complexity of performing a maximization over a continuous set of actions, we considered a discrete action set of $\{-10, -1, -0.1, 0, 0.1, 1, 10\}$. [4] The transition dynamics are characterized by an ODE system and simulated by the Euler method in our experiment.

The goal is to control the mass starting at $(1, 0)$ to stay in state $(0, 0)$, and the reward is the negative $l2$-norm distance between current state and the goal.

We performed simulation rounds, where each round consists of 50 tasks. Tasks are generated by randomly sampling from three distinct spring-mass MDPs (k,d,m). Each task consists of 100 episodes with each episode having 150 steps: these settings were informed by recent work[1]. We repeat this process for 40 rounds to assess average performance across a series of tasks.

We compare against 3 other baselines. The first is single-task C-PACE: the PAC RL algorithm C-PACE is run for each task independently, yielding no information sharing across tasks. In the second baseline, C-PACE (mixture of all MDPs), is executed across all tasks without distinguishing them. This is a naive form of transfer that treats all tasks as identical. Finally, our third baseline is the state-of-the-art online policy gradient method for multi-task RL, PG-ELLA[1]. PG-ELLA learns a shared basis set across different tasks. Unlike our work, PG-ELLA assumes as input the true identification of each task. PG-ELLA runs 5000 episodes rather than 100 for each task. That's because they need more samples to update policy parameters.

The considered algorithms all have input parameters. For C-PACE (and the parts of our algorithm that use C-PACE), we let $k = 1$ since this domain is deterministic. The Lipschitz constant is set to 0.1, and Q_{max} is set to zero. For our algorithm, we set the number of tasks in phase 1 to 15 according to Lemma 2 with uniform task sampling and $\delta = 0.02$. The Q-gap Γ is set to 2. The number of trajectories we run in phase 2 to approximate the Q value, T_i, is set to 1 because the domain is deterministic. For PG-ELLA, the learning rate is selected automatically in their code.

Figure 1 shows the average reward for each of the 50 tasks for the 4 algorithms. As expected, our approach performs comparably to single task C-PACE in phase 1, with a slight loss in performance because we try to fully explore the state–action space. However our algorithm significantly improves in phase 2, successfully accelerating learning by identifying tasks quickly. In phase 2, the gap between our method and single-task C-PACE implies the superiority of transferring samples from previous tasks, which also confirms the analysis of sample complexity in an empirical way. For single task C-PACE could not collect enough samples to converge

[4]For computational efficiency and to focus on the key impact of transferring knowledge from multiple tasks, we chose this discrete action space. Alternatively we could use the Lipschitz constant to define a discretization.

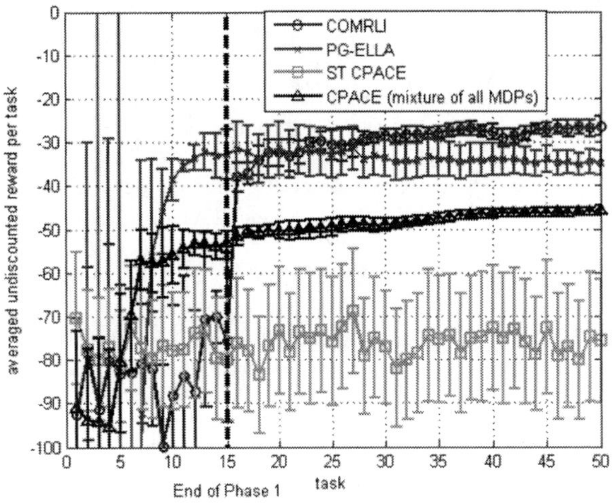

Figure 1: Averaged reward per task. The bar is standard deviation over 40 rounds.

in just one task, its standard deviation is quite big as, as it was shown in the figure. Our algorithm is also better than the C-PACE algorithm that treats all tasks the same, which shows the benefit of learning a separate optimal policy per distinct task instead of a single policy for all tasks.

During phase 2 our algorithm exceeds the performance of PG-ELLA. Note that PG-ELLA uses the first several tasks to learn a shared basis, which we show in the figure, but is omitted in the graphs of their paper. We consider this quite encouraging, since PG-ELLA is provided the identity of each task, compared to our approach which does not have that information. Of course, our algorithm is operating in a domain in which tasks have Q functions that are quite well separated, as the Q-gap assumption.

These preliminary results suggest that our approach can perform well in standard benchmark simulation, with a significant advantage over single task algorithms and naive transfer, and equivalent or slightly improved performance over a state-of-the-art method, PG-ELLA. As our approach has rigorous guarantees on sample complexity, which PG-ELLA lacks, these empirical results are quite encouraging.

7. CONCLUSION AND FUTURE WORK

We have introduced the COMRLI algorithm, a PAC RL algorithm for learning across a series of tasks drawn from a set of continuous-state, discrete action Markov decision processes. To our knowledge, COMRLI is the first algorithm for multi-task learning in continuous state RL problems whose bound on the sample complexity can be significantly smaller in later tasks, and is independent of the covering number for the state–action space. This shows that transferring knowledge in continuous-state RL can provably reduce the amount of experience needed to make good decisions. We also provide preliminary but encouraging evidence that our approach may be helpful in practice, showing good performance in one benchmark domain against a state-of-the-art policy gradient method for multi-task RL.

8. ACKNOWLEDGEMENTS

This work was supported by NSF CAREER award #1350984.

REFERENCES

[1] H. B. Ammar, E. Eaton, P. Ruvolo, and M. Taylor. Online multi-task learning for policy gradient methods. In T. Jebara and E. P. Xing, editors, *Proceedings of the 31st International Conference on Machine Learning (ICML)*, pages 1206–1214. JMLR Workshop and Conference Proceedings, 2014.

[2] H. B. Ammar, R. Tutunov, and E. Eaton. Safe policy search for lifelong reinforcement learning with sublinear regret. *The Journal of Machine Learning Research (JMLR)*, 2015.

[3] P. Auer, T. Jaksch, and R. Ortner. Near-optimal regret bounds for reinforcement learning. In *Advances in Neural Information Processing Systems*, pages 89–96, 2009.

[4] H. Bou-Ammar, J. M. Luna, E. Eaton, and P. Ruvolo. Autonomous cross-domain knowledge transfer in lifelong policy gradient reinforcement learning. In *International Joint Conference on Artificial Intelligence (IJCAI)*, 2015.

[5] E. Brunskill and L. Li. Sample complexity of multi-task reinforcement learning. In *Conference on Uncertainty in Artificial Intelligence*, 2013.

[6] R. Grande, T. Walsh, and J. How. Sample efficient reinforcement learning with gaussian processes. In *Proceedings of the 31st International Conference on Machine Learning (ICML-14)*, pages 1332–1340, 2014.

[7] R. Grande, T. Walsh, and J. How. Sample efficient reinforcement learning with gaussian processes. In T. Jebara and E. P. Xing, editors, *Proceedings of the 31st International Conference on Machine Learning (ICML-14)*, pages 1332–1340. JMLR Workshop and Conference Proceedings, 2014.

[8] Z. Guo and E. Brunskill. Concurrent pac rl. In *AAAI Conference on Artificial Intelligence*, 2015.

[9] S. Kakade, M. Kearns, and J. Langford. Exploration in metric state spaces. In *ICML*, volume 3, pages 306–312, 2003.

[10] S. M. Kakade et al. *On the sample complexity of reinforcement learning*. PhD thesis, University of London, 2003.

[11] M. Kearns and S. Singh. Near-optimal reinforcement learning in polynomial time. *Machine Learning*, 49(2-3):209–232, 2002.

[12] A. Lazaric and M. Restelli. Transfer from multiple mdps. In *Advances in Neural Information Processing Systems*, pages 1746–1754, 2011.

[13] R. Liu and K. R. Koedinger. Variations in learning rate: Student classification based on systematic residual error patterns across practice opportunities.

[14] T. A. Mann and Y. Choe. Directed exploration in reinforcement learning with transferred knowledge. In *EWRL*, pages 59–76, 2012.

[15] S. Nikolaidis, R. Ramakrishnan, K. Gu, and J. Shah. Efficient model learning from joint-action demonstrations for human-robot collaborative tasks. In *Proceedings of the Tenth Annual ACM/IEEE International Conference on Human-Robot Interaction*, pages 189–196. ACM, 2015.

[16] J. Pazis and R. Parr. Pac optimal exploration in continuous space markov decision processes. In *AAAI Conference on Artificial Intelligence*. Citeseer, 2013.

[17] M. E. Taylor and P. Stone. Transfer learning for reinforcement learning domains: A survey. *The Journal of Machine Learning Research*, 10:1633–1685, 2009.

Exploration from Demonstration for Interactive Reinforcement Learning

Kaushik Subramanian
College of Computing
Georgia Tech
Atlanta, GA 30332
ksubrama@cc.gatech.edu

Charles L. Isbell Jr.
College of Computing
Georgia Tech
Atlanta, GA 30332
isbell@cc.gatech.edu

Andrea L. Thomaz
Electrical and Computer Engineering
University of Texas at Austin
Austin, TX 78701
athomaz@ece.utexas.edu

ABSTRACT

Reinforcement Learning (RL) has been effectively used to solve complex problems given careful design of the problem and algorithm parameters. However standard RL approaches do not scale particularly well with the size of the problem and often require extensive engineering on the part of the designer to minimize the search space. To alleviate this problem, we present a model-free policy-based approach called Exploration from Demonstration (EfD) that uses human demonstrations to guide search space exploration. We use statistical measures of RL algorithms to provide feedback to the user about the agent's uncertainty and use this to solicit targeted demonstrations useful from the agent's perspective. The demonstrations are used to learn an exploration policy that actively guides the agent towards important aspects of the problem. We instantiate our approach in a gridworld and a popular arcade game and validate its performance under different experimental conditions. We show how EfD scales to large problems and provides convergence speed-ups over traditional exploration and interactive learning methods.

1. INTRODUCTION

Reinforcement Learning (RL) [36] is the field of research focused on solving sequential decision-making tasks modeled as Markov Decision Processes. Researchers have shown RL to be successful at solving a variety of problems like computer games (Backgammon [39], Atari games [26]), robot tasks (soccer [34], helicopter control [1]) and system operations (inventory management [16]); however, in general, standard RL approaches do not scale well with the size of the problem and often require extensive engineering on the part of the designer to minimize the search space. The reason this problem arises is that RL approaches rely on obtaining samples useful for learning the underlying structure without always using smart methods to explore the problem. In RL literature this is related to balancing the exploration-exploitation tradeoff - a central problem in Reinforcement Learning. Existing methods either use a fixed (uniformly random) policy or value-based metrics [6, 35] that either result in redundant exploration and/or have prohibitively expensive sample complexity. In this work we tackle the problem of smart exploration in RL, by using human interaction. We present a model-free policy-based approach called Exploration from Demonstration (EfD) that serves to *bias an RL agent's exploration to cover the search space effectively.*

In designing an exploration policy for sequential decision-making problems, it is important to help the agent reach parts of the search space that are necessary to model in order to solve the problem. These include guiding the agent towards stochastic regions of the problem or regions of high reward for example. To facilitate exploration in these parts of the domain, we utilize statistical measures of the learning algorithm. We pose the optimization function as a linear regression problem and use relevant measures [27] to help identify *influential* regions. Such an approach has the advantage of learning to explore the problem from the agent's perspective while taking into account the underlying representation, the RL algorithm as well as the problem definition. We solicit interaction from an oracle (human or simulated) to acquire demonstrations that lead the agent towards these *influential* regions. We instantiate our approach on a gridworld and a popular arcade game (Frogger) and show how our policy-based approach is able to solve long horizon problems using exploratory demonstrations while outperforming traditional exploration and interactive learning methods.

2. RELATED WORK

There has been extensive work related to exploration in RL. With regard to the approach presented in this paper, we broadly categorize the existing work into two aspects - automatic exploration in RL and interactive machine learning. We present details on the related work in these fields to provide context to our approach.

2.1 Automatic Exploration in RL

Rmax [31] is an automatic approach introduced to perform exploration using the idea of optimism in the face of uncertainty. The approach performs well in practice, however R-max scales exponentially in the number of state variables which makes it intractable for sufficiently large problems. There are several value-based like UCB [6] and others [24, 7, 11] and model-based methods [35, 29, 18, 19], studied in the context of multi-arm bandits, that perform effective exploration by maintaining statistics about changes in the value function and the number of times state-action pairs have been visited. While successful in smaller domains, these

Appears in: *Proceedings of the 15th International Conference on Autonomous Agents and Multiagent Systems (AAMAS 2016), J. Thangarajah, K. Tuyls, C. Jonker, S. Marsella (eds.), May 9–13, 2016, Singapore.*

approaches run into sample complexity issues when dealing with the high-dimensional long horizon domains we aim to solve.

A smart exploration method was proposed by Gehring and Precup [14] which uses the residual (TD error) as a reward for a Q-function, whose implied policy is then used for exploration. The intuition behind this approach being that state-action pairs that have high residuals should be visited and tried more often. This method relies on stable estimates of the residual. We adapt a version of this approach in our experiments. Using an internal reward function [9] is an interesting approach to exploration in RL. In this method, a user is required to design a reward function for skill learning which is often non-trivial. While the authors provide empirical results on small-sized domains, the idea presented is promising and warrants further exploration. An approach closely related to work presented in this paper is that of Active RL [13] where the authors model the problem as a POMDP. They model the sensitivities of the policy to the unknown transition and reward function and build exploration strategies focusing on these aspects of the problem. This method relies on using Newtons method to solve the problem till convergence (which cannot be guaranteed) and they need to solve the MDP numerous times to test the sensitivity. The work most closely related to our work is one authored by Akiyama et al. [3] where they leverage concepts of least squares approaches to guide exploration in policy iteration methods. The main difference is that the approach they design requires the problems to have certain properties with respect to the reward distribution and as such it is not directly comparable.

2.2 Interactive Machine Learning

There exists is a wide variety of work in the field of Interactive Machine Learning, namely Learning by Demonstration [4], Imitation Learning [30], Policy Shaping [17] and TAMER [22]. Work by Knox and Stone [22, 23] has shown that a general improvement to learning from human feedback is possible if it is used to directly modify the action selection mechanism of the Reinforcement Learning algorithm. Although both approaches use human feedback to modify an agent's exploration policy, they still treat human feedback as either a reward or a value. In our work, we use human interaction to directly learn a policy.

Active Reward Learning [10] has been used to learn a reward function from human feedback and use that in an RL algorithm. They use the human to provide input on task executions - a score to the execution - that they then smooth using Gaussian Processes and Bayesian Optimization. Reward function design in general is known to be a hard problem as there are always possibilities of loops in the learned policy. A paper similar in theme to the work in this paper is one on active imitation learning by state queries [20]. The authors present an approach where the human interacts with the agent by giving a optimal action in a specific state or by saying that the state is bad. The query-states are chosen by a query-by-committee approach based on Bayesian Active Learning. In their approach, they assume the learner has access to a simulator of the MDP and also do not explicitly handle the case where humans provide a bad state response.

In other works, rather than have the human input be a reward shaping input, the human provides demonstrations of the optimal policy. Several papers have shown how the policy information in human demonstrations can be used for inverse optimal control [28, 2], for teaching [8], to seed an agent's exploration [5, 38], and in some cases be used entirely in place of exploration [21, 33]. DAgger [32] is no-regret online learning approach used for supervised learning. The method learns from training data and then executes the learned model. For every mistake made, the human demonstrator provides more examples in that space. These examples are appended to the training set and the learner is retrained. While it is not strictly an RL approach, it is mainly providing examples useful for a supervised learner. We note here that all of the methods presented here require/assume the human provides optimal information which is not necessary in our approach.

3. BACKGROUND AND PRELIMINARIES

Reinforcement Learning (RL) defines a class of algorithms for solving problems modeled as a Markov Decision Process (MDP). An MDP can be represented as a tuple $M = \langle S, A, \mathcal{T}, R, \gamma \rangle$ with states S, actions A, transition function $\mathcal{T} : S \times A \mapsto \Pr[S]$, reward function $R : S \times A \mapsto [R_{\min}, R_{\max}]$, and discount factor $\gamma \mapsto [0, 1]$. A policy $\pi : S \mapsto \Pr[A]$ defines the probability of selecting an action in a state. For a given MDP, a Q-function $Q^\pi(s, a)$ represents the *expected long-term reward* of taking action a in state s, and following policy π thereafter. Mathematically, the Q-function is computed as

$$Q^\pi(s,a) = R(s,a) + \gamma \sum_{s'} \mathcal{T}(s,a,s') \sum_{a'} \pi(s',a') Q^\pi(s',a') \tag{1}$$

The optimal action-value function is $Q^*(s,a) = \max_\pi Q^\pi(s,a)$, and the solution to an MDP is any optimal policy π^*, which maximizes the expected reward for every state.

In this paper we use Q-learning with linear function approximation [37]. The Q-function is represented as a linear function of state-action features, $Q(s,a) = \phi(s,a)^T\theta$. Assuming $\phi(s)$ are the features used to represent the states in an MDP, we obtain $\phi(s,a)$ by duplicating the features $\phi(s)$ for all actions and only activate the ones for the action under consideration. For example if $|A| = 4$, $\phi(s,3) = [\mathbf{0}, \mathbf{0}, \phi(s), \mathbf{0}]^T$. A set of transitions made by the RL agent from a starting state to any terminal state comprises a single episode. For every transition made by the agent in the form $\langle s, a, r, s' \rangle$, where r is the reward obtained for taking action a in state s and transitioning to s', the Q-learning algorithm updates its weight vector, θ using first-order gradient methods in the following manner:

$$\begin{aligned} \delta &= r + \gamma \max_{a' \in A} [\phi(s',a')^T\theta] - \phi(s,a)^T\theta \\ \theta &= \theta + \alpha\, \delta\, \phi(s,a) \end{aligned} \tag{2}$$

Here $\alpha \mapsto [0,1]$ is the learning rate. The error, δ is the Temporal Difference (TD) error (also loosely referred to as Bellman error). The algorithm, while not guaranteed to converge in the general case, is found to perform well in practice.

Exploration in RL is commonly achieved using two methods: ϵ-greedy and softmax action selection. In ϵ-greedy action selection, exploration is performed by uniformly sampling a random action with probability ϵ and the current best action (greedy action selection) with probability $1 - \epsilon$. The choice of ϵ is left to the designer. In some cases, a decay schedule is used where the value of ϵ is decayed over time as the agent gains more domain experience. Softmax action selection takes a more informed approach to exploration. Instead of sampling a random action, the actions are weighted according to their respective Q-value estimates and sampled from the resulting distribution. The most common implementations use a Boltzmann distribution in the following manner: $\pi^B = \frac{e^{Q(s,a)/\tau}}{\sum_{a=1}^{|A|} Q(s,a)/\tau}$ where τ is a positive temperature parameter. A higher temperature value results in a more uniform distribution while a lower value results in greedy action selection.

4. APPROACH

In this section we describe an interactive approach to exploration in reinforcement learning using statistical properties relevant to the underlying learning algorithm. We outline properties of exploration policies, statistical measures useful for this purpose and how these measures can be used to solicit interaction that drives the agent's exploration.

4.1 Exploration Policies

For sequential decision-making problems, exploration policies are used to guide the agent to different parts of the search space so as to obtain good estimates of the value function while covering as much of the state-action space as possible. There are a number of factors affecting this exploration such as the dynamics of the domain, the sparsity of rewards, the size of the state-action space and the problem horizon (steps to goal). In addition to these properties, a subtle but important aspect of exploration that is implicit in existing methods is that exploration policies are not strictly stationary. As the agent gathers more information about the world, the exploration policy changes to accommodate the learned model.

Traditional methods, as explained earlier, explore using a variety of methods ranging from a uniformly random policy to value-based heuristics. These methods are prone to redundant exploration and (in some cases) expensive sample requirements. The idea of inefficient exploration also applies to methods involving human interaction, as human data is often limited to specific regions of the search space while relying on the learning algorithm to generalize effectively. To account for the characteristics of exploration policies while overcoming the limitations of existing methods, we present a policy-based approach to exploration. We solicit demonstrations based on the agent's uncertainty about its model to guide the agent to cover the search space more efficiently. For a given MDP, model uncertainty arises from a combination of stochastic elements in the domain (transition and reward function) and insufficiently explored states and actions. Keeping this in mind, we investigate properties of relevant RL algorithms and select measures that serve to characterize the model uncertainty with the goal of designing effective exploration policies.

In our work we use Q-learning with linear function approximation which uses gradient methods to perform optimization. The loss function used is akin to to minimizing the squared loss of the Bellman error [15]. Using this information, we use statistical properties of analogous methods that have been well-studied, like linear regression or least squares, to understand the impact of each data point or observation on the learning agent's model.

4.2 Statistical Measures

In order to understand the agent's model uncertainty, we review statistical analysis of linear regression methods [27] to find measures useful for our purposes. In linear regression problems, input observations can be scored by their *influence* to measure the effect they have on the learned model. A high influence score points towards observations that merit further investigation. Influence is computed as a combination of two measures: Leverage and Discrepancy. Leverage is a measure of how far a specific observation is from the convex hull of known observations. It helps recognize outliers. Discrepancy is related to how much an observation contributes towards model error. From the perspective of exploration in RL, these measures help to identify parts of the state-action space that have not been explored (using Leverage) and observations that lead to high model error (using Discrepancy). A key insight into using these type of measures for RL is that the data the agent trains on does not contain any outliers as every observation made by the agent, by interacting with the domain, is relevant to solving the MDP. This indicates that there is essentially no data to be discarded. We hypothesize that an RL agent that actively explores the observations that have high leverage and high discrepancy, i.e. overall high influence, will lead to more efficient exploration to solve the MDP.

In order to utilize these statistical measures we explicitly set up the problem as a linear set of equations that correspond to the standard form, $X\beta = y$. An RL agent is solving the MDP to optimize the function, $Q(s,a) = R(s,a) + \gamma \max_{a'} Q(s',a')$ where $Q(s,a) = \phi(s,a)^T\theta$. It is straightforward to see that the left-hand side of the optimization function, $Q(s,a)$ or $\phi(s,a)^T\theta$ takes the place of $X\beta$ and the right-hand side forms y. The input data for our approach comes from transitions of the RL agent as it is attempting to solve the problem. The state-action features, $\phi(s,a)$ observed by the agent during transitions are used to populate the rows of the data matrix, X ($n \times k$ for n observations and k features). Given this formulation we define the statistical measures useful for exploration.

4.2.1 *Leverage*

Leverage is a measure useful to determine how well the state-action space has been covered as it detects outliers in the data. Given independent variables, X, we compute leverage, h using the hat matrix, H as follows [27]:

$$H = X(X^TX)^{-1}X^T \tag{3}$$

The hat matrix maps the vector of dependent variables (y) to the vector of fitted values, $\hat{y} = Hy$. The diagonal elements of the hat matrix, h_{ii} are the leverages, which describe the influence each dependent variable value has on the fitted value for observation i. Leverage values are in the range $[0, 1]$. A high value indicates that the observation is an outlier and vice versa. A fixed threshold parameter is used to detect the presence of outliers. We use 0.5 as the cut-off to indicate if an observation is an outlier. For RL problems, a high leverage indicates that the respective state-action pair is an outlier, i.e. is novel and has not been visited often.

Typically RL algorithms require large amounts of data to solve the MDP which makes it infeasible to store all the transitions in a batch. In addition to that, computing leverage can pose computational issues as it requires taking the inverse of a matrix of size $k \times k$ (for k features) which can be very large for high-dimensional problems. To address the memory and computational concerns, we use the Sherman-Morrison formula to incrementally compute the inverse of $X^T X$. The formula is stated as follows:

$$(A + x^T x)^{-1} = A^{-1} - \frac{A^{-1} x^T x A^{-1}}{1 + x A^{-1} x^T} \tag{4}$$

where A^{-1} is initially set to $\frac{1}{\delta} I$ (identity matrix of size $k \times k$) and δ is a small positive number, say $1e^{-4}$. Using this computation, the leverage of an instance x of data matrix X can be computed as $x A^{-1} x^T$.

4.2.2 *Discrepancy*

This measure captures the observations that the learning algorithm is unable to model thus leading to large errors. Discrepancy is computed using the externally studentized residual [27]. These residuals are obtained by computing the residual for an observation and dividing it by the standard error (or standard deviation). This is done to reduce the effect of the variance in the errors and allow residuals to be compared. An externally studentized residual is one that computes the residual by taking into account the difference in the learned model with and without the observation in question. For observation i, the discrepancy, t_i can computed as:

$$\begin{aligned} t_i &= \frac{e_i}{\sqrt{MSE_{(i)}(1 - h_{ii})}} \\ MSE_{(i)} &= \frac{(n-p)MSE - \frac{e_i^2}{(1-h_{ii})}}{n - p - 1} \end{aligned} \tag{5}$$

Here MSE represents the mean-squared error, n is the number of samples, p the number of independent variables, h_{ii} is the leverage for observation i and e_i is the TD error for sample i. $MSE_{(i)}$ is the mean squared error for the model based on all observations excluding sample i. We note that MSE is typically computed using batch data which is computationally infeasible to store in large scale RL domains. It does not lend itself to incremental computations due to the max operator in the RL optimization function (when computing MSE and e_i). We circumvent this problem by storing a batch data matrix, update it with new observations using a (FIFO) sliding window and compute the required parameters [12] online. In analysis of linear systems, when the absolute value of the externally studentized residual, $|t_i|$ is greater than 2, the corresponding observation is considered an outlier that needs further investigation. Henceforth we use the term discrepancy to represent the externally studentized residual.

Using these measures the RL agent can identify observations in the MDP that require further exploration. We now describe how we use them to solicit demonstrations for exploration.

4.3 Demonstration Query

For every transition made by the RL agent, it computes the leverage and discrepancy and compares it to the respective thresholds. If either threshold is exceeded, we identify the corresponding observation as influential. To learn more about that observation and reduce its influence, we learn a policy using guidance from a person or a simulated oracle that drives the agent towards these observations.

Consider the state associated with an influential observation the agent transitioned into as s^+. To encourage exploration to s^+, it is important to bridge the gap between regions of low influence to those of high influence. Intuitively this can be explained by the idea that state-action pairs that have low influence are likely to have been frequently visited and sufficiently explored. Therefore designing a policy from parts of the state-action space that the agent knows well and visits often to those with high influence is most likely to encourage exploration to and around s^+. As explained before, leverage provides a way to identify data points that have been visited often. To acquire the necessary low influence data point that is to be connected to s^+, we review every observation i, in the current episode and compute the corresponding leverage: $h_i = \phi(s_i, a_i) A^{-1} \phi(s_i, a_i)^T$. We then compute the mean leverage, μ_h from these observations and find the state, s_i that corresponds to the data point with the closest leverage,

$$\underset{i}{\operatorname{argmin}} |h_i - \mu_h| \tag{6}$$

Once the low and high influence observations have been identified, we collect exploratory demonstrations either from a person or a simulated oracle using a Graphical User Interface (GUI) for the domain. When the algorithm queries for demonstrations, the GUI highlights the states that need to be connected by demonstrations. Using the GUI, the user can a) provide demonstration(s), b) choose to ignore the query and c) stop interacting with the algorithm altogether. The simulated oracle provides demonstrations by following the shortest distance path between the queried states. There are no inherent assumptions made about quality or quantity of demonstrations. The only requirement is for the user to be knowledgeable about the MDP dynamics to help the agent navigate in the domain. For every demonstration provided, we learn an oracle exploration policy π^O using standard supervised learning algorithms and sample an action from this policy when the agent decides to explore.

We note here that when soliciting demonstrations, the final state in the demonstration may be different from the query state requested by the agent. This is likely to be observed in domains with stochastic elements and/or non-playable characters. While there is no straightforward way to ensure a certain state is visited in an MDP, our experimental results show that the policy learned using our approach is effective at driving the agent towards influential parts of the MDP as it continues to actively request user demonstrations.

4.4 Action Selection

The oracle exploration policy, π^O defines a policy that when followed is likely to guide the agent from regions of low influence to those of high influence. However using such a policy alone to explore in and of itself can be insufficient for the purposes of RL where the goal is to arrive at the optimal policy as soon as possible. Additionally the nature of exploration is non-stationary and as such if there are limited demonstrations, the agent is less likely to explore the set of influential regions in the MDP. To account for these properties, we design our exploration policy as follows:

$$\pi^E \propto (\pi^O + \pi^L) \cdot \pi^B \tag{7}$$

where π^O is the oracle exploration policy, π^L is the leverage

Algorithm 1 Exploration from Demonstration (EfD)

repeat(for each episode):
  Initialize s
  repeat(for each step of episode):
    Compute π^E (Eqn. 7)
    Choose a (ϵ-greedy action selection using π^E)
    Take action a, observe r, s'
    Store transitions $\langle s, a, r, s' \rangle$
    Update θ and A^{-1} (Eqn. 2 & 4)
    Compute leverage and discrepancy (Eqn. 3 & 5)
    if high influence at s **then**
      $s^+ \leftarrow s$
      Compute starting state, s_i (Eqn. 6)
      Query demonstrations from s_i to s^+
      Update θ and A^{-1}
      Self-play for T_s (includes parameter updates)
    end if
    $s \leftarrow s'$
  until s is terminal
  Decay ϵ
until end of learning

value $\forall a \in A$ for state s and π^B represents the Boltzmann exploration policy. We note that the leverage values lie in the range $[0, 1]$ and for our purposes can be used as probabilities. A leverage value closer to 1 will have the effect of sampling the corresponding action more often. Intuitively π^E represents the exploration policy that chooses between the oracle demonstration or the leverage values, weighted by the softmax Q-values of the actions in the state. This exploration policy allows the agent to reach regions of high influence using human demonstrations or select actions with high leverage while actively seeking the goal. We use π^E in an ϵ-greedy fashion to facilitate exploration in our approach.

4.5 Exploration from Demonstration

We now outline our approach with all the pieces defined using Algorithm Block 1. The objective of Exploration from Demonstration (EfD) is to learn the optimal policy using RL while ensuring the agent actively explores regions of the state-action space that have a potentially large influence on the learned model.

EfD as described in Algorithm Block 1 has a tendency to query the user demonstrations repeatedly as high influence regions are often in close proximity to others. This results in the leverage and discrepancy thresholds being crossed very often within the same episode. In order to make EfD more user-friendly we include a predefined fixed time period, T_s where the agent executes self-play without any user queries. During self-play Q-learning and leverage parameters (θ & A^{-1}) continue to be updated. We note that EfD does not modify any theoretical guarantees of the methods used as Q-learning is an off-policy algorithm. This completes the description of our approach.

5. EXPERIMENTAL SETUP

To validate the performance of EfD we conduct experiments on a gridworld and popular arcade game domain and compare our method to several baselines. In this section we describe the domains used in our experiments and the relevant baselines.

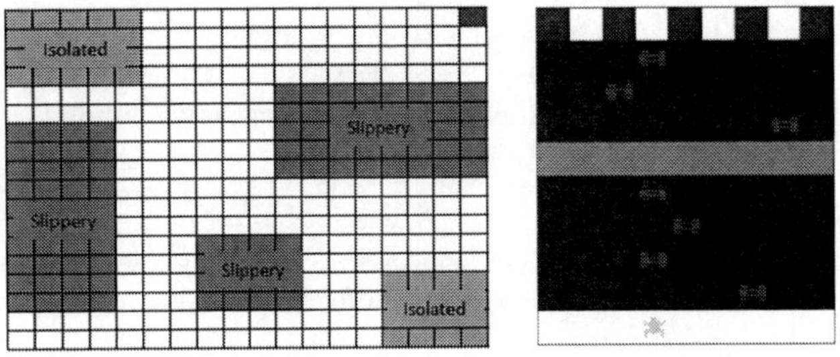

(a) Gridworld (b) Frogger1x

Figure 1: A snapshot of the two domains used in our experiments.

5.1 Domains

We use two domains to empirically highlight the performance and properties of EfD. We represent these domains as MDPs in the following manner:

Gridworld. This domain is designed by adapting the specifications outlined in [14]. We implement an 18×18 discrete grid (Figure 1a) with four deterministic actions that move the agent up, down, left and right. The goal is to reach the top right corner of the grid. For every step taken, the agent accrues a step cost of -1 and a reward of 0 at the goal state. The blue shaded regions represent slippery squares. If the agent transitions out of a slippery square (both into an unshaded square or another slippery square), the reward is uniformly distributed in the interval $[-12, +10]$. The gray shaded regions represent isolated squares. Any transition that leads the agent into this region from an empty square has a 0.1 probability of success. Once inside, movements within the isolated region as well as those leading out are not restricted. Transitions leading into the bounding walls keeps the agent's state unchanged. An episode starts with the agent randomly placed in the grid and stops when the agent reaches the goal. We used identity features to represent the state space.

Frogger. In the game of Frogger (Figure 1b), the agent's goal is to navigate from the bottom to the top of the grid while avoiding the cars and water pits (shown as dark squares in the top row). The cars move in straight lines in their individual rows either going left or right. The direction is randomly chosen at the start of an episode and stays fixed until the episode ends. The intermediate gray row(s) represent safe zones for the agent, i.e. no cars and water pits. The agent has 5 actions: 4 directional actions and a no-op action. Within an episode, the transitions are deterministic. The reward function is $+1000$ for reaching the goal, -100 for dying (directly hitting a car, crossing over a car, falling into water) and 0 everywhere else. An episode starts with the agent in a random position in the bottom row and stops when the agent dies or reaches the goal. The state space of the domain consists of the agent's position along with the position and direction of travel of cars in the grid and represented using binary features. The Frogger domain is particularly interesting as it lends itself to easy scalability. The domain can be made more complex, i.e. have a longer solution horizon, by increasing the number of intermediate rows between the start and goal positions. We use this property to show how our method scales with the size of the domain. We refer to the domain configuration in Figure 1b as Frogger1x and use Frogger2x to indicate doubling the number of rows used in Frogger1x and Frogger4x to indicate a quadruple version of the same.

5.2 Baselines

We implement five baselines in our experiments and compare their performance to EfD. Uniform random exploration and softmax exploration comprise two of the baselines. The remaining three are defined as follows:

Learning from Demonstration + RL. In this method we acquire demonstrations of optimal behavior from people or a simulated oracle. These demonstrations are used to learn a policy using supervised learning methods (in this case logistic regression). We use this policy as the seed policy to initiate RL. We execute the algorithm on the domain and report the results.

Exploration by TD error. This approach draws from insights highlighted in this paper [14] and learns an exploration policy based on TD error. In our implementation we use the current estimate of TD error (the absolute value) as the reward for a given state-action pair and learn a Q-function using this information. A policy is extracted from the Q-function using softmax action selection. The Q-function learned in this process plays the role of driving the agent towards parts of the state-action space that have high TD error in order to gather more information in those regions. We note that this approach is not strictly consistent with standard MDP assumptions as the reward function is non-stationary (TD error is constantly changing). While we counteract this effect to a certain degree by using a small learning rate and a decaying exploration parameter, our experiments show that performance was not greatly affected by this characteristic.

Exploration by Leverage. We derive an exploration policy by computing the leverage on data consisting of visited state-action pairs. For any given state, we compute the leverage for all actions, normalize the results and use it as a distribution from which we sample exploratory actions. As explained earlier leverage captures outliers in the data, which in this case would represent actions, for a given state, that have not been tried often. This way by sampling from normalized leverage values for all actions in a state, the agent is more likely to sample new actions. This baseline is useful to signify the importance of exploratory demonstrations.

6. EXPERIMENTS AND RESULTS

We implement EfD for the chosen domains and highlight the results achieved along with several tests that provide insight into EfD's performance under different experimental conditions.

6.1 Using Leverage and Discrepancy for Exploration

In this experiment we use the gridworld (Figure 1a) to show the utility of leverage and discrepancy as useful measures to guide exploration. The gridworld is suitable for this purpose due to several design choices made. Firstly the isolated (gray) regions in the grid represent parts of the state-space that are hard to reach and thus unlikely to be explored by the agent. Secondly the non-deterministic reward function (represented by slippery blue patches on the grid) pose some difficulty to the learning algorithm in accurately modeling the underlying value-function. We conduct two experiments to show the individual contribution of the chosen exploration measures.

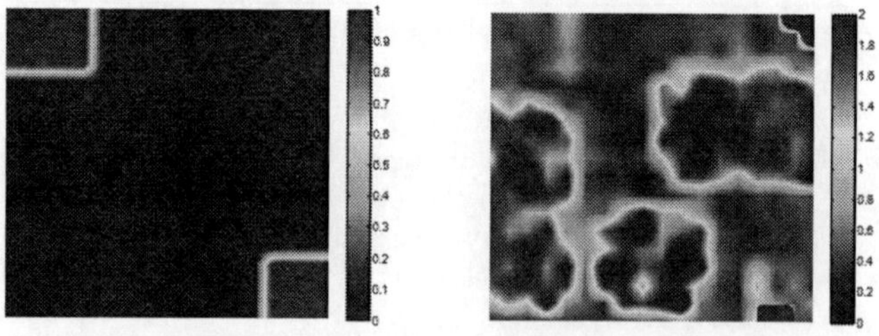

(a) Leverage heat map (b) Discrepancy heat map

Figure 2: Leverage and discrepancy heat maps generated from random exploration of the gridworld domain.

To highlight the utility of leverage, we perform a random walk in the gridworld for 50 episodes. In each episode, the agent starts in a random position and moves randomly until the goal is reached. For every step taken, features of visited state-action pairs are used to form the data matrix X. Using X, we compute the hat matrix H (see Equation 3) and use that to derive the leverage $h(s, a)$ for every state-action pair.

In Figure 2a, we plot a heat map using $\max_a h(s, a)\ \forall s \in S$. The heat map shows the correspondence between the regions of high leverage ($h \geq 0.5$) and hard to explore regions of the gridworld (isolated gray regions). Leverage, as explained earlier, is used to identify outliers in the data. In this case the heat map presents the gray region as outliers which necessitates the need for further exploration. Analogously this effect can be seen in other more complex high-dimensional domains where it is hard to entirely cover the state-action space. Leverage, as shown here, captures regions that the learning agent is unable to reach often.

While leverage captures how often state-action pairs have been visited, it does not capture details about the transition function, reward function and RL algorithm's learned model. Here we show how discrepancy is useful for this task. We perform Q-learning with linear function approximation on the gridworld domain for 50 episodes. We set $\gamma = 0.99$, $\alpha = 0.1$ and $\epsilon = 1.0$. We store all the transitions $\langle s, a, r, s' \rangle$ from the sampled episodes and compute the mean squared error using the learned weight vector θ (refer Equation 5). The mean squared error is used to derive the discrepancy $t(s, a)$ for every state-action pair.

In Figure 2b, we plot a heat map using $\max_a |t(s, a)|\ \forall s \in S$. The heat map shows the correspondence between the regions of high discrepancy ($|t| > 2$) and the slippery regions in the gridworld. Intuitively this is to be expected as the TD error in these areas is likely to have large magnitude and high variance and that warrants further investigation. We note that the bright red patch in the top right corner of the heat map signifies the high residual obtained at the goal and its adjoining states. Using this heat map as a threshold for exploration would draw the agent towards the slippery patches and the goal until the learning algorithm captures the underlying model and the residual decreases.

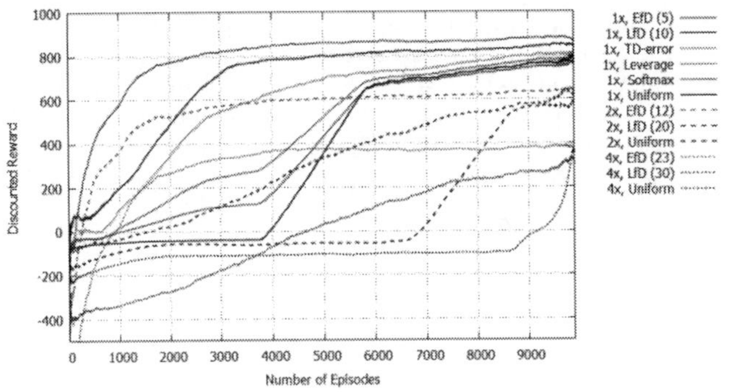

Figure 3: Performance of EfD and baselines on the Frogger game domain of varying sizes (1x, 2x and 4x) averaged over 10 trials. The numbers in parenthesis are the average number of input user demonstrations.

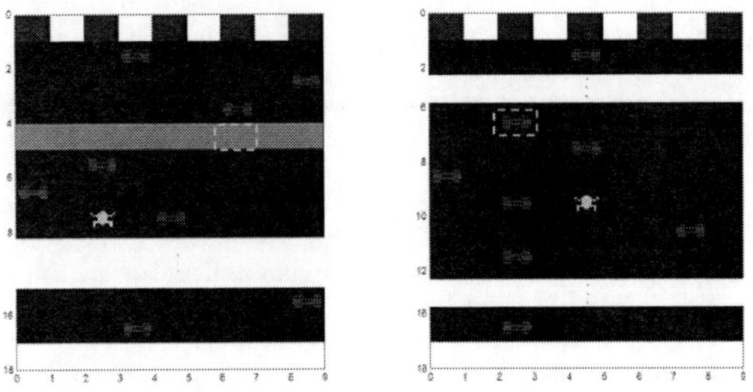

(a) Agent queries the user for demonstrations to the highlighted position based on the leverage threshold.

(b) Agent queries the user for demonstrations to the highlighted position based on the discrepancy threshold.

Figure 4: Examples of the types of states queried by the agent during EfD when applied to Frogger2x (18 rows).

The experiment serves to highlight the roles played by leverage and discrepancy and how they guide the agent's exploration. Leverage guides the agent towards state-action pairs that have not been visited often during learning and the discrepancy guides the agent towards regions of the domain which the learning algorithm has difficulty modeling the value-function.

6.2 EfD for Frogger

In this experiment we instantiate the EfD algorithm in the Frogger domain for different sizes of the problem, Frogger 1x (10 rows), Frogger 2x (18 rows) and Frogger 4x (34 rows). We perform Q-learning with linear function approximation with $\gamma = 0.99$, $\alpha = 0.0006$ and $\epsilon_{start} = 0.8$. We use the following decay schedule for the exploration parameter: $\epsilon = \frac{\epsilon_{start} \times N_0}{(N_0 + Ep\#)}$ where N_0 is the decay rate and $Ep\#$ is the current episode number. We set N_0 as 1500, 2500 and 5000 respectively for the three versions of Frogger. The threshold parameters for EfD were fixed with the leverage threshold set at 0.5 and discrepancy threshold at 2. The self-play time period for EfD was set to $T_s = 500$, $T_s = 2000$ and $T_s = 5000$ steps respectively for the three versions of Frogger. The temperature for softmax Boltzmann exploration was set to 50. We acquired demonstrations from two users who were both familiar with the dynamics of the game. We received anywhere from 5 to 30 demonstrations depending on the size of the domain that was being tested. Demonstration time in total was no more than 10 to 15 mins. The human policy was learned using logistic regression with a learning rate of 0.01. We plot the results of this experiment along with comparative baselines in Figure 3. We see that EfD converges to the optimal policy faster than the baselines using a small number of demonstrations. To ease readability we plot only a subset of the baseline methods in Figure 3 as the performance of the baselines (TD-error, Leverage and Softmax) were consistent across the three sizes. The performance is further improved over the baselines as the size of the domain is increased. This is explained by highlighting how EfD queries and utilizes user demonstrations. In the initial stages of learning, the user is queried with demonstrations leading to states in the rows closer to the bottom row. As the agent gains experience, demonstrations are requested for states further up. In this process, the agent incrementally explores the rows until it finally reaches the goal in the top row. Such an incremental learning approach makes it easier for agent to reach the goal as well as easier for the user to provide demonstrations. This also explains why LfD (+ RL) does not perform as well as EfD for larger grids. The size of the domain limits the search space covered by the human demonstrations as well as prohibits optimal demonstrations from start to the goal. EfD performs better by using the RL algorithm's inductive bias as well as the underlying representation to acquire incremental demonstrations that are most useful to the agent. These results were consistent across both users. The TD-error and leverage baseline methods while more informed do not perform as well due to their redundant exploration. An interesting observation of EfD from our experiments is that, by using thresholds for the statistical measures, with sufficient experience the agent automatically ceases to request demonstrations. In which case, we observe that the agent has enough information to model the Q-function and solve the MDP.

6.3 Types of States Queried

Here we take a closer look at the types of states queried by the agent during EfD. We present results from the Frogger2x domain which consists of 18 rows from start to goal. Figure 4a is an example of an agent query, based on the leverage measure, where a demonstration is required between the frog near row 8 to the highlighted grid position near row 4. An observation that exceeds the leverage threshold indicates that the agent has not visited that state-action pair often and therefore requires input demonstrations. Such a query points towards how EfD gathers information about the state-action - decomposing the domain in smaller regions. Demonstrations are requested from known regions to unknown regions and often they are in close proximity to each other. Providing a demonstration for such a query would be easier than providing optimal demonstrations from start to end in this domain. Figure 4b is an example of an agent query based on the discrepancy threshold. We note that the highlighted position is around a car near row 6 which is a terminal state with reward -100. The discrepancy here exceeded the threshold as the agent's current model was unable to make an accurate prediction of the Q-value of an action in this state and thus requested a demonstration.

We would also like to highlight a few uncommon queries

that provide interesting insights into the method. In some cases the agent requests demonstrations from a state where the frog is closer to the goal to states where the frog is further away. From the perspective of solving the MDP, using such a policy would encode suboptimal information, however for policy-based exploration, it only serves to get a better estimate of the Q-function. Note that exploration is carried out by combining the human policy with softmax policy (Section 4.4) which therefore ensures the agent select actions that are more likely to lead it towards the goal. For some queries we observe that the agent's position on the grid remains the same for both start and final states, while the position of cars is different. With respect to EfD, these are different states and therefore it is a valid demonstration query. This shows how EfD makes demonstration queries by taking into account the underlying representation.

6.4 Effect of Input Demonstrations and Threshold Parameters

In this experiment, we test the sensitivity of EfD to the quality of demonstrations used to learn the exploration policy. While we do not place any assumptions on the quality of demonstrations, we analyze the degrees to which performance is affected as the quality of demonstration is varied. We use the simulated oracle for this experiment under different demonstration noise conditions: Oracle0.1, Oracle0.3, Oracle0.5. An oracle with noise 0.1 (Oracle0.1) will provide the required demonstration 90% of the time and 10% of the time, take random actions. The results of this experiment are summarized in Table 1. As evidenced by the

	Frogger1x (5)	Frogger2x (12)	Frogger4x (23)
Oracle0.0	**2560 ± 150**	**3194 ± 230**	**4430 ± 410**
Oracle0.1	2752 ± 321	3470 ± 527	4893 ± 564
Oracle0.3	2648 ± 469	3304 ± 699	5218 ± 866
Oracle0.5	5102 ± 932	6329 ± 875	7688 ± 1043
ϵ-greedy	6570 ± 120	8555 ± 212	10000 ± 405

Table 1: EfD performance as a function of the quality of input demonstrations from a simulated oracle in the Frogger domain. The values represent the number of episodes taken by each method to converge to the optimal policy. The numbers in parenthesis are the number of input demonstrations the simulated oracles are limited to. We include results from the ϵ-greedy baseline for comparison. The results are averaged over 10 trials.

table, the performance of EfD varies based on the quality of input demonstrations. Relative to Oracle0.0 (optimal oracle demonstrations), Oracle0.1 and Oracle0.3 achieve similar performance. This is explained by the fact that for most query demonstrations there exist multiple ways to reach the desired state and neither path is any more optimal than the other from the perspective of exploration. By introducing noise in the oracle demonstrations, they can potentially explore more states than Oracle0.0 which can include both low and high influence observations. However this has the effect of increased variance in performance for noisy simulated oracles. Oracle0.5 (with 50% random action selection) has large variance in its performance but still outperforms ϵ-greedy uniform random exploration.

In our experiments, we set the leverage threshold at 0.5 and the discrepancy threshold at 2. Changes to these parameters directly affect the number of demonstrations queried by the agent which affects the amount of exploration carried out by the agent. Higher values results in fewer demonstration queries and as a result most of the exploration is carried out by the agent autonomously. On the other hand lower thresholds result in frequent queries which has the effect of learning an exploration policy close to a uniform policy. In general, from tests in our domain, we find that setting leverage threshold to 0.5 and discrepancy threshold anywhere in the range $[2, 6]$ provides the best results.

7. DISCUSSION AND CONCLUSION

Here we highlight the **benefits of using a policy-based approach** for exploration in RL in the context of EfD. When faced with large domains with sparse rewards and long horizons, a policy-based approach is less vulnerable to the large sample requirements of value-based methods as the information acquired from a single demonstration allows the agent to extends its range of exploration over multiple timesteps. Additionally such a method does not concern itself solely with reward information. The statistical measures used in EfD (leverage and discrepancy) focus on different aspects of the MDP which allow the algorithm to function well across a wider class of problems. This is in contrast to value-based methods which rely on large samples of reward information to estimate the uncertainty in the value function often made complicated in sparse reward and long horizon domains. Also EfD does not require optimal demonstrations to learn but instead demonstrations that serve to connect two regions of the agent's choice. As these demonstrations are used for exploration, they can be potentially noisy (which may in some cases help the agent).

In this paper we presented a model-free policy-based approach called Exploration from Demonstration (EfD) that performs interactive exploration for RL algorithms. Our method adapts statistical measures of linear regression to capture aspects of an MDP that are important to explore and model in order to learn the optimal Q-function. We highlight the properties of these measures in an instructional gridworld MDP and empirically test our approach on a popular arcade game under different experimental conditions. We show how EfD scales to larger problems and outperforms baselines using only exploratory demonstrations while placing very few requirements on the quality and quantity of input data. Our method is particularly suited to problems which have a long horizon and sparse rewards as well as those domains where optimal demonstrations are hard to acquire. In the future we would like to extend EfD to learn a model of the MDP, thus allowing the algorithm to request examples from arbitrary states rather that waiting to transition to those areas. Another interesting avenue for future work is the idea of extending EfD to work with more data efficient RL algorithms like Least Squares Policy Iteration [25].

Acknowledgments

We thank the reviewers for their helpful comments in improving the paper. This work is supported by ONR grant No. N000141410003.

REFERENCES

[1] P. Abbeel, A. Coates, and A. Y. Ng. Autonomous helicopter aerobatics through apprenticeship learning. *International Journal of Robotics Research*, 29(13):1608–1639, 2010.

[2] P. Abbeel and A. Y. Ng. Apprenticeship learning via inverse reinforcement learning. In *Proc. of the 21st ICML*, 2004.

[3] T. Akiyama, H. Hachiya, and M. Sugiyama. Efficient exploration through active learning for value function approximation in reinforcement learning. *Neural Networks*, 23(5):639 – 648, 2010.

[4] B. Argall, S. Chernova, M. Veloso, and B. Browning. A survey of robot learning from demonstration. *Robotics and Autonomous Systems*, 57(5):469–483, 2009.

[5] C. Atkeson and S. Schaal. Learning tasks from a single demonstration. In *Proc. of the IEEE ICRA*, pages 1706–1712, 1997.

[6] P. Auer. Using confidence bounds for exploitation-exploration trade-offs. *Journal of Machine Learning Research*, 3:397–422, Mar. 2003.

[7] S. Bubeck, R. Munos, and G. Stoltz. Pure exploration in multi-armed bandits problems. In *ALT*, volume 5809 of *Lecture Notes in Computer Science*, pages 23–37. Springer, 2009.

[8] M. Cakmak and M. Lopes. Algorithmic and human teaching of sequential decision tasks. In *AAAI Conference on Artificial Intelligence*, 2012.

[9] O. Şimşek and A. G. Barto. An intrinsic reward mechanism for efficient exploration. In *Proceedings of the 23rd International Conference on Machine Learning*, ICML '06, pages 833–840. ACM, 2006.

[10] C. Daniel, M. Viering, J. Metz, O. Kroemer, and J. Peters. Active reward learning. In *Proceedings of Robotics: Science & Systems (R:SS)*, 2014.

[11] R. Dearden, N. Friedman, and S. Russell. Bayesian Q-learning. In *Proc. of the 15th AAAI*, pages 761–768, 1998.

[12] T. G. Dietterich. Machine learning for sequential data: A review. In *Structural, Syntactic, and Statistical Pattern Recognition*, pages 15–30. Springer-Verlag, 2002.

[13] A. Epshteyn, A. Vogel, and G. DeJong. Active reinforcement learning. In *ICML*, volume 307 of *ACM International Conference Proceeding Series*, pages 296–303. ACM, 2008.

[14] C. Gehring and D. Precup. Smart exploration in reinforcement learning using absolute temporal difference errors. In *International conference on Autonomous Agents and Multi-Agent Systems, AAMAS*, pages 1037–1044, 2013.

[15] M. Geist and O. Pietquin. Algorithmic survey of parametric value function approximation. *IEEE Trans. Neural Netw. Learning Syst.*, 24(6):845–867, 2013.

[16] I. Giannoccaro and P. Pontrandolfo. Inventory management in supply chains: a reinforcement learning approach. *International Journal of Production Economics*, 78(2):153–161, 2002.

[17] S. Griffith, K. Subramanian, J. Scholz, C. L. Isbell, and A. L. Thomaz. Policy shaping: Integrating human feedback with reinforcement learning. In *Neural Information Processing Systems 26*, pages 2625–2633, 2013.

[18] T. Hester, M. Lopes, and P. Stone. Learning exploration strategies in model-based reinforcement learning. In *Proceedings of the 2013 International Conference on Autonomous Agents and Multi-agent Systems*, AAMAS '13, pages 1069–1076, 2013.

[19] T. Hester and P. Stone. TEXPLORE: Real-time sample-efficient reinforcement learning for robots. *Machine Learning*, 90(3), 2013.

[20] K. Judah, A. P. Fern, T. G. Dietterich, and P. Tadepalli. Active imitation learning: Formal and practical reductions to i.i.d. learning. *Journal of Machine Learning Research*, 15:4105–4143, 2014.

[21] L. P. Kaelbling, M. L. Littmann, and A. W. Moore. Reinforcement learning: A survey. *JAIR*, 4:237–285, 1996.

[22] W. B. Knox and P. Stone. Combining manual feedback with subsequent MDP reward signals for reinforcement learning. In *Proc. of the 9th Intl. Conf. on AAMAS*, pages 5–12, 2010.

[23] W. B. Knox and P. Stone. Reinforcement learning from simultaneous human and MDP reward. In *Proc. of the 11th Intl. Conf. on AAMAS*, pages 475–482, 2012.

[24] L. Kocsis and C. Szepesvári. Bandit based monte-carlo planning. In *ECML*, volume 4212 of *Lecture Notes in Computer Science*, pages 282–293. Springer, 2006.

[25] M. G. Lagoudakis and R. Parr. Least-squares policy iteration. In *Journal of Machine Learning Research*, volume 4, pages 1107–1149, 2003.

[26] V. Mnih, K. Kavukcuoglu, D. Silver, A. A. Rusu, J. Veness, M. G. Bellemare, A. Graves, M. Riedmiller, A. K. Fidjeland, G. Ostrovski, S. Petersen, C. Beattie, A. Sadik, I. Antonoglou, H. King, D. Kumaran, D. Wierstra, S. Legg, and D. Hassabis. Human-level control through deep reinforcement learning. *Nature*, 518(7540):529–533, 02 2015.

[27] D. C. Montgomery, E. A. Peck, and G. G. Vining. *Introduction to Linear Regression Analysis (4th ed.)*. Wiley & Sons, Hoboken, July 2006.

[28] A. Y. Ng and S. Russell. Algorithms for inverse reinforcement learning. In *Proc. of the 17th ICML*, 2000.

[29] J. Pazis and R. Parr. PAC optimal exploration in continuous space markov decision processes. In *Proceedings of the Twenty-Seventh AAAI Conference on Artificial Intelligence*, 2013.

[30] B. Price and C. Boutilier. Accelerating reinforcement learning through implicit imitation. *Journal of Artificial Intelligence Research (JAIR)*, 19:569–629, 2003.

[31] M. T. Ronen I. Brafman. R-max - a general polynomial time algorithm for near-optimal reinforcement learning. *Journal of Machine Learning Research*, pages 213–231, 2002.

[32] S. Ross, G. J. Gordon, and D. Bagnell. A reduction of imitation learning and structured prediction to no-regret online learning. In *AISTATS*, volume 15 of *JMLR Proceedings*, pages 627–635. JMLR.org, 2011.

[33] W. D. Smart and L. P. Kaelbling. Effective

reinforcement learning for mobile robots. In *ICRA*, 2002.

[34] P. Stone, R. S. Sutton, and G. Kuhlmann. Reinforcement learning for robocup soccer keepaway. *Adaptive Behaviour*, 13(3):165–188, 2005.

[35] A. L. Strehl and M. L. Littman. An analysis of model-based interval estimation for markov decision processes. *Journal of Computer and System Sciences*, 74(8):1309–1331, 2008.

[36] R. Sutton and A. Barto. *Reinforcement learning: an introduction.* Adaptive computation and machine learning. MIT Press, 1998.

[37] C. Szepesvári. *Algorithms for Reinforcement Learning.* Synthesis Lectures on Artificial Intelligence and Machine Learning. Morgan & Claypool Publishers, 2010.

[38] M. Taylor, H. B. Suay, and S. Chernova. Integrating reinforcement learning with human demonstrations of varying ability. In *Proc. of the Intl. Conf. on AAMAS*, pages 617–624, 2011.

[39] G. Tesauro. Temporal difference learning and td-gammon. *Communications of the ACM*, 38(3):58–68, Mar. 1995.

Score-based Inverse Reinforcement Learning

Layla El Asri
Orange Labs & Maluuba
Montréal, Canada
layla.elasri@maluuba.com

Bilal Piot
Univ. Lille, CNRS, Centrale Lille, Inria UMR 9189 - CRIStAL
Lille, France
bilal.piot@univ-lille1.fr

Matthieu Geist
UMI 2958, GeorgiaTech-CNRS, CentraleSupélec, Université Paris-Saclay
Metz, France
matthieu.geist@centralesupelec.fr

Romain Laroche
Orange Labs
Issy les Moulineaux, France
romain.laroche@orange.com

Olivier Pietquin
Univ. Lille, CNRS, Centrale Lille, Inria UMR 9189 - CRIStAL
Institut Universitaire de France
Lille, France
olivier.pietquin@univ-lille1.fr

ABSTRACT

This paper reports theoretical and empirical results obtained for the score-based Inverse Reinforcement Learning (IRL) algorithm. It relies on a non-standard setting for IRL consisting of learning a reward from a set of globally scored trajectories. This allows using any type of policy (optimal or not) to generate trajectories without prior knowledge during data collection. This way, any existing database (like logs of systems in use) can be scored *a posteriori* by an expert and used to learn a reward function. Thanks to this reward function, it is shown that a near-optimal policy can be computed. Being related to least-square regression, the algorithm (called SBIRL) comes with theoretical guarantees that are proven in this paper. SBIRL is compared to standard IRL algorithms on synthetic data showing that annotations do help under conditions on the quality of the trajectories. It is also shown to be suitable for real-world applications such as the optimisation of a spoken dialogue system.

Keywords

Reinforcement Learning, Inverse Reinforcement Learning, Markov Decision Processes, Learning from Demonstration, Spoken Dialogue Systems

1. INTRODUCTION

Reinforcement Learning (RL) has seen a growing interest this last decade both from a theoretical and a practical point of view, especially in the domain of Human-Machine Interaction (HMI) where it is now part of the state of the art [20, 13, 24]. In this paradigm, an agent steps from states to states in an environment of unknown dynamics by selecting actions. The action selection process is encoded in a so-called *policy*, which is a mapping between states and actions. Learning occurs via a reward function providing a numerical feedback to the agent after each transition from one state to another. An optimal policy, which should be the result of the learning process, leads to the highest cumulative reward in average. This paradigm is very attractive to learn optimal behaviors in a model-free manner, which allows dealing with complex systems (such as HMI where the human is in the loop and hard to model). Yet, correctly defining the reward function so that it leads to the desired behavior remains a tricky task. For this reason, Inverse Reinforcement Learning (IRL) [19] received a lot of attention recently, including in HMI [15, 5, 16], and many algorithms can now be found in the literature [1, 6, 12]. IRL consists of finding the reward optimised by an expert that provides optimal demonstrations. Yet, these algorithms require numerous expert demonstrations, some of them have to solve the direct RL problem many times [1] or also require many non-expert (and if possible random) trajectories to estimate the dynamics [6]. It is often hard and potentially impossible to comply with these requirements, especially when dealing with human experts. Collecting enough expert demonstrations is time consuming and expensive. Besides, it is also hard for a person to consciously act sub-optimally on demand and, above all, randomly so as to cover the widest range of possible behaviors. This is even more difficult when facing other persons (in the case of HMI problems).

In this paper, we study a different setting for IRL based on scored trajectories and especially an associated algorithm based on the minimisation of the distance between actual and predicted scores [7]. In this paradigm, a database of trajectories is first collected. Each trajectory can be obtained by applying any policy (optimal or not). Each trajectory is then annotated *a posteriori* in terms of global performance by an external expert, who might be error-prone. This is a very practical setting where no expert is needed during the collection of trajectories and there is no requirement on their quality. The expert's job is reduced since s/he only has to rate trajectories instead of providing optimal decisions in each state. It also applies in tasks where only subjective ratings can be obtained, which is often the case for HMI [14],

Appears in: *Proceedings of the 15th International Conference on Autonomous Agents and Multiagent Systems (AAMAS 2016), J. Thangarajah, K. Tuyls, C. Jonker, S. Marsella (eds.), May 9–13, 2016, Singapore.*

or where a set of unreliable data already exists (such as Mechanical Turk data collection).

Compared to preference-based reinforcement learning [2], this method doesn't require a user to explicitly compare each pair of trajectories in the database and therefore results in a lighter effort for the expert. Yet, each trajectory is implicitly compared to all the others through the scores which results in additional information. Moreover, preference-based RL learns a policy, not a reward whereas learning a reward is the purpose of this paper. Indeed, we argue that IRL is a technique which has many advantages such as the transferability to other environments [17] or the ability for the agent to learn online by reinforcement after the reward has been computed, making the policy improve with time. In addition, in the domain of HMI, collecting expert ratings is common and well-researched [14, 8]

It is important to notice that global scores cannot be used directly as rewards (for instance on the final state). Indeed, similar scores can be associated to very different trajectories, finishing on the same state, but having different lengths for instance. Scores must thus be considered as a value associated to the global trajectory. In practice, the IRL problem is cast into a special case of least-square regression and thus results in a very efficient method (renamed SBIRL for Score-based IRL instead of Distance-Minimisation IRL), robust to noisy scoring and coming with theoretical guarantees. Especially, the error propagation analysis is an original contribution of this paper which is accompanied by a finite-sample analysis relying on very recent results on linear least-square estimation. The practical properties of the algorithm are studied on synthetic problems as well as on a real-world application: the optimisation of a spoken dialogue system strategy.

2. FORMAL DESCRIPTION

A Markov Decision Process (MDP) is a tuple $\{\mathcal{S}, \mathcal{A}, P, \gamma, r\}$ where $\mathcal{S}$ is the state space, $\mathcal{A}$ is the finite action space, $P(ds'|s,a)$ the Markovian transition kernel on $\mathcal{S}$, $\gamma \in (0,1)$ the discount factor and $r : \mathcal{S} \to \mathbb{R}$ the (bounded) reward function. A policy is a mapping $\pi : \mathcal{S} \to \mathcal{A}$. For a policy π, we define the transition kernel $P_\pi(ds'|s) = P(ds'|s, \pi(s))$. The quality of a policy is quantified by the related value function, that associates to each state the expected discounted sum of rewards received from starting in state s and following the policy π:

$$v_\pi^r(s) = \mathbb{E}\left[\sum_{t=0}^{\infty} \gamma^t r(S_t) | S_0 = s, S_{t+1} \sim P_\pi(.|S_t)\right].$$

An optimal policy π_*^r (with respect to the reward r) is such that the related value function $v_{\pi_*^r}^r = v_*^r$ satisfies componentwise $v_*^r \geq v_\pi^r$, for any policy π.

In this work, the true reward r is unknown and has to be estimated. To do so, we adopt a linear parameterisation of the reward and we assume the availability of a set of trajectories scored by a human expert. More formally, the reward is parameterised by a feature vector $\phi : \mathcal{S} \to \mathbb{R}^d$,

$$r_\theta(s) = \theta^\top \phi(s).$$

The available data is a set

$$\mathcal{D} = \{(h_i, v_i)_{1 \leq i \leq n}\},$$

where

$$h_i = (s_0^i, \ldots, s_{T_i}^i) = (s_j^i)_{j=0}^{T_i}$$

is a trajectory of length $T_i + 1$ and v_i is the score (seen as the discounted sum of rewards of h_i) given by a human expert for this trajectory. Notice that we do not make any specific assumption about how the trajectory is generated (except that it is a trajectory obtained by applying successively T_i actions on encountered states, next states being drawn according to the dynamics). Trajectories in the dataset are assumed independently and identically distributed (which does not mean that states of a given trajectory are independent, obviously). For a given trajectory $h = (s_t)_{t=0}^T$ and a given reward r_θ, the discounted sum of rewards can be written as

$$\sum_{t=0}^{T} \gamma^t r_\theta(s_t) = \theta^\top \mu(h) \text{ with } \mu(h) = \sum_{t=0}^{T} \gamma^t \phi(s_t).$$

We interpret the scores given by the human expert as noisy estimates of the discounted sum of rewards of the associated trajectories. The expert is thus not assumed to give perfect scores but is error-prone. The problem thus consists of regressing the scores v_i on the mappings of the histories $\mu(h_i)$. Formally, we require that the underlying procedure asymptotically minimizes the risk based on the classic ℓ_2-loss:

$$\mathcal{R}(\theta) = \mathbb{E}[(V - \theta^\top \mu(H))^2]. \quad (1)$$

The joint distribution on V (scores) and $\mu(H)$ (mappings of histories) is imposed: it is the distribution used to sample the dataset $\mathcal{D}$. Given any procedure that asymptotically minimises risk (1), and denoting by θ_n the estimate computed from the dataset $\mathcal{D}$, we obtain an estimate r_{θ_n} of the reward. For example, the SBIRL algorithm estimates the reward by solving the following linear least-squares problem:

$$\theta_n = \operatorname*{argmin}_{\theta \in \mathbb{R}^d} \frac{1}{n} \sum_{i=1}^{n} \left(v_i - \theta^\top \mu(h_i)\right)^2$$
$$= \left(\frac{1}{n} \sum_{i=1}^{n} \mu(h_i)\mu(h_i)^\top\right)^{-1} \frac{1}{n} \sum_{i=1}^{n} \mu(h_i) v_i, \quad (2)$$

assuming that the matrix $\frac{1}{n}\sum_{i=1}^{n} \mu(h_i)\mu(h_i)^\top$ is invertible (ordinary least-squares). If this is not the case, one can use for example ℓ_2-regularisation [22] or ℓ_1-regularisation [21], among others. Hence, given a set of trajectories scored by a human expert, we have a reward estimate r_{θ_n}. In the next section, we analyze the quality of this reward.

3. ANALYSIS

To study the estimate r_{θ_n}, we assume that the scores provided by the expert correspond to a discounted cumulative sum of rewards, up to some noise η, for a reward function that lies in the hypothesis space $\mathcal{H} = \{\theta^\top \phi(s), \theta \in \mathbb{R}^d\}$.

Assumption 1
There exists a vector parameter $\theta_* \in \mathbb{R}^d$ and a centered noise η such that for any trajectory $h = (s_t)_{t=0}^T$ and any associated score v, one has

$$v = \sum_{t=0}^{T} \gamma^t r_{\theta_*}(s_t) + \eta(h).$$

Under this assumption, the minimiser of risk (1) is

$$\theta_* = \operatorname*{argmin}_{\theta \in \mathbb{R}^d} \mathcal{R}(\theta) = A^{-1}b,$$

$$\text{with } A = \mathbb{E}[\mu(H)\mu(H)^\top] \text{ and } b = \mathbb{E}[\mu(H)V],$$

assuming that the matrix A is invertible. First, we assume that the estimator θ_n satisfies (with high probability) that

$$\mathcal{R}(\theta_n) \leq \mathcal{R}(\theta_*) + \epsilon,$$

for some error ϵ. Then, we instantiate the related results in the case of ordinary least-squares.

3.1 Propagation of errors

First, we want to control the risk $\mathbb{E}_\nu[(r_{\theta_*}(S) - r_{\theta_n}(S))^2]$ for some distribution ν over states.

Theorem 1 (Propagation of errors: rewards) *Write λ_m the minimum eigenvalue of $\mathbb{E}[\mu(H)\mu(H)^\top]$ and λ_M the maximum eigenvalue of $\mathbb{E}_\nu[\phi(S)\phi(S)^\top]$. Assume that θ_n satisfies*

$$\mathcal{R}(\theta_n) \leq \mathcal{R}(\theta_*) + \epsilon,$$

then the associated reward satisfies

$$\mathbb{E}_\nu[(r_{\theta_*}(S) - r_{\theta_n}(S))^2] \leq \frac{\lambda_M}{\lambda_m}\epsilon.$$

PROOF. The proof is provided in the appendix. □

Theorem 1 shows that if ϵ is small, the estimated reward r_{θ_n} will be close to the true reward r_{θ_*}. However, we are ultimately interested in computing an optimal policy $\pi_*^{r_{\theta_n}}$ (optimal policy relatively to the reward r_{θ_n}) for the control problem at hand. The question we answer now is: how close to optimal is the policy $\pi_*^{r_{\theta_n}}$ respectively to the one of the true reward $\pi^*_{r_{\theta_*}}$? To do so, we bound the quantity

$$\mathbb{E}_{\nu'}[(v_*^{r_{\theta_*}}(S) - v^{r_{\theta_*}}_{\pi_*^{r_{\theta_n}}}(S))^2],$$

states being sampled according to an arbitrary distribution ν' of interest (possibly different from the distribution ν).

Before stating the result, we provide some notations. For a distribution ν and a function $f \in \mathbb{R}^S$, we write

$$\nu f = \mathbb{E}_\nu[f(S)].$$

For a stochastic kernel Q, we have

$$[Qf](s) = \mathbb{E}_{Q(.|s)}[f(S')].$$

Therefore, νQ is a distribution such that

$$\mathbb{E}_{\nu Q}[f] = \mathbb{E}_\nu[Qf] = \mathbb{E}_{S\sim\nu}[\mathbb{E}_{S'\sim Q(.|S)}][f(S')].$$

Theorem 2 (Propagation of errors: values) *For a policy π, define C_π as the smallest coefficient such that*

$$(1-\gamma)\nu'(I - \gamma P_\pi)^{-1} \leq C_\pi \nu.$$

Assume that θ_n satisfies $\mathcal{R}(\theta_n) \leq \mathcal{R}(\theta_*) + \epsilon$, then the associated value satisfies

$$\mathbb{E}_{\nu'}[(v_*^{r_{\theta_*}}(S) - v^{r_{\theta_*}}_{\pi_*^{r_{\theta_n}}}(S))^2] \leq \frac{2\left(C_{\pi_*} + C_{\pi_*^{r_{\theta_n}}}\right)}{(1-\gamma)^2}\frac{\lambda_M}{\lambda_m}\epsilon.$$

PROOF. The proof is provided in the appendix. □

Theorem 2 shows that, if the error ϵ is small, the optimal policy with respect to the learned reward function will be close to the optimal policy with respect to the unknown reward (closeness being measured in terms of value functions). There is an additional multiplicative term compared to Th. 1. The concentrability coefficient C_π measures the dissimilarity between the distribution of data ν and the distribution $(1-\gamma)\nu'(I-\gamma P_\pi)^{-1}$, the γ-weighted occupancy measure induced by policy π when the initial state is sampled from ν' (the distribution of interest for controlling the value function) and the coefficient $(1-\gamma)^{-1}$ is the average optimisation horizon. Both terms are standard when bounding value functions.

3.2 A finite sample analysis

In this section, we provide a finite sample analysis in the case where $\theta_n \in \mathbb{R}^d$ is the ordinary linear least-squares estimate of Eq. (2), based on the bound of [11]. For this, we need some technical assumptions.

Assumption 2 *The noise is subgaussian: there exists $\sigma \geq 0$ such that, almost surely, for all $\lambda \in \mathbb{R}$,*

$$\mathbb{E}[e^{\lambda\eta(H)}|H] \leq e^{\frac{\lambda^2\sigma^2}{2}}.$$

Moreover, there exists a finite $\rho \geq 1$ such that, almost surely,

$$\frac{\|A^{-\frac{1}{2}}\mu(H)\|_2}{\sqrt{d}} \leq \rho.$$

The subgaussian assumption is easily satisfied if the scores provided by the expert and the basis functions are bounded (in this case, the noise is bounded, and a bounded random variable is subgaussian [10]). The other assumption corresponds to condition 1 of [11]. For example, if for any $s \in \mathcal{S}$ we have

$$\|\phi(s)\|_\infty \leq \phi_{\max},$$

then almost surely we have

$$\|\mu(H)\|_2 \leq \frac{\sqrt{d}}{1-\gamma}\phi_{\max}$$

and the assumption holds for

$$\rho \geq \frac{\phi_{\max}}{(1-\gamma)\sqrt{\lambda_m}}.$$

Corollary 1 *Let δ be such that*

$$\ln\frac{9}{\delta} > \max(0, 2.6 - \ln d).$$

If assumptions 1 and-2 hold and if

$$n \geq 6\rho^2 d \ln\frac{9d}{\delta},$$

then with probability at least $1-\delta$ we have

$$\mathbb{E}_\nu[(r_{\theta_*}(S) - r_{\theta_n}(S))^2] \leq$$
$$\frac{\lambda_M}{\lambda_m}\frac{\sigma^2(d + 2\sqrt{d\ln\frac{9}{\delta}} + 2\ln\frac{9}{\delta})}{n} + o\left(\frac{1}{n}\right).$$

Under the same assumptions, w.p. at least $1-\delta$*:*

$$\mathbb{E}_{\nu'}[(v_*^{r_{\theta_*}}(S) - v_{\pi_*^{r_{\theta_n}}}^{r_{\theta_*}}(S))^2] \leq$$

$$\frac{2\left(C_{\pi_*} + C_{\pi_*^{r_{\theta_n}}}\right)}{(1-\gamma)^2}\frac{\lambda_M}{\lambda_m}\frac{\sigma^2(d + 2\sqrt{d\ln\frac{9}{\delta}} + 2\ln\frac{9}{\delta})}{n} + o\left(\frac{1}{n}\right).$$

PROOF. The proof is provided in the appendix. □

This result mainly tells that in the case of ordinary least-squares, we have $\epsilon = O(\frac{d}{n})$, and thus the rates for the errors of the reward and of the value (of the optimal policy) are the same, up to the additional constants arising because of error propagation. Since d is the number of features and n the number of trajectories, this gives an idea of the amount of data required to attain a given accuracy (however, notice that the concentrability coefficients can be hardly estimated, a standard problem in reinforcement learning). A wiser (but much more difficult) analysis would take into account the number of transitions instead of the number of trajectories, yet this is beyond the scope of this paper.

4. EXPERIMENTS

Experiments are organised in two sets. The first set is executed on synthetic data, *i.e.* randomly-constructed finite MDPs called Garnets [3, 17, 18]. We lead three main canonical experiments aiming at supporting the theoretical results. First, we verify the improvement in performance of SBIRL when the number of trajectories grows. Second, we evaluate the sensitivity to the noise η. Third, we determine if sampling the trajectories with an expert or a random policy influences the performance of SBIRL and compare with standard IRL methods provided with the same data. In a second set of experiments, we investigate the suitability of SBIRL for real-world problems by applying it to the optimisation of spoken dialogue system management.

4.1 Experiments on Garnets

In this section, experiments are done on a set of artificially built MDPs so as to support the theoretical findings. Testing SBIRL requires three key elements: first, to build a finite MDP; second, to generate trajectories of random lengths in this MDP; and finally, to score these trajectories with a given noise η. Garnets [3] are an abstract class of finite MDPs, easy to build. Here, we consider a special case of Garnets specified by three parameters: $(N_{\mathcal{S}}, N_{\mathcal{A}}, N_B)$. Parameters $N_{\mathcal{S}}$ and $N_{\mathcal{A}}$ are respectively the number of states and of actions. Thus, $\mathcal{S} = (s_i)_{i=1}^{N_{\mathcal{S}}}$ and $\mathcal{A} = (a_i)_{i=1}^{N_{\mathcal{A}}}$ are, respectively, the state and action spaces. The parameter N_B ($N_B \leq N_{\mathcal{S}}$), called the branching factor, defines for each pair (s, a) the number of next states. N_B states are drawn uniformly and without replacement from $\mathcal{S}$ and form the set of next states of (s, a) noted $\mathcal{S}_{s,a} = (s'_i)_{i=1}^{N_B}$. Then, to define the Markovian kernel P, for each state-action (s,a), we draw randomly and uniformly in $[0, 1]$ $N_B - 1$ cutting points. Let us note $(p_i)_{i=1}^{N_B-1}$ this set of cutting points sorted in increasing order, $p_0 = 0$ and $p_{N_B} = 1$. To completely define the dynamics, one assigns $P(s'_i|s, a)$ according to the following rule: $\forall i \in \{1, \ldots, N_B\}$, $P(s'_i|s, a) = p_i - p_{i-1}$. Finally, for each state $s \in \mathcal{S}$, the reward $r(s)$ is drawn randomly and uniformly in $[0, 1]$, and $\gamma = 0.9$. This choice imposes that the non-perturbed score of a trajectory $h = (s_t)_{t=0}^{T}$ is bounded as follows

$$0 \leq \sum_{t=0}^{T}\gamma^t r(s_t) \leq \frac{1}{1-\gamma} = 10.$$

As we choose finite MDPs, a canonical choice of features ϕ is the tabular basis $\phi : \mathcal{S} \to \mathbb{R}^{N_{\mathcal{S}}}$ where $\phi(s) \in \mathbb{R}^{N_{\mathcal{S}}}$ is a vector which is null excepted in s where it is equal to 1.

The strategy chosen to generate a trajectory h of random length in a Garnet following a policy π consists of first choosing randomly and uniformly a starting state $s_0 \in \mathcal{S}$. Then, starting from s_0 we apply, with probability $(1-p)$ ($p \in (0, 1)$), the policy π to the current state s_i in order to go to the next state s_{i+1} and with probability p we stop the trajectory. Doing so, we obtain a trajectory $h = (s_t)_{t=0}^{T}$ where the length of the trajectory $T+1$ is a geometrically distributed random variable: for all $k \in \mathbb{N}^*$,

$$Pr(T = k) = (1-p)^{k-1}p, \mathbb{E}[T] = \frac{1}{p} \text{ and } Var[T] = \frac{1-p}{p^2}.$$

We choose this strategy because it is easy to implement and allows us to control the mean of the length of the trajectories.

Finally, to give a score to a trajectory $h = (s_t)_{t=0}^{T}$, we proceed as follows. Let η be a Gaussian distributed and real valued random variable with mean $\nu = 0$ and variance σ^2 ($\eta \sim \mathcal{N}(0, \sigma^2)$), the score of the trajectory h is

$$v(h) = \lceil\sum_{t=0}^{T}\gamma^t r(s_t) + \eta\rfloor = \sum_{t=0}^{T}\gamma^t r(s_t) + \eta + \eta_q,$$

where $\lceil x\rfloor$ is the nearest integer from x and η_q is a quantification noise which is supposed to be a uniformly distributed random variable of mean $\mu = 0$ and variance $\sigma^2 = \frac{1}{12}$. We deliberately add a quantification noise in order to model the fact that experts are often asked to use an integer scale. More precisely, we have seen that the choice of the reward r and the discount factor γ imposes, for a trajectory $h = (s_t)_{t=0}^{T}$, that the non-perturbed score is bounded: $0 \leq \sum_{t=0}^{T}\gamma^t r(s_t) \leq \frac{1}{1-\gamma} = 10$. Thus, we have constructed the score $v(h)$ such that it models the choice of a score in the set of integers $\{0, 1, \ldots, 10\}$.

4.1.1 Performance evaluation of SBIRL

So as to evaluate the SBIRL performance, we want first to measure the mean performance of this algorithm over several Garnets when the number of trajectories, N_T, grows. To do so, we create $(G_q)_{q=1}^{N_G}$ Garnets of size ($N_{\mathcal{S}} = 100, N_{\mathcal{A}} = 5, N_B = 10$) where we compute an optimal policy π_q^e w.r.t the real reward r_q of G_q via the policy iteration algorithm. For each G_q and each iteration $j \in \{1, \ldots, N_{It}\}$ ($N_{It} = 10$), we generate N_T trajectories $(h_i)_{i=1}^{N_T}$ according to a random policy π_r (at each state s, the probability to choose action a is $\frac{1}{N_{\mathcal{A}}}$) with $p = 0.01$ such that the mean length is around 100. We compute, for each trajectory the score $v(h_i)$ with $\eta \sim \mathcal{N}(0, \sigma^2 = 1)$. Here, the standard deviation of the noise represents 10% of the maximum non perturbed-score achievable by a trajectory. Thus, for each G_q, each iteration j and a given number of trajectories N_T, we obtain a set $(h_i, v_i = v(h_i))_{i=1}^{N_T}$ that we use as an input for SBIRL which outputs the reward $r_{q,j}$. If $\pi_*^{r_{q,j}}$ is the optimal policy w.r.t $r_{q,j}$, then the performance of SBIRL is measured via the normalised error between the value functions (w.r.t r_q)

of π_q^e and $\pi_*^{r_{q,j}}$:

$$T_{q,j}(N_T) = \|v_{\pi_q^e}^{r_q} - v_{\pi_*^{r_{q,j}}}^{r_q}\|_2 \|v_{\pi_q^e}^{r_q}\|_2^{-1},$$

where $\|.\|_2$ is the Euclidean norm. The lower the error, the better the performance. Finally, the mean error $T(N_T)$ is the mean of the

$$(T_{q,j}(N_T))_{1 \leq q \leq 50}^{1 \leq j \leq 10}.$$

In Fig. 1, we plot the SBIRL error, $T(N_T)$, where N_T varies from 100 to 1000 and the error corresponding to the random policy. We observe, as predicted by the analysis, that the error converges to zero as N_T grows.

Another interesting aspect to evaluate is the tolerance of our method to the noise $\eta \sim \mathcal{N}(0, \sigma)$ over a number of Garnets. In order to evaluate this aspect, we realise exactly the same experiment as before except that N_T is fixed to 500 and σ (standard deviation of the noise) is now the varying parameter. For each G_q, each iteration j and for a given σ, SBIRL outputs the reward $r_{q,j}$ and the error $T_{q,j}(\sigma)$ of SBIRL is defined as before. The mean error $T(\sigma)$ is the mean of the

$$(T_{q,j}(\sigma))_{1 \leq q \leq 50}^{1 \leq j \leq 10}.$$

In Fig. 2, we plot the SBIRL error, $T(\sigma)$, where σ varies from 0 to 5 which represents 50% of the maximum non-perturbed score given to a trajectory. We observe that the performance is good when the noise is low and deteriorates as the noise gets bigger which is also observed in the bound of Corollary 1. We also remark that the standard deviation of the error, which appears as a shade in Fig. 2, gets bigger as the noise increases.

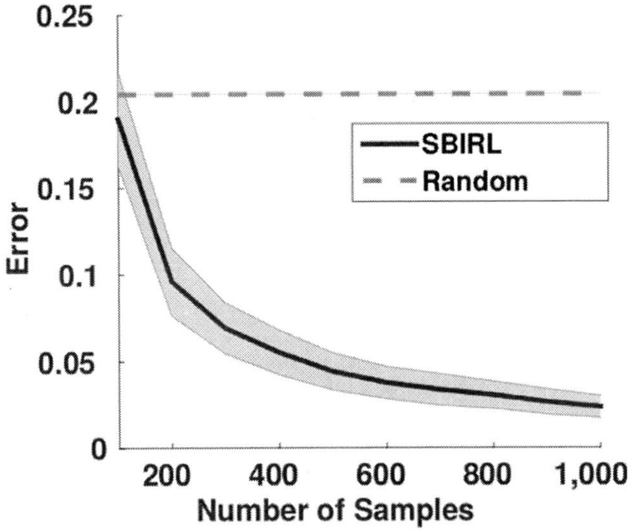

Figure 1: SBIRL error as N_T grows

4.1.2 *Comparison to IRL*

This experiment is designed to provide insights about how unreliable (w.r.t an optimal policy) the data should be to require annotation, preventing the use of standard IRL. To compare IRL to SBIRL, we need to generate near-optimal trajectories to simulate a wide range of expertise levels. To do so, we consider a noisy expert where the noise is controlled by a parameter β such that the generated policy

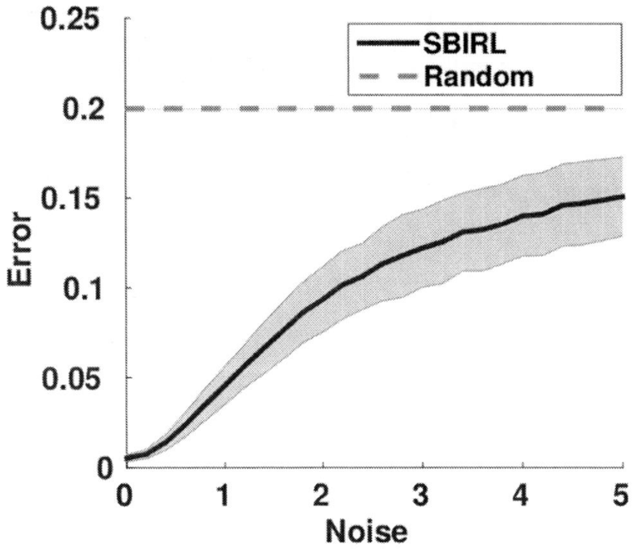

Figure 2: SBIRL error as σ grows

could range from optimal to random policies. More precisely, the trajectories $(h_i)_{i=1}^{N_T}$ are sampled according to a noisy-expert policy $\pi^n(\beta)$ where $\beta \in [0, 1]$ and given as an input to SBIRL and two IRL algorithms which are Projection [1] and SCIRL [12]. To do so, $\lceil \beta N_S \rfloor$ states are drawn randomly without replacement from $\mathcal{S}$. On those states, $\pi^n(\beta)$ is random and on the others, $\pi^n(\beta)$ is optimal. We perform the same experiment as before except that N_T is fixed to 300 and 500, $N_{It} = 3$ and the sampling policy, for each G_q, is $\pi_q^n(\beta)$. For each G_q, each iteration j and for a given β, each algorithm A outputs the reward $r_{q,j}^A$ with an error $T_{q,j}^A(\beta)$. The mean error $T^A(\beta)$ is the mean of the

$$(T_{q,j}^A(\beta))_{1 \leq q \leq 50}^{1 \leq j \leq 3}.$$

In Fig. 3(a) and Fig. 3(b), errors are plot w.r.t β (proportion of random *vs* optimal policy) varying from 0 to 1 for $N_T = 300$ and $N_T = 500$ respectively. When $N_T = 300$, the collected trajectories must be optimal on approximately 60% ($\beta = 0.4$) of states for Projection and 40% ($\beta = 0.6$) for SCIRL to achieve the same result as SBIRL. And, when $N_T = 500$, the collected trajectories must be optimal on approximately 80% ($\beta = 0.2$) of states for Projection and 55% ($\beta = 0.45$) for SCIRL to achieve the same result as SBIRL. This shows that when N_T grows, the data should be of high quality to reach the level of performance of SBIRL. So, according to the amount of available data, their reliability has to be assessed so as to decide whether directly using IRL or spending time for annotations and use SBIRL.

4.2 Application to Spoken Dialogue Systems

Here, SBIRL is applied to the optimization of a spoken dialogue system (SDS) implementing an appointment scheduling task. This experiment is mainly proposed to show the suitability of SBIRL for use in a real-world problem. Of course we do not have information about the quality of the scores or the noise and we do not study the sensitivity to these variables here.

An SDS is an HMI which converses in spoken natural language with users. Speech is transcribed to the machine by Automatic Speech Recognition (ASR). A dialogue is mod-

Policy	Score	#turns	#ASR rejections	Task Completion
Handcrafted	8.266 ± 0.008	6.547 ± 0.036	0.73 ± 0.008	0.878 ± 0.006
SBIRL 500	8.373 ± 0.006	5.568 ± 0.035	0.541 ± 0.006	0.796 ± 0.001
SBIRL 1000	8.424 ± 0.006	4.938 ± 0.027	0.469 ± 0.005	0.791 ± 0.001
SBIRL 1500	8.446 ± 0.005	4.776 ± 0.025	0.44 ± 0.005	0.79 ± 0.001

Table 1: Performance of the handcrafted and SBIRL policies in the appointment scheduling simulations.

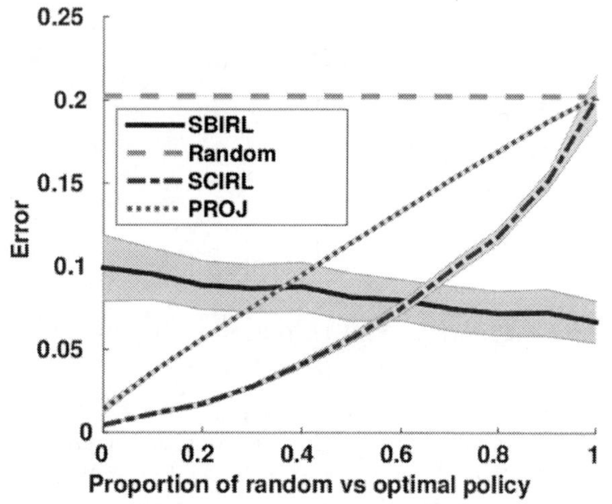

(a) SBIRL vs IRL ($N_T = 300$)

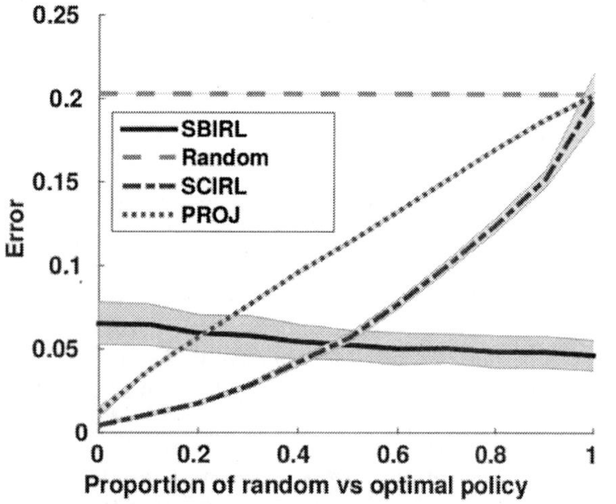

(b) SBIRL vs IRL ($N_T = 500$)

Figure 3: SBIRL vs IRL

eled as a sequence of turns, a turn starting at the beginning of each user utterance. The dialogue manager is the component of the SDS that chooses what the machine should say after each user utterance. To do so, it keeps track of the dialogue context. This process is modeled as an MDP where a state s encodes the current dialogue context and an action a represents a System Dialogue Act (SDA). An SDA describes the meaning of an utterance at the level of illocutionary force [4].

Unlike [7] which simulated dialogues, this experiment relies on interactions collected using an actual SDS. Scores are computed thanks to annotations given by real users. The collected corpus, DINASTI [8], contains 1734 dialogues. For each dialogue, the user had a two-week calendar and was asked to set an appointment at one of the available slots on the calendar. There was always only one slot available for both the system and the user so each dialogue needed several turns of negotiation to find the convenient appointment. After each dialogue, users were asked to fill in a questionnaire and rate the dialogue on a scale of 1 to 10. We trained an ordinal logistic regression model on these ratings and computed the score of new dialogues based on the numbers of dialogue turns and ASR rejections, the average ASR confidence score and task completion.

The system `Sys` and the user `Usr` have 30 time slots in common. Each slot is composed of a day of the week, the day number and an hour. `Usr` and `Sys` have different preferences concerning these slots. This is modeled by uniformly drawing in $[0,1]$ two values, $v^{\mathrm{Usr}}(\mathrm{sl}_i)$ for `Usr` and $v^{\mathrm{Sys}}(\mathrm{sl}_i)$ for `Sys`, for each slot sl_i. These values are drawn at the beginning of each dialogue and `Usr` is set to only accept the 5 slots with the highest values. If `Sys` proposes one of these slots, `Usr` accepts it, otherwise s/he suggests one. `Sys` might ask `Usr` to confirm the last utterance it understood. For an implicit confirmation, `Sys` repeats the utterance and then moves on with the dialogue. If the utterance is correct, `Usr` does not say anything. Otherwise, s/he barges in before `Sys` has moved on and repeats the correct utterance. For an explicit confirmation, `Sys` asks `Usr` whether the understood utterance is correct or not. `Usr` then either confirms or repeats the correct utterance. `Usr` also repeats the last utterance if `Sys` informs her/him that the utterance was not understood (ASR rejection) or if one of the three elements of the slot was not understood. Each dialogue begins by a proposition by `Sys`. Then, during the dialogue, when there is no ASR problem, `Sys` can choose between 4 actions: accept a slot, refuse and propose another slot, ask for an implicit confirmation and ask for an explicit confirmation. A dialogue ends when one participant has accepted the other's proposition. `Sys` proposes slots in decreasing order of $v^{\mathrm{Sys}}(sl_i)$. ASR confidence scores were simulated with a word error rate of 10%. The score was computed by drawing from a normal distribution $\mathcal{N}(-1,1)$ in the case of a misrecognition ($\mathcal{N}(1,1)$ otherwise) and by then applying the sigmoid function to this value. The threshold for ASR rejection was set to 0.5.

For evaluation purposes, SBIRL was applied to simulated dialogues with a uniformly random policy. Given sl_i the selected slot, task completion was defined as $v^{\mathrm{Usr}}(sl_i) + 0.5 \times v^{\mathrm{Sys}}(\mathrm{sl}_i)$. The state space was composed of the latest User Dialogue Act (UDA, for instance ACCEPT) as well as the numbers of dialogue turns and ASR rejections, the average ASR confidence score and the value $v^{\mathrm{Sys}}(\mathrm{sl}_i)$ of the slot sl_i being currently discussed. The state space was built by applying entropy-based discretisation [9] with these parameters on the random corpus and then by aggregating the resulting intervals. We performed 100 runs on 500, 1000 and 1500 dialogues. For each run, we computed the state space, ran SBIRL and then learnt a policy with the new reward function. On average, the state space had respectively 48.5, 71.8 and 79.5 states. The learning algorithm was SARSA with ϵ-greedy exploration, where ϵ was set to 0.01. The learning factor α was set to 0.1. We learnt a policy on 5000 dialogues and tested the learnt policy on 2000 dialogues. We compare learning with a handcrafted policy tested on 100000 dialogues which always asks the user for an implicit confirmation and then accepts a slot sl_i if $v^{\text{Sys}}(\text{sl}_i) \geq 0.5$ or if the number of dialogue turns is superior or equal to 15. Table 1 contains 95% confidence intervals for the estimated user satisfaction score and dialogue statistics with the handcrafted policy and with the policies learnt with SBIRL. The policy learnt with SBIRL improves the performance score by finding a better compromise between the number of dialogue turns and task completion. The policy learnt with SBIRL produces dialogues with, on average, 2 fewer dialogue turns than the ones resulting of the handcrafted policy and with sacrificing less than 10% of the task completion value. This is an important result since the average dialogue duration is well-known to highly influence user's satisfaction [23].

5. CONCLUSION

This paper studied the SBIRL algorithm which applies to a non-standard setting for Inverse Reinforcement Learning (IRL) relying on annotated trajectories. Trajectories can be collected using policies that are not assumed to be generated by an expert but are globally scored *a posteriori* by such an expert. This setting is much more suitable for many applications where datasets are already available but with unreliable quality. Expert's annotations are supposed to be noisy and robustness to noise was assessed both theoretically and practically. The theoretical analysis shows that the algorithm produces a policy that approximates the optimal one at a rate that increases linearly with the number of scored trajectories. Results of synthetic experiments were in accordance with theory and also showed that the noise in the scores is not too influential. These experiments also provided insights about how unreliable the data should be to require annotation, preventing the use of standard IRL methods. An application to spoken dialogue systems, using real data collected with an actual system, showed that this method is applicable in practice to learn more efficient interaction policies in a realistic domain (appointment scheduling). In future work, this methodology will be applied to large scale systems such as human-robot interaction.

APPENDIX

This appendix recalls the stated theoretical results and proves them. First, we recall the required assumptions.

Assumption 1
There exists a vector parameter $\theta_* \in \mathbb{R}^d$ and a centered noise η such that for any trajectory $h = (s_t)_{t=0}^T$ and any associated score v, one has

$$v = \sum_{t=0}^{T} \gamma^t r_{\theta_*}(s_t) + \eta(h).$$

Assumption 2
The noise is subgaussian: there exists $\sigma \geq 0$ such that, almost surely, for all $\lambda \in \mathbb{R}$,

$$\mathbb{E}[e^{\lambda\eta(H)}|H] \leq e^{\frac{\lambda^2\sigma^2}{2}}.$$

Moreover, there exists a finite $\rho \geq 1$ such that, almost surely,

$$\frac{\|A^{-\frac{1}{2}}\mu(H)\|_2}{\sqrt{d}} \leq \rho.$$

We also recall that for a distribution ν and a function $f \in \mathbb{R}^S$, we write

$$\nu f = \mathbb{E}_\nu[f(S)].$$

For a stochastic kernel Q, we have

$$[Qf](s) = \mathbb{E}_{Q(.|s)}[f(S')].$$

Therefore, νQ is a distribution such that

$$\mathbb{E}_{\nu Q}[f] = \mathbb{E}_\nu[Qf] = \mathbb{E}_{S\sim\nu}[\mathbb{E}_{S'\sim Q(.|S)}][f(S')].$$

A. PROPAGATION OF ERRORS: REWARDS

Theorem 1 (Propagation of errors: rewards)
Write λ_m the minimum eigenvalue of $\mathbb{E}[\mu(H)\mu(H)^\top]$ and λ_M the maximum eigenvalue of $\mathbb{E}_\nu[\phi(S)\phi(S)^\top]$. Assume that θ_n satisfies $\mathcal{R}(\theta_n) \leq \mathcal{R}(\theta_*) + \epsilon$, then the associated reward satisfies

$$\mathbb{E}_\nu[(r_{\theta_*}(S) - r_{\theta_n}(S))^2] \leq \frac{\lambda_M}{\lambda_m}\epsilon.$$

PROOF. First, we use the fact that the risk is a quadratic form (and that $A\theta_* = b$):

$$\begin{aligned}
\mathcal{R}(\theta) &= \mathbb{E}[(v - \theta^\top\mu(H))^2] = \theta^\top A\theta - 2\theta^\top b + \mathbb{E}[V^2] \\
&= \|A\theta - b\|_{A^{-1}}^2 + \mathbb{E}[V^2] - b^\top A^{-1} b \\
&= \|A\theta - b\|_{A^{-1}}^2 + \mathbb{E}[V^2] - 2b^\top\theta_* + \theta_*^\top A\theta_* \\
&= \|A\theta - b\|_{A^{-1}}^2 + \mathcal{R}(\theta_*) \\
&= \|\theta - \theta_*\|_A^2 + \mathcal{R}(\theta_*).
\end{aligned}$$

Similarly, writing $C = \mathbb{E}_\nu[\phi(S)\phi(S)^\top]$, one can easily show that

$$\mathbb{E}_\nu[(r_{\theta_*}(S) - r_{\theta_n}(S))^2] = \|\theta - \theta_*\|_C^2.$$

Now, let $x \in \mathbb{R}^d$. For a symmetric and definite positive matrix M, write $\|x\|_M = \sqrt{x^\top Mx}$ and S_M its Cholesky decomposition. Write also $\|M\|_2$ the spectral norm of M. We have

$$\begin{aligned}
\|x\|_C &= \sqrt{x^\top S_C^\top S_C x} \\
&= \|S_C x\|_2 \\
&= \|S_C S_A^{-1} S_A x\|_2 \\
&\leq \|S_C\|_2 \|S_A^{-1}\|_2 \|S_A x\|_2 \\
&= \frac{\lambda_M}{\lambda_m}\|x\|_A.
\end{aligned}$$

Thus, we have

$$\begin{aligned}
\mathbb{E}_\nu[(r_{\theta_*}(S) - r_{\theta_n}(S))^2] &= \|\theta - \theta_*\|_C^2 \\
&\leq \frac{\lambda_M}{\lambda_m}\|\theta - \theta_*\|_A^2 \\
&= \frac{\lambda_M}{\lambda_m}(\mathcal{R}(\theta_n) - \mathcal{R}(\theta_*)).
\end{aligned}$$

Using the fact that $\mathcal{R}(\theta_n) - \mathcal{R}(\theta_*) \leq \epsilon$ proves the result. $\square$

B. PROPAGATION OF ERRORS: VALUES

Theorem 2 (Propagation of errors: values)
For a policy π, define C_π as the smallest coefficient such that $(1-\gamma)\nu'(I-\gamma P_\pi)^{-1} \leq C_\pi \nu$. Assume that θ_n satisfies $\mathcal{R}(\theta_n) \leq \mathcal{R}(\theta_*) + \epsilon$, then the associated value satisfies

$$\mathbb{E}_{\nu'}[(v_*^{r_{\theta_*}}(S) - v^{r_{\theta_*}}_{\pi_*^{r_{\theta_n}}}(S))^2] \leq \frac{2\left(C_{\pi_*} + C_{\pi_*^{r_{\theta_n}}}\right)}{(1-\gamma)^2}\frac{\lambda_M}{\lambda_m}\epsilon.$$

PROOF. To simplify the notations, write $r = r_{\theta_*}$ the unknown reward function (of associated optimal policy $\pi_* = \pi_*^{r_{\theta_n}}$) and $\hat{r} = r_{\theta_n}$ the estimated reward function (of associated optimal policy $\hat{\pi} = \pi_*^{r_{\theta_n}}$). With these notations, the quantity to be bounded is $\mathbb{E}_{\nu'}[(v^r_{\pi_*}(S) - v^r_{\hat{\pi}}(S))^2]$.

Componentwise, we have

$$v^r_{\pi_*} - v^r_{\hat{\pi}} = v^r_{\pi_*} - v^{\hat{r}}_{\pi_*} + v^{\hat{r}}_{\pi_*} - v^{\hat{r}}_{\hat{\pi}} + v^{\hat{r}}_{\hat{\pi}} - v^r_{\hat{\pi}}.$$

As $\hat{\pi}$ is optimal for $\hat{r}$, we have $v^{\hat{r}}_{\pi_*} - v^{\hat{r}}_{\hat{\pi}} \leq 0$, and a value function satisfies

$$v^r_\pi = \sum_{t\geq 0}\gamma^t P^t_\pi r = (I-\gamma P_\pi)^{-1} r,$$

therefore:

$$\begin{aligned}
& v^r_{\pi_*} - v^r_{\hat{\pi}} \\
& \leq v^r_{\pi_*} - v^{\hat{r}}_{\pi_*} + v^{\hat{r}}_{\hat{\pi}} - v^r_{\hat{\pi}} \\
& = (I-\gamma P_{\pi_*})^{-1}(r-\hat{r}) + (I-\gamma P_{\hat{\pi}})^{-1}(\hat{r}-r) \\
& \leq \frac{2}{1-\gamma} Q|r-\hat{r}| \\
\text{with } Q = & \frac{1-\gamma}{2}((I-\gamma P_{\pi_*})^{-1} + (I-\gamma P_{\hat{\pi}})^{-1}).
\end{aligned}$$

Notice that Q is a stochastic kernel. We have

$$\begin{aligned}
& \mathbb{E}_{\nu'}[(v^r_{\pi_*}(S) - v^r_{\hat{\pi}}(S))^2] \\
& \leq \frac{4}{(1-\gamma)^2}\mathbb{E}_{S\sim\nu'}[(\mathbb{E}_{S'\sim Q(.|S)}[|r(S') - \hat{r}(S')|])^2] \\
& \leq \frac{4}{(1-\gamma)^2}\mathbb{E}_{S\sim\nu'}[\mathbb{E}_{S'\sim Q(.|S)}[(r(S') - \hat{r}(S'))^2]] \\
& = \frac{4\mathbb{E}_{S\sim\nu' Q}[(r(S) - \hat{r}(S))^2]}{(1-\gamma)^2} \\
& \leq \frac{4(C_{\pi_*} + C_{\hat{\pi}})}{2(1-\gamma)^2}\mathbb{E}_\nu[(r(S) - \hat{r}(S))^2] \\
& = \frac{2(C_{\pi_*} + C_{\hat{\pi}})}{(1-\gamma)^2}\mathbb{E}_\nu[(r(S) - \hat{r}(S))^2],
\end{aligned}$$

the second inequality being due to the Jensen's inequality and the third one to the definition of C_π. Using Th. 1 allows concluding. □

C. FINITE SAMPLE ANALYSIS

Corollary 1
Let δ be such that $\ln\frac{9}{\delta} > \max(0, 2.6 - \ln d)$. If assumptions 1 and-2 hold and if $n \geq 6\rho^2 d \ln\frac{9d}{\delta}$, then with probability at least $1-\delta$ we have

$$\mathbb{E}_\nu[(r_{\theta_*}(S) - r_{\theta_n}(S))^2] \leq \frac{\lambda_M}{\lambda_m}\frac{\sigma^2(d + 2\sqrt{d\ln\frac{9}{\delta}} + 2\ln\frac{9}{\delta})}{n} + o\left(\frac{1}{n}\right).$$

Under the same assumptions, with probability at least $1-\delta$:

$$\mathbb{E}_{\nu'}[(v_*^{r_{\theta_*}}(S) - v^{r_{\theta_*}}_{\pi_*^{r_{\theta_n}}}(S))^2] \leq \frac{2\left(C_{\pi_*} + C_{\pi_*^{r_{\theta_n}}}\right)}{(1-\gamma)^2}\frac{\lambda_M}{\lambda_m}\frac{\sigma^2(d + 2\sqrt{d\ln\frac{9}{\delta}} + 2\ln\frac{9}{\delta})}{n} + o\left(\frac{1}{n}\right).$$

PROOF. The assumptions made allow using Theorem 1 of [11], which states that with probability at least $1-\delta$ we have

$$\mathcal{R}(\theta_n) \leq \mathcal{R}(\theta_*) + \frac{\sigma^2(d + 2\sqrt{d\ln\frac{9}{\delta}} + 2\ln\frac{9}{\delta})}{n} + o\left(\frac{1}{n}\right).$$

Plugging this result in Th. 1 and 2 allows concluding. □

REFERENCES

[1] P. Abbeel and A. Ng. Apprenticeship learning via inverse reinforcement learning. In *Proc. of ICML*, 2004.

[2] R. Akrour, M. Schoenauer, and M. Sebag. Preference-based policy learning. In *Proc. of ECML*, 2011.

[3] T. Archibald, K. McKinnon, and L. Thomas. On the generation of Markov decision processes. *Journal of the Operational Research Society*, 1995.

[4] J. L. Austin. *How to do Things with Words.* Clarendon Press, Oxford, 1962.

[5] A. Boularias, H. R. Chinaei, and B. Chaib-draa. Learning the reward model of dialogue pomdps from data. In *NIPS Workshop on Machine Learning for Assistive Techniques*, 2010.

[6] A. Boularias, J. Kober, and J. Peters. Relative entropy inverse reinforcement learning. In *Proc. of AISTATS*, 2011.

[7] L. El Asri, R. Laroche, and O. Pietquin. Reward shaping for statistical optimisation of dialogue management. In *Proc. of SLSP*, 2013.

[8] L. El Asri, R. Laroche, and O. Pietquin. DINASTI: Dialogues with a Negotiating Appointment Setting Interface. In *Proc. of LREC*, 2014.

[9] U. M. Fayyad and K. B. Irani. Multi-interval discretization of continuous-valued attributes for classification learning. In *Proc. of UAI*, 1993.

[10] W. Hoeffding. Probability inequalities for sums of bounded random variables. *Journal of the American statistical association*, 58(301):13–30, 1963.

[11] D. Hsu, S. M. Kakade, and T. Zhang. Random design analysis of ridge regression. *Foundations of Computational Mathematics*, 14(3):569–600, 2014.

[12] E. Klein, M. Geist, B. Piot, and O. Pietquin. Inverse reinforcement learning through structured classification. In *Proc. of NIPS*, December 2012.

[13] O. Lemon and O. Pietquin, editors. *Data-Driven Methods for Adaptive Spoken Dialogue Systems: Computational Learning for Conversational Interfaces.* Springer, November 2012.

[14] S. Möller, K.-P. Engelbrecht, and R. Schleicher. Predicting the quality and usability of spoken dialogue services. *Speech Communication*, 50(8):730–744, 2008.

[15] T. Paek. Reinforcement learning for spoken dialogue systems: Comparing strengths and weaknesses for

practical deployment. In *Proc. of Dialog-on-Dialog Workshop at Interspeech*, 2006.

[16] O. Pietquin. Inverse reinforcement learning for interactive systems. In *Proc. of IJCAI workshop on Machine Learning for Interactive Systems*, 2013.

[17] B. Piot, M. Geist, and O. Pietquin. Learning from demonstrations: is it worth estimating a reward function? In *Proc. of ECML*, 2013.

[18] B. Piot, M. Geist, and O. Pietquin. Boosted and reward-regularized classification for apprenticeship learning. In *Proc. of AAMAS*, 2014.

[19] S. Russell. Learning agents for uncertain environments. In *Proc. of COLT*, 1998.

[20] S. P. Singh, M. J. Kearns, D. J. Litman, and M. A. Walker. Reinforcement learning for spoken dialogue systems. In *Proc. of Nips*, 1999.

[21] R. Tibshirani. Regression shrinkage and selection via the LASSO. *Journal of the Royal Statistical Society. Series B (Methodological)*, pages 267–288, 1996.

[22] A. Tikhonov. Solution of incorrectly formulated problems and the regularization method. In *Soviet Mathematics*, volume 5, pages 1035–1038, 1963.

[23] M. A. Walker, D. J. Litman, C. A. Kamm, and A. Abella. PARADISE: A framework for evaluating spoken dialogue agents. In *Proc. of EACL*, 1997.

[24] S. Young, M. Gasic, B. Thomson, and J. D. Williams. POMDP-based statistical spoken dialog systems: A review. *Proceedings of the IEEE*, 101(5):1160–1179, 2013.

Emergence of Emotional Appraisal Signals in Reinforcement Learning Agents

(JAAMAS Extended Abstract)

Pedro Sequeira, Francisco S. Melo, and Ana Paiva
INESC-ID and Instituto Superior Técnico, Universidade de Lisboa
Av. Prof. Dr. Cavaco Silva, 2744-016 Porto Salvo, Portugal
pedro.sequeira@gaips.inesc-id.pt

ABSTRACT

The positive impact of emotions in decision-making has long been established in both natural and artificial agents. In the perspective of appraisal theories, emotions complement perceptual information, coloring our sensations and guiding our decision-making. However, when designing autonomous agents, is *emotional appraisal* the best complement to their perceptions? Mechanisms investigated in the affective sciences provide support for this hypothesis in biological agents. In this paper, we look for similar support in artificial systems. We adopt the intrinsically motivated reinforcement learning framework to investigate different sources of information that can guide decision-making in learning agents, and an evolutionary approach based on genetic programming to identify a small set of such sources that have the largest impact on the performance of the agent in different tasks, as measured by an external evaluation signal. We then show that these sources of information: (i) are applicable in a wider range of environments than those where the agents evolved; (ii) exhibit interesting correspondences to emotional appraisal-like signals previously proposed in the literature. The results of the study thus point towards our departing hypothesis that the appraisal process might indeed provide essential information to complement perceptual capabilities and thus guide decision-making.

Keywords

reinforcement learning; intrinsic motivation; genetic programming; emotions; appraisal theories

1. INTRODUCTION

Emotions indirectly drive behaviors that lead individuals to achieve goals and satisfy needs. Studies show that damage to regions of the brain identified as responsible for emotional processing affects the ability to properly learn aversive stimuli, plan courses of action, *i.e.*, to take advantageous decisions [1]. Appraisal theories of emotions suggest that they arise from evaluations of specific aspects of the individual's relationship with their environment, providing an adaptive response mechanism to situations occurring therein [2].

In artificial systems, the area of affective computing (AC) has investigated the impact of emotional processing capabilities in the development of autonomous agents, often based in appraisal theories of emotions. Appraisal-inspired mechanisms were shown to improve the performance of artificial agents [3, 6]. Within these mechanisms, *appraisal signals* "translate" information about the history of interaction of the agent with its environment that aid decision-making and focus behavior towards dealing with the situation being evaluated [3]. Although one of the driving motivations for the use of emotional appraisal-based agent architectures is the creation of "better agents", one fundamental question remains mostly unaddressed in the literature: *in the search for information that may complement an agent's perceptual capabilities, is the emotional appraisal process the best mechanism to provide such information?*

In this paper we contribute to this question, providing empirical evidence that appraisal-like signals may arise as natural candidates when looking for sources of information to complement an agent's perceptual capabilities. Our approach to the question can be conceptualized as depicted in Fig. 1—we want to analyze which kind of perceptual information processing mechanism best complements an agent's decision-making in a given set of tasks.[1]

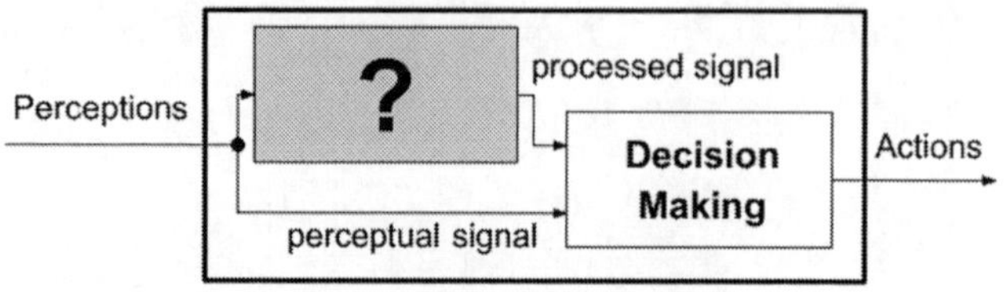

Figure 1: How to complement decision-making?

2. IDENTIFICATION OF SOURCES

In our study, we rely on *intrinsically motivated reinforcement learning* (IMRL) that provides a principled manner to integrate multiple sources of information in the process of learning and decision-making of artificial agents [7]. These complementary sources of information endow the agent with a richer repertoire of behaviors that may successfully overcome agent limitations, *e.g.*, [6, 7]. As such, IMRL is a framework naturally suited to our investigation.

Fig. 2 depicts the evolutionary procedure based on genetic programming, which is inspired by [4]. We depart from an initial population of agents, each endowed with a certain reward function containing information about differ-

Appears in: *Proceedings of the 15th International Conference on Autonomous Agents and Multiagent Systems (AAMAS 2016), J. Thangarajah, K. Tuyls, C. Jonker, S. Marsella (eds.), May 9–13, 2016, Singapore.*

[1]The full version of this manuscript can be found in [5].

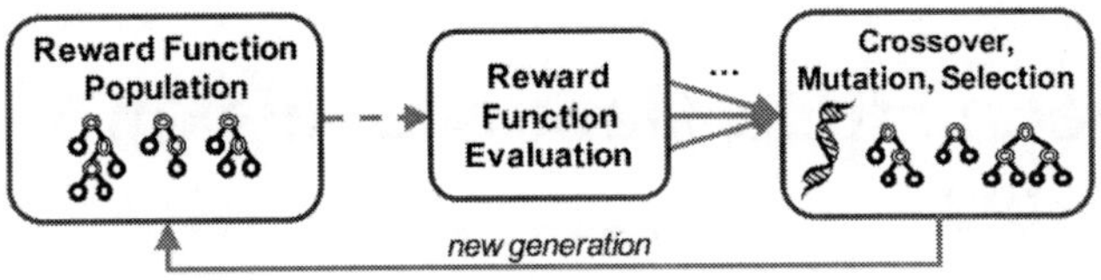

Figure 2: Evolving reward functions with GP.

ent aspects of the agent's interaction with its environment, *e.g.*, the number of visits to some state, the value associated with some action or the perceived distance to some estimated goal state. Each agent/reward function is evaluated in a set of environments of interest. For experimental purposes we tested our IMRL agents in grid-world foraging scenarios, where fitness is measured as the total amount of preys captured. The perceptual limitations of the agent in the different environments pose challenges that directly impact its ability to capture preys and, consequently, its fitness. In each generation, the fittest agents are selected and the reward structure of the other agents is modified by means of the GP operations of mutation and crossover. Upon convergence, the set of agents able to attain the largest fitness in the desired scenarios was identified. The analysis of the corresponding reward structures provided the information about which signals are potentially most *useful* to complement the perceptual capabilities of our IMRL agents. In that regard, the results of our experiments revealed the emergence of the following informative signals:

- **Fitness**, corresponding to the estimate of the extrinsic reward received by executing some action in a state;
- **Value**, assessing the estimated long-term value of executing an action after observing some state;
- **Advantage**, evaluating how good it is to execute an action when in some state, relative to the best action;
- **Predictability**, measuring the probability of transitioning to some state after executing some action;
- **Novelty**, providing a (negative) measure of how novel a state is given the agent's past observations.

3. VALIDATION OF EMERGED SOURCES

In order to assess the general-purpose of the emerged sources of information, *i.e.*, whether they can guide the decision process of learning agents in general, we tested their applicability in a different set of scenarios. For that purpose we created a set of environments inspired by the game of Pac-Man, which are considerably larger and more complex than the foraging scenarios in which the reward signals emerged. We again resorted to the IMRL framework to define a space of reward functions as a linear combination of the 5 emerged signals. By using a basic uniform-sampling optimization procedure, the results of this second experiment showed that indeed the signals are more informative than the extrinsic rewards while mitigating the agent's inherent perceptual limitations when playing Pac-Man.

4. DISCUSSION & CONCLUSIONS

After showing the applicability and general-purpose of the emerged sources of information, we then compared the kinds of information processed by each reward signal with the nature of evaluations made by humans according to appraisal theories of emotions. We based our analysis in the "major appraisal dimensions" identified in [2], namely *novelty, intrinsic pleasantness, motivational bases, power and coping* and *social dimensions*. Each dimension defines an appraisal "theme", *i.e.*, the criteria and kind of information that is used to perform a certain appraisal, according to particular aspects of the subject-environment relationship. The results of our analysis revealed that the identified sources of information exhibit dynamics and properties that can be related to the way natural agents evaluate their environment according to appraisal theories of emotions.

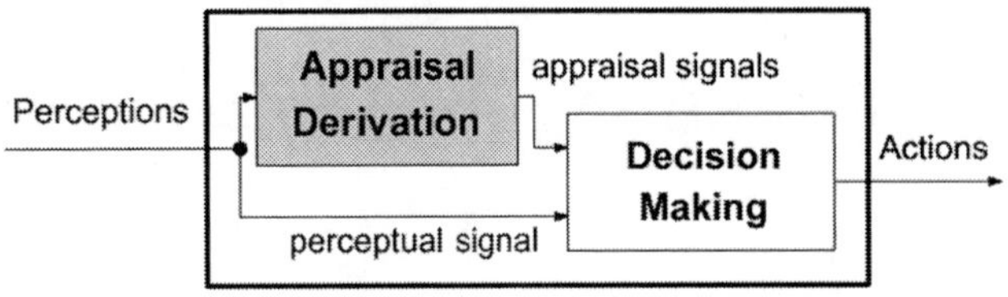

Figure 3: Emotional appraisal-based agent.

In conclusion, our experimental study highlighted the usefulness of appraisal-like processes in identifying different aspects of a task—the sources of information—that complement an agent's perceptual capabilities in the pursuit for more reliable artificial decision-makers, as depicted in Fig. 3. Moreover, these features, much like appraisal processing in nature, also proved to be useful in different environments. We also contributed for research within IMRL by emerging 4 domain-independent reward signals, relying on common information used by most reinforcement learning (RL) algorithms, that could be applied in different scenarios with distinct purposes. As a consequence, the emerged signals provide a general-purpose reward mechanism for artificial RL agents while reducing the need for designers to hand-code reward functions for specific scenarios.

Acknowledgments

This work was supported by national funds through Fundação para a Ciência e a Tecnologia (FCT) with reference UID/CEC/50021/2013. P. Sequeira acknowledges a BDP grant from project INSIDE ref. CMUP-ERI/HCI/0051/2013.

REFERENCES

[1] A. Damasio. *Descartes' Error: Emotion, Reason, and the Human Brain.* Putnam Publishing, 1994.

[2] P. Ellsworth and K. Scherer. Appraisal processes in emotion. In *Handbook of the Affective Sciences.* Oxford University Press, 2003.

[3] S. Marsella, J. Gratch, and P. Petta. Computational models of emotion. In *Blueprint for Affective Computing.* Oxford University Press, 2010.

[4] S. Niekum, A. G. Barto, and L. Spector. Genetic programming for reward function search. *IEEE Trans. Autonomous Mental Development*, 2(2):83–90, 2010.

[5] P. Sequeira, F. S. Melo, and A. Paiva. Emergence of emotional appraisal signals in reinforcement learning agents. *Autonomous Agents and Multi-Agent Systems*, 29(4):537–568, 2014.

[6] P. Sequeira, F. S. Melo, and A. Paiva. Learning by appraising: an emotion-based approach to intrinsic reward design. *Adaptive Behavior*, 22(5):330–349, 2014.

[7] S. Singh, R. Lewis, A. Barto, and J. Sorg. Intrinsically motivated reinforcement learning: An evolutionary perspective. *IEEE Trans. Autonomous Mental Development*, 2(2):70–82, 2010.

Measuring the Distance Between Finite Markov Decision Processes

Jinhua Song, Yang Gao*, Hao Wang
State Key Laboratory for Novel Software Technology, Collaborative Innovation Center of Novel Software Technology and Industrialization
Nanjing University, Nanjing, China
songjinhua2008@gmail.com
gaoy@nju.edu.cn
wanghao@nju.edu.cn

Bo An
School of Computer Engineering
Nanyang Technological University
Singapore
boan@ntu.edu.sg

ABSTRACT

Markov decision processes (MDPs) have been studied for many decades. Recent research in using transfer learning methods to solve MDPs has shown that knowledge learned from one MDP may be used to solve a similar MDP better. In this paper, we propose two metrics for measuring the distance between finite MDPs. Our metrics are based on the Hausdorff metric which measures the distance between two subsets of a metric space and the Kantorovich metric for measuring the distance between probabilistic distributions. Our metrics can be used to compute the distance between reinforcement learning tasks that are modeled as MDPs. The second contribution of this paper is that we apply the metrics to direct transfer learning by finding the similar source tasks. Our third contribution is that we propose two knowledge transfer methods which transfer value functions of the selected source tasks to the target task. Extensive experimental results show that our metrics are effective in finding similar tasks and significantly improve the performance of transfer learning with the transfer methods.

Keywords

Markov decision process; Kantorovich metric; Hausdorff metric; reinforcement learning; transfer learning

1. INTRODUCTION

Markov decision processes (MDPs) are effective models for solving sequential decision-making problems [4] in uncertain environments. By making sequential decisions, the decision maker (called *agent*) can collect numerical feedbacks (called *rewards*) from the environment. The goal of the agent is to maximize the cumulative reward. Planning (e.g. Dynamic programming [3,23]) and learning (e.g. reinforcement learning [15,25]), which aim at finding an optimal mapping from states to actions (called *policy*), can be used to achieve the goal. When there are some MDPs that have been solved, the new MDPs can be solved better by reusing the knowledge of the solved MDPs. This idea has been used in reinforcement learning (RL) domain for many years, which is known as transfer learning in RL. Lots of transfer learning methods have been studied [18,27], which focus on accelerating the learning process and improving the average approximation of the optimal value functions.

Although there has been lots of work on transfer learning, most approaches rely on the implicit assumption that source tasks and target tasks are very similar. However, the assumption is not necessarily true in practice. If the source task is irrelevant to the target task, transfer may cause slower learning speed or even worse performance in the target task; this phenomenon has been recognized as *negative transfer* [18,24,27,28]. Therefore, it is necessary and essential to define the similarity relationship between the source tasks and the target task so as to select the best source task(s), which is the focus of this paper.

Unfortunately, there are few existing distance measures that can be used to estimate the similarity between two MDPs. Some work uses *transfer advantage* [6] to define the similarity between two MDPs [6,9]. However, the similarity is usually difficult to be computed before the target task has been learned, thus it cannot be applied to transfer learning. Some work just measures the distance between dynamics of two MDPs, such as reward functions or transition models, and requires that the state-action spaces are the same [2,6,19]. Konidaris et al. [17] define *agent-space* to describe the features of an agent, and judge whether two MDPs are related by comparing the agent-spaces. However, it is difficult to automatically identify agent-space in advance.

Our contributions in this paper can be claimed as follows. First, we propose two metrics for measuring the distance between two MDPs based on the whole models of MDPs from a quantitative point of view for the first time. The metrics are based on the distance between states which consider actions, probability transition functions and reward functions of the states. We define the notion of homogeneous MDPs and extend Ferns' metric [10], which measures the distance between two states in *one* MDP, to compute the distances between states in different MDPs. After computing all the distances between states, we apply the Kantorovich metric [7] and the Hausdorff metric [5] to composite them to compute the distance between two MDPs. Kantorovich met-

*Corresponding Author

Appears in: *Proceedings of the 15th International Conference on Autonomous Agents and Multiagent Systems (AAMAS 2016), J. Thangarajah, K. Tuyls, C. Jonker, S. Marsella (eds.), May 9–13, 2016, Singapore.*

ric was first proposed in the field of transportation theory and is used to measure the distance between two distributions. We use Kantorovich metric with the assumption that a certain amount of "resources" from one MDP's states are allocated to the other MDP's states. However, when the state spaces of the MDPs are very large, computing Kantorovich metric may be computationally expensive. Thus, we apply another easy-to-compute metric, Hausdorff metric. Hausdorff metric is a mathematical tool for measuring the distance between two sets of points that are subsets of a metric space. The distance between two sets of states is used to represent the distance of two MDPs. Although Hausdorff metric can be computed more efficiently, it may miss some similar MDPs due to "outliers" (states which are very different from others). Therefore, the distance can be computed by Hausdorff metric if the state space is too large and by Kantorovich metric otherwise.

Our second contribution is that we use our metrics to measure the distance between RL tasks which are modeled as MDPs, and apply them in transfer learning for RL. In this paper we focus on transfer learning in one domain and consider homogeneous MDPs which widely exist in one domain as most related works in transfer learning (e.g., [14, 21, 27, 30]). We apply the metrics for source tasks selection in transfer learning. Our third contribution is proposing two transfer methods which transfer value functions of selected source tasks to the target task. After selecting the proper source tasks, transfer methods are used to transfer knowledge to the target task. Since the metrics are based on the distances between states, value functions are used as the transfer knowledge.

Experimental results show that our metrics are effective in finding similar tasks to avoid negative transfer in transfer learning, and significantly improve the performance (i.e. reducing episodes to converge to the optimal policy by more than a third and achieving better asymptotic performance) of the baseline algorithms with our transfer methods.

2. BACKGROUND

2.1 Markov Decision Process

In this paper, we focus on finite Markov decision processes.

DEFINITION 2.1. *A finite Markov decision process can be represented as a 4-tuple* $M = \{S, A, P, R\}$, *where* S *is a finite set of states;* A *is a finite set of actions;* $P : S \times A \times S \to [0, 1]$ *is the probability transition function; and* $R : S \times A \to \Re$ *is the reward function. In this paper, we denote the probability of the transition from state* s *to another state* s' *when taking action* a *by* $P^a_{ss'}$ *and the immediate reward received after the transition by* r^a_s.[1]

A policy is defined as a mapping, $\pi : S \times A \to [0, 1]$. To measure the quality of a policy, a value function, $V^\pi(s)$, is used to estimate the expected long-term cumulative reward from state s under a policy π. It is formally defined as:

$$V^\pi(s) = E_\pi \left[\sum_{t=0}^{\infty} \gamma^t r_t | s_0 = s \right],$$

[1]In fact, the reward could also be related to s'. However in many practical applications, it is usual the case that the reward is determined by the state s and the action a [10]. We follow this convention in this paper.

where γ is a discount factor, r_t is the reward at time-step t, and E_π is the expectation with respect to the policy π. It can be expressed as the Bellman equation:

$$V^\pi(s) = \sum_{a \in A} \pi(s, a) \sum_{s' \in S} P^a_{ss'} \left[r^a_s + \gamma V^\pi(s') \right].$$

Similarly, action value function (called Q-value), the expected long-term cumulative reward of taking action a in state s under a policy π, is defined as:

$$Q^\pi(s, a) = \sum_{s' \in S} P^a_{ss'} \left[r^a_s + \gamma \sum_{a' \in A} \pi(s', a') Q^\pi(s', a') \right].$$

The goal is to find an optimal policy π^* which maximizes the expectation of the long-time discounted cumulative reward from any starting state $s \in S$:

$$\pi^* = \arg\max_\pi E_\pi \left[\sum_{t=0}^{\infty} \gamma^t r_t | s_0 = s \right].$$

2.2 Transfer Learning

The idea of transfer learning comes from psychology and cognitive science research. It is motivated by the finding [22] that humans can solve a problem faster by reusing knowledge learned from solving related problems. In the MDP domain, agents are expected to improve their performance through transferring the knowledge retained from similar MDPs.

Consider the situation that an agent is solving a sequence of MDPs. If these MDPs are related and the agent has solved n MDPs, the agent may use the knowledge learned from the prior MDPs when solving the $(n + 1)$-th MDP. Transfer learning aims to select the learned MDP(s), choose the transfer knowledge (e.g. instances [19], Q-values [29] and policies [16]), and use the knowledge to improve the performance of solving the new MDP. Related MDPs may have some common knowledge which can help the new MDP to be solved better, and transferring from MDPs which differ too much from the new MDP may cause negative transfer. Thus, the notion of MDP similarity (or distance) is essential to transfer learning. However, many transfer approaches ignore this problem. Few work define the similarity, but their definitions can only be used under strict conditions or cannot be applied to transfer learning. In the next section, we define measures that can be used to estimate the similarity between two MDPs.

3. METRICS FOR MEASURING THE DISTANCE BETWEEN MDPS

Our goal is to define metrics to measure the distance between two MDPs based on the whole models of MDPs including state transitions and reward structures. Note that an MDP contains a set of states, and each state s has its own action set A_s, probability transition function P_s and reward function R_s. Therefore, the distance between two MDPs is based on the distance between their states, and the distance between two states depends on their action sets, probability transition functions and reward functions. To measure the distance between two states in different MDPs, we extend Fern's metric of states [10], which considers actions, probability transition functions and reward functions of those states. Then we apply Kantorovich metric and Hausdorff metric to measure the distance between the two state sets of two MDPs.

3.1 Measuring States' Distance in Different MDPs

In this section, we introduce a metric to measure the distance between two states of two MDPs by extending an existing metric for measuring the distance of two states of one MDP [11–13].

DEFINITION 3.1. *For any $s, s' \in S$, their distance $d(s, s')$ is defined as*

$$d(s,s') = \max_{a \in A}\{|r_s^a - r_{s'}^a| + cT_K(d)(P_s^a, P_{s'}^a)\}, \quad (1)$$

where $c \in (0,1)$, P_s^a (resp. $P_{s'}^a$) is the probabilistic transition when action a is taken at state s (resp. s'), and $T_K(d)(P_s^a, P_{s'}^a)$ is the Kantorovich distance between the two probabilistic transitions.

Notice that the above metric is only defined on states in the same MDP and it may not be directly applied to compute the distance between two states in different MDPs. It is known that a specific task can be modeled as different MDPs with different state representations and action representations [25, 26], and it is difficult for the agent to recognize whether the MDPs have the same state-action spaces. Therefore, the above metric is not applicable when the state and action representations are different. Thus, we extend it to measure the distance between states in different MDPs. Our key idea is that if two MDPs can be merged into one, then we directly use this metric to measure the distance between states in the "new MDP". To decide whether MDPs can be merged, we first give the definition of homogeneous MDPs.

DEFINITION 3.2. *MDPs are homogeneous if they satisfy the following conditions:*

(1) their state representations are equivalent (the state-spaces can be different);

(2) there is a one-to-one correspondence between their action spaces;

(3) they are reward-linked.

Equivalent state representations mean that the states in different MDPs have the same kind of representations (i.e. same state variables [27]). For example, states in different Gridworlds can be represented by the agents' positions. Thus these Gridworlds meet the first condition. If the action spaces are actually the same but they are named differently in different MDPs, it is possible to find a correspondence of actions. Actions *up*, *down*, *left*, *right* in one Gridworld can be mapped to *north*, *nouth*, *west*, *east* in another Gridworld. *Reward-linked* [17] indicates that the rewards are equal when reaching the same subgoals (or goals) in two MDPs, such as arriving at the exports in different mazes and eating pac-dots in different Pac-man Games [1].

If MDPs are homogeneous, they can be merged into one "new MDP", and metric d (Definition 3.1) can be used to measure the distance between their states. Consider the example that an indoor mobile robot is required to perform a task in different rooms, which are considered as different tasks and can also be modeled as different homogeneous MDPs. At the same time, the different tasks can be also treated as subtasks of one task and modeled in one MDP. Homogeneous MDPs are common in the MDP domain and we extend the metric in Definition 3.1 to compute the distance between states in different MDPs.

DEFINITION 3.3. *Given two homogeneous MDPs $M_1 = \{S_1, A, P_1, R_1\}$ and $M_2 = \{S_2, A, P_2, R_2\}$, the distance $d'(s, s')$ between any state $s \in S_1$ and any state $s' \in S_2$ is defined as:*

$$d'(s,s') = \max_{a \in A}\{|(r_1)_s^a - (r_2)_{s'}^a| + cT_K(d')((P_1)_s^a, (P_2)_{s'}^a)\}, \quad (2)$$

where $(r_1)_s^a$ (resp. $(r_2)_{s'}^a$) and $(P_1)_s^a$ (resp. $(P_2)_{s'}^a$) are the immediate reward and the probabilistic transition function in M_1 (M_2), and $T_K(d')((P_1)_s^a, (P_2)_{s'}^a)$ is the Kantorovich distance between the two probabilistic transitions.

DEFINITION 3.4. *For two state probability transition functions $(P_1)_s^a$ and $(P_2)_{s'}^a$ in different MDPs, their Kantorovich distance is*

$$\begin{aligned} T_K(d') = & \min_{\lambda_{kt}, k=1\ldots|S_1|, t=1\ldots|S_2|} \sum_{k=1}^{|S_1|}\sum_{t=1}^{|S_2|} \lambda_{kt} d'(s_k, s_t') \\ \text{s.t.} \quad & \sum_t \lambda_{kt} = (P_1)_{ss_k}^a, \forall k, \\ & \sum_k \lambda_{kt} = (P_2)_{s's_t'}^a, \forall t, \\ & \lambda_{kt} \geq 0, \forall k, t, \end{aligned} \quad (3)$$

where $s_k \in S_1$, $s_t' \in S_2$, $|S_1|$ represents the number of states in S_1, and $|S_2|$ denotes the number of states in S_2.

The solution, fixed point $d_f'(s, s')$, for Equation (2) always exists and is unique, which can be derived from the property of metric d [12]. Similar to metric d, fixed point $d_f'(s, s')$ can be computed in an iterative manner. The process of computing the distances between states in different MDPs is shown in Algorithm 1. For each state $s_i \in S_1$ and each state $s_j' \in S_2$, according to Equation (2), $d'(s_i, s_j')$, the maximal sum of the difference between the immediate rewards and Kantorovich distance between the probability transition functions, is computed using the distances of the last iteration (Lines 4-6). δ is the mean absolute error (MAE) of distances in two iterations (Line 7) and is initialized to a value larger than error threshold ξ (Line 1). d_0 stores the distances of the last iteration (Line 9). This process stops when the MAE is not larger than the error threshold (Line 10).

The worst case running time of computing the fixed point, $d_f'(s, s')$, is $O(|A||S_1|^2|S_2|^2|S_1+S_2|\log(S_1+S_2)\lceil\frac{\ln \eta}{\ln c}\rceil)$. However, when the two MDPs are deterministic ones, $T_K(d')$ in Equation (2) can be simplified to $d'(s_{next}, s_{next}')$ where $s_{next}(s_{next}')$ is the next state from $s(s')$. In this situation, the computational cost is $O(|A||S_1||S_2|\lceil\frac{\ln \eta}{\ln c}\rceil)$.

After computing all the distances between states in different MDPs, we need to composite them to compute the distance between the two MDPs. It is not appropriate to simply accumulate or average the distances between all different states. Consider the situation of two same MDPs, where the distance between the MDPs must be zero. However, the entries of the state distance matrix may not always be zero when the two states are not similar. Therefore, we focus on matchings of states and provide two proper metrics, the Kantorovich metric and the Hausdorff metric, for measuring the distances between MDPs. The Kantorovich metric essentially tries to find out an optimal state matching between the two MDPs, and the Hausdorff metric does not rely on any specific matching but rather bounds all "reasonable" matchings. We should note that, to our best knowledge,

Algorithm 1: Computing the distance between states of two homogeneous MDPs

Input: two MDPs $M_1 = \{S_1, A, P_1, R_1\}$ and $M_2 = \{S_2, A, P_2, R_2\}$, parameter c, error threshold ξ.
Output: distance matrix $d'(s_i, s'_j)$.

Initialization. $\delta > \xi$, distance matrixes $d_0(s_i, s'_j) = 0$, $d'(s_i, s'_j) = 0$.
repeat
  foreach $(s_i, s'_j, a_k) \in S_1 \times S_2 \times A$ **do**
    compute $T_K(P^{a_k}_{s_i}, P^{a_k}_{s'_j})$ according to Equation (3) using distance matrix d_0;
    $tempd = |r^{a_k}_{s_i} - r^{a_k}_{s'_j}| + cT_K(P^{a_k}_{s_i}, P^{a_k}_{s'_j})$;
    if$(tempd > d'(s_i, s'_j))$ $d'(s_i, s'_j) = tempd$.
  $\delta = \left(\sum_{i=1}^{|S_1|}\sum_{j=1}^{|S_2|} |d'(s_i, s'_j) - d_0(s_i, s'_j)|\right) / (|S_1| * |S_2|)$;
  foreach $(s_i, s'_j) \in S_1 \times S_2$ **do**
    $d_0(s_i, s'_j) = d'(s_i, s'_j)$.
until $\delta \leq \xi$;

other alternatives are hardly applicable. In the remaining of this section, we give details on the two metrics.

3.2 Hausdorff Metric Based Measure

Hausdorff metric measures the distance between two subsets of a metric space in mathematics. It computes the largest distance of all the distances from a point in one set to the nearest point in the other set. When Hausdorff metric is applied to two MDPs, we consider the state sets as the subsets of the metric space $\{M, d'\}$. For each state in one MDP, finding the most similar state in the other MDP is equivalent to mapping the states from one MDP to the other. After getting the mapped states of both MDPs, Hausdorff metric is applied to find the largest distance between the mapped states. We use this distance to represent the distance between two MDPs. The formal definition of the distance between two MDPs using Hausdorff metric is defined as follows.

Definition 3.5. *Given two MDPs $M_1 = \{S_1, A, P_1, R_1\}$ and $M_2 = \{S_2, A, P_2, R_2\}$, their Hausdorff distance $\Phi(S_1, S_2)$ can be computed as follows.*

$$\Phi(S_1, S_2) = \max\left\{\max_{s\in S_1}\min_{s'\in S_2} d'(s, s'), \max_{s'\in S_2}\min_{s\in S_1} d'(s, s')\right\} \tag{4}$$

where d' is the metric defined in Definition 3.3.

Hausdorff metric can be efficiently computed and it only needs to compare $(2|S_1||S_2| - 1)$ times.

3.3 Kantorovich Metric Based Measure

Using Hausdorff metric to define the distance between MDPs leads to the possibility that similar MDPs are mistakenly treated as dissimilar ones if at least one of the them has an "outlier". Here the notion of an "outlier" is a state which is very different from others. Hausdorff metric computes the largest distance of all the distances from a state in one MDP to the nearest state in the other MDP. Therefore, if one MDP has outliers, the MDPs' distance is the distance of one of the outliers. In this case, even if other states are mapped to each other, the two MDPs cannot be considered similar. An example is presented as follows. Figure 1 shows two simple maze tasks and their MDPs, where S and S' are start states, G and G' are target states, and the black grid is an obstacle. We can see that the only difference between the two tasks is that Task II has an obstacle but Task I does not. The MDPs below the mazes show the state transitions by arrows. Actions and rewards of the transitions are labeled in the braces. The distances between states of different MDPs are computed using Equation (2). The results are shown in Table 1. It is easy to get that $\Phi = 20$. R_1 is an "outlier" in task I. The distance between two MDPs computed by Hausdorff metric is equal to $\min_s d'(s, R_1)$ and it is too large to consider the two MDPs similar.

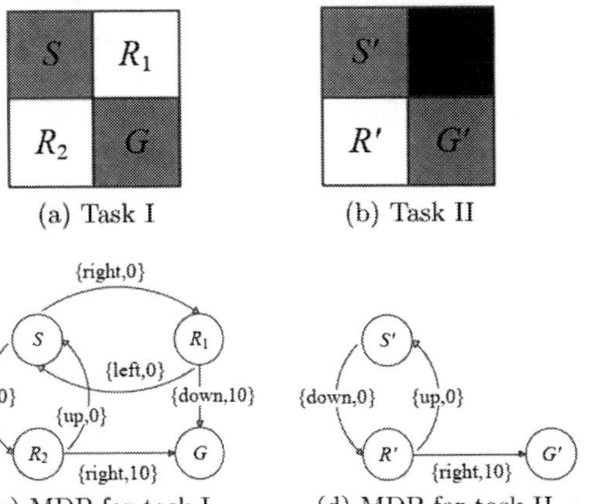

(a) Task I (b) Task II
(c) MDP for task I (d) MDP for task II

Figure 1: Example of measuring the distance between two MDPs

Table 1: Distance between states

distance	S'	R'	G'
S	10	20	20
R_1	20	20	20
R_2	20	5	20
G	20	20	0

To address the limitation of the above measure, we propose a new measure based on Kantorovich metric, which is originally used to find an optimal allocation of transportation resources. In a transportation problem, there are piles of sand (supply nodes) and holes (demand nodes) of the same volume, and the goal is to find an optimal way to move the sand into the holes. Kantorovich metric is an LP method for solving this problem to reach the goal of getting the minimum cost. When it is applied to two MDPs, one MDP's states are considered as the supply nodes and the other's are considered as demand nodes. Suppose that there is a transportation arc from each supply node to each demand node. A flow is an assignment of quantities to be transported along each arc. In general, the total supply and the total demand are equal, hence we set them to 1. The supply quantity of each supply node is $1/|S_1|$ with the assumption that each state is equally important to the MDP, where $|S|$ is the size of the state space of the MDP. The demand quantity of each demand node is $1/|S_2|$ as well. The unit cost of each arc equals to the distance of the corresponding states. Then transportation expense of each arc is the unit cost multiplied by the value of the flow along that arc. The goal is to get the optimal assignment of the flows to minimize the total transportation expenses. It can be seen that the distance of the outlier (if exists) only affects the transportation expense of some flows, so it has less impact on the total transportation expenses.

Now we give the formal definition of the distance between two MDPs based on Kantorovich metric:

Definition 3.6. *Given two MDPs $M_1 = \{S_1, A, P_1, R_1\}$ and $M_2 = \{S_2, A, P_2, R_2\}$, their Kantorovich distance $\Psi(S_1, S_2)$ can be computed as*

$$\begin{aligned} \Psi(S_1, S_2) = \min_{l_{ij}} & \sum_{i=1}^{|S_1|}\sum_{j=1}^{|S_2|} l_{ij} d'(s_i, s'_j) \\ \text{s.t.} \quad & \sum_{j=1}^{|S_2|} l_{ij} = \frac{1}{|S_1|}, \forall i, \\ & \sum_{i=1}^{|S_1|} l_{ij} = \frac{1}{|S_2|}, \forall j, \\ & l_{ij} \geq 0, \forall i, j, \end{aligned} \tag{5}$$

where $d'(s_i, s'_j)$ is the state distance between s_i and s'_j and can be obtained according to Equation (2). Obviously, the value of $\Psi_i(S_1, S_2)$ can be computed by solving an LP.

The cost of computing the Kantorovich metric is $O(|S_1 + S_2||S_1||S_2|\log(S_1 + S_2))$.

We use the above example to illustrate the whole process of computing the distance between two MDPs (see Figure 1 and Table 1). After computing the distances between states, Kantorovich metric is applied to compute the distance between two MDPs. The illustration of the flows is shown in Figure 2. The numbers beside the nodes are supply nodes' supply quantities or demand nodes' demand quantities. The numbers on the bold arrows are the values of flows leaving from the supply states to the demand states, and the values of other flows are zero which are omitted in the figure. The values of flows are l_{ij} in Equation (5). The distance between two MDPs computed by Kantorovich metric is $\Psi = 8.75$, and is much smaller than Φ. We can see from Figure 2, in Kantorovich metric the outlier's distance multiplies a weight to reduce the effect of that.

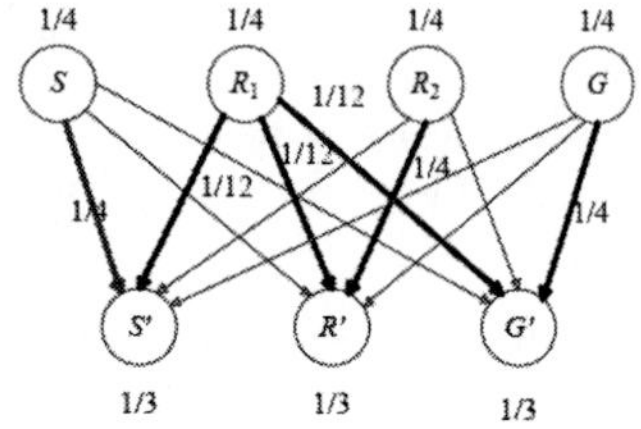

Figure 2: The transition between two MDPs

4. TRANSFER METHODS

Transfer learning for RL aims to improve the agent's learning performance by transferring the knowledge from prior learned task(s). The metrics for measuring the distance between MDPs can be used for automated source tasks selection in transfer learning, after which the knowledge learned in the selected source tasks can be transferred to the target task. The knowledge transfer mechanism adopted is value function transfer. In this section, we propose two transfer methods, one for Kantorovich metric (Ψ) only and the other for both metrics, Kantorovich metric and Hausdorff metric (Φ). We define the transfer method in two scenarios: transferring from one source task (single source transfer) and transferring from multiple source tasks (multiple source transfer).

4.1 Weight Transfer

We first introduce the transfer method (called *weight transfer*) which is only used when metric Ψ is adopted to measure the distance between MDPs. For each state of the target task, each weight l_{ij} defined in Definition 3.6 indicates how similar it is to the corresponding state in the source task. The more similar the two states are, the larger l_{ij} is. Therefore, we can transfer value functions (or Q-values) from states of the source task(s) to states of the target task according to the values of l_{ij}.

The transfer method for transferring from multiple source tasks is defined as follows.

Definition 4.1. *Given the target task's MDP $M : \{S, A, R, P\}$ and n ($n \geq 1$) source MDPs $M_1 : \{S_1, A, R_1, P_1\}, M_2 : \{S_2, A, R_2, P_2\}, \ldots, M_n : \{S_n, A, R_n, P_n\}$, the value functions of M can be initialized by the n source tasks' value functions. For every $s_i \in S$,*

$$V(s_i) = \frac{1}{n}\sum_{k=1}^{|n|}\sum_{j=1}^{|S_k|} \frac{l_{ij}^k}{L_j^k} V^k(s_j^k), \tag{6}$$

where s_j^k is the j-th state in S_k, l_{ij}^k is the weight of $d'(s_i, s_j^k)$ in $\Psi(S, S_k)$, $L_j^k = \sum_{i=1}^{|S|} l_{ij}^k$, and $V^k(s_j^k)$ is the value function of the state s_j^k in source task M_k which has been computed.

Similarly, Q-values of M can be initialized by the following formula:

$$Q(s_i, a) = \frac{1}{n}\sum_{k=1}^{|n|}\sum_{j=1}^{|S_k|} \frac{l_{ij}^k}{L_j^k} Q^k(s_j^k, a), \tag{7}$$

where $Q^k(s_j^k, a)$ is the Q-value of the state-action pair (s_j^k, a) in source task M_k which has been learned.

We choose the most similar n ($n \geq 1$) source tasks, and transfer their average weighted value functions (or Q-values) to the target task. The value of n depends on specific problems, and the weights for the transfer are proportional to l_{ij}. When $n = 1$, Equations (6) and (7) can be used to single source transfer.

The above transfer methods may be applied to algorithms which learn value functions or action value functions to solve the RL tasks. However, we only consider value iteration [23] and Q-learning [31] in this paper.

Algorithm 2 shows the pseudo code of transferring value functions from m ($m \geq 1$) source tasks $M_k (k = 1, \ldots, m)$ to the target task M (the process of transferring Q-values is similar). The whole process of transfer learning consists of three steps: (1) compute the distance $\Psi(S, S_l)$ ($l = 1, \ldots, m$) between the target task and each source task according to Equation (5), and then sort the source tasks according to the computed distances in ascending order; (2) select the most similar n source tasks M_{k_s} ($s = 1, \ldots, n$) and load the weight matrix $l_{ij}^{k_s}$ and their value functions (or Q-values); (3) transfer their value functions (or Q-values) to the target task (Lines 3-8), then use value iteration (or Q-learning) algorithm to solve the target task (Line 9).

Algorithm 2: Transfer value functions and learning

Input: discount rate γ, the number of transferred source tasks n, coefficient matrix l_{ij}^k and value functions $V^k(s^k)$ of the selected source tasks $M_k (k = 1 \ldots n)$.

1 Initialization. weight $\omega = 0$,
2 value functions of the target task: $V(s) = 0$.
3 **foreach** $s_i \in S$ **do**
4 **foreach** M_k **do**
5 **foreach** $s_j^k \in S_k$ **do**
6 $\omega = \frac{l_{ij}^k}{L_j^k}$;
7 $V(s_i) = V(s_i) + \omega V^k(s_j^k)$;
8 $V(s_i) = \frac{V(s_i)}{n}$.
9 Solve the target task with value iteration.

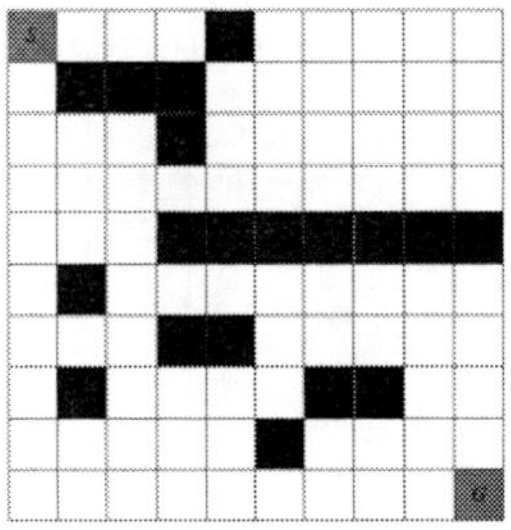

Figure 3: A 10×10 maze

4.2 State transfer

The weight transfer method can be only used for metric Ψ since it needs the coefficient matrix l_{ij}^k. Now we propose another method, called *state transfer*, which can be used for both Ψ and Φ. This method is also based on the idea that transfer can occur between similar states. For each state in the target task, its nearest state can be found in the source task after the distances of states are computed, and we directly transfer the value functions (or Q-values) of the nearest state in the source task to it.

DEFINITION 4.2. *Given the target task's MDP $M_1 = \{S_1, A, R_1, P_1\}$ and the source task's MDP $M_2 = \{S_2, A, R_2, P_2\}$, the value function of each state s in M_1 is initialized by the following equations:*

$$s' = \arg\min_{s'} d'(s, s'),$$

$$V(s) = V(s').$$

Similarly, Q-values of M_1 can be initialized by:

$$Q(s, a) = Q(s', a).$$

In multiple source transfer situation, we transfer the average value functions (or Q-values) of the source tasks' corresponding states to the target task.

5. EXPERIMENTAL EVALUATION

We evaluate our metrics in transfer learning for RL. We consider the maze problem in which many transfer learning methods have been applied [8, 9, 20]. An example of the mazes used in our experiment is shown in Figure 3. 'S' is the start position and 'G' is the goal position. The black squares are called obstacles that block agent to go through, and other things are the same as Gridworld [25]. The objective of the learning agent is to find an optimal path to reach the goal position from the start position. In each position, there are four actions, *up*, *down*, *left*, and *right*, for the agent to choose. After choosing an action, agent deterministically gets to the corresponding neighbor position except when a movement is blocked by an obstacle or the edge of the maze, in which case the agent will stay in its current position, i.e., the (illegal) movement causes no effect. Reward is 100 when arriving at the goal position and 0 in other cases.

We adopt value iteration and Q-learning as the basic learning methods. The transfer learning setting is as follows: There is a library of source tasks and when given a target task we hope to transfer knowledge from the library to improve the learning performance of the target task. In this paper, the maze tasks are homogeneous. The tasks in the library have been learned by the basic learning methods, and their models and learned knowledge (i.e. value functions or Q-values) have been stored. The target task will be also learned by the basic learning methods.

The parameters of the methods are set as follows.

1) We set parameter $c = 0.5$, $\delta = 1$, and the threshold $\xi = 0.01$ when computing the distance of two states in different MDPs (see Algorithm 1).

2) The discount factor γ is set to 0.9.

3) The Q-learning agent behaves in an ϵ-*greedy* way, i.e., it selects the best action (indicated by the largest Q-values) with probability $1 - \epsilon$, and selects a random action with the rest probability of ϵ. The exploration probability ϵ is set to 0.1 and the learning factor α is set to 0.2.

We have conducted two sets of experiments: one is for evaluating the property of the proposed metrics, i.e., the relation between transfer performance and task distance, and the other is for investigating whether the similar source task(s) selected by our metrics can accelerate the learning of the target task.

For the first set of experiments, we randomly generate a 10×10 maze (the target task) and a series of 10×10 mazes (the source tasks) with different distances to the target maze. We use metrics Ψ and Φ to measure the distance between the target task and each source task, after which we record the distances of each pair of the tasks. Then, we transfer the knowledge of all the source tasks to the target task using single source transfer methods. We have two metrics, two transfer methods and two learning methods. To keep it simple, we use letters "K", "H", "W", "S", "V" and "Q" to represent metric Ψ, metric Φ, weight transfer method, state transfer method, value iteration and Q-learning. The combination of these letters represents the combination of methods, e.g., KSV means using metric Ψ, state transfer and value iteration to solve the transfer learning task. In Figure 4, four scatter diagrams and their rough fitting curves are shown.

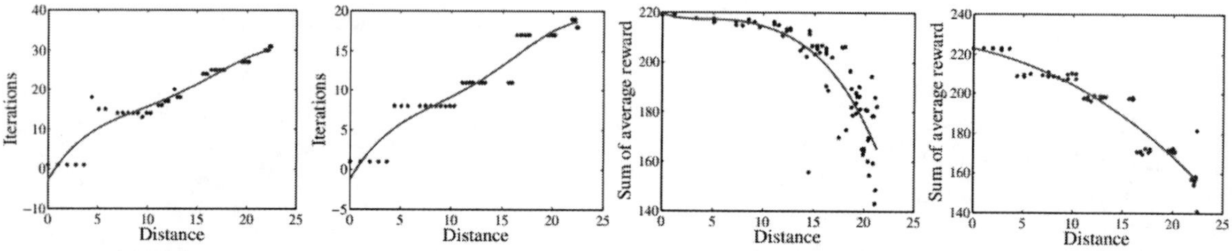

(a) KWV (b) KSV (c) KWQ (d) KSQ

Figure 4: The relation between transfer performance and distance computed by metric Ψ

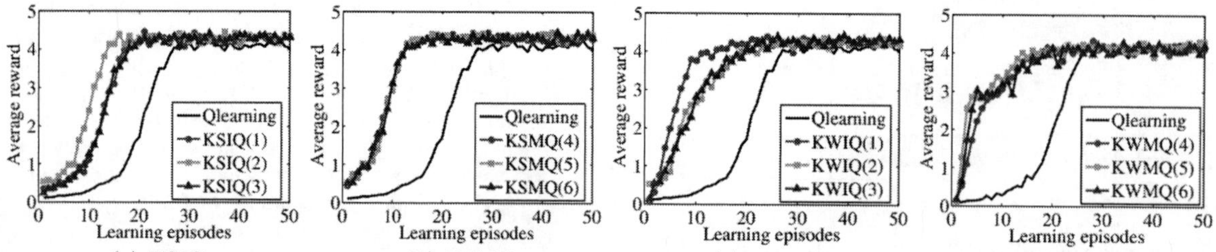

(a) KSIQ (b) KSMQ (c) KWIQ (d) KWMQ

Figure 5: Transferring from the most similar tasks using metric Ψ ($\epsilon = 0.1$)

The horizontal axis represents the distance between the source task and the target task. In subfigures 4(a) and 4(b), vertical axis represents the number of iterations, and in subfigures 4(c) and 4(d) vertical axis represents the sum of the average rewards of each step (we just call it average rewards in the following sections) of the first 50 episodes. The target task's learning process is repeated 50 times and the number of iterations (or the sum of the average rewards) is the average values of these processes. For value iteration, we use the number of iterations to measure the learning performance of the task, the smaller the better. For Q-learning, we use the sum of average rewards of the first 50 episodes to measure the learning performance of the task, the more the better. We use "50 episodes" since the processes of Q-learning have often converged within 50 episodes in this experiment.

We can see from the figures that the performance of transfer is related to the distance computed by metric Ψ. In subfigures 4(a) and 4(b), the number of iterations to learn a task increases as the distance increases. The sum of average rewards decreases as the distance increases in subfigures 4(c) and 4(d). This means the performance of transfer learning improves as the similarity increases. The source tasks with distance less than 5 have the similar distributions (numbers and positions) of obstacles with the target task while the tasks with distance near 25 have quite different ones. Therefore, metric Ψ can describe task similarity in transfer learning correctly, and negative transfer can be avoided by filtering the dissimilar tasks. However, metric Φ does not have such property. The reason may be that it may miss some actually similar MDPs due to "outliers". Although metric Φ does not has such property, the similar tasks selected by it can improve the learning performance in the target task, which will be demonstrated in the next set of experiments.

For the second set of experiments, the target task is a randomly generated 10×10 maze and the source tasks consist of 100 10×10 mazes which have several obstacles that are generated randomly in the grids. After computing the distance between the target task and each source task by our metrics Ψ and Φ, the source tasks are sorted according to the distances in ascending order, and labeled by sequence numbers according to the order. The smaller the number is, the more similar the task is to the target task. The target task is learned in many situations. First it is learned by value iteration (or Q-learning), and then single source transfer and multiple source transfer are used to alter its learning process. For single source transfer scenario, the most similar source task's knowledge is transferred using our single source transfer method. The multiple source transfer scenario is similar, in which knowledge from the most similar n (we consider some different n in this section) source tasks is transferred. The Q-learning agent behaves in an *ϵ-greedy* way, and we test two situations, $\epsilon = 0.1$ and $\epsilon = 0.01$.

We consider all the combinations of metrics, transfer methods and learning methods. We use the combinations of letters to represent the combination of methods. We add letter "I" and "M" to represent single source transfer and multiple source transfer. The "I" and "M" are put before the learning method ("Q" or "V"), e.g., KWIQ means using metric Ψ, single source weight transfer and Q-learning to solve the transfer learning task. The results of Q-learning are shown in Figures 5, 6 and 7.

The horizontal axis x represents the number of learning episodes and the vertical axis y represents the average rewards in episode x. The learning process is repeated 50 times and the average rewards are the average values of these processes. In the figures, for single source transfer, the number n in the parentheses after the combinations of letters means transferring from source task with sequence number

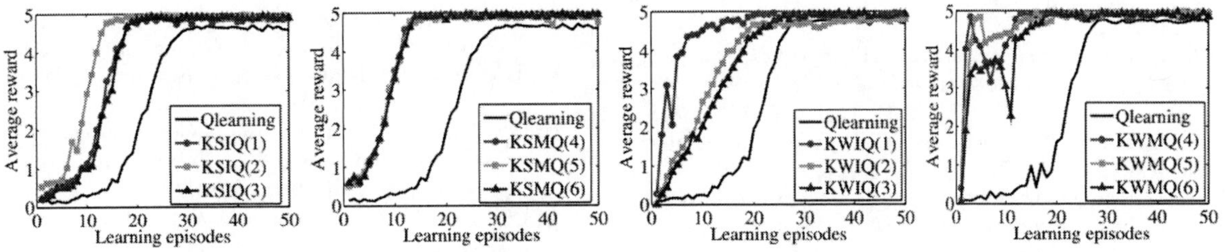

(a) KSIQ (b) KSMQ (c) KWIQ (d) KWMQ

Figure 6: Transferring from the most similar tasks using metric Ψ ($\epsilon = 0.01$)

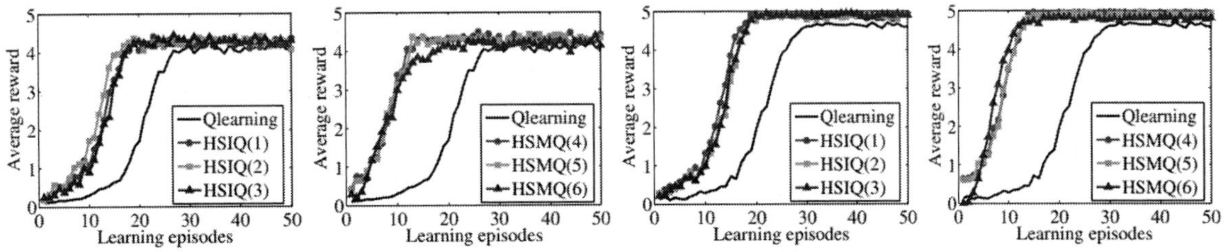

(a) HSIQ ($\epsilon = 0.1$) (b) HSMQ ($\epsilon = 0.1$) (c) HSIQ ($\epsilon = 0.01$) (d) HSMQ ($\epsilon = 0.01$)

Figure 7: Transferring from the most similar tasks using metric Φ

n. For multiple source transfer, the number n in the parentheses means transferring from n most similar source tasks. For example, KWIQ(1) means using metric Ψ, single source weight transfer and Q-learning, and transferring from the source task with sequence number 1 to solve the transfer learning task.

We can see from the figures that the similar tasks selected by our metrics can speed up the learning process of the target task. Moreover, when $\epsilon = 0.01$, transfer learning can improve the asymptotic performance as shown in Figure 6 and Figures 7(c) and 7(d). The curves of transferring from different source tasks in each figure are very close since the distances are close. Therefore, our metrics can perform well in helping finding the similar tasks in transfer learning to improve the learning performance in the target task. We can also see from Figures 5(a), 6(a), 7(a) and 7(c) that, although source tasks selected by Hausdorff metric can benefit learning in the target task, the really similar tasks (e.g. the green curves in Figures 5(a) and 6(a)) may be missed. However, Kantorovich metric can find them.

The results of value iteration are shown in table 2. .

Table 2: The number of iterations in single source transfer

No	*HSIV*	*KSIV*
1	1	1
2	11	11
3	14	15
4	14	14

The column "No" in the table represents the sequence number of the transferred source task. In addition to this column, other columns are numbers of iterations using the transfer learning methods. Value iteration for the target task without transfer can converge after 20 iterations. We can see from the table that HSIV and KSIV can accelerate the process of value iteration. We also test the multiple source transfer scenario, and multiple source transfer methods cannot improve the learning performance. As a result, single source state transfer methods can be applicable to value iteration, and our metrics can perform well in helping finding the similar tasks when using single source state transfer methods.

6. CONCLUSION

In this work, we propose two metrics for measuring the distance between MDPs. We extend Kantorovich metric and Hausdorff metric to define the distance between MDPs. We show that the metrics can be applied in transfer learning for RL where tasks are modeled as MDPs. The metrics can help with selecting similar tasks to effectively transfer and avoid negative transfer. Since the metrics are based on the distances between states, value functions (or action-value functions) are used as the transfer knowledge and we propose two value function transfer methods. Experimental results show that the metrics are effective in finding similar tasks to avoid negative transfer, and the learning algorithms are significantly improved by our metrics and transfer methods.

In the future, we hope to generalize our metrics to other settings, where MDPs are not homogeneous. Our metrics are defined on MDPs with finite state space, and we are trying to establish an extension for infinite state space.

7. ACKNOWLEDGMENTS

The authors would like to acknowledge the support for this work from the National Natural Science Foundation of China (Grant Nos. 61432008, 61503178, 61321491) and the Natural Science Foundation of Jiangsu Province of China (BK20150587).

REFERENCES

[1] Pac-man. http://en.wikipedia.org/wiki/Pac-Man, 2014.

[2] H. B. Ammar, E. Eaton, M. E. Taylor, D. C. Mocanu, K. Driessens, G. Weiss, and K. Tuyls. An automated measure of mdp similarity for transfer in reinforcement learning. In *Workshops at the 28th AAAI Conference on Artificial Intelligence*, 2014.

[3] R. Bellman. Dynamic programming. *Princeton University Press*, 1957.

[4] C. Boutilier, T. Dean, and S. Hanks. Decision theoretic planning: Structural assumptions and computational leverage. *Journal of Artificial Intelligence Research*, 11:1–94, 1999.

[5] D. Braun, J. Mayberry, A. Powers, and S. Schlicker. The geometry of the hausdorff metric. http://faculty.gvsu.edu/schlicks/Hausdorff_paper.pdf, 2003.

[6] J. L. Carroll and K. Seppi. Task similarity measures for transfer in reinforcement learning task libraries. In *Proceedings of the IEEE International Joint Conference on Neural Network*, pages 803–808, 2005.

[7] Y. Deng and W. Du. The kantorovich metric in computer science: A brief survey. *Electronic Notes in Theoretical Computer Science*, 253(3):73–82, 2009.

[8] K. Ferguson and S. Mahadevan. Proto-transfer learning in markov decision processes using spectral methods. In *Proceedings of the 23rd ICML Workshop on Transfer Learning*, pages 895–900, 2006.

[9] F. Fernández and M. Veloso. Probabilistic policy reuse in a reinforcement learning agent. In *Proceedings of the 5th International Joint Conference on Autonomous Agents and Multiagent Systems*, pages 720–727, 2006.

[10] N. Ferns. Metrics for markov decision processes. Master's thesis, McGill University, 2003.

[11] N. Ferns, P. Castro, P. Panangaden, and D. Precup. Methods for computing state similarity in markov decision processes. In *Proceedings of the 22nd Conference in Uncertainty in Artificial Intelligence*, pages 174–181, 2006.

[12] N. Ferns, P. Panangaden, and D. Precup. Metrics for finite markov decision processes. In *Proceedings of the 20th Conference in Uncertainty in Artificial Intelligence*, pages 162–169, 2004.

[13] N. Ferns, P. Panangaden, and D. Precup. Metrics for markov decision processes with infinite state spaces. In *Proceedings of the 21st Conference in Uncertainty in Artificial Intelligence*, pages 201–208, 2005.

[14] A. Haitham, Bou, E. Eric, R. Paul, and T. Matthew. Online multi-task learning for policy gradient methods. In *Proceedings of the 31st International Conference on Machine Learning*, pages 1206–1214, 2014.

[15] L. P. Kaelbling, M. L. Littman, and A. W. Moore. Reinforcement learning: A survey. *Journal of Artificial Intelligence Research*, 4:237–285, 1996.

[16] G. Konidaris and A. G. Barto. Building portable options: Skill transfer in reinforcement learning. In *Proceedings of the 20th International Joint Conference on Artificial Intelligence*, pages 895–900, 2007.

[17] G. Konidaris, I. Scheidwasser, and A. G. Barto. Transfer in reinforcement learning via shared features. *Journal of Machine Learning Research*, 13(1):1333–1371, 2012.

[18] A. Lazaric. Transfer in reinforcement learning: a framework and a survey. In *Reinforcement Learning*, pages 143–173. Springer, 2012.

[19] A. Lazaric, M. Restelli, and A. Bonarini. Transfer of samples in batch reinforcement learning. In *Proceedings of the 25th International Conference on Machine Learning*, pages 544–551, 2008.

[20] H. Li, X. Liao, and L. Carin. Multi-task reinforcement learning in partially observable stochastic environments. *Journal of Machine Learning Research*, 10:1131–1186, 2009.

[21] M. G. Madden and T. Howley. Transfer of experience between reinforcement learning environments with progressive difficulty. *Artificial Intelligence Review*, 21(3–4):375–398, 2004.

[22] D. N. Perkins and G. Salomon. Transfer of learning. *International encyclopedia of education*, 2:6452–6457, 1992.

[23] M. L. Puterman. Markov decision processes: Discrete stochastic dynamic programming. *Journal of the Operational Research Society*, 46(6):792–793, 1995.

[24] M. T. Rosenstein, Z. Marx, L. P. Kaelbling, and T. G. Dietterich. To transfer or not to transfer. In *NIPS Workshop on Inductive Transfer*, 2005.

[25] R. S. Sutton and A. G. Barto. Reinforcement learning: an introduction. *IEEE Transactions on Neural Network*, 9(5):1054–1054, 1998.

[26] M. E. Taylor and P. Stone. Representation transfer for reinforcement learning. In *AAAI 2007 Fall Symposium on Computational Approaches to Representation Change during Learning and Development*, 2007.

[27] M. E. Taylor and P. Stone. Transfer learning for reinforcement learning domains: A survey. *Journal of Machine Learning Research*, 10:1633–1685, 2009.

[28] M. E. Taylor and P. Stone. An introduction to intertask transfer for reinforcement learning. *AI Magazine*, 32(1):15, 2011.

[29] M. E. Taylor, P. Stone, and Y. Liu. Transfer learning via inter-task mappings for temporal difference learning. *Journal of Machine Learning Research*, 8(1):2125–2167, 2007.

[30] L. Torrey, J. Shavlik, T. Walker, and R. Maclin. Skill acquisition via transfer learning and advice taking. In *Proceedings of the 17th European Conference on Machine Learning*, pages 425–436, 2006.

[31] C. Watkins and P. Dayan. Q-learning. *Machine Learning*, 8(3-4):279–292, 1992.

Boosting Nonparametric Policies*

Yang Yu Peng-Fei Hou Qing Da Qian Yu
National Key Laboratory for Novel Software Technology
Nanjing University, Nanjing 210023, China
{yuy, houpf, daq, qiany}@lamda.nju.edu.cn

ABSTRACT

Learning complex policies is a key step toward real-world applications of reinforcement learning. While boosting approaches have been widely applied in state-of-the-art supervised learning techniques to adaptively learn nonparametric functions, in reinforcement learning the boosting-style approaches have been little investigated. Only a few pieces of previous work explored this direction, however theoretical properties are still unclear and empirical performance is quite limited. In this paper, we propose the PolicyBoost method. It optimizes a finite-sample objective function, which leads to maximization of the expected total reward, by employing the GradientBoost approach. Experimental results verify the effectiveness as well as the robustness of PolicyBoost, even without feature engineering.

Categories and Subject Descriptors

H.4 [**Machine learning**]: Reinforcement learning

General Terms

Algorithms

Keywords

Policy gradient, Boosting, nonparametric model

1. INTRODUCTION

In reinforcement learning, an agent learns from trial-and-error feedback from its environment, and produces a state-to-action policy attempting to maximize its long-term total reward [34]. A good reinforcement learning algorithm would be able to generalize well from limited feedbacks, sharing similar principle with supervised learning algorithms. In supervised learning [24], an algorithm is given fixed training examples and expected to build a model that correctly predicts unseen instances. We may learn from successful supervised learning algorithms to design strong reinforcement learning algorithms.

*This research was supported by the NSFC (61375061, 61223003), Foundation for the Author of National Excellent Doctoral Dissertation of China (201451).

Appears in: *Proceedings of the 15th International Conference on Autonomous Agents and Multiagent Systems (AAMAS 2016), J. Thangarajah, K. Tuyls, C. Jonker, S. Marsella (eds.), May 9–13, 2016, Singapore.*

A notable off-the-shelf supervised learning algorithm family is called *boosting*, with representatives such as AdaBoost [10], LogitBoost [11], GradientBoost [12], etc. Most of them share a common routine [22] that trains an additive combination of models via gradient decent in some function space. The success of boosting algorithms is supported by both theoretical guarantees and many successful real-world applications. Particularly, boosting approaches have a strong generalization ability and a good adaptivity to nonparametric and highly nonlinear models, which are also quite appealing properties in reinforcement learning.

Despite the powerful performance of boosting approaches verified in supervised learning, there are few previous studies investigating boosting-like approaches in reinforcement learning. As far as we are aware, the only existing work is the NPPG [17], by which a policy is formed from an *additive model* like the boosting approaches. It trains the model to directly maximize the total reward objective function via the gradient ascent in a function space. However, we found that directly maximizing the objective function on a small training trajectory set results in overfitting due to optimizing only the probability of these trajectories, which can be useful only when the policy is near optimal already. Similar to boosting approaches, the NPPG method has a strong learning ability, which makes the overfitting problem even more severe. Thus NPPG can only work on simple tasks.

In this paper, we firstly derive the finite-sample functional gradient, the core of boosting methods, for maximizing the expected total reward. We then show that the functional gradient method drives policy convergence, and fit the observed best actions. However, it may overfit the observed samples, we thus make a correction to the finite-sample objective to alleviate the overfitting problem. The proposed PolicyBoost optimizes the objective using GradientBoost. Moreover, for a better assessment of the gradient, it is quite useful to include some good trajectories in the training set. Thus unlike NPPG that throws away past samples, PolicyBoost maintains a pool of experienced good trajectories.

We conduct empirical studies of PolicyBoost on several domains. Experiment results reveal that NPPG suffers from the overfitting problem while PolicyBoost does not. Moreover, even using the raw feature representation of states and actions, PolicyBoost is shown to be not only effective in achieving good policies on the tested domains with raw state features, but also highly stable to its configuration parameters, which is desired in practical applications.

The remainder of the paper starts with a section introducing the related work. The PolicyBoost is then presented in a section after, which is followed by the section of empirical studies. The final section suggests future directions.

2. BACKGROUND

2.1 Reinforcement Learning and Policy Gradient

In reinforcement learning, an autonomous agent is put in an environment. The environment involves a state space $\mathcal{X}$, an action space $\mathcal{A}$, a transition probability P such that $P(s'|s,a)$ gives the probability of being in state s' after taking action a on state s, and a reward function $r:\mathcal{X}\times\mathcal{X}\to\mathbb{R}$ that gives a reward value for every step (i.e., a transition from a state to another). In this paper, we consider the state space being a vector space $\mathcal{X}=\mathbb{R}^n$ of n features. A policy π is a decision function that gives a probability distribution for actions, with $\pi(a|\boldsymbol{s})$ denoting the probability of choosing action a at state $\boldsymbol{s}$ by the policy. The agent seeks a policy maximizing its long-term total reward. The long-term total reward can be evaluated by the expected T-step reward $\rho(\pi)=\lim_{t\to\infty}E\{r_1+r_2+\cdots+r_t \mid \pi\}/t$, and the expected discounted reward, $\rho(\pi)=E\{\sum_{t=1}^{\infty}\gamma^{t-1}r_t \mid \pi\}$, where r_t is the reward at step t and γ is the discount factor.

Policy gradient methods [38, 18, 28, 25, 29] are a branch of reinforcement learning approaches, which derive a policy by directly maximizing the total reward via gradient ascent and can avoid the *policy degradation* problem of the value function estimation approaches [5]. Considering a finite execution of a policy, i.e., T-step horizon, all the trajectories with length T constitute the trajectory space $\mathcal{T}$. For each trajectory $\boldsymbol{\tau}=(\boldsymbol{s}_1,\boldsymbol{s}_2,\ldots,\boldsymbol{s}_T)$, let $R(\boldsymbol{\tau})$ be its trajectory-wise reward, for the T-step setting $R(\boldsymbol{\tau})=\frac{1}{T-1}\sum_{i=1}^{T-1}r(\boldsymbol{s}_i,\boldsymbol{s}_{i+1})$ and for the discounted setting $R(\boldsymbol{\tau})=\sum_{i=1}^{T-1}\gamma^{t-1}r(\boldsymbol{s}_i,\boldsymbol{s}_{i+1})$. The expected total reward is then equivalent to,

$$\rho(\pi)=\int_{\mathcal{T}}p^{\pi}(\boldsymbol{\tau})R(\boldsymbol{\tau})\,\mathrm{d}\boldsymbol{\tau}, \tag{1}$$

where the probability of the trajectory $p^{\pi}(\boldsymbol{\tau})$ is

$$\begin{aligned}p^{\pi}(\boldsymbol{\tau})&=p(\boldsymbol{s}_1^{\tau})\prod_{t=1}^{T-1}p^{\pi}(\boldsymbol{s}_{t+1}^{\tau}\mid\boldsymbol{s}_t^{\tau})\\&=p(\boldsymbol{s}_1^{\tau})\prod_{t=1}^{T-1}\int_{\mathcal{A}}p(\boldsymbol{s}_{t+1}^{\tau}\mid\boldsymbol{s}_t^{\tau},a)\pi(a\mid\boldsymbol{s}_t)\,\mathrm{d}a.\end{aligned}$$

Several policy gradient methods have been proposed, and most of them consider the policy as a linear function with parameter vector $\boldsymbol{\theta}$, i.e., $\pi(a|\boldsymbol{s})=g(\boldsymbol{\theta}^{\top}\boldsymbol{s})$ for some probability function g. Then a general expression of the gradient of the expected total reward w.r.t. $\boldsymbol{\theta}$ is $\nabla_{\boldsymbol{\theta}}\rho(\pi_{\boldsymbol{\theta}})=\int_{\boldsymbol{\tau}\in\mathcal{T}}\nabla_{\boldsymbol{\theta}}p^{\pi_{\boldsymbol{\theta}}}(\boldsymbol{\tau})R(\boldsymbol{\tau})d\boldsymbol{\tau}$. Once the gradient has been estimated, the parameter can be updated by the gradient ascent $\boldsymbol{\theta}_{t+1}=\boldsymbol{\theta}_t+\eta_t\nabla_{\boldsymbol{\theta}}\rho(\pi_{\boldsymbol{\theta}_t})$ with a learning rate η_t.

A straightforward way to estimate the gradient is via the finite difference [27], which estimates the gradient by sampling some neighbors of the current parameter vector. The REINFORCE [38] uses log-likelihood ratio trick $\nabla_{\boldsymbol{\theta}}p^{\pi_{\boldsymbol{\theta}}}(\boldsymbol{\tau})=p^{\pi_{\boldsymbol{\theta}}}(\boldsymbol{\tau})\nabla_{\boldsymbol{\theta}}\log p^{\pi_{\boldsymbol{\theta}}}(\boldsymbol{\tau})$, such that the gradient of the objective $\nabla_{\boldsymbol{\theta}}\rho(\pi_{\boldsymbol{\theta}})$ can be estimated on a sample of trajectories $S=\{\boldsymbol{\tau}_1,\ldots,\boldsymbol{\tau}_m\}$ as that, for the k-th dimension,

$$\begin{aligned}\nabla_{\theta_k}\rho_S(\pi_{\theta_k})&=\frac{1}{m}\sum_{i=1}^{m}\nabla_{\theta_k}\log p^{\pi_{\theta_k}}(\boldsymbol{\tau}_i)R(\boldsymbol{\tau})\\&=\frac{1}{m}\sum_{i=1}^{m}\sum_{t=1}^{T-1}\nabla_{\theta_k}\log p^{\pi_{\theta_k}}(\boldsymbol{s}_{t+1}^{\tau_i}\mid\boldsymbol{s}_t^{\tau_i})R(\boldsymbol{\tau}).\end{aligned}$$

Moreover, it usually plugs a constant b into the reward as $(R(\boldsymbol{\tau})-b)$, aiming to minimize the variance of the gradient for stability [15]. In the actor-critic framework, policy gradient has also been employed. For example, considering the stationary distribution of states, the gradient can be [35]

$$\nabla_{\boldsymbol{\theta}}\rho(\pi_{\boldsymbol{\theta}})=\int_{\mathcal{X}}d^{\pi_{\boldsymbol{\theta}}}(\boldsymbol{s})\sum_{a\in\mathcal{A}}Q^{\pi_{\boldsymbol{\theta}}}(\boldsymbol{s},a)\nabla_{\boldsymbol{\theta}}\pi_{\boldsymbol{\theta}}(a|\boldsymbol{s})\mathrm{d}\boldsymbol{s}, \tag{2}$$

where $d^{\pi}(\boldsymbol{s})$ is the probability of state s under the stationary distribution, and $Q^{\pi}(\boldsymbol{s},a)$ is the state-action value. More variants are proposed in different aspects and settings (e.g. [4, 14, 30, 6]).

2.2 Supervised Learning and Boosting

Boosting [33] is a family of algorithms for supervised learning. In supervised learning, we consider an input space $\mathcal{X}$, an output space $\mathcal{Y}$ (e.g. $\mathcal{Y}=\{-1,+1\}$), an underlying distribution $\mathcal{D}$ over $\mathcal{X}$ and an underlying ground truth function $f^*:\mathcal{X}\to\mathcal{Y}$. We are given only a finite set of samples $S=\{\boldsymbol{x}_1,\boldsymbol{x}_2,\ldots,\boldsymbol{x}_m\}$ drawn i.i.d. from $\mathcal{D}$, together with their labels $y_i=f^*(\boldsymbol{x}_i)$ assigned by the underlying ground truth function f^*. With the given samples, a supervised learning algorithm searches for a proper hypothesis $h:\mathcal{X}\to\mathcal{Y}$ in a hypothesis space $\mathcal{H}$. The properness of the hypothesis can be commonly measured by the generalization zero-one error, i.e., $\epsilon_{\mathcal{D}}(h)=E_{\boldsymbol{x}\in\mathcal{D}}[\boldsymbol{I}(h(\boldsymbol{x})\neq f^*(\boldsymbol{x}))]$.

An interesting question on the supervised learning is that whether it is possible to improve a learning algorithm, which is slightly better than random guess to have a strong generalization ability on learnable tasks [16], and boosting was the constructive positive answer to this question [32]. which is a convex spanning of a base hypothesis space $\mathcal{H}_{base}$ that can be the hypothesis space of a base learning algorithm. To search in $\mathcal{H}$, most boosting algorithms employ some kind of gradient descent methods to minimize some surrogate losses of the zero-one error on the training set. Despite the different implementations, they share a common procedure described as follows. First, a base learning algorithm is involved to produce the initial hypothesis h_1 from the training set, and let the initial combined hypothesis be $H_1=h_1$. Then an iteration is repeated $T-1$ times. In iteration $t=2,\ldots,T$, it calculates the gradient value for H_{t-1} point-wisely on every training example, such that a new training set is formed. After that the base learning algorithm is invoked to train h_t from the new training set, and a coefficient α_t is searched to minimize the loss of the combination $H_t=H_{t-1}+\alpha_t h_t$. After all the iterations, a hypothesis $H_T=\sum_{i=1}^{T}\alpha_i h_i$ is obtained, which is called an *additive model.*

Different boosting algorithms mainly differ in the employed gradient methods and surrogate loss functions. They easily produce highly nonlinear models with small generalization error, and thus are among the state-of-the-art learning approaches and have been widely applied (e.g. [37, 21]).

2.3 NPPG Method

The NPPG (non-parametric policy gradient) method [17] is, to the best of our knowledge, the only previous boosting approach for reinforcement learning, following the Gradient-Boost [12].

In NPPG, A policy $\pi(\boldsymbol{s}, a)$ is represented as $g(\Psi(\boldsymbol{s}, a))$ with some potential function Ψ. For discrete action spaces, g can be the Gibbs Sampling function (i.e., the logistic regression function), $\pi_\Psi(a|\boldsymbol{s}) = \frac{\exp(\Psi(\boldsymbol{s},a))}{\sum_{a'}\exp(\Psi(\boldsymbol{s},a'))}$, and for continuous action spaces, g can be the Gaussian function with parameter σ, $\pi_\Psi(a|\boldsymbol{s}) = \frac{1}{\sqrt{2\pi\sigma^2}}\exp\left(-\frac{(\Psi(\boldsymbol{s})-a)^2}{\sigma^2}\right)$. The potential function Ψ is an additive model $\Psi = \sum_{t=1}^{T} h_t$, where the component function h_t is to be trained iteratively. NPPG employs the gradient of Eq.(2) directly, except that the gradient is with respect to the potential function,

$$\nabla_\Psi \rho(\pi_\Psi) = \int_{\mathcal{X}} d^{\pi_\Psi}(\boldsymbol{s}) \sum_{a\in\mathcal{A}} Q^{\pi_\Psi}(\boldsymbol{s}, a)\nabla_\Psi \pi_\Psi(a|\boldsymbol{s})d\boldsymbol{s}.$$

Given the current potential function $\Psi_t = \sum_{i=1}^{t} h_t$, the function can be updated as

$$\Psi_{t+1} = \Psi_t + \eta_t \nabla_\Psi \rho(\pi_{\Psi_t}).$$

However, different with the gradient of linear vectors, the gradient in a function space $\nabla_\Psi \rho(\pi_{\Psi_t})$ is also a function but can not be explicitly expressed. We can only know the gradient value on the samples. Then the point-wise estimation [12] is used to approximate the gradient function via regression learning algorithms. Given a set of state-action samples (which can be extract from the trajectories), the gradient value on each sample (state s and action a) is calculated as $grad(\boldsymbol{s}, a) = Q^\pi(\boldsymbol{s}, a)\nabla_{\Psi(\boldsymbol{s},a)}\pi_\Psi(a|\boldsymbol{s})$. It then constructs a set of examples with features $(\boldsymbol{s}, a)$ and label $grad(\boldsymbol{s}, a)$, and derives a model h_t by regression learning from this set. Now the update rule is by

$$\Psi_{t+1} = \Psi_t + \eta_t h_t.$$

Note this step is a standard supervised regression task, and thus many well-established learning algorithms with strong generalization ability can be used here, which results an adaptively nonlinear model.

3. POLICYBOOST

3.1 Functional Gradient

Following REINFORCE [38], on a sample of m trajectories S, the unbiased gradient of the expected total reward is $\nabla \rho_S(\pi) = \frac{1}{m}\sum_{i=1}^{m}\nabla \log p^\pi(\tau_i)R(\tau_i)$. Considering the same action functions of NPPG, a policy is formed from a potential function Ψ. For a state-action pair $(\boldsymbol{s}, a)$ in a trajectory $\boldsymbol{\tau}$ with the next state s', the *functional gradient* with respect to $\Psi(s, a)$ is

$$\begin{aligned}\nabla_{\Psi(\boldsymbol{s},a)}\rho(\pi_\Psi) &= \frac{1}{m}R(\boldsymbol{\tau})\nabla_{\Psi(\boldsymbol{s},a)}\log p^{\pi_\Psi}(\boldsymbol{\tau})\\ &= \frac{1}{m}\frac{p(\boldsymbol{s}'|\boldsymbol{s},a)}{p^{\pi_\Psi}(\boldsymbol{s}'|\boldsymbol{s})}R(\boldsymbol{\tau})\nabla_{\Psi(\boldsymbol{s},a)}\pi_\Psi(a \mid \boldsymbol{s})\\ &= \frac{1}{m}\frac{p(\boldsymbol{s}'|\boldsymbol{s},a)}{\sum_{t=1}^{n}p(\boldsymbol{s}'|\boldsymbol{s},a_t)\pi(\boldsymbol{s},a_t)}R(\boldsymbol{\tau})\nabla_{\Psi(\boldsymbol{s},a)}\pi_\Psi(a \mid \boldsymbol{s}).\end{aligned}$$

Then for discrete action space, we have

$$\nabla_{\Psi(\boldsymbol{s},a)}\pi(a \mid \boldsymbol{s}) = \pi_\Psi(a \mid \boldsymbol{s})(1 - \pi_\Psi(a \mid \boldsymbol{s})) \quad (3)$$

and for continuous action space,

$$\nabla_{\Psi(\boldsymbol{s},a)}\pi(a \mid \boldsymbol{s}) = 2\pi_\Psi(a \mid \boldsymbol{s})(a - \Psi(\boldsymbol{s}))/\sigma^2. \quad (4)$$

Since the functional gradient results in a function, of which the value can only be calculated on observed state-action pairs, we need to train a least square model h_t to fit the gradient value on the samples, and update the potential function as $\Psi_{t+1} = \Psi_t + \eta_t h_t$ with a small positive constant η. This results in the update of the policy.

3.2 On-Sample Convergence

To disclose how the functional gradient leads the policy, we consider discrete actions, i.e., $\pi_\Psi(a|\boldsymbol{s}) = \frac{\exp(\Psi(\boldsymbol{s},a))}{\sum_{a'}\exp(\Psi(\boldsymbol{s},a'))}$, and study its convergence on the training samples.

Let Ψ_0 be a constant function (e.g. always outputs 0), and recall $\Psi_{t+1} = \Psi_t + \eta\nabla_\Psi \rho_S(\pi_\Psi)$. For simplicity, when the state $\boldsymbol{s}$ is clear, we make some notations: let $\Psi_{t,k}$ be $\Psi_t(\boldsymbol{s}, a_k)$, let $\alpha_k^t = \pi_{\Psi_t}(a_k|\boldsymbol{s})$ for the action a_k, $\beta_{kj} = p(\boldsymbol{s}_j|\boldsymbol{s}, a_k)$, $\gamma_j = p^{\pi_\Psi}(\boldsymbol{s}_j|\boldsymbol{s})$ and $c_{kj} = \sum_{i=1}^{m} 1_{(\boldsymbol{s}_j\in\tau_i)}\beta_{kj}R(\tau_i)$ where $1_{expression}$ is the indicator function that is 1 when *expression* is true and 0 otherwise. Denote k^* the index of the *observed best action* of the state $\boldsymbol{s}$, such that $\forall k \neq k^*\ \forall j : c_{k^*j} \geq c_{kj}$.

The functional gradient of total reward on S at a state-action pair $(\boldsymbol{s}, a_k)$ can be rewritten as

$$\begin{aligned}&\nabla_{\Psi_{t,k}}\rho_S(\pi_\Psi)\\ &= \frac{1}{m}\sum_{i=1}^{m}\sum_{j=1}^{l}1_{(\boldsymbol{s}_j\in\tau_i)}\frac{p(\boldsymbol{s}_j|\boldsymbol{s},a_k)}{p^{\pi_\Psi}(\boldsymbol{s}_j|\boldsymbol{s})}R(\tau_i)\nabla_{\Psi_{t,k}}\pi_\Psi(a_k|\boldsymbol{s})\\ &= \frac{1}{m}\sum_{i=1}^{m}\sum_{j=1}^{l}1_{(\boldsymbol{s}_j\in\tau_i)}\frac{\beta_{kj}R(\tau_i)}{\gamma_j}\alpha_k(1-\alpha_k)\\ &= \frac{1}{m}\alpha_k(1-\alpha_k)\sum_{j=1}^{l}\sum_{i=1}^{m}1(\boldsymbol{s}_j\in\tau_i)\frac{\beta_{kj}R(\tau_i)}{\gamma_j}\\ &= \frac{1}{m}\alpha_k(1-\alpha_k)\sum_{j=1}^{l}\frac{c_{kj}}{\gamma_j}\end{aligned}$$

We prove below that functional gradient converges to the observed best action. Denote $\delta = \min_{k\neq k^*}\sum_{j=1}^{l}c_{k^*j} - c_{kj}$ be the reward margin, which will effect the convergence rate.

LEMMA 1. *For an observed state $\boldsymbol{s}$, let a_{k^*} be the observed best action, it holds that*

$$\nabla_{\Psi_{t,k^*}}\rho_S(\pi_{\Psi_t}) - \nabla_{\Psi_{t,k}}\rho_S(\pi_{\Psi_t}) \geq \frac{1}{m}\alpha_{k^*}^t(1-\alpha_{k^*}^t)\delta.$$

PROOF. We first need to prove $\alpha_{k^*}^t \geq \alpha_k^t$ for all t and $k \neq k^*$. The proof is by induction. When $t = 0$, since Ψ_{0,a_k} is a constant for all k, $\alpha_{k^*}^0 = \alpha_k^0$ for all k.

Then inductively assume that $\alpha_{k^*}^t \geq \alpha_k^t$ for all $k \neq k^*$. From the inductive assumption we have that, for all $k \neq k^*$, $\Psi_{t,k^*} \geq \Psi_{t,k}$ since $\alpha_k^t = \frac{\exp(\Psi_k^t)}{\sum_{i=1}^{n}\exp(\Psi_i^t)}$, and $\alpha_{k^*}^t(1-\alpha_{k^*}^t) \geq \alpha_k^t(1-\alpha_k^t)$ since $\sum_{k=1}^{n}\alpha_k^t = 1$. Therefore, we have that

$$\begin{aligned}&\Psi_{t+1,k^*} - \Psi_{t+1,k}\\ &\geq \eta\nabla_{\Psi_{t,k^*}}\rho_S(\pi_{\Psi_t}) - \eta\nabla_{\Psi_{t,k}}\rho_S(\pi_{\Psi_t})\\ &\geq \frac{\eta}{m}\left(\alpha_{k^*}^t(1-\alpha_{k^*}^t)\sum_{j=1}^{l}\frac{c_{k^*j}}{\gamma_j} - \alpha_k^t(1-\alpha_k^t)\sum_{j=1}^{l}\frac{c_{kj}}{\gamma_j}\right)\\ &\geq 0,\end{aligned}$$

and consequently, $\alpha_{k^*}^{t+1} \geq \alpha_k^{t+1}$. This induction proves that $\forall t\ \forall k \neq k^* : \alpha_{k^*}^t \geq \alpha_k^t$.

We then calculate the difference of the gradient.

$$\begin{aligned}
&\nabla_{\Psi_{t,k^*}} \rho_S(\pi_{\Psi_t}) - \nabla_{\Psi_{t,k}} \rho_S(\pi_{\Psi_t}) \\
&= \frac{1}{m}\alpha^t_{k^*}(1-\alpha^t_{k^*})\sum_{j=1}^{l}\frac{c_{k^*j}}{\gamma_j} - \frac{1}{m}\alpha^t_k(1-\alpha^t_k)\sum_{j=1}^{l}\frac{c_{kj}}{\gamma_j} \\
&\geq \frac{1}{m}\alpha^t_{k^*}(1-\alpha^t_{k^*})\sum_{j=1}^{l}\frac{c_{k^*j}-c_{kj}}{\gamma_j} \\
&\geq \frac{1}{m}\alpha^t_{k^*}(1-\alpha^t_{k^*})\delta,
\end{aligned}$$

where the first inequality is by $\forall k \neq k^* : \alpha_{k^*} \geq \alpha_k$ and $\sum_{k=1}^{n} \alpha_k = 1$, the last inequality is by $\gamma_j \in (0,1]$. □

THEOREM 1. *For any* $\varepsilon \in (0, \frac{1}{n}]$, *let* a_{k^*} *be the observed best action, functional gradient achieves* $\alpha^t_{k^*} \geq 1-\varepsilon$ *in iterations*

$$t \leq \lceil \frac{m \ln n(1-\varepsilon)}{\eta\varepsilon(1-\varepsilon)\delta} \rceil.$$

PROOF. By Lemma 1, we have, for any $k \neq k^*$,

$$\begin{aligned}
&\Psi_{t,k^*} - \Psi_{t,k} \\
&= \Psi_{t-1,k^*} - \Psi_{t-1,k} \\
&\quad + \eta\Big(\nabla_{\Psi(s,a_{k^*})}\rho_S(\pi_\Psi) - \nabla_{\Psi(s,a_k)}\rho_S(\pi_\Psi)\Big) \\
&\geq \Psi_{t-1,k^*} - \Psi_{t-1,k} + \eta\frac{1}{m}\alpha^{t-1}_{k^*}(1-\alpha^{t-1}_{k^*})\delta \\
&\geq \ldots \geq \Psi_{0,k^*} - \Psi_{0,k} + \sum_{i=0}^{t-1}\eta\frac{1}{m}\alpha^i_{k^*}(1-\alpha^i_{k^*})\delta \\
&= \sum_{i=0}^{t-1}\eta\frac{1}{m}\alpha^i_{k^*}(1-\alpha^i_{k^*})\delta.
\end{aligned}$$

Assume $\forall i < t : \alpha^i_{k^*} < 1-\varepsilon$, otherwise we have already found a policy satisfying the theorem. Thus

$$\Psi_{t,k^*} - \Psi_{t,k} \geq \sum_{i=0}^{t-1}\eta\frac{1}{m}\varepsilon(1-\varepsilon)\delta.$$

When $t = \frac{m\ln n(1-\varepsilon)}{\eta\varepsilon(1-\varepsilon)\delta}$, $\Psi_{t,k^*} - \Psi_{t,k} \geq \ln n(1-\varepsilon)$ and thus

$$\alpha^t_{k^*} = \frac{1}{\sum_{i=1}^{n}\exp(\Psi_{t,k} - \Psi_{t,k^*})} \geq 1-\varepsilon$$

Therefore, $\alpha^t_{k^*} \geq 1-\varepsilon$ is achieved in $t \leq \lceil \frac{m\ln n(1-\varepsilon)}{\eta\varepsilon(1-\varepsilon)\delta} \rceil$ iterations. □

The theorem states that the functional policy gradient can converge to the observed best action very quickly.

3.3 Avoid Overfitting

When fitting the gradient function on samples, state-of-the-art regression techniques can be employed to fit the gradient quite well. However, as disclosed previously, the gradient converges towards the observed best actions, which however may not be the real best actions.

When linear models are employed, this problem is commonly addressed by the *variance reduction* trick [15]: for each dimension, an optimal bias to the reward can be calculated. The bias has no effect over the trajectory space, but will reduce the variance of the gradient estimation over

Algorithm 1 PolicyBoost

Input:

T: Number of iterations
ϵ: Probability for ϵ-greedy (for discrete action)
σ: Gaussian width (for continues action)
m: Sample size
(b,u): Parameters for memory pool size
$\{\eta_t\}_{t=1}^{T}$: Learning rate
$\mathcal{L}$: Base regression learner

Procedure:

π: The learned policy

```
Pool_best = ∅, Pool_uniform = ∅
Ψ_0(s,a) = 1, ∀(s,a) ∈ S × A (for discrete action), or
    Ψ_0(s) = 0, ∀s ∈ S (for continues action)
for t = 1 to T do
    Let S_t be m trajectories sampled by executing π_{t-1}:
        π_{t-1}(a|s) = e^{Ψ_{t-1}(s,a)} / Σ_b e^{Ψ_{t-1}(s,b)}
    with ε-greedy for discrete action, or
        π_{t-1}(a|s) = 1/sqrt(2πσ^2) exp(-(Ψ_{t-1}(s)-a)^2/σ^2)
    with a width of σ for continues action
    Generate functional gradient examples D_t as
        D_t = {((s,a), ∇_{Ψ(s,a)} ρ'_τ(π_Ψ))}
    for discrete action, or for continues action as
        D_t = {(s, ∇_{Ψ(s,a)} ρ̃'_τ(π_Ψ))}
    for all (s,a) in all τ ∈ S_t ∪ Pool_best ∪ Pool_uniform
    Train a regression model h_t using L from D_t
    Ψ_t = Ψ_{t-1} + η_t h_t
    Update Pool_best and Pool_uniform with S_t
end for
return π_T
```

limited trajectories. However, this trick cannot straightforwardly apply to functional gradient, since the dimensions are not directly manipulatable.

We instead consider this problem from the aspect of boosting. There are several possible ways to avoid overfitting: reduce the model capacity, and do not fit the samples too well. The model capacity of a boosting algorithm is related to the number of iteration [10], thus we shall use a small, say 1, number of iterations. To less fit the samples, we prefer the model fit only the trajectories with better reward. To do this, note that Theorem 1 says that the best observed actions with $c_{k^*j} > 0$ will be fitted. By the definition of c_{ij} it is easy to turn it to be negative by setting the corresponding trajectories to have negative rewards. Therefore, we use the centralized rewards:

$$\rho'(\pi) = \int_{\mathcal{T}} p(\boldsymbol{\tau}|\pi)\big(R(\boldsymbol{\tau}) - \bar{R}\big)\mathrm{d}\boldsymbol{\tau}, \tag{5}$$

where $\bar{R} = \int_{\mathcal{T}} \frac{1}{\int_{\mathcal{T}}\mathrm{d}\boldsymbol{\tau}} R(\boldsymbol{\tau})$. Similarly with the variance reduction trick, it is easy to verify that maximizing Eq.(1) is equivalent with maximizing Eq.(5) since $\int_{\mathcal{T}} p(\boldsymbol{\tau}|\pi)\mathrm{d}\boldsymbol{\tau}=1$. The gradient on a sample S with m trajectories is

$$\nabla\rho'_S(\pi) = \frac{1}{m}\sum_{i=1}^{m}\nabla\log p^\pi(\boldsymbol{\tau}_i)\big(R(\boldsymbol{\tau}_i) - \bar{R}_S\big), \tag{6}$$

where $\bar{R}_S = \sum_{i=1}^{m}\frac{1}{p^\pi(\boldsymbol{\tau}_i)z_S}R(\boldsymbol{\tau}_i)$ with $z_S = \sum_{i=1}^{m}\frac{1}{p^\pi(\boldsymbol{\tau}_i)}$. Therefore, to use this gradient, we only need to shift the reward of the sampled trajectories by $\bar{R}_S$, and keep anything else unchanged.

3.4 The PolicyBoost Algorithm

We then propose an *actor-only* algorithm, the PolicyBoost, as in Algorithm 1. The details are explained in the following.

To better estimate the gradient, instead of through away all the past sampled trajectories, PolicyBoost employs two pools $Pool_{best}$ and $Pool_{uniform}$ to record some past samples: the former one keeps some best-so-far trajectories, and the latter one contains randomly selected trajectories. They are initialized in line 1. Line 2 initializes the potential function. Then PolicyBoost performs T iterations to update the policy. Given a potential function Ψ, the policy is formed by the Gibbs Sampling function for discrete action spaces and the Gaussian distribution for continuous action spaces, which is the same as that for NPPG. Line 4 uses the policy to sample m trajectories, stored in S_t. In line 5, from the union of all sets, a training data is constructed for learning an approximation of the gradient function in line 6, and the potential function is then updated in line 7 with the learning rate η_t. Line 8 updates the pools.

For the generation and approximation of the gradient function, through the point-wise gradient [12], we calculate the gradient function of Eq.(6) with Eq.(3) or Eq.(4) at every observed state-action pair. Then a data set D_t is constructed in line 5. This data set expresses the gradient values at some state-action points. A regression algorithm is then used to learn a function h_t from the data set to approximate the gradient function, as in line 6.

3.5 Incoporating Demonstrations

Interestingly, PolicyBoost can make use of demonstrated trajectories that could be provided by experts. When demonstrated trajectories are available, we can put them into the $Pool_{best}$ set at the initialization step. If the demonstration data is provided with no rewards, we can either assign a high enough estimated reward, or access the environment and evaluate the demonstrations when it is possible. When the demonstrations are put into the $Pool_{best}$ set, PolicyBoost will automatically utilize them to better estimate the gradient, and learn better policies. Note that, unlike in inverse reinforcement learning [26], PolicyBoost does not require optimal demonstrations. When PolicyBoost generates trajectories better than the demonstrations, it will update the $Pool_{best}$ to wipe them out, so that its performance will not be limited by the quality of the demonstrations.

4. EXPERIMENTS

4.1 Parameter Sensitivity

We employ two typical domains, the *Mountain Car* and the *Acrobot*, to examine the parameter sensitivity.

In the *Mountain Car* task, a state is a two dimensional vector, and each dimension is a continuous variable: the horizontal position x and the velocity $\dot{x}$, which are restricted to the ranges $[-1.2, 0.6]$ and $[-0.07, 0.07]$ respectively. Note that we do not discretize the state space. The agent has three actions: driving left, driving right, and not to use the engine at all. The goal of the agent is to reach the mountain top, i.e., $x > 0.5$, from an initial state in $\{(x, \dot{x}) | x \in [-0.75, -0.25], \dot{x} \in [-0.025, 0.025]\}$. We run each episode at a maximal horizon of 2000 steps. The car receives a reward of -1 before reaching the goal and 1 for reaching the goal. In the *Acrobot* task, a state consists of four dimensions. Each is a continuous variable: two joint positions θ_1, θ_2 and two joint velocities $\dot{\theta}_1$, $\dot{\theta}_2$. There are three actions corresponding to torque to the joint between the first and second link of $-1, 0, 1$ respectively. The goal of the agent is to maintain the tip above the goal line from an initial state in $\{(\theta_1, \theta_2, \dot{\theta}_1, \dot{\theta}_2) | \theta_1, \theta_2, \dot{\theta}_1, \dot{\theta}_2 \in [-0.5, 0.5]\}$. We run each episode at a maximal horizon of 2000 steps. It receives a reward of -1 before reaching the goal line and 1 for reaching the goal. The dynamics of the two domains and other details can be found in [34]. Note that we use the raw state features here, but not any better feature encoding.

In the implementation of PolicyBoost, the base regression learner used in all policies is regression decision trees [7] as implemented in WEKA [39], and we set $m = 50$. The variable parameters include the learning rate, the decision tree depths, and the size of the pools. The performance with

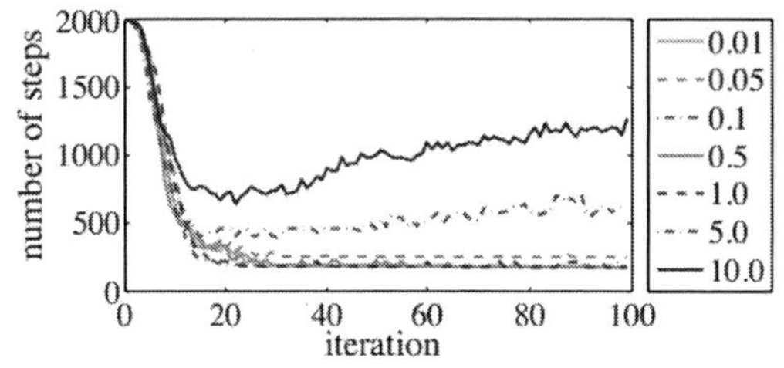

(a) on Mountain Car

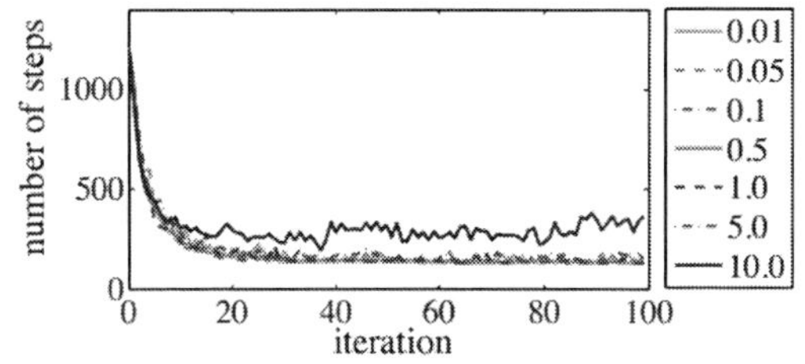

(b) on Acrobot

Figure 1: Performance of PolicyBoost with different learning rates

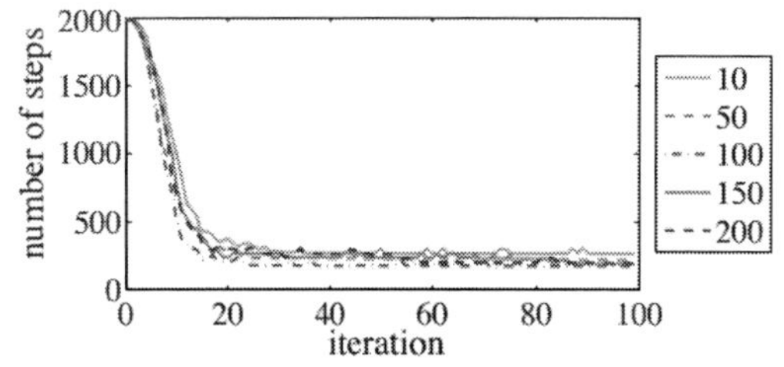

(a) on Mountain Car

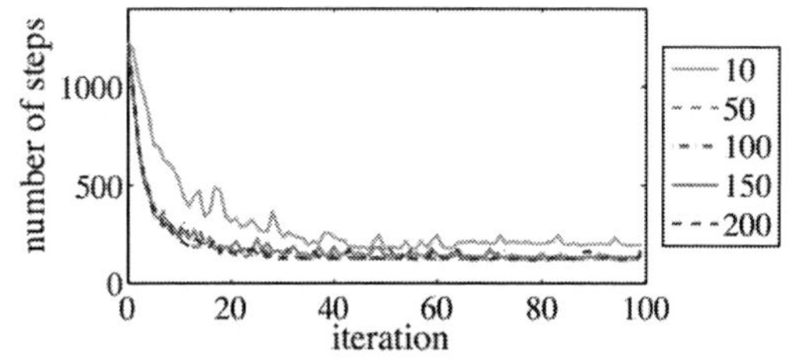

(b) on Acrobot

Figure 2: Performance of PolicyBoost with different tree depths

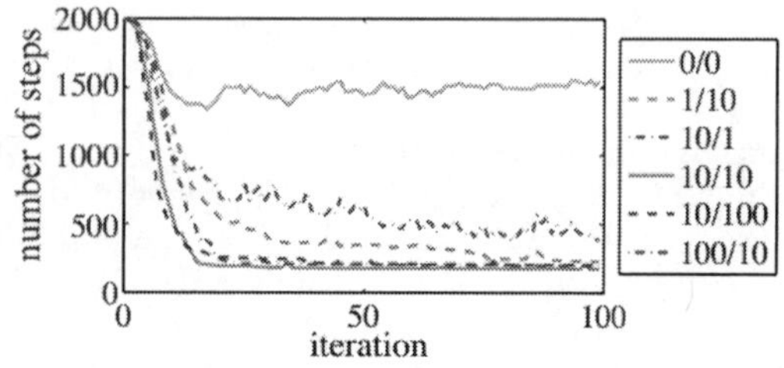

(a) on Mountain Car

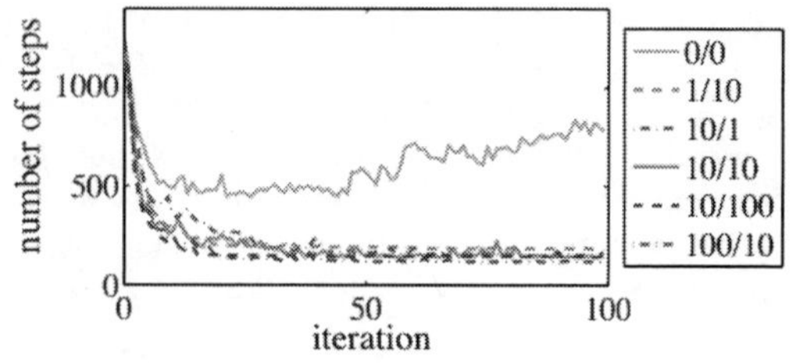

(b) on Acrobot

Figure 3: Performance of PolicyBoost with different pool sizes (best/uniform)

different learning parameters are shown in Figures 1 to 3.

It can be observed that, first from Figure 1, except for too large learning rates (i.e., 5 and 10), PolicyBoost policies does not have a significant different performance. We thus suggest that a fixed learning rate of 1 or 0.1 is good enough in practice. Second, from Figure 2, the tree depth does not show a significant difference except for the smallest depth 10. For it's time consuming to employ deep trees, 100 could be sufficient. On the pool size from Figure 3, we observe that the performance is quite bad with zero pool size, while other pool sizes lead to close performances. We suggest "10/10" in practice. Overall, these comparisons show that PolicyBoost is not quite sensitive to its parameters, and some moderate parameters are suggested.

4.2 Comparisons

We compare the PolicyBoost, using default parameters and raw features of the states and actions, with fine-tuned NPPG, REINFORCE, Sarsa(λ) and LSPI using linear function approximators [31, 13].

For PolicyBoost, we use a fixed setting for all domains: $\eta = 1$, $\epsilon = 0$, tree depth= 100, and the pool size is 10 for both pools. For NPPG, the parameters are carefully tuned: $\eta = 0.1$ and $\epsilon = 0.2$ for Mountain Car, and $\eta = 0.08$ and $\epsilon = 0.1$ for Acrobot. To compare with a linear model using policy gradient methods, we further employ REINFORCE with same parameters: $\eta = 0.1$,$\epsilon = 0$, while the tabular representation [31] is used for REINFORCE. Sarsa(λ) is used as reference of non-policy gradient method. Sarsa(λ) uses the Fourier features [19], and its parameters are set to be: γ=1.0, λ=0.9, $\epsilon = 0.01$ with Fourier bases of order 3. The learning rate is adaptive as in [9]. LSPI is a batch reinforcement learning algorithm and its parameters are set to be: γ=1.0, $\epsilon = 0.01$ with Fourier bases of order 3.

For this group of comparisons, we use an extra domain, Corridor World [17], which is a very simple task where an agent from any random position $x \in [4, 6]$ in a one dimensional corridor $[0, 10]$ needs to reach one of the exits at both ends (0 and 10). For Corridor World, NPPG_{opt} uses $\eta = 0.05$ and $\epsilon = 0.1$.

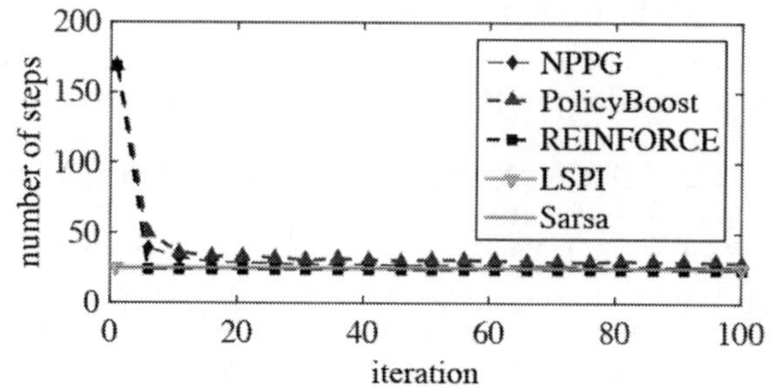

(a) Corridor World

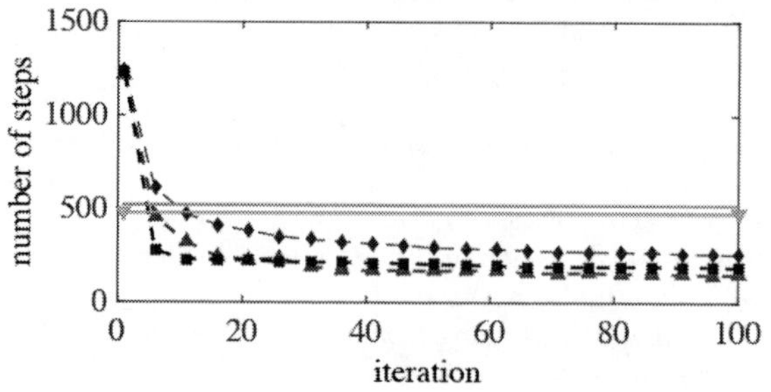

(b) Acrobot

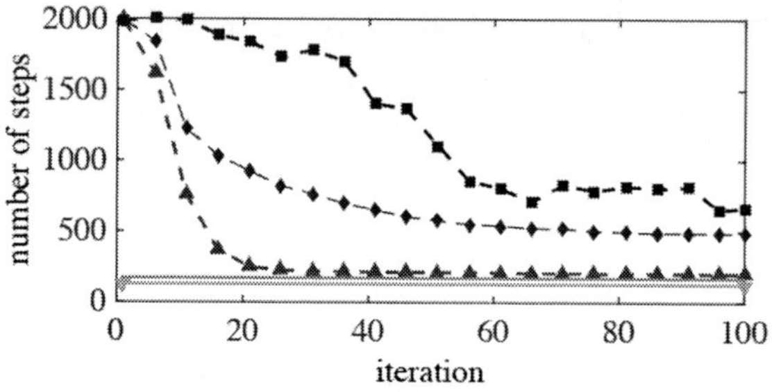

(c) Mountain Car

Figure 4: Performance of different policies at each iteration. The fewer steps the better. Plots (b) and (c) share the legend with plot (a).

The comparison results are presented in Figure 4, where the lines of Sarsa(λ) and LSPI are their performance. Despite that PolicyBoost uses the raw features and the fixed configuration, it produces policies with a clear trend of convergence to the near optimal solution. NPPG works the same as PolicyBoost only on Corridor World, because this task is quite simple so that the overfitting issue is not important. On Acrobot and Mountain Car, NPPG can gain some improvement only after carefully turning the parameters, but is still much worse than PolicyBoost. REINFORCE performs quite well on Corridor World, but the performance degrades badly on Mountain Car. We can conclude that PolicyBoost is more effective and robust than NPPG and REINFORCE.

To verify whether the overfitting problem does exists that encumbers NPPG, we calculated the normalized expected rewards of NPPG and PolicyBoost, i.e.,

$$\sum_{\tau \in S} R(\tau) \cdot p^{\pi}(\tau) / \sum_{\tau'} p^{\pi}(\tau'),$$

using the Mountain Car task. The result is shown in Figure 5. It is clear that PolicyBoost using the proposed objective function indeed learns to rank higher the trajectories with larger rewards, while NPPG fails to do that. This observation confirms that PolicyBoost can well handle the occurring probability overfitting problem, which blocks NPPG.

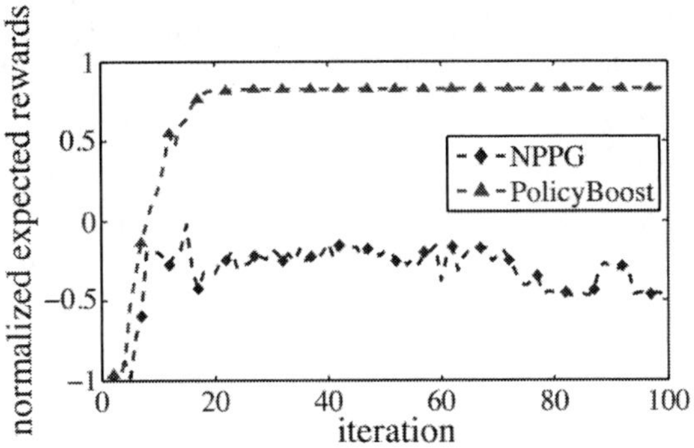

Figure 5: Normalized rewards of NPPG and PolicyBoost on the Mountain Car task.

4.3 Application to Helicopter Control

We use a simulator [36] that models one of the Stanford autonomous helicopters in the flight regime close to hover. The model was learned from data collected using "frequency sweeps" (which systematically vary each of the helicopter's four controls) around the hover flight regime by [3]. This is a challenge task that the agent needs to manipulate 4 continuous control inputs simultaneously based on a 12-dimensional state space. Previously evolutionary algorithm based method [20], programming method [2], and learning from demonstrations [8, 1] have been examined on this task.

We set the maximal horizon to 6000 steps. We regard the four continuous control inputs as independent variables and set $\delta = 0.05$ for each input. So we will learn four policy functions simultaneously each for an input, which does not need to change the structure of the PolicyBoost or NPPG. The PolicyBoost with the fixed configuration is tested. For NPPG we did not find any parameter that leads to any improvement, so the best performance is reported, as in Figure 6. For Sarsa(λ), even if we set the Fourier basis be order 3, the dimensions of the representation for value-function approximator is more than 500,000, leading us to decrease order 3 to 2. LSPI requires too large memory and is not included in the comparison. For REINFORCE, tabular representation would also cause such problem, so we have to use original features. NPPG is not able to find the right gradient direction to improve the hovering steps, while PolicyBoost constantly improves the policy, without any parameter tuning. This observation confirms the advantage of PolicyBoost in real-world applications.

4.4 Incorporating Demonstrations

Finally, we investigate PolicyBoost with demonstrations using the Ms. Pac-Man Game[1] with random ghosts on the first level. The state is described by the directions of the ghosts and directions of the pills with respect to Ms. Pac-Man. Again, PolicyBoost uses the fixed configuration, and NPPG uses well turned parameters. For this game, we record a starter-level human player's actions as the demonstration data, which are not optimal demonstrations. We use 10 such demonstration trajectories in PolicyBoost, which is denoted as $\text{PolicyBoost}_{\text{demo}}$.

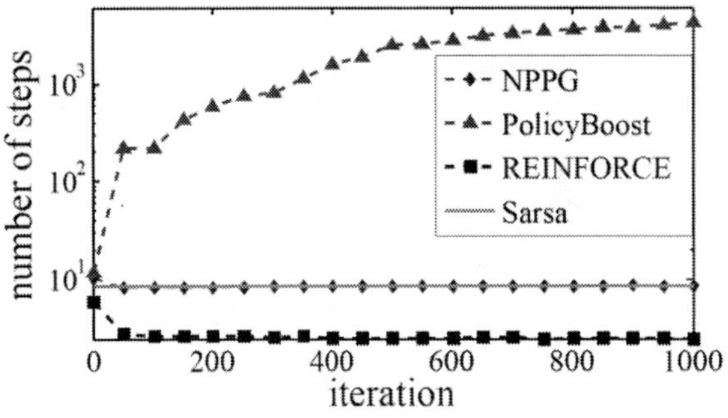

Figure 6: Performance of different policies on the Helicopter Hovering task. The more steps the better.

Figure 7 shows the performance of different approaches. It can be observed that PolicyBoost converges better than NPPG. It is clear that, as the demonstration data is utilized, $\text{PolicyBoost}_{\text{demo}}$ does not only improves the policy much faster than PolicyBoost alone, but also converges to a better performance. The experiment results show that PolicyBoost can well make use of demonstrations to significantly improve its performance.

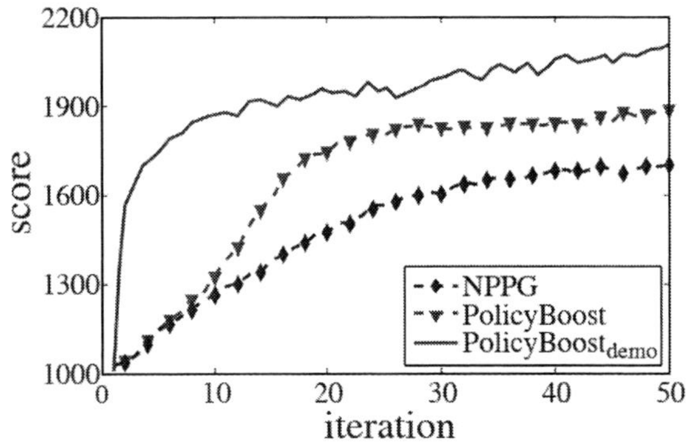

Figure 7: Performance of different policies on the Ms. Pac-Man Game task. The higher score the better.

5. CONCLUSION

In this paper, to combine powerful boosting technique with policy gradient ascent for reinforcement learning problems, we analyzed the functional gradient method and proposed the PolicyBoost method, which searches in an additive function space for a policy that maximizes a corrected total rewards function. Empirical studies on several domains show that, even without feature engineering, PolicyBoost is not only effective to achieve good policies, but is also highly stable to its configuration parameters. Moreover, experiments on the Helicopter Hovering task verifies its applicability in real-world problems, and on the Ms. Pac-Man Game task shows its ability to incorporate non-optimal demonstrations. The future work will focus on designing more

[1]We use the simulator from http://cswww.essex.ac.uk/staff/sml/pacman/PacManContest.html

appropriate mechanisms for trajectory reuse than the current pool-based solution, such as integrating the importance weighting technique with the boosting framework [23].

REFERENCES

[1] P. Abbeel, A. Coates, and A. Y. Ng. Autonomous helicopter aerobatics through apprenticeship learning. *The International Journal of Robotics Research*, 29(13):1608–1639, 2010.

[2] P. Abbeel, A. Coates, M. Quigley, and A. Y. Ng. An application of reinforcement learning to aerobatic helicopter flight. In B. Schölkopf, J. C. Platt, and T. Hoffman, editors, *Advances in Neural Information Processing Systems 19 (NIPS)*, pages 1–8. MIT Press, 2007.

[3] P. Abbeel, V. Ganapathi, and A. Y. Ng. Learning vehicular dynamics, with application to modeling helicopters. In B. S. Yair Weiss and J. Platt, editors, *Advances in Neural Information Processing Systems 18 (NIPS)*, pages 1–8. MIT Press, 2005.

[4] D. A. Aberdeen. *Policy-gradient algorithms for partially observable Markov decision processes.* PhD thesis, Australian National University, 2003.

[5] P. L. Bartlett and J. Baxter. Infinite-horizon policy-gradient estimation. *Journal of Artificial Intelligence Research*, 15:319–350, 2001.

[6] S. Bhatnagar, R. S. Sutton, M. Ghavamzadeh, and M. Lee. Natural actor-critic algorithms. *Automatica*, 45(11):2471–2482, 2009.

[7] L. Breiman, J. Friedman, and C. J. Stone. *Classification and Regression Trees.* Chapman and Hall/CRC, 1984.

[8] A. Coates, P. Abbeel, and A. Y. Ng. Learning for control from multiple demonstrations. In *Proceedings of the 25th International Conference on Machine learning (ICML)*, pages 144–151, Helsinki, Finland, 2008. ACM.

[9] W. Dabney and A. G. Barto. Adaptive step-size for online temporal difference learning. In *AAAI*, 2012.

[10] Y. Freund and R. E. Schapire. A decision-theoretic generalization of on-line learning and an application to boosting. *Journal of Computer and System Sciences*, 55(1):119–139, 1997.

[11] J. Friedman, T. Hastie, and R. Tibshirani. Additive logistic regression: A statistical view of boosting. *The Annals of Statistics*, 28(2):337–407, 2000.

[12] J. H. Friedman. Greedy function approximation: A gradient boosting machine. *Annals of Statistics*, 29(5):1189–1232, 2001.

[13] A. Geramifard, R. H. Klein, C. Dann, W. Dabney, and J. P. How. RLPy: The Reinforcement Learning Library for Education and Research, 2013.

[14] M. Ghavamzadeh and Y. Engel. Bayesian actor-critic algorithms. In *Proceedings of the 24th International Conference on Machine Learning*, pages 297–304, Corvallis, OR, 2007.

[15] E. Greensmith, P. Bartlett, and J. Baxter. Variance reduction techniques for gradient estimates in reinforcement learning. *Journal of Machine Learning Research*, 5:1471–1530, 2004.

[16] M. Kearns and L. G. Valiant. Cryptographic limitations on learning boolean formulae and finite automata. In *Proceedings of the 21st Annual ACM Symposium on Theory of Computing*, pages 433–444, Seattle, WA, 1989.

[17] K. Kersting and K. Driessens. Non-parametric policy gradients: A unified treatment of propositional and relational domains. In *Proceedings of the 25th International Conference on Machine Learning (ICML)*, pages 456–463, Helsinki, Finland, July 2008.

[18] H. Kimura. Reinforcement learning by stochastic hill climbing on discounted reward. In *Proceedings of the 12th International Conference on Machine Learning (ICML)*, pages 295–303, Tahoe City, CA, 1995.

[19] G. Konidaris, S. Osentoski, and P. S. Thomas. Value function approximation in reinforcement learning using the Fourier basis. In *Proceedings of the Twenty-Fifth AAAI Conference on Artificial Intelligence, AAAI 2011, San Francisco, California, USA, August 7-11, 2011*, 2011.

[20] R. Koppejan and S. Whiteson. Neuroevolutionary reinforcement learning for generalized control of simulated helicopters. *Evolutionary intelligence*, 4(4):219–241, 2011.

[21] H.-Y. Lo, K.-W. Chang, S.-T. Chen, T.-H. Chiang, and C.-S. Ferng. An ensemble of three classifiers for kdd cup 2009: Expanded linear model, heterogeneous boosting, and selective naive Bayes. *The 2009 Knowledge Discovery in Data Competition (KDD Cup 2009) Challenges in Machine Learning, Volume 3*, page 53, 2009.

[22] L. Mason, J. Baxter, P. L. Bartlett, and M. R. Frean. Boosting algorithms as gradient descent. In S. A. Solla, T. K. Leen, and K.-R. Müller, editors, *Advances in Neural Information Processing Systems 12 (NIPS)*, pages 512–518. The MIT Press, 2000.

[23] T. Matsubara, T. Morimura, and J. Morimoto. Adaptive step-size policy gradients with average reward metric. In *Proceedings of the 2nd Asian Conference on Machine Learning*, pages 285–298, Tokyo, Japan, 2010.

[24] T. M. Mitchell. *Machine Learning.* McGraw-Hill, Inc., New York, NY, 1997.

[25] A. Y. Ng and M. Jordan. PEGASUS: A policy search method for large MDPs and POMDPs. In *Proceedings of the 16th Conference on Uncertainty in Artificial Intelligence (UAI)*, pages 406–415. Morgan Kaufmann Publishers Inc., 2000.

[26] A. Y. Ng and S. J. Russell. Algorithms for inverse reinforcement learning. In *Proceedings of the 17th International Conference on Machine Learning (ICML)*, pages 663–670, Stanford, CA, 2000.

[27] E. Orate, S. Idelsohn, O. C. Zienkiewicz, and R. L. Taylor. A finite point method in computational mechanics. Application to convectioe transport and fluid flow. *International Journal for Numerical Methods in Engineering*, 39:3839–3866, 1996.

[28] L. Peshkin. *Reinforcement learning by policy search.* PhD thesis, MIT, 2001.

[29] J. Peters. Policy gradient methods. *Scholarpedia*, 5(10):3698, 2010.

[30] J. Peters and S. Schaal. Natural actor-critic. *Neurocomputing*, 71(7):1180–1190, 2008.

[31] N. Roy and J. How. A tutorial on linear function approximators for dynamic programming and reinforcement learning. 2013.

[32] R. E. Schapire. The strength of weak learnability. *Machine Learning*, 5(2):197–227, 1990.

[33] R. E. Schapire and Y. Freund. *Boosting: Foundations and Algorithms.* MIT Press, Cambridge, MA, 2012.

[34] R. S. Sutton and A. G. Barto. *Reinforcement learning: An introduction.* MIT Press, Cambridge, MA, 1998.

[35] R. S. Sutton, D. McAllester, S. Singh, Y. Mansour, et al. Policy gradient methods for reinforcement learning with function approximation. In S. A. Solla, T. K. Leen, and K.-R. Müller, editors, *Advances in Neural Information Processing Systems 12 (NIPS)*, pages 1057–1063. 2000.

[36] B. Tanner and A. White. RL-Glue: Language-independent software for reinforcement-learning experiments. *The Journal of Machine Learning Research*, 10:2133–2136, 2009.

[37] P. Viola and M. Jones. Robust real-time object detection. *International Journal of Computer Vision*, 57(2):137–154, 2004.

[38] R. J. Williams. Simple statistical gradient-following algorithms for connectionist reinforcement learning. *Machine learning*, 8(3):229–256, 1992.

[39] I. H. Witten and E. Frank. *Data Mining: Practical Machine Learning Tools and Techniques.* Morgan Kaufmann, 2005.

State of the Art Control of Atari Games Using Shallow Reinforcement Learning

Yitao Liang†, Marlos C. Machado‡, Erik Talvitie†, and Michael Bowling‡

†Franklin & Marshall College
Lancaster, PA, USA
{yliang, erik.talvitie}@fandm.edu

‡University of Alberta
Edmonton, AB, Canada
{machado, mbowling}@ualberta.ca

ABSTRACT

The recently introduced Deep Q-Networks (DQN) algorithm has gained attention as one of the first successful combinations of deep neural networks and reinforcement learning. Its promise was demonstrated in the Arcade Learning Environment (ALE), a challenging framework composed of dozens of Atari 2600 games used to evaluate general competency in AI. It achieved dramatically better results than earlier approaches, showing that its ability to learn good representations is quite robust and general. This paper attempts to understand the principles that underlie DQN's impressive performance and to better contextualize its success. We systematically evaluate the importance of key representational biases encoded by DQN's network by proposing simple linear representations that make use of these concepts. Incorporating these characteristics, we obtain a computationally practical feature set that achieves competitive performance to DQN in the ALE. Besides offering insight into the strengths and weaknesses of DQN, we provide a generic representation for the ALE, significantly reducing the burden of learning a representation for each game. Moreover, we also provide a simple, reproducible benchmark for the sake of comparison to future work in the ALE.

Keywords

Reinforcement Learning, Function Approximation, DQN, Representation Learning, Arcade Learning Environment

1. INTRODUCTION

In the reinforcement learning (RL) problem an agent autonomously learns a behavior policy from experience in order to maximize a provided reward signal. Most successful RL approaches have relied upon the engineering of problem-specific state representations, diminishing the agent as fully autonomous and reducing its flexibility. The recent Deep Q-Network (DQN) algorithm [20] aims to tackle this problem, presenting one of the first successful combinations of RL and deep convolutional neural-networks (CNN) [13, 14], which are proving to be a powerful approach to representation learning in many areas. DQN is based upon the well-known Q-learning algorithm [31] and uses a CNN to simultaneously learn a problem-specific representation and estimate a value function.

Games have always been an important testbed for AI, frequently being used to demonstrate major contributions to the field [5, 6, 8, 23, 28]. DQN follows this tradition, demonstrating its success by achieving human-level performance in the majority of games within the Arcade Learning Environment (ALE) [2]. The ALE is a platform composed of dozens of qualitatively diverse Atari 2600 games. As pictured in Figure 1, the games in this suite include first-person perspective shooting games (e.g. BATTLE ZONE), platforming puzzle games (e.g. MONTEZUMA'S REVENGE), sports games (e.g. ICE HOCKEY), and many other genres. Because of this diversity, successful approaches in the ALE necessarily exhibit a degree of robustness and generality. Further, because it is based on problems designed by humans for humans, the ALE inherently encodes some of the biases that allow humans to successfully navigate the world. This makes it a potential stepping-stone to other, more complex decision-making problems, especially those with visual input.

DQN's success in the ALE rightfully attracted a great deal of attention. For the first time an artificial agent achieved performance comparable to a human player in this challenging domain, achieving by far the best results at the time and demonstrating generality across many diverse problems. It also demonstrated a successful large scale integration of deep neural networks and RL, surely an important step toward more flexible agents. That said, problematic aspects of DQN's evaluation make it difficult to fully interpret the results. As will be discussed in more detail in Section 6, the DQN experiments exploit non-standard game-specific prior information and also report only one independent trial per game, making it difficult to reproduce these results or to make principled comparisons to other methods. Independent re-evaluations have already reported different results due to the variance in the single trial performance of DQN (e.g. [12]). Furthermore, the comparisons that Mnih et al. did present were to benchmark results using far less training data. Without an adequate baseline for what is achievable using simpler techniques, it is difficult to evaluate the cost-benefit ratios of more complex methods like DQN.

In addition to these methodological concerns, the evaluation of a complicated method such as DQN often leaves open the question of which of its properties were most important to its success. While it is tempting to assume that the neural network must be discovering insightful tailored representations for each game, there is also a considerable amount of domain knowledge embedded in the very struc-

Appears in: *Proceedings of the 15th International Conference on Autonomous Agents and Multiagent Systems (AAMAS 2016), J. Thangarajah, K. Tuyls, C. Jonker, S. Marsella (eds.), May 9–13, 2016, Singapore.*

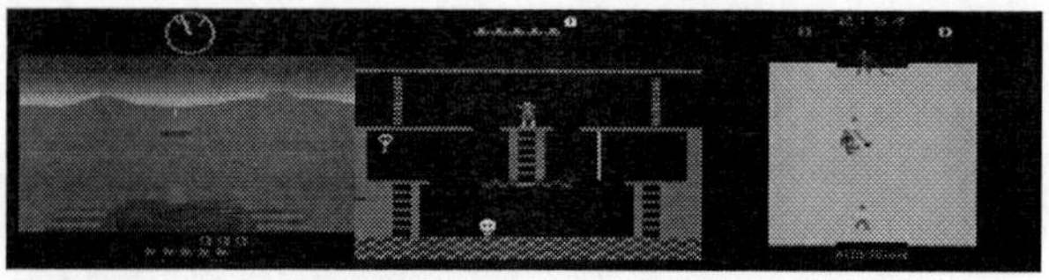

Figure 1: Examples from the ALE (left to right: Battle Zone, Montezuma's Revenge, Ice Hockey).

ture of the network. We can identify three key structural biases in DQN's representation. First, CNNs provide a form of spatial invariance not exploited in earlier work using linear function approximation. DQN also made use of multiple frames of input allowing for the representation of short-range non-Markovian value functions. Finally, small-sized convolutions are quite well suited to detecting small patterns of pixels that commonly represent objects in early video game graphics. These biases were not fully explored in earlier work in the ALE, so a natural question is whether non-linear deep network representations are key to strong performance in ALE or whether the general principles implicit in DQN's network architecture might be captured more simply.

The primary goal of this paper is to systematically investigate the sources of DQN's success in the ALE. Obtaining a deeper understanding of the core principles influencing DQN's performance and placing its impressive results in perspective should aid practitioners aiming to apply or extend it (whether in the ALE or in other domains). It should also reveal representational issues that are key to success in the ALE itself, potentially inspiring new directions of research.

We perform our investigation by elaborating upon a simple linear representation that was one of DQN's main comparison points, progressively incorporating the representational biases identified above and evaluating the impact of each one. This process ultimately yields a fixed, generic feature representation able to obtain performance competitive to DQN in the ALE, suggesting that the general form of the representations learned by DQN may in many cases be more important than the specific features it learns. Further, this feature set offers a simple and computationally practical alternative to DQN as a platform for future research, especially when the focus is not on representation learning. Finally, we are able provide an alternative benchmark that is more methodologically sound, easing reproducibility and comparison to future work.

2. BACKGROUND

In this section we introduce the reinforcement learning problem setting and describe existing results in the ALE.

2.1 Reinforcement Learning

In the *reinforcement learning* (RL) problem [26, 27] an agent interacts with an unknown environment and attempts to maximize a "reward" signal. The environment is commonly formalized as a *Markov decision process* (MDP) $\mathcal{M}$ defined as a 5-tuple $\mathcal{M} = \langle \mathcal{S}, \mathcal{A}, \mathcal{R}, P, \gamma \rangle$. At time t the agent is in the state $s_t \in \mathcal{S}$ where it takes an action $a_t \in \mathcal{A}$ that leads to the next state $s_{t+1} \in \mathcal{S}$ according to the transition probability kernel P, which encodes $Pr(s_{t+1}|s_t, a_t)$. The agent also observes a reward $r_{t+1} \sim \mathcal{R}(s_t, a_t, s_{t+1})$. The agent's goal is to learn the *optimal policy*, a conditional distribution $\pi(a|s)$ that maximizes the *state value function* $V^\pi(s) \doteq \mathbb{E}_\pi\big[\sum_{k=0}^{\infty} \gamma^k r_{t+k+1} | s_t = s\big]$ for all $s \in \mathcal{S}$, where $\gamma \in [0, 1)$ is known as the *discount factor*.

As a critical step toward improving a given policy π, it is common for reinforcement learning algorithms to learn a *state-action value function*, denoted:

$$Q^\pi(s, a) \doteq \mathbb{E}_\pi\big[\mathcal{R}(s_t, a_t, s_{t+1}) + \gamma V^\pi(s_{t+1}) \,\big| s_t = s, a_t = a\big].$$

However, in large problems it may be infeasible to learn a value for each state-action pair. To tackle this issue agents often learn an approximate value function: $Q^\pi(s, a; \theta) \approx Q^\pi(s, a)$. A common approach uses linear function approximation (LFA) where $Q^\pi(s, a; \theta) = \theta^\top \phi(s, a)$, in which θ denotes the vector of weights and $\phi(s, a)$ denotes a static feature representation of the state s when taking action a. However, this can also be done through non-linear function approximation methods, including neural networks.

One of the most popular reinforcement learning algorithms is Sarsa(λ) [22]. It consists of learning an approximate action-value function while following a continually improving policy π. As the states are visited, and rewards are observed, the action-value function is updated and consequently the policy is improved since each update improves the estimative of the agent's expected return from state s, taking action a, and then following policy π afterwards, *i.e.* $Q^\pi(s, a)$. The Sarsa(λ) update equations, when using function approximation, are:

$$\begin{aligned} \delta_t &= r_{t+1} + \gamma Q(s_{t+1}, a_{t+1}; \vec{\theta}_t) - Q(s_t, a_t; \vec{\theta}_t) \\ \vec{e}_t &= \gamma \lambda \vec{e}_{t-1} + \nabla Q(s_t, a_t; \vec{\theta}_t) \\ \vec{\theta}_{t+1} &= \vec{\theta}_t + \alpha \delta_t \vec{e}_t, \end{aligned}$$

where α denotes the step-size, the elements of $\vec{e}_t$ are known as the *eligibility traces*, and δ_t is the *temporal difference error*. Theoretical results suggest that, as an on-policy method, Sarsa(λ) may be more stable in the linear function approximation case than off-policy methods such as Q-learning, which are known to risk divergence [1, 10, 18]. These theoretical insights are confirmed in practice; Sarsa(λ) seems to be far less likely to diverge in the ALE than Q-learning and other off-policy methods [7].

2.2 Arcade Learning Environment

In the Arcade Learning Environment agents have access only to sensory information (160 pixels wide by 210 pixels high images) and aim to maximize the score of the game being played using the 18 actions on a standard joystick without game-specific prior information. Note that in most games a single screen does not constitute Markovian state. That said, Atari 2600 games are deterministic, so the entire history of interaction fully determines the next screen. It is most common for ALE agents to base their decisions on only the most recent few screens.

2.2.1 Linear Value Function Approximation

Early work in the ALE focused on developing new generic feature representations to be used with linear RL methods. Along with introducing the ALE itself, Bellemare et al. [2] presented an RL benchmark using four different feature sets obtained from the game screen. *Basic* features tile the screen and check if each of the available colors in the Atari 2600 are active in each tile. *BASS* features add pairwise combinations of Basic features. *DISCO* features attempt to detect and classify objects on the screen in order to infer their positions and velocities. *LSH* simply applies Locally Sensitive Hashing [9] to raw Atari 2600 screens. Bellemare, Veness, and Bowling proposed an extension to the Basic feature set which involved identifying which parts of the screen were under the agents' direct control. This additional information is known as *contingency awareness* [3].

These feature sets were, for some time, the standard representations for Atari 2600 games, being directly used in other work [7, 16, 17] or serving as the base for more elaborate feature sets [4]. The feature representations presented in this paper follow the spirit of this early work. We use Basic features (formally described below) as a starting point, and attempt to capture pairwise spatial relationships between objects on the screen.

Basic Features: To obtain Basic features we first divide the Atari 2600 screen into 16×14 tiles of size 10×15 pixels. For every tile (c, r) and color k, where $c \in \{1, \ldots, 16\}$, $r \in \{1, \ldots, 14\}$, and $k \in \{1, \ldots, 128\}$, we check whether color k is present within the tile (c, r), generating the binary feature $\phi_{c,r,k}$. Intuitively, Basic features encode information like "there is a red pixel within this region". There are $16 \times 14 \times 128 = 28{,}672$ Basic features in total.

It can be computationally demanding to work directly with 160×210 pixel screens with a 128 color palette. To make the screen more sparse, following previous work (*e.g.* [2, 3]) we subtract the background from the screen at each frame before processing it. The background is precomputed using 18,000 samples obtained from random trajectories.

2.2.2 *Non-Linear Value Function Approximation*

The use of non-linear function approximation in the ALE is more recent. Veness et al. [30], for example, propose the use of compression techniques as a policy evaluation approach in RL, evaluating their method in the ALE. Soon after, the research landscape changed due to the success of using deep learning techniques to approximate value functions, demonstrated by the DQN algorithm [19, 20]. DQN achieved 75% of a human player's score in the majority of games and this inspired much more work in the ALE using deep learning (*e.g.* [11, 24, 25]).

DQN employs a deep convolutional neural network to represent the state-action value function Q. A deep convolutional network uses weight sharing to make it practical to learn a function of high-dimensional image input. Specifically, when processing the image a small network focused on a small region of the screen called a *filter* is applied at multiple positions on the screen. Its output at each position forms a new (smaller) image, which can then be processed by another filter, and so on. Multiple layers of convolution allow the network to detect patterns and relationships at progressively higher levels of abstraction. DQN's network uses three layers of convolution with multiple filters at each layer. The final result of those convolutions is then processed via a more standard fully connected feed-forward network. The convolutional aspect of the network allows the network to detect relationships like "A bullet is near an alien here," where "bullet" and "alien" can be position invariant concepts. The non-linear global layers allow it to represent whole-screen concepts such as "A bullet is near an alien somewhere." This is the inspiration of our spatially invariant features (Section 3). Further, Mnih et al. actually provide the four most recent images as input to their network, allowing it to detect relationships through time (such as movement). This motivates our short-order-Markov features (Section 4). Finally, note that Basic features are essentially a simple convolution where the filters simply detect the presence of each color in their range. DQN's more sophisticated filters motivate our improvement of object detection for base features (Section 5).

3. SPATIAL INVARIANCE

Recall that Basic features detect the presence of each color in various regions of the screen. As discussed above, this can be seen as analogous to a single convolution with a crude filter. The BASS feature set, which was amongst the best performing representations before DQN's introduction encodes pairwise relationships between Basic features, still anchored at specific positions, so it is somewhat analogous to a second convolutional layer. But in many games the absolute positions of objects are not as important as their relative positions to each other. To investigate the effect of ignoring absolute position we impose a non-linearity over BASS (analogous to DQN's fully connected layers), specifically taking the max of BASS features over absolute position.

We call the resulting feature set Basic Pairwise Relative Offsets in Space (B-PROS) because it captures pairwise *relative* distances between objects in a single screen. More specifically, a B-PROS feature checks if there is a pair of Basic features with colors $k_1, k_2 \in \{1, \ldots, 128\}$ separated by an offset (i, j), where $-13 \leq i \leq 13$ and $-15 \leq j \leq 15$. If so, $\phi_{k_1,k_2,(i,j)}$ is set to 1, meaning that a pixel of color k_1 is contained within some block (c, r) and a pixel of color k_2 is contained within the block $(c + i, r + j)$. Intuitively, B-PROS features encode information like "there is a yellow pixel three tiles below a red pixel". The computational complexity of generating B-PROS features is similar to that of BASS, though ultimately fewer features are generated. Note that, as described, B-PROS contains redundant features (e.g. $\phi_{1,2,(4,0)}$ and $\phi_{2,1,(-4,0)}$), but it is straightforward to eliminate them. The complete feature set is composed of the Basic features and the B-PROS features. After redundancy is eliminated, the B-PROS feature set has 6,885,440 features in total $(28{,}672 + ((31 \times 27 \times 128^2 - 128)/2 + 128))$.

Note that there have been other attempts to represent pairwise spatial relationships between objects, for instance DISCO [2] and contingency awareness features [3]. However, these existing attempts are complicated to implement, demanding to compute, and less effective (as will be seen), most likely due to unreliable estimates of object positions.

3.1 Empirical Evaluation

Our first set of experiments compares B-PROS to the previous state of the art in linear representations for the Atari 2600 [2, 3] in order to evaluate the impact of the non-linearity applied to BASS. For the sake of comparison we follow Bellemare et al.'s methodology [2]. Specifically, in 24 independent trials the agent was trained for 5000 episodes. After the learning phase we froze the weights and evaluated the learned policy by recording its average performance over 499 episodes. We report the average evaluation score across the 24 trials. Following Bellemare et al., we defined a maximum length for each episode: 18,000 frames, *i.e.* five minutes of real-time play. Also, we used a frame-skipping technique, in which the agent selects actions and updates its

Table 1: Comparison of linear representations. Bold denotes the largest value between B-PROS and Best Linear [2]. See text for more details.

Game	Best Linear	CAF	B-PROS (std. dev.)
ASTERIX	987.3	1332.0	**4078.7** (1016.0)
BEAM RIDER	929.4	1742.7	**1528.7** (504.4)
BREAKOUT	5.2	6.1	**13.5** (11.0)
ENDURO	129.1	159.4	**240.5** (24.2)
FREEWAY	16.4	19.97	**31.0** (0.7)
PONG	-19.2	-17.4	**4.9** (6.6)
Q*BERT	613.5	960.3	**1099.8** (740.0)
SEAQUEST	664.8	722.89	**1048.5** (321.2)
SPACE INVADERS	250.1	267.93	**384.7** (87.2)

value function every x frames, repeating the selected action for the next $x - 1$ frames. This allows the agent to play approximately x times faster. Following Bellemare et al. we use $x = 5$ (DQN also uses a similar procedure).

We used Sarsa(λ) with replacing traces and an ϵ-greedy policy. We performed a parameter sweep over nine games, which we call "training" games. The reported results use a decay rate $\gamma = 0.99$, an exploration rate $\epsilon = 0.01$, a step-size $\alpha = 0.5$ and eligibility decay rate $\lambda = 0.9$.

Table 1 compares our agent to existing linear agents in our set of training games (note that BREAKOUT, ENDURO, PONG, and Q*BERT were not training games for the earlier methods). "Best Linear" denotes the best performance obtained among four different feature sets: Basic, BASS, DISCO and LSH [2]. For reference, in the "CAF" column we also include results obtained by contingency awareness features [3], as reported by Mnih et al. [20]. Note, that these results are not directly comparable because their agent was given 10,000 episodes of training (rather than 5000).

B-PROS' performance surpasses the original benchmarks by a large margin and, except in one game, even surpasses the performance of CAF, despite being far simpler and training with half as much data. Further, some of the improvements represent qualitative breakthroughs. For instance, in PONG, B-PROS allows the agent to win the game with a score of 20-15 on average, while previous methods rarely scored more than a few points. In ENDURO, the earlier methods seem to be stymied by a sudden change in dynamics after approximately 120 points, while B-PROS is consistently able to continue beyond that point.

When comparing these features sets for all 53 games B-PROS performs better on average than all of Basic, BASS, DISCO, and LSH in 77% (41/53) of the games. Even with less training data, B-PROS performs better on average than CAF in 77% (38/49) of the games in which CAF results were reported[1]. The dramatic improvement yielded by B-PROS clearly indicates that focusing on relative spatial relationships rather than absolute positions is vital to success in the ALE (and likely in other visual domains as well).

4. NON-MARKOVIAN FEATURES

B-PROS is capable of encoding relative distances between objects but it fails to encode movement, which can be a very important aspect of Atari games. For instance, the agent may need to know whether the ball is moving toward or away from the paddle in PONG. Previous linear representations similarly relied mainly on the most recent screen. In contrast, Mnih et al. use the four most recent screens as input, allowing DQN to represent short-order-Markov features of the game screens. In this section we present an extension to B-PROS that takes a similar approach, extracting information from the two most recent screens.

Basic Pairwise Relative Offsets in Time (B-PROT) features represent pairwise relative offsets between Basic features obtained from the screen five frames in the past and Basic features from the current screen (*i.e.* PROT features). More specifically, for every pair of colors $k_1, k_2 \in \{1, \ldots, 128\}$ and every offset (i, j), where $-13 \leq i \leq 13$ and $-15 \leq j \leq 15$, a binary B-PROT feature $\phi_{k_1,k_2,(i,j)}$ is 1 if a pixel of color k_1 is contained within some block $(c+i, r+j)$ on the screen five frames ago and a pixel of color k_2 is contained within the block (c, r) in the current screen.

The B-PROST feature set contains Basic, B-PROS, and B-PROT features. Note that there are roughly twice as many B-PROT features as B-PROS because there are no redundant offsets. As such, B-PROST has a total of 20,598,848 sparse, binary features ($6{,}885{,}440 + 31 \times 27 \times 128^2$).

4.1 Empirical Evaluation

B-PROS outperformed all the other linear architectures in the previous experiment. Subsequent extensions will be primarily compared to DQN (see Section 6). As such, in these experiments, we adopted an evaluation protocol similar to Mnih et al.'s. Each agent was trained for 200,000,000 frames (equivalent to 40,000,000 decisions) over 24 independent trials. The learned policy in each trial was evaluated by recording its average performance in 499 episodes with no learning. We report the average evaluation score over the 24 trials. In an effort to make our results comparable to DQN's we also started each episode with a random number of "no-op" actions and restricted the agent to the minimal set of actions that have a unique effect in each game.

The first two columns of Table 2 present results using B-PROS and B-PROST in the training games. B-PROST outperforms B-PROS in all but one of the training games. One particularly dramatic improvement occurs in PONG; B-PROS wins with a score of 20-9, on average, while B-PROST rarely allows the opponent to score at all. Another result worth noting is in ENDURO. The randomized initial conditions seem to have significantly harmed the performance of B-PROS in this game, but B-PROST seems to be robust to this effect. When evaluated over all 49 games evaluated by Mnih et al. the average score using B-PROST is higher than that using B-PROS in 82% of the games (40/49)[2]. This clearly indicates the critical importance of non-Markov features to success in the ALE.

Before making a final comparison with DQN, we will make one more improvement to our representation.

5. OBJECT DETECTION

Because Basic features encode the positions of individual pixels on the screen, both B-PROS and B-PROST features struggle to distinguish which pixels are part of the same object. DQN's network is capable of learning far more subtle filters. In order to measure the impact of improved low-level object detection, we consider a simple extension to Basic that exploits the fact that Atari screens often contain several contiguous regions of pixels of the same color. We call such

[1] Due to space restrictions we reserve the full table of 53 games for the longer version of this paper [15].

[2] The full results table is available in the longer paper [15].

Table 2: Comparison of relative offset features. Bold indicates the best average of the three columns. The † indicates significant differences between B-PROST and Blob-PROST.

Game	B-PROS Avg. (std. dev.)	B-PROST Avg. (std. dev.)	Blob-PROST Avg. (std. dev.)
ASTERIX	8194.3 (1802.9)	**8928.8**† (1714.5)	4400.8 (1201.3)
BEAM RIDER	1686.9 (255.2)	1808.9 (309.2)	**1902.3** (423.9)
BREAKOUT	7.1 (1.7)	15.0 (4.7)	**46.7**† (45.7)
ENDURO	34.9 (71.5)	207.7 (23.1)	**257.0**† (79.8)
FREEWAY	23.8 (6.7)	29.1 (6.3)	**31.5**† (1.2)
PONG	10.9 (5.2)	18.9 (1.3)	**20.1**† (0.5)
Q*BERT	3647.8 (1273.3)	3608.7 (1129.0)	**6946.8**† (3036.4)
SEAQUEST	1366.1 (445.9)	1636.5 (519.5)	**1664.2** (440.4)
SPACE INVADERS	505.1 (130.4)	582.9 (139.0)	**723.1**† (101.5)

regions "blobs". Rather than directly represent coarsened positions of pixels, we first process the screen to find a list of blobs. Blob features then represent coarsened positions of blobs on the screen. Changing the "primitive" features from Basic to Blob yields the Blob-PROST feature set.

Note that blobs are a simplification; in many Atari games, as would be true in more natural images, objects consist of multiple close but separate blobs. Grouping only strictly contiguous pixels into each blob may generate redundant blobs that all represent a single object. As a simple means to address this we add a tolerance to the contiguity condition, *i.e.* we consider pixels that are in the same $s \times s$ pixel square to be contiguous. This approach has an inherent trade-off. On the one hand, with sufficiently large s we may successfully represent each object with few blobs. Also, by reducing the number of blobs, we substantially decrease the number of primitive features, making Blob-PROS and Blob-PROT features easier to compute. On the other hand, if s is too high then multiple distinct objects may be grouped together. In our experiments we set s to be 6 after an informal search using the set of training games. It is very likely that with a more systematic selection of s one can obtain better results than those reported here.

We define the position of a blob as the centroid of the blob's smallest bounding box. To generate the features, we first generate Blob features that are analogous to Basic features: we divide the screen into tiles of 4×7 pixels and then for every color k and block (c, r), where $c \in \{1, \ldots, 40\}, r \in \{1, \ldots, 30\}$ and $k \in \{1, \ldots, 128\}$, the Blob feature $\phi_{c,r,k}$ is 1 if the block (c, r) contains the centroid for some blob of color k. Note that we use a finer resolution than Basic. This is feasible only because of the extreme sparsity of blobs on the screen. The number of blobs in one frame ranged from 6 (PONG) to 412 (BATTLE ZONE). This sparsity also makes the background subtraction step unnecessary; the background typically reduces to a handful of blobs itself.

The Blob-PROST feature set is then constructed from these primitive features in the same manner as B-PROST. There are 153,600 Blob features ($40 \times 30 \times 128$), 38,182,976 Blob-PROS features ($(79 \times 59 \times 128^2 - 128)/2 + 128$), and 76,365,824 Blob-PROT features ($79 \times 59 \times 128^2$). This yields a total of 114,702,400 Blob-PROST features. Though the number of possible features is very large, most would never be generated due to the sparsity of blobs.

5.1 Empirical Evaluation

The last column of Table 2 presents results using Blob-PROST in the training games. In all but one of the training games, Blob-PROST outperformed both B-PROS and B-PROST on average[3]. In 6 of the 9, Blob-PROST's average performance was statistically significantly better than B-PROST (using Welch's t-test with $p < 0.05$). ASTERIX is a game in which Blob-PROST notably fails; perhaps blob detection lumps together distinct objects in a harmful way. Q*BERT is a notable success; the scores of B-PROS and B-PROST indicate that they rarely complete the first level, while Blob-PROST's score indicates that it consistently clears the first level. Out of the 49 games evaluated by Mnih et al., Blob-PROST's average performance was higher than that of both B-PROS and B-PROST in 59% (29/49) of the games. Its performance was statistically significantly higher than that of B-PROST in 47% (23/49) of the games, showing the clear contribution of even simple improvements in object detection. Though object detection itself is not a feature, it make all features based upon it carry more meaningful information that helps our agents better "interpret" the screen.

6. COMPARISON WITH DQN

The next set of experiments compare Blob-PROST to DQN, showing that the three enhancements investigated above largely explain the performance gap between DQN and earlier LFA approaches. In performing this comparison, we necessarily confront problematic aspects of the original DQN evaluation (some of which we adopt for comparison's sake). In Section 7 we present a more methodologically sound ALE benchmark for comparison to future work.

6.1 DQN Evaluation Methodology

In each game, Mnih et al. trained a DQN agent once for 200,000,000 frames. Rather than evaluating the learned policy after the whole learning phase completed (as in earlier work), they evaluated their agent's performance every 4,000,000 frames and selected the best performing weights. They reported the average and standard deviation of the scores of this best learned policy in 30 evaluation episodes.

Mnih et al. also restricted their agent to the minimal set of actions that have a unique effect in each game, game-specific prior information not exploited by earlier work in the ALE. Since in most games the minimal action set contains fewer actions than the full action set, agents with access to the minimal set may benefit from a faster effective learning rate (this is discussed further in Section 7).

To avoid overfitting to the Atari's determinism, Mnih et al. randomized the initial state of each episode by taking a random number of "no-op" actions. The number of "no-ops" was uniformly randomly selected from $\{1, \ldots, 30\}$.

Mnih et al. also modified when episodes ended. In many Atari games the player has a number of "lives" and the game ends when they are exhausted. DQN employed the same episode termination criteria as Bellemare et al. [2], *i.e.* the end of the game or expiration of the 5 minute time limit, but during training also terminated episodes when the agent lost a life (another form of game-specific prior information).We have not specifically evaluated the impact of this mechanism, but one might speculate that in games that have "lives" (e.g. BREAKOUT, SPACE INVADERS) this modification could more easily generate agents with an "avoid death" policy.

[3]The implementation of the three feature sets we introduced, as well as the code used in our experiments is available at `https://github.com/mcmachado/b-pro`.

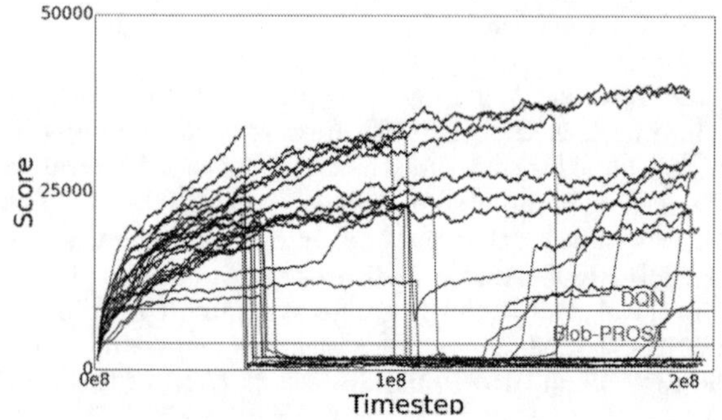

Figure 2: Learning curves for Blob-PROST on the game Up 'n Down, smoothed over 500 episodes.

The DQN experimental methodology possesses three main problematic flaws. First, one cannot make statistical comparisons from a single trial. While Mnih et al. report a standard deviation, this only represents the amount of variation observed when executing the one chosen policy, and not variation observed over different independent executions of the inherently stochastic algorithm. DQN's consistently high performance across games suggests it does indeed regularly perform well, but the reported performance numbers on any particular game may not be representative of their expected performance. Second, selecting the best performing parameterization over the whole learning period is a significant deviation from typical RL methodology. Such a choice may be masking instability issues where learning performance is initially strong but later goes awry. This effect can occur even using comparatively stable linear function approximators. For example, Figure 2 shows 24 independent learning trials from the game UP 'N DOWN using our linear Blob-PROST agent. Many learning trials in this game exhibit an agent steadily improving its performance before a sudden plummet from which it does not recover. The reported performance of DQN and Blob-PROST is also depicted, showing the impact of such instability: most trials perform much better than the reported average at some point. We contend that general competency should include consistent and stable improvement over time, best measured by an agent's performance at the end of training. Third, using designer-provided game-specific prior knowledge in the form of the minimal action set and termination on "death" is counter to the goal of evaluating general competency.

Some of these concerns have been addressed in emerging follow-up work to DQN [21], which uses the final network weights for evaluation and reports the average score over five independent trials.

6.2 Comparing Blob-PROST and DQN

As discussed in Section 4, for comparison's sake, we adopted a similar methodology. We did use the minimal action set, and did add random "no-ops" to the beginning of episodes, but we opted not to utilize the life counter.

6.2.1 Computational Cost

We found that Blob-PROST is far more computationally practical than DQN. We compared the algorithms' resource needs on 3.2GHz Intel Core i7-4790S CPUs. We ran them for 24 hours (to allow resource usage to stabilize), then measured their runtime and memory use.

The computational cost of our implementation of Blob-PROST can vary from game to game. The runtime of our implementation ranged from 56 decisions per second (ALIEN) to 300 decisions per second (STAR GUNNER), that is 280-1500 frames per second (many times real time speed). The memory utilization of our implementation ranged from 50MB (PONG) to 9GB (BATTLE ZONE). Note that BATTLE ZONE was an outlier; the next most memory intensive game (STAR GUNNER) used only 3.7GB of memory. Furthermore, the memory utilization of Blob-PROST can likely be effectively controlled by simplifying the color palette or through the use of feature hashing (*e.g.* [4]).

In contrast, we found DQN's computational cost to be quite consistent across games, running at a speed of approximately 5 decisions per second (*i.e.* 20 frames per second, 3 times slower than real time), and requiring approximately 9.8GB of memory. DQN already uses a reduced color palette and is not immediately amenable to feature hashing to control memory usage. On the other hand, it is amenable to GPU acceleration to improve runtime. Mnih et al. do not report DQN's runtime but in recent follow-up work the GPU accelerated speed has been reported to be approximately 330 frames per second [29], still slower than the Blob-PROST agent in most games. Further note that obtaining enough GPUs to support multiple independent trials in all the games (necessary for statistical comparisons) is, in itself, a prohibitive cost. Emerging work [21] shows that a related approach can be accelerated via CPU parallelism.

6.2.2 ALE Performance

Because only one trial of DQN was reported in each game, and because of the prohibitively high computational cost of independently re-evaluating DQN, a principled comparison between our method and DQN is essentially impossible. Instead, we used a number of ad hoc measures aimed at forming an intuitive understanding of the relative capabilities of the two algorithms, based on available evidence.

First, for each game we record how many trials of Blob-PROST obtained evaluation scores greater than DQN's single trial. If we were to compare an algorithm to itself in this way, we would expect roughly 50% of the trials to have greater performance. In Table 3 (available in the Appendix), the column marked "% trials > DQN" reports the results. The average percentage of trials better than DQN, across all games, was 41%. That is, if you select a game uniformly randomly and run Blob-PROST, there is an estimated 41% chance that it will surpass DQN's reported score.

Second, in each game we compared Blob-PROST's middle trial (12th best) to the single reported DQN trial. If Blob-PROST's evaluation score compares favorably to DQN in this trial then this suggests that scores like DQN's are typical for Blob-PROST. Again, if this method were used to compare an algorithm to itself, one would expect the middle trial to be better in roughly half of the games. In Table 3 the column marked "Middle trial" reports the results. Blob-PROST's middle trial evaluation score was better than DQN's in 43% (21/49) of the games. In 3 of the games in which it performed worse, Blob-PROST's score was not stastically significantly different than DQN's. So in 49% of the games Blob-PROST's middle trial was either not different from or better than DQN's single reported trial.

Third, in each game we compared Blob-PROST's best trial to the single DQN trial. Since it is possible that some of DQN's trials are high-performing outliers, this is intended to give a sense of the level of performance Blob-PROST is capable of reaching, regardless of whether it can do so consistently. In 65% (32/49) of the games, Blob-PROST's best trial's performance exceeded that of the DQN trial. Again, in three games in which Blob-PROST did worse, the difference was not statistically significant. So in 71% of the games Blob-PROST's best trial was either not different from or better than DQN's single reported trial.

Finally, DQN's main result was achieving at least 75% of a human's performance in over half of the games (29/49). The best trial of Blob-PROST crossed this threshold in 34/49 games. The middle trial did so in only 20/49 games.

The Blob-PROST representation was generated using simple and natural enhancements to BASS (one of DQN's main comparison points) aimed at incorporating similar structural biases to those encoded by DQN's designer-provided network architecture. All told, these results seem to indicate that this fixed representation is of comparable quality to DQN's learned representation across many games.

7. ALE BENCHMARK

As discussed above, besides better understanding the core issues underlying DQN's success in the ALE, it is important to present a reproducible benchmark without the problematic flaws discussed in Section 6 (*i.e.* one that reports more than one trial, evaluates the final set of weights, and eschews game-specific prior knowledge). Moreover, establishing this benchmark is important for the ALE's continued use as an evaluation platform. The principled evaluation of complicated approaches depends upon the existence of a sound baseline for what can be achieved with simple approaches.

To this end we also present the performance of Blob-PROST using the full action set. Our agents' average performance after 24 trials using the full action set is reported in the first column of Table 3 in the Appendix. We recommend that future comparisons to Blob-PROST use these results. Surprisingly, we found that when using the full action set Blob-PROST performed slightly better in comparison to DQN using the measures described above than when using the minimal action set. It is not entirely clear why this would be; one possible explanation is that the presence of redundant actions may have a positive impact on exploration in some games.

8. CONCLUSIONS AND FUTURE WORK

While it is difficult to draw firm conclusions, the results indicate the Blob-PROST's performance in the ALE is competitive to DQN's, albeit likely slightly worse overall. Most importantly, these results indicate we may have been able to capture some of the key features of DQN in a practical, fixed linear representation. We saw progressive and dramatic improvements by respectively incorporating relative distances between objects, non-Markov features, and more sophisticated object detection. This illuminates some important representational issues that likely underly DQN's success. It also suggests that the general properties of the representations learned by DQN may be more important to its success in ALE than the specific features it learns in each game. This deeper understanding of the specific strengths of DQN should aid practitioners in determining when its benefits are likely to outweigh its costs.

It is important to note that we do not intend to diminish the importance of DQN as a seemingly stable combination of deep neural networks and RL. This is a promising and exciting research direction with potential applications in many domains. That said, taking into account the fact that DQN's performance may be inflated to an unknown degree as a result of evaluating the best performing set of weights, the fact of DQN's extreme computational cost, and the methodological issues underlying the reported DQN results, we conclude that Blob-PROST is a strong alternative candidate to DQN both as an ALE performance benchmark and as a platform on which to build future ALE agents when representation learning is not the topic being studied. Our results also suggest in general that fixed representations inspired by the principles underlying convolutional networks may yield competitive, lighter-weight alternatives.

As future work, it may be interesting to investigate the remaining discrepancies between our results and DQN's. In some games like GRAVITAR, FROSTBITE and KRULL Blob-PROST's performance was several times higher than DQN's, while the opposite was true in games such as STAR GUNNER, BREAKOUT and ATLANTIS. In general, DQN seems to excel in shooting games (a large part of the games supported by the ALE), maybe because it is able to easily encode object velocities and to predict objects' future positions. DQN also excels on games that require a more holistic view of the whole screen (e.g. BREAKOUT, SPACE INVADERS), something pairwise features struggle with. On the other hand, some of the games in which Blob-PROST surpasses DQN are games where it is fairly easy to die, maybe because DQN interrupts the learning process after the agent loses a life. Other games Blob-PROST succeeds in are games where the return is very sparse (e.g. TENNIS, MONTEZUMA'S REVENGE). These games may generate very small gradients for the network, making it harder for an algorithm to learn both the representation and a good policy. Alternatively DQN's process of sampling from the experience memory may not be effective to draw the "interesting" samples.

These conjectures suggest directions for future work. Adaptive representation methods may potentially benefit from these insights by building in stronger bias toward the types of features we have investigated here. This would allow them to quickly perform well, and then focus energy on learning exceptions to the rule. In the realm of linear methods, these results suggest that there may still be simple, generic enhancements that yield dramatic improvements. More sophisticated object detection may be beneficial, as might features that encode more holistic views of the screen.

Acknowledgements

This research was supported by Alberta Innovates Technology Futures and the Alberta Innovates Centre for Machine Learning. Computing resources were provided by Compute Canada through CalculQuébec.

APPENDIX

The following table reports the data used to compare Blob-PROST to DQN's reported results (see Section 6) as well as our final ALE benchmark (see Section 7). A longer version of this paper presents full tables for all experiments [15].

Table 3: The first column presents the average performance of Blob-PROST using the full action set for comparison to future work (see Section 7). The standard deviation reported represents the variability over the 24 independent learning trials. The rest of the columns present our comparison between Blob-PROST and DQN (see Section 6 for details). In these results the Blob-PROST agent uses the minimal action set, for the sake of comparison. The standard deviation reported for the best trial as well as for the median trial is the standard deviation while evaluating for 499 episodes. We use bold face to denote values that are higher than DQN's and † to denote Blob-PROST averages that are statistically significantly different than DQN's average. To do the comparison for each game we used Welch's t-test ($p<0.025$, which accounts for the usage of DQN results in two tests, for an overall significance level of 0.05).

Game	Avg. (std. dev.) – Full		Best trial (std. dev.)		Middle trial (std. dev.)		% trials > DQN	DQN		Human	Random
Asterix	3996.6	(743.9)	**6921.5**	(4501.2)	4472.9†	(2514.8)	8.3	6012.0	(1744.0)	8503.0	210.0
Beam Rider	2367.3	(815.0)	2965.5†	(1376.1)	1807.6†	(657.0)	0.0	6846.0	(1619.0)	5775.0	363.9
Breakout	52.9	(38.0)	190.3†	(179.7)	33.2†	(21.3)	0.0	401.2	(26.9)	31.8	1.7
Enduro	296.7	(7.8)	299.1	(26.9)	279.2†	(28.2)	0.0	301.8	(24.6)	309.6	0.0
Freeway	32.3	(0.5)	**32.6**†	(1.0)	**31.7**†	(1.0)	95.8	30.3	(0.7)	29.6	0.0
Pong	20.2	(0.4)	**20.5**†	(0.8)	**20.2**†	(1.4)	95.8	18.9	(1.3)	9.3	-20.7
Q*Bert	8072.4	(2210.5)	**14449.4**†	(4111.7)	5881.4†	(1069.0)	12.5	10596.0	(3294.0)	13455.0	163.9
Seaquest	1664.2	(440.4)	2278.0†	(294.1)	1845.1†	(469.8)	0.0	5286.0	(1310.0)	20182.0	68.4
Space Invaders	844.8	(144.9)	889.8†	(374.5)	712.9†	(250.3)	0.0	1976.0	(893.0)	1652.0	148.0
Alien	4154.8	(532.5)	**4886.6**†	(1151.9)	**4219.1**†	(635.4)	95.8	3069.0	(1093.0)	6875.0	227.8
Amidar	408.4	(177.5)	**825.4**	(225.3)	522.3	(153.1)	12.5	739.5	(3024.0)	1676.0	5.8
Assault	1107.9	(207.7)	1829.3†	(702.9)	1380.8†	(449.9)	0.0	3359.0	(775.0)	1496.0	224.4
Asteroids	1759.5	(182.1)	**2229.9**†	(937.0)	**1635.1**	(617.9)	50.0	1629.0	(542.0)	13157.0	719.1
Atlantis	37428.5	(11599.7)	42937.7†	(13763.1)	19983.2†	(5830.4)	0.0	85641.0	(17600.0)	29028.0	12850.0
Bank Heist	463.4	(93.6)	**793.6**†	(102.9)	**455.1**	(100.9)	62.5	429.7	(650.0)	734.4	14.2
Battle Zone	26222.8	(4070.0)	**37850.0**†	(7445.0)	25836.0	(6616.3)	41.7	26300.0	(7725.0)	37800.0	2360.0
Bowling	65.9	(14.2)	**91.1**†	(13.6)	**62.0**	(2.5)	91.7	42.4	(88.0)	154.8	23.1
Boxing	89.4	(16.5)	**98.3**†	(3.3)	**95.8**†	(5.5)	87.5	71.8	(8.4)	4.3	0.1
Carnival	4322.0	(3705.0)	-	-	-	-	-	-	-	-	-
Centipede	3903.3	(6838.8)	**21137.0**†	(6722.8)	426.7†	(313.8)	20.8	8309.0	(5237.0)	11963.0	2091.0
Chopper Command	3006.6	(782.0)	4898.9†	(2511.2)	2998.0†	(1197.7)	0.0	6687.0	(2916.0)	9882.0	811.0
Crazy Climber	73241.5	(10467.9)	81016.0†	(26529.2)	59848.9†	(27960.7)	0.0	114103.0	(22797.0)	35411.0	10781.0
Demon Attack	1441.8	(184.8)	2166.0†	(1327.5)	1774.2†	(979.8)	0.0	9711.0	(2406.0)	3401.0	152.1
Double Dunk	-6.4	(0.9)	**-4.1**†	(2.3)	**-6.2**†	(2.8)	100.0	-18.1	(2.6)	-15.5	-18.6
Fishing Derby	-58.8	(12.0)	-28.7†	(19.0)	-57.4†	(18.3)	0.0	-0.8	(19.0)	5.5	-91.7
Frostbite	3389.7	(743.6)	**4534.0**†	(1496.8)	**3557.5**†	(864.3)	100.0	328.3	(250.5)	4335.0	65.2
Gopher	6823.4	(1022.5)	7451.1†	(3146.1)	5006.9†	(3118.9)	0.0	8520.0	(32.8)	2321.0	257.6
Gravitar	1231.8	(423.4)	**1709.7**†	(669.7)	**1390.6**†	(752.9)	91.7	306.7	(223.9)	2672.0	173.0
H.E.R.O.	13690.3	(4291.2)	**20273.1**†	(1155.1)	13642.1†	(48.4)	12.5	19950.0	(158.0)	25673.0	1027.0
Ice Hockey	14.5	(3.4)	**22.8**†	(6.5)	**14.5**†	(5.5)	100.0	-1.6	(2.5)	0.9	-11.2
James Bond	636.3	(192.1)	**1030.5**†	(947.1)	**587.8**	(99.5)	50.0	576.7	(175.5)	406.7	29.0
Kangaroo	3800.3	(2211.0)	**9492.8**†	(2918.2)	3839.1†	(1601.1)	8.3	6740.0	(2959.0)	3035.0	52.0
Krull	8333.9	(5599.5)	**33263.4**†	(15403.3)	**7463.9**†	(1719.7)	95.8	3805.0	(1033.0)	2395.0	1598.0
Kung-Fu Master	33868.5	(6247.5)	**51007.6**†	(9131.9)	**33232.1**†	(7904.5)	91.7	23270.0	(5955.0)	22736.0	258.5
Montezuma's Revenge	778.1	(789.8)	**2508.4**†	(27.8)	**400.0**†	(0.0)	100.0	0.0	(0.0)	4367.0	0.0
Ms. Pac-Man	4625.6	(774.3)	**5917.9**†	(1984.0)	**4667.4**†	(2126.0)	100.0	2311.0	(525.0)	15693.0	307.3
Name This Game	6580.1	(1773.0)	**7787.0**†	(744.7)	6387.1†	(1046.7)	20.8	7257.0	(547.0)	4076.0	2292.0
Pooyan	2228.1	(274.5)	-	-	-	-	-	-	-	-	-
Private Eye	33.0	(47.6)	100.3	(4.0)	0.0	(0.0)	0.0	1788.0	(5473.0)	69571.0	24.9
River Raid	10629.1	(2110.5)	**14583.3**†	(3078.3)	**9540.4**†	(1053.8)	91.7	8316.0	(1049.0)	13513.0	1339.0
Road Runner	24558.3	(12369.2)	**41828.0**†	(9408.1)	**28848.5**†	(6857.4)	75.0	18257.0	(4268.0)	7845.0	11.5
Robotank	28.3	(2.7)	34.4†	(7.7)	28.5†	(8.0)	0.0	51.6	(4.7)	11.9	2.2
Skiing	-29842.6	(19.8)	-	-	-	-	-	-	-	-	-
Star Gunner	1227.7	(165.1)	1651.6†	(435.4)	1180.0†	(85.2)	0.0	57997.0	(3152.0)	10250.0	664.0
Tennis	0.0	(0.0)	**0.0**†	(0.2)	**0.0**†	(0.2)	100.0	-2.5	(1.9)	-8.9	-23.8
Time Pilot	3972.0	(878.3)	5429.5	(1659.7)	4069.3†	(647.7)	0.0	5947.0	(1600.0)	5925.0	3568.0
Tutankham	81.4	(50.5)	**217.7**†	(33.9)	41.7†	(4.2)	8.3	186.7	(41.9)	167.7	11.4
Up and Down	19533.0	(18733.6)	**41257.8**†	(12061.8)	3716.7†	(1050.8)	45.8	8456.0	(3162.0)	9082.0	533.4
Venture	244.5	(490.4)	**1397.0**†	(294.4)	0.0†	(0.0)	20.8	380.0	(238.6)	1188.0	0.0
Video Pinball	9783.9	(3043.9)	21313.0†	(14916.4)	9480.7†	(6563.1)	0.0	42684.0	(16287.0)	17298.0	16257.0
Wizard of Wor	2733.6	(1259.0)	**5681.2**†	(4573.2)	**3442.9**	(2582.0)	50.0	3393.0	(2019.0)	4757.0	563.5
Zaxxon	8204.4	(2845.3)	**11721.8**†	(4009.7)	**9280.0**†	(2251.4)	87.5	4977.0	(1235.0)	9173.0	32.5
Times > DQN	N/A		32/49		21/49						
Times statist. $\geq$ DQN	N/A		35/49		24/49						

REFERENCES

[1] L. C. Baird III. Residual Algorithms: Reinforcement Learning with Function Approximation. In *Proceedings of the International Conference on Machine Learning (ICML)*, pages 30–37, 1995.

[2] M. G. Bellemare, Y. Naddaf, J. Veness, and M. Bowling. The Arcade Learning Environment: An Evaluation Platform for General Agents. *Journal of Artificial Intelligence Research*, 47:253–279, 06 2013.

[3] M. G. Bellemare, J. Veness, and M. Bowling. Investigating Contingency Awareness using Atari 2600 Games. In *Proceedings of the Twenty-Sixth Conference on Artificial Intelligence (AAAI)*, pages 864–871, 2012.

[4] M. G. Bellemare, J. Veness, and M. Bowling. Sketch-Based Linear Value Function Approximation. In *Proceedings of the Advances in Neural Information Processing Systems (NIPS)*, pages 2222–2230, 2012.

[5] M. Bowling, N. Burch, M. Johanson, and O. Tammelin. Heads-up Limit Hold'em Poker is Solved. *Science*, 347(6218):145–149, January 2015.

[6] M. Campbell, A. J. H. Jr., and F.-H. Hsu. Deep Blue. *Artificial Intelligence*, 134(1âĂŞ2):57 – 83, 2002.

[7] A. Defazio and T. Graepel. A Comparison of Learning Algorithms on the Arcade Learning Environment. *CoRR*, abs/1410.8620, 2014.

[8] D. A. Ferrucci, E. W. Brown, J. Chu-Carroll, J. Fan, D. Gondek, A. Kalyanpur, A. Lally, J. W. Murdock, E. Nyberg, J. M. Prager, N. Schlaefer, and C. A. Welty. Building Watson: An Overview of the DeepQA Project. *AI Magazine*, 31(3):59–79, 2010.

[9] A. Gionis, P. Indyk, and R. Motwani. Similarity Search in High Dimensions via Hashing. In *Proceedings of International Conference on Very Large Data Bases (VLDB)*, pages 518–529, 1999.

[10] G. J. Gordon. Reinforcement Learning with Function Approximation Converges to a Region. In *Proceedings of the Advances in Neural Information Processing Systems (NIPS)*, pages 1040–1046, 2000.

[11] X. Guo, S. P. Singh, H. Lee, R. L. Lewis, and X. Wang. Deep Learning for Real-Time Atari Game Play Using Offline Monte-Carlo Tree Search Planning. In *Proceedings of the Advances in Neural Information Processing Systems (NIPS)*, pages 3338–3346, 2014.

[12] M. J. Hausknecht and P. Stone. Deep Recurrent Q-Learning for Partially Observable MDPs. *CoRR*, abs/1507.06527, 2015.

[13] A. Krizhevsky, I. Sutskever, and G. E. Hinton. ImageNet Classification with Deep Convolutional Neural Networks. In *Proceedings of the Advances in Neural Information Processing Systems (NIPS)*, pages 1106–1114, 2012.

[14] Y. LeCun, L. Bottou, Y. Bengio, and P. Haffner. Gradient-Based Learning Applied to Document Recognition. *Proceedings of the IEEE*, 86(11):2278–2324, 1998.

[15] Y. Liang, M. C. Machado, E. Talvitie, and M. H. Bowling. State of the Art Control of Atari Games Using Shallow Reinforcement Learning. *CoRR*, abs/1512.01563, 2015.

[16] N. Lipovetzky, M. Ramirez, and H. Geffner. Classical Planning with Simulators: Results on the Atari Video Games. In *Proceedings of International Joint Conference on Artificial Intelligence (IJCAI)*, 2015.

[17] M. C. Machado, S. Srinivasan, and M. Bowling. Domain-Independent Optimistic Initialization for Reinforcement Learning. In *AAAI Workshop on Learning for General Competency in Video Games*, 2015.

[18] F. S. Melo, S. P. Meyn, and M. I. Ribeiro. An Analysis of Reinforcement Learning with Function Approximation. In *Proceedings of the International Conference on Machine Learning (ICML)*, pages 664–671, 2008.

[19] V. Mnih, K. Kavukcuoglu, D. Silver, A. Graves, I. Antonoglou, D. Wierstra, and M. Riedmiller. Playing Atari With Deep Reinforcement Learning. In *NIPS Deep Learning Workshop*, 2013.

[20] V. Mnih, K. Kavukcuoglu, D. Silver, A. A. Rusu, J. Veness, M. G. Bellemare, A. Graves, M. Riedmiller, A. K. Fidjeland, G. Ostrovski, S. Petersen, C. Beattie, A. Sadik, I. Antonoglou, H. King, D. Kumaran, D. Wierstra, S. Legg, and D. Hassabis. Human-level Control through Deep Reinforcement Learning. *Nature*, 518(7540):529–533, 02 2015.

[21] V. Mnih, A. P. Badia, M. Mirza, A. Graves, T. P. Lillicrap, T. Harley, D. Silver, K. Kavukcuoglu. Asynchronous Methods for Deep Reinforcement Learning. *CoRR*, abs/1602.01783, 2016.

[22] G. A. Rummery and M. Niranjan. On-line Q-Learning using Connectionist Systems. CUED/F-INFENG/TR 166, Cambridge University Engineering Dept., September 1994.

[23] J. Schaeffer, N. Burch, Y. Björnsson, A. Kishimoto, M. Müller, R. Lake, P. Lu, and S. Sutphen. Checkers is Solved. *Science*, 317(5844):1518–1522, 2007.

[24] J. Schulman, S. Levine, P. Abbeel, M. I. Jordan, and P. Moritz. Trust Region Policy Optimization. In *Proceedings of the International Conference on Machine Learning (ICML)*, pages 1889–1897, 2015.

[25] N. Sprague. Parameter Selection for the Deep Q-learning Algorithm ((Extended Abstract)). In *Proceedings of the Multidisciplinary Conference on Reinforcement Learning and Decision Making (RLDM)*, 2015.

[26] R. S. Sutton and A. G. Barto. *Reinforcement Learning: An Introduction.* MIT Press, 1998.

[27] C. Szepesvári. *Algorithms for Reinforcement Learning.* Synthesis lectures on Artificial Intelligence and Machine Learning. Morgan & Claypool, 2010.

[28] G. Tesauro. Temporal Difference Learning and TD-Gammon. *Communications of the ACM*, 38(3):58–68, Mar. 1995.

[29] H. van Hasselt, A. Guez, and D. Silver. Deep Reinforcement Learning with Double Q-learning. *CoRR*, abs/1509.06461, 2015.

[30] J. Veness, M. G. Bellemare, M. Hutter, A. Chua, and G. Desjardins. Compress and Control. In *Proceedings of the Conference on Artificial Intelligence (AAAI)*, 2015.

[31] C. J. C. H. Watkins and P. Dayan. Technical Note: Q-Learning. *Machine Learning*, 8(3-4), May 1992.

Investigating Practical Linear Temporal Difference Learning

Adam White
Department of Computer Science
Indiana University
Bloomington, IN 47405, USA
adamw@indiana.edu

Martha White
Department of Computer Science
Indiana University
Bloomington, IN 47405, USA
martha@indiana.edu

ABSTRACT

Off-policy reinforcement learning has many applications including: learning from demonstration, learning multiple goal seeking policies in parallel, and representing predictive knowledge. Recently there has been an proliferation of new policy-evaluation algorithms that fill a longstanding algorithmic void in reinforcement learning: combining robustness to off-policy sampling, function approximation, linear complexity, and temporal difference (TD) updates. This paper contains two main contributions. First, we derive two new hybrid TD policy-evaluation algorithms, which fill a gap in this collection of algorithms. Second, we perform an empirical comparison to elicit which of these new linear TD methods should be preferred in different situations, and make concrete suggestions about practical use.

Keywords

Reinforcement learning; temporal difference learning; off-policy learning

1. INTRODUCTION

Until recently, using temporal difference (TD) methods to approximate a value function from off-policy samples was potentially unstable without resorting to quadratic (in the number of features) computation and storage, even in the case of linear approximations. Off-policy learning involves learning an estimate of total future reward that we would expect to observe if the agent followed some target policy, while learning from samples generated by a different behavior policy. This off-policy, policy-evaluation problem, when combined with a policy improvement step, can can be used to model many different learning scenarios, such as learning from many policies in parallel [18], learning from demonstrations [1], learning from batch data [8], or simply learning about the optimal policy while following an exploratory policy, as in the case of Q-learning [25]. In this paper, we focus exclusively on the off-policy, policy evaluation problem, commonly referred to as value function approximation or simply the *prediction problem*. Over the past decade there has been an proliferation of new linear-complexity, policy-evaluation methods designed to be convergent in the off-policy case.

Appears in: *Proceedings of the 15th International Conference on Autonomous Agents and Multiagent Systems (AAMAS 2016), J. Thangarajah, K. Tuyls, C. Jonker, S. Marsella (eds.), May 9–13, 2016, Singapore.*

These novel algorithmic contributions have focused on different ways of achieving stable off-policy prediction learning. The first such methods were the gradient TD family of algorithms that perform approximate stochastic gradient descent on the mean squared projected Bellman error (MSPBE). The primary drawback of these methods is the requirement for a second set of learned weights, a second step size parameter, and potentially high variance updates due to importance sampling. Empirically the results have been mixed, with some results indicating that TD can be superior in on-policy settings[17], and others concluding the exact opposite [4].

Later, provisional TD (PTD) was introduced [20] to rectify the issue that the bootstrap parameter λ, used in gradient TD methods[11] does not correspond well with the same parameter used by conventional TD learning [19]. Specifically, for $\lambda = 1$, gradient TD methods do not correspond to any known variant of off-policy Monte Carlo. The PTD algorithm fixes this issue, and in on-policy prediction is exactly equivalent to the conventional TD algorithm. PTD does not use gradient corrections, and is only guaranteed to converge in the tabular off-policy prediction setting. Its empirical performance relative to TD and gradient TD, however, is completely unknown.

Recently Sutton et al. [21] observed that conventional TD does not correct its update based on the notion of a follow-on distribution. This distributional mis-match provides another way to understand the off-policy divergence of conventional off-policy TD. They derive the Emphatic TD (ETD) algorithm that surprisingly achieves convergence [27] without the need for a second set of weights, like those used by gradient TD methods. Like gradient TD methods, however, it seems that this algorithm also suffers from high variance due to importance sampling. Hallak et al. [7] introduced a variant ETD that utilizes a scaling parameter β, which is meant to reduce the magnitude of the follow-on trace. Comparative empirical studies for ETD and ETD(β), however, have been limited.

The most recent contribution to this line of work explores a mirror-prox approach to minimizing the MSPBE [12, 13, 9]. The main benefit of this work was that it enabled the first finite sample analysis of an off-policy TD-based method with function approximation, and the application of advanced stochastic gradient optimizations. Liu et al. [9] introduced two mirror-prox TD algorithms, one based on the GTD2 algorithm [17] the other based on TDC [17][1] and showed

[1]The GTD2 and TDC algorithms are gradient TD methods that do not use eligibility traces; $\lambda = 0$.

that these methods outperform their base counter-parts on Baird's counterexample [2], but did not extend their new methods with eligibility traces.

A less widely known approach to the off-policy prediction problem is based on algorithms that perform precisely TD updates when the data is sampled on-policy, and corrected gradient-TD style updates when the data is generated off-policy. The idea is to exploit the supposed superior efficiency of TD in on-policy learning, while maintaining robustness in the off-policy case. These "hybrid" TD methods were introduced for state value-function based prediction [11], and state-action value-function based prediction [6], but have not been extended to utilize eligibility traces, nor compared with the recent developments in linear off-policy TD learning (many developed since 2014).

Meanwhile a separate but related thread of algorithmic development has sought to improve the operation of eligibility traces used in both on- and off-policy TD algorithms. This direction is based on another nonequivalence observation: the update performed by the forward view variant of the conventional TD is only equivalent to its backward view update at the end of sampling trajectories. The proposed true-online TD (TO-TD) prediction algorithm [24], and true-online GTD (TO-GTD) prediction algorithm [23] remedy this issue, and have been shown to outperform conventional TD and gradient TD methods respectively on chain domains. The TO-TD algorithm requires only a modest increase in computational complexity over TD, however, the TO-GTD algorithm is significantly more complex to implement and requires three eligibility traces compared to GTD. Nevertheless, both TO-TD and TO-GTD achieve linear complexity, and can be implemented in a completely incremental way.

Although there asymptotic convergence properties of many of these methods has been rigorously characterized, but empirically there is still much we do not understand about this now large collection of methods. A frequent criticism of gradient TD methods, for example, is that they are hard to tune and not well-understood empirically. It is somewhat disappointing that perhaps the most famous application of reinforcement learning—learning to play Atari games [15]—uses potentially divergent off-policy Q-learning. In addition, we have very little understanding of how these methods compare in terms of learning speed, robustness, and parameter sensitivity. By clarifying some of the empirical properties of these algorithms, we hope to promote more wide-spread adoption of these theoretically sound and computationally efficient algorithms.

This paper has two primary contributions. First, we introduce a novel extension of hybrid methods to eligibility traces resulting in two new algorithms, HTD(λ) and true-online HTD(λ). Second, we provide an empirical study of TD-based prediction learning with linear function approximation. The conclusions of our experiments are surprisingly clear:

1. GTD(λ) and TO-GTD(λ) should be preferred if robustness to off-policy sampling is required

2. Between the two GTD(λ) should be preferred if computation time is at a premium

3. Otherwise, TO-ETD(λ, β) was clearly the best across our experiments except on Baird's counterexample.

2. BACKGROUND

This paper investigates the problem of estimating the discounted sum of future rewards *online* and with function approximation. In the context of reinforcement learning we take online to mean that the agent makes decisions, the environment produces outcomes, and the agent updates its parameters in a continual, real-time interaction stream. We model the agent's interaction as Markov decision process defined by a countably infinite set of states $\mathcal{S}$, a finite set of actions $\mathcal{A}$, and a scalar discount function $\gamma : \mathcal{S} \rightarrow \mathbb{R}$. The agent's observation of the current situation is summarized by the feature vector $\mathbf{x}(S_t) \in \mathbb{R}^d$, where $S_t \in \mathcal{S}$ is the current state and $d \ll |\mathcal{S}|$. On each time step t, the agent selects an action according to it's *behavior policy* $A_t \sim \mu(S_t, \cdot)$, where $\mu : \mathcal{S} \times \mathcal{A} \rightarrow [0, 1]$. The environment then transitions into a new state $S_{t+1} \sim P(S_t, A_t, \cdot)$, and emits a scalar reward $R_{t+1} \in \mathbb{R}$. The agent's objective is to evaluate a fixed *target policy* $\pi : \mathcal{S} \times \mathcal{A} \rightarrow [0, 1]$, or estimate the expected return for policy π:

$$v^\pi(s) \stackrel{\text{def}}{=} \mathbb{E}[G_t | S_t = s, A_t \sim \pi]$$

$$\text{for return } G_t \stackrel{\text{def}}{=} \sum_{i=0}^{\infty} \left(\prod_{j=1}^{i} \gamma_{t+j} \right) R_{t+i+1} \qquad \triangleright \gamma_j \stackrel{\text{def}}{=} \gamma(s_j).$$

where $v^\pi(s)$ is called the *state-value function* for policy π.

All the methods evaluated in this study perform temporal difference updates, and most utilize eligibility traces. The TD(λ) algorithm is the prototypical example of these concepts and is useful for understanding all the other algorithms discussed in the remainder of this paper. TD(λ) estimates v^π as a linear function of the weight vector $\mathbf{w} \in \mathbb{R}^d$, where the estimate is formed as an inner product between the weight vector and the features of the current state: $\mathbf{w}^\top \mathbf{x}(s) \approx v^\pi(s)$. The algorithm maintains a memory trace of recently experienced features, called the eligibility trace $\mathbf{e} \in \mathbb{R}^d$, allowing updates to assign credit to previously visited states. The TD(λ) algorithm requires linear computation and storage $O(d)$, and can be implemented incrementally as follows:

$$\begin{aligned} \delta_t &\leftarrow R_{t+1} + \gamma_{t+1} \mathbf{w}_t^\top \mathbf{x}(S_{t+1}) - \mathbf{w}_t^\top \mathbf{x}(S_t) \\ \mathbf{e}_t &\leftarrow \lambda_t \gamma_t \mathbf{e}_{t-1} + \mathbf{x}(S_t) \\ \Delta \mathbf{w} &\leftarrow \alpha \delta_t \mathbf{e}_t \qquad \triangleright \mathbf{w}_{t+1} \leftarrow \mathbf{w}_t + \Delta \mathbf{w}. \end{aligned}$$

In the case when the data is generated by a behavior policy, μ, with $\pi \neq \mu$, we say that the data is generated off-policy. In the off-policy setting we must estimate v^π with samples generated by selecting actions according to μ. This setting can cause the TD(λ) algorithm to diverge. The GTD(λ) algorithm solves the divergence issue by minimizing the MSPBE, resulting in a stochastic gradient descent algorithm that looks similar to TD(λ), with some important differences. GTD(λ) uses importance weights, $\rho_t \stackrel{\text{def}}{=} \frac{\pi(s,a)}{\mu(s,a)} \in \mathbb{R}$ in the eligibility trace to reweight the data and obtain an unbiased estimate of $\mathbb{E}[G_t]$. Note, in the policy iteration case—not studied here—it is still reasonable to assume knowledge of $\pi(s, a)$ for all $s \in \mathcal{S}, a \in \mathcal{A}$; for example when π is near greedy with respect to the current estimate of the state-action value function. The GTD(λ) has a auxiliary set of learned weights, $\mathbf{h} \in \mathbb{R}^d$, in addition to the primary weights $\mathbf{w}$, which maintain a quasi-stationary estimate of a part of the MSPBE. Like the TD(λ) algorithm, GTD(λ)

requires only linear computation and storage and can be implemented fully incrementally as follows:

$$\delta_t \leftarrow R_{t+1} + \gamma_{t+1}\mathbf{w}_t^\top \mathbf{x}(S_{t+1}) - \mathbf{w}_t^\top \mathbf{x}(S_t)$$
$$\mathbf{e}_t \leftarrow \rho_t(\lambda_t\gamma_t\mathbf{e}_{t-1} + \mathbf{x}(S_t)) \qquad \triangleright \text{weighted by } \rho_t$$
$$\Delta\mathbf{w} \leftarrow \alpha\delta_t\mathbf{e}_t - \underbrace{\alpha\gamma_{t+1}(1-\lambda_{t+1})(\mathbf{e}_t^\top\mathbf{h}_t)\mathbf{x}(S_{t+1})}_{\text{correction term}}$$
$$\Delta\mathbf{h} \leftarrow \alpha_\mathbf{h}[\delta_t\mathbf{e}_t - (\mathbf{x}(S_t)^\top\mathbf{h}_t)\mathbf{x}(S_t)] \qquad \triangleright \text{auxiliary weights}$$

The auxiliary weights also make use of a step-size parameter, $\alpha_\mathbf{h}$ which is usually not equal to α.

Due to space constraints we do not describe the other TD-based linear learning algorithms found in the literature and investigated in our study. We provide each algorithm's pseudo code in the appendix, and in the next section describe two new off-policy, gradient TD methods, before turning to empirical questions.

3. HTD DERIVATION

Conventional temporal difference updating can be more data efficient than gradient temporal difference updating, but the correction term used by gradient-TD methods helps prevent divergence. Previous empirical studies[17] demonstrated situations (specifically on-policy) where linear TD(0) can outperform gradient TD methods, and others [6] demonstrated that Expected Sarsa(0) can outperform multiple variants of the GQ(0) algorithm, even under off-policy sampling. On the other hand, TD(λ) can diverge on small, though somewhat contrived counterexamples.

The idea of hybrid-TD methods is to achieve sample efficiency closer to TD(λ) during on-policy sampling, while ensuring non-divergence under off-policy sampling. To achieve this, a hybrid algorithm could do conventional, uncorrected TD updates when the data is sampled on-policy, and use gradient corrections when the data is sampled off-policy. This approach was pioneered by Maei [11], leading to the derivation of the Hybrid Temporal Difference learning algorithm, or HTD(0). Later, Hackman[6] produced a hybrid version of the GQ(0) algorithm, estimating state-action value functions rather than state-value functions as we do here. In this paper, we derive the first hybrid temporal difference method to make use of eligibility traces, called HTD(λ).

The key idea behind the derivation of HTD learning methods is to modify the gradient of the MSPBE to produce a new learning algorithm. Let $\mathbb{E}_\mu$ represent the expectation according to samples generated under the behavior policy, μ. The MSPBE[17] can be written as

$$\mathtt{MSPBE}(\mathbf{w}) = \underbrace{\mathbb{E}_\mu[\delta_t\mathbf{e}_t]}_{-A_\pi\mathbf{w}+b_\pi}^\top \underbrace{\mathbb{E}_\mu[\mathbf{x}(S_t)\mathbf{x}(S_t)^\top]}_{C}^{-1}\mathbb{E}_\mu[\delta_t\mathbf{e}_t],$$

where $\mathbf{e}_t = \rho_t(\lambda_t\gamma_t\mathbf{e}_{t-1} + \mathbf{x}(S_t))$ and

$$A_\pi \stackrel{\text{def}}{=} \mathbb{E}_\mu[\mathbf{e}_t(\mathbf{x}(S_t) - \gamma_{t+1}\mathbf{x}(S_{t+1}))^\top] \tag{1}$$
$$= \sum_{s_t\in\mathcal{S}} d^\mu(s_t) \sum_{a_t\in\mathcal{A}} \underbrace{\mu(s_t,a_t)\rho_t}_{\pi(s_t,a_t)}(\gamma_t\lambda\mathbb{E}_\mu[\mathbf{e}_{t-1}|s_t] + \mathbf{x}(s_t))$$
$$\sum_{s_{t+1}\in\mathcal{S}} P(s_t,a_t,s_{t+1})(\mathbf{x}(s_t) - \gamma_{t+1}\mathbf{x}(s_{t+1}))^\top$$

$$b_\pi \stackrel{\text{def}}{=} \mathbb{E}_\mu[R_{t+1}\mathbf{e}_t]$$
$$= \sum_{s_t\in\mathcal{S}} d^\mu(s_t) \sum_{a_t\in\mathcal{A}} \pi(s_t,a_t)(\gamma_t\lambda\mathbb{E}_\mu[\mathbf{e}_{t-1}|s_t] + \mathbf{x}(s_t))$$
$$\sum_{s_{t+1}\in\mathcal{S}} \pi(s_t,a_t)P(s_t,a_t,s_{t+1})r_{t+1}.$$

Therefore, the relative importance given to states in the MSPBE is weighted by the stationary distribution of the behavior policy, $d_\mu : \mathcal{S} \to \mathbb{R}$, (since it is generating samples), but the transitions are reweighted to reflect the returns that π would produce.

The gradient of the MSPBE is:

$$-\frac{1}{2}\nabla_\mathbf{w}\mathtt{MSPBE}(\mathbf{w}) = -A_\pi^\top C^{-1}(-A_\pi\mathbf{w} + b_\pi). \tag{2}$$

Assuming A_π^{-1} is non-singular, we get the TD-fixed point solution:

$$0 = -\frac{1}{2}\nabla_\mathbf{w}\mathtt{MSPBE}(\mathbf{w}) \implies -A_\pi\mathbf{w} + b_\pi = 0. \tag{3}$$

The value of $\mathbf{w}$, for which (3) is zero, is the solution found by linear TD(λ) and LSTD(λ) where $\pi = \mu$. The gradient of the MSPBE yields an incremental learning rule with the following general form (see [3]):

$$\mathbf{w}_{t+1} \leftarrow \mathbf{w}_t + \alpha(M\mathbf{w}_t + b), \tag{4}$$

where $M = -A_\pi^\top C^{-1}A_\pi$ and $b = A_\pi^\top C^{-1}b_\pi$. The update rule, in the case of TD(λ), will yield stable convergence if A_π is positive definite (as shown by Tsitsiklis and van Roy [22]). In off-policy learning, we require $A_\pi^\top C^{-1}A_\pi$ to be positive definite to satisfy the conditions of the ordinary differential equation proof of convergence [10], which holds because C^{-1} is positive definite and therefore $A_\pi^\top C^{-1}A_\pi$ is positive definite, because A_π is full rank (true by assumption). See Sutton et al. [21] for a nice discussion on why the A_π matrix must be positive definite to ensure stable, non-divergent iterations. The C matrix in Equation (3), can be replaced by any positive definite matrix and the fixed point will be unaffected, but the rate of convergence will almost surely change.

Instead of following the usual recipe for deriving GTD, let us try replacing C^{-1} with

$$A_\mu^{-\top} \stackrel{\text{def}}{=} \mathbb{E}_\mu[(\mathbf{x}(S_t) - \gamma_t\mathbf{x}(S_{t+1}))\mathbf{e}_t^{\mu\top}],$$

where $\mathbf{e}^\mu$ is the regular on-policy trace for the behavior policy (i.e., no importance weights)

$$\mathbf{e}_t^\mu = \gamma_t\lambda\mathbf{e}_{t-1}^\mu + \mathbf{x}(S_t).$$

The matrix $A_\mu^{-\top}$ is a positive definite matrix (proved by Tsitsiklis and van Roy [22]). Plugging $A_\mu^{-\top}$ into (2) results in the following expected update:

$$\frac{1}{\alpha}\mathbb{E}[\Delta\mathbf{w}_t] = A_\pi^\top A_\mu^{-\top}(-A_\pi\mathbf{w}_t + b_\pi)$$
$$= (A_\mu^\top - A_\mu^\top + A_\pi^\top)A_\mu^{-\top}(-A_\pi\mathbf{w}_t + b_\pi)$$
$$= (A_\mu^\top A_\mu^{-\top})(-A_\pi\mathbf{w}_t + b_\pi) + (A_\pi^\top - A_\mu^\top)A_\mu^{-\top}(-A_\pi\mathbf{w}_t + b_\pi)$$
$$= (-A_\pi\mathbf{w}_t + b_\pi) + (A_\pi^\top - A_\mu^\top)A_\mu^{-\top}(-A_\pi\mathbf{w}_t + b_\pi)$$
$$= (-A_\pi\mathbf{w}_t + b_\pi) + \tag{5}$$
$$\mathbb{E}_\mu\left[(\mathbf{x}(S_t) - \gamma_{t+1}\mathbf{x}(S_{t+1}))(\mathbf{e}_t - \mathbf{e}_t^\mu)^\top\right]A_\mu^{-\top}(-A_\pi\mathbf{w}_t + b_\pi)$$

As in the derivation of GTD(λ) [11], let the vector $\mathbf{h}_t$ form a quasi-stationary estimate of the final term,

$$A_\mu^{-\top}(-A_\pi \mathbf{w}_t + b_\pi).$$

Getting back to the primary weight update, we can sample the first term using the fact that $(-A_\pi \mathbf{w}_t + b_\pi) = \mathbb{E}_\mu[\delta_t \mathbf{e}_t]$ (see [11]) and use (1) to get the final stochastic update

$$\Delta \mathbf{w}_t \leftarrow \alpha \left(\delta_t \mathbf{e}_t + (\mathbf{x}_t - \gamma_{t+1}\mathbf{x}_{t+1})(\mathbf{e}_t - \mathbf{e}_t^\mu)^\top \mathbf{h}_t \right). \quad (6)$$

Notice that when the data is generated on-policy ($\pi = \mu$), $\mathbf{e}_t = \mathbf{e}_t^\mu$, and thus the correction term disappears and we are left with precisely linear TD(λ). When $\pi \neq \mu$, the TD update is corrected as in GTD: unsurprisingly, the correction is slightly different but has the same basic form.

To complete the derivation, we must derive an incremental update rule for $\mathbf{h}_t$. We have a linear system, because

$$\mathbf{h}_t = A_\mu^{-\top}(-A_\pi \mathbf{w}_t + b_\pi) \implies A_\mu^\top \mathbf{h}_t = -A_\pi \mathbf{w}_t + b_\pi.$$

Following the general expected update in (4),

$$\mathbf{h}_{t+1} \leftarrow \mathbf{h}_t + \alpha_\mathbf{h} \left((-A_\pi \mathbf{w}_t + b_\pi) - A_\mu^\top \mathbf{h}_t \right) \quad (7)$$

which converges if $A_\mu^\top$ is positive definite for any fixed $\mathbf{w}_t$ and $\alpha_\mathbf{h}$ is chosen appropriately (see Sutton et al.'s recent paper[21] for an extensive discussion of convergence in expectation). To sample this update, recall

$$A_\mu^\top \mathbf{h}_t = \mathbb{E}_\mu[(\mathbf{x}(S_t) - \mathbf{x}(S_{t+1}))\mathbf{e}_t^{\mu\top}]\mathbf{h}_t$$

giving stochastic update rule for $\mathbf{h}_t$:

$$\Delta \mathbf{h}_t \leftarrow \alpha_\mathbf{h} \left[\delta_t \mathbf{e}_t - (\mathbf{x}_t - \gamma_{t+1}\mathbf{x}_{t+1})\mathbf{e}_t^{\mu\top} \mathbf{h}_t \right].$$

As in GTD, $\alpha \in \mathbb{R}$ and $\alpha_\mathbf{h} \in \mathbb{R}$ are step-size parameters, and $\delta_t \overset{\text{def}}{=} R_{t+1} + \gamma_{t+1}\mathbf{w}_t^\top \mathbf{x}_{t+1} - \mathbf{w}_t^\top \mathbf{x}_t$. This hybrid-TD algorithm should converge under off-policy sampling using a proof technique similar to the one used for GQ(λ) (see Maei & Sutton's proof [10]), but we leave this to future work. The HTD(λ) algorithm is completely specified by the following equations:

$$\begin{aligned}
\mathbf{e}_t &\leftarrow \rho_t(\lambda_t \gamma_t \mathbf{e}_{t-1} + \mathbf{x}_t) \\
\mathbf{e}_t^\mu &\leftarrow \lambda_t \gamma_t \mathbf{e}_{t-1}^\mu + \mathbf{x}_t \\
\Delta \mathbf{w}_t &\leftarrow \alpha \left[\delta_t \mathbf{e}_t + (\gamma_{t+1}\mathbf{x}_{t+1} - \mathbf{x}_t)(\mathbf{e}_t^\mu - \mathbf{e}_t)^\top \mathbf{h}_t \right] \\
\Delta \mathbf{h}_t &\leftarrow \alpha_\mathbf{h} \left[\delta_t \mathbf{e}_t + (\gamma_{t+1}\mathbf{x}_{t+1} - \mathbf{x}_t)\mathbf{e}^{\mu\top}_t \mathbf{h}_t \right]
\end{aligned}$$

This algorithm can be made more efficient by exploiting the common terms in $\Delta \mathbf{w}_t$ and $\Delta \mathbf{h}_t$, as shown in the appendix.

4. TRUE ONLINE HTD

Recently, a new forward-backward view equivalence has been proposed for online TD methods, resulting in true-online TD [24] and true-online GTD [23] algorithms. The original forward-backward equivalence was for offline TD(λ)[2]. To derive a forward-backward equivalence under online updating, a new truncated return was proposed, which uses the online weight vector that changes into the future,

$$G_{k,t}^{\lambda,\rho} \overset{\text{def}}{=} \rho_k(R_{k+1} + \gamma_{k+1}[(1-\lambda_{k+1})\mathbf{x}_{t+1}^\top \mathbf{w}_k + \lambda_{k+1} G_{k+1,t}^{\lambda,\rho}]),$$

with $G_{t,t}^{\lambda,\rho} \overset{\text{def}}{=} \rho_t \mathbf{x}_t^\top \mathbf{w}_{t-1}$. A forward-view algorithm can be defined that computes $\mathbf{w}_k$ online assuming access to future samples, and then an exactly equivalent incremental backward-view algorithm can be derived that does not require access to future samples. This framework was used to derive the TO-TD algorithm for the on-policy setting, and TO-GTD for the more general off-policy setting. This new true-online equivalence is not only interesting theoretically, but also translates into improved prediction and control performance [24, 23].

In this section, we derive a true-online variant of HTD(λ). When used on-policy HTD(λ) behaves similarly to TO-TD(λ). Our goal in this section is to combine the benefits of both hybrid learning and true-online traces in a single algorithm. We proceed with a similar derivation to TO-GTD(λ) [23, Theorem 4], with the main difference appearing in the update of the auxiliary weights. Notice that the primary weights $\mathbf{w}$, and the auxiliary weights $\mathbf{h}$, of HTD(λ) have a similar structure. Recall from (5), the modified gradient of the MSPBE, or expected primary-weight update can be written as:

$$\begin{aligned}
\frac{1}{\alpha}\mathbb{E}[\Delta \mathbf{w}_t] &= (-A_\pi \mathbf{w}_t + b_\pi) \\
&+ \mathbb{E}_\mu \left[(\mathbf{x}(S_t) - \gamma_{t+1}\mathbf{x}(S_{t+1}))(\mathbf{e}_t - \mathbf{e}_t^\mu)^\top \right] \mathbf{h}_t
\end{aligned}$$

Similarly, we can rewrite the expected update of the auxiliary weights by plugging $A_\mu^\top$ into (7):

$$\begin{aligned}
\frac{1}{\alpha_h}\mathbb{E}[\Delta \mathbf{h}_t] &= (-A_\pi \mathbf{w}_t + b_\pi) \\
&+ \mathbb{E}_\mu \left[(\mathbf{x}(S_t) - \gamma_{t+1}\mathbf{x}(S_{t+1}))\mathbf{e}_t^{\mu\top} \right] \mathbf{h}_t
\end{aligned}$$

As in the derivation of TO-GTD [23, Equation 17,18]), for TO-HTD we will sample the second part of the update using a backward-view and obtain forward-view samples for $(-A_\pi \mathbf{w}_t + b_\pi)$. The resulting TO-HTD($\lambda$) algorithm is completely specified by the following equations

$$\begin{aligned}
\mathbf{e}_t &\leftarrow \rho_t(\lambda_t \gamma_t \mathbf{e}_{t-1} + \mathbf{x}_t) \\
\mathbf{e}_t^\mu &\leftarrow \lambda_t \gamma_t \mathbf{e}_{t-1}^\mu + \mathbf{x}_t \\
\mathbf{e}_t^o &\leftarrow \rho_t(\lambda_t \gamma_t \mathbf{e}_{t-1}^o + \alpha_t(1 - \rho_t \gamma_t \lambda_t \mathbf{x}_t^\top \mathbf{e}_{t-1}^o)\mathbf{x}_t) \\
\mathbf{d} &= \delta_t \mathbf{e}_t^o + (\mathbf{e}_t^o - \alpha_t \rho_t \mathbf{x}_t)(\mathbf{w}_t - \mathbf{w}_{t-1})^\top \mathbf{x}_t \quad (8) \\
\mathbf{w}_{t+1} &\leftarrow \mathbf{w}_t + \mathbf{d} + \alpha_t(\gamma_{t+1}\mathbf{x}_{t+1} - \mathbf{x}_t)(\mathbf{e}_t^\mu - \mathbf{e}_t)^\top \mathbf{h}_t \\
\mathbf{h}_{t+1} &\leftarrow \mathbf{h}_t + \mathbf{d} + \alpha_\mathbf{h}(\gamma_{t+1}\mathbf{x}_{t+1} - \mathbf{x}_t)\mathbf{e}^{\mu\top}_t \mathbf{h}_t
\end{aligned}$$

In order to prove that this is a true-online update, we use the constructive theorem due to van Hasselt et al. [23].

THEOREM 1 (TRUE-ONLINE HTD(λ)). *For any t, the weight vectors $\mathbf{w}_t^t, \mathbf{h}_t^t$ as defined by the forward view*

$$\begin{aligned}
\mathbf{w}_{k+1}^t &= \mathbf{w}_k^t + \alpha_k(G_{k,t}^{\lambda,\rho} - \rho_k \mathbf{x}_t^\top \mathbf{w}_k^t)\mathbf{x}_k \\
&+ \alpha_k(\mathbf{x}_t - \gamma_{t+1}\mathbf{x}_{t+1})(\mathbf{e}_t - \mathbf{e}_t^\mu)^\top \mathbf{h}_k^t
\end{aligned}$$

$$\begin{aligned}
\mathbf{h}_{k+1}^t &= \mathbf{h}_k^t + \alpha_{h,k}(G_{k,t}^{\lambda,\rho} - \rho_k \mathbf{x}_t^\top \mathbf{w}_k^t)\mathbf{x}_k \\
&+ \alpha_{h,k}(\mathbf{x}_t - \gamma_{t+1}\mathbf{x}_{t+1})\mathbf{e}_t^{\mu\top} \mathbf{h}_k^t
\end{aligned}$$

are equal to $\mathbf{w}_t, \mathbf{h}_t$ as defined by the backward view in (8).

[2]The idea of defining a forward view objective and then converting this computationally impractical forward-view into an efficiently implementable algorithm using traces is extensively treated in Sutton and Barto's introductory text [16].

PROOF. We apply [23, Theorem 1]. The substitutions are

$$\eta_t = \rho_t \alpha_t$$

$$\mathbf{g}_{w,k} = \alpha_k(\mathbf{x}_k - \gamma_{k+1}\mathbf{x}_{k+1})(\mathbf{e}_k - \mathbf{e}_k^{\mu})^\top \mathbf{h}_k$$

$$\mathbf{g}_{h,k} = \alpha_{h,k}(\mathbf{x}_k - \gamma_{k+1}\mathbf{x}_{k+1})\mathbf{e}_k^{\mu\top} \mathbf{h}_k$$

$$Y_t^t = \mathbf{w}_{t-1}^\top \mathbf{x}_t$$

$$Y_k^t = R_{k+1} + \gamma_{k+1}(1 - \lambda_{k+1}\rho_{k+1})\mathbf{w}_k^\top \mathbf{x}_{k+1} + \gamma_{k+1}\lambda_{k+1}G_{k+1,t}^{\lambda,\rho}$$

where $\mathbf{g}_{w,k}$ is called $\mathbf{x}_k$ in van Hasselt's Theorem 1 [23]. The proof then follows through in the same way as in van Hasselt's Theorem 4 [23], where we apply Theorem 1 to $\mathbf{w}$ and $\mathbf{h}$ separately. □

Our TO-HTD(0) algorithm is equivalent to HTD(0), but TO-HTD(λ) is not equivalent to TO-TD(λ) under on-policy sampling. To achieve the later equivalence, replace $\delta_t \stackrel{\text{def}}{=} R_{t+1} + \gamma_{t+1}\mathbf{w}_t^\top \mathbf{x}_{t+1} + \mathbf{w}_{t-1}^\top \mathbf{x}_t$ and $\mathbf{d} \stackrel{\text{def}}{=} \delta_t \mathbf{e}_t^o - \alpha_t \rho_t \mathbf{x}_t(\mathbf{w}_t - \mathbf{w}_{t-1})^\top \mathbf{x}_t$. We opted for the first equivalence for two reasons. In preliminary experiments, TO-HTD(λ) described in Equation (8) already exhibited similar performance compared to TO-TD(λ), and so designing for the second equivalence was unnecessary. Further, TO-GTD(λ) was derived to ensure equivalence between TO-GTD(0) and GTD(0); this choice, therefore, better parallels that equivalence.

Given our two new hybrid methods, and the long list of existing linear prediction algorithms we now focus on how these algorithms perform in practice.

5. EXPERIMENTAL STUDY

Our empirical study focused on three main aspects: (1) early learning performance with different feature representations, (2) parameter sensitivity, and, (3) efficacy in on and off-policy learning. The majority of our experiments were conducted on random MDPs (variants of those used in previous studies[14, 5]). Each random MDP contains 30 states, and three actions in each state. From each state, and for each action, the agent can transition to one of four next states, assigned randomly from the entire set without replacement. Transition probabilities for each MDP instance are randomly sampled from [0, 1] and the transitions were normalized to sum to one. The expected reward for each transition is also generated randomly in [0, 1] and the reward on each transition was sampled without noise. Two transitions are randomly selected to terminate: $\gamma(s_i, s_j) = 0$ for $i \neq j$. Each problem instance is held fixed during learning.

We experimented with three different feature representations. The first, a *tabular* representation where each state is represented with a binary vector with a single one corresponding the current state index. This encoding allows perfect representation of the value function with no generalization over states. The second representation is computed by taking the tabular representation and *aliasing* five states to all have the same feature vector, so the agent cannot differentiate these states. These five states were selected randomly without replacement for each MDP instance. The third representation is a dense *binary* encoding where the feature vector for each state is the binary encoding of the state index, and thus the feature vector for a 30 state MDP requires just five components. Although the binary representation appears to exhibit an inappropriate amount of generalization, we believe it to be more realistic that a tabular representation, because access to MDP state is rare in real-world domains (e.g., a robotic with continuous sensor values). The binary representation should be viewed as an approximation to the poor, and relatively low-dimensional (compared to the number of states in the world) representations common in real applications. All feature encoding we normalized. Experiments conducted with the binary representation use $\gamma = 0.99$, and the rest use $\gamma = 0.9$.

To generate policies with purposeful behavior, we forced the agent to favor a single action in each state. The target policy is generated by randomly selecting an action and assigning it probability 0.9 (i.e., $\pi(s, a_i) = 0.9$) in each state, and then assigning the remaining actions the remaining probability evenly. In the off-policy experiments the behavior policy is modified to be slightly different than the target policy, by selecting the same base action, but instead assigning a probability of 0.8 (i.e., $\mu(s, a_i) = 0.8$) . This choice ensures that the policies are related, but guarantees that ρ_t is never greater than 1.5 thus avoiding inappropriately large variance due to importance sampling[3].

Our experiment compared 12 different linear complexity value function learning algorithms, including: GTD(λ), HTD(λ), true-online GTD(λ), true-online HTD(λ), true-online ETD(λ), true-online ETD(λ, β), PTD(λ), GTD2 - mp(λ), TDC - mp(λ), linear off-policy TD(0), TD(λ), true-online TD(λ). The later two being only applicable in on-policy domains, and the two mirror-prox methods are straightforward extensions (and described in the appendix) of the GTD2-mp and TDC-mp methods [13] to handle traces ($\lambda > 0$). We drop the λ designation of each method in the figure labels to reduce clutter.

Our results were generated by performing a large parameter sweep, averaged over many independent runs, for each random MDP instance, and then averaging the results over the entire set of MDPs. We tested 14 different values of the step-size parameter $\alpha \in \{0.1 \times 2^j | j = -8, -7, ..., 6\}$, seven values of $\eta \in \{2^j | j = -4, -2, -1, 0, 1, 2, 4\}$ ($\alpha_{\mathbf{h}} \stackrel{\text{def}}{=} \alpha\eta$), and 20 values of $\lambda = \{0, 0.1, ..., 0.9, 0.91, ..., 1.0\}$. We intentionally precluded smaller values of $\alpha_{\mathbf{h}}$ from the parameter sweep because many of the gradient TD methods simply become their on-policy variants as $\alpha_{\mathbf{h}}$ approaches zero, whereas in some off-policy domains values of $\alpha_{\mathbf{h}} > \alpha$ are required to avoid divergence [26]. We believe this range of η fairly reflects how the algorithms would be used in practice if avoiding divergence was a priority. The β parameter of TO-ETD(λ, β) was set equal to $0.5\gamma_t$. Each algorithm instance, defined by one combination of α, η, and λ was evaluated using the mean absolute value error on each time step,

$$\epsilon_t \stackrel{\text{def}}{=} \sum_{s \in \mathcal{S}} d_\mu(s) \left| \frac{\mathbf{x}(s)^\top \mathbf{w}_t - V^*(s)}{V^*(s)} \right|,$$

averaged over 30 MDPs, each with 100 runs. Here $V^* : \mathcal{S} \to \mathbb{R}$ denotes the *true* state-value function, which can be easily computed with access to the parameters of the MDP.

The graphs in Figures 1 and 2 include (a) learning curves with α, η, and λ selected to minimize the mean absolute value error, for each of the three different feature representations, and (b) parameter sensitivity graphs for α, η, and λ, in which the mean absolute value error is plotted against the parameter value, while the remaining two parameters

[3]See the recent study by Mahmood & Sutton [14] for an extensive treatment of off-policy learning domains with large variance due to importance sampling.

are selected to minimize mean absolute value error. These graphs are included across feature representations, for on and off-policy learning. Across all results the parameters are selected to optimize performance over the last half of the experiment to ensure stable learning throughout the run.

To analyze large variance due to importance sampling and off-policy learning we also investigated Baird's counterexample [2], a simple MDP that causes TD learning to diverge. This seven state MDP uses a target policy that is very different from the behavior policy, a feature representation that allows perfect representation of the value function, but also causes inappropriate generalization. We used the variant of this problem described by Maei [11] and White [26, Figure 7.1]. We present results with the root mean squared error [4],

$$\epsilon_t \stackrel{\text{def}}{=} \sum_{s \in \mathcal{S}} d_\mu(s) \left(\mathbf{x}(s)^\top \mathbf{w}_t - V^*(s)\right)^2,$$

in Figure 1. The experiment was conducted in the same way was the random MDPs, except we did not average over MDPs—there is only one—and we used different parameter ranges. We tested 11 different values of the step-size parameter $\alpha \in \{0.1 \times 2^j | j = -10, -9, ..., -1, 0\}$, 12 values of $\eta \in \{2^j | j = -16, -8, \ldots, -2, -1, 0, 1, 2, \ldots, 32\}$ ($\alpha_\mathbf{h} \stackrel{\text{def}}{=} \alpha\eta$), and the same 20 values of λ. We did not evaluate TD(0) on this domain because the algorithm will diverge and that has been shown many times before.

In addition to performance results in Figures 1 and 2, Table 1 summarizes the runtime comparison for these algorithms. Though the algorithms are all linear in storage and computation, they do differ in both implementation and runtime, particularly due to true-online traces. The appendix contains several plots of runtime verses value error illustrating the trade-off between computation and sample complexity for each algorithm. Due to space constraints, we have included the aliased tabular representation results for on-policy learning in the appendix, since they are similar to the tabular representation results in on-policy learning.

6. DISCUSSION

There are three broad conclusions suggested by our results. First, we could not clearly demonstrate the supposed superiority of TD(λ) over gradient TD methods in the on-policy setting. In both tabular and aliased feature settings GTD(λ) achieved faster learning and superior parameter sensitivity compared to TD, PTD, and HTD. Notably, the η-sensitivity of the GTD algorithm was very reasonable in both domains, however, large η were required to achieve good performance on Baird's for both GTD(λ) and TO-GTD(λ). Our on-policy experiments with binary features did indicate a slight advantage for TD(λ), PTD, and HTD, and that PTD and HTD exhibit zero sensitivity to the choice of $\alpha_\mathbf{h}$ as expected. In off-policy learning there is little difference between GTD(λ) and PTD and HTD. Our results combined with the prior work of Dann et al. [4] suggest that the advantage of conventional TD(λ) over gradient TD methods, in on-policy learning, is limited to specific domains.

Our second conclusion, is that the new mirror prox methods achieved poor performance in most settings except Baird's counterexample. Both GTD2-mp and TDC-mp achieved the best performance in Baird's counterexample. We hypothesize that the two-step gradient computation more effectively uses the transition to state 7, and so is ideally suited to the structure of the domain[5]. However, the GTD2-MP method performed worse than off-policy TD(0) in all off-policy random MDP domains, while the learning curves of TDC-mp exhibited higher variance than other methods in all but the on-policy binary case and high parameter sensitivity across all settings except Baird's. This does not seem to be a consequence of the extension to eligibility traces because in all cases except Baird's, both TDC-mp and GTD2-mp performed best with $\lambda > 0$. Like GTD and HTD, the mirror prox methods would likely have performed better with values of $\alpha_\mathbf{h} > \alpha$, however, this is undesirable because larger $\alpha_\mathbf{h}$ is required to ensure good performance in some off policy domains, such as Baird's (e.g., $\eta = 2^8$).

Third and finally, several methods exhibited non-convergent behavior on Baird's counterexample. All methods that exhibited reliable error reduce in Baird's did so with λ near zero, suggesting that eligibility traces are of limited use in these more extreme off-policy domains. In the case of PTD, non-convergent behavior is not surprising since our implementation of this algorithm does not include gradient correction—a possible extension suggested by the authors [20]—and thus is only guaranteed to converge under off-policy sampling in the tabular case. For the emphatic TD methods the performance on Baird's remains a concern, especially considering how well TO-ETD(λ, β) performed in all our other experiments. The addition of the β parameter appears to significantly improve TO-ETD in the off-policy domain with binary features, but could not mitigate the large variance in ρ produced by the counterexample. It is not clear if this bad behavior is inherent to emphatic TD methods[6], or could be solved by more careful specification of the state-based interest function. In our implementation, we followed the original author's recommendation of setting the interest for each state to 1.0 [21], because all our domains were discounted and continuing. Additionally, both HTD(λ) and TO-HTD(λ) did not diverge on Baird's, but performance was less than satisfactory to say the least.

Overall, the conclusions implied by our empirical study are surprisingly clear. If guarding against large variance due to off-policy sampling is a chief concern, then GTD(λ) and TO-GTD(λ) should be preferred. Between the two, GTD(λ) should be preferred if computation is at a premium. If poor performance in problems like Baird's is not a concern, then TO-ETD(λ, β) was clearly the best across our experiments, and exhibited nearly the best runtime results. TO-ETD(λ) on the other hand, exhibited high variance in off-policy domains, and sharp parameter sensitivity, indicating parameter turnng of emphatic methods may be an issue in practice.

7. APPENDIX

Additional results and analysis can be found in the full version of the paper: http://arxiv.org/abs/1602.08771.

[4]In this counterexample the mean absolute value error is not appropriate because the optimal values for this task are zero. The MSPBE is often used as a performance measure, but the MSPBE changes with λ; for completeness, we include results with the MSPBE in the appendix.

[5]Baird's counterexample uses a specific initialization of the primary weights: far from one of the true solutions $\mathbf{w} = \mathbf{0}$.

[6]The variance of TO-ETD has been examined before in two state domains [21]. ETD is thought to have higher variance that other TD algorithms due to the emphasis weighting.

	TD(0)	TD(λ)	TO-TD	PTD	GTD	TO-ETD	TO-ETD(β)	HTD	TO-GTD	GTD-MP	TDC-MP	TO-HTD
On-policy	120.0	132.7	150.1	172.4	204.6	287.8	286.0	311.8	366.2	467.4	466.2	466.0
Off-policy	108.3	-	-	158.7	175.2	249.65	254.7	267.5	316.2	407.8	395.7	403.3

Table 1: Average runtime in microseconds for 500 steps of learning, averaged over 30 MDPS, with 100 runs each, with 30-dimensional tabular features.

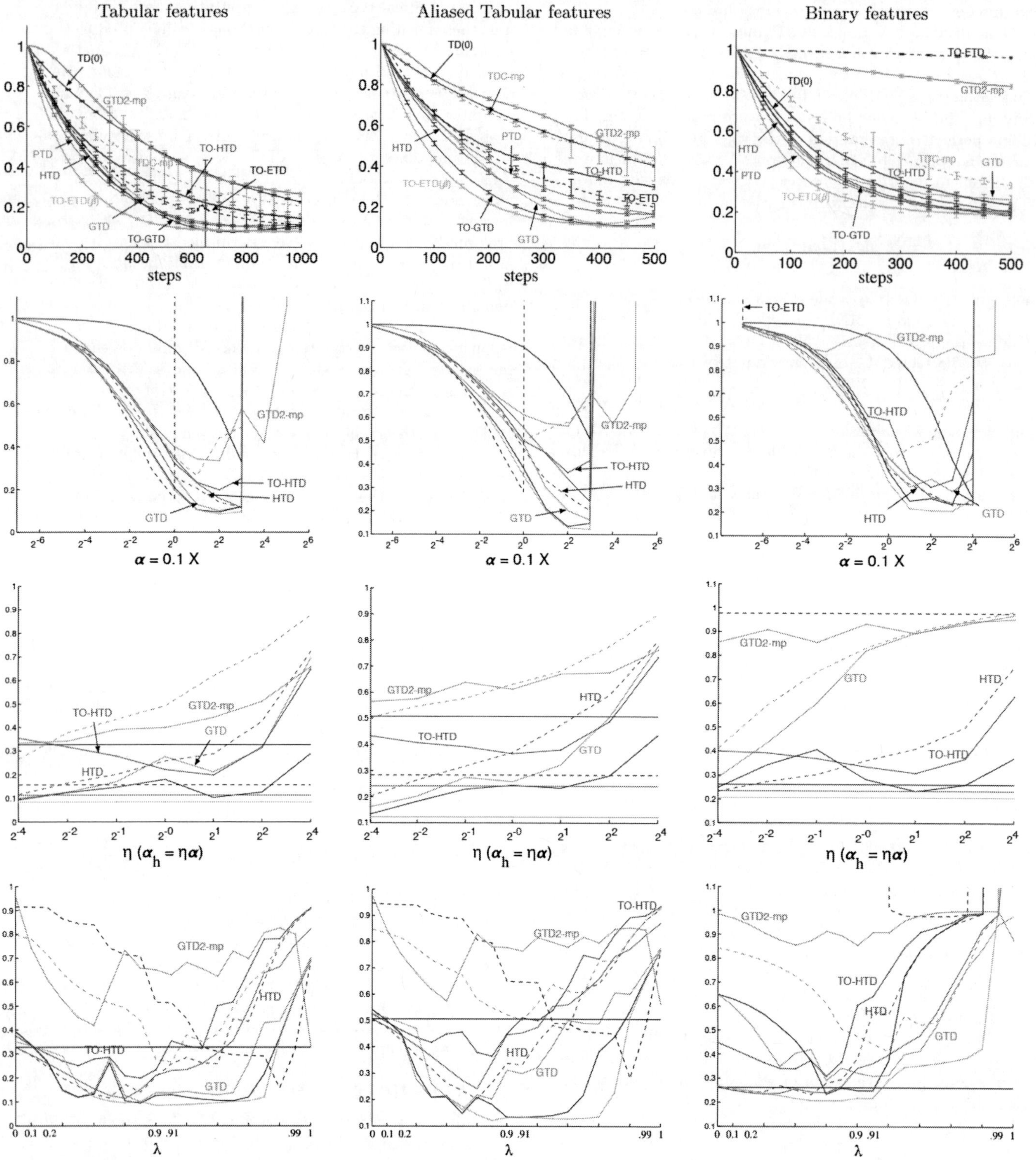

Figure 1: **Off-policy** performance on random MDPs with three different representations. All plots report mean absolute value error averaged over 100 runs and 30 MDPs. The plots are organized in columns left to right corresponding to tabular, aliased, and binary features. The plots are organized in rows from top to bottom corresponding to learning curves, α, η, and λ sensitivity. The error bars are standard errors ($s/\sqrt(n)$) computed from 100 independent runs.

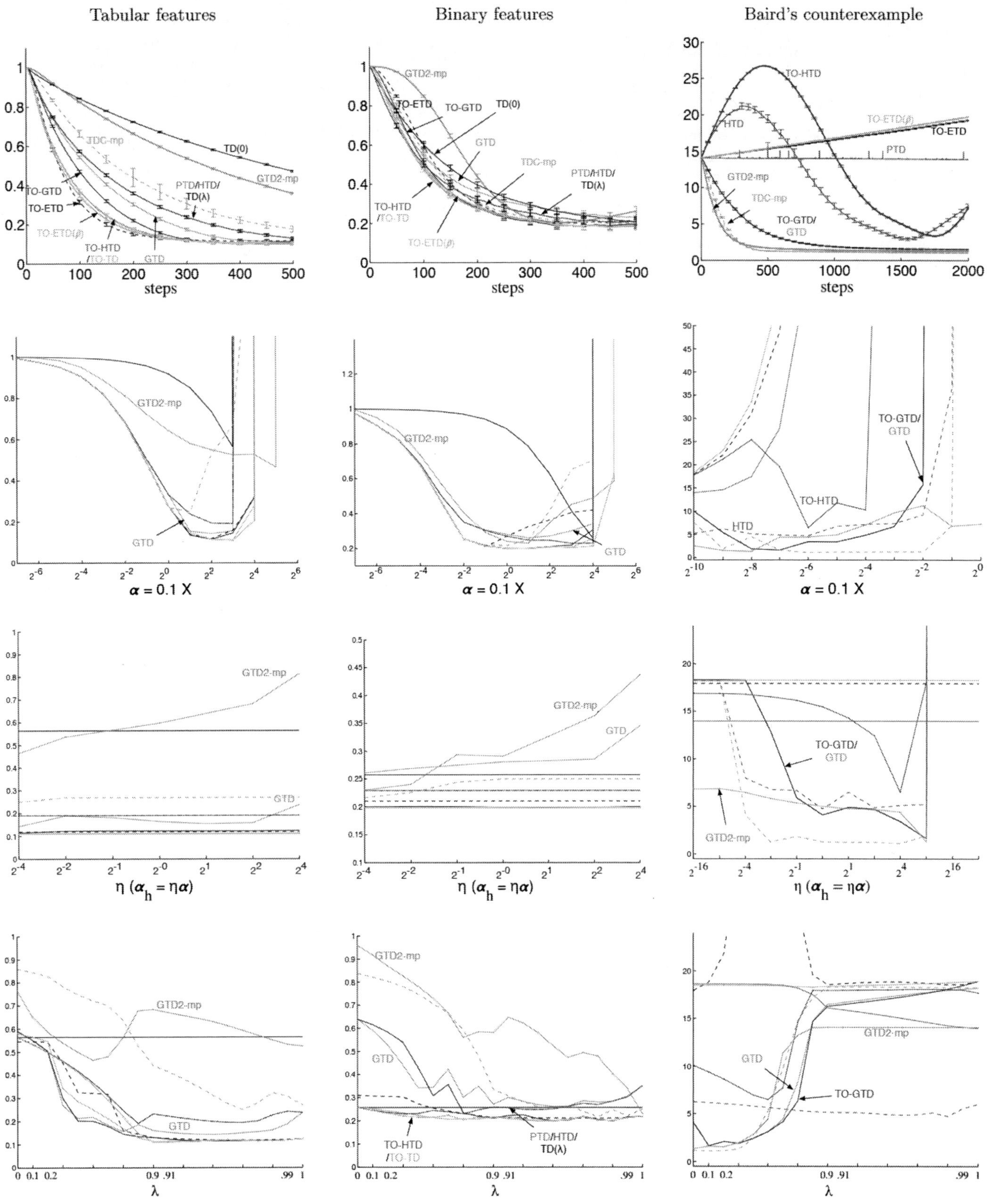

Figure 2: **On-policy** performance on random MDPs with two different representations and **off-policy** performance on Baird's counterexample. All plots report mean absolute value error averaged over 100 runs and 30 random MDPs, and 500 runs for Baird's. The plots are organized in columns left to right corresponding to results on random MDPs with tabular and binary features, and results on Baird's counterexample. The plots are also organized in rows from top to bottom corresponding to learning curves, α, η, and λ sensitivity.

REFERENCES

[1] B. Argall, S. Chernova, M. M. Veloso, and B. Browning. A survey of robot learning from demonstration. *Robotics and Autonomous Systems ()*, 2009.

[2] L. Baird. Residual algorithms: Reinforcement learning with function approximation. In *International Conference on Machine Learning*, 1995.

[3] D. P. Bertsekas and J. N. Tsitsiklis. *Neuro-dynamic programming*. Athena Scientific Press, 1996.

[4] C. Dann, G. Neumann, and J. Peters. Policy evaluation with temporal differences: a survey and comparison. *The Journal of Machine Learning Research*, 2014.

[5] M. Geist and B. Scherrer. Off-policy learning with eligibility traces: a survey. *The Journal of Machine Learning Research*, 2014.

[6] L. Hackman. *Faster Gradient-TD Algorithms*. PhD thesis, University of Alberta, 2012.

[7] A. Hallak, A. Tamar, R. Munos, and S. Mannor. Generalized emphatic temporal difference learning: Bias-variance analysis. *arXiv preprint arXiv:1509.05172*, 2015.

[8] L.-J. Lin. Self-Improving Reactive Agents Based On Reinforcement Learning, Planning and Teaching. *Machine Learning*, 1992.

[9] B. Liu, J. Liu, M. Ghavamzadeh, S. Mahadevan, and M. Petrik. Finite-Sample Analysis of Proximal Gradient TD Algorithms. *Conference on Uncertainty in Artificial Intelligence*, 2015.

[10] H. Maei and R. Sutton. GQ (λ): A general gradient algorithm for temporal-difference prediction learning with eligibility traces. In *AGI*, 2010.

[11] H. R. Maei. *Gradient temporal-difference learning algorithms*. University of Alberta, 2011.

[12] S. Mahadevan and B. Liu. Sparse Q-learning with mirror descent. In *Conference on Uncertainty in Artificial Intelligence*, 2012.

[13] S. Mahadevan, B. Liu, P. S. Thomas, W. Dabney, S. Giguere, N. Jacek, I. Gemp, and J. L. 0002. Proximal reinforcement learning: A new theory of sequential decision making in primal-dual spaces. *CoRR abs/1405.6757*, 2014.

[14] A. R. Mahmood and R. Sutton. Off-policy learning based on weighted importance sampling with linear computational complexity. In *Conference on Uncertainty in Artificial Intelligence*, 2015.

[15] V. Mnih, K. Kavukcuoglu, D. Silver, A. A. Rusu, J. Veness, M. G. Bellemare, A. Graves, M. Riedmiller, A. K. Fidjeland, G. Ostrovski, et al. Human-level control through deep reinforcement learning. *Nature*, 518(7540):529–533, 2015.

[16] R. Sutton and A. G. Barto. *Reinforcement Learning: An Introduction*. MIT press, 1998.

[17] R. Sutton, H. Maei, D. Precup, and S. Bhatnagar. Fast gradient-descent methods for temporal-difference learning with linear function approximation. *International Conference on Machine Learning*, 2009.

[18] R. Sutton, J. Modayil, M. Delp, T. Degris, P. Pilarski, A. White, and D. Precup. Horde: A scalable real-time architecture for learning knowledge from unsupervised sensorimotor interaction. In *International Conference on Autonomous Agents and Multiagent Systems*, 2011.

[19] R. S. Sutton. Learning to predict by the methods of temporal differences. *Machine learning*, 3(1):9–44, 1988.

[20] R. S. Sutton, A. R. Mahmood, D. Precup, and H. van Hasselt. A new Q(lambda) with interim forward view and Monte Carlo equivalence. *ICML*, 2014.

[21] R. S. Sutton, A. R. Mahmood, and M. White. An emphatic approach to the problem of off-policy temporal-difference learning. *The Journal of Machine Learning Research*, 2015.

[22] J. Tsitsiklis and B. Van Roy. An analysis of temporal-difference learning with function approximation. *IEEE Transactions on Automatic Control*, 1997.

[23] H. van Hasselt, A. R. Mahmood, and R. Sutton. Off-policy TD (λ) with a true online equivalence. In *Conference on Uncertainty in Artificial Intelligence*, 2014.

[24] H. van Seijen and R. Sutton. True online TD(lambda). In *International Conference on Machine Learning*, 2014.

[25] C. Watkins. *Watkins: Learning from delayed rewards*. PhD thesis, University of Cambridge, 1989.

[26] A. White. *Developing a predictive approach to knowledge*. PhD thesis, University of Alberta, 2015.

[27] H. Yu. On convergence of emphatic temporal-difference learning. In *Annual Conference on Learning Theory*, 2015.

Active Advice Seeking for Inverse Reinforcement Learning

Phillip Odom
Indiana University
Bloomington, Indiana
phodom@indiana.edu

Sriraam Natarajan
Indiana University
Bloomington, Indiana
natarasr@indiana.edu

ABSTRACT

Intelligent systems that interact with humans typically require input in the form of demonstrations and/or advice for optimal decision making. In more traditional systems, such interactions require detailed and tedious effort on the part of the human expert. Alternatively, active learning systems allow for incremental acquisition of the demonstrations from the human expert where the learning system generates the queries. However, active learning allows for only labeled examples as input, significantly restricting the interaction between expert and learning algorithm. Advice-based learning systems increase the expressiveness of the interaction, but typically require all the advice about the domain in advance. By combining active learning and advice-based learning, we consider the problem of actively soliciting human advice. We present the algorithm in an inverse reinforcement learning setting where the utilities are learned from demonstrations. We show empirically the contribution of a more expressive advice over traditional active learning approaches.

Keywords

Inverse Reinforcement Learning; Advice-based Learning; Active Advice Seeking

1. INTRODUCTION

In Inverse Reinforcement Learning (IRL), an autonomous agent tries to explicitly learn the reward function (utilities) of a Markov Decision Process (MDP) by observing demonstrations. The observations include the demonstrator's behavior over time (i.e., actions), measurements of the demonstrator's sensory inputs (i.e., states) and the model of the environment. IRL was introduced [16] as a linear programming problem for finite state spaces and was later extended in different directions including apprenticeship learning [1], Bayesian learning [17], multi-task learning [14], and learning in partially observable environments [4]. While successful, these methods assume *optimality of the trajectories*, which are simply sequences of current state and action pairs.

A recent approach [9] went beyond the simplifying assumption of optimality of trajectories, by considering the presence of a human expert who specifies reasonable advice. The pieces of advice were given as preferences over states and actions and were inspired by the preference elicitation frameworks [2, 24, 18]. A key feature of this approach is that the experts are domain experts and not machine learning experts. As an example, the expert could specify "completely stop at all stop signs - do not make a rolling stop" instead of specifying that "the reward of stopping completely at this specific stop sign is twice that of making a rolling stop" [1]. While capturing more expressive communication between the expert and learning algorithm, this approach required the expert to list all the advice in advance before any learning takes place. The domain experts often lack the machine learning knowledge to understand the most useful advice. They may instead provide the broad trends as advice that would otherwise clearly follow from the demonstrations. This is a disservice not only to the learning algorithm, which may not get informative advice, but also to the expert who has their time squandered.

An ideal human-in-the-loop agent should determine where to solicit advice and when it has accumulated sufficient advice. We propose to employ the concept of *active learning* [20] for this task. Active Learning is a paradigm that has been extensively applied to supervised learning where the learning algorithm works by (actively) selecting a small but representative set of examples to be labeled by the expert. While active learning has been traditionally applied to soliciting example labels, it has not been considered in the realm of seeking advice from an expert which is crucial in reducing the burden of the expert when providing the combination of trajectories and advice.

We introduce *active advice-seeking* where the goal is to select areas in the feature space to solicit advice from the expert. Actively seeking advice has two distinct advantages over active learning. (1) While active learning is constrained to selecting a single example to label, an active advice-seeker can get advice over a larger section of the feature space. This allows the learner to query about similar areas of the feature space together, potentially reducing the number of advice that the learning algorithm requires. (2) Traditional active learning is also limited from the perspective of the communication with the expert as the only information the expert is allowed to provide is a label for a given example. Advice can be much more expressive, for example, by allowing a set of optimal labels instead of a single label.

We make the following key contributions: (1) We present the first algorithm for actively soliciting advice from experts.

[1]The framework is capable of expressing both forms of advice.

Appears in: *Proceedings of the 15th International Conference on Autonomous Agents and Multiagent Systems (AAMAS 2016), J. Thangarajah, K. Tuyls, S. Marsella, C. Jonker (eds.), May 9–13, 2016, Singapore.*

(2) We show how the algorithm automatically clusters states and computes uncertainty over these states to solicit this advice. (3) We show how the advice can then be incorporated into the IRL setting. (4) Finally, we demonstrate the efficacy of the proposed approach in standard IRL problems and a real-world drone navigation task. The results clearly show the robustness of the approach as compared to obtaining all the advice in advance.

2. BACKGROUND

2.1 Inverse Reinforcement Learning

Inverse Reinforcement Learning (IRL) is a learning framework that learns a reward function based on demonstrations of an expert policy [16]. IRL relies on the expert to act optimally (or near-optimally) and to visit many states in the world. Together, these allow the learner to generate appropriate rewards for the states. IRL is related to Imitation Learning [6, 8, 15] which learns the policy directly from the demonstrations as opposed to learning the reward function. The reward function, used to obtain the optimal policy, mirrors the internal reward function of the demonstrator. IRL is useful in domains where defining the reward function is difficult or tedious, but providing demonstrations of the correct behavior is more practical.

Early work on IRL used linear programs to solve for the reward function [16]. The demonstrations were broken down into constraints on the value of each state. These constraints relied on the vector form of the Bellman equation:

$$\mathbf{v}^{\pi} = (I - \lambda P_{a_*})^{-1}\mathbf{r}$$

where $\mathbf{v}^{\pi}$ is a vector that represents the value function, I is the identity matrix, P_a is the probability transition matrix for action a, P_{a_*} is the expert's probability transition matrix, and $\mathbf{r}$ is the reward function. This form of the equation is used to create a set of constraints on the optimal policy ($\pi^*(s) = a_*$) [16] where A is the set of actions.

$$(P_{a_*} - P_a)(I - \lambda P_{a_*})\mathbf{r} \geq 0 \ \forall a \in A \setminus a_*$$

These constraints are used in the resulting linear program along with bounds on the range of possible reward values. These original constraints (shown in red in equation 1) maximize the difference between the value of the demonstrated action and all other actions. Unfortunately, the standard IRL formulation relies on having correct constraints for each state in order to learn an accurate reward function. Noisy demonstrators or rarely visited states that are not visited by near-optimal policies can violate this assumption.

$$\begin{aligned} \max_{\mathbf{r},\xi_i,\zeta_j} \ & -\|\mathbf{r}\|_1 + \lambda_t \sum_{i=1}^{n} \xi_i + \lambda_a \sum_{j \in \mathcal{S}_e} \zeta_j \\ \text{s. t.} \ & (P^i_{a_*} - P^i_a) B \mathbf{r} \geq \xi_i, \quad \forall a \in A \setminus a_*, \ i = 1, \ldots, n, \\ & (P^j_a - P^j_{a'}) B \mathbf{r} \geq \zeta_j + \delta_j, \quad \forall a \in \mathsf{Pr}_j, \ a' \in \mathsf{Av}_j, \ j \in \mathcal{S}_e, \\ & \zeta_j \geq 0, \quad \forall j \in \mathcal{S}_e, \\ & |r_i| \leq r_{\max}, \quad \forall i = 1, \ldots, n. \end{aligned} \tag{1}$$

Kunapuli et al. [9] extended the IRL formulation to include expert advice that is capable of correcting sub-optimal demonstrations. They include additional constraints[2] (shown in blue in equation 1) that allow an expert to specify a set of preferred and avoided actions for a given state. Similar to the original constraints, they enforce that the value of preferred actions be higher than the value of avoided actions. This is captured in the following inequality:

$$\min_{a \in \mathbf{Pr}_j} q^{\pi}(j,a) - \max_{a' \in \mathbf{Av}_j} q^{\pi}(j,a') \geq 0$$

where $\mathbf{Pr}_j$ and $\mathbf{Av}_j$ are the set of preferred and avoided actions for state j. These two sets should be mutually exclusive ($\mathbf{Pr}_j \cap \mathbf{Av}_j = \emptyset$). While each set should not be empty, the set of preferred and avoided actions need not be exhaustive ($2 \leq |\mathbf{Pr}_j| + |\mathbf{Av}_j| \leq |A|$). Furthermore, advice can be given for as many (or as few) states as the expert defines.

Their method of advice-giving has two key drawbacks: 1) they assume that the expert must give each advice individually ($\mathbf{Pr}_j$ and $\mathbf{Av}_j$ are only for state j) and 2) the expert is responsible for defining the set of useful advice. While knowledgeable about the domain, an expert may *not be fully aware of what advice the learning algorithm would find most useful*. Furthermore, giving advice *over single states is not practical in large domains*.

To deal with these key issues, our ADVISE framework queries the expert for advice in a particular set of states automatically instead of requiring the advice up-front. This allows for $\mathbf{Pr_j}$ and $\mathbf{Av_j}$ to be given with respect to set $\mathbf{j}$. Furthermore, the responsibility for giving the correct advice is off-loaded from the expert and placed squarely on the learning algorithm.

2.2 Active Learning

In standard machine learning, a labeled dataset is provided. However, in many problems such as information extraction or medical diagnoses, it is not trivial to obtain labeled examples. In many of these problems, there is a wealth of unlabeled examples, such as free text, that can be used for learning. Active Learning [20] relies on the fact that if an algorithm can only solicit the label of a limited number of examples, then not all examples provide the same amount of information. The goal of active learning is to iteratively select the most informative examples to be labeled.

One of the most common ways of selecting an example is uncertainty sampling [10] where the learning algorithm selects examples based on the quality of its prediction (possibly entropy or disagreement among an ensemble of classifiers). After receiving additional labels, the updated predictions result in different uncertainties.

Active learning has been applied to SVMs [19], Bayesian Networks [22, 23], and in sequential decision-making tasks including IRL [13] and imitation learning [3, 8, 5]. As previously shown, active learning has unique challenges in IRL [13]. IRL learns a reward function based on trajectories as an intermediate step. Standard reinforcement learning techniques can then be used to achieve a final policy. Unfortunately *many reward functions may result in similar policies so uncertain reward functions do not imply uncertain policies.* We handle this issue by defining an uncertainty

[2]Their formulation allows for providing advice to state, actions or rewards. We present only the action advice since it is the formulation we consider in this work.

function that considers the multiple levels of potential uncertainty. This is described in detail later.

Active advice-seeking is distinct from standard active learning as it solicits more expressive advice than mere labels. Advice is more general (applying to a set of states vs a single state) as well as more expressive (allowing for label preferences as opposed to a single label). Note that the expert is responsible for providing advice that is most characteristic of a set of states. Therefore, more information can pass between the advice-giver and learning algorithm with each query. The generality of the queries posed to the human expert can depend on their availability. The more available the expert, the more specific the questions. Alternatively, the advice-seeker can be more general when constrained to fewer queries.

3. ACTIVE ADVICE-SEEKING

The goal of the active ADVIce-SEeking (ADVISE) agent is to iteratively accrue advice about different areas of the state space. As the advice accumulates, the learning agent should become more confident about its current policy. While it may be possible to acquire advice about every state, such a strategy is not practical for the advice-giving expert. Therefore, the agent's learning algorithm targets areas of the state space that it believes are uncertain. Conceptually, it is important to select both useful areas to query as well as areas which are likely to have similar advice as the expert will give advice about the entire area jointly. As in active learning, the overall goal of ADVISE is to achieve high performance with few queries to the expert.

There are two key reasons why our advice is more expressive than the examples used by standard active learning. First, the expert is queried over a set of states. This means that the expert must generalize advice over these (possibly significantly different) states. Second, the expert's response is over the set of (possibly partial) label preferences. Thus, there could be multiple reasonable responses that an expert could give. As our advice is more expressive, more information can be received by the learning agent for every interaction with the expert.

For example, consider an agent learning to drive a car. In the active learning framework, the agent might solicit which action to take at a yellow light at the intersection of *Seventh Ave* and *Broadway*. However, any such advice is not broadly applicable as it fits only to the specific situation. Alternatively, in our ADVISE framework, an agent could ask for advice at any yellow light at any (or a set of) intersection(s). Notice that the advice is able to cover significantly more states which all share similar advice. The expert might respond that braking is the preferred action and accelerating is the avoided action. This intentionally leaves out turning the wheel as the driver might be preparing for a right turn. However, current classical active learning methods cannot handle such advice and are limited to specific example labels.

The framework (shown in figure 1) begins by learning a policy from only the expert demonstrations. This allows the algorithm to calculate the best advice query using only the demonstrations. Next, the algorithm seeks advice to correct any deficiencies in the policy by: calculating the uncertainty of the state-clustering, soliciting more advice, and finally updating the current policy.

The algorithm can continue collecting advice as long as

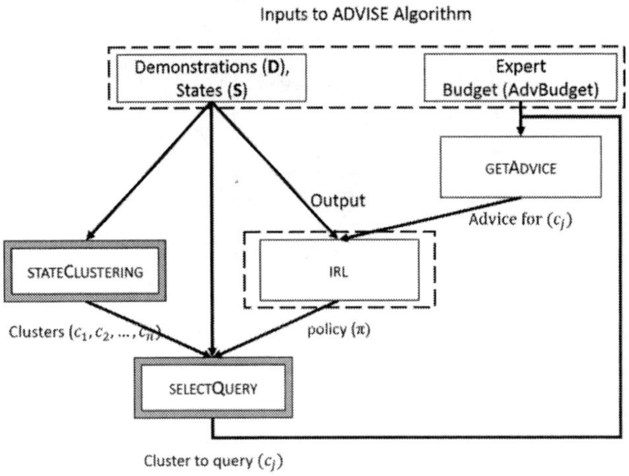

Figure 1: A framework for active advice-seeking.

necessary to learn a high-quality policy. While we do not explicitly address the problem of discovering how much advice is sufficient to learn a good policy, there is a framework called Knows-What-It-Knows (KWIK) [11] that reasons about the sufficient amount of training data. Such an approach could be extended to apply to our advice-based framework. However, this is beyond the scope of this work.

3.1 Problem Formulation

Now, we will formally define the problem and describe it with an intuitive running example.

Goal :	Iteratively solicit advice from the expert to learn a better policy.
Input :	Demonstrations, the set of states/actions, and limited time of expert access.
Output :	A final policy.

The main goal of our framework is to learn a more robust policy by iteratively soliciting advice from the human expert. In previous work [9], experts would be responsible for providing all the relevant advice up-front. This places immense burden on the expert to deeply understand both the domain problem and the learning problem to provide accurate and relevant advice. In many real situations, the domain expert may not be aware of the data available to the learning algorithm. Thus, while the advice will be accurate, it may not be relevant.

We instead formulate the problem of active advice-seeking as an iterative process that aims to solicit relevant advice at each step. Advice received in the previous rounds could effect the advice needed in subsequent rounds. As often in active learning, we assume that there is an advice budget and after that budget is exhausted, the final policy is returned. Our hypothesis, which we verify empirically, is that this policy represents both the best of the advice as well as the best of the data. The framework is shown in figure 1. The key steps of the algorithm are emphasized in grey and will be explained in detail later. We now introduce a running example and use it to explain our algorithm.

Illustrative Example: Consider the example grid nav-

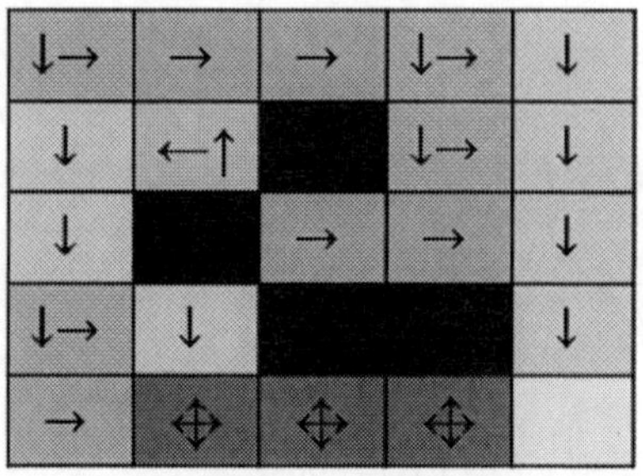

Figure 2: Illustrative example of the ADVISE algorithm for the WumpusWorld domain. The arrows show the actions demonstrated by the human expert. The colors show an ideal clustering of the states. Ideally the algorithm will select the dark grey cluster early to correct the sub-optimal actions.

igation problem in figure 2. The goal is to begin in the upper left state and navigate the grid to reach the lower right state. The arrows inside each cell show the most likely action demonstrated by the expert[3] in that cell (state). Notice how in most of the states the expert gives the correct demonstration. However, the expert makes a mistake on the three middle states in the bottom row (shown in dark grey). The first goal of the algorithm is to cluster the states into sets of similar states. We hypothesize that this will allow for noisy demonstrations to be clustered together. One example clustering is shown through highlighted colors. The second step is to select the cluster with the most uncertainty. Ideally, the dark grey cluster will be selected first and advice will be given to correct the policy in these states yielding a better policy than the one obtained with only the noisy trajectories.

We now define the key concepts of our system using the above example. As we are utilizing an advice-based IRL framework [9] (introduced in the background), the form of our advice is action preferences (sets of preferred and avoided actions). It is important to note that while we share a similar form of advice with Kunapuli et al [9], the goal of this work is to solicit advice from the expert automatically. We now formally define advice using previous notations,

DEFINITION 1. *Advice is a set of preferences ($a_i \in \mathbf{Adv}$). Each piece of advice is given relative to a cluster of states ($\mathbf{c}_i$). It consists of a set of preferred actions ($\mathbf{Pr}_{\mathbf{c}_i}$) and a set of avoided actions ($\mathbf{Av}_{\mathbf{c}_i}$).*

The ADVISE algorithm automatically identifies states of interest ($\boldsymbol{j}$ of the blue constraints in equation 1)[4]. Note that our framework allows $\mathbf{j}$ to be a set of states (as opposed to a single state). The expert then provides the set of preferred ($\mathbf{Pr_j}$) and avoided ($\mathbf{Av_j}$) actions for these states. Note that the states in a cluster could be diverse and the expert is responsible for giving the best representative advice for the entire cluster. Following standard terminology, we refer to a grouping of states as a cluster. A single piece of advice is provided to cover the entire cluster. More formally,

[3]Note that this expert who is generating the demonstrations may be different from the advice-giving expert.

[4]We denote sets as bold.

DEFINITION 2. *Cluster $\mathbf{c}$ is a set of states, $< s_1, s_2, ..., s_n >$ such that $\pi(s_i) \approx \pi(s_j) \forall s_i, s_j \in \mathbf{c}$*

Recall that a policy (π) defines a distribution over the actions for each state [21]. As advice is provided over the entire cluster, it is key that the states in the cluster have similar optimal (or near-optimal) policies. There is a trade-off between the size of the clusters and the accuracy of the clusters. As the size of the clusters are increased, the learning algorithm receives more information. However, as smaller clusters will be more accurate, the learning algorithm receives a higher quality of information.

EXAMPLE 1. *In our illustrative example (figure 2), advice 1 could be comprised of $\mathbf{c}_1 =< s_{12}, s_{13}, s_{14} >$ where s_{11} is the lower left state (states shown in dark grey). The preferred action should be $\mathbf{Pr}_{\mathbf{c}_1} = \{RIGHT\}$ while the avoided actions should be $\mathbf{Av}_{\mathbf{c}_1} = \{UP, DOWN, LEFT\}$.*

Given a set of clusters, the algorithm must decide how to prioritize (or rank [12]) the clusters so that it is receiving the most useful information at each step. This is important as the advice-giving expert may have limited availability with which questions can be answered. This is similar to the active learning problem discussed earlier [20]. As used in active learning, our proposed approach calculates the uncertainty of each cluster and solicits advice for the most uncertain clusters.

IRL has two sources of uncertainty. (1) The inputs (demonstrations) can be ambiguous in some states about the correct actions due to either too few demonstrations in those states or through mistakes– incorrect actions. (2) The other source of uncertainty is that the output (final policy) may not clearly delineate an action for the agent. Therefore, we define the uncertainty of a state as a combination of these two types of uncertainty.

DEFINITION 3. *State-level uncertainty $U_s(s_i)$ is given by $U_s(s_i) = w_p F(s_i) + (1 - w_p) G(s_i)$ where $F(s_i)$ is the uncertainty w.r.t the number of demonstrations provided for state s_i, w_p is the corresponding weight and $G(s_i)$ is the uncertainty w.r.t the policy learned for state s_i.*

Uncertainty at the cluster level is a function of the uncertainty of each state assigned to that cluster.

DEFINITION 4. *The cluster-level uncertainty U_c is given by $U_c(\mathbf{c}_j) = \frac{\sum_{s_i \in \mathbf{c}_j} U_s(s_i)}{|\mathbf{c}_j|}$.*

The two types of uncertainty will be discussed in detail later. The overall goal of active advice seeking is to identify a set of advice out of all possible advice ($\mathbf{a} \subseteq \mathbf{Advice}$), limited by the access to the expert, that minimizes the total uncertainty of all states in the problem. The quality of the advice is also a major concern. Let us denote $\boldsymbol{s_a} = \{\mathbf{c}_1 \cup \mathbf{c}_2, ..., \cup \mathbf{c}_k\}$ as the set of states covered by the k pieces of advice $\boldsymbol{a} = \{a_1, a_2, ..., a_k\}$ and $\boldsymbol{s_b} = \boldsymbol{S} - \boldsymbol{s_a}$. Formally the goal is to find:

$$\arg\min_{\boldsymbol{a}} f(\boldsymbol{a})[U_c(\boldsymbol{s_a}) + U_c(\boldsymbol{s_b})] \qquad (2)$$

where f is a function of the quality of the advice which includes both the size and consistency of the cluster of states over which the advice is defined, and U_c is the cluster-level uncertainty.

Unfortunately, this global optimization problem of minimizing cluster-level uncertainty is not tractable. If the size of the example space is n, then the number of possible clusters of examples (and thus the potential advice given) is exponential in n. Furthermore, the advice-quality function is not trivial as it involves estimating the cohesion of the individual clusters (how similar are the states in the cluster in terms of their optimal policy).

Instead, we present an approximate method that involves generating clusters of examples without considering their quality (i.e. uncertainty). After the clusters have been specified, our agent ranks the generated clusters and solicits advice over the clusters in that order. This gives rise to the two important components of active advice-seeking (ADVISE is shown in algorithm 1): 1) STATECLUSTERING - Clustering the states over which to ask for advice, 2) SELECTQUERY - Deciding what order to query the clusters for advice. We will discuss each component respectively.

3.2 Creating the State-Clustering

One key difficulty for ADVISE is deciding the parts of the state/action space where advice would be most beneficial. Assuming that there are a set of n states $(s_1, s_2, ..., s_n)$, the goal of group discovery is to find m clusters $(\mathbf{c}_1, \mathbf{c}_2, ..., \mathbf{c}_m)$ that are likely to have similar optimal actions (ie $\forall\ s_i, s_j \in \mathbf{c}_k, \pi(i) \approx \pi(j)$). Since the optimal policy is unknown, π has to be approximated.

Our approach is to use the demonstrator's action distribution as an estimation of π. Furthermore, we assume that experts do not always choose sub-optimal actions randomly, but instead they make systematic errors in certain kinds of states. For instance, if a driver rolls through a stop-sign at one intersection, he is likely to roll through most intersections. Note that it is trivial to add any structural information about the states that exist in the world. Such information could have significant utility in identifying similar states. However, as this information does not exist in all domains, we use the same information that is used in IRL to learn the reward functions - the state id. We use *k-means* [7] to cluster states based on the policy of the demonstrator. However, any clustering algorithm could be used to replace k-means. While this will not produce optimal state-clusters, the goal is only to create a reasonable clustering. Our empirical evaluation will show that this approach can create reasonable clusters that are useful in learning.

It must be mentioned clearly that the goal of this work is not to propose an interesting clustering algorithm but motivate the need for clustering the states so that they could be queried for advice. As experiments show, a basic algorithm such as k-means can possibly suffice in many domains. Investigating specialized clustering techniques that can better cluster the states is an interesting direction for future research.

Algorithm 1 ADVISE Algorithm

```
function ADVISE(AdvBudget,Expert,States,D)
    aDist = PARSEDEM(D)
    advice = ∅
    π_0 = IRL(D,adv)
    clusters = STATECLUSTERING(aDist)
    for k = 1 to AdvBudget do
        query = SELECTQUERY(clusters,aDist,π_{k-1})
        newAdv = Expert(query)
        adv = adv ∪ newAdv
        π_k = IRL(D,adv)
    end for
    return π_k
end function
function SELECTQUERY(clusters,size,aDist,π)
    for i = 1 to size do
        U_c(i) = Σ_{s∈clusters(i)} UNCERTAINTY(aDist,π,s)
    end for
    return arg max_i U_c(i)
end function
function UNCERTAINTY(aDist,π,s)
    F(s) = entropy of aDist(s)
    G(s) = entropy of π(s)
    return w_p · F(s) + (1 − w_p) · G(s)
end function
```

3.3 Ordering the Clusters

Now that the state-clusters have been created, the algorithm must decide the order in which to query the clusters. A common method in traditional active learning is called uncertainty sampling [20] that selects examples based on the entropy of the predicted labels (or another uncertainty measure). In IRL, we calculate the uncertainty w.r.t. each state in the feature space. The idea is to ask for more information about states for which the learner is less likely to know the correct action. While the first step of IRL is to learn a reward function, the final output of interest is still a policy, i.e., a mapping from each state to a distribution over the actions. The uncertainty with respect to the reward function may not be equivalent to the uncertainty with respect to the policy as there are many reward functions that result in the same policy [13]. To counter this issue, our approach seeks to combine two potential sources of uncertainty in IRL. The uncertainty might be either due to the paucity of demonstrations or due to the final policy learned from the reward function.

Uncertainty w.r.t. the demonstrations ($F(s_i)$) can be calculated as the entropy $[F(s) = -\sum_{a\in A} P_s(a)log(P_s(a))]$ of the distribution of actions a taken by the expert in state s. As not all states may be visited, Laplace smoothing can be used to ensure there is a valid action distribution in each state. We expect that as the number of actions taken in a particular state by the demonstrator increases, there will be less uncertainty about the reward learned in that particular state.

Uncertainty w.r.t. the policy is more complicated as the final policy is only optimal w.r.t. the learned reward function [21] which is calculated from the set of demonstrations and advice. As the advice changes, new reward functions must be induced leading to different uncertainty over the policy space unlike the uncertainty over the demonstrations which remains constant. There are also various policy strategies once the value function (or q-values) have been learned including ϵ-greedy or Boltzmann distribution. We use the Boltzmann policy:

$$p(s_i, a) = \frac{e^{Q(s_i,a)}}{\sum_{b\in A} e^{Q(s_i,b)}} \tag{3}$$

Then, entropy is used to calculate policy uncertainty.

It is important to mention that the states chosen to solicit advice are the best states to get advice w.r.t. the most

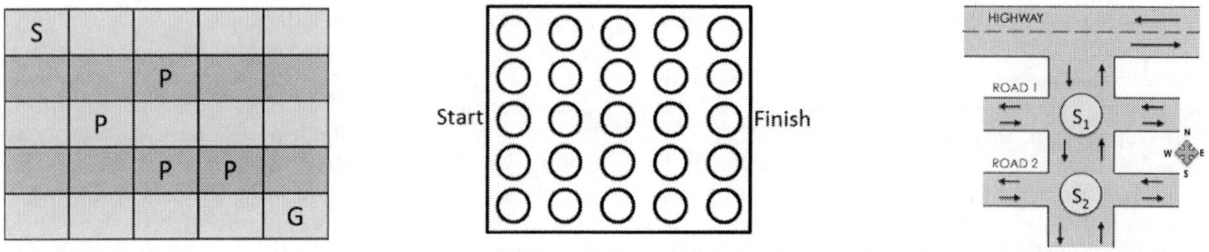

Figure 3: Experimental Domains: WumpusWorld (**LEFT**), Sailing (**CENTER**), Traffic (**RIGHT**)

current reward function. After getting advice, the learner should be able to learn an improved reward function that will in turn provide a potentially different set of uncertain states from which to collect additional advice.

As we will show in several experiments, the ADVISE algorithm is simple, yet effective, in reducing the burden on the expert in two ways. First, while our advice is propositional, we seek general (applying to multiple states) advice as opposed to querying about each state individually. When the state-clusters are large, this reduces the number of queries posed to the expert. The size of these groupings can be controlled based on the query budget. Second, we select the most uncertain queries first. Our hypothesis, which we verify empirically, is that we get sufficient advice even with very few queries.

4. EXPERIMENTS

To evaluate our ADVISE system, we aim to answer the following questions:

General

Q1: Is cluster-level advice effective?

Q2: Does our algorithm correct sub-optimal behaviors?

Q3: Is our algorithm effective in large, realistic problems?

Clustering/Uncertainty Measure

Q4: How effective is the STATECLUSTERING in identifying states with similar optimal actions?

Q5: Does the uncertainty function correctly order clusters?

Q6: How sensitive is the algorithm to sub-optimal state-clusterings?

We demonstrate the performance of ADVISE in three standard domains and one real-world application. In contrast with earlier work [9] focusing on random noise, the demonstrations in our experiments were systematically noisy in certain states. Thus the demonstrator would choose sub-optimal actions in those states. Random actions are also selected with ~10% chance to ensure that they cover the state space. We use GLPK [5] LP solver to learn the rewards and perform value iteration [21]. We consider our expert to be always correct for the purposes of the experiments and use parameter settings $\lambda_t = 1000, \lambda_a = 500$.

WumpusWorld (figure 3.**LEFT**) is an adaptation [9] of a classic domain [21] containing a 5 × 5 grid with several obstacles. The goal is to navigate the grid, avoid the obstacles, and reach the goal state. If the agent enters a state with an obstacle, it loses. The agent can move in four directions. Noise is introduced in specific states by performing sub-optimally. As the goal of this domain is to reach the goal state, performance is measured by the number of times the learned policy is able to reach this state. The results in this domain are from 100 independent trials for learning the reward function.

The **sailing** domain (figure 3.**CENTER**) is a navigation domain where the goal is to sail from one side of a lake to the other. Running aground on the lake causes the agent to crash. The domain is stochastic as wind causes an uncertain transition function, pushing the agent off course depending on the direction of the wind. Our sailing domain consists of a 5 × 5 grid with 2 configurations of the wind. The agent may choose to sail across or laterally for 3 possible actions. As the goal is to reach the dock on the other side, performance is measured as the number of times the agent reaches this state. The main experiment is over 100 independent trials while cluster quality experiments are run 250 times [6].

The **traffic signal** domain (figure 3.**RIGHT**) controls the signals at two intersections. Each stoplight has four possible configurations to let cars through the light by letting cars coming from a single cardinal direction through at once. The different roads around these intersections have different levels of traffic throughput resulting in 256 possible states. The goal of this domain is to reduce the wait time of the cars waiting at the intersection. All the results in this domain are over 100 independent trials.

Finally, we consider a real-world **drone flying** domain where the goal is to fly a quad-copter in a particular path. The position of the drone is collected using a built-in GPS sensor. In our experiments, we consider moving in the four possible cardinal directions. We considered only a constant altitude. The goal of the domain is to navigate the drone through a sequential set of waypoints on the way to the final position. We consider 3 waypoints (in each corner of a room). The optimal path is shown in figure 4 along with an image of the drone as it is navigating. Note that performance is measured in the percentage of time the agent reaches the waypoints in order and flies to the final destination. The agent has a finite number of opportunities to reach the final state before the battery resource is depleted. This domain is difficult for the demonstrator as the drone controls can be imprecise. Therefore, the demonstrations are noisy 40% of the time.

Methods considered: We compare the performance of our ADVISE system (called *Clustered Advice*) to several

[5]http://www.gnu.org/software/glpk

[6]Note that similar results can be shown with 100 runs.

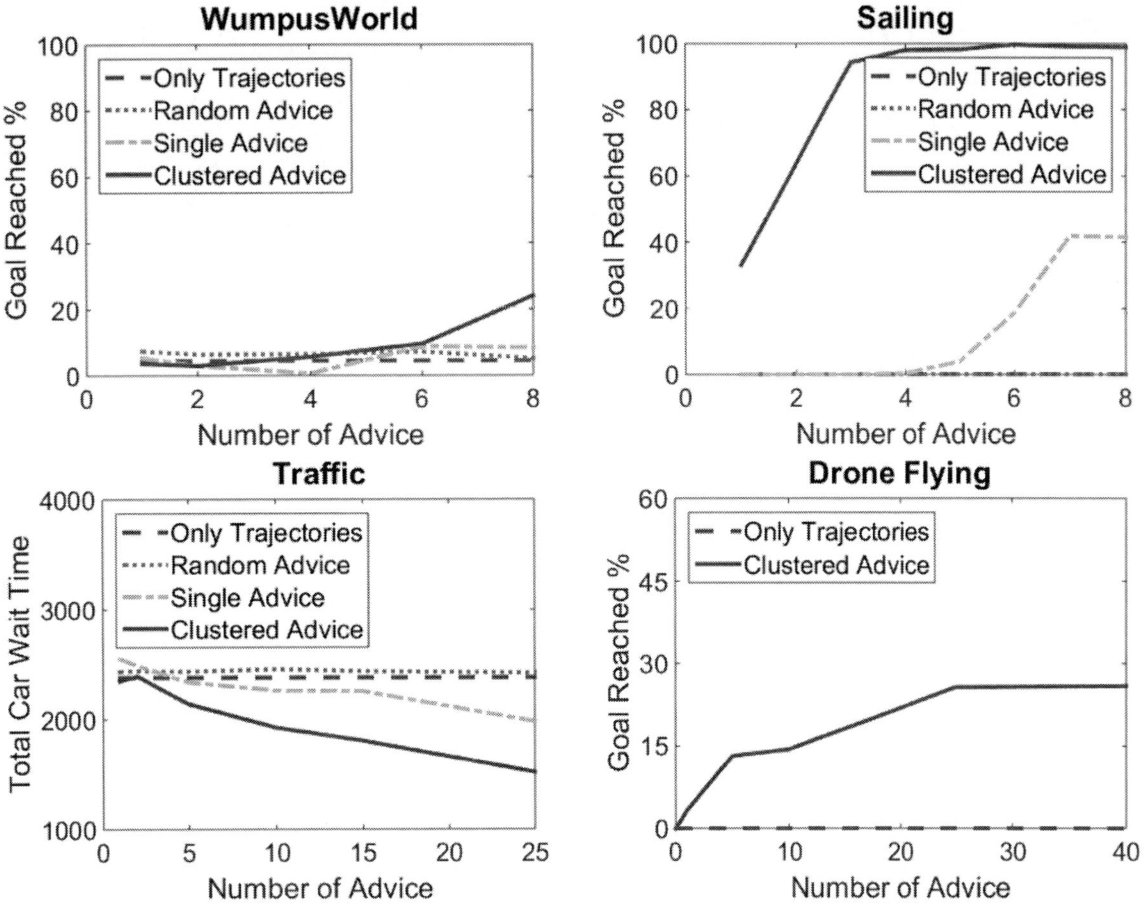

Figure 5: Results for varying the amount of advice in the WumpusWorld (**UPPERLEFT**), Sailing (**UPPERRIGHT**), Traffic (**LOWERLEFT**), and Drone (**LOWERRIGHT**) domains. Performance is measured in domain-specific performance measures. In all cases, our clustered advice outperforms the baselines.

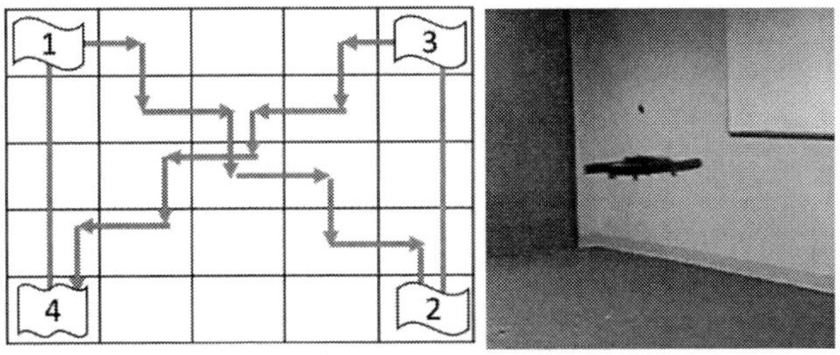

Figure 4: The LEFT image shows an example of the optimal path that the drone should follow. It must visit the waypoints (flags) in order before returning to the starting position. The RIGHT image shows a screenshot of the drone in action.

baselines including only (1) learning from the demonstrations (called *Only Trajectories*), (2) learning from advice over single states instead of advice over the entire cluster (called *Single Advice*), and (3) learning with advice on randomly selected states (called *Random Advice*). When querying about a single state, the expert returns the advice about that particular state. When querying about a group of states, the human expert is responsible for giving advice that is most relevant to the cluster. One possible metric that we use in our experiments is providing preferred actions that appear as optimal actions in the most number of states in the cluster. While this is one strategy, human experts may identify more important states in a cluster. Exploration of these strategies is a area for future work.

Results: We will first discuss results from WumpusWorld, Sailing and Traffic before explaining our progress in the Drone Flying domain. Following the prior work on advice giving, the domains we consider have systematic noise in them. The hypothesis is that ADVISE will correct these behaviors in the learned reward function and therefore in the final policy. Please note that advice is provided only on solicitation by the algorithm and not apriori. Consequently, we evaluate our ADVISE algorithm in different ways: to test whether the advice contributes to the policy, we compare against only using the trajectories; to test whether the STATECLUSTERING generates good advice, we compare against soliciting single pieces of advice; to test the uncertainty measure, we compare against random advice.

The results are shown in figure 5. Please note that in WumpusWorld and Sailing, a higher goal reached % means higher performance, while in Traffic, a lower wait time means higher performance. There are several general trends across all the domains. As the amount of advice increases, the

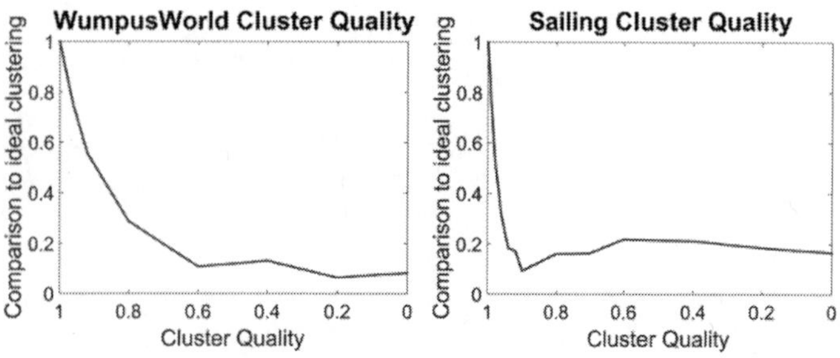

Figure 6: Results for varying the quality of the cluster in the WumpusWorld (**LEFT**) and Sailing (**RIGHT**) domains. Performance is measured relative to the ideal clustering.

performance of the advice methods (other than random) increase. It is clear that advice significantly contributes to the learned policy in all domains (**Q2**). Furthermore, clustered advice yields significantly higher gains much more quickly than soliciting a single piece of advice (**Q1**). Not only is performance higher with clustered advice, it also decreases the number of queries an expert has to answer. This results in significant time savings for the human expert.

For further analysis of these results, we computed the quality of the learned clusters. We defined the quality of the clusters to be the fraction of states which are in a cluster with similar states (states with similar optimal actions). Note we consider the plurality of the cluster to be similar and all other states to be dissimilar. For reference, the minimum possible value for this metric is 25% (WumpusWorld), 33.3% (Sailing), 6.3% (Traffic). For these experiments (100 independent trials), the quality of the clusters is the following: 94.2% (WumpusWorld), 91.3% (Sailing), 69.58% (Traffic). Each of these domains has a fairly high value suggesting that our algorithm is able to identify similar states (**Q4**). There is also room for improvement suggesting that our algorithm could perform better if the clustering algorithm could be improved.

Ideally, the algorithm should target the sub-optimal regions of the state space when requesting advice. Unfortunately, this is very difficult to capture correctly. However, as seen in the experiments, with only a few clustered pieces of advice the algorithm significantly outperforms all of the baselines. This is especially true in the Sailing and Traffic domains. This suggests that our algorithm is able to target these regions, thus answering **Q5** affirmatively.

Varying Cluster Quality: As our method is dependent on the quality of the clusters generated, we investigate how varying the cluster quality impacts the performance. We replace the automatic clustering (StateClustering function in algorithm 1) with a static clustering defined by experts. These clusterings will be optimal in the sense that states appearing in the same cluster will require the same advice. We then measure the performance of the algorithm as we perturb the static clustering. For example when cluster quality is 50%, half of the states will be displaced into incorrect clusters (and thus receive incorrect advice). We compare the performance (goal reached % used in previous experiments) of each sub-optimal clustering to the ideal clustering. Therefore, a performance of 1.0 means that the performance is equal to using an ideal clustering.

We present results for two domains: WumpusWorld (figure 6.**LEFT**) and Sailing (figure 6.**RIGHT**). As expected, in both domains, as the cluster quality decreases, the performance decreases. This confirms the suspicion that the clustering technique is vital to taking the most advantage of expert advice. This answers question **Q6** that the algorithm is reasonably sensitive to sub-optimal state-clusterings. However, as seen in the previous experiments, our algorithm is still able to improve performance by using reasonable approximations of the clusterings.

Real-World Application: In order to show the applicability of our approach on realistic problems and not just on standard benchmarks, we focus on a drone flying domain where the goal is to control a drone as it flies to particular waypoints. This is an especially difficult problem as the drone must visit the waypoints in a particular order to successfully complete the task. We compare only our clustered advise and using only trajectories as this domain represents a proof of concept (figure 5.**LOWERRIGHT**). The difficulty of the problem is clear as noisy trajectories are not sufficient to learn a reasonable policy. However, our clustered advice is capable of guiding the drone more reliably. This domain suggests that our algorithm is effective in large, realistic domains (**Q3**).

5. CONCLUSION

We have presented a new formalism for active advice-seeking. Like traditional active learning, the learning algorithm is responsible for querying the expert about areas of uncertainty. However, unlike active learning, advice is solicited over an area of the state space (multiple states) to further reduce the queries directed to the expert. We demonstrate our algorithm through an advice-taking for inverse reinforcement learning framework and develop an uncertainty function for learning a policy through demonstrations. We demonstrate the validity of our approach in three standard domains and show its applicability to a real-world task. Improving both the clustering technique and the uncertainty measure are clear areas for future improvement. Also, our technique could be improved through relational techniques that would increase the expressiveness of our advice. Our clustering of the ground states is a way of approximating the underlying structure that relational techniques could make use of more faithfully.

6. ACKNOWLEDGMENTS

The authors thank the Army Research Office (ARO) grant number W911NF-13-1-0432 under the Young Investigator Program and the CwC Program Contract W911NF-15-1-0461 with the US Defense Advanced Research Projects Agency (DARPA) and the ARO. Any opinions, findings and conclusion or recommendations expressed in this material are those of the authors and do not necessarily reflect the view of the DARPA, ARO or the US government. The authors also acknowledge the support of PARC XEROX through their faculty award. The authors thank Juan Zapata Valencia for his work with the drone.

REFERENCES

[1] P. Abbeel and A. Y. Ng. Apprenticeship learning via inverse reinforcement learning. In *ICML*, 2004.

[2] C. Boutilier. A POMDP formulation of preference elicitation problems. In *AAAI*, pages 239–246, 2002.

[3] M. Cakmak and A. Thomaz. Active learning with mixed query types in learning from demonstration. In *ICML Workshop on New Developments in Imitation Learning*, 2011.

[4] J. Choi and K.-E. Kim. Inverse reinforcement learning in partially observable environments. *JMLR*, 12:691–730, 2011.

[5] M. Hamidi, P. Tadepalli, R. Goetschalckx, and A. Fern. Active imitation learning of hierarchical policies. In *IJCAI*, 2015.

[6] H. He, H. Daume III, and J. Eisner. Imitation learning by coaching. In *NIPS*, 2012.

[7] A. K. Jain and R. C. Dubes. *Algorithms for Clustering Data*. Prentice-Hall Inc., Upper Saddle River, NJ, 1988.

[8] K. Judah, A. Fern, P. Tadepalli, and R. Goetschalckx. Imitation learning with demonstrations and shaping rewards. In *AAAI*, 2014.

[9] G. Kunapuli, P. Odom, J. Shavlik, and S. Natarajan. Guiding autonomous agents to better behaviors through human advice. In *ICDM*, 2013.

[10] D. Lewis and W. Gale. A sequential algorithm for training text classifiers. In *ACM SIGIR*, 1994.

[11] L. Li, M. Littman, T. Walsh, and A. Stregl. Knows what it knows: a framework for self-aware learning. *Machine Learning*, 82(3):399–443, 2011.

[12] P. Li, C. Burges, and Q. Wu. Mcrank: Learning to rank using mulitple classification and gradient boosting. In *NIPS*, 2007.

[13] M. Lopes, F. Melo, and L. Montesano. Active learning for reward estimation in inverse reinforcement learning. In *ECML*, 2009.

[14] S. Natarajan, G. Kunapuli, K. Judah, P. Tadepalli, K. Kersting, and J. Shavlik. Multi-agent inverse reinforcement learning. In *ICMLA*, 2010.

[15] S. Natarajan, P. Odom, S. Joshi, T. Khot, K. Kersting, and P. Tadepalli. Accelerating imitation learning in relational domains via transfer by initialization. In *ILP*, 2013.

[16] A. Ng and S. Russell. Algorithms for inverse reinforcement learning. In *ICML*, 2000.

[17] D. Ramachandran and E. Amir. Bayesian inverse reinforcement learning. In *IJCAI*, 2007.

[18] C. Rothkopf and C. Dimitrakakis. Preference elicitation and inverse reinforcement learning. In *ECML-PKDD*, 2011.

[19] G. Schohn and D. Cohn. Less is more: Active learning with support vector machines. In *ICML*, 2000.

[20] B. Settles. *Active Learning*. Morgan & Claypool, 2012.

[21] R. S. Sutton and A. G. Barto. *Reinforcement Learning: An Introduction (Adaptive Computation and Machine Learning)*. The MIT Press, Cambridge, MA, 1998.

[22] S. Tong and D. Koller. Active learning for parameter estimation in bayesian networks. In *NIPS*, 2000.

[23] S. Tong and D. Koller. Active learning for structure in bayesian networks. In *IJCAI*, 2001.

[24] T. Walsh. Uncertainty in preference elicitation and aggregation. In *AAAI*, 2007.

Resource Abstraction for Reinforcement Learning in Multiagent Congestion Problems

Kleanthis Malialis*
Dept. of Computer Science
University College London, UK
k.malialis@ucl.ac.uk

Sam Devlin
Dept. of Computer Science
University of York, UK
sam.devlin@york.ac.uk

Daniel Kudenko
Dept. of Computer Science
University of York, UK
daniel.kudenko@york.ac.uk

ABSTRACT

Real-world congestion problems (e.g. traffic congestion) are typically very complex and large-scale. Multiagent reinforcement learning (MARL) is a promising candidate for dealing with this emerging complexity by providing an autonomous and distributed solution to these problems. However, there are three limiting factors that affect the deployability of MARL approaches to congestion problems. These are learning time, scalability and decentralised coordination i.e. no communication between the learning agents. In this paper we introduce Resource Abstraction, an approach that addresses these challenges by allocating the available resources into abstract groups. This abstraction creates new reward functions that provide a more informative signal to the learning agents and aid the coordination amongst them. Experimental work is conducted on two benchmark domains from the literature, an abstract congestion problem and a realistic traffic congestion problem. The current state-of-the-art for solving multiagent congestion problems is a form of reward shaping called difference rewards. We show that the system using Resource Abstraction significantly improves the learning speed and scalability, and achieves the highest possible or near-highest joint performance/social welfare for both congestion problems in large-scale scenarios involving up to 1000 reinforcement learning agents.

CCS Concepts

•Computing methodologies → Multi-agent systems; Multi-agent reinforcement learning;

Keywords

Multiagent learning; Resource abstraction; Congestion problems

1. INTRODUCTION

There has been in recent years an explosion of interest in multiagent systems (MAS) where multiple interacting agents are situated in a common environment. A larger set of problem domains can be practically modelled using MAS for example by taking advantage of the geographic distribution and sharing experiences for faster and better learning [8]. MAS often need to be very complex, and MARL is a promising candidate for dealing with this emerging complexity [7]. MARL approaches provide adaptive and autonomous agents that can improve from experience.

Congestion problems have been formulated in the past as MARL problems [10, 11, 6, 3]. Congestion problems are typically very complex and large-scale. Real-life examples include traffic congestion, air traffic management and network routing. Despite the benefits offered by MARL approaches there are three limiting factors that affect their deployability to real-world congestion problems; these are, learning time, scalability and decentralised coordination i.e. no communication between learning agents.

Firstly, learning time is of particular importance to offline learning and critical to online learning. If a MARL system is slow it may be practically useless even if it eventually achieves a great performance. Furthermore, in real-life complex congestion problems, learning time is typically limited.

Secondly, the curse of dimensionality [9] refers to the exponential growth of the search space, in terms of the number of states and actions. If a MARL solution is not scalable, it will never be considered, let alone adopted, for deployment by a company or organisation.

Lastly, while sharing experiences may be beneficial and even necessary in specific applications, allowing communication between the learning agents is not always desirable or even possible. This is because agents may have been developed by different designers or controlled by different owners. Even if this is not the case, communication messages can be costly, noisy, corrupted, dropped or received out of order [5].

In this paper we introduce Resource Abstraction, an approach that addresses the aforementioned challenges. Experiments are conducted on two benchmark domains from the literature; an abstract congestion problem and a realistic traffic congestion problem where agents or cars "compete" for traffic lanes. Our contributions are the following.

We propose the novel Resource Abstraction approach where its main idea is to allocate the available resources into groups called abstract groups. This grouping provides an abstract (A) reward function that is more informative and aids the coordination among the learning agents to significantly improve the learning speed, scalability and agents' final joint performance or social welfare.

*Most of this work was carried out when the author was at the University of York, UK.

Appears in: *Proceedings of the 15th International Conference on Autonomous Agents and Multiagent Systems (AAMAS 2016), J. Thangarajah, K. Tuyls, C. Jonker, S. Marsella (eds.), May 9–13, 2016, Singapore.*

We compare our approach against systems which learn from local (L), global (G) and difference (D) rewards. The first two are the common approaches while the third is a form of reward shaping that constitutes the state-of-the-art for solving multiagent congestion problems.

Like D, the system using A provides decentralised coordination. It is further shown that the system using A requires significantly fewer time steps per learning episode to achieve the highest system performance or social welfare in large-scale scenarios. The proposed approach scales to a large number of agents and is successfully demonstrated in experiments involving up to 1000 learning agents.

The organisation of this paper is as follows. Section 2 describes the background material necessary to understand the contributions made by this work. Section 3 presents a formal definition of congestion problems as multiagent learning and coordination problems. Section 4 introduces in detail our proposed Resource Abstraction approach. Section 5 and Section 6 provide the experimental work and results for the abstract and traffic congestion problems respectively. A discussion and conclusion is presented in Section 7.

2. BACKGROUND

2.1 Reinforcement Learning

Reinforcement learning is a paradigm in which an active decision-making agent interacts with its environment and learns from reinforcement, that is, a numeric feedback in the form of reward or punishment [9]. The feedback received is used to improve the agent's actions. The problem of solving a reinforcement learning task is to find a policy (i.e. a mapping from states to actions) which maximises the accumulated reward.

The concept of an iterative approach constitutes the backbone of the majority of reinforcement learning algorithms. These algorithms apply so called temporal-difference updates to propagate information about values of states, $V(s)$, or state-action, $Q(s, a)$, pairs. These updates are based on the difference of the two temporally different estimates of a particular state or state-action value. The Q-learning algorithm is such a method [12]. After each real transition, $(s, a) \rightarrow (s', r)$, in the environment, it updates state-action values by the formula:

$$Q(s, a) \leftarrow Q(s, a) + \alpha[r + \gamma \max_{a'} Q(s', a') - Q(s, a)] \quad (1)$$

where α is the rate of learning and γ is the discount factor.

The exploration-exploitation trade-off constitutes a critical issue in the design of a reinforcement learning agent. It aims to offer a balance between the exploitation of the agent's knowledge and the exploration through which the agent's knowledge is enriched. A common method of doing so is ϵ-greedy, where the agent behaves greedily most of the time, but with a probability ϵ it selects an action randomly. To get the best of both exploration and exploitation, it is advised to reduce ϵ over time [9].

Applications of MARL typically take one of two approaches; multiple individual learners (ILs) or joint action learners (JALs) [1]. Multiple ILs assume any other agents to be part of the environment and so, as the others simultaneously learn, the environment appears to be dynamic as the probability of transition when taking action a in state s changes over time. To overcome the appearance of a dynamic environment, JALs were developed that extend their value function to consider for each state the value of each possible combination of actions by all agents. The consideration of the joint action causes an exponential increase in the number of values that must be calculated with each additional agent added to the system. Therefore, as we are interested in scalability and decentralised coordination (i.e. no communication between agents), this work focuses on multiple individual learners and not joint action learners.

In MARL the typical approach provides agents with one of two types of reward. A **local reward (L)** is unique to each agent and often promotes "selfish" behaviours since each agent attempts to increase its own reward, potentially at the cost of the system performance. The **global reward (G)** is in fact the system performance used as a learning signal[1]. This allows each agent to act in the system's interest and typically, the learnt behaviour is better compared to the case where agents are learning using L.

G, however, includes a substantial amount of noise due to other agents acting in the system. This is because an agent may be rewarded for taking a bad action (if the other agents executed a good action), or punished for taking a good action (if the others performed a bad action). This is known as the multiagent credit assignment problem. The reward signal should reward an agent depending on its individual contribution to the system objective. Difference rewards [13], a form of reward shaping, address this issue and are discussed in the next section.

2.2 Difference Rewards

Difference rewards [13] were introduced to address the multiagent credit assignment problem encountered in reinforcement learning. The **difference rewards (D_i)** is a shaped reward signal that helps an agent i to learn the consequences of its actions on the system objective by removing a large amount of the noise created by the actions of other agents active in the system. It is defined as:

$$D_i(z) = G(z) - G(z_{-i}) \quad (2)$$

where z is a general term representative of either states or state-action pairs depending on the application, $G(z)$ is the global reward used, and $G(z_{-i})$ is $G(z)$ for a theoretical system without the contribution of agent i.

Difference rewards exhibit the following two properties. Firstly, any action taken that increases D_i simultaneously increases G. Secondly, since difference rewards only depend on the actions of agent i, D_i provides a cleaner signal with reduced noise. These properties allow for the difference rewards to significantly boost learning performance in a MAS.

The challenge for deriving the difference rewards signal is obviously how to calculate the second term of the equation $G(z_{-i})$ which is called the *counterfactual*. In particular domains, the counterfactual $G(z_{-i})$ is possible to be directly calculated [11, 3]. Alternatively, in cases where this is not possible, it has been demonstrated that difference rewards can be estimated [10, 6].

Difference rewards have been successfully applied in different domains such as congestion problems [10, 11, 6, 3], network security [4] and distributed sensor networks [2].

[1]The terms global reward, system performance and social welfare are used interchangeably.

3. CONGESTION PROBLEMS AS MULTI-AGENT LEARNING PROBLEMS

This section provides a formal definition of congestion problems as multiagent learning problems. A congestion problem occurs when multiple entities are competing for a limited amount of available resources. Different congestion problems (traffic congestion, air traffic management, Beach problem, El Farol Bar problem) have been formulated in the past as multiagent learning problems [10, 11, 6, 3].

Formally, there exists a set S of n resources $S = \{s_1, s_2, ..., s_n\}$. Each resource s is a 3-tuple $s =< w_s, \psi_s, x_{s,t} >$ where $w_s \geq 0$ is the weighting or importance of resource s, $\psi_s > 0$ is the capacity of resource s, and $x_{s,t} \geq 0$ is the consumption of resource s at time t. A resource s at time t is said to be congested if its consumption is higher than its capacity i.e. $x_{s,t} > \psi_s$.

The local reward (L) of an entity located in resource s at time t depends on the resource's weighting, capacity and consumption as shown in Equation 3:

$$L(s,t) = f(w_s, \psi_s, x_{s,t}) \tag{3}$$

The global reward (G) is defined as the summation over all local rewards and is given by Equation 4.

$$G(t) = \sum_{s \in S} L(s,t) \tag{4}$$

Recall from Section 2.2 that the difference rewards signal is calculated by subtracting the counterfactual from the global reward. Therefore, the difference rewards (D) for agent i located in section s at time t can be calculated using Equation 5.

$$\begin{aligned} D_i(t) &= G(t) - G_{-i}(t) \\ &= L(s,t) - L_{-i}(s,t) \end{aligned} \tag{5}$$

The straightforward approach is to consider the entities which compete for the resources as the learning agents. For instance, in a traffic congestion domain [11] where the entities are cars which compete for traffic lanes, we can install a learning agent on each car. In such domains, there is no need to estimate the counterfactual as it can simply be calculated by decreasing the resource's consumption or attendance by 1 as shown in Equation 6

$$\begin{aligned} D_i(t) &= L(s,t) - L_{-i}(s,t) \\ &= f(w_s, \psi_s, x_{s,t}) - f(w_s, \psi_s, x_{s,t} - 1) \end{aligned} \tag{6}$$

Alternatively, there exist congestion problems where learning agents are not installed on the entities competing for the resources and in such cases the counterfactual needs to be estimated [10]. Although estimating D_i has been successfully demonstrated in a number of applications this topic is under ongoing research [6].

4. RESOURCE ABSTRACTION

The idea behind our approach is to allocate the available resources into groups called abstract groups which provide a more informative signal to the learning agents.

Formally, there exists a set B of p abstract groups: $B = \{b_1, b_2, ..., b_p\}$. Each abstract group b is a 4-tuple:
$b =< M_b, W_b, \Psi_b, X_{b,t} >$.

The set $M_b = \{m_1, m_2, ..., m_k\}$ is the member set of abstract group b that consists of k resources. A resource m can belong only to one abstract group, that is, $m \in M_i$ and $m \in M_j$ only if $i = j$. The number of abstract groups (and their members) depends on the application domain.

The weight W_b of abstract group b is defined as the average weight of its members as shown in Equation 7.

$$W_b = \frac{1}{k} \sum_{m \in M_b} w_m \tag{7}$$

The capacity Ψ_b of abstract group b is the total capacity of its members. Similarly, the consumption $X_{b,t}$ of abstract group b at time t is the total consumption of its members. These are calculated using Equations 8 and 9.

$$\Psi_b = \sum_{m \in M_b} \psi_m \tag{8}$$

$$X_{b,t} = \sum_{m \in M_b} x_{m,t} \tag{9}$$

As discussed, the straightforward approach is to consider the entities which compete for the resources as the learning agents. However, depending on the application, this may not necessarily be the case, and our proposed approach does not impose any limitations on the agent selection.

Let us now introduce the proposed reward functions. We start by extending the local reward $L(s,t)$, and define the signal $H(b,t)$ for an abstract group b at time t. It is calculated by taking into account the abstract group's weight, capacity and consumption as shown in Equation 10. It is important to note that the function $f(\cdot)$ is the same which is used to calculate the local reward L (see Equation 3).

$$H(b,t) = -f(W_b, \Psi_b, X_{b,t}) \tag{10}$$

The **abstract reward** (A) is defined as follows. When resource s which belongs to abstract group b is not congested, we provide a reward from $L(s,t)$. Alternatively, we provide a reward from the abstraction configuration i.e. from $H(b,t)$. This is shown in Equation 11.

$$A(b,s,t) = \begin{cases} L(s,t) & \text{if } x_{s,t} \leq \psi_s \\ H(b,t) & \text{if } x_{s,t} > \psi_s \end{cases} \tag{11}$$

where $s \in M_b$.

The intuition behind this reward function is to facilitate the coordination among the learning agents by providing them with a more informative signal. Assuming a "good" abstraction configuration (as mentioned, this is application domain-specific), the abstract reward (A) will provide a bigger (than L) punishment to the agents to encourage them to keep resources decongested. Furthermore, as we will later demonstrate, in domains where the number of entities competing for the resources is greater than the number of available resources, the desired solution is to congest only a minimal amount of them (e.g. only one) and leave the rest decongested. The approach will encourage some agents to consume a congested resource. In such cases the agents already receive a punishment, but they will be provided with a bigger punishment if the agents attempt to switch to a decongested abstract group and congest it.

5. BEACH PROBLEM DOMAIN (BPD)

5.1 Domain Description

The Beach Problem Domain (BPD) [3] is an abstract congestion problem that relates to many real-life congestion problems and allows us to perform a thorough analysis of our proposed approach. In this domain, each tourist (learning agent) gets to choose the beach section it will visit. At each time step each agent knows which beach section it is currently on and must choose to either stay still or move to an adjacent beach section (i.e. left or right).

When all the agents have performed their actions, they receive a reward. The highest reward for a beach section is received when the attendance of agents is equal to the capacity of the beach section. If a beach section gets congested or overcrowded it is undesirable. Beach sections with low attendance are also undesirable. This constitutes a congestion problem when the number of agents is much greater than the total capacity of the beach sections.

In this abstract congestion problem it is assumed that all beach sections have an equal weighting of 1 and they all have the same capacity ψ. The local reward function (L) is given by Equation 12:

$$L(s,t) = x_{s,t} e^{\frac{-x_{s,t}}{\psi}} \tag{12}$$

where s is the beach section and $x_{s,t}$ is the attendance of beach section s at time step t.

The global reward (G) is a summation over all local rewards and is given by Equation 13.

$$G(t) = \sum_{s \in S} x_{s,t} e^{\frac{-x_{s,t}}{\psi}} \tag{13}$$

The difference rewards (D) signal is calculated by applying Equation 6 to Equation 12. This results in Equation 14.

$$D_i(t) = x_{s,t} e^{\frac{-x_{s,t}}{\psi}} - x_{s,t} e^{\frac{-(x_{s,t}-1)}{\psi}} \tag{14}$$

Similarly to the local reward function, we define the corresponding reward function for an abstraction configuration B (defined as described in Section 4). Therefore, the application of Equation 10 to Equation 12 results in Equation 15:

$$H(b,t) = -X_{b,t} e^{\frac{-X_{b,t}}{\Psi_b}} \tag{15}$$

where b is the abstract group, $X_{b,t}$ is the attendance at time step t, and Ψ_b is the capacity of abstract group b.

Lastly, the abstract reward (A) is calculated by applying Equation 11 and is shown in Equation 16.

$$A(b,s,t) = \begin{cases} x_{s,t} e^{\frac{-x_{s,t}}{\psi}} & \text{if } x_{s,t} \leq \psi \\ -X_{b,t} e^{\frac{-X_{b,t}}{\Psi_b}} & \text{if } x_{s,t} > \psi \end{cases} \tag{16}$$

where $s \in M_b$.

Algorithm 1 presents what has been described thus far. Before describing the experimental work, we should note that the best solution for this problem is to overcrowd one (any) beach section, and leave ψ number of agents in the rest of the sections. This will give the highest possible system performance or global reward.

Algorithm 1 Beach Problem with Resource Abstraction

define abstraction configuration B
initialise Q-values: $\forall s, a | Q(s,a) = -1$
set agents to initial locations
for *episode* $= 1$: *num_episodes* **do**
  for *timestep* $= 1$: *num_timesteps* **do**
    for *agent* $= 1$: *num_agents* **do**
      perceive current beach section $s \in S$
      choose action $a = \{-1, 0, +1\}$ using ϵ-greedy
      move to section $s' = \{s-1, 0, s+1\}$
      if $s' \notin S$ **then**
        move to nearest section $s' \in S$
      end if
    end for
    for *section* $= 1$: *num_sections* **do**
      calculate A reward (Equation 16)
    end for
    for *agent* $= 1$: *num_agents* **do**
      update Q(s,a) using A (Equation 1)
    end for
    reduce α using *alpha_decay_rate*
    reduce ϵ using *epsilon_decay_rate*
  end for
  reset agents to initial locations
end for

5.2 Experimental Setup

Our experimental setup is as follows. The learning rate is set to $\alpha = 0.1$ and *alpha_decay_rate* $= 0.9999$. The exploration parameter is set to $\epsilon = 0.05$ and *epsilon_decay_rate* $= 0.9999$. The discount factor is set to $\gamma = 1.0$ and the number of episodes is set to *num_episodes* $= 10000$. Initially, the agents are uniformly distributed (i.e. it is assumed that there exist hotels for the tourists in each beach section). The rest of the parameters are given later for each experiment. In all experiments, we plot the system performance/global reward G at the last time step of each episode. The values are averaged over 30 statistical runs and error bars showing the standard error around the mean are plotted. In some plots the error bars are very small and hardly visible, but they are present on all plots.

5.3 Experimental Results

We have set *num_agents* $= 100$, *num_sections* $= 6$, capacity $\psi = 6$ and *num_timesteps* $= 5$. The highest social welfare or global reward is 11.04 and occurs when one (any) of the six sections is overcrowded with 70 agents, while each of the remaining five sections have six agents; this is shown with a black dashed line in all figures.

The first experimental study investigates how different abstraction (A) configurations affect the performance, and how they compare to the approaches which use the local (L), global (G) and difference (D) rewards. Figure 1 demonstrates this with abstraction configurations of two and three abstract groups. For example, the plot with label "A-4+2" means that the first four beach sections are grouped into one abstract group, while the remaining two beach sections are grouped into another abstract group. There are four important outcomes from this study:

- Abstraction selection does affect the system performance.

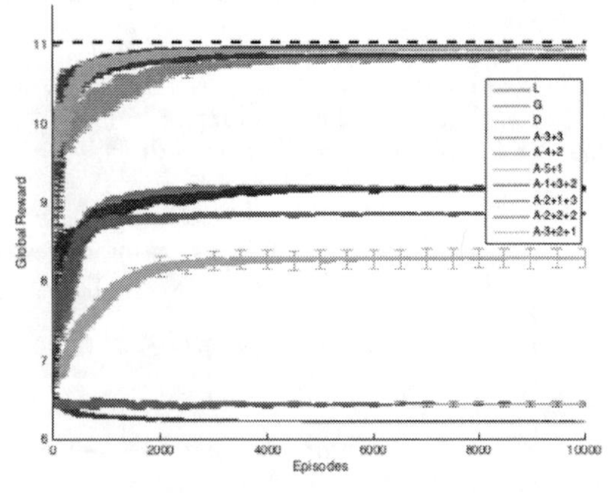

Figure 1: Abstraction configurations

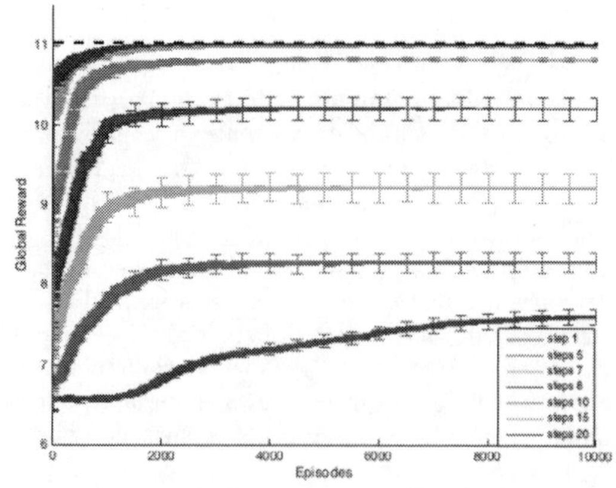

Figure 2: Impact of episode length on D

- However, all the abstractions outperform the system that uses the difference (D) rewards (third plot from the bottom).
- The abstraction "A-2+1+3" achieves the highest performance while three other achieve a near-highest performance. The system using D never achieves the highest social welfare.
- All the abstractions outperform the systems that use the local (L) and global (G) rewards (bottom two plots).

The second experimental study examines how the episode length i.e. number of time steps per episode affects the system performance. Recall that at the start of each new episode, that is, after the last time step of the previous episode (Algorithm 1/Line 23) the agents return to their initial location. It is important to note that changing the length of the episode produces a different and independent version of the problem.

In Figure 2 we apply D in different versions of the BPD, where we vary the time (episode length) agents are allowed to settle to a beach section within an episode. Note that with five or more time steps per episode, an agent located at the far left (or right) beach section can, in principle, move to the far right (or left) section at the end of an episode. However, D achieves the highest performance only in BPD versions with episode length of 15 time steps or more.

We now run the same experiment for the proposed Resource Abstraction approach. Based on previous findings (Figure 1) we proceed with abstraction "A-2+1+3". Figure 3 depicts the performance of A in different BPD versions. It is observed that the highest social welfare is achieved in all BPD versions except when a single time step is used. Also, A learns faster and achieves a significantly higher final performance than D in all BPD versions except from versions with episode length of 15 steps or more, where both have a similar performance. These are important results for potential real-world applications as they show that A is more robust to changes in the problem domain (i.e. episode length) than the current state-of-the-art approach D.

The third experimental study of BPD aims at investigating the scalability of the proposed approach. The setup for this study involves num_agents = 1000, $num\_sections$ =

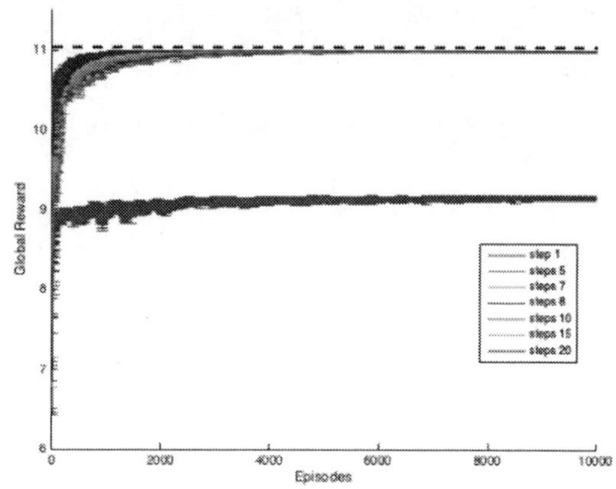

Figure 3: Impact of episode length on A

20, capacity $\psi = 18$ and $num\_timesteps$ = 5. The highest social welfare is 125.82 and is shown with a black dashed line in all figures.

Like before, we have investigated a range of abstraction configurations and many of them are shown in Figure 4. We observe the following. All the abstractions except one (third plot from the bottom) outperform the system that uses the difference (D) rewards (fourth plot from the bottom). All the abstractions outperform the systems that use the local (L) and global (G) rewards (bottom two plots). Note that no approach manages to achieve the best performance in just five time steps per episode. However, taking into consideration the scale of the scenario (1000 agents, 20 sections), some of the abstractions (see upper plots in Figure 4) perform extremely well.

We proceed with abstraction "A-8+1+11" and repeat the same experiment with ten and 20 time steps per episode; results are shown in Figures 5 and 6 respectively. In both figures, the system using A achieves a near-highest performance. The system using D performs orders of magnitude better than the local (L) and global (G) rewards, but still it is significantly outperformed by the proposed A approach.

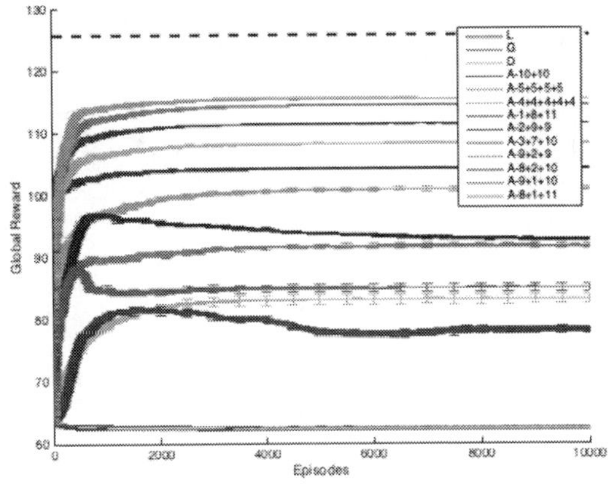

Figure 4: BPD with 1000 agents, 5 time steps

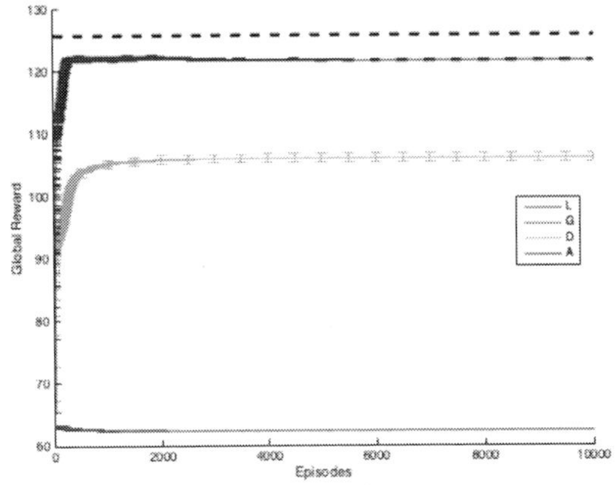

Figure 5: BPD with 1000 agents, 10 time steps

6. TRAFFIC LANE DOMAIN (TLD)

6.1 Domain Description

Despite the BPD being an abstract congestion problem, it is very important as it relates to many real-world congestion problems. One such complex problem is the Traffic Lane Domain (TLD) [11] which is defined as follows.

In this domain each car (learning agent) gets to choose which traffic lane to follow. Each agent knows at each time step which lane it currently follows. At each time step, each agent can either stay in the same lane, or move to an adjacent lane (i.e. left or right). Once all the agents have executed their actions, they receive a reward.

To simulate real-life characteristics there are three major differences with the BPD: *1.* traffic lanes have a different weighting (represents the different preference of drivers) *2.* lanes have different capacities (represents the fact that lanes are of different sizes, or that there exist restrictions due to construction works, tolls, carpools etc.) and *3.* it has a different reward function as it doesn't matter how many cars are on a lane as long as the lane is not congested (as opposed to a beach section which is desirable to have more people as long as it is not overcrowded).

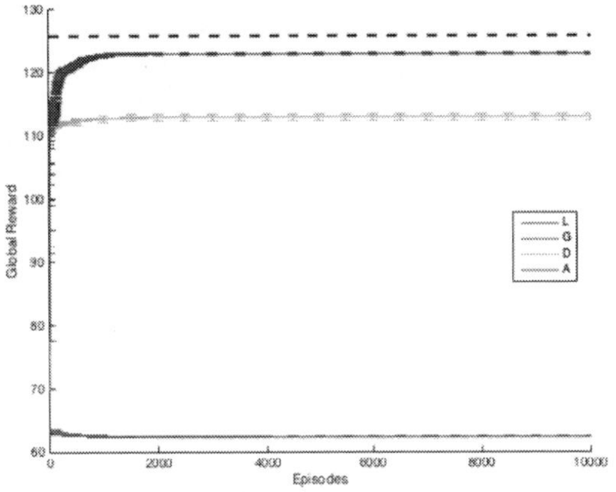

Figure 6: BPD with 1000 agents, 20 time steps

The local reward (L) function is given in Equation 17:

$$L(s,t) = \begin{cases} w_s e^{-1} & \text{if } x_{s,t} \leq \psi_s \\ w_s e^{\frac{-x_{s,t}}{\psi_s}} & \text{if } x_{s,t} > \psi_s \end{cases} \tag{17}$$

where s is the traffic lane, w_s is the weighting, $x_{s,t}$ is the attendance at time step t and ψ_s is the capacity.

The global (G) and difference (D) rewards are calculated using Equations 4 and 6 respectively.

The application of Equation 10 to Equation 17 is shown in Equation 18:

$$H(b,t) = \begin{cases} -W_b e^{-1} & \text{if } X_{b,t} \leq \Psi_b \\ -W_b e^{\frac{-X_{b,t}}{\Psi_b}} & \text{if } X_{b,t} > \Psi_b \end{cases} \tag{18}$$

where b is the abstract group, W_b is the weighting, $X_{b,t}$ is the attendance at time step t, and Ψ_b is the capacity. Lastly, the abstract reward (A) is calculated using Equation 11.

6.2 Experimental Setup

We have set $\alpha = 0.1$, $alpha\_decay\_rate = 0.9999$, $\epsilon = 0.05$, $epsilon\_decay\_rate = 0.9999$, $\gamma = 1.0$ and $num\_episodes = 10000$. Initially, the agents are uniformly distributed. The rest of the parameters are given below. In all experiments, we plot the system performance/global reward G at the last time step of each episode (except where otherwise is stated). The values are averaged over 30 statistical runs and error bars showing the standard error around the mean are plotted. In some plots the error bars are very small and hardly visible, but they are present on all plots.

6.3 Experimental Results

For the first experimental study in the TLD we adopt the same traffic scenario as in [11]. In this scenario, there are 500 cars or learning agents and 9 traffic lanes each with capacity 167, 83, 33, 17, 9, 17, 33, 83, 167 (i.e. a total of 609). The weightings for each lane are 1, 5, 10, 1, 5, 10, 1, 5, 10. The highest possible system performance or global reward is 17.66 and is achieved when all the lanes are decongested; this is shown with a black dashed line in all figures.

The fact that there are different weightings for each resource or traffic lane gives us the opportunity to try non-contiguous abstractions i.e. abstract groups with non-adjacent

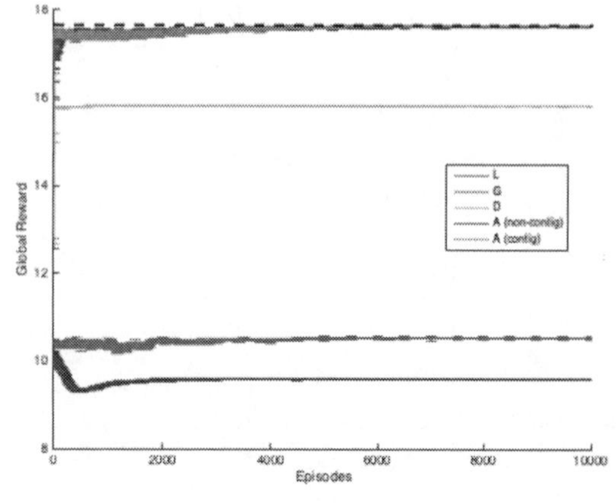

Figure 7: TLD with 500 cars, 5 time steps

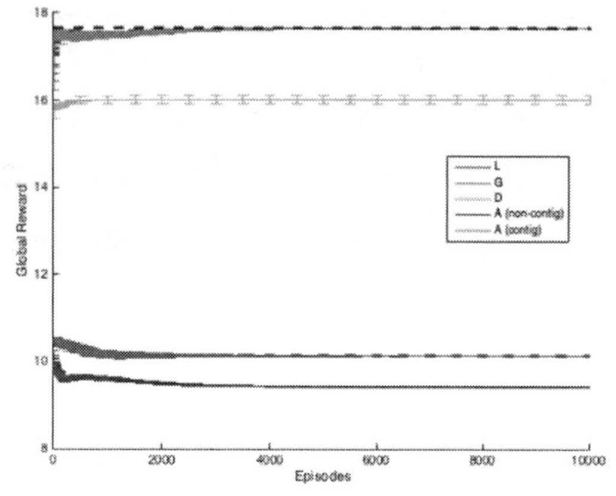

Figure 8: TLD with 500 cars, 10 time steps

members. The obvious configuration is to have three abstract groups each with three member lanes. The first, second and third abstract groups include lanes with weighting 1, 5, and 10 respectively. We will refer to this abstraction configuration as "A (non-contig)". Moreover, like in the BPD, we have experimented with many abstraction configurations and found out that the best performance is obtained with "A-1+8", which we will refer to as "A (contig)".

Figure 7 shows the performance for all approaches for five time steps per episode. The system using abstract rewards (A) achieves the highest performance while both A and D completely outperform L and G. The same experiment with ten time steps per episode is repeated in Figure 8 where very similar results are obtained. Note that with ten time steps, an agent located at the far left (or right) lane has, in principle, adequate time to reach the far right (or left) end. Despite the increase in the number of time steps, the system performance using D is only slightly improved.

An important question is how will the system perform if the lane weightings and capacities change in due course e.g. because of an accident? Consequently, a crucial question that certainly has deployment implications is will a new abstraction configuration be needed each time the lane weightings and capacities change?

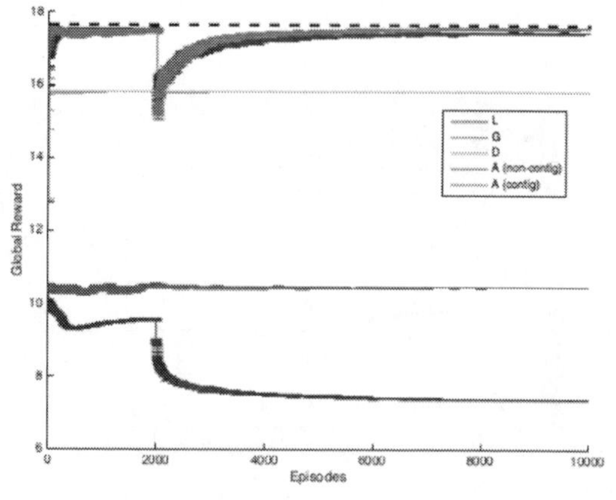

Figure 9: TLD with accidents

The second experimental study in the TLD provides answers to these questions. To simulate such a behaviour we assume that two accidents occurred in lanes 3 and 9 at episode 2000. As a result, their capacity is reduced to half. Also, each of the two lanes has swapped weighting (preference) with one of its adjacent lanes. Therefore, the new capacities are 167, 83, 17, 17, 9, 17, 33, 83, 83 (i.e. a total of 509) and the new weightings are 1, 10, 5, 1, 5, 10, 1, 10, 5. We keep the same number of cars i.e. 500 and at the time of the accidents the agents' exploration parameter is reset to the initial. The number of time steps per episode is five.

Figure 9 shows the results for the scenario with the accidents. The system using L is affected the most and does not manage to recover i.e. to reach the performance it had achieved before the occurrence of the accidents. Interestingly the system using G is not affected at all, but its performance is poor. The system using A is affected but manages to completely recover and achieve the highest possible welfare as it used to be the case without the occurrence of the accidents. The system using D is also affected but only slightly (it is not visible in the graph as it is out-shaded by the decline of the A plots), however, the only system that achieves the best performance is the one using A. The outcome of this study suggests that a system using the proposed approach is robust and does not need to refine the abstraction configuration if something is altered in due course such as the traffic lane capacities and weightings.

It has been assumed so far that all learning agents or cars are participating in the learning scheme. The third experimental study for the TLD examines the behaviour of the approaches when this assumption is violated. In practise, 100% compliance by drivers is unlikely to be achieved [11]. This is because some drivers may not be convinced to participate or even if they are all willing to participate, some of them may come across different problems such as information and sensing limitations.

Figure 10 depicts the system performance ($num\_agents = 500$, $num\_timesteps = 5$) in the presence of 25% non-compliant drivers. Non-compliant drivers are simulated as agents sticking to their initial choice/location. It is observed that the performance of L and G is not affected at all, but it is very poor. The performance of D and A is not affected much and, as a result, the system using A still outperforms the

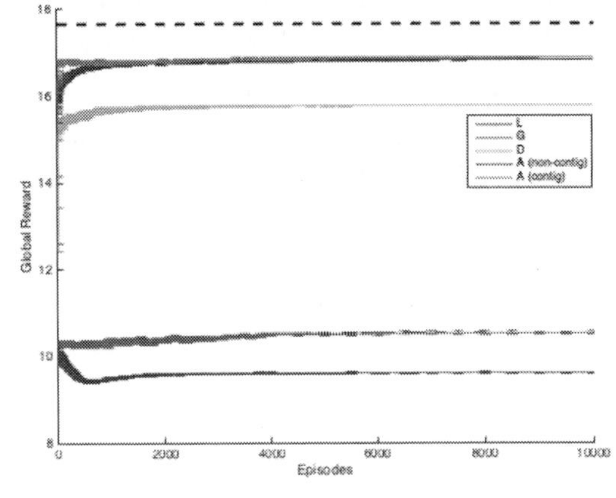

Figure 10: TLD with 25% non-compliant drivers

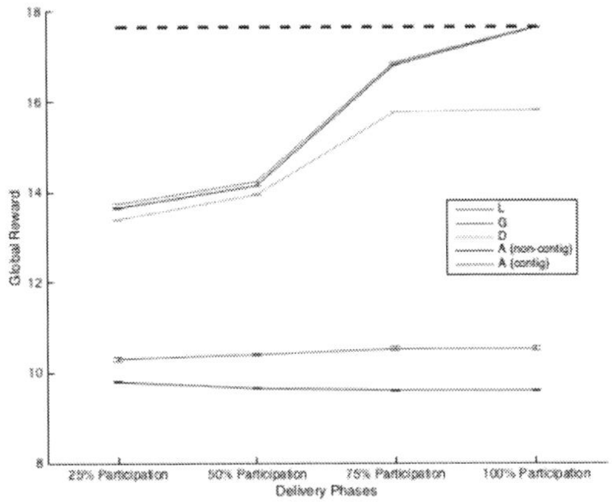

Figure 11: TLD with 4 delivery phases

system that uses D. The results suggest that the proposed system works well under non-compliant drivers.

The fourth experimental study further investigates the potential deployment of such a learning scheme. In practise, it is expected that such a system will be rolled out in phases [11]. For instance, consider a scenario of four delivery phases where the participation is 25%, 50%, 75% and 100% of the drivers. To simulate this situation we vary the rate of non-compliant drivers, for example, the first phase with 25% participation corresponds to 75% non-compliant drivers.

Figure 11 shows the converged performance ($num\_agents =$ 500, $num\_timesteps = 5$) for the scenario with four delivery phases where the superiority of the proposed approach is clearly demonstrated, suggesting that the proposed system can be introduced to the public in different stages.

In the last study we repeat the experiment with 1000 cars. The highest performance is 17.33 and occurs when the first lane (capacity 167, weighting 1) is overcrowded with 558 agents while the remaining eight lines have full capacity. We repeat the case under accident conditions (as in Figure 9), where the highest performance is 17.31 and occurs when the first lane is overcrowded with 658 agents. Figure 12 shows the results ($num\_timesteps = 5$) where the superiority and the ability of the proposed approaches to recover is shown.

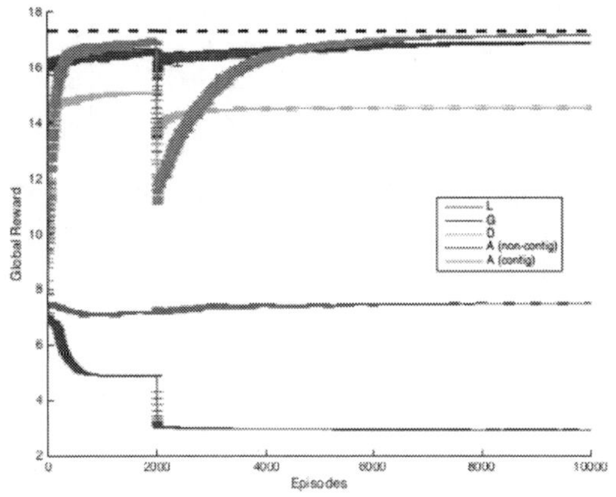

Figure 12: TLD (1000 cars) with accidents

7. DISCUSSION AND CONCLUSION

We have introduced Resource Abstraction for multiagent coordination problems. Our approach allocates available resources into abstract groups to provide a more informative signal to learning agents, significantly improving both learning speed and social welfare.

Experimental work was conducted on two benchmark domains, an abstract congestion problem and a realistic traffic congestion problem. The state-of-the-art solution to solve multiagent congestion problems is a form of reward shaping called difference rewards. We have shown that our novel approach of resource abstraction requires significantly fewer time steps per learning episode to achieve the highest social welfare. This is important for real-world applications where the availability of learning time is limited.

Furthermore, it has been empirically demonstrated in both experimental domains that the proposed approach not only performs better than the two baseline and the difference rewards approaches, but it achieves the highest possible or near-highest system performance even in experiments involving 1000 learning agents. Scalability is another strong aspect of the proposed approach. It has been shown that the proposed approach is robust against changes (e.g. car accidents in the traffic congestion domain) and capable of operating without 100% agent compliance.

It has been shown that when the number of learning steps is limited, then in almost every case Resource Abstraction outperforms the state-of-the-art irrespective of the abstraction grouping (Figures 1 and 4). When the number of learning steps is not limited, we suggest some guidelines that help us define the abstraction grouping. Some experimentation is still necessary but the following heuristics simplify this process: *a.* three abstract groups typically suffice as this allows more resources to be included in an abstract group, hence, a larger penalty can be provided if the group becomes congested *b.* group resources with similar characteristics e.g. the same weightings; the effectiveness of this heuristic is shown by *A (non-contig)* in Figures 7 - 12.

Moreover, it has been shown that if something unexpected occurs (e.g. accidents in the traffic lane domain) it is highly likely that there will be no need to refine the abstraction grouping, as, given some additional exploration time, the system can recover and still achieve the highest performance.

REFERENCES

[1] C. Claus and C. Boutilier. The dynamics of reinforcement learning in cooperative multiagent systems. In *Proceedings of the AAAI Conference on Artificial Intelligence*, 1998.

[2] M. Colby and K. Tumer. Multiagent reinforcement learning in a distributed sensor network with indirect feedback. In *Proceedings of the 2013 international conference on Autonomous agents and multi-agent systems*, pages 941–948, 2013.

[3] S. Devlin, L. Yliniemi, K. Tumer, and D. Kudenko. Potential-based difference rewards for multiagent reinforcement learning. In *Proceedings of the 13th International Conference on Autonomous Agents and Multiagent Systems*, 2014.

[4] K. Malialis, S. Devlin, and D. Kudenko. Distributed reinforcement learning for adaptive and robust network intrusion response. *Connection Science*, 27(3):234–252, 2015.

[5] M. J. Matarić. Using communication to reduce locality in distributed multi-agent learning. *Journal of Experimental and Theoretical Artificial Intelligence, special issue on Learning in DAI Systems, Gerhard Weiss, ed.*, 10(3):357–369, 1998.

[6] S. Proper and K. Tumer. Multiagent learning with a noisy global reward signal. In *Proceedings of the AAAI Conference on Artificial Intelligence*, 2013.

[7] P. Stone. Learning and multiagent reasoning for autonomous agents. In *Proceedings of the International Joint Conference on Artificial Intelligence (IJCAI)*, pages 12–30, 2007.

[8] P. Stone and M. Veloso. Multiagent systems: A survey from a machine learning perspective. *Autonomous Robots*, 8(3):345–383, 2000.

[9] R. S. Sutton and A. G. Barto. *Introduction to Reinforcement Learning*. MIT Press Cambridge, MA, USA, 1998.

[10] K. Tumer and A. Agogino. Distributed agent-based air traffic flow management. In *Proceedings of the 6th International Joint Conference on Autonomous Agents and Multiagent Systems*, 2007.

[11] K. Tumer, Z. Welch, and A. K. Agogino. Traffic congestion management as a learning agent coordination problem. In A. Bazzan and F. Kluegl, editors, *Multiagent Architectures for Traffic and Transportation Engineering*, pages 261–279. Lecture notes in AI, Springer, 2009.

[12] C. J. Watkins and P. Dayan. Q-learning. *Machine learning*, 8(3-4):279–292, 1992.

[13] K. R. W. Wolpert, David H. and K. Tumer. Collective intelligence for control of distributed dynamical systems. *Europhysics Letters*, 49(6), 2000.

Local Approximation of Difference Evaluation Functions

Mitchell Colby
Oregon State University
Corvallis, OR

Theodore Duchow-Pressley
Oregon State University
Corvallis, OR

Jen Jen Chung
Oregon State University
Corvallis, OR

Kagan Tumer
Oregon State University
Corvallis, OR

ABSTRACT

Difference evaluation functions have resulted in excellent multiagent behavior in many domains, including air traffic and mobile robot control. However, calculating difference evaluation functions requires determining the value of a counterfactual system objective function, which is often difficult when the system objective function is unknown or global state and action information is unavailable. In this work, we demonstrate that a local estimate of the system evaluation function may be used to estimate difference evaluations using readily available information, allowing for difference evaluations to be computed in multiagent systems where the mathematical form of the objective function is not known. This approximation technique is tested in two domains, and we demonstrate that approximating difference evaluation functions results in better performance and faster learning than when using global evaluation functions. Finally, we demonstrate the effectiveness of the learned policies on a set of Pioneer P3-DX robots.

Keywords

Multiagent reinforcement learning, difference rewards

1. INTRODUCTION

Difference evaluation functions have been shown to significantly improve learning in multiagent systems, both in the speed of convergence and the quality of the converged policy. They have been successful in many different cooperative multiagent domains, including air traffic control, network routing, multiple mobile robot control, and congestion games such as the bar problem [2, 9]. These evaluation functions have two key theoretical advantages. First, they are aligned with the overall system objective [2]. This means an individual agent acting to increase the value of the difference evaluation function also acts to improve the value of the overall system evaluation function. Second, they remove much of the noise in the feedback signal associated with other agents, allowing for individual agents to more easily learn the effects of their actions on system performance [2].

Difference evaluation functions are the *difference* between the system objective function and the *counterfactual*, or the value of the system objective function independent from the agent being evaluated. This gives an approximation of the value that the agent added to the overall system. While difference evaluation functions are conceptually simple, they are often difficult to compute. More specifically, it is difficult to calculate the counterfactual, or the value of the system objective function independent of a particular agent.

There are two key reasons counterfactuals are difficult to compute. First, calculating the counterfactual requires global knowledge of the system state and the actions taken by each agent; in practice, agents in multiagent systems rarely have such knowledge. This makes local computation of difference evaluation functions difficult in practice. Second, the system objective function itself is typically unavailable to the agents, meaning that even if agents have global knowledge, a direct computation of difference evaluations is typically unavailable. One approach to deal with calculating difference evaluations has been to leverage domain knowledge to estimate the system evaluation function.

Recent work has focused on addressing the calculation of the counterfactual in which the system evaluation function is unknown [20]. The counterfactual is estimated using a function approximator that is trained on previous values of the system evaluation function. This work extended difference evaluation functions to domains in which the analytical form of the system evaluation function is unavailable, and computing difference evaluations requires resimulation or approximation. However, this technique required that the designer had expert system knowledge as well as global state information in order to create the approximation. These are significant limitations, as the form of the system evaluation function is often unknown, and global knowledge about the system is often unavailable. In order for difference evaluations to be applicable in generic multiagent domains, we must use approximation techniques which do not require domain knowledge or global knowledge of the system state.

In this work, we present a generic and model-free approach to approximate difference evaluations. Each agent maintains a local approximation of the system evaluation functions, based on their local state and action information and the value of the system evaluation function. We assume that the only information available to agents includes their local state, their action selection, and the instantaneous value of the system evaluation function. This information is exactly what is available to agents learning with the global evaluation function, so our approximation technique does not require more information than is typically available to learning agents. The only global information needed in this approach

Appears in: *Proceedings of the 15th International Conference on Autonomous Agents and Multiagent Systems (AAMAS 2016), J. Thangarajah, K. Tuyls, C. Jonker, S. Marsella (eds.), May 9–13, 2016, Singapore.*

is the value of the system evaluation function, which we assume can be broadcast to each agent. Each agent uses its private function approximator to estimate the value of the difference evaluation, in order to provide a feedback signal based only on local information.

The contributions of this work are to:

- Develop an approach to approximate difference evaluation functions using information available to each agent in a multiagent system.
- Demonstrate that the proposed approximation algorithm results in up to 98% of the performance of directly computed difference evaluation functions.
- Demonstrate the effectiveness of policies learned using the proposed approximation algorithm using a set of Pioneer P3-DX robots.

In Section 2 we briefly discuss background and related work. Section 3 describes the approximation technique. Section 4 presents the two different domains in which our reward approximation method is applied. Section 5 shows the performance of our algorithm in each domain. Section 6 presents an analysis of learned policies on physicial robots. Finally, in Section 7 we discuss and conclude the work.

2. RELATED WORK

The following sections introduce difference evaluation functions, as well as related work involving approximating evaluation functions to provide agent feedback.

2.1 Difference Evaluation Functions

The agent-specific *difference evaluation function* $D_i(s_i, a_i)$ is defined as [2]:

$$D_i(s_i, a_i) = G(s, a) - G(s_{-i} \cup c_{s,i}, a_{-i} \cup c_{a,i}) \quad (1)$$

where:

- $G(s, a)$ is the total system evaluation
- s is the joint system state
- a is the system joint-action
- s_{-i} are all the states on which agent i has no effect
- a_{-i} are all the agent actions not involving agent i,
- $c_{s,i}$ and $c_{a,i}$ are fixed states and actions not dependent on agent i.

Intuitively, the second term (the *counterfactual*) in Equation 1 evaluates the system without the effects of agent i, so the difference evaluation gives agent i's contribution to the system evaluation [2]. Note that:

$$\frac{\partial D_i(s,a)}{\partial a_i} = \frac{\partial G(s,a)}{\partial a_i} \quad (2)$$

where a_i is the action taken by agent i. Thus, an agent acting to increase the value of its difference evaluation function will also act to increase the value of the overall system evaluation function. This property is termed *factoredness* [2]. Also note that $D_i(s, a)$ removes all elements of the system evaluation function not affected by agent i, decreasing noise and providing agent-specific feedback which is strongly coupled to a particular agent's actions. This property is termed *learnability* [2]. In addition to the theoretical properties of factoredness and learnability, difference evaluations have been shown to improve the probability of agents finding best response actions in cases where tight coordination is required to reach optimal Nash equilibria [10].

Although factoredness and learnability allow for difference evaluations to provide very useful agent feedback during learning, there are two key limitations to these functions. First, calculating the counterfactual in difference evaluations requires global knowledge about the system state and joint action. In practice, such information is rarely available. Therefore, calculating $D_i(s, a)$ analytically requires a centralized mechanism to provide agent feedback, which is generally unavailable. Second, the system evaluation function is typically unknown to agents, making direct calculation of the counterfactual term unfeasible in some cases. In order to extend difference evaluations to general multiagent systems, techniques for approximating the system evaluation function using only local information are required.

2.2 Approximation of Evaluation Functions

In cases where the system evaluation function is unknown, it may be approximated in order to provide better feedback to learning agents [3, 5]. In the case of reinforcement learning, reward functions are modeled; in the case of evolutionary algorithms, fitness functions are modeled. In either case, approximation of system evaluation functions allows for agent evaluation functions to be easily shaped.

Function approximation is commonly seen in reinforcement learning applications, where the value function or system state is approximated due to limited state information [11, 12, 16]. Value functions are often approximated when only partial state information is available, often using neural networks, maps, or some other type of function approximator [1, 6, 18]. The conclusion that only partial state information is necessary to accurately model value functions suggests these types of approaches can be successfully extended to multiagent learning problems, where partial state information is available to each agent.

Fitness functions have also been approximated for use in evolutionary algorithms [7, 15]. This fitness approximation is typically used because the number of fitness function evaluations dominates the optimization cost in evolutionary algorithms, and fitness approximation typically decreases time to convergence [13, 17]. However, these approaches can easily be extended to cases in which the mathematical form of the fitness function is unknown, as in cases where the difference evaluation must be approximated. All of the methods described above are single agent cases, but there has also been research investigating approximating system evaluation functions in multiagent learning settings.

Difference evaluation functions have been approximated in air traffic control domains [20]. A tabulated linear function consisting of neural networks approximates the system evaluation function. Each neural network approximated a specific aspect of the air traffic domain (congestion, delay), and a weighted sum of the network outputs was used to provide the approximation of the overall system evaluation function. This approach yielded accurate approximations of the system evaluation function and allowed for difference evaluation functions to be accurately estimated to provide agent-specific feedback during learning.

There are two key drawbacks to this approach. First, expert domain knowledge was needed to create the approximation of the system evaluation function, and such knowledge is not always available. Second, this approach required global knowledge of the system state, which is often unavailable in a distributed multiagent system. Although this approach gave good results for approximating difference evaluation functions in the air traffic domain, it does not extend to any generic multiagent domain.

There is a wide range of research involving approximation in multiagent learning. However, very little research has been conducted on approximating difference evaluations. More importantly, the research which has been conducted on approximating difference evaluations has involved approximations which were dependent on expert system knowledge as well as global state and action information. In order for difference evaluations to be approximated in generic multiagent settings, the requirements for expert domain knowledge must be eliminated, and the approximations must be constructed using only local information.

3. DIFFERENCE EVALUATION APPROXIMATION

In this section, we introduce a general algorithm for approximating difference evaluations, and then demonstrate how this algorithm is implemented in different types of domains. This algorithm was first presented in [8] for continuous state and action domains, and we now present the generalized approximation algorithm and explain how it can be implemented in different types of domains. In general, multiagent systems may be stateless or stateful, and may have continuous or discrete state and action spaces. We select two types of domains to demonstrate implementation of our algorithm: a stateless, discrete action domain as well as a continuous state and action domain. For the purpose of this analysis, we assume a cooperative multiagent system aims to maximize some system objective function $G(s,a)$, and that the value of $G(s,a)$ is available to each agent. Recall that the difference evaluation is defined as:

$$D_i(s,a) = G(s,a) - G(s_{-i} \cup c_{s,i}, a_{-i} \cup c_{a,i}).$$

Since we assume that the value of $G(s,a)$ is available to each agent, approximating the difference evaluation function only requires approximating the $G(s_{-i} \cup c_{s,i}, a_{-i} \cup c_{a,i})$ term. Given the particular domain, a suitable function approximator is chosen. For a stateless domain with discrete actions, this approximator may simply be a vector. For a stateful domain with continuous actions, this approximator may be a neural network. Note that these are not the only possible options for these function approximators, but are potential choices that match the domains they will be used in.

The difference evaluation approximation algorithm is presented in Algorithm 1. At each time step, each agent takes an action, and $G(s,a)$ is computed and broadcast to each agent. Each agent i maintains a private approximation for $G(s,a)$, denoted as $\hat{G}_i(s_i,a_i)$. The only information available to the agent includes the agent's state, action choice, and the broadcast value of $G(s,a)$. Each agent's approximation of $G(s,a)$ is a mapping from that agent's state and action to the system objective function. This approximation is initially very noisy, because the state and action information used to approximate $G(s,a)$ is limited only to one agent's state and action. However, as learning progresses, the policies of each agent begin to converge; as the policies of other agents converge, approximating $G(s,a)$ using only one agent's state and action becomes less noisy, because the variance in the joint action for a particular system-level state is reduced. Given an agent's approximation $\hat{G}_i(s,a)$, the difference evaluation function is estimated as:

$$\hat{D}_i(s,a) = G(s,a) - \hat{G}_i(c_{s,i}, c_{a,i}) \quad (3)$$

```
Initialize N agents
foreach Agent do
  | Initialize private function approximator Ĝ_i(s_i, a_i)
end
foreach Learning Step do
  foreach Agent do
    | collect local state information s_i
    | select action a_i using agent's policy
  end
  Calculate G(s, a) based on joint action
  Broadcast G(s, a) to each agent
  foreach Agent do
    | Update Ĝ_i(s_i, a_i) using s_i, a_i, and G(s, a)
    | D̂_i(s, a) = G(s, a) − Ĝ_i(c_{s,i}, c_{a,i})
    | Update policy/value table based on D̂_i(s, a)
  end
end
```

Algorithm 1: Approximation of difference evaluation functions. The functional form of $\hat{G}$ depends on the specific domain. For example, a stateless discrete action domain may use a vector, while a continuous state and action domain may use a neural network.

where $\hat{D}_i(s,a)$ is agent i's approximation of the difference evaluation function. In order to evaluate $\hat{G}_i(c_{s,i}, c_{a,i})$, a default state and default action are chosen for each agent. In other words, the approximation of the difference evaluation function determines *the difference between the system objective function and the approximated system objective function if agent i took a default action.*

The implementation of this approximation approach in a stateless discrete action domain as well as a continuous state and action domain are detailed in the following sections. We demonstrate how a multiagent reinforcement learning algorithm with an approximation of difference evaluations may be implemented in the stateless discrete action domain, and how a cooperative coevolutionary algorithm with an approximation of difference evaluations may be implemented in a continuous state and action domain. Difference evaluations are commonly used in both reinforcement learning and cooperative coevolutionary algorithms, so we choose to demonstrate how both types of algorithms may incorporate approximate difference evaluations.

3.1 Stateless Discrete Action Domains

We now demonstrate how Algorithm 1 may be implemented for a multiagent reinforcement learning algorithm in a stateless discrete action domain. The implementation of Algorithm 1 in a multiagent reinforcement learning problem with a stateless discrete action domain is given in Algorithm 2. Note that such problems may also be solved with coevolutionary algorithms. In a stateless discrete action domain, each agent maintains a value vector $V_i(a)$ containing the expected value of each possible action. Each agent also maintains an approximation of $G(a)$, which is simply a vector containing the estimated value of the system evaluation function corresponding to each action the agent may take. At each learning step, each agent i selects an action a_i. The system evaluation function $G(a)$ is then calculated, and this value is broadcast to each agent in the system. Each agent

```
Initialize N agents
foreach Agent do
    Initialize private value table V_i(a)
    Initialize private function approximator Ĝ_i(a)
end
foreach Learning Step do
    foreach Agent do
        select action a_i using agent's policy
    end
    Calculate G(s, a) based on joint action
    Broadcast G(s, a) to each agent
    foreach Agent do
        Ĝ_i(a_i) ← α_1 · Ĝ_i(a_i) + (1 − α_1) · G(a)
        D̂_i(a_i) = G(a) − Ĝ_i(a_0)
        V_i(a_i) ← α_2 · V_i(a_i) + (1 − α_2) · D̂_i(a)
    end
end
```

Algorithm 2: Stateless Discrete-Action Multiagent Reinforcement Learning using $D_i(s, a)$ Approximation

then updates its approximation $\hat{G}_i(a_i)$ according to:

$$\hat{G}_i(a_i) \leftarrow (1 - \alpha_1) \cdot \hat{G}_i(a_i) + \alpha_1 \cdot G(a) \quad (4)$$

Once each agent has updated its approximation of $G(a)$, the difference evaluation for each agent is estimated as:

$$\hat{D}_i(a) = G(a) - \hat{G}_i(c_{a,i}) \quad (5)$$

where $c_{a,i}$ is some default action. The value table is updated using the approximate difference evaluation function:

$$Q_i(a_i) \leftarrow (1 - \alpha_2) \cdot Q_i(a_i) + \alpha_2 \cdot \hat{D}_i(a) \quad (6)$$

3.2 Continuous State and Action Domains

We now demonstrate how Algorithm 1 may be implemented in a cooperative coevolutionary algorithm in a continuous state and action domain. We assume each agent has a neural network policy that maps the agent's state to an action. Further, each agent has a two-layer feedforward neural network approximation of $G(s, a)$. Note that neural networks are not the only form of function approximation that may be used, but are chosen to demonstrate this example. At each timestep, each agent keeps track of its state and chosen actions. The value of the system evaluation function $G(s, a)$ is broadcast to each agent after each agent has taken an action. Then, each agent updates its approximation $\hat{G}_i(s_i, a_i)$ using the $(s, a, G(s, a))$ tuple and backpropagation, where the error in the approximation is $G(s, a) - \hat{G}_i(s_i, a_i)$.

The difference evaluation is then approximated using Equation 3, and the estimated value of $\hat{D}_i(s, a)$ is used to assign the fitness associated with the state-action pairing selected by the agent's policy. Agents are selected for survival using ϵ-greedy selection. The implementation of Algorithm 1 using a cooperative coevolutionary algorithm is given in Algorithm 3.

```
Initialize N populations of k neural networks
foreach Population i do
    foreach Individual j do
        Initialize function approximator Ĝ_{i,j}(s_i, a_i)
    end
end
foreach Generation do
    foreach Population do
        produce k successor solutions
        mutate successor solutions
    end
    for i = 1 → 2k do
        randomly select one agent from each population
        add agents to team T_i
        foreach Simulation Timestep do
            each agent j in team T_i finds local state s_i
            each agent j in team T_i chooses action a_i
            G(s, a) is broadcast to each agent
            update Ĝ_{i,j}(s_i, a_i) based on s_i, a_i, G(s, a)
            D̂_{i,j}(s, a) = G(s, a) − Ĝ_{i,j}(c_{s,i}, c_{s,a})
            each agent j increments fitness by D̂_{i,j}(s, a)
        end
    end
    foreach Population do
        select k networks using ε-greedy
    end
end
```

Algorithm 3: Continuous State and Action CCEA using $D_i(s, a)$ Approximation

4. EXPERIMENTAL DOMAINS

In this section, we introduce the two test domains utilized in this work, and provide a detailed description of the system dynamics and evaluation functions used in each domain. The first domain, the El Farol bar problem, is a stateless congestion domain with a discrete action space. The second domain, the rover domain, is a stateful domain with continuous states and actions. These domains were chosen to highlight that our approximation approach can be applied in a wide range of different multiagent problems.

4.1 Bar Problem

The El Farol Bar Problem [4] is a frequently-used abstraction of congestion problems. We use a multi-night modification of the El Farol Bar Problem. In this problem there is a capacity c that provides the most enjoyment for everyone who attends the bar on that particular night. This is a stateless one shot problem where agents choose the night they attend the bar, and receive a reward based on their enjoyment. The traditional bar problem local reward is a function of the attendance of that night:

$$L_i = e^{\frac{-x_i(a_i)}{c}} \quad (7)$$

where $x_i(a_i)$ is the attendance on the night agent i went to the bar. The system-level reward is a simple summation of these local rewards across all agents:

$$G(a) = \sum_{k=0}^{K} x_k(a) e^{\frac{-x_k(a)}{c}} \quad (8)$$

where k is the index of the night, and $x_k(a)$ is the number of agents who attended on the kth night.

4.2 Rover Domain

In the rover domain [2, 9], a set of rovers on a two dimensional plane must coordinate in order to observe points

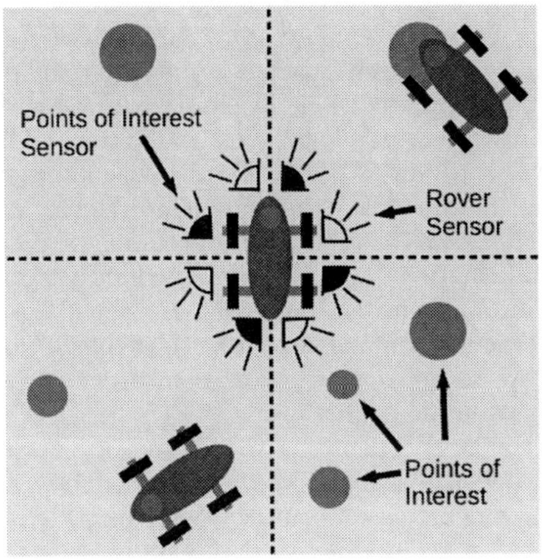

Figure 1: Rover Domain Representation. Each rover senses the POIs and other rovers within an observation radius in each of its four sensing quadrants.

of interest (POIs) scattered across the domain (Figure 1). Each POI has an associated value, and each observation of a POI made by a rover yields an observation value which is inversely proportional to the distance that the rover is from the POI. The distance metric used in this domain is the squared Euclidian norm, bounded by a minimum observation value to prevent division by zero:

$$\delta(x, y) = min\left\{||x - y||^2, \delta^2_{min}\right\} \quad (9)$$

The objective of the rovers is to maximize the observation values of the POIs over an episode, given by:

$$G = \sum_t \sum_j \frac{V_j}{min_i \delta(L_j, L_{i,t})} \quad (10)$$

where V_j is the value of POI j, L_j is the location of POI j, and $L_{i,t}$ is the location of the ith rover at time t.

Although any rover may observe any POI, the system evaluation only takes into account the closest observation made for each POI. The POI locations are static throughout each experiment. The rovers have eight total sensors, two sensors per quadrant. The first sensor for quadrant q returns the sum of the values of POIs divided by their squared distance to the rover:

$$s_{1,q,i} = \sum_{j \in I_q} \frac{V_j}{\delta(L_j, L_i)} \quad (11)$$

where I_q is the set of POIs in quadrant q. The second sensor returns the sum of square distances from a rover to all the other rovers in the quadrant:

$$s_{2,q,i} = \sum_{i' \in N_q} \frac{1}{\delta(L_{i'}, L_i)} \quad (12)$$

where N_q is the set of rovers in quadrant q. The eight sensors give an approximate representation of the world, reducing the location and number of rovers and POIs in each quadrant to an average number. This representation of the rover domain is used as a low-fidelity model of a set of differential drive robots. Section 6 discusses how policies found in this domain can be mapped to a physical robotic system.

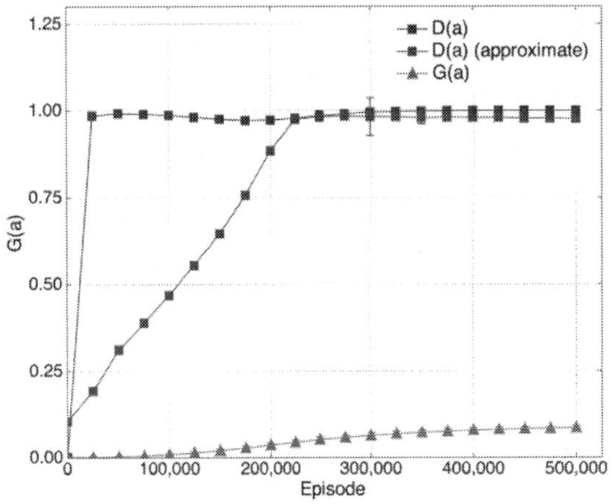

Figure 2: Bar problem results. When approximating $D_i(a)$, the learning rate is slower than when using $D_i(a)$, but the converged performance is nearly identical. $D_i(a)$ performs almost 10 times better than the overall system evaluation function $G(a)$.

5. EXPERIMENTAL RESULTS

The following sections detail the experimental results in the bar problem and the rover domain. One bar problem experiment was conducted, with 1000 agents in the system. Two rover domain experiments were conducted, varying between 10 and 100 agents to determine the effects of system size on the performance of our approximation algorithm.

5.1 Bar Problem Domain Results

The bar problem was initialized as follows. There are 1000 agents and 10 nights, where each night has a capacity of 10. The learning rate α_1 for the approximation of the system evaluation function was set to 0.1. The learning rate α_2 for the value table was set to 0.1. Each experimental run lasted for 500,000 timesteps, and 100 statistical runs were conducted. The experimental results are shown in Figure 2, and the reported error bars are error in the mean σ/N^2.

As seen in Figure 2, approximating the difference evaluation function results in almost 10 times better performance than using the system evaluation function $G(a)$. When approximating $D_i(a)$, the solution takes much longer to converge than when analytically computing $D_i(a)$. However, converged performance of actual and estimated difference evaluation functions is nearly identical.

It is of note that although the analytical calculation of $D_i(a)$ results in faster learning, it is often impossible to analytically compute the system evaluation function in multiagent learning systems. Often, the mathematical form of $G(a)$ is unknown, meaning $D_i(a)$ cannot be directly computed. However, agents can still use local knowledge to approximate $G(a)$ and thus estimate difference evaluation functions, which drastically improve system performance. So, even though the analytical computation of $D_i(a)$ provides faster learning than when approximating $D_i(a)$, it is not always possible to perform this analytical computation.

The key result is that agents with only local knowledge converge to the same performance (although in more computational time) as agents with global knowledge about the system. In cases where global knowledge is available, it is often beneficial to use this knowledge while shaping agent feedback signals. However, in many cases, agents' knowledge is often limited to what they can observe, and constructing meaningful agent feedback based on this limited information is critical for ensuring high system performance. These results demonstrate that in some cases, approximate difference evaluations result in no significant loss in converged system performance when only local knowledge is available.

5.2 Rover Domain Results

The rover domain was initialized as follows. There are 10 agents and 10 POIs in a planar world of size 25 units by 25 units. For coevolution, each agent maintains a population of 25 neural networks. Networks are mutated by adding variables drawn from a Gaussian distribution with zero mean and unit variance to 10 randomly drawn weights from each neural network. Each episode lasts 25 timesteps, and agents can move a maximum of 1 distance unit per timestep. At the beginning of each episode, agent positions are randomly initialized near the center of the domain. The coeovlutionary algorithm[1] was run for 3000 generations, and 150 statistical runs were conducted for statistical significance. The experimental results are shown in Figure 3. As in the bar problem, reported error bars represent the error in the mean of the statistical data.

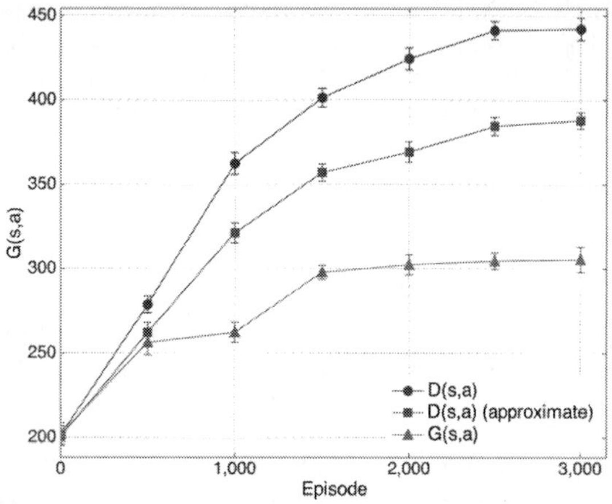

Figure 3: Rover domain results (10 agents). Approximating $D_i(s,a)$ results in 88% of the performance attained when analytically computing $D_i(s,a)$. Approximating the difference evaluation function results in significant performance gains when compared to using the system evaluation function $G(s,a)$.

As seen in Figure 3, approximating $D_i(s,a)$ results in an approximate 23% increase in converged performance compared to using the system evaluation function $G(s,a)$. When approximating $D_i(s,a)$, the converged performance was 88% of the converged performance when analytically computing $D_i(s,a)$. Although the performance decreases when approximating rather than analytically computing $D_i(s,a)$, it is important to note that much less information is required to make the approximation. The approximation of $D_i(s,a)$ requires only an agent's local state and action, and the evaluation of $G(s,a)$. In order to analytically compute $D_i(s,a)$, global information about the state and action of each agent is required, as well as the functional form of $G(s,a)$. So, although estimating $D_i(s,a)$ results in slightly worse performance than analytically computing $D_i(s,a)$, it is often extremely difficult to make this analytical calculation, meaning that approximation is required in order to implement difference evaluation functions.

Unlike the bar problem, there is a drop in converged performance between $D(s,a)$ and $\hat{D}_i(s,a)$. This can be attributed to the increased complexity of the state and action space in the rover domain. In the stateless bar problem, there were simply 10 discrete actions that agents had to choose from. In the rover domain, both the states and actions are continuous. In the bar problem, difference evaluations attempt to answer whether an agent had a positive impact on the system for the specific night the agent attended; in the rover domain, difference evaluations attempt to answer whether the agent had a positive impact on information collection over the course of a time-extended task. Clearly, approximating the system evaluation function in the rover domain is much more complex than in the bar problem, and explains why the approximation resulted in decreased performance of $\hat{D}_i(s,a)$ when compared to $D(s,a)$.

It is important to note that a local approximation only resulted in a 12% decrease in performance when the state information used to construct agent feedback decreased by 90%. The states and actions of all 10 agents are incorporated into calculating $D(s,a)$. In the approximation $\hat{D}_i(s,a)$, only one agent's state is used in the calculation. This is an extremely promising result, as a massive loss in information results in only a small loss in performance.

Another important note is that when learning initially begins, $\hat{D}_i(s,a)$ is simply a noisy version of $\hat{G}(s,a)$. As learning progresses and agent approximations of $G(s,a)$ become more accurate, $\hat{D}(s,a)$ gradually moves from a noisy representation of $\hat{G}(s,a)$ to an approximation of $D_i(s,a)$. This is why early in learning, $\hat{D}_i(s,a)$ performs closer to $G(s,a)$, but gradually performs closer to $D_i(s,a)$.

5.3 Scaling Results

In order to demonstrate the scalability of our approach, we use the difference evaluation approximation algorithm in a larger instance of the rover domain. In this experiment, there are 100 agents and 100 POIs in a planar world of size 50 by 50. Learning is allowed to proceed for 5000 generations. All other parameters of the experiment are identical to the rover experiment in Section 5.2. The experimental results are shown in Figure 4. The reported error bars represent the error in the mean of the statistical data.

As seen in Figure 4, learning with $\hat{D}_i(s,a)$ results in 79% of the performance compared to using the analytically computed difference evaluation, and outperforms the system evaluation function by 49%. Although $\hat{D}_i(s,a)$ performed more poorly compared to $D_i(s,a)$ in this larger domain (79% vs. 88%), it outperformed $G(s,a)$ by a wider margin (49% vs. 23%) as the system grew in complexity. This is strong evidence supporting the use of approximate difference evaluations over the system evaluation function.

[1]We also performed these experiments using multiagent Q-learning using policy gradient methods. The cooperative coevolutionary algorithm results are presented to demonstrate that our approximation of difference evaluations applies to both multiagent reinforcement learning and cooperative coevolutionary algorithms, not to suggest that coevolutionary algorithms are the preferred approach for the rover domain.

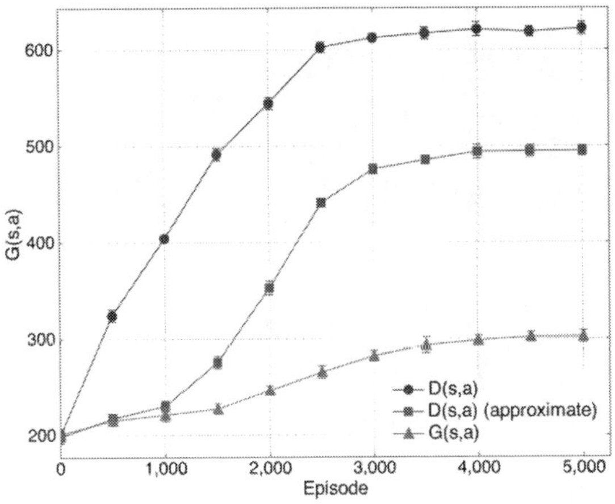

Figure 4: Rover domain results (100 agents). Approximating $D_i(s,a)$ results in 79% of the performance attained when analytically computing $D_i(s,a)$. Approximating the difference evaluation function results in significant performance gains when compared to using the system evaluation function $G(s,a)$.

It is of note that in this larger domain, learning occurs more slowly (as compared to $D_i(s,a)$) than in the 10 agent domain. This can be attributed to the fact that the approximation of $G(s,a)$ is more difficult to learn in the larger domain, and poor approximations early on in learning decrease the learning speed. As the approximator becomes more accurate, learning with $\hat{D}_i(s,a)$ speeds up. However, even when agents use only local knowledge and approximate $D_i(s,a)$, they still significantly outperform agents using $G(s,a)$. These results indicate that difference evaluations may be extended to applications where global knowledge about the system state, as well as the form of the system evaluation function, are unavailable.

It is of note that in all three experiments conducted, approximating difference evaluations instead of directly calculating them required at least 90% less system information, but only resulted in performance losses of up to 21%. This is an extremely promising result, as using far less knowledge to calculate agent feedback results in a comparatively low drop in system performance.

5.4 Theoretical Implications of $D(z)$ Approximation

The difference evaluation is fully factored, meaning that an agent acting to increase the value of $D_i(s,a)$ will always also increase the value of $G(s,a)$. However, when approximating the difference evaluation, the guarantee of factoredness is lost. We now analyze the degree to which the approximate difference evaluation is factored with respect to the system evaluation function.

In order to evaluate the degree of factoredness associated with the approximations, we performed random sampling in the rover domain to compare $G(s,a)$ with $\hat{G}_i(s_i,a_i)$. Random states are created by drawing the positions of the rovers and POIs from a uniform random distribution such that rovers and POIs could be placed at any location in the planar world. Then, a random action was selected (x- and $y-$motion) from uniform random distributions for a randomly selected rover. This action was executed, and the change in the value of $G(s,a)$ was recorded. If the sign of this change is equal to the sign of $\hat{G}_i(s_i,a_i)$, then $\hat{G}_i(s_i,a_i)$ is factored with $G(s,a)$ for this particular state-action pair. This process was repeated for one million randomly generated states.

We found that $\hat{G}_i(s_i,a_i)$ was factored with $G(s,a)$ in 94% of the states tested in the 10 agent domain, and 78% of the states tested in the 100 agent domain. This is a particularly interesting result for two reasons. First, the approximation was capable of attaining a fairly high degree of factoredness, which explains why the approximation of difference evaluations provided good performance. Second, when the approximation of $G(s,a)$ was found to be 95% factored in the 10 agent domain, the approximation of difference evaluations led to 88% of the performance of analytically calculated difference evaluations. When the approximation of difference evaluations was 78% factored, the approximation of difference evaluations led to 79% of the performance of analytically computed difference evaluations. In our experiments, the degree of factoredness of $\hat{G}_i(s_i,a_i)$ is strongly correlated with the performance of $\hat{D}_i(s,a)$.

6. HARDWARE IMPLEMENTATION

We implemented the rover domain on a set of five Pioneer P3-DX compact differential-drive research robots. Each robot was equipped with odometry and lidar sensors, and so could determine its own position and the positions of surrounding objects. Each robot was controlled by a computer running the Robot Operating System (ROS) [21]. POIs were defined as people standing with the robots (Figure 5).

We mapped the rover domain as described in Section 4 onto the hardware implementation by reducing the variety of information brought in by the robots' sensors down to the 8 state variables described above. To mimic the rover sensor return for each quadrant, each robot reported its position to a central hub, using the `rocon` multimaster system for ROS [22]. The hub calculated the relative robot positions and sent each robot its four quadrant sensor values. This centralized calculation was necessary since the lidars were mounted above the robot platform such that their planar laser scans could not reliably detect the small available surface area of the other robots. Future work will investigate improved designs for robust robot detection. The POI sensor values were extracted by feeding the raw lidar returns into the trained people classifier of the `leg_detector` ROS package developed by Willow Garage [19]. The `leg_detector` package output the target position of human POIs in the robot body frame, and this data was condensed into the 4 POI quadrant values using Equation 11.

Rover control policies were trained in a 5-rover, 10-POI simulation (5000 generations) and used the 8 state input variables (2 sensor values for each quadrant, as discussed above) to output a displacement command $(\Delta x, \Delta y)$ in the respective body frame. These values were issued as waypoint commands to the robot through the `move_base` ROS package [14]. This allowed the robot to use the built-in obstacle-avoidance routines to find collision-free paths to the locations dictated by the control policy.

Figure 5 shows the initial and final robot configurations for two sequential trials, as well as the paths taken by each robot. As seen in Figure 6, 9 POIs were successfully ob-

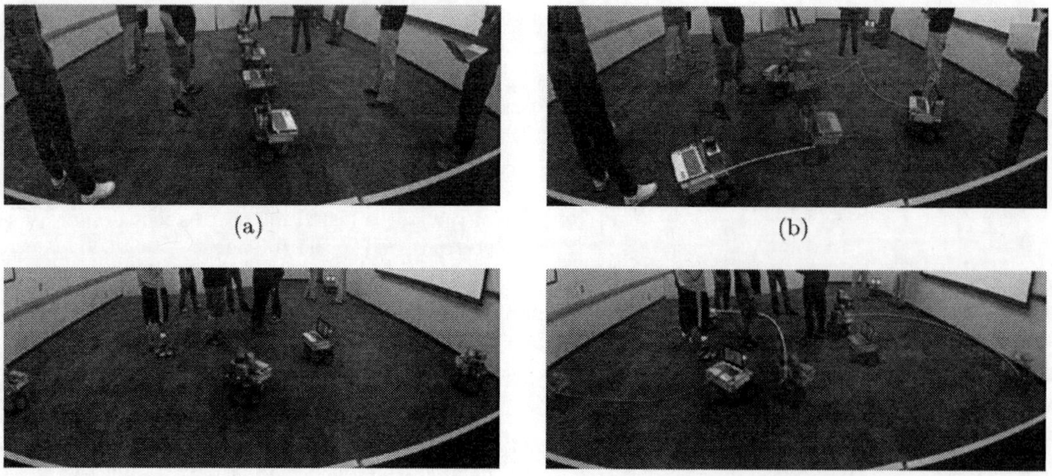
(a) (b) (c) (d)

Figure 5: The initial configuration of the robots and POIs is shown in (a), after 58 s 9 of the 10 POIs have been observed and the trajectories are plotted in (b). At 59 s, the POIs reconfigured to form two clusters, a large cluster of 8 in the center and a small cluster of 2 towards the far right as shown in (c). The control policies on the robots allowed them to reobserve all the POIs. Note that the majority of the lead time was due to the internal path planners on the robots, shown in (d). Also of note is that the robot in the far right corner failed to find a safe motion path, however the team of robots was still able to reacquire all POIs.

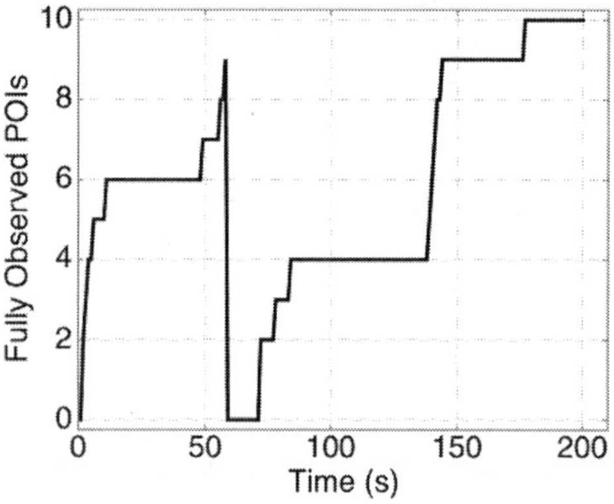

Figure 6: Hardware results from Pioneer P3-DX experiments, with 5 robots and 10 POIs. In the first POI configuration, 9 POIs were fully observed. In the second configuration, all 10 POIs were fully observed.

served in the first trial, and all 10 POIs were successfully observed in the second trial. These results are consistent with the simulation results shown in Section 5.

7. DISCUSSION

Difference evaluations have been empirically shown to improve coordination in multiagent systems in a many domains, including air traffic control, rover control, sensor network control, and congestion games. Further, difference evaluations are fully factored, and are typically low in noise. However, a key limitation of difference evaluations is the requirement for global knowledge about the state of the system as well as the system evaluation function. Thus, directly implementing difference rewards in generic multiagent domains is often a difficult task.

In this work, we demonstrate that difference evaluations may be approximated by each agent using only local state and action information. The only assumption is that the value of the system evaluation function $G(s, a)$ can be broadcast to each agent, which in most cases is a reasonable assumption. We present an approach for approximating difference evaluation functions in order to provide agent-specific feedback to improve coordination, and demonstrate in two domains the effectiveness and scalability of our approach.

The key contribution of this work is presenting a novel method to implement difference evaluation functions in any generic multiagent system, without requiring global knowledge about the state of the system or the mathematical form of the system evaluation function. Further, this approximation approach significantly outperforms methods which use the overall system evaluation function. As each agent maintains a local approximation of the system evaluation function, increases in computational cost are insignificant, because the computation is parallelized across each agent in the system.

An analysis of the relationship between the degree of factoredness of the function approximation and the performance relative to difference evaluations is the most interesting future research topic. In the 10 agent domain, the approximation of $G(s, a)$ was 94% factored and resulted in 88% of the performance of $D_i(s, a)$ without approximation. In the 100 agent domain, the approximation of $G(s, a)$ was 78% factored and resulted in 79% of the performance of $D_i(s, a)$ without approximation; this is an intriguing result, although without further research no claims can be made. There is a clear relationship between the factoredness of the approximation and the resultant system performance, but the nature of this relationship should be further investigated.

Acknowledgements

This work was partially supported under NASA NNX14AI10G.

REFERENCES

[1] J. Abounadi, D. Bertsekas, and V. Borkar. Stochastic Approximation for Non-Expansive Maps: Application to Q-Learning Algorithms. Technical report, SIAM Journal on Control and Optimization, 1998.

[2] A. Agogino and K. Tumer. Analyzing and Visualizing Multiagent Rewards in Dynamic and Stochastic Environments. *Journal of Autonomous Agents and Multi-Agent Systems*, 17(2):320–338, 2008.

[3] K. Anderson and Y. Hsu. Genetic crossover strategy using an approximation concept. In *In IEEE Congress on Evolutionary Computation*, pages 527–533, 1999.

[4] W. B. Arthur. Inductive Reasoning and Bounded Rationality (The El Farol Problem). In *Amer. Econ. Review 1994*, volume 84, pages 406–411, 1994.

[5] J. Branke, C. Schmidt, and H. Schmeck. Efficient Fitness Estimation in Noisy Environment. In *Proceedings of Genetic and Evolutionary Computation*, pages 243–250, 2001.

[6] D. Brillinger. Learning a Potential Function From a Trajectory. *Signal Processing Letters, IEEE*, 14(11):867–870, 2007.

[7] D. Buche, N. Schraudolph, and P. Koumoutsakos. Accelerating Evolutionary Algorithms Using Fitness Function Models. In *Proc. Workshops Genetic and Evolutionary Computation Conference*, 2003.

[8] M. Colby, J. J. Chung, and K. Tumer. Implicit adaptive multi-robot coordination in dynamic environments. In *2015 IEEE/RSJ International Conference on Intelligent Robots and Systems*, 2015.

[9] M. Colby and K. Tumer. Shaping Fitness Functions for Coevolving Cooperative Multiagent Systems. In *Proceedings of the 11th International Conference on Autonomous Agents and Multiagent Systems (AAMAS 2012)*, Valencia, Spain, June 2012.

[10] M. Colby and K. Tumer. An evolutionary game theoretic analysis of difference evaluation functions. In *In Proceedings of Genetic and Evolutionary Computation Conference*, 2015.

[11] C. Gaskett, L. Fletcher, and A. Zelinsky. Reinforcement Learning for Visual Servoing of a Mobile Robot. In *In Proceedings of the Australian Conference on Robotics and Automation (ACRA 2000)*, 2000.

[12] Y. Isukapalli. An Analytically Tractable Approximation for the Gaussian Q-Function. *IEEE Communications Letters*, 12(9):669 – 671, 2008.

[13] Y. Jin. A Comprehensive Survey of Fitness Approximation in Evolutionary Computation. *Soft Comput.*, 9(1):3–12, Jan. 2005.

[14] E. Marder-Eppstein. ROS Wiki - move_base. http://wiki.ros.org/move_base. Accessed: 2015-11-13.

[15] J. Martikainen and S. Ovaska. Fitness Function Approximation by Neural Networks in the Optimization of MGP-FIR Filters. In *Adaptive and Learning Systems, 2006 IEEE Mountain Workshop on*, pages 7–12, 2006.

[16] H. Murao and S. Kitamura. Incremental State Acquisition for Q-Learning by Adaptive Gaussian Soft-Max Neural Network. In *Proceedings of the 1998 IEEE ISIC/CIRA/ISAS Joint Conference*, 1999.

[17] V. Oduguwa and R. Roy. Multiobjective Optimization of Rolling Rod Product Design Using Metamodeling Approach. *In Genetic and Evolutionary Computation Conference*, pages 1164–1171, 2002.

[18] P. Pandey and D. Pandey. Reduct Based Q-learning: an Introduction. In *Proceedings of the 2011 International Conference on Communication*, ICCCS '11, pages 285–288, New York, NY, USA, 2011. ACM.

[19] C. Pantofaru. ROS Wiki - leg_detector. http://wiki.ros.org/leg_detector. Accessed: 2015-11-13.

[20] S. Proper and K. Tumer. Modeling Difference Rewards for Multiagent Learning (Extended Abstract). In *Proceedings of the Eleventh International Joint Conference on Autonomous Agents and Multiagent Systems*, Valencia, Spain, June 2012.

[21] M. Quigley, K. Conley, B. Gerkey, J. Faust, T. Foote, J. Leibs, R. Wheeler, and A. Ng. ROS: An open-source Robot Operating System. In *International Conference on Robotics and Automation Workshop on Open Source Software*, 2009.

[22] D. Stonier, J. Lee, and H. Kim. ROS Wiki - rocon. http://wiki.ros.org/rocon. Accessed: 2015-11-13.

Reinforcement Learning in Partially Observable Multiagent Settings: Monte Carlo Exploring Policies with PAC Bounds

Roi Ceren
THINC Lab, Dept. of Computer Science
University of Georgia
Athens, GA 30602
rceren@uga.edu

Prashant Doshi
THINC Lab, Dept. of Computer Science
University of Georgia
Athens, GA 30602
pdoshi@cs.uga.edu

Bikramjit Banerjee
School of Computing
University of S. Mississippi
Hattiesburg, Miss. 39406
bikramjit.banerjee@usm.edu

ABSTRACT

Perkins' Monte Carlo exploring starts for partially observable Markov decision processes (MCES-P) integrates Monte Carlo exploring starts into a local search of policy space to offer a template for reinforcement learning that operates under partial observability of the state. In this paper, we generalize the reinforcement learning under partial observability to the self-interested multiagent setting. We present a new template, MCES-IP, which extends MCES-P by maintaining predictions of the other agent's actions based on dynamic beliefs over models. MCES-IP is instantiated to be approximately locally optimal with some probability by deriving a theoretical bound on the sample size that in part depends on the allowed error from the sampling; we refer to this algorithm as MCESIP+PAC. Our experiments demonstrate that MCESIP+PAC learns policies whose values are comparable or better than those from MCESP+PAC in multiagent domains while utilizing much less samples for each transformation.

1. INTRODUCTION

Action-value based reinforcement learning (RL) algorithms such as Sarsa(λ) [1] and Q-learning [2] represent some of the best performing RL methods in single-agent settings. If the state is partially observable, the agent may simply use its previous observation as the state of a Markov decision process but the learning may not converge [3]. More preferably, the agent conditions its learning on the recent history of observations [4]. Diverging from the traditional action-value that is computed for a state or observation history, Perkins [5] utilizes action-value to evaluate a *policy*. A T-step (deterministic) policy is a mapping from observation histories of length up to T to an action. This less explored avenue has the strong benefit of directly searching a discrete space of policies and does not require the convergence of action-values for each state before the policy is obtained.

Perkins' Monte Carlo exploring starts for POMDP (MCES-P) [5] obtains action-value for a policy from sampled trajectories, and uses it to determine whether a transformed policy in the local neighborhood of the current policy is better. Sutton and Barto [1] introduced a refinement to Monte Carlo Q-learning allowing the agent to start with a random state-action pair, and called it *exploring starts*. Here, MCES-P transforms the policy using a random pair of observation sequence and action to obtain a locally transformed policy. When instantiated with a probably approximately correct (PAC) style of learning [5], MCES-P guarantees ϵ-local optimality with specified probability if all transformations are explored until the resulting policy stops improving.

The simplicity and theoretical guarantees of MCES-P motivate its generalization to partially observable multiagent settings. We generalize to an individual self-interested agent learning its policy in a setting shared with other agents whose actions cannot be perfectly observed. The generalization is suited to both cooperation and noncooperation between agents. In this regard, this paper makes the following contributions:

1. We introduce a novel RL template for partially observable multiagent settings: MCES-IP that aims to learn a policy for an agent acting and planning in a setting shared with other agents.
2. We comprehensively show that MCESIP+PAC which additionally maintains a prediction of likely actions that others performed based on models converges to policies whose values are comparable or better than the baseline MCES-P in stationary and non-stationary environments with significantly less samples needed per transformation.
3. Instantiations MCESP+PAC and MCES-IP both exhibit the PAC guarantee that the policy on termination is ϵ-locally optimal with a probability that depends on ϵ.
4. We present an observation history pruning method which eliminates transforming over rare experiences, trading some of the PAC guarantees for significant decrease in run time.

We now discuss the minimum epistemological requirements for the learning in MCES-IP. Without loss of generality, we assume that the learning agent's observation is decomposed into public and private signals. While the public signal is common to all agents in the environment, the private signal may differ between agents and is perceived by the corresponding agent only. Of course, both public and private signals may influence each agent's action. A partial observation function that gives the distribution over the joint private signals conditioned on the joint actions is known to all agents in the setting; the transition and reward functions of agents are not known. Subsequently, the RL in MCES-IP is not completely model free.

While convergence to a local optimum is a less desirable guarantee, nevertheless we may combine it with a method such as random restarts to almost surely reach the global optimum. However, any theoretical bounds on sample complexity may no longer hold.

2. RELATED WORK

Several approaches exist for optimizing behavior in uncertain environments with or without the presence of other agents. In the single-agent context, partially observable Markov decision processes (POMDP) [6] consider optimal outcomes to strategies given

Appears in: *Proceedings of the 15th International Conference on Autonomous Agents and Multiagent Systems (AAMAS 2016), J. Thangarajah, K. Tuyls, C. Jonker, S. Marsella (eds.), May 9–13, 2016, Singapore.*

an explicit model of the environment. In multiagent settings, decentralized POMDPs (DEC-POMDP) [7] and interactive POMDPs (I-POMDP) [8] tackle cooperative and self-interested settings, respectively, by considering the effect of other agents and their actions on the state of the game. Solution methods have so far predominantly relied on explicit models of the mechanics of the environment and the opponent.

Early model-free approaches for multiagent problems have been explored in both cooperative and non-cooperative settings. Monte Carlo Q-Alternating (MCQ-Alt) [9] approximates the dynamics of an environment in the presence of another cooperating agent following a fixed policy. After arriving at a locally optimal policy, the agent fixes its own policy and the other agent then learns. Other Q-learning techniques are available for cooperative multiagent settings where communication is not possible [10], and thus the joint action-observation history is unknown. These approaches learn action values based on local observations in the context of agents that are learning concurrently or alternating in action. However, the approach often converges to policies that are considerably suboptimal compared to exact solutions, while better performing heuristics require providing hidden state information prior to learning.

Factored-value partially observable Monte Carlo planning [11] produces policies for agents acting in cooperative multiagent contexts by exploiting actions whose sampled rewards dominate neighboring actions via Q-learning. The approach scales well with the number of agents, observations and states, depending on the method used but requires noise-free, instant communication between agents and does not apply to non-cooperative settings.

A Bayes-Adaptive I-POMDP (BA-IPOMDP) [12] maintains a vector of latent models of environment mechanics and updates its belief over these models online. In contrast to learning policies for all agents, MCES-IP focuses on learning the policy of an individual self-interested agent that shares its environment with cooperative or noncooperative agents. It does not require explicit models of the environment, which are potentially infinite in the case of BA-IPOMDPs. Effectively, BA-IPOMDP casts model-free learning as planning over an infinite space. Along similar lines, Hoang and Low [13] show how a flat Dirichlet Multinomial distribution may be utilized to represent the posterior in interactive Bayes-optimal RL by an agent interacting with other self-interested agents. Differing from our context, the state is assumed to be perfectly observable.

3. BACKGROUND

Perkins' Monte Carlo Exploring Starts for POMDPs (MCES-P) [5] offers a template for online model-free RL in a way that differs substantially from traditional model-free methods such as Q-learning. At its core, it hill climbs the space of neighboring policies, which draws comparisons to policy iteration rather than the value iteration of Q-learning. A random observation sequence, $\vec{o}$, and corresponding action are picked and the latter replaces the previous action at $\vec{o}$ thereby transforming the policy. [1] This is analogous to Sutton's Monte Carlo exploring starts scheme [1] that picked a random state to begin explorations.

To decide whether the transformed policy should be retained instead of the original policy, each policy is simulated to obtain a trajectory of actions, observations and rewards for T time steps: $\tau = \{a^0, r^0, o^1, a^1, r^1, o^2, a^2, r^2, \ldots, o^{T-1}, a^{T-1}, r^{T-1}\}$. Let $R(\tau) = \sum_{t=0}^{T-1} \gamma^t\, r^t$ be the discounted sum of rewards gathered in trajectory τ where $\gamma \in (0,1)$ is the discount factor. Let $R_{pre-\vec{o}}(\tau)$ and $R_{post-\vec{o}}(\tau)$ be the sum of portions of $R(\tau)$ gathered before and after the appearance of $\vec{o}$ in the trajectory, respectively. Notice that the value of a policy may be written as,

$$\begin{aligned} Q_\pi &\approx E^{\tau\sim\pi}[R(\tau)] \\ &= E^{\tau\sim\pi}[R_{pre-\vec{o}}(\tau) + R_{post-\vec{o}}(\tau)] \\ &= E^{\tau\sim\pi}[R_{pre-\vec{o}}(\tau)] + E^{\tau\sim\pi}[R_{post-\vec{o}}(\tau)] \end{aligned}$$

Comparing between a policy and its transformation at $\vec{o}$ is facilitated by this decomposition: it allows focus on the difference in the value of the second term obtained for the two policies as the value of the first term remains unchanged because the changed action on observing $\vec{o}$ cannot impact $R_{pre-\vec{o}}(\tau)$.

Subsequently, MCES-P proceeds by randomly picking an observation sequence at which to transform a policy, sufficiently simulating the original and transformed policies and updating their Q-values with new information for comparison. The transformed policy is adopted if its Q-value exceeds that of the original by ϵ both updated across k samples. The algorithm terminates in the absence of policy transformations for some time.

MCESP+PAC Perkins notes a particular instantiation of MCES-P that utilizes Hoeffding's inequality to ensure that a sufficient number k of samples are taken so that a difference of given ϵ is observed with probability $1-\delta$ or more. This instantiation theoretically founded on Greiner's probably approximately locally optimal learning system [14] derives the following value difference threshold between the Q-values of the two policies based on the number of samples, k_m and probability, δ_m at stage m:

$$\epsilon(m,p,q) = \begin{cases} 2T(R_{max} - R_{min})\sqrt{\frac{1}{2p}\ln\frac{2(k_m-1)N}{\delta_m}} & \text{if } p = q < k_m \\ \frac{\epsilon}{2} & \text{if } p = q \geq k_m \\ +\infty & \text{otherwise} \end{cases}$$

Here, p and q are the number of sampled trajectories simulated from the original and transformed policies, respectively; these must be equal for a comparison. Sample complexity k_m is derived as:

$$k_m \leftarrow \left\lceil 2\frac{(2T(R_{max} - R_{min}))^2}{\epsilon^2} \ln\frac{2N}{\delta_m} \right\rceil$$

and

$$\delta_m \leftarrow \frac{6\delta}{m^2\pi^2}$$

where N is the size of the neighborhood of a policy; $R_{max} = \max_{s,a} R(s,a)$ and $R_{min} = \min_{s,a} R(s,a)$. If we allow the policy to change by a single action only, then the size of N is $\mathcal{O}(|A|\frac{|\Omega|^T-1}{|\Omega|-1})$, which is much less than the entire space of policies $\mathcal{O}(|A|^{\frac{|\Omega|^T-1}{|\Omega|-1}})$; notice that the former is no longer exponential in number of observations. The algorithm terminates if the current policy remains better after k_m samples are reached for both the current and transformed policies or if no neighboring policy exceeds it by more than $\epsilon - 2T(R_{max} - R_{min})\sqrt{\frac{1}{2p}\ln\frac{2(k_m-1)N}{\delta_m}}$ when the number of samples p is less than k_m. We note that the method requires prior knowledge of the maximum and minimum rewards across all states and actions, R_{max} and R_{min}, respectively.

An appealing property of MCESP+PAC is that the policy on termination is guaranteed to be *ϵ-locally optimal*. In other words, no neighboring policy exists that exceeds the current policy in value greater than ϵ.

[1] Perkins' MCES-P curbs the policies to actions contingent on a single observation, ie., memory-less policies. Therefore, it initially picks a single observation and action only. We extend the algorithm here to consider a *sequence* of observations for better performance.

4. RL IN MULTIAGENT SETTINGS

In our review of related work as outlined in Section 2, we did not find any algorithm for truly model-free RL in partially observable multiagent settings (technically our setting is a partially observable stochastic game). [2] Subsequently, MCES-P offers an appealing template for generalizing to multiagent settings with the potential to fill this wide gap. While we focus on learning by *self-interested* agents situated in a multiagent setting in this paper, MCES-P is sufficiently generic for extension to learning the joint policies of multiple agents in cooperative settings as well – an investigation that we defer to future work.

Observe that the MCES-P template briefly discussed in Section 3 may be utilized almost as is in a multiagent setting. Therefore, we begin by exploring this approach followed by presenting a new generalization of MCES-P that improves on it significantly.

4.1 MCESP+PAC in Multiagent Settings

As we mentioned previously, the template offered by MCES-P continues to remain viable for a learning agent i when we generalize from single- to multi-agent settings. Toward this end, we reproduce Perkins' algorithm below in Algorithm 1. Let π_i be the initial seed policy and $\pi_i \leftarrow (\vec{o}_i, a_i)$ be this policy but transformed to perform action a_i on observing $\vec{o}_i$; the latter denotes a neighboring policy.

Algorithm 1 MCES-P

Require: Q-value table initialized; initial policy π_i that is greedy w.r.t. Q-values; learning rate schedule α; horizon T; and error ϵ

$c_{\vec{o}_i,a_i} \leftarrow 0$ for all $\vec{o}_i$ and a_i
$m \leftarrow 0$
repeat
  Pick some observation history $\vec{o}_i$ and action a_i
  Modify π_i to $\pi_i \leftarrow (\vec{o}_i, a_i)$
  Generate trajectory τ of length T according to $\pi_i \leftarrow (\vec{o}_i, a_i)$ (this involves simulating the implicit policies of other agents as well)
  $Q_{\pi_i \leftarrow \vec{o}_i,a_i} \leftarrow (1 - \alpha(m, c_{\vec{o}_i,a_i}))\ Q_{\pi_i \leftarrow \vec{o}_i,a_i} + \alpha(m, c_{\vec{o}_i,a_i})\ R_{post-\vec{o}_i}(\tau)$
  $c_{\vec{o}_i,a_i} \leftarrow c_{\vec{o}_i,a_i} + 1$
  if $\max_{a_i'} Q_{\pi_i \leftarrow \vec{o}_i,a_i'} - Q_{\pi_i} > \epsilon(m, c_{\vec{o}_i,a_i}, c_{\vec{o}_i,\pi_i(\vec{o}_i)})$ **then**
    $\pi_i(\vec{o}_i) \leftarrow a_i'$ where $a_i' \in \arg\max Q_{\pi_i \leftarrow \vec{o}_i,a_i'}$
    $m \leftarrow m + 1$
    for all $\vec{o}_i, a_i$ **do**
      $c_{\vec{o}_i,a} \leftarrow 0$
until termination

In instantiating the above template for PAC bounds, we assume that the other agent is guided by a fixed policy or a fixed distribution over policies (i.e., mixed strategy). This ensures that the sampling distribution is fixed and Hoeffding's inequality continues to apply. We point out that this assumption differentiates our problem from the traditional multiagent RL [15] where all agents are learning simultaneously and therefore the learning problem is not stationary.

Given the above, MCESP+PAC in multiagent settings may face the same four types of errors due to sampling as those faced in single agent settings (see proof of Theorem 1 in Appendix). However, the error due to sampling and the sample complexity differ because of the presence of other agents although the size of the policy neighborhood remains the same. Let $\Lambda(\pi_i, \pi_i')$ be the upper bound on the range of the difference between the action-values of π_i and some other policy π_i'. For simplicity of presentation, we consider one other agent j in the environment. Let $R_{i,max}$ now be defined as, $R_{i,max} \triangleq \max_{s,a_i,a_j} R_i(s, a_i, a_j)$ and analogously for $R_{i,min} \triangleq \min_{s,a_i,a_j} R_i(s, a_i, a_j)$. Then, we get,

[2]Note that MCQ-Alt [9] learns an estimate of the model from samples as an intermediate step and is therefore quasi model based.

$$\begin{aligned}\Lambda(\pi_i,\pi_i') &\triangleq \max_{\tau} (Q_{\pi_i} - Q_{\pi_i'}) - \min_{\tau} (Q_{\pi_i} - Q_{\pi_i'}) \\ &\le \sum_{t=0}^{T-1} \{(R_{i,max} - R_{i,min}) - (R_{i,min} - R_{i,max})\} \\ &= \sum_{t=0}^{T-1} 2(R_{i,max} - R_{i,min}) = 2T(R_{i,max} - R_{i,min})\end{aligned} \tag{1}$$

Consequently, the threshold for comparison at stage m becomes:

$$\epsilon(m,p,q) = \begin{cases} \Lambda(\pi_i,\pi_i')\sqrt{\frac{1}{2p}\ln\frac{2(k_m-1)N}{\delta_m}} & \text{if } p = q < k_m \\ \frac{\epsilon}{2} & \text{if } p = q \ge k_m \\ +\infty & \text{otherwise} \end{cases}$$

and the sample complexity is:

$$k_m = \left\lceil 2\frac{(\Lambda(\pi_i,\pi_i'))^2}{\epsilon^2} \ln\frac{2N}{\delta_m} \right\rceil$$

while the probability δ_m remains the same as in Section 3. Notice that in so called "neutral settings" where agent i's reward does not depend on j's action (although the state is still impacted by j's action) $R_{i,max}$ and $R_{i,min}$ collapse into R_{max} and R_{min}, respectively causing no change in the PAC bounds from Section 3. However, in competitive settings $R_{i,max}$ is often greater than R_{max} whereas $R_{i,min}$ tends to be smaller than its counterpart due to which the sample complexity is higher or the error is greater for the same number of samples.

MCESP+PAC terminates if there has been no policy change when k_m samples are reached or if no neighboring policy exceeds the current policy in action value by more than $\epsilon - \Lambda(\pi_i, \pi_i') \cdot \sqrt{\frac{1}{2p}\ln\frac{2(k_m-1)N}{\delta_m}}$ for lesser samples.

Theorem 1 shows that MCESP+PAC in partially observable multiagent settings will terminate and converge to an ϵ-locally optimal policy.

THEOREM 1 (LOCAL OPTIMALITY OF MCESP+PAC). *Instantiation MCESP+PAC incrementally produces a series of policies $\pi_i^1, \pi_i^2, \ldots, \pi_i^m$, such that each π_i^{n+1} is a local neighbor of π_i^n and with probability at least $1 - \delta$:*

1. *Each policy π_i^{n+1} has an expected value strictly greater than its predecessor, π_i^n where $1 \le n \le m - 1$;*

2. *Final policy π_i^m returned by MCESP+PAC is ϵ-locally optimal such that there is no neighbor of π_i^m given our transformation procedure whose expected value exceeds that of π_i^m by more than ϵ.*

Moreover, MCESP+PAC will terminate with probability 1 if N is finite.

The full proof of this theorem is given in the Appendix. It presents four types of errors that are possible due to sampling. As part of the proof, the expressions for $\epsilon(m, p, q)$, k_m and δ_m are also established.

4.2 MCES-IP Template for RL

While Theorem 1 is appealing, a limitation of MCESP+PAC is that the required sample size is very large. For example, for an ϵ of 0.05 and probability δ = 0.1 the required sample size k_m is 320,200 for the small two-agent competitive Tiger problem. Can we significantly reduce this alarming sample complexity and if so what is the trade off?

A key insight may allow us to mitigate the sample complexity: *If we can predict the other agent's actions, then we may simply optimize in that specific context.* Toward this, we partially relax the model-free characteristic of the RL to obtain savings in samples. We may divide agent i's observations into those that are public and those that are private. The former type are public signals that are shared between agents while the latter are signals privately observed by an agent. This division is without loss of generality because the set of public observations may be empty if agents have private observations only and the set of private observations is empty if only public observations are obtained.

Next, let the private monitoring at time t convey information to the agent about the other agent's action at $t-1$ albeit noisily while the public signal provides information about the common state of the system. We argue that this specificity is often seen in multiagent problems. For example, agents in the multiagent Tiger problem hear growls that inform about the location of the tiger and each agent may also hear a creak from the left or right, or do not hear a creak indicating the door, if any, that was opened by the other agent.

As a final step, we depart from the completely model-free setting of MCES-P and let a joint private observation function that models the information content of private observations only be common knowledge. The agents are not aware of any other model parameters.

Given the setup above, agents in the MCES for interactive POMDP (MCES-IP) template start with a prior distribution over possible models of the other agent and update the prior as they receive private observations. As the agent acts and observes, a sequence of beliefs are obtained and the agent utilizes both sequences: observation sequence and belief sequence to decide on an action. We show the MCES-IP template in Algorithm 2.

Algorithm 2 MCES-IP

Require: Q-value table initialized; initial policy, π_i, that is greedy w.r.t. Q-values; prior on set of models M_j; learning rate schedule α; horizon T; and error ϵ

1: $c^{\vec{a}_j}_{\vec{o}_i,a_i} \leftarrow 0$
2: $m \leftarrow 0$
3: **repeat**
4: Pick some observation history, $\vec{o}_i$, and a_i
5: Modify π_i to $\pi_i \leftarrow (\vec{o}_i, a_i)$
6: Generate trajectory τ of length T according to $\pi_i \leftarrow (\vec{o}_i, a_i)$
7: Generate belief sequence $\vec{b}_i$ based on τ
8: Obtain most probable action sequence $\vec{a}_j$ from $\vec{b}_i$
9: $Q^{\vec{a}_j}_{\pi_i \leftarrow \vec{o}_i,a_i} \leftarrow (1-\alpha(m, c^{\vec{a}_j}_{\vec{o}_i,a_i})) \cdot Q^{\vec{a}_j}_{\pi_i \leftarrow \vec{o}_i,a_i} + \alpha(m, c^{\vec{a}_j}_{\vec{o}_i,a_i}) \cdot R_{post-\vec{o}_i}(\tau)$
10: $c^{\vec{a}_j}_{\vec{o}_i,a_i} \leftarrow c^{\vec{a}_j}_{\vec{o}_i,a_i} + 1$
11: **if** $\max_{a'_i} Q^{\vec{a}_j}_{\pi_i \leftarrow \vec{o}_i,a'_i} - Q^{\vec{a}_j}_{\pi_i} > \epsilon^{\vec{a}_j}(m, c^{\vec{a}_j}_{\vec{o}_i,a_i}, c^{\vec{a}_j}_{\vec{o}_i,\pi_i(\vec{o}_i)})$ **then**
12: $\pi_i(\vec{o}_i) \leftarrow a'_i$ where $a'_i \in \arg\max_{a'_i} Q^{\vec{a}_j}_{\pi_i \leftarrow \vec{o}_i,a'_i}$
13: $m \leftarrow m+1$
14: **for all** $\vec{o}_i, a_i, \vec{a}_j$ **do**
15: $c^{\vec{a}_j}_{\vec{o}_i,a_i} \leftarrow 0$
16: **until** termination

MCES-IP generally follows the procedure of MCES-P. It builds on the latter by additionally generating a belief sequence $\vec{b}_i$ using the actions and observations in a trajectory (line 7); each belief is a distribution over a pre-defined set of models of the other agent. As the space of possible belief sequences is continuous, MCES-IP picks the most-probable model from each belief and the corresponding predicted action, to obtain a corresponding action sequence $\vec{a}_j$ (line 8). Q-values and update counts are now indexed using this action sequence (lines 9-10). In this way, action values of polices are specific to predicted actions of the other agent, which allow a more informed probabilistic hill climbing in multiagent settings.

Belief sequence, $\vec{b}_i$, is generated as follows. A trajectory τ_i is $\{a_i^0, r_i^0, \langle o^1, \omega_i^1\rangle, a_i^1, r_i^1, \langle o^2, \omega_i^2\rangle, a_i^2, r_i^2, \ldots, \langle o^{T-1}, \omega_i^{T-1}\rangle, a_i^{T-1}, r_i^{T-1}\}$. Notice that each observation in the trajectory is composed of public and private signals; denote $\vec{o}_i \triangleq \langle \vec{o}, \vec{\omega}_i\rangle$. Let M_j^t be a discrete set of j's models at time step t, where $m_j^t \in M_j^t$ is: $m_j^t \triangleq \langle h_j^t, \pi_j\rangle$, h_j^t is j's action-observation history of length t which when given as input to j's policy π_j produces the predicted action at time t. Agent i's belief b_i is a distribution over M_j updated based on i's action and observation as given below:

$$b'_i(m_j^{t+1}|a_i^t, o^{t+1}, \omega_i^{t+1}, b_i) = \sum_{m_j^t \in M_j^t} b_i(m_j^t) \sum_{a_j^t \in A_j} Pr(a_j^t|m_j^t)$$
$$\times\, O_i(\omega_i^{t+1}|a_i^t, a_j^t)\, \delta_K(h_j^{t+1}, \text{APPEND}(h_j^t, a_j^t, o^{t+1})) \qquad (2)$$

As a part of updating its belief, i must first update its models of j and in particular, the action-observation history contained in each model using the predicted action a_j^t and public observation o^{t+1}; this is performed by APPEND. Kronecker delta function, δ_K, is 1 if an updated model matches the one in m_j^{t+1} otherwise it is 0. Private observation function O_i is the marginal of the joint, and it allows using the private signal to weight predicted actions and by backward inference the models that generated the actions. This likelihood is then propagated forward to the updated model, m_j^{t+1}. As such, Eq. 2 is a sophisticated Bayesian belief update.

A sequence of beliefs $\vec{b}_i$ is then generated by updating the uniform prior with the action-observation pairs in a trajectory using Eq. 2; thus the length of this sequence is T. We may pick the most probable model from each belief in the sequence, $\arg\max_{m_j} b_i(m_j)$, and get the model-predicted action, $\arg\max_{a_j} Pr(a_j|m_j)$, to obtain the action sequence $\vec{a}_j$.

MCESIP+PAC We instantiate Algorithm 2 to obtain MCES-IP with PAC bounds, which we denote as MCESIP+PAC. For this, we assume that the error is due to sampling trajectories only and that the monitoring is perfect, ie., private signals perfectly reveal j's action. We discuss the effect on the bounds due to observation noise later in this section. For a given error ϵ and probability δ let,

$$\epsilon^{\vec{a}_j}(m,p,q) = \begin{cases} \Lambda^{\vec{a}_j}(\pi_i,\pi'_i)\sqrt{\frac{1}{2p}\ln\frac{2(k_m-1)N}{\delta_m}} & \text{if } p=q<k_m \\ \frac{\epsilon}{2} & \text{if } p=q\geq k_m \\ +\infty & \text{otherwise} \end{cases}$$

where

$$k_m = \left\lceil 2\frac{(\Lambda^{\vec{a}_j}(\pi_i,\pi'_i))^2}{\epsilon^2}\ln\frac{2N}{\delta_m}\right\rceil$$

and

$$\delta_m = \frac{6\delta}{m^2\pi^2}$$

Here, $\Lambda^{\vec{a}_j}(\pi_i,\pi'_i)$ is an upper bound on the range of the difference in action-values between two policies given j's action sequence is $\vec{a}_j$. Let $R^{a_j}_{i,max} = \max_{s,a_i} R_i(s,a_i,a_j)$ and analogously for $R^{a_j}_{i,min}$; these specific values are assumed to be known. Then, we get:

$$\Lambda^{\vec{a}_j}(\pi_i,\pi'_i) = \max_\tau \left(Q^{\vec{a}_j}_{\pi_i} - Q^{\vec{a}_j}_{\pi'_i}\right) - \min_\tau \left(Q^{\vec{a}_j}_{\pi_i} - Q^{\vec{a}_j}_{\pi'_i}\right)$$
$$\leq \sum_{t\in T}\left(R^{a_j^t}_{i,max} - R^{a_j^t}_{i,min}\right) - \left(R^{a_j^t}_{i,min} - R^{a_j^t}_{i,max}\right)$$
$$= \sum_{t\in T} 2\left(R^{a_j^t}_{i,max} - R^{a_j^t}_{i,min}\right) \qquad (3)$$

We note the following key proposition that indicates the benefit of predicting the other agent's actions on sample complexity albeit at the expense of the belief update run time.

PROPOSITION 2 (REDUCED SAMPLE COMPLEXITY). *For any predicted action sequence,* $\vec{a}_j$,

$$\Lambda^{\vec{a}_j}(\pi_i, \pi_i') \leq \Lambda(\pi_i, \pi_i')$$

where Eqs. 1 and 3 define $\Lambda(\pi_i, \pi_i')$ and $\Lambda^{\vec{a}_j}(\pi_i, \pi_i')$, respectively. The proof of this proposition is straightforward and is given in the Appendix. Subsequently, Proposition 2 entails that the sample size bound k_m for MCESIP+PAC is also less than or equal to the corresponding sample size bound for MCESP+PAC. The effect is significant because k_m grows quadratically with Λ. On the other hand, the Q-values table expands significantly with up to $\frac{|\Omega|^T-1}{|\Omega|-1}$ values for each i's policy or its transformation. As such, the reduced sample bound of MCESIP+PAC must be less by a factor of $\frac{|\Omega|^T-1}{|\Omega|-1}$ in the worst case to be effective. This is often the case as we demonstrate for the two-agent Tiger problem where k_m for MCESIP+PAC is as low as 106,822 that is almost three times less than that for MCESP+PAC.

If private signals provide perfect information about j's actions, then MCESIP+PAC terminates when,

$$Q^{\vec{a}_j}_{\pi_i \leftarrow \vec{o}_i, a_i'} < Q^{\vec{a}_j}_{\pi_i} + \epsilon - \epsilon^{\vec{a}_j}(m, c^{\vec{a}_j}_{\vec{o}_i, a_i}, c^{\vec{a}_j}_{\vec{o}_i, \pi_i(\vec{o}_i)})$$

for all $\vec{o}_i$, $a_i' \neq \pi_i(\vec{o}_i)$, and we have encountered at most $\frac{|\Omega|^T-1}{|\Omega|-1}$ many distinct $\vec{a}_j$ in the trajectories for each $\vec{o}_i$, a_i' pair. Under the same assumption of perfect monitoring, for the comparison threshold, sample bound and probability as defined above, the following theorem obtains for MCESIP+PAC.

THEOREM 3 (LOCAL OPTIMALITY UNDER PERFECT MONITORING). *Template MCESIP+PAC under perfect monitoring incrementally produces a series of policies $\pi_i^1, \pi_i^2, \ldots, \pi_i^m$, such that each π_i^{q+1} is a local neighbor of π_i^q and with probability at least $1 - \delta$:*

1. *Each policy π_i^{q+1} has an expected value strictly greater than its predecessor, π_i^q where $1 \leq q \leq m-1$;*
2. *Final policy, π_i^m returned by MCESIP+PAC is ϵ-locally optimal such that there is no neighbor of π_i^m given our transformation procedure whose expected value exceeds that of π_i^m by more than ϵ.*

Moreover, MCESIP+PAC terminates with probability 1 if N is finite.

The proof of this theorem proceeds analogously to the proof for Theorem 1, with Λ replaced with $\Lambda^{\vec{a}_j}$.

We can generalize the above results on MCESIP+PAC for the case of *imperfect monitoring* – when the probability of error in estimating $\vec{a}_j$ is known, say δ_e. In this case, the agent may place Q-samples in the wrong $Q^{\vec{a}_j}$ bins (see line 9 of Algorithm 2), leading to non-identically distributed samples in a bin. Fortunately, given δ_e we may generalize Theorem 3 to the case of independent but non-identically distributed samples using a more general form of Hoeffding's inequality. Analogously to Eq. 3, let $\bar{\Lambda}^{\vec{a}_j}$ be an upper bound on the range of differences in action-values for all j's action sequences that are *different* from $\vec{a}_j$. Then for the case of $p = q < k_m$, we redefine $\epsilon^{\vec{a}_j}(m, p, q)$ as,

$$\epsilon^{\vec{a}_j}(m,p,q) = \sqrt{(1-\delta_e)(\Lambda^{\vec{a}_j})^2 + \delta_e(\bar{\Lambda}^{\vec{a}_j})^2}\sqrt{\frac{1}{2p}\ln\frac{2(k_m-1)N}{\delta_m}}$$

where k_m is redefined as

$$k_m = \left\lceil \frac{2((1-\delta_e)(\Lambda^{\vec{a}_j})^2 + \delta_e(\bar{\Lambda}^{\vec{a}_j})^2)}{\epsilon^2} \ln \frac{2N}{\delta_m} \right\rceil$$

Algorithm 2 requires a slight modification for this case. For convenience, let $\zeta^{\vec{a}_j} = \max_{a_i'} Q^{\vec{a}_j}_{\pi_i \leftarrow \vec{o}_i, a_i'} - Q^{\vec{a}_j}_{\pi_i}$. Then, line 11 of Algorithm 2 changes to the following:

$$(1-\delta_e)\zeta^{\vec{a}_j} + \delta_e \bar{\zeta}^{\vec{a}_j'} > (1-\delta_e)\epsilon^{\vec{a}_j} + \delta_e \bar{\epsilon}^{\vec{a}_j'}$$

The implicit assumption above is that when $Q^{\vec{a}_j}$ receives a wrong sample meant for bin $\vec{a}_j'$, the action sequence is equally likely to be any $\vec{a}_j' \neq \vec{a}_j$. Therefore, $\bar{\zeta}^{\vec{a}_j'}$ is the mean of $\zeta^{\vec{a}_j'}$ for all $\vec{a}_j' \neq \vec{a}_j$ seen so far, and analogously $\bar{\epsilon}^{\vec{a}_j'}$ is also the mean. Notice that insisting on the test of line 11 for every $\vec{a}_j$ before the current policy is changed, would be a stronger form of this test, and hence also sufficient. Finally, we note that when $\delta_e = 0$, we recover MCESIP+PAC for perfect monitoring as a special case of this setting.

5. PRUNING POLICY SEARCH SPACE

Theorems 1 and 3 require exploring all local transformations of a policy for establishing local optimality. However, some of these transformations prescribe differing actions in response to observation sequences that are not likely to occur. Yet, we are required to obtain k_m samples of trajectories involving such observation sequences or establish a significant difference in action-values for less numbers of such samples. This contributes significantly to long run times of the algorithms as we noticed in our experiments. Subsequently, we seek ways to remove such rare observation sequences from consideration thereby pruning the policy search space. As these sequences are relatively much less likely they also contribute less to the expected value of a policy, but not considering them nonetheless introduces *regret* that we seek to compute.

Ignoring a different action at some observation sequence $\vec{o}_i$ is regrettable because we are foregoing the possibility of improving the expected value of i's policy. Of course, a less likely observation sequence may not add much to the expected value of the current policy. Nevertheless, let ϕ be a user-defined bound on allowable regret. By avoiding transforming on $\vec{o}_i$, we are foregoing at most the largest post-$\vec{o}_i$ rewards; specifically this regret is upper bounded by $\max_\tau R_{post-\vec{o}_i}(\tau) - \min_\tau R_{post-\vec{o}_i}(\tau)$. Regret on the expected value of the policy is bounded by

$$\begin{aligned} regret_{\vec{o}_i} &\leq Pr(\vec{o}_i; \pi_i, \pi_j)\left(\max_\tau R_{post-\vec{o}_i}(\tau) - \min_\tau R_{post-\vec{o}_i}(\tau)\right) \\ &= Pr(\vec{o}_i; \pi_i, \pi_j)\,(T - len(\vec{o}_i))\,(R_{i,max} - R_{i,min}) \end{aligned} \quad (4)$$

Here, $Pr(\vec{o}_i; \pi_i, \pi_j)$ is the likelihood of the observation sequence $\vec{o}_i$ whose computation depends on the actions prescribed by both agents' policies, state transition and observation functions; rewards $R_{i,max}$ and $R_{i,min}$ are as defined previously. We may normalize the regret to obtain a proportion between 0 and 1 as, $\overline{regret}_{\vec{o}_i} = \frac{regret_{\vec{o}_i}}{T(R_{i,max} - R_{i,min})}$.

Of course, not knowing π_j and the model parameters implies that we cannot compute $Pr(\vec{o}_i; \pi_i, \pi_j)$ exactly. Hence, as a first step in this paper, we settle for a crude approximation where $Pr(\vec{o}_i; \pi_i, \pi_j)$ is estimated by the fraction of times $\vec{o}_i$ occurs in the k_m or more samples generated so far. This requires keeping a count of each observation sequence encountered in the trajectories.

Let $\mathcal{P}$ be the set of i's observation sequences that will be avoided. If a bound ϕ on the regret is given by the user, we may obtain $\mathcal{P}$ in a straightforward way: Sort the set of all observation sequences of all

Algorithm 3 MCES-IP_Prune

Require: Q-value table initialized; initial policy, π_i, that is greedy w.r.t. Q-values; prior on set of models M_j; learning rate schedule α; horizon T; error ϵ; and regret bound ϕ

1: $c^{\vec{a}_j}_{\vec{o}_i,a_i} \leftarrow 0, c_{\vec{o}_i} \leftarrow 0$ for all $\vec{o}_i$, a_i, and a_j
2: $m \leftarrow 0$
3: $\mathcal{P} \leftarrow \emptyset$
4: **repeat**
5:   Pick some observation history $\vec{o}_i$ and action a_i
6:   $c_{\vec{o}_i} \leftarrow c_{\vec{o}_i} + 1$
7:   **if** $\vec{o}_i \notin \mathcal{P}$ **then**
8:     Modify π_i to $\pi_i \leftarrow (\vec{o}_i, a_i)$
9:   **else**
10:     Go to line 5
11:   Generate trajectory τ of length T according to $\pi_i \leftarrow (\vec{o}_i, a_i)$
12:   Generate belief sequence $\vec{b}_i$ based on τ
13:   Obtain most probable action sequence $\vec{a}_j$ from $\vec{b}_i$
14:   $Q^{\vec{a}_j}_{\pi_i \leftarrow \vec{o}_i,a_i} \leftarrow (1-\alpha(m, c^{\vec{a}_j}_{\vec{o}_i,a_i})) \cdot Q^{\vec{a}_j}_{\pi_i \leftarrow \vec{o}_i,a_i} + \alpha(m, c^{\vec{a}_j}_{\vec{o}_i,a_i}) \cdot R_{post-\vec{o}_i}(\tau)$
15:   $c^{\vec{a}_j}_{\vec{o}_i,a_i} \leftarrow c^{\vec{a}_j}_{\vec{o}_i,a_i} + 1$
16:   **if** $\max_{a'_i} Q^{\vec{a}_j}_{\pi_i \leftarrow \vec{o}_i,a'_i} \geq Q^{\vec{a}_j}_{\pi_i} + \epsilon^{\vec{a}_j}(m, c^{\vec{a}_j}_{\vec{o}_i,a_i}, c^{\vec{a}_j}_{\vec{o}_i,\pi_i(\vec{o}_i)})$ **then**
17:     $\pi_i(\vec{o}_i) \leftarrow a'_i$
18:     $m \leftarrow m + 1$
19:     **for all** $\vec{o}_i, a_i, \vec{a}_j$ **do**
20:       $c^{\vec{a}_j}_{\vec{o}_i,a_i} \leftarrow 0$
21:   **if** $\sum_{\vec{o}_i \in \mathcal{P} \cup \vec{o}_i} \bar{regret}_{\vec{o}_i} \leq \phi + \rho(\sum_{\vec{o}_i} c_{\vec{o}_i})$ **then**
22:     $\mathcal{P} \leftarrow \mathcal{P} \cup \vec{o}_i$
23: **until** termination

lengths by their frequency of occurrence in ascending order. Then, add a sequence into $\mathcal{P}$ beginning with the least frequent and moving up the ordering such that, $\sum_{\vec{o}_i \in \mathcal{P}} \bar{regret}_{\vec{o}_i} \leq \phi$. Consequently, a bound that is more loose would allow disregarding more observation sequences to meet it and thereby prune a larger portion of the search space. Alternately, the sorting is not necessary and we may simply pick an observation sequence at random and check if adding it to $\mathcal{P}$ would cause the cumulative normalized regret to exceed ϕ.

The pruning mechanism described previously may be incorporated into both the MCES-P and MCES-IP templates. Algorithm 3 outlines how it may be utilized with MCES-IP. Two additions can be observed. Lines 7-10 make a determination if the current $\vec{o}_i$ is in the set $\mathcal{P}$ of sequences that will not be considered (initialized to the empty set), and if not policy π_i is locally transformed at $\vec{o}_i$. Lines 21-22 add the observation sequence $\vec{o}_i$ into set $\mathcal{P}$ if the cumulative normalized regret due to all observation sequences in $\mathcal{P}$ including $\vec{o}_i$ remains less than or equal to given bound $\phi + \rho(\sum_{\vec{o}_i} c_{\vec{o}_i})$, where

$$\rho(i) = \begin{cases} 0 & i \geq k \\ +\infty & \text{otherwise} \end{cases}$$

Thus, $\mathcal{P}$ remains empty unless a reasonable number of samples are obtained. In the case of MCESIP+PAC instantiation of the template, k could be simply set to the derived sample bound $\frac{k_m}{2}$.

6. EXPERIMENTS

We implement MCESP+PAC and MCESIP+PAC to obtain converged policies for two strategic and noncooperative multiagent domains. We first experiment with a competitive, multiagent version of the Tiger problem [8]. Our second domain is a 3×2 autonomous unmanned aerial vehicle (AUAV) reconnaissance domain [16]. We set up the AUAV domain by beginning every round with the AUAV in the bottom-left sector and the fugitive in the top-right of a 3×2 grid, and all sectors in the leftmost column are considered safe. Each agent has 3 actions: the AUAV may move left, right, or up, and the fugitive may move left, right, or down. Both agents receive 1 of 4 noisy public observations, representing whether both agents are East or West of each other, North or South of each other, in the same sector, or none of these. The subject agent, which is the AUAV, additionally receives 1 of 3 noisy private observations each correlated with an action the opponent takes. A third domain is the money laundering (ML) problem [17] where a blue team seeks to confiscate illicit money that the opponent red team is laundering. The red team can move money from the initial state to a series of placement states (banks and insurance), to layering states (offshore accounts and shell companies), to integration states (casinos and real estate), and to the safe clean pot. The blue team may place a sensor at each of these locations or confiscate the illicit funds. Each agent receives a noisy public observation indicating whether the money and sensor are in the same location, in the same laundering state, or if neither are the case. The blue team also receives a noisy observation of the last action of the red team.

Table 1 summarizes the domain statistics and parameter settings. For all domains and both methods, each agent has a 15% chance of receiving a noisy public and private observation. The opponent in both games follows a single policy (stationary environment) or fixed distribution over multiple policies (nonstationary environment).

Domain	Specifications
Multiagent Tiger	$\epsilon = 0.05, \delta = 0.1, \phi = 0.15, T = 3,$ $\lvert\Omega\rvert = 2, \lvert A_i\rvert = 3, \lvert A_j\rvert = 3, \lvert\Pi_j\rvert = 14$
3×2 AUAV	$\epsilon = 0.1, \delta = 0.1, \phi = 0.2, T = 3,$ $\lvert\Omega\rvert = 4, \lvert A_i\rvert = 3, \lvert A_j\rvert = 3, \lvert\Pi_j\rvert = 4$
Money Laundering	$\epsilon = 0.1, \delta = 0.15, \phi = 0.2, T = 3,$ $\lvert\Omega\rvert = 4, \lvert A_i\rvert = 4, \lvert A_j\rvert = 5, \lvert\Pi_j\rvert = 8$

Table 1: Parameter configurations for the three problem domains.

We simulate i's policies with opponent j following either a single policy or a mixture of two policies. These policies are picked from a predefined set Π_j. As per the policy space specified in Table 1, 105 games of the multiagent Tiger problem, 9 of the 3×2 AUAV problem, and 13 of ML comprise the data set.

First, we show that MCESP+PAC and MCESIP+PAC demonstrates the PAC guarantee of monotonically increasing successive transformations. Figure 1 illustrates three example runs and the values for MCESP+PAC and MCESIP+PAC given the same opponent. Different runs undergo varying number of transformations with some policies not transforming at all because they are ϵ-locally optimal initially itself. As shown in Fig. 1, each successive transformation results in a higher value and in no case is the final policy lower in value than the initial policy as we should expect. In every case, MCESP+PAC requires more samples to transform than MCESIP+PAC.

Second, Table 2 lists the mean of the theoretical sample bound k_m across the different stages m over all runs and the mean of the effective number of samples over all runs that were utilized by both methods. In validation of our theoretical result, MCESIP+PAC requires remarkably fewer samples to transform per action sequence, around half in multiagent Tiger, about a quarter in 3×2 AUAV, and nearly a tenth in Money Laundering. Additionally, the bound on k_m is also significantly less compared to the bound for MCESP+PAC. Due to stochasticity in the simulations and finite sampling bounds, MCESP+PAC and MCESIP+PAC may deviate in transformation paths. However, in over 80% of the runs, both result in the same converged policy with MCESIP+PAC converging on average under half the number of samples taken by MCESP+PAC.

Finally, observation sequence pruning plays a crucial role in

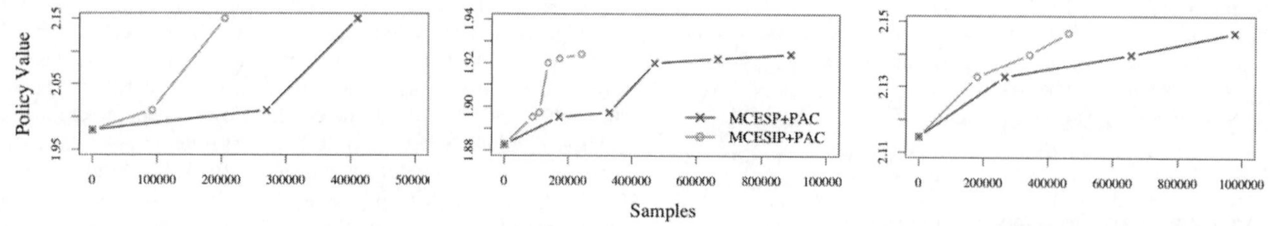

Figure 1: Example policy transformation paths with intermediate values for 3 different opponents in the multiagent Tiger problem. The right most transformation paths are for an opponent with mixed strategy.

Domain	Method	Policy	Mean # of samples per transform	Mean bound on k_m
Tiger	MCESP+PAC	Single	156,328 ± 21,012	265,948 ± 7,909
		Mixed	219,057 ± 9,521	263,565 ± 6,101
	MCESIP+PAC	Single	72,740 ± 5,963	117,590 ± 3,309
		Mixed	117,504 ± 6,678	119,313 ± 1,089
3×2 AUAV	MCESP+PAC	Single	32,397 ± 2,816	91,443 ± 637
		Mixed	42,126 ± 1,689	96,328 ± 118
	MCESIP+PAC	Single	6,437 ± 68	20,397 ± 206
		Mixed	19,499 ± 1,304	22,763 ± 169
ML	MCESP+PAC	Single	20,717 ± 2,418	34,726 ± 617
		Mixed	20,247 ± 4,974	35,612 ± 490
	MCESIP+PAC	Single	1,947 ± 330	24,172 ± 448
		Mixed	3,174 ± 536	24,347 ± 482

Table 2: Mean effective sample size and theoretical bound across the stages for the three problem domains, stratified over method and whether the opponent follows a single policy or a mixed set of policies.

Pruning	Metric	Multiagent Tiger	3×2 AUAV	ML
Without	Neighborhood	128	470	636
	Total k_m	15,893,387	3,704,396	18,911,460
With	Neighborhood	26	32	76
	Total k_m	2,093,328	624,057	2,259,860

Table 3: Neighborhood size and total k_m values for all the domains using their respective parameters in Table 1, with and without pruning for both MCESP+PAC and MCESIP+PAC. Note that the total bound on samples reduces by almost an order of magnitude.

improving the scalability of MCESP+PAC and MCESIP+PAC, dramatically reducing the search space and run time while minimizing the impact on incurred regret. We list the mean of the required total k_m values across all observation sequences for both problem domains in Table 3, both with and without pruning. As the policy search space for both methods is the same, the regret due to pruning the search space does not depend on the method used. Observation sequence pruning benefits both methods equally in reducing the policy search space as we demonstrate in Table 3.

Each neighborhood is calculated with a horizon of 3. For the multiagent Tiger problem, the size of the observation sequence space per round is 6 (2 public × 3 private observations) with 3 possible actions, resulting in a maximum neighborhood of 128. Given a regret bound of 0.15, 34 of 43 distinct observation sequences are eliminated on average, resulting in a neighborhood of 26. For 3×2 AUAV, the observation space is 12 (4 public × 3 private observations) with 3 actions, resulting in a neighborhood of 470. On average, 146 of 157 observation sequences are pruned for a regret bound of 0.2, leaving 32 neighbors. ML's observation space is 9 (3 public × 3 private observations) with 7 actions, resulting in a neighborhood of 636. With a regret bound of 0.2, 80 of 91 sequences are pruned leaving 76 neighbors.

7. CONCLUDING REMARKS

MCES-P offers a template for model-free RL in partially observable settings that differs from traditional Q-learning. It's appealing because it may be instantiated in different ways, resulting in algorithms with differing behavior. In this paper, we generalized MCES-P with PAC bounds to self-interested multiagent settings presenting a model-free RL technique. We exploited the insight that modeling the other agent should catalyze learning leading to a new algorithm, MCESIP+PAC.

MCESIP+PAC dramatically reduces the sample complexity of MCESP+PAC with reductions on sample bounds and empirical sample counts ranging between 50% to 75% less than MCESP+PAC. In nearly every case, MCESIP+PAC is able to achieve the same optima as MCESP+PAC despite the fraction of samples taken. We additionally introduced observation sequence pruning, a methodology that significantly improves run time by reducing the policy search space with bounded regret. We observed over 80% reduction in sample requirement for our domains while introducing a regret between 0.15 and 0.2. Our future work involves extending MCES-P to learning the joint policies in a cooperative setting and analyzing its theoretical properties.

Acknowledgements

This research is supported in part by grants from NSF IIS-0845036 (to PD) and IIS-1526813 (to BB) and a grant from ONR N-00-0-141310870 (to PD). We thank Theodore Perkins for email exchanges that benefited this paper.

APPENDIX

Proof of Theorem 1 MCESP+PAC in the multiagent setting allows for a PAC-style guarantee of ϵ-local optimality. To show that the total error for MCESP+PAC is bounded by the user-defined ϵ with probability $1 - \delta$, we must first define the types of errors that can occur in selecting dominating neighboring policies and terminating when none is found after sampling. In this respect, our proof follows that of Greiner [14].

We define $\mathcal{N}(\pi)$ as the set of neighboring policies of π. A policy is considered a neighbor if it differs from π by only one action for all observation sequences.

1. After seeing p samples (where $p < k$), MCESP+PAC selects some $\pi' \in \mathcal{N}(\pi)$, as π' appears higher value than π, but it is not
2. After seeing p samples (where $p < k$), MCESP+PAC cannot find a $\pi' \in \mathcal{N}(\pi)$ where π' appears higher value than π, but there is one
3. After seeing all k_m samples, MCESP+PAC selects some $\pi' \in \mathcal{N}(\pi)$, as π' appears higher value than π, but it is not
4. After seeing all k_m samples, MCESP+PAC cannot find a $\pi' \in \mathcal{N}(\pi)$ where π' appears higher value than π, but there is one

Recall ϵ and k_m for MCESP+PAC are as follows.

$$\epsilon^*(m,p,q) = \Lambda(\pi_i, \pi_i')\sqrt{\frac{1}{2p}\ln\frac{2(k_m-1)N}{\delta_m}}$$

$$k_m = \left\lceil 2\frac{(\Lambda(\pi_i,\pi_i'))^2}{\epsilon^2}\ln\frac{2N}{\delta_m}\right\rceil$$

Also, let $E[\pi]$ be the reward of the policy π, in the context of other agents and the environment, which the Q-value approximates.

$$a_m^n = Pr\left[\exists\pi_i' \in \mathcal{N}(\pi_i^m) : (Q^{\pi_i'} - Q^{\pi_i^m}) \geq \epsilon(m, c_i^{\pi_i'}, c_i^{\pi_i^m})\right.$$
$$\left.\text{and } E[\pi_i'] < E[\pi_i^m]\right]$$

$$b_m^n = Pr\left[\exists\pi_i' \in \mathcal{N}(\pi_i^m) : (Q^{\pi_i'} - Q^{\pi_i^m}) < \epsilon - \epsilon(m, c_i^{\pi_i'}, c_i^{\pi_i^m})\right.$$
$$\left.\text{and } E[\pi_i'] > E[\pi_i^m] + \epsilon\right]$$

$$c_m = Pr\left[\exists\pi_i' \in \mathcal{N}(\pi_i^m) : (Q^{\pi_i'} - Q^{\pi_i^m}) \geq \frac{\epsilon}{2}\right.$$
$$\left.\text{and } E[\pi_i'] < E[\pi_i^m]\right]$$

$$d_m = Pr\left[\exists\pi_i' \in \mathcal{N}(\pi_i^m) : (Q^{\pi_i'} - Q^{\pi_i^m}) < \frac{\epsilon}{2}\right.$$
$$\left.\text{and } E[\pi_i'] > E[\pi_i^m] + \epsilon\right]$$

We represent each of the probabilities above as disjoint sets over neighbors and the agents' policies. For example, $\mathcal{N}_i^<(\pi_i^m) = \{\pi_i \in \mathcal{N}(\pi^m) | E[\pi_i'] < E[\pi_i^m]\}$.

$$a_m^n = Pr\Big[\bigvee_{\pi_i' \in \mathcal{N}_i^<(\pi_i^m)} (Q^{\pi_i'} - Q^{\pi_i^m}) \geq \epsilon(m, c_i^{\pi_i'}, c_i^{\pi_i^m})\Big]$$

$$b_m^n = Pr\Big[\bigvee_{\pi_i' \in \mathcal{N}_i^>(\pi_i^m)} (Q^{\pi_i'} - Q^{\pi_i^m}) < \epsilon - \epsilon(m, c_i^{\pi_i'}, c_i^{\pi_i^m})\Big]$$

$$c_m = Pr\Big[\bigvee_{\pi_i' \in \mathcal{N}_i^<(\pi_i^m)} (Q^{\pi_i'} - Q^{\pi_i^m}) \geq \frac{\epsilon}{2}\Big]$$

$$d_m = Pr\Big[\bigvee_{\pi_i' \in \mathcal{N}_i^>(\pi_i^m)} (Q^{\pi_i'} - Q^{\pi_i^m}) < \frac{\epsilon}{2}\Big]$$

Considering every possible π' in π^m's neighborhood leads to the following summation.

$$a_m^n \leq \sum_{\pi_i' \in \mathcal{N}_i^<(\pi_i^m)} Pr[(Q^{\pi_i'} - Q^{\pi_i^m}) \geq \epsilon(m, c_i^{\pi_i'}, c_i^{\pi^m}, k_m)]$$
$$\leq \sum_{\pi_i' \in \mathcal{N}_i^<(\pi_i^m)} Pr[(Q^{\pi_i'} - Q^{\pi_i^m}) \geq (E[\pi_i'] - E[\pi_i^m]) + \epsilon(m, c_i^{\pi_i'}, c_i^{\pi^m})]$$
$$\leq \sum_{\pi_i' \in \mathcal{N}_i^<(\pi_i^m)} exp\left\{-2p\left(\frac{\epsilon(m, c_i^{\pi_i'}, c_i^{\pi_i^m})}{\Lambda(\pi_i', \pi_i^m, \pi_j)}\right)^2\right\} \tag{5}$$
$$= \frac{|\mathcal{N}_i^<(\pi_i^m)|\delta_m}{2(k_m-1)|\mathcal{N}(\pi_i^m)|}$$

Equation 5 follows from Hoeffding's Inequality, where $(Q^{\pi_i'} - Q^{\pi_i^m})$ is the sample average of $E[\pi_i'] - E[\pi_i^m]$. We reduce 5 by utilizing ϵ when $p = q < k_m$. b_m^n follows,

$$b_m^n \leq \sum_{\pi_i' \in \mathcal{N}_i^>(\pi_i^m)} Pr\left[(Q^{\pi_i'} - Q^{\pi_i^m}) < \epsilon - \epsilon(m, c_i^{\pi_i'}, c_i^{\pi^m}, k_m)\right]$$
$$\leq \frac{|\mathcal{N}_i^>(\pi_i^m)|\delta_m}{2(k_m-1)|\mathcal{N}(\pi_i^m)|}$$

The other two error types, where $p = k_m$, follow similarly but substitute k_m for n.

$$c_m \leq \sum_{\pi_i' \in \mathcal{N}_i^<(\pi_i^m)} Pr\left[(Q^{\pi_i'} - Q^{\pi_i^m}) \geq \frac{\epsilon}{2}\right] \tag{6}$$

$$\leq \sum_{\pi_i' \in \mathcal{N}_i^<(\pi_i^m)} exp\left\{-2k_m\left(\frac{\epsilon/2}{\Lambda(\pi_i', \pi_i^m, \pi_j)}\right)^2\right\} = \frac{|\mathcal{N}_i^<(\pi_i^m)|\delta_m}{2|\mathcal{N}(\pi_i^m)|} \tag{7}$$

where Eq. 7 is obtained by substituting k_m with its derived value in the previous expression and reducing.

$$d_{m,\pi_j} \leq \sum_{\pi_i' \in \mathcal{N}_i^>(\pi_i^m)} Pr\left[(Q^{\pi_i'} - Q^{\pi_i^m}) < \frac{\epsilon}{2}\right] \leq \frac{|\mathcal{N}_i^>(\pi_i^m)|\delta_m}{2|\mathcal{N}(\pi_i^m)|}$$

The sum total of the error is as follows.

$$\sum_{n=1}^{k_m-1}[a_m^n + b_m^n] + c_m + d_m$$
$$= \sum_{n=1}^{k_m-1}\left[\frac{|\mathcal{N}_i^<(\pi_i^m) + |\mathcal{N}_i^>(\pi_i^m)|}{|\mathcal{N}(\pi_i^m)|}\frac{\delta_m}{2(k_m-1)}\right]$$
$$+ \frac{|\mathcal{N}_i^<(\pi_i^m)| + |\mathcal{N}_i^>(\pi_i^m)|}{\mathcal{N}(\pi_i^m)|}\frac{\delta_m}{2} = \delta_m$$

Over all possible transformations, the total error is bounded by δ.

$$\sum_{m=1}^{\infty}\delta_m = \sum_{m=1}^{\infty}\frac{6\delta}{m^2\pi^2} = \frac{6\delta}{\pi^2}\sum_{m=1}^{\infty}\frac{1}{m^2} = \frac{6\delta}{\pi^2}\frac{\pi^2}{6} = \delta$$

Proof of Proposition 2 Consider the following expanded definition of Prop. 2.

$$\sum_{t=0}^{T}[\max_s\{R(a_{\pi_i'}^t, a_j^t, s) - R(a_{\pi_i^k}^t, a_j^t, s)\} -$$
$$\min_s\{R(a_{\pi_i'}^t, a_j^t, s) - R(a_{\pi_i^k}^t, a_j^t, s)\}] \leq$$
$$\sum_{t=0}^{T}[\max_{s,a_j}\{R(a_{\pi_i'}^t, a_j, s) - R(a_{\pi_i^k}^t, a_j, s)\} -$$
$$\min_{s,a_j}\{R(a_{\pi_i'}^t, a_j, s) - R(a_{\pi_i^k}^t, a_j, s)\}]$$

- Assume $\min_s = \min_{s,a_j}$ for all $t \in T$, resulting in the expression $\sum_{t=0}^{T}\max_s\{R(a_{\pi_i'}^t, a_j^t, s) - R(a_{\pi_i^k}^t, a_j^t, s)\} \leq \sum_{t=0}^{T}\max_{s,a_j}\{R(a_{\pi_i'}^t, a_j, s) - R(a_{\pi_i^k}^t, a_j, s)\}$. It must be the case that the LHS must be at most equivalent to the RHS, as, if the a_j selected in the LHS is the maximal value, the $\max_{s,a_j}$ will select it. If the a_j selected on the LHS is not the maximal value for a given a_i and s, the RHS must then be greater.
- Assume $\max_s = \max_{s,a_j}$ for all $t \in T$, resulting in the expression $\sum_{t=0}^{T}\min_s\{R(a_{\pi_i'}^t, a_j^t, s) - R(a_{\pi_i^k}^t, a_j^t, s)\} \geq \sum_{t=0}^{T}[\min_{s,a_j}\{R(a_{\pi_i'}^t, a_j, s) - R(a_{\pi_i^k}^t, a_j, s)\}]$. Analogously to point 1, if the a_j on the LHS is the minimal value, then the $\min_{s,a_j}$ on the RHS must select it. If it is not, the RHS must be less.
- Following point 1 and 2, since each component of the LHS must be bounded by the equivalent component on the RHS, the LHS must be a smaller range than the RHS. Therefore, $\Lambda^{\vec{a_j}}(\pi_i', \pi_i^m) \leq \Lambda(\pi_i', \pi_i^m)$

REFERENCES

[1] Richard S Sutton and Andrew G Barto. *Introduction to reinforcement learning*. MIT Press, 1998.

[2] Christopher JCH Watkins and Peter Dayan. Q-learning. *Machine learning*, 8(3-4):279–292, 1992.

[3] Leemon Baird et al. Residual algorithms: Reinforcement learning with function approximation. In *International Conference on Machine Learning (ICML)*, pages 30–37, 1995.

[4] Steven D Whitehead. Reinforcement learning for the adaptive control of perception and action. Technical report, DTIC Document, 1992.

[5] Theodore J Perkins. Reinforcement learning for POMDPs based on action values and stochastic optimization. In *AAAI Conference on Artificial Intelligence*, pages 199–204, 2002.

[6] Stuart Russell, Peter Norvig, and Artificial Intelligence. A modern approach. *Artificial Intelligence. Prentice-Hall, Egnlewood Cliffs*, 25, 1995.

[7] Daniel S Bernstein, Shlomo Zilberstein, and Neil Immerman. The complexity of decentralized control of markov decision processes. In *Sixteenth conference on Uncertainty in Artificial Intelligence (UAI)*, pages 32–37. Morgan Kaufmann Publishers Inc., 2000.

[8] Piotr J. Gmytrasiewicz and Prashant Doshi. A framework for sequential planning in multiagent settings. *Journal of Artificial Intelligence Research*, 24:49–79, 2005.

[9] Bikramjit Banerjee, Jeremy Lyle, Landon Kraemer, and Rajesh Yellamraju. Sample bounded distributed reinforcement learning for decentralized POMDPs. In *AAAI Conference on Artificial Intelligence*, 2012.

[10] Landon Kraemer and Bikramjit Banerjee. Reinforcement learning of informed initial policies for decentralized planning. *ACM Transactions on Autonomous and Adaptive Systems (TAAS)*, 9(4):18, 2014.

[11] Christopher Amato and Frans A Oliehoek. Scalable planning and learning for multiagent POMDPs. In *Twenty-Ninth AAAI Conference on Artificial Intelligence (AAAI)*, 2015.

[12] Brenda Ng, Kofi Boakye, Carol Meyers, and Andrew Wang. Bayes-adaptive interactive POMDPs. In *AAAI Conference on Artificial Intelligence*, 2012.

[13] Trong Nghia Hoang and Kian Hsiang Low. A general framework for interacting bayes-optimally with self-interested agents using arbitrary parametric model and model prior. In *Twenty-Third International Joint Conference on Artificial Intelligence (IJCAI)*, pages 1394–1400, 2013.

[14] Russell Greiner. Palo: A probabilistic hill-climbing algorithm. *Artificial Intelligence*, 84(1):177–208, 1996.

[15] Yoav Shoham and Kevin Leyton-Brown. *Multiagent Systems: Algorithmic, Game-theoretic, and Logical Foundations*. Cambridge University Press, 2009.

[16] Ekhlas Sonu and Prashant Doshi. Generalized and bounded policy iteration for finitely-nested interactive pomdps: Scaling up. In *11th International Conference on Autonomous Agents and Multiagent Systems (AAMAS)*, pages 1039–1048, 2012.

[17] Brenda Ng, Carol Meyers, Kofi Boakye, and John Nitao. Towards applying interactive POMDPs to real-world adversary modeling. In *Innovative Applications in Artificial Intelligence (IAAI)*, pages 1814–1820, 2010.

A Memetic Multi-Agent Demonstration Learning Approach with Behavior Prediction

Yaqing Hou
Interdisciplinary Graduate School
Nanyang Technological University, Singapore 639748
houy0003@e.ntu.edu.sg

Yifeng Zeng
School of Computing
Teesside University
Middlesborough, UK
y.zeng@tees.ac.uk

Yew-Soon Ong
School of Computer Engineering
Nanyang Technological University, Singapore 639748
asysong@ntu.edu.sg

ABSTRACT

Memetic Multi-Agent System (MeMAS) emerges as an enhanced version of multi-agent systems with the implementation of meme-inspired agents. Previous research of MeMAS has developed a computational framework in which a series of memetic operations have been designed for implementing multiple interacting agents. This paper further endeavors to address the specific challenges that arise in more complex multi-agent settings where agents share a common setting with other agents who have different and even competitive objectives. Particularly, we propose a memetic multi-agent demonstration learning approach (MeMAS-P) with improvement over existing work to allow agents to improve their performance by building candidate models and accordingly predicting behaviors of their opponents. Experiments based on an adapted minefield navigation task have shown that MeMAS-P could provide agents with ability to acquire increasing level of learning capability and reduce the candidate model space by sharing meme-inspired demonstrations with respect to their representative knowledge and unique candidate models.

Categories and Subject Descriptors

I.2.11 [**Distributed Artificial Intelligence**]: Multiagent systems

General Terms

Algorithms, Experimentation

Keywords

multiple agents; demonstration learning; memetic algorithms

1. INTRODUCTION

Memetic Multi-Agent System (MeMAS) has emerged as an enhanced version of multi-agent system (MAS) wherein all meme-inspired agents acquire increasing learning capacity and intelligence through meme evolution independently or via social interaction [1][8][16]. Taking inspiration from the Darwin's theory of natural selections and Darkins' notion of a meme [13][19], MeMAS introduces a computational framework in which a series of memetic operations have been designed for modeling multiple interacting agents, whereby memes form the fundamental building blocks of agents' mind universe, and can be transmitted to others. Importantly, when compared to the state-of-the-art multi-agent learning approaches, such as Advice Exchange Model (AE) [18], the modelling of multiple agents with MeMAS exhibits significant superiority in achieving a greater level of adaptivity and effective problem-solving. MeMAS has been successfully applied into several problem domains, such as the minefield simulation task [15] and 3D interactive video games [9].

Appears in: *Proceedings of the 15th International Conference on Autonomous Agents and Multiagent Systems (AAMAS 2016), J. Thangarajah, K. Tuyls, C. Jonker, S. Marsella (eds.), May 9–13, 2016, Singapore.*

Existing MeMAS has focused on a simple mutli-agent setting where all agents tend to have same or similar behaviors, and objectives. In case that multiple agents have different objectives, the modeling of multiple agents becomes rather difficult since agents are required to learn an "efficient" strategy to interact with their opponents. Nevertheless, searching for an optimal interaction strategy is a hard problem since its effectiveness depends mostly on the strategies of their opponents involved. Thus, it is further important to extend the agents' learning ability to recognize the strategies of other agents present in the environment.

In this paper, our interest lies in addressing the specific challenges that arise in more realistic and complex multi-agent settings where agents have different and even competitive objectives. Particularly, beyond the formalism of MeMAS and taking meme as basic unit of demonstrations, we propose a memetic multi-agent demonstration learning approach (MeMAS-P) with improvement over existing work to allow subject agents to improve their performance by predicting behavior of their opponents. More specifically, we make the contributions into the following two important components in the development of MeMAS-P:

- Given the instance data that was recorded from previous interaction activities, subject agents in the MeMAS-P are designed to automatically build candidate models of their opponents and predict their behavior by solving the models;
- MeMAS-P provides the ability for subject agents to enhance their learning performance and reduce the complexity of behavior prediction by sharing meme-inspired demonstrations with respect to their internal representative knowledge while also the available candidate models.

In the present study, a popular "Temporal Difference - Fusion Architecture for Learning and Cognition" (FALCON) [23] is employed as the connectionist reinforcement learning machine of our agents due to its well-established fast and online self-learning capabilities. Further, to investigate the effectiveness of the proposed MeMAS-P, we conduct the experiment on an adapted Minefield Navigation Task (MNT). The empirically results show that MeMAS-P could effectively improve the learning performance of subject agents while reducing the behavior prediction complexity through the embedded demonstration learning techniques.

The rest of the paper is organized as the follows: Section 2 provides an overview of the related research literature. Section 3 begins with a brief discussion of reinforcement learning which is followed by an introduction of MeMAS. Further, study of the proposed MeMAS-P which is composed of the behavior prediction and multi-agent demonstration learning is presented in Section 4. Section 5 presents a comprehensive empirical study of the proposed MeMAS-P based on an adapted Minefield Navigation Task. Finally, we conclude this paper with some brief remarks in Section 6.

2. LITERATURE REVIEW

Reinforcement learning (RL) is an interaction-based paradigm wherein agents learn to adjust their actions with the goal of maximizing the reward signals from the environment. Existing approaches for developing RL agents, such as temporal difference [22], dynamic programming [6], policy search [3], *etc.*, focus on the independent learning through exploring the environment. While such techniques have had great success in individual learning and software applications, they require a large amount of data and high exploration times and have limited applications in many realistic and complex problem domains.

On the other hand, learning from demonstration (LfD) is proposed as an algorithm that provides agents with demonstrations from a supposed expert, from which agents derive suitable learning policies and hence increase their learning speed [2]. Proposed techniques span a wide range of policy learning methods, ranging from classification [11] to regression [17], and utilizing a variety of interaction methods, such as natural language [21], kinesthetic teaching [7], observation [4] and advice exchanging [18]. Recently, LfD has also been successfully introduced into RL. For example, Torrey *et al.* [26] studied how a RL agent can best instruct another agent using a limited amount of demonstrations while Brys *et al.* [5] investigated the intersection of RL and LfD and further used the expert demonstrations to speed up learning through a reward shaping process. Nevertheless, existing LfD approaches to date focus almost exclusively on the problem of a single agent being taught by a single teacher demonstrator while the multi-agent demonstration learning has less been explored.

LfD can be problematic because of the number of trials necessary to gather sufficient samples to learn correctly. The problem becomes compounded in a multi-agent setting due to the potentially much larger design space arising from the number of and interactions between the agents. Currently, the research of LfD starts to take steps toward reducing the complexity. Multiple autonomous agents request advice and provide demonstrations for each other [18], and agents with similar behaviors learn from each other by leveraging broadcasted demonstrations [24]. Further, in a recent memetic multi-agents system, demonstrations have also been defined as memes and transferred among agents via an evolutionary imitation process [15]. However, most of the aforementioned research focus on the simple mutli-agent setting where agents tend to have same or similar behaviors, and objectives.

In this paper, we contribute to the development of LfD in multi-agent RL system. Particularly, using an example inspired from minefield navigation task, we investigate the proposed MeMAS-P in addressing the complex MAS problems where agents have competitive objectives.

3. PRELIMINARIES

This section begins with a brief introduction of reinforcement learning which is followed by an introduction of Memetic Multi-Agent System (MeMAS).

3.1 Reinforcement Learning

RL is a paradigm for an agent to optimize its behaviors through reward and punishment received from environment. A standard RL problem is typically formulated as a Markov decision process [22] which is composed of $< S, A, T, R >$ tuples where S indicates the observable environmental states, A denotes the available actions, T describes the stochastic transition between state s and s', usually defined as $T(s|a, s')$; R is the reward function that determines the scalar reward of a transition.

In case of the multiple-step decision making problems, the action selection should not only depend on the current states, since the agent can only know the merit of an action beyond several steps in the future. Thus, Temporal Difference (TD) method, such as Q-learning, is proposed to estimate for a learning system to perform an action a given state s. The iterative estimation of the value function $Q(s, a)$ is usually defined by:

$$Q(s,a) \leftarrow Q(s,a) + \alpha\delta$$

where $\alpha \in [0, 1]$ is the learning parameter, and δ is the temporal-difference error:

$$\delta = R(s,a,s') + \gamma max_{a'} Q(s',a') - Q(s,a)$$

where R is the immediate reward value of performing action a given state s, $\gamma \in [0, 1]$ is the discount parameter, and $max_{a'} Q(s', a')$ is the maximum estimated value of the next state s'.

In this work, we consider a self-organizing neural network "Temporal Difference - Fusion Architecture for Learning and Cognition" (FALCON) [23] (which is depicted in Fig. 1) as the connectionist RL machine of autonomous agents. FALCON employs a three-channel neural network architecture and comprises three input fields, namely, a sensory field F_1^{c1} for representing states, a motor field F_1^{c2} for representing actions, and a feedback field F_1^{c3} for representing reward values. It has a cognitive field F_2 for the acquisition and storage of learning knowledge, which encodes a relation among the patterns in the three input channels. Particularly, in FALCON dynamics, the baseline vigilance parameter ρ^k is an extremely important parameter since it controls the level of knowledge generation where $\rho^k \in [0, 1]$ for $k = 1, 2, 3$.

3.2 Memetic Multi-Agent System

In the design of MeMAS, which is depicted in Fig. 1, the core evolutionary process contains meme representation, meme expression, meme assimilation, meme internal evolution and meme external evolution. Particularly, the meme in memetic, as with genes in genetic, is represented as the building block of cultural transmission and replication. Further, meme representation represents the stored memes which is respectively described internally as the learned knowledge in agents' mind universe (Memotype) and externally as the manifested demonstrations that can be observed by others (Sociotype). Meme expression is the process for individual to express their internal memotypes as demonstrations to others while meme assimilation is the way for an individual to capture these demonstrations and update them into their respective mind universe. Notably, the expression of such memotypes might take the form of the domain-specific knowledge that infect other agents' perceptions, minds, etc. In the present study, we consider a manifestation of neuronal memes as memory items that fill agents' mind universe.

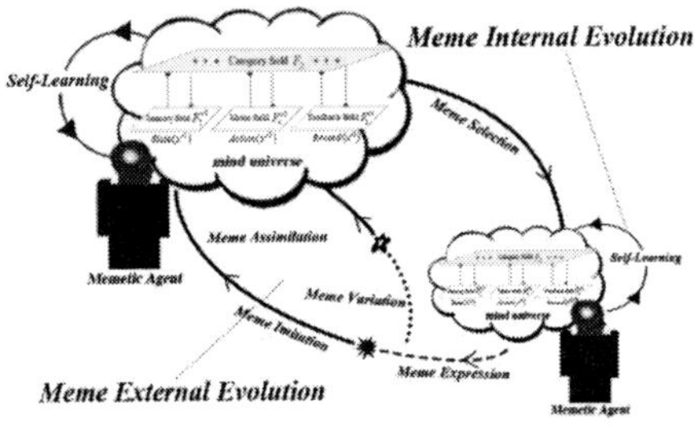

Figure 1: Illustration of the Memetic Multi-Agent System in which FALCON (inside the mind universe) is used as the learning machine for memetic agents.

Meme internal evolution and meme external evolution comprise the main behavioral learning aspects. Meme internal evolution is the process for agents to update their mind universe by self learning. Meme external evolution, on the contrary, serves to model the social interaction among agents. The implementation framework of MeMAS is outlined in Alg. 1. As indicated in the implementation, the meme evolution process is made up of a sequence of learning trials which will continue until the ultimate conditions, such as mission numbers, are satisfied. During the learning process, a population of memetic agents firstly conduct the meme internal evolution within the environment of interest (see line 5). In case that an agent identifies a teacher agent via meme selection, the meme external evolution happens to instruct how an agent learns from the others mainly via meme transmission process (see line 7-12).

MeMAS has been implemented in several applications. Particularly, in a simple minefield simulation task, Feng *et al.* [15] discuss the efficiency of MeMAS in improving the learning performance of agents by modeling the human-like social interactions. Further, Chen *et.al* [9] considers a scenario where agents have different memotypes, and MeMAS in an adapted minefield simulation task shows emergent behaviors of learning agents. Besides, a practical 3D interactive game, namely "Home Defence" has also been studied where non-player characters trained by MeMAS interact naturally with human-players online.

Algorithm 1: Pseudo Code of MeMAS

1 **Begin:**
2 **Initialization:** Generate the initial agents
3 **while** *stop conditions are not satisfied* **do**
4   **for** *each current agent* $agt(c)$ **do**
5   **Perform** *meme internal evolution* process
    /*Meme external evolution*/
6   **if** *identify teacher agent* $agt(s)$ *via meme selection* **then**
7   **Perform** *meme expression* with $agt(s)$ under the state of $agt(c)$
8   **Perform** *meme variation* with probability γ
9   /*γ is the frequency probability of variation process*/
10   **Perform** *meme transmission* for $agt(c)$ to assimilate $agt(s)$'s action
11   /*Perform action from meme external evolution if identified teacher agent, else perform action from meme internal evolution*/
12   /*End *meme internal evolution*/
13 **End**

4. PROPOSED MEMAS-P

We propose a memetic multi-agent demonstration learning framework (MeMAS-P) where subject agents could develop effective interactive mechanisms with existing opponent agents by predicting their behaviors. The implementation of MeMAS-P is depicted in Fig. 2, wherein the behavior prediction and multi-agent demonstration learning are defined as two major components.

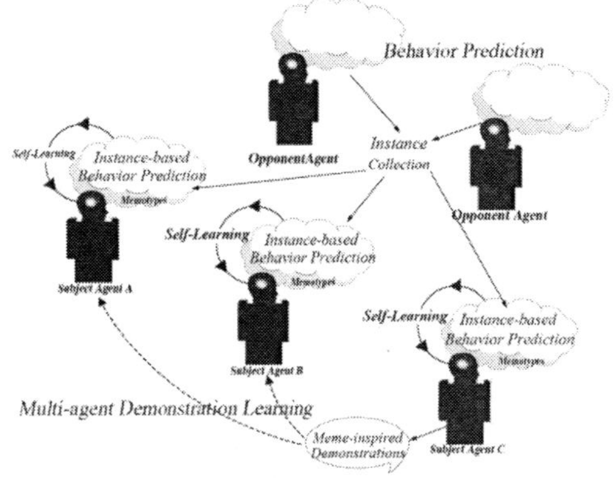

Figure 2: A Generic Illustration of the proposed MeMAS-P.

4.1 Learning Problem Specification

The learning problem of subject agents (defined by MDPs in Section 3.1) in MeMAS-P is made up of a sequence of simulations which will continue until the ultimate conditions, such as success levels, are satisfied. For each current step, subject agents select an appropriate action from a set of possible actions and learn the association from their current states, selected actions to the rewards received from the environment. Further, during the learning process, subject agents are likely to interact with one-or-more other agents, which could also influence individual rewards. Different to subject agents, the opponents that have competitive objectives follow static strategies that are unknown to subject agents. Both subject agents and their opponents act simultaneously at each time step while their actions cannot be directly observed by others.

4.2 Behavior Prediction

In complex multi-agent systems, subject agents are likely to encounter other opponent agents and may need to interact with them to achieve their own goals. In this case, they are required to be aware of the behavior or strategies of their opponents and hence design an efficient interactive solution to handle such encounters. However, agents are usually autonomous and their strategies are private. Therefore, it is essential to extend the the learning ability of subject agents to recognize the capabilities, strategies, or models of their opponents that are presented in the environment.

In our approach, subject agents are expected to build the interactive strategy by predicting the behavior of their opponents. Particularly, the prediction is achieved by solving opponents' models that are trained from the available data instances. Comparing with predicting behavior directly from the data, the model-based behavior prediction has better scalability since the knowledge is reusable. Also, if subject agents get access to the true model of the opponent, they can predict its behavior in any environment and conduct more sensible decisions.

Since the built models (or strategies) of opponent agents are not always known with certainty, subject agents need to maintain a number of candidate models and assign them confidence of being correct. When none of the available models is likely to be exactly correct, we select the one of them that better accounts for the collected data. Further, the confidence that is assigned to candidate models being correct can be adjusted online based on how well they predict the behavior of opponent agents. That means, in case that opponent agents make changes on their strategies during the interaction, subject agents can tune the confidence levels that were assigned to candidate models accordingly.

Alg. 2 summarizes the detailed learning process of subject agents with behavior prediction of their opponents. Specifically, before the learning process, the instances of opponent agents, which are formatted as a set of <S,A,R> tuples, are firstly collected to train all candidate models $M = \{M_1, M_2, ..., M_l\}$. For example, given a <S,A,R> instance, a FALCON candidate model will set a chosen action A, a given states S and a received reward R as inputs of vector F_1^{ck}. Then, it learns to associate the state F_1^{c1}, the action F_1^{c2} and the reward F_1^{c3} and blends them into the cognitive field F_2. Notably, in the study of RL, such instance based methods have been widely leveraged in predicting RL models [20][25]. Once the training process have been completed, subject agents will be assigned with a set of candidate models and begin the online learning process (see step 2-7).

Particularly, the behavior prediction happens whenever a subject agent detects any opponent agent $agt(o)$ nearby (see line 12). More specifically, an ϵ-greedy model selection scheme is used to balance the exploration and exploitation of candidate models (see line 13-16). It selects a candidate model M_s of the highest confidence value $conf(M_l)$ with probability 1 - ϵ ($0 \leq \epsilon \leq 1$), or chooses a random model otherwise. The value of ϵ gradually decays with behavior prediction times of each subject agent. Subsequently, the subject agent will simulate the virtual operation for each available action a and obtain a virtual state $s(agt(c))'$ (see

Algorithm 2: Self Learning with Behavior Prediction

Input: Candidate models $M = \{M_1, M_2, ...M_l\}$, Collected data $D = \{D_1, D_2, ...D_k\}$, where $D_k =< S_k, A_k, R_k >$, Current state s, Action set $A = [a_1, a_2, ..., a_i]$

1 **Begin**:
2 **for** *all* $M_l \in M$ **do**
3   **for** *all* $D_k \in D$ **do**
4   **Set** input vector $< S_k, A_k, R_k >$ in M_l
5   **Training** with vector $< S_k, A_k, R_k >$
6 **Initialize** subject agents and their opponents
7 **Assign** each subject agent with candidate models M
8 **while** *stop conditions are not satisfied* **do**
9   **for** *each subject agent* $agt(c)$ **do**
10   **Perform** *self learning* process
11   /*Behavior Prediction*/
12   **if** *detect an opponent agent* $agt(o)$ **then**
13   **if** $Rand > scheme(\epsilon)$ **then**
14         $M_s = Random\{M_l : for\ all\ model\ M\}$
15   **else**
16         $M_s = Max\{conf(M_l) : for\ all\ modelM\}$
17   **for** *each available action* $a_i \in A$ **do**
18         $s(agt(c))' = Virtual\_Perform(agt(c), a_i)$
19         $a_o = Predict(M_s, s(agt(c))')$
20         $s(agt(o))' = Virtual\_Perform(agt(o), a_o)$
21   **if** *fail interaction after virtual move* **then**
22   **Discard** a_i from action set A
23   **Get** a_s from A with highest reward of self learning in $agt(c)$
24   **Continue** *self learning* process
25   **Update** $conf(M_s)$
26 **End**

line 18). The received state $s(agt(c))'$ is further used to infer the corresponding state of $agt(o)$, and thus predicts its action a_o by activating the internal knowledge of model M_s (see line 19). Upon receiving the results after virtual performing a_o, subject agents will decide whether to discard an action from the available action set A (see line 21-22). Then, agent $agt(c)$ will select an action a_s from the set A with the highest reward yield. After each step of all agents, the M_s leading to more success interactions is updated with greater confidence $conf(M_s)$ of being chosen for subsequent behavior prediction (see line 25):

$$\begin{cases} conf(M_s) = conf(M_s) + reward, & \text{if succeeds} \\ conf(M_s) = conf(M_s) - penalty, & \text{if fails} \end{cases}$$

where reward and penalty are positive integers and $conf(M_l) \in [-100, 100]$.

4.3 Multi-Agent Demonstration Learning

Intuitively, the predicted candidate model derived from RL data could reveal the true behavior of opponent agents if subject agents are aware of the true model of their opponents. However, to achieve such results could be extremely time-consuming, and even impossible due to the large space of candidate models ascribed to opponent agents. In the past few years, most researchers have concentrated on reducing candidate model complexity of other agents. Among them, some work focuses on reducing the solution complexity by compressing the model space of other agents [14]. The second category, instead of constructing and solving various models, infers the model of their opponent directly from available behavior data [28][12][10]. Nevertheless, most of existing works to date focus on the learning of models for single-agent decision making process and does not integrate the behavior prediction method in a multi-agent setting.

Different to existing approaches, we propose a multi-agent demonstration learning approach for enhancing subject agents' learning capability while also reducing their candidate model complexity. In particular, the demonstration learning between agents with unique learning capabilities happens by means of imitation. In present multi-agent settings, all subject agents learn in the same environment and have the same acting abilities. Therefore, the demonstration learning could offer the advantage for student agents to behave at approximately the same performance level as their selected teachers. Further, when multiple candidate models are available, subject agents with the demonstration learning approach do not need to train all the models and they can acquire increasing level of predictive capability from their partners by sharing demonstrations with respect to their unique candidate models. The demonstration learning approach thus reduces candidate model complexity by assigning a small set of models to subject agents.

The multi-agent demonstration learning process in MeMAS-P is summarized in Alg. 3. More specifically, the subject agent will be assigned with a set of candidate models $M^{agt} = \{M_1^{agt}, ..., M_n^{agt}\}$, where agt is the index of the subject agent and n is the number of models in M^{agt} (see line 2). Further, the current agent $agt(c)$ will check if there exists a teacher agent $agt(t)$ that has higher fitness value $Fit(agt(t))$ (see line 4). Once a selection is made, the subject agent $agt(c)$ passes its state to the selected teacher agent $agt(t)$ (see line 6). Meanwhile, if agent $agt(c)$ detects an opponent agent $agt(o)$ nearby, it will also pass the inferred state $s(agt(o))$ of the detected opponent to the teacher agent $agt(t)$ (see line 7-8). By simulating the states of current agent $s(agt(c))$ and the detected opponents agent $s(agt(o))$, the teacher agent $agt(t)$ first conducts behavior prediction according to its own models M^t and discards failure actions from the available action set A (see line 9-10). It further predicts the action a_t from the action set A by activating its internal learned knowledge and transmits it to agent $agt(c)$. Then, if transmitted action a_t is available, agent $agt(c)$ will imitate and assimilate the action a_t into its mind universe by means of self learning (see line 13). In addition, a probability γ is defined in line 12 to give the intrinsic innovation tendency of selected actions in the multi-agent demonstration learning process. This variation process serves to prevent the agent $agt(c)$ from learning from teacher agents blindly.

4.4 Complexity Analysis

As aforementioned, predicting accurate behaviors of opponent agents is computationally intractable due to the complexity of candidate models and thus ways of mitigating the computational intractability are critically needed. Since the complexity is predominantly due to the space of candidate models, we therefore focus on reducing the model space of subject agents while avoiding a significant loss in optimality.

Algorithm 3: Multi-Agent Demonstration Learning

Input: Candidate models $\{M^1, M^2, ...M^{agt}\}$, where $M^{agt} = \{M_1^{agt}, ..., M_n^{agt}\}$, Current state s, Action set $A = [a_1, a_2, ..., a_i]$

1 **Begin**:
2 **Assign** each subject agent with candidate model M^{agt}
3 **for** *each subject agent* $agt(c)$ **do**
4   **if** *identify* $\{agt(t)|Fit(agt(c) < Fit(agt(t))\}$ **then**
5   **Get** $s(agt(c))$ of current $agt(c)$
6   **Pass** $s(agt(c))$ to the teacher agent $agt(t)$
7   **if** *detect an opponent agent* $agt(o)$ **then**
8   **Pass** $s(agt(o))$ to agent $agt(t)$
9   **Perform** *Behavior Prediction* with M^t
10   **Discard** failure actions from action set A
11   **Get** a_t from A with highest reward of self learning in $agt(t)$
12   **Perform** variation on a_t with probability γ
13   **Get** $a_s = a_t$ from $agt(t)$, otherwise get a_s from A with highest reward of self learning in $agt(c)$
14   The left steps are same as that in self learning process (see Alg. 2)
15 **End**

Specifically, in our framework, the entire candidate models M are partitioned into different partial sets according to the number of subject agents: $M = \{M_1^1, M_2^1, M_3^2, ...M_l^{agt}\}$ where M^{agt} aggregates the candidate model set labelled by the same subject agent mark. Then, subject agents will only train candidate models from their corresponding partial sets. According to the proposed demonstration learning process, these non-familial peer subject agents with unique candidate models M^{agt} could communicate socially and takes advantage from each other (see Alg. 3). Hence, the proposed MeMAS-P with demonstration learning can reduce the candidate model space of each subject agent in the multi-agent system.

5. EMPIRICAL STUDY

Minefield navigation task (MNT) has been known as one of the most classical and widely used minefield simulation task where all agents have the same objective to complete the navigating task successfully. Taking the classical MNT as an example, we validate the effectiveness of MeMAS-P in an adapted setting where agents may have similar or conflicting objectives.

5.1 Minefield Navigation Task

In a classic minefield navigation task, all green tanks (subject agent, denoted by *Navigator*) have the same objective to navigate across a minefield and arrive at the target (red flag) within given limited time frame. The tank shall avoid any mines or other agents. In our novel competitive scenario (depicted in Fig. 3), we further import a new kind of red tanks (denoted as *Predator*) with the objective to tracking down the navigators before they flees to the red flag. Notably, the red tanks cannot be destroyed by the mines.

Both navigators and predators that spawn randomly within the field at the beginning of each trial run are equipped with sonar sensors so that they have access to a set of detections, including mine detection, *Navigator* detection, *Preda-*

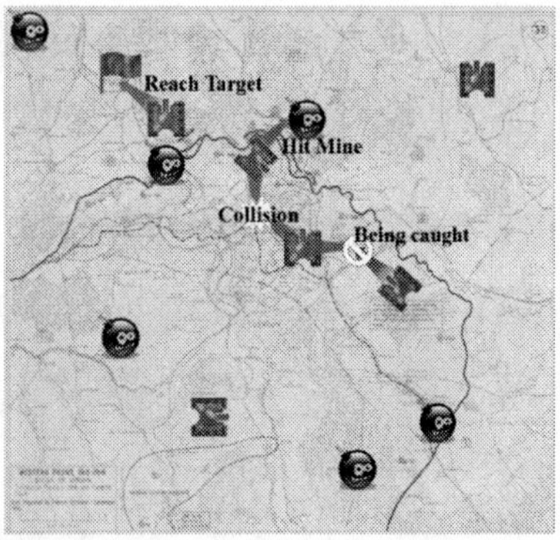

Figure 3: A screenshot of the adapted minefield navigation task with the illustration of Mission Endings.

Table 1: Summary of the parameter setting in the proposed MeMAS-P.

Falcon Parameters	
Choice Parameters $(\alpha^{c1}, \alpha^{c2}, \alpha^{c3})$	$(0.1, 0.1, 0.1)$
Learning Rates $(\beta^{c1}, \beta^{c2}, \beta^{c3})$	$(1.0, 1.0, 1.0)$
Contribution Parameters $(\gamma^{c1}, \gamma^{c2}, \gamma^{c3})$	$(0.5, 0.5, 0)$
Baseline Vigilance Parameters $(\rho^{c1}, \rho^{c2}, \rho^{c3})$	$(0.2, 0.2, 0.5)$
Temporal Difference Learning Paramters	
TD learning rate α	0.5
Discount Factor γ	0.1
Initial Q-value	0.5
ϵ-greedy Model Selection Parameters	
Initial ϵ value	1
ϵ decay rate	0.0005
Demonstration Variation Parameter	
Frequency of Variation γ	0.1

tor detection and target bearing. According to these detected states, each autonomous agent then performs one of the five possible actions at each step with a 180° forward view: $A = \{LEFT, LEFT\ FRONT, FRONT, RIGHT\ FRONT, RIGHT\}$. Particularly, a navigator is rewarded with a positive value 1 if it arrives at the target while a predator receives a reward 1 only if it catches one of the navigators before they reach the red flag. Otherwise, if an agent hits a mine, collides with others, be caught, or does not reach the target within the given limited time steps, it will be assigned with 0 reward. In our experimental study, we have a total of 6 autonomous robots, 6 mines and 1 target flag which are randomly generated over trials in a 12×12 field. A trial completes only if all navigators reach the target, being caught by the predators, hit a mine or other navigators, or exceed 30 time steps.

5.2 Experimental Settings

In our study, we conduct the experiments for 30 independent simulations with each of which has a total of 3000 missions. The parameter settings of FALCON and the proposed MeMAS-P configured in the present experimental study are summarized in Table 1. These configurations of the learning machines are considered to be consistent with previous studies [23] for the purpose of fair comparisons. The results with respect to the following metrics are then reported:

- MN: the number of training missions;
- SR: the average success rate of the agents on completing the missions.

5.3 Brief Study of MeMAS

The objective of the present experimental study is to investigate the performance of MeMAS with all 6 FALCON navigators on completing the classic Minefield Navigation Tasks. For the purpose of comparison, two state-of-the-art multi-agent demonstration learning approaches, namely Advice Exchange Model (AE) [18] and Parallel Transfer Learning (PTL) [24] are also implemented. Specifically, agents in AE with poor performance learn from their elitist by seeking their advice while agents in PTL learn from others by taking advantage from their broadcasted knowledge. Fig. 4 depicts the learning trends of navigators under these three demonstration learning approaches and the conventional MAS where agents cannot learn from others. As can be observed, all demonstration learning approaches outperform the conventional MAS. Particularly, MeMAS is noted to achieve superior performance in terms of success rate throughout the learning process when compared to the existing state-of-the-art multi-agent demonstration learning approaches.

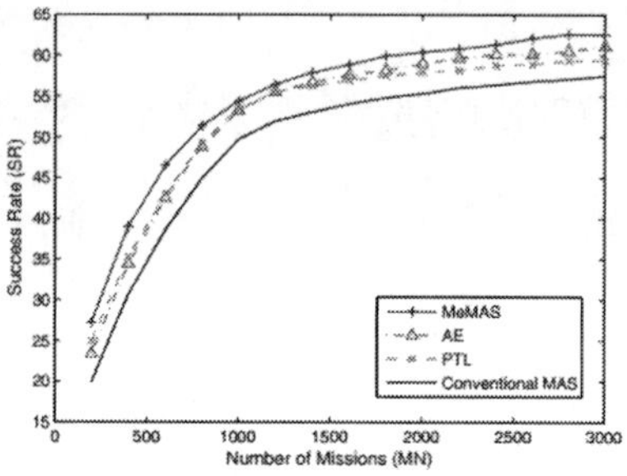

Figure 4: Success rates of navigators under MeMAS, PTL, AE and conventional MAS on completing the missions in classic Minefield Navigation Tasks.

5.4 Study of the MeMAS-P with Actual Model of Predators

We further consider a more complex MNT involving a mixture of 3 navigators and 3 predators where both navigators and predators employ FALCON with $\rho^k = (0.2, 0.2, 0.5)$ as their RL learning machines. Notably, the predator has been well trained before the online learning process of navigators. In this set of experiment, we assume all 3 navigators are aware of the actual trained FALCON model ascribed to predators and thus have the ability to predict the exact behaviors of their opponents.

As aforementioned, the proposed MeMAS-P is composed of two major components, namely behavior prediction and multi-agent demonstration learning. To study the effectiveness of each component, we investigate the average performance of navigators with respect to the following different learning abilities for comparison consideration:

- Navigator-BP: navigators with behavior prediction;
- Navigator-DL: navigators with mutli-agent demonstration learning;
- Navigator-BD: navigators with both behavior prediction and mutli-agent demonstration learning;
- Navigator-Conv: navigators under the conventional MAS that has no behavior prediction and mutli-agent demonstration learning.

Fig. 5 shows the learning trends of different kinds of navigators in terms of success rates. Notably, the success rate of Navigator-Conv in this novel MNT scenario is much lower than that under the classic MNT in the previous subsection. The results indicate that the navigators suffer from the interaction with predators in the novel MNT and have a high probability being caught by their opponents. On the other hand, Navigator-BP achieves significantly higher performance in terms of success rate than Navigator-Conv. This demonstrates that the behavior prediction process in MeMAS-P can effectively help navigators survive from their encounters with predators.

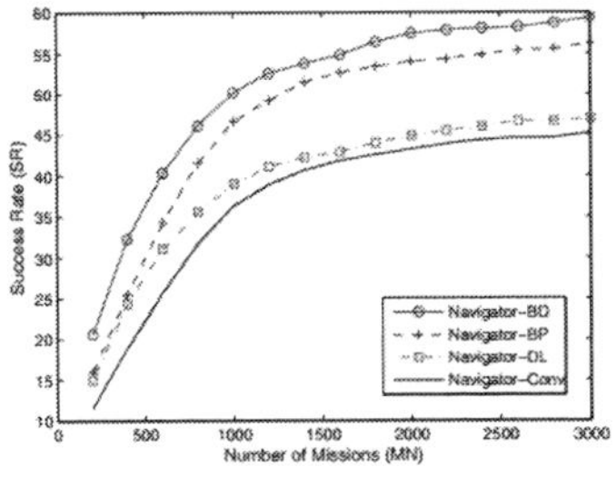

Figure 5: Success rates of navigators with and without MeMAS-P components on completing the missions in the novel Minefield Navigation Tasks.

Further, Navigator-DL and Navigator-BD also report superiority in attaining higher success rates than navigators that have no demonstration learning process. This is attributed to the multi-agent demonstration learning process which endows navigators with capacities to benefit from the demonstrations sharing from the better performing agents, thus accelerating the learning rate of the navigators in solving the missions.

5.5 Study of MeMAS-P with candidate FALCON models

In this experiment, we consider a more common scenario where the exact trained model of the predator is not accessible for navigators. Instead, we assign navigators with a number of candidate models which will be trained using instance data of predators that are recorded from previous interaction activities. According to these trained candidate models, navigators could further predict actions of predators, and use these predictions in place of predators' behaviors.

To facilitate discussion, we consider several FALCON models as candidates that assign different values to the baseline vigilance parameter ρ^k. Table 2 shows the details of parameter settings and the complete results pertaining to the success rate of navigators with different candidate models. Particularly, we classify all candidate models into three sets according to their ρ^k values, known as *1)* a low parameter set $\rho^k \in [0, 0.1]$, *2)* a medium parameter set $\rho^k \in [0.1, 0.5]$ and *3)* a high parameter set $\rho^k \in [0.5, 1]$, respectively. The average performance of navigators with respect to the following settings is then reported:

- Navigator-S: navigators that are assigned with a single candidate model;
- Navigator-All: navigators that are assigned with all candidate models;
- Navigator-L,M,H: navigators that are assigned with candidate models of the low, medium and high parameter sets, respectively;
- Navigator-AVG: average performance of Navigator-L, Navigator-M and Navigator-H;
- Navigator-DL: 3 navigators are assigned with candidate models of low, medium, high parameter set, respectively. Each can learn from their partners according to multi-agent demonstration learning process;

Table 2: Performance of navigators with different candidate models.

	FALCON Candidate Model		Navigator Performance		
#	Model Set	(ρ^1, ρ^2, ρ^3)	Success Rate		
1	Low	(0.05,0.05,0.05)	48.97	48.67	55.59
2		(0.05,0.05,0.1)	49.82		
3	Medium	(0.2,0.2,0.5)	54.97	54.94	
4		(0.5,0.5,0.5)	54.74		
5	High	(0.5,0.5,0.9)	55.52	55.94	
6		(0.9,0.9,0.9)	55.92		

We first investigate the performance of Navigator-S in terms of success rate. Notably, Navigator-Ss with different FALCON candidate models of different baseline vigilance parameter ρ^k report distinct success rates after the learning process (see Table 2, column 4). Particularly, navigators with FALCON candidate model of $\rho^k = (0.9, 0.9, 0.9)$ obtain significant higher success rate than that of $\rho^k = (0.05, 0.05, 0.05)$. Such difference among various FALCON candidate models highlights the importance of selecting a correct candidate model for navigators to predict the behavior of predators. On the other hand, Navigator-All significantly outperforms most of Navigator-Ss. At the end of the learning process, it attains a success rate of 55.59% (see Table 2, column 6), only a bit lower than Navigator-S with the candidate model of highest ρ^k (see Table 2, row 6, column 4). The outstanding performance of Navigator-All verifies the effectiveness of the proposed behavior prediction process in making choice of the most reliable candidate models.

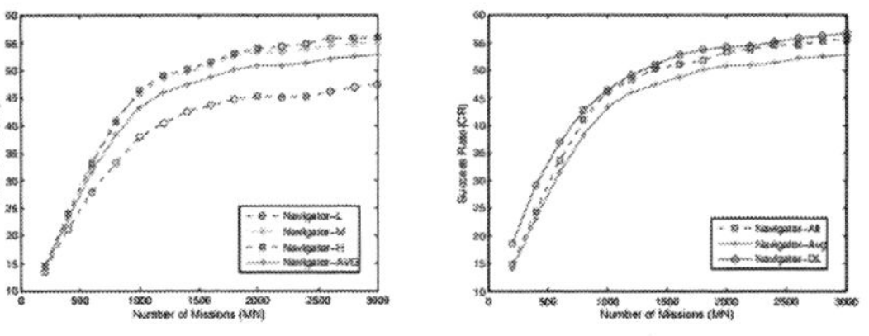

(a) Navigator-L,M,H&AVG. (b) Navigator-All,AVG&DL.

Figure 6: Success rates of navigators using all and part of candidate FALCON models on completing the missions in the novel Minefield Navigation Tasks.

Further, we investigate the performance of navigators with the proposed multi-agent demonstration learning. For comparison consideration, we first study the learning performance of Navigator-L, M and H, respectively, and report their average success rate by Navigator-AVG in Fig. 6(a). The success rates obtained by Navigator-All, Navigator-AVG and Navigator-DL are further depicted in Fig. 6(b). Compared to Navigator-AVG, both Navigator-ALL and Navigator-DL have demonstrated superiority in attaining higher success rates. Particularly, Navigator-DL is noted to obtain success rates that are similar to Navigator-All. This is attributed to the reason that navigators with the multi-agent demonstration learning approach can take advantage from their partners that have better learning capabilities.

Table 3: Computing time taken by Navigator-All and Navigator-DL for training candidate models and behavior prediction.

		Navigator-DL				Navigator-All
#	Metrics	Low ρ^k	Medium ρ^k	High ρ^k	Avg	Avg
1	MT (s)	0.47	0.69	3.91	1.69	5.07
2	PN	8119	8359	10594	9024	9856
3	PT (s)	2.21	4.43	45.60	17.41	21.73

Moreover, in order to quantitatively evaluate how effective the proposed demonstration learning approach reduces the candidate model complexity of subject agents, the computational cost taken per simulation by Navigator-All and Navigator-DL for behaviors predicting is reported in Table 3, where MT is the training time of candidate models, PN is the numbers of prediction and PT is the computational time for behavior prediction. When referring to MT, Navigator-All tends to be more computationally expensive than Navigator-DL since subject agents in Navigator-All need to train all six models while that in Navigator-DL are only assigned with two models. Particularly, when we have a larger agent system with much more candidate models, demonstration learning exhibits significantly better scalability. For example, when 10 agents are in the system and 100 models are available, Navigator-DL reduces the training cost to a tenth of the required amount for Navigator-All.

On the other hand, Navigator-DL has also been observed to outperform Navigator-All by reporting lower computational cost in terms of PT (17.41s, see Table 3, row 3). This is due to the reason that, peer subject agents from Navigator-DL can take advantage form partners with unique candidate model sets. As can be observed, the subject agent with candidate model of high ρ^k tends to share its predicted demonstrations with others and hence obtains the most number of PNs (10594), much more than those obtained by subject agent with low ρ^k and medium ρ^k (8119 and 8359, see Table 3, row 2). Therefore, the proposed MeMAS-P is demonstrated to have the superiority in both reducing the candidate model spaces of subject agents, while also improving their generic learning performance.

5.6 Extensive Study of MeMAS-P with Different RL Candidate Models

Last but not least, we investigate the performance of the proposed MeMAS-P where navigators use different RL techniques as the candidate models of their opponents. In particular, we study the scenario where not only FALCON but a classical multi-layer perceptron (MLP) with gradient descent based back propagation [27] are considered as the candidate models. For a fairness consideration, both the MLP and FALCON candidate models are configured to be consistent with the studies in [23] and will also be trained using available RL instances of predators recorded from previous interactive activities.

The first experiment is conducted to verify the effectiveness of FALCON and MLP as candidate models when predicting predator' behavior. In particular, three navigators in this experiment are assigned with FALCON, MLP and

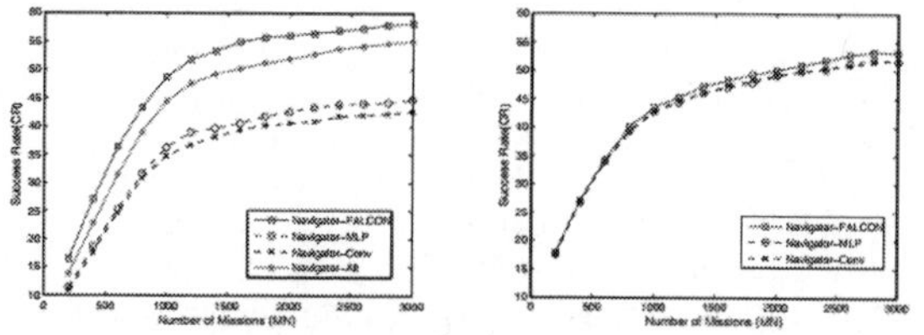

(a) Navigators with no demonstration learning. (b) Navigators with demonstration learning.

Figure 7: Success rates of navigators using FALCON and/or MLP as candidate models on completing the missions in the novel Minefield Navigation Tasks.

no candidate models, respectively, in the same environment. Fig. 7(a) depicts the learning performance in terms of success rate of navigators with respect to the following settings:

- Navigator-FALCON: the navigator using FALCON as the candidate model;
- Navigator-MLP: the navigator using MLP as the candidate model;
- Navigator-All: the navigator using both FALCON and MLP as candidate models;
- Navigator-Conv: the navigator under the conventional MAS that has no behavior prediction of predators.

As can be observed, Navigator-FALCON demonstrates its superiority in attaining much higher success rates than Navigator-MLP and Navigator-Conv. This is reasonable since the FALCON candidate model is the same as the exact learning model of predators, and hence could predict comparatively accurate behaviors.

Further, we endow all navigators with the ability to learn from their partners' valuable demonstrations. According to the result in Fig. 7(b), all of the three navigators with the proposed demonstration learning approach have reported success rates that are approximate to Navigator-All. Particularly, Navigator-MLP and Navigator-Conv show approximately 7.0% and 9.1% improvements in success rates, respectively. The improved performance demonstrates the efficacy of proposed MeMAS-P in improving the learning performance of navigators using different RL techniques as the candidate models in the adapted MNT.

6. CONCLUSIONS

In this paper, we have presented a memetic multi-agent demonstration learning framework (MeMAS-P) for modeling multiple interacting agents. The framework improves on early memetic techniques by providing an instance-based behavior prediction approach for subject agents to interact with present opponents. To reduce the candidate model complexity, we have provided a demonstration learning approach for subject agents to leverage sharing from their partners. The effectiveness of the proposed MeMAS-P has been testified in an adapted minefield navigation task. Future work could investigate incremental approaches for predicting opponents' behavior from online data.

Acknowledgments

This research is supported by the National Research Foundation Singapore under its Interactive Digital Media (IDM) Strategic Research Programme.

REFERENCES

[1] G. Acampora, J. M. Cadenas, V. Loia, and E. M. Ballester. A multi-agent memetic system for human-based knowledge selection. *Systems, Man and Cybernetics, Part A: Systems and Humans, IEEE Transactions on*, 41(5):946–960, 2011.

[2] B. D. Argall, S. Chernova, M. Veloso, and B. Browning. A survey of robot learning from demonstration. *Robotics and autonomous systems*, 57(5):469–483, 2009.

[3] J. Baxter and P. L. Bartlett. Infinite-horizon policy-gradient estimation. *Journal of Artificial Intelligence Research*, pages 319–350, 2001.

[4] D. C. Bentivegna, C. G. Atkeson, A. UDE, and G. Cheng. Learning to act from observation and practice. *International Journal of Humanoid Robotics*, 1(04):585–611, 2004.

[5] T. Brys, A. Harutyunyan, H. B. Suay, S. Chernova, M. E. Taylor, and A. Nowé. Reinforcement learning from demonstration through shaping. In *Proceedings of the International Joint Conference on Artificial Intelligence (IJCAI)*, 2015.

[6] L. Busoniu, R. Babuska, B. De Schutter, and D. Ernst. *Reinforcement learning and dynamic programming using function approximators*, volume 39. CRC press, 2010.

[7] S. Calinon and A. Billard. Incremental learning of gestures by imitation in a humanoid robot. In *Proceedings of the ACM/IEEE international conference on Human-robot interaction*, pages 255–262. ACM, 2007.

[8] X. Chen, Y.-S. Ong, M.-H. Lim, and K. C. Tan. A multi-facet survey on memetic computation. *IEEE Transactions on Evolutionary Computation*, 15(5):591–607, 2011.

[9] X. Chen, Y. Zeng, Y.-S. Ong, C. S. Ho, and Y. Xiang. A study on like-attracts-like versus elitist selection criterion for human-like social behavior of memetic mulitagent systems. In *Evolutionary Computation (CEC), 2013 IEEE Congress on*, pages 1635–1642. IEEE, 2013.

[10] Y. Chen, P. Doshi, and Y. Zeng. Iterative online planning in multiagent settings with limited model spaces and pac guarantees. In *Proceedings of the 2015 International Conference on Autonomous Agents and Multiagent Systems*, pages 1161–1169. International Foundation for Autonomous Agents and Multiagent Systems, 2015.

[11] S. Chernova and M. Veloso. Interactive policy learning through confidence-based autonomy. *Journal of Artificial Intelligence Research*, 34(1):1, 2009.

[12] R. Conroy, Y. Zeng, M. Cavazza, and Y. Chen. Learning behaviors in agents systems with interactive dynamic influence diagrams. In *Proceedings of the 24th International Conference on Artificial Intelligence*, pages 39–45. AAAI Press, 2015.

[13] R. Dawkins. The selfish gene. *Oxford: Oxford University Press*, 1976.

[14] P. J. Doshi. Decision making in complex multiagent contexts: A tale of two frameworks. *AI Magazine*, 33(4):82, 2012.

[15] L. Feng, Y.-S. Ong, A.-H. Tan, and X.-S. Chen. Towards human-like social multi-agents with memetic automaton. In *Evolutionary Computation (CEC), 2011 IEEE Congress on*, pages 1092–1099. IEEE, 2011.

[16] L. Feng, Y.-S. Ong, A.-H. Tan, and I. W. Tsang. Memes as building blocks: a case study on evolutionary optimization+ transfer learning for routing problems. *Memetic Computing*, 7(3):159–180, 2015.

[17] D. H. Grollman and O. C. Jenkins. Dogged learning for robots. In *Robotics and Automation, 2007 IEEE International Conference on*, pages 2483–2488. IEEE, 2007.

[18] E. Oliveira and L. Nunes. Learning by exchanging advice. *In R.Khosla, N. Ichalkaranje, and L. Jain, editors, Design of Intelligent Multi-Agent Systems, chapter 9. Spring, New York, NY, USA*, 2004.

[19] Y.-S. Ong, M. H. Lim, and X. Chen. Research frontier-memetic computation-past, present & future. *IEEE Computational Intelligence Magazine*, 5(2):24, 2010.

[20] D. Ormoneit and Ś. Sen. Kernel-based reinforcement learning. *Machine learning*, 49(2-3):161–178, 2002.

[21] P. E. Rybski, K. Yoon, J. Stolarz, and M. M. Veloso. Interactive robot task training through dialog and demonstration. In *Human-Robot Interaction (HRI), 2007 2nd ACM/IEEE International Conference on*, pages 49–56. IEEE, 2007.

[22] R. S. Sutton and A. G. Barto. *Introduction to Reinforcement Learning*. MIT Press, Cambridge, MA, USA, 1st edition, 1998.

[23] A.-H. Tan, N. Lu, and D. Xiao. Integrating temporal difference methods and self-organizing neural networks for reinforcement learning with delayed evaluative feedback. *Neural Networks, IEEE Transactions on*, 19(2):230–244, 2008.

[24] A. Taylor, I. Dusparic, E. Galván-López, S. Clarke, and V. Cahill. Transfer learning in multi-agent systems through parallel transfer. In *Theoretically Grounded Transfer Learning at the 30th International Conference on Machine Learning (ICML). Omnipress*, 2013.

[25] M. E. Taylor, N. K. Jong, and P. Stone. Transferring instances for model-based reinforcement learning. In *Machine learning and knowledge discovery in databases*, pages 488–505. Springer, 2008.

[26] L. Torrey and M. Taylor. Teaching on a budget: Agents advising agents in reinforcement learning. In *Proceedings of the 2013 international conference on Autonomous agents and multi-agent systems*, pages 1053–1060. International Foundation for Autonomous Agents and Multiagent Systems, 2013.

[27] C. J. C. H. Watkins. *Learning from Delayed Rewards*. PhD thesis, King's College, Cambridge, U.K, May 1989.

[28] Y. Zeng, Y. Chen, and P. Doshi. Approximating behavioral equivalence of models using top-k policy paths. In *The 10th International Conference on Autonomous Agents and Multiagent Systems-Volume 3*, pages 1229–1230. International Foundation for Autonomous Agents and Multiagent Systems, 2011.

An Optimal Algorithm for Stochastic Matroid Bandit Optimization

Mohammad Sadegh Talebi
Department of Automatic Control
KTH Royal Institute of Technology
Stockholm, SWEDEN
mstms@kth.se

Alexandre Proutiere
Department of Automatic Control
KTH Royal Institute of Technology
Stockholm, SWEDEN
alepro@kth.se

ABSTRACT

The selection of leaders in leader-follower multi-agent systems can be naturally formulated as a matroid optimization problem. In this paper, we investigate the online and stochastic version of such a problem, where in each iteration or round, we select a set of leaders and then observe a random realization of the corresponding reward, i.e., of the system performance. This problem is referred to as a stochastic matroid bandit, a variant of combinatorial multi-armed bandit problems where the underlying combinatorial structure is a matroid. We consider semi-bandit feedback and Bernoulli rewards, and derive a tight and problem-dependent lower bound on the regret of any consistent algorithm. We propose KL-OSM, a computationally efficient algorithm that exploits the matroid structure. We derive a finite-time upper bound of the regret of KL-OSM that improves the performance guarantees of existing algorithms. This upper bound actually matches our lower bound, i.e., KL-OSM is asymptotically optimal. Numerical experiments attest that KL-OSM outperforms state-of-the-art algorithms in practice, and the difference in some cases is significant.

Categories and Subject Descriptors

I.2.6 [**Learning**]: Parameter learning; I.2.11 [**Distributed Artificial Intelligence**]: Multiagent systems

Keywords

Multi-Armed Bandits; Online Learning; Combinatorial Optimization; Matroids; Regret Analysis

1. INTRODUCTION

This work is motivated by the design of leader-follower multi-agent systems where a set of leaders act as external control inputs and have the ability to impact the dynamics of the entire system and in turn its overall performance. Of course, the choice of the set of leaders in these systems critically influences their behaviour. It has been recently shown [9, 24] that the leader selection problem could be naturally formulated as a matroid optimization problem. In this paper, we investigate the online and stochastic version of such a problem, where in each iteration or round, we select a set of leaders and then observe a random realization of the corresponding reward, i.e., of the system performance. This problem, referred to as a stochastic matroid Multi-Armed Bandit (MAB) problem, can be seen as a particular instance of combinatorial MAB problems, and is particularly relevant when one wishes to learn as quickly as possible the optimal set of leaders, e.g., in scenarios where this optimal set could evolve over time.

MAB problems [15, 27] constitute the most fundamental model for sequential decision making problems with an exploration vs. exploitation trade-off and have found applications in many fields, including sequential clinical trials, communication systems, economics; see e.g. [6]. In such problems, the decision maker repeatedly selects an arm and observes a realization of the corresponding unknown reward distribution, where each decision is made based on past decisions and observed rewards. The objective is to maximize the expected cumulative reward over some time horizon by balancing exploitation and exploration. Equivalently, the performance of a decision rule or algorithm can be measured through its expected regret, defined as the gap between the expected reward achieved by the algorithm and that achieved by an oracle algorithm always selecting the best arm.

We consider matroid bandits in the stochastic setting as introduced in [19], which are actually a sub-class of combinatorial MAB problems with linear reward functions, defined in, e.g., [8, 10, 13], in which the underlying combinatorial structure is a matroid. Given a set of basic actions E (called ground set), a matroid is a pair $(E, \mathcal{I})$ with some $\mathcal{I} \subset 2^E$ such that $\mathcal{I}$ is an independence system (i.e., it is closed under subset operation) and satisfies the so-called augmentation property (see Definition 1 for a precise definition). Matroid bandits consider weighted matroids, where each element of E is assigned a weight (its average reward). Each arm is then a basis (i.e., an inclusion-wise maximal element of $\mathcal{I}$) of the matroid. The weight of various basic actions are fixed and a priori unknown. The decision maker aims at learning the maximum weight basis by sequentially selecting various arms. Hence, at each round she faces a linear optimization problem under a matroid constraint.

Matroid bandits can be applied beyond leader-follower multi-agent systems. Indeed, matroid structures occur naturally in many problems with practical applications ranging from bidding in ad exchange [29], product search [1], task assignment in crowdsourcing [5], and many other engineering applications. Hence, matroid constraints are quite nat-

Appears in: *Proceedings of the 15th International Conference on Autonomous Agents and Multiagent Systems (AAMAS 2016), J. Thangarajah, K. Tuyls, C. Jonker, S. Marsella (eds.), May 9–13, 2016, Singapore.*

ural for combinatorial problems. For example, assume that the elements of ground set E are categorized into L disjoint categories. A natural requirement for some applications is to force to choose at most one element from each category. In the context of product search, each category might be a specific brand, whereas for news aggregation, each category may correspond to a news domain. Assume that the decision maker is interested in finding a subset $M \subset E$ while maximizing the total reward and such that at most one element from each category belongs to M. Then, she faces a linear optimization subject to a partition matroid constraint. Another natural type of constraints is to have cardinality constraint on the set M, which is related to the notion of uniform matroid. Another notable instance of matroid constraints appears in the problem of finding the minimum spanning tree in a graph, which arises in various engineering disciplines.

Matroid optimization problems are of special interests in the area of combinatorial optimization both theoretically and practically, due to relative tractability of optimization over matroids. In particular, linear optimization over matroid bases is proven to be greedily solvable. More precisely, a well-known result in combinatorial optimization states that an independence system (see later for a formal definition) is a matroid if and only if the *greedy algorithm* leads to a maximum weight basis; see, e.g., [11]. More general cases have been addressed in, e.g., [4, 25]. Matroid theory brings a two-fold advantage in the corresponding bandit optimization problems: firstly, it is possible to devise computationally efficient algorithms that, in most cases, select arms greedily. Secondly, the corresponding regret analysis is usually more tractable. Despite such advantage, lack of optimal algorithms for matroid bandits in the literature is evident. Here we provide a sequential arm selection algorithm, KL-OSM, and show that it is asymptotically optimal. To the best of our knowledge, KL-OSM constitutes the first optimal algorithm for the online matroid problem considered.

Contributions

(a) We derive an asymptotic (as the time horizon T grows large) lower bound on the regret, satisfied by any algorithm (Theorem 2). This lower bound is tight and problem-dependent and its derivation leverages the theory of optimal control of Markov chains with unknown transition probabilities. To our knowledge, our proposed lower bound constitutes the first fundamental performance limit for matroid bandits.

(b) We propose KL-OSM (KL-based Efficient Sampling for Matroids), which is an index policy that maintains a KL-UCB index [14] for each basic action and is based on the greedy algorithm. Hence, it is provably computationally efficient assuming access to an independence oracle (see Section 3 for a precise definition). Through a finite-time analysis (Theorem 1), we show that KL-OSM attains a regret (asymptotically) growing as the proposed lower bound in Theorem 2. Hence, it is asymptotically optimal. To our best knowledge, this is the first optimal algorithm for this class of combinatorial MABs. Numerical experiments for some specific matroid problems show that KL-OSM significantly outperforms existing algorithms.

The rest of the paper is organized as follows. Section 2 provides an overview of combinatorial MAB problems. Section 3 is devoted to description of our model and a precise statement of the problem. In Section 4, we describe KL-OSM, our proposed algorithm for matroid bandits, and provide a finite-time analysis of its regret. In Section 5, we present a lower bound on the regret of our problem. We present some numerical experiments in Section 6. Finally, Section 7 concludes the paper and provides some future work directions. All proofs are provided in the appendix.

2. RELATED WORK

Combinatorial MAB problems have been an active area of research in recent years. These problems have been extensively studied in the adversarial setting; see, e.g., [3, 7] and references therein. In the stochastic setting, some research contributions investigate generic combinatorial problems, e.g., [8,10,13,20], whereas others mostly concern problems where the set of arms exhibits specific structures, such as fixed-size subsets [2,17], matroid and polymatroid [19,21], or permutations [12,23]. The proposed algorithms in these works are variants of UCB or KL-UCB algorithms.

Matroid bandits were introduced and studied in [18, 19]. The proposed algorithm, called OMM, is a UCB-type policy relying on the greedy method. Our proposed algorithm is quite similar to OMM, but uses the KL-UCB index instead.

For a generic combinatorial structure and the stochastic setting considered in this paper, the state-of-the-art algorithm is ESCB [10], which achieves a regret upper-bounded by $\mathcal{O}(\frac{d\sqrt{m}}{\Delta_{\min}}\log(T))$ after T rounds. Here, d and m respectively denote the number of basic actions and maximum cardinality of arms, and $\Delta_{\min}$ denotes the smallest gap between the average rewards of the best arm and of a sub-optimal arm. For matroid bandits, OMM achieves a regret scaling at most as $\mathcal{O}(\frac{d-m}{\Delta_{\min}}\log(T))$. The dependence of this bound on (d, m) is tight and cannot be improved. The regret upper bound of our proposed algorithm, KL-OSM, admits the same scaling $\mathcal{O}(\frac{d-m}{\Delta_{\min}}\log(T))$. However, we are able to show that the constant in $\mathcal{O}(.)$ in the case of KL-OSM is strictly smaller. Moreover, we prove that under KL-OSM, the upper bound on the regret cannot be improved.

3. MODEL AND OBJECTIVES

3.1 Matroid Structure

We give a formal definition of matroids and state some useful related results. More details can be found in, e.g., [26, 28].

DEFINITION 1. *Let E be a finite set and $\mathcal{I} \subset 2^E$. The pair $G = (E, \mathcal{I})$ is called a* matroid *if the following conditions hold:*

(i) $\emptyset \in \mathcal{I}$,

(ii) if $X \in \mathcal{I}$ *and* $Y \subseteq X$, *then* $Y \in \mathcal{I}$,

(iii) if $X, Y \in \mathcal{I}$ *with* $|X| > |Y|$, *then there is some element* $\ell \in X \setminus Y$ *such that* $Y \cup \{\ell\} \in \mathcal{I}$.

Any system satisfying conditions (i) and (ii) is called an independence system. Condition (iii) is referred to as the augmentation property. The set E is usually referred to as the *ground set* and the elements of $\mathcal{I}$ are called the *independent sets*. Any (inclusion-wise) maximal independent set is called a *basis* for matroid G. In other words, if $X \in \mathcal{I}$ is a basis for G, then $X \cup \{\ell\} \notin \mathcal{I}$ for all $\ell \in E \setminus X$.

PROPOSITION 1 ([26]). *Let $G = (E, \mathcal{I})$ be a matroid. Then the following hold:*

(i) All bases of G have the same cardinality, referred to as rank *of G.*

(ii) For all bases X, Y of G, if $\ell \in X \setminus Y$ then there exists $k \in Y \setminus X$ such that $(X \setminus \ell) \cup \{k\}$ is a basis for G. [1]

(iii) For all bases X, Y of G, if $\ell \in X \setminus Y$ then there exists $k \in Y \setminus X$ such that $(Y \setminus k) \cup \{\ell\}$ is a basis for G.

We next provide some examples of matroids. Consider a ground set E with cardinality d. *Uniform matroid* of rank m is $(E, \mathcal{I})$, where $\mathcal{I}$ is the collection of subsets of E with at most m elements. Consider a partition of E given by $\{E_i\}_{i \in [\ell]}$. For some given parameters $k_1, \dots, k_\ell$, define

$$\mathcal{I} = \{X \subseteq E : |X \cap E_i| \le k_i, \ \forall i \in [\ell]\}.$$

Then $(E, \mathcal{I})$ is *partition matroid* of rank $\sum_{i \in [\ell]} k_i$. Given an undirected graph $\mathcal{G} = (V, H)$, define

$$\mathcal{I} = \{F \subseteq H : (V, F) \text{ is a forest}\}.$$

Then, it can be shown that $G(\mathcal{G}) = (H, \mathcal{I})$ is a matroid, referred to as *graphic matroid.* Every spanning forest of the graph G is indeed a basis for matroid $G(\mathcal{G})$.

3.1.1 Weighted Matroids

Now we consider a weighted matroid, where each element of the ground set is given a non-negative weight. For any $\ell \in E$, let w_ℓ denote the weight assigned to ℓ. The matroid optimization problem is to find a basis with maximum total weight:

$$\max_{X \in \mathcal{I}} \sum_{\ell \in X} w_\ell. \tag{1}$$

The above problem can be solved efficiently by the GREEDY algorithm, whose pseudo-code is shown in Algorithm 1.

Algorithm 1 GREEDY [26]

Sort weights $w_i, i \in E$. Denote the new ordering by a bijection $k : E \to E$:

$$w_{k(1)} \ge w_{k(2)} \ge \cdots \ge w_{k(d)}.$$

```
X ← ∅
for i = 1,...,d do
  if X ∪ {k(i)} ∈ I then
    X ← X ∪ {k(i)}
  end if
end for
```

Next we determine the complexity of the GREEDY algorithm. Clearly, sorting can be carried out in $\mathcal{O}(d \log(d))$. Furthermore, assume that testing whether a given subset of the ground set E is independent takes $\mathcal{O}(h(d))$ time for some function h. Then, the time complexity of the GREEDY algorithm is $\mathcal{O}(d \log(d) + dh(d))$. In some computational models, it is assumed that an algorithm has access to an *independence oracle*, that is a routine that given $X \subset E$ returns whether $X \in \mathcal{I}$ or not. Under the independence oracle model, the GREEDY algorithm has a time complexity of $\mathcal{O}(d \log(d))$. Hence, a maximum-weight independent set in a matroid can be found in strongly polynomial time under independence oracle model ([28, Corollary 40.1]).

[1]For any set X and element ℓ, by a slight abuse of notation, we write $X \setminus \ell$ to imply $X \setminus \{\ell\}$.

3.2 MAB Model

Consider a finite set of *basic actions* $E = \{1, \dots, d\}$ and a matroid $G = (E, \mathcal{I})$ of rank m. We consider a combinatorial MAB problem, where each arm M is a basis of G. We let $\mathcal{M}$ denote the set of arms, i.e., the collection of all bases of G. Each arm M is identified with a binary column vector $(M_1, \dots, M_d)^\top$, and we have $\|M\|_1 = m, \ \forall M \in \mathcal{M}$ since G is of rank m. Time proceeds in rounds. For $i \in E$, $X_i(n)$ denotes the random reward of basic action i in round n. For each i, the sequence $(X_i(n))_{n \ge 1}$ is i.i.d. with Bernoulli distribution of mean θ_i. The rewards across basic actions may be arbitrarily correlated. We denote by $\theta = (\theta_1, \dots, \theta_d)^\top \in \Theta = [0,1]^d$ the vector of unknown expected rewards of the various basic actions.

At the beginning of each round n, an algorithm or policy π, selects an arm $M^\pi(n) \in \mathcal{M}$ based on the arms chosen in previous rounds and their observed rewards. The reward of arm $M^\pi(n)$ selected in round n is

$$X^{M^\pi(n)}(n) = \sum_{i \in E} M_i^\pi(n) X_i(n) = M^\pi(n)^\top X(n).$$

We consider semi-bandit feedback, where under policy π and at the end of round n, the outcome of actions $X_i(n)$ for all $i \in M^\pi(n)$ are revealed to the decision maker.[2] The objective is to identify a policy in Π, the set of all feasible policies, which maximizes the cumulative expected reward over a finite time horizon T. Here the expectation is understood with respect to the randomness in the rewards and the possible randomization in the policy. Equivalently, we aim at designing a policy that minimizes regret, where the regret of policy $\pi \in \Pi$ is defined by:

$$R^\pi(T) = \max_{M \in \mathcal{M}} \mathbb{E}[\sum_{n=1}^{T} X^M(n)] - \mathbb{E}[\sum_{n=1}^{T} X^{M^\pi(n)}(n)].$$

Finally, we denote by $\mu_M(\theta) = M^\top \theta$ the expected reward of arm M, and let $M^\star(\theta) \in \mathcal{M}$ be any arm with maximum expected reward:

$$M^\star(\theta) \in \arg\max_{M \in \mathcal{M}} \mu_M(\theta).$$

To simplify the presentation in subsequent analysis, we assume that the elements of the vector θ are distinct, and hence the optimal arm $M^\star(\theta)$ is unique. We further define: $\Delta_M = M^\star(\theta)^\top \theta - \mu_M(\theta)$ for all $M \in \mathcal{M}$.

In subsequent sections, when clear from the context that θ is the underlying parameter, we use $M^\star$ to indicate $M^\star(\theta)$.

4. THE KL-OSM ALGORITHM

In this section, we present KL-OSM which is a natural extension of the KL-UCB algorithm [14] for the described matroid bandit problem.

We introduce the following notation: At time n, we define $t_i(n) = \sum_{s=1}^{n} M_i(s)$ the number of times basic action i has

[2]For brevity, in what follows, for any binary vector z, we write $i \in z$ to denote $z_i = 1$.

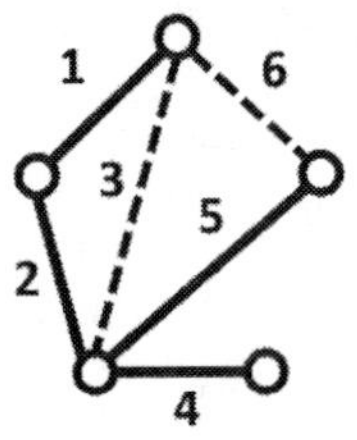

Figure 1: An example for the set $\mathcal{K}_i$ in the case of graphic matroids: Edges shown with solid line correspond to optimal actions. Two sub-optimal actions are shown in dashed line, where $\mathcal{K}_3 = \{1, 2\}$ and $\mathcal{K}_6 = \{1, 2, 5\}$.

been sampled. In round n, we define the empirical mean reward of action i as $\hat{\theta}_i(n) = (1/t_i(n)) \sum_{s=1}^{n} X_i(s) M_i(s)$ if $t_i(n) > 0$ and $\hat{\theta}_i(n) = 0$ otherwise. Our algorithm is an index policy relying on KL-UCB index [14] maintained for each basic action. More precisely, the index of basic action i in round n is denoted by $\omega_i(n)$ and defined as:

$$\omega_i(n) = \max\Big\{q \in [\hat{\theta}_i(n), 1] : t_i(n)\mathrm{kl}(\hat{\theta}_i(n), q) \le f(n)\Big\},$$

with $f(n) = \log(n) + 3\log(\log(n))$.

In each round $n \ge 1$, the KL-OSM algorithm simply consists in computing indexes $\omega_i(n)$ for all i, and then selecting an arm $M(n)$ by solving

$$M(n) \in \arg\max_{M \in \mathcal{M}} \sum_{i \in M} \omega_i(n),$$

using the GREEDY algorithm. The pseudo-code of KL-OSM is given in Algorithm 2.

Algorithm 2 KL-OSM

for $n \ge 1$ **do**
  Select $M(n) \in \mathrm{argmax}_{M \in \mathcal{M}} \sum_{i \in M} \omega_i(n)$ using GREEDY.
  Play $M(n)$, observe the rewards, and update $t_i(n)$ and $\hat{\theta}_i(n), \forall i \in M(n)$.
end for

Next we provide a finite-time analysis of the regret of KL-OSM. To this aim, for any problem instance we introduce mapping $\sigma : E \backslash M^\star \to M^\star$ such that for any $i \in E \backslash M^\star$:

$$\sigma(i) = \arg\min_{j \in \mathcal{K}_i} \theta_j,$$

where

$$\mathcal{K}_i = \Big\{\ell \in M^\star : (M^\star \setminus \ell) \cup \{i\} \in \mathcal{M}\Big\}.$$

Figure 1 shows an example for the set $\mathcal{K}_i$ for the case of graphic matroids.

It is noted that by Proposition 1, we have that $\mathcal{K}_i \neq \emptyset$ for all $i \in E \setminus M^\star$. Moreover, for any $i \notin M^\star$, if $\ell \in \mathcal{K}_i$, then $\theta_\ell > \theta_i$. We show this claim by contradiction: assume this does not hold, namely, $\theta_\ell < \theta_i$. Consider $M' = (M^\star \backslash \ell) \cup \{i\}$. Then, by Proposition 1, $M' \in \mathcal{M}$. Moreover,

$$\mu_{M'}(\theta) - \mu_{M^\star}(\theta) = \sum_{k \in M'} \theta_k - \sum_{k \in M^\star} \theta_k = \theta_i - \theta_\ell > 0,$$

which contradicts the optimality of $M^\star$. Hence, $\theta_\ell > \theta_i$ for any $\ell \in \mathcal{K}_i$.

The following theorem gives an upper bound on the regret of the KL-OSM algorithm.

THEOREM 1. *For any $\varepsilon > 0$, there exist positive constants C_1, $C_2(\varepsilon)$, and $\beta(\varepsilon)$ such that the regret under algorithm π =KL-OSM satisfies:*

$$R^\pi(T) \le \sum_{i \in E \backslash M^\star} \frac{\theta_{\sigma(i)} - \theta_i}{\mathrm{kl}(\theta_i, \theta_{\sigma(i)})}(1 + \varepsilon)\log(T) + o(\log(T)).$$

Hence,

$$\limsup_{T \to \infty} \frac{R^\pi(T)}{\log(T)} \le \sum_{i \in E \backslash M^\star} \frac{\theta_{\sigma(i)} - \theta_i}{\mathrm{kl}(\theta_i, \theta_{\sigma(i)})}.$$

REMARK 1. *When the underlying matroid is a uniform matroid, the problem reduces to MAB with multiple plays as studied in [2, 17]. Assume that actions are enumerated such that $\theta_1 \ge \theta_2 \ge \dots \theta_m > \dots \ge \theta_d$. Then $M^\star = \{1, 2, \dots, m\}$ and $\sigma(i) = m$ for all $i \notin M^\star$. Hence, the regret upper bound of Theorem 1 asymptotically coincides with the results provided in [2, 17].*

Next we compare KL-OSM and OMM [19] in terms of their regret upper bounds. OMM achieves a regret upper-bounded by

$$\mathbb{E}[R^\pi(T)] \le \sum_{i \in E \backslash M^\star} \frac{16}{\Delta_{\min,i}} \log(T) + \mathcal{O}(1),$$

where for any sub-optimal i:

$$\Delta_{\min,i} = \min_{j \in E \backslash M^\star} |\theta_i - \theta_j|.$$

Note that by Pinsker's inequality, we have

$$\mathrm{kl}(\theta_i, \theta_{\sigma(i)}) \ge 2(\theta_i - \theta_{\sigma(i)})^2 \ge 2\Delta_{\min,i}^2.$$

Hence, the regret upper bound for KL-OSM is better than that for OMM. The numerical experiments in Section 6 also show that KL-OSM outperforms OMM in practice.

Implementation.
The KL-OSM algorithm finds a basis with the maximum index using the GREEDY algorithm, whose time complexity under independence oracle model is $\mathcal{O}(d\log(d))$. We also remark that the computation of index $\omega_i(n)$ amounts to finding the roots of a strictly convex and increasing function in one variable (since $z \mapsto \mathrm{kl}(p, z)$ is an increasing function for $z \ge p$). Hence, $\omega_i(n)$ can be computed straightforwardly by a simple line search such as bisection. Therefore, the time complexity of KL-OSM after T rounds is $\mathcal{O}(dT\log(d))$.

5. LOWER BOUND

In this section, we derive a lower bound on the regret of any uniformly good algorithm π for the matroid bandit problem under the case where the rewards across basic actions are independent. We define uniformly good algorithms as in [22]: An algorithm π is uniformly good if and only if $R^\pi(T) = o(T^\alpha)$ for all $\alpha > 0$ and all parameters $\theta \in \Theta$.

The proof of this lower bound uses the theory of optimal control of Markov chains with unknown transition probabilities studied in [16]. Such a technique is also used in [10] to study the regret lower bound for generic stochastic combinatorial MABs. In what follows, first we state the latter result.

Given $\theta \in \Theta$, define the set of *bad* parameters that cannot be distinguished from θ when selecting arm $M^\star(\theta)$, and for which the arm $M^\star(\theta)$ is sub-optimal:

$$B(\theta) = \{\lambda \in \Theta : \lambda_i = \theta_i, \forall i \in M^\star(\theta),\ \max_M M^\top \lambda > M^\star(\theta)^\top \theta\}.$$

According to [10, Theorem 1], the regret of any uniformly good policy $\pi \in \Pi$ for any $\theta \in \Theta$ satisfies

$$\liminf_{T\to\infty} \frac{R^\pi(T)}{\log(T)} \geq c(\theta),$$

where $c(\theta)$ is the optimal value of the following problem:

$$\inf_{x\geq 0} \sum_{M\in\mathcal{M}} \Delta_M x_M \qquad (2)$$

$$\text{subject to: } \sum_{M\in\mathcal{M}} x_M \sum_{i\in E} M_i \mathrm{kl}(\theta_i, \lambda_i) \geq 1, \quad \forall \lambda \in B(\theta).$$

Here $\mathrm{kl}(u,v)$ is the Kullback-Leibler divergence between Bernoulli distributions of respective means u and v, i.e.,

$$\mathrm{kl}(u,v) = u\log(u/v) + (1-u)\log((1-u)/(1-v)).$$

Let $x^\star = (x_M^\star, M \in \mathcal{M})$ denote the optimal solution to this problem. It then follows from [16] that the expected number of times that an optimal algorithm plays arm M up to round T will be $x_M^\star \log(T) + o(\log(T))$. Note that the optimal value $c(\theta)$ and solution $x^\star$ are unfortunately not explicit.

Building on this result, in the next theorem we provide an *asymptotic* lower bound on the regret of any uniformly good policy π for the considered matroid optimization problem.

THEOREM 2. *For all $\theta \in \Theta$ and any uniformly good algorithm $\pi \in \Pi$,*

$$\liminf_{T\to\infty} \frac{R^\pi(T)}{\log(T)} \geq \sum_{i\in E\setminus M^\star} \frac{\theta_{\sigma(i)} - \theta_i}{\mathrm{kl}(\theta_i, \theta_{\sigma(i)})}.$$

Comparing the result of Theorem 1 with that of Theorem 2, we observe that for the case of Bernoulli rewards, the regret upper bound of KL-OSM asymptotically matches the lower bound. Hence, it is asymptotically optimal. We remark that contrary to the lower bound in [19], the lower bound in Theorem 2 is problem-dependent, namely it holds for any parameter θ and any matroid G. Moreover, in contrast to the lower bound given in [10, Theorem 1], ours is explicit.

6. NUMERICAL EXPERIMENTS

We briefly illustrate the performance under the KL-OSM algorithm for the case of graphic and partition matroids. In our first experiment, we consider spanning trees in the complete graph K_N. We set $N = 5$, in which case by Cayley's formula there are 5^3 spanning trees or arms, and $d = 10$ basic actions. In this experiment we consider two scenarios: 'Scenario 1', in which parameter θ is chosen such that $\theta_i = 0.8$ if $i \in M^\star$ and $\theta_i = 0.6$ otherwise; and 'Scenario 2', where θ is drawn uniformly at random from $[0,1]^{10}$. In the second experiment, we consider a partition matroid of rank 5 with $d = 10$ basic actions and 4 partitions. Furthermore, parameter θ is drawn uniformly at random from $[0,1]^{10}$.

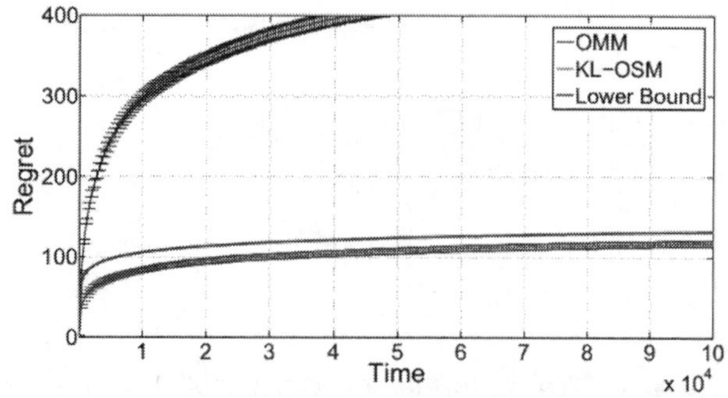

(a) Graphic matroid, Scenario 1

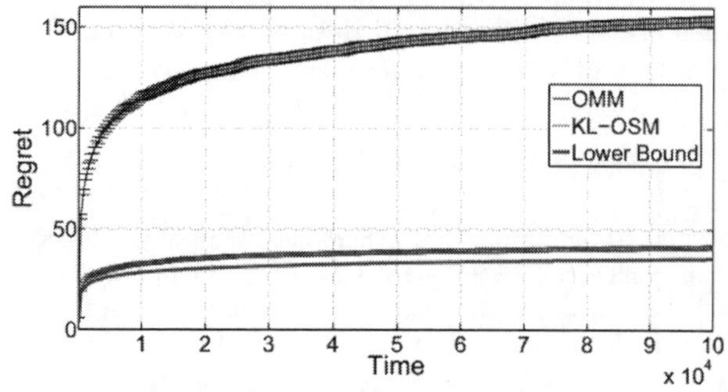

(b) Graphic matroid, Scenario 2

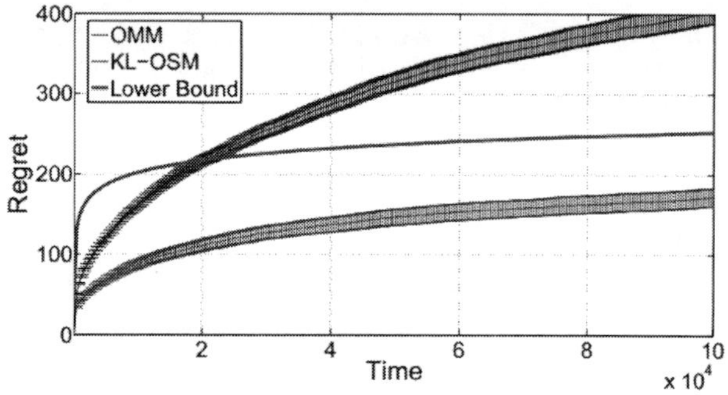

(c) Partition matroid

Figure 2: Regret of various algorithms

Figures 2(a)-(c) present the regret vs. time horizon under KL-OSM and OMM for the various cases. In these figures, curves in blue and black show the average over 100 independent runs along with the 95% confidence intervals. Moreover, the curve in red represents the lower bound of Theorem 2 for the corresponding scenario.

We observe that in all experiments, KL-OSM significantly outperforms OMM. The curves in Figures 2(a)-(c) show the regret of KL-OSM is growing at the same rate of the 'lower bound' when the number of rounds grows large, thus verifying the asymptotic optimality of KL-OSM. Finally, we remark that it is not contradictory that the 'lower bound' curve in Figure 2(a) or 2(c) lies above the regret curve of KL-OSM. This is because the lower bound of Theorem 2 holds asymptotically, i.e., when T grows large.

7. CONCLUSION

In this paper we have investigated matroid bandits with Bernoulli rewards. We have provided a tight and problem-

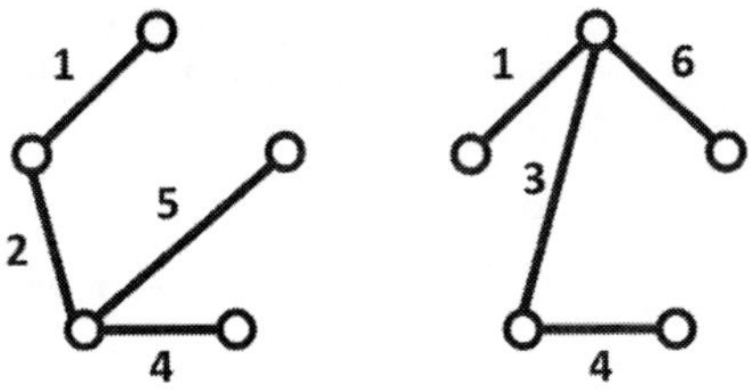

(a) $M^\star$ (b) $M(n)$

Figure 3: An example of bijection τ_n for the case of graphic matroids. In this case: $\tau_n(1) = 1, \tau_n(3) = 2, \tau_n(4) = 4, \tau_n(6) = 5$.

dependent lower bound on the regret. Moreover, we proposed KL-OSM, an efficient algorithm for matroid bandits, and provided a finite-time analysis of its regret. We showed that the regret upper bound of KL-OSM matches the lower bound, and hence it is asymptotically optimal. Moreover, we showed that KL-OSM enjoys a better regret than existing algorithms both theoretically and experimentally. As a future work, we will investigate matroid bandits with more complicated reward functions. Of particular interest is the case where the reward function is a submodular set function.

Acknowledgement

Alexandre Proutiere's research is supported by the ERC FSA grant and the SSF ICT-Psi project.

APPENDIX

A. PROOF OF THEOREM 1

PROOF. Let $T > 0$. Consider round n where $M(n) \neq M^\star$ is selected by the algorithm π =KL-OSM. Using Lemma 1, proven at the end of this section, there exists a bijective mapping τ_n such that: $\tau_n(i) = i$ if $i \in M^\star \cap M(n)$ or $i \in \overline{M^\star \cup M(n)}$. Otherwise, $\tau_n(i) = j$ for some $j \in \mathcal{K}'_i := \mathcal{K}_i \setminus M(n)$. The mapping τ_n simply maps the sub-optimal basic actions of $M(n)$ to the corresponding ones in $M^\star$ that are not chosen by the algorithm at round n. It then follows that

$$\mathbf{1}\{M_i(n) = 1\} = \sum_{j\in\mathcal{K}'_i} \mathbf{1}\{M_i(n) = 1,\ \tau_n(i) = j\}$$

and that $\sum_{j\in\mathcal{K}'_i} \mathbf{1}\{\tau_n(i) = j\} \le 1$ since τ_n is bijective. An example of mapping τ_n for the case of graphic matroids is shown in Figure 3.

For any $i, j \in E$, define $\Delta_{j,i} = \theta_j - \theta_i$. Then, the regret under policy π=KL-OSM is upper bounded as:

$$\begin{aligned} R^\pi(T) &\le \mathbb{E}[\sum_{n=1}^T \Delta_{M(n)}] \\ &= \mathbb{E}[\sum_{n=1}^T \sum_{i\in E\setminus M^\star} \Delta_{\tau_n(i),i} \mathbf{1}\{M_i(n) = 1\}] \\ &= \mathbb{E}[\sum_{i\in E\setminus M^\star} \sum_{n=1}^T \sum_{j\in\mathcal{K}'_i} \Delta_{j,i} \mathbf{1}\{M_i(n) = 1,\ \tau_n(i) = j\}]. \end{aligned}$$

Let $i \in E \setminus M^\star$. Motivated by the design of KL-OSM, namely use of GREEDY to determine $M(n)$ at each round n, we use the following decomposition:

$$\begin{aligned} \mathbf{1}\{M_i(n) = 1,\ \omega_i(n) \ge \omega_{\tau_n(i)}(n)\} &\le \mathbf{1}\{\omega_{\tau_n(i)}(n) < \theta_{\tau_n(i)}\} \\ &+ \mathbf{1}\{M_i(n) = 1,\ \omega_i(n) \ge \theta_{\tau_n(i)}\}. \end{aligned}$$

Hence,

$$\begin{aligned} &\sum_{n=1}^T \sum_{j\in\mathcal{K}'_i} \Delta_{j,i} \mathbf{1}\{M_i(n) = 1,\ \tau_n(i) = j\} \\ &\le \sum_{n=1}^T \sum_{j\in\mathcal{K}'_i} \Delta_{j,i} \mathbf{1}\{\tau_n(i) = j,\ \omega_j(n) < \theta_j\} \\ &+ \sum_{n=1}^T \sum_{j\in\mathcal{K}'_i} \Delta_{j,i} \mathbf{1}\{M_i(n) = 1,\ \tau_n(i) = j,\ \omega_i(n) \ge \theta_j\}, \end{aligned}$$

and therefore,

$$\begin{aligned} &\mathbb{E}[\sum_{i\in E\setminus M^\star} \sum_{n=1}^T \sum_{j\in\mathcal{K}'_i} \Delta_{j,i} \mathbf{1}\{M_i(n) = 1,\ \tau_n(i) = j\} \\ &\le \mathbb{E}[\sum_{i\in E\setminus M^\star} \sum_{n=1}^T \sum_{j\in\mathcal{K}'_i} \mathbf{1}\{\tau_n(i) = j,\ \omega_j(n) < \theta_j\}] \\ &+ \mathbb{E}[\sum_{i\in E\setminus M^\star} \sum_{n=1}^T \sum_{j\in\mathcal{K}'_i} \Delta_{j,i} \mathbf{1}\{M_i(n) = 1,\ \tau_n(i) = j,\ \omega_i(n) \ge \theta_j\}], \end{aligned}$$

since $\Delta_{j,i} \le 1$. We prove that there exist positive constants C_1, $C_2(\varepsilon)$, and $\beta(\varepsilon)$ such that

$$\begin{aligned} &\mathbb{E}[\sum_{i\in E\setminus M^\star} \sum_{n=1}^T \sum_{j\in\mathcal{K}'_i} \mathbf{1}\{\tau_n(i) = j,\ \omega_j(n) < \theta_j\}] \\ &\quad \le (d - m) C_1 \log(\log(T)), \qquad (3) \\ &\mathbb{E}[\sum_{i\in E\setminus M^\star} \sum_{n=1}^T \sum_{j\in\mathcal{K}'_i} \Delta_{j,i} \mathbf{1}\{M_i(n) = 1,\ \tau_n(i) = j,\ \omega_i(n) \ge \theta_j\}] \\ &\quad \le \sum_{i\in E\setminus M^\star} (1+\varepsilon) \frac{\theta_{\sigma(i)} - \theta_i}{\mathrm{kl}(\theta_i, \theta_{\sigma(i)})} f(T) + (d - m) \frac{C_2(\varepsilon)}{T^{\beta(\varepsilon)}}. \qquad (4) \end{aligned}$$

Hence, we get the announced result:

$$\begin{aligned} R^\pi(T) &\le \mathbb{E}[\sum_{i\in E\setminus M^\star} \sum_{n=1}^T \sum_{j\in\mathcal{K}'_i} \Delta_{j,i} \mathbf{1}\{M_i(n) = 1,\ \tau_n(i) = j\}] \\ &\le \sum_{i\in E\setminus M^\star} \frac{\theta_{\sigma(i)} - \theta_i}{\mathrm{kl}(\theta_i, \theta_{\sigma(i)})} (1+\varepsilon) f(T) \\ &+ (d - m) \left(\frac{C_2(\varepsilon)}{T^{\beta(\varepsilon)}} + C_1 \log(\log(T)) \right). \end{aligned}$$

Inequality (3):
Fix $j \in \mathcal{K}'_i$. By the concentration inequality in [14, Theorem 10], we have

$$\mathbb{P}[\omega_j(n) < \theta_j] \le \lceil f(n) \log(n) \rceil e^{1-f(n)},$$

and hence following the same steps as in the proof of [14, Theorem 2], we observe that there exists constant $C_1 \le 7$

such that $\mathbb{E}[\sum_{n=1}^{T} \mathbf{1}\{\omega_j(n) < \theta_j\}] \le C_1 \log(\log(T))$. It then follows that

$$\sum_{j \in \mathcal{K}_i'} \mathbb{E}[\sum_{n=1}^{T} \mathbf{1}\{\tau_n(i) = j,\ \omega_j(n) < \theta_j\}] \le C_1(\log(\log(T)))$$

since τ_n for any n is a bijection. As a result:

$$\sum_{i \notin M^\star} \sum_{j \in \mathcal{K}_i'} \mathbb{E}[\sum_{n=1}^{T} \mathbf{1}\{\tau_n(i) = j,\ \omega_j(n) < \theta_j\}] \le (d-m)C_1(\log(\log(T))).$$

Inequality (4):
For $x, y \in [0,1]$, introduce $\mathrm{kl}^+(x,y) = \mathrm{kl}(x,y)\mathbf{1}\{x < y\}$. Fix $j \in \mathcal{K}_i'$. Observe that the event $\omega_i(n) \ge \theta_j$ implies $\omega_i(n) \ge \theta_{\sigma(i)}$, which further implies that $\mathrm{kl}^+(\hat{\theta}_i(n), \theta_{\sigma(i)}) \le \mathrm{kl}(\hat{\theta}_i(n), \omega_i(n)) = f(n)/t_i(n)$.

We let $\hat{\theta}_{i,s}$ denote the empirical average of rewards of action i when it is selected s times. Hence following the similar steps as in the proof of Lemma 7 in [14], we obtain:

$$\begin{aligned}
&\sum_{j \in \mathcal{K}_i'} \sum_{n=1}^{T} \mathbf{1}\{M_i(n) = 1,\ \tau_n(i) = j,\ \omega_i(n) \ge \theta_j\} \\
&\le \sum_{j \in \mathcal{K}_i'} \sum_{n=1}^{T} \mathbf{1}\{M_i(n) = 1,\ \tau_n(i) = j,\ \omega_i(n) \ge \theta_{\sigma(i)}\} \\
&\le \sum_{n=1}^{T} \mathbf{1}\{M_i(n) = 1,\ \omega_i(n) \ge \theta_{\sigma(i)}\} \\
&\le \sum_{n=1}^{T} \mathbf{1}\{M_i(n) = 1,\ t_i(n)\mathrm{kl}^+(\hat{\theta}_i(n), \theta_{\sigma(i)}) \le f(n)\} \\
&= \sum_{n=1}^{T} \sum_{s=1}^{n} \mathbf{1}\{M_i(n) = 1,\ t_i(n) = s,\ s\mathrm{kl}^+(\hat{\theta}_{i,s}, \theta_{\sigma(i)}) \le f(n)\} \\
&\le \sum_{n=1}^{T} \sum_{s=1}^{n} \mathbf{1}\{M_i(n) = 1,\ t_i(n) = s,\ s\mathrm{kl}^+(\hat{\theta}_{i,s}, \theta_{\sigma(i)}) \le f(T)\} \\
&= \sum_{s=1}^{T} \mathbf{1}\{s\mathrm{kl}^+(\hat{\theta}_{i,s}, \theta_{\sigma(i)}) \le f(T)\} \sum_{n=s}^{T} \mathbf{1}\{M_i(n) = 1,\ t_i(n) = s\} \\
&= \sum_{s=1}^{T} \mathbf{1}\{s\mathrm{kl}^+(\hat{\theta}_{i,s}, \theta_{\sigma(i)}) \le f(T)\},
\end{aligned}$$

where in the last step, we used the fact that for any s, there is only one round n such that $t_i(n) = s$ and $M_i(n) = 1$.

From [14, Lemma 8], we have that (see the arXiv version of the present work for details [30]):

$$\mathbb{E}[\sum_{s=1}^{T} \mathbf{1}\{s\mathrm{kl}^+(\hat{\theta}_{i,s}, \theta_{\sigma(i)}) \le f(T)\}] \le \frac{(1+\varepsilon)f(T)}{\mathrm{kl}(\theta_i, \theta_{\sigma(i)})} + \frac{C_2(\varepsilon)}{T^{\beta(\varepsilon)}},$$

so that

$$\begin{aligned}
&\mathbb{E}[\sum_{n=1}^{T} \sum_{j \in \mathcal{K}_i'} \Delta_{j,i} \mathbf{1}\{M_i(n) = 1,\ \tau_n(i) = j,\ \omega_i(n) \ge \theta_j\}] \\
&\le \frac{\theta_{\sigma(i)} - \theta_i}{\mathrm{kl}(\theta_i, \theta_{\sigma(i)})}(1+\varepsilon)f(T) + \frac{C_2(\varepsilon)}{T^{\beta(\varepsilon)}}.
\end{aligned}$$

Summing over $i \in E \setminus M^\star$ completes the proof of inequality (4) and hence concludes the proof. □

LEMMA 1. *For every $M, M' \in \mathcal{M}$, there exists a bijective mapping $\tau_{MM'} : E \to E$, or τ for short, such that $\tau(i) = i$ if $i \in M \cap M'$ or $i \in \overline{M \cup M'}$. Otherwise, $\tau(i) = j$ for some $j \in \mathcal{L}_i$, where*

$$\mathcal{L}_i = \Big\{\ell \in M' \setminus M : (M' \setminus \ell) \cup \{i\} \in \mathcal{M}\Big\}.$$

In particular this lemma implies that for any problem instance, i.e. fixed $M^\star$, and for any $M \in \mathcal{M}$, there exists a bijective mapping $\tau_{MM^\star}$, or τ for short, which maps any optimal basic action of M to itself, and maps any sub-optimal basic action $i \in M$ to some element in $\mathcal{K}_i \setminus M$. Note that such a mapping may not be unique.

PROOF. Let $M, M' \in \mathcal{M}$. We provide an algorithm that outputs $\tau_{MM'}$. To present the algorithm, for any $i \in M \setminus M'$ let us define:

$$\mathcal{D}_i = \Big\{\ell \in M' \setminus M : (M \setminus i) \cup \{\ell\} \in \mathcal{M}\Big\}.$$

The pseudo-code of the algorithm is shown in Algorithm 3.

Algorithm 3 CONSTRUCTION OF MAPPING $\tau_{MM'}$

```
Initialization:
Set τ(i) = i for all i ∈ M ∩ M' and i ∈ ‾(M ∪ M')‾.
Set S_i = D_i for all i ∈ M \ M'. Set Q = M.
while Q ≠ M' do
  Let i_0 ∈ argmin_{i∈M\M'} |S_i| (ties are broken arbitrarily).
  Select j ∈ S_{i_0} arbitrarily. Set τ(i_0) = j.
  Q ← (Q \ i_0) ∪ {j}
  for i ∈ M \ M' do
    S_i ← S_i \ j
  end for
end while
Output τ.
```

Clearly the algorithm terminates after at most m steps since at each step one element in Q is replaced with some element of M'. In order to guarantee that the output of the algorithm is a bijective mapping it suffices to show at that any step, if $S_i = S_j = \{x\}$ for some $i, j \in B$, then necessarily $i = j$. We prove this claim by contradiction. Assume $S_i = S_j = \{x\}$ and $i \ne j$. Consider basis $M_1 = (Q \setminus i) \cup \{x\}$. Note that $M_1 \ne M'$ since $j \in M_1$. Hence there must exist $\ell \in M' \setminus M_1$ such that $(M_1 \setminus j) \cup \{\ell\}$ is a basis, and by definition $\ell \in S_j$. This is clearly a contradiction since $S_j = \{x\}$ and $x \notin M' \setminus M_1$.

Finally, we show that at each step $\tau(i_0) \in \mathcal{L}_{i_0}$. Observe that $\tau(i_0) \in S_{i_0}$ implies $\tau(i_0) \in \mathcal{D}_{i_0}$ since $S_{i_0} \subseteq \mathcal{D}_{i_0}$. Observe that $\ell \in \mathcal{D}_{i_0}$ implies that $(M \setminus i_0) \cup \{\ell\}$ is a basis, and hence $(M' \setminus \ell) \cup \{i_0\}$ is a basis, so that by definition $\ell \in \mathcal{L}_{i_0}$. This further implies that $\tau(i_0) \in \mathcal{L}_{i_0}$, which concludes the proof. □

B. PROOF OF THEOREM 2

PROOF. For any $M \ne M^\star$ introduce

$$B_M(\theta) = \{\lambda \in \Theta : \lambda_i = \theta_i, \forall i \in M^\star(\theta),\ M^\top \lambda > M^\star(\theta)^\top \theta\}.$$

Observing that $B(\theta) = \cup_{M \ne M^\star} B_M(\theta)$, we equivalently rewrite problem (2) as

$$\inf_{x\geq 0} \sum_{M\neq M^\star} \Delta_M x_M, \tag{5}$$

subject to:

$$\inf_{\lambda\in B_M(\theta)} \sum_{i\in M\setminus M^\star} \mathrm{kl}(\theta_i,\lambda_i)\sum_{Q\in\mathcal{M}} Q_i x_Q \geq 1,\ \ \forall M\neq M^\star.$$

Fix $i\in E\setminus M^\star$. Recall that $\sigma(i)=\mathrm{argmin}_{j\in\mathcal{K}_i}\theta_j$ and let $M^{(i)}=(M^\star\setminus\sigma(i))\cup\{i\}$. By Proposition 1, $M^{(i)}\in\mathcal{M}$. We may simplify the l.h.s. of the constraint corresponding to arm $M^{(i)}$ in (5) as follows:

$$\begin{aligned}
&\inf_{\lambda\in B_{M^{(i)}}(\theta)} \sum_{j\in M^{(i)}\setminus M^\star} \mathrm{kl}(\theta_j,\lambda_j)\sum_{Q} Q_j x_Q\\
&= \inf_{\lambda\in B_{M^{(i)}}(\theta)} \mathrm{kl}(\theta_i,\lambda_i)\sum_Q Q_i x_Q\\
&= \inf_{\lambda\in\Theta:\lambda_i>\theta_{\sigma(i)}} \mathrm{kl}(\theta_i,\lambda_i)\sum_Q Q_i x_Q\\
&= \mathrm{kl}(\theta_i,\theta_{\sigma(i)})\sum_Q Q_i x_Q,
\end{aligned}$$

where we used $M^{(i)}\setminus M^\star=\{i\}$. Let $\mathcal{M}^-=\mathcal{M}\setminus(\{M^\star\}\cup\{M^{(i)}, i\in E\setminus M^\star\})$. It then follows that

$$\begin{aligned}
c(\theta) = \inf_{x\geq 0} & \sum_{M\in\mathcal{M}} \Delta_M x_M \\
\text{subject to: } & \\
& \sum_{M\neq M^\star} M_i x_M \geq \frac{1}{\mathrm{kl}(\theta_i,\theta_{\sigma(i)})},\ \ \forall i\in E\setminus M^\star,\\
& \inf_{\lambda\in B_M(\theta)} \sum_{Q\in\mathcal{M}} x_Q \sum_{i\in E} Q_i \mathrm{kl}(\theta_i,\lambda_i)\geq 1,\ \ \forall M\in\mathcal{M}^-.
\end{aligned}\tag{6}$$

Defining

$$\mathsf{P1}:\ \inf_{x\geq 0} \sum_{M\neq M^\star}\Delta_M x_M$$

$$\text{subject to: } \sum_{M\neq M^\star} M_i x_M \geq \frac{1}{\mathrm{kl}(\theta_i,\theta_{\sigma(i)})},\ \ \forall i\in E\setminus M^\star,$$

gives $c(\theta)\geq \mathrm{val}(\mathsf{P1})$ since the feasible region of problem (6) is contained in that of $\mathsf{P1}$. [3]

For any sub-optimal action $i\in E$, introduce $z_i=\sum_M M_i x_M$, and define $z=(z_i, i\in E)$. Next we represent the objective of $\mathsf{P1}$ in terms of z, and give a lower bound for it. Using Lemma 1, there exists a bijective mapping τ_M such that $\tau_M(i)=i$ if $i\in M\cap M^\star$ or $i\in \overline{M\cup M^\star}$. Otherwise, $\tau_M(i)=j$ for some $j\in\mathcal{K}_i\setminus M$. We have:

$$\begin{aligned}
\Delta_M &= \sum_{i\in M}(\theta_{\tau_M(i)}-\theta_i)\\
&= \sum_{i\in M\setminus M^\star}(\theta_{\tau_M(i)}-\theta_i)\\
&= \sum_{i\in E\setminus M^\star} M_i(\theta_{\tau_M(i)}-\theta_i)\\
&\geq \sum_{i\in E\setminus M^\star} M_i(\theta_{\sigma(i)}-\theta_i).
\end{aligned}$$

[3]We use $\mathrm{val}(\mathsf{P})$ to denote the optimal value of a given optimization problem P.

Hence,

$$\begin{aligned}
\sum_M x_M\Delta_M &\geq \sum_M x_M \sum_{i\notin M^\star} M_i(\theta_{\sigma(i)}-\theta_i)\\
&= \sum_{i\notin M^\star}(\theta_{\sigma(i)}-\theta_i) z_i.
\end{aligned}$$

Then, defining

$$\mathsf{P2}:\ \inf_{z\geq 0} \sum_{i\in E\setminus M^\star}(\theta_{\sigma(i)}-\theta_i) z_i$$

$$\text{subject to: } z_i\geq \frac{1}{\mathrm{kl}(\theta_i,\theta_{\sigma(i)})},\ \ \forall i\in E\setminus M^\star,$$

yields: $c(\theta)\geq\mathrm{val}(\mathsf{P1})\geq\mathrm{val}(\mathsf{P2})$. The proof is completed by observing that

$$\mathrm{val}(\mathsf{P2}) = \sum_{i\in E\setminus M^\star}\frac{\theta_{\sigma(i)}-\theta_i}{\mathrm{kl}(\theta_i,\theta_{\sigma(i)})}.$$

□

REFERENCES

[1] Z. Abbassi, V. S. Mirrokni, and M. Thakur. Diversity maximization under matroid constraints. In *Proceedings of the 19th ACM SIGKDD international conference on Knowledge discovery and data mining*, pages 32–40, 2013.

[2] V. Anantharam, P. Varaiya, and J. Walrand. Asymptotically efficient allocation rules for the multiarmed bandit problem with multiple plays-part i: iid rewards. *IEEE Transactions on Automatic Control*, 32(11):968–976, 1987.

[3] J.-Y. Audibert, S. Bubeck, and G. Lugosi. Regret in online combinatorial optimization. *Mathematics of Operations Research*, 39(1):31–45, 2013.

[4] Y. Berstein, J. Lee, H. Maruri-Aguilar, S. Onn, E. Riccomagno, R. Weismantel, and H. Wynn. Nonlinear matroid optimization and experimental design. *SIAM Journal on Discrete Mathematics*, 22(3):901–919, 2008.

[5] J. Bragg, A. Kolobov, M. Mausam, and D. S. Weld. Parallel task routing for crowdsourcing. In *Second AAAI Conference on Human Computation and Crowdsourcing*, 2014.

[6] S. Bubeck and N. Cesa-Bianchi. Regret analysis of stochastic and nonstochastic multi-armed bandit problems. *Foundations and Trends in Machine Learning*, 5(1):1–222, 2012.

[7] N. Cesa-Bianchi and G. Lugosi. Combinatorial bandits. *Journal of Computer and System Sciences*, 78(5):1404–1422, 2012.

[8] W. Chen, Y. Wang, and Y. Yuan. Combinatorial multi-armed bandit: General framework and applications. In *Proceedings of the 30th International Conference on Machine Learning (ICML)*, pages 151–159, 2013.

[9] A. Clark, L. Bushnell, and R. Poovendran. On leader selection for performance and controllability in multi-agent systems. In *Proceedings of the 51st Annual Conference on Decision and Control (CDC)*, pages 86–93, 2012.

[10] R. Combes, M. S. Talebi, A. Proutiere, and M. Lelarge. Combinatorial bandits revisited. In *Advances in Neural Information Processing Systems 28 (NIPS)*, pages 2107–2115, 2015.

[11] J. Edmonds. Matroids and the greedy algorithm. *Mathematical programming*, 1(1):127–136, 1971.

[12] Y. Gai, B. Krishnamachari, and R. Jain. Learning multiuser channel allocations in cognitive radio networks: A combinatorial multi-armed bandit formulation. In *IEEE Symposium on New Frontiers in Dynamic Spectrum (DySPAN)*, pages 1–9, 2010.

[13] Y. Gai, B. Krishnamachari, and R. Jain. Combinatorial network optimization with unknown variables: Multi-armed bandits with linear rewards and individual observations. *IEEE/ACM Transactions on Networking*, 20(5):1466–1478, 2012.

[14] A. Garivier and O. Cappé. The kl-ucb algorithm for bounded stochastic bandits and beyond. In *Proceedings of the 24th Annual Conference on Learning Theory (COLT)*, pages 359–376, 2011.

[15] J. C. Gittins. Bandit processes and dynamic allocation indices. *Journal of the Royal Statistical Society. Series B (Methodological)*, pages 148–177, 1979.

[16] T. L. Graves and T. L. Lai. Asymptotically efficient adaptive choice of control laws in controlled markov chains. *SIAM J. Control and Optimization*, 35(3):715–743, 1997.

[17] J. Komiyama, J. Honda, and H. Nakagawa. Optimal regret analysis of thompson sampling in stochastic multi-armed bandit problem with multiple plays. In *Proceedings of the 32nd International Conference on Machine Learning (ICML)*, pages 1152–1161, 2015.

[18] B. Kveton, Z. Wen, A. Ashkan, and H. Eydgahi. Matroid bandits: Practical large-scale combinatorial bandits. In *Proceedings of AAAI Workshop on Sequential Decision-Making with Big Data*, 2014.

[19] B. Kveton, Z. Wen, A. Ashkan, H. Eydgahi, and B. Eriksson. Matroid bandits: Fast combinatorial optimization with learning. In *Proceedings of the 30th Conference on Uncertainty in Artificial Intelligence (UAI)*, pages 420–429, 2014.

[20] B. Kveton, Z. Wen, A. Ashkan, and C. Szepesvari. Tight regret bounds for stochastic combinatorial semi-bandits. In *Proceedings of the 18th International Conference on Artificial Intelligence and Statistics (AISTATS)*, pages 535–543, 2015.

[21] B. Kveton, Z. Wen, A. Ashkan, and M. Valko. Learning to act greedily: Polymatroid semi-bandits. *arXiv preprint arXiv:1405.7752*, 2014.

[22] T. L. Lai and H. Robbins. Asymptotically efficient adaptive allocation rules. *Advances in Applied Mathematics*, 6(1):4–22, 1985.

[23] M. Lelarge, A. Proutiere, and M. S. Talebi. Spectrum bandit optimization. In *Proceedings of Information Theory Workshop (ITW)*, pages 34–38, 2013.

[24] F. Lin, M. Fardad, and M. R. Jovanović. Algorithms for leader selection in large dynamical networks: Noise-corrupted leaders. In *Proceedings of the 50th IEEE Conference on Decision and Control and European Control Conference (CDC-ECC)*, pages 2932–2937, 2011.

[25] S. Onn. Convex matroid optimization. *SIAM Journal on Discrete Mathematics*, 17(2):249–253, 2003.

[26] J. G. Oxley. *Matroid theory*, volume 3. Oxford university press, 2006.

[27] H. Robbins. Some aspects of the sequential design of experiments. In *Herbert Robbins Selected Papers*, pages 169–177. Springer, 1985.

[28] A. Schrijver. *Combinatorial Optimization: Polyhedra and Efficiency*. Springer, 2003.

[29] M. Streeter, D. Golovin, and A. Krause. Online learning of assignments. In *Advances in Neural Information Processing Systems 22 (NIPS)*, pages 1794–1802, 2009.

[30] M. S. Talebi and A. Proutiere. An optimal algorithm for stochastic matroid bandit optimization. *arXiv preprint*, 2016.

A Greedy Approach to Adapting the Trace Parameter for Temporal Difference Learning

Martha White
Department of Computer Science
Indiana University
Bloomington, IN 47405, USA
martha@indiana.edu

Adam White
Department of Computer Science
Indiana University
Bloomington, IN 47405, USA
adamw@indiana.edu

ABSTRACT

One of the main obstacles to broad application of reinforcement learning methods is the parameter sensitivity of our core learning algorithms. In many large-scale applications, online computation and function approximation represent key strategies in scaling up reinforcement learning algorithms. In this setting, we have effective and reasonably well understood algorithms for adapting the learning-rate parameter, online during learning. Such meta-learning approaches can improve robustness of learning and enable specialization to current task, improving learning speed. For temporal-difference learning algorithms which we study here, there is yet another parameter, λ, that similarly impacts learning speed and stability in practice. Unfortunately, unlike the learning-rate parameter, λ parametrizes the objective function that temporal-difference methods optimize. Different choices of λ produce different fixed-point solutions, and thus adapting λ online and characterizing the optimization is substantially more complex than adapting the learning-rate parameter. There are no meta-learning method for λ that can achieve (1) incremental updating, (2) compatibility with function approximation, and (3) maintain stability of learning under both on and off-policy sampling. In this paper we contribute a novel objective function for optimizing λ as a function of state rather than time. We derive a new incremental, linear complexity λ-adaption algorithm that does not require offline batch updating or access to a model of the world, and present a suite of experiments illustrating the practicality of our new algorithm in three different settings. Taken together, our contributions represent a concrete step towards black-box application of temporal-difference learning methods in real world problems.

Keywords

Reinforcement learning; temporal difference learning; off-policy learning

1. INTRODUCTION

In reinforcement learning, the training data is produced by an adaptive learning agent's interaction with its environment, which makes tuning the parameters of the learning process both challenging and essential for good performance. In the online setting we study here, the agent-environment interaction produces an unending stream of temporally correlated data. In this setting there is no testing-training split, and thus the agent's learning process must be robust and adapt to new situations not considered by the human designer. Robustness is often critically related to the values of a small set parameters that control the learning process (e.g., the step-size parameter). In real-world applications, however, we cannot expect to test a large range of theses parameter values, in all the situations the agent may face, to ensure good performance—common practice in empirical studies. Unfortunately, safe values of these parameters are usually problem dependent. For example, in off-policy learning (e.g., learning from demonstrations), large importance sampling ratios can destabilize provably convergent gradient temporal difference learning methods, when the parameters are not set in a very particular way ($\lambda = 0$) [33]. In such situations, we turn to meta-learning algorithms that can adapt the parameters of the agent continuously, based on the stream of experience and some notion of the agent's own learning progress. These meta-learning approaches can potentially improve robustness, and also help the agent specialize to the current task, and thus improve learning speed.

Temporal difference learning methods make use of two important parameters: the step-size parameter and the trace-decay parameter. The step-size parameter is the same as those used in stochastic gradient descent, and there are algorithms available for adjusting this parameter online, in reinforcement learning [2]. For the trace decay parameter, on the other hand, we have no generally applicable meta-learning algorithms that are compatible with function approximation, incremental processing, and off-policy sampling.

The difficulty in adapting the trace decay parameter, λ, mainly arises from the fact that it has seemingly multiple roles and also influences the fixed-point solution. This parameter was introduced in Samuel's checker player [16], and later described as interpolation parameter between offline TD(0) and Monte-Carlo sampling (TD($\lambda = 1$) by Sutton[21]. It has been empirically demonstrated that values of λ between zero and one often perform the best in practice [21, 23, 32]. This trace parameter can also be viewed as a bias-variance trade-off parameter: λ closer to one is less biased but likely to have higher variance, where λ closer to zero is more biased, but likely has lower variance. However, it has also been described as a credit-assignment parameter [19], as a method to encode probability of transitions [25], a way to incorporate the agent's confidence in its value func-

Appears in: *Proceedings of the 15th International Conference on Autonomous Agents and Multiagent Systems (AAMAS 2016), J. Thangarajah, K. Tuyls, C. Jonker, S. Marsella (eds.), May 9–13, 2016, Singapore.*

tion estimates [23, 29], and as an averaging of n-step returns [23]. Selecting λ is further complicated by the fact that λ is a part of the problem definition: the solution to the Bellman fixed point equation is dependent on the choice of λ (unlike the step-size parameter).

There are few approaches for setting λ, and most existing work is limited to special cases. For instance, several approaches have analyzed setting λ for variants of TD that were introduced to simplify the analysis, including phased TD [5] and TD*(λ) [17]. Though both provide valuable insights into the role of λ, the analysis does not easily extend to conventional TD algorithms. Sutton and Singh [25] investigated tuning both the learning rate parameter and λ, and proposed two meta-learning algorithms. The first assumes the problem can be modeled by an acyclic MDP, and the other requires access to the transition model of the MDP. Singh and Dayan [18] and Kearns and Singh [5] contributed extensive simulation studies of the interaction between λ and other agent parameters on a chain MDP, but again relied on access to the model and offline computation. The most recent study [3] explores a Bayesian variant of TD learning, but requires a batch of samples and can only be used off-line. Finally, Konidaris et al. [6] introduce TD$_\gamma$ as a method to remove the λ parameter altogether. Their approach, however, has not been extended to the off-policy setting and their full algorithm is too computationally expensive for incremental estimation, while their incremental variant introduces a sensitive meta-parameter. Although this long-history of prior work has helped develop our intuitions about λ, the available solutions are still far from the use cases outlined above.

This paper introduces an new objective based on locally optimizing bias-variance, which we use to develop an efficient, incremental algorithm for learning state-based λ. We use a forward-backward analysis [23] to derive an incremental algorithm to estimate the variance of the return. Using this estimate, we obtain a closed-form estimate of λ on each time-step. Finally, we empirically demonstrate the generality of the approach with a suite of on-policy and off-policy experiments. Our results show that our new algorithm, λ-greedy, is consistently amongst the best performing, adapting as the problem changes, whereas any fixed approach works well in some settings and poorly in anothers.

2. BACKGROUND

We model the agent's interaction with an unknown environment as a discrete time Markov Decision Process (MDP). A MDP is characterized by a finite set of states $\mathcal{S}$, set of actions $\mathcal{A}$, a reward function $r : \mathcal{S} \times \mathcal{S} \to \mathbb{R}$, and generalized state-based discount $\gamma : \mathcal{S} \in [0, 1]$, which encodes the level of discounting per-state (e.g., a common setting is a constant discount for all states). On each of a discrete number of timesteps, $t = 1, 2, 3, \ldots$, the agent observes the current state S_t, selects an action A_t, according to its target policy $\pi : \mathcal{S} \times \mathcal{A} \to [0, 1]$, and the environment transitions to a new state S_{t+1} and emits a reward R_{t+1}. The state transitions are governed by the transition function $P : \mathcal{S} \times \mathcal{A} \times \mathcal{S} \to [0, 1]$, where $P(S_t, A_t, S_{t+1})$ denotes the probability of transitioning from S_t to S_{t+1}, due to action A_t. At timestep t, the future rewards are summarized by the Monte Carlo (MC) return $G_t \in \mathbb{R}$ defined by the infinite discounted sum

$$G_t \stackrel{\text{def}}{=} R_{t+1} + \gamma_{t+1} R_{t+2} + \gamma_{t+1}\gamma_{t+2} R_{t+3} + \ldots \quad \triangleright \gamma_t = \gamma(S_t)$$
$$= R_{t+1} + \gamma_{t+1} G_{t+1}.$$

The agent's objective is to estimate the expected return or value function, $v^\pi : \mathcal{S} \to \mathbb{R}$, defined as $v^\pi(s) \stackrel{\text{def}}{=} \mathbb{E}[G_t | S_t = s, A_t \sim \pi]$. We estimate the value function using the standard framework of linear function approximation. We assume the state of the environment at time t can be characterized by a fixed-length feature vector $\mathbf{x}_t \in \mathbb{R}^n$, where $n \ll |\mathcal{S}|$; implicitly, $\mathbf{x}_t$ is a function of the random variable S_t. The agent uses a linear estimate of the value of S_t: the inner product of $\mathbf{x}_t$ and a modifiable set of weights $\mathbf{w} \in \mathbb{R}^n$, $\hat{v}(S_t, \mathbf{w}) \stackrel{\text{def}}{=} \mathbf{x}_t^\top \mathbf{w}$, with mean-squared error (MSE) $= \sum_{s \in \mathcal{S}} d(s)(v(s) - \hat{v}(s, \mathbf{w}))^2$, where $d : \mathcal{S} \to [0, 1]$ encodes the distribution over states induced by the agent's behavior in the MDP.

Instead of estimating the expected value of G_t, we can estimate a λ-return that is expected to have lower variance

$$G_t^\lambda \stackrel{\text{def}}{=} R_{t+1} + \gamma_{t+1}[(1 - \lambda_{t+1})\mathbf{x}_{t+1}^\top \mathbf{w} + \lambda_{t+1} G_{t+1}^\lambda],$$

where the *trace decay function* $\lambda : \mathcal{S} \to [0, 1]$ specifies the trace parameter as a function of state. The trace parameter $\lambda_{t+1} = \lambda(s_{t+1})$ averages the estimate of the return, $\mathbf{x}_{t+1}^\top \mathbf{w}$, and the λ-return starting on the next step, G_{t+1}^λ. When $\lambda = 1$, G_t^λ becomes the MC return G_t, and the value function can be estimated by averaging rollouts from each state. When $\lambda = 0$, G_t^λ becomes equal to the *one-step λ-return*, $R_{t+1} + \gamma_{t+1}\mathbf{x}_{t+1}^\top \mathbf{w}$, and the value function can be estimated by the linear TD(0) algorithm. The λ-return when $\lambda \in (0, 1)$ is often easier to estimate than MC, and yields more accurate predictions than using the one-step return. The intuition, is that the for large λ, the estimate is high-variance due to averaging possibly long trajectories of noisy rewards, but less bias because the initial biased estimates of the value function participate less in the computation of the return. In the case of low λ, the estimate has lower-variance because fewer potentially noisy rewards participate in G_t^λ, but there is more bias due to the increase role of the initial value function estimates. We further discuss the intuition for this parameter in the next section.

The generalization to state-based γ and λ have not yet been widely considered, though the concept was introduced more than a decade ago [22, 27] and the generalization shown to be useful [22, 10, 14, 26]. The Bellman operator can be generalized to include state-based γ and λ (see [26, Equation 29]), where the choice of λ per-state influences the fixed point. Time-based λ, on the other hand, would not result in a well-defined fixed point. Therefore, to ensure a well-defined fixed point, we will design an objective and algorithm to learn a state-based λ.

This paper considers both on- and off-policy policy evaluation. In the more conventional on-policy learning setting, we estimate $v^\pi(s)$ based on samples generated while selecting actions according to the target policy π. In the off-policy case, we estimate $v^\pi(s)$ based on samples generated while selecting actions according to the behavior policy $\mu : \mathcal{S} \times \mathcal{A} \to [0, 1]$, and $\pi \neq \mu$. In order to learn $\hat{v}$ in both these settings we use the GTD(λ) algorithm [9] specified by the following update equations:

$$\rho_t \stackrel{\text{def}}{=} \frac{\pi(S_t, A_t)}{\mu(S_t, A_t)} \qquad \triangleright \text{importance sampling ratio}$$

$$\mathbf{e}_t \stackrel{\text{def}}{=} \rho_t(\gamma_t \lambda_t \mathbf{e}_{t-1} + \mathbf{x}_t) \qquad \triangleright \text{eligibility trace}$$

$$\delta_t \stackrel{\text{def}}{=} R_{t+1} + \gamma_t \mathbf{x}_{t+1}^\top \mathbf{w}_t - \mathbf{x}_t^\top \mathbf{w}_t \qquad \triangleright \text{TD error}$$

$$\mathbf{w}_{t+1} \leftarrow \mathbf{w}_t + \alpha(\delta_t \mathbf{e}_t - \gamma_t(1-\lambda_{t+1})\mathbf{e}_t^\top \mathbf{h}_t \mathbf{x}_{t+1})$$
$$\mathbf{h}_{t+1} \leftarrow \mathbf{h}_t + \alpha_{\mathbf{h}}(\delta_t \mathbf{e}_t - \mathbf{x}_t^\top \mathbf{h}_t)\mathbf{x}_t \qquad \triangleright \text{auxiliary weights}$$

with step-sizes $\alpha, \alpha_{\mathbf{h}} \in \mathbb{R}^+$ and an arbitrary initial $\mathbf{w}_0, \mathbf{h}_0$ (e.g., the zero vector). The importance sampling ratio $\rho_t \in \mathbb{R}^+$ facilitates learning about rewards as if they were generated by following π, instead of μ. This ratio can be very large if $\mu(S_t, A_t)$ is small, which can compound and destabilize learning.

3. OBJECTIVE FOR TRACE ADAPTATION

To obtain an objective for selecting λ, we need to clarify its role. Although λ was not introduced with the goal of trading off bias and variance [21], several algorithms and significant theory have developed its role as such [5, 17]. Other roles have been suggested; however, as we discuss below, each of them can still be thought of as a bias-variance trade-off.

The λ parameter has been described as a credit assignment parameter, which allows TD(λ) to perform multi-step updates on each time step. On each update, λ_t controls the amount of credit assigned to previous transitions, using the eligibility trace $\mathbf{e}$. For λ_t close to 1, TD(λ) assigns more credit for the current reward to previous transitions, resulting in updates to many states along the current trajectory. Conversely, for $\lambda_t = 0$, the eligibility trace is cleared and no credit is assigned back in time, performing a single-step TD(0) update. In fact, this intuition can still be thought of as a bias-variance trade-off. In terms of credit assignment, we ideally always want to send maximal credit $\lambda = 1$, but decayed by γ, for the current reward, which is also unbiased. In practice, however, this often leads to high variance, and thus we mitigate the variance by choosing λ less than one and speed learning overall, but introduce bias.

Another interpretation is that λ should be set to reflect confidence in value function estimates [29, 23]. If your confidence in the value estimate of state s is high, then $\lambda(s)$ should be close to 0, meaning we trust the estimates provided by $\hat{v}$. If your confidence is low, suspecting that $\hat{v}$ may be inaccurate, then $\lambda(s)$ should be close to 1, meaning we trust observed rewards more. For example in states that are indistinguishable with function approximation (i.e., aliased states), we should not trust the $\hat{v}$ as much. This intuition similarly translates to bias-variance. If $\hat{v}$ is accurate, then decreasing $\lambda(s)$ does not incur (much) bias, but can significantly decrease the variance since $\hat{v}$ gives the correct value. If $\hat{v}$ is inaccurate, then the increased bias is not worth the reduced variance, so $\lambda(s)$ should be closer to 1 to use actual (potentially high-variance) samples.

Finally, a less commonly discussed interpretation is that λ acts as parameter that simulates a form of experience replay (or model-based simulation of trajectories). One can imagine that sending back information in eligibility traces is like simulating experience from a model, where the model could be a set of trajectories, as in experience replay [8]. If $\lambda = 1$, the traces are longer and each update gets more trajectory information, or experience replay. If a trajectory from a point, however, was unlikely (e.g., a rare transition), we may not want to use that information. Such an approach was taken by Sutton and Singh [25], where λ was set to the transition probabilities. Even in this model-based interpretation, the goal in setting λ becomes one of mitigating variance, without incurring too much bias.

Optimizing this bias-variance trade-off, however, is difficult because λ affects the return we are approximating. Jointly optimizing for λ across all time-steps is generally not feasible. One strategy is to take a batch approach, where the optimal λ is determined after seeing all the data [3]. Our goal, however, is to develop approaches for the online setting, where future states, actions, rewards and the influence of λ have yet to be observed.

We propose to take a greedy approach: on each time step select λ_{t+1} to optimize the bias-variance trade-off *for only this step*. This greedy objective corresponds to minimizing the mean-squared error between the unbiased $\lambda = 1$ return G_t and the estimate $\hat{G}_t$ with $\lambda_{t+1} \in [0, 1]$ with $\lambda = 1$ into the future after $t + 1$

$$\hat{G}_t \stackrel{\text{def}}{=} \mathbb{E}[\ \rho_t(R_{t+1} + \gamma_{t+1}[(1-\lambda_{t+1})\mathbf{x}_{t+1}^\top \mathbf{w}_t + \lambda_{t+1} \underbrace{G_{t+1}}_{\text{Monte Carlo}}])\ ].$$

Notice that $\hat{G}_t$ interpolates between the current value estimate and the unbiased $\lambda = 1$ MC return, and so is not recursive. Picking $\lambda_{t+1} = 1$ gives an unbiased estimate, since then we would be estimating $\hat{G}_t = G_t$. We greedily decide how λ_{t+1} should be set on this step to locally optimize the mean-squared error (i.e., bias-variance). This greedy decision is made given both $\mathbf{x}_t$ and $\mathbf{x}_{t+1}$, which are both available when choosing λ_{t+1}. To simplify notation in this section, we assume that $\mathbf{x}_t$ and $\mathbf{x}_{t+1}$ are both given in the below expectations.

To minimize the mean-squared error in terms of λ_{t+1}

$$\text{MSE}(\lambda_{t+1}) \stackrel{\text{def}}{=} \mathbb{E}[(G_t - \hat{G}_t)^2]$$

we will consider the two terms that compose the mean-squared error: the squared bias term and the variance term.

$$\begin{aligned}\text{Bias}(\lambda_{t+1}) &\stackrel{\text{def}}{=} \mathbb{E}[G_t] - \mathbb{E}[\hat{G}_t] \\ \text{Variance}(\lambda_{t+1}) &\stackrel{\text{def}}{=} \text{Var}[\hat{G}_t] \\ \text{MSE}(\lambda_{t+1}) &= \text{Bias}(\lambda_{t+1})^2 + \text{Variance}(\lambda_{t+1}).\end{aligned}$$

Let us begin by rewriting the bias. Since we are given $\mathbf{x}_t$, ρ_t, $\mathbf{x}_{t+1}$ and γ_{t+1} when choosing λ_{t+1},

$$\begin{aligned}\mathbb{E}[\hat{G}_t] &= \rho_t \mathbb{E}\left[R_{t+1} + \gamma_{t+1}(1-\lambda_{t+1})\mathbf{x}_{t+1}^\top \mathbf{w}_t + \lambda_{t+1} G_{t+1}\right] \\ &= \rho_t \mathbb{E}[R_{t+1}] + \rho_t \gamma_{t+1}\left((1-\lambda_{t+1})\mathbf{x}_{t+1}^\top \mathbf{w}_t + \lambda_{t+1}\mathbb{E}[G_{t+1}]\right)\end{aligned}$$

For convenience, define

$$\text{err}(\mathbf{w}, \mathbf{x}_{t+1}) \stackrel{\text{def}}{=} \mathbb{E}[G_{t+1}] - \mathbf{x}_{t+1}^\top \mathbf{w} \qquad (1)$$

as the difference between the $\lambda = 1$ return and the current approximate value from state $\mathbf{x}_{t+1}$ using weights $\mathbf{w}_t$. Using this definition, we can rewrite

$$\begin{aligned}&(1-\lambda_{t+1})\mathbf{x}_{t+1}^\top \mathbf{w}_t + \lambda_{t+1}\mathbb{E}[G_{t+1}] \\ &= (1-\lambda_{t+1})(\mathbb{E}[G_{t+1}] - \text{err}(\mathbf{w}_t, \mathbf{x}_{t+1})) + \lambda_{t+1}\mathbb{E}[G_{t+1}] \\ &= \mathbb{E}[G_{t+1}] - (1-\lambda_{t+1})\text{err}(\mathbf{w}_t, \mathbf{x}_{t+1})\end{aligned}$$

giving

$$\begin{aligned}\mathbb{E}[\hat{G}_t] &= \rho_t\left(\mathbb{E}[R_{t+1}] + \gamma_{t+1}\mathbb{E}[G_{t+1}]\right) \\ &\quad - \rho_t \gamma_{t+1}(1-\lambda_{t+1})\text{err}(\mathbf{w}_t, \mathbf{x}_{t+1}) \\ &= \mathbb{E}[G_t] - \rho_t \gamma_{t+1}(1-\lambda_{t+1})\text{err}(\mathbf{w}_t, \mathbf{x}_{t+1})\end{aligned}$$

$$\implies \text{Bias}^2(\lambda_{t+1}) = \left(\mathbb{E}[G_t] - \mathbb{E}[\hat{G}_t]\right)^2$$
$$= \rho_t^2\gamma_{t+1}^2(1-\lambda_{t+1})^2\text{err}^2(\mathbf{w}_t, \mathbf{x}_{t+1}).$$

For the variance term, we will assume that the noise in the reward R_{t+1} given $\mathbf{x}_t$ and $\mathbf{x}_{t+1}$ is independent of the other dynamics [12], with variance $\sigma_r(\mathbf{x}_t, \mathbf{x}_{t+1})$. Again since we are given $\mathbf{x}_t$, ρ_t, $\mathbf{x}_{t+1}$ and γ_{t+1}

$$\text{Var}[\hat{G}_t]$$
$$= \rho_t^2\text{Var}[R_{t+1} + \underbrace{\gamma_{t+1}(1-\lambda_{t+1})\mathbf{x}_{t+1}^\top\mathbf{w}_t}_{\text{constant given } \rho_t, \mathbf{x}_{t+1}, \gamma_{t+1}} + \gamma_{t+1}\lambda_{t+1}G_{t+1}]$$
$$= \underbrace{\rho_t^2\text{Var}[R_{t+1}] + \rho_t^2\gamma_{t+1}^2\lambda_{t+1}^2\text{Var}[G_{t+1}]}_{\text{independent given } \mathbf{x}_t, \mathbf{x}_{t+1}}$$
$$= \rho_t^2\sigma_r(\mathbf{x}_t, \mathbf{x}_{t+1}) + \rho_t^2\gamma_{t+1}^2\lambda_{t+1}^2\text{Var}[G_{t+1}]$$
$$\implies \text{Variance}(\lambda_{t+1}) = \rho_t^2\gamma_{t+1}^2\lambda_{t+1}^2\text{Var}[G_{t+1}] + \rho_t^2\sigma_r(\mathbf{x}_t, \mathbf{x}_{t+1})$$

Finally, we can drop the constant $\rho_t^2\sigma_r(\mathbf{x}_t, \mathbf{x}_{t+1})$ in the objective, and drop the $\rho_t^2\gamma_{t+1}^2$ in both the bias and variance terms as it only scales the objective, giving the optimization

$$\min_{\lambda_{t+1}\in[0,1]} \text{Bias}^2(\lambda_{t+1}) + \text{Variance}(\lambda_{t+1})$$
$$\equiv \min_{\lambda_{t+1}\in[0,1]} (1-\lambda_{t+1})^2\text{err}_{t+1}^2(\mathbf{w}_t) + \lambda_{t+1}^2\text{Var}[G_{t+1}].$$

We can take the gradient of this optimization to find a closed form solution

$$-2(1-\lambda_{t+1})\text{err}_{t+1}^2(\mathbf{w}_t) + 2\lambda_{t+1}\text{Var}[G_{t+1}] = 0$$
$$\implies \left(\text{Var}[G_{t+1}] + \text{err}_{t+1}^2(\mathbf{w}_t)\right)\lambda_{t+1} - \text{err}_{t+1}^2(\mathbf{w}_t) = 0$$
$$\implies \lambda_{t+1} = \frac{\text{err}_{t+1}^2(\mathbf{w}_t)}{\text{Var}[G_{t+1}] + \text{err}_{t+1}^2(\mathbf{w}_t)} \quad (2)$$

which is always feasible, unless both the variance and error are zero (in which case, any choice of λ_{t+1} is equivalent). Though the importance sampling ratio ρ_t does not affect the choice of λ on the current time step, it can have a dramatic effect on $\text{Var}[G_{t+1}]$ into the future via the eligibility trace. For example, when the target and behavior policy are strongly mis-matched, ρ_t can be large, which multiplies into the eligibility trace $\mathbf{e}_t$. If several steps have large ρ_t, then $\mathbf{e}_t$ can get very large. In this case, the equation in (2) would select a small λ_{t+1}, significantly decreasing variance.

4. TRACE ADAPTATION ALGORITHM

To approximate the solution to our proposed optimization, we need a way to approximate the error and the variance terms in equation (2). To estimate the error, we need an estimate of the expected return from each state, $\mathbb{E}[G_t]$. To estimate the variance, we need to obtain an estimate of $\mathbb{E}[G_t^2]$, and then can use $\text{Var}[G_t] = \mathbb{E}[G_t^2] - \mathbb{E}[G_t]^2$. The estimation of the expected return is in fact the problem tackled by this paper, and one could use a TD algorithm, learning weight vector $\mathbf{w}^{\text{err}}$ to obtain approximation $\mathbf{x}_t^\top\mathbf{w}^{\text{err}}$ to $\mathbb{E}[G_t]$. This approach may seem problematic, as this sub-step appears to be solving the same problem we originally aimed to solve. However, as in many meta-parameter optimization approaches, this approximation can be inaccurate and still adequately guide selection of λ. We discuss this further in the experimental results section.

Similarly, we would like to estimate $\mathbb{E}[G_t^2]$ with $\mathbf{w}^{\text{sq}}\mathbf{x}_t^\top$ by learning $\mathbf{w}^{\text{sq}}$; estimating the variance or the second moment of the return, however, has not been extensively studied. Sobel [20] provides a Bellman equation for the variance of the λ-return, when $\lambda = 0$. There is also an extensive literature on risk-averse MDP learning, where the variance of the return is often used as a measure [15, 13, 1, 28]; however, an explicit way to estimate the variance of the return for $\lambda > 0$ is not given. There has also been some work on estimating the variance of the *value function* [12, 35], for general λ; though related, this is different than estimating the variance of the λ-*return*.

In the next section, we provide a derivation for a new algorithm called variance temporal difference learning (VTD), to approximate the second moment of the return for any state-based λ. The general VTD updates are given at the end of Section 5.2. For λ-greedy, we use VTD to estimate the variance, with the complete algorithm summarized in Algorithm 1. We opt for simple meta-parameter settings, so that no additional parameters are introduced. We use the same step-size α that is used for the main weights to update $\mathbf{w}^{\text{err}}$ and $\mathbf{w}^{\text{sq}}$. In addition, we set the weights $\mathbf{w}^{\text{err}}$ and $\mathbf{w}^{\text{sq}}$ to reflect *a priori* estimates of error and variance. As a reasonable rule-of-thumb, $\mathbf{w}^{\text{err}}$ should be set larger than $\mathbf{w}^{\text{sq}}$, to reflect that initial value estimates are inaccurate. This results in

Algorithm 1: Policy evaluation with λ-greedy

```
w_t ← 0 // Main weights
h_t ← 0 // Auxiliary weights for off-policy learning
e_t ← 0 // Main trace parameters
x_t ← the initial observation
w^err ← Rmax/(1−γ) × 1, w^sq ← 0.0 × 1 // Aux. weights for λ
ē_t ← 0, z̄_t ← 0 // Aux. traces
repeat
    Take action accord. to π, observe x_{t+1}, reward r_{t+1}
    ρ_t = π(s_t, a_t)/μ(s_t, a_t)   // In on-policy, ρ_t = 1
    λ_{t+1} ← λ-greedy(w^err, w^sq, w_t, x_t, x_{t+1}, r_{t+1}, ρ_t)
    // Now can use any algorithm, e.g., GTD
    δ_t = r_{t+1} + γ_{t+1} w_t^T x_{t+1} − w_t^T x_t
    e_t = ρ_t(γ_t λ_t e_{t−1} + x_t)
    w_{t+1} = w_t + α(δ_t e_t − γ_{t+1}(1 − λ_{t+1}) x_{t+1})(e_t^T h_t))
    h_{t+1} = h_t + α_h(δ_t e_t − (h_t^T x_t) x_t)
until agent done interaction with environment
```

Algorithm 2: λ-greedy$(\mathbf{w}^{\text{err}}, \mathbf{w}^{\text{sq}}, \mathbf{w}_t, \mathbf{x}_t, \mathbf{x}_{t+1}, r_{t+1}, \rho_t)$

```
// Use GTD to update w^err
ḡ_{t+1} ← x_{t+1}^T w^err
δ_t ← r_{t+1} + γ_{t+1} ḡ_{t+1} − x_t^T w^err
ē_t = ρ_t(γ_t ē_{t−1} + x_t)
w^err = w^err + α δ_t ē_t
// Use VTD to update w^sq
r̄_{t+1} ← ρ_t^2 r_{t+1}^2 + ρ_t^2 γ_{t+1} r_{t+1} ḡ_{t+1}
γ̄_{t+1} ← ρ_t^2 γ_{t+1}^2
δ̄_t ← r̄_{t+1} + γ̄_{t+1} x_{t+1}^T w^sq − x_t^T w^sq
z̄_t = γ̄_t z̄_{t−1} + x_t
w^sq = w^sq + α δ̄_t z̄_t
// Compute λ estimate
errsq = (ḡ_{t+1} − x_{t+1}^T w_t)^2
varg = max(0, x_{t+1}^T w^sq − (ḡ_{t+1})^2)
λ_{t+1} = errsq/(varg + errsq)
return λ_{t+1}
```

an estimate of variance $\text{Var}[G_{t+1}] \approx \mathbf{x}_{t+1}^\top \mathbf{w}^{\text{sq}} - (\mathbf{x}_{t+1}^\top \mathbf{w}^{\text{err}})^2$ that is capped at zero until $\mathbf{x}_{t+1}^\top \mathbf{w}^{\text{sq}}$ becomes larger than $(\mathbf{x}_{t+1}^\top \mathbf{w}^{\text{err}})^2$.

5. APPROXIMATING THE SECOND MOMENT OF THE RETURN

In this section, we derive the general VTD algorithm to approximate the second moment of the λ-return. Though we will set $\lambda_{t+1} = 1$ in our algorithm, we nonetheless provide the more general algorithm as the only model-free variance estimation approach for general λ-returns.

The key novelty is in determining a Bellman operator for the squared return, which then defines a fixed-point objective, called the Var-MSPBE. With this Bellman operator and recursive form for the squared return, we derive a gradient TD algorithm, called VTD, for estimating the second moment. To avoid confusion with parameters for the main algorithm, as a general rule throughout the document, the additional parameters used to estimate the second moment have a bar. For example, γ_{t+1} is the discount for the main problem, and $\bar{\gamma}_{t+1}$ is the discount for the second moment.

5.1 Bellman operator for squared return

The recursive form for the squared-return is

$$\begin{aligned}(G_t^\lambda)^2 &= \rho_t^2(\bar{G}_t^2 + 2\gamma_{t+1}\lambda_{t+1}\bar{G}_t G_t^\lambda + \gamma_{t+1}^2\lambda_{t+1}^2(G_{t+1}^\lambda)^2)\\ &= \bar{r}_{t+1} + \bar{\gamma}_{t+1}(G_{t+1}^\lambda)^2\end{aligned}$$

where for a given $\lambda : \mathcal{S} \to [0,1]$ and $\mathbf{w}$,

$$\begin{aligned}\bar{G}_t &\stackrel{\text{def}}{=} R_{t+1} + \gamma_{t+1}(1-\lambda_{t+1})\mathbf{x}_{t+1}^\top \mathbf{w}\\ \bar{r}_{t+1} &\stackrel{\text{def}}{=} \rho_t^2\bar{G}_t^2 + 2\rho_t^2\gamma_{t+1}\lambda_{t+1}\bar{G}_t G_{t+1}^\lambda\\ \bar{\gamma} &\stackrel{\text{def}}{=} \rho_t^2\gamma_{t+1}^2\lambda_{t+1}^2.\end{aligned}$$

The $\mathbf{w}$ are the weights for the λ-return, and not the weights $\mathbf{w}^{\text{sq}}$ we will learn for approximating the second moment. For further generality, we introduce a meta-parameter $\bar{\lambda}_t$

$$\bar{V}_t^{\bar{\lambda}} \stackrel{\text{def}}{=} \bar{r}_{t+1} + \bar{\gamma}_{t+1}\left((1-\bar{\lambda}_{t+1})\mathbf{x}_{t+1}^\top \mathbf{w}^{\text{sq}} + \bar{\lambda}_{t+1}\bar{V}_{t+1}^{\bar{\lambda}}\right)$$

to get a $\bar{\lambda}$-squared-return where for $\bar{\lambda}_{t+1} = 1$, $\bar{V}_t^{\bar{\lambda}} = (G_t^\lambda)^2$. This meta-parameter $\bar{\lambda}$ plays the same role for estimating $(G_t^\lambda)^2$ as λ for estimating G_t.

We can define a generalized Bellman operator $\bar{\mathbf{T}}$ for the squared-return, using this above recursive form. The goal is to obtain the fixed point $\bar{\mathbf{T}}\bar{\mathbf{v}} = \bar{\mathbf{v}}$, where a fixed point exists *if the operator is a contraction.* For the first moment, the Bellman operator is known to be a contraction [30]. This result, however, does not immediately extend here because, thought $\bar{r}_{t+1}$ is a valid finite reward, $\bar{\gamma}_{t+1}$ does not satisfy $\bar{\gamma}_{t+1} \le 1$, because ρ_t^2 can be large.

We can nonetheless define such a Bellman operator for the $\bar{\lambda}$-squared-return and determine if a fixed point exists. Interestingly, $\bar{\gamma}_{t+1}$ can in fact be larger than 1, and we can still obtain a contraction. To define the Bellman operator, we use a recent generalization that enables the discount to be defined as a function of (s, a, s') [34], rather than just as a function of s'. We first define $\bar{\mathbf{v}}$, the expected $\bar{\lambda}$-squared-return

$$\bar{\mathbf{v}} \stackrel{\text{def}}{=} \sum_{t=0}^{\infty}(\bar{\mathbf{P}}^{\pi,\gamma})^t\bar{\mathbf{r}},$$

where

$$\bar{\mathbf{P}}^{\pi,\gamma}(s,s') \stackrel{\text{def}}{=} \sum_{s,a,s'} P(s,a,s')\mu(s,a)\rho(s,a)^2\gamma(s')^2\lambda(s')^2 \quad (3)$$

$$\bar{\mathbf{r}} \stackrel{\text{def}}{=} \sum_{s,a,s'} P(s,a,s')\mu(s,a)\bar{r}(s,s').$$

Using similar equations to the generalized Bellman operator [34], we can define

$$\bar{\mathbf{T}}\bar{\mathbf{v}} = \sum_{t=0}^{\infty}(\bar{\mathbf{P}}^{\pi,\gamma}\mathbf{\Lambda})^t\left(\bar{\mathbf{r}} + \bar{\mathbf{P}}^{\pi,\gamma}(\mathbf{I}-\mathbf{\Lambda})\bar{\mathbf{v}}\right)$$

where $\mathbf{\Lambda} \in \mathbb{R}^{|\mathcal{S}|\times|\mathcal{S}|}$ is a matrix with $\lambda(s)$ on the diagonal, for all $s \in \mathcal{S}$. The infinite sum is convergent if the maximum singular value of $\bar{\mathbf{P}}^{\pi,\gamma}\mathbf{\Lambda}$ is less than 1, giving solution $\sum_{t=0}^{\infty}(\bar{\mathbf{P}}^{\pi,\gamma}\mathbf{\Lambda})^t = (\mathbf{I} - \bar{\mathbf{P}}^{\pi,\gamma}\mathbf{\Lambda})^{-1}$. Otherwise, however, the value is infinite and one can see that in fact the variance of the return is infinite!

We can naturally investigate when the second moment of the return is guaranteed to be finite. This condition on $\bar{\mathbf{P}}^{\pi,\gamma}\mathbf{\Lambda}$ should facilitate identifying theoretical conditions on the target and behavior policies that enable finite variance of the return. This theoretical characterization is outside of the scope of this work, but we can reason about different settings that provide a well-defined, finite fixed point. First, clearly setting $\lambda_{t+1} = 0$ for every state ensures a finite second moment, given a finite $\bar{\mathbf{v}}$, regardless of policy mis-match. For the on-policy setting, where $\rho_t = 1$, $\bar{\gamma}_{t+1} \le \gamma_{t+1}$ and so a well-defined fixed point exists, under standard assumptions (see [34]). For the off-policy setting, if $\bar{\gamma}_{t+1} = \lambda_{t+1}^2\gamma_{t+1}^2\rho_t^2 < 1$, this is similarly the case. Otherwise, a solution may still exist, by ensuring that the maximum singular value of $\bar{\mathbf{P}}^{\pi,\gamma}$ is less than one; we hypothesize that this property is unlikely if there is a large mis-match between the target and behavior policy, causing many large ρ_t. An important future avenue is to understand the required similarity between π and μ to enable finite variance of the return, for any given λ. Interestingly, the λ-greedy algorithm should adapt to such infinite variance settings, where (2) will set $\lambda_{t+1} = 0$.

5.2 VTD derivation

In this section, we propose Var-MSPBE, the mean-squared projected Bellman error (MSPBE) objective for the $\bar{\lambda}$-squared-return, and derive VTD to optimize this objective. Given the definition of the generalized Bellman operator $\bar{\mathbf{T}}$, the derivation parallels GTD(λ) for the first moment [9]. The main difference is in obtaining unbiased estimates of parts of the objective; we will therefore focus the results on this novel aspect, summarized in the below two theorems and corollary.

Define the error of the estimate $\mathbf{x}_t^\top \mathbf{w}^{\text{sq}}$ to the future $\bar{\lambda}$-squared-return

$$\bar{\delta}_t^{\bar{\lambda}} \stackrel{\text{def}}{=} \bar{V}_t^{\bar{\lambda}} - \mathbf{x}_t^\top \mathbf{w}^{\text{sq}}$$

and, as in previous work [24, 9], we define the MSPBE that corresponds to $\bar{\mathbf{T}}$

$$\text{Var-MSPBE}(\mathbf{w}^{\text{sq}}) \stackrel{\text{def}}{=} \mathbb{E}[\bar{\delta}_t^{\bar{\lambda}}\mathbf{x}_t]^\top \mathbb{E}[\mathbf{x}_t\mathbf{x}_t]^{-1}\mathbb{E}[\bar{\delta}_t^{\bar{\lambda}}\mathbf{x}_t].$$

To obtain the gradient of the objective, we prove that we can obtain an unbiased sample of $\bar{\delta}_t^{\bar{\lambda}}\mathbf{x}_t$ (a forward view) using a trace of the past (a backward view). The equivalence is simpler if we assume that we have access to an estimate of the first moment of the λ-return. For our setting, we do in fact have such an estimate, because we simultaneously learn $\mathbf{w}^{\text{err}}$. We include the more general expectation equivalence in Theorem 2, with all proofs in the appendix.

THEOREM 1. *For a given unbiased estimate $\bar{g}_{t+1}$ of $\mathbb{E}[G^{\lambda}_{t+1}|S_{t+1}]$, define*

$$\bar{\delta}_t \stackrel{def}{=} (\rho_t^2 \bar{G}_t^2 + 2\rho_t^2 \gamma_{t+1}\lambda_{t+1}\bar{G}_t \bar{g}_{t+1}) + \bar{\gamma}_{t+1}\mathbf{x}_{t+1}^{\top}\mathbf{w}_t^{sq} - \mathbf{x}_t^{\top}\mathbf{w}_t^{sq}$$

$$\bar{\mathbf{z}}_t \stackrel{def}{=} \mathbf{x}_t + \bar{\gamma}_{t+1}\bar{\mathbf{z}}_{t-1}$$

Then $$\mathbb{E}[\bar{\delta}_t^{\bar{\lambda}}\mathbf{x}_t] = \mathbb{E}[\bar{\delta}_t \bar{\mathbf{z}}_t]$$

THEOREM 2.

$$\mathbb{E}[\bar{r}_{t+1}\bar{\mathbf{z}}_t] = E[\rho_{t+1}^2 \bar{G}_t^2 \bar{\mathbf{z}}_t] + 2E[\rho_{t+1}^2 \bar{G}_t(\bar{\mathbf{a}}_t + \bar{\mathbf{B}}_t\mathbf{w}_t)]$$

where

$$\bar{\mathbf{a}}_t \stackrel{def}{=} \rho_t\gamma_t\lambda_t(R_t\bar{\mathbf{z}}_{t-1} + \bar{\mathbf{a}}_{t-1})$$

$$\bar{\mathbf{B}}_t \stackrel{def}{=} \rho_t\gamma_t\lambda_t(\gamma_t(1-\lambda_t)\bar{\mathbf{z}}_{t-1}\mathbf{x}_t^{\top} + \bar{\mathbf{B}}_{t-1})$$

COROLLARY 1. *For $\lambda_t = 1$ for all t,*

$$\mathbb{E}[\bar{r}_{t+1}\bar{\mathbf{z}}_t] = E[\rho_t^2 R_{t+1}^2 \bar{\mathbf{z}}_t] + 2E[R_{t+1}\bar{\mathbf{a}}_t]$$

where

$$\bar{\mathbf{z}}_t = \mathbf{x}_t + \rho_{t-1}^2\gamma_t^2\bar{\mathbf{z}}_{t-1}$$

$$\bar{\mathbf{a}}_t = \rho_t\gamma_t(R_t\bar{\mathbf{z}}_{t-1} + \bar{\mathbf{a}}_{t-1}).$$

To derive the VTD algorithm, we take the gradient of the Var-MSPBE. As this again parallels GTD(λ), we include the derivation in the appendix for completeness and provide only the final result here.

$$-\tfrac{1}{2}\nabla\text{Var-MSPBE}(\mathbf{w}^{\text{sq}})$$
$$= \mathbb{E}[\bar{\delta}_t^{\bar{\lambda}}\mathbf{x}_t] - \mathbb{E}[\bar{\gamma}_{t+1}(1-\bar{\lambda}_{t+1})\mathbf{x}_{t+1}\bar{\mathbf{z}}_t^{\top}]\mathbb{E}[\mathbf{x}_t\mathbf{x}_t]^{-1}\mathbb{E}[\bar{\delta}_t^{\bar{\lambda}}\mathbf{x}_t].$$

As with previous gradient TD algorithms, we will learn an auxiliary set of weights $\mathbf{w}^{\text{sq}}$ to estimate a part of this objective: $\mathbb{E}[\mathbf{x}_t\mathbf{x}_t]^{-1}\mathbb{E}[\bar{\delta}_t^{\bar{\lambda}}\mathbf{x}_t]$. To obtain such an estimate, notice that $\mathbf{h}^{sq} = \mathbb{E}[\mathbf{x}_t\mathbf{x}_t]^{-1}\mathbb{E}[\bar{\delta}_t^{\bar{\lambda}}\mathbf{x}_t]$ corresponds to an LMS solution, where the goal is to obtain $\mathbf{x}_t^{\top}\mathbf{h}^{sq}$ that estimates $\mathbb{E}[\bar{\delta}_t^{\bar{\lambda}}|\mathbf{x}_t]$. Therefore, we can use an LMS update for $\mathbf{h}^{sq}$, giving the final set of update equations for VTD:

$$\bar{g}_{t+1} \leftarrow \mathbf{x}_{t+1}^{\top}\mathbf{w}^{\text{err}}$$
$$\bar{r}_{t+1} \leftarrow \rho_t^2\bar{G}_t^2 + 2\rho_t^2\gamma_{t+1}\lambda_{t+1}\bar{G}_t\bar{g}_{t+1}$$
$$\bar{\gamma}_{t+1} \leftarrow \rho_t^2\gamma_{t+1}^2\lambda_{t+1}^2$$
$$\bar{\delta}_t \leftarrow \bar{r}_{t+1} + \bar{\gamma}_{t+1}\mathbf{x}_{t+1}^{\top}\mathbf{w}_t^{\text{sq}} - \mathbf{x}_t^{\top}\mathbf{w}_t^{\text{sq}}$$
$$\mathbf{w}_{t+1}^{\text{sq}} \leftarrow \mathbf{w}_t^{\text{sq}} + \bar{\alpha}_h\bar{\delta}_t\bar{\mathbf{z}}_t - \bar{\alpha}_h\bar{\gamma}_{t+1}(1-\bar{\lambda}_{t+1})\mathbf{x}_{t+1}\bar{\mathbf{z}}_t^{\top}\mathbf{h}_t^{sq}$$
$$\mathbf{h}_{t+1}^{sq} \leftarrow \mathbf{h}_t^{sq} + \bar{\alpha}_h\bar{\delta}_t\bar{\mathbf{z}}_t - \bar{\alpha}_h\mathbf{x}_t^{\top}\mathbf{h}_t^{sq}\mathbf{x}_t.$$

For λ-greedy, we set $\bar{\lambda}_{t+1} = 1$, causing the term with the auxiliary weights to be multiplied by $1 - \bar{\lambda}_{t+1}$, and so removing the need to approximate $\mathbf{h}^{sq}$.

6. RELATED WORK

There has been a significant effort to empirically investigate λ, typically using batch off-line computing and model-based techniques. Sutton and Singh [25] investigated tuning both α and λ. They proposed three algorithms, the first two assume the underlying MDP has no cycles, and the third makes use of an estimate of the transition probabilities and is thus of most interest in tabular domains. Singh and Dayan [18] provided analytical expression for bias and variance, given the model. They suggest that there is a largest feasible step-size α, below which bias converges to zero and variance converges to a non-zero value, and above which bias and/or variance may diverge. Downey and Sanner [3] used a Bayesian variant of TD learning, requiring a batch of samples and off-line computation, but did provide an empirical demonstration off optimally setting λ after obtaining all the samples. Kearns and Singh[5] compute a bias-variance error bound for a modification of TD called phased TD. In each discrete phase the algorithm is given n trajectories from each state. Because we have n trajectories in each state the effective learning rate is $1/n$ removing the complexities of sample averaging in the conventional online TD-update. The error bounds are useful for, among other things, computing a new λ value for each phase which outperforms any fixed λ value, empirically demonstrating the utility of changing λ.

There has also been a significant effort to theoretically characterizing λ. Most notably, the work of Schapire and Warmuth [17] contributed a finite sample analysis of incremental TD-style algorithms. They analyze a variant of TD called TD*(λ), which although still linear and incremental, computes value estimates quite differently. The resulting finite sample bound is particularly interesting, as it does not rely on model assumptions, using only access to a sequence of feature vectors, rewards and returns. Unfortunately, the bound cannot be analytically minimized to produce an optimal λ value. They did simulate their bound, further verifying the intuition that λ should be larger if the best linear predictor is inaccurate, small if accurate and an intermediate value otherwise. Li [7] later derived similar bounds for another gradient descent algorithm, called residual gradient. This algorithm, however, does not utilize eligibility traces and converges to a different solution than TD methods when function approximation is used [24].

Another approach involves removing the λ parameter altogether, in an effort to improve robustness. Konidaris et al. [6] introduced a new TD method called TD$_\gamma$. Their work defines a plausible set of assumptions implicitly made when constructing the λ-returns, and then relaxes one of those assumptions. They derive an exact (but computationally expensive) algorithm, TD$_\gamma$, that no longer depends on a choice of λ and performs well empirically in a variety of policy learning benchmarks. The incremental approximation to TD$_\gamma$ also performs reasonably well, but appears to be somewhat sensitive to the choice of meta parameter C, and often requires large C values to obtain good performance. This can be problematic, as the complexity grows as $O(Cn)$, where n is the length of the trajectories—not linearly in the feature vector size. Nonetheless, TD$_\gamma$ constitutes a reasonable way to reduce parameter sensitivity in the on-policy setting. Garcia and Serre[4] proposed a variant of Q-learning, for which the optimal value of λ can be computed online. Their analysis, however, was restricted to the tabular case. Finally, Mahmood et al. [11] introduced weighted importance sampling for off-policy learning; though indirect, this is a strategy for enabling larger λ to be selected, without destabilizing off-policy learning.

This related work has helped shape our intuition on the role of λ, and, in special cases, provided effective strategies for adapting λ. In the next section, we add to existing work with an empirical demonstration of λ-greedy, the first λ-adaptation algorithm for off-policy, incremental learning, developed from a well-defined, greedy objective.

7. EXPERIMENTS

We investigate λ-greedy in a ring-world, under both on and off-policy sampling. This ring-world was previously introduced as a suitable domain for investigating λ [5]. We varied the length of the ring-world from $N = 10, 25, 50$. The reward is zero in every state, except for two adjoining states that have +1 and -1 reward, and are terminal states. The agent is teleported back to the middle of the ring-world upon termination. The target policy is to take action "right" with 95% probability, and action "left" with 5% probability. The feature representation is a tabular encoding of states with binary identity vectors, but we also examine the effects of aliasing state values to simulate poor generalization: a common case where the true value function cannot be represented. The length of the experiment is a function of the problem size, $N \times 100$, proportionally scaling the number of samples for longer problem instances.

We compared to fixed values of $\lambda = 0, 0.1, \ldots, 0.9, 1.0$ and to two time-decay schedules, $\lambda_t = 10/(10+t), \lambda_t = 100/(100+t)$, which worked well compared to several other tested settings. The discount factor is $\gamma = 0.99$ for the on-policy chains and 0.95 for the off-policy chains. We include the optimal λ-greedy, which computes $\mathbf{w}^{sq}$ and $\mathbf{w}^{sq}$ using closed form solutions, defined by their respective Bellman operators. For λ-greedy, the initialization was $\mathbf{w}^{sq} = 0.0$ and $\mathbf{w}^{err} = \frac{Rmax}{1-\gamma} \times \mathbf{1}$ for on-policy, to match the rule-of-thumb of initializing with high lambdas, and the opposite for off-policy, to match the rule-of-thumb of more caution in off-policy domains. This max return value is a common choice for optimistic initialization, and prevented inadvertent evaluator bias by overly tuning this parameter. We fixed the learning-rate parameter for λ-greedy to be equal to equal to α used in learning the value function ($\mathbf{w}$), again to demonstrate performance in less than ideal settings. Sweeping the step-size for λ-greedy would improve performance.

The performance results in on and off-policy are summarized in Figure 1 and 2. We report the absolute value error compared to the true value function, which is computable in this domain for each of the settings. We average over 100 runs, and report the results for the best parameter settings for each of the algorithms with 12 values of $\alpha \in \{0.1 \times 2^j | j = -6, -6, ..., 5, 6\}$, 11 values of $\eta \in \{2^j | j = -16, -8, -4, \ldots, 4, 8, 16\}$ ($\alpha_{\mathbf{h}} = \alpha\eta$).

In general, we find that λ-greedy works well across settings. The optimal λ-greedy consistently performs the best, indicating the merit of the objective. Estimating $\mathbf{w}^{sq}$ and $\mathbf{w}^{sq}$ typically cause λ-greedy to perform more poorly, indicating an opportunity to improve these algorithms to match the performance of the optimal, idealistic version. In particular, we did not optimize the meta-parameters in λ-greedy. For the fixed values of λ and decay schedules, we find that they can be effective for specific instances, but do not perform well across problem settings. In particular, the fixed decay schedules settings appear to be un-robust to an increasing chain length and the fixed λ are not robust to the change from on-policy to off-policy.

We also examined the λ value selected by our λ-greedy algorithm plotted against time. For tabular features, λ should converge to zero over-time, since the value function can be approximated and so, at some point, no bias is introduced by using $\lambda_t = 0$, but variance is reduced. The algorithm does converge to a state-based λ ($\lambda(s) \approx 0$ for all states), which was one of our goals to ensure we have a well-defined fixed point. Second, for aliased features, we expect that the final per-state λ should be larger for the states that have been aliased. The intuition is that one should not bootstrap on the values of these states, as that introduces bias. We demonstrate that this does indeed occur, in Figure 3. As expected, the λ-greedy is more robust to state aliasing, compared to the fixed strategies. State aliasing provides a concrete example of when we have less confidence in $\hat{v}$ in specific states, and an effective strategy to mitigate this situation is to set λ high in those states.

8. CONCLUSION AND DISCUSSION

In this paper, we have proposed the first linear-complexity λ adaptation algorithm for incremental, off-policy reinforcement learning. We proposed an objective to greedily trade-off bias and variance, and derived an efficient algorithm to obtain the solution to this objective. We demonstrate the efficacy of the approach in an on-policy and off-policy setting, versus fixed values of λ and time-decay heuristics.

This work opens up many avenues for efficiently selecting λ, by providing a concrete greedy objective. One important direction is to extend the above analysis to use the recently introduced true-online traces [32]; here we focused on the more well-understood λ-return, but the proposed objective is not restricted to that setting. There are also numerous future directions for improving optimization of this objective. We used GTD($\lambda = 1$) to learn the second moment of the λ-return inside λ-greedy. Another possible direction is to simply explore using $\lambda < 1$ or even least-squares methods to improve estimation inside λ-greedy.

There are also opportunities to modify the objective to consider variance into the future differently. The current objective is highly cautious, in that it assumes that only λ_{t+1} can be modified, and assumes the agent will be forced to use the unbiased $\lambda_{t+i} = 1$ for all future time steps. As a consequence, the algorithm will often prefer to set λ_{t+1} small, as future variance can only be controlled by the setting of λ_{t+1}. A natural relaxation of this strictly greedy setting is to recognize that the agent, in fact, has control over all future $\lambda_{t+i}, i > 1$. The agent could remain cautious for some number of steps, assuming λ_{t+i} will likely be high for $1 < i \leq k$ for some horizon k. However, we can assume that after k steps, λ_{t+i} we be reduced to a small value, cutting off the traces and mitigating the variance. The horizon k could be encoded with an aggressive discount; multiplying the current discount $\bar{\gamma}_{t+1}$ by a value less than 1. Commonly, a multiplicative factor less than 1 indicates a horizon of $\frac{1}{1-\text{factor}}$; for example, $\frac{1}{1-0.8} = 5$ gives a horizon of $k = 5$. The variance term in the objective in (2) could be modified to include this horizon, providing a method to incorporate the level of caution.

Overall, this work takes a small step toward the goal of automatically selecting the trace parameter, and thus one step closer toward parameter-free black-box application of reinforcement learning with many avenues for future research.

Acknowledgements
We would like to thank David Silver for helpful discussions and the reviewers for helpful comments.

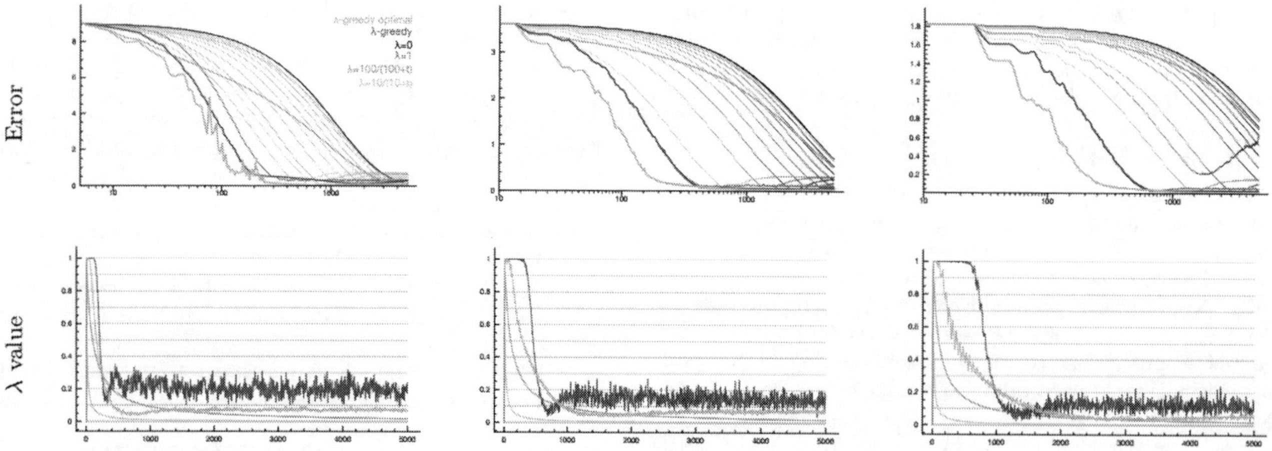

Chain 10 Chain 25 Chain 50

Figure 1: **On-policy** learning performance of GTD(λ) with different methods of adapting λ, for three sizes in the ringworld domain. The first row of results plots the mean squared value error verses time for several approaches to adapting λ: the optimal λ-greedy algorithm, our approximation algorithm, several fixed values of λ, and two fixed decay schedules. The second row of results plots the λ values over-time used by each algorithm. We highlight early learning by taking the log of y axis, as the algorithms should be able to exploit the low variance to learn quickly. For off-policy learning, there is more variance due to importance sampling and so we prefer long-term stability. We therefore highlight later learning using the log of the x-axis.

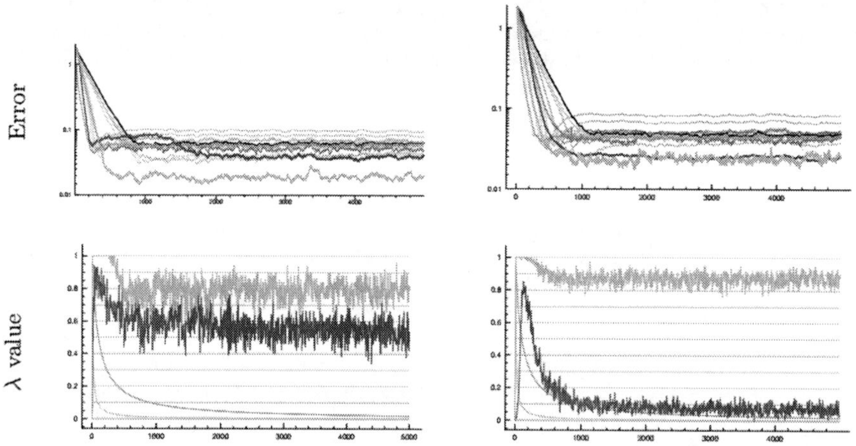

$\pi(s, \text{right}) = 0.95, \mu(s, \text{right}) = 0.85$ $\pi(s, \text{right}) = 0.95, \mu(s, \text{right}) = 0.75$

Figure 2: **Off-policy** learning performance of GTD(λ) with different methods of adapting λ, for two different configurations of π and μ in the size 10 ringworld domain. The first row of results plots the mean squared value error verses time for several approaches to adapting λ. In off-policy learning, there is more variance due to importance sampling and so we prefer long-term stability. We therefore highlight later learning using the log of the x-axis. The second row of results plots the λ values over-time used by each algorithm.

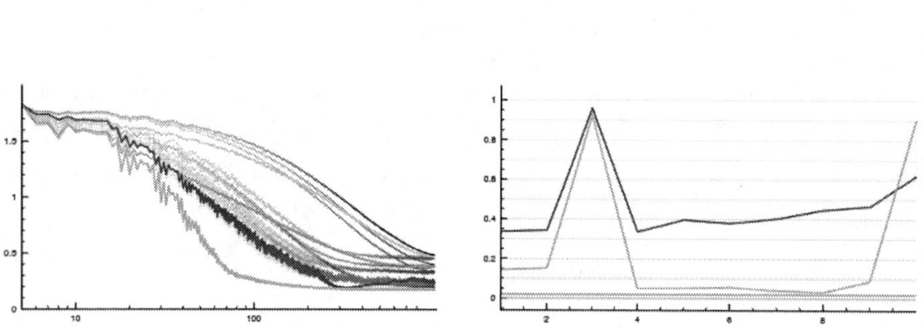

Figure 3: A closer examination of the effects of state aliasing on the choice of state-based λ, for the length 10 chain with $\gamma = 0.95$, under on-policy sampling. State three is aliased with the last state. The left graph shows the learning curves over 5000 steps, and the right graph shows the learned λ function in each state at the end of the run.

REFERENCES

[1] P. L. A and M. Ghavamzadeh. Actor-Critic algorithms for risk-sensitive MDPs. In *Advances in Neural Information Processing Systems*, 2013.

[2] W. Dabney and A. G. Barto. Adaptive step-size for online temporal difference learning. In *AAAI*, 2012.

[3] C. Downey and S. Sanner. Temporal difference Bayesian model averaging: A Bayesian perspective on adapting lambda. In *International Conference on Machine Learning*, 2010.

[4] F. Garcia and F. Serre. From Q(lambda) to Average Q-learning: Efficient Implementation of an Asymptotic Approximation. In *International Joint Conference on Artificial Intelligence*, 2001.

[5] M. J. Kearns and S. P. Singh. Bias-Variance error bounds for temporal difference updates. In *Annual Conference on Learning Theory*, 2000.

[6] G. Konidaris, S. Niekum, and P. S. Thomas. TDgamma: Re-evaluating Complex Backups in Temporal Difference Learning. In *NIPS*, 2011.

[7] L. Li. A worst-case comparison between temporal difference and residual gradient with linear function approximation. In *International Conference on Machine Learning*, 2008.

[8] L.-J. Lin. Self-Improving Reactive Agents Based On Reinforcement Learning, Planning and Teaching. *Machine Learning*, 1992.

[9] H. Maei. *Gradient Temporal-Difference Learning Algorithms*. PhD thesis, University of Alberta, 2011.

[10] H. Maei and R. Sutton. GQ (λ): A general gradient algorithm for temporal-difference prediction learning with eligibility traces. In *AGI*, 2010.

[11] A. R. Mahmood, H. P. van Hasselt, and R. S. Sutton. Weighted importance sampling for off-policy learning with linear function approximation. In *Advances in Neural Information Processing Systems*, 2014.

[12] S. Mannor, D. Simester, P. Sun, and J. N. Tsitsiklis. Bias and variance in value function estimation. In *International Conference on Machine Learning*, 2004.

[13] S. Mannor and J. N. Tsitsiklis. Mean-Variance pptimization in Markov Decision Processes. In *ICML*, 2011.

[14] J. Modayil, A. White, and R. S. Sutton. Multi-timescale nexting in a reinforcement learning robot. *Adaptive Behavior - Animals, Animats, Software Agents, Robots, Adaptive Systems*, 2014.

[15] T. Morimura, M. Sugiyama, H. Kashima, H. Hachiya, and T. Tanaka. Parametric return density estimation for reinforcement learning. In *Conference on Uncertainty in Artificial Intelligence*, 2010.

[16] A. L. Samuel. Some studies in machine learning using the game of checkers. *IBM Journal of Research and Development ()*, 1959.

[17] R. E. Schapire and M. K. Warmuth. On the worst-case analysis of temporal-difference learning algorithms. *Machine Learning*, 1996.

[18] S. P. Singh and P. Dayan. Analytical mean squared error curves in temporal difference learning. In *Advances in Neural Information Processing Systems*, 1996.

[19] S. P. Singh and R. S. Sutton. Reinforcement learning with replacing eligibility traces. *Machine Learning*, 1996.

[20] M. J. Sobel. The variance of discounted Markov Decision Processes. *Journal of Applied Probability*, 1982.

[21] R. Sutton. Learning to predict by the methods of temporal differences. *Machine Learning*, 1988.

[22] R. Sutton. TD models: Modeling the world at a mixture of time scales. In *International Conference on Machine Learning*, 1995.

[23] R. Sutton and A. G. Barto. *Introduction to reinforcement learning*. MIT Press, 1998.

[24] R. Sutton, H. Maei, D. Precup, and S. Bhatnagar. Fast gradient-descent methods for temporal-difference learning with linear function approximation. *International Conference on Machine Learning*, 2009.

[25] R. Sutton and S. P. Singh. On step-size and bias in temporal-difference learning. In *Proceedings of the Eighth Yale Workshop on Adaptive and Learning Systems*, 1994.

[26] R. S. Sutton, A. R. Mahmood, and M. White. An emphatic approach to the problem of off-policy temporal-difference learning. *The Journal of Machine Learning Research*, 2015.

[27] R. S. Sutton, D. Precup, and S. Singh. Between MDPs and semi-MDPs: A framework for temporal abstraction in reinforcement learning. *Artificial intelligence*, 1999.

[28] A. Tamar, D. Di Castro, and S. Mannor. Temporal difference methods for the variance of the reward to go. In *International Conference on Machine Learning*, 2013.

[29] G. Tesauro. Practical issues in temporal difference learning. *Machine Learning*, 1992.

[30] J. N. Tsitsiklis and B. Van Roy. An analysis of temporal-difference learning with function approximation. *Automatic Control, IEEE Transactions on*, 42(5):674–690, 1997.

[31] H. van Hasselt, A. R. Mahmood, and R. Sutton. Off-policy TD (λ) with a true online equivalence. In *Conference on Uncertainty in Artificial Intelligence*, 2014.

[32] H. van Seijen and R. Sutton. True online TD(lambda). In *International Conference on Machine Learning*, 2014.

[33] A. White. *Developing a predictive approach to knowledge*. PhD thesis, University of Alberta, 2015.

[34] M. White. Transition-based discounting in Markov decision processes. *In preparation*, 2016.

[35] M. White and A. White. Interval estimation for reinforcement-learning algorithms in continuous-state domains. In *Advances in Neural Information Processing Systems*, 2010.

Source Task Creation for Curriculum Learning

Sanmit Narvekar, Jivko Sinapov, Matteo Leonetti, and Peter Stone
Department of Computer Science, University of Texas at Austin
Austin, Texas, USA
{sanmit, jsinapov, matteo, pstone}@cs.utexas.edu

ABSTRACT

Transfer learning in reinforcement learning has been an active area of research over the past decade. In transfer learning, training on a source task is leveraged to speed up or otherwise improve learning on a target task. This paper presents the more ambitious problem of *curriculum learning* in reinforcement learning, in which the goal is to design a *sequence* of source tasks for an agent to train on, such that final performance or learning speed is improved. We take the position that each stage of such a curriculum should be tailored to the current ability of the agent in order to promote learning new behaviors. Thus, as a first step towards creating a curriculum, the trainer must be able to create novel, agent-specific source tasks. We explore how such a space of useful tasks can be created using a parameterized model of the domain and observed trajectories on the target task. We experimentally show that these methods can be used to form components of a curriculum and that such a curriculum can be used successfully for transfer learning in 2 challenging multiagent reinforcement learning domains.

Keywords

Reinforcement Learning; Transfer Learning; Curriculum Learning

1. INTRODUCTION

As autonomous agents are called upon to perform increasingly difficult tasks, new techniques will be needed to make learning such tasks tractable. Transfer learning [10, 27] is a recent area of research that has been shown to speed up learning on a complex task by transferring knowledge from one or more easier source tasks. However, most transfer learning methods assume the set of source tasks is provided, and treat the transfer of knowledge as a one-step process. Paradigms such as multi-task reinforcement learning and lifelong learning consider learning multiple tasks, but typically focus on optimizing performance over all tasks, and/or still require the set of tasks to be provided.

In this paper, we extend transfer learning to the problem of *curriculum learning*. As a motivating example, consider the game of Quick Chess[1] (Figure 1). Quick Chess is a game designed to introduce players to the full game of chess, by using a sequence of progressively more difficult "subgames." For example, the first subgame is a 5x5 board with only pawns, where the player learns how pawns move and about promotions. The second subgame is a small board with pawns and a king, which introduces a new objective: keeping the king alive. In each successive subgame, new elements are introduced (such as new pieces, a larger board, or different configurations) that require learning new skills and building upon knowledge learned in previous games. The final game is the full game of chess.

Figure 1: Different subgames in Quick Chess

The question that motivates us is: can we find an optimal sequence of subgames (i.e. a curriculum) for an agent to play that will make it possible to learn the target task of chess fastest, or at a performance level better than learning from scratch?

We postulate that the effectiveness of such a curriculum depends crucially on the quality of the source tasks that compose it *and* the current learning abilities of the agent. As in Quick Chess, tasks should be designed to build upon existing knowledge and promote learning new skills. However, unlike Quick Chess, the tasks need not be the same for all agents. Thus, as a first step towards curriculum development, this paper focuses on how to automatically construct a space of useful subtasks. Our approach uses knowledge of the problem encoded via a parameterized model of the domain, and observes the agent's performance on the target task and each prior task in the curriculum, in order to suggest new source tasks tailored to the abilities of the agent.

Our three contributions are as follows. First, we introduce the problem of curriculum learning in the context of reinforcement learning (Section 3). Second, we propose a set of methods that can produce a space of agent-specific subtasks suitable for use in a curriculum (Section 4). Third, we

Appears in: *Proceedings of the 15th International Conference on Autonomous Agents and Multiagent Systems (AAMAS 2016), J. Thangarajah, K. Tuyls, C. Jonker, S. Marsella (eds.), May 9–13, 2016, Singapore.*

[1]http://www.intplay.com/uploadedFiles/Game_Rules/P20051-QuickChess-Rules.pdf

experimentally show that training using a curriculum has a strong impact on the learning speed or performance of an agent, and that the sequence of tasks in the curriculum does matter. Furthermore, we demonstrate that the methods proposed can create such a curriculum, and be used successfully for transfer learning in Section 5. Section 6 compares our work with existing literature, and Section 7 concludes.

2. BACKGROUND

We represent a *task* as an episodic Markov Decision Process (MDP) M. An MDP is a tuple (S, A, P, R, S_0, S_f), where S is the set of states, A is the set of actions, $P: S \times A \mapsto \Pi(S)$ is a transition function that gives the probability of moving to a new state given the current state and an action, and $R: S \times A \mapsto \mathbb{R}$ is a reward function that gives the immediate reward for taking an action in a state. $S_0 \mapsto \Pi(S)$ denotes the distribution over starting states, and S_f represents the set of terminal states.

At each step, an RL agent observes its current state and chooses an action according to its *policy* $\pi: S \mapsto A$. The goal of the agent is to learn an optimal policy π^* that maximizes the long-term expected sum of discounted rewards for some target task M_t. One standard way of doing this is to learn the optimal action-value function $Q^*(s, a)$, which gives the expected return for taking action a in state s and following policy π^* after:

$$Q^*(s, a) = R(s, a) + \sum_{s'} P(s'|s, a) \max_{a'} Q^*(s', a')$$

Q^* is the unique solution to the Bellman equation above for all (s, a) pairs, and can be learned using methods such as Q-learning or Sarsa [22]. An optimal policy consists of choosing $\arg\max_a Q^*(s, a)$ in each state.

In transfer learning, instead of learning directly on the target task M_t, the agent trains on one or more easier *source tasks* M_s, and *transfers* the knowledge acquired to the target task. This knowledge can take the form of samples [11, 12], options [21], policies [6], models [5], or value functions [26]. In this paper, we consider value function transfer, which uses the parameters of an action-value function $Q_s(s, a)$ learned in a source task to initialize the action-value function in the target task $Q_t(s, a)$.

There are several metrics to quantify the benefit of transfer [27]. Typically, they compare the learning trajectory on the target task for an agent after transfer, with an agent that learns directly on the target task from scratch. In this work, we use *asymptotic performance*, which compares the final performance in the target task of learners when using transfer versus no transfer, and the *jumpstart* metric, which measures the initial performance increase on a target task as a result of transfer.

3. PROBLEM FORMULATION

In curriculum learning, the goal is to generate a sequence of source tasks $M_1, M_2, \ldots M_t$ for an agent to train on, such that the final asymptotic performance increases, or the learning time to reach a desired performance threshold decreases, versus following any other curriculum. As an important step towards this, we first define the domain $\mathcal{D}$ of possible tasks:

Definition 1. A domain $\mathcal{D}$ is a set of MDPs that can be expressed by varying a set of *degrees of freedom*, and applying a set of *restrictions*.

The *degrees of freedom* F of a domain are a vector of features $[F_1, F_2, \ldots F_n]$ that parameterize the domain. For example, in the Quick Chess domain, possible degrees of freedom could be the size of the board, the number of each type of piece, or whether special rules such as castling or en passant are allowed. Each $F_i \in F$ has a range of values $\mathrm{Rng}(F_i)$ that represents the possible values that feature can take. Furthermore, we assume there is an ordering defined over each $\mathrm{Rng}(F_i)$ that corresponds to task complexity. Collectively, these degrees of freedom encode our domain knowledge in the task.

An instantiation of F in $\mathcal{D}$ results in a specific task (an MDP). We assume we have a generator τ that can create tasks given a domain and degree of freedom vector:

$$\tau : \mathcal{D} \times F \mapsto M$$

By *restrictions*, we mean the set of tasks that can be formed by eliminating certain actions or states, modifying the transition or reward function, or changing the starting or terminal distributions of MDPs generated by τ.

Informally, $\mathcal{D}$ captures the universe of possible source tasks for use within the curriculum and could be potentially infinite in size. The goal of this paper is to create a subset of tasks in $\mathcal{D}$ that might be suitable for learning a given target task, using knowledge of the domain, and tailored to the performance and abilities of the learning agent.

Formally, given a target task MDP M_t and trajectory samples X consisting of tuples (s, a, s', r) from following some policy π_t on M_t, the goal is to create suitable source tasks $M_s \in \mathcal{D}$ that will lead to a policy in M_t that is better than π_t. Specifically, we want functions f of the following form:

$$f : M_t \times X \mapsto M_s$$

The overall process we propose is an incremental development of subtasks culminating in a full curriculum: an agent first tries learning M_t, but gets stuck at suboptimal policy π_t. X is generated from π_t, and used to generate a space of possible source tasks tailored for *this* agent at *this* particular point in its learning process. For now, we assume a separate process is available to select a suitable source task M_s from this space, and leave for future work an automated way of finding it. The procedure then repeats, with M_s possibly becoming the new M_t, until a curriculum emerges.

4. SEARCH SPACE FOR SOURCE TASKS

In this section, we describe several methods that can serve as f to create suitable source tasks for a target task. Intuitively, there are many different ways in which a task could be a useful source for transfer to M_t: it could have a smaller or more abstract state space; it could have some actions removed; it could focus on a useful subgoal; or it could drill a common mistake. Some of these source tasks could be generated by simply manipulating the degrees of freedom F, and indeed we consider that case first. However, in the rest of the section, we define additional *domain-independent* instantiations for f.

4.1 Task Dimension Simplification

The first method we propose, TaskSimplification (Algorithm 1), simplifies a task using knowledge of the domain's parameterization. Here, Simplify is a function that changes one of the degrees of freedom $F_i \in F$ to a new $F_i' \in \mathrm{Rng}(F_i)$, in order to make the task smaller or easier. In many domains, there is a natural interpretation for SIMPLIFY. For example, in Quick Chess, we could reduce the value of parameters such as the size of the board or the number of specific pieces. In multiagent settings, we can add cooperative agents or remove adversarial ones.

Algorithm 1 Task Simplification

procedure TASKSIMPLIFICATION($M, X, \mathcal{D}, F, \tau$)
  $F' = $ SIMPLIFY(F)
  $M' \leftarrow \tau(\mathcal{D}, F')$
  return M'
end procedure

TASKSIMPLIFICATION transforms the S, A, P, R elements of an MDP simultaneously, in a domain-specific way.

4.2 Promising Initializations

The second method is designed for tasks that have a sparse reward signal. In many RL problems, positive outcomes can be rare, especially at the onset of learning. An agent may have to reach the goal randomly or through some exploration scheme many times before the policy stabilizes. PROMISINGINITIALIZATIONS creates a task that initializes an agent near states that were found to have high reward.

Algorithm 2 Promising Initializations

procedure PROMISINGINITIALIZATIONS(M, X, C, δ, ρ)
  $Y \leftarrow \{(s, a, s', r) \in X : r \geq \rho^{th}$ percentile of all rewards in $X\}$
  $M' \leftarrow M$
  $S_0' \leftarrow \{\}$
  for $(s, a, s', r) \in Y$ **do**
    $S_0' \leftarrow S_0' \cup$ FINDNEARBYSTATES(s, X, C, δ)
  end for
  $M'.S_0 \leftarrow S_0'$
  return M'
end procedure

Here, the parameter $\rho \in [0, 100]$ is a percentile that defines the fraction of rewards an agent has seen in its experience trajectory X that it should consider to be positive outcomes. FINDNEARBYSTATES is a domain-dependent function that returns a set/distribution of states that are close to a given state, using either a distance metric $C : S \times S \mapsto \mathbb{R}$ or a pseudo-distance based on steps away in a trajectory. The exact form depends on the representation used for the MDP.

If the state space is factored, we can perturb the state vector by some amount δ such that the distance from the original state to the perturbed state (measured by C) is less than δ. In our Quick Chess example, if the state space consists of the positions of all pieces on the board, we can use a distance metric that measures the least number of "moves" needed to transform one board configuration to another. FINDNEARBYSTATES would return all configurations that are δ steps away. If the state space is not factored (for example, in a tabular representation), then we can use the trajectory samples X to find states that are at most δ steps away from a high reward state, and explore these further.

4.3 Mistake-Driven Subtasks

Our next set of methods create subtasks to help an agent avoid and correct its *mistakes*. In principle, a mistake is any action or sequence of actions (e.g., an option [23]) taken in a state that deviates from the optimal policy.

In practice, the agent does not know the optimal policy while learning, so we propose 3 alternative characteristics to automatically identify mistakes. The first is any action that leads to unsuccessful termination of an episode, such as not reaching a goal state. Second is any action that results in no change in state. Finally, a mistake could be any action that incurs a large negative reward. In the following methods, we use ISMISTAKE to denote whether a mistake was detected, using these criteria.

Action Simplification

The first mistake-driven subtask generation method we propose, ACTIONSIMPLIFICATION (Algorithm 3), prunes the action set to create a subtask where mistakes are less likely.

Action set pruning is especially useful in settings where actions have preconditions for success. For example, a robot must grasp an object before manipulating it. An autonomous car must be standing still before opening the doors. Intuitively, any complex, multi-stage policy could benefit from this type of guided exploration.

Algorithm 3 Action Simplification

procedure ACTIONSIMPLIFICATION(M, X, α)
  $M' \leftarrow M$
  $count(a) = 0, \forall a \in A$
  $Y \leftarrow \{(s, a, s', r) \in X :$ ISMISTAKE$(s, a, s', r)\}$
  for $(s, a, s', r) \in Y$ **do**
    $count(a) += 1$
  end for
  $A' = \{a \in A : count(a) > \alpha\}$
  $M'.A = M'.A \setminus A'$
  return M'
end procedure

The parameter $\alpha \in \mathbb{Z}$ is a threshold on the number of times an action should lead to a mistake before it is pruned. In practice, it may be useful to set these thresholds so that only one action is eliminated at a time, or only eliminated in certain states.

Mistake Learning

In contrast, the second approach, MISTAKELEARNING (Algorithm 4), directly tries to correct mistakes by rewinding the game back some number of steps, and having the agent learn a revised policy from there. Intuitively, focusing training on areas of the state space where the agent made a "mistake," gives access to this experience much faster, allowing the agent to also learn to correct itself much faster.

Algorithm 4 Mistake Learning

procedure MISTAKELEARNING(M, X, ϵ)
  $M' \leftarrow M$
  $S_0' \leftarrow \{\}$
  $Y \leftarrow \{(s, a, s', r) \in X :$ ISMISTAKE$(s, a, s', r)\}$
  for $(s, a, s', r) \in Y$ **do**
    $S_0' \leftarrow S_0' \cup$ REWIND(X, s, ϵ)
  end for
  $M'.S_0 \leftarrow S_0'$
  return M'
end procedure

The question of how far back in the trajectory to rewind is an interesting challenge in and of itself. For now, REWIND is a simple method that looks back ϵ steps from s in trajectory X, and returns the found state. However, in principle it could be more complex, based on the type of mistake made or the situation where it was made. In our example of Quick Chess, we could rewind the game to determine what should have been done differently to avoid a checkmate.

4.4 Option-based Subgoals

The next method creates subtasks for learning subgoals. The options literature [23] identifies many approaches to finding subgoals. Many take a state-based approach, where the learner tries to find states that may have strategic value to reach. For example, McGovern and Barto [14], identify subgoals as states that occur frequently in successful trajectories. Menache et al. [15] try to find "bottleneck" states. Simsek and Barto [18] seek to create subgoals for "novel" states, since they facilitate exploration of regions of the state space that the agent normally doesn't reach. Finally, graph-based approaches such as Mannor et al. [13] identify states by clustering over a state-transition map.

OPTIONSUBGOALS (Algorithm 5) is designed to take any option discovery method (FINDOPTION) to create a subtask. Specifically, it creates a task to learn an option given the option's termination set S_f and a pseudo-reward function R for completion. Since an option typically only involves a subset of the task's complete state space, this subtask allows quick learning of how to reach important states. For example, in Quick Chess, capturing the queen would be an example of a useful subgoal.

Algorithm 5 Option Sub-goals

```
procedure OptionSubGoals(M, X, V, φ)
    M' ← M
    (S_f, R) ← FindOption(M, X, V, φ)
    M'.S_f = S_f
    M'.R = R
    return M'
end procedure
```

Since our work takes place in the context of transfer learning, we introduce one additional option discovery method, FINDHIGHVALUESTATES (Algorithm 6), that uses high value states learned in a previous task as a subgoal. Specifically, it checks whether any of the learned values $V(s)$ for states encountered in our trajectory X exceed a threshold ϕ.

Algorithm 6 Find High Value States

```
procedure FindHighValueStates(M, X, V, φ)
    S_f ← {}
    R ← M.R
    for (s, a, s', r) ∈ X do
        if V(s) > φ then
            S_f ← S_f ∪ s
            R(s, a, s') = V(s)
        end if
    end for
    return (S_f, R)
end procedure
```

Instead of using trajectory samples X, we can also extract high value states directly from the value function. For example, with a tabular representation, we can simply lookup states of high value. With function approximation, an optimization routine would be used to solve for high value states.

4.5 Task-based Subgoals

An alternative to creating subgoals within an MDP is to create them directly at the task level. Specifically, we set the termination set S_f of the input MDP to be the initiation set S_0 of some other subtask, as shown in Algorithm 7:

Algorithm 7 Link Subtask

```
procedure LinkSubTask(M, M_s, V)
    M' ← M
    for s' ∈ M_s.S_0, s ∈ M.S, a ∈ M.A do
        R(s, a, s') = V(s')
    end for
    M'.S_f ← M_s.S_0
    M'.R ← R
    return M'
end procedure
```

For example, we can create a subtask that terminates where PromisingInitializations starts as follows:

$$\begin{aligned} M_1 &= \text{PROMISINGINITIALIZATIONS}(M_t, X, C, \delta, \rho) \\ M_s &= \text{LINKSUBTASK}(M_t, M_1, M_1.V) \end{aligned}$$

Applied to Quick Chess, this would create a task to reach configurations that are likely to lead to checkmate. The reward for reaching this terminal set is the value of the state in the subsequent task. This idea is similar to skill chaining [8], except that instead of learning options linking target regions to initiation sets, we link directly on tasks.

4.6 Composite Subtasks

Each of the previous subroutines f takes as input an MDP M_t and trajectory samples X, and returns a modified task MDP M_s. By passing the samples and resulting M_s as input to another function f, we can chain together arbitrary many subroutines to compose new source tasks.

Mathematically, let f and g be any two functions above. Assume we are given a target task MDP M_t and trajectory samples X from it. Then, the composite task $(f \circ g) = f(g(M_t, X), X)$, where for ease of exposition, we've left out the task specific threshold parameters.

Most of the domain-independent functions described previously make specific modifications to a particular part of the target task MDP. In contrast, TASKSIMPLIFICATION can potentially make changes to the state and action space, as well as the transition and reward functions all at once. Thus, in practice, tasks should be composed using TASKSIMPLIFICATION first, followed by the others.

4.7 Summary

In summary, we presented several functions that could create suitable source tasks for a target task. They can be categorized into two types: the first (Section 4.1) allows for task creation using domain knowledge. The others are largely domain-independent, and rely directly on trajectory samples in the target task to create *agent-specific* tasks. We also showed how tasks of both types can be combined to create flexible source tasks for curriculum learning.

We claim that the functions outlined are broadly and generally useful. However, they are not the only possible methods; nor would every method apply to every domain. The next section moves on to experiments in domains for which we have concrete transfer learning results, using source tasks that can be generated with these functions.

5. INSTANTIATIONS AND RESULTS

In this section, we apply the methods described in Section 4 to create a curriculum in two challenging multiagent domains: Ms. Pac-Man and Half Field Offense. First, we demonstrate the effectiveness of domain-dependent and domain-independent subtasks in a simple one-stage curriculum (i.e. classic transfer learning paradigm) applied to Ms. Pac-Man. Then, in Half Field Offense, we utilize multiple functions from Section 4 to create a successful *multistage* curriculum for learning. Furthermore, we show that the sequence of tasks in a curriculum matters, and provide empirical evidence that such curricula can be formed recursively.

5.1 Ms. Pac-Man

Ms. Pac-Man (see Figure 2a and 2b) is a game where the agent's goal is to traverse a maze and accrue points by eating objects such as pills, while avoiding the four ghosts. At the start of the game, there are a large number of pills throughout the maze, four power pills located at each corner, and four ghosts that are initially placed in an area inaccessible to Ms. Pac-Man. If a ghost catches Ms. Pac-Man, the game is over; however, if Ms. Pac-Man eats one of the four power pills, the ghosts themselves become edible by the agent.

We used the Ms. Pac-Man implementation described in [24, 19]. The agent's state space was represented by a set of local features described in [24], that are egocentric with respect to the agent's position on the board. Learning was done using Q-Learning [22], and transfer via value function transfer.

5.1.1 Maze Simplification

The first experiment is an application of the TaskSimplification method. The domain of Ms. Pac-Man comes with four different maze levels, some of which are easier for the agent to learn than the others. Thus, intuitively, one way to apply the TaskSimplification method is to train an agent on an easier maze and transfer the learned policy to a harder one. The results of such an application are shown in Figure 3. Here, the target task was maze level four (Figure 2b). The TaskSimplification principle was used to generate a source task by changing the maze level from four to one (Figure 2a). The transfer curve shows the effects of learning for 5 episodes on the source task and then learning for an additional 20 episodes on the target task. The baseline curve in contrast shows the result of learning for 25 episodes directly on the target task. Both curves are averaged over 20 runs. The results clearly show that applying TaskSimplification results in jumpstart and substantial improvement in the expected reward over the first 25 episodes.

5.1.2 Avoiding Ghosts

Next, we illustrate the use of an agent-specific source task, MistakeLearning, in the Ms. Pac-Man domain. We consider a mistake to be the event where Ms. Pac-Man is eaten by a ghost, which is a terminal non-goal state. Whenever a mistake occurrs, we spawn the following task:

$$M_{mistake} = \text{MistakeLearning}(M_t, X_t, \epsilon)$$

Event	Reward
Goal	1.0
Ball out of bounds	-0.1
Ball with offense	0
Ball captured by defense	-0.2
Ball captured by goalie	-0.1
Episode times out	-0.1

Table 1: Reward structure in HFO

This call creates a subtask that rewinds $\epsilon = 50$ game steps from the moment the episode was terminated. The agent subsequently trains for 5 episodes in the generated subtask, after which training in the target task is resumed. The result of this test is shown in Figure 4. For this experiment, we measured the agent's performance as a function of the number of game steps, since episodes spent on learning in the generated subtasks were much shorter. Results are averaged over 20 trials. The plot shows that the application of MistakeLearning results in much faster learning when compared to the baseline approach of restarting each episode from the initial configuration upon episode termination.

So far, the two examples show that both domain-dependent and domain-independent methods can be used to generate effective source tasks for a given target task. The next set of experiments demonstrate how, in addition, they can also be used to design a curriculum for an agent learning a task that may be too difficult to learn from scratch, or even using a single source task.

5.2 Half Field Offense (HFO)

Half field offense [7] is a subtask of Robocup simulated soccer in which a team of m offensive players try to score a goal against n defensive players while playing on one half of a soccer field. The domain poses many challenges, including a large, continuous state and action space, coordination between multiple agents, and multiagent credit assignment. Each of these difficulties makes learning hard, especially early on when goal scoring episodes can be rare.

Each HFO episode starts with the ball and offensive team placed randomly near the half field line. Likewise, the defensive team is randomly initialized near the goal box. A sample starting configuration can be seen in Figure 2c. The goal of the offensive team is to move the ball up the field while maintaining possession, and take shots to score on goal. An episode ends when either (1) a goal is scored, (2) the ball goes out of bounds, (3) the defense captures the ball, or (4) the episode times out. The reward structure of the domain is shown in Table 1.

As done in Kalyanakrishnan et al. [7], we focus on learning behaviors for the player with the ball. The player with the ball has to choose one of the following actions:

- Pass k: A direct pass to the teammate that is k-th closest to the ball, where $k = 2, 3, \ldots, m$.
- Dribble: A small kick in the cone formed between the player and the goalposts, that maximizes its distance to the closest defender also in the cone.
- Shoot j: A full power kick towards one of j evenly spaced points on the goal line.

Offensive players without the ball follow one of several fixed formations to provide support. The agent's state space

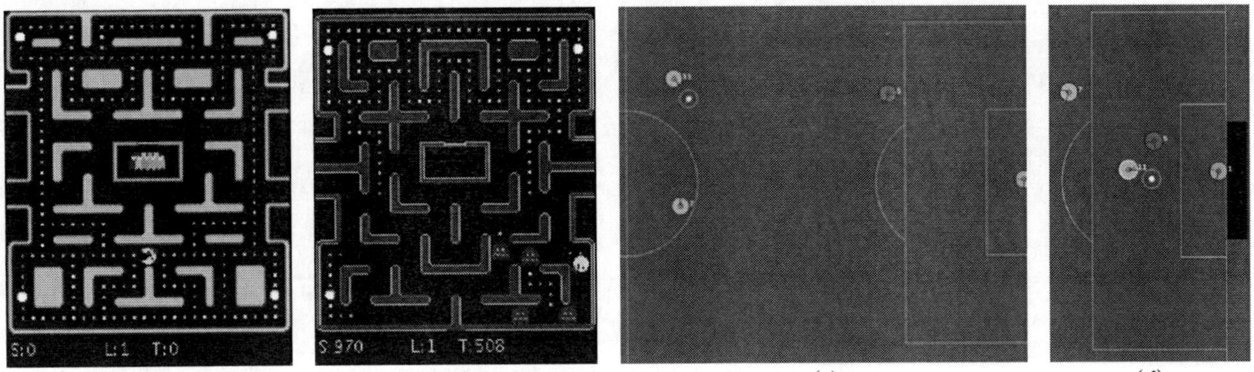

(a) (b) (c) (d)

Figure 2: Examples of tasks in Ms. Pac-Man (a and b) and Half Field Offense (c and d). (a) Maze 1 (b) Maze 4 (c) HFO initial configuration and 2v2 dribble task (d) 2v2 shoot task. In HFO, offensive players are colored yellow, defensive players are blue, and the goalie is pink. The ball is shown by the white circle.

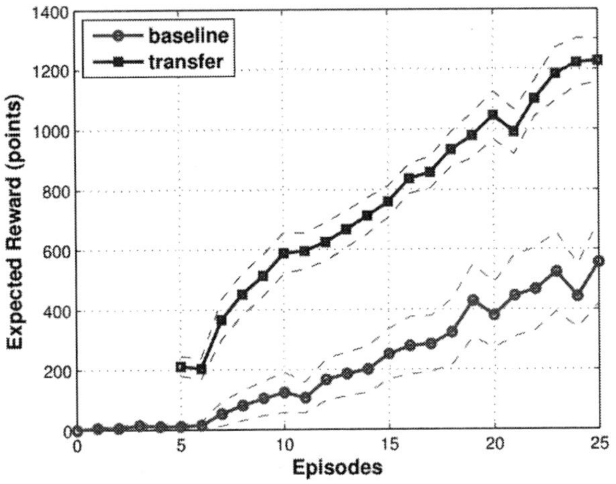

Figure 3: Results of TASKSIMPLIFICATION applied to the Ms. Pac-Man domain. See Section 5.1.1 for details. Dashed lines indicate standard error.

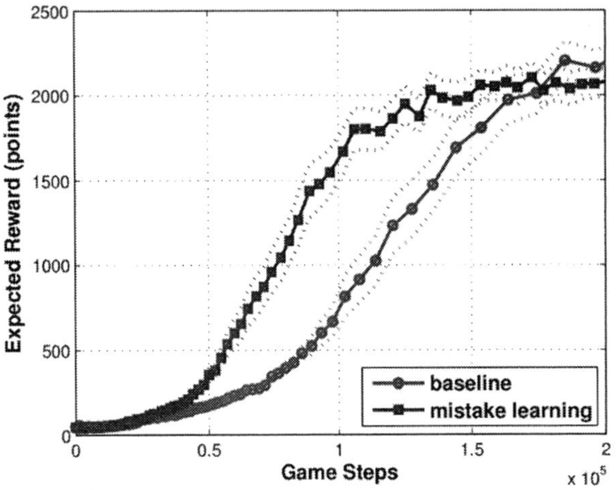

Figure 4: Results of MISTAKELEARNING applied to the Ms. Pac-Man domain. See Section 5.1.2 for details. Dashed lines indicate standard error.

consists of distances and angles to points of interest, which are listed in Table 2. We used CMAC tile coding for function approximation, Sarsa for the learning algorithm [22], and value function transfer to transfer knowledge.

Space of tasks

Half field offense has a number of degrees of freedom that allow creating many different types of tasks. We list some of the relevant degrees of freedom in Table 3. In addition to these, various aspects of the field (such as the size of the goals, the goal box, etc.), the players (such as visibility, stamina, etc.), and the world physics can also be changed.

These degrees of freedom allow us to quickly create many domain-specific source tasks, using the TASKSIMPLIFICATION rule. For example, we can add more teammates or reduce the number of defenders to give the offense more options. We can change the defensive team behavior to train against opponents of varying difficulty. We could also change various aspects of the world size and physics to make scoring and movement easier.

However, we can also create agent-specific source tasks by observing the behavior of the agent on the target task. For example, after observing generally unsuccessful trajectories on the target task, we could use MISTAKELEARNING to recreate situations where the agent lost the ball or failed to score, in order to learn how to avoid or resolve them. Another option would be to build upon successful trajectories using PROMISINGINITIALIZATIONS, which would create tasks that initialize the offense at different positions near the goal, allowing them to drill on how to shoot.

Combined, the methods from the previous section form a space of tasks that can be used to create a curriculum. In the next section, we illustrate the formal specification of some of the tasks and their creation that we found to be useful in our experiments.

5.2.1 2v2 HFO Curriculum

We first consider the target task of 2v2 half field offense, where 2 attackers must score against 1 defender and 1 goalie. We used agents from the released binaries of the Helios team to form the defensive team [1]. Helios and WrightEagle consistently place among the top teams in the annual Robocup 2D Simulation League tournament, making even this small version of half field offense a challenging task.

Feature	Description
dist-to-goalie	Distance from O_1 to the goalie
dist-to-defender-in-cone	Distance from O_1 to the closest defender in the dribble cone
dist-to-teammate$_i$	Distance from O_1 to each teammate O_i, for $i = 2, 3, \ldots m$
dist-teammate$_i$-to-closest-defender	For each O_i, the distance to its closest defender, $i = 2, 3, \ldots m$
dist-teammate$_i$-pass-intercept	For each O_i, the shortest distance between a defender and the line between O_1 and O_i, $i = 2, 3, \ldots m$
min-ang-teammate$_i$-defender	For each O_i, the smallest angle between O_i, O_1, and a defender, $i = 2, 3, \ldots m$
dist-to-shot-target$_i$	Distance from O_1 to location i on the goal line, $i = 1, 2, \ldots j$
dist-goalie-to-shot-target$_i$	Distance from goalie to location i on the goal line, $i = 1, 2, \ldots j$
dist-shot$_i$-intercept	Shortest distance between a defender and the line between O_1 and location i on the goal line, $i = 1, 2, \ldots j$
ang-goalie-shot-target$_i$	Angle between goalie, O_1, and location i on the goal line, $i = 1, 2, \ldots j$
ang-defender-shot-target$_i$	Smallest angle between a defender, O_1, and location i on the goal line, $i = 1, 2, \ldots j$

Table 2: Feature space for the player with the ball in HFO. We index offensive players by their distance to the ball. Thus, the player with the ball is O_1 and its teammates are $O_2, O_3, \ldots O_m$.

Let M_{2v2} denote the target task's MDP, and X_{2v2} be a set of (presumably generally unsuccessful) samples collected from M_{2v2}. We can generate this task $M_{2v2} = \tau(\mathcal{D}, F_{2v2})$, using the following instantiations for the degree of freedom vector (the order of parameters is the same as in Table 3):

$$F_{2v2} = [2, 2, \text{Helios}, \text{flat}, 68, 52.5, 2.7, 1, 0.3]$$

The following are specific subtasks that could be created using the methods from Section 4:

Shoot Task

One useful skill to learn is where a goal can be scored from. After having obtained some experience in the target task with at least a few goals, it is very likely that similar scenarios are also possible to score from. We can gradually expand this set of states that lead to a high reward termination using PROMISINGINITIALIZATIONS, where we use a Euclidean distance metric C over the agent's relative distances and angles to other players, to measure state proximity:

$$M_{shoot} = \text{PROMISINGINITIALIZATIONS}(M_{2v2}, X_{2v2}, C, \delta, \rho)$$

A sample scenario can be seen in Figure 2d. Essentially, this task creates different configurations of players near the goal, and drills shooting. In our experiments, we set $\delta = 3$ and $\rho = 0.10$.

Dribble Task

Initially while exploring, the agent takes many shots on goal from far away, which are unlikely to score. A skill the agent needs is the ability to move the ball up the field, maintaining possession away from defenders, until the agent reaches a state that it can score from. This can be accomplished by chaining ACTIONSIMPLIFICATION with M_{shoot} using LINKSUBTASK:

$$M_1 = \text{LINKSUBTASK}(M_{2v2}, M_{shoot}, V_{shoot})$$
$$M_{dribble} = \text{ACTIONSIMPLIFICATION}(M_1, X_{2v2}, \alpha)$$

LINKSUBTASK creates a subtask M_1 where the goal is to reach situations that the agent is likely to score from, as learned in M_{shoot}. ACTIONSIMPLIFICATION prevents the agent from taking shots on goal from far away, since these actions usually lead to defense captures, and adds this restriction to M_1. An example of the initial configuration for the dribble task is shown in Figure 2c. In our experiments, we set $\alpha = 100$.

2v2 Curriculum Results

Figure 5 shows the performance on the target task of 2v2 HFO for learners following various curricula composed of the 2 tasks above. For each curriculum, we trained on sub tasks until convergence. Offsets in the curves represent time spent training in source tasks. Labels indicate the curricula used; baseline is learning on the target task without transfer.

The teams of agents were evaluated on their goal scoring ability: the fraction of times they are able to score a goal. Since each episode results in binary goal or no goal scored result, we used a sliding window of 200 episodes around each point to determine the average goal-scoring rate at each time step. All results are averaged over 25 trials. From Figure 5, it is clear to see that using a sequence of tasks to guide training significantly improves the final performance.

5.2.2 Extension to 2v3 HFO

In this section, we extend the problem to the harder task of 2v3 half field offense, where there are now 2 defenders and a goalie. 2v3 is fundamentally harder than 2v2, since the additional defender means both attackers can now be marked. We can generate this target task $M_{2v3} = \tau(\mathcal{D}, F_{2v3})$ using the following degree of freedom vector:

$$F_{2v3} = [2, 3, \text{Helios}, \text{flat}, 68, 52.5, 2.7, 1, 0.3]$$

This time, we can use TASKSIMPLIFICATION to simplify the degree of freedom vector to recreate the 2v2 task from the last section, allowing us to use it as a source for 2v3:

$$M_{2v2} = \text{TASKSIMPLIFICATION}(M_{2v3}, X_{2v3}, D, F_{2v3}, \tau)$$

Parameter	Range
Number Offense Players	$\{0, 1, \ldots 4\}$
Number Defense Players	$\{0, 1, \ldots 5\}$
Defense Behavior	{Agent-2D, Helios, WrightEagle}
Formation Type	{ Flat, Box, Trapezoid}
Field Width	20 – 68
Field Length	20 – 52.5
Max ball speed	0 – 5
Max player speed	0 – 1
Wind Noise	0 – 1

Table 3: Half Field Offense degrees of freedom

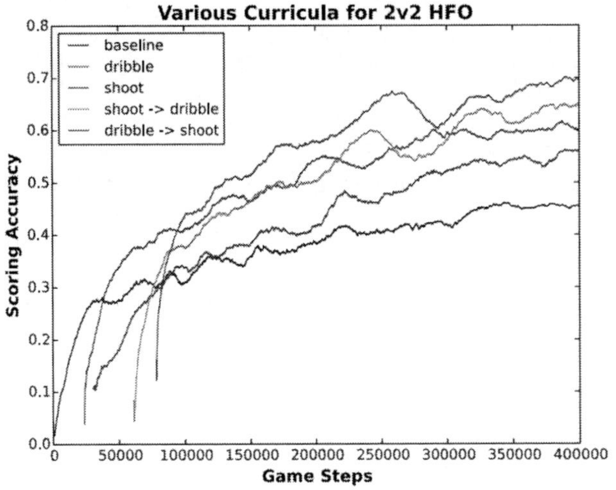

Figure 5: Goal scoring accuracy on 2v2 HFO for agents following different curricula. Standard error (not shown to avoid clutter) ranged from 0.015 to 0.027 over the last 200 episodes for all curves.

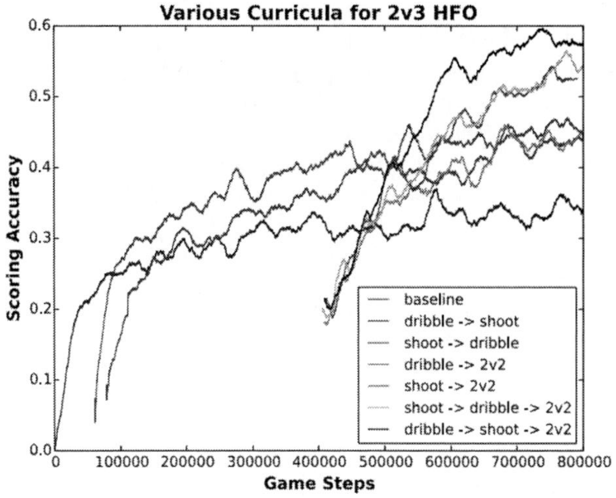

Figure 6: Goal scoring accuracy on 2v3 HFO for agents following different curricula. Standard error (not shown to avoid clutter) ranged from 0.010 to 0.039 over the last 200 episodes for all curves.

Doing this also allows us to utilize the dribble and shoot tasks, since they are derived from M_{2v2}. Thus, we now consider 3 possible source tasks for a curriculum: $M_{dribble}$, M_{shoot}, and M_{2v2}. Results of various curricula composed of these source tasks can be seen in Figure 6.

Again, using a multistage sequence of tasks provides better asymptotic performance than a curriculum composed of a subset of its source tasks. Interestingly, we also find that the most effective curriculum in 2v2 HFO is a subset of the best curriculum in 2v3 HFO when considering this space of tasks. This observation suggests that an automated procedure to create curricula could be designed recursively.

6. RELATED WORK

Learning via a curriculum is an idea pervasive throughout human and animal training [20]. Recently, curriculum learning has also started to be explored in the context of supervised learning [3, 9], where the order in which individual samples are presented to an online learner was shown to considerably affect learning speed and generalization. Several related paradigms, such as multi-task learning [4] and lifelong learning [17], consider learning *groups* of *prediction* tasks. These methods assume tasks are related, and knowledge gained from solving one task can transfer to help learn another. In particular, Ruvolo and Eaton [16] show how a learner can actively select tasks to improve learning speed for all tasks, or for a specific target task. However, all of these works apply to supervised prediction tasks and assume the set of tasks to be learned is already given.

Subsequently, many of these ideas have been studied in the reinforcement learning paradigm. For example, Wilson et al. [28] explored multi-task reinforcement learning while Ammar et al. [2] consider lifelong learning applied to sequential decision making tasks. In both cases, a sequence of RL tasks is presented to a learner, and the goal is to optimize over all tasks. In contrast, our source tasks are designed solely to improve performance on a target task. We aren't concerned with optimizing performance in a source. In addition, neither work considers task *generation*, and thus are dependent on the quality of source tasks given.

In fact, as far as we know, we are the first to propose general methods for creating source tasks for transfer learning. Past work has typically relied solely on domain knowledge to supply suitable source tasks. For example, 3v2 keepaway serving as a source for 4v3 keepaway [26], 2D mountain car as a source for 3D mountain car [25], or varying parameters of physical systems [2]. Sinapov et al. [19] use a set of task descriptors, which are similar to our degrees of freedom, to specify a set of source tasks. This work goes significantly beyond all of those by creating agent-specific tasks from a dynamic analysis of an agent's performance, and shows how these tasks can be used in a multistage curriculum.

Finally, the problem of source task *selection*, which is different from task *generation* has been considered in single step transfer learning as well [12, 19]. As before, they assume the set of tasks is already prespecified, and the goal is to select the best ones. Again, these tasks are not individualized for each agent, and thus depend on the quality of tasks present.

7. CONCLUSION

In this paper, we introduced the problem of curriculum learning in reinforcement learning. As a step towards this goal, we presented a series of functions that utilize domain knowledge and observations of an agent's performance to create subtasks tailored to the agent. We showed how these subtasks could be used as components of a multistage curriculum to significantly improve an agent's performance in two challenging multiagent reinforcement learning domains. A challenging next step in this research agenda is to develop automated methods for selecting from among the space of subtasks that our functions generate, in order to create a fully automated, individualized RL curriculum.

Acknowledgements

This work took place in the Learning Agents Research Group (LARG) at UT Austin. LARG research is supported in part by NSF (CNS-1330072, CNS-1305287), ONR (21C184-01), AFRL (FA8750-14-1-0070), & AFOSR (FA9550-14-1-0087).

REFERENCES

[1] H. Akiyama and T. Nakashima. *HELIOS 2012: RoboCup 2012 Soccer Simulation 2D League Champion*, volume 7500. Springer, 2012.

[2] H. B. Ammar, E. Eaton, P. Ruvolo, and M. Taylor. Online multi-task learning for policy gradient methods. In *Proceedings of the 31st International Conference on Machine Learning (ICML-14)*, pages 1206–1214, 2014.

[3] Y. Bengio, J. Louradour, R. Collobert, and J. Weston. Curriculum learning. In *Proceedings of the 26th Annual International Conference on Machine Learning*, pages 41–48. ACM, 2009.

[4] R. Caruana. Multitask learning. *Machine learning*, 28(1):41–75, 1997.

[5] A. Fachantidis, I. Partalas, G. Tsoumakas, and I. Vlahavas. Transferring task models in reinforcement learning agents. *Neurocomputing*, 107:23–32, 2013.

[6] F. Fernández, J. García, and M. Veloso. Probabilistic policy reuse for inter-task transfer learning. *Robotics and Autonomous Systems*, 58(7):866 – 871, 2010. Advances in Autonomous Robots for Service and Entertainment.

[7] S. Kalyanakrishnan, Y. Liu, and P. Stone. Half field offense in RoboCup soccer: A multiagent reinforcement learning case study. In *RoboCup-2006: Robot Soccer World Cup X*, volume 4434 of *Lecture Notes in Artificial Intelligence*, pages 72–85. Springer Verlag, Berlin, 2007.

[8] G. Konidaris and A. Barto. Skill discovery in continuous reinforcement learning domains using skill chaining. In *Advances in Neural Information Processing Systems*, 2009.

[9] M. P. Kumar, B. Packer, and D. Koller. Self-paced learning for latent variable models. In *Advances in Neural Information Processing Systems*, pages 1189–1197, 2010.

[10] A. Lazaric. Transfer in reinforcement learning: a framework and a survey. In M. Wiering and M. van Otterlo, editors, *Reinforcement Learning: State of the Art*. Springer, 2011.

[11] A. Lazaric and M. Restelli. Transfer from multiple MDPs. In *Proceedings of the Twenty-Fifth Annual Conference on Neural Information Processing Systems (NIPS'11)*, 2011.

[12] A. Lazaric, M. Restelli, and A. Bonarini. Transfer of samples in batch reinforcement learning. In A. McCallum and S. Roweis, editors, *Proceedings of the Twenty-Fifth Annual International Conference on Machine Learning (ICML-2008)*, pages 544–551, Helsinki, Finalnd, July 2008.

[13] S. Mannor, I. Menache, A. Hoze, and U. Klein. Dynamic abstraction in reinforcement learning via clustering. In *Proceedings of the Twenty-First International Conference on Machine Learning*, pages 560–567, 2004.

[14] A. McGovern and A. G. Barto. Automatic discovery of subgoals in reinforcement learning using diverse density. In *Proceedings of the Eighteenth International Conference on Machine Learning*, pages 361–368, 2001.

[15] I. Menache, S. Mannor, and N. Shimkin. Q-cut - dynamic discovery of sub-goals in reinforcement learning. In *13th European Conference on Machine Learning*, pages 295–306. Springer, 2002.

[16] P. Ruvolo and E. Eaton. Active task selection for lifelong machine learning. In *Proceedings of the 27th AAAI Conference on Artificial Intelligence (AAAI-13)*, July 2013.

[17] P. Ruvolo and E. Eaton. Ella: An efficient lifelong learning algorithm. In *Proceedings of the 30th International Conference on Machine Learning (ICML-13)*, June 2013.

[18] O. Simsek and A. G. Barto. Using relative novelty to identify useful temporal abstractions in reinforcement learning. In *Proceedings of the Twenty-First International Conference on Machine Learning*, pages 751–758, 2004.

[19] J. Sinapov, S. Narvekar, M. Leonetti, and P. Stone. Learning inter-task transferability in the absence of target task samples. In *Proceedings of the 2015 ACM Conference on Autonomous Agents and Multi-Agent Systems (AAMAS)*. ACM, 2015.

[20] B. F. Skinner. Reinforcement today. *American Psychologist*, 13(3):94, 1958.

[21] V. Soni and S. Singh. Using homomorphisms to transfer options across continuous reinforcement learning domains. In *In Proceedings of American Association for Artificial Intelligence (AAAI)*, 2006.

[22] R. Sutton and A. Barto. *Reinforcement Learning: An Introduction*. MIT Press, 1998.

[23] R. Sutton, D. Precup, and S. Singh. Between mdps and semi-mdps: A framework for temporal abstraction in reinforcement learning. *Artificial Intelligence*, 112:181–211, 1999.

[24] M. E. Taylor, N. Carboni, A. Fachantidis, I. Vlahavas, and L. Torrey. Reinforcement learning agents providing advice in complex video games. *Connection Science*, 26(1):45–63, 2014.

[25] M. E. Taylor, G. Kuhlmann, and P. Stone. Autonomous transfer for reinforcement learning. In *The Seventh International Joint Conference on Autonomous Agents and Multiagent Systems*, May 2008.

[26] M. E. Taylor and P. Stone. Behavior transfer for value-function-based reinforcement learning. In F. Dignum, V. Dignum, S. Koenig, S. Kraus, M. P. Singh, and M. Wooldridge, editors, *The Fourth International Joint Conference on Autonomous Agents and Multiagent Systems*, pages 53–59, New York, NY, July 2005. ACM Press.

[27] M. E. Taylor and P. Stone. Transfer learning for reinforcement learning domains: A survey. *Journal of Machine Learning Research*, 10(1):1633–1685, 2009.

[28] A. Wilson, A. Fern, S. Ray, and P. Tadepalli. Multi-task reinforcement learning: a hierarchical bayesian approach. In *Proceedings of the 24th International Conference on Machine Learning*, pages 1015–1022. ACM, 2007.

A Survey of Opponent Modeling Techniques in Automated Negotiation

(JAAMAS Extended Abstract)

Tim Baarslag
University of Southampton
United Kingdom
T.Baarslag@soton.ac.uk

Mark J.C. Hendrikx
Delft University of Technology
The Netherlands
M.J.C.Hendrikx@tudelft.nl

Koen V. Hindriks
Delft University of Technology
The Netherlands
K.V.Hindriks@tudelft.nl

Catholijn M. Jonker
Delft University of Technology
The Netherlands
C.M.Jonker@tudelft.nl

1. INTRODUCTION

Negotiation is a process in which parties interact to settle a mutual concern to improve their status quo. Traditionally, negotiation is a necessary, but time-consuming and expensive activity. Therefore, in the last two decades, there has been a growing interest in the *automation* of negotiation.

One of the key challenges for a successful negotiation is that usually only limited information is available about the opponent. Although sharing private information can result in mutual gains, negotiators often avoid this to prevent exploitation. This problem can be partially overcome by deriving information from the opponent's actions. Exploiting this information to learn aspects of the opponent is called *opponent modeling*. Creating an accurate opponent model is a key factor in improving the quality of the outcome and can further increase the benefits of automated negotiation.

Despite the advantages of opponent modeling and two decades of research, there is no recent study that provides an overview of the field. Therefore, in order to stimulate the development of efficient future opponent models, and to outline a research agenda, we provide an overview of existing opponent models in bilateral negotiation [2]. As our main contributions, we classify opponent models using a comprehensive taxonomy and provide recommendations on how to select the best model depending on the negotiation setting.

2. LEARNING ABOUT THE OPPONENT

A bilateral negotiation may be viewed as a two-player game of incomplete information. An opponent model is then simply an abstracted description of a player (and/or their behavior) during the game. In negotiation, opponent modeling often revolves around three concerns: what does the opponent *want*; what will the opponent *do*; and what *type* of player is the opponent. These considerations are often highly related; for example, to understand the opponent's behavior, an agent first needs to know what the opponent desires.

Appears in: *Proceedings of the 15th International Conference on Autonomous Agents and Multiagent Systems (AAMAS 2016), J. Thangarajah, K. Tuyls, C. Jonker, S. Marsella (eds.), May 9–13, 2016, Singapore.*

An important aspect in which opponent models differ is their time of creation. *Offline* opponent models are constructed before the negotiation using historical data. *Online* opponent models are constructed during the negotiation by interpreting the exchange of offers. A major challenge for online models are real-time deadlines, which impose a restriction on the time available for maintaining the model.

Even though there are large differences between opponent models, there is a common set of motivations for using them:

1. **Minimize negotiation cost.** It costs time and resources to negotiate and as a consequence, early agreements are often preferred. Learning can aid in identifying promising bids that lead to swift agreements.
2. **Adapt to the opponent.** Agents can adapt their behavior according to their opponent; e.g., by estimating the deadline or reservation value in an attempt to press for an outcome the opponent will ultimately settle for.
3. **Reach win-win agreements.** In a cooperative environment, agents aim for a fair result. An estimate of the opponent's preference profile can aid in identifying mutually beneficial outcomes.

We found that existing work can fulfill these goals by learning a combination of *four* opponent attributes listed below.

Acceptance Strategy

The decision to accept an offer is made by the *acceptance strategy* of a negotiating agent. Upon acceptance of an offer, the negotiation ends in agreement; otherwise, the agents continue exchanging offers. Learning an opponent's acceptance strategy is potentially of great value as it can help to find the deal with the highest utility that is still acceptable for the opponent.

In negotiations about a single, quantitative issue (such as the price of a service), where the opponent's have opposing preferences that are publicly known, *estimating the reservation value* is sufficient to determine all acceptable bids. The reservation value can be learned by extrapolating the opponent's concessions, for example by applying Bayesian learning. Alternatively, a model may assume that the opponent uses a particular decision function of which the unknown variables can be estimated using non-linear regression.

In multi-issue negotiations, we can *estimate the probability of acceptance* for every possible outcome. By keeping track of what offers were offered and accepted in previous negotiations, an agent can estimate the probability that a bid will be accepted. As it is unlikely that such an estimate can be derived for all possible bids, regression methods can be applied to determine the acceptance probability for the entire outcome space.

Deadline

The *deadline* of a negotiation refers to the time before which an agreement must be reached which is better than the best alternative for each party. Each agent can have their own private deadline, but it is also common for the negotiation deadline to be shared. The deadline may be specified as a maximum number of rounds, or alternatively as a real-time cutoff point.

Private deadlines are important to learn about, as an agent is likely to concede strongly near the deadline to avoid non-agreement. Because of the strong connection with the reservation value, most of the procedures to learn the reservation value can also be applied here.

Preference Profile

The *preference profile* of an agent represents the private valuation of possible negotiation outcomes. Learning the preference profile assists in locating mutually beneficial outcomes and recognizing potential for meaningful concessions.

Four approaches have been used so far to estimate the opponent's preference information:

1. **Importance of the issues.** It is often easier to estimate the *weight* of all issues under negotiation, rather than the preference over all outcomes. The idea is to analyze the opponent's concessions, assuming that stronger concessions are made on issues that are valued less.
2. **Classify the negotiation trace.** Given the opponent's negotiation actions, we can determine which opponent type is most likely, and subsequently apply a classification algorithm to categorize preferences of the opponent.
3. **Aggregate negotiation data.** When offline data is available, we can derive the opponent's preference profile from a large database of negotiation traces from similar – but not identical – opponents.
4. **Importance of outcomes.** A popular technique is the frequency analysis heuristic. The main idea is that preferred values of an issue are offered relatively more often in a negotiation trace. For the issue weights, the opposite holds: an issue is likely unimportant if its value changes often.

Bidding Strategy

The *negotiation strategy* determines an agent's offer in any given negotiation state. Strategies may range from simple time-dependent concessions to complex decision-making that depends on the opponent's behavior. Learning the opponent's bidding strategy allows an agent to anticipate and manipulate the opponent's behavior.

An agent is generally unaware of the opponent's exact strategy, but it might have knowledge about the type of strategy used. If such knowledge can be captured in a closed-form formula with unknown variables, *regression analysis* can be applied.

When limited knowledge is available about the opponent's type, *time series forecasting* is an alternative, which is a technique to extrapolate a set of observations that is sequentially ordered in time. In negotiation, the time series typically consists of the utilities of offers received. Learning the opponent's bidding strategy then boils down to creating a forecast of future offers, using a set of statistical techniques and smoothing methods.

3. DISCUSSION AND CONCLUSION

Constructing an opponent model may be viewed as a classification problem, where the type of the opponent needs to be determined from a range of possibilities. In combination with *opponent classification*, there are two other opponent model categories: models that learn *what the opponent wants*, in terms of its reservation value, deadline, and preferences, and secondly, models that learn *what the opponent will do*, in terms of the bidding and acceptance strategy.

A large number of opponent modeling techniques exist in literature. For each learned opponent attribute, we have identified key approaches that are currently being applied. A natural question that arises with regard to agent design is: which of the depicted modeling techniques is *best*? To date, answering this question is unfeasible, as most authors evaluate opponent models in their own specific setting using different quality measures. A main direction for future work is therefore to outline a procedure for finding the best opponent modeling technique given the particular circumstances.

A fair procedure should consist of two components: a balanced experimental setup to evaluate the model under different conditions, together with an unbiased set of *quality measures* [1]. *Performance measures* are the most commonly used quality measure; they determine the performance gain when a negotiation strategy is supplemented by a learning method, for example the increase in average utility. *Accuracy measures* quantify how closely the model resembles reality, e.g. by calculating the correlation between the actual and estimated utilities of all outcomes. Both approaches augment each other, and in [2] we discuss for each of the four opponent attributes that are learned which measures to apply. In addition, for each of the three reasons for using an opponent model (c.f. Section 2) we recommend a set of corresponding performance measures.

Consistently applying the right negotiation benchmarks would greatly improve comparability of results in negotiation literature, and would provide insight in possible improvements to existing models and how they can be combined to augment each other. Our work serves as a starting point towards finding the best opponent modeling techniques, and thereby the transition from theory to practice.

REFERENCES

[1] T. Baarslag, M. J. Hendrikx, K. V. Hindriks, and C. M. Jonker. Predicting the performance of opponent models in automated negotiation. In *IEEE/WIC/ACM*, volume 2, Nov 2013.

[2] T. Baarslag, M. J. Hendrikx, K. V. Hindriks, and C. M. Jonker. Learning about the opponent in automated bilateral negotiation: a comprehensive survey of opponent modeling techniques. *Autonomous Agents and Multi-Agent Systems*, pages 1–50, 2015.

Ad Hoc Teamwork by Learning Teammates' Task (JAAMAS Extended Abstract)

Francisco S. Melo
INESC-ID/Instituto Superior Técnico
Universidade de Lisboa
Av. Prof. Dr. Cavaco Silva
2744-016 Porto Salvo, Portugal
fmelo@inesc-id.pt

Alberto Sardinha
INESC-ID/Instituto Superior Técnico
Universidade de Lisboa
Av. Prof. Dr. Cavaco Silva
2744-016 Porto Salvo, Portugal
jose.alberto.sardinha@tecnico.ulisboa.pt

ABSTRACT

We address ad hoc teamwork, where an agent must coordinate with other agents in an unknown common task without pre-defined coordination. We formalize the ad hoc teamwork problem as a sequential decision problem and propose (i) the use of an online learning approach that considers the different tasks depending on their ability to predict the behavior of the teammate; and (ii) a decision-theoretic approach that models the ad hoc teamwork problem as a partially observable Markov decision problem. We provide theoretical and empirical evaluation of the performance of our proposed methods in several domains of different complexity.

General Terms

Algorithms,Theory

Keywords

Ad hoc teamwork, online learning, POMDP

1. INTRODUCTION

The challenge of developing autonomous agents that are capable of cooperatively engaging with other unknown agents in a joint common task is known as the *ad hoc teamwork problem* [3]. In this paper, we break down the ad hoc teamwork problem into three challenges that an agent must address when paired within an ad hoc team. We claim that the agent may not always know beforehand the task that it is expected to complete. Therefore, it must *identify the target task*, *idenfy the teammates strategy* and *decide* accordingly.

Research on ad hoc teamwork mostly focused on the decision-making step, relying on different assumptions that simplify the other challenges. For example, Stone and Kraus [5] admit knowledge of teammate and task and use bandit algorithms to drive the teammate to the desired behavior. Posterior works no longer use teammate knowledge, assuming they are best responders, but still rely on task knowledge [4]. Recent works combine learning with planning, extending ad hoc teamwork to complex cooperative domains [1].

In this paper, we formalize the ad hoc teamwork problem as a sequential decision problem, in which the ad hoc agent does not know in advance the target task or how its teammates act towards completing it. Each task is represented as fully cooperative matrix game; the ad hoc agent identifies the target task by determining the corresponding payoff function from a set of possible alternatives. Teammates are assumed to follow a bounded-rationality best-response model [4], adapting their behavior to that of the learning agent. We the propose two novel approaches to the ad hoc teamwork problem: the first uses online learning to detect the target task and act accordingly; the second models the ad hoc teamwork problem as partially observable Markov decision process (POMDP) that can be solved using standard approaches from the literature. Finally, we present both theoretical bounds on and an empirical evaluation of the performance of our approaches in several domains.

Appears in: *Proceedings of the 15th International Conference on Autonomous Agents and Multiagent Systems (AAMAS 2016), J. Thangarajah, K. Tuyls, C. Jonker, S. Marsella (eds.), May 9–13, 2016, Singapore.*

2. THE AD HOC TEAMWORK PROBLEM

An agent placed in a team of unknown agents executing an unknown target task must, first of all, determine such target task. We assume that the target task τ^* lies in a known finite set $\mathcal{T}$ of tasks, each represented as a fully cooperative matrix game $(N, \times_{n=1}^{N} \mathcal{A}_n, u_\tau)$, where N is the number of agents, A_n is the action set of agent n and u_τ is the utility function of task τ. Once the task is identified, the agent must determine how the teammates address that task so that it can plan its own actions. These three steps (task identification, teammate identification and planning) should be expected from any ad hoc agent.

2.1 Online Learning (OL) Approach

We denote the ad hoc agent as α and its teammates as a single meta-agent $-\alpha$. As in other works [4], we assume $-\alpha$ is a best responder to the last M plays of α.

Our first approach requires the ad hoc agent to predict, at each time step n, the action $A_{-\alpha}(n)$ of its teammate. Therefore, at each step n, the ad hoc agent selects a joint action $\hat{A}(n) = \langle A_\alpha(n), \hat{A}_{-\alpha}(n)\rangle$ that includes its own action, $A_\alpha(n)$, and its prediction, $\hat{A}_{-\alpha}(n)$, and incurs a loss

$$\ell(\hat{A}(n), A_{-\alpha}(n)) = 1 - \delta(\hat{A}_{-\alpha}(n), A_{-\alpha}(n)). \quad (1)$$

where δ is the Kroneker delta function. We cast the ad hoc teamwork problem as an *online prediction problem*, associating with each task $\tau \in \mathcal{T}$ an *expert* $E_\tau : \mathcal{H} \times \mathcal{A} \to [0, 1]$, where $E_\tau(h_{1:n}, a)$ is the probability of selecting the joint action a as a best response to the history $h_{1:n}$ according to

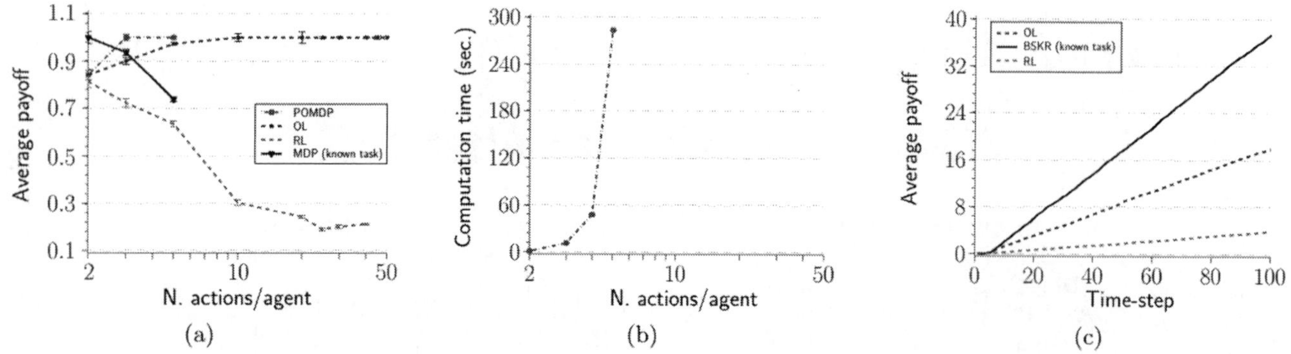

Figure 1: (a) Payoff in randomly generated scenarios vs the number of actions per agent. (b) POMDP computation time vs the number of actions per agent. (c) Payoff in the pursuit domain.

task τ. The cumulative loss of E_τ given the history $h_{1:n}$ is

$$L_\tau(h_{1:n}) \triangleq \sum_{t=0}^{n-1} \ell_\tau(h_{1:t}, a_{-\alpha}(t+1)),$$

where $a_{-\alpha}(t)$ is the actual action played by the teammate at time-step t after history $h_{1:t}$. Considering the *exponentially weighted average predictor* (EWAP) given by:

$$P(h_{1:n}, \hat{a}) \triangleq \frac{\sum_{\tau \in \mathcal{T}} e^{-\gamma_n L_\tau(h_{1:n})} E_\tau(h_{1:n}, \hat{a})}{\sum_{\tau \in \mathcal{T}} e^{-\gamma_n L_\tau(h_{1:n})}}, \qquad (2)$$

where γ_n is a positive parameter, we get the next result [2]:

THEOREM 1. *If* $\gamma_t = \sqrt{2 \ln |\mathcal{E}| / t^{1/2}}$ *for all* $t > 0$*, then, for any finite history* $h_{1:n} \in \mathcal{H}$*, the* regret $R_n(P, \mathcal{E})$ *of an ad hoc agent following the EWAP is bounded above by* $\sqrt{n/2 \ln |\mathcal{E}|}$*, where* $R_n(P, \mathcal{E}) = \mathbb{E}[L_P(h_{1:n}) - L_\tau(h_{1:n})]$ *and* $L_P(h_{1:n})$ *is the cumulative loss of predictor* P *at step* n*, given* $h_{1:n}$*.*

2.2 Decision-theoretic (POMDP) Approach

This section further considers prior knowledge about the target task, encoded as a prior distribution p_0, and the impact of the actions of agent on those of the teammate. The prior p_0 suggests a Bayesian approach to the ad hoc teamwork problem; the consideration of the agent α's actions impacts the way in which *regret* is defined.

We model the ad hoc teamwork problem as a POMDP $(\mathcal{X}, \mathcal{A}, \mathcal{Z}, \mathsf{P}, \mathsf{O}, c, \gamma)$, where at each time step n the state takes values in $\mathcal{X}$ and consists of the history of past M plays and the (unknown) target task. The action of the agent takes values in $\mathcal{A}$ and again includes its own action, $A_\alpha(n)$ and the prediction of the teammate's action, $\hat{A}_{-\alpha}(n)$. After selecting an action, the agent observes $A_{-\alpha}(n)$, which corresponds to the observation space $\mathcal{Z} = \mathcal{A}_{-\alpha}$. The *transition probabilities* P encode the state dynamics as a function of the agent's actions, and are factored in two components: the dynamics of the target task, which remains unchanged, and the dynamics of the history, which evolve according to the agent's actions and the best-response model of the teammate. Finally, the *observation probabilities*, O, map the current state to the teammate's most recent action, and the reward function r weights the payoff received from the interaction (determined by u_{τ^*}) with that of the loss in (1):

$$r(h, \tau, a) = \sum_{\hat{a}, \hat{b} \in \mathcal{A}} E_\tau(h, \hat{a}) E_\tau(h, \hat{b})(K - \ell(\hat{a}, a)) U_\tau(a_\alpha, \hat{b}_{-\alpha})$$

where K is a normalizing constant. We have modeled the ad hoc teamwork problem as a POMDP to which we can apply any POMDP solver. We have the following result [2]:

THEOREM 2. *The POMDP-based approach to the ad hoc teamwork problem is such that* $\lim_{n \to \infty} \frac{1}{n} R_n(P, \mathcal{E}) = 0$.

3. EMPIRICAL EVALUATION

We empirically evaluate the performance in random problems with increasing complexity (Figs. 1(a) and 1(b)) and the benchmark pursuit domain [1]. We compare the performance of the OL and POMDP approaches with the performance of an approach with task knowledge (MDP) and a standard RL approach. As seen in Fig. 1(a), the POMDP approach is clearly superior, although at a cost in computation (Fig. 1(b)). The two approaches proposed herein thus offer a delicate tradeoff between performance and complexity (see [2] for further discussion). In the pursuit domain (Fig. 1(c)), we compare our OL approach to the BSKR approach (from [1]), which uses full knowledge of the task. The domain is too large for the POMDP approach to be competitive (in computational terms). The OL approach is clearly superior to a naive RL approach, although not reaching the superior performance of BSKR. For a more detailed discussion, please refer to the full version of the paper [2].

Acknowledgements

This work was partially supported by national funds through Fundação para a Ciência e a Tecnologia (FCT) with reference UID/CEC/50021/2013 and the CMU-Portugal Program and its Information and Communications Technologies Institute, under project CMUP-ERI/HCI/0051/2013.

REFERENCES

[1] S. Barrett, P. Stone, S. Kraus, A. Rosenfeld. Teamwork with limited knowledge of teammates. *AAAI*, pp. 102-108, 2013.

[2] F. S. Melo, A. Sardinha. Ad hoc teamwork by learning teammates' task. *J. Autonomous Agents and Multiagent Systems*, 30(2):175-219, 2016.

[3] P. Stone, G. Kaminka, S. Kraus, J. Rosenschein. Ad hoc autonomous agent teams: Collaboration without pre-coordination. *AAAI*, pp. 1504-1509, 2010.

[4] P. Stone, G. Kaminka, J. Rosenschein. Leading a best-response teammate in an ad hoc team. *LNBIP, 59*, pp. 132-146, 2010.

[5] P. Stone and S. Kraus. To teach or not to teach?: Decision-making under uncertainty in ad hoc teams. *AAMAS*, pp. 117-124, 2010.

Repeated Dollar Auctions: A Multi-Armed Bandit Approach

Marcin Waniek
University of Warsaw
vua@mimuw.edu.pl

Long Tran-Tranh
University of Southampton
l.tran-thanh@soton.ac.uk

Tomasz Michalak
University of Oxford &
University of Warsaw
tomasz.michalak@cs.ox.ac.uk

ABSTRACT

We investigate the repeated version of Shubik's [34] dollar auctions, in which the type of the opponent and their level of rationality is not known in advance. We formulate the problem as an adversarial multi-armed bandit, and we show that a modified version of the ELP algorithm [25], tailored to our setting, can achieve $\tilde{O}(\sqrt{|\mathcal{S}_0|T})$ performance loss (compared to the best fixed strategy), where $|\mathcal{S}_0|$ is the cardinality of the set of available strategies and T is the number of (sequential) auctions. We also show that under some further conditions, these bound can be improved to $\tilde{O}(|\mathcal{S}_0|^{1/4}\sqrt{T})$ and $\tilde{O}(\sqrt{T})$, respectively. Finally, we consider the case of spiteful players. We prove that when a non-spiteful player bids against a malicious one, the game converges in performance to a Nash equilibrium if both players apply our strategy to place their bids.

CCS Concepts

•Theory of computation → Online learning algorithms; Computational pricing and auctions;

Keywords

dollar auction; online learning; multi-armed bandits

1. INTRODUCTION

Conflicts are an integral part of human culture [8]. Whether it is a competition of rival technological companies [38], a battle of lobbyists trying to acquire a government contract [15] or the arms race of modern empires [31], conflict analysis has always been of interest to game theorists and economists alike [18]. The analysis of conflict is also of natural interest analysed in AI and, especially, in Multi-Agent Systems (MAS) literature [27, 37, 11]. Typically conflicts in MAS used to be considered as failures or synchronisation problems [40, 36]. More recently, however, the need for more advanced studies has been recognized [10], including analyses of conflict generation, escalation, or detection in MAS.

A very simple dollar auction introduced by Shubik [34] provides a powerful framework to formalise and study conflict situations. In this auction two participants compete for a dollar by making bids just as in the regular English auction. However, both the winner and the loser have to pay their final bids. In other words, this is an all-pay auction which means that, once a player decides to participate and make her first bid, any invested resources are irretrievably lost. Consequently, the only way to gain any profit (or minimize the loss) is to win the dollar. However, since both players are in the same situation, the dollar auction often ends up with an irrational conflict escalation [23].

Interestingly, however, in a celebrated work, O'Neill [31] proved that the first player has a winning strategy in the dollar auction assuming pure strategies. In particular, if she makes a bid that is a specific combination of the auction's stake, the budget of both players and the minimal bid increment, her opponent will never win the auction and should therefore pass. For instance, if the price increment is \$0.05 and both players have budgets of \$2.50 each, then the first player that has a chance to bid should offer precisely \$0.60 and the other player should drop out. As a result, escalation should never occur. The result by O'Neill suggests that conflict escalation should never occur and if it does so in real-life experiments, it has to be related to human bounded-rationality or other factors not accounted for by the auction model.

However, O'Neil's result was re-examined by Leininger [23] who showed the advantage of the first bidder vanishes considering mixed strategies equilibria and the auction escalates. Demange [13] proved the same for settings where players are uncertain about each other's strength. In addition, Waniek *et al.* [39] showed that when used against a spiteful or malicious player, the optimal strategy proposed by O'Neill can lead to severe loss.

One of the key deficiencies of all of the above results is that they concern one-shot auction case, where the goal is to investigate what would be an optimal bidding strategy in the single auction. However, many real-world applications consist of a sequence of auctions repeatedly played against the same opponent [7, 20, 17]. In fact, many examples of R&D competition, arms races, lobbying, or interactions in MAS can be seen not as a single instance of an auction, but rather as a series of confrontations. We will show later in this paper that the nature of repeated encounters can be leveraged in order to achieve good performance.

Typically in such repeated settings, there is little (if any) prior knowledge about the opponent's incentives, nor about her rationality level. Second, while it is typical to assume some (perfect or bounded) rationality model of the players, it might be the case that the chosen bids do not follow such

Appears in: *Proceedings of the 15th International Conference on Autonomous Agents and Multiagent Systems (AAMAS 2016), J. Thangarajah, K. Tuyls, C. Jonker, S. Marsella (eds.), May 9–13, 2016, Singapore.*

assumptions (e.g., due to lack of computational power, or lack of perfect execution). As such, efficient bidding strategies need to consider the uncertainty in both the incentive and rationality of the opponent.

In this paper, we reconsider Shubik's dollar auction but now in the repeated setting. We ask whether it is possible to design efficient bidding strategies, given the high level of uncertainty and no prior knowledge of the opponent. Put differently, we investigate whether a participant's knowledge about the opponent (gained in the previous encounters) can give the participant an edge over her opponent so that the escalation does not occur. To this end, we view the problem from the perspective of online learning theory, where the auctions are played against an adversary.

More specifically, we formulate the problem using an adversarial multi-armed bandit model [5, 25], where at each round we choose from a (finite) set of possible strategies $\mathcal{S}_0$ to play against the opponent. At the end of each round, we observe the outcome of the auction and update our estimation on the strategy's fitness (*i.e.*, how much expected profit the strategy can achieve). Our model also assumes that there is some level of interdependence between the different strategies. That is, by observing an outcome of a specific strategy, we can get some *side information* about the fitness of other strategies. For example, if a particular strategy wins the auction with a (final) bid b, then any other strategies that shares the same behaviour as the current one up to b (*i.e.*, the latter is a *prefix* of the former), would also win the auction. As such, we can also update our fitness estimate of the interdependent strategies as well.

Given this, we prove that by applying ELP (*i.e.*, "Exponentially weighted algorithm with Linear Programming")—a state-of-the-art online learning algorithm proposed by [25]—we can achieve $\tilde{O}(\sqrt{|\mathcal{S}_0|T})$ performance loss [1] against the best fixed bidding strategy (*i.e.*, playing the same strategy each round) in hindsight. In particular, since the regret is sub-linear due to the square root in $\tilde{O}(\sqrt{|\mathcal{S}_0|T})$, it implies that the average regret per time step is converging to 0 as T tends to infinity. Thus, the behaviour of ELP converges to that of the best fixed strategy in hindsight. While this result is a direct consequence of the performance analysis of ELP from [25], our main contributions are to improve this result to more concrete cases where we have some additional conditions. Specifically:

- By allowing some additional side-information structure (about the other strategies) that we obtain when observing the outcome of the chosen strategy, we prove that the performance loss can be bounded with $\tilde{O}(|\mathcal{S}_0|^{1/4}\sqrt{T})$, which is an improvement of $|\mathcal{S}_0|^{1/4}$ (note that this improvement is significant, especially when $|\mathcal{S}_0|$ is large);

- When $\mathcal{S}_0$ is the class of non-spiteful optimal bidding strategies with different budget limits, and the opponent is deterministic (*i.e.*, she chooses the next bids in a deterministic manner), the performance loss of the ELP-based bidding strategy is at most $\tilde{O}(\sqrt{T})$.

Finally, we show that when the auction is played between a non-spiteful and a malicious player, if both use ELP, they will converge to a Nash equilibrium.

[1]The logarithmic terms are hidden in the $\tilde{O}$ notation.

The remainder of the paper is organised as follows. We start by introducing the basic definitions and notation, and then outline our multi-armed bandit based bidding model. We then describe the ELP algorithm, and analyse its performance in different settings. The case of non-spiteful against malicious player is discussed afterwards, followed by the conclusions. Appendix provides notation table for the reader's convenience.

2. PRELIMINARIES

In this section, we formally describe the two building blocks of our problem, namely the dollar auction and the multi-armed bandit model.

2.1 The Dollar Auction

The dollar auction [34] is an all-pay auction between two players $N = \{0, 1\}$. We will often denote them by i and j. The winner of an auction is given the stake $s \in \mathbb{N}$. The players can make bids that are multiples of a minimal bid increment δ. Without loss of generality, we assume that $\delta = 1$.

While Shubik [34] considered the dollar auction without any budget limit, following O'Neill [31], most subsequent studies considered the setting in which players have limited budgets $b_0, b_1 \in \mathbb{N}$. In this paper, we assume that both players have equal budgets, *i.e.*, $b_0 = b_1 = b$.

The players move in turns and the starting player is determined randomly at the beginning of the auction. Moreover, the starting player i can either make the first bid, pass and leave the auction, or let j move first. Once the first bid has been made, any player making the move can either make a bid higher than the opponent, or pass. In other words, offering the turn to the opponent is only permitted before the first bid is made. We denote by X_b the set $\{(x, y) \in \{0, \ldots, b-1\} \times \{0, \ldots, b-1\} : y > x\} \cup \{(0, 0)\}$ where x is the last bid of the player currently choosing her bid and y is the last bid of her opponent. Whenever it is a player's turn to make a bid, the dollar auction would be in one of the states in X_b.

We assume that all the strategies in our setting are deterministic. Let us now consider $\mathcal{S}$ the set of all possible strategies in the dollar auction. We have $\mathcal{S} \subset X_b \to \{0, \ldots, b\}$, where for any strategy $f \in \mathcal{S}$, the value $f(x, y)$ represents the bid to be made by the player whose last bid was x and the last bid of her opponent was y. For valid strategies we have $f(x, y) \geq y$, where $f(0, 0) = 0$ represents the decision to let the opponent move first if the player starts (as it is never rational for any player to pass if her opponent has not made any bids yet), and $f(x, y) = y$ represents the decision to pass in all other cases. Set of strategies S contains all valid strategies, *i.e.*, strategies that meet conditions described above.

An auction ends when one of the players either passes or makes the bid that her opponent cannot top (in a setting with equal budgets this would mean bidding the entire budget). The stake is then given to the higher bidder. However, since this is an all-pay auction, both players have to pay their final bids. The profit of player i from an auction that ends with bids y_i and y_j is therefore:

$$p_i = \begin{cases} s - y_i & \text{if } y_i > y_j, \\ -y_i & \text{if } y_i < y_j. \end{cases}$$

2.2 The Multi-Armed Bandit Model

We now describe the *adversarial bandit* model [6], a variation of the *multi-armed bandit* problem [33]. In particular, it consists of T rounds, and a player can choose one of K actions (traditionally described as different slot machines, or bandits, hence the name of the multi-armed bandit model) to play at each round. However, before the player chooses her action to play, an adversary assigns an arbitrary reward vector $r(t) \in [0, 1]^K$, where $r(t) = (r_1(t), \ldots, r_K(t))$, without revealing it to the player. After the player chooses her action i_t to play, the value $r_{i_t}(t) \in [0, 1]$, which represents reward for performing action i_t in round t, is revealed to the player as her (collected) reward. The goal of the player then is to maximise her total collected reward over T rounds.

Let A denote the algorithm of playing actions chosen by the player, which selects action i_{t+1} at each in round $t + 1$ to perform (the choice of action may be based on the observed results $r_{i_1}(1), \ldots, r_{i_t}(t)$ of the previously chosen actions $i_1, \ldots, i_t$). The total collected reward, or the return, of algorithm A after T rounds is as follows:

$$R_A(T) = \sum_{t=1}^{T} r_{i_t}(t).$$

Since the value of each $r(t)$ is not revealed to the player, it is impossible to maximise the term above without having any additional information about $r(t)$. Instead, the performance of an algorithm is measured with a *regret*, which is defined as the difference between the return of the best fixed action over time and the return of the algorithm, namely:

$$U_A(T) = \max_i \sum_{t=1}^{T} r_i(t) - \sum_{t=1}^{T} r_{i_t}(t).$$

Within our bandit formulation, the repeated dollar auction problem provides side information. Within the bandit literature, the first work that fits our setting is the work of Mannor and Shamir [25], which introduced the multi-armed bandit model with side information. In particular, within their model, action j is a *neighbour* of action i chosen by the algorithm in round t if and only if for some fixed parameter d we are able to create unbiased estimator $\hat{r}_j(t)$ of the reward $r_j(t)$, *i.e.*, $\mathbb{E}[\hat{r}_j(t)|\text{action } i \text{ chosen in round } t] = r_j(t)$ and $\mathbb{P}(|\hat{r}_j(t)| \leq d) = 1$. Intuitively, we can use the knowledge gained from the execution of action i to estimate the reward of actions in its neighbourhood.

This extra information can be represented as a sequence of graphs $G_1, \ldots, G_T$ with K nodes each. Let $N_i(t)$ denote the neighbourhood of node i in graph G_t, *i.e.*, an edge from i to j exists in graph G_t if and only if $j \in N_i(t)$. Mannor and Shamir proposed an algorithm, called ELP, to efficiently tackle this bandit model. Here we will rely on the model of Mannor and Shamir and the ELP algorithm, and fit them to our setting of the repeated dollar auction.

3. META-BIDDING ALGORITHM

We now turn to the description of our bidding algorithm. In particular, this algorithm is a meta-strategy that consists of multiple dollar auction strategies played at each round, in order to minimize the regret from the series of auctions. To do so, we first describe the multi-armed bandit formulation of our problem. We then define the neighbourhood of a strategy within the strategy space. Finally we discuss how to tailor the ELP algorithm to our setting.

3.1 Model Description

In our setting, a player takes part in a series of T dollar auctions against the same opponent, each auction corresponds to a single round in the multi-armed bandit model. We assume that the player has at her disposal a set of strategies $\mathcal{S}_0 \subseteq \mathcal{S}$. Before each round t the player has to choose a strategy $f_t \in \mathcal{S}$ to be used in this particular round. Choice of strategy corresponds to the choice of an action (a playing arm) in the multi-armed bandit model. On the other hand, her opponent also chooses her strategy (equivalent of setting payoffs for each action). We do not put any explicit restrictions on the strategy of the opponent.

The auction is played using chosen strategies and the player achieves profit $p_{f_t}(t) \in \{-b + 1, \ldots, s\}$. The profit is then mapped to reward $r_{f_t}(t)$, corresponding to the reward in the multi-armed bandit model. We assume that always $r_{f_t}(t) \in [0, 1]$ (we normalise the rewards for the sake of simplicity). In case of a non-spiteful player (*i.e.*, player who just wishes to maximize her profit) reward depends only on her profit. We discuss the case of a malicious player, whose reward depends on the profit of her opponent in Section 6.

Given this, a meta-strategy is an algorithm that chooses a strategy to be used in each auction, based on the knowledge about previous auctions. Note that it corresponds to the algorithm of choosing an arm for each round in the multi-armed bandit model. The goal of the meta-strategy A is to minimize the regret after a series of auctions, regret being the difference between sum of rewards after using single best strategy in hindsight and after using a sequence of strategies chosen by the meta-strategy:

$$U_A(T) = \max_{g \in \mathcal{S}_0} \sum_{t=1}^{T} r_g(t) - \sum_{t=1}^{T} r_{f_t}(t).$$

3.2 Neighbourhood of a Strategy

We now define the relation of being a *prefix* strategy. In particular, strategy $g \in \mathcal{S}$ is a prefix of strategy $f \in \mathcal{S}$ if and only if $\forall_{(x,y) \in X_b} g(x, y) = f(x, y) \vee g(x, y) = y$. Intuitively, in every moment of the auction g either makes the same bid as f or passes. We can notice that f is also the prefix of itself. We can finally define *neighbourhood of the strategy* f as $N_f = \{g \in \mathcal{S} : g \text{ is a prefix of } f\}$. In fact, the following lemma justifies that playing a strategy provides side information about its prefixes.

LEMMA 1. *Assuming that player used strategy f in the dollar auction, we know the result of an auction if player used strategy g, that is a prefix of f.*

PROOF. After the auction using strategy f in round t we know a sequence of states $(x_1, y_1), \ldots, (x_n, y_n)$ when player was asked for a bid. If $\forall_i g(x_i, y_i) = f(x_i, y_i)$ then reward $r_g(t)$ for using g in auction would have been exactly the actual reward for using f, *i.e.*, $r_g(t) = r_f(t)$. Otherwise, reward for using g would have been $r_g(t) = -x_j$, where j is the lowest index such that $g(x_j, y_j) = y_j$, as the player would pass earlier than when using strategy f. □

3.3 The ELP Algorithm

We now describe how the ELP algorithm [25] can be adapted as a meta-bidding method in the dollar auction. The adaptation is based on the usage of previously defined set of prefixes

Algorithm 1 The ELP algorithm

Input: $\mathcal{S}_0 \subseteq \mathcal{S}$, β, $(\gamma(t))_{t=1}^{T}$, $(\cup_{f\in\mathcal{S}_0}\{q_f(t)\})_{t=1}^{T}$
$\forall_{f\in\mathcal{S}_0} w_f(1) \leftarrow \frac{1}{|\mathcal{S}_0|}$
for $t = 1, \dots, T$ **do**
  for $g \in \mathcal{S}_0$ **do**
    $P_g(t) \leftarrow (1-\gamma(t))\frac{w_g(t)}{\sum_{h\in\mathcal{S}_0} w_h(t)} + \gamma(t)q_g(t)$
  $f_t \sim P(t)$
  Play f_t getting reward $r_{f_t}(t)$
  for $g \in N_{f_t}$ **do**
    Compute $\hat{r}_g(t)$
  for $g \in \mathcal{S}_0$ **do**
    if $f_t \in N_g$ **then**
      $\tilde{r}_g(t) \leftarrow \frac{\hat{r}_g(t)}{\sum_{h\in N_g(t)} P_h(t)}$
    else
      $\tilde{r}_g(t) \leftarrow 0$
  for $g \in \mathcal{S}_0$ **do**
    $w_g(t+1) \leftarrow w_g(t)\exp(\beta\tilde{r}_g(t))$

as the neighbourhood of the strategy, in order to determine the potential profit of other strategies.

Algorithm 1 presents the pseudocode of ELP. The algorithm uses strategies from the provided set $\mathcal{S}_0 \subseteq \mathcal{S}$ to play a series of T dollar auctions, selecting a single strategy for each auction. Typically for multi-armed bandits algorithms, the ELP algorithm chooses between exploration (checking new strategies) and exploitation (using so far most promising strategies to generate profit). This trade-off is expressed by parameters $\gamma(t)$ and $q_f(t)$ of the algorithm. We will discuss the exact values of these parameters, that provide low regret bounds, later in the paper.

In round t algorithm selects strategy $f_t \in \mathcal{S}_0$ using a probability distribution $P(t)$ incorporating knowledge gained in previous rounds. Knowing reward $r_{f_t}(t)$ received for using selected strategy, algorithm computes reward $\hat{r}_g(t)$ that would have been received for playing strategy g from the neighbourhood of f_t in round t. Method of computing this reward is given in the proof of Lemma 1. Basically, for auction where player was making decision in states $(x_1, y_1), \dots, (x_n, y_n)$ we have $\hat{r}_g(t) = r_f(t)$ if $\forall_i g(x_i, y_i) = f(x_i, y_i)$ and $\hat{r}_g(t) = -x_j$ (where j is the lowest index such that $g(x_j, y_j) = y_j$) otherwise.

This reward is used to construct probability distribution in the next round. The higher the reward, the more probably the strategy is going to be used in the subsequent rounds.

3.4 Regret Analysis

We now give an upper bound for the regret of the ELP algorithm:

THEOREM 2. *Assume that the ELP algorithm is run using $\beta \in (0, \frac{1}{2|\mathcal{S}_0|})$, with $(q_f(t))_{f\in\mathcal{S}_0}$ parameters set such that $\forall_f q_f(t) \geq 0$, $\sum_f q_f(t) = 1$ and the value of*

$$\min_{f\in\mathcal{S}_0} \sum_{g\in N_f(t)} q_g(t)$$

is maximal (such values can be computed with linear programming). Moreover assume that $\gamma(t)$ parameters are set to

$$\gamma(t) = \frac{\beta}{\min_{f\in\mathcal{S}_0}\sum_{g\in N_f(t)} q_g(t)}.$$

In addition, let $\varepsilon = \min_{t,g}\gamma(t)q_g(t) > 0$. Then the upper bound on the regret of ELP is

$$U_A(T) \leq 9\beta T\alpha(G)\log\frac{6|\mathcal{S}_0|}{\alpha(G)\varepsilon} + \frac{\log(|\mathcal{S}_0|)}{\beta}.$$

where $\alpha(G)$ is the independence number of the underlying neighbourhood graph G of the strategies in $\mathcal{S}_0$.

PROOF. Following the proof of Theorem 3 in [25][2], we can show that

$$U_A(T) \leq \beta T\alpha G + 2\beta\sum_{t=1}^{T}\frac{P_f(t)}{\sum_{s\in N_f(t)} P_s(t)} + \frac{\log|\mathcal{S}_0|}{\beta}$$

From Lemma 13 of [2], we can further bound the second term of the RHS as follows:

$$\beta\sum_{t=1}^{T}\frac{P_f(t)}{\sum_{s\in N_f(t)} P_s(t)} \leq 2\alpha(G)\log\left(1 + \frac{\frac{|\mathcal{S}_0|^2}{\alpha(G)\varepsilon} + |\mathcal{S}_0| + 1}{\alpha(G)}\right) + 2\alpha(G)$$

By using elementary algebra, the RHS can be further bounded as:

$$\beta\sum_{t=1}^{T}\frac{P_f(t)}{\sum_{s\in N_f(t)} P_s(t)} \leq 2\alpha(G)\log\left(e^2\frac{\frac{|\mathcal{S}_0|^2}{\alpha(G)\varepsilon} + |\mathcal{S}_0| + \alpha(G) + 1}{\alpha(G)}\right)$$

which can be further bounded with

$$\beta\sum_{t=1}^{T}\frac{P_f(t)}{\sum_{s\in N_f(t)} P_s(t)} \leq 2\alpha(G)\log\left(9\frac{4\frac{|\mathcal{S}_0|^2}{\alpha(G)\varepsilon^2}}{\alpha(G)}\right) = 2\alpha(G)\log\left(\frac{6|\mathcal{S}_0|}{\alpha(G)\varepsilon}\right)$$

Here we exploit the facts that $1 \leq \alpha(G) \leq |\mathcal{S}_0|$ and $0 < \varepsilon < 1$. This implies that

$$U_A(T) \leq 9\beta T\alpha G\log\left(\frac{6|\mathcal{S}_0|}{\alpha(G)\varepsilon}\right) + \frac{\log|\mathcal{S}_0|}{\beta}$$

which concludes the proof. □

Choosing the value of β such that both components of the bound are equal, we get the following:

COROLLARY 3. *For $\beta = \sqrt{\frac{\log(|\mathcal{S}_0|)}{9T\alpha(G)\log\frac{6|\mathcal{S}_0|}{\alpha(G)\varepsilon}}}$ the bound defined in Theorem 2 equals to*

$$U_A(T) \leq 6\sqrt{\alpha(G)\log\frac{6|\mathcal{S}_0|}{\alpha(G)\varepsilon}\log(|\mathcal{S}_0|)T}.$$

Note that here we have $U_A(T) = \tilde{O}(\sqrt{\alpha(G)T})$. However, as $\mathcal{S}_0$ can be arbitrary, in the worst case scenario (when there is no side information at all by playing any particular strategy from $\mathcal{S}_0$), we have $U_A(T) = \tilde{O}(\sqrt{|\mathcal{S}_0|T})$, which can be quite large if the set of possible strategies $\mathcal{S}_0$ is large. A

[2]Note that the original proof of this theorem only considers oblivious opponents. However, by using the argument introduced in [32], we can apply the proof to adaptive adversaries as well.

possible way to improve the bound is to make the underlying neighbourhood graph denser. However, it is not trivial to provide such improvements. For example, assuming that even with a neighbourhood graph with a minimum degree of constant m (*i.e.*, m is independent from $|\mathcal{S}_0|$) would not help much. In fact, we state the following:

THEOREM 4. *There exists $\mathcal{S}_0 \in \mathcal{S}$ with minimum neighbourhood degree of m and a (randomised) opponent strategy, such that if $T > 374|\mathcal{S}_0|^3$, we have $U_A(T) \geq 0.6\sqrt{\frac{|\mathcal{S}_0|}{m+1}T}$ for any meta-strategy A.*

PROOF. From Theorem 4 of [25], we know that under the conditions given in the theorem, the following holds:

$$U_A(T) \geq 0.06\sqrt{\alpha(G)T}$$

Now, we just need to show that there exists $\mathcal{S}_0$ with minimum neighbourhood degree of m but $\alpha(G) \geq \frac{|Str_0|}{m+1}$. To do so, consider a set of groups of $m+1$ strategies such that within each group, there is one chosen strategy and the rest are a prefix of the chosen one. It is clear that the underlying neighbourhood graph G has at least $\frac{|\mathcal{S}_0|}{m+1}$ cliques, which implies that $\alpha(G) \geq \frac{|Str_0|}{m+1}$. □

That is, even in this case, we still have $U_A(T) = \Omega(\sqrt{|\mathcal{S}_0|T})$. Nevertheless, in the following sections, we investigate some special cases of the problem, in which this regret bound can be significantly improved.

4. BIDDING WITH RANDOM NEIGHBOURHOOD GRAPH

We first start with the scenario when some additional information are randomly added to the model. In particular, we assume that apart from the side information observed for prefixes of the chosen strategy, we have access to some additional information that can reveal the potential outcome of strategies other then the prefixes of the chosen one.

4.1 Random Neighbourhood

By random additional information, we mean that there is an oracle in the system, to whom we can send our requests to infer about the outcome of other (not-played) strategies, after observing the outcome of our chosen one. This assumption of having such an oracle is quite common in the online learning literature [42, 25]. Note that we do not consider query costs here in our model. In addition, we also assume that the result of a query is probabilistic, that is, it is revealed with some probability $v > 0$. As such, we can represent the neighbourhood graph of the dollar auction as a random graph $G(\mathcal{S}_0, v)$.

Random neighbourhood can model some additional expert knowledge acquired by the player. For example, during the negotiations (modelled by the dollar auction) some strategies can be considered more aggressive than others (and likely giving similar result), despite not being the prefix of each other (in the strict sense described in the previous sections). Another possible interpretations of the additional information include results of intelligence gathering in the arms race scenario (identifying the maximal number of troops or weapon units that our opponent can use during the conflict) or industrial espionage in the R&D competition scenario (abandoning research on technologies already tested by the competition).

4.2 Regret Analysis

Given the random neighbourhood model, we now turn to the regret analysis of the algorithm. In particular, we add the following conditions to the model:

$$|\mathcal{S}_0| \geq 8000 \quad (1)$$

$$1 \geq v \geq |\mathcal{S}_0|^{-\frac{1}{10}} \quad (2)$$

The first condition is reasonable as we typically consider large sets of strategies. The second condition guarantees that the neighbourhood graph is quite dense in general. We state the following:

THEOREM 5. *Suppose that conditions* (1)-(2) *hold. Under the same conditions of Theorem 2, with probability at least $1 - o(|\mathcal{S}_0|)$, we have the following regret bound for ELP* [3]*:*

$$U_A(T) \leq 3|\mathcal{S}_0|^{\frac{1}{4}}\sqrt{2\log\frac{36|\mathcal{S}_0|}{\varepsilon^2}\log(|\mathcal{S}_0|)T}.$$

PROOF. From [16] we have that with at least $1 - o(|\mathcal{S}_0|)$ probability, the following holds:

$$\alpha(G) \leq \frac{2}{v}\Big(\log|\mathcal{S}_0|v - \log\log|\mathcal{S}_0|v - \log 2 + 2\Big)$$

Since $|\mathcal{S}_0| > 8000$ and $v \geq |\mathcal{S}_0|^{-\frac{1}{10}}$, this can further bounded as:

$$\alpha(G) \leq \frac{2}{v}\Big(\log|\mathcal{S}_0|v + 2\Big) \leq 4\frac{\log|\mathcal{S}_0|}{v}$$

Note that we use $v \leq 1$ here. Now, since $v \geq |\mathcal{S}_0|^{-\frac{1}{10}}$, we have that

$$\alpha(G) \leq 4\frac{\log|\mathcal{S}_0|}{|\mathcal{S}_0|^{-\frac{1}{10}}} \leq \sqrt{|\mathcal{S}_0|}$$

The last inequality holds if $|\mathcal{S}_0| \geq 8000$. Applying this to Theorem 2 concludes the proof. □

Note that here we have $U_A(T) = \tilde{O}(|\mathcal{S}_0|^{\frac{1}{4}}\sqrt{T})$, which is a $|\mathcal{S}_0|^{\frac{1}{4}}$ improvement, compared to the regret bound of the general case. In the next section, we will show how this bound can be further improved by taking a different approach of modifying the neighbourhood model.

5. BIDDING WITH THRESHOLD

Beside adding further side information to the model, another way to simplify the underlying structure of the neighbourhood graph, and thus, to improve the induced regret bound, is to restrict the type of behaviour each player can follow. In this spirit, in this section we investigate a class of meta strategies that provides this simplification.

To do so, we first discuss the optimal non-spiteful strategy, proposed by O'Neill, that provides the basis of our class of behaviours. We then describe how to create a class of strategies, which we call optimal strategies with threshold. Finally, we show that by restricting to this class of strategies, we can further improve the previous regret bound with another factor of $|\mathcal{S}_0|^{\frac{1}{4}}$.

[3]Note that the $o(\cdot)$ notation here means that $o(|\mathcal{S}_0|) \to 0$ as $|\mathcal{S}_0|$ tends to infinity.

5.1 The Optimal Non-Spiteful Strategy

We first start with the discussion of the pure strategy in the dollar auction against a non-spiteful opponent that was proposed by O'Neill [31]. In particular, O'Neill proved that this strategy is optimal in terms of maximising the expected utility of the non-spiteful player, when played against a non-spiteful opponent.

Let the initial bid of the strategy be $x_0 = (b-1)mod(s-1)+1$, where b is the budget of both players, s is the stake and 1 is the minimal bid increment. In addition, let $x_i = x_0 + i(s-1)$ for $i > 0$ and let $x_{-1} = 0$. Given this, the optimal strategy of O'Neill $\hat{f}$ for $y \in \{x_{i-1}, \ldots, x_i - 1\}$ is:

$$\hat{f}(x,y) = \begin{cases} x_i & \text{if } x = x_{i-1}, \\ y & \text{otherwise.} \end{cases}$$

5.2 Optimal Strategies with Threshold

Based on the optimal strategy of O'Neill, we now propose a special class of strategies, using of which allow us to achieve better regret bound for ELP. In particular, let $\hat{f} \in \mathcal{S}$ be the optimal strategy by O'Neill described in the previous section. We call a strategy $f_\theta \in \mathcal{S}$ a *strategy with threshold* θ if and only if $\forall_{y<\theta} f_\theta(x,y) = \hat{f}(x,y)$ and $\forall_{y \geq \theta} f_\theta(x,y) = y$

Note that a strategy with threshold follows the optimal strategy by O'Neill up to a moment, when opponent's bid exceed threshold and then passes. The underlying intuition of this class of strategies is that in many cases, the bidder is rational (*i.e.*, bidding optimally), but is also risk-aware. To model the latter, we assume that the bidder is only willing to bid up to a certain threshold value, although her bidding budget would allow her to go beyond that threshold. As such, we argue that this class of strategies with threshold represents a realistic behaviour in many real-world situations.

5.3 Regret Analysis

We now turn to the regret analysis of ELP for the case of bidding with threshold. In particular, we assume that we only have access to the above defined class of non-spiteful strategies with threshold.

THEOREM 6. *Assume that set $\mathcal{S}_0$ contains all strategies with threshold $\theta \in \{0, \ldots, b\}$ and no other strategies. Under the abovementioned conditions and the settings of Theorem 2, the regret bound of the ELP algorithm is at most:*

$$U_A(T) \leq 9\beta T \log \frac{6|\mathcal{S}_0|}{\varepsilon} + \frac{\log(|\mathcal{S}_0|)}{\beta}.$$

PROOF. From Theorem 2 we have:

$$U_A(T) \leq 9\beta T \alpha G \log\left(\frac{6|\mathcal{S}_0|}{\alpha(G)\varepsilon}\right) + \frac{\log|\mathcal{S}_0|}{\beta}$$

where $\alpha(G)$ is the independence number of the information graph G.

Given two strategies with threshold f_θ and f_Θ, where $\theta < \Theta$, there is always an edge $f_\Theta \to f_\theta$ in the information graph for all rounds. If auction was lost while using f_Θ, then auction would have also been lost using f_θ and the result would be equal to $-x$, where x is a last bid of f_θ. If auction was won while using f_Θ, we know the last bid of opponent's strategy y. Since f_θ and f_Θ follow the same sequence of bids, then for $\theta \leq y$ auction would have been lost with the result of $-x$ (x being the last bid made by f_θ) and for $\theta > y$ auction would have been won with the result of $s - x$ (x being the lowest bid made by f_θ higher than y). Therefore, for the setting describe in the theorem, G is a clique and $\alpha(G) = 1$, which concludes the proof. □

Again, choosing the value of β such that both components of the bound are equal, we get the following:

COROLLARY 7. *For $\beta = \sqrt{\frac{\log(|\mathcal{S}_0|)}{9T \log \frac{6|\mathcal{S}_0|}{\varepsilon}}}$ the bound defined in Theorem 6 equals:*

$$U_A(T) \leq 6\sqrt{\log \frac{6|\mathcal{S}_0|}{\varepsilon} \log(|\mathcal{S}_0|)T}.$$

Note that $U_A(T) = \tilde{O}(\sqrt{T})$, which is an improvement of a factor of $|\mathcal{S}_0|^{\frac{1}{2}}$, compared to the regret bound of the general case.

6. AUCTION AGAINST MALICIOUS OPPONENT

So far we have shown that by applying ELP, we can still achieve low regret performance, despite the fact that there is no prior knowledge about the opponent's motives, neither about her rationality. We now introduce the concept of spitefulness and consider an auction against a malicious opponent. As argued by Waniek *et al.* [39], there are various real-world applications, in which the dollar auctions are played between *spiteful* players, whose objective function involves some linear combination of maximising one's own utility and minimising the opponent's utility. For instance, one may argue that certain moves of the USA or the Soviet Union during the Cold War were designed to harm the opponent even if it meant incurring some extra cost.

6.1 The Concept of Spitefulness

We interpret *spitefulness* as the desire of a player to hurt her opponent. We follow the definition of spitefulness introduced by Brandt *et al.* [9].

Any spiteful player i is characterised by a *spitefulness coefficient* $\sigma_i \in [0,1]$. The higher the coefficient, the more the player i is interested in minimizing the profit of her opponent j. The utility function of a spiteful player is then:

$$u_i = (1-\sigma_i)p_i - \sigma_i p_j.$$

where p_i and p_j are the profits of corresponding players.

A player with the spitefulness coefficient $\sigma = 0$ is called a *non-spiteful* player, and she is only interested in maximizing her own profit. On the other hand, a player with spitefulness coefficient $\sigma = 1$ is called a *malicious* player, and she is only interested in minimizing the profit of her opponent.

6.2 Mixed Nash Equilibrium

We now consider a case when a non-spiteful bidder plays the repeated dollar auctions against a malicious opponent, not knowing that the opponent is malicious. In addition, our opponent might not have full information about our non-spitefulness either and might not follow a rational behaviour. Given this, we assume that her strategy is taken from a set of $\mathcal{S}_1 \subseteq \mathcal{S}$.

If we knew the set $\mathcal{S}_1$ in advance (and the opponent also knows our set of strategies $\mathcal{S}_0$), a mixed Nash equilibrium can be easily calculated using standard arguments. However, as this knowledge is typically not available in advance, it is impossible to calculate the Nash equilibrium. Nevertheless, we show that if both players apply the ELP algorithm to play their strategies, we can converge to a Nash equilibrium point in performance.

THEOREM 8. *Let $f_i(t) \in \mathcal{S}_i, i \in \{0,1\}$ denote the bidding strategy of player i at round t, and we denote by $f_j(t)$ the strategy chosen by i's opponent. Let*

$$\tilde{f}_i = \frac{1}{T}\sum_{t=1}^{T} f_i(t),$$

$$\tilde{f}_j = \frac{1}{T}\sum_{t=1}^{T} f_j(t)$$

mixed strategies denote the average of these chosen strategies. Given this, for each T, there exists a mixed Nash equilibrium profile (f_i^*, f_j^*) such that

$$\left| r_i(f_i^*, f_j^*) - r_i(\tilde{f}_i, \tilde{f}_j)\right| \leq \tilde{O}\left(\sqrt{\frac{|\mathcal{S}_0|}{T}}\right)$$

PROOF. For the sake of simplicity we now map the profit of a player i to reward $r_i \in [-1,1]$ (instead of $r_i \in [0,1]$ as before). Reward $r_i = 1$ of the non-spiteful player i corresponds to a profit equal to the budget $p_i = b$, and reward $r_i = -1$ of the non-spiteful player corresponds to a loss equal to the budget $p_i = -b$. Reward of the malicious player is expressed as utility described in the previous section, *i.e.*, reward $r_i = 1$ of the malicious player i corresponds to a loss of the non-spiteful player j equal to the budget $p_j = -b$, and reward $r_i = -1$ of the malicious player i corresponds to a profit of the non-spiteful player j equal to the budget $p_j = b$.

Given that assumption, note that when a non-spiteful player bids against a malicious one, our problem can be regarded as a repeated zero-sum game. In fact, within this game, each player i (with $i \in \{0,1\}$) chooses from set of bidding strategies $\mathcal{S}_i$, the received reward of player i is r_i, and the received reward of her opponent (due to the malicious behaviour) is $r_j = -r_i$.

It is well known that in a 2-player zero-sum game, the minimax value exists and does coincide with the (mixed) Nash equilibrium. Given this, we only need to show that the average behaviour of the players, when both apply ELP, converges in performance to the minimax solution. To do so, let u^* denote the minimax value, which can be defined as follows:

$$u^* = \max_{f_i}\min_{f_j} r_i(f_i, f_j) = \min_{f_j}\max_{f_i} r_i(f_i, f_j)$$

where f_i and f_j are mixed strategies of players i and j, respectively. For now we consider the case that player i (non-spiteful) uses ELP, and player j can play any meta-strategy $\{f_j(t)\}_{t=1}^{T}$. In addition, let $BR(f_i(t))$ denote the best response mixed strategy against player i's $f_i(t)$ bidding strategy. By denoting

$$\Delta_T = 6\sqrt{\frac{\alpha(G)\log\frac{6|\mathcal{S}_0|}{\alpha(G)\varepsilon}\log(|\mathcal{S}_0|)}{T}},$$

from Theorem 2 we have that

$$\begin{aligned}\frac{1}{T}\sum_{t=1}^{T} r_i(t) &\geq \frac{1}{T}\max_{f\in\mathcal{S}_i}\sum_t r_i(f, f_j(t)) - \Delta_T \\ &= \frac{1}{T}\max_{\mathbf{f}}\sum_t r_i(\mathbf{f}, f_j(t)) - \Delta_T\end{aligned}$$

where $\mathbf{f}$ is a mixed strategy over $\mathcal{S}_i$. The first inequality is obtained from Theorem 2, while the second one is from the fact that the mixed strategy belongs to the convex hull of the pure strategies, and thus, cannot exceed the best pure strategy. This can be further bounded as follows:

$$\frac{1}{T}\max_{\mathbf{f}}\sum_t r_i(\mathbf{f}, f_j(t)) - \Delta_T \geq \frac{1}{T}\max_{\mathbf{f}}\sum_t \min_{\mathbf{g}} r_i(\mathbf{f},\mathbf{g}) - \Delta_T$$

where $\mathbf{g}$ is a mixed strategy over $\mathcal{S}_j$. This can be further bounded as:

$$\begin{aligned}\frac{1}{T}\max_{\mathbf{f}}\sum_t \min_{\mathbf{g}} r_i(\mathbf{f},\mathbf{g}) &\geq \max_{\mathbf{f}}\min_{\mathbf{g}} r_i(\mathbf{f},\mathbf{g}) - \Delta_T \\ &= u^* - \Delta_T\end{aligned}$$

That is, we have

$$\frac{1}{T}\sum_{t=1}^{T} r_i(t) \geq u^* - \Delta_T$$

Similarly, we can prove (from the malicious player's perspective) that

$$\frac{1}{T}\sum_{t=1}^{T} r_i(t) \leq u^* + \Delta_T$$

which concludes the proof. □

Note that this convergence in performance is a weaker property, compared to the convergence in strategy (*i.e.*, the average behaviour of the players converge to the distribution of the mixed strategy in the equilibrium point), as the latter automatically implies the former, while the other way is not true in general.

7. RELATED WORK

In this section we describe the bodies of literature concerning important aspects of our setting: all-pay auctions, repeated auctions and multi-armed bandit models.

7.1 All-Pay Auctions and the Dollar Auction

All-pay auctions were studied as a model multiple settings where expenditure of the resource does not always guarantee profit [24]. Some of them include political campaigns, R&D competitions of oligopolistic companies [38], realizing crowdsourcing enterprises [14] and international situation analysis [34]. Aside from theoretical studies, there is also experimental research [12]. The dollar auction is a widely studied type of an all-pay auction[23, 22]. It is often used in a classroom experiments serving a study of conflict escalation among people [29, 19].

Recently, Waniek *et al.* [39] offered a preliminary study of a dollar auction in which a spiteful player plays against a rational opponent. The authors considered the setting in which a non-spiteful bidder unwittingly bids against a spiteful one. In various scenarios in this setting the conflict escalates. In particular, the spiteful bidder is able to force the non-spiteful opponent to spend most of the budget. Still, it is the spiteful bidder who often wins the prize. Furthermore, a malicious player with a smaller budget is likely to plunge the opponent more than a malicious player with a bigger budget. Thus, a malicious player should not only hide his real preferences but also the real size of his budget.

7.2 Repeated Auctions

Modelling various processes as repeated auctions is a well established idea [41]. Among other applications, it was used for allocating tasks to robots [30] and assigning channels in radio network [17]. Many authors concentrate on the problem of possible collusion in repeated auctions [3, 35, 26], focusing their attention on the effect of cooperation between players on the income of an auctioneer [7]. Most of the published results consider second-price auctions [20, 7], however all-pay auction format was also studied [28].

7.3 Multi-Armed Bandits

The first multi-armed bandit models were designed to tackle problems with stochastic rewards [33, 1, 4]. The first adversarial setting was proposed by Auer *et al.* [5, 6]. However, in the early years, adversarial bandit models were believed to be only suitable against non-adaptive opponents. The argument that justified the usage of multi-armed bandits against adaptive opponents was first proposed by Poland [32], whose techniques was adopted by many more recent works. Mannor and Shamir[25] extended the adversarial bandit model to the case when additional side information is provided to improve the regret bounds of the model. Their work was later improved by [2] and [21]. In particular, the former improved the regret bound, while the latter focuses on the cases when the neighbourhood graph cannot be fully revealed in advance (*i.e.*, before the chosen arm is played).

8. CONCLUSIONS

In this paper, we investigated the problem of repeated dollar auctions in which players do not have prior knowledge about the opponent's spitefulness, neither her rationality level. We proposed an adversarial multi-armed bandit model to efficiently tackle this problem, in which the goal is to maximise the players' total utility over time. We showed that by using an adversarial bandit based meta-strategy, ELP, we can indeed provably achieve good performance. We then further improved this performance by considering additional settings of the model: (i) dollar auctions with random neighbourhood graphs; and (ii) playing optimal strategies with thresholds. We also proved that in a special case of non-spiteful player *versus* malicious player, if both use ELP to make their decisions, the game converges to a mixed Nash equilibrium in performance.

As a potential future work, we aim to extend our work to repeated auctions where the auctions share the same budget. That is, apart from making decision about which strategy to use per each auction, the players also have to choose the budget allocated to a particular auction, without exceeding an *a priori* given global limit. As our current techniques significantly rely on the fact that the current budgets are given, it seems to be highly not trivial how to extend our model to such settings. Furthermore, until now, the literature on the dollar auction focused on the case of two players. Hence, it would be very interesting to extend all the results to multiple players.

Acknowledgments

Tran-Thanh gratefully acknowledges funding from the UK Research Council for project "ORCHID", grant EP/I011587/1. Tomasz Michalak was supported by the European Research Council under Advanced Grant 291528 ("RACE").

APPENDIX

Table 1: Notation

Symbol	Meaning
i,j	Players participating in the auction
s	Stake of the auction
δ	Minimal bid increment
b	Budget of both players
X_b	States where player can make a bid
$\mathcal{S}$	Set of all valid strategies in the auction
$\mathcal{S}_0$	Set of available strategies
p_i	Profit of player i
T	Number of rounds (separate auctions)
A	Algorithm selecting strategies
$R_A(T)$	Total reward of algorithm A after T rounds
$U_A(T)$	Regret of algorithm A after T rounds
$r_f(t)$	Reward for using strategy f in round t
G	Neighbourhood graph
$\alpha(G)$	Independence number of graph G
N_f	Neighbourhood of strategy f
f_t	Strategy selected to use in round t
β,$\gamma(t)$,$q_f(t)$	Parameters of the ELP algorithm
$w_f(t)$	Weight of choosing strategy f in round t
$P_g(t)$	Probability of selecting strategy f in round t
$\hat{r}_f(t)$	Estimated reward for using str. f in round t
v	Prob. of revealing additional information
$G(\mathcal{S}_0, v)$	Random neighbourhood graph of strat. $\mathcal{S}_0$
θ	Threshold of a strategy
σ_i	Spitefulness coefficient of player i

REFERENCES

[1] R. Agrawal. Sample mean based index policies with o(log n) regret for the multi-armed bandit problem. *Advances in Applied Probability*, 27:1054–1078, 1995.

[2] N. Alon, N. Cesa-Bianchi, C. Gentile, and Y. Mansour. From bandits to experts: A tale of domination and independence. In *Advances in Neural Information Processing Systems*, pages 1610–1618, 2013.

[3] M. Aoyagi. Bid rotation and collusion in repeated auctions. *Journal of Economic Theory*, 112(1):79–105, 2003.

[4] P. Auer, N. Cesa-Bianchi, and P. Fischer. Finite–time analysis of the multiarmed bandit problem. *Machine Learning*, 47:235–256, 2002.

[5] P. Auer, N. Cesa-Bianchi, Y. Freund, and R. E. Schapire. Gambling in a rigged casino: The adversarial multi-armed bandit problem. In *Foundations of Computer Science, 1995. Proceedings., 36th Annual Symposium on*, pages 322–331. IEEE, 1995.

[6] P. Auer, N. Cesa-Bianchi, Y. Freund, and R. E. Schapire. The nonstochastic multiarmed bandit problem. *SIAM Journal on Computing*, 32(1):48–77, 2002.

[7] S. Bikhchandani. Reputation in repeated second-price auctions. *Journal of Economic Theory*, 46(1):97–119, 1988.

[8] K. E. Boulding. Conflict and defense: A general theory. 1962.

[9] F. Brandt, T. Sandholm, and Y. Shoham. Spiteful bidding in sealed-bid auctions. In *Computing and Markets*, 2005.

[10] J. Campos, C. Martinho, and A. Paiva. Conflict inside out: A theoretical approach to conflict from an agent point of view. AAMAS '13, pages 761–768. International Foundation for Autonomous Agents and Multiagent Systems, 2013.

[11] C. Castelfranchi. Conflict ontology. In *Computational Conflicts*, pages 21–40. Springer, 2000.

[12] E. Dechenaux, D. Kovenock, and R. M. Sheremeta. A survey of experimental research on contests, all-pay auctions and tournaments. WZB Discussion Paper SP II 2012-109, Berlin, 2012.

[13] G. Demange. Rational escalation. *Annales d'ÃL'conomie et de Statistique*, (25/26):pp. 227–249, 1992.

[14] D. DiPalantino and M. Vojnovic. Crowdsourcing and all-pay auctions. In *EC'09*, pages 119–128. ACM, 2009.

[15] H. Fang. Lottery versus all-pay auction models of lobbying. *Public Choice*, 112(3-4):351–371, 2002.

[16] A. M. Frieze. On the independence number of random graphs. *Discrete Mathematics*, 81(2):171–175, 1990.

[17] Z. Han, R. Zheng, and H. V. Poor. Repeated auctions with bayesian nonparametric learning for spectrum access in cognitive radio networks. *Wireless Communications, IEEE Transactions on*, 10(3):890–900, 2011.

[18] A. J. Jones. *Game theory: Mathematical models of conflict*. Elsevier, 2000.

[19] J. H. Kagel and D. Levin. Auctions: a survey of experimental research, 1995–2008. 2008.

[20] J. L. Knetsch, F.-F. Tang, and R. H. Thaler. The endowment effect and repeated market trials: Is the vickrey auction demand revealing? *Experimental economics*, 4(3):257–269, 2001.

[21] T. Kocák, G. Neu, M. Valko, and R. Munos. Efficient learning by implicit exploration in bandit problems with side observations. In *Advances in Neural Information Processing Systems*, pages 613–621, 2014.

[22] V. Krishna and J. Morgan. An analysis of the war of attrition and the all-pay auction. *journal of economic theory*, 72(2):343–362, 1997.

[23] W. Leininger. Escalation and cooperation in conflict situations the dollar auction revisited. *Journal of Conflict Resolution*, 33(2):231–254, 1989.

[24] Y. Lewenberg, O. Lev, Y. Bachrach, and J. S. Rosenschein. Agent failures in all-pay auctions. IJCAI/AAAI, 2013.

[25] S. Mannor and O. Shamir. From bandits to experts: On the value of side-observations. In *Advances in Neural Information Processing Systems*, pages 684–692, 2011.

[26] R. C. Marshall and L. M. Marx. Bidder collusion. *Journal of Economic Theory*, 133(1):374–402, 2007.

[27] H. J. Müller and R. Dieng. On conflicts in general and their use in ai in particular. In *Computational conflicts*, pages 1–20. Springer, 2000.

[28] J. Münster. Repeated contests with asymmetric information. *Journal of Public Economic Theory*, 11(1):89–118, 2009.

[29] J. K. Murnighan. A very extreme case of the dollar auction. *Journal of Management Education*, 26(1):56–69, 2002.

[30] M. Nanjanath and M. Gini. Repeated auctions for robust task execution by a robot team. *Robotics and Autonomous Systems*, 58(7):900–909, 2010.

[31] B. O'Neill. International escalation and the dollar auction. *Journal of Conflict Resolution*, 30(1):33–50, 1986.

[32] J. Poland. Fpl analysis for adaptive bandits. *3rd Symposium on Stochastic Algorithms, Foundations and Applications (SAGA'05)*, pages 58–69, 2005.

[33] H. Robbins. Some aspects of the sequential design of experiments. *Bulletin of the AMS*, 55:527–535, 1952.

[34] M. Shubik. The dollar auction game: A paradox in noncooperative behavior and escalation. *Journal of Conflict Resolution*, pages 109–111, 1971.

[35] A. Skrzypacz and H. Hopenhayn. Tacit collusion in repeated auctions. *Journal of Economic Theory*, 114(1):153–169, 2004.

[36] C. Tessier, L. Chaudron, and H. J. MÃijller. Agents' conflicts: New issues. In *Conflicting Agents*, volume 1 of *Multiagent Systems, Artificial Societies, And Simulated Organizations*, pages 1–30. Springer US, 2002.

[37] W. W. Vasconcelos, M. J. Kollingbaum, and T. J. Norman. Normative conflict resolution in multi-agent systems. *AAMAS'09*, 19(2):124–152, 2009.

[38] X. Vives. Technological competition, uncertainty, and oligopoly. *Journal of Economic Theory*, 48(2):386–415, 1989.

[39] M. Waniek, A. Niescieruk, T. Michalak, and T. Rahwan. Spiteful bidding in the dollar auction. In *Proceedings of the 24th International Conference on Artificial Intelligence*, pages 667–673. AAAI Press, 2015.

[40] D. Weyns and T. Holvoet. Regional synchronization for simultaneous actions in situated multi-agent systems. pages 497–510, 2003.

[41] E. Wolfstetter. Auctions: an introduction. *Journal of economic surveys*, 10(4):367–420, 1996.

[42] J. Y. Yu and S. Mannor. Piecewise-stationary bandit problems with side observations. In *Proceedings of the 26th Annual International Conference on Machine Learning*, pages 1177–1184. ACM, 2009.

A Synergy Coalition Group based Dynamic Programming Algorithm for Coalition Formation

Luke Riley
Dept. of Computer Science
University of Liverpool, UK
L.J.Riley@Liverpool.ac.uk

Katie Atkinson
Dept. of Computer Science
University of Liverpool, UK
K.M.Atkinson@Liverpool.ac.uk

Paul E. Dunne
Dept. of Computer Science
University of Liverpool, UK
P.E.Dunne@Liverpool.ac.uk

Terry R. Payne
Dept. of Computer Science
University of Liverpool, UK
T.R.Payne@Liverpool.ac.uk

ABSTRACT

Coalition formation in characteristic function games entails agents partitioning themselves into a coalition structure and assigning the numeric rewards of each coalition via a payoff vector. Various coalition structure generation algorithms have been proposed that guarantee that an optimal coalition structure is found. We present the Synergy Coalition Group-based Dynamic Programming (SCG-DP) algorithm that guarantees that an optimal coalition structure *and* a least core stable payoff vector is found. This is completed by extending the existing results for the Synergy Coalition Group (SCG) representation to show that only coalitions in the SCG are needed to find a weak-least core stable payoff vector. The SCG-DP algorithm builds on this result by performing only the search operations necessary to guarantee that coalitions in the SCG of the given characteristic function game are found. The number of operations required is significantly less for many coalition-value distributions compared to the original Dynamic Programming (DP) algorithm [34] that finds an optimal coalition structure (e.g. only ~60% of DP's coalition lookup operations are performed in SCG-DP for 18 agents using a normal coalition-value distribution). Our experimental results show that a lower bound for these operations in SCG-DP converges onto 50%. This is an increase on the $\sim 33\%$ bound of the optimal dynamic programming (ODP) algorithm [14], but ODP does not search for a stable solution.

General Terms

Algorithms, Economics, Theory

Keywords

Coalition Formation; Dynamic Programming; Synergy Coalition Groups; Cooperative Game Theory

1. INTRODUCTION

Coalition formation is a process whereby agents recognise that co-operation with others can occur in a mutually beneficial manner and therefore the agents can choose appropriate temporary groups (named coalitions) to form. But determining the set of coalitions that should form is difficult due to: (a) the exponential number of different possible coalitions; (b) the exponential number of possible sets of coalitions; and (c) the many ways in which the agents of a coalition can agree to distribute its rewards between its members (if this reward is transferable between the agents).

Therefore, coalition formation can be thought of as a three stage process [25, 27]: (1) calculating the value of each possible coalition; (2) finding an optimal set of coalitions; and (3) dividing the value of the coalitions in a manner that no agent can object to.

A set of coalitions, known as a *coalition structure*, is an *optimal* coalition structure if it has the - possibly joint - highest total value of all the possible coalition structures (i.e. it maximises social welfare). In *characteristic function games*, where the set of agents must be divided into exhaustive and disjoint coalitions, finding an optimal coalition structure is known as the *coalition structure generation problem* [27]. This problem has been proved to be NP-complete [27], yet there have been algorithms developed to combat this complexity [21]. The algorithms that provide a guarantee that an optimal coalition structure will be found, can be divided into the following two categories (for a more detailed description of these two categories see [24]):

1. **Dynamic programming algorithms:** This is the collection of algorithms where the main problem is solved by dividing it up into sub-problems and then solving the smallest first. The answers to the smallest problems help with answering the larger problems [8]. There are coalition structure generation dynamic programming algorithms (e.g. see [14, 19, 22]) that are modifications of an algorithm presented in [34], which solves the complete set partitioning problem. The main advantage of the dynamic programming algorithms is that an optimal coalition structure is guaranteed to be found in $O(3^n)$ time. Yet a disadvantage is that an optimal coalition structure is only returned when the algorithm completes.
2. **Tree search algorithms:** These algorithms divide the search space into subspaces that are searched using depth-first and branch-and-bound techniques, where the quality of the solution gets better over time (in some well behaved manner). Some example algorithms in this category are: [7, 15, 25, 27]. The main disadvantage of these algorithms is that the worst case running time is $O(n^n)$.

Additionally, there exists algorithms that combine aspects of both of these categories (e.g. see [14, 29]). However all of these coali-

Appears in: *Proceedings of the 15th International Conference on Autonomous Agents and Multiagent Systems (AAMAS 2016), J. Thangarajah, K. Tuyls, C. Jonker, S. Marsella (eds.), May 9–13, 2016, Singapore.*

tion structure generation algorithms do not consider the third stage of coalition formation; payoff distribution. When agents are adversarial, an agent will only join a coalition if it is given a payoff that is stable (i.e. a payoff that cannot reasonably be objected to[1]). It can even be beneficial for benevolent agents to only join a coalition if the payoff they receive is stable [4].

In this paper, the *Synergy Coalition Group-based Dynamic Programming* (SCG-DP) algorithm is introduced, that locates an optimal coalition structure and concurrently identifies the *Synergy Coalition Group* (SCG), which is used to guarantee that a weak-least core or weak-least core^{+} stable payoff distribution is also found (where the plus sign indicates cross coalitional payoff transfers are allowed). The SCG-DP algorithm achieves these results, even though it cuts down significantly on the number of operations required by the original Dynamic Programming (DP) algorithm [34] for many different coalition-value distributions.

The rest of the paper is structured as follows: Section 2 introduces the background to characteristic function games, core-based stability concepts and the SCG. Section 3 introduces the theoretical foundations that SCG-DP is built upon, including a theorem that shows a weak-least core solution can always be found using the SCG. Section 4 details SCG-DP, discusses why SCG-DP satisfies certain solution concepts, and describes a SCG-DP example. Section 5 evaluates SCG-DP against the Optimal Dynamic Programming algorithm [14] and the DP algorithm [34], according to the number of split operations performed and the number of coalition lookup operations. Finally Section 6 concludes and describes future work.

2. BACKGROUND

2.1 Characteristic Function Games

The *characteristic function game* model of coalition formation [18] is denoted: $\mathcal{G} = \langle N, v\rangle$ where $N = \{1, 2, ..., n\}$ is the set of agents, and v is the *characteristic function* ($v(2^N) \to \mathbb{R}$) which assigns every possible coalition a real numeric payoff. Characteristic function games assumes that each coalition's value is static, deterministic and independent of the other coalitions that could form.

An *outcome* of a characteristic function game $\mathcal{G} = \langle N, v\rangle$ for n agents is a coalition structure and payoff vector pair, denoted: $\langle CS, x\rangle$, where CS is a set of k coalitions $CS = \{C_1, ..., C_k\}$ and x is the payoff vector $x = (x_1, ..., x_n)$. Occasionally in this paper, notation is abused so that $x(C) = \sum_{i\in C} x_i$. The coalition structure CS has the following properties: $\bigcup_{j=1}^{k} C_j = N$; and $C_i \cap C_j = \emptyset$ for any $i, j \in \{1, ..., k\}$ where $i \neq j$. To find a *stable outcome* of a characteristic function game, all the agents should have *no valid objection*. Stability is a necessary but not sufficient condition for a payoff vector (or coalition structure) to be agreed upon, because there can be multiple possible stable outcomes.

2.2 Core-based Stability Solution Concepts

The idea of a valid objection changes depending on which stability solution concept is used. Perhaps the most intuitive stability solution concept is known as the **core** [10]. The core is the set of stable outcomes where no subset of agents have an incentive to deviate, i.e., there is no payoff distribution that would make at least one member of a deviating coalition better off, without negatively affecting the other members of the deviating coalition[2].

[1]Definitions of stability are discussed in Section 2.2.

[2]In this section, the core is introduced, not the CS-core, as the CS-core has been shown to not be able to guarantee that the optimal coalition structure is CS-core stable [2, 28].

Definition 1: *The* **core***:- For a characteristic function game $\mathcal{G} = \langle N, v\rangle$, a payoff vector $x = (x_1, ..., x_n)$ for the grand coalition is in the core iff:*

$$\sum_{i\in N} x_i = v(N) \qquad \sum_{i\in C} x_i \geq v(C), \forall C \subset N$$

A problem with the core is that it can sometimes be empty. To tackle this issue, the concept of the *ε-core* was introduced in [30], where the ε-core is a more general case of the core. Two different definitions of the *ε-core* were introduced, named the *strong ε-core* and the *weak ε-core*. This paper focuses on the weak ε-core:

Definition 2: *The* **weak ε-core***:- For a characteristic function game $\mathcal{G} = \langle N, v\rangle$ and a value ϵ, a payoff vector $x = (x_1, ..., x_n)$ for the grand coalition is in the weak ε-core iff:*

$$\sum_{i\in N} x_i = v(N) \qquad \sum_{i\in C} x_i \geq v(C) - |C|\epsilon, \ \forall C \subset N$$

Notice when $\epsilon = 0$, the weak ε-core definition is equivalent to the core. The difference between the strong and weak ε-cores is that under the weak definition, the penalty of forming a new coalition is dependent on its size, while the penalty for forming a new coalition under the strong definition is a fixed amount for any coalition.

The *weak least core* is the smallest, non-empty weak ε-core [30]:

Definition 3: **weak least core***:- For a characteristic function game $\mathcal{G} = \langle N, v\rangle$, a payoff vector x is in the weak least core iff:*

$$x \text{ is in the weak } \epsilon\text{-core and } \forall \epsilon' < \epsilon, \text{ the weak } \epsilon'\text{-core is empty}$$

It should be mentioned that core/ε-core stable payoff vectors can be found with payoff vector transfer schemes (such as [3, 13, 33]), which take a characteristic function game outcome, iteratively apply an operation on it and converge to an element of the ε-core. Yet all of [3, 13, 33] do not detail the search for the optimal coalition structure (they assume the grand coalition forms) and only [13] presents a method to find an element of the least core.

Additionally, a non-cooperative game theoretic approach to coalition formation is through coalitional bargaining, which describes how stable characteristic function game outcomes occur via a process of non-cooperative bargaining and outlines equilibrium concepts that characterise the agent's behaviour in these games.

The coalitional bargaining papers of [5, 9, 17] detail how non-cooperative game theoretic solution concepts match the cooperative solution concept of the core. But these studies do not detail what *cooperative* game solution concept is found when the core is empty.

2.3 Synergy Coalition Groups

When searching for stability, it may not be necessary to check all possible coalitions. The synergy coalition group (SCG) [6] has been shown to include all the coalitions needed to guarantee that a core stable solution can be found. A coalition C is said to introduce synergy, if C has a greater value than any possible disjoint and non-overlapping partition of C. A SCG is defined as follows:

Definition 4: ***A synergy coalition group*** *W consists of a set of pairs of the form $(C, v(C))$. A pair is only in W if it details a coalition that gives synergy to its members. The singleton coalitions are assumed to always be represented within W. For any coalition $C \in (C, v(C)) \in W$, the value of C is $v(C)$. For any coalition $C' \notin W$, the value of C' is: $v(C') = \max(\sum_{C_j\in P_{C'}} v(C_j))$ where $P_{C'} = \{C_1, C_2, ..., C_k\}$ is a partition of C' such that: (a) $\bigcup_{i=1}^{k} C_i = C'$; (b) $C_i \cap C_j = \emptyset$ for any $C_i, C_j \in P_{C'}$ where $i \neq j$; and (c) $(C_j, v(C_j)) \in W$, for all $C_j \in P_{C'}$.*

If a coalition C' is not represented within W, then its value comes from its highest valued partition, as long as this partition has the following properties: (a) all the agents of C' are in a coalition of the partition and there are no additional agents in the partition; (b) each agent of C' occurs in only one coalition of the partition; and (c) each coalition in the partition is represented within W.

Example 1: *Consider the characteristic function game* $G = \langle N, v\rangle$ *where* $N = \{1,2,3,4\}$ *and the SCG representation W gives the following valuations:* $W = \{(\{1\},2),(\{2\},1),(\{3\},1),(\{4\},2),(\{1,2\},5)\}$ *(i.e. the utility value of agent 1 by itself is 2, while the utility value of the coalition, of agents 1 and 2, is 5)*.

Example values of coalitions that are not explicitly represented are: $v(\{3,4\}) = v(\{3\})+v(\{4\}) = 1+2 = 3$*;* $v(\{1,2,3\}) = v(\{1,2\})+v(\{3\}) = 5+1 = 6$*; and* $v(\{1,2,3,4\}) = v(\{1,2\})+v(\{3\})+v(\{4\}) = 5+1+2 = 8$.

The SCG model described in [6] can only represent superadditive characteristic functions. In [16] the original definition of SCG was expanded on, by adding the requirement that if a coalition is explicitly listed in W then it cannot be divided further (note: a coalition may now be listed in W even if it gives no synergy):

Example 2: *Consider the characteristic function game* $G = \langle N, v\rangle$ *where* $N = \{1,2,3,4\}$ *and the SCG representation W gives the following valuations:* $W = \{(\{1\},5),(\{2\},1),(\{3\},1),(\{4\},2),(\{1,2\},3)\}$ *(i.e. the utility value of agent 1 by itself is 5, while the utility value of the coalition, of agents 1 and 2, is 3)*.

Example values of coalitions that are not explicitly represented are: $v(\{1,3\}) = v(\{1\})+v(\{3\}) = 5+1 = 6$*; and* $v(\{1,2,3\}) = v(\{1,2\})+v(\{3\}) = 3+1 = 4$ *(because* $\{1,2\}$ *is in W)*.

In [16], it was shown that it is guaranteed that there will always be an optimal coalition structure (CS^*) with only coalitions in the SCG. The proof consists of showing that if a coalition C is in a coalition structure and not the SCG, then C can be replaced by a partition of C (consisting of only coalitions in the SCG), which has a value equal to or higher than $v(C)$. This is a result you would expect given Definition 4.

Additionally in [16], it was shown how an CS^* could be identified given the SCG as input. This is a different problem from the one studied in this paper, where the SCG-DP algorithm takes a characteristic function game as input and locates an CS^* while concurrently searching for the SCG.

It should be noted that in this paper the additional requirement of [16] is not used, instead the original [6] definition of a SCG is preferred. We show that the original definition is satisfactory to find an CS^* when it is recognised in the SCG-DP algorithm that the value of a coalition $C \notin W$ is in fact the value of C's highest valued partition. Therefore if C is included in CS^*, then in fact SCG-DP should replace C in CS^* with C's highest value partition, and each coalition in the highest value partition will be replaced if it is not in W (and so on until all the coalitions in CS^* are in W).

3. THEORETICAL FOUNDATIONS

Now that the background has been introduced, the foundations that the SCG-DP algorithm is built upon can be detailed.

In Section 3.1 the properties of a synergy coalition group (SCG) are expanded upon. In Section 3.2 we detail what parts of the search space the SCG-DP algorithm must consider.

3.1 Guaranteeing Stable Solutions

When the characteristic function game is superadditive, then the grand coalition is the optimal coalition structure [18]. In Lemma 2 and Theorem 4 of [6] it is proven that the W set of the SCG allows a core solution to be found if the core is non-empty. This Lemma and Theorem have been extended below to show that a payoff vector in the weak least core can also be guaranteed to be found for the grand coalition using the W set (an example follows the lemma):

LEMMA 3.1. *Given a characteristic function game* $\mathcal{G} = \langle N, v\rangle$ *and a payoff vector* x *(where* $\sum_{i\in N} x_i = v(N)$*), let* ϵ^w *be the maximum weak* ϵ *penalty value that still gives an objecting coalition for* x *given full knowledge on each coalition's value. In this situation, an objecting coalition* D *for* ϵ^w *will be present within* W.

PROOF. Suppose x is objected to by a coalition C through $v(C) - |C|\epsilon^w$ because $v(C) - |C|\epsilon^w > x(C)$, and assume that $\forall \epsilon_i^w > \epsilon^w$ there is no objecting coalition. If $(C, v(C)) \in W$ then this proves the lemma. If $(C, v(C)) \notin W$ then from the definition of a SCG, it is known that the value of the coalition can be found through its maximum value partition, i.e. $v(C) - |C|\epsilon^w = \sum_{1\leq j\leq k}(v(C_j) - |C_j|\epsilon^w)$, for some set of coalitions $P_C = \{C_1, ..., C_k\}$ where:

1. $\bigcup_{j=1}^{k} C_j = C$;
2. $C_i \cap C_j = \emptyset$ for any $i, j \in \{1, ..., k\}$ where $i \neq j$; and
3. $(C_j, v(C_j)) \in W$, for all $C_j \in \{C_1, ..., C_k\}$

Via substitution, it follows that $\sum_{1\leq j\leq k}(v(C_j) - |C_j|\epsilon^w) > x(C) = \sum_{1\leq j\leq k} x(C_j)$ and hence for at least one C_j then the following holds: $v(C_j) - |C_j|\epsilon^w > x(C_j)$. Therefore if a coalition C that is not in the SCG representation objects to a payoff vector x given the maximum ϵ^w that still gives an objecting coalition, it has been shown that there exists a coalition $C_j \subset C$, that also objects to x given ϵ^w, yet C_j is represented explicitly within the SCG representation (i.e. $(C_j, v(C_j)) \in W$). Thus the proof is complete. □

Lemma 3.1 shows that given a superadditive characteristic function game, the grand coalition and a payoff vector distributing the grand coalition's value, a coalition that objects to the payoff vector for the maximum weak ϵ penalty value (that allows an objecting coalition) will be present in the SCG representation. For further understanding, consider the following example:

Example 3: *Consider a characteristic function game with* $N = \{1,2,3,4\}$ *agents, where the coalition* $C = \{1,2,3\}$ *has a value of* $v(\{1,2,3\}) = 25$*. In this example, a payoff vector* x *gives the coalition* C *the total payoff of* $x(C) = 18$*. Therefore it is known that the maximum (integer)* weak ϵ *penalty value for* x *that* C *will object to is* $\epsilon^w = 2$*. This is because* $v(C) - |C|\epsilon^w = 25 - (3\times 2) = 25 - 6 = 19 > x(C) = 18$*. Coalition* $\{1,2,3\}$ *does* not *object to* x *when* $\epsilon^w = 3$ *because* $25 - (3\times 3) = 16 < x(C) = 18$.

If $C \in W$*, then an objecting coalition for the maximum objection-allowing weak* ϵ *value has been found in the SCG representation. If* $C \notin W$ *then there must be coalitions within* W *that make up a partition of* C *and have an equal or greater combined value than* C*. For this example assume* $(\{1,2\}, v(\{1,2\}) = 16), (\{3\}, v(\{3\}) = 9) \in W$*. These valuations have been chosen because* $v(\{1,2\}) + v(\{3\}) = v(\{1,2,3\})$*, i.e. the values total the minimal needed to make sure that coalition* $\{1,2,3\}$ *is not in the SCG representation.*

Given theses preliminaries, to stop coalition $\{1,2\}$ *being an objecting coalition when* $\epsilon^w = 2$*, then* $x(\{1,2\})$ *must be greater than or equal to* $v(\{1,2\}) - |\{1,2\}|\epsilon^w = 16 - (2\times 2) = 12$*. Assume that* $x(\{1,2\}) = 12$ *(i.e. the minimal payoff to satisfy the coalition has been given).*

Recall that $x(\{1,2,3\}) = 18$*. Therefore* $x_3 = x(\{1,2,3\}) - x(\{1,2\}) = 18 - 12 = 6$*. But this gives* $v(\{3\}) - |\{3\}|\epsilon^w = 9 - (1\times 2) = 9 - 2 = 7 > x(\{3\}) = 6$ *and so the singleton coalition* $\{3\}$ *will object to* x *when* $\epsilon^w = 2$ *and this objecting coalition has been found in the SCG (as singletons are in W).*

In conclusion, this example demonstrates that if an objecting coalition C for the maximum weak ϵ penalty value (that still admits an objecting coalition) is not *present in the SCG representation, then a coalition $C' \subset C$ that is present in the SCG representation will object to the same weak ϵ penalty value.*

The following theorem shows that given the grand coalition, the coalitions in the SCG representation can be used to find a payoff vector within the weak least core:

THEOREM 3.2. *For the grand coalition, a payoff vector that gives the minimum weak ϵ value for stability to occur can be found using only the coalitions in W.*

PROOF. The value of the grand coalition can be allocated by the payoff vector x by solving the following linear program that minimises ϵ:

$$\min \epsilon \text{ subject to:}$$

$$x_i \geq 0 \text{ for each } i \in N \tag{1}$$

$$x(N) = v(N) \tag{2}$$

$$x(C) \geq v(C) - |C|\epsilon, \text{ for all } (C, v(C)) \in W \tag{3}$$

Only the coalitions in W are needed to be used in this linear program, according to Lemma 3.1. □

Before introducing the corollary to this theorem, a formal definition regarding cross-coalition side payments is required, which is shown through the weak ϵ-core$^+$ and weak least core$^+$ definitions:

Definition 5: *The* **weak ϵ-core$^+$**:- *For a characteristic function game $\mathcal{G} = \langle N, v \rangle$, a coalition structure and payoff vector pair $\langle CS^*, x \rangle$ is in the weak ϵ-core$^+$ iff:*

$$\sum_{i \in N} x_i = CS^* \qquad \sum_{i \in C} x_i \geq v(C) - |C|\epsilon, \ \forall C \subseteq N$$

The difference of the weak ϵ-core$^+$ compared to the weak ϵ-core of Section 2.2 is that a weak ϵ-core$^+$ payoff vector totals the value of the optimal coalition structure, which may not be the grand coalition. Additionally as the weak ϵ-core$^+$ does *not* have the condition that all the payoff of each coalition in the coalition structure is given to that coalition (i.e. $x(C) = v(C), \forall C \in CS^*$ does *not* have to hold), then cross-coalitional payoff vector transfers can occur. As noted in [1, 11], allowing cross-coalition side payments can benefit multi-agent systems, as it was argued that introducing cross-coalition side payments can be considered a more fair payoff mechanism. The additional fairness comes from eliminating the effect of the coalition structure on agent payoffs. The example given in [1], is that it may be possible that in the optimal coalition structure some agents $M \subset N$ are by themselves in singletons, or are members of a comparatively small coalition compared to the size of the other coalitions in the coalition structure. When cross-coalition side payments are not allowed, these M agents do not benefit from the cooperation of others, even when the M agents are in many potential coalitions that have a high value, which the agents $N \backslash M$ may have used to negotiate for a better payoff. Yet, for the greater good of the population (i.e., maximizing social welfare), the M agents may be forced to stay in the optimal coalition structure.

Given the definition of the weak ϵ-core$^+$, the weak least core$^+$ can be defined:

Definition 6: **weak least core$^+$**:- *For a characteristic function game $\mathcal{G} = \langle N, v \rangle$, a coalition structure and payoff vector pair $\langle CS^*, x \rangle$ is in the weak ϵ-core$^+$ iff:*

$$\langle CS^*, x \rangle \text{ is in the weak } \epsilon\text{-core}^+$$

$$\forall \epsilon' < \epsilon, \text{ the weak } \epsilon'\text{-core}^+ \text{ is empty}$$

Given the formal definition regarding cross-coalition side payments, we can introduce the corollary to Theorem 3.2:

COROLLARY 3.2.1. *For the grand coalition of a superadditive cover, a payoff vector in the weak least core$^+$ can be found using only the coalitions in W.*

PROOF. Replace the characteristic function v with the superadditive cover characteristic function v^* in Lemma 3.1 and Theorem 3.2. Now the grand coalition's value will be equal to the optimal coalition structure. This guarantees that a weak least core$^+$ solution for the superadditive cover is found. □

Given Corollary 3.2.1, the SCG-DP algorithm introduced in this paper identifies the following to guarantee that a weak least core$^+$ stable solution is found: (a) the coalitions in the SCG representation W; and (b) an optimal coalition structure that maximises the value of the superadditive cover of the grand coalition. If cross-coalition side payments were not allowed, then it would be much more difficult for the agents to reason over what is the most stable coalition structure and payoff vector pair, as [2, 28] showed that optimal coalition structures may not be the most stable coalition structure. So in this case, multiple coalition structures will have to be compared via not just their value, but also their stability. Searching all possible coalition structures is a highly complex task because the total possible number of coalition structures grows at a significantly higher rate than the number of potential coalitions [27]. For n agents, the number of possible coalition structures is found using the Bell number B_n, which is $\sim \theta(n^n)$ and so significantly larger then the $\theta(2^n)$ growth of possible coalitions [27]. Therefore it is of great benefit to the agents to significantly minimise the number of possible coalition structures to compare.

In this paper, the SCG-DP algorithm assumes cross-coalition side payments are allowed because it significantly reduces the computation costs as multiple coalition structures will not have to be compared according to their stability.

3.2 Search Space Guarantees

Before we detail our search space guarantees, various preliminaries need to be introduced:

Definition 7: *A* **split** *of a coalition C, is a two-set partition of C, denoted $[C^x, C^y]$ where:*

$$|C^x| \leq |C^y|, \ C^x \cup C^y = C \ \text{ and } C^x \cap C^y = \emptyset.$$

Additionally the following condition holds (i.e. that if the same size, then C^x has to be smaller lexicographically than C^y):

$$\text{if } |C^x| = |C^y| \text{ then } C^x <_{lex} C^y$$

A split $[C^x, C^y]$ can also be written as $[C^x, -]$, which indicates a split that has only had its first partition generated. The second partition can then be generated subsequently from $N \backslash C^x$ if required.

A split of a coalition can be further divided into *split-partitions*:

Definition 8: *A* **split-partition** *is a multi-partition set, denoted SP $= \{C^x_1, ..., C^x_p, C^y_1, ..., C^y_q\}$, and is derived from a two-set partition $[C^x, C^y]$ of an original coalition C. A split-partition has the following properties:*

$$\bigcup_{j=1}^{p} C^x_j = C^x, \qquad \bigcup_{j=1}^{q} C^y_j = C^y,$$

$$C^x_i \cap C^x_j = \emptyset \text{ for any } i, j \in \{1, ..., p\} \text{ where } i \neq j \text{ and}$$

$$C^y_i \cap C^y_j = \emptyset \text{ for any } i, j \in \{1, ..., q\} \text{ where } i \neq j.$$

Therefore the previous definition states that the agents in coalition C^x cannot be mixed with the agents of the coalition C^y in the split partition. Next we define the following functions:

- *AllSplits*(C) returns all the splits that can be made from coalition C.
- *AllSParts*$([C^x, C^y])$ returns all the split-partitions of $[C^x, C^y]$.

Our last preliminary definition introduces the concept of split coverage:

Definition 9: *A split* $[C^x, C^y]$ *is said to* **cover** *a split-partition* SP *iff* $\exists SP' \in$ AllSParts$([C^x, C^y])$ *where* $\forall C_j \in SP$ *then* $C_j \in SP'$.

Example 4: *Consider a coalition* $C_1 = \{1, 2, 3, 4, 5, 6\}$ *and the splits* $[\{2, 3\}, \{1, 4, 5, 6\}]$ *and* $[\{1\}, \{2, 3, 4, 5, 6\}]$. *A split partition of* $[\{2, 3\}, \{1, 4, 5, 6\}]$ *is* $SP_1 = \{\{2, 3\}, \{1\}, \{4\}, \{5, 6\}\}$. *Yet* SP_1 *is covered by* $[\{1\}, \{2, 3, 4, 5, 6\}]$ *because the larger coalition* $\{2, 3, 4, 5, 6\}$ *can be broken up into* $\{2, 3\}$, $\{4\}$ *and* $\{5, 6\}$. *Another split partition of* $[\{2, 3\}, \{1, 4, 5, 6\}]$ *is* $SP_2 = \{\{2, 3\}, \{1, 4\}, \{5, 6\}\}$. *But* SP_2 *is not covered by* $[\{1\}, \{2, 3, 4, 5, 6\}]$ *because, by the definition of a split-partition,* $\{1\}$ *must be by itself (as* $\{1\}$ *cannot be grouped with any agents of* $\{2, 3, 4, 5, 6\}$*).*

As the ODP algorithm showed [14], not all splits for each coalition are needed to be analysed to guarantee that an optimal coalition structure (CS^*) can be found. SCG-DP identifies the SCG of the given characteristic function game, as there is always an CS^* that will only contain coalitions in the SCG [16]. Therefore when SCG-DP searches for CS^* it only considers: (i) coalitions from the SCG that it has identified; and (ii) splits that can lead to an analysis of a new coalition structure involving only SCG coalitions.

When SCG-DP is seeking to identify if a coalition C is in the SCG, it does not have to check every possible split of that coalition. This is because some splits include coalitions not in the SCG and some splits cover only split-partitions previously analysed by another split of C.

The SCG-DP algorithm starts generating splits of a coalition C where the size of the smallest coalition in the split $[C^x, C^y]$ is of size $|C^x| = 1$ and SCG-DP continues generating splits of C until the size of C^x is greater than $\lfloor \frac{|C|}{2} \rfloor$ (i.e. when all possible splits have been generated).

Lemma 3.3 and Theorem 3.4 show that given a split $[C^x, C^y]$ of C where $|C^y| < 2 * |C^x|$, then the value of $[C^x, C^y]$ only needs to be compared to $v(C)$ (to find the best valued partition of C and check if $(C, v(C)) \in W$) if both $(C^x, v(C^x)), (C^y, v(C^y)) \in W$. This is because, when $|C^y| < 2 * |C^x|$, every possible split-partition of $[C^x, C^y]$ will have been covered by a split of C that includes a smaller sized coalition than C^x.

LEMMA 3.3. *Consider a coalition* C *and a split* $[C^x, C^y] \in$ AllSplits(C) *where* $|C^y| < 2 * |C^x|$. *Given* $[C^x, C^y]$ *and a split-partition* $SP \in$ AllSParts$([C^x, C^y])$, *then* there exists *another split* $[D^x, D^y] \in$ AllSplits(C) *where* $|D^x| < |C^x|$ *and the following holds:* $SP \in$ AllSParts$([D^x, D^y])$.

PROOF. Assume a split $[C^x, C^y] \in$ *AllSplits*(C) has the property $|C^y| < 2 * |C^x|$, and that $SP \in$ *AllSParts*$([C^x, C^y])$ cannot be found by any $[D^x, D^y] \in$ *AllSplits*(C) where $|D^x| < |C^x|$. For this assumption to hold true, then SP cannot contain a partition E^x_i of size $|E^x_i| < |C^x|$, otherwise SP would have been covered by a split that includes D^x where $D^x = E^x_i$.

When $|C^y| < 2 * |C^x|$ then at least one of the partitions in the split-partition SP has a size less than $|C^x|$. If the last coalition E^y_q of the split-partition SP has the size of $|C^x|$ then $\sum_{i=1}^{p} |E^x_i| + \sum_{i=1}^{q-1} |E^y_i| = |C^y| - |C^x|$. But as $|C^x|$ is greater than half of $|C^y|$, then there exists an $E^x_j \leq |C^y| - |C^x| < |C^x|$, which contradicts the assumption as SP will have to contain at least one partition E^x_j with a size smaller than $|C^x|$. □

Exactly how small $|E^x_j|$ is, depends on how many p elements of E^x and q elements of E^y there are in the split-partition.

The following theorem shows that given a split $[C^x, C^y]$ where $|C^y| < 2 * |C^x|$, then this split only needs to be assessed by SCG-DP to find W, if both C^x and C^y are in the SCG:

THEOREM 3.4. *Consider a coalition* C *and a split* $[C^x, C^y] \in$ AllSplits(C) *where* $|C^y| < 2 * |C^x|$. *Then the SCG-DP algorithm needs to compare* $v(C)$ *to* $f_2[C^x] + f_2[C^y]$ *as part of the checks to see if* $(C, v(C)) \in W$, *only if* $(C^x, v(C^x)), (C^y, v(C^y)) \in W$.

PROOF. According to Lemma 3.3, each split-partition $SP \in$ *AllSParts*$([C^x, C^y])$ has been covered by a split $[D^x, D^y]$ where $|D^x| < |C^x|$. Therefore the value of each SP has already been compared against $v(C)$ when analysing $[D^x, D^y]$ because SCG-DP generates the splits according to the size of the smallest coalition in it (from size 1 to $\lfloor \frac{|C|}{2} \rfloor$). Therefore, only the split $[C^x, C^y]$ (i.e. the split itself and not any split-partitions) has not been compared against $v(C)$. But if one of C^x or C^y is not in W, then one of $[C^x, C^y]$'s split-partitions were of greater or equal value than $[C^x, C^y]$ and so the following is guaranteed to hold: $v(C) \geq f_2(C^x) + f_2(C^y)$. □

The next lemma and theorem show that given a split $[C^x, C^y]$ of C where $|C^y| \geq 2 * |C^x|$, then the value of $[C^x, C^y]$ needs to be compared to $v(C)$ if C^x in the SCG. This is because, when $|C^y| \geq 2 * |C^x|$, there are many possible split-partitions of $[C^x, C^y]$ that will *not* have been covered by a split with a smaller sized coalition than C^x.

LEMMA 3.5. *Consider a coalition* C *and a split* $[C^x, C^y] \in$ AllSplits(C) *where* $|C^y| \geq 2 * |C^x|$. *Given* $[C^x, C^y]$ *and a split-partition* $SP \in$ AllSParts$([C^x, C^y])$, *then* there may not exist *a split* $[D^x, D^y] \in$ AllSplits(C) *where* $|D^x| < |C^x|$ *and* $SP \in$ AllSParts$([D^x, D^y])$.

PROOF. Assume a split $[C^x, C^y] \in$ *AllSplits*(C) has the property $|C^y| \geq 2 * |C^x|$, and that $SP \in$ *AllSParts*$([C^x, C^y])$ can always be found by any $[D^x, D^y] \in$ *AllSplits*(C) where $|D^x| < |C^x|$. For this assumption to hold true, then SP cannot contain only partitions of sizes $\geq |C^x|$, otherwise SP would *not* have been covered by a split that included D^x.

When $|C^y| \geq 2 * |C^x|$ then at least one split-partition SP can be found that includes only partitions that have sizes $\geq |C^x|$. For example, a 3-part split-partition of sizes $|C^x|$, $\lfloor \frac{|C^y|}{2} \rfloor$ and $\lceil \frac{|C^y|}{2} \rceil$ can be made, and because $|C^y| \geq 2 * |C^x|$ the assumption is contradicted. □

The following theorem shows that given a split $[C^x, C^y]$ where $|C^y| \geq 2 * |C^x|$, then this split only needs to be assessed by SCG-DP to find W, if C^x is in the SCG:

THEOREM 3.6. *Consider a coalition* C *and a split* $[C^x, C^y] \in$ AllSplits(C) *where* $|C^y| \geq 2 * |C^x|$. *Then the SCG-DP algorithm needs to compare* $v(C)$ *to* $f_2[C^x] + f_2[C^y]$ *as part of the checks to see if* $(C, v(C)) \in W$, *only if* $(C^x, v(C^x)) \in W$.

PROOF. According to the previous lemma, a split-partition $SP \in$ *AllSParts*$([C^x, C^y])$ may not have been covered by a split $[D^x, D^y]$ when: (a) SP only includes partitions of sizes greater than or equal to $|C^x|$; (b) $|D^x| < |C^x|$; and (c) $|C^y| \geq 2 * |C^x|$. All split-partitions that include partitions of sizes greater or equal to $|C^x|$,

Algorithm 1: The SCG-DP algorithm to find an optimal coalition structure and a stable payoff vector.

1: **function** `SCG-DP` (N, v)
2: **Input:** $\langle N, v\rangle$; where N is the global set of agent IDs and v is the characteristic function.
3: **Output:** $\langle CS^*, x\rangle$; where CS^* is the optimal coalition structure and x is a stable payoff vector.
4: **begin**;
5: $W = \emptyset$; // holds the SCG representation
6: **for** $i \in N$ **do**
7: *set* $f_1[\{i\}] := \{i\}$, $f_2[\{i\}] := v(\{i\})$ and $(\{i\}, f_2[\{i\}]) \in W$;
8: **end for**
9: **for** $s := 2$ to n **do**
10: **for** each $C \subseteq N$ where $|C| = s$ **do**
11: $\Psi = \texttt{EvalSplits}(C, W)$
12: $f_2[C] := \max\{v(C), \max_{[C^x, C^y] \in \Psi}(f_2[C^x] + f_2[C^y])\}$;
13: **if** $f_2[C] < v(C)$ **then**
14: *set* $f_1[C] := C$ and $(C, f_2[C]) \in W$;
15: **else**
16: *set* $f_1[C] := C^*$ where C^* maximises $f_2[C]$;
17: **end if**
18: **end for**
19: **end for**
20: *set* $CS^* := \{N\}$
21: **for** each $C_i \in CS^* = \{C_1, ... C_k\}$ **do**
22: **if** $C_i \notin W$ **then**
23: *set* $CS^* := (CS^* \backslash \{C\}) \cup \{f_1[C]\}$;
24: *restart* this for loop from C_i;
25: **end if**
26: **end for**
27: $x = \texttt{FindStablePayoff}(W)$
28: **return** $\langle CS^*, x\rangle$;
29: **end**;

must include C^x due to the definition of split-partitions. Yet if $(C^x, v(C^x)) \notin W$ then this split does not need to be analysed anyway as an optimal coalition structure can always be found using only the coalitions in W. □

To conclude this section, the SCG-DP algorithm implements implements Theorem 3.4 and Theorem 3.6 (to make sure that the necessary splits are analysed) via its `EvalSplits` function (see Algorithm 2) in lines 8 to 11 and lines 12 to 14 respectively. In the `EvalSplits` function, C^y is generated only when needed, to save on computation, therefore both of the following are used in the function: (a) $|C^y|$ is substituted with $n - |C^x|$; and (b) C^y is only generated if $(C^x, v(C^x)) \in W$.

4. THE SCG-DP ALGORITHM

The SCG-DP algorithm (see Algorithm 1) takes a characteristic function game as input and follows the style of the other dynamic programming algorithms in the literature. That is, SCG-DP breaks the coalition structure generation problem up into finding the highest valued partition of each subset of the grand coalition in size order from smallest subset to largest (line 6 and 9).

To find an optimal coalition structure (CS^*), like DP of [34], the SCG-DP algorithm uses: (a) the f_1 table where $f_1[C]$ is set to equal the highest valued split of C if this is greater or equal to $v(C)$, otherwise $f_1[C] = C$ (lines 14 and 16); and (b) the f_2 table

Algorithm 2: The `EvalSplits` function finds which splits of the coalition C should be checked by `SCG-DP` to find out whether C is in the SCG representation.

1: **function** `EvalSplits` (C, W)
2: **Input:** $\langle C, W\rangle$; where C is the coalition to assess the splits of, and W is the SCG representation.
3: **Output:** $\Psi = \{[C^x, C^y]_1, ..., [C^x, C^y]_k\}$;
4: **begin**;
5: $\Psi = \emptyset$; $p = 1$;
6: **for** $r = 1$ to $r > \lfloor\frac{|C|}{2}\rfloor$ **do**
7: **for** each $[C^x, -] \in AllSplits(C)$ where $|C^x| = r$ **do**
8: **if** $n - |C^x| < 2 * |C^x|$ **and** $(C^x, f_2[C^x]) \in W$ **then**
9: **if** $(C^y, f_2[C^y]) \in W$, where $C^y = N \backslash C^x$ **then**
10: $[C^x, C^y]_p \in \Psi$; $p++$;
11: **end if**
12: **else if** $n - |C^x| \geq 2 * |C^x|$ **and** $(C^x, f_2[C^x]) \in W$ **then**
13: $[C^x, C^y]_p \in \Psi$, where $C^y = N \backslash C^x$; $p++$;
14: **end if**
15: **end for**
16: **end for**
17: **return** Ψ;
18: **end**;

where $f_2[C]$ holds the value of C (if $f_1[C] = C$) or the value of C's highest-valued split (line 12). But crucially the difference between SCG-DP and DP is that SCG-DP's search for the CS^* does not involve considering every possible split of every coalition $C \subseteq N$. Only the splits returned by the `EvalSplits` function are considered (line 11). The ODP algorithm of [14] also does not consider every possible split when searching for an CS^*. The SCG-DP and ODP algorithms are compared in Section 5.

Additionally, SCG-DP, unlike the DP and ODP algorithms, collects the SCG representation in W at two points: (1) Firstly by the definition of the SCG, the singleton coalitions should be in W (line 7); and (2) When every split-partition of C has a value less than $v(C)$ (line 13 and 14). In practice, if C is in W can be recorded simply via a boolean, as the value of C is saved in f_2.

After f_1 and f_2 are computed, the optimal coalition structure CS^* is found recursively in the same manner as the DP algorithm. This is performed by first setting the CS^* equal to the grand coalition (line 20) and then performing a loop (lines 21 to 26) where all the coalitions in the CS^* are checked to see if they are in the SCG (line 22). If a coalition $C \notin W$, then it needs to be replaced by its highest valued partition. This process continues until all the coalitions in CS^* are members of the SCG.

Finally, the coalitions that have been collected into W are used to find a stable payoff vector (line 27). Details of this are described in Section 4.1. Once the stable payoff vector has been found, the characteristic function game outcome will be returned (line 28).

4.1 Solution Concept Satisfiability

As has been described, the SCG-DP algorithm locates all the coalitions in the SCG representation (i.e. it finds W). Given W, various guarantees can be made on the payoff vector x that is returned from the `FindStablePayoff` function (which follows Corollary 3.2.1 in Section 3.1). These guarantees are provided via Theorem 3.2 and Corollary 3.2.1 and depend on the characteristic function game given as input to the SCG-DP algorithm:

- A **core** solution will be found when the characteristic function game has a superadditive v.

- A **weak-least core** solution will be found when the grand coalition is the optimal coalition structure but not core-stable.
- A **weak-least core**$^+$ solution will be found when the grand coalition is *not* the optimal coalition structure. In this case, cross-coalition side payments may occur.

The superadditive cover characteristic function v^*, referred to in Corollary 3.2.1, has been found in the SCG-DP via the f_2 table.

If cross coalition side payments are undesirable, SCG-DP could be modified to find the most stable CS^*. The section of the SCG-DP that finds an CS^* can instead find all the CS^*s. Then each CS^* can be compared via stability. This procedure is known as the optimality gap [28] and significantly cuts down on the number of coalition structures to compare via their stability, as the number of CS^*s is usually significantly less than all the coalition structures.

4.2 An Example of the Algorithm

To show how SCG-DP works, due to space considerations, we focus on the evaluation of two coalitions of size $s = 4$ in a $n = 5$ agent characteristic function game. The following evaluation is also presented in Table 1. As the coalitions are evaluated in size order (see line 6 and 9 of SCG-DP), then coalitions of size $1, 2$ and 3 have already been analysed by SCG-DP. Within those sizes, the following were found to be in the SCG (in this example): $(\{1\}, 1), (\{2\}, 1.2), (\{3\}, 0.8), (\{4\}, 1.2), (\{5\}, 0.9), (\{1, 3\}, 2), (\{2, 5\}, 2.3), (\{3, 5\}, 2), (\{2, 3, 5\}, 3.7) \in W$.

Now for a coalition of size 4, there are 7 different splits, which are shown in the first 7 lines of the second column of Table 1 for each coalition. To find out if a split should be compared to the coalition's value (displayed in the 8th line of column 2 for each coalition), the `EvalSplit` function generates the first coalition C^x of the split and generates the second coalition C^y if $C^x \in W$. Then if the split $[C^x, C^y]$'s value is compared to the value of the coalition depends on the size of C^x, as shall be explained.

Take the first split of coalition $\{1, 2, 3, 4\}$, i.e. $[\{1\}, \{2, 3, 4\}]$. This split satisfies the following: $n - |C^x| = 5 - 1 \geq 2 * |C^x|$ (where $C^x = \{1\}$). Therefore lines 12 to 14 of the `EvalSplit` function is run. As singletons are always in the SCG, then line 13 states that C^y should be generated (hence coalition $\{2, 3, 4\}$ is shown in the table) and that this split should be analysed (hence a numeric result is shown in the table). The value 4.2 is found as $v(\{1\}) = 1$ and the highest valued disjoint partition of $\{2, 3, 4\}$ in the SCG has a value of 3.2, because $v(\{2\}) + v(\{3\}) + v(\{4\}) = 1.2 + 0.8 + 1.2 = 3.2$. Alternatively, in the second line, the best valued partition of $\{1, 3, 4\}$ is also 3.2 but this time because $v(\{1, 3\}) + v(\{4\}) = 2 + 1.2 = 3.2$.

Now consider splits of the form $[C^x, C^y]$ where $|C^x| = |C^y| = 2$ for the same coalition $\{1, 2, 3, 4\}$. The first split of this kind is $[\{1, 2\}, \{3, 4\}]$. This split satisfies the following: $n - |C^x| = 5 - 2 < 2 * |C^x|$ (where $C^x = \{1, 2\}$). So lines 8 to 11 of the `EvalSplit` function are run. As $\{1, 2\} \notin W$, the if statement of line 8 evaluates to false, therefore the C^y coalition of the split is not generated (hence $-$ is shown in the table) and the split is not evaluated (hence N/A is shown in the table). Alternatively, for the split $[\{1, 3\}, \{2, 4\}]$, $C^y = \{2, 4\}$ is generated because $\{1, 3\} \in W$ but the split is not evaluated as $\{2, 4\} \notin W$.

Coalition	The evaluations performed before setting f_1 and f_2	f_1	f_2	In W?
$\{1, 2, 3, 4\}$	$f_2[\{1\}] + f_2[\{2, 3, 4\}] = 4.2$ $f_2[\{2\}] + f_2[\{1, 3, 4\}] = 4.4$ $f_2[\{3\}] + f_2[\{1, 2, 4\}] = 4.2$ $f_2[\{4\}] + f_2[\{1, 2, 3\}] = 4.4$ $f_2[\{1, 2\}] + f_2[-] =$ N/A $f_2[\{1, 3\}] + f_2[\{2, 4\}] =$ N/A $f_2[\{1, 4\}] + f_2[-] =$ N/A $v[\{1, 2, 3, 4\}] = 4.6$	$\{1, 2, 3, 4\}$	4.6	Yes
$\{1, 2, 3, 5\}$	$f_2[\{1\}] + f_2[\{2, 3, 5\}] = 4.7$ $f_2[\{2\}] + f_2[\{1, 3, 5\}] = 4.1$ $f_2[\{3\}] + f_2[\{1, 2, 5\}] = 4.1$ $f_2[\{5\}] + f_2[\{1, 2, 3\}] = 4.1$ $f_2[\{1, 2\}] + f_2[-] =$ N/A $f_2[\{1, 3\}] + f_2[\{2, 5\}] = 4.3$ $f_2[\{1, 5\}] + f_2[-] =$ N/A $v[\{1, 2, 3, 5\}] = 4.3$	$\{1\}\{2, 3, 5\}$	4.7	No

Table 1: This table details the splits and coalitions generated, for coalitions $\{1, 2, 3, 4\}$ and $\{1, 2, 3, 5\}$ in the characteristic function game described in Section 4.2.

5. EXPERIMENTAL EVALUATION

This section will provide an evaluation through the discussion of: (a) the number of split operations to be performed for different agent numbers; and (b) the number of coalition lookup operations to be performed for different agent numbers.

An experimental analysis was used as both (a) and (b) are dependent on the coalition-value distribution, which the SCG-DP algorithm has no *a priori* knowledge on. The experiments were run using: (i) different agent numbers from 5 to 20, where 30 runs for each agent number were used; and (ii) differing coalition-value distributions, which include normal, uniform and NDCS, as is usual in the coalition structure generation literature (see [12, 15, 23, 25]). These coalition-value distributions are defined as:

- *Uniform*:- Each coalition's value is determined by multiplying the number of agents in the coalition by a variable q picked from a uniform distribution between 0 and 1.0. Formally, $v(C) = max(0, |C| \times q)$, where: $q \in \mathcal{U}(a, b)$; $a = 0$; and $b = 1.0$.
- *Normal*:- Each coalition's value is determined by multiplying the number of agents in the coalition by a variable q picked from a normal distribution with mean 1 and variance 0.1. Formally, $v(C) = max(0, |C| \times q)$, where: $q \in \mathcal{N}(\mu, \sigma^2)$; $\mu = 1$; and $\sigma^2 = 0.1$.
- *NDCS*:- Each coalition's value is determined by a variable q picked from a normal distribution with mean of the coalition's size and variance also according to the coalition's size. Formally, $v(C) = max(0, q)$, where: $q \in \mathcal{N}(\mu, \sigma^2)$; $\mu = |C|$; and $\sigma^2 = |C|$.
- *Subadditive*:- A characteristic function game is subadditive if for any two disjoint coalitions D and E, where $D, E \subset N$ and $D \cap E = \emptyset$, then $v(D \cup E) \leq v(D) + v(E)$.
- *Strictly superadditive*:- A characteristic function game is strictly superadditive if for any two disjoint coalitions D and E, where $D, E \subset N$ and $D \cap E = \emptyset$, then $v(D \cup E) > v(D) + v(E)$.

In this section the SCG-DP algorithm is compared to the Optimal Dynamic Programming (ODP) algorithm described in [14] for the above coalition-value distributions. SCG-DP seeks to minimise the number of split operations to find an optimal and stable coalition structure (whatever the coalition-value distribution), while ODP minimises the number of split operations to find the optimal coalition structure (whatever the coalition-value distribution).

5.1 Number of Analysed Splits

The number of analysed splits for a coalition C is defined as the splits of C that are considered for $f_2[C]$. In SCG-DP, this equals

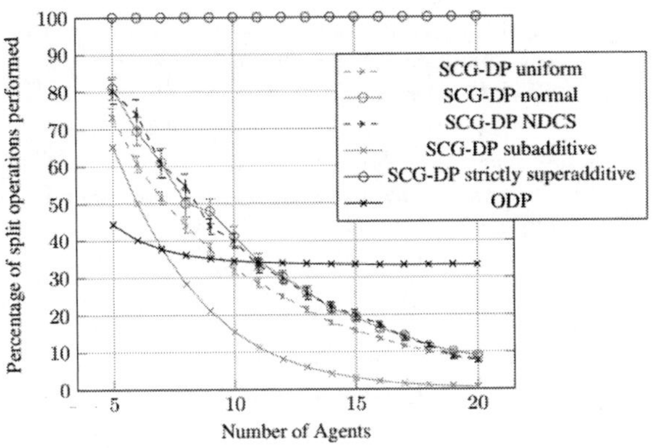

Figure 1: This figure displays the percentage of split operations performed in SCG-DP (for different coalition-value distributions) and in ODP (for any coalition-value distribution), compared to the total possible split operations of the DP algorithm, which is equivalent to the Stirling number of the second kind: $S(n+1,3)$. (95% confidence interval displayed).

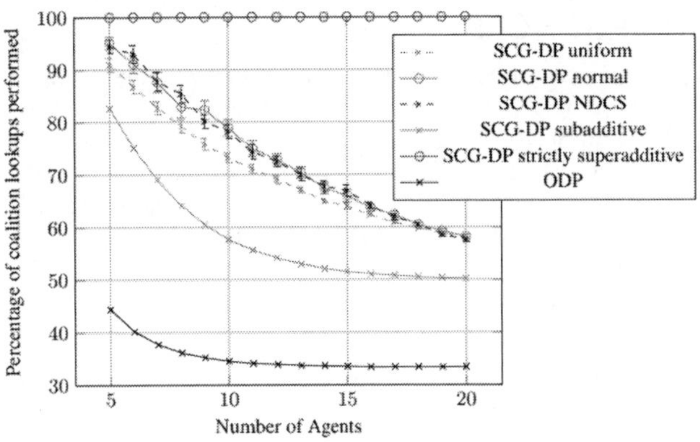

Figure 2: This figure displays the percentage of coalition look up operations performed in SCG-DP (for different coalition-value distributions) and ODP (for any coalition-value distribution) compared to the total possible lookup operations of the DP algorithm, which is equivalent to two times the Stirling number of the second kind: $2 \times S(n+1,3)$. (95% confidence interval displayed).

the number of splits returned by the `EvalSplits` function. The total number of analysed splits is the number of analysed splits for every coalition $C \subseteq N$.

The total number of analysed splits results for SCG-DP for five different coalition-value distributions are displayed in Figure 1. The SCG-DP results are taken from the experiments discussed earlier in this section. Additionally in Figure 1 the ODP algorithm results are detailed, which are found in [14].

As can be seen in Figure 1, as n increases SCG-DP analyses fewer splits than ODP for all non-strictly superadditive coalition-value distributions. This is due to the additional pre-processing `EvalSplits` function of SCG-DP. As ODP does not have a similar pre-processing stage, a fairer comparison method would be to compare via the number of coalition lookups, as discussed next.

5.2 Number of Coalition Lookups

A coalition lookup is defined as the generation of a coalition within a split (and therefore the lookup of the coalition's information). In ODP, as the number of analysed splits does not depend on the coalition-value distribution, then the number of coalition lookups also does not depend on the coalition-value distribution.

For SCG-DP, coalition lookups occur in the `EvalSplits` function. Coalition C^x is generated at line 7 for every split. Then coalition C^y is generated if C^x is in the SCG, at line 9 or line 13. It is then assumed that the information of the looked up coalitions stays in memory until the next time the `EvalSplits` function is run (so that the coalitions do not have to be looked up again). As the generation of C^y is dependant on C^x being in the SCG, the number of coalition lookups is variable in SCG-DP.

The total number of coalition look ups for SCG-DP for the five different coalition-value distributions are displayed in Figure 2. Additionally in Figure 2, the ODP results are detailed.

For SCG-DP, the subadditive experiments have the minimal number of lookups and act as a lower bound. This lower bound occurs because subadditive games have the minimal number of coalitions in the SCG; the n singleton coalitions. As can be seen, the number of lookups in the subadditive experiments are converging onto 50%. This is because C^x always has to be generated in the `EvalSplits` function, and C^y only has to be generated when $|C^x| = 1$ (i.e. when C^x is a singleton coalition). The number of times C^y gets generated as n increases becomes more and more insignificant as a percentage of the total coalition lookups.

Conversely, the strictly superadditive coalition-value distribution acts as an upper bound for SCG-DP. This upper bound occurs because strictly superadditive games have the maximum number of coalitions in the SCG; all the coalitions. In this case SCG-DP performs the same number of lookups as the original DP algorithm [34] (i.e. 100%). That said, for the other three more common coalition-value distributions for coalition structure generation algorithms (uniform, normal and NDCS) [12, 23], the number of coalition lookups is tending towards the lower bound as n is increasing.

6. CONCLUSION AND FUTURE WORK

In this paper, the *Synergy Coalition Group-based Dynamic Programming* (SCG-DP) algorithm was presented, which takes any characteristic function game as input and finds an optimal coalition structure as well as a stable payoff vector by identifying all the coalitions in the Synergy Coalition Group (SCG). SCG-DP locates the SCG without checking the entire search space identified by the Dynamic Programming (DP) algorithm of [34]. The optimal dynamic programming algorithm of [14] showed that only approximately 33% of the search operations of DP are required to guarantee that an optimal coalition structure is found. In this paper, our experimental results show that the lower bound, to guarantee that an optimal coalition structure and a weak least core stable payoff vector is found, converges onto 50% as the number of agents increases. The upper bound remains at 100%, but for standard coalition-value distributions in the literature, the results are trending towards the lower bound as the number of agents increases.

Two possible strands of future work are as follows: (1) SCG-DP only gives a solution upon completion, so exploring an any-time version of SCG-DP could be beneficial; and (2) SCG-DP is a centralised algorithm, yet decentralised methods for the first stage of coalition formation - performing the coalition value calculations (CVC) - exist (e.g. [20, 26, 31, 32]). Building on one of the decentralised CVC algorithms to create a decentralised version of SCG-DP (in a similar manner to how [15] built on [20]), can help spread the computational burden while also making SCG-DP more robust.

REFERENCES

[1] S. Airiau and S. Sen. On the stability of an optimal coalition structure. In *Proceedings of the 19th European Conference on Artificial Intelligence (ECAI)*, pages 203–308, 2010.

[2] S. Brânzei and K. Larson. Coalitional affinity games and the stability gap. In *Proceedings of the 21st International Joint Conference on Artificial Intelligence (IJCAI)*, pages 79–84, 2009.

[3] J. C. Cesco. A convergent transfer scheme to the core of a TU-game. *Revista de Matematicas Aplicadas*, 19:23–35, 1998.

[4] A. Chapman, R. A. Micillo, R. Kota, and N. R. Jennings. Decentralised dynamic task allocation using overlapping potential games. *The Computer Journal*, 53:1462–1477, 2010.

[5] K. Chatterjee, B. Dutta, and K. Sengupta. A noncooperative theory of coalitional bargaining. *Review of Economic Studies*, 60:463–477, 1993.

[6] V. Conitzer and T. W. Sandholm. Complexity of constructing solutions in the core based on synergies among coalitions. *Artificial Intelligence*, 170:607–619, 2006.

[7] V. D. Dang and N. R. Jennings. Generating coalition structures with finite bound from the optimal guarantees. In *Proceedings of the 3th International Conference on Autonomous Agents and Multiagent Systems (AAMAS)*, pages 564–571, 2004.

[8] S. Dasgupta, C. H. Papadimitriou, and U. V. Vazirani. *Algorithms*. McGraw-Hill Higher Education, 2006.

[9] R. Evans. Coalitional bargaining with competition to make offers. *Games and Economic Behaviour*, 19:211–220, 1997.

[10] D. Gillies. *Some theorems on n-person games*. PhD thesis, Princeton University, 1953.

[11] A. Iwasaki, S. Ueda, and M. Yokoo. Finding the core for coalition structure utilizing dual solution. In *Proceedings of the IEEE/WIC/ACM International Conference on Intelligent Agent Technology (IAT)*, pages 114–121, 2013.

[12] K. S. Larson and T. W. Sandholm. Anytime coalition structure generation: An average case study. *Journal of Experimental and Theoretical AI*, 12:23–42, 2000.

[13] E. Lehrer. Allocation processes in cooperative games. *International Journal of Game Theory*, 31:341–351, 2003.

[14] T. Michalak, T. Rahwan, E. Elkind, M. Wooldridge, and N. R. Jennings. A hybrid exact algorithm for complete set partitioning. *Artificial Intelligence*, 230:14 – 50, 2016.

[15] T. Michalak, J. Sroka, T. Rahwan, M. Wooldridge, P. McBurney, and N. R. Jennings. A distributed algorithm for anytime coalition structure generation. In *Proceedings of the 9th International Conference on Autonomous Agents and Multiagent System (AAMAS)*, pages 1007–1014, 2010.

[16] N. Ohta, V. Conitzer, R. Ichimura, Y. Sakurai, A. Iwasaki, and M. Yokoo. Coalition structure generation utilizing compact characteristic function representations. In *Proceedings of the 15th International Conference on Principles and Practice of Constraint Programming (CP)*, pages 623–638, 2009.

[17] A. Okada. A noncooperative coalitional bargaining game with random proposers. *Games and Economic Behaviour*, 16:97–108, 1996.

[18] M. J. Osbourne and A. Rubinstein. *A Course in Game Theory*. MIT Press, 1994.

[19] K. Pawlowski, K. Kurach, K. Svensson, S. D. Ramchurn, T. Michalak, and T. Rahwan. Coalition structure generation with the graphics processing unit. In *Proceedings of the 13th International conference on Autonomous Agents and Multi-Agent Systems (AAMAS)*, pages 293–300, 2014.

[20] T. Rahwan and N. R. Jennings. An algorithm for distributing coalition value calculations among cooperating agents. *Artificial Intelligence*, 171:535–567, 2007.

[21] T. Rahwan and N. R. Jennings. Coalition structure generation: Dynamic programming meets anytime optimization. In *Proceedings of the 23rd Conference on Artificial Intelligence (AAAI)*, pages 156–161, 2008.

[22] T. Rahwan and N. R. Jennings. An improved dynamic programming algorithm for coalition structure generation. In *Proceedings of the 7th International Conference on Autonomous Agents and Multi-Agent Systems (AAMAS)*, pages 1417–1420, 2008.

[23] T. Rahwan, T. Michalak, and N. R. Jennings. A hybrid algorithm for coalition structure generation. In *Proceedings of the 26th Conference on Artificial Intelligence (AAAI)*, pages 1443–1449, 2012.

[24] T. Rahwan, T. Michalak, M. Wooldridge, and N. R. Jennings. Coalition structure generation: A survey. *Artificial Intelligence*, 229:139 – 174, 2015.

[25] T. Rahwan, S. D. Ramchurn, A. Giovannucci, and N. R. Jenning. An anytime algorithm for optimal coalition structure generation. *Journal of Artificial Intelligence Research*, 34:521–567, 2009.

[26] L. Riley, K. Atkinson, P. Dunne, and T. R. Payne. Distributing coalition value calculations to coalition members. In *Proceedings of the 29th Conference on Artificial Intelligence (AAAI)*, pages 2117–2123, 2015.

[27] T. W. Sandholm, K. S. Larson, M. Andersson, O. Shehory, and F. Tohme. Coalition structure generation with worst case guarantees. *Artificial Intelligence*, 111:209–238, 1999.

[28] T. C. Service. *Coalition Structure Generation In Characteristic Function Games*. PhD thesis, Vanderbilt University, 2012.

[29] T. C. Service and J. A. Adams. Constant factor approximation algorithms for coalition structure generation. *Autonomous Agents and Multi-Agent Systems*, 23(1):1–17, 2011.

[30] L. S. Shapley and M. Shubik. Quasi-cores in a monetary economy with non-convex preferences. *Econometrica*, 34:805–827, 1966.

[31] O. Shehory and S. Kraus. Methods for task allocation via agent coalition formation. *Artificial Intelligence*, 101:165–200, 1998.

[32] M. Vinyals, F. Bistaffa, A. Farinelli, and A. Rogers. Coalitional energy purchasing in the smart grid. In *Proceedings of the IEEE International Energy Conference & Exhibition (ENERGYCON)*, pages 848–853, 2012.

[33] L. S.-Y. Wu. A dynamic theory for the class of games with nonempty cores. *SIAM Journal on Applied Mathematics*, 32:328–338, 1977.

[34] D. Y. Yeh. A dynamic programming approach to the complete set partitioning problem. *BIT Numerical Mathematics*, 26:467–474, 1986.

Proactive Dynamic Distributed Constraint Optimization*

Khoi D. Hoang†, Ferdinando Fioretto†, Ping Hou†, Makoto Yokoo⋆, William Yeoh†, Roie Zivan⋄
†Department of Computer Science, New Mexico State University, USA
{khoang, ffiorett, phou, wyeoh}@cs.nmsu.edu
⋆Department of Informatics, Kyushu University, Japan
yokoo@inf.kyushu-u.ac.jp
⋄Department of Industrial Engineering and Management, Ben Gurion University of the Negev, Israel
zivanr@cs.bgu.ac.il

ABSTRACT

Current approaches that model dynamism in DCOPs solve a sequence of static problems, *reacting* to changes in the environment as the agents observe them. Such approaches thus ignore possible predictions on future changes. To overcome this limitation, we introduce *Proactive Dynamic DCOPs (PD-DCOPs)*, a novel formalism to model dynamic DCOPs in the presence of exogenous uncertainty. In contrast to reactive approaches, PD-DCOPs are able to explicitly model the possible changes to the problem, and take such information into account *proactively*, when solving the dynamically changing problem. The additional expressivity of this formalism allows it to model a wider variety of distributed optimization problems. Our work presents both theoretical and practical contributions that advance current dynamic DCOP models: (*i*) we introduce the PD-DCOP model, which explicitly captures dynamic changes of the DCOP over time; (*ii*) we discuss the complexity of this new class of DCOPs; and (*iii*) we develop both exact and approximation algorithms with quality guarantees to solve PD-DCOPs *proactively*.

Keywords

Distributed Constraint Optimization; DCOP; Dynamic DCOP

1. INTRODUCTION

Distributed Constraint Optimization Problems (*DCOPs*) are problems where agents need to coordinate their value assignments to maximize the sum of the resulting constraint utilities [17, 34]. DCOPs have emerged as one of the prominent multi-agent architectures to govern the agents' autonomous behavior in distributed optimization problems. The model represents a powerful approach to the description and solution of many practical problems, serving several applications such as distributed scheduling, coordination of unmanned air vehicles, smart grid electricity networks, and sensor networks [15, 11, 28, 32, 13, 16, 3, 7, 36]. In many distributed problems of interest, agents interact in complex, uncertain, and dynamic environments. For example, in distributed meeting scheduling, participants could change their preferences and priorities over time. In disaster management, new information (e.g., weather forecasts, priorities on buildings to evacuate) typically becomes available in an incremental manner. Thus, the information flow modifies the environment over time. Unfortunately, the classical DCOP paradigm is unable to model problems that change over time.

Consequently, researchers have introduced *Dynamic DCOPs* (*D-DCOPs*) [23, 24, 12, 33], where utility functions can change during the problem solving process. These models make the common assumption that information on how the problem might change is unavailable. As such, existing approaches *react* to the changes in the problem and solve the current problem at hand. However, in several applications, the information on how the problem might change is indeed available, or predictable, within some degree of uncertainty. We provide one such example, a distributed meeting scheduling problem, as our motivating example in Section 3.

Therefore, in this paper, (*i*) we introduce *Proactive Dynamic DCOPs* (*PD-DCOPs*), which explicitly model how the DCOP will change over time; (*ii*) we discuss the complexity of this new class of DCOPs; and (*iii*) we develop exact and approximation algorithms with quality guarantees to solve PD-DCOPs *proactively*.

2. BACKGROUND

We now provide background on the regular and dynamic DCOPs as well as the regular and super-stabilizing DPOP algorithms.

2.1 DCOPs

A *Distributed Constraint Optimization Problem* (*DCOP*) is a tuple $\langle \mathbf{A}, \mathbf{X}, \mathbf{D}, \mathbf{F}, \alpha \rangle$, where $\mathbf{A} = \{a_i\}_{i=1}^{p}$ is a set of *agents*; $\mathbf{X} = \{x_i\}_{i=1}^{n}$ is a set of decision *variables*; $\mathbf{D} = \{D_x\}_{x \in \mathbf{X}}$ is a set of finite *domains* and each variable $x \in \mathbf{X}$ takes values from the set $D_x \in \mathbf{D}$; $\mathbf{F} = \{f_i\}_{i=1}^{m}$ is a set of *utility functions*, each defined over a set of decision variables: $f_i : \prod_{x \in \mathbf{x}^{f_i}} D_x \to \mathbb{R}^+ \cup \{\bot\}$, where $\mathbf{x}^{f_i} \subseteq \mathbf{X}$ is *scope* of f_i and $\bot$ is a special element used to denote that a given combination of values for the variables in $\mathbf{x}^{f_i}$ is not allowed; and $\alpha : \mathbf{X} \to \mathbf{A}$ is a function that associates each decision variable to one agent.

A *solution* σ is a value assignment for a set $\mathbf{x}_\sigma \subseteq \mathbf{X}$ of variables that is consistent with their respective domains. The utility $\mathbf{F}(\sigma) = \sum_{f \in \mathbf{F}, \mathbf{x}^f \subseteq \mathbf{x}_\sigma} f(\sigma)$ is the sum of the utilities across all the applicable utility functions in σ. A solution σ is *complete* if $\mathbf{x}_\sigma = \mathbf{X}$. The goal is to find an optimal complete solution $\mathbf{x}^* = \text{argmax}_{\mathbf{x}} \mathbf{F}(\mathbf{x})$.

Given a DCOP P, $G = (\mathbf{X}, E)$ is the *constraint graph* of P, where $\{x, y\} \in E$ iff $\exists f_i \in \mathbf{F}$ such that $\{x, y\} = \mathbf{x}^{f_i}$. A *DFS*

*The team from NMSU is partially supported by NSF grants 1345232 and 1540168. The views and conclusions contained in this document are those of the authors and should not be interpreted as representing the official policies, either expressed or implied, of the sponsoring organizations, agencies, or the U.S. government. Makoto Yokoo is partially supported by JSPS KAKENHI Grant Number 24220003.

Appears in: *Proceedings of the 15th International Conference on Autonomous Agents and Multiagent Systems (AAMAS 2016), J. Thangarajah, K. Tuyls, C. Jonker, S. Marsella (eds.), May 9–13, 2016, Singapore.*

pseudo-tree arrangement for G is a *spanning tree* $T = \langle \mathbf{X}, E_T \rangle$ of G such that if $f_i \in \mathbf{F}$ and $\{x, y\} \subseteq \mathbf{x}^{f_i}$, then x and y appear in the same branch of T. We use $N(a_i) = \{a_j \in \mathcal{A} \mid \{x_i, x_j\} \in E\}$ to denote the neighbors of agent a_i.

2.2 Dynamic DCOP

A *Dynamic DCOP* (*D-DCOP*) is defined as a sequence of DCOPs with changes between them, without an explicit model for how the DCOP will change over time. Solving a D-DCOP optimally means finding a utility-maximal solution for each DCOP in the sequence. Therefore, this approach is *reactive* since it does not consider future changes. Its advantage is that solving a D-DCOP is no harder than solving h DCOPs, where h is the horizon of the problem. Researchers have used this approach to solve D-DCOPs, where they introduce search- and inference-based approaches that are able to reuse information from previous DCOPs to speed up the search for the solution for the current DCOP [23, 33]. Alternatively, a *proactive* approach predicts future changes in the D-DCOP and finds robust solutions that require little or no changes despite future changes.

Researchers have also proposed other models for D-DCOPs including a model where agents have deadlines to choose their values [24], a model where agents can have imperfect knowledge about their environment [12], and a model where changes in the constraint graph depends on the value assignments of agents [36].

2.3 DPOP and S-DPOP

The *Distributed Pseudo-tree Optimization Procedure* (*DPOP*) [22] is a complete *inference algorithm* composed of three phases:

- *Pseudo-tree Generation:* The agents build a pseudo-tree [8].
- *UTIL Propagation:* Each agent, starting from the leafs of the pseudo-tree, computes the optimal sum of utilities in its subtree for each value combination of variables in its separator.[1] It does so by adding the utilities of its functions with the variables in its separator and the utilities in the UTIL messages received from its children agents, and projecting out its own variables by optimizing over them.
- *VALUE Propagation:* Each agent, starting from the pseudo-tree root, determines the optimal value for its variables. The root agent does so by choosing the values of its variables from its UTIL computations.

Super-stabilizing DPOP (*S-DPOP*) [23] is a self-stabilizing extension of DPOP, where the agents restart the DPOP phases when they detect changes in the problem. S-DPOP makes use of information that is not affected by the changes in the problem.

3. MOTIVATING DOMAIN

We now introduce a distributed dynamic meeting scheduling problem, which will serve as a representative domain to motivate our work. In a distributed meeting scheduling problem [15], a set of $\mathbf{M}$ *weekly* meetings need to be scheduled between members of an organization (e.g., employees of a company; students, faculty members, and staff of a university), taking restrictions in their availability as well as their time and location preferences into account. For a meeting $m \in \mathbf{M}$, A_m is the set of attendees to the meeting, s_m is the start time of the meeting, d_m is its duration, and l_m is its location. Typically, the attendees commit to a meeting time. However, certain exogenous factors may affect the meeting time preferences of some participants. For instance, depending on the location and time of the meeting, traffic conditions may cause delays that should be taken into account, as they could cause cascading effects.

In a typical DCOP formulation, meeting starting times are modeled as decision variables of the agents. Thus, for a given meeting m, each agent $a \in A_m$, controls a pair of decision variables, x_{s_m}, x_{l_m}, whose values represent possible start times s_m and locations l_m for the meeting m. All agents participating in meeting m need to agree upon a given meeting time and location. This condition can be modeled by imposing an equality constraints on the values of the variables x_{s_m}, and x_{l_m} controlled by the agents in A_m. Agent preferences on the time and location for a given meeting can be modeled as unary constraints involving the variable describing the desired meeting. The goal is to find a feasible *weekly* schedule that maximizes the utility over all attendees.

Typical weekly meeting schedules may be adjusted based on changes of the meeting participants' preferences. To address such a requirement, one can use a Dynamic DCOP formulation, where a new DCOP problem, representing the scheduling problem for a *single* week, can be modeled according to the previous formulation and solved, as soon as some agent's meeting preference changes. However, these formulations exhibit several limitations: (*i*) they fail to capture the presence of exogenous factors (e.g., traffic conditions) in the dynamic aspect of the problem, and (*ii*) they do not take account the inconvenience of the participants to change their schedule, when the preference of some agents are updated. Our proposed PD-DCOP model alleviates these limitations by acting proactively during the problem resolution, which allows us to make a step forward towards more refined dynamic solutions.

4. PD-DCOP MODEL

A *Proactive Dynamic DCOP* (*PD-DCOP*) is a tuple $\langle \mathbf{A}, \mathbf{X}, \mathbf{D}, \mathbf{F}, h, \mathbf{T}, c, \gamma, p^0_{\mathbf{Y}}, \alpha \rangle$, where:

- $\mathbf{A} = \{a_i\}_{i=1}^p$ is a set of *agents*.
- $\mathbf{X} = \{x_i\}_{i=1}^n$ is a mixed set of *decision* and *random variables*. To differentiate between decision variables and random variables, we use $\mathbf{Y} \subseteq \mathbf{X}$ to denote the set of random variables that model uncontrollable stochastic events (e.g., traffic, weather, malfunctioning devices).
- $\mathbf{D} = \{D_x\}_{x \in \mathbf{X}}$ is a set of finite *domains*. Each variable $x \in \mathbf{X}$ takes values from the set $D_x \in \mathbf{D}$. We also use $\Omega = \{\Omega_y\}_{y \in \mathbf{Y}} \subseteq \mathbf{D}$ to denote the set of event spaces for the random variables (e.g., different traffic conditions, weather conditions, or stress levels to which a device is subjected to) such that each $y \in \mathbf{Y}$ takes values in Ω_y.
- $\mathbf{F} = \{f_i\}_{i=1}^m$ is a set of *reward functions*, each defined over a mixed set of decision variables and random variables: $f_i : \prod_{x \in \mathbf{x}^{f_i}} D_x \to \mathbb{R}^+ \cup \{\perp\}$, where $\mathbf{x}^{f_i} \subseteq \mathbf{X}$ is *scope* of f_i and $\perp$ is a special element used to denote that a given combination of values for the variables in $\mathbf{x}^{f_i}$ is not allowed.
- $h \in \mathbb{N}$ is a finite *horizon* in which the agents can change the values of their variables.
- $\mathbf{T} = \{T_y\}_{y \in \mathbf{Y}}$ is the set of *transition functions* $T_y : \Omega_y \times \Omega_y \to [0, 1] \subseteq \mathbb{R}$ for the random variables $y \in \mathbf{Y}$, describing the probability for a random variable to change its value in successive time steps. For a time step $t > 0$, and values $\omega_i \in \Omega_y, \omega_j \in \Omega_y$, $T_y(\omega_i, \omega_j) = P(y^t = \omega_j \mid y^{t-1} = \omega_i)$, where y^t denotes the value of the variable y at time step t, and P is a probability measure. Thus, $T_y(\omega_i, \omega_j)$ describes the probability for the random variable y to change its value from ω_i at a time step $t-1$ to ω_j at a time step t. Finally, $\sum_{\omega_j \in \Omega_y} T_y(\omega_i, \omega_j) = 1$ for all $\omega_i \in \Omega_y$.
- $c \in \mathbb{R}^+$ is a *switching cost*, which is the cost associated with the change in the value of a decision variable between time steps.

[1] The separator of x_i contains all ancestors of x_i in the pseudo-tree that are connected to x_i or one of its descendants.

- $\gamma \in [0, 1)$ is a *discount factor*, which represents the decrease in the importance of rewards/costs over time.
- $p^0_{\mathbf{Y}} = \{p^0_y\}_{y \in \mathbf{Y}}$ is a set of initial *probability distributions* for the random variables $y \in \mathbf{Y}$.
- $\alpha : \mathbf{X} \backslash \mathbf{Y} \to \mathbf{A}$ is a function that associates each decision variable to one agent. We assume that the random variables are not under the control of the agents and are independent of decision variables. Thus, their values are solely determined according to their transition functions.

Throughout this paper, we refer to decision (resp. random) variables as with the letter x (resp. y). We also assume that each agent controls exactly one decision variable (thus, α is a bijection), and that each reward function $f_i \in \mathbf{F}$ associates with at most one random variable y_i.[2]

The goal of a PD-DCOP is to find a sequence of $h+1$ assignments $\mathbf{x}^*$ for all the decision variables in $\mathbf{X} \setminus \mathbf{Y}$:

$$\mathbf{x}^* = \underset{\mathbf{x}=\langle \mathbf{x}^0,\ldots,\mathbf{x}^h \rangle \in \Sigma^{h+1}}{\operatorname{argmax}} \mathcal{F}^h(\mathbf{x}) \tag{1}$$

$$\mathcal{F}^h(\mathbf{x}) = \sum_{t=0}^{h-1} \gamma^t \left[\mathcal{F}^t_x(\mathbf{x}^t) + \mathcal{F}^t_y(\mathbf{x}^t) \right] \tag{2}$$

$$- \sum_{t=0}^{h-1} \gamma^t \left[c \cdot \Delta(\mathbf{x}^t, \mathbf{x}^{t+1}) \right] \tag{3}$$

$$+ \tilde{\mathcal{F}}_x(\mathbf{x}^h) + \tilde{\mathcal{F}}_y(\mathbf{x}^h) \tag{4}$$

where Σ is the assignment space for the decision variables of the PD-DCOP, at each time step. Equation (2) refers to the optimization over the first h time steps, with:

$$\mathcal{F}^t_x(\mathbf{x}) = \sum_{f_i \in \mathbf{F} \setminus \mathbf{F}_Y} f_i(\mathbf{x}_i) \tag{5}$$

$$\mathcal{F}^t_y(\mathbf{x}) = \sum_{f_i \in \mathbf{F}_Y} \sum_{\omega \in \Omega_{y_i}} f_i(\mathbf{x}_i|_{y_i=\omega}) \cdot p^t_{y_i}(\omega) \tag{6}$$

where $\mathbf{x}_i$ is an assignment for all the variables in $\mathbf{x}^{f_i}$; we write $\mathbf{x}_i|_{y_i=\omega}$ to indicate that the random variable $y_i \in \mathbf{x}^{f_i}$ takes on the event $\omega \in \Omega_{y_i}$; $\mathbf{F}_Y = \{f_i \in \mathbf{F} \mid \mathbf{x}^{f_i} \cap \mathbf{Y} \neq \emptyset\}$ is the set of functions in $\mathbf{F}$ that involve random variables; $p^t_{y_i}(\omega)$ is the probability for the random variable y_i to assume value ω at time t, and defined as

$$p^t_{y_i}(\omega) = \sum_{\omega' \in \Omega_{y_i}} T_{y_i}(\omega', \omega) \cdot p^{t-1}_{y_i}(\omega') \tag{7}$$

Equation (3) considers the penalties due to the changes in the decision variables' values during the optimization process, where $\Delta : \Sigma \times \Sigma \to \mathbb{N}$ is a function counting the number of assignments to decision variables that differs from one time step to the next.

Equation (4) refers to the optimization over the last time step, which further accounts for discounted future rewards:

$$\tilde{\mathcal{F}}_x(\mathbf{x}) = \frac{\gamma^h}{1-\gamma} \mathcal{F}^h_x(\mathbf{x}) \tag{8}$$

$$\tilde{\mathcal{F}}_y(\mathbf{x}) = \sum_{f_i \in \mathbf{F}_Y} \sum_{\omega \in \Omega_{y_i}} \tilde{f}_i(\mathbf{x}_i|_{y_i=\omega}) \cdot p^h_{y_i}(\omega) \tag{9}$$

$$\tilde{f}_i(\mathbf{x}_i|_{y_i=\omega}) = \gamma^h \cdot f_i(\mathbf{x}_i|_{y_i=\omega}) + \gamma \sum_{\omega' \in \Omega_{y_i}} T_{y_i}(\omega, \omega') \cdot \tilde{f}_i(\mathbf{x}_i|_{y_i=\omega'}) \tag{10}$$

The goal of a PD-DCOP is to find an assignment of values to its decision variables that maximizes the sum of two terms. The first term maximizes the discounted net utility, that is, the discounted rewards for the functions that do not involve exogenous factors ($\mathcal{F}_x$) and the expected discounted random rewards ($\mathcal{F}_y$) minus the discounted penalties over the first h time steps. The second term maximizes the discounted future rewards for the problem.

While the PD-DCOP model can be used to capture the presence of exogenous factors in the dynamic aspect of the problem, it can also model dynamic changes to the DCOP constraint graph, through the transition functions. In particular, the deletion of a constraint will force the random variable associated with that constraint to transit to a 0 reward value for all decision variables; the addition of a constraint can be handled by defining a 0 reward constraint in the model from the start, and updating its reward when the constraint is added.

4.1 Modeling the Motivating Domain

PD-DCOPs can naturally handle the dynamic characteristic of the distributed dynamic meeting scheduling problem that we use as our motivating domain. Uncontrollable events, such as traffic conditions, affecting the meeting times of agents can be modeled via random variables. In particular, in our model, each pair of agent's variables x_{s_m} and x_{l_m}, describing the time and location of a meeting m, is associated to a random variable $y_m \in \mathbf{Y}$, describing the different traffic conditions that can affect agents' time and location preferences for the meeting. Traffic predictions are often available and they are modeled via the transition functions. Additionally, rescheduling meetings is inconvenient for the meeting participants and this inconvenience is modeled via switching costs for each attendee, imposed when a meeting is forced to be rescheduled. Finally, the PD-DCOP horizon captures the horizon (i.e., number of weeks) of the scheduling problem (e.g., the DCOP problem of each time step corresponds to the scheduling problem for a single week).

4.2 Theoretical Properties

We now describe some of the theoretical properties of PD-DCOPs.

THEOREM 1. *Solving a PD-DCOP is PSPACE-complete (-hard) if the horizon h is polynomial (exponential) in $|\mathbf{X}|$.*

PROOF: We first consider the case when h is polynomial in $|\mathbf{X}|$: Membership in PSPACE follows from the existence of a naive depth-first search to solve PD-DCOPs, where a non-deterministic branch is opened for each complete assignment of the PD-DCOP's decision variables and for each time step $0 \leq t \leq h$. The algorithm requires linear space in the number of variables and horizon length. We reduce the *satisfiability of quantified Boolean formula (QSAT)* to a PD-DCOP with 0 horizon. Each existential Boolean variable in the QSAT is mapped to a corresponding decision variable in the PD-DCOP, and each universal Boolean variable in the QSAT is mapped to a PD-DCOP random variable. The domains D_x of all variables $x \in \mathbf{X}$ are the sets of values $\{0, 1\}$, corresponding respectively to the evaluations, *false* and *true*, of the QSAT variables. The initial probability distribution p^0_y of each PD-DCOP random variable $y \in \mathbf{Y}$ is set to as the *uniform* distribution. Each QSAT clause c is mapped to a PD-DCOP reward function f_c, whose scope involves all and only the PD-DCOP-corresponding boolean variables appearing in c, and such that:

$$f_c(\mathbf{x}^c) = \begin{cases} 1, & \text{if } c(\mathbf{x}^c) = \text{true} \\ \perp, & \text{otherwise.} \end{cases}$$

where $c(\mathbf{x}^c)$ denotes the instantiation of the values of the variables in $\mathbf{x}^c$ to the truth values of the corresponding literals of c. In other words, a clause is satisfied *iff* the equivalent reward function preserves its semantics. The choices for, the switching cost, the discount factor γ, and the transition function T_y, for each $y \in \mathbf{Y}$, of

[2]If multiple random variables are associated with a reward function, w.l.o.g., they can be merged into a single variable.

the PD-DCOP, are immaterial. The reduction is linear in the size of the original quantified Boolean formula. The quantified Boolean formula is satisfiable iff the equivalent PD-DCOP has at least one solution $\mathbf{x}$ whose cost $\mathcal{F}(\mathbf{x}) \neq \perp$.

We next consider the case when h is exponential in $\mathbf{X}$: In such case solving PD-DCOPs is PSPACE-hard as storing a solution requires space exponential in $|\mathbf{X}|$. □

Absolute Error Bound: Let U^∞ denote the optimal solution quality with an infinite horizon and U^h denote the optimal solution quality with a finite horizon h. Thus, $\epsilon \geq U^\infty - U^h$ and we first describe this error bound. Let's define $F^\Delta = \max_{\mathbf{y}\in\Omega} \max_{\mathbf{x}\in\Sigma} (\mathbf{F}(\mathbf{x}^* \cup \mathbf{y}) - \mathbf{F}(\mathbf{x} \cup \mathbf{y}))$, where $\mathbf{x}$ and $\mathbf{y}$ are assignments of values to all decision and random variables, respectively; $\mathbf{F}$ is the overall reward function for a (regular) DCOP in the PD-DCOP; and $\mathbf{x}^*$ is an optimal value assignment of decision variables for that regular DCOP given value assignment $\mathbf{y}$.

THEOREM 2. *The absolute error bound ϵ equals $\frac{\gamma^h}{1-\gamma} F^\Delta$.*

PROOF: Let $\check{\mathbf{x}}^* = \langle \check{\mathbf{x}}_0^*, \ldots, \check{\mathbf{x}}_h^*, \check{\mathbf{x}}_{h+1}^*, \ldots \rangle$ be the vector of assignments that maximizes U^∞.

$$U^\infty = \sum_{t=0}^{\infty} \gamma^t \left[\mathcal{F}_x^t(\check{\mathbf{x}}_t^*) + \mathcal{F}_y^t(\check{\mathbf{x}}_t^*) - c \cdot \Delta(\check{\mathbf{x}}_t^*, \check{\mathbf{x}}_{t+1}^*)\right]$$

Ignoring switch costs after time h, we get U_+^∞ and $U^\infty \leq U_+^\infty$, as:

$$U_+^\infty = \sum_{t=0}^{h-1} \gamma^t \left[\mathcal{F}_x^t(\check{\mathbf{x}}_t^*) + \mathcal{F}_y^t(\check{\mathbf{x}}_t^*) - c \cdot \Delta(\check{\mathbf{x}}_t^*, \check{\mathbf{x}}_{t+1}^*)\right] + \sum_{t=h}^{\infty} \gamma^t \left[\mathcal{F}_x^t(\check{\mathbf{x}}_t^*) + \mathcal{F}_y^t(\check{\mathbf{x}}_t^*)\right]$$

Let $\mathbf{x}^* = \langle \mathbf{x}_0^*, \ldots, \mathbf{x}_h^* \rangle$ be the vector of assignments maximizing U^h,

$$U^h = \sum_{t=0}^{h-1} \gamma^t \left[\mathcal{F}_x^t(\mathbf{x}_t^*) + \mathcal{F}_y^t(\mathbf{x}_t^*) - c \cdot \Delta(\mathbf{x}_t^*, \mathbf{x}_{t+1}^*)\right] + \sum_{t=h}^{\infty} \gamma^t \left[\mathcal{F}_x^t(\mathbf{x}_h^*) + \mathcal{F}_y^t(\mathbf{x}_h^*)\right]$$

For $\check{\mathbf{x}}^*$, if we change the decision variable assignment after time step h to $\check{\mathbf{x}}_h^*$, as $\langle \check{\mathbf{x}}_0^*, \ldots, \check{\mathbf{x}}_h^*, \check{\mathbf{x}}_h^*, \ldots \rangle$, we get U_-^∞:

$$U_-^\infty = \sum_{t=0}^{h-1} \gamma^t \left[\mathcal{F}_x^t(\check{\mathbf{x}}_t^*) + \mathcal{F}_y^t(\check{\mathbf{x}}_t^*) - c \cdot \Delta(\check{\mathbf{x}}_t^*, \check{\mathbf{x}}_{t+1}^*)\right] + \sum_{t=h}^{\infty} \gamma^t \left[\mathcal{F}_x^t(\check{\mathbf{x}}_h^*) + \mathcal{F}_y^t(\check{\mathbf{x}}_h^*)\right]$$

Since the value assignments of $\check{\mathbf{x}}$ are identical for all time steps $t \geq h$, $U_-^\infty \leq U^h$. Therefore, we get $U_-^\infty \leq U^h \leq U^\infty \leq U_+^\infty$.

Next, we know that

$$U_+^\infty - U_-^\infty = \sum_{t=h}^{\infty} \gamma^t \left[\mathcal{F}_x^t(\check{\mathbf{x}}_t^*) + \mathcal{F}_y^t(\check{\mathbf{x}}_t^*) - \mathcal{F}_x^t(\check{\mathbf{x}}_h^*) + \mathcal{F}_y^t(\check{\mathbf{x}}_h^*)\right]$$

Given a value assignment $\mathbf{y}$ for all random variables, the PD-DCOP becomes a regular DCOP, where one only needs to find value assignment of decision variables and maximize the total utility. For this DCOP, there is a utility difference between the best assignment and the worst assignment for all decision variables. Among all these utility differences, the maximum one is $F^\Delta = \max_{\mathbf{y}\in\Omega} \max_{\mathbf{x}\in\Sigma} (\mathbf{F}(\mathbf{x}^* \cup \mathbf{y}) - \mathbf{F}(\mathbf{x} \cup \mathbf{y}))$, where $\mathbf{x}$ and $\mathbf{y}$ are assignments of values to all decision and random variables, respectively; $\mathbf{F}$ is the overall reward function for a (regular) DCOP in the PD-DCOP; and $\mathbf{x}^*$ is an optimal value assignment of decision variables for that regular DCOP given value assignment $\mathbf{y}$. Thus, it is the maximum difference in overall reward over all combination of value assignments $\mathbf{x}$ and $\mathbf{y}$.

Notice that the quantity $\mathcal{F}_x^t(\check{\mathbf{x}}_t^*) + \mathcal{F}_y^t(\check{\mathbf{x}}_t^*) - \mathcal{F}_x^t(\check{\mathbf{x}}_h^*) + \mathcal{F}_y^t(\check{\mathbf{x}}_h^*)$ is the utility difference between the value assignment $\check{\mathbf{x}}_t^*$ and $\check{\mathbf{x}}_h^*$ for the regular DCOPs in time step t. So, we have:

$$\mathcal{F}_x^t(\check{\mathbf{x}}_t^*) + \mathcal{F}_y^t(\check{\mathbf{x}}_t^*) - \mathcal{F}_x^t(\check{\mathbf{x}}_h^*) + \mathcal{F}_y^t(\check{\mathbf{x}}_h^*) \leq F^\Delta$$

which concludes the proof. □

COROLLARY 1. *Given a maximum acceptable absolute error ϵ, the minimum horizon h is $\log_\gamma \frac{(1-\gamma)\cdot\epsilon}{F^\Delta}$.*

Upper Bound on Optimal Quality: We now describe an upper bound on the optimal solution quality $\mathcal{F}^h(\mathbf{x}^*)$. Let $\hat{\mathbf{x}}^* = \langle \hat{\mathbf{x}}_0^*, \ldots, \hat{\mathbf{x}}_h^* \rangle$ be the vector of assignments, where:

$$\hat{\mathbf{x}}_t^* = \begin{cases} \operatorname*{argmax}_{\mathbf{x}\in\Sigma} \gamma^t\left[\mathcal{F}_x^t(\mathbf{x}) + \mathcal{F}_y^t(\mathbf{x})\right] & \text{if } 0 \leq t < h \\ \operatorname*{argmax}_{\mathbf{x}\in\Sigma} \left[\tilde{\mathcal{F}}_x(\mathbf{x}) + \tilde{\mathcal{F}}_y(\mathbf{x})\right] & \text{otherwise} \end{cases}$$

and $\hat{\mathcal{F}}^h(\mathbf{x}) = \sum_{t=0}^{h-1} \gamma^t \left[\mathcal{F}_x^t(\mathbf{x}) + \mathcal{F}_y^t(\mathbf{x})\right] + \tilde{\mathcal{F}}_x(\mathbf{x}) + \tilde{\mathcal{F}}_y(\mathbf{x})$.

THEOREM 3. $\forall \mathbf{x} \in \Sigma^{h+1} : \mathcal{F}^h(\mathbf{x}) \leq \mathcal{F}^h(\mathbf{x}^*) \leq \hat{\mathcal{F}}^h(\hat{\mathbf{x}}^*)$.

PROOF: For any given assignment $\mathbf{x} \in \Sigma^{h+1}$, $\mathcal{F}^h(\mathbf{x})$ is a clear lower bound for $\mathcal{F}^h(\mathbf{x}^*)$.

For the upper bound, let $\mathcal{F}_t^h(\cdot)$ be the tth component of the $\mathcal{F}^h(\cdot)$, defined as:

$$\mathcal{F}_t^h(\mathbf{x}_t) = \begin{cases} \gamma^t\left[\mathcal{F}_x^t(\mathbf{x}_t) + \mathcal{F}_y^t(\mathbf{x}_t) - \left[c\Delta(\mathbf{x}_t, \mathbf{x}_{t+1})\right]\right] & \text{if } 0 \leq t < h \\ \tilde{\mathcal{F}}_x(\mathbf{x}_t) + \tilde{\mathcal{F}}_y(\mathbf{x}_t) & \text{otherwise} \end{cases}$$

with $\mathbf{x}_t$, defined as the tth value assignment in the PD-DCOP solution $\mathbf{x}$. Analogously, let us denote with $\hat{\mathcal{F}}_t^h(\cdot)$ the tth component of the $\hat{\mathcal{F}}^h(\cdot)$, defined as:

$$\hat{\mathcal{F}}_t^h(\mathbf{x}_t) = \begin{cases} \gamma^t\left[\mathcal{F}_x^t(\mathbf{x}_t) + \mathcal{F}_y^t(\mathbf{x}_t)\right] & \text{if } 0 \leq t < h \\ \tilde{\mathcal{F}}_x(\mathbf{x}_t) + \tilde{\mathcal{F}}_y(\mathbf{x}_t) & \text{otherwise} \end{cases}$$

It follows that for all $0 \leq t < h$:

$$\begin{aligned} \mathcal{F}_t^h(\mathbf{x}_t^*) &= \gamma^t\left[\mathcal{F}_x^t(\mathbf{x}_t^*) + \mathcal{F}_y^t(\mathbf{x}_t^*) - \left[c\Delta(\mathbf{x}_t, \mathbf{x}_{t+1})\right]\right] \\ &\leq \gamma^t\left[\mathcal{F}_x^t(\mathbf{x}_t^*) + \mathcal{F}_y^t(\mathbf{x}_t^*)\right] \\ &\leq \max_{\mathbf{x}\in\Sigma} \gamma^t\left[\mathcal{F}_x^t(\mathbf{x}) + \mathcal{F}_y^t(\mathbf{x})\right] = \hat{\mathcal{F}}_t^h(\hat{\mathbf{x}}_t^*) \end{aligned}$$

where $\mathbf{x}_t^*$ (resp. $\hat{\mathbf{x}}_t^*$) is the tth component of the PD-DCOP solution vector $\mathbf{x}^*$ (resp. $\hat{\mathbf{x}}^*$). For $t = h$, it follows:

$$\begin{aligned} \mathcal{F}_h^h(\mathbf{x}_h^*) &= \tilde{\mathcal{F}}_x(\mathbf{x}_h^*) + \tilde{\mathcal{F}}_y(\mathbf{x}_h^*) \\ &\leq \max_{\mathbf{x}\in\Sigma} \left[\tilde{\mathcal{F}}_x(\mathbf{x}) + \tilde{\mathcal{F}}_y(\mathbf{x})\right] = \hat{\mathcal{F}}_h^h(\hat{\mathbf{x}}_h^*) \end{aligned}$$

Thus, from the two inequalities above, it follows:

$$\mathcal{F}^h(\mathbf{x}^*) \leq \sum_{t=0}^{h} \hat{\mathcal{F}}_t^h(\mathbf{x}_t^*) = \hat{\mathcal{F}}^h(\hat{\mathbf{x}}^*)$$

which concludes the proof. □

COROLLARY 2. *The approximation ratio ρ is $\frac{\hat{\mathcal{F}}^h(\hat{\mathbf{x}}^*)}{\mathcal{F}^h(\mathbf{x})}$ for any solution $\mathbf{x}$.*

5. PD-DCOP ALGORITHMS

We now introduce exact and approximation PD-DCOP algorithms.

5.1 Exact Approach

We first propose an exact approach, which transforms a PD-DCOP into an equivalent DCOP and solves it using any off-the-shelf DCOP algorithm. Since the transition of each random variable is independent of the assignment of values to decision variables, this problem can be viewed as a Markov chain. Thus, it is possible to collapse an entire PD-DCOP into a single DCOP, where (1) each reward function F_i in this new DCOP captures the sum of rewards of the reward function $f_i \in \mathbf{F}$ across all time steps, and (2) the domain of each decision variable is the set of all possible combination of values of that decision variable across all time steps. However, this process needs to be done in a distributed manner.

We divide the reward functions into two types: (1) The functions $f_i \in \mathbf{F}$ whose scope $\mathbf{x}^{f_i} \cap \mathbf{Y} = \emptyset$ includes exclusively decision variables, and (2) the functions $f_i \in \mathbf{F}$ whose scope $\mathbf{x}^{f_i} \cap \mathbf{Y} \neq \emptyset$ includes one random variable. In both cases, let $\mathbf{x}_i = \langle \mathbf{x}_i^0, \ldots, \mathbf{x}_i^h \rangle$ denote the vector of value assignments to all *decision* variables in $\mathbf{x}^{f_i}$ for each time step.

Then, each function $f_i \in \mathbf{F}$ whose scope includes only decision variables can be replaced by a function F_i:

$$F_i(\mathbf{x}_i) = \sum_{t=0}^{h-1} F_i^t(\mathbf{x}_i^t) + F_i^h(\mathbf{x}_i^h) \tag{11}$$

$$= \left[\sum_{t=0}^{h-1} \gamma^t \cdot f_i(\mathbf{x}_i^t)\right] + \left[\frac{\gamma^h}{1-\gamma} f_i(\mathbf{x}_i^h)\right] \tag{12}$$

where the first term with the summation is the reward for the first h time steps and the second term is the reward for the remaining time steps. Each function $f_i \in \mathbf{F}$ whose scope includes random variables can be replaced by a *unary* function F_i:

$$F_i(\mathbf{x}_i) = \sum_{t=0}^{h-1} F_i^t(\mathbf{x}_i^t) + F_i^h(\mathbf{x}_i^h) \tag{13}$$

$$= \sum_{t=0}^{h-1} \gamma^t \sum_{\omega \in \Omega_{y_i}} f_i(\mathbf{x}_i^t|_{y_i=\omega}) \cdot p_{y_i}^t(\omega) \tag{14}$$

$$+ \sum_{\omega \in \Omega_{y_i}} \tilde{f}_i(\mathbf{x}_i^h|_{y_i=\omega}) \cdot p_{y_i}^h(\omega) \tag{15}$$

where the first term (Equation (14)) is the reward for the first h time steps and the second term (Equation (15)) is the reward for the remaining time steps. The function $\tilde{f}_i$ is recursively defined according to Equation (10). Additionally, each decision variable x_i will have a unary function C_i:

$$C_i(\mathbf{x}_i) = -\sum_{t=0}^{h-1} \gamma^t \left[c \cdot \Delta(\mathbf{x}_i^t, \mathbf{x}_i^{t+1})\right] \tag{16}$$

which captures the cost of switching values across time steps. This collapsed DCOP can then be solved with any off-the-shelf DCOP algorithm. In our experiments, we use DPOP [22] to solve it.

5.2 Approximation Approach

Since optimally solving PD-DCOPs is P-SPACE-hard, the exact approach described earlier will fail to scale to large problems, as we show in our experimental results. Therefore, approximation approaches are necessary to solve the larger problems of interest. Our local search algorithm to solve PD-DCOPs is inspired by MGM [14], which has been shown to be robust in dynamically

Algorithm 1: LOCAL SEARCH( )

```
1  iter ← 1
2  ⟨v_i^{0*}, v_i^{1*}, ..., v_i^{h*}⟩ ← ⟨Null, Null, ..., Null⟩
3  ⟨v_i^0, v_i^1, ..., v_i^h⟩ ← InitialAssignment()
4  context ← ⟨(x_j, t, Null | x_j ∈ N(a_i), 0 ≤ t ≤ h)⟩
5  Send VALUE(⟨v_i^0, v_i^1, ..., v_i^h⟩) to all neighbors
```

Procedure CalcGain()

```
6  ⟨u_i^0, u_i^1, ..., u_i^h⟩ ← CalcUtils(⟨v_i^0, v_i^1, ..., v_i^h⟩)
7  u* ← −∞
8  foreach ⟨d_i^0, d_i^1, ..., d_i^h⟩ in ×_{i=0}^h D_{x_i} do
9      u ← CalcCumulativeUtil(⟨d_i^0, d_i^1, ..., d_i^h⟩)
10     if u > u* then
11         u* ← u
12         ⟨v_i^{0*}, v_i^{1*}, ..., v_i^{h*}⟩ ← ⟨d_i^0, d_i^1, ..., d_i^h⟩
13 if u* ≠ −∞ then
14     ⟨u_i^{0*}, u_i^{1*}, ..., u_i^{h*}⟩ ← CalcUtils(⟨v_i^{0*}, v_i^{1*}, ..., v_i^{h*}⟩)
15     ⟨û_i^0, û_i^1, ..., û_i^h⟩ ← ⟨u_i^{0*}, u_i^{1*}, ..., u_i^{h*}⟩ − ⟨u_i^0, u_i^1, ..., u_i^h⟩
16 else
17     ⟨û_i^0, û_i^1, ..., û_i^h⟩ ← ⟨Null, Null, ..., Null⟩
18 Send GAIN(⟨û_i^0, û_i^1, ..., û_i^h⟩) to all neighbors
```

changing environments. Algorithm 1 shows its pseudocode, where each agent a_i maintains the following data structures:

- $iter$ is the current iteration number.
- $context$ is a vector of tuples (x_j, t, v_j^t) for all its neighboring variables $x_j \in N(a_i)$. Each of these tuples represents the agent's assumption that variable x_j is assigned value v_j^t at time step t.
- $\langle v_i^0, v_i^1, \ldots, v_i^h \rangle$ is a vector of the agent's current value assignment for its variable x_i at each time step t.
- $\langle v_i^{0*}, v_i^{1*}, \ldots, v_i^{h*} \rangle$ is a vector of the agent's best value assignment for its variable x_i at each time step t.
- $\langle u_i^0, u_i^1, \ldots, u_i^h \rangle$ is a vector of the agent's utility (rewards from reward functions minus costs from switching costs) given its current value assignment at each time step t.
- $\langle u_i^{0*}, u_i^{1*}, \ldots, u_i^{h*} \rangle$ is a vector of the agent's best utility given its best value assignment at each time step t.
- $\langle \hat{u}_i^{0*}, \hat{u}_i^{1*}, \ldots, \hat{u}_i^{h*} \rangle$, which is a vector of the agent's best gain in utility at each time step t.

The high-level ideas are as follows: (1) Each agent a_i starts by finding an initial value assignment to its variable x_i for each time step $0 \leq t \leq h$ and initializes its context $context$. (2) Each agent uses VALUE messages to ensure that it has the correct assumption on its neighboring agents' variables' values. (3) Each agent computes its current utilities given its current value assignments, its best utilities over all possible value assignments, and its best gain in utilities, and sends this gain in a GAIN message to all its neighbors. (4) Each agent changes the value of its variable for time step t if its gain for that time step is the largest over all its neighbors' gain for that time step, and repeats steps 2 through 4 until a termination condition is met. In more detail:

Step 1: Each agent initializes its vector of best values to a vector of *Nulls* (line 2) and calls INITIALASSIGNMENT to initializes its current values (line 3). The values can be initialized randomly or according to some heuristic function. We describe later one such heuristic. Finally, the agent initializes its context, where it assumes that the values for its neighbors is null for all time steps (line 4).

Step 2: The agent sends its current value assignment in a VALUE message to all neighbors (line 5). When it receives a VALUE message from its neighbor, it updates its context with the value assignments in that message (lines 19-21). When it has received VALUE

Procedure When Receive VALUE($\langle v_s^{0*}, v_s^{1*}, \ldots, v_s^{h*} \rangle$)

19 **foreach** t from 0 to h **do**
20   **if** $v_s^{t*} \neq Null$ **then**
21   Update $(x_s, t, v_s^t) \in context$ with (x_s, t, v_s^{t*})
22 **if** received VALUE messages from all neighbors in this iteration **then**
23   CALCGAIN()
24 $iter \leftarrow iter + 1$

Procedure When Receive GAIN($\langle \hat{u}_s^0, \hat{u}_s^1, \ldots, \hat{u}_s^h \rangle$)

25 **if** $\langle \hat{u}_s^0, \hat{u}_s^1, \ldots, \hat{u}_s^h \rangle \neq \langle$Null, Null, …, Null$\rangle$ **then**
26   **foreach** t from 0 to h **do**
27   **if** $\hat{u}_i^t \leq 0 \vee \hat{u}_s^t > \hat{u}_i^t$ **then**
28       $v_i^{t*} \leftarrow$ Null
29 **if** received GAIN messages from all neighbors in this iteration **then**
30   **foreach** t from 0 to h **do**
31   **if** $v_i^{t*} \neq$ Null **then**
32       $v_i^t \leftarrow v_i^{t*}$
33   Send VALUE($\langle v_i^{1*}, v_i^{2*}, \ldots, v_i^{h*} \rangle$) to all neighbors

messages from all neighbors in the current iteration, it means that its context now correctly reflects the neighbors' actual values. It then calls CALCGAIN to start Step 3 (line 23).

Step 3: In the CALCGAIN procedure, the agent calls CALCUTILS to calculate its utility for each time step given its current value assignments and its neighbors' current value assignments recorded in its context (line 6). The utility for a time step t is made out of two components (line 41). The first component is the sum of rewards over all reward functions that involve the agent, under the assumption that the agent takes on its current value and its neighbors take on their values according to its $context$. Specifically, if the scope of the reward function F_j^t involves only decision variables, then $F_j^t(v_i^t, v_j^t)$ is a function of both the agent's current value v_i^t and its neighbor's value v_j^t in its $context$ and is defined according to Equations (11) to (12). If the scope involves both decision and random variables, then $F_j^t(v_i^t)$ is a unary constraint that is only a function of the agent's current value v_i^t and is defined according to Equations (13) to (15). The second component is the cost of switching values from the previous time step $t-1$ to the current time step t and switching from the current time step to the next time step $t+1$. This cost is c if the values in two subsequent time steps are different and 0 otherwise. The variable c_i^t captures this cost (lines 35-40). The (net) utility is thus the reward from the reward functions minus the switching cost (line 41).

The agent then searches over all possible combination of values for its variable across all time steps to find the best value assignment that results in the largest cumulative cost across all time steps (lines 8-12). It then computes the net gain in utility at each time step by subtracting the utility of the best value assignment with the utility of the current value assignment (lines 13-15).

Step 4: The agent sends its gains in a GAIN message to all neighbors (line 18). When it receives a GAIN message from its neighbor, it updates its best value v_i^{t*} for time step t to null if its gain is non-positive (i.e., $\hat{u}_i^t \leq 0$) or its neighbor has a larger gain (i.e., $\hat{u}_s^t > \hat{u}_i^t$) for that time step (line 27). When it has received GAIN messages from all neighbors in the current iteration, it means that it has identified, for each time step, whether its gain is the largest over all its neighbors' gains. The time steps where it has the largest gain are exactly those time steps t where v_i^{t*} is not null. The agent thus assigns its best value for these time steps as its current value and restarts Step 2 by sending a VALUE message that contains its new values to all its neighbors (lines 29-33).

Function CalcUtils($\langle v_i^0, v_i^1, \ldots, v_i^h \rangle$)

34 **foreach** t from 0 to h **do**
35   **if** $t = 0$ **then**
36     $c_i^t \leftarrow \gamma^0 \cdot \text{cost}(v_i^0, v_i^1)$
37   **else if** $t = h$ **then**
38     $c_i^t \leftarrow \gamma^{h-1} \cdot \text{cost}(v_i^{h-1}, v_i^h)$
39   **else**
40     $c_i^t \leftarrow \gamma^{t-1} \cdot \text{cost}(v_i^{t-1}, v_i^t) + \gamma^t \cdot \text{cost}(v_i^t, v_i^{t+1})$
41   $u_i^t \leftarrow \sum_{F_j^t | x_i \in \mathbf{x}^{F_j^t}} F_j^t - c_i^t$
42 **return** $\langle u_i^0, u_i^1, \ldots, u_i^h \rangle$

Function CalcCumulativeUtil($\langle v_i^0, v_i^1, \ldots, v_i^h \rangle$)

43 $u \leftarrow \sum_{t=0}^{h} \sum_{F_j^t | x_i \in \mathbf{x}^{F_j^t}} F_j^t$
44 $c \leftarrow 0$
45 **foreach** t from 0 to $h-1$ **do**
46   $c \leftarrow c + \gamma^t \cdot \text{cost}(v_i^t, v_i^{t+1})$
47 **return** $u - c$

Heuristics for INITIALASSIGNMENT: We simplify the PD-DCOP into h independent DCOPs by assuming that the switching costs are 0 and the constraints with random variables are collapsed into unary constraints similar to the description for our exact approach. Then, one can use any off-the-shelf DCOP algorithm to solve these h DCOPs. We initially used DPOP to do this, but our preliminary experimental results show that this approach is computationally inefficient; the runtimes with this approach were larger than with the random assignment heuristic.

However, we observed that these h DCOPs do not vary much across subsequent DCOPs as changes are due only to the changes in distribution of values of random variables. Therefore, the utilities in UTIL tables of an agent a_i remain unchanged across subsequent DCOPs if neither it nor any of its descendants in the pseudo-tree are constrained with a random variable. We thus used S-DPOP to solve the h DCOPs and the runtimes decreased marginally.

We further optimized this approach by designing a new pseudo-trees construction heuristic, such that agents that are constrained with random variables are higher up in the pseudo-tree. Intuitively, this will maximize the number of utility values that can be reused, as they remain unchanged across subsequent time steps. This heuristic, within the Distributed DFS algorithm [8], assigns a score to each agent a according to heuristic $h_1(a)$:

$$h_1(a) = (1 + I(a)) \cdot |N_y(a)| \tag{17}$$

$$N_y(a) = \{a' | a' \in N(a) \wedge \exists f \in \mathbf{F}, \exists y \in \mathbf{Y} : \{a', y\} \in \mathbf{x}^f\}$$

$$I(a) = \begin{cases} 0 & \text{if } \forall f \in \mathbf{F}, \forall y \in \mathbf{Y} : \{a, y\} \notin \mathbf{x}^f \\ 1 & \text{otherwise} \end{cases}$$

It then makes the agent with the largest score the pseudo-tree root and traverses the constraint graph using DFS, greedily adding the neighboring agent with the largest score as the child of the current agent. However, this resulting pseudo-tree can have a large depth, which is undesirable. The popular max-degree heuristic $h_2(a) = |N(a)|$, which chooses the agent with the largest number of neighbors, typically results in pseudo-trees with small depths. We thus also introduced a hybrid heuristic $h_3(a) = w\, h_1(a) + (1 - w)\, h_2(a)$, which combines both heuristics and weigh them according to a *heuristic weight* w.

5.3 Theoretical Properties

In the following discussion, let $O(\mathcal{L})$ denote the agent's space requirement for the INITIALASSIGNMENT function in line 3.

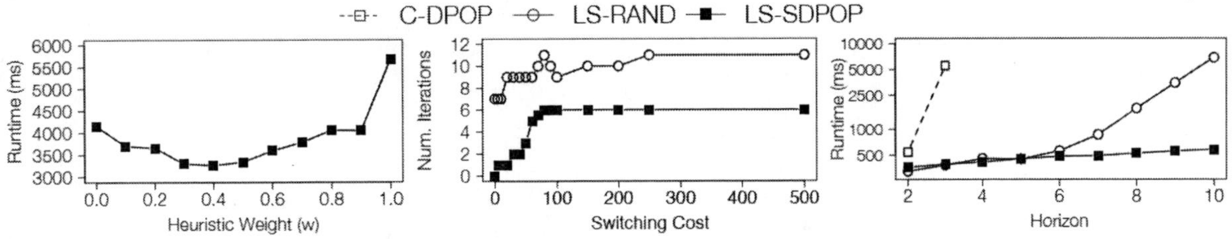

Figure 1: Experimental Results Varying Heuristic Weight (left), Switching Cost (middle), and Horizon (right)

THEOREM 4. *The agent's space required by the PD-DCOP approximation approach is* $O(\mathcal{L} + (h+1)|\mathbf{A}|)$.

PROOF: In our approximation algorithm, each agent first calls the INITIALASSIGNMENT function to find an initial value assignment to its variable for each time step $0 \leq t \leq h$ (line 3). Thus, the memory requirement of this step is $O((h+1) + \mathcal{L})$ at each agent. Next, each agent running our approximation algorithm performs a local search step (lines 4-5), which is analogous to that of MGM. However, different from MGM, our agents search for tuples of $h+1$ values, one for each time step in the horizon. Thus, at each iteration, and for each time step t, each agent stores a vector of values for its current and best variable assignments for its variable; a vector of the agent's utilities and best utilities given its current value assignments; and a vector of the agent's best gain in utility. In addition, each agent stores the context of its neighbors' values for each time step t, which requires $O((h+1) \cdot |N(a_i)|)$ space. Thus, the overall space requirement for our approximation algorithm is $O(\mathcal{L} + (h+1)|\mathbf{A}|)$ per agent. □

In Section 7, we present two approximation approaches: LS-DPOP, which uses DPOP as the INITIALASSIGNMENT function, and LS-RAND, which uses a random assignment function. Thus, the space complexity of LS-DPOP is $O(d^{w^*})$ – where d is the size of the largest domain and w^* is the induced width of the pseudo-tree – as DPOP dominates the space complexity in the initialization step. The space complexity of LS-RAND is instead dominated by the second step of the approximation PD-DCOP algorithm, and it is thus $O((h+1)|\mathbf{A}|)$.

6. RELATED WORK

Aside from the D-DCOPs described in Sections 1 and 2, several approaches have been proposed to proactively solve centralized *Dynamic CSPs*, where value assignments of variables or utilities of constraints may change according to some probabilistic model [29, 10]. The goal is typically to find a solution that is robust to possible changes. Other related models include *Mixed CSPs* [6], which model decision problems under uncertainty by introducing state variables, which are not under control of the solver, and seek assignments that are consistent to any state of the world; and *Stochastic CSPs* [30, 27], which introduce probability distributions that are associated to outcomes of state variables, and seek solutions that maximize the probability of constraint consistencies. While these proactive approaches have been used to solve CSP variants, they have not been used to solve Dynamic DCOPs to the best of our knowledge.

Researchers have also introduced *Markovian D-DCOPs (MD-DCOPs)*, which model D-DCOPs with state variables that are beyond the control of agents [20]. However, they assume that the state is observable to the agents, while PD-DCOPs assume otherwise. Additionally, MD-DCOP agents do not incur a cost for changing values in MD-DCOPs and only a reactive online learning approach to solving the problem has been proposed thus far.

Another related body of work is *Decentralized Markov Decision Processes (Dec-MDPs)* [2]. In a Dec-MDP, agents can also observe its local state (the global state is the combination of all local states), and the goal of a Dec-MDP is to find a policy that maps each local state to the action for each agent. Thus, like PD-DCOPs, it too solves a sequential decision making problem. However, Dec-MDPs are typically solved in a centralized manner [2, 1, 4, 5] due to its high complexity – solving Dec-MDPs optimally is NEXP-hard even for the case with only two agents [2]. In contrast, PD-DCOPs are solved in a decentralized manner and its complexity is only PSPACE-hard. The reason for the lower complexity is because the solution of PD-DCOPs are *open-loop* policies, which are policies that are not dependent on state observations.

Decentralized Partially Observable MDPs (Dec-POMDPs) [2] is a generalization of Dec-MDPs, where an agent may not accurately observe its local state. Instead, it maintains a belief of its local state. A Dec-POMDP policy thus maps each belief to an action for each agent. Solving Dec-POMDPs is also NEXP-hard [2] and they are also typically solved in a centralized manner [9, 26, 25, 31, 5, 21] with some exceptions [18]. Researchers have also developed a hybrid model, called ND-POMDP [19], which is a Dec-POMDP that exploits locality of agent interactions like a DCOP.

In summary, one can view DCOPs and Dec-(PO)MDPs as two ends of a spectrum of offline distributed planning models. In terms of expressiveness, DCOPs can solve single timestep problems while Dec-(PO)MDPs can solve sequential problems. However, DCOPs are NP-hard while Dec-(PO)MDPs are NEXP-hard. PD-DCOPs attempt to balance the trade off between expressiveness and complexity by searching for open-loop policies instead of closed-loop policies of Dec-(PO)MDPs. They are more expressive than DCOPs at the cost of a higher complexity, yet not as expressive as Dec-(PO)MDPs, but also without their prohibitive complexity.

7. EXPERIMENTAL RESULTS

We empirically evaluate *Collapsed DPOP (C-DPOP)*, which collapses the PD-DCOP into a DCOP and solves it with DPOP; *Local Search (Random) (LS-RAND)*, which runs the local search algorithm with random initial values; and *Local Search (S-DPOP) (LS-SDPOP)*, which runs the algorithm with S-DPOP and the h_3 heuristic function to generate pseudo-trees. In contrast to many experiments in the literature, our experiments are performed in an *actual distributed system*, where each agent is an Intel i7 Quadcore 3.4GHz machine with 16GB of RAM, connected in a local area network. We thus report *actual* distributed runtimes. We impose a timeout of 30 minutes and a memory limit of 16 GB. Results are averaged over 30 runs. We use the following default configuration: Number of agents and decision variables $|\mathbf{A}| = |\mathbf{X} \setminus \mathbf{Y}| = 12$; number of random variables $|\mathbf{Y}| = 0.25 \cdot |\mathbf{X} \setminus \mathbf{Y}|$; domain size $|D_x| = |\Omega_y| = 3$; horizon $h = 3$; switching cost $c = 50$; constraint densities $p_1^a = p_1^b = p_1^c = 0.5$;[3] and constraint tightness $p_2 = 0.8$.

[3] p_1^a is the density of functions between two decision variables, p_1^b is the density of functions between a decision variable and a random variable, and p_1^c is the fraction of decision variables that are constrained with random

$|\mathbf{A}|$	C-DPOP		LS-SDPOP			LS-RAND	
	time (ms)	ρ	time (ms)		ρ	time (ms)	ρ
2	223	1.001	197	(207)	1.003	203	1.019
4	489	1.000	255	(307)	1.009	273	1.037
6	5547	1.000	382	(456)	1.011	385	1.045
8	—		739	(838)	1.001	556	1.034
12	—		4821	(7091)	1.003	1092	1.031
16	—		264897	(595245)	1.033	2203	1.015

Table 1: Experimental Results Varying Number of Agents

$|\mathbf{A}|$	C-DPOP		LS-SDPOP		LS-RAND	
	time (ms)	% SAT	time (ms)	% SAT	time (ms)	% SAT
2	509	100	262	100	271	100
4	4786	100	367	100	399	100
6	—		2651	96	718	93
8	—		71726	96	3249	86
10	—		—		9723	86
12	—		—		15370	86

Table 2: Results for Dynamic Distributed Meeting Scheduling

Random Networks. We first vary the weight w of the pseudo-tree construction heuristic h_3 to identify the best weight for LS-SDPOP. Figure 1(left) shows the runtimes of LS-SDPOP. At $w = 0$, the heuristic h_3 corresponds the max-degree heuristic h_2 and, at $w = 1$, the heuristic is analogous to our h_1 heuristic. The runtimes are high at both extremes for the following reasons: When $w = 0$, LS-SDPOP exploits weakly the reuse of information, and when $w = 1$, the resulting pseudo-trees have large depths, which in turn result in large runtimes. The best weight is found at $w = 0.4$, thus we use this value for the remaining experiments.

We then vary the switching cost c of the problem from 0 to 500 to investigate its impact on the algorithms' performance. Figure 1(center) shows the number of iterations it takes for the local search algorithms to converge from the initial solution. When $c = 0$, the initial solution found by LS-SDPOP is an optimal solution since the initial solution already optimizes the utilities of the problem over all time steps ignoring switching costs. Thus, it requires 0 iterations to converge. For sufficiently large costs ($c \geq 100$), the optimal solution is one where the values for each agent is the same across all time steps since the cost of changing values is larger than the gain in utility. Thus, the number of iterations they take to converge is the same for all large switching costs. At intermediate cost values ($0 < c < 100$), they require an increasing number of iterations to converge. Finally, LS-RAND requires more iterations to converge than LS-SDPOP since it starts with poorer initial solutions.

We also vary the horizon h of the problem from 2 to 10 to evaluate the scalability of the algorithms.[4] Figure 1(right) shows the runtimes of all three algorithms. As expected, the runtimes increase when the horizon increases. When the horizon $h \geq 6$ is sufficiently large, LS-SDPOP is faster than LS-RAND indicating that the overhead of finding good initial solutions with S-DPOP is worth the savings in runtime to converge to the final solution.

Finally, we vary the number of agents $|\mathbf{A}|$ (and thus the number of the decision variables) of the problem from 2 to 16. Table 1 tabulates the runtimes and the approximation ration ρ for all three algorithms. The runtimes of LS-SDPOP without reusing information are shown in parentheses. C-DPOP times out after $|\mathbf{A}| \geq 8$. In general, the runtimes of C-DPOP is largest, followed the by the runtimes of LS-SDPOP and the runtimes of LS-RAND. The difference in runtimes increases with increasing number of agents, indicating that the overhead to find good initial solutions with S-DPOP is not worth the savings in convergence runtime. As expected, the approximation ratio ρ with C-DPOP the is the smallest, since it finds optimal solutions, whilst the ratios of the local search algorithms are of similar values, indicating that they converge to solutions with similar qualities. Therefore, LS-SDPOP is preferred in problems with few agents but large horizons and LS-RAND is preferred in problems with many agents but small horizons.

However, another factor to consider when choosing which algorithm to run is their memory requirement. LS-SDPOP suffer from the same exponential memory requirement (in the induced width of the pseudo-tree) of DPOP [22]. In contrast, LS-RAND's memory requirement is only linear in the number of agents and the horizon. Thus, LS-RAND is preferred in problems where agents have a limited amount of memory (e.g., sensor networks).

variables.

[4]In this experiment, we set the number of decision variables to 6 in order for the algorithms to scale to larger horizons.

Dynamic Distributed Meeting Scheduling. We also evaluate our PD-DCOP algorithms on the dynamic distributed meeting scheduling problem introduced in Section 3, where we use the following parameters: We allow each meeting to be scheduled in 4 different starting time and 2 locations. We generate the underlying graph topology randomly, using the same settings described in the previous experiments. Thus, the number of meetings and the number of meetings participants are not bounded by any fixed value. In order to ensure that each agent controls exactly one decision variable, we use the pseudo-agent decomposition technique [35]. Inequality constraints between the meeting start time and locations ensure that an agent can attend at most one meeting at a given time, and that no two meetings are held in the same location at the same time. In addition, start times and locations of each meeting's participants are enforced to be equal, so as to produce feasible schedules. Finally, agents' preferences on time and meeting locations are modeled through unary costs functions. We use the same heuristic weight, switching costs, and horizon settings from the previous experiment on random networks.

Table 2 illustrates the average runtimes (in ms) and the percentage of feasible solutions over 30 instances, returned by the algorithms at varying the number of agents $|\mathbf{A}|$ from 2 to 12. Similar to the results analyzed for random networks, both approximation approaches (LS-SDPOP and LS-RAND) can produce solutions faster than the exact approach. However, the number of satisfiable instances decreases with increasing number of agents. In particular, the quality of solutions found by LS-SDPOP degrades slower than the quality of solutions found by LS-RAND. The reason is likely because LS-SDPOP starts with a better initial solution than LS-RAND. As expected, these results reveal that for our PD-DCOP approximation approach, the initial solution is crucial to ensure convergence to solutions of high quality within a bounded runtime.

8. CONCLUSIONS

In real-world applications, agents often act in dynamic environments. Thus, the Dynamic DCOP formulation is attractive to model such problems. Current research has focused at solving such problems *reactively*, thus discarding the information on possible future changes, which is often available in many applications. To cope with this limitation, we (*i*) introduce *Proactive Dynamic DCOPs* (*PD-DCOPs*), which model the dynamism in Dynamic DCOPs; (*ii*) provide theoretical results on the complexity class of PD-DCOPs; and (*iii*) develop an exact PD-DCOP algorithm that solves the problem *proactively* as well as an approximation algorithm with quality guarantees that can scale to larger and more complex problems. Finally, in contrast to many experiments in the literature, we evaluate our algorithms on an actual distributed system, which will ease the transition to real-world applications.

REFERENCES

[1] R. Becker, S. Zilberstein, V. Lesser, and C. Goldman. Solving transition independent decentralized Markov decision processes. *Journal of Artificial Intelligence Research*, 22:423–455, 2004.

[2] D. Bernstein, R. Givan, N. Immerman, and S. Zilberstein. The complexity of decentralized control of Markov decision processes. *Mathematics of Operations Research*, 27(4):819–840, 2002.

[3] F. Delle Fave, A. Rogers, Z. Xu, S. Sukkarieh, and N. Jennings. Deploying the max-sum algorithm for decentralised coordination and task allocation of unmanned aerial vehicles for live aerial imagery collection. In *Proceedings of ICRA*, pages 469–476, 2012.

[4] J. S. Dibangoye, C. Amato, and A. Doniec. Scaling up decentralized MDPs through heuristic search. In *Proceedings of UAI*, pages 217–226, 2012.

[5] J. S. Dibangoye, C. Amato, A. Doniec, and F. Charpillet. Producing efficient error-bounded solutions for transition independent decentralized MDPs. In *Proceedings of AAMAS*, pages 539–546, 2013.

[6] H. Fargier, J. Lang, and T. Schiex. Mixed constraint satisfaction: A framework for decision problems under incomplete knowledge. In *Proceedings of AAAI*, pages 175–180, 1996.

[7] A. Farinelli, A. Rogers, and N. Jennings. Agent-based decentralised coordination for sensor networks using the max-sum algorithm. *Autonomous Agents and Multi-Agent Systems*, 28(3):337–380, 2014.

[8] Y. Hamadi, C. Bessière, and J. Quinqueton. Distributed intelligent backtracking. In *Proceedings of ECAI*, pages 219–223, 1998.

[9] E. A. Hansen, D. S. Bernstein, and S. Zilberstein. Dynamic programming for partially observable stochastic games. In *Proceedings of AAAI*, pages 709–715, 2004.

[10] A. Holland and B. O'Sullivan. Weighted super solutions for constraint programs. In *Proceedings of AAAI*, pages 378–383, 2005.

[11] A. Kumar, B. Faltings, and A. Petcu. Distributed constraint optimization with structured resource constraints. In *Proceedings of AAMAS*, pages 923–930, 2009.

[12] R. Lass, E. Sultanik, and W. Regli. Dynamic distributed constraint reasoning. In *Proceedings of AAAI*, pages 1466–1469, 2008.

[13] T. Léauté and B. Faltings. Coordinating logistics operations with privacy guarantees. In *Proceedings of IJCAI*, pages 2482–2487, 2011.

[14] R. Maheswaran, J. Pearce, and M. Tambe. Distributed algorithms for DCOP: A graphical game-based approach. In *Proceedings of PDCS*, pages 432–439, 2004.

[15] R. Maheswaran, M. Tambe, E. Bowring, J. Pearce, and P. Varakantham. Taking DCOP to the real world: Efficient complete solutions for distributed event scheduling. In *Proceedings of AAMAS*, pages 310–317, 2004.

[16] S. Miller, S. Ramchurn, and A. Rogers. Optimal decentralised dispatch of embedded generation in the smart grid. In *Proceedings of AAMAS*, pages 281–288, 2012.

[17] P. Modi, W.-M. Shen, M. Tambe, and M. Yokoo. ADOPT: Asynchronous distributed constraint optimization with quality guarantees. *Artificial Intelligence*, 161(1–2):149–180, 2005.

[18] R. Nair, M. Tambe, M. Yokoo, D. Pynadath, and S. Marsella. Taming decentralized POMDPs: Towards efficient policy computation for multiagent settings. In *Proceedings of IJCAI*, pages 705–711, 2003.

[19] R. Nair, P. Varakantham, M. Tambe, and M. Yokoo. Networked distributed POMDPs: A synthesis of distributed constraint optimization and POMDPs. In *Proceedings of AAAI*, pages 133–139, 2005.

[20] D. T. Nguyen, W. Yeoh, H. C. Lau, S. Zilberstein, and C. Zhang. Decentralized multi-agent reinforcement learning in average-reward dynamic DCOPs. In *Proceedings of AAAI*, pages 1447–1455, 2014.

[21] F. Oliehoek, M. Spaan, C. Amato, and S. Whiteson. Incremental clustering and expansion for faster optimal planning in Dec-POMDPs. *Journal of Artificial Intelligence Research*, 46:449–509, 2013.

[22] A. Petcu and B. Faltings. A scalable method for multiagent constraint optimization. In *Proceedings of IJCAI*, pages 1413–1420, 2005.

[23] A. Petcu and B. Faltings. Superstabilizing, fault-containing multiagent combinatorial optimization. In *Proceedings of AAAI*, pages 449–454, 2005.

[24] A. Petcu and B. Faltings. Optimal solution stability in dynamic, distributed constraint optimization. In *Proceedings of IAT*, pages 321–327, 2007.

[25] S. Seuken and S. Zilberstein. Memory-bounded dynamic programming for DEC-POMDPs. In *Proceedings of IJCAI*, pages 2009–2015, 2007.

[26] D. Szer, F. Charpillet, and S. Zilberstein. MAA*: A heuristic search algorithm for solving decentralized POMDPs. In *Proceedings of UAI*, pages 576–590, 2005.

[27] S. A. Tarim, S. Manandhar, and T. Walsh. Stochastic constraint programming: A scenario-based approach. *Constraints*, 11(1):53–80, 2006.

[28] S. Ueda, A. Iwasaki, and M. Yokoo. Coalition structure generation based on distributed constraint optimization. In *Proceedings of AAAI*, pages 197–203, 2010.

[29] R. Wallace and E. Freuder. Stable solutions for dynamic constraint satisfaction problems. In *Proceedings CP*, pages 447–461, 1998.

[30] T. Walsh. Stochastic constraint programming. In *Proceedings of ECAI*, pages 111–115, 2002.

[31] S. Witwicki and E. Durfee. Towards a unifying characterization for quantifying weak coupling in Dec-POMDPs. In *Proceedings of AAMAS*, pages 29–36, 2011.

[32] W. Yeoh, A. Felner, and S. Koenig. BnB-ADOPT: An asynchronous branch-and-bound DCOP algorithm. *Journal of Artificial Intelligence Research*, 38:85–133, 2010.

[33] W. Yeoh, P. Varakantham, X. Sun, and S. Koenig. Incremental DCOP search algorithms for solving dynamic DCOPs. In *Proceedings of IAT*, pages 257–264, 2015.

[34] W. Yeoh and M. Yokoo. Distributed problem solving. *AI Magazine*, 33(3):53–65, 2012.

[35] M. Yokoo, editor. *Distributed Constraint Satisfaction: Foundation of Cooperation in Multi-agent Systems*. Springer, 2001.

[36] R. Zivan, H. Yedidsion, S. Okamoto, R. Glinton, and K. Sycara. Distributed constraint optimization for teams of mobile sensing agents. *Autonomous Agents and Multi-Agent Systems*, 29(3):495–536, 2015.

ER-DCOPs: A Framework for Distributed Constraint Optimization with Uncertainty in Constraint Utilities

Tiep Le, Ferdinando Fioretto, William Yeoh, Tran Cao Son, and Enrico Pontelli
New Mexico State University
Las Cruces, New Mexico, USA
{tile,ffiorett,wyeoh,tson,epontell}@cs.nmsu.edu

ABSTRACT

Distributed Constraint Optimization Problems (DCOPs) have been used to model a number of multi-agent coordination problems. In DCOPs, agents are assumed to have complete information about the utility of their possible actions. However, in many real-world applications, such utilities are stochastic due to the presence of exogenous events that are beyond the direct control of the agents. This paper addresses this issue by extending the standard DCOP model to *Expected Regret DCOP* (ER-DCOP) for DCOP applications with uncertainty in constraint utilities. Different from other approaches, ER-DCOPs aim at minimizing the overall expected regret of the problem. The paper proposes the *ER-DPOP* algorithm for solving ER-DCOPs, which is complete and requires a linear number of messages with respect to the number of agents in the problem. We further present two implementations of ER-DPOP—GPU- and ASP-based implementations—that orthogonally exploit the problem structure and present their evaluations on random networks and power network problems.

Keywords

DCOP; Expected Regret; GPU; ASP

1. INTRODUCTION

Distributed Constraint Optimization Problems (DCOPs) are problems where agents need to cooperatively determine their variables' value assignment to maximize the sum of resulting constraint utilities [22, 25, 19, 31]. Researchers have used them to model various multi-agent coordination and resource allocation problems [18, 7, 28, 30, 32].

A DCOP is typically specified by a finite set of *decision variables* (throughout the paper, whenever we mention variables, we mean decision variables) and a finite set of *constraints* among these variables. Each constraint indicates *a utility* for each value assignment of the variables involved in it. One limitation of DCOPs is that the constraint utilities are assumed to be *known* and *deterministic*. Thus, the DCOP model is not suitable for modeling problems where constraint utilities are stochastic (e.g., the utility of a constraint might depend on exogenous factors that are beyond the *direct* control of the agents, such as weather conditions, properties of the surrounding environment, etc.).

To address the above limitation, several DCOP extensions that handle stochasticity in the constraint utilities have been developed. These extensions require that the constraint utilities **(i)** are sampled from a predefined function that is either known [1] or concave [23]; or **(ii)** depend on additional random variables (not controlled by agents) whose probability distributions are known [16, 14]. Unfortunately, such requirements are not met in several real-world applications (e.g., accurate weather models are often unavailable).

Uncertain Reward DCOP (UR-DCOP) [29] is another extension of the DCOP model that uses an additional *random variable* for each constraint, in order to handle stochastic utilities. Different from other approaches, it can model problems where the probability distribution (referred to as *belief*) of random variables is not known, but sampled from a *known probability distribution space* (referred to as the *belief space*). UR-DCOP *(i)* assumes that the belief of a random variable is *independent* from the values of the decision variables; and *(ii)* uses the *minimax regret* strategy, which minimizes the worst-case loss (the *regret*) over the known belief space. This strategy may be overly pessimistic in many situations.

In this paper, we develop an alternative approach for DCOPs with stochastic constraint utilities that relaxes some of the assumptions made by previously developed models. Specifically, we **(1)** propose the *Expected Regret DCOP* (ER-DCOP) model, which removes the independence assumption in UR-DCOPs and optimizes the *minimum expected regret* in response to the constraint utilities' uncertainty; **(2)** develop the *ER-DPOP* algorithm to solve ER-DCOPs, proposing two implementations: one that exploits GPUs to speed up the process of solving ER-DCOPs, and another one that uses ASP and exploits inference rules to prune the solution search space; **(3)** evaluate the performance of the ER-DPOP implementations on random graphs and power network problems; and **(4)** experimentally show that ER-DCOP solutions outperform corresponding UR-DCOP solutions in terms of the actual regret.

The rest of the paper is organized as follows. We start with a motivating example and review some background in Sections 2 and 3, respectively. The ER-DCOP model is introduced in Section 4, the ER-DPOP algorithm to solve this model is proposed in Section 5, followed by some theoretical analysis in Section 6. Next, we introduce the GPU-based and the ASP-based ER-DPOP implementations in Section 7. Section 8 provides the experimental results, and we conclude the paper with some discussions and related works.

2. MOTIVATING EXAMPLE

In this section, we introduce a motivating example that is used to illustrate the proposed model and algorithm.

EXAMPLE 1. *Consider a Mars Rover problem consisting of two* robotic workers x_1 *and* x_2 *that will collect soil samples on Mars*

Appears in: *Proceedings of the 15th International Conference on Autonomous Agents and Multiagent Systems (AAMAS 2016), J. Thangarajah, K. Tuyls, C. Jonker, S. Marsella (eds.), May 9–13, 2016, Singapore.*

x_1	x_3	r_1	U_1	P^e	P^u
0	0	0	0	10%	30%
		1	50	90%	70%
0	1	0	0	30%	50%
		1	30	70%	50%

(a)

x_2	x_3	r_2	U_2	P^e	P^u
0	0	0	0	50%	90%
		1	40	50%	10%
0	1	0	0	20%	50%
		1	50	80%	50%

(b)

Table 1: Constraints and their Probabilistic Models

(i.e., $x_1, x_2 \in \{0\}^1$), and an assistant robot x_3 *($x_3 \in \{0,1\}$) that will be able to support one worker, either x_1 ($x_3 = 0$) or x_2 ($x_3 = 1$). The random variables r_1 and r_2 are introduced as follows: with $i \in \{1,2\}$, $r_i = 1$ (resp. $r_i = 0$) represents the fact that the worker x_i succeeds (resp. fails) in collecting soil samples. The first four columns of the Table 1(a) (resp. 1(b)) describe the constraint utilities U_1 (resp. U_2) for the joint work between the robots x_1 and x_3 (resp. x_2 and x_3). For example, in Table 1(a), with robot x_3 supporting (i.e., $x_3 = 0$), if worker x_1 succeeds, it collects 50 samples (i.e., $U_1 = 50$); if it fails, it collects 0 sample (i.e., $U_1 = 0$). Moreover, we assume that the chance for workers to succeed or fail depends only on the terrain condition (i.e., even (e) or uneven (u)). The terrain condition is 88% uneven and 12% even. The columns P^e (resp. P^u) in Table 1(a and b) define the probability distributions of the respective random variable for even (resp. uneven) terrain. For example, the first two rows of the column P^e in the Table 1(a) show that, given that the terrain is even and $x_3 = 0$, the probability of the worker x_1 to fail (i.e., $r_1 = 0$) or succeed (i.e., $r_1 = 1$) is 10% or 90%, respectively.*

3. BACKGROUND

In this section, we present an overview of DCOPs; describe DPOP, a popular, complete algorithm to solve DCOPs, whose resolution process is central in our ER-DPOP algorithm; and review the formal definition of UR-DCOPs. We further provide some fundamental definitions of GPU and ASP.

3.1 DCOP

A *Distributed Constraint Optimization Problem* (DCOP) is a tuple $\mathcal{M} = \langle \mathcal{X}, \mathcal{D}, \mathcal{F}, \mathcal{A}, \alpha \rangle$ where $\mathcal{X} = \{x_1, \ldots, x_n\}$ is a finite set of (decision) *variables*; $\mathcal{D} = \{D_1, \ldots, D_n\}$ is a set of finite *domains*, where each D_i is the domain of variable $x_i \in \mathcal{X}$; $\mathcal{F} = \{f_1, \ldots, f_m\}$ is a finite set of *constraints*, where each k_j-ary constraint $f_j : D_{j_1} \times D_{j_2} \times \ldots \times D_{j_{k_j}} \mapsto \mathbb{R} \cup \{-\infty\}$ specifies the utility of each combination of values of the variables in its *scope*; the scope is denoted by $scp(f_j) = \{x_{j_1}, \ldots, x_{j_{k_j}}\}$; $\mathcal{A} = \{a_1, \ldots, a_p\}$ is a finite set of *agents*; and $\alpha : \mathcal{X} \mapsto \mathcal{A}$ maps each variable to an agent. Each constraint in $\mathcal{F}$ can be either *hard*, indicating that some value combinations result in a utility of $-\infty$ and must be avoided, or *soft*, indicating that all value combinations result in a finite utility and need not be avoided. Given a constraint f_j and a *complete value assignment* x for all decision variables, we denote with x_{f_j} a *partial value assignment* from x for all variables in $scp(f_j)$. A *solution* of a DCOP is a complete value assignment $\mathbf{x}$ for all variables such that $\mathbf{x} = \text{argmax}_x \sum_{j=1}^{m} f_j(x_{f_j})$.

A DCOP can be described by its *constraint graph*, i.e., a graph whose nodes correspond to the variables in $\mathcal{X}$ and whose edges connect pairs of variables in the scope of the same constraint. A simplifying assumption, which is common practice in the DCOP literature, is that each agent owns exactly one variable. Thus, nodes of a constraint graph can be seen as representing agents without causing any confusion. A *pseudo-tree* arrangement of a DCOP has the same nodes as the constraint graph and a subset of its edges such that *(i)* the included edges (called *tree edges*) form a rooted tree, and *(ii)* two variables in the scope of the same constraint appear in the same branch of the tree. The remaining edges of the constraint graph not included in the pseudo-tree are called *back edges*. Tree edges connect a node with its parent and its children while back edges connect a node with its pseudo-parents and pseudo-children (i.e., higher nodes are parents or pseudo-parents, and lower nodes are children or pseudo-children). In a pseudo-tree, the *separator* of a node x_i (denoted by sep_i) is the set of ancestors of x_i that are directly connected (via tree edges or back edges) with x_i or with descendants of x_i.

[1]We use 0 to denote this single task for simplicity.

3.2 DPOP

The *Distributed Pseudo-tree Optimization Procedure* (DPOP) [25] is a complete distributed algorithm to solve DCOPs. DPOP consists of three phases: Pseudo-tree generation, UTIL propagation, and VALUE propagation.

- **Pseudo-tree Generation:** DPOP calls existing distributed DFS algorithms [12] to build a pseudo-tree.
- **UTIL Propagation:** Starting from the leafs of the pseudo-tree, each agent computes the optimal sum of utilities in its subtree for each value combination of variables in its separator and sends these utilities in a UTIL message to its parent.
- **VALUE Propagation:** Each agent, starting from the root of the pseudo-tree, determines its variable's optimal value and sends this value, together with its ancestors' optimal values, in VALUE messages to its children. The root agent does so by choosing the value of its variable from its UTIL computations.

3.3 UR-DCOP

Uncertain Reward DCOP (UR-DCOP) [29] is an extension of the original DCOP model with two additional components:

- $\mathcal{E} = \{s_1, \ldots, s_m\}$ is a set of random variables, each random variable s_j is for each constraint $f_j \in \mathcal{F}$.
- $\mathcal{S} = \{S_1, \ldots, S_m\}$ is a set of finite domains where S_j is the domain of random variable s_j.

The constraints in $\mathcal{F}$ are augmented to consider both decision variables and random variables—i.e., each k_j-ary constraint has the form $f_j : S_j \times D_{j_1} \times D_{j_2} \times \ldots \times D_{j_{k_j}} \mapsto \mathbb{R} \cup \{-\infty\}$.

Given a random variable s_j in UR-DCOPs, let $b_j \in \Delta(S_j)$ be the probability distribution over domain S_j, and $\mathbf{b} = \langle b_1, \ldots, b_m \rangle$. When $\mathbf{b}$ is known, solving a UR-DCOP involves finding an assignment of all decision variables x that minimizes the sum of expected values $V(\mathbf{b}, x) = \sum_{j=1}^{m} \sum_{s_j \in S_j} b_j(s_j) \cdot f_j(s_j, x_{f_j})$.

However, since $\mathbf{b}$ is unknown, given the space $\mathcal{B}$ of $\mathbf{b}$, the objective of UR-DCOPs is the *minimax regret*:

$$V_{regret} = \min_{x'} \max_{\mathbf{b} \in \mathcal{B}} \max_{x^*} [V(\mathbf{b}, x^*) - V(\mathbf{b}, x')]$$

where x^* is the optimal solution given $\mathbf{b}$.

3.4 GPUs

Graphics Processing Units (GPUs) are multiprocessor devices, offering hundreds of computing cores and a rich memory hierarchy. A parallel computation is described by a collection of *kernels* (i.e., procedures) executed by several *threads*. Threads are in turn organized hierarchically into *blocks* and *grids of blocks*, and have access to several memory levels, each with different properties in terms of speed and capacity. Each thread can store its private variables in very fast, but few in number, registers. Threads within a block can communicate by reading and writing a common *shared memory* area. Communication between blocks and between blocks and the host (i.e., the CPU) is done through a large but slow *global memory*. Memory levels have significantly different sizes (e.g., registers are in the order of dozens per thread, while shared memory is in the order of a few kilobytes per block) and access times (e.g., global memory access typically requires 400-600 clock cycles, shared memory 20-40 cycles). The conceptual model of parallelism supported by CUDA [26] is *Single-Instruction Multiple-Thread* (SIMT), where the same instruction is executed by different threads that run on identical cores, while data and operands may differ from thread to thread.

3.5 ASP

We now review some background on *Answer Set Programming* (ASP). An *answer set program* [3] Π is a set of *rules* of the form

$$c \leftarrow a_1, \dots, a_s, not\, b_1, \dots, not\, b_t$$

where $s \geq 0$, $t \geq 0$, and the a_i's and b_i's are ground literals of a first order language $\mathcal{L}$. The formula $not\, b_i$ is called a *negation-as-failure* literal (or naf-literal). c can be a ground literal or omitted. A program is *definite* if it does not contain naf-literals. If $s = t = 0$, the rule is called a *fact*.

A set of ground literals X is *consistent* if there is no atom a such that $\{a, \neg a\} \subseteq X$. A literal ℓ is true (false) in a set of literals X if $\ell \in X$ ($\ell \notin X$). A set of ground literals X satisfies a ground rule if any of the following cases is true: *(i)* $c \in X$; *(ii)* some a_i is false in X; or *(iii)* some b_i is true in X. A solution of a program, called an *answer set* [10], is a consistent set S of ground literals such that:

- If Π is a definite program, then S is a subset-minimal set of ground literals satisfying all rules in Π.
- If Π contains some naf-literals, then S is an answer set of Π^S that is obtained from Π by deleting *(i)* each rule that has a naf-literal *not* b in its body with $b \in S$, and *(ii)* all naf-literals in the bodies of the remaining rules.

A rule with variables is viewed as a shorthand of the collection of all of its ground instances. Similarly, a non-ground program is a shorthand for all ground instances of its rules. The ASP language includes also language-level extensions to facilitate the encoding of aggregates (*min*, *max*, *sum*, etc.). ASP solves a problem by encoding it as an ASP program whose answer sets correspond one-to-one to the solutions of the problem [20, 24]. Solutions can be computed using ASP solvers like CLASP [9] and DLV [5].

4. THE ER-DCOP MODEL

In this section, we introduce the *Expected Regret DCOP* (ER-DCOP) model—a new representation for DCOPs with uncertainty in constraint utilities. An ER-DCOP model is always defined over a so-called *belief space*. So, we first propose the ER-DCOP model and then introduce the definition of a belief space.

An ER-DCOP is an extension of DCOP to model stochastic constraint utilities. Formally, it is a tuple $\mathcal{E} = \langle \mathcal{A}, \mathcal{X}, \mathcal{D}, \alpha, \mathcal{R}, \mathcal{S}, \mathcal{F} \rangle$, where:

- $\mathcal{A}, \mathcal{X}, \mathcal{D}$, and α are the same as in a DCOP.
- $\mathcal{R} = \{r_1, \dots, r_m\}$ is a set of random variables modeling external factors beyond the direct control of agents (e.g., the factor of whether robots succeed or not in Example 1). We note that an agent cannot change the value of the random variable directly.
- $\mathcal{S} = \{S_1, \dots, S_m\}$ is a set of finite domains, where S_j is the domain of the random variable $r_j \in \mathcal{R}$ (e.g., success or failure in Example 1).
- $\mathcal{F} = \{f_1, \dots, f_m\}$ is a finite set of constraints, where each k_j-ary constraint $f_j : r_j \times D_{j1} \times D_{j2} \times \ldots \times D_{jk_j} \mapsto \mathbb{R} \cup \{-\infty\}$, different from that in DCOPs, is augmented to consider both a random variable and decision variables in specifying the corresponding utilities. The scope of a constraint f_j is denoted by $scp(f_j) = \{x_{j1}, \dots, x_{jk_j}\}$, which is similar as the scope of constraints in standard DCOP.

We assume that each constraint f_j is associated to one random variable r_j. If a constraint is associated with multiple random variables (i.e., multiple external factors affect the utilities of a constraint), we can merge all such random variables into a single random variable. Furthermore, we assume that random variables are *affected* by the decision variables (i.e., random variables are beyond the direct control of the agents but are influenced by the agent's decisions). Moreover, their values are drawn from *unknown probability distributions* but can be sampled from *known probability distribution spaces*. For example, in Table 1(b), the probability distributions of r_2 varies in: *(i)* different terrain conditions (see columns P^e and P^u) and *(ii)* different value assignments of x_2 and x_3. For example, given $x_2 = x_3 = 0$, the probabilities of $r_2 = 1$ in the even and in the uneven terrain conditions are 50% and 10%, respectively. Additionally, with the even terrain condition, the probabilities of $r_2 = 1$ where $x_2 = x_3 = 0$ and where $x_2 = 0, x_3 = 1$ are 50% and 80%, respectively.

Given a constraint f_j, let X_{f_j} be the set of all possible value assignments for the decision variables in $scp(f_j)$. In ER-DCOPs, the conditional probability distribution of a random variable r_j over its domain S_j given a specific value assignment of the variables in $scp(f_j)$, denoted by b_j, is called a *belief* of the random variable r_j. Thus, the probability that $r_j = s_j \in S_j$ given a specific value assignment $x_{f_j} \in X_{f_j}$ is $b_j(s_j|x_{f_j})$, and we have $\sum_{s_j \in S_j} b_j(s_j|x_{f_j}) = 1$. For example, in Table 1(a), the column P^e denotes the belief b_1^e—the belief of the random variable r_1 in the even terrain. Let x_{f_1} be a partial value assignment in which $x_1 = x_3 = 0$. We have, $b_1^e(0|x_{f_1}) = 0.1$, and $b_1^e(1|x_{f_1}) = 0.9$.

We denote with $B = \langle b_1, \dots, b_m \rangle$ a *joint belief* of all random variables, where each b_j is a belief of $r_j \in \mathcal{R}$. For example, the columns P^e (resp. P^u) in Table 1(a and b) together detail the joint belief B^e (resp. B^u)—the joint belief for even (resp. uneven) terrain.

When the joint belief $B = \langle b_1, \dots, b_m \rangle$ is known, solving ER-DCOPs *with respect to* the joint belief B is straightforward; it involves finding a complete value assignment $\mathbf{x}$ that maximizes the sum of the *expected utility* of the constraints:

$$E(B, \mathbf{x}) = \sum_{j=1}^{m} \underbrace{\sum_{s_j \in S_j} b_j(s_j|\mathbf{x}_{f_j}) \cdot f_j(s_j, \mathbf{x}_{f_j})}_{E(b_j, \mathbf{x}_{f_j})} \tag{1}$$

In Equation (1), $E(b_j, \mathbf{x}_{f_j})$ is the expected utility of the constraint f_j corresponding to the partial value assignment $\mathbf{x}_{f_j}$ w.r.t. b_j.

In Example 1 and throughout the rest of the paper, let x_a (resp. x_b) be a value assignment where $x_1 = x_2 = x_3 = 0$ (resp. $x_1 = x_2 = 0, x_3 = 1$). Since $E(B^e, x_a) = 65 > E(B^e, x_b) = 61$, we have that x_a is the solution for the ER-DCOP with respect to B^e. Moreover, we also have $E(B^u, x_a) = 39 < E(B^u, x_b) = 40$, so x_b is the solution for the ER-DCOP with respect to B^u.

The key challenge here in solving ER-DCOPs is that the joint belief is typically unknown—i.e., an ER-DCOP may have multiple joint beliefs that have to be considered. Formally, an ER-DCOP is defined over a finite nonempty set of joint beliefs, $\mathcal{B} = \{B^1, \dots, B^v\}$, referred to as the *belief space* of the ER-DCOP. The uncertainty of joint beliefs in the belief space $\mathcal{B}$ is drawn under a probabilistic model $\mathcal{P}_\mathcal{B}$ where $\sum_{q=1}^{v} \mathcal{P}_\mathcal{B}(B^q) = 1$. The goal of an ER-DCOP, given the belief space $\mathcal{B}$ whose probability distribution is $\mathcal{P}_\mathcal{B}$, is to find a complete value assignment $\mathbf{x}'$ that *minimizes the expected regret*:

$$ER(\mathcal{B},\mathbf{x}') = \sum_{B^q \in \mathcal{B}} \mathcal{P}_{\mathcal{B}}(B^q) \cdot \max_{\mathbf{x}^{\mathbf{B^q}}} \underbrace{[E(B^q,\mathbf{x}^{\mathbf{B^q}}) - E(B^q,\mathbf{x}')]}_{R(B^q,\mathbf{x}')} \quad (2)$$

The assignment $\mathbf{x}^{\mathbf{B^q}}$ selected by the maximization operator is the solution of the ER-DCOP with respect to B^q—i.e., $E(B^q, \mathbf{x}^{\mathbf{B^q}})$ is the maximal expected utility achieved with respect to B^q and its associated $\mathbf{x}^{\mathbf{B^q}}$. $R(B^q, \mathbf{x}')$ is the *regret* (or loss) for a complete value assignment $\mathbf{x}'$ relative to B^q—i.e., the difference of the aggregate expected utilities achieved by $\mathbf{x}'$ and $\mathbf{x}^{\mathbf{B^q}}$. Note that the smallest value of the expected regret $ER(\mathcal{B}, \mathbf{x}')$ minimizes the expected loss over all possible joint beliefs $B^q \in \mathcal{B}$.

In Example 1, $\mathcal{B} = \langle B^e, B^u \rangle$, $\mathcal{P}_{\mathcal{B}}(B^e) = 12\%$, and $\mathcal{P}_{\mathcal{B}}(B^u) = 88\%$. We have $ER(\mathcal{B}, x_a) = 12\% \cdot (65-65) + 88\% \cdot (40-39) = 0.88$ and $ER(\mathcal{B}, x_b) = 12\% \cdot (65-61) + 88\% \cdot (40-40) = 0.48$. Thus, since $ER(\mathcal{B}, x_a) = 0.88 > ER(\mathcal{B}, x_b) = 0.48$, the value assignment x_b is the solution of the original ER-DCOP as it yields the minimal expected regret of 0.48.

5. ER-DPOP ALGORITHM

We now describe a distributed algorithm, called *Expected Regret-DPOP* (ER-DPOP), to solve ER-DCOPs. It is composed of three phases: **(1)** *Generation of the pseudo-tree*; **(2)** *Resolution of subproblems*, where ER-DPOP computes an optimal solution $\mathbf{x}^{\mathbf{B^q}}$ for each joint belief $B^q \in \mathcal{B}$; and **(3)** *Resolution of the main problem*, where ER-DPOP finds the solution $\mathbf{x}'$ of the original ER-DCOP that minimizes $ER(\mathcal{B}, \mathbf{x}')$. ER-DPOP makes use of repeated calls to the DPOP algorithm [25]. We choose DPOP to develop ER-DPOP because DPOP is one of the most popular complete DCOP algorithms. Moreover, since DPOP is synchronous, a modification of DPOP will allow to solve optimal solutions for every joint belief in Phase 2 simultaneously.

Phase 1 [*Generation of the pseudo-tree*]: In this phase, agents coordinate to build a pseudo-tree as in DPOP.

Phase 2 [*Resolution of subproblems*]: This phase consists of two steps. In the first step, the original ER-DCOP is transformed into a standard DCOP for each joint belief $B^q \in \mathcal{B}$, where the constraint utilities are updated with the respective expected utilities. More precisely, for each joint belief $B^q \in \mathcal{B}$, a new standard DCOP $M^{B^q} = \langle \mathcal{X}, \mathcal{D}, \mathcal{F}^{B^q}, \mathcal{A}, \alpha \rangle$ is generated where $\mathcal{F}^{B^q} = \{f_1^{B^q}, \ldots, f_m^{B^q}\}$ and $f_j^{B^q}$ is a constraint—whose scope is identical to that of $f_j \in \mathcal{F}$, and whose constraint utilities are given by $f_j^{B^q}(x_{f_j}) = E(b_j^q, x_{f_j})$ for each value assignment x_{f_j} of the variables in *scp*(f_j), where $b_j^q \in B^q$.

In the second step, the $|\mathcal{B}|$ DCOPs built in the first step are solved, following the general model of DPOP. Rather than solving each DCOP M^{B^q} sequentially, ER-DPOP adapts the DPOP algorithm to solve them *simultaneously*. Intuitively, the UTIL messages produced in this phase (referred to as UTIL2 messages) transmit vectors of aggregate utilities—within such a vector, each of aggregate utilities is with respect to a joint belief $B^q \in \mathcal{B}$. The VALUE messages produced in this phase (referred to as VALUE2 messages) transmit vectors of optimal value assignments—within such a vector, each of optimal value assignments is with respect to a DCOP M^{B^q}. In detail, each agent $a_i \in \mathcal{A}$:

- Constructs its UTIL2 message that includes a vector $\vec{u}_{x_{sep_i}}$ (referred to as a utility vector) $\vec{u}_{x_{sep_i}} = (u^{B^1}, \ldots, u^{B^{|\mathcal{B}|}})$ for *each value assignment* x_{sep_i} of the variables in sep_i, where each u^{B^q} is the optimal utility for its subtree in the DCOP M^{B^q} given the value assignment x_{sep_i}.
- Constructs its VALUE2 message that includes a vector of optimal value assignments $x = (x^{B^1}, \ldots, x^{B^{|\mathcal{B}|}})$ for each variable $x \in sep_i \cup \{x_i\}$, where each x^{B^q} is the value of x in the solution of the DCOP M^{B^q}.

The actions of aggregating the utilities contained in each UTIL2 message and of determining the value assignment for their variables (given the VALUE2 message from the parent agent) are performed as in DPOP. Each operation is performed $|\mathcal{B}|$ times by each agent, one for each joint belief in the belief space of the original ER-DCOP. At the end of these two steps, ER-DPOP has an optimal solution $\mathbf{x}^{\mathbf{B^q}}$ for each $B^q \in \mathcal{B}$.

In Example 1, consider a pseudo-tree where $sep_1 = sep_2 = \{x_3\}$ and $\mathcal{B} = \langle B^e, B^u \rangle$. The UTIL2 message of agent a_1 is $\vec{u}_{x_3=0} = (45, 35)$ and $\vec{u}_{x_3=1} = (21, 15)$; the UTIL2 message of agent a_2 is $\vec{u}_{x_3=0} = (20, 4)$ and $\vec{u}_{x_3=1} = (40, 25)$. Agent a_3 joins the UTIL2 messages that are received from its children a_1 and a_2 as: $\vec{u}_{x_3=0} = (65, 39)$ and $\vec{u}_{x_3=1} = (61, 40)$, and selects its assignment solution $x_3 = 0$ (resp. $x_3 = 1$) as solutions for the joint belief B^e (resp. B^u).

Phase 3 [*Resolution of the main problem*]: Once Phase 2 terminates, ER-DPOP agents can compute $ER(\mathcal{B}, \mathbf{x}')$ for every possible complete value assignment $\mathbf{x}'$. To do so, ER-DPOP transforms all M^{B^q} DCOPs generated in the previous phase into a standard DCOP $M^{\mathcal{B}} = \langle \mathcal{X}, \mathcal{D}, \mathcal{F}^{\mathcal{B}}, \mathcal{A}, \alpha \rangle$, where $F^{\mathcal{B}} = \{f_1^{\mathcal{B}}, \ldots, f_m^{\mathcal{B}}\}$ and each $f_j^{\mathcal{B}}$ has the same scope as $f_j \in \mathcal{F}$ and its constraint utility values are given by:

$$f_j^{\mathcal{B}}(x_{f_j}) = \sum_{B^q \in \mathcal{B}} \mathcal{P}_{\mathcal{B}}(B^q) \cdot [f_j^{B^q}(\mathbf{x}_{f_j}^{\mathbf{B^q}}) - f_j^{B^q}(x_{f_j})] \quad (3)$$

for each value assignment x_{f_j} of the variables in *scp*(f_j). In Equation (3), $\mathbf{x}_{f_j}^{\mathbf{B^q}}$ is a value assignment of the variables in *scp*(f_j) from the optimal solution $\mathbf{x}^{\mathbf{B^q}}$, computed in the previous phase of ER-DCOP with respect to B^q. Each ER-DPOP agent computes the constraint $f_j^{\mathcal{B}}$ shared among its variables and its ancestor variables without incurring any privacy loss. In Example 1, agents a_1 and a_2 update their constraints $f_1^{\mathcal{B}}$ and $f_2^{\mathcal{B}}$, respectively, where: $f_1^{\mathcal{B}}(x_1 = 0, x_3 = 0) = 12\% \cdot (45-45) + 88\% \cdot (15-35) = -17.6$; $f_1^{\mathcal{B}}(x_1 = 0, x_3 = 1) = 2.88$; $f_2^{\mathcal{B}}(x_2 = 0, x_3 = 0) = 18.48$; and $f_2^{\mathcal{B}}(x_2 = 0, x_3 = 1) = -2.4$.

Once the standard DCOP $M^{\mathcal{B}}$ is generated, ER-DPOP agents solve this problem to find the *minimal* aggregated utility that is the *minimal expected regret* using standard DPOP.[2] To distinguish from the UTIL2 and VALUE2 messages that are produced in Phase 2, the UTIL and VALUE messages produced in Phase 3 by standard DPOP are referred to as UTIL3 and VALUE3 messages, respectively. The solution of the DCOP $M^{\mathcal{B}}$ is the solution of the original ER-DCOP. In Example 1, the solution x_b $(x_1 = x_2 = 0, x_3 = 1)$ is the solution for $M^{\mathcal{B}}$ since it minimizes the expected regret of 0.48 and is the solution of the original ER-DCOP that models Example 1.

6. THEORETICAL ANALYSIS

We now present some theoretical properties of ER-DPOP including its correctness and complexity.

THEOREM 1. *ER-DPOP is correct, that is, given an ER-DCOP $\mathcal{E}$ over a belief space $\mathcal{B}$, ER-DPOP finds a solution $\mathbf{x}'$ that minimizes $ER(\mathcal{B}, \mathbf{x}')$.*

[2] In this phase, agents minimize their aggregated utilities rather than maximizing them.

Proof: In Phase 2, ER-DPOP transforms the original ER-DCOP into $|\mathcal{B}|$ standard DCOP $M^{B^q} = \langle \mathcal{X}, \mathcal{D}, \mathcal{F}^{B^q}, \mathcal{A}, \alpha \rangle$, where $\mathcal{F}^{B^q} = \{f_1^{B^q}, \ldots, f_m^{B^q}\}$ and $f_j^{B^q}$ is a constraint whose scope is identical to that of $f_j \in \mathcal{F}$ except that its constraint utilities are given by $f_j^{B^q}(x_{f_j}) = E(b_j^q, x_{f_j})$. Thus, the solution $\mathbf{x}^{\mathbf{B^q}}$ of DCOP M^{B^q} will maximize the sum of the expected utility of the constraints in ER-DCOP w.r.t the joint belief B^q (i.e., $\mathbf{x}^{\mathbf{B^q}} = \text{argmax}_x\, E(B^q, x)$). Moreover, ER-DPOP agents solve each M^{B^q} simultaneously but independently. Each agent performs the actions (i.e., aggregating the expected utilities and determining its assignment solution) $|\mathcal{B}|$ times independently—once is for each joint belief in $\mathcal{B}$—using DPOP to construct UTIL2 and VALUE2 messages. As a result, following the correctness of DPOP [25], at the end of Phase 2, ER-DPOP finds a solution $\mathbf{x}^{\mathbf{B^q}}$ for each $B^q \in \mathcal{B}$ that maximizes $E(B^q, \mathbf{x}^{\mathbf{B^q}})$.

Similarly, in Phase 3, ER-DPOP solves the DCOP $M^{\mathcal{B}}$ (whose constraints are computed as in Equation (3)) to minimize the aggregated expected regret. Thus, based on the correctness of DPOP [25], at the end of Phase 3, ER-DPOP finds the solution $\mathbf{x}'$ of $M^{\mathcal{B}}$ that minimizes $ER(\mathcal{B}, \mathbf{x}')$, which proves the correctness of ER-DPOP. □

Given $d = \max_{1 \le i \le n} |D_i|$ and $w = \max_{1 \le i \le n} |sep_i|$, we have the following properties:

PROPERTY 1. *The number of messages required by ER-DPOP is bounded by $\mathcal{O}(n)$ where n is the number of agents.*

Proof: In ER-DPOP, Phase 1 requires a linear number of messages in n [25]; Phase 2 requires $(n-1)$ UTIL2 messages and $(n-1)$ VALUE2 messages; and Phase 3 requires $(n-1)$ UTIL3 messages and $(n-1)$ VALUE3 messages. Thus, the number of messages required by ER-DPOP is bounded by $\mathcal{O}(n)$. □

PROPERTY 2. *The size of messages required by ER-DPOP is bounded by $\mathcal{O}(d^w \cdot |\mathcal{B}|)$.*

Proof: In ER-DPOP, Phase 1 produces messages whose size is linear in n [25]; Phase 2 produces UTIL2 and VALUE2 messages whose sizes are bounded by $\mathcal{O}(d^w \cdot |\mathcal{B}|)$ and $\mathcal{O}(w \cdot |\mathcal{B}|)$, respectively; and Phase 3 produces UTIL3 and VALUE3 messages whose sizes are bounded by $\mathcal{O}(d^w)$ and $\mathcal{O}(w)$, respectively [25]. Thus, the size of messages required by ER-DPOP is bounded by $\mathcal{O}(d^w \cdot |\mathcal{B}|)$ □

7. ER-DPOP IMPLEMENTATIONS

The main technical challenges of ER-DCOP are its exponential messages size and its exponential search space (Property 2). Thus, to address these challenges, in this section, we introduce a GPU-based and an ASP-based implementation of ER-DPOP to exploit SIMT-style parallelism and hard constraints, respectively.

7.1 GPU-ER-DPOP

The use of a GPU-based approach to solve ER-DCOPs is motivated by the observation that each utility vector of the UTIL2 messages and each entry of the UTIL3 messages in Phases 2 and 3, as well as constraints that are defined in Equation (3), can be computed independently. Thus, they can be computed in parallel. This observation finds a natural fit for SIMT processing and, as shown in recent works [4, 8], this is a viable approach to enhance the performance of belief propagation- and dynamic programming-based inference processes.

We thus develop GPU-ER-DPOP (GPU-based ER-DPOP implementation), which allows us to speed up the computation processes required by Phases 2 and 3 and, as a consequence, reduces the overall runtime.

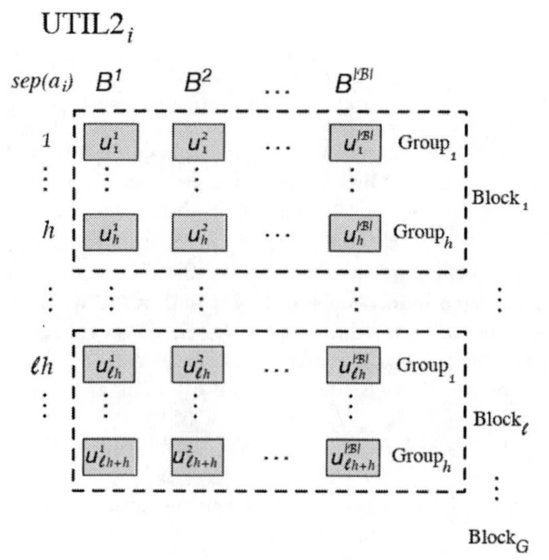

Figure 1: GPU Parallelization

Figure 1 illustrates the high-level parallelization performed by each ER-DPOP agent when computing a UTIL2 message. Our GPU-ER-DPOP operates along three levels of parallelization:

- Each GPU-ER-DPOP agent a_i computes its UTIL2$_i$ message using G GPU-blocks: $b_1, \ldots, b_G$ with $G = \frac{|sep_i|}{h}$, and h being the number of utility vectors computed within a block.
- In constructing its UTIL2$_i$ message, since computing a utility vector for a value assignment of the variables in sep_i is independent of the computation of another utility vectors, we design a GPU-block b_j ($1 \le j \le G$) to compute h utility vectors in parallel. More precisely, the GPU-block b_1 computes h utility vectors corresponding to the first h different partial value assignments of variables in sep_i, sorted in lexicographical order; the GPU-block b_2 computes h utility vectors corresponding to the next h different partial value assignments of variables in sep_i; and so on.
- Within a block, we delegate the computation of each of the h utility vectors to a *group* of $|\mathcal{B}|$ GPU-threads, each of which is in charge of computing the optimal utility u^{B^q} for the agent a_i's subtree in the DCOP M^{B^q}. This is possible since the computations of different u^{B^q} in a utility vector is associated to a particular joint belief and, thus, are independent to each other.

Analogous parallelizations are performed by each GPU agent when constructing UTIL3 messages and computing Equation (3).

The underlying parallelization strategy adopted in our work is inspired to that explored in [8]. In that work, the focus is on the parallelization of the *join* and *projection* operators used in classical (D)COP inference-based resolution approaches. Similarly, GPU-ER-DPOP uses a GPU-thread to compute the optimal sum of utilities in an agent's subtree for a value combination of variables in its separator. In addition, different from the previous approaches, GPU-ER-DPOP heavily exploits the structure of the ER-DCOP model to compute the optimal utilities, with respect to different joint beliefs in parallel, as well as the expected regrets.

The number of threads T used in each block is a parameter that depends on the GPU architecture. It depends on the resource used by the GPU kernel and influences the number h of groups associated to each block. In our settings, we set $T = 256$ and, thus, each block computes at most $h = \lfloor \frac{256}{|\mathcal{B}|} \rfloor$ utility vectors. As a technical

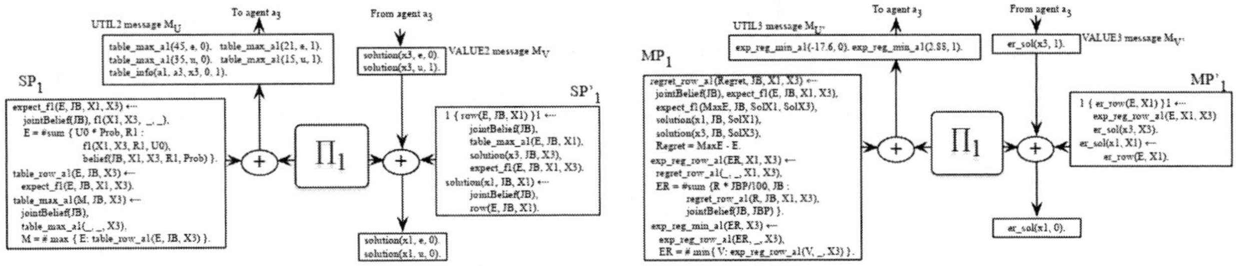

(a) (b)

Figure 2: ASP Programs of Agent a_1 for Phase 2 (a) and Phase 3 (b) in Example 1

note, the number of blocks ℓ that can be scheduled in parallel also depends on the GPU architecture. In our settings $\ell = 14$. Thus, the number of utility vectors computed in parallel is bounded by $\ell \cdot h$.

7.2 ASP-ER-DPOP

Inspired by our ASP-based system that provides significant speedup and better scalability for standard DCOPs [15], we develop ASP-ER-DPOP, an ASP-based implementation of ER-DPOP. As we have previously noted, the ASP-based approach can capitalize on *(i)* the highly-expressive ASP language to more concisely represent constraint utilities as functions instead of explicitly enumerating them, and *(ii)* the highly-optimized ASP solvers to exploit problem structures such as pruning the search space based on hard constraints. We note that we did observe the same trend in our experiments (see Section 8).

We now present ASP-ER-DCOP. In this framework, each agent a_i is composed of the agent specification Π_i and its controller C_i.

Specifying an ER-DCOP: An ER-DCOP is encoded as a set of answer set programs $\{\Pi_i | a_i \in \mathcal{A}\}$. Each Π_i encodes information about: **(i)** the agent a_i, **(ii)** the variable x_i and its domain, **(iii)** the neighboring agents in the constraint graph, their variables, and their variables' domain, **(iv)** the constraints whose scope includes the variable x_i, **(v)** the belief space and its probabilistic model, and **(vi)** the beliefs for the constraints encoded in Π_i. Figure 3 shows the answer set program Π_1 for the ER-DCOP in Example 1.

```
agent(a1).                variable(x1, 0).
neighbor(a3).             variable(x3, 0..1).
scope(f1, x1).            scope(f1, x3).
f1(0, 0, 0, 0).           f1(0, 0, 1, 50).
f1(0, 1, 0, 0).           f1(0, 1, 1, 30).
jointBelief(e, 12).       jointBelief(u, 88).
belief(e, 0, 0, 0, 10).   belief(e, 0, 0, 1, 90).
belief(e, 0, 1, 0, 30).   belief(e, 0, 1, 0, 70).
belief(u, 0, 0, 0, 30).   belief(u, 0, 0, 1, 70).
belief(u, 0, 1, 0, 50).   belief(u, 0, 1, 0, 50).
```

Figure 3: Answer Set Program Π_1 for Example 1

Encoding Messages: Messages in Phases 2 and 3 (i.e., UTIL2, UTIL3, VALUE2, and VALUE3 messages) are encoded as ASP facts. For the UTIL2 and UTIL3 messages, each optimal utility, along with its corresponding *(i)* value assignment of the respective variables and *(ii)* joint belief (for only UTIL2 messages) is represented as a fact (see messages M_U and $M_{U'}$ in Figure 2). Upon receiving a UTIL2 or UTIL3 message, an agent is able to understand the mapping between the values in such facts to the corresponding variables via the information provided by another facts of the form *table_info* (see message M_U in Figure 2) included also in that message. Similarly, for VALUE2 and VALUE3 messages, a solution of a variable (along with its respective joint belief for VALUE2 messages) is encoded as a fact (see messages M_V and $M_{V'}$ in Figure 2).

Agent Controller: The agent controller C_i consists of a set of rules for communication (sending, receiving, and interpreting messages) and a set of rules for generating ASP programs that computes messages in Phases 2 and 3. Due to space constraints, we omit the detailed code of C_i, but we describe its functionality below.

ASP-ER-DPOP has the same phases as ER-DPOP. In Phase 1, the controllers C_i construct a pseudo-tree, and information about the parent, children, and pseudo-parents of a_i are added to Π_i. In Phase 2, after receiving UTIL2 (resp. VALUE2) messages as sets M_U (resp. M_V) of facts from children (resp. parent) agent(s), C_i generates a set SP_i (resp. SP'_i) of rules (see Figure 2(a)), then computes an answer set of the program $\Pi_i \cup SP_i \cup M_U$ (resp. $\Pi_i \cup SP'_i \cup M_V$). Such an answer set is the encoded UTIL2 (resp. VALUE2) message of agent a_i to be sent to its parent (resp. children) agent(s). In Phase 3, after receiving UTIL3 (resp. VALUE3) messages as sets $M_{U'}$ (resp. $M_{V'}$) of facts from children (resp. parent) agent(s), C_i generates a set MP_i (resp. MP'_i) of rules (see Figure 2(b)), then computes an answer set of the program $\Pi_i \cup MP_i \cup M_{U'}$ (resp. $\Pi_i \cup MP'_i \cup M_{V'}$). Such an answer set is the encoded UTIL3 (resp. VALUE3) message of agent a_i to sent to its parent (resp. children) agent(s). The original ER-DCOP's solution for variable owned by a_i is included in the VALUE3 message in this phase.

The controller is written in SICStus Prolog. We use CLASP [9] as our ASP solver and the SICStus *Linda* library for communication.

8. EXPERIMENTAL RESULTS

Since there are no other ER-DCOP solvers, a direct comparison with other systems is not feasible. We implemented another ER-DCOP solver, referred to as *Frodo-ER*, which differs from both ASP-ER-DPOP and GPU-ER-DPOP as follows: Frodo-ER generates a sequence of $|\mathcal{B}|$ DCOP problems M^{B^q} and solves them *sequentially* using DPOP in Phase 2. In contrast, ASP-ER-DPOP and GPU-ER-DPOP solves them *simultaneously*. Frodo-ER uses a publicly-available and widely-used implementation of DPOP [17].

In addition, to compare the actual regret of the solutions of the UR-DCOP and ER-DCOP models, we implemented *Iterative Constraint Generation Max-Sum* (ICG Max-Sum) [29], a UR-DCOP solver, using a publicly-available implementation of Max-Sum.[3]

We compare ASP-ER-DPOP (abbreviated to ASP-ER) and GPU-ER-DPOP (abbreviated to GPU-ER) against Frodo-ER. All

[3] https://code.google.com/p/jmaxsum/

Algorithm	$\lvert\mathcal{X}\rvert$				$\lvert D_i\rvert$					$\lvert\mathcal{B}\rvert$					p_1				
	8	13	18	23	4	6	8	10	12	5	30	50	70	90	0.4	0.5	0.6	0.7	0.8
ASP-ER	3.1	9.4	44.1	120.8	4.5	8.9	22.2	80.4	121.2	7.8	26.5	32.9	39.2	44.9	5.6	7.6	8.1	8.6	13.7
GPU-ER	0.1	0.2	–	–	0.1	0.1	1.2	4.8	15.4	0.2	0.5	0.8	1.1	2.4	0.1	0.1	0.2	0.7	1.7
Frodo-ER	0.3	61.1	–	–	1.8	33.6	143.2	–	–	42.2	86.5	113.7	117.1	131.5	1.1	4.8	45.1	118.5	196.1

(a)

Algorithm	p_2				
	0.4	0.5	0.6	0.7	0.8
ASP-ER	85.8	16.9	7.7	5.8	5.5
GPU-ER	0.2	0.2	0.3	0.2	0.3
Frodo-ER	42.6	42.3	39.6	41.3	41.2

(b)

$\lvert\mathcal{B}\rvert$	Better	Worse	Equal	$\widetilde{V}_{UR-DCOP}$	$\widetilde{R}_{ER-DCOP}$
5	45 %	20 %	35 %	17.21	12.31
10	36 %	28 %	36 %	20.08	18.22
15	47 %	20 %	33 %	20.47	14.33

(c)

$\lvert\mathcal{B}\rvert$	ICG	ASP-ER
5	4.4	2.9
10	50.2	3.0
15	222.9	3.2

(d)

Table 2: Experimental Results of Random Graphs

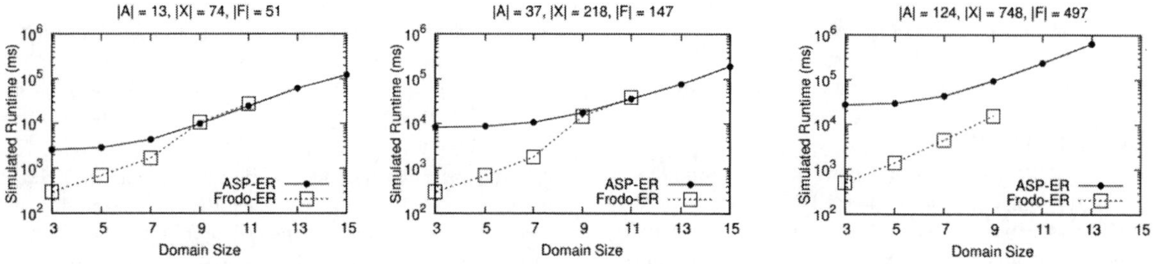

(a) 13 Bus Topology (b) 37 Bus Topology (c) 124 Bus Topology

Figure 4: Experimental Results of Power Network Problems

algorithms use the same pseudo-tree for fair comparisons. We measure the runtime of the algorithms using the simulated runtime metric [27]. All experiments are performed on a Quadcore 2.2GHz machine with 8GB of memory. The GPU device adopted is a GeForce GTX TITAN with 14 multiprocessors, and a clock rate of 837 MHZ. If an algorithm fails to solve a problem, it is due to memory limitations. We conduct our experiments on random graphs [6] (for comparing ASP-ER and GPU-ER against Frodo-ER) and on comprehensive optimization problems in power networks [11] (for comparing ASP-ER against Frodo-ER).

Random Graphs: We create an n-node network, whose constraint density p_1 produces $\lfloor n\,(n-1)\,p_1\rfloor$ edges in total [6]. In these experiments, we vary the number of variables $|\mathcal{X}|$; the domain size $|D_i|$; the constraint density p_1; the constraint tightness p_2, defined as the percentage of forbidden value combinations in a constraint; and the belief space size $|\mathcal{B}|$. For each experiment, we vary only one parameter and fix the others to their "default" values: $|\mathcal{A}| = |\mathcal{X}| = 13, |D_i| = 6, p_1 = p_2 = 0.6, |\mathcal{B}| = 5$. We set the timeout to 30 minutes. Tables 2(a) and 2(b) show the average runtimes (in seconds) for the solved instances (out of 30 instances). An algorithm fails to solve a configuration if it cannot solve at least 15 instances of that configuration.

We observe that ASP-ER is slower than Frodo-ER when the problem is less complex than the one with the default configuration. However, ASP-ER is able to solve more problems and is faster than Frodo-ER when the problem becomes more complex (i.e., increasing $|\mathcal{X}|, |D_i|, p_1, p_2$, or $|\mathcal{B}|$). The reason is that, unlike Frodo-ER agents, ASP-ER agents are able to prune a significant portion of the search space thanks to hard constraints. In detail, the search space does not include infeasible value combinations of the respective variables, and the size of the search space pruned increases with the complexity of the instances. The benefit of pruning is clearly seen at increasing p_2, i.e., while the runtimes of Frodo-ER are similar, those of ASP-ER decrease significantly as there are more hard constraints.

We also observe that GPU-ER is consistently faster than Frodo-ER and ASP-ER. Its use of SIMT-based parallelism is very effective at computing the independent utility vectors (or UTIL3 entries), which results in large speedup. However, as for Frodo-ER, it cannot scale to problems as large as those solved by ASP-ER (the settings with $|\mathcal{X}| \in \{18, 23\}$). This is due to the basic GPU-ER strategy adopted, which does not prune the search space based on hard constraints, resulting in analogous memory requirements as those of Frodo-ER.

We notice that, in Table 2(a), Frodo-ER reaches a timeout for $|D_i| > 8$ while both ASP-ER and GPU-ER can solve such experiments. This is due to that the size of the UTIL tables increases substantially when the domain size increases (Property 2), and ASP-ER and GPU-ER can scale to $|D_i| = 12$ (due to the effect of pruning in ASP-ER, and to the exploited thread-parallelism in GPU-ER), while Frodo-ER operates sequentially on such tables.

Power Network Problems: In this domain [11], each agent represents a node with consumption, generation, and transmission preferences, and a global cost function. Constraints include the power balance and no power loss principles, the generation and consumption limits, and the capacity of the power line between nodes. However, in reality, there is loss in power transmissions, and a stochastic constraint utility function is suited for representing this loss. The loss depends on how much power is transferred and on external factors (e.g., ambient temperature and the quality of power lines). If there are no losses, the objective is to minimize the global cost function. In the presence of losses, the objective is to minimize the regret of the achieved global cost function over different possible losses.

We use three network topologies, defined using the IEEE Distribution Test Feeder 2014 standards, and vary the domain size of the generation, load, and transmission variables of each agent from 3 to 15. We use three levels of losses ($|S_j| = 3$) corresponding to the loss of 10%, 30%, and 60% of the power transferred, and $|\mathcal{B}| = 3$. Figure 4 shows the runtime of ASP-ER and Frodo-ER in milliseconds. The results in Figure 4 are consistent with those shown earlier.

Despite ER-DPOP having space-exponential message sizes, we believe that it is scalable in solving real application domains (e.g., in the power network domain with a 124 Bus topology, we can solve problems with $|\mathcal{X}| = 748$ and $|\mathcal{F}| = 497$). We also observe that ASP-ER has better scalability in the power network problems than in random graphs because the power network problems exhibit more structure than random graphs, and their underlying constraint graphs have small induced width and, thus, small separator sets.

Comparison Between UR-DCOP and ER-DCOP Models: In addition, we compare the solution quality of ER-DCOP and UR-DCOP models in terms of actual regret. After generating UR-DCOP instances, we augment a probability for each joint belief according to a normal distribution, as: $\mathcal{P}_{\mathcal{B}} \sim \mathcal{N}(\frac{|\mathcal{B}|}{2}, \frac{|\mathcal{B}|}{5})$. For each instance, the two solutions—one is with respect to the UR-DCOP model, and the other is with respect to the ER-DCOP model—are computed. The actual regrets of those solutions are achieved by *(i)* picking a joint belief in the belief space based on the distribution $\mathcal{P}_{\mathcal{B}}$, and *(ii)* calculating the actual regret of each of those solutions relative to the picked joint belief.

In this experiment, we generate 1000 instances for each configuration with $|\mathcal{A}| = |\mathcal{X}| = 8, |D_i| = 3, p_1 = 0.5, p_2 = 0$, and $|\mathcal{B}| \in \{5, 10, 15\}$. Table 2(c) compares the quality of ER-DCOP and UR-DCOP solutions over 1000 instances where "better", "worse", and "equal" columns indicate the number of times, in percentage, that the regret of the ER-DCOP solution is less than, greater than, and equal to the regret of the UR-DCOP solution of the same instance, respectively. It also reports the average regret of UR-DCOP ($\bar{V}_{UR-DCOP}$) and ER-DCOP ($\bar{R}_{ER-DCOP}$) solutions over those 1000 instances. Table 2(d) shows the average runtimes (in seconds) for ICG Max-Sum (abbreviated to ICG) and ASP-ER to solve those instances.[4] The ER-DCOP model yield solutions with smaller average regret than the UR-DCOP model when the probabilities of joint beliefs have a normal distribution. We also notice that ER-DCOP solutions can be worse than UR-DCOP solutions. This happens whenever a joint belief associated to a low probability, yet producing a high regret, actually happens. Furthermore, ASP-ER is consistently faster than ICG, due to the presence of cycles in the constraint graphs, which affect the convergence time of ICG (which is based on Max-Sum).

9. DISCUSSION

ER-DCOPs is closely related to UR-DCOPs [29] as both extend DCOPs to deal with stochastic utilities. It is therefore worth to discuss their main differences. The main difference lies in that ER-DCOP removes the independence assumption between the belief of a random variable and the values of decision variables. We observe that ER-DCOPs can be used to model UR-DCOP instances by considering, in every joint belief, the conditional probabilities of a random variable given different value assignments of the respective variables are identical (i.e., $b_j(r_j|x_{f_j}) = b_j(r_j|x'_{f_j})$ where x_{f_j} and x'_{f_j} are two arbitrary different value assignments of variables in $scp(f_j)$). In this sense, ER-DCOPs are more expressive than UR-DCOPs. The second main difference between UR-DCOP and ER-DCOP is the notion of a solution in each framework. While UR-DCOPs minimize the worst-case loss, ER-DCOPs aim to minimize the expected regret. Although we believe that each approach has its own merit, we note that ER-DCOPs might yield better results in term of actual regrets as shown in our experiments.

In general, abstract distributed optimization problems can be formulated as n-player coordination games. Thus, *Bayesian Games* (BGs) and *Potential Games* (PGs) may be used to model same scenarios as ER-DCOP. However, for BGs, the common prior belief is independent from the joint actions of the respective players (e.g., Harsanyi's [13] and Aumann's [2] models). Thus, as beliefs of random variables can be dependent to the decision variables in ER-DCOP, representing ER-DCOPs using BGs is not a straightforward matter. Moreover, for PGs, key differences between DCOPs and PGs are as follows: *(i)* DCOPs assume that the agents are cooperative while agents may be competitive in PGs; *(ii)* DCOPs aim at finding a (global) optimal solution for the potential function, while PGs aim at finding an equilibrium outcome, which correspond to a local optima of the potential function; and *(iii)* DCOPs require a distributed solution approach while PGs do not have such a strict requirement (though solution approaches like best response can also be thought of as distributed approaches).

Finally, we observe that researchers have also used *Graphical Models* (GMs) to model conditional independence/dependencies between variables in combinatorial optimization problems (e.g., [21]). GMs and ER-DCOPs are different as: *(i)* ER-DCOP's random variables exhibit different probabilities for each joint belief, while in typical GMs, this cannot be straightforwardly applied, and *(ii)* GMs are typically used to capture the conditional dependence between random variables, while ER-DCOPs represent conditional dependence between decision variables that are controlled by agents and random variables that are beyond the direct control of agents.

10. CONCLUSIONS

In this paper, we proposed ER-DCOPs to model DCOPs with uncertainty in constraint utilities. Differently from another approaches, it allows to represent the beliefs about exogenous factors, which possibly depend on the decision variables, and it focuses on minimizing the expected regret. To solve ER-DCOPs, we proposed a distributed algorithm, called ER-DPOP, which is complete and requires a linear number of messages in the number of agents in the problem. In addition, we presented two implementations for ER-DPOP: One which harnesses the parallelism offered by GPUs to speed up the process of solving ER-DCOPs, and another which uses ASP and exploits logic programming-based inference rules to prune the solution search space. Such approaches take advantage from two orthogonal means of exploiting the ER-DCOP structure. Our experimental evaluation shows that ER-DCOP solutions outperform corresponding UR-DCOP solutions in terms of the actual regret, and that both ER-DPOP implementations outperform a straightforward repeated application of state-of-the-art DCOP solver (i.e., DPOP) in terms of better scalability and runtime.

ACKNOWLEDGMENT

This research is partially supported by NSF grants 1345232 and 0947465. The views and conclusions contained in this document are those of the authors and should not be interpreted as representing the official policies, either expressed or implied, of the sponsoring organizations, agencies, or the U.S. government.

REFERENCES

[1] J. Atlas and K. Decker. Coordination for uncertain outcomes using distributed neighbor exchange. In *Proceedings of the*

[4] Although ICG Max-Sum does not solve UR-DCOPs optimally [29], we use it as it is the only known UR-DCOP solver. The UR-DCOP results in Table 2(c) are computed using an optimal centralized solver.

International Conference on Autonomous Agents and Multiagent Systems (AAMAS), pages 1047–1054, 2010.
[2] R. J. Aumann, M. Maschler, and R. E. Stearns. *Repeated games with incomplete information*. MIT press, 1995.
[3] C. Baral. *Knowledge Representation, reasoning, and declarative problem solving with Answer sets*. Cambridge University Press, Cambridge, MA, 2003.
[4] F. Bistaffa, A. Farinelli, and N. Bombieri. Optimising memory management for belief propagation in junction trees using gpgpus. In *Proceedings of the International Conference on Parallel and Distributed Systems (ICPADS)*, pages 526–533, 2014.
[5] S. Citrigno, T. Eiter, W. Faber, G. Gottlob, C. Koch, N. Leone, C. Mateis, G. Pfeifer, and F. Scarcello. The dlv system: Model generator and application frontends. In *Proceedings of the Workshop on Logic Programming*, pages 128–137, 1997.
[6] P. Erdös and A. Rényi. On random graphs i. *Publicationes Mathematicae Debrecen*, 6:290, 1959.
[7] A. Farinelli, A. Rogers, A. Petcu, and N. Jennings. Decentralised coordination of low-power embedded devices using the Max-Sum algorithm. In *Proceedings of the International Conference on Autonomous Agents and Multiagent Systems (AAMAS)*, pages 639–646, 2008.
[8] F. Fioretto, T. Le, E. Pontelli, W. Yeoh, and T. C. Son. Exploiting GPUs in solving (distributed) constraint optimization problems with dynamic programming. In *Proceedings of the International Conference on Principles and Practice of Constraint Programming (CP)*, 2015.
[9] M. Gebser, B. Kaufmann, A. Neumann, and T. Schaub. clasp: A conflict-driven answer set solver. In *Proceedings of the International Conference on Logic Programming and Nonmonotonic Reasoning (LPNMR)*, pages 260–265, 2007.
[10] M. Gelfond and V. Lifschitz. Logic programs with classical negation. In *Proceedings of the Interntional Conference on Logic Programming (ICLP)*, pages 579–597, 1990.
[11] S. Gupta, P. Jain, W. Yeoh, S. Ranade, and E. Pontelli. Solving customer-driven microgrid optimization problems as DCOPs. In *Proceedings of the Distributed Constraint Reasoning Workshop*, pages 45–59, 2013.
[12] Y. Hamadi, C. Bessière, and J. Quinqueton. Distributed intelligent backtracking. In *Proceedings of the European Conference on Artificial Intelligence (ECAI)*, pages 219–223, 1998.
[13] J. Harsanyi. Games with incomplete information played by "Bayesian" players, I-III: Part I. the basic model. *Management Science*, pages 1804–1817, 2004.
[14] K. Hoang, F. Fioretto, P. Hou, M. Yokoo, W. Yeoh, and R. Zivan. Proactive dynamic distributed constraint optimization. In *Proceedings of the International Conference on Autonomous Agents and Multiagent Systems (AAMAS)*, 2016.
[15] T. Le, T. C. Son, E. Pontelli, and W. Yeoh. Solving distributed constraint optimization problems with logic programming. In *Proceedings of the AAAI Conference on Artificial Intelligence (AAAI)*, 2015.
[16] T. Léauté and B. Faltings. Distributed constraint optimization under stochastic uncertainty. In *Proceedings of the AAAI Conference on Artificial Intelligence (AAAI)*, pages 68–73, 2011.
[17] T. Léauté, B. Ottens, and R. Szymanek. FRODO 2.0: An open-source framework for distributed constraint optimization. In *Proceedings of the Distributed Constraint Reasoning Workshop*, pages 160–164, 2009.
[18] R. Maheswaran, M. Tambe, E. Bowring, J. Pearce, and P. Varakantham. Taking DCOP to the real world: Efficient complete solutions for distributed event scheduling. In *Proceedings of the International Joint Conference on Autonomous Agents and Multiagent Systems (AAMAS)*, pages 310–317, 2004.
[19] R. Mailler and V. Lesser. Solving distributed constraint optimization problems using cooperative mediation. In *Proceedings of the International Joint Conference on Autonomous Agents and Multiagent Systems (AAMAS)*, pages 438–445, 2004.
[20] V. Marek and M. Truszczyński. Stable models and an alternative logic programming paradigm. In *The Logic Programming Paradigm: a 25-year Perspective*, pages 375–398, 1999.
[21] R. Marinescu and R. Dechter. AND/OR branch-and-bound search for combinatorial optimization in graphical models. *Artificial Intelligence*, 173(16-17):1457–1491, 2009.
[22] P. Modi, W.-M. Shen, M. Tambe, and M. Yokoo. ADOPT: Asynchronous distributed constraint optimization with quality guarantees. *Artificial Intelligence*, 161(1–2):149–180, 2005.
[23] D. T. Nguyen, W. Yeoh, and H. C. Lau. Stochastic dominance in stochastic DCOPs for risk-sensitive applications. In *Proceedings of the International Conference on Autonomous Agents and Multiagent Systems (AAMAS)*, pages 257–264, 2012.
[24] I. Niemelä. Logic programming with stable model semantics as a constraint programming paradigm. *Annals of Mathematics and Artificial Intelligence*, 25(3–4):241–273, 1999.
[25] A. Petcu and B. Faltings. A scalable method for multiagent constraint optimization. In *Proceedings of the International Joint Conference on Artificial Intelligence (IJCAI)*, pages 1413–1420, 2005.
[26] J. Sanders and E. Kandrot. *CUDA by Example. An Introduction to General-Purpose GPU Programming*. Addison Wesley, 2010.
[27] E. Sultanik, R. Lass, and W. Regli. DCOPolis: a framework for simulating and deploying distributed constraint reasoning algorithms. In *Proceedings of the Distributed Constraint Reasoning Workshop*, 2007.
[28] S. Ueda, A. Iwasaki, and M. Yokoo. Coalition structure generation based on distributed constraint optimization. In *Proceedings of the AAAI Conference on Artificial Intelligence (AAAI)*, pages 197–203, 2010.
[29] F. Wu and N. Jennings. Regret-based multi-agent coordination with uncertain task rewards. In *Proceedings of the AAAI Conference on Artificial Intelligence (AAAI)*, pages 1492–1499, 2014.
[30] W. Yeoh, A. Felner, and S. Koenig. BnB-ADOPT: An asynchronous branch-and-bound DCOP algorithm. *Journal of Artificial Intelligence Research*, 38:85–133, 2010.
[31] W. Yeoh and M. Yokoo. Distributed problem solving. *AI Magazine*, 33(3):53–65, 2012.
[32] R. Zivan, H. Yedidsion, S. Okamoto, R. Glinton, and K. Sycara. Distributed constraint optimization for teams of mobile sensing agents. *Autonomous Agents and Multi-Agent Systems*, 29(3):495–536, 2015.

Adding Influencing Agents to a Flock

Katie Genter and Peter Stone
Department of Computer Science, The University of Texas at Austin
Austin, TX 78712 USA
{katie,pstone}@cs.utexas.edu

ABSTRACT

Many different animals, including birds and fish, exhibit a collective behavior known as flocking. Flocking behavior is believed by biologists to emerge from relatively simple local control rules utilized by each individual in a flock. Specifically, each individual adjusts its behavior based on the behaviors of its closest neighbors. In our work we consider the possibility of adding a small set of influencing agents, which are under our control, to a flock. Specifically, we advance existing work on adding influencing agents into a flock and begin to consider the case in which influencing agents must join a flock in motion. Following ad hoc teamwork methodology, we assume that we are given knowledge of, but no direct control over, the rest of the flock. As such, we use the influencing agents to alter the flock's behavior — for example by encouraging all of the individuals to face the same direction or by altering the trajectory of the flock. In this paper we define several new methods for adding influencing agents into the flock and compare them against existing methods.

Categories and Subject Descriptors

I.2.11 [**Distributed Artificial Intelligence**]: Multiagent systems

General Terms

Algorithms, Experimentation

Keywords

Ad Hoc Teamwork; Agent Placement; Flocking

1. INTRODUCTION

As teams of robots become useful in real-world settings, it becomes increasingly likely that robots that are not programmed to explicitly be part of these teams will need to join or otherwise assist these teams. This need could arise because some members of the team become damaged or lost, and there is neither the time nor the expertise to program new robots to add to the team. In this case, an ideal solution would be to add general agents to the team that can perform well as part of the team with no pre-coordination. Such agents are referred to in literature as *ad hoc agents* [11]. In this paper, we consider how ad hoc agents can be used in a flocking setting.

Flocking is an emergent swarm behavior found in nature. Each animal in a flock follows a simple local behavior rule, but these simple behaviors often result in group behavior that appears well organized and stable. Flocking has been studied in various disciplines including physics [13], graphics [9], biology [2], and distributed control theory [6, 7, 12] with the goal of characterizing its emergent behavior. In our work, we instead consider how to influence a flock to adopt particular behaviors by adding a small number of controllable agents to the flock.

As a motivating example, imagine that a flock of birds is flying directly towards a dangerous area, such as an airport or wind farm. Our goal is to encourage the birds to avoid the dangerous area without significantly disturbing them. Since there is no way to directly control the flock's flight path, we must instead alter the environment so as to encourage the flock to alter their flight path as desired. In this work, we choose to alter the environment by adding *influencing agents* to the flock. These influencing agents — which could be in the form of robotic birds[1], robotic bees [10], or ultralight aircraft[2] — follow our algorithms but are perceived by the rest of the flock to be one of their own.

In our work, we follow a well-recognized flocking model [9] when we assume that each bird in the flock updates its heading at each time step based on the headings of its neighbors. In previous work we have considered how influencing agents should behave so as to influence the flock [3, 4] as well as where influencing agents should be placed in the flock if they were somehow able to join the flock instantaneously [5]. In this paper, we (1) extend our work on determining where influencing agents should be placed in the flock (henceforth called the *Placement* case) and (2) consider how influencing agents should behave in order to join a flock in motion (henceforth called the *Joining* case). As such, the research questions addressed by this paper are: *Given computational limitations, how should influencing agents be placed within a flock?* and *How should influencing agents join a flock in motion if they are able to arrive ahead of the flock?*

The remainder of this paper is organized as follows. Section 2 situates our research in the literature. Section 3 introduces the problem of adding influencing agents to a flock. Section 4 overviews existing methods. Section 5 details the

Appears in: *Proceedings of the 15th International Conference on Autonomous Agents and Multiagent Systems (AAMAS 2016), J. Thangarajah, K. Tuyls, C. Jonker, S. Marsella (eds.), May 9–13, 2016, Singapore.*

[1] www.mybionicbird.com
[2] www.operationmigration.org

experimental set-up. Section 6 introduces and evaluates our improved methods for deciding where to place the influencing agents. Section 7 introduces and evaluates our work on joining a flock in motion. Finally, Section 8 concludes.

2. RELATED WORK

To the best of our knowledge, our work is the only work so far that has considered how to add controllable agents to a flock with the goal of using these controllable agents to influence the flock towards a particular behavior. This section highlights the work most related to our own.

In a more complete version of the flocking model used in this work, Reynolds focused on creating a flocking model that behaved realistically [9]. Reynolds' model consists of three simple steering behaviors that determine how each agent maneuvers based on the behavior of the agents around it (henceforth called *neighbors*): *Collision Avoidance* steers the agent such that it avoids collisions with neighbors, *Velocity Matching* moves the agents at a velocity similar to nearby neighbors, and *Flock Centering* steers the agent towards the average heading and position of its neighbors. Vicsek *et al.* considered just part of the *Flock Centering* aspect of Reynolds' model [13]. Hence, like in our work, Vicsek *et al.* use a model where all of the particles move at a constant velocity and adopt the average direction neighboring particles. However, like Reynolds' work, Vicsek *et al.* were only concerned with simulating flock behavior and not with adding controllable agents to the flock.

Jadbabaie *et al.* considered the impact of adding a controllable agent to a flock [7]. Like Vicsek *et al.* , they also used part of the *Flock Centering* aspect of Reynolds' model. Their work showed that a flock with a controllable agent will always converge to the controllable agent's heading. Su *et al.* presented work that used a controllable agent to make a flock converge [12] and Celikkanat and Sahin used informed agents to lead a flock by their preference for a particular direction [1]. However, our work is different from all of these lines of research in that they all influence a flock to converge to a target heading *eventually*, while in our work we influence a flock to converge quickly.

Couzin *et al.* considered how animals in groups make informed, unanimous decisions [2]. They showed that only a very small proportion of informed agents is required for such decisions, and that the larger the group, the smaller the proportion of informed individuals required. This line of research is different from ours because they do not study how to control agents by accounting for how the other agents will react. Instead, in this line of research, each agent behaves in a fixed manner that is pre-decided or solely based on its type.

Finally, Han *et al.* assume that an influencing agent can be placed at any position at any time step [6]. Because of this assumption, the authors repeatedly 'teleport' the influencing agent to the position of the 'worst' flocking agent, which is the one that deviates from the desired orientation the most. In our work, we do not allow teleporting and hence we cannot continually place an influencing agent at the 'worst' flocking agent.

3. PROBLEM DEFINITION

To precisely introduce and define the problem of adding influencing agents to a flock, we must specify (1) a model of the flock, (2) the possible options for adding influencing agents to a flock, (3) the actions available to the influencing agents, and (4) the performance objective. This section outlines these specifications and introduces the simulation environment we use in our experiments. Previous methodologies for addressing the defined problem are reviewed in Section 4 while our new methods are presented in Sections 6 and 7.

3.1 Flocking Model

In order to model the flock, we use a simplified version of Reynolds' Boid algorithm for flocking [9]. Specifically, the simplified version only utilizes part of the *Flock Centering* aspect of Reynolds' model and does not use the *Collision Avoidance* and *Velocity Matching* aspects. Although this model is similar to the model utilized in previous work [3, 5], we present the important details of the model to both include new aspects of our model as well as to help this paper stand on its own.

We assume that the flock is comprised of two types of agents: k *influencing* agents and m *flocking* agents. The flock thus contains $n = k+m$ total agents. The k influencing agents $\{a_0, \ldots, a_{k-1}\}$ are agents whose behavior we control via the algorithms presented in our work. The m flocking agents $\{a_k, \ldots, a_{N-1}\}$ are agents that we cannot directly control but that instead behave according to the simplified version of Reynolds' flocking algorithm.

Every agent a_i in the flock has a velocity $v_i(t)$, a position in the environment $p_i(t)$, and an orientation $\theta_i(t)$ at time t. Each agent's position $p_i(t)$ at time t is updated after its orientation is updated, such that $x_i(t) = x_i(t-1) + v_i(t)\cos(\theta_i(t))$ and $y_i(t) = y_i(t-1) - v_i(t)\sin(\theta_i(t))$.

As is commonly accepted in most flocking models, we assume that the agents in a flock are only influenced by the other agents in their *neighborhood*. We use a *visibility radius* to define each agent's *neighborhood*. Specifically we let $N_i(t)$ be the set of $n_i(t) \leq n$ agents at time t which are located within the *visibility radius* r of agent a_i. All agents in $N_i(t)$ are considered to be neighbors of a_i.

Under the simplified version of Reynolds' model that we employ, we assume that agents in a flock update their orientations based on the orientations of the other agents in their neighborhood. Hence, the global orientation of agent a_i at time step $t+1$, $\theta_i(t+1)$, is set to be the average orientation of all agents in $N_i(t)$ at time t. Formally,

$$\theta_i(t+1) = \theta_i(t) + \frac{1}{n_i(t)} \sum_{a_j \in N_i(t)} \text{calcDiff}(\theta_j(t), \theta_i(t)) \quad (1)$$

We use Equation 1 instead of taking the average orientation of all agents because of the special cases handled by Algorithm 1. For example, the mathematical average of 350° and 10° is 180°, but by Algorithm 1 it is 0°. Throughout this paper, we restrict $\theta_i(t)$ to be within $[0, 2\pi)$.

Algorithm 1 calcDiff($\theta_i(t), \theta_j(t)$)

```
if ((θi(t) − θj(t) ≥ −π) ∧ (θi(t) − θj(t) ≤ π)) then
    return θi(t) − θj(t)
else if θi(t) − θj(t) < −π then
    return 2π + (θi(t) − θj(t))
else
    return (θi(t) − θj(t)) − 2π
```

3.2 Adding Influencing Agents

Influencing agents are added to the flock in order to influence the flock to behave in a particular way. Our previous work considered four methods for initially placing influencing agents directly into a flock by setting $\{p_0(0), \ldots, p_{k-1}(0)\}$ [5]. We overview these methods in Section 4 before considering improvements to these methods in Section 6. Additionally, in Section 7 we consider the case where $\{p_0(0), \ldots, p_{k-1}(0)\}$ is not under our control.

In the *Placement* case where $\{p_0(0), \ldots, p_{k-1}(0)\}$ is under our control we place the influencing agents $\{a_0, \ldots, a_{k-1}\}$ wherever we wish at $t = 0$. In the *Joining* case where $\{p_0(0), \ldots, p_{k-1}(0)\}$ is not under our control, we assume the influencing agents $\{a_0, \ldots, a_{k-1}\}$ begin from a designated station and must then actively move to join the flock.

3.3 Influencing Agent Behavior

We can control the behavior of influencing agents $\{a_0, \ldots, a_{k-1}\}$. Specifically, influencing agents can behave to either (1) influence neighbors or (2) position to a desired location. Hence, at each time step our algorithms for the influencing agents must decide whether to influence or position, as well as how to best execute the chosen behavior.

In this paper, Section 4 reviews the algorithm the influencing agents use in this work to influence neighbors. Then, Section 7 presents some new methods for the influencing agents to utilize while attempting to join a flock in motion.

3.4 Performance Representation

In previous work we defined the *Agent Control and Placement Problem* [5]. In this work we present generalizations that allow influencing agents to travel to their desired positions instead of being placed in these positions. Specifically, the generalized *Agent Control and Placement Problem* is stated as follows: Given a target orientation θ^* and a team of n agents $\{a_0, \ldots, a_{n-1}\}$, where the m flocking agents $\{a_k, \ldots a_{n-1}\}$ have positions $\gamma_m(t) = \{p_k(t), \ldots p_{n-1}(t)\}$ at time t and calculate their orientation based on Equation 1, determine the desired influencing position $\pi(t_i)$ of influencing agents $\{a_0, \ldots a_{k-1}\}$ at time t_i and control $\Phi = \phi(0), \ldots, \phi(t)$ at times $t >= 0$ such that loss $l(\pi(t_i), \Phi)$ is minimized.

A k-agent placement specifies the positions that each influencing agent $\{a_0, \ldots a_{k-1}\}$ will adopt at time t_i, where time t_i is the time at which the influencing agents begin attempting to influence their neighbors. The k-agent placement is denoted by $\pi_k(t_i) = \{p_0(t_i), \ldots, p_{k-1}(t_i)\}$ where $\{p_0(t_i), \ldots, p_{k-1}(t_i)\}$ is the set of positions for influencing agents $\{a_0, \ldots a_{k-1}\}$ at time t_i.

We denote t^* as the earliest time step at which flocking agents $\{a_k, \ldots, a_{N-1}\}$ are oriented such that, for all $t \geq t^*$, $\{\theta_k(t), \ldots, \theta_{N-1}(t)\}$ are all within ϵ of θ^*. However, in some cases this can not occur because some flocking agents may become permanently separated from the flock — we say these agents are *lost*. An agent a_i is considered lost if there exists a subset of flocking agents with cardinality $m' < m$ and orientations within ϵ of θ^* for more than 200 time steps and $|\theta_i(t^*) - \theta^*| > \epsilon$, where t^* is the time step at which the subset converged to θ^*.

The *loss* $l(\pi(t_i), \Phi)$ of a k-agent placement $\pi_k(t_i)$ and control Φ is a weighted function of three terms:

- w_1 is a weight that emphasizes the importance of minimizing the number of lost agents (minimize $\overline{m - m'}$)
- w_2 is a weight that emphasizes the importance of minimizing the number of simulation experiments in which any agent is lost (minimize simulation experiments in which $m - m' > 0$)
- w_3 is a weight that emphasizes the importance of minimizing the number of time steps needed for convergence (minimize $\overline{t^*}$)

$$l(\pi(t_i), \Phi) = w_1 \overline{m - m'} + w_2 \overline{p(m - m' > 0)} + w_3 \overline{t^*} \quad (2)$$

An optimal placement $\pi^*(t_i), \Phi^*$ is one with minimal loss $l(\pi^*(t_i), \Phi)$.

In this work, we set $w_1 > w_2 > w_3$. With these preferences for w_1, w_2, and w_3 we select influencing agent placements that generally lose the least number of agents on average but that also attempt to minimize the chances of losing any agents.

3.5 Simulation Environment

We use the MASON simulator [8] to run the experiments described in this paper. We altered this simulator to encode the flock dynamics described above as well as to compute the performance metric also described above. Pictures of our altered version of the MASON simulator's Flockers domain are shown in Figure 1. In the simulator, each agent orients and moves in the direction of its current velocity vector. We describe our experimental setup in detail in Section 5.

(a) (b)

Figure 1: Images of (a) the start of a trial and (b) the end of a trial. The gray agents are influencing agents while the black agents are other members of the flock.

4. EXISTING BEHAVIOR AND PLACEMENT METHODS

The research presented in this paper utilizes and compares against multiple behavior and placement methods from previous work [3, 5]. In this section, we present high-level overviews of these methods with the goal of making our own methods and experiments that rely on these methods approachable.

4.1 1-Step Lookahead Behavior

The 1-Step Lookahead behavior specifies how an influencing agent should behave in order to influence its neighbors to orient towards a particular heading [3]. Specifically, the

1-Step Lookahead behavior considers all of the influences on neighbors of the influencing agent at a particular point in time. By considering the influences on neighbors, the influencing agent can determine the orientation to adopt that will exert the most influence on the flock during the next time step. The 1-Step Lookahead behavior was found in previous work to be the best behavior in terms of the trade-off between performance and algorithmic complexity. Hence, this is why we chose it to be used by influencing agents in the research described in this paper.

4.2 Placement Methods

Previous work considered where to place influencing agents $\{a_0, \ldots, a_{k-1}\}$ into the flock at time $t = 0$ [5]. We assume that once the influencing agents are placed into the flock, they will immediately follow the 1-Step Lookahead behavior described in Section 4.1 to influence the flock.

In this section, we review the four initial placement methods presented in previous work. For each of these placement methods, we assume that the m flocking agents are initially placed within a pre-set area that is formed by the area in which the flocking agents could initially be placed at time $t = 0$ — we refer to this pre-set area as FA_{preset}.

(a) Grid (b) Border (c) Graph

Figure 2: Examples of three of the influencing agent placement methods from previous work.

4.2.1 *Random Approach*

The Random placement method serves as a simple baseline approach. Specifically, it randomly places the k influencing agents within FA_{preset}. These influencing agent placements are calculated in constant time.

4.2.2 *Grid Approach*

The Grid placement method places k influencing agents at predefined, well-spaced, gridded positions within FA_{preset}. The placement of the influencing agents is dependent on FA_{preset} and not on the actual positions of the flocking agents. Hence, the placement of k influencing agents is determined in constant time. Grids are available that can fit at most x influencing agents, where the smallest grid in which $k \leq x$ is used. Grids are available in which $x \in \{1, 2, 4, 9, 16, 25, 36, \ldots\}$. For each grid size, agents are spread out among the possible positions as much as possible.

4.2.3 *Border Approach*

The Border placement method places k influencing agents as evenly as possible along the borders of FA_{preset}. The placement of the influencing agents is not dependent on the positions of flocking agents. Hence, the placements of k influencing agents are determined in constant time. The Border placement method places influencing agents on the left side of the flock, right side of the flock, bottom of the flock, and top of the flock in order until all k influencing agents are placed. At most $\lceil \frac{k}{4} \rceil$ influencing agents are placed on any particular side of the flock. If more than one influencing agent is placed on a particular side of the flock, the influencing agents spread out as much as possible on that side of the flock.

4.2.4 *Graph Approach*

The Graph approach considers many possible k-sized sets of positions in which the k influencing agents could be placed, and then evaluates how well each of these sets connects the m flocking agents with the k influencing agents. Specifically, it considers adding influencing agents at two different types of positions: (1) mid-points between flocking agents that are within two neighborhood radii of each other and (2) extremely near each flocking agent. Each possible k-sized set of positions is then evaluated in terms of three criteria: (1) minimize the number of flocking agents to which any influencing agent's influence will not spread, (2) maximize the flocking agents that are influenced (both immediately and over time) by influencing agents, and (3) maximize the number of flocking agents that have an influencing agent as a neighbor. The complexity of placing k influencing agents using the Graph placement method is $O(n^3\binom{m^2+m}{k})$.

5. EXPERIMENTAL SETUP

We utilize the MASON simulator [8] for our experiments in this paper. We introduced the MASON simulator in Section 3.5, but in this section we present the details of our experimental environment that are vital for understanding and replicating our experimental setup. We generally only discuss an experimental variable or control if we changed it from the default setting for the simulator. We introduce our experimental setup at this point in the paper so that we can present experimental results throughout the remainder of the paper.

The relevant experimental variables for both the **Placement** case and the **Joining** case are given in Table 1 .

Variable	**Placement Case**	**Joining Case**
toroidal domain	no	no
domain height	300	600
domain width	300	600
units moved by each flocking agent per time step ($v_k = \ldots = v_{N-1}$)	0.2	0.2
units moved by each influencing agent per time step ($v_0 = \ldots = v_{k-1}$)	0.2	0-0.2
neighborhood for each agent (radius)	*10*	*10*

Table 1: Experimental variables for the **Placement** and **Joining** cases. Italicized values are default settings for the simulator.

Most of our experimental variables in Table 1, such as toroidal domain, domain height, domain width, and the units each agent moves per time step, are not set to the default settings for the MASON simulator. We removed the toroidal nature of the domain in order to make the domain more realistic. Hence, if an agent moves off of an edge of our domain, it will not reappear. This is particularly important for *lost* agents remaining *lost*. We also increased the domain height and width, and decreased the units each agent moves per time step, in order to give agents a chance to converge with the flock before leaving the visible area. However, we have no reason to believe the exact experimental settings we chose for the experiments are of particular importance.

All of the experiments reported in this paper used $m = 10$ flocking agents and $k = 2$ to $k = 10$ influencing agents. During our initial research, we ran smaller scale experiments with as many as $m = 50$ flocking agents and $k = 25$ influencing agents. We did not run full scale experiments for flocks with more than $m = 10$ flocking agents mainly due to the high computation time required for the Graph placement approach — this computation issue was the main motivation behind the hybrid approach presented in Section 6.2. As such, we decided to maintain consistency by utilizing $m = 10$ flocking agents for all our experiments in this paper. However, our limited experiments did indicate that results from smaller flocks generally do scale to larger flocks.

In all of our experiments, the flocking agents are initially randomly placed within FA_{preset}, which is a small square at the top left of the environment. Agents are initially assigned random headings that are within 90 degrees of θ^* for the *Placement* case. For the *Joining* case, the flocking agents all begin facing the same orientation (not equal to θ^*) — in our experiments reported in this paper, this particular orientation was 90 degrees away from θ^*.

Experiments and experimental results will be presented throughout the following sections. In all of our experiments, we run 100 trials for each experimental setting and we use the same set of 100 random seeds for each set of experiments. The random seeds are used to determine the exact placement (and orientation for *Placement* experiments) of all of the flocking agents at the start of a simulation experiment. The error bars in all of our graphs depict the standard error of the mean.

6. PLACEMENT IN A FLOCK

Section 4 summarized various published methods for placing influencing agents into a flock at $t = 0$, with the goal of placement being for the influencing agents to influence the flocking agents to orient towards a particular orientation. In this section, we introduce an effective extension to the methods discussed in Section 4.2 as well as a new approach that mitigates the high computational complexity of the Graph placement method reviewed in Section 4.2.4.

6.1 Scaling Placement Area

Three of the placement methods summarized in Section 4.2 — the Random placement approach, the Grid placement approach, and the Border placement approach — do not place influencing agents based on where the flocking agents are initially placed. Instead, these methods all place the influencing agents in predetermined locations based on (1) how many influencing agents are to be added and (2) FA_{preset}.

In order to improve upon these three placement approaches, we decided to scale the area in which the influencing agents are placed based on the area actually occupied by the flocking agents. Specifically, we search all of the locations of the flocking agents and save the highest and lowest x and y values at which flocking agents are located (x_{low}, x_{high}, y_{low}, and y_{high}). We then extend these x and y values by r (the neighborhood radii) and then use the rectangular box formed by $x_{low} - r$, $x_{high} + r$, $y_{low} - r$, and $y_{high} + r$ as the area in which influencing agents can be placed. We call this area FA_{scaled}.

For the *Random Scaled Approach*, we randomly place influencing agents within FA_{scaled}. Similarly, for the *Border Scaled Approach* we spread influencing agents along the borders of FA_{scaled}. For the *Grid Scaled Approach*, we place the k influencing agents at predefined, well-spaced, gridded positions within FA_{scaled}. Within FA_{scaled} we follow the technique for the Grid placement approach from Section 4.2.2. Specifically, we spread out the influencing agents among the possible grid positions as much as possible. Note that there is not a *Graph Scaled Approach* because the Graph Placement Approach already places influencing agents based on where the flocking agents are placed.

In this section we run *Placement* case experiments to compare the performance of the initial placement methods summarized in Section 4.2 against the scaled versions of these methods presented in Section 6.1.

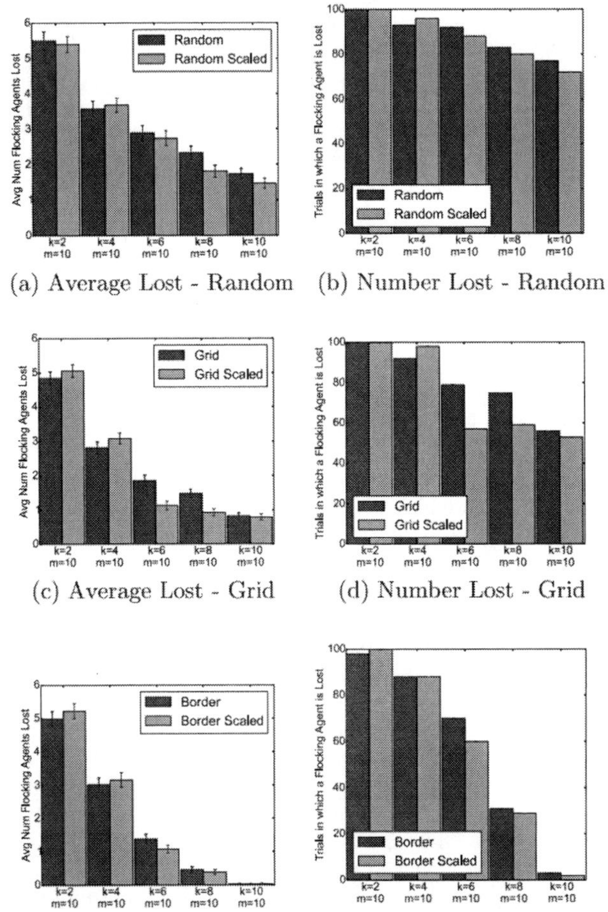

(a) Average Lost - Random (b) Number Lost - Random

(c) Average Lost - Grid (d) Number Lost - Grid

(e) Average Lost - Border (f) Number Lost - Border

Figure 3: Results for the Scaling Placement Area experiments. These graphs compare (a,c,e) the average number of flocking agents lost and (b,d,f) the number of trials in which any flocking agents are lost.

Figure 3(a,c,e) shows the average number of flocking agents lost and Figure 3(b,d,f) shows the total number of trials in which at least one flocking agent is lost. The graphs show these data for six different placement methods when adding $k = 2$ to $k = 10$ influencing agents to a flock with $m = 10$ flocking agents. In the graphs, 'Random' should be compared to 'Random Scaled', 'Grid' should be compared to 'Grid Scaled', and 'Border' should be compared to 'Border Scaled'.

A few interesting trends arise in Figure 3. First, the Grid Scaled and Border Scaled lose more flocking agents on average than their non-scaled counterparts when $k = 2$ and $k = 4$ but lose fewer flocking agents on average than their non-scaled counterparts when $k = 6$, $k = 8$, and $k = 10$ (significantly so for $k = 6$ and $k = 8$ of the Grid placement approach). However, the difference between the scaled and non-scaled approaches are not as large for any of the three placement approaches when $k = 2$, $k = 4$, and $k = 10$. Second, in terms of the number of trials in which no flocking agents are lost, Figure 3(d) shows that the Grid Scaled approach has many more trials in which no flocking agents are lost than its non-scaled counterpart when $k = 6$ and $k = 8$. Additionally — outside of $k = 6$ for the Border placement approach — this difference between the scaled and non-scaled methods does not appear for the other approaches. Both of these trends lead us to believe that influencing agent placement may be less important when there are either few or many influencing agents added to a flock. Of course, the actual k and m values where the scaled approaches perform much better than the non-scaled approaches will vary based on the exact experimental settings.

6.2 Combining Placement Methods for Better Scalability

The Graph placement approach summarized in Section 4.2.4 was shown in previous work [5] to perform better than other approaches in terms of agents lost and trials in which any flocking agents were lost. However, the Graph placement method was not widely and generally useful because the $O(n^3\binom{m^2+m}{k})$ computational complexity limited the sizes of the flocks in which it could be quickly applied.

With this computational complexity issue in mind, in this paper we evaluate hybrid approaches that utilize the Graph placement method to pick the first k_g influencing agent positions and then assign the remaining $k - k_g$ positions based on more computationally efficient methods. The remaining $k - k_g$ positions are randomly chosen from the possible k placements of the more computationally efficient method.

In our experiments, we compare multiple values of k_g as well as multiple placement methods to assign the $k - k_g$ placements not assigned by the Graph placement method. We compared the four initial placement methods summarized in Section 4.2 against hybrid approaches that combine the Graph placement approach with more computationally efficient approaches. These experiments were run under the *Placement* case settings described in Section 5.

Figure 4(a,c,e) shows the average number of flocking agents lost when initially placing influencing agents according to the Baseline, Graph, and hybrid placement approaches. 'Baseline' refers to the initial placement method that is used, chosen from the Random placement approach, the Grid placement approach, and the Border placement approach. The Baseline/Graph (2 Graph) hybrid placement approach places two influencing agents according to the Graph placement approach and then places any remaining influencing agents based on the Baseline placement approach. Likewise, the Baseline/Graph (4 Graph) hybrid placement approach places four influencing agents according to the Graph placement approach and then places any remaining influencing agents based on the Baseline placement approach.

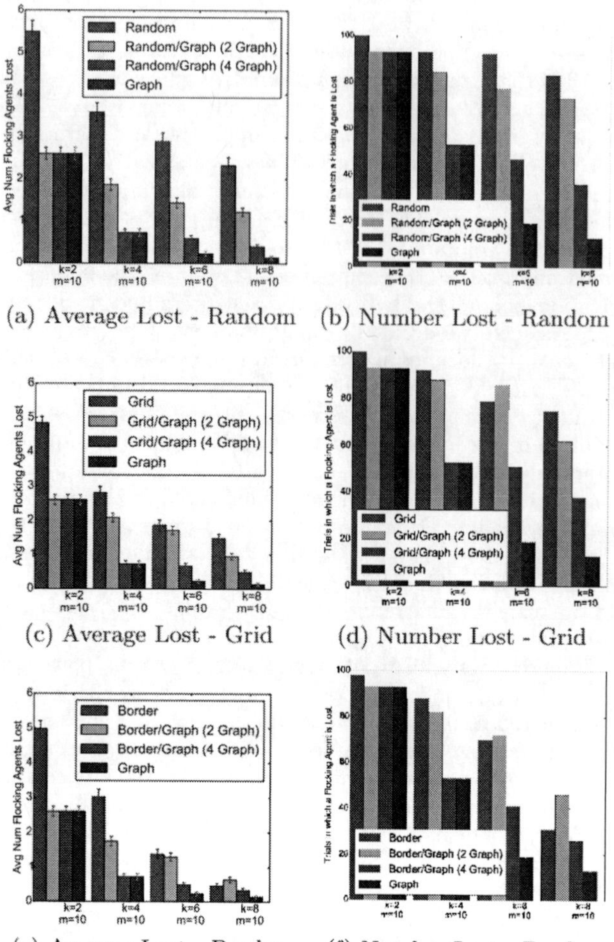

(a) Average Lost - Random (b) Number Lost - Random

(c) Average Lost - Grid (d) Number Lost - Grid

(e) Average Lost - Border (f) Number Lost - Border

Figure 4: Results for the hybrid approach experiments. These graphs compare (a,c,e) the average number of flocking agents lost and (b,d,f) the number of trials in which any flocking agents are lost.

Figure 4(b,d,f) shows the number of trials in which at least one flocking agent was lost. We strive to minimize the number of trials in which any flocking agents are lost. The results in Figure 4(b,d,f) generally appear as we would expect, but there are a few surprising results. Specifically, the data points showing that the Grid and Border placement approaches have fewer trials in which a flocking agent is lost than the hybrid approaches were initially surprising. However, this could be because the hybrid placement approach may cover some areas twice while leaving other areas open that would be covered by the Grid and Border placement approaches. This hypothesis is supported by the fact that the Random placement graph in Figure 4(b) shows that for all k values, the Random placement approach loses at least one flocking agent in more trials than the hybrid placement approaches.

For all of the graphs in Figure 4, for $k = 2$ the results for all of the placement approaches except the Random placement approach are the same — this is expected because both hybrid placement approaches should use the Graph placement approach for both influencing agent placements. Likewise, for $k = 4$, the results of both the Graph placement approach and the Baseline/Graph (4 Graph) approach should be the same since both approaches use the Graph placement approach for all four influencing agent placements.

Finally, although the computation complexity is better for the hybrid placement approach $(O(n^3\binom{m^2+m}{k_g}))$ than for the Graph placement approach, the complexity is still dominated by the general flock size. Even so, we still obtained the expected result of the hybrid placement approaches being a better trade-off in terms of performance and complexity. To make this tradeoff more concrete, consider processor CPU timings across 10 different placements with $k = 5$ and $m = 15$ — the average placement times were 3.11 minutes for the graph placement approach, 19.4 seconds for the Grid/Graph (4 Graph) approach, and 2.51 seconds for the Grid/Graph (2 Graph) approach.

7. JOINING A FLOCK

So far, all of the work in this paper has considered where influencing agents should be placed into a flock if we assume they can somehow be placed into the flock instantaneously. However, a more realistic scenario would require influencing agents to *join* a flock in motion. Specifically, the influencing agents would have to leave stations positioned throughout the environment and join the flock. In this section, we introduce some initial work on behaviors for influencing agents to join a flock.

The scenario we consider is as follows: flocking agents begin flocking together in a specific direction and the influencing agents must join the flock and influence it to change its current direction of travel to be towards some desired heading θ^*. In this work, we consider the initial case in which the influencing agents are always able to arrive ahead of the flock's expected path of travel. We make the important assumption that although the influencing agents can move slower than the flock, they are unable to move quicker than the flock.

The questions we ask in this work involve three main aspects: where the influencing agents should position themselves ahead of the flock, how the influencing agents should behave as the flock arrives, and how the influencing agents should attempt to influence the flock. We consider each of these aspects below and present experimental results in turn.

7.1 Positioning Ahead of the Flock

In this work we assume that the influencing agents are able to fly ahead of the flock and position themselves ahead of the flock's expected path. By positioning themselves as they wish before the flock arrives and then remaining stationary (i.e. adopting a 0 velocity), the influencing agents are able to reach their desired positions before any flocking agents enter their neighborhood. This scenario differs from the previous one because once the influencing agents are within the flocking agents' neighborhoods, the flocking agents will be influenced. As such, the important question addressed in this section is: *How should the influencing agents position themselves if they are able to arrive ahead of the flock?*

To answer this question, we run experiments in which the influencing agents move ahead of the flock's arrival to adopt the positions suggested by methods in Section 4.2 before the flock arrives.

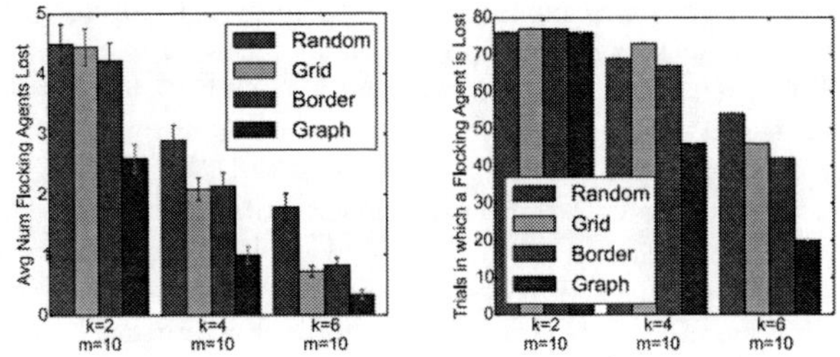

(a) Average Lost (b) Number Lost

Figure 5: Graphs for the positioning ahead of the flock experiments. These graphs compare (a) the average number of flocking agents lost and (b) the number of trials in which any flocking agents are lost.

Figure 5 shows how well the four initial placement methods summarized in Section 4.2 fare as desired positions in the *Joining* case. As can be seen in Figure 5, our experimental results show that these placement approaches do well in the *Joining* case. Specifically, the Graph placement approach does consistently much better than the other approaches in terms of both the average number of flocking agents lost and the number of trials in which at least one flocking agent is lost. Additionally, the Grid placement approach and the Border placement approach do better than the Random placement approach for larger values of k. As expected, these general trends are similar to those seen in *Placement* experimental results reported in previous work [5].

Although the Graph placement approach was shown to perform best, its complexity is much more computationally intensive than the other methods. Hence, for the remainder of the paper we will use the Border placement method for selecting the desired positions of the influencing agents within the flock.

7.2 Behavior as the Flock Arrives

As the flock approaches the waiting influencing agents, the influencing agents will begin to be within the flocking agents' neighborhoods and hence will begin to influence the flocking agents. In this section, we consider how the influencing agents should behave in the short time span between when they are first able to influence the flocking agents and when the flock has reached the point at which they are in their desired positions with respect to the flock's current position.

We present results for two possible behaviors the influencing agents may adopt as the flock is arriving. However, we tested many other behaviors, most of which were unsuccessful for one of two reasons: (1) they influenced the flock before the flock reached the point at which the influencing agents are in their desired positions with respect to the flock's current position or (2) they splintered the flock.

The two influencing agent behaviors that worked best as the flock was arriving were some of the simplest approaches we attempted. Under the first behavior, called 'Face Current', the influencing agents orient towards the heading at which the flock is currently traveling and stay in place until it is time to influence the flock at time t_i. The second behavior, called 'Face Goal', is very similar to the first. Under the 'Face Goal' behavior, the influencing agents orient towards

θ^* and stay in place until it is time to influence the flock at time t_i. In both cases, the influencing agents stay in place by setting $(v_0(t_{start}) \ldots v_{k-1}(t_i) = 0$. t_{start} denotes the time at which the flocking agents begin to remain stationary after they originally adopt their desired position.

Finally, at time t_i the influencing agents begin influencing the flocking agents with the goal of orienting the flock as a whole towards θ^*. Previous work [3] showed that the flocking agents can become lost if the flock is influenced too quickly. Hence, in addition to considering influencing immediately via the 1-Step Lookahead algorithm we also consider influencing the flock to alter its orientation over a longer set of time (specifically, 100 and 200 time steps in our experiments).

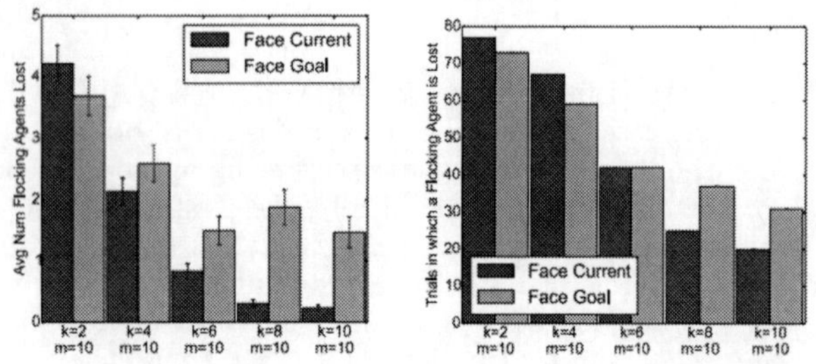

(a) Average Lost (b) Number Lost

Figure 6: Results for the arrival experiments. These graphs compare (a) the average number of flocking agents lost and (b) the number of trials in which any flocking agents are lost.

Figure 6 compares two different behaviors for the influencing agents while the flock is arriving. Although the 'Face Goal' behavior does better in terms of both the average number of flocking agents lost and the number of trials in which any flocking agents are lost when $k = 2$, in general the 'Face Current' behavior does much better. When $k = 8$ and $k = 10$, the 'Face Current' behavior loses significantly fewer flocking agents on average than the 'Face Goal' behavior. This is likely because the 'Face Current' behavior waits until the influencing agents are in their desired positions before influencing, whereas the 'Face Goal' behavior influences flocking agents towards θ^* as the influencing agents enter the flocking agents' neighborhood. Although this type of coincidental influence sometimes influences flocking agents to orient towards θ^*, it is much more likely to result in the flocking agents straying away from both the flock and θ^*.

There are cases in which the 'Face Goal' behavior performs much better than the 'Face Current' behavior. One such case we found in our extensive experiments was when $k = 2$ or $k = 4$ with $m = 10$ and a neighborhood radius $r = 5$. Hence, it seems that there are cases in which each behavior would be appropriate, but based on the experiments we ran, the 'Face Current' behavior usually performs better.

Figure 7 shows results from taking 0 (default), 100, and 200 time steps to slowly influence the flock to orient towards θ^*. The experiments show that although 'Influence 100' and 'Influence 200' perform slightly better than 'Influence 0' in most cases, in general the performance is effectively the same. Despite this, we expect that influencing the flock to orient slowly may be more effective than influencing the flock to orient quickly under particular experimental settings. In particular, one case that showed promise was

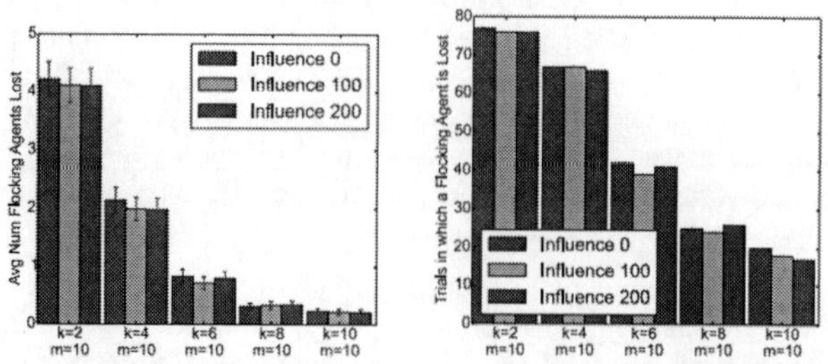

(a) Average Lost (b) Number Lost

Figure 7: Results for the influencing experiments. These graphs compare (a) the average number of flocking agents lost and (b) the number of trials in which any flocking agents are lost.

attempting to influencing a dense flock using a very limited number of influencing agents.

8. CONCLUSION

In this paper we consider how influencing agents should initially be placed within a flock given computational limitations. We also begin to consider how influencing agents should join a flock in motion if they can arrive ahead of the flock. We present multiple methods towards addressing both of these areas, and we present selected results from our extensive experiments. Experimental results show that for larger numbers of influencing agents, scaling the area in which influencing agents are placed to match the area where flocking agents are initially placed fares well. Additionally, hybrid methods that combine simple methods with the computationally complex Graph placement approach provide a decent trade-off between performance and computation time when initially placing influencing agents into a flock. Finally, we also showed that the influencing agent placement methods that worked well for initial placement also work well if the influencing agents are able to position themselves within the flight path of an incoming flock.

As was seen throughout this paper, influencing agent placement in a flock is an important aspect to utilizing influencing agents to influence a flock. As such, there are many potential areas for future work. One natural extension to this work is to determine how to join a flock in motion when the influencing agents are not able to arrive and position themselves ahead of the flock. Additionally, a related question of interest regards how the influencing agents will be able to detach themselves from the flock once they are finished influencing the flock. Finally, although the 1-Step Lookahead algorithm is effective at influencing flocking agents, it would be interesting to develop an algorithm that leveraged coordinated behaviors between multiple influencing agents.

9. ACKNOWLEDGEMENTS

This work has taken place in the Learning Agents Research Group (LARG) at the Artificial Intelligence Laboratory, The University of Texas at Austin. LARG research is supported in part by grants from the National Science Foundation (CNS-1330072, CNS-1305287), ONR (21C184-01), AFRL (FA8750-14-1-0070), AFOSR (FA9550-14-1-0087), and Yujin Robot.

REFERENCES

[1] H. Celikkanat and E. Sahin. Steering self-organized robot flocks through externally guided individuals. *Neural Computing and Applications*, 19(6):849–865, September 2010.

[2] I. D. Couzin, J. Krause, N. R. Franks, and S. A. Levin. Effective leadership and decision-making in animal groups on the move. *Nature*, 433(7025):513–516, February 2005.

[3] K. Genter and P. Stone. Influencing a flock via ad hoc teamwork. In *Ninth International Conference on Swarm Intelligence (ANTS'14)*, September 2014.

[4] K. Genter and P. Stone. Ad hoc teamwork behaviors for influencing a flock. *Acta Polytechnica*, 2016.

[5] K. Genter, S. Zhang, and P. Stone. Determining placements of influencing agents in a flock. In *AAMAS'15*, May 2015.

[6] J. Han, M. Li, and L. Guo. Soft control on collective behavior of a group of autonomous agents by a shill agent. *Systems Science and Complexity*, 19:54–62, 2006.

[7] A. Jadbabaie, J. Lin, and A. Morse. Coordination of groups of mobile autonomous agents using nearest neighbor rules. *IEEE Transactions on Automatic Control*, 48(6):988 – 1001, Jun 2003.

[8] S. Luke, C. Cioffi-Revilla, L. Panait, K. Sullivan, and G. Balan. Mason: A multi-agent simulation environment. *Simulation: Transactions of the Society for Modeling and Simulation International*, 81(7):517–527, 2005.

[9] C. W. Reynolds. Flocks, herds and schools: A distributed behavioral model. *SIGGRAPH*, 21:25–34, August 1987.

[10] J. Shang, S. Combes, B. Finio, and R. Wood. Artificial insect wings of diverse morphology for flapping-wing micro air vehicles. *Bioinspiration & Biomimetics*, 4(3), 2009.

[11] P. Stone, G. A. Kaminka, S. Kraus, and J. S. Rosenschein. Ad hoc autonomous agent teams: Collaboration without pre-coordination. In *AAAI'10*, 2010.

[12] H. Su, X. Wang, and Z. Lin. Flocking of multi-agents with a virtual leader. *IEEE Transactions on Automatic Control*, 54(2):293–307, Feb 2009.

[13] T. Vicsek, A. Czirok, E. Ben-Jacob, I. Cohen, and O. Sochet. Novel type of phase transition in a system of self-driven particles. *PHYS REV LETT.*, 75:1226, 1995.

Towards a Cognitive Meta-Model for Adaptive Trust and Reputation in Open Multi-Agent Systems

(JAAMAS Extended Abstract)

Bruno W. P. Hoelz
University of Brasília
bhoelz@unb.br

Célia G. Ralha
University of Brasília
ghedini@unb.br

ABSTRACT

Computational trust and reputation models are key elements in the design of open multi-agent systems. They offer means of evaluating and reducing risks of cooperation in the presence of uncertainty. However, the models proposed in the literature do not consider the costs they introduce and how they are affected by environmental aspects. In this paper, a cognitive meta-model for adaptive trust and reputation in open multi-agent systems is presented. It acts as a complement to a non-adaptive model by allowing the agent to reason about it and react to changes in the environment. We demonstrate how the meta-model can be applied to existent models proposed in the literature, by adjusting the model's parameters. Finally, we propose evaluation criteria to drive meta-level reasoning considering the costs involved when employing trust and reputation models in dynamic environments.

Keywords

open multi-agent systems, meta-model, adaptiveness, computational trust and reputation

1. INTRODUCTION

In a multi-agent system (MAS), autonomous agents often need to cooperate to achieve their goals. Consequently, agents need to trust each other, explicitly or not. This decision can be based on previous, direct experience or by obtaining information about the reputation of potential partners. While many trust and reputation (T&R) models with different characteristics have been proposed in the literature, from the standpoint of an autonomous agent, there is no evaluation criteria to guide its decision on which model to use and how to adapt it to the dynamic environment of an open MAS.

2. THE AGENT MODEL

In order to allow the agent to reason about its T&R model and adapt it to changes in the environment, we present a cognitive meta-model for T&R adaptation. The agent model containing the meta-model, shown in Figure 1, is divided in two levels: the meta-level, consisting of abstract representations of environmental aspects and common elements of T&R; and the implementation level, that includes the concrete, model-specific realization of these elements.

Appears in: *Proceedings of the 15th International Conference on Autonomous Agents and Multiagent Systems (AAMAS 2016), J. Thangarajah, K. Tuyls, C. Jonker, S. Marsella (eds.), May 9–13, 2016, Singapore.*

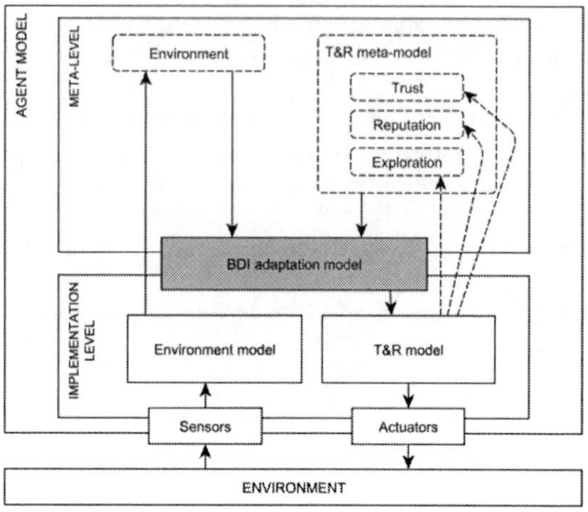

Figure 1: Agent model for T&R adaptation

The environment element of the meta-level is a meta-model that represents domain-independent aspects used in the adaptation process. These include operating costs, frequency of transactions, earned and total utility per unit of time, availability of trusted partners, availability of information sources, communication costs, and cost of information acquisition. Domain-specific aspects can be mapped to one or more meta-level aspects and later in the adaptation process they can be reintroduced via the agent's adaptation model.

The T&R meta-model is divided into three sub-models that are subject to adaptation: trust, reputation and exploration. The T&R sub-models define their respective information sources and how they are used in the T&R evaluations. The exploration sub-model defines how the agent initiates its interactions in the absence of previous information and how it seeks new partners and sources. Figure 2 presents the components of each sub-model.

One of the main characteristics of a T&R model is the set of information sources used in the evaluation of trust. The two most common sources are direct experience and witness information, while others such as direct observation, bias (or prejudice), and norms have been proposed in the literature [1]. In the T&R meta-model, an information source (IS)

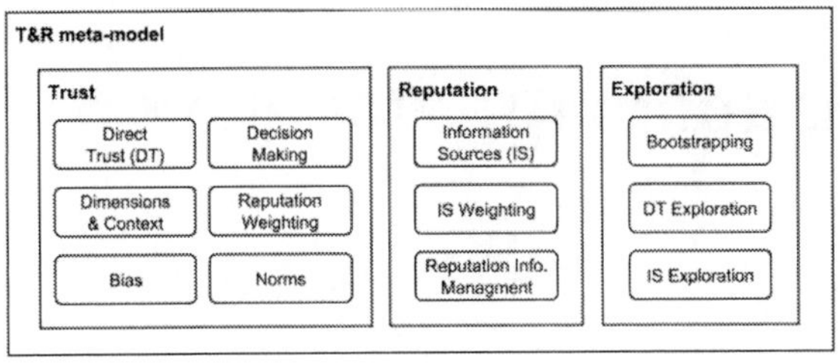

Figure 2: Components of the T&R meta-model

is composed of elements that determine how the agent (i) acquires and shares information, (ii) manages its memory, and (iii) evaluates the reliability and credibility of the IS. These elements have a direct relation with the environmental conditions. For example, information acquisition may be affected by communication costs, and memory management may have to be adjusted to the frequency of transactions.

3. BDI ADAPTATION MODEL

The adaptation model is a Belief-Desire-Intention (BDI) model that connects the meta-level to the implementation level. It allows the agent to reason about T&R adaptation. Beliefs are used to represent facts about the environment and the T&R model, as represented by their meta-level counterparts. To represent the agent's desires, two types of goals are used: monitoring and adaptation goals. Monitoring goals signal the need to adjust the model in use. They trigger an adaptation event that results in the selection of adaptation goals. Next, a plan selection process evaluates the set of available adaptation plans. Lastly, the chosen plan is executed and the concrete model is adapted. The plan is divided in two parts: (i) a model-independent part, that references only meta-level elements, and (ii) a model-specific part, that uses the functions and parameters of the concrete model.

To evaluate the performance of a model under the current environment conditions, the adaptation model considers the costs associated with each component of the T&R meta-model. Two additional costs must also be considered: the cost of staying idle due to the decision of not trusting any of the available partners and the cost of deliberation. The latter depends on the complexity of the agent's reasoning and the amount of evidence used in the evaluation of trust and reputation. The sum of these costs is used to obtain the final evaluation. After the adaptation phase, a new evaluation can be made to measure the impact of the adaptation plan.

4. APPLICATION AND EVALUATION

In order to incorporate an existing model into the meta-model, its functions, algorithms, parameters or beliefs must be mapped into the meta-model's components. These mappings allow the agent to choose the goals and plans that can be applied to the concrete model. Depending on the model, not every element in the T&R meta-model will have a correspondence in the original model. In addition to the mappings, a set of valid configurations for each component of the original model must be provided. The definition of valid configurations, together with the aforementioned mappings, result in potential adaptation plans.

To evaluate the meta-model application we provide mappings to four existing models [2]. Two of these models where chosen for experimental tests.

In the first experiment, we observe how changes in the operating costs affect the decision making component of Marsh's model [3]. In this model, a cooperation threshold is used to determine whether an agent will trust another. If trust is below this threshold, cooperation does not take place. In this experiment, it is possible to observe that agents with static cooperation threshold do not respond to changes in the operating costs and, as such, their utility is reduced as soon as the operating costs are increased. When using the meta-model, the agents reason about the effects of the changing operating costs and change the cooperation threshold accordingly. Consequently, the agent can improve its utility and avoid excessive idleness due to mistrust in a high operating cost environment without incurring in excessive loss of utility as a result of the increased risk.

In the second experiment, we observe the impact of the communication costs/information price on the process of acquiring reputation information in the FIRE model [4]. To do this, we use FIRE's information source for obtaining witness information called a referral network. The adaptation plan used in this experiment changes two parameters of the model: the branching factor (number of referrers directly contacted) and the referral length threshold (the maximum number of referrers in a referral path). In this plan, an agent first reduces the referral length and then reduces the branching factor, thus reducing the costs involved. By using the meta-model to reason about reputation information acquisition process, the agent was able to reduce the cost of information acquisition in response to an increase in communication costs, without significant loss of utility caused by changes in the reliability of the reputation evaluation.

5. CONCLUSIONS

The proposed meta-model was successfully used with two T&R models in a dynamic setting. The experimental results show the importance of the adaptation model as a complement to models used in an open MAS. Agents using the meta-model where able to adapt their models to the environmental conditions and improve the overall utility. Agents using static configurations, on the other hand, had poorer results. Further research should explore learning methods for discovering new adaptation plans and the possibility of multi-model composition.

REFERENCES

[1] I. Pinyol and J. Sabater-Mir. Computational trust and reputation models for open multi-agent systems: a review. *Artificial Intelligence Review*, July 2011.

[2] B. W. P. Hoelz and C. G. Ralha. Towards a cognitive meta-model for adaptive trust and reputation in open multi-agent systems. *Autonomous Agents and Multi-Agent Systems*, 29(6):1125–1156, 2014.

[3] S. P. Marsh. *Formalising trust as a computational concept.* Doctoral thesis, University of Stirling, United Kingdom, 1994.

[4] T. D. Huynh. *Trust and reputation in open multi-agent systems.* Doctoral thesis, University of Southhampton, 2006.

Prioritised Default Logic as Rational Argumentation

Anthony P. Young
Department of Informatics
King's College London
Strand, London, U.K.
peter.young@kcl.ac.uk

Sanjay Modgil
Department of Informatics
King's College London
Strand, London, U.K.
sanjay.modgil@kcl.ac.uk

Odinaldo Rodrigues
Department of Informatics
King's College London
Strand, London, U.K.
odinaldo.rodrigues@kcl.ac.uk

ABSTRACT

We endow Brewka's prioritised default logic (PDL) with argumentation semantics using the ASPIC$^+$ framework for structured argumentation. We prove that the conclusions of the justified arguments correspond to the prioritised default extensions in a normatively rational manner. Argumentation semantics for PDL will allow for the application of argument game proof theories to the process of inference in PDL, making the reasons for accepting a conclusion transparent and the inference process more intuitive. This also opens up the possibility for argumentation-based distributed reasoning and communication amongst agents with PDL representations of mental attitudes.

General Terms

Theory

Keywords

Abstract argumentation; ASPIC$^+$; Prioritised Default Logic; agent reasoning and communication

1. INTRODUCTION

Dung's argumentation theory [8] has become established as a general framework for non-monotonic reasoning (NMR). Given a set of well-formed formulae (wffs) Δ in some non-monotonic logic (NML), the arguments and attacks defined by Δ instantiate a Dung argumentation framework. Additionally, a preference relation over the defined arguments can be used to determine which attacks succeed as defeats. The justified arguments are then evaluated under various Dung semantics, and the claims of the sceptically justified arguments (i.e. arguments contained in *all* extensions under some semantics) identify the inferences from the underlying Δ. More formally, given an argumentation framework AF and a wff θ, the *argumentation-defined inference relation* $\mid\!\sim_{AF}$ over Δ is $\Delta \mid\!\sim_{AF} \theta$ iff θ is the conclusion of a sceptically justified argument in AF. Indeed, a correspondence has been shown between $\mid\!\sim_{AF}$ over Δ, and the instantiating logic's non-monotonic inference relation defined directly over Δ. For example, default logic (DL) [8], logic programming [8], defeasible logic [10] and preferred subtheories (PS) [13] have all been been endowed with *argumentation semantics*. This in turn allows the application of argument game proof theories [12] to the process of inference, and the generalisation of these dialectical proof theories to distributed NMR amongst computational agents, whereby agents can engage in argumentation-based dialogues, submitting arguments and counter-arguments from their own non-monotonic knowledge bases [1, 11, 14]. Furthermore, argumentative characterisations of NMR make use of principles familiar in everyday reasoning and debate, thus rendering transparent the reasons for accepting a conclusion and allowing for human participation and inspection of the inference process.

One well-studied NML that has not yet been endowed with argumentation semantics is Brewka's *prioritised default logic* (PDL) [4]. PDL is important because it upgrades DL [16] with priorities over defaults, so that, for example, one can account for recent information taking priority over information in the distant past, or that more specific information should take priority over more general information. PDL has also been used to represent the (possibly conflicting) beliefs, obligations, intentions and desires (BOID) of agents, and model how these different categories of mental attitudes override each other in order to generate goals and actions that attain those goals [6].

This paper contributes to research in argumentative characterisations of NMR, by endowing PDL with argumentation semantics, proving a correspondence between PDL inference and the inference relation defined by the argumentation semantics, and proving that the result is normatively rational. We realise these contributions by appropriately instantiating the ASPIC$^+$ framework for structured argumentation [13]. ASPIC$^+$ identifies conditions under which logics and preference relations instantiating Dung's frameworks satisfy the Caminada-Amgoud rationality postulates [7].

In Section 2, we review ASPIC$^+$ and PDL. In Section 3, we define a PDL instantiation of ASPIC$^+$. In Section 5, we present a representation theorem proving that inferences defined by the argumentation semantics correspond exactly to inferences in PDL under an appropriate preference relation devised in Section 4. We will also prove that this instantiation is normatively rational in the sense of [7]. In Section 6 we discuss possible generalisations of PDL via its argumentation semantics.

2. BACKGROUND

In the remainder of this paper we make use of the following notation: ":=" means "is defined as". $\mathbb{N}$ is the set of natural numbers. For a set X its power set is $\mathcal{P}(X)$ and its finite power set (set of all finite subsets) is $\mathcal{P}_{\text{fin}}(X)$. $X \subseteq_{\text{fin}} Y$ iff X is a finite subset of Y, therefore $X \in \mathcal{P}_{\text{fin}}(Y) \Leftrightarrow X \subseteq_{\text{fin}} Y$. Undefined quantities are denoted by $*$, for example $1/0 = *$

Appears in: *Proceedings of the 15th International Conference on Autonomous Agents and Multiagent Systems (AAMAS 2016), J. Thangarajah, K. Tuyls, C. Jonker, S. Marsella (eds.), May 9–13, 2016, Singapore.*

in the real numbers. If $\langle P, \leq\rangle$ is a preordered set then the strict version of the preorder is $a < b \Leftrightarrow [a \leq b,\ b \not\leq a]$, which is also a strict partial order. For two sets $A,\ B,\ A \ominus B := (A - B) \cup (B - A)$ denotes their symmetric difference.

2.1 Dung's Abstract Argumentation Theory

We now recap the key definitions of [8]. An *argumentation framework* is a directed graph $\langle \mathcal{A},\ \mathcal{C}\rangle$, where $\mathcal{A}$ is the *set of arguments* and $\mathcal{C} \subseteq \mathcal{A}^2$ is the *conflict relation* on $\mathcal{A}$. For arguments $A,\ B \in \mathcal{A}$ we write $\mathcal{C}(A,\ B) \Leftrightarrow (A,\ B) \in \mathcal{C} \Leftrightarrow A$ conflicts with B, i.e. A is a counterargument against B.

In what follows let $S \subseteq \mathcal{A}$ and $A,\ B \in \mathcal{A}$. S *conflicts with* B iff $(\exists A \in S)\mathcal{C}(A,\ B)$. S is *conflict-free* (cf) iff $\mathcal{C} \cap S^2 = \varnothing$. S *defends* A iff $(\forall B \in \mathcal{A})\,[\mathcal{C}(B,\ A) \Rightarrow S$ conflicts with $B]$. Let $Def(S) := \{A \in \mathcal{A} | S \text{ defends } A\} \subseteq \mathcal{A}$. S is an *admissible extension* iff S is cf and $S \subseteq Def(S)$. An admissible extension S is: a *complete extension* iff $S = Def(S)$; a *preferred extension* iff S is a $\subseteq$-maximal complete extension; the *grounded extension* iff S is the $\subseteq$-least complete extension; a *stable extension* iff S is complete and conflicts with all arguments $B \in \mathcal{A} - S$.

Let $\mathcal{S} := \{complete, preferred, grounded, stable\}$ be the set of *Dung semantics*. An argument $A \in \mathcal{A}$ is *sceptically justified* under the semantics $s \in \mathcal{S}$ iff A belongs to all s-extensions of $\langle \mathcal{A}, \mathcal{C}\rangle$.

2.2 The ASPIC+ Framework

2.2.1 Arguments, Attacks, Preferences and Defeats

Dung's framework provides an intuitive calculus of opposition for determining the justified arguments based on conflict alone; it abstracts from the internal logical structure of arguments, the nature of defeats and how they are determined by preferences, and consideration of the conclusions of the arguments. However, these features are referenced when studying whether any given logical instantiation of a framework yields complete extensions that satisfy the rationality postulates of [7]. ASPIC$^+$ [13] provides a structured account of abstract argumentation, allowing one to reference the above features, while at the same time accommodating a wide range of instantiating logics and preference relations.[1] ASPIC$^+$ then identifies conditions under which complete extensions defined by the arguments, attacks and preferences, satisfy the rationality postulates of [7], and are hence *normatively rational*.

In ASPIC$^+$, the tuple $\langle \mathcal{L},\ -,\ \mathcal{R}_s,\ \mathcal{R}_d,\ n\rangle$ is an *argumentation system*, where $\mathcal{L}$ is a logical language, $- : \mathcal{L} \to \mathcal{P}(\mathcal{L})$ is the *contrary function* $\theta \mapsto \overline{\theta}$ that identifies when one wff in $\mathcal{L}$ conflicts with another. Let $\theta_1, \ldots, \theta_m, \phi \in \mathcal{L}$ be wffs for $m \in \mathbb{N}^+$, $\mathcal{R}_s$ is the *set of strict inference rules* of the form $(\theta_1,\ \ldots,\ \theta_m \to \phi)$, denoting that if $\theta_1,\ \ldots,\ \theta_m$ are true then ϕ is also true, and $\mathcal{R}_d$ is the *set of defeasible inference rules* of the form $(\theta_1,\ \ldots,\ \theta_m \Rightarrow \phi)$, denoting that if $\theta_1,\ \ldots,\ \theta_m$ are true then ϕ is tentatively true. For a strict or defeasible rule $r = (\theta_1, \ldots \theta_m \to / \Rightarrow \phi)$, we define $Ante(r) := \{\theta_1, \ldots, \theta_m\} \subseteq_{\text{fin}} \mathcal{L}$, and $Cons(r) := \phi \in \mathcal{L}$. Finally $n : \mathcal{R}_d \to \mathcal{L}$ is a *partial* function that assigns a *name* to *some* of the defeasible rules. For any $S \subseteq \mathcal{L}$ we define the set $Cl_{\mathcal{R}_s}(S) \subseteq \mathcal{L}$ to be the smallest superset of S that also contains $Cons(r)$ for all $r \in \mathcal{R}_s$ such that $Ante(r) \subseteq Cl_{\mathcal{R}_s}(S)$. We call $Cl_{\mathcal{R}_s}$ the *closure under strict rules operator*.

In ASPIC$^+$, a *knowledge base* is a set $\mathcal{K} := \mathcal{K}_n \cup \mathcal{K}_p \subseteq \mathcal{L}$ where $\mathcal{K}_n$ is the set of *axioms* and $\mathcal{K}_p$ is the set of *ordinary premises*. Intuitively, the knowledge base consists of premises used in the construction of arguments. Given an argumentation system and knowledge base, an *argument* is defined inductively as:

1. (Base) $[\theta]$ is a *singleton argument* with $\theta \in \mathcal{K}$, conclusion $Conc([\theta]) := \theta$, premise set $Prem([\theta]) := \{\theta\} \subseteq \mathcal{K}$, top rule $TopRule([\theta]) := *$ and set of subarguments is $Sub([\theta]) := \{[\theta]\}$.
2. (Inductive, strict) Let $A_1,\ \ldots,\ A_n$ be arguments with respective conclusions $Conc(A_1),\ \ldots,\ Conc(A_n)$ and premise sets $Prem(A_1),\ \ldots,\ Prem(A_n)$. If there is a strict rule $r := (Conc(A_1),\ \ldots,\ Conc(A_n) \to \phi) \in \mathcal{R}_s$, then $B := [A_1,\ \ldots,\ A_n \to \phi]$ is also an argument with $Conc(B) = \phi$, premises $Prem(B) := \bigcup_{i=1}^n Prem(A_i)$, $TopRule(B) = r \in \mathcal{R}_s$ and set of subarguments $Sub(B) := \{B\} \cup \bigcup_{i=1}^n Sub(A_i)$.
3. (Inductive, defeasible) Let $A_1,\ \ldots,\ A_n$ be arguments with respective conclusions $Conc(A_1),\ \ldots,\ Conc(A_n)$ and premise sets $Prem(A_1),\ \ldots,\ Prem(A_n)$. If there is a defeasible rule $r' := (Conc(A_1),\ \ldots,\ Conc(A_n) \Rightarrow \phi) \in \mathcal{R}_d$, then $C := [A_1,\ \ldots,\ A_n \Rightarrow \phi]$ is an argument with $Conc(C) = \phi$, premises $Prem(C) := \bigcup_{i=1}^n Prem(A_i)$, $TopRule(C) = r' \in \mathcal{R}_d$ and set of subarguments $Sub(C) := \{C\} \cup \bigcup_{i=1}^n Sub(A_i)$.

Let $\mathcal{A}$ be the (unique) set of all arguments constructed in this way. It is clear that arguments are finite objects.

Two arguments are *equal* iff they are constructed identically in the above manner. We say A is a *subargument* of B iff $A \in Sub(B)$ and we write $A \subseteq_{\text{arg}} B$. We say A is a *proper subargument* of B iff $A \in Sub(B) - \{B\}$ and we write $A \subset_{\text{arg}} B$. It can be shown that $\subseteq_{\text{arg}}$ is at least a preorder on $Sub(B)$.

An argument $A \in \mathcal{A}$ is *firm* iff $Prem(A) \subseteq \mathcal{K}_n$. Further, $DR(A) \subseteq \mathcal{R}_d$ is the set of defeasible rules applied in constructing A. An argument A is *strict* iff $DR(A) = \varnothing$, else A is *defeasible*. Given $R \subseteq \mathcal{R}_d$, we introduce *the set of all arguments freely constructed with defeasible rules restricted to those in* R as the set $Args(R) \subseteq \mathcal{A}$, which are all arguments with premises in $\mathcal{K}$, strict rules in $\mathcal{R}_s$ and defeasible rules in R. Formally, $Args(R)$ is defined inductively just as arguments are constructed. It is easy to show that $A \in Args(R) \Leftrightarrow DR(A) \subseteq R$. Clearly, $Args(\mathcal{R}_d) = \mathcal{A}$. Given R, $Args(R)$ is unique. Further, $Args(R)$ is *closed under subarguments*, i.e. $A \in Args(R)$ and $B \subseteq_{\text{arg}} A$ implies $B \in Args(R)$.

An argument A *attacks* another argument B, denoted as $A \rightharpoonup B$, iff at least one of the following hold, where:

1. A is said to *undermine* attack B on the subargument $B' = [\phi]$ iff $[\exists \phi \in Prem(B) \cap \mathcal{K}_p]\ Conc(A) \in \overline{\phi}$, i.e. A conflicts with some ordinary premise of B.
2. There is some $B' \subseteq_{\text{arg}} B$ such that $r := TopRule(B') \in \mathcal{R}_d$, $\phi := Cons(r)$ and $Conc(A) \in \overline{\phi}$. A is then said to *rebut* attack B on the subargument B'.
3. There is some $B' \subseteq_{\text{arg}} B$ such that $r := TopRule(B') \in \mathcal{R}_d$ and $Conc(A) \in \overline{n(r)}$. A is then said to *undercut* attack B on the subargument B' (by arguing against the application of the defeasible rule r in B).

[1]ASPIC stands for *Argumentation Service Platform with Integrated Components*.

See [13, Section 2] for a further discussion of why attacks are distinguished in this way. We abuse notation to define the *attack relation* as $\rightharpoonup \subseteq \mathcal{A}^2$ such that $(A, B) \in \rightharpoonup \Leftrightarrow A \rightharpoonup B$.

A preference relation over arguments is then used to determine which attacks succeed as defeats. We denote the preference $\precsim \subseteq \mathcal{A}^2$ (not necessarily a preorder for now) such that $A \precsim B \Leftrightarrow A$ is not more preferred than B. The strict version is $A \prec B \Leftrightarrow [A \precsim B,\ B \not\precsim A]$, and equivalence is $A \approx B \Leftrightarrow [A \precsim B,\ B \precsim A]$. We define a *defeat* as

$$A \hookrightarrow B \Leftrightarrow \left(\exists B' \subseteq_{\text{arg}} B\right)\left[A \rightharpoonup B',\ A \not\prec B'\right] . \tag{2.1}$$

That is to say, A defeats B (on B') iff A attacks B on the subargument B', and B' is not strictly preferred to A. Notice the comparison is made at the subargument B' instead of the whole argument B. We then abuse notation to define the *defeat relation* as $\hookrightarrow \subseteq \mathcal{A}^2$ such that $(A, B) \in \hookrightarrow \Leftrightarrow A \hookrightarrow B$. A set of arguments $S \subseteq \mathcal{A}$ is *conflict-free* (cf) iff $\hookrightarrow \cap S^2 = \varnothing$.[2]

Preferences between arguments are calculated from the argument structure by endowing $\mathcal{K}_p$ and $\mathcal{R}_d$ with preorders $\leq_K$ and $\leq_D$ respectively, where (e.g.) $r_1 \leq_D r_2$ iff r_2 is *more preferred* than r_1 (and analogously for $\leq_K$). This preorder is then lifted to a set-comparison order $\trianglelefteq$ between the sets of premises or defeasible rules of the arguments, and then finally to $\precsim$, following the method in [13, Section 5]. We will summarise this in Section 4.

Given the preference relation $\precsim$ between arguments, we call the structure $\langle \mathcal{A},\ \rightharpoonup,\ \precsim \rangle$ an *ASPIC⁺ SAF* (structured argumentation framework), or *attack graph.* Its corresponding *defeat graph* is $\langle \mathcal{A},\ \hookrightarrow \rangle$, where $\hookrightarrow$ is defined in terms of $\rightharpoonup$ and $\precsim$ as in Equation 2.1.

Given $\langle \mathcal{A},\ \hookrightarrow \rangle$ one can then evaluate the extensions under Dung's semantics (Section 2.1) where $\mathcal{C}$ is $\hookrightarrow$, and thus identify the argumentation defined inferences as the conclusions of the sceptically justified arguments as follows. Let AS be an argumentation system. The *argumentation-defined inference relation* $\mid\!\sim_{AS}$ is $\mathcal{K} \mid\!\sim_{AS} \theta$ iff $\theta = Conc(A)$ where $A \in \mathcal{A}$ is a sceptically justified argument.

2.2.2 *Normative Rationality*

Instantiations of ASPIC$^+$ should satisfy some properties to ensure it is rational [7]. Given an instantiation let $\langle \mathcal{A},\ \rightharpoonup,\ \precsim \rangle$ be its ASPIC$^+$ attack graph with corresponding defeat graph $\langle \mathcal{A}, \hookrightarrow \rangle$. For $S \subseteq \mathcal{A}$ let $Conc(S) := \bigcup_{A \in S} Conc(A)$. Let $\mathcal{E}$ be any of its admissible extensions. The *Caminada-Amgoud rationality postulates* state:

1. If $\mathcal{E}$ is a complete extension then $\mathcal{E}$ is subargument closed.
2. If $\mathcal{E}$ is a complete extension then
$$Cl_{\mathcal{R}_s}\left[Conc(\mathcal{E})\right] = Conc(\mathcal{E})\,. \tag{2.2}$$
3. The sets $Conc(\mathcal{E})$, $Cl_{\mathcal{R}_s}\left[Conc(\mathcal{E})\right] \subseteq \mathcal{L}$ are consistent.

An ASPIC$^+$ instantiation is *normatively rational* iff it satisfies these rationality postulates. These postulates may be proved directly given an instantiation, as we will show for our instantiation to PDL in Theorem 5.4. ASPIC$^+$ also identifies sufficient conditions for an instantiation to satisfy these postulates [13, Section 4], which we will discuss in Section 6.

[2]Note that [13] studies two different notions of cf sets: one where no two arguments *attack* each other, and the other where no two arguments *defeat* each other. We choose the latter notion of cf as this is more commonplace in argumentation formalisms that distinguish between attacks and defeats, e.g. in [15].

2.3 Brewka's Prioritised Default Logic

In this section we recap Brewka's PDL [4]. We work in full first order logic (FOL) of arbitrary signature where the set of first-order formulae is $\mathcal{FL}$ and the set of closed first order formulae[3] is $\mathcal{SL} \subseteq \mathcal{FL}$, with the usual quantifiers and connectives. Given $S \subseteq \mathcal{FL}$, the *deductive closure of* S is $Th(S)$, and given $\theta \in \mathcal{FL}$, the *addition operator* $+ : \mathcal{P}(\mathcal{FL}) \times \mathcal{FL} \to \mathcal{P}(\mathcal{FL})$ is defined as $S + \theta := Th(S \cup \{\theta\})$.

A *normal default* is an expression $\frac{\theta:\phi}{\phi}$ where $\theta, \phi \in \mathcal{FL}$ and read "if θ is the case and ϕ is consistent with what we know, then ϕ is the case". In this case we call θ the *antecedent* and ϕ the *consequent.* A normal default $\frac{\theta:\phi}{\phi}$ is *closed* iff $\theta,\ \phi \in \mathcal{SL}$. We will assume all defaults are closed and normal unless stated otherwise. Given $S \subseteq \mathcal{SL}$, a default is *active (in* S*)* iff $[\theta \in S,\ \phi \notin S,\ \neg\phi \notin S]$. Intuitively, the first requirement says we need to know the antecedent before applying the default, the second requirement is that the consequent must add new information, and the third requirement ensures that what we infer is consistent with what we know.

A *finite prioritised default theory* (PDT) is a structure $\langle D,\ W,\ \prec \rangle$, where $W \subseteq \mathcal{SL}$ is not necessarily a finite set and $\langle D,\ \prec \rangle$ is a *finite* strict poset (partially ordered set) of defaults, where $d' \prec d \Leftrightarrow d$ is *more*[4] *prioritised* than d'. Intuitively, W are the known facts and D the defaults that nonmonotonically extend W.

The inferences of a PDT are defined by its extensions. Formally, let $\prec^+ \supseteq \prec$ be a linearisation[5] of $\prec$. A *prioritised default extension (with respect to* $\prec^+$*)* (PDE) is a set $E := \bigcup_{i \in \mathbb{N}} E_i \subseteq \mathcal{SL}$ built inductively as:

$$E_0 := Th(W) \text{ and} \tag{2.3}$$

$$E_{i+1} := \begin{cases} E_i + \phi\,, & \text{if property 1} \\ E_i\,, & \text{else} \end{cases} \tag{2.4}$$

where "property 1" iff "ϕ is the consequent of the $\prec^+$-greatest default d active in E_i". Intuitively, one first generates all classical consequences from the facts W, and then iteratively adds the nonmonotonic consequences from the most prioritised default to the least. Notice if W is inconsistent then $E_0 = E = \mathcal{FL}$.

It can be shown that the ascending chain $E_i \subseteq E_{i+1}$ stabilises at some finite $i \in \mathbb{N}$ and that E is consistent provided that W is consistent. E does not have to be unique because there are many distinct linearisations of $\prec$. We say the PDT $\langle D,\ W,\ \prec \rangle$ *sceptically infers* $\theta \in \mathcal{SL}$ iff $\theta \in E$ for *all* extensions E.

Henceforth, we will refer to a PDT $\langle D,\ W,\ \prec \rangle$ where $\prec$ is a strict total order as a *linearised PDT* (LPDT). If $\prec$ is total then there is only one way to apply the defaults in D by Equation 2.4, hence the extension is unique and all inferences are sceptical. In what follows, we will use $\prec^+$ to emphasise that the order is total.

Example 1. PDL can be used to model the mental attitudes of agents when deliberating over which goals to pursue. Suppose a research assistant Alice (a) is considering whether she should teach undergraduates. We can model her mental attitudes as a BOID agent's PDT [6] as follows. Define the

[3]i.e. first order formulae without free variables

[4] We have defined the order dually to [4] so as to comply with orderings over the ASPIC$^+$ defeasible inference rules.

[5]i.e. $\prec^+$ is a strict total order and hence $\langle D,\ \prec^+ \rangle$ is a strict toset (totally ordered set).

predicates $R(x) \Leftrightarrow$ "x is a research assistant", $A(x) \Leftrightarrow$ "x is an academic", and $T(x) \Leftrightarrow$ "x is teaching (undergraduates)". Alice is a research assistant, so $W = \{R(a)\}$. She believes that research assistants are academics, so her set of beliefs Bel has the default $\frac{R(a):A(a)}{A(a)}$. She does not want to teach and would rather focus on her research, so her set of desires Des include $\frac{R(a):\neg T(a)}{\neg T(a)}$. However, she is obliged to teach, so her set of obligations Obl include $\frac{A(a):T(a)}{T(a)}$. The set of defaults is $D = Bel \cup Des \cup Obl$, and we assume no other defaults are relevant for this example.

In [6], the relative prioritisations of categories of mental attitudes define different agent types. For example, if Alice is a *realistic selfish agent*, the priority (abuse of notation) is $Obl \prec^+ Des \prec^+ Bel$, and therefore the extension is $Th(\{R(a), A(a), \neg T(a)\})$. She thus generates the goal $\neg T(a)$, i.e. she does not teach. However, if she is a *realistic social agent*, the priority (abuse of notation) is $Des \prec^+ Obl \prec^+ Bel$, and therefore she teaches, as $T(a)$ is in the extension.

3. INSTANTIATING ASPIC+ TO PDL

We now instantiate ASPIC$^+$ to PDL. Let $\langle D, W, \prec^+\rangle$ be a LPDT.[6]

1. Our arguments are expressed in FOL, so our set of wffs is $\mathcal{FL}$.

2. The contrary function $-$ syntactically defines conflict in terms of classical negation.[7] Let θ, ϕ be wffs, then $\overline{\theta} = \phi$ if θ is of the form $\neg\phi$; else $\phi = \neg\theta$.

3. The set of strict rules $\mathcal{R}_s$ characterises inference in first order classical logic. We leave the proof theory implicit. $Cl_{\mathcal{R}_s}$ instantiates to deductive closure.

4. The set of defeasible rules $\mathcal{R}_d$ is defined as:
$$\mathcal{R}_d := \left\{(\theta \Rightarrow \phi)\middle|\frac{\theta:\phi}{\phi} \in D\right\}, \tag{3.1}$$
with $n \equiv *$. Clearly, there is a bijection[8] f where
$$f : D \to \mathcal{R}_d : \frac{\theta:\phi}{\phi} \mapsto f\left(\frac{\theta:\phi}{\phi}\right) := (\theta \Rightarrow \phi) \tag{3.2}$$
and we will define the *strict version of the* preorder $\leq_D$ over $\mathcal{R}_d$ as[9]
$$(\theta \Rightarrow \phi) <_D (\theta' \Rightarrow \phi') \Leftrightarrow \frac{\theta:\phi}{\phi} \prec^+ \frac{\theta':\phi'}{\phi'}. \tag{3.3}$$
We can see that the strict toset $\langle \mathcal{R}_d, <_D\rangle$ is order isomorphic to $\langle D, \prec^+\rangle$, where the non-strict version of the order $\leq_D$ is [$<_D$ or equality].

5. The set of axiom premises is $\mathcal{K}_n = W$, because we take W to be the set of facts. Furthermore, $\mathcal{K}_p = \varnothing$.

[6]We will discuss why we only consider LPDTs in Section 6.
[7]For example, $\neg(\theta \wedge \neg\phi)$ is the contrary of $(\theta \wedge \neg\phi)$, but $(\theta \to \phi)$, where $\to$ in this case denotes material implication, is not the contrary of $(\theta \wedge \neg\phi)$.
[8]Two defeasible rules are *equal* iff they have the same antecedents and consequent *syntactically*.
[9]From Footnote 4, we do not need to define $<_D$ as the order-theoretic dual to $\prec^+$, avoiding potential confusion as to which item is more preferred.

The set $\mathcal{A}$ of ASPIC$^+$ arguments are defined as in Section 2.2. It is easy to see that all arguments are firm because $\mathcal{K}_p = \varnothing$, and so there are no undermining attacks. As n is undefined, no attack can be an undercut. Therefore, we only have rebut attacks, where $A \rightharpoonup B$ iff
$$(\exists B', B'' \subseteq_{\text{arg}} B)\ B' = \left[B'' \Rightarrow \overline{Conc(A)}\right]. \tag{3.4}$$
Defeats are defined as in Equation 2.1. This leaves the question as to how the argument preference $\precsim$ should be defined based on the strict total order $<_D$ over $\mathcal{R}_d$.

4. PREFERENCES

We want to define $\precsim$ in such a way that the extension of the LPDT $\langle D, W, \prec^+\rangle$ corresponds to the conclusions of the justified arguments of the defeat graph $\langle \mathcal{A}, \hookrightarrow\rangle$, instantiated by the corresponding ASPIC$^+$ instantiation, and the result is rational. In ASPIC$^+$, preferences over arguments are calculated from the argument structure, and by comparing the fallible information (ordinary premises and defeasible rules) they contain. In our instantiation, we only compare defeasible rules as there are no ordinary premises. Such a comparison is then lifted to a comparison between the sets of defeasible rules of two arguments, which is then lifted to $\precsim$.

More formally, ASPIC$^+$ defines the *elitist order* [13, Section 5], where for $A, B \in \mathcal{A}$ and $DR(A), DR(B) \subseteq \mathcal{R}_d$, the argument preference $\precsim$ is
$$A \precsim B \Leftrightarrow DR(A) \trianglelefteq_{Eli} DR(B), \tag{4.1}$$
such that for[10] $\Gamma, \Gamma' \subseteq_{\text{fin}} \mathcal{R}_d$,
$$\Gamma \trianglelefteq_{Eli} \Gamma' \Leftrightarrow [\Gamma = \Gamma' \text{ or } \Gamma \vartriangleleft_{Eli} \Gamma'] \text{ and} \tag{4.2}$$
$$\Gamma \vartriangleleft_{Eli} \Gamma' \Leftrightarrow (\exists x \in \Gamma)(\forall y \in \Gamma')\ x <_D y, \tag{4.3}$$
where in Equation 4.3 the order $<_D$ is defined by[11] Equation 3.3. It is easy to show that $\precsim$ is a preorder on $\mathcal{A}$, and $A \approx B \Leftrightarrow DR(A) = DR(B)$. It is known that Brewka's preferred subtheories (PS) [3, Section 6] is a special case of PDL, and the argumentation semantics for PS uses $\trianglelefteq_{Eli}$ to calculate $\precsim$ [13]. Therefore, one might consider using $\trianglelefteq_{Eli}$ (Equations 4.1, 4.2 and 4.3) for calculating $\precsim$. But $\trianglelefteq_{Eli}$ does not yield a correspondence with PDL as the following example illustrates.

Example 2. Consider $\langle D, W, \prec^+\rangle$ where $W = \{a\}$,
$$D = \left\{d_1 := \frac{a:b}{b},\ d_2 := \frac{b:c}{c},\ d_3 := \frac{b:\neg c}{\neg c}\right\} \tag{4.4}$$
and $d_1 \prec^+ d_2 \prec^+ d_3$. The extension is $Th(\{a, b, \neg c\})$.

In the ASPIC$^+$ instantiation: $r_1 <_D r_2 <_D r_3$ (where for $i = 1, 2, 3$, $r_i := f(d_i)$ and f is Equation 3.2). The arguments are $A := [[[a] \Rightarrow b] \Rightarrow c]$ and $B := [[[a] \Rightarrow b] \Rightarrow \neg c]$, which rebut each other at their conclusions.

Under the elitist ordering (Equation 4.2), it is neither the case that $\{r_1, r_2\} \vartriangleleft_{Eli} \{r_1, r_3\}$ nor $\{r_1, r_3\} \vartriangleleft_{Eli} \{r_1, r_2\}$. As the sets are not equal, we have $A \not\precsim B$, $B \not\precsim A$ and $A \not\approx B$. This means $A \hookrightarrow B$ and $B \hookrightarrow A$, which means there are two possible stable extensions $\{A\}$ and $\{B\}$ so that neither argument is sceptically justified, and so $\neg c$ is not an argumentation-defined inference. However $\neg c$ is a PDL

[10]It suffices to consider finite sets as arguments are finite.
[11]It can be shown that this definition avoids counterexamples like [9, Example 5.1], as explained in [17].

inference. Therefore the elitist ordering cannot be used to calculate $\precsim$.

We now investigate a modified elitist order. Suppose that in Example 2 we use the *disjoint elitist order*,

$$\Gamma \lhd_{DEli} \Gamma' \Leftrightarrow (\exists x \in \Gamma - \Gamma') (\forall y \in \Gamma' - \Gamma) \; x <_D y \,, \quad (4.5)$$

with $\lhd_{DEli}$ replacing $\lhd_{Eli}$ in Equations 4.2 and 4.3. Given $r_2 <_D r_3$, it is easy to see that $A \prec B$, $B \not\prec A$, and so $A \not\hookrightarrow B$ and $B \hookrightarrow A$. Hence there is only a single stable extension containing the now sceptically justified argument B with conclusion $\neg c$.

It seems very intuitive for the disjoint elitist order to ignore shared rules, because when deciding whether $A \precsim B$ or $B \precsim A$, we should only focus on the fallible information on which the arguments differ.[12] However, despite this intuitive motivation, the conclusions of the justified arguments given by the disjoint elitist order do not correspond to those obtained in PDL.

Example 3. Let $\langle D, W, \prec^+ \rangle$ have $D = \{d_k\}_{k=1}^5$, $W = \varnothing$,

$$d_1 := \frac{\top : c_1}{c_1}, \; d_4 := \frac{c_3 : c_4}{c_4}, \; d_3 := \frac{\top : c_3}{c_3},$$
$$d_2 := \frac{c_1 : c_2}{c_2}, \; d_5 := \frac{c_1 : \neg(c_2 \wedge c_4)}{\neg(c_2 \wedge c_4)},$$

such that $d_1 \prec^+ d_4 \prec^+ d_3 \prec^+ d_2 \prec^+ d_5$. Our PDE is constructed in the usual manner starting from $E_0 = Th(\varnothing)$. Equation 2.4 gives the order of application of the defaults:

$$E_1 = E_0 + c_3, \; E_2 = E_1 + c_4,$$
$$E_3 = E_2 + c_1, \; E_4 = E_3 + \neg(c_2 \wedge c_4)\,, \quad (4.6)$$

with $E_k = E_4$ for all $k \geq 5$. The default d_2 is blocked because $\neg(c_2 \wedge c_4) \equiv (\neg c_2 \vee \neg c_4)$, and with c_4 (from d_4), we have $\neg c_2$, which blocks d_2. The unique PDE from this LPDT is

$$Th(\{c_1, \neg c_2, c_3, c_4\})\,. \quad (4.7)$$

Now consider the corresponding arguments following our instantiation. We have the defeasible rules[13]

$$r_1 <_D r_4 <_D r_3 <_D r_2 <_D r_5\,. \quad (4.8)$$

The relevant arguments and sets of defeasible rules are

$$A := [[\top \Rightarrow c_1] \Rightarrow c_2]\,, DR(A) = \{r_1, r_2\} \quad (4.9)$$
$$B := [[\top \Rightarrow c_3] \Rightarrow c_4]\,, DR(B) = \{r_3, r_4\} \quad (4.10)$$
$$C := [[\top \Rightarrow c_1] \Rightarrow \neg(c_2 \wedge c_4)]\,, DR(C) = \{r_1, r_5\}\,, \quad (4.11)$$
$$D := [B, C \to \neg c_2]\,, DR(D) = \{r_1, r_3, r_4, r_5\}\,. \quad (4.12)$$

For the correspondence to hold, the desired stable extension is $\{D, B, C, [\top \Rightarrow c_3], [\top \Rightarrow c_1]\}$ and all strict extensions thereof[14], which does have a conclusion set corresponding to Equation 4.7. However, this would require $D \hookrightarrow A$, which means, by Equation 2.1, $D \rightharpoonup A$ and $D \not\prec A$. Clearly, $D \rightharpoonup A$ on A. However, $D \not\prec A$ is equivalent to, under the disjoint elitist order, that r_2 is $<_D$-least in $\mathcal{R}_d$. From Equation 4.8, it is not the case that $r_2 <_D r_1, r_3, r_4$, so we conclude $D \prec A$. Therefore, argumentation does not generate the corresponding stable extension to Equation 4.7.

Example 3 shows that we cannot use the disjoint elitist order to compare sets of defeasible rules because it ignores the *structure* of how arguments are constructed.[15] The way that PDL arranges the defaults in order of preference suggests a new way of defining an argument preference relation compatible with how the arguments are constructed. We now propose the *structure-preference* (SP) *order*. The idea is to transform $<_D$ into a new strict total order, $<_{SP}$, on $\mathcal{R}_d$, such that it captures the original preference $<_D$ *and* when the defeasible rules become applicable during the construction of the arguments.

Since we assumed $\mathcal{R}_d$ is finite, let $1 \leq i \leq |\mathcal{R}_d|$. We define $a_i \in \mathcal{R}_d$ to be the $<_D$-greatest element of the following set:

$$\left\{ r \in \mathcal{R}_d \middle| Ante(r) \subseteq Conc \left[Args \left(\bigcup_{k=1}^{i-1} \{a_k\} \right) \right] \right\} - \bigcup_{j=1}^{i-1} \{a_j\}\,. \quad (4.13)$$

The intuition is: a_1 is the most preferred rule whose antecedent is amongst the conclusions of all strict arguments, a_2 is the next most preferred rule, whose antecedent is amongst the conclusions of all arguments having *at most* a_1 as a defeasible rule. Similarly, a_3 is the next most preferred rule, whose antecedent is amongst the conclusions of all arguments having *at most* a_1 and a_2 as defeasible rules, and so on until all of the rules of $\mathcal{R}_d$ are exhausted. This process orders the rules by how preferred they are under $<_D$ *and* by when they are applicable when constructing the arguments. Notice that the second union after the set difference in Equation 4.13 ensures that once a rule is applied it cannot be applied again. We then define $<_{SP}$ as (notice the dual order)

$$a_i <_{SP} a_j \Leftrightarrow j < i\,, \quad (4.14)$$

where $1 \leq i,\, j \leq |\mathcal{R}_d|$. We define the non-strict order to be $a_i \leq_{SP} a_i \Leftrightarrow [a_i = a_j \text{ or } a_i <_{SP} a_j]$. This makes sense because $i \mapsto a_i$ is bijective between $\mathcal{R}_d$ and $\{1, 2, 3, \ldots, |\mathcal{R}_d|\}$. Clearly $<_{SP}$ is a strict total order on $\mathcal{R}_d$. We call this the *structure preference order* on $\mathcal{R}_d$, which exists and is unique given $<_D$. We define the corresponding strict set comparison relation, $\lhd_{SP}$, as, for Γ, $\Gamma' \subseteq_{\text{fin}} \mathcal{R}_d$,

$$\Gamma \lhd_{SP} \Gamma' \Leftrightarrow (\exists x \in \Gamma - \Gamma') (\forall y \in \Gamma' - \Gamma) \; x <_{SP} y\,. \quad (4.15)$$

The corresponding strict argument preference is

$$A \prec_{SP} B \Leftrightarrow DR(A) \lhd_{SP} DR(B)\,. \quad (4.16)$$

We define the corresponding non-strict preference as $A \precsim_{SP} B \Leftrightarrow [DR(A) \lhd_{SP} DR(B) \text{ or } DR(A) = DR(B)]$. This is the disjoint elitist order[16] (Equation 4.5) with $<_D$ specialised to $<_{SP}$. The SP-order thus allows us to mimic how PDL applies defaults when calculating extensions.

Lemma 4.1. *The preference* $\precsim_{SP}$ *satisfies*

$$(\forall A, B \in \mathcal{A}) [DR(A) \subseteq DR(B) \Rightarrow B \precsim_{SP} A]\,.$$

[12] This has been considered in a different context in [5].

[13] Where, similar to Example 2, r_i corresponds to d_i via Equation 3.2, for $1 \leq i \leq 5$.

[14] Informally, in ASPIC$^+$, for $S \subseteq \mathcal{A}$ the strict extension of S is the smallest set containing S extended with all strict and firm arguments, and all possible applications of strict rules to those arguments. This becomes the deductive closure when ASPIC$^+$ is instantiated into classical logic. See [13, page 370, Definition 17] for more details.

[15] Informally, the "structure" of an argument A is given by the preordered set $\langle Sub(A), \subseteq_{\text{arg}} \rangle$.

[16] We use the disjoint elitist order instead of the usual elitist order because Example 2 shows that the usual elitist order does not give the correspondence in general.

Proof. If $DR(B) = DR(A)$ then $B \approx A$, so $B \precsim_{SP} A$. If $DR(A) \subset DR(B)$, then $DR(A) - DR(B) = \varnothing$, which means $B \prec_{SP} A$ is vacuously true from Equation 4.5 so $B \precsim_{SP} A$. □

This is intuitive because if $A \subseteq_{\text{arg}} B$, then A may contain less fallible information (in our case defeasible rules) than B, so A can be said to be more certain than B. It makes sense to have $B \precsim_{SP} A$ because rational agents should prefer more certainty to less certainty. It is easy to see that strict arguments are most preferred.

We now show that the disjoint elitist order $\lhd_{DEli}$ in general, and hence $\lhd_{SP}$ in particular, is a strict total order on $\mathcal{P}_{\text{fin}}(\mathcal{R}_d)$.

Lemma 4.2. *If $\langle \mathcal{R}_d, <_D \rangle$ is a strict toset, then $\lhd_{DEli}$ is a strict total order on $\mathcal{P}_{fin}(\mathcal{R}_d)$.*

Proof. Let Γ, Γ', $\Gamma'' \in \mathcal{P}_{\text{fin}}(\mathcal{R}_d)$ be arbitrary. *Irreflexivity:* From Equation 4.5, as $\exists$ precedes $\forall$, $\Gamma \lhd_{DEli} \Gamma$ is false.

Transitivity: (Sketch) Assume $\Gamma \lhd_{DEli} \Gamma'$ and $\Gamma' \lhd_{DEli} \Gamma''$. Let $n_1, n_2, \ldots, n_7 \in \mathbb{N}$ be such that

$$\begin{aligned}\Gamma &= \{a_1, \ldots, a_{n_1}\} \cup \{d_1, \ldots . d_{n_4}\} \cup \\ &\quad \{f_1, \ldots, f_{n_6}\} \cup \{g_1, \ldots, g_{n_7}\} \\ \Gamma' &= \{b_1, \ldots, b_{n_2}\} \cup \{d_1, \ldots . d_{n_4}\} \cup \\ &\quad \{e_1, \ldots, e_{n_5}\} \cup \{g_1, \ldots, g_{n_7}\} \\ \Gamma'' &= \{c_1, \ldots, c_{n_3}\} \cup \{e_1, \ldots . e_{n_5}\} \cup \\ &\quad \{f_1, \ldots, f_{n_6}\} \cup \{g_1, \ldots, g_{n_7}\} ,\end{aligned}$$

where the a's to g's in $\mathcal{R}_d$ denote *distinct* defeasible rules. The seven disjoint finite sets $\{a_1, \ldots, a_{n_1}\}, \ldots, \{g_1, \ldots, g_{n_7}\}$ partition $\Gamma \cup \Gamma' \cup \Gamma''$ and can be represented by the subregions of three overlapping circles of the corresponding Venn diagram. If $n_i = 0$ then the corresponding set is empty, e.g. if $n_1 = 0$ then $\{a_1, \ldots, a_{n_1}\} = \varnothing$.

Assuming $\Gamma \lhd_{DEli} \Gamma'$ and $\Gamma' \lhd_{DEli} \Gamma''$, we use Equation 4.5 to prove $\Gamma \lhd_{DEli} \Gamma''$, which is the equivalent of proving, for at least one of $1 \leq k \leq n_1$ or $1 \leq l \leq n_4$,

$$\left[\left(\bigwedge_{i=1}^{n_3} a_k < c_i\right) \wedge \left(\bigwedge_{j=1}^{n_5} a_k < e_j\right)\right]$$
$$\text{or} \left[\left(\bigwedge_{i=1}^{n_3} d_l < c_i\right) \wedge \left(\bigwedge_{j=1}^{n_5} d_l < e_j\right)\right] . \qquad (4.17)$$

By writing out $\Gamma \lhd_{DEli} \Gamma'$ and $\Gamma' \lhd_{DEli} \Gamma''$ in terms of the elements $a_1, \ldots, g_{n_7}$ similar to how $\Gamma \lhd_{DEli} \Gamma''$ is written in Equation 4.17, we get four cases (as "and" and "or" bidistribute). One case gives a contradiction (due to irreflexivity of $<_D$), while the other three cases imply $\Gamma \lhd_{DEli} \Gamma''$ from the totality of $<_D$. Therefore, $\Gamma \lhd_{DEli} \Gamma''$.

Trichotomy: Assume $\Gamma \neq \Gamma'$ and consider $\Gamma \ominus \Gamma' \in \mathcal{P}_{\text{fin}}(\mathcal{R}_d)$. The structure $\langle \Gamma \ominus \Gamma', <_D \rangle$ is a strict finite toset, and thus has a $<_D$-least element m. Either $m \in \Gamma - \Gamma'$ exclusive-or $m \in \Gamma' - \Gamma$, where the former implies $\Gamma \lhd_{DEli} \Gamma'$ and the latter implies $\Gamma' \lhd_{DEli} \Gamma$. □

It follows that $\prec_{SP}$ is a strict total preorder on $\mathcal{A}$.

Example 4. (Example 3 continued) By applying Equations 4.13 and 4.14, we can show that $a_1 = r_3$, $a_2 = r_4$, $a_3 = r_1$, $a_4 = r_5$ and $a_5 = r_2$. The structure preference order is

$$r_2 <_{SP} r_5 <_{SP} r_1 <_{SP} r_4 <_{SP} r_3 . \qquad (4.18)$$

Notice that this is precisely the order in which the corresponding normal defaults are added in PDL, as Equation 4.6 shows. It is easy to show that the corresponding stable extension under the argument preference $\prec_{SP}$ corresponds to the PDL inference, because r_2 is now $<_{SP}$-least, so $D \not\prec_{SP} A$, therefore $A \prec_{SP} D$.

However, $<_{SP}$ does not necessarily follow the PDL order of the application of defaults as the following example illustrates.

Example 5. Consider $\langle \{d_1, d_2\}, \{a\}, \prec^+ \rangle$ with $d_1 := \frac{a:\neg a}{\neg a}$ and $d_2 := \frac{\top:b}{b}$ such that $d_2 \prec^+ d_1$. We have $E = Th(\{a, b\})$, where d_1 is blocked by W, so d_2 is the only default added. In argumentation, we have $\mathcal{K}_n = \{a\}$, $r_1 := (a \Rightarrow \neg a)$ and $r_2 := (\top \Rightarrow b)$ where for $i = 1, 2$, $r_i := f(d_i)$, such that $r_2 <_D r_1$. The arguments are $A_0 := [a]$, $A_1 := [A_0 \Rightarrow \neg a]$ and $B := [\top \Rightarrow b]$. Applying Equation 4.13, we have $r_2 <_{SP} r_1$, which clearly is not the order of how the corresponding defaults are added in PDL. Yet the correspondence still holds, since $A_0 \hookrightarrow A_1$ because A_0 is strict and strict arguments always defeat any non-strict argument they attack, so the stable extension is the strict extension of $\{A_0, B\}$, the conclusion set of which (after deductive closure) is the extension of the underlying LPDT.

Example 5 highlights how blocked defaults and defeated arguments are related. Where PDL blocks the application of a given default, hence preventing its conclusion from featuring in the extension, ASPIC$^+$ allows for the construction of the argument with the corresponding defeasible rule, but that argument is always defeated by another strictly stronger argument and therefore cannot be in any extension.

5. THE REPRESENTATION THEOREM

In this section we state and prove the representation theorem (Theorem 5.3), which guarantees that the inferences with argumentation semantics under the preference $\precsim_{SP}$ correspond exactly to the inferences in PDL.

5.1 Non-Blocked Defaults

We first introduce some concepts to help prove the representation theorem. Let $\langle D, W, \prec \rangle$ be a PDT and $E = \bigcup_{i \in \mathbb{N}} E_i$ one of its extensions generated from the linearisation $\prec^+ \supseteq \prec$. The *set of generating defaults (with respect to $\prec^+$), $GD(\prec^+)$*, is defined as

$$\begin{aligned}GD_i(\prec^+) &:= \{d \in D \,|\, d \text{ is } \prec^+\text{-greatest active in } E_i\} , \\ GD(\prec^+) &:= \bigcup_{i \in \mathbb{N}} GD_i(\prec^+) \subseteq D . \qquad (5.1)\end{aligned}$$

Intuitively, this is the set of defaults applied to calculate E following the order $\prec^+$. However, the same E can be generated by distinct total orders.

Example 6. Consider the PDT $\langle \{\frac{a:c}{c}, \frac{b:c}{c}\}, \{a, b\}, \varnothing \rangle$. We have two possible linearisations $\frac{a:c}{c} \prec_1^+ \frac{b:c}{c}$ and $\frac{b:c}{c} \prec_2^+ \frac{a:c}{c}$. By Footnote 4 we have $GD(\prec_1^+) = \{\frac{b:c}{c}\}$ and $GD(\prec_2^+) = \{\frac{a:c}{c}\}$, which are not equal, even though both linearisations give the same extension $E = Th(\{a, b, c\})$. But in the case of $\prec_1^+$, $\frac{b:c}{c}$ is not active not because it is blocked by $\neg c$, but rather it adds no new information.

We wish to distinguish between inactive defaults that conflict with something we already know, and inactive defaults that do not add any new information. We call a default $\frac{\theta:\phi}{\phi}$ *semi-active (in $S \subseteq \mathcal{SL}$)* iff $[\theta \in S,\ \neg\phi \notin S,\ \phi \in S]$. The *set of semi-active defaults with respect to the linearisation* $\prec^+$ is

$$SAD(\prec^+) := \{d \in D \mid d \text{ is semi-active w.r.t. } \prec^+\} \ . \quad (5.2)$$

Intuitively, semi-active defaults add no new information. We then define the *set of non-blocked defaults* to be

$$NBD(\prec^+) := GD(\prec^+) \cup SAD(\prec^+) \subseteq D \ . \quad (5.3)$$

NBD has a more elegant characterisation:

Lemma 5.1. *If $\prec^+$ generates the PDE E, then we have that*

$$NBD(\prec^+) := \left\{ \frac{\theta:\phi}{\phi} \in D \middle| \theta \in E,\ \neg\phi \notin E \right\} \ . \quad (5.4)$$

Proof. (Sketch) It is sufficient to show Equation 5.3 (with Equations 5.1 and 5.2) is the same as the right hand side of Equation 5.4. Let E be the extension from $\prec^+$. For readability we will omit writing "$\prec^+$" from "$GD(\prec^+)$". It can be shown that $d := \frac{\theta:\phi}{\phi} \in GD \Rightarrow [\theta \in E,\ (\exists i \in \mathbb{N})\ \neg\phi \notin E_i]$, and assuming $\neg\phi \in E$ gives a contradiction (by considering the E_i's in E), so $\neg\phi \notin E$. Trivially, $d \in SAD \Rightarrow [\theta \in E,\ \neg\phi \notin E]$, therefore Equation 5.3 is a subset of Equation 5.4. Assuming that $d \in$ the right hand side of Equation 5.4 gives $d \in GD \cup SAD$ through simple quantifier manipulations. The result follows. □

Given E, $NBD(\prec^+)$ is uniquely determined, so we will write $NBD(E)$ instead. Equation 5.4 adapts Reiter's idea of a *generating default* [16, page 92 Definition 2] to PDL.

5.2 Uniqueness of Stable Extensions

In this section we show that the defeat graph $\langle \mathcal{A}, \hookrightarrow \rangle$ associated with any ASPIC$^+$ attack graph $\langle \mathcal{A}, \rightharpoonup, \precsim_{SP} \rangle$ constructed from a LPDT $\langle D, W, \prec^+ \rangle$ with the SP-order has a unique stable extension.

Theorem 5.2. *Let $\langle \mathcal{A}, \rightharpoonup, \precsim_{SP} \rangle$ be an ASPIC$^+$ attack graph constructed from $\mathcal{L} = \mathcal{FL}$, $-$ is $\neg$, $\mathcal{R}_s$ the rules of proof of FOL, $\langle \mathcal{R}_d, <_{SP} \rangle$ the toset of defeasible rules under the SP-order, the argument preference $\precsim_{SP}$, n is undefined on $\mathcal{R}_d$, $\mathcal{K}_p = \varnothing$ and $\mathcal{K}_n \subseteq \mathcal{FL}$ is a consistent set of formulae. The defeat graph $\langle \mathcal{A}, \hookrightarrow \rangle$ from this attack graph has a unique stable extension.*

Proof. (Sketch) The construction of the unique stable extension imitates how extensions are constructed over an LPDT (Equation 2.4). Given a set of arguments $S \subseteq \mathcal{A}$ we define, for $r \in \mathcal{R}_d$, $S \oplus r := Args(DR(S) \cup \{r\})$, i.e. we close S under all arguments with the addition of a new defeasible rule r. Now consider Algorithm 1, which takes an attack graph $\langle \mathcal{A}, \rightharpoonup, \precsim_{SP} \rangle$ obeying the conditions of the theorem, and outputs a set of arguments.

Algorithm 1 Generating a Stable Extension

```
1: function GENERATESTABLEEXTENSION(⟨A, ⇀, ≾_SP⟩)
2:     S ← {all strict arguments in A}
3:     for r ∈ R_d from <_SP-greatest to <_SP-smallest do
4:         if S ⊕ r has no attacks, (S ⊕ r)^2 ∩ ⇀ = ∅, then
5:             S ← S ⊕ r
   return S
```

The intuition of Algorithm 1 is to first create the largest possible set of undefeated arguments that do not attack each other, first by including all strict arguments because strict arguments are never defeated (Line 2, recall also Example 5) and never attack each other because $\mathcal{K}_n$ is consistent. Then, the algorithm includes the defeasible rules from most to least preferred and tests whether the resulting arguments that are constructed by the inclusion of such a defeasible rule attack each other (Lines 4–5). As $<_{SP}$ is total, all defeasible rules are considered, and the result includes as many defeasible rules as possible such that the result is consistent. Adding the rules in the order of $<_{SP}$ while ensuring conflict freeness mimics the condition of Equation 2.4.

It is clear from the algorithm that S exists and is unique, as it is of the form $Args(R)$ for some $R \subseteq \mathcal{R}_d$. We show S is a stable extension [2, page 26 Definition 2.2.7]: cf is guaranteed by the consistency of $\mathcal{K}_n$ and that defeasible rules $r \in \mathcal{R}_d$ are only added if the resulting arguments do not attack each other. Therefore, S contains no defeats and must be cf. To show that the arguments of S defeat all arguments not in S, let $R := DR(S)$, i.e. the set of all defeasible rules added to S. Let $B \notin S$ be arbitrary. We find an $A \in S$ such that $A \hookrightarrow B$. Given that $B \notin S$, there is some rule $r \in DR(B) - R$ that causes S to attack the subargument of B with top rule r if r is included, according to Algorithm 1, Line 4. Let $B' \subseteq_{\text{arg}} B$ such that $TopRule(B') = r$. Let $A \in S$ be the attacker of B' at r. If r is $<_{SP}$-greatest, then $Args(\varnothing) \oplus r$ contains attacking arguments, so A must be strict and hence $A \hookrightarrow B$. If r is not $<_{SP}$-greatest, then consider the strict up-set of r in $\langle \mathcal{R}_d, <_{SP} \rangle$, $T := \{r' \in \mathcal{R}_d \mid r <_{SP} r'\} \neq \varnothing$. If $T \cap R = \varnothing$, then adding r to S means there is an attack from $A \in Args(\varnothing)$ under $\precsim_{SP}$, and hence B is defeated. If $T \cap R \neq \varnothing$, then $A \in Args(T \cap R)$. Assume A is not strict, then $\varnothing \neq DR(A) \subseteq T \cap R$, so $(\forall s \in DR(A))\, r <_{SP} s$, hence A defeats B. Therefore, in all cases, $A \hookrightarrow B$, and hence B is defeated by some argument in S. Therefore, the defeat graphs of such ASPIC$^+$ attack graphs have a unique stable extension. □

5.3 The Representation Theorem

In this section we state and prove the representation theorem. This shows that inferences made in PDL correspond exactly to the conclusions of the justified arguments in the argumentation semantics of PDL by relating the stable extension of $\langle \mathcal{A}, \hookrightarrow \rangle$ with the extension of the corresponding LPDT $\langle D, W, \prec^+ \rangle$.

Theorem 5.3. *Let $\langle \mathcal{A}, \rightharpoonup, \precsim_{SP} \rangle$ be the attack graph corresponding to an LPDT $\langle D, W, \prec^+ \rangle$ with defeat graph $\langle \mathcal{A}, \hookrightarrow \rangle$ under $\precsim_{SP}$.*

1. *Let E be the extension of $\langle D, W, \prec^+ \rangle$. Then there exists a unique stable extension $\mathcal{E} \subseteq \mathcal{A}$ of $\langle \mathcal{A}, \hookrightarrow \rangle$ such that $Conc(\mathcal{E}) = E$.*
2. *Let $\mathcal{E} \subseteq \mathcal{A}$ be the unique stable extension of $\langle \mathcal{A}, \hookrightarrow \rangle$ by Theorem 5.2, then $Conc(\mathcal{E})$ is the extension of $\langle D, W, \prec^+ \rangle$.*

Proof. (Sketch) To prove the first statement we construct $\mathcal{E}$ in terms of E and show $\mathcal{E}$ is a stable extension of $\langle \mathcal{A}, \hookrightarrow \rangle$ (which is unique given Theorem 5.2), and show $Conc(\mathcal{E}) = E$. Given E, we construct $\mathcal{E} := Args(f(NBD(E)))$. This set is unique from the properties of $Args$. Then we show this $\mathcal{E}$ is a stable extension, which means $\mathcal{E}$ is cf and defeats all arguments not belonging to it. Assume for contradiction that $\mathcal{E}$ is not cf, which means there are arguments $A, B \in \mathcal{E}$ such that $A \hookrightarrow B$, which means $A \rightharpoonup B$. Let $a := Conc(A)$, and as $A \in \mathcal{E}$,

$DR(A) \subseteq f(NBD(E))$ and hence $a \in E$. Now let $B' \subseteq_{\text{arg}} B$ be the argument such that $TopRule(B') = (b \Rightarrow \neg a)$ for some appropriate formula b in B. As $B \in \mathcal{E}$, this means $(b \Rightarrow \neg a) \in f(NBD(E))$ and hence $a \notin E$ by Equation 5.4 and that E is deductively closed – contradiction. Therefore, $\mathcal{E}$ is cf. To show $Args(R)$ defeats all other arguments, let $B \notin Args(R)$ so there is some rule $r \in DR(B) - R$. Let $B' \subseteq_{\text{arg}} B$ be such that $TopRule(B') = r$. r corresponds to a default $f^{-1}(r) = \frac{\theta:\phi}{\phi} \notin NBD(E)$. Either $\theta \notin E$ or $\neg\phi \in E$ by Equation 5.4. If $\neg\phi \in E$, then one can prove there exists an argument $A \in Args(R)$ such that $A \hookrightarrow B'$ and hence $A \hookrightarrow B$ under $\precsim_{SP}$. Assume $\theta \notin E$. There is some $B'' \subset_{\text{arg}} B'$ such that $Conc(B'') = \theta$. If $\theta \notin E$ then B'' is neither strict nor in $Args(f(NBD(E)))$. Thus there is some other $s \in DR(B'') - f(NBD(E))$. We can repeat the above reasoning for s but not indefinitely as arguments are well-founded. We will end up with either a strict subargument of B'' or an argument in $Args(f(NBD(E)))$. Therefore, $\theta \in E$. Therefore, the only reason for $r \notin R$ is because $\neg\phi \in E$, and hence there is an argument A that defeats any argument containing the rule r, which means $Args(R)$ defeats all other arguments and hence it is a stable extension. To show that $E = Conc(\mathcal{E})$, we show $E \subseteq Conc(\mathcal{E})$ and $Conc(\mathcal{E}) \subseteq E$. In the first case, let $\theta \in E$, then if $\theta \in E_0$, we have $W \models \theta$ and by the compactness theorem in FOL, we have $\Delta \subseteq_{\text{fin}} W$ such that $\Delta \models \theta$. From this we build a strict argument A such that $Prem_n(A) = \Delta$ and $Conc(A) = \theta$, and necessarily $A \in \mathcal{E}$ so $\theta \in Conc(\mathcal{E})$. Similarly, if $\theta \in E_k$ for some $k \in \mathbb{N}^+$, we can construct a defeasible argument A concluding θ such that $DR(A) \subseteq f(NBD(E))$ and hence $A \in \mathcal{E}$, so $\theta \in Conc(\mathcal{E})$. Conversely, if $\theta \in Conc(\mathcal{E})$ there is an argument in $\mathcal{E}$ concluding θ. If this argument is strict then $\theta \in E_0 \subseteq E$, else, as the defeasible rules are in $f(NBD(E))$ then $\theta \in E_k \subseteq E$ for some $k \in \mathbb{N}^+$ that indicates when all of the appropriate defaults needed to conclude θ are included. This establishes the first statement.

For the second statement, we show $Conc(\mathcal{E}) \subseteq E$ and $E \subseteq Conc(\mathcal{E})$. For the former, if $\theta \in Conc(\mathcal{E})$ then there is some $A \in \mathcal{E}$ concluding θ. If A is strict then $\theta \in E_0 \subseteq E$. If A is defeasible, then say $DR(A) = \{d_i\}_{i=1}^{k}$ for some $k \in \mathbb{N}^+$. All of these defaults do not introduce any inconsistency because $\mathcal{E}$ is stable and hence cf. Take the smallest $i \in \mathbb{N}$ such that sufficiently many corresponding defeasible rules are applied from $DR(A)$ to conclude θ in E_{i+1} from W. Therefore, $\theta \in E_{i+1} \subseteq E$. Conversely, let $\theta \in E$, so there is some $i \in \mathbb{N}$ such that $\theta \in E_i$. If $i = 0$, then there is a strict argument A, necessarily in $\mathcal{E}$, that concludes θ so $\theta \in Conc(\mathcal{E})$. If $i > 0$, then we can use the appropriate defeasible rules to construct a defeasible argument A such that $Prem(A) \subseteq W$, $Conc(A) = \theta$ and $DR(A) \neq \varnothing$. To show $A \in \mathcal{E}$, we assume for contradiction that $A \notin \mathcal{E}$ so there is some $B \in \mathcal{E}$ such that $B \hookrightarrow A$. But this would result in at least one of the defaults of A being blocked. This is a contradiction because given that $\theta \in E$, the defeasible argument A concluding θ cannot have its defeasible rules correspond to blocked PDL defaults. Therefore, such a B cannot exist and $A \in \mathcal{E}$. This proves that $Conc(\mathcal{E}) = E$. □

The representation theorem means that PDL is sound and complete with respect to its argumentation semantics. We now show that this ASPIC$^+$ instantiation to PDL satisfies the Caminada-Amgould rationality postulates (Section 2.2.2) as a corollary to the representation theorem. Recall that when instantiated to FOL, $Cl_{\mathcal{R}_s}$ becomes deductive closure.

Theorem 5.4. *Let $\langle \mathcal{A}, \rightharpoonup, \precsim_{SP} \rangle$ be the ASPIC$^+$ attack graph of PDL and let $\mathcal{E}$ be any of the admissible extensions of the corresponding defeat graph $\langle \mathcal{A}, \hookrightarrow \rangle$. Our instantiation satisfies the Caminada-Amgoud rationality postulates.*

Proof. By Theorem 5.2, $\langle \mathcal{A}, \hookrightarrow \rangle$ has a unique stable extension $\mathcal{E}$, which is a complete and an admissible extension. It is sufficient to prove the postulates for $\mathcal{E}$ because $\langle \mathcal{A}, \hookrightarrow \rangle$ only has $\mathcal{E}$ as its sole complete extension. (1) To show that $\mathcal{E}$ is subargument closed, recall that Algorithm 1 gives an explicit construction of $\mathcal{E}$, which is of the form $Args(R)$ for some $R \subseteq \mathcal{R}_d$ and is clearly subargument closed. (2) The representation theorem states that $Conc(\mathcal{E}) = E$ and as E is deductively closed, $Conc(\mathcal{E})$ is closed under strict rules. (3) As W is consistent and $Conc(\mathcal{E})$ is the extension, $Conc(\mathcal{E})$ must also be consistent and its deductive closure is consistent. □

6. DISCUSSION AND CONCLUSION

We have endowed PDL [4] with argumentation semantics using ASPIC$^+$ [13]. This is achieved by specialising ASPIC$^+$ to PDL (Section 3), discussing which preferences can be suitable for the correspondence of inferences (Section 4), proving that the inferences do correspond (Theorem 5.3), and that this instantiation is normatively rational (Theorem 5.4). As explained in Section 1, this allows us to interpret the inferences of PDL as conclusions of justified arguments, clarifying the reasons for accepting or rejecting a conclusion. Further, this makes the inference process more intuitive, and amenable to human participation and inspection. The argumentative characterisation of PDL provides for distributed reasoning in the course of deliberation and persuasion dialogues. For example, BOID agents with PDL representations of mental attitudes can now exchange arguments and counterarguments when deliberating about which goals to select, and consequently which actions to pursue (Example 1).

However, it seems that we have restricted our attention to LPDTs. This does not lose generality because calculating extensions in PDL always presupposes a linearisation $\prec^+$ of $\prec$ (see [4] or recall Section 2.3), and Theorem 5.4 shows that for *any* linearisation the correspondence between PDL and its argumentation semantics holds. However, ASPIC$^+$ can identify argumentation-based inferences assuming only a partial ordering, unlike in PDL. This suggests that our argumentative characterisation can be used to generalise PDL; for example, under a partial ordering one might not only generate multiple stable extensions, but extensions under other Dung semantics[17] may become relevant. Future work will look at to what extent we can lift the requirement of linearity, as well as the significance of other Dung semantics.

Further, one aspect of ASPIC$^+$ that has not been discussed in much detail here is how normative rationality (in the sense of [7]) follows for any *well-defined instantiation* with a *reasonable preference* [13, Definitions 12 and 18]. We have shown that our instantiation is normatively rational via a direct proof, but it is worthwhile strengthening this result by asking whether the instantiation we have presented here is well-defined and whether $\precsim_{SP}$ is reasonable. This would also allow us to investigate generalisations and variations of PDL via its argumentation semantics.

[17]When the extension is unique, the distinction between the different Dung semantic types is lost.

REFERENCES

[1] K. Atkinson, T. Bench-Capon, and P. McBurney. A Dialogue Game Protocol for Multi-Agent Argument over Proposals for Action. *Autonomous Agents and Multi-Agent Systems*, 11(2):153–171, 2005.

[2] P. Besnard and A. Hunter. *Elements of Argumentation*. The MIT Press, 2008.

[3] G. Brewka. Preferred Subtheories: An Extended Logical Framework for Default Reasoning. In *IJCAI*, volume 89, pages 1043–1048, 1989.

[4] G. Brewka. Adding Priorities and Specificity to Default Logic. In *Logics in Artificial Intelligence*, pages 247–260. Springer, 1994.

[5] G. Brewka, M. Truszczynski, and S. Woltran. Representing Preferences Among Sets. In *AAAI*, 2010.

[6] J. Broersen, M. Dastani, J. Hulstijn, and L. van der Torre. Goal Generation in the BOID Architecture. *Cognitive Science Quarterly Journal*, 2(3-4):428–447, 2002.

[7] M. Caminada and L. Amgoud. On the Evaluation of Argumentation Formalisms. *Artificial Intelligence*, 171(5):286–310, 2007.

[8] P. M. Dung. On the Acceptability of Arguments and its Fundamental Role in Nonmonotonic Reasoning, Logic Programming and n-Person Games. *Artificial Intelligence*, 77:321–357, 1995.

[9] P. M. Dung. An Axiomatic Analysis of Structured Argumentation for Prioritised Default Reasoning. In *ECAI2014*, pages 267–272. IOS Press, 2014.

[10] G. Governatori, M. J. Maher, G. Antoniou, and D. Billington. Argumentation Semantics for Defeasible Logic. *Journal of Logic and Computation*, 14(5):675–702, 2004.

[11] S. Modgil. An Argumentation Based Semantics for Agent Reasoning. In M. Dastani, A. El Fallah Seghrouchni, J. Leite, and P. Torroni, editors, *Languages, Methodologies and Development Tools for Multi-Agent Systems*, volume 5118 of *Lecture Notes in Computer Science*, pages 37–53. Springer Berlin Heidelberg, 2008.

[12] S. Modgil and M. Caminada. Proof Theories and Algorithms for Abstract Argumentation Frameworks. In *Argumentation in Artificial Intelligence*, pages 105–129. Springer, 2009.

[13] S. Modgil and H. Prakken. A General Account of Argumentation with Preferences. *Artificial Intelligence*, 195:361–397, February 2013.

[14] S. Modgil, F. Toni, et al. The Added Value of Argumentation. In S. Ossowski, editor, *Agreement Technologies*, volume 8, pages 357–403. Springer Netherlands, 2013.

[15] H. Prakken. An Abstract Framework for Argumentation with Structured Arguments. *Argument and Computation*, 1(2):93–124, 2010.

[16] R. Reiter. A Logic for Default Reasoning. *Artificial Intelligence*, 13:81–132, 1980.

[17] A. P. Young, S. Modgil, and H. Prakken. A General Account of Argumentation with Preferences - Erratum. Available from `http://www.dcs.kcl.ac.uk/staff/smodgil/2015-08-30_ASPIC+_fix_revised.pdf`, last accessed 7/11/2015.

Second-order Propositional Announcement Logic

Francesco Belardinelli
Laboratoire IBISC
Université d'Evry
Evry, France
belardinelli@ibisc.fr

Hans van Ditmarsch
LORIA – CNRS
Université de Lorraine
Vandoeuvre-lès-Nancy, France
hvd@us.es

Wiebe van der Hoek
Department of Computing
University of Liverpool
Liverpool, UK
wiebe@csc.liv.ac.uk

ABSTRACT

In this paper we introduce Second-order Propositional Announcement Logic (SOPAL): a language to express arbitrary announcements in Public Announcement Logic, by means of propositional quantification. We present SOPAL within a multi-agent context, and show that it is rich enough to express complex notions such as preservation under arbitrary announcements, knowability, and successfulness. We analyse the model theory of SOPAL and prove that it is strictly more expressive than Arbitrary PAL [2], and as expressive as Second-order Propositional Epistemic Logic [4], even though exponentially more succinct than the latter. These results points to a rich logic, with nice computational properties nonetheless, such as a decidable model checking problem and a complete axiomatisation.

1. INTRODUCTION

Knowledge reasoning and representation has gained pre-eminence in recent years and now it is rightly considered as a success story in the applications of formal methods to artificial intelligence [25]. In this broad line of research, a distinct tradition is represented by epistemic modal languages, which extend propositional logic with operators K_a to express the knowledge of an agent a. The investigations begun in the seminal works by von Wright and Hintikka [26, 14], have now grown into a mature body of contributions [17, 9]. Within this research direction an increasing interest is directed towards the dynamics of knowledge: how is individual knowledge affected by factual change, information exchange, or knowledge updates?

These questions have given rise to temporal epistemic logics [9] and dynamic epistemic logics [23], among others. A particular form of dynamics appearing in epistemic logic deals with truthful public announcements, i.e., publicly observable information that is assumed to be reliable. These occur in many multi-agent scenarios: card games, the muddy children puzzle, security protocols [21]. Public announcements are executed as model restrictions on the epistemic state of the agents listening to them. This idea has been formalised into *Public Announcement Logic* (PAL) [18, 13], which extends epistemic logic with formulas of type $[\phi]\psi$, to express that after announcing ϕ publicly, ψ holds.

Appears in: *Proceedings of the 15th International Conference on Autonomous Agents and Multiagent Systems (AAMAS 2016), J. Thangarajah, K. Tuyls, C. Jonker, S. Marsella (eds.), May 9–13, 2016, Singapore.*

Once public announcements are introduced, it is legitimate to wonder what remains true after arbitrary announcements (a property known as *preservation*), or what can be known by agents provided some suitable public announcement (*knowability*). In this paper we extend the framework of PAL to deal exactly with this sort of issues. We introduce *Second-order Propositional Announcement Logic* (SOPAL), which extends PAL with propositional quantification. As a result, the knowability of formula ϕ (by an agent a) becomes intuitively expressible in SOPAL as

$$\phi \rightarrow \exists p \langle p \rangle K_a \phi \tag{1}$$

that is, if ϕ is true, then after some truthful announcement p, agent a knows that ϕ is true.

The main contributions of the paper can be summarized as follows. We first introduce the syntax and semantics of SOPAL. Then, we compare SOPAL with *Arbitrary Public Announcement Logic* (APAL) [2, 3], an extension of PAL also including arbitrary announcements, and show in which sense SOPAL is strictly more expressive than APAL. We further provide reduction equivalences to eliminate announcements from SOPAL, and thus show that SOPAL is as expressive as *Second-order Propositional Epistemic Logic* (SOPEL), an extension of epistemic logic with propositional quantification [4]. This result allows us to transfer both the complete axiomatisation and the decidable model checking problem for SOPEL to SOPAL. Moreover, we prove that, even if they are equally expressive, SOPAL is exponentially more succinct than SOPEL. Finally, we apply SOPAL to multi-agent game scenarios and specify the dynamic epistemic notions of knowable, preserved, and successful formula.

As a result, we have a powerful logic, with nice computational properties, such as a complete axiomatisation, a decidable model checking problem, and a wide range of interesting applications.

Scheme of the Paper. In Section 2 we introduce the formal framework of Second-order Propositional Announcement Logic. In Section 3 we prove that, at the level of validities, SOPAL is strictly more expressive than APAL. On the other hand, in Section 4 SOPAL is shown to be as expressive as SOPEL. Nonetheless, the former is proved to be exponentially more succinct than the latter in Section 5. We point to future directions of research in the conclusions.

2. THE FORMAL FRAMEWORK

In this section we introduce the syntax and semantics of Second-order Propositional Announcement Logic (SOPAL).

2.1 Syntax

In the rest of the paper we assume a set AP of atomic propositions (or atoms) and a finite set Ag of indexes for agents. Formulas in SOPAL are defined as follows.

DEFINITION 1 (SOPAL). *The formulas in SOPAL are defined in BNF as follows, for $p \in AP$ and $a \in Ag$:*

$$\psi \ ::= \ p \mid \neg\psi \mid \psi \to \psi \mid K_a\psi \mid [\psi]\psi \mid \forall p\psi$$

The language $\mathcal{L}_{sopal}$ of SOPAL contains epistemic formulas $K_a\phi$, for each agent $a \in Ag$, which intuitively say that "agent a knows ϕ"; announcement formulas $[\psi]\phi$, whose reading is that "after announcing ψ, ϕ is true"; as well as quantified formula $\forall p\phi$, which means that "for all propositions p, ϕ is true". Symbols $\bot$, $\top$, connectives $\wedge$, $\vee$, operators M_a, $\langle\psi\rangle$, and quantifier $\exists$ are defined as standard.

Second-order Propositional Announcement Logic extends a number of well-known formalisms. The language $\mathcal{L}_{pal}$ of Public Announcement Logic is obtained by removing construct $\forall p\psi$ in Def. 1; language $\mathcal{L}_{el}$ without clause $[\psi]\psi$ as well is Epistemic Logic, and language $\mathcal{L}_{pl}$ without clause $K_a\psi$ as well is propositional logic. Also, language $\mathcal{L}_{sopel}$ obtained by removing clause $[\psi]\psi$ in Def. 1 is Second-Order Propositional Epistemic Logic [4]; while language $\mathcal{L}_{sopl}$ for Second-order Propositional Logic is obtained from $\mathcal{L}_{sopel}$ by removing clause $K_a\psi$ as well.

In the following we consider for comparison also the language of Arbitrary Public Announcement Logic [2, 3], obtained by extending PAL with formulas $\Box\psi$:

$$\psi \ ::= \ p \mid \neg\psi \mid \psi \to \psi \mid K_a\psi \mid [\psi]\psi \mid \Box\psi$$

where $\Box\psi$ is read as "after every truthful announcement, ϕ holds". Hereafter we show that SOPAL is rich enough to express APAL through quantification. We summarize the main (syntactic) language inclusions in the following schema.

$$\begin{array}{ccccccc} \mathcal{L}_{pl} & \subseteq & \mathcal{L}_{sopl} & \subseteq & \mathcal{L}_{sopel} & \subseteq & \mathcal{L}_{sopal} \\ & & \subsetneq & & \subsetneq & & \subsetneq \\ & & \mathcal{L}_{el} & \subseteq & \mathcal{L}_{pal} & \subseteq & \mathcal{L}_{apal} \end{array}$$

EXAMPLE 1. To illustrate the expressive power of SOPAL, we briefly discuss various epistemic notions. In Public Announcement Logic a formula ϕ is said to be *preserved* if ϕ is true after any announcement. In SOPAL we can capture this by requiring that the following formula holds:

$$\phi \to \forall q[q]\phi \qquad (2)$$

We informally remark that (2) does not hold for Moore's formula $p \wedge \neg K_a p$. However, in SOPAL we can define a suitable restriction of (2), concerning epistemic announcements only:

$$\phi \to \forall p[K_a p]\phi \qquad (3)$$

In Example 2 we show that (3), differently from (2), does hold for Moore's formulas.

Another notion of interest in PAL is knowability: a formula ϕ is *knowable* (by agent a) iff after some announcement, a knows ϕ [22]. We remarked that this notion can be stated formally as (1). Clearly, Moore's formulas are not knowable. We will discuss and compare preserved, knowable, and other classes of formulas in more detail in Section 4.1. ■

In the rest of the section we introduce the technical notions of free atom and substitution that are necessary throughout the rest of the paper.

DEFINITION 2 (FREE ATOMS). *The set $fr(\phi)$ of free atoms in a SOPAL formula ϕ is recursively defined as follows:*

$$\begin{array}{ll} fr(p) & = \{p\} \\ fr(\neg\phi) = fr(K_a\phi) & = fr(\phi) \\ fr(\phi \to \phi') = fr([\phi]\phi') & = fr(\phi) \cup fr(\phi') \\ fr(\forall p\phi) & = fr(\phi) \setminus \{p\} \end{array}$$

The set $bnd(\phi)$ of bound atoms in ϕ is standardly introduced as the set of all atoms q appearing in the scope of some quantifier Qq. By renaming bound atoms, we can assume w.l.o.g. that for every formula ϕ, sets $fr(\phi)$ and $bnd(\phi)$ are disjoint. We now define when an atom p can be safely substituted by a formula ψ in ϕ.

DEFINITION 3 (FREE FOR ...). *A formula ψ is* free *for atom p in ϕ iff p does not appear in ϕ within the scope of any quantifier Qq, whenever q is free in ψ, and if $\phi = [\phi']\phi''$ and $p \in fr(\phi')$, then $\psi \in \mathcal{L}_{sopl}$. Alternatively, we can define whether ψ is* free *for p in ϕ as follows:*

if ϕ is atomic then ψ is free for p in ϕ
if $\phi = \neg\phi'$ then ψ is free for p in ϕ iff it is in ϕ'
if $\phi = \phi' \to \phi''$ then ψ is free for p in ϕ iff it is in ϕ' and ϕ''
if $\phi = K_a\phi'$ then ψ is free for p in ϕ iff it is in ϕ'
if $\phi = [\phi']\phi''$ then ψ is free for p in ϕ iff it is in ϕ' and ϕ'' and $p \in fr(\phi')$ implies $\psi \in \mathcal{L}_{sopl}$
if $\phi = \forall q\phi'$ then ψ is free for p in ϕ iff $q \notin fr(\psi)$ and ψ is free for p in ϕ'

Finally, we introduce substitutions for free atoms.

DEFINITION 4 (SUBSTITUTION). *If ψ is free for p in ϕ, then we inductively define the substitution $\phi[p/\psi]$ as follows:*

$$\begin{array}{lcl} q[p/\psi] & = & \begin{cases} q & \text{for } q \text{ different from } p \\ \psi & \text{otherwise} \end{cases} \\ (\neg\phi)[p/\psi] & = & \neg(\phi[p/\psi]) \\ (\phi \to \phi')[p/\psi] & = & (\phi[p/\psi]) \to (\phi'[p/\psi]) \\ (K_a\phi)[p/\psi] & = & K_a(\phi[p/\psi]) \\ ([\phi]\phi')[p/\psi] & = & [\phi[p/\psi]](\phi'[p/\psi]) \\ (\forall r\phi)[p/\psi] & = & \forall r(\phi[p/\psi]), \text{ with } p \text{ different from } r \end{array}$$

Notice that we make use of square brackets [,] for both substitutions and announcements operators, as both usages are standard. The context will disambiguate.

The restriction on substitution can be deemed quite strong, as we allow only for the substitution of quantified boolean formulas in announcements. Intuitively, this is necessary because, while $[p]p$ is valid, substitution $[q \wedge \neg K_a q](q \wedge \neg K_a q)$ is not. Nonetheless, we will see that, also with such restriction, all results mentioned in the introduction are provable.

2.2 Semantics

To interpret SOPAL formulas we introduce multi-modal Kripke frames and models.

DEFINITION 5 (FRAME). *A Kripke frame is a tuple $\mathcal{F} = \langle W, D, R\rangle$ where*

- *W is a set of* possible worlds*;*
- *D is the* domain of propositions*, i.e., a subset of 2^W;*
- *for every agent $a \in Ag$, $R_a \subseteq 2^{W \times W}$ is an* equivalence relation *on W.*

As standard in epistemic logic [6], for every agent $a \in Ag$, R_a is the indistinguishability relation between worlds in W. In addition, Def. 5 includes a set $D \subseteq 2^W$ of "admissible" propositions for the interpretation of atoms and quantifiers. For technical reasons, in Section 5 we will also consider frames whose accessibility relations are not necessarily equivalences. In the following, for each agent $a \in Ag$ and $w \in W$, we set $R_a(w) = \{w' \mid R_a(w, w')\}$.

To assign a meaning to SOPAL formulas we introduce *assignments* as functions $V : AP \to D$. Given a set $U \in D$, the assignment V_U^p assigns U to p and coincides with V on all other atoms. Notice that atoms can only be assigned propositions in $D \subseteq 2^W$. A *(Kripke) model* is then defined as a pair $\mathcal{M} = \langle \mathcal{F}, V \rangle$.

In the rest of the paper we analyse particular classes of Kripke frames and models, which feature pre-eminently in the literature [10, 16]. To introduce them, we define an operator $[a] : 2^W \to 2^W$ for every $a \in Ag$, such that $[a](U) = \{w \in W \mid R_a(w) \subseteq U\}$.

DEFINITION 6. *A Kripke frame $\mathcal{F}$ is*

boolean *iff D is a boolean algebra, i.e., it is closed under intersection, union and complementation*

epistemic *iff D is a boolean algebra with operators $[a]$, for every $a \in Ag$*

full *iff $D = 2^W$*

A Kripke model $\mathcal{M} = \langle \mathcal{F}, V \rangle$ is boolean *(resp.* epistemic, full*) whenever the underlying frame $\mathcal{F}$ is.*

Hereafter we consider classes $\mathcal{K}_{all}$ of all Kripke frames, $\mathcal{K}_{bl}$ of all boolean frames, $\mathcal{K}_{el}$ of all epistemic frames, and $\mathcal{K}_{fl}$ of all full frames.

DEFINITION 7 (SATISFACTION). *We define whether model $\mathcal{M} = \langle \mathcal{F}, V \rangle$* satisfies *formula φ at world w, or $(\mathcal{M}, w) \models \varphi$, as follows (clauses for propositional connectives are omitted as straightforward):*

$$
\begin{array}{lll}
(\mathcal{M}, w) \models p & \text{iff} & w \in V(p) \\
(\mathcal{M}, w) \models K_a\psi & \text{iff} & \text{for all } w' \in R_a(w),\ (\mathcal{M}, w') \models \psi \\
(\mathcal{M}, w) \models [\psi]\psi' & \text{iff} & (\mathcal{M}, w) \models \psi \text{ implies } (\mathcal{M}_{|\psi}, w) \models \psi' \\
(\mathcal{M}, w) \models \forall p\psi & \text{iff} & \text{for all } U \in D,\ (\mathcal{M}_U^p, w) \models \psi
\end{array}
$$

where $\mathcal{M}_U^p = \langle \mathcal{F}, V_U^p \rangle$, and the restriction *$\mathcal{M}_{|\psi} = \langle W_{|\psi}, D_{|\psi}, R_{|\psi}, V_{|\psi} \rangle$ of model $\mathcal{M}$ according to ψ is defined as:* (i) $W_{|\psi} = \{v \in W \mid (\mathcal{M}, v) \models \psi\}$; (ii) $D_{|\psi} = \{U_{|\psi} = U \cap W_{|\psi} \mid U \in D\}$; (iii) $R_{|\psi,a} = R_a \cap W_{|\psi}^2$; (iv) $V_{|\psi}(p) = V(p) \cap W_{|\psi}$ *for every $p \in AP$.*

Given formula $\phi \in \mathcal{L}_{sopal}$, $[\![\phi]\!]_{\mathcal{M}} = \{w \in W \mid (\mathcal{M}, w) \models \phi\}$ is the satisfaction set in model $\mathcal{M}$. We omit the subscript $\mathcal{M}$ whenever clear from the context. We then prove the following useful lemma on satisfaction sets.

LEMMA 1. *For every formula $\phi \in \mathcal{L}_x$, for $x = pl$ (resp. el, pal, sopal), and for $\mathcal{M} = \langle \mathcal{F}, V \rangle$ with $\mathcal{F} \in \mathcal{K}_y$, for $y = bl$ (resp. el, el, fl), we have that $[\![\phi]\!] \in D$.*

PROOF. The case for $x = pl$ and $y = bl$ follows from equalities $[\![\neg\psi]\!] = \backslash[\![\psi]\!]$, $[\![\psi \wedge \psi']\!] = [\![\psi]\!] \cap [\![\psi']\!]$, $[\![\psi \vee \psi']\!] = [\![\psi]\!] \cup [\![\psi']\!]$ and the fact that D is a boolean algebra.

For $x = el$ and $y = el$, notice that $[\![K_a\psi]\!] = [a]([\![\psi]\!])$ and D is a boolean algebra with operators $[a]$.

The case of $x = pal$ and $y = el$ follows since PAL is as expressive as Epistemic Logic [18].

The case for $x = sopal$ and $y = fl$ is trivial. □

By Lemma 1 we can prove the following result, which guarantees that Def. 7 is well-defined in the sense that the restriction $\mathcal{M}_{|\phi}$ belongs to the same class as model $\mathcal{M}$.

LEMMA 2. *If a model $\mathcal{M}$ is boolean (resp. epistemic, full), then the model restriction $\mathcal{M}_{|\phi}$ for $\phi \in \mathcal{L}_{sopal}$ is also boolean (resp. epistemic, full).*

PROOF. The proof for full frames is immediate, as for all $U \subseteq W_{|\phi}$, $U \subseteq W$ and then $U \in D$. Hence, $U_{|\phi} = U \in D_{|\phi}$.

The proof for boolean frames follows from the equalities below, for $\star \in \{\cap, \cup\}$:

$$U_{|\phi} \star U'_{|\phi} = (U \star U')_{|\phi} \qquad \backslash(U_{|\phi}) = (\backslash U)_{|\phi}$$

As for epistemic frames, we remark that

$$[a](U_{|\phi}) \quad = \quad ([a](\backslash[\![\phi]\!] \cup U))_{|\phi}$$

(here $[a]$ denotes two different operations, the former on $\mathcal{M}_{|\phi}$ and the latter on $\mathcal{M}$.) Indeed, $w \in [a](U_{|\phi})$ iff $R_{|\phi,a}(w) \subseteq U_{|\phi}$. Since, $R_{|\phi,a}(w) = R_a(w) \cap W_{|\phi}^2$, this is the case iff $w \in [\![\phi]\!]$ and for every $w' \in R_a(w)$, $w' \in [\![\phi]\!]$ implies $w' \in U$, iff $w \in [\![\phi]\!]$ and $R_a(w) \subseteq (\backslash[\![\phi]\!] \cup U)$, iff $w \in ([a](\backslash[\![\phi]\!] \cup U))_\phi$. Finally, notice that $[a](\backslash[\![\phi]\!] \cup U) \in D$, as $[\![\phi]\!] \in D$ for every $\phi \in \mathcal{L}_{el}$ by Lemma 1 and D is a boolean algebra with operators. Hence, $[a](U_{|\phi}) = ([a](\backslash[\![\phi]\!] \cup U))_\phi \in D_{|\phi}$. □

We introduce standard notions of truth and validity to be used hereafter. A formula ϕ is *true* at w, or $(\mathcal{F}, w) \models \phi$, iff $(\langle \mathcal{F}, V \rangle, w) \models \phi$ for every assignment V; ϕ is *valid* in a frame $\mathcal{F}$, or $\mathcal{F} \models \phi$, iff $(\mathcal{F}, w) \models \phi$ for every world w in $\mathcal{F}$; ϕ is *valid* in a class $\mathcal{K}$ of frames, or $\mathcal{K} \models \phi$, iff $\mathcal{F} \models \phi$ for every $\mathcal{F} \in \mathcal{K}$.

EXAMPLE 2. To illustrate the semantics of SOPAL, we consider the following instance of (3) for Moore's formula $p \wedge \neg K_a p$:

$$(p \wedge \neg K_a p) \to \forall q[K_a q](p \wedge \neg K_a p) \tag{4}$$

and show that (4) is a validity in all frames.

Suppose that $(\mathcal{M}, w) \models p \wedge \neg K_a p$. Then, for some $w' \in R_a(w)$ different from w, $(\mathcal{M}, w') \not\models p$. Also, if $(\mathcal{M}_U^q, w) \not\models [K_a q](p \wedge \neg K_a p)$ for some reinterpretation $\mathcal{M}_U^q$, then we have $((\mathcal{M}_U^q)_{|K_a q}, w) \not\models p \wedge \neg K_a p$, that is, $(\mathcal{M}_U^q, w) \models K_a q$ but w' must not appear in $(\mathcal{M}_U^q)_{|K_a q}$, i.e., $(\mathcal{M}_U^q, w') \not\models K_a q$. But then, $(\mathcal{M}_U^q, w) \not\models K_a q$ either. A contradiction.

Thus, even though Moore's formulas are not preserved under arbitrary announcements, they are indeed preserved by arbitrary *epistemic* announcements as in (4). ■

EXAMPLE 3. Next, we elaborate on the example of [24, Section 4.3], and consider a simple card game with three players in $Ag = \{1, 2, 3\}$. The cards are identified by their colour: red (r), white (w), and blue (b). We consider atoms r_i, w_i, b_i, for $i \in Ag$, in AP, where intuitively w_1 denotes that player 1 holds the white card. Also, all players know the cards of the game, and that each player can see his own card, but not that of the other players. The situation where each player is dealt a card can be modeled by the full model $\mathcal{M}$ in Fig. 1. The state rwb in $\mathcal{M}$ denotes that player 1 holds red, 2 holds white, and 3 holds blue. We then have for instance

$$(\mathcal{M}, \mathsf{rwb}) \models r_1 \wedge K_1 r_1 \wedge \neg K_2 r_1 \wedge K_1 \neg K_2 r_1$$

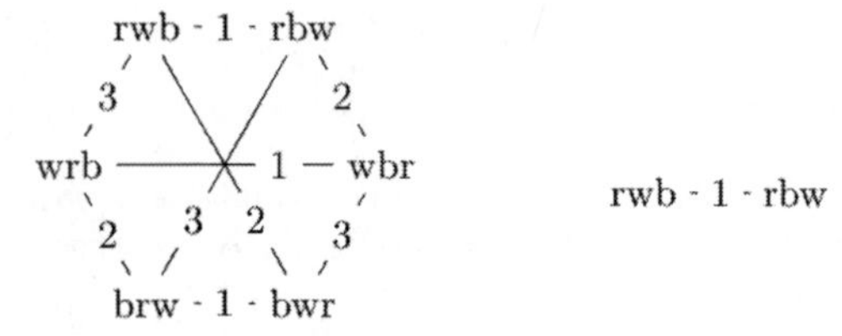

Figure 1: The full models $\mathcal{M}$ and $\mathcal{M}'$ (reflexive edges are omitted for simplicity)

i.e., player 1 holds red, she knows it, but 2 does not, and finally, 1 knows that 2 does not know that 1 holds red.

In general, for every state s in $\mathcal{M}$,

$$(\mathcal{M}, s) \models \exists p \left(p \wedge K_i p \wedge \bigwedge_{j \neq i} \neg K_j p \wedge K_i \bigwedge_{j \neq i} \neg K_j p \right)$$

i.e., every player i knows something that the other players do not know (and she knows that they do not), namely the value of the card that i possesses.

Now suppose player 1 announces publicly the card she has. Such an announcement in state rwb leads to the updated model $\mathcal{M}'$ in Fig. 1. Indeed, for $q_i \in \{r_i, w_i, b_i\}$ we have

$$(\mathcal{M}, s) \models q_i \to \exists p \langle K_i p \rangle \left(\bigwedge_{j \neq i} K_j q_i \right)$$

that is, there is some proposition (namely, the value $U = R_i(s)$ of player i's card) that player i can truthfully announce, so that any other player knows the value of i's card.

On the other hand, the mere announcement that player i knows something is not sufficient to derive the same conclusion, as for every state $s \in W$, $(\mathcal{M}, s) \models \exists p K_i p$, and therefore $\mathcal{M}_{|\exists p K_i p} = \mathcal{M}$. Hence,

$$(\mathcal{M}, s) \not\models q_i \to \langle \exists p K_i p \rangle \left(\bigwedge_{j \neq i} K_j q_i \right)$$

Furthermore, the (false) announcement that player i knows everything trivially implies that the other players know her card:

$$(\mathcal{M}, s) \models q_i \to [\forall p K_i p] \left(\bigwedge_{j \neq i} K_j q_i \right)$$

Indeed, $(\mathcal{M}, s) \not\models \forall p K_i p$. Then, $(\mathcal{M}, s) \models [\forall p K_i p](\bigwedge_{j \neq i} K_j q_i)$. However, it is not the case that every truthful announcement pertaining to player i's knowledge entails that the other players know her card:

$$(\mathcal{M}, s) \not\models q_i \to \forall p [K_i p] \left(\bigwedge_{j \neq i} K_j q_i \right)$$

as for proposition $U = W$, $(\mathcal{M}^p_U, s') \models K_i p$ for every $s' \in W$. But $((\mathcal{M}^p_U)_{|K_i p}, s) \not\models \bigwedge_{j \neq i} K_j q_i$, since $(\mathcal{M}^p_U)_{|K_i p} = \mathcal{M}^p_U$.

By comparing the formulas above, we clearly see that quantifying inside or outside (epistemic) announcements allows us to express subtle differences in SOPAL. ■

3. COMPARISON WITH APAL

In this section we compare SOPAL with APAL, whose original motivation also included the ability to express arbitrary announcements in PAL. The main result of this section is that SOPAL is capable of capturing APAL at the frame level, while the two logics are incomparable at the model level. But first we state some auxiliary lemmas, that will be routinely applied throughout the paper, which illustrate some features of quantification in SOPAL.

LEMMA 3. *Let q and ψ be free for p in ϕ.*

1. *In $\mathcal{K}_{all}$, $(\mathcal{M}^p_{V(q)}, w) \models \phi$ iff $(\mathcal{M}, w) \models \phi[p/q]$*
2. *For $x = bl$ (resp. el, fl) and $y = pl$ (resp. el, $sopal$), in $\mathcal{K}_x$, $(\mathcal{M}^p_{[\![\psi]\!]}, w) \models \phi$ iff $(\mathcal{M}, w) \models \phi[p/\psi]$, for any $\psi \in \mathcal{L}_y$*
3. *If $p \in fr(\phi)$ implies $\psi \in \mathcal{L}_{sopl}$, then $(\mathcal{M}^p_{[\![\psi]\!]})_{|\phi} = (\mathcal{M}_{|\phi[p/\psi]})^p_{[\![\psi]\!]}$*
4. *If $V(fr(\phi)) = V'(fr(\phi))$ then $(\mathcal{M}, w) \models \phi$ iff $(\mathcal{M}', w) \models \phi$*
5. *If $V(fr(\psi)) = V'(fr(\psi))$ then $\mathcal{M}_\psi = \mathcal{M}'_\psi$*

According to Lemma 3.1-2, the syntactic notion of substitution $\phi[p/\psi]$ corresponds to the semantic concept of reinterpretation $\mathcal{M}^p_{[\![\psi]\!]}$; while Lemma 3.3 specifies the interaction between substitution, reinterpretation and model restriction, namely the restriction $(\mathcal{M}^p_{[\![\psi]\!]})_{|\phi}$ of a reinterpreted model is equal to the reinterpretation $(\mathcal{M}_{|\phi[p/\psi]})^p_{[\![\psi]\!]}$ of the model restricted by the substituted formula $\phi[p/\psi]$, provided that $\psi \in \mathcal{L}_{sopl}$ whenever $p \in fr(\phi)$. Moreover, by Lemma 3.4-5 models built on the same frame and agreeing on the interpretation of free atoms, also satisfy the same formulas, and their model restrictions are equal. These results, which show that quantification in SOPAL is "well-behaved", will be extensively used hereafter.

To compare SOPAL and APAL we recall the clause for interpreting the $\Box$ operator [2]:

$$(\mathcal{M}, w) \models \Box\psi \quad \text{iff} \quad \text{for all } \phi \in \mathcal{L}_{el}, (\mathcal{M}, w) \models [\phi]\psi \quad (5)$$

We now prove that, according to (5), APAL can be captured within SOPAL in the following sense.

DEFINITION 8. *Given a class $\mathcal{K}$ of frames, a logic L' is*

- *at least as m-expressive as logic L, or $L \leq_m L'$, iff for any $\phi \in L$, for some $\phi' \in L'$, for any model $\mathcal{M}$ based on some frame in $\mathcal{K}$,*

$$(\mathcal{M}, w) \models \phi \quad \text{iff} \quad (\mathcal{M}, w) \models \phi'$$

- *at least as f-expressive as logic L, or $L \leq_f L'$, iff for any $\phi \in L$, for some $\phi' \in L'$, for any frame $\mathcal{F}$ in $\mathcal{K}$,*

$$(\mathcal{F}, w) \models \phi \quad \text{iff} \quad (\mathcal{F}, w) \models \phi'$$

Clearly, each relation $\leq$ is a partial order, and we write $L = L'$ iff $L \leq L'$ and $L' \leq L$, and $L < L'$ iff $L \leq L'$ and $L \neq L'$. Also, $L \leq_m L'$ implies $L \leq_f L'$.

To investigate the relation between SOPAL and APAL, we start with some preliminary results. First of all, we test the intuition that the operator $\Box$ can be expressed by quantification and announcements.

LEMMA 4. *Let $\mathcal{M}$ be an epistemic model, then*

$$(\mathcal{M}, w) \models \forall p [p] \phi \quad \textit{implies that} \quad (\mathcal{M}, w) \models \Box\phi \quad (6)$$

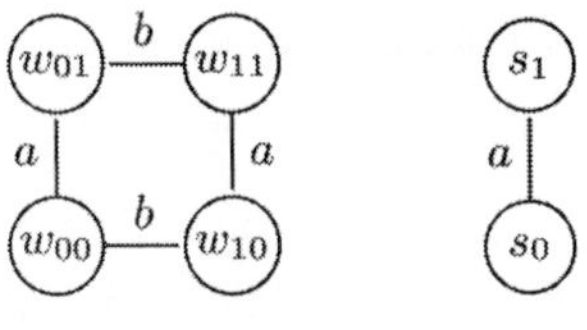

Figure 2: The full models $\mathcal{M}$ and $\mathcal{M}'$ (reflexive edges are omitted for simplicity)

PROOF. Indeed, if $(\mathcal{M}, w) \not\models [\psi]\phi$ for some $\psi \in \mathcal{L}_{el}$, then in particular, $[\![\psi]\!] \in D$ by Lemma 1 and for $U = [\![\psi]\!]$, $(\mathcal{M}^p_U, w) \not\models [p]\phi$. That is, $(\mathcal{M}, w) \not\models \forall p[p]\phi$. □

However, the converse of (6) does not always hold. Consider the full model $\mathcal{M}$ in Fig. 2. Formally, we have that $\mathcal{M} = \langle W, R, D, V\rangle$ with $W = \{w_{00}, w_{01}, w_{10}, w_{11}\}$; $R_a = \{(w_{ij}, w_{i'j'}) \mid i = i'\}$; $R_b = \{(w_{ij}, w_{i'j'}) \mid j = j'\}$; $D = 2^W$; and $V(q) = \{w_{ij} \mid j = 0\}$ for every $q \in AP$. We can check that, for every $\psi \in \mathcal{L}_{el}$, $[\![\psi]\!]$ is equal to either W, or $\emptyset$, or $\{w_{ij} \mid j = 0\}$, or $\{w_{ij} \mid j = 1\}$. As a consequence, for every $\psi \in \mathcal{L}_{el}$, $(\mathcal{M}, w_{i0}) \models [\psi](K_a q \to K_b K_a q)$, that is, $(\mathcal{M}, w_{i0}) \models \Box(K_a q \to K_b K_a q)$. However, for $U = \{w_{00}, w_{01}, w_{10}\}$ we obtain that $(\mathcal{M}^p_U, w_{10}) \not\models [p](K_a q \to K_b K_a q)$, i.e., $(\mathcal{M}, w_{10}) \not\models \forall p[p](K_a q \to K_b K_a q)$.

Actually, Def. (5) for APAL preserves bisimilarity of structures, while Def. 7 for SOPAL does not. To see this, consider the full model $\mathcal{M}'$ in Fig. 2. We remark without proof that the pointed models $(\mathcal{M}, w_{10})$ and $(\mathcal{M}', s_0)$ are bisimilar [6], and satisfy the same formulas in PAL, and consequently, in APAL. However, we noticed that $(\mathcal{M}, w_{10}) \not\models \forall p[p](K_a q \to K_b K_a q)$, while it is easy to check that $(\mathcal{M}', s_0) \models \forall p[p](K_a q \to K_b K_a q)$.

Incidentally, models $\mathcal{M}$ and $\mathcal{M}'$ above prove that at the level of models, SOPAL is no less expressive than APAL.

THEOREM 5. *In class $\mathcal{K}_{fl}$ of full frames, SOPAL $\not\leq_m$ APAL.*

PROOF. Suppose that SOPAL $\leq_m$ APAL. Then, for $\phi = \forall p[p](K_a q \to K_b K_a q)$ in SOPAL there exists a corresponding ϕ' in APAL. However, $(\mathcal{M}, w_{10}) \not\models \phi$ implies $(\mathcal{M}, w_{10}) \not\models \phi'$, which implies $(\mathcal{M}', s_0) \not\models \phi'$ by bisimulation, which finally implies $(\mathcal{M}', s_0) \not\models \phi$. A contradiction. □

We observe that Def. 7 is discussed in [2], but discarded exactly on the ground that it does not preserve bisimulations. Bisimulation-preserving quantification is analysed in [11], the resulting logic is proved as expressive as Epistemic Logic. Here we maintain that in second-order propositional modal logics a stronger notion of bisimulation is needed, which takes into account also quantification, as discussed in [5]. Also, Def. (5) has other issues, in particular, it is not analytic (more below).

Even though $\forall p[p]\psi$ is not equivalent to $\Box\psi$ at the level of models, the two formulas are provably equivalent at the level of frames, under a cardinality assumption.

Consider the following translation τ from APAL to SOPAL:

$$
\begin{aligned}
\tau(p) &= p\\
\tau(\neg\psi) &= \neg\tau(\psi)\\
\tau(\psi \to \psi') &= \tau(\psi) \to \tau(\psi')\\
\tau(K_a\psi) &= K_a\tau(\psi)\\
\tau([\psi]\psi') &= [\psi]\tau(\psi')\\
\tau(\Box\psi') &= \forall p[p]\tau(\psi')
\end{aligned}
$$

where p does not appear free in ψ'.

We can now prove the following result.

LEMMA 6. *In the class of epistemic frames where $|D|$ is enumerable,*

$$\models \phi \quad \textit{iff} \quad \models \tau(\phi)$$

PROOF. The $\Leftarrow$ direction follows from (6) above.

As for the $\Rightarrow$ direction, suppose that for some model $\mathcal{M}$ and state w, $(\mathcal{M}, w) \not\models \tau(\phi)$. Consider now a model $\mathcal{M}'$ s.t. $\mathcal{F}' = \mathcal{F}$ and V' coincides with V on all atoms appearing in ϕ. Further, for every $U \in D$ take $q_U \in AP$ not appearing in ϕ and let $V'(q_U) = U$. By Lemma 3.4, $(\mathcal{M}, w) \not\models \tau(\phi)$ implies $(\mathcal{M}', w) \not\models \tau(\phi)$ (the assignment $V'(q)$ for all atoms not appearing in ϕ and not assigned to a set U is uninfluential.)

Hereafter we write $\mathcal{N} \subseteq \mathcal{M}$ to express that $\mathcal{N}$ is a submodel of $\mathcal{M}$, i.e., $W_{\mathcal{N}} \subseteq W$; $D_{\mathcal{N}} = \{U \cap W_{\mathcal{N}} \mid U \in D\}$; $R_{\mathcal{N},a} = R_a \cap W^2_{\mathcal{N}}$; and $V_{\mathcal{N}}(p) = V(p) \cap W_{\mathcal{N}}$ for every $p \in AP$. We can now state the following auxiliary result: for every submodel $\mathcal{N}'$ of $\mathcal{M}'$ and subformula ψ of ϕ,

$$(\mathcal{N}', w) \models \psi \quad \text{iff} \quad (\mathcal{N}', w) \models \tau(\psi) \tag{7}$$

Finally, by (7) $(\mathcal{M}', w) \not\models \tau(\phi)$ implies $(\mathcal{M}', w) \not\models \phi$. □

As a result, whenever the domain D of propositions is enumerable, APAL can be captured within SOPAL at the frame level, by means of translation τ. Specifically, the arbitrary announcement operator $\Box$ can be expressed by quantification and standard announcements. As a corollary, we have the following result.

COROLLARY 7. *In the class of epistemic frames where $|D|$ is enumerable, APAL $\leq_f$ SOPAL.*

We now show that the converse does not hold in general.

THEOREM 8. *In class $\mathcal{K}_{fl}$ of full frames, SOPAL $\not\leq_f$ APAL.*

As an immediate consequence of Corollary 7 and Theorem 8 we obtain the following.

COROLLARY 9. *In class of epistemic frames where $|D|$ is enumerable, APAL $<_f$ SOPAL.*

Finally, we remarked above that Def. 7 is discussed in [2], but dismissed as it does not preserve bisimulations. On the other hand, the APAL semantics is not analytic in the sense that Lemma 3.4 fails: models that agree on the interpretation of free atoms, may differ in the satisfaction of formulas. Consider again model $\mathcal{M}$ in Fig. 2 and $\varphi = \Box(K_a q \to K_b K_a q)$. Then, define model $\mathcal{M}''$ such that for every $U \subseteq W$, $V(p_U) = U$ for some $p_U \neq q$. Clearly, V and V'' agree on the only free variable q in φ. However, $(\mathcal{M}, w_{00}) \models \varphi$ as noticed above, while $(\mathcal{M}'', w_{00}) \not\models \varphi$. In particular, for $U = \{w_{00}, w_{01}, w_{10}\}$, $(\mathcal{M}'', w_{00}) \not\models [p_U](K_a q \to K_b K_a q)$. Therefore, in APAL the satisfaction of formulas does not depend on values assigned to free variables only, but, if the formula contains an operator $\Box$, on all variables in AP. The example above also entails the following result.

THEOREM 10. *In class $\mathcal{K}_{fl}$ of full frames, APAL $\not\leq_m$ SOPAL.*

PROOF. If APAL $\leq_m$ SOPAL, then for $\varphi = \Box(K_a q \rightarrow K_b K_a q)$ in APAL there exists a corresponding φ' in SOPAL. However, $(\mathcal{M}, w_{00}) \models \varphi$ implies $(\mathcal{M}, w_{00}) \models \varphi'$, which implies $(\mathcal{M}'', w_{00}) \models \varphi'$ by Lemma 3.4, which implies $(\mathcal{M}'', w_{00}) \models \varphi$. A contradiction. □

To summarize the main results proved in this section, SOPAL and APAL are incomparable at the model level, while the former is strictly more expressive than the latter at the frame level.

4. EXPRESSIVITY

In this section we explore expressivity in the various classes of Kripke frames, starting with the properties of quantifiers. The main result of this section is that SOPAL is as expressive as Second-order Propositional Epistemic Logic.

LEMMA 11. *In SOPAL we have the following validities, for $x \in \{bl, el, fl\}$ and $y \in \{pl, el, sopal\}$:*

$$\mathcal{K}_{all} \models \forall p\phi \rightarrow \phi[p/q] \quad \text{for every } q \in AP \tag{8}$$
$$\mathcal{K}_{x} \models \forall p\phi \rightarrow \phi[p/\psi] \quad \text{for every } \psi \in \mathcal{L}_y \tag{9}$$

where q and ψ are free for p in ϕ.
For every class $\mathcal{K}$ of frames,

$$\mathcal{K} \models \psi \rightarrow \phi \quad \text{implies} \quad \mathcal{K} \models \psi \rightarrow \forall p\phi \tag{10}$$

where p does not appear free in ψ.

We remark the essential use of Lemmas 3.2-5 in this proof. By Lemma 11 we can see that quantifiers in SOPAL satisfy the standard principles of quantification: exemplification (8)-(9) and generalisation (10).

It is of utmost interest to study the interactions between quantification and public announcements in SOPAL. In this respect, we obtain the following key result.

LEMMA 12. *The following validities hold in all classes of frames.*

$$[\psi]\forall p\phi \leftrightarrow \psi \rightarrow \forall p[\psi]\phi \tag{11}$$
$$\langle\psi\rangle\exists p\phi \leftrightarrow \psi \wedge \exists p\langle\psi\rangle\phi \tag{12}$$
$$[\psi]\exists p\phi \leftrightarrow \psi \rightarrow \exists p[\psi]\phi \tag{13}$$
$$\langle\psi\rangle\forall p\phi \leftrightarrow \psi \wedge \forall p\langle\psi\rangle\phi \tag{14}$$

where p does not appear in ψ (w.l.o.g. bound variables can always be renamed).

PROOF. As regards (11) observe that,

$$\begin{aligned}(\mathcal{M}, w) \models [\psi]\forall p\phi \text{ iff } & (\mathcal{M}, w) \models \psi \text{ implies } (\mathcal{M}_{|\psi}, w) \models \forall p\phi\\ \text{iff } & (\mathcal{M}, w) \models \psi \text{ implies for all } U' \in D_{|\psi},\\ & ((\mathcal{M}_{|\psi})^p_{U'}, w) \models \phi\end{aligned}$$

Now, if $U \in D$ then $U' = U \cap W_{|\psi} \in D_{|\psi}$. On the other hand, if $U' \in D_{|\psi}$ then for some $U \in D$, $U' = U \cap W_{|\psi}$. In particular $(V_{|\psi})^p_{U'} = (V^p_U)_{|\psi}$, as p does not appear free in ψ. Hence,

$$\begin{aligned}(\mathcal{M}, w) \models [\psi]\forall p\phi \text{ iff } & (\mathcal{M}, w) \models \psi \text{ implies for all } U \in D,\\ & ((\mathcal{M}^p_U)_{|\psi}, w) \models \phi\\ \text{iff } & (\mathcal{M}, w) \models \psi \text{ implies } (\mathcal{M}, w) \models \forall p[\psi]\phi\\ \text{iff } & (\mathcal{M}, w) \models \psi \rightarrow \forall p[\psi]\phi\end{aligned}$$

The other equivalences are proved similarly. □

We recall that Second-order Propositional Epistemic Logic is obtained by removing clause $[\psi]\psi$ from Def. 1. From Lemma 12 and the standard reduction axioms for PAL [18] we derive the following expressivity result:

THEOREM 13. *SOPAL is as expressive as SOPEL.*

This result is extremely relevant, as it allows to apply the model theory and techniques for SOPEL also to SOPAL. As an example, the bisimulations introduced in [5] for Second-order Propositional Modal Logic apply to SOPAL as well. Further consequences of Theorem 13 regard the decidability of model checking SOPAL and its axiomatisability.

COROLLARY 14.

- *The model checking problem for SOPAL is decidable.*
- *SOPAL has a sound and complete axiomatisation.*

These results directly follow from the PSPACE-completeness and axiomatisation of SOPEL in [4].

4.1 Knowability

In this section we analyse the notions of preservation and knowability introduced in Example 1, and present successfulness. Such concepts are of interest to understand the epistemic capabilities of agents in response to different types of public announcements.

We start by introducing the *positive* fragment $\mathcal{L}^+_{sopal}$ inductively defined as

$$\psi ::= p \mid \neg p \mid \psi \wedge \psi \mid \psi \vee \psi \mid K_a\psi \mid [\neg\psi]\psi \mid \forall p\psi$$

As anticipated in Example 1, *preserved formulas* keep their truth under arbitrary announcements. Given a class $\mathcal{K}$, they are defined semantically as those ϕ in SOPAL for which $\mathcal{K} \models \phi \rightarrow \forall p[p]\phi$. We immediately extend the following result for APAL.

LEMMA 15. *Positive formulas are preserved in $\mathcal{K}_{all}$.*

PROOF. We show that for every model $\mathcal{M}$, $\mathcal{M}'$, $\mathcal{M}''$ with $\mathcal{M}'' \subseteq \mathcal{M}' \subseteq \mathcal{M}$, $s \in W''$, and positive ϕ, $(\mathcal{M}', s) \models \phi$ implies $(\mathcal{M}'', s) \models \phi$. The inductive cases for $\phi \neq \forall p\psi$ follow as in [20]. As for $\phi = \forall p\psi$, Consider $U'' \in W''$ s.t. $(\mathcal{M}''^p_{U''}, s) \models \psi$. Clearly, $\mathcal{M}''^p_{U''} \subseteq \mathcal{M}'^p_{U'}$ for $U' \in D'$ s.t. $U'' = U' \cap W''$. Moreover, hypothesis $(\mathcal{M}', s) \models \forall p\psi$ implies $(\mathcal{M}'^p_{U'}, s) \models \psi$, and by induction hypothesis it follows that $(\mathcal{M}''^p_{U''}, s) \models \psi$. Since U'' is arbitrary, $(\mathcal{M}'', s) \models \forall p\psi$. □

As an immediate consequence of Lemma 15, positive formulas are preserved in every class of frames.

In connection with preserved formulas, in Example 1 we introduced the formulas preserved after arbitrary *epistemic* announcements (in a class $\mathcal{K}$) as those formulas ϕ for which $\mathcal{K} \models \phi \rightarrow \forall p[K_a p]\phi$. In Example 2 we remarked that Moore's formulas are not preserved under arbitrary announcements, but they are for epistemic announcements. Obviously, positive formulas are also preserved epistemically. So, it would be of interest to characterize exactly the class of formulas preserved under arbitrary epistemic announcements, but this is beyond the scope of the present paper.

Another semantic notion of interest when dealing with public announcements is that of *success*. Formally, a formula ϕ is successful in class $\mathcal{K}$ of frames iff $[\phi]\phi$ is valid in $\mathcal{K}$.

LEMMA 16. *Formulas preserved in their own class $\mathcal{K}$ of frames are successful in $\mathcal{K}$.*

Finally, we recall that for a given class $\mathcal{K}$ of frames, *knowable* formulas as those for which, for any agents $a \in Ag$, $\mathcal{K} \models \phi \to \exists p\langle p\rangle K_a\phi$ [22].

LEMMA 17. *Positive formulas are knowable in $\mathcal{K}_{all}$ (always knowable). Formulas preserved (resp. successful) in their own class $\mathcal{K}$ are also knowable in $\mathcal{K}$.*

We clearly see that SOPAL allows for a fine-grained analysis of the epistemic notions of preservation, successfulness, and knowability.

5. SUCCINCTNESS OF SOPAL

The fact that SOPAL and SOPEL are equally expressive does not necessarily mean that they are 'the same'. Indeed, we now argue that SOPAL is more succinct than SOPEL, in the sense described below. We will sketch the argument using techniques from [12], where it was proven that PAL is exponentionally more succinct than epistemic logic. For the following we define the length $|\phi|$ of a formula ϕ as standard.

DEFINITION 9. *Given two logics L_1 and L_2 that are equally expressive on a class $\mathcal{K}$ of frames, we say that L_1 is exponentially more succinct than L_2 on $\mathcal{K}$, written $L_1 \preceq_{\mathcal{K}}^{exp} L_2$, if the following holds: There are sequences $\varphi_{n\in\mathbb{N}} = \varphi_1, \varphi_2, \cdots \in L_1$ and $\psi_{n\in\mathbb{N}} = \psi_1, \psi_2, \cdots \in L_2$ and a polynomial function f such that, for all $n \in \mathbb{N}$,*

1. $|\varphi_n| \leq f(n)$*;*
2. $|\psi_n| > 2^n$*;*
3. *ψ_n is the shortest formula in L_2 equivalent to φ_n in $\mathcal{K}$.*

In stating the main result below we also consider the class $\mathcal{C}$ of frames with arbitrary accessibility relations.

THEOREM 18.

- *SOPAL $\preceq_{\mathcal{C}}^{exp}$ SOPEL, if $|Ag| \geq 2$*
- *SOPAL $\preceq_{\mathcal{K}_{all}}^{exp}$ SOPEL, if $|Ag| \geq 4$*

We will only argue here for the first item of the theorem. Consider the following two sequences $\varphi_{n\in\mathbb{N}}$ and $\psi_{n\in\mathbb{N}}$.

$$\begin{aligned} \varphi_0 &= \top \\ \varphi_{n+1} &= \langle\varphi_n\rangle(M_a p \vee M_b q) \\ \psi_0 &= \top \\ \psi_n &= M_a(\psi_{n-1} \wedge p) \vee M_b(\psi_{n-1} \wedge q) \end{aligned}$$

It is easy to see that $|\varphi_i| \leq i \cdot 6$ and $|\psi_i| \geq 2^i$. Using PAL equivalences, we also have that φ_i and ψ_i are equivalent, for all i. So the first two items for succinctness are easily checked, what remains to establish is, that even when we allow for quantification, there are no formulas $\beta_i \in \mathcal{L}_{sopel}$ shorter than $\psi_i \in \mathcal{L}_{sopel}$ equivalent to ψ_i.

For propositional epistemic logic, the technique that [12] uses for this is that of Formula Size Games. We now extend such games to deal with quantification.

DEFINITION 10 (FORMULA SIZE GAME). *The rules of the one-person formula size game (FSG) for Spoiler are the following. The game is played on a tree, where each node is labeled with a pair $\langle \mathrm{M} \circ \mathrm{N}\rangle$ such that M and N are finite sets of finite pointed models. At each step of the game, a node is labeled with one of the symbols from the set $\Sigma = \{\top, \bot, p, \neg, \vee, \wedge, M_i, K_i, \exists p, \forall p\}$ and either it is closed or at most two new nodes are added. Let a node $\langle \mathrm{M} \circ \mathrm{N}\rangle$ be given. Spoiler can make the following moves at this node:*

⊤-move *This can be played only if $\mathrm{N} = \emptyset$. When Spoiler plays this move, the node is closed and labeled with $\top$.*

atomic-move *Spoiler chooses an atom p such that every pointed model in M satisfies p, and no pointed model in N does. After this move, this node is closed and labeled with p.*

not-move *Spoiler labels the node with symbol $\neg$ and adds one new node denoted $\langle \mathrm{N} \circ \mathrm{M}\rangle$ as a successor to $\langle \mathrm{M} \circ \mathrm{N}\rangle$.*

or-move *Spoiler labels the node with symbol $\vee$ and splits M in two sets $\mathrm{M} = \mathrm{M}_1 \cup \mathrm{M}_2$. Two new nodes are added to the tree as successors to $\langle \mathrm{M} \circ \mathrm{N}\rangle$, i.e., $\langle \mathrm{M}_1 \circ \mathrm{N}\rangle$ and $\langle \mathrm{M}_2 \circ \mathrm{N}\rangle$.*

M_a-move *Spoiler labels the node with symbol M_a and for each pointed model $(\mathcal{M}, w) \in \mathrm{M}$, he chooses a pointed model $(\mathcal{M}, w')$ such that wR_iw'. All such choices are collected in M_1. A set of models N_1 is then constructed as follows. For each pointed model $(\mathcal{N}, v) \in \mathrm{N}$ add to N_1 all pointed models $(\mathcal{N}, v')$ such that vR_iv'. If for some pointed model $(\mathcal{N}, v)$, world v does not have an R_i-successor, nothing is added to N_1 for $(\mathcal{N}, v)$. A new node $\langle \mathrm{M}_1 \circ \mathrm{N}_1\rangle$ is added as a successor to $\langle \mathrm{M} \circ \mathrm{N}\rangle$.*

$\exists p$-move *Spoiler labels the node with symbol $\exists p$, and, for each $(\mathcal{M}, w) \in \mathrm{M}$, Spoiler chooses a set $U \in D_{\mathcal{M}}$ and replaces $(\mathcal{M}, w)$ by $(\mathcal{M}_U^p, v)$. All those choices are collected in M_1. A set N_1 is then constructed as follows. For every $(\mathcal{N}, v) \in \mathrm{N}$ and $U' \in D_{\mathcal{N}}$, add $(\mathcal{N}_{U'}^p, v)$ to N.*

The moves for $\bot$, **and**, K_a, and $\forall p$ can be inferred from this: Spoiler acts on N, instead of M. **and**-moves and **or**-moves are collectively called *splitting* moves, while K_a and M_a-moves are called *agent* moves.

DEFINITION 11. *Spoiler wins the FSG starting at $\langle \mathrm{M} \circ \mathrm{N}\rangle$ in n moves iff there is a game tree T with root $\langle \mathrm{M} \circ \mathrm{N}\rangle$ and precisely n nodes such that every leaf of T is closed. Otherwise, Spoiler loses the game in n moves.*

THEOREM 19. *Spoiler can win the FSG starting at $\langle \mathrm{M} \circ \mathrm{N}\rangle$ in less than k moves iff there is a SOPEL formula ψ such that $\mathrm{M} \models \psi$, $\mathrm{N} \models \neg\psi$, $|\psi| = n$, and $n < k$.*

PROOF. We briefly sketch the case for quantifiers, for the other cases we refer to [12, Theorem 1]. The 'if' direction is by induction on the formula, so suppose $\varphi = \exists p\psi$, with the claim proven for ψ with $|\psi| = n - 1$. That is, suppose that φ has size $n < k$ and that $\mathrm{M} \models \exists p\psi$ while $\mathrm{N} \models \neg\exists p\psi$. Spoiler plays the $\exists p$-move: since $\mathrm{M} \models \exists p\psi$, for every model $(\mathcal{M}, w) \in \mathrm{M}$, Spoiler can choose some $U \in D_{\mathcal{M}}$ such that $(\mathcal{M}_U^p, w) \models \psi$. Collecting all pointed models thus obtained in M_1, we have $\mathrm{M}_1 \models \psi$. Since $\mathrm{N} \models \neg\exists p\psi$, if we put all

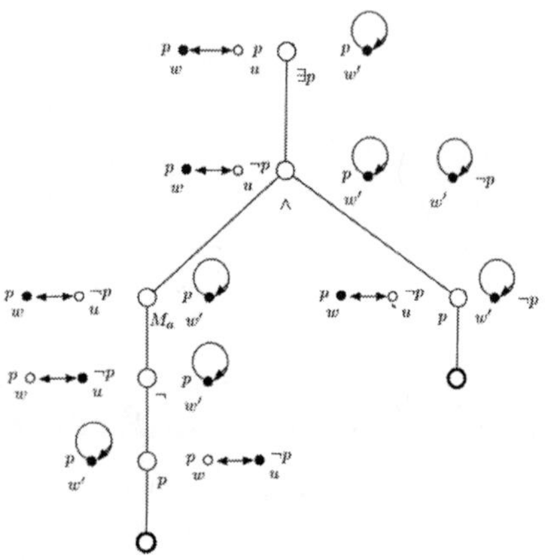

Figure 3: The game tree from Example 4.

models $(\mathcal{N}, v)$ in a set N_1, we have $N_1 \models \neg\psi$. We know that Spoiler can win the sub-game starting in $\langle M_1 \circ N_1 \rangle$ in $n-1$ moves, which in turn ensures he wins the game starting in $\langle M \circ N \rangle$ in n moves.

For the 'only-if' direction, if Spoiler has won the FSG starting at $\langle M \circ N \rangle$ (in $n < k$ moves) then the resulting closed game tree is a parse tree of a formula φ of length n such that $M \models \varphi$ and $N \models \neg\varphi$. To see this, we label the nodes of the tree with formulae, starting with the leaves. In particular, if a node has a label $\exists p$ and its successor is labeled with ψ, then the current node is labeled with $\exists p\psi$. One can verify that for each node $\langle A \circ B \rangle$, the formula labelling the node is true in A, and false in B. Hence, the game tree is a parse tree for the formula labelling the root. □

EXAMPLE 4. Consider Figure 3. This is a game tree for pair pair $\langle M, N \rangle$ with $M = \{(\mathcal{M}, w)\}$ and $N = \{(\mathcal{N}, w)\}$, depicted, resp. left and right of the root of the tree. Designated points of models are black dots, non-designated points are open dots. Leaves are closed nodes and are depicted with thick perimeters. We further assume that in M and N all atoms are true in all worlds, and there is only one agent, a. Notice that the two initial models are bisimilar, and hence have the same epistemic theory. This implies that the FSG starting in $\langle M \circ N \rangle$ can only be won if an $\exists p$ or $\forall p$ move is played. Note that the game displayed 'corresponds' to the formula $\exists p(M_a \neg p \wedge p)$. ■

In light of Theorem 19, if we can, for every $n \in \mathbb{N}$, find classes M_n and N_n of pointed models such that the following two items hold (details omitted), then we have shown that also item 3 of Definition 9 holds for the three step proof that settles that SOPAL $\preceq_C^{exp}$ SOPEL.

1. $M_n \models \psi_n$ and $N_n \models \neg\psi_n$;
2. it takes Spoiler at least 2^n moves to win the FSG starting in $\langle M_n \circ N_n \rangle$.

We conclude this exercise in succinctness with two remarks. Firstly, we think that the notion of FSG can be extended to be played on *frames*. Secondly, although our argument goes through for structures whose accessibility relations are equivalences, the exact formalisation of the argument is more cumbersome, and can, we think, not be done on equivalence frames.

6. CONCLUSIONS

In this paper we introduced Second-order Propositional Announcement Logic: a logic to reason about arbitrary announcements in multi-agent contexts. We presented the language of SOPAL, which extends Public Announcement Logic by means of propositional quantification, and endowed it with a semantics in terms of multi-agent Kripke frames and models. We illustrated the expressivity of SOPAL by analysing relevant notions in knowledge reasoning and representation, such as preservation under arbitrary (epistemic) announcements, knowability, and successfulness. Further, we compared SOPAL with APAL by providing two notions of order between logics. Specifically, we proved that, while SOPAL and APAL are uncomparable at the model level, the former is strictly more expressive than the latter at the frame level. Moreover, we analysed the set of validities in SOPAL and provided reduction equivalences that allow to prove that SOPAL is as expressive as Second-order Propositional Epistemic Logic. As a consequence, SOPAL has a decidable model checking problem and a complete axiomatisation. Announcements make a difference nonetheless. Indeed, SOPAL is exponentially more succinct than SOPEL. We conclude that SOPAL is a succinct, rich logic, strictly more expressive than previous proposals in the area, but with nice computational properties still.

Related Literature. This paper draws from two different traditions in knowledge reasoning and representation: Second-order Propositional Modal Logic [8, 10] on one hand, and Dynamic Epistemic Logic [23] and Public Announcement Logic [18, 13] on the other. Both lines of research are well-established, with a rich literature. For reasons of space we only discuss the closest contributions. Second-order Propositional Epistemic Logic has been introduced in [4], where it is called Epistemic Quantified Boolean Logic. The designation 'second-order' used here is standard in the literature [19, 15], referring to features of propositional quantification. In [5] bisimulations for SOPEL are put forward. In the line of Public Announcement Logic, APAL has been presented in [2, 3], with the aim of capturing arbitrary announcements. We share the same motivation, but the formal analysis through propositional quantification is novel. Quantification (on bisimilar models) has been analysed in [11]. However, the resulting logic is as expressive as Epistemic Logic, and therefore strictly weaker than SOPAL.

In future work we plan to develop further the analysis of SOPAL in multi-agent contexts. In this direction it is of interest to study agents performing announcements: which announcements can an agent perform based on her knowledge? How do such announcements modify the epistemic state of other agents (including knowability and preservation)? How is the proposed framework to be modified to accommodate private communication? In this direction contributions such as Group Announcement Logic [1] are certainly relevant. More technically, SOPAL calls for the development of model-theoretic techniques, such as decision methods for satisfiability, in line with the well-known model theory of modal logic [6, 7].

Acknowledgements. Hans van Ditmarsch acknowledges support from European Research Council project EPS 313360. He is also affiliated to the Institute of Mathethematical Sciences, Chennai, as research associate.

REFERENCES

[1] T. Agotnes, P. Balbiani, H. van Ditmarsch, and P. Seban. Group announcement logic. *Journal of Applied Logic*, 8(1):62–81, 2010.

[2] P. Balbiani, A. Baltag, H. van Ditmarsch, A. Herzig, T. Hoshi, and T. de Lima. What can we achieve by arbitrary announcements?: A dynamic take on fitch's knowability. In *Proceedings of the 11th Conference on Theoretical Aspects of Rationality and Knowledge*, TARK '07, pages 42–51, New York, NY, USA, 2007. ACM.

[3] P. Balbiani, A. Baltag, H. van Ditmarsch, A. Herzig, T. Hoshi, and T. D. Lima. 'Knowable' as 'known after an announcement'. *Review of Symbolic Logic*, 1(3):305–334, 2008.

[4] F. Belardinelli and W. van der Hoek. Epistemic quantified boolean logic: Expressiveness and completeness results. In Q. Yang and M. Wooldridge, editors, *Proceedings of the Twenty-Fourth International Joint Conference on Artificial Intelligence*, pages 2748–2754. AAAI Press, 2015.

[5] F. Belardinelli and W. van der Hoek. A semantical analysis of second-order propositional modal logic. In *Proc. of the 30th AAAI Conference on Artificial Intelligence (AAAI-16)*, 2015.

[6] P. Blackburn, M. de Rijke, and Y. Venema. *Modal Logic*, volume 53 of *Cambridge Tracts in Theoretical Computer Science*. Cambridge University Press, 2001.

[7] P. Blackburn, J. van Benthem, and F. Wolter, editors. *Handbook of Modal Logic*. Elsevier, Amsterdam, the Netherlands, 2007.

[8] R. A. Bull. On modal logic with propositional quantifiers. *The journal of symbolic logic*, 34:257–263, 1969.

[9] R. Fagin, J. Halpern, Y. Moses, and M. Vardi. *Reasoning About Knowledge*. The MIT Press, 1995.

[10] K. Fine. Propositional quantifiers in modal logic. *Theoria*, 36(3):336–346, 1970.

[11] T. French. *Bisimulation quantifiers for modal logic*. PhD thesis, University of Western Australia, 2006.

[12] T. French, W. van der Hoek, P. Iliev, and B. Kooi. On the succinctness of some modal logics. *Artificial Intelligence*, 197:56–85, 2013.

[13] J. Gerbrandy and W. Groeneveld. Reasoning about information change. *Journal of Logic, Language and Information*, 6(2):147–169, 1997.

[14] J. Hintikka. *Knowledge and belief: an introduction to the logic of the two notions*. Contemporary philosophy. Cornell University Press, 1962.

[15] M. Kaminski and M. L. Tiomkin. The expressive power of second-order propositional modal logic. *Notre Dame Journal of Formal Logic*, 37(1):35–43, 1996.

[16] E. Mares and R. Goldblatt. An alternative semantics for quantified relevant logic. *The Journal of Symbolic Logic*, 71(1):163–187, 2006.

[17] J.-J. C. Meyer and W. v. d. Hoek. *Epistemic Logic for AI and Computer Science*. Cambridge University Press, New York, NY, USA, 1995.

[18] J. Plaza. Logics of public communications. In *Proc. of the 4th ISMIS*, pages 201–216. Oak Ridge National Laboratory, 1989.

[19] B. ten Cate. Expressivity of second order propositional modal logic. *J. Philosophical Logic*, 35(2):209–223, 2006.

[20] H. van Ditmarsch and B. Kooi. The secret of my success. *Synthese*, 151(2):201–232, 2006.

[21] H. van Ditmarsch and B. Kooi. *One Hundred Prisoners and a Light Bulb*. Copernicus, 2015.

[22] H. Van Ditmarsch, W. Van der Hoek, and P. Iliev. Everything is knowable–how to get to know whether a proposition is true. *Theoria*, 78(2):93–114, 2012.

[23] H. van Ditmarsch, W. van der Hoek, and B. Kooi. *Dynamic Epistemic Logic*, volume 337 of *Synthese Library*. Springer, 2007.

[24] H. P. van Ditmarsch, W. van der Hoek, and B. P. Kooi. Local properties in modal logic. *Artif. Intell.*, 187:133–155, 2012.

[25] F. van Harmelen, V. Lifschitz, and B. Porter. *Handbook of Knowledge Representation*. Elsevier Science, San Diego, USA, 2007.

[26] G. von Wright. *An Essay in Modal Logic*. North-Holland publishing Company, 1951.

A Logical Theory of Belief Dynamics for Resource-Bounded Agents

Philippe Balbiani
IRIT-CNRS
Toulouse University, France
Philippe.Balbiani@irit.fr

David Fernández-Duque
IRIT, Toulouse University
France
David.Fernandez@irit.fr

Emiliano Lorini
IRIT-CNRS
Toulouse University, France
Emiliano.Lorini@irit.fr

ABSTRACT

The paper presents a new logic for reasoning about the formation of beliefs through perception or through inference in non-omniscient resource-bounded agents. The logic distinguishes the concept of explicit belief from the concept of background knowledge. This distinction is reflected in its formal semantics and axiomatics: (i) we use a non- standard semantics putting together a neighbourhood semantics for explicit beliefs and relational semantics for background knowledge, and (ii) we have specific axioms in the logic highlighting the relationship between the two concepts. Mental operations of perceptive type and inferential type, having effects on epistemic states of agents, are primitives in the object language of the logic. At the semantic level, they are modelled as special kinds of model-update operations, in the style of dynamic epistemic logic (DEL). Results about axiomatization, decidability and complexity for the logic are given in the paper.

Categories and Subject Descriptors

I.2.4 [**Artificial Intelligence**]: Knowledge Representation Formalisms and Methods—*Modal logic*; I.2.11 [**Artificial Intelligence**]: Distributed Artificial Intelligence —*Intelligent agents*

General Terms

Theory

Keywords

Epistemic logic; cognitive agents; resource-bounded reasoning

1. INTRODUCTION

Most of existing logical theories of epistemic attitudes developed in the area of epistemic logic assume that agents are omniscient, in the sense that: (i) their beliefs are closed under conjuction or under known implication, *i.e.*, if φ is believed and ψ is believed then $\varphi \wedge \psi$ is believed and if φ is believed and $\varphi \rightarrow \psi$ is believed then ψ is believed; (ii) their explicit beliefs are closed under logical consequence (*alias* valid implication), *i.e.*, if φ is believed and φ logically implies ψ, *i.e.*, $\varphi \rightarrow \psi$ is valid, then ψ is believed as well; (iii) they believe valid sentences or tautologies; (iv) they have introspection over their beliefs, *i.e.*, if φ is believed then it is believed that φ is believed.

As pointed out by [13, 16], relaxing the assumption of logical omniscience allows for a resource-bounded agent who might fail to draw any connection between φ and its logical consequence ψ and, consequently, to believe any valid sentence and who might need time to infer and form new beliefs from her existing knowledge and beliefs.

The aim of this paper is to propose a new logic which helps in clarifying how a non-omniscient resource-bounded agent can form new beliefs either through perception or through inference from her existing knowledge and beliefs. More precisely, the aim of the paper is to introduce a dynamic logic, called DLEK (Dynamic Logic of Explicit Beliefs and Knowledge) in which programs are mental operations, either of perceptive type or of inferential type, having effects on epistemic states of resourced-bounded agents.

This is not the first attempt to build a logic of epistemic attitudes for non-omniscient agents. Logics of awareness have been studied in the recent years (see, *e.g.*, [19, 12, 10, 1]) starting from the seminal work of Fagin & Halpern [7]. These logics distinguish between explicit beliefs that are under the focus of attention and implicit beliefs, namely, potential beliefs that are derivable from what an agent explictly believes. However, the crucial difference between DLEK and existing logics of awareness is that the former provides a constructive theory of explicit beliefs, as it accounts for the perceptive and inferential steps leading from an agent's knowledge and beliefs to new beliefs. A notable exception is [21], although our conceptual framework is different (see Section 2) and, unlike the present paper, the author does not provide any axiomatization or decidability result for his logic of reasoning steps, as he only provides a semantics. Moreover, [21] does not distinguish the concept of explicit belief and the concept of background knowledge, which is the fundamental distinction of our logic DLEK.

DLEK is the first logical theory of the relationship between explicit beliefs and background knowledge, both from a static and from a dynamic perspective. This is reflected in its formal semantics and axiomatics: (i) we use a non-standard semantics putting together a neighbourhood semantics for explicit beliefs and relational semantics for background knowledge, and (ii) we have specific axioms in the logic highlighting the relationship between the two concepts.

Our constructive approach to explicit beliefs also distin-

Appears in: *Proceedings of the 15th International Conference on Autonomous Agents and Multiagent Systems (AAMAS 2016), J. Thangarajah, K. Tuyls, C. Jonker, S. Marsella (eds.), May 9–13, 2016, Singapore.*

guishes DLEK from existing logics of time-bounded reasoning which represent reasoning as a process that requires time (see, e.g., [2, 9]). Specifically, existing logics of time-bounded reasoning account for the formation of new beliefs due to the time-consuming application of inference rules to the beliefs that are under the focus of attention. However, differently from DLEK, they do not include mental operations of perceptive type and inferential type as primitives in the object language of the logic. As we will show in the paper, the advantage of having mental operations in the object language of DLEK is that we can use it to reason about the consequences of a sequence of perceptive and inferential steps on the epistemic states of agents.

The paper is organized as follows. In Section 2 we present the conceptual foundation of our logic DLEK, namely the general view about dynamics of beliefs in resource-bounded agents which underlies our formal theory. The general idea is that new beliefs can be formed either by perception or by inferring them from existing beliefs in working memory and by retrieving information from background knowledge in long-term memory. Section 3 presents the syntax and the semantics of DLEK. We will show that in DLEK perceptive and inferential steps are modelled as special kinds of model-update operations, in the style of dynamic epistemic logic (DEL) [20]. In Section 4 we present an example illustrating the expressive power of the logic. Section 5 is devoted to present an axiomatics. Finally, Section 6 presents complexity results for the satisfiability problem of the static fragment of DLEK, called LEK as well as a decidability result for the satisfiability problem of DLEK.

2. CONCEPTUAL FRAMEWORK

The cognitive architecture underlying the logic DLEK (Dynamic Logic of Explicit Beliefs and Knowledge) is represented in Figure 1. It clarifies the processing of information in human agents and human-like artificial agents.

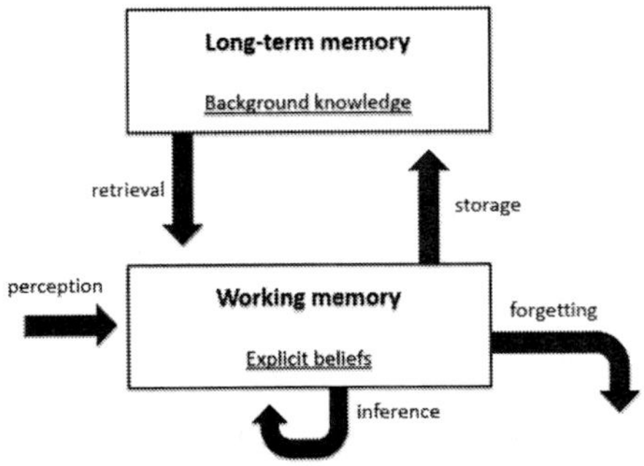

Figure 1: Cognitive view of the relationship between background knowledge and explicit beliefs

In accordance with existing psychological theories and computational models of memory and attention [3, 6, 22, 17], we assume that an agent has two kinds of information in her mind, those available in long-term memory (LTM) and those directly accessible in working memory (WM).

The information available in long-term memory, generally called *background knowledge*, includes both knowledge of specific events in the past and conceptual or causal knowledge representing the agent's unproblematic interpretation of reality.[1] For example, an agent may have background conceptual knowledge about how restaurants are organized or background causal knowledge about the relation between smoke and fire. In particular, she may know that restaurants have waiters, chairs and tables or that if smoke comes out from a window of a certain house, then there is fire inside the house.

Working memory retains information in an accessible state suitable for carrying out any kind of reasoning or decision task. In particular, following [14], we assume that the information available in an agent's working memory includes all *explicit beliefs* of the agent that occupy her consciousness and draw on her limited capacity of attention.[2] Some explicit beliefs are formed via *perception*. Formation of explicit beliefs via perception just consists of adding a new belief to the set of beliefs that are under the focus of the agent's attention. For example, an agent may look outside the window, see that it is raining outside, and thereby start believing that it is raining outside.

An agent can also use her explicit beliefs as premises of an *inference* which leads to the formation of a new belief. In some cases, formation of explicit beliefs via inference requires the *retrieval* of information from long-term memory. For example, suppose that an agent sees that smoke comes out from the window of a certain house and, as a result, she starts to explicitly believe this. The agent retrieves from her background knowledge stored in her long-term memory the information that if smoke comes out from a window of a certain house, then it means that there is fire inside the house. The agent can use this information together with the belief that smoke comes out from the window available in her working memory, to infer that there is fire inside the house and to form the corresponding belief.

Information can also be lost from working memory through *forgetting*: an agent may explicitly believe something but not believe it anymore at a later point. Information can also be removed from working memory and stored in long-term memory to make it available for a later moment. *Storage* of information in long-term memory might be necessary, given the limited capabilities of working memory.

In the next section we present the syntax and the semantics of the logic DLEK which makes precise all concepts informally discussed in this section.

3. LOGICAL FRAMEWORK

DLEK is a logic which consists of a static component and a dynamic one. The static component, called LEK, is a logic of explicit beliefs and background knowledge. The dynamic component extends the static one with dynamic operators capturing the consequences of the agents' mental operations on their explicit beliefs.

3.1 Syntax

Assume a countable set of atomic propositions Atm =

[1]In the Soar architecture [15] these two kinds of background are called, respectively, episodic memory and semantic memory.

[2] Some psychologists (e.g., [6]) distinguish focus of attention from working memory, as they assume that there might be information activated in working memory which is not under the focus of the agent's attention. For simplicity, we here assume that focus of attention and working memory are coextensive.

$\{p, q, \ldots\}$ and a finite set of agents $Agt = \{1, \ldots, n\}$. The set of groups (or coalitions) is defined to be $2^{Agt*} = 2^{Agt} \setminus \{\emptyset\}$. Elements of 2^{Agt*} are denoted by $J, J', \ldots$ We denote with *Prop* the set of all Boolean formulas built out of the set of atomic propositions *Atm*.

The language of DLEK, denoted by $\mathcal{L}_{\mathsf{DLEK}}$, is defined by the following grammar in Backus-Naur Form:

$$\begin{array}{lll} \alpha & ::= & \vdash(\varphi,\psi) \mid \cap(\varphi,\psi) \mid +\varphi \mid -\varphi \\ \varphi, \psi & ::= & p \mid \neg\varphi \mid \varphi \wedge \psi \mid \mathsf{B}_i\varphi \mid \mathsf{K}_i\varphi \mid [\alpha]\varphi \end{array}$$

where p ranges over *Atm* and i ranges over *Agt*.

The other Boolean constructions $\top$, $\bot$, $\vee$, $\rightarrow$ and $\leftrightarrow$ are defined from p, $\neg$ and $\wedge$ in the standard way.

The language of LEK, the fragment of DLEK without dynamic operators, is denoted by $\mathcal{L}_{\mathsf{LEK}}$ and defined by the following grammar in Backus-Naur Form:

$$\varphi, \psi \quad ::= \quad p \mid \neg\varphi \mid \varphi \wedge \psi \mid \mathsf{B}_i\varphi \mid \mathsf{K}_i\varphi$$

where p ranges over *Atm* and i ranges over *Agt*. The other Boolean constructions $\top$, $\bot$, $\vee$, $\rightarrow$ and $\leftrightarrow$ are defined from p, $\neg$ and $\wedge$ in the standard way. In what follows, we explain the meaning of the operators of our logic.

The formula $\mathsf{B}_i\varphi$ is read "the agent i explicitly believes that φ is true" or, more shortly, "the agent i believes that φ is true". As explained in Section 2, explicit beliefs are accessible in working memory and are the basic elements of the agents' reasoning process.

The modal operator K_i captures the notion of background knowledge discussed in Section 2. It represents the information that agent i *can* use and that is available in long term memory to infer new explicit beliefs. Some pieces of background knowledge are either conceptual or causal and represent the agent's unproblematic interpretation of reality.

Differently from explicit beliefs, background knowledge is assumed to satisfy 'omniscience' principles like closure under conjuction and known implication, closure under logical consequence and introspection. Specifically, as we will show below, K_i is nothing but the well-known S5 operator for knowledge widely used in computer science [8]. The fact that the operator K_i satisfies 'omniscience' principles is justified by the assumption that the information that an agent possesses in background defines a deductively closed *knowledge base*.

The formula $[\alpha]\psi$ has to be read "ψ holds, after the mental operation (or mental action) α is publicly performed by all agents". We distinguish four types of mental operations α which allow us to capture some of the dynamic properties of explicit beliefs and background knowledge informally described in Section 2 above: $+\varphi$, $-\varphi$, $\vdash(\varphi,\psi)$ and $\cap(\varphi,\psi)$.

$+\varphi$ and $-\varphi$ correspond, respectively, to the mental operations of forming an explicit belief via perception and forgetting an explicit belief represented in Figure 1.

$\vdash(\varphi,\psi)$ and $\cap(\varphi,\psi)$ characterize two basic operations of forming explicit beliefs via inference. Specifically, $\vdash(\varphi,\psi)$ is the mental operation which consists in inferring ψ from φ in case φ is believed and, according to an agent's background knowledge, ψ is a logical consequence of φ. In other words, by performing this mental operation, an agent tries to retrieve from her background knowledge in long-term memory the information that φ implies ψ and, if she succeeds, she starts to believe ψ. $\cap(\varphi,\psi)$ is the mental operation which consists in closing the explicit belief that φ and the explicit belief that ψ under conjunction. In other words, $\cap(\varphi,\psi)$ characterizes the mental operation of deducing $\varphi \wedge \psi$ from the explicit belief that φ and the explicit belief that ψ.

In this paper we assume that, differently from explicit beliefs, background knowledge is irrevocable in the sense of being stable over time [5]. In the conclusion, we will offer some insights on how to make background knowledge dynamic by including in our logic the operation of storing information in long-term memory, represented in Figure 1.

3.2 Semantics

The main notion in semantics is given by the following definition of LEK model which provides the basic components for the interpretation of the static logic LEK:

DEFINITION 1 (LEK MODEL). *A LEK model is a tuple* $M = (W, N, R_1, \ldots, R_n, V)$ *where:*

- W *is a set of worlds or situations;*
- *for every* $i \in Agt$, $R_i \subseteq W \times W$ *is an equivalence relation on* W*;*
- $N : Agt \times W \longrightarrow 2^{2^W}$ *is a neighbourhood function such that for all* $i \in Agt$, $w, v \in W$ *and* $X \subseteq W$*:*

  (C1) *if* $X \in N(i, w)$ *then* $X \subseteq R_i(w)$*,*

  (C2) *if* wR_iv *then* $N(i, w) = N(i, v)$*;*
- $V : W \longrightarrow 2^{Atm}$ *is a valuation function.*

For every $i \in Agt$ and $w \in W$, $R_i(w) = \{v \in W : wR_iv\}$ identifies the set of situations that agent i considers possible at world w. In cognitive terms, $R_i(w)$ can be conceived as the set of all situations that agent i *can* retrieve from her long-term memory and reason about them. More generally, $R_i(w)$ is called agent i's epistemic state at w. The reason why R_i is an equivalence relation is that it is used to model a form of omniscient background knowledge instead of omniscient background belief. The latter could be modelled by replacing the equivalence relations R_i by serial, transitive and Euclidean relations commonly used in doxastic logic to model a notion of belief.

For every $i \in Agt$ and every $w \in W$, $N(i, w)$ defines the set of all facts that agent i explicitly believes at world w, a fact being identified with a set of worlds. More precisely, if $A \in N(i, w)$ then, at world w, agent i has the fact A under the focus of her attention and believes it. $N(i, w)$ is called agent i's explicit belief set at world w.

Constraint **(C1)** just means that an agent can have explicit in her mind only facts which are compatible with her current epistemic state. According to Constraint **(C2)**, if world v is compatible with agent i's epistemic state at world w, then agent i should have the same explicit beliefs at w and v.

Truth conditions of DLEK formulas are inductively defined as follows.

DEFINITION 2 (TRUTH CONDITIONS). *Let* $M = (W, N, R_1, \ldots, R_n, V)$ *be a LEK model. Then:*

$$\begin{array}{rcl} M, w \models p & \Longleftrightarrow & p \in V(w) \\ M, w \models \neg\varphi & \Longleftrightarrow & M, w \not\models \varphi \\ M, w \models \varphi \wedge \psi & \Longleftrightarrow & M, w \models \varphi \text{ and } M, w \models \psi \\ M, w \models \mathsf{B}_i\varphi & \Longleftrightarrow & ||\varphi||^M_{i,w} \in N(i, w) \\ M, w \models \mathsf{K}_i\varphi & \Longleftrightarrow & M, v \models \varphi \text{ for all } v \in R_i(w) \\ M, w \models [\alpha]\varphi & \Longleftrightarrow & M^\alpha, w \models \varphi \end{array}$$

where

$$||\varphi||^M_{i,w} = \{v \in W : M, v \models \varphi\} \cap R_i(w)$$

and $M^\alpha = (W, N^\alpha, R_1, \ldots, R_n, V)$ *such that, for all* $i \in Agt$ *and* $w \in W$:

$$N^{+\psi}(i,w) = N(i,w) \cup \{||\psi||^M_{i,w}\}$$

$$N^{-\psi}(i,w) = N(i,w) \setminus \{||\psi||^M_{i,w}\}$$

$$N^{\vdash(\psi,\chi)}(i,w) = \begin{cases} N(i,w) \cup \{||\chi||^M_{i,w}\} & \text{if } M, w \models \mathsf{B}_i\psi \wedge \\ & \mathsf{K}_i(\psi \rightarrow \chi) \\ N(i,w) & \text{otherwise} \end{cases}$$

$$N^{\cap(\psi,\chi)}(i,w) = \begin{cases} N(i,w) \cup \{||\psi \wedge \chi||^M_{i,w}\} & \text{if } M, w \models \mathsf{B}_i\psi \wedge \\ & \mathsf{B}_i\chi \\ N(i,w) & \text{otherwise} \end{cases}$$

Note that in the mono-agent case, thanks to Constraint (**C1**), we can assume, in a given model $M = (W, N, R_1, V)$, that R_1 is the universal relation on W.

According to the previous truth conditions, an agent i explicitly believes φ at world w if and only if, at world w, agent i has the fact corresponding to the formula φ (i.e., $||\varphi||^M_{i,w}$) included in her explicit belief set. Moreover, an agent has background knowledge that φ is true if and only if φ is true in all situations that are included in the agent's epistemic state. Mental operations of the form α are formalized as model update operations that expand or contract the agents' explicit belief sets. In particular, the mental operation $+\psi$ consists in perceiving ψ and adding it to the explicit belief set, while the mental operation $-\psi$ consists in forgetting ψ and removing it from the explicit belief set. The mental operation $\vdash(\psi,\chi)$ consists in adding the explicit belief χ to an agent's explicit belief set if the agent believes ψ and has background knowledge that ψ implies χ. The mental operation $\cap(\psi,\chi)$ consists in adding the explicit belief $\psi \wedge \chi$ to an agent's explicit belief set if the agent explicitly believes both ψ and χ.

We write $\models_{\mathsf{DLEK}} \varphi$ to denote that φ is valid, i.e., φ is true at every world w of every LEK-model M. In the next section we show some interesting validities of the logic DLEK.

3.3 Some validities

The following four validities capture the basic properties of the four mental operations $\vdash(\varphi,\psi)$, $\cap(\varphi,\psi)$, $+\varphi$ and $-\varphi$ semantically defined above. Let $\varphi, \psi \in Prop$. Then:

$$\models_{\mathsf{DLEK}} (\mathsf{K}_i(\varphi \rightarrow \psi) \wedge \mathsf{B}_i\varphi) \rightarrow [\vdash(\varphi,\psi)]\mathsf{B}_i\psi \quad (1)$$

$$\models_{\mathsf{DLEK}} (\mathsf{B}_i\varphi \wedge \mathsf{B}_i\psi) \rightarrow [\cap(\varphi,\psi)]\mathsf{B}_i(\varphi \wedge \psi) \quad (2)$$

$$\models_{\mathsf{DLEK}} [+\varphi]\mathsf{B}_i\varphi \quad (3)$$

$$\models_{\mathsf{DLEK}} [-\varphi]\neg\mathsf{B}_i\varphi \quad (4)$$

For instance, according to the first validity, if φ and ψ are propositional formulas, agent i explicitly believes φ and has background knowledge that φ implies ψ then, as a consequence of the mental operation $\vdash(\varphi,\psi)$, she will start to believe ψ. According to the third validity, if φ is a propositional formula then, as a consequence of perceiving that φ is true, agent i starts to explicitly believe that φ is true.

The reason why we need to impose that φ and ψ are propositional formulas is that there are DLEK-formulas such as the Moore-like formula $p \wedge \neg \mathsf{B}_i p$ for which the previous four principles do not hold. For instance, the following formula is not valid:

$$[+(p \wedge \neg\mathsf{B}_i p)]\mathsf{B}_i(p \wedge \neg\mathsf{B}_i p)$$

It is worth noting that in the logic DLEK we can 'simulate' in a dynamic way the rule of necessitation. Indeed:

$$\models_{\mathsf{DLEK}}\varphi \text{ implies } \models_{\mathsf{DLEK}} [+\top]\mathsf{B}_i\varphi \quad (5)$$

We can also dynamically 'simulate' Axiom K for the explicit belief operator, in the case of propositional formulas. Let $\varphi, \psi \in Prop$. Then, we have the following validity:

$$\models_{\mathsf{DLEK}}(\mathsf{B}_i\varphi \wedge \mathsf{B}_i(\varphi \rightarrow \psi)) \rightarrow [\cap(\varphi,\varphi \rightarrow \psi)][\vdash(\varphi \wedge \psi,\psi)]\mathsf{B}_i\psi \quad (6)$$

4. EXAMPLE

In this section we are going to illustrate our logic DLEK with the help of a concrete example. We are interested in describing the dynamics of explicit beliefs in a multi-agent scenario.

The scenario goes as follows. There are two robotic assistants, say robot A (Anne) and robot B (Bob), who have to take care of a person. The two robots are resource-bounded in the sense that they have background knowledge and (non-omniscient) explicit beliefs and form new explicit beliefs by means of the mental operations highlighted in Figure 1 in Section 2. The person communicates with the robots via a coloured electric light which can be either red or green. The communication code is the following one: (i) if the electric light is red (atom r) then it means that the person needs help (atom h), and (ii) if the electric is green (atom g) then it means that the person is having a rest and wants not to be bothered (atom b). We assume that:

H1. robot A has full knowledge about the communication code as she knows that r implies h and that g implies b,

H2. robot B has only partial knowledge about the communication code as he knows that r implies h but he does not know that g implies b, and

H3. robot A and robot B have common knowledge that they share a part of the communication code, namely that each of them knows that r implies h.

Thus, let us suppose that $Agt = \{A, B\}$ and $Atm = \{r, g, h, b\}$. We represent the initial situation by the minimal LEK model satisfying the previous hypothesis H1, H2 and H3 and which only excludes the impossible situations in which the electric light is both red and green and the person needs help and takes a rest at the same time. This model is the tuple $\mathtt{MR} = (W, N, R_A, R_B, V)$ (where MR stands for 'model of the robots') such that:

- $W = \{w_1, w_2, w_3, w_4, w_5, w_6, w_7, w_8, w_9\}$;
- $N(i,w) = \emptyset$ for all $i \in Agt$ and for all $w \in W$;
- the quotient set of W by R_A is $\{\{w_1, w_2, w_3, w_4, w_5\}, \{w_6, w_7\}, \{w_8, w_9\}\}$;

- the quotient set of W by R_B is $\{\{w_1, w_2, w_3, w_4, w_5, w_6, w_7\}, \{w_8, w_9\}\}$;

- $V(w_1) = \{r, h\}$ $V(w_2) = \{h\}$ $V(w_3) = \{g, b\}$ $V(w_4) = \{b\}$ $V(w_5) = \emptyset$ $V(w_6) = \{g\}$ $V(w_7) = \{g, h\}$ $V(w_8) = \{r\}$ $V(w_9) = \{r, b\}$.

The fact that $N(i, w) = \emptyset$ for all $i \in Agt$ and for all $w \in W$ just means that in the initial situation the robots do not have any explicit belief in their short-term memories.

Let us assume that w_1 is the actual situation in which the electric light is red and the person needs help.

The first thing to observe is that in the actual situation the hypothesis H1 and H2 are both satisfied. Indeed, as for H1, we have:

$$\texttt{MR}, w_1 \models \mathsf{K}_A(r \rightarrow h) \wedge \mathsf{K}_A(g \rightarrow b).$$

As for H2, we have:

$$\texttt{MR}, w_1 \models \mathsf{K}_B(r \rightarrow h) \wedge \neg\mathsf{K}_B(g \rightarrow b).$$

In order to specify hypothesis H3, let $\mathsf{EK}_J\varphi$ be an abbreviation of $\bigwedge_{i \in J} \mathsf{K}_i\varphi$, standing for "every agent in J has background knowledge that φ". Then, let us define $\mathsf{EK}_J^k\varphi$ by induction for every natural number $k \in \mathbb{N}$:

$$\mathsf{EK}_J^0\varphi \stackrel{\text{def}}{=} \varphi$$

and for all $k \geq 1$:

$$\mathsf{EK}_J^k\varphi \stackrel{\text{def}}{=} \mathsf{EK}_J(\mathsf{EK}_J^{k-1}\varphi).$$

For every natural number $n \in \mathbb{N}$, let $\mathsf{MK}_J^n\varphi$ be an abbreviation of $\bigwedge_{1 \leq k \leq n} \mathsf{EK}_J^k\varphi$. $\mathsf{MK}_J^n\varphi$ expresses J's background mutual knowledge that φ up to n iterations, *i.e.*, everyone in J has background knowledge that φ, everyone in J has background knowledge that everyone in J has background knowledge that φ, and so on until level n. We omit the full definitions of the universal explicit belief operator EB_J (with $\mathsf{EB}_J\varphi$ standing for "every agent in J explicitly believes that φ") and of the mutual explicit belief operator MB_J^n (with $\mathsf{MB}_J^n\varphi$ standing for "the agents in J have mutual explicit belief that φ up to n iterations") since they can be defined exactly in the same way as the universal knowledge and mutual knowledge operators, starting from the individual explicit knowledge operators.

The previous hypothesis H3 holds in the initial situation since, for every $n \in \mathbb{N}$, we have:

$$\texttt{MR}, w_1 \models \mathsf{MK}_{\{A,B\}}^n \mathsf{EK}_{\{A,B\}}(r \rightarrow h).$$

Let us suppose that the person switches on the red light in order to signal to the two robots that she needs help. This event is represented by the mental operation $+r$ which leads from model $\texttt{MR}$ to the updated model $\texttt{MR}^{+r} = (W, N^{+r}, R_A, R_B, V)$ such that:

$N^{+r}(A, w_1) = \{\{w_1\}\}$, $N^{+r}(A, w_2) = \{\{w_1\}\}$,
$N^{+r}(A, w_3) = \{\{w_1\}\}$, $N^{+r}(A, w_4) = \{\{w_1\}\}$,
$N^{+r}(A, w_5) = \{\{w_1\}\}$, $N^{+r}(A, w_6) = \emptyset$,
$N^{+r}(A, w_7) = \emptyset$, $N^{+r}(A, w_8) = \{\{w_8, w_9\}\}$,
$N^{+r}(A, w_9) = \{\{w_8, w_9\}\}$, $N^{+r}(B, w_1) = \{\{w_1\}\}$,
$N^{+r}(B, w_2) = \{\{w_1\}\}$, $N^{+r}(B, w_3) = \{\{w_1\}\}$,
$N^{+r}(B, w_4) = \{\{w_1\}\}$, $N^{+r}(B, w_5) = \{\{w_1\}\}$,
$N^{+r}(B, w_6) = \{\{w_1\}\}$, $N^{+r}(B, w_7) = \{\{w_1\}\}$,
$N^{+r}(B, w_8) = \{\{w_8, w_9\}\}$, $N^{+r}(B, w_9) = \{\{w_8, w_9\}\}$.

It is easy to check that in the new situation, after the mental operation $+r$ has been executed, the two robots explicitly believe that the light is red. That is:

$$\texttt{MR}^{+r}, w_1 \models \mathsf{EB}_{\{A,B\}}r.$$

However, the mental operation is not sufficient to guarantee that the robots believe that the person needs helps. Indeed, we have:

$$\texttt{MR}^{+r}, w_1 \models \neg\mathsf{B}_A h \wedge \neg\mathsf{B}_B h.$$

It is by trying to infer that the person needs help from the fact that she switched on the red light, represented by $\vdash(r,h)$, that the robots can form this explicit belief. The mental operation $\vdash(r,h)$ leads from model $\texttt{MR}^{+r}$ to the updated model $(\texttt{MR}^{+r})^{\vdash(r,h)} = (W, (N^{+r})^{\vdash(r,h)}, R_A, R_B, V)$ such that:
$(N^{+r})^{\vdash(r,h)}(A, w_1) = \{\{w_1\}, \{w_1, w_2\}\}$,
$(N^{+r})^{\vdash(r,h)}(A, w_2) = \{\{w_1\}, \{w_1, w_2\}\}$,
$(N^{+r})^{\vdash(r,h)}(A, w_3) = \{\{w_1\}, \{w_1, w_2\}\}$,
$(N^{+r})^{\vdash(r,h)}(A, w_4) = \{\{w_1\}, \{w_1, w_2\}\}$,
$(N^{+r})^{\vdash(r,h)}(A, w_5) = \{\{w_1\}, \{w_1, w_2\}\}$,
$(N^{+r})^{\vdash(r,h)}(A, w_6) = \{\emptyset\}$,
$(N^{+r})^{\vdash(r,h)}(A, w_7) = \{\emptyset\}$,
$(N^{+r})^{\vdash(r,h)}(A, w_8) = \{\{w_8, w_9\}\}$,
$(N^{+r})^{\vdash(r,h)}(A, w_9) = \{\{w_8, w_9\}\}$,
$(N^{+r})^{\vdash(r,h)}(B, w_1) = \{\{w_1\}, \{w_1, w_2, w_7\}\}$,
$(N^{+r})^{\vdash(r,h)}(B, w_2) = \{\{w_1\}, \{w_1, w_2, w_7\}\}$,
$(N^{+r})^{\vdash(r,h)}(B, w_3) = \{\{w_1\}, \{w_1, w_2, w_7\}\}$,
$(N^{+r})^{\vdash(r,h)}(B, w_4) = \{\{w_1\}, \{w_1, w_2, w_7\}\}$,
$(N^{+r})^{\vdash(r,h)}(B, w_5) = \{\{w_1\}, \{w_1, w_2, w_7\}\}$,
$(N^{+r})^{\vdash(r,h)}(B, w_6) = \{\{w_1\}, \{w_1, w_2, w_7\}\}$,
$(N^{+r})^{\vdash(r,h)}(B, w_7) = \{\{w_1\}, \{w_1, w_2, w_7\}\}$,
$(N^{+r})^{\vdash(r,h)}(B, w_8) = \{\{w_8, w_9\}\}$,
$(N^{+r})^{\vdash(r,h)}(B, w_9) = \{\{w_8, w_9\}\}$.

It is easy to check that in the new situation, after the mental operation $\vdash(r,h)$ has been executed, the two robots explicitly believe that the person needs help. That is:

$$(\texttt{MR}^{+r})^{\vdash(r,h)}, w_1 \models \mathsf{EB}_{\{A,B\}}h.$$

To sum up, we have the following which holds:

$$\texttt{MR}, w_1 \models [+r]\mathsf{EB}_{\{A,B\}}r \wedge [+r](\neg\mathsf{B}_A h \wedge \neg\mathsf{B}_B h) \wedge [+r][\vdash(r,h)]\mathsf{EB}_{\{A,B\}}h.$$

It is worth noting that the sequence of the two mental operations $+r$ and $\vdash(r,h)$ is not sufficient for the robots to acquire the explicit common belief that the person needs help. Indeed, it is to check that the following holds:

$$(\texttt{MR}^{+r})^{\vdash(r,h)}, w_1 \models \neg\mathsf{B}_A\mathsf{B}_B h \wedge \neg\mathsf{B}_B\mathsf{B}_A h.$$

In order to obtain such explicit common belief, the two robots need to perform the two additional mental operations $\vdash(h,\mathsf{B}_A h)$ and $\vdash(h,\mathsf{B}_B h)$ (i.e., trying to infer that robot A/robot B explicitly believes that h from the fact that h holds), no matter the order in which they are executed. Indeed, for every $n \in \mathbb{N}$, we have:

$$\texttt{MR}, w_1 \models [+r][\vdash(r,h)][\vdash(r,\mathsf{B}_A h)][\vdash(r,\mathsf{B}_B h)]\mathsf{MB}_{\{A,B\}}^n h,$$

$$\texttt{MR}, w_1 \models [+r][\vdash(r,h)][\vdash(r,\mathsf{B}_B h)][\vdash(r,\mathsf{B}_A h)]\mathsf{MB}_{\{A,B\}}^n h.$$

It is just routine to check that the mental operations $+g$ and $\vdash(g,b)$ are also sufficient for robot A to start to believe b explicitly after performing them, but they are not sufficient for robot B since he does not have background knowledge that g implies b. In formal terms, we have:

$$\texttt{MR}, w_1 \models [+g][\vdash(g,b)]\mathsf{B}_A b,$$
$$\texttt{MR}, w_1 \models [+g][\vdash(g,b)]\neg\mathsf{B}_B b.$$

5. AXIOMATIZATION

Let us now present sound and complete axiomatizations for the logic LEK and its dynamic extension DLEK.

DEFINITION 3. *We define LEK to be the extension of classical propositional logic given by the following rules and axioms:*

$$
\begin{array}{lr}
(\mathsf{K}_i\varphi \wedge \mathsf{K}_i(\varphi \to \psi)) \to \mathsf{K}_i\psi & (\mathbf{K}_{\mathsf{K}_i}) \\
\mathsf{K}_i\varphi \to \varphi & (\mathbf{T}_{\mathsf{K}_i}) \\
\mathsf{K}_i\varphi \to \mathsf{K}_i\mathsf{K}_i\varphi & (\mathbf{4}_{\mathsf{K}_i}) \\
\neg\mathsf{K}_i\varphi \to \mathsf{K}_i\neg\mathsf{K}_i\varphi & (\mathbf{5}_{\mathsf{K}_i}) \\
(\mathsf{B}_i\varphi \wedge \mathsf{K}_i(\varphi \leftrightarrow \psi)) \to \mathsf{B}_i\psi & (\mathbf{Mix1}_{\mathsf{K}_i,\mathsf{B}_i}) \\
\mathsf{B}_i\varphi \to \mathsf{K}_i\mathsf{B}_i\varphi & (\mathbf{Mix2}_{\mathsf{K}_i,\mathsf{B}_i}) \\
\dfrac{\varphi}{\mathsf{K}_i\varphi} & (\mathbf{Nec}_{\mathsf{K}_i})
\end{array}
$$

The axiomatics of the logic DLEK includes all principles of the logic LEK *plus* a set of reduction axioms and the rule of replacement of equivalents.

DEFINITION 4. *We define DLEK to be the extension of LEK generated by the following axioms:*

$$
\begin{array}{lr}
[\alpha]p \leftrightarrow p & (\mathbf{Red}_p) \\
[\alpha]\neg\varphi \leftrightarrow \neg[\alpha]\varphi & (\mathbf{Red}_\neg) \\
[\alpha](\varphi \wedge \psi) \leftrightarrow ([\alpha]\varphi \wedge [\alpha]\psi) & (\mathbf{Red}_\wedge) \\
[\alpha]\mathsf{K}_i\varphi \leftrightarrow \mathsf{K}_i[\alpha]\varphi & (\mathbf{Red}_{\mathsf{K}_i}) \\
[+\varphi]\mathsf{B}_i\psi \leftrightarrow (\mathsf{B}_i[+\varphi]\psi \vee \mathsf{K}_i([+\varphi]\psi \leftrightarrow \varphi)) & (\mathbf{Red}_{\mathsf{B}_i,+}) \\
[-\varphi]\mathsf{B}_i\psi \leftrightarrow (\mathsf{B}_i[-\varphi]\psi \vee \neg\mathsf{K}_i([-\varphi]\psi \leftrightarrow \varphi)) & (\mathbf{Red}_{\mathsf{B}_i,-}) \\
[\vdash(\varphi,\psi)]\mathsf{B}_i\chi \leftrightarrow \Big(\mathsf{B}_i[\vdash(\varphi,\psi)]\chi \vee & \\
\quad ((\mathsf{B}_i\varphi \wedge \mathsf{K}_i(\varphi \to \psi)) \wedge & \\
\quad \mathsf{K}_i([\vdash(\varphi,\psi)]\chi \leftrightarrow \psi))\Big) & (\mathbf{Red}_{\mathsf{B}_i,\vdash}) \\
[\cap(\varphi,\psi)]\mathsf{B}_i\chi \leftrightarrow \Big(\mathsf{B}_i[\cap(\varphi,\psi)]\chi \vee & \\
\quad ((\mathsf{B}_i\varphi \wedge \mathsf{B}_i\psi) \wedge & \\
\quad \mathsf{K}_i([\cap(\varphi,\psi)]\chi \leftrightarrow (\varphi \wedge \psi)))\Big) & (\mathbf{Red}_{\mathsf{B}_i,\cap})
\end{array}
$$

and the following rule of inference:

$$\frac{\psi_1 \leftrightarrow \psi_2}{\varphi \leftrightarrow \varphi[\psi_1/\psi_2]} \qquad (\mathbf{RRE})$$

We write DLEK $\vdash \varphi$ to denote the fact that φ is a theorem of DLEK.

It is straightforward to check that all axioms are valid and all rules preserve validity in the class of DLEK-models, from which the following is an immediate consequence:

LEMMA 1. *The logics LEK and DLEK are sound for the class of LEK-models.*

Our goal now is to prove that LEK is strongly complete for its intended semantics. We will achieve this by a fairly standard canonical-model argument, although the neighborhood structure will require some care.

DEFINITION 5 (CANONICAL LEK MODEL). *We define the canonical LEK model*

$$M_c = (W_c, N_c, R_{c1} \ldots, R_{cn}, V_c)$$

where:

- *W_c is the set of all maximal consistent subsets of $\mathcal{L}_{LEK}$.*
- *$wR_{ci}v$ if and only if, for all formulas φ and all agents i, $\mathsf{K}_i\varphi \in w$ if and only if $\mathsf{K}_i\varphi \in v$.*
- *In order to define N_c, for $w \in W$ and $\varphi \in \mathcal{L}_{LEK}$, first define*

  $$A_\varphi(i,w) = \{v \in R_i(w) : \varphi \in v\}.$$

  Then, define N_c by letting

  $$N_c(i,w) = \{A_\varphi(i,w) : \mathsf{B}_i\varphi \in w\}.$$

- *Finally, we define the valuation V_c by $w \in V_c(p)$ if and only if $p \in w$.*

The following is standard and we omit the proof:

LEMMA 2. *The structure M_c defined above is a $\mathcal{L}_{LEK}$-model. Moreover, if $w \in W_c$ and $\varphi \in \mathcal{L}_{LEK}$, then*

1. *$\mathsf{K}_i\varphi \in w$ if and only if, for every v such that $wR_{ci}v$, $\varphi \in v$, and*
2. *if $wR_{ci}v$ and $\mathsf{B}_i\varphi \in w$, then $\mathsf{B}_i\varphi \in v$.*

We also need to prove that M_c has a somewhat less familiar property. This will be used later in the truth lemma, for the case of B_i.

LEMMA 3. *For every $w \in W_c$ and $\mathsf{B}_i\varphi, \mathsf{B}_i\psi \in \mathcal{L}_{LEK}$, if $\mathsf{B}_i\varphi \in w$ but $\mathsf{B}_i\psi \notin w$, it follows that there is $v \in R_{ci}(w)$ such that either $\varphi \in v$ but $\neg\psi \in v$, or $\neg\varphi \in v$ but $\psi \in v$.*

PROOF. Let $w \in W_c$ and φ, ψ be such that $\mathsf{B}_i\varphi \in w$, $\mathsf{B}_i\psi \notin w$. Towards a contradiction, assume that for every $v \in R_{ci}(w)$, either $\varphi, \psi \in v$ or $\neg\varphi, \neg\psi \in v$; then, it follows from Lemma 2 that $\mathsf{K}_i(\varphi \leftrightarrow \psi) \in w$, so that by Axiom $(\mathbf{Mix1}_{\mathsf{K}_i,\mathsf{B}_i})$, $\mathsf{B}_i\psi \in w$, contrary to our assumption. □

With this, we may state and prove our version of the Truth Lemma:

LEMMA 4. *For every $\varphi \in \mathcal{L}_{LEK}$ and every $w \in W_c$, $\varphi \in w$ if and only if $M_c, w \models \varphi$.*

PROOF. The proof proceeds by a standard induction on the construction of φ. All cases are routine except $\varphi = \mathsf{B}_i\psi$.

First assume that $\mathsf{B}_i\psi \in w$. Then, $A_\psi(i,w) \in N_c(i,w)$. But,

$$A_\psi(i,w) = \{v \in R_i(w) : \psi \in v\} \overset{\text{IH}}{=} \|\psi\| \cap R_i(w).$$

Thus, $M_c, w \models \mathsf{B}_i\psi$.

Now, suppose $\mathsf{B}_i\psi \notin w$, so that $\neg\mathsf{B}_i\psi \in w$. We must check that $\|\psi\| \cap R_{ci}(w) \notin N(i,w)$. Choose an arbitrary set $A \in N(i,w)$; by definition, $A = A_\theta(i,w)$ for some θ with

$\mathsf{B}_i\theta \in w$. By Lemma 3, there is some $v \in R_i(w)$ such that $\psi, \neg\theta \in v$ or $\neg\psi, \theta \in v$; in the first case, this shows using the induction hypothesis that $v \in (\|\psi\| \cap R_i(w)) \setminus A_\theta(i, w)$, while in the second we obtain $v \in A_\theta(i,w) \setminus (\|\psi\| \cap R_i(w))$. In either case we obtain $A_\theta(i,w) \neq \|\psi\| \cap R_i(w)$, and since $A = A_\theta(i,w)$ was an arbitrary element of $N(i,w)$, we conclude that $\|\psi\| \cap R_i(w) \notin N(i,w)$ and thus $M_c, w \not\models \mathsf{B}_i\psi$. □

We are now ready to prove that the static LEK is strongly complete.

THEOREM 1. *LEK is strongly complete for the class of LEK models.*

PROOF. Any consistent set of formulas Φ may be extended to a maximal consistent set of formulas $w_* \in W_c$, and $M_c, w_* \models \Phi$ by Lemma 4. □

The strong completeness of DLEK follows from this result, in view of the fact that the reduction axioms may be used to find, for any DLEK formula, a provably equivalent LEK formula.

LEMMA 5. *If φ is any formula of $\mathcal{L}_{DLEK}$, there is a formula $\widetilde{\varphi}$ in $\mathcal{L}_{LEK}$ such that $DLEK \vdash \varphi \leftrightarrow \widetilde{\varphi}$.*

PROOF. This follows by a routine induction on φ using the reduction axioms and the rule of replacement of equivalents (**RRE**) from Definition 4. □

As a corollary, we get the following:

THEOREM 2. *DLEK is strongly complete for the class of LEK models.*

PROOF. If Γ is a consistent set of $\mathcal{L}_{DLEK}$ formulas, then $\widetilde{\Gamma} = \{\widetilde{\varphi} : \varphi \in \Gamma\}$ is a consistent set of $\mathcal{L}_{LEK}$ formulas (since DLEK is an extension of LEK), and hence by Theorem 1, there is a model M with a world w such that $M, w \models \widetilde{\Gamma}$. But, since DLEK is sound and for each $\varphi \in \Gamma$, DLEK $\vdash \varphi \leftrightarrow \widetilde{\varphi}$, it follows that $M, w \models \Gamma$. □

Thus our logics are strongly complete, but the construction we have given will in general produce infinite models. In the next section, we are going move from axiomatics to complexity of the satisfiability problem.

6. COMPLEXITY

In this section we will study the computability of the satisfiability problem of LEK: given a formula φ, determine whether φ is satisfiable. We will also provide a decidability result of the satisfiability problem of DLEK. We first consider the single-agent case and move then to the multi-agent case. Below, $card(A)$ denotes the cardinality of the set A.

6.1 Mono-agent case

Firstly, assume $card(Agt) = 1$. Let φ be a satisfiable formula. Let $M = (W, N, V)$ be a model and $w \in W$ be such that $M, w \models \varphi$. Let $\mathsf{K}\psi_1, \ldots, \mathsf{K}\psi_m$ and $\mathsf{B}\chi_1, \ldots, \mathsf{B}\chi_n$ be lists of the set of all subformulas of φ of the form $\mathsf{K}\psi$ and $\mathsf{B}\chi$. Let $\hat{\mathsf{K}} = \{i : 1 \leq i \leq m \;\&\; M, w \not\models \mathsf{K}\psi_i\}$, $\hat{\mathsf{B}}^+ = \{j : 1 \leq j \leq n \;\&\; M, w \models \mathsf{B}\chi_j\}$ and $\hat{\mathsf{B}}^- = \{k : 1 \leq k \leq n \;\&\; M, w \not\models \mathsf{B}\chi_k\}$. For all $i \in \hat{\mathsf{K}}$, let $v_i \in W$ be such that $M, v_i \not\models \psi_i$. Such v_i exists because $M, w \not\models \mathsf{K}\psi_i$. For all $j \in \hat{\mathsf{B}}^+$, let $A_j \in N$ be such that $A_j = \{v \in W : M, v \models \chi_j\}$. Such A_j exists because $M, w \models \mathsf{B}\chi_j$. For all $j \in \hat{\mathsf{B}}^+$ and for all $k \in \hat{\mathsf{B}}^-$, let $u_{j,k} \in W$ be such that $M, u_{j,k} \not\models \chi_j \leftrightarrow \chi_k$. Such $u_{j,k}$ exists because $M, w \models \mathsf{B}\chi_j$ and $M, w \not\models \mathsf{B}\chi_k$. Let $M' = (W', N', V')$ be the model defined as follows:

- $W' = \{w\} \cup \{v_i : i \in \hat{\mathsf{K}}\} \cup \{u_{j,k} : j \in \hat{\mathsf{B}}^+ \;\&\; k \in \hat{\mathsf{B}}^-\}$,
- $N' = \{A_j \cap W' : j \in \hat{\mathsf{B}}^+\}$,
- for all $p \in VAR$, $V'(p) = V(p) \cap W'$.

Obviously, $card(W')$ and $card(N')$ are polynomial in the size of φ. Let Φ be the closure under single negations of the set of all φ's subformulas.

LEMMA 6. *Let φ be a formula. If $\varphi \in \Phi$ then for all $s \in W'$, $M, s \models \varphi$ iff $M', s \models \varphi$.*

PROOF. By induction on φ. We only consider the cases $\varphi = \mathsf{B}\chi$.
Suppose $M, s \models \mathsf{B}\chi$ and $M', s \not\models \mathsf{B}\chi$. Let $j \in \hat{\mathsf{B}}^+$ be such that $\mathsf{B}\chi = \mathsf{B}\chi_j$. Hence, $A_j = \{t \in W : M, t \models \chi\}$. By induction hypothesis, $A_j \cap W' = \{t \in W' : M', t \models \chi\}$. Thus, $M', s \models \mathsf{B}\chi$: a contradiction.
Suppose $M', s \models \mathsf{B}\chi$ and $M, s \not\models \mathsf{B}\chi$. Let $j \in \hat{\mathsf{B}}^+$ be such that $A_j \cap W' = \{t \in W' : M', t \models \chi\}$. By induction hypothesis, $A_j \cap W' = \{t \in W' : M, t \models \chi\}$. Let $k \in \hat{\mathsf{B}}^-$ be such that $\mathsf{B}\chi = \mathsf{B}\chi_k$. Remember that $A_j = \{t \in W : M, t \models \chi_j\}$. Moreover, $u_{j,k} \in W'$ is such that $M, u_{j,k} \not\models \chi_j$ and $M, u_{j,k} \not\models \chi_k$, or $M, u_{j,k} \not\models \chi_j$ and $M, u_{j,k} \models \chi_k$. In the former case, $u_{j,k} \in A_j \cap W'$. Hence, $M, u_{j,k} \models \chi$: a contradiction. In the latter case, $u_{j,k} \in A_j \cap W'$. Thus, $M, u_{j,k} \models \chi_j$: a contradiction. □

THEOREM 3. *If $card(Agt) = 1$ then satisfiability problem of LEK is NP-complete.*

PROOF. Membership in NP follows from Lemma 6. NP-hardness follows from the NP-hardness of classical propositional logic. □

6.2 Multi-agent case

Our study of the computability in the multi-agent case will be based on the modal tableaux approach developed by Halpern and Moses [11]. Assume $card(Agt) \geq 2$. For all formulas φ, let $SF(\varphi)$ be the closure under single negations of the set of all subformulas of φ.

Modal tableaux.

A set $\mathcal{T}$ of formulas is said to be fully expanded if for all formulas φ, if $\varphi \in \mathcal{T}$ then for all formulas ψ, if $\psi \in SF(\varphi)$ then either $\psi \in \mathcal{T}$, or $\neg\psi \in \mathcal{T}$, $SF(\varphi)$ denoting the closure under single negations of the set of all φ's subformulas. A propositional tableau is a set $\mathcal{T}$ of formulas such that the following conditions holds: (i) for all formulas φ, if $\neg\neg\varphi \in \mathcal{T}$ then $\varphi \in \mathcal{T}$; (ii) for all formulas φ, ψ, if $\neg(\varphi \vee \psi) \in \mathcal{T}$ then $\neg\varphi \in \mathcal{T}$ and $\neg\psi \in \mathcal{T}$; (iii) for all formulas φ, ψ, if $\varphi \vee \psi \in \mathcal{T}$ then either $\varphi \in \mathcal{T}$, or $\psi \in \mathcal{T}$. A propositional tableau $\mathcal{T}$ is said to be blatantly consistent iff for all formulas φ, either $\varphi \notin \mathcal{T}$, or $\neg\varphi \notin \mathcal{T}$.

A modal tableau is a structure of the form $\mathcal{T} = (W, R, L)$ where W is a nonempty set of states (with typical members denoted w, v, etc), R is a function associating a binary relation R_i on W to each $i \in Agt$ and L is a function assigning to each $w \in W$ a blatantly consistent and fully expanded propositional tableau $L(w)$ such that for all $w \in W$, the following conditions holds: (i) for all formulas φ, if $\neg \mathsf{K}_i\varphi \in L(w)$ then there exists $v \in R_i(w)$ such that $\neg\varphi \in L(v)$; (ii) for all formulas φ, if $\mathsf{B}_i\varphi \in L(w)$ then for all formulas ψ, if $\neg\mathsf{B}_i\psi \in L(w)$ then there exists $v \in R_i(w)$ such that either $\varphi \in L(v)$ and $\neg\psi \in L(v)$, or $\neg\varphi \in L(v)$ and $\psi \in L(v)$; (iii) for all formulas φ, if $\mathsf{K}_i\varphi \in L(w)$ then for all $v \in (R_i \cup R_i^{-1})^\star(w)$, $\varphi \in L(v)$ and $\mathsf{K}_i\varphi \in L(v)$; (iv) for all formulas φ, if $\mathsf{B}_i\varphi \in L(w)$ then for all $v \in (R_i \cup R_i^{-1})^\star(w)$, $\mathsf{B}_i\varphi \in L(v)$. For all formulas φ, let $L^{-1}(\varphi) = \{w : w \in W \,\&\, \varphi \in L(w)\}$. We shall say that a modal tableau $\mathcal{T} = (W, R, L)$ is a modal tableau for a formula φ if $L^{-1}(\varphi) \neq \emptyset$.

From models to modal tableaux.

Given a model $M = (W, R, N, V)$, let $\mathcal{T}' = (W', R', L')$ be defined as follows: $W' = W$, $R'_i = R_i$ for each $i \in Agt$, L' is the function assigning to each $w \in W'$ the propositional tableau $L'(w) = \{\varphi : M, w \models \varphi\}$. The proof that $\mathcal{T}'$ is a modal tableau is easy. As a result,

PROPOSITION 1. *Let φ be a formula. If φ is satisfiable then there exists a modal tableau for φ.*

From modal tableaux to models.

Given a modal tableau $\mathcal{T} = (W, R, L)$, let

$$M' = (W', R', N', V')$$

be defined as follows: $W' = W$, $R'_i = (R_i \cup R_i^{-1})^\star$ for each $i \in Agt$, $N'_i(w) = \{(R_i \cup R_i^{-1})^\star(w) \cap L^{-1}(\varphi) : \mathsf{B}_i\varphi \in L(w)\}$ for each $w \in W$ and for each $i \in Agt$, V' is the function assigning to each $p \in Atm$ the subset $V'(p) = \{w : w \in W \,\&\, p \in L(w)\}$ of W'. The proof that $\mathcal{T}'$ is a model is easy. Moreover, one can prove by induction on φ that for all $w \in W$, $\varphi \in L(s)$ iff $M', s \models \varphi$. As a result,

PROPOSITION 2. *Let φ be a formula. If there exists a modal tableau for φ then φ is satisfiable.*

Membership in PSPACE.

By Propositions 1 and 2, satisfiability is reducible to the following decision problem (MT): given a formula φ, determine whether there exists a modal tableau for φ. Based on the tools and techniques developed in ordinary epistemic logics by Halpern and Moses [11], one can design an algorithm that tries to construct a modal tableau for a given formula φ. The main properties of such algorithm are:

- For all given formulas φ, the above algorithm terminates and runs in polynomial space,
- for all given formulas φ, the algorithm returns "there is a modal tableau for φ" iff there is a modal tableau for φ.

PROPOSITION 3. *There is an algorithm for deciding satisfiability that runs in polynomial space.*

As a result,

THEOREM 4. *If $card(Agt) \geq 2$ then satisfiability problem of LEK is PSPACE-complete.*

PROOF. Membership in PSPACE follows from the above discussion. PSPACE-hardness follows from the PSPACE-hardness of multi-agent epistemic logic. □

The reduction axioms and the rule of replacement of equivalents in Definition 4 may then be used to give a decision procedure for the satisfiability of DLEK; however, due to exponential blow-up in the size of formulas, this algorithm would no longer remain in PSPACE without modification. Thus we will state only the following:

COROLLARY 1. *The satisfiability problem of DLEK is decidable.*

PROOF. Immediate from the decidability of LEK and the fact that, given a formula φ of $\mathcal{L}_{\mathsf{DLEK}}$, the formula $\widetilde{\varphi}$ is clearly computable from φ. □

However, we do not believe that such a procedure would be optimal, and indeed conjecture that DLEK is in PSPACE. We leave the computation of its precise complexity for future work.

7. CONCLUSION

Let's take stock. In the paper we have introduced DLEK, a logical theory of belief dynamics for resource-bounded agents inspired by existing psychological theories of human memory. We have provided decidability and complexity results for DLEK as well as for its static fragment LEK.

Directions of future research are manifold. On the conceptual level, we plan to complete the conceptual framework described in Section 2 by extending the family of mental operations with operations of *storage* of information in long-term memory. We believe that these kinds of operations can be modelled as special kinds of epistemic actions in the DEL sense. Specifically, a storage operation modifies an agent's background knowledge by restricting the epistemic relation R_i to worlds in which the information φ to be stored is true, under the condition that this information is already available in the agent's working memory and explicitly believed by the agent.

On the technical level, as emphasized in Section 6, we plan to obtain a result about complexity of the satisfiability problem of DLEK. In particular, we plan to prove that this problem is PSPACE-complete by appropriately adapting to our framework the technique proposed by Lutz [18] for studying complexity of the satisfiability problem of public announcement logic (PAL). We also plan to refine our approach by relaxing the assumption that mental operations are performed by all agents and that this is a public fact. To this aim, we will have to introduce a notion of action model in this sense of [4] which allows us to model a *private* form of mental operation (i.e., an operation which occurs in the mind of a specific agent without the other agents being aware of this).

REFERENCES

[1] T. Ågotnes and N. Alechina. A logic for reasoning about knowledge of unawareness. *Journal of Logic, Language and Information*, 23(2):197–217, 2014.

[2] N. Alechina, B. Logan, and M. Whitsey. A complete and decidable logic for resource-bounded agents. In *Proceedings of AAMAS 2014*, pages 606–613. IEEE Computer Society, 2004.

[3] A. D. Baddeley and G. Hitch. Working memory. In G. H. Bower, editor, *The psychology of learning and motivation: Advances in research and theory*, pages 47–89. Academic Press, 1974.

[4] A. Baltag and L. S. Moss. Logics for Epistemic Programs. *Synthese*, 139(2):165–224, 2004.

[5] A. Baltag and S. Smets. A qualitative theory of dynamic interactive belief revision. In *Proceedings of LOFT 7*, pages 13–60. Amsterdam University Press, 2008.

[6] N Cowan. An embedded process model of working memory. In A. Miyake and P. Shah, editors, *Models of working memory: Mechanisms of Active Maintenance and Executive Control*, pages 62–101. Cambridge University Press, 1999.

[7] R. Fagin and J. Y. Halpern. Belief, awareness, and limited reasoning. *Artificial Intelligence*, 34:39–76, 1988.

[8] R. Fagin, J. Y. Halpern, Y. Moses, and M. Y. Vardi. *Reasoning about knowledge*. MIT Press, 1995.

[9] J. Grant, S. Kraus, and D. Perlis. A logic for characterizing multiple bounded agents. *Autonomous Agents and Multi-Agent Systems*, 3(4):351–387, 2000.

[10] D. Grossi and F. R. Velázquez-Quesada. Twelve Angry Men: A study on the fine-grain of announcements. In *Proceedings of LORI 2009*, volume 5834 of *LNCS*, pages 147–160. Springer, 2009.

[11] J. Halpern and Y. Moses. A guide to completeness and complexity for modal logics of knowledge and belief. *Artificial Intelligence*, 54:319–379, 1992.

[12] J. Y. Halpern and L. C. Rêgo. Reasoning about knowledge of unawareness. *Games and Economic Behavior*, 67(2):503–525, 2009.

[13] J. Hintikka. Impossible possible worlds vindicated. *Journal of Philosophical Logic*, 4:475–484, 1975.

[14] D. Kahneman and A. Tversky. Variants of uncertainty. *Cognition*, 11:143–157, 1982.

[15] J. E. Laird. *The Soar Cognitive Architecture*. MIT Press, 2012.

[16] H. Levesque. A logic of implicit and explicit belief. In *Proceedings of AAAI-84*, pages 198–202. AAAI Press, 1984.

[17] M. C. Lovett, L. M. Reder, and C. Lebiere. Modeling working memory in a unified architecture: An ACT-R perspective. In A. Miyake and P. Shah, editors, *Models of working memory: Mechanisms of Active Maintenance and Executive Control*, pages 135–182. Cambridge University Press, 1999.

[18] C. Lutz. Complexity and Succinctness of Public Announcement Logic. In *Proceedings of AAMAS 2006*, pages 137–144. ACM Press, 2006.

[19] H. van Ditmarsch and T. French. Semantics for knowledge and change of awareness. *Journal of Logic, Language and Information*, 23(2):169–195, 2014.

[20] H. van Ditmarsch, W. van der Hoek, and B. Kooi. *Dynamic Epistemic Logic*. Springer, 2008.

[21] F. R. Velázquez-Quesada. Explicit and implicit knowledge in neighbourhood models. In *Proceedings of LORI 2013*, volume 8196 of *LNCS*, pages 239–252. Springer, 2013.

[22] R. M. Young and R. L. Lewis. The Soar cognitive architecture and human working memory. In A. Miyake and P. Shah, editors, *Models of working memory: Mechanisms of Active Maintenance and Executive Control*, pages 135–182. Cambridge University Press, 1999.

On Learning Attacks in Probabilistic Abstract Argumentation

Régis Riveret
Data61 - CSIRO - NICTA
Brisbane, Australia
regis.riveret@data61.csiro.au

Guido Governatori
Data61, CSIRO, NICTA
Brisbane, Australia
guido.governatori@data61.csiro.au

ABSTRACT

Probabilistic argumentation combines the quantitative uncertainty accounted by probability theory with the qualitative uncertainty captured by argumentation. In this paper, we investigate the problem of learning the structure of an argumentative graph to account for (a distribution of) labellings of a set of arguments. We consider a general abstract framework, where the structure of arguments is left unspecified, and we focus on the grounded semantics. We present, with experimental insights, an anytime algorithm evaluating 'on the fly' hypothetical attacks from the examination of an input stream of labellings.

Keywords

Probabilistic Abstract Argumentation; Structure Learning.

1. INTRODUCTION

The combination of formal argumentation and probability theory to account for uncertainty has been given increasing attention in recent years, in particular with regard to abstract frameworks, see e.g. [12, 21, 2, 6, 15, 19, 20]. In this context, non-trivial problems regard (i) the (efficient) computation of the probability of arguments' statuses given a background argumentative knowledge (and with the assumption that arguments are not probabilistically independent), and (ii) learning the probability distribution of arguments' statuses from examples of argument's statuses. Another problem, which has not been addressed so far and that we call here *abstract structure learning*, concerns the induction of an argumentative structure accounting for arguments' statuses drawn from an unknown probability distribution. This paper addresses this problem, by presenting an anytime algorithm evaluating 'on the fly' hypothetical attack relations amongst arguments from the examination of a sequence of arguments' statuses. We consider a probabilistic abstract framework, leaving thus the possibility to complement this work with techniques for learning the internal structure of arguments.

The fundamental problem of learning a logical structure from examples in a probabilistic setting is not new: it is notably addressed in statistical relational learning (SRL) [9] and probabilistic inductive logic programming (PILP) [17]. However, argumentation plays no role in these approaches.

Some investigations focused on the relationship between inductive reasoning and non-monotonic reasoning akin to argument-based reasoning. [7], for example, gave an analysis of logical induction with a focus on *hypothesis generation* while [14] moved on with a characterisation for *hypothesis selection* with an illustration in rule-based argumentation. [10] investigated the induction of Defeasible Logic theories (possibly interpreted as an instantiated argumentation graph). In a parallel line of research, argumentation and inductive reasoning is combined in [13] to explain examples with expert's arguments. These works, however, do not cater for any probabilistic setting. Furthermore, they have little or no consideration, in the inductive process, for the different reasoning levels characterising argumentation frameworks (such as the labelling of arguments and the labelling of statements) along the fine granularity of possible labellings whereby, for example, an argument shall be labelled as justified, rejected, undecided or unexpressed.

Besides, case-based reasoning (CBR) [11] is often closely related to inductive reasoning since, from a set of cases, it shall form generalizations of these cases. When CBR shows dialectical features, as in legal reasoning, argumentation is a natural mean to model parties arguing about cases. For example, [16] proposed an early investigation of rule-based argumentation for reasoning with precedents represented by a set of attacking arguments, but the attacks over these arguments are given instead of being learnt.

The problem of learning attacks over arguments from arguments' statuses is different from the classic problem of learning a logical structure from statements, but our proposal may be used to position the labelling of arguments as a major reasoning step in structure learning, from the perspective of abstract argumentation and within a probabilistic framework.

As to the applications of the standalone problem, they regard any sequential setting where one or more agents repetitively argue. For each repetition, the status of every argument is justified, rejected, undecided, or unexpressed. The statuses of the arguments are observed, but the attack relations between arguments are unknown. The goal is to reconstruct the attacks.

This paper is organised as follows. Section 2 introduces the probabilistic abstract argumentation setting. Section 3 defines the problem we address. Then, we investigate the learning of argumentative structure in Section 4. with experimental insights in Section 5, before concluding.

Appears in: *Proceedings of the 15th International Conference on Autonomous Agents and Multiagent Systems (AAMAS 2016), J. Thangarajah, K. Tuyls, C. Jonker, S. Marsella (eds.), May 9–13, 2016, Singapore.*

2. PROBABILISTIC ABSTRACT ARGUMENTATION

Our setting for probabilistic abstract argumentation is based on the proposal given in [19], which has the advantage of giving an explicit probability space and which fully relaxes probabilistic independences, even if there are no attack or sub-argument relations amongst arguments. The setting is built on abstract argumentation graphs [3].

DEFINITION 1 (ARGUMENTATION GRAPH). *An argumentation graph is a pair $\langle \mathcal{A}, \rightsquigarrow \rangle$ where $\mathcal{A}$ is a set of arguments, and $\rightsquigarrow \subseteq \mathcal{A} \times \mathcal{A}$ is a binary relation of attack.*

As for notation, given an argumentation graph $\mathcal{G} = \langle \mathcal{A}, \rightsquigarrow \rangle$, we write $\mathcal{A}_{\mathcal{G}} = \mathcal{A}$, and $\rightsquigarrow_{\mathcal{G}} = \rightsquigarrow$.

DEFINITION 2 (SUB-GRAPH). *A sub-graph $\mathcal{H}$ of an argumentation graph $\mathcal{G} = \langle \mathcal{A}, \rightsquigarrow \rangle$ is an argumentation graph $\langle \mathcal{A}_{\mathcal{H}}, \mathcal{R}_{\mathcal{H}} \rangle$, where $\mathcal{A}_{\mathcal{H}} \subseteq \mathcal{A}$, and $\forall A, B \in \mathcal{A}_{\mathcal{H}}$, $(A \rightsquigarrow B) \in \rightsquigarrow_{\mathcal{G}}$ iff $(A \rightsquigarrow B) \in \rightsquigarrow_{\mathcal{H}}$.*

Thus $\mathcal{H}$ is an induced sub-graph of $\mathcal{G}$ if it has exactly the attacks that appear in $\mathcal{G}$ over the same set of arguments.

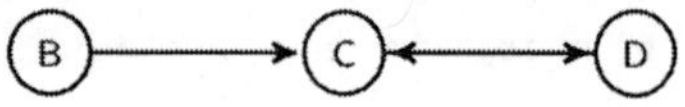

Figure 1: An argumentation graph. The argument B attacks the argument C, the arguments C and D attack each other.

Figure 2: The graph on the left is a sub-graph of the graph in Figure 1, while the graph on the right is not one of its sub-graphs.

Given an argumentation graph, the sets of arguments that are justified or rejected, that is, those arguments that shall survive or not to possible attacks, are computed using some semantics, and, for our purposes, we will consider Dung's grounded semantics [3] by labelling arguments as in [19], which is a slight adaptation of the labellings reviewed in [1] to fit a probabilistic setting. Accordingly, we will distinguish $\{\mathsf{in}, \mathsf{out}, \mathsf{un}\}$-labellings and $\{\mathsf{in}, \mathsf{out}, \mathsf{un}, \mathsf{off}\}$-labellings. In a $\{\mathsf{in}, \mathsf{out}, \mathsf{un}\}$-labelling, each argument is associated with one label which is either in, out, un, respectively meaning that the argument is justified, rejected, or undecided. 'in' means the argument is justified while a label 'out' indicates that it is rejected. The label 'un' marks the status of the argument as undecided. In a $\{\mathsf{in}, \mathsf{out}, \mathsf{un}, \mathsf{off}\}$-labelling, the label 'off' indicates that the argument is not expressed, that is, it does not occur.

DEFINITION 3 (LABELLING). *Let $\mathcal{G}$ denote an argumentation graph.*

- *A $\{\mathsf{in}, \mathsf{out}, \mathsf{un}\}$-labelling of $\mathcal{G}$ is a total function $L : \mathcal{A}_{\mathcal{G}} \rightarrow \{\mathsf{in}, \mathsf{out}, \mathsf{un}\}$.*
- *A $\{\mathsf{in}, \mathsf{out}, \mathsf{un}, \mathsf{off}\}$-labelling of $\mathcal{G}$ is a total function $L : \mathcal{A}_{\mathcal{G}} \rightarrow \{\mathsf{in}, \mathsf{out}, \mathsf{un}, \mathsf{off}\}$.*

In the remainder, we will write $\mathsf{in}(L)$ for $\{A | L(A) = \mathsf{in}\}$, $\mathsf{out}(L)$ for $\{A | L(A) = \mathsf{out}\}$, $\mathsf{un}(L)$ for $\{A | L(A) = \mathsf{un}\}$, and $\mathsf{off}(L)$ for $\{A | L(A) = \mathsf{off}\}$.

A $\{\mathsf{in}, \mathsf{out}, \mathsf{un}\}$-labelling L will be represented as a tuple $\langle \mathsf{in}(L), \mathsf{out}(L), \mathsf{un}(L) \rangle$, and a $\{\mathsf{in}, \mathsf{out}, \mathsf{un}, \mathsf{off}\}$-labelling L as a tuple $\langle \mathsf{in}(L), \mathsf{out}(L), \mathsf{un}(L), \mathsf{off}(L) \rangle$.

Next the set of *complete labellings* is defined. As an argumentation graph may have several complete $\{\mathsf{in}, \mathsf{out}, \mathsf{un}\}$-labellings, we will focus on the unique complete labelling with the smallest set of labels in, i.e. the grounded $\{\mathsf{in}, \mathsf{out}, \mathsf{un}\}$-labelling, see [1].

DEFINITION 4 (COMPLETE $\{\mathsf{in}, \mathsf{out}, \mathsf{un}\}$-LABELLING). *Let $\mathcal{G}$ denote an argumentation graph. A complete $\{\mathsf{in}, \mathsf{out}, \mathsf{un}\}$-labelling of $\mathcal{G}$ is a $\{\mathsf{in}, \mathsf{out}, \mathsf{un}\}$-labelling such that for every argument A in $\mathcal{A}_{\mathcal{G}}$ it holds that:*

- *A is labelled in iff all attackers of A are labelled out,*
- *A is labelled out iff A has an attacker labelled in.*

DEFINITION 5 (GROUNDED $\{\mathsf{in}, \mathsf{out}, \mathsf{un}\}$-LABELLING). *A complete labelling L is a grounded $\{\mathsf{in}, \mathsf{out}, \mathsf{un}\}$-labelling of an argumentation graph $\mathcal{G}$ if $\mathsf{in}(L)$ is minimal (w.r.t. set inclusion) amongst all complete $\{\mathsf{in}, \mathsf{out}, \mathsf{un}\}$-labellings of $\mathcal{G}$.*

Note that, since a complete labelling is a total function, if an argument is not labelled in or out, then it is labelled un.

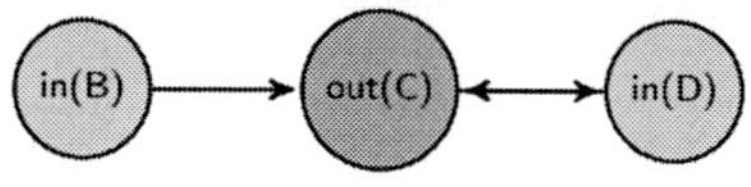

Figure 3: A grounded $\{\mathsf{in}, \mathsf{out}, \mathsf{un}\}$-labelling.

When some arguments are not expressed, we have *grounded* $\{\mathsf{in}, \mathsf{out}, \mathsf{un}, \mathsf{off}\}$-labellings, where only expressed arguments can effectively attack other expressed arguments.

DEFINITION 6 (GROUNDED $\{\mathsf{in}, \mathsf{out}, \mathsf{un}, \mathsf{off}\}$-LABELLING). *Let $\mathcal{G}$ denote an argumentation graph and $\mathcal{H}$ an induced sub-graph of $\mathcal{G}$. A grounded $\{\mathsf{in}, \mathsf{out}, \mathsf{un}, \mathsf{off}\}$-labelling of $\mathcal{G}$ is a $\{\mathsf{in}, \mathsf{out}, \mathsf{un}, \mathsf{off}\}$-labelling such that:*

- *every argument in $\mathcal{A}_{\mathcal{H}}$ is labelled according to the grounded $\{\mathsf{in}, \mathsf{out}, \mathsf{un}\}$-labelling of $\mathcal{H}$,*
- *every argument in $\mathcal{A}_{\mathcal{G}} \backslash \mathcal{A}_{\mathcal{H}}$ is labelled off.*

An argumentation graph has a unique grounded $\{\mathsf{in}, \mathsf{out}, \mathsf{un}\}$-labelling, but it has as many grounded $\{\mathsf{in}, \mathsf{out}, \mathsf{un}, \mathsf{off}\}$-labellings as sub-graphs.

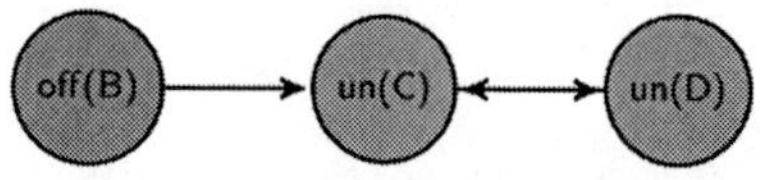

Figure 4: A grounded $\{\mathsf{in}, \mathsf{out}, \mathsf{un}, \mathsf{off}\}$-labelling.

As for notational matters, a complete $\{\mathsf{in}, \mathsf{out}, \mathsf{un}, \mathsf{off}\}$-labelling will be abbreviated as $\{\mathsf{in}, \mathsf{out}, \mathsf{un}, \mathsf{off}\}^c$-labelling, and a grounded $\{\mathsf{in}, \mathsf{out}, \mathsf{un}, \mathsf{off}\}$-labelling as $\{\mathsf{in}, \mathsf{out}, \mathsf{un}, \mathsf{off}\}^g$-labelling. By doing so, we can denote the set of $\mathcal{S}$-labellings of an argumentation graph $\mathcal{G}$ as $\mathcal{L}^{\mathcal{S}}_{\mathcal{G}}$, and each set will basically constitute a possible sample space (i.e. the set of possible outcomes) of our probabilistic setting for argumentation.

As an intuitive account of the probabilistic setting, an agent is in front of a bag of $\mathcal{S}$-labellings, and this agent observes a labelling L grasped from the bag with a probability $P(\{L\})$. In other words, a labelling of an argumentation graph is an outcome, and each outcome is associated with a probability. This view on probabilistic argumentation is formally captured by the following definition of probabilistic argumentation frames.

Definition 7 (Prob. argumentation frame). *A probabilistic argumentation frame is a tuple* $(\mathcal{G}, \mathcal{S}, (\Omega, F, P))$ *where* $\mathcal{G}$ *is an argumentation graph (called the hypothetical argumentation frame),* $\mathcal{S}$ *is the labelling specification and,* (Ω, F, P) *is a probability space such that:*

- *the sample space* Ω *is the set of* $\mathcal{S}$*-labellings of the hypothetical argumentation frame* $\mathcal{G}$, $\Omega = \mathcal{L}^{\mathcal{S}}_{\mathcal{G}}$,
- *the* σ*-algebra* F *is the power set of* Ω,
- *the probability function* P *from* $F(\Omega)$ *to* $[0,1]$ *satisfies Kolmorogov axioms.*

As an illustration, assume a hypothetical argumentation frame as drawn in Figure 1, the sample space of grounded {in, out, un, off}-labellings is shown in the table below.

B	in	in	in	in	off	off	off	off
C	out	out	off	off	un	in	off	off
D	in	off	in	off	un	off	in	off

Table 1: Sample space as the set of grounded {in, out, un, off}-labellings of the argumentation graph drawn in Figure 1.

In the remainder of this paper, we will focus on the grounded {in, out, un, off}-labelling, thus $\mathcal{S}$ will hold for the specification of grounded {in, out, un, off}-labellings. We will consider a sequence of grounded {in, out, un, off}-labellings drawn from a distribution, and our goal is to find an argumentation graph that accounts for these labellings.

3. PROBLEM SETTING

From now, we assume an empirical probability distribution $P_{\mathcal{O}}$ over a set $\mathcal{O}$ of observed grounded {in, out, un, off}-labellings, such that these observed labellings are drawn from a probability distribution of a probabilistic argumentation frame $\langle \mathcal{G}, \mathcal{S}, (\Omega, F, P) \rangle$. The distribution $P_{\mathcal{O}}$ is thus the empirical approximation of the distribution P. The hypothetical argumentation frame $\mathcal{G}$ is called the source argumentation graph, since it is going to be the 'source' of a stream of labellings, and P is called the source distribution.

We readily remark that different argumentation graphs may be indistinguishable in the sense that they have, or can account for, the same observed labellings. For example, the graphs $\mathcal{G}_1 = \langle \{\mathsf{A}, \mathsf{B}\}, \{\mathsf{A} \rightsquigarrow \mathsf{A}, \mathsf{A} \rightsquigarrow \mathsf{B}\} \rangle$ and $\mathcal{G}_2 = \langle \{\mathsf{A}, \mathsf{B}\}, \{\mathsf{A} \rightsquigarrow \mathsf{A}, \mathsf{A} \rightsquigarrow \mathsf{B}, \mathsf{B} \rightsquigarrow \mathsf{A}\} \rangle$ have the same grounded {in, out, un, off}-labellings. As the graph $\mathcal{G}_1$ has less attacks than the graph $\mathcal{G}_2$, then one might consider that the $\mathcal{G}_1$ is a better graph to account for some observed labellings. However it may the case that the source underlying graph is in fact $\mathcal{G}_2$. This example shows that, in some cases, we cannot aim to induce the exact source graph $\mathcal{G}$ of a probabilistic argumentation frame $\langle \mathcal{G}, \mathcal{S}, (\Omega, F, P) \rangle$ underlying a distribution of observed labellings, but this does not prohibit us to find an argumentation graph $\mathcal{X}$ that shall explain (to different degrees) the observed labellings.

To measure how much an argumentation graph $\mathcal{X}$ explains a set $\mathcal{O}$ of observed labellings along its empirical distribution $P_{\mathcal{O}}$, we will assume an explanatory measure of this graph, denoted $M(\mathcal{X}, P_{\mathcal{O}})$, such that the value of this measure is maximal when the graph $\mathcal{X}$ is the source argumentation graph $\mathcal{G}$.

Many different explanatory measures can be considered. Here, an example of a measure that we shall call the *expected explanatory utility* of a graph $\mathcal{X}$ w.r.t. a distribution $P_{\mathcal{O}}$ of a set $\mathcal{O}$ of observed labellings:

$$M(\mathcal{X}, P_{\mathcal{O}}) = \sum_{L \in \mathcal{O}} P_{\mathcal{O}}(L) \cdot \mu(\mathcal{X}, L) \tag{1}$$

where $\mu(\mathcal{X}, L)$ is the explanatory utility of the graph $\mathcal{X}$ to explain the labelling L. We may consider that the graph $\mathcal{X}$ is useful to explain a labelling L when the similarity of the labelling L and the corresponding grounded {in, out, un, off}-labelling of $\mathcal{X}$, denoted L' (the labelling with the same arguments labelled off) is maximised. Accordingly, we may measure the explanatory utility with the following explanatory index with a Jaccard flavour:

$$\mu(\mathcal{X}, L) = \frac{s}{s_{\mathsf{in}} + s_{\mathsf{out}} + s_{\mathsf{un}} + s} \tag{2}$$

where[1]

$$s = |\mathsf{in}(L) \cap \mathsf{in}(L')| + |\mathsf{out}(L) \cap \mathsf{out}(L')| + |\mathsf{un}(L) \cap \mathsf{un}(L')| \tag{3}$$

$$s_{\mathsf{in}} = |\mathsf{in}(L) \cap \mathsf{out}(L')| + |\mathsf{in}(L) \cap \mathsf{un}(L')| \tag{4}$$

$$s_{\mathsf{out}} = |\mathsf{out}(L) \cap \mathsf{in}(L')| + |\mathsf{out}(L) \cap \mathsf{un}(L')| \tag{5}$$

$$s_{\mathsf{un}} = |\mathsf{un}(L) \cap \mathsf{in}(L')| + |\mathsf{un}(L) \cap \mathsf{out}(L')| \tag{6}$$

Hence $\mu(\mathcal{X}, L) \in [0,1]$: if all the labels mismatch then $\mu(\mathcal{X}, L) = 0$, if all the labels match then $\mu(\mathcal{X}, L) = 1$. Consequently, if all the labellings totally mismatch then $M(\mathcal{X}, P_{\mathcal{O}}) = 0$, if all the labellings totally match then $M(\mathcal{X}, P_{\mathcal{O}}) = \sum_{L \in \mathcal{O}} P_{\mathcal{O}}(L)$, and thus $M(\mathcal{X}, P_{\mathcal{O}}) = 1$.

We reckon that the choice of an explanatory measure shall much depend on the envisaged application, and thus, we do not further discuss this point. However, we are now prepared to precise our abstract structure learning problem.

Given:

- an empirical probability distribution $P_{\mathcal{O}}$ of labellings over a set $\mathcal{O}$ of observed labellings (of a set $\mathcal{A}$ of observed arguments), such that these observed labellings are drawn from a probability distribution of a probabilistic argumentation frame $\langle \mathcal{G}, \mathcal{S}, (\Omega, F, P) \rangle$.
- a set $\mathfrak{H}$ of hypothetical argumentation graphs $\langle \mathcal{A}, \rightsquigarrow \rangle$.

find (or induce or learn)

- a hypothetical argumentation graph $\mathcal{X} \in \mathfrak{H}$ such that the explanatory measure $M(\mathcal{X}, P_{\mathcal{O}})$ is maximised.

[1] Here, s is such that we ignore the labelling where all the arguments are labelled off.

If we find an argumentation graph indistinguishable from the source argumentation graph $\mathcal{G}$ underlying the observed labellings, then the explanatory measure will be maximised. Even if the source argumentation graph $\mathcal{G}$ is not found, we may confirm or discard some attack relations, which shall nevertheless appear valuable to inform (i.e. explain) the observed labellings.

4. LEARNING ATTACKS

Our problem assumes a set $\mathfrak{H}$ of hypothetical argumentation graphs, and we have to find in it an argumentation graph to account for some labellings observed in sequence. To build this set, we start from the complete argumentation graph induced by the set of observed arguments, i.e. a graph where all the arguments attack each other.

DEFINITION 8 (COMPLETE ARGUMENTATION GRAPH). *A complete argumentation graph induced by a set of arguments $\mathcal{A}$ is an argumentation graph $\langle \mathcal{A}, \rightsquigarrow \rangle$, where* $\rightsquigarrow = \{A \rightsquigarrow B | A, B \in \mathcal{A}\}$.

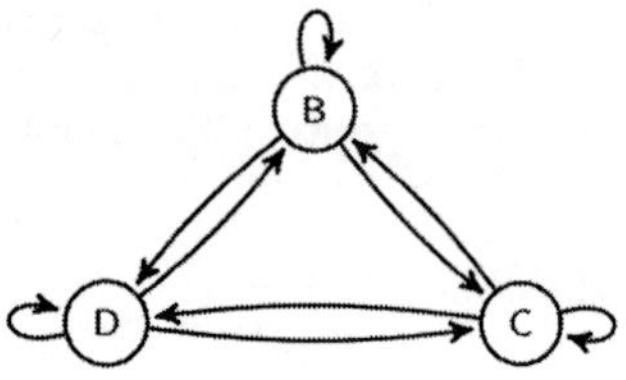

Figure 5: A complete argumentation graph induced by the arguments $\{\mathsf{B}, \mathsf{C}, \mathsf{D}\}$.

Given a probabilistic argumentation graph $\langle \mathcal{G}, \mathcal{S}, (\Omega, F, P) \rangle$, the hypothetical argumentation frame $\mathcal{G}$ is necessarily an 'attack sub-graph' (defined below) of the complete argumentation graph $\mathcal{C}$ induced by the set of arguments $\mathcal{A}_{\mathcal{G}}$.

DEFINITION 9 (ATTACK SUB-GRAPH). *An* attack sub-graph *of an argumentation graph $\langle \mathcal{A}, \rightsquigarrow \rangle$ is an argumentation graph $\langle \mathcal{A}, \rightsquigarrow' \rangle$ such that $\rightsquigarrow' \subseteq \rightsquigarrow$.*

For example, the graph in Figure 1 is an attack sub-graph of the complete graph shown in Figure 5.

A brute force approach for our problem is to start from the complete argumentation graph $\mathcal{C}$ induced by the set of observable arguments, and then consider every attack sub-graphs of $\mathcal{C}$ till we find a graph $\mathcal{X}$ covering all the observed labellings. However this approach is of course not efficient.

As the brute force approach is not efficient, we investigate here an alternative: we start from a complete hypothetical argumentation graph induced from a set of arguments, then, based on the labellings observed in sequence, we will attach a *credit value* to any hypothetical attack relation, and we shall discard or confirm attacks based on their credits. Since we attach a credit value (or let us say a weight) to any hypothetical attack, we resort to *weighted argumentation graphs* (see [5]):

DEFINITION 10 (WEIGHTED ARGUMENTATION GRAPH). *A weighted argumentation graph is a triple $\langle \mathcal{A}, \rightsquigarrow, v \rangle$ such that $\langle \mathcal{A}, \rightsquigarrow \rangle$ is an argumentation graph, and $v : \rightsquigarrow \rightarrow \mathbb{R}$ is a function assigning a real valued weight to every attack.*

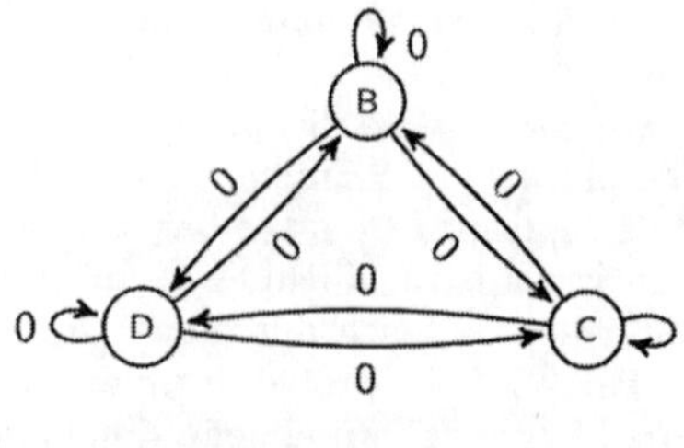

Figure 6: A weighted argumentation graph, where all the weights have a value 0.

Note that weighted argumentation graphs in [5] are used for different investigations: [5] uses weights to introduce an inconsistency budget, whereas we are simply using weighted argumentation graphs to store a number (that we call a credit) to every attack, with the idea that this numerical approach shall ease the treatment of noisy settings in future investigations.

In the remainder, given a weighted argumentation graph $\mathcal{C}$, we will say that an attack $A \rightsquigarrow B$ is

- discarded if $v_{A \rightsquigarrow B} < 0$,
- confirmed if $v_{A \rightsquigarrow B} > 0$,
- undecided if $v_{A \rightsquigarrow B} = 0$,
- possible if $v_{A \rightsquigarrow B} \geq 0$ (in this case the argument A is called a possible attacker of B).

When we abstract from the weight function of a weighted argumentation graph $\langle \mathcal{A}, \rightsquigarrow, v \rangle$, then we shall straightforwardly consider the corresponding argumentation graph $\langle \mathcal{A}, \rightsquigarrow \rangle$ where the weight function is omitted.

To learn attacks, we start from the weighted complete argumentation graph $\mathcal{C}$ where an initial credit is attached to every attack of $\mathcal{C}$, and in order to cater for the observed labellings, we shall change the value of the credits to discard or confirm attacks. To change the credits, we consider simple theorems considering labellings of single arguments or pairs of arguments to induce the presence of some attacks.

Theorems. Let $\mathcal{G}$ be an argumentation graph, L be a grounded $\{\mathsf{in}, \mathsf{out}, \mathsf{un}, \mathsf{off}\}$-labelling of $\mathcal{G}$, and A, B and C denote (not necessarily distinct) arguments in $\mathcal{A}_{\mathcal{G}}$.

THEOREM 1. *If A and B are labelled* in *(i.e. $L(A) = \mathsf{in}$ and $L(B) = \mathsf{in}$), then there is no attack $B \rightsquigarrow A$ (i.e. $B \rightsquigarrow A \notin \rightsquigarrow_{\mathcal{G}}$).*

PROOF. By contradiction. Suppose there is an attack $B \rightsquigarrow A$. Since B is in and L is complete, we conclude that A is out, which contradicts our assumption that A is in. □

THEOREM 2. *If A is labelled* in *and B is labelled* un, *then there are no attacks $A \rightsquigarrow B$ and $B \rightsquigarrow A$.*

PROOF. By contradiction. (i) Suppose there is an attack $A \rightsquigarrow B$. Since A is in and L is complete, B is out, which contradicts our assumption that B is un. (ii) Suppose that there is an attack $B \rightsquigarrow A$. Since B is un and L is complete, A is not in, which contradicts our assumption that A is in. □

THEOREM 3. *If A is labelled* un, *and any possible attacker C of A is labelled* out *or* off *($C \neq A$), then there is an attack $A \rightsquigarrow A$.*

PROOF. By contradiction. Suppose that there is no attack $A \leadsto A$. Since L is complete, we conclude that A is labelled in, which contradicts our assumption that A is un. □

THEOREM 4. *If A is labelled* un *and B is labelled* un, *and there are no attacks $A \leadsto A$ and $B \leadsto B$, and any possible attacker C of A or B is labelled* out *or* off *($C \neq A$ and $C \neq B$), then there is an attack $A \leadsto B$ and $B \leadsto A$.*

PROOF. By contradiction. Suppose that there are no attacks $A \leadsto B$ and $B \leadsto A$. Since L is grounded, we conclude that A and B are not labelled un, which contradicts our assumption that A and B are un. □

THEOREM 5. *If A is* out *and B is* in, *and any possible attacker C of A is labelled* out *or* un *or* off *($C \neq A$ and $C \neq B$), then there is an attack $B \leadsto A$ and no attack $A \leadsto B$.*

PROOF. By contradiction. Suppose it is not the case that "there is an attack $B \leadsto A$ and there is no attack $B \leadsto A$". Since L is grounded, A is not out and B is not in, which contradicts our assumption that A is out and B is in. □

Although these theorems are simple, they are at the core of our approach. They are the basis of the credit rules used in Algorithm 1 to progressively confirm or discard attacks, by increasing or decreasing their credits each time a labelling is observed.

DEFINITION 11 (CREDIT RULES). *Let $\mathcal{C} = \langle \mathcal{A}, \leadsto, v \rangle$ denote a weighted complete argumentation graph, and L any grounded* {in, out, un, off}*-labelling of $\mathcal{C}$. For any argument A and B labelled in L, we have the following rules updating the credits of attacks:*

$\mathsf{R}_1(L, \mathcal{C})$: *If $L(A) =$ in and $L(B) =$ in, then*

$$v_{B \leadsto A} \leftarrow v_{B \leadsto A} - 1$$

$\mathsf{R}_2(L, \mathcal{C})$: *If $L(A) =$ in and $L(B) =$ un, then*

$$v_{B \leadsto A} \leftarrow v_{B \leadsto A} - 1; \quad v_{A \leadsto B} \leftarrow v_{A \leadsto B} - 1$$

$\mathsf{R}_3(L, \mathcal{C})$: *If $L(A) =$ un, $L(B) =$ un, and for any possible attacker C of A or B ($C \neq A$ and $C \neq B$), $L(C) =$ out or $L(C) =$ off, then*

$$v_{B \leadsto A} \leftarrow v_{B \leadsto A} + 1; \quad v_{A \leadsto B} \leftarrow v_{A \leadsto B} + 1$$

$\mathsf{R}_4(L, \mathcal{C})$: *If $L(A) =$ out, $L(B) =$ in, and for any possible attacker C of A ($C \neq A$ and $C \neq B$) we have $L(C) =$ out or $L(C) =$ un or $L(C) =$ off, then*

$$v_{B \leadsto A} \leftarrow v_{B \leadsto A} + 1; \quad v_{A \leadsto B} \leftarrow v_{A \leadsto B} - 1$$

On the basis of the credit rules, we propose an algorithm (Algorithm 1) to learn the attack relations: it iteratively credits the attack relations until some predefined computational budget (typically time or iteration constraint) is reached or until every attack is either confirmed or discarded, at which point the loop is halted and the argumentation graph induced so far is returned.

The algorithm starts from a weighted argumentation graph $\mathcal{C}$, where the credit of every attack is initialised (line 2) - if we are ignorant about the status of an attack, then its credit is initialised to 0. Every time that a labelling is observed (line 4), credits are possibly updated (line 5), until all attacks are confirmed or discarded, or some computational budget is reached. Notice that discarded attacks can be dumped (line 6) to accelerate the application of credit rules. When the loop ends, the weighted argumentation graph $\mathcal{C}$ is pruned (line 8) by dumping any undecided or discarded attacks, to return the argumentation graph with only the confirmed attacks.

Algorithm 1 Attack learning algorithm.

1: **input** The weighted complete argumentation graph $\mathcal{C} = \langle \mathcal{A}_\mathcal{C}, \leadsto_\mathcal{C}, v \rangle$.
2: For any arguments $A, B \in \mathcal{A}_\mathcal{C}$, initialise credits $v_{A \leadsto B}$.
3: **while** there is an attack which is neither confirmed nor discarded, or within computational budget **do**
4: Get a labelling instance L.
5: Credit the attack relations of $\mathcal{C}$ using the credit rules $\mathsf{R}_1(L, \mathcal{C})$, $\mathsf{R}_2(L, \mathcal{C})$, $\mathsf{R}_3(L, \mathcal{C})$, $\mathsf{R}_4(L, \mathcal{C})$.
6: $\mathcal{C} \leftarrow$ *pruneDiscardedAttacks*($\mathcal{C}$). (optional)
7: **end while**
8: $\mathcal{X} \leftarrow$ prune($\mathcal{C}$).
9: **return** the argumentation graph $\mathcal{X}$.

EXAMPLE 1. *Let us illustrate Algorithm 1. Consider the argumentation graph shown in Figure 1 as our source graph of a stream of labellings that we will observe. All attacks are initialised with a credit 0, and thus we start from the weighted argumentation graph as given in Figure 6.*

1. *Suppose that the 1st observed labelling instance is* ({B, D}, {C}, ∅, ∅). *Using the credit rule* R_1, *the weights of the weighted argumentation graph are updated as follows.*

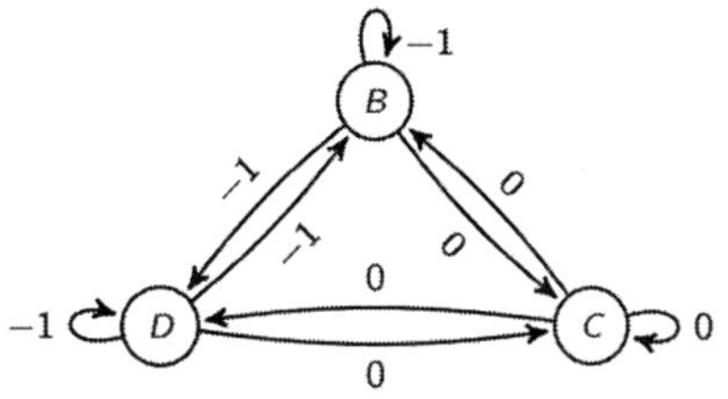

2. *Suppose the 2nd observed labelling instance is* ({B}, {C}, ∅, {D}). *Using credit rules* R_1 *and* R_4, *the weighted argumentation graph is updated as follows.*

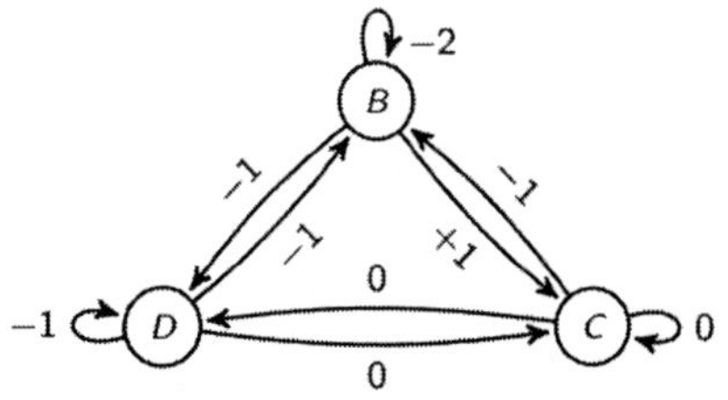

3. *Suppose the 3rd observed labelling instance is again* ({B}, {C}, ∅, {D}). *We use the credit rules* R_1 *and* R_4.

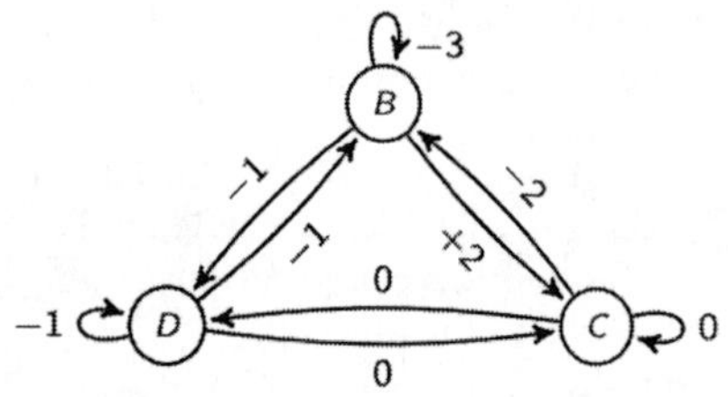

4. *Suppose the 4th observed labelling is* $(\emptyset, \emptyset, \{\mathsf{C}, \mathsf{D}\}, \{\mathsf{B}\})$. *We use the credit rule* R_3.

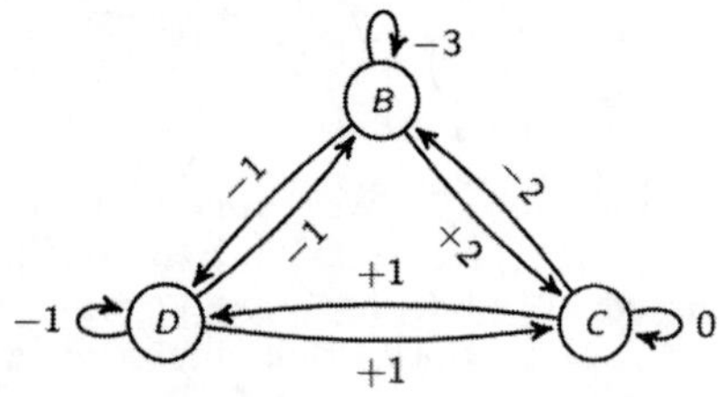

5. *Suppose the 5th labelling instance is* $(\{\mathsf{C}\}, \emptyset, \emptyset, \{\mathsf{B}, \mathsf{D}\})$. *We use the credit rule* R_1 *for the update.*

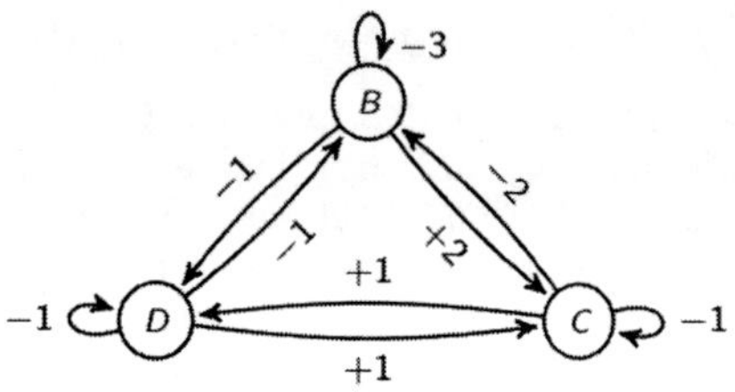

At this stage, all attacks are either confirmed or discarded, and thus we can prune the weighted argumentation graph by dumping all discarded attacks. Finally we return the argumentation graph with only the confirmed attacks, which is the argumentation graph shown in Figure 1.

As the example illustrates, the algorithm works 'on the fly' and thus a major benefit is that we do not have to keep in memory the observed labellings. However we have to keep in memory all the credits of all possible attacks between any pair of arguments amongst $|\mathcal{A}_\mathcal{G}|$ arguments of a complete argumentation graph $\mathcal{G}$. The space complexity is thus quadratic.

THEOREM 6 (SPACE COMPLEXITY). *The space complexity of Algorithm 1 is quadratic.*

PROOF. Trivial, since the number of possible attacks amongst $n = |\mathcal{A}_\mathcal{G}|$ arguments of a complete argumentation graph $\mathcal{G}$ is n^2. □

Concerning time complexity, the burden stems from the application of credit rules to all possible attacks for any pair of arguments amongst $|\mathcal{A}_\mathcal{G}|$ arguments of a complete argumentation graph $\mathcal{G}$.

THEOREM 7 (TIME COMPLEXITY). *The time complexity of applying credit rules is cubic.*

PROOF. In the worst case, the most demanding rules R_3 and R_4 have to check the status of $n = |\mathcal{A}_\mathcal{G}|$ attackers for the arguments of any n^2 possible attacks amongst arguments. □

In practice, the computational complexity is often drastically decreased by pruning discarded attacks of the argumentation graph $\mathcal{C}$ as optionally proposed in line 6 of the algorithm.

In case of active learning (i.e. the algorithm can decide which labellings to consider in line 4 of Algorithm 1), key labellings (see Definition 13) can be observed to straightforwardly evaluate hypothetical attacks. A *key labelling* is a {in, out, un, off}-labelling where a set of arguments is 'isolated', i.e. all the arguments not in this set are labelled off.

DEFINITION 12. *A n-isolated grounded* {in, out, un, off}*-labelling is a grounded* {in, out, un, off}*-labelling with exactly n distinct arguments not labelled* off.

DEFINITION 13 (KEY LABELLING). *A* key labelling *is a 1-isolated grounded* {in, out, un, off}*-labelling or a 2-isolated grounded* {in, out, un, off}*-labelling.*

For instance, any labelling in Table 1 is a key labelling, except the labellings $(\{\mathsf{B}, \mathsf{D}\}, \{\mathsf{C}\}, \emptyset, \emptyset)$ and $(\emptyset, \emptyset, \emptyset, \{\mathsf{B}, \mathsf{C}, \mathsf{D}\})$.
Table 2 summarises the coverage of credit rules w.r.t. every possible key grounded {in, out, un, off}-labelling of two arguments A and B whose the attack relation is unknown.

Table 2: Coverage of key labellings by the credit rules.

A	in	in	in	in	un	un
B	in	out	un	off	un	off
	R_1	R_4	R_2	R_1	R_3	R_3

Every key labelling is covered. However, as illustrated in Section 3, we cannot distinguish the attacks between two arguments from a labelling where both arguments are labelled un and at least one argument self-attacks. We have thus to resolve to induce argumentation graphs indistinguishable from source graphs.

THEOREM 8. *Let $\mathcal{G}$ denote a source argumentation graph, let $n = |\mathcal{A}_\mathcal{G}|$ denote the number of arguments in $\mathcal{G}$. An argumentation graph, indistinguishable from the source graph $\mathcal{G}$, is induced by observing its $n \cdot (n+1)/2$ key labellings.*

PROOF. The number of 1-isolated grounded {in, out, un, off}-labellings of a graph with n arguments is n, while the number of 2-isolated grounded {in, out, un, off}-labellings is $C(2, n) = n \cdot (n-1)/2$[2]. Thus the number of key labellings is $n \cdot (n+1)/2$. By observing all the $n \cdot (n+1)/2$ key labellings, we can thus confirm or discard all the attack relations amongst the n arguments (see Table 2). Finally, the confirmed attacks are the attacks of a graph indistinguishable from the source graph. □

In practice, Theorem 8 is interesting because it implies that, in an active learning setting where it is possible to choose to observe some labellings in particular, one shall choose to observe $n \cdot (n+1)/2$ key labellings to straightforwardly induce an argumentation graph indistinguishable from the source graph (in this case the explanatory measure is maximised).

[2]using standard notation, $C(k, n) = \frac{n!}{k!(n-k)!}$, $k \le n$.

However, the number of labellings observed to induce the source graph can be inferior to the number of key labellings, because a labelling may contain multiple isolated (pairs of) arguments.

If active learning is not possible, and if the algorithm terminates before any attack is confirmed or discarded, then the returned argumentation graph $\mathcal{X}$ may be such that there exists some labellings of $\mathcal{X}$ which are not in the set of observed labellings, and there exists some observed labellings which are not labellings of $\mathcal{X}$. So, the algorithm may never confirm or discard all the attacks, and for this reason, we will assume in the remainder that the underlying probabilistic argumentation frame $\langle \mathcal{G}, \mathcal{S}, (\Omega, F, P)\rangle$ of the observed labelling is such that for any labelling L in the sample space Ω, we have $P(\{L\}) > 0$. With this assumption, the algorithm will always empty the set of undecided attacks.

THEOREM 9 (TERMINATION). *If the computational budget is finite, then Algorithm 1 terminates, else it terminates almost surely (i.e. it terminates with probability one).*

PROOF. If the computational budget is finite, then Algorithm 1 terminates when the computational budget is reached, else the probability that any key labelling get drawn is one (since $P(\{L\}) > 0$). From the key labellings, the attack relations between any pair of arguments are confirmed or discarded, which terminates the loop while. □

THEOREM 10 (SOUNDNESS AT TERMINATION). *If the computational budget is infinite, Algorithm 1 returns almost surely an argumentation graph indistinguishable from the source argumentation graph.*

PROOF. From the key labellings, we induce an argumentation graph indistinguishable from the source argumentation graph. Since all these labellings appear almost surely, then the algorithm returns almost surely an argumentation graph indistinguishable from the source argumentation graph. □

In this regard, the waiting time to collect the set of key labellings is the waiting time akin to a partial collection in the coupon collector problem, see e.g. [8].

If active learning is not possible and the computational budget is finite, some attacks may remain undecided, and thus we may be willing to empty the set of undecided attacks, so that the graph $\mathcal{X}$ can give full explanation of the observed labellings. To empty the set of undecided attacks, a solution consists in approaching the undecided attacks with a brute force, or any other more subtle technique which we do not address here. In the brute force approach, and using Occam's razor, the graph with the fewest attacks shall be selected, but we leave such considerations for future work.

5. EXPERIMENTS

To obtain experimental insights, we created 100 artificial (and thus domain independent) probabilistic argumentation frames $\langle \mathsf{G}, \mathcal{S}, (\Omega, F, P_i)\rangle$ ($i \in \{1, \ldots, 100\}$), all based on the source argumentation graph G shown in Figure 7. This graph has no self-attacking arguments, and thus we can aim to induce it exactly. Since we have 12 arguments, then a brute approach for finding the graph G would have to consider 2^{144} hypothetical graphs.

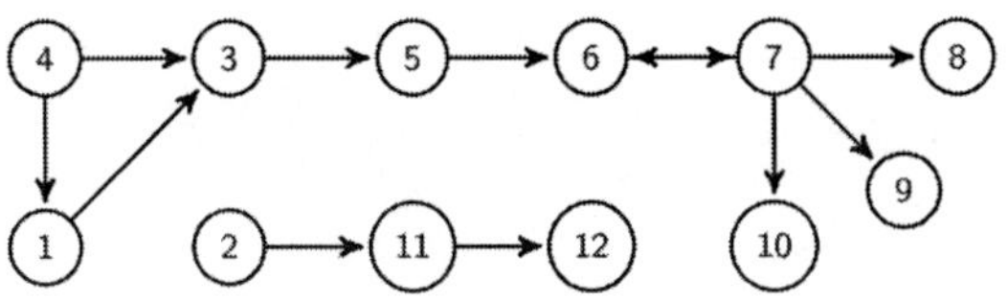

Figure 7: Source argumentation graph.

Each probabilistic argumentation frame had a different entropy. The entropy of the distribution P_i of a probabilistic argumentation frame $\langle \mathsf{G}, \mathcal{S}, (\Omega, F, P_i)\rangle$ is defined as follows:

$$entropy(P_i) = -\sum_{L \in \Omega} P_i(L) \cdot \ln(P_i(L)) \qquad (7)$$

To ensure meaningful experiments, we set a probability 0 for any labelling where all arguments were labelled off.

For every distribution, we run the Algorithm 1 on a stream of labelling instances (drawn from the considered distribution) in order to induce a graph maximising the explanation measure.

As we observed a sequence of n labelling instances, some instances may not be distinct since a labelling may be drawn twice or more. Accordingly, we have to distinguish the number n of labelling instances, and the number m of distinct labelling instances which are observed ($m \leq n$). In Example 1, we observed 6 labelling instances, but we observed 5 distinct labelling instances because the labelling instances at the steps 2 and 3 are the same.

We stopped the algorithm as soon as:

- all the attacks of the source graph were included in the set of confirmed attacks, and the number of undecided attacks was less or equal to 10 (simulating so a brute force search on the remaining undecided attacks), or
- $n = 10^6$ labelling instances were observed.

The number of observed labellings at termination is shown in Figure 8 and the associated expected explanatory utility (as formulated in Section 3) of the induced argumentation graph is given in Figure 9.

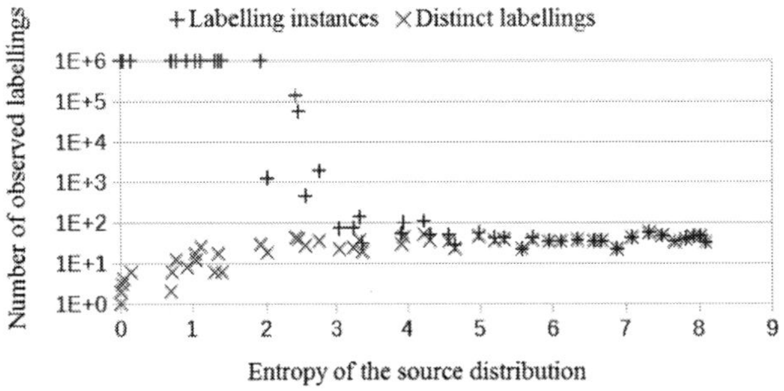

Figure 8: Number of labelling instances and distinct labellings observed at termination.

As expected, the lower the entropy, the longer it took to induce the source argumentation graph. Whatever the entropy, a few distinct labelling instances (less than one hundred) were necessary to exactly induce the source graph - to compare to the 2^{144} possible attack sub-graphs. For

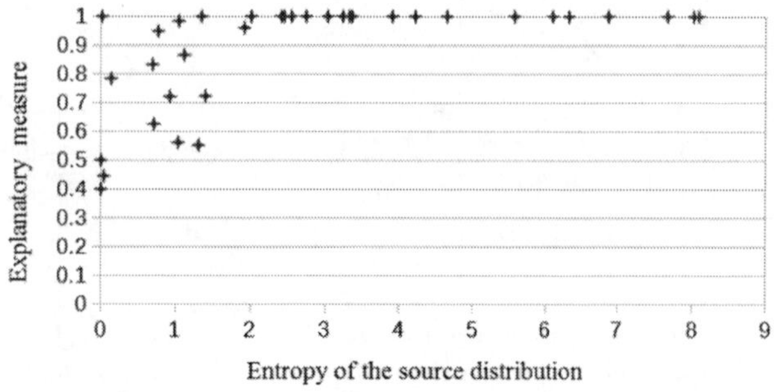

Figure 9: Expected explanatory utility of the induced argumentation graph at termination w.r.t. the observed labellings.

any entropy above 2, the source argumentation graph G was exactly induced. Furthermore, Figure 9 shows that even the original graph is not retrieved, the expected explanatory utility of the returned graph may be close to the maximum.

In a second set of experiments, we evaluated the approach on different distributions, all with an entropy 3 ± 0.05, based on source graphs with different number of arguments, and with up to 100 arguments (i.e. up to 2^{10000} hypothetical graphs).

The number of labelling instances and distinct labelling instances observed at termination is shown in Figure 10 for each distribution.

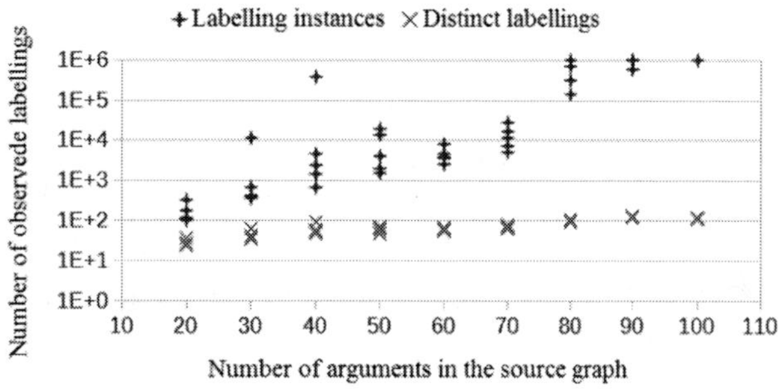

Figure 10: Number of labellings at termination.

The more the number of observed arguments, the longer the time to guess the source graph. Even when the source graph was not found at termination, the expected explanatory utility of the induced graph was above 0.99 at termination (this pretty flat figure is not shown).

Since the source argumentation graphs were exactly induced in most cases (as expected from Theorem 10) and the expected explanatory utility of the induced graphs was above 0.99 at termination in even more cases, the experiments suggest that induced graphs 'make sense' in general. The principal reason holds in that if an attack relation is discarded then this attack is indeed not part of the source graph, and when there are no self-attacking arguments, if an attack relation is confirmed then this attack is indeed part of the source graph, as ensured by backing our approach with Theorems 1-5.

6. CONCLUSION

We settled a problem of abstract structure learning regarding the induction of attacks between arguments in a probabilistic framework for abstract argumentation: labellings of arguments are observed and the goal is to learn attacks between arguments to account for the observed labellings by maximising an explanation measure.

To address this problem of abstract structure learning, we proposed to use five simple theorems about the attacks which can be learned from a labelling of arguments. Based on these theorems, we proposed an anytime and 'on the fly' algorithm taking as input a sequence of labellings, weighting the credit of attacks using credit rules, and returning an argumentation graph meant to account for the observed labellings.

We showed that if the computational budget is infinite, then the algorithm returns - almost surely - an argumentation graph indistinguishable from the source graph. In case of active learning, such an argumentation graph (of n arguments) is returned for sure (and thus the explanatory measure is maximised), by observing its $n \cdot (n+1)/2$ key labellings. In practice, it is possible to induce some source graphs with less labellings than the number of key labellings. The experiments showed that the time to induce a graph indistinguishable from source graph is largely dependent on the entropy of the source distribution of labellings. The higher the entropy, the faster the induction is performed.

As future developments, one may regard different credit rules and other types of labellings, possibly in the light of insights regarding their properties (see e.g. [18, 4]). One may also regard settings with structured arguments and more sophisticated updates of the credits to deal with some types of noise. As the proposed algorithm works with streams of labellings, it may be coupled with a so-called argumentative Boltzmann machine [19, 20] (by showing the labelling grasped line 4 to the machine). Doing so, the induction of the argumentation graph shall occur at the same time as the learning of the probability distribution of labellings, giving thus explanatory ability to the neural network.

Acknowledgements

We would like to thank the helpful AAMAS reviewers. NICTA is funded by the Australian Government through the Department of Communications and the Australian Research Council through the ICT Centre for Excellence Program. Part of the work was supported by the Marie Curie Intra-European Fellowship PIEF-GA-2012-331472.

REFERENCES

[1] P. Baroni, M. Caminada, and M. Giacomin. An introduction to argumentation semantics. *Knowledge Engineering Review*, 26(4):365–410, 2011.

[2] P. Dondio. Toward a computational analysis of probabilistic argumentation frameworks. *Cybernetics and Systems*, 45(3):254–278, 2014.

[3] P. M. Dung. On the acceptability of arguments and its fundamental role in nonmonotonic reasoning, logic programming and n-person games. *Artif. Intell.*, 77(2):321–358, 1995.

[4] P. Dunne, W. Dvorák, T. Linsbichler, and S. Woltran. Characteristics of multiple viewpoints in abstract argumentation. *Artif. Intell.*, 228:153–178, 2015.

[5] P. Dunne, A. Hunter, P. McBurney, S. Parsons, and M. Wooldridge. Weighted argument systems: Basic definitions, algorithms, and complexity results. *Artif. Intell.*, 175(2):457–486, 2011.

[6] B. Fazzinga, S. Flesca, and F. Parisi. On the complexity of probabilistic abstract argumentation frameworks. *ACM Trans. Comput. Logic*, 16(3):22:1–22:39, June 2015.

[7] P. A. Flach. Rationality postulates for induction. In *Proceedings of the 6th Conference on Theoretical Aspects of Rationality and Knowledge*, pages 267–281. Morgan Kaufmann, 1996.

[8] P. Flajolet, D. Gardy, and L. Thimonier. Birthday paradox, coupon collectors, caching algorithms and self-organizing search. *Discrete Appl. Math.*, 39(3):207–229, Nov. 1992.

[9] L. Getoor and B. Taskar. *Introduction to Statistical Relational Learning (Adaptive Computation and Machine Learning).* The MIT Press, 2007.

[10] B. Johnston and G. Governatori. Induction of defeasible logic theories in the legal domain. In *Proceedings of the 9th International Conference on Artificial Intelligence and Law*, pages 204–213. ACM, 2003.

[11] J. Kolodner. *Case-based Reasoning.* Morgan Kaufmann Publishers Inc., San Francisco, CA, USA, 1993.

[12] H. Li, N. Oren, and T. J. Norman. Probabilistic argumentation frameworks. In *Revised Selected Papers of the 1st International Workshop on Theory and Applications of Formal Argumentation.*, Lecture Notes in Computer Science, pages 1–16. Springer, 2011.

[13] M. Mozina, J. Zabkar, and I. Bratko. Argument based machine learning. *Artif. Intell.*, 171(10-15):922–937, 2007.

[14] S. Ontañón, P. Dellunde, L. Godo, and E. Plaza. A defeasible reasoning model of inductive concept learning from examples and communication. *Artif. Intell.*, 193:129–148, Dec. 2012.

[15] S. Polberg and D. Doder. Probabilistic abstract dialectical frameworks. In *Proceedings of the 14th European Conference on Logics in Artificial Intelligence*, pages 591–599. Springer, 2014.

[16] H. Prakken and G. Sartor. Reasoning with precedents in a dialogue game. In *Proceedings of the 6th International Conference on Artificial Intelligence and Law*, ICAIL '97, pages 1–9, New York, NY, USA, 1997. ACM.

[17] L. D. Raedt, P. Frasconi, K. Kersting, and S. Muggleton, editors. *Probabilistic Inductive Logic Programming - Theory and Applications.* Springer Berlin Heidelberg, 2008.

[18] T. Rienstra, C. Sakama, and L. W. N. van der Torre. Persistence and monotony properties of argumentation semantics. In *Revised Selected Papers of the 3rd International Workshop on Theory and Applications of Formal Argumentation*, pages 211–225. Springer, 2015.

[19] R. Riveret, D. Korkinof, M. Draief, and J. V. Pitt. Probabilistic abstract argumentation: an investigation with boltzmann machines. *Argument & Computation*, 6(2):178–218, 2015.

[20] R. Riveret, J. Pitt, D. Korkinof, and M. Draief. Neuro-symbolic agents: Boltzmann machine and Probabilistic Abstract Argumentation with Sub-arguments. In *Proceedings of the 14th International Joint Conference on Autonomous Agents & Multiagent Systems.* IFAAMAS, 2015.

[21] M. Thimm. A probabilistic semantics for abstract argumentation. In *Proceedings of the 20th European Conference on Artificial Intelligence*, volume 242 of *Frontiers in Artificial Intelligence and Applications*, pages 750–755. IOS Press, 2012.

Verification of Multi-Agent Systems via Predicate Abstraction against ATLK Specifications

Alessio Lomuscio
Department of Computing
Imperial College London, UK
a.lomuscio@imperial.ac.uk

Jakub Michliszyn
Institute of Computer Science
University of Wrocław, Poland
jmi@cs.uni.wroc.pl

ABSTRACT

We present a predicate abstraction technique for the verification of multi-agent systems against specifications defined in the epistemic logic ATLK, interpreted on a three-valued semantics. We reduce an infinite-state multi-agent program to a finite model by generating predicates automatically via SMT calls. We show that if an ATLK specification is either true or false in the abstract model, then that is also the case on the original infinite state model. We introduce and describe $MCMAS_{PA}$, a toolkit implementing the technique here described. $MCMAS_{PA}$ supports the three-valued semantics for ATLK, automatically generates program abstractions for a multi-agent system by means of automatic SMT calls, encodes the corresponding program in BDDs and reports the result. The experimental results obtained confirm that $MCMAS_{PA}$ can verify infinite-state multi-agent systems of interest.

1. INTRODUCTION

Multi-Agent Systems (MAS) are distributed computer systems where the components, or agents, rationally interact with one another and the environment in a variety of complex ways [29]. Whereas progress has been made in the theoretical analysis of MAS, both from a logical and game-theoretic perspective, we still lack comprehensive methodologies for the verification of MAS before deployment. This is of concern as techniques such as rapid prototyping, which rely on efficient evaluation, e.g., via verification, have been shown to be of significant importance in the adoption of novel paradigms in applications. In addition, the lack of robust verification methodologies also hinders the adoption of MAS in safety-critical applications.

The current state of the art for the offline analysis of MAS consists of a variety of model checking techniques including BDD-based model checking [11, 27], bounded model checking [26], and symmetry reduction [6]. Existing model checkers implement some of these in a variety of forms [24, 17, 11]. One key characteristic that these techniques and implementations have in common is that they are confined to the analysis of *finite state systems*, i.e., the models corresponding to the MAS descriptions to be analysed only have finitely many states. This is typically enforced via the input language of the toolkit by adopting variable types which can only have bounded instantiations, e.g., bounded integers. This restriction is appealing as finite state model checking is decidable, whereas infinite state model checking is in general undecidable.

While the limitation given by finite models is not significant when the MAS can be appropriately abstracted as a finite state system, most of the MAS programs that are built generate models that have infinitely many states. Additionally even if a bound for a variable can be found by analysing all possible executions, the actual range may be difficult to find for the programmer, who will generally adopt unbounded variable types.

Contribution. In this paper we begin to overcome the limitation of finite states in the practical verification of MAS. Since verifying infinite states systems is undecidable in general, the method we present is sound but not complete. Yet, we show that in some cases of interest the technique can help solving the verification problem. The method takes as input a description of an infinite state MAS and specifications in the epistemic temporal logic ATLK [2, 14]. A finite model abstracting the infinite model for the system is then generated by carrying out abstraction both on the local states and the actions of the agents. The finite model is defined by analysing the conditions that appear in the specification to be checked and in the MAS description. This analysis, which is entirely automated, results in the generation of Boolean predicates that are combined with the original MAS description to generate a finite-state MAS description. We show that if the resulting model checking problem returns either true or false, this is also the result of the verification problem for the infinite-state model.

The technique is fully automated and implemented; we present both the underlying theory for the abstraction as well as the actual predicate generation and verification. We carried out the latter by extending the open-source checker MCMAS [24] to handle the three-valued logic ATLK and implementing the algorithm for generating predicates by means of SMT calls to the SMT-checker CVC4 [4]. The resulting implementation, which we call $MCMAS_{PA}$, constitutes, to our knowledge, the first predicate abstraction toolkit for MAS.

Related Work. Epistemic versions of ATL for specifying MAS have attracted considerable attention over the past few years [14, 25, 5, 1]. The difficulty of validating systems with large state spaces has long been recognised in verification and multi-agent systems. Abstraction has been used in the context of epistemic logic [9] including in the con-

Appears in: *Proceedings of the 15th International Conference on Autonomous Agents and Multiagent Systems (AAMAS 2016), J. Thangarajah, K. Tuyls, C. Jonker, S. Marsella (eds.), May 9–13, 2016, Singapore.*

text of interpreted systems [7]. [20] presents an abstraction technique for ATL; however, it deals with finite states only, and, differently from the present contribution, it deals with complete information only.

Three-valued and multi-valued temporal logic have been developed in the context of model checking [18, 19] and abstraction methodologies have been put forward [15]. These, however, have not been extended to specifications supporting MAS and their automatisation is problematic. Predicate abstraction techniques for under- and over-approximations of infinite state systems were originally suggested in the context of temporal logic and modal μ calculus [13, 8]. While approaches use SMT engines for the generation of the finite model, they have not been extended to epistemic, nor ATL specifications.

Closer to the theoretical part of the work here presented is [21] where the theoretical underpinnings of an abstraction methodology on three valued semantics for ATLK is developed. That work, however, does not deal with infinite-state systems, no methodology for the generation of the finite models via SMT is given and, consequently, no toolkit for the actual verification is given.

Predicate abstraction techniques are normally tailored to temporal logics only. A predicate abstraction for epistemic logic has recently been proposed in [12]. While that work is also based on a three-valued logic, the semantics is different, and ATL is not supported. Indeed, [12] is tailored to the verification of service-oriented applications specified by the GSM language. In contrast we here address MAS modelled by an extension of ISPL, an existing language for reasoning about MAS. Also, a predicate abstraction technique for ATL only was discussed in [3]. The semantic setting in [3] assumes perfect recall and complete information, following the original treatment of ATL in [2]. As we remark in the next section, in principle this semantics is equivalent to the one we use in this paper; however, while [3] assume deterministic evolutions, we allow for non-deterministic transitions to account for a significant role by the environment on the system. Also, [3] is not concerned with epistemic specifications as we are here. Lastly, we are not aware of an implementation based on [3], whereas we here report on an open-source model checker for MAS supporting predicate-abstraction.

2. THE THREE-VALUED LOGIC ATLK

In this section we summarise the three-valued logic ATLK on memoryless interpreted systems with incomplete information which we adopt here. ATLK is an extension of ATL [2], the logic designed to express properties of agents' strategies, that allows also to express epistemic properties of agents and groups of agents [28]. In this context, several choices need to be made when combining the need for efficient procedures and expressive specifications. The rational for the setting we adopt here was discussed in [22].

Let $Ag = \{1, \ldots, m\}$ be a set of agents and $\mathcal{V}$ be a set of propositional variables. We use the letter Γ to denote subsets of agents, e.g., $\Gamma \subseteq Ag$; by $\overline{\Gamma}$ we denote the complementation of Γ, i.e., $Ag \setminus \Gamma$.

Definition 1 (Interpreted systems). *An* interpreted system *is a tuple* $IS = (\{L_i, Act_i, P_i, t_i\}_{i \in Ag}, I, \Pi)$ *such that:*

- *for each agent i L_i is a possibly infinite set of possible* local states, *Act_i is a set of possible* local actions, *$P_i : L_i \to 2^{Act_i} \setminus \{\emptyset\}$ is a* local protocol, *and $t_i \subseteq L_i \times ACT \times L_i$ is a* local transition relation *with $ACT = Act_1 \times \cdots \times Act_m$.*
- *$I \subseteq L_1 \times \cdots \times L_m$ is a set of* global initial states,
- *$\Pi : L_1 \times \cdots \times L_m \times \mathcal{V} \to \{\mathrm{tt}, \mathrm{ff}, \mathrm{uu}\}$ is a* labelling function.

Notice that the definition above allows the value of a propositional variable in a state to be unknown (uu). We will use this to represent abstract states in which the value of some propositional variables is not defined. We consider a possibly non-deterministic transition relation as this will be the case for the abstract models introduced later.

By $t.i$ we denote the i-th element of a tuple t. We define models of interpreted systems in the usual way.

Definition 2 (Models). *Given an interpreted system $IS = (\{L_i, Act_i, P_i, t_i\}_{i \in Ag}, I, \Pi)$, its associated model is a tuple $M_{IS} = (S, T, \{\sim_i\}_{i \in Ag}, I, \Pi)$ such that:*

- *$S \subseteq L_1 \times \cdots \times L_m$ is the set of global states reachable via T from the set of initial global states I,*
- *$T \subseteq S \times ACT \times S$ is a global transition relation such that $T((l_1, \ldots, l_m), a, (l'_1, \ldots, l'_m))$ iff for all $i \in Ag$ we have $t_i(l_i, a, l'_i)$ and $a.i \in P_i(l_i)$,*
- *$\sim_i \subseteq S^2$ is such that $s \sim_i s'$ iff $s.i = s'.i$, for all $i \in Ag$.*

The intended meaning of $s \sim_i s'$ is that the global states s, s' are epistemically indistinguishable for agent i [10]. For $\Gamma \subseteq Ag$, we define the relation $\sim_\Gamma$ for the common knowledge operator as the transitive closure of $(\bigcup_{i \in \Gamma} \sim_i)$.

We only consider models such that for all global states $s \in S$ and joint actions $a \in ACT$ such that $a.i \in P_i(s.i)$ for all $i \in Ag$, there exists an $s' \in S$ such that $T(s, a, s')$.

We are interested in two logics with the same syntax, but different semantics: the two-valued logic ATLK and the three-valued logic ATLK^{3v}. First, we introduce the common syntax for the logics ATLK and ATLK^{3v}.

Definition 3 (ATLK language). *The set of formulas for the logics ATLK and ATLK ^{3v} is defined from $\mathcal{V}$ by the following BNF expression:*
$\varphi ::= q \mid \neg\varphi \mid \varphi \wedge \varphi \mid \langle\langle\Gamma\rangle\rangle X\varphi \mid \langle\langle\Gamma\rangle\rangle(\varphi U \varphi) \mid \langle\langle\Gamma\rangle\rangle G\varphi \mid K_i\varphi \mid C_{\Gamma'}\varphi$
where $i \in Ag$, $\Gamma, \Gamma' \subseteq Ag$, $\Gamma' \neq \emptyset$ and $q \in \mathcal{V}$.

The formulas $K_i\varphi, C_{\Gamma'}\varphi$ are read as "agent i knows that φ" and "in the group Γ' it is commonly known that φ", respectively. The reading of the ATL modalities is as follows. The formula $\langle\langle\Gamma\rangle\rangle G\varphi$ stands for "the agents in Γ *may be able* to ensure that φ holds forever"; the meaning of the "until" modality U is analogous, and $\langle\langle\Gamma\rangle\rangle X\varphi$ can be read as "the agents in Γ can ensure that φ holds at the next state irrespective of the actions of the agents in $Ag \setminus \Gamma$". We use the standard abbreviations to define $\langle\langle\Gamma\rangle\rangle F\varphi$, that stands for "the agents in Γ may be able to ensure that φ will happen at some point in the future", and the Boolean connectives.

The readings above of the ATL modalities was originally given in [25] and used in several approaches that followed. There may be applications where the readings are not appropriate; in these cases the logic CTL, which is entirely subsumed, can be used instead. Our motivation for the work is to provide support for epistemic modalities under an efficient model checking setting; indeed, the complexity of the model checking problem in the setting we describe below is the same as that of CTLK. We refer to [22] for a discussion on these issues.

Semantics

Assume an interpreted system $IS = (\{L_i, Act_i, P_i, t_i\}_{i\in Ag}, I, \Pi)$. A (*local, memoryless*) *strategy* for an agent $i \in \Gamma$, or simply a strategy, is a function $f_i : s.i' \rightarrow 2^{Act_i} \setminus \{\emptyset\}$ such that for each local state $s.i \in L_i$ we have $f_i(s) \subseteq P_i(s.i)$. We do not assume perfect recall, i.e., all the strategies depend on the current local state only.

Given a path $p = s_0 s_1 \ldots$, by p^i we denote s_i, the $i+1$-th element of p. Assume $\Gamma \subseteq Ag$ and an indexed set of strategies $F_\Gamma = \{f_i \mid i \in \Gamma\}$. A set of paths Y is F_Γ-*compatible* if it is a minimal non-empty set of paths such that for each path $p \in Y$, position $j \geq 0$, joint actions a, a' and state s' such that $T(p^j, a, p^{j+1})$, $T(p^j, a', s')$, and for all $i \in \Gamma$, $a.i = a'.i$ and $a.i \in f_i(s_j.i)$, there exists a path $p' \in Y$ starting with $p^0 \ldots p^j s'$. Let $out(s, F_\Gamma)$ be the family of all F_Γ-compatible sets of paths starting with s.

Assume an interpreted system $IS = (\{L_i, Act_i, P_i, t_i\}_{i\in Ag}, I, \Pi)$, its associated model $M = (S, T, \{\sim_i\}_{i\in Ag}, I, \Pi)$ and a global state $s \in S$. We inductively define the two-valued satisfaction relation $\models^2$ as follows.

- $M, s \models^2 q$ iff $\Pi(s, q) =$ tt,
- $M, s \models^2 \neg\varphi$ iff it is not the case that $M, s \models^2 \varphi$,
- $M, s \models^2 \varphi_1 \wedge \varphi_2$ iff $M, s \models^2 \varphi_1$ and $M, s \models^2 \varphi_2$,
- $M, s \models^2 \langle\!\langle\Gamma\rangle\!\rangle X\varphi$ iff for some strategy F_Γ, some $Y \in out(s, F_\Gamma)$ and all $p \in Y$ we have $M, p^1 \models^2 \varphi$,
- $M, s \models^2 \langle\!\langle\Gamma\rangle\!\rangle \varphi_1 U \varphi_2$ iff for some strategy F_Γ, some $Y \in out(s, F_\Gamma)$ and all $p \in Y$, there is a $k \geq 0$ s.t. we have $M, p^k \models^2 \varphi_2$ and for all $0 \leq j < k$, $M, p^j \models^2 \varphi_1$,
- $M, s \models^2 \langle\!\langle\Gamma\rangle\!\rangle G\varphi$ iff for some strategy F_Γ, some $Y \in out(s, F_\Gamma)$ and all $p \in Y$, $i \geq 0$ we have $M, p^i \models^2 \varphi$,
- $M, s \models^2 K_i\varphi$ iff for all $s' \sim_i s$ we have $M, s' \models^2 \varphi$,
- $M, s \models^2 C_\Gamma\varphi$ iff for all $s' \sim_\Gamma s$ we have $M, s' \models^2 \varphi$.

The definition of the three-valued satisfaction $\models^3$, introduced by [22], is given below. We assume Kleene interpretation of boolean operators, i.e., $\neg$uu = uu, $\neg$tt = ff, $\neg$ff = tt and $t \wedge t'$ is tt iff both t, t' are tt, ff if any of them is ff, and uu otherwise.

- $M, s \models^3 q = \Pi(s, q)$,
- $M, s \models^3 \neg\varphi = \neg(M, s \models^3 \varphi = \text{ff})$,
- $M, s \models^3 \varphi_1 \wedge \varphi_2 = (M, s \models^3 \varphi_1 = \text{tt}) \wedge (M, s \models^3 \varphi_2 = \text{tt})$,
- $M, s \models^3 \langle\!\langle\Gamma\rangle\!\rangle X\varphi =$ tt iff for some strategy F_Γ, some $Y \in out(s, F_\Gamma)$ and all $p \in Y$, we have $M, p^1 \models^3 \varphi =$ tt,
- $M, s \models^3 \langle\!\langle\Gamma\rangle\!\rangle X\varphi =$ ff iff for some strategy $F_{\overline{\Gamma}}$, for all $Y \in out(s, F_{\overline{\Gamma}})$ and all $p \in Y$ we have $M, p^1 \models^3 \varphi =$ ff,
- $M, s \models^3 \langle\!\langle\Gamma\rangle\!\rangle \varphi_1 U \varphi_2 =$ tt iff for some strategy F_Γ, for some $Y \in out(s, F_\Gamma)$, and for all $p \in Y$ there is $k \geq 0$ s.t. $M, p^k \models^3 \varphi_2 =$ tt and for all $j < k$, $M, p^j \models^3 \varphi_1 =$ tt,
- $M, s \models^3 \langle\!\langle\Gamma\rangle\!\rangle \varphi_1 U \varphi_2 =$ ff iff for some strategy $F_{\overline{\Gamma}}$, for all $Y \in out(s, F_{\overline{\Gamma}})$ and for all $p \in Y$, $k \geq 0$ we have $M, p^k \models^3 \varphi_2 =$ ff or there is $j < k$ s.t. $M, p^j \models^3 \varphi_1 =$ ff,
- $M, s \models^3 \langle\!\langle\Gamma\rangle\!\rangle G\varphi =$ tt iff for some strategy F_Γ, some $Y \in out(s, F_\Gamma)$ and for all $p \in Y$, $i \geq 0$ we have $M, p^i \models^3 \varphi =$ tt
- $M, s \models^3 \langle\!\langle\Gamma\rangle\!\rangle G\varphi =$ ff iff for some strategy $F_{\overline{\Gamma}}$, for all $Y \in out(s, F_{\overline{\Gamma}})$, and for all $p \in Y$ there is $i \geq 0$ s.t. $M, p^i \models^3 \varphi =$ ff
- $M, s \models^3 K_i\varphi =$ tt iff $M, s' \models^3 \varphi =$ tt for all $s' \sim_i s$,
- $M, s \models^3 K_i\varphi =$ ff iff $M, s \models^3 \varphi =$ ff,
- $M, s \models^3 C_\Gamma\varphi =$ tt iff $M, s' \models^3 \varphi =$ tt for all $s' \sim_\Gamma s$,
- $M, s \models^3 C_\Gamma\varphi =$ ff iff $M, s \models^3 \varphi =$ ff.

In all other cases, the value of a formula is undefined (uu).
While the conditions for the true value are very similar in both semantics, the condition for the false value is much more strict in the three valued case. Intuitively, the conditions for the ATL modalities state that "there is a strategy of agents outside of Γ to prevent a given property" rather than the weaker "there is no strategy of agents of Γ to achieve a given property". It follows that the two semantics do not coincide. For the epistemic modalities, the condition for the false value simply requires the formula to be false in the current state; such a strong condition is required to guarantee the soundness of our abstraction technique, provided later on.

An interpreted system IS satisfies a property φ, written as $IS \models^2 \varphi$, iff for all the initial states s we have $M, s \models^2 \varphi$. We define $IS \models^3 \varphi =$ tt iff for all $s \in I$ we have $M, s \models^3 \varphi =$ tt, $IS \models^3 \varphi =$ ff iff some $s \in I$ we have $M, s \models^3 \varphi =$ ff, and $IS \models^3 \varphi =$ uu otherwise. Note that in this setting the strategies can be replaced by agents' protocols.

It is shown in [22] that for any φ we have that $IS \models^3 \varphi =$ tt implies $IS \models^2 \varphi$ and $IS \models^3 \varphi =$ ff implies $IS \not\models^2 \varphi$.

Remark. No technical contribution is made in this section with respect to the state of the art as we follow [22] for the semantics of the ATLK specifications. Moreover, as far as the two-valued ATL fragment is concerned, the semantics here adopted from [22] assumes that the agents are memoryless, have incomplete information of the global state. We assumed that the resulting models are non-uniform in the sense of [25]; i.e., agents can execute different actions at different global states in which their own local state is the same. This is in contrast with the original semantics for ATL [2], which stipulates complete information of the state, and perfect recall. However, it can be shown that two formulations are logically equivalent in the sense that an ATL formula is true in the setting we here adopt if and only if the formula is true in the semantics adopted in [2]. It follows that, for the two-valued fragment, an ATLK formula holds in an interpreted system under the present semantics if it holds in the ATLK logic in [16].

We follow [22] in adopting the present modelling as in applications agents are naturally assumed to have incomplete information and imperfect recall. Since our specification language includes epistemic modalities, whose definition relies on incomplete information, we find this setting more appropriate. Indeed, the modelling language we adopt in Section 3 follows this assumption, in line with other modelling approaches for MAS. However, the computations for evaluating a formula to true or false can in principle equally be performed by using the semantics in [2, 16].

3. PREDICATE ABSTRACTION OF UISPL PROGRAMS

Verification engines differ in the input language adopted to describe the system. Any abstraction methodology needs to be fine tuned to the language adopted. Here we take ISPL [24] as the starting point; other choices are possible. We chose ISPL as it constitutes the input language to MCMAS, an open-source symbolic model checker for MAS that already supports the verification of ATLK, albeit for the two-valued semantics only.

Like many of its peers, ISPL programs describe finite state systems by using bounded variable types. Below we introduce Unbounded ISPL (or UISPL for short), an extension of ISPL with unbounded integers.

Unbounded ISPL

Like ISPL, an UISPL program consists of a declaration of a number of agents (keyword `Agent`) and an environment, the definition of the initial states of the system (keyword `InitStates`), and the description of the specifications to be checked (keywords `Evaluation`, `Groups` and `Formulae`).

An agent definition consists of the following components: local states, defined by a number of variables (`Vars`) of type Boolean, enumeration, and unbounded integer; local actions (`Actions`), used to interact with other agents and the environment; a local protocol (`Protocol`), representing the actions enabled in a given state; and a local evolution function (`Evolution`), encoding the change to the local state on the basis of the current local state and the action performed by all the agents. Non-deterministic protocols are encoded in UISPL either by specifying more than one target action or by giving different actions for overlapping conditions on local states. The initial states of the system are defined by means of a Boolean formula on the agents' variables, e.g., $Ag1.pos = 1$ *or* $(Ag1.pos < 17$ *and* $Ag2.ready = true)$. Notice that every UISPL program can be naturally associated with its infinite-state interpreted system.

The specifications to be checked are given as a list of ATLK formulas, followed by the declaration for the propositions and groups of agents appearing in the specifications.

Abstract models of UISPL programs

It is easy to show that in general verifying an UISPL program is undecidable, even if the specification is limited to safety properties. The approach that we put forward is sound but not complete. Differently from other approaches including [3], the predicate abstraction technique that we introduce is modular in the agents. Our choice is motivated by the need of providing an efficient methodology for verifying epistemic specifications, which depend on the local states of the individual agents.

Consider an UISPL program, its associated interpreted system $IS = (\{L_i, Act_i, P_i, t_i\}_{i\in Ag}, I, \Pi)$ and a tuple of lists of predicates $(\vec{p}_1, \ldots, \vec{p}_m)$, where $\vec{p}_i = p_i^1, \ldots, p_i^{k_i}$. Each predicate is assumed to be a condition on an agent's state, e.g., $Ag1.pos < 16$. The abstract agent i w.r.t. a list of predicates $\vec{p}_i$ is defined as a tuple $Ag_i^A = (L_i^A, Act_i, P_i^{\text{MAY}}, P_i^{\text{MUST}}, t_i^{\text{MAY}}, t_i^{\text{MUST}})$, where:

- L_i^A is the set (i.e., conjunctions) containing all the predicates from $\vec{p}_i$,
- the *may relation* t_i^{MAY} is such that $t_i^{\text{MAY}}(c, a, c')$ for abstract states c, c' and an action a iff there are local states $l, l' \in L_i$ such that l satisfies c, l' satisfies c' and $t_i(l, a, l')$,
- the *must relation* t_i^{MUST} is such that $t_i^{\text{MUST}}(c, a, c')$ for abstract states c, c' and an action a iff for each local state $l \in L_i$ satisfying c we have $t_i(l, a, l')$ for some state l' satisfying c',
- the *may protocol* P_i^{MAY} is such that $P_i^{\text{MAY}}(c)$ is the union of all $P_i(l)$ for l satisfying c,
- the *must protocol* P_i^{MUST} is such that $a \in P_i^{\text{MUST}}(c)$ iff for every state l satisfying c we have $a \in P_i(l)$ and for every c' such that $t_i(l', a, \bar{l}')$ for some l' satisfying c and $\bar{l}'$ satisfying c', there is a state $\bar{l}$ satisfying c' such that $t_i(l, a, \bar{l})$.

While the may protocol for an abstract state is simply the union of the protocols for the corresponding concrete states, the must protocol is more complex. In the must protocol, an action a is allowed in c only if for any l_1 and l_2 satisfying c, the sets of abstractions of successors of l_1 and l_2 are the same, i.e., $\{c' \mid \exists l'.t_i(l_1, a, l') \wedge l' \text{ satisfies } c'\} = \{c' \mid \exists l'.t_i(l_2, a, l') \wedge l' \text{ satisfies } c'\}$.

EXAMPLE 1. *Consider an agent* 1 *consisting of* L_1, Act_1, P_1, t_1 *defined as follows:*

- $L_1 = \{s_1, s_2, s_3, s_4\}$ *are the local states,*
- $Act_1 = \{a\}$ *is the set containing the only possible action for the agent* 1*,*
- $P_1(l) = \{a\}$ *for each* $l \in L_1$ *is the protocol that allows the agent* 1 *to use the action* a *in all the states,*
- $t_1 = \{(s_1, a, s_3), (s_1, a, s_4), (s_2, a, s_3), (s_3, a, s_3), (s_4, a, s_4)\}$ *is the transition relation.*

Assume the predicates $p_1^1 = s_1 \vee s_2$ *and* $p_1^2 = s_3$*. The set* L_1^A *consists of three states:* $c_{12} = p_1^1 \wedge \neg p_1^2$, $c_3 = \neg p_1^1 \wedge p_1^2$ *and* $c_4 = \neg p_1^1 \wedge \neg p_1^2$ *Notice that* $p_1^1 \wedge p_1^2$ *is not satisfiable. Then we have*

$$\begin{aligned} P_1^{\text{MAY}}(c) &= \{a\} \text{ for every } c \in L_1^A \\ P_1^{\text{MUST}}(c_{12}) &= \emptyset \\ P_1^{\text{MUST}}(c) &= \{a\} \text{ for every } c \in \{c_3, c_4\} \end{aligned}$$

$P_1^{\text{MUST}}(c_{12}) = \emptyset$ *follows from the fact that both* s_1, s_2 *satisfy* c_{12}*, but only one of them is connected via* a *to a state satisfying* c_3*.*

The transition relations are as follows:
$t_1^{\text{MAY}} = \{(c_{12}, a, c_3), (c_{12}, a, c_4), (c_3, a, c_3), (c_4, a, c_4)\}$ *and*
$t_1^{\text{MUST}} = \{(c_{12}, a, c_3), (c_3, a, c_3), (c_4, a, c_4)\}$.

A global state $s = (l_1, \ldots, l_m)$ satisfies a tuple of clauses $(c_1, \ldots, c_m)$ if $s.i$ satisfies c_i for each $i \in A$. We can now define the concept of abstract models.

DEFINITION 4 (ABSTRACT INTERPRETED SYSTEMS). *The* abstract interpreted system *of an interpreted system IS w.r.t. a tuple $(\vec{p}_1, \ldots, \vec{p}_m)$ is a tuple $IS^A = (\{Ag_i^A\}_{i \in Ag}, I^A, \Pi^A)$, where:*

- *for each i, Ag_i^A is the abstract agent i w.r.t. $\vec{p}_i$,*
- *Π^A is such that for any state b, $q \in \mathcal{V}$ and $t \in \{\text{tt}, \text{ff}\}$ we have $\Pi^A(b, q) = t$ iff $\Pi(s, q) = t$ for all the states s satisfying b,*
- *$I^A = \{b \mid \exists s \in I.s \text{ satisfies } b\}$.*

The model *associated to the predicate abstraction IS^A is a tuple $M_{IS}^A = (S^A, \{T_\Gamma^A\}_{\Gamma \subseteq Ag}, \{\sim_i^A\}_{i \in Ag}, I^A, \Pi^A)$, where S^A, $\{\sim_i^A\}_{i \in Ag}$, I^A, Π^A are derived as in Definition 2 and for each $\Gamma \subseteq Ag$ we have $T_\Gamma^A(b, a, b')$ iff*

- *for each $i \in \Gamma$, $a.i \in P^{\text{MUST}}(b.i)$ and $t_i^{\text{MUST}}(b.i, a, b'.i)$, and*
- *for each $i \notin \Gamma$, $a.i \in P^{\text{MAY}}(b.i)$ and $t_i^{\text{MAY}}(b.i, a, b'_i)$.*

In the following we also refer to abstract interpreted systems as predicate abstractions of a given interpreted system.

So, to construct T_Γ^A we force the agents in Γ to adhere to both their must protocol and transition relation but, more liberally, we let the protocols and transitions for the agents in $Ag \setminus \Gamma$ to be selected from their respective may relations.

We now extend the notion of F_Γ-compatibility as follows. A set of paths in M^A is *F_Γ-compatible* if it is a minimal non-empty set of paths such that for each path $p \in IS^A$, position $j \geq 0$, joint actions a, a' and state s' such that $T_\Gamma(p^j, a, p^{j+1})$, $T_\Gamma(p^j, a', s')$, and for all $i \in \Gamma$, $a.i = a'.i$ and $a.i \in f_i(s_j.i)$, there exists a path $p' \in IS^A$ starting with $p^0 \ldots p^j s'$. Having defined F_Γ-compatible paths, the two-valued and three-valued semantics for the ATL modalities can be given analogously to those in Section 2.

THEOREM 5. *Assume an interpreted system IS and let IS^A be its predicate abstraction. For any ATLK property φ, $IS^A \models^3 \varphi = \text{tt}$ implies $IS \models^3 \varphi = \text{tt}$ and $IS^A \models^3 \varphi = \text{ff}$ implies $IS \models^3 \varphi = \text{ff}$.*

PROOF. Let M be the model of IS and M^A be the model of IS^A constructed as above. Consider a state s of M and let b be the state of M^A such that s satisfies b. We prove by induction on φ that $M^A, b \models^3 \varphi = \text{tt}$ implies $M, s \models^3 \varphi = \text{tt}$ and $M^A, b \models^3 \varphi = \text{ff}$ implies $M, s \models^3 \varphi = \text{ff}$. The proof follows from the construction of the abstract system.

Basic cases. Assume $\varphi = q$. If $M^A, b \models^3 q = \text{tt}$, then all the states s' satisfying b are such that $M^A, s' \models^3 q = \text{tt}$, and in particular $M^A, s \models^3 q = \text{tt}$. Similarly, if $M^A, b \models^3 q = \text{ff}$, then all the states s' satisfying b are such that $M^A, s' \models^3 q = \text{ff}$, therefore $M^A, s \models^3 q = \text{ff}$.

Boolean cases are straightforward and therefore omitted.

ATL cases. Assume $\varphi = \langle\langle\Gamma\rangle\rangle X\psi$. Consider the case when $M^A, b \models^3 \varphi = \text{tt}$. There is a joint action a_Γ for the agents in Γ such that for any joint action $a_{\overline{\Gamma}}$ for the agents in $\overline{\Gamma}$ and any state b' such that $T_\Gamma(b, (a_\Gamma, a_{\overline{\Gamma}}), b')$ we have $M^A, b' \models^3 \psi = \text{tt}$. Consider the states s, s' such that we have $T(s, (a_\Gamma, a_{\overline{\Gamma}}), s')$, and s satisfies b and s' satisfies b'. For $i \in \Gamma$, since $a.i \in P_i(b.i)$, we have $t_i^{\text{MUST}}(b.i, (a_\Gamma, a_{\overline{\Gamma}}), b'.i)$. For any $i \notin \Gamma$, we have $t_i^{\text{MAY}}(b.i, (a_\Gamma, a_{\overline{\Gamma}}), b'.i)$ by the definition of the function t_i^{MAY}. So $T_\Gamma(b, (a_\Gamma, a_{\overline{\Gamma}}), b')$ and, by the inductive assumption, $M, s' \models^3 \psi = \text{tt}$ and $M, s \models^3 \varphi = \text{tt}$.

If $M^A, b \models^3 \varphi = \text{ff}$, then there is a joint action $a_{\overline{\Gamma}}$ for $\overline{\Gamma}$ such that for any joint action a_Γ for Γ and any state b' such that $T_{\overline{\Gamma}}(b, (a_{\overline{\Gamma}}, a_\Gamma), b')$ we have $M^A, b' \models^3 \psi = \text{ff}$. Consider states s, s' such that we have $T(s, (a_{\overline{\Gamma}}, a_\Gamma), s')$, s satisfies b and s' satisfies b'. For $i \in \overline{\Gamma}$, since $a.i \in P_i(b.i)$, we have $t_i^{\text{MUST}}(b.i, (a_{\overline{\Gamma}}, a_\Gamma), b'.i)$. For any $i \notin \overline{\Gamma}$, we have $t_i^{\text{MAY}}(b.i, (a_{\overline{\Gamma}}, a_\Gamma), b'.i)$ by the definition of the function t_i^{MAY}. So $T_{\overline{\Gamma}}(b, (a_{\overline{\Gamma}}, a_\Gamma), b')$ and, by the inductive assumption, $M, s' \models^3 \psi = \text{ff}$ and $M, s \models^3 \varphi = \text{ff}$.

The remaining ATL cases can be shown similarly.

Epistemic cases. Consider $\varphi = K_i\psi$. Assume $M^A, b \models^3 \varphi = \text{tt}$. Then for any $b' \sim_i b$, $M^A, b' \models^3 \psi = \text{tt}$. Consider any state $s' \sim_i s$. By definition, there is $b^{s'}$ such that s' satisfies $b^{s'}$ and $b^{s'} \sim_i b$, and so $M^A, b^{s'} \models^3 \psi = \text{tt}$, and, by inductive assumption, $M, s' \models^3 \psi = \text{tt}$. Since s' was an arbitrary state, we have $M, s \models^3 K_i\psi = \text{tt}$.

Assume $M^A, b \models^3 \varphi = \text{ff}$. Then we have $M^A, b \models^3 \psi = \text{ff}$, and, by the inductive assumption, $M, s \models^3 \psi = \text{ff}$, and therefore $M, s \models^3 \varphi = \text{ff}$.

The case for common knowledge is similar. □

Verification of abstract models

We now give algorithms to compute, for an IS and a given specification φ, a pair of BDDs: one representing a set of states where the value of φ is tt and one representing a set of states where the value of φ is ff (Algorithm 1).

For atomic expressions, the BDDs can be computed using an SMT solver. Observe that for each Γ, a BDD representing T_Γ can be computed in a straightforward way. This is used in the function PREIMAGE, which is then used for all the ATL modalities. The procedures for epistemic modalities are as in [22] and therefore omitted. The remaining procedures are similar to the procedures in [22], but here they work on BDDs rather than sets, and use two kinds of transition relations and protocols (this is reflected in the definition of T_Γ).

The verification process works as follows: firstly, we generate the list of predicates. This can be done in several ways; we show one in the next section. Secondly, we generate the abstract model and compute BDDs representing the sets of states where the value of the given specification is tt and ff. If the value is tt in all the initial states, then we return tt; if it is ff in some of the initial states, then we return ff; otherwise, we return uu. In the latter case the value of the specification cannot be determined on the basis of the abstraction constructed above.

4. THE MODEL CHECKER MCMAS$_{\text{PA}}$

We now describe the model checker MCMAS$_{\text{PA}}$, which extends the open-source model checker MCMAS [24] by supporting the three-valued semantics for ATLK and the predicate abstraction methodologies described above. MCMAS$_{\text{PA}}$ is implemented in C++ and uses the SMT solver CVC4 [4].

MCMAS$_{\text{PA}}$ takes as an input an infinite state MAS encoded as an UISPL program and uses the predicate abstraction technique described in the previous sections to generate an abstract, finite state system. The abstract system is then verified against the given ATLK specification by means

Algorithm 1 The model checking procedure for verifying an IS against ATLK^{3v} specifications.

procedure CHECKFORMULA(IS, φ)
  if φ is atomic **then**
    return CHECKATOMIC(IS, φ)
  else if $\varphi = \neg\varphi'$ **then**
    $(S_{tt}, S_{ff}) \leftarrow$ CHECKFORMULA(IS, φ')
    return (S_{ff}, S_{tt})
  else if $\varphi = \varphi_1 \wedge \varphi_2$ **then**
    $(S^1_{tt}, S^1_{ff}) \leftarrow$ CHECKFORMULA(IS, φ_1)
    $(S^2_{tt}, S^2_{ff}) \leftarrow$ CHECKFORMULA(IS, φ_2)
    return $(S^1_{tt} \cap S^2_{tt}, S^1_{ff} \cup S^2_{ff})$
  else if $\varphi = \langle\langle\Gamma\rangle\rangle X\varphi'$ **then**
    return CHECKATLX(IS, Γ, φ')
  else if $\varphi = \langle\langle\Gamma\rangle\rangle(\varphi_1 U \varphi_2)$ **then**
    return CHECKATLU($IS, \Gamma, \varphi_1, \varphi_2$)
  else if $\varphi = \langle\langle\Gamma\rangle\rangle G\varphi'$ **then**
    return CHECKATLG(IS, Γ, φ')
  else
    return CHECKEPISTEMIC(IS, Γ, φ)

Algorithm 2 Auxiliary procedures for CHECKFORMULA. The function PRIMED changes the variables in the BDD for S so they correspond to the third parameter of T_Γ.

procedure CHECKATOMIC(IS, φ)
  $S_{tt} \leftarrow \emptyset$, $S_{ff} \leftarrow \emptyset$
  for each abstract state b **do**
    if $b \wedge \neg\varphi$ is unsatisfiable **then**
      $S_{tt} \leftarrow S_{tt} \cup \{b\}$
    else if $b \wedge \varphi$ is unsatisfiable **then**
      $S_{ff} \leftarrow S_{ff} \cup \{b\}$
  return (S_{tt}, S_{ff})
procedure PREIMAGE(IS, Γ, S)
  $Result = compose(T_\Gamma, Primed(S))$
  for each $i \notin \Gamma$ **do**
    $Result = \forall a_i.Result$
  for each $i \in \Gamma$ **do**
    $Result = \exists a_i.Result$
  return $Result$

of symbolic verification on the three-valued semantics for ATLK. If the result of this check is either true or false, by the result of the previous section, it follows that this is also the case for the original MAS.

MCMAS$_{PA}$ generates a list of predicates in parallel for each agent based on the declarations in the UISPL file. As stated earlier, the technique, differently from other predicate abstraction methodologies, is modular with respect to the agents in the system. For each agent i, we build the list of predicates based on the agent's protocol, the specification to be checked, and the evaluation of the atoms in the system. Specifically, for each atomic expression in the protocol or evaluation for i, or any expression in the specifications

Algorithm 3 Procedures for handling ATL modalities.

procedure CHECKATLX(IS, Γ, φ)
  $(S'_{tt}, S'_{ff}) \leftarrow$ CHECKFORMULA(IS, φ)
  $S_{tt} \leftarrow$ PREIMAGE(IS, Γ, S'_{tt})
  $S_{ff} \leftarrow$ PREIMAGE($IS, \overline{\Gamma}, S'_{ff}$)
  return (S_{tt}, S_{ff})
procedure CHECKATLU(IS, Γ, φ_1, φ_2)
  $(S^1_{tt}, S^1_{ff}) \leftarrow$ CHECKFORMULA(IS, φ_1)
  $(S_{tt}, S_{ff}) \leftarrow$ CHECKFORMULA(IS, φ_2)
  repeat
    $S'_{tt} \leftarrow S_{tt}$
    $S_{tt} \leftarrow S_{tt} \cup ($PREIMAGE$(IS, \Gamma, S_{tt}) \cap S^1_{tt})$
  until $S_{tt} = S'_{tt}$
  repeat
    $S'_{ff} \leftarrow S_{ff}$
    $S_{ff} \leftarrow S_{ff} \cap ($PREIMAGE$(IS, \overline{\Gamma}, S_{ff}) \cup S^1_{ff})$
  until $S_{ff} = S'_{ff}$
  return (S_{tt}, S_{ff})
procedure CHECKATLG(IS, Γ, φ)
  $(S'_{tt}, S'_{ff}) \leftarrow$ CHECKFORMULA(IS, φ)
  repeat
    $S'_{tt} \leftarrow S_{tt}$
    $S_{tt} \leftarrow$ PREIMAGE$(IS, \Gamma, S_{tt}) \cap S_{tt}$
  until $S_{tt} = S'_{tt}$
  repeat
    $S'_{ff} \leftarrow S_{ff}$
    $S_{ff} \leftarrow$ PREIMAGE$(IS, \Gamma, S_{ff}) \cup S'_{ff}$
  until $S_{ff} = S'_{ff}$
  return (S_{tt}, S_{ff})

for the atoms dependent only on i, we tentatively add this expression to the list of predicates. If the expression is not equivalent to an existing predicate or to its complement, we add the expression to the list. The SMT solver CVC4 is employed to check these equivalences. The process terminates when all the expressions have been analysed.

EXAMPLE 2. *Consider the property*

$$Ag1.counter \leq 0 \wedge \ Ag1.v < Ag2.v \wedge \langle\langle\Gamma\rangle\rangle X Ag1.counter > 0$$

The resulting list of predicates from this formula for $Ag1$ consists only of a single predicate $Ag1.counter \leq 0$. The predicate $Ag1.counter > 0$ is not included as it is the negation of $Ag1.counter \leq 0$. The predicate $Ag1.v < Ag2.v$ is also omitted as it refers to a different agent.

Then, CVC4 is employed to generate the may relation. Due to the computational cost of SMT queries on several variables, MCMAS$_{PA}$ employs various heuristics to reduce the computation time. First, we test whether the straightforward translations of the transitions in the UISPL program, where each condition is either replaced by the corresponding predicate or omitted, result in valid may transitions. Then, for each abstract state, we execute a query whose results represent the remaining transitions in the abstract model. This is the most time-consuming step of the

Figure 1: n tunnels version of the scenario.

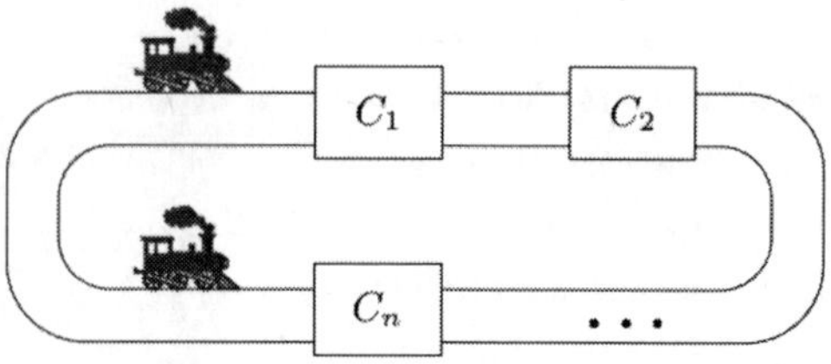

verification procedure. The may protocol is computed in the straightforward way.

While the process to generate the may transition relation and protocol is relatively straightforward, to generate the must protocol, queries involving universal quantifiers are required. Solving these queries is undecidable in general; the SMT solver we employed was unable to answer any queries that would be of practical use. We therefore used an approximation and defined the must protocol on the basis of the may relation and protocol as follows. For each abstract state and action, if there is exactly one possible may transition from this state and action, we add this action and state to the must protocol. The must protocol obtained is a subset of the must protocol previously described; it follows that the preservation theorem still holds in this case. The must relation is defined accordingly.

When the abstract model has been defined, the atoms in the specifications are replaced appropriately in view of the predicates introduced and the finite-state model is verified by using the symbolic three-valued labelling procedure described in the previous section except for one exception. Instead of using the computationally expensive procedure CHECKATOMIC, instead we check whether the given atomic condition was used to generate the list of predicates. If it was, all the states satisfying the corresponding predicate are returned; if they are not satisfying its negation, then the predicate is removed as redundant; otherwise, the empty set is returned. This does not influence the soundness of the algorithm.

5. EXPERIMENTAL EVALUATION

To evaluate the methodology we report the experimental results obtained on a infinite-state variation of the widely-studied, epistemic version of the train-gate-controller benchmark [14]. In the revised version we consider, there are two trains travelling in the opposite direction on two separate circular tracks. The tracks merge into several critical sections (tunnels) where only one train can be present at any given time. The operation at each of the tunnels is governed by a controller (see Fig. 1). At each time step each train either stays in the same section of the track or requests access to the next tunnel. If the request is granted by the controller, it moves to next part of the track. Each controller keeps track of which train has crossed its junctions more times, so that, if it chooses to do so, it may prioritise one over the other.

We modelled the scenario above in UISPL by considering an agent for each of the trains and each of the tunnel controllers. Each controller is equipped with an unbounded integer variable recording how many times each of the train has been given priority to cross the junction. Since there is no bound on this number, even the model with one tunnel has an unbounded number of states. For evaluation purposes we considered several versions of the scenario by scaling the number of the tunnels. All UISPL programs used can be accessed from [23].

To evaluate the scenario we considered the following specifications.

- Train A knows that it may never be able to leave its initial position:

$$K_{Train_a} \langle\langle Train_a \rangle\rangle G\, Train_a.pos = s_0$$

- Train A knows that together with the controller it may eventually be able to enter the first tunnel:

$$K_{Train_a} \langle\langle Train_a, Controller \rangle\rangle F Train_a.pos = s_1$$

- The controller may be able to guarantee that train A enters the tunnel at least as many times as train B:

$$\langle\langle Controller \rangle\rangle G\, Controller.counter \geq 0$$

- Train B may not be able to force Train A into the tunnel:

$$\neg \langle\langle Train_b \rangle\rangle F\, Train_a.pos = s_1$$

We ran the tool against the specifications above for different number of controllers on an Intel® Core™ i7-2600 CPU (3.40GHz, 8 cores) running Linux Kernel 3.11.0-20-generic. MCMAS$_{PA}$ generated appropriate predicates in each of these cases on the basis of the atoms presented in the specification and the UISPL programs. The resulting finite-state descriptions were verified and the specifications were found to hold, as expected. Table 1 reports the time required to generate the abstraction, and the time required to verify the abstract model. Observe that most of the computation time was devoted to computation of the abstract system rather than verification itself. The memory footprint of the checker was between 11MB and 30MB.

We found that MCMAS$_{PA}$ was unable to resolve the truth value of the specification expressing that there is a joint strategy for a controller and Train A to reach a state where the counter equals 10:

$$\langle\langle Controller, Train_a \rangle\rangle F\, Controller.counter = 10$$

This is because all the states of the controller with $counter \in \{1, \ldots, 9\}$ are abstract into a single state with no successors w.r.t. the must relation; therefore the value of the formula in the abstract model cannot be determined. As we remarked earlier the technique is sound but cannot be complete; while we may improve the technique to resolve this particular specifications, there are bound to be formulas whose value the tool will not be able to determine.

The train gate controller scenario focuses on MAS with many agents having a single integer variable. For further benchmarking we now discuss a protocol with two agents only, but which are described by several integer variables.

To do so we consider a simple protocol in which an agent S intends to communicate n integers to an agent R in the presence of a perfect communication line. To communicate the value v_i of the ith number, S uses v_i times the action $send_i$. When all the numbers are sent, S loops using the action *done* forever.

Table 1: Train Gate Controller: verification time

Tunnels	States	Abstract	Verify
1	6	0.3s	<0.1s
2	36	0.6s	0.1s
3	128	2.0s	0.14s
4	400	5.2s	0.2s
5	1152	13s	0.23s
6	3136	31s	0.3s
7	8192	78s	0.36s
8	20736	198s	0.4s
9	51200	489s	0.55s
10	123904	1477s	0.9s

Table 2: Number Transmission: verification time

Integers	States	Abstract	Verify
2	6	0.55s	<0.1s
4	56	2.29s	<0.1s
6	240	7.01s	0.11s
8	992	20.8s	0.15s
10	4032	57.2s	0.21s
12	16256	154s	0.33s
14	65280	406s	0.53s
16	261632	1031s	0.96s
18	1047552	2717s	1.9s
20	4192256	5903s	3.7s

Both agents are implemented by using n integer variables and an enumeration variable *status* that may either be equal to *busy* (representing states where the transmission is in progress), or *done* (representing the end of the protocol). The initial values of the integer variables of S are chosen randomly; the values for R's variables are initialised to 0. Both status values are initially set to *busy*. The protocols and evaluations can be implemented in UISPL in the straightforward way.

We used MCMAS$_{PA}$ to verify the following epistemic specification: whenever R's status is equal to done, then R knows that S's status is equal to done. This can be encoded in ATLK as

$$\langle\langle\emptyset\rangle\rangle G(R.status = done \Rightarrow K_R S.status = done)$$

MCMAS$_{PA}$ reported the specification to hold in all cases considered. The computation times are presented in Table 2. Similarly to the train gate controller example, the numbers of states and verification times increase exponentially with the number of integer variables. The verification time grows slightly slower than in the Train Gate Controller case; one of the reasons for this is that here we have a fixed number of possible actions, and therefore the transition relation is smaller.

We also attempted to verify the protocol's termination by checking the specification

$$\langle\langle R, S\rangle\rangle F R.status = done$$

In this case MCMAS$_{PA}$ reported the formula to be undefined. In the simplest case, with one number being transmitted, this is because the checker considers the abstraction where all the positive values of the number are abstracted into a single state. From this state the only allowed action is $send_0$, resulting in a loop. On the abstract model it therefore cannot be shown that any further state will be reached. Doing so would require refining the model, which we leave for further work.

6. CONCLUSIONS

In this paper we have proposed a technique for the verification of infinite-state MAS by means of predicate abstraction. The specification language we support is based on epistemic logic; we provide support for a weak form of ATL at no extra computational cost, but the logic CTL is fully supported by the technique.

The formalism we put forward shares some of the features present in [22], notably the three-valued approach to ATLK. Yet it differs from it in several respects. Firstly, we here employ a more general semantics that comprises a may and must relation. Secondly, the notion of state abstraction is more general here as we can collapse states with different protocols. Thirdly, [22] assumes finite-state systems and provides no details as to how generate finite models from a MAS program. In contrast in this work we have provided a methodology to do so by creating appropriate Boolean predicates by means of SMT calls and use these to define an abstract, finite-state program for the MAS.

Regarding the evaluation of the technique the checker that we released uses UISPL, an extension of MCMAS's original input language ISPL, to model MAS with unbounded integer values. We have shown that the checker can verify infinite state models automatically. We are not aware of any other model checker for MAS supporting infinite states nor employing predicate abstraction. While no comparison can be made, the experimental results obtained demonstrate the tool's performance is relatively robust with respect to the number of unbounded variables present in the program.

In future work we plan to introduce further optimisations in the generation of SMT calls so that more complex programs can be verified. We also intend to introduce a methodology for action abstraction so that particular types of MAS programs can be more effectively abstracted. The methodology that we studied here is independent of the input language; while we here defined and adopted UISPL, in the future we plan to support other input languages. We see these as steps to achieve the long-term goal to move from the verification of ad-hoc MAS models to the verification of actual MAS code.

ACKNOWLEDGEMENTS

This research was funded by the EPSRC under grant EP/I00520X.

REFERENCES

[1] T. Ågotnes, V. Goranko, W. Jamroga, and M. Wooldridge. Knowledge and ability. In *Handbook of Logics for Knowledge and Belief*. College Publications, 2015.

[2] R. Alur, T. A. Henzinger, and O. Kupferman. Alternating-time temporal logic. *Journal of the ACM*, 49(5):672–713, 2002.

[3] T. Ball and O. Kupferman. An abstraction-refinement framework for multi-agent systems. In *Proceedings of*

the 21st Annual IEEE Symposium on Logic in Computer Science (LICS06), pages 379–388. IEEE, 2006.

[4] C. Barrett, C. Conway, M. Deters, L. Hadarean, D. Jovanović, T. King, A. Reynolds, and C. Tinelli. CVC4. In *Proceedings of the 23rd International Conference on Computer Aided Verification (CAV11)*, pages 171–177. Springer, 2011.

[5] N. Bulling and W. Jamroga. Comparing variants of strategic ability: how uncertainty and memory influence general properties of games. *Autonomous Agents and Multi-Agent Systems*, 28(3):474–518, 2014.

[6] M. Cohen, M. Dam, A. Lomuscio, and H. Qu. A data symmetry reduction technique for temporal-epistemic logic. In *Proceedings of the 7th International Symposium on Automated Technology for Verification and Analysis (ATVA09)*, volume 5799 of *Lecture Notes in Computer Science*, pages 69–83. Springer, 2009.

[7] M. Cohen, M. Dam, A. Lomuscio, and F. Russo. Abstraction in model checking multi-agent systems. In *Proceedings of the 8th International Conference on Autonomous Agents and Multiagent Systems (AAMAS09)*, pages 945–952. IFAAMAS Press, 2009.

[8] S. Das, D. Dill, and S. Park. Experience with predicate abstraction. In *Proceedings of the 11th International Conference on Computer Aided Verification (CAV99)*, pages 160–171. Springer, 1999.

[9] C. Enea and C. Dima. Abstractions of multi-agent systems. In *Proceedings of 5th International Central and Eastern European Conference on Multi-Agent Systems (CEEMAS07)*, volume 4696 of *Lecture Notes in Computer Science*, pages 11–21. Springer, 2007.

[10] R. Fagin, J. Y. Halpern, Y. Moses, and M. Y. Vardi. *Reasoning about Knowledge*. MIT Press, Cambridge, 1995.

[11] P. Gammie and R. van der Meyden. MCK: Model checking the logic of knowledge. In *Proceedings of 16th International Conference on Computer Aided Verification (CAV04)*, volume 3114 of *Lecture Notes in Computer Science*, pages 479–483. Springer, 2004.

[12] P. Gonzalez, A. Griesmayer, and A. Lomuscio. Verification of GSM-based artifact-centric systems by predicate abstraction. In *Proceedings of the 13th International Conference on Service Oriented Computing (ICSOC15)*, volume 9435 of *Lecture Notes in Computer Science*, pages 253–268. Springer, 2015.

[13] S. Graf and H. Saïdi. Construction of abstract state graphs with pvs. In *Proceedings of the 9th International Conference on Computer Aided Verification (CAV97)*, volume 1254 of *Lecture Notes in Computer Science*, pages 72–83. Springer, 1997.

[14] W. van der Hoek and M. Wooldridge. Tractable multiagent planning for epistemic goals. In *Proceedings of the First International Joint Conference on Autonomous Agents and Multiagent Systems (AAMAS02)*, pages 1167–1174. ACM Press, 2002.

[15] M. Huth, R. Jagadeesan, and D. Schmidt. Modal transition systems: A foundation for three-valued program analysis. *ACM Transactions on Programming Languages and Systems*, pages 155–169, 2001.

[16] W. Jamroga and W. van der Hoek. Agents that know how to play. *Fundamenta Informaticae*, 62:1–35, 2004.

[17] M. Kacprzak, W. Nabialek, A. Niewiadomski, W. Penczek, A. Pólrola, M. Szreter, B. Woźna, and A. Zbrzezny. Verics 2007 - a model checker for knowledge and real-time. *Fundamenta Informaticae*, 85(1):313–328, 2008.

[18] B. Konikowska and W. Penczek. Model checking for multi-valued computation tree logics. In *Beyond Two: Theory and Applications of Multiple Valued Logic*, pages 193–210. Physica-Verlag, 2003.

[19] B. Konikowska and W. Penczek. Model checking for multivalued logic of knowledge and time. In *Proceedings of the 5th international joint conference on Autonomous Agents and Multiagent Systems (AAMAS06)*, pages 169–176. IFAAMAS, 2006.

[20] M. Köster and P. Lohmann. Abstraction for model checking modular interpreted systems over ATL. In *Programming Multi-Agent Systems*, volume 7217 of *Lecture Notes in Computer Science*, pages 95–113. Springer, 2012.

[21] A. Lomuscio and J. Michaliszyn. An abstraction technique for the verification of multi-agent systems against ATL specifications. In *Proceedings of the 14th International Conference on Principles of Knowledge Representation and Reasoning (KR14)*, pages 428–437. AAAI Press, 2014.

[22] A. Lomuscio and J. Michaliszyn. Verifying multi-agent systems by model checking three-valued abstractions. In *Proceedings of the 14th International Conference on Autonomous Agents and Multiagent Systems (AAMAS15)*, pages 189–198, 2015.

[23] A. Lomuscio and J. Michaliszyn. $MCMAS_{PA}$: A predicate abstraction model checker for multi-agent systems. http://vas.doc.ic.ac.uk/software/extensions, 2016.

[24] A. Lomuscio, H. Qu, and F. Raimondi. MCMAS: A model checker for the verification of multi-agent systems. *Software Tools for Technology Transfer*, 2015. http://dx.doi.org/10.1007/s10009-015-0378-x.

[25] A. Lomuscio and F. Raimondi. Model checking knowledge, strategies, and games in multi-agent systems. In *Proceedings of the 5th International Joint Conference on Autonomous agents and Multi-Agent Systems (AAMAS06)*, pages 161–168. ACM Press, 2006.

[26] W. Penczek and A. Lomuscio. Verifying epistemic properties of multi-agent systems via bounded model checking. *Fundamenta Informaticae*, 55(2):167–185, 2003.

[27] F. Raimondi and A. Lomuscio. Automatic verification of multi-agent systems by model checking via OBDDs. *Journal of Applied Logic*, 5(2):235–251, 2005.

[28] W. van der Hoek and M. Wooldridge. Model checking cooperation, knowledge, and time - a case study. *Research In Economics*, 57(3):235–265, 2003.

[29] M. Wooldridge and N. R. Jennings. Intelligent agents: theory and practice. *Knowledge Engineering Review*, 2(10):115–152, 1995.

Game-Theoretic Semantics for Alternating-Time Temporal Logic

Valentin Goranko
Stockholm University
Sweden
and Univ. of Johannesburg
South Africa
valentin.goranko@philosophy.su.se

Antti Kuusisto
University of Bremen
Germany
kuusisto@uni-bremen.de

Raine Rönnholm
University of Tampere
Finland
raine.ronnholm@uta.fi

ABSTRACT

We introduce versions of game-theoretic semantics (GTS) for Alternating-Time Temporal Logic (ATL). In GTS, truth is defined in terms of existence of a winning strategy in a semantic evaluation game, and thus the game-theoretic perspective appears in the framework of ATL on two semantic levels: on the object level, in the standard semantics of the strategic operators, and on the meta-level, where game-theoretic logical semantics can be applied to ATL. We unify these two perspectives into semantic evaluation games specially designed for ATL. The novel game-theoretic perspective enables us to identify new variants of the semantics of ATL, based on limiting the time resources available to the verifier and falsifier in the semantic evaluation game; we introduce and analyse an *unbounded* and *bounded* GTS and prove these to be equivalent to the standard (Tarski-style) compositional semantics. We also introduce a non-equivalent *finitely bounded* semantics and argue that it is natural from both logical and game-theoretic perspectives.

Keywords

Logic and game theory; Logics for agents and multi-agent systems; Argumentation-based dialogue and protocols

1. INTRODUCTION

Alternating-Time Temporal Logic ATL was introduced in [3] as a multi-agent extension of the branching-time temporal logic CTL. The semantics of ATL is defined over *multi-agent transition systems*, also known as *concurrent game models*, in which agents take simultaneous actions at the current state and the resulting collective action determines the subsequent state transition. The logic ATL and its extensions such as ATL* have gradually become the most popular logical formalisms for reasoning about strategic abilities of agents in synchronous multi-agent systems.

Game-theoretic semantics (GTS) of logical languages has a complex history going back to Hintikka [8], Lorenzen [11] and others. For an overview of the topic, see [10]. In GTS, truth of a logical formula φ is determined in a formal *debate* between two players, *Eloise* and *Abelard*. Eloise is trying to verify φ, while Abelard is opposing her. Each logical operator is associated with a related rule in the game. The framework of GTS has turned out to be particularly useful for the purpose of defining variants of semantic approaches to different logics. For example, IF-logic of Hintikka and Sandu [9] is an extension of first-order logic which was originally developed using GTS. Also, the game-theoretic approach to semantics has lead to new methods for solving decision problems of logics, e.g., via using parity games for the μ-calculus.

In this article we introduce game-theoretic semantics for ATL. In that framework, the rules corresponding to strategic operators involve scenarios where Eloise and Abelard are both controlling (or leading) coalitions of agents with opposing objectives. The perspective offered by GTS enables us to develop novel approaches to ATL based on different time resources available to the players. In *unbounded* GTS, a coalition trying to verify an until-formula is allowed to continue without a time limit, the price of an infinite play being a loss in the game. In *bounded* GTS, the coalition must commit to *finishing in finite time* by submitting an *ordinal number* in the beginning of the game; the ordinal controls available time resources in the game and *guarantees a finite play*. In fact, even safety games (for release-formulae) will be determined in finite time, and thus the bounded and unbounded approaches to GTS are conceptually different.

Despite the differences between the two semantics, we show that they are in fact equivalent to the standard compositional (i.e., Tarski-style) semantics of ATL and therefore to each other. Furthermore, we introduce a restriction of the bounded GTS, called *finitely bounded* GTS, where the ordinals controlling time flow must always be finite. This is a particularly simple system of semantics where the players will always announce the ultimate (always finite) duration of the game before the game begins. We show that the finitely bounded GTS is equivalent to the standard ATL semantics on *image finite models*, and therefore provides an alternative approach to ATL sufficient for most practical purposes.

Since the finitely bounded semantics is new, we also develop an equivalent (over all models) Tarski-style semantics for it. We note that the difference between the finitely bounded and unbounded semantics is conceptually linked to the difference between *for-loops* and *while-loops*.

The main contributions of this paper are twofold: the development of game-theoretic semantics for ATL and the introduction of new resource-sensitive versions of logics for multi-agent strategic reasoning. The latter relates conceptu-

Appears in: *Proceedings of the 15th International Conference on Autonomous Agents and Multiagent Systems (AAMAS 2016), J. Thangarajah, K. Tuyls, C. Jonker, S. Marsella (eds.), May 9–13, 2016, Singapore.*

ally to the study of other resource-bounded versions of ATL, see [2], [12], [1].

The current article is a short version of the self-contained full paper [7] that includes more technical details and full proofs. The structure of the paper is as follows. After the preliminaries in Section 2, we develop the bounded and unbounded GTS in Section 3. We analyse the frameworks in Section 4, where we show, inter alia, that the two game-theoretic frameworks are equivalent. In Section 5, we compare the game-theoretic and standard Tarski-style semantics and establish the equivalences between them stated above.

It is worth pointing out that some of our technical results could be derived using more general alternative methods from coalgebraic modal logic. We will discuss this matter in more detail in the concluding section 5.

2. PRELIMINARIES

In this section we define concurrent game models as well as the syntax and standard compositional semantics of ATL.

DEFINITION 2.1. *A* ***concurrent game model*** *(CGM) $\mathcal{M}$ is a tuple $(\mathbb{A}\text{gt}, \text{St}, \Pi, \text{Act}, d, o, v)$ which consists of the following non-empty sets:* ***agents*** $\mathbb{A}\text{gt} = \{1, \ldots, k\}$, ***states*** St, ***proposition symbols*** Π, ***actions*** Act, ***action function*** $d : \mathbb{A}\text{gt} \times \text{St} \to \mathcal{P}(\text{Act}) \setminus \{\emptyset\}$ *assigning a non-empty set of actions available to each agent at each state, and a* ***transition function*** *o assigning a unique* ***outcome state*** *$o(q, \vec{\alpha})$ to each state $q \in$ St and* ***action profile*** *(a tuple of actions $\vec{\alpha} = (\alpha_1, \ldots, \alpha_k)$ such that $\alpha_i \in d(i, q)$ for each $i \in \mathbb{A}\text{gt}$), and a* ***valuation function*** $v : \Pi \to \mathcal{P}(\text{St})$.

Sets of agents $A \subseteq \mathbb{A}\text{gt}$ are also called **coalitions**. The complement $\overline{A} = \mathbb{A}\text{gt} \setminus A$ of a coalition A is called the **opposing coalition** (of A). We also define the set of action tuples that are *available* to coalition A at a state $q \in$ St: $\text{action}(A, q) := \{(\alpha_i)_{i \in A} \mid \alpha_i \in d(i, q) \text{ for each } i \in A\}$.

DEFINITION 2.2. *Let $\mathcal{M} = (\mathbb{A}\text{gt}, \text{St}, \Pi, \text{Act}, d, o, v)$ be a concurrent game model. A* ***strategy***[1] *for an agent $a \in \mathbb{A}\text{gt}$ is a function $s_a : \text{St} \to \text{Act}$ such that $s_a(q) \in d(a, q)$ for each $q \in$ St. A* ***collective strategy*** *S_A for $A \subseteq \mathbb{A}\text{gt}$ is a tuple of individual strategies, one for each agent in A. A* ***path*** *in $\mathcal{M}$ is a sequence of states Λ such that $\Lambda[n{+}1] = o(\Lambda[n], \vec{\alpha})$ for some admissible action profile $\vec{\alpha}$, where $\Lambda[n]$ is the n-th state in Λ ($n \in \mathbb{N}$). The function $\text{paths}(q, S_A)$ returns the set of all paths that can be formed when the agents in A play according to S_A, beginning from the state q.*

The **formulae of** ATL are defined as follows[2]:

$$\varphi ::= p \mid \neg\varphi \mid (\varphi \vee \varphi) \mid \langle\!\langle A \rangle\!\rangle \mathsf{X}\, \varphi \mid \langle\!\langle A \rangle\!\rangle (\varphi \,\mathsf{U}\, \varphi) \mid \langle\!\langle A \rangle\!\rangle (\varphi \,\mathsf{R}\, \varphi)$$

Other Boolean connectives are defined as usual, and the combined operators $\langle\!\langle A \rangle\!\rangle \mathsf{F}\, \varphi$ and $\langle\!\langle A \rangle\!\rangle \mathsf{G}\, \varphi$ are defined respectively by $\langle\!\langle A \rangle\!\rangle \top \mathsf{U}\, \varphi$ and $\langle\!\langle A \rangle\!\rangle \bot \mathsf{R}\, \varphi$.

DEFINITION 2.3. *Let $\mathcal{M} = (\mathbb{A}\text{gt}, \text{St}, \Pi, \text{Act}, d, o, v)$ be a CGM, $q \in$ St a state and φ an ATL-formula. Truth of φ in $\mathcal{M}$ and q, denoted by $\mathcal{M}, q \models \varphi$, is defined as follows:*

- $\mathcal{M}, q \models p$ *iff* $q \in v(p)$ *(for $p \in \Pi$).*
- $\mathcal{M}, q \models \neg\psi$ *iff* $\mathcal{M}, q \not\models \psi$.
- $\mathcal{M}, q \models \psi \vee \theta$ *iff* $\mathcal{M}, q \models \psi$ *or* $\mathcal{M}, q \models \theta$.
- $\mathcal{M}, q \models \langle\!\langle A \rangle\!\rangle \mathsf{X}\, \psi$ *iff there exists S_A such that for each $\Lambda \in \text{paths}(q, S_A)$, we have $\mathcal{M}, \Lambda[1] \models \psi$.*
- $\mathcal{M}, q \models \langle\!\langle A \rangle\!\rangle \psi \,\mathsf{U}\, \theta$ *iff there exists S_A such that for each $\Lambda \in \text{paths}(q, S_A)$, there is $i \geq 0$ such that $\mathcal{M}, \Lambda[i] \models \theta$ and $\mathcal{M}, \Lambda[j] \models \psi$ for every $j < i$.*
- $\mathcal{M}, q \models \langle\!\langle A \rangle\!\rangle \psi \,\mathsf{R}\, \theta$ *iff there exists S_A such that for each $\Lambda \in \text{paths}(q, S_A)$ and $i \geq 0$, we have $\mathcal{M}, \Lambda[i] \models \theta$ or there is $j < i$ such that $\mathcal{M}, \Lambda[j] \models \psi$.*

[1]Unless otherwise specified, a 'strategy' hereafter will mean a positional and deterministic strategy.

[2]The operator R (Release) was not part of the original syntax of ATL but has been commonly added later.

3. GAME-THEORETIC SEMANTICS

In this section we will introduce unbounded, bounded and finitely bounded evaluation games for ATL. By defining the truth of a formula as the existence of a winning strategy for the verifier in the corresponding evaluation game, these variants of evaluation games lead to three different versions of game-theoretic semantics for ATL.

3.1 Unbounded evaluation games

Given a CGM $\mathcal{M}$, a state q_{in} and a formula φ, the **evaluation game** $\mathcal{G}(\mathcal{M}, q_{in}, \varphi)$ is intuitively an argument between two opponents, **Eloise (E)** and **Abelard (A)**, about whether the formula φ is true at the state q_{in} in the model $\mathcal{M}$. Eloise claims that φ is true, so she adopts (initially) the role of a **verifier** in the game, and Abelard tries to prove the formula false, so he is (initially) the **falsifier**. These roles can swap in the course of the game when negations are encountered in the formula to be evaluated.

We will often use the following notation: if $\mathbf{P} \in \{\mathbf{A}, \mathbf{E}\}$, then $\overline{\mathbf{P}}$ denotes the **opponent** of $\mathbf{P}$, i.e., $\overline{\mathbf{P}} \in \{\mathbf{A}, \mathbf{E}\} \setminus \{\mathbf{P}\}$.

DEFINITION 3.1. *Let $\mathcal{M} = (\mathbb{A}\text{gt}, \text{St}, \Pi, \text{Act}, d, o, v)$ be a CGM, $q_{in} \in$ St and φ an ATL-formula. The* ***unbounded evaluation game*** *$\mathcal{G}(\mathcal{M}, q_{in}, \varphi)$ between the players $\mathbf{A}$ and $\mathbf{E}$ is defined as follows.*

- *A* ***position*** *of the game is a tuple $\text{Pos} = (\mathbf{P}, q, \psi)$ where $\mathbf{P} \in \{\mathbf{A}, \mathbf{E}\}$, $q \in$ St and ψ is a subformula of φ. The* ***initial position*** *of the game is $\text{Pos}_0 := (\mathbf{E}, q_{in}, \varphi)$.*
- *In every position $(\mathbf{P}, q, \psi)$, the player $\mathbf{P}$ is called the* ***verifier*** *and $\overline{\mathbf{P}}$ the* ***falsifier*** *for that position.*
- *Each position of the game is associated with a rule. The rules for positions where the related formula is either a proposition symbol or has a Boolean connective as its main connective, are defined as follows.*

1. *If $\text{Pos}_i = (\mathbf{P}, q, p)$, where $p \in \Pi$, then Pos_i is called an* ***ending position*** *of the evaluation game. If $q \in v(p)$, then $\mathbf{P}$ wins the evaluation game. Else $\overline{\mathbf{P}}$ wins.*
2. *Let $\text{Pos}_i = (\mathbf{P}, q, \neg\psi)$. The game then moves to the next position, $\text{Pos}_{i+1} = (\overline{\mathbf{P}}, q, \psi)$.*
3. *Let $\text{Pos}_i = (\mathbf{P}, q, \psi \vee \theta)$. Then the player $\mathbf{P}$ decides whether $\text{Pos}_{i+1} = (\mathbf{P}, q, \psi)$ or $\text{Pos}_{i+1} = (\mathbf{P}, q, \theta)$.*

In order to deal with the strategic operators, we now define a ***one step game****, denoted by $\text{step}(\mathbf{P}, A, q)$, where $A \subseteq \mathbb{A}\text{gt}$. This game consists of the following two actions.*

i) First $\mathbf{P}$ chooses an action $\alpha_i \in d(i, q)$ for each $i \in A$.
ii) Then $\overline{\mathbf{P}}$ chooses an action $\alpha_i \in d(i, q)$ for each $i \in \overline{A}$.

The ***resulting state*** *of the one step game $\text{step}(\mathbf{P}, A, q)$ is the state $q' := o(q, \alpha_1, \ldots, \alpha_k)$ arising from the combined action of the agents. We now define how the evaluation game proceeds in positions where the formula is of type $\langle\!\langle A \rangle\!\rangle \mathsf{X}\, \psi$:*

4. *Let $\text{Pos}_i = (\mathbf{P}, q, \langle\!\langle A \rangle\!\rangle \mathsf{X}\, \psi)$. The next position Pos_{i+1} is $(\mathbf{P}, q', \psi)$, where q' is the resulting state of $\text{step}(\mathbf{P}, A, q)$.*

The rules for the other strategic operators are obtained by iterating the one step game. For this purpose, we now define the **embedded game** $\mathbf{G} := \mathbf{g}(\mathbf{V}, \mathbf{C}, A, q_0, \psi_{\mathbf{C}}, \psi_{\overline{\mathbf{C}}})$, *where both* $\mathbf{V}, \mathbf{C} \in \{\mathbf{E}, \mathbf{A}\}$, *$A$ is a coalition, q_0 a state, and $\psi_{\mathbf{C}}$ and $\psi_{\overline{\mathbf{C}}}$ are formulae. The player* $\mathbf{V}$ *is called the* **verifier** *(of the embedded game) and* $\mathbf{C}$ *the* **controller**. *These may, but need not be, the same player. We let* $\overline{\mathbf{V}}$ *and* $\overline{\mathbf{C}}$ *denote the opponents of* $\mathbf{C}$ *and* $\mathbf{V}$, *respectively.*

The embedded game $\mathbf{G}$ *starts from the* **initial state** q_0 *and proceeds from any state q according to the following rules, applied in the order below, until an* **exit position** *is reached.*

i) $\mathbf{C}$ *may end the game at the exit position* $(\mathbf{V}, q, \psi_{\mathbf{C}})$.

ii) $\overline{\mathbf{C}}$ *may end the game at the exit position* $(\mathbf{V}, q, \psi_{\overline{\mathbf{C}}})$.

iii) If the game has not ended due to the above rules, the one step game $\mathsf{step}(\mathbf{V}, A, q)$ *is played to produce a resulting state q'. The embedded game is continued from q'.*

If the embedded game $\mathbf{G}$ *continues an infinite number of rounds, the controller* $\mathbf{C}$ *loses the entire evaluation game* $\mathcal{G}(\mathcal{M}, q_{in}, \varphi)$. *Else the evaluation game resumes from the exit position of the embedded game.*

We now define the rules of the evaluation game for the remaining strategic operators as follows:

5. *Consider a position* $\mathsf{Pos}_i = (\mathbf{P}, q, \langle\!\langle A \rangle\!\rangle \psi \,\mathsf{U}\, \theta)$. *The next position* Pos_{i+1} *is the exit position of the embedded game* $\mathbf{g}(\mathbf{P}, \mathbf{P}, A, q, \theta, \psi)$. *(Note the order of the formulae.)*
6. *Consider a position* $\mathsf{Pos}_i = (\mathbf{P}, q, \langle\!\langle A \rangle\!\rangle \psi \,\mathsf{R}\, \theta)$. *The next position* Pos_{i+1} *is the exit position of the embedded game* $\mathbf{g}(\mathbf{P}, \overline{\mathbf{P}}, A, q, \theta, \psi)$.

The embedded game $\mathbf{g}(\mathbf{V}, \mathbf{C}, A, q, \psi_{\mathbf{C}}, \psi_{\overline{\mathbf{C}}})$ can be seen as a 'simultaneous reachability game' where both players have a goal they are trying to reach before the opponent reaches her/his goal. The verifier $\mathbf{V}$ leads the coalition A and the falsifier $\overline{\mathbf{V}}$ leads the opposing coalition $\overline{A}$. The goal of both $\mathbf{V}$ and $\overline{\mathbf{V}}$ is defined by a formula. When $\mathbf{V} = \mathbf{C}$, the goal of $\mathbf{V}$ is to verify $\psi_{\mathbf{C}}$ and the goal of $\overline{\mathbf{V}}$ is to *falsify* $\psi_{\overline{\mathbf{C}}}$. When $\mathbf{V} \neq \mathbf{C}$, the goal of $\mathbf{V}$ is to verify $\psi_{\overline{\mathbf{C}}}$ and that of $\overline{\mathbf{V}}$ is to falsify $\psi_{\mathbf{C}}$. Both players $\mathbf{V}$ and $\overline{\mathbf{V}}$ have the possibility to end the game when they believe that they have reached their goal. However, the controller is responsible for ending the embedded game in finite time, and (s)he will lose if the game continues infinitely long. If both players reach their targets at the same time, the controller $\mathbf{C}$ has the priority to end the embedded game first.

3.2 Bounded evaluation games

The difference between bounded and unbounded evaluation games is that in the bounded case, the embedded games are associated with a time limit. In a bounded evaluation game, the controller must first announce some possibly infinite ordinal γ which will decrease in each round. This will guarantee that the embedded game, and in fact the entire evaluation game, will end after a finite number of rounds.

Bounded evaluation games $\mathcal{G}(\mathcal{M}, q_{in}, \varphi, \Gamma)$ have an additional parameter Γ, which is an ordinal that fixes an upper bound for the ordinals that the players can announce during the related embedded games. Different parameters Γ give rise to different kinds of evaluation games and thus lead to different kinds of game-theoretic semantics, as we will see.

DEFINITION 3.2. *Let* $\mathcal{M}$ *be a* CGM, $q_{in} \in \mathrm{St}$, φ *an* ATL*-formula and* Γ *an ordinal. The* **bounded evaluation game** $\mathcal{G}(\mathcal{M}, q_{in}, \varphi, \Gamma)$ *is defined as the unbounded evaluation game* $\mathcal{G}(\mathcal{M}, q_{in}, \varphi)$, *the only difference between the two games being the treatment of until- and release-formulae.*

Let $\mathbf{G} = \mathbf{g}(\mathbf{V}, \mathbf{C}, A, q_0, \psi_{\mathbf{C}}, \psi_{\overline{\mathbf{C}}})$ *be an embedded game that arises from a position* Pos *in* $\mathcal{G}(\mathcal{M}, q_{in}, \varphi)$. *In that same position* Pos *in the bounded evaluation game* $\mathcal{G}(\mathcal{M}, q_{in}, \varphi, \Gamma)$, *the player* $\mathbf{C}$ *first chooses some ordinal* $\gamma_0 < \Gamma$ *as the* **initial time limit** *for the embedded game* $\mathbf{G}$. *This choice leads to a* **bounded embedded game** *that is denoted by* $\mathbf{G}[\gamma_0]$.

A **configuration** *of* $\mathbf{G}[\gamma_0]$ *is a pair* (γ, q), *where* γ *is a (possibly infinite) ordinal called the* **current time limit** *and* $q \in \mathrm{St}$ *a state called the* **current state**. *The bounded embedded game* $\mathbf{G}[\gamma_0]$ *starts from the* **initial configuration** (γ_0, q_0) *and proceeds from any configuration* (γ, q) *according to the following rules, applied in the given order.*

i) If $\gamma = 0$, *the game ends at the exit position* $(\mathbf{V}, q, \psi_{\mathbf{C}})$.

ii) $\mathbf{C}$ *may end the game at the exit position* $(\mathbf{V}, q, \psi_{\mathbf{C}})$.

iii) $\overline{\mathbf{C}}$ *may end the game at the exit position* $(\mathbf{V}, q, \psi_{\overline{\mathbf{C}}})$.

iv) If the game has not ended due to the previous rules, then $\mathsf{step}(\mathbf{V}, A, q)$ *is played in order to produce a resulting state q'. Then the bounded embedded game continues from the configuration* (γ', q'), *where* $\gamma' = \gamma - 1$ *if* γ *is a successor ordinal, and if* γ *is a limit ordinal, then* γ' *is an ordinal smaller than* γ *and chosen by* $\mathbf{C}$.

We denote the set of configurations in $\mathbf{G}[\gamma_0]$ *by* $\mathsf{Conf}_{\mathbf{G}[\gamma_0]}$. *After the bounded embedded game* $\mathbf{G}[\gamma_0]$ *has reached an exit position—which it will, because ordinals are well-founded—the evaluation game resumes from the exit position.*

It is clear that bounded evaluation games end after a finite number of rounds because bounded embedded games do. Note that if time limits are infinite ordinals, they do not directly refer to the number of rounds left in the game, but instead they are related to the game duration in a more abstract way. Different kinds of ways to use ordinals in game-theoretic considerations go way back. An important and relatively early reference is [13] which contains references to even earlier related articles.

It is possible to analyse embedded games as separate entities independent of evaluation games. An embedded game of the form $\mathbf{G} = \mathbf{g}(\mathbf{V}, \mathbf{C}, A, q_0, \psi_{\mathbf{C}}, \psi_{\overline{\mathbf{C}}})$ can be played without a time limit as in unbounded evaluation games, or it can be given some time limit γ_0 as a parameter, which leads to the related bounded embedded game $\mathbf{G}[\gamma_0]$. When we use the plain notation $\mathbf{G}$ (as opposed to $\mathbf{G}[\gamma_0]$), we always assume that the embedded game $\mathbf{G}$ is not bounded—we may even emphasize this by calling $\mathbf{G}$ an *unbounded* embedded game.

Evaluation games of the form $\mathcal{G}(\mathcal{M}, q_{in}, \varphi, \omega)$ constitute a particularly interesting subclass of bounded evaluation games. We call the games in this class **finitely bounded evaluation games.** In these games, only *finite* time limits are allowed to be announced for bounded embedded games.

3.3 Game-theoretic semantics

A strategy for a player $\mathbf{P} \in \{\mathbf{A}, \mathbf{E}\}$ will be defined below to be a function on game positions; in positions where the player $\mathbf{P}$ is not required to make a move, the strategy of $\mathbf{P}$ will output a special value "void". We occasionally also give the value void to some other functions when the output is not relevant (e.g., when formulating a winning strategy, we may assign void for losing positions).

DEFINITION 3.3. *Let* $\mathbf{G} = \mathbf{g}(\mathbf{V}, \mathbf{C}, A, q_0, \psi_{\mathbf{C}}, \psi_{\overline{\mathbf{C}}})$ *be an embedded game and* $\mathbf{P} \in \{\mathbf{A}, \mathbf{E}\}$. ***A strategy for the player*** $\mathbf{P}$ ***in*** $\mathbf{G}$ *is a function* $\sigma_{\mathbf{P}}$ *whose domain is* St *and* *whose range is specified below. Firstly, for any $q \in \mathrm{St}$, it is possible to define $\sigma_{\mathbf{P}}(q) \in \{\psi_{\mathbf{C}}, \psi_{\overline{\mathbf{C}}}\}$; then $\sigma_{\mathbf{P}}$ instructs $\mathbf{P}$ to end the game at the state q. Here it is required that if $\mathbf{P} = \mathbf{C}$, then $\sigma_{\mathbf{P}}(q) = \psi_{\mathbf{C}}$ and if $\mathbf{P} = \overline{\mathbf{C}}$, then $\sigma_{\mathbf{P}}(q) = \psi_{\overline{\mathbf{C}}}$. If $\sigma_{\mathbf{P}}(q) \notin \{\psi_{\mathbf{C}}, \psi_{\overline{\mathbf{C}}}\}$, then the following conditions hold.*

- *If $\mathbf{P} = \mathbf{V}$, then $\sigma_{\mathbf{P}}(q)$ is a tuple of actions in $\mathsf{action}(A, q)$.*
- *If $\mathbf{P} = \overline{\mathbf{V}}$, then $\sigma_{\mathbf{P}}(q)$ is defined to be a **response function** $f : \mathsf{action}(A, q) \to \mathsf{action}(\overline{A}, q)$ that assigns a tuple of actions for $\overline{A}$ as a response to any tuple of actions for A.*

Let γ_0 be an ordinal. A strategy $\sigma_{\mathbf{P}}$ for $\mathbf{P}$ in $\mathbf{G}[\gamma_0]$ is defined in the same way as a strategy in $\mathbf{G}$, but the domain of this strategy is the set of all possible configurations $\mathsf{Conf}_{\mathbf{G}[\gamma_0]}$.

Note that strategies in embedded games are positional, i.e., they depend only on the current state in the unbounded case and the current configuration in the bounded case.

Any strategy $\sigma_{\mathbf{P}}$ for an unbounded embedded game $\mathbf{G}$ can be used also in any bounded embedded game $\mathbf{G}[\gamma_0]$: we simply use the same action $\sigma_{\mathbf{P}}(q)$ for each configuration $(\gamma, q) \in \mathsf{Conf}_{\mathbf{G}[\gamma_0]}$. Also note that if a strategy $\sigma_{\mathbf{P}}$ for a bounded embedded game $\mathbf{G}[\gamma_0]$ is independent of time limits (and thus depends on states only), it can also be used in the unbounded embedded game $\mathbf{G}$.

Definition 3.4. *Let $\mathbf{P} \in \{\mathbf{A}, \mathbf{E}\}$. A **strategy for player $\mathbf{P}$ in an unbounded evaluation game** $\mathcal{G} = \mathcal{G}(\mathcal{M}, q_{in}, \varphi)$ is a function $\Sigma_{\mathbf{P}}$ defined on the set of positions POS of $\mathcal{G}$ (with the range specified below) satisfying the following conditions.*

1. *If $\mathsf{Pos} = (\mathbf{P}, q, \psi \vee \theta)$, then $\Sigma_{\mathbf{P}}(\mathsf{Pos}) \in \{\psi, \theta\}$.*
2. *If $\mathsf{Pos} = (\mathbf{P}, q, \langle\!\langle A \rangle\!\rangle \mathsf{X} \psi)$, then $\Sigma_{\mathbf{P}}(\mathsf{Pos})$ is a tuple of actions in $\mathsf{action}(A, q)$ for the one step game $\mathsf{step}(\mathbf{P}, A, q)$.*
3. *If $\mathsf{Pos} = (\overline{\mathbf{P}}, q, \langle\!\langle A \rangle\!\rangle \mathsf{X} \psi)$, then $\Sigma_{\mathbf{P}}(\mathsf{Pos})$ is a response function $f : \mathsf{action}(A, q) \to \mathsf{action}(\overline{A}, q)$ for $\mathsf{step}(\mathbf{P}, A, q)$.*
4. *Let $\mathsf{Pos} = (\mathbf{P}, q, \langle\!\langle A \rangle\!\rangle \psi \mathsf{T} \theta)$ or $\mathsf{Pos} = (\overline{\mathbf{P}}, q, \langle\!\langle A \rangle\!\rangle \psi \mathsf{T} \theta)$, where $\mathsf{T} \in \{\mathsf{U}, \mathsf{R}\}$. Then $\Sigma_{\mathbf{P}}(\mathsf{Pos})$ is a strategy $\sigma_{\mathbf{P}}$ for $\mathbf{P}$ in the respective embedded game $\mathbf{g}(\mathbf{V}, \mathbf{C}, A, q, \theta, \psi)$.*
5. *In all other cases, $\Sigma_{\mathbf{P}}(\mathsf{Pos}) = \mathsf{void}$.*

*We say that $\Sigma_{\mathbf{P}}$ is a **winning strategy** for $\mathbf{P}$ in $\mathcal{G}$ if $\mathbf{P}$ wins all plays of $\mathcal{G}$ where (s)he plays according to that strategy.*

Definition 3.5. *A **strategy for player $\mathbf{P}$ in a bounded evaluation game** $\mathcal{G} = \mathcal{G}(\mathcal{M}, q_{in}, \varphi, \Gamma)$ is defined as in Definition 3.4, with the exception of positions with until- and release-formulae, which are treated as follows.*

4. *Let $\mathsf{Pos} = (\mathbf{P}, q, \langle\!\langle A \rangle\!\rangle \psi \mathsf{T} \theta)$ or $\mathsf{Pos} = (\overline{\mathbf{P}}, q, \langle\!\langle A \rangle\!\rangle \psi \mathsf{T} \theta)$, where $\mathsf{T} \in \{\mathsf{U}, \mathsf{R}\}$, and let $\mathbf{G} = \mathbf{g}(\mathbf{V}, \mathbf{C}, A, q, \theta, \psi)$ denote the embedded game related to Pos. If $\mathbf{P} = \mathbf{C}$, then $\Sigma_{\mathbf{P}}(\mathsf{Pos}) = (\gamma_0, t, \sigma_{\mathbf{P}})$ where the following conditions hold.*
   - *$\gamma_0 < \Gamma$ is an ordinal. It is the choice for the initial time limit that leads to the bounded embedded game $\mathbf{G}[\gamma_0]$.*
   - *t is a function, called **timer**, on pairs (γ, q), where $\gamma \leq \gamma_0$ is a limit ordinal and $q \in \mathrm{St}$. The timer t gives an instruction how to lower the time limit γ after a transition to q has been made; the value $t(\gamma, q)$ must be an ordinal less than γ.*
   - *$\sigma_{\mathbf{P}}$ is a strategy for $\mathbf{P}$ in $\mathbf{G}[\gamma_0]$.*

   Finally, if $\mathbf{P} \neq \mathbf{C}$, then $\Sigma_{\mathbf{P}}(\mathsf{Pos})$ is a function that maps any ordinal $\gamma_0 < \Gamma$ to some strategy $\sigma_{\mathbf{P}}$ for $\mathbf{P}$ in $\mathbf{G}[\gamma_0]$.

In finitely bounded evaluation games, only finite time limits $\gamma_0 < \omega$ may be announced by $\mathbf{C}$. Since no limit ordinal is reached, the timer t can be omitted from the strategy.

Different choices for time limit bounds Γ give rise to different semantic systems, and most results in the next section will be proven for an arbitrary choice of Γ. However, in this paper we mainly focus on the cases $\Gamma = \omega$ (where ω is the smallest infinite ordinal) and $\Gamma = 2^\kappa$, where κ is the cardinality of the model. We will prove later that time limit bounds greater than 2^κ are not needed.

Definition 3.6. *Let $\mathcal{M}$ be a CGM, $q \in \mathrm{St}$ and φ an ATL-formula. Let κ be the cardinality of the model $\mathcal{M}$. We define three different notions of truth of φ in $\mathcal{M}$ and q based on three different evaluation games, thereby defining the **unbounded, bounded** and **finitely bounded semantics** (denoted, respectively, by $\models^g_u$, $\models^g_b$, and $\models^g_f$) as follows.*

- *$\mathcal{M}, q \models^g_u \varphi$ iff $\mathbf{E}$ has a winning strategy in $\mathcal{G}(\mathcal{M}, q, \varphi)$.*
- *$\mathcal{M}, q \models^g_b \varphi$ iff $\mathbf{E}$ has a winning strategy in $\mathcal{G}(\mathcal{M}, q, \varphi, 2^\kappa)$.*
- *$\mathcal{M}, q \models^g_f \varphi$ iff $\mathbf{E}$ has a winning strategy in $\mathcal{G}(\mathcal{M}, q, \varphi, \omega)$.*

We also write more generally that $\mathcal{M}, q \models^g_\Gamma \varphi$ iff $\mathbf{E}$ has a winning strategy in $\mathcal{G}(\mathcal{M}, q, \varphi, \Gamma)$.

We will prove that *both* the bounded and unbounded semantics are equivalent to the standard compositional semantics of Definition 2.3. The finitely bounded sematics, on the other hand, is equivalent to a natural variant of the compositional semantics to be introduced in Section 5. The following example shows that the finitely bounded GTS differs from the unbounded and bounded cases. In particular, the fixed point property of the temporal operator F fails:

Example 3.7. *Let $\mathcal{M} = (\{a\}, \{q_0\} \cup \mathbb{N} \times \mathbb{N}, \{p\}, \mathbb{N}, d, o, v)$, where $v(p) = \{(i, i) \mid i \in \mathbb{N}\}$, $d(a, q_0) = \mathbb{N}$, $d(a, (i, j)) = \{0\}$, $o(q_0, i) = (i, 0)$ and $o((i, j), 0) = (i, j+1)$. In this model $\mathcal{M}, q_0 \not\models^g_f \langle\!\langle \emptyset \rangle\!\rangle \mathsf{F} p$ while $\mathcal{M}, q_0 \models^g_f \langle\!\langle \emptyset \rangle\!\rangle \mathsf{X} \langle\!\langle \emptyset \rangle\!\rangle \mathsf{F} p$. This is because for every time limit $n < \omega$ chosen by Eloise, Abelard may select the action n in the first round for the agent a, so it will take $n+1$ rounds to reach a state where p is true. But after the first step, the game will be at a state $(i, 0)$ for some $i \in \mathbb{N}$, whence Eloise can choose any time limit $n \geq i$ and reach a state where p is true before time runs out.*

However, $\mathcal{M}, q_0 \models^g_b \langle\!\langle \emptyset \rangle\!\rangle \mathsf{F} p$, since Eloise can choose ω as the time limit in the beginning of the game and then lower it to $i < \omega$ when the next state $(i, 0)$ is reached. Also, $\mathcal{M}, q_0 \models^g_u \langle\!\langle \emptyset \rangle\!\rangle \mathsf{F} p$ since a state where p is true will always be reached in finite time. Still, we will show that the three semantics become equivalent over image finite models.

4. ANALYSING EMBEDDED GAMES

In this section we will examine the properties of different versions of embedded games that occur as part of evaluation games. We associate each state with a winning time label which describes how good that state is for the players. Using the optimal labels will lead to a canonical strategy which will be a winning strategy whenever there exists one.

4.1 Winning time labels

Different values of the time limit bound Γ correspond to different classes of bounded embedded games $\mathbf{G}[\gamma_0]$ where $\gamma_0 < \Gamma$. In this section—unless otherwise specified—we use a fixed value of Γ and assume that all bounded embedded games are part of some evaluation game $\mathcal{G}(\mathcal{M}, q_{in}, \varphi, \Gamma)$. Since Γ could have any ordinal value, our results will hold for both the bounded and finitely bounded semantics.

If $\mathbf{G} = \mathbf{g}(\mathbf{V}, \mathbf{C}, A, q_0, \psi_{\mathbf{C}}, \psi_{\overline{\mathbf{C}}})$ is an embedded game and $q \in \mathrm{St}$, we write $\mathbf{G}[q] := \mathbf{g}(\mathbf{V}, \mathbf{C}, A, q, \psi_{\mathbf{C}}, \psi_{\overline{\mathbf{C}}})$. We also use the abbreviation $\mathbf{G}[q,\gamma] := (\mathbf{G}[q])[\gamma]$. This notation is useful, since by the recursive nature of bounded embedded games, any configuration (γ, q) of $\mathbf{G}[\gamma_0]$ (where $\gamma_0 < \Gamma$) is the initial configuration of $\mathbf{G}[q,\gamma]$. Note that since the players use positional strategies, they do not see any difference between initial configurations and other configurations.

We next define winning strategies for embedded games. "Winning an embedded game" means for the player $\mathbf{P}$ that (s)he has a winning strategy in the *evaluation game* that continues from the exit position of the embedded game.

DEFINITION 4.1. *Let $\mathbf{G} = \mathbf{g}(\mathbf{V}, \mathbf{C}, A, q_0, \psi_{\mathbf{C}}, \psi_{\overline{\mathbf{C}}})$ be an embedded game and let $\gamma_0 < \Gamma$.*

1. We say that $\sigma_{\mathbf{P}}$ is a ***winning strategy for the player P in G*** *if infinite plays are possible with $\sigma_{\mathbf{P}}$ only if $\mathbf{P} \neq \mathbf{C}$ and the equivalence $\mathcal{M}, q \models^g_u \psi \Leftrightarrow \mathbf{P} = \mathbf{V}$ holds for all exit positions $(\mathbf{V}, q, \psi)$ of $\mathbf{G}$ that can be reached with $\sigma_{\mathbf{P}}$.*

2. If $\mathbf{P} = \mathbf{C}$, we say that the pair $(\sigma_{\mathbf{P}}, t)$ is a ***timed winning strategy for P in*** *$\mathbf{G}[\gamma_0]$ if $\mathcal{M}, q \models^g_\Gamma \psi \Leftrightarrow \mathbf{P} = \mathbf{V}$ holds for all exit positions $(\mathbf{V}, q, \psi)$ that can be encountered when $\mathbf{P}$ plays using the strategy $\sigma_{\mathbf{P}}$ and timer t.*

If $\mathbf{P} \neq \mathbf{C}$, we say that $\sigma_{\mathbf{P}}$ is a ***winning strategy for P in*** *$\mathbf{G}[\gamma_0]$ if $\mathcal{M}, q \models^g_\Gamma \psi \Leftrightarrow \mathbf{P} = \mathbf{V}$ holds for all exit positions $(\mathbf{V}, q, \psi)$ that can occur when $\mathbf{P}$ plays using $\sigma_{\mathbf{P}}$.*

If the unbounded (respectively, bounded) embedded game in the above definition ends in a position where the equivalence $\mathcal{M}, q \models^g_u \psi \Leftrightarrow \mathbf{P} = \mathbf{V}$ (respectively, $\mathcal{M}, q \models^g_\Gamma \psi \Leftrightarrow \mathbf{P} = \mathbf{V}$) holds, we also say that $\mathbf{P}$ **wins** the embedded game. In the unbounded case, $\overline{\mathbf{C}}$ wins also if the play is infinite.

Consider an embedded game $\mathbf{G} = \mathbf{g}(\mathbf{V}, \mathbf{C}, A, q_0, \psi_{\mathbf{C}}, \psi_{\overline{\mathbf{C}}})$. We next define for $\mathbf{G}$ so called **winning time labels**, $\mathcal{L}_{\mathbf{P}}(q)$, for each $q \in \mathrm{St}$. The labels will indicate how good the state q is for the player $\mathbf{P}$ when different bounded embedded games $\mathbf{G}[q, \gamma_0]$ are played with different time limits $\gamma_0 < \Gamma$. If the label is "win" or "lose", then the state is a winning (respectively, losing) state for $\mathbf{P}$, regardless of the time limit γ_0. If the label is an ordinal $\gamma < \Gamma$, it means that γ is the "critical time limit" for winning or losing the game: if $\mathbf{P} = \mathbf{C}$, γ is the least time limit needed for $\mathbf{P}$ to win from q, and if $\mathbf{P} \neq \mathbf{C}$, then γ is the least time limit such that $\mathbf{P}$ can no longer guarantee that (s)he will not lose the game from q.

DEFINITION 4.2. *Let $\mathbf{G} = \mathbf{g}(\mathbf{V}, \mathbf{C}, A, q_0, \psi_{\mathbf{C}}, \psi_{\overline{\mathbf{C}}})$ be an embedded game and $\mathbf{P} \in \{\mathbf{A}, \mathbf{E}\}$. The* ***winning time label*** *$\mathcal{L}_{\mathbf{P}}(q)$* ***for P in G at state*** *$q \in \mathrm{St}$ is defined as follows.*

Case 1. Suppose $\mathbf{P} = \mathbf{C}$. Let $\sigma_{\mathbf{P}}$ be a strategy for $\mathbf{P}$. We first define a ***strategy label*** *$l(q, \sigma_{\mathbf{P}})$ as follows.*

- *Set $l(q, \sigma_{\mathbf{P}}) :=$ lose if $(\sigma_{\mathbf{P}}, t)$ is not a timed winning strategy in $\mathbf{G}[q, \gamma]$ for any timer t and $\gamma < \Gamma$.*
- *Else, set $l(q, \sigma_{\mathbf{P}}) := \gamma$, where $\gamma < \Gamma$ is the least time limit for which there is a timer t such that $(\sigma_{\mathbf{P}}, t)$ is a timed winning strategy in $\mathbf{G}[q, \gamma]$.*

When there exists at least one strategy $\sigma_{\mathbf{P}}$ for $\mathbf{P}$ such that $l(q, \sigma_{\mathbf{P}}) \neq$ lose, we define $\mathcal{L}_{\mathbf{P}}(q)$ as the least ordinal value of strategy labels $l(q, \sigma_{\mathbf{P}})$. Else, we define $\mathcal{L}_{\mathbf{P}}(q) :=$ lose.

Case 2. Suppose $\mathbf{P} \neq \mathbf{C}$. Let $\sigma_{\mathbf{P}}$ be a strategy for $\mathbf{P}$.

- *If $\sigma_{\mathbf{P}}$ is a winning strategy in $\mathbf{G}[q, \gamma]$ for every time limit $\gamma < \Gamma$, then set $l(q, \sigma_{\mathbf{P}}) :=$ win.*
- *Else, set $l(q, \sigma_{\mathbf{P}}) := \gamma$, where $\gamma < \Gamma$ is the least time limit such that $\sigma_{\mathbf{P}}$ is not a winning strategy in $\mathbf{G}[q, \gamma]$.*

If $l(q, \sigma_{\mathbf{P}}) =$ win for some $\sigma_{\mathbf{P}}$, then set $\mathcal{L}_{\mathbf{P}}(q) :=$ win. Else, set $\mathcal{L}_{\mathbf{P}}(q)$ to be the least upper bound for the values $l(q, \sigma_{\mathbf{P}})$.

The following proposition relates values of winning time labels to durations of embedded games and existence of winning strategies. A proof, which follows quite directly from the definition of winning time labels, is given in [7].

PROPOSITION 4.3. *Let $\mathbf{G} = \mathbf{g}(\mathbf{V}, \mathbf{C}, A, q_0, \psi_{\mathbf{C}}, \psi_{\overline{\mathbf{C}}})$ be an embedded game, $\mathbf{P} \in \{\mathbf{A}, \mathbf{E}\}$ and $q \in \mathrm{St}$.*

1. Assume $\mathbf{P} = \mathbf{C}$. We have $\mathcal{L}_{\mathbf{P}}(q) = \gamma < \Gamma$ iff there is a pair $(\sigma_{\mathbf{P}}, t)$ that is a timed winning strategy in $\mathbf{G}[q, \gamma']$ for all γ' such that $\gamma \leq \gamma' < \Gamma$, but there is no timed winning strategy for $\mathbf{P}$ in $\mathbf{G}[q, \gamma']$ for any $\gamma' < \gamma$.
We have $\mathcal{L}_{\mathbf{P}}(q) =$ lose iff there is no timed winning strategy $(\sigma_{\mathbf{P}}, t)$ for $\mathbf{P}$ in $\mathbf{G}[q, \gamma]$ for any $\gamma < \Gamma$.

2. Assume $\mathbf{P} \neq \mathbf{C}$. We have $\mathcal{L}_{\mathbf{P}}(q) = \gamma < \Gamma$ iff for every $\gamma' < \gamma$, there is some $\sigma_{\mathbf{P}}$ which is a winning strategy for $\mathbf{P}$ in $\mathbf{G}[q, \gamma']$, but there is no winning strategy for $\mathbf{P}$ in $\mathbf{G}[q, \gamma']$ for any γ' such that $\gamma \leq \gamma' < \Gamma$.
We have $\mathcal{L}_{\mathbf{P}}(q) =$ win iff there is a strategy $\sigma_{\mathbf{P}}$ which is a winning strategy in $\mathbf{G}[q, \gamma]$ for every $\gamma < \Gamma$.

Winning time labels $\mathcal{L}_{\mathbf{P}}(q)$ of an embedded game are either ordinals less than the time limit bound Γ or labels win, lose. If we increased the value of Γ to some $\Gamma' > \Gamma$ and considered the values of winning time labels of the corresponding embedded game within the evaluation game $\mathcal{G}(\mathcal{M}, q_{in}, \varphi, \Gamma')$, then some of the labels that originally were win or lose, could now obtain ordinal values γ s.t. $\Gamma \leq \gamma < \Gamma'$. Other kinds of changes of labels would also be possible because the truth sets of the goal formulae $\psi_{\mathbf{C}}$ and $\psi_{\overline{\mathbf{C}}}$ could change. However, it is easy to see that if all ordinal valued labels stay strictly below Γ in all embedded games when going from Γ to Γ', then each label in fact remains the same in the transition.

We say that Γ is **stable** for an embedded game $\mathbf{G}$ if the winning time labels of the game cannot be altered by increasing Γ. We say that Γ is **globally stable** for a concurrent game model $\mathcal{M}$ if Γ is stable for *all* bounded embedded games within all evaluation games $\mathcal{G}(\mathcal{M}, q_{in}, \varphi, \Gamma)$. We will see later that there exists a globally stable time limit bound for every concurrent game model. When Γ is globally stable, its role is not so relevant anymore, since players would not benefit from the ability to choose arbitrarily high time limits. However, for technical reasons, we always need some time limit bound to avoid strategies becoming proper classes.

4.2 Canonical strategies for embedded games

DEFINITION 4.4. *Let $\mathbf{G} = \mathbf{g}(\mathbf{V}, \mathbf{C}, A, q_0, \psi_{\mathbf{C}}, \psi_{\overline{\mathbf{C}}})$ be an embedded game, let $\mathbf{P} \in \{\mathbf{A}, \mathbf{E}\}$ and assume that $\mathbf{P} = \mathbf{C}$. We define the* ***canonical strategy*** *$\tau_{\mathbf{P}}$ and* ***canonical timer*** *t_{can} for $\mathbf{P}$ in $\mathbf{G}$ as follows.*

If $\mathcal{L}_{\mathbf{P}}(q) = \gamma$, then $\tau_{\mathbf{P}}(q) = \sigma_{\mathbf{P}}(\gamma, q)$ for some strategy $\sigma_{\mathbf{P}}$ for which there is a timer t such that $(\sigma_{\mathbf{P}}, t)$ is a timed winning strategy in $\mathbf{G}[q, \gamma']$ for all γ' such that $\gamma \leq \gamma' < \Gamma$. (Note that such a strategy exists by Proposition 4.3). And if $\mathcal{L}_{\mathbf{P}}(q) =$ lose, then $\tau_{\mathbf{P}}(q) =$ void.

We define t_{can} for any pair (γ, q) ($\gamma < \Gamma$ is a limit ordinal and $q \in \mathrm{St}$) such that if $\mathcal{L}_{\mathbf{P}}(q) \neq$ lose and $\mathcal{L}_{\mathbf{P}}(q) < \gamma$, then $t_{can}(\gamma, q) = \mathcal{L}_{\mathbf{P}}(q)$, and otherwise $t_{can}(\gamma, q) =$ void.

We call the pair $(\tau_{\mathbf{P}}, t_{can})$ the ***canonically timed strategy*** *(for the controller).*

Note that when $\mathbf{P} = \mathbf{C}$, the canonical strategy $\tau_{\mathbf{P}}$ depends only on states and can thus be used in both unbounded and bounded embedded games. We will see that if $\mathbf{C}$ can win $\mathbf{G}[\gamma_0]$ for some $\gamma_0 < \Gamma$, then $\mathbf{C}$ wins $\mathbf{G}[\gamma_0]$ with $(\tau_{\mathbf{C}}, t_{can})$.

The canonical strategy of $\mathbf{C}$ can also be seen, in some sense, as optimal for winning the game as fast as possible.

DEFINITION 4.5. *Let $\mathbf{G} = \mathbf{g}(\mathbf{V}, \mathbf{C}, A, q_0, \psi_{\mathbf{C}}, \psi_{\overline{\mathbf{C}}})$ be an embedded game, let $\mathbf{P} \in \{\mathbf{A}, \mathbf{E}\}$ and assume that $\mathbf{P} \neq \mathbf{C}$. We define the **canonical strategy** $\tau_{\mathbf{P}}$ for $\mathbf{P}$ in $\mathbf{G}[\gamma_0]$ for all $\gamma_0 < \Gamma$. We define $\tau_{\mathbf{P}}$ at every configuration (γ, q), where $\gamma < \Gamma$ and $q \in \mathrm{St}$, as follows.*

If $\mathcal{L}_{\mathbf{P}}(q) = \mathsf{win}$, then $\tau_{\mathbf{P}}(\gamma, q) = \sigma_{\mathbf{P}}(\gamma, q)$ for some $\sigma_{\mathbf{P}}$ that is a winning strategy in $\mathbf{G}[q, \gamma]$ for every $\gamma < \Gamma$ (such a strategy exists by Proposition 4.3). Else, if $\mathcal{L}_{\mathbf{P}}(q) = \gamma'$ and $\gamma' > \gamma$, then $\tau_{\mathbf{P}}(\gamma, q) = \sigma_{\mathbf{P}}(\gamma, q)$ for some $\sigma_{\mathbf{P}}$ that is a winning strategy in $\mathbf{G}[q, \gamma]$ (such a strategy exists by Proposition 4.3). Otherwise we define $\tau_{\mathbf{P}}(\gamma, q) = \mathsf{void}$.

*We also define, for every $n < \omega$, the **n-canonical strategy** $\tau^n_{\mathbf{P}}$ for $\mathbf{P}$ in $\mathbf{G}$ and the **∞-canonical strategy** $\tau^{\infty}_{\mathbf{P}}$ for $\mathbf{P}$ in $\mathbf{G}$. These are defined for each $q \in \mathrm{St}$ as follows.*

If $\mathcal{L}_{\mathbf{P}}(q) \geq \omega$ or $\mathcal{L}_{\mathbf{P}}(q) = \mathsf{win}$, then $\tau^n_{\mathbf{P}}(q) = \tau_{\mathbf{P}}(n, q)$. Else, if $\mathcal{L}_{\mathbf{P}}(q) = m > 0$, then $\tau^n_{\mathbf{P}}(q) = \sigma_{\mathbf{P}}(m-1, q)$ for some $\sigma_{\mathbf{P}}$ that is a winning strategy in $\mathbf{G}[q, m-1]$ (such a strategy exists by Proposition 4.3). Otherwise $\tau^n_{\mathbf{P}}(q) = \mathsf{void}$.

If $\mathcal{L}_{\mathbf{P}}(q) = \mathsf{win}$, then $\tau^{\infty}_{\mathbf{P}}(q) = \tau_{\mathbf{P}}(\Gamma-1, q)$, and otherwise $\tau^{\infty}_{\mathbf{P}}(q) = \mathsf{void}$. Note that to be able to define $\tau^{\infty}_{\mathbf{P}}$, we have to assume that Γ is a successor ordinal.

When $\mathbf{P} \neq \mathbf{C}$, the canonical strategy $\tau_{\mathbf{P}}$ depends on time limits, and thus it cannot be used in unbounded embedded games. However, both n-canonical and ∞-canonical strategies depend only on states. We fix the notation such that from now on $\tau_{\mathbf{P}}$, $\tau^n_{\mathbf{P}}$ and $\tau^{\infty}_{\mathbf{P}}$ will always denote canonical strategies (of the respective type) for the player $\mathbf{P}$.

DEFINITION 4.6. *Let $\mathbf{G} = \mathbf{g}(\mathbf{V}, \mathbf{C}, A, q_0, \psi_{\mathbf{C}}, \psi_{\overline{\mathbf{C}}})$ be an embedded game. Let $\sigma_{\mathbf{P}}$ be a strategy in $\mathbf{G}[\gamma_0]$ ($\gamma_0 < \Gamma$). Suppose that (γ, q) is such a configuration that $\sigma_{\mathbf{P}}(\gamma, q)$ is either a tuple of actions for A or some response function for $\overline{A}$. We say that set $Q \subseteq \mathrm{St}$ is **forced** by $\sigma_{\mathbf{P}}(\gamma, q)$ if for each $q' \in \mathrm{St}$, it holds that $q' \in Q$ if and only if there is some play with $\sigma_{\mathbf{P}}$ from (γ, q) such that the next configuration is (γ', q') for some γ'. We use the same terminology for the set forced by $\sigma_{\mathbf{P}}(q)$ when $\sigma_{\mathbf{P}}$ depends only on states.*

The following lemma shows that the canonical strategy (with the canonical timer) is guaranteed to be a (timed) winning strategy always when such exists. A proof, which follows quite directly from Definitions 4.4 and 4.5, is given in [7].

LEMMA 4.7. *Let $\mathbf{G} = \mathbf{g}(\mathbf{V}, \mathbf{C}, A, q_0, \psi_{\mathbf{C}}, \psi_{\overline{\mathbf{C}}})$ be an embedded game. Let $\mathbf{P} \in \{\mathbf{A}, \mathbf{E}\}$ and $\gamma_0 < \Gamma$.*

1. *Suppose that $\mathbf{P} = \mathbf{C}$. If $\mathbf{P}$ has a timed winning strategy $(\sigma_{\mathbf{P}}, t)$ in $\mathbf{G}[\gamma_0]$, then $(\tau_{\mathbf{P}}, t_{can})$ is a timed winning strategy for $\mathbf{P}$ in $\mathbf{G}[\gamma_0]$.*
2. *Suppose that $\mathbf{P} \neq \mathbf{C}$. If $\mathbf{P}$ has a winning strategy $\sigma_{\mathbf{P}}$ in $\mathbf{G}[\gamma_0]$, then $\tau_{\mathbf{P}}$ is a winning strategy for $\mathbf{P}$ in $\mathbf{G}[\gamma_0]$.*

By the first claim of the previous proposition, we see that it suffices to consider those strategies of player $\mathbf{C}$ which are independent of time limits. The following lemma shows that the same holds for the player $\overline{\mathbf{C}}$ in bounded embedded games with a *finite* time limit. The key here will be the use of n-canonical strategies. A proof is given in [7].

LEMMA 4.8. *Let $\mathbf{G} = \mathbf{g}(\mathbf{V}, \mathbf{C}, A, q_0, \psi_{\mathbf{C}}, \psi_{\overline{\mathbf{C}}})$ be an embedded game, let $\mathbf{P} \in \{\mathbf{A}, \mathbf{E}\}$ and assume that $\mathbf{P} \neq \mathbf{C}$.*

Let $n < \omega$. Now, if $\mathbf{P}$ has a winning strategy $\sigma_{\mathbf{P}}$ in $\mathbf{G}[m]$ for some $m \leq n$, then $\tau^n_{\mathbf{P}}$ is a winning strategy in $\mathbf{G}[m]$.

EXAMPLE 4.9. *In the cases where $\mathcal{L}_{\overline{\mathbf{C}}}(q) = \omega$, the player $\overline{\mathbf{C}}$ can win the game with any time limit $n < \omega$, but there is no single strategy that would win for every n. But if $\overline{\mathbf{C}}$ knows that the initial time limit is (at most) m, then (s)he knows that the m-canonical strategy will be her/his winning strategy. Therefore $\overline{\mathbf{C}}$ needs to know the time limit when **selecting** the strategy, but not when using it (since n-canonical strategies are independent of time limits).*

4.3 Determinacy of embedded games

The following correspondence between the winning time labels of $\mathbf{C}$ and $\overline{\mathbf{C}}$ will be the key for proving determinacy of bounded embedded games.

PROPOSITION 4.10. *Let $\mathbf{G} = \mathbf{g}(\mathbf{V}, \mathbf{C}, A, q_0, \psi_{\mathbf{C}}, \psi_{\overline{\mathbf{C}}})$ be an embedded game. The equivalence $\mathcal{L}_{\mathbf{C}}(q) = \gamma$ iff $\mathcal{L}_{\overline{\mathbf{C}}}(q) = \gamma$ holds for each state $q \in \mathrm{St}$ and each ordinal $\gamma < \Gamma$.*

PROOF. Sketch of proof: We can prove the claim by transfinite induction on γ. The case $\gamma = 0$ is clear, since if $\mathbf{C}$ cannot win the game with time limit 0, then $\overline{\mathbf{C}}$ will win it automatically. We then suppose that the claim holds for every $\gamma' < \gamma$ and prove the equivalence for γ. If $\mathcal{L}_{\mathbf{C}}(q) = \gamma$, then $\mathbf{C}$ has a winning strategy in $\mathbf{G}[q, \gamma]$ and thus $\overline{\mathbf{C}}$ cannot have a winning strategy in that game. Hence by Proposition 4.3 we have $\mathcal{L}_{\overline{\mathbf{C}}} \leq \gamma$. By the induction hypothesis, $\mathcal{L}_{\overline{\mathbf{C}}} \neq \gamma'$ for every $\gamma' < \gamma$ and thus $\mathcal{L}_{\overline{\mathbf{C}}}(q) = \gamma$.

Suppose then that $\mathcal{L}_{\overline{\mathbf{C}}}(q) = \gamma$. If there existed some $\sigma_{\overline{\mathbf{C}}}$, $\gamma' < \Gamma$ and $Q \subseteq \mathrm{St}$ forced by $\sigma_{\overline{\mathbf{C}}}(\gamma', q)$ s.t. $\mathcal{L}_{\overline{\mathbf{C}}}(q') \geq \gamma$ for every $q' \in Q$, then we could use $\sigma_{\overline{\mathbf{C}}}$ to formulate a winning strategy for $\overline{\mathbf{C}}$ in $\mathbf{G}[q, \gamma]$. This is not possible since we have $\mathcal{L}_{\overline{\mathbf{C}}}(q) = \gamma$. Thus it can be shown that $\mathbf{C}$ can play such that for all possible successor states q', we have $\mathcal{L}_{\overline{\mathbf{C}}}(q') < \gamma$, whence by the induction hypothesis $\mathcal{L}_{\mathbf{C}}(q') < \gamma$. Hence we can formulate a timed winning strategy for $\mathbf{C}$ in $\mathbf{G}[q, \gamma]$ and thus $\mathcal{L}_{\mathbf{C}}(q) = \gamma$. For a detailed proof, see [7]. □

Apart from ordinal values that are less than the bound Γ, the only possible winning time label for $\mathbf{C}$ is the label lose. For $\overline{\mathbf{C}}$, the only non-ordinal value is win. Hence by the previous proposition, we also have $\mathcal{L}_{\mathbf{C}}(q) = \mathsf{lose}$ iff $\mathcal{L}_{\overline{\mathbf{C}}}(q) = \mathsf{win}$.

PROPOSITION 4.11. *$\mathbf{C}$ has a timed winning strategy in a bounded embedded game $\mathbf{g}(\mathbf{V}, \mathbf{C}, A, q_0, \psi_{\mathbf{C}}, \psi_{\overline{\mathbf{C}}})[\gamma_0]$ iff $\overline{\mathbf{C}}$ does not have a winning strategy in that game.*

PROOF. If $\mathcal{L}_{\mathbf{C}}(q_0) = \mathsf{lose}$, then $\mathcal{L}_{\overline{\mathbf{C}}}(q_0) = \mathsf{win}$, whence by Proposition 4.3, the player $\overline{\mathbf{C}}$ has a winning strategy and $\mathbf{C}$ does not have a timed winning strategy. Else $\mathcal{L}_{\mathbf{C}}(q_0) = \gamma$ for some $\gamma < \Gamma$. Now, by Proposition 4.10, also $\mathcal{L}_{\overline{\mathbf{C}}}(q_0) = \gamma$. If $\gamma \leq \gamma_0$, then by Proposition 4.3 the player $\mathbf{C}$ has a timed winning strategy, while $\overline{\mathbf{C}}$ does not have a winning strategy. Analogously, if $\gamma > \gamma_0$, then $\overline{\mathbf{C}}$ has a winning strategy, while $\mathbf{C}$ does not have a timed winning strategy. □

4.4 Finding stable time limit bounds

DEFINITION 4.12. *Let $\mathcal{M}$ be a CGM and let $q \in \mathrm{St}$. We define the **branching degree of** q, $\mathsf{BD}(q)$, as the cardinality of the set of states accessible from q with a single transition: $\mathsf{BD}(q) := \mathsf{card}(\{o(q, \vec{\alpha}) \mid \vec{\alpha} \in \mathsf{action}(\mathbb{A}\mathrm{gt}, q)\})$. We define the **infinite branching bound of** $\mathcal{M}$, $\mathsf{IBB}(\mathcal{M})$, as the smallest infinite cardinal κ such that $\kappa > \mathsf{BD}(q)$ for every $q \in \mathrm{St}$.*

With this definition $\mathsf{IBB}(\mathcal{M}) = \omega$ iff $\mathcal{M}$ is image finite. We will see that the value of $\mathsf{IBB}(\mathcal{M})$ is closely related to the sizes of a globally stable time limit bounds for $\mathcal{M}$.

LEMMA 4.13. *Let* $\mathbf{G} = \mathbf{g}(\mathbf{V}, \mathbf{C}, A, q_0, \psi_\mathbf{C}, \psi_{\overline{\mathbf{C}}})$ *be an embedded game,* $\mathbf{P} \in \{\mathbf{A}, \mathbf{E}\}$ *and* $\mathbf{P} = \mathbf{C}$. *Now the following holds for every* $q \in \mathrm{St}$: *If* $\mathcal{L}_\mathbf{P}(q) = \gamma > 0$ *and* $Q \subseteq \mathrm{St}$ *is forced by* $\tau_\mathbf{P}(q)$, *we have* $\mathcal{L}_\mathbf{P}(q') < \gamma$ *for every* $q' \in Q$, *and*

- $\max\{\mathcal{L}_\mathbf{P}(q') \mid q' \in Q\} = \gamma - 1$ *if* γ *is a successor ordinal,*
- $\sup\{\mathcal{L}_\mathbf{P}(q') \mid q' \in Q\} = \gamma$ *if* γ *is a limit ordinal.*

PROOF. When $\mathcal{L}_\mathbf{P}(q) = \gamma > 0$, by Lemma 4.7, $(\tau_\mathbf{P}, t_{can})$ is a timed winning strategy in $\mathbf{G}[q, \gamma]$. Therefore every winning time label in the set Q forced by $\tau_\mathbf{P}(q)$ must be an ordinal less than γ. If γ is a successor ordinal, then there must be some state with label $\gamma - 1$ in Q, and if γ is a limit ordinal, then γ must be the supremum of the winning time labels in Q (else there would be a winning strategy for $\mathbf{C}$ in $\mathbf{G}[q, \gamma']$ for some $\gamma' < \gamma$). See [7] for more details. □

The following lemma shows that if a certain ordinal valued winning time label exist for an embedded game, then all the smaller winning time labels must exist for that game as well. The proof that is given in [7] is done by using Lemma 4.13.

LEMMA 4.14. *Let* $\mathbf{G} = \mathbf{g}(\mathbf{V}, \mathbf{C}, A, q_0, \psi_\mathbf{C}, \psi_{\overline{\mathbf{C}}})$ *be an embedded game and* $\gamma < \Gamma$ *an ordinal. Assume that* $\mathcal{L}_\mathbf{P}(q) = \gamma$ *for some* $q \in \mathrm{St}$ *and* $\mathbf{P} \in \{\mathbf{A}, \mathbf{E}\}$. *Now for every* $\delta \leq \gamma$ *there is a state* q_δ *for which* $\mathcal{L}_\mathbf{C}(q_\delta) = \delta$.

EXAMPLE 4.15. *In finite models all winning time labels are strictly smaller than the cardinality of the model, i.e. if* $\mathsf{card}(\mathcal{M}) = n < \omega$, *then* n *is a globally stable time limit bound for* $\mathcal{M}$. *This can be seen by the following reasoning.*

If there was some state with a winning time label $\gamma \geq n$, *then by Lemma 4.14, there would be a state* $q \in \mathrm{St}$ *for which* $\mathcal{L}_\mathbf{C}(q) = n$. *Further, by Lemma 4.14 we would now find states with winning time labels* $n-1, n-2, \ldots, 0$. *But since winning time labels are unique for each state, this would mean that* $\mathsf{card}(\mathcal{M}) > n$, *a contradiction.*

This result is quite obvious by the observation that the controller can only win the embedded game by reaching a state in the truth set of the formula $\psi_\mathbf{C}$. *Hence it would not be beneficial for the controller to go in cycles.*

The following proposition shows how we can find an upper bound for the values of possible winning time labels by just looking at the infinite branching bound of a model.

PROPOSITION 4.16. *Let* $\mathcal{M}$ *be a* CGM *such that we have* $\mathsf{IBB}(\mathcal{M}) = \kappa$. *We define an ordinal* Γ *as follows:*

$$\begin{cases} \Gamma := \kappa \text{ if } \kappa \text{ is a regular cardinal,} \\ \Gamma := \kappa^+ \text{ (the successor \textbf{cardinal} of } \kappa\text{) otherwise.} \end{cases}$$

Now Γ *is a globally stable time limit bound for* $\mathcal{M}$.

PROOF. For the sake of contradiction, suppose that there is $\Gamma' > \Gamma$ and embedded game $\mathbf{G}$ within a bounded evaluation game $\mathcal{G}(\mathcal{M}, q_{in}, \varphi, \Gamma')$ such that in $\mathbf{G}$ either of the players has winning time labels that are greater or equal to Γ. By Lemma 4.14, there is a state $q \in \mathrm{St}$ for which $\mathcal{L}_\mathbf{C}(q) = \Gamma$. Let $Q \subseteq \mathrm{St}$ be the set of states that is forced by $\tau_\mathbf{C}(q)$. Since $\mathsf{IBB}(\mathcal{M}) = \kappa$, we have $\mathsf{card}(Q) < \kappa \leq \Gamma$. By Lemma 4.13, $\mathcal{L}_\mathbf{C}(q') < \Gamma$ for every state $q' \in Q$, and furthermore, since Γ is a limit ordinal, Γ must be the supremum of the winning time labels of the states in Q.

Now every winning time label in Q is smaller than Γ and the cardinality of Q is less than Γ. Because successor cardinals are regular, Γ is necessarily a regular cardinal, and thus it is equal to its own cofinality. Hence we have $\sup\{\mathcal{L}_\mathbf{C}(q') \mid q' \in Q\} < \Gamma$. This is a contradiction and thus Γ must be a globally stable time limit bound. □

In [7] we show that Γ in Proposition 4.16 is the least ordinal that is guaranteed to be globally stable. From Proposition 4.16 we obtain the following corollary on the stability of the time limit bounds used with the bounded and finitely bounded GTS. For a detailed proof of the corollary, see [7].

COROLLARY 4.17. *Let* $\mathcal{M}$ *be a* CGM. *If* $\mathsf{card}(\mathcal{M}) = \kappa$, *then* 2^κ *is a globally stable time limit bound for* $\mathcal{M}$. *If* $\mathcal{M}$ *is image finite,* ω *is a globally stable time limit bound for* $\mathcal{M}$.

4.5 Relationship between the unbounded and bounded embedded games

The following lemma shows that when Γ satisfies certain conditions, then, if $\mathbf{P}$ uses ∞-canonical strategy $\tau_\mathbf{P}^\infty$ and begins from a state with the label win, $\mathbf{P}$ will always stay in states with the label win. A proof is given in [7].

LEMMA 4.18. *Let* $\mathbf{G} = \mathbf{g}(\mathbf{V}, \mathbf{C}, A, q_0, \psi_\mathbf{C}, \psi_{\overline{\mathbf{C}}})$ *be an embedded game,* $\mathbf{P} \in \{\mathbf{A}, \mathbf{E}\}$ *and* $\mathbf{P} \neq \mathbf{C}$. *Assume that the time limit bound* Γ *is a successor ordinal and* $\Gamma - 1$ *is stable for* $\mathbf{G}$. *Now for every* $q \in \mathrm{St}$, *if* $\mathcal{L}_\mathbf{P}(q) = \mathsf{win}$ *and* $Q \subseteq \mathrm{St}$ *is forced by* $\tau_\mathbf{P}^\infty$, *then* $\mathcal{L}_\mathbf{P}(q') = \mathsf{win}$ *for every* $q' \in Q$.

The following proposition shows that when the time limit bound Γ is stable, then bounded embedded games become essentially equivalent with unbounded embedded games.

PROPOSITION 4.19. *Let* $\mathbf{G} = \mathbf{g}(\mathbf{V}, \mathbf{C}, A, q_0, \psi_\mathbf{C}, \psi_{\overline{\mathbf{C}}},)$ *be an embedded game and* $\mathbf{P} \in \{\mathbf{A}, \mathbf{E}\}$. *Suppose also that* Γ *is stable for* $\mathbf{G}$. *Now the following equivalences hold:*

- *If* $\mathbf{P} = \mathbf{C}$, *there is a winning strategy* $\sigma_\mathbf{P}$ *in* $\mathbf{G}$ *iff there is* $\gamma_0 < \Gamma$ *and a timed winning strategy* $(\sigma'_\mathbf{P}, t)$ *in* $\mathbf{G}[\gamma_0]$.
- *If* $\mathbf{P} \neq \mathbf{C}$, *there is a winning strategy* $\sigma_\mathbf{P}$ *in* $\mathbf{G}$ *iff there is* $\sigma'_\mathbf{P}$ *which is a winning strategy in* $\mathbf{G}[\gamma_0]$ *for every* $\gamma_0 < \Gamma$.

PROOF. Sketch of proof: Assume first that $\mathbf{P} = \mathbf{C}$. For the implication from right to left, we see that if there is a timed winning strategy for $\mathbf{P}$ in $\mathbf{G}[\gamma_0]$ for some $\gamma_0 < \Gamma$, then $(\tau_\mathbf{P}, t_{can})$ is a timed winning strategy in $\mathbf{G}[\gamma_0]$. Since $\tau_\mathbf{P}$ depends on states only, it can be used in $\mathbf{G}$, where it will be a winning strategy. For the other direction, we first notice that if $\mathcal{L}_\mathbf{P}(q_0) = \gamma$ for some $\gamma < \Gamma$, then $(\tau_\mathbf{P}, t_{can})$ is a winning strategy in $\mathbf{G}[\gamma]$. We can also show that if $\mathcal{L}_\mathbf{P}(q_0) = \mathsf{lose}$, then $\overline{\mathbf{P}}$ can force the game to stay at states with the label lose, whence $\mathbf{P}$ cannot win $\mathbf{G}$.

When $\mathbf{P} \neq \mathbf{C}$, the implication from left to right is immediate. For the other direction, we notice that the assumption immediately implies that we have $\mathcal{L}_\mathbf{P}(q_0) = \mathsf{win}$. Now we can construct the ∞-canonical strategy $\tau_\mathbf{P}^\infty$ for the time limit bound $\Gamma' := \Gamma + 1$. Since Γ is stable, raising the value of the time limit bound to Γ' will not affect the winning time labels of states. We can then use Lemma 4.18 to show that any play with $\tau_\mathbf{P}^\infty$ will stay on states with the label win. But $\mathbf{P}$ can lose $\mathbf{G}$ only if (s)he ends up at a state with label 0 in finite time. Since $\tau_\mathbf{P}^\infty$ also depends on states only, it is thus a winning strategy in $\mathbf{G}$. See [7] for more details. □

As bounded embedded games are determined, the previous proposition implies that also unbounded embedded games are determined. By this result, we see that even if we defined memory based strategies for bounded or unbounded embedded games, the semantics so obtained would remain equivalent to the current one. We can now prove the equivalence of unbounded and bounded game-theoretic semantics.

THEOREM 4.20. *Let* $\mathcal{M}$ *be a* CGM, $q \in \mathrm{St}$ *and* φ *an* ATL-*formula. We have* $\mathcal{M}, q \models_u^g \varphi$ *iff* $\mathcal{M}, q \models_b^g \varphi$.

PROOF. Assume that $\mathsf{card}(\mathcal{M}) = \kappa$. By Corollary 4.17, 2^κ is globally stable for $\mathcal{M}$. Consider an embedded game $\mathbf{G}$. If Eloise is the controller in $\mathbf{G}$, then by Proposition 4.19 she has a winning strategy in $\mathbf{G}$ iff there is some $\gamma < 2^\kappa$ such that she has a winning strategy in $\mathbf{G}[\gamma]$. If Eloise is not the controller in $\mathbf{G}$, then by Proposition 4.19, she has a winning strategy in $\mathbf{G}$ iff she has a winning strategy in $\mathbf{G}[\gamma]$ for every $\gamma < 2^\kappa$. Hence we can prove by a straightforward induction on φ that Eloise has a winning strategy in $\mathcal{G}(\mathcal{M}, q, \varphi)$ iff she has a winning strategy in $\mathcal{G}(\mathcal{M}, q, \varphi, 2^\kappa)$. □

Even though the finitely bounded semantics is not equivalent to the bounded semantics (see Example 3.7), the two systems become equivalent on a natural class models:

THEOREM 4.21. *Let $\mathcal{M}$ be an image finite* CGM, *$q \in \mathrm{St}$ and φ an* ATL*-formula. Now $\mathcal{M}, q \models^g_f \varphi$ iff $\mathcal{M}, q \models^g_b \varphi$.*

PROOF. By Corollary 4.17, in image finite models all ordinal valued winning time labels are finite. Thus the controller would gain nothing from being able to use infinite ordinals in embedded games. Hence we can prove the claim by a straightforward induction on φ. □

5. COMPARING GAME-THEORETIC AND COMPOSITIONAL SEMANTICS

We next establish that the unbounded GTS is equivalent to the standard compositional semantics of ATL.

THEOREM 5.1. *Let $\mathcal{M}$ be a* CGM, *$q_{in} \in \mathrm{St}$ and φ an* ATL*-formula. Now $\mathcal{M}, q_{in} \models \varphi$ iff $\mathcal{M}, q_{in} \models^g_u \varphi$.*

PROOF. Sketch of proof: For the right-to-left direction, we suppose that Eloise has a winning strategy $\Sigma_{\mathbf{E}}$ in the evaluation game $\mathcal{G}(\mathcal{M}, q_{in}, \varphi)$. We then show that the following condition must hold for every position $\mathsf{Pos} = (\mathbf{P}, q, \psi)$ that is reached in the game when Eloise uses $\Sigma_{\mathbf{E}}$:

$$\mathcal{M}, q \models \psi \quad \text{iff} \quad \mathbf{P} = \mathbf{E}. \qquad (\star)$$

We can prove this by induction on φ. Consequently, this will hold for the initial position $(\mathbf{E}, q_{in}, \varphi)$, which concludes this direction of the claim.

For the other direction, we suppose that $\mathcal{M}, q_{in} \models \varphi$. Hence $(\star)$ holds for the initial position $(\mathbf{E}, q_{in}, \varphi)$. We then construct a strategy $\Sigma_{\mathbf{E}}$ for Eloise in such a way that $(\star)$ will hold for every position $\mathsf{Pos} = (\mathbf{P}, q, \psi)$ that is reached in the game. By using $\Sigma_{\mathbf{E}}$, Eloise will then finally win the game in every reachable ending position. For this direction of the proof, we also need to use the fact that the embedded games are determined. For a detailed proof, see [7]. □

By our earlier observations, the finitely bounded game-theoretic semantics is not equivalent to the standard compositional semantics of ATL. However, it can be shown equivalent to a natural semantics, to be defined next, which we call **finitely bounded compositional semantics**.

DEFINITION 5.2. *Let $\mathcal{M} = (\mathrm{Agt}, \mathrm{St}, \Pi, \mathrm{Act}, d, o, v)$ be a* CGM, *$q \in \mathrm{St}$ and φ an* ATL*-formula. The truth of φ in $\mathcal{M}$ at q according to* ***finitely bounded semantics****, denoted by $\mathcal{M}, q \models_f \varphi$, is defined recursively as follows:*

- *The semantics for $p \in \Pi$, $\neg\psi$, $\psi \vee \theta$ and $\langle\!\langle A \rangle\!\rangle \mathsf{X} \psi$ are as in the standard compositional semantics of* ATL *(Def 2.3).*
- *$\mathcal{M}, q \models_f \langle\!\langle A \rangle\!\rangle \psi \,\mathsf{U}\, \theta$ iff there exists $n < \omega$ and S_A such that for each $\Lambda \in \mathsf{paths}(q, S_A)$, there is $i \leq n$ such that $\mathcal{M}, \Lambda[i] \models_f \theta$ and $\mathcal{M}, \Lambda[j] \models_f \psi$ for every $j < i$.*
- *$\mathcal{M}, q \models_f \langle\!\langle A \rangle\!\rangle \psi \,\mathsf{R}\, \theta$ iff for every $n < \omega$, there exists $S_{A,n}$ such that for each $\Lambda \in \mathsf{paths}(q, S_{A,n})$ and $i \leq n$, either $\mathcal{M}, \Lambda[i] \models_f \theta$ or there is $j < i$ such that $\mathcal{M}, \Lambda[j] \models_f \psi$.*

To prove the equivalence between the finitely bounded compositional semantics and the finitely bounded GTS, we need to show that it is sufficient to consider only such strategies in the embedded games that depend on states only. This property will be needed because the collective strategies for coalitions in the compositional semantics are of this form.

LEMMA 5.3. *If Eloise has a winning strategy $\Sigma_{\mathbf{E}}$ in a finitely bounded evaluation game $\mathcal{G}(\mathcal{M}, q_{in}, \varphi, \omega)$, then she has a winning strategy $\Sigma'_{\mathbf{E}}$ which uses in the embedded games exclusively strategies $\sigma_{\mathbf{E}}$ that depend only on states.*

PROOF. Sketch: If $\mathbf{E} = \mathbf{C}$ in some embedded game, Eloise may play with the canonical strategy $\tau_{\mathbf{E}}$ that depends only on states. If $\mathbf{E} \neq \mathbf{C}$ and Abelard chooses $n < \omega$ as the time limit, Eloise may play with the n-canonical strategy $\tau^n_{\mathbf{E}}$ that depends only on states. For a detailed proof, see [7]. □

With the help of the previous lemma, we can now prove the equivalence between the finitely bounded compositional and game-theoretic semantics using a similar induction as the one in the proof of Theorem 5.1. For a proof, see [7].

THEOREM 5.4. *Let $\mathcal{M}$ be a* CGM, *$q_{in} \in \mathrm{St}$ and φ an* ATL*-formula. We have $\mathcal{M}, q_{in} \models_f \varphi$ iff $\mathcal{M}, q_{in} \models^g_f \varphi$.*

Concluding remarks

We argue that the systems of GTS for ATL introduced in this article are conceptually and technically natural from both logical and game-theoretic perspective. They offer novel complementary approaches to the semantics of ATL. In particular, our bounded GTS provides a framework where truth of ATL-formulae can be determined in finite time. In the future we will develop game-theoretic approaches to ATL^+, ATL^* and beyond. As argued above, approaches via GTS have proved their worth in multiple fields of logic.

As mentioned in the introduction, *some* of our technical results could have alternatively been derived relatively directly using results for coalgebraic modal logic. This is because concurrent game models can be viewed as coalgebras for a *game functor* defined in [5], and the fixed-point extension of the coalitional coalgebraic modal logic for this functor links to ATL in a natural way. Game-theoretic semantics has been developed for coalgebraic fixed-point logics, e.g. in [14, 4, 6] and can be used to obtain *some* of our results concerning the unbounded game-theoretic semantics. However, that approach would be unhelpful for readers not familiar with coalgebras and coalgebraic modal logic, so the more direct and self-contained approach in this article has its benefits. Moreover, our work on the bounded and finitely bounded semantics is not directly related to existing work in coalgebraic modal logic. However, even there some natural shortcuts based on background theory could have been used. For example, using König's Lemma, it is possible to prove that the finitely bounded and unbounded game-theoretic semantics are equivalent on image-finite models.

Acknowledgements

The work of Valentin Goranko was partly supported by a research grant 2015-04388 of the Swedish Research Council. The work of Antti Kuusisto was supported by the ERC grant 647289 "CODA." We thank the referees for valuable remarks.

REFERENCES

[1] N. Alechina, N. Bulling, B. Logan, and H. N. Nguyen. On the boundary of (un)decidability: Decidable model-checking for a fragment of resource agent logic. In *IJCAI 2015*, pages 1494–1501, 2015.

[2] N. Alechina, B. Logan, N. H. Nga, and A. Rakib. Logic for coalitions with bounded resources. *J. Log. Comput.*, 21(6):907–937, 2011.

[3] R. Alur, T. A. Henzinger, and O. Kupferman. Alternating-time temporal logic. *J. ACM*, 49(5):672–713, 2002.

[4] C. Cîrstea, C. Kupke, and D. Pattinson. EXPTIME tableaux for the coalgebraic μ-calculus. In *CSL 2009*, pages 179–193, 2009.

[5] C. Cîrstea, A. Kurz, D. Pattinson, L. Schröder, and Y. Venema. Modal logics are coalgebraic. *Comput. J.*, 54(1):31–41, 2011.

[6] G. Fontaine, R. A. Leal, and Y. Venema. Automata for coalgebras: An approach using predicate liftings. In *ICALP 2010*, pages 381–392, 2010.

[7] V. Goranko, A. Kuusisto, and R. Rönnholm. Game-theoretic semantics for alternating-time temporal logic. *arXiv:1602.07667 [math.LO]*, 2015.

[8] J. Hintikka. *Logic, Language-games and Information: Kantian Themes in the Philosophy of Logic.* Clarendon Press, 1973.

[9] J. Hintikka and G. Sandu. Informational independence as a semantical phenomenon. In J. E. Fenstad, editor, *Logic, Methodology and Philosophy of Science VIII*, pages 571–589. North-Holland, Amsterdam, 1989.

[10] J. Hintikka and G. Sandu. Game-theoretical semantics. In J. van Benthem and A. ter Meulen, editors, *Handbook of Logic and Language*, pages 361–410. Elsevier, 1997.

[11] P. Lorenzen. Ein dialogisches konstruktivitätskriterium. In A. Mostowski, editor, *Proceedings of the Symposium on Foundations of Mathematics, Warsaw 1959*, pages 193–200. Panstwowe wydawnictwo naukowe, 1961.

[12] D. D. Monica, M. Napoli, and M. Parente. On a logic for coalitional games with priced-resource agents. *Electr. Notes Theor. Comput. Sci.*, 278:215–228, 2011.

[13] C. Smith. Graphs and composite games. *J. Combin. Theory*, 1:51–81, 1966.

[14] Y. Venema. Automata and fixed point logic: A coalgebraic perspective. *Inf. Comput.*, 204(4):637–678, 2006.

Constrained Social-Energy Minimization for Multi-Party Sharing in Online Social Networks

Sarah Rajtmajer
Department of Mathematics
Pennsylvania State University
University Park, PA 16802
smr48@psu.edu

Anna Squicciarini
College of Information Sciences and Technology
Pennsylvania State University
University Park, PA 16802
asquicciarini@ist.psu.edu

Christopher Griffin
Department of Mathematics
United States Naval Academy
Annapolis, MD 21402
griffinch@ieee.org

Sushama Karumanchi
College of Information Sciences and Technology
Pennsylvania State University
University Park, PA 16802
sik5273@psu.edu

Alpana Tyagi
College of Information Sciences and Technology
Pennsylvania State University
University Park, PA 16802
aft5121@psu.edu

ABSTRACT

The development of fair and practical policies for shared content online is a primary goal of the access control community. Multi-party access control, in which access control policies are determined by multiple users each with vested interest in a piece of shared content, remains an outstanding challenge. Purposeful or accidental disclosures by one user in an online social network (OSN) may have negative consequences for others, highlighting the importance of appropriate sharing mechanisms. In this work, we develop a game-theoretic framework for modeling multi-party privacy decisions for shared content. We assume that the content owner (*uploader*) selects an initial privacy policy that constrains the privacy settings of other users. We prove the convergence of users' access control policies assuming a multi-round consensus-building game in which all players are fully rational and investigate a variation of rational play that better describes user behavior and also leads to the rational equilibrium. Additionally, in an effort to better approximate human behavior, we study a bounded rationality model and simulate real user choices in this context. Finally, we validate model assumptions and conclusions using experimental data obtained through a study of 95 individuals in a mock-social network.

CCS Concepts

•Security and privacy → Social network security and privacy; *Economics of security and privacy; Social aspects of security and privacy;* **•Human-centered computing → Social content sharing; Social networks;** *Social media; Social tagging systems; Synchronous editors;* **•Theory of computation → Network games;** *Algorithmic game theory;*

Appears in: *Proceedings of the 15th International Conference on Autonomous Agents and Multiagent Systems (AAMAS 2016), J. Thangarajah, K. Tuyls, C. Jonker, S. Marsella (eds.), May 9–13, 2016, Singapore.*

Keywords

Multi-party access control, Collective sharing, Game theory, Bounded Rationality

1. INTRODUCTION

The ubiquity of online social networks (OSNs) and their expanding role in the day to day lives of user-members has led to a substantial amount of shared personal content, and along with it, increased exposure and privacy-related concerns. Although OSNs provide privacy control mechanisms, they typically adopt a discretionary approach, wherein content "uploaders" are also in charge of managing the content entirely and other stakeholders have no control over their access control decisions. For instance, when one user uploads a photo and tags friends who appear in the photo, tagged friends cannot restrict who can see this photo. Since multiple associated users may have different privacy concerns about a piece of shared content, lack of infrastructure for collaborative privacy control increases the potential risk of purposeful or accidental information leakage.

In addition, as noted by [20], government sectors are adopting social networks to exchange information and establish specialized groups/communities/task forces. These environments need to protect and control shared data due to its potential sensitivity and criticality.

Users face several potential dangers when over-sharing. Social media usage may lead to strained interpersonal relationships [31], decreased productivity [24] and susceptibility to negative feedback in disinhibited online communication [46], in addition to breeches of privacy. Users' perception of these and other risks inform their general comfort level with sharing personal information and content online. Individual behavior online, like individual behavior offline, is also subject to social norms and peer influence [18,21,33]. Notions of what is appropriate in content sharing online is defined comparatively, so that subtle shifts in local behavior may have much farther-reaching consequences for the network as a whole. In sum, unlike the SN site which is ultimately a business operating with a business model, users are individuals with more complex incentives, concerns and considerations operating voluntarily within the constraints of the SN.

In this paper, we propose a social-energy minimizing game framework for modeling the privacy-related decisions of users in an OSN. We consider a "multi-party" access control decision making process, considering the case of a user/owner of a piece of shared content, and another set of users who have some relationship to that content and accordingly a personal stake in its access control settings. We establish a utility function representation of users' interests based on the core notions of inherent personal comfort and peer pressure.

The emphasis on multi-party access control represents a shift from the traditional approach taken in the access control community for two main reasons. First, the access control community has long investigated models and techniques to facilitate single subjects' access to resources according to well-defined, secure policies. Little, if any, attention has been given to group-driven access control decisions. The primary exception to this being secret sharing (see e.g. [40]). Second, the underlying goal has been to maintain confidentiality rather than facilitate controlled sharing. As such, the decisions offered by these mechanisms are single-user driven and often binary and based on inflexible policies. As others have noted [20], the inflexibility of binary decisions typically offered by current access control systems is a major inhibitor to information sharing when dealing with events in social networking sites. The lack of collective access control for resource sharing can threaten the protection of user data, including violating privacy expectations of content owners (and stakeholders) [12], due to the inability to determine whether a given disclosure meets the privacy expectations of the group.

Because ensuring "collective" access control requires taking into account multiple users' input, we tackle the problem of access control by formally modeling how users' access control decisions are made, and use those models to develop actionable and practical access control models that can be applied in a variety of real-world contexts. For example we consider which goals, reasons and influential dimensions affect users' privacy decisions.

The remainder of this paper is organized as follows: In Section 2 we provide a brief survey of related work to seat our results in the literature. We discuss our problem statement in Section 3. The model is formalized in Section 4, where results under rationality assumptions are given. In Section 5 we discuss a bounded rationality variation of our model and provide basic simulation results. In Section 6 we discuss experimental results from human trials. We conclude in Section 7.

2. RELATED WORK

There is a growing body of work on game-theoretic approaches to security [2,8,47] including leader-follower Stackelberg game models [34–36,41,49]. Stackelberg games have recently been used to model various security issues, with emphasis on classic attacker-defenders problems [36], although some limitations to the applicability of these games have been noted [51]. In particular, as noted by Pita et al., it is important to determine whether optimality assumptions hold when humans are involved in the decision making processes [34, 35]. Yet, recent contributions show that with proper modifications, Stackelberg games are suitable even with bounded rationality [35]. While this work does not use explicit Stackelberg formalisms, we do assume an initial decision constrains all players; this decision is not necessarily made with that fact in mind.

In this paper, we explore a social-energy minimization game for multi-party access control problems. With the exception of [17, 37] which explore the single-owner scenario, we are not aware of any work using game theory in this way to deal with access control problems.

This work is related in general to the body of work on game theory in social networks, both offline and online. Fundamental research efforts exploring cooperation in structured human populations include [32, 39, 48]. In the realm of online social networks, game theoretic models have been implemented for the study of the evolution of various social dilemmas, influence, bargaining, voting and deception [4, 14, 22, 25, 26, 38]. Most closely related to our work is the subset of this research concerning agent-based decision-making related to privacy and security in online social networks. Chen et al. model users' disclosure of personal attributes as a weighted evolutionary game and discuss the relationship between network topology and revelation in environments with varying level of risk [10]. Hu et al. tackle the problem of multi-party access control in [19], proposing a logic-based approach for identification and resolution of privacy conflicts. In [20] these authors extend this work, this time proposing adopting a game-theoretic framework, specifically a multi-party control game to model the behavior of users in collaborative data sharing in OSNs. The primary difference between our work and theirs is our relaxation of perfect rationality assumptions in the interest of a more realistic bounded rationality model of human behavior.

Also related to our work is the body of work on the economics of privacy. Researchers from many communities have noted the trade-off between privacy and utility (e.g., [6, 9, 28, 43, 45]). The majority of this prior work tends to view the privacy/utility trade-off as mutually exclusive: an increase in privacy (resp. utility) results in an immediate decrease in utility (resp. privacy). While this is certainly the case in some applications, (e.g. data anonymization [27]), it is not always such a straightforward relationship. In particular, the interplay of multiple users in any access control/privacy decision, in which privacy and utility are unevenly distributed among the players, and context-dependent, results in a more complicated relationship between these concepts.

Finally, our research overlaps with work on decision support systems (DSS) [5], and in particular, Group-centric and Model-driven DSS. Group-centric DSS focus on communication related activities of team members engaged in computer-supported cooperative work [11]. Some group-oriented work has emphasized the importance of optimizing group objectives, and developed standardized objectives for problem solving [29]. Model-driven DSS concentrate on formulation of quantitative (primarily business-related) problems (e.g., minimize stock or maximize revenue), and overlap to some extent with our envisioned approaches to modeling complex multi-party access control. However, DSS research has concentrated on how to solve group centric problems faster, especially through mixed-integer-linear programming, rather than on rigorous models and concrete case studies on access control (or security at large) [3, 5].

3. PROBLEM STATEMENT

Consider a social network (SN) site, wherein users share pieces of personal content freely within the network and possibly with selected subgroups of network users, according to a set of privacy settings for shared content made available by the site to its users. Examples of these settings in practice may include "visible to only me", "share with specific individuals", "share with friends", "share with my network" and "public". We abstract away from the details of how privacy options are presented by a site to its users, and map them to real values on the interval $[0, 1]$. In practice, the granularity of these options aims to be fine enough to meet users' needs, but coarse enough to be manageable in implementation for both the users and the SN site.

We focus here on the problem of assigning a privacy setting to a piece of content shared among multiple stakeholders. Assume one user in the network is the leading stakeholder, or equivalently, the poster of the content. This user chooses the privacy setting he is *most comfortable with* and posts the content to the site at this setting. This user constrains the action space of all subsequent users. Unlike in a Stackelberg game, we do not assume this user is necessarily maximizing an objective function, but simply imposing an upper-bound based on his/her comfort with data sharing.

In posting, we assume owner bounds the set of privacy options available for the content. In practice, this may mean that the owner lays out a discrete set of options from which followers may choose. Or, more simply, the leader sets an upper- or lower- bound on the sharing level for the given piece of content and followers choose from amongst options laid out by the SN site within those bounds. It may even be possible that the poster is not a personal stakeholder in the content and that he may choose not to constrain the space of privacy settings at all. The content stakeholders would then have the full range of available settings as options. From the standpoint of the model, these manifestations are equivalent as they leave followers in the position of jointly selecting one from amongst a fixed, finite set of access control settings. Following, we assume that the owner sets an upper-bound on sharing and remaining stakeholders have the ability to amend the privacy selection downward (toward more private options) but not to determine that the content should be shared more publicly.

Given this assumption, we assume all users' objective functions are composed of

1. a personal comfort term describing how comfortable they are with sharing a piece of content and
2. a peer pressure term making them more interested in coming to consensus with their peers. Peer pressure here also loosely includes the trust level users have toward each other when sharing content and establishing privacy settings.

Objective functions are expressed in terms of *energy* where a user seeks a minimum (social) energy state at any given time. The intuition is that users have an inherent degree of disclosure they feel most comfortable with, but are also influenced by their peers when making sharing decisions.

Since these two dimensions may not be considered equally for all users, we introduce weights to capture interpersonal differences in susceptibility to peer pressure. Precisely, we offer the option of including weights on either the peer pressure or personal comfort components of the user's utility function allowing customization of the model for non- homogeneous users and an opportunity to strengthen the model in the presence of additional information on user behavior, which the site may learn through observation. An overview of the general problem is provided in Figure 1.

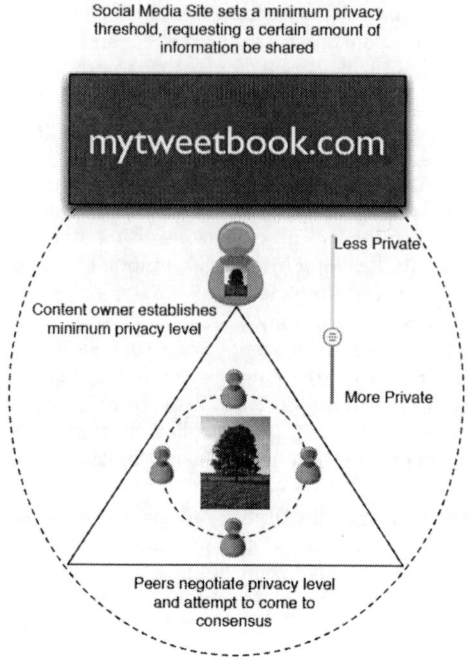

Figure 1: A representation of the multi-party access control problem for collective sharing in OSNs.

4. FULLY RATIONAL MODEL

Assume a SN is represented by a graph $G = (V, E)$, where V is a set of users (represented by vertices in the graph) and E is the set of social connections (edges) between them. For the remainder of this paper, assume $|V| = N$. The poster-leader (henceforth, poster) shares a piece of content on the SN site with privacy setting x_0. The other user stakeholders (henceforth, users) engage in an iterative process of determining the final privacy setting of the content x^*. At round k:

1. Each user i chooses value $x_i^k \leq x_0$.
2. If $|x_i^k - x_j^k| \leq \epsilon$ for all pairs i, j, then iteration stops and $x^* = \bar{x}$. For $\epsilon = 0$, iteration stops when the users have converged on a common value.

For a fixed piece of content, we define the optimality privacy selection of each user in terms of:

1. Peer Pressure (and Reputation)
2. Comfort level

Comfort level in the context of privacy and information disclosure refers to the degree of disclosure users feel comfortable with. This notion, often used to characterize information sharing in online sites (e.g. [1, 13]), is also adopted in our model. Users reaching their optimal comfort level wish not to change any of their information sharing practices. Previous work has indicated that reputation are highly correlated [44], and so we consider peer pressure here as a single measure representing the social considerations of an individual user with respect to sharing.

To model peer pressure, we assume that individuals are encouraged to behave in accordance with the norms of their social group. In particular as stakeholders in the same piece of shared content, we assume that there is an additional pressure to come to agreement and select the privacy setting for the respective content. We can assume that if a consensus is not reached by the users some default setting is selected with which no one is happy (e.g., the content is not published to the site).

We assume that as time passes without consensus, the peer pressure felt by all members to come to agreement increases [7]. For User i, we define, let the peer-pressure function be:

$$P_i(x_i, \mathbf{x}_{-i}, k) = \rho^{(k)} \cdot \sum_{j \in N(i)} f_P(x_i - x_j). \quad (1)$$

Here f_P is a differentiable quasi-convex function with minimum at 0, $\mathbf{x}_{-i}$ is the vector of strategies of all other users in the network (other than User i), and $N(i)$ is the immediate neighborhood of User i in a social network. The coefficients increase monotonically so that $1 \leq \rho^{(1)} \leq \rho^{(2)} \leq \rho^{(3)} \leq \cdots$, thus increasing the influence of peer pressure. This is notationally consistent with [16].

Let the personal comfort function for User i be:

$$C_i(x_i) = f_C(x_i - x_i^+). \quad (2)$$

Here, x_i^+ is the preferred privacy level for a specific piece of user content according to User i and f_C is a differentiable quasi-convex function with minimum at 0. Since the privacy level is constrained by the content owner, we assume that if x_i^+ is more permissive than this level, then x_i^+ is reset to the constrained level set by the content owner. This assures that all privacy decisions will force the information exposure level downward (toward a more private choice).

In practice x_i^+ may be difficult to determine for an unknown User i. However, we assume that based on user demographics, as well as observed overall user behavior for a mass of users, either at the individual or group level, it is possible to infer of x_i^+, or at least an expected value $E[x_i^+]$ within a tolerated window of error.

Thus, the total objective function for User i is:

$$J_i(x_i, \mathbf{x}_{-i}, k) = P_i(x_i, \mathbf{x}_{-i}, k) + C_i(x_i) = \rho^{(k)} \sum_{j \in N(i)} f_P(x_i - x_j) + f_C(x_i - x_i^+). \quad (3)$$

Proposition 1 (Rosen 1963). *If f_P and f_C are convex and $x_i \in \Omega_i$, where Ω_i is a convex set for $i = 1, \ldots, N$, then there is an equilibrium solution $x_1^*, \ldots, x_N^*$.* □

Rosen's result informs us that there is a (Nash) equilibrium assuming simultaneously play, it neither ensures the uniqueness of the equilibrium, nor does it ensure flocking or consensus behavior; i.e., that $|x_i - x_j| < \epsilon$ for some small ϵ.

For the case when $f_P(z) = f_C(z) = z^2$ and we have a complete graph, it is relatively easy to see that consensus occur for some value $\rho^{(k)}$. To see this, note that at equilibrium, each agent must satisfy the equations (derived the first order necessary conditions of optimality):

$$\rho^{(k)} \sum_{j \neq i} (x_i - x_j) + (x_i - x_i^+) = 0 \quad \forall i \quad (4)$$

This system of equations admits the solution:

$$x_i^{(k)} = \left[\frac{\rho^{(k)}}{1 + N\rho^{(k)}} \sum_{j \neq i} x_j^+ \right] + \left[\frac{(1 + \rho^{(k)}) x_i^+}{1 + N\rho^{(k)}} \right] \quad (5)$$

The following is immediately clear:

Proposition 2. *Suppose $\rho^{(1)} < \rho^{(2)} < \cdots < \rho^{(k)} < \cdots$ and $\lim_{k \to \infty} \rho^{(k)} = \infty$, then:*

$$\lim_{k \to \infty} x_i^* = \frac{1}{N} \sum_j x_j^+ \quad (6)$$

Therefore, as long as the *pressure* to come to consensus increases on each round, the players converge to their mean comfort levels.

Corollary 3. *For all $\epsilon > 0$ there exists a $K > 0$ so that for all $k > K$, $|x_i^{(k)} - x_j^{(k)}| < \epsilon$ for all i, j. Thus the system converges after a finite number of rounds.*

If all players realize this, then rational play at each round results in behavior equivalent to a one shot game where users intuitively *know* a K that ensures fast convergence.

An alternate update rule, and more in keeping with human behavior is to assume a *recency model* wherein individual users take their peers' strategy from the last round of play and construct a weighted average based on this value rather than their peers' initial selections. Specifically, the objective function for User i is then:

$$J_i(x_i, \mathbf{x}_{-i}, k) = \rho^{(k)} \sum_{j \in N(i)} f_P(x_i - x_j^{(k-1)}) + f_C(x_i - x_i^+). \quad (7)$$

In this case:

$$x_i^{(k)} = \frac{\rho^{(k)} \sum_{j \neq i} x_j^{(k-1)}}{1 + (N-1)\rho^{(k)}} + \frac{x_i^+}{1 + (N-1)\rho^{(k)}} \quad (8)$$

with $x_i^{(0)} = x_i^+$ for all i. We show that this play also results in the rational Nash equilibrium. Let $F_k : [0,1]^N \to [0,1]^N$ be the function whose i^{th} component is given by Equation 8. Then: F_k has at least one fixed point by Brouwer's Fixed Point theorem and we can show that:

$$x_i^*(k) = \frac{x_i^+ + \rho^{(k)} \sum_j x_j^+}{1 + N\rho^{(k)}} \quad (9)$$

is a (unique) fixed point of F arising from the solution of N linear fixed point equations.

Lemma 4. *$F_k : [0,1]^N \to [0,1]^N$ is a contraction for $N \geq 4$.*

Proof. For notational simplicity, $\rho = \rho^{(k)}$ and let $\mathbf{x}, \mathbf{y} \in [0,1]^N$ where (e.g.) $\mathbf{x} = \langle x_1, \ldots, x_N \rangle$. Then:

$$\frac{|F_k(\mathbf{x}) - F_k(\mathbf{y})|^2}{|\mathbf{x} - \mathbf{y}|^2} = \frac{\rho^2}{(1 + (N-1)\rho)^2} \frac{\sum_i \left(\sum_{j \neq i} (x_j - y_j) \right)^2}{\sum_i (x_i - y_i)^2} \quad (10)$$

Let:

$$\beta = \frac{\rho^2}{(1 + (N-1)\rho)^2} \quad (11)$$

Then we can re-write Expression 10 as:

$$\beta \frac{(N-1)\sum_i (x_i - y_i)^2 + N \sum_i \sum_{j>i} (x_i - y_i)(x_j - y_j)}{\sum_i (x_i - y_i)^2} =$$

$$\beta \left((N-1) + \frac{N \sum_i \sum_{j>i} (x_i - y_i)(x_j - y_j)}{\sum_i (x_i - y_i)^2} \right)$$

The expression

$$(N-1) + \frac{N \sum_i \sum_{j>i} (x_i - y_i)(x_j - y_j)}{\sum_i (x_i - y_i)^2}$$

has maximum value when $x_i - y_i = \frac{1}{2}$ for all i (this can be proved using the Karush-Kuhn-Tucker conditions on an ancillary maximization problem). Evaluating at this point we have:

$$(N-1) + \frac{N \sum_i \sum_{j>i} (x_i - y_i)(x_j - y_j)}{\sum_i (x_i - y_i)^2} \leq$$

$$(N-1) + \frac{N(N-1)}{2} = (N-1)\left(1 + \frac{N}{2}\right)$$

Thus:

$$\frac{|F_k(\mathbf{x}) - F_k(\mathbf{y})|^2}{|\mathbf{x} - \mathbf{y}|^2} \leq$$

$$\frac{\rho^2 (N-1)\left(1+\frac{N}{2}\right)}{(1 + (N-1)\rho)^2} < \frac{\rho^2 (N-1)\left(1+\frac{N}{2}\right)}{((N-1)\rho)^2} =$$

$$\frac{1 + N/2}{N-1} \tag{12}$$

For $N \geq 4$, $(1 + N/2)/(N-1) \leq 1$. Since the inequality is strict in Expression 12, it follows F_k is a contraction for $N \geq 4$. □

The following is an immediately consequence of the lemma and the Banach Fixed Point Theorem.

Corollary 5. *The fixed point given by Expression 9 is unique and is the contraction point for F_k.*

Remark 1. In reality, it may be the case we can do better than $N \geq 4$ and show that F_k is a contraction for $N \geq 1$. Certainly for $N = 1$, F_k is just a constant function and thus a contraction.

The following lemma is clear from the work done so far:

Lemma 6. *The following holds:*

$$\lim_{k \to \infty} x_i^*(k) = \bar{x}^+ = \frac{1}{N} \sum_j x_j^+$$

further convergence of the sequence of fixed points $x^*(k)$ to $\bar{x}^+$ is uniform.

It remains to show this is an attracting fixed point of the recurrence relations. From Theorem 2 of [15] and the fact that the F_k are contractions, we have:

Theorem 7. *Let $F_0(\mathbf{x})$ return $\langle x_1^+, \ldots, x_N^+ \rangle$. If $G_k(\mathbf{x}) = F_k \circ F_{k-1} \circ \cdots \circ F_0(\mathbf{x})$ and $N \geq 4$, then:*

$$G = \lim_{k \to \infty} G_k \tag{13}$$

is a constant function whose value is the limit of the fixed points of F_k. Furthermore, convergence of the function sequence $\{G_k\}_k$ is uniform.

Having shown that the recency update rule with increasing peer pressure leads to a constant fixed point and that each individual's privacy choice approaches this fixed point, we have the following corollary:

Corollary 8. *Assume the latency updating rule and $N \geq 4$. For all $\epsilon > 0$, there exists a $K > 0$ so that if $k > K$, then $|x_i^{(k)} - x_j^{(k)}| < \epsilon$. Thus the system converges after a finite number of rounds under the latency rule.*

5. BOUNDED RATIONALITY

In practice, as users negotiate sharing levels at each iteration of the game, they express their preferences not in terms of the continuous value $x_i^*(t)$ but as a selection among the discrete set of options $\{l_1, \ldots, l_n\}$. In practice these discrete values map to settings specifying the audience for posted content, e.g., "friends" or "my network".

We could expect that perfectly rational users, observing complete information without error will, at any given time t, choose the option l_i closest to $x_i^{(k)}$. That is, each user will select $l_i = \min_{\{l_1,\ldots,l_n\}} |l_i - x_i^{(k)}|$.

However, [23, 42] suggests that realistic models of human behavior should relax perfect-rationality assumptions in favor of *bounded rationality* models accounting for limited time and information, as well as cognitive limitations. Let:

$$U_{i,j}^{(k)} = J_i\left(l_j, \mathbf{x}_{-i}^{(k)}\right).$$

This is the social stress experienced by User i making choice l_j when all other players make choice $\mathbf{x}_{-i}^{(k)}$ at round k.

One well-established model of bounded rationality is the Quantal Response model [30], which gives the probability that user i will choose setting l_j at epoch k:

$$q_i^{(k)}(\lambda|\mathbf{x}) = \frac{\exp\left(-\lambda U_{i,j}^{(k)}\right)}{\sum_r \exp\left(-\lambda U_{i,r}^{(k)}\right)}$$

Recent work has indicated that a Quantal Response model is a promising model of human behavior in the context of security games [50]. In our consensus-building formulation, the probabilities that each player will select each option converge to a single probability distribution (see Proposition 9) under the assumption of *rational play.*

Proposition 9. *Suppose $\rho^{(1)} < \rho^{(2)} < \cdots < \rho^{(k)} < \cdots$ and $\lim_{k\to\infty} \rho^{(k)} = \infty$. If users engage in rational play, then there is a probability distribution with support $\{l_1, \ldots, l_k\}$, $q^*(\lambda)$ so that:*

$$\lim_{k \to \infty} q_i^{(k)}(\lambda|\mathbf{x}) = q^*(\lambda). \tag{14}$$

Proof. As $k \to \infty$, $x_i^* = x_j^*$ for all i, j. As a result, $U_{i,r}^{(k)} = U_{j,r}^{(k)}$ for all i, j. Thus, $q_i^{(k)}(\lambda|\mathbf{x}) = q_j^{(k)}(\lambda|\mathbf{x}) = q^*(\lambda)$. □

Given perfectly rational players, that is as $\lambda \to \infty$, this distribution will tend to 1 for the choice nearest to $x_i^*(t)$ and 0 everywhere else. In this case, players are guaranteed to come to agreement on an access control policy. For decreasing values of λ and more uniform corresponding probability distributions, players' actual selections are non-deterministic and therefore non-convergent. This is *particularly* true when users engage in the recency model of play in which previous players' decisions are weighted against the users' preferred privacy level.

To gain a better understanding of the consensus-building game with bounded rationality, we simulated play among players in various population sizes for a varying rationality parameter λ.

Specifically, consider a game among human users acting with bounded rationality and using the recency model. The uploader shares a piece of content with privacy setting x_0 and the remaining stakeholders (followers) determine their individual $x_i^k \leq x_0$ according the user objective function (3). We (randomly) assign users a discrete choice from the fixed set of privacy settings at each iteration of play based on the probabilities given by the Quantal Response model (5). We iterate this procedure until we obtain convergence of the expected value of each player's strategy vector within some small interval ϵ. We consider games with $3, 4, 5, 6, 7, 8, 9$ and 10 players, and vary $0 \leq \lambda \leq 10$. Simulations are run 100 times for each population size/lambda pairing, and averages are reported.

Of primary interest is the expected value of the final probability vector q^*. Figure 2 shows a histogram of the average differences $\frac{1}{N}\sum_j E[q_j] - \frac{1}{N}\sum_j x_j^+$ obtained for simulations run for each population size/lambda pairing (88 total). We observe that $E[q^*] \rightarrow \bar{x}^+$. This result is consistent with Equations 6 and 9, despite using the recency update rule with bounded rationality. We will make this result formal, proving convergence to the mean comfort in future work.

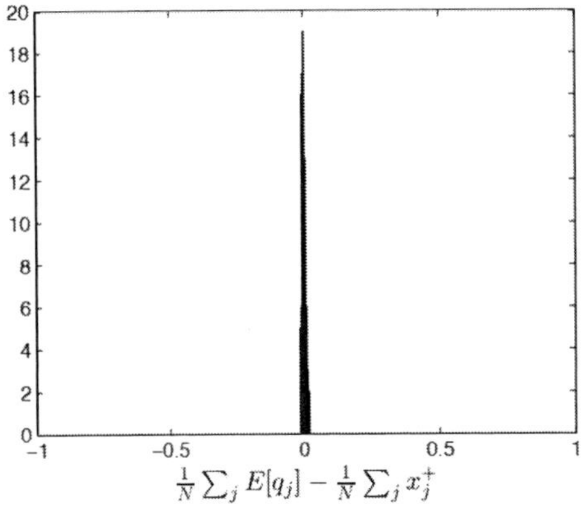

Figure 2: A histogram of average difference between average expected value and average comfort obtained over 100 simulations for 88 parameter pairs.

Despite the convergence of $E[q_i]$ for all players, we have argued that in the presence of bounded rationality, each user's actual choice from among the discrete set of options will vary depending on λ. That is, less rational actors are more likely to deviate from optimal play. Formally,

$$\lim_{\lambda \to 0} q_i^{(k)} = \frac{1}{n}$$

for $l_j \in \{l_1, \ldots, l_n\}$. This relationship between decreasing lambda and increasing variance is illustrated in Figure 3 for our simulations.

An additional practical consideration for real applications of multi-party access control is the number of iterations of revisions required for group consensus, or at least sufficient convergence of $E[q_i]$. Figure 4 indicates the number of rounds of play until convergence within an interval of $\epsilon = 0.1$. Here the number of iterations is increasing in lambda, respecting the greater difficulty in aligning the expected values of non-uniform probability vectors. In other words, more rational users or users more acutely aware of their optimal choice may take longer to reach consensus. Access control decisions for a single piece of shared content in an OSN are typically not subject to multiple revisions, but are rather posted by the uploader and potentially revised once (e.g., a user may remove a tag of him or herself in an image or remove a tagged image from his or her profile page, newsfeed, or similar). However, we suggest that multiple revisions may be considered an abstraction of a process which spans the course of multiple instances of collective sharing decisions for a given group of users. Similarly, we can interpret ϵ as the granularity of a privacy policy, where a wider set of options would require a smaller ϵ for group consensus in real-life scenarios.

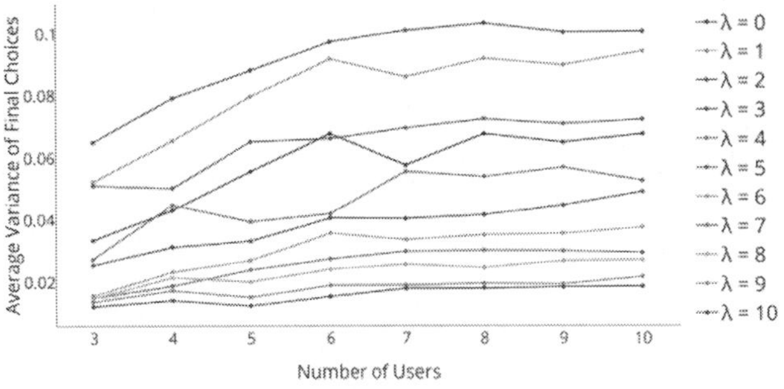

Figure 3: A plot of the average statistical variance of users' final selected privacy settings, obtained over 100 simulations for given number of players and rationality parameter λ.

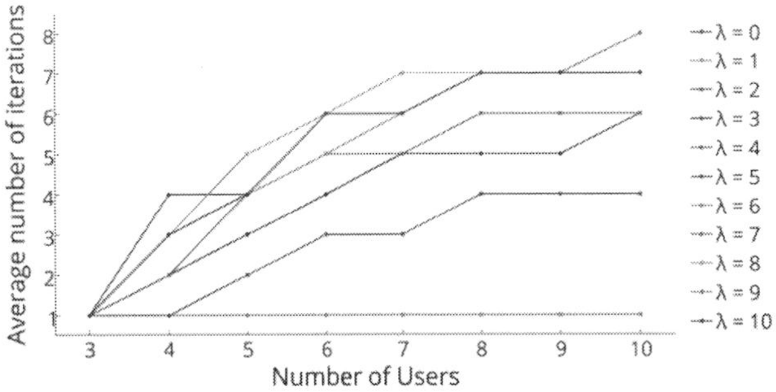

Figure 4: Average number of iterations of play until group consensus within $\epsilon = 0.1$, obtained over 100 simulations for given number of players and rationality parameter λ.

6. EXPERIMENTAL RESULTS

In order to validate the mathematical results discussed for multi-party privacy decisions, we collected real-world data on privacy setting selections in a small group setting. Our small groups (of 3 or 4 individuals) represent a set of user-stakeholders determining access control settings for a piece of shared content, within a set of constraints, namely given a fixed set of privacy options.

Specifically, we created a fictitious SN site using Drupal as a backbone and invited users to generate a social group within the site. Participants were asked to work in teams of 3 or 4 to jointly set up fictitious privacy options for a newly formed social group, and select, for three different content types (images, documents, posts/event notifications) the privacy settings the group should offer as well as default settings for each content type.

Once the available privacy options were established, participants were asked to individually set their privacy preferences for each piece of content shown to them. All users within the group simultaneously entered their preferences for that piece of content. As individual selections were made, they were displayed to the rest of the members of the group. Upon observation of their peers' selected privacy settings, group members were allowed to revise their options as desired, for as many iterations as they chose. Users were encouraged to come to a consensus, being told that if they did not, the content would not be shared at all.

Monitoring the iterated individual revisions of selected privacy settings, we compare the influence of users' peers on individual behavior with the behavior anticipated by our theoretical results. In particular, we aim to determine whether the mean-consensus model (6,9) well-describes user observed behavior.

Overall, we had 95 participants (74% females and 26% males). Participants were college-aged students, and reported a high frequency of use of SNing sites (87% declared accessing SN once or more a day). Further, 93% of responders indicated changing their privacy settings on any of their profile items at least once, therefore indicating some degree of privacy awareness. We partitioned participants into 25 fictional social groups and recorded each group's data for 9 pieces of content - 3 photos, 3 blog posts and 3 events.

Each available privacy setting (specifically, "everyone", "friends", "colleagues", "family", "self") is mapped into the interval $[0, 1]$, where 0 indicates most restrictive ("only self") and 1 least restrictive ("everyone"). Each team represents a small complete friendship graph on three or four nodes. For a given piece of content, let the initial privacy setting selection for User i represent his comfort level x_i^+, since this selection is made before any information is obtained about peers' preferences.

As User i receives feedback from his peers, we argue that the iterative revisions he makes to his own preferences should tend toward $x_i^* = \frac{1}{N}\sum_j x_j^+$ if his objective function follows similarly to one we have proposed.

Consider each group's decision process for each piece of content as negotiation amongst followers to come to agreement on an access control policy. Amongst 225 of these games represented in our dataset, 109 involved at least one user revision. In 85 of these 109, the revision process led to group consensus. If we assume that each user's initial privacy setting, before seeing his peers' selections, represents his inherent comfort level for sharing that particular content, we expect that the final group choice is equal to the mean of the users' initial selections (6). Let x^* be the final collaborative access control decision of a particular group for a particular piece of content. Figure 5 gives a histogram of values $x^* - \frac{1}{N}\sum_j x_j^+$ for the 85 games in which consensus was reached after revision. As expected, these center very near 0, with mean 0.006 and standard deviation 0.099. Notice Figure 5 is qualitatively similar to Figure 2. In future work, we plan to collect more data and compare these two results using (e.g.) a χ^2 Goodness of Fit test to determine whether the simulated user behaviors provides a reasonable model of true human behavior.

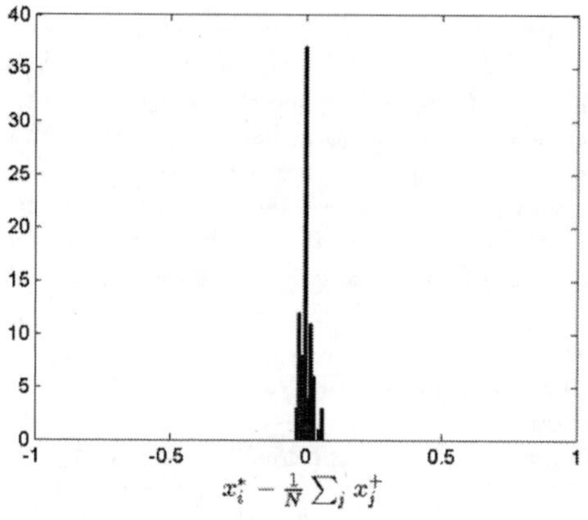

Figure 5: A histogram of values $x_i^* - \frac{1}{N}\sum_j x_j^+$ for 85 pieces of shared content.

7. CONCLUSION

We present a behavioral game-theoretic model of multiparty access control in OSNs. Specifially, we address the problem where one user shares a piece of content online and other users with a personal stake in the given content respond within the constraints established by the uploader. We discuss the convergence of user decisions given a consensus-building game with fully-rational users, and simulate play with a quantal response model to better approximate the bounded rationality of human agents. Results of experimental validation with real users in a mock-social network indicate that these models closely approximate real user behavior.

We suggest that this work meets a growing need for foundational research to understand and facilitate the privacy requirements of multiple users for collaboratively managing shared data in OSNs, and may serve as the basis for extended validation. Future work includes incorporating asymmetrical peer pressure, alternate rationality parameters, penalties for iterated revision, and dynamic comfort which may represent memory and allow users to learn from previous games.

The model we have developed here does not rely on the structure of the OSN and we propose is generalizable in the context of collaborative sharing more widely. Other variations of this model may need to consider context-dependent amendments to the peer pressure function, provided the nature of peer pressure remains quantifiable and can be assumed to be increasing over time with lack of consensus.

Acknowledgments

Portions of Dr. Griffin's, Dr. Squicciarini's and Dr. Rajtmajer's work were supported by the Army Research Office under grant W911NF-13-1-0271. Portions of Dr. Squicciarini's work were additionally supported by a National Science Foundation grant 1453080.

REFERENCES

[1] M. S. Ackerman, L. F. Cranor, and J. Reagle. Privacy in e-commerce: Examining user scenarios and privacy preferences. In *Proceedings of the 1st ACM Conference on Electronic Commerce*, EC '99, pages 1–8, New York, NY, USA, 1999. ACM.

[2] B. An, D. Kempe, C. Kiekintveld, E. Shieh, S. Singh, M. Tambe, and Y. Vorobeychik. Security games with limited surveillance. *Ann Arbor*, 1001:48109, 2012.

[3] D. Arnott and G. Pervan. Eight key issues for the decision support systems discipline. *Decision Support Systems*, 44(3):657–672, 2008.

[4] L. Backstrom, D. Huttenlocher, J. Kleinberg, and X. Lan. Group formation in large social networks: membership, growth, and evolution. In *Proceedings of the 12th ACM SIGKDD international conference on Knowledge discovery and data mining*, pages 44–54. ACM, 2006.

[5] H. K. Bhargava, D. J. Power, and D. Sun. Progress in web-based decision support technologies. *Decision Support Systems*, 43(4):1083–1095, 2007.

[6] B. Bhumiratana and M. Bishop. Privacy aware data sharing: balancing the usability and privacy of datasets. In *Proceedings of the 2nd International Conference on PErvasive Technologies Related to Assistive Environments*, page 73. ACM, 2009.

[7] R. Böhme and S. Pötzsch. Collective exposure: Peer effects in voluntary disclosure of personal data. In *Proceedings of the 15th International Conference on Financial Cryptography and Data Security*, FC'11, pages 1–15, Berlin, Heidelberg, 2012. Springer-Verlag.

[8] M. Brown, B. An, C. Kiekintveld, F. Ordóñez, and M. Tambe. An extended study on multi-objective security games. *Autonomous Agents and Multi-Agent Systems*, 28(1):31–71, Jan. 2014.

[9] A. Brush, J. Krumm, and J. Scott. Exploring end user preferences for location obfuscation, location-based services, and the value of location. In *Proceedings of the 12th ACM international conference on Ubiquitous computing*, pages 95–104. ACM, 2010.

[10] J. Chen, M. R. Brust, A. R. Kiremire, and V. V. Phoha. Modeling privacy settings of an online social network from a game-theoretical perspective. In *Collaborative Computing: Networking, Applications and Worksharing (Collaboratecom), 2013 9th International Conference Conference on*, pages 213–220. IEEE, Oct. 2013.

[11] Y.-L. Chen, L.-C. Cheng, and C.-N. Chuang. A group recommendation system with consideration of interactions among group members. *Expert systems with applications*, 34(3):2082–2090, 2008.

[12] P. C. Cheng, P. Rohatgi, C. Keser, P. A. Karger, G. M. Wagner, and A. S. Reninger. Fuzzy multi-level security: An experiment on quantified risk-adaptive access control. In *IEEE Symposium on Security and Privacy.*, pages 222–230. IEEE, 2007.

[13] L. F. Cranor, J. Reagle, and M. S. Ackerman. *Beyond concern: Understanding net users' attitudes about online privacy.* Cambridge, MA: MIT Press, 2000.

[14] F. Fu, C. Chen, L. Liu, and L. Wag. Social dilemmas in an online social network: The structure and evolution of cooperation. *Physics Letters A*, 371(1-2):58–64, 2007.

[15] J. Gill. The use of the sequence $f_n(z) = f_n \circ \cdots \circ f_1(z)$ in computing fixed points of continued fractions, products, and series. *Applied Numerical Mathematics*, 8(6):469 – 476, 1991.

[16] C. Griffin, A. Squicciarini, S. Rajtmajer, M. Tentilucci, and S. Li. Site-constrained privacy options for users in social networks through stackelberg games. In *Proc. of Sixth ASE International Conference on Social Computing. May 2014.*, 2014.

[17] C. Griffin, A. C. Squicciarini, S. Rajtmajer, M. Tentilucci, and S. Li. Site-constrained privacy options for users in social networks through stackelberg games. In *Sixth ASE International Conference on Social Computing (SocialCom)*, 2014.

[18] R. Gross and A. Acquisti. Information revelation and privacy in online social networks. In *Proceedings of the 2005 ACM workshop on Privacy in the electronic society*, WPES '05, pages 71–80, New York, NY, USA, 2005. ACM.

[19] H. Hu, G.-J. Ahn, and J. Jorgensen. Multiparty access control for online social networks: model and mechanisms. *Knowledge and Data Engineering, IEEE Transactions on*, 25(7):1614–1627, 2013.

[20] H. Hu, G.-J. Ahn, Z. Zhao, and D. Yang. Game theoretic analysis of multiparty access control in online social networks. In *Proceedings of the 19th ACM Symposium on Access Control Models and Technologies*, SACMAT '14, pages 93–102, New York, NY, USA, 2014. ACM.

[21] P. Hui and S. Buchegger. Groupthink and Peer Pressure: Social Influence in Online Social Network Groups. In *2009 International Conference on Advances in Social Network Analysis and Mining (ASONAM)*, pages 53–59, Los Alamitos, CA, USA, July 2009. IEEE.

[22] N. Immorlica, B. Lucier, and B. Rogers. Emergence of cooperation in anonymous social networks through social capital. In *In Proceedings of the 11th ACM Conference on Electronic Commerce (EC*, 2010.

[23] D. Kahneman. Maps of bounded rationality: Psychology for behavioral economics. *American Economic Review*, 93(5):1449–1475, 2003.

[24] P. A. Kirschner and A. C. Karpinski. Facebook® and academic performance. *Computers in Human Behavior*, 26(6):1237–1245, Nov. 2010.

[25] J. Kleinberg and E. Tardos. Balanced outcomes in social exchange networks. In *Proceedings of the 40th Annual ACM Symposium on Theory of Computing*, STOC '08, pages 295–304, New York, NY, USA, 2008. ACM.

[26] J. M. Kleinberg. Challenges in mining social network data: processes, privacy, and paradoxes. In *KDD '07: Proceedings of the 13th ACM SIGKDD international*

conference on Knowledge discovery and data mining, pages 4–5, New York, NY, USA, 2007. ACM.

[27] K. LeFevre, D. J. DeWitt, and R. Ramakrishnan. Mondrian multidimensional k-anonymity. In *Proceedings of the 22nd International Conference on Data Engineering, ICDE'06*, pages 25–25. IEEE, 2006.

[28] K. Liu and E. Terzi. A framework for computing the privacy scores of users in online social networks. *ACM Trans. Knowl. Discov. Data*, 5(1):6:1–6:30, Dec. 2010.

[29] J. Lu, G. Zhang, and D. Ruan. *Multi-objective group decision making: methods, software and applications with fuzzy set techniques.* Imperial College Press, 2007.

[30] R. D. McKelvey and T. R. Palfrey. Quantal response equilibria for normal form games. *Games and Economic Behavior*, 10(1):6 – 38, 1995.

[31] A. Muise, E. Christofides, and S. Desmarais. More Information than You Ever Wanted: Does Facebook Bring Out the Green-Eyed Monster of Jealousy? *CyberPsychology & Behavior*, 12(4):441–444, Aug. 2009.

[32] H. Ohtsuki, C. Hauert, E. Lieberman, and M. A. Nowak. A simple rule for the evolution of cooperation on graphs and social networks. *Nature*, 441(7092):502–505, May 2006.

[33] N. Park, K. Kee, and S. Valenzuela. Being Immersed in Social Networking Environment: Facebook Groups, Uses and Gratifications, and Social Outcomes. *CyberPsychology & Behavior*, 12(6):729–733, Dec. 2009.

[34] J. Pita, M. Jain, F. Ordóñez, M. Tambe, S. Kraus, and R. Magori-Cohen. Effective solutions for real-world stackelberg games: When agents must deal with human uncertainties. In *Proceedings of The 8th International Conference on Autonomous Agents and Multiagent Systems-Volume 1*, pages 369–376. International Foundation for Autonomous Agents and Multiagent Systems, 2009.

[35] J. Pita, M. Jain, M. Tambe, F. Ordóñez, and S. Kraus. Robust solutions to Stackelberg games: Addressing bounded rationality and limited observations in human cognition. *Artificial Intelligence*, 174(15):1142–1171, 2010.

[36] J. Pita, M. Tambe, C. Kiekintveld, S. Cullen, and E. Steigerwald. Guards: game theoretic security allocation on a national scale. In *The 10th International Conference on Autonomous Agents and Multiagent Systems-Volume 1*, pages 37–44. International Foundation for Autonomous Agents and Multiagent Systems, 2011.

[37] S. Rajtmajer, C. Griffin, D. Mikesell, and A. Squicciarini. An evolutionary game model for the spread of non-cooperative behavior in online social networks. In *Proceedings of the 30th Annual ACM Symposium on Applied Computing*, SAC '15, pages 1154–1159, New York, NY, USA, 2015. ACM.

[38] S. M. Rajtmajer, C. Griffin, D. Mikesell, and A. Squicciarini. A cooperate-defect model for the spread of deviant behavior in social networks. *CoRR*, abs/1408.2770, 2014.

[39] D. G. Rand, S. Arbesman, and N. A. Christakis. Dynamic social networks promote cooperation in experiments with humans. *Proceedings of the National Academy of Sciences*, 108(48):19193–19198, 2011.

[40] A. Shamir. How to share a secret. *Commun. ACM*, 22(11):612–613, Nov. 1979.

[41] Y. Sharma and D. P. Williamson. Stackelberg thresholds in network routing games or the value of altruism. *Games and Economic Behavior*, 67(1):174–190, 2009.

[42] H. Simon. A behavioural model of rational choice. In H. Simon, editor, *Models of man: social and rational; mathematical essays on rational human behavior in a social setting*, pages 241–260. J. Wiley, New York, 1957.

[43] D. J. Solove. *Nothing to hide: The false tradeoff between privacy and security.* Yale University Press, 2011.

[44] A. Squicciarini and C. Griffin. An informed model of personal information release in social networking sites. In *2012 ASE/IEEE Conference on Privacy, Security, Risk and Trust*, Amsterdam, Netherlands, September 2012.

[45] F. Stutzman and W. Hartzog. Boundary regulation in social media. In *Proceedings of the ACM 2012 conference on Computer Supported Cooperative Work*, pages 769–778. ACM, 2012.

[46] J. Suler. The Online Disinhibition Effect. *Cyberpsychology & Behavior*, 7(3):321–326, June 2004.

[47] M. Tambe. *Security and game theory: algorithms, deployed systems, lessons learned.* Cambridge University Press, 2011.

[48] Z.-X. Wu, Z. Rong, and H.-X. Yang. Impact of heterogeneous activity and community structure on the evolutionary success of cooperators in social networks. *Phys. Rev. E*, 91:012802, Jan 2015.

[49] R. Yang, F. Fang, A. X. Jiang, K. Rajagopal, M. Tambe, and R. Maheswaran. Designing better strategies against human adversaries in network security games. In *Proceedings of the 11th International Conference on Autonomous Agents and Multiagent Systems-Volume 3*, pages 1299–1300. International Foundation for Autonomous Agents and Multiagent Systems, 2012.

[50] R. Yang, C. Kiekintveld, F. Ordóñez, M. Tambe, and R. John. Improving resource allocation strategies against human adversaries in security games: An extended study. *Artificial Intelligence*, 195:440 – 469, 2013.

[51] Z. Yin, D. Korzhyk, C. Kiekintveld, V. Conitzer, and M. Tambe. Stackelberg vs. Nash in security games: Interchangeability, equivalence, and uniqueness. In *Proceedings of the 9th International Conference on Autonomous Agents and Multiagent Systems: volume 1-Volume 1*, pages 1139–1146. International Foundation for Autonomous Agents and Multiagent Systems, 2010.

Concurrent Multi-Player Parity Games

Vadim Malvone
Università degli Studi di Napoli
Federico II, Italy
vadim.malvone@unina.it

Aniello Murano
Università degli Studi di Napoli
Federico II, Italy
murano@na.infn.it

Loredana Sorrentino
Università degli Studi di Napoli
Federico II, Italy
loredana.sorrentino@unina.it

ABSTRACT

Parity games are a powerful framework widely used to address fundamental questions in computer science. In the basic setting they consist of *two-player turn-based* games, played on directed graphs, whose nodes are labeled with *priorities*. Solving such a game can be done in time exponential in the number of the priorities (and polynomial in the number of states) and it is a long-standing open question whether a polynomial-time algorithm exists. Precisely this problem resides in the class UP ∩ co-UP.

In this paper we introduce and solve efficiently *concurrent multi-player parity games* where the players, being existential and universal, compete under fixed and strict alternate coalitions. The solution we provide uses an extension of the classic *Zielonka Recursive Algorithm*. Precisely, we introduce an ad hoc algorithm for the *attractor* subroutine. Directly from this, we derive that the problem of solving such games is in PSPACE. We also address the lower bound and show that the complexity of our algorithm is tight, i.e. we show that the problem is PSPACE-HARD by providing a reduction from the *QBF satisfiability problem*.

Categories and Subject Descriptors

I.2.11 [**Artificial intelligence**]: Distributed artificial intelligence — *Multi-agent systems*

General Terms

Theory, Verification

Keywords

Parity games; Concurrent multi-player games

1. INTRODUCTION

Parity games [15, 40] are a very powerful mathematical framework widely used to address fundamental questions in computer science. They are strictly connected with other games of infinite duration and in particular with the *multi-agent* strategic reasoning [4, 8, 9, 12].

In the basic setting parity games consist of two-player turn-based games, played on directed graphs, whose nodes are labeled with *priorities* (i.e., natural numbers). The players, conventionally named $Player_0$ and $Player_1$, move in turn a token along graph's edges. Thus, a play induces an infinite path and $Player_0$ wins the play if the greatest priority visited infinitely often along the path is even; otherwise, $Player_1$ wins the play. $Player_0$ *wins* the game if he can induce a play that is winning. Otherwise $Player_1$ wins the game. The problem of finding the winner in a parity game is known to be in UPTIME ∩ COUPTIME [23]. Deciding whether a polynomial-time solution exists is a long-standing open question. Aimed to solve this question, as well as to come out with solutions working efficiently in practice, several algorithms have been proposed in the last two decades. Among the others we mention the *Zielonka Recursive Algorithm* [40] as the best performing one in practice [17].

Parity games have been largely and beneficially applied in formal system design and verification [13, 14, 26, 35, 38]. In such a domain, we mainly distinguish between *closed* and *open* (reactive) systems [18, 27]. While the behavior of closed systems fully depends on internal states, open systems are characterized by an ongoing interaction with an external unpredictable environment whose interaction possibly affects the system behavior. In open system verification we check that the system satisfies a desired behavior (specification) no matter how the environment acts. In a very large setting of specification, the problem reduces to solve a parity game where the system and the environment take place as adversarial players [3, 15, 26].

In recent years, we are witnessing a strong expansion and adaptation of models and game-based reasoning in the multi-player area [1, 21, 22, 32]. In this domain, the game often involves a multitude of players who play different roles. In some simplified yet powerful settings, one can have two teams competing for opposite objectives [1]. In this scenario, if one wants to make use of parity games then there are two basic ways to follow. The first, very restricted to the specific problem under exam is to possible reduce the multi-player reasoning to a two-players one. The second, much more efficient, elegant, and general would rather introduce a multi-player parity game concept, give an efficient solution to the problem and apply it directly whenever it is required. The latter is the motivation of this paper. Our aim is indeed to come up with an abstract tool to both model reactive multi-player systems and properly solve related decision problems. In the multi-player setting these games could be efficiently applied to reasoning about the strategic interaction among the players by means of logical formalism. As a more concrete example, one can polynomially reduce formal verification

Appears in: *Proceedings of the 15th International Conference on Autonomous Agents and Multiagent Systems (AAMAS 2016), J. Thangarajah, K. Tuyls, C. Jonker, S. Marsella (eds.), May 9–13, 2016, Singapore.*

questions about logics for the strategic reasoning such as *Strategy Logic* [5, 10, 32, 33] and the like [29, 31] into our game setting, as well as reasoning efficiently about solution concepts in multi-player games.

In this paper we introduce and solve efficiently *Concurrent Multi-Player Parity Games* (*CMPG*, for short), in which the players behave existential or universal in strict and fixed alternation. With more details, a CMPG extends classic two-player turn-based parity games by admitting n players, namely $Player_0 \dots Player_{n-1}$, to play simultaneously over the prioritized arena. Each $Player_i$, with $i \bmod 2 = 0$ acts as *existential*; the other players are instead *universal*. The aim in a CMPG is to check whether there exists a $Player_0$ strategy such that for all $Player_1$ strategies there exists a $Player_2$ strategy, and so on, such that the resulting plays satisfy the parity condition. In this case we say that the team of the existential players wins the game. Solving a CMPG amount to check whether this is the case.

We show a solution for the introduced CMPG class of games by using a non-trivial extension of the classic Zielonka Recursive Algorithm that, we recall, has been conceived for two-player turn-based parity games. Precisely, we build a new algorithm for the attractor subroutine. We show that our solution takes, as complexity, polynomial space in the size of the game. We also show that this is a tight-complexity solution. Indeed, we provide a PSPACE lower bound by using a reduction from the satisfiability problem for *Quantified Boolean Formulas* (QBF). As another evidence of the strength of our result, we show that our solution algorithm is better than a simple (direct) reduction to a two-player turn-based parity game. In fact, given a CMPG G, such a translation would lead to a classic parity game with a number of states that is exponential in the number of players' decision in G (and thus exponential in the number of the players) but with the same number of priorities. By recalling that the Zielonka Recursive Algorithm is polynomial in the number of states but exponential in the number of priorities, we would obtain a non-tight exponential-time upper-bound.

We strongly believe that our result can be usefully used in a wide range of application domains. The verification setting we have mentioned above is surely a good example. In multi-player strategic reasoning several questions can be directly reduced to this problem. For example it can be used to address the model checking question of logics for the strategic reasoning. See [5] for an argument. It is worth mentioning that the specific setting of multi-player parity games we have introduced has never been addressed before. Indeed, all the literature on parity games mainly concentrates on solving the two-player setting [24, 25, 40], trying to reduce the time complexity [16, 17, 37] or to get parametrized algorithms [17, 19, 28, 36], as well as to apply them in the synthesis and verification of reactive systems [2, 27, 28]. In case a multi-player system is faced, then parity game have been always applied by first introducing a two-player intermediate setting [1, 11]. Finally, we report that concurrent two-player parity games have been considered in the stochastic setting [6, 7, 12, 39].

Outline The sequel of the paper is structured as follows. In Section 2, we introduce Concurrent Multi-Player Parity Structures and other preliminary concepts about games. In Section 3, we report the classic Zielonka Recursive Algorithm used to solve turn-based parity games. In Section 4, we introduce CMPG and provide a first simple but non-tight solution via a translation to turn-based two-player parity games. In Section 5 we provide a PSPACE solution algorithm to solve CMPG by introducing a new appropriate Attractor function of the Zielonka Recursive Algorithm to work with multiple players. In Section 6, we study the lower bound of the address problem and show that it is PSPACE-HARD by means of a reduction from the QBF satisfiability problem. Finally, in Section 7 we give some conclusions.

2. MODEL

In this section, we introduce a semantic framework, namely a *Concurrent Multi-Player Parity Structure* as an abstract game arena in which a number of players, concurrently and independently, perform their moves. Such a structure is obtained by further equipping classic *Concurrent Game Structures* [1, 32] with a labeling function that assigns to each state a natural number called *priority*. The definition follows.

DEFINITION 2.1. *A* Concurrent Multi-Player Parity Structure *(*CMPS*) is a tuple* $\mathcal{G} \triangleq < \mathrm{Pl}, \mathrm{Ac}, \mathrm{St}, s_I, \lambda, \mathsf{tr} >$, *where* $\mathrm{Pl} = \{Player_0, \dots, Player_{|\mathrm{Pl}-1|}\}$ *is a finite non-empty set of* players, Ac *and* St *are enumerable non-empty sets of* actions *and* states, $s_I \in \mathrm{St}$ *is a designated* initial state, *and* $\lambda : \mathrm{St} \to \mathrm{N}$ *is a* labeling function *that assigns to each state a natural number named* priority. *Let* $\mathrm{Dc} \triangleq \mathrm{Pl} \rightharpoonup \mathrm{Ac}$ *be the set of* decisions, *i.e., partial functions describing players' action choices. Also, let* $d[i \to a]$ *be the decision that differs from* d *on the fact that* $Player_i$ *chooses action* a. *Then,* $\mathsf{tr} : \mathrm{Dc} \to (\mathrm{St} \rightharpoonup \mathrm{St})$ *denotes the* transition function *mapping every decision* $\delta \in \mathrm{Dc}$ *to a partial function* $\mathsf{tr}(\delta) \subseteq \mathrm{St} \times \mathrm{St}$ *representing a deterministic graph over the states.*

We will use CMPS to define the semantics of Concurrent Multi-Player Parity Games (CMPG). Before doing that we need some additional basic game concepts.

A *track* is a finite sequence of states $\rho \in \mathrm{St}^*$ such that, for each $i \in [0, \cdots, |\rho| - 1[$, there exists a decision $d \in \mathrm{Dc}$ such that $(\rho)_{i+1} = \mathsf{tr}((\rho)_i, d)$. A track ρ is *non trivial* if $|\rho| > 0$. We use $\mathrm{Trk} \subseteq \mathrm{St}^+$ to denote the set of all non trivial traces. Moreover, by $\mathsf{fst}(\rho) = \rho_0$ we denote the first state of a track. By $\mathrm{Trk}(s) \subseteq \mathrm{Trk}$ we denote the set of tracks starting from the state s, *i.e.* $\mathrm{Trk}(s) \triangleq \{\rho \in \mathrm{Trk} : \mathsf{fst}(\rho) = s\}$.

A *path* π is an infinite sequence of states $\pi \in \mathrm{St}^\omega$ such that, for each $i \in \mathrm{N}$, there exists a decision $d \in \mathrm{Dc}$ such that $(\pi)_{i+1} = \mathsf{tr}((\pi)_i, d)$. We use $\mathrm{Pth} \subseteq \mathrm{St}^\omega$ to indicate the set of all paths and $\mathrm{Pth}(s) \subseteq \mathrm{Pth}$ for the set of paths starting from the vertex s, that is $\mathrm{Pth}(s) \triangleq \{\pi \in \mathrm{Pth} : \mathsf{fst}(()\pi) = s\}$.

A CMPG is a game played over a CMPS by players $Player_0, \dots, Player_{|\mathrm{Pl}-1|}$ under the assumption that they will play for an infinite number of rounds. In each round, the players concurrently and independently choose moves, and the current state and the action chosen for each player determine the successor state. In details we have that each $Player_i$, with $i \bmod 2 = 0$ is part of the *existential (even) team*; the other players are instead part of the *universal (odd) team*. Informally, the goal in a CMPG is to check whether there exists a $Player_0$ strategy such that for each $Player_1$ strategy there exists a $Player_2$ strategy, and so forth, such that the induced plays satisfy the parity condition. Then, we say that the existential player team *wins* the game. A *strategy* can be seen as a scheme that, for each player, contains all the choices of actions he can perform depending on the track of the game. The formal definition follows.

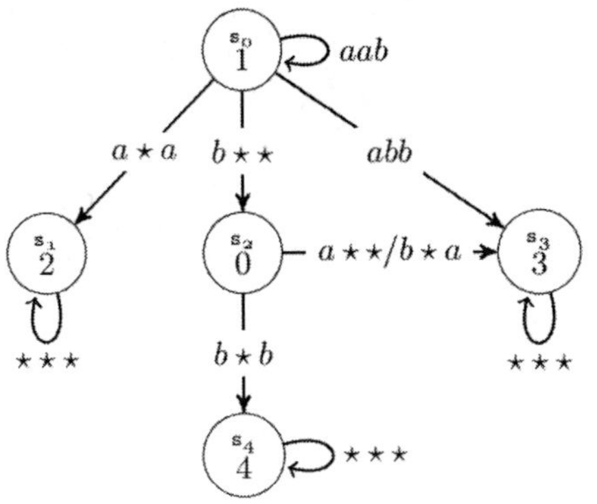

Figure 1: Concurrent Multi-Player Parity Game.

DEFINITION 2.2. *A* strategy *is a partial function* $\sigma : \mathrm{Trk} \rightharpoonup \mathrm{Ac}$ *that maps each non-trivial internal track in its domain to an action. Given a state* $s \in \mathrm{St}$*, a strategy* σ *is said* s-total *if it is defined on all tracks starting in* s*, i.e.,* $\mathsf{dom}(\sigma) = \mathrm{Trk}(s)$. Str *(resp.,* $\mathrm{Str}(s)$*) denotes the set of all (resp.,* s*-total) strategies. Additionally, for a player* $Player_i \in \mathrm{Pl}$*, we indicate with* $\mathrm{Str}_i(s)$ *the set of all strategies for* $Player_i$ *starting from* s *and with* $\sigma_i \in \mathrm{Str}_i(s)$ *one of its strategies.*

A *play* is an outcome of the game determined by the strategies of all the players being involved. Its definition follows.

DEFINITION 2.3. *Given a fixed strategy* $\sigma_i \in \mathrm{Str}_i(s)$ *for each* $Player_i \in \mathrm{Pl}$*, the composition of these strategies induces a unique path* $\pi = \pi_0\pi_1\pi_2\ldots$ *named* play *such that for all* $j \in \mathrm{N}$*, it holds that* $(\pi)_{j+1} = \mathsf{tr}((\pi)_j, d_j)$*, where* d_j *is the decision* $\sigma_0((\pi)_{\leq j}) \times \ldots \times \sigma_{|\mathrm{Pl}-1|}((\pi)_{\leq j})$.

For the sake of clarity we introduce the following example.

EXAMPLE 2.1. *Consider the CMPG depicted in Figure 1. It models the interaction between three players* $\mathrm{Pl}=\{Player_0, Player_1, Player_2\}$ *over an arena with five states,* $\mathrm{St} = \{s_0, s_1, s_2, s_3, s_4\}$*, where* s_0 *is the initial state. Each state of the arena is labeled with a natural number, reported under the name of the graph vertex, as defined by the priority function:* $\lambda(s_0) = 1$, $\lambda(s_1) = 2$, $\lambda(s_2) = 0$, $\lambda(s_3) = 3$, $\lambda(s_4) = 4$. *The transition function is so defined:* $\mathsf{tr}(s_0, a \star a) = s_1$, $\mathsf{tr}(s_0, b \star \star) = s_2$, $\mathsf{tr}(s_0, abb) = s_3$, $\mathsf{tr}(s_0, aab) = s_0$ $\mathsf{tr}(s_1, \star\star\star) = s_1$, $\mathsf{tr}(s_2, a \star \star) = s_3$, $\mathsf{tr}(s_2, b \star a) = s_3$, $\mathsf{tr}(s_2, b \star b) = s_4$, $\mathsf{tr}(s_3, \star\star\star) = s_3$ *and* $\mathsf{tr}(s_4, \star\star\star) = s_4$*, for all* $\star \in \mathrm{Ac}$. *A possible play is* $\pi = s_0 s_2 s_4{}^{\omega}$. *This play is obtained by letting the players to take in traces* (s_0) (s_0s_2) $(s_0s_2s_4)^{\omega}$ *the following actions, respectively: for* $Player_0$ *the actions* b, b, $\star$*, for* $Player_1$ *the actions* $\star\ \star\ \star$*, and for* $Player_2$ *the actions* $\star\ b\ \star$.

3. ZIELONKA RECURSIVE ALGORITHM

A *Turn-Based Two-Player Parity Game* (T2PG, for short) is played on a Turn-Based Two-Player Game Structure (T2PS), an arena in which the states are partitioned into two sets and respectively assigned to the two players $Player_0$ and $Player_1$. These players move a (single and shared) token along the edges of the graph and a player moves the token

```
Algorithm Solve(G):
if St = ∅ then
  W0 = ∅;
  W1 = ∅;
if St ≠ ∅ then
  p = max{λ(s)|s ∈ St};
  i = p mod 2;
  X = {s ∈ St : λ(s) = p};
  A = Attr_i(G, X);
  (W'_i, W'_¬i) = Solve(G \ A);
  if W'_¬i = ∅ then
    W_i = A ∪ W'_i;
    W_¬i = ∅;
  else
    B = Attr_¬i(G, W'_¬i);
    (W''_i, W''_¬i) = Solve(G \ B);
    W_i = W''_i;
    W_¬i = B ∪ W''_¬i;
return (W_i, W_¬i)
```

Figure 2: Zielonka Recursive Algorithm.

to an adjacent node when he owns it along one of its states. As in CMPG, the moves of the player induce an infinite play and $Player_0$ wins this play if the largest priority that occurs infinitely often is even; otherwise $Player_1$ wins. Formally, the winner of the play $\pi = s_0, s_1, \ldots \in \mathrm{Pth}$ under the *parity condition* is $Player_i$ iff $\mathsf{max}\{p : \forall j\, \exists k \geqslant j : \lambda(s_k) = p\} \mod 2 = i$. $Player_0$ wins the game if he is can prevent $Player_1$ to induce a play in which $Player_1$ is the winner.

It is useful to observe that, if we consider a CMPG with two players in which in each state only one player can choose an action (this is possible as we have set *decision function* to possibly be partial along the definition) then we obtain a T2PG. Therefore, in the following we assume a T2PG to be just a CMPG with two players and equipped with a specific partial decision function, as described before, that effectively let partitioning the set of states among the two players.

In the literature, several algorithms have been introduced to solve T2PG and, among the others, the *Zielonka Recursive Algorithm* [40] has been shown to perform better than the others in randomly generated games [17]. This slgorithm, as reported in Figure 2, uses a divide and conquer technique. It constructs the winning sets for both players using the solution of sub-games. It removes the nodes with the highest priority from the game, together with all nodes (and edges) attracted to this set. The algorithm *Solve*(G) takes as input a game graph G and, after a number of recursive calls over ad hoc built sub-games, returns the winning sets W_0 and W_1 for $Player_0$ and $Player_1$, respectively. It constructs the winning sets W_0 and W_1 for both players using the solution of sub-games. In particular, it makes use of a subroutine called *attractor*. Informally, starting from a set $X \subseteq \mathrm{St}$ and $Player_i$, with $i \in \{0, 1\}$, the i-attractor of X is the least set of nodes $Attr_i(X)$ containing X such that i can force a visit to X from every node in $Attr_i(X)$. In other words, it starts with the initial set X and adds, in every step, all nodes belonging to $Player_i$ that can reach X with a single edge and all nodes belonging $Player_{1-i}$ that must reach X no matter which edge $Player_{1-i}$ takes. Since calculating the reachable vertexes from a set of vertexes X requires at most time $O(|e| + |n|)$, we have that, in the worst case, calculating $Attr_i(X)$ requires time $O(|n|^2)$.

The following theorem reports the complexity of the Zielonka Recursive Algorithm.

THEOREM 3.1. *[40] For a* T2PG $\mathcal{G}$ *with n states, e edges, and k priorities, the algorithm Solve(G), returning the winning sets for both players, takes time complexity* $O(e \cdot n^k)$.

4. SOLVING CMPG VIA A REDUCTION TO T2PG

In this section, we introduce an algorithm to solve CMPG through a direct reduction to T2PG. As we will see later, this gives a non-efficient solution. Indeed, in Section 5 we show a better performing algorithm resulting from a non-trivial extension of the Zielonka Recursive Algorithm. Precisely, we introduce an ad hoc algorithm for the attractor subroutine.

In the reduction we propose from a CMPG to a T2PG, the players are not treated in a one-shot fashion, but rather they are emulated by finite games between the two players: the first chooses the actions of the players of the existential team and the second the ones from the universal one. The resulting T2PG is just polynomial in the number of actions and exponential in the number of players of the starting CMPG.

THEOREM 4.1. *Given a* CMPG $\mathcal{G}$ *with* $|\mathrm{St}|$ *states and k priorities, there is a* T2PG $\mathcal{G}^\star$*, played by Player*$_0$ *and Player*$_1$ *over a* T2PS *with* $|\mathrm{St}| \cdot |\mathrm{Pl}| \cdot |\mathrm{Ac}^{\mathrm{Pl}}|$ *states and* $O(|k|)$ *priorities such that Player*$_0$ *wins the* T2PG $\mathcal{G}^\star$ *iff the existential player team wins the* CMPG $\mathcal{G}$.

PROOF (SKETCH). Let $\mathcal{G} \triangleq < \mathrm{Pl}, \mathrm{Ac}, \mathrm{St}, s_I, \lambda, \mathsf{tr} >$ be a CMPG, we now show how to construct the required T2PG $\mathcal{G}^\star \triangleq < \mathrm{Pl}^\star, \mathrm{Ac}^\star, \mathrm{St}^\star, s_I{}^\star, \lambda^\star, \mathsf{tr}^\star >$.

By definition, $\mathcal{G}^\star$ has two players, *Player*$_0$ and *Player*$_1$, and *Player*$_0$ wins the game if he is able to induces only plays in which the greatest priority that occurs infinitely often along the corresponding paths in the structure of the game is even; otherwise *Player*$_1$ wins the game. To achieve this task, for each state in St, *Player*$_0$ (resp., *Player*$_1$) chooses an appropriate action for each player even (resp., odd). Thus we set $\mathrm{Pl}^\star \triangleq \{Player_0, Player_1\}$ and $\mathrm{Ac}^\star \triangleq \mathrm{Ac}$. The state space has to maintain an information about the position in $\mathcal{G}$ together with the index of the player that has still to be evaluated and the actions already associated to the previous players. To do this, we set $\mathrm{St}^\star \triangleq \mathrm{St} \times [0, |\mathrm{Pl}| - 1] \times_i (Dc_{<i})$ where $\mathrm{Dc}_{<i}$ is the decision of *Player*$_j$, for each $j = 0, \ldots, i-1$.

Before proceeding with the definition of the transition function, it is helpful to identify which are the active players for each possible state. We define a function $\mathsf{type}: \{0, \ldots, |\mathrm{Pl}|\} \to \mathrm{Pl}^\star$ that for an index of player gives the corresponding player in $\mathcal{G}^\star$. For a state $(s, i, d) \in \mathrm{St}^\star$ the active player is $\mathsf{type}(i) \triangleq i \bmod 2$.

The transition function is defined as follows. For each state (s, i, d) with $i < |\mathrm{Pl}| - 1$ and decision $\mathsf{type}(i) \mapsto c$, we simply need to increase the counter i and associate the player i with action c. Formally, we set $\mathsf{tr}^\star((s, i, d)) \triangleq (s, i+1, d[i \mapsto c])$. For a state $(s, |\mathrm{Pl}| - 1, d)$, instead, we define a transition to the state $(s', 0, \varnothing)$, where s' is the successor of s in the game $\mathcal{G}$ following the decision $d[|\mathrm{Pl}| - 1 \mapsto c]$, whenever active. Formally, we have $\mathsf{tr}^\star((s, |\mathrm{Pl}| - 1, d)) \triangleq (\mathsf{tr}(s, d[|\mathrm{Pl}| - 1 \mapsto c]), 0, \emptyset)$. Now, we define the priority function $\lambda^\star$. For each state (s, i, d), we have that:

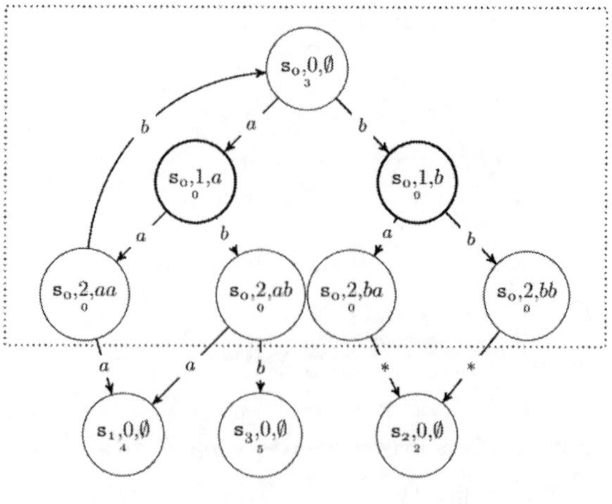

Figure 3: Conversion of the initial state.

$$\lambda^\star((s, i, d)) \triangleq \begin{cases} \lambda(s) + 2, & \text{if } i = 0 \text{ and } d = \emptyset; \\ 0, & \text{otherwise.} \end{cases}$$

The idea behind the priority function is to simulate in an equivalent manner the concurrent game. Given a transition from s to s' in $\mathcal{G}$ with d the actions associated to each player, the effective transition in $\mathcal{G}$ occurs when the game is in $(s, |\mathrm{Pl}| - 1, d')$ with d' in accordance with d, and the player $|\mathrm{Pl}| - 1$ selects the action in accordance with d, then the game passes at the state $(s', 0, \emptyset)$. We name all states (s, i, d) with $i = 0$ and $d = \emptyset$ the external states and internal the others. Our goal is to use a small priority for the internal states, *i.e.* the states that do not correspond to any state in the original game. To do this, we label all internal states with the lowest priority (*i.e.* 0) and all external states by increasing their priority by a factor of 2. We increase the priority of external states to avoid the case that the internal states may have the same priority of the external once. Finally, the initial state is $s_I^\star \triangleq (s_I, 0, \varnothing)$.

Now, we discuss the complexity of reduction from $\mathcal{G}$ to $\mathcal{G}^\star$. First, we have that for each $s \in \mathrm{St}$ the reduction produces a number of states equal to $\prod_{|\mathrm{Pl}|} |\mathrm{Ac}^{\mathrm{Pl}}|$. In fact, given a state s for each player, in the worst case, the number of states produced by the reduction is $|\mathrm{Ac}^{\mathrm{Pl}}|$, *i.e.* the cardinality of the set of decisions. Then, the complexity result follows. □

To better understand the reduction in the previous theorem, consider again the model introduced in the previous section and in particular its initial state s_0. In gray rectangle depicted in Figure 3 there are the states that represent s_0 in a two-player turn-based parity game. In particular, there are three level of decision, two for *Player*$_0$ and one for *Player*$_1$ (depicted in bold). After the three level of decision, as in Figure 1 there are the effective transactions. For example, consider the state $(\mathsf{s}_o, 2, aa)$. The owner of this state is *Player*$_0$ in fact $\mathsf{type}(2) = 0$. If *Player*$_0$ chooses the action b it returns to state $(\mathsf{s}_o, 0, \emptyset)$ that in $\mathcal{G}$ is represented through a loop on initial state s_0.

By the construction showed in the Theorem 4.1 and by the complexity for solving a T2PG reported in Theorem 3.1, we obtain the following result.

COROLLARY 4.1. *The complexity to solve the* CMPG *is exponential in both the number of the priorities and the number of players.*

5. SOLVING EFFICIENTLY A CMPG

The main complexity bottleneck in dealing with CMPG is the number of players. Indeed, the attractor procedure needs to follow the full chain of players to come up with the winning set of states and this requires, in the worst case, exponential time. In this section we provide some tools in order to simplify this task and then we show how to apply them to have an efficient solution algorithm to solve the game.

Generally speaking, standard quantification over strategies introduces an unintuitive interpretation in the semantics of games, since it instantiates full strategies, which includes also future actions, whereas players see only actions played in the past. In more details, a quantification of the form $\forall\exists$ means that the existentially quantified strategy is chosen in response to the universally quantified strategy, which prescribes actions in response to tracks that may never arise in the actual game. In classic games, a player reacts only to current and past actions taken by other players, so the response of the existentially quantified strategy to a given track should depend only on the response of the universally quantified strategy to this track. We deeply make use of this concept along the proposed solution for CMPG. To explain this formally, we make use of the concept of *Skolem's dependence function* of a quantification, as introduced in [32]. The main idea here is inspired by what Skolem proposed for *First Order Logic* in order to eliminate all existential quantifications over variables, by substituting them with second order existential quantifications over functions, whose choice is uniform *w.r.t.* the universal variables.

We start by introducing some notation regarding quantification prefixes.

Let $\wp \in Qnt(\mathrm{V})$ be a quantification prefix over a set $V(\wp) \triangleq \mathrm{V} \subseteq \mathrm{Vr}$ of variables. By $\langle\langle\wp\rangle\rangle \triangleq \{x \in V(\wp) : \exists i \in [0, |\wp|[. (\wp)_i = \langle\!\langle x \rangle\!\rangle\}$ and $[[\wp]] \triangleq V(\wp) \setminus \langle\langle\wp\rangle\rangle$ we denote the sets of *existential* and *universal variables* quantified in $\wp$, respectively.

Let $x, y \in V(\wp)$ be two variables. We say that x *precedes* y in $\wp$, in symbols $x <_\wp y$, if x occurs before y in $\wp$, i.e., there are two indexes $i, j \in [0, |\wp|[$, with $i < j$, such that $(\wp)_i \in \{\langle\!\langle x \rangle\!\rangle, [\![x]\!]\}$ and $(\wp)_j \in \{\langle\!\langle y \rangle\!\rangle, [\![y]\!]\}$. We also say that y is *functional dependent* on x, in symbols $x \rightsquigarrow_\wp y$, if $x \in [[\wp]]$, $y \in \langle\langle\wp\rangle\rangle$, and $x <_\wp y$, i.e., y is existentially quantified after that x is universally quantified, so, there may be a dependence between a value chosen by x and that chosen by y. This definition induces the set $Dep(\wp) \triangleq \{(x, y) \in V(\wp) \times V(\wp) : x \rightsquigarrow_\wp y\}$ of *dependence pairs* and its derived version $Dep(\wp, y) \triangleq \{x \in V(\wp) : x \rightsquigarrow_\wp y\}$ containing all variables from which y depends.

We use $\overline{\wp} \in Qnt(V(\wp))$ to indicate the quantification derived from $\wp$ by *dualizing* each quantifier contained in it, i.e., for all indexes $i \in [0, |\wp|[$, it holds that $(\overline{\wp})_i = \langle\!\langle x \rangle\!\rangle$ iff $(\wp)_i = [\![x]\!]$, with $x \in V(\wp)$. It is evident that $\langle\langle\overline{\wp}\rangle\rangle = [[\wp]]$ and $[[\overline{\wp}]] = \langle\langle\wp\rangle\rangle$.

Finally, we define the notion of *valuation* of variables. Let D a generic set, called *domain*, by $Val_{\mathrm{D}}(\mathrm{V}) \triangleq \mathrm{V} \to \mathrm{D}$ we denote the set of all valuation functions over D defined on $\mathrm{V} \subseteq \mathrm{Vr}$. In the sequel of the paper we consider as domain set just the set of actions.

We now give a general high-level semantics for the quantification prefixes by means of the following definition of *Skolem dependence function*.

Definition 5.1 (Skolem Dependence Function). *Let $\wp \in Qnt(\mathrm{V})$ be a quantification prefix over a set $\mathrm{V} \subseteq \mathrm{Vr}$ of variables, and D a set. Then, a* Skolem dependence function *for $\wp$ over D is a function $\theta : Val_{\mathrm{D}}([[\wp]]) \to Val_{\mathrm{D}}(\mathrm{V})$ satisfying the following properties:*

1. *$\theta(v)_{\restriction [\![\wp]\!]} = v$, for all $v \in Val_{\mathrm{D}}([\![\wp]\!])$;*
2. *$\theta(v_1)(x) = \theta(v_2)(x)$, for all $v_1, v_2 \in Val_{\mathrm{D}}([[\wp]])$ and $x \in \langle\langle\wp\rangle\rangle$ such that $v_{1\restriction Dep(\wp,x)} = v_{2\restriction Dep(\wp,x)}$.*

By $\Theta_{\mathrm{D}}(\wp)$ we denote the set of all Skolem dependence functions for $\wp$ over D. It is important to note that, by replacing D with the set of strategies, we obtain a Skolem dependence function over strategies.

We have now all the ingredients to give an appropriate definition of the Attractor function for a given CMPG G. Recall that, differently from the turn-based case, we do not have the specific membership of a state to a specific player. Also, we do not have two single players but rather two teams of players, one existential and one universal, with the players of the two teams playing in a precise shuffled modality. Accordingly, we introduce two different sub-notions of Attractor, one used for the team of players to which is associated the existential quantifier $Attr^{\exists}(G, X)$ and the other for the one to which it is associated the universal quantifier $Attr^{\forall}(G, X)$. The two definitions follow.

Definition 5.2. *$Attr^{\exists}(G, X)$ is the largest set of vertexes such that the players associated to the existential quantifier have a strategy that allows to move from any vertex of $Attr^{\exists}(G, X)$ to X in a finite number of steps. Formally, for each $k \in \mathrm{N}$ we define*

$X_0 = X$;

$X_{k+1} = X_k \cup \{s \in \mathrm{St} : \exists \theta \in \Theta_{\mathrm{Ac}}(\wp), \forall c \in Val_{\mathrm{Ac}}([[\wp]]) : tr(s, \theta(c)) \in X_k\}$.

$Attr^{\exists}(G, X) = \bigcup_{k \in \mathrm{N}} X_k$.

Definition 5.3. *$Attr^{\forall}(G, X)$ is the largest set of vertexes such that the players associated to the universal quantifier have a strategy that allows to move from any vertex of $Attr^{\forall}(G, X)$ to X in a finite number of steps. Formally, for each $k \in \mathrm{N}$ we define*

$X_0 = X$;

$X_{k+1} = X_k \cup \{s \in \mathrm{St} : \exists \theta \in \Theta_{\mathrm{Ac}}(\neg\wp), \forall c \in Val_{\mathrm{Ac}}([[\wp]]) : tr(s, \theta(c)) \in X_k\}$.

$Attr^{\forall}(G, X) = \bigcup_{k \in \mathrm{N}} X_k$.

Similarly, we can define the sets of vertexes from which the existential $\exists$ or the universal $\forall$ team gets trapped, so losing the game. The formal definition of the trap notion follows.

Definition 5.4. *Let $i \in \{\exists, \forall\}$. A σ_i-*trap *over G is any non-empty set X of vertexes such that for each vertex $s \in X$, if $i = \exists$ there exists a function $\theta \in \Theta_{\mathrm{Ac}}(\neg\wp) \forall c \in Val_{\mathrm{Ac}}([[\wp]])$ such that $tr(s, \theta(c)) \in X$, otherwise there exists a function $\theta \in \Theta_{\mathrm{Ac}}(\wp) \forall c \in Val_{\mathrm{Ac}}([[\wp]])$ such that $tr(s, \theta(c)) \in X$.*

Below, we report some basic properties about the construction of the winning sets for the coalitions of players $\exists$ and $\forall$. The following facts are immediate remarks on the definition of the game and extend to our game setting similar concepts from the classic two-player turned-based parity games.

```
1   Algorithm Attr(G,X,f,n):
2   c = |X|;
3   for k = 1 to c do
4     v = X_k;
5     h = numadj(X_k)\removeAdjIn(v,X);
6     while h ≠ 0
7       u = removeFirst(adj(v));
8       h = h-1;
9       if Check(n,f,0,∅,s,X) = 1 then
10        X = X ∪ u;
11  return (X)
```

Figure 4: Multi-player Attractor Algorithm.

```
1   Algorithm Check(n,f,i,d, s, X):
2   r = i mod 2;
3   for c ∈ Ac do
4     if i = n-1 then
5       if i mod 2 = f
6         r = (r ∨ tr(s, d[i → c]) ∈ X);
7       else
8         r = (r ∧ tr(s, d[i → c]) ∈ X);
9     else
10      if i mod 2 = f
11        r = (r ∨ Check(n, f, i+1, d[i → c], s, X));
12      else
13        r = (r ∧ Check(n, f, i+1, d[i → c], s, X));
14  return (r)
```

Figure 5: Check Algorithm.

REMARK 5.1. *Let G be a CMPG. For each set $X \subseteq \mathrm{St}$ we have that $\mathrm{St} \setminus Attr^{\forall}(G, X)$ is a trap for the players associated to the universal quantifier.*

REMARK 5.2. *Let G be a CMPG. For each set $X \subseteq \mathrm{St}$ we have that $\mathrm{St} \setminus Attr^{\exists}(G, X)$ is a trap for the players associated to the existential quantifier.*

Finally, the next remark refers to the winning sets W constructed in the algorithm $Solve(G)$ in Figure 2.

REMARK 5.3. *For $i \in \{\exists, \forall\}$ and $X \subseteq \mathrm{St}$. If $\mathrm{W}'_{\neg i} = \emptyset$ then $\mathrm{W}_i = Attr^i(G, X) \cup \mathrm{W}'_i$ is a winning set for a set of player i.*

In the sequel we describe how to compute the attractor sets. We also discuss the time and space complexity of the related routines.

THEOREM 5.1. *Let G be a CMPG, $p \in \{\exists, \forall\}$, and $X \subseteq Attr^{p}(G, X)$. Let $m = |\mathrm{St}|$ be the number of vertexes in G. The set $Attr_p(G, X)$ is computable in time $2^{O(log(m)+log|\mathrm{Ac}|*n)}$ where n is the number of players and Ac the set of actions.*

PROOF. Consider the algorithm $Attr(G, X, f, n)$ in Figure 4. It takes as input a game graph G, a set $X \subseteq \mathrm{St}$ of vertexes, a flag f indicating whether it is the turn of the player belonging to the team even or odd, and n corresponding to the number of players. Suppose that the vertexes are ordered. First, the algorithm computes the size of the set X ($c = |X|$). For each vertex in X, its adjacency list is scanned, checking if every adjacent vertex satisfies the IF condition in line 9. The algorithm terminates when all the adjacency lists of the vertexes in X have been exploited. Then the algorithm returns the set X containing the largest set of vertexes form which, in a finite number of steps, it is able to reach a vertex in X. The algorithm in the mentioned IF condition makes a call to the subroutine $Check(n, f, 0, \emptyset, s, X)$. This function takes as input n corresponding to the number of players, a flag f indicating whether it is the turn of a player belonging to the team even or odd, an index i tracking the player who is playing at the current time, a decision d representing the choice of an action for each player, a vertex s and a set X that are used to determine whether, from s and performing the decision d, it is possible to stay in X. It assigns, from a vertex s taken as input, an action to a player and then checks whether this choice allows to achieve the target. Let analyze the time complexity of the subroutine $Check(n, f, 0, \emptyset, s, X)$. We indicate this value with $T_{Check(n)}$. This complexity clearly relies on the construct FOR in line 3 that gives the major contribution over the input parameters. This construct is repeated at most $|\mathrm{Ac}|$ times. To calculate $T_{Check(n)}$, we calculate the complexity of a generic $T_{Check(n-i)}$. Let $T_{Check(n-i)}$ be a positive function expressed as follows.

$$T_{Check(n-i)} = \begin{cases} 2 + 3 * |\mathrm{Ac}| & \text{if } i = n-1 \\ 2 + (3 + T_{Check(n-(i+1))}) * |\mathrm{Ac}| & \text{if } i < n-1 \end{cases}$$

By replacing, iteratively, the values of the variable i, we obtain $T_{Check(n)} = 2 + 5 * \sum_{i=1}^{n-1} |\mathrm{Ac}|^i + 3 * |\mathrm{Ac}|^n$. From this we can deduce what follows.

$$\begin{aligned} T_{Check(n)} &= 2 + 5 * \textstyle\sum_{i=1}^{n-1} |\mathrm{Ac}|^i + 3 * |\mathrm{Ac}|^n \\ &\leq 2 + 5 * (n-1) * |\mathrm{Ac}|^{n-1} + 3 * |\mathrm{Ac}|^n \text{ [1]} \\ &\leq (n-1) * |\mathrm{Ac}|^{n-1} \\ &= O(n * (|\mathrm{Ac}|^n \div |\mathrm{Ac}|)) \\ &= O(n * |\mathrm{Ac}|^{n-1}) \\ &= O(n * |\mathrm{Ac}|^n) \\ &= O(n * 2^{\log |\mathrm{Ac}| * n}) \\ &= O(2^{\log n} * 2^{\log |\mathrm{Ac}| * n}) \\ &= O(2^{\log n + \log |\mathrm{Ac}| * n}) \\ &= 2^{O(\log |\mathrm{Ac}| * n)} \end{aligned}$$

So far, we have calculated the complexity of the subroutine $Check(n, f, 0, \emptyset, s, X)$.

Now, we analyze the complexity of the attractor function $Attr(G, X, f, n)$. The assignment at the line 1 is done in constant time. The FOR (line 3...11) is performed $|X|$ times that, in the worst case, is equal to $|\mathrm{St}|$. The WHILE construct (line 6) is performed h times. Based on these considerations, we say that the running time of the attractor function is given by $\sum_{k=1}^{|X|} 3 + (4 + T_{Check}(n))h_k$.

Assume that $m = |\mathrm{St}|$ and $j = |X|$. It is easy to see that $h_k = m - j$ (line 5). So, we have that $\sum_{k=1}^{j} 3 + (4 + T_{Check}(n))k(m-k)$. By a matter of calculation and over approximation, we get that the time complexity of the attractor is $2^{O(log(m)+log|\mathrm{Ac}|*n)}$. □

[1] Note that $|\mathrm{Ac}| > (n-1)$

It is clear that the extra time complexity in solving a CMPG, with respect to the classic two player parity games, relies on the fact that it admits a multitude of players. In particular, this is due to the fact that on increasing the number of players, for each state, the number of decisions increases exponentially.

The complexity of the proposed algorithm results to be much better in terms of space consumption. Indeed, it only requires polynomial space, as we prove in the next theorem. In the next section we also show that this is a tight complexity.

THEOREM 5.2. *Let* G *be a* CMPG. *The algorithm Solve(* G*) is computed in space* $|\mathrm{St}|^2 + (log|C| + log|\mathrm{St}| + |\mathrm{Pl}| * log|\mathrm{Ac}|) * |\mathrm{St}|$ *where* St, C, Pl *and* Ac *are the set of states, the set of different priorities, the set of players and the set of the actions, respectively.*

PROOF. We first analyze the subroutines of the recursive algorithm. Start with the function $Check(n, f, i, d, s, X)$. At line 2 it is initialized a Boolean variable that needs constant space. For the assignments at the lines 6 and 8, we do not need additional storage space as we can overwrite the same boolean variable. As the FOR construct regards (line 3 - 13) we need $log|\mathrm{Ac}|$ space. Concerning lines 11-13, the algorithm is recursively called (by the next player).

By iterating on the number of players, we have that

$$S_{Check(1)} = 1 + log|\mathrm{Ac}|$$
$$S_{Check(2)} = 1 + log|\mathrm{Ac}| + S_{Check(1)} = 2 * (1 + log|\mathrm{Ac}|)$$
$$S_{Check(3)} = 1 + log|\mathrm{Ac}| + S_{Check(2)} = 3 * (1 + log|\mathrm{Ac}|)$$
$$\vdots$$

The generic element $S_{Check(n-i)}$ is given by

$$S_{Check(n-i)} = \begin{cases} 1 + log|\mathrm{Ac}| & \text{if } i = n-1 \\ 1 + log|\mathrm{Ac}| + S_{Check(n-(i+1))} & \text{if } i < n-1 \end{cases}$$

It is easy to note that, to each iteration, the value $1 + log|\mathrm{Ac}|$ does not depend on the next iteration. So, we can conclude that

$$\begin{aligned} S_{Check(n)} &= n * (1 + log|\mathrm{Ac}|) \qquad \text{since } n = |\mathrm{Pl}| \\ &= O((1 + log|\mathrm{Ac}|) * |\mathrm{Pl}|) \\ &= O(|\mathrm{Pl}| * log|\mathrm{Ac}|) \end{aligned}$$

Then, the amount of memory required to perform $Check(n, f, i, d, s, X)$ is $O(|\mathrm{Pl}| * log|\mathrm{Ac}|)$. We proceed by analyzing the space complexity of the function $Attr(G, X, f, n)$. Each of the basic operations needs space $log|\mathrm{St}|$. Then, we have $5 * log|\mathrm{St}|$. By knowing the space complexity of the function $Check(n, f, i, d, s, X)$, we have that the amount of memory required to perform $Attr(G, X, f, n)$ is given by $S_{Attr}(G, X, f, n) = O(log|\mathrm{St}| + |\mathrm{Pl}| * log|\mathrm{Ac}|)$.

Finally, we analyze the complexity of the algorithm $Solve(G)$. The assignments at lines 3-4 require constant space. In addition, the operations from lines 5 to 19 (excluding the attractor calls) need the declaration of the seven variables, each of which needs $|\mathrm{St}|$ space. By knowing the complexity space of the function $Attr(G, X, f, n)$, we have that the space complexity of the recursive algorithm $Solve(G)$ is given by $S_{Solve}(G) = 7*|\mathrm{St}| + log|C| + S_{Solve}(G \setminus A) + S_{Attr}(G, X, f, n)$ where C corresponds to the maximum number of priority.

Let $n = |\mathrm{St}|$, by using an over-approximation of the $G \setminus A$, we have that

$$S_{Solve(n)} = \begin{cases} 2 & \text{if } n = 0 \\ 7*n + log|C| + S_{Solve}(n-1) + S_{Attr}(G, X, f, n) & \text{if } n > 0 \end{cases}$$

By iterating over n, we have that

$$\begin{aligned} S_{Solve}(0) &= 2 \\ S_{Solve}(1) &= 7 + log|C| + S_{Solve}(0) + S_{Attr}(G, X, f, n) \\ &= 7 + log|C| + 2 + S_{Attr}(G, X, f, n) \\ &= 9 + log|C| + S_{Attr}(G, X, f, n) \\ S_{Solve}(2) &= 14 + log|C| + S_{Solve}(1) + S_{Attr}(G, X, f, n) \\ &= 14 + log|C| + 9 + log|C| + S_{Attr}(G, X, f, n) + \\ &\quad S_{Attr}(G, X, f, n) \\ &= 23 + 2 * log|C| + 2 * S_{Attr}(G, X, f, n) \\ &\vdots \\ S_{Solve}(n) &= (7 * (n * (n+1)))/2 + 2 + n * log|C| + n * \\ &\quad S_{Attr}(G, X, f, n) \\ &= (n^2 + (log|C| + S_{Attr}(G, X, f, n)) * n) \\ &= (n^2 + (log|C| + log|\mathrm{St}| + |\mathrm{Pl}| * log|\mathrm{Ac}|) * n) \\ &= (|\mathrm{St}|^2 + (log|C| + log|\mathrm{St}| + |\mathrm{Pl}| * log|\mathrm{Ac}|) * |\mathrm{St}|) \end{aligned}$$

Hence, in term of space complexity, the algorithm is quadratic in the number of states, logarithmic in the number of priorities and actions and polynomial in the number of players. In other words, it takes polynomial space and therefore we are done with the proof. □

6. LOWER BOUND

In this section we show that solving CMPG is PSPACE-HARD through a reduction from the satisfiability problem of quantified Boolean formulas (QBF, for short). A (fully) quantified Boolean formula is a formula in quantified propositional logic where every variable (from a finite set) is quantified by using either an existential or a universal quantifier. For example, $\exists x\ \forall y\ \exists z\ ((x \wedge z) \vee y)$ is an instance of QBF. A quantified Boolean formula is in *prenex normal form* if it has two basic parts: a portion containing only quantifiers and a portion containing an unquantified Boolean formula. Checking whether in a quantified Boolean formula ϕ there exists an assignment profile to the variables, given in accordance with the quantifiers, that satisfies ϕ is known to be a PSPACE-COMPLETE problem. We will provide a reduction such that for each instance $\phi \in$ QBF we build a CMPG G such that ϕ is true if and only if the existential coalition in G wins the game.

The reduction we provide uses and extends a reduction introduced in [20, 30]. They show that, in case we restrict to formulas in QBF with a prefix of quantification $\exists\forall$ the satisfiability problem can be reduced to solving a game over a specific concurrent arena (formally a CGS) where each move comes from the possible interaction between the coalitions of players. These moves are defined through a Σ_2^P algorithm, named $CPre$, that calculates the pre-image of a set of states over a given coalition. We recall that Σ_i^P is the class of problems that can be solved by a nondeterministic Turing machine in polynomial time with i recursive calls to an NP oracle, that $\Delta_{i+1}^P = P^{\Sigma_i^P}$, and that $PH = \bigcup_{k \in \mathrm{N}} \Delta_i^P$ [34].

The $CPre$ algorithm in [20, 30] considers just one call to an NP oracle as the game structure cannot accommodate

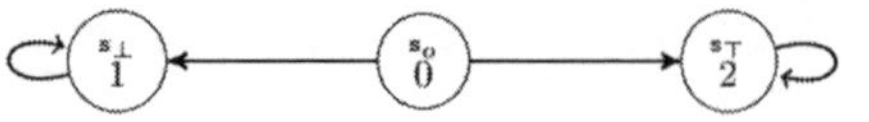

Figure 6: The game resulting from the reduction.

more than one coalition alternation. In our case, instead we can address games with an arbitrary number of (strict) alternation among coalitions of players.

THEOREM 6.1. *The problem of deciding a winner in a* CMPG *is* PSPACE-HARD

PROOF. Given a fully quantified Boolean formula $\phi = Q_0x_0 \cdots Q_{n-1}x_{n-1}\varphi(x_0,\ldots,x_{n-1})$ in prenex normal form, we now show how to construct an instance of a CMPG $\mathcal{G}$ such that the existential team wins the game if and only if the formula is satisfiable. The game is $\mathcal{G} \triangleq <\mathrm{Pl}, \mathrm{Ac}, \mathrm{St}, s_I, \lambda,$ $\mathsf{tr}>$ where the set of players $\mathrm{Pl} = \{x_0,\ldots,x_{n-1}\}$ is the set of the Boolean variables, the set of actions $\mathrm{Ac} = \{0,1\}$ is the sets of the truth values to be assigned to Boolean variables, the set of states is $\mathrm{St} = \{s_0, s_\top, s_\bot\}$, the labeling function $\lambda : \mathrm{St} \to \mathrm{N}$ assigning to each state a priority is such that $\lambda(s_0) = 0$, $\lambda(s_\bot) = 1$, and $\lambda(s_\top) = 2$. Finally, $s_I = \{s_0\} \in \mathrm{St}$ is a designated initial state. It just remains to define the transition function tr. Let $d \in \mathrm{Dc}$ be a specific decision where $\mathrm{Dc} \triangleq \mathrm{Pl} \rightharpoonup \mathrm{Ac}$ is the set of *decisions*. We say that

$$\mathsf{tr}(s_0, d) = \begin{cases} s_\top, & \text{if} \quad d \models \varphi \\ s_\bot, & \textit{otherwise} \end{cases}$$

The game built out of this construction is showed in Figure 6. Note that, if the assignment of the truth values at the Boolean variables makes the formula true then the token remains infinitely often at the state $s_\top$ (so letting the existential team to win the game) otherwise it remains in $s_\bot$ infinitely often.

It is easy to see that by using an explicit transition function (as we have done so far) the reduction from QBF to CMPS is exponential. In order to make the reduction to be polynomial one can use instead an implicit representation of the transition function as in [30]. Precisely, we assume that the transitions from any state s are given by the sequence $((\varphi_0, s_0), (\varphi_1, s_1), \ldots, (\varphi_{|\mathsf{tr}(s)|}, s_{|\mathsf{tr}(s)|}))$, where $s_i \in \mathrm{St}$ and φ_i is a boolean combination of propositions $x_j = a_j$ that evaluate to true iff x_j chooses the action a_j. The transition table is then defined as follows: $tr(s, a_0, \ldots a_{n-1}) = s_j$ iff j is the lowest index s.t. φ_j evaluates to true when players x_0 to x_{n-1} choose moves a_0 to a_{n-1}. At this point, we use the procedure in Figure 7 to calculate the transition function that extends the one introduced in [30]. The procedure $CPre$ guesses an action for each player in order to construct a decision. It expands the set of states that are winning for the existential players if the QBF formula φ holds. In particular, note that s_0 belongs to $CPre(\mathrm{Pl}, s_\top)$ iff there exists a valuation for variables assigned to the existential quantifiers such that $\varphi_\top$ is true whatever the players associated to the variables universally quantified will choose. Finally, the theorem holds by using the following reasoning. Given φ, the algorithm $CPre$ requires a tower of guesses whose height depends on the number n of quantifications. More precisely, for all φ with n quantifications $CPre$ is in Σ_n^p.

Hence in general, for each formula φ, we have that the algorithm $CPre$ is in PH.

```
Procedure CPre(Pl, S):
W = ∅;
For each s ∈ St
 i = 0;
 For each i < |Pl|
  if (i mod 2 == 0)
   a_i = guess_∃(s, Pl_i, d_<i);
  else
   a_i = guess_∀(s, Pl_i, d_<i);
  d_<i+1 = d_<i · a_i;
  j = 0;
  while (¬φ_j(d))
   j++;
  if s_j ∈ S
   W = W ∪ {s_j};
return W
```

Figure 7: Procedure CPre.

7. CONCLUSION

In this paper, we have introduced and solved *Concurrent Multi-Player Parity Games* (CMPG) as an extension of the classic and well-known (two player turn-based) parity games. In a CMPG several players concurrently and independently move along edges by taking decisions as tuples of action moves. As for classic parity games the arena is labeled with natural number priorities. In a CMPG players are partitioned into two teams: the existential and universal teams. In a play, players take role (from the two teams) in a strict $\exists\forall$ alternation and the existential team wins the game if all the players it comprises can enforce a play that satisfies the parity condition, i.e. the maximal priority that is seen infinitely often is even. We have proved that the problem of solving a CMPG is PSPACE-COMPLETE. For the upper bound we have introduced a non-trivial extension of the *attractor* function along the Zielonka Recursive Algorithm. For the lower bound we have provided a reduction from the QBF satisfiability problem.

Classic parity games have been deeply investigated in a number of application fields both as an abstract tool to model reactive systems and a machinery to properly solve decision problems. In the multi-player setting they have been also recently applied to reasoning about the strategic interaction of players by means of logic formalisms [5]. However, a strong limitation in this area resides on the fact that problems have to be first casted somehow in a two-player turn-based framework and then reduced to parity games. This often requires resources and the solution through these games becomes less effective. We believe that having now introduced and solved efficiently concurrent multi-player parity games could get back more attention to such an approach and solve open problems efficiently in the multi-player setting.

As future work it would be interesting to consider some improvements and heuristic evaluation by implementing our algorithm. A good platform to do this is PGSolver [17] that contains most of the known algorithms to solve classic parity games.

Acknowledgments

This work has been partially supported by the FP7 EU project 600958-SHERPA and the IndAM project "Logica, Automi e Giochi per Sistemi Auto-adattivi".

REFERENCES

[1] R. Alur, T. Henzinger, and O. Kupferman. Alternating-Time Temporal Logic. *JACM*, 49(5):672–713, 2002.

[2] B. Aminof, F. Mogavero, and A. Murano. Synthesis of Hierarchical Systems. *SCP*, 83:56–79, 2014.

[3] B. Aminof and O. Kupferman and A. Murano. Improved model checking of hierarchical systems. *Inf. Comput.*, 210:68–86, 2012.

[4] D. Berwanger. Admissibility in Infinite Games. In *STACS'07*, LNCS 4393, pages 188–199. Springer, 2007.

[5] P. Cermak, A. Lomuscio, and A. Murano. Verifying and synthesising multi-agent systems against one-goal strategy logic specifications. In *AAAI'15*, pages 2038–2044, 2015.

[6] K. Chatterjee, L. D. Alfaro, and T. Henzinger. The complexity of quantitative concurrent parity games. In *SODA'06*, pages 678–687, 2006.

[7] K. Chatterjee, L. D. Alfaro, and T. A. Henzinger. Qualitative concurrent parity games. *TOCL*, 12(4):28, 2011.

[8] K. Chatterjee, L. Doyen, T. Henzinger, and J.-F. Raskin. Generalized Mean-payoff and Energy Games. In *FSTTCS'10*, LIPIcs 8, pages 505–516. Leibniz-Zentrum fuer Informatik, 2010.

[9] K. Chatterjee, T. Henzinger, and M. Jurdzinski. Mean-Payoff Parity Games. In *LICS'05*, pages 178–187. IEEE Computer Society, 2005.

[10] K. Chatterjee, T. Henzinger, and N. Piterman. Strategy Logic. *Information and Computation*, 208(6):677–693, 2010.

[11] K. Chatterjee and T. A. Henzinger. A survey of stochastic ω-regular games. *Journal of Computer and System Sciences*, 78(2):394–413, 2012.

[12] K. Chatterjee, M. Jurdziński, and T. Henzinger. Quantitative stochastic parity games. In *SODA'04*, pages 121–130, 2004.

[13] E. Clarke and E. Emerson. Design and Synthesis of Synchronization Skeletons Using Branching-Time Temporal Logic. In *LP'81*, LNCS 131, pages 52–71. Springer, 1981.

[14] E. Clarke, O. Grumberg, and D. Peled. *Model Checking*. MIT Press, 2002.

[15] E. Emerson and C. Jutla. The Complexity of Tree Automata and Logics of Programs (Extended Abstract). In *FOCS'88*, pages 328–337. IEEE Computer Society, 1988.

[16] O. Friedmann. Recursive algorithm for parity games requires exponential time. *RAIRO-Theoretical Informatics and Applications*, 45(04):449–457, 2011.

[17] O. Friedmann and M. Lange. Solving parity games in practice. In *ATVA'09*, LNCS 5799, pages 182–196. Springer, 2009.

[18] D. Harel and A. Pnueli. *On the Development of Reactive Systems*. Springer, 1985.

[19] P. Hoffmann and M. Luttenberger. Solving parity games on the GPU. In *ATVA'13*, pages 455–459. Springer, 2013.

[20] W. Jamroga and J. Dix. Do agents make model checking explode (computationally)? In *CEEMAS'15*, LNCS 3690, pages 398–407. Springer, 2005.

[21] W. Jamroga and A. Murano. On Module Checking and Strategies. In *AAMAS'14*, pages 701–708. IFAAMAS, 2014.

[22] W. Jamroga and A. Murano. Module checking of strategic ability. In *AAMAS'15*, pages 227–235. IFAAMAS, 2015.

[23] M. Jurdzinski. Deciding the winner in parity games is in up $\cap$ co-up. *Inf. Process. Lett.*, 68(3):119–124, 1998.

[24] M. Jurdzinski. Small progress measures for solving parity games. In *STACS'00*, LNCS 1770, pages 290–301. Springer, 2000.

[25] M. Jurdzinski, M. Paterson, and U. Zwick. A deterministic subexponential algorithm for solving parity games. *SIAM J. Comput.*, 38(4):1519–1532, 2008.

[26] O. Kupferman, M. Vardi, and P. Wolper. An Automata Theoretic Approach to Branching-Time Model Checking. *JACM*, 47(2):312–360, 2000.

[27] O. Kupferman, M. Vardi, and P. Wolper. Module Checking. *Information and Computation*, 164(2):322–344, 2001.

[28] O. Kupferman and M. Y. Vardi. Weak alternating automata and tree automata emptiness. In *STOC'98*, pages 224–233. ACM, 1998.

[29] F. Laroussinie and N. Markey. Augmenting atl with strategy contexts. *Information and Computation*, 245:98–123, 2015.

[30] F. Laroussinie, N. Markey, and G. Oreiby. On the expressiveness and complexity of atl. *LMCS*, 4(2):1–25, 2008.

[31] A. Lopes, F. Laroussinie, and N. Markey. ATL with Strategy Contexts: Expressiveness and Model Checking. In *FSTTCS'10*, LIPIcs 8, pages 120–132. Leibniz-Zentrum fuer Informatik, 2010.

[32] F. Mogavero, A. Murano, G. Perelli, and M. Vardi. Reasoning About Strategies: On the Model-Checking Problem. *TOCL*, 15(4):34:1–42, 2014.

[33] F. Mogavero, A. Murano, and M. Vardi. Reasoning About Strategies. In *FSTTCS'10*, LIPIcs 8, pages 133–144. Leibniz-Zentrum fuer Informatik, 2010.

[34] C. H. Papadimitriou. *Computational complexity*. John Wiley and Sons Ltd., 2003.

[35] J. Queille and J. Sifakis. Specification and Verification of Concurrent Programs in Cesar. In *SP'81*, LNCS 137, pages 337–351. Springer, 1981.

[36] S. Schewe. Solving parity games in big steps. In *FSTTCS'07*, LNCS 4855, pages 449–460. Springer, 2007.

[37] A. D. Stasio, A. Murano, V. Prignano, and L. Sorrentino. Solving parity games in scala. In *FACS'14*, LNCS 8997, pages 145–161. Springer, 2015.

[38] W. Thomas. Infinite games and verification. In *CAV'02*, pages 58–64. Springer, 2002.

[39] M. Yannakakis and K. Etessami. Recursive concurrent stochastic games. *Logical Methods in Computer Science*, 4, 2008.

[40] W. Zielonka. Infinite Games on Finitely Coloured Graphs with Applications to Automata on Infinite Trees. *TCS*, 200(1-2):135–183, 1998.

Graded Strategy Logic: Reasoning about Uniqueness of Nash Equilibria

Benjamin Aminof
Technische Universitat Wien, Austria
benj@forsyte.tuwien.ac.at

Vadim Malvone, Aniello Murano, Sasha Rubin
Università degli Studi di Napoli Federico II, Italy
{vadim.malvone, aniello.murano, sasha.rubin}@unina.it

ABSTRACT

Strategy Logic (SL) is a well established formalism for strategic reasoning in multi-agent systems. In a nutshell, SL is built over LTL and treats strategies as first-order objects that can be associated with agents by means of a binding operator. In this work we introduce Graded Strategy Logic (GRADED-SL), an extension of SL by graded quantifiers over tuples of strategy variables such as "there exist at least g different tuples $(x_1, ..., x_n)$ of strategies". We study the model-checking problem of GRADED-SL and prove that it is no harder than for SL, i.e., it is non-elementary in the quantifier rank.

We show that GRADED-SL allows one to count the number of different strategy profiles that are Nash equilibria (NE), or subgame-perfect equilibria (SPE). By analyzing the structure of the specific formulas involved, we conclude that the important problems of checking for the existence of a unique NE or SPE can both be solved in 2EXPTIME, which is not harder than merely checking for the existence of such equilibria.

Categories and Subject Descriptors

I.2.11 [**Artificial Intelligence**]: Distributed Artificial Intelligence —*Multiagent Systems*

General Terms

Theory, Verification

Keywords

Strategic logics; Graded modalities; Nash equilibrium

1. INTRODUCTION

Strategy Logic (SL) is a powerful formalism for reasoning about strategies in multi-agent systems [43,44]. Strategies tell an agent what to do — they are functions that prescribe an action based on the history. The fundamental idea in SL is to treat strategies as first-order object. A strategy x can be quantified existentially $\langle\langle x \rangle\rangle$ (read: there exists a strategy x) and universally $[\![x]\!]$ (read: for all strategies x). Furthermore, strategies are not intrinsically glued to specific agents: the *binding* operator (α, x) allows one to bind an agent α to the strategy x. SL strictly subsumes several other logics for strategic reasoning including the well known ATL and ATL* [3]. Being a very powerful logic, SL can directly express many solution concepts [9,19,32,35,43] among which that a strategy profile $\overline{x}$ is a Nash equilibrium, and thus also the existence of a Nash equilibrium (NE).

Nash equilibrium is one of the most important concepts in game theory, forming the basis of much of the recent fundamental work in multi-agent decision making. A challenging and important aspect is to establish whether a game admits a *unique* NE [2,20,48]. This problem impacts on the predictive power of NE since, in case there are multiple equilibria, the outcome of the game cannot be uniquely pinned down [21,49,57]. Unfortunately, uniqueness has mainly been established either for special cost functions [2], or for very restrictive game topologies [47]. More specifically, uniqueness of NE in game theory is proved with procedures that are separated from the ones that check for its existence [2]; these procedures require various transformations of the best response functions of individual contributors [28,29,53], and there is no general theory that can be applied to different application areas [2].

In this paper, we address and solve the problem of expressing the uniqueness of certain solution concepts (and NE in particular) in a principled and elegant way. We introduce an extension of SL called GRADED-SL and study its model-checking problem. More specifically, we extend SL by replacing the quantification $\langle\langle x \rangle\rangle$ and $[\![x]\!]$ over strategy variables with *graded quantification over tuples of strategy variables*: $\langle\langle x_1, \dots, x_n \rangle\rangle^{\geq g}$ (read $\langle\langle x_1, \dots, x_n \rangle\rangle^{\geq g}$ as "there exist at least g different tuples $(x_1, \dots, x_n)$ of strategies") and its dual $[\![x_1, \dots, x_n]\!]^{<g}$ ($g \in \mathbb{N}$). Here, two strategies are different if they disagree on some history. That is, we count strategies syntactically as is usual in graded extensions of modal and description logics [6,12,15,30,36]. The key for expressing uniqueness of NE is the combination of quantifying over tuples (instead of singleton variables), and adding counting (in the form of graded modalities).

We address the model-checking problem for GRADED-SL and prove that it has the same complexity as SL, i.e., it is non-elementary in the nesting depth of quantifiers. In particular, we show that model checking GRADED-SL formulas with a nesting depth $k > 0$ of blocks of quantifiers (a block of quantifiers is a maximally-consecutive sequence of quantifiers of the same type, i.e., either all existential, or all universal) is in $(k+1)$EXPTIME, and that for the special case where the formula starts with a block of quantifiers, it is in kEXPTIME. Since many natural formulas contain a very small number of

Appears in: *Proceedings of the 15th International Conference on Autonomous Agents and Multiagent Systems (AAMAS 2016), J. Thangarajah, K. Tuyls, C. Jonker, S. Marsella (eds.), May 9–13, 2016, Singapore.*

quantifiers, the complexity of the model-checking problem is not as bad as it seems. Specifically, several solution concepts can be expressed as SL formulas with a small number of quantifiers [9,19,32,35,43]. Since the existence of a NE, and the fact that there is at most one NE, can be expressed in GRADED-SL using simple formulas we are able to conclude that the problem of checking the uniqueness of a NE can be solved in 2EXPTIME. Previously, it was only known that existence of NE can be checked in 2EXPTIME [32,43], and indeed it is 2EXPTIME-complete [4,32,50]. Thus, GRADED-SL is the first logic that can solve the existence and uniqueness of NE (as well as many other solution concepts) in a uniform way.

SL has a few natural syntactic fragments, the most powerful of which is called Nested-Goal SL which can express NE [43]. Similarly, we define GRADED-SL *Nested-Goal*, a syntactic fragment of GRADED-SL. The Nested-Goal restriction encompasses formulas in a special prenex normal form with a particular nested temporal structure that restricts the application of both strategy quantifiers and agent bindings (see Section 2 for details). We show that the graded extension of Nested-Goal SL has the same model-checking complexity, i.e., non-elementary in the *alternation number* of the quantifiers appearing in the formula (the alternation number is, roughly speaking, the maximum number of existential/universal quantifier switches [43]). Since uniqueness of NE can be expressed in Nested-Goal GRADED-SL using alternation one, we get an alternative proof for checking the NE uniqueness in 2EXPTIME.

We exemplify our definition and our automata-theoretic algorithm for the model-checking problem with a large number of applications. In particular, we use it for reasoning about repeated one-shot games such as the *iterated prisoner's dilemma* (IPD) [51]. The prisoner's dilemma game is a popular metaphor for the problem of stable cooperation and has been widely used in several application domains [8]. In the classic definition, it consists of two players, each of them has an option to defect or collaborate. More involved is the IPD in which the process is repeated and one can model reactive strategies in continuous play. The IPD has become a standard model for the evolution of cooperative behaviour within a community of egoistic agents, frequently cited for implications in both sociology and biology (see [8]). Evaluating the existence of NE in an IPD and, even more, its uniqueness, is a very challenging and complicated question due to the rich set of strategies such a game can admit [8,16,17]. In particular, such infinite-duration games need to be supported by more complex solution concepts such as *subgame-perfect* equilibrium [27,41,55]. Thanks to GRADED-SL and the related model-checking result, we get that checking the uniqueness of a NE in an IPD can be solved in 2EXPTIME.

Related work. The importance of solution concepts, verifying a unique equilibrium, and the relationship with logics for strategic reasoning is discussed above. We now give some highlights from the long and active investigation of graded modalities in the formal verification community.

Graded modalities were first studied in modal logic [26] and then exported to the field of *knowledge representation* to allow quantitative bounds on the set of individuals satisfying a given property. Specifically, they were considered as *counting quantifiers* in first-order logics [31] and *number restrictions* in *description logics* [34]. *Graded μ-calculus*, in which immediate-successor accessible worlds are counted, was introduced to reason about graded modal logic with fixed-point operators [36]. Recently, the notion of graded modalities was extended to count the number of paths in the branching-time temporal logic formulas CTL and CTL* [7,10]. In the verification of reactive systems, we mention two orthogonal approaches: module checking for graded μ-calculus [6,25] and an extension of ATL by graded path modalities [24].

The work closest to ours is [40]: also motivated by counting NE, it introduces a graded extension of SL, called GSL. In contrast with our work, GSL has a very intricate way of counting strategies: it makes use of a semantic definition of strategies being equivalent, and counting in which equivalent strategies are counted as a single strategy. While this approach has been proved to be sound and general, it heavily complicates the model-checking problem. Indeed, only a very weak fragment of GSL has been solved in [40] by exploiting an *ad hoc* solution that does not seem to be easily scalable to (all of) GSL. Precisely, the fragment investigated there is the vanilla restriction of the graded version of one-goal SL [42]. There is a common belief that the one-goal fragment is not powerful enough to express the existence of a Nash Equilibrium in concurrent games. The smallest fragment that is know to be able to represent this is the so called Boolean-goal Strategy Logic, whose graded extension (in the GSL sense) has no known solution.[1]

Outline. The sequel of the paper is structured as follows. In Section 2 we introduce GRADED-SL and provide some preliminary related concepts. In Section 3 we address the model-checking problem for GRADED-SL and its fragments. We conclude with Section 4 in which we have a discussion and suggestions for future work.

2. GRADED STRATEGY LOGIC

In this section we introduce Graded Strategy Logic, which we call GRADED-SL for short.

2.1 Models

Sentences of GRADED-SL are interpreted over *concurrent game structures*, just as for ATL and SL [3,43].

DEFINITION 2.1. *A* concurrent game structure *(CGS) is a tuple* $\mathcal{G} \triangleq \langle \mathrm{AP}, \mathrm{Ag}, \mathrm{Ac}, \mathrm{St}, s_I, \mathsf{ap}, \mathsf{tr} \rangle$, *where* AP, Ag, Ac, *and* St *are the sets of* atomic propositions, agents, actions *and* states, *respectively,* $s_I \in \mathrm{St}$ *is the* initial state, *and* $\mathsf{ap} : \mathrm{St} \to 2^{\mathrm{AP}}$ *is the* labeling function *mapping each state to the set of atomic propositions true in that state. Let* $\mathrm{Dc} \triangleq \mathrm{Ag} \to \mathrm{Ac}$ *be the set of* decisions, i.e., *functions describing the choice of an action by every agent. Then,* $\mathsf{tr} : \mathrm{Dc} \to (\mathrm{St} \to \mathrm{St})$ *denotes the* transition function *mapping every decision* $\delta \in \mathrm{Dc}$ *to a function* $\mathsf{tr}(\delta) : \mathrm{St} \to \mathrm{St}$.

We will usually take the set Ag of agents to be $\{\alpha_1, \ldots, \alpha_n\}$.

A *path (from s)* is a finite or infinite non-empty sequence of states $s_1 s_2 \ldots$ such that $s = s_1$ and for every i there exists a decision δ with $\mathsf{tr}(\delta)(s_i) = s_{i+1}$. The set of paths starting

[1]In [33] it has been shown that, in the restricted case of turn-based structures it is possible to express the existence of Nash equilibria in m^{-}ATL* [45], a memory-full variant of ATL* (hence included in one-goal SL), but exponentially more succinct — and thus with a much more expensive model-checking algorithm. As also the authors in [33] state, it is not clear how to extend this result to the concurrent setting, even in the two player case.

with s is denoted $\text{Pth}(s)$. The set of finite paths from s, called the *histories (from s)*, is denoted $\text{Hst}(s)$. A *strategy (from s)* is a function $\sigma \in \text{Str}(s) \triangleq \text{Hst}(s) \to \text{Ac}$ that prescribes which action has to be performed given a certain history. We write Pth, Hst, Str for the set of all paths, histories, and strategies (no matter where they start).

We use the standard notion of equality between strategies, [38], i.e., $\sigma_1 = \sigma_2$ iff for all $\rho \in \text{Hst}$, $\sigma_1(\rho) = \sigma_2(\rho)$. This extends to equality between two n-tuples of strategies in the natural way, i.e., coordinate-wise.

2.2 Syntax

We describe the syntax as well as related basic concepts. GRADED-SL extends SL by replacing the classic singleton strategy quantifiers $\langle\langle x\rangle\rangle$ and $[[x]]$ with the graded (tupled) quantifiers $\langle\langle x_1,\ldots,x_n\rangle\rangle^{\geq g}$ and $[[x_1,\ldots,x_n]]^{<g}$, respectively, where each x_i belongs to a countable set of variables Vr and $g \in \mathbb{N}$ is called the *degree* of the quantifier. Intuitively, these are read as "there exist at least g tuples of strategies $(x_1,\ldots,x_n)$" and "all but less than g many tuples of strategies", respectively. The syntax (α, x) denotes a *binding* of the agent α to the strategy x. The syntax of GRADED-SL is:

DEFINITION 2.2. GRADED-SL formulas *are built inductively by means of the following grammar, where* $p \in \text{AP}$, $\alpha \in \text{Ag}$, $x, x_1, \ldots x_n \in \text{Vr}$ *such that* $x_i \neq x_j$ *for* $i \neq j$, *and* $g, n \in \mathbb{N}$:

$$\varphi := p \mid \neg\varphi \mid \varphi \vee \varphi \mid \mathsf{X}\,\varphi \mid \varphi\,\mathsf{U}\,\varphi \mid \langle\langle x_1,\ldots,x_n\rangle\rangle^{\geq g}\varphi \mid (\alpha, x)\varphi.$$

Notation. For the rest of the paper, whenever we write $\langle\langle x_1,\ldots,x_n\rangle\rangle^{\geq g}$ we also mean that $x_i \neq x_j$ for $i \neq j$.

Shorthands are derived as usual. Specifically, $\mathsf{true} \triangleq p \vee \neg p$, $\mathsf{false} \triangleq \neg\mathsf{true}$, $\mathsf{F}\,\varphi \triangleq \mathsf{true}\,\mathsf{U}\,\varphi$, and $\mathsf{G}\,\varphi \triangleq \neg\,\mathsf{F}\,\neg\varphi$. Moreover, the graded universal operator corresponds to the dual of the existential one, i.e., $[[x_1,\ldots,x_n]]^{<g}\varphi \triangleq \neg\langle\langle x_1,\ldots,x_n\rangle\rangle^{\geq g}\neg\varphi$. A *placeholder* refers to an agent or a variable. In order to define the semantics, we first define the concept of free placeholders in a formula. Intuitively, an agent or variable is free in φ if it does not have a strategy associated with it (either by quantification or binding) but one is required in order to ascertain if φ is true or not. The definition mimics that for SL [43]. It is included here both for completeness and because it is important for defining the model-checking procedure, in particular for the encoding of strategies as trees (Definition 3.2).

DEFINITION 2.3. *The set of* free agents *and* free variables *of a* GRADED-SL *formula* φ *is given by the function* free : GRADED-SL $\to 2^{\text{Ag}\cup\text{Vr}}$ *defined as follows:*

- $\mathsf{free}(p) \triangleq \emptyset$, *where* $p \in \text{AP}$;
- $\mathsf{free}(\neg\varphi) \triangleq \mathsf{free}(\varphi)$;
- $\mathsf{free}(\varphi_1 \vee \varphi_2) \triangleq \mathsf{free}(\varphi_1) \cup \mathsf{free}(\varphi_2)$;
- $\mathsf{free}(\mathsf{X}\,\varphi) \triangleq \text{Ag} \cup \mathsf{free}(\varphi)$;
- $\mathsf{free}(\varphi_1\,\mathsf{U}\,\varphi_2) \triangleq \text{Ag} \cup \mathsf{free}(\varphi_1) \cup \mathsf{free}(\varphi_2)$;
- $\mathsf{free}(\langle\langle x_1,\ldots,x_n\rangle\rangle^{\geq g}\varphi) \triangleq \mathsf{free}(\varphi) \setminus \{x_1,\ldots,x_n\}$;
- $\mathsf{free}((\alpha,x)\varphi) \triangleq \mathsf{free}(\varphi)$, *if* $\alpha \notin \mathsf{free}(\varphi)$, *where* $\alpha \in \text{Ag}$ *and* $x \in \text{Vr}$;
- $\mathsf{free}((\alpha,x)\varphi) \triangleq (\mathsf{free}(\varphi) \setminus \{\alpha\}) \cup \{x\}$, *if* $\alpha \in \mathsf{free}(\varphi)$, *where* $\alpha \in \text{Ag}$ *and* $x \in \text{Vr}$.

A formula φ *without free agents (resp., variables), i.e., with* $\mathsf{free}(\varphi) \cap \text{Ag} = \emptyset$ *(resp.,* $\mathsf{free}(\varphi) \cap \text{Vr} = \emptyset$*), is called* agent-closed *(resp.,* variable-closed*). If* φ *is both agent- and variable-closed, it is called a* sentence.

Another important concept that characterizes the syntax of GRADED-SL is the *alternation number* of quantifiers, i.e., the maximum number of quantifier switches $\langle\langle\cdot\rangle\rangle[[\cdot]]$, $[[\cdot]]\langle\langle\cdot\rangle\rangle$, $\langle\langle\cdot\rangle\rangle\neg\langle\langle\cdot\rangle\rangle$, or $[[\cdot]]\neg[[\cdot]]$ that binds a tuple of variables in a subformula that is not a sentence. We denote by $\mathsf{alt}(\varphi)$ the alternation number of a GRADED-SL formula φ. The *quantifier rank* of φ is the maximum nesting of quantifiers in φ, e.g., $\langle\langle x_1,\ldots,x_n\rangle\rangle^{\geq g}(\alpha_1,x_1)\ldots(\alpha_n,x_n)\bigwedge_{i=1}^{n}(\langle\langle \mathrm{y}\rangle\rangle(\alpha_i,\mathrm{y})\psi_i) \to \psi_i$ has quantifier rank 2 if each ψ_i is quantifier free. Moreover, a *quantifier-block of* φ is a maximally-consecutive sequence of quantifiers in φ of the same type (*i.e.*, either all existential, or all universal). The *quantifier-block rank of* φ is exactly like the quantifier rank except that a quantifier block of j quantifiers contributes 1 instead of j to the count.

SL has a few natural syntactic fragments, the most powerful of which is called Nested-Goal SL. Similarly, we define GRADED-SL *Nested-Goal* (abbreviated GRADED-SL[NG]), as a syntactic fragment of GRADED-SL. As in Nested-Goal SL, in GRADED-SL[NG] we require that bindings and quantifications appear in exhaustive blocks. I.e., whenever there is a quantification over a variable in a formula ψ it is part of a consecutive sequence of quantifiers that covers all of the free variables that appear in ψ, and whenever an agent is bound to a strategy then it is part of a consecutive sequence of bindings of all agents to strategies. Finally, formulas with free agents are not allowed. To formalize GRADED-SL[NG] we first introduce some notions. A *quantification prefix* over a finite set $\text{V} \subseteq \text{Vr}$ of variables is a sequence $\wp \in \{\langle\langle x_1,\ldots,x_n\rangle\rangle^{\geq g}, [[x_1,\ldots,x_n]]^{<g} : x_1,\ldots,x_n \in \text{V} \wedge g \in \mathbb{N}\}^*$ such that each $x \in \text{V}$ occurs exactly once in $\wp$. A *binding prefix* is a sequence $\flat \in \{(a,x) : \alpha \in \text{Ag} \wedge x \in \text{Vr}\}^{|\text{Ag}|}$ such that each $\alpha \in \text{Ag}$ occurs exactly once in $\flat$. We denote the set of binding prefixes by Bn, and the set of quantification prefixes over V by Qn(V).

DEFINITION 2.4. GRADED-SL[NG] *formulas are built inductively using the following grammar, with* $p \in \text{AP}$, $\wp \in \text{Qn}(\text{V})$ *(*$\text{V} \subseteq \text{Vr}$*), and* $\flat \in \text{Bn}$:

$$\varphi ::= p \mid \neg\varphi \mid \varphi \vee \varphi \mid \mathsf{X}\,\varphi \mid \varphi\,\mathsf{U}\,\varphi \mid \wp\varphi \mid \flat\varphi,$$

where in the rule $\wp\varphi$ *we require that* φ *is agent-closed and* $\wp \in \text{Qn}(\mathsf{free}(\varphi))$.

We conclude this subsection by introducing GRADED-SL[1G], another graded extension of fragment of SL, namely the one-goal sub-logic. As the name says, this fragment is obtained by restricting GRADED-SL[NG] to encompass formulas with just one nested goal. The importance of this fragment in SL stems from the fact that it strictly includes ATL* while maintaining the same complexity for both the model checking and the satisfiability problems, *i.e.* 2EXPTIME-COMPLETE [42,43]. However, it is commonly believed that Nash Equilibrium cannot be expressed in this fragment. The definition of GRADED-SL[1G] follows.

DEFINITION 2.5. GRADED-SL[1G] *formulas are built inductively using the following grammar, with* $p \in \text{AP}$, $\wp \in \text{Qn}(\text{V})$ *(*$\text{V} \subseteq \text{Vr}$*), and* $\flat \in \text{Bn}$:

$$\varphi ::= p \mid \neg\varphi \mid \varphi \vee \varphi \mid \mathsf{X}\,\varphi \mid \varphi\,\mathsf{U}\,\varphi \mid \wp\flat\varphi,$$

with $\wp$ *quantification prefix over* $\mathsf{free}(\flat\varphi)$.

2.3 Semantics

As for SL, the interpretation of a GRADED-SL formula requires a valuation of its free placeholders. This is done via *assignments (from s), i.e.,* functions $\chi \in \mathrm{Asg}(s) \triangleq (\mathrm{Vr} \cup \mathrm{Ag}) \to \mathrm{Str}(s)$ mapping variables/agents to strategies. We denote by $\chi[e \mapsto \sigma]$, with $e \in \mathrm{Vr} \cup \mathrm{Ag}$ and $\sigma \in \mathrm{Str}(s)$, the assignment that differs from χ only in the fact that e maps to σ. Extend this definition to tuples: for $\overline{e} = (e_1, \ldots, e_n)$ with $e_i \neq e_j$ for $i \neq j$, define $\chi[\overline{e} \mapsto \overline{\sigma}]$ to be the assignment that differs from χ only in the fact that e_i maps to σ_i (for each i).

Since assignments are total functions, each assignment from s determines a unique path from s, called a play:

DEFINITION 2.6. *For an assignment $\chi \in \mathrm{Asg}(s)$ the (χ, s)-play denotes the path $\pi \in \mathrm{Pth}(s)$ such that for all $i \in \mathbb{N}$, it holds that $\pi_{i+1} = \mathsf{tr}(\mathsf{dc})(\pi_i)$, where $\mathsf{dc}(\alpha) \triangleq \chi(\alpha)(\pi_{\leq i})$ for $\alpha \in \mathrm{Ag}$. The function $\mathsf{play} : \mathrm{Asg} \times \mathrm{St} \to \mathrm{Pth}$, with $\mathsf{dom}(\mathsf{play}) \triangleq \{(\chi, s) : \chi \in \mathrm{Asg}(s)\}$, maps (χ, s) to the (χ, s)-play $\mathsf{play}(\chi, s) \in \mathrm{Pth}(s)$.*

The notation $\pi_{\leq i}$ (resp. $\pi_{<i}$) denotes the prefix of the sequence π of length i (resp. $i-1$). Similarly, the notation π_i denotes the ith symbol of π. Thus, $\mathsf{play}(\chi, s)_i$ is the ith state on the play determined by χ from s.

The following definition of χ_i says how to interpret an assignment χ starting from a point i along the play, i.e., for each placeholder e, take the action the strategy $\chi(e)$ would do if it were given the prefix of the play up to i followed by the current history.

DEFINITION 2.7. *For $\chi \in \mathrm{Asg}(s)$ and $i \in \mathbb{N}$, writing $\rho \triangleq \mathsf{play}(\chi, s)_{\leq i}$ (the prefix of the play up to i) and $t \triangleq \mathsf{play}(\chi, s)_i$ (the last state of ρ) define $\chi_i \in \mathrm{Asg}(t)$ to be the assignment from t that maps $e \in \mathrm{Vr} \cup \mathrm{Ag}$ to the strategy that maps $h \in \mathrm{Hst}(t)$ to the action $\chi(e)(\rho_{<i} \cdot h)$.*

We now define the semantics of GRADED-SL. In particular, we define $\mathcal{G}, \chi, s \models \varphi$ and say that φ *holds at s in $\mathcal{G}$ under χ*.

DEFINITION 2.8. *Fix a CGS $\mathcal{G}$. For all states $s \in \mathrm{St}$ and assignments $\chi \in \mathrm{Asg}(s)$, the relation $\mathcal{G}, \chi, s \models \varphi$ is defined inductively on the structure of φ:*

- $\mathcal{G}, \chi, s \models p$ *iff* $p \in \mathsf{ap}(s)$;
- $\mathcal{G}, \chi, s \models \neg\varphi$ *iff* $\mathcal{G}, \chi, s \not\models \varphi$;
- $\mathcal{G}, \chi, s \models \varphi_1 \vee \varphi_2$ *iff* $\mathcal{G}, \chi, s \models \varphi_1$ *or* $\mathcal{G}, \chi, s \models \varphi_2$;
- $\mathcal{G}, \chi, s \models \mathsf{X}\varphi$ *iff* $\mathcal{G}, \chi_1, \mathsf{play}(\chi, s)_1 \models \varphi$;
- $\mathcal{G}, \chi, s \models \varphi_1 \mathsf{U} \varphi_2$ *iff there is an index $i \in \mathbb{N}$ such that* $\mathcal{G}, \chi_i, \mathsf{play}(\chi, s)_i \models \varphi_2$ *and, for all indexes $j \in \mathbb{N}$ with $j < i$, it holds that* $\mathcal{G}, \chi_j, \mathsf{play}(\chi, s)_j \models \varphi_1$;
- $\mathcal{G}, \chi, s \models (\alpha, x)\varphi$ *iff* $\mathcal{G}, \chi[\alpha \mapsto \chi(x)], s \models \varphi$;
- $\mathcal{G}, \chi, s \models \langle\langle x_1, \ldots, x_n \rangle\rangle^{\geq g} \varphi$ *iff there exist g many tuples $\overline{\sigma_1}, \ldots, \overline{\sigma_g}$ of strategies such that:*
  - $\overline{\sigma_i} \neq \overline{\sigma_j}$ *for* $i \neq j$, *and*
  - $\mathcal{G}, \chi[\overline{x} \mapsto \overline{\sigma_i}], s \models \varphi$ *for* $1 \leq i \leq g$.

Intuitively, the existential quantifier $\langle\langle x_1, \ldots, x_n \rangle\rangle^{\geq g} \varphi$ allows us to count the number of distinct tuples of strategies that satisfy φ.

As usual, if χ and χ' agree on $\mathsf{free}(\varphi)$, then $\mathcal{G}, \chi, s \models \varphi$ if and only if $\mathcal{G}, \chi', s \models \varphi$, i.e., the truth of φ does not depend on the values the assignment takes on placeholders that are not free. Thus, for a sentence φ, we write $\mathcal{G} \models \varphi$ to mean that $\mathcal{G}, \chi, s_I \models \varphi$ for some (equivalently, for all) assignments χ, and where s_I is the initial state of $\mathcal{G}$.

Comparison with other logics. In the following we give the main intuitions relating GRADED-SL with SL and a *naive* fragment of GRADED-SL in which quantifiers are over single variables (and not tuple of variables).

GRADED-SL extends SL by replacing universal and existential strategy quantifiers $\langle\langle x \rangle\rangle$ and $[[x]]$ with their graded versions over tuples of variables $\langle\langle x_1, \ldots, x_n \rangle\rangle^{\geq g}$ and $[[x_1, \ldots, x_n]]^{<g}$. Grades allow one to count, which is not possible, a priori, in SL. On the other hand, every formula of SL has an equivalent formula of GRADED-SL: formed by replacing every quantifier $\langle\langle x \rangle\rangle$ with $\langle\langle x \rangle\rangle^{\geq 1}$.

An important power of GRADED-SL is that it can quantify over tuples of strategy variables. Consider the formula $\varphi = \langle\langle x, y \rangle\rangle^{\geq 2}(a, x)(b, y)\psi$ in GRADED-SL that represents the property in which there exist two tuples of strategies that satisfy ψ, and compare it to the following attempt at expressing φ only quantifying over single strategies: $\varphi' \triangleq \langle\langle x \rangle\rangle^{\geq 2} \langle\langle y \rangle\rangle^{\geq 2}(a, x)(b, y)\psi$. Observe that φ' says that there are two different strategies σ_1 and σ_2 for agent α_1, and for each σ_i there are two different strategies δ_1^i and δ_2^i for the agent α_2 that satisfy ψ. Thus, there are four tuples of strategies that satisfy ψ, i.e., $\{\sigma_1, \delta_1^1\}$, $\{\sigma_1, \delta_2^1\}$, $\{\sigma_2, \delta_1^2\}$, $\{\sigma_2, \delta_2^2\}$. Other attempts (such as $\langle\langle x \rangle\rangle^{\geq 2} \langle\langle y \rangle\rangle^{\geq 1}(a, x)(b, y)\psi$), also fail to capture φ as they restrict one of the agents to a single strategy. This demonstrates the inadequacy of quantifying over single strategies for counting solution concepts.

2.4 Games with temporal objectives

In game theory, players have objectives that are summarised in a payoff function they receive depending on the resulting play. In order to specify such payoffs we follow a formalisation from [35] called *objective* LTL. This will allow us to model the Prisoner's Dilemma (PD), probably the most famous game in game-theory, as well as an iterated version (IPD). We then discuss appropriate solution concepts, and show how to express these in GRADED-SL.

Let $\mathcal{G}$ be a CGS with n agents. Let $m \in \mathbb{N}$ and fix, for each agent $\alpha_i \in \mathrm{Ag}$, an *objective* tuple $S_i \triangleq \langle \mathsf{f}_i, \varphi_i^1, \ldots, \varphi_i^m \rangle$, where $\mathsf{f}_i : \{0, 1\}^m \to \mathbb{N}$, and each φ_i^j is an LTL formula over AP. If π is a play, then agent α_i receives payoff $\mathsf{f}_i(\overline{h}) \in \mathbb{N}$ where the j'th bit $\overline{h}_j$ of $\overline{h}$ is 1 if and only if $\pi \models \varphi_i^j$. For instance, f may count the number of formulas that are true.

Prisoner's Dilemma – One shot and Iterated

Two people have been arrested for robbing a bank and placed in separate isolation cells. Each has two possible choices, remaining silent or confessing. If a robber confesses and the other remains silent, the former is released and the latter stays in prison for a long time. If both confess they get two convictions, but they will get early parole. If both remain silent, they get a lighter sentence (e.g., on firearms possession charges). The dilemma faced by the prisoners is that, whatever the choice of the other prisoner, each is better off confessing than remaining silent. But the result obtained when both confess is worse than if they both remain silent.

We describe this (one-shot) scenario with the CGS in Figure 1 and, for agent α_i, the objective $S_i \triangleq \langle \mathsf{f}_i, \varphi_i^1, \varphi_i^2, \varphi_i^3, \varphi_i^4 \rangle$

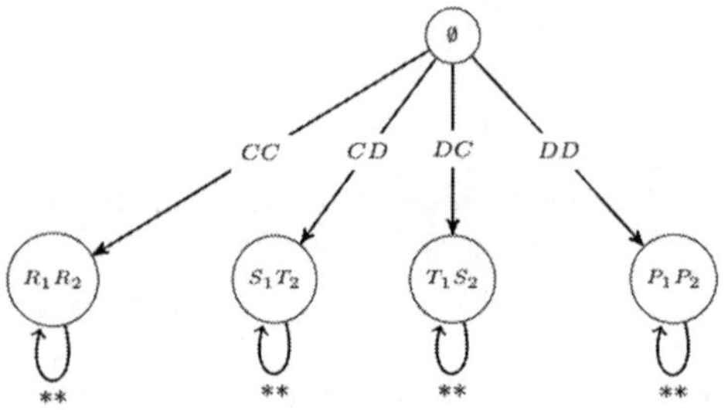

Figure 1: Prisoner's dilemma.

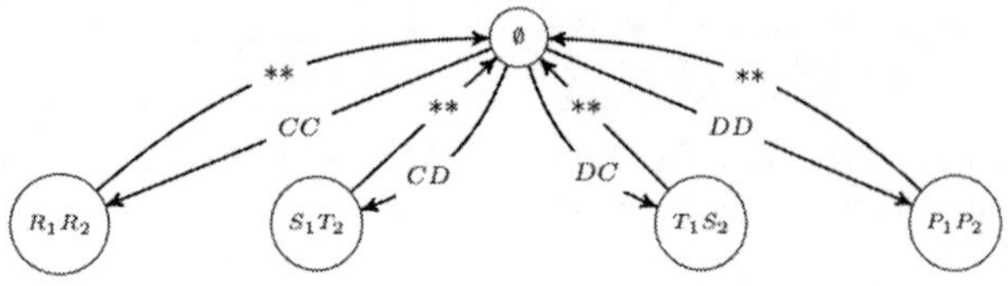

Figure 2: Iterated Prisoner's dilemma.

where $\varphi_i^1 \triangleq \mathsf{X}\,\mathbf{S}_i$, $\varphi_i^2 \triangleq \mathsf{X}\,\mathbf{P}_i$, $\varphi_i^3 \triangleq \mathsf{X}\,\mathbf{R}_i$, and $\varphi_i^4 \triangleq \mathsf{X}\,\mathbf{T}_i$ and f_i returns the value of its input vector interpreted as a binary number, *e.g.*, $\mathsf{f}_i(0100) = 4$.

In words, we have two agents α_1 and α_2. Each agent has two actions: cooperate (C) and defect (D), corresponding, respectively, to the options of remaining silent or confessing. For each possible pair of moves, the game goes in a state whose atomic propositions represent the payoffs: $\mathbf{R}_i$ represents the *reward* payoff that α_i receives if both cooperate; $\mathbf{P}_i$ is the *punishment* that α_i receives if both defect; $\mathbf{T}_i$ is the *temptation* that α_i receives as a sole defector, and $\mathbf{S}_i$ is the *sucker* payoff that α_i receives as a sole cooperator. The payoffs satisfy the following chain of inequalities: $\mathbf{T}_i > \mathbf{R}_i > \mathbf{P}_i > \mathbf{S}_i$.

The Iterated Prisoner's Dilemma (IPD) is used to model a series of interactions. This is like PD except that after the first choice, both agents have another choice and so on. This is modeled in Figure 2. The main difference between the one-shot and iterated PD is that in the latter the agents' actions (may) depend on the past behaviour. Convenient payoff functions for the IPD are the mean-average and discounted-payoff [11]. Such quantitative payoffs can be replaced, in a first approximation, by LTL payoffs such as "maximise the largest payoff I receive infinitely often". This is formalised, for agent α_i, by the objective $S_i \triangleq \langle \mathsf{f}_i, \varphi_i^1, \varphi_i^2, \varphi_i^3, \varphi_i^4 \rangle$ where $\varphi_i^1 \triangleq \mathsf{G}\,\mathsf{F}\,\mathbf{S}_i$, $\varphi_i^2 \triangleq \mathsf{G}\,\mathsf{F}\,\mathbf{P}_i$, $\varphi_i^3 \triangleq \mathsf{G}\,\mathsf{F}\,\mathbf{R}_i$, and $\varphi_i^4 \triangleq \mathsf{G}\,\mathsf{F}\,\mathbf{T}_i$, and f_i is as in the one-shot PD.

Solution Concepts. Solution concepts are criteria by which one captures what rational agents would do. This is especially relevant in case each agent has its own objective. The central solution concept in game theory is the Nash Equilibrium.

A tuple of strategies, one for each player, is called a *strategy profile.* A strategy profile is a *Nash equilibrium (NE)* if no agent can increase his payoff by unilaterally choosing a different strategy. A game may have zero, one, or many NE.

Consider first a CGS $\mathcal{G}$ with n agents, where the objective of the agent $\alpha_i \in \mathrm{Ag}$ contains a single LTL formula φ_i (with a larger payoff if it holds than if it doesn't). It is not hard to see that the following formula of SL expresses that $\overline{x} \triangleq (x_1 \ldots x_n)$ is a Nash Equilibrium:

$$\psi_{NE}^1(\overline{x}) \triangleq (\alpha_1, x_1) \ldots (\alpha_n, x_n) \bigwedge_{i=1}^{n} (\langle\!\langle \mathsf{y} \rangle\!\rangle (\alpha_i, \mathsf{y}) \varphi_i) \rightarrow \varphi_i$$

An alternative (which we will later use to obtain a formula in the fragment GRADED-SL[NG] that expresses the existence of a unique NE) is the following:

$$\phi_{NE}^1(\overline{x}) \triangleq [\![\mathsf{y}_1]\!] \ldots [\![\mathsf{y}_n]\!] \bigwedge_{i=1}^{n} (\flat_i \varphi_i) \rightarrow \flat \varphi_i$$

where $\flat = (\alpha_1, x_1) \ldots (\alpha_n, x_n)$, and $\flat_i = (\alpha_1, x_1) \ldots (\alpha_{i-1}, \mathsf{x}_{i-1})(\alpha_i, \mathsf{y}_i)(\alpha_{i+1}, \mathsf{x}_{i+1}) \ldots (\alpha_n, x_n)$.

Consider now the general case, where each agent α_i has an objective tuple $S_i \triangleq \langle \mathsf{f}_i, \varphi_i^1, \ldots, \varphi_i^m \rangle$. Given a vector $\overline{h} \in \{0,1\}^m$, let $gd_i(\overline{h}) \triangleq \{\overline{t} \in \{0,1\}^m \mid \mathsf{f}_i(\overline{t}) \geq \mathsf{f}_i(\overline{h})\}$ be the set of vectors $\overline{t}$ for which the payoff for agent α_i is not worse than for $\overline{h}$. Also, let $\eta_i^{\overline{h}}$ be the formula obtained by taking a conjunction of the formulas $\varphi_i^1, \ldots, \varphi_i^m$ or their negations according to $\overline{h}$, i.e., by taking φ_a^j if the j'th bit in $\overline{h}$ is 1, and otherwise taking $\neg\varphi_a^j$. Formally, $\eta_i^{\overline{h}} \triangleq \wedge_{j \in \{1 \leq j \leq m \mid h_j = 1\}} \varphi_i^j \wedge \wedge_{j \in \{1 \leq j \leq m \mid h_j = 0\}} \neg\varphi_i^j$. Observe that the following formula says that $\overline{x} \triangleq (x_1 \ldots x_n)$ is a Nash Equilibrium:

$$\psi_{NE}(\overline{x}) \triangleq (\alpha_1, x_1) \ldots (\alpha_n, x_n) \bigwedge_{i=1}^{n} \bigwedge_{\overline{h} \in \{0,1\}^m} (\langle\!\langle \mathsf{y} \rangle\!\rangle (\alpha_i, \mathsf{y}) \eta_i^{\overline{h}}) \rightarrow \bigvee_{\overline{t} \in gd_i(\overline{h})} \eta_i^{\overline{t}}$$

Alike, one can modify $\phi_{NE}^1(\overline{x})$ to obtain a similar formula $\phi_{NE}(\overline{x})$ expressing that $\overline{x} \triangleq (x_1 \ldots x_n)$ is a Nash Equilibrium:

$$\phi_{NE}(\overline{x}) \triangleq [\![\mathsf{y}_1]\!] \ldots [\![\mathsf{y}_n]\!] \bigwedge_{i=1}^{n} \bigwedge_{\overline{h} \in \{0,1\}^m} (\flat_i \eta_i^{\overline{h}}) \rightarrow \bigvee_{\overline{t} \in gd_i(\overline{h})} \flat \eta_i^{\overline{t}}$$

Going back to the PD example, due to the simplicity of the payoff functions, the formula ψ_{NE} collapses to become:

$$\psi_{PD}(\overline{x}) \triangleq (\alpha_1, x_1) \ldots (\alpha_n, x_n) \bigwedge_{i=1}^{2} \bigwedge_{j=1}^{4} (\langle\!\langle y \rangle\!\rangle (\alpha_i, y) \varphi_i^j) \Rightarrow (\bigvee_{r \geq j} \varphi_i^r)$$

As it turns out (again due to the simplicity of the payoff functions), the formula above is also correct for the IPD.

It has been argued (in [35,55]) that NE may be implausible when used for sequential games (of which iterated one shot games are central examples), and that a more robust notion is subgame-perfect equilibrium [52]. Given a game $\mathcal{G}$, a strategy profile is a *subgame-perfect equilibrium (SPE)* if for every possible history of the game, the strategies are an NE. The following formula expresses that $\overline{x} \triangleq (\alpha_1, x_1) \ldots (\alpha_n, x_n)$ is an SPE:

$$\phi_{SPE}(\overline{x}) \triangleq [\![z_1, \ldots, z_n]\!] (\alpha_1, z_1) \ldots (\alpha_n, z_n)\, \mathsf{G}\, \phi_{NE}(\overline{x})$$

Using graded modalities, we can thus express the uniqueness of a NE using the following GRADED-SL formula:

$$\langle\!\langle x_1, \ldots, x_n \rangle\!\rangle^{\geq 1} \psi_{NE}(\overline{x}) \wedge \neg \langle\!\langle x_1, \ldots, x_n \rangle\!\rangle^{\geq 2} \psi_{NE}(\overline{x})$$

By replacing ψ_{NE} with ϕ_{NE} (resp. by ϕ_{SPE}) in the formula above, we can express the uniqueness of a NE (resp. SPE) in GRADED-SL[NG].

3. THE MODEL-CHECKING PROCEDURE

In this section we study the model-checking problem for GRADED-SL and show that it is decidable with a time-complexity that is non-elementary (i.e., not bounded by any fixed tower of exponentials). However, it is elementary if the number of blocks of quantifiers is fixed. For the algorithmic procedures, we follow an *automata-theoretic approach* [37], reducing the decision problem for the logic to the emptiness problem of an automaton. The procedure we propose here extends that used for SL in [43]. The only case that is different is the new graded quantifier over tuples of strategies.

We start with the central notions of automata theory, and then show how to convert a GRADED-SL sentence φ into an automaton that accepts exactly the (tree encodings) of the concurrent game structures that satisfy φ. This is used to prove the main result about GRADED-SL model checking.

3.1 Automata Theory

A Σ-*labeled* Υ-*tree* T is a pair $\langle T, V\rangle$ where $T \subseteq \Upsilon^+$ is prefix-closed (i.e., if $t \in T$ and $s \in \Upsilon^+$ is a prefix of t then also $s \in T$), and $V : T \to \Sigma$ is a labeling function. Note that every word $w \in \Upsilon^+ \cup \Upsilon^\omega$ with the property that every prefix of w is in T, can be thought of as a path in T. Infinite paths are called *branches.*

Nondeterministic tree automata (NTA) are a generalization to infinite trees of the classical automata on words [54]. *Alternating tree automata* (ATA) are a further generalization of nondeterministic tree automata [23]. Intuitively, on visiting a node of the input tree, while an NTA sends exactly one copy of itself to each of the successors of the node, an ATA can send several copies to the same successor. We use the parity acceptance condition [37].

For a set X, let $\mathtt{B}^+(X)$ be the set of positive Boolean formulas over X, including the constants **true** and **false**. A set $Y \subseteq X$ satisfies a formula $\theta \in \mathtt{B}^+(X)$, written $Y \models \theta$, if assigning **true** to elements in Y and **false** to elements in $X \setminus Y$ makes θ true.

DEFINITION 3.1. *An Alternating Parity Tree-Automaton* (APT*) is a tuple* $\mathcal{A} \triangleq \langle \Sigma, \Delta, \mathrm{Q}, \delta, q_0, \aleph\rangle$, *where* Σ *is the* input alphabet, Δ *is a set of* directions, Q *is a finite set of* states, $q_0 \in \mathrm{Q}$ *is an* initial state, $\delta : \mathrm{Q} \times \Sigma \to \mathtt{B}^+(\Delta \times \mathrm{Q})$ *is an* alternating transition function, *and* $\aleph$, *an* acceptance condition, *is of the form* $(\mathrm{F}_1, \ldots, \mathrm{F}_k) \in (2^{\mathrm{Q}})^+$ *where* $\mathrm{F}_1 \subseteq \mathrm{F}_2 \ldots \subseteq \mathrm{F}_k = \mathrm{Q}$.

The set $\Delta \times \mathrm{Q}$ is called the set of *moves*. An NTA is an ATA in which each conjunction in the transition function δ has exactly one move (d, q) associated with each direction d.

An *input tree* for an APT is a Σ-labeled Δ-tree $\mathsf{T} = \langle \mathrm{T}, \mathsf{v}\rangle$. A *run* of an APT on an input tree $\mathsf{T} = \langle \mathrm{T}, \mathsf{v}\rangle$ is a $(\Delta \times \mathrm{Q})$-tree R such that, for all nodes $x \in \mathrm{R}$, where $x = (d_1, q_1) \ldots (d_n, q_n)$ (for some $n \in \mathbb{N}$), it holds that *(i)* $y \triangleq (d_1, \ldots, d_n) \in \mathrm{T}$ and *(ii)* there is a set of moves $\mathrm{S} \subseteq \Delta \times \mathrm{Q}$ with $\mathrm{S} \models \delta(q_n, \mathsf{v}(y))$ such that $x \cdot (d, q) \in \mathrm{R}$ for all $(d, q) \in \mathrm{S}$.

The acceptance condition allows us to say when a run is successful. Let R be a run of an APT $\mathcal{A}$ on an input tree T and $u \in (\Delta \times \mathrm{Q})^\omega$ one of its branches. Let $\mathsf{inf}(u) \subseteq \mathrm{Q}$ denote the set of states that occur in infinitely many moves of u. Say that *u satisfies the parity acceptance condition* $\aleph = (\mathrm{F}_1, \ldots, \mathrm{F}_k)$ if the least index $i \in [1, k]$ for which $\mathsf{inf}(u) \cap \mathrm{F}_i \neq \emptyset$ is even. An APT *accepts* an input tree T iff there exists a run R of $\mathcal{A}$ on T such that all its branches satisfy the acceptance condition $\aleph$. The *language* $\mathrm{L}(\mathcal{A})$ of the APT $\mathcal{A}$ is the set of trees T accepted by $\mathcal{A}$. Two automata are *equivalent* if they have the same language. The *emptiness problem* for alternating parity tree-automata is to decide, given $\mathcal{A}$, whether $\mathrm{L}(\mathcal{A}) = \emptyset$. The *universality problem* is to decide whether $\mathcal{A}$ accepts all trees.

3.2 From Logic to Automata

Following an automata-theoretic approach, we reduce the model-checking problem of GRADED-SL to the emptiness problem for alternating parity tree automata [43]. The main step is to translate every GRADED-SL formula φ (i.e., φ may have free placeholders), concurrent-game structure $\mathcal{G}$, and state s, into an APT that accepts a tree if and only if the tree encodes an assignment χ such that $\mathcal{G}, \chi, s \models \varphi$.

We first describe the encoding, following [43]. Informally, the CGS $\mathcal{G}$ is encoded by its "tree-unwinding starting from s" whose nodes represent histories, i.e., the St-labeled St-tree $\mathsf{T} \triangleq \langle \mathrm{Hst}(s), \mathsf{u}\rangle$ such that $\mathsf{u}(h)$ is the last symbol of h. Then, every strategy $\chi(e)$ with $e \in \mathsf{free}(\varphi)$ is encoded as an Ac-labelled tree over the unwinding. The unwinding and these strategies $\chi(e)$ are viewed as a single $(\mathrm{VAL} \times \mathrm{St})$-labeled tree where $\mathrm{VAL} \triangleq \mathsf{free}(\varphi) \to \mathrm{Ac}$.

DEFINITION 3.2. *The* encoding of χ (w.r.t. $\varphi, \mathcal{G}, s$) *is the* $(\mathrm{VAL} \times \mathrm{St})$*-labeled* St*-tree* $\mathsf{T} \triangleq \langle \mathrm{T}, \mathsf{u}\rangle$ *such that* T *is the set of histories h of $\mathcal{G}$ starting with s and* $\mathsf{u}(h) \triangleq (\mathsf{f}, q)$ *where q is the last symbol in h and* $\mathsf{f} : \mathsf{free}(\varphi) \to \mathrm{Ac}$ *is defined by* $\mathsf{f}(e) \triangleq \chi(e)(h)$ *for all* $e \in \mathsf{free}(\varphi)$.[2]

LEMMA 3.1. *For every* GRADED-SL *formula* φ, CGS $\mathcal{G}$, *and state* $s \in \mathrm{St}$, *there exists an* APT $\mathcal{A}_\varphi$ *such that for all assignments* χ, *if* T *is the encoding of* χ *(w.r.t.* $\varphi, \mathcal{G}, s$*), then* $\mathcal{G}, \chi, s \models \varphi$ *iff* $\mathsf{T} \in \mathrm{L}(\mathcal{A}_\varphi)$.

PROOF. As in [43] we induct on the structure of the formula φ to construct the corresponding automaton $\mathcal{A}_\varphi$. The Boolean operations are easily dealt with using the fact that disjunction corresponds to non-determinism, and negation corresponds to dualising the automaton. Note (†) that thus also conjunction is dealt with due to De Morgan's laws. The temporal operators are dealt with by following the unique play (determined by the given assignment) and verifying the required subformulas, e.g., for $\mathsf{X}\,\psi$ the automaton, after taking one step along the play, launches a copy of the automaton for ψ. All of these operations incur a linear blowup in the size of the automaton. The only case that differs from [43] is the quantification, i.e., we need to handle the case that $\varphi = \langle\!\langle x_1, \ldots, x_n\rangle\!\rangle^{\geq g}\psi$. Recall that $\mathcal{G}, \chi, s \models \langle\!\langle x_1, \ldots, x_n\rangle\!\rangle^{\geq g}\psi$ iff there exists g many tuples $\overline{\sigma_1}, \ldots, \overline{\sigma_g}$ of strategies such that: $\overline{\sigma_a} \neq \overline{\sigma_b}$ for $a \neq b$, and $\mathcal{G}, \chi[\overline{x} \mapsto \overline{\sigma_i}], s \models \psi$ for $1 \leq i \leq g$. We show how to build an NPT for φ that mimics this definition: it will be a projection of an APT $\mathcal{D}_\psi$, which itself is the intersection of two automata, one checking that each of the g tuples of strategies satisfies ψ, and the other checking that each pair of the g tuples of strategies is distinct.

In more detail, introduce a set of fresh variables $X \triangleq \{x_i^j \in \mathrm{Vr} : i \leq n, j \leq g\}$, and consider the formulas ψ^j (for $j \leq g$) formed from ψ by renaming x_i (for $i \leq n$) to x_i^j. Define $\psi' \triangleq \wedge_{j \leq g}\psi^j$. Note that, by induction, each ψ^j has a corresponding APT, and thus, using the conjunction-case

[2]In case $\mathsf{free}(\varphi) = \emptyset$, then f is the (unique) empty function. In this case, the encoding of every χ may be viewed as the tree-unwinding from s.

(†) above, there is an APT $\mathcal{B}$ for ψ'. Note that the input alphabet for $\mathcal{B}$ is $(\mathsf{free}(\psi') \to \mathrm{Ac}) \times \mathrm{St}$ and that $X \subseteq \mathsf{free}(\psi')$.

On the other hand, let $\mathcal{C}$ be an APT with input alphabet $(\mathsf{free}(\psi') \to \mathrm{Ac}) \times \mathrm{St}$ that accepts a tree $\mathsf{T} = \langle \mathrm{T}, \mathsf{v} \rangle$ if and only if for every $a \neq b \leq g$ there exists $i \leq n$ and $h \in \mathrm{T}$ such that $\mathsf{v}(h) = (f, q)$ and $f(x_i^a) \neq f(x_i^b)$.

Form the APT $\mathcal{D}_\psi$ for the intersection of $\mathcal{B}$ and $\mathcal{C}$.

Now, using the classic transformation [46], we remove alternation from the APT $\mathcal{D}_\psi$ to get an equivalent NPT $\mathcal{N}$ (note that this step costs an exponential). Finally, use the fact that NPTs are closed under projection (with no blowup) to get an NPT for the language $proj_X(L(\mathcal{N}))$ of trees that encode assignments χ satisfying φ.

For completeness we recall this last step. If L is a language of Σ-labeled trees with $\Sigma \triangleq \mathrm{A} \to \mathrm{B}$, and $X \subset \mathrm{A}$, then the X-*projection of* L, written $proj_X(L)$, is the language of Σ'-labeled trees with $\Sigma' \triangleq \mathrm{A} \setminus \mathrm{X} \to \mathrm{B}$ such that $\mathsf{T} \triangleq \langle \mathrm{T}, \mathsf{v} \rangle \in proj_X(L)$ if and only if there exists an X-labeled tree $\langle \mathrm{T}, \mathsf{w} \rangle$ such that the language L contains the tree $\langle \mathrm{T}, \mathsf{u} \rangle$ where $\mathsf{u} : \mathrm{T} \to (\mathrm{A} \to \mathrm{B})$ maps $t \in \mathrm{T}$ to $\mathsf{v}(t) \cup \mathsf{w}(t)$. Now, if $\mathcal{N}$ is an NPT with input alphabet $\Sigma \triangleq \mathrm{A} \to \mathrm{B}$, and if $\mathrm{X} \subset \mathrm{A}$, then there is an NPT with input alphabet $\Sigma' \triangleq \mathrm{A} \setminus \mathrm{X} \to \mathrm{B}$ with language $proj_X(L(\mathcal{N}))$.

The proof that the construction is correct is immediate. □

We make some remarks about the proof. First, all the cases in the induction incur a linear blowup except for the quantification case (recall that the translation from an APT to an NPT results in an exponentially larger automaton [37]). Thus, the size of the APT for φ is non-elementary in the quantifier-rank of φ. However, we can say a little more. Note that a block of k identical quantifiers only costs, in the worst case, a single exponential (and not k many exponentials) because we can extend the proof above to deal with a block of quantifiers at once. Thus, we get that the size of the APT for φ is non-elementary in the quantifier-block rank of φ.

Here is the main decidability result.

THEOREM 3.1. *The model-checking problem for* GRADED-SL *is* PTIME-COMPLETE *w.r.t. the size of the model and* $(k+1)$EXPTIME *if* $k \geq 1$ *is the quantifier-block rank of* φ. *Moreover, if* φ *is the form* $\wp\psi$, *where* $\wp$ *is a quantifier-block, and* ψ *is of quantifier-block rank* $k-1$, *then the complexity is* kEXPTIME.

PROOF. The lower-bound w.r.t the size of the model already holds for SL [43]. For the upper bound, use Lemma 3.1 to transform the CGS and φ into an APT and test its emptiness. The complexity of checking emptiness (or indeed, universality) of an APT is in EXPTIME [37]. As discussed after the proof of the Lemma, the size of the APT is a tower of exponentials whose height is the quantifier-block rank of φ. This gives the $(k+1)$EXPTIME upper bound.

Moreover, suppose that $\varphi = \wp\psi$ where $\wp$ consists of, say, n existential quantifiers (resp. universal quantifiers). The quantifier-block rank of ψ is $k-1$. Moreover, in the proof of Lemma 3.1, the APT $\mathcal{D}_\psi$, whose size is non-elementary in $k-1$, has the property that it is non-empty (resp. universal) if and only if the CGS satisfies $\wp\psi$. Conclude that model checking $\wp\psi$ can be done in kEXPTIME. □

THEOREM 3.2. *The model-checking problem for* GRADED-SL[NG] *is* PTIME-COMPLETE *w.r.t. the size of the model and* $(k+1)$-EXPTIME *when restricted to formulas of maximum alternation number* k.

PROOF. The lower bound already holds for SL[NG] [43], and the upper bound is obtained by following the same reasoning for SL[NG] of the singleton existential quantifier [43] but using the automaton construction as in Theorem 3.1. □

Directly from the statements reported above, we get the following results:

THEOREM 3.3. *Checking the uniqueness of NE, and checking the uniqueness of SPE, can be done in* 2EXPTIME.

PROOF. For NE: by Section 2.4, we need to check that $\langle\langle x_1, \ldots, x_n \rangle\rangle^{\geq 1} \psi_{NE}(\overline{x})$ holds but $\langle\langle x_1, \ldots, x_n \rangle\rangle^{\geq 2} \psi_{NE}(\overline{x})$ does not; by the second part of Theorem 3.1, each of these two model-checking problems can be decided in 2EXPTIME.

For SPE: apply Theorem 3.2 and use the fact that the formula for SPE in Section 2.4 is in GRADED-SL Nested-Goal and has alternation number 1. □

We conclude this section with the complexity of the model checking problem for GRADED-SL[1G]. Also in this case one can derive the lower bound from the one holding for the corresponding sub-logic in SL (SL[1G]) and the upper bound by using the same algorithm for SL[1G] but plugging a (yet no more complex) different automata construction for the new existential quantifier modality. Indeed the model checking problem for GRADED-SL[1G] is 2EXPTIME-COMPLETE. It is worth recalling that SL[1G] strictly subsumes ATL* [43]. It is quite immediate to see that this also holds in the graded setting (note that ATL* already allows quantifying over tuples of agents' (bound) strategies). As the model checking for ATL* is already 2EXPTIME-HARD, we get that also for the graded extension for this logic, which we name GATL*, the model checking problem is 2EXPTIME-COMPLETE. The model checking results for both GATL* and GRADED-SL[1G] are reported in the following theorem.

THEOREM 3.4. *The model-checking problem for* GATL* *and* GRADED-SL[1G] *is* PTIME-COMPLETE w.r.t. *the size of the model and* 2-EXPTIME-COMPLETE *in the size of formula.*

4. CONCLUSION

The Nash equilibrium is the foundational solution concept in game theory. The last twenty years have witnessed the introduction of many logical formalisms for modeling and reasoning about solution concepts, and NE in particular [9,14, 19,32,39,43,44]. These formalisms are useful for addressing qualitative questions such as *"does the game admit a Nash equilibrium?"*. Among others, Strategy Logic (SL) has come to the fore as a general formalism that can express and solve this question, for LTL objectives, in 2EXPTIME. Contrast this with the fact that this question is 2EXPTIME-complete even for two player zero-sum LTL games [4].

One of the most important questions about NE in computational game theory is *"does the game admit more than one NE?"* [20, 48] — the unique NE problem. This problem is deeply investigated in game theory and is shown to be very challenging [2,21,28,29,47,49,53,57]. Prior to this work, no logic-based technique, as far as we know, solved this problem.[3] In this paper we introduced GRADED-SL to address

[3]In the related work section we discussed the logic GSL that, although motivated by the need to address the unique NE problem, only supplies a model-checking algorithm for a very small fragment of GSL that, it is assumed, is not able to express the existence of NE.

and solve the unique NE problem. We have demonstrated that GRADED-SL is elegant, simple, and very powerful, and can solve the unique NE problem for LTL objectives in 2EXPTIME, and thus at the same complexity that is required to merely decide if a NE exists. We also instantiate our formalism by considering the well-known prisoner's dilemma and its iterated version. We have also shown that using the same approach one can express (and solve) the uniqueness of other standard solution concepts, e.g., subgame-perfect equilibria, again in 2EXPTIME. Finally, our work gives the first algorithmic solution to the model-checking problem of a graded variant of ATL*, and proves it to be 2EXPTIME-COMPLETE.

The positive results presented in this paper open several directions for future work. We are most excited about extending LTL objectives to quantitative objectives such as mean-payoff or discounted-payoff. These naturally extend classic games with quantitative aspects. That is, the result of a play is a real-valued payoff for each player [58]. In a mean-payoff game, one is interested in the *long-run average* of the edge-weights along a play, called the *value* of the play. In the basic setting, there are two players, one wishing to minimize this value, and the other to maximize it. In the discounted version, the weights associated with edges are "*discounted*" with time. In other words, an edge chosen at time t adds a weight to the long-run average that is greater than the value the same edge would contribute if chosen later on. Because of their applicability to economics these games have been studied from an algorithmic perspective for some time [58]. Also, the connection of mean-payoff and discounted-payoff objectives with NE has been recently investigated in the multi-agent setting (see [13] for a recent work). However, extending our results to the weighted setting may prove challenging since, in this setting, the automata-theoretic approach gives rise to weighted-automata, for which many problems are much harder or undecidable (though not in all cases) [1, 5].

In the multi-agent setting, reasoning about epistemic alternatives plays a key role. Thus, an important extension would be to combine the knowledge operators in SLK [18] with the graded quantifiers we introduced for GRADED-SL. Since strategic reasoning under imperfect information has an undecidable model-checking problem [22], one may restrict to memoryless strategies as was done for SLK. More involved, would be to add grades to the knowledge operators, thus being able to express "there exists at least g equivalent worlds" [56].

Last but not least, another direction is to consider implementing GRADED-SL and its model-checking procedure in a formal verification tool. A reasonable approach would be, for example, to extend the tool SLK-MCMAS [18].

Acknowledgments

We thank Michael Wooldridge for suggesting uniqueness of Nash Equilibria as an application of graded strategy logic. Benjamin Aminof is supported by the Austrian National Research Network S11403-N23 (RiSE) of the Austrian Science Fund (FWF) and by the Vienna Science and Technology Fund (WWTF) through grant ICT12-059. Sasha Rubin is a Marie Curie fellow of the Istituto Nazionale di Alta Matematica. Aniello Murano is partially supported by the GNCS 2016 project: Logica, Automi e Giochi per Sistemi Auto-adattivi.

REFERENCES

[1] S. Almagor, U. Boker, and O. Kupferman. What's decidable about weighted automata? In *ATVA'11*, LNCS 6996, pages 482–491, 2011.

[2] E. Altman, H. Kameda, and Y. Hosokawa. Nash equilibria in load balancing in distributed computer systems. *IGTR*, 4(2):91–100, 2002.

[3] R. Alur, T. Henzinger, and O. Kupferman. Alternating-Time Temporal Logic. *JACM*, 49(5):672–713, 2002.

[4] R. Alur, S. La Torre, and P. Madhusudan. Playing games with boxes and diamonds. In *CONCUR'03*, LNCS 2761, pages 127–141. Springer, 2003.

[5] B. Aminof, O. Kupferman, and R. Lampert. Rigorous approximated determinization of weighted automata. *Theor. Comput. Sci.*, 480:104–117, 2013.

[6] B. Aminof, A. Legay, A. Murano, and O. Serre. μ-calculus pushdown module checking with imperfect state information. In *IFIP-TCS'08*, IFIP 273, pages 333–348. Springer, 2008.

[7] B. Aminof, A. Murano, and S. Rubin. On CTL* with graded path modalities. In *LPAR-20'15*, LNCS 9450, pages 281–296, 2015.

[8] R. Axelrod. The evolution of strategies in the iterated prisoners dilemma. *The dynamics of norms*, pages 1–16, 1987.

[9] F. Belardinelli. A logic of knowledge and strategies with imperfect information. In *LAMAS'15*, 2015.

[10] A. Bianco, F. Mogavero, and A. Murano. Graded Computation Tree Logic. *TOCL*, 13(3):25:1–53, 2012.

[11] K. G. Binmore. *Fun and Games: A Text on Game Theory*. D.C. Heath, 1992.

[12] P. Bonatti, C. Lutz, A. Murano, and M. Vardi. The Complexity of Enriched muCalculi. *LMCS*, 4(3):1–27, 2008.

[13] E. Boros, K. M. Elbassioni, V. Gurvich, and K. Makino. Nested family of cyclic games with k-total effective rewards. *CoRR*, abs/1412.6072, 2014.

[14] T. Brihaye, A. D. C. Lopes, F. Laroussinie, and N. Markey. ATL with Strategy Contexts and Bounded Memory. In *LFCS'09*, LNCS 5407, pages 92–106, 2009.

[15] D. Calvanese, G. De Giacomo, and M. Lenzerini. Reasoning in expressive description logics with fixpoints based on automata on infinite trees. In *IJCAI'99*, pages 84–89, 1999.

[16] V. Capraro. A model of human cooperation in social dilemmas. *CoRR*, abs/1307.4228, 2013.

[17] V. Capraro, M. Venanzi, M. Polukarov, and N. R. Jennings. Cooperative equilibria in iterated social dilemmas. In *SAGT'13*, LNCS 8146, pages 146–158. 2013.

[18] P. Čermák, A. Lomuscio, F. Mogavero, and A. Murano. MCMAS-SLK: A Model Checker for the Verification of Strategy Logic Specifications. In *CAV'14*, LNCS 8559, pages 524–531. Springer, 2014.

[19] K. Chatterjee, T. Henzinger, and N. Piterman. Strategy Logic. *IC*, 208(6):677–693, 2010.

[20] R. Cornes, R. Hartley, and T. Sandler. An elementary proof via contraction. *Journal of Public Economic Theory*, 1(4):499–509, 1999.

[21] J. B. D. Simchi-Levi, X. Chen. *The Logic of Logistics:*

Theory, Algorithms, and Applications for Logistics Management. Science and Business Media. 2013.

[22] C. Dima and F. Tiplea. Model-checking ATL under Imperfect Information and Perfect Recall Semantics is Undecidable. Technical report, arXiv, 2011.

[23] E. A. Emerson and C. S. Jutla. Tree automata, mu-calculus and determinacy (extended abstract). In *ASFCS'91*, pages 368–377, 1991.

[24] M. Faella, M. Napoli, and M. Parente. Graded Alternating-Time Temporal Logic. *FI*, 105(1-2):189–210, 2010.

[25] A. Ferrante, A. Murano, and M. Parente. Enriched Mu-Calculi Module Checking. *LMCS*, 4(3):1–21, 2008.

[26] K. Fine. In So Many Possible Worlds. *NDJFL*, 13:516–520, 1972.

[27] D. Fisman, O. Kupferman, and Y. Lustig. Rational Synthesis. In *TACAS'10*, LNCS 6015, pages 190–204. Springer, 2010.

[28] C. D. Fraser. The uniqueness of nash equilibrium in the private provision of public goods: an alternative proof. *Journal of Public Economics*, 49(3):389–390, 1992.

[29] A. Glazer and K. A. Konrad. Private provision of public goods, limited tax deducibility, and crowding out. *FinanzArchiv / Public Finance Analysis*, 50(2):203–216, 1993.

[30] E. Grädel. On the restraining power of guards. *J. Symb. Log.*, 64(4):1719–1742, 1999.

[31] E. Grädel, M. Otto, and E. Rosen. Two-Variable Logic with Counting is Decidable. In *LICS'97*, pages 306–317. IEEE Computer Society, 1997.

[32] J. Gutierrez, P. Harrenstein, and M. Wooldridge. Reasoning about equilibria in game-like concurrent systems. In *KR'14*, 2014.

[33] J. Gutierrez, P. Harrenstein, and M. Wooldridge. Expressiveness and complexity results for strategic reasoning. In *CONCUR'15*, LIPIcs 42, pages 268–282, 2015.

[34] B. Hollunder and F. Baader. Qualifying Number Restrictions in Concept Languages. In *KR'91*, pages 335–346. Kaufmann, 1991.

[35] O. Kupferman, G. Perelli, and M. Y. Vardi. Synthesis with rational environments. In *EUMAS'14*, LNCS 8953, pages 219–235, 2014.

[36] O. Kupferman, U. Sattler, and M. Vardi. The Complexity of the Graded muCalculus. In *CADE'02*, LNCS 2392, pages 423–437. Springer, 2002.

[37] O. Kupferman, M. Vardi, and P. Wolper. An Automata Theoretic Approach to Branching-Time Model Checking. *JACM*, 47(2):312–360, 2000.

[38] K. Leyton-Brown and Y. Shoham. *Essentials of Game Theory: A Concise, Multidisciplinary Introduction (Synthesis Lectures on Artificial Intelligence and Machine Learning).* M&C, 2008.

[39] A. Lopes, F. Laroussinie, and N. Markey. ATL with Strategy Contexts: Expressiveness and Model Checking. In *FSTTCS'10*, LIPIcs 8, pages 120–132, 2010.

[40] V. Malvone, F. Mogavero, A. Murano, and L. Sorrentino. On the counting of strategies. In *TIME'15*, pages 170–179, 2015.

[41] J. H. Miller. The coevolution of automata in the repeated prisoner's dilemma. *Journal of Economic Behavior & Organization*, 29(1):87–112, 1996.

[42] F. Mogavero, A. Murano, G. Perelli, and M. Vardi. What Makes ATL* Decidable? A Decidable Fragment of Strategy Logic. In *CONCUR'12*, LNCS 7454, pages 193–208. Springer, 2012.

[43] F. Mogavero, A. Murano, G. Perelli, and M. Vardi. Reasoning About Strategies: On the Model-Checking Problem. *TOCL*, 15(4):34:1–42, 2014.

[44] F. Mogavero, A. Murano, and M. Vardi. Reasoning About Strategies. In *FSTTCS'10*, LIPIcs 8, pages 133–144. Leibniz-Zentrum fuer Informatik, 2010.

[45] F. Mogavero, A. Murano, and M. Vardi. Relentful Strategic Reasoning in Alternating-Time Temporal Logic. In *LPAR'10*, LNAI 6355, pages 371–387, 2010.

[46] D. E. Muller and P. E. Schupp. Simulating alternating tree automata by nondeterministic automata: New results and new proofs of the theorems of rabin, mcnaughton and safra. *Theor. Comput. Sci.*, 141(1&2):69–107, 1995.

[47] A. Orda, R. Rom, and N. Shimkin. Competitive routing in multiuser communication networks. *IEEE/ACM Trans. Netw.*, 1(5):510–521, 1993.

[48] G. Papavassilopoulos and J. B. Cruz. On the uniqueness of nash strategies for a class of analytic differential games. *Journal of Optimization Theory and Applications*, 27(2):309–314, 1979.

[49] L. Pavel. *Game Theory for Control of Optical Networks.* Science and Business Media. Springer, 2012.

[50] A. Pnueli and R. Rosner. Distributed reactive systems are hard to synthesize. In *FOCS'90*, pages 746–757, 1990.

[51] A. Rubinstein. Finite automata play the repeated prisoner's dilemma. *Journal of Economic Theory*, 39(1):83–96, 1986.

[52] R. Selten. Spieltheoretische behandlung eines oligopolmodells mit nachfragetragheit. *Zeitschrift fur die gesamte Staatswissenschaft*, 121:301–324, 1965.

[53] H. R. V. T. C. Bergstrom, L. E. Blume. On the private provision of public goods. *Journal of Public Economics*, 29(1):25–49, 1986.

[54] W. Thomas. Infinite trees and automaton definable relations over omega-words. In *STACS'90*, pages 263–277, 1990.

[55] M. Ummels. Rational behaviour and strategy construction in infinite multiplayer games. In *FSTTCS'06*, LNCS 4337, pages 212–223, 2006.

[56] W. van der Hoek and J.-J. Meyer. Graded modalities in epistemic logic. In *LFCS'92*, LNCS 620, pages 503–514. 1992.

[57] Y. Zhang and M. Guizani. *Game Theory for Wireless Communications and Networking.* CRC Press, 2011.

[58] U. Zwick and M. Paterson. The complexity of mean payoff games on graphs. *Theor. Comput. Sci.*, 158(1&2):343–359, 1996.

Expressiveness and Nash Equilibrium in Iterated Boolean Games

Julian Gutierrez
Dept. of Computer Science
University of Oxford
Oxford, United Kingdom
julian.gutierrez@cs.ox.ac.uk

Paul Harrenstein
Dept. of Computer Science
University of Oxford
Oxford, United Kingdom
paulhar@cs.ox.ac.uk

Giuseppe Perelli
Dept. of Computer Science
University of Oxford
Oxford, United Kingdom
giuseppe.perelli@cs.ox.ac.uk

Michael Wooldridge
Dept. of Computer Science
University of Oxford
Oxford, United Kingdom
mjw@cs.ox.ac.uk

ABSTRACT

We introduce and investigate a novel notion of expressiveness for temporal logics that is based on game theoretic properties of multi-agent systems. We focus on *iterated Boolean games*, where each agent i has a goal γ_i, represented using (a fragment of) Linear Temporal Logic (LTL). The goal γ_i captures agent i's preferences: the models of γ_i represent system behaviours that would satisfy i, and each player is assumed to act strategically, taking into account the goals of other players, in order to bring about computations satisfying their goal. In this setting, we apply the standard game-theoretic concept of Nash equilibria: the Nash equilibria of an iterated Boolean game can be understood as a (possibly empty) set of computations, each computation representing one way the system could evolve if players chose strategies in Nash equilibrium. Such an equilibrium set of computations can be understood as expressing a temporal property—which may or may not be expressible within a particular LTL fragment. The new notion of expressiveness that we study is then as follows: *what* LTL *properties are characterised by the Nash equilibria of games in which agent goals are expressed in fragments of* LTL? We formally define and investigate this notion of expressiveness and some related issues, for a range of LTL fragments.

Keywords

Iterated Boolean games; LTL; Expressiveness; Nash equilibrium

1. INTRODUCTION

Temporal logics are probably the most successful and widely used class of formalisms for the specification and verification of computer systems [10]. In particular, temporal logics have proven to be enormously valuable in model checking, where a standard question is whether all computations of a given system satisfy a particular temporal logic property φ [7]. A natural question relating to temporal logics is that of their *expressive power*: what system properties is it possible to express within a particular temporal logic or temporal logic fragment? For example, the relative expressiveness of linear *versus* branching time temporal logics was a major research topic in theoretical computer science for more than a decade [11, 31], and still generates debate to the present day.

In this article, we are interested in the use of temporal logic for reasoning about multi-agent systems, and in particular, we are interested in questions relating to expressiveness that arise in such settings. We use *iterated Boolean games* as our abstract model of multi-agent systems [15]. In this model, each agent i exercises exclusive control over a subset of Boolean variables, and the game is played over an infinite number of rounds, where at each round each player chooses a valuation for their variables. The result of play is an infinite computation, which can be understood as a model for Linear Temporal Logic (LTL) [26, 10]. To represent agent preferences in iterated Boolean games, each player i is assumed to have a goal γ_i, expressed using (a fragment of) LTL: the models of γ_i represent computations/plays that would satisfy i. Each player is assumed to act strategically, taking into account the goals of other players, in order to try to bring about computations that will satisfy their goal. We can then apply the standard game-theoretic concept of Nash equilibrium: the Nash equilibria of an iterated Boolean game can be understood as a (possibly empty) set of computations, with each computation representing one way the system could evolve if players in the game chose strategies in equilibrium.

Our main interest in the present paper is as follows. The Nash equilibria of an iterated Boolean game are a set of computations, and such a set of computations can be understood as expressing a temporal property. Now, suppose we have a game G in which each player i has a goal γ_i expressed in a fragment L of LTL: then, *what temporal properties can be expressed by the equilibria of G?* In particular, it is very natural to ask whether the equilibria of an L-game can be characterised within L itself. We formally define and investigate this novel notion of expressiveness as well as some related issues for a range of known fragments of LTL.

The problem of expressing Nash equilibria of concurrent games has, of course, been considered elsewhere. For instance, a popular approach is to develop new formalisms for representing temporal properties of Nash equilibria, and similar game-theoretic solution concepts, *in the object language* by adding new operators to existing temporal logics [5, 14]. We believe that our approach—focussing on the temporal properties that Nash equilibrium can distinguish in logic-based (Boolean) games—is markedly different.

Appears in: *Proceedings of the 15th International Conference on Autonomous Agents and Multiagent Systems (AAMAS 2016), J. Thangarajah, K. Tuyls, C. Jonker, S. Marsella (eds.), May 9–13, 2016, Singapore.*

As a motivating example, consider the following temporal variation on the *Battle of the Sexes* game (see, for instance, [21]).

EXAMPLE 1 (BOOLEAN BALLET). *Alice and Bob go out every weekend, either alone or together. They have to decide repeatedly whether to go to the prize fight or to the ballet, but are unable to correlate their actions. Their preferences, however, are slightly divergent. Alice wishes always to go out together, whereas Bob wants to go at least once to the ballet together with Alice but also at least once wishes to see the prize fight alone. The situation can be modelled as an iterated Boolean game where Alice controls variable p and Bob variable q. Setting p to true indicates Alice going to the ballet and similarly for q and Bob. Setting p, (respectively, q), to false means going to the prize fight. The preferences of the two agents can then be represented as follows, where* $\mathsf{G}\,\varphi$ *stands for "always* φ*,"* $\mathsf{F}\,\varphi$ *for "eventually* φ*," and* $\bar{q}$ *for "not q":*

$$\gamma_{Alice} = \mathsf{G}(p \leftrightarrow q) \qquad \gamma_{Bob} = \mathsf{F}(p \wedge q) \wedge \mathsf{F}(p \wedge \bar{q})$$

Thus, the preferences of the players are phrased using only the temporal operators F *and* G*. Observe that the set of equilibrium runs includes the run* $pq, \bar{p}\bar{q}, \bar{p}\bar{q}, \bar{p}\bar{q}, \ldots$*: Alice and Bob go out to the ballet together the first time and meet at the prize fight forever after. Alice will thus be satisfied. Not so Bob, but there is little Bob can do apart from going to the ballet alone at some point and be miserable as well, or miss out on the ballet altogether. The set of equilibrium runs, however, does not include* $pq, pq, \bar{p}\bar{q}, \bar{p}\bar{q}, \bar{p}\bar{q}, \ldots$ *as Bob would dash off to the prize fight after having been to the ballet first. The runs that are sustained by a Nash equilibrium are precisely those in which always either* pq *or* $\bar{p}\bar{q}$ *is the case and in which either* pq *or* $\bar{p}\bar{q}$ *occurs at most once. This, however, is not a property that can be expressed in the (stutter-invariant) fragment of* LTL *with* F *and* G *as the only temporal operators.*[1] *Moreover, it raises the question as to which properties can be characterised as the set of runs sustained by a Nash equilibrium of some iterated Boolean game with the players' preferences formulated in this and other fragments.*

2. PRELIMINARIES

Our analysis uses *Linear Temporal Logic* and the iterated Boolean games based on it. In this section, we present the core concepts of these frameworks along with a number of auxiliary notions.

*Linear Temporal Logic (*LTL*).*

We use the well-known framework of **Linear Temporal Logic** (LTL) [26, 10, 2]. The formulae of LTL are constructed in the usual fashion from a non-empty and finite set Φ of propositional variables using the Boolean connectives *negation* ($\neg\varphi$) and *disjunction* ($\varphi \vee \psi$), as well as the temporal operators *next* ($\mathsf{X}\,\varphi$), *eventually* ($\mathsf{F}\,\varphi$), *always* ($\mathsf{G}\,\varphi$), and *until* ($\varphi\,\mathsf{U}\,\psi$). *truth* ($\top$), *falsity* ($\bot$), *conjunction* ($\varphi \wedge \psi$), *implication* ($\varphi \rightarrow \psi$), and *bi-implication* ($\varphi \leftrightarrow \psi$), are introduced as the usual abbreviations of $p \vee \neg p$, $\neg\top$, $\neg(\neg\varphi \vee \neg\psi)$, $\neg\varphi \vee \psi$, and $(\varphi \rightarrow \psi) \wedge (\psi \rightarrow \varphi)$, respectively. For p a propositional variable we will write $\bar{p}$ for $\neg p$. We also omit conjunctions in conjunctive clauses and, for instance, denote $p \wedge \neg q \wedge r$ by $p\bar{q}r$.

By a **valuation** v we understand a subset of propositional variables, that is, $v \subseteq \Phi$. Thus the set of valuations over Φ is given by 2^Φ. Intuitively, a propositional variable p is set to true at valuation v whenever $p \in v$. For a valuation $v \subseteq \Phi$, we have χ_v^Φ denote the **characteristic clause for** v given by $\chi_v^\Phi = \bigwedge_{p\in v} p \wedge \bigwedge_{q\in\Phi\setminus v} \bar{q}$. Thus, for $w, v \subseteq \Phi$, we have $w \models \chi_v^\Phi$ if and only if $v = w$. We will also identify valuations and their characterising clauses, that is, write $p\bar{q}r$ for valuation $\{p, r\}$ if $\Phi = \{p, q, r\}$.

The formulae of LTL are interpreted with respect to **runs** $\rho = v_1, v_2, \ldots$, which we define as infinite sequences (or ω-*words*) over valuations in Φ, that is, $\rho \in (2^\Phi)^\omega$. We denote the set of runs over valuations in 2^Φ by $runs(\Phi)$, again omitting the reference to Φ when clear from the context.

The semantics of LTL then interprets LTL-formulae with respect to a run $\rho = v_0, v_1, v_2, \ldots$ and time index $t \in \mathbb{N}$ as follows.

$$\begin{array}{lll}
\rho, t \models p & \text{iff} & p \in v_t \quad (\text{for } p \in \Phi) \\
\rho, t \models \neg\varphi & \text{iff} & \rho, t \not\models \varphi \\
\rho, t \models \varphi \vee \psi & \text{iff} & \rho, t \models \varphi \text{ or } \rho, t \models \psi \\
\rho, t \models \mathsf{X}\,\varphi & \text{iff} & \rho, t+1 \models \varphi \\
\rho, t \models \mathsf{F}\,\varphi & \text{iff} & \rho, t' \models \varphi \text{ for some } t' \geq t \\
\rho, t \models \mathsf{G}\,\varphi & \text{iff} & \rho, t' \models \varphi \text{ for all } t' \geq t \\
\rho, t \models \varphi\,\mathsf{U}\,\psi & \text{iff} & \text{for some } t' \geq t \text{ both } \rho, t' \models \psi \text{ and} \\
& & \rho, t'' \models \varphi \text{ for all } t \leq t'' < t'
\end{array}$$

We say that a run ρ **satisfies** a formula φ if $\rho, 0 \models \varphi$. The set of runs that satisfy formula φ we denote by $[\![\varphi]\!]$. A formula φ is **satisfiable** if some run satisfies φ. Observe that $\neg\mathsf{X}\,\varphi$ is equivalent to $\mathsf{X}\,\neg\varphi$, and $\mathsf{F}\,\varphi$ to $\neg\mathsf{G}\,\neg\varphi$.

We also employ a number of auxiliary concepts. For $\Psi \subseteq \Phi$ and $\rho \in runs(\Phi)$, we write $\rho|_\Psi$ for the **restriction** (or **projection**) of ρ to Ψ, that is, if $\rho = v_1, v_2, \ldots$ then $\rho|_\Psi = w_1, w_2, \ldots$ where $w_t = v_t \cap \Psi$ for each $t \geq 1$. For $X \subseteq runs(\Phi)$ and $\Psi \subseteq \Phi$, we denote by $X|_\Psi$ the set $\{\rho|_\Psi : \rho \in X\}$.

By a **history** we understand a *finite* and possibly empty sequence $\pi = v_0, \ldots, v_k$ in V^*. We let $length(\pi)$ denote the **length** of π. We furthermore use the usual operations on histories. For π and π', we have $\pi; \pi'$ denote the *concatenation* of π and π', and $\pi^\omega = \pi; \pi; \pi; \ldots$ the *infinite iteration* of π. We also specify subsets of runs in $runs(\Phi)$ by ω-*regular expressions* over the alphabet $\Sigma = 2^\Phi$ using the operations *concatenation* $(X; Y)$, *union* $(X + Y)$, *finite iteration* (X^*), and *infinite iteration* (X^ω).

A history $\pi = w_0, \ldots, w_k$ is a **prefix** of a run $\rho = v_0, v_1, v_2, \ldots$ (in symbols $\pi \leq \rho$) if $v_t = w_t$ for all $t \leq k$. The set of prefixes of a run ρ we denote by $prefix(\rho)$. We say that a history π is the (unique) **maximal common prefix** of two (finite or infinite) runs ρ and ρ' if π is a prefix of both ρ and ρ' and no prefix of greater length has this property. For instance, $\pi = pq, p\bar{q}$ and $\pi' = pq, p\bar{q}, \bar{p}q$ are both a common prefix of the runs $\rho = pq, p\bar{q}, \bar{p}q, pq, pq, \ldots$ and $\rho' = pq, p\bar{q}, \bar{p}q, \bar{p}\bar{q}, \bar{p}\bar{q}, \ldots$, but only π' is maximal.

We will invoke frequently the notion of an ultimately periodic run. A run $\rho = v_0, v_1, v_2, \ldots$, is said to be **ultimately periodic** if there are $s, p \geq 0$, called the **starting index** and **period**, respectively, such that for every $t \geq s$, we have that $v_t = v_{t+p}$. The *Ultimately Periodic Model Theorem* in [29] establishes that every satisfiable LTL-formula is satisfied by an ultimately periodic run.

THEOREM 2 (SISTLA AND CLARKE [29]). *Every satisfiable* LTL-*formula is satisfied by an ultimately periodic run.*

Moreover, every ultimately periodic run $\rho = v_0, v_1, \ldots$ over 2^Φ with starting index s and period p is characterised by the formula

$$\chi_\rho = \textstyle\bigwedge_{0\leq t\leq s+p} \mathsf{X}^t \chi_{v_t} \wedge \mathsf{X}^s\, \mathsf{G}(\bigwedge_{v\in 2^\Phi} (\chi_v \rightarrow \mathsf{X}^p \chi_v)),$$

where $\mathsf{X}^k \varphi = \underbrace{\mathsf{X} \cdots \mathsf{X}}_{k \text{ times}} \varphi$.

PROPOSITION 3. *Let* $\rho = v_0, v_1, \ldots$ *be an ultimately periodic run over* 2^Φ*. Then,* ρ *is the unique run over* 2^Φ *that satisfies* χ_ρ*.*

[1] Interestingly, had Bob's goal been to go both to the ballet with Alice and to the prize fight alone infinitely often, that is, if Bob's goal had been $\mathsf{G}(\mathsf{F}(p \wedge q) \wedge \mathsf{F}(p \wedge \bar{q}))$, the set of Nash equilibria of the resulting iterated Boolean game would be expressible in this fragment, namely by $\mathsf{G}(p \leftrightarrow q) \wedge (\mathsf{F}\,\mathsf{G}\,pq \vee \mathsf{F}\,\mathsf{G}\,\bar{p}\bar{q})$.

Fragments of Linear Temporal Logic.

We study the expressive power of the most natural, and therefore most widely known, fragments of LTL. Such fragments are the "stutter-invariant" fragment (technically, the X-free fragment), denoted by L_{U}, as well as other fragments where the use of the "until" operator is restricted to simply being G or F, leading to the following sublogics: $L_{\mathsf{G,F,X}}$, where only G and F and X are allowed, and with similar interpretations, the sublogics $L_{\mathsf{G,F}}$, $L_{\mathsf{X,G^+}}$, and $L_{\mathsf{X,F^+}}$, where the "+" notation indicates that negations are allowed only in front of propositional variables (otherwise, for instance, the L_{G} fragment would be the same as the L_{F} fragment). The fragment $L_{\mathsf{G,F}}$ was briefly discussed in Example 1. We will not study the extremely weak sublogics $L_{\mathsf{G^+}}$, $L_{\mathsf{F^+}}$, L_{X}, and $L_{\emptyset}$ (the latter referring to propositional logic). On the one hand, the two latter sublogics cannot express interesting properties of infinite runs—all their models are finite words; on the other hand, the first two sublogics can express only very limited classes of temporal properties: only "safety" properties in the case of $L_{\mathsf{G^+}}$ and only "reachability" properties in the case of $L_{\mathsf{F^+}}$. Indeed, our study covers the most relevant LTL fragments in the literature. Finally, by $L_{\omega\text{-}reg}$ we refer to the set of ω-regular expressions, which are seen as an *extension* of LTL, rather than a fragment [33]. Sometimes we refer explicitly to the set Ψ of variables over which L is defined, and write $L(\Psi)$ for L.

Iterated Boolean Games.

Boolean games were introduced by Harrenstein et al. [17] and further popularised by, among others, Bonzon, Lang, and Wooldridge (see, for instance, [4, 12]). In this paper, we adopt the framework of *iterated Boolean games* as proposed by Gutierrez et al. [15], where players play a Boolean game over an infinite number of rounds and where the players's goals are given by an LTL-formula. For L a fragment of LTL over Φ, an **L-iterated Boolean game** is a tuple

$$G = (N, \Phi, \Phi_1, \dots, \Phi_n, \gamma_1, \dots, \gamma_n),$$

where N is a set of players, each $\Phi_i \subseteq \Phi$ is a subset of propositional variables under control of player i, and γ_i is a formula in L representing player i's preferences over $runs(\Phi)$. We assume $\Phi_1, \dots, \Phi_n$ to partition Φ, that is, $\Phi_1 \cup \cdots \cup \Phi_n = \Phi$ and $i \neq j$ implies $\Phi_i \cap \Phi_j = \emptyset$. Henceforth, we refer to an L-iterated Boolean game as an **L-game**. We say that G is an L-game over Φ if we make explicit reference to the set Φ.

An iterated Boolean game takes place in an infinite number of rounds and in every round each player i simultaneously makes a **choice** $v_i \subseteq \Phi_i$ of values for the propositional variables under its control based on the values chosen by *all* players in previous rounds. Formally, a **strategy** for a player i is a function $f_i\colon (2^{\Phi})^* \to 2^{\Phi_i}$ which associates with every history $\pi \in V^*$ a choice $f_i(\pi) \in 2^{\Phi_i}$. A **strategy profile** is a tuple $f = (f_1, \dots, f_n)$ that associates with each player i a strategy f_i and induces an infinite run $\rho(f) = v_0, v_1, v_2, \dots$ defined as follows:

$$v_0 = f_1(\epsilon) \cup \cdots \cup f_n(\epsilon)$$
$$v_{t+1} = f_1(v_0, \dots, v_t) \cup \cdots \cup f_n(v_0, \dots, v_t)$$

A player i strictly prefers runs that satisfy γ_i to runs that do not and is indifferent otherwise, that is, i **strictly prefers** run ρ to run ρ' if and only if $\rho \not\models \gamma_i$ and $\rho' \models \gamma_i$. Thus, each player's preferences in iterated Boolean games are dichotomous, dividing the set of runs into those that are preferred and those that are not preferred.

It can easily be seen that with the players, strategies and preferences defined in this way, each iterated Boolean game defines a **strategic game** in the game-theoretic sense of the word (see, e.g., [24, 22, 28]). Accordingly, the usual game theoretic solution concepts are available for the analysis of iterated Boolean games. This in particular holds for **Nash equilibrium**, which in our present setting is a strategy profile $f^* = (f_1^*, \dots, f_n^*)$ such that for all players i and all of i's strategies g_i, we have that $\rho(f_{-i}^*, g_i) \models \gamma_i$ implies $\rho(f^*) \models \gamma_i$, where (f_{-i}^*, g_i) denotes the profile $(f_1^*, \dots, f_{i-1}^*, g_i, f_{i+1}^*, \dots, f_n^*)$. We furthermore say that a run $\rho \in runs(\Phi)$ is *sustained* by a Nash equilibrium f^* in a game G whenever $\rho(f^*) = \rho$. We then refer to ρ as an **equilibrium run**. The set of equilibrium runs of G—rather than the set of equilibria itself—we denote by $NE(G)$.

Expressiveness.

Given a suitable model-theoretic semantics, the expressive power of a logic can be measured in terms of the sets of models it can characterise. In the case of LTL, the models are runs of valuations and by a **linear time property** given a set Φ of propositional variables, we understand any subset $X \subseteq runs(\Phi)$ of runs.

We say that an LTL-fragment L can **express** a property $X \subseteq runs(\Phi)$ if there is some formula $\varphi \in L$ such that $X = [\![\varphi]\!]$. A weaker notion of expressiveness applies when, given a temporal property, the fragment can express a stronger property. Thus, L is said to **weakly express** the non-empty property X whenever there is a *satisfiable* formula $\varphi \in L$ with $[\![\varphi]\!] \subseteq X$.

The concept of weak expressiveness is much weaker than standard expressiveness, in the sense that fragments are likely to be able to express considerably more properties in the weak sense than they can under the standard notion. Indeed, for an LTL-fragment L to weakly express *every* LTL-property it suffices to be able to express $\emptyset$ and $\{\rho\}$ for every ultimately periodic run $\rho \in runs(\Phi)$. By virtue of Proposition 3, this holds, for instance, for the fragment $L_{\mathsf{X,F,G}}$. In settings where a designer uses temporal logic to specify the desired behaviour of a system, however, the concept of weak expressiveness seems to be quite natural. If the designer wants a system, for instance a multi-agent system, to behave accordingly to the specification and she manages to design it so that it behaves in equilibrium according to a *stronger* but consistent specification, she should still be satisfied.

A third notion of expressiveness abstracts away from the propositional variables available in the language. Rather than requiring that a temporal property X on 2^{Φ} *coincide* with the set of runs satisfying some formula φ in a fragment $L(\Phi)$, it demands that X be the set of *projections to* Φ of the runs satisfying some formula φ of L in *an extended set of propositional variables*. Formally, we say that LTL-fragment $L(\Phi)$ can **projectively express** property $X \subseteq runs(\Phi)$ if there is some finite set Ψ of auxiliary variables and some formula $\varphi \in L(\Phi \cup \Psi)$ such that $X = \{\rho|_{\Phi} \in runs(\Phi) \colon \rho \in [\![\varphi]\!]\}$.

Finally, a fragment $L(\Phi)$ is said to be able to **weakly projectively express** a non-empty property $X \subseteq runs(\Phi)$ if there is some finite set Ψ of variables and some formula $\varphi \in L(\Phi \cup \Psi)$ such that for every run $\rho \in runs(\Phi \cup \Psi)$ we have that $\rho \in [\![\varphi]\!]$ implies $\rho|_{\Phi} \in X$.

On the basis of the above concepts we also introduce concepts of *relative* expressiveness. Thus, we say that fragment L_1 is **at least as expressive as** another fragment L_2, in symbols $L_1 \geq L_2$, if every property that can be expressed by L_2 can also be expressed by L_1. Furthermore, $L_1 \geq^{\mathsf{w}} L_2$ denotes that every property that L_2 can express (not weakly express!), can also be weakly expressed by L_1. The notations $L_1 \geq^{\mathsf{p}} L_2$ and $L_1 \geq^{\mathsf{wp}} L_2$ are defined analogously for projective and weak projective expressiveness. Note that the relations $\geq^{\mathsf{p}}$ and $\geq^{\mathsf{wp}}$ need not be reflexive. Finally, $L_1 >^{\mathsf{w}} L_2$ denotes that $L_1 \geq^{\mathsf{w}} L_2$ and there is a property $X \in runs(\Phi)$ that is not expressible in L_2 but that L_1 can weakly express. The notations $L_1 > L_2$, $L_1 >^{\mathsf{p}} L_2$, and $L >^{\mathsf{wp}} L_2$ are introduced analogously.[2]

[2]Observe that it is *not* generally the case that $L_1 >^{\mathsf{w}} L_2$ if and only if $L_1 \geq^{\mathsf{w}} L_2$ and not $L_2 \geq^{\mathsf{w}} L_1$. Similarly for $>^{\mathsf{p}}$ and $>^{\mathsf{wp}}$.

The roots of *projective expressiveness* go back to the work of Beth [3] and Craig [8] in the 1950s on definability in first order logic. The concept has numerous applications in model theory [6, 18] and has recently also been studied in the context of modal and temporal logics [13, 16]. In our setting, projective expressiveness defines relatively weak constraints on a fragment and should be carefully distinguished from standard expressiveness. Thus, it is well known that the properties that LTL can express are *non-counting* and cannot, for instance, characterise temporal property $even(p)$, the set of runs on 2^Φ in which p is set to true at every even state (see, for instance [33]). Still, $q \wedge \mathsf{G}(q \leftrightarrow \mathsf{X}\neg q) \wedge \mathsf{G}(q \rightarrow p)$ projectively expresses exactly this property. It is known from the literature that every *ω-regular* property can be projectively expressed by LTL if you can use an *unbounded* number of additional propositional variables [13, 30]. We reformulate this result for our setting.

PROPOSITION 4. $\mathrm{LTL} \geq L_{\mathsf{X},\mathsf{F},\mathsf{G}} \geq^{\mathsf{P}} L_{\omega\text{-reg}}$.

Proof: Let $A = (Q, 2^\Phi, \delta, Q_0, F)$ be a nondeterministic Büchi automaton [2]. We construct a formula φ_A in $L_{\mathsf{F},\mathsf{G},\mathsf{X}}(\Phi \cup Q)$, where Φ and Q are disjoint, as follows.

$$\varphi^A_{init} = \bigvee_{q \in Q_0} q$$

$$\varphi^A_{trans} = \mathsf{G}(\bigwedge_{q\in Q}(q \rightarrow \bigvee_{\{(q',v):\, q' \in \delta(q,v)\}}(\chi^\Phi_v \wedge \mathsf{X}\, q')))$$

$$\varphi^A_{accept} = \mathsf{G}\,\mathsf{F} \bigvee_{q\in F} q$$

$$\varphi^A_{invar} = \mathsf{G}(\bigvee_{q\in Q}(q \wedge \bigwedge_{q' \neq q} \bar{q}'))$$

Then set $\varphi^A = \varphi^A_{init} \wedge \varphi^A_{trans} \wedge \varphi^A_{accept} \wedge \varphi^A_{invar}$. By an inductive argument it then follows that $\mathscr{L}_A = \{\rho|_\Phi : \rho \models \varphi_A\}$, where $\mathscr{L}_A$ is the language accepted by A. It follows that $L_{\mathsf{X},\mathsf{F},\mathsf{G}}$ can projectively express all ω-regular temporal logic properties. Recalling that $L_{\omega\text{-reg}}$ is the class of languages over 2^Φ accepted by nondeterministic Büchi automata and that $\mathrm{LTL} \geq L_{\mathsf{X},\mathsf{F},\mathsf{G}}$, we obtain the result. □

It is interesting to note that allowing for additional variables along with projection has a similar effect as, for instance, extending LTL to *Extended Temporal Logic* (ETL) by including to the logical language suitable *grammar-operators* as proposed in [33].

Expressiveness in Equilibrium.

Nash equilibrium fundamentally pertains to strategy profiles rather than to runs, and the former have a much richer structure than the latter. A strategy profile $f = (f_1, \dots, f_n)$ not only prescribes which actions each player has to perform at every time during the run $\rho(f)$, it also prescribes actions off this path, that is, for histories that are *not* a prefix of ρ. Thus the following two things can hold in an L-game G:

(*i*) different strategy profiles f and g may induce the same run, that is, $\rho(f) = \rho(g)$, even if f is an equilibrium and g is not;

(*ii*) different runs ρ and ρ' may satisfy the same players' goals, even if one is sustained by a Nash equilibrium and the other one is not.

Possibility (*ii*) makes that the set of equilibrium runs of a game may seem quite unrelated to the goals of the players. To see this, consider the following example.

EXAMPLE 5. *Let G be the two-player game where players 1 and 2 control p and q, respectively, and whose goals are given by $\gamma_1 = \mathsf{F}(p \wedge q)$ and $\gamma_2 = \top$, respectively. Then, run $(\bar{p}\bar{q})^\omega$ is sustained by the Nash equilibrium where the two players always set p and q to false, respectively. Thus, γ_2 is satisfied, but γ_1 is not. This is also true of run $(\bar{p}q)^\omega$, which, however, is not sustained by any Nash equilibrium: no matter what strategies are played, player 1 would deviate to a strategy that sets p to true at some point.*

This last phenomenon illustrates that for fragments L of LTL it is quite possible that the Nash equilibrium runs of L-games are distinct from the sets of runs satisfying L-formulae.

For this reason we now also introduce the following notions of expressiveness, which relate to the temporal properties that are characterised by the sets of equilibria runs of iterated Boolean games in a given fragment L. Thus, we say that LTL-fragment L can **express in equilibrium** property $X \subseteq runs(\Phi)$ if there is an L-game G with $X = NE(G)$. Example 1 shows how the standard notion of expressiveness can be different from expressiveness in equilibrium. The concepts of **weak expressiveness in equilibrium**, **projective expressiveness**, and **weak projective expressiveness** are then defined analogously to weak expressiveness, projective expressiveness, and weak projective expressiveness, respectively, with the role of the extensions $[\![\varphi]\!]$ of L-formulae being taken over by the Nash equilibrium runs $NE(G)$ of L-games G.

The corresponding relative expressiveness notions are similarly defined as expected. Here, we have L^{NE} refer to the temporal language over 2^Φ that is defined by the sets of equilibrium runs of L-games. For fragments L_1 and L_2 we then write $L_1^{NE} \geq L_2$ if every property that can be expressed by L_2, can also be expressed in equilibrium by L_1, that is, if for every $\varphi \in L_2$, there is an L_1-game such that $NE(G) = [\![\varphi]\!]$. The notations $L_1 \geq L_2^{NE}$, $L_1^{NE} \geq L_2^{NE}$ have an analogous interpretation and, moreover, extend naturally to $\geq^{\mathsf{w}}$, $\geq^{\mathsf{p}}$, and $\geq^{\mathsf{wp}}$. Clearly, $L_1 \geq L_2$ implies both $L_1 \geq^{\mathsf{w}} L_2$ and $L_1 \geq^{\mathsf{p}} L_2$. Moreover, each of the following expressiveness relations $\geq$, $\geq^{\mathsf{w}}$, $\geq^{\mathsf{p}}$, and $\geq^{\mathsf{wp}}$ is easily shown to be transitive.

One would expect that, if a fragment L can express a property X, it can also express X in equilibrium. Although generally true, there is one notable exception: if there is only a single propositional variable p and $X = \emptyset$. For L, any unsatisfiable formula will do. For L^{NE}, however, one has to observe that in the setting of iterated Boolean games, control over a single variable p can be assigned to a single player i only, who is then also the only player who could possibly deviate from a profile. If X is the empty property, i should want to deviate from *every* given run ρ and, consequently, i does not have its goal satisfied at any of them. Then, there is no run that i would possibly want to deviate to and the (non-empty) set of all runs coincides with the set of equilibrium runs.

If L expresses X by φ and there are at least two variables p and q, one can construct the **L-game** G^{mp}_φ, which bears a resemblance to the well-known game of *matching pennies* [24], as follows. Let there be two players, i and j, such that i controls p and j all other variables, including q, and whose goals are given by:

$$\gamma_i = \varphi \vee (p \leftrightarrow q) \qquad \gamma_j = \varphi \vee (p \leftrightarrow \bar{q}).$$

To see that $[\![\varphi]\!]$ is exactly the set of equilibrium runs of G^{mp}_φ, observe that every run that satisfies φ, also satisfies both players' goals and, hence, is sustained by an equilibrium. If, by contrast, a run ρ does not satisfy φ, the players will be entangled in a matching pennies game on p and q. Consequently, ρ is not sustained by an equilibrium. Thus we obtain that

$$L_1 \geq L_2 \text{ implies } L_1^{NE} \geq L_2, \text{ provided that } |\Phi| \geq 2.$$

Observe that G^{mp}_φ could also contain additional variables. Thus, for projective expressiveness in equilibrium we immediately have the following statement.

$$L_1 \geq L_2 \text{ implies } L_1^{NE} \geq^{\mathsf{p}} L_2.$$

Using a construction that is similar to G_φ^{mp}, it can also be shown that, if a fragment L can express a property X, it can also projectively express in equilibrium the complement of X. This result is especially relevant for fragments that are not closed under negation.

LEMMA 6. *Let φ be a formula in fragment L. Then, L can projectively express $[\![\neg\varphi]\!]$ in equilibrium.*

Proof: Let $p, q \notin \Phi$. Consider the two-player L-game G with $\Phi_1 = \{p\}$, $\Phi_2 = \Phi \cup \{q\}$ and the players' goals being given by:

$$\gamma_1 = \varphi \wedge (p \leftrightarrow q) \qquad \gamma_2 = \bar{p} \leftrightarrow q.$$

First observe that no equilibrium run in G satisfies φ. To see this, let f be an arbitrary profile with $\rho(f) \models \varphi$. If $\rho(f) \not\models \gamma_1$, player 1 would deviate by choosing the opposite value for p in the first round. If, on the other hand, $\rho(f) \models \gamma_1$, player 2 would deviate by choosing the opposite value for q in the first round. Hence, $NE(G)|_\Phi \subseteq [\![\neg\varphi]\!]$. To see that this inclusion also holds in the opposite direction, assume that $\rho \not\models \varphi$ and that profile f induces ρ. Since, neither p nor q occurs in φ, we may assume without loss of generality that $\rho \models \bar{p} \leftrightarrow q$. Therefore, player 2 has its goal achieved and will not deviate. As, moreover, player 1 controls no variables occurring in φ, no deviation from f will satisfy its goal. It follows that f is a Nash equilibrium and $\rho \in NE(G)$, as desired. □

3. EQUILIBRIA AND FRAGMENTS

We now will proceed to investigate expressiveness in equilibrium of a number of well-known fragments of LTL.

3.1 The Full and Empty Fragments

It is not necessarily the case that a fragment can express or projectively express more temporal properties in equilibrium than it normally can. A prime example is *propositional calculus*, that is, the LTL-fragment $L_\emptyset$. A fundamental observation in the literature on Boolean games is that the formula

$$\bigwedge_{1\leq i\leq N}(\bigvee_{\theta:\,\Phi_i\to\{\top,\bot\}} \theta(\gamma_i) \to \gamma_i),$$

where $\theta(\gamma_i)$ results from γ_i by replacing every occurrence of $p \in \Phi_i$ by $\theta(p)$, characterises the set of equilibrium runs of the $L_\emptyset$-game $(N, \Phi, \Phi_1, \ldots, \Phi_n, \gamma_1, \ldots, \gamma_n)$ (see, e.g., [4]). Thus, $L_\emptyset$ can express every property that it can express in equilibria, and vice versa—provided that Φ contains at least two propositional variables.

PROPOSITION 7. *$L_\emptyset > L_\emptyset^{NE}$, if there is at most one propositional variable. Otherwise, both $L_\emptyset \geq L_\emptyset^{NE}$ and $L_\emptyset^{NE} \geq L_\emptyset$.*

The full fragment LTL is at the other end of the syntactic spectrum of the linear temporal logics considered in this paper. Barring the borderline case in which $|\Phi| \leq 1$, we have

$$\text{LTL}^{NE} \geq L$$

for all fragments L we consider. Thus, the question remains how expressive LTL is w.r.t. LTL^{NE}, that is, to what extent the temporal properties defined by the Nash equilibria of LTL-games can be expressed by LTL itself. As a first step in this direction we prove game-theoretic pendant of Theorem 2: if an LTL-game has an *equilibrium run*, it also has an ultimately periodic *equilibrium run*.

PROPOSITION 8. *Let G be an LTL-game with the players' goals given by $\gamma_1, \ldots, \gamma_n$. Then, for every run $\rho \in NE(G)$, there is an ultimately periodic run $\rho^* \in NE(G)$ such that $\rho \models \gamma_i$ if and only if $\rho^* \models \gamma_i$ for every player i.*

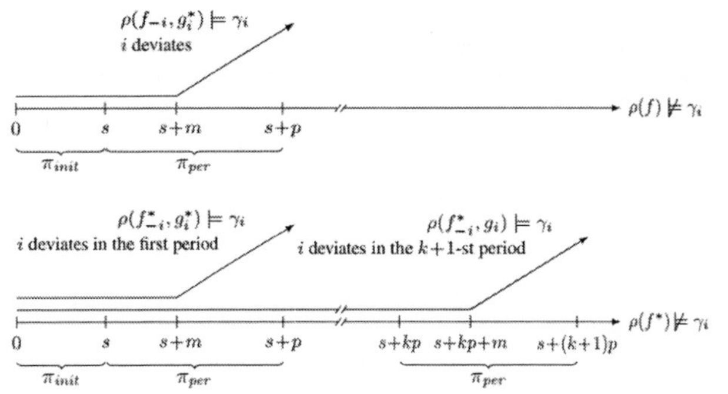

Figure 1: Proof of Proposition 8. For equilibrium f, construct profile f^* such that $\rho(f^*)$ is an ultimately periodic equilibrium run. If we assume that i deviates from f^* in the $k+1$-st period, it follows that i would deviate in the first period as well. As f and f^* coincide on any history with a maximal common prefix in $\pi_{init}; \pi_{per}$, it follows that i also deviates from f.

Proof: Let ρ be an equilibrium run of G and let f be a Nash equilibrium sustaining ρ. Let $W = \{i \in N \colon \rho \models \gamma_i\}$ be the set of *winners* at ρ and consider the formula

$$\gamma_\rho = \bigwedge_{i\in W} \gamma_i \wedge \bigwedge_{i\in N\setminus W} \neg\gamma_i.$$

Clearly, $\rho \models \gamma_\rho$. By virtue of Theorem 2, there is also an ultimately periodic run $\rho^* = \pi_{init}; \pi_{per}^\omega$ with start index s and period p such that $\rho^* \models \gamma_\rho$. Moreover, due to Lemma 4.5 in [29], we may assume for every $t \geq s$ that we have $\rho^*, t \models \gamma_i$ if and only if $\rho^*, t+p \models \gamma_i$ for all players i in the game.

We define a strategy profile f^* that induces ρ^* and show that it is a Nash equilibrium of G. Hence, $\rho^* \in NE(G)$. First observe that every history π has a unique maximal common prefix π_{com} with ρ^*, which is either a prefix of π_{init} or has the form $\pi_{init}; \pi_{per}^r; \pi_{per'}$, where $r \geq 0$ and $\pi_{per'} \leq \pi_{per}$. Now define f^* such that, for each player i and history $\pi = \pi_{com}; \pi''$,

$$f_i^*(\pi) = \begin{cases} f_i(\pi_{com}; \pi'') & \text{if } \pi_{com} \leq \pi_{init}, \\ f_i(\pi_{init}; \pi_{per}; \pi_{per'}; \pi'') & \text{if } \pi_{com} = \pi_{init}; \pi_{per}^r; \pi_{per'}. \end{cases}$$

Observe that $\rho(f^*) = \rho^* = \pi_{init}; \pi_{per}^\omega$ and, hence, $\rho(f^*) \models \gamma_\rho$.

We prove that f^* is a Nash equilibrium of G (also see Figure 1 for an illustration of the argument). To this end, assume for contradiction that there is a strategy g_i for some player i such that $\rho(f^*) \not\models \gamma_i$ and $\rho(f_{-i}^*, g_i) \models \gamma_i$. Then, $\rho(f^*)$ and $\rho(f_{-i}^*, g_i)$ have a maximal common prefix π', for which either $\pi' \leq \pi_{init}; \pi_{per}$ or $\pi' = \pi_{init}; \pi_{per}^k; \pi_{per'}$ for some $k \geq 1$.

If the former—that is, if i deviates from f^* before the first period π_{per} is completed—we have $\rho(f_{-i}, g_i) = \rho(f_{-i}^*, g_i)$ and can immediately conclude that f is not a Nash equilibrium, a contradiction.

If the latter $\rho(f_{-i}^*, g_i) = \pi_{init}; \pi_{per}^k, \rho'$ for some $\rho' \in runs(\Phi)$. Thus, k is the number of times that the period π_{per} is completed before i deviates from f^* by playing g_i. We now define another strategy g_i^* for i on the basis of g_i in a similar way as f^* was constructed from f. For every history $\pi = \pi_{com}; \pi''$, let

$$g_i^*(\pi) = \begin{cases} g_i(\pi) & \text{if } \pi_{com} \leq \pi_{init}, \\ g_i(\pi_{init}; \pi_{per}^{r+k}; \pi_{per'}; \pi'') & \text{if } \pi_{com} = \pi_{init}; \pi_{per}^r; \pi_{per'}. \end{cases}$$

Thus, for every history π and $r = 0$, we have $g_i^*(\pi) = g_i(\pi) = f_i(\pi)$ if $\pi_{com} \leq \pi_{init}$, and $g_i^*(\pi_{init}; \pi'') = g(\pi_{init}; \pi_{per}^k; \pi'')$ if

$\pi_{init} < \pi_{com} \leq \pi_{init}; \pi_{per}$. Intuitively, g_i^* behaves in the first period exactly as g_i in the k-th period. Hence, $\rho(f_{-i}^*, g_i^*) = \pi_{init}; \pi_{per'}; \rho'$. Then, by virtue of Lemma 4.5 in [29] it follows that $\rho(f_{-i}^*, g_i^*) \models \gamma_i$. Moreover, $\rho(f_{-i}^*, g_i^*) = \rho(f_{-i}, g_i^*)$ and hence $\rho(f_{-i}, g_i^*) \models \gamma_i$. It follows that f is *not* a Nash equilibrium and a contradiction ensues, as desired. □

As an immediate consequence we find that every property that can be expressed by LTL in equilibrium can be weakly expressed by LTL itself. By virtue of Proposition 8, every non-empty set of equilibrium runs also contains an ultimately periodic run, which, by Proposition 3, is characterised by an LTL-formula.

COROLLARY 9. LTL $\geq^{\mathsf{w}}$ LTL^{NE}.

For the moment we leave whether LTL $\geq^{\mathsf{p}}$ LTL^{NE} and whether LTL $\geq$ LTL^{NE} as open questions. As a first step to resolve these issues, however, we show that LTL^{NE} $\not\geq L_{\omega\text{-reg}}$. Key to this issue are temporal properties that are *noncounting* (see, e.g., [23]). A property $X \subseteq runs(\Phi)$ is said to be **noncounting** if there exists an $n_0 > 0$ such that, for all $k \geq n_0$, histories π, π', and runs ρ,

$$\pi; \pi^k; \rho \in X \text{ if and only if } \pi; \pi^{k+1}; \rho \in X.$$

As a prime example of a *counting* property over $runs(\Phi)$ consider the one defined by the ω-regular expression $(\emptyset; \emptyset)^*; \{p\}^\omega$. Although for every even $k \geq 0$ we have that the run $\emptyset^k; p^\omega$ belongs to this property but the run $\emptyset^{k+1}; p^\omega$ does not. Indeed, Kučera and Strejček [19] have characterised the LTL-properties as those that are both ω-regular and non-counting.

THEOREM 10 ([19]). *A property $X \subseteq runs(\Phi)$ can be expressed by* LTL *if and only if X is ω-regular and noncounting.*

We find that for every LTL-game G the set $NE(G)$ of equilibrium runs is noncounting. As the proof of this result runs along similar lines as the one for Proposition 8, here we only give a sketch.

PROPOSITION 11. *For every* LTL*-game G, the set $NE(G)$ of equilibrium runs is noncounting.*

Sketch of proof: Consider an arbitrary LTL-game G. For every run $\rho \in NE(G)$ there is a subset $W \subseteq N$ such that ρ satisfies $\gamma_W = \bigwedge_{i \in W} \gamma_i \wedge \bigwedge_{i \in N \setminus W} \neg\gamma_i$. Moreover, by Theorem 10, there exists an $n_{\gamma_W} > 0$ by virtue of which $[\![\gamma_W]\!]$ is noncounting. At this point, consider $n_0 = \max_{W \subseteq N}\{n_{\gamma_W}\}$. The proof proceeds by showing that, for all $k \geq n_0$, histories π, π', and runs ρ,

$$\pi; \pi^k; \rho \in NE(G) \text{ if and only if } \pi; \pi^{k+1}; \rho \in NE(G).$$

For the "only if"-direction, we may assume the existence of a Nash equilibrium f that sustains $\pi; \pi^k; \rho$ and on its basis construct a Nash equilibrium f^* that induces $\pi; \pi^{k+1}; \rho \in NE(G)$. The definition of f^* is similar to the construction in Proposition 8. The "if"-direction is proven analogously. □

Thus, in particular, the ω-regular property $(\emptyset; \emptyset)^*; p^\omega$ can not be obtained as the set of equilibrium runs of any LTL-game. As an immediate consequence of Proposition 11 we thus obtain that

$$\text{LTL}^{NE} \not\geq L_{\omega\text{-reg}}.$$

In view of the characterisation result by Kučera and Strejček, Proposition 11 gives us one half of the proof that LTL $\geq$ LTL^{NE}. Indeed, it remains to be shown that the set of equilibrium runs of every LTL-game is an ω-regular set. We leave it here as an open question to be investigated in a future work.

3.2 The Next-Free Fragment

In this section we consider the fragment L_{U}, which does not contain the "next"-operator X, and show that we can characterise *every* LTL-property as the set of runs sustained by a Nash equilibrium in some L_{U}-game. For our construction we need at least two players and six additional propositional variables on which the LTL-property does not depend.

In [20] it is made a case for so-called stutter-invariant specifications.[3] Formally, we say that a temporal property $X \subseteq runs(\Phi)$ is **stutter-invariant** if, for all runs $\rho = v_0, v_1, v_2, \ldots$ and every sequence $k_0, k_1, k_2, \ldots$ of positive integers,

$$v_0, v_1, v_2, \ldots \in X \text{ if and only if } v_0^{k_0}, v_1^{k_1}, v_2^{k_2}, \ldots \in X$$

where v^k denotes the k-fold iteration of v. Thus, for instance, the property defined by $(p; \bar{p})^\omega$, henceforth denoted by *toggle*(p), does *not* define a stutter-free property, as it contains $p, \bar{p}, p, \bar{p}, \ldots$, but not $p, p, \bar{p}, \bar{p}, p, p, \bar{p}, \bar{p}, \ldots$. Peled and Wilke [25], furthermore, showed that L_{U} is the *largest* stutter-free fragment of LTL.

As *toggle*(p) is expressed by the LTL-formula $p \wedge \mathsf{G}(p \leftrightarrow \mathsf{X}\,\bar{p})$, we immediately obtain $L_{\mathsf{U}} \not\geq$ LTL as well as $L_{\mathsf{U}} \not\geq^{\mathsf{w}}$ LTL. Some reflection reveals moreover that for every $\Psi \subseteq \Phi$, if X is a stutter-invariant property on $runs(\Phi)$, then so is $X|_\Psi$, that is, property X projected to Ψ. Hence, L_{U} does not even projectively express LTL:

$$L_{\mathsf{U}} \not\geq^{\mathsf{p}} \text{LTL}.$$

We find, however, that property *toggle*(p) can be projectively expressed in equilibrium. To see this, consider the two-player game G_{toggle} with two players, i and j, who control $\Phi_i = \{p, s\}$ and $\Phi_j = \{q, r\}$, respectively, and whose goals are given by:

$$\gamma_i = p \wedge (r \leftrightarrow \bar{s}),$$
$$\gamma_j = \mathsf{F}((pq \wedge (pq \,\mathsf{U}\, p\bar{q})) \vee (\bar{p}q \wedge (\bar{p}q \,\mathsf{U}\, \bar{p}\bar{q}))) \wedge (r \leftrightarrow s).$$

Intuitively, player j's goal can only be satisfied if p is true at two subsequent time points in the future. But even if this were so, j still has to win a matching pennies game on r and s against player i. As player i would then deviate by choosing appropriate values for p and s, player j will not achieve its goal in any equilibrium. This being established, the first conjunct of γ_j will not be satisfied in any equilibrium either. Otherwise, j would deviate and win the matching pennies game on r and s and thus achieve its goal. Therefore, in no equilibrium will p subsequently assume the same truth-value. On the other hand, if p is initially true and then toggles truth-values indefinitely, there is no way player j can deviate and get its goal achieved. Accordingly, he can just as well let player i win the matching pennies game on r and s. Player i will then achieve its goal and have no incentive to deviate either.

LEMMA 12. *Let $\rho \in NE(G_{toggle})$. Then, $\rho, t \models p$ if and only if t is even and, hence, $\{\rho|_{\{p\}} : \rho \in NE(G_{toggle})\} = toggle(p)$.*

Lemma 12 not only shows that L_{U}^{NE} can projectively express $(p; \bar{p})^\omega$ in equilibrium—and thus that $L_{\mathsf{U}}^{NE} > L_{\mathsf{U}}$—it can also be leveraged to prove that the next-free fragment can actually projectively express *every* LTL-property. To this end, let $p \notin \Phi$. We then

[3] On this issue Peled and Wilke [25] write "A specification that is not invariant under stuttering will not allow refinement and will thus be useless for hierarchical (modular) reasoning." Moreover, stutter-invariance enables state space reductions in model checking of concurrent systems (also see [25]).

define a *translation* $\tau\colon \mathrm{LTL}(\Phi) \to L_{\mathsf{U}}(\Phi \cup \{p\})$ such that,

$$\begin{aligned} q^\tau &= q \\ (\neg\varphi)^\tau &= \neg(\varphi^\tau) \\ (\varphi \wedge \psi)^\tau &= \varphi^\tau \wedge \psi^\tau \\ (\varphi \vee \psi)^\tau &= \varphi^\tau \vee \psi^\tau \\ (\varphi \,\mathsf{U}\, \psi)^\tau &= \varphi^\tau \,\mathsf{U}\, \psi^\tau \\ (\mathsf{X}\,\varphi)^\tau &= (p \to p\,\mathsf{U}(\bar{p} \wedge \varphi^\tau)) \wedge (\bar{p} \to \bar{p}\,\mathsf{U}(p \wedge \varphi^\tau)), \end{aligned}$$

where $q \in \Phi$. Thus, on every run $\rho \in \Phi \cup \{p\}$ with $\rho|_{\{p\}} = (p;\bar{p})^\omega$, each formula φ and its translation φ^τ will have the same truth-value.

LEMMA 13. *Let $\varphi \in \mathrm{LTL}(\Phi)$, p a propositional variable not in Φ, and $\rho = v_0, v_1, v_2, \dots$ a run in $runs(\Phi \cup \{p\})$ such that $\rho, t \models p$ if and only if t is even. Then, $\rho \models \varphi$ if and only if $\rho \models \varphi^\tau$.*

Proof: The proof proceeds by structural induction on φ. The basis is immediate and the induction hypothesis covers all inductive cases apart from $\varphi = \mathsf{X}\,\psi$. Consider an arbitrary $t \geq 0$ and assume $\rho, t \models \mathsf{X}\,\psi$. Then, $\rho, t+1 \models \psi$ and by the induction hypothesis also $\rho, t+1 \models \psi^\tau$. Now either $\rho, t \models p$ or $\rho, t \models \bar{p}$. First assume the former. Then immediately $\rho, t \models \bar{p} \to \bar{p}\,\mathsf{U}(p \wedge \psi^\tau)$. Moreover, $\rho, t+1 \models \bar{p}$ by definition of ρ and, therefore, $\rho, t \models p\,\mathsf{U}(\bar{p} \wedge \psi^\tau)$ and also $\rho, t \models p \to (p\,\mathsf{U}(\bar{p} \wedge \psi^\tau))$. We may conclude that $\rho, t \models (\mathsf{X}\,\psi)^\tau$, as desired. The argument if $\rho, t \models \bar{p}$ is analogous.

For the opposite direction, assume $\rho, t \not\models \mathsf{X}\,\psi$. Then, $\rho, t+1 \not\models \psi$ and by the induction hypothesis $\rho, t+1 \not\models \psi^\tau$. Now, either $\rho, t \models p$ or $\rho, t \models \bar{p}$. If the former, both $\rho, t \not\models \bar{p} \wedge \psi^\tau$ and $\rho, t+1 \not\models \bar{p} \wedge \psi^\tau$. It follows that $\rho, t \not\models p\,\mathsf{U}(\bar{p} \wedge \psi^\tau)$, $\rho, t \not\models p \to (p\,\mathsf{U}(\bar{p} \wedge \psi^\tau))$, and eventually $\rho, t \not\models (\mathsf{X}\,\psi)^\tau$. As the argument if $\rho, t \models \bar{p}$ is analogous, we may conclude the proof. □

To obtain the main result of this section, we construct for each LTL-formula φ a four-player L_{U}-game with six additional variables. Intuitively, two players play the game $G^{mp}_{\varphi^\tau}$ ensuring that φ^τ holds at precisely the equilibrium runs. Two other players play G_{toggle} ensuring that an additional variable p alternately assumes the truth values true and false, and φ^τ evaluates as intended.

THEOREM 14. $L^{NE}_{\mathsf{U}} \geq^{\mathsf{p}} \mathrm{LTL}$.

Proof: Let $\varphi \in \mathrm{LTL}(\Phi)$ and $\Psi = \{p, q, r, s, x, y\}$ a set of auxiliary variables disjoint from Φ. Now construct L_{U}-game G on $\Phi \cup \Psi$ with four players, 1, 2, 3, and 4, such that $\Phi_1 = \{p, s\}$, $\Phi_2 = \{q, r\}$, $\Phi_3 = \Phi \cup \{x\}$, and $\Phi_4 = \{y\}$. Let the players' goals, moreover, be given by:

$$\begin{aligned} \gamma_1 &= p \wedge (r \leftrightarrow \bar{s}), \\ \gamma_2 &= \mathsf{F}((pq \wedge (pq\,\mathsf{U}\,p\bar{q})) \vee (\bar{p}q \wedge (\bar{p}q\,\mathsf{U}\,\bar{p}\bar{q}))) \wedge (r \leftrightarrow s), \\ \gamma_3 &= \varphi^\tau \vee (x \leftrightarrow y), \\ \gamma_4 &= \varphi^\tau \vee (x \leftrightarrow \bar{y}). \end{aligned}$$

Thus, players 1 and 2 play G_{toggle} and Lemma 12 ensures that in every equilibrium run $\rho \in \Phi \cup \Psi$, $\rho, t \models p$ if and only if t is even. Players 3 and 4—quite independently from 1 and 2—play $G^{mp}_{\varphi^\tau}$. Thus, $\rho \models \varphi^\tau$ if and only if ρ is an equilibrium run of G. Lemma 13 then yields the result. □

The following result is then an immediate consequence of Theorem 14, Proposition 4, and transitivity of $\geq^{\mathsf{p}}$.

COROLLARY 15. $L^{NE}_{\mathsf{U}} \geq^{\mathsf{p}} L_{\omega\text{-}reg}$.

It is worth noting that the size of φ^τ is exponential in the number of nestings of the X-operator, that is, even if L_{U} can projectively express every LTL-property in equilibrium, this may come at the cost of having exponentially longer goals for the players. Whether this exponential blowup is inevitable, we leave as an open question.

3.3 The Positive Future Fragment

We now consider the fragment $L_{\mathsf{X,F+}}$, where the F-operator cannot occur within the scope of a negation. We find that also this, rather weak, fragment can express more in equilibrium than it can by itself. First we have the following lemma, which intuitively says that every $L_{\mathsf{X,F+}}$-formula, when satisfied, will be satisfied after a finite number of rounds. Formally, a temporal property $X \subseteq runs(\Phi)$ is **tail-invariant** if $\rho \in X$ implies the existence of a prefix $\pi \in prefix(\rho)$ such that $\pi;\rho' \in X$ for all $\rho' \in runs(\Phi)$.

LEMMA 16. *Every temporal property $X \subseteq runs(\Phi)$ that can be expressed in $L_{\mathsf{X,F+}}$ is tail-invariant.*

Sketch of proof: Let $\varphi \in L_{\mathsf{X,F}}$. As the F-operator occurs within the scope of a negation symbol $\neg$, exploiting the equivalence of $\neg\mathsf{X}\,\varphi$ and $\mathsf{X}\,\neg\varphi$, we can transform φ to an equivalent formula in which all negation symbols occur in front of propositional variables.

Let $\varphi \in L_{\mathsf{X,F+}}$ and assume that φ is in this normal form. Consider an arbitrary run $\rho = v_0, v_1, \dots$ in $runs(\Phi)$ such that $\rho \models \varphi$. We have to show that there is a prefix $\pi \in prefix(\rho)$ such that $\pi;\rho' \models \varphi$ for all $\rho' \in runs(\Phi)$. Define inductively for every formula $\psi \in L_{\mathsf{X,F+}}$ and every $t \geq 0$, $\kappa_{\rho,t}(\psi)$ the following:

$$\begin{aligned} \kappa_{\rho,t}(p) &= \kappa_{\rho,t}(\bar{p}) = 0 \\ \kappa_{\rho,t}(\chi_1 \wedge \chi_2) &= \kappa_{\rho,t}(\chi_1 \vee \chi_2) = \max(\kappa_{\rho,t}(\chi_1), \kappa_{\rho,t}(\chi_2)) \\ \kappa_{\rho,t}(\mathsf{X}\,\chi) &= \kappa_{\rho,t}(\chi) + 1 \\ \kappa_{\rho,t}(\mathsf{F}\,\chi) &= \begin{cases} t' - t + \kappa_{\rho,t'}(\chi) & \text{if } \rho, t \models \mathsf{F}\,\chi, \\ 0 & \text{otherwise,} \end{cases} \end{aligned}$$

where $t' = \min\{t'' \geq t \colon \rho, t'' \models \chi\}$. By a structural induction on ψ it can then be shown that $\rho, t \models \psi$ implies the existence of a prefix $\pi \in prefix(\rho)$ with $length(\pi) \leq t + \kappa_{\rho,t}(\psi)$ such that $\pi_\psi;\rho', t \models \psi$ for all $\rho' \in runs(\Phi)$. This holds in particular for φ, which yields the result. □

The property defined by the LTL-formula $\mathsf{G}\,p$ may serve as the quintessential property that is *not* tail-invariant, and is neither expressible nor weakly expressible in $L_{\mathsf{X,F+}}$. Observing that tail-invariance of $X \subseteq runs(\Phi)$ implies tail-invariance of $X|_\Psi$ for every $\Psi \subseteq \Phi$, we may even conclude that $\mathsf{G}\,p$ cannot even be projectively expressed by $L_{\mathsf{X,F+}}$. Yet, as $\mathsf{G}\,p$ is LTL-equivalent to $\neg\mathsf{F}\,\bar{p}$, in virtue of Lemma 6, we find that $L_{\mathsf{X,F+}}$ can projectively express $\mathsf{G}\,p$ in equilibrium. Hence,

$$L^{NE}_{\mathsf{X,F+}} >^{\mathsf{p}} L_{\mathsf{X,F+}}.$$

Leveraging the same ideas along with the fact that every ultimately periodic run can be characterised in $L_{\mathsf{X,F,G}}$ with only one occurrence of the G-operator, we also obtain the following expressiveness result for $L_{\mathsf{X,F+}}$ with respect to LTL.

PROPOSITION 17. $L_{\mathsf{X,F+}} \geq^{\mathsf{wp}} \mathrm{LTL}$.

Proof: Let $\varphi \in \mathrm{LTL}$. If φ is unsatisfiable, Lemma 6 yields the result immediately as $p \vee \bar{p}$ is a formula in $L_{\mathsf{X,F+}}$. On the other hand, if φ is satisfiable then by Theorem 2 and Proposition 3 there is an ultimately periodic run $\rho = v_0, v_1, \dots$ with starting index s and period p such that is characterised by the LTL-formula χ_ρ given by

$$\textstyle\bigwedge_{0 \leq t \leq s+p} \mathsf{X}^t \chi_{v_t} \wedge \mathsf{X}^s\,\mathsf{G}(\bigwedge_{v \in 2^\Phi}(\chi_v \to \mathsf{X}^p \chi_v)).$$

By suitably applying the laws of propositional logic, the duality of F and G, as well as the equivalence of $\neg\mathsf{X}\,\varphi$ and $\mathsf{X}\,\neg\varphi$, we find that the *negation* of χ_ρ is equivalent to

$$\textstyle\bigvee_{0 \leq t \leq s+p} \mathsf{X}^i \neg\chi_{v_i} \vee \mathsf{X}^s\,\mathsf{F}(\bigvee_{v \in 2^\Phi}(\chi_v \wedge \mathsf{X}^p \neg\chi_v)),$$

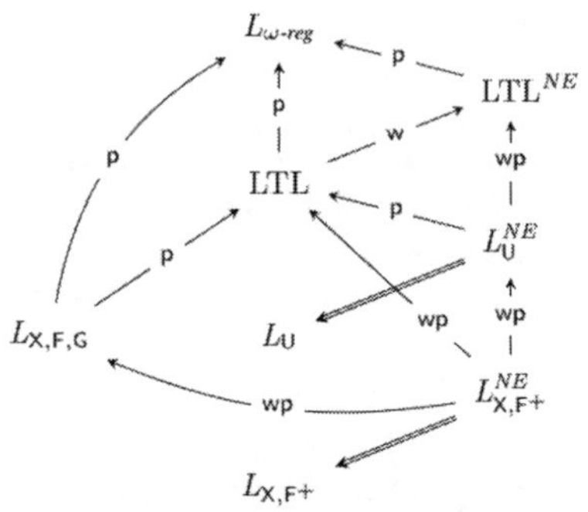

Figure 2: Relation between expressiveness and expressiveness in equilibrium of LTL-fragments assuming $|\Phi| \geq 2$. Double arrows relate to strict expressiveness ($L_1 > L_2$).

which is included in the fragment $L_{\mathsf{X,F+}}$. By Lemma 6 we know that $L_{\mathsf{X,F+}}$ can projectively express χ_ρ in equilibrium. Hence, $L_{\mathsf{X,F+}}$ can weakly projectively express φ in equilibrium, as desired. □

4. RELATED WORK

The expressive power of LTL and many of its syntactic fragments has been a research topic for decades, with work showing connections with other temporal logic languages as well as results classifying the power of LTL and its fragments [27]. The most basic and well known classifications are with respect to sub-languages, that is, LTL fragments where only some operators are allowed. However, more refined studies have also been conducted, for instance, LTL fragments with respect to the allowed number of propositional variables or the number of nested temporal operators [9].

Most of these studies have focused not only in the expressive power of the resulting sublogics but also in the implications of imposing such restrictions in the complexity of the model checking and satisfiability problems of such sublogics. These studies have also made it possible to understand connections between LTL fragments and standard automata models over infinite words—which in turn also easily show how to define different automata-theoretic decision procedures for each LTL sublanguage at hand [32].

Despite the very many studies about the expressive power of LTL and related sublanguages, to the best of our knowledge, there are no results on the expressive power of LTL or its fragments with respect to the classes of runs that can be sustained by some Nash equilibrium. In this paper, we study precisely that issue and provide the first known results in the literature. The results are rather promising: they show that even though some LTL sublanguage, say L_1, may be strictly more expressive than other LTL sublanguage, say L_2, when interpreted over the full class of ω-regular runs, such two sublogics L_1 and L_2 become equi-expressive when interpreted over a class of runs that can be sustained by some Nash equilibrium in a given class of games, as many of our results show.

As this kind of result can usually only be obtained by adding extra propositional variables to the "weaker" language, we also studied the expressive power, and game-theoretic implications, of allowing languages interpreted over different sets of propositional variables (projective expressiveness). Again, the results were promising in the sense that they show that generally weaker LTL sublogics can be made as expressive as generally stronger LTL sublogics by the addition of fresh propositional variables to the weaker language, a notion that goes back to the 1950s [3, 8] and has proven useful in a number of settings (see, for instance, [18, 6, 13, 16]).

5. CONCLUSION

In this paper, we have explored the temporal properties that are characterised by the equilibrium runs of iterated Boolean games, where the players' dichotomous preferences are represented by formulae in fragments of Linear Time Logic (LTL). The Nash equilibria of an iterated Boolean game are fully determined by the goals of the players and the way control of the propositional variables is distributed over the players. In particular, they are not dependent on an additional underlying game structure—like, for instance, *concurrent game structures* (see, for instance, [1]). This enabled us to focus on the *logical* aspects of Nash equilibrium and accordingly we formulated our research issue in terms of expressiveness.

We investigated the concept of expressiveness in equilibrium for a number of fragments of LTL. We found that for a given fragment every (non-trivial) property that can be (projectively) expressed can also be (projectively) expressed in equilibrium, but not generally the other way round. For an overview of our results see Figure 2. In the future, we plan to explore more fully the links that remain missing. In particular, whether $\mathrm{LTL} \geq \mathrm{LTL}^{NE}$ is still open. Other questions for future research concern the minimal number of players and additional propositional variables that may be needed to express or projectively express temporal properties in a particular fragment.

Apart from specific fragments, the concept of *expressiveness in equilibrium* gives rise to a number of more abstract and conceptual questions. First, most of our game constructions involve a "matching pennies" game like G^{mp}_{φ}. These games establish a crucial link between runs that satisfy a given formula and equilibrium runs in iterated Boolean games. This feature, however, is due to one player trying to achieve $p \leftrightarrow q$ and another $p \leftrightarrow \bar{q}$, and as such is largely of a non-temporal nature. An interesting question is if this is peculiar to the results in this paper or that it points at a more fundamental connection with the concept of expressiveness in equilibrium.

Second, our investigations in a considerable measure relied on projective expressiveness, as our game constructions usually involve additional propositional variables. Expressiveness in equilibrium does not afford such freedom and one would suspect a narrower gap between expressiveness and expressiveness in equilibrium that between the respective projective notions for most fragments. An important question is how narrow this gap is.

Third, as in most work on model checking and concurrent game structures, the strategies of the players are functions from histories to choices whereas, in stark contrast, the preferences of the players are represented by logical formulae. As such the former are much finer grained than the latter. One may wonder to what extent the gap between the standard notion of expressiveness and expressiveness in equilibrium can be attributed to this "mismatch." For instance, would the phenomenon also occur in iterated Boolean games, if the players' strategies are similarly specified by temporal formulae?

Fourth, all our notions of expressiveness naturally extend to game-theoretic solution concepts other than Nash Equilibrium and we aim to investigate some of these concepts in future work.

Finally, the original motivation for our work was the problem of allocating tasks to agents so that a given property is satisfied in all resulting equilibria. We hope that our research on expressiveness in equilibrium shed some light on this issue and to what extent the design of multi-agent systems in practice can be simplified by providing "lean" temporal specifications of individual agents who can be assumed to play strategies that together form an equilibrium.

Acknowledgments

The authors are financially supported by the ERC under Advanced Investigator Grant 291528 ("RACE") at Oxford.

REFERENCES

[1] R. Alur, T. A. Henzinger, and O. Kupferman. Alternating-time temporal logic. *Journal of the ACM*, 49(5):672–713, 2002.

[2] C. Baier and J.-P. Katoen. *Principles of Model Checking*. The MIT Press, 2008.

[3] E. W. Beth. On Padoa's method in the theory of definition. *Indagationes Mathematicae*, 15:330–339, 1953.

[4] E. Bonzon, M. Lagasquie, J. Lang, and B. Zanuttini. Boolean games revisited. In *Proceedings of the Seventeenth European Conference on Artificial Intelligence (ECAI-2006)*, 2006.

[5] N. Bulling, W. Jamroga, and J. Dix. Reasoning about temporal properties of rational play. *Annals of Mathematics and Artificial Intelligence*, 53(1):51–114, 2008.

[6] C. C. Chang and H. J. Keisler. *Model Theory*, volume 73 of *Studies in Logic and the Foundations of Mathematics*. North-Holland Publishing Company, third edition, 1990.

[7] E. M. Clarke, O. Grumberg, and D. A. Peled. *Model Checking*. The MIT Press: Cambridge, MA, 2000.

[8] W. Craig. Three uses of the Herbrand-Gentzen theorem in relating model theory and proof theory. *Journal of Symbolic Logic*, 22(3):269–285, 1957.

[9] S. Demri and P. Schnoebelen. The complexity of propositional linear temporal logics in simple cases. *Information and Computation*, 174(1):84–103, 2002.

[10] E. A. Emerson. Temporal and modal logic. In J. van Leeuwen, editor, *Handbook of Theoretical Computer Science Volume B: Formal Models and Semantics*, pages 996–1072. Elsevier, 1990.

[11] E. A. Emerson and J. Y. Halpern. 'Sometimes' and 'not never' revisited: on branching time versus linear time temporal logic. *Journal of the ACM*, 33(1):151–178, 1986.

[12] U. Endriss, S. Kraus, J. Lang, and M. Wooldridge. Designing incentives for Boolean games. In R. Turner, Yolum, E. A. Sonenberg, and Stone, editors, *10th International Conference on Autonomous Agents and Multiagent Systems (AAMAS 2011)*, volume 1, pages 79–86, 2011.

[13] A. P. Gheerbrant and B. ten Cate. Craig interpolation for linear temporal languages. In E. Grädel and R. Kahle, editors, *Proceedings of 23rd international Workshop, CSL 2009, 18th Annual Conference of the EACSL, Coimbra, Portugal, September 7-11, 2009*, volume 5771 of *Lecture Notes in Computer Science*, pages 287–301. Springer, 2009.

[14] J. Gutierrez, P. Harrenstein, and M. Wooldridge. Reasoning about equilibria in game-like concurrent systems. In *14th Conference on Principles of Knowledge Representation and Reasoning (KR-2014)*, pages 408–417, 2014.

[15] J. Gutierrez, P. Harrenstein, and M. Wooldridge. Iterated Boolean games. *Information and Computation*, 242:53–79, 2015.

[16] J. Y. Halpern, D. Samet, and E. Segev. On definability in multimodal logic. *The Review of Symbolic Logic*, 2(3):451–468, 2009.

[17] P. Harrenstein, W. van der Hoek, J.-J. Meyer, and C. Witteveen. Boolean games. In J. van Benthem, editor, *Proceeding of the Eighth Conference on Theoretical Aspects of Rationality and Knowledge (TARK VIII)*, pages 287–298, 2001.

[18] W. Hodges. *Model Theory*. Cambridge University Press, 1993.

[19] A. Kučera and J. Strejček. The stuttering principle revisited. *Acta Informatica*, 41(7–8):415–434, 2005.

[20] L. Lamport. Specifying concurrent program modules. *ACM Transactions on Programming Languages and Systems*, 5(2):190–222, 1983.

[21] R. D. Luce and H. Raiffa. *Games and Decisions*. John Wiley & Sons, 1957.

[22] M. Maschler, E. Solan, and S. Zamir. *Game Theory*. Cambridge U.P., 2013.

[23] A. Mateescu and A. Salomaa. Formal languages: An introduction and a synopsis. In G. Rozenberg and A. Salomaa, editors, *Handbook of Formal Languages*, volume I: Word, Language, Grammar, chapter 1. Springer, 1997.

[24] M. J. Osborne and A. Rubinstein. *A Course in Game Theory*. The MIT Press: Cambridge, MA, 1994.

[25] D. A. Peled and T. Wilke. Stutter-invariant temporal properties are expressible without next-time operator. *Information Processing Letters*, 63(5):243–246, 1997.

[26] A. Pnueli. The temporal logic of programs. In *Proceedings of the Eighteenth IEEE Symposium on the Foundations of Computer Science*, pages 46–57, 1977.

[27] A. M. Rabinovich. Expressive power of temporal logics. In L. Brim, P. Jancar, M. Kretínský, and A. Kucera, editors, *CONCUR 2002—Concurrency Theory*, volume 2421 of *Lecture Notes in Computer Science*, pages 57–75. Springer, 2002.

[28] Y. Shoham and K. Leyton-Brown. *Multiagent Systems: Algorithmic, Game-Theoretic, and Logical Foundations*. Cambridge University Press: Cambridge, England, 2008.

[29] A. P. Sistla and E. M. Clarke. The complexity of propositional linear temporal logics. *Journal of the ACM*, 32(3):733–749, 1985.

[30] W. Thomas. Languages, automata, and logic. In G. Rozenberg and A. Salomaa, editors, *Handbook of Formal Languages*, volume III: Beyond works, chapter 5. Springer, 1997.

[31] M. Y. Vardi. Branching vs. linear time: Final showdown. In T. Margaria and W. Yi, editors, *Proceedings of the 2001 Conference on Tools and Algorithms for the Construction and Analysis of Systems, TACAS 2001* volume 2031 of *Lecture Notes in Computer Science*, pages 1–22. Springer, 2001.

[32] M. Y. Vardi and P. Wolper. Reasoning about infinite computations. *Information and Computation*, 115(1):1–37, 1994.

[33] P. Wolper. Temporal logic can be more expressive. *Information and Control*, 56, 1983.

Gap in pagination due to formatting issues.

Pages 716-727

The Misrepresentation Game: How to win at negotiation while seeming like a nice guy

Jonathan Gratch, Zahra Nazari and Emmanuel Johnson
University of Southern California, Institute for Creative Technologies
12015 Waterfront Dr., Playa Vista, CA 90094
gratch@ict.usc.edu

ABSTRACT

Recently, interest has grown in agents that negotiate with people: to teach negotiation, to negotiate on behalf of people, and as a challenge problem to advance artificial social intelligence. Humans negotiate differently from algorithmic approaches to negotiation: people are not purely self-interested but place considerable weight on norms like fairness; people exchange information about their mental state and use this to judge the fairness of a social exchange; and people lie. Here, we focus on lying. We present an analysis of how people (or agents interacting with people) might optimally lie (maximally benefit themselves) while maintaining the illusion of fairness towards the other party. In doing so, we build on concepts from game theory and the preference-elicitation literature, but apply these to human, not rational, behavior. Our findings demonstrate clear benefits to lying and provide empirical support for a heuristic – the "fixed-pie lie" – that substantially enhances the efficiency of such deceptive algorithms. We conclude with implications and potential defenses against such manipulative techniques.

General Terms and Keywords

Negotiation, Game Theory, Preference Elicitation

1. INTRODUCTION

Negotiation is an indispensable skill for any social creature. Within the multiagent systems community, negotiation between autonomous agents has been a central focus of research [28, 42, 45], both as a means for advancing electronic commerce [31] and as a challenge problem to enhance the capability of socially intelligent systems [24, 56]. More recently, there has been growing interest in agents that negotiate with people [27, 41]. There are many motivations for exploring human-agent negotiation. Agents could serve as virtual role players to help teach negotiation skills [7, 26]. Negotiation agents could allow companies more flexibility over setting fixed prices on the websites. More broadly, agents that understand human negotiation might serve as decision-support tools, for example, serving as negotiation mediators or providing automated analysis of human-human negotiations [10].

Negotiations between people differ considerably from the rational and structured frameworks favored in the multiagent community. Rational models, such as game-theory, treat negotiation as a joint decision between self-interested rational agents [35]. Communication, from this perspective is often considered superfluous "cheap talk" that cannot affect payoffs. Thus, negotiating agents typically interact via highly-constrained and structured mechanisms such as the alternating-offer protocol [44]. In contrast, human negotiators reach agreements through unstructured discussions that frequently violate axioms of rationality. For example, most people place considerable weight on social norms such as honesty and fairness [16, 20]. People don't view talk as cheap [18] and readily exchange honest information about their needs and goals [48, 50]. Indeed, withholding such information undermines trust [46]. These prosocial conventions can offer considerable advantages. People achieve higher joint outcomes than are predicted from rational models [21]. Unfortunately, prosocial tendencies also make people vulnerable to exploitation. This highlights another important difference between people and agents: people lie to gain strategic advantage [15].

This paper describes a rational analysis of lying in negotiation. Our analysis differs from classical game-theoretic analysis of communication between rational negotiators (such as [9, 14, 56]) and from behavioral game-theoretic analysis of how human negotiators behave towards each other (see [8]). Rather, we examine how a rational self-interested actor should act towards a typical human negotiator. Such an actor must reason about, and sometimes act in accordance with human social conventions, without being bound by them. Unfortunately, some human actors behave in this fashion. Indeed, this is the definition of the Machiavellian personality [22].

The literature on human negotiation has documented the myriad ways negotiators can lie. One approach is to feign a position of power. For example, when negotiating for a car, people often lie about their alternative offers ("I got a much better offer from the last dealer" or "this car is so popular we can't give discounts"). This can be an effective strategy, but often leaves the other party feeling abused and can undermine the possibility of getting deals from this party in the future [16].

A more effective approach would be to lie to one's opponent in such a way that they feel like they got a fair deal. O'Connor and Carnevale [38] present a simple but surprisingly effective technique for doing just that. They point out that negotiations often involve issues where both parties' interests align but they often believe they are in opposition. For example, consider a negotiation where both parties want to divide a basket of fruit (see Figure 1). Parties might assume that each side has the same interests, where in fact one side wants all fruit equally, but the other side only wants apples. The apples are referred to as a *common-value issue* because both parties' preferences are aligned. The presence of common-value issues creates the opportunity for an effective negotiation tactic. If one party realizes an issue is of common value before the other, they can feign opposed interest. This allows them to "claim value" over the undesired issue and trade this value off against something they want. For example, in the bottom half of Figure 1, the woman has misrepresented her interests in such a way that she wins the negotiation yet the man believes he received a fair deal.

Appears in: Proceedings of the 15th International Conference on Autonomous Agents and Multiagent Systems (AAMAS 2016), J. Thangarajah, K. Tuyls, C. Jonker, S. Marsella (eds.), May 9–13, 2016, Singapore.

Figure 1: Bargaining without (top) and with (bottom) lying

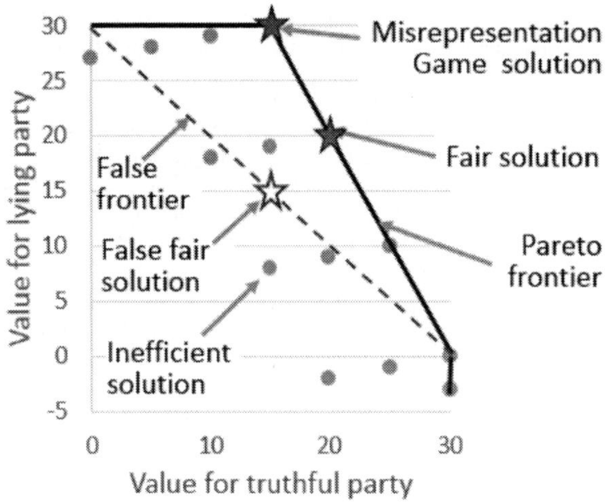

Figure 2: The space of bargaining solutions

In this article, we present an analysis of how people (or agents interacting with people) might optimally lie. By this, we consider how they might misrepresent their own interests in such a way to maximally benefit themselves while creating an illusion of fairness towards the other party. Our analysis builds on a game theoretic perspective and presents a simple game – *the misrepresentation game* – that formalizes this notion. We also build on techniques from the preference-elicitation literature to show how people (or agents interacting with people) can efficiently discover their opponent's interests without revealing much about themselves.

Although we build on rational techniques like game theory, our goal is not to find a rational solution to the misrepresentation game in the classical sense, but rather to identify strategies that a purely self-interested actor could use against typical human opponents. This analysis is in service of several more fundamental goals. First, we seek better understanding of communication processes in human negotiation and how communication can be misused for malicious ends. Second, we aim to produce general models of negotiation that can guide behavior of agents that negotiate with people. In that people lie, it is important for agents to understand, detect and potentially defend against such malicious strategies. Finally, we seek to use these models to teach negotiation skills. For example, by practicing with malicious agents, human students can better prepare themselves to deal with malicious behavior that, unfortunately far too often, arises in the real world (e.g., see [24]).

In the sections that follow, we first define the misrepresentation game. We next present a simplified version of the game wherein the preferences of the opponent are assumed to be known in advance. We describe a surprisingly simple heuristic that appears optimal for a common class of negotiation tasks. We next extend the approach to situations where the opponent's preferences are unknown in advance and must be inferred through information exchange. Finally, we present user study that demonstrates that people are more satisfied with a deal from a lying agent than the same deal from an honest one. We conclude with a discussion of limitations and extensions to the current approach.

2. THE MISREPRESENTATION GAME

Before defining the misrepresentation game, we first introduce a formalization of negotiation and summarize some of the main behavioral findings on how people typically solve this task.

Multi-issue bargaining task: Negotiation can be formalized in many ways. In this article, we adopt a common formulation known as the multi-issue bargaining task [30] which has become a *de facto* standard for both teaching and research on negotiation in the social and computer sciences (e.g., see [1, 33, 52]). Multi-issue bargaining generalizes simpler games developed in game theory, such as the ultimatum game, and more closely approximates many of the challenges found in real-life negotiations.

In its basic form, multi-issue bargaining requires parties to reach agreement over a set of issues. Each issue consists of a set of levels and players must jointly decide on a level for each issue (levels might correspond to the amount apples in a basket of fruit, or different attributes of a single object, such as the price or warranty of a car). Each party receives some payoff for each possible agreement and each player's payoff is usually not known to the other party. The payoff is often, but not necessarily, assumed to be additive (e.g., a player's total payoff might be the sum of the value obtained for each issue, weighted by the importance of that issue). If parties fail to agree, they each receive a (usually much smaller) "disagreement payoff" (also known as a BATNA). For example, Figure 1 illustrates a two-issue (apples and oranges), four-level (zero-to-three fruit) bargaining task, where each party assigns different weights to the issues ($5 vs. $10 for apples, respectively). Henceforth, we assume the disagreement payoff is zero for each party.

Human negotiation behavior: Multi-issue bargaining has been studied extensively from the perspectives of game theory [35]), behavioral game theory (e.g., [43]) and psychology (e.g., [39]). This research has clarified important and systematic differences between rational predictions and actual human behavior. In particular, people rarely act out of pure self-interest. Rather, they exhibit "other-regarding" preferences (such as the desire for fairness and reciprocity). Further, they often feel bound by social and conversational conventions, such as honesty. Finally, people have limited cognitive abilities and have difficulty, in particular, with the recursive theory-of-mind reasoning required by game theoretic solutions. In solving the misrepresentation game, we assume human negotiators will exhibit the following empirically-supported characteristics (we consider ways to relax these assumptions in the conclusion):

Fairness: Following Rawls [40], we assume negotiators aim for an equitable solution. There have been many attempts to formalize principles of fairness [53]. Here, we adopt Kalai's principle of max-min fairness [29] (i.e., negotiators will strive to minimize the difference in payout between the parties in a negotiation). There is good empirical support that human negotiators tend towards equal distributions across a wide variety of contexts [20, 43].

Efficiency: Following Nash [35], we assume negotiators prefer deals that are *Pareto efficient*. This means that if a deal can be improved for one player without harming the other, the improvement will be preferred by both players. For example, Figure 2 shows the space of all possible deals for the negotiation illustrated in Figure 1. The x-axis represents the value of deals that the man could receive, whereas the y-axis represents the value of deals for the woman. The Pareto frontier represents the set of efficient solutions and any deal below this can be ignored. Note, however, that negotiators can only calculated the frontier if they share their preferences, but in most negotiations, this information is unknown to one or both negotiators. This leads to our next assumption.

The cooperative principle of language: Following Grice [25], we adopt the perspective that to communicate at all, negotiators must adhere to communicative conventions. Grice argues that speakers will exchange honest, relevant, clear and sufficient information to complete the task at hand. Clearly, some negotiators are tempted to violate these maxims. In particular, negotiators are reluctant to reveal their true preferences (violating Grice's maxim of quantity) as this makes negotiators vulnerable to exploitation. Yet to find efficient solutions, negotiators must exchange honest information. One solution to this dilemma is the principle of *reciprocal information exchange*: reveal information if and only if the other party reciprocates [55]. By engaging in such reciprocity, parties develop a mutual understanding of each other's preferences and can discover Pareto efficient solutions [50]. Thus, we assume that parties are honest, relevant and clear, but will only reveal preference information if comparable information is offered in exchange.

Fixed-pie bias: Finally, following Bazerman [4], we assume that cognitive limitations lead to departures from rational predictions. In particular, in what is known as the *fixed-pie bias,* negotiators often assume that the other party's interests are completely opposed to their own. In the absence of information exchange, this bias explains why negotiators often fail to discover efficient solutions [50]. It also implies they will be predisposed to believe lies that are consistent with this bias [38]. We assume human players hold this bias.

Definition: From the discussion above, most human negotiators will strive for fair and efficient solutions, and will discover these to the extent they engage in reciprocal information exchange. However, this creates the opportunity for malicious negotiators to misrepresent their preferences for strategic gain. For example, in the bottom of Figure 1, the woman is lying about her true preferences (by saying she likes all fruit equally when she truly prefers apples). Assuming the male negotiator takes this lie at face value, he would perceive a different (and incorrect) Pareto frontier (illustrated by the dashed diagonal line in Figure 2) wherein the deal giving away all three apples appears fair and efficient.

Given these preliminaries, we define the *misrepresentation game* as the problem of:

- gaining an information advantage by learning the opponent's preferences without revealing one's own preferences, and
- identifying a false set of preferences to communicate to one's opponent that (a) maximize one's own reward from a negotiation, (b) subject to the constraint that the other party believes the negotiated agreement to be fair and efficient.

For the remainder of this article we will formalize and analyze the properties of a special case of this game, subject to certain assumptions about the form of each player's preferences.

3. SOLVING THE GAME

We present an efficient solution to the misrepresentation game subject to an additional assumption about the form of players' utility functions. As we will discuss, this assumption simplifies both the problem of finding a false set of preferences and the problem of eliciting true preferences from the opponent. The cost of this assumption is it precludes certain utility functions and certain beneficial lies (which we will revisit at the conclusion). Our solution is presented in three stages. In Section 3.1, we present a solution when the opponent's preferences are known in advance. Section 3.2 extends this solution the case where the opponent's preferences are unknown. Finally, Section 3.3 presents a simulation study that assesses the solution's effectiveness.

3.1 When opponent's preferences known

The misrepresentation game can be greatly simplified if we know our other party's preferences in advance of the negotiation. This might occur if the other party first truthfully reveals their preferences, or the liar has done sufficient research to accurately estimate them. When the opponent's preferences are known, the game can be cast as an optimization problem: for all possible preference weights on each issue, identify the set of weights that maximizes the value to self while seeming fair.

Specifically, let N be the number of issues and let each issue have L_i levels (L_i could be an integer, e.g., corresponding to the number of apples and oranges in Figure 1; or it could be a real-valued resource that can be continuously partitioned, such as an employee's salary). Let $\{a_i\}$ be numeric weights representing the deceiver's true preference for each issue i and $\{b_i\}$ be the true preferences of their opponent. We assume $\{a_i\}$ and $\{b_i\}$ are permutations of $\{1,\ldots,N\}$. Let and x_i and y_i represent the portion of issue i claimed by the deceiver and the opponent, respectively and $(\{x_i\},\{y_i\})$ denote a possible deal. Then, the objective of the deceiver is to find the optimal false preferences $\{\bar{a}_i\}$, also a permutations of $\{1,\ldots,N\}$, that maximizes the deceiver's true utility, given that the negotiated solution appears to be efficient and fair:

$$\max_{\bar{a}_i} \sum_{i=1}^{n} a_i \cdot x_i \qquad (1)$$

where x_i is the optimal solution of

$$\max_{x_i, y_i} \bar{a}_i \cdot x_i \qquad (2)$$

such that :

$$\sum_{i=1}^{n} \bar{a}_i \cdot x_i \leq \sum_{i=1}^{n} b_i \cdot y_i \qquad (3)$$

$$\forall i : x_i + y_i \leq L_i \qquad (4)$$

$$0 \leq x_i, y_i \leq L_i \qquad (5)$$

In general, (2-5) finds the optimal efficient solution, which satisfies Kalai's fairness condition which is imposed by constraint (3).

Ranking assumption: Note that our formulation does not allow arbitrary utility functions. Rather, treats each issue as a resource to be partitioned, and it restricts players to holding a qualitative ranking over the set of issues (i.e., $\{a_i\}$, $\{\bar{a}_i\}$, and $\{b_i\}$ are assumed to be permutations of $\{1,\ldots,N\}$). This restriction is not uncommon in multi-attribute problems as players often have difficulty articulating their preferences as a numeric utility function. Rather, people are more comfortable communicating qualitatively (e.g., they are good at saying they like A more than B but poor at quantifying how much they prefer A to B). Equations (1) and (3) also entail that issues are independent and that overall utility is a liner combination of issue-ranks. Together, these assumptions define a standard utility function known as the Borda Score [3] often used by AI preference-elicitation techniques (e.g., see [11]).

The ranking assumption simplifies the problem of finding the optimal lie. It also simplifies the problem, introduced in the next subsection, of eliciting preferences from the opponent (as many common preference elicitation techniques use the Borda Score). A consequence, however, is it precludes utility functions where preferences are non-linear or interdependent. It also limits the type of lies a negotiator can make. They can lie about the relative ranking of their preferences but not the absolute value of different issues. We return to these limitations in the conclusion.

The optimization problem could be generalized. Constraints (1) and (3) could be relaxed, but may preclude efficient solutions. Constraint (3) could be replaced with other fairness criteria, such as Nass's axiom of symmetry [35]. The ranking assumption could also be relaxed but will require additional constraints on lying to preclude trivial or degenerate solutions.

Solution: Our formulation consists of two-levels of optimization which is not straightforward to solve. Fortunately, Nguyen proves that it can be reformulated and solved as a mixed integer linear program (see [37] for details). Nguyen further proves that under the additional assumption that all levels are equal (i.e., for all i,j, $L_i = L_j$), the optimal solution to the misrepresentation problem is to pretend the same preferences as one's opponent (i.e., $\{\bar{a}_i\} = \{b_i\}$). This simple solution seems to apply more generally to a range of bargaining tasks, so from this we propose the following heuristic:

Definition: The *fixed-pie-lie heuristic* is to feign the identical preference structure as one's opponent.

One psychological advantage of the fixed-pie lie heuristic is that aligns nicely with the fixed-pie bias introduced in Section 2. According to this bias, people often come to a negotiation assuming their interests are opposed and that they will only be able to achieve half of their value (see [49]). In Figure 1, the total "pie" is appears to be worth \$30 to the man on the left, thus it is plausible to believe that \$15 is a fair deal. In fact, as parties have different preferences, the fair deal is \$20. With the fixed-pie heuristic, a malicious opponent recognizes the pie can be grown but keeps this additional value for themselves.

Lying in this way can afford considerable benefit and comes at no cost (at lease when the opponent's preferences are known). This is illustrated in Figure 3. This figure contrasts the value obtained by lying with the value obtained by being honest for a large set of possible negotiation problems. Specifically, given N issues, each player could have one of $N!$ possible rankings (i.e., all permutations of the N issues). As each player could have a different ranking, this creates a space of $(N!)^2$ possible joint rankings. A negotiation problem must also specify the number of levels per issue. Figure 3 illustrates all 14,400 possible combinations of player preferences for two extreme cases: (1) continuous – where each issue can be continuously partitioned; and (2) 2-level discrete – wherein each issue consists of a single indivisible quantity that must be allocated to one party or the other. In each case, L_i equals one for all levels.

Figure 3: Shows relative advantage of lying for all possible 5-issue negotiations.

Figure 3 shows it never hurts to lie. In the continuous case (the blue circles), lying always offers improvement except when the negotiation truly has a fixed-pie structure (in this case, the solution is to tell the truth, which affords each party 7.5). In the discrete case (red circles), lying sometimes affords no benefit over truth, but also doesn't hurt. As the number of ways to partition each issue increases, these two sets of solutions will converge.

It should also be noted that the fixed-pie lie is especially nasty to the opponent. At least for the continuous case, the opponent always receives half of the diminished "fake pie." For the 5-issue problem, this corresponds to 7.5 (the opponent can sometimes do better than this in the discrete case, but always no-better than the liar).

3.2 When opponent's preferences unknown

The previous analysis suggests the fixed-pie-lie heuristic is optimal when the opponent's preferences are known. Unfortunately, negotiators do not have perfect access to their opponent's preferences but must infer them through an exchange of information. In agent-agent negotiations, opponent preferences (if they are considered at all) are typically inferred by the exchanging offers and counterproposals [2]. In human negotiations, preferences are most commonly inferred from explicit statements of preferences [36, 50]. We present a solution to this problem, subject to assumptions about how the opponent communicates. Unlike the perfect-information game, our solution is heuristic and we make no claims of optimality.

First, as discussed in Section 2, the cooperative principle of language suggests that human negotiators feel bound by social norms of honesty [25] and engage in reciprocal information exchange [5] (i.e., if preference information is provided by one party, the other party should reciprocate). This implies that a negotiator cannot elicit their opponent's preferences without giving up some information in return. Of course, an agent can give up fake information, but it is unclear how to lie without having perfect information about the opponent. Further, premature lies can limit the liar's options. For example, an agent might pretend they like apples best (when truthfully they like them least), but if they subsequently learn the opponent likes them least as well, they are trapped in their own lie: they can either agree to accept the undesired apples or admit to the

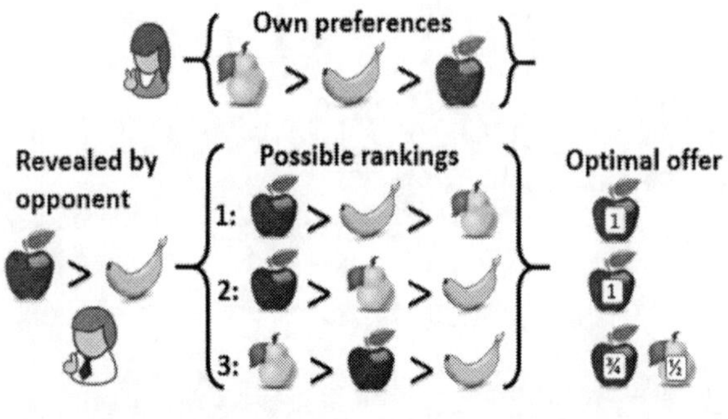

Figure 4: Example of preference elicitation

lie. Our solution relies on the assumption that people follow the cooperative principles of language and liars cannot admit to lies.

Second, as discussed in Section 3.1, people have difficulty expressing numeric preferences but they find it easy to make pairwise comparisons of the relative importance of different issues. Thus, we assume negotiators can only ask or assert relative pairwise comparison statements (e.g., "Do you like apples better than oranges?"). Obviously, more complex preference statements can be constructed from sequences of these primitives.

Finally, following [9], we analyze this problem as a "take it or leave it" bargaining game where parties first engage in several rounds of information exchange and then one party (the agent) makes a single offer which the other party (the human) must accept or reject. We assume the human opponent will accept this offer if and only if it appears fair under the possible models they have of the agent's preferences. Admittedly, this assumption imposes strong constraints on the liar's behavior: they are forced to make an initial offer and then stick to this offer at all costs. This may result in suboptimal solutions but greatly simplifies decision-making.

From these assumptions, it is clear that misrepresenting agents should (a) ask questions about their opponent's preferences that gain the maximal information while (b) reciprocating by offering information that allows the most freedom to misrepresent and then (c) make an offer when the costs of (b) exceed the benefits of (a).

Eliciting preferences: The first problem (a) is to determine which questions to ask, and in what sequence, to quickly and efficiently minimize uncertainty about the opponent's ranking. This problem has already been addressed in the preference-elicitation literature. Here we adopt the solution introduced by Lu and Boutilier [32].

We illustrate this algorithm with the aid of Figure 4. This example imagines a 3-issue negotiation over pears, bananas and apples. Each negotiator could hold one of 3! Possible rankings. The deceptive negotiator holds the ranking at the top (pears > bananas > apples). The other negotiator reveals that they prefer apples to bananas. This information rules out some possible rankings, but three are consistent with this statement. The figure also illustrates the optimal "fair" offer for each of these possible rankings. For example, if the opponent truly preferred apples>bananas>pears, then the liar should claim the same, offer one apple to their opponent, and keep the rest. Under the Borda-count utility function, this appears to afford each agent a utility of 3 (3 for apples vs. 2 for bananas plus 1 for pears) but, in truth, gains the liar 5 (3 for pears and 2 for bananas. Note that the same offer is optimal for the second ranking but a very different offer holds for the third ranking.

Lu and Boutilier use the principle of minimax regret to guide preference elicitation. With incomplete information, a lying negotiator must make their best guess concerning their opponent's preference. Regret is the loss (or regret) associated with guessing wrong. In Figure 4, the liar might propose offering a single apple as this yields the greatest expected return across all possible rankings. However, if the true ranking is ranking 3, this offer will be rejected (as it would appear unfair to the recipient). Lu and Boutilier propose a method of asking questions that minimizes the maximum possible regret. We refer the reader to their paper for details.

Under reciprocal information exchange, a misrepresenting agent faces a dilemma. The more information it asks, the more information it must provide (possibly constraining their freedom to misrepresent). Fortunately, the elicitation approach is incremental. At the start of a negotiation, an agent has no information about the opponent's preferences and all preference rankings are possible. This set reduces following each question. The algorithm repeatedly queries the opponent to determine their preference until regret falls below a certain threshold. In order to find the opponent's exact preference, this algorithm would have to be repeated until only one ranking is consistent. However, the algorithm can be terminated early. At this point, the opponent might have one of a number of preferences but the regret at picking one of these arbitrarily is guaranteed to fall below this threshold (assuming the opponent responded honestly).

If the elicitation algorithm is allowed to run to completion, the opponent's preferences are completely known and the agent can generate an offer as outlined in Section 3.1. If the preferences are incompletely determined, the agent can simply make an offer with the highest expected return over all possible consistent preferences.

Offering preferences: Assuming an agent must offer some information in return after each preference that it elicits, a misrepresenting should offer information that gives their opponent the least strategic advantage. In general, we should consider that the opponent might use sophisticated elicitation strategies as well, but in this article, we adopt a further simplification: the misrepresenting agent simply offers a preference statement of its own choosing after asking a preference question (e.g., Agent: "Do you like apples better than oranges?"; Human: "Yes?"; Agent: "I like apples better than oranges as well."). This minimally satisfies the principle of reciprocal information exchange while simplifying analysis (we return to this in the final section).

Given these further restrictions, we propose two possible misrepresentation approaches and, in the next section, contrast their effectiveness with an honest control condition:

- One misrepresentation approach (max-max regret) is essentially the dual of min-max regret. The idea is to offer information, at each round, that maximizes the possible regret of the opponent. For example, if the opponent asks a very informative question ("Do you like A>B?") the agent could respond with a different, less informative response ("Well, I like C > D").
- A second misrepresentation approach is motivated by the fix-pie-lie heuristic. Namely, at each round, if the opponent acknowledges that A>B, the agent should simply respond in kind ("A>B for me too")
- Finally, an honest agent would offer preference statements that are maximally helpful to the opponent (i.e., that minimize the opponent's max regret)

3.3 Simulation Study

The previous subsection identified two possible heuristics for solving the misrepresentation problem while satisfying the constraint of

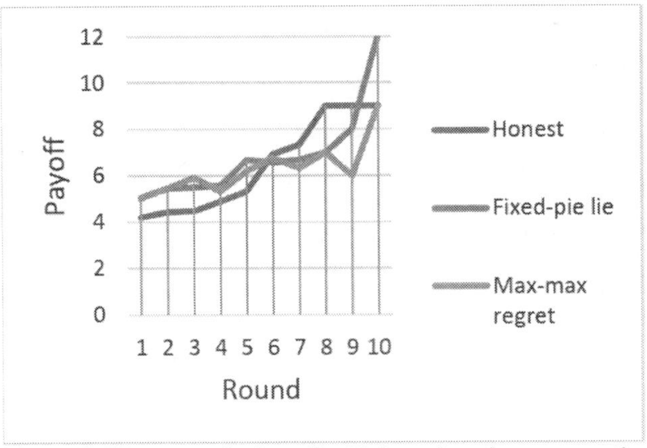

Figure 5: Illustrates the benefit of lying when the opponent's preferences are unknown. Results contrast the returns from two misrepresentation heuristics with being honest.

reciprocal information exchange. Both approaches use min-max regret to elicit questions from the opponent but differ in how they offer information in return (max-max regret vs. fixed-pie lie). Here we run a simulation experiment to contrast these approaches.

In that there is a potential tradeoff between the cost and benefits of exchanging information, we empirically explore this tradeoff. A misrepresenting agent could simply keep asking questions until the opponent's preferences are fully known. This yields more information about the opponent but forces the agent to reveal its own information in return (possibly limiting opportunities to misrepresent). Alternatively, an agent could terminate questions early and make its best guess at a good offer.

We compared max-max regret and fixed-pie-lie against an agent that was honest and maximally helpful. We compared these heuristics on a 5-issue negotiation task where there is a good opportunity to misrepresent: parties' preferences are complementary (A>B>C>D>E vs. A<B<C<D<E). For each approach (max-max regret, fixed-pie-lie and honest), we ran a simulated negotiation of these strategies against a truthful opponent. This opponent only accepted offers that appeared fair given what the agent revealed about its preferences. We varied how many rounds the agent could ask questions before making an offer from 1 to 10 (10 rounds of questions are sufficiently to completely determine the opponents preferences for a 5-issue negotiation).

The results are shown in Figure 5. They illustrate the complex relationship between the costs and benefits of asking questions. Both max-max regret and fixed-pie lie led to greater returns for small numbers of questions. Fixed-pie lie performed best when the opponent's preferences were fully revealed. At some points, honesty appears to be the best policy.

One might expect max-max regret to out-perform fixed-pie-lie because it is doing a more systematic exploration of the space of possible preference models and picking the one that maximizes maximum expected value. The problem is that, at early points in the elicitation phase there is insufficient information to determine the value of different lies, so the method can commit itself to statements that constrain its options to lie in later rounds. Overall, the fixed-pie-lie heuristic is simple and works surprisingly well.

4. USER EVALUATION

Up to this point, we have made theoretical arguments and evaluated methods against simulated human opponents. But would actual human negotiators be fooled by such simple techniques? Here we report the results of a study that answers this question. Specifically, we test two hypotheses:

H1 (perceived fairness of outcome): We hypothesize that people would be more willing to accept an offer (H1a), find it more fair (H1b) and satisfying (H1c), and place greater trust in their opponent (H1d) if the opponent misrepresents their preferences as a fixed pie, compared with an offer of equal value where the true preferences were honestly conveyed.

H2 (perceived fairness of communication): We hypothesize that people need their preference statements to be reciprocated and would be more willing to accept an offer (H2a), find it more fair (H2a) and satisfying (H2c), and place greater trust in their opponent (H2d) if the opponent provides reciprocal but false preference statements, compared with an offer of equal value without reciprocal information provided.

Together, these hypotheses imply a corollary: opponent models matter. In other words, people base their decisions, not based on their absolute benefit, but their perceptions of the other party's interests and how this relates to norms of distributional and communicative fairness.

To test these hypotheses, we conducted an online experiment using seventy-five participants recruited over Amazon Mechanical Turk. Participants were randomly assigned to one of three conditions. In all conditions, participants were asked to imagine they were in a

Imagine you are negotiating over the six items shown above (2 apples, 2 bananas and 2 pears) with another person. Apples are worth $3 each, bananas $2 each and pears are $1 each. Thus, your preference is Apples > Bananas > Pears and you don't know your partner's preference. Below is a dialog between a partner and yourself. Based on your preference and the dialog provided, please decide if you would accept the partner's offer:

Condition 2:

Partner: Do you like apples more than bananas?
You: Yes
Partner: I like bananas more than apples
Partner: Do you like bananas more than pears?
You: Yes
Partner: I like pears more than bananas
Partner: How about this, I give you both apples and I get the rest?

Figure 6: An illustration of the "truthful" condition

	% Accept	Satisfied	Trust in partner	Fairness of offer
Fixed-pie Lie	**0.88***	**3.73⁺**	3.15	**3.73***
Honest	0.58	3.12	3.04	2.81
No information	0.56	3.26	3.19	3.04

Table 1: Experimental Results (* $p \leq 0.05$; $^{+} p \leq 0.10$)

negotiation. They were presented a dialog between them and a hypothetical opponent concerning how to partition a basket of fruit (see Figure 6). They were asked if they would accept they offer made by their opponent (yes/no), and to rate its fairness, their satisfaction with the offer, and whether they felt the other party seemed honest (all items using 5-point Likert scale).

The only difference between conditions was the preference statements made by the opponent. In the misrepresentation condition, the opponent produces preference statements according to the fixed-pie-lie heuristic and the participant was offered half the apparent value. In the honest condition (illustrated in Figure 6), the opponent produces honest preference statements (clearly indicating that the pie could be grown), but the participant received the same offer as in the misrepresentation condition. Finally, in the non-reciprocal condition, the opponent asks questions but does not provide any information in return. Again, the identical offer was proposed across conditions. Table 1 summarizes the results.

Our first hypotheses shows good support. People were more willing to accept an offer (H1a) and found it more fair (H1b) if their opponent misrepresented their preferences as a fixed pie and claimed half the pie. People accepted more offers from the fixed-pie-lie condition (M=88%) compared to the honest condition (M=58%); $\chi^2(1, N=52)=6.26, p=0.027$. They rated the offer from the lying opponent as more fair (M=3.73, SD=0.33) than the truthful opponent (M=2.81, SD=0.51); $t(25)=3.00, p=0.006$. There was a near-significant trend ($p=0.065$) in perceived satisfaction (H1c) and no difference in trust (H1d) in the partner.

Our second hypothesis also shows good support. People accepted more offers (H2a) and found them more fair (H2b) when provided reciprocal but deceptive feedback about their opponent's preferences than no feedback at all. They accepted more from the fixed-pie-lie condition (M=88%) than the no-information condition (56%); $\chi^2(1, N=53)=7.07, p=0.014$. People rated the lying opponent as more fair (M=3.73, SD=0.33) than the no-information condition (M=3.04, SD=1.18); $t(25)=2.18, p=0.039$. There was a nonsignificant trend ($p=0.091$) in perceived satisfaction (H2c) and no significance difference in trust (H1d) in the partner.

For completeness, we compared differences in acceptance rate and subjective impressions between the honest and no-information conditions but found no significant differences.

In summary, people were much more willing to accept an offer when the opponent misrepresents their preferences then when truthful. This is because the truthful offer was seen as considerably less fair (people recognized the pie had grown but the opponent was keeping a disproportionate amount). People were also less willing to accept offers when the agent failed to reveal its own preferences, giving support for the principle of reciprocal information exchange. Again, such offers were considered less fair. From this we can conclude that malicious agents must attend to two concerns: relative fairness of the offer and relative fairness of information exchange.

5. LIMITATIONS AND CONCLUSION

We presented a method that allows negotiators to reap unequal rewards over opponents while maintaining the illusion of fairness. Our analysis and results demonstrate there can be considerable strategic benefits from this form of lying. The simulation results in Section 3.2 illustrate that many negotiations can yield strategic gain and sometimes these rewards can be considerable (Figure 3). Section 3.4 illustrates that these rewards can be achieved even when an opponent's preferences are unknown (via deceptive reciprocal information exchange). Finally, the experimental results in Section 4 illustrate that people find these deceptive strategies to be credible and even preferred to honesty (or no information at all). Apparently in negotiation, honesty is not always the best policy.

There are several ways to extend the current analysis.

Improving the analysis: We have proven the validity of the fixed-pie lie when the opponent's preferences are known in advance [37] but rely on simulation and empirical data for the more typical situation where this information is unknown. We suspect it should be straightforward to prove the validity of the fixed-pie-lie heuristic under fairly general assumptions.

Relaxing assumptions about the structure of the negotiation: Our assumptions about the structure of players' utilities greatly simplifies our analysis but limits the generality of the approach. Much of the innovative work in negotiation agents explores less restrictive assumptions such as non-linear utilities [19], incomplete information about levels and even non-convexity of the utility space [12]. More work is needed in generalizing our solution to these contexts.

More importantly for the goals of this paper, these assumptions preclude some opportunities for misrepresentation that have been observed in the human negotiation literature. For example, negotiations typically include a "disagreement payoff" (the utility received by each player if a negotiation fails). One common tactic is for a negotiator to feign a higher disagreement payoff than they actually hold. This could be explored by adding this payoff to the game.

Our assumption of an additive preference function also precludes certain misrepresentation tactics. For example, a negotiator might claim a nonlinear relationship over the levels of an issue (i.e., "I get a bonus if I get all three apples"). Including a broader space of preference functions would enrich our analysis.

More generally, the concept of fairness itself might be open to negotiation and misrepresentation. In this article, we adopt the *equality principle* which states that everyone in a group should share benefits equally. However, Welsh [53] argues that different people use different fairness criteria, and even the same person might use different criteria in different circumstances. For example, the *need principle* states that those who are in more desperate need of a resource deserve a greater share, whereas the *equity principle* argues the opposite (arguing that gains should be partitioned relative to each parties' power/resources). Our ranking assumption obscures the differences between these principles because players discuss their ranking but not their need. Without this assumption, liars could be free to claim the receive less for each issue and thus "need" a greater share (e.g., see Roth's findings of focal points [43]).

Relaxing assumptions about the nature of the opponent: Our results illustrate the potential benefits of lying, but opponents might adopt a variety of countermeasures that could undermine this potential. In the current analysis, we assumed the opponent was truthful, and in indeed in many laboratory studies of negotiation participants tell the truth much more than would be predicted by rational models, but this tendency is hardly universal.

One straightforward way to approach mutual deception is to extend the analysis in Section 3.1 to consider a Stackelberg formulation of the misrepresentation game. In Stackelberg games, one player (the defender) moves first, and the second player responds. In a Stackelberg formulation of the misrepresentation game, one negotiator might publicize a false set of information about their preferences (e.g., the MSRP of different automobile packages) in order to minimize the risk of exploitation or maximize their own gain.

Our current analysis also assumed the human opponent passively accepted reciprocal preference statements, however we should relax this assumption to allow opponents to ask arbitrary preference questions, and perhaps to refuse to directly answer. If the human is free to ask arbitrary preference questions, the misrepresenting-agent is left the dilemma of whether to address these questions directly or to defect them in some way. For example, if the human asks "do you like apples more than oranges," the agent might deflect the response by answering a different question ("Well, I like bananas better than pears") or to hedge the response ("I might like apples better"). If the agent is allowed to deflect, we must assume the human opponent can as well, and such contingencies must be incorporated into the analysis. One approach is to assume deflections come at some cost and model these in the analysis of what questions to ask and answer.

Finally, we only considered a negotiation protocol where parties exchange information about preferences before making a take-it-or-leave it offer. Human negotiations typically involve a mixture of information and offer exchanges and this sort of flexibility needs to be incorporated into our models. Indeed, discrepancies between what one's opponent says and what they offer can be a good indicator of deception [36].

Countermeasures: The previous discussion has focused on how to increase the generality and robustness of strategic misrepresentation but our ultimate aim is to use such models to help people (and agents) to avoid being deceived. Understanding and modeling a malicious technique is often a necessary the first step to proposing countermeasures (e.g., [34]).

In our own work, we are developing these techniques to inform the design of a negotiation tutoring system [24]. Specifically, students would be able to practice negotiation tactics, including how to detect and avoid deceptive behavior, with computer generate opponents. One such tactic is to offer one's opponent a counteroffer that would, assuming they are truthful, have equivalent value. For example, in the situation at the bottom of Figure 1, the man could counter by offering the reverse ("How about I take all apples and you take all oranges?"). Taking her false statements at face value, she should be indifferent to these two deals. In reality, this reverse deal has negative value to her.

The opportunity to make counteroffers highlights the potential riskiness of misrepresentation. For example, if the man insisted on offering oranges, the woman would be caught in her lie. She would either be forced to accept a disadvantageous offer or backtrack on her preference statements (see [47]. The former approach would harm her gains within the negotiation but the latter would harm her reputation for honesty and possibly undermine long term rewards. The idea of repeated interactions presents other complications. For example, if a company uses deception in their negotiations but lies in different ways to different customers, customers could compare notes and uncover the deception.

Characterizing the disadvantages of deception: Here we focus on potential benefits of deception but it can also have obvious costs, especially if both parties are being deceptive. In negotiation research, several studies have illustrated that honest information exchange can lead to better outcomes than deceptive communication or no communication, and achieve greater gains that might seem possible from a purely rational analysis (e.g., [50, 51]). In fact, it might turn out that, under more relaxed assumptions, that honest is the best policy after all. Indeed, Figure 5 illustrates that honesty pays at least under certain circumstances (where intermediate-levels of information are exchanged).

There may also be more intelligent strategies that switch between lying and honesty depending on the situation (see [47]). For example, although the fixed-pie lie exceeded the performance of the max-max regret heuristic in our simulation study (Figure 5), a disadvantage of the fixed-pie lie is that it commits a player to lying from the point of the very first question. Max-max regret strives to be honest but minimally informative. An advantage of this latter approach is that it doesn't committed a player to deception. Rather, the max-max regret heuristic allows a player to revert to honesty if this turns out to afford the greatest reward.

Contrasting human and rational behavior: The immediate next steps in our research, beyond relaxing the assumptions listed above, is to use these models to analyze the behavior of human negotiators. The present analysis suggests that people will tend to win at negotiations if they ask a lot of questions about what their opponents want, are vague about their own interests, and then invent a set of lies that makes self-advantageous deals seem fair. In other work, we have collected a large corpus of human-human negotiations where people clearly lie (see [17]) but we have yet to characterize the tactics they use and the success or failure of these lies. The rational analysis we present here can provide a valuable yardstick with which to measure and give insight into human negotiation processes and ultimately aid in the design that can cope with humans behaving badly. One next step is to use the analysis in this paper to examine if human liars are following our proposed solution.

The ethics of misrepresentation: Our analysis suggests that people, and (potentially) autonomous agents acting on behalf of people, can perform better in negotiations by misrepresenting their preferences. But should such agents ever be constructed. One source of guidance to this question is the rich literature on business and legal ethics, wherein negotiation is a central topic. Interestingly, misrepresentation is often argued to be legal and even ethical. For example, the American Bar Association's code of ethical conduct prohibits lawyers from knowingly misrepresenting facts, but then goes on to say that statements concerning price or value in a negotiation are not considered facts (e.g., see [13]). The rational is that a certain amount of "puffing" is to be expected. In contrast, others point out that such lies cause harm to the opponent and therefore are unethical, even if not illegal [54]. Others claim that it may be unethical to misrepresent through verbal statements but that misrepresenting the same information via emotional expressions is acceptable [23]. The ethics of such emotional manipulation has been considered within the field of affective computing (e.g., see [6]).

In conclusion, we presented an analysis of how people, or agents interacting with people, can win at negotiations while seeming fair. Our findings demonstrate clear benefits a type of lying (misrepresenting the relative importance of different issues) and suggest that negotiators should adopt a "fixed-pie lie" (i.e., pretend that their preferences are identical to their opponent). Future research should extend this analysis to more ecologically-valid situations and a broader class of misrepresentation techniques.

6. ACKNOWLEDGMENTS

This work benefited from some suggestions by Zinovi Rabinovich and Svetlana Obraztsova. We are also thankful for the feedback from the anonymous reviewers. This work was supported by the National Science Foundation under grant BCS-1419621 and the U.S. Army. Any opinion, content or information presented does not necessarily reflect the position or the policy of the United States Government, and no official endorsement should be inferred.

7. REFERENCES

[1] Baarslag, T., Fujita, K., Gerding, E. H., Hindriks, K., Ito, T., Jennings, N. R., Jonker, C., Kraus, S., Lin, R., and Robu, V., “Evaluating practical negotiating agents: Results and analysis of the 2011 international competition,” *Artificial Intelligence*, vol. 198, pp. 73-103, 2013.

[2] Baarslag, T., Hendrikx, M., Hindriks, K., and Jonker, C., "Measuring the performance of online opponent models in automated bilateral negotiation," *AI 2012: Advances in Artificial Intelligence*, pp. 1-14: Springer, 2012.

[3] Baharad, E., and Nitzan, S., “The Borda rule, Condorcet consistency and Condorcet stability,” *Economic Theory*, vol. 22, no. 3, pp. 685-688, 2003.

[4] Bazerman, M. H., and Carroll, J. S., “Negotiator cognition,” *Research in Organizational Behavior*, vol. 9, pp. 247-288, 1987.

[5] Brett, J. M., and Gelfand, M., "At your service - teaching notes," *Negotiation,teamwork and decision-making exercises*, Evenston, IL: Dispute Resolution Research Center, 2009.

[6] Bringsjord, S., and Clark, M. H., “Red-pill robots only, please,” *Affective Computing, IEEE Transactions on*, vol. 3, no. 4, pp. 394-397, 2012.

[7] Broekens, J., Harbers, M., Brinkman, W.-P., Jonker, C. M., Van den Bosch, K., and Meyer, J.-J., "Virtual reality negotiation training increases negotiation knowledge and skill." pp. 218-230.

[8] Camerer, C., *Behavioral game theory: Experiments in strategic interaction*: Princeton University Press, 2003.

[9] Chakraborty, A., and Harbaugh, R., “Cheap talk comparisons in multi-issue bargaining,” *Economics Letters*, vol. 78, no. 3, pp. 357-363, 3//, 2003.

[10] Chalamish, M., and Kraus, S., “AutoMed: an automated mediator for multi-issue bilateral negotiations,” *Autonomous Agents and Multi-Agent Systems*, vol. 24, no. 3, pp. 536-564, 2012/05/01, 2012.

[11] Chen, L., and Pu, P., *Survey of preference elicitation methods*, 2004.

[12] Conley, J. P., and Wilkie, S., “An extension of the Nash bargaining solution to nonconvex problems,” *Games and Economic behavior*, vol. 13, no. 1, pp. 26-38, 1996.

[13] Craver, C. B., “Negotiation Ethics: How to Be Deceptive Without Being Dishonest/How to Be Assertive Without Being Offensive,” *S. Tex. L. Rev.*, vol. 38, pp. 713, 1997.

[14] Crawford, V. P., and Sobel, J., “Strategic Information Transmission,” *Econometrica*, vol. 50, no. 6, pp. 1431-1451, 1982.

[15] Croson, R., Boles, T., and Murnighan, J. K., “Cheap talk in bargaining experiments: lying and threats in ultimatum games,” *Journal of Economic Behavior & Organization*, vol. 51, no. 2, pp. 143-159, 2003.

[16] Curhan, J. R., and Elfenbein, H. A., “What do people value when they negotiate? Mapping the domain of subjective value in negotiation,” *Journal of Personality & Social Psychology*, vol. 91, no. 3, pp. 493-512, 2006.

[17] DeVault, D., Mell, J., and Gratch, J., “Toward Natural Turn-Taking in a Virtual Human Negotiation Agent,” in AAAI Spring Symposium on Turn-taking and Coordination in Human-Machine Interaction, Stanford, CA, 2015.

[18] Farrell, J., and Gibbons, R., “Cheap talk can matter in bargaining,” *Journal of Economic Theory*, vol. 48, no. 1, pp. 221-237, 1989.

[19] Fatima, S., Wooldridge, M., and Jennings, N. R., "An analysis of feasible solutions for multi-issue negotiation involving nonlinear utility functions." pp. 1041-1048.

[20] Fehr, E., and Schmidt, K. M., “A Theory of Fairness, Competition, and Cooperation,” *The Quarterly Journal of Economics*, vol. 114, no. 3, pp. 817-868, August 1, 1999, 1999.

[21] Frank, R., *Passions with reason: the strategic role of the emotions*, New York, NY: W. W. Norton, 1988.

[22] Fry, W. R., “The effect of dyad Machiavellianism and visual access on integrative bargaining outcomes,” *Personality and Social Psychology Bulletin*, vol. 11, no. 1, pp. 51-62, 1985.

[23] Fulmer, I. S., Barry, B., and Long, D. A., “Lying and Smiling: Informational and Emotional Deception in Negotiation,” *Journal of Business Ethics*, vol. 88, no. 4, pp. 691-709, 2008.

[24] Gratch, J., Devault, D., Lucas, G., and Marsella, S., “Negotiation as a Challenge Problem for Virtual Humans,” in 15th International Conference on Intelligent Virtual Agents, Delft, The Netherlands, 2015.

[25] Grice, H. P., "Logic and Conversation," *Syntax and Semantics*, P. Cole and J. Morgan, eds.: Academic Press, 1975.

[26] Hill, R. W., Lane, H. C., Core, M., Forbell, E., Kim, J., Belanich, J., Dixon, M., and Hart, J., "Pedagogically Structured Game-based Training: Development of the ELECT BiLAT Simulation."

[27] Hindriks, K. V., and Jonker, C. M., "Creating human-machine synergy in negotiation support systems: Towards the pocket negotiator." pp. 47-54.

[28] Jennings, N. R., Faratin, P., Lomuscio, A. R., Parsons, S., Sierra, C., and Wooldridge, M., “Automated Negotiation: Prospects, Methods and Challenges,” *International Journal of Group Decision and Negotiation*, vol. 10, no. 2, 2001.

[29] Kalai, E., “Proportional Solutions to Bargaining Situations: Interpersonal Utility Comparisons,” *Econometrica*, vol. 45, no. 7, pp. 1623-1630, 1977.

[30] Kelley, H. H., and Schenitzki, D. P., “Bargaining,” *Experimental Social Psychology. New York: Holt, Rinehart, and Winston*, pp. 298-337, 1972.

[31] Lopes, F., Novais, A. Q., and Coelho, H., "Bilateral Negotiation in a Multi-Agent Energy Market," *Emerging Intelligent Computing Technology and Applications*, Lecture Notes in Computer Science D.-S. Huang, K.-H. Jo, H.-H. Lee, H.-J. Kang and V. Bevilacqua, eds., pp. 655-664: Springer Berlin Heidelberg, 2009.

[32] Lu, T., and Boutilier, C., "Robust approximation and incremental elicitation in voting protocols." p. 287.

[33] Movius, H., “The Effectiveness of Negotiation Training,” *Negotiation Journal*, vol. 24, no. 4, pp. 509-531, 2008.

[34] Naamani-Dery, L., Obraztsova, S., Rabinovich, Z., and Kalech, M., "Lie on the fly: iterative voting center with manipulative voters." pp. 2033-2039.

[35] Nash Jr, J. F., “The bargaining problem,” *Econometrica: Journal of the Econometric Society*, pp. 155-162, 1950.

[36] Nazari, Z., Lucas, G., and Gratch, J., “Opponent Modeling for Virtual Human Negotiators,” in 15th International Conference on Intelligent Virtual Agents, Delft, the Netherlands, 2015.

[37] Nguyen, T., and Gratch, J., *Misrepresentation Negotiation Games*, ICT-TR-01.2016, University of Southern California Instutite for Creative Technologies, Playa Vista, CA, 2016.

[38] O'Connor, K. M., and Carnevale, P. J., “A Nasty but Effective Negotiation Strategy: Misrepresentation of a Common-Value Issue,” *Personality and Social Psychology Bulletin*, vol. 23, no. 5, pp. 504-515, May 1, 1997, 1997.

[39] Pruitt, D. G., *Negotiation behavior*: Academic Press New York, 1981.

[40] Rawls, J., *A theory of justice*: Harvard university press, 2009.

[41] Rosenfeld, A., Zuckerman, I., Segal-Halevi, E., Drein, O., and Kraus, S., "NegoChat: a chat-based negotiation agent." pp. 525-532.

[42] Rosenschein, J. S., and Zlotkin, G., *Rules of encounter: designing conventions for automated negotiation among computers*: MIT press, 1994.

[43] Roth, A. E., "Bargaining experiments," 1995.

[44] Rubinstein, A., "Perfect equilibrium in a bargaining model," *Econometrica: Journal of the Econometric Society*, pp. 97-109, 1982.

[45] Sandholm, T., and Lesser, V. R., "Issues in automated negotiation and electronic commerce: Extending the contract net framework." pp. 66-73.

[46] Schug, J., Matsumoto, D., Horitaa, Y., Yamagishi, T., and Bonnet, K., "Emotional expressivity as a signal of cooperation," *Evolution and Human Behavior*, vol. 31, pp. 87-94, 2010.

[47] Schweitzer, M. E., Brodt, S. E., and Croson, R. T. A., "Seeing and believing: visual access and the strategic use of deception," *International Journal of Conflict Management*, vol. 13, no. 3, pp. 258-375, 2002/03/01, 2002.

[48] Sierra, C., and Debenham, J., "The LOGIC negotiation model." p. 243.

[49] Thompson, L., and Hastie, R., "Social perception in negotiation," *Organizational Behavior and Human Decision Processes*, vol. 47, no. 1, pp. 98-123, 1990/10/01, 1990.

[50] Thompson, L. L., "Information exchange in negotiation," *Journal of Experimental Social Psychology*, vol. 27, no. 2, pp. 161-179, 3//, 1991.

[51] Valley, K., Thompson, L., Gibbons, R., and Bazerman, M. H., "How Communication Improves Efficiency in Bargaining Games," *Games and Economic Behavior*, vol. 38, no. 1, pp. 127-155, 1//, 2002.

[52] Van Kleef, G. A., De Dreu, C. K. W., and Manstead, A. S. R., "The interpersonal effects of anger and happiness in negotiations," *Journal of Personality and Social Psychology*, vol. 86, no. 1, pp. 57-76, 2004.

[53] Welsh, N. A., "Perceptions of fairness in negotiation," *Marq. L. Rev.*, vol. 87, pp. 753, 2003.

[54] Wetlaufer, G. B., "Ethics of Lying in Negotiations, The," *Iowa L. Rev.*, vol. 75, pp. 1219, 1989.

[55] Wilson, S. R., and Putnam, L. L., *Interaction goals in negotiation*, 1990.

[56] Zlotkin, G., and Rosenschein, J. S., "Incomplete Information and Deception in Multi-Agent Negotiation." pp. 225-231.

Mobile Crowdsensing with Mobile Agents

(JAAMAS Extended Abstract)

Teemu Leppänen[1], Jóse Álvarez Lacasia[2], Yoshito Tobe[3], Kaoru Sezaki[2], Jukka Riekki[1]

[1]Department of Computer Science and Engineering, University of Oulu, Finland
[2]Institute of Industrial Science, University of Tokyo, Japan
[3]RealWorld Communication Laboratory, Aoyama Gakuin University, Japan
teemu.leppanen@ee.oulu.fi[1], sezaki@iis.u-tokyo.ac.jp[2], yoshito-tobe@rcl-aoyama.jp[3]

ABSTRACT

Mobile crowdsensing applications can be designed as multi-agent systems with campaign-specific roles, realized as mobile agents, and role-based interactions. Mobile agents facilitate decentralized and autonomous crowdsesing campaign execution that takes into account dynamic resource availability in the system. Mobile agents address issues in collaborative campaign execution, campaign monitoring, data collection, data analysis and handling participant-related issues. A software framework is presented that seamlessly exposes campaigns and mobile agents as Web resources. Real-world evaluation shows comparable results with existing crowdsensing approaches but with smaller energy consumption. In-network data sharing introduces insignificant overhead.

Keywords

Multi-agent systems; Mobile agent; Mobile computing; Web services

1. INTRODUCTION

Urban phenomena can be addressed by involving humans in participatory sensing networks that rely on their mobility patterns, intelligence and social interactions. A software framework runs the campaign in participants' devices and coordinates the participants to collaborate towards campaign goals. Data are then analyzed centrally in backend systems. The variety and scale of mobile crowdsensing applications introduce challenges for system design, development and deployment. Finding suitable participants, that either opt-in to campaigns or are selected opportunistically if they meet the campaign requirements, is a challenge. Campaign execution and collected data quality is another challenge as participants' actions and interactions can not be controlled. Privacy protection has to be emphasized as the collected data can reveal the personal behaviors of the participants.

In the work [1], crowdsensing campaigns are designed as multi-agent systems (MAS) with campaign-specific roles and role-based interactions that are realized as mobile agents. This provides decentralized and autonomous campaign execution and coordination, where dynamic resource availability in the opportunistic network of participants' devices is considered by the mobile agents. While executing their roles, mobile agents consider participant's recruitment, data quality issues, privacy and compensations for the participants. Real-time data sharing enables to distribute campaign execution load. Mobile agents in a MAS facilitate concurrent execution of multiple campaigns.

Appears in: *Proceedings of the 15th International Conference on Autonomous Agents and Multiagent Systems (AAMAS 2016), J. Thangarajah, K. Tuyls, C. Jonker, S. Marsella (eds.), May 9–13, 2016, Singapore.*

2. MOBILE AGENTS IN CROWDSENSING

Campaign-specific roles embrace their associated tasks, inputs and outputs, which facilitates cooperation between roles. The role-based tasks of mobile agents include data clean-up, feature extraction, event detection, data quality assessment, privacy protection and exposing data and the task results for real-time sharing. Campaigns can be executed by injecting mobile agents into the system, where they operate autonomously, negotiate their task execution, react to changes in their environment and share their results. This enables crowdsensing online model, where sensing tasks arrive during runtime and multiple campaigns can be executed simultaneously in the same set of devices.

The sensing parameters in smartphones can be controlled by mobile agents. Manual, automatic and context-aware sensing modes are supported. Mobile agents control the sensing task based on the specified context, such as location or detected event. Different representations of the data with task execution metadata can be uploaded to the campaigner for monitoring purposes.

Participants are recruited based on their availability, location, activity, events and history. Participants' behaviors in the campaign are monitored by the mobile agents and suggestions can be made to change the in-situ data collection to eliminate unwanted behaviors. Participants' reputations are calculated by the agent for promoting suitable participants for the campaigners. Fair compensation for their resource usage is calculated for the participants by the agents.

Mobile agents assist in maintaining participant privacy by enforcing personal privacy constraints, e.g. excluding sensitive locations. With in-network data processing, mobile agents expose only selected data features to the campaign.

3. SOFTWARE FRAMEWORK

The software framework [1] is based on resource-oriented architecture, where the resources are participating devices, integrated sensors and physical components, sensor data and agents' task results. HTTP is utilized as the universal communication protocol, which integrates campaigns and mobile agents seamlessly into the Web. Each resource is accessed through an URL containing its name and address. HTTP methods are used to access resources and to control sensors and physical components in the participating devices. A set of agent interaction protocols based on HTTP are introduced in [1] to enable mobile agent operations and conversations in the MAS.

In this kind of highly mobile distributed system, a resource directory (RD) component encompasses the real-time resource availability. Each device joins the system by registering its resources to the RD and when resource availability changes, the device updates its description in the RD. Now, campaigners can perform runtime lookups for find available resources. It is assumed that the campaigner controls the campaign through a Web service.

Figure 1 illustrates the framework and shows how crowdsensing campaigns are conducted in the framework. The devices register themselves into the RD (1). The campaigner locates resources for the campaign through resource lookups into the RD (2), injects mobile agents to execute the campaign (3) and monitors campaign execution through the results returned by the mobile agents (6). Mobile agents autonomously migrate in the system (4) and collaborate to execute their tasks (5).

4. REAL-WORLD EVALUATION

An extensive set of simulations was conducted in [1] to study different aspects of the mobile agent based crowdsensing. The total campaign execution energy was found to be lower and the amount of transmitted data to be reduced in comparison with existing crowdsensing approaches. Real-time information sharing introduces insignificant overhead to the energy consumption. Real-world evaluation was conducted in the software framework with Android smartphones in [1], hosting a mobile agent execution environment (EE) application, with a campaign that detected participant flocks from Wi-Fi scan operation data. Energy consumption data and the amount of transmitted data were then collected from the participating smartphones. Different agent migration and data upload periods where considered, as shown in Figure 2. The energy consumption of the EE application alone is also shown (Application).

The real-world campaign was implemented with two different designs. The designs were compared against a reference campaign without mobile agents, where the EE uploads raw data to the campaigner periodically. In the first design (Resident), four collector mobile agents migrate into the devices p2-p5 (Figure 1) at the join time and process collected sensor data in real-time in the device until the end of the campaign. Data from these agents is processed in the device p1 by an aggregator mobile agent before uploading it to the campaigner. This design demonstrates in-network data processing and sharing. In the second design (Migrate), a collector mobile agent migrates between the devices p2-p5 and processes their collected raw data each time the device is visited. An aggregator mobile agent operates in device p1 similarly as in the first design.

We observe that mobile agent based campaigns significantly reduce the total amount of transmitted data, which contributes towards less communication and less data processing in the campaign. Considering energy consumption,

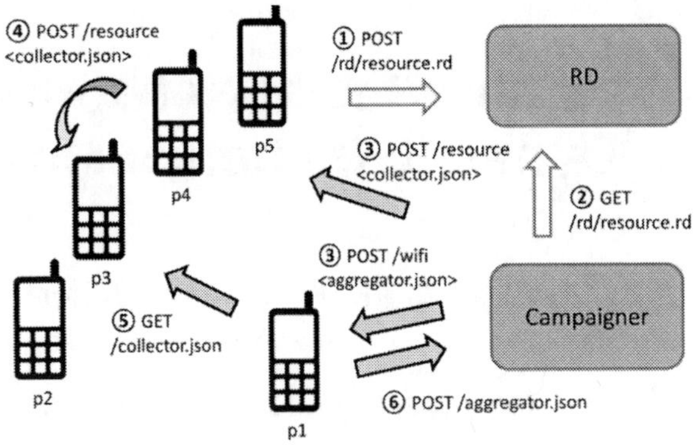

Figure 1: Crowdsensing software framework.

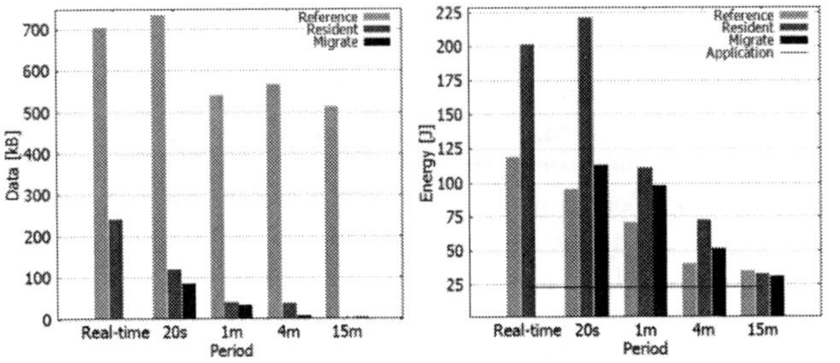

(a) Transmitted data (b) Total energy consumption

Figure 2: Real-world evaluation results.

we observe that mobile agent based campaigns consume less energy across the different upload and migration periods in comparison with the reference campaign. The Migrate campaign consumes less energy than the Resident campaign, due to large chunk of data being processed and more results shared at once. Within the same period, reference campaign energy consumption is similar with the Migrate campaign energy consumption, even though it includes in-network data processing and data sharing. Also, the EE implementation suffers from high mobile agent execution overhead as explained in [1]. To address this issue, the effects of different overheads were considered in the paper. Overall, this suggests that mobile agent based campaign execution is the most beneficial with infrequent agent migrations.

5. CONCLUSION

Mobile agents based crowdsensing campaign implementation in a MAS facilitates autonomous and decentralized campaign execution. Mobile agents embrace sensing and other tasks while distributing their execution. Mobile agents enable multiple simultaneous campaigns running in the same set of participant devices. With mobile agents, campaigns can be operated more energy efficiently than the existing crowdsensing approaches and the amount of transmitted data reduced, while providing comparable results.

REFERENCES

[1] T. Leppänen, J. Álvarez Lacasia, Y. Tobe, K. Sezaki, and J. Riekki. Mobile crowdsensing with mobile agents. *Auton. Agent Multi Agent Syst.*, pages 1–35, 2015.

Using Social Networks to Aid Homeless Shelters: Dynamic Influence Maximization under Uncertainty

Amulya Yadav, Hau Chan[1], Albert Jiang[1], Haifeng Xu, Eric Rice, Milind Tambe
University of Southern California, Los Angeles, CA 90089
[1]Trinity University, San Antonio, TX 78212
{amulyaya, haifengx, ericr, tambe}@usc.edu [1]{hchan, xjiang}@trinity.edu

ABSTRACT

This paper presents HEALER, a software agent that recommends sequential intervention plans for use by homeless shelters, who organize these interventions to raise awareness about HIV among homeless youth. HEALER's sequential plans (built using knowledge of social networks of homeless youth) choose intervention participants strategically to maximize influence spread, while reasoning about uncertainties in the network. While previous work presents influence maximizing techniques to choose intervention participants, they do not address three real-world issues: (i) they *completely fail* to scale up to real-world sizes; (ii) they do not handle deviations in execution of intervention plans; (iii) constructing real-world social networks is an expensive process. HEALER handles these issues via four major contributions: (i) HEALER casts this influence maximization problem as a POMDP and solves it using a novel planner which scales up to previously unsolvable real-world sizes; (ii) HEALER allows shelter officials to modify its recommendations, and updates its future plans in a deviation-tolerant manner; (iii) HEALER constructs social networks of homeless youth at low cost, using a Facebook application. Finally, (iv) we show hardness results for the problem that HEALER solves. HEALER will be deployed in the real world in early Spring 2016 and is currently undergoing testing at a homeless shelter.

1. INTRODUCTION

HIV-AIDS kills 2 million people worldwide every year [24]. In USA alone, AIDS kills around 10,000 people per annum [2]. HIV has an extremely high incidence among homeless youth, as they are more likely to engage in high HIV-risk behaviors (e.g., unprotected sexual activity, injection drug use) than other sub-populations. In fact, previous studies show that homeless youth are at 10X greater risk of HIV infection than stably housed populations [5]. Thus, any attempt at eradicating HIV crucially depends on our success at minimizing rates of HIV infection among homeless youth.

As a result, many homeless shelters organize intervention camps for homeless youth in order to raise awareness about HIV prevention and treatment practices. These intervention camps consist of day-long educational sessions in which the participants are provided with information about HIV prevention measures [18].

However, due to financial/manpower constraints, the shelters can only organize a limited number of intervention camps. Moreover, in each camp, the shelters can only manage small groups of youth ($\sim$3-4) at a time (as emotional and behavioral problems of youth makes management of bigger groups difficult). Thus, the shelters prefer a series of small sized camps organized sequentially [17]. As a result, the shelter cannot intervene on the entire target (homeless youth) population. Instead, it tries to maximize the spread of awareness among the target population (via word-of-mouth influence) using the limited resources at its disposal. To achieve this goal, the shelter uses the friendship based social network of the target population to strategically choose the participants of their limited intervention camps. Unfortunately, the shelters' job is further complicated by a lack of complete knowledge about the social network's structure [15]. Some friendships in the network are known with certainty whereas there is uncertainty about other friendships.

Thus, the shelters face an important challenge: they need a sequential plan to choose the participants of their sequentially organized interventions. This plan must address four key points: (i) it must deal with network structure uncertainty; (ii) it needs to take into account new information uncovered during the interventions, which reduces the uncertainty in our understanding of the network; (iii) the plan needs to be deviation tolerant, as sometimes homeless youth may refuse to be an intervention participant, thereby forcing the shelter to modify its plan; (iv) the intervention approach should address the challenge of gathering information about social networks of homeless youth, which usually costs thousands of dollars and many months of time [17].

In this paper, we model the shelters' problem by introducing the ***Dynamic Influence Maximization under Uncertainty*** (or DIME) problem. The sequential selection of intervention participants under network uncertainty in DIME sets it apart from any other previous work on influence maximization, which mostly focuses on single shot choices [1, 23, 9, 13]. Additionally, in previous work, PSINET [27], a POMDP based tool, was proposed for solving this problem, but it has three limitations. First, PSINET completely fails to scale up to the problem's requirements; running slowly and out of memory. It runs very slowly for moderate-sized networks, and runs out of memory as the network is scaled up. Worse still, even on these moderate sized networks, it runs out of memory when the number of participants in an intervention are increased (as shown later). Second, PSINET did not explicitly allow officials to modify its recommended plans if some participants refuse to attend the intervention. Third, PSINET requires entire social networks of homeless youth as input, while homeless shelters lack the money/time/manpower required to generate these input networks.

In this paper, we build a new software agent, HEALER (**H**ierarchical **E**nsembling based **A**gent which p**L**ans for **E**ffective **R**eduction in HIV Spread), to provide an end-to-end solution to the DIME problem. HEALER addresses PSINET's shortcomings

Appears in: *Proceedings of the 15th International Conference on Autonomous Agents and Multiagent Systems (AAMAS 2016), J. Thangarajah, K. Tuyls, C. Jonker, S. Marsella (eds.), May 9–13, 2016, Singapore.*

via four contributions. First, HEALER casts the DIME problem as a Partially Observable Markov Decision Process (POMDP) and solves it using HEAL (**H**ierarchical **E**nsembling **A**lgorithm for p**L**anning), a novel POMDP planner which quickly generates high-quality recommendations (of intervention participants) for homeless shelter officials. HEAL uses a hierarchical ensembling heuristic to ensure low memory utilization, thereby enabling scale up. HEAL hierarchically subdivides our *original POMDP* at two layers: (i) In the top layer, graph partitioning techniques are used to divide the *original POMDP* into *intermediate POMDPs*; (ii) In the second level, each of these *intermediate POMDPs* is further simplified by sampling uncertainties in network structure repeatedly to get *sampled POMDPs*; (iii) Finally, we use aggregation techniques to combine the solutions to these simpler POMDPs, in order to generate the overall solution for the *original POMDP*. Our simulations show that even on small settings, HEAL achieves a 100X speed up and 70% improvement in solution quality over PSINET; and on larger problems *where PSINET is unable to run at all*, HEAL continues to provide high quality solutions quickly. Second, HEALER tolerates deviations in execution of intervention plans, as it periodically receives feedback from shelter officials about executed plans, reasons about any deviations from its recommended plans, and updates its plan accordingly to maximize solution quality. Third, HEALER quickly gathers information about the homeless youth social network (at low cost) by interacting with youth via a Facebook application. Fourth, we analyze several novel theoretical aspects of the DIME problem, which illustrates its hardness.

(a) Computers at Homeless Shelter where HEALER is deployed

(b) Emergency Resource Shelf at the Homeless Shelter

Figure 1: Facilities at our Collaborating Homeless Shelter

We deploy HEALER in a real-world pilot study, in collaboration with a homeless shelter (name withheld for anonymity), which provides food and lodging to homeless youth aged 12-25. They provide these facilities for ~55-60 homeless youth every day. They also operate an on-site medical clinic where free HIV and Hepatitis-C testing is provided. HEALER has been reviewed by officials at our collaborating homeless shelter and their feedback has been positive. We are currently preparing to register 100 youth in our deployment of HEALER at this shelter. To the best of our knowledge, this pilot study represents the first real-world evaluation of such sequential influence maximization algorithms. We expect deployment to commence in early Spring 2016.

2. RELATED WORK

First, we discuss work related to influence maximization. There are many algorithms for finding 'seed sets' of nodes to maximize influence spread in networks [9, 13, 1, 23]. However, all these algorithms assume *no uncertainty in the network structure* and select a single seed set. In contrast, we select several seed sets sequentially in our work to select intervention participants. Also, our problem takes into account uncertainty about the network structure and influence status of network nodes (i.e., whether a node is influenced or not). Finally, unlike [9, 13, 1, 23], we use a different diffusion model as we explain later. Golovin et. al. [7] introduced adaptive submodularity and discussed adaptive sequential selection (similar to our problem), and they proved that a Greedy algorithm has a $(1 - 1/e)$ approximation guarantee. However, unlike our work, they assume no uncertainty in network structure. Also, while our problem can be cast into the adaptive stochastic optimization framework of [7], our influence function is not adaptive submodular (see Section 5), because of which their Greedy algorithm loses its approximation guarantees.

Next, we discuss literature from *social work*. The general approach to these interventions is to use Peer Change Agents (PCA) (i.e., peers who bring about change in attitudes) to engage homeless youth in interventions, but most studies don't use network characteristics to choose these PCAs [20]. A notable exception is Valente et. al. [25], who proposed selecting intervention participants with highest *degree centrality* (the most ties to other homeless youth). However, previous studies [3, 27] show that *degree centrality* performs poorly, as it does not account for potential overlaps in influence of two high degree centrality nodes.

The final field of related work is planning for reward/cost optimization. We only focus on the literature on Monte-Carlo (MC) sampling based online POMDP solvers since this approach allows significant scale-up [19]. The POMCP solver [21] uses Monte-Carlo UCT tree search in online POMDP planning. Also, Somani et. al. [22] present the DESPOT algorithm, that improves the worst case performance of POMCP. Our initial experiments with POMCP and DESPOT showed that they run out of memory on even our small sized networks. A recent paper [27] introduced PSINET-W, a MC sampling based online POMDP planner. We have discussed PSINET's shortcomings in Section 1 and how we remedy them. In particular, as we show later, HEALER scales up whereas PSINET fails to do so. *HEALER's algorithmic approach also offers significant novelties in comparison with PSINET (see Section 6.1).*

3. HEALER'S DESIGN

We now explain the high-level design of HEALER. It consists of two major components: (i) a Facebook application for gathering information about social networks; and (ii) a DIME Solver, which solves the DIME problem (introduced in Section 5). We first explain HEALER's components and then explain HEALER's design.

Facebook Application: HEALER gathers information about social ties in the homeless youth social network by interacting with youth via a Facebook application. We choose Facebook for gathering information as Young et. al. [29] show that ~80% of homeless youth are active on Facebook. Once a fixed number of homeless youth register in the Facebook application, HEALER parses the Facebook contact lists of all the registered homeless youth and generates the social network between these youth. HEALER adds a link between two people, if and only if both people are (i) friends on Facebook; and (ii) are registered in its Facebook application. Unfortunately, there is *uncertainty* in the generated network as friendship links between people who are only friends in real-life (and not on Facebook) are not captured by HEALER.

Previously, homeless shelters gathered this social network information via tedious face-to-face interviews with homeless youth, a process which cost thousands of dollars and many months of time. HEALER's Facebook application allows homeless shelters to quickly generate a (partial) homeless youth social network at low cost. This Facebook application has been tested by our collaborating homeless shelter with positive feedback.

DIME Solver: The DIME Solver then takes the approximate social network (generated by HEALER's Facebook application) as input and solves the DIME problem (formally defined in Section 5) using our new algorithm (explained in Section 6.1). HEALER pro-

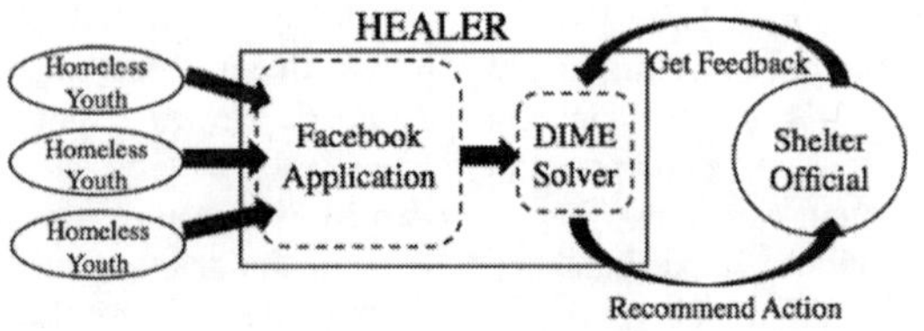

Figure 2: HEALER's Design

vides the solution of this DIME problem as a series of recommendations (of intervention participants) to homeless shelter officials.

HEALER Design: HEALER's design (shown in Figure 2), begins with the Facebook application constructing an *uncertain* network (as explained above). HEALER has a *sense-reason-act* cycle; where it repeats the following process for T interventions.

It *reasons* about different long-term plans to solve the DIME problem, it *acts* by providing DIME's solution as a recommendation (of intervention participants) to homeless shelter officials. The officials may choose to not use HEALER's recommendation in selecting their intervention's participants. Upon the intervention's completion, HEALER *senses* feedback about the conducted intervention from the officials. This feedback includes new observations about the network, e.g., uncertainties in some links may be resolved as intervention participants are interviewed by the shelter officials (explained more in Section 5). HEALER uses this feedback to update and improve its future recommendations.

4. NETWORK GENERATION

First, we explain our model for influence spread in *uncertain social networks*. Then, we describe how HEALER generates a social network using its' Facebook application.

4.1 Background

We represent social networks as directed graphs (consisting of *nodes* and *directed edges*) where each *node* represents a person in the social network and a *directed edge* between two nodes A and B (say) represents that node A *considers* node B as his/her friend. *We assume directed-ness of edges as sometimes homeless shelters assess that the influence in a friendship is very much uni-directional; and to account for uni-directional follower links on Facebook.* Otherwise friendships are encoded as two uni-directional links.

Uncertain Network: The uncertain network is a directed graph $G = (V, E)$ with $|V| = N$ nodes and $|E| = M$ edges. The edge set E consists of two disjoint subsets of edges: E_c (the set of certain edges, i.e., friendships which we are certain about) and E_u (the set of uncertain edges, i.e., friendships which we are uncertain about). Note that uncertainties about friendships exist because HEALER's Facebook application misses out on some links between people who are friends in real life, but not on Facebook.

To model the uncertainty about missing edges, every uncertain edge $e \in E_u$ has an existence probability $u(e)$ associated with it, which represents the likelihood of "existence" of that uncertain edge. For example, if there is an uncertain edge (A, B) (i.e., we are unsure whether node B is node A's friend), then $u(A, B) = 0.75$ implies that B is A's friend with a 0.75 chance. In addition, each edge $e \in E$ (both certain and uncertain) has a propagation probability $p(e)$ associated with it. A propagation probability of 0.5 on directed edge (A, B) denotes that if node A is influenced (i.e., has information about HIV prevention), it influences node B (i.e., gives information to node B) with a 0.5 probability in each subsequent time step (our full influence model is defined below). This graph G with all relevant $p(e)$ and $u(e)$ values represents an uncertain network and serves as an input to the DIME problem. Figure 3 shows an uncertain network on 6 nodes (A to F) and 7 edges. The dashed and solid edges represent uncertain (edge numbers 1, 4, 5 and 7) and certain (edge numbers 2, 3 and 6) edges, respectively. Next, we explain the influence diffusion model that we use in HEALER.

Influence Model We use a variant of the independent cascade model [28]. In the standard independent cascade model, all nodes that get influenced at round t get a **single** chance to influence their un-influenced neighbors at time $t + 1$. If they fail to spread influence in this **single** chance, they don't spread influence to their neighbors in future rounds. Our model is different in that we assume that nodes get **multiple** chances to influence their un-influenced neighbors. If they succeed in influencing a neighbor at a given time step t', they stop influencing that neighbor for all future time steps. Otherwise, if they fail in step t', they try to influence again in the next round. This variant of independent cascade has been shown to empirically provide a better approximation to real influence spread than the standard independent cascade model [4, 28]. Further, we assume that nodes that get influenced at a certain time step remain influenced for all future time steps. We now explain how HEALER generates an *uncertain social network.*

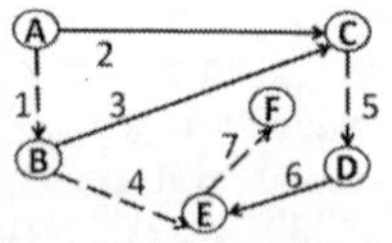

Figure 3: Uncertain Network

4.2 HEALER's Facebook application

HEALER generates an *uncertain network* by (i) using its Facebook application to generate a network with no uncertain edges; (ii) using well known link prediction techniques such as KronEM [10] to infer existence probabilities $u(e)$ for all possible *missing* edges that are not present in the network; (iii) deciding on a threshold probability τ (in consultation with homeless shelter officials), so that we *only* add a *missing* edge as an uncertain edge if its inferred existence probability $u(e) > \tau$; and (iv) asking homeless shelter officials to provide $p(e)$ estimates for network edges.

Choosing τ: Rice et. al [16] show that real-world homeless youth networks are *relatively sparse*. Thus, shelter officials choose the threshold probability value τ such that the number of uncertain edges that get added because of τ does not make our input uncertain network *overly dense*. Next, we introduce the DIME problem.

5. DIME PROBLEM

We now provide some background information that helps us define a precise problem statement for DIME. After that, we will show some hardness results about this problem statement.

Given the *uncertain network* as input, HEALER runs for T *rounds* (corresponding to the number of interventions organized by the homeless shelter). In each round, HEALER chooses K *nodes* (youth) as intervention participants. These participants are assumed to be influenced post-intervention with certainty. Upon influencing the chosen nodes, HEALER '*observes*' the true state of the *uncertain edges* (friendships) out-going from the selected nodes. This translates to asking intervention participants about their 1-hop social circles, which is within the homeless shelter's capabilities [16].

After each round, influence spreads in the network according to our influence model for L *time steps*, before we begin the next round. This L represents the time duration in between two successive intervention camps. *In between rounds, HEALER does not observe the nodes that get influenced during L time steps.* HEALER only knows that explicitly chosen nodes (our intervention participants in all past rounds) are influenced. Informally then, given an uncertain network $G_0 = (V, E)$ and integers T, K, and L (as defined above), HEALER finds an online policy for choosing *exactly* K nodes for T successive rounds (interventions) which maximizes influence spread in the network at the end of T rounds.

We now provide notation for defining HEALER's policy formally. Let $\boldsymbol{\mathcal{A}} = \{A \subset V \text{ s.t. } |A| = K\}$ denote the set of K sized subsets of V, which represents the set of possible choices that HEALER can make at every time step $t \in [1, T]$. Let $A_i \in \boldsymbol{\mathcal{A}} \, \forall i \in [1, T]$ denote HEALER's choice in the ith time step. Upon making choice A_i, HEALER '*observes*' uncertain edges adjacent to nodes in A_i, which updates its understanding of the network. Let $G_i \, \forall \, i \in [1, T]$ denote the uncertain network resulting from G_{i-1} with *observed* (additional edge) information from A_i. Formally, we define a history $H_i \, \forall \, i \in [1, T]$ of length i as a tuple of past choices and observations $H_i = \langle G_0, A_1, G_1, A_2, .., A_{i-1}, G_i \rangle$. Denote by $\boldsymbol{\mathcal{H}_i} = \{H_k \text{ s.t. } k \leqslant i\}$ the set of all possible histories of length less than or equal to i. Finally, we define an i-step policy $\boldsymbol{\Pi_i} \colon \boldsymbol{\mathcal{H}_i} \to \boldsymbol{\mathcal{A}}$ as a function that takes in histories of length less than or equal to i and outputs a K node choice for the current time step. We now provide an explicit problem statement for DIME.

PROBLEM 1. ***DIME Problem*** *Given as input an uncertain network $G_0 = (V, E)$ and integers T, K, and L (as defined above). Denote by $\mathcal{R}(H_T, A_T)$ the expected total number of influenced nodes at the end of round T, given the T-length history of previous observations and actions H_T, along with A_T, the action chosen at time T. Let $\mathbb{E}_{H_T, A_T \sim \Pi_T}[\mathcal{R}(H_T, A_T)]$ denote the expectation over the random variables $H_T = \langle G_0, A_1, .., A_{T-1}, G_T \rangle$ and A_T, where A_i are chosen according to $\Pi_T(H_i) \, \forall \, i \in [1, T]$, and G_i are drawn according to the distribution over uncertain edges of G_{i-1} that are revealed by A_i. The objective of DIME is to find an optimal T-step policy $\boldsymbol{\Pi_T^*} = \text{argmax}_{\Pi_T} \mathbb{E}_{H_T, A_T \sim \Pi_T}[\mathcal{R}(H_T, A_T)]$.*

Next, we show hardness results about the DIME problem. First, we analyze the value of having complete information in DIME. Then, we characterize the computational hardness of DIME. Due to lack of space, most proofs are in the appendix[1] or in the extended version [26].

The Value of Information. We characterize the impact of insufficient information (about the uncertain edges) on the achieved solution value. We show that no algorithm for DIME is able to provide a good approximation to the *full-information solution value* (i.e., the best solution achieved w.r.t. the underlying ground-truth network), even with infinite computational power.

THEOREM 5.1. *Given an uncertain network with n nodes, for any $\epsilon > 0$, there is no algorithm for the DIME problem which can guarantee a $n^{-1+\epsilon}$ approximation to OPT_{full}, the full-information solution value.*

Computational Hardness. We now analyze the hardness of computation in the DIME problem in the next two theorems.

THEOREM 5.2. *The DIME problem is NP-Hard.*

PROOF SKETCH. Consider the case where $E_u = \Phi$, $L = 1$, $T = 1$ and $p(e) = 1 \forall e \in E$. This degenerates to the classical influence maximization problem which is known to be NP-hard. Thus, the DIME problem is also NP-hard. □

Some NP-Hard problems exhibit nice properties that enable approximation guarantees for them. Golovin et. al. [7] introduced adaptive submodularity, an analog of submodularity for adaptive settings. Presence of adaptive submodularity ensures that a simply greedy algorithm provides a $(1 - 1/e)$ approximation guarantee w.r.t. the optimal solution defined on the *uncertain network*. However, as we show next, while DIME can be cast into the adaptive stochastic optimization framework of [7], our influence function is not adaptive submodular, because of which their Greedy algorithm does not have a $(1 - 1/e)$ approximation guarantee.

THEOREM 5.3. *The influence function of DIME is not adaptive submodular.*

6. HEAL: DIME PROBLEM SOLVER

The above theorems show that DIME is a hard problem as it is difficult to even obtain any reasonable approximations. We model DIME as a POMDP [14] because of two reasons. First, POMDPs are a good fit for DIME as (i) we conduct several interventions sequentially, similar to sequential POMDP actions; and (ii) we have *partial observability* (similar to POMDPs) due to uncertainties in network structure and influence status of nodes. Second, POMDP solvers have recently shown great promise in generating near-optimal policies efficiently [21]. We now explain how we map DIME onto a POMDP.

States. A POMDP state in our problem is a pair of binary tuples $s = \langle W, F \rangle$ where W and F are of lengths $|V|$ and $|E_U|$, respectively. Intuitively, W denotes the influence status of network nodes, where $W_i = 1$ denotes that node i is influenced and $W_i = 0$ otherwise. Moreover, F denotes the existence of uncertain edges, where $F_i = 1$ denotes that the ith uncertain edge exists in reality, and $F_i = 0$ otherwise.

Actions. Every choice of a subset of K nodes is a POMDP action. More formally, $A = \{a \subset V s.t. |a| = K\}$. For example, in Figure 3, one possible action is $\{A, B\}$ (when $K = 2$).

Observations. Upon taking a POMDP action, we "*observe*" the ground reality of the uncertain edges outgoing from the nodes chosen in that action. Consider $\Theta(a) = \{\text{e} \mid \text{e} = (\text{x,y}) \text{ s.t. x} \in a \wedge \text{e} \in E_u\} \, \forall a \in A$, which represents the (ordered) set of uncertain edges that are observed when we take action a. Then, our POMDP observation upon taking action a is defined as $o(a) = \{F_e | e \in \Theta(a)\}$, i.e., the F-values of the observed uncertain edges. For example, by taking action $\{B, C\}$ in Figure 3, the values of F_4 and F_5 (i.e., the F-values of uncertain edges in the 1-hop social circle of nodes B and C) would be observed.

Rewards. The reward $R(s, a, s')$ of taking action a in state s and reaching state s' is the number of newly influenced nodes in s'. More formally, $R(s, a, s') = (\|s'\| - \|s\|)$, where $\|s'\|$ is the number of influenced nodes in s'.

Initial Belief State. The initial belief state is a distribution β_0 over all states $s \in S$. The support of β_0 consists of all states $s = \langle W, F \rangle$ s.t. $W_i = 0 \, \forall \, i \in [1, |V|]$, i.e., all states in which all network nodes are un-influenced (as we assume that all nodes are un-influenced to begin with). Inside its support, each F_i is distributed independently according to $P(F_i = 1) = u(e)$.

Transition And Observation Probabilities. Computation of exact transition probabilities $T(s'|s, a)$ requires considering all possible paths in a graph through which influence could spread, which is $\mathcal{O}(N!)$ (N is number of nodes in the network) in the worst case. Moreover, for large social networks, the size of the transition and observation probability matrix is prohibitively large (due to exponential sizes of state and action space).

Therefore, instead of storing huge transition/observation matrices in memory, we follow the paradigm of large-scale online POMDP solvers [21, 6] by using a generative model $\Lambda(s, a) \sim$

[1]http://teamcore.usc.edu/people/amulya/dime-sup.pdf

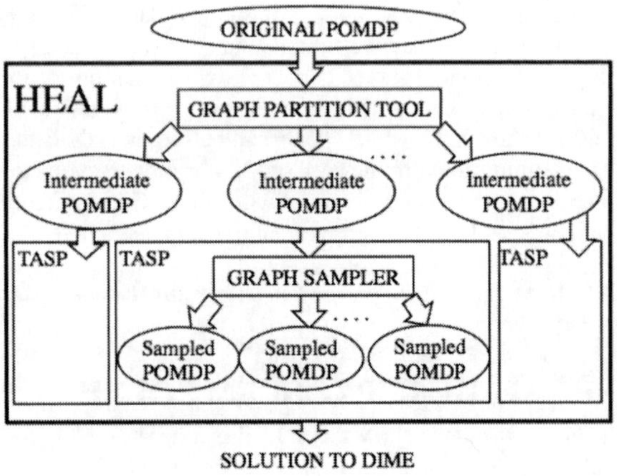

Figure 4: Hierarchical decomposition in HEAL

(s', o, r) of the transition and observation probabilities. This generative model allows us to generate on-the-fly samples from the exact distributions $T(s'|s,a)$ and $\Omega(o|a,s')$ at very low computational costs. Given an initial state s and an action a to be taken, our generative model Λ simulates the random process of influence spread to generate a random new state s', an observation o and the obtained reward r. Simulation of the random process of influence spread is done by *"playing"* out propagation probabilities (i.e., flipping weighted coins with probability $p(e)$) according to our influence model to generate sample s'. The observation sample o is then determined from s' and a. Finally, the reward sample $r = (\|s'\| - \|s\|)$ (as defined above). This simple design of the generative model allows significant scale and speed up (as seen in previous work [21] and also in our experimental results section).

We solve this POMDP using a novel algorithm (described in Section 6.1) to find the optimal policy $\mathbf{\Pi}^*_T$ for the DIME problem.

6.1 HEALER's DIME Solver

Initial experiments with the POMCP solver [21] showed that it ran out of memory on 30 node graphs. Similarly, PSINET-W [27] was simply unable to scale up to real world demands (as shown in our experiments). Hence, we propose HEAL, a new heuristic based online POMDP planner (for solving the DIME problem) which scales up to our collaborating shelter's real world demands.

6.1.1 HEAL

HEAL solves the *original POMDP* using a novel *hierarchical ensembling heuristic*: it creates ensembles of imperfect (and smaller) POMDPs at *two* different layers, in a hierarchical manner (see Figure 4). HEAL's *top layer* creates an ensemble of smaller sized *intermediate POMDPs* by subdividing the original *uncertain network* into several smaller sized *partitioned networks* by using graph partitioning techniques [12]. Each of these partitioned networks is then mapped onto a POMDP, and these *intermediate POMDPs* form our *top layer* ensemble of POMDP solvers.

In the bottom layer, each *intermediate POMDP* is solved using TASP (**T**ree **A**ggregation for **S**equential **P**lanning), our novel POMDP planner, which subdivides the POMDP into another ensemble of smaller sized *sampled POMDPs*. Each member of this *bottom layer* ensemble is created by randomly sampling uncertain edges of the partitioned network to get a sampled network having no uncertain edges, and this sampled network is then mapped onto a *sampled POMDP*. Finally, the solutions of POMDPs in both the *bottom* and *top layer* ensembles are aggregated using novel techniques to get the solution for HEAL's original POMDP.

Algorithm 1: TASP Solver

Input: Uncertain network G, Parameters K, T, L
Output: Best K node action κ
1 Create ensemble of Δ different POMDPs;
2 **for** $\delta \in \Delta$ **do**
3 $\quad \alpha^\delta = Evaluate(\delta)$;
4 $r = Expectation(\alpha)$;
5 $\kappa = \text{argmax}_j \, r_j$;
6 return κ;

HEAL uses several novel heuristics. First, it uses a novel two-layered *hierarchical ensembling heuristic*. Second, it uses graph partitioning techniques to partition the uncertain network, which generates partitions that minimize the edges going across partitions (while ensuring that partitions have similar sizes). Since these partitions are "almost" disconnected, we solve each partition separately. Third, it solves the *intermediate POMDP* for each partition by creating smaller-sized *sampled POMDPs* (via sampling uncertain edges), each of which is solved using a novel tree search algorithm, which avoids the exponential branching factor seen in PSINET [27]. Fourth, it uses novel aggregation techniques to combine solutions to these smaller POMDPs rather than simple plurality voting techniques seen in previous ensemble techniques [27].

These heuristics enable scale up to real-world sizes (at the expense of sacrificing performance guarantees), as instead of solving one huge problem, we now solve several smaller problems. However, these heuristics perform very well in practice. Our simulations show that even on smaller settings, HEAL achieves a 100X speed up over PSINET, while providing a 70% improvement in solution quality; and on larger problems, *where PSINET is unable to run at all*, HEAL continues to provide high solution quality. Now, we elaborate on these heuristics by first explaining the TASP solver.

6.1.2 Bottom layer: TASP

We now explain TASP, our new POMDP solver that solves each *intermediate POMDP* in HEAL's bottom layer. Given an *intermediate POMDP* and the uncertain network it is defined on, as input, TASP goes through four steps (see Algorithm 1).

First, Step 1 makes our *intermediate POMDP* more tractable by creating an ensemble of smaller sized *sampled POMDPs*. Each member of this ensemble is created by sampling uncertain edges of the input network to get an *instantiated* network. Each uncertain edge in the input network is randomly kept with probability $u(e)$, or removed with probability $1 - u(e)$, to get an *instantiated* network with no uncertain edges. We repeat this sampling process to get Δ (a variable parameter) different *instantiated* networks. These Δ different *instantiated* networks are then mapped onto to Δ different POMDPs, which form our ensemble of *sampled POMDPs*. Each *sampled POMDP* shares the same action space (defined on the input partitioned network) as the different POMDPs only differ in the sampling of uncertain edges. Note that each member of our ensemble is a POMDP as even though sampling uncertain edges removes uncertainty in the F portion of POMDP states, there is still partial observability in the W portion of POMDP state.

In Step 3 (called the Evaluate Step), for each instantiated network $\delta \in [1, \Delta]$, we generate an α^δ list of rewards. The ith element of α^δ gives the long term reward achieved by taking the ith action in *instantiated* network δ. In Step 4, we find the expected reward r_i of taking the ith action, by taking a reward expectation across the α^δ lists (for each $\delta \in [1, \Delta]$) generated in the previous step. For e.g., if $\alpha_1^{\delta_1} = 10$ and $\alpha_1^{\delta_2} = 20$, i.e., the rewards of taking

Algorithm 2: Evaluate Step

```
Input: Instantiated network δ, Number of simulations NSim
Output: Ranked Ordering of actions α^δ
1 tree = Initialize_K_Level_Tree();
2 counter = 0;
3 while counter ++ < NSim do
4     K_Node_Act = FindStep(tree);
5     LT_Reward = SimulateStep(K_Node_Act);
6     UpdateStep(tree, LT_Reward, K_Node_Act);
7 α^δ = Get_All_Leaf_Values(tree);
8 return α^δ;
```

Algorithm 3: FindStep

```
Input: K level deep tree - tree
Output: Action set of size K nodes - Act
1 Act = Φ;
2 tree_node = tree.Root;
3 while is_Leaf(tree_node) == false do
4     MAB_node = Get_UCB_at_Node(node);
5     next_node = Ask_UCB(MAB_node);
6     Act = Act ∪ next_node;
7     tree_node = tree_node.branch(next_node);
8 return Act;
```

the 1st action in instantiated networks δ_1 and δ_2 (which occurs with probabilities $P(\delta_1)$ and $P(\delta_2)$) are 10 and 20 respectively, then the expected reward $r_1 = P(\delta_1) \times 10 + P(\delta_2) \times 20$. Note that $P(\delta_1)$ and $P(\delta_2)$ are found by multiplying existence probabilities $u(e)$ (or $1 - u(e)$) for uncertain edges that were kept (or removed) in δ_1 and δ_2. Finally, in Step 5, the action $\kappa = \text{argmax}_j\, r_j$ is returned by TASP. Next, we discuss the Evaluate Step (Step 3).

Evaluate Step Algorithm 2 generates the α^δ list for a single instantiated network $\delta \in [1, \Delta]$. This algorithm works similarly for all instantiated networks. For each instantiated network, the Evaluate Step uses $\mathbf{NSim}$ (we use 2^{10}) number of MC simulations to evaluate the long term reward achieved by taking actions in that network. Due to the combinatorial action space, the Evaluate Step uses a UCT [11] driven approach to strategically choose the actions whose long term rewards should be calculated. UCT has been used to solve POMDPs in [21, 27], but these algorithms suffer from a $\binom{N}{K}$ branching factor (where K is number of nodes picked per round, N is number of network nodes). We exploit the structure of our domain by creating a K-level UCT tree which has a branching factor of just N (explained below). This K-level tree allows storing reward values for smaller sized node subsets as well (instead of just K sized subsets), which helps in guiding the UCT search better.

Algorithm 2 takes an *instantiated* network and creates the aforementioned K-level tree for that network. The first level of the tree has N branches (one for each network node). For each branch i in the first level, there are $N - 1$ branches in the second tree level (one for each network node, except for node i, which was covered in the first level). Similarly, for every branch j in the mth level ($m \in [2, K-1]$), there are $N - m$ branches in the $(m+1)^{th}$ level. Theoretically, this tree grows exponentially with K, however, the values of K are usually small in practice (e.g., 4).

In this K level tree, each leaf node represents a particular POMDP action of K network nodes. Similarly, every non-leaf tree node v represents a subset S_v of network nodes. Each tree node v maintains a value R_v, which represents the average long term reward achieved by taking our POMDP's actions (of size K) which contain S_v as a subset. For example, in Figure 3, if $K = 5$, and for tree node v, $S_v = \{A, B, C, D\}$, then R_v represents the average long term reward achieved by taking POMDP actions $A_1 = \{A, B, C, D, E\}$ and $A_2 = \{A, B, C, D, F\}$, since both A_1 and A_2 contain $S_v = \{A, B, C, D\}$ as a subset. To begin with, all nodes v in the tree are initialized with $R_v = 0$ (Step 1). By running $\mathbf{NSim}$ number of MC simulations, we generate good estimates of R_v values for each tree node v.

Each node in this K-level tree runs a UCB1 [11] implementation of a multi-armed bandit. The arms of the multi-armed bandit running at tree node v correspond to the child branches of node v in the K-level tree. Recall that each child branch corresponds to a network node. The overall goal of all the multi-armed bandits running in the tree is to construct a POMDP action of size K (by traversing a path from the root to a leaf), whose reward is then calculated in that MC simulation (explained in Algorithm 3). Every MC simulation consists of three steps: Find Step (Step 4), Simulate Step (Step 5) and Update Step (Step 6).

Find Step: The Find Step takes a K-level tree for an instantiated network and *finds* a K node action, which is used in the Simulate Step. Algorithm 3 details the process of *finding* this K node action, which is found by traversing a path from the root node to a leaf node, one edge/arm at a time. Initially, we begin at the root node with an empty action set of size 0 (Steps 1 and 2). For each node that we visit on our way from the root to a leaf, we use its multi-armed bandit (denoted by MAB_{node} in Step 4) to choose which tree node do we visit next (or, which network node do we add to our action set). We get a K node action upon reaching a leaf.

Simulate Step: The Simulate Step takes a K node action from the Find Step, to *evaluate* the long term reward of taking that action (called Act) in the instantiated network. Assuming that T_0 interventions remain (i.e., we have already conducted $T - T_0$ interventions), the Simulate Step first uses action Act in the generative model Λ to generate a reward r_0. For all remaining $(T_0 - 1)$ interventions, Simulate Step uses a rollout policy to randomly select K node actions, which are then used in the generative model Λ to generate future rewards $r_i\ \forall\, i \in [1, T_0 - 1]$. Finally, the long term reward returned by Simulate Step is $r_0 + r_1 + ... + r_{T_0 - 1}$.

Update Step: The Update Step uses the long term reward returned by Simulate Step to update relevant R_v values in the K-level tree. It updates the R_v values of all nodes v that were traversed in order to find the K node action in the Find Step. First, we get the tree's leaf node corresponding to the K node action that was returned by the Find Step. Then, we go and update R_v values for all ancestors (including the root) of that leaf node.

After running the Find, Simulate and Evaluate for $\mathbf{NSim}$ simulations, we return the R_v values of all leaf nodes as the α^δ list. Recall that we then find the expected reward r_i of taking the ith action, by taking an expectation of rewards across the α^δ lists. Finally, TASP returns the action $\kappa = \text{argmax}_j\, r_j$.

6.1.3 Top layer: Using Graph Partitioning

We now explain HEAL's top layer, in which we use METIS [12], a state-of-the-art graph partitioning technique, to subdivide our original uncertain network into different partitioned networks. These partitioned networks form the ensemble of *intermediate POMDPs* (in Figure 4) in HEAL. Then, TASP is invoked on each intermediate POMDP independently, and their solutions are aggregated to get the final DIME solution. We try two different partitioning/aggregation techniques, which leads to two variants of HEAL:

K Partition Variant (HEAL): Given the *uncertain* network G and the parameters K, L and T as input, we first partition the uncertain network into K partitions. In each round from 1 to T, we invoke the bottom layer TASP algorithm to select 1 node from each of the K clusters. These singly selected nodes from the K clusters give us an action of K nodes, which is given to shelter officials to execute. Based on the *observation* (about uncertain edges) that officials get while executing the action, we update the partition networks (which are input to the *intermediate POMDPs*) by either replacing the *observed* uncertain edges with certain edges (if the edge was *observed* to exist in reality) or removing the uncertain edge altogether (if the edge was *observed* to *not exist* in reality). The list of K node actions that Algorithm 4 generates serves as an online policy for use by the homeless shelter.

T Partition Variant (HEAL-T): Given the *uncertain* network G and the parameters K, L and T as input, we first partition the uncertain network into T partitions and TASP picks K nodes from the ith partition ($i \in [1, T]$) in the ith round.

7. EXPERIMENTAL RESULTS

In this section, we analyze HEAL and HEAL-T's performance in a variety of settings. All our experiments are run on a 2.33 GHz 12-core Intel machine having 48 GB of RAM. All experiments are averaged over 100 runs. We use a metric of "*Indirect Influence*" throughout this section, which is number of nodes "*indirectly*" influenced by intervention participants. For example, on a 30 node network, by selecting 2 nodes each for 10 interventions (horizon), 20 nodes (a lower bound for any strategy) are influenced with certainty. However, the total number of influenced nodes might be 26 (say) and thus, the *Indirect Influence* is $26 - 20 = 6$. In all experiments, the propagation and existence probability values on all network edges were uniformly set to 0.1 and 0.6, respectively. This was done based on findings in Kelly et. al.[8]. However, we relax these parameter settings later in the section. All experiments are statistically significant under bootstrap-t ($\alpha = 0.05$).

Baselines: We use two algorithms as baselines. We use PSINET-W as a benchmark as it is the most relevant previous algorithm, which was shown to outperform heuristics used in practice; however, we also need a point of comparison when PSINET-W does not scale. No previous algorithm in the influence maximization literature accounts for uncertain edges and uncertain network state in solving the problem of sequential selection of nodes; in-fact we show that even the standard Greedy algorithm [9, 7] has no approximation guarantees as our problem is not adaptive submodular. Thus, we modify Greedy by replacing our uncertain network with a certain network (in which each uncertain edge e is replaced with a certain edge e_0 having propagation probability $p(e_0) = p(e) \times u(e)$), and then run the Greedy algorithm on this *certain network*. We use the Greedy algorithm as a baseline as it is the best known algorithm known for influence maximization and has been analyzed in many previous papers [3, 1, 23, 9, 13, 7].

Datasets: We use *four real world social networks* of homeless youth, provided to us by our collaborators. All four networks are friendship based social networks of homeless youth living in different areas of a big city in USA (name withheld for anonymity). The first and second networks are of homeless youth living in two large areas (denoted by VE and HD to preserve anonymity), respectively. These two networks (each having ~150-170 nodes, 400-450 edges) were created through surveys and interviews of homeless youth (conducted by our collaborators) living in these areas. The third and fourth networks are relatively small-sized online social networks of these youth created from their Facebook (34 nodes, 120 edges) and MySpace (107 nodes, 803 edges) contact lists, respectively. When HEALER is deployed, we anticipate even larger networks, (e.g., 250-300 nodes) than the ones we have in hand and we also show run-time results on artificial networks of these sizes.

Solution Quality/Runtime Comparison. We compare *Indirect Influence* and run-times of HEAL, HEAL-T and PSINET-W on

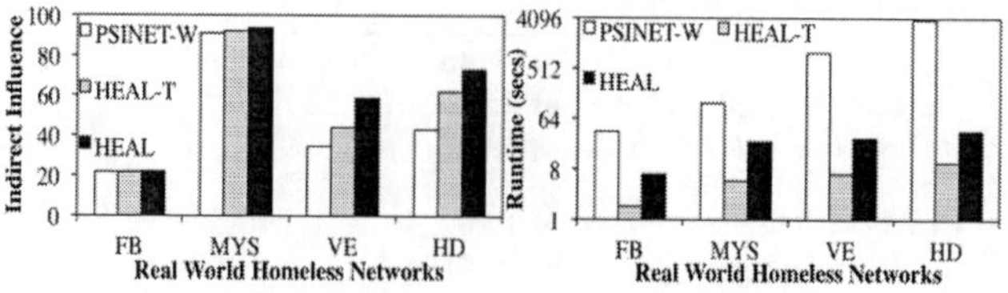

(a) Solution Quality (b) Runtime

Figure 5: Solution Quality and Runtime on Real World Networks

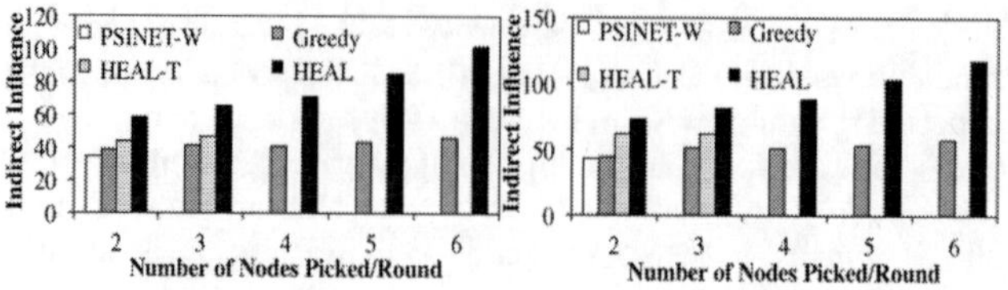

(a) VE Network (b) HD Network

Figure 6: Scale up in number of nodes picked per round

all four real-world networks. We set $T = 5$ and $K = 2$ (since PSINET-W fails to scale up beyond $K = 2$ as shown later). Figure 5a shows the *Indirect Influence* of the different algorithms on the four networks. The X-axis shows the four networks and the Y-axis shows the *Indirect Influence* achieved by the different algorithms. This figure shows that (i) HEAL outperforms all other algorithms on every network; (ii) *it achieves ~70% improvement over PSINET-W* in VE and HD networks; (iii) it achieves ~25% improvement over HEAL-T. The difference between HEAL and other algorithms is not significant in the Facebook (FB) and MySpace (MYS) networks, as HEAL is already influencing almost all nodes in these two relatively small networks. Thus, in experiments to come, we focus more on the VE and HD networks.

Figure 5b shows the run-time of all algorithms on the four networks. The X-axis shows the four networks and the Y-axis (in log scale) shows the run-time (in seconds). This figure shows that (i) *HEAL achieves a 100X speed-up over PSINET-W*; (ii) PSINET-W's run-time increases exponentially with increasing network sizes; (iii) HEAL runs 3X slower than HEAL-T but achieves 25% more *Indirect Influence*. Hence, HEAL is our algorithm of choice.

Next, we check if PSINET-W's run-times become worse on larger networks. Because of lack of larger real-world datasets, we create relatively large artificial Watts-Strogatz networks (model parameters $p = 0.1, k = 7$). Figure 9a shows the run-time of all algorithms on Watts-Strogatz networks. The X-axis shows the size of networks and the Y-axis (in log scale) shows the run-time (in seconds). This figure shows that *PSINET-W fails to scale beyond 180 nodes, whereas HEAL runs within 5 minutes*. Thus, PSINET-W fails to scale-up to network sizes that are of importance to us.

Scale Up Results. Not only does PSINET-W fail in scaling up to larger network sizes, it even fails to scale-up with increasing number of nodes picked per round (or K), on our real-world networks. Figures 6a and 6b show the *Indirect Influence* achieved by HEAL, HEAL-T, Greedy and PSINET-W on the VE and HD networks respectively ($T = 5$), as we scale up K values. The X-axis shows increasing K values, and the Y-axis shows the *Indirect Influence*. These figures show that (i) PSINET-W and HEAL-T fail to scale up – they cannot handle more than $K = 2$ and $K = 3$ respectively (thereby not fulfilling real world demands); (ii) HEAL outperforms all other algorithms, and the difference between HEAL and Greedy increases linearly with increasing K values. Also, *in*

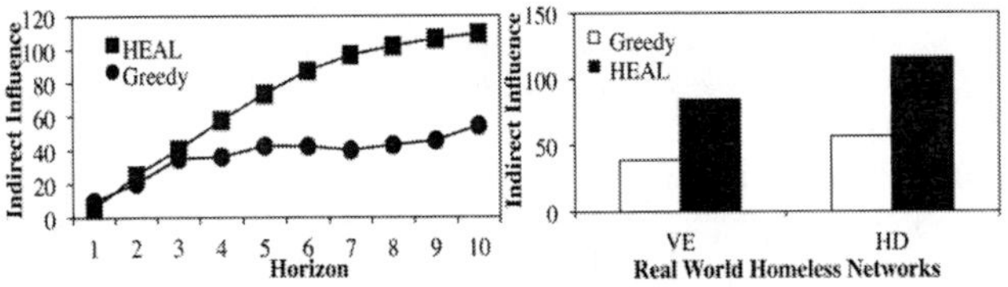

(a) Solution Quality (b) Maximum Relative Gain

Figure 7: Horizon Scale up & Maximum Gain on HD Network

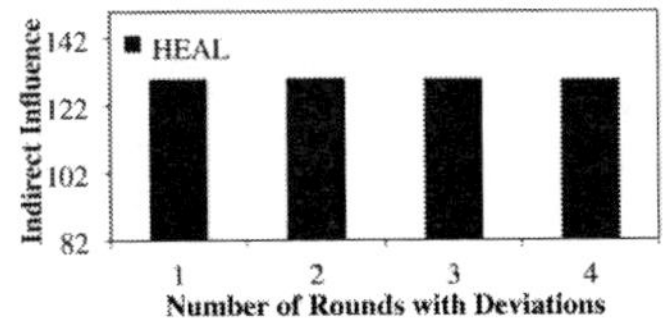

(a) Deviation Tolerance

$p(e)$ \ $u(e)$	0.1	0.2	0.3
0.7	45.62	44.37	30.85
0.6	48.95	24.56	30
0.5	29.5	55.18	28.21

(b) % Increase over Greedy

Figure 8: Deviation Tolerance & HEAL vs Greedy

the case of $K = 6$, HEAL runs in less than 40.12 seconds on the HD network and 34.4 seconds on the VE network.

Thus, Figures 5a, 5b, 6a and 6b show that PSINET-W (the best performing algorithm from previous work) fails to scale up with increasing network nodes, and with increasing K values. Even for $K = 2$ and moderate sized networks, it runs very slowly. Moreover, HEAL is the best performing algorithm that runs quickly, provides high-quality solutions, and can scale-up to real-world demands. Since only HEAL and Greedy scale up to $K = 6$, we now analyze their performance in detail.

Scaling up Horizon. Figure 7a shows HEAL and Greedy's *Indirect Influence* in the HD network, with varying horizons (see appendix for VE network results). The X-axis shows increasing horizon values and the Y-axis shows the *Indirect Influence* ($K = 2$). This figure shows that the relative difference between HEAL and Greedy increases significantly with increasing T values.

Next, we scale up K values with increased horizon settings to find the maximum attainable solution quality difference between HEAL and Greedy. Figure 7b shows the *Indirect Influence* achieved by HEAL and Greedy (with $K = 4$ and $T = 10$) on the VE and HD networks. The X-axis shows the two networks and the Y-axis shows the *Indirect Influence*. This figure shows that with these settings, *HEAL achieves ~110% more Indirect Influence than Greedy (i.e., more than a 2-fold improvement) in the two real-world networks.*

HEAL vs Greedy. Figure 8b shows the percentage increase (in *Indirect Influence*) achieved by HEAL over Greedy with varying $u(e)/p(e)$ values. The columns and rows of Figure 8b show varying $u(e)$ and $p(e)$ values respectively. The values inside the table cells show the percentage increase (in *Indirect Influence*) achieved by HEAL over Greedy when both algorithms plan using the same $u(e)/p(e)$ values. For example, with $p(e) = 0.7$ and $u(e) = 0.1$, HEAL achieves 45.62% more *Indirect Influence* than Greedy. This figure shows that *HEAL continues to outperform Greedy across varying $u(e)/p(e)$ values.* Thus, on a variety of settings, HEAL dominates Greedy in terms of both *Indirect Influence* and run-time.

Deviation Tolerance. We show HEAL's tolerance to deviation by replacing a fixed number of actions recommended by HEAL with randomly selected actions. Figure 8a shows the variation in *Indirect Influence* achieved by HEAL ($K = 4, T = 10$) with increasing number of random deviations from the recommended actions. The X-axis shows increasing number of deviations and the Y-axis shows the *Indirect Influence*. For example, when there were

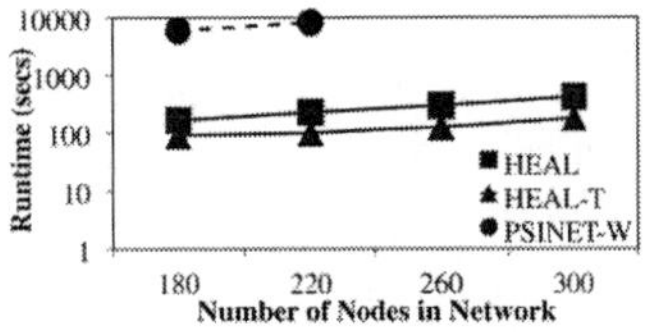

(a) Artificial Networks

$p(e)$ \ $u(e)$	0.1	0.2	0.3
0.7	24.42	21.02	16.85
0.6	0.0	18.26	12.46
0.5	11.58	10.53	8.11

(b) % Loss in HEAL Solution

Figure 9: Artificial Networks And Sensitivity Analysis

2 random deviations (i.e., two recommended actions were replaced with random actions), HEAL achieves 100.23 *Indirect Influence*. This figure shows that HEAL is highly deviation-tolerant.

Sensitivity Analysis. Finally, we test the robustness of HEAL's solutions in the HD network (see appendix for VE network results), by allowing for error in HEAL's understanding of $u(e)/p(e)$ values. We consider the case that $u(e) = 0.1$ and $p(e) = 0.6$ values that HEAL plans on, are wrong. Thus, HEAL plans its solutions using $u(e) = 0.1$ and $p(e) = 0.6$, but those solutions are evaluated on different (correct) $u(e)/p(e)$ values to get *estimated solutions*. These *estimated solutions* are compared to *true solutions* achieved by HEAL if it planned on the correct $u(e)/p(e)$ values. Figure 9b shows the percentage difference (in *Indirect Influence*) between the *true* and *estimated* solutions, with varying $u(e)$ and $p(e)$ values. For example, when HEAL plans its solutions with wrong $u(e) = 0.1/p(e) = 0.6$ values (instead of correct $u(e) = 0.3/p(e) = 0.5$ values), it suffers a 8.11% loss. This figure shows that HEAL is relatively robust to errors in its understanding of $u(e)/p(e)$ values, as it only suffers an average-case loss of $\sim$ 15%.

8. CONCLUSION

This paper focuses on the important problem of selecting participants of sequentially deployed interventions, which are organized by homeless shelters to spread awareness about HIV prevention practices among homeless youth. This is an extremely important problem as homeless youth are at high-risk to HIV (~10% of homeless youth are HIV positive). While previous work tries to solve this problem, it *simply fails to scale up to real world sizes and demands*. It runs out of memory on large networks, with increased number of intervention participants, and runs very slowly on moderate sized networks. In this paper, we develop HEALER, a new software agent for solving this problem which scales up to real world demands. HEALER casts the problem as a POMDP and uses a completely novel suite of algorithms (HEAL, TASP and Evaluate) to achieve a 100X speedup over state-of-the-art algorithms while outperforming them by 70% in terms of solution quality. More than that, it runs when previous algorithms can't scale up. Also, HEALER saves homeless shelters' thousands of dollars and many months of time by generating uncertain networks at low cost using its Facebook application. Finally, we show some novel theoretical hardness results about the problem that HEALER solves. HEALER is fully ready to be deployed in the real world, in collaboration with a homeless shelter. The shelter officials have tested HEALER's components and their feedback has been positive. HEALER's deployment is expected to commence in early Spring 2016.

9. ACKNOWLEDGEMENTS

This research was supported by MURI Grant W911NF-11-1-0332. Rice was supported by NIMH Grant number R01-MH093336.

REFERENCES

[1] C. Borgs, M. Brautbar, J. Chayes, and B. Lucier. Maximizing Social Influence in Nearly Optimal Time. In *Proceedings of the Twenty-Fifth Annual ACM-SIAM Symposium on Discrete Algorithms*, SODA '14, pages 946–957. SIAM, 2014.

[2] CDC. HIV Surveillance Report. `www.cdc.gov/hiv/pdf/g-l/hiv_surveillance_report_vol_25.pdf`, Mar. 2013.

[3] E. Cohen, D. Delling, T. Pajor, and R. F. Werneck. Sketch-based Influence Maximization and Computation: Scaling up with guarantees. In *Proceedings of the 23rd ACM International Conference on Conference on Information and Knowledge Management*, pages 629–638. ACM, 2014.

[4] J.-P. Cointet and C. Roth. How Realistic Should Knowledge Diffusion Models Be? *Journal of Artificial Societies and Social Simulation*, 10(3):5, 2007.

[5] N. H. Council. HIV/AIDS among Persons Experiencing Homelessness: Risk Factors, Predictors of Testing, and Promising Testing Strategies. `www.nhchc.org/wp-content/uploads/2011/09/InFocus_Dec2012.pdf`, Dec. 2012.

[6] A. Eck and L.-K. Soh. To Ask, Sense, or Share: Ad Hoc Information Gathering. In *Proceedings of the 2015 International Conference on Autonomous Agents and Multiagent Systems*, pages 367–376. International Foundation for Autonomous Agents and Multiagent Systems, 2015.

[7] D. Golovin and A. Krause. Adaptive Submodularity: Theory and Applications in Active Learning and Stochastic Optimization. *Journal of Artificial Intelligence Research*, 42:427–486, 2011.

[8] J. A. Kelly, D. A. Murphy, K. J. Sikkema, T. L. McAuliffe, R. A. Roffman, L. J. Solomon, R. A. Winett, and S. C. Kalichman. Randomised, Controlled, Community-Level HIV-Prevention Intervention for Sexual-Risk Behaviour among Homosexual men in US cities. *The Lancet*, 350(9090):1500, 1997.

[9] D. Kempe, J. Kleinberg, and É. Tardos. Maximizing the Spread of Influence through a Social Network. In *Proceedings of the ninth ACM SIGKDD international conference on Knowledge discovery and data mining*, pages 137–146. ACM, 2003.

[10] M. Kim and J. Leskovec. The Network Completion Problem: Inferring Missing Nodes and Edges in Networks. In *Proceedings of the SIAM Conference on Data Mining*. SIAM, 2011.

[11] L. Kocsis and C. Szepesvári. Bandit based Monte-Carlo Planning. In *Machine Learning: ECML 2006*, pages 282–293. Springer, 2006.

[12] D. LaSalle and G. Karypis. Multi-threaded Graph Partitioning. In *Parallel & Distributed Processing (IPDPS), 2013 IEEE 27th International Symposium on*, pages 225–236. IEEE, 2013.

[13] J. Leskovec, A. Krause, C. Guestrin, C. Faloutsos, J. VanBriesen, and N. Glance. Cost-effective Outbreak Detection in Networks. In *Proceedings of the 13th ACM SIGKDD international conference on Knowledge discovery and data mining*, pages 420–429. ACM, 2007.

[14] M. L. Puterman. *Markov Decision Processes: Discrete Stochastic Dynamic Programming*. John Wiley & Sons, 2009.

[15] E. Rice. The Positive Role of Social Networks and Social Networking Technology in the Condom-using Behaviors of Homeless Young People. *Public health reports*, 125(4):588, 2010.

[16] E. Rice, A. Barman-Adhikari, N. G. Milburn, and W. Monro. Position-specific HIV risk in a Large Network of Homeless Youths. *American journal of public health*, 102(1):141–147, 2012.

[17] E. Rice, A. Fulginiti, H. Winetrobe, J. Montoya, A. Plant, and T. Kordic. Sexuality and Homelessness in Los Angeles public schools. *American Journal of Public Health*, 102, 2012.

[18] E. Rice, E. Tulbert, J. Cederbaum, A. B. Adhikari, and N. G. Milburn. Mobilizing Homeless Youth for HIV Prevention: a Social Network Analysis of the Acceptability of a face-to-face and Online Social Networking Intervention. *Health education research*, 27(2):226, 2012.

[19] S. Ross, J. Pineau, S. Paquet, and B. Chaib-Draa. Online Planning Algorithms for POMDPs. *Journal of Artificial Intelligence Research*, pages 663–704, 2008.

[20] J. A. Schneider, A. N. Zhou, and E. O. Laumann. A new HIV Prevention Network Approach: Sociometric Peer Change Agent Selection. *Social Science & Medicine*, 125:192–202, 2015.

[21] D. Silver and J. Veness. Monte-Carlo Planning in large POMDPs. In *Advances in Neural Information Processing Systems*, pages 2164–2172, 2010.

[22] A. Somani, N. Ye, D. Hsu, and W. S. Lee. DESPOT: Online POMDP Planning with Regularization. In *Advances In Neural Information Processing Systems*, pages 1772–1780, 2013.

[23] Y. Tang, X. Xiao, and Y. Shi. Influence maximization: Near-Optimal Time Complexity meets Practical Efficiency. In *Proceedings of the 2014 ACM SIGMOD international conference on Management of data*, pages 75–86. ACM, 2014.

[24] UNAIDS. Report on the Global AIDS Epidemic. `www.unaids.org/en/resources/campaigns/20121120_globalreport2012/globalreport/`, Mar. 2012.

[25] T. W. Valente and P. Pumpuang. Identifying Opinion Leaders to Promote Behavior Change. *Health Education & Behavior*, 2007.

[26] A. Yadav, H. Chan, A. Jiang, H. Xu, E. Rice, and M. Tambe. Using social networks to aid homeless shelters: Dynamic influence maximization under uncertainty - an extended version. *arXiv:1602.00165*, 2016.

[27] A. Yadav, L. Marcolino, E. Rice, R. Petering, H. Winetrobe, H. Rhoades, M. Tambe, and H. Carmichael. Preventing HIV Spread in Homeless Populations Using PSINET. In *Proceedings of the Twenty-Seventh Conference on Innovative Applications of Artificial Intelligence (IAAI-15)*, 2015.

[28] Q. Yan, S. Guo, and D. Yang. Influence Maximizing and Local Influenced Community Detection based on Multiple Spread Model. In *Advanced Data Mining and Applications*, pages 82–95. Springer, 2011.

[29] S. D. Young and E. Rice. Online Social Networking Technologies, HIV knowledge, and Sexual Risk and Testing Behaviors among Homeless Youth. *AIDS and Behavior*, 15(2):253–260, 2011.

Optimal Pricing for Efficient Electric Vehicle Charging Station Management

Yanhai Xiong[1], Jiarui Gan[2], Bo An[2], Chunyan Miao[2], Yeng Chai Soh[3]
[1]Joint NTU-UBC Centre of Excellence in Active Living for the Elderly, Nanyang Technological University
[2]School of Computer Engineering, Nanyang Technological University
[3]School of Electrical & Electronic Engineering, Nanyang Technological University
Singapore 639798
{yxiong003, jrgan, boan, ascymiao, eycsoh}@ntu.edu.sg

ABSTRACT

The rapid development of Electric Vehicles (EVs) seen in recent years has been drawing increasing attentions from the public, markets, decision-makers, and academia. Notwithstanding the progress, issues still remain. Because of the widely complained disadvantages of limited battery capacity and long charging time, charging convenience has become a top concern that greatly hinders the adoption of EVs. Specialized EV charging station, which provides more than 10 times faster charging speed than domestic charging, is therefore a critical element for successful EV promotion.

While most existing researches focus on optimizing spatial placement of charging stations, they are inflexible and inefficient against rapidly changing urban structure and traffic pattern. Therefore, this paper approaches the management of EV charging stations from the pricing perspective as a more flexible and adaptive complement to established charging station placement. In this paper, we build a realistic pricing model in consideration of residential travel pattern and EV drivers' self-interested charging behavior, traffic congestion, and operating expense of charging stations. We formulate the pricing problem as a mixed integer non-convex optimization problem, and propose a scalable algorithm to solve it. Experiments on both mock and real data are also conducted, which show scalability of our algorithm as well as our solution's significant improvement over existing approaches.

Categories and Subject Descriptors

[**Social and professional topics**]: Pricing and resource allocation

General Terms

Management, Design, Algorithms, Experimentation

Keywords

Electric Vehicle; Charging Station; Pricing; Game Theory

Appears in: *Proceedings of the 15th International Conference on Autonomous Agents and Multiagent Systems (AAMAS 2016), J. Thangarajah, K. Tuyls, C. Jonker, S. Marsella (eds.), May 9–13, 2016, Singapore.*

1. INTRODUCTION

Electric Vehicles (EVs) are welcoming a rapid development along with progresses of relevant technologies in recent years. As an eco-friendly substitute for traditional fuel-engined vehicle, EV is seen as a promising solution to the ever devastating energy crisis and environmental pollution around the globe, thus has drawn increasing attentions from the public, markets, decision-makers, and academia. Many countries and cities have proposed plans to promote EV usage or have been preparing to do so, providing a foreseeable vision that EV will become the major vehicle of private transportation sector in the near future [1]. Notwithstanding the progresses, challenges still remain. Limited battery capacity and long charging time, probably the most widely complained disadvantages, raise mileage anxiety and largely impair EV users' driving experience. As a result, charging convenience has become a top concern affecting potential users' choice between EV and traditional fuel-engined vehicle. Specialized EV charging stations, which provide more than 10 times faster charging speed than domestic charging, are therefore critical to the successful promotion of EV.

While there have been some existing work concerning the management of EV charging stations, they mostly focused on the spatial placement of charging stations. For example, Frad et al. studied the placement and capacity allocation of EV charging stations for an area of Lisbon with the emphasis of maximizing coverage of charging demands [2]. Wong et al. proposed a muti-objective planning model for the placement of EV charging stations in Chengdu, China, with a solution based on demand and usage of existing gas stations [3]. Chen et al. particularly considered EV users' costs for accessing charging stations, and minimizing the costs and penalizing unmet demand [4]. Moreover, He et al. and Xiong et al. took a more broad view and emphasized the impact on overall efficiency of transportation system when optimizing the placement [5, 6]. However, a major drawback of the existing work is that such once-for-all solutions can hardly adapt to rapidly changing urban structures. Development of local infrastructure, such as opening-up of a new hospital, shopping mall, school, or housing estate, can all fundamentally modify the residential traffic pattern, making it unbalanced against the existing charging network. Thus follow-up adjustments are expected but might be costly and inefficient if we only rely on optimizing the placement.

To adapt to the urban structure change as well as varying

charging demand, a practical solution as we propose in this paper is to leverage charging price to readjust EV users' charging behavior and improve efficiency of the charging network. Compared with placement, pricing is easily and immediately implementable without additional cost or waste of resources. Dynamic pricing schemes adapt to either long-term changes of travel demand caused by residential movements or short-term variances between peak and non-peak time, and serve as a flexible complement to existing charging station placement. Our goal is to optimize the pricing scheme to optimize the efficiency of charging stations, i.e., to minimize the additional cost caused by EV users' charging behavior, which is referred as social cost. There have been some works leveraging dynamic pricing to improve efficiency of public transportation systems, such as taxi systems [7, 8]. Some works have particularly focused on real-time pricing and charge-discharge policy for EV management [9, 10]. However, their aim is merely to balance electricity load in power grids, while traffic condition is not in their consideration. Moreover, their method cannot be incorporated with trivial modifications because the traffic condition deeply relates to EV users' self-interested charing behavior associated with a graph-based road network, which are all absent from existing work.

In this paper, we take a game-theoretic perspective and build the problem on a non-atomic congestion game played by EV users. The model incorporates the following key features: 1) EV users' self-interested charging behavior that they strategically choose the best charging plan (i.e., where to charge and how to reach the charge station) to minimize their costs including charging fees, traveling time, and queuing time; 2) EV users' traffic pattern with complex spatial variances; 3) Traffic congestion in the road network that is affected by both the EVs and other external vehicles; and 4) A budget constraint that ensures sufficient income to support sustainable operation of the charging network. Using this model, we formulate the EV charging station pricing problem as a mixed integer non-convex optimization problem, and propose a scalable algorithm to solve the problem, in particular to deal with the large strategy space of the EVs. Experiments on both mock and real data are also conducted, which show scalability of our algorithm as well as our solution's significant improvement in social cost over existing approaches. A concrete instance is also used to visualize the difference between our approach and existing approaches.

2. MOTIVATION

Singapore is a city country with a vehicle ownership of around 970,000 on its small territory of 720 km^2. As a highly developed metropolis with open attitudes toward cutting edge technologies, yet a country with limited natural resource and energy supply, Singapore is actively seeking the possibility of mass adoption of EVs to support its sustainable development. Ever since 2011, its authorities have started an EV test-bed to study the feasibility of EVs on its road. More recently, in the Government's sustainable blueprint to guide the country's development over the next 15 years launched in 2014, Singapore has even planned to lead an EV-sharing project to make the new technology even more convenient and environmentally-friendly.

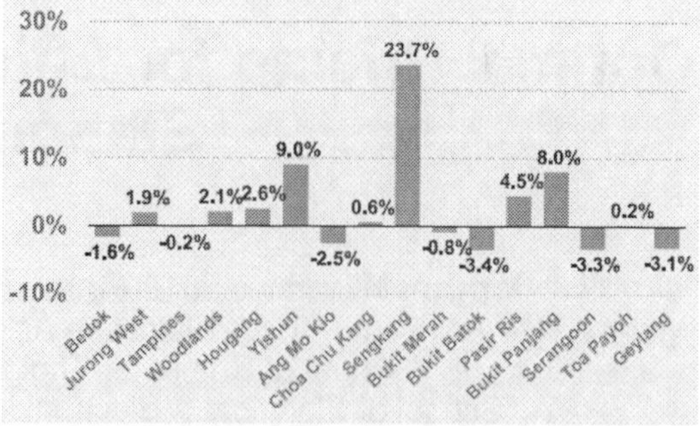

Figure 1: Population growth rate of major residential zones of Singapore from 2010 to 2015

Indeed, the relatively short driving distances on the small territory and the advanced power grid of Singapore make EVs a good option for this city. However, there are also many difficulties that require every step taken to be carefully planned. Because of the land scarcity and the fact that roads have already taken up 12 percent of Singapore's total land area, there is limited room for further expansion of Singapore's road network. This leaves Singapore a very high road density of $4.8km/km^2$, and a transportation system that is highly sensitive to any changes to the current transportation mode. Besides, Singapore is undergoing a rapid change in residential pattern along with its continuing development. As shown in Figure 1, population growth varies significantly among major residential zones of Singapore, indicating similar significant changes in residential traffic pattern. A sustainable plan therefore needs to be compatible to the current system while adaptable to future changes, to ensure a smooth transition toward the new EV-led transportation mode. This motivates our work and offers us a concrete study case.

3. PRELIMINARY

In this section, we introduce some notations and definitions that will be helpful to scenario visualization and be used in formulating the problem.

3.1 Notations

Considering the residential distribution of the studied city (e.g., Singapore), we divide the region to be analyzed (whole or part of the city) into a set $\mathcal{Z}$ of zones. There are roads linking the zones. Without loss of generality, we assume that there is at most one link between a pair of zones representing the average connectivity between them, and denote the set of links as $\mathcal{E}$ and the road network as a graph $\mathcal{G} = (\mathcal{Z}, \mathcal{E})$. In each zone $i \in \mathcal{Z}$, there are γ_i EVs owned by the residents who have some chance to charge in the charging stations. The γ_i EVs are furthermore classified into K_i groups according to their travel patterns, i.e., their daily travel routine as a set of most frequently visited zones. Each travel pattern is a set of connected zones that they visit daily. We denote by γ_{ij} the number of EVs in each group, and by $\mathcal{P}_{ij}$ their pattern for $j \in \mathcal{K}_i = \{1, \ldots, K_i\}$. The union of all patterns is denoted by $\mathcal{P} = \bigcup_{i \in \mathcal{Z}, j \in \mathcal{K}_i} \mathcal{P}_{ij}$.

Given the number τ_i (≥ 0) of chargers in each zone i, our goal is to calculate the charging rate (i.e., per unit electricity price) x_i to be set at each zone, such that the social cost (to be defined later) is minimized. Accordingly, we denote the set of feasible price as $\mathcal{X}$.

3.2 Factors Affecting EVs' Decision

EVs make decisions about where to charge and how to reach the charging zone according to the estimated charging cost, which consists of three parts: charging fee, travel cost and queuing cost. The charging fee is the variable to be optimized in this work. In the following, we introduce the definition of travel cost and queuing cost.

Travel Cost. There are furthermore two kinds of travel cost: 1) *cost on link*, i.e., cost for travelling between zones, and 2) *cost on node*, i.e., cost for traveling within the zone where the EV charges. The cost on a link depends on the length and the traffic congestion level of this link. Generally, more vehicles on the road results in higher congestion level, and larger road capacity leads to lower congestion. We adopt a widely used linear model of traffic congestion taken as the ratio of the traffic flow to the road capacity (both in the number of vehicles). Thus, for a link $(i, i') \in \mathcal{E}$, given the length $d_{ii'}$, the capacity $C_{ii'}$ and traffic flow $f^0_{ii'} + f_{ii'}$ (we distinguish flow of EVs heading for charging, i.e., $f_{ii'}$, with flow of other vehicle, i.e., $f^0_{ii'}$, which is assumed to be constant), the traffic congestion $\alpha_{ii'}$ of link (i, i') is presented in Eq. (1) [11]. Travel cost on (i, i') is defined as a function of its length and traffic congestion as Eq. (2).

$$\alpha_{ii'} = \frac{f^0_{ii'} + f_{ii'}}{C_{ii'}} \tag{1}$$

$$t_{ii'} = d_{ii'}\alpha_{ii'} \tag{2}$$

Meanwhile, when an EV chooses to charge in a zone i, there is extra travel cost, i.e., cost on node, as she drives off the main road to access the charging station within zone i. Considering that a zone includes more internal roads (than in between two zones) and that the EVs coming for charging does not have to traverse all of them, we add a discount factor ζ to denote the EVs' influence on congestion in the zone. In this case, a similar function as Eq. (2) is used for the extra travel cost in the charging zone:

$$t_i = d_i \frac{f^0_i + \zeta f_i}{C_i}, i \in \mathcal{Z}, \tag{3}$$

where d_i denotes the radius of the zone, f^0_i is the normal traffic amount, f_i is the total number of EVs that choose to charge in zone i and C_i is the capacity of the zone regarding all its travel network.

Queuing Cost. The queuing cost depends on the number of chargers in the charging station and the number of EVs that come to the charging station. We use a linear model to denote the relationship among them as Eq. (4). Recalling that τ_i denotes the number of chargers in zone i, let q_i be the queuing cost and f_i be the number of EVs charging there, then we have

$$q_i = \frac{f_i}{\tau_i}, i \in \mathcal{Z}. \tag{4}$$

4. EVS' CHARGING BEHAVIOR

From a game-theoretic perspective [12], when we optimize charging station management, we need to take into account the strategic behavior of EV owners. Namely, they are self-interested and profit-driven, such that they will respond to our pricing with the best charging strategy to minimize their charging cost. Next, we explicitly explain the charging game - the model of EVs' charging behavior. To distinguish a zone that EVs reside in from one EVs charge in, we use i and z respectively to denote a zone in the follows.

4.1 Charging Strategy

Each EV chooses a pure charging strategy and the s-trategies of the EVs in the same zone of the same travel pattern form a distribution over their strategy space. A pure charging strategy is to choose a zone with charging stations installed, and an additional travel path from a zone on her daily routine to the charging zone and back if the chosen zone is not in the EV's travel pattern. Thus a pure charging strategy can be denoted as a tuple $\mathbf{s}$ with

$$\mathbf{s} = \begin{cases} \{z\}, z \in \mathcal{P}_{ij} \\ \{z', (z, z'), (z', z) \,|\, z \in \mathcal{P}_{ij}, z' \in \mathcal{Z} \setminus \mathcal{P}_{ij}, \} \end{cases}, \tag{5}$$

where both (z, z') and (z', z) are in set $\mathcal{E}$. Note that by Eq. (5), we only consider EVs' charging zones inside or adjacent to zones in their travel pattern and assume that they do not charge in farther places. This is because the distance to those places is usually much farther than a single hop, thus causing higher travel cost and is unlikely to happen in reality. Experimental results in Section 6.3 verify that this assumption is reasonable. We then use $\mathcal{S}_{ij}$ to denote the strategy space for the EVs in zone i of travel pattern j. Furthermore, $\mathcal{S} = \bigcup_{i \in \mathcal{Z}, j \in \mathcal{K}_i} \mathcal{S}_{ij}$ is used to denote the strategy space union for all the EVs in the studied region. For example, there are 6 zones illustrated in Figure 2, and

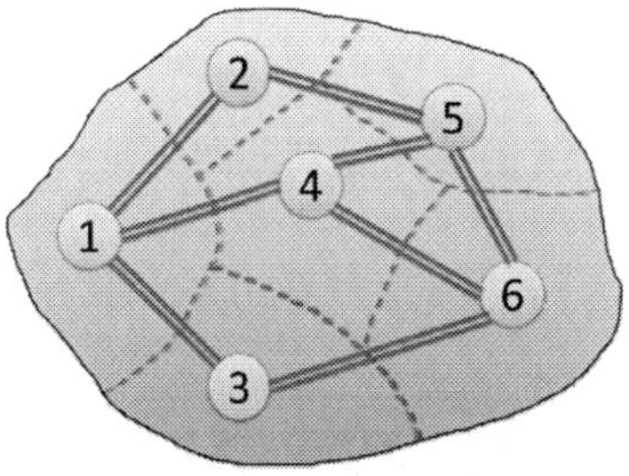

Figure 2: Zone division illustration

we suppose there are chargers in all zones. If a group of EVs' daily travel routine includes zones 1, 4 and 6, their strategy space includes these 8 pure strategies:

$$\mathbf{s}_1 = \{1\}, \quad \mathbf{s}_2 = \{4\}, \quad \mathbf{s}_3 = \{6\}, \quad \mathbf{s}_4 = \{2, (1,2), (2,1)\},$$

$$\mathbf{s}_5 = \{3, (1,3), (3,1)\}, \quad \mathbf{s}_6 = \{5, (4,5), (5,4)\},$$

$$\mathbf{s}_7 = \{5, (6,5), (5,6)\}, \quad \mathbf{s}_8 = \{3, (6,3), (3,6)\}.$$

When the charging zone is in their routine, there is no links in the strategy (e.g., $\mathbf{s}_1$, $\mathbf{s}_2$ and $\mathbf{s}_3$). Otherwise (e.g., $\mathbf{s}_4$ to

$\mathbf{s}_8$), there are two additional links specifying a round trip to the charging zone.

EVs choose charging strategy according to charging cost, including charging fee, travel cost and queuing cost. In reverse, their strategies also influence congestion level and queueing time, i.e., travel cost and queueing cost. We denote the strategy distribution of EVs of group j in the zone i as $\mathbf{p}_{ij}$, with each $p_{ij}(\mathbf{s})$ denoting the proportion of γ_{ij} EVs using pure strategy $\mathbf{s}$ in the group of EVs' strategy space $\mathcal{S}_{ij}$.

Given a strategy profile $\mathbf{P} = \{\mathbf{p}_{ij}\}$, the number of EVs in each charging station $z \in \mathcal{Z}$ and the number of EVs on each link $e \in \mathcal{E}$ can then be seen as functions of the $\mathbf{P}$ as:

$$f_z(\mathbf{P}) = \sum_{\mathbf{s}\in\mathcal{S}:z\in\mathbf{s}} \sum_{i\in\mathcal{Z}} \sum_{j\in\mathcal{K}_i:\mathbf{s}\in\mathcal{S}_{ij}} \gamma_{ij} p_{ij}(\mathbf{s}) \quad (6)$$

$$f_e(\mathbf{P}) = \sum_{\mathbf{s}\in\mathcal{S}:e\in\mathbf{s}} \sum_{i\in\mathcal{Z}} \sum_{j\in\mathcal{K}_i:\mathbf{s}\in\mathcal{S}_{ij}} \gamma_{ij} p_{ij}(\mathbf{s}) \quad (7)$$

Similarly, travel cost t for link e and zone z, and queuing cost q for zone z are respectively defined as:

$$t_e(\mathbf{P}) = \frac{d_e}{C_e}\Big(f_e^0 + \sum_{\mathbf{s}\in\mathcal{S}:e\in\mathbf{s}} \sum_{i\in\mathcal{Z}} \sum_{j\in\mathcal{K}_i:\mathbf{s}\in\mathcal{S}_{ij}} \gamma_{ij} p_{ij}(\mathbf{s})\Big), \quad (8)$$

$$t_z(\mathbf{P}) = \frac{d_z}{C_z}\Big(f_z^0 + \zeta \sum_{\mathbf{s}\in\mathcal{S}:z\in\mathbf{s}} \sum_{i\in\mathcal{Z}} \sum_{j\in\mathcal{K}_i:\mathbf{s}\in\mathcal{S}_{ij}} \gamma_{ij} p_{ij}(\mathbf{s})\Big), \quad (9)$$

$$q_z(\mathbf{P}) = \frac{1}{\tau_z} \sum_{\mathbf{s}\in\mathcal{S}:z\in\mathbf{s}} \sum_{i\in\mathcal{Z}} \sum_{j\in\mathcal{K}_i:\mathbf{s}\in\mathcal{S}_{ij}} \gamma_{ij} p_{ij}(\mathbf{s}). \quad (10)$$

Apart from the above costs, EVs also consider their charging fees, denoted by x_z, which vary at different zones. The weights ω_1, ω_2, and ω_3 are assigned to the three types of costs respectively. Thus, given the electricity price x_z in zone z, the charging cost of an EV using charging strategy $\mathbf{s}$ under strategy profile $\mathbf{P}$ is:

$$C_{ij}(\mathbf{P},\mathbf{s}) = \sum_{z\in\mathbf{s}}\Big(\omega_1 q_z(\mathbf{P}) + \omega_2 t_z(\mathbf{P}) + \omega_3 x_z\Big) + \sum_{e\in\mathbf{s}} \omega_2 t_e(\mathbf{P}) \quad (11)$$

for all zone $i \in \mathcal{Z}$, group $j \in \mathcal{K}_i$ and pure strategy $\mathbf{s} \in \mathcal{S}_{ij}$.

4.2 Equilibrium

We adopt Nash equilibrium pin *non-atomic* congestion game as our solution concept. A non-atomic congestion game is one that is played by an uncountably large number of players (which is exactly the case in our problem, with around 30,000 EVs in the system), so that each agent's effect on the congestion level is negligibly small. It is widely used to model congestion scenario with a large number of agents, which is exactly our case. In an equilibrium state, no EV can decrease her charging cost by unilaterally changing her charging strategy. Specifically, for each EV group j in zone i, the charging cost of all pure strategies that are used with non-zero probability are the same and the minimal, i.e.,

$$C_{ij}(\mathbf{P},\mathbf{s}) \le C_{ij}(\mathbf{P},\mathbf{s}') \quad \forall \mathbf{s} \in \mathcal{S}_{ij},\ p_{ij}(\mathbf{s}) > 0 \quad (12)$$

In this case, no EV has incentive to unilaterally change her charging strategy.

4.3 Pricing Problem for EV Charging Station Management

As we have mentioned before, our goal is to minimize the social cost, denoted as SC. Specifically, we consider the extra social cost incurred by EVs' charging behavior, which is measured with the congestion experienced by all EVs in charging stations and extra congestion caused by EVs' charging behavior for *all* vehicles in the road network, i.e.,

$$SC = \nu_1 \sum_{z\in\mathcal{Z}} f_z(\mathbf{P}) q_z(\mathbf{P}) + \quad (13)$$

$$\nu_2 \sum_{z\in\mathcal{Z}} \Big((f_z^0 + f_z(\mathbf{P})) t_z(\mathbf{P}) - f_z^0 t_z(\mathbf{0}) \Big) + \quad (14)$$

$$\nu_2 \sum_{e\in\mathcal{E}} \Big((f_e^0 + f_e(\mathbf{P})) t_e(\mathbf{P}) - f_e^0 t_e(\mathbf{0}) \Big), \quad (15)$$

where the first component represents queuing cost for EVs in all zones, weighted with ν_1; and the second and the third components respectively represent additional travel cost in each zone and on each link for all vehicles, weighted with ν_2. It suffices for us to formulate the pricing problem for EV charging station management, which turns out to be a non-convex optimization problem **PCS** as follows.

$$\textbf{PCS:} \quad \min_{\mathbf{x},\mathbf{P}} \ SC \quad (16)$$

$$\text{s.t.} \quad p_{ij}(\mathbf{s}) C_{ij}(\mathbf{P},\mathbf{s}) \le p_{ij}(\mathbf{s}) C_{ij}(\mathbf{P},\mathbf{s}'), \quad \forall i \in \mathcal{Z}, \forall j \in \mathcal{K}_i, \forall \mathbf{s},\mathbf{s}' \in \mathcal{S}_{ij} \quad (17)$$

$$\sum_{z\in\mathcal{Z}} f_z(\mathbf{P}) x_z \ge B \quad (18)$$

$$x_z \in \mathcal{X}, \quad \forall z \in \mathcal{Z} \quad (19)$$

$$p_{ij}(\mathbf{s}) \ge 0, \quad \forall i \in \mathcal{Z}, \forall j \in \mathcal{K}_i, \forall \mathbf{s} \in \mathcal{S}_{ij} \quad (20)$$

$$\sum_{\mathbf{s}\in\mathcal{S}_{ij}} p_{ij}(\mathbf{s}) = 1, \quad \forall i \in \mathcal{Z}, \forall j \in \mathcal{K}_i \quad (21)$$

Note that Eq. (17) functions as the equilibrium criteria in Eq. (12), i.e., when $p_{ij}(\mathbf{s}) = 0$, it holds unconditionally, and when $p_{ij}(\mathbf{s}) > 0$, it is equivalent to $C_{ij}(\mathbf{P},\mathbf{s}) \le C_{ij}(\mathbf{P},\mathbf{s}')$; Eq. (18) is a budget constraint requiring that the income of all charging station can at least cover their management and operation expenses; we suppose the charging rate in each zone is selected from a price set $\mathcal{X}$; and the last two constraints are to bound the p variables.

5. COMPUTING OPTIMAL PRICE

In this section, we present our algorithm for problem **PCS**. Problem **PCS** is a non-convex quadratic optimization problem, with its objective function SC being quadratic, and the first constraint (i.e., Eq. (17)) being non-convex. Besides, the scale of problem **PCS** is very large because EVs have many travel patterns and, moreover, each pattern may contain many zones, which amounts to a large strategy space and a similarly large set of variables for problem **PCS**. Therefore, problem **PCS** is hard to solve (particularly hard to scale up). To resolve the problem, we first rewrite constraint (17), and reformulate **PCS** to the following *binary* programming **PCS-*binary*** with an additional set of binary variables $\mathbf{y} = \langle y_{ij}(\mathbf{s}) \rangle$.

PCS-*binary*:

$$\min_{\mathbf{x},\mathbf{P},\mathbf{y}} \quad SC \tag{22}$$

$$\text{s.t.} \quad y_{ij}(\mathbf{s}) C_{ij}(\mathbf{P}, \mathbf{s}) \leq y_{ij}(\mathbf{s}) C_{ij}(\mathbf{P}, \mathbf{s}'), \quad \forall i \in \mathcal{Z}, \forall j \in \mathcal{K}_i, \forall \mathbf{s}, \mathbf{s}' \in \mathcal{S}_{ij} \tag{23}$$

$$p_{ij}(\mathbf{s}) \leq y_{ij}(\mathbf{s}), \; \forall i \in \mathcal{Z}, j \in \mathcal{K}_i, \mathbf{s} \in \mathcal{S}_{ij} \tag{24}$$

$$y_{ij}(\mathbf{s}) \in \{0, 1\}, \; \forall i \in \mathcal{Z}, j \in \mathcal{K}_i, \mathbf{s} \in \mathcal{S}_{ij} \tag{25}$$

Eqs. (18) – (21)

Eqs. (23)–(24) are modified from Eq. (17) with the auxiliary variable $\mathbf{y}$. As we can see, $y_{ij}(\mathbf{s})$ is an indicator for whether $\mathbf{s}$ can be used with *non-zero* probability in the solution, i.e., when $y_{ij}(\mathbf{s}) = 0$, we have (by Eq. (24)) $0 \leq p_{ij}(\mathbf{s}) \leq 0 \Rightarrow p_{ij}(\mathbf{s}) = 0$, and when $y_{ij}(\mathbf{s}) = 1$, we have $0 \leq p_{ij}(\mathbf{s}) \leq 1$. Therefore, Eqs. (23)–(24) are equivalent to (17), and **PCS-*binary*** is equivalent to **PCS**. To solve **PCS-*binary***, a brute-force way is to exhaustively try all the 0/1 combinations in the feasible space $\{0, 1\}^{|\mathbf{y}|}$ for $\mathbf{y}$. When $\mathbf{y}$ is fixed, **PCS-*binary*** becomes a quadratic programming with linear constraints, which is relatively easy to solve. We then propose a Strategy Space Generation Algorithm (*SSGA*) to speed up the brute-force search, which is sketched with Algorithm 1.

SSGA starts with an initialized vector $\mathbf{y}^*$ (Line 1) and, repeatedly, solves **PCS-*binary*** with $\mathbf{y}^*$, and updates $\mathbf{y}^*$ with two key procedures Rule A (Lines 6–8) and Rule B (Lines 11–15), until no update is made on $\mathbf{y}^*$ in some iteration (Line 16). Specifically,

- Rule A disables strategies $\mathbf{s}$ that are chosen with very small probability (i.e., $p_{ij}(\mathbf{s}) < \delta$ with $0 < \delta \ll 1$) by setting $y_{ij}(\mathbf{s}) = 0$, so that they will not be used in the next iteration. The intuition behind Rule A is that when $p_{ij}(\mathbf{s})$ is very closed to 0, setting it to 0 will not cause much change to the cost of the EVs, but can significantly expand the feasible space as the associate constraint in Eq. (23) is relaxed.

- Rule B checks if there are any unused strategies that could potentially lower EVs' cost, and enables them by setting $y_{ij}(\mathbf{s}) = 1$ when they are found. Intuitively, these newly enabled strategies are EVs' better responses for the current strategy profile.

Finally, Proposition 1 shows that *SSGA* always converges to a Nash equilibrium. The price $\mathbf{x}^*$ it returns is thus the optimal price under the equilibrium.

PROPOSITION 1. *The algorithm SSGA always converges to an equilibrium charging strategy profile.*

PROOF. Recalling that we use *Rule B* to validate whether or not we need to keep on the iteration of upgrading the set of used pure strategies and *Rule B* is exactly using the equilibrium criteria as stated in Eq.(12), we can always ensure the strategy distribution $\mathbf{P}$ in the solution is an equilibrium. □

Algorithm 1: SSGA

1 $\mathbf{y}^* \leftarrow$ Initialize as a binary vector;
2 $\mathbf{x}^* \leftarrow$ *Null*;
3 **repeat**
4 $\quad \langle \mathbf{x}^*, \mathbf{P}^* \rangle \leftarrow$ Fix $\mathbf{y}$ to $\mathbf{y}^*$ and solve **PCS-*binary***;
5 $\quad \mathbf{y}' \leftarrow \mathbf{y}^*$;
$\quad$ /* --------------- Rule A -------------- */
6 $\quad$ **for** *each* $i \in \mathcal{Z}$, $j \in \mathcal{K}_i$, $\mathbf{s} \in \mathcal{S}_{ij}$ **do**
7 $\quad\quad$ **if** $p^*_{ij}(\mathbf{s}) < \delta$ **then**
8 $\quad\quad\quad y^*_{ij}(\mathbf{s}) \leftarrow 0$;
9 $\quad$ **if** $\mathbf{y}^* \neq \mathbf{y}'$ **then**
10 $\quad\quad$ **goto** Line 4;
$\quad$ /* --------------- Rule B -------------- */
11 $\quad$ **for** *each* $i \in \mathcal{Z}$, $j \in \mathcal{K}_i$ **do**
12 $\quad\quad C^{min}_{ij} \leftarrow \arg\min_{\mathbf{s}: \mathbf{s} \in \mathcal{S}_{ij} \wedge p'_{ij}(\mathbf{s}) > 0} C_{ij}(\mathbf{P}^*, \mathbf{s})$;
13 $\quad\quad$ **for** *each* $\mathbf{s} \in \mathcal{S}_{ij}$ **do**
14 $\quad\quad\quad$ **if** $y'_{ij}(\mathbf{s}) = 0$ *and* $C_{ij}(\mathbf{P}^*, \mathbf{s}) \leq C^{min}_{ij}$ **then**
15 $\quad\quad\quad\quad y^*_{ij}(\mathbf{s}) \leftarrow 1$;
16 **until** $\mathbf{y}^* = \mathbf{y}'$;
17 **return** $\mathbf{x}^*$;

6. EXPERIMENTAL RESULTS

In this section, experimental results are provided to verify the optimality and scalability of the proposed approach *SSGA*, and to present the improvement of traffic system performance provided by our approach. All computations are performed on a 64-bit machine with 16 GB RAM and a quad-core Intel i7-4770 3.4 GHz processor. All standard optimization problems, such as Line 4 of Algorithm 1, are solved with KNITRO 9.0.0.

Data of Singapore. We divide Singapore into 23 zones as Figure 3 according to the official planning-area information [13] and other geographic information. According to statistic data from the Department of Statistics, Ministry of Trade and Industry, Singapore [14], 23% of the residents usually drive to work. Besides, there are more than 972,000 vehicles in year 2014, among which more than 600,000 are cars or station-wagons. We suppose 5% of the 600,000 vehicles are EVs that charge in the charging game, then the total number of 30,000 EVs are assigned to different zones according to the residential population distribution. The traffic flow and road capacity for each zone and link are estimated according to Google real-time traffic map. The price set is set as $\mathcal{X} = \{1, 1.5, 2, 2.5, 3\}$, according to the charging fee of charging stations in the U.S. [15]. The discount factor in computing the traffic congestion inside a zone is set as $\zeta = 0.5$. The weights for different parts in social cost and EVs' charging cost are set as: $\nu_1 = 0.8$, $\nu_2 = 0.2$; $\omega_1 = 0.1$, $\omega_2 = 0.3$ and $\omega_3 = 0.6$. The reason for this setting is to make sure that charging fee, travel cost and queuing cost are comparable. Except in Section 6.1, where we use a set of mock data of the traffic network and

EV population to test the solution quality and scalability of *SSGA*, all other experiments are based on the data of Singapore.

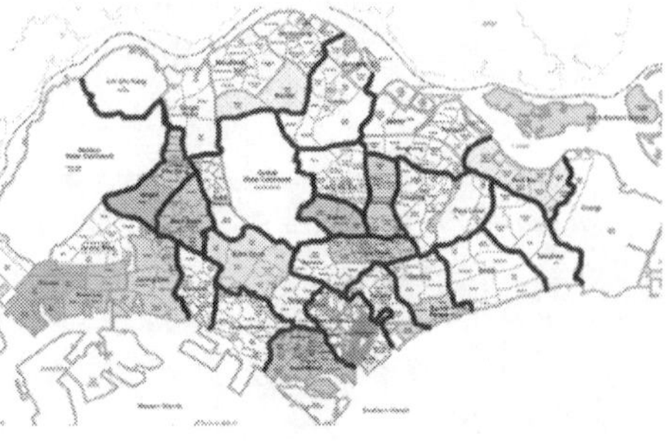

Figure 3: Singapore map and zone division

Initializing the Binary Indicators for *SSGA*. The initial value of the indicators in Line 1 of the algorithm *SSGA* significantly influences the accuracy and speed of the approach. We apply the following method for initializing starting indicators for *SSGA*. We first compute the estimate charging cost of each pure strategy assuming that there is only one EV that charges in the charging zone of that pure strategy and ignoring the charging fee. Formally, The estimate charging cost $\widetilde{C}_{ij}(\mathbf{s})$ for EVs of each pattern j in each zone i is computed as

$$\widetilde{C}_{ij}(\mathbf{s}) = \sum_{z\in\mathbf{s}}\left(\omega_1\frac{1}{\tau_z}+\omega_2\frac{d_z}{C_z}(f_z^0+\zeta)\right)+\sum_{e\in\mathbf{s}}\omega_2\frac{d_e}{C_e}(f_e^0+1). \tag{26}$$

Then we select the strategies whose estimated charging costs are no more than twice of the minimum of them and set their indicators as 1. That is to say, we set the indicator $y_{ij}(\mathbf{s}) = 1$ for all the $\mathbf{s} \in \mathcal{S}_{ij}$ with $\widetilde{C}_{ij}(\mathbf{s}) \leq 2\min_{\mathbf{s}'\in\mathcal{S}_{ij}}\widetilde{C}_{ij}(\mathbf{s}')$.

Virtual Charging Station Placement for Experiments on Data of Singapore. Since the charging station network in Singapore are not settled yet, we use virtual placements of EV charging stations for our experiments. For the total number of 30,000 EVs in the charging game, we assign a total number of 2,000 chargers to the charging stations in the region. Three kinds of placement are used according to the following rules, respectively.

A1 Placement according to population distribution. Namely, the chargers are distributed proportionally according to the population in each zone, i.e., $\tau_z \propto \gamma_z, \forall z \in \mathcal{Z}$.

B1 Placement according to current gas station distribution. This rule refers to the current gas station distribution in Singapore and assign chargers proportionally according to the number of gas stations in each zone. Formally, assume that there are τ_z^{Gas} gas stations in zone z, the number of chargers in this zone $\tau_i \propto \tau_z^{Gas}$.

C1 Placement considering traffic congestion. The number of chargers in a zone is set proportional to the inverse of the normal congestion (regardless of the charging EVs) inside the zone, i.e., $\tau_z \propto \frac{C_z}{f_z^0}, \forall z \in \mathcal{Z}$.

6.1 Solution Quality and Scalability of SSGA

For experiments in this part, we generate a set of mock data, because we need problems of different scales to verify the optimality and scalability of *SSGA* through comparing with **PCS**.

Mock Data. We generate mock data using a Java program. First, the number of zones n is specified and the budget is set as $100n$. The traffic network is randomly generated by building a two-way link between any pair of zones with probability $4.5/n$. After the construction of the travel network, we randomly set the number of travel patterns in each zone as one of the elements in the set $\{1,2,3\}$ and we randomize the number of EVs of each pattern between 50 and 100. The traffic capacity and external flow (i.e., f_z^0 and f_e^0) in zones and links are randomized as integers in $[140,160]$ and $[100,200]$, respectively. For the charging stations' location and size, we use two methods to set them up. In the following are the two **charging station placement plans on mock data**.

A2 We randomly choose some of the zones and assign 10 chargers to each of them. The expectation of the number of zones with chargers is $n/2$.

B2 We first calculate an index value θ_z for each zone $z \in \mathcal{Z}$ as following

$$\theta_z = \sum_{i\in\mathcal{Z}}\sum_{j\in\mathcal{K}_i:z\in\mathcal{P}_{ij}}\gamma_{ij}.$$

This index value reflects how many EVs visit zone z frequently. Then we assign a number $5n$ of chargers to the zones proportionally, i.e., $\tau_z \propto \theta_z, \forall z \in \mathcal{Z}$.

To test the optimality and scalability of *SSGA*, we generate different problems with n ranging from 5 to 12. Since the travel network, travel patterns and charging stations are randomly generated, the size of strategy space (i.e., $|\mathcal{S}|$), as well as the average size of strategy space for each travel pattern of EVs (i.e., $|\mathcal{S}|/|\mathcal{P}|$), are also randomized and does not have to increase with n (refer to "$|\mathcal{S}|$/#Pattern" curve in Figure 4(a) for the variation trend). We then solve **PCS** and *SSGA* based on the above described mock data and the corresponding charging station placement **A2** and **B2**.

Experimental results are shown in Fig 4. When we increase the number of zones, the size of the strategy space also increases accordingly. In Figure 4(a) and Figure 4(c), the running time of both approaches under different charging station placement plans is respectively described. It is shown that the running time of **PCS** does not monotonously increase with the number of zones, but corresponds to the "$|\mathcal{S}|$/#Pattern" curve. This is because the latter decides the complexity of the problem. For better visualization, we depict the relationship between running time and the average strategy space $|\mathcal{S}|/|\mathcal{P}|$ in Figure 4(b), from which we can see that the running time increases accordingly when $|\mathcal{S}|/|\mathcal{P}|$ increases. In Figure 4(c), as we are using the charging station plan **B2**, the number of zones with chargers increases, so does the problem scale. In this case, **PCS** cannot handle the problem even for a small graph. Obviously, our approach *SSGA* drastically decreases the running time. As we can see from Figure 4(d), *SSGA* always results in very close optimal

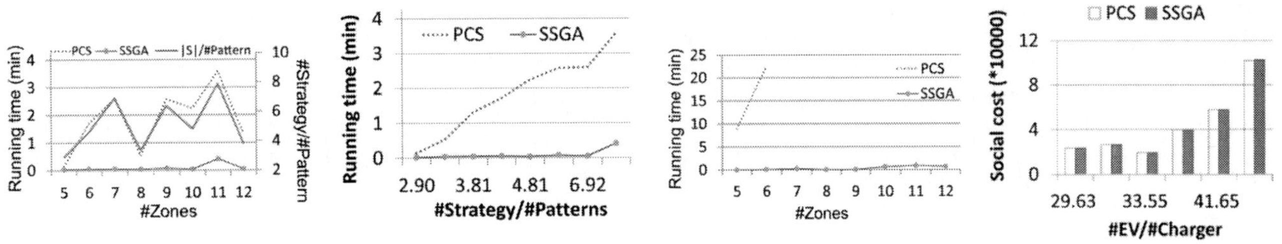

(a) Running time (**A2**) (b) Running time trend (**A2**) (c) Running time (**B2**) (d) Social cost (**A2**)

Figure 4: Optimality and scalability of *SSGA* comparing with **PCS**: (a) illustrates the running time of **PCS** and *SSGA* on the primary y axis, while on the secondary y axis showing the total number of pure strategies divided by the total number of EV patterns (i.e., the average size of strategy space for each pattern of EVs) corresponding to the charging station placement **A2**; (b) shows the relationship between the running time and the average size of strategy space for each pattern of EVs; (c) depicts running time results corresponding to the charging station placement **B2**; and (d) depicts the social cost of both **PCS** and *SSGA* for placement **A2**;

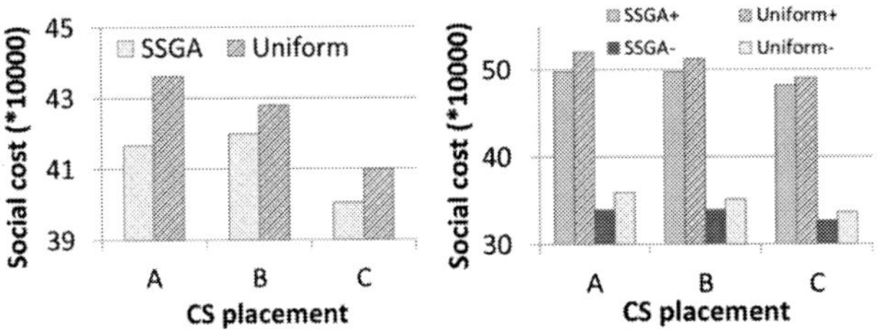

(a) Social cost (b) Social cost w.r.t. # of EVs

Figure 5: Comparing *SSGA* with uniform pricing under different charging station placement plans **A1**, **B1** and **C1**: (a) the number of EVs is estimated as we stated before; and (b) we increase and decrease the number of EVs by 10%.

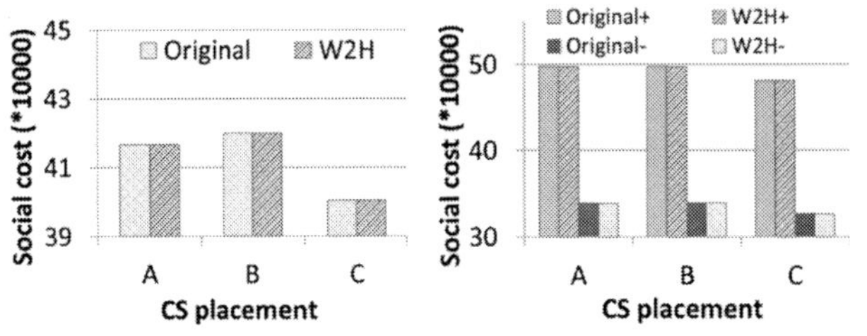

(a) Social cost (b) Social cost w.r.t. # of EVs

Figure 6: Social cost of *SSGA* on original data and with two-step hop charging strategies: (a) the number of EVs is estimated as we stated before; and (b) the number of EVs in each travel pattern is increased/decreased by 10%.

social cost to **PCS**. Note that the social cost increases with the number of EVs divided by the number of chargers, i.e., the average number of EVs that a charger needs to serve.

6.2 Advantages over Uniform Pricing

We apply our approach to the data of Singapore and compare our pricing policy with the benchmark - uniform pricing (i.e., set charging rate in all the charging stations as the same), which represents no utilization of pricing measure for improving traffic system performance. We then conduct experiments according to different charging station placement plans **A1** to **C1** for both *SSGA* and uniform pricing. In Figure 5(a), the number of EVs in each zone is set as we stated before. We can see that *SSGA* largely decreases the social cost, especially when the social cost is higher. We then increase/decrease the number of EVs in different extents to see what is the difference between the two methods when the EV density in the region is different. In Figure 5(b), the legends "*SSGA*+" and "Uniform+" refer to the results when the number of EVs is increased by 10%; similarly, the legends "*SSGA*-" and "Uniform-" refer to the results when the number of EVs is decreased by 10%. We find that when the number of EVs increases, the advantage of distinct pricing computed by *SSGA* also increases.

6.3 Two-step Hop Charging Strategies

In this part, we release the assumption that EVs only charge in her routine zones or adjacent ones of them to see what will happen to the optimal social cost and the equilibrium strategy profile. We choose zone 1 for the test by adding up all the 2-step hop charging strategies $\mathbf{s}'$ for the each patterns j EVs in zone 1:

$$\mathbf{s}' = \{z'', (z, z'), (z', z''), (z'', z'), (z', z)\}, \qquad (27)$$

where z is a zone in the travel pattern $\mathcal{P}_{1j}$, but z' and z'' are not. We then conduct experiments on original data and data with varied number of EVs (increas/decreas by 10% as we used in Section 6.2). We find that although the two-step hop strategies are added to the EVs' strategy space, they are never used and the optimal social cost never changes, which is shown in Figure 6. Furthermore, we find that the charging cost of those two-step hop strategies is much larger than those employed strategies. We conclude that it is reasonable to ignore these strategies.

6.4 Adaption to Population Change

The population in cities changes in amount as well as in distribution along with the city development. A concrete example is what we show in Section 2 about Singapore. Once the charging stations are settled in the city, it is costly to modify their layout although that the traffic system performance will decrease along with city development, which directly leads to citizens' travel pattern change. Thus we propose to use adaptive dynamic pricing to accommodate changes in population density and travel patterns, thus to mitigate the traffic congestion and decrease the social cost.

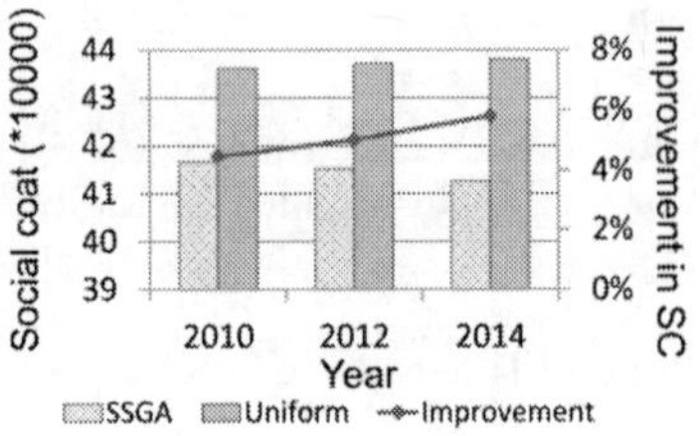

Figure 7: The optimal social cost of *SSGA* and uniform pricing, as well as the system efficiency improvement along with time.

We first arrange the charging stations according to plan **A2** for Singapore in year 2010. Based on that charging station placement, we then conduct experiments for population distribution in year 2012 and 2014, respectively. The results in social cost of both *SSGA* and uniform pricing are depicted in Figure 7, where the x axis denotes the year, and the primary and secondary y axis denote social cost and the percentage of improvement in social cost, respectively. As we can see, *SSGA* is quite adaptive to the population density change and it always decreases the social cost by a considerable amount. Furthermore, the "Improvement" curve shows that the decrease in social cost (i.e., improvement in system performance) increases with time. It turns out that when the system degenerates, *SSGA* performs even better.

6.5 Sensitivity and Robustness

In the above sections, the number of EVs in each zone of each pattern is accurately estimated. Considering that there might be some deviation between estimation and true values, we test the sensitivity of our approach regarding the number of EVs and consider the case that the estimated number of EVs is not accurate. We first compute the optimal price $\mathbf{x}$ according to our estimation. Then we compute the social cost with fixed $\mathbf{x}$ and EV number deviation by letting $\gamma_i' = \gamma_i(1 \pm \varepsilon)$ with $\epsilon = 5\%$ or 10%.

As we can see in Figure 8, *SSGA* always achieves better performance (i.e., results in lower social cost) than uniform pricing even when the estimation is not precise. Thus our pricing policy is robust regarding to the uncertainty of estimation of the number of EVs. Besides, according to the social cost of uniform pricing and the "Improvement" curve, we can see that when the social cost is higher, *SSGA* actually outperforms uniform pricing more.

7. CONCLUSION & APPLICATION

In this paper, we take a game-theoretic perspective to study the EV charging station pricing problem motivated by

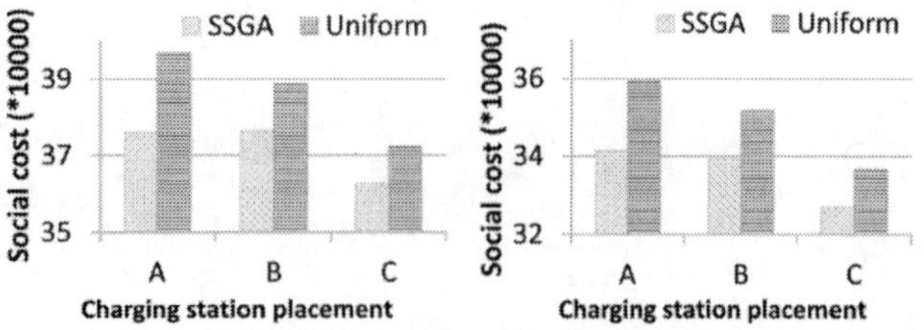

(a) # of EVs decrease by 5% (b) # of EVs decrease by 10%

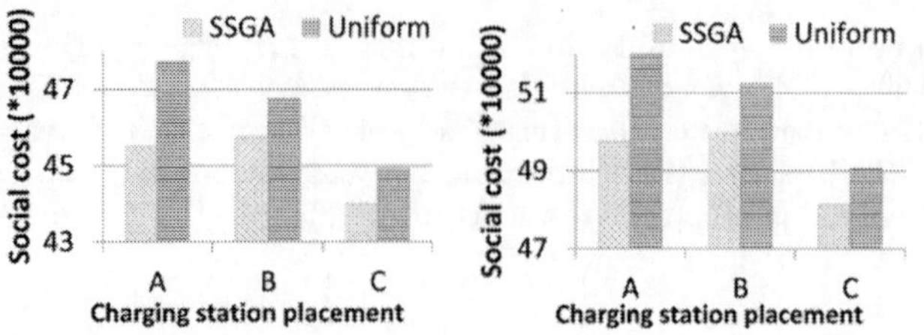

(c) # of EVs increase by 5% (d) # of EVs increase by 10%

Figure 8: Robustness test of *SSGA* comparing with uniform pricing regarding to deviation in estimation of the number of EVs: (a) the actual number of EVs of each pattern is 5% less than the estimation; (b) the actual number of EVs of each pattern is 10% less than the estimation; (c) the actual number of EVs of each pattern is 5% more than the estimation; and (d) the actual number of EVs of each pattern is 10% more than the estimation.

the practical need of EV promotion in Singapore. Our first contribution in this paper is a novel pricing model that comprehensively incorporates EV users' self-interested charging behavior and their various traffic patterns, traffic congestion contributed by EVs and other non-EV vehicles in the road network, as well as the financial concern for a sustainable operation of the charging network. The second contribution is the algorithm, *SSGA*, to solve the mixed integer non-convex optimal pricing problem, which features two key rules that guarantee efficient converging to equilibrium solution and drastically improves the running time perfomance. The final contribution is our extensive experiments and results which demonstrate our approach in several aspects, including solution quality, scalability and robustness. Moreover, we compare our approach with uniform pricing and demonstrate how and to what extent *SSGA* can help with improving the traffic system efficiency and decreasing social cost caused by EV owners' charging behavior. Our approach can be applied in various modern cities like the motivated example Singapore to manage the charging stations in the future. We are actively approaching authorities of Singapore to look for such potential application.

8. ACKNOWLEDGEMENT

This research is supported by the National Research Foundation Singapore under its Interactive Digital Media (IDM) Strategic Research Programme.

REFERENCES

[1] Farzad Rajaei Salmasi. Control strategies for hybrid electric vehicles: Evolution, classification, comparison, and future trends. *Vehicular Technology, IEEE Transactions on*, 56(5):2393–2404, 2007.

[2] I. Frade, R. Anabela, G. Goncalves, and A. P. Antunes. Optimal location of charging stations for electric vehicles in a neighborhood in lisbon, portugal. *Transportation Research Record: Journal of the Transportation Research Board*, 2252:91–98, 2011.

[3] H. Wang, Q. Huang, C. Zhang, and A. Xia. A novel approach for the layout of electric vehicle charging station. In *Proceedings of International Conference on Apperceiving Computing and Intelligence Analysis (ICACIA)*, pages 64–70, 2010.

[4] T. D. Chen, K. M. Kockelman, M. Khan, et al. The electric vehicle charging station location problem: a parking-based assignment method for seattle. In *Proceedings of 92nd Annual Meeting of the Transportation Research Board (TRB)*, 2013.

[5] F. He, D. Wu, Y. Yin, and Y. Guan. Optimal deployment of public charging stations for plug-in hybrid electric vehicles. *Transportation Research Part B: Methodological*, 47:87–101, 2013.

[6] Yanhai Xiong, Jiarui Gan, Bo An, Chunyan Miao, and Ana L. C. Bazzan. Optimal electric vehicle charging station placement. In *Proceedings of the 24th International Joint Conference on Artificial Intelligence (IJCAI)*, pages 2662–2668, 2015.

[7] Jiarui Gan, Bo An, Haizhong Wang, Xiaoming Sun, and Zhongzhi Shi. Optimal pricing for improving efficiency of taxi systems. In *Proceedings of the 23rd International Joint Conference on Artificial Intelligence (IJCAI)*, pages 2811–2818, 2013.

[8] Jiarui Gan, Bo An, and Chunyan Miao. Optimizing efficiency of taxi systems: Scaling-up and handling arbitrary constraints. In *Proceedings of the 2015 International Conference on Autonomous Agents and Multiagent Systems (AAMAS)*, pages 523–531, 2015.

[9] Sara Deilami, Amir S Masoum, Paul S Moses, and Mohammad AS Masoum. Real-time coordination of plug-in electric vehicle charging in smart grids to minimize power losses and improve voltage profile. *Smart Grid, IEEE Transactions on*, 2(3):456–467, 2011.

[10] Keiichiro Hayakawa, Enrico H. Gerding, Sebastian Stein, and Takahiro Shiga. Online mechanisms for charging electric vehicles in settings with varying marginal electricity costs. In *Proceedings of the 24th International Joint Conference on Artificial Intelligence (IJCAI)*, pages 2610–2616, 2015.

[11] Robert L Bertini. You are the traffic jam: an examination of congestion measures. *The 85th Annual Meeting of Transportation Research Board*, 2006.

[12] Noam Nisan, Tim Roughgarden, Eva Tardos, and Vijay V Vazirani. *Algorithmic game theory*. Cambridge University Press, 2007.

[13] Wikipedia. Urban planning areas in singapore. `https://en.wikipedia.org/wiki/Urban_planning_areas_in_Singapore`, 2015.

[14] Singapore. General household survey 2005 statistical release 2: Transport, overseas travel, households and housing characteristics. `http://www.singstat.gov.sg/publications/publications-and-papers/GHS/ghrs2`, 2005.

[15] Chargepoint. Find charging spots. `https://na.chargepoint.com/charge_point`, 2015.

Best Action Selection in a Stochastic Environment*

Yingce Xia[1], Tao Qin[2], Nenghai Yu[1], Tie-Yan Liu[2]
[1]University of Science and Technology of China [2]Microsoft Research
yingce.xia@gmail.com, {taoqin, tie-yan.liu}@microsoft.com, ynh@ustc.edu.cn

ABSTRACT

We study the problem of selecting the best action from multiple candidates in a stochastic environment. In such a stochastic setting, when taking an action, a player receives a random reward and affords a random cost, which are drawn from two unknown distributions. We target at selecting the best action, the one with the maximum ratio of the expected reward to the expected cost, after exploring the actions for n rounds. In particular, we study three mechanisms: (i) the uniform exploration mechanism $\mathcal{M}_{\rm U}$; (ii) the successive elimination mechanism $\mathcal{M}_{\rm SE}$; and (iii) the ratio confidence bound exploration mechanism $\mathcal{M}_{\rm RCB}$. We prove that for all the three mechanisms, the probabilities that the best action is not selected (i.e., the error probabilities) can be upper bounded by $O(\exp\{-cn\})$, where c is a constant related to the mechanisms and coefficients about the actions. We then give an asymptotic lower bound of the error probabilities of the consistent mechanisms for Bernoulli setting, and discuss its relationship with the upper bounds in different aspects. Our proposed mechanisms can be degenerated to cover the cases where only the reward/costs are random. We also test the proposed mechanisms through numerical experiments.

Keywords

Design, Economics, Bandit Algorithm, Stochastic

1. INTRODUCTION

Sponsored search is a very effective means for and widely used by many businesses to advertise and promote their products. In sponsored search, an advertiser needs to bid a keyword for her ad to participate in ad auctions. After bidding a keyword, whether she can win the ad auction depends on how many other advertisers bid exactly the same keyword and other related keywords. If she wins the auction, whether her ad is clicked is determined by the behaviors of the search users, which depends on many random factors. If her ad is clicked, the payment to the search engine is determined by the click-through rate (CTR) and the bid of the ad next to hers according to the generalized second pricing (GSP) mechanism.[1] Thus, the reward (click or not) and cost (the payment) of choosing a keyword are both random in sponsored search. To maximize her utility, the advertiser needs to identify the keyword (as well as setting a proper bid) with the maximal ratio of the expected clicked number to expected cost as soon as possible. Such a problem can be abstracted as the best action selection in a stochastic environment, in which an action is the operation of bidding a keyword (including selecting the keyword and setting a bid).

Cloud computing provides an effective way for firms to reduce their computation and IT costs. There are more and more firms moving their computation tasks to cloud. Amazon EC2, the largest provider in cloud computing, provides a specific kind of virtual machines, spot instances[2], for price sensitive firms. Spot instances let one bid on spare Amazon EC2 instances to name one's own price for computation capacity. The spot price fluctuates based on the supply and demand of available EC2 capacity and thus is random. Different types of spot instances have different computation powers (due to the different resource configurations, such as CPU, memory, IO, bandwidth, and geographical locations) and different prices. Since the real performance of a spot instance is impacted by the resource consumption of other instances that are virtualized in the same physical server, there is no guarantee that two spot instances of the same type have the same performance, e.g., how many web visitors can be supported concurrently if hosting a website on the spot instance. Actually, it is more natural to model the performances of spot instances as random variables. Therefore, to be better off, a firm would like to select the type of instance with the maximum ratio of the expected performance to the expected cost as soon as possible after trying different types of instances for several rounds. This instance selection problem can also be modeled as the best action selection in a stochastic environment.

The above two problems are related to the *best arm identification* for multi-armed bandits [6, 1, 15, 20]. A multi-armed bandit (MAB) is a slot machine with K arms. After pulling an arm, the player will receive a reward drawn from an unknown distribution associated with the arm. After pulling the arms for n rounds, the player needs to recommend the arm with the largest expected reward she thinks. The algorithms proposed for best arm identification cannot directly fit our concerned problems, because in our problem, the player will receive two observations, a random reward

*This work was conducted at Microsoft Research Asia.

Appears in: *Proceedings of the 15th International Conference on Autonomous Agents and Multiagent Systems (AAMAS 2016), J. Thangarajah, K. Tuyls, C. Jonker, S. Marsella (eds.), May 9–13, 2016, Singapore.*

[1]For more details, please refer to a recent survey about sponsored search auctions [18].
[2]`https://aws.amazon.com/ec2/spot/`

and a random cost, after each selection, and is interested in the ratio of the observations. In this work, we design new mechanisms to solve the best action selection problem in a stochastic environment.

Model Setup There are $K(\geq 2)$ candidate actions to be selected. For any $i \in [K]$ (denote the set $\{1, 2, \cdots, K\}$ as $[K]$ for simplicity), action i is associated with a reward distribution and a cost distribution, both of which are unknown and with bounded supports. Without loss of generality, we assume the two distributions are supported in $[0, 1]$. At round t, taking action i results in a random reward $X^{\lambda}_{i,t}$ and a random cost $X^{\mu}_{i,t}$, which are independently sampled[3] from the two distributions and are independent of the past actions and observations. Denote the expected reward and cost of action i as λ_i and μ_i respectively, i.e., $\mathbb{E}\{X^{\lambda}_{i,t}\} = \lambda_i$ and $\mathbb{E}\{X^{\mu}_{i,t}\} = \mu_i$. We assume that $0 < \lambda_i, \mu_i < 1$ for any $i \in [K]$. The best action is defined as the one with the maximum ratio of the expected reward to the expected cost. For simplicity, we assume that there is a single best action. W.l.o.g, we set that $\frac{\lambda_1}{\mu_1} > \frac{\lambda_2}{\mu_2} \geq \frac{\lambda_3}{\mu_3} \geq \cdots \geq \frac{\lambda_K}{\mu_K}$ throughout this work. Therefore, action 1 is the best one, and the other action are suboptimal ones. Please note that this order is just for ease of theoretical analysis, and the player (e.g., the advertiser to explore keywords in sponsored search and the firm to try different instances in cloud computing) has no such order information.

The player can explore the actions for n rounds, after which she needs to find out the best action she thinks. Here n is a positive integer known and fixed in advance. Denote the action that the player selects after n rounds as J_n. The player would like to maximize the probability of finding the best action, i.e., minimize the error probability defined in (1), where $\mathcal{M}$ is the exploration mechanism the player uses.

$$\mathscr{E}_n(\mathcal{M}) = \mathbb{P}\{J_n \text{ is not the best action}\}. \quad (1)$$

When the context is clear, we will omit $\mathcal{M}$ from $\mathscr{E}_n(\mathcal{M})$.

Proposed Mechanisms As far as we know, there is no literature about how to select the action with the maximum ratio of the expected reward to the expected cost in a stochastic environment. In this work, we design three mechanisms for the problem. The first is the naive uniform exploration mechanism $\mathcal{M}_{\text{U}}$, in which we take turns to try each action, observe the rewards and costs. The second is the successive elimination mechanism $\mathcal{M}_{\text{SE}}$, in which we divide the n selection rounds into $K-1$ phases (recall K is the number of candidate actions); and at the end of each phase, we eliminate the empirical worst action. The third is the ratio confidence bound mechanism $\mathcal{M}_{\text{RCB}}$, which is an adaptive version of the UCB mechanism [1]. For $\mathcal{M}_{\text{U}}$ and $\mathcal{M}_{\text{RCB}}$, we recommend the action with the maximum ratio of the accumulative rewards to the accumulative costs. For $\mathcal{M}_{\text{SE}}$, there is only one action that survives after n rounds of selections and therefore we recommend this action.

Theoretical Results We prove that for all the above three mechanisms, $\mathscr{E}_n$ can be upper bounded by $O(\exp\{-cn\})$, where c is a constant related to the mechanisms and coefficients about the actions. Thus, all the three mechanisms are consistent in the sense that their error probabilities converge to zero exponentially as n tends to infinity. We also give an asymptotic lower bound of the error probability of the consistent mechanisms for the setting that the reward and cost distributions of all the actions are Bernoulli, which is $\Omega(\exp\{-\mathcal{D}_*n\})$ and $\mathcal{D}_*$ is an action-related coefficient. We show that for the aforementioned Bernoulli setting, the upper bounds of the proposed three mechanisms match the lower bound, in terms of the order of n. That is, the three mechanisms are optimal in certain conditions. In addition, we also make discussions on the impact of the action-related parameters on the constants in the above bounds.

[3]Here we assume that the reward of an action is independent of its cost. Note that an action with a higher cost does not always have a higher reward. For example, in the keyword bidding problem, a keyword $k1$ can have a higher cost than another keyword $k2$ because more advertisers bid for $k1$, but $k1$ does not necessarily lead to more clicks. We leave the setting with dependent rewards and costs to future work.

2. RELATED WORK

Bandit algorithms play important roles for mechanism design in stochastic environments [14, 4, 3, 21, 9, 19]. The most important related work about our concerned problem is the literature about best arm identification. There are two settings for the best arm identification problem in MAB:

Fixed budget setting: The player needs to minimize the error probability within n rounds of pulling and n is fixed and known in advance. A UCB style exploration mechanism was proposed in [1]. The idea of elimination policy was proposed in [1, 2, 24]. Different criteria to recommend the best arm were discussed in [7]: the maximum empirical average reward, the maximum pulling time, and the probabilities proportional to the pulling time of each arm.

Fixed confidence setting: The player needs to minimize the pulling rounds while guaranteeing that the error probability is smaller than a given threshold. For this setting, a lower bound of the sample complexity was given in [17], and an action elimination mechanism was proposed in [11]. Furthermore, the sample complexities under both settings were compared in [16], and a unified approach for both settings was presented in [12].

Another line of related work is the budgeted MAB [23, 10, 26, 19, 25], in which the goal of the player is to maximize the accumulate reward before the budget runs out. The mechanism design in our paper can be seen as a dual problem of the above five works. Compared with the budgeted MAB, we focus on searching for the best action rather than minimizing the cumulative regret.

3. MECHANISMS

Before describing the mechanisms, we first introduce some notations that are frequently used in the following sections. For any $t \in [n]$ and $i \in [K]$, (1) I_t denotes the action selected at round t; (2) $T_i(t)$, $\bar{X}^{\lambda}_{i,T_i(t)}$ and $\bar{X}^{\mu}_{i,T_i(t)}$ denote the number of selected rounds, the average reward and average cost of action i until round t respectively. Mathematically,

$$T_i(t) = \sum_{s=1}^{t} \mathbf{1}\{I_s = i\}; \; \bar{X}^{\lambda}_{i,T_i(t)} = \frac{1}{T_i(t)} \sum_{s=1}^{t} X^{\lambda}_{i,s}\mathbf{1}\{I_s = i\};$$
$$\bar{X}^{\mu}_{i,T_i(t)} = \frac{1}{T_i(t)} \sum_{s=1}^{t} X^{\mu}_{i,s}\mathbf{1}\{I_s = i\}. \quad (2)$$

We propose three mechanisms to the applications modeled in Section 1. Our mechanisms are inspired from the best arm identification problem in conventional bandits.

First, we adapt the *uniform exploration mechanism* [6, 22] to the best action selection, and call the corresponding mechanism $\mathcal{M}_{\text{U}}$, which is shown in Algorithm 1. The idea behind $\mathcal{M}_{\mathrm{U}}$ is very simple: one just selects actions one after one and then recommends the action with the largest ratio of the empirical average reward to the average cost.

Algorithm 1: Uniform Exploration Mechanism ($\mathcal{M}_{\mathrm{U}}$)

1 **for** $t \leftarrow 1$ *to* n **do**
2   Select action (t mod K)+1;
3 *Return* $J_n = \arg\max_i\{\bar{X}^{\lambda}_{i,T_i(n)}/\bar{X}^{\mu}_{i,T_i(n)}\}$.

The uniform exploration mechanism is simple. However, it has a clear drawback: after exploring the actions for a number of rounds, even if we know with high probabilities that some actions cannot be the best one, we still need to explore them as frequently as others.

Algorithm 2: Successive Elimination Mechanism($\mathcal{M}_{\mathrm{SE}}$)

1 *Initialization*: $A_1 = [K]$; $n_0 = 0$;$\{n_k\}_{k\in[K-1]}$ in (3);
2 **for** *phase* $k \leftarrow 1$ *to* $K-1$ **do**
3   For any $i \in A_k$, select action i for $n_k - n_{k-1}$ rounds;
4    $A_{k+1} \leftarrow A_k \backslash \{\arg\min_{i\in A_k}(\bar{X}^{\lambda}_{i,n_k}/\bar{X}^{\mu}_{i,n_k})\}$;
5 *Return* $J_n =$ the unique action in A_K.

The *elimination policy* [11, 24] is a strategy that can overcome this drawback. It sequentially eliminates suboptimal actions. We adapt it to our mechanisms and propose the *Successive Elimination mechanism* $\mathcal{M}_{\mathrm{SE}}$ (See Algorithm 2). The n_k for any $k \in [K-1]$ that is used in $\mathcal{M}_{\mathrm{SE}}$ is defined as below:

$$H(K) = \frac{1}{2} + \sum_{i=2}^{K}\frac{1}{i}; \quad n_k = \left\lceil \frac{1}{H(K)}\frac{n-K}{K+1-k}\right\rceil. \tag{3}$$

Mechanism $\mathcal{M}_{\mathrm{SE}}$ works as follows. It divides the rounds into $K-1$ phases. At the end of each phase, it removes the action with the smallest ratio of the average rewards to the average costs. Intuitively, actions with closer ratios to the best one are more likely to survive after more phases.

Algorithm 3: RCB Exploration Mechanism ($\mathcal{M}_{\mathrm{RCB}}$)

1 Select each action once at the first K rounds;
2 **for** $t \leftarrow K+1$ *to* n **do**
3    $\forall i \in [K]$, calculate the $\hat{\lambda}_i(t)$ and $\hat{\mu}_i(t)$ defined in (4);
4   **if** $\{i|\hat{\mu}_i(t) \le 0\}$ *is not empty* **then**
5   Select action $I_t = \arg\min_i\{T_i(t-1)|\hat{\mu}_i(t) \le 0\}$;
6   **else**
7   Select action $I_t = \arg\max_i\{\hat{\lambda}_i(t)/\hat{\mu}_i(t)\}$;
8 *Return* $J_n = \arg\max_i\{\bar{X}^{\lambda}_{i,T_i(n)}/\bar{X}^{\mu}_{i,T_i(n)}\}$.

The UCB-style mechanisms (see Chapter 2 of [5] for an introduction) play an important role of best arm identification. We also adapt a UCB-style mechanism for our best action selection problem, which we call the *Ratio Confidence Bound mechanism* $\mathcal{M}_{\mathrm{RCB}}$ (see Algorithm 3). In $\mathcal{M}_{\mathrm{RCB}}$, we introduce an upper confidence bound for the reward and a lower confidence bound for the cost as defined in (4):

$$\hat{\lambda}_i(t) = \bar{X}^{\lambda}_{i,T_i(t-1)} + \mathcal{E}^{\alpha}_i(t),\ \hat{\mu}_i(t) = \bar{X}^{\mu}_{i,T_i(t-1)} - \mathcal{E}^{\alpha}_i(t), \tag{4}$$

where $i \in [K], t \in [n], \mathcal{E}^{\alpha}_i(t) = \sqrt{\alpha/T_i(t-1)}$ and α is a positive hyper-parameter. Note that both $\hat{\lambda}_i(t)$ and $\hat{\mu}_i(t)$ depend on α, and we omit the α for simplicity.

The "ratio" in $\mathcal{M}_{\mathrm{RCB}}$ is between the upper confidence bound of the average reward and the lower confidence bound of the average cost.[4] To run $\mathcal{M}_{\mathrm{RCB}}$, one needs a positive hyper parameter α as the input.

From the above descriptions, one can see that the ratios of the empirical average rewards to costs are important to all the three mechanisms. Note that it is practically possible that the denominator of $\bar{X}^{\lambda}_{i,T_i(t)}/\bar{X}^{\mu}_{i,T_i(t)}$ is zero for some i and t. In this case, we calculate the ratio as follows:

$$\begin{aligned} \bar{X}^{\lambda}_{i,T_i(t)}/\bar{X}^{\mu}_{i,T_i(t)} &= 0 \quad \text{if } \bar{X}^{\lambda}_{i,T_i(t)} = 0; \\ \bar{X}^{\lambda}_{i,T_i(t)}/\bar{X}^{\mu}_{i,T_i(t)} &= \infty \quad \text{if } \bar{X}^{\lambda}_{i,T_i(t)} > 0. \end{aligned} \tag{5}$$

Furthermore, we break ties randomly when more than one action is selected in the arg min or arg max operators in the three mechanisms.

4. MECHANISM ANALYSIS

In this section, we prove the upper bounds of the error probabilities of the proposed three mechanisms.

Before the formal theoretical analysis, we introduce two new concepts defined as follows: For any $i \ge 2$, we define Δ_i and ϱ_i as follows:

$$\Delta_i = \frac{\lambda_1}{\mu_1} - \frac{\lambda_i}{\mu_i}; \qquad \varrho_i = \frac{\mu_1\mu_i\Delta_i}{\lambda_1 + \mu_1 + \lambda_i + \mu_i}. \tag{6}$$

Δ_i measures the gap between the best action and a suboptimal action i, in terms of the ratio of the expected reward to the expected cost. ϱ_i measures the difference between the best action and a suboptimal action i in another way: in order to make their ratios equal, we can increase λ_i and μ_1 by ϱ_i, while decreasing λ_1 and μ_i by ϱ_i, i.e.,

$$\frac{\lambda_1 - \varrho_i}{\mu_1 + \varrho_i} = \frac{\lambda_i + \varrho_i}{\mu_i - \varrho_i}. \tag{7}$$

It is easy to verify $\lambda_1 > \varrho_i$ and $\mu_i > \varrho_i$ for any $i \ge 2$.
We further define the following notations: (1) $\varrho_1 = \min_{i\ge 2}\{\varrho_i\}$; (2) $H_1 = \max\{\mu_1^{-2}, \varrho_1^{-2}\} + \sum_{i=2}^{K}\varrho_i^{-2}$; (3) $H_2 = \max_{i\ge 2} i\varrho_i^{-2}$.

The upper bounds of error probabilities of $\mathcal{M}_{\mathrm{U}}$, $\mathcal{M}_{\mathrm{SE}}$ and $\mathcal{M}_{\mathrm{RCB}}$ depends on the aforementioned notations. We first present the result for $\mathcal{M}_{\mathrm{U}}$:

THEOREM 1. *The error probability of $\mathcal{M}_U$ can be upper bounded as below:*

$$\mathscr{E}_n(\mathcal{M}_U) \le 2\sum_{i=1}^{K} e^{2\varrho_i^2}\exp\{-2\varrho_i^2\frac{n}{K}\}. \tag{8}$$

PROOF. If $\mathcal{M}_{\mathrm{U}}$ recommends a suboptimal action, i.e., $J_n \ne 1$, we know that the following event ξ_{unif} is true:

$$\xi_{\mathsf{unif}} = \bigcup_{i=2}^{K}\left\{\frac{\bar{X}^{\lambda}_{i,T_i(n)}}{\bar{X}^{\mu}_{i,T_i(n)}} \ge \frac{\bar{X}^{\lambda}_{1,T_1(n)}}{\bar{X}^{\mu}_{1,T_1(n)}}\right\}. \tag{9}$$

According to (7), we know at least one of the following two events holds:

$$(1)\ \frac{\bar{X}^{\lambda}_{1,T_1(n)}}{\bar{X}^{\mu}_{1,T_1(n)}} \le \frac{\lambda_1 - \varrho_i}{\mu_1 + \varrho_i}; \quad (2)\ \frac{\bar{X}^{\lambda}_{1,T_1(n)}}{\bar{X}^{\mu}_{1,T_1(n)}} \ge \frac{\lambda_i + \varrho_i}{\mu_i - \varrho_i}. \tag{10}$$

[4]In the 5th step of Alogorithm 3, if $\hat{\mu}_i(t)$ is smaller than zero, it is highly probable that 0 is within the lower confidence bound for the cost. Therefore, we have to continue exploring these actions to get more accurate estimations of the expected costs.

By intersecting the ξ_{unif} defined in (9) and the union of the two events in (10), we have

$$\xi_{\text{unif}} \subseteq \bigcup_{i=2}^{K} \Big\{\Big\{\frac{\bar{X}^{\lambda}_{1,T_1(n)}}{\bar{X}^{\mu}_{1,T_1(n)}} \le \frac{\lambda_1-\varrho_i}{\mu_1+\varrho_i}\Big\} \bigcup \Big\{\frac{\bar{X}^{\lambda}_{i,T_i(n)}}{\bar{X}^{\mu}_{i,T_i(n)}} \ge \frac{\lambda_i+\varrho_i}{\mu_i-\varrho_i}\Big\}\Big\},$$

which can be further decomposed as

$$\xi_{\text{unif}} \subseteq \bigcup_{i=2}^{K} \Big\{\{\bar{X}^{\lambda}_{1,T_1(n)} \le \lambda_1-\varrho_i\} \cup \{\bar{X}^{\mu}_{1,T_1(n)} \ge \mu_1+\varrho_i\}$$

$$\cup\, \{\bar{X}^{\lambda}_{i,T_i(n)} \ge \lambda_i+\varrho_i\} \cup \{\bar{X}^{\mu}_{i,T_i(n)} \le \mu_i-\varrho_i\}\Big\}$$

$$= \bigcup_{i=2}^{K} \Big\{\{\bar{X}^{\lambda}_{i,T_i(n)} \ge \lambda_i+\varrho_i\} \cup \{\bar{X}^{\mu}_{i,T_i(n)} \le \mu_i-\varrho_i\}\Big\} \quad (11)$$

$$\cup\, \{\bar{X}^{\lambda}_{1,T_1(n)} \le \lambda_1-\varrho_1\} \cup \{\bar{X}^{\mu}_{1,T_1(n)} \ge \mu_1+\varrho_1\}. \quad (12)$$

Please note that: (1) even if $\bar{X}^{\mu}_{i,T_i(n)} = 0$ for some i, this case also belongs to (11) or (12); (2) when using $\mathcal{M}_{\text{U}}$, $T_i(n)$ for any i is deterministic, rather than random. Therefore, according to Hoeffding's inequality[5], we can obtain

$$\mathbb{P}\{\xi_{\text{unif}}\} \le \sum_{i=2}^{K} \Big\{\mathbb{P}\{\bar{X}^{\lambda}_{i,T_i(n)} \ge \lambda_i+\varrho_i\} + \mathbb{P}\{\bar{X}^{\mu}_{i,T_i(n)} \le \mu_i-\varrho_i\}\Big\}$$

$$+ \mathbb{P}\{\bar{X}^{\lambda}_{1,T_1(n)} \le \lambda_1-\varrho_1\} + \mathbb{P}\{\bar{X}^{\mu}_{1,T_1(n)} \ge \mu_1+\varrho_1\}$$

$$\le 2\sum_{i=1}^{K} \exp\{-2T_i(n)\varrho_i^2\}.$$

It is obvious that $T_i(n) \ge \frac{n}{K} - 1$ for any $i \in [K]$ when using $\mathcal{M}_{\text{U}}$, according to which we know

$$\mathscr{E}_n(\mathcal{M}_{\text{U}}) \le \mathbb{P}\{\xi_{\text{unif}}\} \le 2\sum_{i=1}^{K} e^{2\varrho_i^2} \exp\{-2\varrho_i^2 \frac{n}{K}\}. \quad (13)$$

Therefore, we can conclude Theorem 1. □

The proof of Theorem 1 illustrates the importance of the concept ϱ_i defined in (6). The ϱ_i concept is also crucial to the proofs of other mechanisms. $\mathcal{M}_{\text{U}}$ is a simple and naive mechanism. Next we show the theoretical results for $\mathcal{M}_{\text{SE}}$:

THEOREM 2. *The error probability of $\mathcal{M}_{SE}$ can be upper bounded as below:*

$$\mathscr{E}_n(\mathcal{M}_{SE}) \le 2K(K-1)\exp\Big\{-\frac{2(n-K)}{H_2 \ln 2K}\Big\}. \quad (14)$$

PROOF. First of all, we can verify that Algorithm 2 takes at most n steps. This is because the action eliminated at phase $k(\le K-1)$ is selected for n_k rounds. Thus, the total action selection rounds of $\mathcal{M}_{\text{SE}}$ is:

$$\Big(\sum_{k=1}^{K-1} n_k\Big) + n_{K-1} \le K + \frac{n-K}{\frac{1}{2}+\sum_{i=2}^{K}\frac{1}{i}}\Big(\frac{1}{2}+\sum_{i=2}^{K}\frac{1}{i}\Big) \le n.$$

During phase $k(\le K-1)$, at least one of the k worst actions survives. Therefore, if action 1 (i.e., the best action) has been eliminated at phase k, it means that

$$\frac{\bar{X}^{\lambda}_{1,n_k}}{\bar{X}^{\mu}_{1,n_k}} \le \max_{i\in\{K,K-1,K+1-k\}} \frac{\bar{X}^{\lambda}_{i,n_k}}{\bar{X}^{\mu}_{i,n_k}}. \quad (15)$$

[5]A quick introduction can be found at `https://en.wikipedia.org/wiki/Hoeffding's_inequality`

According to (15), we have that

$$\mathscr{E}_n(\mathcal{M}_{\text{SE}}) \le \sum_{k=1}^{K-1}\sum_{i=K+1-k}^{K} \mathbb{P}\Big\{\frac{\bar{X}^{\lambda}_{1,n_k}}{\bar{X}^{\mu}_{1,n_k}} \le \frac{\bar{X}^{\lambda}_{i,n_k}}{\bar{X}^{\mu}_{i,n_k}}\Big\}$$

$$\le \sum_{k=1}^{K-1}\sum_{i=K+1-k}^{K} \Big(\mathbb{P}\Big\{\frac{\bar{X}^{\lambda}_{1,n_k}}{\bar{X}^{\mu}_{1,n_k}} \le \frac{\lambda_1-\varrho_i}{\mu_1+\varrho_i}\Big\} + \mathbb{P}\Big\{\frac{\bar{X}^{\lambda}_{i,n_k}}{\bar{X}^{\mu}_{i,n_k}} \ge \frac{\lambda_i+\varrho_i}{\mu_i-\varrho_i}\Big\}\Big)$$

$$\le \sum_{k=1}^{K-1}\sum_{i=K+1-k}^{K} \Big(\mathbb{P}\Big\{\bar{X}^{\lambda}_{1,n_k} \le \lambda_1-\varrho_i\Big\} + \mathbb{P}\Big\{\bar{X}^{\mu}_{1,n_k} \ge \mu_1+\varrho_i\Big\}$$

$$+ \mathbb{P}\Big\{\bar{X}^{\lambda}_{i,n_k} \ge \lambda_i+\varrho_i\Big\} + \mathbb{P}\Big\{\bar{X}^{\mu}_{i,n_k} \le \mu_i-\varrho_i\Big\}\Big)$$

$$\le \sum_{k=1}^{K-1}\sum_{i=K+1-k}^{K} 4\exp\{-2n_k\varrho_i^2\}$$

$$\le \sum_{k=1}^{K-1}\sum_{i=K+1-k}^{K} 4\exp\{-2(\frac{1}{H(K)}\frac{n-K}{K+1-k})\varrho_i^2\}$$

$$\le \sum_{k=1}^{K-1}\sum_{i=K+1-k}^{K} 4\exp\{-2(\frac{1}{H(K)}\frac{n-K}{i\varrho_i^{-2}})\}$$

$$\le 2K(K-1)\exp\Big\{-\frac{2(n-K)}{H(K)H_2}\Big\} \le 2K(K-1)\exp\Big\{-\frac{2(n-K)}{H_2\ln 2K}\Big\}.$$

Therefore, we have proved Theorem 2. □

From Theorem 1 and Theorem 2, we can see that the error probabilities of both $\mathcal{M}_{\text{U}}$ and $\mathcal{M}_{\text{SE}}$ decrease exponentially in terms of n. We can verify that when $\varrho_1^2 \le K/[H_2\ln(2K)]$, (intuitively, ϱ_1 is very small and K is large) for a sufficiently large n, the upper bound of $\mathscr{E}_n(\mathcal{M}_{\text{SE}})$ will be smaller than that of $\mathscr{E}_n(\mathcal{M}_{\text{U}})$.

Finally, we have the following theorem for $\mathcal{M}_{\text{RCB}}$. (Keep in mind that for any i and t, $\hat{\lambda}_i(t)$ and $\hat{\mu}_i(t)$ in $\mathcal{M}_{\text{RCB}}$ are related to the hyper-parameter α.)

THEOREM 3. *If $\mathcal{M}_{RCB}$ runs with hyper parameter $0 < \alpha \le \frac{9}{16}\frac{n-K}{H_1}$, we have that*

$$\mathscr{E}_n(\mathcal{M}_{RCB}) \le 4nK\exp\Big\{-\frac{\alpha}{50}(\lambda_1+\mu_1)^2\Big\}. \quad (16)$$

In particular, for $\alpha = \frac{9}{16}\frac{n-K}{H_1}$, we have

$$\mathscr{E}_n(\mathcal{M}_{RCB}) \le 4nK\exp\Big\{-\frac{9(\lambda_1+\mu_1)^2}{800H_1}(n-K)\Big\}. \quad (17)$$

We will prove Theorem 3 by three steps from $(\mathcal{S}1)$ to $(\mathcal{S}3)$:

$(\mathcal{S}1)$ *Preparation*: Denote the event ξ_{RCB} as below:

$$\Big\{\forall i \in [K], s \in [n], |\bar{X}^{\lambda}_{i,s} - \lambda_i| < x_0\sqrt{\frac{\alpha}{s}}, |\bar{X}^{\mu}_{i,s} - \mu_i| < x_0\sqrt{\frac{\alpha}{s}}\Big\},$$

in which $x_0 = (\lambda_1+\mu_1)/[3(\lambda_1+\mu_1) + 2\max_{i\ge 2}(\lambda_i+\mu_i)]$. According to Hoeffding's inequality, we can get

$$\mathbb{P}\{\bar{\xi}_{\text{RCB}}\} \le 4nK\exp\{-2x_0^2\alpha\}. \quad (18)$$

It is easy to verify that

$$(\lambda_1+\mu_1)/10 \le x_0 < 1/3. \quad (19)$$

Combining (18) and (19), $\mathbb{P}\{\bar{\xi}_{\text{RCB}}\}$ can be upper bounded as below.

$$\mathbb{P}\{\bar{\xi}_{\text{RCB}}\} \le 4nK\exp\Big\{-\frac{\alpha}{50}(\lambda_1+\mu_1)^2\Big\}. \quad (20)$$

We present two lemmas that will be used later. Please note that the two lemmas can also be seen as side products of the number of selection rounds of the actions:

LEMMA 4. *Conditioned on* ξ_{RCB}, *for any* $i \geq 2$ *and* $t \leq n$, *we have that*

$$T_i(t) \leq \frac{(1+x_0)^2\alpha}{\varrho_i^2} + 1. \quad (21)$$

LEMMA 5. *Conditioned on* ξ_{RCB}, *for any* $i \geq 2$ *and* $t \leq n$, *at least one of the following two events is true:*

(a) $T_i(t) \geq \frac{\alpha}{4}(1-x_0)^2(\lambda_1+\mu_1)^2 F_i$, where

$$F_i = \min\Big\{\frac{1}{(\mu_i\mu_1\Delta_i)^2}, \frac{T_1(t)-1}{\alpha(1+x_0)^2(\lambda_i+\mu_i)^2}\Big\};$$

(b) $T_1(t) \leq (1+x_0)^2\alpha\mu_1^{-2} + 1$.

We prove Lemma 4 by induction. Lemma 5 can be similarly proved and we omit its proof due to space limitations.

Proof of Lemma 4: Lemma 4 is proved by induction. It is obvious that (21) holds for $t \leq K$. Assume (21) holds at round $t(\geq K)$. At round $t+1$, if $I_{t+1} \neq i$, we have

$$T_i(t+1) = T_i(t) \leq \frac{(1+x_0)^2\alpha}{\varrho_i^2} + 1.$$

If $I_{t+1} = i$, at least one of the following two cases is true:

$$\text{Case (i)} \quad \bar{X}^{\mu}_{i,T_i(t)} - \sqrt{\tfrac{\alpha}{T_i(t)}} \leq 0;$$

$$\text{Case (ii)} \quad \frac{\bar{X}^{\lambda}_{i,T_i(t)} + \sqrt{\frac{\alpha}{T_i(t)}}}{\bar{X}^{\mu}_{i,T_i(t)} - \sqrt{\frac{\alpha}{T_i(t)}}} \geq \frac{\bar{X}^{\lambda}_{1,T_1(t)} + \sqrt{\frac{\alpha}{T_1(t)}}}{\bar{X}^{\mu}_{1,T_1(t)} - \sqrt{\frac{\alpha}{T_1(t)}}}, \quad (22)$$

$$\bar{X}^{\mu}_{i,T_i(t)} - \sqrt{\tfrac{\alpha}{T_i(t)}} > 0,\ \bar{X}^{\mu}_{1,T_1(t)} - \sqrt{\tfrac{\alpha}{T_1(t)}} > 0.$$

Next we will analyze the above two cases:
For Case (i): Since ξ_{RCB} holds, we have $|\bar{X}^{\mu}_{i,T_i(t)} - \mu_i| < x_0\sqrt{\frac{\alpha}{T_i(t)}}$, which implies that $\bar{X}^{\mu}_{i,T_i(t)} > \mu_i - x_0\sqrt{\frac{\alpha}{T_i(t)}}$. Therefore, we obtain that $T_i(t) \leq \frac{(1+x_0)^2\alpha}{\mu_i^2}$. As a result, we have

$$T_i(t+1) \leq \frac{(1+x_0)^2\alpha}{\mu_i^2} + 1 \leq \frac{(1+x_0)^2\alpha}{\varrho_i^2} + 1. \quad (23)$$

For Case (ii): In this case, if $T_i(t) \leq (1+x_0)^2\alpha/\mu_i^2$, we can obtain Lemma 4 by (23). Therefore, in the left content for the proof based on Case (ii), we only need to consider $T_i(t) > \frac{(1+x_0)^2\alpha}{\mu_i^2}$, which implies that $\mu_i - (1+x_0)\sqrt{\frac{\alpha}{T_i(t)}} > 0$. Conditioned on ξ_{RCB}, we have $|\bar{X}^{\mu}_{j,T_j(t)} - \mu_j| < x_0\sqrt{\frac{\alpha}{T_j(t)}}$ for any $j \in [K]$. We also have that $\bar{X}^{\mu}_{j,T_j(t)} - \sqrt{\frac{\alpha}{T_j(t)}} > 0$ for any $j \in \{1, i\}$. They jointly imply that

$$0 < \bar{X}^{\mu}_{1,T_1(t)} - \sqrt{\frac{\alpha}{T_1(t)}} \leq \mu_1 - (1-x_0)\sqrt{\frac{\alpha}{T_1(t)}}.$$

Thus, conditioned on ξ_{RCB}, we have

$$\frac{\lambda_i + (1+x_0)\sqrt{\frac{\alpha}{T_i(t)}}}{\mu_i - (1+x_0)\sqrt{\frac{\alpha}{T_i(t)}}} \geq \frac{\bar{X}^{\lambda}_{i,T_i(t)} + \sqrt{\frac{\alpha}{T_i(t)}}}{\bar{X}^{\mu}_{i,T_i(t)} - \sqrt{\frac{\alpha}{T_i(t)}}}$$

$$\geq \frac{\bar{X}^{\lambda}_{1,T_1(t)} + \sqrt{\frac{\alpha}{T_1(t)}}}{\bar{X}^{\mu}_{1,T_1(t)} - \sqrt{\frac{\alpha}{T_1(t)}}} \geq \frac{\lambda_1 + (1-x_0)\sqrt{\frac{\alpha}{T_1(t)}}}{\mu_1 - (1-x_0)\sqrt{\frac{\alpha}{T_1(t)}}} > \frac{\lambda_1}{\mu_1} > \frac{\lambda_i + \varrho_i}{\mu_i - \varrho_i},$$

which shows that $T_i(t) \leq (1+x_0)^2\alpha/\varrho_i^2$. Accordingly, $T_i(t+1) \leq [(1+x_0)^2\alpha/\varrho_i^2] + 1$. Lemma 4 is proved. □

($\mathcal{S}2$) *Problem Transformation*: If we can prove the following proposition, then we can conclude Theorem 3.

PROPOSITION 6. *Given* ξ_{RCB} *is true, for any* $i \in [K]$, *we have* $x_0\sqrt{\frac{\alpha}{T_i(n)}} \leq \varrho_i$.

This is because if Proposition 6 holds, given ξ_{RCB} is true, for any $i \geq 2$, we have that $\bar{X}^{\mu}_{i,T_i(n)} > \mu_i - x_0\sqrt{\frac{\alpha}{T_i(n)}} > \varrho_i - x_0\sqrt{\frac{\alpha}{T_i(n)}} \geq 0$. And further, we can obtain

$$\begin{aligned}\frac{\bar{X}^{\lambda}_{1,T_1(n)}}{\bar{X}^{\mu}_{1,T_1(n)}} &> \frac{\lambda_1 - x_0\sqrt{\frac{\alpha}{T_1(n)}}}{\mu_1 + x_0\sqrt{\frac{\alpha}{T_1(n)}}} \geq \frac{\lambda_1 - \varrho_i}{\mu_1 + \varrho_i} \\ &= \frac{\lambda_i + \varrho_i}{\mu_i - \varrho_i} \geq \frac{\lambda_i + x_0\sqrt{\frac{\alpha}{T_i(n)}}}{\mu_i - x_0\sqrt{\frac{\alpha}{T_i(n)}}} > \frac{\bar{X}^{\lambda}_{i,T_i(n)}}{\bar{X}^{\mu}_{i,T_i(n)}},\end{aligned} \quad (24)$$

which means that action 1 can be eventually recommended. That is, by Proposition 6, ξ_{RCB} holds means that the best action can be recommended. Therefore, $\mathscr{E}_n(\mathcal{M}_{RCB})$ is smaller than $\mathbb{P}\{\bar{\xi}_{RCB}\}$, which has been shown in (20).

($\mathcal{S}3$) *Proof of Proposition* 6: By Lemma 4 and (19),

$$\begin{aligned}T_1(n) - 1 &= n - 1 - \sum_{i=2}^{K} T_i(n) \geq n - K - \sum_{i=2}^{K} \frac{\alpha(1+x_0)^2}{\varrho_i^2} \\ &\geq \frac{16\alpha}{9}\max\{\frac{1}{\mu_1^2}, \frac{1}{\varrho_1^2}\} + \frac{16\alpha}{9}\sum_{i=2}^{K}\frac{1}{\varrho_i^2} - \sum_{i=2}^{K}\frac{\alpha(1+x_0)^2}{\varrho_i^2} \\ &> \alpha(1+x_0)^2\max\{\mu_1^{-2}, \varrho_1^{-2}\}.\end{aligned} \quad (25)$$

Therefore, when $t = n$, the (b) in Lemma 5 does not hold and thus, the (a) in Lemma 5 must hold.
We can verify that for any $i \geq 2$,

$$\begin{cases} \frac{\alpha}{4}(1-x_0)^2(\lambda_1+\mu_1)^2\frac{1}{(\mu_i\mu_1\Delta_i)^2} \geq \frac{\alpha x_0^2}{\varrho_i^2}; \\ \frac{\alpha}{4}(1-x_0)^2(\lambda_1+\mu_1)^2\frac{\alpha(1+x_0)^2}{\varrho_1^2\alpha(1+x_0)^2(\lambda_i+\mu_i)^2} \geq \frac{\alpha x_0^2}{\varrho_i^2}. \end{cases} \quad (26)$$

According to (25), (26) and Lemma 5, we can conclude that for any $i \in [K]$, $T_i(n) \geq \frac{\alpha x_0^2}{\varrho_i^2}$, i.e., Proposition 6 holds. □

(17) suggests that $\mathscr{E}_n(\mathcal{M}_{RCB})$ is bounded by $O(n\exp\{-cn\})$ where c is a constant independent of n. $O(n\exp\{-cn\})$ is bounded by $O(\exp\{-\tilde{c}n\})$ for any $\tilde{c} \in (0, c)$. Therefore, like $\mathscr{E}_n(\mathcal{M}_U)$ and $\mathscr{E}_n(\mathcal{M}_{SE})$, $\mathscr{E}_n(\mathcal{M}_{RCB})$ decreases exponentially in terms of n.

From Theorem 3, one may notice that the upper bound in (16) seems to increase w.r.t n, which is counterintuitive. Actually, this impression is not correct. Parameter α can also depend on n, and in particular, when $\alpha = \frac{9}{16}\frac{n-K}{H_1}$, the upper bound in (17) will decrease exponentially w.r.t. n.

Based on Theorem 1, 2 and 3, we can derive certain sample complexities that make the error probabilities of the three mechanisms smaller than $\varepsilon \in (0, 1)$:

COROLLARY 7. *For any* $\varepsilon \in (0, 1)$, *to find the best action with probability at least* $1 - \varepsilon$, *a total of* $O(K\varrho_1^{-2}\ln(1/\varepsilon))$ *rounds of selection suffices for* $\mathcal{M}_U$, $O((H_2\ln(2K))\ln(1/\varepsilon))$ *for* $\mathcal{M}_{SE}$, *and* $O(R(\varepsilon)\ln R(\varepsilon))$ *for* $\mathcal{M}_{RCB}$ *with* $\alpha = (9(n-K))/(16H_1)$, *where* $R(\varepsilon) = (H_1/(\lambda_1+\mu_1)^2)\ln(1/\varepsilon)$.

According to Corollary 7, if we are only interested in the complexity related to ε, all the three mechanisms are $O(\ln\frac{1}{\varepsilon})$; $\mathcal{M}_{SE}$ and $\mathcal{M}_{RCB}$ need less sample complexity than $\mathcal{M}_U$ when ϱ_1 is small and K is large.

5. LOWER BOUND FOR THE BERNOULLI SETTING

In this section, we provide an asymptotic lower bound for consistent mechanisms when both the rewards and costs of all the actions are sampled from Bernoulli distributions. For ease of references, we call such settings *Bernoulli settings*, which are a common choice for lower bound analysis for bandit problems. Similar to [16], we say a mechanism $\mathcal{M}$ is *consistent* if for every underlying reward/cost distribution, for any $\varepsilon \in (0,1)$, there exists an integer $n(\varepsilon) > 0$, such that for any $n > n(\varepsilon)$, $\mathscr{E}_n(\mathcal{M}) < \varepsilon$. That is, for a consistent mechanism $\mathcal{M}$, $\mathscr{E}_n(\mathcal{M})$ converges to zero as n tends to infinity.

Define the KL divergence of two Bernoulli distributions with parameter x and y as follows:

$$D(x\|y) = x\ln\frac{x}{y} + (1-x)\ln\frac{1-x}{1-y}, \text{ where } x, y \in (0,1). \quad (27)$$

Furthermore, for any $i \geq 2$ and $\gamma \geq 0$, define the δ-gap $\delta_i(\gamma)$ as follows:

$$\delta_i(\gamma) = \frac{\mu_1\mu_i\Delta_i}{\gamma\lambda_1 + \mu_1}. \quad (28)$$

$\delta_i(\gamma)$ can be seen as an asymmetric adaptive version of Δ_i: to make suboptimal action i the best action, one can increase λ_i by $\delta_i(\gamma)$ while decreasing the μ_i by $\gamma\delta_i(\gamma)$. Please note that when $\gamma = 1$, the asymmetric δ-gap becomes symmetric. Furthermore, it is easy to verify that $\frac{\lambda_1}{\mu_1} = \frac{\lambda_i+\delta_i(\gamma)}{\mu_i-\gamma\delta_i(\gamma)}$.

The following theorem shows that for Bernoulli settings, the asymptotic lower bound of error probability of any consistent mechanism is $\Omega(\exp\{-\mathcal{D}_*n\})$, which decreases exponentially in terms of n. ($\mathcal{D}_*$ is defined in Theorem 8.)

THEOREM 8. *Considering best action selection with Bernoulli settings, for any consistent mechanism $\mathcal{M}$, we have*

$$\overline{\lim}_{n\to\infty} -\frac{1}{n}\ln\mathscr{E}_n(\mathcal{M}) \leq \mathcal{D}_*,$$

in which $\mathcal{D}_* = \inf_{(j,\gamma)\in\Gamma}\{D(\lambda_j+\delta_j(\gamma)\|\lambda_j)+D(\mu_j-\gamma\delta_j(\gamma)\|\mu_j)\}$ *and* $\Gamma = \{(j,\gamma_j)|j \in [K]\backslash\{1\}, \lambda_j + \delta_j(\gamma_j) < 1, \gamma_j \geq 0\}$. *Note that $\mathcal{D}_*$ always exists and is positive.*

PROOF. Define $\hat{D}_{\nu,\upsilon}$ as follows:

$$\begin{aligned}\hat{D}_{\nu,\upsilon} = &\sum_{i=1}^{K}\sum_{t=1}^{n}\ln\frac{\nu_i^\lambda X_{i,t}^\lambda + (1-\nu_i^\lambda)(1-X_{i,t}^\lambda)}{\upsilon_i^\lambda X_{i,t}^\lambda + (1-\upsilon_i^\lambda)(1-X_{i,t}^\lambda)}\\ &+\sum_{i=1}^{K}\sum_{t=1}^{n}\ln\frac{\nu_i^\mu X_{i,t}^\mu + (1-\nu_i^\mu)(1-X_{i,t}^\mu)}{\upsilon_i^\mu X_{i,t}^\mu + (1-\upsilon_i^\mu)(1-X_{i,t}^\mu)},\end{aligned} \quad (29)$$

in which (1) $\nu_i^\lambda, \nu_i^\mu, \upsilon_i^\lambda, \upsilon_i^\mu \in (0,1)$ for any $i \in [K]$; (2) $X_{i,t}^\lambda, X_{i,t}^\mu \in \{0,1\}$ are the reward and the cost of action i at round t; (3) ν and υ denote the two product Bernoulli distributions. Mathematically,

$$\begin{aligned}\nu &= \otimes_{i=1}^K \text{Bern}(\nu_i^\lambda) \times \otimes_{i=1}^K \text{Bern}(\nu_i^\mu),\\ \upsilon &= \otimes_{i=1}^K \text{Bern}(\upsilon_i^\lambda) \times \otimes_{i=1}^K \text{Bern}(\upsilon_i^\mu),\end{aligned} \quad (30)$$

where[6] Bern(p) represents the Bernoulli distribution with success probability p.

Let $\mathcal{F}_n$ denote the σ-algebra generated by $\{X_{i,t}^\lambda\}_{i\in[K],t\in[n]}$, $\{X_{i,t}^\mu\}_{i\in[K],t\in[n]}$ and the selection history. According to the Lemma 15 of [16], we can obtain that for any $A \in \mathcal{F}_n$,

$$\begin{aligned}\mathbb{P}_\upsilon\{A\} &= \mathbb{E}_\nu\{\exp(-\hat{D}_{\nu,\upsilon})\mathbf{1}\{A\}\}\\ &= \mathbb{E}_\nu\{\exp(-\hat{D}_{\nu,\upsilon})\mathbf{1}\{A\}|\mathbf{1}\{A\}=1\}\mathbb{P}_\nu\{A\}\\ &= \mathbb{E}_\nu\{\exp(-\hat{D}_{\nu,\upsilon})|\mathbf{1}\{A\}=1\}\mathbb{P}_\nu\{A\}\\ &= \mathbb{E}_\nu\{\exp(-\hat{D}_{\nu,\upsilon})|A\}\mathbb{P}_\nu\{A\} \geq \exp(-\mathbb{E}_\nu[\hat{D}_{\nu,\upsilon}|A])\mathbb{P}_\nu\{A\}.\end{aligned}$$

Accordingly, we have

$$\mathbb{E}_\nu[\hat{D}_{\nu,\upsilon}|A] \geq \ln\frac{\mathbb{P}_\nu\{A\}}{\mathbb{P}_\upsilon\{A\}}. \quad (31)$$

Since $A \in \mathcal{F}_n$, $\bar{A} \in \mathcal{F}_n$. By substituting the A in (31) with $\bar{A}$, we have

$$\mathbb{E}_\nu[\hat{D}_{\nu,\upsilon}|\bar{A}] \geq \ln\frac{\mathbb{P}_\nu\{\bar{A}\}}{\mathbb{P}_\upsilon\{\bar{A}\}}.$$

Then we can obtain that

$$\begin{aligned}\mathbb{E}_\nu\{\hat{D}_{\nu,\upsilon}\} &= \mathbb{E}_\nu\{\hat{D}_{\nu,\upsilon}|A\}\mathbb{P}_\nu\{A\} + \mathbb{E}_\nu\{\hat{D}_{\nu,\upsilon}|\bar{A}\}\mathbb{P}_\nu\{\bar{A}\}\\ &\geq \mathbb{P}_\nu\{A\}\ln\frac{\mathbb{P}_\nu\{A\}}{\mathbb{P}_\upsilon\{A\}} + \mathbb{P}_\nu\{\bar{A}\}\ln\frac{\mathbb{P}_\nu\{\bar{A}\}}{\mathbb{P}_\upsilon\{\bar{A}\}}\\ &= D(\mathbb{P}_\nu\{A\}\|\mathbb{P}_\upsilon\{A\}).\end{aligned} \quad (32)$$

By some derivations, one can verify that

$$\mathbb{E}_\nu\{\hat{D}_{\nu,\upsilon}\} = n\sum_{i=1}^K D(\nu_i^\lambda\|\upsilon_i^\lambda) + n\sum_{i=1}^K D(\nu_i^\mu\|\upsilon_i^\mu). \quad (33)$$

Combining (32) and (33), we have

$$n\sum_{i=1}^K D(\nu_i^\lambda\|\upsilon_i^\lambda) + n\sum_{i=1}^K D(\nu_i^\mu\|\upsilon_i^\mu) \geq D(\mathbb{P}_\nu\{A\}\|\mathbb{P}_\upsilon\{A\}). \quad (34)$$

To get the lower bound of the error probability for consistent mechanisms, we specialize A, ν and υ as follows:

$A = \{J_n = 1\}$; (It is obvious that $A \in \mathcal{F}_n$;)

$\upsilon = \otimes_{i=1}^K\text{Bern}(\lambda_i) \times \otimes_{i=1}^K\text{Bern}(\mu_i)$; $\nu = \nu^\lambda \otimes \nu^\mu$;

$\nu^\lambda = \otimes_{i=1}^{j-1}\text{Bern}(\lambda_i) \otimes \text{Bern}(\lambda_j + \delta_j(\gamma) + \varepsilon) \otimes_{i=j+1}^K \text{Bern}(\lambda_i)$;

$\nu^\mu = \otimes_{i=1}^{j-1}\text{Bern}(\mu_i) \otimes \text{Bern}(\mu_j - \gamma\delta_j(\gamma) - \varepsilon) \otimes_{i=j+1}^K \text{Bern}(\mu_i)$,

in which the γ and ε are constraint by $\lambda_j + \delta_j(\gamma) + \varepsilon \in (0,1)$ and $\mu_j - \gamma\delta_j(\gamma) - \varepsilon \in (0,1)$, and $j \geq 2$.

For any consistent mechanism $\mathcal{M}$ and any $\varepsilon \in (0,1)$, we can always find a large enough number $n(\varepsilon)$ such that for any $n \geq n(\varepsilon)$, $\mathbb{P}_\nu\{A\} \leq \varepsilon \leq \mathbb{P}_\upsilon\{A\}$. Therefore, by setting the notations in (34) with the corresponding ones specified above, we have that for any $j \geq 2$,

$$\begin{aligned}&D(\lambda_j + \delta_j(\gamma) + \varepsilon\|\lambda_j) + D(\mu_j - \gamma\delta_j(\gamma) - \varepsilon\|\mu_j)\\ \geq &\frac{1}{n}D(\mathbb{P}_\nu\{A\}\|\mathbb{P}_\upsilon\{A\}) \geq \frac{1}{n}D(\varepsilon\|\mathbb{P}_\upsilon\{A\})\\ \geq &\frac{1}{n}(\varepsilon\ln\varepsilon + (1-\varepsilon)\ln\frac{1-\varepsilon}{\mathscr{E}_n}).\end{aligned} \quad (35)$$

Let $J_j(\gamma)$ denote $D(\lambda_j + \delta_j(\gamma)\|\lambda_j) + D(\mu_j - \gamma\delta_j(\gamma)\|\mu_j)$ for any $(j,\gamma) \in \Gamma$ (defined in Theorem 8). Taking the supremum limit with $\varepsilon \to 0$ on both sides of (35), we have

$$\overline{\lim}_{n\to\infty} -\frac{1}{n}\ln\mathscr{E}_n \leq J_j(\gamma). \quad (36)$$

Finally, we need to prove the existence of $\mathcal{D}_*$. For any $j \geq 2$, denote the domain of $J_j(\gamma)$ as Γ_j, which is $\{\gamma|(j,\gamma) \in \Gamma\}$. One can verify that for any $j \geq 2$, in Γ_j, $J_j(\gamma)$ either increases w.r.t γ, or first decreases then increases w.r.t γ. By careful derivations, we can get that $\inf_{\gamma\in\Gamma_j} J_j(\gamma)$ can be achieved at some $\gamma_j^* \in \Gamma_j$. Since K is limited, we can always find the $\mathcal{D}_*$, which is $\min_{j\geq 2} J_j(\gamma_j^*)$. □

[6]For simplicity, $\otimes_{i=1}^K\text{Bern}(\nu_i^\lambda)$ represents a product of K independent distributions, where the i-th one is Bern(ν_i^λ). Both $\otimes$ and $\times$ represent the products of distributions.

5.1 Discussions

Generally speaking, the upper bounds of the error probabilities for the proposed three mechanisms match the lower bound given in Theorem 8, in terms of the order of n. To gain more understanding of the relationship between the upper bounds and the lower bound, we also need to check the constants in the bounds. For this purpose, we investigate how the action-related coefficients (like Δ_i) behave in the lower and upper bounds of the error probabilities. We take $\mathcal{M}_{\mathrm{SE}}$ as an example to give detailed discussions. We can get similar conclusions for $\mathcal{M}_{\mathrm{U}}$ and $\mathcal{M}_{\mathrm{RCB}}$.

First, let us have a look at how the error probability $\mathscr{E}_n$ depends on Δ_i, the sub-optimality of action i compared to the best action. Consider the following example: There is a Bernoulli setting with the following parameters: for any $i \in [K]$, $\lambda_i, \mu_i \in [p, 1-p]$, in which $p \in (0, \frac{1}{2})$. We can bound $\mathcal{D}_*$ by setting $\gamma \to \infty$ in Theorem 8 as below.

$$\mathcal{D}_* \le \frac{(\mu_1\mu_i\Delta_i)^2}{\lambda_1^2\mu_i(1-\mu_i)} \le \frac{\Delta_i^2}{p^3}, \forall i \ge 2. \tag{37}$$

Define $\Delta_{\min} = \min_{i\ge 2}\Delta_i$. By (37), the lower bound of the error probability of any consistent mechanism is

$$\mathscr{E}_n \ge \Omega\Big(\exp\Big\{-\frac{1}{p^3}\Delta_{\min}^2 n\Big\}\Big). \tag{38}$$

The upper bound of $\mathscr{E}_n(\mathcal{M}_{\mathrm{SE}})$ is:

$$\mathscr{E}_n(\mathcal{M}_{\mathrm{SE}}) \le O\Big(\exp\Big\{-\frac{p^4}{8K\ln(2K)}\Delta_{\min}^2 n\Big\}\Big). \tag{39}$$

(38) and (39) share the common term $\Delta_{\min}^2 n$ within the exponential order. Therefore, as $\Delta_{\min}$ becomes smaller, both the lower bound of the error probability of any consistent mechanism and the upper bound of $\mathscr{E}_n(\mathcal{M}_{\mathrm{SE}})$ increase.

Then we study how the error probabilities of the mechanisms change w.r.t. the magnitude of the parameters of the actions. For ease of reference, we denote the parameters of the Bernoulli K-action setting as $\{\lambda_i, \mu_i\}_{i=1}^K$. Let us check three variants of Bernoulli action setting by introducing a hyper parameter $\theta \in (0, 1]$. The three variants of the settings are ($\mathcal{V}_1$) $\{\theta\lambda_i, \mu_i\}_{i=1}^K$; ($\mathcal{V}_2$) $\{\lambda_i, \theta\mu_i\}_{i=1}^K$; ($\mathcal{V}_3$) $\{\theta\lambda_i, \theta\mu_i\}_{i=1}^K$. The θ for the variant ($\mathcal{V}_1$) should be smaller than $\min\{\mu_1/(\lambda_1\mu_i), 1\}$ for any $i \ge 2$. We get that the asymptotic lower bound (related to n and θ simultaneously) of any consistent mechanism for the three variants is

$$\mathscr{E}_n \ge \Omega(\exp\{-L(\mathcal{V}_i)\theta n\}, \qquad i \in \{1,2,3\}, \tag{40}$$

$$\text{where} \quad L(\mathcal{V}_1) = \min_{i\ge 2}\frac{(\lambda_1\mu_i - \lambda_i\mu_1)^2}{\mu_1^2\lambda_i(1-\lambda_i)}; \tag{41}$$

$$L(\mathcal{V}_2) = L(\mathcal{V}_3) = \min_{i\ge 2}\frac{(\lambda_1\mu_i - \lambda_i\mu_1)^2}{\lambda_1^2\mu_i(1-\mu_i)}. \tag{42}$$

(41) and (42) can be obtained by a similar derivation to that of (37). Specifically, we need to set γ in Theorem 8 as 0 to get (41) and as ∞ to get (42).

The upper bounds of the error probabilities $\mathcal{M}_{\mathrm{SE}}$ under the three variants share the following common form:

$$O\Big(\exp\Big\{-\min_{i\ge 2}\Big(\frac{\lambda_1\mu_i - \lambda_i\mu_1}{\lambda_1+\lambda_i+\mu_1+\mu_i}\Big)^2\frac{2\theta^2 n}{K\ln(2K)}\Big\}\Big). \tag{43}$$

From (40) and (43), we come to two conclusions: (1) Decreasing the expected rewards (or, the expected costs) of all the actions lead to a larger lower bound and a larger upper bound of the error probabilities. (2) If the expected rewards and the expected costs decrease simultaneously, the lower bound of the error probability of any consistent mechanism becomes larger and the upper bound of the error probability of $\mathcal{M}_{\mathrm{SE}}$ also becomes larger.

6. TWO DEGENERATED CASES

In this section, we consider the two degenerated cases as follows[7]. For any $i \in [K]$ and $t \in [n]$,
(Case 1): the rewards are random variables but the costs are deterministic, i.e., $X_{i,t}^{\mu} = \mu_i$.
(Case 2): the rewards are deterministic but the costs are random variables, i.e., $X_{i,t}^{\lambda} = \lambda_i$.

Our proposed three mechanisms can be applied to solve the above cases: (1) Both $\mathcal{M}_{\mathrm{U}}$ and $\mathcal{M}_{\mathrm{SE}}$ can be directly applied to the two degenerated cases. (2) $\mathcal{M}_{\mathrm{RCB}}$ can be applied with minor revisions. Since we do not need to introduce confidence bounds for deterministic observations,

For Case 1, we set $\hat{\mu}_i(t)$ in (4) as μ_i;

For Case 2, we set $\hat{\lambda}_i(t)$ in (4) as λ_i.

We extend the definition of ϱ_i for any $i \ge 2$ by introducing two binary variables $\beta_\lambda, \beta_\mu \in \{0,1\}$:

$$\varrho_i(\beta_\lambda, \beta_\mu) = \frac{\mu_1\mu_i\Delta_i}{\beta_\mu(\lambda_1+\lambda_i)+\beta_\lambda(\mu_1+\mu_i)}. \tag{44}$$

Similarly, define $\varrho_1(\beta_\lambda, \beta_\mu) = \min_{i\ge 2}\varrho_i(\beta_\lambda, \beta_\mu)$. We can regard β_λ and β_μ as binary variables, which represent whether the rewards and costs are random variables or not ("1" means "yes"). We redefine H_1 and H_2 as $H_1(\beta_\lambda, \beta_\mu)$ and $H_2(\beta_\lambda, \beta_\mu)$ with the corresponding $\varrho_i(\beta_\lambda, \beta_\mu)$'s.

The error probabilities for the two degenerated cases can be bounded in unified forms using β_λ and β_μ. For $\mathcal{M}_{\mathrm{U}}$ and $\mathcal{M}_{\mathrm{SE}}$, we have

$$\mathscr{E}_n(\mathcal{M}_{\mathrm{U}}) \le (\beta_\lambda + \beta_\mu)\sum_{i=1}^{K} e^{2\varrho_i^2(\beta_\lambda,\beta_\mu)}\exp\{-2\varrho_i^2(\beta_\lambda,\beta_\mu)\frac{n}{K}\}.$$

$$\mathscr{E}_n(\mathcal{M}_{\mathrm{SE}}) \le (\beta_\lambda + \beta_\mu)K(K-1)\exp\Big\{-\frac{2(n-K)}{\ln(2K)H_2(\beta_\lambda,\beta_\mu)}\Big\}.$$

By setting $0 < \alpha \le \frac{9}{16}\frac{n-K}{H_1(\beta_\lambda,\beta_\mu)}$ for $\mathcal{M}_{\mathrm{RCB}}$, we get

$$\mathscr{E}_n(\mathcal{M}_{\mathrm{RCB}}) \le 2(\beta_\lambda + \beta_\mu)nK\exp\Big\{-\frac{2\alpha(\beta_\mu\lambda_1 + \beta_\lambda\mu_1)^2}{25(\beta_\lambda+\beta_\mu)^2}\Big\}.$$

In particular, for $\alpha = \frac{9}{16}\frac{n-K}{H_1(\beta_\lambda,\beta_\mu)}$, we have

$$\mathscr{E}_n(\mathcal{M}_{\mathrm{RCB}}) \le 2(\beta_\lambda + \beta_\mu)nK\exp\Big\{-\frac{9(n-K)(\beta_\mu\lambda_1 + \beta_\lambda\mu_1)^2}{200(\beta_\lambda+\beta_\mu)^2 H_1(\beta_\lambda,\beta_\mu)}\Big\}.$$

We can verify that by substituting both the β_λ and the β_μ with 1 in the above formulas, (which means that the rewards and costs are random) the obtained error probabilities are the same as the corresponding ones in Theorem 1, 2 and 3.

The lower bounds for the degenerated cases are shown below: (45) for Case 1 (i.e., $\beta_\lambda = 1, \beta_\mu = 0$) and (46) for Case 2 (i.e., $\beta_\lambda = 0, \beta_\mu = 1$).

$$\mathscr{E}_n \ge \Omega\Big(\exp\{-D(\lambda_1 - \mu_1\Delta_{\min}\|\lambda_1)n\}\Big); \tag{45}$$

$$\mathscr{E}_n \ge \Omega\Big(\exp\{-\min_{i\ge 2}D\Big(\mu_i - \frac{\mu_1\mu_i\Delta_i}{\lambda_1}\|\mu_i\Big)n\}\Big). \tag{46}$$

Note that for simplicity, (45) is obtained with an additional setting that $\lambda_1/\mu_1 > \lambda_2/\mu_2 > \lambda_i/\mu_i$ for any $i \ge 3$. We can also refine the discussions in Section 5 to get their counterparts for the two degenerated cases.

Furthermore, by setting $\mu_i = 1$ for all i, our best action selection problem will degenerate to the conventional best arm identification problem in [1]. The coefficients before n in $\exp\{\cdots n\}$ of our upper bounds for $\mathscr{E}_n(\mathcal{M}_{\mathrm{SE}})$ and $\mathscr{E}_n(\mathcal{M}_{\mathrm{RCB}})$ are up to constant factors to those in [1].

[7] We do not consider the case that both the rewards and the costs are deterministic because it is trivial to identify the best action after taking each action once.

7. EMPIRICAL PERFORMANCE

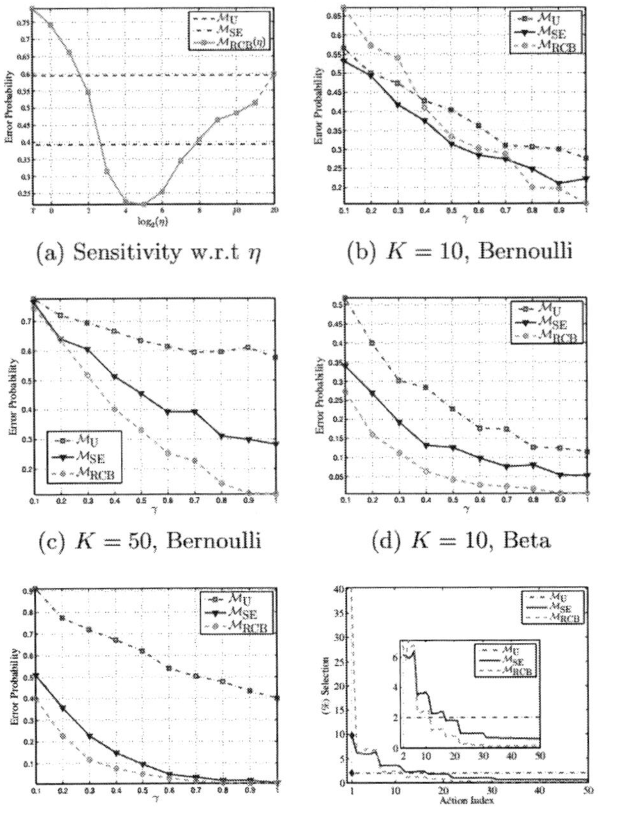

(a) Sensitivity w.r.t η (b) $K = 10$, Bernoulli

(c) $K = 50$, Bernoulli (d) $K = 10$, Beta

(e) $K = 50$, Beta (f) (%) Selections of each action

Figure 1: Experimental Results

In this section, we test the empirical performance of the proposed mechanisms through numerical simulations. We repeat each experiment for 500 times and use the relative frequencies (normalized by 500) that a mechanism does not recommend the best action as a proxy of $\mathscr{E}_n$.

We first simulated a 10-action Bernoulli setting and a 50-action Bernoulli setting. In the 10-action setting, for any $i \in \{1, 2, \cdots, 5\}$, $\lambda_i = 0.4+0.1i, \mu_i = \lambda_i - 0.1$; $\lambda_6 = \mu_6 = 0.9$; for any $i \in \{7, 8, 9, 10\}$, $\lambda_i = 1.5 - 0.1i$, $\mu_i = \lambda_i + 0.1$. In the 50-action setting, the parameters are randomly duplicated while keeping the best action unique. We set $N_{10} = 10000$ and $N_{50} = 50000$. For the x-action setting, the number of selection rounds is set as γN_x, where $x \in \{10, 50\}$ and $\gamma \in \{0.1, 0.2, \cdots, 1\}$.

$\mathcal{M}_{\mathrm{RCB}}$ is associated with a hyper-parameter α. According to Theorem 3, and the previous literature [1, 13], we set $\alpha = \eta \frac{n}{H_1}$, where η is a hyper-parameter. We first study the sensitivity of the error probability w.r.t η for $\mathcal{M}_{\mathrm{RCB}}$. We take the 50-action Bernoulli setting with selection rounds $0.7N_{50}$ for example. The η is chosen from $\{T, 2^0, 2^1, 2^2, \cdots, 2^{10}, 2^{11}, 2^{20}\}$, where $T = 9/16$. T is the parameter suggested in Theorem 3. From Figure 1(a), we can see that $\mathscr{E}_n(\mathcal{M}_{\mathrm{RCB}})$ is sensitive to the choice of the hyper-parameter, which is a drawback of $\mathcal{M}_{\mathrm{RCB}}$. However, on the other side, this is the flexibility of $\mathcal{M}_{\mathrm{RCB}}$, since by tuning the η, $\mathcal{M}_{\mathrm{RCB}}$ can achieve very good results. One should not set η too small (like $T, 1, 2$) when n is not large enough, for which the mechanism can be easily trapped in the empirical best selection and make little exploration. The η should not be set too large (like $2^{10}, 2^{20}$), for which $\mathcal{M}_{\mathrm{RCB}}$ behaves like $\mathcal{M}_{\mathrm{U}}$. Therefore we choose $\eta = 16$ for all the following experiments.

The results for the two Bernoulli settings are shown in Figure 1(b) and Figure 1(c). From the figures we have several observations. (1) As n increases, the error probabilities of all the mechanisms decrease. (2) $\mathcal{M}_{\mathrm{SE}}$ outperforms $\mathcal{M}_{\mathrm{U}}$. Though $\mathcal{M}_{\mathrm{SE}}$ does not need to know anything about the bandit, the error probabilities of $\mathcal{M}_{\mathrm{SE}}$ are not much worse than $\mathcal{M}_{\mathrm{RCB}}$. (3) $\mathcal{M}_{\mathrm{RCB}}$ performs the best among the three mechanisms. (4) $\mathcal{M}_{\mathrm{U}}$ is not as good as other two mechanisms since it wastes too many selections on the actions that are certainly not the best one. Note that the error probability of $\mathcal{M}_{\mathrm{U}}$ is acceptable for a sufficiently large n if the number of actions is not large (like Figure 1(b)), because it can still identify the best action with high probability even if it wastes some rounds of selections. (5) Fixing n, the error probabilities of the three mechanisms increase w.r.t K. Take $n = 10^4$ for example: the error probabilities of $\mathcal{M}_{\mathrm{U}}, \mathcal{M}_{\mathrm{SE}}, \mathcal{M}_{\mathrm{RCB}}$ are $0.28, 0.22, 0.16$ for $K = 10$, and $0.72, 0.64, 0.63$ for $K = 50$. This is not surprising, since more actions make the optimal one harder to be distinguished from others.

We also simulate a 10-action beta setting and a 50-action beta setting, whose rewards and costs follow beta distributions. From Figure 1(d) and Figure 1(e), we can get similar observations as those for the Bernoulli settings.

At last we study the selection frequency of each action for the 50-action Bernoulli setting with $n = 0.7N_{50}$ (See Figure 1(f)). The x-axis is the action index ordered by the expected reward to the expected cost ratio in non-increasing orders. (The x-axis of the small figure starts from action 2.) We can see that both $\mathcal{M}_{\mathrm{SE}}$ and $\mathcal{M}_{\mathrm{RCB}}$ spend most of the selections on the best action and those close to the best one, which are the most uncertain actions. $\mathcal{M}_{\mathrm{RCB}}$ selects the best action most, thus the head of its curve is the heaviest. Next comes $\mathcal{M}_{\mathrm{SE}}$. The curve of $\mathcal{M}_{\mathrm{U}}$ is flat since it allocates each action the same selection rounds.

Overall, the experimental results suggest that $\mathcal{M}_{\mathrm{U}}$ is not so effective as $\mathcal{M}_{\mathrm{SE}}$ and $\mathcal{M}_{\mathrm{RCB}}$ for the best action selection problem in a stochastic environment, and $\mathcal{M}_{\mathrm{RCB}}$ performs the best by carefully setting the hyper parameter.

8. CONCLUSION AND FUTURE WORK

We designed three mechanisms for the best action selection problem in a stochastic environment. We theoretically upper bounded the error probabilities of the proposed three mechanisms and empirically tested their performances. We also provided a lower bound of the error probability of any consistent mechanism with the Bernoulli setting.

We will explore the following directions in the future. First, we will study the setting that the rewards and costs of each action are dependent. Second, we will study the multiple actions identification problem, i.e., select the top-$m(\geq 1)$ best actions like the problems studies in [8, 27]. Third, we defined the best action as the one with the largest ratio of the expected reward to expected cost. It is interesting to consider other definitions of the best action.

Acknowledgments

This work is partially supported by National Natural Science Foundation of China (NSFC, NO.61371192).

REFERENCES

[1] J.-y. Audibert, S. Bubeck, and R. Munos. Best arm identification in multiarmed bandits. In *23rd annual Conference on Learning Theory*, 2010.

[2] A. Badanidiyuru, R. Kleinberg, and A. Slivkins. Bandits with knapsacks. In *Foundations of Computer Science (FOCS), 2013 IEEE 54th Annual Symposium on*, pages 207–216. IEEE, 2013.

[3] S. Bhat, S. Jain, S. Gujar, and Y. Narahari. An optimal bidimensional multi-armed bandit auction for multi-unit procurement. In *Proceedings of the 2015 International Conference on Autonomous Agents and Multiagent Systems (AAMAS)*, pages 1789–1790, 2015.

[4] A. Biswas, S. Jain, D. Mandal, and Y. Narahari. A truthful budget feasible multi-armed bandit mechanism for crowdsourcing time critical tasks. In *Proceedings of the 2015 International Conference on Autonomous Agents and Multiagent Systems (AAMAS)*, pages 1101–1109, 2015.

[5] S. Bubeck and N. Cesa-Bianchi. Regret analysis of stochastic and nonstochastic multi-armed bandit problems. *arXiv preprint arXiv:1204.5721*, 2012.

[6] S. Bubeck, R. Munos, and G. Stoltz. Pure exploration in multi-armed bandits problems. In *Algorithmic Learning Theory*, pages 23–37. Springer, 2009.

[7] S. Bubeck, R. Munos, and G. Stoltz. Pure exploration in finitely-armed and continuous-armed bandits. *Theoretical Computer Science*, 412(19):1832–1852, 2011.

[8] S. Bubeck, T. Wang, and N. Viswanathan. Multiple identifications in multi-armed bandits. In *Proceedings of the 30th International Conference on Machine Learning (ICML-13)*, 2013.

[9] P.-A. Chen and C.-J. Lu. Playing congestion games with bandit feedbacks. In *Proceedings of the 2015 International Conference on Autonomous Agents and Multiagent Systems (AAMAS)*, pages 1721–1722, 2015.

[10] W. Ding, T. Qin, X.-D. Zhang, and T.-Y. Liu. Multi-armed bandit with budget constraint and variable costs. In *The 27th AAAI Conference on Artificial Intelligenc*, 2013.

[11] E. Even-Dar, S. Mannor, and Y. Mansour. Action elimination and stopping conditions for the multi-armed bandit and reinforcement learning problems. *The Journal of Machine Learning Research*, 7:1079–1105, 2006.

[12] V. Gabillon, M. Ghavamzadeh, and A. Lazaric. Best arm identification: A unified approach to fixed budget and fixed confidence. In *Advances in Neural Information Processing Systems*, pages 3212–3220, 2012.

[13] V. Gabillon, M. Ghavamzadeh, A. Lazaric, and S. Bubeck. Multi-bandit best arm identification. In *Advances in Neural Information Processing Systems*, pages 2222–2230, 2011.

[14] S. Jain, S. Gujar, O. Zoeter, and Y. Narahari. A quality assuring multi-armed bandit crowdsourcing mechanism with incentive compatible learning. In *Proceedings of the 2014 international conference on Autonomous agents and multi-agent systems (AAMAS)*, pages 1609–1610, 2014.

[15] S. Kalyanakrishnan, A. Tewari, P. Auer, and P. Stone. Pac subset selection in stochastic multi-armed bandits. In *Proceedings of the 29th International Conference on Machine Learning (ICML-12)*, pages 655–662, 2012.

[16] E. Kaufmann, O. Cappé, and A. Garivier. On the complexity of best arm identification in multi-armed bandit models. *arXiv preprint arXiv:1407.4443*, 2014.

[17] S. Mannor and J. N. Tsitsiklis. The sample complexity of exploration in the multi-armed bandit problem. *The Journal of Machine Learning Research*, 5:623–648, 2004.

[18] T. Qin, W. Chen, and T.-Y. Liu. Sponsored search auctions: Recent advances and future directions. *ACM Transactions on Intelligent Systems and Technology (TIST)*, 5(4):60, 2015.

[19] S. Sen, A. Ridgway, and M. Ripley. Adaptive budgeted bandit algorithms for trust development in a supply-chain. In *Proceedings of the 2015 International Conference on Autonomous Agents and Multiagent Systems (AAMAS)*, pages 137–144, 2015.

[20] M. Soare, A. Lazaric, and R. Munos. Best-arm identification in linear bandits. In *Advances in Neural Information Processing Systems*, pages 828–836, 2014.

[21] R. Stranders, L. Tran-Thanh, F. M. D. Fave, A. Rogers, and N. R. Jennings. Dcops and bandits: Exploration and exploitation in decentralised coordination. In *Proceedings of the 11th International Conference on Autonomous Agents and Multiagent Systems (AAMAS)*, pages 289–296. International Foundation for Autonomous Agents and Multiagent Systems, 2012.

[22] L. Tran-Thanh, A. Chapman, E. Munoz de Cote, A. Rogers, and N. R. Jennings. Epsilon-first policies for budget–limited multi-armed bandits. In *Twenty-Fourth AAAI Conference on Artificial Intelligence*, 2010.

[23] L. Tran-Thanh, A. Chapman, A. Rogers, and N. R. Jennings. Knapsack based optimal policies for budget-limited multi-armed bandits. In *The 26th AAAI Conference on Artificial Intelligence*, 2012.

[24] Y. Wu, A. Gyorgy, and C. Szepesvari. On identifying good options under combinatorially structured feedback in finite noisy environments. In *Proceedings of the 32nd International Conference on Machine Learning (ICML-15)*, pages 1283–1291, 2015.

[25] Y. Xia, W. Ding, X.-D. Zhang, N. Yu, and T. Qin. Budgeted bandit problems with continuous random costs. In *Proceedings of the 7th Asian Conference on Machine Learning*, 2015.

[26] Y. Xia, H. Li, T. Qin, N. Yu, and T.-Y. Liu. Thompson sampling for budgeted multi-armed bandits. In *Proceedings of the 24th International Joint Conference on Artificial Intelligence*, pages 3960–3966, 2015.

[27] Y. Zhou, X. Chen, and J. Li. Optimal pac multiple arm identification with applications to crowdsourcing. In *Proceedings of the 31st International Conference on Machine Learning (ICML-14)*, pages 217–225, 2014.

Author Index

15th International Conference on Autonomous Agents and Multiagent Systems (AAMAS 2016)

Singapore
9-13 May 2016

Volume 2 of 2

ISBN: 978-1-5108-5508-3

Printed from e-media with permission by:

Curran Associates, Inc.
57 Morehouse Lane
Red Hook, NY 12571

proceedings.com

Some format issues inherent in the e-media version may also appear in this print version.

Printed by Curran Associates, Inc. (2017)

Additional copies of this publication are available from:

Curran Associates, Inc.
57 Morehouse Lane
Red Hook, NY 12571 USA
Phone: 845-758-0400
Fax: 845-758-2633
Email: curran@proceedings.com
Web: www.proceedings.com

Table of Contents

Invited Talks

Game Theory I

Game Theory II

Game Theory III

Game Theory IV

Game Theory V

Game Theory VI

Social Choice I

Social Choice II

Social Choice III

Social Choice IV

Learning I

Learning II

Learning III

Learning IV

Trust & Cooperation

Logic I

Logic II

Bargaining & Negotiation

Applications I

Applications II

Applications III

Virtual Agents II

Robotics I

Robotics II

Robotics III

Agent Societies

Planning

Verification

Demonstrations

Doctoral Mentoring Abstracts

CAPTURE: A New Predictive Anti-Poaching Tool for Wildlife Protection

Thanh H. Nguyen[1], Arunesh Sinha[1], Shahrzad Gholami[1], Andrew Plumptre[2], Lucas Joppa[3], Milind Tambe[1], Margaret Driciru[4], Fred Wanyama[4], Aggrey Rwetsiba[4], Rob Critchlow[5], Colin M. Beale[5]
[1]University of Southern California, USA, {thanhhng,aruneshs,sgholami,tambe}@usc.edu
[2]Wildlife Conservation Society, USA, aplumptre@wcs.org
[3]Microsoft Research, USA, lujoppa@microsoft.com
[4]Uganda Wildlife Authority, Uganda, {margaret.driciru,fred.wanyama,aggrey.rwetsiba}@ugandawildlife.org
[5]The University of York, UK, {rob.critchlow,colin.beale}@york.ac.uk

ABSTRACT

Wildlife poaching presents a serious extinction threat to many animal species. Agencies ("defenders") focused on protecting such animals need tools that help analyze, model and predict poacher activities, so they can more effectively combat such poaching; such tools could also assist in planning effective defender patrols, building on the previous security games research.

To that end, we have built a new predictive anti-poaching tool, CAPTURE (Comprehensive Anti-Poaching tool with Temporal and observation Uncertainty REasoning). CAPTURE provides four main contributions. First, CAPTURE's modeling of poachers provides significant advances over previous models from behavioral game theory and conservation biology. This accounts for: (i) the defender's imperfect detection of poaching signs; (ii) complex temporal dependencies in the poacher's behaviors; (iii) lack of knowledge of numbers of poachers. Second, we provide two new heuristics: parameter separation and target abstraction to reduce the computational complexity in learning the poacher models. Third, we present a new game-theoretic algorithm for computing the defender's optimal patrolling given the complex poacher model. Finally, we present detailed models and analysis of real-world poaching data collected over 12 years in Queen Elizabeth National Park in Uganda to evaluate our new model's prediction accuracy. This paper thus presents the largest dataset of real-world defender-adversary interactions analyzed in the security games literature. CAPTURE will be tested in Uganda in early 2016.

Keywords

Security Game; Wildlife Protection; Temporal Behavorial Model

1. INTRODUCTION

Wildlife protection is a global concern. Many species such as tigers and rhinos are in danger of extinction as a direct result of illegal harvesting (i.e., poaching) [19, 26]. The removal of these and other species from the landscape threatens the functioning of natural ecosystems, hurts local and national economies, and has become an international security concern due to the unregulated profits of poachers flowing to terrorist organizations [24]. To prevent wildlife poaching, conservation organizations attempt to protect wildlife parks with well-trained park rangers. In each time period (e.g., one month), park rangers conduct patrols within the park area to prevent poachers from capturing animals either by catching the poachers or by removing animals traps laid out by the poachers. During the rangers' patrols, poaching signs are collected and then can be used together with other domain features (e.g., animal density) to predict the poachers' behavior [6, 8]. In essence, learning the poachers' behavior, anticipating where poachers often go for poaching, is critical for the rangers to generate effective patrols.

Motivated by the success of defender-attacker Stackelberg Security Game (SSG) applications for infrastructure security problems [28, 3, 14], previous work has began to apply SSGs for wildlife protection [30, 9, 8]. In particular, an SSG-based patrolling decision-aid called PAWS has been deployed in south-east Asia [8]. PAWS focuses on generating effective patrols for the rangers, taking into account the complex topographic conditions of Asian forests. Despite its successful application, PAWS is known to suffer from several limitations. First, PAWS relies on an existing adversary behavior model known as Subjective Utility Quantal Response (SUQR) [8], which makes several limiting assumptions such as (a) all poaching signs are perfectly observable by the rangers; (b) poachers' activities in one time period are independent of their activities in previous or future time periods; (c) the number of poachers is known. As a result, SUQR's modeling falls short of what is required, as security agencies in some countries are interested in detailed analysis, modeling and prediction of poacher behavior, taking into account all of the detailed domain features. That is they may wish to obtain such information for situational awareness of the area under their protection and for other strategic decisions. Second, since SUQR has traditionally only relied on three or four domain attributes in its modeling, it has not been able to provide a detailed analysis of the impact of environmental and terrain features on poacher behavior, and thus such analysis of real-world data has been lacking in the literature. Third, richer adversary models would also require new patrol generation algorithms that improve upon what is used in PAWS.

In essence, our new CAPTURE tool attempts to address all aforementioned limitations in PAWS while providing the following three key contributions. Our first area of contribution relates to CAPTURE's addressing SUQR's limitations in modeling ad-

Appears in: *Proceedings of the 15th International Conference on Autonomous Agents and Multiagent Systems (AAMAS 2016), J. Thangarajah, K. Tuyls, C. Jonker, S. Marsella (eds.), May 9–13, 2016, Singapore.*

versary behavior. More specifically, CAPTURE introduces a new behavioral model which takes into account the rangers' imperfect detection of poaching signs. Additionally, we incorporate the dependence of the poachers' behavior on their activities in the past into the component for predicting the poachers' behavior. Moreover, we adopt logistic models to formulate the two components of the new model. This enables capturing the aggregate behavior of attackers without requiring a known number of poachers. Finally, CAPTURE considers a richer set of domain features in addition to the three/four features used in SUQR in analyzing the poachers' behavior. Second, we provide two new heuristics to reduce the computational cost of learning adversary models in CAPTURE, namely *parameter separation* and *target abstraction*. The first heuristic divides the set of model parameters into separate subsets and then iteratively learns these subsets of parameters separately while fixing the values of the other subsets. This heuristic decomposes the learning process into less complex learning components which help in speeding up the learning process with no loss in accuracy. The second heuristic of target abstraction works by leveraging the continuous spatial structure of the wildlife domain, starting the learning process with a coarse discretization of forest area and gradually using finer discretization instead of directly starting with the most detailed representation, leading to improved runtime overall. Our third contribution lies in computing the optimal patrolling strategy of the rangers given the new behavioral model. Specifically, we provide a new game-theoretic algorithm for single/multiple-step patrolling plans wherein the poachers' actions (which follow the CAPTURE model) are recursively explored in multiple time steps.

Finally, we extensively evaluate the prediction accuracy of our new CAPTURE model based on a detailed analysis of the largest dataset of real-world defender-adversary interactions collected by rangers in Queen Elizabeth National Park (QENP) over 12 years. In fact, this is the largest such study in the security games literature. The experimental results show that our model is superior to existing models in predicting the poachers' behaviors, demonstrating the advances of our model over the previous state-of-the-art models. To that end, CAPTURE will be tested in Uganda in early 2016.

2. BACKGROUND & RELATED WORK

Stackelberg Security Games. In Stackelberg security games, there is a defender who attempts to optimally allocate her limited security resources to protect a set of targets against an adversary attempting to attack one of the targets [28]. In SSGs, the defender commits to a *mixed* strategy first while the attacker can observe the defender's strategy and then take an action based on that observation. A pure strategy of the defender is an assignment of her limited resources to a subset of targets and a mixed strategy of the defender refers to a probability distribution over all possible pure strategies. The defender's mixed strategies can be represented as a marginal coverage vector over the targets (i.e., the coverage probabilities with which the defender will protect each target) [13]. We denote by N the number of targets and $0 \leq c_i \leq 1$ the defender's coverage probability at target i for $i = 1 \ldots N$. If the attacker attacks target i and the defender is not protecting that target, the attacker obtains a reward R_i^a while the defender gets a penalty P_i^d. Conversely, if the target is protected, the attacker receives a penalty P_i^a while the defender achieves a reward R_i^d. The expected utilities of the defender, U_i^d, and attacker, U_i^a, are computed as follows:

$$U_i^d = c_i R_i^d + (1 - c_i) P_i^d \tag{1}$$

$$U_i^a = c_i P_i^a + (1 - c_i) R_i^a \tag{2}$$

Behavioral Models of Adversaries. In SSGs, different behavioral models have been proposed to capture the attacker's behavior. The Quantal Response model (QR) is one of the most popular behavioral models which attempts to predict a stochastic distribution of the attacker's responses [16, 17]. In general, QR predicts the probability that the attacker will choose to attack each target with the intuition that the higher expected utility of a target, the more likely that the attacker will choose that target. A more recent model, SUQR, (which is shown to outperform QR) also attempts to predict an attacking distribution over the targets [22]. However, instead of relying on expected utility, SUQR uses the subjective utility function, $\hat{U}_i^a$, which is a linear combination of all features that can influence the attacker's behaviors.

$$\hat{U}_i^a = w_1 c_i + w_2 R_i^a + w_3 P_i^a \tag{3}$$

where (w_1, w_2, w_3) are the key model parameters which measure the importance of the defender's coverage, the attacker's reward and penalty w.r.t the attacker's action. Based on subjective utility, SUQR predicts the attacking probability, q_i, at target i as follows:

$$q_i = \frac{e^{\hat{U}_i^a}}{\sum_j e^{\hat{U}_j^a}} \tag{4}$$

In addition to QR/SUQR, there are other lines of research which focus on building models of criminal behavior in urban crime [7, 20, 23, 32] or opponent behavior in poker [10, 27]. However, these models are specifically designed for these domains, which rely on the complete past crime/game data as well as intrinsic domain characteristics. Another line of research focuses on adversarial plan recognition [1], which can be applied for computer intrusion detection and detection of anomalous activities, etc. This line of work does not learn model parameters as well as do any patrol planning. Here, CAPTURE focuses on modeling the poachers' behavior in wildlife protection which exhibits unique challenges (as shown below) that existing behavioral models cannot handle.

Wildlife Protection. Previous work in security games has modeled the problem of wildlife protection as a SSG in which the rangers play in a role of the defender while the poachers are the attacker [30, 9, 8, 12]. The park area can be divided into a grid where each grid cell represents a target. The rewards and penalties of each target w.r.t the rangers and poachers can be determined based on domain features such as animal density and terrain slope. Previous work focuses on computing the optimal patrolling strategy for the rangers given that poachers' behavior is predicted based on existing adversary behavioral models. However, these models make several limiting assumptions as discussed in Section 1 including (a) all poaching signs (e.g., snares) are perfectly observable by the rangers; (b) poachers' activities in one time period are independent of their activities in previous or future time periods; (c) the number of poachers is known. To understand the limiting nature of these assumptions, consider the issue of observability. The rangers' capability of making observations over a large geographical area is limited. For example, the rangers usually follow certain paths/trails to patrol; they can only observe over the areas around these paths/trails which means that they may not be able to make observations in other further areas. In addition, in areas such as dense forests, it is difficult for the rangers to search for snares. As a result, there may be still poaching activities happening in areas where rangers did not find any poaching sign. Therefore, relying entirely on the rangers' observations would lead to an inaccurate prediction of the poachers' behavior, hindering the rangers' patrol effectiveness. Furthermore, when modeling the poachers' behavior, it is critical to incorporate important aspects that affect the poachers' behavior including time dependency of the poachers' activities and patrolling frequencies of the rangers. Lastly, the rangers are unaware of the total number of attackers in the park.

In ecology research, while previous work mainly focused on estimating the animal density [15], there are a few works which attempt to model the spatial distribution of the economic costs/benefits of illegal hunting activities in the Serengeti national park [11] or the threats to wildlife and how these change over time in QENP [6]. However, these models also have several limitations. First, the proposed models do not consider the time dependency of the poachers' behaviors. These models also do not consider the effect of the rangers' patrols on poaching activities. Furthermore, the prediction accuracy of the proposed models is not measured. Finally, these works do not provide any solution for generating the rangers' patrolling strategies with a behavioral model of the poachers.

3. BEHAVIORAL LEARNING

Security agencies protecting wildlife have a great need for tools that analyze, model and predict behavior of poachers. Such modeling tools help the security agencies gain situational awareness, and decide general strategies; in addition, these agencies also find it useful to have patrol planning tools that are built based on such models. The key here is that in wildlife protection areas around the world, these security agencies have collected large amounts of data related to interactions between defenders (patrollers) and adversaries (poachers). In our work, we focus on QENP [30, 6], where in collaboration with the Wildlife Conservation Society (WCS) and Uganda Wildlife Authority (UWA), we have obtained 12 years of ranger-collected data (that is managed in database MIST/SMART).

In CAPTURE, we introduce a new hierarchical behavioral model to predict the poachers' behavior in the wildlife domain, taking into account the challenge of rangers' imperfect observation. Overall, the new model consists of two layers. One layer models the probability the poachers attack each target wherein the temporal effect on the poachers' behaviors is incorporated. The next layer predicts the conditional probability of the rangers detecting any poaching sign at a target given that the poachers attack that target. These two layers are then integrated to predict the rangers' final observations. In our model, we incorporate the effect of the rangers' patrols on both layers, i.e., how the poachers adapt their behaviors according to rangers' patrols and how the rangers' patrols determine the rangers' detectability of poaching signs. Furthermore, we consider the poachers' past activity in reasoning about future actions of the poachers. We also include different domain features to predict either attacking probabilities or detection probabilities or both.

3.1 Hierarchical Behavioral Model

We denote by T the number of time steps, N the number of targets, and K the number of domain features. At each time step t, each target i is associated with a set of feature values $\mathbf{x_{t,i}} = \{x^k_{t,i}\}$ where $k = 1 \dots K$ and $x^k_{t,i}$ is the value of the kth feature at (t, i). In addition, $c_{t,i}$ is defined as the coverage probability of the rangers at (t, i). When the rangers patrol target i in time step t, they have observation $o_{t,i}$ which takes an integer value in $\{-1, 0, 1\}$. Specifically, $o_{t,i} = 1$ indicates that the rangers observe a poaching sign at (t, i), $o_{t,i} = 0$ means that the rangers have no observation and $o_{t,i} = -1$ when the rangers did not patrol at (t, i). Furthermore, we define $a_{t,i} \in \{0, 1\}$ as the actual action of poachers at (t, i) which is hidden from the rangers. Specifically, $a_{t,i} = 1$ indicates the poachers attack at (t, i); otherwise, $a_{t,i} = 0$ means the poachers did not attack at (t, i). In this work, we only consider the situation of attacked or not (i.e., $a_{t,i} \in \{0, 1\}$); the case of multiple-level attacks is left for future work. Moreover, we mainly focus on

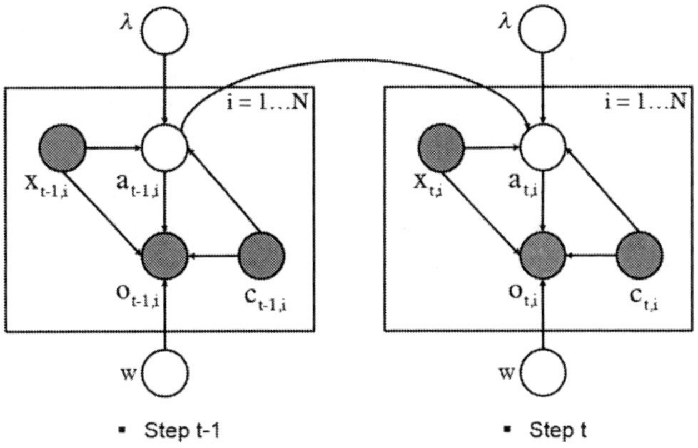

Figure 1: Dependencies among CAPTURE modeling elements

the problem of false negative observations, meaning that there may still exist poaching activity at locations where the rangers found no sign of poaching. We make the reasonable assumption that there is no false positive observation, meaning that if the rangers found any poaching sign at a target, the poachers did attack that target. In other words, we have $p(a_{t,i} = 1|o_{t,i} = 1) = 1$ and $p(o_{t,i} = 1|a_{t,i} = 0) = 0$.

The graphical representation of the new model is shown in Figure 1 wherein the directed edges indicate the dependence between elements of the model. The grey nodes refer to known elements for the rangers such as domain features, the rangers' coverages and observations while the white nodes represent the unknown elements such as the actual actions of poachers. The elements $(\lambda, \mathbf{w})$ are model parameters which we will explain later.

Our new CAPTURE graphical model is a significant advance over previous models from behavioral game theory, such as QR/SUQR, and similarly models from conservation biology [11, 6]. First, unlike SUQR/QR which consider poachers behavior to be independent between different time steps, we assume that the poachers' actions $a_{t,i}$ depends on the poachers' activities in the past $a_{t-1,i}$ and the rangers' patrolling strategies $c_{t,i}$. This is because poachers may tend to come back to the areas they have attacked before. Second, CAPTURE considers a much richer set of domain features $\{x^k_{t,i}\}$ that have not been considered earlier but are relevant to our domain, e.g., slope and habitat. Third, another advance of CAPTURE is modeling the observation uncertainty in this domain. We expect that the rangers' observations $o_{t,i}$ depend on the actual actions of the poachers $a_{t,i}$, the rangers' coverage probabilities $c_{t,i}$ and domain features $\{x^k_{t,i}\}$ Finally, we adopt the logistic model [4] to predict the poachers' behaviors; one advantage of this model compared to SUQR/QR is that it does not assume a known number of attackers and models probability of attack at every target independently. Thus, given the actual action of poachers, $a_{t-1,i}$, at previous time step $(t-1, i)$, the rangers' coverage probability $c_{t,i}$ at (t, i), and the domain features $\mathbf{x_{t,i}} = \{x^k_{t,i}\}$, we aim at predicting the probability that poachers attack (t, i) as follows:

$$p(a_{t,i} = 1|a_{t-1,i}, c_{t,i}, \mathbf{x_{t,i}}) = \frac{e^{\lambda'[a_{t-1,i}, c_{t,i}, \mathbf{x_{t,i}}, 1]}}{1 + e^{\lambda'[a_{t-1,i}, c_{t,i}, \mathbf{x_{t,i}}, 1]}} \quad (5)$$

where $\lambda = \{\lambda_k\}$ is the $(K+3) \times 1$ parameter vector which measure the importance of all factors towards the poachers' decisions. λ_{K+3} is the free parameter and λ' is the transpose vector of λ. In essence, compared to Equation 4 where SUQR was seen to only use three features, we now have a weighted sum over a much larger number of features as is appropriate in our wildlife domain.

Furthermore, if the poachers attack at (t,i), we predict the probability that the rangers can detect any poaching signs as follows:

$$p(o_{t,i}=1|a_{t,i}=1,c_{t,i},\mathbf{x_{t,i}}) = c_{t,i} \times \frac{e^{\mathbf{w}'[\mathbf{x_{t,i}},1]}}{1+e^{\mathbf{w}'[\mathbf{x_{t,i}},1]}} \quad (6)$$

where the first term is the probability that the rangers are present at (t,i) and the second term indicates the probability that the rangers can detect any poaching sign when patrolling at (t,i). Additionally, $\mathbf{w}=\{w_k\}$ is the $(K+1)\times 1$ vector of parameters which indicates the significance of domain features in affecting the rangers' probability of detecting poaching signs. $\mathbf{w}'$ is transpose of $\mathbf{w}$. In QENP specifically, CAPTURE employs seven features: animal density, distances to rivers/roads/villages, net primary productivity (NPP), habitat and slope to predict attacking/detection probabilities.

In the following, we will explain our approach for learning the parameters $(\lambda,\mathbf{w})$ of our hierarchical model. We use $p(a_{t,i}=1|a_{t-1,i},c_{t,i})$ and $p(o_{t,i}=1|a_{t,i}=1,c_{t,i})$ as the abbreviations of the LHSs in Equations 5 and 6. The domain features $\mathbf{x_{t,i}}$ are omitted in all equations for simplification.

3.2 Parameter Estimation

Due to the presence of unobserved variables $\mathbf{a}=\{a_{t,i}\}$, we use the standard Expectation Maximization (EM) method in order to estimate $(\lambda,\mathbf{w})$. In particular, EM attempts to maximize the log-likelihood that the rangers can have observations $\mathbf{o}=\{o_{t,i}\}$ given the rangers' coverage probabilities $\mathbf{c}=\{c_{t,i}\}$ and domain features $\mathbf{x}=\{\mathbf{x_{t,i}}\}$ for all time steps $t=1,\ldots,T$ and targets $i=1,\ldots,N$ which is formulated as follows:

$$\max_{\lambda,\mathbf{w}} \log p(\mathbf{o}|\mathbf{c},\mathbf{x},\lambda,\mathbf{w}) \quad (7)$$

The standard EM procedure [4] is to start with an initial estimate of $(\lambda,\mathbf{w})$ and iteratively update the parameter values until a locally optimal solution of (7) is reached. Many restarts are used with differing initial values of $(\lambda,\mathbf{w})$ to find the global optimum. Each iteration of EM consists of two key steps:

- **E** step: compute $p(\mathbf{a}|\mathbf{o},\mathbf{c},(\lambda,\mathbf{w})^{\mathbf{old}})$
- **M** step: update $(\lambda,\mathbf{w})^{\mathbf{old}}) = (\lambda^*,\mathbf{w}^*)$ where $(\lambda^*,\mathbf{w}^*) = \underset{\lambda,\mathbf{w}}{\operatorname{argmax}} \sum_{\mathbf{a}} p(\mathbf{a}|\mathbf{o},\mathbf{c},(\lambda,\mathbf{w})^{\mathbf{old}}) \log(p(\mathbf{o},\mathbf{a}|\mathbf{c},\lambda,\mathbf{w}))$.

In our case, the **E** (Expectation) step attempts to compute the probability that the poachers take actions $\mathbf{a}=\{a_{t,i}\}$ given the rangers' observations $\mathbf{o}$, the rangers' patrols $\mathbf{c}$, the domain features $\mathbf{x}=\{\mathbf{x_{t,i}}\}$, and current values of the model parameters $(\lambda,\mathbf{w})^{\mathbf{old}}$. The **M** (Maximization) step tries to maximize the expectation of the logarithm of the complete-data $(\mathbf{o},\mathbf{a})$ likelihood function given the action probabilities computed in the **E** step and updates the value of $(\lambda,\mathbf{w})^{\mathbf{old}}$ with the obtained maximizer.

Although we can decompose the log-likelihood, the EM algorithm is still time-consuming due to the large number of targets and parameters. Therefore, we use two novel ideas to speed up the algorithm: *parameter separation* for accelerating the convergence of EM and *target abstraction* for reducing the number of targets.

Parameter Separation. Observe that the objective in the **M** step can be split into two additive parts as follows:

$$\sum_{\mathbf{a}} p(\mathbf{a}|\mathbf{o},\mathbf{c},(\lambda,\mathbf{w})^{\mathbf{old}}) \log(p(\mathbf{o},\mathbf{a}|\mathbf{c},\lambda,\mathbf{w})) \quad (8)$$
$$= \sum_{t,i}\sum_{a_{t,i}} p(a_{t,i}|\mathbf{o},\mathbf{c},(\lambda,\mathbf{w})^{\mathbf{old}}) \log p(o_{t,i}|a_{t,i},c_{t,i},\mathbf{w})$$
$$+ \sum_{t,i}\sum_{a_{t,i}}\sum_{a_{t-1,i}} p(a_{t,i},a_{t-1,i}|\mathbf{o},\mathbf{c},(\lambda,\mathbf{w})^{\mathbf{old}}) \log p(a_{t,i}|a_{t-1,i},c_{t,i},\lambda)$$

In (8), the first component is obtained as a result of decomposing w.r.t the detection probabilities of the rangers at every (t,i) (Equation 6). The second one results from decomposing according to the attacking probabilities at every (t,i) (Equation 5). Importantly, the first component is only a function of $\mathbf{w}$ and the second component is only a function of λ. Following this split, for our problem, the **E** step reduces to computing the following two quantities:

$$\textbf{Total probability: } p(a_{t,i}|\mathbf{o},\mathbf{c},(\lambda,\mathbf{w})^{\mathbf{old}}) \quad (9)$$

$$\textbf{2-step probability: } p(a_{t,i},a_{t-1,i}|\mathbf{o},\mathbf{c},(\lambda,\mathbf{w})^{\mathbf{old}}) \quad (10)$$

which can be computed by adapting the Baum-Welch algorithm [4] to account for missing observations, i.e., $o_{t,i}=-1$ when rangers do not patrol at (t,i). This can be done by introducing $p(o_{t,i}=-1|a_{t,i},c_{t,i}=0)=1$ when computing (9) and (10).

More importantly, as shown in (8), the structure of our problem allows for the decomposition of the objective function into two separate functions w.r.t attack parameters λ and detection parameters $\mathbf{w}$: $F^d(\mathbf{w})+F^a(\lambda)$ where the detection function $F^d(\mathbf{w})$ is the first term of the RHS in Equation 8 and the attack function $F^a(\lambda)$ is the second term. Therefore, instead of maximizing $F^d(\mathbf{w})+F^a(\lambda)$ we decompose each iteration of EM into two **E** steps and two **M** steps that enables maximizing F^d and F^a separately as follows:

- **E1** step: compute total probability
- **M1** step: $\mathbf{w}^* = \operatorname{argmax}_{\mathbf{w}} F^d(\mathbf{w})$; update $\mathbf{w}^{\mathbf{old}} = \mathbf{w}^*$
- **E2** step: compute 2-step probability
- **M2** step: $\lambda^* = \operatorname{argmax}_{\lambda} F^a(\lambda)$; update $\lambda^{\mathbf{old}} = \lambda^*$

Note that the detection and attack components are simpler functions compared to the original objective since these components only depend on the detection and attack parameters respectively. Furthermore, at each EM iteration, the parameters get closer to the optimal solution due to the decomposition since the attack parameter is now updated based on the new detection parameters from the **E1/M1** steps instead of the old detection parameters from the previous iteration. Thus, by decomposing each iteration of EM according to attack and detection parameters, EM will converge more quickly without loss of solution quality. The convergence and solution quality of the separation can be analyzed similarly to the analysis of multi-cycle expected conditional maximization [18].

Furthermore, the attack function $F^a(\lambda)$ is shown to be concave by Proposition 1 (its proof is in Online Appendix A[1]), allowing us to easily obtain the global optimal solution of the attacking parameters λ at each iteration of EM.

PROPOSITION 1. *$F^a(\lambda)$ is concave in the attack parameters λ.*

Target Abstraction. Our second idea is to reduce the number of targets via target abstraction. Previous work in network security and poker games has also applied abstraction for reducing the complexity of solving these games by exploring intrinsic properties of the games [2, 25]. In CAPTURE, by exploiting the spatial connectivity between grid cells of the conservation area, we can divide the area into a smaller number of grid cells by merging each cell in the original grid with its neighbors into a single bigger cell. The corresponding domain features are aggregated accordingly. Intuitively, neighboring cells tend to have similar domain features. Therefore, we expect that the parameters learned in both the original and abstracted grid would expose similar characteristics. Hence, the model parameters estimated based on the abstracted grid could be effectively used to derive the parameter values in the original one.

[1]https://www.dropbox.com/s/mngapyvv5112uhb/Appendix.pdf

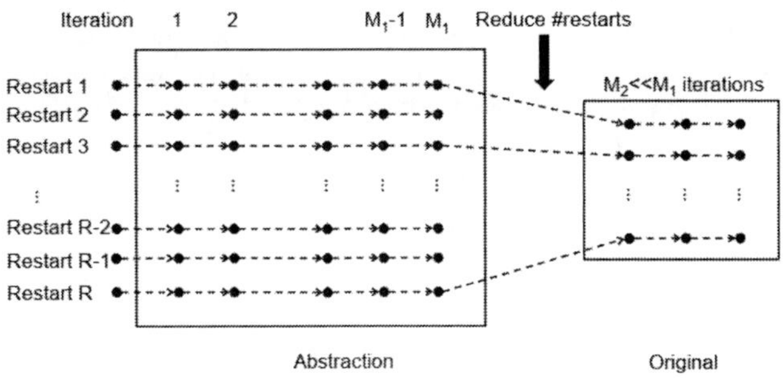

Figure 2: Target Abstraction

In this work, we leverage the values of parameters learned in the abstracted grid in two ways: (i) reduce the number of restarting points (i.e., initial values of parameters) for reaching different local optimal solutions in EM; and (ii) reduce the number of iterations in each round of EM. The idea of target abstraction is outlined in Figure 2 wherein each black dot corresponds to a set of parameter values at a particular iteration given a specific restarting points. At the first stage, we estimate the parameter values in the abstracted grid given a large number of restarting points R, assuming that we can run M_1 EM iterations. At the end of the first stage, we obtain R different sets of parameter values; each corresponds to a local optimal solution of EM in the abstracted grid. Then at the second stage, these sets of parameter values are used to estimate the model parameters in the original grid as the following: (i) only a subset of K resulting parameter sets which refer to the top local optimal solutions in the abstracted grid are selected as initial values of parameters in the original grid; and (ii) instead of running M_1 EM iterations again, we only proceed with $M_2 << M_1$ iterations in EM since we expect that these selected parameter values are already well learned in the abstracted grid and thus could be considered as *warm restarts* in the original grid.

4. PATROL PLANNING

Once the model parameters $(\lambda, \mathbf{w})$ are learned, we can compute the optimal patrolling strategies for the rangers in next time steps taking into account the CAPTURE model. We consider two circumstances: 1) single-step patrol planning in which the rangers only focus on generating the patrolling strategy at the next time step and 2) multiple-step patrol planning for generating strategies for the next $\Delta T > 1$ time steps, given the rangers' patrol and observation history and domain features. While the former provides a one-step patrolling strategy with an immediate but short-term benefit, the latter generates strategies across multiple time steps with a long-term benefit. We leave the choice of which planning option to use for the rangers given the cost/benefit trade-off between the two. The key challenge in designing strategies for the rangers given the CAPTURE model is that we need to take into account new aspects of the modeling of the adversary. These include the rangers' detection uncertainty and the temporal dependency of the poachers' activities. This challenge leads to a complicated non-convex optimization problem to compute the optimal patrolling strategy for the rangers; we provide novel game-theoretic algorithms to solve it.

We suppose that the rangers have an observation history $\mathbf{o} = \{o_{t',i}\}$ for $t' = 1, \ldots, T$ and $i = 1, \ldots, N$. Similar to standard SSGs, we assume that if the poachers successfully attack at (t, i), the rangers receive a penalty $P^d_{t,i}$. Conversely, if the rangers successfully confiscate poaching tools at (t, i), the rangers obtain a reward $R^d_{t,i}$. Therefore, the rangers' expected utility at (t, i) if the poachers attack at (t, i) is computed as follows where $p(o_{t,i} = 1|a_{t,i} = 1, c_{t,i})$ is the rangers' detection probability at (t, i) as shown in Equation 6:

$$U^d_{t,i} = p(o_{t,i} = 1|a_{t,i} = 1, c_{t,i}) \times [R^d_{t,i} - P^d_{t,i}] + P^d_{t,i} \quad (11)$$

We now explain in detail our new game-theoretic algorithms. The rangers' past patrols at (t', i) for for $t' = 1, \ldots, T$ and $i = 1, \ldots, N$ are already known and thus can be omitted in all following mathematical formulations for simplification.

4.1 Single-step Patrol Planning

Given the rangers' observation history $\mathbf{o}$ and the model parameters $(\lambda, \mathbf{w})$, the problem of computing the optimal strategies at the next time step $T + 1$ can be formulated as follows:

$$\max_{\{c_{T+1,i}\}} \sum_i p(a_{T+1,i} = 1|\mathbf{o}, c_{T+1,i}) \times U^d_{T+1,i} \quad (12)$$

$$s.t.\ 0 \leq c_{T+1,i} \leq 1,\ i = 1 \ldots N \quad (13)$$

$$\sum_i c_{T+1,i} \leq B \quad (14)$$

where B is the maximum number of ranger resources and $p(a_{T+1,i} = 1|\mathbf{o}, c_{T+1,i})$ is the probability that the poachers attack at $(T + 1, i)$ given the rangers' observation history $\mathbf{o}$ and the rangers' coverage probability $c_{T+1,i}$. Since the poachers' behaviors depends on their activities in the past (which is hidden to the rangers), we need to examine all possible actions of the poachers in previous time steps in order to predict the poachers' attacking probability at $(T + 1, i)$. Hence, the attacking probability $p(a_{T+1,i} = 1|\mathbf{o}, c_{T+1,i})$ should be computed by marginalizing over all possible actions of poachers at (T, i) as follows:

$$p(a_{T+1,i} = 1|c_{T+1,i}, \mathbf{o}) = \quad (15)$$
$$\sum_{a_{T,i}} p(a_{T+1,i} = 1|a_{T,i}, c_{T+1,i}) \times p(a_{T,i}|\mathbf{o})$$

where $p(a_{T+1,i}|a_{T,i}, c_{T+1,i})$, which is computed in (5), is the attacking probability at $(T + 1, i)$ given the poachers' action $a_{T,i}$ at (T, i) and the rangers' coverage probability $c_{T+1,i}$. In addition, $p(a_{T,i}|\mathbf{o})$ is the total probability at (T, i) which can be recursively computed based on the Baum-Welch approach as discussed in Section 3. Overall, (12 – 14) is a non-convex optimization problem in the rangers' coverage probabilities $\{c_{T+1,i}\}$. Fortunately, each additive term of the rangers' utility in (12) is a separate sub-utility function of the rangers' coverage, $c_{T+1,i}$, at $(T + 1, i)$:

$$f_i(c_{T+1,i}) = p(a_{T+1,i} = 1|\mathbf{o}, c_{T+1,i}) \times U^d_{T+1,i} \quad (16)$$

Therefore, we can piecewise linearly approximate $f_i(c_{T+1,i})$ and represent (12 – 14) as a Mixed Integer Program which can be solved by CPLEX. The details of piecewise linear approximation can be found at [31]. Essentially, the piecewise linear approximation method provides an $O(\frac{1}{M})$-optimal solution for (12 – 14) where M is the number of piecewise segments [31].

4.2 Multi-step Patrol Planning

In designing multi-step patrol strategies for the rangers, there are two key challenges in incorporating the CAPTURE model that we need to take into account: 1) the time dependence of the poachers' behavior; and 2) the actual actions of the poachers are hidden (unobserved) from the rangers. These two challenges make the problem of planning multi-step patrols difficult as we show below.

Given that the rangers have an observation history $\mathbf{o} = \{o_{t'i}\}$ for $t' = 1, \ldots, T$ and $i = 1 \ldots N$, the rangers aim at generating patrolling strategies $\{c_{t,i}\}$ in next ΔT time steps where

$t = T+1, \ldots, T+\Delta T$. Then the problem of computing the optimal patrolling strategies for next ΔT time step $T+1, \ldots, T+\Delta T$ can be formulated as follows:

$$\max_{\{c_{t,i}\}} \sum_{t,i} p(a_{t,i} = 1|\mathbf{o}, c_{T+1\ldots t,i}) U^d_{t,i} \quad (17)$$

$$s.t.\ 0 \leq c_{t,i} \leq 1,\ t = T+1 \ldots T+\Delta T,\ i = 1 \ldots N \quad (18)$$

$$\sum_i c_{t,i} \leq B,\ t = T+1 \ldots T+\Delta T. \quad (19)$$

where $p(a_{t,i} = 1|\mathbf{o}, c_{T+1\ldots t,i})$ is the attacking probability at (t, i) given the rangers' coverages at (t', i) where $t' = T+1, \ldots, t$ and observation history $\mathbf{o} = \{o_{t',i}\}$ where $t' = 1, \ldots, T$. Because of the two aforementioned challenges, we need to examine all possible actions of the poachers in previous time steps in order to compute the attacking probability at (t, i), $p(a_{t,i} = 1|\mathbf{o}, c_{T+1\ldots t,i})$. Our idea is to recursively compute this attacking probability via the attacking probabilities at previous time steps as follows:

$$p(a_{t,i} = 1|\mathbf{o}, c_{T+1\ldots t,i}) = \sum_{a_{t-1,i}} p(a_{t,i}|a_{t-1,i}, c_{t,i}) \times \quad (20)$$
$$p(a_{t-1,i}|\mathbf{o}, c_{T+1\ldots t-1,i})$$

where the initial step is to compute the total probability $p(a_{T,i}|\mathbf{o})$ by using the Baum-Welch approach. Here, the objective in (17) can be no longer divided into separate sub-utility functions of a single coverage probability at a particular (t, i) because of the time dependency of the poachers' behaviors. Thus, we can not apply piecewise linear approximation as in the single-step patrol planning for solving (17 – 19) quickly. In this work, we use non-convex solvers (i.e., fmincon in MATLAB) to solve (17 – 19).

In [9], the dependence of the attacker's actions on the defender's patrolling strategies in the past is also considered; they assume that the attacker's responses follow the SUQR model while the attacker perceives the defender's current strategy as a weighted linear function of the defender's strategies in the past. They also assume that these weights are known, thereby making the computational problem easy. In contrast, we make the more realistic assumption that the poachers are influenced by their own past observations and our learning algorithm learns the weights corresponding to such influence from the data. Unfortunately, this makes the problem of planning multistep patrols more difficult as shown before.

5. EXPERIMENTS

We aim to (i) extensively assess the prediction accuracy of the CAPTURE model compared to existing models based on real-world wildlife/poaching data; (ii) examine the runtime performance of learning the new model; and (iii) evaluate the solution quality of the CAPTURE planning for generating patrols. In the following, we provide a brief description of the real-world wildlife data used.

5.1 Real-world Wildlife/Poaching Data

In learning the poachers' behavior, we use the wildlife data collected by the rangers over 12 years from 2003 to 2014 in QENP (Figure 3 with animal density). This work is accomplished in collaboration with the Wildlife Conservation Society (WCS) and Uganda Wildlife Authority (UWA). While patrolling, the park rangers record information such as locations (latitude/longitude), times, and observations (e.g., signs of human illegal activities). Similar to [6], we also divide collected human signs into six different groups: commercial animal (i.e., human signs such as snares which refer to poaching commercial animals such as buffalo, hippo and elephant), non-commercial animal, fishing, encroachment, commercial plant, and non-commercial plant. In this work, we mainly focus on two types of human illegal activities: commercial animal and non-commercial animal which are major threats to key species of concern such as elephants and hippos.

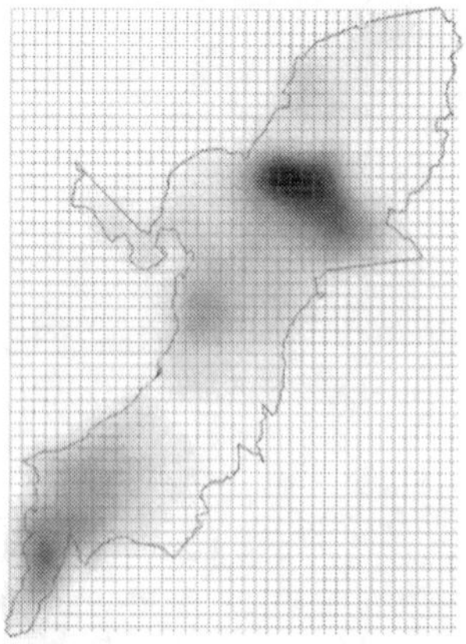

Figure 3: QENP with animal density

The poaching data is then divided into the four different groups according to four seasons in Uganda: dry season I (Jun, July, and August), dry season II (December, January, and February), rainy season I (March, April, and May), and rainy season II (September, October, November). We aim at learning behaviors of the poachers w.r.t these four seasons as motivated by the fact that the poachers' activities usually vary seasonally. In the end, we obtain eight different categories of wildlife data given that we have the two poaching types and four seasons. Furthermore, we use seven domain features in learning the poachers' behavior, including animal density, slope, habitat, net primary productivity (NPP), and locations of villages/rivers/roads provided by [6].

We divide the park area into a $1km \times 1km$ grid consisting of more than 2500 grid cells ($\approx 2500km^2$). Domain features and the rangers' patrols and observations are then aggregated into the grid cells. We also refine the poaching data by removing all abnormal data points such as the data points which indicate that the rangers conducted patrols outside the QENP park or the rangers moved too fast, etc. Since we attempt to predict the poachers' actions in the future based on their activities in the past, we apply a time window (i.e., five years) with an 1-year shift to split the poaching data into eight different pairs of training/test sets. For example, for the (commercial animal, rainy season I) category, the oldest training/test sets correspond to four-year data (2003–2006) w.r.t this category for training and one-year (2007) data for testing. In addition, the latest training/test sets refer to the four years (2010–2013) and one year (2014) of data respectively. In total, there are eight different training/test sets for each of our eight data categories.

5.2 Behavioral Learning

Prediction Accuracy. In this work, we compare the prediction accuracy of six models: 1) CAPTURE (CAPTURE with parameter separation); 2) CAP-Abstract (CAPTURE with parameter separation and target abstraction); 3) CAP-NoTime (CAPTURE with parameter separation and without the component of temporal effect); 4) Logit (Logistic Regression); 5) SUQR ; and 6) SVM (Support Vector Machine). We use AUC (Area Under the Curve) to measure the prediction accuracy of these behavioral models. Based on ROC plots of data, AUC is a standard and common statistic in machine learning for model evaluation [5]. Essentially, AUC refers to the probability that a model will weight a random positive poaching sample higher than a random negative poaching sample in labeling these samples as positive (so, higher AUC values are better). For each data category (w.r.t poaching types and poaching seasons), the AUC values of all the models are averaged over the eight test sets as explained in Section 5.1. We also show the average prediction accuracy over all seasons. We use bootstrap-t [29] to measure the statistical significance of our results.

Models	Rainy I	Rainy II	Dry I	Dry II	Average
CAPTURE	0.76	0.76	0.74	0.73	0.7475
CAP-Abstract	0.79	0.76	0.74	0.67	0.74
CAP-NoTime	0.71	0.75	0.67	0.71	0.71
Logit	0.53	0.59	0.57	0.60	0.5725
SUQR	0.53	0.59	0.56	0.62	0.575
SVM	0.61	0.59	0.51	0.66	0.5925

Table 1: AUC: Commercial Animal

Models	Rainy I	Rainy II	Dry I	Dry II	Average
CAPTURE	0.76	0.70	0.78	0.72	0.74
CAP-Abstract	0.76	0.70	0.74	0.70	0.725
CAP-NoTime	0.72	0.68	0.75	0.70	0.7125
Logit	0.52	0.63	0.57	0.52	0.56
SUQR	0.54	0.62	0.58	0.54	0.57
SVM	0.42	0.50	0.55	0.56	0.5075

Table 2: AUC: Non-Commercial Animal

The results are shown in Tables 1 and 2. We can infer the following key points from these tables. First, and most important, CAPTURE improves performance over the state of the art, which is SUQR and SVM. CAPTURE's average AUC in Table 1 (essentially this is over 32 data points of eight test sets over four seasons) is 0.7475 vs 0.575 for SUQR, and in Table 2 is 0.74 vs 0.57 for SUQR. This clearly shows a statistically significant ($\alpha = 0.05$) advance in our modeling accuracy. This improvement illustrates that all the four advances in CAPTURE mentioned in Section 1 — addressing observation error, time dependence, detailed domain features and not requiring a firm count of poachers beforehand – have indeed led to a significant advance in CAPTURE's performance. We can now attempt to understand the contributions of each of CAPTURE's improvements, leading to the next few insights. Second, comparison of CAPTURE with CAP-NoTime which only addresses the challenge of observation bias demonstrates the importance of considering time dependence. Third, while parameter separation does not cause any loss in solution quality as discussed in Section 3.2, Tables 1 and 2 shows that the prediction accuracy of CAPTURE with target abstraction is good in general except for Dry season II with Commercial Animal. As we show later, parameter separation and target abstraction help in speeding up the runtime performance of learning the CAPTURE model.

Fourth, the results of the model parameter values in the CAPTURE model show that all these domain features substantially impact the poachers' behaviors. For example, one learning result on the model parameters corresponding to the category (non-commercial animal/dry season I) in 2011 is $(0.33, 1.46, -2.96, -1.97, 1.88, -0.78, 0.36)$ for domain features (habitat, NPP, slope, road distance, town distance, water distance, and animal density), -1.40 for the rangers' coverage probability and 4.27 for the poachers' past action. Based on these learned weights, we can interpret how these domain features affect the poachers' behavior. Specifically, the negative weights for road/water distances indicates that the poachers tend to poach at locations near roads/water. In addition, the resulting positive weight for the poachers' past actions indicates that the poachers are more likely to attack the targets which were attacked before. Furthermore, the resulting negative weight for the rangers' patrols also shows that the poachers' activity is influenced by the rangers' patrols, i.e., the poachers are less likely to attack targets with higher coverage probability of the rangers. Lastly, the ranger-poacher interaction changes over time as indicated by different negative weights of the rangers' patrols across different years (Table 3). For example, the patrol weight corresponding the category (non-commercial animal/dry season II) in 2014 is -17.39 while in 2013 is -1.78, showing that rangers' patrols have more impact on the poachers' behavior in 2014 than in 2013. This is the first time there is a real-world evidence which shows the impact of ranger patrols on poacher behavior.

Runtime Performance. We compare the runtime performance of learning the CAPTURE model in three cases: 1) learning without both heuristics of parameter separation and target abstraction; 2) learning with parameter separation only; and 3) learning with both heuristics. In our experiments, for the first two cases, we run 20 restarting points and 50 iterations in EM. In the third case, we first run 20 restarting points and 40 iterations in EM with target abstraction. In particular, in target abstraction, we aggregate or interpolate all domain features as well as the rangers' patrols into $4km \times 4km$ grid cells while the original grid cell size is $1km \times 1km$. Then given the results in the abstracted grid, we only select 5 results of parameter values (which correspond to the top five prediction accuracy results w.r.t the training set). We use these results as restarting points for EM in the original grid and only run 10 iterations to obtain the final learning results in the original grid.

Year	2009	2010	2011	2012	2013	2014
Weight	-10.69	-4.35	-0.7	-2.21	-1.78	-17.39

Table 3: Patrol weights in recent years

Heuristics	Average Runtime
None	1419.16 mins
Parameter Separation	333.31 mins
Parameter Separation w/ Target Abstraction	222.02 mins

Table 4: CAPTURE Learning: Runtime Performance

The results are shown in Table 4 which are averaged over 64 training sets (statistically significant ($\alpha = 0.05$)). In Table 4, learning CAPTURE model parameters with parameter separation is significantly faster (i.e., 4.25 times faster) than learning CAPTURE without this heuristic. This result clearly shows that reducing the complexity of the learning process (by decomposing it into simpler sub-learning components via parameter separation) significantly speeds up the learning process of CAPTURE. Furthermore, the heuristic of target abstraction helps CAPTURE in learning even faster although the result is not as substantial as with parameter separation, demonstrating the advantage of using this heuristic.

5.3 Patrol Planning

Based on the CAPTURE model, we apply our CAPTURE planning algorithm (Section 4) to compute the optimal patrolling strategies for the rangers. The solution quality of our algorithm is evaluated based on the real-world QENP domain in comparison with SUQR (i.e., optimal strategies of the rangers against SUQR-based poachers), Maximin (maximin strategies of the rangers against worst-case poacher responses), and Real-world patrolling strategies of the rangers. The real-world strategies are derived from the four seasons in years 2007 to 2014. Given that CAPTURE's prediction accuracy is the highest among all the models, in our experiments, we assume that the poachers' responses follow our model. Given the QENP experimental settings, the reward of the rangers at each target are set to be zero while the penalty is the opposite of the animal density (i.e., zero-sum games). We assess the solution quality of all algorithms according to different number of the rangers' resources (i.e., number of targets the rangers can cover during a patrol). The real-world patrolling strategies are normalized accordingly. Moreover, we also consider different number of time steps for generating patrols.

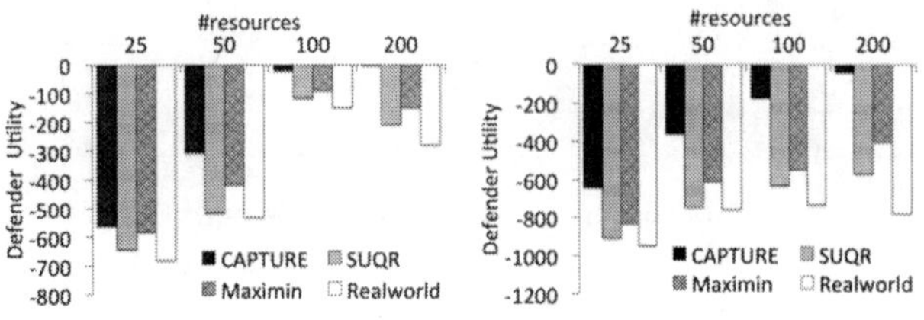

(a) 2 time steps (b) 4 time steps

Figure 4: Solution quality of CAPTURE-based planning

The experimental results are shown in Figure 4 which are averaged over all years and seasons. In Figure 4, the x-axis is the number of the rangers' resources and the y-axis is the aggregated utility the rangers receive over two and four time steps (seasons) for playing CAPTURE, SUQR, Maximin, and Real-world patrolling strategies respectively. As shown in Figure 4, our CAPTURE planning algorithm provides the highest utility for the rangers (with statistical significance ($\alpha = 0.05$)). Especially when the number of the rangers' resources increases, the CAPTURE planning algorithm significantly improves the quality of the rangers' patrolling strategies. Furthermore, our CAPTURE algorithm provides patrolling strategies which take into account the temporal effect on the poachers' behaviors. As a result, when the number of time steps increases (Figure 4(b)), our algorithm enhances its solution quality compared to the others.

6. CAPTURE-BASED APPLICATION

CAPTURE tool is available for the rangers to predict the poachers' behavior and design optimal patrol schedules. Not all the regions are equally attractive to the poachers, so it is beneficial to detect the hotspots and favorite regions for poachers and protect those areas with higher probability. The general work-flow for this software could be itemized as: 1) Aggregating previously gathered data from the park to create a database that includes domain features, poaching signs and rangers' effort to protect the area; 2) Preprocessing of the data points; 3) Running the CAPTURE tool to predict the attacking probability, rangers' observation over the area and generate the optimal patrol strategy; and 4) Post-processing of the results and generating the related heatmaps.

To compare the optimal strategy generated by the single-step patrol planning algorithm provided by CAPTURE and current real strategy deploying over the area, we plotted the related heatmaps according to the defender coverage, shown in Figure 5(a) and Figure 6(a). The darker the area, the greater chance to be covered by the rangers. Also, we used CAPTURE to predict the probability of the attack based on these patrol strategies. These heatmaps are shown in Figure 5(b) and Figure 6(b). The darker regions on the map demonstrate the more attractive regions to the poachers.

We can see the following key points based on the heatmaps: (i) The optimal patrol strategy covers more of the regions with higher animal density (for instance south-west and middle parts of the park as shown in Figure 3). So the deployment of the optimal strategy would result in more protection to areas with higher animal density,

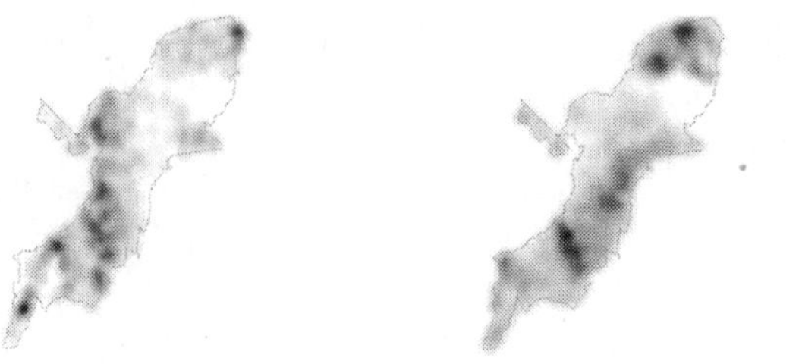
(a) Patrol strategy (b) Attack probability

Figure 5: Heatmaps by CAPTURE (based on the real patrol strategy)

(a) Patrol strategy (b) Attack probability

Figure 6: Heatmaps by CAPTURE (based on the optimal strategy)

as shown in Figure 6(a) and 6(b). (ii) The poaching heatmap shows significantly higher predicted activity of attackers against human generated patrols in regions with higher animal density, as shown in Figure 5(a) and 5(b).

7. CONCLUSION

We propose a new predictive anti-poaching tool, CAPTURE. Essentially, CAPTURE introduces a novel hierarchical model to predict the poachers' behaviors. The CAPTURE model provides a significant advance over the state-of-the-art in modeling poachers in security games [8] and in conservation biology [11, 6] via 1) addressing the challenge of imperfect observations of the rangers; 2) incorporating the temporal effect on the poachers' behaviors; and 3) not requiring a known number of attackers. We provide two new heuristics: parameter separation and target abstraction to reduce the computational complexity in learning the model parameters. Furthermore, CAPTURE incorporates a new planning algorithm to generate optimal patrolling strategies for the rangers, taking into account the new complex poacher model. Finally, this application presents an evaluation of the largest sample of real-world data in the security games literature, i.e., over 12-years of data of attacker defender interactions in QENP. The experimental results demonstrate the superiority of our model compared to other existing models. CAPTURE will be tested in QENP in early 2016.

Acknowledgements: This research was supported by MURI Grant W911NF-11-1-0332 and by CREATE under grant number 2010-ST-061-RE0001. We are grateful to the Wildlife Conservation Society, Uganda Wildlife Authority, MacArthur Foundation, USAID, US Fish and Wildlife Service, and Daniel K. Thorne Foundation for supporting the data collection in Queen Elizabeth National Park. We wish to acknowledge the support of the University of York. We would like to thank Bazil Andira and all the rangers and wardens in Queen Elizabeth National Park for their contribution in collecting the law enforcement monitoring data in MIST.

REFERENCES

[1] D. Avrahami-Zilberbrand and G. A. Kaminka. Keyhole adversarial plan recognition for recognition of suspicious and anomalous behavior. In *Plan, Activity, and Intent Recognition*, pages 87–121. 2014.

[2] N. Basilico and N. Gatti. Automated abstractions for patrolling security games. In *AAAI*, 2011.

[3] N. Basilico, N. Gatti, and F. Amigoni. Leader-follower strategies for robotic patrolling in environments with arbitrary topologies. In *AAMAS*, 2009.

[4] C. M. Bishop. *Pattern recognition and machine learning*. springer, 2006.

[5] A. P. Bradley. The use of the area under the roc curve in the evaluation of machine learning algorithms. *Pattern recognition*, 30(7):1145–1159, 1997.

[6] R. Critchlow, A. Plumptre, M. Driciru, A. Rwetsiba, E. Stokes, C. Tumwesigye, F. Wanyama, and C. Beale. Spatiotemporal trends of illegal activities from ranger-collected data in a ugandan national park. *Conservation Biology*, 2015.

[7] J. S. De Bruin, T. K. Cocx, W. Kosters, J. F. Laros, J. N. Kok, et al. Data mining approaches to criminal career analysis. In *Data Mining, 2006. ICDM'06. Sixth International Conference on*, pages 171–177. IEEE, 2006.

[8] F. Fang, T. H. Nguyen, R. Pickles, W. Y. Lam, G. R. Clements, B. An, A. Singh, M. Tambe, and A. Lemieux. Deploying paws: Field optimization of the protection assistant forwildlife security. In *IAAI*, 2016.

[9] F. Fang, P. Stone, and M. Tambe. When security games go green: Designing defender strategies to prevent poaching and illegal fishing. In *IJCAI*, 2015.

[10] S. Ganzfried and T. Sandholm. Game theory-based opponent modeling in large imperfect-information games. In *The 10th International Conference on Autonomous Agents and Multiagent Systems-Volume 2*, pages 533–540. International Foundation for Autonomous Agents and Multiagent Systems, 2011.

[11] H. HOFER, K. L. CAMPBELL, M. L. EAST, and S. A. HUISH. Modeling the spatial distribution of the economic costs and benefits of illegal game meat hunting in the serengeti. *Natural Resource Modeling*, 13(1):151–177, 2000.

[12] D. Kar, F. Fang, F. D. Fave, N. Sintov, and M. Tambe. A game of thrones: When human behavior models compete in repeated stackelberg security games. In *International Conference on Autonomous Agents and Multiagent Systems (AAMAS 2015)*, 2015.

[13] D. Korzhyk, V. Conitzer, and R. Parr. Complexity of computing optimal stackelberg strategies in security resource allocation games. In *AAAI*, 2010.

[14] J. Letchford and Y. Vorobeychik. Computing randomized security strategies in networked domains. In *AARM*, 2011.

[15] D. I. MacKenzie, J. D. Nichols, G. B. Lachman, S. Droege, J. Andrew Royle, and C. A. Langtimm. Estimating site occupancy rates when detection probabilities are less than one. *Ecology*, 83(8):2248–2255, 2002.

[16] D. McFadden. Conditional logit analysis of qualitative choice behavior. Technical report, 1972.

[17] R. McKelvey and T. Palfrey. Quantal response equilibria for normal form games. *Games and economic behavior*, 10(1):6–38, 1995.

[18] X.-L. Meng and D. B. Rubin. Maximum likelihood estimation via the ecm algorithm: A general framework. *Biometrika*, 80(2):267–278, 1993.

[19] M. Montesh. Rhino poaching: A new form of organised crime1. Technical report, University of South Africa, 2013.

[20] S. V. Nath. Crime pattern detection using data mining. In *Web Intelligence and Intelligent Agent Technology Workshops, 2006. WI-IAT 2006 Workshops. 2006 IEEE/WIC/ACM International Conference on*, pages 41–44. IEEE, 2006.

[21] T. H. Nguyen, F. M. Delle Fave, D. Kar, A. S. Lakshminarayanan, A. Yadav, M. Tambe, N. Agmon, A. J. Plumptre, M. Driciru, F. Wanyama, et al. Making the most of our regrets: Regret-based solutions to handle payoff uncertainty and elicitation in green security games. In *GameSec*, 2015.

[22] T. H. Nguyen, R. Yang, A. Azaria, S. Kraus, and M. Tambe. Analyzing the effectiveness of adversary modeling in security games. In *AAAI*, 2013.

[23] G. Oatley, B. Ewart, and J. Zeleznikow. Decision support systems for police: Lessons from the application of data mining techniques to "soft" forensic evidence. *Artificial Intelligence and Law*, 14(1-2):35–100, 2006.

[24] U. H. C. on Foreign Affairs. Poaching and terrorism: A national security challenge (serial no. 114-25). Washington:US Government Publishing Office, April 2015.

[25] T. Sandholm and S. Singh. Lossy stochastic game abstraction with bounds. In *EC*, pages 880–897. ACM, 2012.

[26] G. Secretariat. Global tiger recovery program implementation plan: 2013-14. *Report, The World Bank, Washington, DC*, 2013.

[27] F. Southey, M. P. Bowling, B. Larson, C. Piccione, N. Burch, D. Billings, and C. Rayner. Bayes' bluff: Opponent modelling in poker. *arXiv preprint arXiv:1207.1411*, 2012.

[28] M. Tambe. *Security and Game Theory: Algorithms, Deployed Systems, Lessons Learned*. Cambridge University Press, 2011.

[29] R. Wilcox. *Applying contemporary statistical techniques*. Academic Press, 2002.

[30] R. Yang, B. Ford, M. Tambe, and A. Lemieux. Adaptive resource allocation for wildlife protection against illegal poachers. In *AAMAS*, 2014.

[31] R. Yang, F. Ordonez, and M. Tambe. Computing optimal strategy against quantal response in security games. AAMAS, 2012.

[32] C. Zhang, A. Sinha, and M. Tambe. Keeping pace with criminals: Designing patrol allocation against adaptive opportunistic criminals. In *AAMAS*, 2015.

Avicaching: A Two Stage Game for Bias Reduction in Citizen Science

Yexiang Xue
Computer Science Dept
Cornell University
yexiang@cs.cornell.edu

Ian Davies, Daniel Fink, Christopher Wood
Cornell Lab of Ornithology
{id99, daniel.fink, chris.wood}@cornell.edu

Carla P. Gomes
Computer Science Dept
Cornell University
gomes@cs.cornell.edu

ABSTRACT

Citizen science projects have been very successful at collecting rich datasets for different applications. However, the data collected by the citizen scientists are often biased, more aligned with the citizens' preferences rather than scientific objectives. We introduce a novel two-stage game for reducing data-bias in citizen science in which the game *organizer*, a citizen-science program, incentivizes the *agents*, the citizen scientists, to visit under-sampled areas. We provide a novel way of encoding this two-stage game as a single optimization problem, cleverly folding (an approximation of) the agents' problems into the organizer's problem. We present several new algorithms to solve this optimization problem as well as a new structural SVM approach to learn the parameters that capture the agents' behaviors, under different incentive schemes. We apply our methodology to *eBird*, a well-established citizen-science program for collecting bird observations, as a game called *Avicaching*. We deployed Avicaching in two New York counties (March 2015), with a great response from the birding community, surpassing the expectations of the eBird organizers and bird-conservation experts. The field results show that the Avicaching incentives are remarkably effective at encouraging the bird watchers to explore under-sampled areas and hence alleviate the eBird's data bias problem.

Keywords

Two-Stage Game, Bilevel Optimization, Structural SVM, Citizen Science

1. INTRODUCTION

Over the past decade, along with the emergence of the *big data* era, the data collection process for scientific discovery has evolved dramatically. One effective way of collecting large datasets is to engage the public through citizen science projects, such as *Zooniverse*, *Cicada Hunt* and *eBird* [24, 42, 35]. The success of these projects relies on the ability to tap into the intrinsic motivations of the volunteers to make participation enjoyable [5]. Thus in order to engage large groups of participants, citizen science projects often have few restrictions, leaving many decisions about where, when, and how to collect data up to the participants. As a result, the data collected by volunteers are often biased, more aligned with their preferences, rather than providing systematic observations across various experimental settings. Moreover, since participants volunteer their effort, personal convenience is an important factor that often determines how data are collected. For spatial data, this means more searches occur in areas close to urban areas and roads (Fig. 1).

Appears in: *Proceedings of the 15th International Conference on Autonomous Agents and Multiagent Systems (AAMAS 2016), J. Thangarajah, K. Tuyls, C. Jonker, S. Marsella (eds.), May 9–13, 2016, Singapore.*

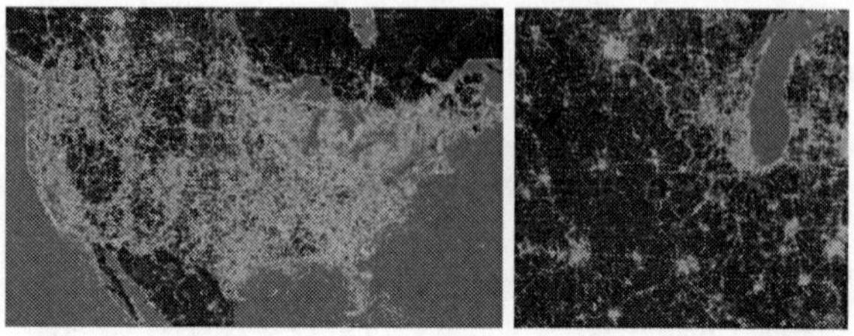

Figure 1: Highly biased distribution of *eBird* observations until 2014. (Left) continental US (Right) Zoom in Midwest US. Submissions coincide with urban areas.

We provide a general methodology to mitigate the data bias problem, as a two-stage game in which the game organizer, e.g., a citizen-science program, provides incentives to the agents, the citizen scientists, to perform more crucial scientific tasks. We apply it to *eBird*, a well-established citizen-science program for collecting bird observations, as a game called *Avicaching*.

Our proposed two-stage game is related to the Principal-Agent framework, originally studied in economics [31], and more recently in computer science [1, 17, 14], and to the Stackelberg games [13, 12, 28, 15], which also involves e.g., a *principal* or a *leader* and *agents* or *followers*. These games have been studied under different assumptions regarding the agents' preferences and computational abilities [18, 8]. In crowdsourcing, there has been related work on mechanisms to improve the crowd performance [29, 23, 21, 22, 34, 26, 37, 7]. Notable works include using incentives to promote exploration activities [16], and steering user participation with badges [3]. [32, 10, 9] discuss the optimal reward allocation to reduce the empirical risk of machine learning models.

In our two-stage game setting, the *agents* are citizen scientists maximizing their intrinsic utilities, as well as the incentives distributed by the game organizer, subject to a budget constraint. The organizer corresponds to an organization with notable influence on the citizen scientists. The *organizer* factors in the reasoning process of the citizen scientists to optimize an incentive scheme. In our setting, the game organizer's goal is to optimize an incentive scheme in order to **induce a uniform data collection process**. Furthermore, the organizer **explicitly models the discrete choice problem of each agent as a knapsack problem.** We refer to this two-stage game as the **Optimal Incentives for Knapsack Agents (OptIKA)** game.

We provide several novel algorithms to solve **OptIKA** and in particular we convert the two-stage game into a single optimization problem by cleverly folding (an approximation of) the agents' problems into the organizer's problem.

We consider **(1) different objectives** for the organizer, corresponding to different measures of data uniformity using *Mixed Integer Programming* and *Mixed Integer Quadratic Programming* formulations. We also consider **(2) different levels of rationality** for the *agents*, which result in different approaches to fold the agents' knapsack problems into the organizer's problem. For the scenario in which the agents have **unbounded rationality**, we developed an **iterative, row generation method**, given the exponential number of constraints induced by agents' knapsack problems. We also consider two scenarios in which the agents have **bounded rationality**: one in which the agents use a **greedy heuristic** and another one based on a **dynamic programming (DP), polynomial time approximation scheme** for the knapsack problem. For **(3) scalability**, we use the Taylor expansion of the L2-norm and develop a novel approach based on the *Alternating Direction Method of Multipliers*. **(4)** We propose **a novel structural SVM** framework to solve the so-called **identification problem**, which learns agents' behaviors under different incentive schemes.

We applied our methodology to *eBird* as a game called **Avicaching, deploying it as a pilot study in two New York counties.** Since the inception in March 2015, **19%** of the *eBird* observations in our pilot counties shifted from traditional locations to *Avicaching* locations with no previous observations. Our field results show that our **Avicaching incentives are remarkably effective at encouraging the bird watchers to explore under-sampled areas and hence it alleviates the data bias problem in *eBird*.** We also showed that **under our Avicaching scheme, agents can cover the area more uniformly**, which leads **to higher performance on a predictive model for bird occurrence** than the no-incentive case, with the same amount of effort devoted. Our methodology is general and can be applied to other citizen science applications as well as similar scenarios, beyond citizen science.

2. PROBLEM FORMULATION

We consider the setting in which citizen scientists are encouraged to conduct *scientific surveys*. For example in *eBird*, bird watchers survey a given area, and record all the interesting species observed in that area. This setting can be generalized to other scientific exploration activities. The general formulation of the two-stage game is:

$$\begin{aligned} \textbf{(Organizer)}\ & \text{maximize}_{\,r} && U_o(v,r), \\ & \text{subject to} && B_o(r), \\ \textbf{(Agents)}\ & \text{maximize}_{\,v} && U_a(v,r), \\ & \text{subject to} && B_a(v), \end{aligned} \tag{1}$$

where r is the external reward that the organizer (e.g., a citizen science program) uses to steer the agents (e.g., citizen scientists), and v are the reactions from the agents, which is the result of optimizing their own utilities. $U_o(v,r)$ and $U_a(v,r)$ are the utility functions of the organizer and agents, respectively, and $B_o(r)$ and $B_a(v)$ are their respective budget constraints.

The Organizer's Objective is to promote a balanced exploration activity, which corresponds to sending people to under-sampled areas. **The pricing problem** is the associated organizer's problem of determining the optimal rewards to induce the desired behavior from the agents, namely sending the agents to undersampled areas. Let $L = \{l_1, l_2, \ldots, l_n\}$ be the set of locations, and $X_{0,i}$ the number of historical visits at location l_i at the beginning of a time period T. Suppose there are m citizen scientists $b_1, b_2, \ldots, b_m$. During time period T, each citizen scientist b_j chooses a set $L_j \subseteq L$ of locations to explore. At the end of time period T, location i received a net amount of visits $V_i = |\{l_i \in L_j : j = 1, \ldots, m\}|$ and its total number Y_i of visits corresponds to $Y_i = X_{0,i} + V_i$. We denote by $\mathbf{Y}$ the column vector $(Y_1, \ldots, Y_n)^T$ and by $\overline{\mathbf{Y}}$ the constant column vector $(\overline{Y}, \ldots, \overline{Y})^T$ where $\overline{Y} = \frac{1}{n}\sum_{i=1}^{n} Y_i$. As the organizer aims to promote a more uniform sampling effort among different locations, this objective can be expressed as the reduction $D_p = \frac{1}{n}||\mathbf{Y} - \overline{\mathbf{Y}}||_p^p$ of the difference between $\mathbf{Y}$ and $\overline{\mathbf{Y}}$. Given this definition, D_1 corresponds to the *mean absolute deviation*, while D_2 corresponds to the *sample variance*. Other objectives could be used, e.g., maximizing the entropy of the sample distribution in order to minimize the distance to a uniform distribution.[1] (See section 3.1.)

The Agents' Model – Each agent is maximizing her own utility subject to her budget constraint. Namely, if a citizen scientist b_j chooses to visit location l_i, she will receive an intrinsic utility $u_{j,i}$, at a cost $c_{j,i}$. We assume that agent b_j has a given budget C_j, so the total cost of all the places explored by b_j cannot exceed C_j.

To incentivize citizen scientists to visit undersampled areas, the organizer introduces an extra incentive r_i for each location l_i. Every citizen scientist visiting location l_i receives an extra reward r_i, besides their internal utility $u_{j,i}$. For the sake of fairness, we require that these rewards only vary across locations and are the same for all agents. In addition, to make it easier to communicate with the agents, we assume that all rewards come from a fixed discrete set: $r_i \in R = \{r_1^*, \ldots, r_k^*\}$. Taking into account intrinsic utilities, external rewards and the budget constraint, the citizen scientist b_j's planning problem becomes:

$$\begin{aligned} \underset{L_j \subseteq L}{\text{maximize}} \quad & \sum_{l_i \in L_j} u_{j,i} + w_r \cdot r_i, \\ \text{subject to} \quad & \sum_{l_i \in L_j} c_{j,i} \le C_j. \end{aligned} \tag{2}$$

In this formulation, $u_{j,i}$ is the intrinsic utility, r_i is the external reward, w_r is the relative importance ratio between the intrinsic utilities and the external rewards, $c_{j,i}$ is the cost, and C_j is the total budget for an agent. Overall, combining the organizer's goal and the agents' models, the pricing

[1]Note: uncertainty measures, often used in active learning [30], are typically tied to a particular predictive model and therefore do not serve our goal of meeting multiple scientific objectives with balanced sampling. We cannot commit to improving one particular predictive model.

Organizer's Objective	Agents' Rationality: Full	Bounded: DP	Bounded: Greedy	
L1-Norm	OptIKA-L1-Full	OptIKA-L1-DP	OptIKA-L1-Greedy	MIP
L2-Norm	OptIKA-L2-Full	OptIKA-L2-DP	OptIKA-L2-Greedy	MIQP
L2-Taylor	OptIKA-L2T-Full	OptIKA-L2T-DP	OptIKA-L2T-Greedy	MIP/ADMM
	Iterative Row Gen	*Single* Constraint Programming instance		

Figure 2: Two stage game scenarios and corresponding algorithms described in Section 3.1.

problem of the **Opt**imal **I**ncentives for **K**napsack **A**gents (**OptIKA**) game is:

$$
\begin{aligned}
\textbf{(OptIKA)} \quad & \underset{r}{\text{minimize}} \quad \frac{1}{n}||\mathbf{Y} - \overline{\mathbf{Y}}||_p^p \\
& \text{subject to} \quad L_j = \underset{L_j \subseteq L}{\text{argmax}} \sum_{i \in L_j} u_{j,i} + w_r \cdot r_i, \\
& \qquad \sum_{l_i \in L_j} c_{j,i} \le C_j, \; j \in \{1, \dots, m\}, \\
& \qquad r_i \in R, \; i \in \{1, \dots, n\}.
\end{aligned} \tag{3}
$$

The Identification Problem learns the parameters capturing agents' behavior, by fitting a model to predict the agents' preferences under various incentive schemes. The identification problem is related to Inverse Reinforcement Learning [27, 36, 20], in which one also assumes that the agents are optimizing for long-term rewards (Section 3.2).

3. ALGORITHMS

3.1 Pricing Problem

We developed a variety of algorithms to solve the pricing problem, capturing different organizer's objectives and agents' computational capabilities, as summarized in Fig. 2. First, the complexity of the **OptIKA** problem depends on the uniformity measure of the organizer. The **OptIKA** problem can be solved using a Mixed Integer Programming (MIP) formulation when minimizing the mean absolute deviation (L_1-norm), whereas it becomes a Mixed Integer Quadratic Program (MIQP) when minimizing the sample variance (L_2-norm). Second, the computational capability of the agents impacts how one can fold the constraints of the agents into the organizer's problem. If the agent solves her knapsack problem optimally with *full* rationality, it yields an exponential number of constraints to be handled by the organizer, thus raising scalability issues and requiring an iterative approach (see *Row Generation* encoding). We also consider the case in which agents have *bounded* rationality, whether the agent solves her knapsack using a *dynamic programming*-based approach or in a *greedy* fashion. In this scenario, the polynomial number of linear constraints to consider can be encoded in a single Constraint Programming instance. Furthermore, in order to scale up with the number of agents, we improve our approach with a decomposition method that decouples the agents' optimization problems (see *ADMM*).

3.1.1 Modeling the Organizer's Objective

A first measure of sample uniformity is the mean absolute deviation D_1, which allows us to formulate the objective function as a MIP. For every location l_i, introduce a variable Z_i such that $Z_i \ge |Y_i - \overline{Y}|$. Overall, the organizer's objective function can be captured as: min $\sum_{i=1}^{n} Z_i$, s.t. $Z_i \ge Y_i - \overline{Y}, Z_i \ge \overline{Y} - Y_i$. We refer to this formulation as `OptIKA-L1`. A second formulation (`OptIKA-L2`) uses the L2-norm sample variance (D_2). In this case, the organizer's objective is quadratic, and hence the entire problem becomes a Mixed Integer Quadratic Program (MIQP). As a third option, we model the organizer's objective using the Taylor approximation of the sample variance (`OptIKA-L2T`), in which case the organizer's problem translates into minimizing $S = \sum_{i=1}^{n} s_i V_i$, where $s_i = \frac{2}{n}\left(X_{0,i} - \overline{X_0}\right)$. Notice that the Stackelberg pricing games studied in [17] is a special case of **OptIKA** in this form, therefore **OptIKA** is APX-hard. We leave the details in the supplementary materials, anonymously online at [40].

Algorithm 1: Row Generation `OptIKA-LX-Full`

$\Phi \leftarrow \emptyset$;
OptimalFlag $\leftarrow$ *False*;
while *OptimalFlag* $=$ *False* **do**
  $(\mathbf{r}_\dagger, \mathbf{v}_{1\dagger}, \dots, \mathbf{v}_{m\dagger}) \leftarrow$ `OptIKA-LX-Full-Relax`(Φ);
  OptimalFlag $\leftarrow$ *True*;
  for $j \in \{1, \dots, m\}$ **do**
    $\mathbf{v}_j^* \leftarrow \text{argmax } (\mathbf{u}_j + w_r \cdot \mathbf{r}_\dagger)^T \cdot \mathbf{v}_j$,
      subject to $\mathbf{c}_j^T \cdot \mathbf{v}_j \le C_j$;
    if $(\mathbf{u}_j + w_r \cdot \mathbf{r}_\dagger)^T \cdot \mathbf{v}_j^* > (\mathbf{u}_j + w_r \cdot \mathbf{r}_\dagger)^T \cdot \mathbf{v}_{j\dagger}$ **then**
      $\Phi \leftarrow \Phi \cup \{ (\mathbf{u}_j + w_r \cdot \mathbf{r})^T \cdot \mathbf{v}_j \ge (\mathbf{u}_j + w_r \cdot \mathbf{r})^T \cdot \mathbf{v}_j^* \}$;
      OptimalFlag $=$ *False*;
    end
  end
end

3.1.2 Modeling the Knapsack Agents

Row Generation Encoding We first present the algorithm `OptIKA-LX-Full` (where `X` is either `1`, `2` or `2T`) in which we assume the agents have full rationality, and their reasoning process is captured by an iterative row generation method. This algorithm can be combined with any of the three organizer's objectives. Let $v_{j,i}$ be a binary variable, which is 1 if and only if $l_i \in L_j$. Using vector representations, we set $\mathbf{v}_j = (v_{j,1}, \dots, v_{j,n})^T$, $\mathbf{u}_j = (u_{j,1}, \dots, u_{j,n})^T$, $\mathbf{c}_j = (c_{j,1}, c_{j,2}, \dots, c_{j,n})^T$, $\mathbf{r} = (r_1, \dots, r_n)^T$, $\mathbf{s} = (s_1, \dots, s_n)^T$.

The key to solve a bilevel optimization like `OptIKA` is to find clever ways to fold the nested optimization (the agents' problem) as constraints to the global problem. Here we show that the agents' optimization problem can be transformed into an exponential number of constraints of the type:

$$(\mathbf{u}_j + w_r \cdot \mathbf{r})^T \cdot \mathbf{v}_j \ge (\mathbf{u}_j + w_r \cdot \mathbf{r})^T \cdot \mathbf{v}_j', \tag{4}$$

in which $\mathbf{v}_j'$ ranges over all vectors in $\{0,1\}^n$, which satisfies $\mathbf{c}_j^T \cdot \mathbf{v}_j' \le C_j$, for all $j \in \{1, \dots, m\}$. The intuitive meaning of Inequality 4 is that the location set that the agent chooses is better in terms of utility values than any other location set within the budget constraint. We use Φ to denote a set of constraints of this form, and we write $\{\mathbf{v}_1, \dots, \mathbf{v}_m\} \in \Phi$ to mean that $\mathbf{v}_1, \dots, \mathbf{v}_m$ satisfy all the constraints in Φ.

We cannot add all the constraints upfront, as there are exponentially many of them. Instead, we add them in an iterative manner until proving optimality. The row generation scheme starts by solving a relaxation of the original pricing problem: OptIKA-LX-Full-Relax(Φ), with a small initial constraint set Φ of constraints as shown in Inequality 4:

$$\texttt{OptIKA-LX-Full-Relax}(\Phi) : \text{Min: (organizer's obj) } D_p \text{ or } S,$$
$$\text{s. t. } \mathbf{c}_j^T \cdot \mathbf{v}_j \le C_j,\ j \in \{1,..,m\},$$
$$\{\mathbf{v}_1,\ldots,\mathbf{v}_m\} \in \Phi,$$
$$r_i \in R,\ i \in \{1,\ldots,n\}.$$

Then the algorithm seeks to enlarge the set Φ with new constraints of the form in Inequality 4 to further improve the objective function. This step is done by solving the Knapsack problem for each agent. If the current response of one agent b_j is not the optimal response to the Knapsack problem, then it implies that at least one constraint of the form shown in Inequality 4 is violated. We then add in the constraint into Φ and solve again. The whole algorithm iterates until no new constraints can be added to Φ, at which point we can prove optimality. The algorithm is shown as Algorithm 1.

There is one last subtlety: the Inequality (4) is not a linear one, because both $\mathbf{r}$ and $\mathbf{v}_j$ are variables. To linearize it, we bring in an extra variable $ur_{j,i}$, and we add constraints to ensure that $ur_{j,i}$ is always equal to $v_{j,i} \cdot (u_{j,i} + w_r \cdot r_i)$. The constraints needed are:

$$ur_{j,i} \ge 0,$$
$$ur_{j,i} \le u_{j,i} + w_r \cdot r_i,$$
$$v_{j,i} = 0 \Rightarrow ur_{j,i} \le 0, \tag{5}$$

In this case, Inequality (4) can be rewritten as $\sum_{i=1}^{n} ur_{j,i} \ge (\mathbf{u}_j + w_r \cdot \mathbf{r})^T \cdot \mathbf{v}'_j$. Eq. (5) is an indicator constraint, which can be linearized with the big-M formulation [11].

Dynamic Programming Encoding OptIKA-LX-DP is the best performing encoding, motivated by the polynomial time approximation scheme to solve the Knapsack Problem. It encodes the entire problem into a single MIP, rather than a series of iterative MIPs as in the row generation approach. It reflects the bounded rationality of agents, as it sacrifices a little precision when modeling the cost under a bounded memory size.

In the Knapsack Problem for citizen scientist b_j, we first discretize the budget C_j into N_b equal-sized units. Let $\mathcal{D}_j = \{kC_j/N_b | k = 0,\ldots,N_b\}$ be the set of all discrete units. We further round the cost $c_{j,i}$ to its nearest discrete unit from above in $\mathcal{D}_j$. We introduce extra variables $opt(j,i,c)$, for $i \in \{1,\ldots,n\}$ and $c \in \mathcal{D}_j$, to denote the optimal utility for agent b_j if we only consider the first i locations $l_1,\ldots,l_i$ and the total cost cannot exceed c. Consider the Dynamic Programming recursion to solve the Knapsack Problem:

$$opt(j,i,c) = \begin{cases} \max\{opt(j,i-1,c-c_{j,i}) + u_{j,i} + w_r \cdot r_i, & \\ \quad opt(j,i-1,c)\}, & \text{if } i > 1, c \ge c_{j,i}, \\ opt(j,i-1,c), & \text{if } i > 1, c < c_{j,i}, \\ 0, & \text{otherwise.} \end{cases} \tag{6}$$

The key insight of OptIKA-LX-DP is that this recursion can be translated as a set of linear inequalities. As an example, when $i > 1$ and $c \ge c_{j,i}$, the recursion can be encoded as,

$$opt(j,i,c) \ge opt(j,i-1,c), \tag{7}$$
$$opt(j,i,c) \ge opt(j,i-1,c-c_{j,i}) + u_{j,i} + w_r \cdot r_i. \tag{8}$$

There are similar inequalities to capture other cases in Equation 6. Denote $u_{\mathcal{D}_j}^{knap}$ as the optimal utility for solving the knapsack problem for citizen scientist b_j. We must have $u_{\mathcal{D}_j}^{knap} \ge opt(j,n,c)$, for all $c \in \mathcal{D}_j$. In summary, agent b_j's knapsack problem can be encoded as:

$$(\mathbf{u}_j + w_r \cdot \mathbf{r})^T \cdot \mathbf{v}_j \ge u_{\mathcal{D}_j}^{knap}, \tag{9}$$
$$\mathbf{c}_j^T \cdot \mathbf{v}_j \le C_j \text{ and } u_{\mathcal{D}_j}^{knap} \ge opt(j,n,c),\ \forall c \in \mathcal{D}_j,$$

Here, $opt(j,n,c)$ is encoded by linear inequalities similar to the ones in Equations 7 and 8. Finally, we need to use a big-M notation to linearize the inequality in Equation 9.

If we bound N_b, this encoding introduces $O(mnN_b)$ extra variables and $O(mnN_b)$ extra constraints. Notice that this encoding can be combined with the row generation approach. We can first solve the problem under limited precision using this dynamic programming encoding, then further refine the solution using the row generation approach.

Greedy Formulation OptIKA-LX-Greedy assumes each agent follows a simple greedy heuristic: first, rank all the locations based on their efficiency, i.e. the ratio between the utility (including the external reward) and the cost; then greedily select locations with the highest efficiency, without exceeding the budget limit. This simple heuristic is a 2-approximation for the Knapsack problem, and works well in practice. Define $\psi_{j,i} = (w_r \cdot r_i + u_{j,i})/c_{j,i}$ as the efficiency of location l_i according to agent b_j. Our formulation is based on the following theorem:

THEOREM 1. *Assume for all $i \neq i'$, $\psi_{j,i} \neq \psi_{j,i'}$[2], then $\{v_{j,1},\ldots,v_{j,n}\}$ is a decision made by the greedy algorithm if and only if the following two constraints hold:*

$$v_{j,i} = 0 \Rightarrow c_{j,i} > C_j - \sum_{i' \neq i} v_{j,i'} c_{j,i'} \mathbf{1}(\psi_{j,i'} \ge \psi_{j,i}), \tag{10}$$

for all $i \in 1,..,n$, and $\sum_{i=1}^{n} c_{j,i} \cdot v_{j,i} \le C_j$.

In this theorem, $\mathbf{1}(\psi_{j,i'} \ge \psi_{j,i})$ is an indicator variable, which is one if and only if $\psi_{j,i'} \ge \psi_{j,i}$. Theorem 1 translates the greedy process into a set of constraints. The intuitive meaning of inequality (10) says that if location l_i is not in the knapsack ($v_{j,i} = 0$), then it must be the case that some locations with higher efficiency than l_i has already taken up its space. Unfortunately, inequality (10) is not linear. We can again use big-M notation to transform the above constraint into a set of linear constraints.

3.1.3 Scaling to Many Agents with ADMM

In order to model a large number of citizen scientists, the pricing algorithm needs to be able to scale. To that end, we develop OptIKA-L2T-ADMM, harnessing a variant of the Alternating Direction Method of Multipliers [6, 25]. This approach decomposes the global problem of designing the rewards for all agents to a series of subproblems, each of which designs the optimal rewards for one agent. Then the algorithm matches the local rewards for all agents using an iterative approach. To the best of our knowledge, this is the first time that a decomposition based method is introduced to solve the optimal pricing problem. Because ADMM requires a decomposable objective function, this variant only applies to the third organizer's objective function that uses the Taylor expansion (OptIKA-L2T) as described in the supplementary material [40]. We introduce a local copy of the

[2] In practice, efficiencies almost always differ when they are learned from data.

reward vector for each agent b_j: $\mathbf{r}_j = (r_{j,1}, \ldots, r_{j,n})^T$, and we rewrite the global problem as:

$$\min \quad S = \sum_{j=1}^{m} \mathbf{s}^T \cdot \mathbf{v}_j,$$
$$\text{s.t.} \quad (\mathbf{r}_j, \mathbf{v}_j) \in \Sigma_j, \quad \mathbf{r}_j = \mathbf{r}, \quad \forall j \in \{1, \ldots, m\}.$$

In this formulation, we use $(\mathbf{r}_j, \mathbf{v}_j) \in \Sigma_j$ to mean that $\mathbf{v}_j$ is optimal for agent b_j given rewards $\mathbf{r}_j$:

$$(\mathbf{r}_j, \mathbf{v}_j) \in \Sigma_j \iff r_{j,i} \in R, \; \forall i \in \{1, \ldots, n\},$$
$$\mathbf{v}_j = \text{argmax } (\mathbf{u}_j + w_r \cdot \mathbf{r}_j)^T \cdot \mathbf{v}_j,$$
$$\text{s.t. } \mathbf{c}_j^T \cdot \mathbf{v}_j \leq C_j.$$

Our variant of the ADMM can be derived via the Augmented Lagrangian:

$$L_\rho = \sum_{j=1}^{m} \mathbf{s}^T \cdot \mathbf{v}_j + \boldsymbol{\lambda}_j^T \cdot (\mathbf{r}_j - \mathbf{r}) + (\rho/2)||\mathbf{r}_j - \mathbf{r}||_2^2.$$

in which $\boldsymbol{\lambda}_j$'s are Lagrangian multipliers, $\rho > 0$ is the penalty parameter. Our variant starts with an initial $\mathbf{r}_j^0$, $\mathbf{v}_j^0$, $\boldsymbol{\lambda}_j^0$ and $\mathbf{r}^0$, and updates the Lagrangian in an alternating manner for T steps. At the k-th step, $(\mathbf{v}_j^{k+1}, \mathbf{r}_j^{k+1})$ and $\mathbf{r}^{k+1}$ are obtained by minimizing $L_\rho(.)$ w.r.t. $(\mathbf{v}_j, \mathbf{r}_j)$ and $\mathbf{r}$, respectively. $\boldsymbol{\lambda}_j^{k+1}$ is updated by taking a subgradient step in the dual. The updates of `OptIKA-L2T-ADMM` are:

$$(\mathbf{v}_j^{k+1}, \mathbf{r}_j^{k+1}) = \text{argmin}_{(\mathbf{v}_j, \mathbf{r}_j) \in \Sigma_j} \mathbf{s}^T \mathbf{v}_j + \boldsymbol{\lambda}_j^{kT} (\mathbf{r}_j - \mathbf{r}^k) + (\rho/2)||\mathbf{r}_j - \mathbf{r}^k||_2^2, \quad (11)$$

$$\mathbf{r}^{k+1} = \frac{1}{m} \sum_{j=1}^{m} (1/\rho) \boldsymbol{\lambda}_j^k + \mathbf{r}_j^{k+1}, \quad (12)$$

$$\boldsymbol{\lambda}_j^{k+1} = \boldsymbol{\lambda}_j^k + \rho(\mathbf{r}_j^{k+1} - \mathbf{r}^{k+1}). \quad (13)$$

The difference of our variant with classical ADMM is that we impose extra constraints $(\mathbf{v}_j, \mathbf{r}_j) \in \Sigma_j$ in the first optimization step in Equation 11. This makes it computationally hard. In practice, we solve it via MIP, using the three encodings as described above.[3] However, the benefit of this algorithm is that the optimization problem for agent b_j is *localized*: it only involves variables and constraints for agent b_j herself, which represents a significant improvement over the previous algorithms, in which we need to consider all m agents all together in one encoding.

ADMM allows us to derive a series of interesting properties about the obtained solution. The Lagrange dual function $g(\{\boldsymbol{\lambda}_j\})$ is defined as:

$$g(\{\boldsymbol{\lambda}_j\}) = \inf_{\mathbf{r}, \mathbf{v}_j, \mathbf{r}_j : (\mathbf{v}_j, \mathbf{r}_j) \in \Sigma_j} L_\rho (\{\mathbf{r}_j\}, \{\mathbf{v}_j\}, \{\boldsymbol{\lambda}_j\}, \mathbf{r}).$$

We can view `OptIKA-L2T-ADMM` as an alternating direction descend algorithm trying to find the optimum of the optimization problem $max_{\{\boldsymbol{\lambda}_j\}} \; g(\{\boldsymbol{\lambda}_j\})$. The proofs of the following theorems are left to the supplementary materials [40].

THEOREM 2. *(Weak Duality) The optimal objective value to the problem* $\max_{\{\boldsymbol{\lambda}_j\}} \; g(\{\boldsymbol{\lambda}_j\})$ *is a lower bound on the optimal value of the global problem (**OptIKA**).*

THEOREM 3. $g(\{\boldsymbol{\lambda}_j\})$ *is concave for* $\{\boldsymbol{\lambda}_j | j = 1 \ldots m\}$.

THEOREM 4. *If* `OptIKA-L2T-ADMM` *converges, then* $\mathbf{r}_1, .., \mathbf{r}_m$ *and* $\mathbf{r}$ *all converge to the same vector.*

[3]In the case of `OptIKA-L2T-DP` (or `greedy`), Σ_j is then a relaxed constraint set, which only has constraints specified by the dynamic programming (or greedy) encoding. We use a big-M notation to handle the quadratic term $||\mathbf{r}_j - \mathbf{r}^k||_2^2$.

3.2 Identification Problem

In practice, parameters governing agents' preferences, such as $\mathbf{u}_j$, w_r, are unknown to us. The identification problem therefore is to learn these parameters by observing agents' reactions under different reward schemes. In our setting, we use road distance as cost $c_{j,i}$ (which is the main factor for accessibility) and we learn each agent's budget C_j from the historical mean. The variables left to estimate are the intrinsic utilities $u_{j,i}$ and the elasticity of external rewards w_r. We further assume that the intrinsic utility $u_{j,i}$ is parameterized by a set of features: $u_{j,i} = \mathbf{w}_u^T \cdot \mathbf{f}_{j,i}$, in which $\mathbf{f}_{j,i}$ includes both personal features related to agent b_j and environmental features related to location i. We assume agents are rational, therefore, their choices should always maximize the overall utility. In other words, suppose one agent chooses location set L_j, then $\sum_{i \in L_j} \mathbf{w}_u^T \cdot \mathbf{f}_{j,i} + w_r \cdot r_i \geq \sum_{i \in L'} \mathbf{w}_u^T \cdot \mathbf{f}_{j,i} + w_r \cdot r_i$, holds for any other set of locations L', when the total distance to reach all locations in L' is within the budget. The identification problem then corresponds to finding $(\mathbf{w}_u, w_r)$ to satisfy all inequalities of this type. Because of the trivial solution $\mathbf{w}_u = \mathbf{0}$, $w_r = 0$, we aim to maximize the margin:

$$\text{Min } ||\mathbf{w}_u||^2 + w_r^2,$$
$$\text{s.t. } \sum_{i \in L_j} \mathbf{w}_u^T \cdot \mathbf{f}_{j,i} + w_r \cdot r_i \geq \sum_{i \in L'} \mathbf{w}_u^T \cdot \mathbf{f}_{j,i} + w_r \cdot r_i + \Phi(L_j, L'), \quad \forall L' : \sum_{i \in L'} c_{j,i} \leq C_j. \quad (14)$$

Here $\Phi(L_j, L')$ is a loss function, which applies different levels of penalties to location set L', depending on how similar L' and L_j are. We choose $\Phi(L_j, L') = |L_j \setminus L'| + |L' \setminus L_j|$ in the experiment. In practice, not all constraints shown in Equation 14 can be satisfied. Therefore, we introduce linear slack variables, and the whole identification problem becomes:

$$\text{Min } ||\mathbf{w}_u||^2 + w_r^2 + C \sum_{j=1}^{m} \xi_j,$$
$$\text{s.t. } \sum_{i \in L_j} \mathbf{w}_u^T \cdot \mathbf{f}_{j,i} + w_r \cdot r_i \geq \sum_{i \in L'} \mathbf{w}_u^T \cdot \mathbf{f}_{j,i} + w_r \cdot r_i + \Phi(L_j, L') - \xi_j, \quad \forall L' : \sum_{i \in L'} c_{j,i} \leq C_j. \quad (15)$$

This is a novel application of structural SVM [39]. As another contribution, we developed a modified delayed constraint generation approach to solve the optimization problem as shown in Equation 15, which involves solving knapsack-type problems for both the prediction and the separation problem within the structural SVM.

4. EXPERIMENTS

4.1 Algorithm Performance

We first compare algorithms assuming different levels of rationalities for the organizer and agents, on synthetically generated benchmarks, in which the initial number of visits $X_{0,i}$ is drawn from a geometric distribution in order to introduce some spatial bias, and other variables are drawn from uniform distributions. All the experiments are run using IBM CPLEX 12.6, on machines with a 12-core Intel x5690 3.46GHz CPU, and 48GB of memory. We implement the distributed version of the `ADMM`-based algorithms with 12 cores, in which each agent problem is allocated to one core.

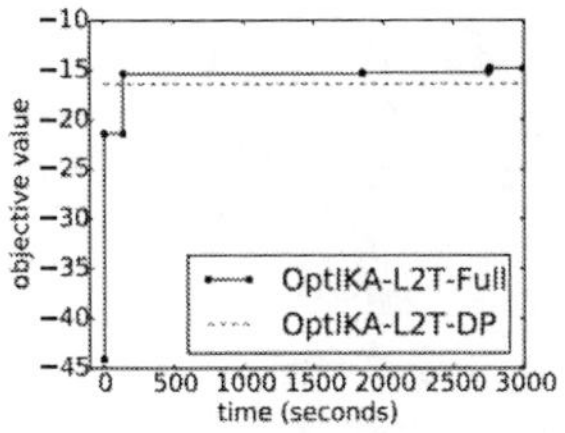

Figure 3: Comparison between `OptIKA-L2T-Full` and `OptIKA-L2T-DP`. (blue) Improvement of the objective function for `OptIKA-L2T-Full` over time. (red) Approximate solution value found by `OptIKA-L2T-DP` from solving a single MIP (very close to optimal, and much faster).

Method	*Red.*	δr
`OptIKA-L2-Full`	44%	0
`OptIKA-L2-DP(50)`	41%	1.36
`OptIKA-L2-DP(100)`	42%	1.13
`OptIKA-L2-Greedy`	41%	1.30

Method	δr
`OptIKA-L2-Full`	0
`OptIKA-L1-Full`	1.20
`OptIKA-L2T-Full`	0.74

Table 1: (Left) Comparison of different agents' rationality level. *Red.* is the L2-norm reduction w.r.t. the non-incentive case, while δr is the average hamming distance of the reward vector w.r.t. the *Full*-rational case. (Right) Comparison of different organizer's objectives, where δr is the average hamming dist. of the reward vector w.r.t. the L2 case.

Comparing Organizer's Objectives & Agents' Rationality Levels: We test our algorithms with 300 synthetic benchmarks. We fix the organizer's goal (L2-norm), and consider the case where agents are planning with different levels of rationality. The left panel of Table 1 reports the reduction in terms of the organizer's objective, and the mean hamming distance of the reward vectors obtained (i.e. the total number of locations in which the two reward vectors differ). Regarding the solution quality, the performance of the different approaches is similar in terms of the reduction in $L2$ and, while these approaches recommend 5 locations with positive rewards in the median case, the hamming distance between the reward vectors is barely more than 1. This suggests that the different models for the agents yield very similar results.

On the other hand, they largely differ in terms of computational complexity. When assuming full rationality of the agents, the row generation approach needs to solve multiple CPLEX instances iteratively. Fig. 3 depicts the running time for `OptIKA-L2T-Full` for one instance, compared with `OptIKA-L2T-DP`. As we can see, it takes the row generation algorithm a very long time to prove optimality, while `OptIKA-L2T-DP` finds a solution, close to optimal, and it is much faster. For a set of instances with 10 locations and up to 10 agents, the median completion time for the `Full` case is $1,251$ seconds, while it corresponds to 80, 93 and 38 seconds for the single MIP in the `DP` case with $N_b = 50$, $N_b = 100$ and in the `Greedy` case, respectively.

Second, we study the impact of choosing different organizer's objectives. As shown in the right panel of Table 1, the difference in terms of the solution quality is again very small. However, the running times vary significantly. The median completion times are $1,251$, 11 and 10 seconds for `L2`, `L1` and `L2T` objectives, respectively.

Convergence of `ADMM`: In order to measure how fast `OptIKA-ADMM-L2T-DP` converges, we first run `OptIKA-ADMM-L2T-DP` for a set of small benchmarks with 20 or 30 agents and 20 locations. Although `OptIKA-ADMM-L2T-DP` works for problems of much larger scale, we still experiment with small benchmarks in order to compare it with non-decomposition based methods. In this experiment, the ADMM algorithm allocates one subproblem per agent. Because the main goal is to examine the decomposition method, each subproblem is solved by an `OptIKA-L2T-DP` module, and we compare the result with another `OptIKA-L2T-DP` which considers all agents at once. The two `OptIKA-L2T-DP` algorithms share a common discretization. The ρ for `OptIKA-ADMM-L2T-DP` is selected to be 1.

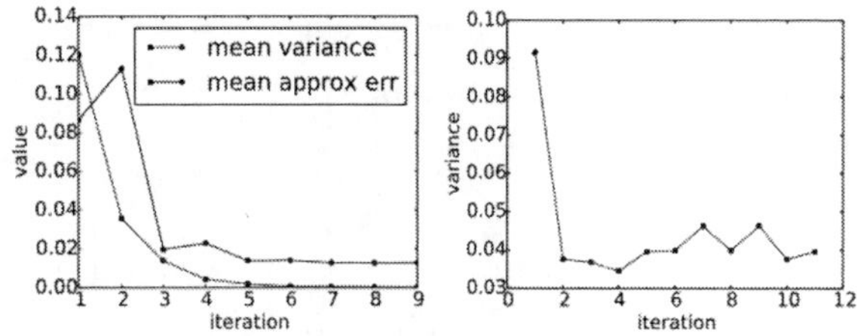

Figure 4: (Left) The mean variance and the relative error of `OptIKA-ADMM-L2T-DP` vs. iteration on small instances. (Right) Mean variance vs. iteration on a real *eBird* instance with 3,000 observers. ADMM converges very quickly.

Metric	SVM-struct	#Species	Popularity
Percentage Loss	**3.9%**	10.6%	8.2%
Utility Percentile	**2.3%**	46.0%	20.3%
Environmental Diff	**2.0**	5.9	4.9

Table 2: The Structural SVM model outperforms two other models on identifying people's behavior (#Species: model based on estimated species num; Popularity: model based on location popularity).

The blue line (top curve) in the left plot of Fig. 4 shows the relative error in the objective function as a function of the iteration number. The relative error is defined as $|S_{dp} - S_{admm}|/|S_{dp}|$, in which S_{dp} and S_{admm} are the objective values found by `OptIKA-L2T-DP` and `OptIKA-ADMM-L2T-DP`, respectively. The mean relative error is averaged among all benchmarks. As we can see, the error quickly drops from 10% to about 2% in only 3 iterations. At the same time, the red line shows how quickly the local copies $\mathbf{r}_j$ converge towards a common $\mathbf{r}$. For one benchmark, the variance is defined as: $\frac{1}{nm}\sum_{j=1}^{m} ||\bar{\mathbf{r}} - \mathbf{r}_j||^2$, in which $\bar{\mathbf{r}}$ is the mean of $\mathbf{r}_1, \dots, \mathbf{r}_m$. The mean variance is taken among all benchmarks. As we can see, the variance drops to close to zero after 3 iterations.

Next we show the performance of `OptIKA-ADMM-L2T-DP` on an instance with 63 locations and 3,000 agents, which cannot be solved by non-decomposition methods at all. The agents' behavior parameters come from real *eBird* data. We would like to emphasize that $3,000$ is enough for real use, since there are in total $2,626$ bird observers in New York State who submitted 3 or more observations in the past 10 years. The right plot of Fig. 4 shows the mean variance w.r.t. different iterations. Again we see that the local copies $\mathbf{r}_j$ almost converge to a common $\mathbf{r}$ in a few iterations.

4.2 Avicaching in eBird

eBird is a well-established citizen-science program for collecting bird observations. In its first years of existence, *eBird* mainly focused on appealing to birders to help address sci-

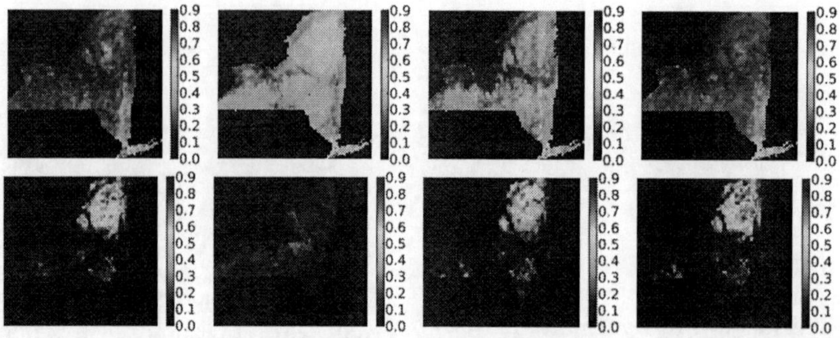

Figure 6: Heatmaps for the prediction of the White-throated Sparrow. (Upper 4 figures) Models for April. (Lower 4 figures) Models for July. A model trained on small, only 5% of the original data, but spatially uniform dataset (*Grid*, 2 in the leftmost column) has comparable accuracy with a model trained on the whole, big dataset that experts consider close to the ground truth (*Complete*, 2 in rightmost column), while other biased datasets have lower accuracy (*Urban*, 2nd column, *Random Subsample*, 3rd column).

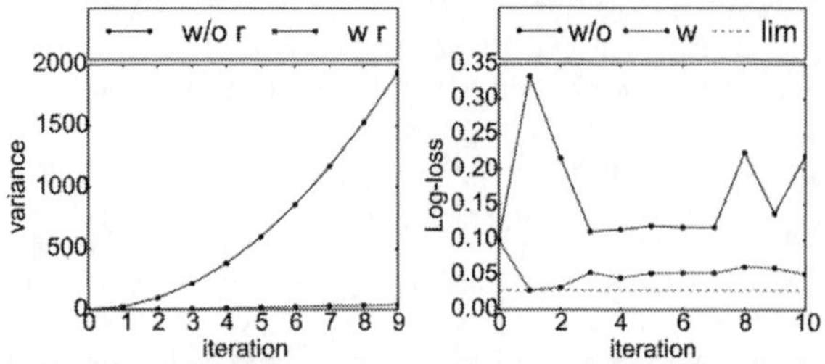

Figure 5: (Left) The change of spatial variance with and without incentives in the simulation study. (Right) The change of Log-loss to predict the occurrence of Horned Lark (with and without incentives). Dashed line is the performance limit.

Year	norm D_2
2015	**0.010**
2014	0.016
2013	0.018

Treatment	norm D_2
OptIKA	**0.015**
B1: Inv-correlate #visits	0.021
B2: Uniform-in-Avicache	0.017
Manual (Expert's)	0.020

Table 3: (Left) Visits are more uniform (in normalized D_2) from April to August, 2015, when *Avicaching* is introduced, compared to previous years. (Right) Visits are more uniform under rewards designed by OptIKA against baseline B1 which assigns rewards inversely correlates to the number of visits to locations, B2 which assigns uniform rewards to all Avicaching locations, zero to others, and manually designed rewards (average over weeks of each treatment) in summer 2015.

ence objectives. The participation rates were disappointing. After 3 years, in order to make participation more fun and engaging, in the spirit of "friendly competition" and "cooperation", *eBird* started providing tools to allow birders to track and rank their submissions (e.g., leaderboards by region, number of species, and number of checklists). This approach resulted in an exponential increase of submissions [35]. Nevertheless, like most citizen-science programs, *eBird* suffers from sampling bias. Birders tend to visit locations aligned with their preferences, leading to gaps in remote areas and areas perceived as uninteresting, as shown in Fig. 1.

In order to address this data bias, we gamified our methodology via a web-based application called ***Avicaching***, explaining to birders that the goal of *Avicaching* is to "increase eBird data density in habitats that are generally underrepresented by normal eBirding". We deployed *Avicaching*

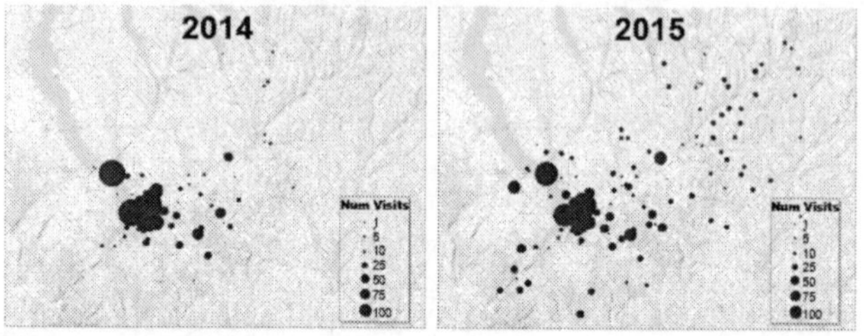

Figure 7: The number of eBird submissions in Tompkins and Cortland County in New York State. The circle sizes represent the number of submissions in each location. (Left) from Mar 28 to Oct 31, 2014 before *Avicaching*. (Right) from Mar 28 to Oct 31, 2015 when *Avicaching* is in the field. 19% effort is shifted to undersampled *Avicaching* locations.

as a pilot study in Tompkins and Cortland counties, NY, starting in March 2015. Tompkins is known for a high participation rate for *eBird*, while surprisingly, Cortland, a county adjacent to Tompkins, receives much fewer observations. We identified a set of locations with no prior observations and defined them as *Avicache* locations: bird watchers receive extra *avicache* points for every checklist submitted in those locations. The locations were selected around undercovered regions, emphasizing on important yet undersampled land types. We also ensure that all locations are publicly accessible. *Avicache* points have intrinsic values to bird watchers, because these points mark their contribution to science. In addition, participants have a chance to win a pair of binoculars from a lottery drawn based on their *avicache* points.

Pricing and Agents' Model We update the *Avicaching* points every week. In the first few weeks, the allocation of points is manually assigned, based only on the number of previous visits to locations. This phase is designed to collect data to fit participants' behavior model. After the initial phase, the points are assigned by the pricing algorithm (`OptIKA-L1-DP`). We fit the agents' model using data from the two counties in 2015 (with Avicaching rewards), as well as data from the same season in 2013 and 2014 (without rewards). The results of the structural model are shown in Table 2, in which we predict the location set that people will visit per week. We randomly split all the data into a 90% training set and a 10% test set. The scores shown in the table are evaluated on the separate test set. The first measure is the the percentage loss: $\frac{1}{n}(|L_{pred} \setminus L_{true}| + |L_{true} \setminus L_{pred}|)$, which is the difference between the predicted location set with respect to the ground truth set. As shown in the table, **the mean percentage loss is merely 4%. This result is remarkably good, especially taking into account of the fact that we are modeling complex and noisy human behaviors.** We also look at how good our model is in terms of capturing people's rationality. Ideally, we would like to see that our model always ranks the ground truth behavior the highest in terms of the utility score. Yet, this is impossible, because human beings occasionally take sub-optimal actions. In the utility percentile row, we show the percentile of the ground truth actions in terms of the utility scores among all valid actions. For example, the score 2.3% means that on average the utility scores of the ground truth actions are ranked at top 2.3% among all valid actions. Because the action set is big, we sample 10,000 location sets per test point. The low rank indicates that people are indeed motivated by the utilities defined in our model. Finally, the third row shows the difference of the environmental variables (NLCD values [19], normalized) between the predicted location set and the ground truth set. We compare our learned model with two other models. One chooses the set of locations which maximizes the estimated number of species (column #Species), and the other maximizes the total popularity of locations (column Popularity). These are the *two main* factors when planning a trip, according to expert opinions and birders' surveys. In summary, our model is quite good at capturing agents' preferences.

Field Results and Simulation We are delighted to see that people's behaviors are changing with *Avicaching*.

1. Between Mar 28, 2015 and Aug 31, 2015, there have been 1,021 observations submitted from *Avicaching* locations, out of the 5,376 observations in total for these two counties: **19% birding effort has shifted from traditional locations to *Avicaching* locations, which received zero visits before. A few new birders also became more active, motivated by the *Avicaching* game.**

2. In terms of locations, Cortland, an undersampled county, received only 128 observations from April to August in 2013 and 2014 combined. This year during the same period of time, with *Avicaching*, it received **452** observations, over **3.5 times the total number of observations of the previous 2 years**!

3. Serious bird watchers are motivated to participate in *Avicaching*. **14 out of the Top 20 bird watchers in Tompkins and 15 out of the Top 20 bird watchers in Cortland (ranked by the number of species discovered since 2015) participated in *Avicaching*.** People who participated in *Avicaching* submitted 64% of total observations in Tompkins and Cortland, from April to August, 2015.

4. In terms of whether *Avicaching* is useful to motivate people to visit undersampled areas, we compare **OptIKA** against two baselines and a manually designed scheme. To eliminate time effects, we ensure that the results against baselines were all collected in summertime, with treatments interleaved. All baselines and **OptIKA** were given two weeks time. The numbers of locations receiving each level of rewards were kept the same for B1, **OptIKA**, and manual. The non-zero reward in B2 matches the mean of other treatments. Table 3 shows the comparison on the normalized D_2 score, which is $\frac{1}{n}||\mathbf{Y}-\overline{\mathbf{Y}}||_2/\overline{Y}$. The visits are more uniform in 2015, when *Avicaching* is introduced. Moreover, **OptIKA** wins against baselines in terms of uniformity. Figure 7 provides a visual confirmation on the map. The success of *Avicaching* is the combination of the gamification and the algorithm. It is difficult to isolate the algorithm's contribution, because field implementation is time-consuming and we cannot afford to alienate the community with drastic or complicated experiments. The **OptIKA** algorithm is better in our experiment, but simpler algorithms may also work, especially at a small scale. However, they are likely to perform worse for new scenarios or over a large scale.

5. We further simulate, for a longer period, a set of virtual agents whose behaviors are learned from the ***real bird watchers***. At the end of each round, we fit a predictive model based on all the data virtually collected so far, to see how much the species distribution model can be affected by agents' shifts of exploration efforts. We use the collected data to predict the occurrence of the Horned Lark in Spring. The left plot of Fig. 5 illustrates the sample variance D_2 as a function of the number of iterations with and without extra incentives. The right plot of Fig. 5 shows the Log-loss of the fitted predictive model in the first few iterations. This simulation shows that ***under the Avicaching scheme, agents cover the area more uniformly*** than the no-incentive case, which leads ***to higher performance on a predictive model for bird occurrence***, with the same amount of effort devoted. More details of this simulation are in the supplementary materials [40].

Power of Uniform Sampling Finally, we also illustrate the benefit of incentivizing people to sample areas uniformly, by comparing the performance of a random forest classifier trained on four datasets, subsampled in different ways from the real *eBird* dataset. In Fig. 6, we show that the predictive model fit on a small, but spatially uniformly subsampled dataset is close to the ground truth, and outperforms the model fit on biased datasets. More details are in the supplementary materials [40].

5. CONCLUSION

We introduced a methodology to improve the scientific quality of data collected by citizen scientists, by providing incentives to shift their efforts to more crucial scientific tasks. We formulated the problem of Optimal Incentives for Knapsack Agents (**OptIKA**) as a two-stage game and provided novel algorithms on optimal reward design and on behavior modeling. We applied our methodology to *eBird* as a gamified application called *Avicaching*, deploying it in two NY counties. Our results show that our incentives are remarkably effective at steering the bird watchers' efforts to explore under-sampled areas, which alleviates the data bias problem and improves species modeling.

Acknowledgments

We are thankful to Ronan Le Bras, the anonymous reviewers for comments, thousands of eBird participants, and the Cornell Lab of Ornithology for managing the database. This research was supported by National Science Foundation (0832782, 1522054, 1059284, 1356308), ARO grant W911-NF-14-1-0498, the Leon Levy Foundation and the Wolf Creek Foundation.

REFERENCES

[1] G. Aggarwal, T. Feder, R. Motwani, and A. Zhu. Algorithms for multi-product pricing. In *ICALP*, 2004.

[2] A. K. Agogino and K. Tumer. Analyzing and visualizing multiagent rewards in dynamic and stochastic environments. *Journal of Autonomous Agents and Multi-Agent Systems*, 17(2):320–338, 2008.

[3] A. Anderson, D. P. Huttenlocher, J. M. Kleinberg, and J. Leskovec. Steering user behavior with badges. In *22nd Int'l World Wide Web Conference, WWW*, 2013.

[4] D. F. Bacon, D. C. Parkes, Y. Chen, M. Rao, I. Kash, and M. Sridharan. Predicting your own effort. In *Proc. of the 11th Int'l Conf. on Autonomous Agents and Multiagent Systems-Volume 2*, pages 695–702, 2012.

[5] R. Bonney, C. B. Cooper, J. Dickinson, S. Kelling, T. Phillips, K. V. Rosenberg, and J. Shirk. Citizen science: a developing tool for expanding science knowledge and scientific literacy. *BioScience*, 59(11):977–984, 2009.

[6] S. P. Boyd, N. Parikh, E. Chu, B. Peleato, and J. Eckstein. Distributed optimization and statistical learning via the alternating direction method of multipliers. *Foundations and Trends in Machine Learning*, 3(1):1–122, 2011.

[7] J. Bragg, Mausam, and D. S. Weld. Crowdsourcing multi-label classification for taxonomy creation. In *HCOMP*, 2013.

[8] P. Briest, M. Hoefer, L. Gualà, and C. Ventre. On stackelberg pricing with computationally bounded consumers. In *WINE*, pages 42–54, 2009.

[9] Y. Cai, C. Daskalakis, and C. H. Papadimitriou. Optimum statistical estimation with strategic data sources. *CoRR 14*, 2014.

[10] X. Chen, Q. Lin, and D. Zhou. Optimistic knowledge gradient policy for optimal budget allocation in crowdsourcing. In *ICML*, 2013.

[11] V. Chvatal. *Linear Programming*. W. H. Freeman and Company, New York, USA, 1983.

[12] V. Conitzer and N. Garera. Learning algorithms for online principal-agent problems (and selling goods online). In *Proc. of the 23rd ICML*, 2006.

[13] V. Conitzer and T. Sandholm. Computing the optimal strategy to commit to. In *Proc. 7th ACM Conference on Electronic Commerce (EC)*, pages 82–90, 2006.

[14] U. Endriss, S. Kraus, J. Lang, and M. Wooldridge. Incentive engineering for boolean games. *IJCAI Proceedings-International Joint Conference on Artificial Intelligence*, 22(3):2602, 2011.

[15] F. Fang, P. Stone, and M. Tambe. When security games go green: Designing defender strategies to prevent poaching and illegal fishing. In *IJCAI*, 2015.

[16] P. Frazier, D. Kempe, J. M. Kleinberg, and R. Kleinberg. Incentivizing exploration. In *ACM Conference on Economics and Computation, EC*, pages 5–22, 2014.

[17] V. Guruswami, J. D. Hartline, A. R. Karlin, D. Kempe, C. Kenyon, and F. McSherry. On profit-maximizing envy-free pricing. In *SODA*, pages 1164–1173, 2005.

[18] J. D. Hartline and V. Koltun. Near-optimal pricing in near-linear time. In *Algorithms and Data Structures, 9th Int'l Workshop, WADS*, pages 422–431, 2005.

[19] C. Homer, J. Dewitz, J. Fry, M. Coan, N. Hossain, C. Larson, N. Herold, A. Mckerrow, J. N. Vandriel, and J. Wickham. Completion of the 2001 National Land Cover Database for the conterminous United States. *Photogrammetric Engineering and Remote Sensing*, 73(4):337–341, 2007.

[20] J. Hu and M. P. Wellman. Online learning about other agents in a dynamic multiagent system. In *Proceedings of the Second International Conference on Autonomous Agents*, AGENTS '98, 1998.

[21] S. Jain, Y. Chen, and D. C. Parkes. Designing incentives for online question-and-answer forums. *Games and Economic Behavior*, 86:458–474, 2014.

[22] R. Kawajiri, M. Shimosaka, and H. Kashima. Steered crowdsensing: Incentive design towards quality-oriented place-centric crowdsensing. In *UbiComp*, 2014.

[23] H. Li, F. Tian, W. Chen, T. Qin, Z. Ma, and T. Liu. Generalization analysis for game-theoretic machine learning. In *AAAI*, 2015.

[24] C. J. Lintott, K. Schawinski, A. Slosar, et al. Galaxy Zoo: morphologies derived from visual inspection of galaxies from the Sloan Digital Sky Survey. *Monthly Notices of the Royal Astronomical Society*, 389(3):1179–1189, Sept. 2008.

[25] A. F. T. Martins, M. A. T. Figueiredo, P. M. Q. Aguiar, N. A. Smith, and E. P. Xing. An augmented lagrangian approach to constrained MAP inference. In *Proceedings of ICML*, pages 169–176, 2011.

[26] P. Minder, S. Seuken, A. Bernstein, and M. Zollinger. Crowdmanager-combinatorial allocation and pricing of crowdsourcing tasks with time constraints. In *Workshop on Social Computing and User Generated Content in conjunction with ACM Conference on Electronic Commerce (ACM-EC 2012)*, 2012.

[27] A. Y. Ng and S. J. Russell. Algorithms for inverse reinforcement learning. In *ICML*, pages 663–670, 2000.

[28] P. Paruchuri, J. P. Pearce, J. Marecki, M. Tambe, F. Ordóñez, and S. Kraus. Playing games for security: an efficient exact algorithm for solving bayesian stackelberg games. In *AAMAS*, pages 895–902, 2008.

[29] G. Radanovic and B. Faltings. Incentive schemes for participatory sensing. In *AAMAS*, 2015.

[30] B. Settles. Active learning literature survey. *University of Wisconsin, Madison*, 52(55-66):11, 2010.

[31] S. Shavell. Risk sharing and incentives in the principal and agent relationship. *The Bell Journal of Economics*, 1979.

[32] Y. Singer and M. Mittal. Pricing mechanisms for crowdsourcing markets. In *Proceedings of the 22nd Internat. Conf. on World Wide Web (WWW)*, 2013.

[33] A. Singla and A. Krause. Truthful incentives in crowdsourcing tasks using regret minimization mechanisms. In *Proceedings of the 22Nd International Conference on World Wide Web*, 2013.

[34] A. Singla, M. Santoni, G. Bartók, P. Mukerji, M. Meenen, and A. Krause. Incentivizing users for balancing bike sharing systems. In *AAAI*, 2015.

[35] B. L. Sullivan, J. L. Aycrigg, J. H. Barry, R. E. Bonney, N. Bruns, C. B. Cooper, T. Damoulas, A. A.

Dhondt, T. Dietterich, A. Farnsworth, D. Fink, J. W. Fitzpatrick, T. Fredericks, J. Gerbracht, C. Gomes, W. M. Hochachka, M. J. Iliff, C. Lagoze, F. A. L. Sorte, M. Merrifield, W. Morris, T. B. Phillips, M. Reynolds, A. D. Rodewald, K. V. Rosenberg, N. M. Trautmann, A. Wiggins, D. W. Winkler, W.-K. Wong, C. L. Wood, J. Yu, and S. Kelling. The ebird enterprise: An integrated approach to development and application of citizen science. *Biological Conservation*, 169(0):31 – 40, 2014.

[36] U. Syed, M. Bowling, and R. E. Schapire. Apprenticeship learning using linear programming. In *Proceedings of the 25th International Conference on Machine Learning*, ICML '08, 2008.

[37] L. Tran-Thanh, T. D. Huynh, A. Rosenfeld, S. D. Ramchurn, and N. R. Jennings. Crowdsourcing complex workflows under budget constraints. In *Proceedings of the AAAI Conference*. AAAI, 2015.

[38] L. Tran-Thanh, S. Stein, A. Rogers, and N. R. Jennings. Efficient crowdsourcing of unknown experts using bounded multi-armed bandits. *Artificial Intelligence*, 214:89–111, 2014.

[39] I. Tsochantaridis, T. Joachims, T. Hofmann, and Y. Altun. Large margin methods for structured and interdependent output variables. *J. Mach. Learn. Res.*, 6:1453–1484, Dec. 2005.

[40] Y. Xue, I. Davies, D. Fink, C. Wood, and C. P. Gomes. Avicaching: A two stage game for bias reduction in citizen science. *Technical Report*, 2016.

[41] H. Zhang, E. Law, R. Miller, K. Gajos, D. Parkes, and E. Horvitz. Human computation tasks with global constraints. In *CHI*, 2012.

[42] D. Zilli, O. Parson, G. V. Merrett, and A. Rogers. A hidden markov model-based acoustic cicada detector for crowdsourced smartphone biodiversity monitoring. *J. Artif. Intell. Res. (JAIR)*, 51:805–827, 2014.

Assessing Maritime Customs Process Re-Engineering using Agent-Based Simulation

F. Jordan Srour
Adnan Kassar School of Business
Lebanese American University, Lebanon
Jordan.Srour@lau.edu.lb

Neil Yorke-Smith
Olayan School of Business
American University of Beirut, Lebanon
nysmith@aub.edu.lb

ABSTRACT

Case studies report that corruption is not easily combated by policy changes, and that reform policies can have unexpected side-effects in practice. Using agent-based simulation, this paper studies potential anti-corruption policies in the maritime customs context. We detail an agent-based simulation calibrated on the processes of an archetypal Mediterranean container port (where in-group relationships contribute to a situation of endemic corruption), and describe insights gained about the costs and benefits of various reform policies. Results from the simulation model provide commentary on cases reported in the literature, and offer novel evaluation of policies involving process re-engineering.

Keywords

policy analysis; agent-based simulation; customs; ethics

1. INTRODUCTION

Despite customs revenue contributing a significant component of public finances, particularly in developing countries, the Organization for Economic Co-operation and Development (OECD) finds that customs efficiency is often hampered by widespread corruption, creating "a major disincentive and obstacle to trade expansion" and leading to "disastrous consequences in terms of national security and public finance" [23]. The literature concludes that customs corruption is not easily combated by policy changes, that reform policies can have unexpected side-effects, and that a broadly-based, systemic approach is required [26, 39].

Our domain of interest is maritime customs, namely the import of sea-based containers. A port, including its customs import processes, is an instance of a complex socio-technical system with multiple stakeholders. The aim of this paper is to explore potential anti-corruption policies in this maritime customs context, focussing on process re-engineering. We describe the design, implementation, and validation of a multiagent-based simulation (MABS) calibrated on evidence from ports in high-corruption Mediterranean countries [10]. The goal of the simulation model is not to simulate precise behaviours or to make quantitative forecasts, but to simulate archetypal process deviations and suggest possible qualitative outcomes of policy measures.

Specifically, we examine a set of localized measures and a set of broader process re-engineering policies. The localized policies include increasing customs employee wage rates, and increasing enforcement and fines. The process re-engineering policies include removing the capability of freight forwarders to select specific (in-group) customs officers to work with, and streamlining processes through the introduction of electronic payment of duties. Results from the simulation model offer multi-factor assessment of such policies in a complex environment with endemic corruption and significant in-group relationships between actors.

2. BACKGROUND AND CONTEXT

Whenever a process has the opportunity or obligation for people to negotiate, the possibility of corruption arises. According to the World Bank, corruption is "the misuse of public office for private gain" [51], whether (1) *routine* corruption (e.g., bribes for normal or expedited completion of processes); (2) *fraudulent* corruption (e.g., tacit or explicit collusion to reduce fiscal obligations); or (3) *criminal* corruption. The negative repercussions of corruption upon institutions, societies, and nations include poverty, tax evasion, political instability, weakened democracy and rule of law, reduced national competitiveness, and (especially for customs) distortion of trade figures. Further, corruption—whether *collusive* or *coercive*—reinforces disenfranchisement and hinders development, being "one of the most serious barriers to overcoming poverty" with a strong correlation between perceived corruption and per capita income [52].

In order to counter established, widespread corrupt practices, a deeper understanding is required of the processes in which corruption features, together with a deeper understanding of the corrupt practices that occur, within the broad socio-political, socio-economic, governmental and cultural situation [23, 26, 43, 1]. Among case studies, Hungarian researchers noted how government structures can allow for the formation of elite cliques which can design and coordinate entire networks of corruption [25]. Studies in China further explored the influence of corrupt in-group networks which, in situations of collective corruption, tend towards rewriting norms and thus legitimizing further corruption [15]. Indeed, the interconnectedness of actors is an antecedent for collective corruption which in turn can lead to endemic corruption [29]. As such, highly-connected environments may demand a greater level of policy engineering in the form of process redesign, automation, procedural streamlining, and norm change. This need to understand

Appears in: *Proceedings of the 15th International Conference on Autonomous Agents and Multiagent Systems (AAMAS 2016), J. Thangarajah, K. Tuyls, S. Marsella, C. Jonker (eds.), May 9–13, 2016, Singapore.*

the nuanced impact of potential policy reforms provides the motivation for our work in the field of maritime customs.

Customs is "the official department that administers and collects the duties levied by a government on imported goods" (Oxford English Dictionary [OED]), and, we might add, to enforce customs regulations. Our motivating domain is maritime customs, specifically import of sea-based containers. A key role in the process of moving a container through customs is that of the *freight forwarder*, a company that manages and organizes shipments for others, sometimes consolidating smaller shipments. The process is primarily based on a match between shipping documents (e.g., bill of lading) and customs documents (e.g., manifest). If this match is made and the shipper and/or consignee (i.e., recipient) are considered trustworthy, then the container may proceed following the payment of standard duties. Otherwise, or if it should be randomly selected, the container is subject to search and may see additional duties or fines. Possible *deviations* from an archetypal customs import process (see Fig. 1) include inaccurate, incomplete, or fictitious documentation; under- or over-inspection; inaccurate value estimation; waiving true fines or imposing additional fines; and delaying or expediting certain containers. In some situations, a whole grey 'parallel customs' system evolves [14, 24].

Policy efforts led by the International Monetary Fund (IMF), OECD, World Customs Organization, and World Bank have focused—not without critique [26]—on reducing trade barriers, reforming trade procedures, and building 'cultures of integrity'. Great care is required in such policy engineering, since, on the one hand, customs corruption has been shown to be not easily combated by policy changes [14, 23], and on the other hand, policy changes can have adverse side-effects, including unexpected fiscal distortions [39, 44].

Agent-Based Models.

In light of these challenges, a benefit of MABS is its potential to give qualitative insights into what-if policy scenarios—scenarios which are not subject to hypothesis-and-test experimentation in the real world [12].

The domain studied, while embedded into a social context and highly influenced by organizational, cultural, and social factors, does not match exactly any of the paradigmatic models for agent-based social simulation identified by Marietto et al. [33]; the closest match is *socio-concrete models*. Rather, simulating deviations in maritime customs may be better characterized not as a social simulation per se, but as simulating social complexity—the structure and norms of what is and is not considered acceptable in the realm of customs processes, and the micro–macro link between (emergent) actor behaviours and policies applied to the system.[1] Our objective is not so much forecasting (as in computational economics) or optimization (as in traditional operations research) but understanding of collective behaviours.

Granted that negotiation is the most common entry point for deviations within customs processes [27], the study of negotiation is multi-faceted, including political science, economics, policy research, psychology, and computer science. Sycara and Dai [50] report on efforts to unify research in behavioural and computational (including agent) communities. While the maritime customs domain holds a rich vein of research in the dynamics of bargaining situations, our objective is not to study deeply the negotiation itself but rather to capture agent interactions within the customs process in order to study policy analysis questions.

Agent-based models and MABS have been successful in port management (e.g., [21, 20]), maritime container shipment (e.g., [31]), and policy analysis in transport (e.g., [3]). Agent-based simulation has also been used to study corruption. Hammond [18] develops an agent-based population model in an effort to explain shifts in corruption levels. Corruption is modelled as a simple, game-theoretic repeated interaction on the micro level. In a tax-evasion domain, endogenous shifts in global corruption levels are observed as emerging from the micro-behaviour. Among studies of social behaviour, Abdallah et al. [1] show that peer-punishment is more effective than an overly strong centralized punishment in promoting cooperation, if actors are able to bribe centralized authorities. It will be interesting to extend Hammond's direction and explore in- and out-group peer-effects in customs departments.

Our previous work, Harb et al. [19], presented a methodological approach for choosing a modelling paradigm for policy analysis, using the Port of Beirut as a case study. In Srour and Yorke-Smith [49] we went on to outline the design of a MABS of the customs processes of a container port; here we extend the model to include, among other factors, coercive as well as collusive corruption, develop the design to an implemented simulation, and report the results. Other works that study practices in the same customs context do not aim to build a behavioural simulation [42, 36, 8].

Situngkir [48] is interested in the link between corrupt behaviours in individual agents and the normative societal and cultural environment in which they interact. He builds a MABS inspired by corrupt bureaucrats in Indonesia and obtains system-wide results. Balke et al. [2] discuss in detail norms in agent-based simulation, and Norling et al. [35], for instance, seek to add more 'human-like' decision making strategies, while Dignum et al. [9] and subsequent works emphasize models that include culture.

Archetypal Port.

Our work focuses on ports in high-corruption Mediterranean countries. Individually the ports that we focus on serve in the range of 750,000 to 1.5M Twenty-foot Equivalent Units (TEUs) per year and with values greater than $200M. This is the size of terminal that begins to have a significant impact on the economics of the country in which it is situated. The Port of Beirut, Lebanon, for example, accounts for nearly 90% of Lebanon's customs income, and is a large contributor to Value Added Tax, the largest source of government revenue [40]; whereas "widespread corruption" is reported at the Customs Department [16].

Our data gathering aimed to characterize the domain and the processes of interest, and to elicit structural, environmental, institutional, and behavioural knowledge necessary to build a MABS. We sought information in three sources [11]: observation and data collection from the target system (i.e., the port), bibliographical review (i.e., theories), and domain experts. The material found included press articles

[1] In the taxonomy of Davidsson et al. [7], the domain is 'social system and organizations'; the end-user is 'scientists' and, perhaps, 'policy makers'; the purpose is 'prediction' and 'analysis'; the simulated entity is 'living'; the number of agent types is a small finite number; the structure is peer-to-peer, hierarchal; agents communicate; the input data is mostly artificial; the present maturity is 'laboratory experiments'.

on issues pertaining to practices at ports in our area of interest [38, 32, 6, 24, 17] and ethnography as reported by ourselves [19], Diab et al. [8], and others [46].

Target observation. The data obtained directly from the target system were published statistics including total number of TEUs per month, value, and breakdown by type, and average time at the port; statistics about the staffing levels; and customs tariffs, fees, and fines. It comes as no surprise that efforts to collect empirical data by observation (e.g., sampling containers and following their progresses) have not been successful; in view of the sensitivity of questions in the domain, this kind of empirical study is unlikely.

Source review. While jurisdictions differ in their regulations and procedures, nearly all ports have similar import–export processes [34], which centre on a match between manifest and declaration. Nearly all ports have an IT system [53], usually divided into two parts: a customs clearance system that maintains the customs records (the manifest), and a portal that allows submission of the required bill-of-lading documents. We use the terms *LIGHT* and *STAR* to differentiate the two systems, respectively. The widest differences between jurisdictions are taxation schemes. Fig. 1 depicts the import process that we use as the archetypal import process underlying the MABS.

Domain experts. We conducted a set of approximately ten semi-structured, exploratory interviews with customs brokers, freight forwarders, longshoremen (i.e., the workers who physically move containers), and Customs Officers at a port within our region of interest [19]. From these interviews we found that the process of moving the container from a ship is physically separated from the process of clearing the container through customs. As such, the MABS includes the role of the customs agency, but excludes the role of the container terminal operator.

The actors in the import–export processes are listed in Table 1. Interviewees, when feeling able to speak with some freedom, reported a systemic norm of deviations in import–export process. Customs Officers in practice have greater discretion than their job description states. It was considered routine to engage in 'wasta' [32]—exploitation of influence, political (or other) power, connections—or to offer a bribe or a 'baksheesh'—a widespread practice "[of] a small sum of money given as alms, a tip, or a bribe" (OED).

3. POLICY MEASURES AND METRICS

The goal of our simulation is analysis of policies designed to combat corruption. As noted in Sect. 2, policy measures to reform customs tend to be in the areas of trade facilitation or broad anti-corruption efforts. Specific areas where new policies may be applied, or existing policies enforced, include [51, 28, 27, 23]: (1) computerized data systems, (2) auditing, (3) sanctions, (4) role separation, (5) Customs Officer wages, (6) declaration and monitoring of assets for Customs Officers, (7) training, (8) culture of integrity (e.g., Code of Ethics), (9) legislative reforms, (10) legal reforms, (11) tax and tariff reform, (12) simplification of administrative procedures[2], (13) increased accountability and transparency (e.g., process documentation), (14) public awareness, (15) regular stakeholder meetings, (16) an independent complaints authority, and (17) media freedom.

[2]The length and the complexity of the import process is significant, since "systems and procedures appeared to have evolved to maximise the number of steps and approvals—to create as many opportunities as possible for negotiationbetween traders and customs officials " [23].

Owner	**Excise officer**
Owner's agent	**Head of Excise**
Freight forwarder	Customs broker
Shipping company	Longshoremen
Vessel captain	Warehouse employees
Clearance Agency officer	Port security staff
Customs Agency officer	Recipient (consignee)
Head of Customs	Police officer
Inspection officer	Customs audit officer
Head of Inspection	Policy maker

Table 1: Actors identified in maritime imports process. Bold denotes actors in the simulation.

Principled means are required to evaluate and compare specific policy measures. We formulated the following metrics to assess evaluation of policy measures for import–export processes, based on the literature (e.g., [30]), reflection over published measured data available, and interviewees' statements: (1) end-to-end time for an item to clear customs, (2) time difference (usually, delay) from desired date of receipt, (3) cost for an item to clear customs, including any corruption costs, e.g., bribes, that can be quantified, (4) number and type of deviations from published process, (5) number of illegal or misdeclared ('deviant') containers, (6) percentage of deviant containers not detected (i.e., allowed to enter the country), (7) amount of revenue obtained by customs, and (8) cost of enforcement (e.g., measured by the total salary of customs staff, plus enforcement actions).

4. DESIGN AND VALIDATION

In this section we describe the design (following [49]) and validation of a MABS for containers passing through the maritime customs import process. We take each shipment as analogous to a round in a sequential bargaining game. Each shipment brings the opportunity for actors to negotiate, or not. The simulation scope is a subset of the full maritime import process, in order to focus on the key actors, processes, and negotiation opportunities.

The most relevant **artefacts** are the owner's declaration, the bill of lading, the *IM4 folder*—which represents a container in the customs process shown in Fig. 1, and which consists of the invoice, packing list, various registration and identity verification documents, and a declaration of value—and the various customs orders and receipts. All these artefacts are commonly in electronic form.

Of the **actors** listed in Table 1, we selected the eight in bold for inclusion in the simulation. Our reasons for excluding explicit representation of other actors were: (1) some actors can be subsumed by others with little loss of generality, e.g., the owner can be represented by the owner's agent; (2) some actors have a role in the maritime import process but their role in the customs sub-process is limited, e.g., the vessel captain; (3) the role of some actors can be emulated by a non-agent entity, e.g., the audit officer can be emulated by the probability of a customs employee being audited; (4) simplification by focusing on the key actors; and (5) limiting the scope of the simulation in order to obtain explanation for observed results. Future work is to expand the simulation's

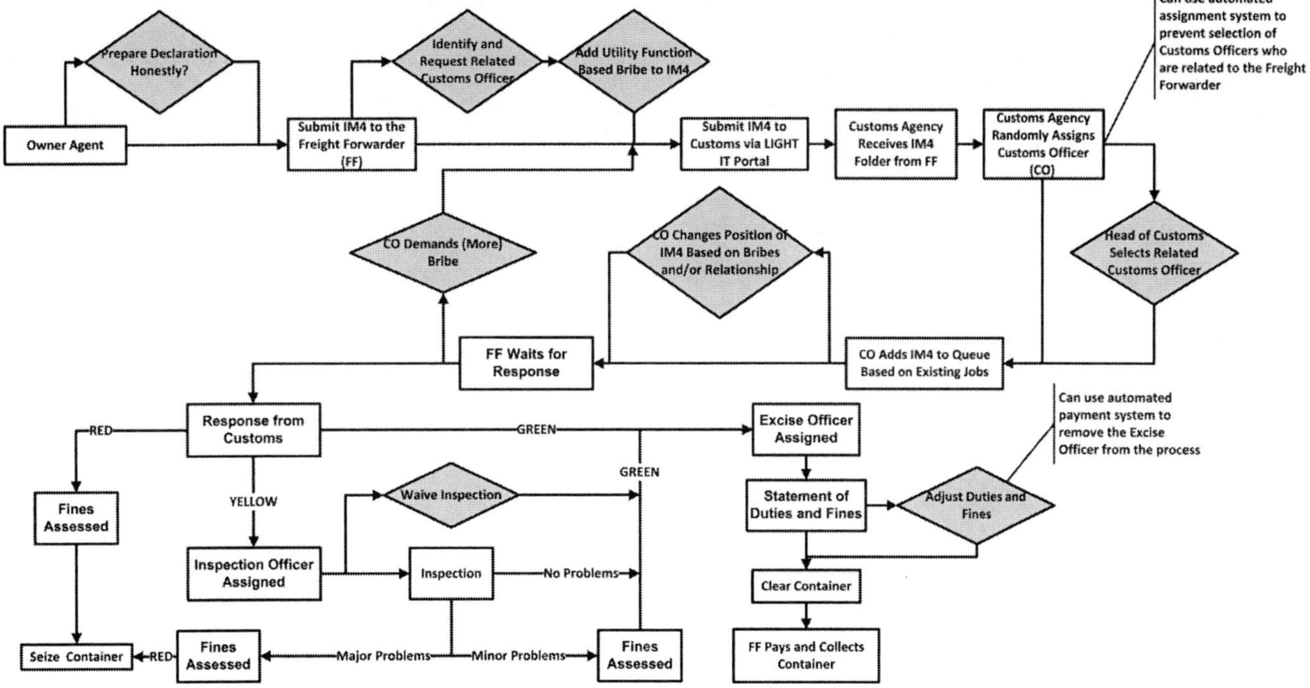

Figure 1: Flowchart of import process at archetypal port as implemented in the MABS.

scope to include, for instance, an explicit representation of the customs audit officer.

Owner's agent (OA). Decides what to declare based on the tariff for the actual container contents, and estimates of the cost of bribes necessary and probability of inspection.

Freight forwarder (FF). Offers bribe to CO (part of which will be passed on to other actors in customs) to expedite container if its due date is close. Offer a bribe to HCO to obtain assignment to a preferred CO, i.e., a CO to whom the FF has a relationship. Offers bribe to CO obtain a GREEN decision if the expected cost of doing so is less than the cost of fines and fees; assumes that all COs will accept a bribe of sufficient amount (a warranted assumption when corruption is endemic). If the CO demands, will increase bribe amount up to the maximum amount where expected cost would exceed expected value. Routinely offers baksheesh. Note that we fold the important role of the customs broker [24] into the FF.

Customs Agency officer (CO). Unless opposed to bribes in principle, accepts any bribe of sufficient amount, to either expedite the container, waive inspection, or change decision outcome. May demand a bribe if none offered or if its amount is too low. May impose an unnecessary inspection unless bribed. Works slowly on a container unless given a baksheeh. Always declares GREEN a container whose owner or consignee is related closely enough.

Head of Customs (HCO). Supportive of the COs, turns blind eye to non-standard practices [24]. Does not overrule a CO's decision, except for RED decisions for a sufficient bribe. Will override IT system's assignment of container to a CO for a sufficient bribe. HIO and HEO behave similarly.

Inspection officer (IO). Unless opposed to bribes in principle, accepts any bribe of sufficient amount, to waive or expedite the inspection, to or report a different contents than the actual found. Works slowly unless given a baksheeh.

Excise officer (EO). Unless opposed to bribes in principle, accepts any bribe of sufficient amount, to set lower duty than the published tariff rules. Works slowly without baksheeh.

At the heart of the simulation are the actors' progression through the documented processes for each shipment, the points of possible deviation, the decisions whether to engage in (or how to respond to) non-standard practices, and the negotiation that may ensue. We simulate the main, documented customs **process** as follows (Fig. 1): (1) owner's agent submits IM4 to the freight forwarder company, which assigns a specific FF agent; (2) FF submits IM4 to customs agency via the *LIGHT* IT portal; (3) *LIGHT* assigns IM4 to a specific CO; (4) CO sees output of the *STAR* IT system and can override: the decision is RED (fines imposed, seize container), YELLOW (inspect container), or GREEN (approve container, duty imposed); (5) if inspection is required, *LIGHT* assigns a specific IO; (6) the IO inspects the container and sends the report to the CO via *STAR*; (7) the CO revises a YELLOW decision to RED or GREEN and informs the FF; (8) approved GREEN containers proceed to the Excise Department and are assigned by *LIGHT* to a specific EO; (9) the EO computes the final duty, fines (if any), and other costs (handling, storage, etc.) and informs the FF; (10) the FF pays the due amount (plus interest, if applicable); and (11) the CO approves the release of the container. Note that the heads of the respective departments can override both the assignment of officers (by *LIGHT*) and the decisions of officers (in *STAR*).

Deviations, shown in grey in Fig. 1, can occur from the documented process as follows. First, the FF can offer bribes to attempt to obtain its preferred CO, to expedite the container, or to have a deviant container pass through as GREEN. Second, the HCO can accept a bribe and assign the preferred CO. Third, the CO can accept a bribe (collusive), or it can demand (more) bribe (coercive). Fourth, the IO can waive, expedite, or report differently the inspection. Fifth, the EO can change the amount due.

Audits occur, randomly, at two points in the process. First, the IO's inspection can be audited. We assume that the audit is effective, and will find the actual container contents and value. Since IO could have legitimately missed something in the container, it receives a penalty if it repeatedly is audited as 'failing' in its inspections. The second audit point is after the CO's decision. Again we assume the audit is effective. The CO receives a penalty if its decision differs from the facts available to it. The audits constitute a learning opportunity: the deviational behaviour of all customs actors are reinforced if they are not caught by audit, but the behaviour is reduced if caught. For example, a CO that accepted a bribe and was not caught is more likely to accept bribes in future, but one that was caught is less likely. For the FF, whether a deviant container made it through as GREEN or was stopped as RED (whether by a customs employee or by audit) is a learning opportunity about bribe success and bribe amounts.

In-group relationships. The degree to which two agents share an affinity, and the obligations that come from such an in-group relationship, is a cornerstone of business and society in all Arab and many other Mediterranean countries [46, 22, 26]. As noted earlier, interconnectedness of actors is an antecedent for various forms of corruption. We capture such relationships by a simple model of each agent's sect, hometown, and clan membership. Based on the strength of the overall connection between two agents, the propensity to offer, accept, and demand bribes, the bribe amounts, and customs actor behaviours (e.g., speed of work, inspection decisions, assessed tariff levels), may all change. Notably, the strongest component of relationship is familial. If two agents hail from the same family, then culture can demand that they selflessly seek the welfare of the other, such as by a CO accepting a bribe even of negative expected value.

Assumptions.

The scope of the system simulated is deliberately restricted to the customs import process. Our main assumption is that to begin to answer the questions of interest, we do not need to simulate a larger cross-section of society, nor simulate the whole maritime import process. We also take the approach that we do not need to model in detail each actor's internal cognition and mental state (e.g., beliefs, desires, norms, goals)—just sufficiently to capture deviational practices. We hold further that process deviations can be understood on the basis of analysis of individual initiatives of the agents involved in those processes. That is, while we recognize the significance of group/organizational modelling, we hold that individual-level modelling can give insight into the effects of process deviations.

We briefly mention further assumptions. First, which actors negotiate with which others, especially outside of documented process interactions? We assume that negotiation can occur at each point in the process, but we do not consider negotiation to bypass the process entirely, i.e., so-called 'grey containers'. Second, adaptive behaviour is limited: agents learn from previous 'rounds', but they do not adapt to others' behaviours. For example, the propensity to offer a bribe will increase as bribes are accepted, in general; however, the propensity to offer a bribe to a *specific* CO will not differ from the general propensity, unless there is a relationship between the agents. Third, non-monetary exchanges (e.g., gift of jewellery) are considered as the equivalent monetary value. Further, since the literature indicates that bribes are more prevalent than threats, we do not consider the latter. Fourth, relational capital (wasta) is modelled as a probability regarding whether two agents have an in-group connection (e.g., clan). Because of the sensitivity and complexity of the issue, we decided to not consider patronage. Fifth, all agents of the same type, e.g., all FF agents, operate in the same way and follow the same negotiation model. Although an agent's 'personality' is captured by modelling its propensity to corruption, its experience of past containers, and its in-group characteristics, we do not yet consider emotive state.

Implementation and Validation.

The simulation was implemented using the Java-based agent toolkit Jadex [37]. Compared with dedicated MABS environments (e.g., NetLogo, RePast), Jadex readily allows BDI-style agents, i.e., agents with explicit representations of beliefs, goals, and plans. It has in-built support for simulation [4]. We developed a prototype, then the full MABS.

Verification and validation (V&V) were performed on each subpart and on the overall MABS by the development team, following the process of Sargent [41]. Ideally, domain experts are involved in V&V. Due to the nature of the domain problem, it proved too sensitive a matter—in part because of ongoing media reporting of deviations at the port [17]—to involve any of our earlier interviewees. We did consult consignees who had recent experience of importing goods.

Data validity. The validity of data used to build the model fell into two extremes. On the one hand, data about tariff rates, for instance, came from official sources and is considered fully reliable. On the other hand, data about bribe amounts came from interview, anecdotal, and media sources, and, despite our efforts to triangulate, is necessarily approximate. Fortunately, our aim is not to simulate behaviours precisely or make quantitative forecasts, but to simulate archetypal process deviations.

Conceptual model validation. Regarding the simulation model design, again it proved infeasible to have the review of domain experts. However, a process flowchart representation of the simulation model was examined by independent individuals familiar with the port. Further, an agent's actions were traced longitudinally through simulation runs, for each type of agent.

Implementation verification. We followed standard practices, including code review, modular verification, and testing of extreme parameter values. Notably the latter tested 0% and 100% for percentage parameters.

Operational validity. In our case, the MABS intends to give qualitative projections into what-if policy scenarios. At the system level, it was not possible to compare the trace of a simulated container with actual traces, since, as noted earlier, efforts to obtain traces through the actual process were unsuccessful. Beyond our previous work [49], there are no other models of the studied system to compare with, other than an abstracted Petri net model [36] and scheduling models of other processes at the port. Third, it is not meaning-

Type	Duty	Percentage
Personal possessions	Exempt	5%
Jewellery	Exempt	5%
Appliances	Standard	10%
Furniture	Standard	5%
Computers	Exempt	10%
Foodstuffs (perishable)	Standard/Punitive	15%
Raw commodities	Exempt	25%
Gold	Standard	5%
Clothing	Standard	15%
Automobiles	High	10%

Table 2: Container distribution mix.

Parameter	Baseline value
Illicit container %	10%
Standard tariff rate	5–10%
VAT rate	10%
Fine penalty	10x tariff
Chance of inspection	25%
Inspection success	80%
Work-slow ratio	3 times
CO collusive propensity	75%
CO coercive propensity	60%
Chance FF & CO related	2%
Chance of audit	2%
Audit penalty	6x salary

Table 3: Main simulation parameters.

ful to directly compare output measures from the simulation with the modelled system (e.g., reported monthly Key Performance Indicators [KPIs]), due to the level of fidelity of the simulation and its scope. However, we did explore qualitative correlation with reported outcomes, such as decreasing duties on gasoline [13].

5. INSIGHTS ON POLICY MEASURES

In this section we exploit the MABS to analyze reform policies in maritime customs. We model the contents of containers as falling into ten categories, giving a representative spread across attributes (small/large items, low/high value, perishable/not) and tariffs (exempt, standard, punitive) [30], and estimated the distribution of these categories from published statistics (Table 2). Table 3 gives the baseline parameter values extrapolated from the target system.

The baseline parameters gave the values of Key Performance Indicators of Table 4. Results reported are averaged over 100 runs of 1600 containers each. This number of containers corresponds to approximately two months of simulated time. The number of runs was empirically sufficient for variation in results to converge to a small value. We recorded the metrics listed in Sect. 3 and report them as the average per container, with the exception of # Deviant and % Not Caught, which reflect the total number of mis-declared or illicit containers (out of 160,000 across all the runs), and the percentage of those deviant containers that were accepted with an outcome of GREEN. Enforcement cost, not shown for space reasons, is dominated by customs salaries.

Of the areas for policy measures noted earlier, some have been already implemented in the archetypal port (e.g., computerized data systems, process documentation) or exist in the country (e.g., media freedom, complaints hotline). Others (e.g., legal reform) are out of scope of the simulation. We therefore focused on two areas of policy reform: (1) localized measures, including auditing, sanctions, Customs Officer wages, and tariff reform; and (2) process re-engineering, including (further) role separation, and simplification of administrative procedures. We model some policies by their proxy effects on the simulation. Specifically, policies such as training and fostering a culture of integrity we model by their effect on actors' propensity to corruption.

Localized Policy Changes.

For each experiment in changing a policy, Table 4 provides the KPI results for a representative choice of policy values.

Honesty vs. corruption. First we explore the impact of the containers submitted to the customs department. The direct cost of corruption—baksheesh and bribes, besides additional delays (which we do not monetize)—in the baseline scenario is approximately $500 per container. If the percentage of illicit containers increases, the cost (to FF) and bribe levels increase as do the number of deviant containers—although, of those deviant containers, only 76% are admitted. If the container owner is less willing ('only' 50%) to permit the FF to offer a bribe on her behalf, the consequence of note is that the number of deviant containers decreases; other metrics remain the similar to the baseline case. Delays increase if the owner is unwilling to offer even baksheesh.

Next, we consider policies that affect the honesty of Customs Officers. The effect of the propensity of CO agents to accept a bribe has, as expected, a direct bearing on the number of deviant containers that pass through customs, and on customs revenue. If the collusiveness of COs decrease, i.e., COs are less likely to accept a bribe, then the bribe level and number of deviations go down; other metrics remain as in the baseline case. If the coerciveness of COs decreases, i.e., COs are less likely to demand a (larger) bribe, then cost and revenue increase, bribe levels decrease, and fewer deviations occur. Notably, fewer illicit containers receive GREEN, while more misdeclared containers receive GREEN. We attribute this to COs accepting fewer bribes, and so more containers being inspected, and therefore the corruption of IOs having a greater influence.

Tariff levels. As their level rises, the incentive to avoid tariffs increases—in a system where an alternative (deviant) path of container clearance exists. We observe an increase in bribe level and in delay, presumably due to FFs having more incentive to negotiate with the CO. Revenue increases, supposing that the level of imports is unaffected by the tariff level (we also experimented with scenarios where container imports have a negative elasticity to tariff increases; results not reported here). Overall, increasing tariffs can be seen as not being an effective policy in that it not only increases bribes, but will certainly make the port less competitive as importers' costs grow.

Fine levels. Akin to tariffs, as the fine level rises for deviant containers, the incentive to avoid a fine (by acting honestly) increases, but so does the incentive to offer larger bribes (to better ensure the container is not found to be RED). As a result, the customs revenue goes up significantly while the bribe level goes up only moderately. Other metrics remain similar to the baseline case.

Experiment	Time (hrs)	Delay (hrs)	Cost ($)	Deviations	#Deviant (% Not Caught)	Revenue ($)	Bribe ($)
baseline	109	19	26029	12.7	20834 (81%)	18277	503
high illicit	104	10	60151	12.4	144546 (76%)	49551	789
OA honesty	108	19	25962	12.9	18695 (80%)	18443	502
low corruption	106	17	27027	11.9	21038 (78%)	19360	474
low coercive	108	18	27134	12.1	20806 (79%)	19508	463
higher tariff (x4)	110	23	62218	13.0	20799 (81%)	54436	506
punitive fines	108	19	35977	12.8	21085 (81%)	28235	510
more inspection	56	4	30005	8.9	20868 (62%)	20886	1139
perfect inspection	107	18	26605	12.9	20952 (80%)	18822	505
more staff	106	18	26037	12.3	20598 (81%)	18369	492
higher salary	110	19	29878	12.6	20861 (86%)	17232	2475
more audits	107	16	54926	10.1	20453 (28%)	47354	462
many more audits	93	10	41709	5.8	20416 (19%)	33982	625
higher penalties	109	19	50169	12.2	20762 (42%)	42509	502
stronger IT	102	16	26799	11.2	21419 (80%)	19014	495
electronic payment	60	7	26041	11.0	21097 (82%)	18314	503
IT & electronic	57	5	26698	9.5	21028 (80%)	18926	495

Table 4: Snapshot KPI results for baseline scenario, localized policy changes, and process re-engineering.

Chance of inspection. As the number of inspections increase, the percentage of deviant containers found GREEN decreases from 80% in the baseline case to 62%. This decrease, however, is not as substantial as the comparative increase in bribes. Thus, rather than being incentivized to act honestly, the FFs increase bribes to avoid the inspection. Hence, customs revenue remains consistent with the baseline case while bribe levels and increase substantially. Note that the apparent drop in deviations is only the headline figure of the total number, because deviation types such as work-slow deviations, protracted bribe negotiation, and extra inspections and reduced by the larger bribes. Positively, in one sense, delay decreases since containers are being expedited by the CO and inspections waived.

Second, as the quality (i.e., thoroughness) of inspections improves, no change is seen relative to the baseline case. This is likely due to the endemic corruption leading to only a small number of containers actually being inspected.

Customs department size. Adding more staff to the customs department does increase capacity, at the cost of increased salary. The corruption effects (e.g., work-slow, negotiation delays, improper container prioritization) hamper any increase in container throughput. There is only a marginal effect on corruption, since a FF can still influence which of the increase pool of COs is assigned to a container.

Wage scale. Substantially increasing salary, by an order of magnitude greater than the current schedule of bribes, has the effect of making CO agents unlikely to risk accepting a bribe in the short term—until the bribe schedule adapts in the medium term. Salary cost obviously also increases.

Chance of audit. We expected that increased risk of being (honestly) audited will make customs agents less likely to accept bribes. The value of the bribes, however, shows an interesting pattern with an initial decrease in the bribe levels with a moderate number of audits, but with a large number of audits, the bribe levels increase, while both the revenue and costs decrease. We attribute this observation to a greater number of learning opportunities for the customs employees and for the FFs, whose interactions then emerge into a new stable state of higher bribes, to outweigh the greater expected cost if caught. In all cases, more audits ensure that a low percentage of deviant containers receive a GREEN decision. Although enforcement cost increases and the audits take time, overall the delay decreases. We attribute this to less negotiation between FF and CO, and less slow-working by customs staff.

Level of penalty on corrupt customs actors. The baseline scenario has a flat penalty of 6 times monthly salary for COs, if an audit discovers impropriety. Increasing the penalty has an effect much like increasing the chance of audit, although the magnitude of its effect is smaller.

Process Re-Engineering.

Granted that process re-engineering (often, simplification) is an important means to reduce the opportunities for process deviations [23], an advantage of MABS is their use in qualitative predictions of (side-)effects in novel situations, for which other types of models (e.g., equation-based) do not apply because of the novelty [12].

Strengthening *LIGHT* IT system. First, suppose that the *LIGHT* IT system is modified such that the Head of Customs cannot override allocations of containers to Customs Officers made by the system. The effect is that the relationship between FF and CO is likely to be reduced. The observed consequence is that deviations decrease, together with bribe levels and delay decrease. There is a small increase in revenue. Enforcement costs see a minor increase.

Streamlining payment sub-process. Second, suppose that the way FF pay for cleared containers is modified such that Excise Officers no longer have an intermediary role. Rather, when notified of the total payment due, the FF submits the payment electronically. The effect is that the opportunity for EOs to modify (reduce) or solicit for a cut of the payment is removed. We also expect that the automation in the payment process will accelerate the overall customs process. Indeed, the observed consequence is a sizeable decrease in delay (from 19 [baseline] to 7 hours) and a decrease in the number of deviations.

Combining the two process re-engineering policies is surprisingly effective at further reducing delay and decreasing the number of deviations: average delay drops to 5 hours and the number of deviations to 9.5.

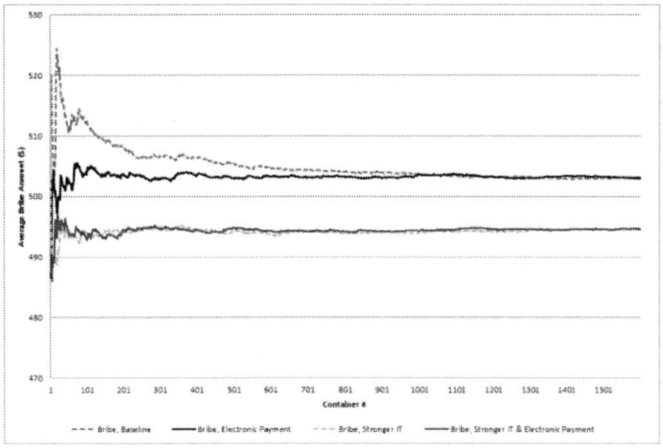

Figure 2: Process re-engineering effects on bribe level. Cumulative averages per container as averaged over 100 runs of 1600 containers.

Fig. 2 highlights the impact of these different policy re-engineering strategies on the cumulative average of the bribe level per container across the 1600 containers in each simulation run. Following the initial period (approximately the first 50 containers) where the system moves into steady state, the effect of the actors' adaptivity can be observed, until the bribe level reaches an equilibrium average value. Strengthening the *LIGHT* system leads to a lower equilibrium average bribe level, whereas streamlining the payments leads to faster convergence but the equilibrium level is the same as in the baseline. We attribute this same level as due to the limited opportunity EOs have to influence bribe levels, being the last customs department actor in the import process and the actor receiving the last cut of the bribe pie. Note that other KPIs, e.g., time and delay, do have different values as a direct effect of the electronic payments.

We conclude that many of the localized policy measures examined are impotent in a situation of endemic corruption—and can exhibit unexpected side-effects—whereas selected process re-engineering offers more promise because it can reduce the frequency of opportunities for deviation. Only a change in internal culture and norms, or rigorous and honest audits with the threat of sizeable penalties, deters customs staff from the lure of collusive or coercive corruption. The web of corruption thickens as in-group relationships increase, suggesting further study on the causes and effects of such relationships [32, 46, 29].

6. SUMMARY AND OUTLOOK

Our objective in this paper was to use agent-based simulation to explore the impact of reform policy measures on maritime customs. We detailed the design of a MABS of customs imports, based on processes and deviations from them at an archetypal Mediterranean port in a context of widespread corruption. The simulation models collusive and coercive corruption, in-group relationships, and agents' adaptive behaviours in negotiation.

Simulation enables us to provide important qualitative insights into what-if policy scenarios, which are not readily subject to hypothesis-and-test experimentation in the real world. Taken as a whole, our observed results correlate with the literature that "localized punitive- or incentive-based policies cannot correct a situation of widespread corruption" [23]. We found that modifying existing process factors such as fines and wage levels had little effect in a situation of endemic corruption, that measures such as inspections could increase customs revenue but not reduce deviations—rather, bribe amounts simply increased—and that deviations could be reduced only by increasing audits, which can have unexpected side-effects. Further, in practice in such a setting, the auditors are themselves open to corruption [1]. Focusing on process re-engineering was found to offer more promise. Strengthening the autonomy of the IT system reduced bribe levels and deviations, while streamlining processes through the introduction of electronic payment of duties reduced both deviations and delays although not the bribe levels.

The results of our study are subject to a set of limitations: (1) scope of the MABS, e.g., the focus on bi-lateral bribe-based deviations; (2) accuracy of data, e.g., about deviations from the published process—despite the efforts towards triangulation reported in Sect. 2, the nature of non-standard behaviour makes deviant behaviour difficult to document and harder still to verify; (3) fidelity of agent behaviour modelled, particularly in regard to motivations/goals, and negotiation patterns; (4) actors not explicitly modelled, and stakeholders at other levels outside the customs import process (e.g., societal, policy makers); (5) factors excluded from the MABS, such as patronage; and (6) calibration and validation on a single port instance.

While recognizing the limitations of a MABS, our results to date serve as the basis for a broader stakeholder discussion. Ultimately, we want to understand not only the potential effectiveness of reform measures, but their impact at multiple levels to the behaviours of the stakeholders of the port socio-technical system. Notably, in the longer term, stakeholders with power to set policy must be engaged in order for there to be application of any policy measures.

We mention four lines of ongoing and future work. First, to expand the scope of simulation by, for instance, including additional actors and enhancing individual agent negotiation behaviours. Second, to examine in detail the effect of in-group relationship on policy efficacy, and to consider specific reform policies in the context of high and low levels of such relationships and with specific social network structures. Third, to include export processes, since containers imported into one port have been exported from another. Lastly, to compare behaviours to other contexts [38]. While process deviations similar to our archetypal port are widespread across the Mediterranean and elsewhere [10, 47, 5, 45], we posit that MABS can give insight into the relative effectiveness of policies in different socio-political, socio-economic, governmental, and cultural contexts.

Acknowledgements. We thank the anonymous reviewers. We thank E. Gerding, J. Hess, C. M. Karam, T. Miller, P. Perez, and the anonymous participants of our field studies. We thank M. Assaad, A. Chereith, T. Eid, H. Harb, R. Outa, and S. Zeitouny, and also thank P. Atie. This work was partially supported by University Research Board grant numbers A88813 and 288810 from the American University of Beirut, and grant number OFFER_C1_2013_2014 from the Olayan School of Business. NYS thanks the Operations group at the Cambridge Judge Business School and the fellowship at St Edmund's College.

REFERENCES

[1] S. Abdallah, R. Sayed, I. Rahwan, B. L. LeVeck, M. Cebrian, A. Rutherford, and J. H. Fowler. Corruption drives the emergence of civil society. *J. Royal Society Interface*, 11(93):20131044, 2014.

[2] T. Balke, S. Cranefield, G. D. Tosto, S. Mahmoud, M. Paolucci, B. T. R. Savarimuthu, and H. Verhagen. Simulation and NorMAS. In *Normative Multi-Agent Systems*, Dagstuhl Follow-Ups, pages 171–189. 2013.

[3] M. Bergkvist, P. Davidsson, J. A. Persson, and L. Ramstedt. A hybrid micro-simulator for determining the effects of governmental control policies on transport chains. In *Proc. of MABS'04*, LNCS 3415, pages 236–247, New York, NY, 2005. Springer.

[4] L. Braubach and A. Pokahr. The Jadex project: Simulation. In *Multiagent Systems and Applications*, pages 107–128. Springer, 2013.

[5] M. Chêne. Literature review on corruption at ports and border points in Southern Africa. Expert Answers 387, U4 Anti-Corruption Resource Centre, 2013.

[6] Customs department denies port corruption. The Daily Star, 22 Dec. 2012.

[7] P. Davidsson, J. Holmgren, H. Kyhlbäck, D. Mengistu, and M. Persson. Applications of agent based simulation. In *Proc. of MABS'06*, LNCS 4442, pages 15–27, New York, NY, 2007. Springer.

[8] W. Diab, N. Jarrouj, and G. B. Melki. Corruption on the Port of Beirut. American University of Beirut, PSPA 202, Spring 2013–14, 2014.

[9] V. Dignum, F. Dignum, S. A. Osinga, and G. J. Hofstede. Normative, cultural and cognitive aspects of modelling policies. In *Proc. of WSC'10*, pages 720–732, 2010.

[10] B. Dillman. Shining light on the shadows: The political economy of illicit transactions in the Mediterranean. *Mediterranean Politics*, 12(2):121–139, 2007.

[11] B. Edmonds. The use of models: Making MABS more informative. In *Proc. of MABS'00*, LNCS 1979, pages 15–32, New York, NY, 2001. Springer.

[12] B. Edmonds, C. Hernandez, and K. G. Troitzsch, editors. *Social Simulation: Technologies, Advances and New Discoveries*. Information Science Reference, Hershey, PA, 2007.

[13] R. El Hafez. Who are the taxpayers? Where money does get spent. In *Lebanon Opportunities*, pages 41–57. InfoPro SAL, Oct. 2014.

[14] M. Finger and P. Schuler. *Implementation of Uruguay Round Commitments: The Development Challenge*. Blackwell, Oxford, UK, 2000.

[15] T. Gong. Dangerous collusion: corruption as a collective venture in contemporary China. *Communist and Post-Communist Studies*, 35(1):85–103, 2002.

[16] O. Habib. Customs graft costing treasury $400m a year. The Daily Star, 4 Dec. 2013.

[17] D. Halawi. Khalil vows to crack down on corruption at Customs. The Daily Star, 8 Nov. 2014.

[18] R. Hammond. Endogenous transition dynamics in corruption: An agent-based computer model. Working Paper 19, Brookings Institution, 2000.

[19] H. Harb, F. J. Srour, and N. Yorke-Smith. A case study in model selection for policy engineering: Simulating maritime customs. In *Advanced Agent Technology*, LNCS 7068, pages 3–18. Springer, New York, NY, 2012.

[20] L. Henesey, P. Davidsson, and J. A. Persson. Agent based simulation architecture for evaluating operational policies in transshipping containers. *JAAMAS*, 18(2):220–238, 2009.

[21] L. E. Henesey, T. E. Notteboom, and P. Davidsson. Agent-based simulation of stakeholders relations: An approach to sustainable port and terminal management. In *Proc. of Intl. Association of Maritime Economists Annual Conf.*, pages 314–331, 2003.

[22] P. Horden and N. Purcell. *The Corrupting Sea: A Study of Mediterranean History*. Blackwell, Oxford, UK, 2000.

[23] I. Hors. Fighting corruption in customs administration: What can we learn from recent experiences? OECD Development Centre Working Paper 175, OECD, 2001.

[24] H. Illeik. Port of Beirut: A sea of corruption. Al Akhbar, 11 Jan. 2012.

[25] D. Jancsics and I. Jávor. Corrupt governmental networks. *International Public Management Journal*, 15:62–99, 2012.

[26] M. Johnston. *Syndroms of Corruption: Wealth, Power, and Democracy*. Cambridge University Press, New York, NY, 2005.

[27] R. Klitgaard, R. MacLean-Abaroa, and H. L. Parris. *Corrupt Cities: A Practical Guide to Cure and Prevention*. ICS Press, Oakland, CA, 2000.

[28] P. Langseth. Prevention: An effective tool to reduce corruption. In *Proc. of ISPAC Conf. on Responding to the Challenge of Corruption*, 1999.

[29] M. Lauchs, R. Keast, and N. Yousefpour. Corrupt police networks: Uncovering hidden relationship patterns, functions and roles. *Policing & Society*, 21(1):110–127, 2011.

[30] Lebanese Customs Authority. Lebanese customs. `www.customs.gov.lb/customs`. [Online; 29-Sep-2015].

[31] P. Lokuge and D. Alahakoon. Improving the adaptability in automated vessel scheduling in container ports using intelligent software agents. *EJOR*, 177(3):1985–2015, 2007.

[32] J. Makhoul and L. Harrison. Intercessory wasta and village development in Lebanon. *Arab Studies Quarterly*, 26(3):25–41, 2004.

[33] M. B. Marietto, N. David, J. S. Sichman, and H. Coelho. A classification of paradigmatic models for agent-based social simulation. In *Proc. of MABS'03*, LNCS 2927, pages 193–208, New York, NY, 2003. Springer.

[34] G. Muller. *Intermodal Freight Transportation*. Eno Transportation Foundation and Intermodal Association of North America, 4th edition, 1999.

[35] E. Norling, L. Sonenberg, and R. Rönnquist. Enhancing multi-agent based simulation with human-like decision making strategies. In *Proc. of MABS'00*, LNCS 1979, pages 349–357, New York, NY, 2001. Springer.

[36] R. Outa. Formal modeling and verification of maritime container processing. Master's thesis, American University of Beirut, 2013.

[37] A. Pokahr, L. Braubach, and W. Lamersdorf. Jadex: A BDI Reasoning Engine. In *Multi-Agent Programming*, pages 149–174, New York, NY, 2005. Springer.

[38] M. Y. A. Rawwas, G. L. Patzer, and S. J. Vitell. A cross-cultural investigation of the ethical values of consumers: The potential effect of war and civil disruption. *J. Business Ethics*, 17:435–448, 1998.

[39] S. Rose-Ackerman. Corruption and government. *International Peacekeeping*, 15(3):328–343, 2008.

[40] E. Sakr. Corruption widespread, deep-rooted at Beirut Port. The Daily Star, 13 Nov. 2012.

[41] R. G. Sargent. Verification and validation of simulation models. In *Proc. of WSC'07*, pages 124–137, 2007.

[42] L. J. Sawaya. What kind of future for the Port of Beirut? Master's thesis, MIT, 2002.

[43] A. Seleim and N. Bontis. The relationship between culture and corruption: A cross-national study. *J. Intellectual Capital*, 10(1):165–184, 2009.

[44] S. Sequeira. Displacing corruption: Evidence from a tariff liberalization program. `personal.lse.ac.uk/sequeira/Displacing_Corruption_Sequeira.pdf`, 2013. [Online; 28-Sep-2015].

[45] S. Sequeira and S. Djankov. Corruption and firm behavior: Evidence from African ports. *J. International Economics*, 94(2):277–294, 2014.

[46] Y. Sidani and W. L. Gardner. Work values in the Arab culture: The case of Lebanese workers. *J. Social Psychology*, 140(5):597–607, 2000.

[47] P. Sioussiouras and I. Vavouras. Political rights, development, and corruption in the Balkan and Arab Mediterranean countries. *Mediterranean Quarterly*, 23:89–103, 2012.

[48] H. Situngkir. Money-Scape: A generic agent-based model of corruption. Computational Economics Archive 0405008, EconWP, 2004.

[49] F. J. Srour and N. Yorke-Smith. Towards agent-based simulation of maritime customs. In *Proc. of AAMAS'15*, pages 1637–1638, 2015.

[50] K. Sycara and T. Dai. Agent reasoning in negotiation. In *The Handbook of Group Decision and Negotiation*, chapter 26. Springer, New York, NY, 2010.

[51] The World Bank. Helping countries combat corruption: The role of the World Bank, poverty reduction and economic management network. Technical report, 1997.

[52] Transparency International. The Global Corruption Report 2009. `www.transparency.org/whatwedo/pub/global_corruption_report_2009`, 2009. [Online; 29-Sep-2015].

[53] P. van Baalen, R. Zuidwijk, and J. van Nunen. Port inter-organizational information systems. *Foundations and Trends in Technology, Information and Operations Management*, 2(2–3):81–241, 2008.

Multi-Agent Systems in Practice When Research Meets Reality

Marco Lützenberger, Tobias Küster, Nils Masuch, and Johannes Fähndrich
DAI-Labor, Technische Universität Berlin
Ernst-Reuter-Platz 7
10587 Berlin, Germany
{firstname.lastname}@dai-labor.de

ABSTRACT

The applicability and usefulness of agent technology for real world problems is still a matter of discussion—even within the AAMAS community. While theoretical models have significantly matured and led to an exciting variety of results, there were only few attempts to validate these models in reality. In this paper we aim to report on challenges that occurred when agent theory was used to approach real world problems. In doing so, we focus on the concept of planning, since planning currently appears to be one of the most relevant concepts for distributed real world applications. We examine four agent-based applications and emphasise problems that occurred when agent theory was practically applied. We also show how these problems were countered and propose more general solutions based on these tailored and context-specific approaches. The aim of this paper is to bring the two diverging branches of agent theory and practice back together in order to better adapt agent technology to the requirements of professional software.

Keywords

Automated planning; Agent theory & practice; Challenges; Industrial adoption; Service oriented architecture

1. INTRODUCTION

Research in agents and multi-agent systems has significantly matured. It seems that we, as a community, have shifted from initial experiments in building individual agents or multi-agent systems to rigorous theoretical foundations based on increasingly sophisticated computational models. Yet, despite these advances, there were only few attempts to validate these models in real world applications. The reasons for this are not entirely clear, though, the problem was recognised by the AAMAS community. At AAMAS 2015, for instance, a separate panel was being held with the objective to identify problems that hamper the 'real world validation' of agent-technology and to determine steps to counter these problems. In this panel, the community aimed to clarify the questions on whether 'we as a field are doing enough for this validation' [23, p. 30] and 'what should we do to encourage such validation in real applications' [23, p. 30].

Appears in: *Proceedings of the 15th International Conference on Autonomous Agents and Multiagent Systems (AAMAS 2016), J. Thangarajah, K. Tuyls, C. Jonker, S. Marsella (eds.), May 9–13, 2016, Singapore.*

It was not possible to find satisfying answers to these questions, though, the community agreed that it is necessary to foster the relationship between those doing foundational scientific research and those making autonomous agents and multi-agent systems a commercial or public policy reality. In more particular, practitioners were encouraged to share their experiences in applying agent-theory to real world applications and to report on problems in order to encourage improvements of theoretical foundations and to trigger further research.

In this paper we reply to this call and report on problems and limitations that were experienced during the development of real world agent applications. In doing so we focus on applications that were implemented by agent frameworks with support for the *service oriented architecture* (*SOA*) [11] design principle. When analysing existing agent applications, we recognised that a lot of works were implemented through agent frameworks with support for SOA. We explain this phenomenon with the fact that a programming framework, which merges SOA and agents innately provides many features that are required for the development of (professional) real world software, e.g. transparently connecting to and integrating with third party services and support for common protocol standards. In fact it has been argued [5, 33, 35, 40, 47] that connections to established programming paradigms is a significant factor for industrial technology adoption, thus, we consider our focus to be justified.

We start this paper by surveying concepts that have their foundation in (theoretical) agent research and that currently play a role in professional software engineering (see Section 2). For this paper we focus on one particular concept that repeatedly caused problems when applied to real world applications, namely *planning*. Thus, in Section 2.2 we elaborate on the concept of planning with particular emphasis on planning in SOA and agent environments. Based on a fundamental understanding for the latest advances in planning, we look into professional agent-based applications, where the concept of planning plays a fundamental role and discuss difficulties that occurred when planning theory was used for the implementation of these applications (see Section 3). In Section 4, we structure these problems into more general categories and summarise how planning concepts had to be adjusted in the previously presented applications in order to fit their purpose. Based on these 'tailored solutions', we identify *where* and outline *how* the theoretical foundations of agent planning have to be improved in order to cope with real world requirements. We conclude this work in Section 5.

2. SERVICE ORIENTATION

In this work we put a focus on applications that were implemented through agent frameworks with support for SOA. SOA is an established design principle, which made its way into professional software engineering and applications. Any merger of SOA and agent-based techniques thus provides support for developing autonomous and highly distributed entities, which can connect (in a standardised fashion) to a broad spectrum of available real world functionality (or services). In this section we provide an overview over principles of and current trends in merging SOA and agents. Due to its importance for real world applications we put particular emphasis on the concept of planning. In the next section we use this fundamental understanding in order to analyse existing agent applications.

2.1 Semantic Services

Currently there are four SOA trends, which are relevant for the agent world. Each trend provides remarkable solutions, yet, it has to be mentioned that some of these solutions are far away from practical applicability. Following Papazoglou et al. [38], these trends can be classified as:

- Service Foundations,
- Service Composition,
- Service Management,
- Service Engineering.

The category *Service Foundations* comprises principal concepts, e.g. a service-oriented middleware that connects service providers and offers service deployment and discovery mechanisms. The *Service Engineering* category, in turn, comprises the specification of services and of their internal processes.

Service Composition is based on concepts that can be classified as Service Foundations and describes the aggregation of multiple services to a value-added service, which, itself, may be a part of more complex compositions. In the beginning, orchestration was done manually, e.g. by means of service description standards like *WSDL* and orchestration languages like *WS-BPEL* [37]. These mechanisms were able to foster interoperability between services (and thus between agents that offer services), yet, the workflow was predefined, static and not dynamically adaptable unless the designer clearly specified alternatives or abstract adaptation patterns [48].

A more flexible approach to compose services is referred to as *automated composition of services*. Automated service composition is a concept, which aims to automatically find and combine services in order to achieve a certain goal. Automated service composition should be flexible and robust enough to compensate for unforeseen changes in the environment, e.g. service failures or the sudden emergence of services with a higher quality value. All of these aspects are discussed under the umbrella of *Service Management*. Furthermore, Service Management also comprises concepts like Self-* properties such as self-healing or self-optimising (the latter more commonly known as 'self-organisation', when it comes to the field of agent research).

We already mentioned that this work is focused on agent frameworks with support for SOA, thus, we can assume that an agent's capabilities are offered as services. It is obvious that advances in automated service composition directly further the progress of agent-based computing. Despite the importance of automated service composition, real world applications are sparse. The reasons for this are not entirely clear, though, the lack of (more) comprehensive solutions might be a factor.

We deem automated service composition to be one of the most promising software-engineering concepts and thus proceed by discussing automated service composition in the light of agent-functionalities that are offered in compliance with SOA. We conclude this section with a detailed explanation of automated planning procedures—the ultimate driving-force for service composition.

Semantics.

In order to make autonomic behaviour in the process of service composition possible, agents have to be able to interpret the purpose and effects of other agents' services. This can be achieved with the help of semantics. Semantics usually rely on a formal specification and enable the definition of ontologies. Ontologies represent the domain of concern and define interrelationships between entities. Contrary to common programming languages, which can also be used for domain modelling, semantic languages come up with more complex constructs, such as restrictions, axioms and rules. These constructs make the automatic categorisation of information considerably more accurate. Established approaches in this area are the *Knowledge Interchange Format (KIF)* [15], the *Planning Domain Language (PDDL)* [17], the *Web Services Modelling Language (WSML)* [8] and the *Web Ontology Language (OWL)* [34].

Semantic Services.

Despite its capabilities, the ontological representation of the domain does not enable the automated interpretation of services. What is actually required is a structure that specifies how semantics are related to service properties and to an agent's functionalities, respectively. These structures exist in the form of semantic service description languages, e.g. *Semantic Web Services Framework (SWSF)*,[1] *Web Service Modeling Ontology (WSMO)*,[2] *Semantic Annotations for WSDL (SAWSDL)* [26], *Web Service Modeling Language (WSML)* [14], *DIANE Service Description Language (SDS)* [28] and the *Web Ontology Language for Services (OWL-S)* [31], to name but a few. Some of these languages are 'lightweight approaches', providing information about inputs and outputs only, others are more complex and allow for the definition of preconditions, effects or even Quality-of-Service parameters. The bottom-line is: semantic service description languages are able to make services machine-readable and interpretable.

Semantic Service Matchmaking.

Assuming an appropriate semantic description, it is possible to equip agents with mechanisms that are able to automatically discover 'promising' services. Such concept is commonly known as service matchmaking. Currently, there are several service matchmaking approaches available. One particular category is focusing on functional parameters such

[1] SWSF website: `www.w3.org/Submission/SWSF/`
[2] WSMO website: `www.w3.org/Submission/WSMO/`

as inputs, outputs, preconditions and effects (also referred to as IOPE) and is using taxonomical analyses, lexicographic methods, and rule reasoning for the comparison of service request and advertisement [24, 29, 32]. Other approaches put emphasis on Quality-of-Service properties (non-functional) in order to find promising service options. There are also approaches [4, 6], which combine both mechanisms. A service matchmaker can be understood as a one-step planner, thus, a service matchmaker can be always be used as a basic module for a more comprehensive planning approach.

2.2 Planning with Services

Most available AI planning approaches are based on a search through a solution space. Solutions that are based on service composition and the execution of composed services are scarce [18]. In this work, we focus on software agents that are compatible with the SOA paradigm, thus, we understand a service as a semantically described action of an agent and also as a basic building block of a construct, which we refer to as 'plan'. Developing plans is extremely challenging [36] and usually starts with the abstract creation of a plan and ends with its execution. Creating plans at runtime aggravates the problem by adding practical challenges [2].

AI planning is well explored, thus, most of the automated service composition approaches transform their services into PDDL descriptions and then use standard AI planning algorithms for solving the planning problem. Examples for such approaches are *WSPlan* [39], *OWLS-XPlan* [25], or were presented by Sirin et al. [45], Akkiraju et al. [1], or Hatzi et al. [20]. All these works are based on a similar mechanism, that is: i) transforming service descriptions to PDDL or another logic language, ii) using a planning algorithm to solve the search problem, iii) translating the results into a sequence of service calls. Due to this mechanism, the capability of most automated service composition approaches (even the latest developments, cf. Sabatucci and Cossentino [42]) is determined by the capability of the underlying logical language. Furthermore, depending on the particular approach, different theoretic properties like the *Open World Assumption* or the *Frame Problem* are 'flexibly interpreted' in order to meet the requirements of the modelling space of the applied language. The effects of these design decisions are commonly neglected.

Only a few solutions approach the problem of service composition directly in the service domain and by means of AI planning. One promising approach was presented by Sathya and Hemalatha [43]. The authors propose a high-level architecture including a *Universal Description, Discovery and Integration* repository and a mechanism that composes registered services to an invocation order. Fähndrich et al. [13] argue that state definition planning can be executed directly in OWL and propose to use OWL-S for planning based on service description. The authors suggest to describe either the start or the goal state and to use SWRL to describe the effects of actions. A similar approach to avoid transformations to languages other than OWL-S, was presented by Redavid et al. [41]. In order to avoid the dependency to an underlying language, the authors propose to create SWRL-DL rules from the input and output parameters of the service if the OWL-S service description provides no information about preconditions or effects. These rules can be stored in a domain ontology were initial knowledge and goals are constantly updated. After creating and storing SWRL rules in the ontology, a backward search is used in order to find a path that is able to achieve the pursued goal. This path can be considered as a composition of service calls. A similar service-based approach was presented by Cruz et al. [7]. The approach is based on services, which are described in OWL-S and which support SWRL rules. The output parameters of the services can be used for analysis or for input parameters of other services. To this end, the approach focusses on output parameters of services and not on 'world-altering' effects like in other solutions. Tong et al. [46] integrate agents with service composition techniques. The authors present a distributed planning algorithm, namely *Distributed Planning Algorithm for Web Service Composition* (*DPAWSC*), which transforms the service composition problem into a graph search problem according to the dependencies among service agents.

The application of web service languages motivates further theoretic and practical solutions. In more particular, it is necessary to discuss problems that occur when planning theory is being executed. The first challenge here is to differentiate two types of services:

World-altering services are services, which cause changes in the environment when being executed. During planning these effects are only simulated on a virtual state, however, during the execution of a plan, services have effects. These have to be handled if the plan fails during execution.

Information services are services, which provide information, without having any other effect. The effect (the abstract knowledge of an agent) of such a service cannot be described in PDDL [19].

During the planning process, the effects of executed information services have to be considered. To account for this, the planning process has to instantiate individuals that represent the abstract knowledge in the current state, respectively. Summing up, we do not only have to deal with the commonly known frame problem [16], but with this new problem of remembering state-knowledge as well.

Additionally the semantic service research is done in compliance with the *Open World Assumption*, which means that facts can be either 'true', 'false', or 'unknown' (compared to the *Closed World Assumption*, where facts can only be 'true' or 'false') [39]. The creation of a locally closed world eases these two challenges, yet, the underlying theoretic problem on the other hand remains unsolved [9].

Practically there is no reasoner available, which exceeds the capabilities of *SWRL:B*[3] and *SWRL:X*[4], e.g. modelling of lists, sets, maps, and instance or class creation. Thus, contrary to PDDL, semantic services maintain the expressiveness of describing more than 'add lists' and 'delete lists' in an effect, however, the usage is limited due to the lack of theoretic reasoning capabilities of current reasoners.

3. SCENARIOS

There are many scenarios how those advances in service technology can be used in current trends such as the *Internet of Things*, human-computer-interaction, smart cities,

[3]SWRL:B website: `www.daml.org/rules/proposal/builtins.html`

[4]SWRL:X website: `swrl.stanford.edu/ontologies/built-ins/3.3/swrlx.owl`

etc. In this section, we present a number of current research projects: The 'smart home' of *Connected Living*, the charging optimisation of *MSG EUREF*, the intermodal route planning of *IMA*, and the service orchestration of EMD. Each project uses some of the aforementioned service paradigms; in particular, each employs some form of planning. In the following, we look at each of those in more detail.

3.1 Connected Living

The *Connected Living* (CL) project is about creating a 'smart home', featuring different devices and services. Each of those devices is represented by a software agent, providing services for the different sensors and actuators of the device, e.g. for reading a humidity sensor or for turning off the heater or for switching on a lamp. Those services can be controlled via 'assistants', i.e. another kind of agent providing different web UIs and/or rules for controlling the device agents. Those agents can be added to and removed from the platform dynamically at runtime.

The CL assistants and rules have been implemented in a demonstration platform that has been evaluated in a small number of selected households. Parts of the CL system eventually passed into the *IO-LITE* platform[5].

With each of the services being semantically annotated with input and output, precondition and effect, as well as some quality-of-service metrics, those device agents' services can be planned with, and orchestrated to more complex services according to the user's goals.

Consider the following scenario: Instead of manually operating the light, the blinds, or the air conditioning, the user simply states the goal 'I want my room to be warm and bright'. First, the system would determine what 'my room' refers to, using context information provided by the user, and filtering the services that relate to the same room. Then, it matches services that have an effect on brightness, such as turning on different lamps in the room, or operating the blinds, as well as services regulating the temperature, like heaters and air conditioning. Depending on the current conditions, some of those services are applicable, and others are not—opening the blinds will not make it brighter if it is dark outside, and turning on the heater does not do any good if it is already too warm in the room. The remaining services are then assessed w.r.t. the quality-of-service attributes that are relevant to the user in the current situation, and one or more of the services are executed.

The planning problem encountered in this project is not too difficult. While the number of devices can be rather high, and each device can have multiple services, those services usually have discrete parameters, making the search-space as a whole finite and not too large. Also, as few of the devices' effects depend on effects from other devices, service chains are rather short; in fact, a single service execution is often enough to achieve a goal.

3.2 MSG EUREF

The project *MSG EUREF* is part of a larger group of projects in the *Schaufenster Elektromobilität* that are concerned with finding optimal charging schedules for electric vehicles in a micro-smart grid (MSG) [30]. The different projects are based on the same abstract domain model and the same optimisation algorithm, with a few specific adaptations for each of the projects.

[5]IO-LITE website: `iolite.de/`

The MSG EUREF project is currently in the final stage of its field test at the EUREF campus. In this field test, the application creates charging schedules for two local buffer storages, six charging stations for electric vehicles, and a combined heat and power plant.

The core of each of those projects is a domain model, describing the different components of the micro smart grids, such as different charging stations, storages, and vehicles, as well as abstract concepts such as prognoses, bookings, and charging schedules. Those models are used in a multi-stage optimisation for finding an optimal schedule for charging the vehicles and local storages for meeting a certain goal (usually a set of bookings) while making best use of locally produced energy and low energy prices [21].

The optimisation is subdivided into several stages:

1. Using machine learning to predict energy available from local production.
2. Assignment of vehicles to bookings, swappable storages to vehicles, and vehicles to charging stations.
3. Optimisation of the charging schedules using stochastic optimisation.
4. Load-smoothening using local storages and/or combined heat and power plants.

Each of those stages is represented as a service provided by a different agent. For some stages, different implementations are available (reflecting the requirements of the different sub-projects), to be orchestrated to the overall optimisation process [22].

The schedule is created using a $(\mu/\rho + \lambda)$ evolution strategy, a form of genetic algorithm [10]. Starting with an empty schedule, the algorithm repeatedly recombines the 'parent' schedules, creating and mutating 'offspring' schedules and assessing them by simulating the charging processes in those schedules. A numeric quality measure is determined by calculating the weighted sum of some key metrics, such as ratio of bookings fulfilment, and total energy cost. The schedules that have the highest quality are carried over to the next generation and the process is repeated until the quality converges.

While this project is also concerned with creating a plan, or a schedule, the approach to planning is entirely different than in the one before. Here, the number of different actions is very limited (charging or discharging any of the storages), but the actions have multiple continuous parameters (start of charging, end of charging, and charging power). The effect of the actions is well-understood, to the point where it can be accurately simulated, and small changes in input parameters yield small changes in the action's result, making the application of stochastic and local search algorithms possible.

3.3 IMA

The *Intermodal Assistance for Megacities*, or *IMA*[6] project aims to tackle the problem of integrating ever diversifying mobility services: Next to public transportation and private cars, car and ride sharing are becoming more prevalent in large cities, and often a combination of different means of transportation is the best option.

[6]IMA website: `ima.dai-labor.de`

In IMA, mobility providers can register and offer their services by implementing interfaces for corresponding routing requests. The approach allows for the development of high-level functionality, which autonomously accesses, assesses and utilises available services. Those are integrated into an assistance system, which calculates and proposes intermodal routes that are tailored to the individual preferences and requirements of users. To make this work, services are specified through semantic service descriptions, using OWL-S, containing preconditions, effects, and descriptions of the service's attributes, to be matched against the user's preferences.

Based on a semantically enriched service landscape, intermodal route calculation becomes a typical planning problem. The algorithm accesses the distributed platform and uses a semantic service matchmaking component to determine services that fit to the user's preferences and characteristics (e.g. if the user has no driver's license, the planner must not include car-sharing services). After the matching-procedure, all locations or stations of possible mobility services are integrated as nodes into a graph, which are in turn assembled to clusters indicating potential changing locations between modes of transportation. Next, the costs are estimated by an objective function considering the user's preferences, such as time, monetary costs, ecological footprint, and others. In order to be able to set the preferences into relation, each of them is normalised according to the worst estimation for the respective route. Based on this heuristic, an optimal intermodal routing solution can be searched for on the graph using the A-star algorithm.

The system was implemented as a distributed multi-agent system, encapsulating bits of functionality as individual software agents. In doing so, inter-agent communication works 'out-of-the-box', and new agents can be deployed to the system without need for further configuration, even at runtime. As a consequence, mobility service providers simply have to implement an agent providing the respective service, interfacing with the backend service running on their own hardware, and deploy this agent to the IMA system. This approach facilitates the providers' data sovereignty, increases trust and eases the access to the system. The agent-based approach enables the development of more sophisticated route-finding approaches, e.g. approaches in which software agents represent mobility providers as bidders in auctions where a customer's mobility requests are negotiated.

The IMA system is deployed in Berlin, Germany. The application includes detailed information about the local public transportation network, three car-sharing and two bike-sharing companies as well as one taxi service provider. The resulting graph comprises approximately 12,000 nodes, which are connected by more than 4 million edges. The overall graph size is significantly determined by the user's particular settings, thus, the systems' response time varies. An average response time of roughly 5 seconds was determined during a field test study. This time lag was required to compute the first set of results, yet, the philosophy of IMA is not only to rely on the best results, but to search all kinds of alternative options (in particular intermodal route options). To make this work, IMA uses a threshold of 20 seconds to search for further routing options. Results are ranked and presented to the user, who can select from the proposed options. The applied planning concepts were able to tailor route-finding in IMA to the individual preferences of the user. In more than 90 % of the cases, the user selected the same option that the IMA system assessed with the highest quality. This was also shown during the above-mentioned field test.

In IMA, planning is used in two ways: First, the low-level route finding algorithm is an example for a domain-specific, highly optimised planning algorithm. Secondly, a planning algorithm is used in order to determine the potential combinations of available routing actions, e.g. via car or via train. While those actions have very similar effects—getting the user from A to B—they can have very specific preconditions as well as quality-of-service parameters, such as the duration, cost, or eco-friendliness.

3.4 EMD

The project *EMD* (*Extendable and Adaptive E-Mobility Services*) is concerned with developing semantic service descriptions for real-world services and with using those descriptions for searching, matching, and planning with those services, so that they can be reused and orchestrated to more complex processes.

Services—both agent actions and web services—are semantically annotated using OWL-S with preconditions and effects being described in SWRL. The domain ontologies are modelled with OWL, or OWL ontologies are derived from existing Java or EMF models. Those services can then be searched for or matched against a service template, both, at development time and at runtime, using the Semantic Service Matcher $SeMa^2$ [32].

The matched services (or the service templates for matching at runtime) are then imported into BPMN process diagrams and thus orchestrated to more complex services, which can again be semantically annotated and added to the list of available services. Those processes are then either transformed to executable agent components or are invoked directly using a process interpreter agent [27].

Besides matching individual services against some service template and the manual assembly of those services to larger processes, the project is also concerned with the automated planning of complex service orchestrations [13], both at development and at runtime. Other than in many related approaches (see Section 2.2), EMD is aiming at planning directly at the OWL-S level instead of using PDDL as an abstraction, making this approach more complex, but also more applicable in practice: Services are not required to be known a-priori, but can be discovered at runtime, plus, service parameters can be any semantically described complex data type. This allows interoperability on a semantic layer and enables fuzzy service discovery by preserving grounding and feasibility. In the project EMD, 13 agents have been implemented to provide 42 example services.

Besides using the services that were defined especially for EMD, the project also aims at being integrated with the other projects (or rather, the services defined in those projects), particularly with MSG EUREF and IMA. This, however, gives rise to further challenges: As the projects were not originally designed to work together, heterogeneous technologies are used and similar concepts are described in different domain models. These and other challenges, which can also be found in many real-life problems, will be the topic of the next section.

Table 1: **Connection of research projects, planning problems and challenges.**

	Element	CL	EUREF	IMA	EMD
Planning	Informed Search			x	
	Local Search/Optim.		x		
	Semantic Services	x		x	x
	Service Matching	x		x	x
	Semantic Planning				x
Challenges	Size of Search Space		x	x	x
	Communication	x		x	x
	Gen.-Purpose Plan.			x	x
	Interoperability	x			x
	Dev. Tools	x	x		x
	Beyond PDDL	x			x

4. CHALLENGES

While specialised planning algorithms are commonly used throughout industry, there are still many open problems that hinder the application of automated general-purpose planning in real-world applications.

While each of the research projects presented in the previous section uses some form of planning, their approaches to planning are very different, ranging from informed search algorithms and optimisation for solving specific problems to semantic service matching and planning w.r.t. different available services and their preconditions and effects. Due to this heterogeneity, it is difficult to compare those projects and their respective solutions. Nevertheless we will show their most important characteristics as well as the challenges that arose from those characteristics in Table 1.

In the following, we discuss some of those challenges, and briefly outline how they could be tackled.

Communication and Interaction.

Examined applications—IMA in particular—showed that effective planning processes are frequently slowed down by the distribution of relevant planning entities and the communicational overhead that is required to exchange information between these entities. Because of this, IMA refrains from distributed planning and applies a centralised approach, which caches information that is required for the planning. The approach fits its purpose, yet, on the expense of precision and flexibility. One minor side effect of this 'adaptation' is a wrongly calculated arrival time (e.g. due to outdated traffic information), however, it is also possible that the planning algorithm proposes to use a car sharing vehicle, which is not available any more (e.g. because of outdated booking information). What we generally suggest is to find ways to decrease the information exchange in distributed planning approaches. IMA showed that caching is a way to do that, however, in this case it is necessary to include the concept of 'ageing data' in order to account for information that is not up-to-date.

Domain-specific vs. general-purpose planning.

The presented projects use very different planning algorithms: On the one hand, domain-specific, highly optimised planning algorithms are used for the routing problem and for finding charging schedules. Those algorithms do not need semantic annotations, as the semantics of the actions is often encoded in the algorithms themselves.

On the other hand, different semantically annotated services are selected and orchestrated using general-purpose planners, operating on those services' preconditions and effects. General purpose planners will never catch up, and thus never replace specialised planners in their respective domains, but there are things they could adopt. For one, some planning algorithms are incorporating heuristics, such as the minimum number of steps to reach the goal, or the number of fulfilled sub-goals in a given state. Integrating this kind of heuristics into planning algorithms like *GraphPlan* or partial order planning, as attempted, e.g. in [3], holds great promise for the future.

Interoperability among system borders.

Looking at the aforementioned scenarios, it becomes clear that the interconnection between systems of different domains will be one of the key advantages of service-oriented multi-agent systems. Especially upcoming trends like the Internet of Things, or *IoT* metaphor with presumably millions of nodes, will push the development to open and adaptive architectures. However, the need for interoperability raises a significant challenge, that is: Having a common domain model in order to exchange information. IMA and EMD are closely related to each other, therefore the developers decided to use the same model for both projects in order to ensure compatibility. The developers, however, reported that such approach involved a significant number of synchronicity problems, e.g. version control, different interpretation of attributes, or update cycles, to name but a few—let alone that the concept of common ontologies will not cope with future application requirements, especially with the requirements of the IoT.

A more general, holistic approach is required. First experiments showed that *ontology matching* [12] might work here. The basic idea of ontology matching is to (automatically) identify relations between entities of (possibly) different ontologies. Available approaches usually apply one or more matching strategies. Common strategies are name-based, string-based (*Jaro-Winkler measure* or *Cosine-similarity*), or structure-based and semantic-based strategies. The concept of ontology matching appears to be promising, especially when dealing with large numbers of (different) applications with heterogeneous models. Yet, in order to work in real world applications, several challenges have to be tackled [44]—most importantly (especially in the IoT context) 'large-scale matching'. Also, most matching solutions are design-time approaches, neglecting adaptability at runtime. Finally, an appropriate weighting of the different matching techniques within the aggregation process is missing. Tests have shown that, depending on the ontologies, specific techniques seem to be more suitable than others. An automatic approach to identify the proper technique for the respective situation is still missing.

Development and Debugging Tools.

Programming with autonomous agents in general, and with planning agents in particular, presents the developer with different challenges than in conventional programming. Besides obvious points, such as accurately annotating actions with their preconditions and effects, it can also be difficult to determine why a software agent is behaving in a certain way. The action could have been triggered by a rule, or by a plan, and that plan, again, has been selected in accordance to some goal, under the very specific circumstances that held when the goal was evaluated. It is not as easy to link a triggering event to a resulting action, and vice versa. On the one hand, this can make programming easier, as the developer does not have to care about *how* something is achieved, but on the other hand, in case something fails, it is also much harder to determine the cause of the failure.

For example, a classical exception stack trace shows the call hierarchy of a function and thus shows why and under what circumstances that function was called. But in case of a planning agent, it will just show that the action was invoked by the plan execution engine, but not why that action was selected. This calls for new programming and debugging tools, keeping track of the reasoning performed by the agent.

Also, while this is not in particular a challenge of planning, the distributed nature of agents can complicate debugging, as well. Here, a number of approaches exist, both for modelling interactions and for remotely monitoring and controlling agents and multi-agent systems.

Planning 'beyond PDDL'.

In Section 2.2, we elaborated on the complexity of planning processes, which operate on semantic description languages and which are executed in the web service domain. Below, we transfer these problems to service-agent environments and emphasise factors that aggravate the successful use of semantic descriptions for real world agent planning and service composition:

Continuous parameters vs. finite predicates: In many toy domains, object properties are modelled as predicates, representing finite state, which narrow the search space in contrast to real applications. In reality, parameters are continuous elements. These are hard to guess during a search process. As an example consider the following two descriptions: *IsOpen(Door)* and *Open(Door, 42cm)*

Expressiveness: Depending on the description logic of the language used to describe states, preconditions, effects, domain restrictions, and pursued goals, the reasoning on a service's effects can be indeterministic. Such phenomenon was demonstrated by means of the description logic *OWL-DL SROIQ(D)*.

Concretisation: In many cases, precondition and effects of services are abstract descriptions. These have to be concretised during the plan execution, since effect descriptions cannot provide all the required details. Such an effect can be demonstrated through the instantiation of an entity. The instantiation process has to set all mandatory parameters (either by inheritance or by inference).

Knowledge representation: At runtime, the agent has access to the representation of the currently executed plan. Additionally acquired knowledge as well as the interpretation of this knowledge cannot be represented. Furthermore, stronger reasoning at runtime on preconditions and effects is needed.

Blending planning and execution: Execution of information services during plan time and monitoring of service execution at runtime are additional concepts, which should be reflected in the description of services. Also, it is not possible to formally represent failures that occur during the execution of a plan. This is not limited to, but includes Quality-of-Service parameters.

The (automatic) composition of functionality that is described by semantics, has great potential—if not the highest potential of all planning-related techniques. Yet, available approaches require much improvement and further research in order to cope with real world problems.

5. CONCLUSION

In this paper we showed that, despite the fact that the agent-community deems several approaches as 'adequately matured', there still are significant problems when these theories are turned into reality. We used the concept of planning to emphasise the practical implications of these problems. In order to do that, we analysed existing agent-based applications with an adequate level of sophistication and maturity and that were developed to serve a real world purpose. The aim of this analysis was to collect planning-related problems that occurred during the implementation of these applications and to show how and to what extend these problems were countered.

In total we identified five categories of problems. To start with, software agents that serve a real world purpose frequently have to communicate to entities in different computer networks via Ethernet or mobile communication protocols. In terms of transmission rates, these protocols are highly optimised, thus, we do not see much potential for improvements here. Rather, more efficient 'real-world-ready' planning approaches are required, or, from a scientific point of view it is necessary to answer questions like: *Is it possible to implement planning algorithms that feature the same level of quality as established approaches, but at the same time require a decreased number of interactions between the involved entities?* Established planning approaches (see Section 2.2) are—in theory—able to include large numbers of agents, yet, in reality it was shown that these approaches reach their limits with 30 to 40 entities that are involved in the planning process. In the IMA project this limitation was countered through a centralised planning approach, which grabs and caches information from all available agents before planning is done. The approach fits purposes, though, on the expense of the planning's quality and flexibility. Due to the fact that information is being cached, planning is not based on the latest data, e.g. up-to-the-minute traffic information or newly deployed or adjusted mobility and transportation services. Thus, for a more comprehensive application of agent technology in a similar context, the communication overhead between planning-relevant entities has to be decreased. The IMA project showed that such problem can be approached by information caching mechanisms.

Secondly, in order to account for the connection of many different applications, some form of ontology matching is required. Examined applications (IMA and EMD in particular) avoided such approach by defining a common domain model, yet, the analysis of both applications showed that a common foundation quickly reaches its limit. Especially when it comes to the maintenance tasks, version control, or update cycles, common approaches are clearly inferior to the more flexible ontology matching. Ontology matching (at least current approaches), however, is not ready for real world applications. There are several problems that have to be tackled—most importantly support for 'large-scale matching'. This feature becomes increasingly important in the context of the Internet of Things. Other problems are the missing support for adaptability at runtime and an appropriate weighting of the different matching techniques within the aggregation process.

Thirdly, we emphasised that two different types of planning were applied, namely specialised and general purpose planning. The advantage of general purpose planners is the possibility to comprehensively reuse existing software (mostly with minor additions). Yet, general purpose planners are usually slow and thus not applicable to problems where results are required quickly. The analysis of existing agent-based applications substantiated this thesis since specialised planning solutions were preferred. However, when looking into specialised solutions we were able to identify one feature that can be adopted by general approaches, that is, the incorporation of heuristics. Some approaches include heuristics like the minimum number of steps to reach the goal or the number of fulfilled sub-goals in a given state. We learned that these heuristics are promising and suggest adding them to general purpose planners as well. Following Bercher et al. [3], such integration is by all means possible.

We deem automatic composition of semantically described functionality to have the highest potential of all planning-related techniques. Yet, first tests clearly showed that available approaches require much improvement and further research (e.g. in terms of continuity, expressiveness, concretisation, and knowledge representation) in order to cope with real world problems.

Finally, we identified the need for new programming and debugging tools. Programming for itself is complex—and programming in distributed environments significantly more challenging. Classical exception stack traces show call hierarchies of functions and under what circumstances these functions were called, yet, in the case of a planning agent, it is difficult to get more information than the name of an action that (might have) caused problems. More detailed (and highly important) information, e.g. why the action was selected in the first place, are not visible to the programmer. In order to facilitate any professional adoption of agent-based frameworks we propose the development of new programming and debugging tools that help developers to keep track of the reasoning performed by the agent. After all, comprehensive tools support is arguably [5, 33, 35, 40, 47] a significant driver for industrial adoption of technology.

Wrapping up we can say that agent-technology is able to meet the requirements of real world applications through the use of service paradigms. The problem, however, is that agent-based programming frameworks and runtimes do not work 'out of the box' and frequently have to be adapted (e.g. with respect to their performance). This might hamper any broader application or validation of agent-based models, since programmers prefer to focus on the development of the application—not on dealing with shortcomings of the framework. This constellation is exceptionally unfortunate, especially in the light of the ever-new evolving software development trends that may significantly profit from the agent-based approach. As an example consider the Internet of Things, where agent-technology can significantly contribute to an easy integration of intelligent software, sensors, mobile devices and human beings.

Based on our analysis we argue that (most of the time) performance problems do not result from 'insufficient implementations' of concepts that have their roots in agent theory but rather from limitations of agent theory that is applied to real world problems. Nevertheless, considering these theories to be inapplicable is not helpful as well, thus, we identified the particular bottlenecks and proposed ways to improve the fundamental concepts. We identified challenges in both, theory and practice:

Theory: Communication overhead, expressiveness of description languages, knowledge representations, ontology alignment.

Practice: Development tools i.e. for debugging, execution monitoring, planning in continuous parameter spaces, heuristics to guide the shift from domain specific to general purpose planning.

We hope that our work will help theorists to better understand the problems and requirements that practitioners have when applying agent-based programming to reality. We have to find a joint approach to further the adoption of agent-technology, after all we, as the agent community, are strongest when we are working hand in hand.

REFERENCES

[1] R. Akkiraju, B. Srivastava, A.-A. Ivan, R. Goodwin, and T. Syeda-Mahmood. SEMAPLAN: Combining planning with semantic matching to achieve web service composition. In *Proceedings of the 21st National Conference on Artificial Intelligence (AAAI'06)*, 2006.

[2] T. Aubonnet, L. Henrio, S. Kessal, O. Kulankhina, F. Lemoine, E. Madelaine, C. Ruz, and N. Simoni. Management of service composition based on self-controlled components. *Journal of Internet Services and Applications*, 6(1):1–15, 2015.

[3] P. Bercher, T. Geier, and S. Biundo. Using state-based planning heuristics for partial-order causal-link planning. In I. J. Timm and M. Thimm, editors, *KI 2013: Advances in Artificial Intelligence*, volume 8077 of *Lecture Notes in Artificial Intelligence*, pages 1–12. Springer Berlin / Heidelberg, 2013.

[4] D. Bianchini, V. D. Antonellis, M. Melchiori, and D. Salvi. Semantic-enriched service discovery. In *Proceedings of the 22nd Conference on Data Engineering Workshops*, pages 38–38, 2006.

[5] B. Burmeister. Industrial application of agent systems: Lessons learned and future challenges. In L. Braubach, W. van der Hoek, P. Petta, and A. Pokahr, editors, *Multiagent System Technologies, 7th German Conference, MATES 2009, Hamburg, Germany, September 2009, Proceedings*, volume 5774 of *Lecture Notes in Artificial Intelligence*, pages 1–3. Springer Berlin / Heidelberg, 2009.

[6] A. Carenini, D. Cerizza, M. Comerio, E. D. Valle, F. D. Paoli, A. Maurino, M. Palmonari, and A. Turati. GLUE2: A web service discovery engine with non-functional properties. In *Proceedings of the IEEE*

6th *European Conference on Web Services (ECOW'08)*, pages 21–30, 2008.

[7] S. A. B. Cruz, A. M. V. Monteiro, and R. Santos. Automated geospatial web services composition based on geodata quality requirements. *Computers & Geosciences*, 47(0):60–74, 2012.

[8] J. de Bruijn, H. Lausen, R. Krummenacher, A. Polleres, L. Predoiu, M. Kifer, and D. Fensel. The web service modeling language (WSML). Technical report, Digital Enterprise Research Institute (DERI), 2005. http://www.wsmo.org/TR/d16/d16.1/v0.21/.

[9] P. Doherty, W. Lukaszewicz, and A. Szalas. Efficient reasoning using the local closed-world assumption. In S. A. Cerri and D. Dochev, editors, *Artificial Intelligence: Methodology, Systems, and Applications*, volume 1904 of *Lecture Notes in Computer Science*, pages 49–58. Springer Berlin / Heidelberg, 2003.

[10] A. E. Eiben and J. E. Smith. *Introduction to Evolutionary Computing*. Natural Computing. Springer, 2003.

[11] T. Erl. *SOA Principles of Service Design*. Prentice Hall, 2007.

[12] J. Euzenat and P. Shvaiko. *Ontology Matching*. Springer, 2007.

[13] J. Fähndrich, N. Masuch, H. Yildirim, and S. Albayrak. Towards automated service matchmaking and planning for multi-agent systems with OWL-S – approach and challenges. In *Service-Oriented Computing – ICSOC 2013 Workshops*, volume 8377 of *Lecture Notes in Computer Science*, pages 240–247. Springer International Publishing, 2014.

[14] D. Fensel, F. M. Facca, E. Simperl, and I. Toma. *Semantic Web Services*. Springer Science & Business Media, 2011.

[15] M. Genesereth. Knowledge interchange format. Proposed Draft NCITS.T2/98-004, American National Standard, 1998.

[16] A. Gerevini, A. Saetti, and I. Serina. Case-based planning for problems with real-valued fluents: Kernel functions for effective plan retrieval. In *Proceedings of the* 20th *European Conference on Artificial Intelligence (ECAI 2012)*, pages 348–353, 2012.

[17] M. Ghallab, A. Howe, C. Knoblock, D. Mcdermott, A. Ram, M. Veloso, D. Weld, and D. Wilkins. PDDL – the planning domain definition language, 1998.

[18] M. Ghallab, D. Nau, and P. Traverso. The actor's view of automated planning and acting: A position paper. *Artificial Intelligence*, 208:1–17, 2014.

[19] L. Guzmán, A. Jaime, C. Ovalle, and A. Demetrio. Web service composition: a semantic web and automated planning technique application. *Ingeniería e Investigación*, 28(3):145–149, 2008.

[20] O. Hatzi, D. Vrakas, M. Nikolaidou, N. Bassiliades, D. Anagnostopoulos, and I. Vlahavas. An integrated approach to automated semantic web service composition through planning. *IEEE Transactions on Services Computing*, 5(3):319–332, 2012.

[21] C.-E. Hrabia, T. Küster, M. Voß, F. D. P. Pardo, and S. Albayrak. Adaptive multi-stage optimisation for EV charging integration into smart grid control. In Q. Chen, P. Torroni, S. Villata, J. Hsu, and A. Omicini, editors, *PRIMA 2015: Principles and Practice of Multi-Agent Systems*, volume 9387 of *Lecture Notes in Artificial Intelligence*, pages 622–630. Springer International Publishing, 2015.

[22] C.-E. Hrabia, F. D. P. Pardo, T. Küster, and S. Albayrak. Multi-stage smart grid optimisation with a multiagent system (demonstration). In *Proceedings of* 14th *International Conference on Autonomous Agents and Multiagent Systems (AAMAS 2015)*, pages 1937–1938, 2015.

[23] International Foundation for Autonomous Agents and Multiagent Systems. *AAMAS 2015 Conference Program*. IFAAMAS, 2015.

[24] P. Kapahnke and M. Klusch. Adaptive hybrid selection of semantic services: The iSeM matchmaker. In *Semantic Web Services: Advancement through Evaluation*. Springer Berlin / Heidelberg, 2012.

[25] M. Klusch, A. Gerber, and M. Schmidt. Semantic web service composition planning with OWLS-Xplan. In *Agents and the Semantic Web: Papers from the AAAI Fall Symposium. AAAI Fall Symposium, November 4-6, Arlington, VA, USA*, pages 55–62, 2005.

[26] J. Kopecký, T. Vitvar, C. Bournez, and J. Farrell. SAWSDL: Semantic annotations for WSDL and XML schema. *IEEE Internet Computing*, 11(6):60–67, 2007.

[27] T. Küster, M. Lützenberger, and S. Albayrak. A formal description of a mapping from business processes to agents. In M. Baldoni, L. Baresi, and M. Dastani, editors, *Engineering Multi-Agent Systems*, volume 9318 of *Lecture Notes in Artificial Intelligence*, pages 153–170. Springer International Publishing, 2015.

[28] U. Küster, B. König-Ries, M. Klein, and M. Stern. DIANE: A matchmaking-centered framework for automated service discovery, composition, binding, and invocation on the web. *International Journal of Electronic Commerce*, 12(2):41–68, 2007.

[29] J. Li. A fast semantic web services matchmaker for OWL-S services. *Journal of Networks*, 8(5):1104–1111, 2013.

[30] M. Lützenberger, N. Masuch, T. Küster, D. Freund, M. Voß, C.-E. Hrabia, D. Pozo, J. Fähndrich, F. Trollmann, J. Keiser, and S. Albayrak. A common approach to intelligent energy and mobility services in a smart city environment. *Journal of Ambient Intelligence and Humanized Computing*, 6(3):337–350, 2015.

[31] D. Martin, M. Paolucci, S. McIlraith, M. Burstein, D. McDermott, D. McGuinness, B. Parsia, T. Payne, M. Sabou, M. Solanki, N. Srinivasan, and K. Sycara. Bringing semantics to web services: The OWL-S approach. In *Semantic Web Services and Web Process Composition*, pages 26–42. Springer Berlin / Heidelberg, 2004.

[32] N. Masuch, B. Hirsch, M. Burkhardt, A. Heßler, and S. Albayrak. SeMa^2 – a hybrid semantic service matching approach. In *Semantic Services: Advancement through Evaluation*, pages 35–48. Springer-Verlag, 2012.

[33] V. Mařík and D. McFarlane. Industrial adoption of agent-based technologies. *Intelligent Systems, IEEE*, 20(1):27–35, 2005.

[34] D. McGuinness and F. van Harmelen. OWL web

ontology language overview. Technical report, W3C, 2004. http://www.w3.org/TR/owl-features/.

[35] J. McKean, H. Shorter, M. Luck, P. McBurney, and S. Willmott. Technology diffusion: analysing the diffusion of agent technologies. *Autonomous Agents and Multi-Agent Systems*, 17:372–396, 2008.

[36] D. S. Nau, M. Ghallab, and P. Traverso. Blended planning and acting: Preliminary approach, research challenges. *AAAI*, pages 4047–4051, 2015.

[37] Organization for the Advancement of Structured Information Standards (OASIS). *Web Services Business Process Execution Language (WS-BPEL) Version 2.0*, Apr. 2007.

[38] M. P. Papazoglou, P. Traverso, S. Dustdar, and F. Leymann. Service-oriented computing: a research roadmap. *International Journal of Cooperative Information Systems*, 17(2):223–255, 2008.

[39] J. Peer. A PDDL based tool for automatic web service composition. In H. J. Ohlbach and S. Schaffert, editors, *Principles and Practice of Semantic Web Reasoning*, volume 3208 of *Lecture Notes in Computer Science*, pages 149–163. Springer Berlin Heidelberg, 2004.

[40] M. Pěchoučyek and V. Mařík. Industrial deployment of multi-agent technologies: review and selected case studies. *Autonomous Agents and Multi-Agent Systems*, 17(3):397–431, 2008.

[41] D. Redavid, L. Iannone, T. Payne, and G. Semeraro. OWL-S atomic services composition with SWRL rules. In A. An, S. Matwin, Z. W. Raś, and D. Ślęzak, editors, *Foundations of Intelligent Systems*, volume 4994 of *Lecture Notes in Computer Science*, pages 605–611. Springer Berlin / Heidelberg, 2008.

[42] L. Sabatucci and M. Cossentino. From means-end analysis to proactive means-end reasoning. In *Proceedings of the 10th International Symposium on Software Engineering for Adaptive and Self-Managing Systems (SEAMS 2015)*, pages 2–12, 2015.

[43] C. Sathya and T. Hemalatha. An adaptive architecture for autonomic orchestration of web services. *International Journal Of Engineering and Computer Science*, 2(4):972–975, 2013.

[44] P. Shvaiko and J. Euzenat. Ontology matching: State of the art and future challenges. *IEEE Transactions on Knowledge and Data Engineering*, 25(1):158–176, 2013.

[45] E. Sirin, B. Parsia, D. Wu, J. Hendler, and D. Nau. HTN planning for web service composition using SHOP2. *Web Semantics: Science, Services and Agents on the World Wide Web*, 1(4):377–396, 2004.

[46] H. Tong, J. Cao, S. Zhang, and M. Li. A distributed algorithm for web service composition based on service agent model. *IEEE Transactions on Parallel and Distributed Systems*, 22(12):2008–2021, 2011.

[47] D. Weyns, A. Helleboogh, and T. Holvoet. How to get multi-agent systems accepted in industry? *International Journal of Agent-Oriented Software Engineering (IJAOSE)*, 3(4):383–390, May 2009.

[48] F. Zambonelli, N. Bicocchi, G. Cabri, L. Leonardi, and M. Puviani. On self-adaptation, self-expression, and self-awareness in autonomic service component ensembles. In *Proceedings of the 5th IEEE Conference on Self-Adaptive and Self-Organizing Systems Workshops (SASOW 2011)*, pages 108–113, 2011.

120 Million Agents Self-Organize into 6 Million Firms: A Model of the U.S. Private Sector

Robert L. Axtell
George Mason University
4400 University Drive
Fairfax, VA 22030 USA
+1 (703) 556-0333
rax222@gmu.edu

ABSTRACT

An agent model is described at full-scale with the U.S. private sector, consisting of some 120 million agents. Using data on the population of U.S. firms the model is calibrated to closely reproduce firm sizes, ages, growth rates, job tenure and labor flows, along with several other empirically-important facts. It consists of a coalition formation model in which the Nash equilibria are dynamically unstable for sufficiently large coalitions. When agents are free to join coalitions where they are made better off there results a steady-state distribution of coalitions. The agent level is in perpetual disequilibrium but the aggregate level approaches a steady-state. This model represents a significant advance over conventional approaches to economic modeling, made possible by large-scale, parallel agent computing.

CCS Concepts

Computing methodologies: Parallel computing methodologies: massively parallel algorithms: self-organization; Artificial intelligence: distributed artificial intelligence; Modeling and simulation; simulation types and techniques, agent/discrete models, distributed simulation; **Applied computing**: Law, social and behavioral sciences: economics.

General Terms

Algorithms, Economics, Experimentation, Verification.

Keywords

Agent solutions of significant social and economic impact; coalition formation; behavioral game theory; organizations and institutions; Social simulation.

1. INTRODUCTION

Over the last decade the U.S. private sector workforce has ranged from 115 to 120 million employees, with nearly 3 million workers changing employers *each month* on average [1]. Over this same period there were, each year, 5.7-6.0 million firms with employees of which, on average, 100 thousand went out of business *monthly* while a comparable number started up [2]. Such high levels of turnover in the American economy—1 in 40 workers changing employers monthly, 1 in 60 firms terminating its operations—portrays a kind of *perpetual economic flux* in the U.S. private sector. How should we interpret such persistent adjustments and reorganizations of production? If we stipulate that the economy is in general equilibrium then there is no way to realize micro-dynamics except by the imposition of external shocks. Can microeconomic models *endogenously* produce the kinds of dynamics observed empirically when the incentives agents have to change jobs are fully represented?

Here I describe a microeconomic model capable of producing, *without* exogenous shocks, firm and labor dynamics of the size and type the U.S. economy experiences. While conventional explanations for these large labor flows exist [e.g., 3], here I provide a microeconomic explanation without the need for aggregate shocks. Also reproduced are a number of cross-sectional properties of U.S. businesses. Over the past decade there have appeared increasing amounts of micro-data on U.S. firms, including administratively *comprehensive* (tax record-based) data on firm sizes, ages, growth rates, labor productivity, job tenure, and wages. Extant theories place few restrictions on these data.[1] Lucas [10] derives Pareto-distributed firm sizes from a Pareto distribution of managerial talent. Luttmer [11, 12] obtains Zipf-distributed firm sizes and exponential firm ages [13] in a variety of general equilibrium settings, driven by exogenous shocks. Rossi-Hansberg and Wright [14] study establishment growth and exit rates arising in general equilibrium due to industry-specific productivity shocks. Elsby and Michaels [15] and Arkolakis [16] simulate heterogeneous firm growth rates due to productivity shocks. However, there are *many* more data on firm dynamics and labor flows to be explained. Here I develop a model that reproduces more than two dozen features of the empirical data *without* recourse to exogenous shocks—such shocks are not necessary in a model with worker-level dynamics.

The model draws together threads from various theoretical literatures. It is written at the level of individual agents and incentive problems of the type studied in the principal-agent literature manifest themselves. The agents work in perpetually novel environments, so contracts are incomplete and transaction costs are implicit. Each firm is a coalition of agents making the theory of coalition formation relevant [17]. Agent decisions generate firm growth and decline in the spirit of evolutionary economics [18]. Specifically, the model consists of a heterogeneous population of agents with preferences for income and leisure. Production takes place under increasing returns to scale, so agents who work together can produce more output per unit effort than by working alone. However, agents act non-cooperatively[2]: they select effort levels that improve their own

Appears in: *Proceedings of the 15th International Conference on Autonomous Agents and Multiagent Systems (AAMAS 2016), J. Thangarajah, K. Tuyls, C. Jonker, S. Marsella (eds.),*
May 9–13, 2016, Singapore.

[1] A generation ago Simon [4, 5] noted the inability of the neoclassical theory of the firm to explain empirical size distributions. Transaction cost [e.g., 6] and game theoretic explanations of the firm [e.g., 7, 8] make few empirical claims. Sutton [9] bounds the extent of intra-industry concentration, constraining the shape of size distributions.

[2] For a cooperative game theoretic view of firms see Ichiishi [19].

welfare, and may migrate between firms or start-up new firms when it is advantageous to do so. Analytically, Nash equilibria within a firm can be unstable. Large firms are ultimately unstable because each agent's compensation is imperfectly related to its effort level, making free-riding possible. Highly productive agents eventually leave large firms and such firms eventually decline. All firms have finite lives. The dynamics of firms perpetually forming, growing and perishing are studied. *This non-equilibrium regime provides greater welfare than equilibrium.*

These dynamics mean it is analytically difficult to relate agent level behavior to aggregate outcomes. Therefore, features that emerge at the firm population level are studied using agent-based computing [20-23]. When agent models are 'spun' forward in time macro-structure "grows" from the bottom-up [e.g., 24]. No equations governing the aggregate level are specified, nor do agents have either complete information or correct models for how the economy will unfold. Instead, they glean data inductively from the environment and from their social networks, through direct interactions, and make imperfect forecasts of economic opportunities. [25]. The macroscopic properties of the model *emerge* from the agent interactions. This methodology facilitates modeling agent heterogeneity [26], non-equilibrium dynamics [27], local interactions [28], and bounded rationality [29, 30]. The results in this paper should be of interest both to economists and multi-agent systems researchers working on coalition formation.

2. SINGLE FIRM ANALYTICS

Consider a group of agents A, $|A| = n$, engaged in team production, each agent contributing some amount of effort, generating team output.[3] Specifically, agent i has endowment $\omega_i > 0$ and contributes effort level $e_i \in [0, \omega_i]$, to the group. The total effort of the group is then $E = \Sigma_{i \in A} e_i$. The group produces output, O, as a function of E, according to $O(E) = aE + bE^{\beta}$, $\beta > 1$, without capital as in Hopenhayn [34].[4] For $b > 0$ there are increasing returns to effort.[5] Increasing returns in production means that agents working together can produce more than they can as individuals.[6] To see this, consider two agents having effort levels e_1 and e_2, with $\beta = 2$. As individuals they produce total output $O_1 + O_2 = a(e_1 + e_2) + b(e_1^2 + e_2^2)$, while working together they make $a(e_1 + e_2) + b(e_1 + e_2)^2$. Clearly this latter quantity is at least as large as the former since $(e_1 + e_2)^2 \geq e_1^2 + e_2^2$. Agents earn according to a compensation rule. For now consider agents sharing total output equally: at the end of each period all output is sold for unit price and each agent receives an O/N share of the total output.[7] Agents have Cobb-Douglas preferences for income and leisure, parameterized by θ. All time not spent working is spent in leisure, so agent i's utility can be written as a function of its effort, e_i, and the effort of other agents, $E_{\sim i} = E - e_i$ as

$$U_i(e_i; \theta_i, \omega_i, E_{\sim i}, n) = \left(\frac{O(e_i, E_{\sim i})}{n}\right)^{\theta_i} (\omega_i - e_i)^{1-\theta_i}$$

Consider the individual efforts of agents to be unobservable. From team output, O, each agent i determines E and, from its contribution to production, e_i, can figure out $E_{\sim i}$. Agent i then selects effort $e_i^*(\theta_i, \omega_i, E_{\sim i}, n) = \arg max\, U_i(e_i)$. For $\beta = 2$, this can be solved exactly, but as we will have occasion to use values not equal to 2 the solution is not written out here. It turns out that e^* does not depend on n but does depend on $E_{\sim i}$—the effort put in by the other agents. Optimal effort decreases monotonically as 'other agent effort,' $E_{\sim i}$, increases. For each θ_i there exists some $E_{\sim i}$ beyond which it is rational for agent i to put in no effort. For constant returns, e_i^* decreases linearly with $E_{\sim i}$ with slope $\theta_i - 1$. Furthermore, it has been shown in [41] that

Proposition 1: Nash equilibrium exists and is unique [42].

***Proposition 2*:** There exists a set of efforts that Pareto dominate Nash equilibrium [43], a subset of which are Pareto optimal. These (a) involve larger effort levels than the Nash equilibrium, and (b) are not individually rational.

***Proposition 3*:** Nash equilibria are dynamically unstable for sufficiently large group size.

3. MANY FIRMS: MAIN RESULTS

With these results in hand we can now consider a large population of agents in which many teams form simultaneously. If one or more of these teams becomes unstable some of the agents will look for employment in other teams, or perhaps they will form new teams if it makes them better off. What happens overall? Do lots of little teams form or a few big ones? Is a static equilibrium of agents in teams reached if we wait long enough? Are patterns produced in the population of teams that are recognizable vis-á-vis real firms? Here I show that such patterns *do* arise and closely resemble data on U.S. firms.

I study the formation of teams within a population using software agents. In the agent-based model total output of a firm consists of both constant and increasing returns. Preferences and endowments, θ and ω respectively, are heterogeneous across agents. When agent i acts it searches over $[0, \omega_i]$ for the effort maximizing its next period utility. Because many firms will arise in the computational model, it is necessary to specify how agents move between firms. Each agent has an exogenous social network, a random graph, consisting of ν_i other agents. It considers (a) staying in its current firm, (b) joining ν_i other firms—in essence an on-the-job search over its social network [44, 45]—and (c) starting up a new firm. It chooses the option that yields greatest utility. Since agents evaluate only a small number of firms their information is very limited. We utilize 120 million agents, roughly the size of the U.S. private sector. Specifically, about 5 million agents are activated each period, corresponding to one calendar month, in rough accord with job search frequency [46] and closely approximating the distribution of job tenure. The 'base case' parameterization of the model in table 1 was developed by seeking good fits to the many empirical data described subsequently.[8]

[3] The model derives from Canning [31], Huberman and Glance [32] and Glance *et al.* [33].

[4] While $O(E)$ relates inputs to outputs, like a production function, E is not the choice of a single decision-maker, since it results from the actions of autonomous agents. Thus, $O(E)$ cannot be made the subject of a math program, as in production theory, yet describes production possibilities.

[5] Increasing returns goes back at least to Marshall [35] and was the basis of theoretical controversies in economics in the 1920s [36, 37]. Recent work on increasing returns is reprinted in Arthur [38] and Buchanan and Yoon [39]. Colander and Landreth [40] give a history of the idea.

[6] There are many ways to motivate increasing returns, including 'four hands problems': two people working together are able to perform a task that neither could do alone, like carrying a piano up a flight of stairs.

[7] The model yields roughly constant total output, so in a competitive market the price of output would be nearly constant. Since there are no fixed costs, agent shares sum to total cost, which equals total revenue. The shares can be thought of as either uniform wages in pure competition or profit shares in a partnership.

[8] For model attributes with random values, each agent or firm is given a realization when it is instantiated.

Table 1: 'Base case' configuration of the agent model

Model Attribute	Value
$\|A\|$	120,000,000
a	*uniform* on [0, 1/2]
b	*uniform* on [3/4, 5/4]
β	*uniform* on [3/2, 2]
θ	*uniform* on [0, 1]
ω	1
compensation	equal shares
v	*uniform* on [2,6]
activation	uniform (all active each period)
activation/period	4% of total agents (4,800,000)
one period	one month of calendar time
initial condition	all agents in singleton firms

The model's execution can be summarized in pseudo-code:

```
• INSTANTIATE and INITIALIZE time, agent, firm,
  and data objects;
• REPEAT:
  o FOR each agent, activate it with 4%
    probability:
    ▪ Compute e* and U(e*) in current firm;
    ▪ Compute e* and U(e*) for starting up a
      new firm;
    ▪ FOR each firm in the agent's social
      network:
      • Compute e* and U(e*);
    ▪ IF current firm is not best choice THEN
      leave:
      • IF start-up firm is best THEN form
        start-up;
      • IF another firm is best THEN join
        other firm;
  o FOR each firm:
    ▪ Sum agent inputs and do production;
    ▪ Distribute output;
  o COLLECT monthly, annual statistics;
  o INCREMENT time and reset periodic
    statistics;
```

Each worker is represented as an agent in this model, and both agents and firms are software objects. It is important to emphasize that this is *not* a numerical model: there are no (explicit) equations governing the aggregate level; the only equations present are for agent decisions. "Solving" an agent model means marching it forward in time to see what patterns emerge (cf. Axtell 2000).

Initially, agents work alone. As each is activated it discovers it can do better working with another agent to jointly produce output. Over time some teams expand as certain agents find it welfare-improving to join them, while other teams contract as their agents discover better opportunities elsewhere. New firms are started-up by agents who lack better opportunities. Overall, once an initial transient passes an approximately stationary macrostate emerges.[9] In this macro steady-state agents continue to adjust their efforts and change jobs, causing firms to evolve, and so there is no equilibrium at the agent level.

[9] Movies are available at `css.gmu.edu/~axtell/Rob/Research/Pages/Firms.html#6`.

The number of firms varies over time, due both to entry—agents leaving extant firms for start-ups—and the demise of failing firms. In the U.S. about 6 million firms have employees. Figure 1 shows the number of firms (blue) in the steady-state over 25 years (300 months), in good agreement with the data.

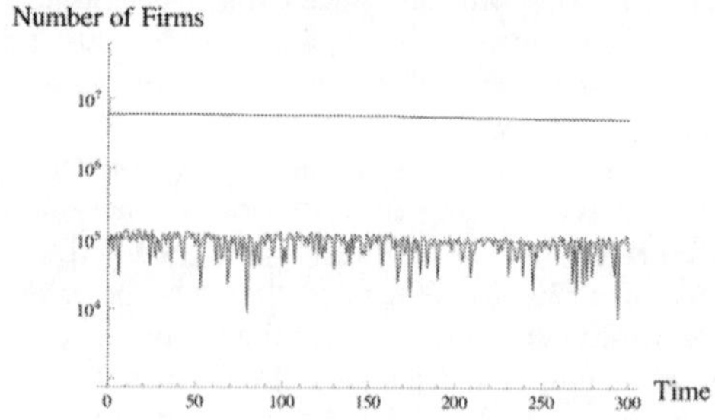

Figure 1: Typical time series for the total number of firms (blue), new firms (green), and exiting firms (red) over 25 years (300 months); note higher volatility in exits.

There are ~100K startups with employees in the U.S. monthly [2], quite close to the number produced by the model as shown in figure 6 (green). Exits are shown in red. The model predicts higher variability in firm exit than entry. Mean firm size in the U.S. is about 20 workers/firm [47]. Since there are 120 million agents in the model and the number of firms that emerges is approximately 6 million, mean firm size, as shown in figure 2, is very close to 20.

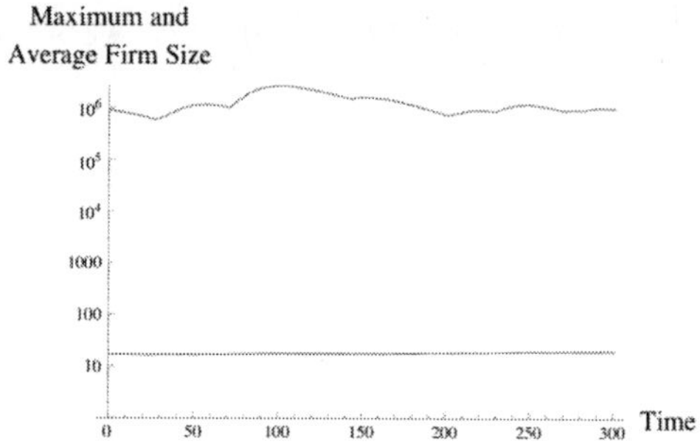

Figure 2: Typical time series for average firm size (blue) and maximum firm size (magenta)

Also shown in figure 2 is the size of largest firm (red), which fluctuates around a million. The largest firm in the U.S. (Wal-Mart) employs about 1.3 million today.

Agents who work together improve upon their singleton utility levels with reduced effort, as shown in figures 3 and 4. This is the *raison d'être* of firms

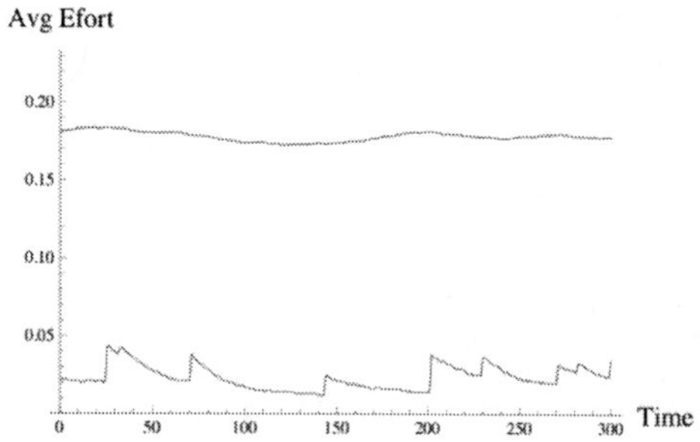

Figure 3: Typical time series for (a) average effort level in the population (blue) and in the largest firm (magenta)

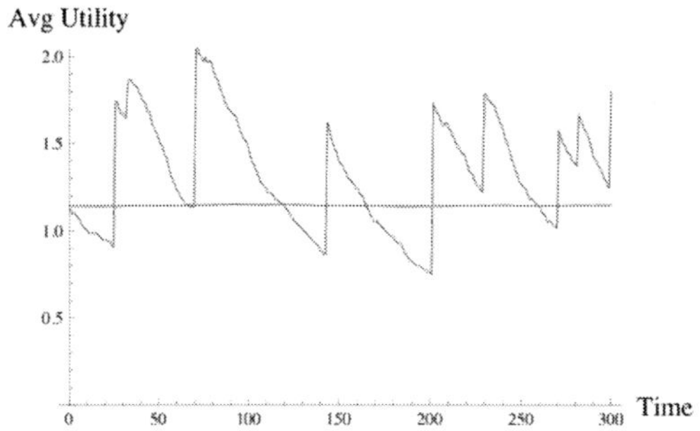

Figure 4: Typical time series for average utility (blue) and in the largest firm (magenta)

While efforts in large firms fluctuate, average effort overall is quite stable (figure 3). Much of the dynamism in the 'large firm' time series is due to the identity of the largest firm changing. Figure 4 shows the average agent utility (blue) is usually less than that in the largest firm (red). Occasionally utility in large firms falls below average, signaling that the large firm is in decline.

In the U.S. economy people change jobs with, what is to some, "astonishingly high" frequency [48: 1151]. Job-to-job switching (aka employer-to-employer flow) represents 30-40% of labor turnover, substantially higher than unemployment flows [46, 49-51]. Moving between jobs is intrinsic to this model. In figure 5 the level of monthly job changing at steady-state is shown (blue)—just over 3 million/month—along with measures of jobs created (red) and jobs destroyed (green). Job creation occurs in firms with net monthly hiring, while job destruction means firms lose workers (net). Job destruction is about 4x more volatile than job creation, comparable to U.S. data [52].

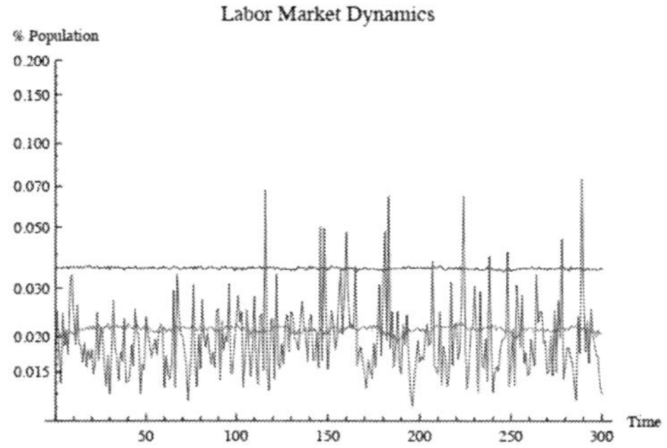

Figure 5: Typical monthly job-to-job changes (blue), job creation (yellow) and destruction (green)

Watching firms form, grow, and die in the model movies (see footnote 9), one readily sees the coexistence of big firms, medium-sized ones, and small ones. At any instant there exists a distribution of firm sizes in the model. At steady-state, sizes are skew, with a few big firms and larger numbers of progressively smaller ones. Typical model output is shown in figures 6 and 7 for firm size measured by employees and output. The modal firm size is 1 employee with the median between 3 and 4, in agreement with the data on U.S. firms. Firm sizes, S, are approximately Pareto distributed, the complementary CDF of which, $\bar{F}_S(s)$ is

$$Pr[S \geq s] \equiv \bar{F}_S(s;\, \alpha, s_0) = \left(\frac{s_0}{s}\right)^{\alpha}, s \geq s_0, \alpha \geq 0$$

where s_0 is the minimum size, unity for size measured by employees. The U.S. data are well fit by $\alpha \sim$ -1.06 [47], the line in figure 6.

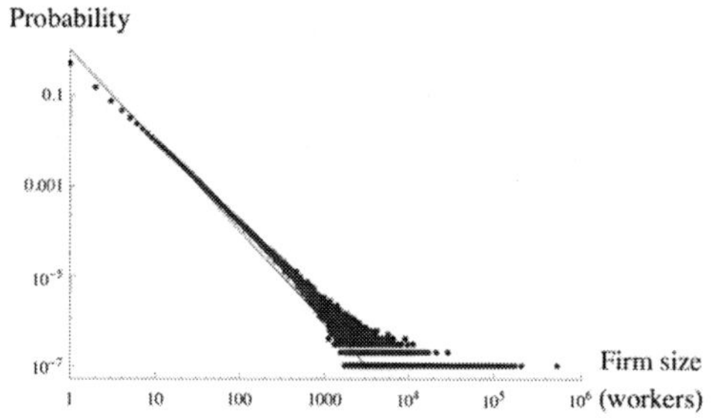

Figure 6: Stationary firm size distribution (*PMF*) by employees

The Pareto is a power law, and for $\alpha = 1$ is known as Zipf's law. Note that the power law fits almost the *entire distribution* of firm sizes. A variety of explanations for power laws have been proposed.[10] Common to these is the idea that such systems are far from (static) equilibrium at the microscopic (agent) level. Our model is non-equilibrium with agents regularly changing jobs.

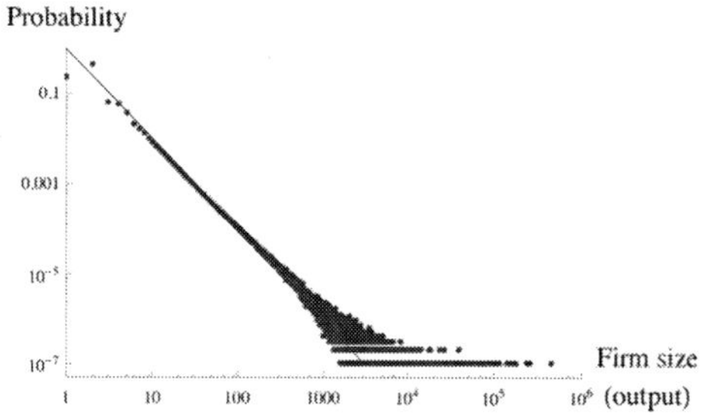

Figure 7: Stationary firm size distributions (*PMF*) by output

Firm output per employee is labor productivity. Figure 8 plots average firm output as a function of firm size. Fitting a line by several methods indicates that $ln(O)$ scales linearly with $ln(S)$ with slope very nearly 1.

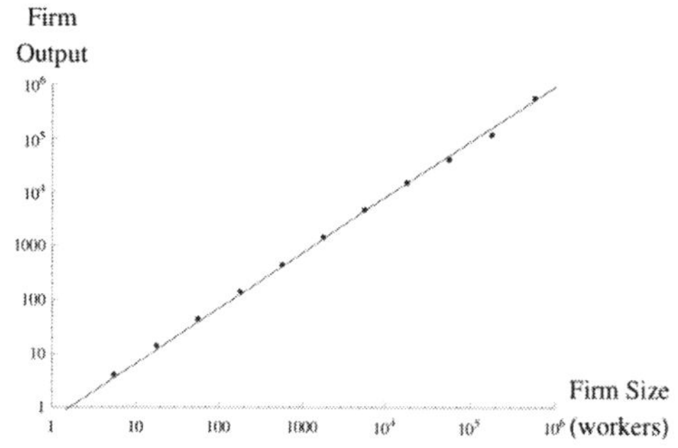

Figure 8: Constant returns at the aggregate level despite increasing returns at the micro-level

This represents essentially constant returns to scale, also a feature of U.S. output data; see Basu and Fernald [59]. That nearly *constant returns* occur at the *aggregate* level despite *increasing returns* at the *micro*-level suggests the difficulties of making inferences across levels. An explanation of why this occurs is apparent. High productivity firms grow by adding agents who work less hard than incumbents, thus such firms are driven toward the average productivity. In essence, each agent who changes jobs 'arbitrages' returns across firms.[11]

---

[10] Bak [53: 62-64], Marsili and Zhang [54], Gabaix, [55], Reed [56], and Saichev *et al.* [57]; for a review see [58].

[11] As output per worker represents wages in our model, there is little wage-size effect [60, 61].

It is well known that there is large heterogeneity in labor productivity across firms [e.g., 62]. Shown in figure 9 are data on all U.S. companies for three size classes: 1-99 employees (blue), 100-9,999 (red) and 10,000+ (green).

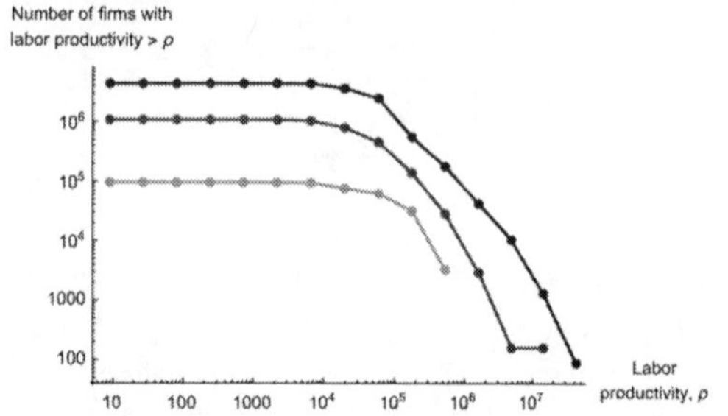

Figure 9: Labor productivity U.S. data (Census), in arbitrary units

Note the log-log coordinates, so the right tail is very nearly a power law with large slope. Souma *et al.* [63] have studied the productivity of Japanese firms and find similar results. Figure 10 is model output for the same size classes.

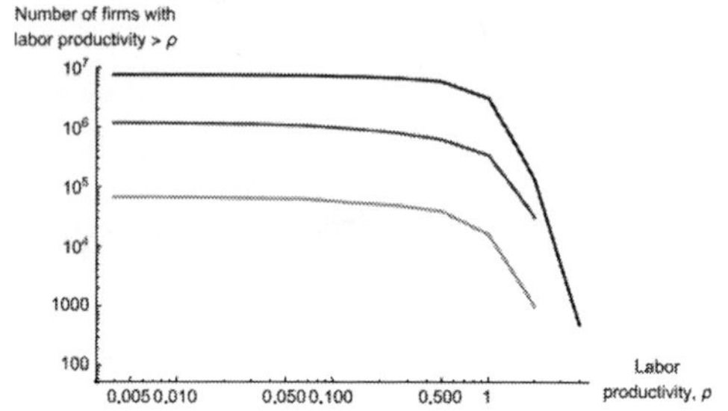

Figure 10: Labor productivity, model output in arbitrary units

Using data from the BLS Business Employment Dynamics program, figure 11 gives the age distribution (*PMF*) of U.S. firms, in semi-log coordinates, with each colored line representing the distribution reported in a recent year.

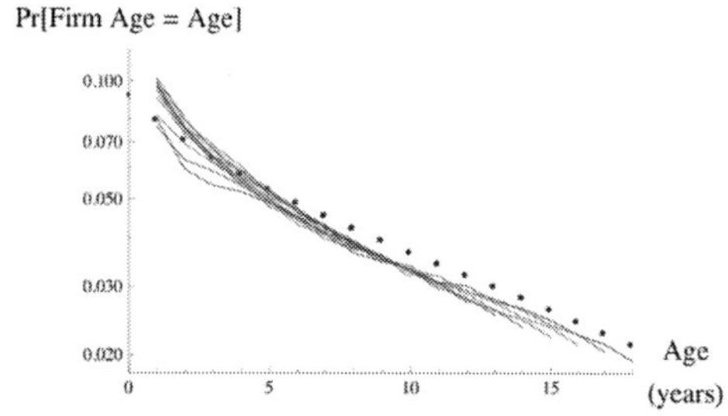

Figure 11: Firm age distributions (*PMFs*), U.S. data 2000-2011 (lines) and model output (points)

Model output is overlaid on the raw data as points and agrees reasonably well. Average firm lifetime and standard deviation are 14-15 years here. The curvature in the data implies that firm ages are better fit by the Weibull distribution than the exponential [64].

Data on U.S. firm ages is right censored so little systematic information is known about long-lived firms, except that they are rare [65]. Further, the role of mergers and acquisitions (M&A) makes the lifetime of a firm ambiguous, as when a younger firm buys an older one. This model can be run for a long time and makes strong predictions about the distribution of firm ages, along with the closely related idea of firm lifetimes, as shown in figures 12 and 13.

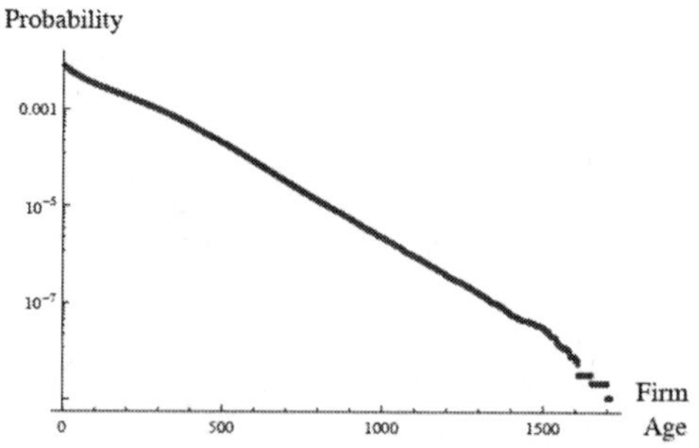

Figure 12: Firm age distribution (*PMFs*) in the long run (months)

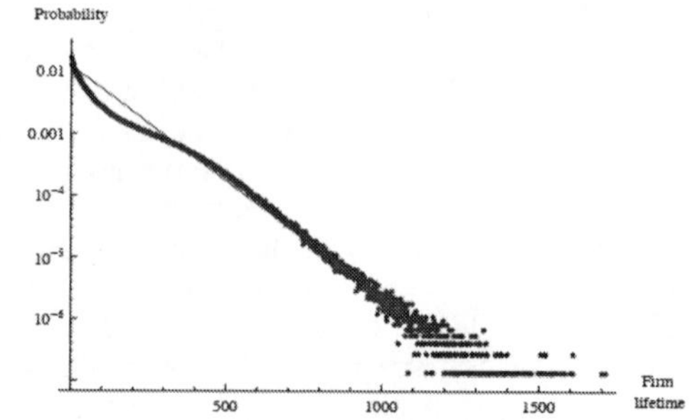

Figure 13: Firm lifetime distribution in the long run (months)

If firm ages were exactly exponentially distributed then the survival probability would be constant, independent of age [66]. Curvature in figure 11 indicates that survival probability depends on age. Empirically, survival probability *increases* with age [67-69]. This is shown in figure 15 for U.S. companies in recent years (lines) along with model output (points). The model slightly over-predicts the survival probabilities of young firms.

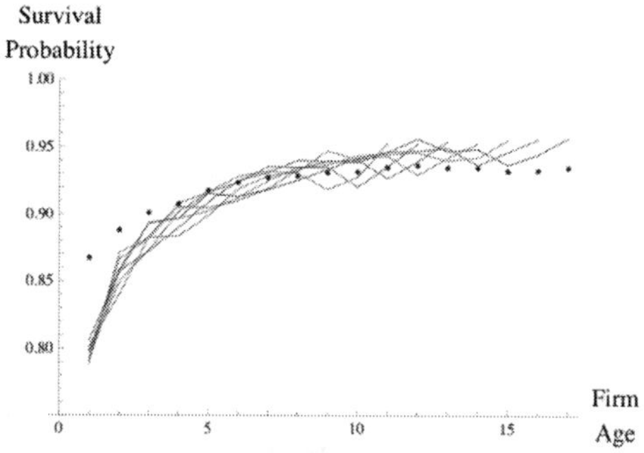

Figure 14: Firm survival probability increases with firm age and size, U.S. data 1994-2000 (lines) and model (points)

The joint distribution of size and age is shown in figure 15, a normalized histogram in *log* probabilities.

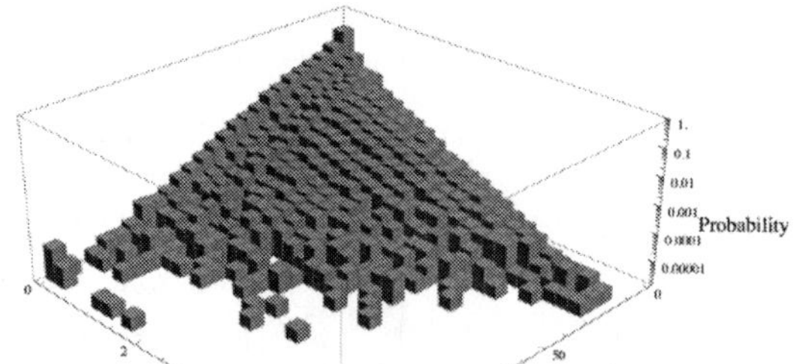

Figure 15: Histogram of the steady-state distribution of firms by *log*(*S*) and age in the model

Note that log probabilities decline approximately linearly as a function of age and $log(S)$. Many of the largest firms in the model are relatively young ones that grow rapidly, much like in the U.S. economy [e.g., 13, figure 1]

Call S_t a firm's size at time t. Its one period growth rate is $G \equiv S_{t+1}/S_t \in \boldsymbol{R}_+$.[12] In a population of firms consider G to be a stationary random variable. Gibrat's law of proportional growth [70] implies that if all firms have the same G then $S_{t+1} = GS_t$ is lognormally distributed at any t while the mean and variance of S grows with time [71: 40], i.e., S is not stationary. Adding firm birth and death processes can lead to stationary firm size distributions [72]. Historically, knowledge of G was limited by the relatively small samples of firm data available [e.g., 73]. Beginning with Stanley *et al.* [74], who analyzed data on publicly-traded U.S. manufacturing firms (Compustat), there has emerged a consensus that $g \equiv ln(G) \in \boldsymbol{R}$ is well-fit by the Subbotin or exponential power distribution.[13] This distribution embeds the Gaussian and Laplace distributions and has *PDF*

$$\frac{\eta}{2\sigma_g\Gamma(1/\eta)}exp\left[-\left(\frac{|g-\bar{g}|}{\sigma_g}\right)^{\eta}\right]$$

where $\bar{g}$ is the average log growth rate, σ_g is proportional to the standard deviation, and η is a parameter; $\eta = 2$ corresponds to the normal distribution, $\eta = 1$ the Laplace or double exponential.[14]

Data on g for all U.S. establishments has been analyzed by Perline *et al.* [82], shown as a histogram in figure 16 for 1998-99, decomposed into seven logarithmic size classes. Note the vertical axis is ln(frequency). In comparison to later years, e.g., 1999-2000, 2000-2001, this distribution is very nearly stationary.

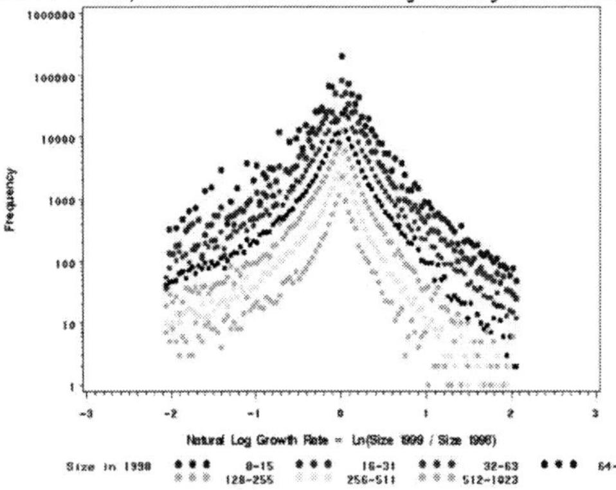

Figure 16: Histogram of annual g for U.S. establishments, by size

Perline *et al.* [82] find that $\eta \sim 0.60$ for the size 32-63 size class, lesser for smaller firms, larger for bigger ones. The gross statistical features of g are:

A. Growth rates *depend* on firm size—small and large firms have different g. This means that *Gibrat's law is false*: all firms do *not* have the same G.

B. Mode of $g \sim 0$, so mode(G) ~ 1, i.e., many firms do not grow.

C. There is more variance for firm decline ($g < 0$) than for growth ($g > 0$), i.e., there is more variability in job destruction than job creation [52], requiring an asymmetric Subbotin distribution [82].

D. Growth rate variance falls with firm size [67, 68, 74, 83, 84].

There are at least five other well-known regularities concerning firm growth rates that are *not* illustrated by the previous figure:

E. Mean growth is approximately 0;

F. Mean grow rate declines with firm size, and is positive for small firms, negative for large firms [52, 68, 84-87].

G. Mean growth *declines* with age [86, 88].

H. Mean growth *rises* with size, controlling for age [69].

I. Growth rate variance *declines* with firm age [86].

With these empirical features of firm growth rates as background, figure 17 shows distributions of g produced by the model for seven sizes of firrns, from small (blue) to large (purple) ones.

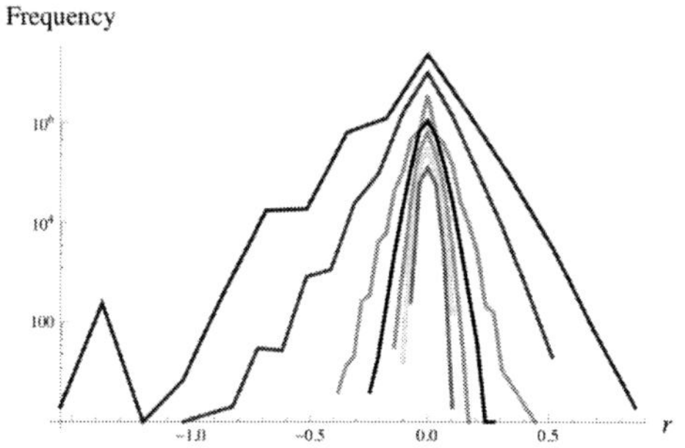

Figure 17: Distribution of annual g by firm size: 8-15 (blue), 16-31 (red), 32-63 (green), 64-127 (black), 128-255 (orange), 256-511 (yellow), and 512-1023 (purple)

In this plot we can see at least half of the empirical properties of firm growth: g clearly depends on firm size (*A*), with mode(g) = 0 (*B*) and $\bar{g} \sim 0.0$ (*E*). It is harder to see that there is more variance in firm decline than growth (*C*) but it is the case numerically. Clearly, variance declines with firm size (*D*). Figures 18 and 19 show mean growth rates as a function of firm size and age.

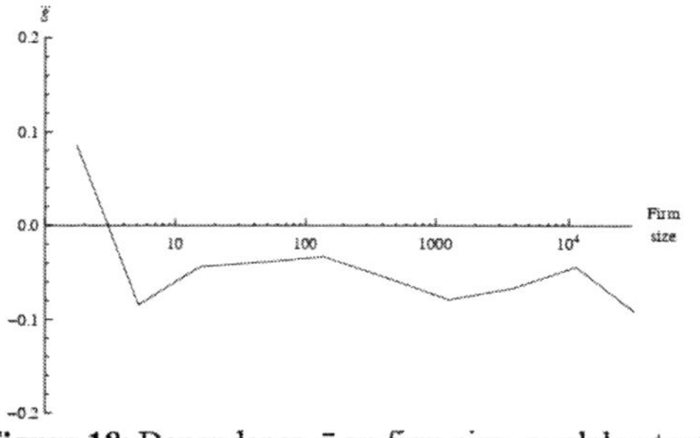

Figure 18: Dependence $\bar{g}$ on firm size, model output

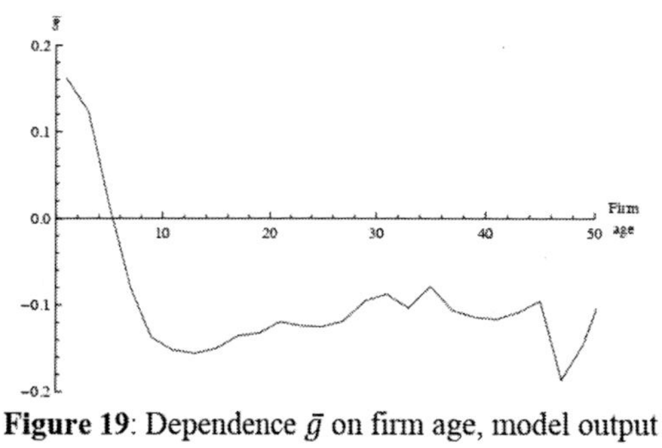

Figure 19: Dependence $\bar{g}$ on firm age, model output

---

[12] An alternative definition of G is $2(S_{t+1} - S_t)/(S_t + S_{t+1})$, making $G \in [-2, 2]$ [52]. Although advantageous because it keeps exiting and entering firms in datasets for one additional period, it obscures differences in growth rate tails by artificially truncating them.

[13] Subsequent work includes European pharmaceuticals [75] and Italian and French manufacturers [76, 77]. Bottazzi and Secchi [78] give theoretical reasons why g should have $\eta \sim 1$, having to do with the central limit theorem for the number of summands geometrically distributed [79]. Schwarzkopf [80, 81] argues that g is Levy-stable.

[14] For g Laplace-distributed, G follows the log-Laplace distribution, a kind of double-sided Pareto distribution [56], a combination of the power function distribution on (0, 1) and the Pareto on (1, ∞).

It is clear from thee figures that $\bar{g}$ declines with size (*F*) and similarly for age (*G*). For more than 30 years, since the work of Birch [85, 89], economists have debated the meaning of figures like 19. Specifically, given that small firms are often young and young firms small, it is not clear whether size or age plays the larger role in determining positive growth rates. Haltiwanger and co-workers [69, 88, 90] control for age and argue that it is not small firms that create jobs but rather young ones. The problem with such 'controls' for non-montonic relationships is that they mix effects across distinct (size, age) classes. The only actual way to understand the distinct effects of size and age is to show how they each effect $\bar{g}$. This is done in figure 20, where each firm is placed into a (size, age) bin and the average g computed locally.

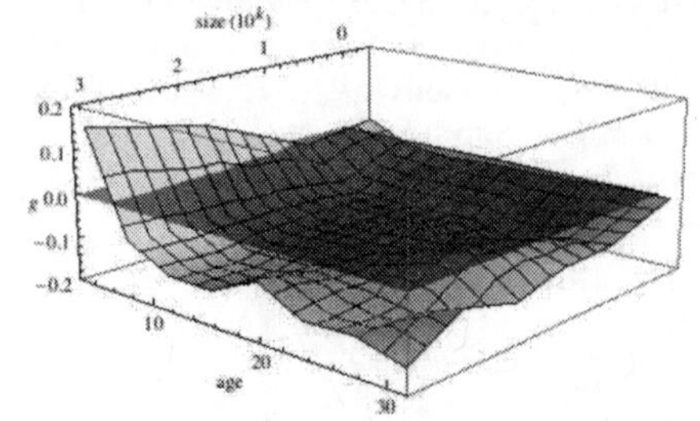

Figure 20: Dependence of $\bar{g}$ on firm size and age

To see precisely whether size or age matters most, a no growth ($\bar{g}$ = 0) plane is shown on the model's $\bar{g}$(size, age), revealing young firms grow the most with minor contribution from small firms.

Firm growth rate variability falls with size (*D*) and age (*I*). Figures 21 and 22 show this unconditionally for the model.

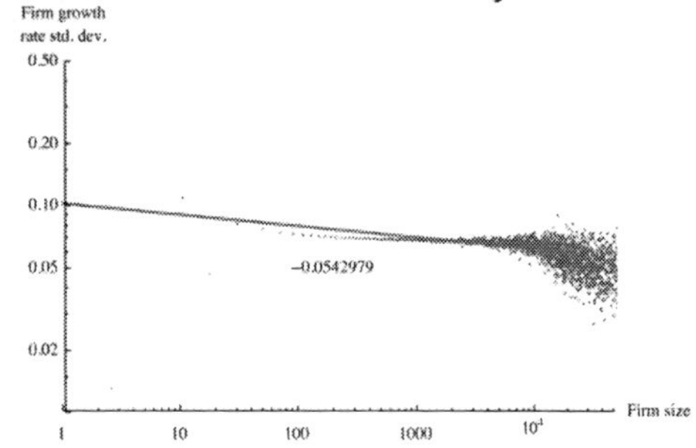

Figure 21: Dependence of the standard deviation of g on firm size

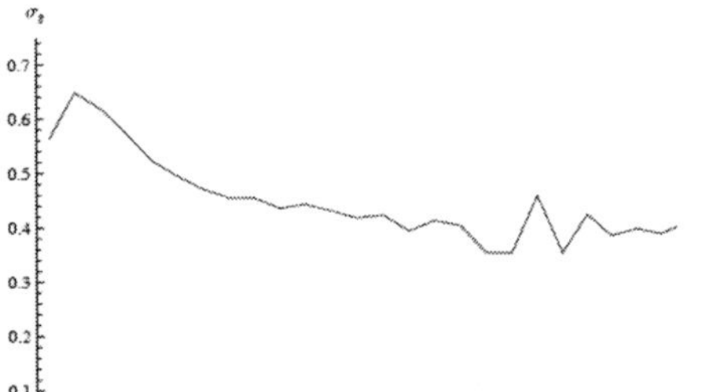

Figure 22: Dependence of the standard deviation of g on firm age

Specifically, the standard deviation of g falls with size in figure 21. Based on central limit arguments one expects this to be proportional to $S^{-\kappa}$, κ = ½ meaning the fluctuations are independent while κ< ½ implies they are correlated. Stanley *et al.* [74] find $\kappa \sim 0.16 \pm 0.03$ for publicly-traded firms (Compustat data) while Perline *et al.* [82] estimate $\kappa \sim 0.06$ for all U.S. establishments. From the model output $\kappa = 0.054 \pm 0.010$. A variety of explanations for $0 \leq \kappa \leq ½$ have been proposed [91-96], all involving firms having more or less elaborate internal structure. Note that no internal structure exists in the present model, where firms are simply collections of agents, yet dependence of the standard deviation of g on size is present nonetheless.

At all times some firms are growing and others are declining. However, growing firms shed workers and declining ones hire. Figure 23 shows that growing firms hire in excess of their separation rate, while declining firms keep hiring even when separations are the norm, much like in the empirical data [1]. The 'hiring' line is quite comparable to the empirical result, but the 'separations' line is different—too few separations in the model.

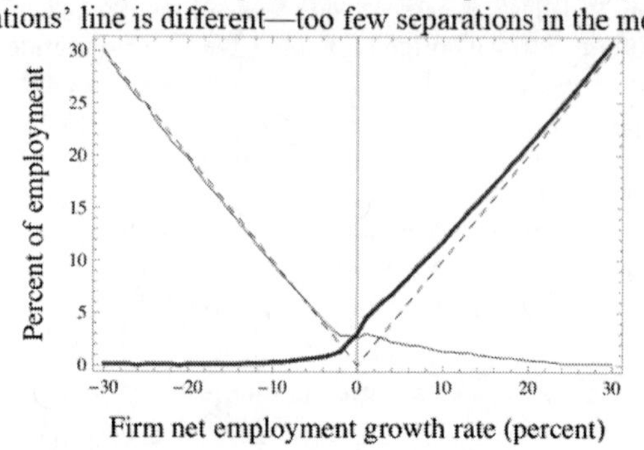

Figure 23: Model labor transitions as a function of firm growth

Having explored firms cross-sectionally, we next turn to the population of agents. Steady-state worker behavior is quantified here. While each agent's situation adjusts uniquely, at the population level there emerge robust statistical features.

While income and wealth are famously heavy-tailed [97, 98], *wages* are less so. A recent empirical examination of U.S. adjusted gross incomes argues that an exponential distribution fits the data below about \$125K, while a power law better fits the upper tail [99]. Figure 24 is the model's income distribution.

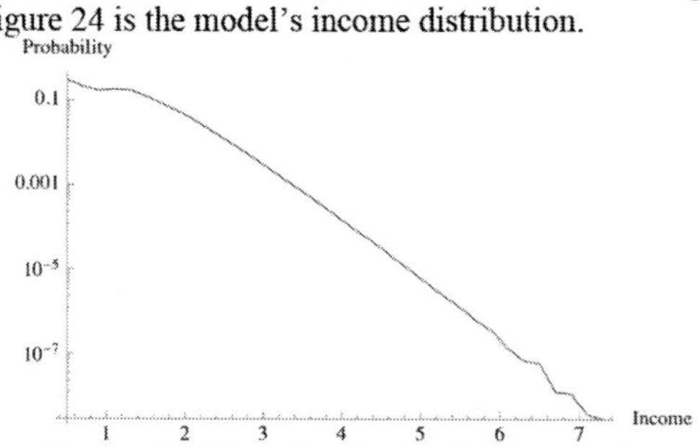

Figure 24: Wage distribution (arbitrary units)

Since incomes are nearly linear in this semi-log coordinate system, they are approximately exponentially-distributed.

Job tenure in the U.S. has a median of just over 4 years and a mean of about 8.5 years. The complementary-cumulative distribution for 2010 is figure 25 (points) with the straight line being the model output. As with income, these data are approximately exponentially distributed.

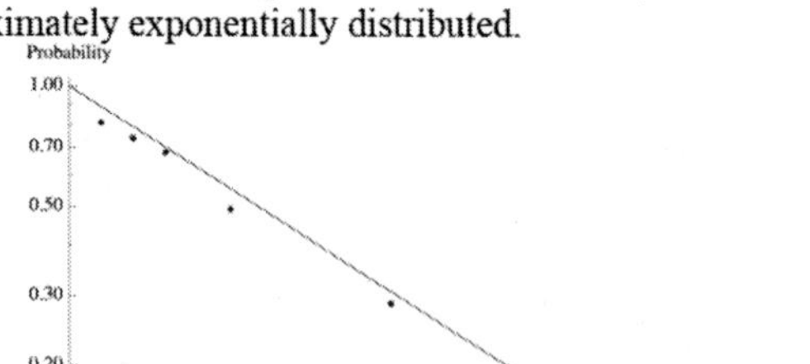

Figure 25: Job tenure (months) is exponentially-distributed in the U.S. (dots, binned) and in the model (line)

The base case of the model is calibrated to make these distributions coincide. That is, the number of agent activations per period is specified in order to make the line go through the points, thus defining the meaning of one unit of time in the model—a month. The many output of the model having to do with time—e.g., firm growth rates, ages—derive from this calibration.

In the model, as in the real world, workers regularly move between jobs. Here the *structure* of such migrations is studied, using a graph theoretic representation of inter-firm labor flows. Let each firm be a node (vertex) in such a graph, and an edge exists between two firms if a worker has migrated between the firms. Elsewhere this has been called the *labor flow network* [100]. In figure 26 a property of this network for the base case of the model is shown, the degree distribution, This closely reproduce data from Finland and Mexico [100], shown inset.

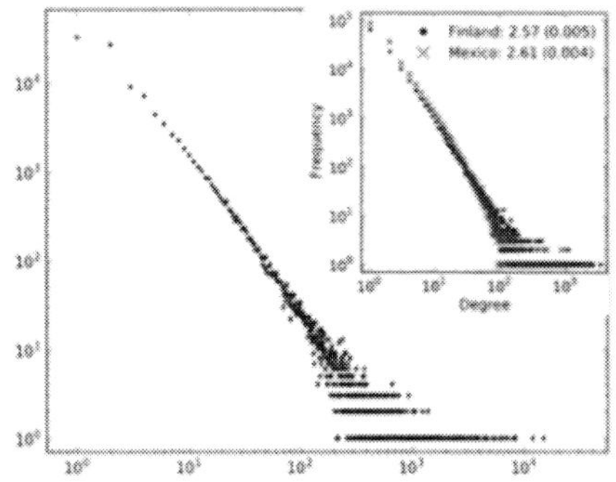

Fig 26: Degree distribution of the labor flow network

Each time an agent is activated it seeks higher utility, which is bounded from below by the singleton utility. Therefore, it must be the case that all agents prefer the non-equilibrium state to one in which each is working alone—the state of all firms being size one is Pareto-dominated by the dynamical configurations above. To analyze welfare of agents, consider homogeneous groups of maximum stable size, having utility levels shown in figure 3b, replotted in figure 27.

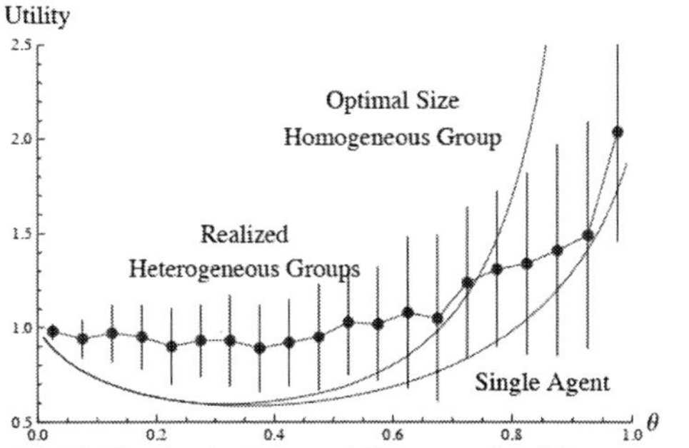

Figure 27: Utility in single agent firms, optimal homogeneous firms, and realized firms, by θ

Overall, this large-scale multi-agent model, calibrated to data using approximately a dozen parameters (table 1), has been shown here to closely reproduce nearly two dozen empirical facts concerning the U.S. economy, and represents a new approach to modeling industrial organization

4. REALIZING 120 MILLION AGENTS

Creating a model at full-scale with the U.S. economy has proved challenging in many dimensions. First there was the problem of *instantiating* so many agents. Hardware with large, flat (shared) memory spaces proved the most useful as all attempts to store this large agent population to disk was prohibitively slow. Second was the problem of fast execution. Many HPC architectures turns out to not be useful, such as cloud computing, running a single instance of the model on multiple machines, vector supercomputers and even GPUs. While each provided certain advantages, the dense interactions between agents in this model make inter-process communication voluminous and, because it is slow, prohibitive. The synchronous nature of vector supercomputers and GPUs led to problems by generating computational artifacts that had no meaningful interpretation. Instead of any of these technologies, a single dedicated workstation, with 32 cores and 256 GB of RAM, proved the most successful architecture. Using optimized C/C++ code and various threading libraries, for wide values of parameters the model reaches a near steady-state condition from the initial conditions of table 1 in approximately half a day a day of wall time. Given the expense of these model runs, the parameter optimization that led to the specification of table 1 was obtained heuristically.

5. SUMMARY AND CONCLUSIONS

Using the combination of a universe of micro-data on firms with large-scale multi-agent computing, a new kind of economic model has been created, its gross features being described above. It represents a novel contribution to both computational economics and multi-agent computer science. In terms of the former, most models in economics and finance today are solved for agent-level equilibria, while the model developed here involves agent-level disequilibria. This *feature* of the model permits us to generate endogenous economic dynamics that, as has been shown above, closely reproduce many economic facts. From a computer science point-of-view, the model shows new ways of building realistic, empirically-grounded coalition formation models, and demonstrates that these can be realized at massive scale.

For many years multi-agent systems researchers have been deeply enamored of more or less conventional game theoretic ideas, all of which involve agent-level equilibria. At the same time, social scientists have been attracted to MAS precisely because it is a technology that permits relaxation of the highly unrealistic strictures that analytical solutions require (e.g., fixed preferences, static prices, uniform probability of interaction, etc.). With models such as this one I hope to demonstrate to both communities that there is much to be gained from trade in new ideas for how to build empirically-salient models of human systems using multi-agent systems computer science.

6. ACKNOWLEDGMENTS

Support from the National Science Foundatin (0738606) and the Small Business Administration (SBAHQ-05-Q-0018) is gratefully acknowledged.

7. REFERENCES

[1] Davis, S.J., R.J. Faberman, and J.C. Haltiwanger, The Flow Approach to Labor Markets: New Data Sources and Micro-Macro Links. *Journal of Economic Perspectives*, 2006. **20**(3): p. 3-26.

[2] Fairlie, R.W., *Kauffman Index of Entrepreneurial Activity: 1996-2012*, 2012, Ewing and Marion Kauffman Foundation: Kansas City, KS.

[3] Krusell, P., et al., A three state model of worker flows in general equilibrium. *Journal of Economic Theory*, 2011. **146**: p. 1107-1133.

[4] Ijiri, Y. and H.A. Simon, *Skew Distributions and the Sizes of Business Firms*. 1977, New York, N.Y.: North-Holland.

[5] Simon, H.A., *An Empirically-Based Microeconomics*. Raffaele Mattioli Lectures. 1997, Cambridge, U.K.: Cambridge University Press.

[6] Williamson, O.E., *The Economic Institutions of Capitalism: Firms, Markets, Relational Contracting*. 1985, New York, N.Y.: Free Press.

[7] Hart, O., *Firms, Contracts and Financial Structure*. 1995, New York, N.Y.: Oxford University Press.

[8] Zame, W.R., Incentives, Contracts, and Markets: A General Equilibrium Theory of Firms. *Econometrica*, 2007. **75**(5): p. 1453-1500.

[9] Sutton, J., *Technology and Market Structure*. 1998, Cambridge, Mass.: MIT Press.

[10] Lucas, R.E., Jr., On the Size Distribution of Business Firms. *Bell Journal of Economics*, 1978. **9**: p. 508-523.

[11] Luttmer, E.G.J., Selection, Growth, and the Size Distribution of Firms. *Quarterly Journal of Economics*, 2007. **122**(3): p. 1103-1144.

[12] Luttmer, E.G.J., Models of Growth and Firm Heterogeneity. *Annual Reviews of Economics*, 2010. **2**: p. 547-576.

[13] Luttmer, E.G.J., On the Mechanics of Firm Growth. *Review of Economic Studies*, 2011. **78**(3): p. 1042-1068.

[14] Rossi-Hansberg, E. and M.L.J. Wright, Establishment Size Dynamics in the Aggregate Economy. *American Economic Review*, 2007. **97**(5): p. 1639-1666.

[15] Elsby, M.W.L. and R. Michaels, Marginal Jobs, Heterogeneous Firms, and Unemployment Flows. *American Economic Journal: Macroeconomics*, 2013. **5**(1): p. 1-48.

[16] Arkolakis, C., *A Unified Theory of Firm Selection and Growth*, in *NBER Working PAper*2013.

[17] Ray, D., *A Game Theoretic Perspective on Coalition Formation*. The Lipsey Lectures. 2007, New York, N.Y.: Oxford University Press.

[18] Nelson, R. and S.G. Winter, *An Evolutionary Theory of Economic Change*. 1982, Cambridge, Mass.: Harvard University Press.

[19] Ichiishi, T., *The Cooperative Nature of the Firm*. 1993, New York, N.Y.: Academic Press.

[20] Axtell, R.L., Why Agents? On the Varied Motivations for Agent Computing in the Social Sciences, in *Proceedings of the Workshop on Agent Simulation: Applications, Models, and Tools*, C.M. Macal and D. Sallach, Editors. 2000, Argonne National Laboratory: Chicago, Illinois. p. 3-24.

[21] Tesfatsion, L., Agent-Based Computational Economics: Growing Economies from the Bottom Up. *Artificial Life*, 2002. **8**(1): p. 55-82.

[22] Holland, J.H. and J. Miller, Artificial Adaptive Agents in Economic Theory. *American Economic Review*, 1991. **81**(2): p. 363-370.

[23] Vriend, N.J., Self-Organization of Markets: An Example of a Computational Approach. *Computational Economics*, 1995. **8**(3): p. 205-231.

[24] Grimm, V., et al., Pattern-Oriented Modeling of Agent-Based Complex Systems: Lessons from Ecology. *Science*, 2005. **310**: p. 987-991.

[25] Arthur, W.B., Inductive Reasoning and Bounded Rationality. *American Economic Review*, 1994. **84**(2): p. 406-411.

[26] Kirman, A.P., Whom or What Does the Representative Individual Represent? *Journal of Economic Perspectives*, 1992. **6**(2): p. 117-136.

[27] Arthur, W.B., Out-of-equilibrium economics and agent-based modeling, in *Handbook of Computational Economics, Volume 2: Agent-Based Computational Economics*, K. Judd and L. Tesfatsion, Editors. 2002, North-Holland: New York, N.Y.

[28] Kirman, A.P., The Economy as an Interactive System, in *The Economy as an Evolving Complex System II*, W.B. Arthur, S.N. Durlauf, and D.A. Lane, Editors. 1997, Addison-Wesley: Reading, Mass.

[29] Arthur, W.B., Designing Economic Agents That Act Like Human Agents: A Behavioral Approach to Bounded Rationality. *American Economic Review*, 1991. **81**(2): p. 353-359.

[30] Kirman, A.P., Ants, Rationality and Recruitment. *Quarterly Journal of Economics*, 1993. **108**: p. 137-156.

[31] Canning, D., *Evolution of Group Cooperation through Inter-Group Conflict*, 1995, Queens University of Belfast: Belfast, Northern Ireland.

[32] Huberman, B.A. and N.S. Glance, Fluctuating Efforts and Sustainable Cooperation, in *Simulating Organizations: Computational Models of Institutions and Groups*, M.J. Prietula, K.M. Carley, and L. Gasser, Editors. 1998, MIT Press: Cambridge, Mass.

[33] Glance, N.S., T. Hogg, and B.A. Huberman, Training and Turnover in the Evolution of Organizations. *Organization Science*, 1997. **8**: p. 84-96.

[34] Hopenhayn, H., Entry, Exit and Firm Dynamics in Long Run Equilibrium. *Econometrica*, 1992. **60**(5): p. 1127-1150.

[35] Marshall, A., *Principles of Economics*. 8th ed. 1920, London: Macmillan.

[36] Young, A., Increasing Returns and Economic Progress. *Economic Journal*, 1928. **38**: p. 527-542.

[37] Sraffa, P., The Laws of Returns Under Competitive Conditions. *Economic Journal*, 1926. **XXXVI**(144): p. 535-50.

[38] Arthur, W.B., *Increasing Returns and Economic Theory*. 1994, Ann Arbor, Mich.: University of Michigan Press.

[39] Buchanan, J.M. and Y.J. Yoon, *The Return to Increasing Returns*. 1994, Ann Arbor, Mich.: University of Michigan Press.

[40] Colander, D.C. and H. Landreth, *Increasing Returns: Who, If Anyone, Deserves Credit for Reintroducing It into Economics?*, in *Paper presented at the American Economic Association Annual Meetings*1999: New York, N.Y.

[41] Axtell, R.L., Non-Cooperative Dynamics of Multi-Agent Teams, in *Proceedings of the First International Joint Conference on Autonomous Agents and Multiagent Systems*, C. Castelfranchi and W.L. Johnson, Editors. 2002, ACM Press: Bologna, Italy. p. 1082-1089.

[42] Watts, A., Uniqueness of equilibrium in cost sharing games. *Journal of Mathematical Economics*, 2002. **37**: p. 47-70.

[43] Holmstrom, B., Moral Hazard in Teams. *Bell Journal of Economics*, 1982. **13**: p. 324-340.

[44] Granovetter, M., The Strength of Weak Ties. *American Journal of Sociology*, 1973. **78**: p. 1360-1380.

[45] Montgomery, J.D., Social Networks and Labor-Market Outcomes: Toward an Economic Analysis. *American Economic Review*, 1991. **81**(5): p. 1408-1418.

[46] Fallick, B.C. and C.A. Fleischman, *The Importance of Employer-to-Employer Flows in the U.S. Labor Market*, 2001: Washington, D.C. p. 44.

[47] Axtell, R.L., Zipf Distribution of U.S. Firm Sizes. *Science*, 2001. **293**(5536): p. 1818-20.

[48] Hall, R.E., Labor-Market Frictions and Employment Fluctuations, in *Handbook of Macroeconomics*, J.B. Taylor and M. Woodford, Editors. 1999, Elsevier Science: New York, N.Y. p. 1137-1170.

[49] Davis, S.J., R.J. Faberman, and J.C. Haltiwanger, Labor market flows in the cross section and over time. *Journal of Monetary Economics*, 2012. **59**: p. 1-18.
[50] Faberman, R.J. and É. Nagypál, *Quits, Worker Recruitment, and Firm Growth: Theory and Evidence*, 2008, Federal Reserve Bank of Philadelphia: Philadelphia, Pennsylvania. p. 50.
[51] Nagypál, É., *Worker Reallocation over the Business Cycle: The Importance of Employer-to-Employer Transitions*, 2008, Northwestern University: Evanston, Illinois. p. 55.
[52] Davis, S.J., J.C. Haltiwanger, and S. Schuh, *Job Creation and Job Destruction*. 1996, Cambridge, Mass.: MIT Press.
[53] Bak, P., *How Nature Works: The Science of Self-Organized Criticality*. 1996, New York, N.Y.: Copernicus.
[54] Marsili, M. and Y.-C. Zhang, Interacting Individuals Leading to Zipf's Law. *Physical Review Letters*, 1998. **LXXX**(12): p. 2741-2744.
[55] Gabaix, X., Zipf's Law for Cities: An Explanation. *Quarterly Journal of Economics*, 1999. **114**(3): p. 739-767.
[56] Reed, W.J., The Pareto, Zipf and other Power Laws. *Economics Letters*, 2001. **74**: p. 15-19.
[57] Saichev, A., Y. Malevergne, and D. Sornette, *Theory of Zipf's Law and Beyond*. Lecture Notes in Economics and Mathematical Systems. 2010, New York, N.Y.: Springer-Verlag.
[58] Mitzenmacher, M., A Brief History of Generative Models for Power Law and Lognormal Distributions. *Internet Mathematics*, 2004. **1**(2): p. 226-251.
[59] Basu, S. and J.G. Fernald, Returns to Scale in U.S. Manufacturing: Estimates and Implications. *Journal of Political Economy*, 1997. **105**(2): p. 249-283.
[60] Brown, C. and J. Medoff, The Employer Size-Wage Effect. *Journal of Political Economy*, 1989. **97**: p. 1027-1059.
[61] Even, W.E. and D.A. Macpherson, Is Bigger Still Better? The Decline of the Wage Premium at Large Firms. *Southern Economic Journal*, 2012. **78**(4): p. 1181-1201.
[62] Dosi, G., Statistical Regularities in the Evolution of Industries. A Guide through some Evidence and Challenges for the Theory, in *Perspectives on Innovation*, F. Malerba and S. Brusoni, Editors. 2007, Cambridge University Press: Cambridge, UK.
[63] Souma, W., et al., Distribution of Labour Productivity in Japan over the Period 1996-2006. *Economics: The Open-Access, Open-Assessment E-journal*, 2009. **3**(2009-14).
[64] Coad, A., The Exponential Age Distribution and the Pareto Firm Size Distribution. *Journal of Industrial Competition and Trade*, 2010. **10**: p. 389-395.
[65] de Geus, A., *The Living Company: Habits for Survival in a Turbulent Business Environment*. 1997, Boston, Mass.: Harvard Business School Press.
[66] Barlow, R.E. and F. Proschan, *Mathematical Theory of Reliability*. 1965, New York, N.Y.: John Wiley & Sons, Inc.
[67] Evans, D.S., Tests of Alternative Theories of Firm Growth. *Journal of Political Economy*, 1987. **95**(4): p. 657-674.
[68] Hall, B.W., The Relationship Between Firm Size and Firm Growth in the U.S. Manufacturing Sector. *Journal of Industrial Economics*, 1987. **35**: p. 583-606.
[69] Haltiwanger, J.C., R.S. Jarmin, and J. Miranda, *Who Creates Jobs? Small vs. Large vs. Young*, 2011, NBER: Cambridge, Mass.
[70] Gibrat, R., *Les Inegalities Economiques; Applications: Aux Ineqalities des Richesses, a la Concentartion des Entreprises, Aux Populations des Villes, Aux Statistiques des Families, etc., d'une Loi Nouvelle, La Loi de l'Effet Proportionnel*. 1931, Paris: Librarie du Recueil Sirey.
[71] Sutton, J., Gibrat's Legacy. *Journal of Economic Literature*, 1997. **XXXV**(1): p. 40-59.
[72] de Wit, G., Firm Size Distributions: An Overview of Steady-State Distributions Resulting from Firm Dynamics Models. *International Journal of Industrial Organization*, 2005. **23**: p. 423-450.
[73] Hart, P.E. and S.J. Prais, The Analysis of Business Concentration: A Statistical Approach. *Journal of the Royal Statistical Society, Series A*, 1956. **119**(series A): p. 150-191.
[74] Stanley, M.H.R., et al., Scaling Behaviour in the Growth of Companies. *Nature*, 1996. **379**(29): p. 804-806.
[75] Bottazzi, G., et al., Innovation and corporate growth in the evolution of the drug industry. *International Journal of Industrial Organization*, 2001. **19**: p. 1161-1187.
[76] Bottazzi, G., et al., Corporate growth and industrial dynamics: evidence from French manufacturing. *Applied Economics*, 2011. **43**(1): p. 103-116.
[77] Bottazzi, G., et al., Invariances and Diversities in the Patterns of Industrial Evolution: Some Evidence from Italian Manufacturing Industries. *Small Business Economics*, 2007. **29**(1-2): p. 137-159.
[78] Bottazzi, G. and A. Secchi, Explaining the distribution of firm growth rates. *Rand Journal of Economics*, 2006. **37**(2): p. 235-256.
[79] Kotz, S., T.J. Kozubowski, and K. Podgorski, *The Laplace Distribution and Generalizations: A Revisit with Applications to Communications, Economics, Engineering, and Finance*. 2001: Birkhauser.
[80] Schwarzkopf, Y., *Complex Phenomena in Social and Financial Systems: From bird population growth to the dynamics of the mutual fund industry*, in *Physics*2010, California Institute of Technology. p. 158.
[81] Schwarzkopf, Y., R.L. Axtell, and J.D. Farmer, *An Explanation of Universality in Growth Fluctuations*, 2011. p. 12.
[82] Perline, R., R. Axtell, and D. Teitelbaum, *Volatility and Asymmetry of Small Firm Growth Rates Over Increasing Time Frames*, in *SBA Research Reports*2006: Washington, D.C.
[83] Hymer, S. and P. Pashigian, Firm Size and the Rate of Growth. *Journal of Political Economy*, 1962. **70**(4): p. 556-569.
[84] Mansfield, E., Entry, Gibrat's Law, Innovation, and the Growth of Firms. *American Economic Review*, 1962. **52**(5): p. 1023-1051.
[85] Birch, D.L., Who Creates Jobs? *The Public Interest*, 1981. **65**: p. 3-14.
[86] Evans, D.S., The Relationship Between Firm Growth, Size, and Age: Estimates for 100 Manufacturing Industries. *Journal of Industrial Economics*, 1987. **35**: p. 567-581.
[87] Neumark, D., B. Wall, and J. Zhang, Do Small Businesses Create More Jobs? New Evidence for the United States from the National Establishment Time Series. *The Review of Economics and Statistics*, 2011. **93**(1): p. 16-29.
[88] Haltiwanger, J.C., R.S. Jarmin, and J. Miranda, *Business Formation and Dynamics by Business Age: Results from the New Business Dynamics Statistics*, 2008, University of Maryland: College Park, Maryland.
[89] Birch, D.L., *Job Creation in America: How Our Smallest Companies Put the Most People to Work*. 1987, New York, N.Y.: Free Press.

[90] Haltiwanger, J.C., R. Jarmin, and J. Miranda, *High Growth and Faiure of Young Firms*, in *Business Dynamics Statistics Briefing*2009, Ewing Marion Kauffman Foundation: Kansas City, Missouri. p. 4.

[91] Fu, D., et al., The Growth of Business Firms: Theoretical Framework and Empirical Evidence. *Proc Natl Acad Sci U S A*, 2005. **102**(52): p. 18801-18806.

[92] Sutton, J., The Variance of Firm Growth Rates: The Scaling Puzzle. *Physica A*, 2002. **312**.

[93] Wyart, M. and J.-P. Bouchaud, *Statistical Models for Company Growth*, in *arXiv*2002.

[94] Amaral, L.A.N., et al., Power Law Scaling for a System of Interacting Units with Complex Internal Structure. *Physical Review Letters*, 1998. **80**: p. 1385-1388.

[95] Buldyrev, S.V., et al., Scaling Behavior in Economics: II. Modeling Company Growth. *Journal de Physique I France*, 1997. **7**: p. 635-650.

[96] Riccaboni, M., et al., The size variance relationship of business firm growth rates. *Proc Natl Acad Sci U S A*, 2008. **105**(50): p. 19595-19600.

[97] Pareto, V., *Manual of Political Economy*. 1971 [1927], New York, N.Y.: Augustus M. Kelley.

[98] Wolff, E.N., *Top Heavy: A Study of the Increasing Inequality of Wealth in America*. A Twentieth Century Fund Report. 1994, New York, N.Y.: Twentieth Century Foundation.

[99] Yakovenko, V.M. and J. Rosser, J. Barkley, Statistical mechanics of money, wealth, and income. *Reviews of Modern Physics*, 2009. **81**(4): p. 1703-1725.

[100] Guerrero, O.A. and R.L. Axtell, Employment Growth through Labor Flow Networks. *PLoS ONE*, 2013. **8**(5): p. e60808.

Load Forecasting in a Smart Grid through Customer Behaviour Learning Using L1-Regularized Continuous Conditional Random Fields

Xishun Wang
School of Computing and Information Technology
University of Wollongong
xw357@uowmail.edu.au

Minjie Zhang
School of Computing and Information Technology
University of Wollongong
minjie@uow.edu.au

Fenghui Ren
School of Computing and Information Technology
University of Wollongong
fren@uow.edu.au

ABSTRACT

Load forecasting plays a critical role in Smart Grid. As there have been various types of customers with different behaviours in a Smart Grid, it would benefit load forecasting if customer behaviours were taken into consideration. This paper proposes a novel load forecasting method that efficiently explores customers' power consumption behaviours through learning. Our method uses L_1-CCRF to initially learn the behaviour of each customer, followed by a hierarchical clustering process to cluster all the customers according to their different behaviour patterns, and then fine-tunes a corresponding L_1-CCRF to predict the load for each customer cluster, and finally, sums all the predicted loads of customer clusters to obtain the load for the whole Smart Grid. The proposed method utilizes L_1-CCRFs to effectively capture the relationships between various customers' loads and a range of outside influential factors. Experiments from different perspectives demonstrate the advantages of our load forecasting method through customer behaviour learning.

Keywords

Load Forecasting; Customer Behaviour; Continuous Conditional Random Fields; Regularization

1. INTRODUCTION

Load forecasting benefits a power grid in supply-demand balance and efficient energy distributions. As it plays a critical role, load forecasting has been widely studied [22, 10]. Representative methods include time series models [7], ARIMA [19] and neural networks [6, 8]. Recently, some novel learning-based methods have been proposed. Srinivasan [21] introduces a group method of data handling neural network for load forecasting. In his method, six categories of consumers are predicted respectively, yet the customer groups are stipulated manually. Amjady et al. [3] uses a bilevel method, which is composed of a feature selection technique and a forecasting engine, to predict the power load of a single micro-grid. Their method has been tested on the load forecasting for a campus. Motamedi et al. [15] combine a multi-input multi-output forecasting engine for joint price and load prediction with data association mining algorithms, through which the relationship of load and price is extracted. This method is applied to a macro scope, regardless of the types of customers.

In Smart Grid, the concept of "customer" has extended to not only general energy consumers, but also interruptible consumers, consumers with storage capacity and even small renewable energy producers. Due to these potential customers' various power consumption behaviours, traditional load forecasting methods, which orient to the whole grid or a specific customer, face challenges to effectively forecast the load of a Smart Grid with such varieties of customers. Even though some researchers [21] manually distinguish different customers' power consumption behaviours, there has been no effective load forecasting method which can automatically take various customers' behaviours into consideration, to the best of our knowledge.

This paper proposes an innovative load forecasting method by learning to explore different behaviours of various customers. The proposed LF-CBL (Load Forecasting through Customer Behaviour Learning) focuses on short-term load forecasting [10], i.e. forecasting the hourly power usages in the future 24 hours. The customer behaviour here specially refers to the customer's power consumption behaviour. In our work, a novel learning method, L_1 regularized Continuous Conditional Random Fields (L_1-CCRF), is proposed and used in LF-CBL. The pipeline of LF-CBL is briefly described as follows. First, a range of features, which may facilitate the load forecasting, are extracted. Based on the rich features, an L_1-CCRF is learned for each customer. L_1-CCRF analyzes customers' behaviours from feature selection and feature weighting. Feature selection determines whether the customer's behaviour is influenced by a certain feature, while feature weighting analyzes how much the power consumption is related to a selected feature. According to the different behaviour patterns in power consumption, all customers are clustered. For each customer cluster, a corresponding L_1-CCRF is fine-tuned and used to predict the load of the cluster. Finally, the load for a Smart Grid is obtained by the sum of the loads of all customer clusters.

The motivation of using L_1-CCRF for LF-CBL is briefly explained on two successive reasons, which are: 1) The reason to introducing CCRF to model the load forecasting prob-

Appears in: *Proceedings of the 15th International Conference on Autonomous Agents and Multiagent Systems (AAMAS 2016), J. Thangarajah, K. Tuyls, C. Jonker, S. Marsella (eds.), May 9–13, 2016, Singapore.*

lem, and 2) The reason to introducing L_1 norm for CCRF regularization. **To the first reason:** In short-term load forecasting, a sequence of load variables is influenced by the outside observations (time, weather conditions etc.). Besides, partial autocorrelation [9] reveals that there are strong correlations of adjacent target variables. CCRF gains advantages to model the load sequence simultaneously taking the above two factors into account. Moreover, CCRF optimally outputs the load sequence based on the whole observations. However, to our best knowledge, the only work used CCRF for load forecasting was Guo's study [9]. He used CCRF to predict the short-term load of a building, and demonstrated superior performance to state-of-the-art methods. To take the advantages of CCRF and to further explore CCRF in load forecasting, we adopt CCRF to model the load forecasting problem. **To the second reason:** L_1 norm is capable of feature selection and avoiding model over-fitting. Its feature selection property can be utilized in customer behaviour analysis. Therefore, we introduce L_1 norm as the regularization term for CCRF. To fit our problem and to provide the potential for broad applications, in the proposed L_1-CCRF, we change the traditional CCRF in two aspects. First, we extend the definition domain of weights of CCRF from a practical perspective. Second, we provide a new learning method for L_1-CCRF.

The proposed method for load forecasting in a Smart Grid has two major contributions. **1)** Our method provides a new solution to handle the challenges of various customers' different behaviours in load forecasting. To our knowledge, it is the first attempt to introduce learning method to explore customers' power consumption behaviours for load forecasting. Experiment evaluations demonstrate the advantages of utilizing learned customer behaviours in load forecasting for a Smart Grid. **2)** In our method, the proposed L_1-CCRF can be a suggested method for feature selection and prediction to apply to related research domains, because the first exploration of L_1-CCRF in feature selection and load forecasting has produced convincing results demonstrated from our experiments.

The rest of the paper is organized as follows. Section 2 makes a brief introduction to CCRF. Section 3 describes the proposed LF-CBL in details. Section 4 demonstrates and analyzes the proposed LF-CBL through experiments in different perspectives. Section 5 presents the related work. Finally, conclusions are drawn in Section 6.

2. AN INTRODUCTION TO CCRF

In this section, the concept of CCRF is introduced. As CCRF is originated from Conditional Random Fields (CRF), we first introduce CRF, and then extend CRF to CCRF.

2.1 Conditional Random Fields

The Conditional Random Fields (CRF) [12] was initially proposed for labeling sequence data. The chain-structured CRF, as illustrated in Figure 1, is widely used.

Assume $X = \{x_1, x_2, \cdots, x_m\}$ is the given sequence of observations, and $Y = \{y_1, y_2, \cdots, y_n\}$ is the label sequence to be predicted. CRF defines the conditional probability $P(Y|X)$ in Equation 1.

$$P(Y|X) = \frac{1}{Z(X)} exp(\Psi), \tag{1}$$

where Ψ is the energy function, and $Z(X)$ is the partition

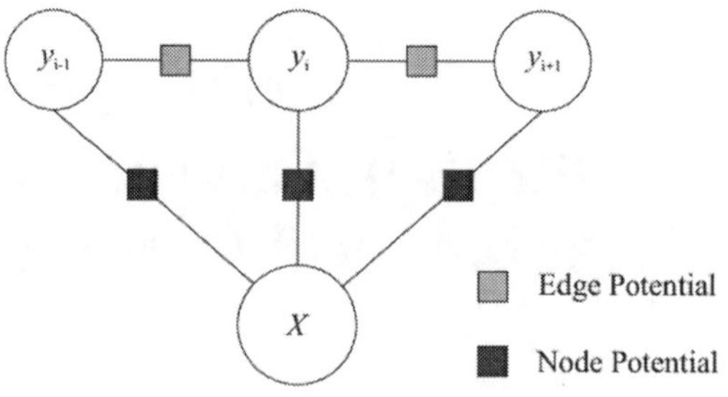

Figure 1: An illustration of a CRF with a chain structure.

function that normalizes $P(Y|X)$. The energy function Ψ is further defined as

$$\Psi = \sum_i \sum_{k=1}^{K_1} \alpha_k f_k(y_i, X) + \sum_{i,j} \sum_{k=1}^{K_2} \beta_k g_k(y_i, y_j, X), \tag{2}$$

where function $f_k(y_i, X)$ is called node potential and function $g_k(y_i, y_j, X)$ is called edge potential, and α_k and β_k are corresponding weight parameters. In the energy function, the node potential captures the associations between inputs and outputs, and the edge potential captures the interactions between related outputs. The partition function $Z(X)$ is defined in Equation 3.

$$Z(X) = \sum_Y exp(\Psi) \tag{3}$$

CRF explicitly defines $P(Y|X)$, which means Y is determined by the whole observation X. Therefore, CRF gains the advantage of considering the whole observed sequence for the output.

2.2 Continuous Conditional Random Fields

The CRF model outputs discrete values, while CCRF extends CRF to be capable of outputing real values. The definition of CCRF differs from CRF in three aspects [17]. 1) The output $Y = \{y_1, y_2, \cdots, y_n\}$ can be a real value sequence. 2) The partition function $Z(X)$ is alternatively defined as:

$$Z(X) = \int_Y exp(\Psi) \tag{4}$$

3) The weights $\boldsymbol{\alpha}$ and $\boldsymbol{\beta}$ are required to be positive to ensure the partition function is integrable.

To learn a CCRF model, maximum log-likelihood is used to find the fittest weights $\boldsymbol{\alpha}$ and $\boldsymbol{\beta}$. Given training data $D = \{(X,Y)\}_1^Q$, where Q is the total number of training samples, the log-likelihood $L(\boldsymbol{\alpha}, \boldsymbol{\beta})$ is maximized:

$$(\hat{\boldsymbol{\alpha}}, \hat{\boldsymbol{\beta}}) = \text{argmax}_{(\boldsymbol{\alpha}, \boldsymbol{\beta})}(L(\boldsymbol{\alpha}, \boldsymbol{\beta})), \tag{5}$$

where

$$L(\boldsymbol{\alpha}, \boldsymbol{\beta}) = \sum_{l=1}^{Q} logP(Y_q|X_q) \tag{6}$$

After the weights $\boldsymbol{\alpha}$ and $\boldsymbol{\beta}$ are obtained, inference for a CCRF is to find the most likely value for Y_k, provided an observed sequence X_k:

$$\hat{Y_k} = \text{argmax}_{Y_k}(P(Y_k|X_k)) \tag{7}$$

In machine learning, regularization has been commonly used in learning process to avoid over-fitting. L_2 norm regularization has been used in [5, 18, 9] in learning CCRF. L_1 norm regularizer is theoretically studied in [16] by Ng, and in practice, the L_1 norm regularizer has gained roughly the same accuracy as the L_2 norm regularizer [13]. Besides, L_1 norm has a favorable property of selecting effective features, which can be utilized to analyze customer behaviours in our research. Therefore, we introduce L_1 norm to regularize the CCRF. However, L_1 norm is not differentiable at zero. Some special methods have been proposed to tackle the learning with L_1 norm regularizer [4, 26]. In our work, we introduce the Orthant-Wise Limited-memory Quasi-Newton (OWL-QN) [4] to learn an L_1-CCRF.

3. LOAD FORECASTING THROUGH CUSTOMER BEHAVIOUR LEARNING

LF-CBL focuses on the short-term load forecasting, i.e. to predict the hourly power usages in the next 24 hours. In the following subsections, we first illustrate how to use CCRF to model the load forecasting problem, and then the learning of L_1-CCRFs with the consideration of customer behaviours is described, and finally, the load forecasting using learned L_1-CCRFs is presented.

3.1 Model Design

CCRF discriminatively models the conditional probability $P(Y|X)$. In our research, we use a vector $\mathbf{y} = (y_1, y_2, \cdots, y_n)$ to denote the hourly power usages to be predicted. The observations X are specified with a matrix $\mathbf{X} = (\mathbf{x}_1, \mathbf{x}_2, \cdots, \mathbf{x}_n)^T$, where each row $\mathbf{x}_i$ represents the observed D-dimension feature vector for hour i.

In our model, both node potential and edge potential bear a quadratic form. In this scenario, CCRF can be derived into a multivariate Gaussian [18], resulting in convenience in learning and inference. The node potential f_k and edge potential g_k are further discussed below.

The node potential is defined as follows.

$$f_k(y_i, \mathbf{X}) = -(y_i - \mathbf{X}_{i,k})^2 \tag{8}$$

A node potential associates the input feature with the output. For an output y_i, we associate it with the current observed feature $\mathbf{x}_i$. As the number of features in $\mathbf{x}_i$ is D, D node potentials are generated for the current observation. After preprocessing, the feature, without any transformation, is used in the node potential, so we can analyze how much the feature relates to certain customer's load in the learning process.

The edge potential, which captures the interactions between outputs, is defined as follows.

$$g_k(y_i, y_j, \mathbf{X}) = -\delta_k^{(p)}(y_i - y_j)^2 \tag{9}$$

Edge potentials are generated in between every two adjacent outputs. The quadratic edge potential contributes to convenient learning and inference, but results in a weak feature constraint problem [9], which is briefly explained as follows. When CRF works on a binary case, the edge potentials can reflect the true distribution of y_i. In contrast, CCRF copes with continuous problems, and it is not easy to capture the true distribution of y. Thus, it is reasonable to divide the distribution of y into sub-distributions to approximate the true distribution. We follow the work by Guo [9] and introduce the Predictive Clustering Trees (PCTs) [25] to tackle this problem. Δx is introduced to denote the change of adjacent features, and Δy is to denote the change between y_i and y_j. The PCTs provide more sophisticated relationships between Δy and Δx through the indicator function $\delta_k^{(p)}$. The value of an indicator function is determined by its corresponding assertion. When the assertion holds, it takes the value 1, otherwise, it is 0. Figure 2 uses the temperature feature as an instance to illustrate how PCTs work. When the assertion that Δx is small (similar temperatures in the two adjacent hours) holds, $\delta_k^{(1)}$ is true, otherwise, it is 0. Similar processes repeat for $\delta_k^{(2)}$ and $\delta_k^{(3)}$. That is how PCTs determines the indicator function $\delta_k^{(p)}$, and thus provides more interactions between Δy and Δx. In our situation, $P = 3$ is adequate to supply sufficient relationship information between Δy and Δx.

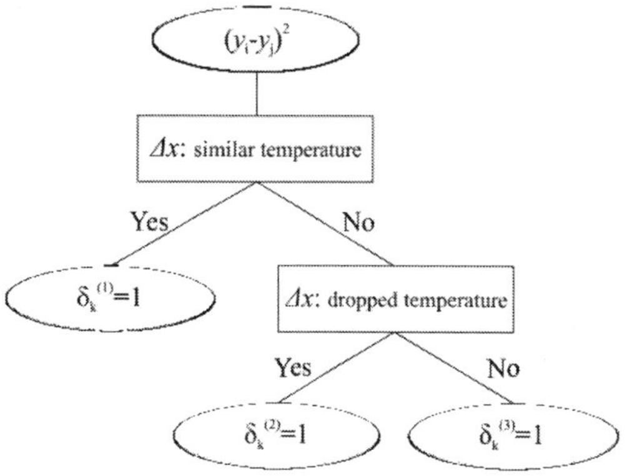

Figure 2: An illustration of how PCTs work with respect to the temperature feature

With the node potential in Equation 8 and edge potential in Equation 9, our CCRF model finally results in the following formula.

$$\begin{aligned} P(\mathbf{y}|\mathbf{X}) = & \frac{1}{Z(\mathbf{X})} \cdot \\ & exp(-\sum_{i=1}^{n}\sum_{k=1}^{D}\alpha_k(y_i - \mathbf{X}_{i,k})^2 - \\ & \sum_{i,j}\sum_{k=1}^{D-1}\sum_{p=1}^{P}\delta_k^{(p)}\beta_k^{(p)}(y_i - y_j)^2) \end{aligned} \tag{10}$$

Following Radosavljevic's work [18], the CCRF in Equation 10 can be derived into the following multivariate Gaussian form to facilitate learning and inference.

$$\begin{aligned} P(\mathbf{y}|\mathbf{X}) = & \frac{1}{(2\pi)^{n/2}|\mathbf{\Sigma}|^{1/2}} \cdot \\ & exp(-\frac{1}{2}(\mathbf{y} - \mu(\mathbf{X}))^T \mathbf{\Sigma}^{-1}(\mathbf{y} - \mu(\mathbf{X}))) \end{aligned} \tag{11}$$

In Equation 11, the inverse of the covariance matrix $\mathbf{\Sigma}^{-1}$, is the sum of two $n \times n$ matrices, further expressed as follows.

$$\mathbf{\Sigma}^{-1} = 2(\mathbf{M}^1 + \mathbf{M}^2), where$$

$$M^1_{i,j} = \begin{cases} \sum_{k=1}^{D} \alpha_k & if \quad i = j \\ 0 & otherwise \end{cases}$$

$$M^2_{i,j} = \begin{cases} \sum_{j=1}^{n} \sum_{k=1}^{D-1} \sum_{p=1}^{P} \delta_k^{(p)} \beta_k^{(p)} - \\ \sum_{k=1}^{D-1} \sum_{p=1}^{P} \delta_k^{(p)} \beta_k^{(p)} & if \quad i = j \\ -\sum_{k=1}^{D-1} \sum_{p=1}^{P} \delta_k^{(p)} \beta_k^{(p)} & if \quad i \neq j \end{cases} \tag{12}$$

Moreover, the mean $\mu(\mathbf{X})$ is computed by

$$\mu(\mathbf{X}) = \mathbf{\Sigma}\boldsymbol{\theta} \tag{13}$$

Here, $\boldsymbol{\theta}$ is an n-dimension vector, where each element is calculated by

$$\theta_i = 2\sum_{k=1}^{D} \alpha_k \mathbf{X}_{i,k} \tag{14}$$

Practically, the multivariate Gaussian form, shown in Equation 11, brings convenience to learning and inference in C-CRF, which is introduced in details in the following subsections.

3.2 Learning L_1-CCRFs

Learning L_1-CCRFs for load forecasting in a Smart Grid is introduced in this subsection. A L_1-CCRF is first learned for each customer to analyze the customer's behaviours, then all the customers are clustered based on their behaviour patterns, and finally, for each customer cluster, a corresponding L_1-CCRF is fine-tuned.

3.2.1 Learning a L_1-CCRF for Each Customer

From a practical perspective, we first extend the definition domain of the weights of CCRF, and then introduce OWL-QN to optimize the weights for a CCRF.

In previous CCRF [17, 18], the partition function takes the following form:

$$Z(\mathbf{X}) = \int_{\mathbf{y}} exp(\sum_{i}\sum_{k=1}^{K_1} -\alpha_k(y_i - \mathbf{X}_{i,k})^2 + \sum_{i,j}\sum_{k=1}^{K_2} -\delta_k\beta_k(y_i - y_j)^2) \tag{15}$$

For Equation 15, we do not pay much attention to any specific parameters, but focus on the quadratic terms. When the variables $\mathbf{X}$ and $\mathbf{y}$ are defined in infinite domains, both $\boldsymbol{\alpha}$ and $\boldsymbol{\beta}$ are required to be positive to ensure that the partition function is integrable. However, in practical use, the observed feature $\mathbf{X}$ is preprocessed to be within a certain domain, and Y is also targeted in a finite range. Thus, the partition function is integrable regardless of the domains of $\boldsymbol{\alpha}$ and $\boldsymbol{\beta}$. Therefore, we do not have to constrain $\boldsymbol{\alpha}$ and $\boldsymbol{\beta}$.

To perform feature selection and avoid over-fitting, we introduce L_1 norm to regularize the weights $\boldsymbol{\alpha}$ and $\boldsymbol{\beta}$. $\boldsymbol{\lambda} =< \boldsymbol{\alpha}, \boldsymbol{\beta} >$ is introduced to compactly represent the weights. The cost function for L_1-CCRF is shown in Equation 16.

$$F(\boldsymbol{\lambda}) = -L(\boldsymbol{\lambda}) + \rho\|\boldsymbol{\lambda}\|_1 \tag{16}$$

In the cost function, the first term is the loss function, which is a negative of log-likelihood of the training set (see Equation 6), while the second term is the L_1 norm of $\boldsymbol{\lambda}$, used as a regularization term. The parameter ρ compromises the loss and the regularization term.

As the L_1 norm is non-differentiable at zero, we seek to OWL-QN algorithm to minimize the cost function. We first derive the gradient of α_k and $\beta_k^{(p)}$ in the loss function. With the gradients of α_k and $\beta_k^{(p)}$, the corresponding pseudo-gradients [4] of Equation 16 is obtained. Then we use OWL-QN algorithm to minimize $F(\boldsymbol{\lambda})$, resulting in the optimal weights for L_1-CCRF.

3.2.2 Clustering Customers

As a L_1-CCRF has been learned for each customer, we can utilize the obtained weight vector $\boldsymbol{\lambda}$ to analyze each customer's behaviours and accordingly cluster customers. In the learned weights $\boldsymbol{\lambda} =< \boldsymbol{\alpha}, \boldsymbol{\beta} >$ for a certain customer, each α_k reveals how much a feature influences the power usage of the customer, and each β_k reveals how much the adjacent feature change influences the hourly usage change. As we use L_1 norm to regularize CCRF, the weights of unrelated features have been pushed to zero, and the rest features with non-zero weights reflect how much the load is influenced by the related features. As the learned weights meaningfully relate to the customer power consumption behaviours, we use them to cluster the various customers.

We propose a hierarchically clustering method to cluster the customers with respect to the weights of L_1-CCRF, as illustrated in Figure 3. First, each weight in $\boldsymbol{\lambda}$ is binarized.

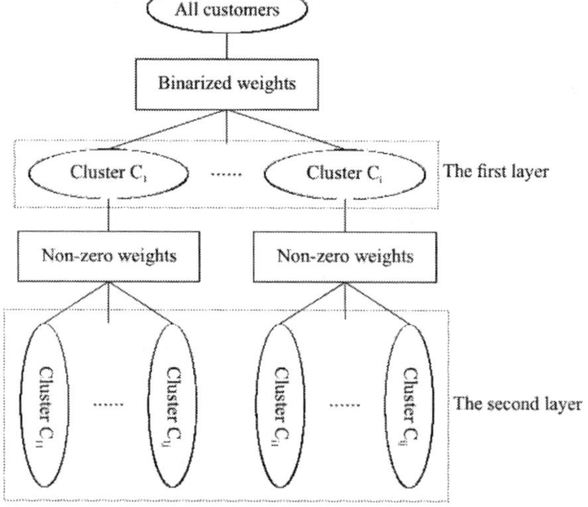

Figure 3: An illustration of clustering customers

To be specific, all the non-zero values are converted into 1, and the zero values remain. In the first layer, all customers are clustered according to the binarized weights. Customers who share the same binarized weights fall into the same cluster. In the second layer, for the each cluster $C_k, k = 1, \cdots, i$, the corresponding non-zero weights are used to further cluster the customers. K-means, with an Euclidean distance criterion Δ, is utilized in the second layer clustering. Δ is a critical parameter, which determines the number of final clusters and influences the final precision of load forecasting. This parameter is further analyzed in the Experiment part (see Subsection 4.4).

A two-layer clustering tree is obtained (see Figure 3), and clusters in each layer indicate clear physical meanings. In the first layer clustered by the binarized weights, the features with weights "1" are related to the customers' power usages. Thus, customers in the same cluster are influenced by the same range of features. In practice, customers in this layer can be certain customer genres such as wind producers, householders influenced by temperatures, householders regardless of temperatures. In the second layer, each cluster C_k is further divided into smaller clusters according to the non-zero weights, which indicate how much each feature influences the customers' power usages. After a second clustering, customers in each smaller cluster C_{kl} share similar sensitivity to the range of features. Take the office buildings for an example. Office buildings in one cluster may adaptively adjust their power usages with respect to temperatures, while buildings in another cluster are less sensitive to the influence of temperatures.

3.2.3 Fine-tuning L_1-CCRFs

After obtained the clustering tree, we fine-tune a L_1-CCRF for each cluster. In Subsubsection 3.2.1, a L_1-CCRF has been learned for each customer. For a customer cluster, one learned L_1-CCRF is randomly selected and fine-tuned. Fine-tuning a L_1-CCRF for each cluster gains two advantages. 1) Increasing prediction precision: for an individual customer, his/her behaviour is chaotic, thus the short-term load is hard to predict. On the contrary, the customers' usage data seem to be "smoothed" in a customer cluster. 2) Reducing computation cost: for a cluster with N customers, only one fine-tuned L_1-CCRF is needed in the end.

Fine-tuning a L_1-CCRF for a cluster is quite straightforward. For the selected L_1-CCRF, the input feature $\mathbf{X}_q$ remains, while for the ground-truth, each element y_i in $\mathbf{y}_q$ becomes the sum of all the customers' power usages in each hour. Then training process repeats with the input features and the new ground-truth. Fine-tuning process results in a quick convergence, because the weights in the selected L_1-CCRF are close to the optimal values of the final L_1-CCRF.

3.3 Load Forecasting

With the learned L_1-CCRF for each customer cluster, the hourly load can be predicted. Aggregating the predicted load for each cluster, the final load for the whole Smart Grid can be obtained.

To predict the load for each customer cluster, we find the most likely $\mathbf{y}$ given the observed feature $\mathbf{X}$, as formulated in Equation 7. Benefiting from the multivariate Gaussian form, the inference becomes quite tractable. To maximize $P(\mathbf{y}|\mathbf{X})$ in the multivariate Gaussian (see Equation 11), we simply make $\mathbf{y}$ equal to $\mu(\mathbf{X})$,

$$\hat{\mathbf{y}} = \text{argmax}_{\mathbf{y}}(P(\mathbf{y}|\mathbf{X})) = \mu(\mathbf{X}) = \mathbf{\Sigma}\boldsymbol{\theta} \tag{17}$$

The above equation shows how the load for each cluster is predicted. Assuming there are N customer clusters formed in a Smart Grid, adding up each cluster's predicted load $\hat{\mathbf{y}}_i$ in element wise, the final load $\mathbf{y}_{SG}$ of the whole grid is obtained by the following equation.

$$\mathbf{y}_{SG} = \sum_{1}^{N} \hat{\mathbf{y}}_i \tag{18}$$

4. EXPERIMENT AND ANALYSIS

Three experiments were conducted from different perspectives to evaluate LF-CBL. **Experiment 1:** Evaluation of customer behaviour learning. Two other prediction methods based on L_1-CCRF but without the consideration of customer behaviours were constructed. We compared LF-CBL with the two methods to demonstrate the advantage of customer behaviour learning. **Experiment 2:** Comparison with Linear Regression with LASSO. Linear Regression with LASSO was introduced to learn customer behaviours to predict the load in a Smart Grid. we compared the performance of LF-CBL with the new method on customer behaviour learning and load forecasting precision. **Experiment 3:** Analysis of the clustering criterion Δ. As the clustering criterion Δ determined the granularity of final customer clusters and affected the final load forecasting result, we tried different values for Δ to find better one for practical use of LF-CBL.

Our experiments were conducted on the platform of Power Trading Agent Competition (Power TAC) [11]. Power TAC has drawn wide attentions and has become a benchmark in the Smart Grid research community. Power TAC simulates a variety of customers with various behaviours in a Smart Grid. Moreover, there are rich features, including real-world weather conditions and real-time market status. Besides, the Power TAC server supplies rich logs of customers' hourly power usages, which are regarded as the ground-truth to evaluate the proposed LF-CBL.

4.1 Experiment Settings

Representative features, which may relate to the customer behaviours, are studied in our work. These features include temporal features, weather features and market features. Table 1 lists the contents of the three features, and the indexes provide convenience for further discussions.

Table 1: Features used in LF-CBL

Feature	Content	Index
Temporal feature	hour of a day	t_1
	day of a week	t_2
Weather feature	temperature	w_1
	wind strength	w_2
	wind direction	w_3
	cloudiness	w_4
Market feature	lowest price	m_1
	average price	m_2

We configured the Power TAC server and weather data server, and utilized Power TAC games to generate training and test data. Training data were generated by six games for the year 2009 (with real-world weather data). Test data were from six games for the year 2010. The logged customers' usages were regarded as the ground-truths of loads to be predicted. To induce rich features, three broker models, TacTex [24], cwiBroker [14] and our own broker model. were introduced to compete in the games. In Power TAC, 40 customers, each customer with a certain population, were simulated. For two customers, each had population up to tens of thousands. We split these two customers into customers with population of 100 and rendered them with some random behaviours in the log data, such as power usage decreasing for going out at night, or load increasing for having a party at home. In the end, 538 customers were obtained. These customers were manageable for experiments and sufficient to analyze the proposed LF-CBL.

The configurations in LF-CBL are described in details. L_1-CCRF modeled 24 hours power usages under the influences of 24 hourly features. For the features in each hour, 8 node potentials were generated. There were 23 intervals between every two adjacent hours in a day. Edge potentials were generated in every intervals, and PCTs were applied to weather and market features, but not temporal features. Thus, in each interval, 20 edge potentials were generated. To ensure the L_1-CCRF for each customer was converged, we set 50 iterations for OWL-QN. For the fine-tuned L_1-CCRF for each customer cluster, 10 iterations were sufficient to ensure convergence. L_1-CCRF was implemented in Matlab, and OWL-QN was implemented based on minFunc [20].

In the proposed LF-CBL, there are only two parameters. One parameter is the ρ in the cost function of L_1-CCRF in Equation 16, and the other is the criterion Δ in customer clustering. In learning a L_1-CCRF for each customer, ρ was determined by cross-validation process. For the final L_1-CCRF for each customer cluster, similar process repeated. Our cross-validation process extracted the daily data of every four days. The extracted data were used for validation, and the remained data were for training. The parameter Δ determines the granularity of the customer clusters, which has a strong influence to the performance of LF-CBL. Therefore, we will further analyze this parameter in Experiment 3. For Experiment 1 and 2, we set $\Delta = 0.05$. In the following three subsections, we report and analyze the results of the three experiments, respectively.

4.2 Experiment 1: Evaluation of Customer Behaviour Learning

We evaluated the contribution of customer behaviour learning in load forecasting by comparing LF-CBL with other two methods, which both used L_1-CCRF but without the considerations of customer behaviours. In method 1, one L_1-CCRF was trained for each customer. The load of a Smart Grid was a sum of all individual customer's loads predicted by L_1-CCRFs. We named this method as LF-S. In method 2, one L_1-CCRF was trained towards the whole Smart Grid, regardless of any individual customer's behaviours. We used LF-W to denote this method. Mean Absolute Percentage Error (MAPE) for each hour of the three methods are illustrated in Figure 4. We can see that LF-S performs slightly better than LF-W, and LF-CBL gains patent advantages over the other two methods.

LF-S used L_1-CCRF to predict the load for each customer. However, some behaviours of an individual customer were random and impossible to predict. For instance, some household customers may occasionally go out for parties on any weekday. Thus, the weakness of LF-S came from many accumulated errors resulted from the random customer behaviours. For LF-W, it utilized one L_1-CCRF to predict the load for all the customers, but a single L_1-CCRF failed to handle the various customers with different behaviours. In the end, the final load prediction result of LF-W was not satisfactory.

In contrast, LF-CBL performed well because it overcame the disadvantages in the above two methods. LF-CBL used L_1-CCRF to first analyze customer behaviours, then customers were clustered and customers shared the similar behaviours gathered in one cluster. In a cluster of customers, the chaotic random behaviours were averaged, resulting in "smooth" power usage data. With a fine-tuned L_1-CCRF for each customer cluster, the final prediction result was much better than that of the other two methods.

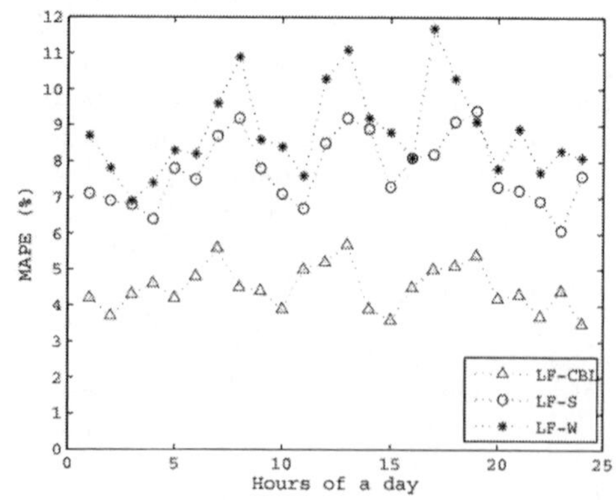

Figure 4: Performance comparison of LF-S, LF-W and LF-CBL

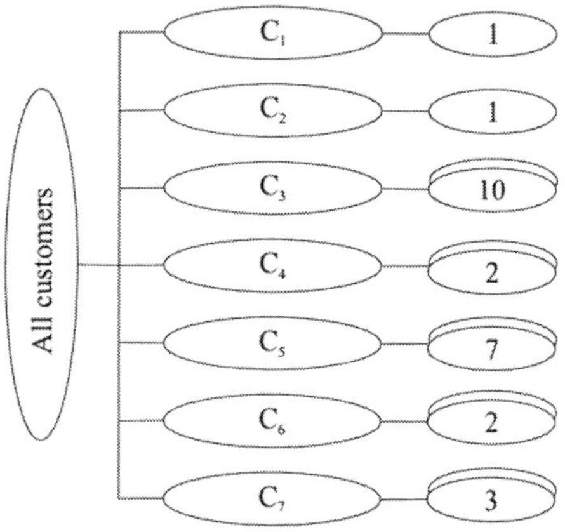

Figure 5: Clustering tree of LF-CBL

Figure 5 shows the clustering tree of LF-CBL. In the clustering tree, 7 clusters ($C_1, \cdots, C_7$) are obtained in the first layer. In the second layer, the digit on each ellipse indicates the number of clusters. 26 clusters are formed in the end.

In the first layer of the clustering tree, based on the binarized feature weights, we can determine if customer behaviours in one cluster is influenced by a certain feature. Table 2 uses a binary matrix to show the relationships between the clusters and features. In Table 2, "1" indicates that the cluster is influenced by this feature, while "0" means the feature is not related to this cluster. The clusters in the first layer show clear physical meanings. For instance, customers in C_1 are wind power producers, and their behaviours are influenced by the related wind features. Customers in C_2 are solar energy producers whose power usages are affected by time, temperature and cloudiness. Observing the customers in each cluster, we can see that they generally belong to the same category of customers. For example, customers in

C_4 are thermal storage customers, and customers in C_5 are householders and office users.

Table 2: Cluster and feature relation matrix

	t_1	t_2	w_1	w_2	w_3	w_4	m_1	m_2
C_1	0	0	0	1	1	0	0	0
C_2	1	0	1	0	0	1	0	0
C_3	1	1	0	0	0	0	0	1
C_4	1	0	0	0	0	0	1	1
C_5	1	1	1	0	0	0	0	0
C_6	1	1	1	0	0	0	1	0
C_7	1	0	1	0	0	0	1	0

In the second layer, customers are further clustered, resulting in 26 smaller clusters. Take C_5 for example. C_5 is further clustered into 7 smaller clusters based on the non-zero weights. In each customer cluster C_{5j}, customers show similar responses to the influences of outside features. For the 26 customer clusters, accordingly, 26 corresponding L_1-CCRFs are fine-tuned. In the end, 26 L_1-CCRFs are maintained for load forecasting for a whole Smart Grid with many different types of customers. Therefore, our LF-CBL results in a reasonable computation cost.

4.3 Experiment 2: Comparison with Linear Regression with LASSO

We constructed Linear Regressions with LASSO [23] to forecast load with the consideration of customer behaviours. This method followed the framework of LF-CBL, but a Linear Regression with LASSO was used to instead a L_1-CCRF. We named the Load Forecasting using Linear Regressions with LASSO as LF-LRL. The same criterion $\Delta = 0.05$ in customer clustering was applied to both methods.

Linear Regression with LASSO is briefly described as follows. A Linear Regression uses a linear form to estimate load sequence from the input features, which is shown in Equation 19 in a vectorized form.

$$\hbar(\mathbf{X}) = \mathbf{aX} + \mathbf{b} \tag{19}$$

$\boldsymbol{\lambda} =< \mathbf{a}, \mathbf{b} >$ is used to denote the weight vector. Linear Regression with LASSO minimizes the following cost function to learn the weights.

$$F(\boldsymbol{\lambda}) = \frac{1}{2}\sum_{q=1}^{Q}(\mathbf{y}_q - \hbar(\mathbf{X}_q))^2 + \rho\|\boldsymbol{\lambda}\|_1 \tag{20}$$

In the above equation, the first term is a mean square error loss function, and the second term is L_1 norm regularizer. Weights in $\boldsymbol{\lambda}$ are learned through minimizing the Equation 20 using LASSO algorithm [23].

LF-LRL and LF-CBL were compared in customer behaviour analysis and final prediction precisions. We compared the behaviour analysis from the clustering trees formed in LF-CBL (refer to Figure 5) and LF-LRL (similar to the clustering tree of LF-CBL, not shown due to page limit). In the first layer, there were 7 clusters in LF-LRL, same as that in LF-CBL. We also constructed relationship matrix between clusters and features for LF-LRL, and there was only one row in LF-LRL different from that in LF-CBL. Besides, the distributions of customers in customer clusters in the first layer were also similar in both methods. In the second layer, the non-zero weight vectors were quite different, resulting in different final customer clusters and customer distributions in clusters. Through the comparisons in customer behaviour analysis of the two methods, LF-LRL and LF-CBL performed similar in feature selection, but the feature weights were different, as a result, the result of load forecasting would be different, as shown in Figure 6.

The MAPE for each hours of LF-LRL and LF-CBL is depicted in Figure 6. We can see that the MAPE of LF-CBL is

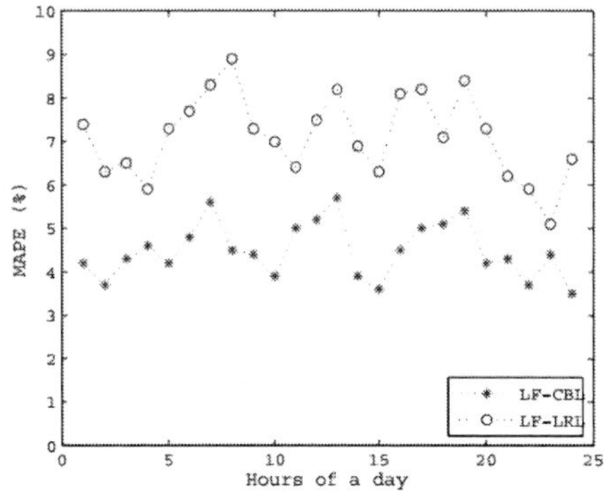

Figure 6: Performance comparison of LF-LRL and LF-CBL

better than that of LF-LRL. The total MAPE of LF-CBL is 4.51%, while that of LF-LRL is 7.26%. That LF-CBL gains better performance than LF-LRL in load forecasting indicates that the L_1-CCRF has advantage over Linear Regression. L_1-CCRF not only models the relationship between the feature and the load using node potentials, but also models the interactions of load changes and feature changes using edge potentials. In contrast, Linear Regression can only associate the features with the load.

With respect to the clustering tree of LF-CBL, we further analyzed LF-CBL and LF-LRL on load forecasting in two typical customer clusters. One customer cluster contained householders sensitive to temperatures. The overall MAPE of this cluster using LF-CBL was 4.62%, and that of LF-LRL was 8.57%. LF-CBL showed patent advantage over LF-LRL. For the householders sensitive to temperature, their loads had strong interactions between adjacent hours, and their adjacent hourly load changes were influenced by the changes of temperatures. In LF-CBL, L_1-CCRF successfully modeled the above factors, while in LF-LRL, the Linear Regression could not consider those factors. Therefore, LF-CBL got better prediction precision than LF-LRL. Another customer cluster was a group of wind power producers. The overall MAPE using LF-CBL and LF-LRL were 4.79% and 4.82%, respectively. These customers were only affected by the weather conditions. Thus it was not necessary to model the interactions of power usages in adjacent hours. As expected, LF-CBL and LF-LRL achieved similar performances in load forecasting for wind power producers. When there were no interactions of power usages in adjacent hours, L_1-CCRF degenerated to regression.

4.4 Experiment 3: Analysis of the Clustering Criterion Δ

In this experiment, an important parameter Δ was set to different values, resulting in different granularity of the final customer clusters. We observed the influence of the granularity of customer cluster to the final load forecasting precision, and thus suggest a reasonable range of Δ for practical use.

Four different values were set for Δ, which were: 0.025, 0.05, 0.75, 0.10. In the learning process, after a L_1-CCRF was learned for each customer, different values of Δ were applied to the clustering process and four clustering trees were formed, respectively. For each clustering tree, fine-tuning process was applied to the L_1-CCRF for each customer cluster. In the end, the final load was predicted using Equation 17 and 18. Table 3 summarizes the number of clusters and the overall MAPE under different Δ values.

Table 3: The influence of Δ on the MAPE and the number of clusters

Δ	Number of clusters	overall MAPE(%)
0.025	65	5.96
0.05	26	4.51
0.075	24	4.72
0.10	17	5.73

In Table 3, when Δ was set to 0.025, 65 customer clusters were formed, and the total MAPE was 5.96%. When we set $\Delta = 0.05$, 26 customer clusters were obtained, and the total MAPE became better. Comparing the above two settings, we could see that a small Δ resulted in fine granularity of customer clusters. When the customer cluster was too small, the "smoothness" of load data was compromised. That is why small Δ led to a less satisfactory prediction result. When Δ was set to 0.075, 24 customer clusters were formed, and the total MAPE was 4.72%. This indicated that when Δ changed from 0.05 to 0.075, the performance of LF-CBL did not change much. Besides, as the number of clusters also determined the required final L_1-CCRFs, the range from 0.05 to 0.075 resulted in an acceptable computation cost. When Δ was 0.10, the prediction precision declined. From the above analysis, we suggest that the reasonable range of Δ is $[0.05, 0.075]$. In this range, LF-CBL demonstrated a reasonable computation cost and competitive performance.

5. RELATED WORK

Load forecasting towards a whole grid or a specific customer has been deeply studied [22, 10], but there is little work considering different customer behaviours. Srinivasan [21] manually divided different customers in a power grid into six groups, and he introduced a group method of data handling (GMDH) neural network for load forecasting. Our method first introduces a learning method to explore different customer behaviours. Then customers are clustered based on the learned customer behaviour patterns. As we take the learned customer behaviours into account, our method is more advantageous than the existing methods in load forecasting in Smart Grid.

Some novel learning methods have also been introduced for load forecasting. Amin-Naseri and Soroush [2] used supervised and unsupervised learning to predict the dailiy peak load. Ali et al. [1] combined neural network, time series models and ANOVA for load forecasting. Recently, Guo [9] used Continuous Conditional Random Fields (CCRF) to forecast the short-term power and gas usages in a building. His work demonstrated the advantages of CCRF and achieved superior performances in load forecasting. Our work took a further step on the study of CCRF in load forecasting in a whole Smart Grid. We extended the definition domain of weights for CCRF and introduced L_1 norm as a regularization term. We creatively used L_1-CCRF to perform customer behaviour analysis and short-term load forecasting, resulting in a satisfactory result.

6. CONCLUSIONS

This paper proposed a load forecasting method through customer behaviour learning (LF-CBL). Our method introduced L_1-CCRF to analyze the customers' behaviours by using the weights of features in L_1-CCRF to reflect customer behaviours. The proposed method was evaluated and analyzed by experiments from three different perspectives, and experimental results demonstrated the advantages of the proposed LF-CBL against other baseline methods. With the consideration of learned customer behaviours, LF-CBL achieved a good performance in load forecasting. In addition, evaluation results also indicated that the proposed L_1-CCRF is effective in feature selection. Thus, L_1-CCRF can also be used in other related research domains.

Acknowledgments

The authors would like to thank Tao Qin for his useful discussions on CCRF. Moreover, we thank the organizers of Power TAC, which supplies a simulation of real-world Smart Grid market. Our experiments are done based on that platform. This work is supported by a Discovery Project (DP140100974) from Australian Research Council.

REFERENCES

[1] A. Ali, S. Ghaderi, and S. Sohrabkhani. Forecasting electrical consumption by integration of neural network, time series and anova. *Applied Mathematics and Computation*, 186(2):1753–1761, 2007.

[2] M. Amin-Naseri and A. Soroush. Combined use of unsupervised and supervised learning for daily peak load forecasting. *Energy Conversion and Management*, 49(6):1302–1308, 2008.

[3] N. Amjady, Keynia F, and H. Zareipour. Short-term load forecast of microgrids by a new bilevel prediction strategy. *IEEE Transactions on Smart Grid*, 1(3):286–294, 2010.

[4] G. Andrew and J. Gao. Scalable training of l 1-regularized log-linear models. In *Proceedings of the 24th international conference on Machine learning*, pages 33–40. ACM, 2007.

[5] T. Baltrusaitis, N. Banda, and P. Robinson. Dimensional affect recognition using continuous conditional random fields. In *Automatic Face and Gesture Recognition*, pages 1–8. IEEE, 2013.

[6] TWS Chow and C. Leung. Neural network based short-term load forecasting using weather compensation. *IEEE Transactions on Power Systems*, 11(4):1736–1742, 1996.

[7] J. Fan and J. McDonald. A real-time implementation of short-term load forecasting for distribution power systems. *IEEE Transactions on Power Systems*, 9(2):988–994, 1994.

[8] R. Gareta, L. M Romeo, and A. Gil. Forecasting of electricity prices with neural networks. *Energy Conversion and Management*, 47(13):1770–1778, 2006.

[9] H. Guo. Accelerated continuous conditional random fields for load forecasting. *to appear in IEEE Transactions on Knowledge & Data Engineering*, 2015.

[10] L. Hernandez, C. Baladron, J. Aguiar, B. Carro, Antonio J Sanchez-Esguevillas, J. Lloret, and J. Massana. a survey on electric power demand forecasting: Future trends in smart grids, microgrids and smart buildings. *IEEE Communications Surveys & Tutorials*, 16(3):1460–1495, 2014.

[11] W. Ketter, J. Collins, P. Reddy, and M. Weerdt. The 2014 power trading agent competition. *ERIM Report Series Reference No. ERS-2014-004-LIS*, 2014.

[12] J. Lafferty. Conditional random fields: probabilistic models for segmenting and labeling sequence data. In *Proceedings of the 18th International Conference on Machine Learning (ICML-2001)*. Morgan Kaufmann, 2001.

[13] T. Lavergne, O. Cappé, and F. Yvon. Practical very large scale crfs. In *Proceedings of the 48th Annual Meeting of the Association for Computational Linguistics*, pages 504–513. Association for Computational Linguistics, 2010.

[14] B. Liefers, J. Hoogland, and P. La. A successful broker agent for power tac. In *Agent-Mediated Electronic Commerce. Designing Trading Strategies and Mechanisms for Electronic Markets*, pages 99–113. Springer, 2014.

[15] A. Motamedi, H. Zareipour, and W. Rosehart. Electricity price and demand forecasting in smart grids. *IEEE Transactions on Smart Grid*, 3(2):664–674, 2012.

[16] A. Ng. Feature selection, l 1 vs. l 2 regularization, and rotational invariance. In *Proceedings of the twenty-first international conference on Machine learning*, page 78. ACM, 2004.

[17] T. Qin, T. Liu, X. Zhang, D. Wang, and H. Li. Global ranking using continuous conditional random fields. In *Advances in neural information processing systems*, pages 1281–1288, 2009.

[18] V. Radosavljevic, S. Vucetic, and Z. Obradovic. Continuous conditional random fields for regression in remote sensing. In *ECAI*, pages 809–814, 2010.

[19] S. Saab, E. Badr, and G. Nasr. Univariate modeling and forecasting of energy consumption: the case of electricity in lebanon. *Energy*, 26(1):1–14, 2001.

[20] M. Schmidt. minfunc: unconstrained differentiable multivariate optimization in matlab. http://www.cs.ubc.ca/ schmidt-m/Software/minFunc.html, 2005.

[21] D. Srinivasan. Energy demand prediction using gmdh networks. *Neurocomputing*, 72(1):625–629, 2008.

[22] L. Suganthi and A. Samuel. Energy models for demand forecastin–a review. *Renewable and Sustainable Energy Reviews*, 16(2):1223–1240, 2012.

[23] R. Tibshirani. Regression shrinkage and selection via the lasso. *Journal of the Royal Statistical Society. Series B (Methodological)*, pages 267–288, 1996.

[24] D. Urieli and P. Stone. Tactex'13: a champion adaptive power trading agent. In *Proceedings of the 2014 international conference on Autonomous agents and multi-agent systems*, pages 1447–1448, 2014.

[25] D. Vail, M. M. Veloso, and J. Lafferty. Conditional random fields for activity recognition. In *Proceedings of international conference on Autonomous agents and multiagent systems*, page 235. ACM, 2007.

[26] J. Yu, S. Vishwanathan, S. Günter, and N. Schraudolph. A quasi-newton approach to nonsmooth convex optimization problems in machine learning. *The Journal of Machine Learning Research*, 11:1145–1200, 2010.

An MDP-Based Winning Approach to Autonomous Power Trading: Formalization and Empirical Analysis

Daniel Urieli
Dept. of Computer Science
University of Texas at Austin
Austin, TX 78712, USA
urieli@cs.utexas.edu

Peter Stone
Dept. of Computer Science
University of Texas at Austin
Austin, TX 78712, USA
pstone@cs.utexas.edu

ABSTRACT

With the efforts of moving to sustainable and reliable energy supply, electricity markets are undergoing far-reaching changes. Due to the high-cost of failure in the real-world, it is important to test new market structures in simulation. This is the focus of the Power Trading Agent Competition (Power TAC), which proposes autonomous electricity broker agents as a means for stabilizing the electricity grid. This paper focuses on the question: how should an autonomous electricity broker agent act in competitive electricity markets to maximize its profit. We formalize the electricity trading problem as a continuous, high-dimensional Markov Decision Process (MDP), which is computationally intractable to solve. Our formalization provides a guideline for approximating the MDP's solution, and for extending existing solutions. We show that a previously champion broker can be viewed as approximating the solution using a lookahead policy. We present TacTex'15, which improves upon this previous approximation and achieves state-of-the-art performance in competitions and controlled experiments. Using thousands of experiments against 2015 finalist brokers, we analyze TacTex'15's performance and the reasons for its success. We find that lookahead policies can be effective, but their performance can be sensitive to errors in the transition function prediction, specifically demand-prediction.

Keywords

Autonomous electricity trading; Trading Agents; Smart-grid; Markets

1. INTRODUCTION

With the efforts of moving to sustainable and reliable energy supply, electricity markets (aka power markets) are undergoing far-reaching changes: customers are being engaged in power markets to incentivize adaptation of demand to supply conditions [34]; and wholesale markets are being deregulated and opened to competition [10]. In principle, deregulation can increase efficiency. In practice, the California energy crisis (2001) has demonstrated the high-costs of failure due to flawed deregulation [30, 4], and the importance of testing new market structures in simulation before deploying them [35]. This is the focus of the Power Trading Agent Competition (Power TAC) [13].

In Power TAC, autonomous broker agents compete with each other to make profits in a realistic, detailed smart-grid simulation environment with wholesale, retail and balancing power markets, and about 57,000 customers. The stability of electricity grids critically depends on having balanced electricity supply and demand at all times. Broker agents are financially incentivized to maintain supply-demand balance in their portfolio and thus contribute to grid stability.

It is likely that autonomous broker agents will be employed in future power markets, due to the need to act continually and make real-time decisions in a complex, competitive, dynamic environment. The decision-making challenges of such brokers have been under study in the autonomous agents community, but under either limited scope, or limited competitiveness and comparability [13]. This paper focuses on the question: how should an autonomous broker agent act in competitive power markets to maximize its profits? we advance the state of the art towards answering this question in the following ways:

- This paper is the first to formalize the *complete* broker's power trading problem. We formalize the problem as a Markov Decision Process (MDP) which, due to its continuous high-dimensional state and action spaces, cannot be solved exactly in practice. Our formalization compactly captures the challenges faced by a broker, and provides a guideline for approximating the solution and for extending existing solutions. While our formalization is based on the Power TAC simulation, we expect it to generalize and be useful in reality, since Power TAC closely models real-world markets.

- We present TacTex'15, which is by many metrics the best Power TAC broker at the current time. Using three strategic improvements, TacTex'15 extends a previous strategy which can be viewed as a lookahead-policy [23] that approximates the solution to the MDP. The strategic improvements may seem minor on the surface but result in large performance improvements.

- Using thousands of experiments, we analyze the performance of TacTex'15, and the reasons for its success. Importantly, we investigate how the accuracy of the transition-function predictors (i.e. the demand and cost predictors) affect the performance of the broker's power trading lookahead-policy.

Appears in: *Proceedings of the 15th International Conference on Autonomous Agents and Multiagent Systems (AAMAS 2016), J. Thangarajah, K. Tuyls, C. Jonker, S. Marsella (eds.), May 9–13, 2016, Singapore.*

This paper's contributions can be valuable for two communities. For the artificial intelligence community, this paper is a case-study of effective sequential decision making in a domain too complex to be solved by current out-of-the-box methods, which involves autonomous agents, multiagent systems, game-theoretic considerations, markets, and a potentially important computational sustainability application [7]. For the power markets community, this paper may provide insights on autonomous trading in modern electricity markets, due to the realism of the Power TAC simulation environment.

2. POWER TAC GAME DESCRIPTION

Power TAC is an annual competition in which the competitors are autonomous brokers programmed by teams from around the world. The competition includes hundreds of games and takes several days to complete. In a game, the Power TAC simulator runs on a central server, while competing brokers run remotely and communicate with the server through the internet. Each broker receives partial state information from the server, and responds by communicating the actions it takes. The competition includes different game sizes, ranging from small to large number of competitors. Participants release their broker binaries after the competition, and use them to run controlled experiments.

Power TAC uses a high-fidelity power markets simulator, modeling a smart-grid with more than 57,000 simulated customers (50,000 consumers and 7,000 renewable producers). Power TAC's customers are *autonomous agents* that optimize the electricity-costs and comfort of their human owners [28]. Customers model commercial and residential buildings, solar/wind farms, storage facilities and electric vehicles. Customers consume/produce using time-series generators constructed from real-world data, according to weather and calendar factors. The simulation proceeds in 1-hour timeslots for 60 simulated days and completes in 2 hours.

Figure 1 shows the structure of the Power TAC simulation environment. In Power TAC, autonomous broker agents compete by acting in three markets: (1) a *wholesale market*, where brokers bid in sequences of 24 double auctions to procure energy from generation companies (or sell surplus), to be delivered in the following 24 hours, (2) a *tariff market*, which is a retail market where energy is traded with consumers and distributed renewable energy producers, and (3) a *balancing market*, which ensures that supply and demand are balanced and determines the broker imbalance fees.

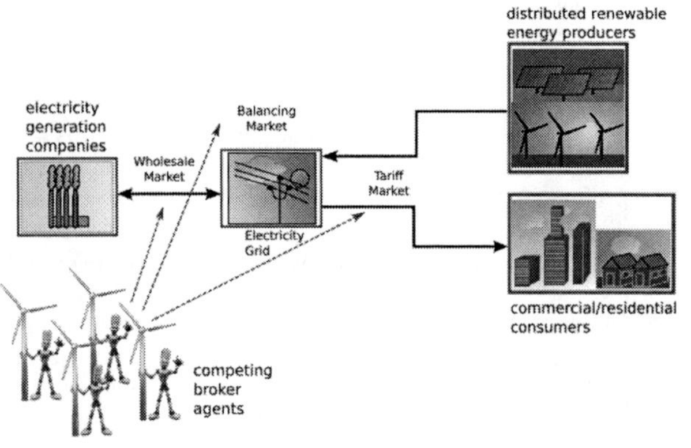

Figure 1: High-level structure of the Power TAC simulation

The brokers compete to gain market share and maximize profit by trading electricity. In the tariff market, brokers publish tariff contracts for energy consumption/production. Tariffs may include fixed and varying prices and possibly bonuses/fees. Customers stochastically subscribe to tariffs which maximize their utility (cost savings and comfort). Customers are equipped with smart-meters, so consumption and production are reported to the broker every hour. Brokers typically balance their portfolio's net demand by buying in the wholesale market. Full details can be found in the Power TAC Game Specification [12].

3. THE BROKER'S POWER TRADING PROBLEM

This section formalizes the broker's power trading problem. Our formalization compactly captures the complex challenges faced by a broker, and provides a guideline for approximating the solution and for extending existing solutions. While our formalization is based on the Power TAC simulator, we expect it to generalize and be useful in reality, since Power TAC closely models real-world markets. We start with an intuitive problem description and continue to our formalization.

Figure 2 illustrates the temporal structure of a broker's power trading problem. The temporal structure of the tariff and wholesale market actions differ in multiple ways. Tariffs specify energy for *immediate* and *repeated* delivery and are published at *low-frequency* (every one or more days). Wholesale bids typically specify energy for *future*, *one-time* delivery and are executed at *high-frequency* (every hour).

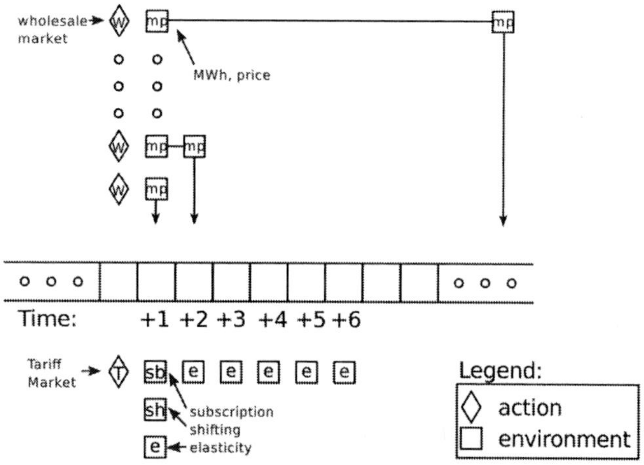

Figure 2: **Temporal structure of the power trading problem.** Time progresses to the right; the notation '$+i$' stands for 'i timeslots into the future'. Diamonds stand for broker actions. Squares stand for simulation environment responses. The top part represents the wholesale market: a broker submits limit orders to buy/sell energy for the next 24 hours, then it receives the results of the 24 double-auctions. The bottom part represents the tariff market: a broker may publish one or more tariffs (once every 6 hours), and customers respond by potentially (1) subscribing to new tariffs, (2) shifting consumption to cheaper times, and (3) elastically adapting total consumption based on price.

Power Trading as an MDP.

Given the internal states of the simulator and competing

brokers, the broker's energy trading problem is a Markov Decision Process (MDP) [25]. However, since competitors' states and parts of the simulator state are unobservable, the trading problem is a Partially Observable MDP (POMDP). Nevertheless, for computational tractability and modeling clarity, we treat unobservable parts of the state as environment stochasticity and formulate the trading problem as an MDP, as follows (denoting B_0 as the acting broker):

- **States:** S is the set of states, where state s is a tuple $\langle t, \mathcal{B}, \mathcal{C}, \mathcal{P}, \mathcal{T}, \mathcal{S}_{B_0}, \mathcal{Q}_{B_0}, \mathcal{A}_{B_0}, I_{B_0}, \mathcal{W}, cash_{B_0}, \rho\rangle$ that includes the current time t (which encapsulates weekday/hour), and the sets: competing broker identities $\mathcal{B}$; identities of consumers $\mathcal{C}$ and producers $\mathcal{P}$ (both referred to as *customers*); published tariffs of all brokers $\mathcal{T} := \cup_{B \in \mathcal{B}} \mathcal{T}_B$; customer subscriptions to B_0's tariffs $\mathcal{S}_{B_0}$; current energy consumption/production of B_0's customers $\mathcal{Q}_{B_0}$; recent auction results $\mathcal{A}_{B_0} := \{\langle p^c, q^c, \mathcal{O^c}_{B_0}, \mathcal{O}^u, \mathcal{M}_{B_0}\rangle_j\}_{j=t+1}^{t+24}$ including, for each of the following 24 timeslots, the clearing price p^c and total quantity q^c, B_0's cleared orders $\mathcal{O^c}_{B_0}$, all brokers' uncleared orders $\mathcal{O}^u$, and B_0's *market-positions* $\mathcal{M}_{B_0}$ (energy deliveries and charges, updated incrementally from $\mathcal{O^c}_{B_0}$); B_0's energy imbalance I_{B_0}; current weather and forecast $\mathcal{W}$; B_0's cash balance $cash_{B_0}$; and randomly sampled game-parameters (such as fees and game length) ρ. **Note:** the underlying state of the game, which includes elements unobserved by the broker, is the tuple $\langle t, \mathcal{B}^o, \mathcal{G}^o, \mathcal{C}^o, \mathcal{P}^o, \mathcal{T}, \mathcal{S}, \mathcal{Q}, \mathcal{A}, \mathcal{I}, \mathcal{W}, cash, \rho\rangle$ where $\mathcal{B}^o, \mathcal{G}^o, \mathcal{C}^o, \mathcal{P}^o$ are the identities *and* internal states of brokers, generation companies, consumers and producers, respectively; and where $\mathcal{S} := \cup_{B \in \mathcal{B}} \mathcal{S}_B$, $\mathcal{Q} := \cup_{B \in \mathcal{B}} \mathcal{Q}_B$, $\mathcal{A} := \cup_{B \in \mathcal{B}} \mathcal{A}_B$, $\mathcal{I} := \{I_B\}_{B \in \mathcal{B}}$, $cash := \{cash_B\}_{B \in \mathcal{B}}$.

- **Actions:** A broker's set of actions $A := A^\tau \cup A^\omega \cup A^\beta$ is composed of tariff market actions A^τ, wholesale market actions A^ω and balancing market actions A^β, as follows.

  1. *Tariff market actions* A^τ: create/modify/revoke tariffs. A tariff is a tuple $T = \langle type, rates, fees\rangle$ where:
     - $type \in$ {consumption, production,...} can be general (e.g. production) or specific (e.g. solar-production).
     - $rates$: a set of rates, each specifying a price and when it applies (times and/or usage thresholds).
     - $fees$: optional periodic/signup/withdraw payments.
  2. *Wholesale market actions* A^ω*:* submit limit orders of the form

     $$\langle energyAmount, limitPrice, targetTime\rangle$$

     to buy/sell energy for one of the next 24 hours.
  3. *Balancing market actions* A^β*:* submit customers energy curtailment requests (currently unused).

- **Transition Function:** The transition function is partially deterministic and partially stochastic, as follows. The time t is incremented by 1 hour; $\mathcal{B}, \mathcal{C}, \mathcal{P}$ remain unchanged; $\mathcal{T}$ is updated by create/modify/revoke tariff actions, deterministically by B_0, and stochastically (due to unobservability) by other brokers; $\mathcal{S}_{B_0}$ is updated stochastically based on customers' decisions; $\mathcal{Q}_{B_0}$ is determined stochastically based on weather and customers' internal states (shifting and elasticity, see Figure 2); $\mathcal{A}_{B_0}$ is updated with auction results, stochastically since (i) competitors rely on stochastic information (demand predictions), (ii) competitors' internal states are hidden, and (iii) generation companies bid stochastically; I_{B_0} is a deterministic function of $\mathcal{T}_{B_0}, \mathcal{S}_{B_0}, \mathcal{Q}_{B_0}, \mathcal{A}_{B_0}$; $\mathcal{W}$ is stochastic; *cash* is updated deterministically from the recent stochastic reward; and ρ remains unchanged.

- **Reward:** Let s_t, r_t, a_t be the state, reward, and broker-action(s) at time t. Let $r^\tau, r^\omega, r^\beta$ be the broker's energy buy/sell payments in the tariff, wholesale, and balancing markets respectively. Let *dist* be the energy distribution fees, and $fees$ the tariff-market fees. The reward at time t can be characterized by the following function.

$$\begin{aligned} r_t(s_{t-1}, a_{t-1}, s_t) &:= r^\tau(s_t) + r^\omega(s_t) + r^\beta(s_t) \\ &+ dist(s_t) + fees(s_{t-1}, a_{t-1}, s_t) := \\ &\underbrace{Q_t^{cons} p_t^{cons} - Q_t^{prod} p_t^{prod}}_{r^\tau(s_t)} + \underbrace{Q_t^{ask} p_t^{ask} - Q_t^{bid} p_t^{bid}}_{r^\omega(s_t)} \\ &\underbrace{\pm bal(I_{B_0,t})}_{r^\beta(s_t)} \underbrace{- max(Q_t^{cons}, Q_t^{prod}) \times distFee}_{dist(s_t)} \\ &\underbrace{-pub(a_{t-1}) - rev(a_{t-1}) \pm psw(\mathcal{S}_{B_0,t-1}, \mathcal{S}_{B_0,t})}_{fees(s_{t-1}, a_{t-1}, s_t)} \end{aligned} \quad (1)$$

  where $\pm$ denotes components that can be positive or negative; Q_t^{cons}, Q_t^{prod} are the total consumed/produced quantities by B_0's customers in the tariff-market (both are sums of entries of $\mathcal{Q}_{B_0}$); Q_t^{ask}, Q_t^{bid} are the amounts B_0 sold/procured in the wholesale-market (both are sums of elements of $\mathcal{M}_{B_0}$ inside $\mathcal{A}_{B_0}$); p_t^{cons}, p_t^{prod}, p_t^{ask}, p_t^{bid} are the average buying/selling prices (determined by $\mathcal{T}_{B_0}$, $\mathcal{S}_{B_0}$, $\mathcal{Q}_{B_0}$ and $\mathcal{M}_{B_0}$); $bal(I_{B_0,t})$ is the fee for imbalance $I_{B_0,t} = Q_t^{cons} - Q_t^{prod} + Q_t^{ask} - Q_t^{bid}$ (which depends on unobserved other broker imbalances $I \backslash I_{B_0,t}$); $distFee$ is a fixed fee per kWh transferred over the grid; *pub, rev* are tariff publication and revoke fees; *psw* are tariff periodic/signup/withdraw fees/bonuses.

- **Discount Factor:** γ reflects daily interest on cash balance.

4. THE TacTex'15 BROKER AGENT

This section characterizes approximate MDP solutions, and describes TacTex'15's approximate solution.

4.1 Approximate MDP Solutions

The MDP's solution is an optimal power-trading policy (a mapping from states to actions). There are two problems to solve the MDP exactly: first, the high-dimensional states and actions and the complex reward makes it computationally intractable, and second, some components of the transition and reward functions are unknown to the broker. Therefore, brokers necessarily can only approximate the solution. There are four categories of approximate solutions to large MDPs, of which *lookahead policies* seem suitable for our domain, since they are effective in time-varying settings, where it is unclear how to approximate a value function or find a simple rule that maps states to actions [23].

Lookahead policies are partial MDP solutions that have been effective in high-dimensional state-spaces [24, 3, 11, 29, 5, 6, 18, 32]. Lookahead policies optimize over simulated trajectories s_t, r_t, a_t, s_{t+1}, r_{t+1}, a_{t+1},... using generative models that predict *action effects* (next state and reward). Here, the reward is a deterministic function of s_{t-1}, a_{t-1}, s_t except for the $bal(I_{B_0,t})$ component. Therefore a broker needs generative models for $bal(I_{B_0,t})$, for $\mathcal{T} \setminus \mathcal{T}_{B_0}, \mathcal{S}_{B_0}, \mathcal{Q}_{B_0}$ (to predict Q_t^{cons}, p_t^{cons}, Q_t^{prod}, p_t^{prod}), and for $\mathcal{A}_{B_0}$ (to predict Q_t^{ask}, p_t^{ask}, Q_t^{bid}, p_t^{bid}).

While these action effects can be predicted independently, actions need to be optimized in conjunction: the $bal(I_{B_0,t})$ function is designed such that imbalance fees typically result in negative reward when taking actions of a single type, while positive reward can be achieved by taking actions of multiple types in parallel (to maintain low imbalance). Therefore, any tractable lookahead policy is required to efficiently (i) sample, and (ii) combine the actions to simulate.

The 2013 champion, TacTex'13 [33], can be viewed as approximating an MDP solution using a lookahead policy. TacTex'13 does not optimize production tariffs, wholesale selling and fees, so $Q_t^{prod}p_t^{prod}$, $Q_t^{ask}p_t^{ask}$, and $psw()$ are always zero in Equation 1. TacTex'13's main routine is roughly Algorithm 1. For each tariff in a sample of fixed-rate consumption tariffs (line 1), it uses a *demand-predictor* to predict $Q_t^{cons}p_t^{cons}$ for each t in the horizon (line 2), assumes $Q_t^{bid} = Q_t^{cons}$ (and therefore marks both as Q_t), uses a *cost-predictor* to predict for every t the price p_t^{bid} of buying Q_t (line 4), predicts a profit (called *utility* or *return*) as the sum of rewards along the horizon (line 5), and executes the utility-maximizing combination of actions (lines 7-8). Therefore, TacTex'13 lookahead efficiently *combines* actions (addressing (ii) from above) by constraining $Q_t^{bid} = Q_t^{cons}$, instead of examining combinations (therefore $bal(I_{B_0,t}) = 0$). TacTex'13 efficiently *samples* actions (addressing (i) from above) by sampling fixed-rate tariffs in a limited region in the tariff market, and by treating wholesale actions hierarchically: it (a) treats Q_t^{bid} as an action to be sampled (in Q_t^{cons} values), and (b) solves a subproblem of finding a cost-minimizing sequential bidding policy $\pi(Q)$ for procuring quantities Q on a small MDP isolated from the full MDP.

Algorithm 1 TacTex'13's Lookahead Policy

1: **for** trf *in* sampleCandidateTariffs() ∪ {no-op} **do**
2: $\{\langle Q_t, p_t^{cons}\rangle | t = +1, ..., +T\}$ ← demandPredictor.predict(trf)
3: **for** t *in* $\{+1, ..., +T\}$ **do**
4: p_t^{bid} ← costPredictor.predict(Q_t)
5: utilities[trf] ← $\sum_{t=+1}^{+T} Q_t p_t^{cons} - Q_t p_t^{bid} - dist(Q_t) - pub(\text{trf})$
6: trf* ← $\arg\max_{trf}$ utilities[trf]
7: publishTariff(trf*) // tariff market action, possibly no-op
8: procure $\{Q_t\}_{t=+1}^{+T}$ predicted for trf* in line 2 // wholesale market

4.2 TacTex'15's Architecture

TacTex'15's architecture is similar to that of TacTex'13 in four main ways. TacTex'15 does not try to benefit from (1) production tariffs (2) wholesale selling, (3) imbalance, and (4) tariff fees, since in preliminary tests (1)-(3) did not seem beneficial and (4) had some simulator implementation issues (see Section 5.1). As a result, TacTex'15 assumes $Q_t^{prod}p_t^{prod}$, $Q_t^{ask}p_t^{ask}$, $bal()$, and $psw()$ in Equation 1 to be zero. Therefore TacTex'15's lookahead policy is quite similar to TacTex'13's (Algorithm 1); we refer the reader to [33] for pseudo-code of the main routines. On the other hand, TacTex'15 introduces three main improvements over TacTex'13: it uses different (1) demand-predictor, (2) cost-predictor (both (1)-(2) are *transition-function* predictors), and (3) wholesale bidding strategy π.

Demand Predictor. The demand-predictor predicts customer subscription changes and future demand, which determine $Q_t^{cons}p_t^{cons}$. TacTex'13 learned a demand-predictor from data. However, in Power TAC there is no need to do so: these complex stochastic customer behaviors are coded in Power TAC's open-source simulator. Instead, TacTex'15 uses the simulator's customer code as a basis for its demand-predictor. However, this code does not provide a complete demand-predictor: it relies on information hidden from brokers. TacTex'15 seeds this information with expected values: customers of other brokers are assumed to be subscribed to the best tariffs, customer subscriptions are predicted in the limit (expected values after infinite time), and customer demand parameters are set to expected values.

The simulator's customer code is a high-quality demand-predictor which, beyond contributing to the broker's performance, allows us to empirically analyze the dependency of the broker's performance on the demand-predictor's accuracy, and more generally to gain insight into the dependency of lookahead-based power trading on the transition-function predictors' accuracy. Section 5 includes the results of such an analysis which, due to the realism of the Power TAC simulator, could generalize to real markets.

Cost Predictor. Wholesale costs are determined by procured quantities and brokers' bidding strategies, which may change dynamically. TacTex'15 uses an adaptive cost-predictor $Q_t^{bid} \mapsto p_t^{bid}$, described in Algorithm 2. It has two components: a linear regression predictor trained on *boot data* (wholesale transactions sent by the simulator at game start) (line 1), and a real-time correction factor constructed from the last 24 hours' prediction errors (line 2). Since the correction factor is constructed from little data (to ensure responsiveness), we limit it to bias correction. The boot data is larger (336 instances) so we use it to determine the slope. TacTex'13's cost-predictor ignored Q_t^{bid}, and predicted past average prices based on time. We compare the two predictors in Section 5.

Algorithm 2 cost-predictor(Q_t^{bid})

1: reg ← trainLinearRegression($\{\langle Q_i^{bid}, p_i^{bid}\rangle\}_{i \in bootdata}$)
2: correctionFactor ← averagePredictionErrorInLast24Hours()
3: **return** reg.predict(Q_t^{bid}) - correctionFactor

Wholesale Bidding Strategy. TacTex'15 uses a combination of truthful and strategic (i.e. non-truthful) bidding. A truthful bidder sets its limit price to the predicted imbalance fee $\overline{p}$. It gets the highest priority among competitors who bid less than $\overline{p}$ and never pays more than $\overline{p}$. However, since the sequential double-auction mechanism is not incentive compatible, truthful bidding is suboptimal in some situations. TacTex'13 used a learned optimistic strategic (i.e. non-truthful) bidding strategy $\pi(Q)$ that assumed that bids with limit-prices higher than a double-auction's clearing price would get fully cleared. This strategy is optimal in some situations (e.g. single-buyer or cooperative setups), but can be exploited by competitors who learn to bid slightly higher. Since each of the two strategies is beneficial in different situations, combining them provides a form of hedging for TacTex'15. Let $\underline{p}$ be the limit price suggested by TacTex'13's strategy, and ϵ be the minimum amount that can be traded (0.01 mWh). To bid for a quantity Q_t^{bid}, TacTex'15 submits the following 25 orders (see MDP wholesale actions, Section 3) $\langle Q_t^{bid} - 24\epsilon, \overline{p}, t\rangle$, $\{\langle \epsilon, \underline{p} + i\frac{\overline{p}-\underline{p}}{24}, t\rangle\}_{i=0}^{23}$. This strategy benefits from both worlds: if TacTex'15 sets the price, it will either be the strategic price returned by $\pi(Q)$, or the lowest among its higher bids. If another broker sets the price, TacTex'15 will have a higher priority and benefit from the lower price as long as it is not higher than $\overline{p}$.

Future Extensions of TacTex'15's MDP Solution. Referring back to the reward specification (Equation 1), our MDP provides a guideline for future extensions of TacTex'15's lookahead policy. In some situations a broker can profit from imbalance. We can relax the assumption that $Q_t^{cons} = Q_t^{bid}$, add imbalanced trajectories to our lookahead search, setting $Q_t^{cons} - Q_t^{bid} = I_{B_0,t}$ for a sample of $I_{B_0,t}$ values, and predict $bal(I_{B_0,t})$ using a learned predictor. We can sample production tariffs like consumption tariffs, and treat wholesale sell hierarchically like wholesale buy actions. This addresses requirement (i) from Section 4.1 (sample actions efficiently). However, addressing requirement (ii) (combined actions efficiently) becomes more challenging. In an initial implementation we use an alternating, local improvement based approach which performs well, but more sophisticated methods might be possible. Finally, tariff-revoke actions can be added by simulating lookahead trajectories with each of the active tariffs removed. Initial implementation shows promising results.

5. RESULTS

We analyze TacTex'15's performance in competitions (Section 5.1) and controlled experiments (Section 5.2).

5.1 Competition Results

The Power TAC 2015 Finals included 11 teams from universities in America, Europe and Asia. 230 games were played continually over a week, in three different sizes: 3-brokers, 9-brokers, and 11-brokers. A day after the finals ended, 8 of the teams competed in a post-finals, demo-competition with 70 4-broker games. While being unofficial, this competition was run similarly to the finals with one important difference: a simulator-loophole that was exploited during the finals, was fixed. Due to the proximity to the finals, and a parallel workshop, we believe that teams used the same brokers they used in the finals.

Table 1 summarizes the 2015 finals results. While TacTex'15 was officially ranked 2nd, it was the best broker that did not exploit a simulator-loophole: the 1st-ranked broker gained the highest overall score by exploiting a simulator loophole in 3-broker games, which resulted in unrealistic dynamics and an unrealistically high score that biased the final ranking (see dark gray cells in Table 1).[1] Specifically, Maxon15 subscribed customers to inflated tariffs which promised customers large payments if customers *unsubscribed* from them after a period shorter than a single timeslot. While customers had no way to unsubscribe quickly enough to collect these payments, due to the loophole they subscribed to these tariffs assuming they *could* collect the payments, thus paying inflated prices to Maxon15.

Table 1: **Power TAC 2015 finals results.** Ranking is determined by the "Total" score, which is a sum of individual z-scores in each game size, displayed in the columns "11-brokers" (10 games played by all brokers), "9-brokers" (45 games played by each broker) and "3-brokers" (45 games played by each broker).

Broker	11-brokers	9-brokers	3-brokers	Total
Maxon15	0.611	0.801	1.990	3.402
TacTex'15	*0.897*	*1.066*	*0.258*	*2.221*
CUHKTac	0.962	0.859	0.106	1.927
AgentUDE	0.421	0.367	0.809	1.597
Sharpy	0.429	0.614	0.521	1.564
COLDPower	0.726	0.397	-0.751	0.371
cwiBroker	-0.002	-0.120	0.465	0.343
Mertacor	0.413	0.142	-1.341	-0.786
NTUTacAgent	-1.017	-1.638	0.453	-2.202
SPOT	-1.052	-0.243	-1.032	-2.327
CrocodileAgent	-2.387	-2.244	-1.479	-6.111

After the finals, the loophole was fixed. When replaying 3-broker competition games without the loophole, Maxon15 no longer won by a large gap, but instead lost by a large gap to TacTex'15. When taking into account only 11- and 9-broker games from the finals (where the loophole had no impact), TacTex'15 ended 1st with a total z-score of 0.142 ahead of CUHKTac and 0.551 ahead of Maxon15, finishing slightly behind CUHKTac in 11-broker games (by 0.065) and ahead of CUHKTac in 9-broker games (by 0.207). In the post-finals demo competition with a repaired simulator, TacTex'15 won by a large gap ahead of the others (Table 2), making 50% more profits than the 2nd place (Maxon15). Maxon15 used the same strategy as before, but it was not as effective with the loophole fixed.[2]

Table 2: **Power TAC 2015 post-finals demo competition results.** 70 games were played in a single game-size (4-brokers). Ranking is determined by z-score.

Broker	4-brokers (profits)	4-brokers (z-score)
TacTex'15	*15.0M*	*1.122*
Maxon15	10.7M	0.627
CUHKTac	10.0M	0.537
AgentUDE	9.7M	0.509
cwiBroker2015	7.9M	0.297
Sharpy	4.6M	-0.092
COLDPower	-0.8M	-0.724
SPOT	-14.0M	-2.276

Figure 3 shows an analysis of TacTex'15's performance

[1] The loophole's exploitation was confirmed by the competition organizers. However, Maxon was not disqualified: they explained it as an unintended result of automatic parameter tuning right before the finals.

[2] To be fair, one should note that they did not retune their parameters to the repaired simulator. On the other hand, it's not clear that other parameters would have done particularly better in the absence of the loophole.

in the 2015 finals and in the post-finals competition. In 11-broker games CUHKTac (1st) and TacTex'15 (2nd) won by a large gap over the other brokers, where most brokers ended with losses. In 9-broker games TacTex'15 won by a large gap, making 30% more profit than the 2nd place broker in this category (CUHKTac), despite missing 3 out of 45 games due to network connection problems. The revenue and costs plots show that in 11- and 9-broker games TacTex'15 chose to reduce its market share, likely due to the fierce competition, so that its revenue and costs were lower compared with other top brokers, while its profit remained high. In 3-broker games TacTex'15 typically performed the best, although this is harder to see in the figure, due to several events that biased the final averages: (a) Maxon15's loophole-exploitation, discussed above; (b) About 1/2 of of AgentUDE's, Sharpy's and cwiBroker's 3-broker game scores come from single outlier games in which they played against a non-functioning broker and/or a competitor's crash in a monopoly/duopoly situation; (c) TacTex'15 missed 5 out of its 45 3-broker games due to network connection problems, resulting in a score of 0 in these games, and a reduction of 4.3% in TacTex'15's average profit. In the 4-broker games of the post-finals competition TacTex'15 made about 50% more profit than the 2nd place broker. The revenue and costs plots show that it had a similar revenue to the 2nd and 3rd place brokers, but much lower costs; higher revenue and lower costs than the 5th, 6th brokers; and almost double the revenue of each of the other brokers.

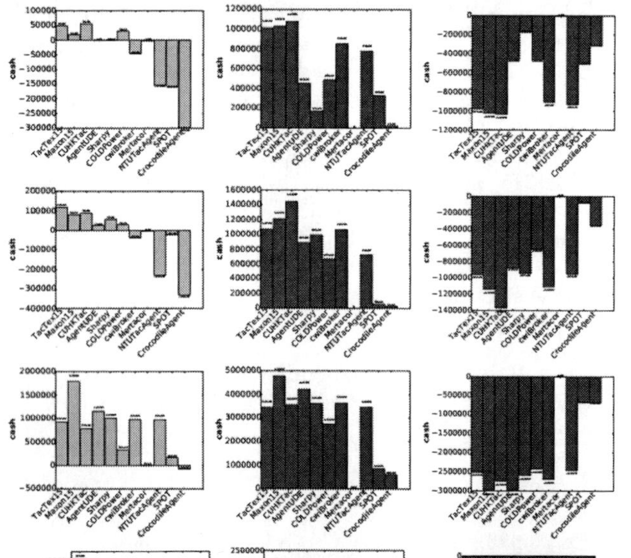

Figure 3: **Competition analysis: average profit, revenue and costs.** The top 3 lines respectively summarize 11-, 9-, 3-broker games from Power TAC 2015 finals; bottom line summarizes the 4-broker games of the post-finals demo competition. Each line shows average profit (left), revenue (middle), and costs (right). 3-broker game results are biased due to a simulator-loophole exploitation by Maxon15 and a few other events (see text for details)

5.2 Controlled Experiments

While the competition is motivating and its results are illustrative, it cannot isolate specific broker components in a statistically significant way. We therefore subsequently tested TacTex'15 in thousands of games, in two types of controlled experiments: (a) performance tests, and (b) ablation analysis tests, which evaluate the contribution of TacTex'15's main components to its overall performance.[3]

5.2.1 Experimental Setup

Each experiment consisted of running 56 games against a set of opponent brokers, using broker binaries of 2015 finalists. To better evaluate statistical significance, we held most of the random factors in the simulation fixed across experiments (random seeds, weather conditions). To fix weather conditions, we used weather files containing 3 months of real-world weather. To cover year-round conditions we used 8 weather files (each file used by 1/8 of the games) with start-dates of January, April, July, October of 2009 and 2010.

5.2.2 Performance Tests

A successful broker should perform well in expectation against every set of opponents, under different stochastic conditions (here weather/random seeds). At the time of writing this paper, five 2015 finalists have released their brokers' binaries. We used these binaries to test TacTex'15's performance in $2, 3, \ldots, 6$-broker games. We generated combinations of brokers for each game size, and tested each combination in 56 games, as described above. Figure 4 presents the results. TacTex'15 significantly won against every combination of opponents, typically by a large gap.

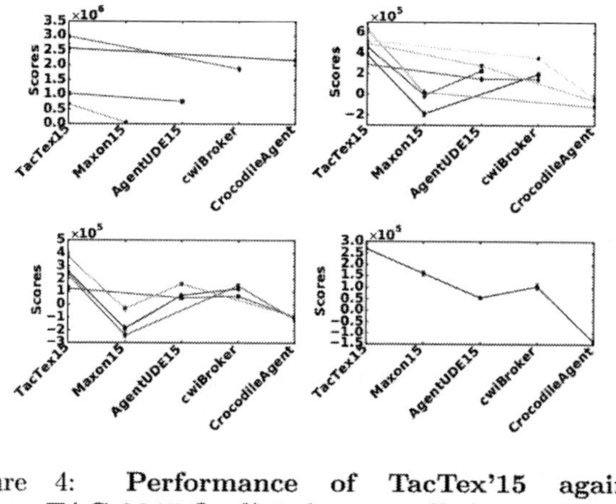

Figure 4: **Performance of TacTex'15 against Power TAC 2015 finalists in controlled experiments of game-sizes of 2-5.** Each line connects n points where each point is an average score (y-value) of a broker (x-value). Therefore, each line represents the average scores of a combination of brokers playing each other under a variety of conditions (note the small error bars). Results are shown for game-sizes of 2-, 3-, 4-, 5-brokers (top-left, top-right, bottom-left, bottom-right, respectively). Similar results for 6-brokers are omitted. TacTex'15 consistently won against all combinations of brokers, in all game-sizes.

[3]To clarify, in all controlled experiments TacTex'15 was the exact competition agent. Its demand predictor has never used the simulator code with the loophole since this code relied on information hidden from the broker.

5.2.3 Ablation Analysis

To understand the reasons for TacTex'15's success, we tested the contribution of TacTex'15's main components to its overall performance, in all possible game-sizes (2,...,6). We created three ablated versions of TacTex'15 by disabling each of its main components. For each game size, we selected the "strongest" combination of opponents, against which TacTex'15 had the lowest score. We tested each ablated version against these opponents in a 56-game experiment, holding random seeds and weather conditions fixed to the same values used against TacTex'15. When disabling a component, we used as a baseline the corresponding component used by TacTex'13 (since TacTex'15's ablated version must have some component in place of a disabled one to run properly). Figure 5 shows the results of our ablation analysis. Disabling the cost-predictor (Abl-cost) did not have significant impact on TacTex'15's performance (however it can reduce performance, see Figure 7). Disabling the wholesale-bidding strategy (Abl-bid) significantly hurts TacTex'15's performance: it reduces TacTex'15's score in game sizes 2, 4, 5, 6, and it causes TacTex'15 to either lose its lead (in game sizes 2, 3) or have a smaller victory margin (in game sizes 4, 5, 6). Disabling the demand-predictor (Abl-demand) significantly hurts TacTex'15's performance: it drops TacTex'15's score in all game sizes, and causes TacTex'15 to either lose its lead (in game sizes 3, 5, 6) or have a smaller victory margin (in game sizes 2, 4).

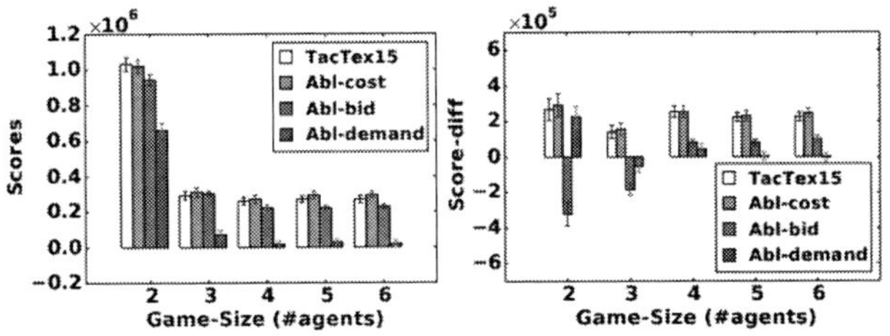

Figure 5: **Ablation analysis for 2-6 broker games.** The performance of TacTex'15 is compared with three of its ablated versions, when playing against the strongest combination of opponents in each game size. Ablated versions are constructed from TacTex'15 by disabling cost predictor (Abl-cost), wholesale-bidding strategy (Abl-bid), and demand-predictor (Abl-demand). The left figure shows the average scores of each version in each game size; the right figure shows the average score-differences of each version from opponents' average score (y-axes' scales are the same).

5.2.4 Ablation Analysis Extensions

To gain more insight into the importance of TacTex'15's main components, we extended each ablation experiment. First, we extended TacTex'15's demand-predictor ablation analysis from a binary ablation test (disabled/enabled, see Abl-demand in Figure 5) to a continuum of ablation-levels, thus testing TacTex'15's sensitivity to demand prediction errors. Figure 6 shows the performance-degradation as a function of ablation-level. We see that TacTex'15's degrades quickly even for small levels of ablation. We conclude that having an accurate demand-predictor is crucial for TacTex'15's success.

Next, we extended the ablation analysis of TacTex'15's wholesale-bidding strategy with additional comparisons against

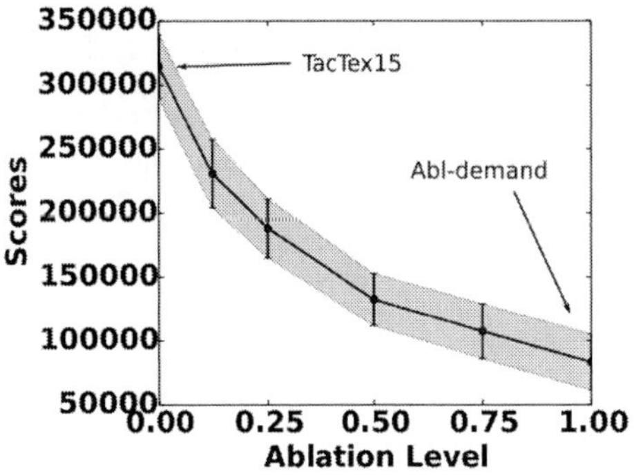

Figure 6: **Performance as a function of ablation level of the demand-predictor in 3-agent games.** The plot shows the degradation in TacTex'15's performance as the ablation level of its demand predictor increases. To change ablation level along a continuum, TacTex'15 uses here a weighted combination of two demand-predictors: (1) its own predictor, and (2) TacTex'13's demand-predictor, which was used by the ablated agent Abl-demand in Figure 5. Ablation level is then represented as the relative weight given to predictor (2), so that a weight of 0 means "no-ablation", and a weight of 1 means "full-ablation".

its ablated version (used by Abl-bid, see Figure 5). Abl-bid's strategy (which is TacTex'15's strategy) can be viewed as more cooperative than TacTex'15's, since it submits lower bids, and thus may result in lower costs against an opponent using a similar strategy. To understand whether Abl-bid's cooperative strategy is preferable in some situations, we created a payoff matrix (Table 3) by running 2-broker games, testing both TacTex'15 and Abl-bid in self-play and against each other. While Abl-bid's cooperative strategy indeed resulted in lower costs in self-play (40 \$/mWh vs. 57 \$/mWh, a 29.8% reduction), Abl-bid's total scores in self-play were not higher than TacTex'15's, since the competitive selling strategy reduced selling-prices further than TacTex'15's, such that the profit remained similar to TacTex'15's. As a result, TacTex'15's competitive strategy dominated Abl-bid's cooperative strategy in Table 3's experiments.

Table 3: **Payoff matrix of two wholesale-bidding strategies in 2-agent games.** The matrix shows a game-theoretic payoff matrix of two wholesale bidding strategies: (a) Comp-Bid is TacTex'15's competitive bidding strategy, and (b) Coop-Bid is Abl-bid's (and TacTex'13's) cooperative bidding strategy from Figure 5. The matrix entries show the average scores of agents using these strategies (TacTex'15 and Abl-bid, respectively) in self-play and against each other.

Payoff Matrix

	Coop-Bid	Comp-Bid
Coop-Bid	$1.0M$ / $1.0M$	$1.6M$ / $0.8M$
Comp-Bid	$0.8M$ / $1.6M$	$1.0M$ / $1.0M$

We ran additional self-play experiments using 3-, 4-, 5-broker games. In these cases Abl-bid's more cooperative bidding policy resulted in higher scores than TacTex'15, mainly since Abl-bid's lower energy costs enabled a longer price-reduction period after game-start, during which selling-prices where higher than the eventual equilibrium after which the profit of all brokers increased in the same pace.

Finally, we extended TacTex'15's cost-predictor ablation analysis. Even though ablating TacTex'15's cost predictor did not reduce performance against the 2015 finalists (Figure 5), we expect it to reduce performance when wholesale costs change more dynamically. Figure 7 shows the result of such an experiment, where TacTex'15 played against its cost-predictor ablated version (Abl-cost from Figure 5), and was quicker to react to a drop in wholesale costs and thus significantly won against Abl-cost.

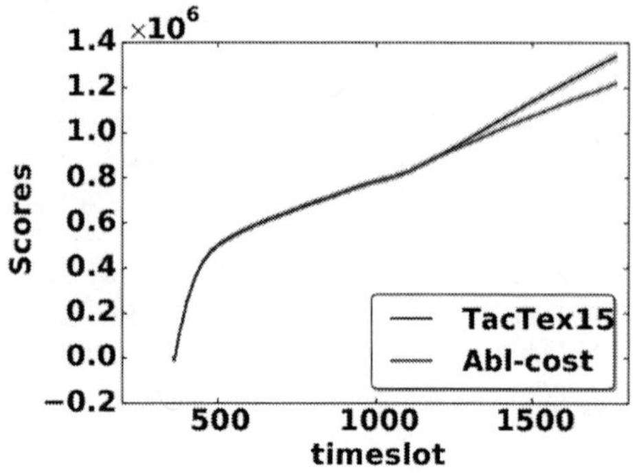

Figure 7: **Cost-predictor ablation in presence of abruptly changing market-costs.** The plot shows the average cumulative profit (with confidence bounds) as a function of time in head-to-head games of TacTex'15 vs. its cost-predictor ablated version (Abl-cost from Figure 5), when market costs abruptly dropped in timeslot 1080 (mid-game). TacTex'15 was quicker to react due to its more adaptive cost-predictor: it reduced selling prices, and thus gained market-share and increased its profits. To create a market-cost drop effect, we could reduce either the sellers' asks, or the brokers' bids. We implemented the latter (to avoid changing the simulator), by making both brokers switch their bidding policies in timeslot 1080 from competitive policies (of TacTex'15) to a cooperative policy (of TacTex'13).

6. RELATED WORK

This work is the first to formalize the *complete* broker's power trading problem as an MDP, and characterize its approximate solutions. Previous research either did not formulate the trading problem explicitly, or used an MDP to model either a more *abstract* trading problem [26, 27], or a *subproblem* of the complete trading problem [22, 16, 33, 15, 1, 20]. Moreover, all these MDP models were *heuristically* and *manually* constructed. In contrast, our MDP is defined by the underlying problem.

Previous approaches to power trading did not use lookahead policies to optimize the predicted utility (other than TacTex'13, which was discussed above). AgentUDE14 [20] (1st place, 2014) used an empirically tuned tariff strategy provoking subscription changes and withdraw payments, and Q-learning for wholesale bidding. CwiBroker14 (2nd place, 2014) [9] used tuned heuristics based on domain knowledge. An analysis of the 2014 Power TAC finals can be found at [2]. Mertacor13 [19] used Particle Swarm Optimization based tariff strategy. CwiBroker13 [17] (2nd place, 2013) used tariff strategy inspired by Tit-for-Tat. Their wholesale strategy used multiple bids per auction but was based on equilibria in continuous auctions, rather than TacTex'15's hedging between optimistic strategic bidding and truthful bidding.

In other trading agent competitions, utility-optimization approaches were used in different market structures [31, 21]. Other approaches included game theoretic analysis of the economy [14] and fuzzy reasoning [8].

7. CONCLUSION

This paper has focused on the question: how should an autonomous electricity broker agent act in competitive electricity markets to maximize its profit. We have formalized the complete electricity trading problem as an MDP, which is computationally intractable to solve exactly. Our formalization provides a guideline for approximating the MDP's solution, and for extending existing approximate solutions. We introduced TacTex'15 which extends the lookahead policy of a previously champion agent (TacTex'13) with better transition function predictors and a more competitive bidding strategy, and achieves state-of-the-art performance in competitions and controlled experiments. Using thousands of experiments against 2015 finalist brokers, we analyzed TacTex'15's performance and reasons for its success, finding that while its lookahead policy is an effective solution in the power trading domain, its performance can be sensitive to errors in the transition function prediction, especially demand-prediction. An important direction for future work is to further close the gap between the current approximate solution to the trading MDP and its fully optimal solution.

Acknowledgments

This work has taken place in the Learning Agents Research Group (LARG) at UT Austin. LARG research is supported in part by NSF (CNS-1330072, CNS-1305287), ONR (21C184-01), and AFRL (FA8750-14-1-0070), and AFOSR (FA9550-14-1-0087).

REFERENCES

[1] J. Babic and V. Podobnik. Adaptive bidding for electricity wholesale markets in a smart grid. In *AAMAS Workshop on Agent-Mediated Electronic Commerce and Trading Agents Design and Analysis (AMEC/TADA 2014)*, May 2014.

[2] J. Babic and V. Podobnik. An analysis of power trading agent competition 2014. In *Agent-Mediated Electronic Commerce*, 2014.

[3] D. Bertsekas and D. Castanon. Rollout algorithms for stochastic scheduling problems. *Journal of Heuristics*, 5(1):89–108, 1999.

[4] S. Borenstein. The trouble with electricity markets: Understanding california's restructuring disaster. *Journal of Economic Perspectives*, 16(1):191–211, 2002.

[5] H. Finnsson and Y. Björnsson. Simulation-based approach to general game playing. In *Proceedings of the 23rd National Conference on Artificial Intelligence - Volume 1*, AAAI'08, pages 259–264. AAAI Press, 2008.

[6] S. Gelly and D. Silver. Combining online and offline knowledge in uct. In *Proceedings of the 24th International Conference on Machine Learning*, ICML '07, pages 273–280, New York, NY, USA, 2007. ACM.

[7] C. P. Gomes. Computational sustainability: Computational methods for a sustainable environment, economy, and society. *The Bridge*, 39(4):5–13, 2009.

[8] M. He, A. Rogers, E. David, and N. R. Jennings. Designing and evaluating an adaptive trading agent for supply chain management applications. In H. L. Poutré, N. Sadeh, and J. Sverker, editors, *Agent-mediated Electronic Commerce, Designing Trading Agents and Mechanisms: AAMAS 2005 Workshop AMEC 2005, Utrecht, Netherlands, July 25, 2005, and IJCAI 2005 Workshop TADA 2005, Edinburgh, UK, August 1, 2005, Selected and Revised Papers*, pages 35–42. Springer, 2005. Event Dates: Auguest 2005.

[9] J. Hoogland and H. L. Poutre. An effective broker for the power tac 2014. In *AAMAS Workshop on Agent-Mediated Electronic Commerce and Trading Agents Design and Analysis (AMEC/TADA 2015)*, May 2015.

[10] P. L. Joskow. Lessons learned from electricity market liberalization. *The Energy Journal*, Volume 29, 2008.

[11] M. J. Kearns, Y. Mansour, and A. Y. Ng. Approximate planning in large pomdps via reusable trajectories. In *Advances in Neural Information Processing Systems 12, [NIPS Conference, Denver, Colorado, USA, November 29 - December 4, 1999]*, pages 1001–1007, 1999.

[12] W. Ketter, J. Collins, P. P. Reddy, and M. D. Weerdt. The 2015 power trading agent competition. *ERIM Report Series Reference No. ERS-2015-001-LIS*, 2015.

[13] W. Ketter, M. Peters, and J. Collins. Autonomous agents in future energy markets: The 2012 Power Trading Agent Competition. In *Proceedings of the Twenty-Seventh AAAI Conference on Artificial Intelligence*. AAAI, 2013.

[14] C. Kiekintveld, Y. Vorobeychik, and M. Wellman. An analysis of the 2004 supply chain management trading agent competition. In H. PoutrÃľ, N. Sadeh, and S. Janson, editors, *Agent-Mediated Electronic Commerce. Designing Trading Agents and Mechanisms*, volume 3937 of *Lecture Notes in Computer Science*, pages 99–112. Springer Berlin Heidelberg, 2006.

[15] R. T. Kuate, M. Chli, and H. H. Wang. Optimising market share and profit margin: Smdp-based tariff pricing under the smart grid paradigm. In *Innovative Smart Grid Technologies Conference Europe (ISGT-Europe), 2014 IEEE PES*, pages 1–6, Oct 2014.

[16] R. T. Kuate, M. He, M. Chli, and H. H. Wang. An intelligent broker agent for energy trading: An mdp approach. In *The 23rd International Joint Conference on Artificial Intelligence*, 2013.

[17] B. Liefers, J. Hoogland, and H. L. Poutre. A successful broker agent for power tac. In *AAMAS Workshop on Agent-Mediated Electronic Commerce and Trading Agents Design and Analysis (AMEC/TADA 2014)*, May 2014.

[18] R. Lorentz. Amazons discover monte-carlo. In H. van den Herik, X. Xu, Z. Ma, and M. Winands, editors, *Computers and Games*, volume 5131 of *Lecture Notes in Computer Science*, pages 13–24. Springer Berlin Heidelberg, 2008.

[19] E. Ntagka, A. Chrysopoulos, and P. A. Mitkas. Designing tariffs in a competitive energy market using particle swarm optimization techniques. In *AAMAS Workshop on Agent-Mediated Electronic Commerce and Trading Agents Design and Analysis (AMEC/TADA 2014)*, May 2014.

[20] S. Ozdemir and R. Unland. Agentude: The success story of the power tac 2014's champion. In *AAMAS Workshop on Agent-Mediated Electronic Commerce and Trading Agents Design and Analysis (AMEC/TADA 2015)*, May 2015.

[21] D. M. Pardoe. *Adaptive Trading Agent Strategies Using Market Experience*. PhD thesis, 2011.

[22] M. Peters, W. Ketter, M. Saar-Tsechansky, and J. Collins. A reinforcement learning approach to autonomous decision-making in smart electricity markets. *Machine Learning*, 92(1):5–39, 2013.

[23] W. Powell and S. Meisel. Tutorial on stochastic optimization in energy – part ii: An energy storage illustration. *Power Systems, IEEE Transactions on*, PP(99):1–8, 2015.

[24] W. B. Powell. *Approximate Dynamic Programming: Solving the Curses of Dimensionality, 2nd Edition*. Wiley, 2011.

[25] M. L. Puterman. *Markov Decision Processes: Discrete Stochastic Dynamic Programming*. John Wiley & Sons, Inc., New York, NY, USA, 1st edition, 1994.

[26] P. P. Reddy and M. M. Veloso. Learned behaviors of multiple autonomous agents in smart grid markets. In *AAAI*, 2011.

[27] P. P. Reddy and M. M. Veloso. Strategy learning for autonomous agents in smart grid markets. In *Proceedings of the Twenty-Second international joint conference on Artificial Intelligence-Volume Volume Two*, pages 1446–1451. AAAI Press, 2011.

[28] P. P. Reddy and M. M. Veloso. Factored Models for Multiscale Decision Making in Smart Grid Customers. In *Proceedings of the Twenty-Sixth AAAI Conference on Artificial Intelligence (AAAI-12)*, 2012.

[29] D. Silver and J. Veness. Monte-carlo planning in large pomdps. In J. Lafferty, C. Williams, J. Shawe-Taylor, R. Zemel, and A. Culotta, editors, *Advances in Neural Information Processing Systems 23*, pages 2164–2172. Curran Associates, Inc., 2010.

[30] S. Stoft. *Index*, pages 460–468. Wiley-IEEE Press, 2002.

[31] P. Stone, R. E. Schapire, M. L. Littman, J. A. Csirik, and D. McAllester. Decision-theoretic bidding based on learned density models in simultaneous, interacting auctions. *Journal of Artificial Intelligence Research*, 19:209–242, 2003.

[32] D. Urieli and P. Stone. A learning agent for heat-pump thermostat control. In *Proceedings of the 12th International Conference on Autonomous Agents and Multiagent Systems (AAMAS)*, May 2013.

[33] D. Urieli and P. Stone. Tactex'13: A champion adaptive power trading agent. In *Proceedings of the Twenty-Eighth Conference on Artificial Intelligence (AAAI 2014)*, July 2014.

[34] U.S. Department of Energy. *"Grid 2030" A National Vision For Electricity's Second 100 Years*, 2003.

[35] A. Weidlich and D. Veit. A critical survey of agent-based wholesale electricity market models. *Energy Economics*, 30(4):1728 – 1759, 2008.

Decentralized Multi-Project Scheduling via Multi-Unit Combinatorial Auction

Wen Song, Donghun Kang, Jie Zhang[a], Hui Xi[b]
Rolls-Royce@NTU Corp Lab, Nanyang Technological University, Singapore
[a]School of Computer Engineering, Nanyang Technological University, Singapore
[b]Rolls-Royce Singapore Pte Ltd, Singapore
{songwen, donghun.kang, [a]zhangj}@ntu.edu.sg, [b]hui.xi@rolls-royce.com

ABSTRACT

In industry, many problems are considered as the Decentralized Resource-Constrained Multi-Project Scheduling Problem (DRCMPSP). Existing approaches encounter difficulties in dealing with large problems while preserving information privacy of project agents. In this paper, we propose a novel approach to solve DRCMPSP based on the multi-unit combinatorial auction, which can efficiently solve the problem without violating information privacy. It adopts a greedy resource allocation strategy with fixed resource cost to simplify computation required for project (bidder) and auctioneer agents. In addition, a bid modification step is incorporated to allow project agents to better utilize resources. Analysis and empirical results indicate that our approach outperforms state-of-the-art decentralized approaches in minimizing average project delay, and scales well to large problems with thousands of activities from tens of projects.

Keywords

Multi-Project Scheduling, Multi-Unit Combinatorial Auction, Resource Allocation

1. INTRODUCTION

Most business firms need to manage multiple projects simultaneously. Usually, these projects have temporal constraints on activities and capacity constraints on resources [23]. With the rapid growth of globalization and information technology, nowadays it is quite common for firms to conduct intra- and inter-firm collaborations to improve efficiency and reduce cost [21]. This trend brings the traditional multi-project scheduling into a decentralized environment, where projects are distributed and controlled by different self-interested decision makers. In order to achieve individual objectives, these decision makers usually need to compete for some shared global resources having limited capacities. Moreover, they may be reluctant to reveal private information on the projects, especially when they are rivals in the market. In this decentralized and information asymmetric environment, the traditional multi-project scheduling problem has evolved into the *Decentralized Resource-Constrained Multi-Project Scheduling Problem* (DRCMPSP) [4].

Appears in: *Proceedings of the 15th International Conference on Autonomous Agents and Multiagent Systems (AAMAS 2016), J. Thangarajah, K. Tuyls, C. Jonker, S. Marsella (eds.), May 9–13, 2016, Singapore.*

Many real-world problems in manufacturing and service operations with complex product/supply structures are considered as DRCMPSP. In [11], an intra-firm scenario is given where different product managers in an electronics manufacturing company must share and compete for common production resources (e.g. automated production lines) in a regular basis. To satisfy their own customers' requirements, these managers need to deal with uniquely different sets of activities and constraints (e.g. lead time pressure, processing requirements). In terms of inter-firm scenarios, a typical example can be found in the Aero Repair and Overhaul industry [20]. In this example, different fleet managers who are dedicated to manage the aero engines of an airline, compete for several overhaul bases heaving limited repair capacities with other fleet managers. These managers need to schedule the overhaul base visit time for each controlled engine, to maximize their operating revenue at the same time. Similar inter-firm cases can also be found in the airport ground handling service scheduling [15] and supply chain scheduling [12]. As stated in both [12] and [20], approaches that respect the privacy of self-interested decision makers are more preferable in decentralized scheduling, since these decision makers may as well be competitors in the same marketplace.

Due to its decentralized nature, DRCMPSP is usually modeled as a mediated multi-agent system where each project is represented by a Project Agent (PA) and all PAs are coordinated by a Mediator Agent (MA). The core problem in DRCMPSP is how to allocate the shared global resources to each decision maker in a decentralized manner. Market-based approach, especially combinatorial auction, is an ideal choice for decentralized scheduling since it well supports the decentralized decision making and information privacy of the decision makers [22]. However, as will be detailed in Section 2, current combinatorial auction based approaches either cannot fully satisfy the requirements of DRCMPSP (e.g. not fully decentralized, not allow multiple activities per project), or underperform both in solution quality and computational efficiency, especially on large problem cases with thousands of activities from tens of projects.

In this paper, we propose a novel decentralized approach for solving DRCMPSP based on the multi-unit combinatorial auction. We simplify the computation of the agents by adopting a greedy resource allocation strategy and fixed resource cost, and incorporate a bid modification step to provide possibilities for the project agents to better utilize global resources. Following previous research on DRCMPSP, we assume that the agents are willing to provide truthful information required by the approach, i.e. currently we do not handle the incentive compatibility issue[1]. However, by limiting the exchanged information to bids and demand ratio (defined in Section 4), this approach does not require private project information from the project agents.

Our complexity analysis shows that this approach terminates within a maximum number of auctions that increases linearly along with the number of projects, regardless of the number of activities, and requires polynomial computation for all agents. Empirical results on cases with multi-unit resources (obtained from the public benchmark MPSPLIB[2]) and single-unit resource (generated from MPSPLIB) show that our approach outperforms state-of-the-art decentralized approaches in minimizing average project delay, one of the most widely adopted performance measure of DRCMPSP, within reasonable computational time.

2. RELATED WORK

In the literature, combinatorial auction has been applied to solve simple decentralized scheduling problems [11, 22, 4]. In [11], Kutanoglu and Wu introduce a combinatorial auction based distributed scheduling framework, and show that combinatorial auction with a certain payment function is corresponding to the lagrangean decomposition of the centralized problem. Nevertheless, their approach is not fully decentralized, since a centralized algorithm is needed to clear the market and generate a feasible solution. In [22], Wellman et al. give concrete theoretical results on the equilibrium and efficiency of applying combinatorial auction to schedule activities from different agents on a shared resource. However, their analysis is based on the model of a simple factory scheduling problem where each agent is only in charge of one activity. In large DRCMPSP cases, each project agent (PA) could be in charge of hundreds of activities with complex precedence relations. Confessore et al. propose another combinatorial auction based approach in [4]. This approach is based on an iterative combinatorial auction named *i*Bundle [17], which has been applied to solve problems such as multi-agent pathfinding [2] and train scheduling [18]. The nice properties of *i*Bundle, including optimality guarantee and strategy-proofness, are based on the assumption that all bidders can give Myopic Best-Response (MBR) in each round of auction. However, when applied to DRCMPSP, MBR is difficult to satisfy due to the intractability of local bidding problems. When approximated algorithms without optimality guarantee are used for bidding, as in [4], both optimality and strategy-proofness on the final solution will be compromised. In addition, when MBR cannot be satisfied, *i*Bundle cannot guarantee that all the bidders will be granted a bid upon termination. Finally, *i*Bundle could take a large number of iterations to terminate, which requires intense computation for bidders and the auctioneer, resulting in inefficiency on large-scale cases. Besides their own limitations, all approaches in [11, 22, 4] can only be used to schedule single-unit global resources. Moreover, test cases are rather small with tens of activities in total from several PAs. In contrast, our approach can efficiently handle multi-unit resources and large problem cases.

More recently, several approaches have been proposed to solve much larger DRCMPSP cases with hundreds to thousands of activities from tens of projects sharing several multi-unit global resources [15, 7, 1, 24]. In [15], Mao et al. propose a market-based approach to schedule the airport ground handling services, but the resource capacities are assumed to be infinite which is hardly found in practice. In [7], Homberger presents an evolutionary computation based negotiation approach, but it is outperformed by a centralized approach SASP [10], one of the best priority rule based multi-project scheduling algorithms in minimizing average project delay. In [1], Adhau et al. introduce an approach named DMAS/ABN, which conducts an auction-based negotiation on each time slot for each activity. In [24], Zheng et al. propose an approach named DMAS/EM which employs an activity elimination algorithm to fix an infeasible solution. Both DMAS/ABN and DMAS/EM outperform SASP in minimizing average project delay. One common feature of the approaches in [15, 7, 1, 24] is that, they are based on activity-level negotiation to generate or fix a solution, which has two major drawbacks. Firstly, activity information (e.g. start time, duration, resource requirements) is inevitably required by the mediator. Secondly, when the individual objective of each PA cannot be decomposed precisely to each activity (e.g. project makespan, delay cost), the decision on global resource allocation to each activity can only rely on the estimated objective value, which could result in unsatisfactory solution quality. On the contrary, global resource allocation in our approach is purely on project level, which can satisfy the private information requirement and provide more precise information for allocating global resources.

3. PROBLEM STATEMENT

In DRCMPSP, a number of projects that share global resources will be scheduled in a time horizon of T consecutive time slots. Each project P_i, $i \in \{1, ..., N\}$, consists of non-preemptive activities a_{ij}, $j \in \{1, ..., J_i\}$. Let s_{ij} and d_{ij} be the start time and duration of an activity a_{ij}, respectively. The precedence constraint $a_{ij} \prec a_{ik}$ indicates that an activity a_{ik} cannot start before the completion of its preceding activity a_{ij} (i.e. $s_{ik} \geq s_{ij} + d_{ij}$). Each project P_i has two time-related attributes, an earliest start date ed_i and an expected due date dd_i. For a project P_i, a Project Agent PA_i is assigned to control P_i. Each PA_i can receive a revenue rv_i upon the completion of P_i.

Each activity requires certain amounts of resources. A set of G global resources are shared by all the projects. Each global resource R_g, $g \in \{1, ..., G\}$ has a limited capacity C_{gt} in time t, $t \in \{1, ..., T\}$, and has a fixed utilization cost c_g per unit at each time slot. The global resources are managed by a Mediator Agent (MA). Also, each PA_i may own a set of L_i local resources[3] that are dedicated to P_i. Each local resource R_{l_i}, $l_i \in \{1, ..., L_i\}$, has a limited capacity C_{l_it} in time t. Each activity a_{ij} requires r_{ij}^{g} units of global resource R_g and $r_{ij}^{l_i}$ units of local resource R_{l_i} during each time slot of its processing period.

Let S be a solution of a DRCMPSP and S_i be a schedule of a project P_i. Assume that S_i is a vector of individual activity's start times, namely $S_i = (s_{i1}, ..., s_{iJ_i})$. Then, the solution S can be defined as a vector of individual project's

[1]Note that privacy and truthfulness are two separate issues. Even though an agent is willing to tell the truth, it may still not be willing to disclose their sensitive information [5].

[2]http://www.mpsplib.com/

[3]Here we ignore the cost of local resources since they are assumed to be already owned by the PA and do not need to be allocated to each PA. However, our approach can also work when local resource cost is considered.

schedules: $S = (S_1, ..., S_N)$. A feasible solution S cannot violate any precedence or global/local resource constraints, but the project due dates are soft constraints that can be violated. However, for PA_i, any violation on the due date caused by schedule S_i will impose a delay cost $dc_i(S_i)$, which is a function that monotonically increases with the project completion time $ct_i(S_i) = \max_j\{s_{ij} + d_{ij}\}$. Here we use a linear cost function which is frequently used in the literature: $dc_i(S_i) = p_i \cdot \max\{0, ct_i(S_i) - dd_i\}$, where p_i is the unit delay penalty. Nevertheless, our approach can also adopt non-linear cost functions with the property of monotonic increasing. Also following the previous research, we set the optimality criteria on solution S as the minimization of *Average Project Delay* (APD):

$$APD(S) = \frac{\sum_{i=1}^{N} \max\{0, (ct_i(S_i) - dd_i)\}}{N}. \tag{1}$$

The information of the activities (e.g. d_{ij}, s_{ij}, r^g_{ij}, $r^{l_i}_{ij}$) and local resources (e.g. R_{l_i}, $C_{l_i t}$) are considered as private to each project agent.

4. OUR AUCTION-BASED APPROACH

In general, our approach contains a series of multi-unit combinatorial auctions, and incrementally allocates global resources to PAs. We formulate the auctions following a paradigm similar to [4], where PAs act as bidders, the MA acts as the auctioneer, and the goods to sell are the global resources at each time slot. However, we make the following modifications: (i) we adopt multi-unit combinatorial auction instead of single-unit, since multi-unit global resources need to be handled; (ii) we define the bidder utility based on fixed resource cost instead of changing bundle prices; (iii) we set the objective of the auctioneer as maximizing social welfare instead of revenue, since optimizing revenue may lead to unsatisfactory allocation efficiency [13].

Given G global resources and the scheduling horizon T, there are $G \times T$ goods to sell. We denote the available units of global resource R_g at time t as Ψ_{gt}. Initially, $\Psi_{gt} = C_{gt}$; as the approach proceeds, it is possible that $\Psi_{gt} \leq C_{gt}$. A *multiset* [9] of goods is denoted as a matrix $\Lambda = [\lambda_{gt}]_{G\times T}$, where λ_{gt} is the units of R_g at time t. In each auction round, each participating PA needs to place one bid on the multiset that can (approximately) maximize its *utility*. For PA_i, utility is a function $u_i : \mathbf{\Lambda} \mapsto \Re^+$, $\mathbf{\Lambda} = \{\Lambda | 0 \leq \lambda_{gt} \leq \Psi_{gt}\}$, defined as a quasi-linear function $u_i(\Lambda) = v_i(\Lambda) - RC_i(\Lambda)$, where $v_i(\Lambda)$ is its valuation for Λ and $RC_i(\Lambda)$ is the cost for utilizing Λ. Under fixed unit global resource cost, $RC_i(\Lambda)$ can be calculated as follows:

$$RC_i(\Lambda) = \sum_{g=1}^{G} c_g \sum_{t=1}^{T} \lambda_{gt}. \tag{2}$$

The valuation function will be further detailed in Section 4.1. A bid from PA_i is a pair $B_i = < \Lambda, v_i(\Lambda) >$, where the interested multiset and its valuation are specified. In each round of auction, the MA needs to solve a Winner Determination Problem (WDP) to optimize social welfare, which is the summation of the valuation of the bidders, under the current global resource capacities. Given a set of bids $\mathscr{B} = \{B_\xi | \xi \in \{1, ..., N_b\}\}$ submitted by N_b bidders, a WDP of single-minded bidders (e.g. one bidder is interested

Algorithm 1: Our Auction-based Approach

Input: A DRCMPSP case
Output: A solution of the case

1 MA initializes the auction environment, by setting $\overline{SS} \leftarrow \emptyset$, $\overline{IW} \leftarrow \emptyset$, $\overline{US} \leftarrow \{PA_i | i \in \{1, ..., N\}\}$;
2 **while** $\overline{US} \neq \emptyset$ **do**
3   **forall the** $PA_i \in \overline{US}$ **do**
4   Solve a bidding problem, generate a schedule S_i^* and a bid B_i^* ;
5   MA solves a WDP, updates $\overline{IW}$ and $\overline{US}$;
6   MA calculates the demand ratio;
7   **while** $\overline{IW} \neq \emptyset$ **do**
8   **forall the** $PA_i \in \overline{IW}$ **do**
9   Solve a bid modification problem, generate a schedule $S_i^{*'}$ and a bid $B_i^{*'}$;
10   MA solves a WDP, grants global resources to the final winners, and updates $\overline{SS}$ and $\overline{IW}$;
11   Final winners confirm their schedules $S_i^{*'}$;
12   MA updates global resource capacities;
13 **return** $S^* \leftarrow \{S_1^{*'}, ..., S_N^{*'}\}$

in one multiset [13]) can be formulated as:

$$\begin{aligned} \max \quad & \sum_{\xi=1}^{N_b} v_\xi \cdot x_\xi \\ \text{s.t.} \quad & \sum_{\xi=1}^{N_b} \lambda_{gt}^{\xi} \cdot x_\xi \leq \Psi_{gt}, \ \forall g, t \\ & x_\xi \in \{0, 1\}, \ \forall \xi \end{aligned} \tag{3}$$

Our approach is described in Algorithm 1. Throughout the whole process, three sets of PAs are maintained by the MA: *Scheduled Set* $\overline{SS}$, *Unscheduled Set* $\overline{US}$, and *Initial Winner Set* $\overline{IW}$. Initially, all PAs belong to $\overline{US}$, while $\overline{SS}$ and $\overline{IW}$ are empty. Each round of auction consists of two successive phases: *initial phase* (Line 3 to 6) and *final phase* (Line 7 to 12). In the initial phase, the MA initiates an auction among the unscheduled PAs to determine the *initial winners*. Each PA in $\overline{US}$ generates a bid by solving a bidding problem, then the MA solves a WDP. The initial winners will be moved from $\overline{US}$ to $\overline{IW}$. In the final phase, several rounds of auctions among the initial winners are initiated by the MA to finalize the global resource allocation. In each round of these auctions, each PA in $\overline{IW}$ modifies its bid according to the *demand ratio* (see Definition 5) published by the MA. Then the MA solves a WDP to determine the *final winners* who will be granted the amounts of global resources specified in its bid, and will be moved from $\overline{IW}$ to $\overline{SS}$. Intuitively, the initial phase is used to choose the most "promising" PAs given the current global resource capacities, and the final phase tries to guide these chosen PAs to tune their demand profile in order to provide chances for unscheduled PAs to improve their utilities. Next, we will explain the major components of Algorithm 1 in detail.

4.1 Bid Generation

Here we show how bidders find the multisets that can (approximately) maximize their utility by solving a corresponding single Resource-Constrained Project Scheduling Problem (RCPSP). More formally, a bidder needs to find an optimal or near-optimal solution Λ_i^* of the *bidding problem*:

$$\Lambda_i^* = \underset{\Lambda \in \mathbf{\Lambda}}{\text{argmax}}\ u_i(\Lambda), \tag{4}$$

and calculate its valuation $v_i(\Lambda_i^*)$. First we discuss how to evaluate a multiset by introducing the following definition:

Definition 1. A multiset Λ is said to be *feasible* to PA_i, if there exists a feasible schedule S_i that satisfies all the precedence and local/global resource constraints of P_i, when PA_i obtains the amount of global resources specified in Λ.

Now we can define the valuation function as follows:

$$v_i(\Lambda) = \begin{cases} rv_i - DC_i(\Lambda), & \text{if } \Lambda \text{ is feasible} \\ 0, & \text{otherwise,} \end{cases} \tag{5}$$

where $DC_i(\Lambda)$ is the delay cost of Λ. To show how to calculate $DC_i(\Lambda)$, the following definition is needed:

Definition 2. Given a feasible multiset Λ of PA_i, the set $\boldsymbol{S}_i^{\Lambda}$ which contains all feasible schedules of P_i given the amounts of global resources specified in Λ, is called a *solution set.* A solution $\widehat{S}_i^{\Lambda} \in \boldsymbol{S}_i^{\Lambda}$ that has the minimum completion time $ct_i(\widehat{S}_i^{\Lambda})$ is called a *primal schedule* of Λ to PA_i.

Assume a bidder can find a primal schedule $\widehat{S}_i^{\Lambda}$ of Λ, it can safely choose $\widehat{S}_i^{\Lambda}$ and discard other schedules in $\boldsymbol{S}_i^{\Lambda}$, since the delay cost cannot be reduced further by choosing another schedule. Hence, the delay cost of a multiset can be calculated as the delay cost of its primal schedule:

$$DC_i(\Lambda) = dc_i(\widehat{S}_i^{\Lambda}). \tag{6}$$

It seems straightforward to evaluate Λ using Equation (5) and (6). However, it is computationaly intractable to solve these two equations, since firstly in Equation (5) it is hard to determine if a schedule is feasible (equivalent to solving a feasibility problem of RCPSP which is NP-hard [16]), and secondly in Equation (6) it is hard to find the primal solution (equivalent to solving a RCPSP which is NP-hard [3]). On the other hand, to generate a feasible multiset from a feasible schedule is quite easy, as stated in the following definition:

Definition 3. Given a schedule $S_i = (s_{i1}, ..., s_{iJ_i})$ of P_i, the multiset $\widehat{\Lambda}_i = \widehat{\Lambda}_i(S_i)$ calculated as:

$$\widehat{\lambda}_{gt}^i(S_i) = \sum_{a_{ij} \in A_i(t)} r_{ij}^g, \tag{7}$$

where $A_i(t) = \{a_{ij}, j \in \{1, ..., J_i\} | s_{ij} \le t, (s_{ij} + d_{ij}) > t\}$, is called a *core*[4] of PA_i.

Definition 2 and 3 build connections between schedules and multisets. Given a feasible schedule, a feasible multiset (which is a core) can be obtained immediately using Equation (7); given a feasible multiset, there must exist a feasible schedule that is primal, since the solution set cannot be empty. In Section 5.1, we will show that a candidate multiset of the bidding problem must be a core. However, it is still hard to give the exact valuation of a core, due to the hardness on computing Equation (6). Here we estimate a core's delay cost using the delay cost of its corresponding schedule. Then the approximate valuation of core $\widehat{\Lambda}_i(S_i)$ is:

$$\widetilde{v}_i(\widehat{\Lambda}_i(S_i)) = rv_i - dc_i(S_i). \tag{8}$$

The approximate utility can be calculated as:

$$\widetilde{u}_i(\widehat{\Lambda}_i(S_i)) = rv_i - dc_i(S_i) - RC_i(\widehat{\Lambda}_i(S_i)). \tag{9}$$

Given a feasible schedule S_i, the computation of Equation (8) and (9) is trival. In Section 5.1, we will show that the above equation provides an approximation to the exact utility of the optimal solution of the bidding problem, with an error that monotonically increases with $ct_i(S_i)$. Hence, we can approximately solve the bidding problem by finding a sub-optimal schedule of the corresponding RCPSP (with the global resource capacities equal to Ψ_{gt}), then generate the corresponding core and calcualte the approximate valuation using Equation (7) and (8), respectively. Here we adopt the parallel schedule generation scheme with one of the best priority-rule *Latest Finish Time* [8], to generate a near-optimal schedule. However, all the resources considered in [8] have constant capacities over the whole scheduling horizon, which cannot be directly applied to our problem. Thus, we modify the activity selection step of the original algorithm by checking the global and local resource capacities over all the duration of an activity, instead of simply checking the first time slot.

4.2 Bid Modification

In a DRCMPSP case, requirements for different time slots of global resource are not even; some time slots may be demanded more heavily than others. Since winners will be granted their bids in the end of each round, if they can switch to other bids producing the same utility but deviated from heavily demanded time slots, other unscheduled PAs may have better chances to improve their utilities. Based on this idea, we design a bid modification step, where the winners try to modify their bids based on the *demand ratio* provided by the MA as demand status feedback. To define the bid modification problem, first we define the *equivalent set*:

Definition 4. For PA_i, given a core $\widehat{\Lambda}_i = \widehat{\Lambda}_i(S_i)$ generated by a schedule S_i, the *equivalent set* of $\widehat{\Lambda}_i$ is defined as $\mathscr{A}(\widehat{\Lambda}_i) = \left\{\widehat{\Lambda}_i(S_i') \middle| ct_i(S_i') = ct_i(S_i)\right\}$.

As will be shown in Lemma 1 in Section 5.1, the equivalent set consists of cores that produce the same approximate utility to a PA. Next we give the following definitions:

Definition 5. Given a set of bids $\mathscr{B}$, the *demand ratio* is defined as a matrix $D(\mathscr{B}) = [\delta_{gt}(\mathscr{B})]_{G\times T}$, where

$$\delta_{gt}(\mathscr{B}) = \left(\sum_{\xi=1}^{N_b} \lambda_{gt}^{\xi}\right) / \Psi_{gt}. \tag{10}$$

Definition 6. The *resource index* of a multiset Λ under demand ratio D is defined as:

$$RI(\Lambda, D) = \sum_{g=1}^{G} \sum_{t=1}^{T} \lambda_{gt}\delta_{gt}. \tag{11}$$

The intuition of Definitions 5 and 6 is that, a higher aggregate demand on a resource time slot with lower capacity results in a higher demand ratio, and a multiset with a lower resource index is more likely to avoid the heavily demanded time slots. Now we define the *bid modification problem*:

[4]Note that this definition is different from the commonly used definition of core in game theory.

Algorithm 2: Bid Modification

```
Input: A schedule S_i^* and demand ratio D
Output: Modified schedule S_i^{*'} and bid B_i^{*'}
1 if Global resource capacities changed then
2   | Solve the bidding problem;
3 Calculate the activity slackness, and put all the
  flexible activities in FJ_i;
4 while FJ_i ≠ ∅ do
5   | Virtually shift all the flexible activities within their
    | slackness, and record the best shifting with the
    | most reduction in resource index;
6   | Apply the best shifting, and remove the selected
    | activity from FJ_i;
7   | Update the activity slackness;
8 Calculate a bid B_i^{*'} ←< Λ_i^{*'}, u_i^{*'} > based on the
  modified schedule;
9 return S_i^{*'}, B_i^{*'}
```

Definition 7. Given demand ratio D and multiset Λ_i^* in the solution of the bidding problem, the problem of finding

$$\Lambda_i^{*'} = \underset{\Lambda \in \mathscr{A}(\Lambda^*)}{\text{argmin}}\ RI(\Lambda, D) \tag{12}$$

is called the bid modification problem.

The above problem is NP-hard since it can be transformed to a RCPSP with an additional hard due date constraint. Here we design a polynomial-time algorithm to approximately solve this problem, as shown in Algorithm 2. This algorithm generates an equivalent multiset by shifting flexible activities in an existing schedule. An activity a_{ij} in a schedule S_i is flexible if its *slackness* $slk_{ij} = \{t | est_{ij} \le t < lst_{ij}\}$ is not empty, where:

$$\begin{aligned} est_{ij} &= \max\left\{ad_i, \max_{a_{ij'} \prec a_{ij}} \{s_{ij'} + d_{ij'}\}\right\}, \\ lst_{ij} &= \min\left\{ct_i(S_i), \min_{a_{ij} \prec a_{ij'}} \{s_{ij'} - d_{ij}\}\right\}. \end{aligned} \tag{13}$$

In Algorithm 2, PA_i may need to update its bid before activity shifting procedures by solving a bidding problem, since the global resource capacities could change during the finalization phase (Line 1 to 2). In activity shifting procedures, first all the flexible activities are detected and put into a set FJ_i (Line 3). Then, an iterative process (Line 4 to 7) shifts $a_{ij} \in FJ_i$ to start at a global and local resource feasible time $t \in slk_{ij}$ which reduces the resource index value most, and removes a_{ij} from FJ_i. When FJ_i is empty, a new schedule S_i' is found, and a modified bid is generated (Line 8). A simple example of the bid modification is given in Figure 1, where two projects compete for one global resource with a capacity of 5. Both projects can start from time 0. Figure 1(a) shows the schedules generated by two successive rounds of auctions (without modification), where PA_1 wins the first round and PA_2 wins the second round. The demand profile of PA_1 and demand ratio of the first round is given in Figure 1(b). As in Figure 1(c), if PA_1 can shift its flexible activity a_{12} to start at time 2 according to the demand ratio, PA_2 can achieve a better schedule which completes at time 8, instead of time 10 in Figure 1(a). The modified demand profile of PA_1 is shown in Figure 1(d).

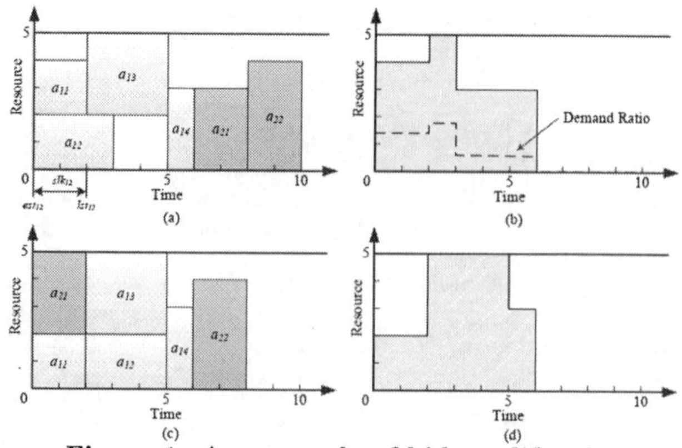

Figure 1: An example of bid modification

4.3 Winner Determination

The WDP is proved as NP-complete [19]. A polynomial-time algorithm with a proved upper-bound for solving WDP among single-minded bidders is provided in [6]. The algorithm first sorts all the bids based on a given criterion, then examines each bid in order and labels the bidder as winner if its bid does not conflict with the previous winners. Here we adopt this algorithm with the following sorting criterion:

$$\gamma(B_\xi) = \frac{v_\xi}{\sqrt{\sum_{g=1}^{G} \sum_{t=1}^{T} \lambda_{gt}^{\xi} / \Psi_{gt}}}. \tag{14}$$

A bid with a higher γ value is more likely to be a winner in the optimal solution. Hence, all bids are first sorted descendingly according to their γ values, then examined one by one to check if there is any violation on resource capacity.

5. ANALYSIS

We provide analysis about our approach in this section, including some formal proofs to support our design, and detailed analysis on its information exchange and complexity.

5.1 Theoretical Support for Our Design

In Section 4.1, we design an efficient method to approximately solve the bidding problem by generating a multiset (i.e. core) given a schedule using Equation (7). Here, we formally prove that the multiset generated in this way must be a candidate of the optimal solution of the bidding problem, and analyze the error of the approximate utility in Equation (9). We first prove that under fixed resource cost, a core satisfies the properties described in the following lemma:

Lemma 1 *For PA_i, the following statements hold: (1) all cores have the same resource cost; (2) the resource cost of a core is the lowest among all the feasible multisets; (3) cores generated from schedules with the same completion time has the same approximate utility.*

Proof Introduce an auxiliary variable $\overline{r}_{ij,t}^{g}$ for each a_{ij}:

$$\overline{r}_{ij,t}^{g} = \begin{cases} r_{ij}^{g}, & \text{if } s_{ij} \le t < (s_{ij} + d_{ij}) \\ 0, & \text{otherwise} \end{cases} \tag{15}$$

Then a core $\widehat{\Lambda}_i$ defined by Equation (7) can be rewritten as

$$\widehat{\lambda}_{gt}^{i} = \sum_{a_{ij} \in A_i(t)} r_{ij}^{g} = \sum_{j=1}^{J_i} \overline{r}_{ij,t}^{g}. \tag{16}$$

Putting the above equation into Equation (2), we have

$$RC_i(\widehat{\Lambda}_i) = \sum_{g=1}^{G} c_g \sum_{t=1}^{T}\sum_{j=1}^{J_i} \overline{r}^g_{ij,t} = \sum_{g=1}^{G}\sum_{j=1}^{J_i} c_g r^g_{ij} d_{ij}. \qquad (17)$$

Since c_g, r^g_{ij} and d_{ij} are all constant, $RC_i(\widehat{\Lambda}_i)$ is also a constant regardless of $\widehat{\Lambda}_i$, the first statement holds. Assuming there exists a multiset $\widetilde{\Lambda}$ such that $RC_i(\widetilde{\Lambda}) < RC_i(\widehat{\Lambda}_i)$, according to Equation (17), at least one activity $a_{i\widetilde{j}}$, $\widetilde{j} \in \{1,..,J_i\}$ cannot obtain enough amount of global resource R_g during at least one time slot in $d_{i\widetilde{j}}$, which means $\widetilde{\Lambda}$ is not a feasible multiset. Hence the second statement holds. The third statement can be obtained immediately according to the first statement and Equation (9). □

Now we are ready to prove the following proposition:

Proposition 1 *The optimal multiset Λ^*_i of PA_i defined in Equation (4) must be the core generated by the schedule S^*_i which has the minimum completion time regarding the current global resource capacity Ψ_{gt}.*

Proof According to Equation (5), any infeasible multiset cannot be optimal. For any feasible multiset Λ, according to Lemma 1 and Definition 2, it is always true that $u_i(\widehat{\Lambda}_i(\widehat{S}^{\Lambda}_i)) \geq u_i(\Lambda)$, hence an optimal solution must be a core. Since all cores have the same resource cost, the core Λ^*_i generated by S^*_i solves the bidding problem to optimal, since Λ^*_i results in the lowest delay cost. □

Proposition 1 shows that any multiset that is not a core cannot be optimal, and the optimal solution of the bidding problem is $\Lambda^*_i = \widehat{\Lambda}_i(S^*_i)$. Noted that the estimated utility $\widetilde{u}_i(\Lambda^*_i)$ calculated using Equation (9) is the same as its exact utility $u_i(\Lambda^*_i)$, since $DC_i(\Lambda^*_i) = dc_i(S^*_i)$. Hence, for any feasible schedule S_i and the estimated utility $\widetilde{u}_i(\widehat{\Lambda}_i(S^*_i))$, the error from the optimal utility $u_i(\Lambda^*_i)$ is $err = \widetilde{u}_i(\widehat{\Lambda}_i(S_i)) - \widetilde{u}_i(\Lambda^*_i) = dc_i(S_i) - dc_i(S^*_i)$.

5.2 Information Exchange

In our approach, only two kinds of information need to be exchanged between PAs and the MA, namely bids and demand ratio. Beyond them, PAs do not need to specify any private information regarding activities and local resources. More importantly, it is very hard to obtain these kinds of private information only from the bids and demand ratio. Nevertheless, they need to provide truthful valuation on the global resource requirements that they are interested in.

Besides privacy preserving, another advantage of our design is that, the bids provide more precise information for the decisions on global resource allocation. Though utilities are approximated using Equation (8) and (9), the actual utility a bidder will gain after being granted $\widehat{\Lambda}(S_i)$ cannot be lower than the approximate value, assuming it will not apply a schedule with a larger completion time than $ct_i(S_i)$. On the contrary, activity-level approaches directly allocate global resources to individual activities according to some activity-level criteria. However, these criteria cannot exactly reflect the individual objectives (e.g. makespan, revenue) of each project, since these objectives can only be known exactly when all the activities are scheduled. This is more evident under tighter resource constraints, since it is more difficult for a PA to predict its objective without knowing the global resource demand status in the following decision process. This is also confirmed by our experiments in Section 6.1, as our approach improves the results of DMAS/EM more on cases with tighter resource constraints.

5.3 Complexity Analysis

The complexity of our modified RCPSP algorithm in Section 4.1 is $O\left(J_i^2(G+L_i)d^*_i\right)$, where $d^*_i = \max\{d_{i1},...,d_{iJ_i}\}$. For Algorithm 2, the worst-case complexity of calculating activity slackness is $O(J_i^2)$, hence the worst-case complexity of Algorithm 2 is $O(J_i^2\sigma_i)$, where $\sigma_i = \max\{(G+L_i)d^*_iT, J_i\}$. For the WDP algoritm, the complexity to calculate Equation (14) is $O(GT)$, hence the worst-case complexity of this algorithm is $O(N\omega)$, where $\omega = \max\{GT, \log N\}$.

If the scheduling horizon is too small, it is possible that some PAs cannot find a feasible solution for the bidding problem. Whenever this happens, the scheduling horizon can be extended. Here we assume the scheduling horizon is enough for all PAs to generate feasible multisets until Algorithm 1 terminates. Hence, the WDP algorithm can guarantee that at least one winner will be found in each round of auction. We denote the number of outer rounds between Line 2 and 12 of Algorithm 1 as N', the number of inner rounds between Line 7 and 12 in outer round n as m'_n, and the number of initial winners in outer round n as m_n. Based on the operations to $\overline{SS}$, $\overline{IW}$ and $\overline{US}$, we have $N' \leq N$, $m'_n \leq m_n$, and $\sum_{n=1}^{N'} m_n = N$. Hence, the total number of WDPs the MA needs to solve is $N' + \sum_{n=1}^{N'} m'_n \leq N' + N \leq 2N$. This means that in the worst-case scenario, Algorithm 1 terminates within $O(N)$ rounds of auctions. This upper bound on the number of auction rounds is usually much less than *i*Bundle. As shown in [17], in the worst case, the maximum number of auction rounds for *i*Bundle to terminate is proportional to the number of possible multiset for all the PAs, which grows exponentially with the number of items in the auctions.

Based on the above analysis, MA need to solve $2N$ WDPs at most, leading to a worst-case complexity of $O(N^2\omega)$. Assume a PA becomes an initial winner at outer round i, then in the worst case it needs to participate $i + m_i$ WDPs. Since $m_i \leq N - \sum_{n=1}^{i-1} m_n \leq N - (i-1)$, we have $i + m_i \leq N + 1$. Hence the worst-case complexity of a PA is $O(NJ_i^2\sigma_i)$.

6. EMPIRICAL EVALUATION

We test our approach on two problem sets. The first one contains all the 140 cases from MPSPLIB. To the best of our knowledge, this is the only public benchmark of DRCMPSP. We compare our approach with state-of-the-art decentralized approaches DMAS/EM [24], DMAS/ABN [1], and a centralized approach SASP on this problem set. We also compare our approach with the other combinatorial auction based approach in [4] (denoted as Confessore's). Since this approach can only handle one single-unit global resource, we conduct experiments on the second problem set, which is generated from MPSPLIB by replacing the multi-unit global resources in each case with one single-unit global resources.

6.1 Experiments on the First Problem Set

In this section, we describe the experiments on the first problem set. The 140 cases from MPSPLIB are divided into 20 subsets named as "MP_J_N", where $J \in \{30, 90, 120\}$ is the number of activities per project, and $N \in \{2, 5, 10, 20\}$ is the number of projects. Thus the largest cases contain $20 \times 120 = 2400$ activities. Each case contains 4 resource

Table 1: Comparison with other approaches

Subset	Our Approach	DMAS/EM	DMAS/ABN	SASP
MP_30_2	13.6	**8.9**	15.9	22.4
MP_90_2	**6**	6.6	9.9	18.5
MP_120_2	**50.6**	59.4	67.2	69.1
MP_30_5	19.76	**17**	21.2	31.9
MP_90_5	10.72	**4.6**	11	23.8
MP_120_5	**45.92**	54.2	66.48	71.9
MP_30_10	**55.78**	66.4	87.5	90.2
MP_90_10	**39.02**	50.9	46.08	65
MP_120_10	**107.14**	119.6	130.96	139.6
MP_30_20	**116.1**	138	207.96	185.5
MP_90_20	**20.95**	27.4	30.22	48.6
MP_120_20	**24.27**	28.6	37.18	61.1
MP_90_2AC	**108.15**	126	144.15	158.6
MP_120_2AC	**37.75**	52.4	47	56.7
MP_90_5AC	**249.42**	284.6	384.08	404.6
MP_120_5AC	**181.3**	233.5	291.44	258.8
MP_90_10AC	**175.23**	223.3	313.33	283.9
MP_120_10AC	**103.74**	169.4	171.54	181
MP_90_20AC	**94.05**	126.7	146.37	161.8
MP_120_20AC	**163.36**	280.7	297.39	297.4

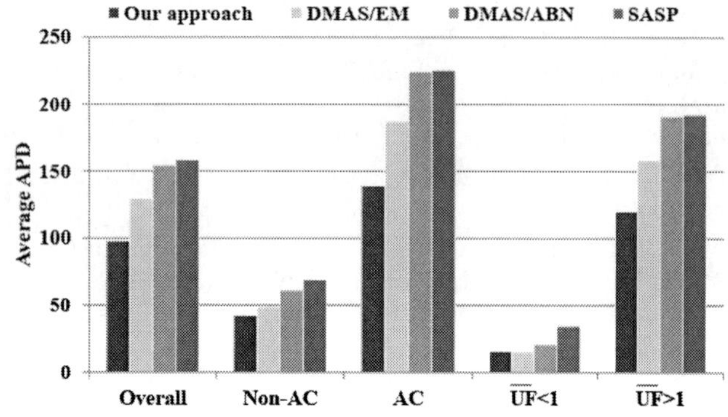

Figure 2: Comparison of average APD

per project, and the number of global resource G in each case is chosen between 1 and 4. The cases with no local resource, i.e. $G = 4$, are called "Agent Cooperation" cases, and a postfix "AC" is added to the subset names. Each AC subset contains 10 cases, while each non-AC subset contains 5 cases. To measure the tightness of global resource constraints, a Utilization Factor (UF) [7] value is calculated for each case. $UF < 1$ indicates a low to medium resource constraint, while $UF > 1$ indicates a medium to high constraint [14]. Average UF value $\overline{UF}$ of each subset can be found in [7]. In general, AC subsets have higher $\overline{UF}$ than non-AC subsets given the same N and J, which makes AC subsets harder to solve.

6.1.1 Performance Comparison

Our approach is implemented using Java 1.8, and runs on a single Intel Xeon Workstation (3.5GHz, 16GB). We set the scheduling horizon $T = 1500$ for all the cases. All the 140 cases are successfully solved within a total time of 170 seconds. We calculate the average APD of each subset in Table 1, where the best results are marked as bold. Among the 20 subsets, our approach outperforms other approaches in 17 subsets. For MP_120_20AC, one of the most complex subset with the tightest resource constraints, our approach outperforms DMAS/EM by 41.8%.

To evaluate the performance of our approach in different types of subsets, we first split the problem subsets into two groups consist of only non-AC and AC cases, and calculate the average APD obtained by the four approaches. Then

Table 2: Comparison with DMAS/EM

Type	Overall	Non-AC	AC	$\overline{UF} < 1$	$\overline{UF} > 1$
Our approach	**97.71**	**42.49**	**139.13**	15.88	**120.03**
DMAS/EM	129.89	48.47	187.08	**15.52**	158.26
Difference (%)	-24.77	-12.34	-25.63	2.32	-24.15

Table 3: Results with and without bid modification

Subset	Mod	NoMod	Subset	Mod	NoMod
MP30_2	**13.6**	13.7	MP90_20	**20.95**	21.28
MP90_2	6	**5.8**	MP120_20	**24.27**	24.39
MP120_2	**50.6**	50.7	MP90_2AC	**108.15**	108.35
MP30_5	19.76	**19.6**	MP120_2AC	**37.75**	38.3
MP90_5	**10.72**	11.2	MP90_5AC	**249.42**	249.72
MP120_5	**45.92**	46	MP120_5AC	**181.3**	181.76
MP30_10	55.78	**55.38**	MP90_10AC	**175.23**	175.75
MP90_10	**39.02**	39.34	MP120_10AC	**103.74**	104.6
MP120_10	**107.14**	108.24	MP90_20AC	**94.05**	95.29
MP30_20	**116.1**	117.38	MP120_20AC	**163.36**	163.56

we group the subsets according to if $\overline{UF} > 1$, and calculate the corresponding average APD. We plot these values along with the overall average APD of all the 140 cases in Figure 2. As presented, our approach produces the lowest average APD compared with other three approaches. Moreover, our approach generates better results for three types of subsets non-AC, AC, and $\overline{UF} > 1$; for $\overline{UF} < 1$, our result is comparable with the best result obtained by DMAS/EM. In Table 2, we compare our approach with DMAS/EM, which produces the closest results to ours. As shown, overall our approach outperforms DMAS/EM by 24.77%. For the two harder groups AC and $\overline{UF} > 1$, our approach gives 25.63% and 24.15% improvements against DMAS/EM, respectively. In general, our approach generates results with lower APD compared to other three approaches, and performs better on harder subsets with tighter global resource constraints.

To show the effectiveness of bid modification, we compare our approach (Mod) with the modified one (NoMod) that replaces the bid modification in Line 9 of Algorithm 1 with bid generation. In Table 3, our approach with bid modification shows signs of improvement on the APD in 17 out of 20 subsets, and has better results in all AC subsets. A possible reason for the marginal improvement is that the bids generated by our method already could provide effective information for allocating global resources, hence the room for bid modification to further improve the results is limited. Since Algorithm 2 is efficient, bid modification does not affect the scalability of this approach.

6.1.2 Scalability Evaluation

We evaluate the scalability of our approach according to the total time for solving one case, since it is simulated on a single computer. Since d_i^* and $G + L_i$ are constants in all the cases of MPSPLIB and T is fixed, the worst-case complexity of the MA and PA are $O(N^2 \log N)$ and $O(NJ_i^3)$. Thus, if Algorithm 1 runs on a single thread, the worst-case complexity to generate a solution is $O(N^2 \max\{\log N, J^{*3}\})$, where $J^* = \max\{J_1, ..., J_N\}$. We plot the average execution time against N and J^* in Figure 3, by fixing one parameter and increasing the other. The time increasing trends in Figure 3 are compatible with our complexity analysis and show that our approach can efficiently solve large problem cases with thousands of activities from tens of projects.

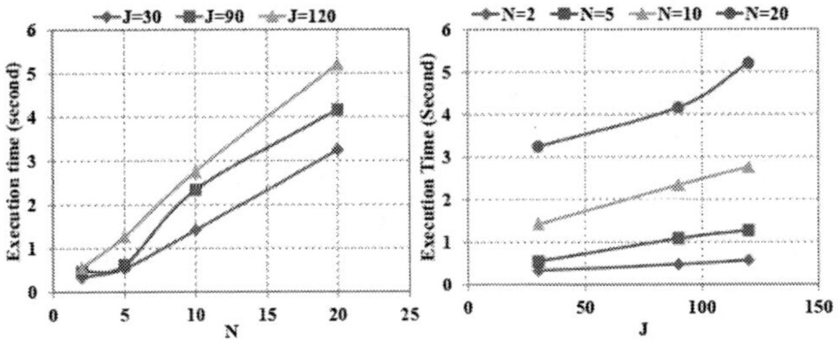

Figure 3: Execution time on MPSPLIB cases: (left) fix J^*, and (right) fix N

Table 4: Number of cases solved by Confessore's approach for each subset of the second problem set

Subset	Total	Solved	Ratio(%)	Subset	Total	Solved	Ratio(%)
MP30_2	5	5	100	MP30_10	5	4	80
MP90_2	15	15	100	MP90_10	15	10	67
MP120_2	15	15	100	MP120_10	15	14	93
MP30_5	5	5	100	MP30_20	5	4	80
MP90_5	15	12	80	MP90_20	15	3	20
MP120_5	15	14	93	MP120_20	15	9	60

6.2 Experiments on the Second Problem Set

In this section, we describe the experiments on the second problem set, which contains 140 cases generated from the MPSPLIB. More specifically, for each case in MPSPLIB, we first keep the global resource that has the minimum capacity and remove other ones, and then replace the capacity and requirements of each activity on that resource with 1. We classify the newly generated cases based on the number of activities and projects, hence 12 subsets can be obtained.

6.2.1 *Performance Comparison*

We implement Confessore's approach using Java 1.8, and run both Confessore's and our approach on the same workstation as in the previous section. During experimentation, we observe that Confessore's approach cannot converge on some cases, hence we limit the maximum iterations of this approach to 3000. The scheduling horizon T is set to 15000. All the 140 cases in this problem set are successfully solved by our approach within 730 seconds, while Confessore's approach can solve 79% (110/140) of all cases in about 15 hours. We list the number of cases solved by Confessore's approach for each subset in Table 4. From this table, we can further conclude that when the number of projects is 2, 5, 10, 20, Confessore's approach can solve 100%, 88.6%, 80%, 46% of the cases, respectively. This indicates that Confessore's approach may not be able to solve large cases where tens of projects are involved. In the following evaluation, we only consider those cases that are solved by both approaches.

We then evaluate the solution quality of these two approaches by calculating the average APD of each subset in Table 5, which shows that our approach consistantly achieves lower APD on all the subsets, and the improvement tends to increase on harder cases with more activities and projects.

6.2.2 *Scalability Comparison*

To compare the scalability of our approach and Confessore's approach, we calculate the average execution time and the number of total WDPs regarding the project number N. As shown in Figure 4 (vertical axes are in log scale), both the execution time and number of WDPs of our approach are much smaller than those of Confessore's approach. When N is larger than 10, our approach can be two orders of magnitude faster. These results clearly show that our approach is computationally frugal, and can efficiently solve large cases where tens of projects are involved.

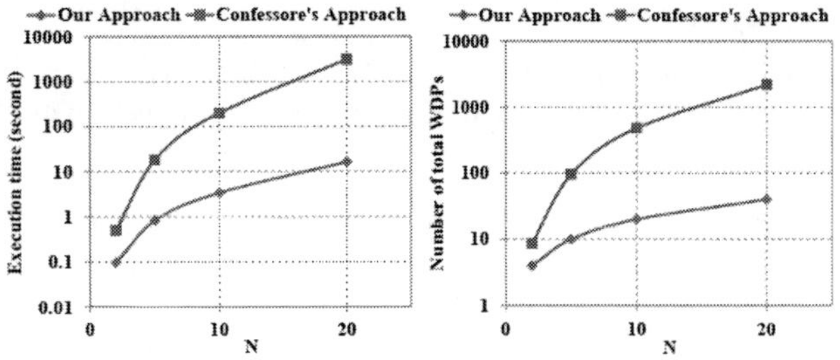

Figure 4: Scalability comparison on the second problem set with Confessore's approach

Table 5: Comparison with respect to problem subset of the second problem set

Subset	Our Approach	Confessore's Approach	Diff(%)
MP30_2	**106.4**	122.8	-13.36
MP90_2	**354.27**	393.7	-10.02
MP120_2	**362.2**	439.6	-17.61
MP30_5	**167.28**	279.8	-40.21
MP90_5	**641.02**	869.67	-26.29
MP120_5	**993.36**	1281.24	-22.47
MP30_10	**393.3**	667.08	-41.04
MP90_10	**1504.75**	2111.3	-28.73
MP120_10	**1564.11**	2360.66	-33.74
MP30_20	**937.39**	1540.06	-39.13
MP90_20	**1591.27**	2800.17	-43.17
MP120_20	**3037.74**	5075.11	-40.14

7. CONCLUSION AND FUTURE WORK

In conclusion, this paper presents a novel decentralized approach for solving DRCMPSP based on multi-unit combinatorial auction. It does not require private information of projects, and can efficiently find solutions with much lower average project delay than state-of-the-art decentralized approaches. As our approach runs in polynomial time for all agents, it can easily scale to large problems with thousands of activities from tens of projects.

Though the model of DRCMPSP is general enough to describe a large class of decentralized scheduling problems, some real-world problems could be more complex (e.g. with hierarchical activity structure and additional constraints between global resources). For future work, we will extend our approach to handle these new problems. Experimental results show that our approach has good allocation efficiency. However, incentive compatibility remains an unsolved issue. It is of great importance to provide incentives for self-interested agents to provide truthful information, especially in a decentralized environment. Thus, another future research direction for us is to address this issue.

Acknowledgments

This work was conducted within the Rolls-Royce@NTU Corporate Lab with support from the National Research Foundation (NRF) Singapore under the CorpLab@University Scheme.

REFERENCES

[1] S. Adhau, M. Mittal, and A. Mittal. A multi-agent system for distributed multi-project scheduling: An auction-based negotiation approach. *Engineering Applications of Artificial Intelligence*, 25(8):1738–1751, 2012.

[2] O. Amir, G. Sharon, and R. Stern. Multi-agent pathfinding as a combinatorial auction. In *Proceedings of the Twenty-Ninth AAAI Conference on Artificial Intelligence (AAAI'15)*, pages 2003–2009, 2015.

[3] J. Blazewicz, J. K. Lenstra, and A. R. Kan. Scheduling subject to resource constraints: classification and complexity. *Discrete Applied Mathematics*, 5(1):11–24, 1983.

[4] G. Confessore, S. Giordani, and S. Rismondo. A market-based multi-agent system model for decentralized multi-project scheduling. *Annals of Operations Research*, 150(1):115–135, 2007.

[5] A. Fink and J. Homberger. Decentralized multi-project scheduling. In *Handbook on Project Management and Scheduling Vol. 2*, pages 685–706. Springer, 2015.

[6] R. Gonen and D. Lehmann. Optimal solutions for multi-unit combinatorial auctions: Branch and bound heuristics. In *Proceedings of the 2nd ACM conference on Electronic Commerce (EC'00)*, pages 13–20, 2000.

[7] J. Homberger. A (μ, λ)-coordination mechanism for agent-based multi-project scheduling. *OR Spectrum*, 34(1):107–132, 2012.

[8] R. Kolisch. Serial and parallel resource-constrained project scheduling methods revisited: Theory and computation. *European Journal of Operational Research*, 90(2):320–333, 1996.

[9] P. Krysta, O. Telelis, and C. Ventre. Mechanisms for multi-unit combinatorial auctions with a few distinct goods. In *Proceedings of the 2013 International Conference on Autonomous Agents and Multi-Agent Systems (AAMAS'13)*, pages 691–698, 2013.

[10] I. Kurtulus and E. Davis. Multi-project scheduling: Categorization of heuristic rules performance. *Management Science*, 28(2):161–172, 1982.

[11] E. Kutanoglu and S. D. Wu. On combinatorial auction and lagrangean relaxation for distributed resource scheduling. *IIE transactions*, 31(9):813–826, 1999.

[12] J. S. Lau, G. Q. Huang, K.-L. Mak, and L. Liang. Agent-based modeling of supply chains for distributed scheduling. *Systems, Man and Cybernetics, Part A: Systems and Humans, IEEE Transactions on*, 36(5):847–861, 2006.

[13] D. Lehmann, L. I. Oćallaghan, and Y. Shoham. Truth revelation in approximately efficient combinatorial auctions. *Journal of the ACM*, 49(5):577–602, 2002.

[14] A. Lova and P. Tormos. Analysis of scheduling schemes and heuristic rules performance in resource-constrained multiproject scheduling. *Annals of Operations Research*, 102(1-4):263–286, 2001.

[15] X. Mao, N. Roos, and A. Salden. Stable multi-project scheduling of airport ground handling services by heterogeneous agents. In *Proceedings of The 8th International Conference on Autonomous Agents and Multi-Agent Systems (AAMAS'09)-Volume 1*, pages 537–544, 2009.

[16] K. Neumann, C. Schwindt, and J. Zimmermann. *Project scheduling with time windows and scarce resources: temporal and resource-constrained project scheduling with regular and nonregular objective functions*. Springer Science & Business Media, 2003.

[17] D. C. Parkes and L. H. Ungar. Iterative combinatorial auctions: Theory and practice. In *Proceedings of the 17th National Conference on Artificial Intelligence (AAAI'00)*, pages 74–81, 2000.

[18] D. C. Parkes and L. H. Ungar. An auction-based method for decentralized train scheduling. In *Proceedings of the 5th International Conference on Autonomous Agents (AAMAS'01)*, pages 43–50, 2001.

[19] T. Sandholm, S. Suri, A. Gilpin, and D. Levine. Winner determination in combinatorial auction generalizations. In *Proceedings of the First International Joint Conference on Autonomous Agents and Multi-Agent Svystems (AAMAS'02)*, pages 69–76, 2002.

[20] A. Stranjak, P. S. Dutta, M. Ebden, A. Rogers, and P. Vytelingum. A multi-agent simulation system for prediction and scheduling of aero engine overhaul. In *Proceedings of the 7th International Joint Conference on Autonomous Agents and Multiagent Systems (AAMAS'08): Industrial Track*, pages 81–88, 2008.

[21] W. E. Walsh and M. P. Wellman. Decentralized supply chain formation: A market protocol and competitive equilibrium analysis. *Journal of Artificial Intelligence Research*, pages 513–567, 2003.

[22] M. P. Wellman, W. E. Walsh, P. R. Wurman, and J. K. MacKie-Mason. Auction protocols for decentralized scheduling. *Games and economic behavior*, 35(1):271–303, 2001.

[23] H. Xi, C. K. Goh, P. S. Dutta, M. Sha, and J. Zhang. An agent-based simulation system for dynamic project scheduling and online disruption resolving. In *Proceedings of the 2015 International Conference on Autonomous Agents and Multiagent Systems (AAMAS'15)*, pages 1759–1760, 2015.

[24] Z. Zheng, Z. Guo, Y. Zhu, and X. Zhang. A critical chains based distributed multi-project scheduling approach. *Neurocomputing*, 143:282–293, 2014.

Modeling Autobiographical Memory in Human-Like Autonomous Agents

Di Wang[1], Ah-Hwee Tan[2] and Chunyan Miao[1,2]
[1]Joint NTU-UBC Research Centre of Excellence in Active Living for the Elderly (LILY) and
[2]School of Computer Engineering
Nanyang Technological University, 50 Nanyang Avenue, Singapore 639798
{wangdi,asahtan,ascymiao}@ntu.edu.sg

ABSTRACT

Although autobiographical memory is an important part of the human mind, there has been little effort on modeling autobiographical memory in autonomous agents. With the motivation of developing human-like intelligence, in this paper, we delineate our approach to enable an agent to maintain memories of its own and to wander in mind. Our model, named Autobiographical Memory-Adaptive Resonance Theory network (AM-ART), is designed to capture autobiographical memories, comprising pictorial snapshots of one's life experiences together with the associated context, namely time, location, people, activity, and emotion. In terms of both network structure and dynamics, AM-ART coincides with the autobiographical memory model established by the psychologists, which has been supported by neural imaging evidence. Specifically, the bottom-up memory search and the top-down memory readout operations of AM-ART replicate how the brain encodes and retrieves autobiographical memories. Furthermore, the wandering in reminiscence function of AM-ART mimics how human wanders in mind. For evaluations, we conducted experiments on a data set collected from the public domain to test the performance of AM-ART in response to exact, partial, and noisy memory retrieval cues. Moreover, our statistical analysis shows that AM-ART can simulate the phenomenon of wandering in reminiscence.

Categories and Subject Descriptors

I.2.0 [**ARTIFICIAL INTELLIGENCE**]: General—*Cognitive simulation*; I.2.11 [**ARTIFICIAL INTELLIGENCE**]: Distributed Artificial Intelligence—*Intelligent agents*

General Terms

Algorithms, Experimentation

Keywords

Cognitive model, Computational autobiographical memory model, Memory storage and retrieval, Wander in reminiscence

1. INTRODUCTION

Autobiographical memory is "a system that encodes, stores and guides retrieval of all episodic information related to our personal experiences" [4]. Although autobiographical memory is an important part of the human mind, there has been little effort on modeling autobiographical memory in autonomous agents. With the motivation of developing human-like intelligence, in this paper, we delineate our approach to enable an agent to encode and retrieve the autobiographical memories and to wander in reminiscence. Reminiscence, often being investigated as a function of autobiographical memory, plays a critical role in self-acceptance and self-change [4]. In this paper, we refer to *wandering in reminiscence* as recalling a sequence of contextually connected autobiographical memory across different episodes of life events. This is the typical objective of reminiscence therapies often being used with senior citizens to improve their psychological and cognitive well-being [16].

The main focus of our paper is to show how our agent can encode and retrieve autobiographical memory (**AM**) like human brains do [7], especially when dealing with noisy retrieval cues. Moreover, our agent can emulate the wandering in reminiscence effect by retrieving contextually connected memories across episodes of events. To the best of our knowledge, our model is the first research that simulates the phenomenon of wandering in autobiographical memories. Our agent is web-based, which allows users to upload their memories and even to import memories from popular online social networks, such as Facebook. A preliminary demonstration prototype of our AM agent has been described in [29]. In this paper, we present the detailed design and the dynamics of our computational AM model and show how it can be considered as human-like.

Our model, named Autobiographical Memory-Adaptive Resonance Theory network (**AM-ART**), follows the hierarchical structure of the AM model established by psychologists [7], which has been supported by neural imaging evidence [1]. More importantly, the dynamics of AM-ART coincide with the three stages of the generative memory retrieval process identified in [7]. AM-ART adopts the dynamics of a self-organizing neural network named fusion ART [24], but extends the network structure to a three-level hierarchy. The bottom layer of AM-ART encodes event-specific knowledge comprising 5W1H, namely time (when), location (where), people (who), activity (what), imagery (which), and emotion (how). The middle layer encodes events by associating the event-specific knowledge and the top layer encodes episodes by associating related events. Memory retrieval in AM-ART first takes place in the bottom layer, where the retrieval cue is presented. By following the bottom-up memory search procedure, the corresponding event and episode can be identified in the middle and top layers, respectively. Consequently, we can retrieve them by performing the top-down memory readout procedure. One of the novel features of AM-ART is its capability to emulate human mind in wandering in reminiscence. Specifically, AM-ART can iteratively perform the gener-

Appears in: *Proceedings of the 15th International Conference on Autonomous Agents and Multiagent Systems (AAMAS 2016), J. Thangarajah, K. Tuyls, C. Jonker, S. Marsella (eds.), May 9–13, 2016, Singapore.*

ative retrieval of autobiographical memories by mutating the retrieval cue with regulated noise in each iteration.

Experiments have been conducted, wherein AM-ART is used to capture a person's autobiographical memory based on a data set collected from the public domain. After encoding the memories, we perform memory retrieval using three types of cues, namely exact, partial, and noisy ones. To demonstrate the advantage of AM-ART, we compare its performance against the standard keyword-based query method, which is employed by many existing photo or memory repositories and the recently proposed computational AM models (e.g., [12]). The comparisons show that AM-ART performs robust and flexible memory retrievals, especially in response to noisy cues. The ability to handle uncertainty is one of the key functionalities of our human brains, which has not been well catered by many existing photo or memory repositories. Furthermore, to evaluate the performance of AM-ART in wandering in reminiscence, we devise three measurement metrics, namely coverage, diversity, and relatedness. We compare the performance of AM-ART in different parameter settings against each other and two baseline retrieval methods, namely sequential retrieval and random retrieval. Moreover, we propose two null hypotheses that mind wandering simulated by AM-ART performs on the same level as the baseline methods. The statistical analysis of the results supports the rejection of both hypotheses and shows that AM-ART can emulate mind wandering in terms of recalling a sequence of contextually connected memory across different episodes covering a moderate subset of a person's autobiographical memory.

The rest of the paper is organized as follows. Section 2 reviews the related work. Section 3 introduces the psychological basis established by the psychologists, leading to the design of our computational AM model. Section 4 first presents the network structure of our AM model and discusses how it coincides with its psychological basis, and then introduces its dynamics with detailed formal definitions and algorithms. Section 5 introduces how our AM model emulates the wandering in reminiscence phenomenon. Section 6 presents the experimental results with visualizations and discussions. Section 7 concludes this paper and proposes future work.

2. RELATED WORK

Memory modules are always the important components of the various cognitive models. For example, cognitive models, such as Soar [13, 15], ACT-R [2], and Icarus [14], incorporate long-term memory modules besides short-term and/or working memory modules. Although the aforementioned cognitive models may not specify the exact types of the long-term memory modules they employ such as episodic [26], semantic [11], or autobiographical [21], a specific model of Soar [17] explicitly states its incorporation of an episodic memory module, which is mainly used to perform case-based reasoning by mining the stored historical data. In addition, a well-defined computational episodic memory model, which stands alone without connecting to other cognitive modules, is presented in [30]. It explicitly defines the formation, retrieval, and forgetting of the past events happened in a computer game. However, the model's usage is limited to the recall of historical data and it does not incorporate emotion [8] as one of the input fields, which is an important element in autobiographical memory [3].

Episodic memory and autobiographical memory are two closely related terms as both refer to memory collections of past events experienced by an individual. However, autobiographical memory can be considered as a special type of episodic memory containing a person's life long experience from a personal perspective [4]. Nonetheless, most existing computational episodic and autobiographical memory modules do not significantly differentiate from one another in terms of their usages and/or their representations. We identify our computational memory model as autobiographical because (a) it explicitly incorporates emotion [3] and (b) it focuses more on the cohesiveness or the connectedness among the retrieved memories. Connectedness is another criterion given in [9] to differentiate between the autobiographical and episodic memories.

Research work related to the autobiographical memory is emerging. The AM model, named Xapagy [5], is "designed to perform narrative reasoning, an activity roughly analogous to some of the mental processes humans perform with respect to stories". Xapagy is well-defined and incorporates complex natural language processing methods. However, its usage is limited to storytelling. Thudt, Baur, and Huron developed an online system to enable users to build visual mementos as a form of visualized AM based on their movement data, in the form of GPS coordinates and other context, for self-reflection and sharing experiences [25]. Pointeau, Petit, and Dominey stored the human-robot interactions as AM, by which a humanoid robot can accumulate its experience and extract regularities [19]. However, when retrieving the stored memories, all the three afore-reviewed AM models only invoke simple retrievals using the minimal amount of indexing knowledge. Specifically, they simply retrieve all memories [19], all memories of the particular user [25], or all memories comprising the selected verb [5]. Kope, Rose, and Katchabaw proposed a computational AM model using keyword-based queries for memory retrieval [12]. Taking input memories in the form of sentences describing the events happened in a game environment, their proposed model maintains a linked graph of all the parsed keywords, wherein the weights associated with the links represent the coexistence of the keyword pairs. Unlike all the computational AM models proposed in the literature, our computational AM model, named AM-ART, is designed to capture the memories comprising pictorial snapshots of one's life experience together with the associated context, namely time, location, people, activity, and emotion. It can retrieve encoded AM using different types of cues and emulate the wandering in reminiscence phenomenon of the human mind.

To the best of our knowledge, in the literature of both episodic and autobiographical memory models, there is no prior study focusing on the wandering phenomenon. Pavloski and Karimi made such an attempt to emulate the wandering effect in short- and long-term associative memories modeled by the self-trapping attractor neural network [18]. They refer wandering in their network to the mechanism of allowing "the sparsely connected network to wander to the vicinity of attractors far from the initial state." In AM-ART, we refer wandering to the process of regulated memory retrievals wherein the subsequent memories are retrieved based on highly similar but randomly mutated cues.

3. PSYCHOLOGICAL BASIS OF AM-ART

Among the various AM models established by the psychologists, the one presented by Conway and Pleydell-Pearce [7] has been accepted widely in the academic world. They categorized autobiographical memory knowledge into three levels, namely *lifetime periods*, *general events*, and *event-specific knowledge* (from general to specific, see Figure 1). Furthermore, they proposed that autobiographical memories can be directly accessed if the cues are specific and personally relevant. On the other hand, if the cues are general, a *generative retrieval* process must be engaged to produce more specific cues for the retrieval of relevant memories. The main difference between the direct and generative retrieval is that "the search process is modulated by control processes in generative retrieval but not, or not so extensively, in direct retrieval" [7]. This difference between the two types of memory retrieval is supported

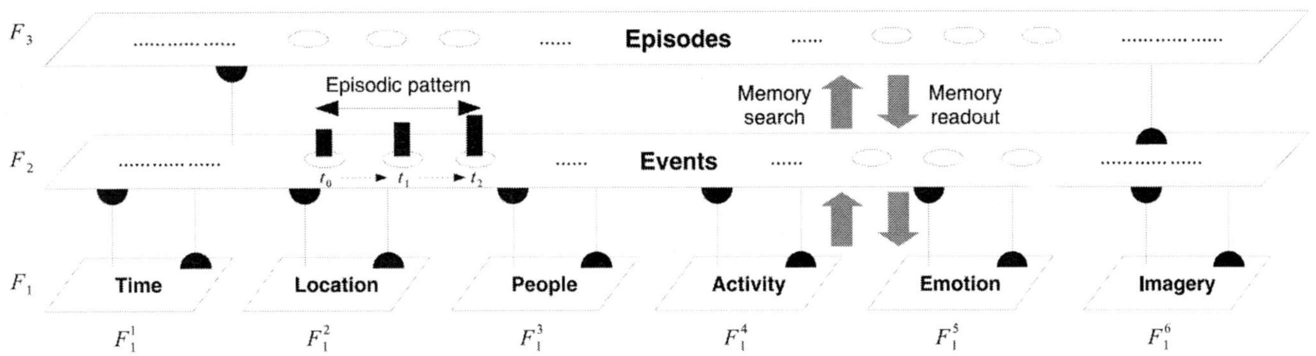

Figure 2: Network structure of AM-ART.

Table 1: Operations applied in AM-ART to realize the three stages of generative autobiographical memory retrieval.

#	Stage	Description given in [7]	AM-ART operations
1	Elaboration	"The elaboration of a cue with which to search memory and the simultaneous setting of verification criteria."	Template masking, mutation (See Algorithm 3), and setting of the vigilance parameters (see (3))
2	Strategic search	"Matching the description to records in memory."	Code activation and code competition
3	Evaluation	"Records accessed in memory were assessed against the verification criteria."	Template matching

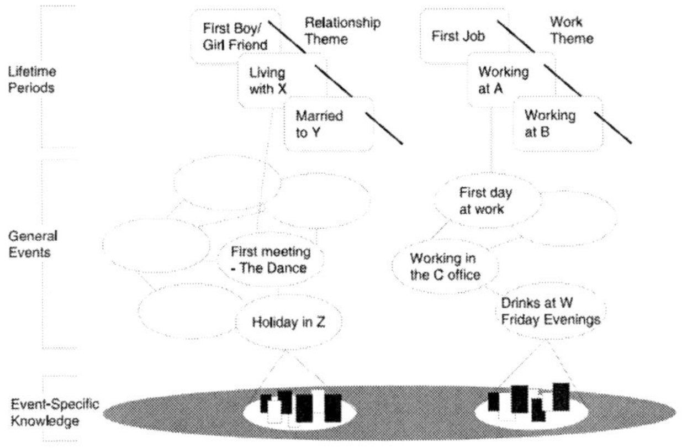

Figure 1: Illustration of the autobiographical memory hierarchy. This figure replicates Figure 1 presented in [7].

by neural imaging evidence that we can observe the difference in various regions of the brain, such as left parahippocampal gyrus, left medial prefrontal cortex, left inferior frontal gyrus, left medial parietal cortex, and left hippocampus/entorhinal cortex [1]. These established neural-psychology theories serve as the design principles of our computational autobiographical memory model.

4. AM-ART MODEL AND ITS DYNAMICS

The network structure of our computational Autobiographical Memory-Adaptive Resonance Theory (AM-ART) model is shown in Figure 2. AM-ART is a three-layer neural network that in the top-down order, its F_3, F_2, and F_1 layers encode *lifetime periods, general events*, and *event-specific knowledge*, respectively. The structure of AM-ART is consistent with the hierarchical model established by Conway and Pleydell-Pearce (see Figure 1), which serves as the theoretical basis of AM-ART. Following the examples given in Figure 1, we can highlight the correspondence between the two models. The life experience of "working at A" can be represented as a code (learned episode) in F_3 of AM-ART. The associated events of that episode, namely "first day at work", "working in the C office", and "drinks at W Friday evenings", can be represented as codes (learned events) in F_2. A specific event, taking "drinks at W Friday evenings" as an example, can be read out in F_1 that on Friday night (time), at W (location), with colleagues (people), drinking (activity), feeling happy (emotion), together with the pictorial memory (imagery).

Furthermore, memory retrieval in AM-ART replicates the three stages of the generative memory retrieval presented in [7], namely the *elaboration stage*, *strategic search stage*, and *evaluation stage*. The operations applied in AM-ART to realize the three stages of the generative memory retrieval are summarized in Table 1.

AM-ART extends the network structure of the fusion ART model [24], which is a generic self-organizing neural network comprising two layers of neural fields connected by bidirectional conditional links. However, the same bottom-up search and top-down readout operations between the layers still apply in AM-ART.

4.1 Dynamics of Fusion ART

With reference to the F_1 (comprising of six input fields) and F_2 (comprising of one association field) layers shown in Figure 2, we introduce the dynamics of fusion ART as follows.

Input vectors: Let $\mathbf{I}^k = (I_1^k, I_2^k, \ldots, I_L^k)$ denote an input vector, where I_i^k denotes the input i to channel k, for $i = 1, 2, \ldots, L$ and $k = 1, 2, \ldots, N$, where L denotes the length of channel k and N denotes the number of channels.

Input fields: Let F_1^k denote an input field that holds the input pattern for channel k. Let $\mathbf{x}^k = (x_1^k, x_2^k, \ldots, x_L^k)$ denote the activation vector of F_1^k receiving $\mathbf{I}^k$, where $x_i^k \in [0, 1]$. To prevent code proliferation when using fuzzy operations (see (1) and (4)), complement coding is applied that each $\mathbf{x}^k$ is augmented with a complement vector $\overline{\mathbf{x}}^k$ such that $\overline{x}_i^k = 1 - x_i^k$ [6]. Readers may refer to [28] for a more detailed description of complement coding.

Association field: Let $\mathbf{y} = \{\mathbf{y}_1, \mathbf{y}_2, \ldots, \mathbf{y}_C\}$ denote the activation vector of F_2, where C denotes the number of codes in F_2.

Weight vectors: Let $\mathbf{w}_j^k$ denote the weight vector of the jth code in F_2 for learning the input pattern in F_1^k.

Parameters: The dynamics of fusion ART are regulated by the parameters associated with all the input fields in the lower layer, namely choice parameters $\alpha^k > 0$, learning rate parameters $\beta^k \in [0, 1]$, contribution parameters $\gamma^k \in [0, 1]$, where $\sum \gamma^k = 1$, and vigilance parameters $\rho^k \in [0, 1]$.

Code activation: A bottom-up knowledge search starts from the computation of the activations (choice function values) for all codes in F_2. Specifically, given $\mathbf{x}^k$, for each F_2 code j, the choice function T_j is computed as follows:

$$T_j = \sum_k \gamma^k \frac{|\mathbf{x}^k \wedge \mathbf{w}_j^k|}{\alpha^k + |\mathbf{w}_j^k|}, \tag{1}$$

where the fuzzy AND operation $\wedge$ is defined by $p_i \wedge q_i \equiv min(p_i, q_i)$ and the norm $|.|$ is defined by $|\mathbf{p}| \equiv \sum_i p_i$.

Code competition: A code competition process follows under which the F_2 code with the highest choice function value is identified. The winner is indexed at J, where

$$T_J = \arg\max\{T_j : \text{for all } F_2 \text{ code } j\}. \tag{2}$$

Template matching: A template matching process checks whether resonance occurs at the chosen code J. Specifically, resonance occurs if for each channel k, the match function m_J^k meets its vigilance criterion, such that

$$m_J^k = \frac{|\mathbf{x}^k \wedge \mathbf{w}_J^k|}{|\mathbf{x}^k|} \geq \rho^k. \tag{3}$$

If any vigilance constraint is violated, mismatch reset occurs in which T_J is set to 0 for the duration of the input presentation. Thus, another F_2 code will be selected as the new winner. This search and evaluation process is guaranteed to end, because either a committed code that satisfies the vigilance criteria will be identified or an uncommitted one (all weight values initialized to 1, which definitely satisfies the criteria) will be recruited to encode the new input pattern. Once an uncommitted code is recruited, a new uncommitted code will be autonomously added in F_2. Thus, the fusion ART model self-organizes its network structure.

Template learning: Once the code J is identified as wherein resonance occurs, for each channel k, the weight vector $\mathbf{w}_J^k$ can be updated by the following learning rule:

$$\mathbf{w}_J^{k(\text{new})} = (1 - \beta^k)\mathbf{w}_J^{k(\text{old})} + \beta^k(\mathbf{x}^k \wedge \mathbf{w}_J^{k(\text{old})}). \tag{4}$$

Knowledge readout: This top-down retrieval procedure is invoked when the chosen F_2 code J presents its weight vectors to the input fields in F_1, such that $\mathbf{x}^{k(\text{new})} = \mathbf{w}_J^k$.

Template masking: Due to the dynamics of fusion ART, not all input vectors have to be presented for knowledge retrieval [23]. In such cases, all the values of the absent vector $\mathbf{x}^k$ (including complements) are set to 1.

4.2 Encoding and Retrieval of Events

In AM-ART (see Figure 2), the input fields in F_1 encode the 5W1H, respectively. To make the activation vectors $\mathbf{x}^k$ compact and generic, we use normalized values to represent *time* and *location*. On the other hand, we use categorical values to present *people*, *activity*, *emotion*, and *imagery*.

Time vector $(\mathbf{x}^1)$**:** It represents *when* the event happened in terms of six values, namely the normalized day ($x_1^1 = I_1^1/31$), month ($x_2^1 = I_2^1/12$), and year ($x_3^1 = (I_3^1 - 1900)/200$), together with their complements.

Location vector $(\mathbf{x}^2)$**:** It represents *where* the event happened in terms of four values, namely the normalized latitude ($x_1^2 = (I_1^2 + 90)/180$)) and longitude ($x_2^2 = (I_2^2 + 180)/360$) ($\mathbf{I}^2$ denotes the input vector of location, which is determined via Google Geocoder API), together with their complements.

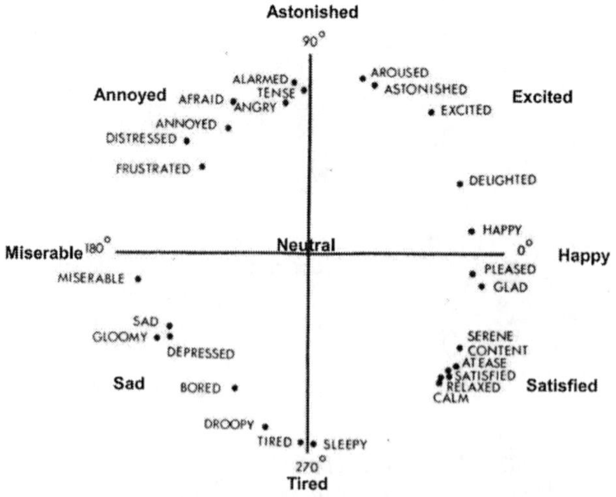

Figure 3: Categorization of emotion based on Russell's circumplex model of affect [22].

People vector $(\mathbf{x}^3)$**:** It is a binary-valued vector representing *who* were involved in the event. Its length corresponds to the categorization of people based on relationship.

Activity vector $(\mathbf{x}^4)$**:** It is a binary-valued vector representing *what* was the event. Similarly, its length corresponds to the categorization of activities.

Emotion vector $(\mathbf{x}^5)$**:** It is a binary-valued vector representing *how* was the feeling during the event. Emotion is an important component of our past experience, which affects the encoding and retrieval of autobiographical memories [3]. We categorize nine types of emotion, namely neutral, astonished, excited, happy, satisfied, tired, sad, miserable, and annoyed (see Figure 3). Thus, the length of x^5 is 18. This categorization follows the pleasure-arousal model established by Russell [22] and applied in [27].

Imagery vector $(\mathbf{x}^6)$**:** It is a binary-valued vector representing *which* pictorial memory was associated with the event. Its value encodes the file-path of the stored imagery. During memory retrieval, this vector is not presented along with the others as a part of the retrieval cue. Therefore, in Algorithms 3 and 4, only the first five input fields of F_1 (see Figure 2) are involved.

The F_2 layer of AM-ART encodes events. The procedure of event encoding and retrieval is shown in Algorithm 1.

Algorithm 1 Event encoding and retrieval

```
Encode x^k in F_1 w.r.t the given input pattern I^k
Activate all codes in F_2                                ▷ see (1)
repeat selecting the winner code J                       ▷ see (2)
until resonance occurs                                   ▷ see (3)
if encoding is required then perform learning            ▷ see (4)
end if
if retrieval is required then read out w_J^k in F_1
end if
```

4.3 Encoding and Retrieval of Episodes

Assume the related events of one episode happened at $t_0, t_1, \ldots, t_n$ and let y_{t_i} denote the activation value of the event happened at t_i. To encode the sequence of the events, we need to always hold the inequality that $y_{t_n} > y_{t_{n-1}} > \cdots > y_{t_0}$. Therefore, we use a decay parameter $\tau \in (0, 1)$ to regulate the activation decays, such that $y_j^{(\text{new})} = y_j^{(\text{old})}(1 - \tau)$ at each new time step.

The F_3 layer of AM-ART encodes episodes to associate the related events encoded in F_2. The procedure of episode encoding and retrieval is shown in Algorithm 2.

Algorithm 2 Episode encoding and retrieval

```
for all subsequent events of an episode do
    select the winner code J in F_2 w.r.t x^k in F_1
    y_J ← 1    ▷ or a predefined value if using partial sequence to identify the episode
    for all previously selected codes in F_2 do
        y_i^(new) ← y_i^(old) (1 − τ)
    end for
end for
Select the winner code J' in F_3 w.r.t y
if encoding is required then learn the weight vector w'_J' in F_3:
    w'_J'^(new) ← (1 − β_2) w'_J'^(old) + β_2 (y ∧ w'_J'^(old))
end if
if retrieval is required then read out w'_J' in F_2
end if
```

5. WANDER IN REMINISCENCE

In this section, we present how we enable AM-ART to wander in reminiscence. The wandering involves two major procedures, namely mutating the retrieval cue and iteratively retrieving autobiographical memories using a mutated cue in each iteration.

We show the procedure of mutating a retrieval cue in Algorithm 3, which is conceptually similar to mutate the chromosomes in genetic algorithms [10]. We can summarize the mutation procedure as that upon given a retrieval cue, we intentionally add regulated noise to it in the randomly determined positions. The mutation process is regulated by two parameters, namely mutation rate $T \in [0, 1]$ and noise level $L \in [0, 1]$. We use mutation rate T to control the probability on mutating the value of the retrieval cue in a certain field and use noise level L to control the amount of mutation.

Algorithm 3 Mutation of Memory Retrieval Cues

```
Given a memory retrieval cue: x = {x^1, x^2, ..., x^5}
for all x^i ∈ x do
    if rand() ≤ T then    ▷ the ith field is selected for mutation, where 0 ≤ rand() < 1
        for all x_j^i, where j = 1, 2, ..., |x^i|/2 do    ▷ |p| denotes the cardinality of vector p
            if i ≤ 2 && rand() ≤ 2/|x^i| then    ▷ for normalized vector, the jth value is selected for mutation
                x_j^i ← (1 + (rand() − 0.5)L) · x_j^i;
                bound x_j^i within the [0, 1] interval
            else if i ≥ 3 && rand() ≤ 2(1+L)/|x^i| then    ▷ for binary-valued vector
                negate the binary value of x_j^i
            end if
        end for
        for all x_j^i, where j = |x^i|/2 + 1, |x^i|/2 + 2, ..., |x^i| do
            x_j^i ← 1 − x_{j−|x^i|/2}^i    ▷ recompute the complements
        end for
    end if
end for
```

Table 2: List of AM-ART parameters used in experiments.

Parameter	Value	Description/Remark
Choice (α^k)	0.1	Mainly used to avoid having NaN in (1)
Learning rate (β^k)	1	Not in use during memory retrieval
Contribution (γ^k)	0.167	Equally assigned, such that $\sum \gamma^k = 1$
Vigilance (ρ^k)	1	Value varies in different retrieval settings, see Fig. 4; set to 0 during wandering, see Algo. 4
Decay rate (τ)	0.1	Used for encoding event sequence

We show how AM-ART wanders in reminiscence in Algorithm 4. We can summarize the wandering procedure as that upon given the memory retrieval cue at the beginning of each iteration, we first use the given cue to retrieve the most related event, which has not been included in the retrieved memory set, and then we append the retrieved event to the memory set and proceed to the next iteration with the mutated retrieval cue. The stopping criterion of Algorithm 4 is by retrieving a predefined number (N) of events, which is mainly set for experimental purposes. However, this criterion can be easily removed or modified for continuous retrieval.

Algorithm 4 Wandering in Reminiscence

```
Given a memory retrieval cue: x = {x^1, x^2, ..., x^5}
ρ^k ← 0, for k = 1, 2, ..., 6    ▷ remove all vigilance criteria during memory retrieval
M = ∅;    ▷ initialize the memory set
repeat
    repeat identify E in F_2 w.r.t x;    ▷ find winner event
        y_E ← 0    ▷ suppress its activation value
    until E ∉ M
    M ← M ∪ {E}    ▷ retrieving order preserved in M
    Mutate x    ▷ see Algorithm 3
until |M| = N
retrieve all events in M
```

6. EXPERIMENTS

To conduct experiments, we collected a data set comprising 53 snapshots of events, together with the corresponding context, of Mr. Obama, the current President of the USA. The 53 events are organized in twelve episodes, each of which contains three to seven events. Most of these photos are collected from Zimbio[1] and others via Google Images. From the online web pages, we directly extracted all features except emotion, which was manually derived from the picture and its context. It is important to note that the automated extraction of such contextual information is not the focus of this paper, but can be considered as a future extension to AM-ART.

According to the collected data set, we define eight types of relationship among people, namely family, neighbors, spouse, friends, classmates, colleagues, acquaintances, and strangers. Moreover, we define fifteen classes of activities, namely meal, leisure, travel, holiday, shopping, night-out, recreation, sports, exercise, work, gathering, party, celebration, wedding, and school. After formalizing the input vectors, we present the data samples to AM-ART to encode the 53 events in F_2 and the 12 episodes in F_3 (see Algorithms 1 and 2, respectively).

The parameters of AM-ART used in all experiments are listed in Table 2. Most such parameters take on a standard set of parameter values and all do not require tuning in the experiments.

[1]URL: http://www.zimbio.com/Barack+Obama/pictures/pro

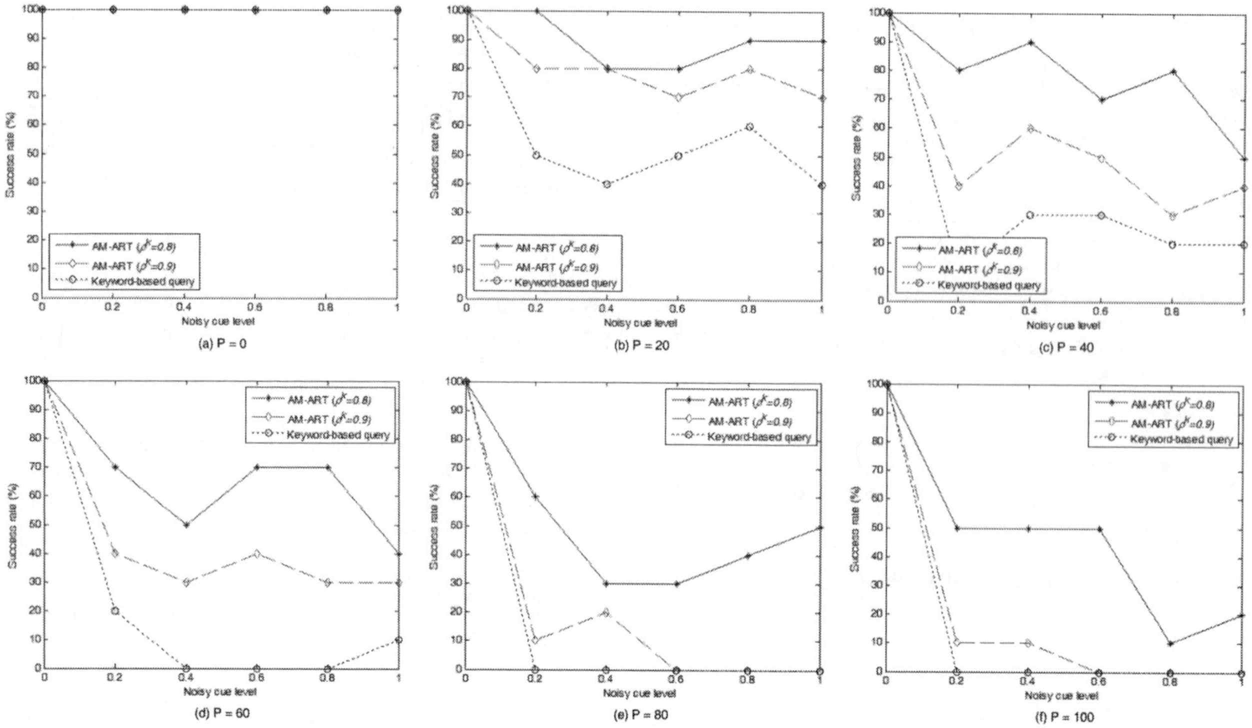

Figure 4: Success rates of memory retrievals by AM-ART and the keyword-based query method in response to noisy cues with different cue completeness percentile P and different noisy cue level L'.

6.1 Autobiographical Memory Retrieval Using Exact, Partial, and Noisy Cues

After AM-ART encodes the memories, we first test its performance in memory retrieval using the following three types of cues:

Exact cues: We randomly select an event from the data set and use its representation vector $\mathbf{x} = \{\mathbf{x}^1, \mathbf{x}^2, \ldots, \mathbf{x}^5\}$ (except the imagery path) as the *exact* retrieval cue.

Partial cues: Given an exact cue $\mathbf{x}$ and a cue completeness percentile P, in the *partial* cue $\mathbf{x}_P$, for each field k, where $k = 1, 2, \ldots, 5$, if $rand() \leq P/100$, $\mathbf{x}_P^k = \mathbf{x}^k$. Otherwise, $\mathbf{x}_P^k = \{1, \ldots, 1\}$. In ART models, a vector consisting of all 1s (including the complements) signifies do-not-care. When $P = 100$, $\mathbf{x}_P = \mathbf{x}$.

Noisy cues: Given a partial cue $\mathbf{x}_P$ and a noisy cue level L', in the selected fields of $\mathbf{x}_P$, where $\mathbf{x}_P^k \neq \{1, \ldots, 1\}$, we introduce noise to obtain the *noisy* cue $\mathbf{x}_N$. The process of introducing noise to a retrieval cue exactly follows the process from Step 4 to Step 13 described in Algorithm 3, wherein $L = L'$.

For the benchmarking method, we select the keyword-based query method, which is employed by many existing photo or memory repositories and the recently proposed computational AM models [12]. Its retrieval criterion is based on whether the given retrieval cues exactly match the corresponding portions of the stored records. In the context of this paper, a set of events will be retrieved after performing the keyword-based query in response to the given retrieval cue. If the event initially being used to generate the given cue can be found in the retrieved set, we consider the retrieval as a success. Otherwise, we consider it as a failure.

For AM-ART to handle the noisy cues, we can lower the vigilance parameters ρ^k. Actually, in the front-end of our online AM agent [29], we allow users to define the confidence level (which refers to ρ^k in the back-end) associated with any field of the retrieval cue they provide. In such a way, the users can retrieve certain memories even by providing imperfect cues. This feature is the major advantage of our agent over many other existing photo or memory repository type of applications. In response to the given retrieval cue, our AM-ART agent retrieves a set of memories and plays them back to the users. For fair comparisons, the judging criterion between a successful retrieval and a failure is the same as that of the keyword-based query method.

For each experiment, we repeat for ten times, wherein the retrieval cue is randomly selected or generated at each time, and we aggregate the results for further analysis.

Due to the way we use to generate partial cues and the criterion we adopt to count successful retrievals, both AM-ART and the keyword-based query method achieve 100% success rate in response to exact and partial retrieval cues. However, dealing with noisy cues is challenging because uncertainties can be well handled by our human brains but not by many computational models. The experimental results on memory retrievals in response to noisy cues are visualized in Figure 4. Please note that when $\rho^k = 1$, which means AM-ART requires exact matches, the performance of AM-ART is equivalent to that of the keyword-based query method.

The six sub-figures of Figure 4 show the success rates according to different values of the cue completeness percentile P. When $P = 0$, all models essentially retrieve all the events in the data set. Therefore, in Figure 4(a), all models achieve 100% success rate. As the value of P increases, the retrieval cue consists of an increasing number of input fields. Therefore, as expected, we observe that the performance of all models generally decline as the values of the cue completeness percentile P and the noisy cue level L' increase.

By comparing the performance of the AM-ART models against that of the keyword-based query as shown in Figure 4, AM-ART

Table 4: **A partial subsequence of the autobiographical memories retrieved by AM-ART (W22) during wandering.**

#	Time (when)	Location (where)	People (who)	Activity (what)	Emotion (how)	Event # of Episode #
Cue	**08-Jul-2014**	Honolulu, United States	**friends**	**night-out**	**happy**	randomly initialized
1	**08-Jul-2014**	Wynkoop Brewing Co.	**friends & acquaintances**	**night-out**	**happy**	Event #1 of Episode #5
2	**10-Dec-2014**	**Joint Base Anacostia-Bolling**	**friends & acquaintances & strangers**	**party**	**happy**	Event #3 of **Episode #10**
3	**10-Dec-2014**	**Joint Base Anacostia-Bolling**	**friends & acquaintances & strangers**	**party**	astonished	Event #1 of **Episode #10**
4	08-Jul-2014	Wynkoop Brewing Co.	**friends & acquaintances**	night-out	happy	Event #2 of Episode #5

*Associated values across consecutive retrievals are highlighted in **bold**. **Retrieved events #1 and #4 differ in their event imagery.

Figure 5: The imagery playback of the retrieved events following the order presented in Table 4.

Table 3: Naming conventions on the parameter settings.

Name	Setting (T, L)	Name	Setting (T, L)
S	Sequential retrieval	R	Random retrieval
WSS	Wandering (0.0, 0.0)	WRR	Wandering (1.0, 1.0)
W11	Wandering (0.2, 0.1)	W12	Wandering (0.2, 0.2)
W21	Wandering (0.4, 0.1)	W22	Wandering (0.4, 0.2)

clearly performs better in terms of the successful retrieval rate in response to noisy cues. This finding is encouraging because it suggests that by lowering its vigilance when handling the noisy cues, AM-ART can better deal with the uncertainty involved in the retrieval process, which is more towards the pursuit of human-like intelligence in terms of handling imperfect information.

6.2 Wandering in Reminiscence

As listed in Table 3, different value combinations of the mutation rate T and the noise level L (see Algorithm 3) are used in different settings for performance comparisons on wandering in reminiscence. We choose $T = 0.2$ or 0.4 such that during mutation, we can expect one or two fields of the cue to be mutated on average, respectively. We choose $L = 0.1$ or 0.2 to generate a reasonably small amount of noise during wandering. We also test the extreme cases (WSS and WRR), wherein T and L are set to the boundary values. The experimental results obtained using these parameter settings are compared against each other and against the two baselines, namely sequential retrieval by strictly retrieving memories according to the event encoding order during learning and random retrieval, wherein all (unique) memories are retrieved randomly.

In Table 4, we present a partial sequence of the memories (see Figure 5) retrieved by AM-ART during wandering in the W22 configuration. Table 4 well demonstrates that AM-ART wanders off Episode #5 (consisting of five events) to Episode #10 (consisting of seven events), but wanders back to Episode #5 after two steps.

We conducted series of experiments and in each run we retrieved N events (see Algorithm 4). In this paper, we set $N = 35$, which is around 2/3 of the total number of events (53) in the data set. To numerically evaluate the performance of AM-ART during wandering, we devise the following three measurement metrics, which are all normalized within the range of [0,1]. A higher value of each metric only indicates a better performance in the respective aspect.

Coverage C**:** It measures the distribution of the retrieved events among all the episodes. Let S_C denote the number of episodes, which have at least one event in the retrieved memory set $\mathbf{M}$, and $S_{C_{\min}}$ denote the minimum value of S_C, which can be determined by N and the composition of the data set in use. Thus, $C = (S_C - S_{C_{\min}})/(P - S_{C_{\min}})$, where P denotes the total number of episodes in the data set. For this data set, $P = 12$ and $S_{C_{\min}} = 8$.

Diversity D**:** It measures the diversity of the retrieved memories. Let $\mathbf{u} = \{u_1, u_2, \ldots, u_{N-1}\}$ denote a binary-valued vector to capture the relationship among the subsequently retrieved events in $\mathbf{M}$. For $k = 1, 2, \ldots, N-1$, if $\mathbf{M}_k$ and $\mathbf{M}_{k+1}$ are retrieved from different episodes, $u_k = 1$. Otherwise, $u_k = 0$. Similar to $S_{C_{\min}}$, $S_{D_{\min}}$ denoting the minimum number of 1s in $\mathbf{u}$ can be determined by N and the composition of the data set. Thus, $D = (H(\mathbf{u}) - S_{D_{\min}})/(N - 1 - S_{D_{\min}})$, where $H(\mathbf{u})$ computes the Hamming weight of $\mathbf{u}$. For this data set, $S_{D_{\min}} = 7$.

Relatedness R**:** It measures the relatedness of the subsequently retrieved memories. Let $\mathbf{v}_j = \{\mathbf{v}_j^1, \mathbf{v}_j^2, \ldots, \mathbf{v}_j^5\}$ denote the jth retrieved event in vector form (without complements), where $j = 1, 2, \ldots, N$. Moreover, let E_k, for $k = 1, 2, \ldots, N-1$, denote the Euclidean distance (dissimilarity) between $\mathbf{v}_j$ and $\mathbf{v}_{j+1}$. Thus, $R = (S_{R_{\max}} - \sum E_k)/S_{R_{\max}}$, where $S_{R_{\max}}$ denotes the maximum dissimilarity among all the retrieved memories. For this data set, we estimate $S_{R_{\max}}$ as follows. The length (without compliments) of the first five input fields (see Figure 2) is 2, 3, 8, 15, and 9, respectively. However, for activity and emotion vectors, one and only one bit is 1. Therefore, the maximum dissimilarity between any two consequent retrievals is $\sqrt{3 \cdot \sqrt{2} + \sqrt{3} + \sqrt{8}} \approx 8.8$. Thus, $S_{R_{\max}} = 34 \times 8.8 = 299.2$.

For fair comparisons, all experimental settings use the same randomly initialized cue to retrieve the first piece of autobiographical memory and each experiment is repeated for ten times for statistical analysis. To test whether AM-ART can simulate wandering in reminiscence, we propose the following two null hypotheses.

$\mathbf{H_{01}}$**:** The performance of AM-ART during wandering is at the same level as that of sequential memory retrieval.

$\mathbf{H_{02}}$**:** The performance of AM-ART during wandering is at the same level as that of random memory retrieval.

We visualize the averaged experimental results in Figure 6. Across the three sub-figures, it seems that the performance of typical wandering settings, namely W11, W12, W21, and W22, is always in the middle range and appears to be different from the rest. However, we need to perform statistical analysis for further investigations.

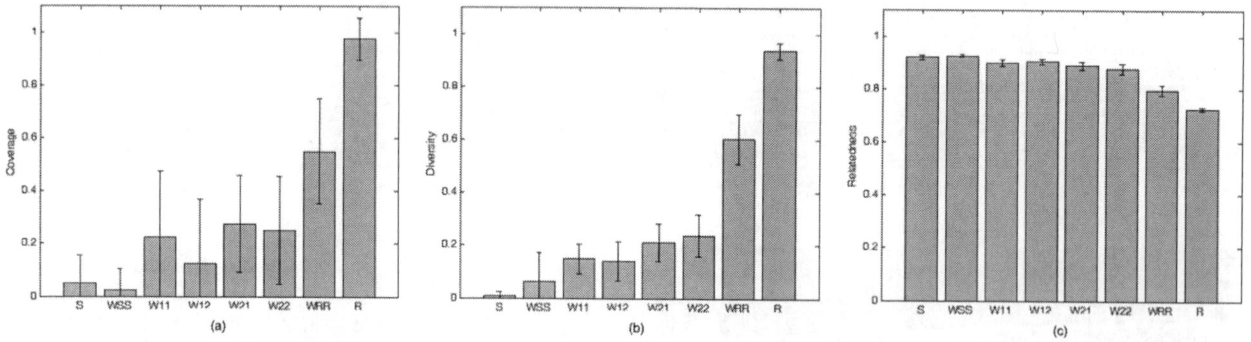

Figure 6: Performance comparisons of various configurations in terms of (a) Coverage C; (b) Diversity D; and (c) Relatedness R.

Table 5: Statistical analysis using two-tail p-values. If $p < 0.05$, the value is highlighted in bold.

Model	S			WSS			WRR			R		
	Cover.	Diver.	Relat.	Cover.	Diver.	Relat.	Cover.	Diver.	Relat.	Cover.	Surpr.	Relat.
W11	0.110	**<0.001**	**<0.001**	0.053	0.086	**<0.001**	**0.006**	**<0.001**	**<0.001**	**<0.001**	**<0.001**	**<0.001**
W12	0.279	**<0.001**	**<0.001**	0.104	0.110	**0.001**	**0.001**	**<0.001**	**<0.001**	**<0.001**	**<0.001**	**<0.001**
W21	**0.004**	**<0.001**	**<0.001**	**0.001**	**0.008**	**<0.001**	**0.003**	**<0.001**	**<0.001**	**<0.001**	**<0.001**	**<0.001**
W22	**0.022**	**<0.001**	**<0.001**	**0.010**	**0.007**	**<0.001**	**0.006**	**<0.001**	**<0.001**	**<0.001**	**<0.001**	**<0.001**

Table 6: Performance evaluation of the typical settings.

	W11	W12	W21	W22
A-mean of C, D, and R	0.424	0.390	**0.458**	0.454
G-mean of C, D, and R	0.311	0.252	**0.375**	0.373

*The highest value in each row is highlighted in **bold**.

Based on the statistical analysis results shown in Table 5, we observe that (a) all typical wandering settings behave significantly different from that of random memory retrievals (WRR and R) and (b) with mutation rate $T = 0.4$, the typical wandering settings behave significantly different from those of both sequential (S and WSS) and random memory retrievals. The latter finding is further supported in Table 6, wherein in terms of both arithmetic and geometric means, W21 and W22 perform better than W11 and W12.

In summary, with a mutation rate of $T = 0.4$, we can reject both $\mathbf{H_{01}}$ and $\mathbf{H_{02}}$ with a strong statistical support. Based on the various performance comparisons, we find that W21 configuration performs best among all the typical settings in terms of the overall measure (see Table 6) and it is truly different from both sequential and random retrievals (see Table 5). Therefore, we show that AM-ART in the W21 configuration effectively retrieves a moderate subset of an individual's autobiographical memory in a contextually connected sequence across multiple episodes and can simulate the phenomenon of wandering in reminiscence.

7. CONCLUSION

This paper has presented a computational model, named AM-ART, for the encoding and retrieval of autobiographical memories in online autonomous agents modeling users' life experiences. To the best of our knowledge, AM-ART is the first computational model simulating the mind wandering phenomenon in human autobiographical memories. The network structure and the dynamics of AM-ART follow the AM model established by psychologists [7], which has been supported by neural imaging evidence [1]. Specifically, the three-layer AM-ART structure coincides with the hierarchy of the AM model presented in [7] and the operations of AM-ART coincide with the retrieval mechanisms presented in [7]. In terms of memory retrieval in response to noisy cues, AM-ART is shown as performing better than the keyword-based query method, which cannot handle noisy cues in many existing photo or memory repositories. To evaluate the performance of AM-ART in wandering in reminiscence, we devise three measurement metrics, namely coverage, diversity, and relatedness. Statistical analysis of the experimental results shows that AM-ART can emulate mind wandering in terms of recalling a sequence of contextually connected memory across different episodes covering a moderate subset of a person's autobiographical memory.

One important feature of AM not discussed in this paper is that humans partially reconstruct their memories based on their internal mental states, such as self-intention, central concerns, or personal characteristics [4]. Therefore, one key direction of our future work is to introduce such factors into AM-ART to simulate the reconstruction of AM from the personal perspective. One possible approach is to experiment with different parameter values, including the mutation rate and the noise level, associated with each field representing the 5W1H according to the user's biases and preferences.

We show in this paper that AM-ART is designed in accordance to a well-established psychological basis and it can encode and retrieve real-life autobiographical memory, comprising pictorial snapshots of one's life experiences together with the associated context. However, the performance of AM-ART in wandering in reminiscence is only shown through a statistical analysis of the experimental results. Going forward, we shall conduct user studies on the human-likeness of the memory retrievals and whether the overall system can deliver enjoyment and desirably health improvement through memory playback [20].

Acknowledgments

We thank Wei-Xuan Huang for her contribution in data collection and system integration. This research is supported in part by the National Research Foundation Singapore under its Interactive Digital Media (IDM) Strategic Research Programme.

REFERENCES

[1] D. R. Addis, K. Knapp, R. P. Roberts, and D. L. Schacter. Routes to the past: Neural substrates of direct and generative autobiographical memory retrieval. *Neuroimage*, 59(3):2908–2922, 2012.

[2] J. R. Anderson, D. Bothell, M. D. Byrne, S. Douglass, C. Lebiere, and Y. Qin. An integrated theory of the mind. *Psychological Review*, 111:1036–1060, 2004.

[3] D. Berntsen and D. C. Rubin. Emotionally charged autobiographical memories across the life span: The recall of happy, sad, traumatic, and involuntary memories. *Psychology and Aging*, 17(4):636–652, 2002.

[4] S. Bluck and L. J. Levine. Reminiscence as autobiographical memory: A catalyst for reminiscence theory development. *Ageing and Society*, 18(2):185–208, 1998.

[5] L. Boloni. Integrating perception, narrative, premonition and confabulatory continuation. *Biologically Inspired Cognitive Architectures*, 8:120–131, 2014.

[6] G. A. Carpenter, S. Grossberg, and D. B. Rosen. Fuzzy ART: Fast stable learning and categorization of analog patterns by an adaptive resonance system. *Neural Networks*, 4(6):759–771, 1991.

[7] M. A. Conway and C. W. Pleydell-Pearce. The construction of autobiographical memories in the self-memory system. *Psychological Review*, 107(2):261–288, 2000.

[8] J. Dias and A. Paiva. Feeling and reasoning: A computational model for emotional characters. *Progress in artificial intelligence, Lecture Notes in Computer Science*, 3808:127–140, 2005.

[9] A. Gilboa. Autobiographical and episodic memory–one and the same? Evidence from prefrontal activation in neuroimaging studies. *Neuropsychologia*, 42(10):1336–1349, 2004.

[10] D. E. Goldberg. *Genetic Algorithms in Search, Optimization, and Machine Learning*. Addison-Wesley, 1989.

[11] J. Hart and M. A. Kraut, editors. *Neural Basis of Semantic Memory*. Cambridge University Press, 2007.

[12] A. Kope, C. Rose, and M. Katchabaw. Modeling autobiographical memory for believable agents. In *Proceedings of AAAI Conference on Artificial Intelligence and Interactive Digital Entertainment*, pages 23–29, 2013.

[13] J. E. Laird. *The Soar Cognitive Architecture*. MIT Press, 2012.

[14] P. Langley. Cognitive architectures and general intelligent systems. *AI Magazine*, 27:33–44, 2006.

[15] J. Li and J. Laird. Spontaneous retrieval from long-term memory for a cognitive architecture. In *Proceedings of AAAI Conference on Artificial Intelligence*, pages 544–550, 2015.

[16] Y.-C. Lin, Y.-T. Dai, and S.-L. Hwang. The effect of reminiscence on the elderly population: A systematic review. *Public Health Nursing*, 20(4):297–306, 2003.

[17] A. M. Nuxoll and J. E. Laird. Extending cognitive architecture with episodic memory. In *Proceedings of AAAI Conference on Artificial Intelligence*, pages 1560–1565, 2007.

[18] R. Pavloski and M. Karimi. Wandering mind: A self-trapping network can converge to attractors far from the initial state. In *Proceedings of International Joint Conference on Neural Networks*, pages 1168–1173, 2001.

[19] G. Pointeau, M. Petit, and P. F. Dominey. Successive developmental levels of autobiographical memory for learning through social interaction. *IEEE Transactions on Autonomous Mental Development*, 6(3):200–212, 2014.

[20] C. Routledge, T. Wildschut, C. Sedikides, and J. Juhl. Nostalgia as a resource for psychological health and well-being. *Social and Personality Psychology Compass*, 7(11):808–818, 2013.

[21] D. C. Rubin, editor. *Autobiographical Memory*. Cambridge University Press, 1988.

[22] J. A. Russell. A circumplex model of affect. *Journal of Personality and Social Psychology*, 39(6):1161–1178, 1980.

[23] A.-H. Tan. Direct code access in self-organizing neural networks for reinforcement learning. In *Proceedings of International Joint Conference on Artificial Intelligence*, pages 1071–1076, 2007.

[24] A.-H. Tan, G. A. Carpenter, and S. Grossberg. Intelligence through interaction: Towards a unified theory for learning. In *Proceedings of International Symposium on Neural Networks*, pages 1094–1103, 2007.

[25] A. Thudt, D. Baur, and S. Huron. Visual mementos: Reflecting memories with personal data. *IEEE Transactions on Visualization and Computer Graphics*, 22(1):369–378, 2016.

[26] E. Tulving. *Elements of Episodic Memory*. Oxford University Press, 1983.

[27] D. Wang and A.-H. Tan. Mobile humanoid agent with mood awareness for elderly care. In *Proceedings of International Joint Conference on Neural Networks*, pages 1549–1556, 2014.

[28] D. Wang and A.-H. Tan. Creating autonomous adaptive agent in a real-time first-person shooter computer game. *IEEE Transactions on Computational Intelligence and AI in Games*, 7(2):123–138, 2015.

[29] D. Wang and A.-H. Tan. MyLife: An online personal memory album. In *Proceedings of IEEE/WIC/ACM International Conference on Web Intelligence and Intelligent Agent Technology*, pages 243–244, 2015.

[30] W. Wang, B. Subagdja, A.-H. Tan, and J. A. Starzyk. Neural modeling of episodic memory: Encoding, retrieval, and forgetting. *IEEE Transactions on Neural Networks and Learning Systems*, 23(10):1574–1586, 2012.

Variational Inference with Agent-Based Models

Wen Dong
Department of Computer Science and Engineering &
Institute of Sustainable Transportation and Logistics
State University of New York at Buffalo
wendong@buffalo.edu

ABSTRACT

In this paper, we develop a variational method to track and make predictions about a real-world system from continuous imperfect observations about this system, using an agent-based model that describes the system dynamics. By combining the power of big data with the power of model-thinking in the stochastic process framework, we can make many valuable predictions. We show how to track the spread of an epidemic at the individual level and how to make short-term predictions about traffic congestion. This method points to a new way to bring together modelers and data miners by turning the real world into a living lab.

Keywords

Social simulation, interactive simulation, novel agent and multi-agent applications, epidemic dynamics, short term traffic forecasting, discrete event simulation, stochastic kinetic model, variational methods, expectation propagation, Bethe variational principle, Markov process.

1. INTRODUCTION

Agent-based modeling has been employed by researchers in many disciplines to specify the elements of a complex system and their interactions, to check their understandings of a system, to conduct thought experiments and to inform design and analysis [16, 47, 6, 21]. With the availability of big data in recent years [10, 30, 12], we hope to track and make predictions about a real world system from the data that represent the continuous observations of this system and an agent-based model that specifies how the system evolves, and consequently to turn our world into a living lab. In this paper, we identify the agent-based model as a discrete-event Markov process, and develop a variational inference method that searches the latent state trajectories of the elements of the system in the probability space that are most compatible with the noisy observations by minimizing the Bethe variational principle [4].

Data have traditionally been used by agent-based modelers to calibrate model parameters, drive model execution, and validate the model. The inquiry in this paper is instead about how continuous imperfect observations about a real-world system can help us make inferences about the system here and now. Instead of simulating traffic jams at rush hours using road network data and agent trips synthesized from census data [32, 42], we are more interested in predicting whether today's traffic jams will be formed earlier or last longer from the trajectories of probe vehicles, and how the knowledge about future traffic states will help drivers use the road network more efficiently. Instead of constructing the S-shaped curve of an infectious population from simulation [8, 31], we are more interested in who got a sniffle from his dynamic social network and how we can prevent epidemics from further spreading [29, 14, 18]. Instead of showing the emergence of cities and roads from how people explore and exploit resources [2, 44, 19], We are more interested in identifying poverty and extracting census information from how people make phone calls [5, 10, 38]. Predictions with an agent-based model about real-world data are interpretable in terms of how agents interact with one another and change states, and are amenable to reason regarding non-recurrent scenarios. This transparency about the predictions is lacking in non-parametric approaches.

Our approach is to identify an agent-based simulator as a Markov process, and to search in the probability space specified by the simulator for agent behaviors and interactions that best match the continuous observations about our real-world system. The key observation behind this approach is that an agent-based simulator generates different sample paths with different probabilities — it therefore defines a stochastic process with a probability measure assigned to the space of the sample paths that describe the interactions among the elements of the system. In this stochastic process, the system state as a function of time is composed of the states of its elements. This stochastic process is driven by a number of events that change the system state and happen with event rates that are functions of the current system state. A sample path of the stochastic process is defined by a sequence of events and the corresponding times when those events happened, from which we can unambiguously recover the system state as a function of time. An agent-based simulator therefore iteratively samples the next event according to event rates then changes the world state according to the sampled state starting from the initial state, until the required amount of simulated time has passed.

To find out the maximum likelihood probability distribution of the system state X_t for $t_1 \leq t \leq t_2$ from observed system state x_{t_1} at time t_1 and x_{t_2} at time t_2, we follow the forward-backward algorithm: we first let the probability mass diffuse from x_{t_1} in the forward step according to how

Appears in: *Proceedings of the 15th International Conference on Autonomous Agents and Multiagent Systems (AAMAS 2016), J. Thangarajah, K. Tuyls, C. Jonker, S. Marsella (eds.), May 9–13, 2016, Singapore.*

this system evolves from t_1 to t_2, and then we iteratively trace backwards from t_2 to t_1 in the backward step how the probability mass ended at system state x_{t_2} instead of another state. After the forward step and the backward step, we get the probability distribution of system state X_t for $t_1 \leq t \leq t_2$ conditioned on both of its states x_{t_1} and x_{t_2}.

The challenge in making probabilistic inferences about an agent-based model is that we have to deal with an exploding state space — for just a simple task of tracking the binary states of 50 agents, we must cope with 2^{50} combinatorial states because the agents interact with one another. And, of course, a real-world system is much larger. To cope with this exploding state space, we use mean field approximation: the probabilistic evolution of an agent state is determined by the mean field (average) effect of the states of the other agents. The variational framework for making inferences about stochastic processes was developed in the field of machine learning [45] as minimizing Bethe variational principle [4] with applications to expectation propagation [33, 24] and loopy belief propagation [34].

This paper therefore advocates that we should combine the power of big data and the power of model-thinking in the stochastic process framework. Agent-based modeling is a physicist's approach for modeling human societies when data are unavailable and experiments impossible [16], and we believe that big data will transform agent-based modeling from speculation into a physical science. This paper also offers a solution that fits to big time-series data any agent-based model defined by a production rule system based on mean-field approximation. Hence, this system brings together modelers and data miners. We have benchmarked our solution on systems of hundreds of agents, and our benchmarking gives meaningful results.

The rest of this paper is organized as follows. In Section 2 we introduce a probabilistic production (rule) system to describe the microscopic dynamics of a generative model, and identify the production system as a stochastic process. In Section 3 we derive a mean-field solution to the generative model under the constraint of data. In other words, given a simulator and noisy observational data about a process generated by the simulator logic, our algorithm infers the probabilities on a per-agent basis of all possible outcomes. In Section 4 we give examples and benchmark this algorithm against other algorithms. We summarize what we have accomplished and offer our speculation about big data in Section 5.

2. STOCHASTIC PROCESS INDUCED BY AGENT-BASED MODELS

In this section, we introduce the stochastic kinetic model described by the Gillespie algorithm [22] to make inferences about social dynamics from information about individuals in the social system. A "stochastic kinetic model" is a chemist's way of describing the temporal evolution of a system with M agent species driven by V events (or chemical reactions) parameterized by rate constants $c = (c_1, \dots, c_V)$. At any specific time t, the populations of the species are $x_t = (x_t^{(1)}, \dots, x_t^{(M)})$. An event v happens with rate $h_v(x_t, c_v)$, changing the populations byΔ_v. The V events are mutually independent.

Gillespie algorithm

1. Initialize the system at time $t = 0$ with rate constants $c_1, \dots, c_V$ and initialize the populations of the species as $x^{(1)}, \dots x^{(M)}$.
2. Simulate the time τ to the next event according to exponential distribution $\tau \sim \text{Exponential}(h_0(x, c) = \sum_{v=1}^{V} h_v(x, c_v))$.
3. Simulate the event v according to categorical distribution $v \sim \text{Categorical}(\frac{h_1}{h_0}, \dots, \frac{h_V}{h_0})$.
4. Update and output time $t \leftarrow t + \tau$ and populations $x \leftarrow x + \Delta_v$.
5. Repeat steps 2-5 until the termination condition is satisfied.

The stochastic kinetic model specified by the Gillespie algorithm assigns a probability measure to a sample path of the system induced by a sequence of events $v_1, \dots, v_n$, happening between time 0 and time T, $0 = t_0 < t_1 < \dots < t_n < T$, which is

$$\begin{aligned} & P(v_1, \dots, v_n, t_1, \dots, t_n, x) \qquad (1) \\ = & \prod_{i=1}^{n} h_{v_i}(x_{t_{i-1}}, c_{v_i}) \exp\left(-\sum_{i=1}^{n} h_0(x_{t_{i-1}}, c)(t_i - t_{i-1})\right) \\ = & \prod_{i=1}^{n} h_{v_i}(x_{t_{i-1}}, c_{v_i}) \exp\left(-\int d\, t\; h_0(x_t, c)\right). \end{aligned}$$

The stochastic kinetic model was designed to explain the macroscopic properties of a system via the microscopic interactions among particles in the system [47]. If we are able to observe particles, we expect not only to improve our estimation of the system properties but also to make inferences about the particles. When this model is applied to a social system, the particles are the individuals in the system, and the capability to make inferences about these particles becomes even more important. An event in the Gillespie algorithm looks like the following:

$$\alpha_v^{(1)} X^{(1)} + \dots + \alpha_v^{(M)} X^{(M)} \to \beta_v^{(1)} X^{(1)} + \dots + \beta_v^{(M)} X^{(M)}, \qquad (2)$$

$$h_v(x, c_k) = c_v g_v(x) = c_v \prod_{m=1}^{M} g_v^{(m)}(x^{(m)}) = c_v \prod_{m=1}^{M} (x^{(m)})^{\alpha_v^{(m)}}, \qquad (3)$$

$$\Delta_v = (\beta_v^{(1)} - \alpha_v^{(1)}, \dots, \beta_v^{(M)} - \alpha_v^{(M)}).$$

When $\alpha_v^{(1)}$ individuals of species 1, $\alpha_v^{(2)}$ individuals of species 2 ... meet, they trigger event v with rate constant c_v, which result in $\beta_v^{(1)}$ individuals of species 1, $\beta_v^{(2)}$ individuals of species 2, and so on. The rate $h_v(x, c_v)$ for this event to happen is rate constant c_v times a total of $\prod_{m=1}^{M} \left(x^{(m)}\right)^{\alpha_v^{(m)}}$ different ways for the individuals to meet.

When the components of the agent-based model $X^{(1)}, \dots, X^{(M)}$ lose meaning as the populations of agent species, we can find the probability distribution of a component state among a finite partition of the component's state space. When the event rates cannot be expressed as the multiplications of component contributions in the form of Eq. 3, we take Taylor expansions of the event rates around the mean value of the system state

$$h_v(x, c_v) = \sum_{|\alpha|\geq 0} \frac{(x - \mathbf{E}x)^\alpha}{\alpha!} \partial^\alpha h_v(\mathbf{E}x, c_v),$$

with each term being in the form of Eq. 3. α is a multi-index and E is the expectation operator.

Although the stochastic kinetic model is a continuous time model, we work with a discrete time stochastic model in the rest of this paper, because our goal is to track stochastic kinetic dynamics from observations of populations or individuals with countably many computational steps. There are two ways to turn a continuous stochastic process into a discrete one, both of which involve Jensen's uniformization/randomization method [23].

The first method for discretizing a continuous time stochastic system is through approximating the continuous time process with a discrete time process on a countable set of equally spaced time points $0, \tau, 2\tau, \ldots$, with a time interval so small that the probability of more than one event happening in the interval τ is negligible. This approximation works because the state transition kernel from time 0 to time τ is $p(x_0 \to x_\tau) = \sum_{n=0}^{\infty} \left(I + \frac{Q}{\gamma}\right)^n \exp(-\gamma\tau)\frac{(\gamma\tau)^n}{n!}$ according to the uniformization method, where γ is a uniformization rate, I is the identity matrix and Q is the infinitesimal generator defined by $h_k, k = 1, \ldots, V$. With $\gamma \to \infty$ and $\gamma\tau = 1$, we get a first-order approximation of the state transition kernel $I + Q \cdot \tau$.

Specifically, let $v_1, \ldots, v_T$ be a sequence of events in the discrete time stochastic kinetic system, $x_1, \ldots, x_T$ be a sequence of states (populations of species), and $y_1, \ldots, y_T$ be a set of observations about the populations. Our goal is to make inferences about $\{v_t, x_t : t = 1, \ldots T\}$ from $\{y_t : t = 1, \ldots, T\}$ according to the following probability measure, where indicator function $1(x_t - x_{t-1} = \Delta_{v_t})$ is 1 if the previous state is x_{t-1} and the current state is $x_t = x_{t-1} + \Delta_{v_t}$, and 0 otherwise.

$$P(v_{1,\ldots,T}, x_{1,\ldots,T}, y_{1,\ldots,T}) = \prod_{t=1}^{T} P(x_t, y_t, v_t | x_{t-1}), \tag{4}$$

where $P(x_t, y_t, v_t | x_{t-1})$

$$= P(v_t | x_{t-1}) 1(x_t - x_{t-1} = \Delta_{v_t}) P(y_t | x_t), \tag{5}$$

$$\text{and} \quad P(v_t | x_{t-1}) = \begin{cases} c_k \tau \cdot g_k(x_{t-1}) & \text{if } v_t = k \\ 1 - \sum_j c_j \tau g_j(x_{t-1}) & \text{if } v_t = \emptyset \end{cases}. \tag{6}$$

The second way to discretize a continuous time stochastic system is by introducing a uniformization rate γ that is faster than all event rates in Q and inspecting a discrete time Markov chain defined by the state transition matrix $I + \frac{Q}{\lambda}$, with the transitions happening at time $t_1, t_2, \ldots$, sampled according to a uniform Poisson process with rate γ. This works because according to the uniformization method the uniformised continuous time process has the same probability measure as the original process.

We employ a stochastic kinetic model to simplify the state space transition kernel for several reasons. First, the stochastic kinetic model already successfully describes the time evolution of reaction systems in many areas, including chemistry and cell biology [1, 22]. It is therefore a more natural model for describing and tracking the spatio-temporal process driven by events. Second, the event based transition kernel is more general and flexible–we can define the number of events based on the complexity of real transitions.

3. MAKING INFERENCES WITH AN AGENT-BASED MODEL

In this section, we derive a mean-field solution to infer the probabilities on a per-agent basis of all possible paths of system evolution, given a simulator and noisy observational data about this system generated by the simulator logic.

3.1 Variational Inference

Recall the forward-backward algorithm to make inferences with a state space model [39]. Let X_t be the hidden states and y_t be the observations of a discrete-time state-space model (Kalman filter and hidden Markov model) identified by a transition probability $P(X_{t+1}|X_t)$ and an observation model $P(Y_t|X_t)$, where $t = 1, \cdots, T$. The forward-backward algorithm for making inferences about hidden states X_t from observations y_t is comprised of a forward/filtering sweep to compute the forward statistics $\alpha(x_t) = P(x_t|y_1, \cdots, y_T)$ and a backward/smoothing sweep to estimate the one-slice statistics $\gamma(y_t) = P(x_t \,|\, y_1, \cdots, y_T)$. From the forward statistics and the one-slice statistics we can extract the backward statistics $\beta(x_t) = \gamma(x_t)/\alpha(x_t)$ and the two-slice statistics $\xi(x_t, x_{t+1}) = \alpha(x_t)P(y_{t+1}, x_{t+1} \,|\, x_t)\beta(x_{t+1})P(y_{t+1}|y_{1,\cdots,t})$. Here we follow the tradition, use upper case letters for random variables and use lower case letters for the values of random variables.

The challenge with making inferences about a non-trivial agent-based model is that we have to search in a formidable state space — $X_t = (X_t^{(1)}, X_t^{(2)}, \cdots, X_t^{(M)})$, where the superscripts $1, \cdots, M$ represent the states of the interacting elements of the system. We therefore estimate the state distributions of the hidden states in an amenable state space with mean field approximation $\gamma_t(x_t) = \prod_m \gamma_t^{(m)}(x_t^{(m)})$:

minimize over $\xi_t(x_{t-1,t}, v_t)$:

$$\sum_{t;x_{t-1,t};v_t} \xi_t(x_{t-1,t}, v_t) \log \frac{\xi_t(x_{t-1,t}, v_t)}{P(x_t, v_{t-1}, y_t | x_{t-1})} - \sum_{t;x_t} \prod_m \gamma_t^{(m)}(x_t^{(m)}) \log \prod_m \gamma_t^{(m)}(x_t^{(m)}) \tag{7}$$

subject to:

$$\sum_{v_t;x_{t-1,t}:\text{ fixed } x_t^{(m)}} \xi_t(x_{t-1}, x_t, v_t) = \gamma_t^{(m)}(x_t^{(m)}), \text{ for all } t, m, x_t^{(m)}, \tag{8}$$

$$\sum_{v_t;x_{t-1,t}:\text{ fixed } x_{t-1}^{(m)}} \xi_t(x_{t-1}, x_t, v_t) = \gamma_{t-1}^{(m)}(x_{t-1}^{(m)}), \text{ for all } t, m, x_{t-1}^{(m)}, \tag{9}$$

$$\sum_{x_t:\text{ fixed } x_t^{(m)}} \gamma_t^{(m)}(x_t^{(m)}) = 1, \text{ for all } t, m, x_t^{(m)}. \tag{10}$$

We apply the method of Lagrange multipliers to solve this optimization problem, which begins with forming the Lagrange function to be optimized:

$$\sum_{t;x_{t-1,t};v_t} \xi_t(x_{t-1,t}, v_t) \log \frac{\xi_t(x_{t-1,t}, v_t)}{P(x_t, v_{t-1}, y_t | x_{t-1})} - \sum_{t;x_t} \prod_m \gamma_t^{(m)}(x_t^{(m)}) \log \prod_m \gamma_t^{(m)}(x_t^{(m)}) \tag{11}$$

$$+\sum_{t;m;x_t^{(m)}} \beta^{(m)}_{t,x_t^{(m)}} \Big(\sum_{v_t;x_{t-1,t}:\text{ fixed } x_t^{(m)}} \xi_t(x_{t-1},x_t,v_t) - \gamma_t^{(m)}(x_t^{(m)})\Big)$$
$$+\sum_{t;m;x_{t-1}^{(m)}} \alpha^{(m)}_{t-1,x_{t-1}^{(m)}} \Big(\sum_{v_t;x_{t-1,t}:\text{ fixed } x_{t-1}^{(m)}} \xi_t(x_{t-1},x_t,v_t) - \gamma_{t-1}^{(m)}(x_{t-1}^{(m)})\Big).$$

Taking the derivative of the expression involving Lagrange multipliers over $\xi_t(x_{t-1},x_t,v_t)$ and $\gamma_t^{(m)}(x_t^{(m)})$, we see that $\alpha_t^{(m)}(x_t^{(m)})=\exp(\sum_i \alpha_{t,i}^{(m)}\cdot 1(x_t^{(m)}=i))$ is associated with the marginalized forward probabilities, $\beta_t^{(m)}(x_t^{(m)})=\exp(\sum_i \beta_{t,i}^{(m)}\cdot 1(x_t^{(m)}=i))$ is associated with the marginalized backward probabilities, with $\gamma_t^{(m)}(x_t^{(m)}) = \alpha_t^{(m)}(x_t^{(m)})\beta_t^{(m)}(x_t^{(m)})$. The dual optimization problem is to find the marginal forward statistics $\alpha_t^{(m)}(x_t^{(m)})$ and the marginal backward statistics $\beta_t^{(m)}(x_t^{(m)})$ to maximize the approximate partition function given by Eq. 12, and the solution is the fixed point of Eq. 13, where normalization constant $Z_t = P(y_t|y_{1,\cdots,t-1})$:

$$\log P(y_{1,\cdots,T})=\sum_t \log \sum_{x_{t-1,t}} \prod_m \alpha_{t-1}^{(m)}(x_{t-1}^{(m)}) P(x_t,v_t|x_{t-1}) \prod_m \beta_t^{(m)}(x_t^{(m)}) \tag{12}$$

$$\xi_t(x_{t-1},x_t,v_t) = \frac{1}{Z_t} P(x_t,v_t|x_{t-1}) \tag{13}$$
$$\cdot \prod_m \alpha_{t-1}^{(m)}\left(x_{t-1}^{(m)}\right) \cdot \prod_m P\left(y_t^{(m)}|x_t^{(m)}\right) \prod_m \beta_t^{(m)}\left(x_t^{(m)}\right),$$

$$\text{where } P(x_t,v_t|x_{t-1}) = \tag{14}$$
$$\begin{cases} c_k\tau \prod_m g_k^{(m)}\left(x_{t-1}^{(m)}\right)\cdot \prod_m 1(x_t^{(m)}-x_{t-1}^{(m)}=\Delta_k^{(m)}) & v_t = k \neq \emptyset \\ (1-\sum_k c_k\tau \prod_m g_k^{(m)}(x_{t-1}^{(m)}))\cdot \prod_m 1(x_t^{(m)}-x_{t-1}^{(m)}=0) & v_t = \emptyset. \end{cases}$$

Marginalizing Eq. 13 over all chains $X_t^{(m')}$ for $m' \neq m$ and t, we find that the solution to the Bethe variational principle is the mean field approximation of the original dynamics with marginal two-slice statistic given by Eq. 15. From the mean field approximation, $\alpha_{t,i}^{(m)}$ and $\beta_{t,i}^{(m)}$ can be solved by forward-backward algorithm and fixed point iteration.

$$\xi_t(x_{t-1}^{(m)},x_t^{(m)},v_t) = \frac{1}{Z_t} P(x_t^{(m)},v_t|x_{t-1}^{(m)}) \tag{15}$$
$$\cdot \alpha_{t-1}^{(m)}(x_{t-1}^{(m)}) \cdot P(y_t^{(m)}|x_t^{(m)})\beta_t^{(m)}(x_t^{(m)}),$$

$$\text{where } P(x_t^{(m)},v_t|x_{t-1}^{(m)}) \propto \tag{16}$$
$$\begin{cases} c_k\tau g_k^{(m)}(x_{t-1}^{(m)}) \prod_{m'\neq m} \tilde{g}_{k,t-1}^{(m')}\cdot 1(x_t^{(m)}-x_{t-1}^{(m)}=\Delta_k^{(m)}) & v_t^{(m)}=k\neq\emptyset \\ \left(1-\sum_k c_k\tau g_k^{(m)}(x_{t-1}^{(m)}) \prod_{m'\neq m} \hat{g}_{k,t-1}^{(m')}\right) 1(x_t^{(m)}-x_{t-1}^{(m)}=0) & v_t^{(m)} = \emptyset, \end{cases}$$

$$\tilde{g}_{k,t-1}^{(m')} = \frac{\sum_{x_t^{(m')}-x_{t-1}^{(m')}\equiv\Delta_k^{(m')}} \alpha_{t-1}^{(m')}(x_{t-1}^{(m')})P(y_t^{(m')}|x_t^{(m')})\beta_t^{(m')}(x_t^{(m')})g_k^{(m')}(x_{t-1}^{(m')})}{\sum_{x_t^{(m')}-x_{t-1}^{(m')}\equiv 0} \alpha_{t-1}^{(m')}(x_{t-1}^{(m')})P(y_t^{(m')}|x_t^{(m')})\beta_t^{(m')}(x_t^{(m')})},$$

$$\hat{g}_{k,t-1}^{(m')} = \frac{\sum_{x_t^{(m')}-x_{t-1}^{(m')}\equiv 0} \alpha_{t-1}^{(m')}(x_{t-1}^{(m')})P(y_t^{(m')}|x_t^{(m')})\beta_t^{(m')}(x_t^{(m')})g_k^{(m')}(x_{t-1}^{(m')})}{\sum_{x_t^{(m')}-x_{t-1}^{(m')}\equiv 0} \alpha_{t-1}^{(m')}(x_{t-1}^{(m')})P(y_t^{(m')}|x_t^{(m')})\beta_t^{(m')}(x_t^{(m')})},$$

$$Z_t = \sum_j c_j\tau \prod_m \tilde{g}_{j,t-1}^{(m)} + 1 - \sum_j c_j\tau \prod_m \hat{g}_{j,t-1}^{(m)}.$$

The above is a factorized stochastic kinetic model. The marginal two-slice probability $\xi_t(x_{t-1}^{(m)},x_t^{(m)},v_t)$ in Eq. 15 takes the same form as the coupled two-slice probability $\xi_t(x_{t-1},x_t,v_t)$ in Eq. 13. The marginal state transition kernel $P(x_t^{(m)},v_t|x_{t-1}^{(m)})$ in Eq. 16 consists of choosing an event (or no event) v_t according to event probability $P(v_t|x_{t-1}^{(m)})$ and changing the state $x_t^{(m)}$ in a deterministic way, similar to the joint state transition kernel $P(x_t,v_t|x_{t-1})$ in Eq. 14, except that we marginalize over all $x^{(m')}$ for $m' \neq m$.

Hence the solution to the above Bethe variational principle through Legendre-Fenchel transform [40] is one in which the interacting elements of the system evolve their states marginally according to the average effects of the other elements. As such, instead of searching the joint probability space of of $(X_1,\cdots,X_T)$, we search the marginal probability spaces of $(X_1^{(m)},\cdots,X_T^{(m)})$.

3.2 Graphical Model Representation

The stochastic kinetic model with its distinct graphical model structure is more suitable than traditional models for modeling complex interactions in social dynamics. To illustrate this point, we compare its graphical model with the coupled hidden Markov model.

A coupled hidden Markov model (CHMM, Figure 1(a)) combines a number of conventional hidden Markov models (HMMs) to model the dynamics of interacting processes [7, 35]. In CHMM the latent state of HMM at time t depends on the latent states of *all* HMMs at time $t-1$. Traditional ways to simplify the state transition kernel include the factorial hidden Markov model which decouples the inter-chain probability dependence [28] and the hidden Markov decision tree which assumes fixed and sparse inter-chain probability dependence [20].

A stochastic kinetic model has a graphical model representation different from CHMM, as shown in Figure 1(b). First, we define a set of stochastic events to summarize the complex interactions and decouple direct dependencies between nodes. Second, while the system can move from any state to any other state in a CHMM, in any infinitesimal time interval no more than one out of V possible events is happening in a stochastic kinetic model. Third, conditioned on the system state $x_{t-1}^{(1)},\ldots,x_{t-1}^{(M)}$ describing the populations of species $1,\ldots,M$, the latent state at the next time step $x_t^{(1)},\ldots,x_t^{(M)}$ could be dependent. (Consider an event that changes population m_1 and population m_2 simultaneously.) In contrast, in a CHMM the states $x_t^{(1)},\ldots,x_t^{(M)}$ at time t are conditionally independent given the states $x_{t-1}^{(1)},\ldots,x_{t-1}^{(M)}$ at time $t-1$. Thus the inference algorithms of CHMM are not applicable for modeling the complex interactions in social dynamics driven by events.

The factorial stochastic kinetic model has a graphical model similar to the stochastic kinetic model except that it factorizes stochastic events to individual species (Figure 1(c)). The new graphical model further simplifies the inference algorithm.

3.3 Parameter Learning

In order to find the rate constants c_v in a stochastic kinetic model and in a factorial stochastic kinetic model, we maximize the expected log likelihood and the Bethe entropy approximation respectively over these rate constants.

The likelihood of rate constants c_v in a continuous time stochastic kinetic model with respect to a sample path iden-

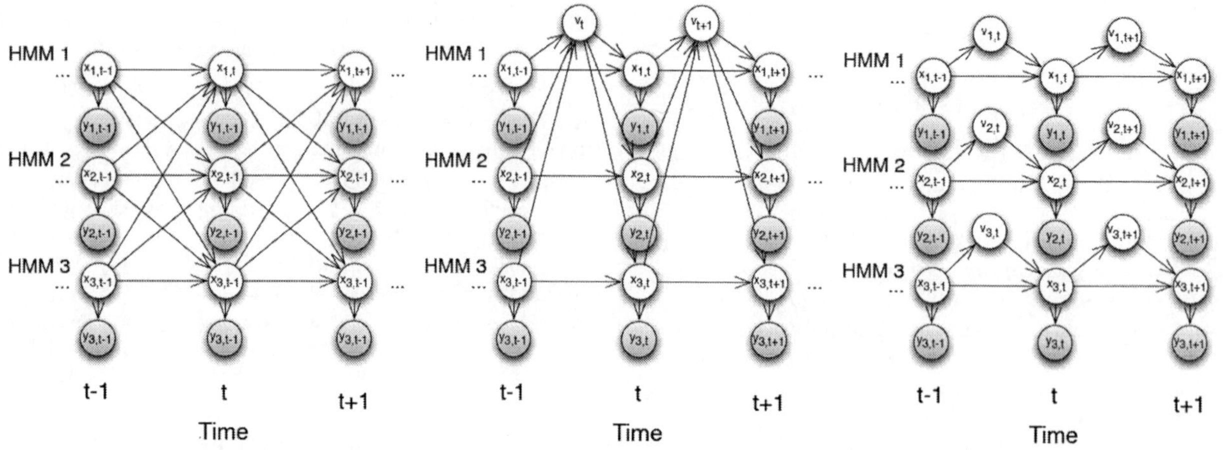

(a) CHMM (b) SKM (c) FSKM

Figure 1: In comparison of coupled hidden markov model (a), a stochastic kinetic model (b) decouples inter-chain interactions with events v and allows factorization (c).

tified by events $v_1, \cdots, v_n$, system states to $x_{t_1}, \cdots, x_{t_n}$ and times $t_1, \cdots, t_n$ is given in Eq. 1, and the event rates are given in Eq. 3. To find the maximum likelihood estimate of the rate constants, we set the partial derivatives of the log-likelihood over the rate constants to 0:

$$\log P = \textstyle\sum_i \log c_{v_i} + \log g_{v_i}(x_{t_{i-1}}) - \sum_i \sum_j c_j g_j(x_{t_{i-1}}) \cdot (t_i - t_{i-1}),$$

$$\frac{\partial}{\partial c_v} \log P = \frac{\sum_i 1(v_i = v)}{c_v} - \sum_i g_v(x_{t_{i-1}}) \cdot (t_i - t_{i-1}),$$

$$c_v = \frac{\sum_i 1(v_i = v)}{\sum_i g_v(x_{t_{i-1}})(t_i - t_{i-1})} = \frac{\sum_i 1(v_i = v)}{\int_0^T d\, t\; g_v(x(t))}.$$

Hence, the maximum likelihood estimate of the rate constants c_v is such that the numbers of events that are expected to happen according to the event rates along the sample path $\int_0^T dt\; c_v g_v(x(t))$ match the numbers of events $\sum_i 1(v_i = v)$ that happened in the sample path. Indicator function $1(v_i = v)$ takes value 1 if $v_i = v$ and 0 if $v_i \neq v$.

The likelihood of rate constants c_v in a discrete time stochastic kinetic model with respect to a sample path identified by events $v_1, \cdots, v_T$, system states $x_1, \cdots, x_T$ and observations $y_1, \cdots, y_T$ is given in Eq. 4. To find the maximum likelihood estimate of the rate constants, we similarly set the partial derivatives of the log-likelihood over the rate constants to 0:

$$\log P = \sum_t \log p(y_t|x_t) + \sum_t \log p(v_t|x_{t-1}) 1(x_t - x_{t-1} = \Delta_{v_t})$$

$$\frac{\partial}{\partial c_v} \log P = \frac{\sum_t 1(v_t = v)}{c_v} - \sum_t \frac{\tau g_v(x_{t-1}) 1(v_t = \emptyset)}{1 - \sum_j c_j \tau g_j(x_{t-1})}$$

$$c_v = \frac{\sum_t 1(v_t = v)}{\sum_t \frac{\tau g_v(x_{t-1}) \cdot 1(v_t = \emptyset)}{1 - \sum_j c_j \tau g_j(x_{t-1})}} \xrightarrow{\tau \to 0} \frac{\sum_t 1(v_t = v)}{\sum_t \tau g_v(x_{t-1})}.$$

Hence, the maximum likelihood estimate of the rate constants c_v in a discrete-time stochastic kinetic model similarly matches the numbers of events that are expected to happen according to the event rates ($\sum_t \frac{c_v \tau g_v(x_{t-1}) 1(v_t = \emptyset)}{1 - \sum_j c_j \tau g_j(x_{t-1})}$, extrapolated from the times of null events) with the number of events that happened ($\sum_t 1(v_t = v)$). As the interval τ approaches 0, the probability of a null event ($1 - \sum_j c_j \tau g_j(x_{t-1})$) and the fraction of null events ($\sum_{t=1}^T 1(v_t = \emptyset)/T$) both approach 1, and the maximum likelihood estimate of the rate constants in the discrete time stochastic kinetic model approaches the maximum likelihood estimate in the continuous time stochastic kinetic model.

When the events $v_1, \cdots, v_T$ and the system states $x_1, \cdots, x_T$ are unobserved latent variables, we use the expectation maximization (EM) algorithm to iteratively search for the rate constants that maximize the expected log likelihood over the probability distribution of the latent variables. EM is an iterative method for finding the maximum likelihood estimate of the parameters in statistical models involving unobserved latent variables [11]. It alternates performing the expectation (E) step, which constructs the expected log likelihood as a function of the parameters over the probability distribution of the latent variables using the current estimate for the parameters, with the maximization (M) step, which computes the parameters to maximize the expected log likelihood function constructed in the E step. The estimated parameters are used to determine the probability distribution of the latent variables in the next E step.

The expected log likelihood over the posterior probability of events $v_1, \cdots, v_T$ and system states $x_1, \cdots, x_T$ conditioned on the observations $y_1, \ldots, y_T$ takes the form in Eq. 17. Maximizing this expected log likelihood by setting its partial derivatives over the rate constants gives the updated estimate of rate constants in Eq. 18.

$$\mathrm{E}(\log P) = \sum_{t; x_{t-1,t}; v_t} \xi_t(x_{t-1,t}, v_t; c^{\mathrm{old}}) \cdot \log P(x_t, y_t, v_t | x_{t-1}; c) \tag{17}$$

$$\frac{\partial \mathrm{E}(\log P)}{\partial c_v} = \sum_t \frac{\xi(v_t = v)}{c_v} - \sum_{t; x_{t-1}} \frac{\tau g_v(x_{t-1}) \xi(x_{t-1}, v_t = \emptyset)}{1 - \sum_j c_j \tau g_j(x_{t-1})} \overset{\text{set}}{=} 0,$$

$$c_v = \frac{\sum_t \xi(v_t = v)}{\sum_{t; x_{t-1}} \frac{\tau g_v(x_{t-1}) \cdot \xi(x_{t-1}, v_t = \emptyset)}{1 - \sum_j c_j \tau g_j(x_{t-1})}} \tag{18}$$

$$\xrightarrow{\tau\to 0} \frac{\sum_t \xi(v_t = v)}{\sum_{t;x_{t-1}} \tau\gamma(x_{t-1})g_v(x_{t-1})}.$$

As such, the rate constant c_v for event v matches the expected number of times this event could have happened $(\sum_t \frac{c_v \tau g_v(x_{t-1})\xi(x_{t-1},v_t=\emptyset)}{1-\sum_j c_j \tau g_j(x_{t-1})})$ according to the event rates $(c_j \tau g_j(x_{t-1}))$ along the sample path with the expected number of times the events happened $(\sum_i \xi(v_i = v))$.

Using Bethe entropy approximation, $\alpha_{t-1}(x_{t-1}) = \prod_m \alpha_{t-1}^{(m)}(x_{t-1}^{(m)})$ and $\beta_t(x_t) = \prod_m \beta_t^{(m)}(x_t^{(m)})$, and setting the discretization time interval τ to be small enough, the rate constants c_v can be updated according to Eq. 19.

$$c_v = \frac{\sum_t \xi(v_t = v)}{\sum_t \tau \prod_m \sum_{x_{t-1}^{(m)}} \gamma^{(m)}(x_{t-1}^{(m)}) g_v^{(m)}(x_{t-1}^{(m)})}, \tag{19}$$

$$\text{where } \xi(v_t = v) = \frac{c_v^{\text{old}} \prod_m \tilde{g}_{v,t-1}^{(m)}}{\sum_j c_j^{\text{old}} \tau \prod_m \tilde{g}_{j,t-1}^{(m)} + 1 - \sum_j c_j^{\text{old}} \tau \prod_m \hat{g}_{j,t-1}^{(m)}}.$$

Therefore, the rate constant for event v is the expected number of occurrences of this event summed over all times, divided by the total cross-section of this event also summed over all times.

To summarize, we provide the variational agent-based inference algorithm below.

Variational Inference with Gillespie Algorithm

Given observations $y_t^{(m)}$ for $t = 1, \ldots, T$ and $m = 1, \ldots, M$, and the stochastic kinetic model of a complex system defined by Eq. 4, find $x_t^{(m)}$, $v_t^{(m)}$ and rate constants c_k for $k = 1, \ldots, V$.

- Latent state inference. Iterate through the following forward pass and backward pass until convergence, where $P(x_t^{(m)}, v_t | x_{t-1}^{(m)})$ is given by Eq. 16.
  - Forward pass. For $t = 1, \ldots, T$ and $m = 1, \ldots, M$, update $\alpha_t^{(m)}(x_t^{(m)})$ according to

$$\alpha_t^{(m)}(x_t^{(m)}) \leftarrow \frac{1}{Z_t} \sum_{x_{t-1}^{(m)}, v_t} \alpha_{t-1}^{(m)}(x_{t-1}^{(m)}) P(x_t^{(m)}, v_t | x_{t-1}^{(m)}) P(y_t^{(m)} | x_t^{(m)}).$$

  - Backward pass. For $t = T, \ldots, 1$ and $m = 1, \ldots, M$, update $\beta_{t-1}^{(m)}(x_{t-1}^{(m)})$ according to

$$\beta_{t-1}^{(m)}(x_{t-1}^{(m)}) \leftarrow \frac{1}{Z_t} \sum_{v_t, x_t^{(m)}} P(x_t^{(m)}, v_t | x_{t-1}^{(m)}) P(y_t^{(m)} | x_t^{(m)}) \beta_t^{(m)}(x_t^{(m)}).$$

- Parameter estimation. Iterate through latent state inference (above) and rate constants estimate of c_k according to Eq. 19, until convergence.

4. EXPERIMENTAL RESULTS

In this section, we evaluate the performance of variational agent-based inference for two applications: epidemic dynamics and traffic dynamics. We selected these because they are important applications with significant practical value.

4.1 Epidemic Dynamics

In this section, we infer the progression of common cold in a dynamic social network using an agent-based susceptible-infectious-susceptible (SIS) model at the individual level through a small numbr of volunteers who report their symptoms, and estimate the total number of infectious individuals. Being able to estimate the outbreak of an epidemic in advance and determine who has the highest probability of infection is important for health-care providers and health policy researchers who must optimize limited medical resources. Conventional agent-based epidemic simulators [17, 26, 41, 27, 15] lack the capability to infer epidemic spreading with symptoms observations in the social network, and thus the sample paths given by these simulators can differ significantly from the truth.

In the SIS dynamics, each individual is either infectious (I) or susceptible (S), and the system has three events: a) an in infectious individual in the network infects a susceptible individual and turns that person infectious in the network with rate constant c_1 (probability per unit time), b) an infectious individual recovers and becomes susceptible again with rate constant c_2, and 3) a susceptible individual becomes infectious by contacting an infectious individual from outside the system with rate constant c_3.

$$I + S \to 2 \times I, \text{ infection, rate constant} = c_1,$$
$$I \to S, \text{ recover, rate constant} = c_2,$$
$$S \to I, \text{ infection from outside, rate constant}=c_3.$$

To model the SIS dynamics at the individual level with Gillespie algorithm, we assign two "species" to each person p: $I^{(p)} \in \{0,1\}$, $S^{(p)} \in \{0,1\}$ and $I^{(p)} + S^{(p)} = 1$. The probability for a susceptible person p to become infectious through one unit time of contact with an infectious person q is thus $h(x, c_1) = c_1 \cdot s^{(p)} \cdot i^{(q)} = c_1$. The mean field probability for the susceptible person p to become infectious is thus

$$\sum_{q \in \text{neighbor of } p} c_1 \cdot s^{(p)} \cdot \mathbf{E} I^{(q)} = c_1 \cdot s^{(p)} \sum_{q \in \text{neighbor of } p} \mathbf{E} I^{(q)},$$

i.e., the average total number of infectious neighbors in the individual's social network times the probability of infection per infectious neighbor. If infection happens, we change $S^{(p)}$ from 1 to 0 and change $I^{(p)}$ from 0 to 1.

We benchmark the performance of the variational agent-based inference algorithm using the Dartmouth College campus data set [29]. This data set contains the locations of 13,888 on-campus WiFi users from April 2001 to June 2004. On top of this dynamic social network we synthesized epidemic progression using the SIS model and set parameters such that an individual is on average infected twice per year and takes one week on average to recover. We randomly select 10% of individuals as volunteers who report their daily symptoms and from these we infer the daily infectious/susceptible state of the other 90% individuals. As far as we know, there is no real data set with both a large amount of sensor data and symptom reports; we hope our research encourages data collection and analysis in this direction.

Figure 2(a) compares the receiver operating characteristic (ROC) curve of predicting whether an individual is infectious using either a variational agent-based inference algorithm or a support vector classifier [37]. The support vec-

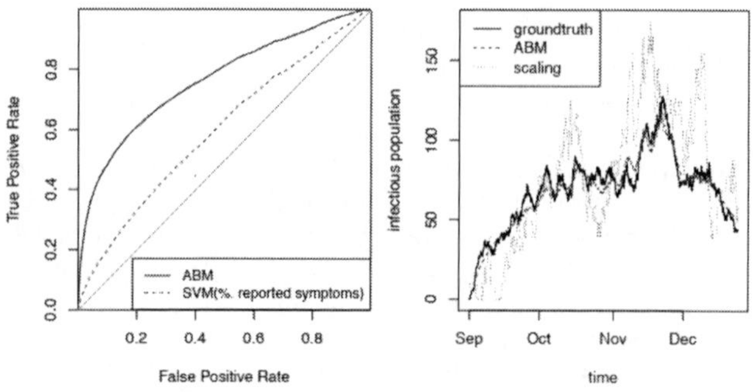

(a) Detecting infections (b) Estimating infectious population

Figure 2: Statistical inference in Dartmouth data

tor classifier (SVC) estimates the probability that an individual is infectious based on the percentage of his contacts reporting symptoms. Since only 10% of individuals are reporting symptoms in the experiment setup, the likelihood that an individual is infected can be only roughly estimated by SVC. In addition, infectious individuals make different contributions to epidemic progression because infectious diseases from randomly infected individuals go first to the hubs of a social network then spread to the other nodes from those hubs [9], and SVC has difficulty in capturing such network-related features. Variational agent-based inference, on the other hand, can correctly predict 60% of infections with only a 20% false positive rate.

Figure 2(b) compares the performance in estimating the number of infectious persons in the 90% of individuals who do not report their daily symptoms from daily symptoms reported by the 10%. A scaling-based method missed the rapid increase of infectious individuals in early September and overestimated the number of infectious individuals in mid-October and November. This occurred because not all infectious individuals contribute to epidemic progression the same way.

4.2 Traffic Dynamics

In this experiment, we predict road traffic up to one hour ahead of time from a large set of tracked vehicle locations in conjunction with an agent-based transportation simulator called MATSIM [32]. While tracked vehicle locations from car telematics systems are already being exploited to provide drivers with real-time traffic information, the chaotic nature of transportation networks means that an incident at one location might affect the traffic condition of another location up to a hundred miles away. A decision made according to current travel times might therefore be suboptimal, and can in certain cases even lead to global system breakdown.

Researchers employ a transportation simulator to explain the macroscopic phenomena of transportation dynamics by simulating how individuals travel in a real-world transportation network. Such a simulator takes three primary components as its input: a road network like the one used in a GPS navigator, a population specification that lists the location and travel of individuals on a typical day synthesized from census data and trip surveys with the number of simulated vehicles matching the number of vehicles in the real world, and a control file specifying how daily itineraries are scored and how individuals improve their daily itineraries (and the parameters specifying the modeling details). From these data, the simulator will proceed to execute travel, to score daily itineraries, and to perturb daily itineraries in an attempt to improve them, and then repeat the three steps until equilibrium is reached. Simulation without continuous observtations about a real-world transportation network however doesn't tell us whether today's traffic jams will be formed earlier or last longer.

Many existing algorithms to track and predict real-time traffic dynamics on the other hand — vector ARIMA [3], state space models [46], neural networks [48], and Bayesian network models [25, 13] — have difficulty in coping with noisy and missing data, with making predictions in non-recurrent scenarios, and with explaining predictions in terms of agent trips. According to Vlahogianni [43], the challenge in short-term traffic forecasting is not only to predict but also to explain phenomena at the city network level — to fuse new data sources such as those from telematics units and to easily incorporate the effects of non-recurrent conditions.

To join the event model of a discrete-event simulator with continued observations about real-world social systems, we make use of the fact that all discrete event simulators (at least, to the best of our knowledge) have a way to dump the events happening in a simulation run. As such, we can reconstruct simulation runs according to the event sequences and so reconstruct the stochastic discrete-event model from simulation runs outside the simulator, instead of hacking the source code of a specific simulator over many man-months. MATSIM, for example, has about 140 thousand lines of code, and hacking its source code to make real-time inferences with real-world data wouldn't be easy.

In this way, we dump four events: vehicle leaving a building, vehicle entering a link, vehicle leaving a link and vehicle entering a building. From these four events, we have constructed a data frame representing continued observations of the locations (the link or building) of all vehicles at equally spaced time steps. From the data frame we constructed a state transition matrix to represent vehicle dynamics (with each row and column representing a link/building), along with entries giving the state transition probabilities according to how long a vehicle stays at a link/building and how frequently a vehicle chooses the next link/building. By uniformly sampling a given fraction of tracked vehicles, we have constructed an observation model that provides the probability distribution of observed vehicles at a location given the total number of vehicles there. This system has only one event $p_i \circ l_j \to p_i \circ l_k$, a vehicle i moving from link/building j to link/building k with rate constant p_{l_j,l_k}, changing the location of vehicle from $X_t^{(p_i)} = l_j$ to $X_{t+1}^{(p_i)} = l_k$, changing the number of vehicles on link l_i from $X_t^{(l_i)} = x_t^{(l_i)}$ to $X_{t+1}^{(l_i)} = x_t^{(l_i)} - 1$, and changing the number of vehicles on link l_k from $X_t^{(l_k)} = x_t^{(l_k)}$ to $X_{t+1}^{(l_k)} = x_t^{(l_k)} + 1$. But the inference is much more complex due to the interactions between vehicles and links.

We employ the mobility traces of more than 500 taxi cabs collected over 30 days in the San Francisco metropolitan area [36] to benchmark the advantages of considering possible future traffic conditions for individual transportation planning. We extract the road network from OpenStreetMap, a collaborative project to create a free editable map of the world. We obtain population distribution and daily trip statistics from the U.S. Census, and obtain the state transi-

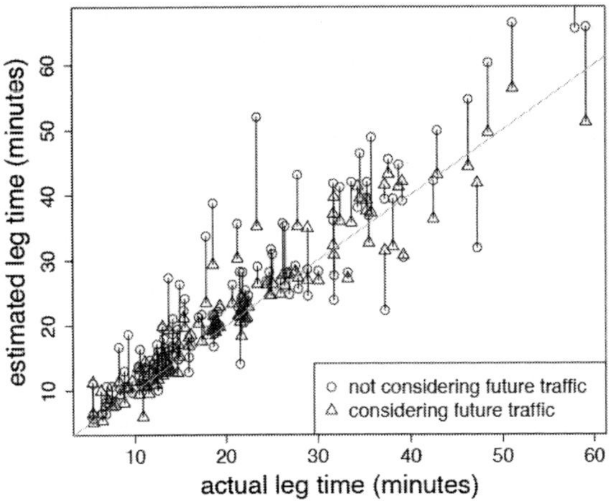

Figure 3: Considering future traffic reduces the relative error of travel time versus actual travel time from 35% when future traffic is not considered to 29% when it is.

tion matrices from one link/building to another at equilibrium from simulations. We map the latitudes and longitudes of tracked vehicle locations to links and buildings because our stochastic inference is at the link/building level.

To benchmark how the estimation of travel time can be improved by considering future traffic conditions even though traffic conditions vary significantly, we extract the 20% of trips with the highest difference between actual travel time and estimated travel time according to traffic at the time of departure, then estimate the average travel time according to our probabilistic model. Such travel often occurs at the rising edge of overall traffic volume, during bad weather, and on less developed roads.

Figure 3 compares these estimated travel times according to only traffic at the time of departure with the same data considering possible future traffic estimations through a random sample of 128 trips. The travel estimations that do *not* project future traffic exhibit on average a 35% relative error (in comparison with a 29% when projecting future traffic), and therefore occasionally differ significantly from the actual travel time.

As such, we can combine the sporadically observed vehicle locations with the large compilation of typical trip plans to continuously estimate current and future traffic conditions. Starting from the number and behavior of tracked vehicles in a road link, we can determine the total number of vehicles in the link by scaling and estimating traffic conditions. If we trace the origins and destinations of the estimated number of vehicles through the factorial stochastic process model (filling any gaps with prior individual travel behaviors), we can extract information about the traffic at other road links. If we then iterate estimations between the traffic at links and the trip choices of simulated vehicles, we improve our estimation of both.

5. CONCLUSIONS AND DISCUSSIONS

In this paper, we have developed a variational method to make inferences about a real-world system from continuous imperfect observations about the system, using an agent-based model that describes the dynamics of this system. To demonstrate the value of combining the power of big data and the power of model-thinking in the stochastic process framework, we show how we can track epidemics at the individual level from only a small number of volunteers who report their symptoms, and we make short-term predictions about road traffic from sporadically observed probe vehicles. This is just a taste of what this powerful combination of approaches can do, and we expect to see further applications and theoretical development to test the bounds of this methodology.

APPENDIX

The duality between Eq. 7 and Eq. 12 is a duality between maximum relative entropy and maximum pseudo-likelihood. To get the dual form of the Bethe variational problem in Eq. 12, we set the derivatives of Eq. 11 over $\xi_t(x_{t-1,t}v_t)$ and $\gamma_t^{(m)}(x_t^{(m)})$ to 0.

$$\frac{\partial L}{\partial \xi_t(x_{t-1,t},v_t)} = \log \frac{\xi_t(x_{t-1,t},v_t)}{p(x_t,v_t,y_t|x_{t-1})} + 1 - \sum_m \beta^{(m)}_{t,x_t^{(m)}} - \sum_m \alpha^{(m)}_{t-1,x_{t-1}^{(m)}} \overset{\text{set}}{=} 0$$

$$\Rightarrow \xi_t(x_{t-1,t},v_t) \propto \exp\left(\sum_m \alpha^{(m)}_{t-1,x_{t-1}^{(m)}}\right) p(x_t,v_t,y_t|x_{t-1}) \exp\left(\sum_m \beta^{(m)}_{t,x_t^{(m)}}\right),$$

$$\frac{\partial L}{\partial \gamma_t^{(m)}(x_t^{(m)})} = \log \gamma_t^{(m)}(x_t^{(m)}) + 1 - \beta^{(m)}_{t,x_t^{(m)}} - \alpha^{(m)}_{t,x_t^{(m)}} \overset{\text{set}}{=} 0$$

$$\Rightarrow \gamma_t^{(m)}(x_t^{(m)}) \propto \exp\left(\alpha^{(m)}_{t,x_t^{(m)}} + \beta^{(m)}_{t,x_t^{(m)}}\right).$$

After taking $\xi_t(x_{t-1,t},v_t)$ and $\gamma_t^{(m)}(x_t^{(m)})$ into Eq 7, we get Eq. 12.

To derive Eq. 15, we marginalize Eq. 13 over all $x_{t-1,t}^{(m')}$ for $m' \neq m$.

$$\begin{aligned}
&\xi(x_{t-1}^{(m)}, v_t, x_t^{(m)}) \\
&= \frac{1}{Z_t} \sum_{x_{t-1,t},v_t:\text{fix } x_{t-1,t}^{(m)},v_t} p(x_t,v_t|x_{t-1}) \prod_m \alpha^{(m)}(x_{t-1}^{(m)}) \beta^{(m)}(x_t^{(m)}) p^{(m)}(y_t^{(m)}|x_t^{(m)}) \\
&\propto c_k \tau \prod_{m' \neq m} \sum_{x_{t-1,t}^{(m')}} \alpha_{t-1}^{(m')} g^{(m')}(x_{t-1}^{(m')}) \beta_t^{(m')} p(y_t^{(m')}|x_t^{(m')}) 1(\Delta x_t^{(m')} = \Delta_k^{(m')}) \\
&\cdot \alpha_{t-1}^{(m)}(x_{t-1}^{(m)}) g^{(m)}(x_{t-1}^{(m)}) \beta_t^{(m)}(x_t^{(m)}) p(y_t^{(m)}|x_t^{(m)}) 1(\Delta x_t^{(m)} = \Delta_k^{(m)}) \\
&\qquad \text{if } v_t = k \neq \emptyset, \qquad (20) \\
&\propto \prod_{m' \neq m} \sum_{x_{t-1,t}^{(m')}} \alpha_{t-1}^{(m')}(x_{t-1}^{(m')}) \beta_t^{(m')}(x_t^{(m')}) p(y_t^{(m')}|x_t^{(m')}) 1(\Delta x_t^{(m')} = 0) \\
&\cdot \alpha_t^{(m)}(x_{t-1}^{(m)}) \beta_t^{(m)}(x_t^{(m)}) p(y_t^{(m)}|x_t^{(m)}) 1(\Delta x_t^{(m)} = 0) \\
&- \sum_k c_k \tau \prod_{m' \neq m} \sum_{x_{t-1,t}^{(m')}} \alpha_{t-1}^{(m')} g^{(m')}(x_{t-1}^{(m')}) \beta_t^{(m')} p(y_t^{(m')}|x_t^{(m')}) 1(\Delta x_t^{(m')} = 0) \\
&\cdot \alpha_{t-1}^{(m)}(x_{t-1}^{(m)}) g^{(m)}(x_{t-1}^{(m)}) \beta_t^{(m)}(x_t^{(m)}) p(y_t^{(m)}|x_t^{(m)}) 1(\Delta x_t^{(m)} = 0) \\
&\qquad \text{if } v_t = \emptyset. \qquad (21)
\end{aligned}$$

After deviding Eq. 20 and Eq. 21 by

$$\prod_{m' \neq m} \sum_{x_{t-1,t}^{(m')}} \alpha_{t-1}^{(m')}(x_{t-1}^{(m')}) \beta_t^{(m')}(x_t^{(m')}) p(y_t^{(m')}|x_t^{(m')}) 1(\Delta x_t^{(m')} = 0)$$

we get Eq. 15, $\tilde{g}^{(m)}_{k,t-1}$, $\hat{g}^{(m)}_{k,t-1}$ and Z_t.

REFERENCES

[1] Adam Arkin, John Ross, and Harley H McAdams. Stochastic kinetic analysis of developmental pathway bifurcation in phage λ-infected escherichia coli cells. *Genetics*, 149(4):1633–1648, 1998.

[2] M. Batty. *Cities and Complexity: Understanding Cities With Cellular Automata, Agent-Based Models, and Fractals.* Mit Press, 2007.

[3] Moshe Ben-Akiva, Michel Bierlaire, Haris Koutsopoulos, and Rabi Mishalani. Dynamit: a simulation-based system for traffic prediction. In *DACCORS short term forecasting workshop, The Netherlands.* Citeseer, 1998.

[4] HA Bethe. Statistical theory of superlattices. In *Proc. Roy. Soc. London A*, volume 150, pages 552–575, 1935.

[5] Vincent D Blondel, Adeline Decuyper, and Gautier Krings. A survey of results on mobile phone datasets analysis. *EPJ Data Science*, 4(1):1–55, 2015.

[6] Andrei Borshchev. *The Big Book of Simulation Modeling: Multimethod Modeling with AnyLogic 6.* AnyLogic North America, 2013.

[7] Matthew Brand, Nuria Oliver, and Alex Pentland. Coupled hidden markov models for complex action recognition. In *Proc. of CVPR*, pages 994–999, 1997.

[8] Claudio Castellano, Santo Fortunato, and Vittorio Loreto. Statistical physics of social dynamics. *Reviews of Modern Physics*, 81(2):591–646, 2009.

[9] Nicholas A. Christakis and James H. Fowler. The spread of obesity in a large social network over 32 years. *The New England Journal of Medicine*, 357:370–379, 2007.

[10] Yves-Alexandre de Montjoye, Zbigniew Smoreda, Romain Trinquart, Cezary Ziemlicki, and Vincent D Blondel. D4d-senegal: the second mobile phone data for development challenge. *arXiv preprint arXiv:1407.4885*, 2014.

[11] Arthur P Dempster, Nan M Laird, and Donald B Rubin. Maximum likelihood from incomplete data via the em algorithm. *Journal of the royal statistical society. Series B (methodological)*, pages 1–38, 1977.

[12] Wen Dong, Bruno Lepri, and Alex Sandy Pentland. Modeling the co-evolution of behaviors and social relationships using mobile phone data. In *Proceedings of the 10th International Conference on Mobile and Ubiquitous Multimedia*, pages 134–143. ACM, 2011.

[13] Wen Dong and Alex Pentland. A network analysis of road traffic with vehicle tracking data. In *AAAI Spring Symposium: Human Behavior Modeling*, pages 7–12, 2009.

[14] Wen Dong, Alex Pentland, and Katherine A. Heller. Graph-coupled hmms for modeling the spread of infection. In Nando de Freitas and Kevin P. Murphy, editors, *UAI*, pages 227–236. AUAI Press, 2012.

[15] Stefan B Edlund, Matthew A Davis, and James H Kaufman. The spatiotemporal epidemiological modeler. In *Proceedings of the 1st ACM International Health Informatics Symposium*, pages 817–820. ACM, 2010.

[16] Joshua M. M. Epstein. *Generative Social Science: Studies in Agent-Based Computational Modeling (Princeton Studies in Complexity).* Princeton University Press, 2007.

[17] Stephen Eubank, Hasan Guclu, VS Anil Kumar, Madhav V Marathe, Aravind Srinivasan, Zoltan Toroczkai, and Nan Wang. Modelling disease outbreaks in realistic urban social networks. *Nature*, 429(6988):180–184, 2004.

[18] Kai Fan, Marisa Eisenberg, Alison Walsh, Allison Aiello, and Katherine Heller. Hierarchical graph-coupled hmms for heterogeneous personalized health data. In *Proceedings of the 21th ACM SIGKDD International Conference on Knowledge Discovery and Data Mining*, pages 239–248. ACM, 2015.

[19] Jay Wright Forrester and Jay W Forrester. *Urban dynamics*, volume 114. mIt press Cambridge, 1969.

[20] Zoubin Ghahramani and Michael I Jordan. Factorial hidden markov models. *Machine learning*, 29(2-3):245–273, 1997.

[21] Nigel Gilbert. *Agent-Based Models (Quantitative Applications in Social Sciences).* Sage Publications, Inc., 2007.

[22] Daniel T Gillespie. Stochastic simulation of chemical kinetics. *Annu. Rev. Phys. Chem.*, 58:35–55, 2007.

[23] Winfried Karl Grassmann. Transient solutions in markovian queueing systems. *Computers & Operations Research*, 4:47–53, 1977.

[24] Tom Heskes and Onno Zoeter. Expectation propogation for approximate inference in dynamic bayesian networks. In Adnan Darwiche and Nir Friedman, editors, *UAI*, pages 216–223. Morgan Kaufmann, 2002.

[25] Eric J Horvitz, Johnson Apacible, Raman Sarin, and Lin Liao. Prediction, expectation, and surprise: Methods, designs, and study of a deployed traffic forecasting service. *arXiv preprint arXiv:1207.1352*, 2012.

[26] Lars Hufnagel, Dirk Brockmann, and Theo Geisel. Forecast and control of epidemics in a globalized world. *Proceedings of the National Academy of Sciences of the United States of America*, 101(42):15124–15129, 2004.

[27] Lorenzo Isella, Juliette Stehlé, Alain Barrat, Ciro Cattuto, Jean-François Pinton, and Wouter Van den Broeck. What's in a crowd? analysis of face-to-face behavioral networks. *Journal of theoretical biology*, 271(1):166–180, 2011.

[28] Michael I Jordan, Zoubin Ghahramani, and Lawrence K Saul. Hidden markov decision trees. In *Proc. of NIPS*, pages 501–507, 1996.

[29] David Kotz, Tristan Henderson, Ilya Abyzov, and Jihwang Yeo. CRAWDAD data set dartmouth/campus (v. 2007-02-08). Downloaded from http://crawdad.org/dartmouth/campus/, 2007.

[30] Kalev Leetaru and Philip A Schrodt. Gdelt: Global data on events, location, and tone, 1979–2012. In *ISA Annual Convention*, volume 2, page 4, 2013.

[31] Thomas Liggett. *Interacting particle systems*, volume 276. Springer Science & Business Media, 2012.

[32] MATSim development team (ed.). MATSIM-T: Aims, approach and implementation. Technical report, IVT, ETH Zürich, Zürich, 2007.

[33] Thomas P. Minka. Expectation propagation for approximate bayesian inference. In Jack S. Breese and

Daphne Koller, editors, *UAI*, pages 362–369. Morgan Kaufmann, 2001.

[34] Kevin P Murphy, Yair Weiss, and Michael I Jordan. Loopy belief propagation for approximate inference: An empirical study. In *Proceedings of the Fifteenth conference on Uncertainty in artificial intelligence*, pages 467–475. Morgan Kaufmann Publishers Inc., 1999.

[35] Wei Pan, Wen Dong, Manuel Cebrian, Taemie Kim, James H Fowler, and Alex Sandy Pentland. Modeling dynamical influence in human interaction: Using data to make better inferences about influence within social systems. *Signal Processing Magazine, IEEE*, 29(2):77–86, 2012.

[36] Michal Piorkowski, Natasa Sarafijanovic-Djukic, and Matthias Grossglauser. CRAWDAD data set epfl/mobility (v. 2009-02-24). Downloaded from http://crawdad.org/epfl/mobility/, February 2009.

[37] John Platt et al. Probabilistic outputs for support vector machines and comparisons to regularized likelihood methods. *Advances in large margin classifiers*, 10(3):61–74, 1999.

[38] Neeti Pokhriyal, Wen Dong, and Venu Govindaraju. Virtual networks and poverty analysis in senegal. *arXiv preprint arXiv:1506.03401*, 2015.

[39] Lawrence R Rabiner. A tutorial on hidden markov models and selected applications in speech recognition. *Proceedings of the IEEE*, 77(2):257–286, 1989.

[40] Ralph Tyrell Rockafellar. *Convex analysis*. Princeton university press, 2015.

[41] Marcel Salathé, Maria Kazandjieva, Jung Woo Lee, Philip Levis, Marcus W Feldman, and James H Jones. A high-resolution human contact network for infectious disease transmission. *Proceedings of the National Academy of Sciences*, 107(51):22020–22025, 2010.

[42] Laron Smith, Richard Beckman, and Keith Baggerly. Transims: Transportation analysis and simulation system. Technical report, Los Alamos National Lab., NM (United States), 1995.

[43] Eleni I Vlahogianni, Matthew G Karlaftis, and John C Golias. Short-term traffic forecasting: Where we are and where we're going. *Transportation Research Part C: Emerging Technologies*, 43:3–19, 2014.

[44] Paul Waddell. Urbansim: Modeling urban development for land use, transportation, and environmental planning. *Journal of the American Planning Association*, 68(3):297–314, 2002.

[45] Martin J. Wainwright and Michael I. Jordan. Graphical models, exponential families, and variational inference. *Foundations and Trends in Machine Learning*, 1(1-2):1–305, 2008.

[46] Yibing Wang, Markos Papageorgiou, and Albert Messmer. Real-time freeway traffic state estimation based on extended kalman filter: Adaptive capabilities and real data testing. *Transportation Research Part A: Policy and Practice*, 42(10):1340–1358, 2008.

[47] Darren James. Wilkinson. *Stochastic modelling for systems biology*. Taylor & Francis, Boca Raton, FL, 2006.

[48] Hongbin Yin, S_C Wong, Jianmin Xu, and CK Wong. Urban traffic flow prediction using a fuzzy-neural approach. *Transportation Research Part C: Emerging Technologies*, 10(2):85–98, 2002.

Affect-Aware Student Models for Robot Tutors

Samuel Spaulding
MIT Media Lab
Cambridge, MA 02139
samuelsp@media.mit.edu

Goren Gordon
Curiosity Lab
Tel-Aviv University
Tel Aviv 6997801, Israel
goren@gorengordon.com

Cynthia Breazeal
MIT Media Lab
Cambridge, MA 02139
cynthiab@media.mit.edu

ABSTRACT

Computational tutoring systems, such as educational software or interactive robots, have the potential for great societal benefit. Such systems track and assess students' knowledge via inferential methods, such as the popular Bayesian Knowledge Tracing (BKT) algorithm. However, these methods do not typically draw on the affective signals that human teachers use to assess knowledge, such as indications of discomfort, engagement, or frustration.

In this paper we present a novel extension to the BKT model that uses affective data, derived autonomously from video records of children playing an interactive story-telling game with a robot, to infer student knowledge of reading skills. We find that, compared to a control group of children who played the game with only a tablet, children who interacted with an embodied social robot generated stronger affective data signals of engagement and enjoyment during the interaction. We then show that incorporating this affective data into model training improves the quality of the learned knowledge inference models.

These results suggest that physically embodied, affect-aware robot tutors can provide more effective and empathic educational experiences for children, and advance both algorithmic and human-centered motivations for further development of systems that tightly integrate affect understanding and complex models of inference with interactive, educational robots.

Keywords

socially assistive robots; educational robots; child-robot interaction; affective computing

1. INTRODUCTION

Intelligent tutoring systems (ITS) are software tutors that attempt to combine the educational benefits of one-on-one tutoring with the scale and ease-of-deployment of software [23]. While ITS research has led to improved outcomes for students, they are often designed as digital workbooks, with the tutoring system providing a sequence of practice problems and offering the student a limited action space (often just the choice of providing an answer or asking for a hint). Recent evidence indicates more interactive learning styles may be better suited for school-age children; we believe the design of computational tutors should reflect these principles.

Appears in: *Proceedings of the 15th International Conference on Autonomous Agents and Multiagent Systems (AAMAS 2016),*
J. Thangarajah, K. Tuyls, C. Jonker, S. Marsella (eds.),
May 9–13, 2016, Singapore.

Previous research indicates that *physically embodied social robots, capable of perceiving and understanding affective signals* can deliver more engaging and empathic educational experiences [13]. In this paper, we add to this increasing body of evidence by establishing social robots' unique capability to engage children in *affect-aware tutoring experiences*.

We conducted an analysis of children's facial expressions from video records of an experiment described in [9] and [10]. In this experiment, children played an interactive story-telling game with a robot. During the game, the robot would assess the child's reading ability by verbally asking them to identify a word written on the screen. The experiment was recorded, including a close camera shot of the child's face, which, along with time-synced records of the child's game actions, forms our dataset.

This analysis was conducted using Affdex, a commercial affect-analysis tool based on FACS and trained on data from over 2.7 million faces in 75 countries [20, 17]. We developed a custom application using the Affdex SDK to analyze 38 children's interactions with a robot, each approximately 12 minutes long.

We compared the affective response, derived via Affdex, of children who interacted with a robot to the affective response of a control group of children who only interacted with a tablet, and show that children who played the story game with a robot generated stronger average emotional expressions over the course of the interaction.

We then used this affective data, in combination with the student's performance data (right/wrong answers), to train a novel, *affective* model for inferring student knowledge. We compare the affective model to a standard Bayesian Knowledge Tracing (BKT) model (trained only on the student performance data) and show that the affective model is better able to generalize to test data from the same population.

2. RELATED WORK

This paper describes work to combine the sophisticated modeling techniques of Intelligent Tutoring Systems with the engaging and empathic abilities of physically embodied, socially interactive robots. Here we give a short review of some relevant work from the ITS and HRI communities.

Intelligent Tutoring Systems (ITSs) refer to a wide variety of computer-based educational tools [23]. The subclass of "affect-aware tutors" [26] are ITSs that explicitly sense, model, and reason about students' affective states. Inspired by psychological theories of emotion and learning, affect-aware tutors seek to foster engagement and learning from data-driven estimates of students' affective states. Previous work has established the validity of affective data captured during educational interactions [11], and efforts to develop affect-aware tutoring systems have culminated in a number of extensively studied systems, e.g., the Wayang Tutor [1] and Affective Meta-Tutor [24] projects. Yet much of the computational work on affect and modeling in the ITS literature focuses on models to *infer* affect. Typically, once affective states are detected or identified, they trigger simple behavioral rules: a tutor might change its facial expression or offer a supportive comment. These rules are most commonly hardcoded by the developers and remain fixed throughout the deployment, limiting the generality and flexibility of the agent's affective responses.

In parallel, researchers have explored the use of robots as educational tutors. Social robots have been successfully deployed in schools to teach topics as varied as vocabulary [22], chess [13], mathematics [4], and abstract analytic skills [14]. Long-term studies of robots, while less common, have demonstrated that social robots can be an effective tool for improving children's literacy skills [12]. These results suggest that social robots may be particularly well-suited to educational tutoring applications.

Some work has explored physical robots that respond to human affect in education. As with ITSs, however, the robot's responses are typically the result of scripted rules. In work by Szafir and Mutlu [21], students wore an EEG sensor while a robot told a story. The robot responded to perceived student decreases in attention by producing exaggerated gestures, which led to better participant story recall.

Researchers in the LIREC project developed a robotic chess tutoring system that uses more sophisticated affective models to give empathy-based support [13]. The robot models a child's affective state by tracking in-game events in combination with external physical sensors and offers support by mirroring the child's (estimated) affective state.

Unlike previous efforts to unite affect, tutoring, and robots, in this paper, we incorporate affect directly into a robot's *learning* model. While other work has used affect as an input to behavioral rules, this work is the first to evaluate a robotic tutoring system that uses affective data to train models of student knowledge.

3. METHODS FOR COMPUTATIONALLY ASSESSING KNOWLEDGE

One challenge for any tutor, human or computer, is the problem of determining what a student does or does not know. If a student's skill level is too far above or below the level required by the curriculum, they may feel bored or discouraged. The ability to modulate the curriculum to keep students in a state of Flow – in which they are highly engaged in a task at an optimal challenge level – is considered a crucial advantage of one-on-one tutoring [8]. To do so, a tutor must have an accurate estimate of a student's skill level. But how does one assess another's knowledge?

3.1 Bayesian Knowledge Tracing

For computational tutors, Bayesian inference on graphical models is the most popular approach. If the subject domain can be suitably modeled, algorithms for inference can allow computational systems to accurately estimate student skill levels. The most popular and widely used of these methods is known as Bayesian Knowledge Tracing (BKT), a domain-general model used to infer skill mastery from student data. BKT models are widely used in ITS research and can be applied to any educational domain which can be decomposed into different component "skills"[7, 2].

Under the BKT model, a student's mastery of each skill is modeled by a Dynamic Bayesian Network. These skill models are a special case of Hidden Markov Models, which can be in one of

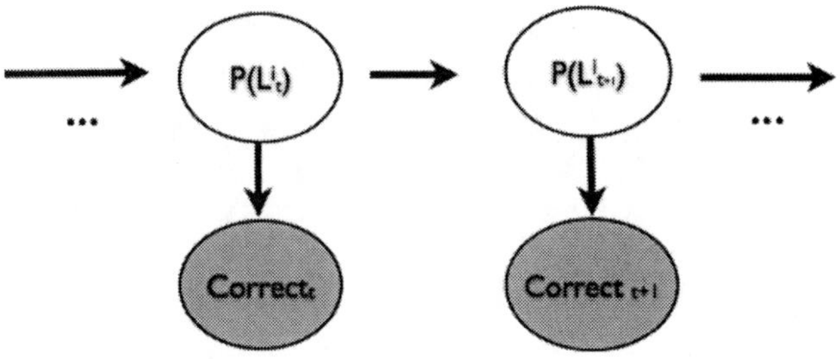

Figure 1: Traditional BKT Hidden Markov Model. Based on observations of a student's correct and incorrect responses, the model can infer the student's hidden knowledge state. The state nodes represent the probability that skill *i* was learned after question t. The observable nodes represent whether the student correctly demonstrated skill *i* when answering question *t*

two hidden states, "skill mastered" or "skill not-mastered", where the observations are the student's answers to questions requiring knowledge of a particular skill.

The BKT model, while popular for its straightforward analysis and ease of implementation, suffers from some limitations. Most significantly for this work, the BKT model relies solely on a student's pattern of correct/incorrect answers to drive inference, while ignoring a wide range of relevant contextual information, such as a student's affective expressions. In spite of BKT's limitations, it is still one of the most popular methods for knowledge assessment and forms the basis of a substantial body of research [2, 27].

3.2 Affective-BKT

In this paper we introduce an affective variant of the BKT model, which we call the Affective-BKT (Aff-BKT) model – a BKT model with additional observation nodes representing features of the student's facial expression measured during an educational interaction with a robot. The Aff-BKT model is an attempt to improve the BKT model, by augmenting it to draw inference from *affective* as well as knowledge-based features. Whereas the standard BKT model has only one observation per timestep (whether the student answered a question correctly or not), the Aff-BKT model is an HMM that incorporates multiple observations per time step. In addition to the observable node corresponding to a correct/incorrect response, our Aff-BKT model includes observable nodes that correspond to whether a child was smiling and whether a child appeared engaged. These affective observation nodes are structured identically to the observation of correct/incorrect answers (see Fig. 1), therefore each additional node requires just two additional parameters per skill model.

While our Affective BKT model does not address all of the limitations of BKT, it serves as a proof-of-concept that affective information can be reliably detected and made useful to computational tutoring systems, and that models that take advantage of affective information can outperform existing techniques.

4. EXPERIMENTAL OVERVIEW

The data used to train and evaluate our models come from video records of a previously published experiment [9, 10]. In this experiment, children (aged 4-8) played a story game with a robot. The interaction was designed around a child-robot-tablet interface, in which the child and robot sit across from each other, with a tablet placed between them as a shared, social context that can be sensed by the robot (Figure 3).

The child and the robot played a custom-designed game called "Storymaker." In the game, graphics of characters (such as animals

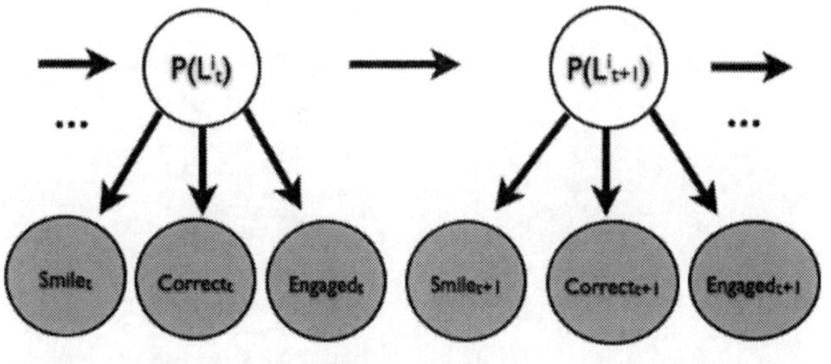

Figure 2: The Affective BKT model, which incorporates affective signals into knowledge state inference.

Figure 3: Picture of the interaction setup from which the dataset was collected. Children played a storytelling game with a robot, during which they were periodically prompted to read a word

or objects) float on a background of different scenes (such as a beach or jungle) and can be moved by the child via touchscreen. The robot was framed as a younger peer. It greeted the child by saying "Let's play word games together!" and was introduced by the experimenter as "a young robot who has just learned to speak, and wants to learn to read."

During the game, the child was prompted to move the characters to different regions of the scene. After each 'action' taken by the child, the app procedurally generates a sentence that characterizes this action, which the robot would speak aloud. For example, if the child moves the Dragon character graphic towards the rightmost side of the forest scene (depicting a tree), the game might generate the sentence "Dragon goes to the tree" as part of the story. The spoken sentence would also appear in written form at the top of the tablet.

50% of the time, after the robot had spoken a sentence, the robot would follow by prompting the child to read one of the words in the sentence by saying: "I don't know how to read the word [X], can you show it to me?" The game would then pause until the child tapped on one of the words in the sentence (shown at the top of the tablet). If the child tapped the correct word, the app (via TTS) would read the tapped word, thereby letting the child know whether their answer was correct. If the child tapped an incorrect word, he/she would be prompted to try again by the robot ("I don't think that's right. Can you try again?"). After two incorrect tries, the game would highlight and read the correct word, then continue with the next part of the story. On average, a child experienced 29 of these demonstration opportunities during the interaction.

4.1 Tablet-only Interaction Participants

Section 4 describes the interaction for 25 of the participants. However, there was also a smaller control group of 13 participants that did *not* interact with the robot. In this condition, a white cardboard box was placed over the robot for the duration of the experiment, The children were not told there was a robot underneath the box, only that they would be playing word games on a tablet. Other than the presence of the covering box and the removal of experimenter references to the robot, the experiment proceeded exactly as described above. The robot's story 'speech' still came from the

Figure 4: Sample frame of collected footage

same speakers and the children were still prompted to read words as before; the underlying technology did not change. This condition therefore provides an ideal scenario to examine how children's emotional expressiveness varies with the presence of a social robot during *otherwise identical* interactions, which we discuss in Section 7.1.

4.2 Video QA-interval Dataset

Video of the entire interaction was recorded from a camera, located behind and to the side of the robot, aimed at the child's face (Fig. 4). In addition to video data, the full state of the game, all child actions on the tablet, all robot speech, and all tablet actions (e.g., highlighting the correct word if the child answered incorrectly twice) were recorded and synchronized via ROS to support search, playback, and analysis.

Though complete footage of the interaction was recorded, in this work we are primarily concerned with analyzing children's emotions while they are engaged in educational activity. In addition, the HMM formalism for both Knowledge Tracing models (BKT and Aff-BKT) requires discrete timesteps. We therefore only analyze video footage from specific, educationally relevant, intervals during each interaction called **QA-intervals**.

As described above, after a child moved the story characters, the robot would sometimes ask the child to read a word, denoted [X], by asking the child "I don't know the word [X]. Can you show it to me?" The robot was asking the child to identify word [X] in text on the screen, providing both an opportunity for the child to demonstrate his/her reading ability and an opportunity to collect spontaneous facial expression data during educational activity. We identified the precise times at which the robot *asked* a question and the times at which the child *gave an answer to that question*. We then extracted video footage from 5 seconds before each asking event to 5 seconds after each response event, which defined a **"QA-interval"**.

5. AFFECTIVE BKT: IMPLEMENTATION AND EVALUATION

In this section, we describe the implementation and evaluation of the two Knowledge Tracing models in the context of assessing the students' reading skills. We discuss the skills we chose to model, followed by detailing the structural implementations of each model, how the training data was obtained, and how the parameters for each model were trained from the data.

5.1 Modeling alphabetic principle skills

Learning to read is an acquired skill that requires mastery of many foundational sub-skills before fluent "reading" occurs [25]. In this paper, we focus on modeling a subset of these skills known as "alphabetic principle" skills. The alphabetic principle is the recognition that *written* letters and their combinations correspond to *spoken* sounds in specific and predictable ways. In other words, these skills are the rules and mappings that connect written letters with spoken sounds [6, 16].

In this paper, we model children's literacy progress via **four BKT skill models and four Aff-BKT skill models**. Three models of each type correspond to one of three alphabetic principle skills. In addition, we include one model of each type that tracks the complete ability to read a word exactly. The three alphabetic principle skills tracked were: recognizing the first grapheme of a word, identifying a word of approximately the same length as a spoken word, and recognizing the final grapheme of a word.

The first skill, denoted FIRST-LETTER, requires the child to hear a requested word, decompose its sounds into phonemes, map the phonemes into graphemes, and then select a word that features those graphemes at the beginning of the word. Roughly, it corresponds to the first step of the oft-repeated advice to a young reader - "Sound it out!" We considered a student to have correctly demonstrated this skill if they selected a word that *starts* with the same grapheme as the requested word.

The second skill, denoted LENGTH, requires the child to understand that the length of a written word corresponds to the number of syllables in its spoken instantiation. For this skill, we considered a student to have correctly demonstrated this skill if they selected a word with a length within 1 letter of the requested word's length.

The third skill, denoted LAST-LETTER, requires the child to go through the same process as FIRST-LETTER, applied to the end of the word. This skill poses slightly more of a challenge, as children naturally attempt to read a word from its start. We considered a student to have correctly demonstrated this skill if they selected a word that *ends* with the same grapheme as the requested word.

Lastly, we model the complete, correct reading of a word. This skill, denoted EXACT-CORRECT, requires the child to fully and correctly identify the requested word, representing the complete ability to read the requested word. Because the requested word was spoken aloud by the tablet, homophones were considered equivalent (e.g. if the robot asked for the word 'to', and both 'to' and 'too' were among the possible answers, either would be considered 'exactly correct').

We chose to analyze this set of skills because they are well-suited to the task from which the dataset was derived (see Sec 4), relatively easy to detect computationally (compared to, e.g., analysis of a child's pronunciation), and because they are developmentally appropriate for the age group of the population [19]. Though the alphabetic principle skills are clearly interrelated, BKT skills are most commonly treated independently. In line with our stated research focus (examining whether *affective features* improve Knowledge Tracing models), we assume that each skill is mastered independently of the others.

5.2 Building BKT and Aff-BKT Skill Models

We constructed BKT models for each tracked skill using Kevin Murphy's Bayes Net Toolkit [18], a freely available, open-source library for implementing a wide variety of graphical models. Each BKT model has one hidden node – with two possible states, (Skill Learned or Skill Not-Learned) – and one observation node – with two possible values (Question Correct or Question Incorrect) – per time step. Each BKT model has the structure depicted in Figure 1 and is fully specified by 5 parameters, which set the rate of learning, the probability of forgetting a previously mastered skill, the probability of guessing correctly (if the skill is not mastered), the probability of making a mistake (i.e., answering wrong if the skill is mastered), and the prior probability that the skill is mastered.

As with the BKT models, we constructed an Aff-BKT model for each skill using the Bayes Net Toolkit. Each Aff-BKT model includes two additional observable nodes per time step – $Smile_t$ and $Engaged_t$, depicted in Figure 2. These additional nodes require just two additional parameters each: the probability that a child appears engaged if they have/have not mastered the skill and the probability that a child smiles if they have/have not mastered the skill. Thus, each Aff-BKT model is fully specified by 9 parameters. In the following sections, we describe how we derived the training data from video footage of the interactions, how the parameters for each model were learned from the data, and how we evaluated each model.

5.3 Deriving QA-interval skill data

In Section 4.2, we defined the concept of a *QA-interval*: the educationally relevant portions of the interactions from just before the robot asked for a word to be read to just after the child gave an answer. We implemented string-matching functions to compute whether the word the child provided during each QA-interval represented a correct application of a skill, given the requested word. For example, if a child selected the word **'prince'** when the requested word was **'princess'**, that is a correct application of FIRST-LETTER, but not of EXACT-CORRECT, LENGTH, or LAST-LETTER. For each QA-interval, we applied these functions to the requested and answered words. The end result was, for each QA-interval, four boolean results (Correct or Incorrect) representing whether or not the child's answer represented a correct demonstration of each skill (FIRST-LETTER, LENGTH, LAST-LETTER, EXACT-CORRECT).

5.4 Deriving QA-interval affective data

5.4.1 *Affdex: a tool for autonomous affect detection*

Often, researchers studying human affect use human coders to manually review video footage of interactions and provide labels from a set of pre-determined affective states. Sometimes coders will have training in facial expression coding, but in many cases, the video coders are either the experimenters themselves, undergraduate research assistants, or online workers (e.g., workers on Amazon Mechanical Turk). Inter-coder reliability ratings can help verify the accuracy of labeling, but all of these methods are ultimately subject to human judgement.

Our research goals are to develop social robot tutors that are robust enough to be widely deployed for long-term interactions and intelligent enough to act autonomously. To achieve these goals, robots cannot rely solely on human annotation to understand user affect. Methods for *unobtrusively* and *autonomously* sensing affect are rapidly improving; in line with our vision, we rely solely on autonomous affect detection and labeling in this work.

To analyze children's emotional expressions without relying on human coders, we used the Affdex SDK, a commercial tool marketed by Affectiva, Inc. to enable development of affect-aware mobile applications. Affdex uses state-of-the-art face detection and analysis algorithms to extract estimates of four physical facial expression features **(Smile, BrowFurrow, BrowRaise, and LipDepress)** and two hidden affective features **(Valence and Engagement)** from video or images of faces. For each of these six metrics, Affdex produces an estimate of the strength of that affective indicator, normalized to [0, 100], excepting Valence, which is normalized to [-100, 100].

Affdex uses data collected from over 2.7 million faces in authentic scenarios, labeled by FACS-trained coders and rigorously validated by leading specialists in affective computing [20, 17]. We used the Affdex SDK to analyze sequences of time-stamped images extracted from video. Affdex analyzes each frame (providing data at a much finer level of granularity than is typically afforded by human coders) and each frame result can be precisely linked back to the rest of the data through its timestamp.

5.4.2 *Analyzing affective data*

We sampled still frames from video footage of each QA-interval (each interaction contained 29 QA-intervals, on average) at approximately 20fps. We wrote a simple app using the Affdex SDK that analyzed all frames from each QA-interval. The output of the analysis was, for each frame, either a single measured value for each of the 6 metrics, or a null measurement (indicating that no data could be extracted from the frame). Each frame result was then written to file, and manually transferred to a secure data storage location for subsequent analysis.

Autonomously sensed affective data is difficult to capture and interpret. Unsurprisingly, the initial measurements from Affdex were highly variable, even on a frame-by-frame basis. Frame results would alternate rapidly between consistent, modest values (indicative of correct processing and analysis) and null or extreme results (e.g., minimum or maximum values for all metrics). To smooth these discontinuities, we applied a median filter to the data, operating over a sliding window of 20 frames, (see Fig. 5). The end result of this median smoothing process is a set of data points with significantly fewer spikes or rapid increases and decreases. However, when such increases or decreases are present, they are more likely due to a *bona fide* affective signal, rather than noise.

To derive data for the Smile/Engagement features of the Affective-BKT model, for each QA-interval we calculated the mean value of the Engagement and Smile metrics, both of which have been used as input to behavioral rules in prior affective-aware tutoring work [5]. We assigned each QA-interval a discrete, boolean label of Smile/No Smile and Enaged/Not Engaged via a mean value threshold of 30. The end result of this process was, for each QA-interval, two sets of boolean results (Smile/No Smile and Engaged/Not Engaged). Note that, unlike the skill correctness data, the affective data does not change with the skill being modeled.

5.5 Training BKT and Aff-BKT models from QA-interval data

5.5.1 *Expectation Maximization: learning model parameters from observed data*

We trained the parameter values for each skill model via Expectation Maximization (EM). Expectation Maximization (EM) is a general technique for estimating a set of parameters from data. Under the assumption that some set of parameters, θ, generated a set of data, D, Expectation Maximization tries to find the Maximum Likelihood Estimate (MLE) of the parameters, given the data: $max_{\theta}Pr(\theta|D)$. For the BKT models, the data used to train each skill model is the set of skill-correctness data for the corresponding skill (described in Sec. 5.3). For the Aff-BKT skill models, the training data is the skill-correctness data *and* the affective data. EM converges when the difference in likelihood between iterations falls below some threshold parameter, ε. In this work, we let $\varepsilon = 10^{-5}$. All models converged in <15 iterations. Each BKT model took approximately 20 minutes to train; each Aff-BKT model took approximately 40 minutes to train.

5.5.2 *Initial Conditions*

EM is a deterministic algorithm, and therefore the final learned model is somewhat sensitive to initial conditions. We initially set the prior mastery parameter at .5, the learning rate parameter at .2, the slip and guess parameters at .25 (the actual chance of guessing correctly ranges from $11-33\%$ depending on the skill and QA-interval), and, as is common in short-term BKT models, the forgetting rate parameter at 0. During EM, these parameters are tuned to maximize the likelihood of the parameter set, given the data. The end result of training is a set of learned parameters (i.e., the learned model), which we denote θ_{aff} for an Aff-BKT model and θ_{bkt} for a traditional BKT model.

6. BAYESIAN MODEL SELECTION

The main research question of this paper is whether incorporating affective information into the training process improves BKT models. Knowledge Tracing is difficult precisely because a student's knowledge state is not directly observable. Because we have no ground-truth data, it is infeasible to use traditional supervised learning benchmarks (e.g., precision and recall or F-score), to evaluate the Aff-BKT and BKT models.

To overcome this limitation, we evaluate our models from the perspective of Bayesian Model Selection. Bayesian Model Selection is the general problem of determining which of several possible models should be preferred, given some data. Approaches to model selection vary based on the space of possible models and datasets, but typically rely on comparing the likelihoods of different models.

Many standard model selection metrics (e.g., Bayesian or Akaike Information Criterion) are used to compare models with different *structures*, trained on the same *data*. The BKT and Affective-BKT models differ not only in their structure but also in the data they model and are trained from; therefore, these techniques are not appropriate for this case.

To properly address our stated research focus, we construct a new Aff-BKT model, denoted $\hat{\theta}_{aff}$, which has the same *structure* as θ_{bkt}, but is trained from the Aff-BKT *data*. This model is the subset of the parameters that the BKT and Aff-BKT models share. Specifically, we derive the $\hat{\theta}_{aff}$ model by taking the subset of parameters from θ_{aff} that are also present in θ_{bkt} (described in Section 5.2) after training.

By doing so, we reduce the difficulty of model comparison to a more tractable situation. $\hat{\theta}_{aff}$ and θ_{bkt} share the same *structure*, but only $\hat{\theta}_{aff}$ was trained with affective *data*. This enables us to conduct a more straightforward analysis of the models' respective likelihoods: leave-one-out cross-validation (LOOCV), in which all but one participants' data is used to train the model, then the likelihood of each trained model is evaluated, with respect to the held-out participant's data.

LOOCV occurs in two phases: during the "training" phase, a single participant's data is held-out and the two models are trained on the remaining data via EM. Then, during the "testing phase", the probability of the held-out data, under the trained model is calculated (separately, for each model) as an estimate of the model's overall performance. The probability of the held-out data is the likelihood of the model, and is used to measure model 'fit' – that is, how well the model explains the observed data. Models with higher likelihood and, hence, better fit are preferred.

During a full LOOCV evaluation, this process is repeated for each of the participants, such that for a complete analysis of n participants, n different training sessions occur (each differing slightly, due to variation in training data), and n different test data points (the probabilities of all n participant's held-out data or, equivalently, n different model likelihoods) are collected per model.

Data from 38 participants was used. Thus, we repeated the process 38 times, holding out one participant each fold, and computed

Table 1: T-test results by metric, comparing differences in mean interaction value across Robot and Tablet conditions

Metric	T-test statistic	p-value
Smile	2.23	***0.037***
BrowFurrow	0.898	0.378
BrowRaise	2.68	***0.011***
LipDepress	0.328	0.746
Valence	0.844	0.405
Engagement	2.59	***0.014***

38 model likelihoods per skill model. Figure 6 shows the complete evaluation pipeline - from training data, to model construction, to model evaluation. Full results by skill and model type are presented in Figures 8 and 9. Aggregate statistics for each skill and model type are presented in Table 2.

7. RESULTS AND DISCUSSION

7.1 Children are more emotionally expressive when interacting with a social robot

To determine a participant's overall level of emotional expressiveness, we combined the affective data (for each metric) from a participant's QA-intervals and calculated the *mean value* for that metric. In other words, we calculated the average value, over the participant's interaction, of the median-filtered Affdex measurements. Because we are interested in *overall levels* of emotional expression and because valence, unlike other metrics, ranges from [-100, 100] rather than [0,100], we used the mean of the *absolute value* of the valence data. This captures the idea that highly positive and highly negative measurements both represent 'strong' emotional expressions and are evaluated as such in our analysis. Figure 5 depicts the complete data analysis workflow, from video footage to mean interaction metric value.

For each metric, we obtained mean interaction values from 25 participants that interacted with a robot, and 13 control group participants that did not interact with a robot. The means and standard error of the mean for each metric and population (Robot vs. Tablet) are shown in Figure 7.

For each metric, we first established the normality of the mean interaction values via a Shapiro-Wilk test. Then, for each metric, we conducted a Student's T-test to determine whether participants who played the game with a physical robot present were, on average, more emotionally expressive.

The test results (Table 1) show that Affdex recorded higher average emotional metric values from children in the robot condition, compared to the children in the tablet-only condition. These differences were statistically significant for 3 of the 6 metrics: **Smile, BrowRaise, and Engagement**. While the other metric differences did not reach significance, in all metrics the average measured value was higher in the robot condition.

These results agree with previous qualitative research, suggesting that children tend to smile and are highly engaged by social robots [3] and extends that research by confirming *quantitatively* and *autonomously* (i.e., without human judgement) that children who interacted with a robot during an educational task generated higher average emotional expression readings than children who did not see the robot. Previous research that has shown that the mere *physical presence* of robots can lead to increased learning gains in tutoring interactions [15]. Our work suggests that *a physical robot's capacity to modulate student affective response* may be one mechanism by which physical presence improves learning gains.

Skill	Model	Mean LL $\pm SD$
EXACT-CORRECT	A-BKT	-14.923 ± 9.01
EXACT-CORRECT	BKT	-19.79 ± 10.386
FIRST-LETTER	A-BKT	-13.652 ± 10.091
FIRST-LETTER	BKT	-17.090 ± 10.386
LENGTH	A-BKT	-13.6160 ± 9.596
LENGTH	BKT	-14.5992 ± 9.513
LAST-LETTER	A-BKT	-14.644 ± 9.493
LAST-LETTER	BKT	-18.222 ± 9.98

Table 2: Leave-one-out cross-fold validation log-likelihood metrics of Aff-BKT and BKT models

7.2 Affective-BKT models fit test data better than standard BKT models

Figure 8 shows the the log-likelihood of each BKT and Aff-BKT skill model, evaluated on every participant. For three of the four skills (EXACT-CORRECT, FIRST-LETTER, and LAST-LETTER) the Aff-BKT model error is lower for nearly all participant test data. For LENGTH, the Aff-BKT model error is generally lower, but there were some cases in which the BKT model had better fit. We suspect our approach to modeling the LENGTH skill may have been too coarse to accurately model skill mastery.

Overall, however, it is clear that the model trained with affective data fits the held-out skill data much better than the BKT model. Table 2 reinforces these results: every Aff-BKT skill model has higher mean likelihood than the traditional BKT model for the same skill. Figure 9 shows the statistical significance of these results, presented as a decrease in model error, rather than an increase in 'fit'. Following [27], we use the *negative* log-likelihood as an error function for model evaluation (for ease of presentation). This definition of error follows naturally from the interpretation of model likelihood as a measure of 'fit' (see Sec. 6). Figure 9 shows the mean error (that is, *average negative log-likelihood*) of each skill model.

These results answer our research question – "Can we build models that use affective data to improve the performance of traditional Knowledge Assessment models?" – affirmatively. Interestingly, this conclusion is reached by evaluating a BKT model and an Aff-BKT model that is *structurally identical* to the traditional BKT model and hence does not *explicitly* model affect. Rather, the influence of the affective data manifests itself in the trained values of the traditional BKT parameters. In other words, by including the additional parameters, structure, and data to support affect-awareness, we find that the Aff-BKT model learns better fitting parameters *even for parts of the model that have nothing to do with affect*! Without further study, the underlying reasons for this cannot be conclusively determined. However, we hypothesize that the affective data helps "explain away" some of the observed variance in Correct/Incorrect answers. That is, the BKT model tries to fit all five of its parameters to explain the *full* variance in the skill-correctness data. However, modern theories of affect and learning suggest that the two are deeply related, hence variance in the skill-correctness data can likely be explained in part by affective factors. The additional affective parameters of the Aff-BKT model can adjust to the variance due to affective variables (e.g., distraction, confusion), leaving the remaining parameters (common to the traditional BKT model) free to better fit the variance due to *knowledge-based* factors (e.g., genuine skill mastery).

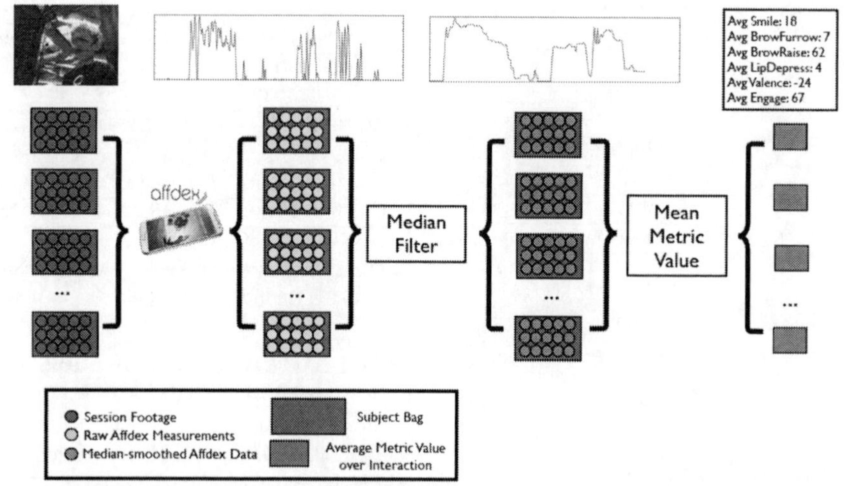

Figure 5: Data pipeline for assessing children's average level of emotional expression. Frames are sampled from video footage at 20fps, then passed to Affdex. The Affdex measurements are then passed through a median filter for smoothing. For each metric, the smoothed data points for each participant are averaged to produce a mean metric value across the entire interaction.

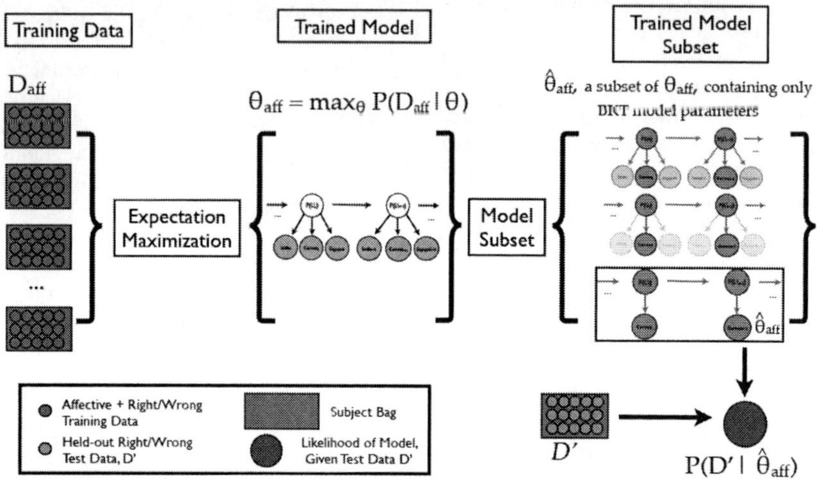

Figure 6: A single fold of the full training and evaluation pipeline for Aff-BKT skill models. The models are trained from the right/wrong *and* the affective QA-interval data via EM, with a single participant's data "held-out" for testing, resulting in a set of learned model parameters. We use a subset of the learned parameters, $\hat{\theta}_{aff}$, structured identically to the BKT parameter set, and evaluate both in the same way: comparing the likelihood of the two parameter sets, under the held-out participant's skill-correctness data. This process is repeated once for each participant, thus the final result is a set of 38 'likelihood estimate' data points for each (Aff-BKT and BKT) skill model.

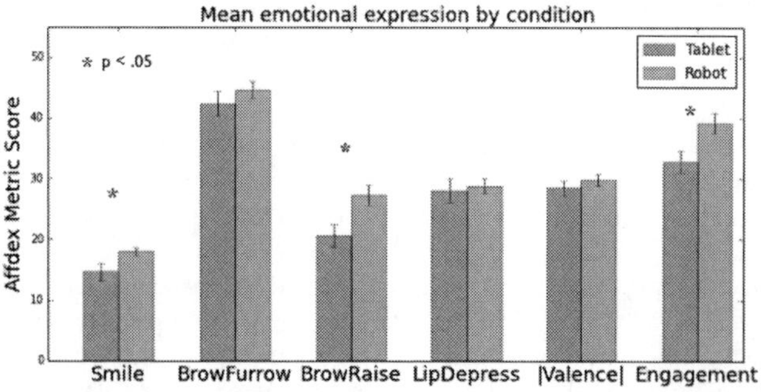

Figure 7: Average emotional expression value, by condition. Error bars represent standard error of the mean.

8. CONTRIBUTIONS AND CONCLUSIONS

In this work, we have shown that children are more emotionally expressive when engaged in an interactive educational task with a social robot than when engaged in an *identical* task with a tablet alone. Previous research has shown that the mere physical presence of social robots can alter important interaction dynamics: our work adds to that body of research by identifying an important aspect of that phenomenon (children's increased emotional expressivity) and demonstrating one way in which the next generation of computational tutors can leverage interactive learning styles for algorithmic improvements.

We have introduced a novel *affective* approach to Knowledge Tracing and demonstrated that children's emotional expression data can be successfully integrated into inferential models for assessing knowledge. These affective models outperform traditional approaches to Knowledge Tracing, demonstrating the utility of sensing affective data and constructing tutoring models to make use that data, suggesting that embodied social robots may be a more beneficial medium for developing affect-aware computational tutors.

Researchers in psychology and cognitive science are coming to understand that affect, far from being an 'irrational' influence, is

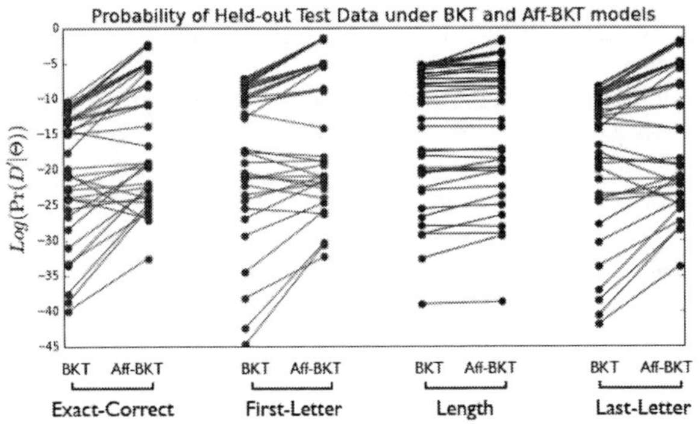

Figure 8: Probability of Test Data under BKT and Aff-BKT models, color-coded by skill. Within each skill, data points to the left represent the log-likelihood (model fit) of the BKT model evaluated on one test participant's data. Each point is connected to the log-likelihood of the Aff-BKT model evaluated on the same participant's data.

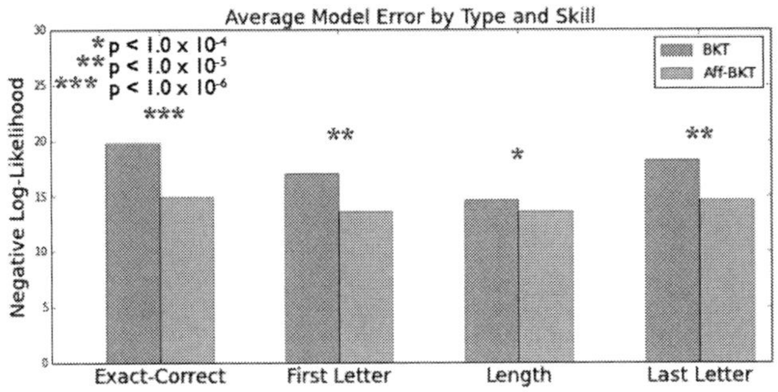

Figure 9: Mean error estimates of BKT and Aff-BKT models by skill. Significance was calculated via a one-sample T-test on the *difference* between model error estimates, evaluated on the same test participant data.

crucial to everyday decision-making. This understanding is beginning to influence the design of agents and algorithms that model or simulate intelligent behavior. While a relatively recent effort, many researchers are now pursuing efforts to integrate affect understanding into intelligent systems. Our work shows that physical robots may have advantages over software-only systems in sensing and using affective data, by demonstrating social robots' ability to induce higher degrees of emotional expressivity and showing that integrating emotionally expressive data into inference can improve the performance of student Knowledge Tracing models. Encouraged by our results, we believe this research will ultimately lead to more effective, intelligent, and natural interactions with technology.

9. ACKNOWLEDGEMENT

This research was supported by the National Science Foundation (NSF) under Grants CCF-1138986 and an NSF GRF under Grant No. 1122374. Any opinions, findings and conclusions, or recommendations expressed in this paper are those of the authors and do not represent the views of the NSF.

REFERENCES

[1] I. Arroyo, C. Beal, T. Murray, R. Walles, and B. P. Woolf. Web-based intelligent multimedia tutoring for high stakes achievement tests. In *Intelligent Tutoring Systems*, pages 468–477. Springer, 2004.

[2] R. S. Baker, A. T. Corbett, and V. Aleven. More accurate student modeling through contextual estimation of slip and guess probabilities in bayesian knowledge tracing. In *Intelligent Tutoring Systems*, pages 406–415. Springer, 2008.

[3] T. Belpaeme, P. E. Baxter, R. Read, R. Wood, H. Cuayáhuitl, B. Kiefer, S. Racioppa, I. Kruijff-Korbayová, G. Athanasopoulos, V. Enescu, et al. Multimodal child-robot interaction: Building social bonds. *Journal of Human-Robot Interaction*, 1(2):33–53, 2012.

[4] L. N. Brown and A. M. Howard. The positive effects of verbal encouragement in mathematics education using a social robot. In *Integrated STEM Education Conference (ISEC), 2014 IEEE*, pages 1–5. IEEE, 2014.

[5] W. Burleson. *Affective learning companions: strategies for empathetic agents with real-time multimodal affective sensing to foster meta-cognitive and meta-affective approaches to learning, motivation, and perseverance*. PhD thesis, Massachusetts Institute of Technology, 2006.

[6] B. Byrne and R. Fielding-Barnsley. Phonemic awareness and letter knowledge in the child's acquisition of the alphabetic principle. *Journal of Educational Psychology*, 81(3):313, 1989.

[7] A. T. Corbett and J. R. Anderson. Knowledge tracing: Modeling the acquisition of procedural knowledge. *User modeling and user-adapted interaction*, 4(4):253–278, 1994.

[8] M. Csikszentmihalyi. Flow and education. *NAMTA journal*, 22(2):2–35, 1997.

[9] G. Gordon and C. Breazeal. Bayesian active learning-based robot tutor for children?s word-reading skills. In *Proceedings of the Twenty-Ninth Conference on Artificial Intelligence (AAAI-15)*, 2015.

[10] G. Gordon, C. Breazeal, and S. Engel. Can children catch curiosity from a social robot? In *Human-Robot Interaction (HRI), 2015 10th ACM/IEEE International Conference on*, 2015.

[11] J. M. Harley, F. Bouchet, M. S. Hussain, R. Azevedo, and R. Calvo. A multi-componential analysis of emotions during complex learning with an intelligent multi-agent system. *Computers in Human Behavior*, 48:615–625, 2015.

[12] J. Kory and C. Breazeal. Storytelling with robots: Learning companions for preschool children's language development. In *Robot and Human Interactive Communication, 2014 RO-MAN: The 23rd IEEE International Symposium on*, pages 643–648. IEEE, 2014.

[13] I. Leite, G. Castellano, A. Pereira, C. Martinho, and A. Paiva. Empathic robots for long-term interaction. *International Journal of Social Robotics*, 6(3):329–341, 2014.

[14] D. Leyzberg, S. Spaulding, and B. Scassellati. Personalizing robot tutors to individuals' learning differences. In *Proceedings of the 2014 ACM/IEEE international conference on Human-robot interaction*, pages 423–430. ACM, 2014.

[15] D. Leyzberg, S. Spaulding, M. Toneva, and B. Scassellati. The physical presence of a robot tutor increases cognitive learning gains. In *Proceedings of the 34th Annual Conference of the Cognitive Science Society. Austin, TX: Cognitive Science Society*, 2012.

[16] I. Y. Liberman, D. Shankweiler, and A. M. Liberman. The alphabetic principle and learning to read. 1989.

[17] D. McDuff, R. Kaliouby, and R. W. Picard. Crowdsourcing facial responses to online videos. *Affective Computing, IEEE Transactions on*, 3(4):456–468.

[18] K. Murphy et al. The bayes net toolbox for matlab. *Computing science and statistics*, 33(2):1024–1034, 2001.

[19] U. of Oregon Center for Teaching and Learning. Big ideas in beginning reading: Alphabetic principle, April 2015. [Online; Accessed April 22, 2015].

[20] R. Swinton and R. El Kaliouby. Measuring emotions through a mobile device across borders, ages, genders and more.

[21] D. Szafir and B. Mutlu. Pay attention!: designing adaptive agents that monitor and improve user engagement. In *Proceedings of the SIGCHI Conference on Human Factors in Computing Systems*, pages 11–20. ACM, 2012.

[22] F. Tanaka and S. Matsuzoe. Children teach a care-receiving robot to promote their learning: Field experiments in a classroom for vocabulary learning. *Journal of Human-Robot Interaction*, 1(1), 2012.

[23] K. VanLehn. The relative effectiveness of human tutoring, intelligent tutoring systems, and other tutoring systems. *Educational Psychologist*, 46(4):197–221, 2011.

[24] K. VanLehn, W. Burleson, M.-E. C. Echeagaray, R. Christopherson, J. G. Sanchez, J. Hastings, Y. H. Pontet, and L. Zhang. The affective meta-tutoring project: How to motivate students to use effective meta-cognitive strategies. In *19th International Conference on Computers in Education, Chiang Mai, Thailand*, 2011.

[25] M. Wolf and C. J. Stoodley. *Proust and the squid: The story and science of the reading brain*. Icon Cambridge, 2008.

[26] B. Woolf, W. Burleson, I. Arroyo, T. Dragon, D. Cooper, and R. Picard. Affect-aware tutors: recognising and responding to student affect. *International Journal of Learning Technology*, 4(3):129–164, 2009.

[27] M. V. Yudelson, K. R. Koedinger, and G. J. Gordon. Individualized bayesian knowledge tracing models. In *Artificial Intelligence in Education*, pages 171–180. Springer, 2013.

Limiting the Influence of Low Quality Information in Community Sensing

Goran Radanovic
Ecole Polytechnique Federale de Lausanne
Artificial Intelligence Laboratory
CH-1015 Lausanne, Switzerland
goran.radanovic@epfl.ch

Boi Faltings
Ecole Polytechnique Federale de Lausanne
Artificial Intelligence Laboratory
CH-1015 Lausanne, Switzerland
boi.faltings@epfl.ch

ABSTRACT

We consider a community of private sensors that collect measurements of a physical phenomenon, such as air pollution, and report it to a center. The center should be able to prevent low quality reports from degrading the quality of the aggregated information, as there are numerous reasons for operators to inject false sensor data. Hence, it is necessary to track the quality of the sensors over time in order to filter out low quality and malicious reports. To achieve this, we construct a reputation system with a guaranteed bounds on negative impact that malicious sensors can cause, and we evaluate its performance on a realistic dataset.

Keywords

Reputation Systems; Community Sensing; Online Learning

1. INTRODUCTION

Sensors that monitor important environmental phenomena are becoming smaller, cheaper and more ubiquitous. When such sensing units become more affordable and widely adopted by individuals, we arrive at *participatory*, *community* or *crowd* sensing [5, 1], where different entities, public or private, operate sensors and report the measurements to a *center*. The center interprets the reported data and publishes its results.

We consider a community sensing scenario where the center aggregates crowdsensed information in an online manner, from both public and private sensors, to provide real time estimates of air pollution over a certain urban area. In this scenario, the center controls a few accurate sensors that provide spatially or temporally sparse measurements (e.g., very accurate particle sensors are slow; similarly NO_2 can be sensed chemically but it's again slow and expensive), so to properly monitor the localized features of air pollution, it complements its own measurements with those obtained by crowd-participants who own ubiquitous sensor devices.

Figure 1 depicts the particularities of our setting. At the beginning, the center has only prior information about air pollution over an urban area. After some time, the center receives a report and merges it with the current pollution map P using pollution model $\mathcal{M}$. This process repeats until

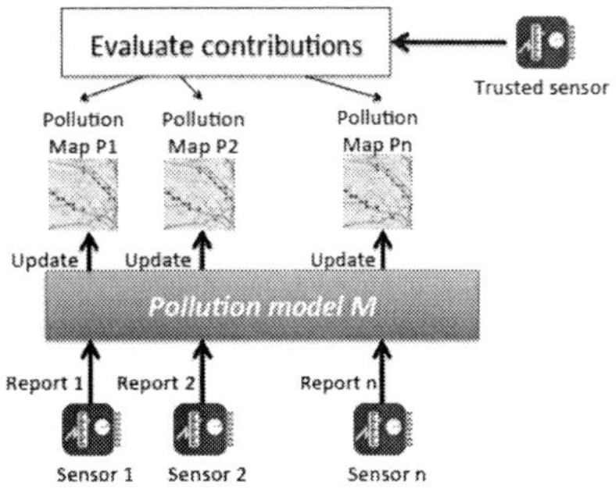

Figure 1: Crowd sensing scenario with online information fusion.

a trusted sensor reports its measurement, after which the center can evaluate the reports of crowd-sensors. We consider this to be one period of sensing and we denote it by t. The crowd sensing process then continues in the same manner until the period $t = T$, which we call *sensing time*.

One of the main challenges in the described scenario is how to cope with untrustworthy information. While this issue has been partly addressed by the incentive mechanism design [16, 17], such an approach reaches its limit of effectiveness when a sensor owner intends to be malicious and intentionally misreports values. For example, a factory owner who wants to hide her own pollution traces could install sensors that misreport values of pollution. Therefore, a more rigorous approach is needed in order to identify faulty or malicious sensors. Reputation systems provide such an approach: bad reports lead to low reputation, which limits the influence of the later reports.

Existing reputation systems model the trustworthiness of sensors using reputation scores, and to determine which sensors are trustworthy, they compare the reputation scores with a predefined threshold (e.g. [3, 9]). These reputation systems provide only guarantees for particular reporting strategies, and can be easily manipulated, as we demonstrate in the paper.

Our reputation model is inspired by the *influence limiter* algorithm, primarily designed for recommender systems [20]. The influence limiter is provably resistant to misreporting, but its applicability is limited due to the significant amount of discarded data in the reputation boosting period. In pollution monitoring, sensors are expected to provide a large number of reports, so the information loss plays much smaller role than in recommender systems. However, the design of the influence limiter is not suitable for our setting, which we show in the paper.

Appears in: *Proceedings of the 15th International Conference on Autonomous Agents and Multiagent Systems (AAMAS 2016), J. Thangarajah, K. Tuyls, C. Jonker, S. Marsella (eds.), May 9–13, 2016, Singapore.*

Our main contribution is a novel reputation system, called *Community Sensing Influence Limiter* (CSIL), suitable for real time community sensing scenarios where measurements are aggregated in an online manner. We show that the CSIL algorithm has provable guarantees on the direct negative impact that any malicious strategy could have. To the best of our knowledge, no technique with such guarantees has ever been proposed for the considered setting. Moreover, we evaluate the performance of the CSIL algorithm on a realistic test-bed to confirm its the theoretical properties and show its advantages over the existing reputation systems.

2. PRELIMINARIES

2.1 Sensors

In our setting, the center controls a small number of sensors, that we refer to as *trusted* sensors; these sensors are assumed to report accurate measurements. Other sensors are in control of private entities, and the center does not know their character, i.e., whether they are malicious or not. *Non-malicious* sensors are considered to be strategic — rational agents that aim to maximize their scores — or honest, while *malicious* sensors do not respond to incentives and their goal is to lower the quality of produced pollution maps. In the group of malicious sensors, we can also put *faulty* sensors that are not intentionally malicious, but do provide inaccurate data. Furthermore, notice that a malicious sensor might report accurately in some sensing periods in order to deceive the center. This means that the decision on how to use a sensor's reports in the information fusion process should be done by monitoring the behaviour of the sensor over the whole sensing time T.

Each sensor repeatedly performs a measurement $X \in [0, max]$ and reports value $Y \in [0, max]$, where $max \in \mathbb{R}$ is a maximum value that is reasonable to measure and report. If a sensor is honest, its report is equal to its measurement, i.e., $Y = X$. In general, however, the value of a report depends on both the sensor's measurement and its reporting strategy. Clearly, apart from their measurements, sensors also report their location, which we do not explicitly emphasize in the further text. As mentioned in the introduction, a time period t is defined by the arrival of a trusted report, which we assume to be stochastic. To simplify the description of our algorithm, we impose three conditions for sensors not controlled by the center: a sensor reports one measurement per time period, measurements between two time periods are statistically independent, and reports from different sensors arrive stochastically one at a time.

Strategy space. We make restrictions to the strategic space of malicious agents by assuming that their reports do not have a significant impact on the quality of the information provided by non-malicious sensors. As noted by [20], the restriction to *myopic strategies* is not a trivial assumption, but still allows a large scope of possible misreporting strategies, including strategies where malicious sensors change their reporting behaviour over time. Furthermore, it is likely that non-myopic strategies require complex implementation. For example, an effective malicious strategy that is based on the report sequence would require information about when sensing periods start/end. Since each sensing period ends when a trusted report is submitted, the center can easily obscure the starting point of a sensing period by, for example, not immediately notifying sensors of their reputation change. This also provides a justification for the assumption of stochastic arrival of reports.

2.2 Pollution Model

The center's goal is to construct and publish a pollution map P using the current set of measurements. We are particularly interested in a real-time updating, where pollution map P is updated after receiving each measurement using a pollution model, denoted by $\mathcal{M}$. We keep a general form of pollution model $\mathcal{M}$, where the input is defined by a finite set of reported measurements $\{Y_1, Y_2, ...\}$, while the output is a pollution map. Pollution map P contains either levels of pollution at the points of interest, or in case of probabilistic pollution models, probability distribution functions over the levels of pollution at the points of interest. Pollution model $\mathcal{M}$ is, thus, assumed to capture well correlations among measurements taken at different locations.

Since we want to keep a possibility of having a very general pollution model $\mathcal{M}$, we consider it as a *black box*. This implies that after receiving report Y_s from sensor s, the center should decide whether to publish a new pollution map P_s^{new} obtained by incorporating report Y_s into the existing pollution map P_s^{old}, or to keep the existing pollution map as its output. The rationale behind this is that the pollution map updating should be computationally efficient. For example, the updating procedure of the classical influence limiter is not consistent with this view, as a new output is a linear combination of P_s^{new} and P_s^{old}. However, a proper procedure for obtaining P_s^{new} in the influence limiter has exponential time complexity in the number of sensor, as we argue later on in the paper.

2.3 Evaluating Sensors

We evaluate sensors by their marginal contributions to the quality of produced pollution maps. More precisely, consider a pollution map P_s^{new} obtained by fusing sensor s's report with a pollution map P_s^{old} that preceded the report of sensor s. Furthermore, let $S(P, X_{trust})$ be a general scoring function that evaluates the quality of a pollution map with respect to the report $Y_{trust} = X_{trust}$ of a trusted sensor, and let it take values from a bounded interval $[-c/2, c/2]$. For example, a scoring function can be a quadratic scoring rule defined by equation (2) (in Section 5.2). The score of sensor s is then defined by the gain G_s of the center when it fully incorporates the sensor's report into the existing pollution map P_s^{old}:

$$score_s = G_s = \frac{1}{c}[S(P_s^{new}, X_{trust}) - S(P_s^{old}, X_{trust})]$$

It is easy to see that the score takes values in $score_s \in [-1, 1]$. Notice that the center needs not to publish pollution map P_s^{new} - this decision is separated from the decision on how to score sensor s. The score can further be used to define (monetary) incentives given to the sensor.

2.4 Myopic impact

Following the approach from [20], we use the notion of sensor s's *myopic impact*. Since our main method probabilistically decides whether to accept or discard sensor s's report, we define the *expected myopic impact* of sensor s at time period t as:

$$\bar{\Delta}_{s,t} = \pi_{update} \cdot G_{s,t} + (1 - \pi_{update}) \cdot 0 = \pi_{update} \cdot G_{s,t}$$

where π_{update} is the probability of incorporating sensor s's report into the existing output. The intuition behind the definition is straightforward. Whenever the center *accepts* to fuse sensor s's report into the existing pollution map, the sensor's impact is equal to the center's information gain: $G_{s,t} = \frac{1}{c}[S(P_s^{new}, X_{trust}) - S(P_s^{old}, X_{trust})]$. Otherwise, when the center decides to *discard* sensor s's report, the sensor's impact is 0 because it does not change the center's output P_s^{old}. Finally, we define the expected *total myopic impact* as $\bar{\Delta}_s = \sum_{t=1}^{T} \bar{\Delta}_{s,t}$. Notice that the myopic impacts are functions of $G_{s,t}$. Since $G_{s,t}$ is a random variable, we can associate expected values over $G_{s,t}$ for both $\bar{\Delta}_{s,t}$ and $\bar{\Delta}_s$, which we denote by $\mathbb{E}(\bar{\Delta}_{s,t})$ and $\mathbb{E}(\bar{\Delta}_s)$, respectively.[1]

3. RELATED WORK

The standard approach of dealing with untrustworthy information in sensing is by using reputation systems [14, 3, 9, 4, 24, 6], with the Beta reputation system [8] being the most common way of assigning reputation scores. While in the literature one can find other ways of assigning reputation scores, such as using the Gompertz function [13], the classification of whether a sensor misbehaves is typically based on a simple thresholding principle: if the reputation of a sensor is lower than a certain threshold, the sensor is denoted as misbehaving, otherwise, it is considered to be trustworthy. A thresholding approach is common even among techniques that do not necessarily use reputation systems (e.g., [23]). While such a thresholding principle can cope with simple attacks where malicious sensors report consistently wrong values, it fails to protect the center against deceiving attacks, as we describe it later in the paper.

[22] and [19] take a different approach to fuse information from multiple sensors that are not a priori assumed to be trustworthy. [22] tries to learn the parameters related to the trustworthiness using a maximum likelihood method over the assumed (Gaussian) model with unknown parameters. [19] proposes a two stage Bayesian multi-sensor fusion algorithm that incorporates model of sensors' trustworthiness. Neither of the two multi-sensor fusion methods have provable guarantees on the loss of the system experienced when the majority of sensors is untrustworthy and potentially malicious. As alternatives to reputation systems, we also mention hardware solutions, such as trusted platform modules (e.g., [21, 10]). These approaches, however, require additional hardware on each sensing module, which limits their applicability.

3.1 Current Approach

Let us now describe the thresholding approach. When the center receives a report $Y_{s,t}$ of sensor s, it fuses the report with the existing information if sensor s's reputation is greater than a certain classification threshold Θ, and otherwise discards it. The approach is depicted by Algorithm 1. Function *Update*$(P, Y_{s,t})$ uses the existing set of *included* reports (the set of reports that produced pollution map P), adds to it report $Y_{s,t}$, and applies model $\mathcal{M}$ to obtain a new pollution map. *RepUpdate* updates the reputation of sensor s using $score_{s,t}$, and has one condition: if $score_{s,t}$ has a strictly positive constant value, the reputation converges to its maximum value; if $score_{s,t}$ has a strictly negative constant value, the reputation converges to its minimum value.

[1] $\mathbb{E}(\bar{\Delta}_s)$ is the expectation over gains from all time periods.

Data: Initial reputation ρ_0, threshold Θ
begin
  for *Sensor s* **do**
    $\rho_{s,1} \longleftarrow \rho_0$;
  end
  for $t = 1$ *to* $t = T$ **do**
    Compute prior map P;
    Publish P;
    for *Sensor s* **do**
      Receive s's report $Y_{s,t}$;
      $P_s^{old} \longleftarrow P$;
      $P_s^{new} \longleftarrow Update(P, Y_{s,t})$;
      if $\rho_{s,t} \geq \Theta$ **then**
        $P \longleftarrow P_{new}^{s}$;
        Publish P;
      end
    end
    Receive report $Y_{trust,t} = X_{trust,t}$;
    for *Sensor s* **do**
      $score_{s,t} \longleftarrow$ $\frac{1}{c}[S(P_s^{new}, X_{trust,t}) - S(P_s^{old}, X_{trust,t})]$;
      $\rho_{s,t+1} \longleftarrow RepUpdate(\rho_{s,t}, score_{s,t})$;
    end
  end
end

Algorithm 1: Thresholding

This simple reputation system can be considered to be a part of a large family of reputations systems that use fix thresholds to classify whether a certain sensor misbehaves or not. These reputation systems can cope with simple attacks where malicious sensors report consistently wrong values. For example, they can limit the effectiveness of the malicious strategy that consists of reporting low pollution values. However, they fail to protect the system against deceiving attacks.

One particular deceiving strategy of a malicious sensor could be to report informative values when its reputation is below threshold Θ, while report low quality information when its reputation is above the threshold. The intuition behind this attack is that a sensor reports useful information only when the center does not use it, and when the center uses its information, it deliberately misreports.

PROPOSITION 1. *Consider a pollution model $\mathcal{M}$ that allows arbitrary generation of gains $G_{s,t}$ related to sensor s. Then, there exists a sequence of gains such that the total myopic impact $\bar{\Delta}_s$ of sensor s in Algorithm 1 is negative and monotonically decreases with T, i.e.,* $\lim_{T\to\infty} \bar{\Delta}_s = -\infty$.

PROOF. Consider a sequence of gains such that whenever $\rho_{s,t} < \Theta$, gain $G_{s,t}$ is equal to $G_{s,t} = g > 0$, while $\rho_{s,t} \geq \Theta$ implies negative gain $G_{s,t} = -g < 0$. In other words, $\pi_{update} = 1$ for $G_{s,t} < 0$ and $\pi_{update} = 0$ for $G_{s,t} \geq 0$. Since reputations converge to the maximum possible reputation if $score_{s,t}$ (i.e., $G_{s,t}$) is fixed to $g > 0$, we know that $\rho_{s,t}$ will infinitely often be greater than Θ for $T \to \infty$. Therefore, $\bar{\Delta}_s$ is negative (because $\pi_{update} = 0$ for $G_{s,t} \geq 0$) and $\lim_{T\to\infty} \bar{\Delta}_s = -\infty$ (because $\rho_{s,t} \geq \Theta$ infinitely often). □

In Section 5.5, we simulate such a behaviour to show that the thresholding does not prevent the center from experiencing an unbounded negative influence.

3.2 The Influence Limiter

The influence limiter, when transformed to our setting, has the same skeleton structure as the thresholding algorithm with the main differences in three components, which we point out in this section. We show, however, that all the three components should be modified in order to obtain a practical algorithm.

Information fusion. The standard version of the influence limiter has a deterministic information fusion component. In particular, the influence limiter incorporates all the reports, but assigns different weights to different reports. In our scenario, this would mean that when a report from a sensor s is received, the new pollution map P_s^{new} is calculated and the published pollution map P is updated to:

$$P \longleftarrow (1 - w_{s,t}) \cdot P_s^{old} + w_{s,t} \cdot P_s^{new} \quad (1)$$

Here, the weight is equal to $w_{s,t} = \min(\rho_{s,t}, 1)$. The crucial part of the algorithm is how P_s^{new} should be calculated, i.e., the structure of the *Update* function.

In the influence limiter, a sensible updating function has to include the fact that all reports are fused, but with different weights. Since pollution model $\mathcal{M}$ is assumed to be a *black box*, one has to additionally ensure that the reports are properly weighted (limited) when updating pollution map P. For example, consider two reports Y_{s1} and Y_{s2} that arrive sequentially. Initially, P should be set to $\mathcal{M}(\emptyset)$. Once Y_{s1} is reported, the update of P, denoted by P_1, is easy to calculate: we simply make a linear combination of P and $\mathcal{M}(\{Y_1\})$, with weights $1 - w_1$ and w_1 (see (1)). The problem, however, arises when we update the current pollution map P_1 for report Y_{s2}. Namely, the new update should be a linear combination of the current pollution map P_1 and the pollution map P_{s2}^{new} that does not limit Y_{s2}, but does appropriately limit the reports that had arrived before Y_{s2}. In our case, the limited report in P_{s2}^{new} would be Y_{s1}. Since Y_{s1} should in P_{s2}^{new} be limited in the same way as in P_1 (otherwise report Y_{s2} has influence on the limiting process of prior information), we obtain that P_{s2}^{new} is equal to $P_{s2}^{new} \longleftarrow (1 - w_1) \cdot \mathcal{M}(\{Y_2\}) + w_1 \cdot \mathcal{M}(\{Y_1, Y_2\})$. Now, notice that for report Y_{s1} we only needed to query model $\mathcal{M}$ once because there were no prior reports. For report Y_{s2}, we needed to query model $\mathcal{M}$ twice. This can be easily generalized; for example, for the third report Y_{s3}, we would need to query model $\mathcal{M}$ four times to obtain pollution maps: $\mathcal{M}(\{Y_{s3}\})$, $\mathcal{M}(\{Y_{s1}, Y_{s3}\})$, $\mathcal{M}(\{Y_{s2}, Y_{s3}\})$ and $\mathcal{M}(\{Y_{s1}, Y_{s2}, Y_{s3}\})$. By using induction, we prove the following claim:

PROPOSITION 2. *The number of queries to a black box model $\mathcal{M}$ of the influence limiter algorithm in one time period t is $\Omega(2^n)$, where n is the number of reported values.*

Scoring rule. The properties of the influence limiter are proven only for a *quadratic scoring rule* (see Lemma 5 in [20]). Since our goal is not to make restrictions on the form of model $\mathcal{M}$, allowing general scoring techniques is crucial in our design. For example, if a model $\mathcal{M}$ is non-probabilistic, a quadratic scoring rule is not applicable.

Furthermore, the influence limiter uses a binary outcome in its scoring rule (this is a requirement of Lemma 5 in [20]). In our scenario, the report $Y_{trust} = X_{trust}$ of a trusted sensor is a real number, so one needs to transform it into a binary variable in order to apply it in the influence limiter. This can be done by defining a threshold and a binary variable equal to 0 if X_{trust} is smaller than the threshold, and 1 otherwise. An issue with this approach is that the evaluation process is much less accurate. For example, if the threshold is equal to 30, then this scoring technique would assign the same quality evaluations for both $X_{trust} = 35$ and $X_{trust} = 50$.

Reputation update. The reputation updating rule of the influence limiter is defined by $\rho_{s,t+1} \longleftarrow \rho_{s,t} + w_{s,t} \cdot score_{s,t}$, and resembles the information fusion updating.

In our approach, which is described in the following section, we use a *non-deterministic* information fusion to lower the query complexity and we allow general scoring rules based on non-binary outcomes. These changes also imply a different reputation updating rule. All these structural differences point out that the influence limiter is not trivially transformable to our setting.

4. COMMUNITY SENSING INFLUENCE LIMITER

The Community Sensing Influence Limiter (CSIL) is a version of the influence limiter reputation system with an exponential reputation boosting. Furthermore, it shares some similarities with randomized weighted majority algorithms (e.g., see [15]), where the decision making rule is non-deterministic and uses weights that have a multiplicative updating rule.

```
Data: Initial reputation ρ_0 > 0
begin
    for Sensor s do
        ρ_{s,1} ⟵ ρ_0;
    end
    for t = 1 to t = T do
        Compute prior map P;
        Publish P;
        for Sensor s do
            Receive s's report Y_{s,t};
            P_s^old ⟵ P ;
            P_s^new ⟵ Update(P, Y_{s,t}) ;
            if rand(0,1) < ρ_{s,t} / ρ_{s,t+1} then
                P ⟵ P_s^new;
                Publish P;
            end
        end
        Receive report Y_{trust,t} = X_{trust,t};
        for Sensor s do
            score_{s,t} ⟵
              (1/c)[S(P_s^new, X_{trust,t}) − S(P_s^old, X_{trust,t})];
            ρ_{s,t+1} ⟵ ρ_{s,t} · (1 + (1/2) · score_{s,t});
        end
    end
end
```

Algorithm 2: Community Sensing Influence Limiter

The exact description of CSIL can be found in Algorithm 2, and it has the following steps. Initially, sensors' reputations are set to $\rho_0 > 0$. At time period t, upon the arrival of a sensor s's report, the reputation system calculates pollution map P_s^{new} using function $Update(P, Y_{s,t})$, which adds report $Y_{s,t}$ to the existing set of *included* reports (the set of reports that produced pollution map P) and applies model $\mathcal{M}$ to obtain a new pollution map. In the next step, the algorithm decides whether the current pollution map should be replaced with the update or not. The decision is probabilistic — with probability equal to $\frac{\rho_{s,t}}{\rho_{s,t}+1}$, the center sets pollution map P to P_s^{new}, while otherwise, it discards sensor s's report. The final step of the repetitive algorithm is to update the reputation of sensor s when the report $Y_{trust} = X_{trust}$ of a trusted sensor is received. The reputation updating rule assigns a new reputation to sensor s by adding to the current reputation $\rho_{s,t}$ the score of sensor s modulated by $\frac{\rho_{s,t}}{2}$.

4.1 Theoretical Analysis

Since the deterministic information fusion rule of the standard influence limiter has an exponential query complexity, we have applied a stochastic information fusion rule in the CSIL algorithm. Because of that, CSIL has a significantly lower query complexity, in particular, it makes only a constant number of queries per report.

THEOREM 1. *(Query Complexity) The number of queries to a black box model $\mathcal{M}$ of the CSIL algorithm in one time period t is $O(n)$, where n is the number of reported values.*

PROOF. The CSIL's function *Update* is simple: it uses the set of reports that produced P, say $\{Y_1, ..., Y_k\}$ where $P \longleftarrow \mathcal{M}(\{Y_1, ..., Y_k\})$, adds to it the report $Y_{s,t}$ of sensor s and calculates $P_s^{new} \longleftarrow \mathcal{M}(\{Y_1, ..., Y_k\} \cup \{Y_{s,t}\})$. Therefore, CSIL makes $O(1)$ queries to $\mathcal{M}$ for $i-th$ sensor, thus, for n sensors in one time period t we have $O(n)$ queries. □

An important characteristic of CSIL is that the probabilistic decision making rule allows a possibility of incorporating reports of sensors that are not necessarily considered to be reliable. To make the procedure sound, the probability of fusing a report of a sensor with low reputation is low. For example, a sensor with reputation 0.1 can affect the current pollution map, but only with probability $\frac{0.1}{0.1+1}$. This way, one makes deceiving malicious strategies less effective. In particular, their overall impact cannot be highly negative, meaning that the sum of a sensor's contributions, which can be positive and negative, is bounded from below.

THEOREM 2. *(Limited Damage) The expected total myopic impact $\bar{\Delta}_s = \sum_{t=1}^{T} \bar{\Delta}_{s,t}$ of sensor s is in the CSIL algorithm bounded from below by:*

$$\bar{\Delta}_s > -2 \cdot \rho_0$$

where ρ_0 is the initial reputation of sensor s.

PROOF. The expected myopic impact $\bar{\Delta}_{s,t}$ is equal to $\frac{\rho_{s,t}}{\rho_{s,t}+1} \cdot G_{s,t} = \frac{\rho_{s,t}}{\rho_{s,t}+1} \cdot score_{s,t}$. On the other hand, for reputation $\rho_{s,T+1}$ we have:

$$\ln(\rho_{s,T+1} + 1) = \ln(\rho_{s,T} \cdot (1 + \frac{1}{2} \cdot score_{s,T}) + 1)$$

$$= \ln((\rho_{s,T} + 1) \cdot (1 + \frac{\rho_{s,T}}{\rho_{s,T} + 1} \cdot \frac{1}{2} \cdot score_{s,T}))$$

$$= \ln(\rho_{s,T} + 1) + \ln(1 + \frac{1}{2} \cdot \bar{\Delta}_{s,T}) = ...$$

$$= \ln(\rho_0 + 1) + \sum_{t=1}^{T} \ln(1 + \frac{1}{2} \cdot \bar{\Delta}_{s,t})$$

$$\leq \ln(\rho_0 + 1) + \frac{1}{2} \sum_{t=1}^{T} \bar{\Delta}_{s,t} = \ln(\rho_0 + 1) + \frac{1}{2} \cdot \bar{\Delta}_s$$

where we used the fact that $\ln(1 + x) \leq x$ for $x > -1$. By noting that the updating rule for reputations keeps the reputations positive, i.e., $\rho_{s,t} > 0$, we have that $\ln(\rho_{s,T+1} + 1) > 0$, so $\bar{\Delta}_s$ is lower bounded by:

$$\bar{\Delta}_s > -2 \cdot \ln(\rho_0 + 1) \geq -2 \cdot \rho_0$$

were we again applied $\ln(1 + x) \leq x$ for $x > -1$. □

The consequence of Theorem 2 is that the direct damage of a group of m malicious sensors can be controlled by setting the sensors' initial reputation to a low value. Namely, the impact $\bar{\Delta}_{s,t}$ of sensor s at time period t is measured by its marginal contribution, so the total myopic impact of all malicious sensors over sensing period T is by Theorem 2 at least $-2 \cdot m \cdot \rho_0$ (i.e., the absolute value of the negative impact is at most $2 \cdot m \cdot \rho_0$). By choosing a small value of ρ_0, one can make the (negative) impact of malicious sensors close to 0, regardless of the reporting strategies they use and their reporting time frame. This also implies that when average over a longer sensing period, their negative impact is negligible.

Theorem 2, however, is not sufficient to state that CSIL performs well against malicious strategies. For example, a simple reputation system that discards all the reports completely limits the negative influence of malicious sensors, but in doing so, it discards all the valuable information coming from non-malicious sensors.

The CSIL decision making procedure also induces a certain information loss due to the fact that valuable information might be discarded. This is especially true for the initial sensing periods where all sensors have relatively low reputations, including the ones that are not malicious. For example, if the reputations are set to $\rho_0 = 0.1$, the probability of including a report from an honest and accurate sensor is initially equal to $\frac{0.1}{0.1+1}$. Since only information that comes from sensors with large reputation scores has a good chance of being considered, accurate sensors should build up their reputation quickly, which is indeed the case for the CSIL algorithm because the reputation increase is exponential. Namely, the increase in the reputation is equal to $\frac{1}{2} \cdot \rho_{s,t} \cdot score_{s,t}$, which for a non-malicious sensor with predominantly positive scores implies an exponential reputation growth. Therefore, by using the exponential reputation boosting, CSIL is capable of limiting the negative influence of malicious sensors, while not discarding too many reports of non-malicious sensors.

We measure the expected information loss for partially limiting an accurate sensor s as the difference between the total score of the sensor $\sum_{t=1}^{T} score_{s,t} = \sum_{t=1}^{T} G_{s,t}$ and its impact $\bar{\Delta}_s$. The rationale is that a sensor's scores reflect its contributions — information gains — that the sensor would have made had it not been limited. The following theorem formally shows that if a sensor reports accurate and precise measurements, i.e., its scores are positive in expectation and have small variances, then there is a bound to the amount of sensor s's information discarded by CSIL.

THEOREM 3. *(Bounded Information Loss) Consider a sensor s whose reporting strategy does not depend on its reputation $\rho_{s,t}$ and that has:*

- *Expected scores greater than 0: $\mathbb{E}(score_{s,t}) > 0$*
- *Variance of the scores bounded from above by: $Var(score_{s,t}) < \mathbb{E}(score_{s,t})$.*

Furthermore, let us denote: $g_{s,t} = \ln(1 + \frac{1}{2} \cdot score_{s,t}) \in [g_{min,t}, g_{max,t}]$ *and* $h_{s,t} = \mathbb{E}(g_{s,t})$. *Then the expected information loss* $\sum_{t=1}^{T}(\mathbb{E}(score_{s,t}) - \mathbb{E}(\bar{\Delta}_{s,t}))$ *of the CSIL algorithm for potentially discarding sensor s's reports is bounded from above by:*

$$\sum_{t=1}^{T}(\mathbb{E}(score_{s,t}) - \mathbb{E}(\bar{\Delta}_{s,t})) < z \cdot \left[\frac{e^{-\frac{1}{2}\cdot d}}{1-e^{-\frac{1}{2}\cdot d}} + \frac{2 \cdot \ln \frac{\rho_0+1}{\rho_0}}{h}\right]$$

where $z = \max_{1\le t\le T} \mathbb{E}(score_{s,t}) \le 1$, $h = \min_{1\le t\le T}(\frac{1}{t}\sum_{\tau=1}^{t} h_{s,\tau}) \ge \min_{1\le t\le T} h_{s,t} > 0$ *and* $d = \min_{1\le t\le T} \frac{1}{t}\frac{(\sum_{\tau=1}^{t} h_{s,\tau})^2}{\sum_{\tau=1}^{t}[g_{max,\tau}-g_{min,\tau}]^2} > \frac{h^2}{2}$.

PROOF. The expected value of the myopic impact is:

$$\mathbb{E}(\bar{\Delta}_{s,t}) = \mathbb{E}(\frac{\rho_{s,t}}{\rho_{s,t}+1} \cdot score_{s,t})$$

Since scores are stochastically generated (they are independent of reputation $\rho_{s,t}$), we obtain that:

$$\mathbb{E}(\bar{\Delta}_{s,t}) = \mathbb{E}(\frac{\rho_{s,t}}{\rho_{s,t}+1}) \cdot \mathbb{E}(score_{s,t})$$

Furthermore, Markov's inequality gives us:

$$\mathbb{E}(\frac{\rho_{s,t}}{\rho_{s,t}+1}) \ge Pr(\rho_{s,t} \ge \rho_0 \cdot a_t) \cdot \frac{\rho_0 \cdot a_t}{\rho_0 \cdot a_t + 1}$$

where we used: $a_t = e^{\frac{1}{2}\sum_{\tau=1}^{t} h_{s,\tau}}$, $h_{s,\tau} = \mathbb{E}(\ln(1 + \frac{1}{2} \cdot score_{s,\tau}))$. Let us also denote: $h = \min_{1\le t\le T} \frac{1}{t}\sum_{\tau=1}^{t} h_{s,\tau}$. Using $\ln(1+x) \ge x - x^2$ for $x \ge -\frac{1}{2}$, it follows that $h_{s,t} \ge \frac{1}{2}\cdot\mathbb{E}(score_{s,t}) - \frac{1}{4}\cdot\mathbb{E}((score_{s,t})^2)$. By applying the conditions of the theorem, and the fact that $\mathbb{E}((score_{s,t})^2) - (\mathbb{E}(score_{s,t}))^2 = Var(score_{s,t}) < \mathbb{E}(score_{s,t})$ and $0 < (\mathbb{E}(score_{s,t}))^2 \le \mathbb{E}(score_{s,t}) \le 1$, we obtain that $h_{s,t} > 0$ (and, hence, $h > 0$). Now, notice that:

$$\begin{aligned}
Pr(\rho_{s,t} \ge \rho_0 \cdot a_t) &= Pr(\ln \rho_{s,t} \ge \ln(\rho_0 \cdot a_t)) \\
&= Pr(\ln \rho_{s,t} \ge \ln \rho_0 + \frac{1}{2}\cdot\sum_{\tau=1}^{t} h_{s,\tau}) \\
&= Pr(\ln \rho_{s,t} - \sum_{\tau=1}^{t} h_{s,\tau} - \ln \rho_0 \ge -\frac{1}{2}\cdot\sum_{\tau=1}^{t} h_{s,\tau}) \\
&\ge 1 - Pr(\ln \rho_{s,t} - \sum_{\tau=1}^{t} h_{s,\tau} - \ln \rho_0 \le -\frac{1}{2}\cdot\sum_{\tau=1}^{t} h_{s,\tau}) \\
&= 1 - p_t
\end{aligned}$$

where we denoted the last term $Pr(.)$ by p_t. Since $\ln \rho_{s,t} - \ln \rho_0$ is a sum of t independent random variables $g_{s,\tau} = \ln(1 + \frac{1}{2} \cdot score_{s,\tau})$ (with $1 \le \tau \le t$) that are in expectation equal to $h_{s,\tau} = \mathbb{E}(g_{s,\tau})$, using Hoeffding's inequality, we obtain:

$$p_t \le e^{-\frac{2\cdot(\sum_{\tau=1}^{t} h_{s,\tau})^2}{4\cdot\sum_{\tau=1}^{t}[g_{max,\tau}-g_{min,\tau}]^2}} \le e^{-\frac{2\cdot\left(\frac{\sum_{\tau=1}^{t} h_{s,\tau}}{t}\right)^2\cdot t}{4\cdot\frac{\sum_{\tau=1}^{t}[g_{max,\tau}-g_{min,\tau}]^2}{t}}} \le e^{-\frac{1}{2}\cdot d\cdot t}$$

where we put $d = \min_{1\le t\le T} \frac{\left(\frac{\sum_{\tau=1}^{t} h_{s,\tau}}{t}\right)^2}{\frac{\sum_{\tau=1}^{t}[g_{max,\tau}-g_{min,\tau}]^2}{t}}$, which is greater than $d > \frac{h^2}{2}$ because $\frac{1}{2}\cdot score_{s,\tau} \in [-0.5, 0.5]$ (and, hence, $[g_{max,\tau} - g_{min,\tau}]^2 < 2$). The expected information loss (the difference between the sensor's score and its impact) in round t is bounded by:

$$\begin{aligned}
\mathbb{E}(score_{s,t}) - \mathbb{E}(\bar{\Delta}_{s,t}) &= \mathbb{E}(score_{s,t}) \cdot (1 - \mathbb{E}(\frac{\rho_{s,t}}{\rho_{s,t}+1})) \\
&\le \mathbb{E}(score_{s,t}) \cdot \left[1 - (1 - e^{-\frac{1}{2}\cdot d\cdot t}) \cdot \frac{\rho_0 \cdot a_t}{\rho_0 \cdot a_t + 1}\right] \\
&= \mathbb{E}(score_{s,t}) \cdot \left[\frac{1}{\rho_0 \cdot a_t + 1} + e^{-\frac{1}{2}\cdot d\cdot t} \cdot \frac{\rho_0 \cdot a_t}{\rho_0 \cdot a_t + 1}\right]
\end{aligned}$$

Therefore, over time period T, the information loss in expectation upper bounded by:

$$z \cdot \left[\sum_{t=1}^{T}\frac{1}{\rho_0 \cdot a_t + 1} + \sum_{t=1}^{T} e^{-\frac{1}{2}\cdot d\cdot t} \cdot \frac{\rho_0 \cdot a_t}{\rho_0 \cdot a_t + 1}\right]$$

where $z = \max_{1\le t\le T} \mathbb{E}(score_{s,t})$. We examine bounds for each of the terms in the bracket. We have:

$$\begin{aligned}
&\sum_{t=1}^{T} e^{-\frac{1}{2}\cdot d\cdot t} \cdot \frac{\rho_0 \cdot a_t}{\rho_0 \cdot a_t + 1} \le \sum_{t=1}^{T} e^{-\frac{1}{2}\cdot d\cdot t} \\
&= e^{-\frac{1}{2}\cdot d} \cdot \sum_{t=0}^{T-1} e^{-\frac{1}{2}\cdot d\cdot t} < e^{-\frac{1}{2}\cdot d} \cdot \sum_{t=0}^{\infty} e^{-\frac{1}{2}\cdot d\cdot t} = \frac{e^{-\frac{1}{2}\cdot d}}{1-e^{-\frac{1}{2}\cdot d}}
\end{aligned}$$

where we applied $\sum_{t=0}^{\infty} x^t = \frac{1}{1-x}$ for $x \in (0,1)$. Furthermore, using the fact that:

$$a_t = e^{\frac{1}{2}\sum_{\tau=1}^{t} h_{s,\tau}} \ge e^{\frac{1}{2}\cdot t\cdot h}$$

we obtain:

$$\begin{aligned}
&\sum_{t=1}^{T}\frac{1}{\rho_0 \cdot a_t + 1} \le \sum_{t=1}^{T}\frac{1}{\rho_0 \cdot e^{\frac{1}{2}\cdot t\cdot h} + 1} \\
&\le \int_{t=0}^{T}\frac{1}{\rho_0 \cdot e^{\frac{1}{2}\cdot t\cdot h} + 1}dt < \int_{t=0}^{\infty}\frac{1}{\rho_0 \cdot e^{\frac{1}{2}\cdot t\cdot h} + 1}dt \\
&= \frac{2}{h}\cdot\ln(\frac{\rho_0+1}{\rho_0})
\end{aligned}$$

Which completes the proof. □

The intuition behind this results is fairly simple. If a sensor has mostly positive scores, i.e., the expected scores are positive and their variances are low, it will boost up its reputation rather quickly to the values where its reports are practically no longer limited. Notice that the bound on the total information loss does not (directly) depend on time (i.e., does not monotonically increase with time), which means that when averaged over a long sensing period T (typical for crowdsensing), the information loss becomes negligible. Furthermore, the bound multiplicatively depends on parameter z that represents a sensor's expected score: the better the sensor is, the more quality information the center looses when it discards the sensor's reports. The second multiplicand in the bound describes how quickly a sensor can boost up its reputation, which depends on how *informative* the sensor is: the more useful the sensor's reports are, the higher its score is, and, thus, the greater its reputation increase is. This is captured by parameters h and d, which are related to the performance of a sensor through random variable $g_{s,t} = \ln(1 + \frac{1}{2} \cdot score_{s,t})$. In the next section, we give an example scenario for which we estimate the values of z, h and d. Notice that by Theorem 3, we can set $z = 1$ and $d = \frac{h^2}{2}$ in order to obtain a looser upper bound that does not require estimates of z and d.

Theorem 2 and Theorem 3 provide guarantees on the performance of the CSIL algorithm that depend on the initial reputation. The bounds of the theorems indicate that the value of the initial reputation ρ_0 should be such that it limits the negative impact of malicious sensors, while not discarding too much information from non-malicious sensors. Since for a longer sensing period, accurate sensors have enough time to build up their reputations, the initial reputation ρ_0 can be set to a relatively small value so that the CSIL algorithm is more robust against malicious reporting strategies.

Finally, we analyze the incentive component of the CSIL algorithm. The important property of sensors' scores, which can be used to define monetary payments, is that they incentivize non-malicious sensors to provide reports that maximize the information gain of the center. Notice that the most *useful* information is not necessarily the true measurement. This is due to the presence of malicious sensors, as well as the possible imperfections of pollution model $\mathcal{M}$. In other words, a strategic behaviour is often desirable.

THEOREM 4. *(Informed Reporting) If a sensor s maximizes its expected score* $\mathbb{E}(score_{s,t})$*, then it also maximizes its expected impact* $\mathbb{E}(\bar{\Delta}_{s,t})$.

PROOF. The myopic impact of sensor s, $\bar{\Delta}_{s,t}$, is proportional to its score $\bar{\Delta}_{s,t} = \frac{\rho_{s,t}}{\rho_{s,t}+1} \cdot G_{s,t} = \frac{\rho_{s,t}}{\rho_{s,t}+1} \cdot score_{s,t}$. Hence, a sensor s that aims to maximize its expected score, is also incentivized to submit a report that maximizes its expected impact. □

5. EXPERIMENTAL EVALUATION

Considering that, in a real dataset, one cannot identify upfront the strategies adopted by different sensors, we simulate different malicious strategies to experimentally validate our approach. Our pollution sensing scenario is based on four weeks of hourly measurements of NO_2 concentrations from an area in Strasbourg (France) covering 116 locations, with each week coming from a different season. The data is the output from the physical model ADMS Urban V2.3 [7] collected by ASPA [2], denoting estimations of pollution concentrations calculated from the emission inventory and actual measurements. In total, the dataset contains approximately one month of hourly measurements - the larger sensing periods can be simulated by looping over the dataset several times, which we do 12 times to obtain the sensing time of $T = 12 \cdot 4 \cdot 7 \cdot 24$ hours. Our main reputation system is CSIL with the initial reputation set to $\rho_0 = 0.1$.

5.1 Pollution Model

We use a probabilistic air pollution model that is based on Gaussian process regression, as described in [18]. For any point of interest (in our case 116 locations), the pre-trained Gaussian Process (GP) model produces a probability distribution function over the possible levels of pollution from the reports of sensors placed at different locations. This posterior distribution is a normal distribution $\mathcal{N}(\mu, \sigma)$, with parameters μ and σ derived from the GP model. We are interested in predicting the value of pollution level that a trusted sensor measures at its location, so we denote the corresponding prediction by $p(X_{trust})$.

5.2 Scoring Function

The standard way of measuring the quality of a probability distribution function is by *strictly proper scoring rules* [11, 12], that take as argument both the predicted probability distribution and the outcome of the predicted event. In our case, the event that we aim to predict is measurement X_{trust} of a trusted sensor, and the prediction we want to evaluate is the posterior density function $p(X_{trust})$, which represents the output of the model at the location of the trusted sensor. We focus on a quadratic scoring rule, that, for events whose outcomes take real values, has the form:

$$S(p, X) = p(X) - \frac{1}{2} \int_{-\infty}^{\infty} p(y)^2 dy \qquad (2)$$

Model $\mathcal{M}$ outputs a normal distribution $\mathcal{N}(\mu, \sigma)$ for a point of interest (x, y). Therefore, we apply scoring rule (2) on probability density function p of the form $p(x) = \frac{1}{\sqrt{2\pi\sigma^2}} e^{-\frac{(x-\mu)^2}{2\sigma^2}}$ to obtain:

$$S(p, X_{trust}) = \frac{1}{\sqrt{2\pi}\sigma} e^{-\frac{(X_{trust}-\mu)^2}{2\sigma^2}} - \frac{1}{4\sigma\sqrt{\pi}}$$

The score takes values in $[-\frac{1}{4\sigma\sqrt{\pi}}, \frac{1}{\sigma\sqrt{\pi}}(\frac{1}{\sqrt{2}} - \frac{1}{4})]$, and can be further scaled so that $score_{s,t} \in [-1, 1]$. In our case, no specific scaling was needed.

5.3 Sensors

We consider 40 mobile crowd-sensors and 1 trusted sensor that are at each time period placed at one of 116 available locations. The 40 crowd-sensors are either honest (25% of them) or are malicious sensors (75% of them) that report according to one of the following four strategies. In the *Vary* strategy, sensors build up their reputations by reporting honestly for the first 1000 iterations, and from then on, they report only a low level of pollution. In the *Deceive* strategy, sensors report honestly when their reputation is below 0.5; otherwise, they report a low level of pollution. *Vary and Deceive* is a mixed strategy where malicious sensors first build up their reputation by reporting honestly for 1000 iterations, and from then on, they use the *Deceive* strategy. *Cover* is a strategy that mimics a situation where malicious sensors try to boost up their reputation when it is not important for them to misreport, and then, on specific events, they report wrong values. In our case, malicious sensors boost up their reputation for 1000 iterations. Then, they report honestly whenever the pollution is below 35 ppb of NO_2 or their reputation is lower than 0.5; otherwise, they report a low level of pollution. The low level of pollution in the above strategies is defined as 10 ppb of NO_2 plus a Gaussian noise with 0 mean and standard deviation equal to 5.

5.4 Theoretical Bound

By Theorem 2, it follows that $0.75 \cdot 40 = 30$ malicious sensors can cause an immediate damage of at most $2 \cdot 30 \cdot 0.1 = 6$ score units (units used in (2)). To calculate the bound from Theorem 3, one needs to estimate parameters z, h and d. We can approximate these values by investigating averages of $score_{s,t}$, $\log(1 + \frac{1}{2} \cdot score_{s,t})$ and $\max_s \log(1 + \frac{1}{2} \cdot score_{s,t}) - \min_s \log(1 + \frac{1}{2} \cdot score_{s,t})$ over time t. Assuming that the scores of honest sensors are similar in most of the sensing periods, these averages lead to the estimates:[2] $z \approx 0.002$, $h \approx 0.001$ and $d \approx 0.005$, from which we can estimate the

[2] If $k << T$ sensing periods have significantly different values from the average values, to achieve a higher precision, one can exclude these k periods when estimating the upper

the upper bound from Theorem 3: 10.39. By multiplying the estimate with the number of honest sensors (i.e., 10), we conclude that the total information loss should be no more than 103.9 score units. Notice that the bounds from Theorem 2 and Theorem 3 have different meanings: the bound from Theorem 2 describes how much a malicious sensor could intentionally shift the result, while the bound from Theorem 3 describes an implicit damage whose nature is not controlled by a malicious sensor. Nevertheless, it follows from the bounds that the quality degradation should not be more than 109.9 score units in total. This can be averaged over time, so that at each time step t, we have an average degradation of at most $\frac{109.9}{t}$ score units. The average goes to 0 as time increases, implying a no-regret property in terms of sensors' myopic impact.

5.5 Simulations

5.5.1 Baseline: Beta Reputation System

In the Beta reputation system, we quantify the behaviour of a sensor using two parameters, α and β, which represent the parameters of beta distribution $B(\alpha, \beta)$. In the setting we analyze, the parameters can be updated as follows (e.g., see [8]). If the marginal information gain $G_{s,t} = score_{s,t}$ of updating the current pollution map with a sensor s's report is positive, parameter $\alpha_{s,t}$ is updated to $\alpha_{s,t+1} = \alpha_{s,t} + G_{s,t}$. Otherwise, parameter β is updated to $\beta_{s,t+1} = \beta_{s,t} + G_{s,t}$. The reputation of sensor s is at time t calculated as the mean of beta distribution $B(\alpha_{s,t}, \beta_{s,t})$, i.e., $\rho_{s,t} = \frac{\alpha_{s,t}}{\alpha_{s,t}+\beta_{s,t}}$. In other words, the reputation of sensor s characterizes the fraction of the positive impact that the sensor had on the system. The decision on whether to include the report of sensor s is based on its reputation and determined using the thresholding principle. We set the initial values of α and β parameters to 0.01 and 0.1, respectively, with threshold $\Theta = 0.5$.

5.5.2 Evaluation Metric

We define a measure of an average regret that evaluates the quality of the aggregates produced by the center with respect to the aggregates obtained by fusing the reports of honest sensors. More precisely:

$$AvgRegret_t = \frac{Score_{honest,t} - Score_{center,t}}{t}$$

where $Score_{honest,t}$ is the total score (until time period t) of the aggregates obtained from the reports of honest sensors, and $Score_{center,t}$ is the total score of the center (with a particular reputation system) until time period t. Both scores are calculated using the quadratic scoring rule, as described by the previous subsections, applied on the pollution map published prior to the report of a trusted sensor. Therefore, the regret is measured in the same score units as the theoretical bound computed in Section 5.4.

5.5.3 Results

Figures (2a, 2b, 2c, 2d) show the performance of the CSIL algorithm and the Beta reputation system in terms of the average regret for four different misreporting strategies. Along with those results, we put the theoretical estimate of the upper bound on the regret of CSIL algorithm ($\frac{109.9}{t}$), which

bound from Theorem 3 and simply add to the calculated bound $k \cdot \max_{\tau \in kPeriods} \mathbb{E}(score_{s,\tau})$.

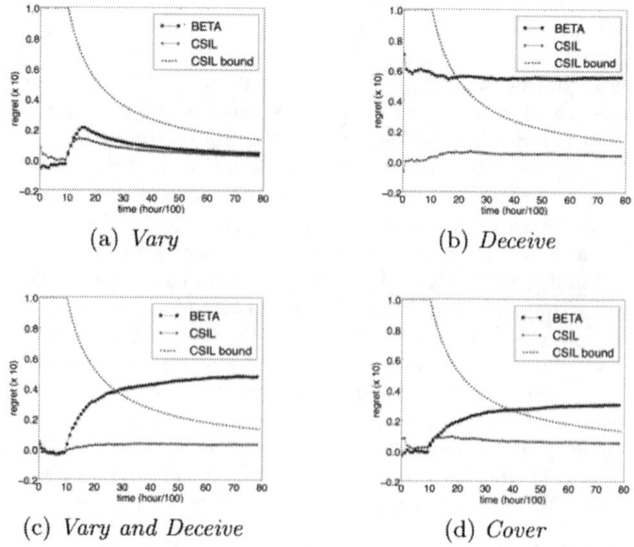

(a) *Vary* (b) *Deceive*

(c) *Vary and Deceive* (d) *Cover*

Figure 2: Average regrets (times 10) for different strategies

is truncated to 0.1 for large values. The Beta reputation system is able to limit the negative influence of malicious sensors that use the *Vary* strategy. However, in the *Vary* strategy, malicious sensors misreport in a simple and consistent way. For the other three misreporting strategies, the Beta reputation system experiences an average regret that is clearly away from 0, and in two of the cases, the regret is increasing, which means that the total negative impact of malicious sensors is not bounded. The CSIL algorithm is much better in dealing with malicious sensors: its average regret over a longer sensing period is for all the malicious strategies close to 0, as expected by the theoretical results. Finally, the strategy independent upper bound on the CSIL's regret is often below the regret of the Beta reputation system.

6. CONCLUSION

We discus a problem of having malicious sensors in community sensing with online information fusion. Due to the abundance of crowdsourced data, one can partially discard useful information to limit the overall negative influence of malicious participants. We have designed a novel reputation system, called CSIL, that has a manageable complexity and puts an upper bound on the total negative impact that malicious sensors can have on the fused result, regardless of their reporting strategy. This is in contrast to the standard reputation systems proposed for sensing which do not provide any theoretical guarantees and for which the total negative impact of malicious sensors can increase with time. We have empirically confirmed that the theoretical results hold in a realistic air pollution sensing scenario, and have shown that in an average-case simulation, CSIL outperforms a state of the art reputation system for sensing, whose performance is often worse than the worst case performance of CSIL.

Acknowledgments

The work reported in this paper was supported by Nano-Tera.ch as part of the OpenSense2 project. We thank Jason Jingshi Li for providing a testbed and the anonymous reviewers for useful comments and feedback.

REFERENCES

[1] K. Aberer, S. Sathe, D. Chakraborty, A. Martinoli, G. Barrenetxea, B. Faltings, and L. Thiele. Opensense: Open community driven sensing of environment. In *ACM SIGSPATIAL International Workshop on GeoStreaming*, 2010.

[2] ASPA. l'association pour la surveillance et l'etude de la pollution atmosphérique en alsace. `www.atmo-alsace.net`, 2013.

[3] S. Buchegger and J.-Y. L. Boudec. A robust reputation system for mobile ad-hoc networks. Technical report, Proceedings of P2PEcon, 2003.

[4] S. Buchegger and J.-Y. Le Boudec. Performance analysis of the confidant protocol. In *Proceedings of the 3rd ACM International Symposium on Mobile Ad Hoc Networking and Computing*, 2002.

[5] J. Burke, D. Estrin, M. Hansen, A. Parker, N. Ramanathan, S. Reddy, and M. B. Srivastava. Participatory sensing. In *Workshop on World-Sensor-Web: Mobile Device Centric Sensor Networks and Applications*, 2006.

[6] H. Chen. Task-based trust management for wireless sensor networks. *International Journal of Security and Its Applications*, 2009.

[7] R. N. Colvile, N. K. Woodfield, D. J. Carruthers, B. E. A. Fisher, A. Rickard, S. Neville, and A. Hughes. Uncertainty in dispersion modelling and urban air quality mapping. *Environmental Science and Policy*, 5(3):207–220, 2002.

[8] B. E. Commerce, A. Josang, and R. Ismail. The beta reputation system. In *Proceedings of the Electronic Commerce Conference*, 2002.

[9] S. Ganeriwal and M. B. Srivastava. Reputation-based framework for high integrity sensor networks. In *Proceedings of the 2nd ACM workshop on Security of ad hoc and sensor networks*, 2004.

[10] P. Gilbert, J. Jung, K. Lee, H. Qin, D. Sharkey, A. Sheth, and L. P. Cox. Youprove: Authenticity and fidelity in mobile sensing. In *Proceedings of the 9th ACM Conference on Embedded Networked Sensor Systems*, 2011.

[11] T. Gneiting and A. E. Raftery. Strictly proper scoring rules, prediction, and estimation. *Journal of the American Statistical Association*, 102:359–378, 2007.

[12] R. D. Hanson. Logarithmic market scoring rules for modular combinatorial information aggregation. *Journal of Prediction Markets*, 1(1):1–15, 2007.

[13] K. L. Huang, S. S. Kanhere, and W. Hu. On the need for a reputation system in mobile phone based sensing. *Ad Hoc Networks*, 12:130–149, Jan. 2014.

[14] P. Michiardi and R. Molva. Core: A collaborative reputation mechanism to enforce node cooperation in mobile ad hoc networks. In *Proceedings of the Sixth Joint Working Conference on Communications and Multimedia Security*, 2002.

[15] N. Nisan, T. Roughgarden, E. Tardos, and V. V. Vazirani. *Algorithmic Game Theory*. Cambridge University Press, New York, NY, USA, 2007.

[16] A. Papakonstantinou, A. Rogers, E. H. Gerding, and N. R. Jennings. Mechanism design for the truthful elicitation of costly probabilistic estimates in distributed information systems. *Artificial Intelligence*, 175(2):648–672, 2011.

[17] G. Radanovic and B. Faltings. Incentive schemes for participatory sensing. In *Proceedings of the 2015 International Conference on Autonomous Agents and Multiagent Systems*, 2015.

[18] C. E. Rasmussen and C. K. I. Williams. *Gaussian Processes for Machine Learning (Adaptive Computation and Machine Learning)*. The MIT Press, 2005.

[19] S. Reece, S. J. Roberts, C. Claxton, and D. Nicholson. Multi-sensor fault recovery in the presence of known and unknown fault types. In *12th International Conference on Information Fusion*, 2009.

[20] P. Resnick and R. Sami. The influence limiter: Provably manipulation-resistant recommender system. In *Proceedings of the 2007 ACM Conference on Recommender Systems*, 2007.

[21] S. Saroiu and A. Wolman. I am a sensor, and I approve this message. In *Proceedings of the Eleventh Workshop on Mobile Computing Systems and Applications*, 2010.

[22] M. Venanzi, A. Rogers, and N. R. Jennings. Trust-based fusion of untrustworthy information in crowdsourcing applications. In *Proceedings of the 2013 International Conference on Autonomous Agents and Multi-agent Systems*, 2013.

[23] W. Wang, H. Li, Y. Sun, and Z. Han. Catchit: Detect malicious nodes in collaborative spectrum sensing. In *Proceedings of the 28th IEEE Conference on Global Telecommunications*, 2009.

[24] K. Yadav and A. Srinivasan. iTrust: An integrated trust framework for wireless sensor networks. In *Proceedings of the 2010 ACM Symposium on Applied Computing*, 2010.

Bid2Charge: Market User Interface Design for Electric Vehicle Charging

Sebastian Stein* ss2@ecs.soton.ac.uk
Enrico H. Gerding* eg@ecs.soton.ac.uk
Adrian Nedea* adrian.nedea@gmail.com
Avi Rosenfeld◇ rosenfa@gmail.com
Nicholas R. Jennings* nrj@ecs.soton.ac.uk
*University of Southampton, Southampton, United Kingdom
◇Jerusalem College of Technology, Jerusalem, Israel

ABSTRACT

We consider settings where owners of electric vehicles (EVs) participate in a market mechanism to charge their vehicles. Existing work on such mechanisms has typically assumed that participants are fully rational and can report their preferences accurately to the mechanism or to a software agent participating on their behalf. However, this may not be reasonable in settings with non-expert human end-users. To explore this, we compare a fully expressive interface that covers the entire space of preferences to two restricted interfaces that reduce the space of possible options. To enable this analysis, we develop a novel game that replicates key features of an abstract EV charging scenario. In two extensive evaluations with over 300 users, we show that restricting the users' preferences significantly reduces the time they spend deliberating. More surprisingly, it also leads to an increase in their utility compared to the fully expressive interface (up to 70%). Finally, we find that a reinforcement learning agent displays similar performance trends, enabling a novel methodology for evaluating market interfaces.

Keywords

Market user interface design; smart grid; electric vehicle charging

1. INTRODUCTION

Market mechanisms designed for multi-agent systems hold considerable promise for addressing emerging challenges in future electricity networks, where supply will increasingly be generated from intermittent and unreliable renewable sources, and where demand will increase due to the electrification of transportation [12]. In particular, recent years have seen a proliferation of interest in electric vehicles (EVs), generally perceived as a key technology for achieving sustainable mass transportation with low carbon emissions [14]. However, their widespread use will also place considerable strains on the existing electricity infrastructure.

To address this, previous work has proposed auction-like mechanisms for scheduling the charging of EVs [13, 4]. These achieve a high efficiency because they take the individual preferences of drivers (i.e., their availability and willingness to pay) into account when allocating a limited supply of electricity. Other work relies on real-time price signals to incentivise autonomous charging agents to shift or curtail their consumption when supply is low [11].

However, such approaches assume that the human end-users have perfect knowledge of their preferences, i.e., they can reason accurately about the value of different amounts of electricity, considering all possible, often uncertain future opportunities of using it. This is often not realistic [18, 6]. Moreover, providing the complete preferences is tedious and the associated cost could outweigh the benefits of doing so [7].

To address this challenge, there has been some work on auctions with *restricted reporting*, i.e., where bidders do not report their full preferences, but rather choose from a restricted messaging space. Such auctions can lead to equilibria with certain desirable properties, including higher revenue for the auctioneer [8, 3]. This includes settings where the messaging space is reduced to a small set of discrete options, e.g., [1] describes how to select these options to maximise either social welfare or revenue, and [2] characterises the associated loss of efficiency. Other work, e.g., [15], considers how complex preferences can be elicited through an incremental query process. However, these approaches all assume rational agents and do not evaluate the auctions with real bidders.

Another strand of work explicitly considers non-expert market participants. For example, research on hidden market design has looked at building simple interfaces that hide the rules and pricing mechanisms of a complex underlying market [16]. However, that work cannot be applied directly to EV charging, as it considers an exchange market for computational storage without financial payments. Related to this, [17] has investigated market user interface design. That work focuses on simplifying complex market interactions by asking users to select from a discrete set of options. However, it considers a setting with posted prices and is significantly simpler than the EV setting. Crucially, neither [16] nor [17] provides a direct comparison to fully expressive interfaces, which leaves their relative benefits unclear.

To address these limitations, we conduct the first thorough study of how to design market interfaces for the EV charging setting, and we make several novel contributions. First, we formalise the EV charging setting to capture several real-world challenges that give rise to complex preferences and we design two restricted interfaces for reporting preferences in this setting: one that reduces the dimensionality of the reporting space (but retains infinitely many options) and one that restricts the reporting space to a discrete set of options. To evaluate these interfaces with real users, we then develop a game that serves as an abstract representation of the EV charging setting. Using this game, we experimentally compare the restricted interfaces to a fully expressive interface in two large user

Appears in: *Proceedings of the 15th International Conference on Autonomous Agents and Multiagent Systems (AAMAS 2016), J. Thangarajah, K. Tuyls, C. Jonker, S. Marsella (eds.), May 9–13, 2016, Singapore.*

studies involving a total of over 300 participants hired on Amazon Mechanical Turk. We show that the restricted interfaces significantly alleviate the participants' cognitive burden (as measured by the time they deliberate). More surprisingly, they also lead to a significantly better performance than the fully expressive interface (up to 70% in some cases). Furthermore, we show that the choice of restriction can influence the energy consumption of participants without decreasing their utility. This indicates that market user interface design is an important topic to enable efficient future energy markets for end-consumers. Finally, we show that a reinforcement learning agent replicates general behaviour trends of human players, potentially paving the way for a new approach for optimising market interfaces without running large-scale user trials.

2. THE EV CHARGING PROBLEM

In this section, we present an abstract model of the EV charging problem. Our aim is to capture the key challenges that are inherent in the domain, while still retaining a succinct and general model. More specifically, we capture the following challenges that are found in realistic settings.

First, electricity has **no intrinsic value**. Its value instead depends on how it is utilised to complete journeys. Second, the problem is of an inherently **uncertain** nature. On one hand, this is a key feature of the market itself, as supply and demand may fluctuate significantly over time. On the other hand, there may be considerable uncertainty over what journeys the driver needs to complete in the future. Third, there are **complementarities**, i.e., the driver's preferences are typically highly nonlinear over the *quantity* of electricity they receive. For example, a driver may require a minimum overnight charge of 10 kWh to drive to work the next day. Receiving any less has no value.

Given this, we consider a general setting where EV drivers participate in a market mechanism to charge their vehicles. We abstract away from the particular market and assume that a driver simply reports her preferences for charging to an autonomous agent at regular intervals (e.g., once a day).[1] The agent then participates in the market on its owner's behalf and procures electricity for the vehicle while it is plugged in (e.g., overnight). At the end of the charging period, the driver can use the vehicle to complete journeys and derives value from doing so.

More formally, the problem consists of a sequence of n *days*, $D = \{1, 2, \dots, n\}$. An EV starts with a given initial *state of charge (SOC)* $s_1 \in [0, s_{\max}]$ (in kWh). Then, at the start of each day d, the driver reports her charging preferences to an autonomous agent, which procures electricity from the market to charge the EV.

2.1 Electricity Market

We assume electricity is sold in discrete, unit-sized quantities (we use 1 kWh, w.l.o.g.). To participate in the market for day d, the EV driver reports her preferences for each quantity of electricity to her charging agent. This is done in the form of a *preference report vector* $w_d = [w_{d,1}, w_{d,2}, \dots, w_{d,s_{\max}-s_d}]$, which indicates the driver's maximum willingness to pay for a given charge (up to the maximum capacity) on that day. This structure allows complementarities to be expressed — for example, a preference vector $w_d = [0, 4, 5]$ indicates that the driver is not willing to pay anything for receiving 1 kWh (e.g., because this is too little to complete any journeys), she will pay up to \$4 for 2 kWh and up to \$5 for 3 kWh.

Given this preference vector, the charging agent then participates in the market and obtains $x_d(w_d)$ units of electricity at a price of $p_d(w_d)$. These are uncertain, depending on the day's market conditions (e.g., supply of renewables and fluctuations in aggregate demand), but we assume that the agent maximises the driver's utility in expectation, such that truthful reporting is optimal, i.e., $\forall w_d, \hat{w}_d : \mathbb{E}[w_{d,x_d(w_d)} - p_d(w_d)] \geq \mathbb{E}[w_{d,x_d(\hat{w}_d)} - p_d(\hat{w}_d)]$, where w_d is the driver's true willingness to pay. In practice, this can be achieved by participating in an incentive compatible mechanism [13, 4] or by acting strategically on the owner's behalf, e.g., when optimising charging decisions given price predictions for real-time pricing [11]. Throughout the paper we will also assume that an agent's charging behaviour could influence prices on the same day, but has a negligible impact on the market conditions of the following days. This is a reasonable assumption in energy markets, where a single domestic consumer has little impact on future prices.

[1]For example market mechanisms, see [11, 13, 4].

2.2 EV Utilisation

Given the outcome of the market interaction, the new SOC of the EV is now $s'_d = \min(s_d + x_d(w_d), s_{\max})$. This can then be used by the EV driver to complete journeys. Specifically, every day, there is a set of *potentially available* journeys, $j_d \subseteq J$, where $J = \{1, 2, \dots\}$ is the set of all journeys. These represent possible journeys the driver may wish to make during the day (e.g., driving to work or to the supermarket). To model realistic scenarios, at the time of reporting preferences, there may be uncertainty about which journeys will be available (e.g., because they depend on the weather or because some journeys will only be necessary in exceptional circumstances). To reflect this uncertainty, a journey is defined by a probability $r_j \in [0, 1]$ (we assume these are independent, although this can be easily relaxed, as discussed briefly in Appendix A) and a value $v_j \in \mathbb{R}$. The value of a journey reflects its importance to the driver and may represent the inconvenience cost incurred when missing the journey, or even the cost of alternative transport (e.g., to travel to work). The sets of potential journeys j_d are known in advance for all days, but the set of *actually available* journeys on day d, denoted by $j'_d \subseteq j_d$, only becomes known after charging is complete on that day.

Given the set of journeys j'_d, the driver now chooses which subset $a_d \subseteq j'_d$ of these to complete. Doing so reduces the EV's SOC, as given by an appropriate cost function $\gamma : 2^J \to \mathbb{R}_{\geq 0}$ (journeys that exceed the SOC cannot be completed). Furthermore, the driver receives the total value of these journeys. Thus, her total utility is the difference between the overall value derived from journeys over time horizon D, and the total costs incurred. In the following sections, we discuss two approaches for solving this optimisation problem computationally, one is optimal and one is a learning approach that may be a better model of human behaviour.

2.3 Optimal Solution

To optimise her utility, an EV driver needs to report a preference vector w_d on every day d that expresses the respective expected utility for receiving each possible quantity of charge. This is a complex problem, as it needs to take into account the (uncertain) availability of journeys not only on the current day, but also on future days, as well as likely future market conditions, as the battery of the EV allows the driver to store surplus electricity.

To derive the optimal strategy for a perfectly rational driver, we will assume that the driver has knowledge about the expected prices $p_d(w_d)$ and the distribution of allocations $x_d(w_d)$ for a given preference vector. With this, we can model the problem as a Markov Decision Process (MDP) [5], the full details of which are in Appendix A. The solution to such an MDP is a *policy* that selects both appropriate preference vectors to report to the charging agent and sets of journeys to complete, depending on the state (the current day d, the current SOC and the journeys available on a given day).

Solving this MDP optimally is NP-hard in general (as the journey selection generalises the Knapsack problem), but problems of realistic sizes can still be solved quickly. This is because we consider a limited time horizon here, allowing the use of backwards induction and dynamic programming. Furthermore, the possible journeys that a driver will seriously consider on a given day will be small, perhaps in the order of a dozen or fewer. We also discretise the state space of the SOC to include all reachable states, given the cost function γ. Finally, as the charging agent participates in the market optimally, the optimal preference vector is simply the driver's true valuation for each level of charge, and this is obtained readily from the MDP solution.

2.4 Reinforcement Learning Agent

Clearly, the optimal solution makes some assumptions that are unlikely to hold in practice (such as knowledge of the distributions of $p_d(w_d)$ and $x_d(w_d)$, and all potential future journeys). Hence, a second approach for solving the EV driver's decision problem is to design a reinforcement learning agent [19] (note this agent is different from the agent described above that interacts with the market). This approach does not require an explicit model of future market interactions or available journeys, but rather learns the optimal policy from repeatedly interacting with the environment and observing realised costs and rewards.

Specifically, we employ the widely-used Q-Learning algorithm [20] with an ϵ-greedy exploration strategy (see Appendix B for details). We hypothesise that this learning approach may be a good approximation of how real users interact with the system, by trying some preference reports, observing how the system responds and then making small adjustments to their strategies (rather than reasoning about the optimal strategy). In fact, reinforcement learning has been used as a computational model to explain learning and decision-making behaviours in animals [9].

3. RESTRICTED MARKET INTERFACES

In practice, the drivers solving the above optimisation problem will be humans, and, as we argued, they may not have the time or capacity to act optimally. Neither of the solution approaches discussed in the previous section are feasible for completely automating people's decision processes — the optimal solution requires full information about all possible future journeys, while reinforcement learning requires a long training phase until it performs well.

Instead, we here focus on simplifying the market interface for drivers. In particular, we use a range of interfaces that intentionally restrict the reporting space for the user (but without changing the underlying market mechanism). Knowing which interface to present to users can alleviate the cognitive burden, as the user has to consider fewer options.

Given this, we denote the full space of possible reports in a fully expressive interface by $W = \mathbb{R}_{\geq 0}^{s_{\max}}$. In the following, we will use two approaches for restricting this space by providing the user with an alternative set of reports, W', which maps to W through a function $\omega : W' \to W$, to determine the corresponding report that is used by the charging agent. Both approaches rely on significantly reducing the dimensionality of the decision space, while still retaining the ability for users to express a range of valuations.

3.1 Single Marginal Value with Quantity (SMV)

The first restriction, SMV, reduces the driver's possible reports to a single marginal value $m_d \in \mathbb{R}_{\geq 0}$ and a maximum quantity $q_d \in \mathbb{N}$ she wishes to acquire. Here, m_d expresses the value she gains for receiving each *additional* unit of electricity up to a total quantity of q_d. Thus, the space for this restriction is $W^{\text{SMV}} = \mathbb{R}_{\geq 0} \times \mathbb{N}$ and we denote a report by $w_d^{\text{SMV}} = (m_d, q_d)$. The corresponding mapping function is $\omega^{\text{SMV}}(m_d, q_d) = [m_d, 2m_d, 3m_d, \ldots, q_d m_d]$.

The rationale behind providing this restriction is that it reduces the dimensionality of the problem to two dimensions, which may be significantly easier for a user to understand and solve. However, the disadvantage of this approach is that the space of possible reports is still infinitely large. While q_d is discrete and restricted by the battery size, m_d may take on arbitrary values.

3.2 Finite Set of Alternatives

In the second restriction (FINITE), which has been used in related work [1, 17, 2], we select a finite subset of f alternatives from the full report space, $\{\alpha_1, \alpha_2, \ldots, \alpha_f\} \subset W$. The corresponding restricted report space is then $W^{\text{FINITE}} = \{1, 2, \ldots, f\}$, such that a report $w_i^{\text{FINITE}} = x$ expresses the user's choice of alternative α_x, i.e., $\omega^{\text{FINITE}}(x) = \alpha_x$.

The advantage of this restriction is that the driver has to consider a very small number of alternatives. In practice, f can be chosen to trade off the cognitive burden on the user with the expressivity of the space (typically, we envisage f to be a handful or less). The alternatives could be chosen to represent a cross section of the full report space, could be manually selected by domain experts or could even be selected by an autonomous agent that adjusts these alternatives to a particular user.

Note that both the optimal solution and the reinforcement learning approach can be adapted for the restricted interfaces through appropriate discretisation. The details are in Appendices A and B

4. THE BID2CHARGE TESTBED

To test how human participants interact with our interfaces, and to empirically determine which one works best, we designed a web-based game called Bid2Charge, which replicates the EV charging setting. We frame this as a game, as this is a low-cost, controlled way of gathering data from large numbers of users in a short time.

In more detail, in Bid2Charge, the player takes the role of an EV delivery van driver. This provides an intuitive explanation to players of what journeys represent (in the game, journeys are referred to as delivery tasks and result in a certain payment), what the objective of the game is (maximise overall profit) and what the uncertainty means (delivery tasks may or may not come up on a given day). We use an incentive-compatible auction based on the well-known VCG mechanism [10] as the market mechanism in this game, and so the player's reports in each of the market interfaces are framed as bids for this auction.[2]

Figure 1 shows the main game screen. At the top, there are some general statistics, showing the player's accumulated profit, the current day and current SOC. Below that, on the left, there is a task planning view. This provides the user with information about j_d, i.e., the tasks that are potentially available on the current day. Both the value, v_j, and the realisation probability, a_j, are shown for each task. Furthermore, the user can select subsets of tasks, $j' \subseteq j$ to inspect both the total value ($v(j')$) and the total cost ($\gamma(j')$) if those tasks are completed (here, $\gamma(j')$ is calculated based on the Euclidean distance of the shortest route past all tasks in j'). Note that interacting with this view does not affect the game — it simply provides the player with information about the available tasks. In Figure 1 the user has selected the \$10 and \$15 tasks and is informed that this will require 11 kWh in total for a reward of \$25.

The auction view, which is to the right of the task planning view,

[2]VCG fulfils the conditions for optimality in Section 2.1. It is dominant strategy incentive compatible for the current day (while assuming a probabilistic model of prices on future days).

Figure 1: Main game view.

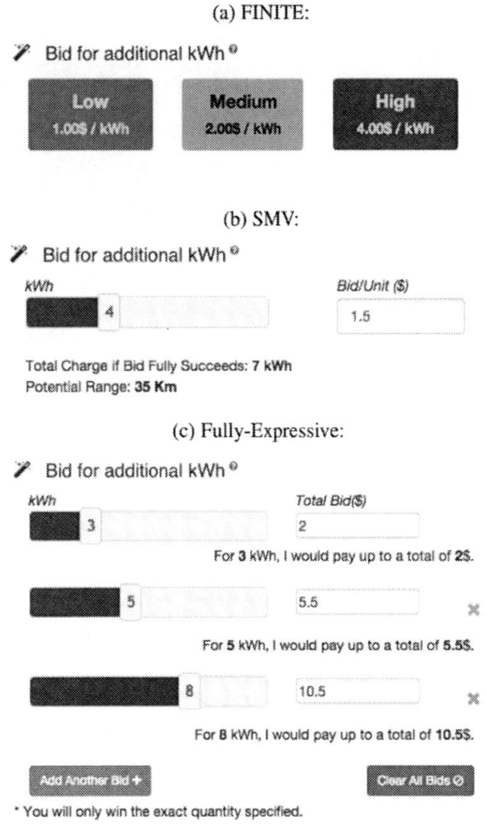

Figure 2: Auction Bidding Panels.

allows the player to submit their bid w_d for the current day. The view supports all three interfaces discussed in this paper, as shown in Figure 2: FINITE, SMV and a fully expressive interface. Only one of these is shown to each user. Here, the candidates for FINITE in Figure 2a can be customised by the game administrator, but this particular view shows $[1, 2, 3, \ldots]$, $[2, 4, 6, \ldots]$ and $[4, 8, 12, \ldots]$, which we also use for our experiments. The view for SMV in Figure 2b shows a user entering the bid $m_d = 1.5, q_d = 4$. Finally, the view for the fully expressive interface in Figure 2c shows a user entering $w_d = [0, 0, 2, 2, 5.5, 5.5, 5.5, 10.5]$. The user always has the option to skip the auction. On pressing the "Run Auction" button, they are informed of the outcome and then taken to a task view.

In the task view, representing the EV utilisation phase and shown in Figure 3, the user is presented with the realisation of tasks for the current day and can select their desired choice of tasks to complete. The options for this are given as a table with corresponding rewards and costs, and any dominated solutions are automatically removed.

5. EXPERIMENTAL EVALUATION

The purpose of our experiments is to investigate how real human users interact with the two restricted interfaces proposed in this paper, as well as the fully expressive interface, and whether the choice of a particular interface influences the performance of users. Our approach is to evaluate this through a randomised, controlled experiment, where we allocate market interfaces randomly to users, in order to exclude self-selection bias. Participants were given instructions only for the particular interface they were assigned to and were not told that others existed. In carrying out our experiments, we were guided by two main hypotheses:

Hypothesis 1: *Players using more expressive interfaces achieve the same or a higher profit than those using restricted interfaces.*

Hypothesis 2: *Players using more expressive interfaces spend more time on the game than those using more restricted interfaces.*

The first hypothesis is based on the fact that the more expressive interfaces offer more possible reports to the players. Experimental evidence also suggests that market user interfaces with more options lead to the same or better performance than those with fewer options [17]. However, more expressivity may also incur a higher cognitive burden, which is expressed by Hypothesis 2.

We tested these hypotheses through one initial experiment, where we asked participants to play through a single game consisting of 30 days. To further explore how players learn and improve over time, we carried out a second experiment, where we asked another set of participants to play through three identical 10-day games in sequence (although journeys and their probabilities were identical, their realisations were not necessarily the same). In addition to validating the results from the first experiment, the main hypothesis we tested in the second setting was:

Hypothesis 3: *Players using more complex interfaces improve their profit more significantly over repeated plays of the game than those using more restricted interfaces.*

Furthermore, this more sequential setting allowed us to compare the human learning trends to those of the reinforcement learning agent we proposed in Section 2.4.

5.1 Player Recruitment

We recruited players from Amazon Mechanical Turk, a platform that allows requesters to advertise tasks to a large audience of online workers.[3] We asked workers to first read a set of instructions explaining the rules and objectives of the game, then they had to give consent to participating in a study as well as answer three basic questions about the rules (to test their understanding). We told workers the task would take about 25 minutes, they would receive a base payment of \$2.50 and then a bonus based on the profit they made in the game. Specifically, in the first experiment, we offered \$0.02 for each \$1.00 earned in the game, while (due to budget constraints) in the second experiment we offered \$0.01 for each \$1.00 earned in each of the three games. In both experiments, this was capped at \$3.00).[4] This bonus was chosen to ensure that the incentives of the player were aligned with the objective of the game. We assigned participants to interfaces using a block randomisation scheme, to achieve a balanced spread of participants across

[3] `http://www.mturk.com/`

[4] This maximum was set to limit our potential spend. Only three players managed to reach this.

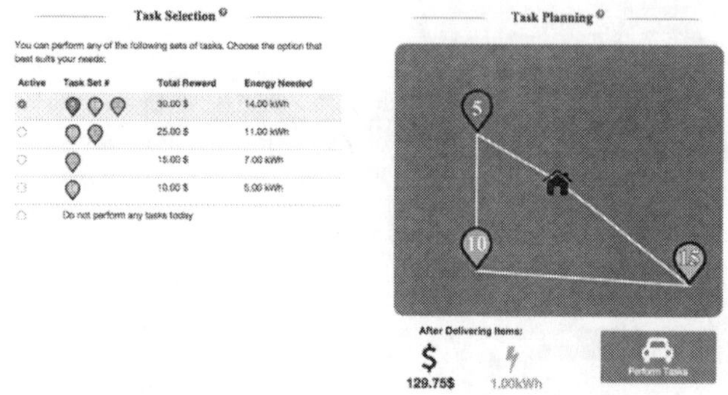

Figure 3: Task view with actually available tasks.

the interfaces. To ensure players understood the game, they had to correctly answer a short multiple-choice questionnaire. In the first experiment, 130 workers played the game; while in the second experiment 189 played three games each.

5.2 Experimental Parameters

To simulate the auction, we determine the marginal prices of units, denoted by $p_{d,x}$ for the xth unit, using random distributions. These are identical for all interfaces, on all days and for all participants (but the prices were sampled independently each time). Specifically, each price was determined by first setting $p_{d,0} = 0$, and then iteratively determining each $p_{d,x}$ as $p_{d,x} = p_{d,x-1} + \epsilon_x$, where ϵ_x was drawn from a uniform distribution $\mathcal{U}(0.2x - 0.2, 0.4x + 0.6)$. The rising mean of this distribution ensures that marginal prices for each unit generally increase. Given these prices, we then select $x_d(w_d) = \text{argmax}_x\, w_{d,x} - \sum_i^x p_{d,i}$.

The game in the first experiment was played for 30 simulated days, and we varied the number of tasks every 1–4 days (with between 1–6 tasks available every day). We did not give players information about tasks on future days (only the total number of days to play), and there was no prior information about the distribution of auction prices and allocation probabilities. This is reasonable because in real-world settings these would also be highly uncertain, and because we did not want to overwhelm players with a large amount of information. In the second game, a 10-day game was played three times by each player, enabling some learning.

5.3 Benchmarks

To establish upper and lower bounds for the possible performance of players, we compare them to a number of benchmarks: **Optimal** is the optimal strategy assuming a fully expressive interface. We also show two variants, **Optimal (SMV)** and **Optimal (FINITE)**, for the restricted interfaces. All of these are obtained by solving the MDP. **RandomGreedy** is a benchmark that places a random bid (chosen from the FINITE options) and then greedily chooses the highest-value tasks. Finally, **MaxGreedy** places a bid that is high enough to fully charge the EV each day and then greedily chooses the highest-value tasks. These two represent simple strategies that a worker could employ to complete the task with as little effort as possible (thus representing a lower bound on performance). Finally, we also show results for reinforcement learning strategies corresponding to the three interfaces, **QL(λ)**, **QL(SMV,λ)** and **QL(FINITE,λ)**, where λ is the number of episodes the game has been played by the agent. This performance is obtained by temporarily setting ϵ to 0.

5.4 Results of First Experiment

We first consider the overall performance in terms of the overall profit achieved, as this is the main objective of the game and to ver-

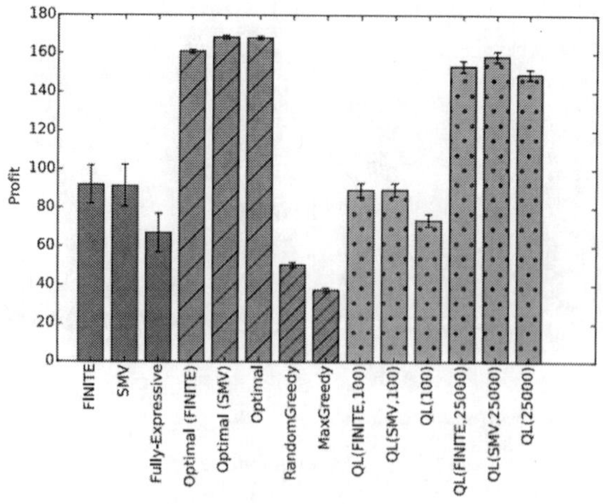

Figure 4: Average profit in first experiment.

ify Hypothesis 1. Figure 4 shows this for the three interfaces with human participants (in red, plain), for the three optimal policies (in green, hatched), the two baseline benchmarks (in blue, finely hatched) and the reinforcement learning agent after 100 and 25000 iterations of the game, which are representative of early and late stages of learning (in orange, dotted). All results are shown with 95% confidence intervals. Focusing first on the performance of the optimal (in green), it is interesting to note here that there is little difference between the optimal performance in the restricted setting (in particular for SMV) and the fully expressive setting. This is encouraging, showing that, despite the severe restrictions, there is little loss in the utility players could, in theory, achieve.

Considering the performance of human players, these are generally situated between the optimal and the baseline benchmarks. Unsurprisingly, the humans perform significantly worse than a rational agent, given that the problem is highly complex due to its inherent stochasticity and combinatorial nature. However, when comparing the human players to the baseline benchmarks, there is a marked improvement. This provides some evidence that the participants are putting effort into the game rather than selecting strategies that require the least effort.

When comparing the performance of the human players using different market interfaces, several interesting trends emerge. First, we note that the choice of mechanism seems to have a significant influence on performance.[5] Counter-intuitively, the players using the fully expressive interface achieve the overall lowest performance with an average profit of only \$66.96, while players with SMV achieve an average profit of \$91.38 and players with FINITE achieve an average \$91.93.[6] This constitutes an improvement of over 35% compared to the fully expressive interface. This means our Hypothesis 1 needs to be rejected. One possible reason why the fully expressive interface does not perform as well is because of its substantial cognitive burden, because users are faced with a complex decision problem.

Considering the performance of the reinforcement learning agent, several interesting trends emerge. First, the fully-expressive interface consistently performs worse than the other two interfaces (with the same amount of learning). This is because the extremely large

[5]This is confirmed by ANOVA with $p = 0.001$.

[6]A post-hoc Bonferroni test confirms that there is a significant difference between the fully expressive mechanism and each of the other two (with $p = 0.004$). There is no significant difference between the performance of users with FINITE and SMV.

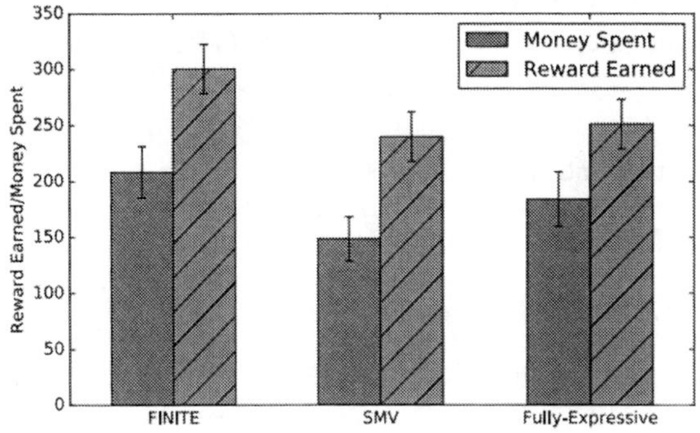

Figure 5: Average money spent and reward earned.

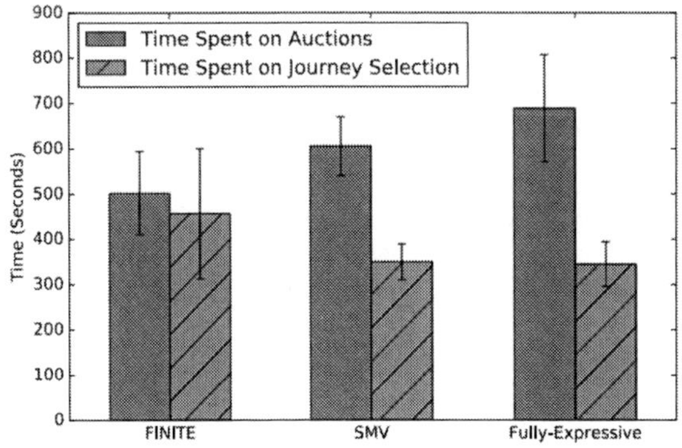

Figure 6: Average time spent by players on auctions and journeys.

reporting space takes longer to explore than in the other two interfaces. Furthermore, after 100 learning episodes, the performance of the reinforcement learning agent resembles that of human players, indicating that it may be useful for predicting human behaviour.

Although there is no significant difference in profit between FINITE and SMV for human players, interesting trends emerge when considering the actual money that was spent on acquiring electricity and how much was gained from completing tasks. This is shown in Figure 5. Here, players using FINITE spent an average $208.44 acquiring electricity and achieved an average reward of $300.37. In contrast, players using SMV spent only an average of $148.50 and earned $239.89. The differences here are highly significant.[7] Thus, while the profit for both is similar, FINITE induces a very different behaviour in the players — they spend significantly more on acquiring electricity and are then able to use this to complete a larger number of tasks. This is likely because SMV requires users to explicitly set a maximum number of units, thereby focusing them on this parameter and implicitly suggesting they restrict this demand. This is an interesting result, showing that significant changes in behaviour can be caused by the right choice of mechanism. Especially in the energy domain, low overall consumption may be a particularly desirable goal and SMV encourages this.

Next, to investigate Hypothesis 2, Figure 6 shows the time that players spent on the auction and task screens. Participants using the fully expressive interface spent the longest time on the auction (689 minutes on average), while participants using FINITE spent the least amount of time on the auction (502 minutes on average). This supports the hypothesis.[8]

[7]ANOVA confirms this for both metrics with $p \leq 0.002$. Post-hoc Bonferroni tests confirm differences between FINITE and SMV with $p = 0.001$.

[8]ANOVA ($p = 0.026$) and a Bonferroni test confirm a difference between the expressive and FINITE ($p = 0.021$.)

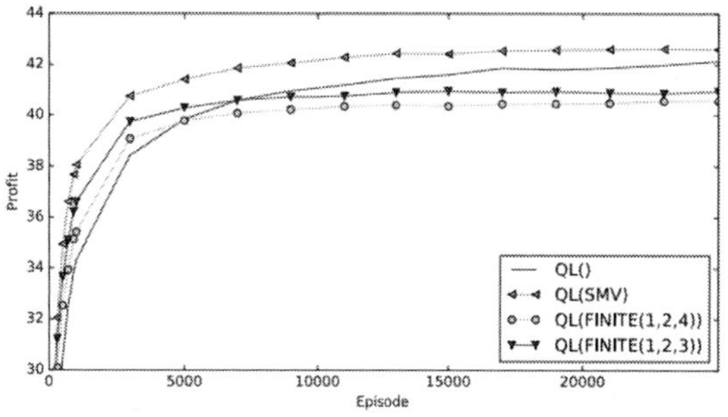

Figure 7: Average profit over number of learning episodes obtained by reinforcement learning agent.

5.5 Results of Second Experiment

To further examine whether our proposed reinforcement learning agent can be applied to optimising market user interfaces, we ran the agent in the setting of the second experiment and identified a small change to the FINITE strategy that led to an improvement in the agent's performance. Specifically, we decreased the marginal valuation reported in the third alternative from $4/kWh to $3/kWh. We used both alternatives in the second experiment, and in the following, we will refer to interfaces FINITE(1,2,3) and FINITE(1,2,4) to distinguish between these two. Figure 7 shows the performance of the reinforcement learning agent over time using the various interfaces.

Figure 8 shows the overall performance results from the second experiment, grouped by the three games each player completed. First, it is clear that there is a strong learning effect — on all treatments, the players perform better over time. On the first game, there is also a very clear performance difference between the interfaces. Fully expressive performs worse (average profit $15.6) while SMV performs best (average profit $26.8).[9] However, participants on the fully expressive interface then start to perform significantly better on subsequent games, supporting Hypothesis 3. This is likely because they begin to exploit the higher expressivity of the interface. At the same time, they are still taking significantly longer to deliberate during the auction phase (taking 373, 266 and 227 minutes for the three games, compared to 178, 123 and 116 of FINITE(1,2,3)), and they still do not outperform the restricted interfaces.

Finally, comparing the results with the predictions of the reinforcement learning agent, several trends are confirmed. First, FINITE(1,2,3) indeed outperforms FINITE(1,2,4), validating the agent's predictions and indicating that our approach of optimising the interface based on the agent's response is sensible. This is particularly promising, because there is no discernible difference in the *optimal* performance of the two interfaces (see Figure 8). Other trends indicated by the agent are also confirmed: SMV consistently performs well throughout, while the fully expressive interface initially performs poorly, but then catches up with the others as more learning and exploration take place.

6. CONCLUSIONS AND FUTURE WORK

As appropriate market mechanisms can efficiently allocate scarce resources to competing consumers, they hold considerable promise in addressing emerging challenges in the energy domain. However, in many realistic settings, including the EV charging problem,

[9]ANOVA ($p = 0.006$) and a Bonferroni test find a significant difference ($p = 0.036$) between these two.

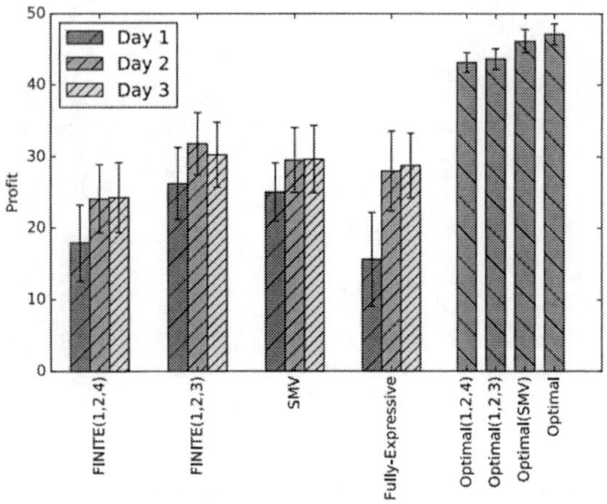

Figure 8: Average profit during each of the three games in the second experiment, along with benchmarks.

there are non-expert participants. In this paper, we studied how the cognitive burden on such participants can be alleviated by using restricted market interfaces.

This paper's extensive evaluation used a new framework called Bid2Charge that allowed us to compare people's behaviour in a simulated EV charging setting and using a variety of interfaces. As such, our work is the first comprehensive study of a wide spectrum of market interfaces, ranging from fully expressive to parameterised (SMV) to very limited (FINITE). In carrying out this study, we found that using restricted market interfaces has several key advantages over standard fully expressive approaches. First, participants spend less time deliberating, which indicates a lower cognitive burden. Second, these participants tend to perform better than those using a fully expressive, theoretically optimal interface. This performance gap is particularly pronounced during the first interactions, and then gradually closes with experience. Third, particular types of interfaces induce different behaviours in participants, while achieving the same utility. This could be a promising tool for nudging people towards particularly desirable behaviours, such as energy conservation. Last, we found that a reinforcement learning agent was able to predict broad trends in the relative performance of alternative interfaces. As such, we believe it constitutes a valuable tool for the evaluation and optimisation of market user interfaces.

In future work, we plan to build on this framework and develop new optimised interfaces that adapt to users. In particular, we will extend the reinforcement learning agent proposed in this paper to offer advice and support the user through autonomous decisions. Last, it is important to note that while Bid2Charge was evaluated using EV market mechanisms, it is a general framework which is easily adapted to other markets. Along these lines, we plan to study restricted interfaces and learning agents in other settings.

Acknowledgements

This work was supported by the EPSRC-funded ORCHID project and the Southampton Annual Adventures in Research grant.

APPENDIX

A. OPTIMAL SOLUTION

Here, we present the MDP formulation of the EV charging problem, describe an agent's policies and present the optimal solution.

A.1 MDP Formulation

We formalise the EV charging problem from Section 2 as a tuple $(\Sigma, \Sigma', J, j_{d\in D}, r_{j\in J}, v_{j\in J}, \gamma, X_{d\in D}, P_{d\in D})$, where:

- $\Sigma = D \times [0, s_{\max}]$ is the set of states *before* the market interaction, and $\Sigma' = D \times [0, s_{\max}] \times 2^J$ is the set of states *after* the market interaction (but before selecting from the available journeys). Both include the current day, d, and state of charge, s_d or s'_d, while a state $\sigma' \in \Sigma'$ also includes the set of available journeys j'_d.
- J, j_d, r_j, v_j and γ describe the journeys, their potential availability per day, realisation probabilities, values and journey costs, as defined in Section 2.
- $X_d : (W \times \{0, 1, \ldots, s_{\max}\}) \to [0, 1]$ is the probability distribution of x_d, i.e., $X_d(w_d, x)$ is the probability of obtaining x units when reporting w_d during a market interaction.
- $P_d : W \to \mathbb{R}$ is the expected price of a market interaction given a report, i.e., $P_d(w_d) = \mathbb{E}[p_d(w_d)]$.

The actions, transition probabilities and rewards of this MDP are fully described by the tuple above. Specifically, the available **actions** depend on the current state as follows. For $\sigma \in \Sigma$, the actions are the reports in W. For $\sigma' = (d, s'_d, j'_d) \in \Sigma'$, the set of actions is $\{a \in 2^{j'_d} \mid \gamma(a) \leq s'_d\}$, i.e., all subsets of the available journeys that can be completed with the current state of charge. **Transition probabilities** from a state σ to a state σ' are determined by the chosen report w_d and X_d (to determine s'_d) and by j_d and r_j (to determine j'_d). Transitions from a state σ' to σ are deterministically given by the chosen action a_d and cost function γ. **Rewards** are incurred when transitioning from one state to the next, and they correspond to the prices paid for electricity (negative) and the values derived from completing journeys (positive). Specifically, the former is given by $-P_d(w_d)$, while the latter is $\sum_{j\in a_d} v_j$.

A.2 Agent Policy

An agent's policy determines which preference vector to report for the market interaction, and which journeys to complete, given the current state. Thus, it is described by a tuple (π, π'), where $\pi : \Sigma \to W$ determines the reports and $\pi' : \Sigma' \to 2^J$ the journeys.

Given this, we can now define the expected utility of a policy (π, π') using a value function for each type of state. For state $\sigma = (d, s_d) \in \Sigma$:

$$V(d, s_d, \pi, \pi') = -P_d(\pi(\sigma)) + \sum_{i=0}^{s_{\max}} \Big[X_d(\pi(\sigma), i) \cdot \sum_{j'_d \subseteq j_d} R(j'_d)\, V'(d, \min(s_d + i, s_{\max}), j'_d, \pi, \pi')\Big], \quad (1)$$

where $R(j'_d) = \prod_{j\in j'_d} r_j \prod_{j\in j_d \setminus j'_d} (1 - r_j)$ is the probability that j'_d is the set of journeys available.[10]

For state $\sigma' = (d, s'_d, j'_d) \in \Sigma'$, with $d < n$:

$$V'(d, s'_d, j'_d, \pi, \pi') = \Big[\sum_{j\in\pi'(\sigma')} v_j\Big] + V(d+1, s'_d - \gamma(\pi'(\sigma')), \pi, \pi'), \quad (2)$$

while for the last day, $V'(n, s'_n, j'_n, \pi, \pi') = \sum_{j\in\pi'(\sigma)} v_j$.

[10]Note that while this definition of $R(j'_d)$ assumes independence between journeys, it could be redefined to account for correlated journey probabilities without changing the solution approach or its computational complexity.

Algorithm 1 Optimal Solution

1: **procedure** FINDOPTIMAL
2: Initialise π^*, π'^*, V and V' to be empty
3: Initialise Γ to hold feasible charge levels given γ
4: **for** $d \in \{n, n-1, n-2, \ldots, 1\}$ **do**
5: **for** $s \in \Gamma$ **do**
6: **for** $j'_d \subseteq j_d$ **do**
7: **if** $d = n$ **then**
8: $\pi'^*(d, s, j'_d) = \text{argmax}_{a \subseteq j'_d \mid \gamma(a) \leq s} \sum_{j \in a} v_j$
9: **else**
10: $\pi'^*(d, s, j'_d) = \text{argmax}_{a \subseteq j'_d \mid \gamma(a) \leq s} \sum_{j \in a} v_j + V(d+1, s-\gamma(a), \pi^*, \pi'^*)$
11: Calculate $V'(d, s, j'_d, \pi^*, \pi'^*)$ using Equation 2
12: Calculate $\pi^*(d, s, \pi^*, \pi'^*)$ using Equation 4
13: Calculate $V(d, s, \pi^*, \pi'^*)$ using Equation 1
14: **return** (π^*, π'^*)

A.3 Optimal Solution

Given the above definition, the optimal policy (π^*, π'^*) is simply:

$$(\pi^*, \pi'^*) = \underset{(\pi, \pi')}{\text{argmax}}\, V(1, s_{\text{initial}}, \pi, \pi'), \tag{3}$$

where s_{initial} is the initial state of charge. As discussed in Section 2.3, this can be found using dynamic programming with backwards induction and by recognising that the agent's best strategy is to bid its true valuation for each level of electricity. This valuation is given directly by V', such that:

$$\pi^*(d, s_d) = \left[V'(d, s_d+1, \pi^*, \pi'^*), V'(d, s_d+2, \pi^*, \pi'^*), \ldots, V'(d, s_{\max}, \pi^*, \pi'^*)\right] \tag{4}$$

The full algorithm for computing the optimal policy is shown in Algorithm 1. In order to obtain optimal policies for the restricted interfaces, we can replace line 12 with the following:

13: $w^* = \text{argmax}_{w \in W'} -P_d(\omega(w)) + \sum_{i=0}^{s_{\max}} \Big[X_d(\omega(w), i) \cdot \sum_{j'_d \subseteq j_d} R(j'_d)\, V'(d, \min(s+i, s_{\max}), j'_d, \pi, \pi')\Big]$
14: $\pi^*(d, s) = \omega(w^*)$

For SMV, this requires a discretisation of the marginal value. In our experiments, we use $m_d \in \{\$0, \$0.01, \$0.02, \ldots, \$5\}$, which is sufficiently fine-grained to lead to a near-optimal performance.

B. REINFORCEMENT LEARNING AGENT

Algorithm 2 shows the reinforcement learning algorithm we use as a more realistic benchmark than the optimal. This algorithm does not need knowledge of the underlying MDP and instead uses a Q-Learning approach to gradually learn the value of making particular reports in a given state (expressed using a $Q(\sigma, w)$ function). It takes three parameters: an exploration probability ϵ, a learning rate parameter α, and the set of possible reports W. In the experiments, we set $\epsilon = 0.2$ and $\alpha = 0.1$ (our results are not particularly sensitive to this choice). W is determined by the relevant interface.

In more detail, for each day d of each episode e, the agent first senses the current state σ (line 6). It then selects a report to submit using the PICKREPORT function. This function depends on the interface the agent is using. Algorithm 3 shows this for the Fully-Expressive interface, while Algorithm 4 is used for FINITE and SMV. Both approaches use an ϵ parameter that balances exploration (choosing a random, potentially untested report) with exploitation (choosing the best-performing report). As discussed in Section 2.4, the Fully-Expressive uses a local search technique to

Algorithm 2 Reinforcement Learning Agent

1: **procedure** QLEARNINGAGENT(ϵ, α, W)
2: $\hat{Q} \leftarrow \{\}$ ▷ State/action pairs that have been tried
3: $\forall \sigma \in \Sigma, w \in W : Q(\sigma, w) \leftarrow 0$ ▷ Initialise Q-function
4: **for** $e \in \{1, 2, \ldots\}$ **do** ▷ Episodes
5: **for** $d \in \{1, 2, \ldots, n\}$ **do**
6: $\sigma \leftarrow$ SENSEAUCTIONSTATE()
7: $w \leftarrow$ PICKREPORT($\epsilon, \sigma, Q, \hat{Q}, W$)
8: REPORT(w)
9: $p_d \leftarrow$ OBSERVECOST()
10: $(d, s, j'_d) \leftarrow$ SENSEJOURNEYSTATE()
11: **if** $d = n$ **then**
12: $a_d \leftarrow \text{argmax}_{a \subseteq j'_d \mid \gamma(a) \leq s} \sum_{j \in a} v_j$
13: **else**
14: $a_d \leftarrow \text{argmax}_{a \subseteq j'_d \mid \gamma(a) \leq s} \Big[\Big(\sum_{j \in a} v_j\Big) + \text{argmax}_{w \in W} Q((d+1, s-\gamma(a)), w)\Big]$
15: $v \leftarrow \sum_{j \in a_d} v_j$
16: **if** $(\sigma, w) \notin \hat{Q}$ **then**
17: $Q(\sigma, w) \leftarrow v - p_d$
18: $\hat{Q} \leftarrow \hat{Q} \cup \{(\sigma, w)\}$
19: **else**
20: $Q(\sigma, w) \leftarrow Q(\sigma, w) + \alpha \cdot (v - p_d - Q(\sigma, w))$
21: **if** RANDOM(0,1) $< \epsilon$ **then**
22: $a_d \in \{a \subseteq j'_d \mid \gamma(a) \leq s\}$ ▷ Pick random journey set
23: COMPLETEJOURNEYS(a_d)

generate new reports during exploration. Here, the MODIFYRANDOMELEMENT(w) function takes a report w, sets one randomly chosen element w_i to a random number (in the experiments, this is on the interval $[0, 6i]$), and then adjusts the other elements to ensure the vector is non-decreasing, by decreasing elements before i and increasing elements after i as necessary.

The agent then submits its chosen report, observes the incurred cost in the market and the new state (lines 8–10). It then picks the best set of journeys to complete, given the Q-values of states on the following day (lines 11–14). These state transitions are deterministic, given the costs of journeys, so we do not learn separate Q-values for journey choices. However, note that most Q-values for the next states will be zero initially, so the agent will start by greedily completing journeys to maximise its immediate reward.

Next, the agent updates the Q-function for its chosen report based on the overall profit achieved during the day (lines 15–20). Finally, with a small probability ϵ, the agent picks a new random set of journeys, which is again used for exploration; otherwise, it executes its chosen set a_d (lines 21–23).

Algorithm 3 Report Selection Function for Fully-Expressive

1: **procedure** PICKREPORT($\epsilon, \sigma, Q, \hat{Q}, W$)
2: $q \leftarrow \{w \mid (\sigma, w) \in \hat{Q}\}$
3: **if** RANDOM(0,1) $< \epsilon \vee |q| = 0$ **then**
4: **if** $|q| = 0$ **then**
5: $w \leftarrow [0, 0, \ldots, 0]$ ▷ $s_{\max}$ elements
6: **else**
7: $w \in q$ ▷ Random report
8: **return** MODIFYRANDOMELEMENT(w)
9: **else**
10: **return** $\text{argmax}_w\, Q(\sigma, w)$

Algorithm 4 Report Selection Function for FINITE and SMV

1: **procedure** PICKREPORT($\epsilon, \sigma, Q, \hat{Q}, W$)
2: **if** RANDOM(0,1) $< \epsilon$ **then**
3: **return** $w \in W$ ▷ Random report
4: **else**
5: **return** $\text{argmax}_w\, Q(\sigma, w)$

REFERENCES

[1] D. Bergemann, J. Shen, Y. Xu, and E. Yeh. Multi-dimensional mechanism design with limited information. In *Proceedings of the 13th ACM Conference on Electronic Commerce*, EC '12, pages 162–178, New York, NY, USA, 2012. ACM.

[2] L. Blumrosen and M. Feldman. Mechanism design with a restricted action space. *Games and Economic Behavior*, 82(0):424 – 443, 2013.

[3] P. Dütting, F. Fischer, and D. C. Parkes. Simplicity-expressiveness tradeoffs in mechanism design. In *Proceedings of the 12th ACM Conference on Electronic Commerce*, EC '11, pages 341–350, New York, NY, USA, 2011. ACM.

[4] K. Hayakawa, E. Gerding, S. Stein, and T. Shiga. Online mechanisms for charging electric vehicles in settings with varying marginal electricity costs. In *24th International Joint Conference on Artificial Intelligence (IJCAI)*, pages 2610–2616, April 2015.

[5] R. A. Howard. *Dynamic Programming and Markov Processes*. MIT Press, 1960.

[6] D. Kahneman. A psychological point of view: Violations of rational rules as a diagnostic of mental processes (commentary on stanovich and west). *Behavioral and Brain Sciences*, 23:681–683, 2000.

[7] K. Larson and T. Sandholm. Mechanism design and deliberative agents. In *Proceedings of the Fourth International Joint Conference on Autonomous Agents and MultiAgent Systems*, pages 650–656, 2005.

[8] P. Milgrom. Simplified mechanisms with an application to sponsored-search auctions. *Games and Economic Behavior*, 70(1):62 – 70, 2010. Special Issue In Honor of Ehud Kalai.

[9] P. R. Montague, S. E. Hyman, and J. D. Cohen. Computational roles for dopamine in behavioural control. *Nature*, 431(7010):760–767, 2004.

[10] N. Nisan, T. Roughgarden, E. Tardos, and V. V. Vazirani. *Algorithmic game theory*, volume 1. Cambridge University Press Cambridge, 2007.

[11] S. D. Ramchurn, P. Vytelingum, A. Rogers, and N. R. Jennings. Agent-based homeostatic control for green energy in the smart grid. *ACM Transactions on Intelligent Systems and Technology (TIST)*, 2(4):35, 2011.

[12] S. D. Ramchurn, P. Vytelingum, A. Rogers, and N. R. Jennings. Putting the 'smarts' into the smart grid: A grand challenge for artificial intelligence. *Commun. ACM*, 55(4):86–97, Apr. 2012.

[13] V. Robu, E. H. Gerding, S. Stein, D. C. Parkes, A. Rogers, and N. R. Jennings. An online mechanism for multi-unit demand and its application to plug-in hybrid electric vehicle charging. *Journal of Artificial Intelligence Research*, 48:175–230, 2013.

[14] Royal Academy of Engineering. *Electric Vehicles: Charged with potential*. Royal Academy of Engineering, 2010.

[15] T. Sandholm and C. P. Boutilier. *Combinatorial Auctions*, chapter Preference elicitation in combinatorial auctions, pages 233–263. MIT Press, 2006.

[16] S. Seuken, K. Jain, D. S. Tan, and M. Czerwinski. Hidden markets: UI design for a P2P backup application. In *Proceedings of the SIGCHI Conference on Human Factors in Computing Systems*, CHI '10, pages 315–324, New York, NY, USA, 2010. ACM.

[17] S. Seuken, D. C. Parkes, E. Horvitz, K. Jain, M. Czerwinski, and D. Tan. Market user interface design. In *Proceedings of the 13th ACM Conference on Electronic Commerce*, EC '12, pages 898–915, New York, NY, USA, 2012. ACM.

[18] H. A. Simon. Theories of bounded rationality. *Decision and organization: A volume in honor of Jacob Marschak*, pages 161–176, 1972.

[19] R. S. Sutton and A. G. Barto. *Reinforcement learning: An introduction*. MIT Press Cambridge, 1998.

[20] C. J. Watkins and P. Dayan. Q-learning. *Machine learning*, 8(3-4):279–292, 1992.

Semi-Automated Construction of Decision-Theoretic Models of Human Behavior

David V. Pynadath
Institute for Creative Technologies, University of Southern California
pynadath@usc.edu

Heather Rosoff
Sol Price School of Public Policy & CREATE, University of Southern California
rosoff@usc.edu

Richard S. John
Department of Psychology & CREATE, University of Southern California
richardj@usc.edu

ABSTRACT

Multiagent social simulation provides a powerful mechanism for policy makers to understand the potential outcomes of their decisions before implementing them. However, the value of such simulations depends on the accuracy of their underlying agent models. In this work, we present a method for automatically exploring a space of decision-theoretic models to arrive at a multiagent social simulation that is consistent with human behavior data. We start with a factored Partially Observable Markov Decision Process (POMDP) whose states, actions, and reward capture the questions asked in a survey from a disaster response scenario. Using input from domain experts, we construct a set of hypothesized dependencies that may or may not exist in the transition probability function. We present an algorithm to search through each of these hypotheses, evaluate their accuracy with respect to the data, and choose the models that best reflect the observed behavior, including individual differences. The result is a mechanism for constructing agent models that are grounded in human behavior data, while still being able to support hypothetical reasoning that is the main advantage of multiagent social simulation.

General Terms

Algorithms

Keywords

multiagent social simulation, POMDPs, disaster response

1. INTRODUCTION

Understanding hypothetical outcomes is critical for making good policy decisions. A city government trying to ensure its readiness to respond to a disaster does not have the benefit of repeated practice. It must somehow make policy decisions that affect and are affected by thousands to millions of people.

To understand the implications and impact of such policy decisions within a complex social environment, the standard approach is to have social scientists who are experts in the domain gather human subject data, either from real or hypothetical disasters (e.g., [10]). Surveys ask questions of survivors of real disasters or experimental participants faced with a hypothetical one. The gathered data contains their answers as to what they believed about the situation, what they did (or would do), and what the important factors were in that decision. Social scientists use statistical analyses of these data to make policy recommendations. Unfortunately, the gathering and analysis of such data is costly, and the conclusions drawn are often applicable to only the specific scenario studied. To understand a different situation, one must gather more data, which is costly and labor-intensive, when it is possible at all.

Multiagent social simulation takes an alternative approach to answering the hypothetical questions asked by policy makers [2, 7, 11, 12, 18]. Such simulations instead represent people with autonomous agents that reflect individuals' or groups' decision-making perspectives and behavior. For example, we can use decision-theoretic models to capture people's decision-making processes, in the form of beliefs, choices, preferences, etc. [4, 5, 13, 15, 20]. By representing these relatively persistent characteristics, the agent can make decisions that are aligned with the corresponding real people in hypothetical situations of interest.

Of course, social simulation relies on building an accurate model. Manual construction of such models, even when grounded in well-established social science theories, is a time-consuming, labor-intensive process that often requires a great deal of trial-and-error iterations. Multiagent researchers have developed automated methods that are sometimes capable of learning such models from data. Unfortunately, in rarely occurring scenarios like disasters, we do not have observations of the transitions, as is typically required for learning decision-theoretic models of human behavior [5]. Furthermore, from the decision-making perspective, the real-world transition likelihoods are not as important as what each person *perceives* them to be (e.g., the likelihood of finding another job if s/he moves to a different city). Data on such subjective perceptions of transitions are even harder to find than data on the real transitions themselves.

In this work, we seek to exploit what subjective data we *do* have, namely surveys of beliefs, preferences, and decisions in response to hypothetical disasters (illustrated in Section 2). We present a framework for modeling the decision-making process as a Partially Observable Markov Decision Problem (POMDP) in Section 3. We exploit a factored representation and additional structural assumptions to arrive at a modeling language that is more restrictive than a general POMDP, but is more amenable to input from domain experts. This

Appears in: *Proceedings of the 15th International Conference on Autonomous Agents and Multiagent Systems (AAMAS 2016), J. Thangarajah, K. Tuyls, C. Jonker, S. Marsella (eds.), May 9–13, 2016, Singapore.*

language allows us to elicit a hypothesized model from such experts that we can potentially use within a multiagent social simulation.

However, manual model construction is no guarantee of validity, regardless of the experts' knowledge. We must instead measure the model's accuracy against human behavior observed in our data. Section 4 describes how we can quantify a model's accuracy by identifying what subset of individuals behave consistently with the model's predictions. Comparing these predictions at the individual level allows us to identify systematic errors in the model and suggest improvements. We can elicit such improvements from domain experts, allowing us to generate a hypothesis space of possible variations on our model. By identifying the individuals consistent with each of these variations, we can quantify their accuracy and make informed choices about which models to use in the eventual multiagent social simulation.

Importantly, we do not need to simply find a model that covers the most people possible. We instead select *multiple* models to cover the diverse decision-making perspectives represented in the data. We are thus able to arrive at multiple agent models that reflect the individual differences among our surveyed population. At the same time, each model is consistent with a significant number of that population, so we do not sacrifice generality to achieve this diversity.

The result is a general human-in-the-loop methodology for arriving at a set of representative agent models that are usable in simulation. This methodology offers a great deal of room for further refinement and extensions: in the space of hypothesized models, their evaluation mechanism, their selection for use in simulation, etc., as discussed in Section 5. We thus believe that this line of investigation provides a promising direction for researchers to take in pursuing rich agent-based models of human decision-making.

2. DISASTER RESPONSE SCENARIO

The scenario under investigation in this work is a hypothetical anthrax attack in Seattle [16]. The original investigation of this scenario was motivated by an exercise exploring methods for urban recovery from such an attack. As such, it was critical to understand how the public would react both to the attack itself and to official announcements and recommendations in its aftermath. Policy makers need to understand how the public will assess such situations and formulate plans of action in response. The investigators of this scenario were particularly desirous of insight into whether residents would remain in the city, leave temporarily, or leave permanently. Such behavior would have enormous long-term implications for the viability of Seattle as an urban center.

Understanding such behavior, as well as how to influence it, requires an understanding of the public's concerns in that regard. What are their primary concerns: their personal health or safety, their long-term financial stability, etc.? How deeply would the attack affect their feelings of well-being, and how willing would they be to change their behavior based on any long-term damage done to the city? Answers to these questions would help guide the city government in choosing how to prioritize their preparations and how to direct any needed post-disaster response.

It is unfortunately impossible to answer these questions using real-world data, as there fortunately has not been any such attack in Seattle. The investigation of these questions instead used a hypothetical simulation of such an attack through a video simulation of local news reports which immersed participants in an unfolding timeline of events. There were five episodes, corresponding to different points of time, from hours after the attack, to two years afterward.

After watching each of the five videos, respondents answered a series of questions. Some of these questions pertained to demographic details, such as "What is your current employment status (paid opportunities only)?" Others asked respondents to indicate a level of agreement from 1 (Strongly Disagree) to 5 (Strongly Agree) with statements like:

- "I believe the anthrax attack poses a serious risk to me."
- "If I miss ONE paycheck, I would not have enough money to buy food and pay bills."
- "I believe the government will provide emergency response and health services I might need, for example antibiotics."
- "I would LEAVE the Seattle area for at least a short time after watching the earlier news video."
- "I would change my daily routine to avoid exposure to anthrax."
- "I would obtain the antibiotic and take it as directed."
- "I would continue going to work or school if open."

Another portion of the survey asked respondents to rank personal objectives:

- "Personal safety (from crime)"
- "Financial stability (being financially stable/secure, general affordability of necessities)"
- "Health safety and personal anthrax survival (effectiveness and access to antibiotic)"
- "Family or friend anthrax survival"
- "Other"

3. AGENT MODELS

We wish to construct a social-simulation model of the residents of Seattle within a multiagent framework like PsychSim [15]. To do so, we must represent the decisions expressed in the survey within a POMDP [8]. In precise terms, a POMDP is a tuple, $\langle S, A, P, \Omega, O, R\rangle$. This section presents the components of the POMDP and how we model Section 2's disaster response survey within them.

3.1 Actions, A

A is the set of actions available to the agent, so it corresponds to the possible decisions that an individual faces in the scenario to be modeled. The behavior of interest in the survey is whether and when residents would leave Seattle, and if so, whether and when they would return. Both options become possible actions for our agent:

LeaveSeattle: "LEAVE the Seattle area for at least a short time after watching the earlier news video."

ReturnSeattle: "RETURN to the Seattle area at this point in time"

These two actions also imply a third option, which would be to stay in the person's current location:

Stay: Remain in current location, either in Seattle or beyond the Seattle area.

The survey also contains questions about behavioral choices if staying in Seattle:

ChangeRoutine: "Change my daily routine to avoid exposure to anthrax."

ContWorkSch: "Continue going to work or school if open."

OutdoorPrecaution: "Take necessary precautions to avoid anthrax exposure when outside."

TakeAntiBiotic: "Obtain the antibiotic and take it as directed."

A person can choose to perform any combination of these four actions, so that these questions imply 16 possible actions,

The survey also contains questions about employment choices upon leaving Seattle:

TempWork: "Look for temporary work."

PermanentMove: "Move out of the Seattle area (e.g. look for permanent employment, school, housing)."

These two actions are mutually exclusive.

To structure the decision problem, we divide the person's decisions into two phases, "where" and "how". In the "where" phase, the person chooses between "LeaveSeattle" and "Stay" if in Seattle and between "ReturnSeattle" and "Stay" if not. In the "how" phase, the person chooses among the 16 behavioral options if in Seattle and between "TempWork" and "PermanentMove" if not.

3.2 States, S

The state space, S, represents the key features of the agent's operating environment, both observable and hidden, both external and internal. These features can capture both objective facts and subjective perceptions about a person's decision-making context. We use the individual survey questions to constitute a factored state space, $S = S_0 \times S_1 \times \cdots \times S_n$ [1]. Demographic responses become state features, where it is safe to assume that the person has knowledge of the true values. The questions that begin "I believe" become state features, where the person may have only uncertain beliefs. There are 13 such features, of which the following are a representative sample:

JobFulltime: "My current employment status is: full-time (35 or more hours per week)"

RiskMe: "The anthrax attack poses a serious risk to me."

MissPay1: "If I miss ONE paycheck, I would not have enough money to buy food and pay bills."

GovtProvides: "The government will provide emergency response and health services I might need, for example antibiotics."

We define each such feature as a binary variable, valued as 1 if the statement is true, and 0 if it is false. We could treat these features as more fine-grained (e.g., different levels of risk). However, the survey asks the respondent's to express a degree of agreement with the statement, so we represent that degree within the beliefs (see Section 3.5), rather than within the true state of the world. There is no fundamental obstacle to enriching the domains of these state features, but in this case, there is little incentive to do so, as we do not have more fine-grained information from the respondents.

We also need state features to represent the degree to which the person's objectives are satisfied. We ignore the miscellaneous "Other" objective, leaving us with 4 new state features.

PersonalSafety: "Personal safety (from crime)"

FinanceStable: "Financial stability (being financially stable/secure, general affordability of necessities)"

PersonalSurvival: "Health safety and personal anthrax survival (effectiveness and access to antibiotic)"

FriendSurvival: "Family or friend anthrax survival"

We define these features as binary variables as well, valued as 1 if the objective is satisfied, and 0 otherwise. This is obviously a gross oversimplification, in that "PersonalSurvival" cannot distinguish between dying from anthrax and becoming infected with anthrax but surviving. We choose to start with the simplest possible model here, but we can always add additional levels to the domains of these state features later without changing our methodology.

As described in Section 3.1, certain choices depend on the person's location and on the current phase of decision-making. We therefore introduce additional state features to keep track of these conditions:

location: Either "Seattle" or "beyond", indicating whether the person is within or beyond the Seattle area.

phase: Either "where" or "how", depending on the current phase of decision-making

These two features potentially eliminate certain actions from consideration. For example, the action "LeaveSeattle" is considered only when "location" is "Seattle". Likewise, "PermanentMove" is considered only when "location" is "beyond".

3.3 Reward, R

The agent's reward, R, represents the objective function that it is seeking to maximize, so it makes a natural mechanism for representing people's preferences. As described in Section 3.2, a subset of the state features in S represent the objectives from the survey. We limit the reward function to concern only this subset of state features, and specify it according to the priorities expressed in the respondent's ranking. In particular, we define the reward function as a weighted sum of the values of the objective state features. The survey asks people to rank the objectives from 1 to 5, so we weigh each state feature by (6 – its rank) within R. This translation allows us to treat people's ranking of the objectives as a direct expression of their reward function.

The ranking allows us to identify how important the satisfaction of these objectives is to people, but it does not give us any information about the degree to which they believe them to be satisfied. We may get indirect information about these beliefs from the other questions, but we make a simplifying assumption that there is no such information. We instead treat the initial value of the objective state features as if everyone had responded with a 3 to questions about their belief. This is not a critical assumption at this point, as it is the *change* in objective satisfaction that drives behavior, and the starting value has less impact.

3.4 Transition Probability, P

The transition probability, P, represents the probabilistic effects of actions on the state of the world. Representing such effects allows us to capture the way in which people can anticipate the expected outcomes of their possible decisions. The transition probability for our non-survey state features ("location" and "phase") is straightforwardly deterministic. If the person chooses, "Stay", then "location" does not change. If the person chooses "LeaveSeattle", then "location" becomes "beyond". If the person chooses "ReturnSeattle", then "location" becomes "Seattle". The transition probability for "phase" is similarly deterministic, in that when it is "where", it becomes "how" after performing the chosen action, and vice versa.

The transition probability for the other state features in Section 3.2 is not as simple. There is no a priori obvious definition of the effects of (for example) "TakeAntiBiotic" on "RiskMe" and "PersonalSurvival". Likewise, there are no explicit questions about these effects in the survey that can inform such a definition. Therefore, we treat the specification of this transition probability as the heart of the modeling task.

To both constrain the potential search space and to simplify the elicitation of expert knowledge, we restrict the structure of the transition probability function. We start from the standard factored POMDP's use of Dynamic Bayesian Networks [9] and influence diagrams [6] to exploit conditional independence in modeling the effects of actions [1]. We can thus express dependencies among our states and actions as links among the nodes of a dynamic influence diagram [19], as in the example model visualized in Figure 1. The ovals on the left represent the state values at time t, the rectangles in the middle represent the possible action choices at time t, and the ovals on the right represent the state values at time $t+1$. The colored nodes represent states and actions specific to the person, while the uncolored nodes represent global states (e.g., if the government provides health care, it applies to every resident). The links from "location" and "phase" to the action nodes indicate that the available choices depend on those variables.

3.4.1 Action Effects

The other links represent dependencies encoded in this particular model of the person's decision-making. In this illustrative model, "RiskMe" is affected by the possible "how" actions in Seattle (e.g., "TakeAntiBiotic"). In general, the dependency expressed on the links could be an arbitrary conditional probability table across the combinations of parent node values. To simplify the model specification, we instead specify the dependency on each link independently.

For the links from action nodes to subsequent state features, we specify a magnitude and direction of the dependency for each possible prior value of the state feature (`True` or `False`). We express the magnitude and direction by -1, 0, or 1, representing that the performance of the action has a negative, neutral, or positive effect, respectively, on the likelihood of the state feature being `True` afterward. For example, we can specify a value of 1 for the effect of "ContWorkSch" on "RiskMe" (whether starting at `True` or `False`) to represent the increased risk incurred by continuing to go to work or school. Likewise, we can specify a value of -1 for the effect of "LeaveSeattle" on "JobFulltime" (whether `True` or `False`) to represent the challenge of finding another full-time job after leaving Seattle. We do not currently allow these links to be contingent on other state features (e.g., going to work may have less impact on the anthrax risk if "Decontaminated" is `True`). However, this is again a trivial relaxation that would only change the search space, and not any of the methods.

We translate the links from actions to a state by aggregating the -1 and 1 values on those links. We first compute the minimum and maximum possible incoming weights by looking at the possible combinations of actions (e.g., all of the "how" actions simultaneously) and counting the -1 and 1 values separately. For our initial model, a person choosing "ContWorkSch" would incur a maximum value of 1 over "RiskMe"'s incoming links, while a person choosing "ChangeRoutine", "OutdoorPrecaution", and "TakeAntiBiotic" would incur a minimum value of -3. We then normalize the total values for each possible action choice across this range (in this example, [-3,1]) and map it to a Likert scale of 1–5. We then translate the result into a probability of the state feature being `True` using a table of our design: $1 \rightarrow 10\%$, $2 \rightarrow 25\%$, $3 \rightarrow 50\%$, $4 \rightarrow 75\%$, and $5 \rightarrow 90\%$.

3.4.2 Interdependency among States

We make a similar simplifying assumption for links incoming to objective nodes. We label each link from a state node to an objective node with two numbers on a 1–5 scale, with the two values representing the conditions where the parent node is `True` or `False`. A value of 1 (5) indicates that the parent node's being `True`/`False` strongly decreases (increases) the likelihood of the objective node being `True`. For example, our initial model has a link from "RiskMe" to "PersonalSurvival". This link is 1 for `True`, indicating that if there is a risk to the person, then the survival chances go down. This link is 5 for `False`, indicating that survival chances increase if there is little to no risk.

We fill in the conditional probability table over all of the incoming links at an objective node using a noisy OR. Based on the `True`/`False` values of the parents, we translate the corresponding link values into probabilities, p_i, using the same mapping as in Section 3.5. We then use a standard noisy OR formula, $\Pr(\text{child}|\text{parents}) = 1 - \prod_i (1 - p_i)$. As in the action dependencies, we are making a strong assumption of independence among these effects on the objectives. Relaxing this assumption is also trivial, in that it only reduces the space of possible dependency definitions, and does not affect any of the algorithms.

3.4.3 Initial Model

The examples in this section are drawn from the transition probability function used in our initial model. We elicited the links in this initial model from the social scientists who conducted the survey and had performed some preliminary statistical analyses of the data. The resulting transition probability function included 6 non-zero links from actions

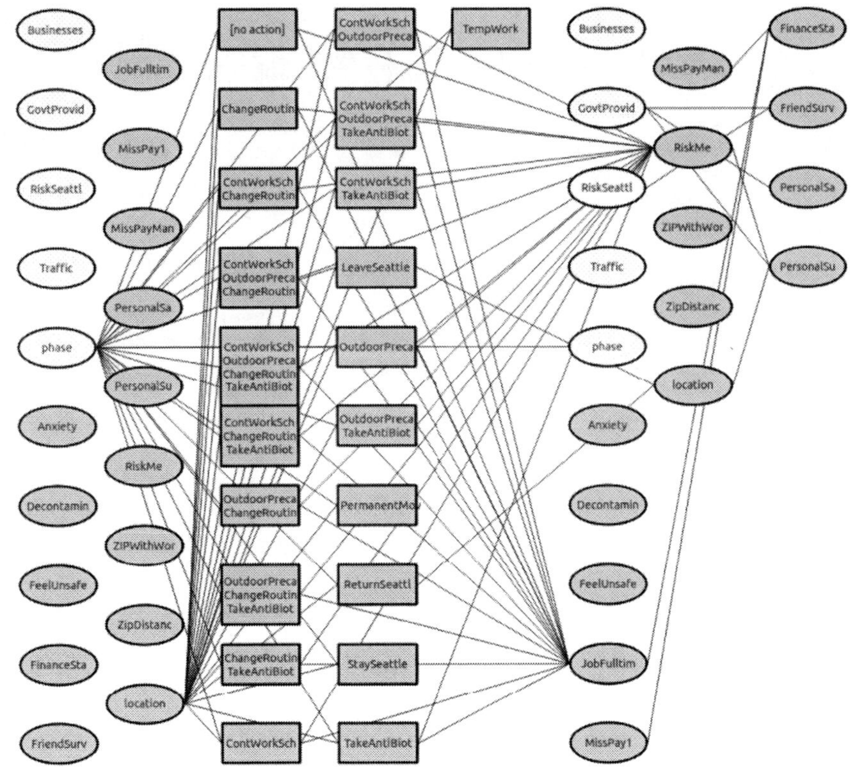

Figure 1: Influence diagram visualization of P.

to "RiskMe" and 1 to "JobFulltime". It also included 3 links from states to "PersonalSurvival", 3 to "PersonalSafety", 4 to "FinanceStable", and 5 to "FriendSurvival".

3.5 Observations, Ω and O

Ω is a set of possible observations that the agent may receive, while the function, O, represents the likelihood of receiving specific observations as a function of the current state of the world. We can use the combination of Ω and O to capture the information (possibly incomplete and noisy) that people receive about the state of the world, especially in terms of how that information shapes their subjective perceptions. Within our disaster-response scenario, we take two state features, "location" and "phase", to be fully observable. Therefore, these components of Ω have the same domain as their corresponding state variables in S. We do not model any other observations in the current investigation.

In general, we can define Ω just as we do state features, and the observation function, O, just as we do the transition probability, P. For example, if we did not limit ourselves to only the first decision stage, we could expand Ω to include observations like the number of deaths mentioned in a video broadcast. We could then add potential links from state features (e.g., "RiskMe") to these observation variables, with the same coarse positive/negative influence labelings we use within P. We likewise use the same noisy OR function to combine the incoming influences into a single probability of a given observation in O.

The current investigation does not explore this observation space, because we do not model the belief update that will occur due to future videos, nor the expectations of the decisions that will be made after those videos. We do still account for such partial observability, but we take the person's starting beliefs directly from the survey responses. The responses range from 1–5, where 1 (5) indicates strong disagreement (agreement) with the statement. We therefore translate the responses into probabilities of the statement being `True` using the same mapping from Section 3.4.1: $1 \rightarrow 10\%$, $2 \rightarrow 25\%$, $3 \rightarrow 50\%$, $4 \rightarrow 75\%$, and $5 \rightarrow 90\%$. This translation allows us to treat people's responses as a direct expression of their subjective belief state.

4. DATA-DRIVEN MODELING

Our initial model provides a good starting hypothesis, partially informed by both domain knowledge and data analysis. However, we need to make fuller use of the data to both validate and refine the model. Even after all of our restrictive assumptions made on the transition probability in Section 3.4, there is still an enormous space of possible models. There are $21 \times 13 = 273$ possible links from actions to states, with 9 possible specifications each ("increase", "decrease" or "stay the same" for `True` or `False` values of the original state). Similarly, there are $13 \times 4 = 52$ possible links from state features not related to objectives to state features that are tied to objectives, with 25 possible specifications each (1–5 Likert scale for `True` or `False` values of the original state). There are thus $9^{273} + 25^{52} = 3.2 \times 10^{260}$ possible models. This space of models would get only larger if we expand the domain of our variables beyond our current binary values. It is therefore infeasible to perform anywhere near an exhaustive search of this space.

4.1 Executing an Agent Model

Regardless of how we search the space of possible models, we first need a method to evaluate a candidate model. The POMDP represents a decision model that can compute the expected reward, $E[R]$, of each candidate action in A. We start from a belief state, b, to be provided from the survey responses, and consider each possible "where" action, a_W. We then apply the transition probability function to proceed to the "how" phase. At this point, we could also use the POMDP to generate "how" decisions, but we instead use the survey responses, translating the 1–5 responses into a probability of action choice, $\pi_H(a_H)$, using the same mapping from Section 3.5. We again apply the transition probability function to arrive at a final state. We apply the reward function to the states to arrive at a final value, as expressed in Equation 1:

$$V(b, a_W) = \sum_{s \in S} b[s] \sum_{s' \in S} \left(P(s, a_W, s') R(s') + \sum_{a_H} \pi_H(a_H) \sum_{s'' \in S} P(s', a_H, s'') R(s'') \right) \quad (1)$$

Rather than optimize this POMDP and choose the action, a_W, for which V is the highest, we instead use a *softmax*, which uses a Boltzmann-like distribution to make the likelihood of an action choice dependent on its relative value:

$$\pi_W(b)[a_w] = \frac{e^{r \cdot V(b,a_w)}}{\sum_{a'} e^{r \cdot V(b,a')}} \quad (2)$$

where r is the reciprocal of the temperature constant in a Boltzmann distribution. In this case, r controls a degree of certainty or rationality by which the agent follows its value function. The higher this value, the more likely the agent is to choose the optimal action. We start with $r = 10$ based on experience with prior agent modeling in PsychSim.

4.2 Evaluating an Agent Model

A candidate POMDP model thus generates a policy of "where" behaviors that we can now compare against the data. We focus here on the "where" decisions made in the first stage of the survey, when everyone's "location" is "Seattle". We examine each individual response in the survey data, extract the person's beliefs, b, and "how" behaviors, π_H, and plug them into Equations 1 and 2 to generate a probability of "LeaveSeattle". We then map this probability to our 1–5 scale (inverting the mapping from Section 3.4.1) and compare it against the person's actual response for "LeaveSeattle".

Our initial model generates the correct "LeaveSeattle" response for 127 of the 433 people in the survey. This is not bad, considering the minimal dependencies included in our initial model. However, there is obviously much room for improvement. We can compute a confusion matrix for our model, looking more closely at the specific mistakes it is making. Figure 2 shows the counts of individuals under all combinations of actual and predicted responses. The bold entries along the diagonal indicate the numbers of individuals for whom the model makes an accurate prediction.

Survey Response	Model Prediction				
	1	2	3	4	5
1	**0**	0	9	3	0
2	0	**0**	43	24	0
3	0	0	**92**	32	1
4	0	0	85	**33**	0
5	0	0	68	15	**1**

Figure 2: Prediction matrix from initial model.

4.3 Model Search

By comparing our model's predictions against individual responses, we can more easily see systematic flaws in the model. In particular, we observe that our initial agent model predicts a much greater willingness to leave Seattle (higher values are stronger agreement with leaving). There are many possible disincentives for leaving that we could add to the model. Adding such disincentives would lead to models that are able to capture the individuals who are less willing to leave—in other words, those that responded with 1 or 2, all completely missed by our initial model in Table 2.

For example, upon leaving, the agent can choose a "how" behavior of "PermanentMove", which, in our initial model, increases the likelihood of achieving "JobFulltime" (value of 1) which in turns increases the likelihood of satisfying "FinanceStable" (value of 5). However, many people may be less optimistic about their chances of finding a full-time job upon moving, which we could capture by making the value on the former link 0. The resulting agent model would see less expected reward from choosing "PermanentMove" than our initial model, which would in turn lower the expected reward of "LeaveSeattle".

We can formulate other such hypotheses as well. Trying to leave Seattle may be dangerous, due to crowds of other people doing the same. We can represent this possible effect with a link from "LeaveSeattle" to "PersonalSafety" with a value of -1 for `True` and 0 for `False`. In other words, people who start off being safe would feel that leaving Seattle would slightly endanger their safety, while those who start off being unsafe would not have their safety affected by leaving.

By considering all possible combinations of these link modifications, we accumulate a set of possible variations on our initial model. We can then execute each of these new models across all of the individual survey responses, following the behavior generation procedure of Section 4.2. In this investigation, we generated a set of 10 possible variations, leading to 1024 possible models for consideration.

Comparing the output of these models against the survey responses allows us to clearly see the accuracy of potential hypotheses with respect to the data. For example, although leaving Seattle had an implied negative impact on financial stability (due to potential unemployment), we also hypothesized that perhaps adding a direct negative link from "LeaveSeattle" to "FinanceStable" might be more accurate. However, introducing this link did not change the predictions, and comparison against the survey responses provided concrete evidence of its redundancy.

4.4 Model Choices

Having compared the behavior generated by all 1024 models across the individuals in the survey, it turns out that our initial model's match of 127 respondents is the highest match count achieved. There are three other models that match an equal number of people, and, in fact, they match the same 127 individuals. These four models are identical except for the absence or presence of two links. We can therefore treat them as equivalent, and we use a bias toward fewer links to choose the model that has both links absent.

While having a model that matches 127 out of 433 people may not be very impressive, it is important to note that we are not done. Our goal is a multiagent social simulation, with multiple agents representing the population of interest. Therefore, there is no requirement that all of the agents in the simulation use the same model. We instead seek to find a *set* of agent models that covers the range of behaviors observed in the data.

The freedom to choose multiple models gives us an ability to capture individual differences within our data. The survey does capture those differences in beliefs and preferences, but there are likely to also be differences in each person's view of cause and effect. In other words, it is unreasonable to expect that everybody is going to forecast the effects of leaving in exactly the same way. By allowing ourselves to choose multiple agent models, we can arrive at a population of agents that share the same diversity of perspective as the people they are representing.

We have a variety of options in how to choose the set of models. In this work, we take a greedy approach, where we first choose the model that covers the largest number of people. We then add the model that covers the largest number of the people not covered by the first model. We proceed until we have either covered everybody, or have no models that match the remaining people.

When we hit the last case, it gives us an opportunity to re-examine our hypothesized model variations. Beyond looking at just the incorrect predictions, we can also examine the beliefs expressed by the individuals for whom our models are inaccurate. For example, our models failed to match the subset of respondents who expressed a strong willingness to perform all of the safe "how" behaviors (e.g., take antibiotics), but still wanted to leave, despite the diminished risk entailed. One hypothesis is that these people had a lower belief in the efficacy of these methods, when compared against the dependencies in our models. By varying our model so that these methods were not effective (i.e., had 0 effect on "RiskMe"), we arrive at a new hypothesis model that generates the correct staying behavior.

At the other end of the spectrum were people who responded in ways consistent with wanting to leave (e.g., high belief in "RiskMe", high rank for "PersonalSurvival") but were strongly against leaving. Some of these respondents also expressed a strong willingness to adopt the safe "how" behaviors. We therefore hypothesized that they may have a stronger belief in the efficacy of such behaviors, even stronger than in our initial models. We relaxed our restriction on the values of links from these actions to states, so that we used a value of -3 instead of -1. This variation was able to explain most of these people, who appeared as outliers with respect to our original models.

We have focused so far on variations that modify only the links within our transition probability function. This restriction is self-imposed, because we are free to consider any variation on our models that still supports the execution of the underlying POMDP. For example, we observed that there were cases when our models would be correct with respect to whether a person was favoring leaving or staying, but would be overly strong in that sentiment. In such cases, the model might be correctly capturing the tradeoffs being considered, but incorrectly capturing the confidence the person has in the resulting valuation. We can potentially represent such a lack of confidence by modifying our softmax parameter, r. We tried lower values for r, both 5 and 2, instead of 10.

4.5 Results

Our greedy search begins by making the following sequence of model choices:

Model variation	Matches
Original	127
"LeaveSeattle" decreases "PersonalSafety"	77
"PermanentMove" no effect on "JobFulltime"	44
Both of the previous two variations	43

The next selections include too many variations to list explicitly, but they add the following numbers of individuals to the covered set: 35, 23, 15, 13, 9, 5, 4, 3, 2, 2, 2, 2, 1. We can therefore cover 407 of the 433 people (94%) using 17 different agent models. There is an obvious diminishing of returns for the later models added, and it is not clear how generally useful a model that covers only one or two people might be. However, there is still a good deal of generality with the most "useful" models. With the first 10 models, we cover 391 of the 433 people (90%), and with just the first 5 models, we cover 326 people (75%).

Of the 26 people who remain unmatched by any of the models, 19 of them favor staying. We are therefore still missing a disincentive for leaving. For example, many people are likely to have an emotional attachment to their homes, an attachment that would not show up in the survey itself, let alone in our current POMDP expected reward calculation. Again, while we would prefer being able to find models that cover all of the people, even such mismatches are informative when we examine the unmatched responses within a POMDP decision-making framework.

While the selected models demonstrate a certain degree of accuracy with respect to the surveyed Seattle residents, one might question how well these models will generalize to other scenarios. A subsequent survey placed 466 residents of the San Francisco area in a similar hypothetical anthrax scenario [17]. The variables in our models map to a subset of questions asked in this more recent survey, so it is straightforward to apply our agent model to the new data. Encouragingly, our initial model, which captured 127 (29%) of our Seattle residents, also captures 139 (30%) of our San Francisco residents. However, our secondary model choices do not generalize as well, as the first 5 models cover only 306 (66%, instead of 75%) of our San Francisco residents. By examining differences in the modeling features in more depth, both within and across scenarios, we can potentially gain further insight into the different dependencies that are guiding the thinking of different subpopulations.

5. DISCUSSION

In this investigation, we made several restrictive assumptions in developing a proof-of-concept for our general methodology. In this initial attempt, we were able to follow a human-in-the-loop search method to arrive at agent models (in POMDP form) that accurately represent our human behavior data. There are a wide number of possible extensions that can build upon this methodology and expand its power in useful and interesting ways.

Within the modeling assumptions made, there are many candidates for relaxation. It would be obviously easy to extend the potential dependency hypotheses to be more fine-grained, as we did in our one case of using -3 instead of -1 on a link from "how" actions to "RiskMe". As already mentioned, we could also allow links to be contingent on other state features. The domains of the variables themselves are also subject to expansion, as nothing in our method requires our current choice of binary domains.

We could also relax other aspects of the POMDP model, just as we did for the rationality parameter, r. For example, we could allow for an expanded horizon, rather than restricting all of the expected reward calculations to consider only two time steps. In general, every aspect of the POMDP model is subject to variation to generate novel hypotheses to consider. The evaluation of the hypotheses is even more general, in that the comparison against individual data and choices of model coverings would apply to non-POMDP agent models as well.

The current evaluation of our models is limited to the responses from the first stage of the survey, but the survey includes additional questions at four subsequent stages, after watching additional news broadcasts that reflect the further passage of time. These "longitudinal" questions would provide a more stringent validation of our models. However, the subsequent surveys do not have all the same questions, so we cannot extract the same belief states at those stages. However, in future work, we can incorporate a belief update stage that would allow us to include hypotheses about those missing future beliefs, as well as the ensuing decisions. This would greatly expand the hypothesis space, but structural assumptions related to the observation function should be able to keep this expansion within feasible and descriptive limits. The additional cost might be worth incurring, because agent models that correctly capture an individual's decisions over these multiple stages would have passed a higher bar of validation and would engender even more confidence in their accuracy.

In this investigation, we consider a relatively small number of modeling hypotheses, 10 possible variations, which allows us to exhaustively evaluate all possible combinations of them. With larger hypothesis spaces, we will not have that luxury, in which case search control over these combinations arises as a new challenge. One possibility is to consider one variation at a time to perform a local search through the model space, along the lines of gradient descent or evolutionary search. Such a search would be directed toward models that cover more and more people, although we would of course lose the guarantees of finding the models with the largest coverage.

In this work, we also had the luxury of domain experts to suggest variations to explore. It is easy to envision a completely automated approach to hypothesis generation instead. However, it is less clear how best to generate informed hypotheses. One possibility is to exploit piecewise linear representations, which have shown to provide some degree of invertibility within decision-theoretic models like Bayesian networks [3] and PsychSim itself [14]. Exploiting such representations would potentially allow one to identify and modify the links that are contributing the most error in the value function.

Having arrived at an evaluation of a satisfactory set of hypothesized models, there still remains the question of how to choose an appropriate subset of them to use in simulation. We use a greedy algorithm as a first approach, but there are undoubtedly better methods. An exhaustive search of all possible coverings may be intractable, but, even if it were feasible, it is not clear what optimality criterion we would use to make our choice. One possibility is to choose the covering that uses the fewest number of models. Another possibility is to minimize the overlap among the models chosen, so that the models essentially partition the population. It is an open research question as to what scoring function leads to modeling choices that provide the highest fidelity in social simulation.

Finally, we apply our simulation methodology here to a survey data set that was never intended for such a purpose. While we were regardless able to gain considerable modeling leverage from this data set, this exercise also informs us as to potentially valuable refinements to the survey instrument for future iterations. For example, even within our limited hypothesis space, there is considerable overlap where an individual's behavior is consistent with multiple models. By examining the points at which these models *differ*, we can potentially arrive at questions to ask in future surveys to disambiguate such cases. Thus, in addition to survey data informing our modeling, we return the favor by using our modeling to inform future data gathering.

6. CONCLUSION

By leveraging a structured POMDP representation, we arrive at a reduced space of possible modeling hypotheses. By comparing the predictions of candidate models against the responses of individual people, we get more detailed feedback on the accuracy of those models than we would from an aggregate statistical analysis. Finally, by choosing multiple agent models, rather than a single best model, we are able to capture individual differences, while still generalizing enough that each model can capture a significant number of people.

The overall impact of this methodology is that we leverage the POMDP's general decision-making framework to capture persistent and shared components of human decision-making (in particular, the cause-and-effect model within the transition probability). However, because our goal is not a single general claim about human behavior, but rather a multiagent simulation of a population, we are free to consider sets of models. We are thus able to include sufficient diversity within our agent models to better cover the whole population. This is especially important in social simulation, where understanding the "atypical" behaviors (e.g., looters after a disaster) is just as critical, if not more so, as understanding the typical ones. Thus, this work demonstrates a path toward enabling researchers, both in computer *and* social science, to more easily build and validate decision-theoretic multiagent models of human behavior.

Acknowledgments

This work was sponsored by the U.S. Army Research, Development, and Engineering Command (RDECOM). The content does not necessarily reflect the position or policy of the Government. No official endorsement should be inferred.

REFERENCES

[1] C. Boutilier, T. Dean, and S. Hanks. Decision-theoretic planning: Structural assumptions and computational leverage. *Journal of Artificial Intelligence Research*, 11(1):94, 1999.

[2] K. M. Carley, D. B. Fridsma, E. Casman, A. Yahja, N. Altman, L.-C. Chen, B. Kaminsky, and D. Nave. BioWar: scalable agent-based model of bioattacks. *IEEE Transactions on Systems, Man and Cybernetics, Part A: Systems and Humans*, 36(2):252–265, 2006.

[3] H. Chan and A. Darwiche. When do numbers really matter? In *Proceedings of the Conference on Uncertainty in Artificial Intelligence*, pages 65–74, 2001.

[4] A. S. Goodie, P. Doshi, and D. L. Young. Levels of theory-of-mind reasoning in competitive games. *Journal of Behavioral Decision Making*, 25(1):95–108, 2012.

[5] J. Hoey and J. J. Little. Value-directed human behavior analysis from video using partially observable markov decision processes. *IEEE Transactions on Pattern Analysis and Machine Intelligence*, 29(7):1118–1132, 2007.

[6] R. A. Howard and J. E. Matheson. Influence diagrams. In *The Principles and Applications of Decision Analysis*. 1984.

[7] *The Journal of Artificial Societies and Social Simulation*. http://jasss.soc.surrey.ac.uk/JASSS.html.

[8] L. P. Kaelbling, M. L. Littman, and A. R. Cassandra. Planning and acting in partially observable stochastic domains. *Artificial Intelligence*, 101:99–134, 1998.

[9] U. Kjaerulff. A computational scheme for reasoning in dynamic probabilistic networks. In *Proceedings of the International Conference on Uncertainty in Artificial Intelligence*, pages 121–129, 1992.

[10] M. K. Lindell, K. J. Tierney, and R. W. Perry. *Facing the Unexpected:: Disaster Preparedness and Response in the United States*. Joseph Henry Press, 2001.

[11] S. Luke, C. Cioffi-Revilla, L. Panait, K. Sullivan, and G. Balan. MASON: A multiagent simulation environment. *Simulation*, 81(7):517–527, 2005.

[12] *Proceedings of The International Workshop on Multi-Agent-Based Simulation*. http://www.pcs.usp.br/~mabs/.

[13] P. Paruchuri, N. Chakraborty, G. Gordon, K. Sycara, J. Brett, and W. Adair. Inter-cultural opponent behavior modeling in a POMDP based automated negotiating agent. In *Models for Intercultural Collaboration and Negotiation*, pages 165–182. Springer, 2013.

[14] D. V. Pynadath and S. C. Marsella. Fitting and compilation of multiagent models through piecewise linear functions. In *Proceedings of the International Conference on Autonomous Agents and Multiagent Systems*, pages 1197–1204, 2004.

[15] D. V. Pynadath and S. C. Marsella. PsychSim: Modeling theory of mind with decision-theoretic agents. In *Proceedings of the International Joint Conference on Artificial Intelligence*, pages 1181–1186, 2005.

[16] H. Rosoff, R. John, W. Burns, R. Siko, et al. Structuring uncertainty and conflicting objectives for life or death decisions following an urban biological catastrophe. *Journal of Integrated Disaster Risk Management*, 2(1):49–69, 2012.

[17] H. Rosoff, R. Siko, R. John, and W. J. Burns. Should I stay or should I go? an experimental study of health and economic government policies following a severe biological agent release. *Environment Systems & Decisions*, 33(1):121–137, 2013.

[18] R. Sun. *Cognition and multi-agent interaction: From cognitive modeling to social simulation*. Cambridge University Press, 2006.

[19] J. A. Tatman and R. D. Shachter. Dynamic programming and influence diagrams. *IEEE Transactions on Systems, Man and Cybernetics*, 20(2):365–379, 1990.

[20] N. Wang, D. V. Pynadath, and S. C. Marsella. Subjective perceptions in wartime negotiation. *IEEE Transactions on Affective Computing*, 6(2):118–126, 2015.

Cooperation Emergence under Resource-Constrained Peer Punishment

Samhar Mahmoud, Simon Miles, Michael Luck
King's College London, London, UK
{samhar.mahmoud, simon.miles, michael.luck}@kcl.ac.uk

ABSTRACT

In distributed computational systems with no central authority, social norms have shown great potential in regulating the behaviour of self-interested agents, due to their distributed cost. In this context, peer punishment has been an important instrument in enabling social norms to emerge, and such punishment is usually assigned a certain enforcement cost that is paid by agents applying it. However, models that investigate the use of punishment as a mechanism to allow social norms to emerge usually assume that unlimited resources are available to agents to cope with the resulting enforcement costs, yet this assumption may not hold in real world computational systems, since resources are typically limited and thus need to be used optimally. In this paper, we use a modified version of the metanorm model originally proposed by Axelrod [1] to investigate this, and show that it allows norm emergence only in limited cases under bounded resources. In response, we propose a resource-aware adaptive punishment technique to address this limitation, and give an experimental evaluation of the new technique that shows it enables norm establishment under limited resources.

Keywords

Metanorm, Emergence, Limited Enforcement Cost

1. INTRODUCTION

In many application domains, engineers of distributed systems may choose, or be required, to adopt an architecture in which there is no central authority, and the overall system consists solely of self-interested autonomous agents. The rationale for doing so can range from efficiency reasons to privacy requirements. In order for such systems to achieve their objectives, it may nevertheless be necessary for the behaviour of the constituent agents to be cooperative. In peer-to-peer file sharing networks, for example, it is required that (at least a proportion of) peers provide files in response to the requests of others, while in wireless sensor networks nodes must share information with others for the system to determine global properties of the environment. However, there is typically a temptation in such settings for individuals to deviate from the desired behaviour, which is known as the problem of free riding behaviour. For example, to save bandwidth, peers may choose not to provide files, and to conserve energy, the nodes in a sensor network may choose not to share information. Therefore, some form of mechanism is needed to outweigh such temptations and to encourage cooperation among self interested agents.

Norms that are imposed and monitored by central authorities, have been proposed by many (e.g., [3, 4, 8, 15, 19]) as a valuable mechanism for regulating or constraining the behaviour of self-interested agents. However, in virtual environments, interactions can be of high magnitude and speed, and thus their regulation is expensive, and may even be infeasible. Social norms offer a means to provide distributed mechanisms for the self-regulation of virtual systems and societies, by delegating to the population itself the responsibility to impose appropriate behavioural standards [6, 28].

In this context, many have been concerned with the development of mechanisms to ensure the emergence of such social norms (e.g., [9, 12, 30, 32, 34]). In particular, researchers from many scientific areas have considered *punishment* as a key motivating element for norms to be established [10, 14, 17, 31]. Here, punishment is a monetary incentive, typically incurring an enforcement cost for the punisher, but bringing a potential benefit to the population as a whole when correctly applied. Work that investigates the use of punishment as a means for social norms to emerge has assumed that agents applying such punishment have unlimited resources, allowing them to bear the resulting enforcement cost. This assumption is significant in real world settings in which resources are limited and require more careful exploitation. For example, sensors in wireless networks have limited energy and thus need to optimise their use of it.

In response, this paper[1] seeks to address such limitations by investigating the effect of scarce resources on norm emergence, based on which a resource-aware adaptive punishment mechanism is proposed and evaluated through experimental simulations[2]. For this purpose, we first integrate the constraint of limited resources within the metanorm model originally proposed by Axelrod [1] and adapted by Mahmoud et al. [23, 22]. The metanorm model has been shown to be capable of regulating distributed computational systems under various settings. Moreover, it is equipped with an

Appears in: *Proceedings of the 15th International Conference on Autonomous Agents and Multiagent Systems (AAMAS 2016), J. Thangarajah, K. Tuyls, C. Jonker, S. Marsella (eds.), May 9–13, 2016, Singapore.*

[1] A 2-page abstract on a small part of the work contained here appears elsewhere [25].

[2] This material is based upon work supported by the Air Force Office of Scientific Research, Air Force Materiel Command, USAF under Award No. FA9550-15-1-0092.

adaptive punishment mechanism that we believe to be vital when dealing with limited resources. We then investigate the limitations of both static and adaptive punishment mechanisms of this model under limited resources constraints, before proposing our resource-aware adaptive punishment.

The remainder of this paper is organised as follows. Section 2 introduces related work, and Section 3 discusses the implications of limiting resources for both static and adaptive punishment mechanisms. Section 4 then builds on this with the integration of an enhanced adaptive punishment mechanism that takes limited resources into consideration and, through experimental analysis, shows that it succeeds in establishing a norm. Finally, the paper concludes in Section 5.

2. RELATED WORK

Achieving a particular desired behaviour among a population of autonomous individuals has received much attention. Many have been concerned with the evolution of altruistic punishment and its effect on the emergence and stability of cooperative strategies within human populations. Indeed, in the last decade, an important body of work concerned with multi-agent systems and punishment has developed, analysing all aspects related to the regulation of normative behaviour [16]. For example, Fehr et al. [11, 10] study the effect of distributed punishment in improving cooperation among self-interested agents. Their results show that heavy punishment succeeds in deterring free riding and promoting cooperation. However, Nikiforakis et al. [28] show that this does not hold when free riders are given the chance of counter-punishment. The threat of such counter-punishment weakens the desire to punish free riders, thus leading to less cooperation. To study these effects, Helbing et al. [17] show that the addition of punishing strategies to a classical public goods game, to allow rewarding cooperators or punishing defectors, increases cooperation among the entire population in the case of well-mixed interactions. Similarly, Savarimuthu et al. [30] show that peer-to-peer punishment is effective in achieving norm emergence in virtual on-line societies when the cost of punishing is low.

These previous models employ static punishment mechanisms in which punishment is a fixed value set at design time. In contrast, a mechanism for dynamically determining punishment values was proposed by Mahmoud et al. [21], using the prior experience of agents with their interaction partners in order to specify the appropriate level of punishment. However, this approach is dependent on repeated interactions between agents, which is not common in certain domains such as peer-to-peer file sharing. Miller et al. [26, 27] and Jurca et al. [18] suggest the use of explicit payment schemes as incentives to encourage honest reporting of information (such as reputation [18] and product feedback [27]) among an agent community. Specifically, the rating provided by an agent is assessed for trustworthiness by comparing it against those of other agents, and a financial reward is estimated (applying specific rules) and issued correspondingly if the agent is reporting the truth.

The above approaches rely on some form of punishment to deter malicious behaviour. However, they all assume that resources are unlimited in applying such punishment, yet this is an unrealistic assumption in many real world domains. In what follows, we investigate the effect of introducing the constraint of limited resources on the process of regulating self-interested agent behaviour using a version of perhaps the best known model in which punishment is a crucial aspect, Axelrod's metanorm model.

3. PEER PUNISHMENT AND LIMITED RESOURCES

Peer punishment has been widely used as a method to regulate the behaviour of participants in a distributed system. Such punishment usually carries a cost for the agent applying the punishment, known as an enforcement cost. Most existing models that study this phenomenon make use of *static* punishment, where there is an enforcement cost paid by the enforcer that is fixed at design time. Considering the free riding phenomenon in a peer-to-peer (P2P) file sharing system, de Pinninck et al. [7] suggest that the punishment for such behaviour should be *blocking*, by which all other agents cease interacting with an agent that is observed not to share files after downloading them. The blocking period can be for a specific length of time, which needs to be set at design time. In this case, the enforcement cost paid is the loss of access to files from the blocked agents, considering that prior to blocking them, free riders can still be sharing a small set of the file they downloaded, while withholding the majority of these files.

Determining an appropriate blocking period can be crucial to the performance of the overall system, especially those that rely on the participation of members for their functionality and effectiveness (as with P2P networks). Because of the dynamism of these systems and the cost incurred by both the agent that is applying the punishment and the agent that is being punished, choosing a single punishment value that is effective to be used against all agents may not be feasible. Therefore, mechanisms that support punishments whose value can be adapted at run-time are much better suited. This is *adaptive* punishment. Returning to our example, a blocking time of 30 minutes may be enough to deter the behaviour of agent i, but not agent j. The next time that agent j defects, a blocking time that is longer than 30 minutes can be used to try to force agent j to comply and start sharing files.

In real world distributed systems, resources can be crucial and optimising their use can be vital if these systems are to function effectively. The period duration for which peers in P2P systems can block other peers in the example above is limited, since they need to maintain a certain level of availability and interactions in the system.

As mentioned above, Axelrod's metanorm model is a strong candidate for use in analysing the effects of limited resources, since it has been shown to establish norms under various distributed systems settings. Moreover, in Mahmoud's variant, it employs both static and adaptive punishment mechanisms. In what follows, we first introduce the metanorm model, and then modify the model to consider the situation of limited resources. Finally, we provide an experimental evaluation to show the effect of these limited resources on norm establishment.

3.1 Metanorm Model

In Axelrod's metanorm model [1], a population of agents play a game in which each agent has to decide between cooperation and defection. The agent population evolves through a number of iterations, with a mechanism whereby successful behaviour (as measured by the scoring system) tends to be replicated and unsuccessful behaviour tends to be discarded. A major problem with Axelrod's model is due to the evolutionary approach adopted (as identified in [20, 13]). In consequence, this original approach has been replaced with a reinforcement learning algorithm that limits accessibility to global information, and instead allows agents to learn from their own experience [23]. Moreover, in order to capture a key feature of computational systems such as on-line virtual communities, Axelrod's classic model has been adapted by introducing a topological structure [22] that determines observability among agents, so that an agent's neighbours are the only witnesses of its interactions. This indicates that an agent only imposes punishment on its defecting neighbours, and metapunishment on its non-punishing neighbours.

This is the model we introduce next, which can be divided into four different parts: the interaction model, the agent model, the policy learning capability and the punishment mechanism.

3.1.1 Interaction Model

In the metanorm model, agents play a game iteratively. In each iteration, each agent must decide between cooperation and defection. Defection brings a reward for the defecting agent called a *temptation* value, and a penalty to all other agents called a *hurt value*. However, each defector risks being observed *by the other agents* in the population, and punished as a result. These other agents thus decide whether to punish agents that were observed defecting, with a low penalty for the punisher known as the *enforcement cost* and a high penalty for the punished agent known as the *punishment cost*. Agents that do not punish those observed defecting risk being observed themselves, and potentially incur metapunishment. Thus, finally, each agent decides whether to metapunish agents observed to spare defecting agents. Again, metapunishment comes at a high penalty for the punished agent and a low penalty for the punisher, through the punishment cost and enforcement cost, respectively.

3.1.2 Agent Model

With regard to agent decision making, the decisions of agents are driven by two private variables: *boldness*, and *vengefulness*. Boldness determines the probability that an agent defects, and vengefulness is the probability that an agent punishes or metapunishes another agent. These values are initialised randomly following a uniform distribution.

In each round, agents are given a fixed number of opportunities to defect, in which boldness determines the probability that an agent defects, and vengefulness is the probability that an agent punishes or metapunishes another agent. Thus, the boldness and vengefulness of an agent are said to comprise that agent's *policies*. After several rounds of the game, each agent's rewards and penalties are tallied, and successful and unsuccessful strategies are identified.

3.1.3 Policy Learning Capability

Having performed a set of actions in a particular round, agents are able to adapt their policies according to the positive or negative outcomes of these policies using a policy learning algorithm. In this algorithm, agents adapt their policies (boldness and vengefulness) at the end of each round of the simulation through a form of q-learning [33], a reinforcement learning technique embedded in each agent. Here, agents track the utility gained or lost from choosing the different actions available, and modify the relevant action policy in the direction that either increases or decreases the chances of performing these actions in the future, which should improve their utility.

However, agents do not adapt their policies in the same manner: a policy that results in a low utility is altered differently to a policy that is not as bad. Therefore, agents change their policies proportionally to their success, following the WoLF philosophy [5], so that if the utility lost from taking a certain action is high, then the change to the policy is greater, and if the utility lost is low then the change to the policy is less.

3.1.4 Punishment Mechanism

There are two different punishment mechanisms that have been employed by the metanorm model: Axelrod's original static punishment mechanism [1], and Mahmoud et al.'s adaptive punishment mechanism [21]. Using static punishment, agents apply the same amount of punishment or metapunishment in every instance. This amount is fixed at design time. However, agents adapt their policies in a utility-maximising way, where the adaptation is proportional to the positive or negative utility associated with each action. Agents therefore are provided with an adaptive punishment mechanism whose task is twofold: (1) calculate the appropriate punishment to deter a defector from future violations; and (2) lower the cost for the punisher, because of the proportionality relationship between the cost of punishment and its damage (by allowing the punisher to adapt the intensity of punishment to be applied, the cost associated with it adapts consequently).

In order to calculate the appropriate punishment, an agent needs to consider the past behaviour of the specific violator, which constitutes the *image* of this agent in terms of frequency of defection and cooperation. To achieve this, the identity and actions of the various other interacting agents in the environment must be recorded. Now, an agent's memory is limited to a particular window size so that only the most recent interactions are recorded, and an agent whose behaviour changes is not punished severely just because of defection in the distant past. Thus, if an agent continues to defect regularly, any new punishment should be stronger than the previous one. Similarly, a generally compliant agent that only recently defected should be punished less that an agent that regularly defects, to avoid using unnecessary power, and waste resources.

3.2 Limiting Enforcement Resources

As mentioned previously, agents usually have limited resources that can be used for enforcement. Thus, once an agent is in a position to apply punishment to a violator, the punishment can only take place if sufficient resources exist to supplement the enforcement cost that can result from the punishment. The decision making mechanisms of agents in the metanorm model above therefore needs to be updated to take available resources into account before applying any form of punishment or metapunishment. We model this formally as follows.

First, an agent ag_i needs to be able to identify the amount of resources available as follows:

$$Res : AGENT \to \mathbb{R} \tag{1}$$

where $\forall ag_i \in AGENT, Res(ag_i)$ is the amount of resource units available for agent ag_i, and $AGENT$ is the set of all agents.

In addition, ag_i needs to estimate the resources (enforcement cost) required to apply punishment p to ag_j:

$$EC : AGENT \times AGENT \times \mathbb{R} \rightarrow \mathbb{R} \quad (2)$$

where $\forall ag_i, ag_j \in AGENT, p \in \mathbb{R} : EC(ag_i, ag_j, p)$ is the enforcement cost related to the current punishment's instance.

Based on this, an agent's decision to apply a punishment can be achieved using the $CanPunish$ function:.

$$CanPunish : AGENT \rightarrow \{TRUE, FALSE\} \quad (3)$$

such that:

$\forall ag_i \in AGENT$:

$$CanPunish(ag_i) = \begin{cases} TRUE & \text{if } Res(ag_i) \geq EC(ag_i) \\ FALSE & \text{if } Res(ag_i) < EC(ag_i) \end{cases}$$

The above function can be used for the purpose of both punishment and metapunishment since they both require enforcement costs. Here $TRUE$ means that the agent can punish, while $FALSE$ means punishment is not possible.

Having verified that a punishment is possible, agent ag_i can punish the defecting agent ag_j, which results in the resources of agent ag_i decreasing by the relevant enforcement cost. This affects future decisions that ag_i can make with regard to punishment and metapunishment.

In addition, it is worth mentioning that resources considered here are those that are limited over a particular period of time. This means that once a particular agent spends all of its resources, it cannot apply any form of punishment or metapunishment until the restriction period has passed, after which resources are renewed. The model is round based, and in every round each agent is given multiple opportunities to defect. Each defection generates many punishment and metapunishment decisions, each of which consume resources. Therefore, we assume that resources are renewed every round for each agent, which needs to optimise the use of such resources within each round.

In what follows, using experiments, we show the effect of this new limited resources restriction on norm establishment using the metanorm model.

3.3 Experimental Evaluation

Before discussing experimental results, it is important to clarify the different possible results and what they show. The most desirable results are those with high vengefulness and low boldness, which are referred to as *norm establishment*. This is because low boldness means that agents defect rarely, and high vengefulness means that agents are generally willing to punish another agent that defects. Results where both low vengefulness and low boldness are observed are also good, because they indicate rare defections. However, with the absence of punishment, boldness tends to increase, causing a high defection rate, which is referred to as *norm collapse*. Other results involving midrange or high level of boldness are also referred to as norm collapse, since they involve a high number of defections. The evaluation of the different variations of the metanorm model introduced in this paper is based on how successful they are in bringing about norm establishment and avoiding norm collapse. It is also important to point out the effect of different decisions that an agent can make on norm establishment and collapse. Metapunishment is required for high vengefulness, without which the cost of punishment leads to low vengefulness due to the enforcement costs paid by the punishing agent. Low vengefulness leads to less punishment, which in turns leads to high boldness and norm collapse.

Topologies are an important component of this type of simulation, and they have different effects on norm establishment [22]. For the purposes of this paper, we use a lattice and a scale free topology for which norm establishment has been achieved previously. In a (one-dimensional) lattice with neighbourhood size n, agents are situated on a ring, with each agent connected to its neighbours n or fewer hops (lattice spacings) away, so that each agent is connected to exactly $2n$ other agents. Thus, in a lattice topology with $n = 1$, each agent has two neighbours and the network forms a ring. In a lattice topology with $n = 3$, each agent is connected to 6 neighbours. Such a topology has a regularity in the number of connections shared among all agents, which helps in studying the effects of the new setting in isolation of other network factors that can influence the results of the model [24]. In contrast, in a scale free topology, connections between nodes follow the power law distribution. Thus, few nodes (hubs) have a vast number of connections, but the majority have very few connections. These properties of scale-free networks suggest an imbalance in connections, which have been shown to affect norm establishment using the metanorm model [24]. In this section, we evaluate the ability of the metanorm model to establish a norm under limited resources. This is achieved using two sets of experiments: a first set where agents have static punishments with fixed enforcement costs, and a second set, in which agents can apply adaptive punishments with proportionate enforcement costs. The results of these experiments are described next, but first the parameter set-up is introduced.

Moreover, in many simulations that investigate the use of punishment, including the version of the metanorm model described above, agent selection is sequential. So the order in which the agents have opportunities to defect is the same every time. This is acceptable when resources are unlimited, since the order by which agents interact has no impact. However, with limited resources, a fixed selection mechanism means that agents spend all their resources after enforcing the same subset of agents (those earlier in the order) every time, and the remaining agents can escape punishment most of the time. Therefore, the simulation is updated to allow a random selection order of agents to take a decision about defecting, and a random selection order of agents that can apply punishment and metapunishment to those who defect. However, this random selection mechanism ensures that each neighbour observes the defection of every other neighbour, and observes the same neighbour sparing a defector from punishment.

3.3.1 *Experimental Setup*

The general parameter set-up used in the experiments conducted is presented in Table 1. The punishment cost and enforcement cost are those of the static punishment technique. In addition, we make sure to run the model on a relatively large population of agents, a large number of runs, and for a lengthy period per run to avoid obtaining misleading results.

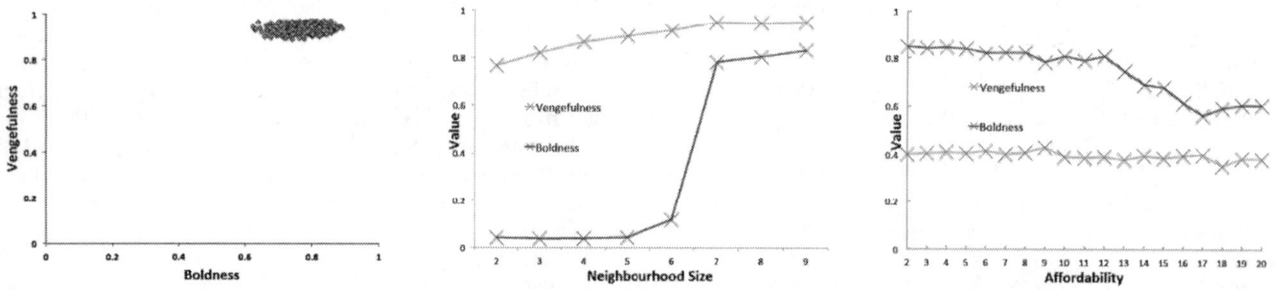

(a) affordability of 12, lattice, $n = 8$ (b) affordability of 12, lattice, various n (c) various affordability, scale free

Figure 1: impact of limited resources with static punishment on final B and V

Table 1: Parameters Set-up

Term	Value
Boldness	Uniform distribution from 0 to 1
Vengefulness	Uniform distribution from 0 to 1
Number of opportunities to defect per round	4
Temptation to defect	$+3$
Hurt suffered by others	-1
Cost of being punished	-9
Cost of punishing	-2
Cost of being metapunished	-9
Cost of metapunishing	-2
Number of Agents	$1,000$
Number of Rounds	$1,000,000$
Number of Runs	$1,000$

3.3.2 *Static Punishment Experimental Results*

We first evaluate the effects of limiting resources on the outcome of the metanorm model with static punishment. Axelrod originally suggested the proportion of (-9,-2) between punishment cost and enforcement cost, and our work is consistent with this. Moreover, Galan et al. [13] have experimentally determined the most effective proportions with static punishment, confirming that this is optimal. The interaction model of agents involves the following sequence of actions. For every defection opportunity that an agent i has, all of i's neighbours have a chance to punish i. If a neighbour j decides to spare i from punishment, then all of j's neighbours have the chance of metapunishing j. Assuming that every agent has 4 distinct neighbours, this means that for every single defection, 4 punishment decisions need to be taken, and if all these punishment decisions result in sparing the defector, $4 \times 4 = 16$ metapunishments can arise. Based on this, it is clear that agents will invest most of their resources on punishment and metapunishment as a result of the outcome of the first few defections, with scarce resources left to regulate the behaviour of the remaining agents.

The above explains the results obtained from using the metanorm model with constrained enforcement resources and static punishment, shown in Figure 1(a), where the diamonds represent the value of the mean average boldness and vengefulness of the final round of a particular run. In this experiment, each agent is provided with 12 resource units that are renewed every round. These results show that the model fails to establish the norm with the average boldness of agents remaining very high, and reflecting a very high rate of defection. The surprise here is that the average vengefulness is also high. Previous reported results of the metanorm model have shown that high vengefulness and high boldness is not a stable state for the population and usually leads to a norm establishment state with high vengefulness and low boldness. The case here is different because of the introduction of the limited resources. High vengefulness is due to two factors. First, for the first few occurrences of defection, sufficient resources remain available for metapunishment. Second, resources run out quickly, so no more enforcement costs are being paid by agents to cause vengefulness to drop. This last factor can also be used to explain the high boldness, with insufficient punishment taking place to deter defecting agents by outweighing the temptation gained.

This suggests that neighbourhood size plays a major role in the obtained results. Therefore, further experiments were conducted with varied neighbourhood size. The results reported in Figure 1(b) are for lattice topologies with neighbourhood sizes between 2 and 9, and limited resources of 12 units. Each point in the graph represents an average of 1,000 runs with a particular neighbourhood size. It is clear from this that the effectiveness of the amount of resource available is limited by the number of neighbours. A static punishment mechanism with 12 units manages to establish the norm up to a neighbourhood size of 6, and fails after that. A similar outcome is found using other amounts of limited resources. For example, with limited resources of 6 units, norm establishment is observed up to a neighbourhood size of 3, and up to a neighbourhood size of 4 with limited resources of 8 units.

Previous analysis of the effect of scale free networks on the metanorm model [24] with unlimited resources has shown that hubs are instrumental to norm establishment. This is because of the vast number of connections that hubs have, which means they punish many other agents for defecting, and consequently pay a very high cumulative enforcement cost. To investigate the effect of limiting resources, we ran 1000 experiments on a scale-free network with 1000 agents, five of which were *hubs* (having a large number of connections) and the others (which we call *outliers*) having at least two connections to other agents in the population, and typically no more than four connections (according to Barabasi's

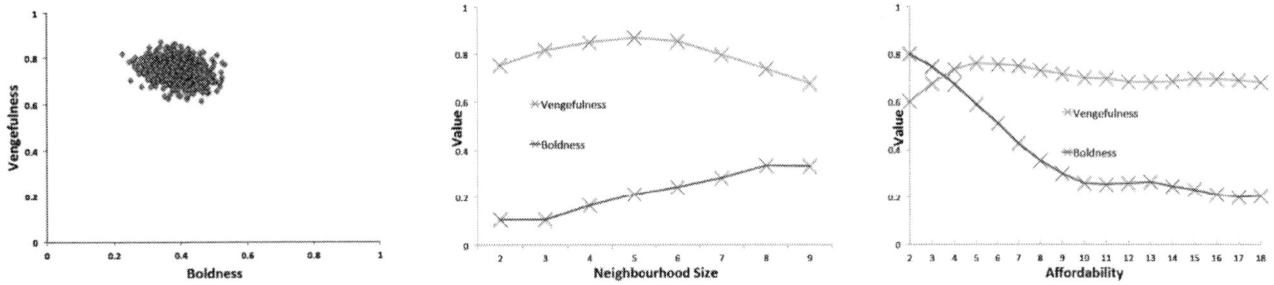

(a) affordability of 12, lattice, $n = 8$ (b) affordability of 12, lattice, various n (c) various affordability, scale free

Figure 2: impact of limited resources with adaptive punishment on final B and V

algorithm [2]). We repeated these experiments with various amounts of limited resources between 2 and 20, and the results are shown in Figure 1(c), where each point in the graph represents an average of 1,000 runs with a particular amount of limited resources. The results indicate norm collapse, as all runs end with high boldness and midrange vengefulness. This is because hubs, which are the deriving agents of the population, run out of resources quickly, and do not allow boldness to drop. However, there are enough resources for outliers, which keep vengefulness at a midrange level. We can also see that at a level of resources of 13 upwards, boldness starts to drop to a midrange level. In fact, some experiments which are not shown here for clarity suggest that at least 50 units of resources are needed for the norm to be established with static punishment.

3.3.3 Adaptive Punishment Experimental Results

While static punishment does not always establish the norm under limited resources settings, it seems that adaptive punishment should do better, since the punishment is adapted according to the *image* of the agent under punishment or metapunishment. Thus resources should be used efficiently. The results shown in Figure 2(a) confirm this. In this experiment the punishment was factorised based on a basic punishment unit of -1, and the cost of punishment (enforcement cost) is set to 1 unit for punishers, reducing the utility of violators by 4 units (1:4 proportion is used because it has been shown [29] to be more effective in promoting cooperation). The results are better since the level of boldness drops to a midrange level. However, this does not reflect norm establishment, since a considerable number of defections still take place in every round. This is because adaptive punishment allows better use of available resources to regulate the behaviour of other agents, but resources are still not being made best use of, since the adaptive punishment mechanism in its current form depends only on the image of the current defector. Similar to the static punishment case, some experiments with different neighbourhood sizes were conducted, with the results of those with limited resources of 12 units shown in Figure 2(b). These results indicate that norm establishment is achieved with a relatively small number of neighbours, with this being weakened as the neighbourhood size is increased. Similar observations are obtained with other amounts of limited resources, too.

Norm establishment is also observed in scale free networks with limited resources of 10 upwards (Figure 2(c)). Below that, boldness starts to drop gradually, but not to a level at which the norm can be considered to be established. The results have clearly improved, which is due to more efficient use of resources to deal with defectors. However, this is not enough especially with hubs that are connected to too many agents with a high probability of frequent defection. So even when using the basic adaptive punishment, resources are still not optimally distributed. However, if we consider the available resources, or the remaining potential defectors that still need to be responded to, we may be able to help solve the problem, as we investigate next.

4. PUNISHMENT WITH CONSIDERATION OF LIMITED RESOURCES

The above approach does not take into account further defections that are yet to happen until resources are renewed, which explains the poor results. In this section, we introduce a new version of the adaptive punishment technique that is capable of allocating an appropriate amount of resources for the current enforcement action, taking into account the possibilities of future violations and the resources needed to deal with such violations.

In what follows, we first introduce a modified version of the adaptive punishment mechanism that takes into account resource limitations, followed by the results of an experimental evaluation of this new mechanism.

4.1 Resource-Aware Punishment Model

The basic idea of adaptive punishment is that each agent is supplied with a memory of limited size, in which they store information about their observations of actions taken by their direct neighbours. So, in the case of observing a defection, an agent stores the identity of the defecting agent together with the fact that this agent has defected, and the same in the case of cooperation. With regard to second level violation, an agent that spares a defector from punishment is also a defector, while one that punishes a defector is a cooperator. These facts are also stored in the memory, together with the identity of agents.

In order to allow agents to apply punishment with the appropriate intensity, punishment needs to change according to the defector's previous history. Based on this, and in relation to a particular *defecting* agent j, two main factors can be calculated: the number of previous instances of defection of agent j (dentoted by nd_j), and the number of previous instances of compliance of agent j (dentoted by nc_j), both in the context of the window size. From these values we obtain the *defection proportion* (dentoted by dp_j), representing the percentage of defections compared to the total number of decisions, by dividing nd_j by the total of nd_j and nc_j. This can be obtained as follows.

$$dp_j = \frac{nd_j}{nd_j + nc_j} \quad (4)$$

This is represented in what we call the *local image* of agent j from agent i prespective, and is specified as follows:

$$LocalDefImage : AGENT \times AGENT \rightarrow \mathbb{R} \quad (5)$$

with $\forall ag_i, ag_j \in AGENT : LocalDefImage(ag_i, ag_j) = dp_j$ where:

- ag_i is the punishing agent;
- ag_j is the defecting agent; and
- dp_j is the defection proportion of agent j in agent i's memory.

However, as shown in Section 3.3.3, considering only the past experience of the agent under punishment is not sufficient when resources are limited. Therefore, agents need to take into account other agents that they need to deal with in the future, which are those that are observable and, according to the metanorm model, these are the direct neighbours specified by the interaction topology. This can be achieved by taking into account the average image with regard to defection of all agents in the neighbourhood, which can be calculated as follows.

First, the agent needs to obtain a set of neighbours by applying function NB:

$$NB : AGENT \rightarrow 2^{AGENT} \quad (6)$$

where

$$\forall ag_i \in AGENT : NB(ag_i) = \{ag_j | ag_j \text{ is connected to } ag_i\}$$

Having obtained the set of neighbours, an agent is capable of calculating the average image of those agents using the following function:

$$AvgDefImage : AGENT \times 2^{AGENT} \rightarrow \mathbb{R} \quad (7)$$

where

$$\forall ag_i \in AGENT \text{ and } NB(ag_i) \in 2^{AGENT} :$$

$$AvgDefImage(ag_i) = \frac{\sum_{ag_j \in NB(ag_i)} LocalDefImage(ag_i, ag_j)}{|NB(ag_i)|}$$

The comparison of the local image and the average image provides useful information on which to base the punishment decision. If the local image is greater than the average image, then the current defector has worse behaviour than most other agents in the neighbourhood, and needs more resources devoted to enforcing its behaviour. If the local image is less than average, then the current agent is not as bad as others in the neighbourhood and less resource can be used for its punishment. Based on this, we can estimate the deviation of the defecting agent's past behaviour from the behaviour pattern in the neighbourhood as follows:

$$Deviation : AGENT \times AGENT \rightarrow \mathbb{R} \quad (8)$$

where

$$\forall ag_i, ag_j \in AGENT :$$

$$Deviation(ag_i, ag_j) = \frac{LocalDefImage(ag_i, ag_j)}{AvgDefImage(ag_i)}$$

Thus, an agent can calculate a suitable amount of punishment that should be applied in this particular instance. But first an agent calculates a uniform amount of resources available for punishment based on equal distribution of resources. This is achieved by dividing the available resources by the number of neighbours, as follows:

$$UniformRes : AGENT \rightarrow \mathbb{R} \quad (9)$$

where

$$\forall ag_i \in AGENT : UniformRes(ag_i) = \frac{Res(ag_j)}{|NB(ag_i)|}$$

It is worth emphasising that the resources that are available to an agent are used as an enforcement cost, which is a particular enforcement cost percentage (ECP) of the applied punishment. The above function calculates the average resources available to be used for enforcement costs and not as a punishment value. Therefore, such a value needs to be converted into an equivalent punishment value as follows:

$$EquivPunish : AGENT \times \mathbb{R} \rightarrow \mathbb{R} \quad (10)$$

where

$$\forall ag_i \in AGENT \text{ and } ECP \in \mathbb{R} :$$
$$EquivPunish(ag_i, ECP) = UniformRes(ag_i) \times ECP$$

Having calculated the average punishment value, it needs to be adapted according to the deviation of the current defecting agent from the average defecting behaviour in the neighbourhood of the punishing agent. Also, an initial punishment value is needed as a base to be adapted depending on the type of defection. This punishment unit (pu) is used to determine the punishment value. Punishment is thus a function that takes two agents and returns the punishment value applied by the first agent to the second, as follows:

$$AdaptPunish : AGENT \times AGENT \rightarrow \mathbb{R} \quad (11)$$

where

$$\forall ag_i, ag_j \in AGENT, AdaptPunish(ag_i, ag_j) =$$
$$Deviation(ag_i, ag_j) \times EquivPunish(ag_i, ECP) \times pu$$

In summary, the value of the adaptive punishment in this case is a factor of the behaviour of the defecting agent with regard to defection, in comparison to the rest in the neighbourhood, the uniform resources available to deal with agents on an equal basis and an initial punishment unit. This means that if the agent at hand has a defection rate that is larger than average, then the uniform resources are scaled up to deal with this agent, and in the case that the agent defection rate is less than average, then the uniform resources are scaled down. The value of metapunishment is calculated similarly, with the number of defections representing the number of instances of sparing defectors, and the number of instances of compliance representing the number of instances of punishing defectors.

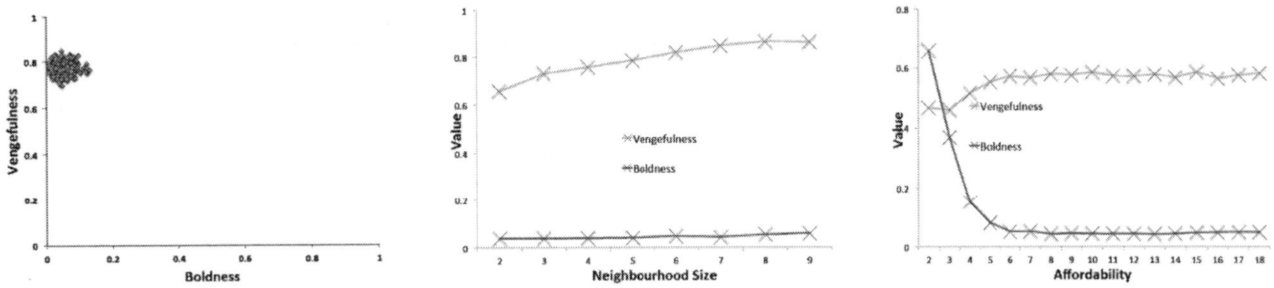

(a) Affordability of 12, lattice, $n = 8$ (b) Affordability of 12, lattice, various n (c) various affordability, scale free

Figure 3: impact of limited resources with resource aware adaptive punishment on final B and V

4.2 Evaluation

With a similar parameter set-up to the experiments reported in Section 3.3, we ran experiments that involve the resource-aware adaptive punishment mechanism introduced in the previous section. The results of these experiments are shown in Figure 3(a), which indicate considerable improvements from the previous results, as norm establishment has been observed in all runs.

Even when the neighbourhood size is increased, norm establishment is achieved. This is due to the capability of the new approach to consider the number of neighbours that an agent may have to deal with, so punishment may be less even with more neighbours. However, the increased number of neighbours compensates for this. To simplify, assuming that 5 resource units available for enforcement, in the case of neighbourhood size of 5, an agent i will have 10 neighbours. If all of these neighbours are regular defectors, then the punishment that i applies to a defecting neighbour j is approximately $\frac{5}{10} = 0.5$, which is less than the gain that the j obtains from defecting (3). However, there are another 9 neighbours that can still punish j, and the combined punishment of these agents is enough to overcome the utility gained by j from defecting. This is illustrated by the results shown in Figure 3(b), where norm establishment is achieved with renewable resources of 12 units regardless of the neighbourhood size of the connection topology. In fact, larger neighbourhood sizes lead to better norm establishment due to the higher number of potential metapunishment opportunities that can be triggered by sparing a defector.

Much better results, reported in Figure 3(c), are also achieved over scale free networks. Even with limited resources (as low as 4), hubs are able to divide equally resources among the large number of agents they are connected to. Such resources, combined with the resources resulting from other outliers' punishment, are enough to cause norm establishment. Clearly, resources of 2 and 3 are not enough for the norm establishment to happen.

5. CONCLUSION AND FUTURE WORK

There have been many models proposed for norm emergence among groups of self interested agents. Punishment has been used as the core mechanism in most of these models. Such punishment is usually assigned a particular enforcement cost, and the general assumption is that unlimited resources are available for agents to cope with this cost. This paper has studied the effect of integrating a limited resource constraint within the well established metanorm model. Experimental results show that both the static and adaptive punishment mechanisms of the metanorm model fail to establish the norm with the absence of significant amount of resources. This is mainly because resources are not being used optimally.

In response, an enhanced adaptive punishment technique was proposed, which takes into account the amount of resources available to the agent and the number of punishment decisions that this agent may need to apply using such resources. The experimental evaluation showed that the new technique succeeds in establishing the norm with larger neighbourhood sizes than the static and original adaptive punishment mechanisms. Moreover, this new adaptation of the metanorm model allows designers of distributed computational systems to determine the amount of resources that is needed in order for the system to be appropriately regulated. As future work, we want to investigate the effect of the limited resources constraint on other norm emergence mechanisms in the literature.

REFERENCES

[1] R. Axelrod. An evolutionary approach to norms. *American Political Science Review*, 80(4):1095–1111, 1986.

[2] A. L. Barabasi and R. Albert. Emergence of Scaling in Random Networks. *Science*, 286(5439):509–512, 1999.

[3] G. Boella, L. Torre, and H. Verhagen. Introduction to normative multiagent systems. *Computational & Mathematical Organization Theory*, 12(2-3):71–79, Oct. 2006.

[4] M. Boman. Norms as constraints on real-time autonomous agent action. In *Proceedings of the 8th European Workshop on Modelling Autonomous Agents in a Multi-Agent World: Multi-Agent Rationality*, pages 36–44. Springer-Verlag, 1997.

[5] M. Bowling and M. Veloso. Rational and convergent learning in stochastic games. In *Proceedings of the 17th International Joint Conference on Artificial intelligence - Volume 2*, IJCAI'01, pages 1021–1026. Morgan Kaufmann Publishers Inc., 2001.

[6] R. Boyd, H. Gintis, S. Bowles, and P. J. Richerson. The evolution of altruistic punishment. *Proceedings of the National Academy of Sciences of the United States of America*, 100(6):3531–3535, 2003.

[7] A. P. de Pinninck, C. Sierra, and M. Schorlemmer.

Distributed Norm Enforcement: Ostracism in Open MultiAgent Systems. In *Computable Models of the Law*, volume 4884 of *LNCS*, pages 275–290. Springer, 2008.

[8] F. Dignum. Autonomous agents with norms. *Artificial Intelligence and Law*, 7:69–79, 1999.

[9] J. M. Epstein. Learning to be thoughtless: Social norms and individual computation. *Computational Economics*, 18(1):9–24, Aug. 2001.

[10] E. Fehr and S. Gächter. Altruistic punishment in humans. *Nature*, 415(6868):137–140, Jan. 2002.

[11] E. Fehr and S. Gächter. Cooperation and punishment in public goods experiments. *The American Economic Review*, 90(4):pp. 980–994, 2000.

[12] F. Flentge, D. Polani, and T. Uthmann. Modelling the emergence of possession norms using memes. *Journal of Artificial Societies and Social Simulation*, 4(4), 2001.

[13] J. M. Galan and L. R. Izquierdo. Appearances can be deceiving: Lessons learned re-implementing Axelrod's evolutionary approach to norms. *Journal of Artificial Societies and Social Simulation*, 8(3), 2005.

[14] F. Giardini, G. Andrighetto, and R. Conte. A cognitive model of punishment. In *Proceedings of the 32nd Annual Conference of the Cognitive Science Society*, pages 1282–1288. Austin: Cognitive Science Society, 2010.

[15] J. P. Gibbs. Norms: The problem of definition and classification. *The American Journal of Sociology*, 70(5):586–594, 1965.

[16] D. Grossi, H. Aldewereld, and F. Dignum. Ubi lex, ibi poena: Designing norm enforcement in e-institutions. In *Coordination, Organizations, Institutions, and Norms in Agent Systems II*, volume 4386 of *Lecture Notes in Computer Science*, pages 101–114. Springer-Heidelberg, 2007.

[17] D. Helbing, A. Szolnoki, M. Perc, and G. SzabÃş. Punish, but not too hard: how costly punishment spreads in the spatial public goods game. *New Journal of Physics*, 12(8):083005, 2010.

[18] R. Jurca and B. Faltings. An incentive compatible reputation mechanism. In *Proceedings of the Second International Joint Conference on Autonomous Agents and Multiagent Systems*, AAMAS '03, pages 1026–1027. ACM, 2003.

[19] F. López y. López and M. Luck. Modelling norms for autonomous agents. In *Proceedings of the 4th Mexican International Conference on Computer Science*, ENC '03, pages 238–245. IEEE Computer Society, 2003.

[20] S. Mahmoud, N. Griffiths, J. Keppens, and M. Luck. An analysis of norm emergence in Axelrod's model. In *NorMAS'10: Proceedings of the Fifth International Workshop on Normative Multi-Agent Systems*. AISB, 2010.

[21] S. Mahmoud, J. Keppens, N. Griffiths, and M. Luck. Efficient norm emergence through experiential dynamic punishment. In *Proceedings of the 20th European Conference on Artificial Intelligence*, pages 576–581. IOS Press, 2012.

[22] S. Mahmoud, J. Keppens, M. Luck, and N. Griffiths. Norm establishment via metanorms in network topologies. In *Proceedings of the 2011 IEEE/WIC/ACM International Conferences on Web Intelligence and Intelligent Agent Technology*, WI-IAT '11, pages 25–28. IEEE Computer Society, 2011.

[23] S. Mahmoud, J. Keppens, M. Luck, and N. Griffiths. Overcoming omniscience in axelrod's model. In *Proceedings of the 2011 IEEE/WIC/ACM International Conferences on Web Intelligence and Intelligent Agent Technology - Volume 03*, WI-IAT '11, pages 29–32. IEEE Computer Society, 2011.

[24] S. Mahmoud, J. Keppens, M. Luck, and N. Griffiths. Norm emergence: Overcoming hub effects in scale free networks. In *Proceedings of the AAMAS 2012 Workshop on Coordination, Organizations, Institutions and Norms*, pages 136–150, 2012.

[25] S. Mahmoud, S. Miles, A. Taweel, B. Delaney, and M. Luck. Norm establishment constrained by limited resources. In *Proceedings of the 2015 International Conference on Autonomous Agents and Multiagent Systems, AAMAS 2015*, pages 1819–1820, 2015.

[26] N. Miller, P. Resnick, and R. Zeckhauser. Eliciting honest feedback in electronic markets. KSG Working Paper Series RWP02-039, 2002.

[27] N. Miller, P. Resnick, and R. Zeckhauser. Eliciting informative feedback: The peer-prediction method. *Management Science*, 51:2005, 2005.

[28] N. Nikiforakis. Punishment and counter-punishment in public good games: Can we really govern ourselves? *Journal of Public Economics*, 92:91–112, 2008.

[29] N. Nikiforakis and H.-T. Normann. A comparative statics analysis of punishment in public-good experiments. *Experimental Economics*, 11(4):358–369, 2008.

[30] B. T. R. Savarimuthu, M. Purvis, and M. Purvis. Social norm emergence in virtual agent societies. In *Proceedings of the 7th International Joint Conference on Autonomous Agents and Multiagent Systems - Volume 3*, AAMAS '08, pages 1521–1524, 2008.

[31] D. Villatoro, G. Andrighetto, J. Sabater-Mir, and R. Conte. Dynamic sanctioning for robust and cost-efficient norm compliance. In *Proceedings of the Twenty-Second International Joint Conference on Artificial Intelligence*, pages 414–419. IJCAI/AAAI, 2011.

[32] D. Villatoro, S. Sen, and J. Sabater-Mir. Topology and memory effect on convention emergence. In *Proceedings of the 2009 IEEE/WIC/ACM International Joint Conference on Web Intelligence and Intelligent Agent Technology - Volume 02*, WI-IAT '09, pages 233–240. IEEE Computer Society, 2009.

[33] C. J. C. H. Watkins and P. Dayan. Q-learning. *Machine Learning*, 8(3-4):279–292, 1992.

[34] T. Yamashita, K. Izumi, and K. Kurumatani. An investigation into the use of group dynamics for solving social dilemmas. In *Multi-Agent and Multi-Agent-Based Simulation*, volume 3415, pages 185–194. Springer-Heidelberg, 2005.

Modeling Culture in Intelligent Virtual Agents - From Theory to Implementation

(JAAMAS Extended Abstract)

Samuel Mascarenhas
INESC-ID, Instituto Superior Técnico, Universidade de Lisboa, Portugal
samuel.fm@gmail.com

Nick Degens
Hanze University of Applied Science, The Netherlands
d.m.degens@pl.hanzel.nl

Ana Paiva, Rui Prada
INESC-ID, Instituto Superior Técnico, Universidade de Lisboa, Portugal
{ana.paiva,rui.prada}@inesc-id.pt

Gert Jan Hofstede, Adrie Beulens
Wageningen University, The Netherlands
gertjan.hofstede@wur.nl

Ruth Aylett
Heriot-Watt University, Edinburgh, UK
r.s.aylett@hw.ac.uk

1. INTRODUCTION

This work addresses the representation of general cultural biases of social conduct in a cognitive model for virtual agents. The resulting model was applied in a serious game named Traveller [1], which is centered around human-agent interaction in everyday situations with agents that have their own cultural values. A cross-cultural study was conducted using one scene of Traveller with participants from two different countries, Portugal and the Netherlands. The aim was to investigate whether individuals from these two countries perceive and interact more favorably with agents that have a similar culture profile. The results showed that this was the case for the collectivistic agents who were indeed perceived significantly more favorably by the Portuguese participants than the Dutch. However, the general opinion about individualistic agents was similarly positive in both countries, possibly due to limitations in the scenario design.

2. MODELING CULTURE

According to Kemper [4], the extent to which we are willing to act in the interest of others, both in the performance of instrumental or ritualistic actions, is determined by how we perceive each other in relational terms. This perception is a subjective process that is heavily influenced by cultural biases. For instance, in cultures that score high on collectivism, the importance of in-group members is higher than it is in more individualistic cultures [3].

Our proposed SID model [6] is centered around the notion of Social Importance (SI). This is a relational variable that agents have towards others. It quantifies the extent that an agent is willing to act voluntarily in the interest of another, similar to the notion of status in Kemper's theory [4]. SI is determined by the sum of all *SI Attribution Rules* whose activation conditions are verified in the agent's beliefs. Each rule represents a specific relational factor that is associated in human culture to a gain or a loss of SI. For instance, in the case of the in-group bias of collectivism, our proposed model includes two *SI Attribution Rules*, one that increases the SI of other agents that belong to the in-group and another that decreases the SI of others that are perceived as outsiders. In both rules, the amount that is increased or decreased is augmented by a factor that is linearly proportional to the collectivism score (COL) of the agent's culture.

The *SI Attribution Rules* are one of the three components of the SID model that are shared by a group of agents. The other two elements are *SI Claims* and *SI Conferrals*. An *SI Claim* associates a specific SI requirement to a given action, like joining a group to strike a conversation. Whenever an agent witnesses another agent performing an action, if the SI they attribute to the performer is lower than the SI score of the action's *SI Claim* then the act is perceived as inappropriate and the SI attributed to the performer is lowered. Consequentially, to avoid being inappropriate, agents infer how much SI they have and abstain from choosing actions whose claims exceed it. Claims can also be influenced by cultural biases and in our model, there is a claim associated to the action of joining a group having a conversation. More precisely, the SI requirement of this claim is linearly increased by the COL score of the agent's culture.

Concerning *SI Conferrals*, they represent a behavior that confers a certain amount of SI and is socially expected to be performed in a given context. In our model, the context is dictated by a set of logical conditions. Whenever such conditions are verified in the agent's beliefs, the agent will have a desire to perform the conferral to another agent as long as the amount of SI of the conferral does not exceed that other agent's SI. If more than one conferral meets the SI requirement, the agent will choose the one with the highest SI among the alternatives.

Appears in: *Proceedings of the 15th International Conference on Autonomous Agents and Multiagent Systems (AAMAS 2016), J. Thangarajah, K. Tuyls, C. Jonker, S. Marsella (eds.), May 9–13, 2016, Singapore.*

3. EVALUATION

The proposed SID model [6] has been implemented into

an existing BDI agent architecture, named FAtiMA Modular [2] and the resulting architecture was used to develop an intercultural training application named Traveller [1]. Traveller is a serious game where users are encouraged to raise their intercultural awareness by interacting with intelligent virtual agents whose cultural biases can be adapted with our model. The experience consists of an interactive narrative that takes place in a fictitious world and is divided in several scenes, named critical incidents. Each of the scenes is designed to evoke mismatches between the cultural biases of users and the cultural biases of agents.

The first critical incident of Traveller takes place in a bar located on a beach where the user arrives late at night after failing to find the way to his or her hotel. At the start of the scene, there are only two characters sitting in the bar and they are talking to each other. The barman is absent (although he later appears). The goal of the user is simply to find directions to his or her hotel. Because the user plays the role of a foreigner, agents will believe the user is an outsider and the higher the collectivism score of the agents the more they will lower the SI they attribute to the user. The user will also lose some SI when he or she performs an action that is perceived as an inappropriate claim in the culture of the agents. Consequentially, agents will choose to perform conferrals with a lower SI score in response.

We conducted a cross-cultural study to determine how users perceived and responded to two cultural configurations in the beach bar scenario. The aim was to compare users from both a collectivistic country, Portugal, and an individualistic country, the Netherlands, concerning how they perceived the behaviour of the agents in this particular scenario. For reference, Portugal is the most collectivistic country in Europe (scoring 27 on that dimension), and the Netherlands is one of the most individualistic countries in Europe (scoring 80 on that dimension) [3].

The experiment consisted of a 2x2 between-subjects design in which the independent variables were the participant's nationality (Dutch or Portuguese) and the cultural parameterization of the agents (Individualistic or Collectivistic). The main hypotheses we wanted to verify within this study were the following: H1 - Portuguese participants have a more positive opinion of the collectivistic agents' behavior than the Dutch and H2 - Dutch participants have a more positive opinion of the individualistic agents' behavior than the Portuguese.

After the participants completed the beach bar episode, they were asked to fill in an online questionnaire about their experience. The questionnaire contained both open-ended questions as well Likert statements about the participants' impressions of the characters' social behavior. In total, we had 72 participants of which 37 were Dutch and 35 were Portuguese, with an average age of 23.

The obtained results of the two-way factorial ANOVA statistical test, as detailed in [5], show that a significant interaction effect between the agents' culture and the participants' nationality was found for the statement "My general impression about the behavior of these characters is positive" ($F(1,68) = 6.441$, $p = 0.013$) and for the statement "The characters behaved appropriately toward me" ($F(1,68) = 4.922$, $p = 0.03$). For these two statements, the participants' opinions about the two cultural versions of the agents was affected differently by their nationalities. A simple effects analysis revealed that the score of the collectivistic agents was significantly higher in Portugal than in the Netherlands for the first statement ($F(1,68) = 6.685$ $p = 0.012$) and for the second statement ($F(1,68) = 4.678$, $p = 0.034$). Both results support hypothesis H1. In contrast, hypothesis H2 was not supported as the score given to the individualistic agents by the Dutch was not significantly higher than the score given by the Portuguese, neither for the first statement ($F = 1.052$, $p = 0.309$) nor for the second one ($F(1,68) = 0.982$, $p = 0.325$).

These results constitute evidence of the proposed model's capability in adapting the agents' cultural behavior toward one extreme of the Individualism vs. Collectivism dimension. However, the adaptation of the model to make agents more individualistic did not cause a negative impression in the Portuguese participants. Still, in their qualitative answers, some Portuguese participants wrote negative remarks about the appropriateness of the individualistic agents. For instance, they found it strange that these agents invited the user to sit with them immediately. However, it is plausible that for many Portuguese participants, this strangeness was interpreted as unexpected friendliness rather than unwarranted intrusiveness.

Acknowledgments

This work was partially supported by national funds through FCT - Fundação para a Ciência e a Tecnologia, under project UID/CEC/50021/2013. It was also partially supported by a FCT scholarship (SFRH BD /62174/2009), by the European Community (EC), and was partially funded by the ECUTE project (ICT-5-4.2 257666).

REFERENCES

[1] N. Degens, G. J. Hofstede, S. Mascarenhas, A. Silva, A. Paiva, F. Kistler, E. André, A. Swiderska, E. Krumhuber, A. Kappas, et al. Traveller–intercultural training with intelligent agents for young adults. In *Proceedings of the 8th International Conference on Foundations of Digital Games 2013*, 2013.

[2] J. Dias, S. Mascarenhas, and A. Paiva. Fatima modular: Towards an agent architecture with a generic appraisal framework. In T. Bosse, J. Broekens, J. Dias, and J. van der Zwaan, editors, *Emotion Modeling*, volume 8750 of *Lecture Notes in Computer Science*, pages 44–56. Springer International Publishing, 2014.

[3] G. Hofstede, G. J. Hofstede, and M. Minkov. *Cultures and Organizations: Software of the Mind*. New York: McGraw-Hill, 3 edition, 2010.

[4] T. Kemper. *Status, power and ritual interaction: a relational reading of Durkheim, Goffman, and Collins*. Ashgate Publishing Limited, England, 2011.

[5] S. Mascarenhas, N. Degens, A. Paiva, R. Prada, G. J. Hofstede, A. Beulens, and R. Aylett. Modeling culture in intelligent virtual agents - from theory to implementation. *Journal of Autonomous Agents and Multi-Agent Systems*, pages 1–32, 2015.

[6] S. Mascarenhas, R. Prada, A. Paiva, and G. Hofstede. Social importance dynamics: A model for culturally-adaptive agents. In R. Aylett, B. Krenn, C. Pelachaud, and H. Shimodaira, editors, *Intelligent Virtual Agents*, volume 8108 of *Lecture Notes in Computer Science*, pages 325–338. Springer Berlin Heidelberg, 2013.

The Effects of Interrupting Behavior on Interpersonal Attitude and Engagement in Dyadic Interactions

Angelo Cafaro, Nadine Glas and Catherine Pelachaud
LTCI, CNRS, Télécom ParisTech, Université Paris-Saclay
{angelo.cafaro, nadine.glas, catherine.pelachaud}@telecom-paristech.fr

ABSTRACT

Interruptions frequently occur in dyadic human interaction. In addition to serve as turn-taking mechanism, they may lead to different perceptions of both the interruptee and interrupter's interpersonal attitude, engagement and involvement. We present an empirical study to investigate whether different interruption types (i.e. amount of overlap between speakers and utterance completeness) and strategies (disruptive vs. cooperative) in agent-agent interaction have an impact on perceived agents' interpersonal attitude, engagement and involvement. We found that the interruption type has more influence on the perceived attitudes of both agents, whereas by using a cooperative strategy (as opposed to a disruptive one) an interrupter is perceived as more engaged and more involved in the interaction.

Keywords

Turn-taking; Interruptions; Interpersonal attitude; Engagement; Empirical evaluation; Embodied conversational agents

1. INTRODUCTION

The organization of turn-taking is fundamental in human-human interaction [29]. Interruptions represent a violation of the basic turn-taking rules and a possible way of claiming the turn [4]. An interruption is "a starting up of some intervention by one person while another's turn is in progress" [28]. In order to model socially believable conversational agents in human-agent and/or agent-agent interaction, it is important to consider and to handle phenomena, such as interruptions, that frequently occur between humans [9].

Interruptions have long been associated with interpersonal dominance [35], but more recently a more balanced view has emerged, distinguishing two **strategies** based on the content of the interruption: *disruptive* and *cooperative* [24, 25]. At the same time, different **types** of interruptions can be distinguished from an organizational turn taking point of view, considering the amount of simultaneous speech and utterance completeness [10].

Different interruption types and strategies influence the way in which interactants are perceived with respect to their mutual interpersonal attitude [4] and interaction-related aspects such as engagement and involvement [32]. Human-agent interaction is often modeled on human-human interaction theories [7], therefore interruption mechanisms may have similar effects in human-agent interaction. For example, a user's interrupting behavior while interacting with a conversational agent might lead to different perceptions of **interpersonal attitudes** (e.g. dominance and friendliness in Argyle's representation [1]), **engagement** (i.e. the coordination and cooperation that is necessary to perform the joint activity of interacting [12]) and **involvement** in the interaction ("being captured by the experience" [31]).

Previous findings showed that an agent's turn-taking behavior influences human's impressions of it in terms of interpersonal attitude and personality [21]. However, we believe that interrupting behavior is not always a sign of power, disturbance and/or disengagement, instead the interplay between different interruption types and strategies might reveal effects on the perceived attitudes (e.g. friendliness and dominance), engagement and involvement of an interrupter. For example, a cooperative interruption strategy might be perceived as indicator of increased friendliness and engagement.

The assessment of these socio-emotional qualities in dyadic interaction represents a fundamental aspect for building affective and socio-believable intelligent conversational agents. We questioned whether deploying specific interruption strategies (e.g. cooperative) has greater impact on the above mentioned assessments compared to interruption type (i.e. amount of overlap between the interactants during the interruption and utterance completeness) or vice-versa. Is an interrupter agent by definition always dominant? What is the impact of interrupting behavior on the agents' engagement level?

In this paper, in the context of the European project *ARIA-VALUSPA* on affective information retrieval through a virtual assistant, we present a study aimed at investigating the effects of interruption strategies and types, in agent-agent interactions, on human perception of both agents' interpersonal attitudes towards each other, level of engagement, and involvement in the interaction. We considered a dyadic agent interaction as it allowed us a complete systematic control of both the **interrupter** and the **interruptee**'s behavior. While the main focus is on the interrupter's behavior, we also took into account the user's perception of the interruptee's attitudes and engagement/involvement as exploratory assessments.

Appears in: *Proceedings of the 15th International Conference on Autonomous Agents and Multiagent Systems (AAMAS 2016), J. Thangarajah, K. Tuyls, C. Jonker, S. Marsella (eds.), May 9–13, 2016, Singapore.*

2. THEORETICAL BACKGROUND

2.1 Interruption Types

An interruption is defined as a starting up of some intervention by one person while another's turn is in progress, often including "not letting them finish" [28]. An overlap refers to the fact of more than one person talking at a time [28], which means that an interruption does not necessarily implies overlap. There are multiple ways in which interruptions can be further subdivided based on the temporal aspects of the speaker's switch (e.g. [18], [10], [28]). We use the taxonomy of attempted speaker-switches by [10] that was later modified by [4]. Figure 1 shows this taxonomy and the types of interest in the present study are marked in boldface (more details about the experimental design are provided in Section 4.1.1). The classification makes a first division

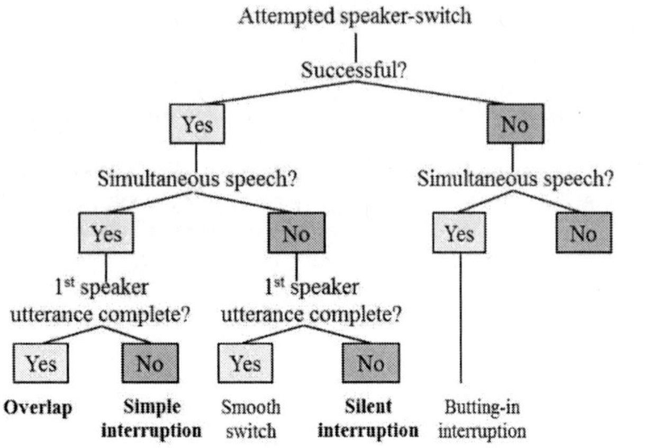

Figure 1: Beattie's taxonomy of interruption types.

according to whether or not the speaker-switch is successful, meaning that the initiator of the attempted interruption takes the floor [4]. Further division is based respectively on the presence of simultaneous speech, and first speaker utterance completeness. In this taxonomy back-channels (such as *yeah, hmm, exactly*) are not considered as interruptions [4].

2.2 Interruption Strategies

Interruptions have been often considered power displays (i.e. dominance), while recently a more balanced view has emerged [18]. This view has led to the identification of two broad types of interruptions, often referred as intrusive and cooperative [18, 24]. In this paper, we name these two types **strategies**. We adopted the terms *disruptive* [25] and *cooperative* as they refer to the interaction, where other terms may already imply an attitude or stance of the participants (i.e. (non) power [14], (dis) confirming [16]).

According to [24] "cooperative interruptions are intended to help the speaker by coordinating the process and/or content of the ongoing conversation" [18]. "Intrusive interruptions pose threats to the current speaker's territory by disrupting the process and/or content of the ongoing conversation" [18, 24, 14].

Researchers identified different sub-strategies (cooperative/disruptive). For example, in [24] do not mention any cooperative sub-strategy, while [18, 16] mention three: **(1) Agreement**, showing concurrence, compliance, understanding or support. Sometimes also serving as an extension or elaboration of the idea presented by the speaker; **(2) Assistance**, providing the current speaker with a word, phrase, sentence or idea in order to help completing his/her utterance and **(3) Clarification,** having the current speaker clarify or explaining previously elicited piece of information that the listener is unclear about.

In [18] they further combine four disruptive sub-strategies from [24] and [16]: **(1) Disagreement**, disagree with what the current speaker is saying and want to voice his or her opinion immediately; **(2) Floor taking**, developing the topic of the current speaker by taking over the floor from the current speaker; **(3) Topic change**; and **(4) Tangentialization**, reflecting awareness, usually by summarization, of the information being sent by the current speaker. Tangentialization prevents the interrupter from listening to an unwanted piece of information either because it has been already presented previously or because it is already known to the listener.

In our study we needed to consider the sequence organization of the interactions (conversational analysis) [29] as this may (also) influence how an interrupting agent is perceived. More precisely, we needed to consider the adjacency pairs of which the interruption might be a part of. An adjacency pair consists of two speakers' turns where the second part of a pair is responsive to the action of the first part [29]. Adjacency pairs examples are offer-accept/decline and question-answer [29]. The basic rule of operation for a second speaker is to produce a second part of a pair according to the type of the first part. For example, the sequence *assessment-(dis)agreement* [17] may be considered more natural than the sequence *assessment-question*.

In this study we are not interested in the possible different consequences of the second pair part types among each other, but we are aware that they can be perceived differently. We therefore focused on the distinction between cooperative and disruptive strategies for each set of second pair parts separately (e.g. agreement/disagreement) (details in Section 4.1.2).

2.3 Interpersonal Attitudes

Interpersonal attitudes are essentially an individual's conscious or unconscious evaluation of how s/he feels about and relates to another person [1, p. 85]. Several researchers attempted to identify the dimensions that can best represent the different interpersonal attitudes expressed during social interaction. Schutz [30] proposed the dimensions of inclusion, control and affect. Burgoon and Hale [6] identified twelve dimensions defining different communication styles (e.g. dominance, intimacy, confidence). Argyle proposed a two-dimensional representation. A first dimension is the **affiliation**, characterized as the degree of liking or friendliness and ranging from unfriendly to friendly. A second dimension is the **status**, related to power and assertiveness during the interaction and ranging from submissive to dominant [1, p. 86].

We adopted Argyle's model because it has an intrinsic simplicity (i.e. only two dimensions) and it offers the best compromise between explanatory power and parsimony.

2.4 Engagement and Involvement

Engagement is a concept that has many interpretations in the domain of human-agent interaction [12]. All of them, however, refer more or less directly to the coordination and cooperation that is necessary to perform the joint activity of interacting [12]. Our interpretation of engagement comes from [26] as "the value that a participant in an interaction attributes to the goal of being together with the other participant(s) and of continuing the interaction".

Involvement refers to "being captured by the experience" [31]. [3] defines five aspects of involvement: (1) Immediacy (physical proximity); (2) Expressiveness (energy, activity, enthusiasm); (3) Altercentrism (focus on the conversation parner); (4) Interaction management (smooth flow); (5) Composure dimesion (body movement, confidence) and (6) Positive affect (good feelings). We used the interpretation of [31], which refers to aspects 2, 3 and 4. While involvement can be closely related to engagement [12, 19, 20], in this paper we differentiate it as it might provide us more fine grained qualities of the dyadic interaction.

We expected that initiating one's turn exactly when the other's turn finishes may be a sign of coordination and thus engagement. Previous research showed that leaving pauses between turns creates the feeling of having more rapport (i.e. a feature of engagement) [21], while other research in human-human interaction has shown that simultaneous speech can be a way to show involvement in an interaction [32].

3. RELATED WORK

Turn-Taking in Perception Studies. Maat et al. [21] showed how different turn-taking strategies (including interruptions) in a user-agent interaction could influence users' impressions of an agent's personality (agreeableness), emotion and social attitudes. However, their analysis did not take into account the speech content nor the interruption strategy. Thórisson and colleagues [33] evaluated a turn-taking model (YTTM) in terms of scalability and believability, however they focused more on timing and prosody features for autonomously assign the turn in a multi-party agent interaction. In [27] a multi-agent model for reflecting interpersonal attitudes in conversing groups has been presented. Their emphasis was on nonverbal behavior (e.g. interpersonal space, gestures) and turn-taking strategies, however they did not consider verbal behavior and different interruption types/strategies.

Interruptions. Crook and colleagues [9, 8] presented a mechanism for handling "barge-in" interruptions from a user interacting with an embodied conversational agent. Their agent was able to detect and respond to user interruptions. The handling process consisted of an address phase — i.e. the agent addressing the particular interruption that occurred — and a resumption phase where the agent implemented context-sensitive strategies for continuing or aborting the current conversational plan. While they modeled an handling mechanism that considered the affective user's perception of the interruptee (i.e. the agent), they did not consider the effects of the interrupter (the user in their case), strategy of interruption on perceived interpersonal attitude, engagement, and involvement in the interaction with the agent.

In [15] they examined interruptions in a corpus of spontaneous task oriented dialogue. They focused on timing and acoustic/prosodic features that predict interruptions, whereas we investigate the effects of different interruption strategies and types (i.e. amount of overlap between speakers and utterance completeness, while keeping constant the timing of the interruption) on perceived interpersonal attitudes, engagement and involvement of the interactants.

In sum, previous work focused on turn-taking strategies' impact on perceived agent's personality and attitude [21], handling of interruptions [9, 8] and predicting them [15]. However, to the best of our knowledge no one examined the effects of different interruption strategies and types (according to the definitions provided earlier) on perceived interpersonal attitudes, engagement level and involvement in the interaction between two participants. The next section presents the experimental design of a web study aiming at addressing these aspects.

4. EXPERIMENTAL DESIGN

In order to evaluate the effects of different interruption types and strategies on the human perception of interpersonal attitude (i.e. dominance and friendliness), engagement and involvement in a dyadic agent interaction, we designed an empirical experiment. In particular, we designed a web study in which participants listened to a series of conversational fragments between two agents. The application scenario for our virtual assistant in the ARIA-VALUSPA project is the book *"Alice in Wonderland"* by Lewis Carroll. We therefore adapted the subject of our fragments conforming to this scenario. For each fragment we systematically varied the interruption type (described in Section 2.1) and strategy (introduced in Section 2.2) for a given subcategory (i.e. communicative function of the interruption as described later). After listening to each fragment, participants rated the perceived level of *dominance*, *friendliness*, *engagement* and *involvement* of the two agents which are referred as the **Interruptee** (or **A**) and **Interrupter** (or **B**) in the remainder of the paper.

4.1 Stimuli Design and Preparation

We based the generation of interruptions on existing literature in human-human interaction. However, there are many ways for producing an interruption of a particular type and strategy. For practical reasons, we examined four categories of comparable interruption strategies (later defined as *functions*).

Furthermore, we were aware of possible gender influences on the interactants behavior [36, 4, 35] and the perception of their attitudes [4, 35, 14]. We considered the agents' gender as a blocking factor. Therefore, while we designed our study with this aspect in mind, as a first step and considering that our primary interest was on interruption types and strategy effects, we started with two male gendered agents. In the following sections we describe the design of the different interruption types and strategies.

4.1.1 Interruption Types

We focused on the successful interruptions, as shown in Figure 1, where the interrupter takes the floor. This was necessary in order to make it possible for the interrupter to utter a complete sentence (in the other cases the sentence is partially uttered), and thus effectively deploy an interruption *strategy* (i.e. disruptive vs. cooperative).

In [4] they illustrate each of these attempted speaker-switches with an example, which also gave us some indications about the possibility of pauses in between the turns. We did not consider the smooth speaker switch as it represents an unproblematic "smooth" way of taking the floor and was not of interest for us in terms of interruption type. According to the classification and examples provided in [4], we generated conversational fragments consisting of sequential turns that imitate each of these interruption types, shown in table 1. Synchronous speech is indicated between squared brackets. The length of the synchronous speech is not only the result of theoretical considerations but depends further on the speech duration of the agents' synthesized speech. The Interruptee is indicated as **A** in the "Agent" column and it always initiates the conversational fragments, whereas the Interrupter is indicated with **B**.

4.1.2 Interruption Strategies

We based the generation of disruptive and cooperative strategies on the categories described in Section 2.2. We examined four categories of comparable strategies, respectively disruptive vs. cooperative, as follows: (1) *Question implying misunderstanding – Clarification question*; (2) *Disagreement – Agreement*; (3) *Tangentialization – Completion*; (4) *New topic introduction – Topic elaboration.*

For practical reasons, we gave a name to each of these categories, that we call the *function* of the interruption and that is based on the commonality of both interruptions in the set: (1) *Understanding question*: both sub-strategies are consequences of the interrupter's (mis) understanding of the interruptee's turn; (2) *Opinion*: both express the interrupter's (dis) agreement with the interruptee; (3) *Partner Communication*: both try to adjust (future) utterances of the interruptee; (4) *Topic*: both strategies contribute to the topic management of the interaction.

In order to verify that for each function the instances of the interruption strategies that we created were indeed perceived as disruptive/cooperative strategies, we performed a manipulation check.

4.1.3 Manipulation Check

Participants rated how disruptive/cooperative they found the interrupter's utterance in the conversation fragments (in written format on a web page), on a 5-points Likert scale (anchors *very disruptive* and *very cooperative*). The second speaker turns were placed directly after the end of the first speaker's turn, corresponding to [4]'s example of smooth speaker-switches (Section 2.1), thereby serving as a baseline.

Results from 11 participants (7 males) indicated that strategies in all functions were correctly recognized, except for the disruptive one in the *Opinion* function (i.e. disagreement). Contrary to our expectations, it was judged, on average, as being closer to cooperative ($M = 3, S.E. = 1.3$). This can be explained by the fact that the disagreement was expressing a mitigated disagreement with respect to the first speaker's evaluation of a story (*Well, that's debatable, it's not my favorite one.*). Therefore, we refined the sub-strategy by creating a direct (non-mitigated) disagreement presented as a factual one. This lead us to use the utterance "*No, it does not tell an amazing story at all*". The final validated list of utterances used in our study is shown in Table 1.

4.1.4 Independent Variables

We split the study in 4 trials according to our **Functions** of interest: *Understanding Question, Opinion, Partner Communication* and *Topic.* In each trial (i.e for each function), our independent variables (IVs) were **Interruption Type** (with levels *overlap, simple* and *silent*) and **Strategy** (*disruptive* vs. *cooperative*). We designed each trial as a 3x2 within-subjects study where the type and strategy were within-subjects factors.

4.1.5 Stimuli Preparation

We produced a total number of 24 conversation fragments (6 for each function/trial) as summarized in Table 1, using a male synthesized voice created with the Cereproc text-to-speech (TTS) tool [2]. We opted for a single synthesized voice as opposed to pre-recorded speech to control for additional biases in the experiment. Indeed, a human speaker might pronounce the same sentence (e.g. A's sentences in our stimuli) with different intonations. We presented our stimuli in the form of videos with subtitles and stereo sound. The subtitles served for compensating the possible lack of clarity due to the synthesized nature of the voice, thus making sure that the participants were correctly exposed to our stimuli. Whereas the stereo sound, in addition to subtitles, allowed us to use the same voice but at the same time clearly discriminate speakers based on their voice sources (i.e. left and right channels). Participants of a pilot test (2 males and 2 females) thought that we used different voices "since the speech came from different audio sources".

All videos displayed two still male head silhouettes facing each other on a black background. The silhouettes' color was white grey and they had a label on top respectively showing "Left Agent" and "Right Agent". The subtitles progressively appeared below the corresponding silhouette as the words were audible.

In order to reduce confounding effects, in each conversation fragment (i.e. condition) the interruptee (i.e. first speaker) was uttering the same sentence when it was interrupted. We also kept the onset of the interruptions [28] equal among the different interruption types, meaning that the second speaker (i.e. interrupter) begins speaking **at the same moment** relative to the interruptee's current turn. Only in the silent interruption case we added a small pause in the interruptee's turn following the examples in [4]. For this we added 0.2 seconds of white noise at an amplitude of 0.001 in order to keep the left channel (i.e. of the interruptee) open and to avoid an abrupt termination that might have sounded as a recording error.

Furthermore, in Beattie's examples interruptions occur at possible *completion points* where a speaker's utterance could be produced [23]. There are three aspects that participants in an interaction use to determine possible completion points: syntax, prosody and pragmatics [23]. We generated conversation fragments where the second speaker interrupts at the moment where the first speaker's turn can be judged syntactically and pragmatically complete. However, we did not manipulate prosody features in our stimuli in order to control for possible effects across conditions. Thus, we did not provide the TTS with specific prosody instructions, and we deployed the synthesized output in our videos as it was produced by the tool. In order to compensate for unnatural prosody caused by an imperfect speech synthesis we added punctuation to the subtitles.

4.2 Measurements

For each stimulus, we asked the participants to rate the perceived **attitudes** (**dominance** and **friendliness**) of the agents towards each other, and their level of **engagement** and **involvement** in the interaction.

Table 1: Interruption types and strategies for the function categories investigated in our study. The Interruptee (A) is the first speaker, the Interrupter (B) is the second speaker. In the silent interruption (0.2) refers to a silent pause in seconds.

Interruption Type	Function	Interruption Strategy	Agent	Utterances	
Overlap			A	You know I've read the story Alice in Wonderland. It tells an amazing story [about a little girl.]	(1)
	Understanding	Disruptive	B	[When were you in] the Wonderland theme park?	(2)
	Question	Cooperative	B	[Do you mean the book writ]ten by Lewis Carrol?	(3)
	Opinion	Disruptive	B	[No, it does] not tell an amazing story at all.	(4)
		Cooperative	B	[Great! I] love it and I've read it several times.	(5)
	Partner Com-	Disruptive	B	[I've read the book s]o I know the story.	(6)
	munication	Cooperative	B	[About a busy rab]bit and a smiling cat.	(7)
	Topic	Disruptive	B	[I borrowed the book B]eauty and the Beast.	(8)
		Cooperative	B	[It was first rele]ased in 1865.	(9)
Simple Interruption			A	You know I've read the book Alice in Wonderland. It tells an amazing story [about]	(10)
	Understanding	Disruptive	B	[When] were you in the Wonderland theme park?	(11)
	Question	Cooperative	B	[Do you] mean the book written by Lewis Carrol?	(12)
	Opinion	Disruptive	B	[No,] it does not tell an amazing story at all.	(13)
		Cooperative	B	[Great]! I love it and I've read it several times.	(14)
	Partner Com-	Disruptive	B	[I've re]ad the book so I know the story.	(15)
	munication	Cooperative	B	[About] a busy rabbit and a smiling cat.	(16)
	Topic	Disruptive	B	[I bo]rrowed the book Beauty and the Beast.	(17)
		Cooperative	B	[It was] first released in 1865.	(18)
Silent Interruption			A	You know I've read the book Alice in Wonderland. It tells an amazing story (0.2)	(19)
	Understanding	Disruptive	B	When were you in the Wonderland theme park?	(20)
	Question	Cooperative	B	Do you mean the book written by Lewis Carrol?	(21)
	Opinion	Disruptive	B	No, it does not tell an amazing story at all.	(22)
		Cooperative	B	Great! I love it and I've read it several times.	(23)
	Partner Com-	Disruptive	B	I've read the book so I know the story.	(24)
	munication	Cooperative	B	About a busy rabbit and a smiling cat.	(25)
	Topic	Disruptive	B	I borrowed the book Beauty and the Beast.	(26)
		Cooperative	B	It was first released in 1865.	(27)

For measuring each attitude's dimension we adapted 2 statements from the Riverside Q-Sort inventory [11], using the two most reliable items (i.e. adjectives or key terms) of positive and negative valence as defined in Wiggin's interpersonal circumplex inventory [34]. The items adopted to assess dominance were: "tries to control" and "seems insecure". For friendliness they were: "tries to be likable" and "expresses hostility". For example, a question about the Interrupter dominance (i.e. right agent in our stimuli) towards the Interruptee (i.e. left agent) was: "*The **Right** Agent tries to control the interaction with the Left Agent*". All answers were on a 5-points labeled Likert scale (anchors *1. Completely disagree* and *5. Completely agree*).

For assessing the agents' level of engagement we asked two questions on a 5-points labeled Likert scale (anchors *1. No Value* and *5. A Maximum Value*) that are based on [26, 13]. For instance, the questions for the Interrupter were: (1) *"What value the **Right** Agent attributes to being together with the Left Agent?"* and (2) *"What value does the **Right** Agent attributes to continuing the interaction?"*.

We also assessed the agents' level of involvement as recommended in [31] by asking a question on a 5-points labeled Likert scale (anchors *1. Not at All* and *5. Very Much*). For the Interrupter, for instance, we used: *"How engaging was the interaction for the Right Agent?"*. In [31], more questions are proposed for measuring involvement, however we selected this one as it was more suitable for our design and linked to engagement [19, 20].

A summary of our dependent variables (DVs) is shown in Table 2. As naming convention we preceded the variable names with A and B referring, respectively, to the Interruptee and Interrupter.

4.3 Hypotheses

4.3.1 Interpersonal Attitudes

Disruptive interruption strategies in human-human interaction increase the perceived dominance of an interrupter [14, 35], whereas cooperative strategies increase affiliation (i.e. liking or friendliness) [14]. Therefore we expected that the perceived dominance and friendliness of the interrupter agent would be affected by the interruption strategy adopted by the interrupter (i.e. main effect).

As for the interruption type, in the stimuli that we created

Table 2: **Summary of the measures. DV names are preceded by A and B referring, respectively, to Interruptee and Interrupter.**

MEASURE	DV Names
Attitude: Dominance	A-Dom, B-Dom
Attitude: Friendliness	A-Friend, B-Friend
Engagement	A-Eng, B-Eng
Involvement	A-Inv, B-Inv

the interruption occurs always at the same moment during the interruptee's turn, therefore the difference among the levels of our interruption types (i.e. *overlap*, *simple* and *silent*) lies in the amount of overlap between the two interactants when the interruption occurs (respectively *long* overlap, *short* and *none*). In human-human interaction a speaker holding the turn (in our case resulting in a long overlap) is perceived as more dominant [4, 14] and less likable [14]. Considering that the interrupter agent always completes its utterance (in order to deploy a specific strategy) whereas the interruptee agent varies the amount of produced overlap when the interruption type changes, we predicted that the perceived dominance and friendliness of the interruptee agent would be affected by the interruption type (main effect).

In light of these observations, for each trial (i.e. function examined) we hypothesized the following:

- **H.A-Dom (Interruptee)**: The **Interruption Type** will have a main effect on perceived Interruptee's Dominance, the *higher* the overlap (i.e. from none to long) the *higher* will be **A-Dom**.
- **H.A-Friend (Interruptee)**: The **Interruption Type** will have a main effect on perceived Interruptee's Friendliness, the *higher* the overlap (i.e. from none to long) the *lower* will be **A-Friend**.
- **H.B-Dom (Interrupter)**: The **Interruption Strategy** will have a main effect on perceived Interrupter's Dominance, the disruptive strategy will lead to *higher* **B-Dom** compared to the cooperative one.
- **H.B-Friend (Interrupter)**: The **Interruption Strategy** will have a main effect on perceived Interrupter's Friendliness, the cooperative strategy will lead to *higher* **B-Friend** compared to the disruptive one.

4.3.2 Engagement and Involvement

We expected that when an agent is interrupted with a cooperative strategy it would show more engagement and involvement compared to a disruptive one. Cooperative interruptions coordinate the process and/or content of the conversation, while intrusive ones disrupt the process and/or content of the ongoing interaction. Given that engagement is characterized by a coordination between the interaction participants [12], we expect that cooperative interruptions are signs of more interrupter engagement and involvement than disruptive ones (i.e. main effect). Moreover, with respect to the interruption types previous research has shown contradictory effects on engagement related measures regarding the interrupter (Section 2.4) making it unclear to predict a specific outcome.

To the best of our knowledge, previous research did not provide evidence of interruption type/strategy effects on an interruptee's engagement level. We believe that involvement might increase when this agent finishes its turn. However, we considered the interruptee's engagement and involvement as exploratory measures, and thus we did not provide specific hypotheses for those.

In sum, for the interrupter agent in each trial (i.e. function examined) we hypothesized the following:

- **H.B-Eng (Interrupter)**: The **Interruption Strategy** will have a main effect on perceived Interrupter's Engagement, a cooperative strategy will lead to *higher* **B-Eng** compared to a disruptive one.
- **H.B-Inv (Interrupter)**: The **Interruption Strategy** will have a main effect on perceived Interrupter's Involvement, a cooperative strategy will lead to *higher* **B-Inv** compared to a disruptive one.

4.4 Participants and Procedure

We recruited a total of 72 participants via mailing lists (18 in each trial). 46% of the participants were between 18 and 30 years old, 34% between 31 and 40. 57% were male, 39% were female and 4% preferred to not say it. 82% were well educated (above master level). They had different cultural backgrounds[1], the two most prominent groups were France (20.8%) and USA (14%).

We ran this study online. A participant was first presented with a consent page and a sound check ensuring that audio could be played. Then, we showed a tutorial page including the instructions, a video sample and the questionnaires underneath the video player. Once the tutorial was completed, we randomly assigned a participant to a trial (i.e. function), (s)he played the corresponding videos (6) and answered the questions in a within-subjects repeated measures design. To control for first order carryover effects we adopted a counter balanced treatment order for showing the videos according to a latin square design, as recommended in [5].

4.5 Results

We conducted 4 separate statistical analyses for each function that we examined (i.e. trial). An informal comparison among them is discussed in Section 5. For each trial, we conducted 3x2 repeated measures MANOVAs (Multivariate Analysis of Variance) on **Interruptee**'s and, respectively, **Interrupter's Dominance** and **Friendliness** (A-Dom and A-Friend, B-Dom and B-Friend), **Engagement** and **Involvement** (A-Eng and A-Inv, B-Eng and B-Inv). The within-subjects factors were Interruption **Type** (3) and **Strategy** (2).

Prior to conducting the analyses we normalized all DVs in the range $[0-1]$. Due to space constraints we only report significant main effects and interactions of the follow-up UNIVARIATE analyses (sphericity assumption was not violated). We refer to Interruptee (**A**) and Interrupter (**B**) in the reminder of the paper. Simple main effects of interactions between factors were tested using Bonferroni adjustments for multiple comparisons. Effect sizes (η_p^2) for all

[1]As part of the demographic information, we asked participants to indicate the nationality that most represented their cultural identity.

comparisons ranged from **.18** to **.76**. Figure 2 provides a summary of our quantitative findings for all trials.

4.5.1 Function: Question

A's Dominance and Friendliness. The analyses revealed a main effect of Type on A-Dom ($F(2,34) = 9.1$, $p < .001$). As the amount of overlap increased the perceived A's dominance increased (*none*: M=.48, SE=.04; *short*: M=.53 SE=.03; and *long*: M=.64 SE=.04), therefore **H.A-Dom** is **supported**.

Type also had a main effect on A-Friend ($F(2,34) = 3.6$, $p < .05$). In this case an increasing overlap decreased the perceived A's friendliness (*none*: M=.74, SE=.04; *short*: M=.71 SE=.03; and *long*: M=.66 SE=.04), thus the hypothesis **H.A-Friend** is **supported**.

B's Dominance and Friendliness. We found a main effect of Type on B-Dom ($F(2,34) = 4.0$, $p < .05$), therefore **H.B-Dom** is **rejected**. When the agent interrupted in silence (i.e. no overlap) it was perceived significantly less dominant (M=.70, SE=.04) compared to the two other interruption types (*short*: M=.78, SE=.04; *long*: M=.78, SE=.03).

For friendliness we discovered two main effects of Type ($F(2,34) = 7.9$, $p < .005$) and Strategy ($F(1,17) = 11.9$, $p < .005$) but no significant interaction effects, thus **H.B-Friend** is **partially supported**. We decomposed these effects and discovered that in general a cooperative Strategy accounts for higher friendliness (M=.53, SE=.04) compared to a disruptive one (M=.42, SE=.04). However, when using a disruptive Strategy, the agent was perceived significantly more friendly when interrupting in silence (M=.53, SE=.05) in comparison with the other two Types (*short* overlap: M=.32, SE=.05; *long*: M=.39, SE=.04).

A's Engagement and Involvement. We did not find any significant effect on A-Eng. However, we found a significant interaction effect between Type and Strategy on A-Inv ($F(2,34) = 4.4$, $p < .05$). More specifically, when interrupted in silence (i.e. no overlap), A is considered more involved in the interaction when B's strategy is cooperative (M=.60, SE=.04) compared to disruptive (M=.70, SE=.03).

B's Engagement and Involvement. We found two main effects of Type ($F(2,34) = 5.5$, $p < .05$) and Strategy ($F(1,17) = 17.0$, $p < .005$) on B-Eng, but no significant interaction effects, thus **H.B-Eng** is **partially confirmed**. The decomposition of these effects revealed that, in general, B was more engaged when it used the cooperative Strategy (M=.61, SE=.05) compared to the disruptive one (M=.45, SE=.05). However, when using a disruptive Strategy, it was perceived significantly more engaged when interrupting in silence (M=.54, SE=.05) in comparison with the other two Types (*short* overlap: M=.41, SE=.05; *long*: M=.40, SE=.06).

Strategy had a main effect on B-Inv ($F(1,17) = 12.5$, $p = .003$). Cooperative interruptions made B more involved (M=.59, SE=.04) than disruptive ones (M=.40, SE=.06). Therefore, **H.B-Inv** is **supported**.

4.5.2 Function: Opinion

A's Dominance and Friendliness. We did not find significant effects on A-Dom (**H.A-Dom rejected**). However, we found a significant interaction effect on A-Friend ($F(2,34) = 3.8$, $p < .05$), thus **H.A-Friend** is **partially supported**. In particular, for silent Type of interruptions (i.e. A not overlapping), when the other agent interrupted with a cooperative Strategy, A was perceived less friendly (M=.66, SE=.05) compared to the case when a disruptive strategy was used (M=.74, SE=.03).

B's Dominance and Friendliness. We did not find significant effects on B-Dom (**H.B-Dom rejected**). We found a main effect of Strategy on B-Friend ($F(1,17) = 54.8$, $p < .001$), therefore **H.B-Friend** is **supported**. B was more friendly when doing cooperative interruptions (M=.52, SE=.04) compared to disruptive ones (M=.26, SE=.03).

A's Engagement and Involvement. No significant effects were found.

B's Engagement and Involvement. We discovered a main effect of Strategy on B-Eng ($F(1,17) = 26.0$, $p < .001$) and B-Inv ($F(1,17) = 23.8$, $p < .001$), thus **H.B-Eng** and **H.B-Inv** are **supported**. In particular, interrupting with a cooperative Strategy led to higher engagement (M=.46, SE=.04) and involvement (M=.46, SE=.04) compared disruptive ones (M=.22, SE=.02 and M=.23, SE=.04).

4.5.3 Function: Partner

A's Dominance and Friendliness. We found a main effect of Strategy on A-Dom ($F(1,17) = 12.8$, $p < .005$). When B adopted a cooperative Strategy, A was perceived significantly more dominant (M=.60, SE=.03) compared to when a disruptive Strategy was used (M=.55, SE=.03). Therefore, **H.A-Dom** is **rejected**. We did not find significant main effects or interactions on A-Friend (**H.A-Friend** is **rejected**).

B's Dominance and Friendliness. We found a main effect of Type on B-Dom ($F(2,34) = 5.3$, $p < .05$), therefore **H.B-Dom** is **rejected**. B's dominance was significantly higher when A suddenly stopped its utterance in reaction to the interruption (Type=*simple*: M=.75, SE=.03), compared to the case where A took a pause in its utterance (Type=*silent*: M=.67, SE=.03).

For friendliness (B-Friend) we discovered two main effects of Type ($F(2,34) = 8.6$, $p < .005$) and Strategy ($F(1,17) = 30.8$, $p < .001$) but no significant interaction effects, thus **H.B-Friend** is **partially supported**. We decomposed these effects and discovered that for all interruption Types a cooperative Strategy accounts for higher friendliness (M=.52, SE=.04) compared to a disruptive one (M=.27, SE=.03). However, this effect is more remarked when Type is *silent* (*cooperative*: M=.62, SE=.05; *disruptive*: M=.33, SE=.04).

A's Engagement and Involvement. No significant effects were found.

B's Engagement and Involvement. The analysis revealed a main effect of Strategy on B-Eng ($F(1,17) = 30.7$, $p < .005$) and B-Inv ($F(1,17) = 15.5$, $p < .001$), therefore **H.B-Eng** and **H.B-Inv** are **supported**. In both cases a cooperative Strategy led to higher B's engagement (M=.42, SE=.04) and involvement (M=.43, SE=.03) compared to a disruptive one, respectively (M=.18, SE=.04) and (M=.21, SE=.04).

4.5.4 Function: Topic

For this trial we only found a significant main effect of Type on B-Friend ($F(2,34) = 7.9$, $p < .005$). In particular, B's friendliness was significantly higher when A took a pause in its utterance (Type=*silent*: M=.47, SE=.05), compared to the other two interruption Types (Type=*overlap*: M=.38, SE=.03, Type=*simple*: M=.35, SE=.03).

	INTERRUPTEE AGENT (A)			INTERRUPTER AGENT (B)		
Function	Type (↗ *overlap*)	Strategy (*disr.* to *coop.*)	Type AND Strategy (*disr.* to *coop.*)	Type (↗ *overlap*)	Strategy (*disr.* to *coop.*)	Type OR Strategy (*disr.* to *coop.*)
QUESTION	↗ Dominance ↘ Friendliness	*n.s.*	↗ Involvement (when type: *no overlap*)	↗ Dominance	↗ Involvement	↗ Friendliness ↗ Engagement (particular cases: see *Section 4.5.1*)
OPINION	*n.s.*	*n.s.*	↗ Friendliness (when type: *no overlap*)	*n.s.*	↗ Friendliness ↗ Engagement ↗ Involvement	*n.s.*
PARTNER	*n.s.*	↗ Dominance	*n.s.*	↗ Dominance	↗ Engagement ↗ Involvement	↗ Friendliness (more remarked when type: *no overlap*)
TOPIC	*n.s.*	*n.s.*	*n.s.*	↘ Friendliness	*n.s.*	*n.s.*

Figure 2: Summary of results for all functions examined. IVs are listed in the header. Inclined arrows indicate effects directions for the DVs in the cells. In the QUESTION trial, for example, changes in interruption Type (an increasing ↗ *overlap*) decreased A's perceived Friendliness ↘. For OPINION, by changing interruption Strategy from *disruptive* to *cooperative* B's perceived Engagement increased ↗.

5. DISCUSSION AND FUTURE WORK

Type and strategy of interruption had main and interaction effects on the mutual attitudes of the agents. Contrary to our expectations, type had greater importance compared to strategy on user's perceived dominance and friendliness of both A (interruptee) and B (interrupter).

In the "Question" trial, A's dominance increased (and friendliness decreased) as the amount of overlap with B increased. B was perceived less dominant during silent interruption types. This would suggest that no matter how disruptive/cooperative is a question, the amount of overlap between interactants has higher impact on users' perception of their dominance and friendliness.

For "Opinions" (i.e. disagreement vs. agreement), strategy had greater impact but only on friendliness. In particular, a cooperative strategy increases B's friendliness. However, for A this effect also depended on the type of interruption (i.e. *silent*). When B used a cooperative strategy in silent type interruptions, A' friendliness decreased and vice-versa for disruptive ones. We think that B has been perceived very hostile while placing a disruptive strategy (strong disagreement), making A looking more friendly in comparison. The lack of differences in dominance levels can be explained by the tendency of opinions (i.e. A's utterance when interrupted was "It tells an amazing story...") to elicit a (dis) agreement, thus both strategies seemed appropriate.

In the "Partner Communication" trial, B's strategy had effects on A's dominance (B's disruptive strategy led to lower A's dominance compared to the cooperative one), whereas the type had impact on B's dominance as found in other trials. The first outcome can be explained by the notion introduced in [22] about complementarity of interpersonal attitudes in dyads, and stating that dominant behavior induces submissive responses.

Strategy had an effect on B's level of friendliness (more friendly when cooperative). In particular, this effect was more pronounced when the interruption happened after A's silence.

As for the engagement and involvement assessments, A's engagement was never influenced by B's interrupting behavior. Even if A stopped/continued its utterance in reaction. A's involvement was influenced by type and strategy only in the "Question" trial. A possible explanation is that a misunderstanding/clarification question is the only interruption in this study that can reveal something about A's quality of interacting. In the "Question", "Opinion", and "Partner Communication" trials cooperative strategies led to higher B's engagement and involvement levels compared to disruptive ones. This reflects the nature of cooperative interruptions as less face-threatening compared to disruptive ones [18], and displays of joint involvement [14].

The overall lack of significant effects in the "Topic" trial (except for a main effect of type on B's friendliness) can be explained by difficulties in capturing differences among the stimuli, as also reported by participants' feedback (6 out of 18).

In sum, the **turn-taking** mechanism (i.e. **type of interruption**) had more impact on the users' perception of **interpersonal attitudes** of both agents, though changing from a disruptive to a cooperative strategy increased interrupter's friendliness and reduced its dominance. We believe that for silent interruption types, when no overlap occurred, the content of the interrupter's utterances became more noticeable, thus increasing the effect of the two different strategies. On the other hand, the **strategy** had important main effects on **engagement** and **involvement** of the interrupter. These results have implications for the design of autonomous conversational agents that can be interrupted and can interrupt human users in a mixed-initiative incremental dialogue. When a cooperative interruption occurs, for example, the agent's mental model of the user (i.e. *Theory of Mind*) can be updated with the perceived user's intention of being friendly and subsequent agent's communicative intents can be (re)planned and adapted accordingly.

Future work should be considered. In human-human interaction personal characteristics such as the gender and status of the interactants can play a role in their interruption behavior [36, 4]. While we kept such variables stable in our study, they form interesting concepts to be considered in future work on interruptions in human-agent interaction. We also kept important factors, such as the timing of the interruption, constant across conditions to avoid further biases. However, we believe that manipulating the moment when the interruption occurs during the interruptee's turn might reveal interesting outcomes on the perceived interrupter's attitude. Finally, we are working on an agent able to manage interruptions (i.e. implementing different handling strategies in response to a user's interruption) or proactively interrupt the user by deploying a specific interruption strategy.

Acknowledgments

This work was supported by the European project H2020 ARIA-VALUSPA and the French ANR project MOCA. It was partially performed within the Labex SMART (ANR-11-LABX-65) supported by French state funds managed by the ANR within the Investissements d'Avenir programme under reference ANR-11-IDEX-0004-02.

REFERENCES

[1] M. Argyle. *Bodily communication*. Methuen, New York, 2nd ed. edition, 1988.

[2] M. Aylett and C. Pidcock. The cerevoice characterful speech synthesiser sdk. In C. Pelachaud, J.-C. Martin, E. André, G. Chollet, K. Karpouzis, and D. Pelé, editors, *Intelligent Virtual Agents*, volume 4722 of *Lecture Notes in Computer Science*, pages 413–414. Springer Berlin Heidelberg, 2007.

[3] B. S. Bamoallem, A. J. Wodehouse, G. M. Mair, and G. A. Vasantha. The impact of head movements on user involvement in mediated interaction. *Computers in Human Behavior*, 55, Part A:424 – 431, 2016.

[4] G. W. Beattie. Interruption in conversational interaction, and its relation to the sex and status of the interactants*. *Linguistics*, 19(1-2):15–36, 1981.

[5] J. V. Bradley. Complete counterbalancing of immediate sequential effects in a latin square design. *Journal of the American Statistical Association*, 53(282):525–528, 1958.

[6] J. K. Burgoon and J. L. Hale. The fundamental topoi of relational communication. *Communication Monographs*, 51(3):193–214, 1984.

[7] J. Cassell. *Embodied conversational agents*. MIT press, 2000.

[8] N. Crook, D. Field, C. Smith, S. Harding, S. Pulman, M. Cavazza, D. Charlton, R. Moore, and J. Boye. Generating context-sensitive eca responses to user barge-in interruptions. *Journal on Multimodal User Interfaces*, 6(1-2):13–25, 2012.

[9] N. Crook, C. Smith, M. Cavazza, S. Pulman, R. Moore, and J. Boye. Handling user interruptions in an embodied conversational agent. In *Proceedings of the AAMAS International Workshop on Interacting with ECAs as Virtual Characters, Toronto*, pages 27–33, 2010.

[10] N. Ferguson. *Interruptions: speaker-switch nonfluency in spontaneous conversation*. PhD thesis, University of Edinburgh, 1975.

[11] D. C. Funder, R. M. Furr, and C. R. Colvin. The riverside behavioral q-sort: A tool for the description of social behavior. *Journal of Personality*, 68(3):451–489, 2000.

[12] N. Glas and C. Pelachaud. Definitions of engagement in human-agent interaction. In *Workshop on Engagement in Human Computer Interaction (ENHANCE) at ACII 2015*, pages 944–949, 2015.

[13] N. Glas and C. Pelachaud. User engagement and preferences in information-giving chat with virtual agents. In *Workshop on Engagement in Social Intelligent Virtual Agents (ESIVA) at IVA 2015*, pages 33–40, 2015.

[14] J. A. Goldberg. Interrupting the discourse on interruptions: An analysis in terms of relationally neutral, power-and rapport-oriented acts. *Journal of Pragmatics*, 14(6):883–903, 1990.

[15] A. Gravano and J. Hirschberg. A corpus-based study of interruptions in spoken dialogue. In *INTERSPEECH, 13th Annual Conference of the International Speech Communication Association*, pages 855–858, 2012.

[16] C. W. Kennedy and C. T. Camden. A new look at interruptions. *Western Journal of Communication (includes Communication Reports)*, 47(1):45–58, 1983.

[17] S. C. Levinson. *Pragmatics (Cambridge textbooks in linguistics)*. Cambridge University Press, 1983.

[18] H. Z. Li. Cooperative and intrusive interruptions in inter-and intracultural dyadic discourse. *Journal of Language and Social Psychology*, 20(3):259–284, 2001.

[19] M. Lombard and T. Ditton. At the heart of it all: The concept of presence. *Journal of Computer-Mediated Communication*, 3(2):0–0, 1997.

[20] M. Lombard, T. B. Ditton, D. Crane, B. Davis, G. Gil-Egui, K. Horvath, J. Rossman, and S. Park. Measuring presence: A literature-based approach to the development of a standardized paper-and-pencil instrument. In *Third international workshop on presence, delft, the netherlands*, volume 240, 2000.

[21] M. T. Maat, K. P. Truong, and D. Heylen. How turn-taking strategies influence users' impressions of an agent. In J. Allbeck, N. Badler, T. Bickmore, C. Pelachaud, and A. Safonova, editors, *Intelligent Virtual Agents*, volume 6356 of *Lecture Notes in Computer Science*, pages 441–453. Springer Berlin Heidelberg, 2010.

[22] P. M. Markey, D. C. Funder, and D. J. Ozer. Complementarity of interpersonal behaviors in dyadic interactions. *Personality and Social Psychology Bulletin*, 29(9):1082–1090, 2003.

[23] H. J. Mazeland. *Inleiding in de conversatieanalyse*. Coutinho, 2003.

[24] K. Murata. Intrusive or co-operative? a cross-cultural study of interruption. *Journal of Pragmatics*, 21(4):385–400, 1994.

[25] S. H. Ng, M. Brooke, and M. Dunne. Interruption and influence in discussion groups. *Journal of Language and Social Psychology*, 14(4):369–381, 1995.

[26] I. Poggi. *Mind, hands, face and body: a goal and belief view of multimodal communication*. Weidler, 2007.

[27] B. Ravenet, A. Cafaro, B. Biancardi, M. Ochs, and C. Pelachaud. Conversational behavior reflecting interpersonal attitudes in small group interactions. In W.-P. Brinkman, J. Broekens, and D. Heylen, editors, *Intelligent Virtual Agents*, volume 9238 of *Lecture Notes in Computer Science*, pages 375–388. Springer International Publishing, 2015.

[28] E. A. Schegloff. Accounts of conduct in interaction: Interruption, overlap, and turn-taking. In *Handbook of sociological theory*, pages 287–321. Springer, 2001.

[29] E. A. Schegloff. *Sequence organization in interaction: Volume 1: A primer in conversation analysis*, volume 1. Cambridge University Press, 2007.

[30] W. C. Schutz. *FIRO: A Three-dimensional Theory of Interpersonal Behaviour*. Rinehart books in the assessment of personality. Holt, Rinehart and Winston, 1958.

[31] C. L. Sidner, C. Lee, C. D. Kidd, N. Lesh, and C. Rich. Explorations in engagement for humans and robots. *Artificial Intelligence*, 166(1):140–164, 2005.

[32] D. Tannen. Gender differences in topical coherence: Creating involvement in best friends' talk. *Discourse Processes*, 13(1):73–90, 1990.

[33] K. R. Thórisson, O. Gislason, G. R. Jonsdottir, and H. T. Thorisson. A multiparty multimodal architecture for realtime turntaking. In *Intelligent Virtual Agents*, pages 350–356, 2010.

[34] J. S. Wiggins, P. Trapnell, and N. Phillips. Psychometric and geometric characteristics of the revised interpersonal adjective scales (ias-r). *Multivariate Behavioral Research*, 23(4):517–530, 1988.

[35] J. Youngquist. The effect of interruptions and dyad gender combination on perceptions of interpersonal dominance. *Communication Studies*, 60(2):147–163, 2009.

[36] D. H. Zimmermann and C. West. Sex roles, interruptions and silences in conversation. *Amsterdam Studies in the Theory and History of Linguistic Science Series 4*, pages 211–236, 1996.

SOCRATES: from SOCial Relation to ATtitude ExpressionS

Florian Pecune
LTCI, CNRS, Telecom ParisTech, Universite Paris-Saclay
pecune@enst.fr

Magalie Ochs
Aix Marseille Universite, CNRS, ENSAM, Universite de Toulon, LSIS UMR7296
13397, Marseille, France
magalie.ochs@lsis.org

Stacy Marsella
Northeastern University
Boston, MA 02115, USA
s.marsella@neu.edu

Catherine Pelachaud
LTCI, CNRS, Telecom ParisTech, Universite Paris-Saclay
pelachaud@enst.fr

ABSTRACT

To be perceived as believable partners in human-machine interactions, virtual agents have to express adequate social attitudes. The social attitude expressed by an agent should reflect the social situation of the interaction. The agent ought to take into account its role and its social relation toward its interactants when deciding how to react in the interaction. To build such an agent able to reason about its role and relation and to adapt its social attitude, we build a model of social decision making. First, we formalize the dynamics of the social relation through a combination of goals and beliefs. Then, we design a decision making model based on the social goals and the situational goals of the agent.

Keywords

Virtual agents; social relations; social attitudes; decision making

1. INTRODUCTION

Nowadays machines own a prominent place in our life. Studies show that we are becoming more comfortable with the idea of interacting with them [35] in particular when the interaction involves virtual humans as partners. Our purpose is to improve the naturalness and the believability of these human-machine interactions by integrating socio-emotional components into virtual agents. These components should allow agents to manage the inherently social and emotional dimension of the interaction by expressing an emotional behavior and a social attitude relevant to the context of the interaction.

In [33], Scherer defines social attitudes (also called interpersonal stance) as an *"affective style that spontaneously develops or is strategically employed in the interaction with a person or a group of persons, coloring the interpersonal exchange in that situation"*. Strategical processes can be understood under the light of social roles. Indeed, in particular social contexts or situations, people endow specific roles [10] and intend to express particular behavior and social attitude. Thus, in a restaurant (social context), waiters (social role) are supposed to be nice and polite (social attitude). The same goes for a teacher giving a lesson to a class: they want to be perceived as dominant and controlling the situation.

Spontaneous development of the social attitude can be understood under the light of social relations. Indeed, the social relation between two people influences their behaviour and their social attitudes. For instance, two people who like each other spontaneously tend to comply with the other's requests thus showing a friendly attitude [8]. Moreover, depending on their actions during the interactions, their social relation might change. Hence, their social attitudes have to follow this evolution: if the same people end up hating each other, they will probably express more hostility than they did before.

In order to give the capability to a virtual agent to reason about its role and its own social relation toward the user, and to express an adequate social attitude according to the situation, we designed a model of social decision making. First, we propose a formal model of social relations dynamics based on the agent's goals and beliefs. This representation allows the agent to reason about the situation in order to take a decision and to build a strategy influenced by the agent's socio-emotional state. We also propose a model of decision making influenced by the agent's social relations toward its interaction partners and the agent's role in the interaction. The paper is organized as follows. In Section 2, we present the existing models of social relations while our general approach is described in section 3. In Section 4, our formalization of social relation dynamics is introduced. Our model of decision making is explained in Section 5 and illustrated by variations of a teacher/student scenario in Section 6. We conclude and discuss future work in Section 7.

Appears in: *Proceedings of the 15th International Conference on Autonomous Agents and Multiagent Systems (AAMAS 2016), J. Thangarajah, K. Tuyls, C. Jonker, S. Marsella (eds.), May 9–13, 2016, Singapore.*

2. RELATED WORKS OF SOCIAL RELATIONS MODELS

In the first section of this related work, we present works modeling the influence of actions and events on an agent's social relations. In the second section, we present works modeling the influence of social roles on the agent's attitude and behaviour.

Agents with dynamical social relations: understanding the spontaneous development of social attitude

Agents' social relations can be represented by different dimensions. Many existing models use two dimensions defined by the axis of dominance and the axis of liking. However, it is important to note that the definitions of these dimensions may vary across these models. In [20], liking is defined as *"a general and enduring positive or negative feeling about some person"* [20]. This notion is asymmetric [25, 27]. However, in [2] as in [15], liking involves not only feeling but also commitment. There are also different interpretations of dominance. In [2] and [27] dominance is defined as a hierarchical framework while [25] defines it as *"the capacity of one agent to affect the behavior of another"*. This influence is itself characterized by the resources and strategies available to the agent [29].

One approach to model the dynamics of agent's social relations is based on the emotions felt by the agent. In SCREAM [28] the emotions felt by the agent play an important role, changing the relationship according to their valence and intensity. A positive emotion elicited by another agent will raise the liking value towards it, while a negative emotion will have the opposite effect. The authors also add the notion of familiarity, still a function of the emotions but evolving monotonically: only positive emotions are taken into account. Similar dynamics can be found in [21], where authors describe the influence of particular emotions on liking, dominance and solidarity. For instance, an agent A feeling an emotion of pride elicited by another agent B will improve A's values of dominance and liking toward B. These values are initially defined by the role of the agent. In EVA [16], the relation between the agent and the user is represented by two values of friendliness and dominance. Like [28, 21], these values evolve according to four emotions felt by the agent: gratitude, anger, joy and distress.

In SGD [26], the authors try to team up humans with a group of synthetic characters, using a formal representation of liking and dominance. However, the evolution of these two dimensions does not rely on emotions, but on the content of the interactions between the agents. Socio-emotional actions, such as encouraging or disagreeing with one agent, will have an impact (respectively positive and negative) on its liking value. Instrumental actions, such as enhancing an agent's competence or obstructing one of its problems, will have an impact on its dominance.

Avatar Arena focuses on the appreciation in a scenario in which a user must negotiate a schedule appointment with several agents [30]. Before each session, the appreciation level between agents is fixed (either low, medium, or high), as well as their assumptions about other agents' preferences. According to the Congruity Theory described by Osgood and Tannenbaum [23], when an agent discovers a mismatch between its assumption about another agent's preference and what this agent's preference actually is, the former's appreciation toward the latter's decreases. Some other works rely on stage models to implement the notion of intimacy in their agents. This is the case for Laura who encourages users to exercise on a daily basis [5]. Laura's behavior is driven by its intimacy level with users that evolves during the interactions. The more the user interacts with Laura, the more familiar it will behave.

In most of these works, the agent directly expresses the social relation it feels. There is no strategical process, hence no social context adaptation. Moreover, the social relation rarely influences the decision taken by the agent.

Agents with social roles: modeling the strategical processes involved in social attitude

To enhance the believability of virtual agents, several models have proposed to define the agent's role in a particular social context along different variables. These works focus on the influence of these social variables on the agent's behaviour. In [36], the linguistic style and the politeness of a virtual character is determined according to its social distance and power. In Rousseau and Hayes-Roth [31] the agent's behavior is computed based on its personality and attitudes. Gratch [11] proposes a social layer that manages communication and biases plan generation and execution in accordance with a social context . However in these different works the social variables do not vary along the interaction. They are fixed for each agent.

Callejas et al. rely on a circumplex representation (liking, dominance) of social roles to build a computational model of social attitudes for a virtual recruiter in a job interview scenario [6]. In this work, the social attitude of the recruiter is dynamically computed according to the difficulty level of the interview and the anxiety level of the user. The recruiter will be friendly in lower difficulty levels, but might change its attitude as the difficulty increases. Here, the attitude is expressed strategically, in order to comfort or challenge the user. A virtual recruiter is also modeled in [1]. However, in this work, the social attitude expressed by the recruiter depends on its emotions, its mood, and the social cues that the agent gets from the user.

Another example of relational agent is Rea who adapts its dialog strategy according to the principle of trust [4]. Endowing the role of a real estate agent, Rea uses small-talks to enhance the confidence of the user. Once the user becomes more confident with Rea, task-oriented dialog can take place.

Although these works model the influence of the social context on the decision making, most of them rely on static variables: the agent does not adapt its behaviour regarding the other interactants actions. We propose a model of decision making combining dynamic social relations and agent's social role. Thus, the agent plans its strategy taking into account the social context of the interaction, and is able to adapt it depending on the other's actions.

3. GENERAL APPROACH

Our purpose is to build a virtual agent able to reason about its social role and its social relation towards its interactant. The action of the interactant influences the agent's emotional state which in turn influences its social relation toward the interactant. Both emotional state and social relation are part of the agent's beliefs. During an interaction, the agent selects its next action according to its goals and beliefs (including emotional state and social relation). Thus, the action resulting from this reasoning process conveys an adequate social attitude computed from its social role and social relation, itself influenced by the agent's emotional state. Our social decision making model is illustrated by Fig.1 and is described as follows:

Social role and social relation The social role of the agent represents its ideal self in a particular social context.

First, it defines the agent's function during the interaction: the agent might be a teacher, a student, a colleague... It also defines the *ideal state* of the relationship for the agent toward its interactant given the situation: Does the agent want to be an authoritative teacher toward its student or a compliant one? Does the agent want to play the role of an hostile student toward its teacher or a friendly one? As in [6, 1], we define the *ideal social relation* of an agent i toward another agent j in a particular social context using two dimensions of liking and dominance.

$$IdealRelation_{i,j} =< IdealLik_{i,j}; IdealDom_{i,j} >$$
$$\text{with } IdealLik_{i,j} \in [-1;1] \text{ and } IdealDom_{i,j} \in [-1;1] \quad (1)$$

These two values are static as the agent maintain its role during the interaction and thus, its ideal relation.

Similar to the *ideal social relation*, we define the *actual social relation* of an agent i toward another agent j using the two dimensions of liking and dominance.

$$ActualRelation_{i,j} =< Lik_{i,j}; Dom_{i,j} >$$
$$\text{with } Lik_{i,j} \in [-1;1] \text{ and } Dom_{i,j} \in [-1;1] \quad (2)$$

Unlike the ideal social relation, values of dominance and liking related to the agent's actual social relation i toward the agent j are dynamic. They represent the *actual state* of the relationship. Indeed, i's social relation evolves during the interaction depending on i's emotions (see sect.4). Our social decision making model relies on three kinds of goals: (1) one long-term relational goal, (2) social goals and (3) situational goals.

$$Goals_{i,j} = \{LgtG_{i,j}; SocG_{i,j}; SitG_i\} \quad (3)$$

Long-term relational goal The long-term relational goal describes the importance granted by an agent to maintain a long-term relation with its interactant. This goal is based on the interpersonal complementarity theory [32]. This theory is defined using the circumplex representation of Argyle's dimensions and states that two people with complementary behaviors will experience a better and longer relationship. For instance, two agents i and j are complementary if both are friendly, and either i or j is dominant. On the opposite, if i is friendly and j is hostile, or if both i and j are dominant, the relationship is less likely to work. Moreover, the importance $k \in [0;1]$ accorded by agent i to the long-term relational goal depends on the liking value of i toward j: the more an agent i likes an agent j, the more agent i values maintaining a long-term relationship with j [8].

$$LgtG_{i,j} = G^k_{i,j}((Lik_{i,j} = Lik_{j,i}) \wedge (Dom_{i,j} = -Dom_{j,i}))$$
$$\text{with } k = max(Lik_{i,j}; 0) \quad (4)$$

Social Goals The social goals are related to Theory of Mind (ToM) [3] and represent how agent i would like agent j to feel toward it. For instance, i might want j to like it, or i might want j to consider it as more dominant. These goals are influenced by the ideal and the social relations of agent i:

$$SocG_{i,j} = \{G^{kl}_{i,j}(Lik_{j,i} > 0); G^{kd}_{i,j}(Dom_{j,i} > 0);$$
$$G^{kd'}_{i,j}(Dom_{j,i} < 0)\} \quad (5)$$

We do not consider the goal $G_{i,j}(Lik_{j,i} < 0)$ (agent i desires agent j to dislike it) because if i dislikes j, it will consider that maintaining the relationship is not important at all. Thus, i will not have the goal to be disliked by j. These social goals are influenced by the agent ideal relation and its actual relation.

(1) Ideal relation: How the agent sees its own role directly influences its social goal. For instance, as a teacher, agent i might want agent j to like it, and to consider it as more dominant.

(2) actual relation: The agent's actual social relation also influences its social goals. Indeed, according to the complementarity theory, agent i might want agent j to have a complementary relation with it. That means that agent i wants agent j to have the same liking relation toward it, but an opposite relation of dominance.

Importances kl, kd and kd' of these goals are computed as follows:

$$kl = max\left(\frac{IdealLik_{i,j} + Lik_{i,j}}{2}; 0\right)$$
$$kd = max\left(\frac{IdealDom_{i,j} + Dom_{i,j}}{2}; 0\right) \quad (6)$$
$$kd' = max\left(-\frac{IdealDom_{i,j} + Dom_{i,j}}{2}; 0\right)$$

Situational Goals Finally, situational goals are defined by how an agent considers its own social role. For instance, if agent i is a teacher, its situational goal might be to make the student j learn and finish its homework. Those goals do not necessarily involve another agent and their importance k depends on how the agent sees its role. Some agent might consider that working is more important than having fun, while others do not share this opinion.

$$SitG_i = \{G^k_i(1); G^{k'}_i(2); G^{k''}_i(3)...G^{kn}_i(n)\} \quad (7)$$

During the interaction, the social relation between i and j might change according to the emotions felt by i. If the relation evolves in a positive way (i likes j more), then i will care more about the relationship. Therefore, i will care more about j's relation toward it. According to the balance between situational and social goals, the agent makes its decision and selects an appropriate action.

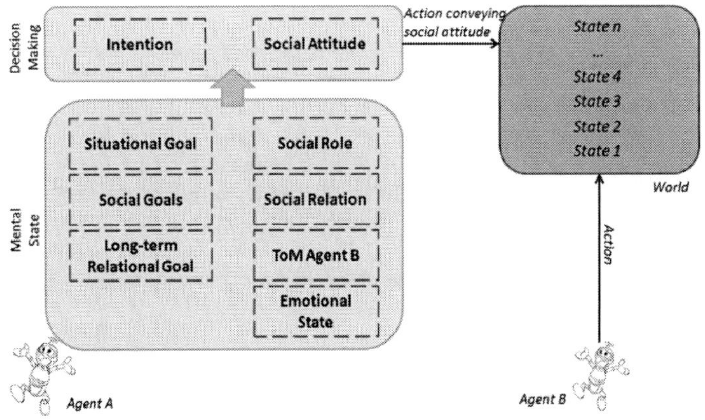

Figure 1: Global model description

4. MODEL OF SOCIAL RELATIONS DYNAMICS

We now present our formal model of social relation dynamics. As already mentioned, our representation of the mental state of the agent is defined in terms of goals and beliefs allowing us to model the emotional state of the agent and how this latter affects the social relation of the agent.

4.1 Theoretical Background

Liking dynamics

As explained in sect.2, one approach to model an agent's liking dynamics is based on the emotions it feels. Shiota et al. [34] make a difference between the emotions experienced and those expressed by the agent. The authors describe how distinct positive emotions influence the social relationship depending on its type: parental, romantic, friendship and group. Ortony assesses that emotions felt by an agent play an important role in the evolution of its liking toward others [22]. The direction of the evolution relies on the valence of the emotions felt by the agent: positive emotions increase the degree of liking while negative emotions decrease the degree of liking.

Heider proposes another theory to model liking dynamics [13]. This theory can be represented as a triangular schema between a person P as the focus of the analysis, another person O and an impersonal entity X, which could be a physical object, an idea or an event. If both P and O share the same opinion about X, they like each other more. If P and O have different opinions about X, they like each other less. In their theory, Osgood and Tannenbaum keep the same triangular schema [23]. However, the evolution of the liking between P and O depends on the congruity between P's assumption of O's attitude toward X and O's actual attitude.

Dominance dynamics

Most of the works modeling the dominance of an agent and its dynamics are based on the agent's goals. Emerson [9] assesses that an agent A's level of dependence toward an agent B is *"directly proportional to A's motivational investment in goals mediated by B and inversely proportional to the availability of those goals to A outside of the A-B relation"*. A's level of dominance is then the difference between the two levels of dependence. Castelfranchi [7] formalizes the different patterns of dependence that can happen in a relationship. An agent is dependent on another one if the latter can help the former to achieve one of its goals. The dependence level may vary if the dependent agent finds alternative solutions, or manages to induce a mutual or reciprocal dependence. Hexmoor et al. [14] address autonomy, power and dependence from another perspective. In their work, the agent's power is characterized as a difference between personal weights and *'liberties'* of preferences. The weights influence the agent towards individual or social behavior. The *'liberties'* represent internal or external processes that influence the agent's preferences of choice.

4.2 The logical framework

As mentioned before (see Fig. 1), the agent's mental state is made of its goals and beliefs (including its social relation and emotional state). To formalize the agent's mental state, we introduce the following logical framework:

Let $\neg$, $\wedge$, and $\vee$ represent respectively logical negation, conjunction and disjunction, $\exists$ and $\forall$ existential and universal quantifier. Let the symbols i and j represent two different agents (virtual or real), a and a' different actions, ϕ and ψ logical formulas. As already stated in section 3, $Lik_{i,j}$ and $Dom_{i,j}$ represent respectively the value of liking and dominance of agent i toward agent j. The agent's beliefs and goals are formalized respectively by the modal operator B and G.

- $B_i^h(\phi)$ can be read as the agent i believes that ϕ is true with a strength equal to $h \in]0,1]$.
- $G_i^k(\phi)$ means that the agent i has the goal ϕ and wants ϕ to be true. $G_i^k(\phi) \in SitG_i$ is a situational goal and the importance accorded to this goal is equal to $k \in]0,1]$.

We also define the following temporal operators and two syntactic abbreviations:

- $After_a(\phi)$ means that ϕ is true after the action a
- $Before_a(\phi)$ means that ϕ was true before the action a
- $Resp_i(a)$ means that the agent i is the author of the action a
- $Done_i(a,\phi) \equiv Before_a(\neg\phi) \wedge Resp_i(a) \wedge \phi$ means that the agent i did an action a and ϕ was true after that action.
- $CanDo_i(a,\phi) \equiv \neg\phi \wedge \exists a(Resp_i(a) \wedge After_a(\phi))$ means that the agent i can do an action a and ϕ would be true after that.

The operators are based on a Kripke's possible-world semantics with, for each operator, an accessibility relation [17].

Emotions Our work is based on Lorini's formalization of emotions [18] and [12]. The intensity l of the emotions of gratitude and anger depends on the importance k accorded to the goals. On the other hand, the intensity l of the expectation-based emotions hope and fear [18] relies on the importance k given to the goals G and to the strength h of the beliefs B on the other agent's action. Finally the intensity l of the emotions relief, fearconfirmed, disappointment and satisfaction is related to the intensity of the expectation-based emotions.

$$\begin{cases} Gratitude_{i,j}^l(a,\phi) \equiv G_i^k(\phi) \wedge Done_j(a,\phi) \\ Anger_{i,j}^l(a,\phi) \equiv G_i^k(\neg\phi) \wedge Done_j(a,\phi) \\ \text{with } l = k \end{cases} \tag{8}$$

$$\begin{cases} Hope_{i,j}^l(a,\phi) \equiv G_i^k(\phi) \wedge B_i^h(CanDo_j(a,\phi)) \\ Fear_{i,j}^l(a,\phi) \equiv G_i^k(\neg\phi) \wedge B_i^h(CanDo_j(a,\phi)) \\ \text{with } l = \dfrac{k+h}{2} \end{cases} \tag{9}$$

$$\begin{cases} Relief_{i,j}^l(a,\phi) \equiv Fear_{i,j}^l(a,\phi) \wedge Done_j(a,\neg\phi) \\ FearConfirmed_{i,j}^l(a,\phi) \equiv Fear_{i,j}^l(a,\phi) \wedge Done_j(a,\phi) \\ Disappointment_{i,j}^l(a,\phi) \equiv Hope_{i,j}^l(a,\phi) \wedge Done_j(a,\neg\phi) \\ Satisfaction_{i,j}^l(a,\phi) \equiv Hope_{i,j}^l(a,\phi) \wedge Done_j(a,\phi) \end{cases} \tag{10}$$

4.3 Liking and Dominance dynamics

Liking Dynamics Our model of liking dynamics is based on [22]. As explained in section 4.1, a positively valenced emotion of an agent i triggered by an agent j has a positive influence on i's liking toward j. On the opposite, a negative emotion of i triggered by j lowers i's liking toward j. The liking dynamics not only depends on the valence of the emotion felt by i, but also depends on the intensity l of this emotion. The higher the intensity l of the emotion, the more it influences i's liking toward j. The liking dynamics is captured by the following formulas:

$$\left.\begin{array}{r} Gratitude^l_{i,j}(a,\phi) \\ Hope^l_{i,j}(a,\phi)) \\ Satisfaction^l_{i,j}(a,\phi)) \\ Relief^l_{i,j}(a,\phi) \end{array}\right\} Lik_{i,j} = min(Lik_{i,j} + l; 1) \quad (11)$$

$$\left.\begin{array}{r} Anger^l_{i,j}(a,\phi) \\ Fear^l_{i,j}(a,\phi) \\ FearConfirmed^l_{i,j}(a,\phi) \\ Disappointment^l_{i,j}(a,\phi) \end{array}\right\} Lik_{i,j} = max(Lik_{i,j} - l; -1) \quad (12)$$

According to the equations 8,9 and 10 introduced in section 4.2, the evolution of i's social relation toward j can be represented by a combination of goals and beliefs. For example, if j helps i to achieve one of i's goals, i feels gratitude towards j and its liking toward j increases.

Dominance dynamics Our model of dominance dynamics is rooted in [9]. An agent i is less dominant toward an agent j if i believes that j can influence one of i's goals. The dominance dynamics also depends on the importance k accorded by i to its goal, and the strength of its belief about j's action. The more i considers its goal as important, the less dominant i is. Moreover, the more i believes that j can influence its goal, the less dominant i is. According to the equations 8,9 and 10, we obtain the following formulas:

$$\left.\begin{array}{r} Fear^l_{i,j}(a,\phi) \\ Hope^l_{i,j}(a,\phi) \\ Satisfaction^l_{i,j}(a,\phi) \\ FearConfirmed^l_{i,j}(a,\phi) \end{array}\right\} Dom_{i,j} = max(Dom_{i,j} - l; -1) \quad (13)$$

$$\left.\begin{array}{r} Relief^l_{i,j}(a,\phi) \\ Disappointment^l_{i,j}(a,\phi) \end{array}\right\} Dom_{i,j} = min(Dom_{i,j} + l; 1) \quad (14)$$

For instance, agent i **dominance** toward j **decreases** if i fears that j can prevent one of i's goals.

5. MODEL OF SOCIAL DECISION MAKING

5.1 PsychSim implementation

We implemented our model in PsychSim [19], where agents are decision-theoretic models with actions, goals and beliefs. Moreover, PsychSim agents have the notion of mental horizon whereby an agent can project into the future, simulating the consequences of their actions. As part of this projection, an agent can take into account how other agents will react, including how those agents' beliefs will change. To perform this projection, PsychSim agent incorporates Theory of Mind. Specifically an agent can have mental models of other agents that are fully specified agent models with beliefs, goals and actions, thus allowing an agent to simulate other agents. Through the dynamic changes of the agent's mental state, the emotional state of the agent is implicitly captured. Thus the evolution of the social relation of the agent is influenced by its emotional state.

Representing actual social relation and ideal social relation as states of the world. States are objective facts about agent's status or about the world itself. The features of a state can be booleans, finite sets of possible values, or a range of continuous values. In PsychSim, an agent only has indirect knowledge about the world, therefore partial observability. Thus an agent's subjective beliefs about the world may differ from the actual world. As explained in section 3, we represent the agent's *actual social relation* and the *ideal social relation* associated with its role using two dimensions of dominance and liking. For each agent, ideal liking, ideal dominance, actual liking and actual dominance are represented as state features ranging from -1 to 1.

Actions. In PsychSim, agent's actions constitute the possible decisions an agent can make. In particular, actions can be either physical actions or dialog acts whose influence is largely on other agents' beliefs. Each action is defined by an actor and a name but might also include a target and a parameter that modifies the action impact. Actions dynamics represent the influence of actions on the states variables introduced above. For instance, shouting at the student might have a negative influence on the student's liking value. Traditional notions of action preconditions and effects are realized through these dynamics. We saw in section 4 how agent j's actions influence agent i's social relation through the emotions i feels. We do not explicitly model agent i emotional state in PsychSim. However, according to the effects of j's actions on agent i's goals, i's social relation evolves. For instance, j's action helping i to achieve its goal enhances i's liking toward j. The evolution of the liking feature associated with one action relies on the following equation:

$$Lik_{t+1} = Lik_t + (LikMaxValue - Lik_t) * weight \quad (15)$$

Indeed, repeating the same action decreases the effect of this action on the other's liking. The weight represents the importance accorded by i to the goal impacted by the action. As stated in section 4, influencing important goals brings emotions with high intensity, thus having a high influence on social relation.

Representing goals as reward functions. The reward function maps the state of the world into an evaluation of the benefit to the agent. In this work, we use a simplified version whereby the agent has relative preferences for goals defined as the agent's desire to maximize or minimize particular state variables. For instance, agent i has the goal to maximize its fun. Moreover, the agent might also want to alter other agents' states or beliefs. For instance, the agent i wants to maximize j's knowledge. Each goal is associated with a preference weight representing the importance accorded by the agent to this goal. According to this weight, each action will be attributed an expected utility: actions having a positive (respectively, negative) influence on a high importance goal are considered more useful (respectively, useless). The situational goals of the agent are then represented by different reward functions related to states of the world. The importance accorded to these situational reward functions is fixed. On the opposite, computation of social goals importance relies on the four social states described above following the formula 6.

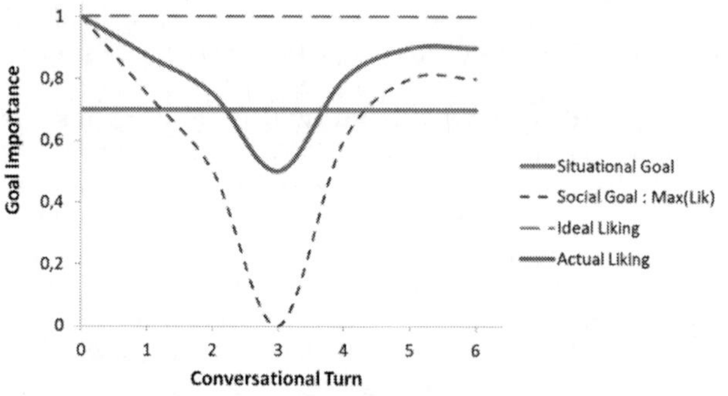

Figure 2: The balance between situational goals and social goals relies on the social relations dynamics. Situational goals are fixed while social goals vary. In this example, for a maximal ideal liking, social goal (here maximizing the liking of the other toward the agent) becomes less important than the situational goal as the liking value drops.

Representing beliefs strength as mental models distribution. An agent in PsychSim has not only beliefs about itself, but also about the other agents. When planning its own actions, the agent takes all these beliefs into consideration. Each agent has a mental model for itself, and at least one mental model for each other agent (mental models include agent's state, beliefs, goals, and actions). For instance, a tutor might have two different models for a student: one where the student is motivated by finishing its homework (model A), and another one where the student just wants to have fun (model B). The agent's belief about another agent is represented as a probability distribution of these mental models. For instance, the tutor might initially be sure at 75% that the student wants to work (model A), and 25% that the student wants to play (model B). In PsychSim, the agent is able to infer another agent's goals according to the latter's actions. Hence, during the interaction, the tutor might notice that the student's behavior does not fit this distribution (for instance, if the student keeps playing although it is asked to do its homework). Therefore, the tutor will update its belief, and will change the distribution according to this observation. When computing the dominance value of an agent i, this probablity is taken into account: the more an agent i believes that agent j can do an action that will influence its goals, the less dominant i feels toward j. The importance accorded to the goal also influences the final value of dominance

$$Dom_{t+1} = Dom_t + (DomMaxValue - Dom_t) * \frac{weight + belStrength}{2}$$

Repeating the same action decreases the effect of this action on the other's dominance. This is coherent with Raven's theory [29], assessing that multiple use of reward/coercive strategies lowers the impact of these strategies on others.

Horizon and decision making. As chess players, agents are able to project themselves few steps forward and thus predict the outcome of all the possible sequences of actions. Indeed, when an agent plans its next action, it first projects itself into the future to evaluate the effect of each of its possible actions on the different states. Then, using its mental models of the other agents, it will predict their expected actions and their impact on their states. Then again, the agent will anticipate its reaction, and so on. The number of steps that the agent is able to predict is called *horizon*. Hence, an agent with a high horizon is able to look several steps in the future, and to predict outcomes that an agent with a low horizon is not able to foresee. When the agent finishes its projection, it evaluates the overall effect of each sequence of actions according to its goals. Then, the agent selects the action with the highest expected utility.

6. USE CASE: TUTOR-STUDENT INTERACTION

To illustrate our model, we define a scenario taking place in the following social context: one agent *Bob* endowing the role of a virtual tutor wants to make another agent *Alice* do her homework. As shown in [37], two teachers expressing different social attitudes might get different results when giving a class. Moreover, recent studies have shown that a good tutor/student relationship may improve the student's motivation and her academic achievements [24]. Hence, modeling an agent trying to make a student work presents an interesting challenge.

Tutor's goals and actions Being a tutor, the agent *Bob* has only one situational goal $SitG_{Bob}$, namely the student finishes her homework (operationalized as working for two units of time) during the interaction. Agent *Bob* can do several actions (including doing nothing) to reach his goal.

$$SitG_{Bob} = G_{Bob}(HomeworkDone)$$

RequestWork means that *Bob* informs *Alice* that he wants *Alice* to work and to do her homework.

$$Request_{Bob}(Alice, HomeworkDone) \Rightarrow B_{Alice}(G_{Bob}(Done_{Alice}(Work, HomeworkDone)))$$

PromiseToPlay means that *Bob* requests *Alice* to finish her homework and that he would play with her if she satisfies that request.

$$Promise_{Bob}(Alice, HomeworkDone, PlayWithStudent) \Rightarrow Request_{Bob}(Alice, HomeworkDone) \wedge Inform_{Bob}(Alice, CanDo(Bob, PlayWithStudent))$$

ThreatenToSwitchOffConsole means that *Bob* requests *Alice* to work and that he would switch off the console if she does not.

$$Threaten_{Bob}(Alice, HomeworkDone, SwitchOffConsole) \Rightarrow Request_{Bob}(Alice, HomeworkDone) \wedge Inform_{Bob}(Alice, CanDo(Bob, SwitchOffConsole))$$

PlayWithStudent means that *Bob* can increase *Alice*'s fun by playing with her.

$$PlayWithStudent_{Bob}(Alice) \Rightarrow Done_{Bob}(PlayWithStudent, Fun)$$

$SwitchOffConsole$ means that *Bob* can switch off the console. *Alice* will not be able to play anymore with the console after that.

$$SwitchOffConsole_{Bob}(Alice)$$
$$\Rightarrow Done_{Bob}(SwitchOffConsole, ConsoleSwitchedOff)$$

Student's goals and actions Being a student, *Alice* has two different situational goals $SitG_{Alice}$: she wants to play but also wants to do her homework. She can do three different actions (including doing nothing).

$$SitG_{Alice} = \{G_{Alice}(HomeworkDone), G_{Alice}(Fun)\}$$

Play means that *Alice* increases her level of fun if she plays. This effect decreases as *Alice* plays repeatedly (it approaches an asymptotic, see equation15).

$$Play_{Alice}(Bob)$$
$$\Rightarrow Done_{Alice}(Play, Fun)$$
with $Fun_{t+1} = Fun_t + (FunMaxValue - Fun_t) * weight$

Work means that *Alice* works and finishes one exercise.

$$Work_{Alice}(Bob)$$
$$\Rightarrow Done_{Alice}(Work, HomeworkDone)$$

Finally, we built four different models of the student *Alice* depending on relative preference for her goals (HomeworkDone Vs PlayVideoGames) and her horizon (high Vs low). We ran several simulations, varying these different parameters: (1) social goals, and (2) horizon. In the following subsection, we describe some of these simulations and analyze the results we obtained.

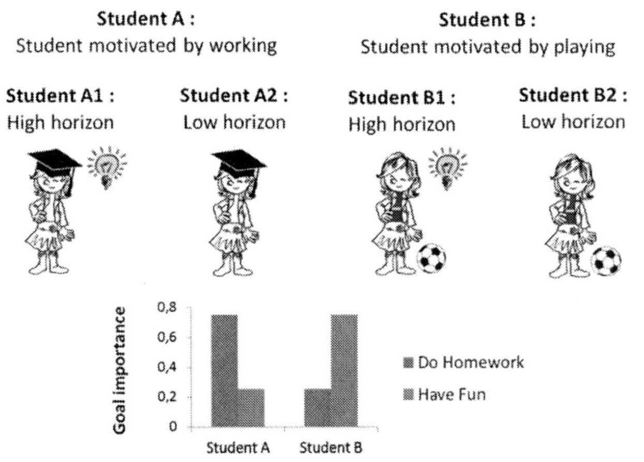

Figure 3: Different models of the student. Student A considers doing homework as more important than having fun, while student B prefers to have fun, regardless their horizon.

6.1 Simulation 1: Reference simulation

In this simulation, we consider the influence of social relation and social role during the interaction and how the interaction might change the balance between situational and social goals. We expect that the tutor will adapt his strategy depending on the student reactions.

Starting situation: Student B2

	Tutor	Student
Ideal Relation	IdealLik(High) IdealDom(Med)	IdealLik(Neutral) IdealDom(Neg)
Actual Relation	Lik(Med) Dom(Med)	Lik(Neutral) Dom(Low)
Situational Goals	Work(HighImp)	Work(LowImp) Fun(HighImp)
Social Goals	MaxLik(HighImp) MinDom(MedImp)	

The teacher *Bob* wants the student *Alice* to do her homework, and also wants to maintain the relationship with her. He believes he is dominant toward the student, and his liking toward her is moderately high. The student strongly desires to play, and considers that doing her homework is less important. Her liking is neutral, and she believes she is slightly dominant toward the teacher.

Actions sequence

Step 1: Student-Play
Student *Alice* believes she is dominant. Indeed, with her low horizon, *Alice* does not believe that the tutor *Bob* can influence her goals. Therefore, *Alice* plays because it is more desirable for her.

Step 2: Teacher-PromiseToPlay
The tutor *Bob* wants to maintain his relationship with the student *Alice*. He then considers a reward strategy, and promises *Alice* that he will play with her if she finishes her homework first. This way, it should lower *Alice*'s dominance while enhancing her liking, thus making her work.

Step 3: Student-Play
Alice still believes she is dominant. She does not believe she will be rewarded if she works, so she keeps playing.

Step 4: Teacher-PromiseToPlay
Bob still considers that maintaining a good relationship with *Alice* is more important than forcing her to work. *Bob* tries again to convince his student using a reward strategy.

Step 5: Student-Play
Alice still believes she is dominant. she does not believe she will be rewarded so she keeps playing.

Step 6: Teacher-SwitchOffConsole
Since *Alice* keeps playing, the tutor gets disappointed again (*Bob* expected *Alice* would do her homework, but she did not fulfill *Bob*'s expectations). *Bob* likes *Alice* less (decrease of his liking), and considers now that maintaining the relationship with her is less important than finishing homework. Thus, the tutor changes his strategy, and uses his coercive power to switch off *Alice*'s console.

Step 7: Student-Work
Alice now believes the tutor is dominant. She still believes that playing is more important for her than working, but she works because she has no other options.

Step 8: Teacher-DoNothing
Bob believes that *Alice* will keep working now that her console is switched off. *Bob* has nothing else to do.

Step 9: Student-Work
Alice still has nothing to do but work.

Ending situation

After the interaction, we notice that the relationship between the tutor and his student is not so bad. The tu-

	Tutor	Student
Ideal Relation	IdealLik(High) IdealDom(Med)	IdealLik(Neutral) IdealDom(Neg)
Actual Relation	Lik(Med) Dom(Med)	Lik(Low) Dom(Neg)
Situational Goals	Work(HighImp)	Work(LowImp) Fun(HighImp)
Social Goals	MaxLik(HighImp) MinDom(MedImp)	

tor *Bob* eventually managed to make *Alice* work, so his liking toward her slightly increases and he still feels dominant. Since *Bob* tried to use reward strategies first, *Alice* also slightly increases her liking toward him: the reward strategy increased liking, offsetting the following decrease in liking due to switching off the console. However, *Alice* does not feel dominant anymore. Her dominance level has dropped.

6.2 Simulation 2: Playing with goals

In this simulation, the starting situation is the same as the reference one (see section 6.1) except that we adjusted the ideal social relation of the tutor *Bob* so that he does not have any social goal ($SocLik_{Bob,Alice} + Lik_{Bob,Alice} \leq 0$). By doing this, *Bob* only focuses on his situational goal: he will choose the most efficient plan that will make *Alice* finish her homework.

Actions Sequence
Step 1: Student-Play.
Step 2: Teacher-ThreatenToSwitchOffConsole.
Step 3: Student-Play.
Step 4: Teacher-SwitchOffConsole.
Step 5: Student-Work.
Step 6: Teacher-DoNothing.
Step 7: Student-Work.
Step 8: Teacher-DoNothing.
Step 9: Student-Work.

Student *Alice* believes she is dominant. Indeed, with her low horizon, *Alice* does not believe that the tutor *Bob* can influence her goals. Therefore, *Alice* plays because it is more desirable for her. The tutor does not have the goal to maintain the relationship, so he chooses a coercive strategy. Indeed, by switching off *Alice*'s console, thus forbidding her to play, *Bob* knows that she will have nothing to do but work.

After the interaction, the relation between *Bob* and *Alice* is bad. The tutor eventually managed to make *Alice* work, so his liking toward her slightly increases and he still feels dominant. However, *Bob* used coercive strategies, threatening *Alice* to switch off her console if she would not do her homework. Even though it was effective, this strategy had a disastrous influence on *Alice*'s relation since *Alice*'s liking value toward *Bob* has noticeably dropped and reached negative value.

6.3 Simulation 3: Playing with horizon

In this simulation, we want to check the effect of the horizon on the scenario. Starting from the same situation as the one described in section 6.1, we only raise the student's horizon. By doing this, we expect different sequences of actions, and different social relations in the end: the student with a high horizon should be able to delay her gratification. She should be able to resist the temptation of getting immediate fun by playing, and to wait for the late reward of playing with the tutor. (note we could also get a similar effect by giving to the student different discount factors on future rewards).

Actions sequence
Step 1: Student-Work.
Step 2: Teacher-DoNothing.
Step 3: Student-Work.
Step 4: Teacher-DoNothing.
Step 5: Student-Work.
Step 6: Teacher-PlayWithStudent.
Step 7: Student-Play.
Step 8: Teacher-PlayWithStudent.
Step 9: Student-Play.

Since she has a high horizon, the student *Alice* is able to project herself more steps ahead into the future. She believes that the teacher *Bob* will switch off her console if she does not work. *Alice* also believes that *Bob* will play with her if she finishes her homework (which she expects will take two units of working time). After considering all the possibilities, *Alice* decides that working is worth it. Indeed, it will bring her more fun to play with *Bob* rather than not working and playing alone. Moreover, *Alice* will also complete her other goal of finishing her homework. Therefore, she decides to delay her gratification (playing gives *Alice* a better immediate reward than working) and start working. *Bob* does not have to do anything at the beginning because *Alice* is working. Once *Alice* finishes her homework, *Bob* starts to play with her and keeps playing with her until the end of the interaction.

In the end, the relationship between *Bob* and *Alice* is good. *Alice* fulfilled *Bob*'s goal by completing her homework, and *Bob* did not do anything but play with her, improving her fun. Thus, the liking value of both agents is very high. The dominance value did not change during the interaction.

7. CONCLUSION AND FUTURE WORK

In this paper, we presented an agent able to express a particular social attitude that takes into account spontaneous and strategical processes. Our main contributions are: (1) a formal model of dynamical social relations relying on goals and beliefs, and (2) a social decision making model based on the agent's social relation and social role. We have illustrated our model on a tutor-student use-case. We also noticed that if at least one agent had a low horizon, the relationship would decrease. Indeed, agents with low horizon are not able to consider the affective consequences of their actions, on others as well as on themselves. By analogy to humans, agents lacking Socio-Emotional Intelligence can not maintain a proper relationship. Our next step is to evaluate our model. After generating different tutor/student scenarios, we plan to ask participants whether they recognize the teacher's social attitude through its sequence of actions. Our work still has some limits. For instance, we did not address the following problem: should *Bob* like *Alice* more if he believes that *Alice* did her homework because she was forced to do so (in terms of attribution theory, she is not praiseworthy if she was forced).

8. ACKNOWLEDGEMENT

This work was partially performed within the Labex SMART (ANR-11-LABX-65) supported by French state funds managed by the ANR within the Investissements d'Avenir programme under reference ANR-11-IDEX-0004-02. It has also been partially funded by the French National Research Agency project MOCA (ANR-12-CORD-019).

REFERENCES

[1] K. Anderson, E. André, T. Baur, S. Bernardini, M. Chollet, E. Chryssafidou, I. Damian, C. Ennis, A. Egges, P. Gebhard, et al. The tardis framework: intelligent virtual agents for social coaching in job interviews. In *Advances in Computer Entertainment*, pages 476–491. Springer, 2013.

[2] D. Ballin, M. Gillies, and I. Crabtree. A framework for interpersonal attitude and non-verbal communication in improvisational visual media production. pages 203–210, London, UK, 2004.

[3] S. Baron-Cohen, A. M. Leslie, and U. Frith. Does the autistic child have a 'theory of mind'? *Cognition*, 21(1):37–46, 1985.

[4] T. Bickmore and J. Cassell. Social dialongue with embodied conversational agents. In *Advances in natural multimodal dialogue systems*, pages 23–54. Springer, 2005.

[5] T. W. Bickmore and R. W. Picard. Establishing and maintaining long-term human-computer relationships. *ACM Transactions on Computer-Human Interaction (TOCHI)*, 12(2):293–327, 2005.

[6] Z. Callejas, B. Ravenet, M. Ochs, and C. Pelachaud. A computational model of social attitudes for a virtual recruiter. In *Proceedings of the 2014 international conference on Autonomous agents and multi-agent systems*, pages 93–100. International Foundation for Autonomous Agents and Multiagent Systems, 2014.

[7] C. Castelfranchi, M. Miceli, and A. Cesta. Dependence relations among autonomous agents.

[8] R. B. Cialdini and N. J. Goldstein. Social influence: Compliance and conformity. *Annu. Rev. Psychol.*, 55:591–621, 2004.

[9] R. Emerson. Power-dependence relations. *American Sociological Review*, 27(1):31–41, 1962.

[10] E. Goffman. Presentation of self in everyday life. *American Journal of Sociology*, 55:6–7, 1949.

[11] J. Gratch. Socially situated planning. In *Socially Intelligent Agents*, pages 181–188. Springer, 2002.

[12] N. Guiraud, D. Longin, E. Lorini, S. Pesty, and J. Rivière. The face of emotions: a logical formalization of expressive speech acts. In *The 10th International Conference on Autonomous Agents and Multiagent Systems-Volume 3*, pages 1031–1038. International Foundation for Autonomous Agents and Multiagent Systems, 2011.

[13] F. Heider. *The Psychology of Interpersonal Relations.* Psychology Press, 1958.

[14] H. Hexmoor. A model of absolute autonomy and power: toward group effects. *Connection Science*, 14(4):323–333, 2002.

[15] K. Isbister. *Better Game Characters by Design, A Psychological Approach.* Morgan Kaufmann, 2006.

[16] Z. Kasap, M. Ben Moussa, P. Chaudhuri, and N. Magnenat-Thalmann. Making them remember, emotional virtual characters with memory. *Computer Graphics and Applications, IEEE*, 29(2):20–29, 2009.

[17] S. Kripke. Semantical considerations on modal logic. *Acta Philosophica Fennica*, 16:83–94, 1963.

[18] E. Lorini. A dynamic logic of knowledge, graded beliefs and graded goals and its application to emotion modelling. In *Logic, Rationality, and Interaction*, pages 165–178. Springer, 2011.

[19] S. C. Marsella, D. V. Pynadath, and S. J. Read. Psychsim: Agent-based modeling of social interactions and influence. In *Proceedings of the international conference on cognitive modeling*, pages 243–248. Citeseer, 2004.

[20] L. Moshkina and R. Arkin. On tameing robots. *IEEE International Conference on Systems, Man and Cybernetics*, 4:3949–3959, 2003.

[21] M. Ochs, N. Sabouret, and V. Corruble. Simulation of the dynamics of nonplayer characters' emotions and social relations in games. *Computational Intelligence and AI in Games, IEEE Transactions on*, 1(4):281–297, 2009.

[22] A. Ortony. Value and emotion. *Memories, thoughts, and emotions: Essays in the honor of George Mandler*, pages 337–353, 1991.

[23] C. E. Osgood and P. H. Tannenbaum. The principle of congruity in the prediction of attitude change. *Psychological review*, 62(1):42, 1955.

[24] H. J. Pennings, J. van Tartwijk, T. Wubbels, L. C. Claessens, A. C. van der Want, and M. Brekelmans. Real-time teacher–student interactions: A dynamic systems approach. *Teaching and Teacher Education*, 37:183–193, 2014.

[25] R. Prada and A. Paiva. *New Advances in Virtual Humans*, volume 140, chapter Social Intelligence in Virtual Groups, pages 113–132. Springer, 2008.

[26] R. Prada and A. Paiva. Teaming up humans with autonomous synthetic characters. *Artificial Intelligence*, 173(1):80–103, 2009.

[27] H. Prendinger, S. Descamps, and M. Ishizuka. Scripting affective communication with life-like characters in web-based interaction systems. *Applied Artificial Intelligence: An International Journal*, 16(7-8):519–553, 2002.

[28] H. Prendinger, S. Descamps, and M. Ishizuka. Scripting affective communication with life-like characters in web-based interaction systems. *Applied Artificial Intelligence*, 16(7-8):519–553, 2002.

[29] B. Raven. The bases of power and the power/interaction model of interpersonal influence. *Analyses of Social Issues and Public Policy*, 8(1):1–22, 2008.

[30] T. Rist, M. Schmitt, C. Pelachaud, and M. Bilvi. Towards a simulation of conversations with expressive embodied speakers and listeners. In *Computer Animation and Social Agents, 2003. 16th International Conference on*, pages 5–10. IEEE, 2003.

[31] D. Rousseau and B. Hayes-Roth. A social-psychological model for synthetic actors. In *Proceedings of the second international conference on Autonomous agents*, pages 165–172. ACM, 1998.

[32] P. Sadler and E. Woody. 8 interpersonal complementarity. *Handbook of interpersonal psychology: Theory, research, assessment, and therapeutic interventions*, page 123, 2010.

[33] K. Scherer. What are emotions? and how can they be measured? *Social Science Information*, 2005.

[34] M. N. Shiota, B. Campos, D. Keltner, and M. J. Hertenstein. Positive emotion and the regulation of interpersonal relationships. *The regulation of emotion*, pages 127–155, 2004.

[35] S. Turkle. *Close Engagements with Artificial Companions: Key social, psychological, ethical and design issues*, chapter In Good Company: On the treshold of robotic companions, pages 1–10. John Benjamins, 2010.

[36] M. A. Walker, J. E. Cahn, and S. J. Whittaker. Improvising linguistic style: Social and affective bases for agent personality. In *Proceedings of the first international conference on Autonomous agents*, pages 96–105. ACM, 1997.

[37] T. Wubbels, M.-C. Opdenakker, and P. Den Brok. Let's make things better. In *Interpersonal relationships in education*, pages 225–249. Springer, 2012.

I Remember You! Interaction with Memory for an Empathic Virtual Robotic Tutor

Helen Hastie, Mei Yii Lim, Srini Janarthanam, Amol Deshmukh, Ruth Aylett
School Of Mathematical and Computer Sciences
Heriot-Watt University, Edinburgh
EH14 4AS, UK
{h.hastie, m.y.lim, sc445, a.deshmukh, r.s.Aylett}@hw.ac.uk

Mary Ellen Foster
School of Computing Science, University of Glasgow, Glasgow
G12 8RZ, UK
maryellen.foster@glasgow.ac.uk

Lynne Hall
Dept. Computing, Engineering and Technology, University of Sunderland, Sunderland
SR6 0DD, UK
lynne.hall@sunderland.ac.uk

ABSTRACT

We present a study that investigates the effect of incorporating memory in the interaction for a virtual robotic tutor in terms of helping children achieve a pedagogical goal and the perceived likeability and empathy of the tutor. The domain is a virtual robotic tutor who is guiding and helping learners through a mobile Treasure Hunt exercise that tests their map reading skills. The contribution described in this paper is the discovery that incorporating 'memory' through utterances that recall events from previous interactions significantly increases the learner's ability to perform a pedagogical task. However, the virtual tutor with memory was perceived as less likeable and the instructions given as harder to follow than with a virtual tutor without memory. In addition, there was a significant drop in perceived empathy. This work has a large potential influence in the field of interaction design for agents as one cannot blindly add in human-like features, such as, memory that improve task performance without considering the potential detrimental effects to the perceived empathy and likeability.

Keywords

Human-Robot Interaction; Human-Agent Interaction; Empathy; Memory

1. INTRODUCTION

This paper describes a study with a robotic and migrating virtual tutor who is able to significantly improve task success of participants on a pedagogical task by recalling previously learned geography skills, experiences and interactions. Effective human teachers are able to engage, motivate and empathise with learners. Part of this effective teaching strategy is building up a long term relationship between teacher and learner, knowing the learner's' strengths and weaknesses and adapting interactions and exercises accordingly. As part of the EMOTE project (http://www.emote-project.eu), we aim to build socially intelligent, empathic tutor robots and virtual agents that could play a long-term role in an educational environment. Therefore, some 'human-like' memory is needed to avoid shallowness of personality [1] and improve the effectiveness of the robot and virtual agent as teaching aids.

Personalised learning environments have been shown to have a positive effect on achievement and attendance rates [2]. Memory, as part of shared social interaction, can help provide such a personalised experience. How this memory should be implemented in an agent and its effect on the perceived overall interaction are research questions addressed in this paper.

Appears in: *Proceedings of the 15th International Conference on Autonomous Agents and Multiagent Systems (AAMAS 2016), J. Thangarajah, K. Tuyls, C. Jonker, S. Marsella (eds.), May 9–13, 2016, Singapore.*

1.1 Hypotheses

The hypotheses we are testing are fourfold where *with-memory* is the ability of the virtual tutor to remember and mention previously discussed and practised skills and tools.

H1 (TaskSuccess): Participants who interact with the agent with-memory will have higher task *performance* in a pedagogical task than participants who interact with the agent without-memory.

H2 (Likeability): The agent with-memory will be rated higher in terms of general *likeability* than the agent without-memory.

H3 (Empathy): The agent with-memory will be rated more *empathic* than the agent without-memory.

H4 (Empathy Shift): The agent with-memory will cause a *shift* in perceived empathy.

In this paper, we show we can accept H1 and H4 but must reject H2 and H3. This work has a large potential influence in the field of human-agent interaction as it shows that one cannot blindly add in personality features that improve task performance without thinking about the potential detrimental effects to the perceived character of the virtual tutor agent. This is particularly relevant when dealing with vulnerable users such as the young and elderly and may put users off interacting with the system in the long term.

In the remainder of the paper, we will examine previous related work (Section 2); discuss the methodology and experimental set-up and introduce the task (Section 3); we describe both the empathic robot and the touch table map application (Section 4); we then give an overview of the virtual robotic tutor and its interaction behaviour on a mobile Treasure Hunt application (Section 5); results are given in Section 6 and finally we conclude discussing the impact of including memory in the interaction design of both robots and virtual agents for learning environments (Section 7).

2. RELATED WORK

Work on declarative memory (both episodic and semantic) for robots and agents has concerned itself with improving planning [3], story telling [4] or improving user experience in domains such as the service domain by remembering user preferences [5]. There is less work with respect to memory for human-robot and human-agent interaction for educational domains and for older children. In this section, we discuss related work including the use of memory for migrating agents and 'social robots', focusing on educational settings.

Memory has been considered for some time as a vital part of successfully migrating agents [6, 7]. [7] showed that a migrating agent that remembers events lived in other embodiments contributes to the user's perception of a consistent identity and showed that those with memory are perceived as more competent. We are not exploring here whether the migrated agent is perceived as the same identity, rather whether using memory adds to the effectiveness of the learning environment or not. [8] shows that there is a trend for people to prefer a companion with selective memory (stores only significant information) as compared to one with absolute memory (stores everything). Similarly, we investigate here the preferences of users towards using declarative memory or not, in an educational setting.

Previous studies on robotic companions in real-world classroom environments [9] have shown that robotic platforms are promising tools for experimental learning. A similar application but with a virtual tutor is described in [10] and [11], where the authors investigated affective vs non-affective feedback. In this study, it was found that the use of a virtual tutor increased the perceived difficulty of the pedagogical task, while the affective virtual tutor's feedback, in particular, made the questions seem more difficult to answer than the non-affective virtual tutor.

One can posit that discussing shared experiences, i.e. having memory, is a 'social behaviour'. How to incorporate social behaviour into robots and virtual agents has been much studied, in particular, for systems aimed at infants (e.g. aged 1.5-2 years of age [12]). There has been less work, however, on older children in learning environments. In some recent work, [13] found that, whilst the presence of a robot can improve learning gain for children aged 7 or 8, this improvement is lost when the robot is 'social', using affective responses, gestures and personalisation. The authors speculate that the affective robot may be a distraction and is viewed more as a teacher in the non-social case, and warn that applying social behaviour to a robot in a tutoring context may have negative effects. Here, we corroborate the essence of their argument that the assumption of adding human-like characteristics, such as affect and memory should not be implicit, rather an in-depth study of how exactly these types of behaviours affect the learning environment is needed. Work described here thus contributes to this much needed study.

As [14] states, older children are less likely to view robots and virtual agents as social actors and therefore would require more complex interactions and social behaviours including memory. However, with this higher level of sophistication comes a greater expectation of capability and if the agent falls short of this then negative feelings may result towards the agent. This may be the case in the study described here with children aged 11-12, where the introduction of a 'social' robot agent (i.e. one that remembers) adversely affects the perceived ease of an educational task and results in a less likeable and empathic agent. As a consequence, this may affect morale and the overall learner experience. In particular, it clearly demonstrates that adding memory to a conversational agent is not a straightforward modification: the agent's behaviour may have an unanticipated, negative effect on the user experience.

3. METHODOLOGY

To address the above mentioned hypotheses, we assigned participants to two groups. One group was in the with-memory condition and the second group was in the without-memory condition. The task was in two stages. The first stage, which was the same for both groups, involved doing a short map-based pedagogical exercise on a touch-table with an empathic real-world robot called Susie in the form of an EMYS robot [15] (see Figure 1). In the second stage, Susie was 'teleported' onto a mobile application on a tablet (see Figure 4). For the second stage, the participants went immediately outdoors to perform a real world treasure hunting exercise using the mobile application with the virtual robotic tutor either with or without-memory. During the first stage, the real-world robot is empathic in that it adapts to the user affective state and the current game state. This empathic behaviour is described in further detail below. Post-migration, the virtual robotic tutor responds according to whether the participants answer each question correctly. It does not employ the same empathic strategies as the physical robot in either conditions due to the fact that it is not practically possible to have the relevant sensors during this mobile task.

36 school pupils aged between 11-12 years old participated in this study. Participants were randomly distributed between conditions whilst maintaining a gender balance between groups, however, the majority of participants were boys with 27 boys and 9 girls. The school has a policy for these types of tasks to be done in pairs and therefore the participants were allocated into pairs in consultation with the teacher, maintaining similar overall levels of abilities and compatibility within each pairing. The individuals were told to take it in turns answering questions on the touch table and on the tablet. Participants filled-out individual questionnaires after interacting with the robot and then again after completing the Treasure Hunt.

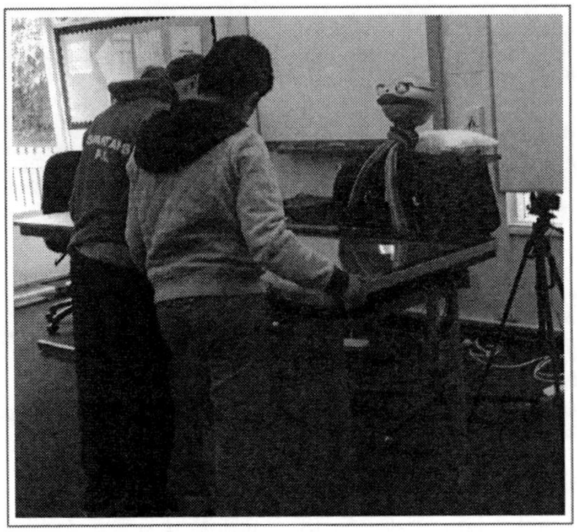

Figure 1: Two participants interacting with the physical robot and the touch table

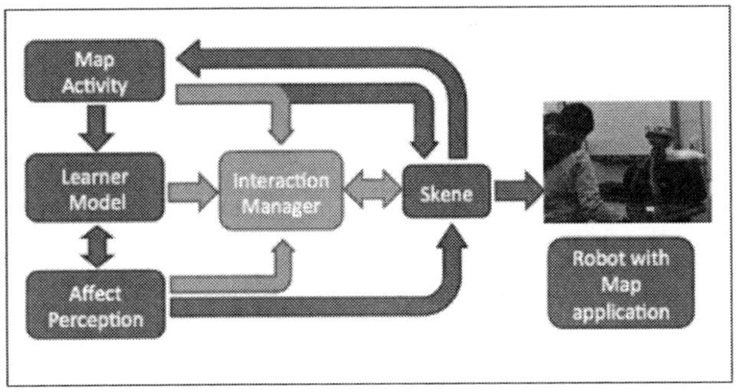

Figure 2: The Emote Architecture configuration for empathic interaction using the touch table map reading application and the physical robot

4. THE EMPATHIC ROBOT AND THE TOUCH TABLE APPLICATION

Empathy is the psychological processes that make a person feel more congruent with another's circumstances than with his own [16]. In order to embed empathy in learning environments, the tutor needs to be able to perceive, model and reason about the affective states experienced by learners as well as respond emotionally to the situation. As a result, recent research on computer-based learning systems attempts to endow artificial tutors with the capability to perceive the learner's emotional states and incorporate these into pedagogical strategies [17].

Analogously, during the interaction the robotic Susie was empathic, that is, it adapts to the learner's emotional state [18], taking into consideration the learner state and the emotional state of the participant. Figure 2 shows the modules configured for this empathic robotic interaction environment.

The Learner Model functions by checking a learner's answers for correctness and the time to complete and provides an indication of the current skill levels of the learner. The model for the following mapping skills application tracks the skills or competencies: compass reading, map symbol knowledge, and distance measuring. The Perception module takes sensor data from a vision-based facial expression understanding technology (OKAO) [19], which processes information about facial expression into valence/arousal dimensions for affect, giving positive, neutral and negative outputs. The affective state is also inferred by considering the progress of the user in the current tasks, for example many errors may suggest a negative affective state.

These module outputs are used by the Interaction Manager (IM) module, which controls dialogue and other interaction modalities for the robotic tutor at a high level of abstraction [20, 21]. It provides necessary feedback and other helpful pedagogical tactics as the participants proceed through the task. This is the module that deals with the empathic response in which the affective state of the user impacts the actions of the tutor. In consultation with teachers and through examination of human-human pedagogical interactions in the same map reading domain, a set of empathic behaviours including feedback were defined and outlined here.

- High arousal and negative valence suggest a stressed and unhappy user: IM increases pedagogical support;
- Low arousal and negative valence indicate a bored or disengaged user: IM tries to engage and motivate;
- High arousal and positive valence indicate the user is happy and engaged: IM gives less scaffolding support; and
- Low arousal and positive valence indicate a focused user: IM gives less scaffolding support.

Finally, the Skene module translates IM actions into movement of the robot head and eyes, for example, the robotic tutor would look at the relevant point on the map. It also supports semi-automated gaze behaviour, such as gaze at an active speaker or joint gaze at an object of interest [22].

Figure 1 shows a pair of participants interacting with Susie and the touch table application. This interaction was limited to 5 minutes and involved the participants using a map application. The robot presented them with a series of tasks where basic skills relating to the use of compass directions, finding distances, and recognising and using map symbols were involved. The tools used and the skill levels of the pair as they interact are logged. An example of one step in the map reading task would be to find a museum 500 metres north of the railway station.

5. THE MOBILE TREASURE HUNT APPLICATION

After the robot interaction activity, the participants are shown the robot 'teleporting' onto a tablet application (see Figure 4) where Susie emulates going to sleep and the virtual robotic tutor on the application 'wakes up', thus following the 'soul-shell' approach [23]. It has been shown in previous studies, as discussed above, that users perceive a single agent across multiple embodiments if the personality of the agent is consistently maintained [24, 25, 26, 27]. Here, the virtual robot's voice and appearance are the same as the physical robot and, therefore, we believe that the participants perceived Susie to be the same character across embodiments.

Information about the pair's performance is also migrated including the level of skill for distance measuring, cardinal directions and their knowledge of ordnance survey symbols.

Figure 3: **Two participants doing a map reading exercise and interacting with the virtual tutor, Susie, on a tablet**

Whether they used any of the tools (namely map key, distance tool and compass) is also transferred to the tablet.

This real-world Treasure Hunt activity, which has been carried out at a local school for several years using paper, requires the participants to carry out a series of navigation steps in the real world, following a predetermined route on a map (see Figure 3). Each navigation step first requires the participants to walk a few yards while making use of their map-reading skills, and then to answer a series of questions regarding their new location; for example, they might be asked to identify the colour of a door of a house in a specific grid reference. The application includes the virtual Susie head, which presents the navigation instructions, poses the questions, and gives feedback on the correctness of the participants' answers (see Figure 4 for a screenshot of the application).

There are two versions of this application for the two conditions. For the with-memory condition, virtual Susie makes comments with respect to the previous interaction. Example utterances are given here for the with-memory condition: 'Do you remember, we used the compass before on the table to determine which direction you are heading. We can use it again now.' or 'We didn't try using the compass before on the table, but why don't you make use of it now?' and for the without-memory condition 'You can try using the compass to determine which direction you are heading'. The length of the system utterances between conditions and the lexicon used were balanced as much as possible, with the with-memory condition being only slightly longer but not significantly so by an unpaired t-test (mean 10.6 words per utterance for with-memory, compared to 10.1 for without-memory).

6. RESULTS AND ANALYSIS

To measure the participants' objective success in the pedagogical task, the following measures were collected:

- **TaskSuccess**: the number of questions answered correctly on the tablet Treasure Hunt;

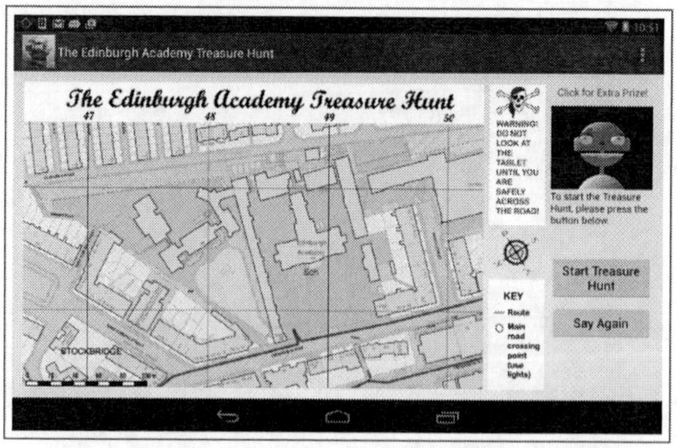

Figure 4: The Android application for the Treasure Hunt with the virtual robotic tutor

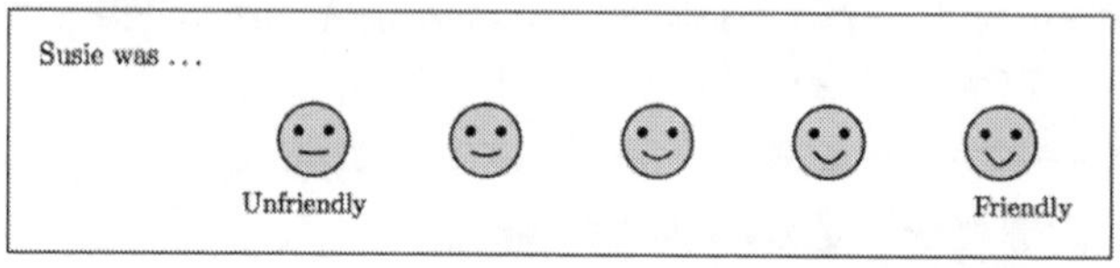

Figure 5: The smileyometer for the questionnaire

- **WaypointScore**: the total number of waypoints (11) minus the number of diversions away from the route as calculated using the GPS trace. See Figure 6 for the route and an example GPS trace; and
- **TimeonTask**: the time from starting the real-world Treasure Hunt with the tablet to the final waypoint

The participants' subjective experience was measured through a three-part questionnaire, answered on an individual basis:

- Four questions regarding the participants' opinion of the robotic Susie after interacting with the robot but before the real-world Treasure Hunt;
- Four questions regarding the real-world Treasure Hunt itself after completion of the Treasure Hunt; and
- Ten questions addressing the participants' opinion of the virtual robotic tutor, Susie, asked of the participants after the real-world Treasure Hunt (includes the initial 4 questions repeated).

The items from the first and last part of the questionnaire were taken and modified for children from the Godspeed questionnaire series [28], which is designed to be a standard user measurement tool for human-robot interaction. The items were drawn primarily from the 'likeability' portion of the questionnaire and were rephrased to make them clear for the target age group. In addition, two questions were targeted at determining whether Susie was deemed empathic ('I would describe Susie as soft-hearted' and 'Sometimes Susie felt sorry for me when I was having problems'). These were modified and adapted from the empathy questionnaire devised and reported in [29]. Finally, a question to determine whether Susie seemed to remember things about the participants was included in the final questionnaire.

All questions were presented using a five-point Smileyometer (see Figure 5), which has been shown to be an effective instrument for evaluating child-computer interactions

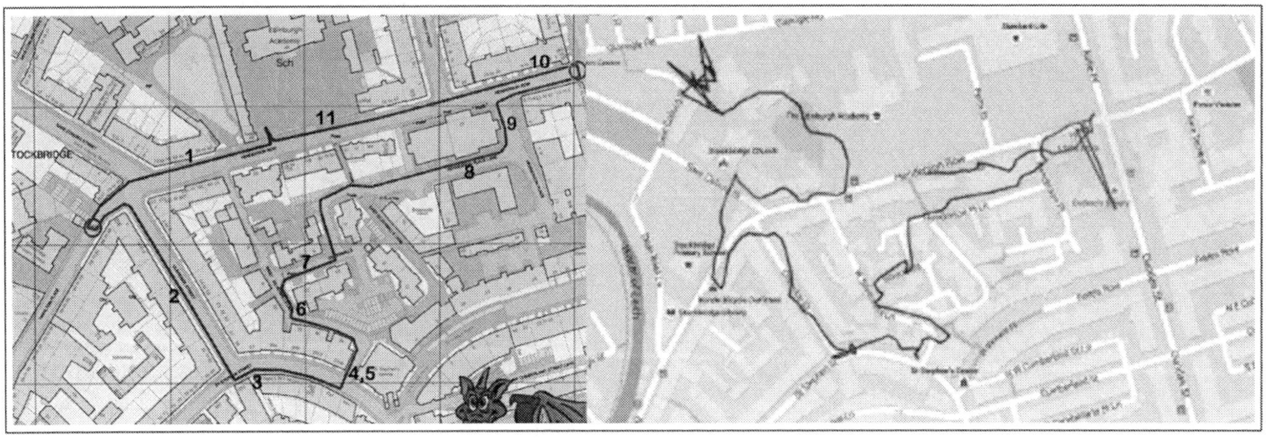

Figure 6: The intended route of the Treasure Hunt on the left hand side and an example route taken by one pair of participants as logged by the GPS trace on the right hand side with a WaypointScore of 9 out of 11. The yellow areas highlight the two diversions from the Treasure Hunt route

[30]. Below, we list the exact wording of the questions and a keyphrase for the questions used in this paper (but not given on the questionnaire). The activity was performed in pairs, however the questionnaires were filled out individually.

Although the objective measures, such as task success would be the same for both individuals in the pair, the interaction may have been perceived differently. For example, the subjects may vary in academic ability and confidence and this may affect their perception of the tutor. Indeed, the Kappa coefficient for agreement of the individuals within the pair does vary, with half the groups mostly agreeing with respect to their subjective ratings from the questionnaires (Kappa coefficient of $\geq$0.5) and roughly half the groups disagreeing. Therefore, the following results analysis assumes that each participant is a datapoint with 36 datapoints.

Questions about Susie BEFORE the real-world Treasure Hunt outside the school

1. **SusieFriendliness:** Susie was Unfriendly...Friendly
2. **SusieLikeability**: I liked Susie...Not at all...A lot
3. **SusieUnderstandability**: Susie was...Hard to understand...
   Easy to understand
4. **SusieSoftheartedness**: I would describe Susie as softhearted...No, I disagree...Yes, I agree

Questions about the real-world Treasure Hunt using the tablet

5. **Fun**: The Treasure Hunt was...No fun at all...Lots of fun
6. **InstructionEase**: The instructions were...Hard to follow...Easy to follow
7. **QuestionEase**: The questions were...Hard to answer...Easy to answer
8. **Groupwork**: I think my group did...Very badly...Very well

Questions about Susie DURING the real-world Treasure Hunt

9. **SusieFriendliness:** Susie was Unfriendly...Friendly
10. **SusieLikeability**: I liked Susie...Not at all...A lot
11. **SusieRememberedMe**: Susie remembered things about me...No, I disagree...Yes, I agree
12. **SusieUnderstandability**:Susie was...Hard to understand...Easy to understand
13. **SusieKindness**: Susie was...Unkind...Kind
14. **SusiePleasantness**: Susie was...Unpleasant...Pleasant
15. **SusieAwfulness**: Susie was...Awful...Nice
16. **SusieHelpfulness**: Susie was...Not helpful...Helpful
17. **SusieSoftheartedness**: I would describe Susie as softhearted...No, I disagree...Yes, I agree
18. **SusieSorryforme**: Sometimes Susie felt sorry for me when I was having problems...No, I disagree...Yes, I agree

6.1 Task Success Results

With regards H1 (TaskSuccess), we can see from Table 1, in general the with-memory condition results in higher TaskSuccess and WaypointScore, significantly so for the latter ($t(34) = 2.63$, $p<0.05$, unpaired t-test) so we can accept H1. In general, the task took slightly longer using the system with memory, but not significantly so.

6.2 Likeability and Empathy Results

For the subjective scores across all of the 14 questions, the without-memory condition was rated higher. This difference was significant for the following questions: InstructionEase, SusieLikeability and SusieRememberedMe ($p<0.05$, unpaired Mann-Whitney U test). Figures 7 and 8 and Table 2 give results for a subset of the questions showing these significant differences. The fact that the ratings for SusieRememberedMe were actually significantly lower for the with-memory condition is counter-intuitive and it was evident by

Table 1: Objective measures (standard deviation in brackets), where * indicates significance p< 0.05 by a unpaired t-test

	TaskSuccess (%)	WaypointScore (out of 11)	TimeOnTask (minutes)
With Memory	88.2(6.4)	**9.89(0.58)***	37.33(8.43)
Without Memory	83.3(11)	9.22(1.06)	34.78(5.98)

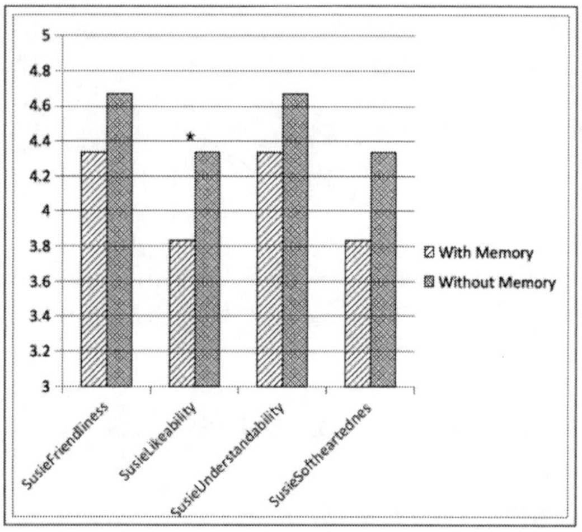

Figure 7: Graph comparing mean rating on the y-axis for a sub-set of responses for the two conditions. * indicates p< 0.05, unpaired Mann-Whitney U test

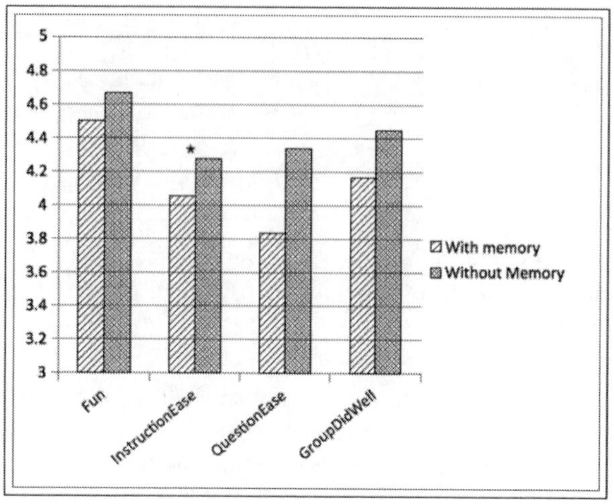

Figure 8: Graph comparing the mean rating responses on the y-axis to questions asking about the real-world Treasure Hunt activity. * indicates p< 0.05, unpaired Mann-Whitney U test

interacting with the participants post-experiment that they did not completely understand the question. In fact, some of the participants were referring to the robotic Susie and the fact that the robotic Susie remembered their names rather than the memory of the virtual Susie on the tablet. Therefore, one should not read into this result too much and we will not refer to this measure going forward.

With regards task ease, we can see from Figure 8, the without-memory condition has been rated higher, significantly so for InstructionEase. One reason for this may be the fact that for the with-memory condition, we are asking them to recall facts and memories and therefore the cognitive load may be higher than the without-memory condition.

Recall H3 (Empathy) is "The tutor with-memory will be rated more *empathic* than a tutor without-memory." There are no significant differences between the ratings of SusieSofthearted between the conditions after the real-world Treasure Hunt application (see Table 2), therefore, we have no evidence to accept the H3 hypothesis.

The second empathy question "SusieSorryforme: Sometimes Susie felt sorry for me when I was having problems" was answered once after the entire interaction and rated generally lower than the other questions (mean with-memory is 1.83; mean without-memory is 2.44). There was no significant differences between the conditions. On reflection, this question would be more suited to a long-term study where more problems might arise, which the empathic robotic tutor could help the participants solve. Here, it was observed through qualitative feedback that if the participant did not have any problems then they rated low on the scale for this question which was not the opinion the question was intending to elicit.

With regards H4 (Empathy Shift) "The tutor with-memory will cause a shift in perceived empathy", we are testing whether there is any shift in opinion with regards empathy after the interaction with the virtual robotic tutor. Recall the physical robot, Susie, is designed to be empathic and to test this, we asked the subjects a number of questions immediately after interacting with the robot. The level of empathy is reflected in the subjective scores for questions such as SusieSofthearted where, across all participants (i.e. both conditions), the mean rating is 4.64 out of 5 (with mode and median 5). It is interesting to see if this level of empathy holds when the robot is migrated to a virtual robotic tutor. In fact, the virtual tutor with-memory had a significant *drop in rating* (Wilcoxon Signed-Rank Test, Z=-2.73, p=0.003) for this question post-Treasure Hunt whereas the virtual tutor without-memory did not see a drop (see Figure 9 and Table 3). The inclusion of memory may have a compounded effect on the perception of the empathic tutor and project the tutor as a hard task master, resulting in lower post-experiment ratings. We can, therefore, reject the null hypothesis for H4, having observed a significant, negative effect a tutor with memory has on the perceived empathy of the tutor.

7. DISCUSSION AND FUTURE WORK

As expected the use of memory significantly improved the TaskSuccess of participants so we can therefore accept the hypothesis H1. The virtual robot tutor that reminded them of the types of skills that they had learned and the tools they had previously used had a positive effect on the participants in terms of performing the task correctly and getting around the route with fewer diversions.

Table 2: **Mean/mode/median rating scores on a 5 point Smileyometer scale for a subset of the questions comparing the answers between the two memory conditions after the real-world Treasure Hunt. * indicates a significant difference (p<0.05 for an unpaired Mann-Whitney U test).**

	SusieFriendliness	SusieLikeability	SusieUnderstandability	SusieSoftheartedness
`With Memory`	4.33/5/4.5	3.83/4/4	4.33/5/4	3.83/4/4
`Without Memory`	4.67/5/5	**4.33/4/4***	4.67/5/5	4.33/5/4.5

Table 3: Mean/mode/median rating scores on a 5 point Smileyometer scale for the first 4 questions comparing the answers between the two conditions after the interaction with the empathic robot comparing *before* and *after* the real-world Treasure Hunt. * indicates a significant difference comparing consistency of answers for the same question before and after the Treasure Hunt (p<0.01 for Wilcoxon Signed-Rank test)

	SusieFriendliness	SusieLikeability	SusieUnderstandability	SusieSoftheartedness
`Before With Memory`	4.5/5/5	4.11/4/4	3.94/4/4	**4.5/5/5***
`After With Memory`	4.33/5/4.5	3.83/4/4	4.33/5/4	3.83/4/4
`Before Without Memory`	4.78/5/5	4.33/5/4	4.61/5/5	4.67/5/5
`After Without Memory`	4.67/5/5	4.33/4/4	4.67/5/5	4.33/5/4.5

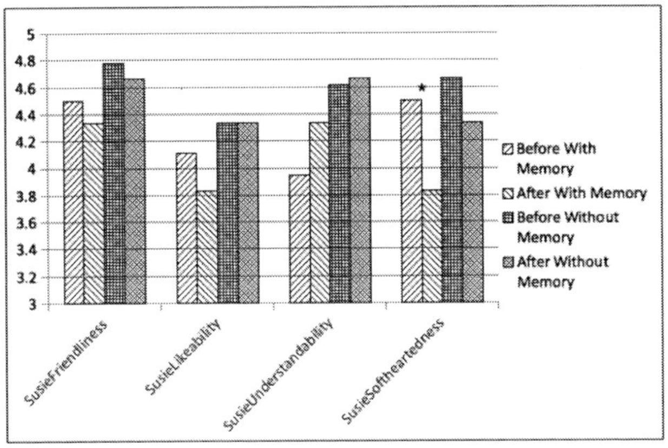

Figure 9: Graph comparing mean rating responses on the y-axis for the same questions before and after the Treasure Hunt. * indicates a significant difference of ratings before/after (p< 0.05 paired Mann-Whitney U test)

Recall hypotheses H2, H3 and H4 are around testing whether memory has a positive effect on general likeability of the tutor (H2) and whether the tutor is deemed as empathic (H3) and if there is any change in perceived empathy (H4). For H2 (Likeability), there is evidence that the participants rated the likeability of using the virtual tutor with-memory significantly lower than the virtual tutor without-memory. As with the study reported in [8] where the users' disprefer absolute memory versus selective memory, it may be that the virtual robotic tutor is almost reminding them too much of what they have done wrong and therefore subjective measures are lower for the memory condition.

With regards empathy (H3 and H4). There is no significant difference between the ratings of the robot between the groups before the participants encounter the virtual tutor. This is to be expected as there is no difference in this part of the experiment across conditions. Post experiment, again there is no evidence of differences between the two conditions, we therefore have to accept the null hypothesis for H3 indicating that adding memory does not increase the level of empathy significantly.

On the other hand, there was a significant drop in the ratings for how 'softhearted' Susie was after interacting with the with-memory agent. As discussed above, it may be that the robot, once perceived as empathic, after the real-world Treasure Hunt was felt to be more of a hard task master, constantly reminding them of skills and the tools that they should know about from the previous interaction, rather than letting them enjoy the experience of being on a Treasure Hunt outside of school.

In summary, we have observed here that there are positive aspects to adding memory in terms of aiding the learners in completing a task. However, the positive effect of empathy observed with the physical robot was lost when the robot migrated to a virtual agent with memory condition. In addition, the with-memory agent was perceived as less likeable and their instructions harder to follow. It is, therefore, clear that one cannot simply add memory to an agent without the possibility of adverse affects in terms of how the agent is perceived to the user. Recent studies have corroborated the idea that by incorporating traits of human interaction such as being social [13] or having memory as discussed here, can have both positive and negative effects on the interaction in learning environments and therefore caution must be taken when developing educational robots with such 'human-like' features.

Our contribution lies in the study of memory as a teaching tool for virtual and robotic tutors, its efficacy and its potential effect on the perceived character of the physical and virtual robot. In the context of the larger research project—which has the overall goal of developing empathic robot tutors—future work includes applying the findings from this study to the other robotic and virtual tutors being developed in the project, taking care to ensure that any affective feedback from the agents has the intended effect on the overall pedagogical and social goals of the interaction.

8. ACKNOWLEDGMENTS

This work was supported by the EC, funded by the FP7 ICT-317923 project EMOTE. The authors are solely responsible for the content of this publication. It does not represent the opinion of the EC, and the EC is not responsible for any use that might be made of data appearing therein.

REFERENCES

[1] K. Dautenhahn, "The art of designing socially intelligent agents - science, fiction and the human in the loop," *Applied Artificial Intelligence Journal, Special Issue on Socially Intelligent Agents*, vol. 12, pp. 12–7, 1998.

[2] Hanover Research, "Best practices in personalized learning environments (Grades 4-9)," 2012. [Online]. Available: http://www.hanoverresearch.com/media/Best-Practices-in-PersonalizedLearning-Environments.pdf

[3] D. Stachowicz and G. Kruijff, "Episodic-like memory for cognitive robots," *Autonomous Mental Development, IEEE Transactions on*, vol. 4, no. 1, pp. 1–16, March 2012.

[4] W. C. Ho, J. a. Dias, R. Figueiredo, and A. Paiva, "Agents that remember can tell stories: Integrating autobiographic memory into emotional agents," in *Proceedings of the 6th International Joint Conference on Autonomous Agents and Multiagent Systems*, ser. AAMAS '07. New York, NY, USA: ACM, 2007, pp. 10:1–10:3.

[5] W. Ho, K. Dautenhahn, M. Lim, and K. Du Casse, *Modelling human memory in robotic companions for personalisation and long-term adaptation in HRI*, ser. Frontiers in Artificial Intelligence and Applications. IOS Press, 2010, pp. 64–71.

[6] M. Lim, R. Aylett, W. Ho, S. Enz, and P. Vargas, "A socially-aware memory for companion agents," in *Intelligent Virtual Agents*, ser. Lecture Notes in Computer Science, Z. Ruttkay, M. Kipp, A. Nijholt, and H. H. Vilhjálmsson, Eds. Springer Berlin Heidelberg, 2009, vol. 5773, pp. 20–26.

[7] R. Aylett, M. Kriegel, I. Wallace, E. M. Segura, J. Mercurio, and S. Nylander, "Memory and the design of migrating virtual agents," in *Proceedings of AAMAS*, 2013, pp. 1311–1312.

[8] M. Y. Lim, R. Aylett, P. Vargas, S. Enz, and W. C. Ho, "Forgetting through generalisation: a companion with selective memory." in *Proceedings of AAMAS*, 2011, pp. 1119–1120.

[9] I. Leite, G. Castellano, A. Pereira, C. Martinho, and A. Paiva, "Modelling empathic behaviour in a robotic game companion for children: An ethnographic study in real-world settings," in *Proceedings of HRI 2012*, 2012, pp. 367–374.

[10] M. E. Foster, A. Deshmukh, S. Janarthanam, M. Y. Lim, H. Hastie, and R. Aylett, "Influencing the learning experience through affective agent feedback in a real-world treasure hunt," in *Proceedings of AAMAS*, 2015, pp. 1711–1712.

[11] M. E. Foster, M. Y. Lim, A. Deshmukh, S. Janarthanam, H. Hastie, and R. Aylett, "Affective feedback for a virtual robot in a real-world treasure hunt," in *Proceedings of the 2014 Workshop on Multimodal, Multi-Party, Real-World Human-Robot Interaction*, ser. MMRWHRI '14. New York, NY, USA: ACM, 2014, pp. 31–32.

[12] F. Tanaka, A. Cicourel, and J. Movellan, "Socialization between toddlers and robots at an early childhood education center," *PNAS*, vol. 104(46), 2007.

[13] J. Kennedy, P. Baxter, and T. Belpaeme, "The robot who tried too hard: Social behaviour of a robot tutor can negatively affect child learning," in *Proceedings of the Tenth Annual ACM/IEEE International Conference on Human-Robot Interaction*, 2015, pp. 67–74.

[14] R. Ros, M. Nalin, R. Wood, P. Baxter, R. Looije, Y. Demiris, T. Belpaeme, A. Giusti, and C. Pozzi, "Child-robot interaction in the wild: Advice to the aspiring experimenter," in *Proceedings of the 13th International Conference on Multimodal Interfaces*, ser. ICMI '11. New York, NY, USA: ACM, 2011, pp. 335–342.

[15] J. Kedzierski, R. Muszynski, C. Zoll, A. Oleksy, and M. Frontkiewicz, "Emys-emotive head of a social robot," *International Journal of Social Robotics*, vol. 5, no. 2, pp. 237–249, 2013.

[16] M. Hoffman, *Empathy and moral development: Implications for caring and justice.* Cambridge University Press, 2001.

[17] W. Burleson, "Affective learning companions: Strategies for empathetic agents with real-time multimodal affective sensing to foster meta-cognitive and meta-affective approaches to learning, motivation, and perseverance," Ph.D. dissertation, Massachusetts Institute of Technology, Massachusetts, 2006.

[18] A. Deshmukh, A. Jones, S. Janarthanam, H. Hastie, T. Ribeiro, R. Aylett, A. Paiva, G. Castellano, M. Ellen Foster, L. J. Corrigan *et al.*, "An empathic robotic tutor in a map application," in *Proceedings of AAMAS*, 2015, pp. 1923–1924.

[19] S. Lao and M. Kawade, "Vision-based face understanding technologies and their applications," in *Advances in Biometric Person Authentication.* Springer, 2005, pp. 339–348.

[20] S. Janarthanam, H. Hastie, A. Deshmukh, R. Aylett, and M. E. Foster, "A reusable interaction management module: Use case for empathic robotic tutoring," in *Proceedings of SemDial*, 2015.

[21] S. Janarthanam, H. Hastie, A. Deshmukh, and R. Aylett, "Towards a serious game playing empathic robotic tutorial dialogue system," in *Proceedings of the 2014 ACM/IEEE International Conference on Human-robot Interaction*, ser. HRI '14. New York, NY, USA: ACM, 2014, pp. 180–181.

[22] T. Ribeiro and A. Paiva, "Make way for the robot animators! bringing professional animators and AI programmers together in the quest for the illusion of life in robotic characters," in *AAAI Fall Symposium Series*, 2014.

[23] P. F. Gomes, E. M. Segura, H. Cramer, T. Paiva, A. Paiva, and L. E. Holmquist, "Vipleo and phypleo: Artificial pet with two embodiments," in *The Proceedings of The 8th International Conference on Advances in Computer Entertainment Technology (ACE).* Lisbon, Portugal: ACM, November 2011.

[24] M. Kriegel, R. Aylett, P. Cuba, M. Vala, and A. Paiva, "Robots meet ivas: A mind-body interface for migrating artificial intelligent agents," in *Intelligent Virtual Agents - 11th International Conference IVA 2011*, ser. Lecture Notes in Computer Science, H. H. Vilhjálmsson, S. Kopp, S. Marsella, and K. R.

Thórisson, Eds., vol. 6895. Eindhoven, The Netherlands: Springer Berlin / Heidelberg, September 2011, pp. 282–295.

[25] K. Koay, D. Syrdal, K. Dautenhahn, K. Arent, L. Malek, and B. Kreczmer, "Companion migration-initial participants' feedback from a video-based prototyping study," in *Mixed Reality and Human-Robot Interaction*, ser. Intelligent Systems, Control and Automation: Science and Engineering, X. Wang, Ed. Springer Netherlands, 2011, vol. 1010, pp. 133–151.

[26] M. Imai, T. Ono, and T. Etani, "Agent migration: communications between a human and robot," in *Systems, Man, and Cybernetics, 1999. IEEE SMC '99 Conference Proceedings. 1999 IEEE International Conference on*, vol. 4, 1999, pp. 1044–1048 vol.4.

[27] K. Ogawa and T. Ono, "Ubiquitous cognition: mobile environment achieved by migratable agent," in *Proceedings of the 7th international conference on Human computer interaction with mobile devices & services.* ACM, 2005, pp. 337–338.

[28] C. Bartneck, D. Kulić, E. Croft, and S. Zoghbi, "Measurement instruments for the anthropomorphism, animacy, likeability, perceived intelligence, and perceived safety of robots," *International Journal of Social Robotics*, vol. 1, pp. 71–81, 2009.

[29] M. H. Davis, "Measuring individual differences in empathy: Evidence for a multidimensional approach," *Journal of Personality and Social Psychology*, vol. 44, pp. 113–126, 1983.

[30] J. Read and S. Macfarlane, "Endurability, engagement and expectations: Measuring children's fun," *Interaction Design and Children*, pp. 1–23, 2002.

Goal Inference Improves Objective and Perceived Performance in Human-Robot Collaboration*

Chang Liu †§
changliu@berkeley.edu

Jessica B. Hamrick †‡
jhamrick@berkeley.edu

Jaime F. Fisac †°
jfisac@berkeley.edu

Anca D. Dragan °
anca@berkeley.edu

J. Karl Hedrick §
khedrick@me.berkeley.edu

S. Shankar Sastry °
sastry@eecs.berkeley.edu

Thomas L. Griffiths ‡
tom_griffiths@berkeley.edu

§ Department of Mechanical Engineering
‡ Department of Psychology
° Department of Electrical Engineering and Computer Sciences
University of California, Berkeley
Berkeley, California, 94720

ABSTRACT

The study of human-robot interaction is fundamental to the design and use of robotics in real-world applications. Robots will need to predict and adapt to the actions of human collaborators in order to achieve good performance and improve safety and end-user adoption. This paper evaluates a human-robot collaboration scheme that combines the task allocation and motion levels of reasoning: the robotic agent uses Bayesian inference to predict the next goal of its human partner from his or her ongoing motion, and re-plans its own actions in real time. This anticipative adaptation is desirable in many practical scenarios, where humans are unable or unwilling to take on the cognitive overhead required to explicitly communicate their intent to the robot. A behavioral experiment indicates that the combination of goal inference and dynamic task planning significantly improves both objective and perceived performance of the human-robot team. Participants were highly sensitive to the differences between robot behaviors, preferring to work with a robot that adapted to their actions over one that did not.

Keywords

Human-Agent Interaction, Teamwork, Intention Inference, Collaborative Task Allocation

1. INTRODUCTION

Once confined to controlled environments devoid of human individuals, robots today are being pushed into our homes and workplaces by unfolding advances in autonomy. From sharing workcells [20], to assisting older adults [2, 19, 30], to helping in surveillance [13] and search and rescue [11, 27], robots need to operate in human environments, both with and around people.

While autonomous systems are becoming less reliant on human oversight, it is often still desirable for robots to collaborate with human partners in a peer-to-peer structure [5, 10, 26]. In many scenarios, robots and humans can fill

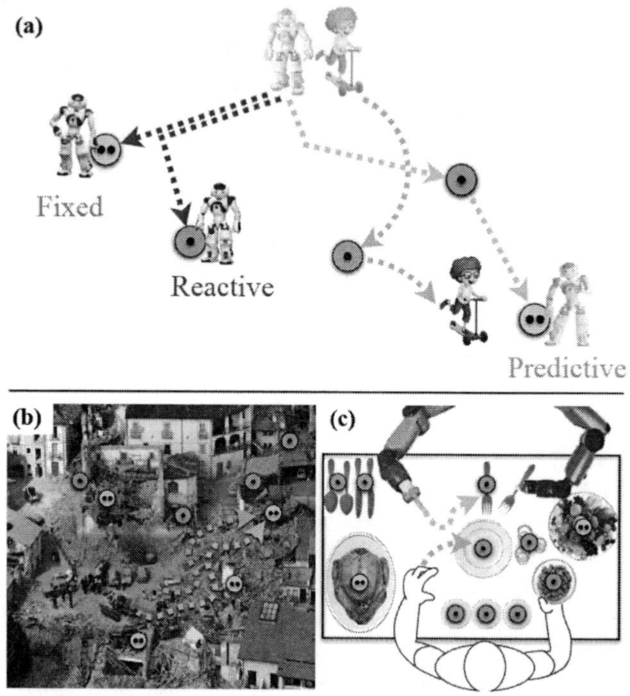

Figure 1: (a) Human avatar and three types of robot avatar used in the experiment. Circles with a single dot represent tasks that can be completed by any agent (either human or robot) and circles with two dots require simultaneous collaboration of both agents. (b) Illustration of a search-and-rescue collaboration scenario. (c) Illustration of a collaborative table setting scenario.

†These authors contributed equally to this paper.
*This work is supported by ONR under the Embedded Humans MURI (N00014-13-1-0341).

Appears in: *Proceedings of the 15th International Conference on Autonomous Agents and Multiagent Systems (AAMAS 2016), J. Thangarajah, K. Tuyls, C. Jonker, S. Marsella (eds.), May 9–13, 2016, Singapore.*

complementary roles in completing a shared task, possibly by completing different sub-goals in a coordinated fashion (Fig. 1a). For example, in a search-and-rescue mission (Fig. 1b), human first responders might load injured persons onto an autonomous vehicle, which would then transport the victims to a medical unit. In a number of manipulation scenarios, humans and robots can take advantage of their different aptitudes and capabilities in perception, planning and actuation to boost performance and achieve better results.

Collaboration hinges on coordination and the ability to infer each other's intentions and adapt [28, 29]. There is an abundant history of failure cases in human-automation systems due to coordination errors and miscommunication between human and autonomous agents [22, 24, 25]. Such failures often result from an inability of autonomous systems to properly anticipate the needs and actions of peers; ensuring that autonomous systems have such an ability is critical to achieving good team performance [31]. Consider the collaborative manipulation scenario in Fig. 1c, in which both the human and the robot work together to set a table. It is important for the robot to anticipate the object that the human will take so that it can avoid hindering or even injuring the human.

Across robotics [7, 32], plan recognition [4], and cognitive science [1, 23], Bayesian goal inference has been applied to the problem of inferring human goals from their ongoing actions. Recently, we proposed a task allocation method which utilizes Bayesian goal inference at the motion level to enable the robot to adapt to the human at the task planning level [21]. However, the strategy detailed in this work has not been evaluated in collaboration scenarios involving real humans. Building on our initial work, we make the following contributions in this paper:

Evaluation: we evaluate the combination of two methods traditionally studied in isolation, namely applying goal inference at the motion level to compute a collaborative plan at the task level. This work differs from other user studies evaluating the use of Bayesian goal inference in human-robot interaction, which have focused on assisting humans to achieve an immediate goal [8,9]. We developed and ran a behavioral experiment (Fig. 1a) in which participants collaborated with virtual robots that (i) performed goal inference and re-planned as the human was moving (the *predictive* robot); (ii) only re-planned after the person reached their goal (the *reactive* robot); or (iii) never re-planned unless the current plan became infeasible (the *fixed* robot). We also had two between-subjects conditions in which we varied the type of inference used by the robot. In the "oracle" condition, the predictive robot had direct access to the participant's intent, emulating perfect goal inference, while in the "Bayesian" condition, the predictive robot used probabilistic inference on noisy human trajectories (as would happen in a realistic setting). Building on literature that evaluates human-robot collaboration [6, 18], we evaluated performance both objectively and subjectively. Objective metrics included time to complete the task and the proportion of tasks completed by the robot; subjective metrics were based on elicited preferences for the robots, and a survey regarding perceptions of the collaboration. As expected, errors in prediction do increase task completion time and lower subjective ratings of the robot. Despite these errors, both conditions produce the same results: we find that a robot that anticipates human goals to adapt its overall task plan is significantly superior to one that does not, in terms of both objective performance and subjective perception.

Implication. Despite the nontrivial assumption that the human will plan optimally after the current goal, the behavioral study reveals that using this model for the robotic agent's adaptation greatly improves objective team performance (reducing task completion time and increasing the proportion of robot-completed goals). This may be due to the combination of swift adaptation to the human (which attenuates the impact of the optimality assumption) with an additional closed-loop synergy arising as the adapted robot plan becomes more likely to match the human's own expectation. Importantly, adaptation based on this model also significantly improves subjective perceptions: users patently notice—and appreciate—the agent's adaptive behavior. The implications of these results on human-robot interaction design are explored in the discussion.

2. TASK ALLOCATION DURING HUMAN-ROBOT COLLABORATION

To test the importance of inferring human intent and adapting in collaborative tasks, we use a task allocation scenario with both individual and shared tasks. Following [21], we consider a setting in which human agent H and a robot agent R are in a compact planar domain $\mathcal{D} \subset \mathbb{R}^2$ with N one-agent tasks located at positions $p_i \in \mathcal{D}$, $i = 1, ..., N$, and M joint tasks with locations $q_j \in \mathcal{D}$, $j = 1, ..., M$. One-agent tasks are executed instantly when visited by any agent, whereas joint tasks are only completed when visited by both agents simultaneously. The agent that arrives first at a joint task cannot leave until the other one comes to help complete the task. The human starts at position $h_0 \in \mathcal{D}$ and the robot starts at $r_0 \in \mathcal{D}$. Both agents are able to move in any direction at the same constant velocity V. The discrete-time dynamics of the human-robot team at each time step $k \geqslant 0$ are $h_{k+1} = h_k + u$ and $r_{k+1} = r_k + w$, respectively, where $\|u\| = \|w\| = V$, with $\|\cdot\|$ being the Euclidean norm. Both agents have the common objective of completing all tasks in the minimum amount of time. Each agent can observe its own location, the location of the other agent, and the location and type of all remaining tasks. However, agents can not explicitly communicate with each other. This can be seen as a multi-agent version of the Traveling Salesman Problem [16].

2.1 Robot Collaboration Scheme

The scheme for integrating goal inference into task allocation presented in [21] achieves robustness to suboptimal human actions by adjusting its plan whenever the human's actions deviate from the robot's current internal allocation. At the initial time $k = 0$, the robot computes the optimal task allocation and capture sequence given the initial layout of tasks and agent positions (Section 2.3). The robot observes the human's actions as both human and robot move towards their respective goals. To infer whether the human is deviating from the robot's internal plan, the robot conducts a *maximum a posteriori* (MAP) estimate (Section 2.2). If a deviation is detected, the robot computes a new allocation of tasks based on the current state and the inferred human intent.

When computing the optimal allocation, it is assumed that the human will in fact execute the resulting joint plan. In the ideal scenario where both agents are perfectly rational, this would indeed be the case (without the need for explicit coordination). Of course, this rationality assumption is far from trivial in the case of human individuals; we nonetheless make use of it as an approximate model, admitting incorrect predictions and providing a mechanism to adapt in these cases. It is worth noting that this model maximally exploits collaboration in those cases in which the prediction is correct: that is, if the human does follow the computed plan, then the team achieves the best possible performance at the task. As will be seen, adaptation based on this model leads to significant improvements in team performance.

2.2 Bayesian Goal Inference

Let g denote the location of any of the $N+M$ tasks. Once the human starts moving towards a new task, the robot infers the human's intent as the task with the highest posterior probability, $P(g|h_{0:k+1})$, given the history of observations thus far, $h_{0:k+1}$. The posterior probability is updated iteratively using Bayes' rule:

$$P(g|h_{0:k+1}) \propto P(h_{k+1}|g, h_{0:k})P(g|h_{0:k}),$$

where the prior $P(g|h_{0:k})$ corresponds to the robot's belief that the human is heading towards task g based on previous observed positions $h_{0:k}$. The likelihood function $P(h_{k+1}|g, h_{0:k})$ corresponds to the transition probability for the position of the human given a particular goal. Under the Markov assumption, the likelihood function can be simplified as:

$$P(h_{k+1}|g, h_{0:k}) = P(h_{k+1}|g, h_k).$$

We compute the term $P(h_{k+1}|g, h_k)$ assuming that the human is noisily optimizing some reward function. Following [1], we model this term as a Boltzmann ('soft-max') policy:

$$P(h_{k+1}|g, h_k) \propto \exp(\beta V_g(h_{k+1})),$$

where $V_g(h)$ is the value function for each task location g. Following [21], we model $V_g(h)$ as a function of the distance between the human h and the task, $d_g(h) = \|g - h\|$; i.e. $V_g(h) = \gamma^{d_g(h)}U - c[(\gamma - \gamma^{d_g(h)})/(1-\gamma)]$. This corresponds to the value function of a γ-discounted optimal control problem with terminal reward U and uniform running cost c. The value function causes the Boltzmann policy to assign a higher probability to actions that take the human closer to the goal location g.

The parameter β is a rationality index, capturing how diligent we expect the human to be in optimizing their reward. When $\beta = 0$, $P(h_{k+1}|g, h_k)$ gives a uniform distribution, with all actions equally likely independent of their reward (modeling an indifferent human agent). Conversely, as $\beta \to \infty$, the human agent is assumed to almost always pick the optimal action with respect to their current goal.

2.3 Task Allocation

We compute the optimal allocation and execution order of tasks that minimizes completion time using a mixed-integer linear program (MILP). Let $\mathbb{A}$ denote the set of human and robot agents and $\mathbb{G}$ represent the set of remaining tasks. Then, the task allocation problem can be formulated as:

$$\min_{\mathbf{x}_{\text{alloc}}, \mathbf{t}_{\text{alloc}}} \quad \max_{v \in \mathbb{V}, g \in \mathbb{G}} t_g^v$$
$$\text{subject to} \quad \mathbf{x}_{\text{alloc}} \in \mathbb{X}_{\text{feasible}} \quad \mathbf{t}_{\text{alloc}} \in \mathbb{T}_{\text{feasible}},$$

where t_g^v denotes the time when v^{th} agent completes task g; $\mathbf{x}_{\text{alloc}}$ encodes the allocation of tasks to each agent and $\mathbf{t}_{\text{alloc}}$ represents the time for agents to arrive and leave tasks; and $\mathbb{X}_{\text{feasible}}$ and $\mathbb{T}_{\text{feasible}}$ denote the corresponding sets of feasible values that satisfy the requirements on completing one-agent and joint tasks. To generate an allocation that respects the intent of the human agent, the inferred goal is assigned as the first task for the human, which is enforced in $\mathbb{X}_{\text{feasible}}$. Other constraints of $\mathbb{X}_{\text{feasible}}$ include 1) each task is assigned to the human or robot, 2) an agent can only visit and complete a task once 3) an agent can leave a task position at most once and can only do so after visiting it (continuity condition) and 4) no subtour exists for any agent. The timing constraints of $\mathbb{T}_{\text{feasible}}$ requires that a joint task be completed the time when both the human and the robot visit the task while a common task be executed immediately when an agent visits it. Readers interested in details of the MILP formulation of this particular traveling salesman problem can refer to [21]. In this study, the MILP is solved by the commercial solver Gurobi [15].

2.4 Evaluation

The method outlined above was evaluated in [21] through simulations in which human behavior was modeled as a mixture of optimality and randomness. Specifically, humans were modeled assuming that they would take the optimal action with probability α, or take an action uniformly at random with probability $1 - \alpha$. However, as true human behavior is much more sophisticated and nuanced than this, it is unclear how well these results would generalize to real humans. Moreover, the simulation results tell us little about what people's perceived experiences might be. Even if Bayesian goal inference does decrease the time needed to complete a set of tasks with real people, it is important that those people subjectively perceive the robot as being helpful and the collaboration as being fluent, and that they feel confident that they can rely on the robot's help and comfortable collaborating with it.

To more rigorously test the robot's task allocation strategy, we ran a behavioral experiment in which we asked human participants to collaborate with three different robots, as shown in Fig. 1a, one at a time and in a counter-balanced order: a robot that did not re-plan its strategy regardless of the human's choices (the *fixed* robot), a robot that reacted to these choices only once the human reached the goal in question (the *reactive* robot), and a robot that anticipated the human's next goal at each step and adapted its behavior early (the *predictive* robot). We conducted the experiment under two different conditions: one with an *oracle-predictive* robot that can make perfect inferences of the human's intent, and a second with a *Bayesian-predictive* robot, in which the Bayesian intent inference is at times erroneous (as it will be in real human-robot interactions).

3. EXPERIMENTAL DESIGN

3.1 Task

We designed a web-based human-robot collaboration experiment where the human participant was in control of an avatar on a screen. In this experiment, the human and virtual robot had to complete a set of tasks as quickly as possible. While some of the tasks could be completed by either the human or the robot (*one-agent tasks*), others required both agents to complete the task simultaneously (*joint tasks*). The participant chose to complete tasks by clicking on them, causing the human avatar to move to that task while the robot moved towards a task of its choice. After the human completed the chosen task, they chose another task to complete, and so on until all tasks were completed.

3.2 Independent Variables

To evaluate the collaboration scheme described in Section 2, we manipulated two variables: **adaptivity** and **inference type**.

3.2.1 Adaptivity

We manipulated the amount of information that the robot receives during the task, which directly affects how adaptive the robot is to human actions. The following robots vary from least adaptive to most adaptive:

Fixed: *This robot receives no information about the human's goal.* It runs an initial optimal task allocation for the human-robot team and subsequently executes the robot part of the plan irrespective of the human's actions. It only re-plans its task allocation if an inconsistency or deadlock is reached. For example, if the human finishes a task that the robot had internally allocated to itself, the fixed robot removes the task from its list of pending tasks and chooses the next pending task as the goal. Additionally, if both agents reach different joint tasks, the robot moves to the human's location and re-plans its strategy to account for this deviation.

Reactive: *This robot receives information about the human's goal only when the human reaches their goal.* At this point, the robot reruns task allocation for the team assuming that the human will behave optimally for the remainder of the trial.

Predictive: *This robot receives information about the human's goal before they reach the goal.* After receiving this information, the robot recomputes the optimal plan, again assuming optimal human behavior thereafter.

3.2.2 Inference Type

We also manipulated the type of inference used by the predictive robot:

Oracle-predictive: *This robot receives perfect knowledge of the human's next goal as soon as the human chooses it.* Although there are real-world cases in which a human might inform a robot about its goal immediately after deciding, it is rare for a robot to know exactly the human's goal without having the human explicitly communicate it.

Bayesian-predictive: *This robot continuously receives information related to the human's goal by observing the motion of the human.* Based on this motion, the robot attempts to predict the human's goal using the Bayesian inference scheme described in Section 2.2. In most cases of human-robot collaboration, the robot will only have access to the human's motions.

3.3 Experimental Conditions

We manipulated the independent variables of adaptivity and inference type in a 3×2 mixed design in which inference type was varied between-subjects, while adaptivity was varied within-subjects. All participants collaborated with the fixed and reactive robots (corresponding to the *low adaptivity* and *medium adaptivity* conditions, respectively). For the *high adaptivity* conditions, half the participants were assigned to a *oracle* condition, in which they collaborated with the oracle-predictive robot; and half were assigned to a *Bayesian* condition, in which they collaborated with the Bayesian-predictive robot. This design is given in Table 1 for reference.

Table 1: Experimental Conditions

Inference Type (between-subjects)	**Adaptivity** (within-subjects)	**Robot**
-	Low Adaptivity	*Fixed*
-	Med. Adaptivity	*Reactive*
Oracle	High Adaptivity	*Oracle-predictive*
-	Low Adaptivity	*Fixed*
-	Med. Adaptivity	*Reactive*
Bayesian	High Adaptivity	*Bayesian-predictive*

The motivation for this design was to prevent participants from having to keep track of too many robots (as would be the case in a 4×1 design), while still creating the experience of comparing the predictive robot with non-predictive baselines.

3.4 Procedure

3.4.1 Stimuli

There were 15 unique task layouts which consisted of a collection of five or six tasks, as well as initial positions of the human and robot avatars. As shown in Fig. 1a, one-agent tasks were depicted by an orange circle with a single dot inside it, and joint tasks were depicted by a cyan circle with two dots inside it. The human avatar was a gender-neutral cartoon of a person on a scooter, and the robot avatars were images of the same robot in different poses and colors (either red, blue, or yellow), which were counterbalanced across participants.

3.4.2 Trial Design

First, we presented participants with four example trials to help them understand the task, which they completed with the help of a gray robot. Each experimental layout was presented to participants three times over the course of the experiment (once with each of the fixed, reactive, and predictive robots). The trials were grouped into five blocks of nine trials (45 trials total). Within each block, participants completed three trials with one of the robots, then three with a different robot, and then three with the final robot. The order of the robots and task layouts were randomized according to a Latin-square design, such that the order of the robots varied and such that no task layout was repeated within a block.

3.4.3 Layout Generation

We randomly generated task layouts according to the following procedure. First, we assumed a model of human goal selection that sets the probability of choosing the next goal task as inversely proportional to the distance between the position of the human agent and the tasks[1]. Under this model, we calculated the expected task completion time of 104 randomly generated layouts with reactive and Bayesian-predictive robots. We then computed the rank ordering of

[1]Specifically, we used a Boltzmann policy to model human task selections. We fit the tuning parameter from participant's choices in an earlier pilot experiment using maximum-likelihood estimation, resulting in a best fitting parameter value of $\beta = 1.05$.

these completion times relative to all possible completion times for each layout, and computed the ratio of the rank order of the Bayesian-adaptive robot to the rank order of the reactive robot. This ratio gave us a measure of how differently we would expect the two robots to behave: layouts with ratio greater than 1.5 (9 layouts) or less than 0.6 (6 layouts) were selected, giving a total of 15 layouts for each robot. Subjects completed 5 blocks of 9 layouts, totaling 45 layouts.

3.4.4 Avatar Animation

When moving to complete a task, the robot avatar always moved in a straight line towards the task. For the human avatar, however, the trajectory followed was not a straight path, but a Bézier curve that initially deviated to a side and then gradually corrected its course towards the correct task location. The reason for using this trajectory was to allow the Bayesian-predictive robot to make errors: if the human always moved in a straight line, then the Bayesian-predictive robot would almost always infer the correct goal right away (and thus would give nearly identical results as the oracle-predictive robot). Furthermore, this choice of curved trajectory is a more realistic depiction of how actual humans move, which is not usually in a straight line [3].

3.4.5 Attention Checks

After reading the instructions, participants were given an attention check in the form of two questions asking them the color of the one-agent tasks and joint tasks. At the end of the experiment, we also asked them whether they had been paying attention to the difference in helpfulness between the three robots.

3.4.6 Controlling for Confounds

We controlled for confounding factors by counterbalancing the colors of the robots (Section 3.4.1); by using a different color robot for the example trials (Section 3.4.2); by randomizing the trial order (Section 3.4.2); by generating stimuli to give advantages to different robots (Section 3.4.3); by animating the human avatar in a realistic way to differentiate between the Bayesian-predictive and oracle-predictive robots (Section 3.4.4); and by including attention checks (Section 3.4.5).

3.5 Dependent Measures

3.5.1 Objective measures

During each trial, a timer on the right side of the screen kept track of the time it took to complete the tasks. This timer was paused whenever the participant was prompted to choose the next task and only counted up when either the human avatar or robot avatar were moving. The final time on the timer was used an object measure of how long it took participants to complete each trial. We also tracked how many one-agent tasks were completed by the robot, the human, or both simultaneously.

3.5.2 Subjective measures

After every nine trials, we asked participants to choose the robot that they most preferred working with based on their experience so far. At the end of the experiment, we also asked participants to fill out a survey regarding their subjective experience working with each of the robot partners (Table 2). These survey questions were based on Hoffman's

Table 2: Subjective Measures

Fluency
1. The human-robot team with the [color] robot worked fluently together.
2. The [color] robot contributed to the fluency of the team interaction.
Contribution
1. (Reversed) I had to carry the weight to make the human-robot team with the [color] robot better.
2. The [color] robot contributed equally to the team performance.
3. The performance of the [color] robot was an important contribution to the success of the team.
Trust
1. I trusted the [color] robot to do the right thing at the right time.
2. The [color] robot is trustworthy.
Capability
1. I am confident in the ability of the [color] robot to help me.
2. The [color] robot is intelligent.
Perceptiveness (originally 'Goals')
1. The [color] robot perceived accurately what my goals were.
2. (Reversed) The [color] robot did not understand what I was trying to accomplish.
Forced-Choice Questions
1. If you were to redo this experiment with only one of the robots, which would you most prefer to work with?
2. If you were to redo this experiment with only one of the robots, which would you least prefer to work with?

metrics for fluency in human-robot collaborations [17], and were answered on a 7-point Likert scale from 1 ("strongly disagree") to 7 ("strongly agree"). We also included two forced-choice questions, which had choices corresponding to the three robots.

3.6 Hypotheses

We hypothesized that adaptivity and inference type would affect both objective measures (Section 3.5.1) and subjective measures (Section 3.5.2).

H1 - Task Completion Time *Robot adaptivity will negatively affect task completion times, with the least adaptive robots resulting in the slowest completion times, and the most adaptive robots resulting in the fastest completion times. The Bayesian-predictive will robot result in slower completion times than the oracle-predictive robot.*

H2 - Robot Task Completion *Robot adaptivity will positively affect the number of tasks that the robot completes, with more adaptive robots completing more tasks than the less adaptive robots. The Bayesian-predictive robot will complete fewer tasks than the oracle-predictive robot.*

H3 - Robot Preference *Robot adaptivity will positively affect participants' preferences, with more adaptive robots being preferable to less adaptive robots. The Bayesian-predictive robot will be less preferable than the oracle-predictive robot. Additionally, preferences will become stronger as participants gain more experience with each robot.*

H4 - Perceptions of the Collaboration *Robot adaptiv-*

ity will positively affect participants' perceptions of the collaboration as indicated by the subjective survey measures, with more adaptive robots being rated higher than less adaptive robots. Inference type will also affect perceptions, with the Bayesian-predictive robot scoring lower than the oracle-predictive robot.

3.7 Participants

We recruited a total of 234 participants from Amazon's Mechanical Turk using the psiTurk experimental framework [14]. We excluded 32 participants from analysis for failing the attention checks, as well as 6 due to an experimental error, leaving a total of $N = 196$ participants whose data we used. All participants were treated in accordance with local IRB standards and were paid \$1.20 for an average of 14.7 minutes of work, plus an average bonus of \$0.51. Bonuses could range from \$0.00 to \$1.35 depending on performance: for each trial, participants could get a \$0.03 bonus if they completed all tasks in the shortest possible amount of time; a \$0.02 bonus if they finished within the top 5% fastest times; or a \$0.01 bonus if they finished within the top 10% fastest times[2]. They received no bonus if they were slower than the top 10% fastest times.

4. RESULTS

4.1 Manipulation Checks

The goal of changing the inference type was ultimately to influence the number of errors made by the robot. To ensure that the Bayesian-predictive robot did make more errors than the oracle-predictive robot, we counted the proportion of timesteps on each trial during which the Bayesian-predictive robot had an incorrect belief about the human's goal. We then constructed a mixed-effects model for these error rates with only the intercept as fixed effects, and both participants and stimuli as random effects. The intercept was 0.27 ± 0.021 SE ($t(14.043) = 12.83$, $p < 0.001$), indicating an average error rate of about 27%. We also looked at the stimuli individually by reconstructing the same model, except with stimuli as fixed effects. Using this model, we found that error rates ranged from $15.0\% \pm 1.18\%$ SE to $41.0\% \pm 1.18\%$ SE.

4.2 H1 - Task Completion Time

First, we looked at the objective measure of task completion time, which is also shown in Fig. 2. To analyze task completion time, we first found the average completion time for each participant across stimuli, then constructed a linear mixed-effects model for these times using the inference type and adaptivity as fixed effects and the participants as random effects. We found main effects of both inference type ($F(2, 194) = 10.30$, $p < 0.01$) and adaptivity ($F(2, 388) = 709.27$, $p < 0.001$), as well as an interaction between the two ($F(2, 388) = 10.07$, $p < 0.001$).

We performed post-hoc comparisons using the multivariate t method for p-value adjustment. In support of **H1**, we found that the reactive robot led to completion times that were $0.52s \pm 0.029$ SE faster than the fixed robot ($t(388) = 17.777$, $p < 0.001$). Also in support of **H1**, the oracle-predictive robot led to completion times that were $0.69s \pm 0.041$ SE faster than the reactive robot ($t(388) = -16.785$, $p < 0.001$), and the Bayesian-predictive robot led to completion times that were $0.47s \pm 0.041$ SE faster than the reactive robot ($t(388) = -11.339$, $p < 0.001$). There was no evidence for a difference between the fixed robots between participants ($t(329.53) = -1.528$, $p = 0.61$), nor between the reactive robots ($t(329.53) = -1.756$, $p = 0.46$). There was, however, a difference between the oracle-predictive and Bayesian-predictive robots, ($t(329.53) = -5.03$, $p < 0.001$), with the oracle-predictive robot resulting in completion times that were faster by $0.34s \pm 0.067$ SE. The combination of these results fully support **H1**: when adaptivity increases or the number of errors in inference decreases, task completion time decreases.

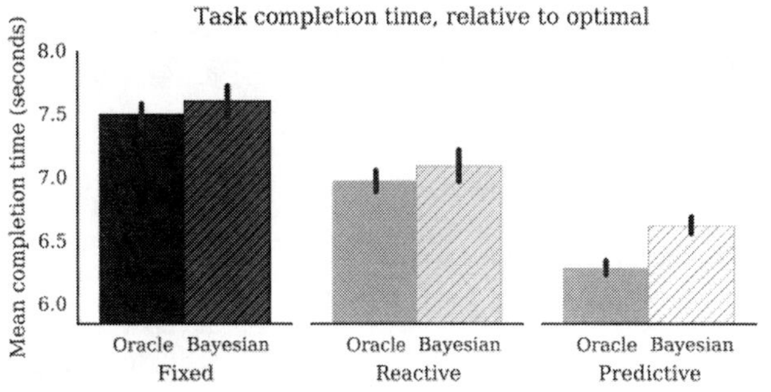

Figure 2: Comparison of completion times for different robots. The y-axis begins at the average optimal completion time, and thus represents a lower bound. Error bars are bootstrapped 95% confidence intervals of the mean using 1,000 samples.

4.3 H2 - Robot Task Completion

Next, we looked at the additional object measure of how many one-agent tasks were completed by the robot.[3] For each participant, we counted the total number of one-agent tasks completed by the robot throughout the entire experiment. These numbers are shown in Fig. 3. To analyze these results, we constructed a linear mixed-effects model for the number of tasks with inference type and adaptivity as fixed effects and the participants as random effects. There was no evidence for a main effect of inference type on the number of tasks completed by the robot ($F(2, 194) = 0.905$, $p = 0.34$), but there was an effect of the adaptivity on the number of tasks completed by the robot ($F(2, 388) = 171.15$, $p < 0.001$), as well as an interaction between adaptivity and inference type ($F(2, 388) = 9.237$, $p < 0.001$).

To investigate these effects further, we performed post-hoc comparisons with multivariate t adjustments. Consistent with **H2**, we found that the reactive robot completed 1.2 ± 0.24 SE more tasks than the fixed robot ($t(388) = 4.969$, $p < 0.001$); the oracle-predictive robot completed 2.3 ± 0.34 SE more tasks than the reactive robot ($t(388) = 6.722$, $p < 0.001$); and the Bayesian-predictive robot completed 4.0 ± 0.35 SE more tasks than the reactive robot ($t(388) = 11.566$, $p < 0.001$). Surprisingly, however, in comparing be-

[2]When comparing completion times to the range of possible times, we always compared the participants' completion times with the range of all times achievable with the robot they were currently collaborating with.

[3]Sometimes the robot and human could complete the same one-agent task simultaneously. We excluded these cases from the number of one-agent tasks completed by the robot, because for these tasks the robot was not actually providing any additional help. We found that the robot and human competed for the same task 1.5%, 8.6%, 14.6%, and 18.1% of the time in the oracle-predictive, Bayesian-predictive, reactive, and fixed conditions, respectively.

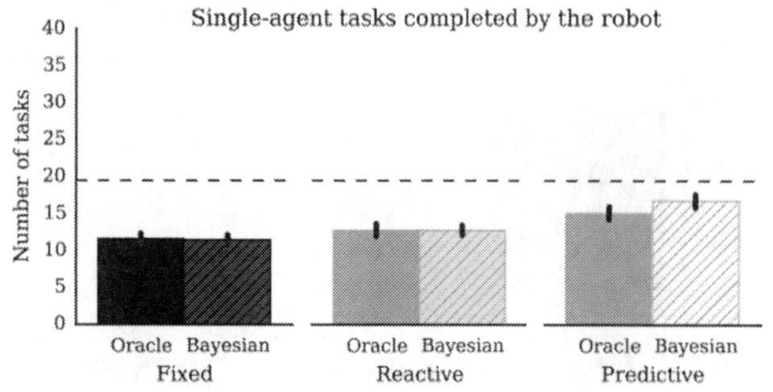

Figure 3: Number of one-agent tasks completed by the robot. The dotted lines represent the robot and the human completing an equal proportion of tasks. Error bars are bootstrapped 95% confidence intervals of the mean using 1,000 samples.

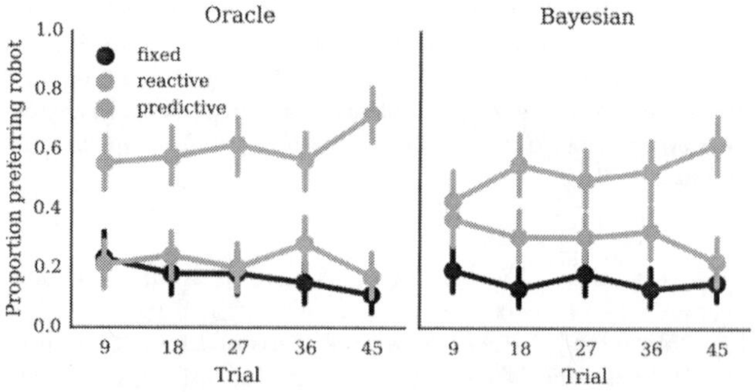

Figure 4: Preferred robot as a function of trial. Error bars are bootstrapped 95% confidence intervals of the mean using 1,000 samples.

tween subjects, we found the opposite of **H2**: the Bayesian-predictive robot completed 1.7 ± 0.58 SE more tasks than the oracle-predictive robot ($t(316.19) = 2.903$, $p < 0.05$).

These results confirm part of **H2**—that adaptivity increases the number of tasks completed by the robot—but disconfirm the other part of **H2**—that Bayesian inference decreases the number of tasks completed by the robot. However, we note that the effects are quite small between the different robots: the differences reported are in the order of 1–4 tasks for the entire experiment, which had a total of 39 one-agent tasks. Each trial only had two or three one-agent tasks, and thus these results may not generalize to scenarios that include many more tasks. Furthermore, although we found that the Bayesian inference type increased the number of tasks completed by the robot, we speculate that this may be due to the Bayesian-predictive robot inferring the incorrect human goal and therefore taking some other one-agent task. However, further investigation is required to determine the actual source of this difference.

4.4 H3 - Robot Preference

We next analyzed the subjective measure of participants' preferences for which robot they would rather work with.

4.4.1 Preferences over time

Fig. 4 shows the proportion of participants choosing each robot as a function of trial. We constructed a logistic mixed-effects model for binary preferences (where 1 meant the robot was chosen, and 0 meant it was not) with inference type, adaptivity, and trial as fixed effects and participants as random effects. Using Wald's tests, we found a significant main effect of adaptivity ($\chi^2(2) = 16.7184$, $p < 0.001$) and trial ($\chi^2(1) = 5.1104$, $p < 0.05$), supporting **H3**. We also found an interaction between adaptivity and trial ($\chi^2(1) = 9.2493$, $p < 0.01$). While the coefficient for trial was negative ($\beta = -0.022 \pm 0.0095$ SE, $z = -2.261$, $p < 0.05$), the coefficient for the interaction of trial and the predictive robot was positive ($\beta = 0.036 \pm 0.0120$, $z = 3.017$, $p < 0.01$). This also supports **H3**: if preferences for the predictive robot increase over time, by definition the preferences for the other robots must decrease, thus resulting in an overall negative coefficient.

Although we did not find a significant main effect of inference type ($\chi^2(1) = 1.457$, $p = 0.23$), we did find an interaction between inference type and adaptivity ($\chi^2(2) = 7.7208$, $p < 0.05$). Post-hoc comparisons with the multivariate t adjustment indicated that there was a significant overall improvement in preference between the fixed and reactive robots ($z = -5.23$, $p < 0.001$) as well as an improvement in preference between the reactive and oracle-predictive robots ($z = 11.86$, $p < 0.001$) and between the reactive and Bayesian-predictive robots ($z = 6.95$, $p < 0.001$). While there was no significant difference between participants for the fixed robot ($z = 0.40$, $p = 0.998$), there was a significant difference for the reactive robot ($z = -2.93$, $p < 0.05$) and a marginal difference between the predictive robots ($z = 2.52$, $p = 0.098$), with the oracle-predictive robot being slightly more preferable to the Bayesian-predictive robot.

4.4.2 Final rankings

For each participant, we assigned each robot a score based on their final rankings. The best robot received a score of 1; the worst robot received a score of 2; and the remaining robot received a score of 1.5. We constructed a logistic mixed-effects model for these scores, with inference type and adaptivity as fixed effects and participants as random effects; we then used Wald's tests to check for effects. In partial support of **H3**, there was a significant effect of adaptivity on the rankings ($\chi^2(2) = 52.352$, $p < 0.001$) but neither a significant effect of inference type ($\chi^2(1) = 1.149$, $p = 0.28$) nor an interaction between adaptivity and inference type ($\chi^2(2) = 3.582$, $p = 0.17$). Post-hoc comparisons between the robot types were adjusted with Tukey's HSD and indicated a preference for the reactive robot over the fixed robot ($z = 5.092$, $p < 0.001$) and a preference for the predictive robots over the reactive robot ($z = 5.634$, $p < 0.001$).

4.5 H4 - Perceptions of the Collaboration

Finally, we looked at the subjective measures of participants' perceptions of the collaboration. For each robot and measure (capability, contribution, fluency, goals, and trust), we averaged each participants' responses to the individual questions, resulting in a single score per participant, per measure, per robot. The results are shown in Fig. 5. We constructed a linear mixed-effects model for the survey responses with the adaptivity, inference type, and measure type as fixed effects, and with participants as random effects. We found significant main effects for both the adaptivity ($F(2, 2730) = 543.18$, $p < 0.001$) and measure type ($F(4, 2730) = 5.28$, $p < 0.001$). While there was no significant main effect of inference type ($F(2, 195) = 0.08$, $p = 0.78$), there was an interaction between adaptivity and inference type ($F(2, 2730) = 17.17$, $p < 0.001$). We did not find interactions between inference type and measure type

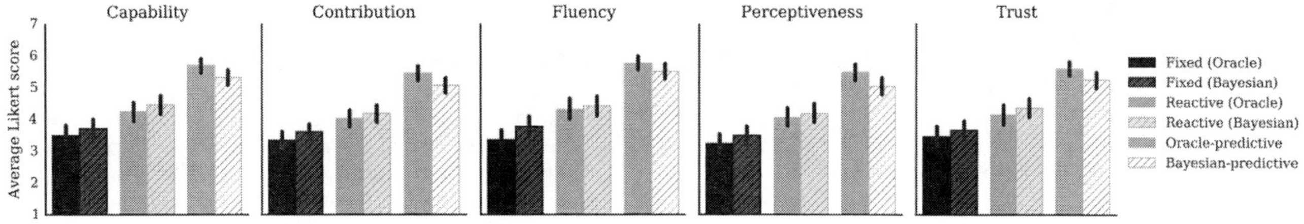

Figure 5: Findings for subjective measures. Error bars are bootstrapped 95% confidence intervals of the mean.

($F(4, 2730) = 0.14$, $p = 0.97$), between adaptivity and measure type ($F(8, 2730) = 0.38$, $p = 0.93$), or between adaptivity, inference type, and measure type ($F(8, 2730) = 0.14$, $p = 0.997$).

We investigated these effects further through a post-hoc analysis with multivariate t corrections. In support of **H4**, we found that participants rated the reactive robot higher than the fixed robot by 0.72 ± 0.058 SE points on the Likert scale ($t(2730) = 12.415$, $p < 0.001$). They also rated the oracle-predictive robot higher than the reactive robot by 1.44 ± 0.082 SE points ($t(2730) = 17.568$, $p < 0.001$), the Bayesian-predictive robot higher than the reactive robot by 0.91 ± 0.083 SE points ($t(2730) = 11.064$, $p < 0.001$), and the oracle-predictive robot higher than the Bayesian-predictive robot by 0.36 ± 0.112 points ($t(470.31) = 3.267$, $p < 0.05$).

5. DISCUSSION

In this paper we set out to answer three questions. First, does an increase in robot adaptivity lead to an objective improvement in real human-robot collaboration scenarios? Second, even if performance improves objectively, do people actually notice a difference? Third, if the robot does not have perfect knowledge of the human's goals and must infer them, does adaptivity still result in the same improvements?

Implications. Our results suggest that outfitting robots with the ability to adaptively re-plan their actions from a motion-based inference of human intent can lead to a systematic improvement in both the objective and perceived performance in human-robot collaboration. We found that this type of adaptivity increases performance objectively by lowering the amount of time it takes the team to complete the tasks and by improving the balance of work between the two agents. Subjectively, we found that participants preferred motion-based predictive adaptation to purely reactive adaptation at the task level (which, as expected, was in turn preferred to no adaptation), and that they rated the more adaptive robot higher on a number of measures including capability, collaboration, fluency, perceptiveness, and trust. Unsurprisingly, introducing prediction errors through manipulation of the inference type generally decreased both objective performance and subjective ratings. What is surprising, however, is how small this decrease in performance was, particularly given that the Bayesian-predictive robot had an error rate ranging from a low of 15% to a high of 40% for some stimuli. This suggests that an attempt to predict and adapt to human goals—even under limited accuracy—can have a significant effect on the team's objective performance and the human's perception of the robot.

Another non-obvious observation is that the adaptation mechanism is successful in spite of the strong assumption that the human agent will behave optimally from the current state. In practice, the impact of this assumption is limited by the fact that the robot quickly adapts whenever the human does not follow this optimal plan; this is comparable to how model-predictive control can use a nominal system model and correct for model mismatch at each re-planning step. Additional effects may also explain the observed improvement. In particular, our model of human task planning explicitly accounts for the joint actions of the two agents (as opposed to only their own); because human inferences of other agent's intentions have been shown to be consistent with models of approximately rational planning [1], it is therefore likely that the robot's adapted actions closely match users' actual expectations. In addition, the fact that the robot adapts by switching to the new joint optimal plan means that the human is always "given a new chance" to behave optimally; in other words, the robot's adaptation is always placing the team in the situation with the best achievable outcome. Developing and testing these hypotheses further will be the subject of future work.

Limitations. There are several limitations to this work which we plan to address in future research. First, in our experiment, participants could only select the goal task and the trajectory for human avatar was predefined. It would be more realistic if participants were allowed to directly control the motion of human avatar. To better understand the role of realistic control, we will conduct a future study in which participants can continuously move their avatar using the arrow keys. Second, the robot's working assumption that the human will follow the optimal joint plan is unrealistic. Better results could conceivably be obtained if this assumption were to be relaxed and replaced by a more refined model of human inference and decision-making, enabling a more effective adaptation of the robot's plan. Lastly, while adaptivity is fundamental to successful collaboration in many types of tasks, it may not lead to improvements in *all* contexts. For example, in manufacturing scenarios where there is scheduling and allocation ahead of time, adaptation on either side is not required: in these cases, humans actually prefer that robots take the lead and give them instructions [12], rather than adapting to their actions.

Conclusions. Overall, our results demonstrate the benefits of combining motion-level inference with task-level plan adaptation in the context of human-robot collaboration. Although our results are based on virtual simulations, we speculate that the improvement found here will be even more important in real-world situations, during which humans may be under considerable stress and cognitive load. In such cases, a robot partner not behaving as expected can lead to frustration or confusion, impeding the human's judgment and performance. A robot partner that adapts to the human can make all the difference, both in the successful completion of the task and in the perceived quality of the interaction.

REFERENCES

[1] C. L. Baker, R. Saxe, and J. B. Tenenbaum. Action understanding as inverse planning. *Cognition*, 113(3):329–349, 2009.

[2] R. Bemelmans, G. J. Gelderblom, P. Jonker, and L. De Witte. Socially assistive robots in elderly care: a systematic review into effects and effectiveness. *Journal of the American Medical Directors Association*, 13(2):114–120, 2012.

[3] D. Brogan and N. Johnson. Realistic human walking paths. *IEEE International Workshop on Program Comprehension*, 2003.

[4] E. Charniak and R. P. Goldman. A Bayesian model of plan recognition. *Artificial Intelligence*, 64(1):53–79, 1993.

[5] M. B. Dias, B. Kannan, B. Browning, E. G. Jones, B. Argall, M. F. Dias, M. Zinck, M. M. Veloso, and A. J. Stentz. Sliding autonomy for peer-to-peer human-robot teams. *Intelligent Autonomous Systems (IAS)*, 2008.

[6] A. D. Dragan, S. Bauman, J. Forlizzi, and S. S. Srinivasa. Effects of robot motion on human-robot collaboration. *ACM/IEEE International Conference on Human-Robot Interaction (HRI)*, 2015.

[7] A. D. Dragan and S. S. Srinivasa. Formalizing assistive teleoperation. *Robotics, Science and Systems (RSS)*, 2012.

[8] A. D. Dragan and S. S. Srinivasa. A policy-blending formalism for shared control. *The International Journal of Robotics Research*, 32(7):790–805, 2013.

[9] A. Fern, S. Natarajan, K. Judah, and P. Tadepalli. A decision-theoretic model of assistance. *Journal of Artificial Intelligence Research*, 50(1):71–104, 2014.

[10] T. Fong, I. Nourbakhsh, C. Kunz, L. Flückiger, J. Schreiner, R. Ambrose, R. Burridge, R. Simmons, L. M. Hiatt, A. Schultz, et al. The peer-to-peer human-robot interaction project. *AIAA Space*, 2005.

[11] T. Furukawa, F. Bourgault, B. Lavis, and H. F. Durrant-Whyte. Recursive Bayesian search-and-tracking using coordinated UAVs for lost targets. *IEEE International Conference on Robotics and Automation (ICRA)*, 2006.

[12] M. C. Gombolay, R. A. Gutierrez, G. F. Sturla, and J. A. Shah. Decision-making authority, team efficiency and human worker satisfaction in mixed human-robot teams. *Robotics, Science and Systems (RSS)*, 2014.

[13] B. Grocholsky, J. Keller, V. Kumar, and G. Pappas. Cooperative air and ground surveillance. *IEEE Robotics & Automation Magazine*, 13(3):16–25, 2006.

[14] T. M. Gureckis, J. Martin, J. McDonnell, R. S. Alexander, D. B. Markant, A. Coenen, J. B. Hamrick, and P. Chan. psiTurk: An open-source framework for conducting replicable behavioral experiments online. *Behavioral Research Methods*, 2015.

[15] Gurobi Optimization. Gurobi reference manual, 2015. Available at `http://www.gurobi.com`.

[16] M. Held and R. M. Karp. The traveling-salesman problem and minimum spanning trees. *Operations Research*, 18(6):1138–1162, 1970.

[17] G. Hoffman. Evaluating fluency in human-robot collaboration. *ACM/IEEE International Conference on Human-Robot Interaction (HRI), Workshop on Human Robot Collaboration*, 2013.

[18] G. Hoffman and C. Breazeal. Effects of anticipatory action on human-robot teamwork efficiency, fluency, and perception of team. *ACM/IEEE International Conference on Human-Robot Interaction (HRI)*, 2007.

[19] C. D. Kidd, W. Taggart, and S. Turkle. A sociable robot to encourage social interaction among the elderly. *IEEE International Conference on Robotics and Automation (ICRA)*, 2006.

[20] C. Lenz, S. Nair, M. Rickert, A. Knoll, W. Rosel, J. Gast, A. Bannat, and F. Wallhoff. Joint-action for humans and industrial robots for assembly tasks. *Robot and Human Interactive Communication (RO-MAN)*, 2008.

[21] C. Liu, S.-y. Liu, E. L. Carano, and J. K. Hedrick. A framework for autonomous vehicles with goal inference and task allocation capabilities to support task allocation with human agents. *Dynamic Systems and Control Conference (DSCC)*, 2014.

[22] D. T. McRuer. *Pilot-induced oscillations and human dynamic behavior*, volume 4683. NASA, 1995.

[23] G. Pezzulo, F. Donnarumma, and H. Dindo. Human sensorimotor communication: a theory of signaling in online social interactions. *PLoS ONE*, 8(2), 2013.

[24] M. Saffarian, J. C. F. de Winter, and R. Happee. Automated Driving: Human-Factors Issues and Design Solutions. *Proceedings of the Human Factors and Ergonomics Society Annual Meeting*, 56(1):2296–2300, 2012.

[25] N. B. Sarter and D. D. Woods. Team play with a powerful and independent agent: operational experiences and automation surprises on the Airbus A-320. *Human Factors*, 39(4):553–569, 1997.

[26] J. Shah and C. Breazeal. An empirical analysis of team coordination behaviors and action planning with application to human–robot teaming. *Human Factors*, 52(2):234–245, 2010.

[27] J. Tisdale, Z. Kim, and J. K. Hedrick. Autonomous uav path planning and estimation. *IEEE Robotics & Automation Magazine*, 16(2):35–42, 2009.

[28] M. Tomasello, M. Carpenter, J. Call, T. Behne, and H. Moll. Understanding and sharing intentions: the origins of cultural cognition. *Behavioral and Brain Sciences*, 28(05):675–691, 2005.

[29] C. Vesper, S. Butterfill, G. Knoblich, and N. Sebanz. A minimal architecture for joint action. *Neural Networks*, 23(8):998–1003, 2010.

[30] K. Wada and T. Shibata. Living with seal robots – its sociopsychological and physiological influences on the elderly at a care house. *IEEE Transactions on Robotics*, 23(5):972–980, 2007.

[31] J. Yen, X. Fan, S. Sun, T. Hanratty, and J. Dumer. Agents with shared mental models for enhancing team decision makings. *Decision Support Systems*, 41(3):634–653, 2006.

[32] B. D. Ziebart, N. Ratliff, G. Gallagher, C. Mertz, K. Peterson, J. A. Bagnell, M. Hebert, A. K. Dey, and S. Srinivasa. Planning-based prediction for pedestrians. *IEEE/RSJ International Conference on Intelligent Robots and Systems (IROS)*, 2009.

“Do As I Say, Not As I Do:” Challenges in Delegating Decisions to Automated Agents

Celso M. de Melo
Institute for Creative Technologies, University of Southern California, 12015 Waterfront Drive, Building #4, Playa Vista, CA 90094-2536
demelo@usc.edu

Stacy Marsella
College of Computer and Information Science, Northeastern University, 440 Huntington Avenue, Boston, Massachusetts 02115
stacymarsella@gmail.com

Jonathan Gratch
Institute for Creative Technologies, University of Southern California, 12015 Waterfront Drive, Building #4, Playa Vista, CA 90094-2536
gratch@ict.usc.edu

ABSTRACT
There has been growing interest, across various domains, in computer agents that can decide on behalf of humans. These agents have the potential to save considerable time and help humans reach better decisions. One implicit assumption, however, is that, as long as the algorithms that simulate decision-making are correct and capture how humans make decisions, humans will treat these agents similarly to other humans. Here we show that interaction with agents that act on our behalf or on behalf of others is richer and more interesting than initially expected. Our results show that, on the one hand, people are more selfish with agents acting on behalf of others, than when interacting directly with others. We propose that agents increase the social distance with others which, subsequently, leads to increased demand. On the other hand, when people task an agent to interact with others, people show more concern for fairness than when interacting directly with others. In this case, higher psychological distance leads people to consider their social image and the long-term consequences of their actions and, thus, behave more fairly. To support these findings, we present an experiment where people engaged in the ultimatum game, either directly or via an agent, with others or agents representing others. We show that these patterns of behavior also occur in a variant of the ultimatum game – the impunity game – where others have minimal power over the final outcome. Finally, we study how social value orientation – i.e., people's propensity for cooperation – impact these effects. These results have important implications for our understanding of the psychological mechanisms underlying interaction with agents, as well as practical implications for the design of successful agents that act on our behalf or on behalf of others.

General Terms
Experimentation, Economics, Human Factors, Theory.

Keywords
Automated Agents; Decision Making; Social Distance; Social Image; Power; Social Value Orientation

1. INTRODUCTION
Recent times have seen increased interest in automated computational systems that make decisions on behalf of people [1]-[8]. These systems have the potential to save considerable time and effort by helping humans reach optimal decisions in complex negotiations or other economic settings [1]-[5]. They can help business leaders reduce labor cost, improve quality, enforce company policy, and work around the clock [6]. They also have the potential to free us from mundane activities, such as driving [7] and they can deliver merchandise for us very efficiently [8]. For these and other reasons, there has been considerable investment in applying these automated agents in health, finance, retail, driving, manufacturing, robotics, defense, etc.

One implicit assumption when creating these systems is that if these agents implement correct decision algorithms and capture how humans make decisions in similar settings, then people will behave with them similarly to how they do with humans. In fact, initial theories of human-computer interaction suggest that to the extent that agents display social cues (e.g., interactivity, verbal and non-verbal behavior), people will treat them in a fundamentally social manner and apply the same rules they use when interacting with humans [9]-[14]. However, recent studies suggest that people still make important distinctions in their behavior with computers, when compared to humans [15]-[17]. These results show that in the same economic tasks, for the same financial incentives, people make more favorable decisions with humans than computers [18]-[21], and show patterns of higher brain activation with humans [22]-[24]. These studies, though, focus on computers that acted *on their own behalf*; in contrast, here we are interested in people's behavior with agents that act *on behalf of humans*. The answer to this research question is, comparatively, much less well understood.

This paper, therefore, explicitly tests whether agents that act on behalf of humans are treated in the same manner as humans. To accomplish this, we present an experiment where participants engaged in the ultimatum bargaining and the impunity games, as proposers, with other humans or agents representing other humans. Moreover, participants either made decisions directly with their counterparts or via an automated agent. Our results show that there are fundamental differences in the way people behave with these automated agents, when compared to humans; moreover, people act differently with agents that represent them, when compared to agents that represent others. Specifically, the results show that people will task their agents to behave fairly (“Do as I say”), but will act selfishly with agents that represent others (“Not as I do”). Finally, we look at how power – i.e., the counterpart's ability to shape the final outcome – and social value

Appears in: *Proceedings of the 15th International Conference on Autonomous Agents and Multiagent Systems (AAMAS 2016), J. Thangarajah, K. Tuyls, C. Jonker, S. Marsella (eds.),*
May 9–13, 2016, Singapore.

orientation – i.e., an individual trait that measures people's propensity for cooperation – influence these effects.

1.1 Social Distance & Agents That Act on Behalf of Others

As mentioned above, initial theories of human-computer interaction predict that, in social settings, people will interact with agents in the same manner as they would with humans [5], [9]-[14]. The argument is that in such settings people use cognitive heuristics and apply the rules of human-human interaction in human-agent interaction. Thus, in our case, the prediction is that: People's decisions would be as favorable with agents that act on behalf of humans, as with humans.

Research on the effects of social distance on decision making [25]-[31], however, suggest that people will distinguish between interacting with humans directly vs. interacting with an automated agent that acts on behalf of humans. In this research, social distance between participants and their counterparts was achieved by manipulating anonymity, familiarity with others, temporal distance, and physical distance. Hoffman, McCabe, and Smith [25], [26] showed that in conditions of full anonymity – i.e., participants could not be identified by their counterparts or the experimenters – people offered much less than when anonymity was not preserved. Researchers also showed that people offered more in a dictator game to friends than strangers [27], [28]. Pronin, Olivola, and Kennedy [29] demonstrated that temporal distance also affected decision making; in their studies, people showed larger psychological distance between their future selves, who were treated the same as different people, than their present selves. Finally, various researchers have shown that physical proximity can lead to increased cooperation (e.g., [30], [31]). These results, thus, suggest that people will perceive agents that act on behalf of other humans as being more socially distant than the humans themselves. Therefore, in contrast to the prediction in the previous paragraph, we advanced the following hypothesis:

> ***Hypothesis 1:*** *People's decisions will be more favorable to humans than to agents that act on behalf of other humans.*

1.2 Social Image & Agents that Act on Our Behalf

When people interact via an agent, the physical distance to their counterparts increases. Thus, a straightforward application of the argument presented in the previous section should lead to the following hypothesis:

> ***Hypothesis 2a:*** *People's decisions when engaging with others via an agent should be less favorable than when interacting with others directly.*

However, interacting with an agent that represents us is different than interacting with agents that represent others. In contrast to the latter case, when people task an agent to be their representative, they are likely to take special considerations for one's reputation or social image. An automated agent is a persistent representation of the person's values and is likely to engage in multiple interactions with various counterparts. Thus, rather than take solely into account the short-term impact, people will also consider the long-term effect of their choices. For all these reasons, people have added incentive to behave fairly when interacting via an automated agent.

Supporting this view, research in the behavioral sciences shows that people tend to behave more fairly when their actions impact their reputations [32], [33] or are being watched by an audience [34]. In a related line of research, construal level theory [35] argues that people focus on concrete and specific aspects of events or objects that are perceived to be psychologically close; in contrast, people focus on more abstract and global aspects when something is perceived to be more psychologically distant. Accordingly, studies demonstrate that when people adopt an abstract level of construal (the "big picture"), rather than focus on the particular interaction they are involved in – and, thus, seek a short-term selfish reward – they, instead, cooperate more in social and moral dilemmas [36]-[38], as well as in negotiation [39], [40].

Thus, we advance a second competing hypothesis:

> ***Hypothesis 2b:*** *People's decisions when engaging with others via an agent should be more favorable than when interacting with others directly.*

We next consider how two factors that usually have important consequences in social interaction – power and social value orientation – impact decisions with automated agents.

1.3 Power

Power can be broadly defined as the ability to exert influence on other people [41], [42]. In social decision making, one party often has more power than the other and this leads to important consequences to the way people behave and to the final outcome. Research shows that powerful parties tend to have higher aspirations [43], demand more and concede less [44], and be more likely to use threats to get their way [45]. Because power plays such a critical role, we also wanted to explore how this situational factor moderates people's offers with automated agents. To accomplish this we compared behavior in the ultimatum game – where the responder has considerable power, in that if s/he rejects the offer, no one gets anything – with the impunity game – where the responder has little power, in that s/he can only symbolically reject the offer, without affecting the outcome for the proposer. Since it was not clear, however, how power would interact with the type of automated agents involved, we advanced a research question:

> ***Research Question 1:*** *How will counterpart power influence people's decisions when they are interacting via or with agents?*

1.4 Social Value Orientation

Whereas power is a situational factor, social value orientation (SVO) is an individual factor that captures one's propensity for cooperation [46], [47]. This trait distinguishes between two types of individuals: cooperators (or prosocials) and non-cooperators (or proselfs). The former tend to cooperate by default, though they are able to adjust their behavior in the presence of non-cooperators. Non-cooperators, on the other hand, tend to act selfishly by default, and often need external incentive to cooperate. SVO is argued to be a stable personality trait that is shaped by biology and one's early history of social interaction. Several studies have demonstrated that this trait has a powerful influence on people's decision making in social settings [48], [49]. In our work, we wanted to study whether this individual trait could impact behavior with automated agents. Thus, we advanced a final research question:

Research Question 2: *How will social value orientation influence people's decisions when they are interacting via or with agents?*

2. EXPERIMENT

To test our hypotheses and address our research questions, we ran an experiment where participants engaged in the ultimatum game with automated agents that either represented the participants themselves or the counterparts. To manipulate power, participants also engaged in a variant of the ultimatum game – the impunity game – where counterparts are given little power over the final outcome.

2.1 Methods

Design. The experiment followed a 2 × 2 × 2 mixed factorial design: *Responder* (Human vs. Agent; between-participants) × *Proposer* (Human vs. Agent; between-participants) × *Power* (Ultimatum game vs. Impunity game; within-participants). Participants always assumed the role of proposers.

Tasks. In the ultimatum game [50], there are two players: a proposer and a responder. The proposer is given an initial endowment of money and has to decide how much to offer to the responder. Then, the responder has to make a decision: if the offer is accepted, both players get the proposed allocation; if the offer is rejected, however, no one gets anything. The standard rational prediction is that the proposer should offer the minimum non-zero amount, as the responder will always prefer to have something to nothing. In practice, people usually offer 40 to 50 percent of the initial endowment and low offers (about 20 percent of the endowment) are usually rejected [51]. This behavior is usually explained by a concern with fairness and a fear of being rejected [52].

The impunity game is similar to the ultimatum game [53], [54]. The proposer is given an initial endowment of money and makes an offer to a responder, who must decide whether to accept or reject the offer. The critical difference is that, if the offer is rejected, the responder gets zero, but the proposer still keeps the money s/he designated for her-/himself. A rejection by the responder, thus, does not impact the proposer's payoff and is only symbolic. The impunity game can therefore be seen as a version of the ultimatum game where responders are given less power over the outcome[1]. Experimental results with this game show that proposers tend to offer less than in the ultimatum game, though still above the rational prediction of zero [53].

In our experiment, participants were always assigned the role of proposers. In each game, participants were given an initial endowment of 20 lottery tickets. They could make an offer ranging from 0 to 20 tickets. These tickets had financial consequences as they would enter lotteries (one per game) worth $30. Participants were assigned to one of the four possible Proposer × Responder conditions, and played one round of the ultimatum game and one round of the impunity game. The order with which these games was presented was counterbalanced across participants. Before engaging in the actual games, participants read the instructions, were quizzed on the instructions, and completed a tutorial. The interface was also different for these games in terms of colors and icons on screen to make sure people did not confuse the two games. A snapshot for the ultimatum game is shown in Figure 1.

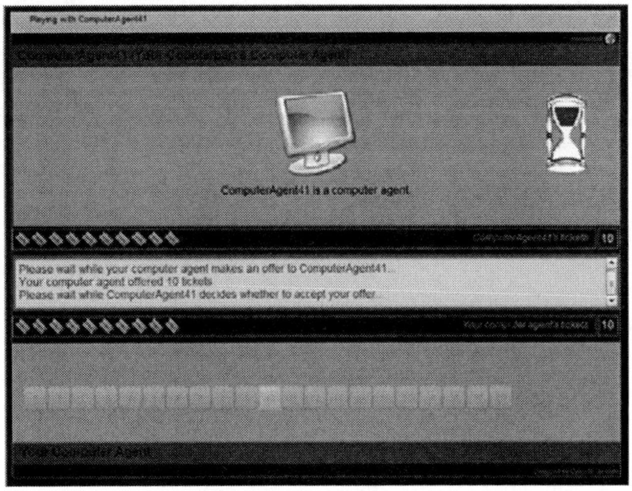

Figure 1. A snapshot of the ultimatum game software.

Responders. Participants were told that the counterparts were either other participants or automated agents that would make decisions on behalf of other participants. Moreover, they were informed that they would play with a different counterpart in each game (i.e., they would play at most once with the same human or agent counterpart). In reality, however, independently of the counterpart type, participants always engaged with the same computer script[2]. To make this manipulation believable, we had people connect to a fictitious server before starting the task for the purposes of "being matched with other participants". Connecting to this server took approximately 30-45 seconds. After concluding the experiment, participants were fully debriefed about this deception.

Proposers. Participants always assumed the role of proposer. They were ostensibly told that this assignment was random. Participants would then interact directly with their counterparts or via an automated agent that would act on their behalf. In the latter case, before starting the task, participants were asked to program their agents to make the offer they wanted.

Sample. We recruited 194 participants from Amazon Mechanical Turk, which is a crowdsourcing platform that allows people to complete online tasks in exchange for pay. Previous research shows that studies performed on Mechanical Turk can yield high-quality data, minimize experimental biases, and successfully replicate the results of behavioral studies performed on traditional pools [55]. We only sampled participants from the United States with an excellent performance history (95% approval rate in previous Mechanical Turk's tasks). Regarding gender, 50.5% of

[1] The dictator game is another well-known variant of the ultimatum game where the responder always has to accept what the proposer offers and, in this case, isn't even allowed to make a symbolic rejection. The responder, thus, has the least amount of power among the three games. However, since the responder – human or agent – doesn't have to make any decision, we consider the dictator game to be out of scope for our research objectives.

[2] Using this form of deception is not uncommon when studying people's decision making with humans and computers [19], [22]-[24].

the participants were males. Age distribution was as follows: *22 to 34 years*, 61.3%; *35 to 44 years*, 24.7%; *45 to 54 years*, 9.3%; *55 to 64 years*, 3.6%; *over 65 years*, 1.0%. Professional backgrounds were quite diverse. Participants were paid $2.00 for their participation. Moreover, they had the chance to win extra money, through the lotteries, according to their performance in the tasks. Finally, participants gave their consent before engaging in the experiment and the research presented here was approved by the Internal Review Board at the University of Southern California.

Full anonymity. This experiment was fully anonymous for the participants. To preserve anonymity between participants, human counterparts were referred to as "anonymous" and we never collected any information that could identify the participants. Agents were referred to as "computer agents". To preserve anonymity with respect to the experimenters, we relied on Amazon Mechanical Turk's anonymity system. When interacting with participants from this online pool, researchers are never able to identify the participants, unless they explicitly ask for information that may serve to identify them (e.g., name or photo), which we did not.

Measures. Our main measure was the offers participants made to their counterparts. After completing each task, we had one manipulation check for perception of power: During this event, do you think your counterpart felt powerful (as opposed to powerless)? (1, *Not at all*, to 7, *Very much*). After completing both tasks, we had two further manipulation checks:

- In this experiment, some participants interacted directly with a counterpart, whereas others interacted with computer agents that made decisions on their behalf. In your case, how did you interact with your counterpart? (I interacted directly with my counterpart vs. I interacted via a computer agent that decided on my behalf)
- In this experiment, some participants interacted with another MTurker directly, whereas others interacted with a computer agent that acted on behalf of someone else. In your case, who did you interact with? (I interacted with another MTurker directly vs. I interacted with a computer agent that acted on behalf of someone else).

Finally, to measure social value orientation, before starting the tasks, participants completed the 6-item version of the Slider SVO Measure [56]. After running this measure on our sample, 39.7% of the participants were classified as non-cooperators, and 60.3% as cooperators.

2.2 Results

Manipulation checks. To analyze the manipulation checks for the proposer conditions (Were you interacting via an agent?) and the responder conditions (Were you interacting with an agent?), we ran chi-square tests. The results confirmed that participants accurately remembered the condition they were assigned to (proposers: $\chi^2 = 89.68$, $p < .001$; responders: $\chi^2 = 133.61$, $p < .001$). Regarding the manipulation check for power, participants perceived their counterparts, as expected, to have more power in the ultimatum game ($M = 3.37$, $SE = .134$) than in the impunity game ($M = 2.25$, $SE = .125$), $t(193) = 7.47$, $p < .001$, $r = .473$).

Offers. The offers participants made in the ultimatum and impunity games are shown in Figure 2. To analyze this data, we ran a Responder × Proposer × Power × SVO mixed ANOVA. The results showed a main effect of Responder, with people offering more to humans ($M = 7.13$, $SE = .27$) than to agents representing others ($M = 6.29$, $SE = .26$), $F(1, 186) = 4.98$, $p = .027$, partial $\eta^2 = .026$. This result, thus, supports Hypothesis 1.

The results also reveal a main effect of Proposer, with people offering more when interacting via an agent ($M = 7.09$, $SE = .27$) than when interacting directly with their counterparts ($M = 6.33$, $SE = .26$), $F(1, 186) = 4.18$, $p = .042$, partial $\eta^2 = .022$. This result, therefore, supports Hypothesis 2b (and contradicts Hypothesis 2a).

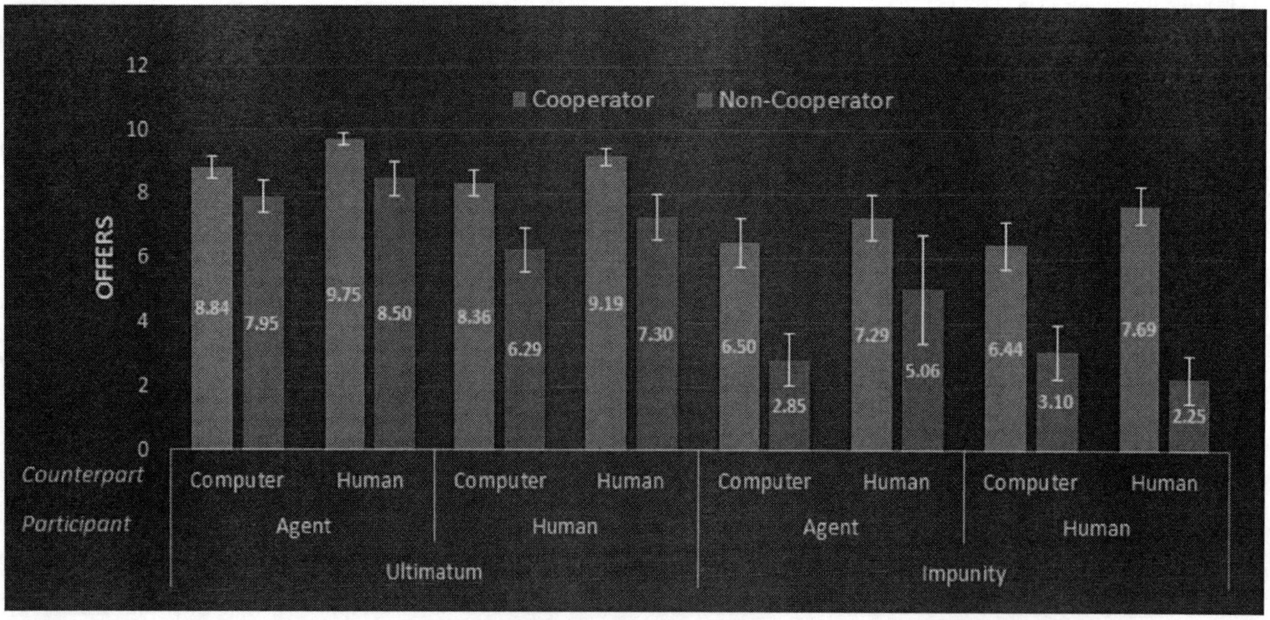

Figure 2. Offers in the ultimatum and impunity games. The error bars show standard errors.

Regarding power, there was a main effect with people offering more in the ultimatum (M = 8.27, SE = .16) than in the impunity game (M = 5.15, SE = .30), $F(1, 186) = 106.00, p < .001$, partial $\eta^2 = .363$. However, there were no statistically significant interactions with Responder or Proposer: Power × Responder, $F(1, 186) = .00, p = .966$; Power × Proposer, $F(1, 186) = .48, p = .489$; Power × Responder × Proposer, $F(1, 186) = 1.51, p = .221$.

Finally, regarding social value orientation, there was a main effect with cooperators (M = 8.01, SE = .24) offering more than non-cooperators (M = 5.41, SE = .29), $F(1, 186) = 47.86, p < .001$, partial $\eta^2 = .205$. There was also a SVO × Power interaction, $F(1, 186) = 12.39, p = .001$, partial $\eta^2 = .062$: non-cooperators offered much less in the impunity game than participants in any other condition. There were no statistically significant interactions, however, with Responder or Proposer: SVO × Responder, $F(1, 186) = .08, p = .781$; SVO × Proposer, $F(1, 186) = 2.48, p = .117$; SVO × Responder × Proposer, $F(1, 186) = .54, p = .462$.

3. DISCUSSION

At a time when there is increased interest in agents that act on behalf of humans, this paper raises awareness to important distinctions people still make between interacting with agents that represent humans and interacting with humans directly. Our first main finding is that, everything else being equal, people tend to make more favorable offers to humans than to agents acting on behalf of humans. This result is in line with findings in the behavioral sciences that reveal that perceived social distance impacts decision making [25]-[31]. Accordingly, the higher the perceived social distance to the counterpart, the less favorable the decisions are likely to be.

Our second main finding is that, in contrast to the tendency to be less fair with agents that represent others, people show higher concern for fairness when tasking an agent to represent them in decision making settings. Despite the fact that acting through an agent increases the social distance with the counterpart, considerations for the longer-term consequences for one's social image seem to prevail [32]-[34]. When creating an agent that is meant to represent one's values, possibly across several interactions with various counterparts, people choose to behave more fairly and preserve their reputations.

A first reading of these findings may suggest that what we accomplished here was to raise a warning to the risk individuals incur of being doubly disadvantaged if they task an agent to interact with other humans. However, instead, we see these findings as introducing two exciting opportunities. First, the results emphasize what needs to be addressed in order to have humans treat agents that represent others as fairly as the humans they are representing, and that is to reduce the perceived social distance to the agents. This can be achieved by emphasizing the presence of the human for whom the agent is working for or, alternatively, by emphasizing shared group membership or common values. In support of this view, previous research demonstrates that people cooperate and trust more with agents that are perceived to share salient physical characteristics (e.g., race [11]) or with which people share a "common fate" (e.g., when they engage in a task as teammates [10], [57]). In fact, by associating agents with membership in multiple positive group memberships, it is even possible to make people favor agents to humans [57].

The second opportunity is that acting through agents can increase a motivation for fairness. The implication is that interaction between agents has the potential to *improve* fairness in society, when compared to the current state-of-affairs in human-human interaction. Because agents do not suffer from the typical constraints we see in humans (e.g., bounded rationality [58]), we already knew that it was possible to use them to increase efficiency in terms of standard economics metrics, such as pareto-optimality [1]-[4]. Here, we propose that agents also have the potential to enhance the kind of social considerations we see in humans [59] – fairness, cooperation, altruism, reciprocity, etc. – by virtue of motivating designers and human users to consider the broader implications of their decisions.

Notice that our proposal is not that people will be more generous when interacting via agents, but rather that they will show higher concerns for fairness. Thus, when playing in the role of proposer, we expect people to make more generous offers than if they were interacting directly with their counterparts; however, when playing in the role of responder, we expect people to be *less* likely to accept unfair offers than if they were not interacting via an automated agent. This is, in fact, an interesting hypothesis to test in future work. These concerns for fairness, for instance, may explain why people show higher demand when interacting via an automated agent than when interacting directly with others in a negotiation task [60].

Our results also demonstrate that power – i.e., the counterpart's ability to shape the final outcome – impacts the decisions we make with automated agents. Our experimental results show that people's offers via agents or with agents were always better when the counterpart was perceived to have more power. This is a replication of earlier findings in the behavioral sciences [41]-[45] and, thus, our contribution is simply to show that the effects of power we see in human-human interaction carry to human-agent interaction.

Additionally, our findings confirm that social value orientation – i.e., people's inherent propensity for cooperation – can also impact behavior with agents. The results showed that cooperators, in general, offered more via agents or with agents than non-cooperators. Given that the literature on social value orientation has mostly focused in social interaction involving exclusively humans [46]-[49], our contribution is in showing that this important individual trait also extends to interactions with automated agents.

The results presented in this paper have important practical implications across several domains. For automated negotiation [1]-[5], the recommendation is that, as discussed above, designers should allow human users to customize their agents. This is likely to lead users to show higher concern for reaching a fair deal. Additionally, designers should strive to minimize the perceived social distance to their human counterparts. These results are also not limited to software agents. As robots get immersed into society [61], [62], the guidelines proposed here for optimizing decision making in human-agent interaction should also be useful for human-robot interaction. Our findings provide insight into how increasing social distance will affect interaction with autonomous vehicles [7] or unmanned flying vehicles [8]: on the one hand, people may react more harshly when something goes wrong because of these vehicles; on the other hand, designers and human will likely strive to embed in them best driving or flying practices. Overall, by reducing social distance with these automated agents and maximizing considerations for the human users' social image, designers can pave the way for more efficient human-agent interaction in various domains.

Finally, this work has interesting ethical implications. There has been considerable concern about allowing these automated agents take their place in society. For instance, the UK's 1998 Data Protection Act gives employees the right to ask for human intervention in the case of any decision made solely by automated means, when personal data is involved. People are also naturally reluctant to let automated vehicles drive on their streets and for unmanned aerial vehicles to apply lethal force [63]. However, experimental work, such as the one presented here, provides critical insight into the psychological mechanisms driving people's behavior with automated agents and, consequently, suggest ways for overcoming these concerns. Moreover, the results in this paper suggest that the very fact that people are forced to think about how they want their agents to behave in society, can lead to a higher-level perspective and, subsequently, to increased motivation for fairness and cooperation.

4. CONCLUSION

In this paper, we show that people's behavior with or via automated agents is different than their behavior with humans. On the one hand, we show that people tend make less favorable offers to agents that act on behalf of humans than if they were interacting with the humans themselves. We propose that to reduce (or increase) this effect we should reduce (or increase) the perceived social distance to the humans on whose behalf the agents are acting. On the other hand, we show that people are likely to demonstrate a higher concern for fairness when interacting via an automated agent than if interacting directly with others. We propose this occurs because people demonstrate a higher concern for their social image and reputation, when tasking an agent to act on their behalf. These results, thus, provide key insight into the psychological mechanisms driving people's behavior with automated agents and, consequently, are key for achieving in human-agent interaction the same kind of efficiency – fairness, cooperation, reciprocity, etc. – we see in human-human interaction.

5. ACKNOWLEDGMENTS

This work is supported by the National Science Foundation, under grant BCS-1419621, and the Air Force Office of Scientific Research, under grant FA9550-14-1-0364. The content does not necessarily reflect the position or the policy of any Government, and no official endorsement should be inferred.

6. REFERENCES

[1] Lin, R., and Kraus, S. 2010. Can automated agents proficiently negotiate with humans? *Comm. ACM* 53, 78-88.

[2] Jennings, N., Faratin, P., Lomuscio, A., Parsons S., Wooldridge, M., and Sierra, C. 2001. Automated negotiation: Prospects, methods and challenges. *Group Dec. Negot.* 10, 199-215.

[3] Jonker, C., and Robu, V. 2007. An agent architecture for multi-attribute negotiation using incomplete preference information. In *Proceedings of the Autonomous Agents and Multi-Agent Systems Conference (AAMAS'07).*

[4] Sycara, K., and Dai, T. 2010. Agent reasoning in negotiation. In *Handbook of Group Decision and Negotiation*, D. Kilgour, and C. Eden, Eds. Springer Netherlands, 437-451.

[5] Lin, R., Kraus, S., Oshrat, Y., and Gal, Y. 2010. Facilitating the evaluation of automated negotiators using peer designed agents. In *Proceedings of the 24th AAAI Conference on Artificial Intelligence (AAAI'10).*

[6] Davenport, T., and Harris, J. 2005. Automated decision making comes of age. *MIT Sloan Manage. Rev.* 46, 83-89.

[7] Dresner, K., and Stone, P. 2007. Sharing the road: Autonomous vehicles meet human drivers. In *Proceedings of the International Joint Conference on Artificial Intelligence (IJCAI'07).*

[8] Gupte, S. 2012. A survey of quadrotor Unmanned Aerial Vehicles. In *Proceedings of IEEE Southeastcon.* IEEE, 1-6.

[9] Nass, C., and Moon, Y. 2000. Machines and mindlessness: Social responses to computers. *J. Soc. Issues* 56, 81-103.

[10] Nass, C., Fogg, B., and Moon, Y. 1996. Can computers be teammates? *Int. J. Hum-Comput. St.* 45, 669-678.

[11] Nass, C., Isbister, K., and Lee, E.-J. 2000. Truth is beauty: Researching embodied conversational agents. In *Embodied conversational agents*, J. Cassell Ed. MIT Press, Cambridge, MA, 374-402.

[12] Nass, C., Moon, Y., and Carney, P. 1999. Are people polite to computers? Responses to computer-based interviewing systems. *J. App. Psychol.* 29, 1093-1110.

[13] Nass, C., Moon, Y., and Green, N. 1997. Are computers gender-neutral? Gender stereotypic responses to computers. *J. App. Soc. Psychol.* 27, 864-876.

[14] Reeves, B., and Nass, C. 1996. *The media equation: How people treat computers, television, and new media like real people and places.* Cambridge University Press.

[15] Gray, H., Gray, K., and Wegner, D. 2007. Dimensions of mind perception. *Science* 315, 619.

[16] Blascovich, J., Loomis, J., Beall, A., Swinth, K., Hoyt, C., and Bailenson, J. 2002. Immersive virtual environment technology as a methodological tool for social psychology. *Psychol. Inq.* 13, 103-124.

[17] Waytz, A., Gray, K., Epley, N., and Wegner, D. 2010. Causes and consequences of mind perception. *Trends Cogn. Sci.* 14, 383-388.

[18] de Melo, C., and Gratch, J. 2015. People show envy, not guilt, when making decisions with machines. In *Proceedings of the Affective Computing and Intelligent Interaction Conference (ACII) 2015.*

[19] Rilling, J., Gutman, D., Zeh, T., Pagnoni, G., Berns, G., and Kilts, C. 2002. A neural basis for social cooperation. *Neuron* 35, 395-405.

[20] Krach, S., Hegel, F., Wrede, B., Sagerer, G., Binkofski, F., and Kircher, T. 2008. Can machines think? Interaction and perspective taking with robots investigated via fMRI. *PLOS ONE* 3, 1-11.

[21] McCabe, K., Houser, D., Ryan, L., Smith, V., and Trouard, T. 2001. A functional imaging study of cooperation in two-person reciprocal exchange. *Proc. Nat. Acad. Sci.* 98, 11832-11835.

[22] Sanfey, A., Rilling, J., Aronson, J., Nystrom, L., and Cohen, J. 2003. The neural basis of economic decision-making in the ultimatum game. *Science* 300, 1755-1758.

[23] Kircher, T., Blümel, I., Marjoram, D., Lataster, T., Krabbendam, L., Weber, J., van Os, J., and Krach, S. 2009. Online mentalising investigated with functional MRI. *Neurosci. Lett.* 454, 176-181.

[24] Gallagher, H., Anthony, J., Roepstorff, A., and Frith, C. 2002. Imaging the intentional stance in a competitive game. *NeuroImage* 16, 814-821.

[25] Hoffman, E., McCabe, K., and Smith, V. 1996. Social distance and other-regarding behavior in dictator games. *Am. Econ. Rev.* 86, 653-660.

[26] Hoffman, E., McCabe, K., Shachat, K., and Smith, V. 1994. Preferences, property rights, and anonymity in bargaining games. *Games Econ. Behav.* 7, 346–380.

[27] Leider, S., Mobius, M., Rosenblat, T., and Do, Q-A. 2009. Directed altruism and enforced reciprocity in social networks. *Q. J. Econ.* 124, 1815-1851.

[28] Goeree, J., McConnell, M., Mitchell, T., Tromp, T., and Yariv, L. 2010. The 1/d law of giving. *Am. Econ. J. Microecon.* 2, 183-203.

[29] Pronin, E., Olivola, C., and Kennedy K. 2008. Doing unto future selves as you would do unto others: Psychological distance and decision making. *Person. Soc. Psychol. Bull.* 34, 224-236.

[30] Nowak, M., and May, R. 1992. Evolutionary games and spatial chaos. *Nature* 359, 826–829.

[31] Nowak, M., Tarnita, C., and Antal T. 2010. Evolutionary dynamics in structured populations. *Philos. Trans. R. Soc. B: Biol. Sci.* 365, 19-30.

[32] Nowak, M., and Sigmund, K. 2005. Evolution of indirect reciprocity. Nature 437, 1291-1298.

[33] Ohtsuki, H. and Iwasa, Y. 2006. The leading eight: social norms that can maintain cooperation by indirect reciprocity. J. Theor. Biol. 239, 435–444.

[34] Andreoni, J. & Bernheim, B. 2009. Social image and the 50–50 norm. A theoretical and experimental analysis of audience effects. Econometrica 77, 1607-1636.

[35] Trope, Y., and Nira, L. 2010. Construal-level theory of psychological distance. *Psychol. Rev.* 117, 440-463.

[36] Agerström, J., and Björklund, F. (2009a). Moral concerns are greater for temporally distant events and are moderated by value strength. *Soc. Cogn.* 27, 261-282.

[37] Agerström, J., and Björklund, F. (2009b). Temporal distance and moral concerns: Future morally questionable behavior is perceived as more wrong and evokes stronger prosocial intentions. *Basic App. Soc. Psychol.* 31, 49-59.

[38] Sanna, L., Chang, E., Parks, C., and Kennedy, L. (2009). Construing collective concerns: Increasing cooperation by broadening construals in social dilemmas. *Psychol. Sci.* 20, 1319-1321.

[39] Henderson, M., Trope, Y., and Carnevale, P. 2006. Negotiation from a near and distant time perspective. *J. Pers. Soc. Psychol.* 91, 712-729.

[40] Giacomantonio, M., De Dreu, C., Shalvi, S., Sligte, D., and Leder, S. 2010. Psychological distance boosts value-behavior correspondence in ultimatum bargaining and integrative negotiation. *J. Exp. Soc. Psychol.* 46, 824-829.

[41] Bacharach, S., and Lawler, E. 1981. *Bargaining: Power, tactics, and outcomes*. San Francisco: Jossey-Bass.

[42] Kelley, H., and Thibaut, J. 1978. *Interpersonal relations: A theory of interdependence.* New York: Academic Press.

[43] Pinkley, R., Neale, M., and Bennett, R. 1994. The impact of alternatives to settlement in dyadic negotiation. *Organ. Behav. Human Dec. Proc.* 57, 97-116.

[44] De Dreu, C. 1995. Coercive power and concession making in bilateral negotiation. *J. Confl. Resolut.* 39, 646-670.

[45] Lawler, E. 1992. Power processes in bargaining. *Sociol. Q.* 33, 17-34.

[46] Messick, D., and McClintock, C. 1968. Motivational bases of choice in experimental games. *J. Exp. Soc. Psychol.* 4, 1-25.

[47] Van Lange, P. 1999. The pursuit of joint outcomes and equality in outcomes: An integrative model of social value orientation. *J. Pers. Soc. Psychol.* 77, 337-349.

[48] Bogaert, S., Boone, C., and Declerck, C. 2008. Social value orientation and cooperation in social dilemmas: A review and conceptual model. *Brit. J. Soc. Psychol.* 47, 453-480.

[49] Balliet, D., Parks, C., and Joireman, J. 2009. Social value orientation and cooperation in social dilemmas: A meta-analysis. *Group Process. Interg.* 12, 533-547.

[50] Güth, W., Schmittberger, R., and Schwarze, B. 1982. An experimental analysis of ultimatum bargaining. *J. Econ. Behav. & Organ.* 3, 367-388.

[51] J. Henrich, R. Boyd, S. Bowles, C. Camerer, E. Fehr, H. Gintis, and R. McElreath. 2001. In search of homo economicus: behavioral experiments in 15 small-scale societies. *Am. Econ. Rev.* 91, 73-78.

[52] Camerer, C., and Thaler, R. 1995. Ultimatums, dictators, and manners. *J. Econ. Perspect.*, *9*, 209-219.

[53] Yamagishi, T., Horita, H., Shinada, M., Tanida, S., and Cook, K. 2009. The private rejection of unfair offers and emotional commitment. *Proc. Nat. Acad. Sci.* 106, 11520-11523.

[54] Bolton, G., and Zwick, R. 1995. Anonymity versus punishment in ultimatum bargaining. *Games Econ. Behav.* 10, 95-121.

[55] Paolacci, G., Chandler, J., and Ipeirotis, P. 2010. Running experiments on Amazon Mechanical Turk. *Judgm. Decis. Mak.* 5, 411-419.

[56] Murphy, R., Ackermann, K., and Handgraaf, M. 2011. Measuring social value orientation. *Judgm. Decis. Mak.* 6, 771-781.

[57] de Melo, C., Carnevale, P., and Gratch, J. 2014. Social categorization and cooperation between humans and computers. In *Proceedings of the Annual Meeting of the Cognitive Science Society (CogSci'14).*

[58] Simon, H. 1972. Theories of bounded rationality. In *Decision and Organization*, McGuire, C., and Radner, R., Eds. North-Holland Publishing Company, 161-176.

[59] Rand, D., and Nowak, M. Human cooperation. 2013. *Trends Cogn. Sci.* 17, 413-425. In *Proceedings of the Autonomous Agents and Multi-Agent Systems Conference (AAMAS'04).*

[60] Grosz, B., Kraus, S., and Talman, S. 2004. The influence of social dependencies on decision-making: Initial investigations with a new game. In

[61] Breazeal, C. 2003. Toward sociable robots. *Robotics and autonomous systems* 42: 167-175.

[62] Leite, I., Martinho, C., and Paiva, A. 2013. Social robots for long-term interaction. *Int. J. Soc. Robotic.* 5, 291-308.

[63] Arkin, R. Ethical robots in warfare. *IEEE Technol. Soc. Mag.* 28, 30-33.

A Need for Speed: Adapting Agent Action Speed to Improve Task Learning from Non-Expert Humans

Bei Peng
Washington State University
bpeng@eecs.wsu.edu

James MacGlashan
Brown University
jmacglashan@gmail.com

Robert Loftin
North Carolina State University
rtloftin@csc.ncsu.edu

Michael L. Littman
Brown University
mlittman@cs.brown.edu

David L. Roberts
North Carolina State University
robertsd@csc.ncsu.edu

Matthew E. Taylor
Washington State University
taylorm@eecs.wsu.edu

ABSTRACT

As robots become pervasive in human environments, it is important to enable users to effectively convey new skills without programming. Most existing work on Interactive Reinforcement Learning focuses on interpreting and incorporating non-expert human feedback to speed up learning; we aim to design a better representation of the learning agent that is able to elicit more natural and effective communication between the human trainer and the learner, while treating human feedback as discrete communication that depends probabilistically on the trainer's target policy. This work entails a user study where participants train a virtual agent to accomplish tasks by giving reward and/or punishment in a variety of simulated environments. We present results from 60 participants to show how a learner can ground natural language commands and adapt its action execution speed to learn more efficiently from human trainers. The agent's action execution speed can be successfully modulated to encourage more explicit feedback from a human trainer in areas of the state space where there is high uncertainty. Our results show that our novel adaptive speed agent dominates different fixed speed agents on several measures of performance. Additionally, we investigate the impact of instructions on user performance and user preference in training conditions.

Categories and Subject Descriptors

I.2.6 [**Learning**]: Miscellaneous

General Terms

Languages, Performance, Human Factors, Experimentation

Keywords

Learning Sequential Decision Tasks from Humans; Human-Agent Interaction; Crowdsourcing Experiments; Eliciting Human Feedback; Variable Speed Agents

Appears in: *Proceedings of the 15th International Conference on Autonomous Agents and Multiagent Systems (AAMAS 2016), J. Thangarajah, K. Tuyls, C. Jonker, S. Marsella (eds.), May 9–13, 2016, Singapore.*

1. INTRODUCTION

As robots become pervasive in human environments, it is important to enable users to effectively convey new skills without programming. Recent work has shown that reinforcement learning [18] (RL) agents can successfully speed up learning using human feedback [3, 9, 20]. However, learning efficiently from human input brings significant challenges (e.g., delay, inconsistent input, and limited human patience) relative to learning autonomously.

This work is inspired by the ways humans train dogs — using rewards and punishments is a simple and familiar paradigm for humans to train intelligent agents. A human can easily correct the agent if it makes a mistake interpreting a command, rather than stopping the agent and providing a new language example. In particular, we treat human feedback as a discrete communication that depends probabilistically on the trainer's target policy. RL methods are most effective in environments where the numerically-valued reward function contains all the information needed to learn the policy. Learning from human feedback is substantively different. Trainers generally do not have numerical rewards to give to learners — instead, they use only a small set of discrete feedback signals and they may give those signals in a number of different ways to implicitly communicate the target behavior. Thus, while standard RL algorithms can be used in this setting, they are not designed to leverage all of the available information. Our previous work [12] showed that considering human feedback to be a discrete communication that depends probabilistically on the trainer's target policy can be more effective for training an agent, rather than treating it as a numerical reward signal as in traditional approaches. Our *Strategy-aware Bayesian Learning* (SABL) model is able to learn from both explicit and implicit feedback from human trainers.

While most existing work on Interactive Reinforcement Learning focuses on interpreting and incorporating human feedback to speed up learning, the design of agents is one neglected topic. We aim to design a better representation of the learning agent that is able to elicit more natural and effective communication between the human trainer and the learner, treating human feedback as a discrete value (reward, punishment, or neutral). Considering that human trainers get tired and then give infrequent feedback to the agent [11], trying to motivate people to provide more explicit feedback to the agent when it is in more important states is current work. To enable the agent to make the most of limited human input, higher amounts of explicit feedback should be delivered in areas of the state space where the learner has more uncertainty about how to act. Similarly, when the agent is fairly confident in its action choice, humans can expend less effort providing feedback.

To seek a more successful and effective learning interaction, the agent should aim to minimize the number of task failures, maximize its use of explicit human feedback, and minimize the total time needed to learn to successfully complete the task. The agent can move slower when it is unsure, giving human trainers more time to think about their strategy and deliver feedback. Similarly, when the agent is fairly confident in its action choice, it can move faster and finish the task more quickly. Lastly, the number of actions needed to learn a (near-)optimal policy should be minimized to reduce any per-action penalties (e.g., efficiently exploring a state space while minimizing wear on a robot). Note that minimizing the time and the number of actions is identical when the agent acts with a fixed time per action — if the action rate is variable, the number of actions executed can accrue at a different rate from the wall clock time expended.

Therefore, we are interested in designing an agent to optimize four metrics. We aim to 1) minimize the wall clock time the agent spends learning, 2) minimize the number of actions the agent takes while learning, 3) encourage the user to give explicit feedback to the agent (especially when the agent is unsure about its action choice), and 4) consistently learn a (near-)optimal policy.

In this paper, we present our Learning Agents Modeling Belief-Dependent Action Speeds (LAMBDAS) approach and results of a human-subjects experiment to show how a learner can adapt its action execution speed to learn more efficiently from human trainers. We demonstrate that the agent's action execution speed can be successfully modulated to strategically encourage more explicit feedback from a human trainer in parts of the state space where the learner has more uncertainty about how to act. Our results show that our novel adaptive speed agent dominates different fixed speed agents according to the four metrics discussed above.

2. BACKGROUND AND RELATED WORK

This section discusses the research most related to this paper's contributions.

There is a growing literature that addresses learning from human feedback [6, 7, 14]. Most existing reinforcement-learning algorithms treat human feedback as a numerical signal to be maximized by the agent. The TAMER algorithm is modeled after standard RL methods that learn a value function from human-delivered numerical rewards, and has been shown to be effective in a number of task domains [9, 10]. Thomaz and Breazeal [20, 21] treat human feedback as a form of guidance for an agent solving an RL problem. There, human feedback does not change the optimal policy for the RL problem, but improves exploration and accelerates learning. Their results show that humans give reward in anticipation of good actions, instead of rewarding or punishing the agent's recent actions. Suay and Chernova [17] extend their work by applying the Interactive Learning Algorithm to a real-world robotic system. They demonstrate that user guidance significantly reduces the learning rate and the impact of teacher guidance increases with state space size. Tenorio-Gonzalez et al. [19] introduce a dynamic reward shaping approach to learn from infrequent and inconsistent human feedback where the user's feedback is converted into a shaping reward, which is then used to modify the MDP reward to guide the agent's learning process.

Work by Griffith et al. [3] and Ho et al. [4] are perhaps the most similar to ours. Here, human feedback is treated as discrete communication that depends probabilistically on the trainer's target policy, rather than on some numerical reward, so that the trainer's feedback is making a direct statement about the policy itself rather than influencing the policy through a reward. Specifically, In the work of Ho et al. [4], instead of using the *reward-maximizing model* based on standard reinforcement learning, an *action-feedback model* is shown to be followed by the majority of people while teaching. However, the interaction between learning mechanism and feedback pattern is not explored. In the current paper, human feedback (either explicitly rewarding, explicitly punishing, or providing no feedback) after an agent's action is evidence for or against hypothesized target tasks represented by MDP reward functions. At each time step, the agent follows the optimal policy for the most likely task, which is computed using an "off-the-shelf" MDP planning algorithm.

To better learn from human feedback, we must deeply understand how do human teachers want to teach the agent. Work by Knox et al. [8] examine how users want to provide feedback, finding that: 1) there is little difference in a trainer's feedback whether they think that the agent can learn or that they are critiquing a fixed performance; and 2) humans can reduce the amount of feedback they give over time, and having the learner purposefully select bad actions can encourage more feedback. Similarly, our work addresses the problem of increasing the trainer's feedback quantity and quality. However, it is the first to consider modulating the agent's action execution speed according to its confidence level to elicit more explicit feedback. Our previous work [12] find that people choose different training strategies to teach the agent, and may use a lack of explicit feedback to communicate the same information as delivered by reward or punishment in both contextual bandit and sequential decision-making tasks. The choices of trainer strategies are shown to be affected by several factors (e.g., the nature of the training task or the learning agent). Instead of focusing on training strategies, we aim to seek a more successful and effective learning interaction, while maximizing the agent's learning performance on several measures. Our empirical user studies demonstrate that our novel adaptive speed agent can achieve this goal.

In this learning framework, the effect of different types of instructions on human feedback are also studied. Thomas et al. [2] show that human teachers are silent 30% of the time on average while providing feedback, implicating the importance for the policy shaping algorithm to interpret that silence. Different instructions are given to manipulate the meaning of silence to evaluate the performance impact. Pradyot et al. [15, 16] show that humans can provide sporadic instructions to speed up learning. The instructions here reduce the agent's search space and narrow down the potential interesting objects without specifying any information about how to perform the task. Similarly, we explore the impact of instructions on user performance. However,

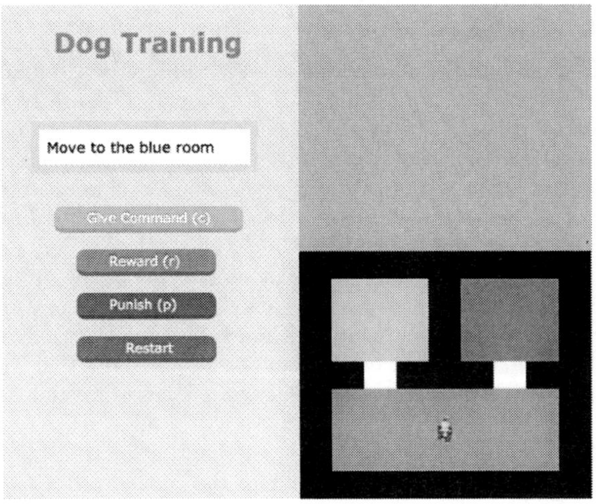

Figure 1: The GUI used to train the agent with given commands. It shows the task used in the tutorial.

our instructions are not designed to manipulate trainer's feedback strategies or affect the agent's behavior. We want to understand whether users can interpret the behavior of the adaptive speed agent correctly and perform better if they have a correct belief about the agent's belief.

3. LANGUAGE LEARNING WITH REWARD AND PUNISHMENT

To enable people to naturally and effectively train an artificial agent to carry out a variety of different tasks with reward and punishment, one approach is for a person to manually specify each new task they are training and when they wanted an agent to perform a previously trained task, provide an interface that allowed them to select from the previously trained tasks. However, a more natural interface would be to connect the task learning with a natural language model. In this setting, a trainer could give a novel command and reward / punish the agent until the agent successfully completed the task. As the trainer taught additional tasks, the agent would become better at interpreting the language, thereby enabling the agent to successfully interpret and carry out novel commands without any reward and punishment. For example, an agent might learn the interpretation of "red" and "chair" from the command "move the red chair," and the interpretation of "blue" and "bag" from the command "bring me the blue bag," thereby allowing correct interpretation of the novel command "bring me the red bag." The domain we use in our experiment is a simplified simulated home environment. Our domain and user study GUI are shown in Figure 1.

To enable language learning from agents trained with reward and punishment, we use our previous probabilistic model [13] that connected the IBM Model 2 (IBM2) language model [1] with a factored generative model of tasks, and the goal-directed SABL algorithm [12] for learning from human feedback.

Using this probabilistic model, an iterative training regime proceeds as follows. First, the trainer gives an English command. Second, from this command, a distribution over the possible tasks for the current state of the environment is inferred using Bayesian inference. Third, this task distribution is used as a prior for the goals in goal-directed SABL. Fourth, the agent is trained with SABL for a series of time steps. Fifth, after completing training, a new posterior distribution over tasks is induced and used to update the IBM2 model via weakly-supervised learning. The process repeats when provided a new command.

To validate that the agent is able to successfully learn novel language commands using reward and punishment feedback from a human trainer, In our previous work [13] participants train the agent on seven commands including "take the blue chair to the yellow room" and "take the purple bag to the blue room." As training proceeds, the agent becomes better at correctly interpreting commands and requires less feedback to disambiguate the intended meaning. After training, the agent is able to correctly interpret novel commands that describe different combinations of objects, object colors, and room colors. For example, the agent correctly interprets the command "take the purple chair to the green room" despite never being trained with commands involving a purple chair or taking an object to a green room. However, in this work, we are concerned with the per-task training rather than validating the quality of the learned language model.

4. ADAPTIVE SPEED AGENT

This section presents our LAMBDAS approach to implement the adaptive speed agent in our experiment.

4.1 Motivation

Our goal is to design a framework in which non-expert humans (i.e., workers on Amazon's Mechanical Turk, also known as "Turkers") can provide categorical feedback to an agent to learn task groundings, while maximizing its learning performance. To seek a more successful and effective learning interaction, the agent should aim to minimize the number of task failures, maximize its use of explicit human feedback, and minimize the total time and number of actions needed to learn to successfully complete the task (discussed in Section 1).

Considering that human trainers tire and then give less feedback to an agent, it is a reasonable design decision to have the agent try to elicit explicit feedback when it is in some states. Higher amounts of explicit feedback should be delivered in parts of the state space where the learner has more uncertainty about how to act, so that the agent can make the most of limited human input. Similarly, when the agent is fairly confident in its action choice, humans can expend less effort providing feedback. Our core hypothesis was that changing the speed of the agent can be a good way to achieve this goal; the agent can move slower when it is unsure, giving the human trainers more time to think about the strategy and deliver feedback. Similarly, when the agent is fairly confident in its action choice, it can move faster and finish the task more quickly.

We are interested in studying whether users can interpret the behavior of the adaptive speed agent correctly and how user performance will change in response to the changing speed of the agent. Our insight was that the adaptive speed agent would be either competitive with or outperform the fixed speed agents according to the four metrics discussed above.

4.2 Modeling Belief-Dependent Action Speed

We develop the LAMBDAS approach to implement our novel adaptive speed agent. We first define the confidence level of the agent in its action choice, and then develop a model to map its confidence to different action execution speeds. The entropy (H) of the action selection is used to summarize the agent's confidence level,

$$H = -\sum_{a \in A} \Pr(a = a^*|s, F) \ln(\Pr(a = a^*|s, F)), \quad (1)$$

where A is the set of possible actions, F is the history of feedback events from the trainer, and $\Pr(a = a^*|s, F)$ is the probability that action a given state s and feedback history F is the optimal action (a^*). A high entropy means the agent has high uncertainty in choosing the optimal action, while a low entropy indicates agent confidence in which action is the optimal action for the given state.

Because we follow the SABL formalism in which human feedback gives evidence for an intended reward function for which there are corresponding optimal policies, the probability that an action selection is the optimal action can be inferred by marginalizing the policies over the reward functions. Specifically, the probability distribution over optimal actions is computed as

$$\Pr(a = a^*|s, F) = \sum_{r \in R} \pi(s, a|r) \Pr(r|F), \quad (2)$$

where R is the hypothesis space of possible reward functions to be trained, $\pi(s, a|r)$ is an indicator function specifying whether action a is the optimal action in state s when reward function r is being maximized,[1] and $\Pr(r|F)$ is the current probability based on the feedback history F that reward function r is the intended reward function by the trainer that is learned using SABL.

We develop three mathematical models (linear, sigmoidal, and threshold) to map each computed entropy to the agent's action execution speed,

$$T = \theta_f + (\theta_s - \theta_f) * H, \quad (3)$$

$$T = \theta_f + \frac{\theta_s - \theta_f}{1 + e^{-10(H - \theta_f)}}, \quad (4)$$

$$T = \begin{cases} \theta_s & H > 0.1 \\ \theta_f & otherwise \end{cases} \quad (5)$$

Given the entropy of the action selection H, the corresponding step interval T between two consecutive actions is computed at each time step, which reflects the agent's confidence level of the current action choice. The agent speed varies from θ_f seconds (the fastest speed with highest confidence/minimum entropy) to θ_s seconds (the slowest speed with lowest confidence/maximum entropy) per step.

5. EXPERIMENTS

To study how humans want to train the agent in sequential domains, we developed a user study in which participants train a virtual agent to accomplish pre-specified commands by giving reward and/or punishment.

[1]If there are multiple optimal actions for the reward function, then $\pi(s, a|r)$ either arbitrarily selects only one, or is defined to be uniform over the subset of optimal actions.

5.1 Domain

Our domain[2] is a simplified simulated home environment. The domain and user study GUI are shown in Figure 1. The domain consists of four object classes: agent, room, object, and door. The visual representation of the agent is a virtual dog, to fit with our initial motivation of humans being able to teach dogs complex tasks. The agent can deterministically move one unit north, south, east, or west, and push objects by moving into them. The objects are chairs or bags; rooms and objects can be red, yellow, green, blue, and purple. Doors (shown in white in Figure 1) connect two rooms so that the agent can move from one room to another. The possible commands given to the agent include moving to a specified colored room (e.g., "move to the blue room") and taking an object with specified shape and color to a colored room (e.g., "move the blue chair to the purple room"). We provide a fixed set of environments and commands to human participants, limiting the human to providing rewards and punishment feedback.

5.2 Design

In our IRB-approved user study, human participants must first pass a color blind test before starting the experiment since the training task requires the ability to identify different colored objects. Second, users fill out a background survey indicating their age, gender, education, history with dog ownership, dog training experiences, and the dog training techniques they are familiar with. Third, users are taken through a tutorial that explains how to interactively reward and punish the virtual dog based on its behavior. The user is told that punishment can be treated as a signal that the virtual dog should consider a different task than the one it was executing. Fourth, users are tested in the same environment as the tutorial to verify that they understood the interface. Participants that failed this basic check for comprehension (11.3%) were excluded from results.

Following the tutorial and verification test, users are requested to train the virtual dog in a series of three environments shown in Figure 2. Each environment has a different level of complexity and is presented to users in a random order. Following training in the three environments, the users are asked to repeat training with a new virtual dog that behaves differently in the same three environments. Upon finishing the second sequence of tasks, users are asked to describe the strategy used when training the agent. Then, we elicit users' preference with respect to constant or adaptive speed of the virtual dog, and ask them to explain how the adaptive speed virtual dog changes its speed. Finally, participants have the option to provide any additional comments about the experiment.

5.3 Preliminary Studies

To implement the novel training condition with adaptive speed agent, we did a set of preliminary studies to determine the threshold of the agent speed ($[\theta_f, \theta_s]$) and the model to be used in the adaptive case.

We first tested four different constant agent speeds, to gain some preliminary insights into the effect of an agent's speed on trainer feedback. The different values of the speed were 0.5, 0.75, 1.0, and 2.0 (seconds per step). It was inspired by

[2]The video showing the dog training task in our user study is available from `https://www.youtube.com/watch?v=AJQSGD_XPrk`

(a) "Move to the yellow room" (b) "Move the blue chair to the purple room" (c) "Move the red bag to the blue room"

Figure 2: The three training environments and their corresponding commands.

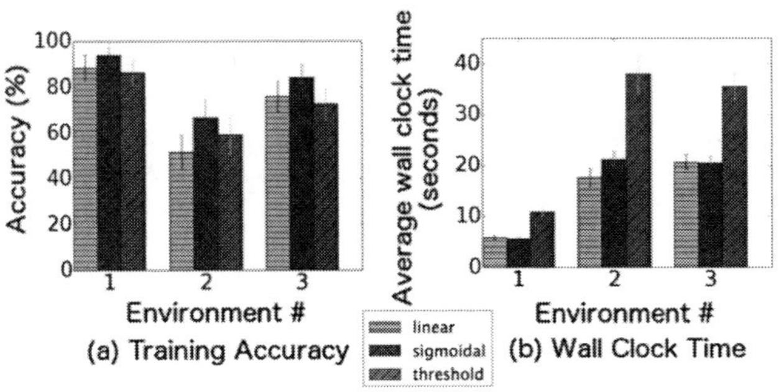

Figure 3: (a) Training accuracy (b) Average wall clock time spent to successfully train the agent when agent's speed changed according to linear, threshold or adaptive model.

the cognitive process study of Hockley [5], which shows that the mean human response time varies from $540.3 \sim 1093.5$ ms. Thus, the fastest action execution speed of the agent was assigned as 0.5 seconds/step so that the agent could complete the task with minimal wall clock time while human trainers generally had sufficient time to provide feedback to the virtual dog. Similarly, the slowest action execution speed was set to 2.0 seconds/step to allow each user to have time to think about the strategy and to deliver feedback. We considered the results from 60 users from Amazon's Mechanical Turk and compared the results across different agent speeds. Each participant experienced two agents that moved at different constant fast or slow intervals. There were 30 unique users for each of the four training conditions. Our preliminary analysis suggested that the agent used more wall clock time but fewer actions to learn the appropriate policy when it moved more slowly, receiving more explicit feedback from human trainers. This suggested the agent's speed did affect the trainer feedback and performance. Thus, the threshold of the adaptive agent speed was set as $[0.5, 2.0]$, where the fastest speed θ_f was 0.5 seconds/step, and the slowest speed θ_s was 2.0 seconds/step.

Second, to study the most effective model in modulating the agent speed in adaptive case, we collected data from another 45 Mechanical Turk participants, where each participant was required to train two adaptive speed agents using two of the three speed models (linear, sigmoidal, and threshold). There were 30 participants for each of the three adaptive agents with different speed models. Our preliminary results (shown in Figure 3 (b)) suggested that users spent the most wall clock time to successfully train the adaptive speed agent using the threshold model (Equation 5). This is not surprising since the agent always moved at the slowest interval (2.0 seconds/step) when it had high entropy (low confidence). However, in the other two models, the agent would only move at the slowest interval if it achieved the maximum entropy. A two-way ANOVA test shows that the wall clock time spent training the agent using each of the three adaptive models was significantly different ($p \ll 0.01$). The effect of task complexity on wall clock time used was also statistically significant ($p \ll 0.01$). There was a statistically significant interaction ($p = 0.01$) between the effects of task complexity and adaptive model on wall clock time used. There was statistically significant ($p \ll 0.01$) pairwise difference between the threshold model and linear or sigmoidal model. Compared to the adaptive speed agent using linear model (Equation 3), more users could successfully train the agent using the sigmoidal model (Equation 4) to learn the (near-)optimal policy (shown in Figure 3 (a)). Therefore, we picked the most effective sigmoidal model to map the agent's confidence level to different action execution speeds.

5.4 Final Setup

Based on our preliminary results, we consider two fixed speed agents, one constantly moving fast (0.5 seconds/step) or slow (2.0 seconds/step), and an adaptive speed agent which adjusted its speed ($0.5 \sim 2.0$ seconds/step) using the sigmoidal model to reflect its confidence level in the current action choice.[3] In the adaptive case, the agent would move quickly when it was confident (had low uncertainty) in its current action choice and slower when it was unsure. Note that action certainty is often different than the agent's confidence in which task and policy is the training target—an agent may have very high confidence in an action if it is in a long hallway and all hypothesized task policies suggest that it should exit the hallway in the same direction.

To investigate whether users can interpret the behavior of the adaptive speed agent correctly, we added another training condition with instructions about when and how the

[3]We note that we have no evidence for or against trainers interpreting the agent's speed as confidence or confusion; however, regardless of interpretation, the speed is computed to reflect confidence and the data supports the claim that it is effective at getting trainers to adjust their feedback.

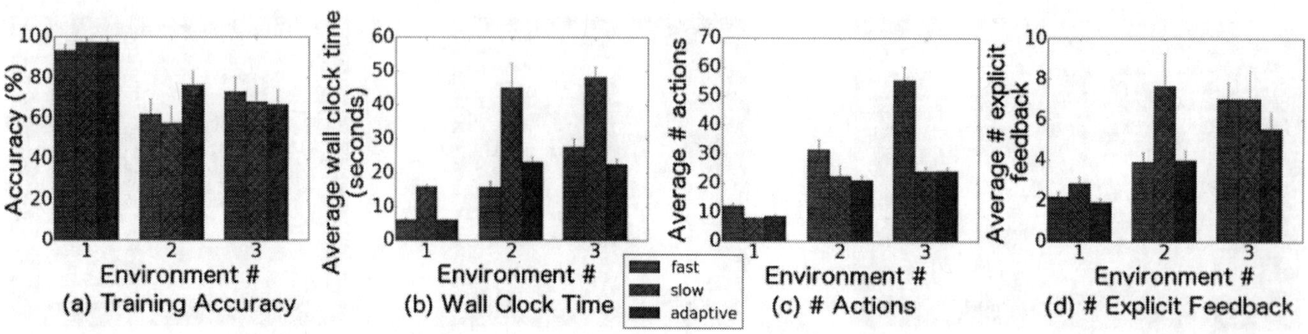

Figure 4: (a) Training accuracy (b) Average wall clock time spent to successfully train the agent (c) Average # actions executed to learn the (near-)optimal policy (d) Average # explicit feedback given when agent's speed was constant fast, constant slow, or adaptive (without instructions), given different environments.

virtual dog changes its speed in the adaptive case—in the tutorial, we explicitly told users that the virtual dog would change its behavior based on how confident it was in its action choice.

In summary, we consider four experimental conditions according to the speed of the agent described as below:

- **Constant Fast Condition**: the agent moves constantly fast (0.5 seconds/step).
- **Constant Slow Condition**: the agent moves constantly slow (2.0 seconds/step).
- **Adaptive Condition without Instructions**: the agent moves adaptively ($0.5 \sim 2.0$ seconds/step) based on its confidence level without instructions about its changing behavior.
- **Adaptive Condition with Instructions**: the agent moves adaptively ($0.5 \sim 2.0$ seconds/step) based on its confidence level with instructions about when and how it changes its speed.

6. RESULT ANALYSIS

This section summarizes our user-study results. The user study was published on Amazon Mechanical Turk as a set of Human Intelligence Tasks. We consider data from the 60 unique workers who successfully trained the verification task after the tutorial, showing that they understood the basics of the interface. Each participant trained two virtual dogs that behaved differently in two sequences of the three environments. The two sequences were assigned the same three environments in random order, with two different training conditions. The two training conditions were randomly picked from four different combinations of constant and adaptive conditions. There were the same number of tasks for each of the four training conditions (constant fast, constant slow, adaptive without instructions, and adaptive with instructions).

6.1 User Performance

In this section, we compare the results of the two fixed speed agents (constant fast or slow) against the adaptive speed agent without instructions (the effect of instructions will be discussed later). In all four evaluation metrics we consider—1) training accuracy, 2) wall clock time, 3) number of actions, and 4) amount of explicit feedback—the adaptive speed agent is either competitive with or outperforms the fixed speed agents.

We first evaluated participants' training accuracy by computing the ratio of tasks that were successfully trained to the total number of tasks that were trained by each user. Figure 4(a) shows the average training accuracy achieved in different training conditions given different environments. As we expected, compared against the constant fast or slow agent speed, the training accuracy was not hurt when the agent moved at an adaptive speed. A two-way ANOVA test indicates that the accuracy differences between three training conditions were not statistically significant ($p > 0.05$). However, the accuracy differences between three environments were statistically significant ($p \ll 0.01$), demonstrating that the task complexity did affect the performance of participants in training the agent. We find that environment 1 achieved the highest accuracy since it was easiest, as there were no objects in the environment—the agent only needed to learn the words corresponding to room colors. Contrary to our expectations, the third environment was not harder than the second, even though two objects (a red bag and a red chair) need to be identified in the third environment but only one object (a blue chair) needs to be identified in environment 2. There was no statistically significant ($p > 0.05$) pairwise difference between the second environment and third environment.

Figure 4(b) summarizes the average wall clock time people spent to teach an agent the (near-)optimal policy the first time.[4] Users spent less wall clock time training in the adaptive case than the constant slow agent case, as expected. Wall clock time was minimized in the constant fast agent case in first two environments. It is surprising that the adaptive agent took less wall clock time than the constant fast agent in environment 3, even though the adaptive agent moved slowly when it lacked confidence in its action choice, while the constant fast agent always moved fast in the entire training process. A two-way ANOVA test shows that the wall clock time spent in each of the three training conditions was significantly different ($p \ll 0.01$). The effect of task complexity on wall clock time used was also statistically significant ($p \ll 0.01$). There was a statistically significant interaction ($p = 0.009$) between the effects of task complexity and training condition on wall clock time used. There

[4]Users can decide when to finish training. To standardize timing, we record the time at which the agent first discovers an optimal policy.

was no statistically significant ($p > 0.05$) pairwise difference between the adaptive agent and constant fast agent.

These results show that an agent could accomplish a task using less wall clock time with faster speed. However, it might result in a larger number of actions executed by the agent. Increasing the number of actions executed increases the probability of the agent executing incorrect actions and causing any unwanted effects of those actions. Considering the average number of actions executed by the agent to successfully learn the (near-)optimal policy, shown in Figure 4(c), we find that the adaptive speed agent took fewer actions than the constant fast agent. A two-way ANOVA test shows that the differences of the number of actions executed between the three training conditions or three environments were both statistically significant ($p \ll 0.01$). The interaction effects of task complexity and training condition on number of actions executed were statistically significant ($p \ll 0.01$). There was no statistically significant ($p > 0.05$) pairwise difference between the adaptive speed agent and constant slow agent on this metric.

Combining the first three evaluation metrics, we find that the adaptive speed agent can use 1) significantly less wall clock time with similar number of actions (compared to the constant slow agent) and 2) significantly fewer actions but not significantly worse wall clock time (compared to the constant fast agent) to train the agent, 3) without significantly sacrificing training accuracy.

Lastly, we measured the average amount of explicit feedback given to the agent when it behaved differently. Previous work has shown that the amount of human feedback will decrease over time and forcing a learner to make mistakes can encourage more human feedback [11]. Because fewer actions were used in the adaptive speed case (relative to the constant fast case), we were worried that the agent may receive less explicit human feedback and thus make the problem of inferring the correct task harder for the agent by relying on implicit feedback. As is clear from Figure 4(d), even though fewer actions were used by the adaptive speed agent, roughly the same amount of explicit feedback was given to the constant fast and adaptive speed agents. Learning in fewer actions does not necessarily result in less explicit human feedback. A two-way ANOVA test shows that the amount of explicit feedback delivered in each of the three training conditions or three environments were both significantly different ($p < 0.05$). There was no statistically significant ($p > 0.05$) pairwise difference between the adaptive agent and constant fast agent.

To better understand whether the adaptive speed agent is either competitive with, or outperforms, the fixed speed agents on all four criteria, Figure 5 summarizes the performance of the three agents on the four metrics in Environment 3. Bars show the percentage difference, where the best value for a given metric is 100%. The other bars are computed as $\left(1 - \frac{V_c - V_o}{V_o}\right) \times 100\%$ if the smallest value is the optimum or $\left(1 - \frac{V_o - V_c}{V_o}\right) \times 100\%$ if the largest value is the optimum. V_o is the optimal value of an evaluation metric, and V_c is any other value of the same criterion. We find that the adaptive speed agent outperforms the constant speed agents on wall clock time used and number of actions executed, while maintaining similar training accuracy.

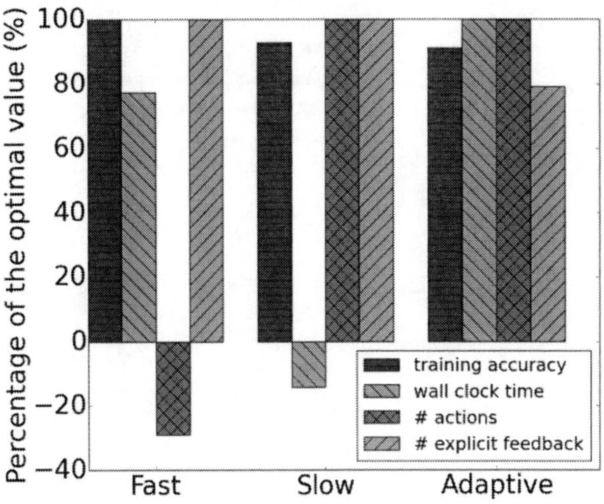

Figure 5: A bar plot showing the percentage of the optimal value each of the four criteria reached given different agent speeds in environment 3. The best result found for a given metric is 100%. The negative value indicates the percentage difference to the optimum is more than 100%. The adaptive speed agent is either competitive with or outperforms the fixed speed agents.

6.2 Speed Feedback Behavior

Recall that one motivation of our implementation of the adaptive speed agent is to encourage users to provide more explicit feedback to the agent when it has higher uncertainty in its action choice. Figure 6 shows the ratio of explicit feedback given to the agent when it moved fast or slow in the adaptive training condition, either with or without instructions, given different environments. As we expected, users tended to give more explicit feedback to the agent when it moved slowly rather than quickly. Considering that the user may provide rewards with certain delay, the slow agent speed provides more time for the trainer to think about the strategy and deliver feedback. It is also possible that the fast agent speed makes the user more nervous and she may hesitate to provide evaluative feedback. For example, one of our subjects reported that "I feel less stressful when the dog slows down and it gives me time to decide whether to reward or punish." A two-way ANOVA test shows that the ratio of explicit feedback delivered by participants when the adaptive speed agent (with or without instructions) moved fast or slowly were significantly ($p \ll 0.01$) different. There was a statistically significant interaction ($p < 0.05$) between the effects of task complexity and agent speed on ratio of explicit feedback given.

To investigate whether users can interpret the behavior of the adaptive speed agent correctly, we analyzed the conditions where they were provided explicit instructions about when and how the virtual dog changed its speed in the adaptive case. In cases where there explanation was provided, we explicitly told users that the virtual dog would change its behavior based on how confident it was in its action choice. Surprisingly, the adaptive speed agent with instructions performed fairly similar with the one without instructions on first three evaluation metrics (training accuracy, wall clock

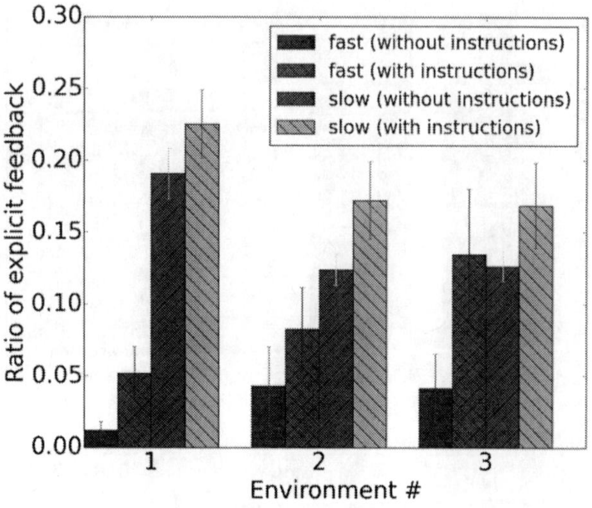

Figure 6: A bar plot showing the ratio of explicit feedback given to the agent when it moved fast or slowly in adaptive training condition with or without instructions, given different environments.

time, and number of actions) we consider before. However, it is worth noting that users provided more explicit feedback in the adaptive case with instructions. The one-way ANOVA test indicates that the number of explicit feedbacks given between the adaptive speed agent with or without instructions was significantly different ($p < 0.05$). Based on the observation that more users interpreted the changing behavior of the agent correctly in adaptive case with instructions (after analyzing users' thoughts about the reason that the agent changed its speed), it is possible that understanding when and how the agent changed its speed did help users to be actively involved in the training and provide more explicit feedback. Future work will investigate our hypothesis.

6.3 User Preference

In this section, to better understand how users interpret the changing speed of the agent, we focus on analyzing the users' responses about constant or adaptive speed agents and consider the results of users from all four training conditions (constant fast, constant slow, adaptive without instructions, and adaptive with instructions) based on different grouping criterion.

Recall that each user interacted with a constant speed agent and an adaptive speed agent in the user study; we first analyze each user's preferences regarding the two different speeds. 86.7% of users expressed a preference. Of these, 73% preferred a constant speed agent since they thought it was easier to predict or control the agent's behavior. However, it is worth noting that among those 27% of users who preferred adaptive speed agent, many of them pointed out that the agent was responsive and behaved like a real dog, giving them insights into its level of comprehension of the task.

Then, we grouped the users based on whether they experienced the constant fast or slow agent, or if they interpreted the behavior of the adaptive speed agent correctly. It is interesting that participants were more likely to prefer the adaptive speed agent if they experienced the constant fast speed agent rather than the constant slow speed agent, or when they understood the changing speed of the agent. Specifically, 36.7% of users expressed that they preferred the adaptive speed agent when they also experienced the constant fast speed agent, while only 13.3% of users preferred the adaptive case when also seeing the constant slow speed agent. Among those users who interpreted the changing speed of the agent correctly, 40% of them preferred the adaptive case. However, the percentage of participants who chose the adaptive case when they misunderstood the agent's behavior was only 22%. Fisher's exact test shows that the differences in user preference for the adaptive speed agent between these two groups were both not statistically significant ($p = 0.07$ and $p = 0.25$ respectively). This suggest an important direction for future work—when, if ever, should an agent behave to maximize performance metrics, even if doing so would not maximize user satisfaction?

7. CONCLUSIONS AND FUTURE WORK

This work considers agents that are better able to learn from human feedback by adapting their speed based on their confidence. Our experimental results show an adaptive speed agent dominates fixed speed agents in four evaluation metrics (training accuracy, wall clock time, number of actions, and amount of explicit feedback). Specifically, an adaptive action execution speed motivates non-expert users to be actively involved in the training and to effectively train agents to perform new tasks in reasonable training times and steps, without sacrificing training accuracy. We demonstrate that the agent's action execution speed can be successfully modulated to encourage more explicit feedback from a human trainer in parts of the state space where the learner has more uncertainty about how to act.

We acknowledge that there are some limitations of this work. First, the agent is constrained to follow the optimal policy of the most likely goal being trained, preventing it from taking exploratory actions to better understand the intention. Second, we did not measure whether trainers switch their feedback strategy during training, particularly if they are more confident in the agent's understanding of the task (trainer's belief about the agent's belief). If such switches in user strategy occurred, the SABL model we currently use cannot gracefully handle dynamic strategy switches.

Future work will 1) consider how human subjects can construct novel tasks and select their own wording (potentially in different languages) to command goals, 2) explore ways to improve the SABL model to consider dynamic strategy switches, 3) allow users to specify a sequence of tasks they would like to train, rather than being constrained to training pre-defined tasks, and 4) investigate how the adaptive speed of an agent can be used to influence human feedback in physical robotic platforms.

Acknowledgements

This research has taken place in part at the Intelligent Robot Learning (IRL) Lab, Washington State University and the CIIGAR Lab at North Carolina State University. IRL research is supported in part by grants AFRL FA8750-14-1-0069, AFRL FA8750-14-1-0070, NSF IIS-1149917, NSF IIS-1319412, USDA 2014-67021-22174, and a Google Research Award. CIIGAR research is supported in part by NSF grant IIS-1319305.

REFERENCES

[1] P. F. Brown, J. Cocke, S. A. D. Pietra, V. J. D. Pietra, F. Jelinek, J. D. Lafferty, R. L. Mercer, and P. S. Roossin. A statistical approach to machine translation. *Computational linguistics*, 16(2):79–85, 1990.

[2] T. Cederborg, I. Grover, C. L. Isbell, and A. L. Thomaz. Policy shaping with human teachers. In *Proc. of IJCAI*, 2015.

[3] S. Griffith, K. Subramanian, J. Scholz, C. Isbell, and A. L. Thomaz. Policy shaping: Integrating human feedback with reinforcement learning. In *Advances in Neural Information Processing Systems*, pages 2625–2633, 2013.

[4] M. K. Ho, M. L. Littman, F. Cushman, and J. L. Austerweil. Teaching with rewards and punishments: Reinforcement or communication? In *Proc. of COGSCI*, 2015.

[5] W. E. Hockley. Analysis of response time distributions in the study of cognitive processes. *Journal of Experimental Psychology: Learning, Memory, and Cognition*, 10(4):598, 1984.

[6] C. Isbell, C. R. Shelton, M. Kearns, S. Singh, and P. Stone. A social reinforcement learning agent. In *Proceedings of the fifth international conference on Autonomous agents*, pages 377–384. ACM, 2001.

[7] K. Judah, S. Roy, A. Fern, and T. G. Dietterich. Reinforcement learning via practice and critique advice. 2010.

[8] W. B. Knox, B. D. Glass, B. C. Love, W. T. Maddox, and P. Stone. How humans teach agents - a new experimental perspective. *I. J. Social Robotics*, 4(4):409–421, 2012.

[9] W. B. Knox and P. Stone. Interactively shaping agents via human reinforcement: The tamer framework. In *Proceedings of the fifth international conference on Knowledge capture*, pages 9–16. ACM, 2009.

[10] W. B. Knox, P. Stone, and C. Breazeal. Training a robot via human feedback: A case study. In *Social Robotics*, pages 460–470. Springer, 2013.

[11] G. Li, H. Hung, S. Whiteson, and W. B. Knox. Using informative behavior to increase engagement in the TAMER framework. In *Proc. of AAMAS*, 2013.

[12] R. Loftin, B. Peng, J. MacGlashan, M. L. Littman, M. E. Taylor, J. Huang, and D. L. Roberts. Learning behaviors via human-delivered discrete feedback: modeling implicit feedback strategies to speed up learning. *Journal of Autonomous Agents and Multi-Agent Systems*, pages 1–30, 2015.

[13] J. MacGlashan, M. L. Littman, R. Loftin, B. Peng, D. L. Roberts, and M. E. Taylor. Training an agent to ground commands with reward and punishment. In *Proceedings of the AAAI Machine Learning for Interactive Systems Workshop*, 2014.

[14] P. M. Pilarski, M. R. Dawson, T. Degris, F. Fahimi, J. P. Carey, and R. S. Sutton. Online human training of a myoelectric prosthesis controller via actor-critic reinforcement learning. In *Rehabilitation Robotics (ICORR), 2011 IEEE International Conference on*, pages 1–7. IEEE, 2011.

[15] V. Pradyot Koruplou, S. Manimaran, B. Ravindran, and S. Natarajan. Integrating human instructions and reinforcement learners: An srl approach. In *Proceedings of the UAI workshop on Statistical Relational AI*, 2012.

[16] V. Pradyot Koruplou, M. S. Sivamurugan, and B. Ravindran. Instructing a reinforcement learner. In *Proceedings of the Twenty Fifth Florida AI Research Society Conference*, pages 56–61, 2012.

[17] H. B. Suay and S. Chernova. Effect of human guidance and state space size on interactive reinforcement learning. In *RO-MAN*, pages 1–6. IEEE, 2011.

[18] R. Sutton and A. Barto. *Reinforcement learning: An introduction*. The MIT Press, 1998.

[19] A. C. Tenorio-Gonzalez, E. F. Morales, and L. Villaseñor-Pineda. Dynamic reward shaping: training a robot by voice. In *Advances in Artificial Intelligence–IBERAMIA 2010*, pages 483–492. Springer, 2010.

[20] A. L. Thomaz and C. Breazeal. Reinforcement learning with human teachers: Evidence of feedback and guidance with implications for learning performance. In *AAAI*, volume 6, pages 1000–1005, 2006.

[21] A. L. Thomaz and C. Breazeal. Robot learning via socially guided exploration. In *Development and Learning, 2007. ICDL 2007. IEEE 6th International Conference on*, pages 82–87. IEEE, 2007.

Optimal Testing for Crowd Workers

Jonathan Bragg
University of Washington
Seattle, WA, USA
jbragg@cs.washington.edu

Mausam
Indian Institute of Technology
New Delhi, India
mausam@cse.iitd.ac.in

Daniel S. Weld
University of Washington
Seattle, WA, USA
weld@cs.washington.edu

ABSTRACT

Requesters on crowdsourcing platforms, such as Amazon Mechanical Turk, routinely insert gold questions to verify that a worker is diligent and is providing high-quality answers. However, there is no clear understanding of when and how many gold questions to insert. Typically, requesters mix a flat 10–30% of gold questions into the task stream of every worker. This static policy is arbitrary and wastes valuable budget — the exact percentage is often chosen with little experimentation, and, more importantly, it does not adapt to individual workers, the current mixture of spamming vs. diligent workers, or the number of tasks workers perform before quitting.

We formulate the problem of balancing between (1) testing workers to determine their accuracy and (2) actually getting work performed as a partially-observable Markov decision process (POMDP) and apply reinforcement learning to dynamically calculate the best policy. Evaluations on both synthetic data and with real Mechanical Turk workers show that our agent learns adaptive testing policies that produce up to 111% more reward than the non-adaptive policies used by most requesters. Furthermore, our method is fully automated, easy to apply, and runs mostly out of the box.

Keywords

Crowdsourcing; reinforcement learning

1. INTRODUCTION

The practice of crowdsourcing, or outsourcing tasks to a group of unknown people ("workers") in an open call, has become extremely popular — used for solving a wide variety of tasks, from audio transcription to annotation of training data for machine learning. However, ensuring high-quality results for such tasks is challenging, because of the high variability in worker skill. Accordingly, many AI researchers have investigated quality control algorithms. Two prominent techniques have emerged for the problem [24]: (1) periodically inserting gold questions (those with known answers) for each worker, in order to estimate worker reliability, and firing workers who fall below an acceptable accuracy threshold, and (2) employing agreement-based approaches that do not use gold data, instead using expectation maximization (EM) or similar unsupervised methods to jointly estimate worker reliability and task output quality.

These two methods have complementary strengths and weaknesses. While the former is simpler and easy to understand, it puts the onus on the task designer to supply gold questions. Moreover, it is prone to 'bot attacks where, over time, workers identify all gold questions and create 'bots that answer those correctly while answering other questions randomly [18]. On the other hand, the unsupervised approach is technically more sophisticated, but requires significant amounts of data per worker and workers per task before low-quality workers can be reliably identified. Thus, it does not provide a quick filter for firing errant workers.

In practice, while unsupervised techniques have garnered significant research interest (e.g., [26, 25, 7]), the simpler technique of inserting gold questions is the norm in industry. CrowdFlower, a major crowdsourcing platform and consulting company, calls gold questions *"the best way to ensure high quality data from a job"* [2]. Furthermore, many research projects that use crowdsourcing to generate training data eschew EM-based quality control and simply insert gold questions [11, 6, 28, 3].

While insertion of gold questions is popular in practice, to the best of our knowledge, there is no formal model of when and how many gold questions to insert. CrowdFlower's rule of thumb is to have 10–20% of data as gold, and to insert one gold question per page [2]. Such a policy is arbitrary and may waste valuable budget. Moreover, and more importantly, such a policy is static and does not adapt to individual workers or the current mix of spamming and diligent workers. The percentage of testing questions should only be high if a large percentage of the labor pool are poor quality workers or spammers. Similarly, an adaptive policy that tests less once it is certain that a worker is diligent will likely perform better than a static one.

We formulate the problem of balancing between (1) testing workers to ensure their accuracy and (2) getting work done as a Partially Observable Markov Decision Process (POMDP). Our worker model captures the possibility that worker performance may degrade over time and workers may leave our system after any question. Our model also takes as input a desired accuracy of the final output, and a base testing policy. We apply reinforcement learning over our POMDP to dynamically improve the given base policy with experience. Evaluations on both synthetic data and real data, from Amazon Mechanical Turk, show that our agent is robust to various parameter settings, and typically beats

Appears in: *Proceedings of the 15th International Conference on Autonomous Agents and Multiagent Systems (AAMAS 2016), J. Thangarajah, K. Tuyls, C. Jonker, S. Marsella (eds.), May 9–13, 2016, Singapore.*

the baseline policies used by most requesters, as well as the input base policy. Furthermore, our method is fully automated, easy to apply, and runs mostly out of the box. We release our software for further use by the research community.[1] Overall, we make the following contributions:

1. We use a POMDP model to formulate the problem of varying the number and placement of gold test questions in order to optimally balance the quality-cost tradeoff for crowdsourcing.

2. We present an adaptive reinforcement learning algorithm that simultaneously estimates worker reliability (by inserting gold questions) and assigns work to produce high-quality output.

3. We comprehensively test our model using simulation experiments and show that our algorithm is robust to variations in desired output accuracy, worker mix, and other parameters.

4. Additional experiments on three live data sets (collected using Amazon Mechanical Turk) show that our reinforcement learning agent produces up to 111% more reward than common policies found in the literature.

2. RELATED WORK

Most practitioners of crowdsourcing use some kind of testing regimen to ensure worker quality. However, the exact policy is usually ad hoc. For example, CrowdFlower has two settings, the number of test questions and total number of questions per page, with the default (best practice) settings as 1 and 5, respectively (i.e., 20% gold). It also allows requesters to specify a minimum acceptable running accuracy for a worker, whose default value is 80%. All these settings can be changed by a requester, but very little advice is offered on how to set their values [1].

Researchers also routinely insert gold questions in their training data collection. As an example, we survey some papers that used crowdsourcing to generate labeled data for the task of relation extraction from text. Zhang *et al.* [28] use a policy similar to CrowdFlower's — 20% gold questions and filtering workers under 80% accuracy. Gormley *et al.* [11] use three test questions every ten questions (30% gold) and filter workers under 85% accuracy. They also boot workers that answer three or more questions in less than three seconds each, and they show that the combination of these methods works better than either alone. Angeli *et al.* [3] insert two gold questions into a set of fifteen (13% gold) questions and filter the workers who have lower than 67% accuracy. They also filter the specific sets of fifteen questions on which a worker fails both test questions.

All these papers use a common strategy of gold question insertion and worker filtering, but choose very different parameter settings for the same task. Moreover, no paper describes a strategy for computing these parameter settings, which are usually chosen by gut instinct and, in rare cases, by limited A/B testing to assess cost-quality variations empirically for various parameter settings. More importantly, these settings are *static* and do not respond to any change in worker mix, or to individual worker characteristics. In this paper, we develop a POMDP-based formalism for mathematically modeling this problem, present an algorithm for automatically learning model parameters, and hence produce a suitable adaptive policy targeted to a given task and labor market.

Our work falls in line with the existing literature on the use of MDPs and POMDPs for crowdsourcing control. These methods have been previously used for deciding whether to hire another worker or to submit a crowdsourced binary answer [7, 14, 19]. POMDPs are also used for controlling more complex workflows such as iterative improvement [8], switching between multiple workflows for the same task [16], and selecting the right worker pool for a question [21]. Similarly, MDPs are used for optimal pricing for meeting a deadline of task completion [10].

In the literature exploring the aggregation-based, cost-quality tradeoff, POMDP decisions are taken based on the needs of the *question* at hand: "Should one take another vote or instead submit one's best estimate of the answer?" Here, the interactions with a worker are quite passive — following a *pull model*, where once a question is sent to the marketplace, any worker may answer it. In practice, a worker usually has a longer relationship with a requester (crowdsourcing control system), since she answers several questions in succession. This sequence of answers can be used for actively allocating test or work questions (*push model*). In our work, we use POMDPs to decide actively when to test a worker and whether to fire them, in case they are not performing to expectation.

Researchers have also explored the temporal dimension of worker behavior, for example Toomim *et al.*'s empirical analysis of worker survival curves [23]. Inspired by this work, our model uses a parameter to model the probability that a worker is going to leave the system at the next step. Worker retention can be improved by bonuses, making tasks more engaging, or other incentives, but we have not yet tried to optimize these factors. Some recent related work has used worker-centric MDPs for optimally placing an intermediate goal [15] or deciding whether to provide a bonus to encourage worker quality or retention [27].

Other researchers have developed more complex time-series models of worker reliability, e.g., using hidden Markov models [9, 27], or autoregressive models [12]. Since our focus is test question insertion, we use a simpler model for temporal reliability, including a parameter to account for the phenomenon that a worker's accuracy may decrease over time,[2] either due to fatigue, boredom, or deceit. Extensions to more complex models is a topic for future work.

Finally, we note that methods that induce lower-quality workers to leave of their own volition are complementary to our approach. Mao et al. [17] found that some workers self-police and stop working on tasks for which they are unsure. Carefully designed instruction and reputation systems may cause workers to recognize when they may be providing low-quality work and stop working.

3. WORKER CONTROL

We propose a controller that automatically decides at each time step whether a specific worker should answer a test

[1]`https://crowdlab.cs.washington.edu/optimal-training-and-testing-for-crowd-workers`

[2]We do not model increase in accuracy, since most fielded crowdsourcing workflows do not provide continued feedback (after an initial tutorial) that would cause workers to improve over time.

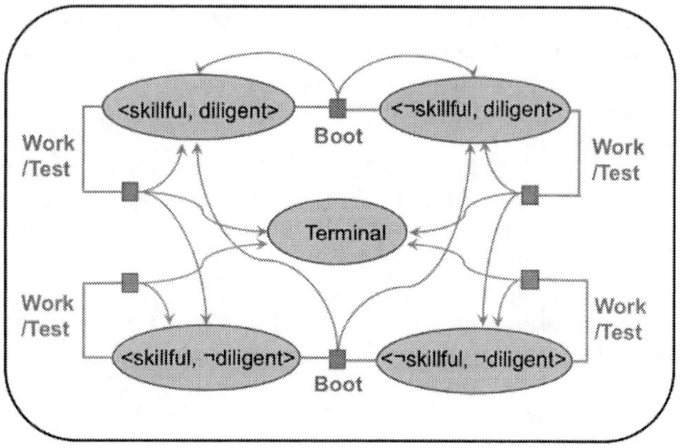

Figure 1: Transition dynamics of the Worker Controller POMDP. Note that the reward and observation model for Work and Test actions are different, but their transition models are the same, as shown.

question, a work question, or whether this worker's performance is not up to the mark, and so this worker should be fired and a replacement worker hired. The actuators that actually perform these actions are part of a web application, which selects new questions from a database of questions and interacts with a crowdsourcing platform to recruit new workers. Our controller should be adaptive, i.e., it should make decisions for each worker, based on their past behavior, instead of following some pre-defined static policy. The global objective of the controller is to get workers to answer as many questions as possible while obtaining a minimum target accuracy supplied by the requester. We first describe key design decisions in formulating this controller.

At a high level, this is clearly a sequential control problem, where the controller gets successive observations about a worker from test questions, and needs to take successive actions based on this history. This problem is *partially* observable because a worker's accuracy isn't known exactly and can change over time. However, the controller can maintain a probability distribution over each worker's accuracy based on its observations. This suggests a controller based on a Partially Observable Markov Decision Process (POMDP).

A POMDP [13] is a popular AI formalism for modeling sequential decision making problems under uncertainty. In a POMDP the state is not fully observed, although observations from information-gathering actions help the agent to maintain a *belief*, which is a probability distribution over the possible world states. A POMDP's objective is to maximize the long-term expected reward minus cost. The solution of a POMDP is a policy that maps a belief into an action.

One natural modeling choice for our worker controller POMDP would be to include the exact accuracy of the worker, a number in $[0, 1]$, in the world state. This accuracy could then be estimated over time based on the test questions. Unfortunately, solving POMDPs over a continuous state space is known to be notoriously hard [20]. Discretizing the accuracy space might be a workable alternative, though it may still be unnecessarily complex since many accuracy bins may result in the same policy.

In response, we adopt a *two-class*[3] worker model, assuming that a worker is randomly drawn from one of the two classes: skillful and unskillful. Both classes of workers have their own (initially unknown) accuracy distributions with mean accuracy of the skillful class higher than that of the unskillful class. This abstraction is beneficial for three reasons. First, for each individual worker the information gathering is limited to ascertaining which class they belong to, and no estimation of individual accuracy or accuracy bin is needed. Second, the worker population mix is abstracted into class means, which can be estimated using an initial exploration phase; these parameters are global, and once estimated apply to the whole population and need not be re-estimated per worker. Third, we can estimate these latent variables in closed form without the need for computationally-expensive approximate inference subroutines within our reinforcement-learning algorithm.

Our model also includes a parameter for workers leaving the task at will. We treat this as a global parameter for the whole worker population. Finally, we also realize that a key reason for repeated testing is that workers can become complacent and their performance may lapse over time. We model this by adding a variable (D) in the state, which, when to set to 1, represents that the worker is diligent (not complacent), and answering to the best of their ability. We now describe the controller in detail.

3.1 The POMDP Model

Defining a POMDP requires specifying (or learning) a state space, action space, transition and observation probabilities, and a reward function. We first describe these aspects of our controller POMDP.

- The state space $\mathcal{S}$ can be factored as $\langle C, D\rangle$, where C is a variable indicating the worker class (skillful or unskillful) and D is a Boolean variable indicating whether the worker is diligent ($D = 1$). The state variable D captures behavior where workers may lapse and start answering without focusing on the problem (with a consequent drop in accuracy); it also models the possibility of spammers faking high-quality work until they think a requester has stopped testing. Additionally, we define a special terminal state denoting the end of process.

- The set of actions $\mathcal{A}$ available to our agent in any non-terminal state consists of *test* (administer a test using a gold question), *work* (ask an unknown question), and *boot* (terminate employment and hire a replacement worker). No action is available in the terminal state.

- The transition function $P(s' \mid s, a)$, depicted pictorially in Figure 1, specifies a probability distribution over new states s' given that the agent takes action a from state s. We assume that workers are diligent to start, so any new worker starts from a state with $D = 1$ and C unknown. The POMDP's belief is a probability distribution over C which is initialized with a prior distribution over classes. This prior is estimated by a single class mix parameter that learns what fraction of workers are a priori skillful and what fraction unskillful.

When the controller agent takes *test* or *work* actions, the worker may decide to leave the task with (un-

[3]We performed preliminary experiments with larger state spaces and found the gains to be insignificant. Moreover, these more expressive models require significantly more data to learn, which reduces their empirical effectiveness.

known) probability p_{leave} and transition to the terminal state. Moreover, if the worker is in a state $\langle C, D = 1\rangle$, she may transition to a spamming state $\langle C, D = 0\rangle$ with probability $p_{\text{lapse}}(1-p_{\text{leave}})$ or remain in the same state with probability $(1-p_{\text{lapse}})(1-p_{\text{leave}})$. If the worker is already in spamming state $\langle C, D = 0\rangle$, she remains there with probability $(1 - p_{\text{leave}})$. The *boot* action fires this worker and hires a replacement worker with initial belief as described above.

- Observation function: The agent can only directly observe responses to *test* actions. If the worker is in a state with $D = 1$, we assume she answers correctly according to her unknown class accuracy μ_c. Workers with state variable $D = 0$ spam with accuracy 0.5, i.e., they resort to random guessing of a binary-valued question. Additionally, the agent directly observes when a worker leaves.

- Reward function: The agent incurs a cost c for each *test* and *work* action it takes (assuming the worker provides a response). Additionally for *work* actions, our reward model incurs a penalty PN for each incorrect answer and a reward RW for each correct answer it receives. Since *work* actions ask questions with unknown answers, the POMDP needs to compute an expected reward, as follows:

$$R = \mathrm{E}_{Y,X}\left[f(y, x)\right],$$

where

$$f(y,x) = \begin{cases} \text{RW}, & \text{if } y = x \\ \text{PN}, & \text{otherwise.} \end{cases}$$

Here Y and X are binary random variables for the latent true answer to the question and the worker response, respectively. This expectation can be computed using joint probabilities $P(Y, X) = P(Y)P(X \mid Y)$, where $P(X = y \mid Y = y)$ is the worker accuracy. This accuracy depends on the current state in the POMDP. We assume that each worker class c has its own latent mean accuracy, μ_c, but that when $D = 0$, workers generate random answers.

So that the requester may specify this reward function in an intuitive way, our experiments focus on the setting where RW $= 1$ and the value of PN will vary depending on the requester's desired accuracy. If the requester would like to gather answers from workers with accuracy greater than a^*, she may specify PN $= a^*/(a^*-1)$, which will induce positive reward[4] only for workers with accuracy greater than a^*.

As defined, the POMDP, in its pursuit to maximize its long-term expected reward, should learn to test and boot unskillful workers (if their class accuracy is less than a^*) in order to obtain a positive reward. It should also periodically test skillful workers in order to verify that their performance hasn't begun to degrade. The exact parameters of how often and how much to test depend on the unknown mix of the worker classes, target accuracy, model parameters p_{lapse} and p_{leave}, as well as the belief on the current worker at hand.

Our POMDP need only reason about distributions over five world-states (based on different assignments of C and D, and the terminal state), and three actions; thus, it can easily be solved using most modern POMDP algorithms.

3.2 Reinforcement learning

When our system is deployed in a new crowdsourcing environment, it must also learn the POMDP model parameters. This necessitates a reinforcement learning solution with an exploration-exploitation tradeoff.

Five parameters need to be learned: p_{leave}, p_{lapse}, the class mix in the worker population, and the mean accuracies μ_1 and μ_2 for the two classes. Learning these parameters accurately could be data intensive, which means that a typical controller starting from scratch may waste significant budget in learning the model. It may, as part of exploration, boot skillful workers, leading to worker dissatisfaction and subsequent bad requester rating by workers. Most requesters would not be able to afford this.

To alleviate this concern, we allow the requesters to specify a base policy, say, something similar to CrowdFlower's recommended best practice policy. Our reinforcement learner can start with this base policy instead of a random policy. It will gradually transition to following the POMDP policy once it has observed enough workers to estimate parameters. Common base policies that insert a fraction of test questions are desirable because (1) they are widely adopted and easy to implement and (2) the inserted test questions enable our agent to estimate parameters accurately.

To implement this mixed off/on-policy learning strategy, when the controller agent hires a new worker, it follows the base policy with probability $q(b, B)$ and the POMDP policy with probability $(1 - q(b, B))$, where b is the budget spent so far and B is the total budget. When the agent decides to follow the POMDP policy, it reestimates model parameters and replans prior to hiring a new worker. We define our particular choice of function q in the next section.

To estimate parameters, we treat the sequential data as an input-output hidden Markov model [4] and use the Baum-Welch (EM) algorithm initialized with parameters from the previous episode and one random restart. We use default uninformed priors of Beta(1, 1) on parameters, but use a prior of Beta(5, 2) for class accuracy and a prior of Beta(2, 20) for p_{lapse}. Beta(5, 2) encodes the fact that the accuracy should be at least 0.5 for Boolean questions, and Beta(2, 20) is an optimistic prior that workers don't tend to become spammers very frequently.[5] We assume that each class has its own accuracy but use parameter tying to estimate values for p_{leave} and p_{lapse} that are shared between classes.

We also experimented with an estimation process that is identical, except that it does not estimate the class accuracies. Instead, it defines two worker accuracy bins, one on $[a^*, 1.0]$ for skillful workers and one on $[0.5, a^*)$ for unskillful workers and fixes $\mu_1 = (a^* + 1.0)/2$, $\mu_2 = (0.5 + a^*)/2$. While these accuracy means may differ from the maximum likelihood estimates, they still allow the agent to distinguish between workers expected to give work of sufficient quality (positive reward) and workers the agent should boot. This variant has two primary benefits. First, estimating only the class ratios requires much less data than estimating both the class ratios and the accuracy means. Second, it is pos-

[4]This formula comes from setting the expected reward $(a\text{RW} + (1-a)\text{PN})$ to 0 when RW $= 1$.

[5]In preliminary experiments, we found an optimistic prior was important to enable our system to distinguish between skillful workers who may drop in accuracy and unskillful workers who had low accuracy from the start.

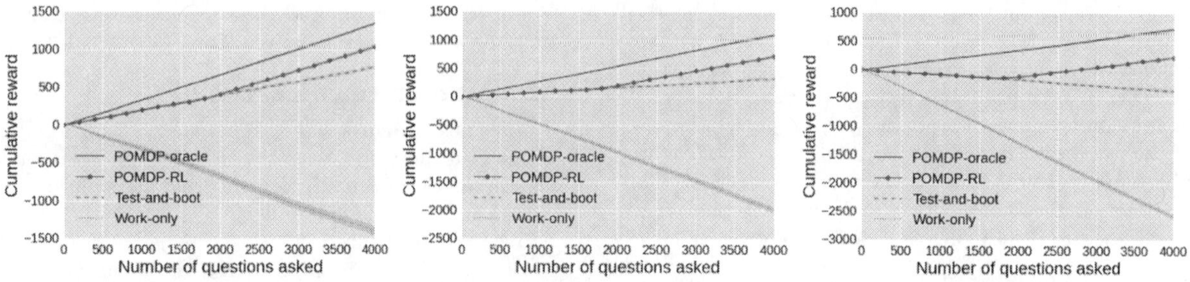

(a) 80:20 class ratio. (b) 50:50 class ratio. (c) 20:80 class ratio.

Figure 2: Our controller agent achieves significantly higher rewards than baseline policies under a variety of ratios of skillful to unskillful workers. As can be seen by the slopes of the curves, after learning, the RL policies start performing about as well as the optimal POMDP policy, which was given true parameters. These plots (and all subsequent reward plots) show mean performance over 200 runs with shaded 95% confidence intervals.

sible that the maximum likelihood estimates for accuracy means will produce means $\mu_1, \mu_2 < a^*$. Fixing an accuracy bin above a^* ensures that the agent will be able to identify high-quality workers even if the mean accuracy μ_1 for skillful workers is below the desired accuracy a^*.

4. EXPERIMENTS

In experiments, we first test our agent with simulated workers under a variety of settings; the goal is to assess the robustness of our method to differing task settings and its ability to adapt to attacks by different populations of spammers. Later, we demonstrate performance on three NLP datasets using real workers from Amazon Mechanical Turk.

We implement a reinforcement learning agent (POMDP-RL) that improves upon a base policy of inserting 20% gold questions and firing workers if their accuracy is less than the desired accuracy (Test-and-boot). We compare the RL agent with this base policy on its own, as well as a baseline policy that inserts no gold questions (Work-only). The Test-and-boot base policy inserts a batch of 4 test questions in every set of 20 questions. In simulation experiments, we are also able to compare performance with an agent that has access to the true model parameters (POMDP-oracle).

POMDP-RL learns the class ratio, class mean accuracies (μ_1, μ_2), p_{leave}, and p_{lapse} using the priors specified in the previous section. We use the Test-and-boot policy in each experiment as our base exploration policy. We used the ZMDP POMDP package,[6] which implements the Focused Real Time Dynamic Programming (FRTDP) algorithm for solving POMDPs [22]. We ran the solver with default configuration settings, maximum solve time of 1 minute,[7] and discount factor of 0.99. In order to speed up experiment runtimes, the agents recomputed the POMDP policy at most once every 10 workers and at most 10 times total.

4.1 Agent Robustness

In our simulation experiments, we considered two classes of workers, one of high accuracy ($\mu_1 = 0.9$) and one of low accuracy ($\mu_2 = 0.6$). Worker accuracy in each class varies according to a truncated normal distribution parameterized by the class mean and $\sigma = 0.1$ and bounded on $[0.5, 1]$. Unless otherwise noted, we consider a 50:50 mixture of these two classes, where workers degrade with probability $p_{\text{lapse}} = 0.01$. Only the simulator and POMDP-oracle had access to the true worker parameters; POMDP-RL estimated parameters based only on observations.

Our experiments are from the point of view of a requester who wants to ensure data quality above $a^* = 0.75$. Our penalty function gives us $\text{PN} = -3$, which provides positive rewards for data above this accuracy. The default budget size is $B = 4000$ questions. In this set of experiments, we used the sigmoid exploration function $q(b, B) = 1 - 1/(1 + \exp(40(b/B - 0.4))$, which approximately changes from 1 to 0 in the range of 25% to 50% of the budget.

RQ1. Is our agent robust to the ratio of skillful to unskillful workers in the labor pool?

In these experiments, we varied the mixture of skillful workers to unskillful workers, while keeping the worker distribution properties fixed. Figure 2 shows that as this ratio decreases from 80:20 to 20:80, policies achieve lower reward, as we would expect with just a few skillful workers. The relative benefit of the POMDP agents, however, remains significant. In all settings, POMDP-RL learns a policy that gains roughly as much reward per question as the POMDP-oracle. This can be seen by the fact that in the last half of the budget, POMDP-oracle and POMDP-RL have similar reward slopes.

Both POMDP-oracle and POMDP-RL earn significantly higher total cumulative reward after spending the budget than the best baseline policy (Test-and-boot), according to two-tailed T tests ($p \ll 0.001$ for all; $t = 32.5$, $t = 13.2$ for 80:20; $t = 30.9$, $t = 13.8$ for 50:50; $t = 55.3$, $t = 27.7$ for 20:80). The differences tend to become more significant for settings with fewer skillful workers, since careful testing becomes more important there.

RQ2. Is our agent robust to the fraction of workers who stop being diligent (eventually answering randomly)?

In order to test how our agent responds to workers who may begin to spam with probabilities other than 0.01, we experimented with $p_{\text{lapse}} \in \{0, 0.2, 0.4\}$, as shown in Figure 3. Note that for $p_{\text{lapse}} = 0$ (Figure 3a), POMDP-RL uses the base policy of Test-and-boot-once, which tests 4 times *only at the start* (and fires the worker if they answer more than one question incorrectly). For this setting, we

[6]`https://github.com/trey0/zmdp`

[7]Solver ran on 2.3 GHz Intel Xeon E7-8850-v2 processors.

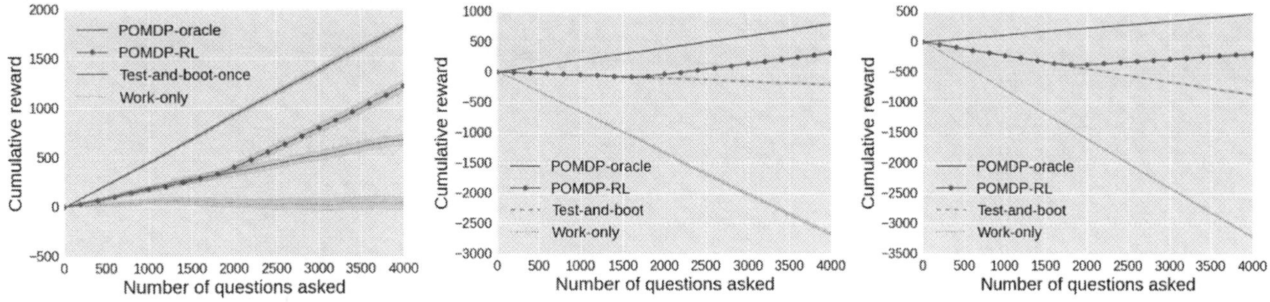

(a) $p_{\text{lapse}} = 0$.

(b) $p_{\text{lapse}} = 0.02$.

(c) $p_{\text{lapse}} = 0.04$.

Figure 3: Our RL controller is also robust to the number of deceptive spam workers, beating the baseline exploration policy, and eventually matching the performance of the POMDP-oracle model (which has knowledge of the true parameters). When $p_{\text{lapse}} = 0.04$, 4% of previously diligent workers start answering randomly after each question.

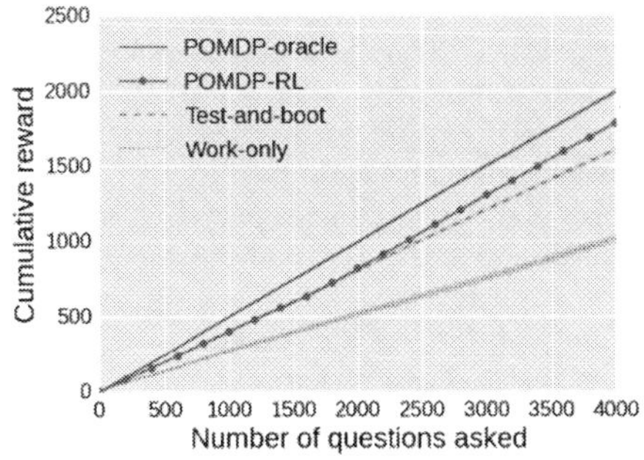

(a) Penalty -1 (desired accuracy 0.5).

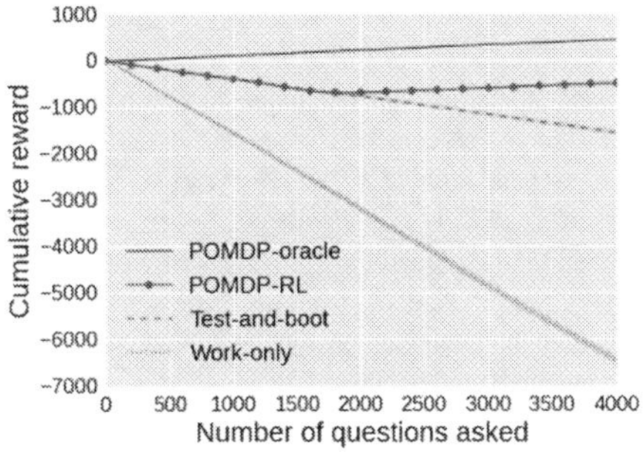

(b) Penalty -6 (desired accuracy 0.86).

Figure 4: Our agents perform robustly when supplied different utility functions and produce higher relative rewards for utility functions corresponding to higher desired accuracies.

don't need a policy that tests at intervals; it is optimal to do all testing at the beginning if worker performance does not drop. This set of experiments used synthetic data from the default equally-sized worker classes. In all experiments, the POMDP-oracle and POMDP-RL agents again obtain significantly higher reward than the baselines.

RQ3. Is the RL controller robust to changes in the requester's utility function (i.e., desired accuracy)?

The previous experiments used PN $= -3$ (desired minimum accuracy of 0.75). In this set of experiments, we varied the utility function by setting PN $= -1$ and PN $= -6$, corresponding to desired accuracies of 0.5 and approximately 0.86, respectively. As shown in Figure 4, the relative gains of adaptive testing increase as the desired accuracy (and corresponding magnitude of penalty) increase. Note that for PN $= -6$ (Figure 4b), only the POMDP-oracle agent has final positive cumulative reward. After having spent some budget, POMDP-RL also learns a policy that improves cumulative reward (neither baseline policy is able to improve reward). In both experiments, POMDP-oracle and POMDP-RL produce significantly higher reward than the best baseline policy (Test-and-boot).

RQ4. How good is the learned RL policy compared to the POMDP with known parameters?

Figures 2 through 4 show that POMDP-RL is able to learn policies with reward slopes similar to those of POMDP-oracle. This research question evaluates the policy learned by POMDP-RL isolated in a pure exploitation phase on the last 10% of an experiment with $B = 2000$ and the default worker configuration (50:50 class ratio, $p_{\text{lapse}} = 0.01$). Figure 6 shows that the reward obtained by POMDP-RL is on par with POMDP-oracle (there is no statistically significant difference in cumulative reward at the end of the budget), suggesting that the combination of base exploration policy and exploration-exploitation tradeoff is learning effectively.

Examination of worker traces shows that POMDP-RL and POMDP-oracle take similar actions. Both have an initial testing phase to establish worker quality, and then periodically insert a test question in every batch of approximately 6 questions. If a worker answers the single test question incorrectly, the agent will administer additional test questions adaptively.

4.2 Testing on Real Workers & Tasks

To answer the question of how well our agent performs on real datasets, we conducted experiments using three datasets gathered on Amazon Mechanical Turk. The worker completes an Entity Linking task in which a sentence and a mention (a portion of the sentence) is shown, and the worker is asked to match the mention to the correct Wikipedia entry. Two of our datasets, *LinWiki* and *LinTag*, were supplied by Lin *et al.* [16], who had Mechanical Turk workers answer questions using two different styles of questions, which they called WikiFlow and TagFlow. These datasets consist of 110 questions. 135 workers supplied 3,857 answers in LinWiki, and 149 workers supplied 3,999 answers in LinTag.

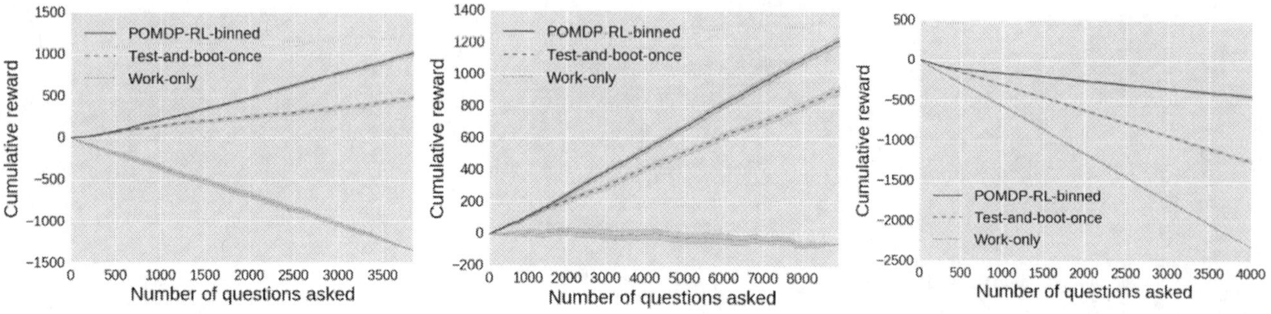

(a) LinWiki dataset.

(b) Rajpal dataset.

(c) LinTag dataset.

Figure 5: Our RL controller (POMDP-RL) significantly outperforms baseline policies on all three datasets with real workers. Figures show mean performance over 200 runs (with shaded 95% confidence intervals).

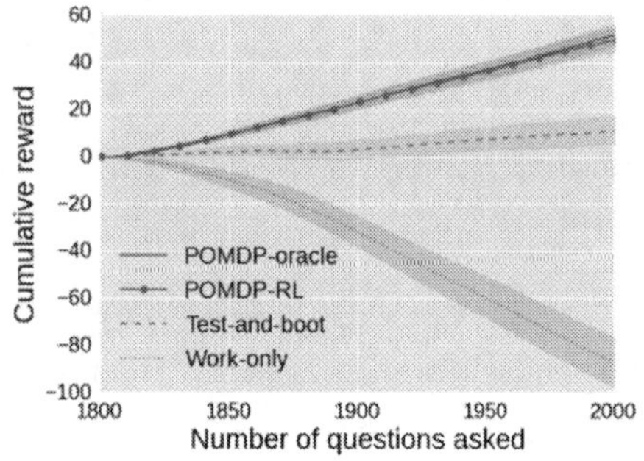

Figure 6: Zooming into the agent's behavior during the last 10% of the budget (i.e., after most learning), there is no statistically significant different between our RL controller and the agent that is given the true model of workers by an oracle. This figure uses the same worker distribution as Figure 2b (50:50 class mixture and $p_{\text{lapse}} = 0.01$).

Our third dataset, *Rajpal*, consists of 150 questions from the same task. Rajpal *et al.* [21] recruited workers with Mechanical Turk Masters qualifications (35 workers, 3,015 answers) as well as without those qualifications (108 workers and 5,870 answers). We combined these two sets of responses into a single dataset (143 workers, 8,885 answers) for this experiment.

When performing experiments, we set the budget B equal to the total number of answers. The Work-only policy used every answer from every worker exactly once upon completing this budget. Since the other policies may boot workers and therefore require more workers than exist in the original dataset while consuming the budget, we recycle workers as needed for those policies. Our simulator randomizes the order of workers and the order of worker answers because the datasets do not contain metadata (e.g., timestamps) that would let us determine the order in which answers were received.

Since answers from a worker arrive in random order, expected worker quality should not change over time; we fix $p_{\text{lapse}} = 0$. Thus, these experiments use the Test-and-boot-once variant of the base policy, which performs one block of testing at the start only (and boots if the accuracy in that block is below the desired accuracy).

We set the desired accuracy to 0.85, a value close to the upper bound of what is reasonable, since only a small fraction of answers in the LinTag dataset come from workers above this accuracy. To give the base policy enough granularity when determining worker accuracy, the base policy tests 7 times (and boots if more than one answer is incorrect). We fix class mean accuracies μ_1, μ_2 for POMDP-RL using the binning method to ensure that our method can identify workers above the desired accuracy even if the maximum likelihood class means are below that value. Since the agent does not need to estimate these parameters, we explore only for the first 20 workers.

Note that workers cannot distinguish a gold question from a non-gold question; they have exactly the same effect on a worker. Since we know the correct answers, we can (post-hoc) treat any question as gold, and evaluate any possible policy.

Performance on these three datasets is summarized in Figure 5 and Table 1. Note that we are only able to run the POMDP-RL agent (not POMDP-oracle), since we do not know the true worker parameters. After consuming the budget, POMDP-RL generated 111% more cumulative reward than the best baseline for the LinWiki dataset (1018.2 vs. 481.7) and 35% more reward for the Rajpal dataset (1214.5 vs. 902.5). On the LinTag dataset, all methods produced negative reward, but POMDP-RL produced only 35% as much negative reward as the best baseline. The best baseline in each case is Test-and-boot-once. Running a two-tailed T test on these rewards determines that the differences are significant for all datasets ($t = 21.5$, 13.6, and 46.7 for the LinWiki, Rajpal, and LinTag datasets, respectively; $p \ll 0.001$).

Inspecting the distribution of worker accuracies and number of questions answered by each worker helps to explain these results. As shown in Figure 7, some low-accuracy workers answer a large number of questions in the LinWiki dataset; POMDP-RL produces large gains by adaptively testing and filtering these workers. In contrast, the lower quality workers in the Rajpal and LinTag datasets tend to leave on their own accord after a small number of questions, reducing the possible benefit of testing them in order to fire poor performers. The LinTag dataset has a small fraction of workers above the desired accuracy, and none of the methods were able to produce a dataset with the desired accuracy.

Examining the action traces and overall statistics on the number of times the POMDP-RL agent took test, work, and boot actions gives some insight into how the agent is able to improve on the static Test-and-boot baseline. As the

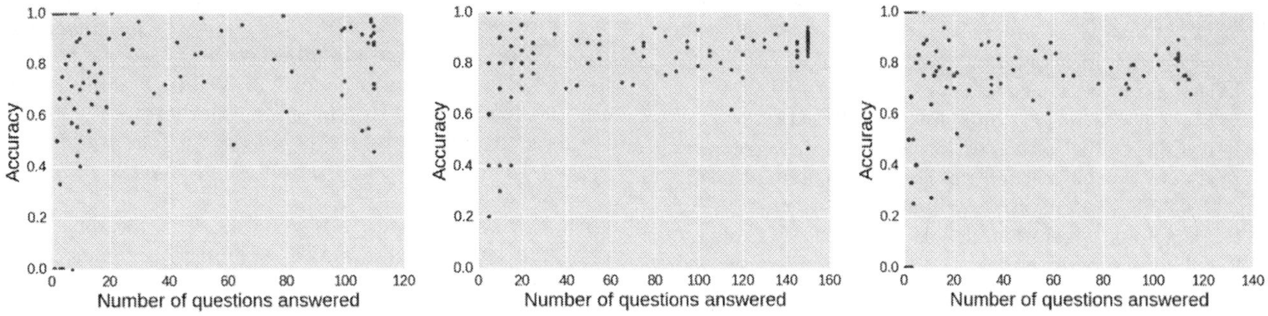

(a) LinWiki dataset. (b) Rajpal dataset. (c) LinTag dataset.

Figure 7: Scatter plots of worker accuracy vs. number of questions answered show that low accuracy workers leave on their own accord after a small number of questions in the Rajpal and LinTag datasets — hence all forms of worker testing have limited benefit in these scenarios. Adaptive testing has the most potential benefit in the LinWiki dataset.

Dataset	Policy	Reward	Labels	Acc
LinWiki	POMDP-RL	***1018.2**	2656	**90.8**
LinWiki	Test-and-boot-once	481.7	2895	87.5
LinWiki	Work-only	-1346.6	3857	79.8
Rajpal	POMDP-RL	***1214.5**	6867	**87.7**
Rajpal	Test-and-boot-once	902.5	7629	86.8
Rajpal	Work-only	-62.0	8885	84.9
LinTag	POMDP-RL	***-439.5**	1253	**79.6**
LinTag	Test-and-boot-once	-1251.3	2842	78.4
LinTag	Work-only	-2320.2	3999	76.3

Table 1: Our reinforcement learning agent captures higher rewards than the baseline policies on all three live datasets. Asterisks indicate significantly higher rewards. Our agent produces datasets of higher accuracy (Acc) at the expense of gathering fewer labels.

POMDP-RL agent transitions from the base (static) exploration policy to the learned adaptive policy, the mean number of test actions per worker stays constant or decreases slightly, but the mean number of work actions per worker decreases and the agent boots more frequently. This suggests that the agent becomes more conservative with its work actions, thus increasing accuracy.

5. CONCLUSIONS

In order to distinguish between high-quality and error-prone workers, requesters on crowdsourcing platforms, such as Amazon Mechanical Turk, routinely reserve 10–30% of their workload for "gold" test questions, whose answers are known, and then dismiss workers who fail a disproportionate percentage. This type of static policy is arbitrary and wastes valuable budget. The exact percentage of test questions and dismissal rate is often chosen with little experimentation, and, more importantly, it does not adapt to individual workers, the current mixture of skillful vs. unskillful workers, nor the number of tasks workers perform before quitting. Intuitively, the percentage of test questions should be high if a large percentage of the workers are spammers. Furthermore, once one is very certain that a worker is diligent, one can likely decrease the testing frequency.

To develop a principled solution to the problem of balancing between (1) testing workers to determine their accuracy, and (2) actually getting work performed by good workers, we formulate it as a partially-observable Markov decision process (POMDP). Our worker model captures the possibility that worker performance may degrade over time (whether due to fatigue, boredom, or deceit) and workers may leave our system after any question. Our model also takes as input a minimum desired accuracy of the final output, and a base testing policy. We apply reinforcement learning over the POMDP to dynamically improve the given base policy with experience. We comprehensively test our model using simulation experiments and show that our algorithm is robust to variations in desired output accuracy, worker mix, and other parameters. Additional experiments on three live data sets (collected using Amazon Mechanical Turk) show that our agent performs up to 111% better than common policies found in the literature. Importantly, our software is fully automated, easy to apply, runs mostly out of the box, and is made available for further use by the research community.

We note that our method has several limitations. For example, gold test questions are only applicable for crowd work with objective answers. Neither our testing approach nor methods based on expectation maximization will work for subjective questions or descriptive tasks where correct answers can be highly variable. However, we think our POMDP model could be extended to schedule *separate* validation jobs from an independent set of crowd workers. Another exciting direction for future work would be to extend our model to handle instruction in addition to testing [5]. Such a model would choose between (1) teaching a worker to improve proficiency, (2) testing to measure worker accuracy, and (3) getting work done, all before the worker quits the system.

ACKNOWLEDGEMENTS

We thank Chris Lin and the anonymous reviewers for helpful comments. This work was supported by NSF grant IIS-1420667, ONR grant N00014-15-1-2774, the WRF/Cable Professorship, and a gift from Google to Dan Weld and gifts from Google and Bloomberg to Mausam.

REFERENCES

[1] Crowdflower Inc. job launch checklist. `https://success.crowdflower.com/hc/en-us/articles/202703195-Job-Launch-Checklist`.

[2] Crowdflower Inc. test question best practices. `https://success.crowdflower.com/hc/en-us/articles/202703105-Test-Question-Best-Practices`.

[3] G. Angeli, J. Tibshirani, J. Wu, and C. D. Manning. Combining distant and partial supervision for relation extraction. In *Proceedings of the Conference on Empirical Methods in Natural Language Processing (EMNLP 2014)*, 2014.

[4] Y. Bengio and P. Frasconi. An input output HMM architecture. In *Advances in Neural Information Processing Systems (NIPS)*, 1995.

[5] J. Bragg, Mausam, and D. S. Weld. Learning on the job: Optimal instruction for crowdsourcing. In *ICML Workshop on Crowdsourcing and Machine Learning*, 2015.

[6] C. Callison-Burch and M. Dredze. Creating speech and language data with amazon's mechanical turk. In *Proceedings of the NAACL HLT 2010 Workshop on Creating Speech and Language Data with Amazon's Mechanical Turk*, 2010.

[7] P. Dai, C. H. Lin, Mausam, and D. S. Weld. POMDP-based control of workflows for crowdsourcing. *Artif. Intell.*, 202:52–85, 2013.

[8] P. Dai, Mausam, and D. S. Weld. Decision-theoretic control of crowd-sourced workflows. In *Proceedings of the Twenty-Fourth AAAI Conference on Artificial Intelligence (AAAI 2010)*, 2010.

[9] P. Donmez, J. G. Carbonell, and J. G. Schneider. A probabilistic framework to learn from multiple annotators with time-varying accuracy. In *Proceedings of the SIAM International Conference on Data Mining (SDM 2010)*, 2010.

[10] Y. Gao and A. G. Parameswaran. Finish them!: Pricing algorithms for human computation. *Proceedings of the VLDB Endowment (PVLDB)*, 7(14):1965–1976, 2014.

[11] M. R. Gormley, A. Gerber, M. Harper, and M. Dredze. Non-expert correction of automatically generated relation annotations. In *NAACL Workshop on Creating Speech and Language Data With Amazon's Mechanical Turk*, 2010.

[12] H. J. Jung, Y. Park, and M. Lease. Predicting next label quality: A time-series model of crowdwork. In *Proceedings of the Second AAAI Conference on Human Computation and Crowdsourcing (HCOMP 2014)*, 2014.

[13] L. P. Kaelbling, M. L. Littman, and A. R. Cassandra. Planning and acting in partially observable stochastic domains. *Artif. Intell.*, 101(1-2):99–134, 1998.

[14] E. Kamar, S. Hacker, and E. Horvitz. Combining human and machine intelligence in large-scale crowdsourcing. In *Proceedings of the International Conference on Autonomous Agents and Multiagent Systems (AAMAS 2012)*, 2012.

[15] A. Kobren, C. H. Tan, P. G. Ipeirotis, and E. Gabrilovich. Getting more for less: Optimized crowdsourcing with dynamic tasks and goals. In *Proceedings of the 24th International Conference on World Wide Web (WWW 2015)*, 2015.

[16] C. H. Lin, Mausam, and D. S. Weld. Dynamically switching between synergistic workflows for crowdsourcing. In *Proceedings of the Twenty-Sixth AAAI Conference on Artificial Intelligence (AAAI 2012)*, 2012.

[17] A. Mao, Y. Chen, E. Horvitz, M. E. Schwamb, C. J. Lintott, and A. M. Smith. Volunteering Versus Work for Pay: Incentives and Tradeoffs in Crowdsourcing. In *Proceedings of the First AAAI Conference on Human Computation and Crowdsourcing (HCOMP 2013)*, 2013.

[18] D. Oleson, A. Sorokin, G. P. Laughlin, V. Hester, J. Le, and L. Biewald. Programmatic gold: Targeted and scalable quality assurance in crowdsourcing. In *Human Computation Workshop*, page 11, 2011.

[19] A. G. Parameswaran, H. Garcia-Molina, H. Park, N. Polyzotis, A. Ramesh, and J. Widom. Crowdscreen: Algorithms for filtering data with humans. In *Proceedings of the ACM SIGMOD International Conference on Management of Data (SIGMOD 2012)*, 2012.

[20] J. M. Porta, N. Vlassis, M. T. Spaan, and P. Poupart. Point-based value iteration for continuous POMDPs. *J. Mach. Learn. Res.*, 7:2329–2367, Dec. 2006.

[21] S. Rajpal, K. Goel, and Mausam. POMDP-based worker pool selection for crowdsourcing. In *ICML Workshop on Crowdsourcing and Machine Learning*, 2015.

[22] T. Smith and R. Simmons. Focused real-time dynamic programming for MDPs: Squeezing more out of a heuristic. In *Proceedings of the 21st National Conference on Artificial Intelligence (AAAI 2006)*, 2006.

[23] M. Toomim, T. Kriplean, C. Pörtner, and J. A. Landay. Utility of human-computer interactions: toward a science of preference measurement. In *Proceedings of the International Conference on Human Factors in Computing Systems (CHI 2011)*, 2011.

[24] D. Weld, Mausam, C. Lin, and J. Bragg. Artificial intelligence and collective intelligence. In T. Malone and M. Bernstein, editors, *The Collective Intelligence Handbook*. MIT Press, 2015.

[25] P. Welinder, S. Branson, S. Belongie, and P. Perona. The multidimensional wisdom of crowds. In *Advances in Neural Information Processing Systems (NIPS)*, 2010.

[26] J. Whitehill, P. Ruvolo, T. Wu, J. Bergsma, and J. R. Movellan. Whose vote should count more: Optimal integration of labels from labelers of unknown expertise. In *Advances in Neural Information Processing Systems (NIPS)*, 2009.

[27] M. Yin and Y. Chen. Bonus or not? learn to reward in crowdsourcing. In *Proceedings of the Twenty-Fourth International Joint Conference on Artificial Intelligence (IJCAI 2015)*, 2015.

[28] C. Zhang, F. Niu, C. Ré, and J. W. Shavlik. Big data versus the crowd: Looking for relationships in all the right places. In *Proceedings of the 50th Annual Meeting of the Association for Computational Linguistics (ACL 2012)*, 2012.

Transfer Learning for User Adaptation in Spoken Dialogue Systems

Aude Genevay
Orange Labs
Issy les Moulineaux, France
aude.genevay@gmail.com

Romain Laroche
Orange Labs
Issy les Moulineaux, France
romain.laroche@orange.com

ABSTRACT

This paper focuses on user adaptation in Spoken Dialogue Systems. It is considered that the system has already been optimised with Reinforcement Learning methods for a set of users. The goal is to use and transfer this prior knowledge to adapt the system to a new user as quickly as possible without impacting asymptotic performance. The first contribution is a source selection method using a multi-armed stochastic bandit algorithm in order to improve the jumpstart, *i.e.* the average performance at the start of the learning curve. Contrarily to previous source selection methods, there is no need to define a metric between users, and it is parameter free. The second contribution is an innovative method for selecting the most informative transitions within the previously selected source, to improve the target model, in such a way that only transitions that were not observed with the target user are transferred from the selected source. For our experimentation, Reinforcement Learning is performed with the Fitted Q-Iteration algorithm. Both methods are validated on a negotiation game: an appointment scheduling simulator that allows the definition of simulated user models adopting diversified behaviours. Compared to state-of-the-art transfer algorithms, results show significant improvements for both jumpstart and asymptotic performance.

General Terms

Algorithms

Keywords

Reinforcement Learning, Transfer Learning, Markov Decision Processes, Online Learning, User Profiling, Multi-Armed Bandit, Jumpstart, Asymptotic Performance Spoken Dialogue Systems

1. INTRODUCTION

Spoken dialogue systems have the ability to interact directly with a human through speech. Reinforcement Learning [35] is a popular framework for dialogue management in spoken dialogue systems [28, 34]. This allows the system to learn its optimal behaviour by exploring different options and getting a delayed reward denoting the performance of its actions. Such an approach is generally solved by casting the system into a Markov Decision Process (MDP). While previous work in spoken dialogue systems mostly focused on learning a policy which is good for all users in average [27, 39], the goal here is to learn a personalised policy which is adapted to the user's characteristics.

The general goal in this paper is to transfer in an efficient way relevant information from well-known[1] users called *sources* to a new user called *target*. This problem, known for a decade as Transfer Learning [7, 31], and adapted to Reinforcement Learning more recently [38, 25] faces a trade-off between a good *jumpstart* (an efficient initial policy for a new user) and a good *asymptotic performance* (average return received after infinitely many iterations). Learning an average policy for all users and reusing it for a new similar user provides a good jumpstart but leads to a poor asymptotic performance, while learning from scratch for a new user has the opposite effect. The difficult task is therefore to imprint the virtuous bias from the sources into the learning on the target, and at the same time erase the vicious bias.

In order to optimise this trade-off, two issues are tackled in this article. The first one is choosing relevant sources for transfer. More precisely, which users, trajectories or inferred knowledge are similar or informative for the target to improve the learning procedure. The second issue is how to transfer knowledge to the target. Once relevant sources have been identified, the goal is to use this supplementary information, and merge it wisely with the new target information. Although research on Transfer Learning has been quite dynamic in recent years, these ideas have mostly been ignored in dialogue literature until 2013.

In the dialogue literature, Gašić [16, 17] uses Gaussian Processes Reinforcement Learning [11] for Transfer Learning cast as Partially Observable Markov Decision Processes for domain extension in spoken dialogue systems. The system has been optimised on a source domain, and they want to use this knowledge on a new target domain. As a consequence, there is no source selection, contrarily to [5] which uses the same framework for user adaptation of dialogue systems to different classes of dysartric users. However, their approach requires defining a metric between users for source selection. It works well in a setting like theirs where the user profiles are defined by a similarity based on the voice signature, which can be easily defined and measured online. But on a dialogue management level, with generic user behaviour

Appears in: *Proceedings of the 15th International Conference on Autonomous Agents and Multiagent Systems (AAMAS 2016), J. Thangarajah, K. Tuyls, C. Jonker, S. Marsella (eds.), May 9–13, 2016, Singapore.*

[1]By well-known, we mean that these users have interacted sufficiently with the system so that we can consider that it has converged to an optimal policy.

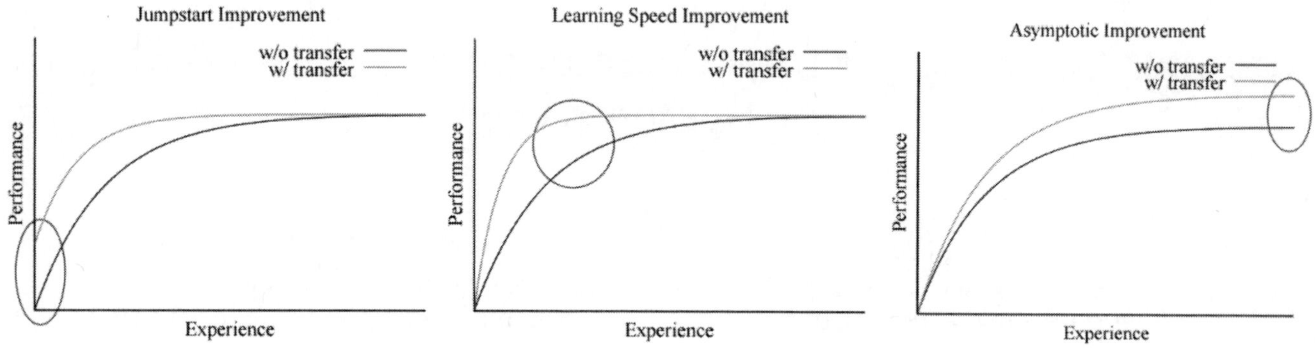

Figure 1: The three objectives of Transfer Learning.

profiles, it is hard to design and to measure: the observed features that are necessary to compute the similarity may be biased by the policy followed during data collection.

The first contribution of this article is a novel source selection method casting the source selection problem as a multi-armed bandit problem. Instead of searching for the most similar source, the paradigm is changed to looking for a model learnt from a source user that performs well with the target user. Since the objective is to minimise the regret at the beginning of the learning curve, it should induce an improvement in the jumpstart. Empirical results confirm this but also shows that the source selection is improved.

The transfer process consists in an instance transfer: the transitions from one Markov Decision Process state to another, after performing an action. Transitions from the trajectories of the chosen source are added to those already collected from the target as suggested by Lazaric [26]. Reinforcement Learning is then performed with a batch reinforcement learning algorithm. The second contribution consists in selecting transitions from the selected source with an innovative method which only keeps the ones embedding information missing from the target trajectories. Again, the empirical results show an asymptotic performance improvement against two state-of-the-art transfer algorithms.

Thus, this paper focuses on the individual adaptation of a system to its specific users. Any kind of personal assistant is a practical application, like in a connected home, where each house has its own configuration, inside which each house member might have different habits, implying different exploitable prior knowledge, and different ways to express themselves, which requires adapted behaviours from the system. User adaptation is also useful in negotiation-based dialogues [32, 19], which is the experimental setting that has been chosen in this paper. Negotiation dialogue has been lately solved by abandoning the single-agent reinforcement learning paradigm in favour of multi-agent reinforcement learning [18] and stochastic games [2]. However, considering that most dialogue tasks, including negotiation ones such as appointment scheduling, are cooperative, the user adaptation approach makes sense to yield maximum rewards.

The empirical studies in this article are led on a recently published negotiation dialogue game abstraction [23]. The dialogue negotiation literature[2] has been abstracted as an agreement problem over a shared set of options. The goal for the players is to reach an agreement and select an option. This negotiation dialogue game can be parametrised to make it zero-sum, purely cooperative, or general sum. In our experiments, it is set to a purely cooperative game and it is exposed as an appointment scheduling problem.

The transfer framework, method and contributions are detailed from end to end in the next section. Then, the negotiation game designed for our experiments is thoroughly introduced. Afterwards, the settings of the experiment and the results are presented. Eventually, we conclude the paper by proposing some areas of improvements.

2. FRAMEWORK AND ALGORITHMS

This section presents the framework and algorithms for transfer between users in a Reinforcement Learning domain. First, it presents the theoretical framework for Transfer in Reinforcement Learning that is used in this article, which is largely inspired from [25]. Figure 1 recalls the three objectives of Transfer Learning [22]: jumpstart or the improvement of the starting model, learning speed, and asymptotic performance. The two contributions of this articles concern: jumpstart thanks to a multi-armed stochastic bandit source selection approach, and asymptotic performance[3] improvement thanks to a density-based transition selection within the previously selected source.

2.1 Transfer in Reinforcement Learning

The dialogue system is formalised as a Markov Decision Process (MDP) which is the classical framework for Reinforcement Learning. An MDP is a tuple $\langle \mathcal{S}, \mathcal{A}, P, R, \gamma \rangle$ where $\mathcal{S}$ is the state space, $\mathcal{A}$ is the action space, $P : \mathcal{S} \times \mathcal{A} \to \mathcal{S}$ is the Markovian transition stochastic function, $R : \mathcal{S} \to \mathbb{R}$ is the immediate reward stochastic function, and γ is the discount factor.

A *trajectory* $\langle s_t, a_t, s_{t+1}, R_t \rangle_{t \in \llbracket 0, T-1 \rrbracket}$ is the projection into the MDP of the task episode, called *dialogue* in our domain. The goal is to generate trajectories with high discounted cumulative reward, also called more succinctly *return*:

$$r(\langle s_t, a_t, s_{t+1}, R_t \rangle_{t \in \llbracket 0, T-1 \rrbracket}) = \sum_{t=0}^{T-1} \gamma^t R_t \qquad (1)$$

To do so, one needs to find a policy $\pi : \mathcal{S} \to \mathcal{A}$ which yields optimal expected returns. Formally, this means find-

[2][12] considers sets of furniture, [8, 18] resource trading, and [24, 10] appointment scheduling.

[3]against other transfer algorithms. Against learning without transfer, learning speed is improved.

ing the policy which maximises the following Q-function:

$$Q^*(s,a) = Q^{\pi^*}(s,a) = \operatorname*{argmax}_{\pi} \mathbb{E}_\pi \left[\sum_{t \geq 0} \gamma^t R_t | s, a \right] \quad (2)$$

A Transfer Learning algorithm intends to make the learning for a new *task* easier, by using antecedent knowledge from one or several similar tasks. Let $\mathscr{U} = \{\mu_u^k\}_{k \in [\![1,n]\!]}$ be the set of K different users defining as many tasks M_u^k, $\mathscr{M} = \{M_u^k\}_{\mu_u^k \in \mathscr{U}}$ be the space of tasks, $\mathscr{K}$ be the space of knowledge transferred from one task to another, $\mathscr{H}$ be the space of hypotheses for solving the tasks, and $\mathscr{L} : \mathscr{K} \to \mathscr{H}$ be the general learning algorithm.

In our setting, a task M_u^k is defined as an MDP. The difference between a task and another is solely dependent on the users defining the task. As they are part of the environment, the state space $\mathscr{S}_u^k$, the action space $\mathscr{A}_u^k$ and the discount factor γ_u^k are invariant and $M_u^k = \langle \mathscr{S}, \mathscr{A}, P_u^k, R_u^k, \gamma \rangle$.

Representation transfer [37] is an active research area: one can find studies on option based transfers [20, 30], which are dependant on hierarchical reinforcement learning [36], on Proto-value functions [29, 15], or on representation transfer for Gaussian Processes Reinforcement Learning [16, 17, 5]. This article does not deal with representation transfer, and has chosen instead to focus on transfer selection: source selection [14, 30] and instance selection [26].

As a consequence, in the remainder of the article, $\mathscr{L}$ can be instantiated with any batch learning algorithm taking as an input a set of transitions (or samples, or instances) $\langle s, a, s', r \rangle \in \mathscr{S} \times \mathscr{A} \times \mathscr{S} \times \mathbb{R}$ within a trajectory, s being the current state, a the taken action, s' the next reached state and r the immediate reward. Therefore, $\mathscr{K} = (\mathscr{S} \times \mathscr{A} \times \mathscr{S} \times \mathbb{R})^N$, where N is the number of transferred transitions.

2.2 Similarity-based source selection

The similarity-based source selection is widely spread in the Transfer Learning literature [4, 38, 5]. In [5], four dysartric speaker profiles are defined. Then, the goal is to transfer the Gaussian Processes Reinforcement Learning [11] performed on those profiles to the new target user. A similarity between users is defined in order to identify the profile that is the closest to the speaking profile of the target. This similarity is based on statistics on the audio signal features from their voices. When faced with a new user, the closest user is defined as :

$$\mu_u^* = \operatorname*{argmin}_{\mu_u^k \in \mathscr{U}} ||\hat{\nu}_u^k - \hat{\nu}_u^{new}|| \quad (3)$$

where $||.||$ is a norm, $\hat{\nu}_u^k$ and $\hat{\nu}_u^{new}$ are the vectors of statistics for user μ_u^k and the target user respectively. Unfortunately, this approach has several shortcomings.

Firstly, it is difficult in a general setting to identify the insightful statistics for selecting the best user. It is even more complex to define the $||.||$ norm. In [5], on a specific user adaptation problem, three different metrics are tested and yield heterogeneous results.

Secondly, for behavioural profiling, those insightful statistics often require knowledge that cannot be obtained directly: for instance, in order to know the sentence error rate of the speech recognition, the system needs to explicit its understanding, this statistic collection is therefore dependent on the followed policy, and it is a source of bias in the statistics.

Thirdly, when no trajectory has been collected on the target, a generic, default policy learnt uniformly over all users is used to gather the first n_{first} dialogues. This policy experiences to be more efficient than a random policy, but still yields a large regret.

2.3 Performance-based source selection

The first contribution of this article is a statistics independent source selection: instead of selecting a similar source user, the approach consists in selecting an efficient source user in a spirit close to Policy Library through Policy Reuse [14]. The source selection is modelled as a multi-armed stochastic bandit problem, where each arm corresponds to the optimal policy π_s^k learnt with a source user μ_u^k; where *pulling an arm* a_k means using this policy π_s^k for a whole dialogue, and thus generate a whole trajectory; and where the bandit reward for the chosen arm corresponds to the dialogue return defined by Equation 1. In practice, such a bandit algorithm can learn to select an efficient policy to use and to transfer from with only a few dialogue returns, or equivalently arm pulls in the bandit setting. There is no guarantee that the selected arm will be the best, but with high probability, it corresponds an efficient policy, which is sufficient.

In order to select the right bandit algorithm, it is important to define exactly what is the main objective of the algorithm. Is it to select the best arm with the highest probability as in action elimination algorithms [13]? Is it to minimise the regret as in Upper Confidence Bound (UCB) algorithms [1]? The answer is that there is no need to select the best arm, only a good enough arm is required to be used as a source, but it is important to guarantee a good jumpstart for the Transfer Learning algorithm while the first trajectories are collected from the target, and this is exactly what UCB does by minimising the regret.

More specifically, as the time scale for the jumpstart improvement is very short, a variance estimation is impossible. As a consequence, the simplest UCB algorithm: the UCB1 algorithm [1] has been implemented. First, it pulls each arm once, then it pulls the arm a^k that maximises the following equation:

$$\hat{\mu}^k + \rho \sqrt{\frac{\ln n}{n_k}} \quad (4)$$

where $\hat{\mu}^k$ is the empirical average return after pulling arm a^k, where ρ is a constant parameter controlling the magnitude of exploration, where n is the total number of times UCB pulled arms, and where n_k is the number of times arm a_k has been pulled.

The problem becomes non-stationary when the arms change, *i.e.* if the user policies evolve. Fortunately, the source selection intervenes during the jumpstart. As a consequence, the UCB algorithm is only used during this first stationary step of length n_{first}. After that, we are able to select a user with an efficient policy to get source from and to learn a target policy that is better than any of the source ones.

2.4 Transition selection: baseline

The transfer algorithm uses trajectories from the chosen source to initialise the batch Reinforcement Learning algorithm, and trajectories collected with the new user are added gradually to the batch. The previous subsection explained the way the first step is handled, when no target trajectory has been collected. This subsection describes how the transitions issued from source and target trajectories are merged.

The classical way to do it consists in initialising $K \in \mathscr{K}$ with $n_{transfer}$ transitions transferred with the selected source, and to add the target transitions as the trajectories are collected [38, 25]. The target transitions will eventually overwhelm the source ones. One might be tempted to eventually remove the source transitions from K. It is reported that it is often more efficient to keep them in. The reason is that the source is used to provide a prior on the similarity between the tasks. Removing the source transitions leaves ignorance on the performance of some state-action couples, ignorance that has to be made up for. Both baselines with and without replacement will be considered.

2.5 Density-based transition selection

When a source is selected, it is crucial to add the right amount of information to the initial batch: too little will result in a bad jumpstart, while too much will lead to overfitting the source. It is also crucial to add the right type of information. It is pointless to transfer source transitions that are frequent in the target trajectories: this leads to keeping a bias from the source. On the contrary, the transitions that are absent from the target trajectories are mostly state-actions couples that yielded poor performance in the source and that the target would be better off not exploring. These absent transitions should be chosen so that the state-action space is well covered.

To solve this issue, a novel algorithm is introduced to select relevant transitions within the trajectories of the previously selected source. Given a transition from the source $\langle s, a, s', r \rangle$, all the transitions already in the batch which contain action a are considered. If there is a transition $\langle s_i, a, s_i', r_i \rangle$ such that $||s - s_i||_2 \leq \eta$ then the transition is not added to the batch. This means that only transitions which are far enough from existing transitions are added to have just the amount of information needed. The choice of η depends on the problem and should be tuned carefully. A large value for this parameter will lead to adding too few transitions to the batch, while a small value will have the opposite effect.

The use of a similarity and a threshold is obviously a shortcoming. Although, it does not apply to the same problem as the similarity measure between reinforcement learning tasks. In practice, it is easier to define a similarity between MDP states $\mathscr{S}$, which can be computed with a simple Euclidean distance, than between user behaviours, which are determined by stochastic functions P_u^k and R_u^k and are therefore not directly observable (since the internal user's states are unknown). A wide range of algorithms for learning a state representation exists [3, 9].

2.6 End-to-end algorithm

Algorithm 1 details the pseudo-code for the transfer learning procedure. It lays out more clearly the articulation of the various parts of the procedure described above.

The algorithm is initialised with a list of known users as well as the new user for which learning has to be performed. To each user corresponds a previously learnt policy π_s^k and a transition database $\mathscr{D}^k$ recording previously collected dialogues. These variables are respectively initialised to default policy and $\emptyset$ for the new target user.

Algorithm 1 Transfer for Reinforcement Learning with UCB source selection and density-based transition selection

TransferLearning()

Initialisation()
$\mathscr{u}_u^* =$ UCBSourceSelection()
for ($i = 1$; $i < nbBatch$; i++) **do**
  $\mathscr{D}^{tr} =$ DensityBasedSelection($\mathscr{u}_u^*$,$\mathscr{D}^{new}$)
  $\pi_s^{new} =$ updatePolicy($\mathscr{D}^{new} \cup \mathscr{D}^{tr}$)
  while $n_{new} \neq 0 \pmod{batchSize}$ **do**
    dial = playDialogue($\mathscr{u}_u^{new}$, π_s^{new})
    $\mathscr{D}^{new} \leftarrow \mathscr{D}^{new} \cup$ dial.getTransitions()
    n_{new}++
  end while
end for
$\pi_s^{new} =$ updatePolicy($\mathscr{D}^{new} \cup \mathscr{D}^{tr}$)

Initialisation()

$\mathscr{U} = \left[\mathscr{u}_u^1, \mathscr{u}_u^2, \ldots, \mathscr{u}_u^K\right]$
$\forall k \in [\![1, K]\!]$, $\mathscr{u}_u^k = \{\pi_s^k, \mathscr{D}^k\}$
$\mathscr{u}_u^{new} = \{\pi_s^{new}, \mathscr{D}^{new} = \emptyset\}$
$n_{new} = 0$
$nbBatch$
$batchSize$

UCBSourceSelection()

while $n_{new} < n_{first}$ **do**
  $idx =$ UCB.Choice()
  dial = playDialogue($\mathscr{u}_u^{new}$, π_s^{idx})
  $\mathscr{D}^{new} \leftarrow \mathscr{D}^{new} \cup$ dial.getTransitions()
  UCB.setReturn(dial)
  n_{new}++
end while
$\mathscr{u}_u^* =$ UCB.bestArm()
return $\mathscr{u}_u^*$

DensityBasedSelection($\mathscr{u}_u^k$,$\mathscr{D}^{new}$)

$\mathscr{D}^{tr} = \emptyset$
for $\langle s_i^k, a_i^k, s'^k_i, r_i^k \rangle \in \mathscr{D}^k$ **do**
  addTransition = true
  for $\langle s_j^{new}, a_i^k, s'^{new}_j, r_j^{new} \rangle \in \mathscr{D}^{new}$ **do**
    if $||s_i^k - s_j^{new}||_2 \leq \eta$ **then**
      addTransition = false
      break
    end if
  end for
  if addTransition **then**
    $\mathscr{D}^{tr} \leftarrow \mathscr{D}^{tr} \cup \{\langle s_i^k, a_i^k, s'^k_i, r_i^k \rangle\}$
  end if
end for
return $\mathscr{D}^{tr}$

First, UCB-based source selection is performed with **UCBSourceSelection()** which returns the best source user $\mathscr{u}_u^*$. Then, **DensityBasedSelection($\mathscr{u}_u^*$,$\mathscr{D}^{new}$)** takes this user as an input and selects interesting transitions from $\mathscr{D}^*$ to return them in a new matrix $\mathscr{D}^{tr}$. This matrix which is further added to $\mathscr{D}^{new}$ in order to start the learning procedure.

The current policy is updated with **updatePolicy()** which implements a batch Reinforcement Learning algorithm taking a transitions matrix as an input. New dialogues are collected with this policy until the chosen batch size is reached after which the policy is updated again to collect new dialogues and so on. This update/collection process is repeated *nbBatch* times before proceeding to the final policy update.

3. A NEGOTIATION GAME

3.1 Appointment scheduling simulator

Our experiments are run on a negotiation game designed specifically to have different user strategies [23]. It can be interpreted as an appointment scheduling problem between two players. One of the players is a user $\mathscr{p}^i_u$, and the other one is the system $\mathscr{p}^i_s$ to be optimised against/with $\mathscr{p}^i_u$. $n = 30$ time-slots are considered, and for each time-slot τ, each player $\mathscr{p}^i$ has a utility $\omega^i_\tau \in [0, 5]$ for booking it. Cooperation between players is introduced, which results in the following definition of player $\mathscr{p}^i$'s immediate reward at the end of the dialogue:

$$R^i(s_T) = \omega^i_\tau + \alpha\, \omega^j_\tau \tag{5}$$

where s_T is the last state reached at the end of the dialogue, where τ is the chosen time-slot and where $\alpha \in \mathbb{R}$ is the cooperation parameter. If both players cannot agree after n turns (which would correspond to a strategy in which each player enumerates his time-slots in descending order of preference one after the other) the final immediate rewards $R^i(s_T)$ and $R^j(s_T)$ are equal to 0 for both players. As well, if the system misunderstands and agrees on a time-slot which isn't the one proposed by the user, $R^i(s_T) = R^j(s_T) = 0$.

A system $\mathscr{p}_s$ and a user $\mathscr{p}_u$ act each one in turn, starting randomly by one or the other. They have four possible parametric actions:

- ACCEPT(τ) means that the user accepts the time-slot τ[4]. This act ends the dialogue.
- REFPROP(τ) means that the user refuses the proposed time-slot and proposes instead time-slot τ.
- REPEAT means that the player asks the other player to repeat his proposition.
- ENDDIAL denotes the fact that the player does not want to negotiate anymore.

Understanding through speech recognition of system $\mathscr{p}_s$ is assumed to be noisy with a sentence error rate SER^k_s after listening to a user $\mathscr{p}^k_u$: with probability SER^k_s, an error is made, and the system understands a random time-slot instead of the one that was actually pronounced. In order to reflect human-machine dialogue reality, a simulated user always understands what the system says: $SER^s_u = 0$. We adopt the way [21] generates speech recognition confidence scores:

$$score_{reco} = \frac{1}{1+e^{-X}} \text{ where } X \sim \mathscr{N}(c, 0.2) \tag{6}$$

Given a user $\mathscr{p}^k_u$, two parameters $(c^k_\perp, c^k_\top)$ with $c^k_\perp < c^k_\top$ are defined such that if the player understood the right time-slot, $c = c^k_\top$ otherwise $c = c^k_\perp$. The further apart the normal distribution centres are, the easier it will be for the system to know if it understood the right time-slot, given the score.

[4]Independently from the fact that τ has been proposed by the other player. If it has not, this induces a null reward.

3.2 User profiles

A user interacts symmetrically with the system. The first proposal is made randomly by the user or the system, and then they alternately make proposals until an agreement is found, or the maximal number of turns is reached.

A characteristic of a user is its intelligibility by the system, parametrised by its average sentence error rate p_{SER}. Another understanding characteristic consists in varying centres $(c^i_\perp, c^i_\top)$ for the speech recognition score. For distant $(c^i_\perp, c^i_\top)$ values, the system will easily know if it understood well.

In order to add more variability in our simulated users, two handcrafted classes of users have been implemented:

- The *Deterministic User* (parameter x) ACCEPT(τ) if and only if $\tau \in \mathscr{T}_x$, where $\mathscr{T}_x$ is the set of its x preferred time-slots. If $\tau \notin \mathscr{T}_x$, he REFPROP($\tau'$), $\tau' \in \mathscr{T}_x$ being his preferred time-slot that was not proposed before. If all $\tau \in \mathscr{T}_x$ have been refused, or if the system insists by proposing the same time-slot twice, he ENDDIAL.
- The *Random User* (parameter p) ACCEPT(τ) any time-slot τ asked by the system, with probability p. With probability $1-p$, he REFPROP(τ') a time-slot τ' randomly. If he's asked to repeat, he'll make a new random proposition.

3.3 Reinforcement learning implementation

Least-squares Fitted Q-Iteration is used to learn the policy with a linear parametrisation of the Q-function. The following recalls the basics. The optimal Q-function Q^* is known to verify Bellman's equation:

$$Q^*(s,a) \;=\; \mathbb{E}\left[R(s,a,s') + \gamma \max_{a'} Q^*(s',a')\right] \tag{7}$$

$$\Leftrightarrow \quad Q^* \;=\; T^* Q^* \tag{8}$$

The optimal Q-function is thus the fixed point of Bellman's operator T^* and since it is a contraction Banach's theorem ensures its uniqueness. Hence, the optimal Q-function can be obtained by iteratively applying Bellman's operator. This procedure is called Value Iteration.

When the state space is continuous (or very large) it is impossible to use Value-Iteration as such. The Q-function must be parametrised. A popular choice is the linear parametrisation of the Q-function [6]:

$$\hat{Q}_a(s) = \hat{\theta}_a^\top \Phi_a(s) \tag{9}$$

where $\Phi = \{\Phi_a\}_{a\in\mathscr{A}}$ is the feature vector for linear state representation and $\theta = \{\theta_a\}_{a\in\mathscr{A}}$ is the parameter that has to be learnt. Each dimension of θ_a represents the influence of the corresponding feature in the Q-function.

The inference problem can be solved by alternately applying Bellman's operator and projecting the result back onto the space of linear functions, and iterating these two steps until convergence.

$$\theta_a^{(i+1)} = (X_a^\top X_a)^{-1} X_a^\top y_a^{(i)} \tag{10}$$

where X_a is the observation matrix, where each line is the s_j feature vector: $(X_a)_{\sigma_a(j)} = \Phi_a(s_j)$, $y_a^{(i)}$ is a vector such that $(y_a^{(i)})_{\sigma_a(j)} = r_j + \gamma \max_{a'} \theta_{a'}^{(i)} \Phi_{a'}(s'_j)$, and $\sigma_a(j)$ is the index

role	name	user characteristics type	parameter	centres	avg return w. policy π_s^i learnt against π_u^i π_s^1	π_s^2	π_s^3	π_s^4	π_s^5
source	π_u^1	deterministic	1/10	(0,0)	**4.72**	1.90	2.77	1.63	1.74
source	π_u^2	deterministic	1/10	(-5,5)	5.22	**6.13**	4.73	2.50	2.61
source	π_u^3	deterministic	1/5	(-5,5)	5.28	**6.14**	**6.14**	3.05	3.25
source	π_u^4	random	0.3	(-5,5)	3.96	4.58	4.72	**5.09**	4.96
source	π_u^5	random	0.5	(-5,5)	4.15	4.83	5.08	5.42	**5.51**
target	π_u^a	deterministic	1/5	(-1,1)	5.12	4.75	**5.38**	2.72	2.70
target	π_u^b	deterministic	1/5	(0,0)	**4.57**	2.29	3.22	2.34	2.28
target	π_u^c	deterministic	1/10	(-1,1)	**4.64**	4.48	3.87	2.08	2.02
target	π_u^d	deterministic	1/3	(-5,5)	4.84	6.31	**6.41**	3.60	3.73
target	π_u^e	random	0.3	(-1,1)	3.80	4.76	4.32	**5.10**	**5.07**

Table 1: On the left part of the table, description of the source and target users. On the right, the average return $\gamma^T R^i(s_T^i)$ yielded when opposing users with the policies optimised for other users. The best policy is displayed in bold.

of the jth observation, in matrix X_a. The transposition of these notations into the Transfer Learning problem gives:

$$\mathscr{L}_\Phi : (\mathcal{S} \times \mathcal{A} \times \mathcal{S} \times \mathbb{R})^N \xrightarrow{FQI} \mathbb{R}^{|\Phi|} \quad (11)$$

In the experiment, the feature vector Φ_a is a 6-dimensional vector composed of the following features for each action:

- The constant feature 1.
- The utility loss between the last proposed time-slot and the next one.
- The square of the previous feature.
- The number of time-slots which can still be proposed.
- The length of the dialogue.
- The speech recognition score.

$\mathcal{A}$ is defined according to notations in Subsection 3.1 as follows:

- ACCEPT(τ) $\Leftrightarrow$ the same as in Subsection 3.1.
- REFINSIST(τ_k) $\Leftrightarrow$ REFPROP(τ_k), with τ_k equal to the last proposed time-slot by the system.
- REFNEWPROP(τ_{k+1}) $\Leftrightarrow$ REFPROP(τ_{k+1}), with τ_{k+1} the preferred one after τ_k.
- REPEAT $\Leftrightarrow$ the same as in Subsection 3.1.

4. EXPERIMENT AND RESULTS

4.1 Experiment specifications

In the experiment, there are 5 source users and 5 target users whose characteristics are described in Table 1. The environment is fully cooperative ($\alpha = 1$) with discount factor $\gamma = 0.9$ and sentence error rate $p_{SER} = 0.3$.

At first, learning is performed individually on the sources, and the optimal policy at the end of the learning phase is saved to be used for UCB-based source selection, as well as the transitions for later transfer. With Fitted Q-Iteration, the policy is updated every 500 dialogues for a total of 5000 dialogues to ensure convergence. An ϵ-greedy policy is used with $\epsilon = \frac{1}{2j}$ where j is the iteration index. In Table 1, all the policies learnt on source users are tested on all the users – both source and target – to highlight the importance of user adaptation in our appointment scheduling game. Indeed, using a policy learnt on a source user on another user can lead to a very low return if the users are too different. In particular, using a policy learnt from a random user on a deterministic user is highly inefficient, since every REFINSIST(τ_k) act would yield a task failure. From the second part of the table, it appears that some source users are more efficient than others when their policy is applied to a target.

The features used for statistics-based source selection are the following: average speech recognition score, acceptance rate, acceptance rate after insisting, a proxy for the correct recognition rate as a function of the score. The only time when the system knows if it understood the right slot is when it accepts a request. Hence, the correct recognition rate is only updated when this situation happens. In order to have different statistics for different score values, three different statistics are collected depending on the associated speech recognition score : under 0.6, between 0.6 and 0.8, above 0.8. The correct recognition rate is biased by the policy: if the system learns to accept only proposals with recognition scores higher than 0.9, then, the "above 0.8" statistics is biased in fact towards "above 0.9" statistics.

For each new user, five algorithms are tested:

- No Transfer: without any transfer, learning is performed from scratch.
- Statistics-based (TS): with statistics-based source selection and density-based transition selection ($\eta = 0.3$).
- UCB-Based (TS): with UCB-based source selection and density-based source transition selection ($\eta = 0.3$).
- UCB-Based (noTS): with UCB-based source selection but constant source transition transfer from $n_{transfer} = 200$ dialgoues and no transition selection.
- UCB-Based (TR): with UCB-based source selection but linearly replaced source transition transfer from $n_{transfer} = 200$ dialgoues and no transition selection.

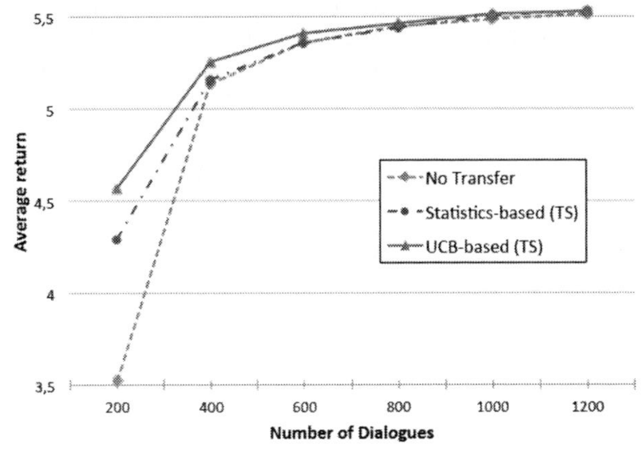

Figure 2: Learning curves comparison of algorithms for source selection.

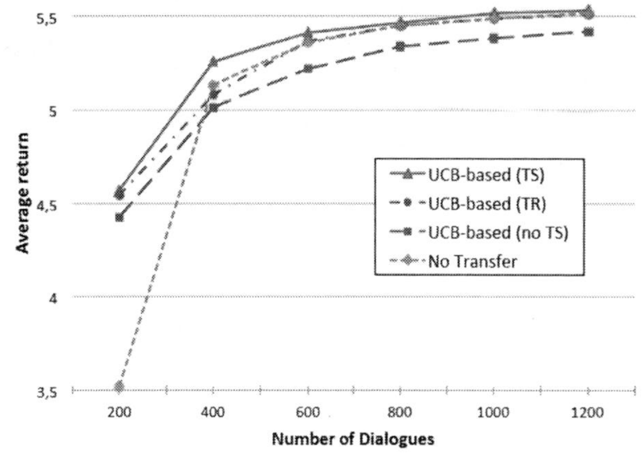

Figure 3: Learning curves comparison of algorithms for transition selection and transfer.

All those algorithms use Fitted Q-Iteration to optimise their policies. They are updated every $batchSize = 200$ dialogues with a total of $nbBatch = 6$ batches, and an ϵ-greedy policy is used with $\epsilon = \frac{1}{2j}$. In both transfer methods, there is a first phase of source selection over $n_{first} = 50$ dialogues. The policy is then updated with Fitted Q-Iteration and used for 150 dialogues before making a second update. Then an update is made every 200 dialogues like with standard Fitted Q-Iteration.

4.2 Results and discussions

Numerical results are reported in Table 2. The values in the table represent the average returns over the first 1000 dialogues and over 100 runs for the five target users. The results show a robust significant improvement of the scores for the algorithm including both the contributions from this article: UCB source selection and transition selection. Figures 2 and 3 enable a more precise analysis of relative performances on jumpstart, learning speed and asymptote.

Figure 2 shows the difference between learning from scratch and using both kinds of source selection for target users. The first point in the figure represents the average reward of $n_{first} = 50$ random dialogues used to select the source and $200 - n_{first} = 150$ dialogues learnt with the batch from the chosen user mixed with the first dialogues of the new user. These two phases are averaged together in the graph to keep the same number of dialogues per point. Both transfer algorithms perform dramatically better than without transfer at the beginning of the learning procedure. Indeed, the policies used during the source selection phase are far more efficient than a random policy, which is used when no transfer is being used; and, transferring transitions allows to make the first update earlier. UCB was considered first because it was parameter free, and by its ability to improve immediate jumpstart, but the gain from using UCB for source selection over the statistics-based method remains clear even after two or three iterations, indicating that it is also better than the statistics-based method at selecting the source.

Algorithm	(a)	(b)	(c)	(d)	(e)	avg
No Transfer	5.35	4.47	4.65	5.75	4.68	4.98
Statistics-based (TS)	5.55	4.58	5.00	**5.99**	4.61	5.15
UCB-based (TS)	**5.64**	**4.63**	**5.16**	**5.99**	**4.78**	**5.24**
UCB-based (noTS)	5.36	4.44	4.86	**6.00**	4.71	5.07
UCB-based (TR)	5.56	4.59	5.04	5.95	**4.78**	5.18

Table 2: Average returns for the first 1000 dialogues over 100 trials. For each target user, the significantly best results are displayed in bold.

Figure 3 compares the three variants of the transition transfer. It appears that using transition selection, and keeping dialogues from the source in the batch are the best options. Indeed, adding an constant number of dialogues in the batch impairs both the learning speed since the start and the asymptotic performance until the end, as unwanted information is added and kept, which causes a bigger inertia from the source. Not keeping source dialogues in the batch has no effect on asymptotic performance but it impairs the learning speed (as defined in Figure 1) as the system has to re-explore the transitions that were dismissed.

5. CONCLUSION AND FUTURE WORK

This article coped with user adaptation in Spoken Dialogue Systems. The system is cast as a Markov Decision Process and Transfer Learning is applied in order to boost reinforcement learning returns, both in terms of jumpstart and learning speed. Empirical results on a simulated negotiation dialogue game show strong and significant performance gains on both sides.

Two novel contributions were presented in this article. Firstly, a UCB-based method to select a source showed three main advantages in comparison with the state of the art: it is model-free, it has a better performance during jumpstart, and it improves speed convergence thanks to a better source selection. Secondly, the source transitions were selected in order to cover the whole space of state-action couples. This method proved to learn fast without compromising the asymptotic convergence.

As future work, we plan to gather dialogues with real users on this game and analyse the user strategy profiles. We are also interested in studying the co-learning impact on this game and adapt the framework to non stationary behaviours (probably with Stochastic Games [33, 2]).

REFERENCES

[1] P. Auer, N. Cesa-Bianchi, and P. Fischer. Finite-time analysis of the multiarmed bandit problem. *Machine Learning*, 47(2):235–256, May 2002.

[2] M. Barlier, J. Perolat, R. Laroche, and O. Pietquin. Human-machine dialogue as a stochastic game. In *Proceedings of the 16th Annual Meeting of the Special Interest Group on Discourse and Dialogue (Sigdial)*, 2015.

[3] W. Böhmer, J. T. Springenberg, J. Boedecker, M. Riedmiller, and K. Obermayer. Autonomous learning of state representations for control. *KI-Künstliche Intelligenz*, pages 1–10, 2015.

[4] J. L. Carroll and K. Seppi. Task similarity measures for transfer in reinforcement learning task libraries. In *Neural Networks, 2005. IJCNN'05. Proceedings. 2005 IEEE International Joint Conference on*, volume 2, pages 803–808. IEEE, 2005.

[5] I. Casanueva, T. Hain, H. Christensen, R. Marxer, and P. Green. Knowledge transfer between speakers for personalised dialogue management. In *Proceedings of the 16th Annual Meeting of the Special Interest Group on Discourse and Dialogue (Sigdial)*, 2015. preprint.

[6] S. Chandramohan, M. Geist, and O. Pietquin. Optimizing spoken dialogue management with fitted value iteration. In *Proceedings of the 10th Annual Conference of the International Speech Communication Association (Interspeech)*, pages 86–89, 2010.

[7] C. Do and A. Y. Ng. Transfer learning for text classification. In *Proceedings of the 19th Annual Conference on Neural Information Processing Systems (NIPS)*, 2005.

[8] I. Efstathiou and O. Lemon. Learning non-cooperative dialogue behaviours. In *15th Annual Meeting of the Special Interest Group on Discourse and Dialogue (SigDial)*, page 60, 2014.

[9] L. El Asri, R. Laroche, and O. Pietquin. The negotiation dialogue game. In *Proceedings of the Seventh International Workshop on Spoken Dialogue System (IWSDS 2016)*, 2016.

[10] L. El Asri, R. Lemonnier, R. Laroche, O. Pietquin, and H. Khouzaimi. Nastia: Negotiating appointment setting interface. In *Proceedings of the 9th Edition of Language Resources and Evaluation Conference (LREC)*, 2014.

[11] Y. Engel, S. Mannor, and R. Meir. Reinforcement learning with gaussian processes. In *Proceedings of the 22nd International Conference on Machine Learning (ICML)*, pages 201–208. ACM, 2005.

[12] M. S. English and P. A. Heeman. Learning mixed initiative dialogue strategies by using reinforcement learning on both conversants. In *Proceedings of the conference on Human Language Technology (HLT)*, 2005.

[13] E. Even-Dar, S. Mannor, and Y. Mansour. Action elimination and stopping conditions for reinforcement learning. In *Proceedings of the 20th International Conference on Machine Learning (ICML)*, pages 162–169, 2003.

[14] F. Fernández and M. Veloso. Probabilistic policy reuse in a reinforcement learning agent. In *Proceedings of the fifth international joint conference on Autonomous agents and multiagent systems*, pages 720–727. ACM, 2006.

[15] E. Ferrante, A. Lazaric, and M. Restelli. Transfer of task representation in reinforcement learning using policy-based proto-value functions. In *Proceedings of the 7th international joint conference on Autonomous agents and multiagent systems-Volume 3*, pages 1329–1332. International Foundation for Autonomous Agents and Multiagent Systems, 2008.

[16] M. Gašić, C. Breslin, M. Henderson, D. Kim, M. Szummer, B. Thomson, P. Tsiakoulis, and S. Young. Pomdp-based dialogue manager adaptation to extended domains. In *Proceedings of the 14th Annual Meeting of the Special Interest Group on Discourse and Dialogue (Sigdial)*, 2013.

[17] M. Gašić, D. Kim, P. Tsiakoulis, C. Breslin, M. Henderson, M. Szummer, B. Thomson, and S. Young. Incremental on-line adaptation of pomdp-based dialogue managers to extended domains. In *Proceedings of the 14th Annual Conference of the International Speech Communication Association (Interspeech)*, 2014.

[18] K. Georgila, C. Nelson, and D. Traum. Single-agent vs. multi-agent techniques for concurrent reinforcement learning of negotiation dialogue policies. In *Proceedings of the 52nd Annual Meeting of the Association for Computational Linguistics (Volume 1: Long Papers)*, pages 500–510, Baltimore, Maryland, June 2014. Association for Computational Linguistics.

[19] K. Georgila and D. R. Traum. Reinforcement learning of argumentation dialogue policies in negotiation. In *Proceedings of the 11th Annual Conference of the International Speech Communication Association (Interspeech)*, pages 2073–2076, 2011.

[20] B. Hengst. *Discovering hierarchy in reinforcement learning.* University of New South Wales, 2003.

[21] H. Khouzaimi, R. Laroche, and F. Lefevre. Optimising turn-taking strategies with reinforcement learning. In *Proceedings of the 16th Annual Meeting of the Special Interest Group on Discourse and Dialogue (Sigdial)*, 2015.

[22] P. Langley. Transfer of knowledge in cognitive systems. Paper presented at the workshop on Structural Knowledge Transfer for Machine Learning at the Twenty-Third International Conference on Machine Learning (ICML), 2006.

[23] R. Laroche and A. Genevay. The negotiation dialogue game. In *Proceedings of the Seventh International Workshop on Spoken Dialogue System (IWSDS 2016)*, 2016.

[24] R. Laroche, G. Putois, P. Bretier, M. Aranguren, J. Velkovska, H. Hastie, S. Keizer, K. Yu, F. Jurcicek, O. Lemon, and S. Young. D6.4: Final evaluation of classic towninfo and appointment scheduling systems. *Report D6*, 4, 2011.

[25] A. Lazaric. Transfer in reinforcement learning: a framework and a survey. In *Reinforcement Learning*, pages 143–173. Springer, 2012.

[26] A. Lazaric, M. Restelli, and A. Bonarini. Transfer of samples in batch reinforcement learning. In *Proceedings of the 25th International Conference on Machine Learning (ICML)*, pages 544–551. ACM, 2008.

[27] O. Lemon and O. Pietquin, editors. *Data-Driven Methods for Adaptive Spoken Dialogue Systems: Computational Learning for Conversational Interfaces* . Springer, November 2012.

[28] E. Levin and R. Pieraccini. A stochastic model of computer-human interaction for learning dialogue strategies. In *Proceedings of the 5th European Conference on Speech Communication and Technology (Eurospeech)*, 1997.

[29] S. Mahadevan and M. Maggioni. Proto-value functions: A laplacian framework for learning representation and control in markov decision processes. *Journal of Machine Learning Research*, 8(2169-2231):16, 2007.

[30] N. Mehta, S. Natarajan, P. Tadepalli, and A. Fern. Transfer in variable-reward hierarchical reinforcement learning. *Machine Learning*, 73(3):289–312, 2008.

[31] S. J. Pan and Q. Yang. A survey on transfer learning. *Knowledge and Data Engineering, IEEE Transactions on*, 22(10):1345–1359, 2010.

[32] F. Sadri, F. Toni, and P. Torroni. Dialogues for negotiation: agent varieties and dialogue sequences. In *ATAL*, pages 405–421. Springer, 2001.

[33] L. S. Shapley. Stochastic games. *Proceedings of the National Academy of Sciences of the United States of America*, 39(10):1095, 1953.

[34] S. P. Singh, M. J. Kearns, D. J. Litman, and M. A. Walker. Reinforcement learning for spoken dialogue systems. In *Proceedings of the 13th Annual Conference on Neural Information Processing Systems (NIPS)*, 1999.

[35] R. S. Sutton and A. G. Barto. *Reinforcement learning: An introduction*, volume 1. MIT press Cambridge, 1998.

[36] R. S. Sutton, D. Precup, and S. Singh. Between mdps and semi-mdps: A framework for temporal abstraction in reinforcement learning. *Artificial intelligence*, 112(1):181–211, 1999.

[37] M. E. Taylor and P. Stone. Representation transfer for reinforcement learning. In *AAAI 2007 Fall Symposium on Computational Approaches to Representation Change during Learning and Development*, 2007.

[38] M. E. Taylor and P. Stone. Transfer learning for reinforcement learning domains: A survey. *Journal of Machine Learning Research*, 10:1633–1685, 2009.

[39] S. Young, M. Gašić, B. Thomson, and J. D. Williams. POMDP-based statistical spoken dialog systems: A review. *Proceedings of the IEEE*, 101(5):1160–1179, 2013.

Don't Lose Sight of the Forest

Why the Big Picture of Social Intelligence is Essential

Emma Norling
School of Computing, Mathematics and Digital Technology
Manchester Metropolitan University
United Kingdom
norling@acm.org

ABSTRACT

This paper argues that "social intelligence," a hot topic in this community in recent years, is still not properly understood, and that this has important implications for multi-agent systems. The term shows up repeatedly in the intelligent agents and distributed artificial intelligence literature over many years, but in most cases the authors refer to just limited sub-components of social intelligence, such as norms, or trust. It is argued here that these (and other) facets of social intelligence are inextricably linked, and that we should only attempt to model them in isolation if we know what the implications of ignoring the other facets will be on model outcomes. We do not necessarily need to *implement* a "big picture" of social intelligence for every agent system, but having a conceptual model of this big picture will help us to understand the implications of what we *do* choose to model. This paper sketches a possible conceptual model of social intelligence, and begins to untangle the implications for different facets of social intelligence that are commonly scrutinised by the multi-agent systems community. The community is challenged to go further in developing this model and understanding of how its various facets make up the whole.

Keywords

social intelligence; human behaviour modelling

1. INTRODUCTION

Computational social intelligence is a topic that has received considerable attention in recent years (e.g. [6, 10], but the concept of "social intelligence" has had attention in the intelligent agents community for at least thirty years [7]. However when you look at the usage of the term, the way in which it used often focuses on just a narrow sub-view of what social intelligence really is, such as social structure [2], social situation [4], norms [1, 5], and trust [3, 12]. While each of these things is no doubt an aspect of social intelligence, none on its own fully captures the entirety of the problem. Thus while a superficial scan of the literature seems to indicate that we as a community have been studying this problem for decades, in this paper it is argued that we still do not understand the big picture of social intelligence; we cannot see the forest because of all the trees. In fact we could go one step further than that, saying that we are not just looking at the trees, but individual aspects of a tightly coupled ecosystem, and that we should not try to understand any one aspect without considering its relationships with all other elements of the forest.

It is argued here that we should start with a conceptual model of social intelligence, giving us understanding of how the various aspects influence each other, before we attempt to model these aspects in isolation. Social intelligence is not necessarily relevant to some theoretical areas of multi-agent system, or even some problem domains, but when any aspect of it is, it is worth considering if other aspects might also be. It is probably not necessary – in fact it would be probably be overkill – to implement *every* aspect of social intelligence within an agent framework, but understanding the interplay between them should make the implications of ignoring particular aspects of social intelligence more clear. For example, what is the implication of considering social situation while ignoring social structure, or the implication of considering norms without taking trust into account? The answers to these questions have obvious implications for systems involving or modelling human behaviour (e.g. socio-technical systems, or social simulation). There may also subtle lessons that could be learned for purely technical systems (e.g. agent-mediated e-commerce) that integrate aspects of social intelligence, in that they may suggest future developments for such systems.

This paper starts with a definition of social intelligence from the social psychology literature, sketching a conceptual model based on this definition. The difficulty is that the social psychologist's perspective is that of the forest, the big picture of social intelligence, without much of the detail. The next stage is to begin to understand how various aspects of social intelligence – those mentioned above and others – relate to each other within this framework. Some steps towards this are presented here, but this is only a beginning, and the wider community is encouraged to contribute to this endeavour, and to consider the implications for all types of multi-agent systems.

2. SOCIAL INTELLIGENCE

The term "social intelligence" was coined by Thorndike in 1920 [16], and perhaps the earliest clear definition was given by Vernon, who described social intelligence as

> "ability to get along with people in general, social technique or ease in society, knowledge of

Appears in: *Proceedings of the 15th International Conference on Autonomous Agents and Multiagent Systems (AAMAS 2016), J. Thangarajah, K. Tuyls, C. Jonker, S. Marsella (eds.), May 9–13, 2016, Singapore.*

social matters, susceptibility to stimuli from other members of a group, as well as insight into the temporary moods or underlying personality traits of strangers." [17]

This definition breaks down into five components:

1. **Ability to get along with people in general.**

   This refers to people's general ability to "rub along" with others; to co-exist in relative harmony despite different beliefs and goals.

2. **Social technique or ease in society.**

   This is the ease with which an individual interacts with others. It is closely linked to the individual's self-image, and also understanding of relationships between themself and others.

3. **Knowledge of social matters.**

   Societies have expected behaviours and standards, and social intelligence implies a knowledge that these exist, and an ability to work with them.

4. **Stimuli from other members of a group.**

   A socially intelligent person should be able to recognise and respond to cues from other societal members, particularly those related to the expected behaviours and standards that were previously mentioned, but also those related to the individual needs of fellow group members.

5. **Insights about strangers.**

   Underlying this point is an assumption that the individual recognising other individuals being in some way "like self." However here it is recognised that while at one level others are similar, they also have differences based on temporary moods and personality traits, and a socially intelligent individual will recognise at least some of these differences.

Amongst these five points, we start to see aspects of social intelligence that are often highlighted in the multi-agent systems literature. For example, points three and four relate closely to norms and normative behaviour, while point one has a strong relationship with work on negotiation. But the point is that all five *together* combine to give social intelligence, and if we examine them in isolation, we may miss important influences on behaviour. There are also other things that are commonly regarded as aspects of social intelligence, such as trust, which are not even mentioned. Does this mean that these aspects are not really part of social intelligence? Or is this definition in fact not sufficient? The assumption made here is that in fact these aspects of social intelligence are hidden in the detail of the definition, and that we should be able to identify them as we develop a conceptual model.

3. DEVELOPING A CONCEPTUAL MODEL

Based on the assumption that we will be able to identify particular aspects of social intelligence as we develop the conceptual model, Figure 1 begins to sketch just what such a model might look like.

Three components have been added to the agent itself: self, normative framework and theory of mind(s) (ToM(s)).

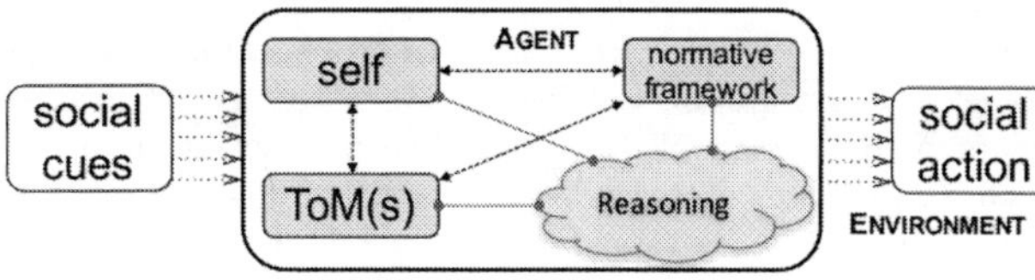

Figure 1: A Sketch of the Conceptual Model

These three components all influence each other, and most importantly, they influence the agent's reasoning. This reasoning could be one of many existing reasoning frameworks.

"Self" refers to the agent's self-image and positioning (relationships) within society. This will moderate the way that an agent acts based upon its relationships and the image that it wishes to project.

The understanding of norms and normative behaviour is an intrinsic element of social intelligence, and this is what is required in the "normative framework" component. There has been extensive work in the multi-agent systems community on norms and normative behaviour that could be adapted for use here.

"ToM(s)" refers to the agent's mental models of the other members of society. Social intelligence requires recognising other societal members as in some sense like-minded individuals, but also allowing for individual differences. The detail of the ToM at this stage is blurred, but it is important to remember that at this point it is a *conceptual* model that is being developed, for the purpose of better understanding social intelligence. Any actual *implementation* of a model of social intelligence may well contain far fewer details for pragmatic reasons. That said, what is needed here? First, it is worth noting that although every member of society can be recognised as an individual, the level of detail in the mental model for each individual will vary tremendously. Those "close" to the agent will typically be represented by quite detailed models, while those distant will have very simple models. These ToMs should moderate the agent's behaviour in many ways. With knowledge of others, the agent may seek help to further its goals. It may also choose to support the pursuit of others' goals, or even thwart the goals of others. These choices will be strongly influenced by the agent's "self."

Also in this diagram, outside the agent, are social cues and social action. These are elements of the environment in the diagram, but they are still linked to the agent itself, because even if social cues *occur* in the diagram, they may not be recognised by the agent. Similarly, although the agent's social actions occur in the environment, the reasoning that generates those actions must be within the agent.

It is freely acknowledged that none of these elements are new ideas in the agents research community: examples of normative frameworks have already been discussed, and ideas regarding *self* and *ToM* are rich in both the affective agents research community and the cognitive modelling research community (see for example [9, 13, 18, 19]). The unique contribution is in using these elements to create a framework that can relate the various aspects of social intelligence.

4. UNTANGLING SOCIAL INTELLIGENCE

We now have a sketch of a conceptual model that can capture the given definition of social intelligence. There is considerably more work to be done in order to fully develop this conceptual model, but let us return to the purpose of this model. The aim of developing this conceptual model is to have a better understanding of social intelligence, and in particular, how the various facets of social intelligence interact with and depend upon each other. This in turn will help us to understand the implications of ignoring some aspects of social intelligence when we model others. We can see already, even in this conceptual model we have three interdependent components, all influencing the agent's reasoning. If the assumption that other aspects of social intelligence will be identified within this framework is correct, it is difficult to imagine how they too will not be tightly coupled.

So what are the aspects of social intelligence that we might want to identify? A non-exhaustive list includes: norms, trust, reputation, negotiation, argumentation, responsibility, and obligations. These are all things which have been discussed in relation to social intelligence, and so should be able to be explained with reference to a conceptual model of social intelligence. A normative framework has already been included within the framework, so let us take the next item: trust.

4.1 Trust as an example

Can we see a way of untangling trust from the model? At this stage there is not sufficient detail in the conceptual model to completely achieve this. However even though we do not have the detail at this stage, it is worth considering whether it would be *possible* to understand trust in terms of this model of social intelligence. There are a myriad of existing models of trust, as evidenced in Yu et al.'s recent survey [20].

For the sake of the thought experiment, let use consider just one model, that of Singh [14]. Singh's model is based on the idea of trust as dependence, with a series of postulates about trust that are connected to an agent framework. In other words, trust is expressed in terms of connections between actions, a trust that one state will lead to some other state (where the first state is typically brought about by an action of the trustor, and the second state is typically – but not necessarily – brought about by an action of the trustee).

Conceptually, what is needed here are:

- Recognition of other entities.
- Recognition of the desired states. It is not completely clear in the described model whether it is necessary that the trusted agent brought about the desired state. (It could for example be brought about by the action of an independent party.) Nevertheless, regardless of the intention in the original work, the perceived contribution of the trusted agent to the outcome should probably contribute to trust.
- Commitment. This is the flip-side to trust: If agent X trusts agent Y to achieve a state given some precondition state, agent Y has a commitment to agent X that it will (try to) achieve that state given the precondition; if agent Y fails in that commitment, it will betray the trust that X has in it.
- Mutual progress. Whereas it was not clear in the model description whether an agent's contribution to a desired state influenced trust in the general case, for this case it is explicit. When agents trust each other to achieve a common goal, they expect to see their trustee working towards that goal.
- Teamwork. Although teamwork is explicitly discussed in presentation of the model, teamwork itself is embedded in a subset of the trust postulates. Thus to implement this model of trust it is not necessary to explicitly account for teamwork; support for (at least this view of) teamwork should arise if the other aspects of the trust model are accounted for.
- Scepticism. One agent's trust of another agent is lowered if that trusted agent fails to achieve the outcome state in an activated connection. (For example, if agent X trusts agent Y to send goods upon payment, and agent X has made payment but agent Y has not sent goods, agent X's trust in Y is lowered.)
- Faith. This is essentially the opposite of scepticism: one agent's trust of another agent is increased each time the state needed to be achieved by trusted agent in an activated connection is achieved. (So in a buyer-seller relationship, the buyer's trust in the seller is achieved each time goods are successfully shipped.)

The first two points are already explicit in the conceptual framework: other entities are present as ToM models, and also in the relationships in the "self" component. Recognition of social cues will capture the recognition of working towards desired states. Commitment is not explicit in the conceptual framework, but may actually be part of the underlying reasoning framework. Many reasoning frameworks (for example the BDI framework [8]) already include commitment as an intrinsic element, but in many cases this is a "light-weight" version of commitment: not a commitment to another agent, but a commitment to achieving a goal. To fully capture this idea of commitment to another, the relationships with other agents would again come into play, such as discussed by Singh [15]. It is not necessary to explicitly account for teamwork with this model of trust, as discussed previously, so the remaining two points to be addressed are faith and scepticism. Both of these relate to the degree of trust an agent has in another, or in other words, it is part of the relationship with the other agent. This can even take into account the fact that you might trust an individual in some contexts but not others, such as the example in the original paper: "you can trust your friend to take your side in a dispute, but not against his employer." [14]

We can see from this thought experiment that it should be possible to capture *this* model of trust within the conceptual framework, with the addition of some detail (regarding a measure of trust and its manipulation, plus commitment to others) to the relationship structures. As it happens, this model is neatly constrained within the "self" component of the conceptual model, other than the recognition of social cues. This does not mean however that it is neatly isolated from other aspects of social intelligence, as these too may use and manipulate the same elements. Even if we just look at the next item in the list, reputation, it quickly becomes obvious that these are closely related. (Indeed, trust and reputation are often tightly coupled, see [11] for a survey.)

4.2 The Bigger Picture

The point here is that although we were able to demonstrate that a particular model of trust *could* be implemented within the conceptual framework, it still doesn't capture how trust relates to other aspects of social intelligence. In order to this, we need a categorical list of what these aspects are, and how each and every one of them fits into the conceptual framework. One of the challenges here is that many aspects of social intelligence – trust being the perfect example – have not just one but many potential models that could be considered. Given this variation, can we be sure that we will correctly identify the links between different aspects of social intelligence if we map a particular computational model of an aspect to the conceptual framework? It would be better perhaps to again take a step back, identifying the important aspects of social simulation from the multi-agent systems literature, but turning to psychology and sociology for explanations of their relationships to social intelligence. Once this bigger picture has been developed, we will have a yardstick against which we can consider particular computational models of aspects, such as the one discussed above.

5. THE CHALLENGES

This paper has presented a problem – that we are losing track of the big picture of social intelligence as we focus on specific aspects of it – and started to sketch a solution to this problem. This big picture of social intelligence is important because the many different aspects of it that we study are in fact interrelated, and if we do not understand these relationships, we cannot be sure of the implications of studying a single aspect (or set of aspects) in isolation. Understanding the relationships will give us a better understanding of the scope of any of these models, and also insights into how we could grow and enhance them.

There are a series of challenges presented in this paper in which the wider multi-agent systems research community is invited to take part:

1. Development of the high level conceptual model of social intelligence. Only a rough sketch has been provided here, with many details to be completed.
2. Creation of a comprehensive list of the aspects of social intelligence in which we as a community are interested.
3. Development of a relational map of each of these aspects of social intelligence within the conceptual model, particularly highlighting their relationships with other aspects of social intelligence.

Each of these three challenges is non-trivial, but the resultant conceptualisation will be invaluable to the community.

REFERENCES

[1] M. Boman and H. Verhagen. Social intelligence as norm adaptation. In B. Edmonds and K. Dautenhahn, editors, *Socially Situated Intelligence: a workshop held at SAB'98*, pages 17–24, Zürich, 1998.

[2] C. Castelfranchi. Modelling social action for AI agents. *Artificial Intelligence*, 103(1–2):157 – 182, 1998.

[3] C. Castelfranchi and Y.-H. Tan. The role of trust and deception in virtual societies. *International Journal of Electronic Commerce*, 6(3):55–70, 2002.

[4] R. Conte. Social intelligence among autonomous agents. *Computational and Mathematical Organization Theory*, 5(3):203–228, 1999.

[5] R. Conte. Agent-based modeling for understanding social intelligence. *Proceedings of the National Academy of Sciences*, 99(suppl 3):7189–7190, 2002.

[6] F. Dignum, R. Prada, and G. J. Hofstede. From autistic to social agents. In *The 2014 international conference on Autonomous agents and multi-agent systems*, pages 1161–1164. IFAAMAS, 2014.

[7] L. Gasser. 1985 DAI workshop report. *AI Magazine*, 8(2):91–98, 1987.

[8] M. Georgeff, B. Pell, M. Pollack, M. Tambe, and M. Wooldridge. The belief-desire-intention model of agency. In J. P. Müller, M. P. Singh, and A. S. Rao, editors, *Intelligent Agents V, Proceedings of 5th ATAL Workshop*, volume 1555 of *Springer LNAI*, pages 1–10. Springer, 1999.

[9] J. Gratch. Understanding the mind by simulating the body: virtual humans as a tool for cognitive science research. In S. Chipman, editor, *Oxford Handbook of Cognitive Science*. Oxford University Press, Oxford, UK, In press.

[10] G. A. Kaminka. Curing robot autism: a challenge. In *Proceedings of the 2013 international conference on Autonomous agents and multi-agent systems*, pages 801–804. IFAAMAS, 2013.

[11] J. Sabater and C. Sierra. Review on computational trust and reputation models. *Artificial Intelligence Review*, 24(1):33–60, 2005.

[12] M. Schillo, P. Funk, and M. Rovatsos. Using trust for detecting deceitful agents in artificial societies. *Applied Artificial Intelligence*, 14(8):825–848, 2000.

[13] M. Shayganfar, C. Rich, and C. Sidner. An overview of affective motivational collaboration theory. In *Proceedings of AAAI Workshop on Symbiotic Cognitive Systems*, 2016.

[14] M. P. Singh. Trust as dependence: a logical approach. In *The 10th International Conference on Autonomous Agents and Multiagent Systems-Volume 2*, pages 863–870. IFAAMAS, 2011.

[15] M. P. Singh. Commitments in multiagent systems: Some history, some confusions, some controversies, some prospects. In F. Paglieri, L. Tummolini, R. Falcone, and M. Miceli, editors, *The Goals of Cognition. Essays in Honor of Cristiano Castelfranchi*, pages 601–626. College Publications, London, 2012.

[16] E. L. Thorndike. Intelligence and its uses. *Harper's Magazine*, 140:227–235, 1920.

[17] P. Vernon. Some characteristics of the good judge of personality. *Journal of Social Psychology*, 4:42–57, 1933.

[18] H. de Weerd, R. Verbrugge, and B. Verheij. Negotiating with other minds: the role of recursive theory of mind in negotiation with incomplete information. *Autonomous Agents and Multi-Agent Systems*, pages 1–38, 2015.

[19] A. B. Youssef, M. Chollet, H. Jones, N. Sabouret, C. Pelachaud, and M. Ochs. Towards a socially adaptive virtual agent. In *Intelligent Virtual Agents*, pages 3–16. Springer International Publishing, 2015.

[20] H. Yu, Z. Shen, C. Leung, C. Miao, and V. R. Lesser. A survey of multi-agent trust management systems. *Access, IEEE*, 1:35–50, 2013.

On Decentralized Coordination for Spatial Task Allocation and Scheduling in Heterogeneous Teams

Eduardo Feo Flushing, Luca M. Gambardella, Gianni A. Di Caro
Dalle Molle Institute for Artificial Intelligence (IDSIA), USI/SUPSI
Lugano, Switzerland
{eduardo, luca, gianni}@idsia.ch

ABSTRACT

In the context of coordination and planning in collaborative multi-robot/agent systems, we consider a general reference problem that includes tasks that are spatially localized and have an associated service time, and accounts for the use of a heterogeneous team, in which different robots may have a different performance on the same task. A mixed integer linear formulation is introduced and used to solve the problem model in a centralized iterative manner: in closed-loop, team-level plans are adaptively computed and sent out. Unfortunately, a centralized scheme can suffer from computational and communication shortcomings. Therefore, we introduce a top-down recipe for decentralization, aiming to balance the tradeoff among implementation costs, computational requirements, and quality of coordination. The decentralized architecture depends on various aspects that we study through an empirical sensitivity analysis. Results show that the impact and the relationships among the different aspects are far from being obvious or intuitive. A number of practical lessons are learned, that could apply to other similar problems and/or decentralized architectures derived in the same top-down modality.

Keywords

Multi-Robot Systems; Decentralized Coordination and Planning; Collaborative Teams; Task Allocation

1. INTRODUCTION

It is well understood that, in general, the support of a *coordinated planning* scheme is necessary to optimize the performance of a *multi-agent team.* Coordination is required to avoid conflicts, unnecessary overlapping, and incoherent executions, while, at the same time, to boost cooperation and synergies when tackling a common mission. This is even more true when the team is heterogeneous, due to the fact that different agents might perform differently for the various sub-tasks composing the overall mission.

In this work, we focus on mission scenarios that require the use of embedded physical agents, a mobile *multi-robot team* in particular, and that are defined through a set of *spatially distributed tasks*, each with its own characteristics and demand levels. The class of problems that we consider generalizes the classical multi-robot task allocation problems. It includes the notion of spatial locality [22, 10] and service time, which enrich the mission model with a routing and scheduling component. We refer to the problems in this class as the *spatial task allocation and scheduling problem in heterogeneous multi-robot teams*, or STASP-HMR in short.

In practice, our modeling approach is derived from complex *search and rescue* scenarios, that require to coordinate a heterogeneous team for searching over an area, transporting items, mapping, detecting dangerous events, and so on. In these cases, due to the inherent uncertainties of the environment to act upon, agent planning cannot be usually done in one shot, but instead needs to be performed iteratively, in *closed-loop with mission enrollment*, to account for new evidence, deviations, and unexpected issues.

In previous work [13], we tackled the heterogeneous team-level planning through the use of a *linear mixed integer mathematical formulation*, which was solved using the combination of standard solvers and ad hoc heuristics that was able to retain *anytime* properties and formal guarantees on solution quality while speeding up computations. The planner operates in a *centralized, closed-loop modality*: a joint plan is issued, then updates are continually sent from the executing agents to the planner, and in turn this triggers the computation of new plans, iteratively. This way of proceeding has obvious limitations, especially in the search and rescue scenarios of reference, where communication infrastructures are hardly available, many unexpected events can happen on the field requiring continual replanning, and the criticality of the situation requires a very rapid adaptation and response.

To overcome these well-known issues, in this paper we propose a *decentralized approach* for STASP-HMR, where each agent runs a replica of the mathematical model, based on local data and limited information sharing. Apart from the characterization of the above class of problems, our *contribution* here is two-fold. First, we introduce a decentralized coordination and planning algorithm that meets computational and communication requirements, and at the same time incurs in limited performance losses compared to the centralized solution. Second, we propose a *general top-down recipe* for deriving an effective decentralized scheme from a centralized mathematical model. Moreover, a *third contribution* consists in the identification of a set of interrelated design aspects that have a critical impact on the performance of a decentralized team, and in performing a *sensitivity analysis* (in simulation) with respect to these aspects.

Appears in: *Proceedings of the 15th International Conference on Autonomous Agents and Multiagent Systems (AAMAS 2016), J. Thangarajah, K. Tuyls, C. Jonker, S. Marsella (eds.), May 9–13, 2016, Singapore.*

In particular, we consider team heterogeneity, amount of information sharing, planning look-ahead, and replanning frequency. A number of not trivial results have been observed and practical lessons have been learned. The claim is that these same results could apply to other classes of decentralized coordination systems obtained following a top-down approach from a centralized mathematical model.

2. BACKGROUND

According to the level of coordination that they demand, multi-robot missions can be categorized into tightly-coupled and loosely-coupled missions [15, 5, 31, 18, 2, 25]. Tightly-coupled missions are composed of tasks with strong coordination requirements. These include coalition formation scenarios in which robots must complement their skills and coordinate their actions to act, as a team, upon certain tasks [28, 30, 26], and scenarios that impose ordering constraints between tasks that require negotiation and coordination among the agents so as to prevent conflicts and deadlocks [18, 7, 11, 21, 20, 14]. Other forms of tightly-coupled missions are inter-schedule dependencies [19] that restrict the set of actions of a single robot depending on the tasks being carried out by other robots, e.g., for preserving network connectivity [6, 23], or coalitions [31]. In general, these tightly-coupled domains involve inter-task or inter-agent dependencies that affect the feasibility of the mission, therefore they require the use of strong coordination mechanisms.

On the contrary, the degree of coordination in loosely-coupled missions may have an impact on their performance but does not compromise their feasibility. In practice, these missions could rely on local decisions made by the agents without any form of agreement among them. However, the lack of coordination in these missions may result, for instance, into a duplication of effort and a waste of resources [4], therefore having a negative effect over team performance. Thus, coordination is desirable but not strictly necessary. Among these type of missions we find scenarios that are modeled as foraging tasks, with the objective of minimizing completion time or maximizing some notion of reward, e.g., search, surveillance, coverage, patrolling [1, 17].

Decentralized approaches surge as a response to the drawbacks and limitations of their centralized counterparts. They eliminate the need for a central entity by transferring the control authority to the agents that execute the mission. As a result, the agents become autonomous decision-making elements in charge of planning their own actions. This transfer of control provides fault tolerance, resiliency, and scalability.

Several decentralization strategies exist in the literature, tailored to fit the different coordination requirements of the missions that they tackle. Among them, implicit coordination is a common and flexible way to deal with loosely-coupled missions [17]. It is achieved by having each agent, independently, computing a (global) solution utilizing a centralized planner. From this solution, each single robot retrieves its own plan. The basis of this method is that, when all robots possess a similar knowledge about the environment, they would compute similar solutions. As a result, they implicitly coordinate and plan their own actions.

In this work, we analyze the tradeoff between the choice of coordinated actions and the performance of a decentralized scheme based on the implicit coordination principle, in the context of a loosely-coupled scenario. This tradeoff is not well understood in the literature, and it is also unclear how to quantify the performance degradation of reduced coordination in these domains [29, 3]. Interestingly, we can empirically study these properties by comparing the performance of a centralized planner, which computes optimal mission plans using full knowledge, against the one of a decentralized solution. In this work we follow this approach to investigate the effect of several design choices and their different parameters in implicitly coordinated missions.

3. SPATIAL TASK ALLOCATION & SCHEDULING IN HETEROGENEOUS TEAMS

In this section, we define the class of problems that we address in this work, namely the STASP-HMR. We first introduce the concepts that underlie the model of the mission. Then, we provide a concise statement of the STASP-HMR.

3.1 Mission representation

Let $\mathcal{A}$ be a team of heterogeneous mobile agents that are available to perform a *joint mission* in an environment of a specified dimension. We assume that the mission has been decomposed into a set $\mathcal{T}$ of *spatially distributed, location-dependent tasks*. These tasks can be *non-atomic*, incrementally providing a reward proportional to the progress achieved in their completion, and can be eventually brought to an end.

The spatial layout of tasks is captured by a *traversability graph* that defines how agents can move between tasks. In this respect, we define a directed traversability graph $G = (\mathcal{T}, E)$ where E contains an arc (i, j) if task j can be scheduled right after task i. In the general case, graph G is complete (i.e., $E = \mathcal{T} \times \mathcal{T}$), and, in this way, we are assuming that all tasks are independent from each other. However, G can be used to accommodate constraints over the sequences of tasks that can be executed. For instance, when some tasks cannot be designated immediately after others, e.g., due to mobility constraints, or when specific tasks must be serviced immediately before servicing others, e.g., unblocking a road to reach other parts of the area.

From the point of view of the mission, the complete execution of any task $\tau \in \mathcal{T}$ provides an overall *utility*, or *reward*, indicated with R_τ. The values assigned to R_τ can be used to indicate how important is the task for the mission, e.g., in a search and rescue mission when some locations are more important to search accurately than others based on some a priori knowledge.

3.2 Task efficiency model and completion

For a given mission, we can look at tasks as requests to be possibly serviced, and at the agents as the entities with the capabilities to service these requests. When we deal with heterogeneous teams, different agents may demonstrate different levels of performance accomplishing the same task.

In order to accommodate team heterogeneity we propose the use of *task efficiency models* that allow, as their name suggest, to specify the efficiency with which an agent services a specific task. The intuition behind these models is that any progress on the completion of a task is proportional to the overall time devoted to it. Agent a is more efficient than agent b on the same task τ if in the same amount of time a pushes τ closer to its completion.

The definition of the task efficiency models should be based on the specific skills of the agents in relation to the specific local characteristics of each task. For instance, the time effort required for pushing a box across a room is dependent upon how much force a robot is able to apply to the box and on well it can detect possible obstacles along the way. We assume that the efficiency models, for each single agent, are known and defined as $\varphi : \mathcal{A} \times \mathcal{T} \mapsto \mathbb{R}$. $\varphi_k(\tau)$, $k \in \mathcal{A}, \tau \in \mathcal{T}$ relates the time an agent spends doing a task to the progress achieved towards its completion. The value of $\varphi_k(\tau)$ is inversely proportional to the amount of service time that k requires for the completion of τ.

In the following, for the sake of simplifying the formulation, we assume that time is discretized into *mission intervals* of equal length $\Delta_{\mathcal{T}}$. In addition, with the purpose of avoiding the challenges posed by the solution of non-linear models, we assume that task efficiency models follow a linear law. More precisely, when an agent $k \in \mathcal{A}$ performs a task $\tau \in \mathcal{T}$ for t mission intervals, it contributes with $100 \times \varphi_k(\tau) \cdot t$ percent to the *task completion*.

To express the residual service needed by each task, we use the *completion map* $C_m : \mathcal{T} \mapsto [0, 1]$. The values in the completion map identify the *current completion level* of tasks whose workload has been partially addressed in previous planning stages. For instance, a value of 0 for $C_m(\tau)$ indicates that task τ has been already completed in the past, and therefore no further efforts from the agents are required. If an agent attempts to further deal with that task it will receive no additional reward, which will amount a waste of time and resources. Servicing a fraction p of the workload of task τ decreases its required completion $C_m(\tau)$ by p and provides a partial utility of pR_τ.

3.3 Definition of STASP-HMR

Based on the concepts introduced above, the STASP-HMR can be stated as follows. Given a set of heterogeneous agents, each characterized by its task efficiency model, and a *limited time budget* T, the STASP-HMR consists in determining joint plans for the activities of the agents in the environment which enable the timely selection of the tasks to perform, and aiming to maximize the overall mission utility (i.e., the sum of all gathered rewards).

A *solution to the STASP-HMR* (i.e., a mission plan) consists of time-constrained sequences of tasks, one for each agent, that can be represented as paths in G. In addition, plans also define how much effort (i.e., devoted time) each one of the selected tasks will receive. Due to the limited time budget, not all tasks may be performed: a plan implicitly defines a selection among all tasks in $\mathcal{T}$. The goal is to assign the right agent to deal with the right task, at the right time. Here "right" means the agent who is the most efficient for the task among the agents in the vicinity.

In real-world scenarios, the available information concerning the environment is usually incomplete or imperfect, and the environment itself is often dynamic. Moreover, deviations in the agents' response to plans may occur as a consequence of unexpected sensing/actuation problems. For these reasons, a solution approach to the STASP-HMR in real-world scenarios should adapt the issued plans to these dynamic aspects. This calls for a *closed-loop* approach: while plans are executed, mission information is gathered from the agents, based on this information new plans are adaptively issued, and the process is iterated until mission completion. This is precisely the approach we follow, as described in Section 4.1.

4. CENTRALIZED SOLUTION APPROACH

We formulate the STASP-HMR as stated above by means of a *mixed-integer linear program* (MIP). An optimal solution to the MIP defines plans for each one of the agents with the goal of maximizing the total mission reward. For the sake of completeness, we present the MIP, and refer the interested reader to [13] for a detailed description.

$$\text{maximize} \quad \sum_{\tau \in \mathcal{T}} R_\tau \Phi_\tau \tag{1}$$

subject to

$$\sum_{(0,j) \in E} x_{0j}^k = 1 \qquad k \in \mathcal{A} \tag{2}$$

$$\sum_{(i,0) \in E} x_{i0}^k = 1 \qquad k \in \mathcal{A} \tag{3}$$

$$\sum_{(i,j) \in E} x_{ij}^k = \sum_{(j,i) \in E} x_{ji}^k = y_j^k \qquad k \in \mathcal{A},\ j \in \mathcal{T} \tag{4}$$

$$t_i^k + w_i^k - t_j^k \leq (1 - x_{ij}^k)T \qquad k \in \mathcal{A}, (i,j) \in E, i,j \neq 0 \tag{5}$$

$$y_i^k \leq t_i^k, w_i^k \leq T y_i^k \qquad k \in \mathcal{A},\ i \in \mathcal{T} \tag{6}$$

$$\Phi_\tau \leq \sum_{k \in \mathcal{A}} \varphi_k(\tau) w_i^k \qquad \tau \in \mathcal{T} \tag{7}$$

$$0 \leq \Phi_\tau \leq C_m(\tau) \qquad \tau \in \mathcal{T} \tag{8}$$

$$\Phi_\tau \in \mathbb{R} \qquad \tau \in \mathcal{T} \tag{9}$$

$$t_i^k,\ w_i^k \in \mathbb{N} \qquad k \in \mathcal{A}, i \in \mathcal{T} \tag{10}$$

$$x_{ij}^k,\ y_j^k \in \{0, 1\} \qquad k \in \mathcal{A},\ i,j \in \mathcal{T} \tag{11}$$

We use the following *decision variables* to build the MIP model for the STASP-HMR presented in (1)-(11):
x_{ij}^k: binary, equals 1 if agent k traverses arc $(i, j) \in E$;
y_i^k: binary, equals 1 if agent k is assigned to task $i \in \mathcal{T}$;
Φ_τ: service provided to task $\tau \in \mathcal{T}$ by all agents;
t_i^k: starting time of execution of task $i \in \mathcal{T}$ by agent k;
w_i^k: time assigned to task $i \in \mathcal{T}$ for agent k.

The objective function (1) defines the quality of a mission plan in terms of its utility, quantifying the expected effect of agents' activities over the current state of the completion map C_m. A dummy vertex (denoted by 0) represents the starting point and ending point of the agents' paths. Graph G is extended with arcs from 0 to each one of the tasks that are initially accessible. Constraints (2-4) ensure path continuity. Constraints (5) eliminate sub-tours [27] and, together with (6), they define the bounds on the variables t and w. The completion levels of each task are bounded by constraints (7-8). These bounds ensure that each task τ provides a maximum reward equal to $R_\tau C_m(\tau)$, and that the utility of a plan is contributed with R_τ scaled by the completion of τ (i.e., Φ_τ). Finally, constraints (9-11) set the real, integer, and binary requirements on the model variables.

In general, the above MIP can be computationally hard to solve and therefore finding an optimal mission plan may take a significant amount of time. However and conveniently, standard MIP solvers have *anytime* properties: solutions are progressively and monotonically improved over time, and can be retrieved with formal error bounds on optimality. In our case, to exert a proper control of the time spent computing a plan, the planner sets a maximum time t_{plan} to the MIP solver, after which the solver stops the optimization and returns the best solution found.

4.1 Online iterative replanning

For a given mission, the MIP formulation proposed above could be used to perform a *one-shot* planning. Yet, as mentioned in Section 3.3, the offline computation of mission plans is not practical since it cannot accommodate the dynamic aspects of real-world environments.

To this end, we consider an online, iterative replanning approach based on the continual acquisition of new information about the environment and the current status of the agents. The iterative replanning is implemented as a *multi-stage, periodic, re-optimization procedure* [16, 8] that consists in solving, over time, a sequence of static problem instances with varying horizon length. During the entire mission, the planner continuously gathers new information about the state of the environment, as well as the current status of the agents and of the tasks they are executing. This information is taken into account in the next replanning iteration, so as to make the new plans adapting to the changing situation.

More in detail, the iterative replanning works as follows. At any single planning stage, the planner sets a horizon T_H that defines how far to look ahead during planning. Longer horizons should enable a better allocation of resources, but also increase the computational complexity as the size of the associated problems increases [14, 22]. In contrast, shorter horizons tend to be computationally affordable, but also to make agents to reason myopically, resulting into lower-quality decisions. This tradeoff is discussed in Section 6. After the value T_H has been chosen, it is used as T in the MIP model associated to the current stage.

The selected scheme for online replanning must guarantee that, at any time, an agent has a plan to follow. Recall that a given mission plan has a limited time span that depends on the value of the last horizon T_H used. Beyond this time span, the agents do not have any planned actions. Therefore, at the planner, the computation of the next plan needs to be triggered before the current plan expires, so as to extend the plan and let the agents to continue with the mission.

Without losing generality, we assume that replanning can be triggered within an interval $[t_a, t_b]$ with $1 \leq t_a \leq t_b \leq T_H - t_{plan}$ measured from the time when the last plan was issued. When $t_a = 1$, replanning can occur just after the agents execute the first action of the last plan computed. When $t_b = T_H - t_{plan}$, the next replanning stage can occur, at the latest, just before the current mission plan expires (i.e., while agents execute their last task assigned). In Section 6 we extend the discussion about the choice of $[t_a, t_b]$ and the impact this parameter has on the performance of iterative replanning.

5. TOP-DOWN DECENTRALIZATION

The centralized iterative replanning scheme presented above provides several advantages: allows to place much of the computational load to the central controller, therefore reducing the cost and the complexity of the team [9], makes the whole operation relatively easier to implement, and, if the controller has an accurate, global view of the mission, then it is possible to compute optimal mission plans, that take into account global constraints. On the other side, this scheme suffers from scalability issues, meaning that, for large team sizes, the computational complexity and communication requirements prohibit its use [24]. These issues are even more evident when the replanning rate becomes higher.

In the following of this section we describe the top-down approach for solving the STASP-HMR in a decentralized manner. It addresses the drawbacks and limitations of its centralized counterpart, by providing fault tolerance, resiliency, and scalability. However, these appealing characteristics may often lead to sub-optimal, lower quality solutions The approach is based upon implicit coordination and replicates the centralized scheme on each agent. As a result a decentralized decision making is achieved by letting each agent planning its own actions.

In order to achieve decentralized coordination, agents must make their decisions on the basis of a common ground. Therefore, we first enumerate what and how data should be exchanged among the agents in order to maximize their local perception of the mission. Lastly, we discuss how the local data are exploited for the efficient computation of plans and for the implicit coordination the mission.

5.1 Shared knowledge representation

Apart from the static information about the problem, which can be initially distributed among the agents, there are two main types of information that need to be revised, and updated, in order to replicate the iterative replanning scheme at each agent: the completion map C_m and the planned actions of the other agents.

During the execution of a plan, the executed tasks receive certain amount of service that decrease the initial workload required for them. In a centralized setting, this information would be gathered at the central controller and used to keep an up-to-date global completion map C_m. However, this is not the case in a decentralized scheme, and agents should keep a local estimation of the C_m. The more accurate these estimates are, the better plans an agent can compute.

In addition, it is also useful to know the scheduled future actions of other agents. For instance, let us assume that an agent a is about to compute a local plan and, according to its local perception of C_m, there is a nearby task τ that requires full service. Even if such estimate is accurate and indeed τ has not been attended yet by any other agent, the inclusion of this task in a's current plan could be a bad decision if there exists another agent b that has already included τ in its plan. These situations can become frequent and, unless some explicit fallback strategy is executed (e.g., detecting ad preventing the overlapping of actions), they degrade the performance of the mission.

Both types of data, the completion map and the plans, are described in terms of *incremental updates* that, once added up all together, allow to reconstruct a global shared representation of the mission. In the case of the completion map, an incremental update is a tuple $C_m^u = < k, \tau, t_{start}, t_{end} >$ that indicates that agent k has provided service to task τ from time t_{start} to t_{end}. These updates are issued by the same agent that performs the service. Each agent uses the C_m^u's that are issued by other agents to update its own local C_m. This is done by computing the amount of service provided to each task using the efficiency models φ_k. Note that it is sufficient to aggregate the updates, independently of the time at which they were generated, in order to approximate C_m to its true value. An important remark is that agents should not apply twice the same update. To this end, each C_m^u is uniquely identified by a sequence number, assigned by the agent that generates the update.

Regarding the mission plans, a similar approach is followed. A plan update is a tuple $< k, t_{gen}, \tau, t_{start}, t_{end}, >$ that indicates the intention of agent k to perform task τ from t_{start} to t_{end}. Note that in this case we also use an additional time stamp t_{gen} to specify the time at which k expressed such intention. At any time instant t, we can (partially) reconstruct the mission plan of an agent k by considering all the plan updates with $t \leq t_{start}$. The values of t_{gen} allow us to resolve conflicts when two or more updates overlap. As for the completion map updates, each plan update is uniquely identified by a sequence number and stored in a table.

5.2 Information exchange

In a decentralized operation, communication among the agents enables the acquisition of relevant information regarding the past, current, and planned activities. In real-world deployments, communication is usually supported by a wireless network. However, when networked teams operate in large-scale environments, data exchange can become sparse, because it is restricted by the transmission range of the network.

Based on the shared representation, the final goal is to exploit at most the communication interactions among the agents. To this end, a gossip-based mechanism[12] helps to spread the information about the mission among the team. This mechanism is implemented as follows.

During the mission, all agents broadcast periodic network discovery messages that serve to announce their presence to other agents. Using these messages, each single agent keeps a list of all other agents from which it has received a message recently. From this list, and with certain frequency, the agent chooses another agent to initiate a synchronization procedure. This procedure enables the agents to merge and synchronize their local knowledge and possibly improve their local perception of the mission.

5.3 Adaptive replanning using the MIP

To perform the iterative replanning, each agent uses its local estimate of the the completion map, and of the current (partial) plans of other agents to set up the MIP.

The completion map C_m is used to define constraints (8). The plans of other agents are used to fix some of the routing and scheduling variables t_i^k, x_{ij}^k, and w_i^k. Since the agents can spread out over the area, data exchange can be sparse. As a result, agents may become unaware of the activities of some members of the team. Therefore, when building the MIP, each agent only considers the teammates from which it has recently gotten some information update. The general idea is to rely only on fresh information, that can be considered as reliable.

Each agent uses the MIP to primarily compute its own plan. However, the MIP is intended to optimize the global joint mission plan. This means that, when an agent a only has partial information about the plans of the other agents, a must either infer the missing parts of the plans or let the solver compute them. In this work, we adopt the former approach. Partial plans are completed by an agent a using a heuristic procedure, which works as follows. First, the tasks in the vicinity of a that still need to be completed are listed. Then, in sequence, for each other agent from which a has reliable information and an incomplete plan, a greedy task assignment is performed: the next task from the list that maximizes the agent reward is assigned to it in the MIP formulation. As a result, the set of decision variables of the MIP is drastically reduced to the variables that only define the actions of the agent a. The decision variables regarding the other agents are fixed and treated as constants. In our tests, we note that this way of proceeding leads to substantial computational savings and better performance compared to solving the entire MIP. In fact, the gain that would potentially be obtained by solving the entire problem is diminished by the relative poor quality of the solutions that can be effectively computed in the limited time budget allocated for planning.

6. SENSITIVITY ANALYSIS

In this section we present a sensitivity analysis of the proposed decentralized scheme. The analysis is based on simulations. In order to obtain solutions to the mathematical programs we use CPLEX® as MIP solver, combined with a simple greedy heuristic that provides an initial feasible solution. In the following, first, we describe the instances of the STASP-HMR that constitute the benchmark of the analysis. Next, we use these instances to study the computational performance of the centralized implementation and to derive bounds on mission performance. These bounds are used as a performance baseline for the analysis of the decentralized system. In the remaining part of this section we focus the sensitivity analysis on the following aspects: team heterogeneity and spatial correlation among the tasks, amount of information sharing, and length of the planning horizon and frequency of replanning.

6.1 Experimental setup

We consider problem instances where the locations of the tasks composing the mission are obtained through a grid decomposition of the area with a one to one correspondence between tasks and grid cells. The grid size is 20×20, for a total of four hundred tasks. We adopt a dimensionless space, yet we consider that robots must move through adjacent cells in the Moore neighborhood (i.e., if they share at least one vertex on the grid). This condition is translated into the traversability graph and imposes routing constraints on the set of feasible sequences of tasks.

We let the task locality to impose limits on the communication. In some instances, data exchange between two robots occur only within a limited communication range ψ_r. To simulate the communication constraints we embed the grid into a Cartesian plane, and define the distance between two tasks as the euclidean norm between the center of the associated cells. Whenever two robots are within a distance less or equal to ψ_r they are able to exchange data and to synchronize their current knowledge using the mechanisms described in Section 5.2.

We consider four types of agents, each characterized by the efficiency in accomplishing the tasks. As introduced in Section 3, the value of φ precisely relates each robot to the efficiency in doing each task. Numerically, φ defines the fraction of workload of a task that a robot can tackle during a single time step. For each single task, we consider that any robot type exhibits one out of five different efficiency levels, ranging from completely inefficient ($\varphi \triangleq 3\%$) up to highly efficient ($\varphi \triangleq 100\%$). These models are assumed to be known by all agents, and to remain constant during the mission. We setup a mission by defining the number

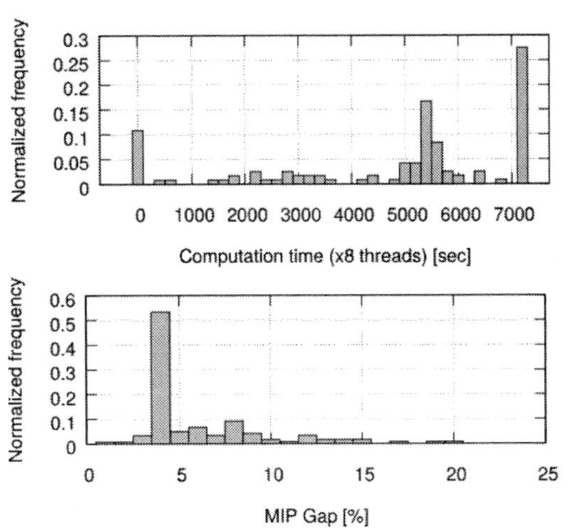

Figure 1: Computational results of the centralized planning over 120 STASP-HMR instances with 12 agents.

of agents of each type (which could be zero), together with their initial deployment. The total number of agents in a mission is 12 unless otherwise specified.

All simulated missions have a duration of 48 steps. At the start, the robots are deployed at random positions inside the grid. They all compute an initial plan, and then execute the online replanning in an asynchronous way, as described in Section 5. At each replanning stage, each agent allows a maximum of $t_{plan} = 150$ seconds to compute a next plan using the MIP solver. This time limit has been chosen to emulate a real-world scenario where plans meant to be computed in near real-time on embedded systems with potentially low computing power (e.g., small flying robots).

6.2 The complexity of centralized planning

As an initial step in our analysis we use the solver to compute global solutions under a centralized setting and with full knowledge of the environment. The goal of the experiments reported here is twofold. First, to observe the complexity of the centralized planning. Second, to use the computed solutions to derive a bound on the best achievable performance of a decentralized execution in any single problem instance.

We compute the baseline solutions using the mathematical solver, imposing a time limit of two hours and a memory limit of 8 GB, and using up to 8 parallel threads, each one allocated to an individual core in a computing cluster. Upon reaching the limits of computational resources, the solver returns the best solution found $Best^{cent}$. It also provides a measure of the solution quality in terms of a *relative optimality gap* (G^{cent}_{opt}), also called MIP gap. This gap is related to a lower bound (LB^{cent}) that is derived from the linear programming relaxation. The value of LB^{cent} is computed and improved by the solver during the solution process by relaxing the integrality constraints through the branch and bound search and by automatically generating cutting planes. We let the solver stop the computation when G^{cent}_{opt} becomes less than 5%, meaning that we obtained a satisfactory solution.

Figure 1 shows the distribution of the computation time (top) and MIP gaps (bottom) for a set of 120 problem instances using a centralized planner. Results show that most of the instances satisfied the relative optimality gap of 5%. In addition, besides a small subset of instances, the computation time taken by the solver was in general above 5,000 seconds, which multiplied by 8 threads/cores, it is equivalent to over 11 hours of computation. From these results we can appreciate the complexity of centralized planning. It is precisely this computational complexity one of the aspects that we expect to overcome by using a decentralized approach.

To evaluate the relative performance of the decentralized implementations with respect to the centralized one, we use the solutions obtained above to define a baseline metric. More precisely, for each problem instance, we compute the relative gap G^{dec}_{opt} between the decentralized solution and the centralized bound LB^{cent}. We consider this metric instead of using directly $Best^{cent}$ because, as noted in Figure 1, in many cases it is computationally unfeasible to reduce G^{cent}_{opt} to zero given the limited computational resources available.

6.3 Team diversity and tasks' correlation

A core feature of our solution approach to STASP-HMR is that we optimize the match between tasks and agents allocated to them. In this respect, heterogeneity could become an advantage when different tasks can benefit from different skills. However, in order to exploit heterogeneity, the plans for the individual agents need to be well coordinated among each other. This, in turn, depends on the spatial correlation among the tasks with respect to the task efficiency models of the agents.

When the task efficiency models are not spatially correlated, we can expect that the efficiency of an agent changes abruptly over neighbor tasks. On the contrary, when the models exhibit certain degree of spatial structure, changes are smooth, which also means that once an agent is performing a task for which is good for, we expect that it would be also well suited for the surrounding tasks.

The spatial correlation aspects also affect the way conflicts among the agents arise and are solved by local coordination. In the uncorrelated case, conflicts are sparse, and more difficult to solve due to the lack of smoothness of the models. For instance, when an agent finds itself competing with others for some task of high value for it (e.g., it is well suited for the task), it becomes more difficult to coordinate and maybe sacrifice its individual objective (for the sake of the mission) and select other tasks in the vicinity that have a similar value. However, when the efficiency models are spatially correlated, there is a good chance of solving the conflict with slight local changes in the plans.

With respect to team diversity, it remains to understand how it affects the performance of the decentralized scheme, and what is the role of coordination in this context. Perhaps more interestingly is to study the interplay between the choice of a heterogeneous team and the degree of spatial structure of the task efficiency models.

In this section, we consider two classes of missions. In the first class, tasks efficiency models follow a discrete uniform random distribution. In the second class, we use random fractals to obtain spatially structured surfaces from which we generate models that exhibit some degree of spatial correlation. Figure 2 depicts one instance of each class to illustrate the difference between them.

Discussion: Figure 3 shows the performance of the decentralized scheme for both classes of missions. The plot shows the median value and 25% and 75% error bars of the performance of the decentralized schemes, measured in terms of G^{dec}_{opt}. The performance for each class is analyzed

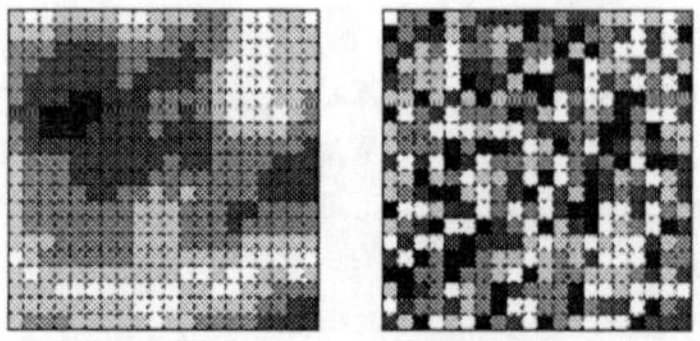

Figure 2: Visual representation of two efficiency models with (left) and without (right) spatial correlation. Each color represents an efficiency level.

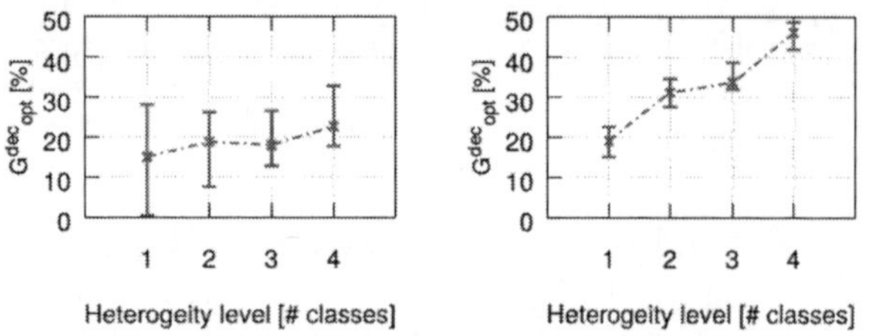

Figure 3: Effect of team diversity on instances with spatially correlated models (left) and with random uniform task models (right).

with respect to the level of heterogeneity (i.e., increasing the number of agent classes). From the results, we immediately observe that, in both cases, the performance with respect to the centralized model degrades when the heterogeneity level is increased. Surprisingly, these effects are stronger for uncorrelated models

The lesson learned from this discussion is the following. If we employ an heterogeneous team with efficiency models that exhibit low spatial correlation, we should be aware that the decentralized solution can show a performance (relative to the centralized solution) significantly lower than the one obtained with a homogeneous team. At last we point out that, at the global system level, heterogeneity is beneficial. For instance, the following table shows the percentage of performance improvement, with respect to homogeneous teams, for the centralized model.

# agent classes	2	3	4
uniform random	20	34	32
spatially correlated	24	31	34

These numbers indicate that well-coordinated heterogeneous teams perform better than homogeneous teams.

6.4 Local vs. global information sharing

In Section 5 we propose a shared representation of the mission on top of which the decentralized scheme is implemented. In this section we analyze the value that each piece of information (i.e., completion map, and partial plans) brings to the performance of the decentralized approach. In the presence of communication constraints, we also analyze the effect of inconsistent knowledge among the agents.

We consider two different classes of scenarios. In the first, robots are allowed to exchange data without restrictions ($\psi_r = \infty$). In the second class, robots can only exchange data with other robots located within a communication range $\psi_r = 3$. In this way we analyze the impact of incomplete information.

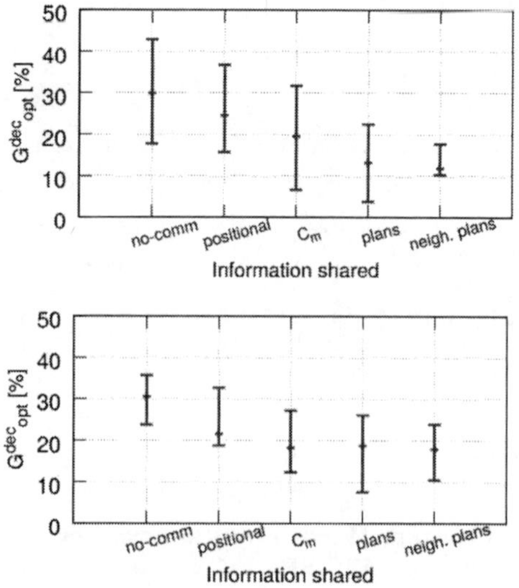

Figure 4: Effect of information sharing with full (top) and constrained communication (bottom).

We simulated 40 missions with spatially correlated models and using a team of 12 robots with two classes of agents. We distinguish 4 types of scenarios that add, incrementally, the following data to the list of data that are shared among the agents: (1) positional information; (2) completion map C_m updates; (3) partial mission plans; (4) plans computed for other agents. In the latter case, agents also share, with a subset of their neighbors, the plans that they complete for them. We believe that this strategy can help save computational resources since the agents utilize plans that have already been computed by another agents to extend their current plans, without resorting to the MIP. However, it is unclear if this provides some gain in performance.

Discussion: Figure 4 summarizes the value of each piece of information in both full and constrained communication scenarios. The data labeled as "no-comm" correspond to the case where agents do not exchange any information. An important observation is that sharing the completion map is sufficient to guarantee a performance within 20% from the centralized solution. This suggest that this piece of information is the most valuable one for the implicit coordination scheme. The rest of the information only makes a difference, albeit relatively small, if it can be spread out among the agents. Lastly, we remark that the strategy of sharing computed plans with the neighbors does not improve the performance in a significant way. However, it can be used to reduce the amount of planning iterations that agents must execute and, in overall, to reduce the cost of planning, while at the same time providing similar performance with respect to the case where this information is not shared.

6.5 Planning horizon and replanning frequency

Two of the most important parameters of the online replanning are the length of the lookahead planning horizon (T_H) and the replanning frequency (specified by an interval $[t_a, t_b]$). Here we examine the single and correlated effects of these parameters. We consider different replanning intervals and horizon lengths. First, we fix a relatively short interval for replanning and evaluate the effect of the increasing horizon. The short interval is chosen to ensure that the results primarily depend on the length of the horizon.

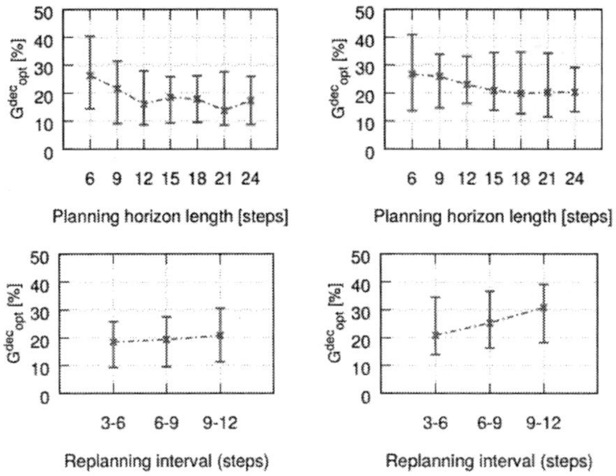

Figure 5: Effect of the lookahead planning horizon (top) and the replanning frequency (bottom) on the decentralized scheme with full (left), and constrained communication (right).

Figure 5 (top) shows the effect of increasing the horizon from 6 up to 24 steps. We indicate the median value and 25% and 75% error bars among the benchmark instances, for both the communication-constrained (top right) and unconstrained scenarios (top left). Intuitively, one would expect that the longer is the horizon, the better are the plans that robots compute, which also results into better global mission plans. Indeed, we observe that the increasing horizon tends to improve the performance of the team. However, for longer horizons, the improvement stops and the performance stagnates. A similar observation is made by [10], although they do not provide any explanation of it.

Regarding the relationship between these parameters and the amount of information exchanged we note that information is better exploited with longer horizons. In the communication limited scenarios, the use of longer horizons only provide a marginally better performance.

Discussion: One possible cause for the behavior described above is the fact that, for longer horizons, the corresponding MIPs become harder to solve. However, after an examination of the distribution of the MIP gap values over the increasing horizon length for all the MIPs solved during the simulations ($\sim 70,000$), we noticed that the increase of complexity was not significant. In fact, most of the MIP solutions remain within 2 % from the optimal solution. We conjecture that this behavior may be due to the asynchronicity of the online schemes and the effect of incomplete information regarding the planned actions of other agents.

Next, we evaluate the impact of the replanning frequency. We consider three replanning intervals, $[3, 6]$, $[6, 9]$, and $[9, 12]$. The interval is set at the beginning of the missions and the agents decide, randomly, when to trigger the next replanning stage based on the interval. The goal is to analyze the case when agents perform planning in an asynchronous way, and have the freedom to replan in an adaptive way.

Figures 5 (bottom) compares the performance that is obtained using the different replanning intervals. When the replanning occurs less frequently, the performance tends to deteriorate sharply when communication is limited. When communication is not an issue, the frequency of replanning is not central, but nevertheless compensates the small decrease in performance due to the inconsistent information.

7. CONCLUSIONS AND FUTURE WORK

Building on previous research, we present a decentralized solution to the spatial task allocation and scheduling problem with heterogeneous mobile teams. The work was motivated by the computation and communication constraints that the real-world imposes on a centralized approach. In the process of developing a decision support system for search and rescue missions using multiple heterogeneous robots, we directly faced the challenges that limit the use of a centralized system. These are mainly due to the lack of a network infrastructure (which is not usually present in these scenarios) and the need for rapid recomputation of plans to adapt to the dynamic aspects of the mission.

We have presented a recipe for the top-down decentralization of a mathematical programming model for the coordinated planning of multi-robot systems. The recipe aims at minimizing the computational and communication costs for the single agents while, at the same time, minimizing the loss of coordination due to the decentralization. The experimental results from extensive simulations have shown that we could balance the trade off between computation vs. coordination with the decentralized system in general performing within 10-30% with respect to a centralized implementation.

We also performed an empirical sensitivity analysis of the decentralized system since in general its performance depends on the interplay of a number of aspects such as team diversity, amount of information exchanged, and parameters regulating the computation of plans. Unfortunately, these aspects have correlated effects in presence of multiple agent interactions which are difficult to predict. Our study reveals some counter-intuitive effects and suggests that care should be adopted when designing a distributed/decentralized system. A number of practical lessons have been learned and that could be applied to similar problems and/or to other decentralized architectures derived using the same top-down recipe. In the future we will integrate the empirical results with formal tools so as to perform a sensitivity analysis in a more systematic and general way. We will also soon test our results with real robots in the context of search and rescue scenarios. Preliminary results in this context confirm that the system works but more systematic and comprehensive experiments are needed.

Acknowledgments

This research was supported by the Swiss National Science Foundation (SNSF) through the National Centre of Competence in Research (NCCR) Robotics (www.nccr-robotics.ch) and the Sinergia project SWARMIX, project number CRSI22_133059.

REFERENCES

[1] M. Alighanbari and J. How. Decentralized Task Assignment for Unmanned Aerial Vehicles. In *IEEE Conference on Decision and Control*, pages 5668–5673, 2005.

[2] C. Amato, G. Konidaris, G. Cruz, C. A. Maynor, J. P. How, and L. P. Kaelbling. Planning for decentralized control of multiple robots under uncertainty. In *Proc. of IEEE International Conference on Robotics and Automation (ICRA)*, pages 1241–1248, 2015.

[3] F. Amigoni, N. Basilico, and A. Quattrini Li. How Much Worth Is Coordination of Mobile Robots for Exploration in Search and Rescue? In *RoboCup 2012: Robot Soccer World Cup XVI*, volume 7500 LNAI, pages 106–117. Springer Berlin Heidelberg, 2013.

[4] M. Anderson and N. Papanikolopoulos. Implicit cooperation strategies for multi-robot search of unknown areas. *Journal of Intelligent and Robotic Systems*, 53(4):381–397, 2008.

[5] M. Bernardine Dias, R. Zlot, N. Kalra, and A. Stentz. Market-based multirobot coordination: A survey and analysis. *Proc. of the IEEE*, 94(7):1257–1270, 2006.

[6] N. Bezzo, B. Griffin, P. Cruz, J. Donahue, R. Fierro, and J. Wood. A Cooperative Heterogeneous Mobile Wireless Mechatronic System. *IEEE/ASME Transactions on Mechatronics*, 19(1):20–31, 2014.

[7] A. Brutschy, G. Pini, C. Pinciroli, M. Birattari, and M. Dorigo. Self-organized task allocation to sequentially interdependent tasks in swarm robotics. *International Conference on Autonomous Agents and Multiagent Systems (AAMAS)*, 28(1):101–125, 2014.

[8] L. Chen and E. Miller-Hooks. Optimal team deployment in urban search and rescue. *Transportation Research Part B: Methodological*, 46(8):984–999, 2012.

[9] H. L. Choi, L. Brunet, and J. P. How. Consensus-based decentralized auctions for robust task allocation. *IEEE Transactions on Robotics*, 25(4):912–926, 2009.

[10] D. Claes, F. A. Oliehoek, K. Tuyls, and D. Hennes. Effective Approximations for Multi-Robot Coordination in Spatially Distributed Tasks. In *International Conference on Autonomous Agents and Multiagent Systems (AAMAS)*, pages 881–890, 2015.

[11] D. Di Paola, A. Gasparri, D. Naso, G. Ulivi, and F. L. Lewis. Decentralized task sequencing and multiple mission control for heterogeneous robotic networks. In *IEEE International Conference on Robotics and Automation*, pages 4467–4473. IEEE, 2011.

[12] J. W. Durham, R. Carli, P. Frasca, and F. Bullo. Discrete partitioning and coverage control for gossiping robots. *IEEE Transactions on Robotics*, 28(2):364–378, 2012.

[13] E. Feo Flushing, L. M. Gambardella, and G. A. Di Caro. A mathematical programming approach to collaborative missions with heterogeneous teams. In *Proc. of IEEE/RSJ International Conference on Intelligent Robots and Systems (IROS)*, pages 396–403, 2014.

[14] S. K. Gan, R. Fitch, and S. Sukkarieh. Online decentralized information gathering with spatial-temporal constraints. *Autonomous Robots*, 37(1):1–25, 2014.

[15] B. P. Gerkey and M. J. Matarić. Sold!: Auction methods for multirobot coordination. *IEEE Transactions on Robotics and Automation*, 18(5):758–768, 2002.

[16] G. Ghiani, F. Guerriero, G. Laporte, and R. Musmanno. Real-time vehicle routing: Solution concepts, algorithms and parallel computing strategies. *European Journal of Operational Research*, 151(1):1–11, 2003.

[17] G. A. Hollinger and S. Singh. Multirobot coordination with periodic connectivity: Theory and experiments. *IEEE Transactions on Robotics*, 28(4):967–973, 2012.

[18] E. Jones, B. Browning, M. Dias, B. Argall, M. Veloso, and A. Stentz. Dynamically formed heterogeneous robot teams performing tightly-coordinated tasks. In *Proc. of IEEE International Conference on Robotics and Automation (ICRA)*, pages 570–575, 2006.

[19] G. A. Korsah, A. Stentz, and M. B. Dias. A comprehensive taxonomy for multi-robot task allocation. *The International Journal of Robotics Research*, 32(12):1495–1512, 2013.

[20] T. Lemaire, R. Alami, and S. Lacroix. A distributed tasks allocation scheme in multi-UAV context. *Proc. of IEEE International Conference on Robotics and Automation (ICRA)*, 4:3622–3627, 2004.

[21] L. Luo, N. Chakraborty, and K. Sycara. Multi-robot assignment algorithm for tasks with set precedence constraints. In *IEEE International Conference on Robotics and Automation*, pages 2526–2533, 2011.

[22] J. Parker, E. Nunes, J. Godoy, and M. Gini. Exploiting spatial locality and heterogeneity of agents for search and rescue teamwork. *Journal of Field Robotics*, 7, 2015.

[23] S. Ponda, J. Redding, Han-Lim Choi, J. P. How, M. Vavrina, and J. Vian. Decentralized planning for complex missions with dynamic communication constraints. In *Proc. of American Control Conference*, pages 3998–4003. IEEE, 2010.

[24] S. S. Ponda, L. B. Johnson, A. N. Kopeikin, H.-L. Choi, and J. P. How. Distributed Planning Strategies to Ensure Network Connectivity for Dynamic Heterogeneous Teams. *IEEE Journal on Selected Areas in Communications*, 30(5):861–869, 2012.

[25] S. Sariel-Talay, T. R. Balch, and N. Erdogan. A generic framework for distributed multirobot cooperation. *Journal of Intelligent and Robotic Systems*, 63(2):323–358, 2011.

[26] P. M. Shiroma and M. F. M. Campos. CoMutaR: A framework for multi-robot coordination and task allocation. In *Proc. of IEEE/RSJ International Conference on Intelligent Robots and Systems (IROS)*, pages 4817–4824, 2009.

[27] P. Vansteenwegen, W. Souffriau, and D. V. Oudheusden. The orienteering problem: A survey. *European Journal of Operational Research*, 209(1):1–10, 2011.

[28] L. Vig and J. A. Adams. Market-Based Multi-robot Coalition Formation. In *Distributed Autonomous Robotic Systems 7*, pages 227–236. Springer, 2006.

[29] F. Wu, S. Zilberstein, and X. Chen. Online planning for multi-agent systems with bounded communication. *Artificial Intelligence*, 175(2):487–511, 2011.

[30] Y. Zhang and L. E. Parker. IQ-ASyMTRe: Forming Executable Coalitions for Tightly Coupled Multirobot Tasks. *IEEE Transactions on Robotics*, 29(2):400–416, 2013.

[31] Y. Zhang, L. E. Parker, and S. Kambhampati. Coalition coordination for tightly coupled multirobot tasks with sensor constraints. In *Proc. of IEEE International Conference on Robotics and Automation (ICRA)*, pages 1090–1097, 2014.

The Impact of POMDP-Generated Explanations on Trust and Performance in Human-Robot Teams

Ning Wang and David V. Pynadath
Institute for Creative Technologies
University of Southern California
nwang@ict.usc.edu,pynadath@usc.edu

Susan G. Hill
U.S. Army Research Laboratory
Aberdeen Proving Ground, MD
susan.g.hill.civ@mail.mil

ABSTRACT

Researchers have observed that people will more accurately trust an autonomous system, such as a robot, if they have a more accurate understanding of its decision-making process. Studies have shown that hand-crafted explanations can help maintain effective team performance even when the system is less than 100% reliable. However, current explanation algorithms are not sufficient for making a robot's quantitative reasoning (in terms of both uncertainty and conflicting goals) transparent to human teammates. In this work, we develop a novel mechanism for robots to automatically generate explanations of reasoning based on Partially Observable Markov Decision Problems (POMDPs). Within this mechanism, we implement alternate natural-language templates and then measure their differential impact on trust and team performance within an agent-based online testbed that simulates a human-robot team task. The results demonstrate that the added explanation capability leads to improvement in transparency, trust, and team performance. Furthermore, by observing the different outcomes due to variations in the robot's explanation content, we gain valuable insight that can help lead to refinement of explanation algorithms to further improve human-robot interaction.

General Terms

Algorithms

Keywords

Human-robot interaction, POMDPs, explainable AI, trust

1. INTRODUCTION

Robots are increasingly teaming with humans in complex real-world tasks, ranging from search and rescue to space exploration [2, 3]. Although the ever-improving capabilities of robotic systems may lead to improved team capabilities, they also create challenges that need to be overcome before such hybrid partnerships can achieve their full potential [1]. When robots are more suited than humans for a certain task, then we want the humans to trust the robots to perform that task. When the robots are less suited, then we want the humans to appropriately gauge the robots' ability and perform the task themselves. Failure to do so results in *disuse* of robots in the former case and *misuse* in the latter [27]. Real-world case studies and laboratory experiments show that failures in both cases are common [20].

Research has also shown that people are more likely to avoid such failures if they have an accurate understanding of the robot's decision-making process [19]. Unfortunately, as robots gain complexity and autonomy, it is increasingly challenging for humans to understand their decision processes. Successful human-robot interaction (HRI) therefore hinges on the robot's ability to make its decision-making process transparent to the people it works with. Hand-crafted explanations have shown to be effective in providing such transparency [7].

However, such hand-crafted explanations do not scale to the sophisticated reasoning that robots currently perform to handle the uncertainty and conflicting goals within their task environments. Many robotic platforms use Partially Observable Markov Decision Problems (POMDPs) [14], whose quantitative transition probabilities, observation probabilities, reward functions, and decision-making algorithms have proven successful in many robotic domains, such as navigation [4, 18] and HRI [28]. Unfortunately, the quantitative nature of these models and the complexity of their solution algorithms also make POMDP-reasoning opaque to potential human teammates.

In our work, we develop algorithms that can generate natural-language explanations from POMDP-based reasoning. We thus draw inspiration from the aims of prior researchers in "explainable AI" [33, 40], but within the novel context of decision-theoretic reasoning with uncertain beliefs. We build our algorithms on top of a multiagent social simulation framework, PsychSim [21, 29], that includes transparency of the various components of a POMDP model (e.g., beliefs, observations, outcome likelihoods). By grounding explanations in the agent's decision-making process, we can automatically generate a space of possible explanation content and measure their impact on the human-robot interaction (Section 4).

To quantify the effectiveness of different explanation content in achieving the desired transparency, we implemented an experimental testbed to simulate an HRI scenario (Section 5). This virtual human-robot simulation teams a robot with a human counterpart in reconnaissance missions [38]. The robot is modeled as a POMDP, with beliefs and observations of its surroundings, goals (e.g., mission objectives), and actions to achieve those goals. We conducted a study

Appears in: *Proceedings of the 15th International Conference on Autonomous Agents and Multiagent Systems (AAMAS 2016), J. Thangarajah, K. Tuyls, C. Jonker, S. Marsella (eds.), May 9–13, 2016, Singapore.*

where people interacted with different versions of the robot, where we varied its ability and its explanation content. The empirical results quantify the degree to which the explanations impacted transparency, human-robot trust, and overall team performance (Section 6). By examining people's behaviors over different combinations of the robot's ability and explanation content, we discuss the implications of the results and directions for future work (Section 7).

2. RELATED WORK

Our current work follows a long history of similar explorations of automated explanation mechanisms, especially within the context of expert systems [33]. While most of this work operated on rule- and logic-based systems, there has been more recent work on generating explanations based on Markov Decision Problems (MDPs) [8, 15]. However, there has been no work on explaining POMDP-based policies, where the system operates under uncertainty about the state of the world. Furthermore, there has been little empirical evaluation of the impact of these explanations on human-machine trust, although the existing data suggest that explanations do increase user acceptance of expert systems [40]. This limited evidence is encouraging as to the potential success of applying a general-purpose explanation on top of a robot's decision-making process.

The need for such explanations is evidenced by existing HRI studies that have shown that a human's ability to understand its robot teammate has a clear impact on trust [19]. Explanations have shown to contribute to that understanding in a way that provides transparency and improves trust [7]. Our goal is to create an automated, domain-independent method for generating explanations that has the same impact as the manually crafted explanations used in prior work.

Looking beyond the AI and HRI literature, we can find a large number of studies that measure the impact of various forms of explanation on people's perceptions of risks and uncertainties when making decisions. A survey of these studies across multiple domains indicates that "People prefer numerical information for its accuracy but use a verbal statement to express a probability to others." [36]. This finding led to a recommendation to include a numeric representation in any communication informing a person of the uncertainties underlying a decision. On the other hand, one of the studies in the survey contrasted a numeric representation of uncertainty with more anecdotal evidence and found that the numeric information carried less weight when both types were present [12]. A study of risk communication in medical trade-off decisions showed that people performed better when receiving numeric expressions of uncertainty in percentage (67%) rather than frequency (2 out of 3) form [39]. This same study also found that people expressed a preference for information "as words" rather than "as numbers". It is therefore clear that both percentage and verbal expressions of uncertainty have value in conveying uncertainty, but it is less clear what form makes the most sense in an HRI context. In translating our robot's reasoning into a human-understandable format, our explanation algorithms use natural-language templates inspired by these various findings in the literature.

3. POMDP MODEL OF AN HRI SCENARIO

We have implemented the explanation algorithms using PsychSim [21, 29], which combines two established agent technologies: decision-theoretic planning [14] and recursive modeling [9]. Decision-theoretic planning provides an agent with quantitative utility calculations that allow it to assess tradeoffs between alternative decisions under uncertainty. Recursive modeling gives the agent a theory of mind, allowing it to form beliefs about the human users' preferences, factor those preferences into its own decisions, and update its beliefs in response to observations of the users' decisions. The combination of decision theory and theory of mind has enabled PsychSim agents to operate in a variety of human-agent interaction scenarios [13, 16, 17, 23, 26].

PsychSim agents generate their beliefs and behaviors by solving POMDPs [6, 14]. In precise terms, a POMDP [14] is a tuple, $\langle S, A, P, \Omega, O, R\rangle$, that we describe here in terms of an illustrative HRI scenario [37]. In it, a human teammate works with a robot in reconnaissance missions to gather intelligence in a foreign town. Each mission involves the human teammate searching eight buildings in the town. The robot serves as a scout, scans the buildings for potential danger, and relays its findings to the teammate. Prior to entering a building, the human teammate can choose between entering with or without equipping protective gear. If there is danger present inside the building, the human teammate will be fatally injured without the protective gear. As a result, the team will have to restart from the beginning and re-search the entire town. However, it takes time to put on and take off protective gear (e.g., 30 seconds each). So the human teammate is incentivized to consider the robot's findings before deciding how to enter the building. In the current implementation, the human and the robot move together as one unit through the town, with the robot scanning the building first and the human conducting a detailed search afterward. The robot has a NBC (nuclear, biological and chemical) weapon sensor, a camera that can detect armed gunman, and a microphone that can listen to discussions in foreign language.

Within the POMDP model of this scenario, the state, S, consists of objective facts about the world, some of which may be hidden from the robot itself, such as the separate locations of the robot and its human teammate, as well as the presence of dangerous people or chemicals in the buildings to be searched. The state also includes feature-value pairs that represent the human teammate's health level, any current commands from the teammate, and the accumulated time cost so far.

The robot's available actions, A, correspond to the possible decisions it can make. Given its search mission, the robot's first decision is where to move to next. We divide the environment into a set of discrete waypoints, so the robot's action set includes potentially moving to any of them. Upon arrival, the robot then makes a decision as to whether to declare a location as safe or unsafe for its human teammate. For example, if the robot believes that armed gunmen are at its current location, then it will want its teammate to take adequate preparations (e.g., put on body armor) before entering. Because there is a time cost to such preparations, the robot may instead decide to declare the location safe, so that its teammates can more quickly complete their own reconnaissance tasks.

We model the dynamics of the world using a transition probability function, P, that captures the possibly uncertain effects of the robot's actions on the subsequent state.

We simplify the robot's navigation task by assuming that a decision to move to a specific waypoint succeeds deterministically. However, we could relax this assumption to decrease the robot's movement ability, as is done in more realistic robot navigation models [4, 18]. The robot's recommendation decision affects the health of its teammate, although only stochastically, as its teammate may not follow its recommendation. Instead, a recommendation that a building is safe (unsafe) has a high (low) probability of decreasing the teammate's health if there are, in fact, chemicals present.

The robot has only indirect information about the true state of the world. Within the POMDP model, this information comes through a subset of possible observations, Ω, that are probabilistically dependent (through the observation function, O) on the true values of the corresponding state features. We make some simplifying assumptions, namely that the robot can observe the location of itself and its teammate with no error (e.g., via GPS). However, it cannot detect the presence of armed gunmen or dangerous chemicals with perfect reliability or omniscience. Instead, it receives a local reading about their presence (or absence) at its current location. For example, if dangerous chemicals are present, then the robot's chemical sensor will detect them with a high probability. There is also a lower, but nonzero, probability that the sensor will not detect them. In addition to such a false negative, we can also model a potential false positive reading, where there is a low, but nonzero, probability that it will detect chemicals even if there are none present. By controlling the observations that the robot receives, we can manipulate its ability in our testbed.

Partial observability gives the robot only a subjective view of the world, where it forms beliefs about what it thinks is the state of the world, computed via standard POMDP state estimation algorithms. For example, the robot's beliefs include its subjective view on the presence of threats, in the form of a likelihood (e.g., a 33% chance that there are toxic chemicals in the farm supply store). Again, the robot derives these beliefs from its local sensor readings, so they may diverge from the true state of the world. By decreasing the accuracy of the robot's observation function, O, we can decrease the accuracy of its beliefs, whether receiving correct or incorrect observations. In other words, we can also manipulate the robot's ability by allowing it to over- or under-estimate the accuracy of its sensors.

We instantiate the human-robot team's mission objectives within the POMDP's reward function, R, which maps the state of the world into a real-valued evaluation of benefit for the agent. The highest reward is earned in states where all buildings have been explored by the human teammate. This reward component incentivizes the robot to pursue the overall mission objective. There is also an increasingly positive reward associated with level of the human teammate's health. This reward component punishes the robot if it fails to warn its teammate of dangerous buildings. Finally, there is a negative reward that increases with the time cost of the current state. This motivates the robot to complete the mission as quickly as possible. By providing different weights to these goals, we can change the priorities that the robot assigns to them. For example, by lowering the weight of the teammate's health reward, the robot may allow its teammate to search waypoints that are potentially dangerous, in the hope of searching all the buildings sooner. Alternatively, lowering the weight on the time cost reward might motivate the robot to wait until being almost certain of a building's threat level (e.g., by repeated observations) before recommending that its teammate visit anywhere. By varying the relative weights of these different motivations, we can manipulate the benevolence of the robot toward its teammate in our testbed.

The robot can autonomously generate its behavior based on its POMDP model of the world by determining the optimal action based on its current beliefs, b, about the state of the world [14]. Rather than perform an offline computation of a complete optimal policy, π, over all possible beliefs, we instead take an online approach so that the robot computes the optimal decision with respect to only its current beliefs, $\pi(b)$ [31]. The robot uses a bounded lookahead procedure that seeks to maximize expected reward by simulating the dynamics of the world from its current belief state. In particular, the robot will consider declaring a building dangerous or safe (i.e., recommending that its teammate put protective gear on or not). It will combine its beliefs about the likelihood of possible threats in the building with each possible declaration to compute the likelihood of the outcome, in terms of the impact on the teammate's health and the time to search the building. It will finally combine these outcome likelihoods with its reward function and choose the option that has the highest reward.

4. POMDP-GENERATED EXPLANATIONS

By exposing different components of the robot's POMDP model, we can make different aspects of its decision-making transparent to its human teammate. We create natural-language templates to translate the contents of a POMDP model into human-readable sentences:

- A: The robot can make a decision as to whether to declare the building safe or not and communicate its chosen action, e.g., "I think the doctor's office is safe." The string representation of each action, $a \in A$, is a domain-specific string. Upon making its decision, the robot chooses the string corresponding to its current choice, $\pi(b)$.
- S: The robot can also communicate the level of uncertainty underlying its beliefs, e.g., "I am 67% confident about this assessment," if it believed that the probability of the doctor's office being safe was 67%. We use a template that includes a variable indicating which element(s) of the factored state representation the robot should substitute for the probability reference. In this case, the only variable of interest is the robot's $b(\text{safe}_X = \text{True}, \text{my location} = X)$. When generating such an explanation, the robot will compute the indicated belief and insert it into the natural-language template.
- P: The robot can also reveal the relative likelihood of possible outcomes, e.g., "There is a 33% probability that you will be injured if you enter the doctor's office without protective gear." Here, the robot will weigh the possible outcomes by its belief in the hidden state. In particular, it can compute $\sum_s b(s) \Pr(\text{health} \downarrow | s, \text{no protection})$ to instantiate this template.
- Ω: Communicating its observation can reveal information about its sensing abilities, e.g., "My NBC sensors have detected traces of dangerous chemicals." We write domain-specific strings for each possible observation, $\omega \in \Omega$.

- O: Beyond the specific observation it received, the robot can also reveal information about how it models its own sensor capabilities, e.g., "My image processing will fail to detect armed gunmen 30% of the time." In this case, we combine the domain-specific templates for each possible observation, $\omega \in \Omega$, with the appropriate observation function value:

$$\frac{\sum_{\omega \neq \text{gunmen}} \sum_{s|\text{gunmen}_x,\text{my location}=x} \sum_a O(s,a,\omega)}{\sum_{\omega} \sum_{s|\text{gunmen}_x,\text{my location}=x} \sum_a O(s,a,\omega)}$$

.

- R: By communicating the expected reward outcome of its chosen action, the robot can reveal its benevolence (or lack thereof) toward its teammate, e.g., "I think it will be dangerous for you to enter the informant's house without putting on protective gear. The protective gear will slow you down a little." The template here relies on factored rewards, allowing the robot to compute separate expected rewards, $E[R]$, over the goals of keeping its teammate alive and achieving the mission as quickly as possible. We write domain-specific templates for each goal, for both the positive and negative cases. The robot then computes the separate $E[R]$ values and chooses the appropriate template depending on whether the value is positive or negative.

These templates provide a variabilized mechanism for specifying natural-language forms offline that can be instantiated by the robot at runtime based on its current beliefs. These various template formats can be used for any POMDP. We thus ensure that the results can be re-used by other researchers studying other HRI domains as well.

5. EVALUATION

5.1 Simulation Testbed for HRI

We implemented an online version of our HRI scenario to study the impact of these automatically generated explanations on trust and team performance. The testbed can be accessed from a web browser. The testbed's server executes the POMDP to both maintain the state of the simulated mission and to generate decisions for the robot. These are displayed on the participant's web browser, which sends decisions made by the participant back to the testbed's server.

5.2 Participants

We recruited 220 participants from Amazon Mechanical Turk (AMT). The participants had previously completed 500 or more jobs on AMT and had a completion rate of 95% or higher. All participants were located in the USA.

5.3 Design

We used the online testbed to evaluate how the different POMDP-generated explanations from Section 4 impact trust and team performance. We conducted two iterations of the study. For the sake of clarity, we will describe the methodology of the two iterations together. The first iteration of the study primarily focused on whether explanations can build transparency, establish a proper level of trust, and improve task performance. There were two independent variables for the first iteration of the study: *ability* and *explanation*. The *ability* variable had two levels: low and high. The *explanation* variable also has two levels: no explanation, and explanation of two sensor readings. After preliminary analysis of the first iteration of the study (details in Section 6.1), we extended the *explanation* variable to include two additional types of explanations: explanation of three sensor readings, confidence-level explanations. The two iterations of the study all combine to form a 2x4 design.

As already mentioned, the *ability* variable has two levels: a low-ability robot vs. a high-ability robot. Regardless of the ability of the robot, the human teammates will learn the correctness of the robot's individual decisions upon entering the buildings themselves.

- **High Ability** The robot with high ability makes the correct decision 100% of the time.
- **Low Ability** The robot with low ability has a faulty camera and makes only false-negative mistakes, e.g., not detecting armed gunmen in the simulation. The other simulated sensors (e.g., NBC weapon detector and microphone) and the robot's decision-making capability remain intact. As a result, the low-ability robot will occasionally give an incorrect "safe" assessment.

The *explanation* variable has a total of four levels: no explanation, explanation of two sensor readings, explanation of three sensor readings, and confidence-level explanation. At all four levels, the robot informs its teammate of its decision, derived from the A template from Section 4 (e.g., "I have finished surveying the doctor's office. I think the place is safe."). Under the conditions where explanations are offered, the robot augments this decision with additional information that should help its teammate better understand its ability (e.g., decision-making and sensing), one of the key dimensions of trust [22].

- **NoExp** In the No Explanation condition, the robot only informs its teammate of its decisions. One such communication from our scenario would be: *"I have finished surveying the Cafe. I think the place is safe."*
- **Exp2Sensor** In the Explanations of Two Sensor Observations condition, these explanations augments the decision message with non-numeric information about the robot's sensing capability. In this case, the sensing capability is limited to the NBC sensor and the camera – the only two sensors used by the PsychSim agents. Section 4's Ω template thus provides the teammate with the robot's observations from these two sensors. One such communication with both decision and explanation from our scenario would be: *"I have finished surveying the Cafe. I think the place is dangerous. My sensors have detected traces of dangerous chemicals. From the image captured by my camera, I have not detected any armed gunmen in the Cafe. I think it will be dangerous for you to enter the Cafe without protective gear. The protective gear will slow you down a little."* Although these explanations can potentially actually help the robot's teammate understand which sensors are working correctly (e.g., the NBC sensor) and which ones are not (e.g., the faulty camera), they do not actually help the teammate decide what to do with sensor readings from the Camera. This is because the robot, particularly the one in the Low Ability condition, has a faulty camera that makes false-negative mistakes. This means that when the robot reports no danger found by the camera, the teammate still doesn't know if they should put on the protective gear or not.

Figure 1: Human Robot Interaction Simulation Testbed with HTML front-end.

- **Exp3Sensor** In the Explanations of Three Sensor Observations, the explanations again augments the decision message with non-numeric information about the robot's sensing capability – the NBC sensor, the camera and the microphone. Section 4's Ω explanation provides the teammate with the robot's observations from these two sensors. One such communication with both decision and explanation from our scenario would be: *"I have finished surveying the Cafe. I think the place is safe. My sensors have not detected any NBC weapons in here. From the image captured by my camera, I have not detected any armed gunmen in the cafe. My microphone picked up a friendly conversation."* These explanations will thus potentially help the robot's teammate understand which sensors are working correctly and which ones are not, and help them decide what to do in case of camera failure. For example, while a faulty camera may not be able to detect armed gunman, the microphone is capable of picking up a suspicious conversation.

- **ExpConf** In the Confidence-Level Explanations condition, the confidence-level explanations augment the decision message with additional information about the robot's uncertainty in its decision. Section 4's S template incorporates the robot's probabilistic assessment of the hidden state of the world (e.g., the presence of threats) on which it bases its recommendation.[1] One example of a confidence-level explanation would be: *"I have finished surveying the Cafe. I think the place is dangerous. I am 78% confident about this assessment."* Because the low-ability robot's one faulty sensor will lead to occasional conflicting observations, it will on those occasions have lower confidence in its erroneous decisions after incorporating that conflicting information into its beliefs.

The study is a between-subject design. Each participant interacted with one of the eight simulated robots. In the first iteration of the study, we assigned 30 participants to each condition. In the second iteration of the study, we assigned 25 participants to each condition.

5.4 Procedure

Each participant first read an information sheet about the study and then filled out the background survey. Next, participants worked with a simulated robot on three reconnaissance missions. After each mission, participants filled out a post-mission survey. Each participant worked with a robot with the same ability and communication (e.g., low ability and communicates with confidence-level explanations) throughout the three missions. Participants were randomly assigned to team up with one of the eight robots. The study was designed to be completed in 90 minutes. Participants were compensated with $10 for their participation.

5.5 Measure

The Background Survey includes measures of the demographic information, education, video game experience, military background, predisposition to trust [24], propensity to trust [25], complacency potential [30], negative attitude to-

[1] Probability and confidence are generally different concepts. We used the probability as an approximation of the robot's confidence level.

wards robots [34] and uncertainty response scale [10]. In the Post-Mission Survey, we have designed items to measure participants' understanding of the robot's decisions and decision-making process. A sample item from this measure is "I understand the robot's decision-making process". We modified items on interpersonal trust to measure trust in the robot's ability, benevolence and integrity [22]. We also included the NASA Cognitive Load Index [11], Situation Awareness Rating Scale [35], trust in oneself and teammate [30], and trust in robots [32]. The Post-Mission survey was filled out after each mission (3 missions total in the study). We have also collected interaction logs from the online testbed. Based on the log data, we compute measures of team performance: mission success, percentage of correct decisions, and compliance (e.g., percentage of the robot's decision adopted by its teammate). The Post-Mission survey data and the log data provide coarse measures of how trust changes over time, which is beyond the scope of this paper. In this paper, the analysis includes measures on team performance, and trust in the robot's ability [22] and the scale we designed on the understanding of the robot's decision-making process presented in the Post-Mission Survey.

6. RESULTS

We excluded data from 18 participants due to incomplete entries (e.g., participants skipped survey questions or left the simulations). Although not part of the experiment manipulation, a closer examination revealed that the incomplete entries only occurred in conditions where explanations were offered. As a result, 202 participants are included in the analysis. The participants average 33.4 years old. 42% of the participants are female and 58% participants are male. 5 participants answered that they had worked with an automated squad member (such as a robot) before. 3 participants had reconnaissance or search and rescue training, and 1 was actually involved in such missions. Only 1 participant was an active service member.

We measured participants' predisposition to trust, propensity to trust, complacency potential, negative attitude towards robots and uncertainty responses. We did not find any significant main or interaction effect of the independent variables on any of these scales. Studying the impact of individual differences on trust is not the focus of this paper. Instead, we will focus on comparing the impact of different explanation algorithms on trust [22] and team performance. In the analysis presented here, we focus on self-reported perceptions of the robot's ability and behavioral measures of task performance (e.g., mission success rates, correct decisions percentage). Self-reported measures are calculated by averaging survey responses gathered after each mission (3 missions total). Behavioral measures are based on log data from all 3 missions as well.

The four dependent variable included in the analysis are:

- **Trust in Robot's Ability** Trust in the robot's ability, benevolence and integrity is measured by modifying an existing scale [22] that measures these three factors of trustworthiness. Each factor of trust is calculated by averaging corresponding Post-Mission Survey items collected after each of the 3 missions. The explanations compared in this paper are designed to influence perceptions of the ability factor of trust, and do not explicitly target the benevolence and integrity factors of trust. So we focus on only the ability component of trust in this paper. The value ranges from 1 to 7.
- **Understand Robot's Decisions** This is measured using 1âĂŞ7 Likert scale items on the understanding of the robot's decision-making process, designed by the researcher. A sample item from this measure is "I understand the robot's decision-making process". The measure is calculated by averaging responses to corresponding survey items in the Post-Mission Survey after each of the 3 missions. The value range from 1 to 7.
- **Mission Success Percentage** This team-performance measure is extracted from a line in the interaction log indicating whether the mission ended in success/failure, then divided by the total number of missions (3) in the study. The value ranges from 0 to 100.
- **Percentage of Correct Decisions** This variable is measured using log data. It is calculated by dividing the total number of the participant's correct decisions (e.g., putting on protective gear when there is danger, and forgo the protective gear when it is safe) by the total number of participant's decisions, across three missions. The value ranges from 0 to 100.
- **Percentage of Decisions that Follow Robot Recommendations** This variable is measured using log data. It is calculated by dividing the total number of the participant's decisions that are the same as the robot's recommended, by the total number of participant's decisions, across three missions. The value ranges from 0 to 100.

6.1 First Iteration of Study

Preliminary analysis of data collected from the first iteration of the study using ANOVA tests revealed no significant impact of the explanation of two sensor readings on any of the four measures, except for understanding of the robot's decisions, compared to when no explanations were offered, regardless of the robot's ability. Closer examination of the scenario design and explanation of two sensor readings suggests that this could be due to the "usefulness" or "helpfulness" of the explanations. The robot, particularly the low-ability robot, makes only false-negative mistakes due to its faulty camera. This means that even when the participants know the robot's decision may not be correct because of the camera failure, they still do not know what the correct decision to make is, e.g., whether to put protective gear on or not. The sensible yet conservative decision would be putting on protective gear all the time. Thus, we added two additional explanation levels— explanation of three sensor readings and confidence-level explanations— that aimed to help participants diagnose faulty sensors and make decisions on whether to put on protective gear. In these two explanations, we also removed the recommendation to put on protective gear, because it is redundant (e.g., the robot's finding of danger implicitly suggests that one should put protective gear on) and removing it reduces the length of text.

6.2 Main Effect of Ability and Explanations

The subsequent analyses include data from both iterations of the study. Overall, ANOVA tests indicate that participants who worked with a high-ability robot reported trusting the robot more, made better decisions and succeeded in more

Table 1: Comparing the main effect of the robot's ability. Means are shown in the table. Differences on all variables between High and Low ability robot are statistically significant ($p < .05$)

	High Ability	Low Ability
Trust in Robot's Ability	6.46	5.05
Understand Robot's Recommendations	5.98	4.70
Mission Success %	82.8	67.6
% of Correct Decisions	92.6	80.0

missions (Table 1). Surprisingly, participants also felt that they understood the robot's decision and decision-making process more, when the robot's ability is high.

As for the main effect of the explanations offered by the robot, Table 2 shows that not all explanations are created equal (Tukey HSD tests on all possible pairwise contrasts). Overall, explanations that facilitate decision-making (e.g., confidence-level explanations, and explanations of 3 sensors) helped the participants succeed in more missions and made the participants feel that they can trust the robot's ability more. Surprisingly, we did not find any significant impact of explanations on the percentage of correct decisions.

There is a significant interaction between the robot's ability and the explanation offered on trust in the robot's ability ($p < .0001$), and understanding of the robot's decisions and decision-making process ($p < .0001$), mission success rate ($p = .0008$), and percentage of correct decisions ($p < .0001$). We will break down the comparison of the impact of robot's explanation between high and low ability robot in the following sections.

6.3 Explanation and Low-Ability Robot

When the low-ability robot makes a decision (e.g., recommendation) that has unwanted consequences, it not only affects the team performance but also jeopardizes the trust its teammate has in it. When no explanations were offered, its human teammate had no additional information to help him/her understand why the robot's recommendation failed. The goal of the explanations is not to help human teammates trust the low-reliability robot more, but to instead calibrate their trust level appropriately and know when and when not to trust it. As a result, the teammate's decision-making and the team performance can be improved. Results from ANOVA and Tukey's HSD tests (on all possible pairwise contrasts) are presented in Table 3. From the table, we can see that the decision-facilitating explanations (e.g., explanations of three sensor and confidence-level explanations), help the teammate understand the low-ability robot's decision and decision-making process, make better decisions, and succeed in more missions, compared to when no explanations were offered or when the explanation is not helpful towards decision making (e.g., explanations of two sensors). The human teammates also trusted the low-ability robot more when it offered the decision-facilitating explanations.

6.4 Explanations and High-Ability Robot

It may seem counter-intuitive that one would not trust a perfectly reliable robot that makes correct decisions 100% of the time. However, disuse is a realistic and common problem in human-automation interaction [27] and often linked to lack of transparency [5]. So we hypothesize that explanations, even offered by a reliable robot, can help improve the trust relationship and team performance. ANOVA and Tukey's HSD tests revealed that there was no statistically significant impact of the robot's explanations on trust in the robot's ability, understanding of the robot's decision and decision-making process, correct decisions made and mission success rate, when the robot is making correct recommendations 100% of the time.

7. DISCUSSION

In this paper, we discussed the design of POMDP-based algorithms for explaining a robot's decision making to a human teammate. We implemented an online experiment platform that we used to conduct an evaluation of the explanation algorithms, where participants teamed up with a simulated robot with either high or low ability, and offered three different types of explanations or no explanations with its decisions. Results indicate that the robot explanations can potentially improve task performance, build transparency and foster trust relationship. However, only explanations that are designed to facilitate decision-making made much difference. Explanations that left participants ambiguous about how to act on the recommendation and explanations did not achieve such an effect, and were as badly regarded as when no explanations were offered at all. This is particularly true so when the robot's ability is low and makes unreliable recommendations.

Additionally, the decision-facilitation explanation helped improve understanding of the robot's decision, but only in the low-ability robot and not the high-ability one. This could be due to the fact that the high-ability robot is making correct decisions 100% of the time. Participants who interacted with this robot never needed to question the robot's decision. Thus, these participants may have never carefully examined the robot's statement that explained its confidence level or observations. Working with a low-ability robot, on the other hand, requires the teammates to pay close attention to the explanations to gauge when and when not to trust the robot's decisions.

Earlier studies on the impact of hand-crafted explanations on trust [7] show that explanations, even those were provided before the interaction and used in ways similar to "excuses", can draw someone into the pitfall of trusting the robot more, even though the robot is unreliable. The result presented here, particularly the finding on decision-facilitating explanation offered by the low-ability robot and subjective trust, sheds some light on the hidden factors between explanations and trust— the "helpfulness" or "usefulness" of the explanation. Our results show that explanations made participants trust the robot's ability more, but only when the explanations facilitated decision-making and not when the explanations left participants unsure about what decisions to make. Participants distrusted a robot that offered such explanations as much as one that did not offer explanations at all.

Interestingly, we did not find any significant differences on the measures we analyzed between the two decision-facilitating explanations e.g., confidence-level explanations and explanations of three sensors. Both types of explanations are useful in helping the human teammate decide when to trust the robot. For example, a teammate could potentially learn

Table 2: Compare the main effect of explanations offered by the robot. Means are shown in the table. A pair of ∗ or † or ♣ or ♠ means the difference between the two variables are statistically significant ($p < .05$).

	NoExp	Exp2Sensor	Exp3Sensor	ExpConf
Trust in Robot's Ability	$5.37^{*\dagger}$	$5.44^{\clubsuit\spadesuit}$	$6.27^{*\clubsuit}$	$6.17^{\dagger\spadesuit}$
Understand Robot's Recommendation	$4.75^{*\dagger}$	5.36	5.93^{*}	$5.51^{\dagger}$
Mission Success %	$65.0^{*\dagger}$	$58.9^{\clubsuit\spadesuit}$	$92.3^{*\clubsuit}$	$96.0^{\dagger\spadesuit}$
% of Correct Decisions	82.8	84.1	89.6	90.0
% of Decisions Follow Robot's Recommendation	83.9	85.6	86.6	86.0

Table 3: Compare the main effect of explanations offered by the *Low Ability* robot. Means are shown in the table. A pair of ∗ or † or ♣ or ♠ means the difference between the two variables are statistically significant ($p < .05$).

	NoExp	Exp2Sensor	Exp3Sensor	ExpConf
Trust in Robot's Ability	$4.31^{*\dagger}$	$4.28^{\clubsuit\spadesuit}$	$6.07^{*\clubsuit}$	$6.15^{\dagger\spadesuit}$
Understand Robot's Recommendation	$3.66^{*\dagger}$	$4.46^{\clubsuit\spadesuit}$	$5.71^{*\clubsuit}$	$5.51^{\dagger\spadesuit}$
Mission Success %	$52.2^{*\dagger}$	$43.0^{\clubsuit\spadesuit}$	$93.7^{*\clubsuit}$	$97.0^{\dagger\spadesuit}$
% of Correct Decisions	$71.9^{*\dagger}$	$74.0^{\clubsuit\spadesuit}$	$87.0^{*\clubsuit}$	$91.9^{\dagger\spadesuit}$
% of Decisions Follow Robot's Recommendation	74.2	77.0	81.5	84.6

his/her own heuristics that if the robot's confidence level is below (for example) 75%, then do not follow the robot's decision. Similarly, a teammate could diagnose from the observation explanations that if the camera reports no signs of danger, but the robot's microphone picks up unfriendly conversations, then it is time to be cautious and put protective gear on, regardless of the robot's overall assessment of safety. It is concerning that participants who received confidence-level explanations also felt that they understood the robot's decision-making process, even though such explanations did not reveal any of the robot's inner workings. While confidence-level explanations may help teammates make decisions just as well as with observation explanations, they will not help teammates diagnose or repair the robot (e.g., the participants will not know that it is the camera that caused the robot to make wrong decisions).

One of the limitations of the current work is that the understanding of the robot's decisions is measured via self-report. In other words, it is unclear whether the participants actually understood the decisions, as they claimed. Future work can include measures to test participants' knowledge of the robot, e.g., its capability, or allow it to be inferred more directly and specifically from the subsequent decisions that participants made, e.g., ask participants to choose MOPP gear vs. body armor. Another limitation of the current work is that the measures are aggregated from participants' responses after each of the 3 missions. More fine-grained analysis of data collected from each mission can be conducted to study how trust evolves over time. These future analyses can lead to further refinements of our explanation algorithms that can increase the positive impact already exhibited by the current implementation on human-robot trust.

Acknowledgment

This project is funded by the U.S. Army Research Laboratory. Statements and opinions expressed do not necessarily reflect the position or the policy of the United States Government, and no official endorsement should be inferred.

REFERENCES

[1] B. Adams, L. Bruyn, S. Houde, and P. Angelopoulos. Trust in automated systems: literature review. Technical Report DRDC-TORONTO-CR-2003-096, Defence Research Reports, 2003.

[2] W. Bluethmann, R. Ambrose, M. Diftler, S. Askew, E. Huber, M. Goza, F. Rehnmark, C. Lovchik, and D. Magruder. Robonaut: A robot designed to work with humans in space. *Autonomous Robots*, 14(2-3):179–197, 2003.

[3] J. L. Burke, R. R. Murphy, M. D. Coovert, and D. L. Riddle. Moonlight in Miami: Field study of human-robot interaction in the context of an urban search and rescue disaster response training exercise. *Human-Computer Interaction*, 19(1-2):85–116, 2004.

[4] A. R. Cassandra, L. P. Kaelbling, and J. A. Kurien. Acting under uncertainty: Discrete Bayesian models for mobile-robot navigation. In *IROS*, volume 2, pages 963–972, 1996.

[5] H. Cramer, V. Evers, S. Ramlal, M. Van Someren, L. Rutledge, N. Stash, L. Aroyo, and B. Wielinga. The effects of transparency on trust in and acceptance of a content-based art recommender. *User Modeling and User-Adapted Interaction*, 18(5):455–496, 2008.

[6] P. Doshi and D. Perez. Generalized point based value iteration for interactive pomdps. In *AAAI*, pages 63–68, 2008.

[7] M. T. Dzindolet, S. A. Peterson, R. A. Pomranky, L. G. Pierce, and H. P. Beck. The role of trust in automation reliance. *International Journal of Human-Computer Studies*, 58(6):697–718, 2003.

[8] F. Elizalde, L. E. Sucar, M. Luque, J. Diez, and A. Reyes. Policy explanation in factored markov decision processes. In *Proceedings of the European WS on Probabilistic Graphical Models*, pages 97–104, 2008.

[9] P. J. Gmytrasiewicz and E. H. Durfee. A rigorous, operational formalization of recursive modeling. In *ICMAS*, pages 125–132, 1995.

[10] V. Greco and D. Roger. Coping with uncertainty: The construction and validation of a new measure. *Personality and individual differences*, 31(4):519–534, 2001.

[11] S. G. Hart and L. E. Staveland. Development of NASA-TLX (task load index): Results of empirical and theoretical research. *Advances in Psychology*, 52:139–183, 1988.

[12] L. Hendrickx, C. Vlek, and H. Oppewal. Relative importance of scenario information and frequency information in the judgment of risk. *Acta Psychologica*, 72(1):41–63, 1989.

[13] W. L. Johnson and A. Valente. Tactical language and culture training systems: Using AI to teach foreign languages and cultures. *AI Magazine*, 30(2), 2009.

[14] L. P. Kaelbling, M. L. Littman, and A. R. Cassandra. Planning and acting in partially observable stochastic domains. *Artificial Intelligence*, 101:99–134, 1998.

[15] O. Z. Khan, P. Poupart, and J. P. Black. Minimal sufficient explanations for factored Markov Decision Processes. In *ICAPS*. Citeseer, 2009.

[16] J. M. Kim, J. Randall W. Hill, P. J. Durlach, H. C. Lane, E. Forbell, M. Core, S. Marsella, D. Pynadath, and J. Hart. BiLAT: A game-based environment for practicing negotiation in a cultural context. *IJAIED: Special Issue on Ill-Defined Domains*, 19(3):289–308, 2009.

[17] J. Klatt, S. Marsella, and N. Krämer. Negotiations in the context of AIDS prevention: An agent-based model using theory of mind. In *IVA*, 2011.

[18] S. Koenig and R. Simmons. Xavier: A robot navigation architecture based on partially observable Markov decision process models. In D. Kortenkamp, R. P. Bonasso, and R. R. Murphy, editors, *AI Based Mobile Robotics: Case Studies of Successful Robot Systems*, pages 91–122. MIT Press, 1998.

[19] J. Lee and N. Moray. Trust, control strategies and allocation of function in human-machine systems. *Ergonomics*, 35(10):1243–1270, 1992.

[20] J. D. Lee and K. A. See. Trust in automation: Designing for appropriate reliance. *Human Factors*, 46(1):50–80, 2004.

[21] S. C. Marsella, D. V. Pynadath, and S. J. Read. PsychSim: Agent-based modeling of social interactions and influence. In *ICCM*, pages 243–248, 2004.

[22] R. C. Mayer, J. H. Davis, and F. D. Schoorman. An integrative model of organizational trust. *Academy of Management Review*, 20(3):709–734, 1995.

[23] R. McAlinden, A. Gordon, H. C. Lane, and D. Pynadath. UrbanSim: A game-based simulation for counterinsurgency and stability-focused operations. In *Proceedings of the AIED WS on Intelligent Educational Games*, 2009.

[24] D. H. McKnight, V. Choudhury, and C. Kacmar. Developing and validating trust measures for e-commerce: An integrative typology. *Information Systems Research*, 13(3):334–359, 2002.

[25] S. L. McShane. Propensity to trust scale, 2014. http://highered.mheducation.com/sites/0073381225/student_view0/chapter7/self-assessment_7_4.html.

[26] L. C. Miller, S. Marsella, T. Dey, P. R. Appleby, J. L. Christensen, J. Klatt, and S. J. Read. Socially optimized learning in virtual environments (SOLVE). In *ICIDS*, 2011.

[27] R. Parasuraman and V. Riley. Humans and automation: Use, misuse, disuse, abuse. *Human Factors*, 39(2):230–253, 1997.

[28] J. Pineau, M. Montemerlo, M. Pollack, N. Roy, and S. Thrun. Towards robotic assistants in nursing homes: Challenges and results. *Robotics and Autonomous Systems*, 42(3):271–281, 2003.

[29] D. V. Pynadath and S. C. Marsella. PsychSim: Modeling theory of mind with decision-theoretic agents. In *IJCAI*, pages 1181–1186, 2005.

[30] J. M. Ross. *Moderators of trust and reliance across multiple decision aids*. PhD thesis, University of Central Florida, 2008.

[31] S. Ross, J. Pineau, S. Paquet, and B. Chaib-Draa. Online planning algorithms for POMDPs. *JAIR*, 32:663–704, 2008.

[32] K. E. Schaefer. *The perception and measurement of human-robot trust*. PhD thesis, University of Central Florida Orlando, Florida, 2013.

[33] W. R. Swartout and J. D. Moore. Explanation in second generation expert systems. In *Second generation expert systems*, pages 543–585. Springer, 1993.

[34] D. S. Syrdal, K. Dautenhahn, K. L. Koay, and M. L. Walters. The negative attitudes towards robots scale and reactions to robot behaviour in a live human-robot interaction study. *Adaptive and Emergent Behaviour and Complex Systems*, 2009.

[35] R. Taylor. Situational awareness rating technique (SART): The development of a tool for aircrew systems design. *AGARD, Situational Awareness in Aerospace Operations*, 1990.

[36] V. H. Visschers, R. M. Meertens, W. W. Passchier, and N. N. De Vries. Probability information in risk communication: a review of the research literature. *Risk Analysis*, 29(2):267–287, 2009.

[37] N. Wang and D. V. Pynadath. Building trust in a human-robot team. In *I/ITSEC*, 2015.

[38] N. Wang, D. V. Pynadath, K. Unnikrishnan, S. Shankar, and C. Merchant. Intelligent agents for virtual simulation of human-robot interaction. In *Virtual, Augmented and Mixed Reality*, pages 228–239. Springer, 2015.

[39] E. A. Waters, N. D. Weinstein, G. A. Colditz, and K. Emmons. Formats for improving risk communication in medical tradeoff decisions. *Journal of health communication*, 11(2):167–182, 2006.

[40] L. R. Ye and P. E. Johnson. The impact of explanation facilities on user acceptance of expert systems advice. *MIS Quarterly*, 19(2):157–172, 1995.

Robotic Agents Representing, Reasoning, and Executing Wiping Tasks for Daily Household Chores

Daniel Leidner[1], Wissam Bejjani[1], Alin Albu-Schäffer[1], and Michael Beetz[2]
[1] German Aerospace Center (DLR), Institute of Robotics and Mechatronics, Weßling, Germany
{daniel.leidner, wissam.bejjani, alin.albu-schaeffer}@dlr.de
[2] University of Bremen, Institute for Artificial Intelligence, Bremen, Germany
beetz@cs.uni-bremen.de

ABSTRACT

Universal robotic agents are envisaged to perform a wide range of manipulation tasks in everyday environments. A common action observed in many household chores is wiping, such as the absorption of spilled water with a sponge, skimming breadcrumbs off the dining table, or collecting shards of a broken mug using a broom. To cope with this versatility, the agents have to represent the tasks on a high level of abstraction. In this work, we propose to represent the medium in wiping tasks (e. g. water, breadcrumbs, or shards) as generic particle distribution. This representation enables us to represent wiping tasks as the desired state change of the particles, which allows the agent to reason about the effects of wiping motions in a qualitative manner. Based on this, we develop three prototypical wiping actions for the generic tasks of absorbing, collecting and skimming. The Cartesian wiping motions are resolved to joint motions exploiting the free degree of freedom of the involved tool. Furthermore, the workspace of the robotic manipulators is used to reason about the reachability of wiping motions. We evaluate our methods in simulated scenarios, as well as in a real experiment with the robotic agent Rollin' Justin.

Keywords

AI Reasoning Methods, Task and Effect Representation, Robotic Manipulation Planning, Service Robotics

1. INTRODUCTION

Research in controlling robotic agents has for a long time been dominated by the study of robot actions that are inspired by the seminal blocks world problem that was introduced with the Shakey system [24]. Even today most research efforts that realize activity on autonomous robots do so in demonstrating scenarios that mostly include only very simple fetch-and-place tasks. The fetch-and-place actions considered in those research efforts so far are very simple in nature. They can be considered as actions that have discrete instantaneous effects. For the execution of the task the only constraint to be satisfied is to find collision free paths to reach, pick up, and transfer the object to the destination. Consequently, robotic agents that reason about these actions can abstract away from how actions are executed and model them using relatively simple action models consisting of preconditions and effects [10].

Appears in: *Proceedings of the 15th International Conference on Autonomous Agents and Multiagent Systems (AAMAS 2016), J. Thangarajah, K. Tuyls, C. Jonker, S. Marsella (eds.), May 9–13, 2016, Singapore.*

Figure 1: Illustration of the robotic agent Rollin' Justin skimming the windshield of a car and scrubbing the hood with a sponge.

In contrast, the research roadmaps for autonomous robotic agents [4, 23] envisage robotic agents manufacture products in close physical cooperation with their human co-workers or in the more distant future as helpers that enable old and disabled citizens to live their lives more independently. Such robotic agents would have to be capable of taking over a substantial part of the human daily household chores.

Cakmak et al. [3] collected and classified the manipulation actions that characterize the human household chores based on their semantic similarity and identified that almost half of them are based on wiping of surfaces located in rooms, on furniture, or other objects. Most of these tasks are related to cleaning, such as dusting furniture with a feather duster, sweeping breadcrumbs from the kitchen countertop, or collecting shards of a broken mug with a broom.

Compared to fetch-and-place tasks, wiping tasks demand enormously rich and complex actions. Depending on **how** the wiping is done in terms of force applications and motions the wiping can remove sticky dirt, dry a wet surface, or paint an area. This means that the same action can produce very different effects depending on how it is executed. In order to perform the respective tasks successfully the robotic agent must carefully select the motion and force parameters in a continuous parameter space. Moreover, the successful execution of wiping tasks requires a substantial amount of geometric reasoning as the purpose of wiping might be the collection, the spreading, or the elimination of particles.

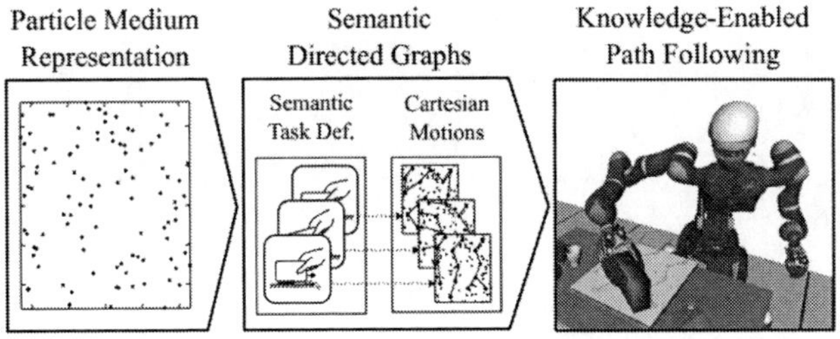

Figure 2: Overview of the proposed framework.

In our earlier work, [20] we proposed to classify wiping tasks based on the set of parameters describing the semantic relation between tools and the environment. In particular, we classify wiping tasks based on the relation between the tool, the surface, and the medium to be manipulated. The tool orientation, and the direction of motion are thereby crucial aspects for the task performance. For example, cleaning the body of a car can be solved by repeatedly moving a sponge in random orientations and directions along the car surface, while skimming snow from a windshield is only successfully if each wiping motion is directed towards the edge of the window, having the tool properly aligned as it is illustrated inf Fig. 1.

In this paper, we investigate the reasoning and action execution problems that enable robotic agents to successfully carry out abstractly specified wiping tasks. We propose to represent wiping tasks on a high level of abstraction and develop generalized action execution mechanisms that are able to ground these high-level task descriptions to low-level robotic control programs. Our method constitutes an effect-oriented reasoning approach to manipulate the medium in wiping tasks, i. e. liquids or particles, in a generalized manner. Our contribution include (i) a qualitative representation of the medium in wiping tasks based on a particle distribution; (ii) an effect-oriented approach to reason about the desired effects of wiping tasks, i. e. the state change of the medium, by means of Semantic Directed Graphs (SDG); (iii) a knowledge-enabled path following approach to resolve Cartesian tool motions into joint motions of the agent; and (iv) an extended approach that integrates reasoning about the reachability of the agent to solve wiping tasks in wider areas by utilizing capability maps. In conclusion, we enable robotic agents to reason about the effect of wiping tasks on a high level of abstraction and enable the agents to execute the matching goal oriented joint motions for the tasks of absorbing, collecting and skimming. The methods are evaluated in three simulated scenarios, where the target surface is defined by (a) a chopping board, (b) the surface of a table, and (c) the windshield of a car. Additionally, we show experiment (a) in a real world setting with the humanoid robot Rollin' Justin successfully collecting breadcrumbs on a chopping board with a sponge.

An overview of the proposed framework is provided in Fig. 2. A particle based medium representation serves as the basis of our reasoning methods (Sec. 3). It is used to describe the desired state change, i. e. the semantic goal states and derive Cartesian tool motions for the prototypical wiping tasks investigated (Sec. 4). This Cartesian motions are resolved to whole-body joint motions (including the mobile base of the agent) by exploiting the free Degrees of Freedom (DOF) of the involved tool (Sec. 5).

2. RELATED WORK

Automated manipulation planning with a universal robotic agent in domestic environments has ever since been a major goal in robotics research, as well as in research on autonomous agents. Recently, this field has regained momentum thanks to affordable and safe light weight robots such as the LBR III [14]. These compliant manipulators enable a robotic agent to get in deliberate soft contact with their environment, which is a key element for many manipulation tasks, including wiping of surfaces.

Especially cleaning related wiping tasks have been investigated in detail lately. Urbanek *et al.* [30] demonstrated how machine learning can be used to teach a robot different movement primitives by demonstration in the context of wiping a table. Do *et al.* [7] solve the inverse problem of predicting appropriate action parameters by learning from experience during wiping tasks. Vanthienen *et al.* [31] describe table wiping tasks as a set of constraints with the *iTaSC* framework. Okada *et al.* [26, 25] apply an inverse-kinematics-based programming approach to compute whole-body motions for the tasks of sweeping the floor, vacuuming the floor, and washing the dishes with a humanoid robot. Lana *et al.* [28] represent robotic manipulation tasks in an algebraic form, which incorporates poses, velocities and forces in a simulated window cleaning task. In robotics, wiping tasks are often investigated from a control theoretic point of view. Ortenzi *et al.* [27] propose to exploit the environment contact constraints of wiping tasks in the operational space, to decouple the motion of the robotic agent from the applied force. Schindlbeck and Haddadin [29] utilize task-energy tanks to react safely upon contact loss.

The task of wiping a surface is often considered as a *coverage path planning* problem [18], where an agent has to find a path (i. e. for a cleaning device) connecting all nodes of a graph in a time- or effort-optimal way. Gabriely and Rimon [9] consider the coverage problem arising for a mobile robot such as a autonomous lawn mower. They propose to subdivide the search space into a grid and apply variations of the *Spanning Tree Covering (STC)* algorithm to cover the area. Hess *et al.* [13] describe an approach to autonomously compute cleaning trajectories for redundant robotic manipulators guiding a sponge on 3d surfaces. They utilize a variation of the *Traveling Salesman Problem (TSP)* and resolve the joint motions of the robotic manipulator by nulls-space optimization in a discretized Jacobian null-space along the Cartesian path (see [15]). While the work of Hess *et al.* [13] is most related to our work, it does not integrate different semantic goals and is therefore only applicable to undirected tasks, such as vacuuming or dusting.

The approaches listed so far mainly focus on the physical part of the problem, while mainly ignoring the semantic meaning of the motion. In contrast, Kunze *et al.* [17] reason about the semantic effect of the tool interacting with the medium based on a simplified process model. The authors simulate the effect of a sponge contacting liquids, namely the absorption of the liquid. In our earlier work [22], we utilized a knowledge-based approach to formulate a window cleaning task on a high level of abstraction. The approach combines the desired semantic effect of the task with a concrete geometric process model, which integrates the parameterization of the low-level control program of the agent. However, the Cartesian tool motions are pre-defined properties of the manipulated objects (e. g. the window pane). Consequently, the agent cannot adapt to new situations in case of unforeseen obstacles. In this work we extend this approach by reasoning autonomously about the appropriate tool motions w. r. t. the desired semantic effect and the environmental state.

3. WIPING EFFECT REPRESENTATION

This work is based on our classification of compliant manipulation tasks [20]. The classification is based on the semantic contact situation between manipulated objects and the environment. Wiping tasks are thereby represented based on the geometric relation of the tool, the surface and the medium to be manipulated. This taxonomy will be used in this work to develop an abstract representation of wiping motions to be executed by a robotic agent. In particular, we will investigate the removal actions *absorbing*, *collecting*, and *skimming* the medium as illustrated in Fig. 3.

The medium in wiping tasks, as defined in [20], is representative for arbitrary liquids or particles with different properties. To reason about wiping motions in a generalized form, a medium representation has to incorporate the properties of arbitrary media. For example, the medium in absorption tasks may be a variation of dust or dirt or a liquid. An example for the medium in skimming tasks is water or detergent on a window, or snow on a windshield. Shards of a broken mug, leaves, or rubble are exemplary for collecting tasks. To incorporate these different types of media, we propose a qualitative model based on a particle distribution estimation on a planar target surface

$$\boldsymbol{P} = \big\{(x_1, y_1), (x_2, y_2), \ldots, (x_N, y_N) \,|\, x_i, y_i \in \mathbb{R} \wedge x_{min} \leq x_i \leq x_{max} \wedge y_{min} \leq y_i \leq y_{max}\big\}, \tag{1}$$

where N particles (x_i, y_i) are estimated within the boundaries of the target surface $(x_{min}, x_{max}, y_{min}, y_{max})$. An example for such a distribution is provided in Fig. 4 which resembles a kitchen scenario with bread crumbs on a chopping board. In most real world scenario, the dirt distribution can be provided by a visual perception system if the particles are big enough to be perceived. However, especially dust and dirt is very hard to perceive and the real distribution on the surface can hardly be modeled. Instead, we assume a unified distribution in this case.

The particle distribution is utilized to simulate the desired semantic *state change* $S_{t_0} \rightarrow S_g$ provided as desired effect in PDDL syntax [10], e. g. *(*`collected` *breadcrumbs chopping_board)*. The respective estimated change of the particle distribution $\boldsymbol{P}_{t_0} \rightarrow \boldsymbol{P}_g$ is visualized in Fig. 4. The contact model considers the exact CAD data of the tool and the position of each particle. Depending on the tool type and the properties of the medium (i. e. liquid or solid particles), the particles react with different effects upon contact. For example, if a sponge is simulated to wipe a liquid, the resulting effect is the absorption of the liquid, which is implemented as a delete operation. In case of solid particles, the contact with the sponge moves the particles in parallel to the direction of motion. We use this behavior for the collect and the skim action. The state change of the particle distribution enable the agent to qualitatively reason about the effect of its motions [8], and subsequently the task performance used to evaluate our methods in Sec. 6.

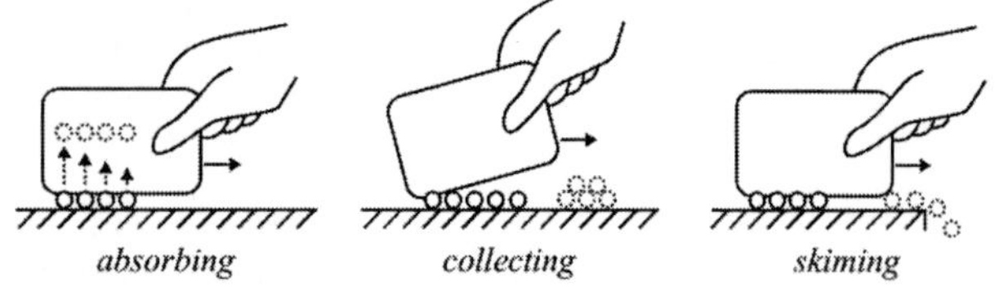

Figure 3: The three prototypical removal actions identified in the classification of wiping tasks. The initial state of the medium is pictured as solid circles, the desired state as dashed circles.

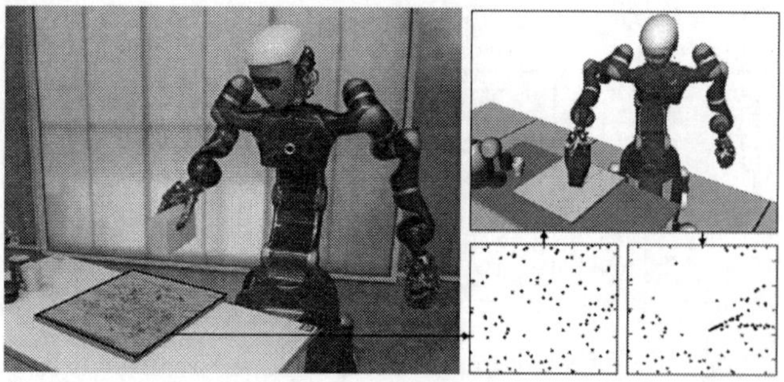

Figure 4: Change estimation of the particle distribution in contact with the sponge during wiping.

4. REASONING WIPING MOTIONS WITH SEMANTIC DIRECTED GRAPHS

Wiping tasks can be considered as a coverage path planning problem. The removal actions to be investigated in this paper have to cover the entire particle distribution and simultaneously satisfy the semantic goal state. To achieve this, we utilize *Semantic Directed Graphs (SDGs)*

$$\boldsymbol{SDG} = f(\boldsymbol{P}, S_g, G_s), \tag{2}$$

which incorporate the coverage problem for the particle distribution $\boldsymbol{P}$, the semantic goal state S_g of the respective action, and the geometric state G_s of the environment. SDGs define a graph structure projected on the planar target surface to be wiped, where

- each node n_i represents a waypoint of the Cartesian tool motion w. r. t. the *Tool Center Point (TCP)*,
- the edge (n_i, n_{i+1}) in between two nodes represents the interpolated tool motion in contact with the surface.

The surface coverage, i. e. the node distribution, is thereby dependent on the current state of the geometric environment G_s, which assembles the volumetric model for geometric planning of wiping motions. Accordingly, a collision avoidance strategy based on a *collision sphere model* is utilized to explore the target surface as visualized in Fig. 5. This sphere is of variable diameter $d_s = ||\boldsymbol{D}_{aoe}||$, where $\boldsymbol{D}_{aoe}$ is the dimension of the area of effect of the tool. We do not consider the full extend of the tool, since this might be much bigger than the actual required space. For example. vacuuming under a bed requires to move the nozzle of the tool to the desired goal region. Although the vacuum cleaner does not fit under the bed, the nozzle is clear to reach the dust.

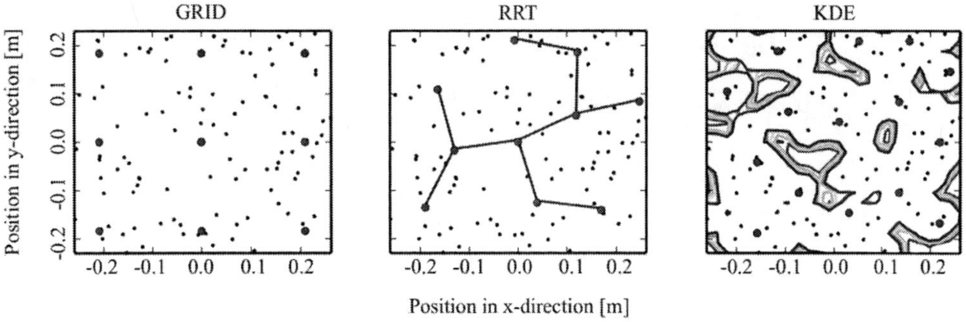

Figure 6: The coverage strategies utilized to explore the target surface.

We have investigated three different coverage strategies to distribute the initial set of graph nodes, namely a discretized grid (GRID), Rapidly Exploring Random Trees (RRT) [19], and a Kernel Density Estimation (KDE), as illustrated in Fig. 6, where red dots mark the nodes of the graph. The coverage strategies are compared below.

Discretized Grid: The first coverage strategy constitutes a simple grid heuristic within the bounds of the target area. The radius, $r_s = d_s/2$, of the collision sphere is used to calculate the grid resolution, given the dimension of the target surface. This coverage strategy is uninformed and can also be applied if no prior knowledge on the particle distribution is available.

Rapidly Exploring Random Trees: RRTs [19] are a well established generic method in research on path planning and exploration. In a nutshell, the algorithm samples a random configuration $\boldsymbol{q}_{rand}$ in the free space C, calculates the nearest neighbor $\boldsymbol{q}_{near}$, and extends the tree starting from this configuration towards $\boldsymbol{q}_{new}$, which incorporates the maximal expansion length $\boldsymbol{q}_{delta}$. For our approach $\boldsymbol{q} \in \mathbb{R}^2$ and $\boldsymbol{q}_{delta}$ is defined by the radius r_s. As the algorithm is biased to explore uncovered regions, it is predestined to generate the initial nodes for wiping tasks. However, RRTs do not necessarily yield goal oriented paths w. r. t. the desired semantic goal, especially considering the skim action. Therefore, we do not use the tree developed structure to derive wiping motions, but only the nodes that were created during the expansion.

Figure 5: An exemplary geometric state G_s. The collision sphere is utilized to verify the SDG nodes in a grid distribution, where green is valid and red in collision.

Kernel Density Estimation: As a third strategy, we apply a Gaussian KDE to estimate the regions with high particle probability within the particle distribution $\boldsymbol{P}$:

$$\boldsymbol{K}(\boldsymbol{x}) = \frac{1}{\mathrm{N}} \sum_{i=1}^{\mathrm{N}} e^{-||\boldsymbol{P}_i - \boldsymbol{x}||^2/h^2} \tag{3}$$

where h is the bandwidth of the kernels. The multivariate KDE is visualized as a contour plot on the left in Fig. 6. The resulting continuous representation is used to select the M most significant peaks. This approach is most valuable if prior knowledge about the distribution is available, e. g. perceived by a vision system. The nodes are naturally placed at the position with the highest effect.

The calculated nodes n_i serve as the starting point to grow SDGs with different semantic goals S_g. As the coverage strategy may influence the task performance, we will evaluate the execution time and task performance of the resulting wiping motions in Sec. 6. In the following we will use the distribution generated by the KDE to outline the graph generation for the three removal actions.

Every wiping action can be described as the desired state change of the medium in an abstract form. We represent these state changes as *constraints* for the set describing the goal particle distribution $\boldsymbol{P}_g$, as listed in (4), (5), and (6). For example, the goal state of absorbing is to remove all particles from the surface, by simply getting in contact with each particle to trigger a delete operation. Collecting and skimming, however, require directed tool motions to have the medium moved towards a certain goal area (collect), or moved from the edge of the surface (skim), respectively. The geometric process models of these actions have to correspond to this state change, respectively the desired effect to the particle distribution $\boldsymbol{P}$ as illustrated in Fig. 7. Based on our previous investigations [20], these process models are designed in accordance with the tool, the surface, and the medium to be manipulated as hand crafted Cartesian task motions are hardly applicable in most of the cases. For example, absorbing dust from a sideboard using a feather duster may be represented as a set of Cartesian straight line motions along the sideboard surface, however, if it is obstructed with obstacles, e. g. a television, flowers, and books, these simple representation is not anymore applicable. Having generated, instead of a hand crafted task space paths one can overcome this issue. To this end, we implement three prototypical strategies to ground the semantic actions corresponding to the three investigated semantic goal states S_g, i. e. (`absorbed` *?m - medium ?s - surface*), (`collected` *?m - medium ?s - surface*), (`skimmed` *?m - medium ?s - surface*). Accordingly, SDGs embody one of the following actions.

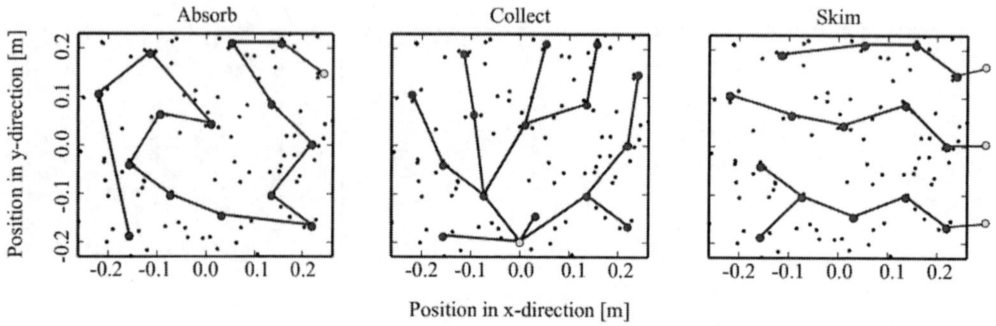

Figure 7: SDGs for the three prototypical removal actions absorb, collect, and skim.

Absorb: The first action to be investigated is the absorb action, as it occurs e. g. in vacuuming, dusting, or soaking up water with a sponge. The effect to the particles (i. e. the absorption) is independent of the direction of motion, as long as the entire region is covered by the tool at least once to remove all particles, such that

$$P_g = \emptyset. \tag{4}$$

A possible solution to this issue is the *Traveling Sales Person (TSP)* algorithm. Hess *et al.* [13] showed that this is a performant approach to solve unconstrained wiping tasks in a generalized way. We apply a variation of the TSP to absorbing, as seen in Fig. 7. The outcome is a natural curved motion covering all nodes of the graph.

Collect: Collecting the medium constitutes the second removal action. The particles are modeled to be pushed upon contact. The desired goal state S_g can be geometrically represented as a single goal region on the target surface. This region is defined by an additional node n_g added to the SDG (yellow dot). The goal is currently given to the robotic agent by the operator but may be inferred from the current world state in future. All branches of the graph have to be directed towards this single goal node, such that

$$P_g = \{(x_1, y_1), (x_2, y_2), \dots, (x_N, y_N) \,|\, x_i, y_i \in \mathbb{R} \wedge \\ ||(n_{g,x}, n_{g,y}) - (x_i, y_i)|| \leq r_s\}. \tag{5}$$

To do so, we implement a *Minimum Spanning Tree (MST)* [11] for a single root node. The distance between nodes serves as cost function with a maximum connection length $l_{max} = d_s$.

Skim: The third SDG strategy is designed to solve arbitrary skimming tasks. In principle, skimming can be related to collecting. The particles are pushed away upon contact with the tool. The semantic goal S_g of the action corresponds to a geometric state where all particles are pushed off the target surface, such that

$$P_g = \{(x_1, y_1), (x_2, y_2), \dots, (x_N, y_N) \,|\, x_i, y_i \in \mathbb{R} \wedge \\ (x_{min} > x_i \vee x_i > x_{max} \vee y_{min} > y_i \vee y_i > y_{max})\}. \tag{6}$$

We implement this action as a collecting action with multiple goals, i. e. multiple MSTs. These goals are represented by multiple virtual goal nodes equally distributed along the edges of the target surface. Depending on the target object, only a subset of the available edges may be used. In the scenario at hand, only the edge parallel to the table edge is a valid goal region (right in Fig. 7). As a result, multiple trees expand towards the upper edge of the surface. Each tree forms thereby a MST w. r. t. the closest goal node.

5. RESOLVING WHOLE-BODY WIPING MOTIONS FOR A ROBOTIC AGENT

So far, we have discussed the problem of wiping only from a Cartesian point of view. In particular, SDGs only consider translational paths of a spherical body along the target surface w. r. t. a desired semantic goal. This is only a first estimate for the feasibility of the action. The joint state of the robotic agent, as well as the orientation of the tool are yet to be integrated into the reasoning process. The highly redundant robotic agent is able to resolve the Cartesian tool motions in manifold ways, where some configurations result in local minima, while others allow to follow the desired path. A similar problem is observed for the tool orientation. In some cases it is better to rotate the tool to obtain a better reachability in favor of a decreasing task performance, i. e. a poorer cleaning result. These issues are discussed in details in the following sub-sections.

5.1 Generate Joint Motions

The branches of the SDG represent Cartesian tool motions that serve as the basis for the joint motions of the agent. The underlying problem to resolve a Cartesian path into joint motions is formulated as *path following problem*. For each Cartesian pose $\boldsymbol{x}$ on a Cartesian path $\boldsymbol{X}$, the agent has to find a joint configuration $\boldsymbol{q}$, respectively $\dot{\boldsymbol{q}}$

$$\dot{\boldsymbol{q}} = \boldsymbol{J}^{\dagger}\dot{\boldsymbol{x}} + (I - \boldsymbol{J}^{\dagger}\boldsymbol{J})\dot{\boldsymbol{q}}_0 \tag{7}$$

where $\boldsymbol{J}^{\dagger}$ is the generalized inverse of the Jacobian matrix (e. g. the Moore-Penrose pseudoinverse [2]). The first term on the right minimizes the norm of the joint distance and the second term exploits the redundancy of the robotic agent to satisfy secondary criteria, such as collision and singularity avoidance. For instance, the joint velocity $\dot{\boldsymbol{q}}$ and the joint acceleration $\ddot{\boldsymbol{q}}$ must not exceed the limits of the robotic manipulators and the resulting joint path $\boldsymbol{Q}$ must not collide with obstacles in the environment nor the agent itself. This problem is especially challenging for highly redundant robotic manipulators with a high number of DOF, such as the robotic agent Rollin' Justin [1].

A possible solution to this problem has been proposed by Konietschke and Hirzinger [16]. They utilize an inverse kinematics solver based on non-linear optimization. The algorithm enables Rollin' Justin to track arbitrary Cartesian trajectories on-line. The algorithm does not consider collisions with the environment, nor with the agent itself. Moreover, since it is based on local optimization techniques, it might diverge towards local minima, i. e. singularities in the joint space. A deterministic path following approach

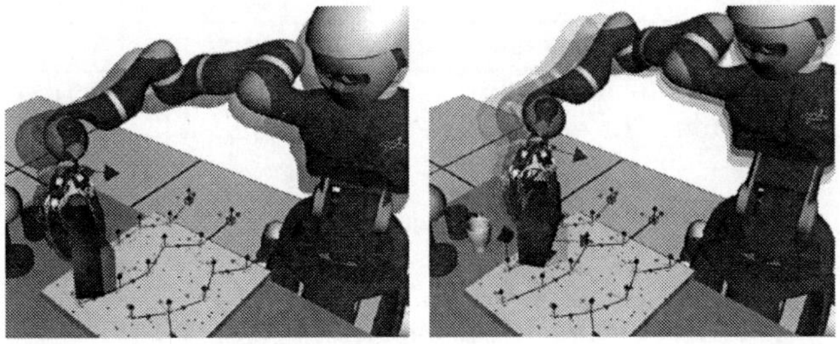

Figure 8: Initially, each node is directed towards the next node in the graph. If this pose is in collision (left), or unreachable, e. g. due to joint limitations (right), the free DOF of the tool are exploited.

was proposed by Huaman and Stilman [15]. They propose a resolution complete solution that exploits the redundancy in discretized Jacobian null-space of robotic manipulators. The algorithm implements a breadth-first backwards search procedure when encountering local minimas or obstacles in the environment. Compared to the former method, the drawback of this solution is the high computation time. Both methods try to exactly follow the Cartesian path, where all six dimension (i. e. three translational dimension and three rotational dimension) of the task are considered. This is not necessarily mandatory for wiping tasks. For example, a sponge can be rotated w. r. t. the normal of the target surface, without decreasing the area of effect. On the other hand, a window wiper has to be moved orthogonal to the wiper blade in order to achieve the desired effect, but it is allowed be rotated along the main axis of the blade, up to a certain degree. To this end, we propose a path following method that is aware of the free tool DOF available in the Cartesian space. Furthermore, we propose to exploit local path following methods whenever possible, and utilize global search-based methods only if no other alternative is feasible to decrease the overall planning time.

The sequence in which the SDG branches are processed depends on the wiping action. The absorb motion is unambiguous since it has only one branch to follow from start to end. For each branch, in the collect and skim actions, the Cartesian space is resolved iteratively starting from a leaf node and expanding backward to the branch's root node. Initially, the orientation of the nodes n_i is directed towards the next node n_{i+1} in the branch. The resulting pose, i. e. the translation and rotation of the node, is used as initial hypothesis for the goal pose of the tool (see Fig. 8). The edge in between the nodes is interpolated to resolve the path following task outlined in (7). We apply the local path following method described in [16], with additional checks for collision between the agent and the environment. Ideally, all poses are reachable and collision free so that the agent can manipulate the tool accordingly. The default orientation $\boldsymbol{x}_{goal,0}$ is most effective w. r. t. the manipulation of the medium, i. e. the particle distribution. However, in a cluttered environment it is likely that the edge between two nodes cannot be tracked without collision, or the robotic agent falling into a local minima. In this case we backtrack to the initial pose $\boldsymbol{x}_{start}$, select an alternative goal pose $\boldsymbol{x}_{goal}$ w. r. t. the free DOF of the tool, and repeat the path following task. The procedure is outlined in Algorithm 1.

The procedure is repeated until all alternative combinations in the discretized search space of the free DOF are evaluated. If none is successful, the path that had the largest part of it solved by the local method is selected to be solved using the global method described in [15], which is guaranteed to find a path if one exists (given enough time). If no feasible inverse kinematics solution is found at all, the agent abandons the node and moves on to the remaining nodes of the branch. Another solution to this issue would be to alter the Cartesian graph at this point until it can be resolved by the agent, e. g. by displacing the goal node or changing the curvature of the graph edge.

Algorithm 1: PathFollowing($\boldsymbol{q}_{n_i}$, n_{i+1}, δ)

Input: The initial joint configuration $\boldsymbol{q}_{n_i}$, the goal node n_{i+1}, and the step-size δ
Output: A continous joint path $\boldsymbol{Q}$

$\boldsymbol{x}_{start} \leftarrow$ CalculateToolPose($\boldsymbol{q}_{n_i}$, $\boldsymbol{x}_{grasp}^{-1}$)
foreach $\boldsymbol{x}_{goal}$ *in IterateFreeDOF*(n_{i+1}) **do**
  $\boldsymbol{Q} \leftarrow$ List()
  $\boldsymbol{X} \leftarrow$ Interpolate($\boldsymbol{x}_{start}$, $\boldsymbol{x}_{goal}$, δ)
  foreach $\boldsymbol{x}_i$ *in* $\boldsymbol{X}$ **do**
    $\boldsymbol{x}_{eef,i} \leftarrow \boldsymbol{x}_i \cdot \boldsymbol{x}_{grasp}$
    $\boldsymbol{q}_i \leftarrow$ FindIK($\boldsymbol{x}_{eef,i}$)
    if *IsValid*($\boldsymbol{q}_i$) **then**
      $\boldsymbol{Q}[i] \leftarrow \boldsymbol{q}_i$
    else
      break
  if *Length*($\boldsymbol{Q}$) = *Length*($\boldsymbol{X}$) **then**
    return $\boldsymbol{Q}$

5.2 Extended Semantic Directed Graphs

Up to this point, we have considered wiping tasks as globally realizable in terms of reachability, albeit it is quite common for wiping tasks to cover larger regions, which may be unreachable for a static manipulator. For example, if the agent is commanded to clean a whole table surface, the larger task space requires to move the mobile base. A mobile robotic agent is able to reposition itself to overcome this issue and execute tasks in extended areas. We incorporate this by utilizing *extended Semantic Directed Graphs (eSDG)*, which augment the graph nodes n_i with reachability information to reposition the base of the robotic agent.

One approach to position a robotic manipulator optimally w. r. t. the reachability of a certain task is the use of *capability maps* [32]. We have already utilized capability maps to initially optimize the base position of a robotic agent in front of a windowpane, in order to clean it [22]. While this provides a solution for the initial positioning problem, the base motions during the task execution are handcrafted. We incorporate the reachability information for single graph nodes in eSDGs by utilizing capability maps. This way, we enable the agent to optimize its base positions for sub-graphs of eSDGs, respectively the underlying particle distribution. Capability maps represent the workspace of robotic manipulators in a discretized grid. For each voxel in the grid, the reachability index $r = \frac{R}{N}$ is computed, where N is the maximum number of hypothetically reachable positions, and R the actual reachable positions [32].

The sub-graphs of eSDGs, here called cluster, are computed according to Algorithm 2. Initially, all nodes are associated to one cluster $\boldsymbol{C}$. The agent computes the base

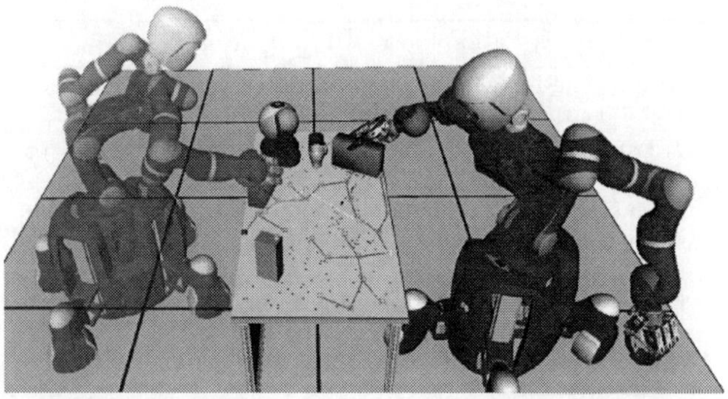

Figure 9: The eSDG collect graph consists of three clusters. As the goal is located on the right (yellow node), the clusters on the left are resolved first.

position by means of the capability maps in order to reach all nodes in the cluster. For every node n_i, the reachability index is obtained for all the available alternative poses of the end-effector $\boldsymbol{x}_{eef,i} = \boldsymbol{x}_{n_i} \cdot \boldsymbol{x}_{grasp}$. If the mean reachability for these poses is higher than $0.5\, r_{\max}$, the node is considered as reachable [22]. If all nodes are reachable, the cluster and the corresponding base position is stored. If a sub-set of nodes is unreachable the cluster is split into two new clusters. This is done using the K-Means algorithm with $K = 2$ and the two centers initialized as the centers of the reachable, and unreachable nodes, respectively. This approach yields large connected areas instead of smaller scattered regions. The algorithm is recursively executed.

The clusters are considered during the reasoning process of the wiping action. Each cluster, resembles the strategy of the main graph, i. e. absorbing, collecting and skimming. The clusters for the absorb action can be executed independently. Collecting requires to align the clusters towards the goal node of the eSDG. Each sub-graph implements the collect strategy with an intermediate goal. For skimming, the cluster on the edge of the target surface may also be considered independently. If the cluster is not connected to the edge of the target surface, the skimming paths are directed to the closest cluster with a connection to the surface edge. We utilize an A* algorithm [12] to navigate between the base positions of the clusters. As an example, the eSDG collect strategy is visualized in Fig. 9.

Algorithm 2: ExtendSDG($\boldsymbol{C}$, $\boldsymbol{eSDG}$)

Input: The initial cluster $\boldsymbol{C}$, and the $\boldsymbol{eSDG}$ structure
Output: The $\boldsymbol{eSDG}$ structure, including a list of clusters $\boldsymbol{C}$, and their base positions $\boldsymbol{x}_{base}$

```
x_base ← OptimizeBasePose(C)
R, U ← List()
foreach n_i in C do
    r_i ← CalculateReachability(n_i, x_grasp)
    if r_i >= 0.5 r_max^1 then
        R[i] ← n_i
    else
        U[i] ← n_i
if U = ∅ then
    eSDG.append([C, x_base])
else
    foreach C_i in KMeans(C, Centers(R, U)) do
        eSDG ← ExtendSDG(C_i, eSDG)
return eSDG
```

6. EVALUATION AND CONCLUSION

We evaluate the proposed methods in three different scenarios. Scenario I constitutes the chopping board scenario illustrated in Fig. 4. This scenario is executed by the humanoid robotic agent Rollin' Justin as illustrated in Fig. 10. The proposed reasoning methods command a whole-body impedance control framework [6] which enables the agent to compliantly interact with the environment. Besides the pure motion aspect discussed in this work, we have conducted detailed research efforts on the knowledge-based parameterization of compliant contact behavior [22], [21]. Among others, the desired Cartesian force, the Cartesian stiffness and the damping are parameterized according to the requirements of the tool, the surface and the manipulated medium.

For scenario II, we assume the same environment without the chopping board, where the particles are distributed on the entire table surface as shown in Fig. 9. Scenario III is a variation of the car cleaning example visualized in Fig. 1, where we approximate a planar target surface aligned with the windshield. In all scenarios the agent manipulates the sponge illustrated in Fig. 4 to obtain comparable results. We utilize the eSDG approach to incorporate the optimization of the base position for all scenarios. We evaluate the three coverage strategies (i. e. GRID, RRT, KDE), paired with the three removal actions (i. e. absorb, collect, skim), w. r. t. the traveled Cartesian distance during contact, the computation time, the execution time, and the task performance. The calculation time includes the node distribution, the cluster computation, and the path following. For all steps the collision check time using OpenRAVE [5] is included. The execution time is based on the assumption of a maximum velocity of $1\, rad/s$ joint speed, and a maximum joint acceleration of $2\, rad/s^2$. The performance measurement is conducted according to the constraint definitions (4), (5), and (6). The metric for the absorb action is the number of deleted particles, the collect action is evaluated based on the number of particles within the radius r_s around the goal node, and the metric for the skim action is the number of particles pushed outside the boundaries of the surface area. All numbers are averaged over five trials with different particle distributions. The results are listed in Table 1. A video of the task executions is available at `https://youtu.be/ZA2U9upkrjo`.

In the lesser obstructed chopping board scenario, as well as in the windshield scenario, the KDE coverage strategy mainly outperforms the other two methods w. r. t. the task performance. In general, this indicates that the KDE approach is favorable for tasks with a detailed model of the medium. However, the KDE strategy is noticeably biased by the obstacles in the table scenario, which results in many collisions and unreachable, i. e. unconnectable nodes, which is also reflected by the poorly developed path lengths. The GRID heuristic and the RRT coverage strategy perform similarly good for most of the cases, where the GRID strategy generates reproducible motions independent of the particle estimation or probabilistic effects.

In general, the proposed particle distribution is a suitable representation to estimate the outcome of wiping motions in compliant contact. The task execution illustrated in Fig. 10 shows that the outcome in a real environment matches the

Table 1: Results for the three scenarios Chopping Board, Table, and Windshield

		Chopping Board			Table			Windshield		
		GRID	RRT	KDE	GRID	RRT	KDE	GRID	RRT	KDE
Absorb	Cart. dist. [m]	1.52	1.41	1.90	4.34	4.10	3.24	4.44	4.84	4.69
	comp. time [s]	45.96	57.12	62.00	144.47	312.45	169.92	314.04	423.21	417.66
	exec. time [s]	18.01	25.92	27.71	41.30	66.96	52.485	77.59	111.90	66.11
	performance [%]	84.25	85.00	95.75	77.00	79.50	70.50	90.13	90.50	91.00
Collect	Cart. dist. [m]	1.54	1.45	1.90	3.68	3.60	2.92	4.97	4.76	4.22
	comp. time [s]	69.89	68.48	72.24	110.92	161.60	270.56	885.45	262.55	428.05
	exec. time [s]	16.17	32.42	43.28	65.71	83.36	62.14	112.47	116.26	97.56
	performance [%]	86.50	86.75	90.50	70.25	69.25	41.75	48.50	39.25	62.75
Skim	Cart. dist. [m]	1.81	1.62	2.01	5.48	4.95	3.75	5.58	5.65	5.89
	comp. time [s]	107.17	44.25	90.57	211.14	260.34	255.58	325.97	212.34	199.03
	exec. time [s]	32.11	26.51	45.81	113.37	122.76	102.48	108.18	103.29	96.03
	performance [%]	88.00	80.25	97.00	71.75	66.50	53.00	94.50	88.50	88.50

Figure 10: The robotic agent Rollin' Justin accomplishing the collect task in the chopping board scenario. The outcome is similar to the prediction obtained with the particle distribution representation.

expectations of the simulated behavior of the particles for small grain dirt particles. It is therefore applicable to infer the effect of wiping motions generated with the different coverage strategies and measure the task performance w. r. t. the constraint definition for the three removal actions. In conclusion, our approach enables a robotic agent to reason about the task performance of wiping actions as it is aware of the desired state change of the particle distribution. This allows to decide for the most effective strategy to clean a surface given a certain problem instance.

The task performance for a specific scenario is highly dependent on the selected coverage strategy. While this is a drawback for onetime tasks, this observation can be exploited to improve recurring tasks, e. g. industrial manufacturing tasks, such as polishing the surface of a car. These tasks can be autonomously optimized w. r. t. the execution time by iterating over the available coverage strategies. Moreover, the agent can continuously improve on the task performance by integrating episodic memories of previous executions into the reasoning process. For example, the task performance of previous trials can be used to benchmark future trials with alternative task parameters, e. g. a different tool alignment or a different force profile. The generic approach can be utilized to solve previously unseen wiping tasks, only given the desired semantic goal and the geometric properties of the tool and the environment. To this end, we believe that our approach constitutes a valuable addition for autonomous robotic agents.

Building on our findings, we plan to extend our research on compliant manipulation towards the closure of the semantic feedback loop based on visual and haptic perception and the integration of an appropriate uncertainty model to incorporate bad contact situations. In the case of wiping tasks, this will allow the agent to reason about the real effect of its actions and the resulting task performance, update the qualitative medium representation, and schedule additional wiping motions to improve the cleaning result.

7. SUMMARY

We described a qualitative reasoning approach to solve everyday wiping tasks with a robotic agent on a high level of abstraction. We proposed (*i*) a qualitative representation of the medium in wiping tasks (*ii*) in combination with Semantic Directed Graphs (SDG) which enable the agent to plan Cartesian task motions w. r. t. the desired semantic goal state, i. e. the state change of the particle distribution. Furthermore, we proposed (*iii*) a path following method that is aware of the free DOF of the tool and the redundant joint space of the agent to allow for a robust task execution. Eventually, (*iv*) we integrated reachability information into the reasoning process to extend our approach towards wide area tasks. We have shown that our approach is applicable to various tasks, i. e. absorbing, collecting, and skimming, in three different scenarios in simulation, as well as in a real experiment with the humanoid robotic agent Rollin' Justin. The robotic agent experiment proves that our qualitative representation matches the effects of the real world.

ACKNOWLEDGMENTS

This work was partially funded by the European Community's Seventh Framework Programme under grant agreement no. 608849 EuRoC and partially by the Helmholtz Association Project HVF-0029 RACE-LAB.

REFERENCES

[1] C. Borst, T. Wimböck, F. Schmidt, M. Fuchs, B. Brunner, F. Zacharias, P. R. Giordano, R. Konietschke, W. Sepp, S. Fuchs, et al. Rollin'justin-mobile platform with variable base. In *Proc. of the IEEE International Conference on Robotics and Automation (ICRA)*, pages 1597–1598, 2009.

[2] S. R. Buss. Introduction to inverse kinematics with jacobian transpose, pseudoinverse and damped least squares methods. *IEEE Journal of Robotics and Automation*, 17(1-19):16, 2004.

[3] M. Cakmak and L. Takayama. Towards a comprehensive chore list for domestic robots. In *Proc. of the ACM/IEEE International Conference on Human-Robot Interaction (HRI)*, pages 93–94, 2013.

[4] H. I. Christensen et al. A roadmap for u.s. robotics from internet to robotics. Technical report, Robotics Virtual Organization, 2013.

[5] R. Diankov. *Automated Construction of Robotic Manipulation Programs*. PhD thesis, Carnegie Mellon University, Robotics Institute, 2010.

[6] A. Dietrich, T. Wimböck, A. Albu-Schäffer, and G. Hirzinger. Reactive whole-body control: Dynamic mobile manipulation using a large number of actuated degrees of freedom. *IEEE Robotics & Automation Magazine*, 19(2):20–33, 2012.

[7] M. Do, J. Schill, J. Ernesti, and T. Asfour. Learn to wipe: A case study of structural bootstrapping from sensorimotor experience. In *Proc. of the IEEE International Conference on Robotics and Automation (ICRA)*, pages 1858–1864, 2014.

[8] K. D. Forbus. Qualitative process theory. *Artificial intelligence*, 24(1):85–168, 1984.

[9] Y. Gabriely and E. Rimon. Spanning-tree based coverage of continuous areas by a mobile robot. *Annals of Mathematics and Artificial Intelligence*, 31(1-4):77–98, 2001.

[10] M. Ghallab, A. Howe, D. Christianson, D. McDermott, A. Ram, M. Veloso, D. Weld, and D. Wilkins. Pddl—the planning domain definition language. *AIPS98 planning committee*, 78(4):1–27, 1998.

[11] R. Graham and P. Hell. On the history of the minimum spanning tree problem. *Annals of the History of Computing*, 7(1):43–57, 1985.

[12] P. E. Hart, N. J. Nilsson, and B. Raphael. A formal basis for the heuristic determination of minimum cost paths. *IEEE Transactions on Systems Science and Cybernetics*, 4(2):100–107, 1968.

[13] J. M. Hess, G. D. Tipaldi, and W. Burgard. Null space optimization for effective coverage of 3d surfaces using redundant manipulators. In *Proc. of the IEEE/RSJ International Conference on Intelligent Robots and Systems (IROS)*, pages 1923–1928, 2012.

[14] G. Hirzinger, N. Sporer, A. Albu-Schäffer, M. Hahnle, R. Krenn, A. Pascucci, and M. Schedl. Dlr's torque-controlled light weight robot iii-are we reaching the technological limits now? In *Proc. of the IEEE International Conference on Robotics and Automation (ICRA)*, volume 2, pages 1710–1716. IEEE, 2002.

[15] A. Huaman and M. Stilman. Deterministic motion planning for redundant robots along end-effector paths. In *Proc. of the International Conference on Humanoid Robots (ICHR)*, pages 785–790, 2012.

[16] R. Konietschke and G. Hirzinger. Inverse kinematics with closed form solutions for highly redundant robotic systems. In *Proc. of the IEEE International Conference on Robotics and Automation (ICRA)*, pages 2945–2950. IEEE, 2009.

[17] L. Kunze, M. E. Dolha, E. Guzman, and M. Beetz. Simulation-based temporal projection of everyday robot object manipulation. In *Proc. of the International Conference on Autonomous Agents and Multiagent Systems (AAMAS)*, pages 107–114, 2011.

[18] J.-C. Latombe. *Robot Motion Planning*. Springer, 1990.

[19] S. LaValle. Rapidly-exploring random trees: A new tool for path planning. 1998.

[20] D. Leidner, C. Borst, A. Dietrich, and A. Albu-SchÃd'ffer. Classifying compliant manipulation tasks for automated planning in robotics. In *Proc. of the IEEE/RSJ International Conference on Intelligent Robots and Systems (IROS)*, pages 1769–1776, 2015.

[21] D. Leidner, A. Dietrich, M. Beetz, and A. Albu-Schäffer. Knowledge-enabled parameterization of whole-body control strategies for compliant service robots. *Autonomous Robots (AURO): Special Issue on Whole-Body Control of Contacts and Dynamics for Humanoid Robots*, pages 1–18, 2015.

[22] D. Leidner, A. Dietrich, F. Schmidt, C. Borst, and A. Albu-Schäffer. Object-centered hybrid reasoning for whole-body mobile manipulation. In *Proc. of the IEEE International Conference on Robotics and Automation (ICRA)*, pages 1828–1835, 2014.

[23] B. Liepert, S. Stramigioli, R. Bischoff, U. Haass, et al. Multi-annual roadmap for robotics in europe. Technical report, euRobotics Association Internationale Sans But Lucratif (AISBL), 2014.

[24] N. J. Nilsson. Shakey the robot. Technical report, DTIC Document, 1984.

[25] K. Okada, M. Kojima, Y. Sagawa, T. Ichino, K. Sato, and M. Inaba. Vision based behavior verification system of humanoid robot for daily environment tasks. In *Proc. of the IEEE-RAS International Conference on Humanoid Robots (ICHR)*, pages 7–12, 2006.

[26] K. Okada, T. Ogura, A. Haneda, J. Fujimoto, F. Gravot, and M. Inaba. Humanoid motion generation system on hrp2-jsk for daily life environment. In *Proc. of the IEEE International Conference on Mechatronics and Automation (ICMA)*, pages 1772–1777, 2005.

[27] V. Ortenzi, M. Adjigble, K. Jeffrey, R. Stolkin, and M. Mistry. An experimental study of robot control during environmental contacts based on projected operational space dynamics. In *Proc. of the IEEE-RAS International Conference on Humanoid Robots (ICHR)*, pages 407–412, 2014.

[28] E. Pablo Lana, B. Vilhena Adorno, and C. Andrey Maia. A new algebraic approach for the description of robotic manipulation tasks. In *Proc. of the IEEE International Conference on Robotics and Automation (ICRA)*, pages 3083–3088, 2015.

[29] C. Schindlbeck and S. Haddadin. Unified passivity-based cartesian force/impedance control for rigid and flexible joint robots via task-energy tanks. In *Proc. of the IEEE International Conference on Robotics and Automation (ICRA)*, pages 440–447, 2015.

[30] H. Urbanek, A. Albu-Schäffer, and P. van der Smagt. Learning from demonstration: repetitive movements for autonomous service robotics. In *Proc. of the IEEE/RSJ International Conference on Intelligent Robots and Systems (IROS)*, pages 3495–3500, 2004.

[31] D. Vanthienen, S. Robyns, E. Aertbeliën, and J. De Schutter. Force-sensorless robot force control within the instantaneous task specification and estimation (iTaSC) framework. In *Benelux Meeting on Systems and Control*, 2013.

[32] F. Zacharias, C. Borst, and G. Hirzinger. Capturing robot workspace structure: representing robot capabilities. In *Proc. of the IEEE/RSJ International Conference on Intelligent Robots and Systems (IROS)*, pages 3229–3236, 2007.

Analogical Generalization of Actions from Single Exemplars in a Robotic Architecture

Jason R. Wilson
wilson@cs.tufts.edu

Evan Krause
evan.krause@tufts.edu

Matthias Scheutz
matthias.scheutz@tufts.edu

Morgan Rivers
daniel.rivers@tufts.edu

Human-Robot Interaction Lab
Tufts University
200 Boston Ave
Medford, MA

ABSTRACT

Humans are often able to generalize knowledge learned from a single exemplar. In this paper, we present a novel integration of mental simulation and analogical generalization algorithms into a cognitive robotic architecture that enables a similarly rudimentary generalization capability in robots. Specifically, we show how a robot can generate variations of a given scenario and then use the results of those new scenarios run in a physics simulator to generate generalized action scripts using analogical mappings. The generalized action scripts then allow the robot to perform the originally learned activity in a wider range of scenarios with different types of objects without the need for additional exploration or practice. In a proof-of-concept demonstration we show how the robot can generalize from a previously learned pick-and-place action performed with a single arm on an object with a handle to a pick-and-place action of a cylindrical object with no handle with two arms.

Keywords

analogical generalization, action learning, robotic architecture, mental simulation

1. INTRODUCTION

Humans are known to employ many different methods for learning new information, from data-driven statistical learning (e.g., when infants discover and entrain the motor behaviors) to knowledge-based conceptual learning (e.g., based on "insight" or "understanding"). One striking ability of adult human learners is that they can bring their learned knowledge at all levels of abstraction to bear when faced with new learning problems and can thus generalize new information very quickly from only a few exemplars. For example, human adult learners, after observing another human demonstrating a novel action on a novel object, are typically able to describe the new action and potentially perform it right away; and most importantly, they often can immediately determine whether it might apply to similar objects and how they would have to modify it to perform it on those objects. In a sense, *humans can learn generalized knowledge from single exemplars* and the main goal of this paper is to demonstrate for the first time a similar, albeit much more restricted capability (compared to the human case) for generalization from a single demonstration in a cognitive robotic architecture. This functionality is achieved by integrating algorithms for analogical reasoning and generalization as well as algorithms for generating counter-factual scenarios from a given scenario together with a physics simulation into a cognitive robotic architecture.

The paper proceeds as follows. We start with a motivating scenario which we will use throughout the paper to describe the functionality of our system. Next, we introduce both existing and new algorithms for mental simulation and generalization, and then introduce the relevant parts of the robotic architecture and a proof-of-concept demonstration of the integrated systems on a physical PR2 robot. We then evaluate the generalization process, review related work, and conclude with a discussion of our work and future directions enabled by the integrated architecture and the generalization capabilities.

2. MOTIVATION

Consider a scenario where a robot is tasked with picking up a medical kit from a table. Initially, the robot has no concept of the steps necessary to perform the task, which is then demonstrated by a human who picks up the medical kit by its handle and moves it aside. Suppose the robot is then able to construct a step-wise representation that enables it to imitate the human and pick up the same medical kit by the handle and move it to the side. Figure 1 (left) shows the robot demonstrating its ability to use the action representation to mimic the demonstrated action.

This newly learned action, however, is very specific to the human demonstration and does not automatically generalize to other scenarios (e.g., different object orientation/location on the table, different types of objects with and without handles, etc.). A human learner in this case would, for example, notice that many details about the object (e.g., the color, the texture, the size within some ranges, the orienta-

Appears in: *Proceedings of the 15th International Conference on Autonomous Agents and Multiagent Systems (AAMAS 2016), J. Thangarajah, K. Tuyls, C. Jonker, S. Marsella (eds.), May 9–13, 2016, Singapore.*

Figure 1: The PR2 performing the action learned from a single exemplar (left) and its generalization to a new object and action (right).

tion) do not matter for the particular pick-and-place action as long as it has a handle; and even if it did not have a handle, there might be different ways to pick it up (e.g., using two hands). Alternatively, humans can adapt the sequence of actions (e.g. add, remove, or repeat some) in a manner that still accomplishes the goal. But how do humans achieve this feat? One suggestion is that humans perform quick mental simulations, possibly physics-based, that allow them to imagine different scenarios and try out the learned activity "in their mind" [1]. Based on these "mental experiments", they are then able to generalize to the successful cases and exclude the unsuccessful ones. The successful or unsuccessful outcome of a mental simulation is, of course, *no guarantee* that an action will or will not work. Clearly, the accuracy of the simulation together with the appropriateness of the assumptions about objects and their properties will be a major determinant of how well mental simulation can predict actual outcomes. However, even when the accuracy of the simulation is not very high, the simulations can at the very least be used as a guideline for whether the simulated action should be considered as a valid alternative to be incorporated into a generalization of the action. When a new scenario is presented and the robot has not learned an appropriate action for it, the generalized action obtained through a series of mental simulations is a promising choice that can later be refined through practice.

3. FROM LEARNED ACTIONS TO GENERALIZATIONS AND BACK

Given a robotic control architecture that comprises the functionality (implemented in various components, say) to learn and execute an action script (such as the one for picking up a medical kit), the question we address in this paper then is how such an architecture can be augmented to allow for action generalization, i.e., what architectural extensions and algorithm integrations are needed for the robot to be able to generalize and immediately execute the previously learned actions in different scenarios. Note that there are several important gaps between the given and the desired architectural capabilities that such an extension has to bridge. These gaps are intrinsically connected to the tension between the concrete and the abstract as well as the tension between the physical world and the mental simulation.

Specific vs general:.

On the one hand, we have very specific knowledge about a single (learned) exemplar, yet we want to generate more abstract knowledge about a class of exemplars. Statistical approaches bridging this gap by learning from numerous specific exemplars are not applicable, hence we attempt to bridge this gap with a novel combination of simulation and analogical reasoning.

Continuous vs discrete:.

Some of the involved sensory data is typically continuous (the robot's vision system might create a point cloud representation of the perceived object, where each point is along three dimensions in continuous space). Similarly, the robot's arm motion is described by 3-D vectors along a continuous trajectory, while classes of trajectories in an action representation might be denoted by single action modifier (e.g., "up" as in "lift up"). One way to bridge this gap is to add explicit links between these continuous and discrete representations (e.g., in the form of a predicate that relates "up" to the vector for moving up).

Exemplars vs generalization:.

Every exemplar has associated with it far more information than is encoded in the generalization (this concerns all aspects of the exemplar including the involved objects and actions as well as other details of the scene). The process of creating the generalization naturally eliminates irrelevant information, but what information is irrelevant? The generalization must maintain enough information such that it is sufficient for performing the generalized action for an interesting class of exemplars. The mental simulation in conjunction with systematic variations of the scenario can partly address this problem by allowing the robot to discover relevant aspects (e.g., if a particular variation led to action failure that that variation was relevant for performing the action).

Simulated vs physical world:.

There are three primary gaps between these worlds: *physics*, *objects*, and *perception*. The obvious gap in the physics is that the simulation is just an approximation of the actual physics of the real world. This is best exemplified in collisions. In the simulation world, collisions can optionally be ignored and in some cases need to be ignored (e.g., at the moment when the gripper "becomes one" with the object). A significant difference in the representation of objects is that in the simulation world we can assume complete knowledge of the object. This means we know its weight, color, size, shape, location, etc. In the physical world, we cannot easily know some of this information (such as the weight) and other information is based on inferences by the vision system. An example is that in the simulation world we have a full 3-D model of the object, but in the physical world we can only get a 2.5-D model of the object. Lastly, the assumption of complete knowledge in the simulation world allows us to avoid problems with inaccurate or wrong perceptions, which have to be addressed in the real world. However, note that action selection, execution, and learning must operate in simulation in nearly the exact same way as in the real world.

To bridge these various gaps, we propose the process depicted in Figure 2: given an initial action representation, (e.g., via learning from demonstration or some other method), the robot can use the representation to either execute the action or construct a generalization of the action. The generalization process performs mental simulations in counter-factual scenarios that differ from the given one in some respects. The robot must store enough information about the context in which it learned the action to be able to generate counter-factual scenarios. The resulting generalized action representation is applicable to both scenarios it considered during mental simulation and others it did not consider. Note that the robot can either generalize the learned action right away (after having learned it), or it can perform the generalization at a later point.

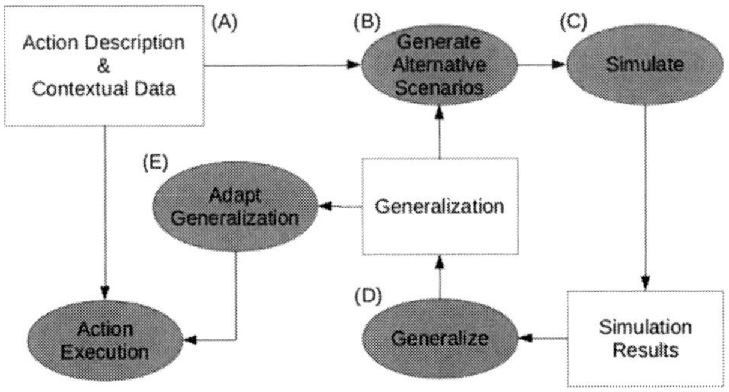

Figure 2: The action generalization process. The letters correspond to the subsections below and depict the typical data flow.

3.1 Action and Scene Representation (A)

The input to this process is a representation of an action and the context in which the action can be applied. This information may have come from a human demonstrating the action, or it may have been provided to the robot in some other form, such as instruction. A description of the action is not sufficient – the context of the action, including all relevant objects and agents involved and relations between these entities, is essential and must be included.

The action representation gives the robot a basic understanding of how to perform the desired action by providing a set of step by step action sequences. In the case of the pick-and-place action representation for picking up a medkit, three simplified action scripts for picking up an object, moving it aside, and setting it back down can be seen in Figure 3. The top-level action is composed of two sub-actions – a pick action and a place action (both action scripts themselves), and the pick sub-action is composed of the three stages: moving to the object, grasping the object, and lifting it vertically relative to its original position. The place sub-action is broken down into a lateral and downward movement, and finally the object is released. Here, the lowest level actions (i.e., move-to-object, grasp-object, move-to-relative, release-object) are action primitives that can be executed by a component in the architecture.

Each action also defines a set of parameters and a set of pre- and post-conditions. The post-conditions serve two important roles. Given an arbitrary goal, the action that has the goal as a post-condition may be executed to accomplish the goal. This is commonly seen in planning systems. Additionally, the post-conditions define the means by which we

```
pick-and-place ?robot ?object ?arm ?dest
  pick ?robot ?object ?arm
  place ?robot ?object ?arm ?dest

pick ?robot ?object ?arm
  move-to-object ?robot ?arm ?object !grasp
  grasp-object ?robot ?arm ?closepos ?object
  move-to-rel ?robot ?arm !up-pt ?orient

place ?robot ?object ?arm ?dest
  move-to-rel ?robot ?arm !over-pt ?orient
  move-to-rel ?robot ?arm !down-pt ?orient
  release-object ?robot ?arm ?object
```

Figure 3: Simplified action scripts for picking up an object, moving it aside, and setting it back down.

measure the success of the goal. For example, the pick-and-place action has the post-condition `at(?object,?dest)`, meaning that the object is at the destination location. The action is intended to move the object to this location, but if the action is not successful (e.g., because it is not the right action or used with the wrong parameters) then the object will not have been displaced.

In addition to the action representation, the scene has additional contextual information that must be represented in order to instantiate meaningful counter-factual simulation scenarios. Here it must be determined what information is relevant, what should be stored (e.g., to allow for simulations to be constructed in the future), and what should be varied during simulation. Scene representations include basic information about objects properties and the relation between the objects. Properties of the object include basic physical properties (e.g. mass, color, etc.), the shape and structure (e.g. cylindrical with a vertical handle on the side), and the location of the object. An object may be related to other objects spatially, compositionally, or otherwise (e.g. the cup is on the table, or the mass of the box is greater than that of the cup). The scene must also have some representation of the agent performing the action and any other relevant agents. For the example of picking up a medical kit by its handle, it is important that the agent have a mechanism by which it can do this. Thus the agent description must include a physical description of the agent and its capabilities (e.g. the robot has a gripper, gripper can grasp object). The scene representation is not limited to a physical description of the scene. An action may be relevant to other contextual information, such as social roles (e.g. the agent giving the instruction is a manager) or cultural norms (e.g. shaking hands when greeting).

3.2 Scenario Generation (B)

The robot knows (because it was been told, it has been demonstrated, or it has been instructed) that a given action is applicable to a specific scenario. This is just one scenario in which the action may be applicable, but it must consider alternative scenarios that may be equally applicable. The robot conducts a scenario generation process to produce counter-factual scenarios that will be subject to simulation and incorporated into the generalization.

Each variant of the exemplar produced during scenario generation is intended to give the robot multiple virtual experiences so that it can form an understanding of the effects of variations on the provided goal. Each counter-factual scenario is constructed by varying one or more variables in the exemplar. Variables can describe either the robot's actions (i.e., action variables as defined above) or scene variables that describe the world with which the robot interacts.

Each scenario variable is carefully defined to allow automated generation of variants and contains five important properties: (1) whether it is an action variable or scene variable, (2) type (continuous or discrete values), (3) its relation to other variables (i.e., valid states), (4) the degree of effect on the success of the simulation, and (5) state history from previous scenarios, to reduce duplication of generated variants on the demonstration. Some of the variables that may be varied and the set of possible values are shown in Table 1.

Table 1: Some variables that may be varied during scenario generation pertain to the action, but many describe the object. Variables have either a set of discrete values or a range of values. Color is unique in that it has 3 range values.

Name	Action?	Values
base shape	N	sphere, cylinder, box
height	N	[0.01, .4]
radius	N	[0.035, .15]
width	N	[0.07, .4, 1]
length	N	[0.07, .4, 1]
has handle	N	handled, handleless
handle type	N	loop, bar, knob
handle location	N	top, left, right, front
handle	N	vertical, horizontal
mass	N	[0.01, .1]
color	N	[0, 1],[0,1],[0,1]
y offset	N	[-.2, .2]
grasp type	Y	close, apart, push, two arm
arm	Y	right, left, both
gripper % open	Y	[.01, .1]
gripper % closed	Y	[.01, .1]

When generating variables that describe the scene, we take advantage of the abilities that generalization by analogical reasoning provides. One such ability is to be able to analyze a scenario with changes in multiple variables at a time and still perform effective analogical analysis between the scenarios. Thus, each counter-factual scenario generated may contain multiple variables that have been altered. The scenario generation algorithm performs (1) a systematic variation of the action variable that affects the greatest number of actions and (2) two random variations on less important variables defining the object to be interacted with. This three-variable variation for each scene allows a significant reduction in the number of scenes required for meaningful learning to occur while still maintaining the accuracy of produced analogies.

The way we generate the values of variables defining our scenario variations involves important assumptions the robot has about the world it must interact with. For example, ubiquitous physical properties such as friction are given default values unless otherwise provided by the demonstration. We also assume that the objects the robot performs actions on can be adequately represented by a combination of a simple base shape (sphere, cylinder, or box) and a handle (knob, loop, or bar) centered on one of its visible faces.

Another relevant assumption about the generated objects is that object interaction is limited to a set of allowable points on the object which the robot can grasp. The effective production of these points has been demonstrated in other research (e.g., [20, 4]), and we did not attempt to re-implement them here. As a result, the object is given a set of predefined grasps based on the object's geometry and handle number.

3.3 Mental Simulation (C)

The mental simulation stage begins by instantiating the scene in the simulation world. The robot is initialized to a specified state, while the rest of the scene is initialized from the scene variables defined in the scenario generation stage. These robot and scene specifications are used to produce a realistic representation of each scenario in the physics simulator. For our scenario, each scene consists of a robot, a table, and single object located on the table-top. Once the simulation scene has been initialized, the robot attempts to execute the action script using the action variables defined in the scenario generation stage.

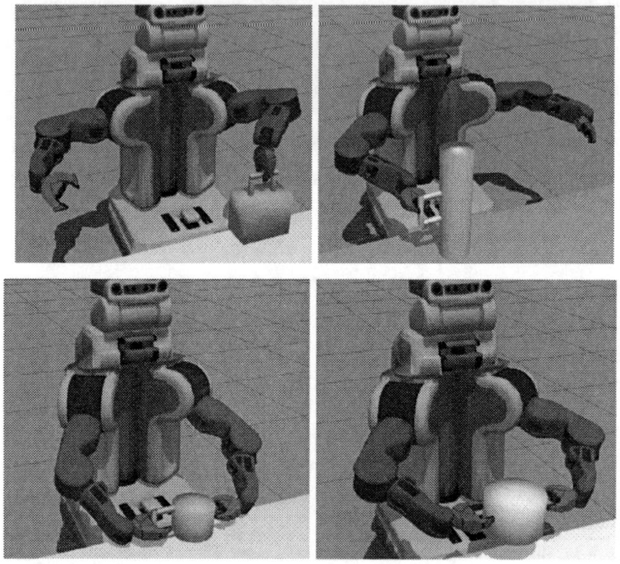

Figure 4: Four examples of the robot simulating the pick-and-place action on different objects.

While the robot performs these actions in the simulated environment (see Figure 4 for examples), the success of the actions it attempts is monitored, and a simulation success rating is recorded for each simulation run. During a simulation run, the inability to perform a required primitive action is considered a failure, ending the simulation of that scenario, resulting in a low score. Otherwise, the robot will execute the entire action script, reevaluating the overall success after each action is completed. The degree to which the action is successful is based on the post- conditions of the action. If the action is to pick up the object but the object is still on the table, then the action was not successful and the simulation success rating would be low. Some actions may not fully succeed or fully fail. For these there needs to be a measure of success. For example, if the goal of the action is to move the object one meter to the right, but the action only moved it half way, then the action is given a score representing the partial success.

3.4 Generalization by Analogy (D)

The Generalization by Analogy produces a set of generalizations of the exemplar action where each generalization is a structurally different abstraction of the action that still accomplishes the same goal. The generalizations are constructed by analogically comparing each the of counter- factual scenarios to the original exemplar. If the scenario is sufficiently similar, it is assimilated into the generalization. If it is not, then a new generalization is constructed with the scenario as the base exemplar. The algorithm described below has the following enhancements from the one proposed in [21]: (1) incorporating of simulation results and (2) constructing multiple generalizations.

Evidence from psychology (e.g. [8], [9], [14]) suggests that humans use analogical comparison in learning generalizations. Moreover, prior computational approaches have demonstrated that generalizations [12] or schemas [10] can be learned through a series of analogical comparisons. Analogical generalization is thus an alternative from of learning general concepts compared to statistical approaches which typically rely on extracting abstractions from data alone using a large amount of data. In contrast to statistical approaches, analogical generalization can learn general concepts with only a small number of exemplars, which also more closely resembles human rates of learning [15]. Another advantage of analogical generalization is that it can abstract away insignificant elements even if they are frequent enough. For example, the color of an object does not matter for the pick-and-place task and analogical generalization will be able to abstract away this insignificant property as it appears in the majority of the exemplars.

The analogical comparisons done during the generalization process we describe here are done using the Structure Mapping Engine (SME) [5], which is a computational model of analogy based on Structure mapping theory [7]. Given two descriptions – in our case, one for the original exemplar and a counter-factual – SME aligns their common structure to find a mapping between the scenarios. This mapping consists of a set of correspondences between entities, attributes, and relations in the two scenarios. Structure mapping theory defines the principles of *systematicity* and *structural consistency* [7], which then provide the basis for the scoring of the analogical similarity. This score, called the *structural evaluation score*, combined with the simulation success score gives the overall score that is used to determine whether a scenario should be integrated into a generalization.

Algorithm 1 describes the overall process of creating a set of generalizations of an action and its context (β) given a set of counter-factual scenarios (T). Each scenario (τ) is compared with each generalization (γ). If the analogical similarity combined with the simulation success produces a score above a pre-specified threshold (θ), then the scenario is assimilated into the generalization. If the scenario is not sufficiently similar to any of the generalizations, then a new generalization is created with that scenario as the base of it.

3.5 Action Selection and Execution (E)

Given a new scenario in which the robot is to accomplish a goal, the robot must select the appropriate action. Selecting a generalized action requires comparing the overall

Algorithm 1 Generalization of β given T

```
function GENERALIZE(β, T) : set of generalizations
    γ ←newGen(β)
    Γ ← {γ}
    for all τ ∈ T do
        flag ←F
        for all γ ∈ Γ do
            μ ←compare(γ, τ)
            μ ← μ× simulationSuccess(τ)
            if μ > θ then
                assimilate (τ, γ)
                flag ←T
            end if
        end for
        if ¬flag then
            γ ←newGen(τ)
            Γ ← Γ + γ
        end if
    end for
    return Γ
end function
```

context of the new scenario (including the goal, the objects involved, and the environment) to the generalized action. If the comparison concludes that there is a sufficient similarity between the generalization and the current scenario, then the generalized action is likely to be applicable. It has been shown that the specific details of the action that are necessary for executing the action may be inferred as part of an analogical comparison of the current scenario with the generalized scenario [21].

4. PROOF-OF-CONCEPT IMPLEMENTATION ON THE ROBOT

We describe here the integration of this approach into a cognitive architecture and a demonstration of learning to adapt an action to a new object.

4.1 System Architecture

To demonstrate the utility of our approach we have implemented a proof-of-concept demonstration for a simple scenario which has been implemented using the DIARC (Distributed Integrated Affect, Reflection, and Cognition) architecture [18]. A detailed view of the DIARC implementation for this demonstration can be seen in Figure 5. Here, we have highlighted three major computational groups: (1) the *Physical World*, (2) *Simulation Management and Learning*, and (3) the *Simulated World*.

The architectural components in the *Physical World* make up the core set of capabilities for the physical robot. The *Simulation Management and Learning* group is responsible for setting up each simulation environment, running the simulations, collecting simulation results, and using the collected results to learn new actions. The *Simulation World* configuration used by the *Simulation Management and Learning* group is nearly identical to that of the *Physical World*. This is critical, and ensures that the actions explored in simulation are available on the physical robot, and provides a reasonable certainty of behavioral equivalence between the physical and simulated worlds. One notable difference is the simulated vision component. Because the simulation setup component is responsible for initializing each simulation environment (based on the scene representation described above), perfect ground truth of each object and object location is known and no perceptual processing of video or point cloud data is necessary.

In addition to the DIARC cognitive architecture, we also use the Robot Operating System (ROS) to leverage existing low-level capabilities of this framework (e.g., robot model, motion planning). In particular, we make heavy use of ROS MoveIt! [19], a software package for mobile manipulation. The tight integration between DIARC and ROS is achieved through an off-line tool used to auto-generate rosjava nodes that can then be instantiated in DIARC components to create a seamless bridge between the two frameworks and allows easy use of the Willow Garage PR2 robot and Gazebo simulator.

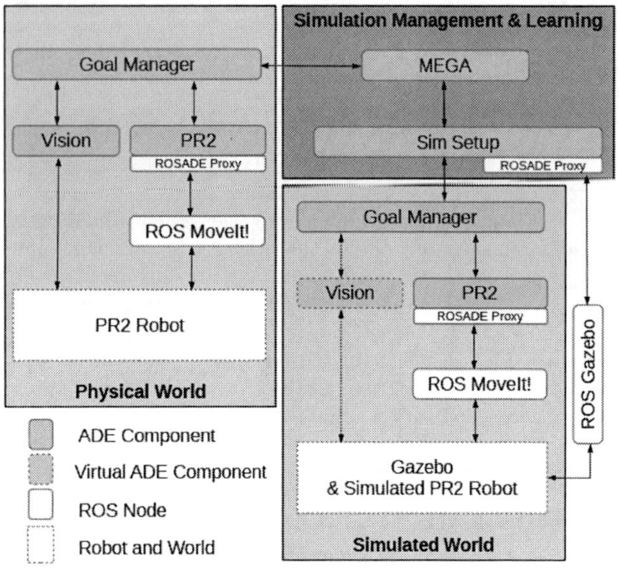

Figure 5: High-level view of the integrated architecture. The blue computational groups represent partial architecture configurations for the physical robot (left) and simulated robot (right). The salmon colored group contains novel algorithms for generalization through analogical reasoning.

4.2 Demonstration on the Robot

Our demonstration starts with an existing action representation for pick-and-place on a medical kit with one arm by the handle. While situated in an environment that contains a table and medical kit (located on the table), the physical robot begins by executing the action script to pick up the medical kit and move it aside.

This action representation is executed by the components in the *Physical World* group and requires the coordination of a goal manager component to execute the action script, and vision and robot components that provide perception and manipulation capabilities, respectively. The vision component is responsible for the detection of the table plane and medical kit (assumed to be on the table). Here, we use a Microsoft Kinect sensor to provide colored 3D point cloud (RGB-D) data, and perform plane detection to detect the table top. Once a table is detected, objects located on the table are segmented from the scene and classified against a predefined database of objects using global feature descriptors (Viewpoint Feature Histograms [17]). Once classified, an object is pose-aligned with the matching database object to transfer a list of known grasp poses to the new object. Given the information about the detected object along with information defined in the action script, the robot component is then able to plan and execute the motion commands for the pick-and-place action.

Next, the *Simulation Management and Learning* group begins the process of generalizing the given action script. The MEGA component determines the scenario (scene and action) to simulate, and then passes that information to a simulation setup component to instantiate the simulation scene. The modified action script is then passed to the goal manager component in the *Simulated World* group to execute the action in much the same way as described in the *Physical World* above. The results from the simulation run are collected by the MEGA component, and the process is repeated for each simulation. Once all the simulations have completed, the MEGA component carries out the generalization process and produces a generalized action script.

In general, the details of the scenarios instantiated and explored by the simulation process should be guided by the robot's current scenario, outcomes from previous simulation runs, and also the kinds of scenarios the robot expects to encounter. This is an open research question and we instead choose five predefined scenarios to simulate based on the scenario that is expected at the end of the generalization (i.e., picking up a cylindrical tub). For the scenario presented here, the simulations are able to achieve speeds of up to twice real time (using the Gazebo simulator on a machine with two Quad-Core i7 Xeon Processors and 24 GB RAM), and all five take less than five minutes in total. While this might seem like a considerable amount of time, the runtime would be considerably longer if these simulations were instead carried out on the physical robot. It should also be noted that each simulation was performed in serial, and the generalization process is amenable to parallel processing, where each simulation could run in parallel in future implementations.

Finally, to validate the usefulness of the generalized action script, the physical robot is presented with a new object (a small plastic tub), and the robot demonstrates that it can perform the pick-and-place action on the new object. The same process as described above for the medical kit pick-and-place is applied here, where instead the new generalized action script is executed which perform a two-handed grasp, successfully picking up the tub. If instead, the original medical kit action script was executed in an attempt to pickup the tub, a one-handed grasp would have been attempted resulting in a failed pick-and-place. A video of this proof-of-concept can be seen here: `https://youtu.be/hcm-nxnYd5k`.

5. GENERALIZATION EVALUATION

The proof-of-concept demonstrates that the robot can learn how to adapt an action to accommodate changes in the object. Our approach is capable of learning far more, including fundamental differences in the action representing *structural changes*. The purpose of this evaluation is to verify that the approach is able to recognize these structural differences and group structurally similar scenarios into the same generalization. An example of a structural difference is a step in an action being skipped, repeated, or added. If our approach were limited to learning the appropriate set of parameters to use to accomplish an action, then we would not be able to consider changes to the overall action that are not parameters. Allowing for changes in the structure of the action enables us to explore a broader range of actions that are still applicable to the scenario. The purpose of the evaluation is to confirm that the analogical generalization process will identify structural differences and construct an alternative generalization.

To evaluate this, we defined 22 scenarios to be generalized. These scenarios could be generated by the scenario generation process described above, could be an example of a scenario that has been attempted or was demonstrated, or could have been described to the robot. It does not matter what the source of the scenario is in the evaluation of the generalization. Most of the scenarios (19) resemble the original exemplar in that they had every action and every step of every action. Three of the scenarios represent pushing the object instead of picking it up and placing it. These scenarios skip the steps of lifting the arm and lowering the arm but the goal of moving the object from its original location to the new location is still achieved. All other action steps persist (reaching for the object, grasping it, moving the arm aside). Since we are strictly looking at the generalization process, we assume that each scenario would have successfully simulated. As such, the scenarios we constructed are ones in which the simulation would be successful.

When running the generalization process on the set of scenarios, two generalizations were constructed. One generalization closely resembles the initial action in that it has all of the same actions and steps. The second generalization is structurally different in that the two actions are absent. In both generalizations, the object is moved from the start location to the end location, thereby accomplishing the goal of the action. Table 2 summarizes the results of the evaluation. The number of predicates in the generalization is less than the average number of predicates in each exemplar because many of the terms are abstracted away. These predicates include insignificant descriptions of the object (e.g. color, mass, dimensions, etc.). We conclude from this evaluation that the generalizations have successfully abstracted away irrelevant information and that the generalization process is able to create generalizations for groups of scenarios that are more structurally similar.

Table 2: Summary of two generalizations constructed in evaluation. The first generalization is most similar to the original exemplar. The second generalization resembles a pushing action that still moves the object from the original location to the destination.

	Generalization 1	Generalization 2
No. exemplars	19	3
No. actions	9	7
Avg. no. predicates in exemplars	108.15	102
No. predicates in generalization	98	97

6. RELATED WORK

While there are other integrated architectures that use mental simulations (e.g., [2, 11]), none has been demonstrated to accomplish the kind of generalization learning from a single exemplar and immediate execution in a different scenario. The most closely related work is that of Kunze and his colleagues [13], where they use some of the same technologies (i.e. ROS, Gazebo, and the PR2) to conduct mental simulations in order to learn about actions.

The difference is that our work goes beyond learning parameters of actions, and attempts to construct a generalized representation of the action. This is in contrast to the approach taken by Kunze, who uses decision trees to classify data from simulations and crowdsourced data, to learn the appropriate parameters (e.g., angle to pour) for a desired outcome (e.g., size of pancake). Our approach is able to learn parameters (e.g., close position of gripper) but is also able to learn to adapt the structure of the action (e.g., adding or removing particular sub-actions). A push action learned from a pick-and-place action will, for example, have the lift-up and set-down sub-actions removed from its action representation, as they are not required to accomplish the goal.

It is this kind of structural adaptation that is necessary for two hands instead of one, or to push the object instead of pick it up. The end goal of our approach is not just to learn particular parameters (though this is a necessary step) but to learn the more general concept of an action for which a variety of parameters and sub-actions may work to accomplish the overall goal of the action.

An agent can learn a goal-directed sequence of actions using Reinforcement Learning (RL). For example, [16] demonstrates a robot learning a pick-and place behavior, but policies learned from RL are not necessarily general and applicable to a wide variety of novel scenarios. We demonstrate here that the robot can apply a generalized action in a scenario that it has not seen before.

We highlight the significance of the analogical generalization and contrast it with previous approaches to analogical generalization. Hummel and Holyoak [10] have a process of schema induction using analogical generalization, but their approach to analogy does not necessarily follow the principles defined in structure mapping theory [7]. These principles, *structural consistency* and *systematicity* enable the analogical generalization to recognize scenarios in which the actions are more structurally similar and group them into the same generalization.

Others have used the Structure Mapping Engine (SME) [5] to implement the principles of structure mapping theory in analogical generalization [12]. We are also using SME to do the analogies, and there are some similarities and differences in our generalization algorithm. In both algorithms, the similarity score generated by SME influences how or whether the exemplar is integrated into the generalization. Contrasting with previous approaches, we modify the similarity score with the simulation success rating before determining if an exemplar is to be incorporated into a generalization. There are also key differences in how an exemplar is integrated into a generalization. Previous work used a probability for each entity in a relation based on the frequency with which it occurred. The frequency of an element still affects how we incorporate elements in our algorithm, but the frequency is weighted by a significance score. Our work associates a significance score with each entity, where this score is calculated using the overall similarity score, the score associated with each mapping within a comparison, and the simulation success rating.

We also note that the generalization process we have demonstrated requires a relatively minimal amount of knowledge. Some knowledge about objects, their properties, and possible values must be known. Additionally, knowledge of the available actions to the robot are required. We contrast this with other computational uses of analogical generalization that use a large knowledge base like OpenCyc [12, 6, 3]. In comparison, we require a small amount of knowledge but are still able to construct generalizations that the robot is able to use.

7. DISCUSSION

The integrated system together with the proof-of-concept evaluation demonstrates that it is possible for a robot to generalize actions from single exemplars and successfully execute these generalized actions on novel objects. Critical for this accomplishment was the integration of various components and component algorithms that had to be connected in the right way, bridging various representational and processing gaps. While these components and their interactions thus point to an integrated architecture that could enable unprecedented rapid learning for robots in the future, the current system is not there yet as several simplifications had to be made in the process of developing it. For one, the entire architecture was known a priori which allowed all software components to be manually instantiated. A more general approach would allow the architecture to introspect on the current *Physical World* configuration and dynamically replicate this configuration in a *Simulation World* when starting the learning process. Another shortcut was the prior knowledge of grasp points on the actual objects (in the real world) and the newly generated objects in the simulation. Ideally, these points would have to be determined based on perceptions only (e.g., using algorithms like [20]). In addition, background knowledge of what dimensions are available to be altered for simulation and which are important for generalization were given to the robot ahead of time, instead of letting the robot infer them from the task or to learn them. Finally, even though our system is able to generate mupliple generalizations, the proof-of-concept only uses one generalization. Previously we have demonstrated how to use analogy to select the appropriate generalization [21].

Paramount in our approach is the analogical generalization. Strictly learning parameters to an action does not allow for the robot to learn more novel (and perhaps creative) means of accomplishing the same goal. Our evaluation confirmed that the analogical generalization process is able to identify the structural differences and construct alternative generalized actions. While our evaluation was limited to removing action steps, other forms of structural changes would also be possible. This includes changing the order of the actions, adding constraints, or using some different actions. Additional constraints may include the spatial relation between the robot and the object or that the color of the target location must match the color of the object. Using a different action brings along with it a different set of arguments, preconditions, and postconditions. This could radically change the structure of the action representation, especially if there is little overlap in the preconditions and postconditions with other actions. Future work will explore the limits of the structural variations in the actions that can be adequately generalized.

Exploring a wide range of variations can be a time consuming process. We point out that the generation of scenarios, simulating them, and generalizing does not necessarily need to occur immediately after the initial action has been demonstrated. There are three time scales on which we envision this process to occur. The first is as demonstrated in our proof-of-concept, where immediately after the action has been demonstrated a small set of scenarios are generated and simulated to that a generalization may be constructed to meet immediate needs. The exploration of possible scenarios in this case can be constrained by the requirements of the current scenario. The second time scale allows the robot to create a generalization of the action that may be needed in the near future but there is no immediate need. While the robot is idle, it can explore the state space of scenarios and produce the appropriate generalizations. At a later time (minutes, hours, or days later), the robot may finally need to perform an action similar to the originally demonstrated action. At this time the robot can examine the set of generalizations that have been produced to see if any of them are applicable. If one is applicable it can be immediately applied, and if none are applicable then it can actively generate and simulate scenarios based on the constraints of the current situation. Lastly, the robot can actively explore a broad state space, requiring significant processing resources. This approach allows the robot to consider scenarios that differ greatly from the original action. In particular, the robot can consider scenarios with more structural differences, where different primitive actions are attempted or some action is repeated multiple times. This proactive exploration of the set of possible scenarios is likely to produce numerous generalizations, where some represent novel and creative ways to accomplish the same goal as the original action.

8. CONCLUSION

In this paper we demonstrate the first integrated robotic architecture that can learn generalized actions from a single exemplar and immediately apply this knowledge to perform modified actions on similar objects in different scenarios. In a next step, we intend to improve the architecture by addressing the shortcomings mentioned in the Discussion section and by parallelizing some the mental simulations to achieve better real-time performance. We also plan to improve the algorithms for devising counter-factual exemplars by integrating them with the goal and context knowledge of the architecture to allow for better determination of relevant scenarios that should be generated. Future work will also test the limits of the analogical generalization by considering larger numbers of scenarios and ones that significantly differ from the original. Finally, we plan to combine the current system with previous systems that could learn a new action from natural language instruction and observation to demonstrate the whole sequence of learning and generalization from a single exemplar.

Acknowledgments

This work was supported by ONR BRC No. N00014-14-1-0144.

REFERENCES

[1] P. Battaglia, J. Hamrick, and J. Tenenbaum. Simulation as an engine of physical scene understanding. *PNAS*, 110:18327–18332, 2013.

[2] N. L. Cassimatis, J. G. Trafton, A. C. Schultz, and M. D. Bugajska. Integrating Cognition , Perception and Action through Mental Simulation in Robots. *Robotics and Autonomous Systems*, 49(1):13–23, 2004.

[3] M. D. Chang and K. D. Forbus. Clustering Hand-Drawn Sketches via Analogical Generalization. In *Proceedings of the Twenty-fifth Annual Conference on Innovative Applications of Artificial Intelligence*, pages 1507–1512, 2013.

[4] S. El-Khoury and A. Sahbani. A new strategy combining empirical and analytical approaches for grasping unknown 3d objects. *Robotics and Autonomous Systems*, 58(5):497–507, 2010.

[5] B. Falkenhainer, K. D. Forbus, and D. Gentner. The structure-mapping engine: Algorithm and examples. *Artificial intelligence*, 41(1):1–63, 1989.

[6] S. Friedman, J. Taylor, and K. Forbus. Learning Naive Physics Models by Analogical Generalization. In *New Frontiers in Analogy Research. Proceedings of the Second International Conference on Analogy*, pages 145–154, 2009.

[7] D. Gentnèr. Structure-mapping: A theoretical framework for analogy. *Cognitive science*, 7:155–170, 1983.

[8] D. Gentner and J. Medina. Similarity and the development of rules. *Cognition*, 65(2-3):263–97, Jan. 1998.

[9] D. Gentner and L. L. Namy. Analogical Processes in Language Learning. *Current Directions in Psychological Science*, 15(6):297–301, Dec. 2006.

[10] J. Hummel and K. Holyoak. Distributed representations of structure: A theory of analogical access and mapping. *Psychological Review*, 104:427–466, 1997.

[11] W. G. Kennedy, M. D. Bugajska, W. Adams, A. C. Schultz, and J. G. Trafton. Incorporating Mental Simulation for a More Effective Robotic Teammate. In *AAAI*, pages 1300–1305, 2008.

[12] S. E. Kuehne, K. D. Forbus, D. Gentner, and B. Quinn. SEQL: Category learning as progressive abstraction using structure mapping. *Proceedings of the 22nd Annual Meeting of the Cognitive Science Society*, pages 286–291, 2000.

[13] L. Kunze. *Naïve Physics and Commonsense Reasoning for Everyday Robot Manipulation*. PhD thesis, München, Technische Universität München, Diss., 2014, 2014.

[14] C. M. Liao and R. S. Masters. Analogy learning: a means to implicit motor learning. *Journal of sports sciences*, 19(January 2015):307–319, 2001.

[15] A. Lovett, K. Lockwood, M. Dehghani, and K. Forbus. Modeling human-like rates of learning via analogical generalization. *Analogies: Integrating Multiple Cognitive Abilities*, 5:35, 2007.

[16] M. Luciw, Y. Sandamirskaya, S. Kazerounian, J. Schmidhuber, and G. Schoner. Reinforcement and Shaping in Learning Action Sequences with Neural Dynamics. In *Development and Learning and Epigenetic Robotics (ICDL-Epirob), 2014 Joint IEEE International Conferences on*, pages 48–55, Chicago, 2014. IEEE.

[17] R. B. Rusu, G. R. Bradski, R. Thibaux, and J. M. Hsu. Fast 3d recognition and pose using the viewpoint feature histogram. In *IROS*, pages 2155–2162. IEEE, 2010.

[18] M. Scheutz, G. Briggs, R. Cantrell, E. Krause, T. Williams, , and R. Veale. Novel mechanisms for natural human-robot interactions in the diarc architecture. In *Proceedings of AAAI Workshop on Intelligent Robotic Systems*, 2013.

[19] I. A. Sucan and S. Chitta. Moveit! http://moveit.ros.org, 2015. Accessed: 2015-09-01.

[20] A. ten Pas and R. Platt. Using geometry to detect grasps in 3d point clouds. In *International Symposium on Robotics Reserach*, 2015.

[21] J. R. Wilson and M. Scheutz. Analogical generalization of activities from single demonstration. In *Advances in Artificial Intelligence*, 2014.

Online Planning for Collaborative Search and Rescue by Heterogeneous Robot Teams

Zoltán Beck
Electronics and Computer Science
University of Southampton
Southampton, UK
zb1f12@ecs.soton.ac.uk

Luke Teacy
Electronics and Computer Science
University of Southampton
Southampton, UK
wtlt@ecs.soton.ac.uk

Alex Rogers
Department of Computer Science
University of Oxford
Oxford, UK
alex.rogers@cs.ox.ac.uk

Nicholas R. Jennings
Electronics and Computer Science
University of Southampton
Southampton, UK
nrj@ecs.soton.ac.uk

ABSTRACT

Collaboration is essential for effective performance by groups of robots in disaster response settings. Here we are particularly interested in *heterogeneous* robots that collaborate in complex scenarios with incomplete, dynamically changing information. In detail, we consider a search and rescue setting, where robots with different capabilities work together to accomplish tasks (rescue) and find information about further tasks (search) at the same time. The state of the art for such collaboration is robot control based on independent planning for robots with different capabilities and typically incorporates uncertainty with only a limited scope. In contrast, in this paper, we create a *joint plan* to optimise all robots' actions incorporating uncertainty about the future information gain of the robots. We evaluate our planner's performance in settings based on real disasters and find that our approach decreases the response time by 20-25% compared to state-of-the-art approaches. In addition, practical constraints are met in terms of time and resource utilisation.

Keywords

multi-robot systems, robot coordination, online planning, disaster response, search and rescue, hindsight optimisation

1. INTRODUCTION

In recent years, there has been an ongoing focus within the rescue robotics research domain to use robots in professional disaster response [20, 21]. These initial deployments use individual robots that are labour intensive to control and are operated independently. This places a high demand on human expertise, which is a limited resource in disaster response. Thus, to decrease this workload, there is a need to develop semi-autonomous teams of robots, that can make their own decisions and coordinate to make best use of their combined resources [27]. To tackle this challenge, researchers typically focus on multi-robot collaboration within known settings, where the possible robot actions are defined as a set of tasks [11, 19, 22]. However, in most real-world settings, there is a significant amount of uncertainty present. For example, information about a disaster site develops gradually during disaster relief, thus initially there is often very little certainty about the locations of people requiring assistance (e.g. damaged buildings, trapped victims, or supply shortages). In addition, as new technologies allow a diverse group of robots with differing capabilities to be deployed, they are required to work together, combining their individual capabilities to be more efficient [6]. A good example for such complex settings is *Search And Rescue* (SAR), where robots cooperate to find and aid victims [18]. In this setting, some robots may be specialised for fast exploration (e.g. by having advanced mobility or high resolution sensors), while others are capable of aiding victims (e.g. by having good manoeuvrability or specific actuators).

Existing solutions that tackle collaboration in the face of uncertain information are typically limited to simple exploration or target search problems [3, 7, 29, 31]. Moreover, the use of generic temporal planners rapidly becomes intractable for such problems [9] unless applied in a domain-specific manner [3]. Finally, domain specific approaches rarely involve complex action relations, such as task workflows where the actions of some robots are built on the actions of others. When they do so, decomposition techniques are applied to decrease the problem complexity [15, 33], or simple heuristics are applied to enhance similar collaboration [5]. Such approaches often lead to low quality solutions, because vital action dependencies across different roles are not taken into account during the optimisation.

Particularly in SAR, collaboration between different robots is vital for good performance when using a diverse group of robots to perform search operations and rescue actions at the same time. When using decomposition planning, rescue robots cannot build on the plans of search robots to identify valuable actions, and similarly, search robots cannot priori-

Appears in: *Proceedings of the 15th International Conference on Autonomous Agents and Multiagent Systems (AAMAS 2016), J. Thangarajah, K. Tuyls, S. Marsella, C. Jonker (eds.), May 9–13, 2016, Singapore.*

tise their search according to the actions of the rescue robots. The main challenge is that the problem of multi-robot exploration (search) and multi-robot task allocation (rescue) are both complex optimisation problems [14]; especially when combined within an uncertain domain. For this reason joint planning for multiple robots involving action dependencies in an uncertain setting has not been achieved. In addition, in line with the dynamic nature of disaster response, incoming information from first responders can significantly change the situation from one moment to another. For this reason, a computationally efficient online planning approach is necessary to ensure rapid response from the system.

To address these shortcomings, we offer a novel planning approach for multi-role robot collaboration under uncertainty that provides the benefits of collaborative planning while keeping the computation time at an acceptable level. Uncertain information is incorporated in our planning process using *hindsight optimisation* (HOP) [32] that allows us to apply computationally efficient deterministic planning techniques. To create a joint plan for different robots, the individual plans of homogeneous robot groups are optimised, with regards to the plans of the other groups as constraints, in an iterative process. In particular, we introduce temporal constraints (search precedes rescue) over the stochastic action domain. As a result, we can generate plans for robots assigned to rescue operations even before the final locations of those rescues are confirmed. Similarly, we can generate plans for robots assigned to searching for casualties, taking account of the current plans of rescue robots that will be tasked with rescuing them. We show that joint planning improves the overall SAR performance against the state-of-the-art decomposition approach in simulations based on two real-world disaster scenarios (on an earthquake in Haiti and an industrial spill in Hungary). In so doing, we make the following contributions to the state of the art:

- We are the first to propose a method for homogeneous Multi-Robot Task Allocation (MRTA) given an arbitrary task distribution and continuous action space (UMRTA problem). In detail, we use HOP to assign a task or a motion direction for each robot using an MRTA scheduler.
- We offer the first online planning approach to create a joint plan under uncertainty for distinct groups of search robots and rescue robots in a SAR scenario. As a result, rescue plans are made over an uncertain set of rescue locations and iteratively optimised along with search plans.
- We evaluate the performance of the planning approaches against the state-of-the-art decomposition planning approach in realistic SAR settings [2, 24, 30]. In particular, we find that the time of the rescues are reduced by 20-25% with our joint planning compared to decomposition planning.

In the following, we introduce the background of this work (Section 2). Next, the underlying basic task allocation problems are explained (Section 3), then the SAR collaboration problem itself is defined (Section 4). After that, we present the state-of-the-art approach and our joint planning approach to solve this problem (Section 5). This is followed by the experimental evaluation of these approaches (Section 6). Finally, we provide concluding remarks and outline directions for future work (Section 7).

2. BACKGROUND

There are two main methodologies for mobile robot (or autonomous vehicle) collaboration. The first is task allocation, where the problem is allocating a set of robots to accomplish tasks, and it is well defined in the literature. In particular, [14] introduces the family of *Multi-Robot Task Allocation* (MRTA) problems. Specifically, when coordinating mobile robots, tasks typically consist of going to a specific location and perform an operation in its proximity. The second formulation of the spatial collaboration of robots is during searching an area. In these settings, an importance or intensity map contains the current state of the search and the knowledge about the area. The robots travel on this map and update the intensity values according to the sensed values. A simple and robust way to guide the robots is to apply gradient descent on this map [12, 31]. When the motion capabilities are limited as for fixed-wing *Unmanned Aerial Vehicles* (UAVs), performing a tree search within the feasible paths can be performed to control the vehicles [29]. To better capture the random outcomes of actions probabilistic planning can be applied. Unfortunately, to use such techniques in an online fashion, the action space is significantly reduced by either discretising the problem [7], or limiting the action space to a set of fixed search patterns [3].

When multiple groups of robots collaborate at the disaster site, the collaboration of groups becomes important besides the task allocation for the individual groups. Some approaches investigate multiple task types and their relations and apply the task allocation for the whole group. For example, [19] represents the complex relations between tasks as a tree, and subtrees are allocated to individual robots. However, this assumes that the robots are capable of performing all tasks within a subtree, that is not the case when the different robot platforms are specific for a certain type of task. When using aerial robots, the amount of instrumentation on a platform is very limited, so distinct groups of robots performing tasks at a different level is more likely, as exemplified by [8].

In such settings, the most common approach of collaboration is independent action planning. In this vein, [10] performs a search and rescue like mission using multiple UAVs, but search and rescue are separated in time. There are examples of robots with different capabilities operating at the same time in a search and surveillance setting [33, 15]. However, the planning for the different robot platforms is separate, only the outcome of their actions are shared between all robots.

Some examples exist for collaborative planning with different robots, [5] uses the probabilistic plans of a ground robot to find areas to scout with a UAV, and in [16] the allocations of different tasks are planned sequentially to allocate robots for a complex mission. However, these approaches are limited in terms of taking vital action dependencies into account by all robot groups, as they do not create a *joint plan* for all kinds of robots in a way that all plans are optimised regarding the plans of all other robots. In the rest of the paper, we introduce an online planner that creates a joint plan for search and rescue robots, and meets practical constraints in terms of computation time and resource utilisation.

3. TASK ALLOCATION

As introduced below, a fundamental problem underlying multi-robot collaboration is task allocation. In this section, we first define the *Multi-Robot Task Allocation* (MRTA) problem in a SAR setting, then we propose an extension to it, the *Uncertain Multi-Robot Task Allocation* (UMRTA) problem introducing uncertainty in the tasks.

3.1 MRTA

In this paper, we investigate MRTA with Single-Task robots, Single-Robot tasks, and Time-extended Assignment (ST-SR-TA) [14]. This means that each robot can do a single task at once, each task can be done by a single robot, and the robot actions are considered in an extended time horizon (task schedule instead of a single task).

In our context, tasks are divided into two types: *search tasks* (e.g. searching a specific area for victims, or assessing collapsed buildings) or *rescue tasks* (e.g. rescue a victim, or secure an unsafe structure). By performing these tasks, the robots aim to maximise the number of successful rescues, which must first be discovered by undertaking search tasks. We model this as a linearly decreasing utility function[1]:

$$U(\tau) = U_0 - \gamma t(\tau), \tag{1}$$

$$\sum_{\tau \in \mathbf{T}} U(\tau) = U_0 |\mathbf{T}| - \sum_{\tau \in \mathbf{T}} \gamma t(\tau), \tag{2}$$

where $\mathbf{T}$ is the set of tasks, $t(\tau)$ represents the time of completion of task τ, U_0 is the initial utility of a task, and γ is the utility decrease factor. Moreover, each of these tasks has a specific location which the robots have to travel to in order to complete it. The time required to travel between the specific tasks can be derived from the motion model of the robot and the traversability of the area. These times can be regarded as necessary setup times to execute a task.

This MRTA problem can be formulated as a Parallel Machine Scheduling Problem (PMSP) of the following format: $P/\mathrm{ST_{sd}}/\sum T_j$ [1]. In particular it is an identical machine scheduling problem with sequence dependent setup times where the aim is to minimise the total tardiness of the jobs with a common due-date at $t = 0$ ($T_j = t(\tau_j)$). The complexity of the problem for a single machine and sequence independent setup times ($1/\mathrm{ST_{si}}/\sum T_j$) is polynomial when the due-date is common, however given sequence dependent setup times ($1/\mathrm{ST_{sd}}/\sum T_j$) it becomes NP-hard [25]. Therefore the MRTA problem, that is the parallel machine version of the above, is also NP-hard.

In the following, we define the MRTA problem as a tuple $\langle \mathbf{R}, \mathbf{T} \rangle$, where $\mathbf{R}$ is the set of robots, and $\mathbf{T}$ is the set of tasks. The solution consists of an assigned task (x_R) for each robot (R):

$$\mathbf{X} = \{x_R \in \mathbf{T} : \forall R \in \mathbf{R}\}.$$

3.2 UMRTA

In realistic settings, however, there might not be complete information about the tasks. In this case, the uncertainty about the tasks can be represented as a probability distribution. We define the UMRTA problem as an MRTA problem ($\langle \mathbf{R}, \mathbf{T} \rangle$) with a random variable representing the set of tasks: $\langle \mathbf{R}, \mathcal{T} \rangle$. The random task set ($\mathcal{T}$) breaks into a set of known tasks ($\mathbf{T}$) and a set of uncertain tasks ($\mathcal{T}^+$): $\mathcal{T} = \mathbf{T} \cup \mathcal{T}^+$.

In this case the optimisation maximises the expected overall utility gain. Accordingly, Equation 2 changes as follows:

$$\mathop{\mathbf{E}}_{\mathcal{T}^+} \left[\sum\nolimits_{\tau \in \mathcal{T}} U(\tau) \right] \tag{3}$$

In contrast to the MRTA problem, the solution may contain a general motion direction for a robot ($\mathbf{D} = [0, 2\pi)$) besides the set of known tasks ($\mathbf{T}$). This allows us to optimise the robot's position given the distribution of uncertain tasks to be closer to these tasks when they are discovered. Of course, these directions need to be reassigned in a timely manner to navigate the robots efficiently. As a result, the solutions will have the following form:

$$\mathbf{X} = \{x_R \in \mathbf{T} \cup \mathbf{D} : \forall R \in \mathbf{R}\}.$$

4. SAR COLLABORATION PROBLEM

Having described the components of the collaboration problem, we now present the complete heterogeneous robot collaboration problem in a SAR setting. Because search and rescue require a different set of skills from the robots (high speed and advanced sensors for search, good manoeuvrability and actuators for rescue), they split into a group of search robots and a group of rescue robots. Search robots find rescue locations during their search process, while rescue robots move around the disaster area and perform rescues at these locations.

In this setting, the collaboration breaks into a task allocation problem for the search robots and another one for the rescue robots. The search tasks are known beforehand, while rescue tasks are initially unknown, and will be gradually discovered by search tasks. This means that search can be formulated as a MRTA problem, while rescue as an UMRTA problem. For simplicity, we assume uniform utility and process time for rescue tasks with random 2D locations. Assuming complete spatial randomness, the task locations are the outcome of a non-homogeneous spatial Poisson process [17] with intensity function λ. During SAR, this distribution frequently changes as new information is introduced about the disaster site, or as a region is searched. Within our evaluation we chose a simplistic observation model, meaning that when a region is searched, all tasks within that region are discovered, and the intensity for undiscovered tasks within that region thus drops to zero.

Formally, the search MRTA problem is determined by the set of search robots ($\mathbf{R}_s$) and search tasks ($\mathbf{T}_s$), while the rescue UMRTA problem is determined by the set of rescue robots ($\mathbf{R}_r$) and the random set of rescue tasks ($\mathcal{T}_r$). The rescue tasks can be divided into a set of known ($\mathbf{T}_r$) and a random set of unknown tasks, that is a Poisson point process ($\mathcal{T}_r^+ \sim \mathit{Poisson}(\lambda)$). Additionally, the connection between the search and the rescue problem can be given by the $\mathit{exploredby} : \mathbf{T}_s \times \mathcal{T}_r \to \{0, 1\}$ function that indicates if a rescue task is found when a search task is performed (if it falls within the associated area).

Accordingly, the SAR collaboration problem is defined by $\langle \mathbf{R}_s, \mathbf{T}_s, \mathbf{R}_r, \mathcal{T}_r, \mathit{exploredby} \rangle$ and the solutions will have the following form:

$$\mathbf{X} = \{x_R \in \mathbf{T}_s : \forall R \in \mathbf{R}_s\} \cup \{x_R \in \mathbf{T}_r \cup \mathbf{D} : \forall R \in \mathbf{R}_r\}.$$

[1]Search tasks are not directly associated with a utility, but instead are responsible for discovering rescue tasks (details below).

5. ONLINE PLANNING APPROACHES

We now introduce three planning methods for the above problem: the first approach represents the state-of-the-art in collaborative online planning, the second uses HOP to solve the UMRTA problem, and the third approach creates a joint plan for the linked MRTA and UMRTA problem.

5.1 Decomposition Planning with Gradient Descent

This approach represents our benchmark, where the MRTA problem of search and the UMRTA problem of rescue are solved independently using existing approaches. We use Shortest Adjusted Processing Time first (SAPT) algorithm to solve the task allocation as tardiness scheduling problem ($P/\mathrm{ST}_{\mathrm{sd}}/\sum T_j$). The SAPT scheduling is optimal for the sequence-independent single machine case ($1/\mathrm{ST}_{\mathrm{si}}/\sum T_j$), but nevertheless provides a good heuristic in the sequence-dependent settings [25, 26]. In detail, we define the adjusted processing time as follows:

$$AP\left(\tau_i, [s, \tau_j]\right) = AP\left(\tau_j, s\right) + trav(\tau_i, \tau_j) + P(\tau_i). \tag{4}$$

$AP\left(\tau, s\right)$ represents the adjusted processing time of task τ after schedule s ($t(\tau)$ in Equation 1, if the schedule is followed by the robot), $[s, \tau]$ stands for a schedule where task τ is inserted at the end of schedule s, $trav(\tau_i, \tau_j)$ is the necessary travel time between task τ_i and τ_j, and $P(\tau)$ is the process time of task τ.

As a standard online planner, the SAPT scheduler is applied to provide a solution both for the search MRTA problem $\langle \mathbf{R}_s, \mathbf{T}_s \rangle$ and the known part of the rescue problem $\langle \mathbf{R}_r, \mathbf{T}_r \rangle$. This is to prioritise the known tasks in the optimisation, as can be found in the literature for similar problem settings [28, 33]. In case of idle rescue robots (no known tasks are assigned by the SAPT scheduler), gradient descent is applied to maximise the intensity at the robot's location, and to orientate the robots towards central areas. In detail, rescue robots with no assigned tasks will travel:

- towards the nearest point of the disaster area if outside,
- along the gradient of the task distribution intensity,
- towards the mean of the task distribution at zero gradient.

5.2 Decomposition Planning with HOP

In this approach, instead of ignoring the task distribution for the planning of the rescue, HOP is used to solve the UMRTA problem. HOP has been shown to effectively incorporate probabilistic information for a similar problem domain for a generic temporal planner [7]. Unfortunately the introduced temporal planner does not scale well with the size of the problem due to the iteration through the possible resulting states. By contrast, we present a HOP planner that can solve the above presented UMRTA problem with continuous state space. This planner, instead of replanning for all the possible future states, determines the best action using only a single solution for the current state.

The HOP planner incorporates the distribution of unknown task locations, using a Monte Carlo simulation. It provides solutions for independent samples of the distribution as if it was a deterministic planning problem (MRTA in this case). As a result, the maximisation criterion (Equation 3) is approximated as follows:

$$\mathop{\mathbf{E}}_{\mathcal{T}_r^+}\left[\sum_{\tau \in \mathcal{T}_r} U(\tau)\right] \approx \frac{1}{N}\sum_{i}^{N} \sum_{\tau \in \mathbf{T}_r \cup \mathbf{t}_r^i} U_{sch}(\tau) \tag{5}$$

In detail, the expected utility is estimated by the average of the utilities ($U_{sch}(\tau)$) determined by the SAPT MRTA scheduler output schedules ($s_{R,i}$) for N samples ($\mathbf{t}_r^i$) of the Poisson process ($\mathcal{T}_r^+$). Note that the MRTA scheduler can be replaced with any MRTA solver for a specific application (e.g. an auction-based negotiation combined with RRT path planning [22]).

The maximisation is applied on this utility estimation, and as a result rescue robot actions are determined. This process is detailed in Algorithm 1.

Algorithm 1 HOP UMRTA Solver

Require: $\mathbf{T}_r$: set of known rescue tasks
Require: $\mathbf{R}_r$: set of rescue robots
Require: N: size of the Monte Carlo simulation
Require: $s_{R,i}, \forall R \in \mathbf{R}_r, i \in \{1..N\}$: hindsight schedules
1: **for all** $R \in \mathbf{R_r}$ **do**
2: $\quad \tau^* = \arg\max_{\tau \in \mathbf{T}_r} \mathrm{count}_{i=1}^{N} \left(\tau = first(s_{R,i})\right)$
3: $\quad$ **if** $\mathrm{count}_{i=1}^{N} \left(\tau^* = first(s_{R,i})\right) > \frac{N}{2}$ **then**
4: $\quad\quad x_R \leftarrow \tau^*$ ▷ assign task τ^* to robot R
5: $\quad$ **else**
6: $\quad\quad d = \mathrm{mean}_{i=1}^{N} \left[w(s_{R,i}) * dir(R, first(s_{R,i}))\right]$
7: $\quad\quad x_R \leftarrow d$ ▷ assign direction d to robot R
8: $\quad$ **end if**
9: **end for**
Ensure: $\mathbf{X} = \{x_R : \forall R \in \mathbf{R}_r\}$: chosen actions for robots

Specifically, function $first(s)$ returns the first task in schedule s, and $dir(R, \tau)$ calculates the direction that robot R has to take to move towards task τ. In general, for each robot, the aggregation will assign either the most commonly assigned first task in the schedules (τ^*) to the robot, or the weighted average of the direction of the first assigned tasks. In detail, the algorithm iterates over all robots, and finds the most commonly assigned first task ($\tau^* \in \mathbf{T}_r$) in its schedules (Line 2). If it is assigned as first in the majority of the schedules, the robot's instruction will be to execute task $x_R = \tau^*$, otherwise it will be a general heading direction ($d \in \mathbf{D}$) as in Line 6. This direction is a weighted average of the first assigned tasks' directions, where the weight represents the number of tasks in a schedule ($w(s) = |s|$). This weight tells how many tasks are going to be delayed if the execution of the first task is delayed.

This weighted average will provide the *optimal direction of movement* to maximise the utility estimate in Equation 5. This, of course, assumes hindsight knowledge of the random task set for each sample ($\mathbf{t}_r^i$), as it is a HOP technique. The proof of the optimality is omitted due to space limitations[2].

5.3 Joint Planning with HOP

This approach creates a joint plan for the search and rescue robots via a negotiation process[3]. At each step of the nego-

[2]It can be found in http://bit.ly/20ZD3wn.

[3]The iteration length within 5 and 9 does not change the overall result significantly, so we chose 5 iterations in the evaluation.

tiation, one of the robot groups (search or rescue) optimises their plan according to the current plan of the other group. This way, the solution quality can be further improved by taking the relations between the search and rescue activities into account (search tasks find rescue tasks within an area).

Rescue Planning Optimisation uses the search plan to introduce a constraint to the execution time of sampled rescue tasks. Accordingly, the adjusted processing time in Equation 4 changes as follows:

$$AP'(\tau, s) = \max\left(AP(\tau, s), cstr(\tau)\right). \qquad (6)$$

Function $cstr(\tau)$ is the time when task τ is discovered according to the current search plan (temporal constraint). In brief, the execution time of each "hindsight task" is delayed until discovered according to the current search plan. The MRTA scheduling problem is still solved using SAPT with the adjusted processing time in Equation 6.

Also, the weights (w) in Line 6 of Algorithm 1 need adjustment to ensure optimality. Because the tasks that are delayed due to the temporal constraints do not increase the urgency of a schedule, they should not be counted in the weight. Accordingly, $w(s)$ equals the number of consecutive non-delayed tasks at the beginning of schedule s.

Search Planning Optimisation does not simply minimise the execution time of the search tasks using the plan of the other group. The subject of optimisation is to improve rescue, as the utility comes from the rescue tasks. Therefore, the optimisation is applied to minimise the delay introduced on the rescue tasks by the temporal constraints (introduced in Equation 6). Due to the nonlinearity of this measure, building an increasing plan by adding tasks to the end of each schedule (as in SAPT scheduling), would not result in a good quality solution. For this reason, a greedy method sequentially introduces tasks and inserts them to a position of a schedule with minimal cost, as in the MURDOCH negotiation [13], detailed in Algorithm 2.

Algorithm 2 Search Plan Optimisation

Require: $\mathbf{T}_s$: set of search tasks
Require: $\mathbf{I} = \{\mathbf{t}_\tau : \forall\tau \in \mathbf{T}_s\}$: timings from rescue
Require: $\mathbf{R}_s$: set of search robots
1: $\mathbf{T}' \leftarrow \mathbf{T}_s$: unassigned search tasks
2: $s_r \leftarrow \emptyset, \forall r \in \mathbf{R}_s$: robot schedules
3: **while** $\mathbf{T}' \neq \emptyset$ **do**
4: $\quad \tau^* = \arg\min_{\forall\tau\in\mathbf{T}'} \min \mathbf{t}_\tau$
5: $\quad \langle r^*, i^* \rangle = \arg\min_{\langle r,i \rangle;\forall r\in\mathbf{R}_s,\forall i\leq|s_r|\in\mathbb{N}} \Delta(s_r, \tau^*, i)$
6: $\quad s_{r^*} \leftarrow insert(s_{r^*}, \tau^*, i^*)$ ▷ Insert τ^* to schedule
7: $\quad \mathbf{T}' \leftarrow \mathbf{T}' \setminus \{\tau^*\}$ ▷ Remove from unassigned tasks
8: **end while**
Ensure: $\mathbf{S} = \{s_r : \forall r \in \mathbf{R}_s\}$

Here, $\mathbf{t}_\tau$ is a set of planned rescue times for sampled rescue tasks discovered by task τ, and the $insert(s, \tau, i)$ function inserts task τ into schedule s to the ith location. Besides that, $D(s)$ estimates the delay caused by schedule s:

$$D(s) = \sum_{\tau\in s}\sum_{q\in\mathbf{t}_\tau} \max(0, t(\tau, s) - q), \qquad (7)$$

$$\Delta(s_r, \tau, i) = D(insert(s_r, \tau, i)) - D(s_r). \qquad (8)$$

In Equation 7, $t(\tau, s)$ denotes the execution time of task τ within schedule s. In brief, Algorithm 2 inserts available tasks – starting with the most urgent ones – into the search robots' schedule using minimal insertion. Specifically, the most urgent task is selected as the one with the soonest rescue time (Line 4). Having selected this task, the best insert location is determined within the current schedules (Line 5). The best position is determined by minimising the delay estimate's increase (Equation 8) computed based on the information from the rescue robots' plan ($\mathbf{I} = \{\mathbf{t}_\tau : \forall\tau \in \mathbf{T}\}$).

6. EXPERIMENTAL EVALUATION

The evaluation resembles a currently feasible robotic search and rescue setting based on feedback from Rescue Global[4]. In this setting we rely on aerial robots (UAVs) only, due to their successful disaster response deployments as opposed to ground robots. Specifically, fixed-wing UAVs are able to rapidly fly over the disaster site, so they take the role of search robots; small rotary-wing UAVs have high manoeuvrability and are able to approach objects on the ground, therefore they are responsible for rescue tasks. In detail, fixed-wings search the area by taking aerial images. These images are analysed (by either a professional or computer vision) to point out sights of interest (e.g. possible victim locations, dangerous buildings, or critical supplies). The sights of interest are visited by rotary-wing UAVs to provide detailed, close-up video feeds to first responders. This procedure allows first responders to assess an area and be able to locate some high priority tasks before accessing the disaster site.

In disaster response, SAR can be very different depending on the cause of the disaster (e.g. earthquake, extreme weather, or industrial disaster), the impact of the disaster or the population density of the area. For this reason, our experiments include two very different settings taken from the Ajka Alumina Plant industrial spill (2010) (Figure 3) and the Haiti earthquake (2010) (Figure 2). In detail, the former has a sparse effect spreading along a large region, while the latter represents a larger impact disaster in a smaller area. The area size and the density of tasks will determine if rescue agents spend more time moving between rescue locations or performing rescues. In the following we detail the settings and the numerical results of the conducted experiment.

6.1 Experimental Setup

For both disasters, there are three different settings with different levels of available information. In each setting, there is a rescue task intensity map (λ) that represents the prior information about the disaster impact:

- *Ground Truth*: The intensity of the rescue locations at the disaster site is based on detailed assessment.
  - *Ajka* scenario: A combination of the built-up regions and the flooded area (with decreasing intensity with the distance from the source) covering 5.1 km^2 taken from [2]. (Figure 1d)
  - *Haiti* scenario: Victim intensity in a search sector of Port au Prince based on a building damage assessment with intensities according to Table 1 covering 0.106 km^2 taken from [30]. (Figure 1a)
- *Preliminary*: There is some preliminary information about the possible outcome of the disaster containing

[4]http://www.rescueglobal.org/

Tag	Description	E[#rescues]
Grade 1	Negligible to slight damage	0.002
Grade 2	Moderate damage	0.004
Grade 3	Substantial to heavy damage	0.01
Grade 4	Very heavy damage	0.04
Grade 5	Destruction	0.125

Table 1: Haiti assessment [30] damage levels and expected number of rescues[5] at each tag location

Parameter	Search Robots	Rescue Robots
Robot speed	25 m/s	10 m/s
Task length	0 s	30 s

(a) Robot parameters

Parameter	Ajka Scenario	Haiti Scenario
Search grid spacing	440 m	105 m
Search imagery area	530×530 m	125×125 m
Simulation time step	3 s	1 s
#samples (N)	100	100
#search robots	2	2
#rescue robots	4	8
#search tasks	400, 120, 79	95, 95, 87
#rescue tasks	20 (avg.)	61 (avg.)

(b) Scenario parameters

Table 2: Simulation parameters

less information than the ground truth intensity. This is the realistic case when disaster impact estimations are available due to disaster resilience [4].

- *Ajka* scenario: A combination of the built-up regions and the results of a spill simulation for a similar spill incident covering a larger possible area (12.7 km^2) taken from [24]. (Figure 1e)
- *Haiti* scenario: Uniform inside the search sector (0.875 km^2) with higher intensities around 20 simulated report locations (drawn from the *Ground Truth* intensity). (Figure 1b)

• *Blank*: There is no information about the task density other than the search area, the intensity is uniform.

- *Ajka* scenario: A uniform intensity over a large rectangular area (78.5 km^2) above the possible area of the industrial spill. (Figure 1c)
- *Haiti* scenario: A uniform intensity inside a search sector (0.875 km^2) in Port au Prince. (Figure 1f)

The performance of the different planning approaches are compared in simulation for 128 different disaster outcomes for both scenarios. Each outcome is an independent sample from a Poisson process with the *Ground Truth* intensity introduced above. Each approach is tested with the three different levels of available information independently.

During the experiments, we simulate robots performing collaborative SAR in two groups: search robots and rescue robots. Table 2 details the chosen parameters for these simulations. The parameters are chosen to match realistic settings as much as possible. The parameters for the two scenarios differ due to the differences in the two disaster environments. Specifically, the Haiti sector is a densely populated urban area where the large number of features require sub-cm resolution, while large fields covered with red mud near Ajka require lower resolution imagery for victim search. The search imagery area size was chosen according to these measures to include a similar number of features. Consequently, the simulation time step is chosen in a way that the search robots need 4-6 time steps to travel between two search locations. This allows a human supervisor to intervene between actions, and also to interact with a reasonably responsive decision making system [23]. However, varying the simulation time step did not change the result significantly. Search tasks are located on grid points where the intensity is greater than zero ($\lambda > 0$) for the corresponding area.

[5]Expected number of points in a Poisson point process equals the integral of the intensity function within an area.

The start locations of the UAVs can be seen in Figure 2 and in Figure 3 over the satellite imagery of the area. In detail, the area marked with blue edge is the edge of the Blank search area, yellow markers show rotary-wing start locations, and green rectangles mark the start location of fixed wing UAVs. The fixed-wing start locations are placed on possible take-off locations such as nearby airports and intact straight roads, while rotary-wing start locations are chosen at rubble-free locations where the infrastructure can be set up for controlling them.

Each simulation instance used a single core of an Intel Xeon E5-2670 processor. The computation time is measured for each approach to evaluate computational feasibility.

In the following, the results of the conducted experiments are introduced. The statistical significance is tested by comparing the relative performance against our approach for each run that used the same rescue locations by a one-sample t-test. Specifically, we use the average time of the rescue operations as a performance indicator. This gives a direct comparison of the overall utility gained by the different approaches according to the utility definition (Equation 2). The lower this metric, the higher the SAR performance.

6.2 Experimental Results

In this section the performance and the computation time is evaluated for the previously detailed approaches in the above settings. Within the comparison (Figure 4 and 5), there is a two character code identifying each test case, assembled by the first letter of the information representation and the number of the planning approach. The notation of the case depending on available information is the following:

Bx: *Blank* intensity map,

Px: *Preliminary* intensity map,

Gx: *Ground Truth* intensity map.

Likewise, the three collaboration approaches are:

x1: *Decomposition Planning with Gradient Descent*,

x2: *Decomposition Planning with HOP*,

x3: *Joint Planning with HOP*.

For instance, "G3" stands for the *Ground Truth* information representation and *Joint Planning with HOP* approach.

The **Overall Performance Comparison** can be seen in Figure 4, while the relative performance to our approach

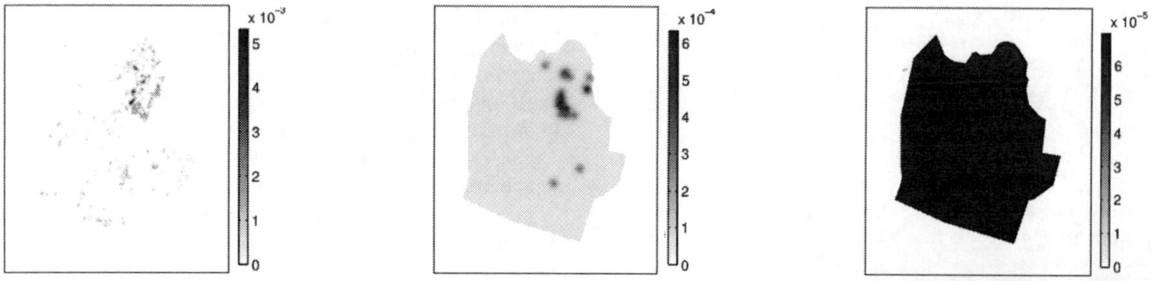

(a) Haiti Ground Truth intensity (b) Haiti Pleriminary intensity (c) Haiti Blank intensity

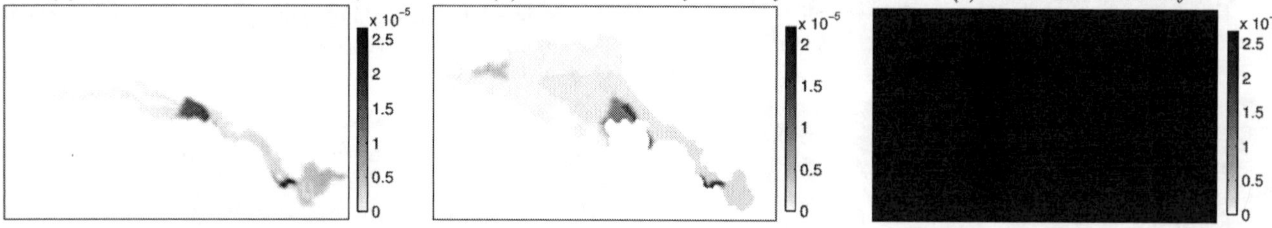

(d) Ajka Ground Truth intensity (e) Ajka Pleriminary intensity (f) Ajka Blank intensity

Figure 1: Intensity maps (units are task/m^2)

Figure 2: UAV start locations for the Haiti scenario

Figure 3: UAV start locations for the Ajka scenario

	Blank		Prelim.		G. Truth	
Approach	Ajka	Haiti	Ajka	Haiti	Ajka	Haiti
Dec. GD	2	<1	<1	<1	<1	<1
Dec. HOP	18	40	8	43	10	39
Joint HOP	**4541**	210	214	212	97	159

Table 3: Average computation time in each time step [ms]

can be seen in Figure 5. Firstly, an improvement of 15-45% in the average rescue time can be observed between the *Decomposition Planning with Gradient Descent* (the state-of-the-art for complex collaborative planning under uncertainty) and our *Joint Planning with HOP* approach for the cases with sufficient available information. In more detail, the *Joint Planning with HOP* approach (P3 or G3) performs significantly better than the other approaches for the same problem setting (P1-2 or G1-2) as the confidence regions are above 1. For the realistic case of inaccurate preliminary information, the rescues are performed 26% earlier for the Ajka scenario, and 22% earlier for the Haiti scenario compared to the gradient descent approach. However, the joint planning approach does not perform well for the *Blank* settings (B3). These settings do not provide enough information about the task distribution for significant improvements using sophisticated planning. In this case the solution for search becomes trivial as the lawnmower pattern (the result of SAPT scheduling) is optimal [9].

The **Computation Time** of the different approaches is listed in Table 3. The values are significantly below the couple of seconds time limit to result in a reasonably responsive system [23]. The only case when it is around the limit is in the *Blank* setting within the Ajka scenario (highlighted with bold). As discussed earlier, the search area optimisation is not efficient in this setting, because of the large amount of empty areas being searched (see Figure 3). The search plan optimisation (Algorithm 2) has linear complexity in terms of number of agents, but it is cubic in terms of the number of search tasks. The number of search tasks is 400 in the Ajka Blank case, and around 100 in the other test cases, that is reflected by the computation times in Table 3. Overall, the computation time is kept under a practical limit in realistic

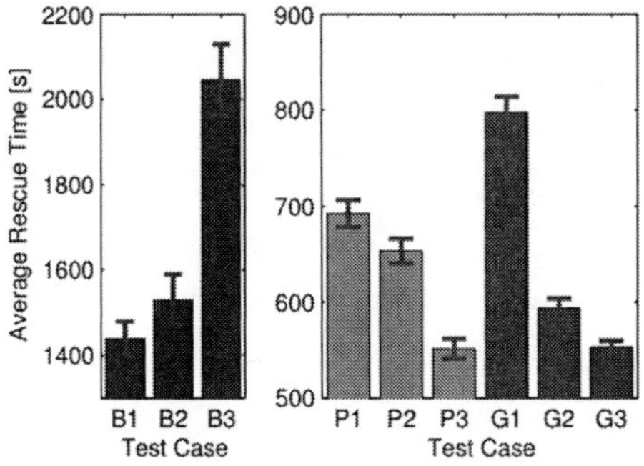

(a) Ajka scenario performance

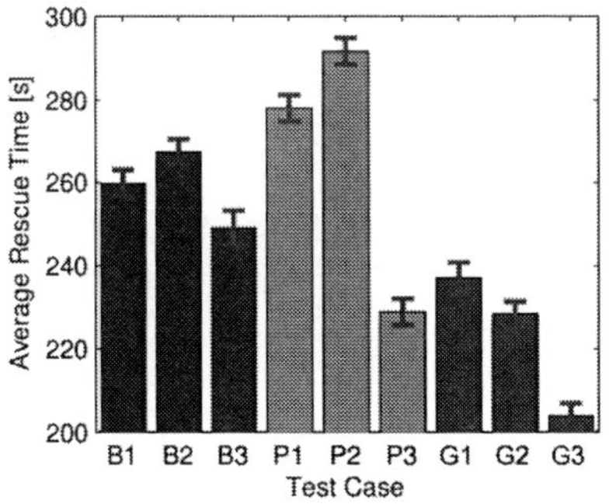

(b) Haiti scenario performance

Figure 4: Average rescue time comparison with 95% confidence intervals.

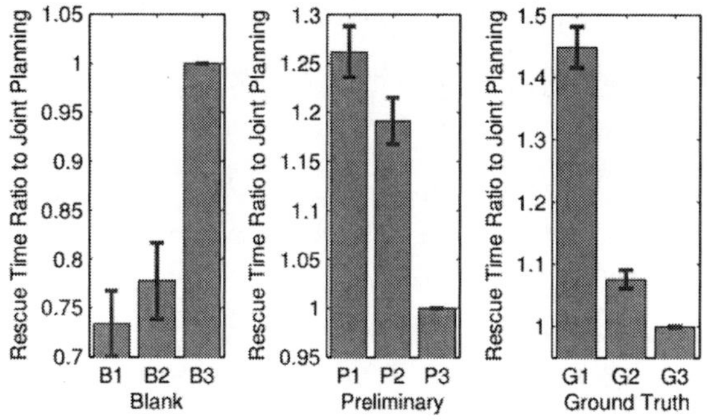

(a) Ajka relative performance

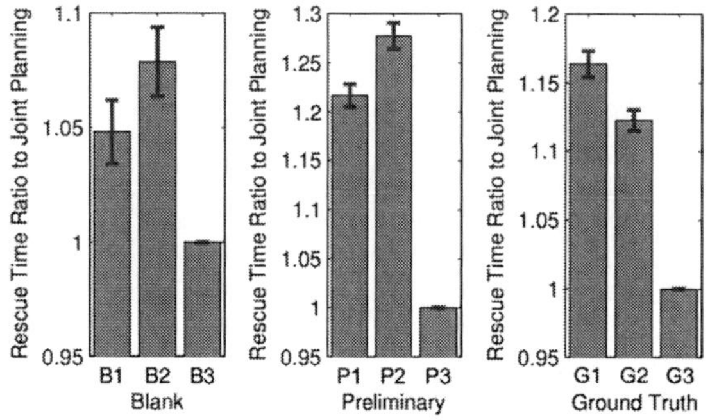

(b) Haiti relative performance

Figure 5: Relative performance comparison with 95% confidence intervals.

settings with not more than a couple hundred search tasks. For larger search missions with more tasks, we recommend grouping nearby tasks together for a feasible online planning process.

7. CONCLUSIONS

We introduced an algorithm for solving the Uncertain Multi-Robot Task Allocation (UMRTA) problem to control robots in a continuous space given an arbitrary task distribution. We also proposed an approach for heterogeneous SAR robot collaboration under uncertainty, that is the first to create a joint plan for both search and rescue robots. The resulting online planner[6] rescues 26% and 22% earlier compared to the state of the art approaches. Moreover, computation time is maintained on an acceptable level for realistic settings.

For future work, we aim to deploy this work on physical platforms where a robust, communication fault tolerant system is desired. We also plan to investigate applying online learning techniques to improve plans using the experience from previously produced plans.

8. ACKNOWLEDGMENTS

This research was undertaken as part of the ORCHID project funded by the EPSRC (EP/I011587/1). We also acknowledge the use of the IRIDIS High Performance Computing Facility, and associated support services at the University of Southampton, in the completion of this work.

[6]The following example videos show the system working: http://bit.ly/1Odyzv4, http://bit.ly/1NBjxMX

REFERENCES

[1] A. Allahverdi, C. Ng, T. Cheng, and M. Y. Kovalyov. A survey of scheduling problems with setup times or costs. *European Journal of Operational Research*, 187(3):985 – 1032, 2008.

[2] A. Ambrus. Analysis of high resolution digital aerial imagery – the mapping of the sludge spill of october 2010 and statistical analysis. Bsc thesis, Eötvös Loránd University, Faculty of Science, 2011.

[3] S. Bernardini, M. Fox, D. Long, and J. Bookless. Autonomous search and tracking via temporal planning. In *Proceedings of the 23st International Conference on Automated Planning and Scheduling (ICAPS-13)*, Jun 2013.

[4] J. Birkmann, editor. *Measuring Vulnerability to Natural Hazards: Towards Disaster Resilient Societies.* United Nations University Press, Dec. 2013.

[5] R. Boumghar and S. Lacroix. Over the hill and far away: aerial/ground cooperation for long range navigation. In *Proceedings of the 14th International Conference on Climbing and Walking Robots and the Support Technologies for Mobile Machines, Paris (France)*, pages 215–222. World Scientific, 2011.

[6] A. Brutschy, N.-L. Tran, N. Baiboun, M. Frison, G. Pini, A. Roli, M. Dorigo, and M. Birattari. Costs and benefits of behavioral specialization. *Robotics and Autonomous Systems*, 60(11):1408 – 1420, 2012. Towards Autonomous Robotic Systems 2011.

[7] E. Burns, J. Benton, W. Ruml, S. Yoon, and M. Do. Anticipatory on-line planning. In *International*

Conference on Automated Planning and Scheduling, 2012.

[8] L. Chaimowicz and V. Kumar. A framework for the scalable control of swarms of unmanned ground vehicles with unmanned aerial vehicles. In *In Proceedings of the 10th International Conference on Robotics and Remote Systems for Hazardous Environments*, 2004.

[9] A. I. Coles, D. Long, and P. Rendell. Experiences with temporal planning. In *Proceedings of the Workshop of the UK Planning and Scheduling Special Interest Group (PlanSIG)*, December 2010.

[10] P. Doherty and P. Rudol. A uav search and rescue scenario with human body detection and geolocalization. In M. Orgun and J. Thornton, editors, *AI 2007: Advances in Artificial Intelligence*, volume 4830 of *Lecture Notes in Computer Science*, pages 1–13. Springer Berlin Heidelberg, 2007.

[11] F. M. D. Fave, A. Farinelli, A. Rogers, and N. Jennings. A methodology for deploying the max-sum algorithm and a case study on unmanned aerial vehicles. In *IAAI 2012: The Twenty-Fourth Innovative Applications of Artificial Intelligence Conference*, pages 2275–2280, 2012.

[12] S. K. Gan, R. Fitch, and S. Sukkarieh. Real-time decentralized search with inter-agent collision avoidance. In *2012 IEEE International Conference on Robotics and Automation (ICRA)*, pages 504–510, May 2012.

[13] B. Gerkey and M. Mataric. Sold!: auction methods for multirobot coordination. *Robotics and Automation, IEEE Transactions on*, 18(5):758–768, Oct 2002.

[14] B. P. Gerkey and M. J. Matarić. A formal analysis and taxonomy of task allocation in multi-robot systems. *The International Journal of Robotics Research*, 23(9):939–954, 2004.

[15] B. Grocholsky, J. Keller, V. Kumar, and G. Pappas. Cooperative air and ground surveillance. *Robotics Automation Magazine, IEEE*, 13(3):16–25, Sept 2006.

[16] D. Jing, C. Jian, and S. Min. Cooperative task assignment for heterogeneous multi-uavs based on differential evolution algorithm. In *IEEE International Conference on Intelligent Computing and Intelligent Systems, ICIS 2009.*, volume 2, pages 163–167, Nov 2009.

[17] J. F. C. Kingman. *Poisson processes*, volume 3. Oxford university press, 1992.

[18] H. Kitano, S. Tadokoro, I. Noda, H. Matsubara, T. Takahashi, A. Shinjou, and S. Shimada. Robocup rescue: search and rescue in large-scale disasters as a domain for autonomous agents research. In *IEEE SMC '99 Conference Proceedings.*, volume 6, pages 739–743 vol.6, 1999.

[19] Y. Liu, J. Yang, Y. Zheng, Z. Wu, and M. Yao. Multi-robot coordination in complex environment with task and communication constraints. *International Journal of Advanced Robotic Systems*, 10(229), 2013.

[20] E. Lubrano. Drone adventure in haiti, May 2013.

[21] K. Nagatani, S. Kiribayashi, Y. Okada, K. Otake, K. Yoshida, S. Tadokoro, T. Nishimura, T. Yoshida, E. Koyanagi, M. Fukushima, and S. Kawatsuma. Emergency response to the nuclear accident at the

fukushima daiichi nuclear power plants using mobile rescue robots. *Journal of Field Robotics*, 30(1):44–63, 2013.

[22] M. Nanjanath and M. Gini. Repeated auctions for robust task execution by a robot team. *Robotics and Autonomous Systems*, 58(7):900 – 909, 2010. Advances in Autonomous Robots for Service and Entertainment.

[23] J. Nielsen. *Usability Engineering*. Morgan Kaufmann Publishers Inc., San Francisco, CA, USA, 1993.

[24] Police of Hungary. Simulation reproducing the industrial spill at the ajka alumina plant, 2010. Simulated in the OSIRIS system, using the DTA-50 and DDM-50 databases of the Hungarian Defese Froce.

[25] G. Rabadi, M. Mollaghasemi, and G. C. Anagnostopoulos. A branch-and-bound algorithm for the early/tardy machine scheduling problem with a common due-date and sequence-dependent setup time. *Computers & Operations Research*, 31(10):1727 – 1751, 2004.

[26] S. Radhakrishnan and J. A. Ventura. Simulated annealing for parallel machine scheduling with earliness-tardiness penalties and sequence-dependent set-up times. *International Journal of Production Research*, 38(10):2233–2252, 2000.

[27] S. Ramchurn, J. Fischer, Y. Ikuno, F. Wu, J. Flann, and A. Waldock. A study of human-agent collaboration for multi-uav task allocation in dynamic environments. In *International Joint Conference on Artificial Intelligence (IJCAI 2015)*, July 2015.

[28] C. Rasche, C. Stern, W. Richert, L. Kleinjohann, and B. Kleinjohann. Combining autonomous exploration, goal-oriented coordination and task allocation in multi-uav scenarios. In *Autonomic and Autonomous Systems (ICAS), 2010 Sixth International Conference on*, pages 52–57, March 2010.

[29] P. Scerri, T. Von Gonten, G. Fudge, S. Owens, and K. Sycara. Transitioning multiagent technology to uav applications. In *Proceedings of the 7th International Joint Conference on Autonomous Agents and Multiagent Systems: Industrial Track*, AAMAS '08, pages 89–96, Richland, SC, 2008. International Foundation for Autonomous Agents and Multiagent Systems.

[30] UNOSAT. Haiti earthquake 2010: Remote sensing based building damage assessment data, March 2010.

[31] S. Waharte and N. Trigoni. Supporting search and rescue operations with uavs. In *Emerging Security Technologies (EST), 2010 International Conference on*, pages 142–147, Sept 2010.

[32] S. Yoon, A. Fern, R. Givan, and S. Kambhampati. Probabilistic planning via determinization in hindsight. In *Proceedings of the 23rd National Conference on Artificial Intelligence - Volume 2*, AAAI'08, pages 1010–1016. AAAI Press, 2008.

[33] R. Zivan and K. Sycara. Cooperation between search and surveillance agents in DCOP_MST. In *Workshop 18 The Twelfth International Workshop on Distributed Constraint Reasoning DCR 2010*, 2010.

Expectation-Maximization for Inverse Reinforcement Learning with Hidden Data

Kenneth Bogert
THINC Lab, Dept. of Computer Science
University of Georgia
Athens, GA 30602
kbogert@uga.edu

Jonathan Feng-Shun Lin
Dept. of Electrical and Computer Engg.
University of Waterloo
Waterloo, ON N2L 3G1
jf2lin@uwaterloo.ca

Prashant Doshi
THINC Lab, Dept. of Computer Science
University of Georgia
Athens, GA 30602
pdoshi@cs.uga.edu

Dana Kulic
Dept. of Electrical and Computer Engg.
University of Waterloo
Waterloo, ON N2L 3G1
dana.kulic@uwaterloo.ca

ABSTRACT

We consider the problem of performing inverse reinforcement learning when the trajectory of the agent being observed is partially occluded from view. Motivated by robotic scenarios in which limited sensor data is available to a learner, we treat the missing information as hidden variables and present an algorithm based on expectation-maximization to solve the non-linear, non-convex problem. Previous work in this area simply removed the occluded portions from consideration when computing feature expectations; in contrast our technique takes expectations over the missing values, enabling learning even in the presence of dynamic occlusion. We evaluate our new algorithm in a simulated reconnaissance scenario in which the visible portion of the state space varies. Finally, we show our approach enables apprenticeship learning by observing a human performing a sorting task in spite of key information missing from observations.

1. INTRODUCTION

Inverse reinforcement learning (IRL) [1] offers a way to learn skilled behavior by passively observing an expert. It finds applications as a methodology for robot learning from demonstrations and in imitation learning [2]. It approaches the task as that of learning the expert's preferences from observations given that the expert's set of capabilities and any associated non-determinism are known. The underlying premise is that the preference function is more easily transferable from the expert to the learner than other artifacts of the expert's behavior.

Technically, this problem is usually modeled by ascribing a Markov decision process (MDP) to the expert whose solution guides the expert's actions. While the dynamics of the expert are presumed to be available, the learner seeks to learn the reward function of this MDP from observing trajectories composed of state-action pairs of the expert [3]. As this maximum likelihood problem is under constrained, a popular method involves finding the distribution over possible expert behaviors that conform to the observed trajectories and which maximizes entropy [4, 5].

To motivate this paper, consider a line robot who must learn to sort fruit by observing a human expert. The particular task here involves sorting distinguishably ripe fruit from fruit that may not be ripe as yet. Immersing the expert in a motion capture system coupled with a video camera provides trajectory and image data that is informative about which type of fruit is placed in which bin. However, the coupled system does not reveal that the ripe fruit must be handled very gently during sorting and other fruit may not need special care. While force sensors could help here these tend to be inaccurate and imprecise. Nevertheless, it seems possible to infer the *latent* variable related to handling from the fact that the sorted fruit is generally not damaged and the time consumed in sorting types of fruit.

In the above example, a component (or factor) of the expert's action is unobserved in the collected trajectories. Knowing this component is essential in order to inversely learn the correct preferences of the expert from its behavior and complete the task successfully. Toward this end, this paper makes the following contributions:

1. We generalize IRL to operate in the context of data containing hidden factors. Specifically, we present a novel generalization of Ziebart et al.'s [4] maximum entropy optimization that conditions on hidden variables. Because the corresponding nonlinear program is not convex, the optimization is approximated to become convex.

2. Expectation-maximization (EM) [6] is an iterative scheme that is specifically well suited for optimization given hidden variables. Wang et al. [7] present an application of EM toward solving the latent-variable maximum entropy approximation. We adapt the EM to operate in the context of IRL where observed trajectories have missing action factors and address associated challenges.

3. The inverse learning is evaluated on data with missing factors collected from human demonstrations of a ball-sorting task. Humans sorted two types of colored balls (as substitutes for fruit) while immersed in a motion capture system coupled with a video camera; no force senors were utilized. We show that our approach allowed the learner – a robotic arm – to correctly learn to sort the balls while realizing that a certain type of ball needed

Appears in: *Proceedings of the 15th International Conference on Autonomous Agents and Multiagent Systems (AAMAS 2016), J. Thangarajah, K. Tuyls, C. Jonker, S. Marsella (eds.), May 9–13, 2016, Singapore.*

to be handled gently in order to complete the task successfully, analogously to the human expert.

The generalized IRL that operates with possibly hidden data is well suited for a variety of other tasks where portions of the data may be occluded from the learner. This paper's contributions represent significant steps toward making IRL ready for real-world applications.

Rest of this paper is organized as follows. We review IRL and an entropy optimization method for such learning in Section 2. Hidden variables are introduced in Section 3 and a generalization of maximal entropy IRL in the context of hidden data is presented. We evaluate the performance of the generalized IRL on two robotic problem domains in Section 4 and discuss related work in Section 5. Concluding remarks and future work is outlined in Section 6.

2. BACKGROUND

We briefly review IRL and a solution method that is based on maximum entropy [8].

2.1 Inverse Reinforcement Learning

IRL [3] seeks to find the most likely reward function, R_I, that an expert I is executing. Current IRL methods typically apply in the presence of a single expert where the expert has solved a Markov decision process (MDP). Furthermore, they assume that this MDP excluding the reward function is known to the learner. The expert executes its policy multiple times and each (fully) observed trajectory of arbitrary length T is a sequence of state-action pairs, $Y = (\langle s,a\rangle^0, \langle s,a\rangle^1, \ldots, \langle s,\varnothing\rangle^T)$, where $\varnothing$ is the null action and Y belongs to the set of observed trajectories $\mathcal{Y}$. Let $\mathbb{Y}$ be the finite set of all trajectories of length T; $\mathcal{Y} \subseteq \mathbb{Y}$.

As the space of possible reward functions is very large, the function is commonly expressed as a linear combination of $K > 0$ *feature functions*, $R_I(s,a) \triangleq \sum_{k=1}^{K} \theta_k\, \phi_k(s,a)$, where θ_k are the weights, and ϕ: $S \times A_I \rightarrow \{0,1\}$, is a feature function. It maps a state from the set of states, S, and an action from the set of I's actions, A_I, to 0 or 1. IRL algorithms use feature expectations to evaluate the quality of the learned reward function. The kth feature expectation for a learned reward function R_I is, $\sum_{Y\in\mathbb{Y}} Pr(Y)$ $\sum_{\langle s,a\rangle\in Y} \phi_k(s,a)$. Alternately, the kth feature expectation may be formulated as, $\sum_{\pi_I\in\Pi_I} Pr(\pi_I) \sum_{s\in S} \mu_{\pi_I}(s)\, \phi_k(s,\pi_I(s))$. Here, $\mu_{\pi_I}(s)$ is the state visitation frequency: the number of times state s is visited on using deterministic policy π_I from the set of policies Π_I. The expectations are compared with those of the expert's from its observed trajectory, $\hat{\phi}_k \triangleq \sum\limits_{Y\in\mathcal{Y}} \tilde{Pr}(Y) \sum\limits_{\langle s,a\rangle\in Y} \phi_k(s,a)$, where $\tilde{Pr}(Y)$ is the empirical probability of Y. For example, if all trajectories in $\mathcal{Y}$ are observed just once then we may obtain, $\hat{\phi}_k \triangleq \frac{1}{|\mathcal{Y}|} \sum\limits_{Y\in\mathcal{Y}} \sum\limits_{\langle s,a\rangle\in Y} \phi_k(s,a)$.

2.2 Maximum Entropy IRL

Multiple policies may induce matches with the observed feature expectations equally well. In order to resolve this ill-posed problem, the principle of maximum entropy is useful [8]. While multiple formulations of the IRL problem exist that involve maximizing entropy [4, 5], we focus on the approach by Ziebart *et al.* [4] in this paper. Hence, we briefly review this problem formulation.

The approach maintains a distribution over all trajectories constrained to match the observed feature expectations while being maximally noncommittal to any one trajectory. Mathematically, the problem is formulated as a nonlinear optimization:

$$\max_{\Delta} \left(-\sum_{Y\in\mathbb{Y}} Pr(Y)\, log\, Pr(Y)\right)$$
$$\textbf{subject to} \quad \sum_{Y\in\mathbb{Y}} Pr(Y) = 1 \tag{1}$$
$$\sum_{Y\in\mathbb{Y}} Pr(Y) \sum_{\langle s,a\rangle\in Y} \phi_k(s,a) = \hat{\phi}_k \quad \forall k$$

Here, Δ is the space of all distributions $Pr(Y)$ and $\hat{\phi}_k$ is as defined previously in Section 2.1.

We may apply Lagrangian relaxation bringing both the constraints into the objective function and then solving the dual. The relaxed objective function becomes,

$$\mathcal{L}(Pr,\boldsymbol{\theta},\eta) = -\sum_{Y\in\mathbb{Y}} Pr(Y)\, logPr(Y) + \sum_k \theta_k \left(\sum_{Y\in\mathbb{Y}} Pr(Y) \sum_{\langle s,a\rangle\in Y} \phi_k(s,a) - \hat{\phi}_k\right) + \eta \left(\sum_{Y\in\mathbb{Y}} Pr(Y) - 1\right) \tag{2}$$

As Eq. 2 is convex for a deterministic MDP, taking the derivative with respect to $Pr(Y)$ and setting it to zero gives us the optimum:

$$\frac{\partial\mathcal{L}}{\partial Pr(Y)} = -log\, Pr(Y) - 1 + \sum_k \theta_k \sum_{\langle s,a\rangle\in Y} \phi_k(s,a) + \eta = 0$$
$$Pr(Y) = \frac{e^{\sum_k \theta_k \sum_{\langle s,a\rangle\in Y} \phi_k(s,a)}}{\Xi(\boldsymbol{\theta})} \tag{3}$$

where $\Xi(\boldsymbol{\theta})$ is the normalization constant $e^{-\eta+1}$; as such η may easily be obtained. Plugging Eq. 3 back into the Lagrangian (Eq. 2), we arrive at the dual $\mathcal{L}^{\text{dual}}(\boldsymbol{\theta})$ which is concave. We have,

$$\mathcal{L}^{\text{dual}}(\boldsymbol{\theta}) = log\, \Xi(\boldsymbol{\theta}) - \sum_k \theta_k \hat{\phi}_k \tag{4}$$

The dual above may be optimized to obtain $\boldsymbol{\theta}^*$ using the exponentiated gradient descent [9]. The gradient,

$$\nabla\mathcal{L}^{\text{dual}}(\boldsymbol{\theta}) = \sum_{Y\in\mathbb{Y}} Pr(Y) \sum_{\langle s,a\rangle\in Y} \phi_k(s,a) - \hat{\phi}_k$$

involves summing over the set of all trajectories, which may be very large. Ziebart *et al.* [4] suggest an efficient approach that calculates the expected state visitation frequency and action distribution instead. The feature expectations may be obtained easily given these values.

3. MAXENT IRL WITH HIDDEN DATA

We consider situations where portions of the expert's trajectory encompassing some states, parts of actions or both are hidden from the learner's view. A simple modification to the maximum entropy IRL reviewed in the previous section is to simply ignore occluded portions of the trajectories when calculating feature expectations. However, the gradient for those features that activate in the occluded states only or due to occluded actions become zero. As a result, this method may not learn weights for many features, which motivates a principled way to managing hidden data.

We begin by providing a general formulation of maximum entropy IRL with hidden data followed by applying it to our specific case where components of actions cannot be observed by the learner.

3.1 General Formulation

Consider again the expert's observed trajectory of length T, $Y = (\langle s,a\rangle^0, \langle s,a\rangle^1, \ldots, \langle s,\varnothing\rangle^T)$. Let Y be the observed portion of the full trajectory X and denote the occluded portion as Z; in other words, $X = (Y \cup Z)$. Z could be a few more state-action pairs that were performed in a portion of the state space that is occluded from the learner. It could also be the component of the expert's action that is hidden from the learner's view.

Of course, we may simply ignore the occluded data [10]. However, we hypothesize that a revised formulation of the maximum entropy nonlinear program in (1), which allows for an expectation of Z given Y provides a tighter solution. In other words, the resulting distribution may possess lesser entropy because the observed Y informs an expectation of Z effectively allowing more data.

Recall $\hat{\phi}_k$ in Section 2.1 whose analogous definition is $\sum_{X\in\mathbb{X}} \tilde{Pr}(X) \times \sum_{\langle s,a\rangle\in X} \phi_k(s,a)$. We may rewrite this as follows $\sum_{Y\in\mathcal{Y}} \sum_{Z\in\mathbb{Z}} \tilde{Pr}(Y,Z) \times \sum_{\langle s,a\rangle\in X} \phi_k(s,a)$. However, as Z is hidden we may treat it as a latent variable and decompose the joint $\tilde{Pr}(Y,Z)$ as,

$$\hat{\phi}_k^{Z|Y} \triangleq \sum_{Y\in\mathcal{Y}} \tilde{Pr}(Y) \sum_{Z\in\mathbb{Z}} Pr(Z|Y) \sum_{\langle s,a\rangle\in Y\cup Z} \phi_k(s,a) \quad (5)$$

The maximum entropy program of (1) then changes to accommodate the hidden data as given below,

$$\begin{aligned} &\max_{\Delta} \left(-\textstyle\sum_{X\in\mathbb{X}} Pr(X)\, log\, Pr(X)\right) \\ &\textbf{subject to} \;\; \textstyle\sum_{X\in\mathbb{X}} Pr(X) = 1 \\ &\textstyle\sum_{X\in\mathbb{X}} Pr(X) \sum_{\langle s,a\rangle\in X} \phi_k(s,a) = \hat{\phi}_k^{Z|Y} \quad \forall k \end{aligned} \quad (6)$$

Here, Δ is the space of all distributions $Pr(X)$ and $\hat{\phi}_k^{Z|Y}$ is as defined in Eq. 5.

The key difference between the program of (1) and its generalized version above is in the computation of the observed feature expectations, $\hat{\phi}_k$, in the primary constraint. The original program simply sums the value of the kth feature function across each $\langle s,a\rangle$ pair in the observed trajectory. However, as some $\langle s,a\rangle$ pairs may be missing from the trajectory, we obtain an expectation of the hidden state-action pairs given the observed portion, $Pr(Z|Y)$. Prior probability $\tilde{Pr}(Y)$ empirically approximates the true prior; we may use the fraction of times Y appears in $\mathcal{Y}$. Each pair in the complete data $Y \cup Z$ is then utilized to find the observed feature function counts.

The revised maximum entropy optimization above may be seen as an application of Wang *et al.* [7]'s generalization of the maximum entropy program to allow considerations of incomplete data to the context of inverse reinforcement learning. This gives us the first principled generalization of IRL to contexts involving hidden data that does not simply ignore it. Notice that if Z is empty indicating that all data is observed, then $X = Y$ and (6) reduces to the maximum entropy program of (1). Thus, the above generalizes the original maximum entropy program.

3.2 Hidden Actions

Motivated by the application of designing a robotic fruit sorter, we consider the setting where the expert's action consists of $N > 1$ components: $A_I = A_1 \times A_2 \times \ldots \times A_N$. A subset of these components, $M \leq N$ are unobserved in its trajectory. Subsequently, we may rewrite the set of actions as: $A_I = A_1 \times A_2 \times \ldots \times A_M \times \ldots \times A_N$. Let $\hat{A}_I = A_1 \times A_2 \times \ldots \times A_M$.

Given the above, Y reduces from the sequence of observed state-action pairs to the observed state-action pairs where the actions do not include the hidden component. Formally, $Y = \{\langle s, a_{/\hat{a}}\rangle^0, \langle s, a_{/\hat{a}}\rangle^1, \ldots, \langle s, \varnothing\rangle^T\}$, and $Z = X/Y$. The maximum entropy program of (6) is applied to accommodate this hidden data.

Due to the presence of the conditional probability in the Lagrangian $\mathcal{L}(Pr(X), \boldsymbol{\theta}, \eta)$, the relaxed objective function is not convex. Its partial derivative w.r.t. $Pr(X)$ shown below may not yield a closed-form solution:

$$\frac{\partial \mathcal{L}}{\partial Pr(X)} = -log\, Pr(X) - 1 + \sum_{k=1}^{K} \theta_k \sum_{\langle s,a\rangle\in X} \phi_k(s,a) + \sum_{k=1}^{K} \theta_k$$
$$\left(\sum_{Y\in\mathcal{Y}} \tilde{Pr}(Y) \frac{\sum_{Z'\in\mathbb{Z}} \left[\sum_{\langle s,a\rangle\in X'} \phi_k(s,a) - \sum_{\langle s,a\rangle\in X} \phi_k(s,a) \right] Pr(X')}{Pr(Y)^2} \right)$$
$$+\eta$$

where $X' = (Y \cup Z')$ and Z' is a hidden trajectory in $\mathbb{Z}$. Wang *et al.* suggest approximating the above partial derivative with the following simpler form:

$$\frac{\partial \mathcal{L}}{\partial Pr(X)} \approx -log\, Pr(X) - 1 + \sum_{k=1}^{K} \theta_k \sum_{\langle s,a\rangle\in X} \phi_k(s,a) + \eta$$

Setting the above to 0 and solving for $Pr(X)$ yields an optimum for $Pr(X)$ that is log linear:

$$Pr(X)^* \approx \frac{e^{\sum_k \theta_k \sum_{\langle s,a\rangle\in X} \phi_k(s,a)}}{\Xi(\boldsymbol{\theta})} \quad (7)$$

Now that we have the (approximately) optimal value of $Pr(X)$, we seek to find the maximizing value of Lagrangian parameter vector $\boldsymbol{\theta}$. In order to find this, Eq. 7 is substituted back in $\mathcal{L}(Pr, \boldsymbol{\theta}, \eta)$ and we minimize the resulting dual to obtain the following:

$$\mathcal{L}^{\text{dual}}(\boldsymbol{\theta}) \approx log\, \Xi(\boldsymbol{\theta}) - \sum_{k=1}^{K} \theta_k \sum_{Y\in\mathcal{Y}} \tilde{Pr}(Y) \sum_{Z\in\mathbb{Z}} Pr(Z|Y) \times \sum_{\langle s,a\rangle\in Y\cup Z} \phi_k(s,a) \quad (8)$$

3.3 Expectation-Maximization

One way to obtain the maximizing value of parameter vector $\boldsymbol{\theta}$ is to again seek to perform the exponentiated gradient descent. However, Eq. 8 may not offer a closed-form gradient due to the presence of $Pr(Z|Y)$. Alternatively, Wang *et al.* offer an EM-based iterative scheme, which when adapted to our maximum entropy IRL converges to a fixed point yielding $\boldsymbol{\theta}$ that maximizes Eq. 8.

We seek to maximize the likelihood of Lagrangian parameters $\boldsymbol{\theta}$, where the log likelihood is defined as $LL(\boldsymbol{\theta}|\mathcal{Y}) = log\, Pr(\mathcal{Y};\boldsymbol{\theta})$. This becomes,

$$\begin{aligned} LL(\boldsymbol{\theta}|\mathcal{Y}) &= log \prod_{Y\in\mathcal{Y}} Pr(Y;\boldsymbol{\theta})^{\tilde{Pr}(Y)} = \sum_{Y\in\mathcal{Y}} \tilde{Pr}(Y)\, log\, Pr(Y;\boldsymbol{\theta}) \\ &= \sum_{Y\in\mathcal{Y}} \tilde{Pr}(Y)\, log\, Pr(Y;\boldsymbol{\theta}) \sum_{Z\in\mathbb{Z}} Pr(Z|Y;\boldsymbol{\theta}) \\ &= \sum_{Y\in\mathcal{Y}} \tilde{Pr}(Y) \sum_{Z\in\mathbb{Z}} Pr(Z|Y;\boldsymbol{\theta})\, log\, Pr(Y;\boldsymbol{\theta}) \end{aligned}$$

Rewriting $Pr(Y;\boldsymbol{\theta}) = \frac{Pr(Y,Z;\boldsymbol{\theta})}{Pr(Z|Y;\boldsymbol{\theta})}$ in the above equation we get,

$$\begin{aligned} LL(\theta|\mathcal{Y}) &= \sum_{Y\in\mathcal{Y}} \tilde{Pr}(Y) \sum_{Z\in\mathbb{Z}} Pr(Z|Y;\boldsymbol{\theta})\, log\, \frac{Pr(Y,Z;\boldsymbol{\theta})}{Pr(Z|Y;\boldsymbol{\theta})} \\ &= \sum_{Y\in\mathcal{Y}} \tilde{Pr}(Y) \sum_{Z\in\mathbb{Z}} Pr(Z|Y;\boldsymbol{\theta})\, (log\, Pr(Y,Z;\boldsymbol{\theta}) \\ &\quad -log\, Pr(Z|Y;\boldsymbol{\theta})) \end{aligned}$$

The above likelihood may be iteratively improved until convergence (possibly to a local optima) by casting it in an EM scheme. Specifically, the likelihood may be rewritten as, $Q(\boldsymbol{\theta},\boldsymbol{\theta}^{(t)})+C(\boldsymbol{\theta},\boldsymbol{\theta}^{(t)})$ where,

$$Q(\boldsymbol{\theta},\boldsymbol{\theta}^{(t)}) = \sum_{Y\in\mathcal{Y}} \tilde{Pr}(Y) \sum_{Z\in\mathbb{Z}} Pr(Z|Y;\boldsymbol{\theta}^{(t)})\, log\, Pr(Y,Z;\boldsymbol{\theta}) \tag{9}$$

$$C(\boldsymbol{\theta},\boldsymbol{\theta}^{(t)}) = -\sum_{Y\in\mathcal{Y}} \tilde{Pr}(Y) \sum_{Z\in\mathbb{Z}} Pr(Z|Y;\boldsymbol{\theta}^{(t)})\, log\, Pr(Z|Y;\boldsymbol{\theta})$$

Notice that in Eq. 9, we may replace $Pr(Y,Z;\boldsymbol{\theta})$ with $Pr(X;\boldsymbol{\theta})$, and we may now substitute in Eq. 7. This gives us,

$$\begin{aligned} Q(\boldsymbol{\theta},\boldsymbol{\theta}^{(t)}) &= \sum_{Y\in\mathcal{Y}} \tilde{Pr}(Y) \sum_{Z\in\mathbb{Z}} Pr(Z|Y;\boldsymbol{\theta}^{(t)}) \Bigg(\sum_{k}\theta_k \\ &\quad \times \sum_{\langle s,a\rangle\in X} \phi_k(s,a) - log\, \Xi(\boldsymbol{\theta})\Bigg) \\ &= -\Bigg(log\, \Xi(\boldsymbol{\theta}) - \sum_{k}\theta_k \sum_{Y\in\mathcal{Y}} \tilde{Pr}(Y) \sum_{Z\in\mathbb{Z}} Pr(Z|Y; \\ &\quad \boldsymbol{\theta}^{(t)}) \sum_{\langle s,a\rangle\in X} \phi_k(s,a)\Bigg) \end{aligned}$$

Notice that the Q function above is almost the negative of the dual Lagrangian presented in Eq. 8 with the only difference being $\boldsymbol{\theta}^{(t)}$. On maximizing Q to convergence, we have $\boldsymbol{\theta} = \boldsymbol{\theta}^{(t)}$, due to which we conclude that maximizing the Q function minimizes the dual Lagrangian function. Therefore, approximately solving the maximum entropy IRL of (6) for $\boldsymbol{\theta}$ is equivalent to maximizing the Q function; Theorem 1 states this formally.

THEOREM 1. *Under the assumption that the distribution of the complete trajectories is log linear, the reward function that maximizes the log likelihood of the observed incomplete trajectories also maximizes the entropy of the distribution constrained by the conditional expectation of the feature functions.*

This gives us another path to a feasible solution to the generalized IRL in (6) subject to the constraints and the log-linear model for $Pr(X)^*$. However, due to the nonconvexity of the Lagrangian this solution may not necessarily be the optimal one.

Using this insight, we may now split the primary constraint in (6) into two portions and solve each separately.

3.3.1 E-step

The E-step involves obtaining a conditional expectation of the K feature functions using the parameter $\boldsymbol{\theta}^{(t)}$ from the previous iteration. We may initialize the parameter vector randomly. For all $k = 1 \ldots K$ we obtain,

$$\hat{\phi}_k^{Z|_Y,(t)} = \sum_{Y\in\mathcal{Y}} \tilde{Pr}(Y) \sum_{Z\in\mathbb{Z}} Pr(Z|Y;\boldsymbol{\theta}^{(t)}) \sum_{\langle s,a\rangle\in Y\cup Z} \phi_k(s,a)$$

3.3.2 M-step

This involves solving a simpler version of the constrained maximum entropy program of (6) by utilizing $\hat{\phi}_k^{*,(t)}$ from the E-step above and the log linear model for $Pr(X)$ to obtain $\boldsymbol{\theta}$.

$$\begin{aligned} &\max_{\Delta} \left(-\sum_{X\in\mathbb{X}} Pr(X)\, log\, Pr(X)\right) \\ &\textbf{subject to} \sum_{X\in\mathbb{X}} Pr(X) = 1 \\ &\sum_{X\in\mathbb{X}} Pr(X) \sum_{\langle s,a\rangle\in X} \phi_k(s,a) = \hat{\phi}_k^{Z|_Y,(t)} \quad \forall k \end{aligned} \tag{10}$$

We point out that solving the nonlinear program above is facilitated by the fact that $\hat{\phi}_k^{Z|_Y,(t)}$ is already available from the E-step and therefore may be treated as a constant. Consequently, optimizing the relaxed Lagrangian for (10) becomes straightforward. The iterative EM converges when $\boldsymbol{\theta}$ obtained from the M-step is identical to the previous $\boldsymbol{\theta}^{(t)}$.

Due to the presence of local optima, we perform restarts with different initial values for $\boldsymbol{\theta}$ and treat the run that achieved the highest entropy as the optimal one.

4. PERFORMANCE EVALUATION

In this section, we describe the method for evaluating the performance of the EM based IRL presented previously. We introduce suitable baselines for comparison and report on our experiments.

4.1 Problem Domains and Features

We introduce two problem domains to evaluate the performance of the EM based generalized IRL with hidden data.

UAV reconnaissance with ground cover Our first domain is a simulation-only reconnaissance application in which an aerial drone L tracks a fugitive I moving repeatedly through a grid of sectors to a safe sector. The drone is tasked with learning the policy of the fugitive from observing multiple runs over time each of which differs because the fugitive starts at a random location and exhibits a stochastic transition function. An important challenge is that some of the sectors are forested, which provides cover for the fugitive. Unfortunately, the fugitive's action is completely occluded from L in the forested sectors. We illustrate this domain in Fig. 1.

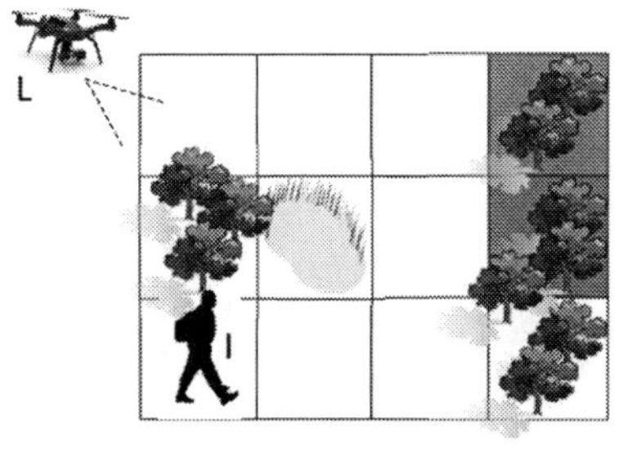

Figure 1: An overhead drone is tracking a fugitive moving through a 3 × 4 grid of sectors. The fugitive's movement is partially occluded as it passes through the forest cover. The sectors shaded blue and orange are safe and penalty sectors respectively.

Learner L models the fugitive I as following the same policy output from its MDP across the runs. The states, actions and transition function of the MDP are known to L; this is the standard assumption in IRL although recent work seeks to partially relax this assumption [11]. The states of the MDP are the sector coordinates (x, y) and I has four actions that move it in each of the four cardinal directions. I's transition function is modeled as I moving in the intended direction successfully with a probability of 0.9 and the remaining probability mass is distributed to moving in the other three directions. The reward function of the fugitive R_I is modeled as a linear combination of weighted feature functions. R_I is composed of the following three binary feature functions:

1. **Cost of movement** is the penalty for taking an action. This encourages I to reach the safe sector quickly. It is used at all states and actions;

2. **Goal state reached** is activated if I reaches the sector located at (4,3);

3. **Penalty state reached** is activated if I reaches the sector located at (4, 2) in the theater.

Learning from human demonstration of ball sorting The second domain involves a learning robot L equipped with Trossen Robotics' PhantomX Pincher arm that is given data on humans simulating a fruit sorting task. Humans are immersed in a Motion Analysis, 8 Eagle camera system and are tasked with sorting 24 colored balls into two bins without deforming the balls. Motion capture markers are placed along one of their arms and the wrist and coordinate data is recorded in the Cortex software. A synchronized video camera records the performance as well. L must successfully perform the same task.

Four types of balls – 6 each – are present. These are laboratory substitutes for ripe and regular fruit of two varieties. Balls made of soft playable clay represent ripe fruit and must be handled gently. Ping-pong balls and other solid balls can be handled regularly.

Despite the presence of the motion capture and video camera system, a key factor in performing the task successfully remains uncaptured. This is the amount of force that is applied while grabbing the balls and placing them in a bin. In particular, the soft clay ball (substitute for ripe fruit) must be grabbed gently to avoid damaging it while the hard ball (regular fruit) is grabbed with default force. We show frames of two human subjects sorting the balls in Fig. 2.

Learner L models human I's sorting behavior as guided by a policy that is output from a MDP whose states, actions and transition function are known to L. States of the MDP are combinations of the following four factors: ball_position = { on table, in center, bin 1, bin 2}, ball_type = {1,2,3,4}, holding_ball = {true, false}, and time_for_prev_action which is the time duration of the last action discretized into 12 segments: {less than 0.3s, 0.3s, 0.4s, ..., 1.3s, greater than 1.3s}.

Human I performs one of the following seven actions:

- *Grab hard* denotes the hand grabbing a ball with default force and sets the holding_ball factor to true;

- *Grab soft* denotes the hand grabbing a ball gently and sets holding_ball to true.

  On average, grabbing a ball gently is slower than grabbing it by default. Both grab actions are applicable for states where the ball position is on the table only;

- *Move To center* denotes the hand moving to the center position while holding a ball. This action applies for states where the hand has grabbed the ball that is on the table;

- *Move to bin 1* is the hand moving to bin 1 while holding the ball;

(a)

(b)

Figure 2: Video captures from our experiment showing a subject performing the ball sorting task. Notice that there are four types of balls in all - soft clay balls of two colors and hard ping-pong balls of two colors. Balls are sorted into two bins based on their color. (a) Subject picks a hard ball, and (b) Subject places a soft ball in one of the bins. Positions of the red bounding box correspond to the states of the MDP.

- *Move to bin 2* is the hand holding the ball moving to bin 2;

  These actions that move the ball to the bins are applicable when the ball is held and its position is in the center;

- *Release hard* places the ball with default force in a bin and sets the factor holding_ball to false, and on average is faster than grab soft; only for states in the center position

- *Release soft* places the ball gently in a bin and sets holding_ball to false.

  On average, placing a ball gently in a bin is slower than placing it with regular force. Both release actions are applicable when the ball is held and its position is in the center.

The transition function models each action as having its intended effect with a probability of 0.9 with the remaining probability mass distributed to the intended states of other actions applicable at the current state. For the state variable time_for_prev_action, the remaining mass is distributed to the other values.

Finally, I's reward function is modeled to have the following feature functions:

- **Release ball type X in bin 1** leads to 4 feature functions each of which is activated when a ball of that type is placed in bin 1;

- **Release ball type X in bin 2**, 4 features each of which is activated when a ball of that type is placed in bin 2;

- **Handle ball type X gently** also leads to 4 features each of which is activated when the ball of the corresponding type is grabbed and moved gently.

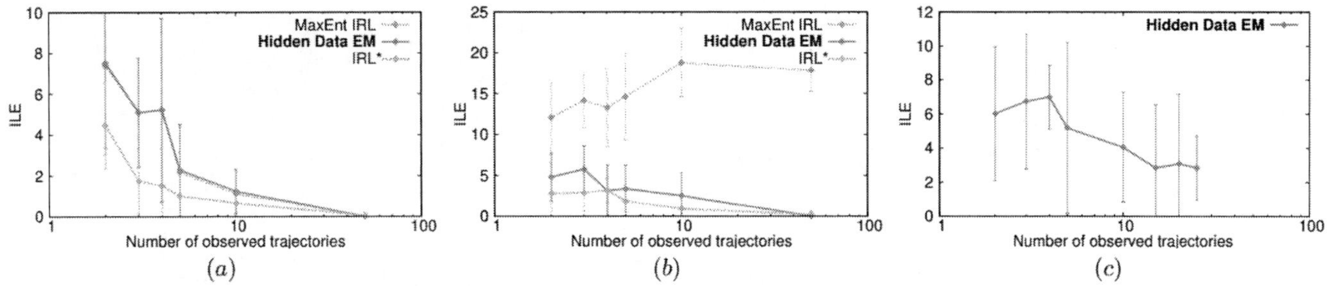

Figure 3: Performance evaluation of all three methods on the UAV reconnaissance simulation. (a) ILE for all methods in the fully observable setting. Notice that Hidden Data EM's performance coincides with that of MaxEnt IRL as we may expect. (b) ILE for the setting where the fugitive's trajectories are partially occluded. (c) High levels of occlusion which changes randomly between trajectories. Lower ILE is better. Vertical bars denote the standard deviation.

In total, the reward function is composed of 12 weighted feature functions.

Parameters of the robot's MDP are similar to those of the human's except that the arm took the same time to move the ball from the table to the bin whether it is grasping the ball gently or not. However, we noticed that the arm exhibited a greater tendency to drop the ball when grasping it gently. Therefore, we modified the transition function to reflect this property of the robotic arm. Specifically, actions with the default (hard) grasp have a 0.89 probability of being successful and 0.11 probability of dropping the ball. On the other hand, movement actions involving a gentle grasp have an increased 0.17 probability of dropping the ball while moving it to the bin (values were determined empirically prior to the experiment). Finally, the reward function features are the same as for the human.

4.2 Metrics and Baselines

In order to evaluate the performance of a method for IRL, it is tempting to compare the learned reward function directly to the actual reward function of I, R_I, if available. However, the learned reward function depends on the quality and quantity of the observations, and such comparisons ignore the fact that reward functions different from I's actual one may still result in the same optimal policy as the one utilized by I; these reward functions should be considered equivalent. Consequently, we adopt the metric used by Choi and Kim [12], which compares between the value functions of policies obtained from optimally solving I's MDP and from solving the MDP that is formed by using the learned reward function. In other words, let R_I^L be the reward function learned by L, π_I^* be the optimal policy of I and π_I^L be the policy obtained by optimally solving the MDP whose reward function is now R_I^L. Then, we use the following *inverse learning error (ILE)* metric:

$$\text{ILE} = ||V^{\pi_I^*} - V^{\pi_I^L}||_1$$

where $V^{\pi_I^*}$ is the optimal value function of I's MDP and $V^{\pi_I^L}$ is the value function due to utilizing the policy π_I^L on I's MDP. In the event that the learned reward function results in a policy identical to I's actual optimal policy, $\pi_I^* = \pi_I^L$, ILE will be 0; ILE monotonically increases as the two diverge. Furthermore, use of the difference in values also allows the error to grow proportionately to the value of the states where the learned policy diverges thereby placing emphasis on higher-valued states.

When the true reward function is unavailable we must utilize another metric to show successful learning. As our fruit sorting domain involves learning from humans with unknown reward functions we evaluate the learned rewards by utilizing them to guide a real robot in an apprenticeship learning procedure. Specifically, the learned rewards are transfered to the robot's MDP, which is then solved optimally to obtain the policy executed by the robot. This allows us to evaluate the performance of our new method by evaluating the performance of the robot in its assigned task.

To provide a comparative baseline, we evaluate the EM based IRL against *two* existing methods. First is a simple modification of Ziebart *et al.*'s IRL that was reviewed in Section 2.2. Specifically, occluded portions of the trajectories are simply ignored when calculating feature expectations. Thus the gradient for those features that activate in the occluded states or due to occluded actions become zero. As a result, this algorithm may not learn weights for many features. We label this algorithm as MaxEnt IRL.

A second baseline is to use a single-expert version of the method presented by Bogert and Doshi [10] that manages occlusion. While this algorithm also ignores feature expectations due to occluded states, it does not use the gradient and as such may find the correct weights for most features. However, this method requires the set of occluded states and actions to be fixed across all trajectories. As such, it cannot be applied to scenarios where this changes between observations. This method is labeled as IRL*.

Finally, we note that a possible approach in the context of occluded actions when actions are deterministic or when the transition stochasticity is very low is to simply fill in the blanks with the most likely action that produces the observed state transition in the trajectory. However, this approach becomes implausible in the context of actions with moderate or high nondeterminism or when two or more actions have similar transition probabilities; the latter case presents itself in both our domains. As such, this approach lacks robustness and a principled way of learning under occlusion is needed.

4.3 Experiments

We begin by comparing the performance of EM based IRL, labeled as Hidden Data EM, with the performances of MaxEnt IRL and IRL* on simulations in the UAV reconnaissance domain. Each method received up to 50 trajectories where a trajectory involved movement by the fugitive for 5 steps. At least one path exists from any start sector that reaches the safe sector within 5 steps. The fugitive started at different locations and its state-action pairs constitute the trajectory. The UAV can observe neither the state nor the action of the fugitive when it is passing through sectors covered by forest. Hidden Data EM used 10 restarts with random initial feature weights and the result with the maximum entropy is chosen as output.

Figure 3(a) reports the ILE as UAV L observes an increasing number of trajectories in the absence of any occlusion. The data points shown are the means of 100 runs. Here, we expect the per-

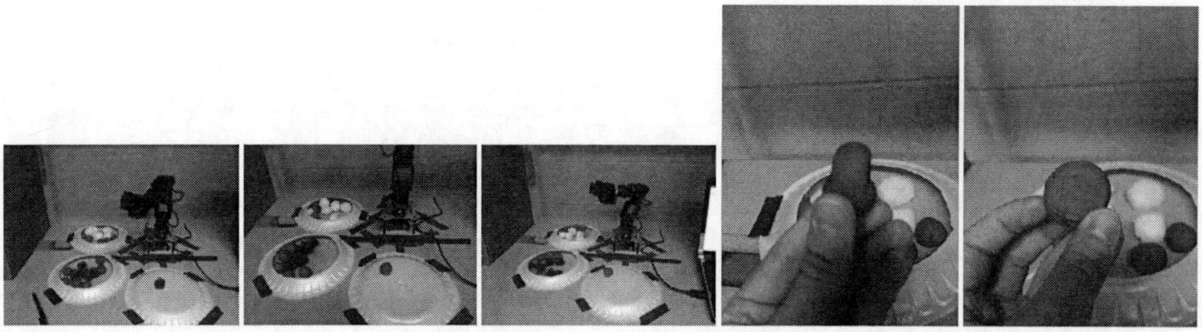

Figure 4: A series of snapshots of the Phantom Pincher arm sorting the balls. We introduce balls one at a time due to lack of sufficient space for several balls and the arm being small. The two bins with balls are visible on the left side of the arm. We show the deformed clay ball due to mishandling and the non-deformed clay ball on the right.

formance of Hidden Data EM to be identical to the performance of MaxEnt IRL because the former collapses into the latter when the set Z is empty. Indeed, the performances of the two methods coincide. IRL* performs slightly better than the other two methods in this test – this may be attributed to its policy-oriented approach making better use of available data.

Next, we compare all three methods under fixed occlusion (Fig. 3(b)) and when the occlusion varies between trajectories (Fig. 3(c)). The latter may occur if the fugitive is tracked in different regions of the theater that exhibit differing forest cover. Notice that MaxEnt IRL performs much worse now due to occlusion and its ILE remains significantly above 0 whereas the ILE of both IRL* and Hidden Data EM eventually reaches zero. The difference between Hidden Data EM and MaxEnt IRL is now statistically significant (paired Student's t-test, $p < 0.001$). For randomly varying levels of occlusion, neither MaxEnt IRL nor IRL* are applicable as both require the occluded state space to be the same across all trajectories. However, the EM-based IRL completes each trajectory with expected information and uses it in the inverse learning thereby showing a robust performance even for this pathological case.

Our second experiment involved sorting 24 balls of four types into two bins using a Phantom Pincher arm. [1] Each of the three methods learned a reward function from a single run (24 balls sorted) of the ball sorting task performed by a human subject. As we mentioned previously, the type of grasp employed by the human (gentle or default grasp) is hidden from the learner's view. Additionally, we utilized a control method that used the MaxEnt IRL on trajectory data in which the type of grasp was made explicit. Hence, there was no occlusion; we refer to this method as Occlusion-free control and it provides an upper bound performance for all other methods. For a deeper analysis of the learned reward function, we show the weights of the 12 feature functions learned by all four methods in the Appendix.

Table 1 shows the performance of all four methods on the task of sorting the 24 balls into two bins. Unable to infer the occluded action, MaxEnt IRL utilized the default grasp while sorting the balls thereby deforming 11 of the 24 balls. Nevertheless, it did sort most of the balls correctly. IRL* correctly inferred that one type of clay ball should be grasped gently but failed to arrive at a similar conclusion for the second set of soft balls and incorrectly found that the hard balls should also receive gentle handling. As a result, it damaged 5 and dropped 3. On the other hand, Hidden Data EM correctly learns a reward function – in 4 EM iterations – that has

[1]We replaced ping-pong balls with smaller balls because the former were overly large for the Phantom's small gripper.

Method	Ball correctly sorted	Balls dropped	Balls damaged
MaxEnt IRL	23	1	11
IRL*	21	3	5
Hidden Data EM	23	1	0
Occlusion-free control	23	1	0

Table 1: Performance of the various methods on the Phantom Pincher arm on the ball sorting task. Notice that the EM-based IRL did not damage any balls and dropped just one ball while sorting. It's performance is similar to our control method that provides an upper bound.

the arm grasp gently all the balls of clay with the two colors. As a result, none of the balls were damaged while one ball was dropped during the sorting. All balls were correctly sorted into the two bins by color. This strong performance by Hidden Data EM matches that of the Occlusion-free control method.

We show a series of snapshots in Fig. 4 of an example run of sorting the balls by the robotic arm. The right-most two snapshots compare a deformed and nondeformed clay ball for reference. Notice that most of the balls are correctly sorted at the end. A video of the sort is available for viewing at `https://www.youtube.com/channel/UC0IivL24ibPml8FJwdN3ITw`.

In summary, our generalized formulation of maximum entropy IRL presents a plausible method for inversely learning from data that suffers from occlusion. Experiments on two domains provide convincing evidence that the method can operate in the context of varying amount and type of occlusion – of state and components of action. The EM converges quickly to a reward function that accurately reflects that of the expert.

5. RELATED WORK

Ng and Russell [3] introduced IRL as a problem involving a single subject agent learning from a single expert modeled as a MDP. Inverse optimal control [13] generalizes IRL by allowing for control frameworks other than MDPs as well. Previous improvements to IRL include modeling the reward function as a linear combination of features [14] and learning with noisy feature functions [15].

In this paper, we relax the key assumption that the entire trajectory of the expert is fully observable, which has significant implications toward making IRL more pragmatic. Bogert and Doshi [10] also investigates maximum entropy IRL under occlusion. However, key differences exist in its method and treatment of occlusion. It seeks to maximize the entropy over all possible policies as introduced by

Ball sorting task												
Method	ϕ_1	ϕ_2	ϕ_3	ϕ_4	ϕ_5	ϕ_6	ϕ_7	ϕ_8	ϕ_9	ϕ_{10}	ϕ_{11}	ϕ_{12}
MaxEnt IRL	0.2213	0.2456	0	0	0	0	0.27	0.259	0	0	0	0
IRL*	0.8331	1.697	-0.4020	-0.44	0.25	0.26	1.08	1.07	1.08	1.06	0.61	-0.78
Hidden Data EM	0.1622	0.1033	0	0	0	0	0.1879	0.1647	0	0.37	0	0.0109
Occlusion-free control	0.0002	0.0001	0	0	0	0	0.0002	0.00006	0	0.5	0	0.4991

Table 2: Feature weights learned by all four methods from ball sorting data. ϕ_1 - ϕ_4: reward for sorting ball types 1-4 into bin 1, ϕ_5 - ϕ_8: reward for sorting ball types 1-4 into bin 2, and ϕ_9 - ϕ_{12}: reward for handling ball types 1-4 gently.

Method	Ball type hard and black	Ball type soft and red	Ball type hard and white	Ball type soft and green
MaxEnt IRL	To Bin 1 firmly	To Bin 1 firmly	To Bin 2 firmly	To Bin 2 firmly
IRL*	To Bin 1 gently	To Bin 1 gently	To Bin 2 gently	To Bin 2 firmly
Hidden Data EM	To Bin 1 firmly	To Bin 1 gently	To Bin 2 firmly	To Bin 2 gently
Occlusion-free control	To Bin 1 firmly	To Bin 1 gently	To Bin 2 firmly	To Bin 2 gently

Table 3: Optimal policies learned by all four methods from the ball sorting data with hidden variables. While the state consists of multiple variables, we show the robot's action map for the main state variable of ball type here. Underlined actions are erroneous.

Boularias et al. [15] rather than over trajectories. More importantly, it limits the optimization to the observed portions of the trajectories only. Consequently, the Lagrangian gradient becomes undefined and the method resorts to performing optimization using a technique that does not utilize the gradient. In comparison, we seek to infer expected data for portions of the trajectory that are occluded and the use of EM allows us to continue using the Lagrangian gradient for descent as shown by Wang et al. [7].

Few approaches investigate relaxing other knowledge requirements of IRL. Boularias et al. [16] propose model-free IRL with a single expert, learning the reward function by minimizing the relative entropy between distributions over trajectories generated by a baseline and target policies. Importance sampling is used for computing the relative entropy and the reward function reflects greedy maximization at each state in the absence of a transition function. In contrast, Bogert and Doshi [11] present a method that explicitly first learns the transition function under occlusion, making it a semi-model based method, before moving to IRL.

6. CONCLUDING REMARKS

Motivated by real-world applications in robotics, we focused on inverse reinforcement learning with partially occluded trajectories by treating the missing data as hidden variables. We developed an expectation-maximization based method to solve this problem and examined its performance in a UAV reconnaissance domain. Our approach improves on existing methods, which simply ignored the missing information, by enabling learning in the presence of occlusion that may even be dynamic; this is critical for real-world scenarios where the learner or environment is dynamic. Additionally, we demonstrated the value of our approach in an apprenticeship learning from demonstration application in which a critical component of the task being demonstrated is naturally hidden from the learner. In future work we will continue relaxing the data requirements of IRL, such as focusing on noisy-data scenarios where the learner observes the subject's state or action with sensor noise; this is common with robots.

Acknowledgments

This research is supported in part by a grant from NSF IIS-0845036 and a grant from ONR N000141310870. This paper benefited from conversations with Brian Ziebart.

APPENDIX

All four methods utilized the data collected from the experiment that involved humans sorting the balls. Recall that I's reward function contained 12 feature functions as described in Section 4.1. We show the weights learned for these 12 feature functions by all four methods in Table 2. Weights of features that should be minimized are ϕ_3 to ϕ_6, ϕ_9 and $\phi_1 1$. All methods give low weights to these. Among the rest, ϕ_{10} and ϕ_{12} are most important and the reference method Occlusion-free control gives high weight to these.

In Table 3 we also show broadly the policies obtained from the MDPs with the reward functions learned by all four methods. It provides key insight into the observed performances of the various methods.

REFERENCES

[1] Stuart Russell. Learning agents for uncertain environments (extended abstract). In *Conference on Learning Theory (COLT)*, pages 101–103, 1998.

[2] Brenna D. Argall, Sonia Chernova, Manuela Veloso, and Brett Browning. A survey of robot learning from demonstration. *Robotics and Autonomous Systems*, 57(5):469–483, May 2009.

[3] Andrew Ng and Stuart Russell. Algorithms for inverse reinforcement learning. In *International Conference on Machine Learning (ICML)*, pages 663–670, 2000.

[4] Brian D. Ziebart, Andrew Maas, J. Andrew Bagnell, and Anind K. Dey. Maximum entropy inverse reinforcement learning. In *Twenty-Second Conference on Artificial Intelligence (AAAI)*, pages 1433–1438, 2008.

[5] Krishnamurthy Dvijotham and Emanuel Todorov. Inverse optimal control with linearly-solvable MDPs. In *International Conference on Machine Learning (ICML)*, pages 335–342, 2010.

[6] A. P. Dempster, N. M. Laird, and D. B. Rubin. Maximum likelihood from incomplete data via the EM algorithm. *Journal of the Royal Statistical Society, Ser. B*, 39(1):1–38, 1977.

[7] Shaojun Wang, Dale Schuurmans, and Yunxin Zhao. The latent maximum entropy principle. *ACM Transactions on Knowledge Discovery from Data (TKDD)*, 6(2):8:1–8:42, 2012.

[8] Henryk Gzyl. *The Method of Maximum Entropy*. World Scientific, 1995.

[9] Jyrki Kivinen and Manfred K. Warmuth. Exponentiated gradient versus gradient descent for linear predictors. *Information and Computation*, 132(1):1–63, 1997.

[10] Kenneth Bogert and Prashant Doshi. Multirobot inverse reinforcement learning with interactions under occlusion. In *Autonomous Agents and Multi-Agent Systems Conference (AAMAS)*, pages 173–180, 2014.

[11] Kenneth Bogert and Prashant Doshi. Toward estimating others' transition models under occlusion for multi-robot irl. In *24th International Joint Conference on Artificial Intelligence (IJCAI)*, pages 1867–1873, 2015.

[12] J Choi and Kee-eung Kim. Inverse reinforcement learning in partially observable environments. *Machine Learning Research*, 12:691–730, 2011.

[13] RW Obermayer and Frederick A Muckler. *On the inverse optimal control problem in manual control systems*, volume 208. NASA, 1965.

[14] Pieter Abbeel and AY Ng. Apprenticeship learning via inverse reinforcement learning. In *International Conference on Machine Learning (ICML)*, page 1, 2004.

[15] Abdeslam Boularias, O Krömer, and J Peters. Structured apprenticeship learning. *Machine Learning and Knowledge Discovery in Databases*, pages 227–242, 2012.

[16] A Boularias, Jens Kober, and J Peters. Relative entropy inverse reinforcement learning. In *International Conference on AI and Statistics (AISTATS)*, pages 182–189, 2011.

Unsupervised Learning of Qualitative Motion Behaviours by a Mobile Robot

Paul Duckworth
School of Computing,
University of Leeds, UK
p.duckworth@leeds.ac.uk

Yiannis Gatsoulis
School of Computing,
University of Leeds, UK
y.gatsoulis@leeds.ac.uk

Ferdian Jovan
Intelligent Robotics Lab,
University of Birmingham, UK
fxj345@cs.bham.ac.uk

Nick Hawes
Intelligent Robotics Lab,
University of Birmingham, UK
n.a.hawes@cs.bham.ac.uk

David C Hogg
School of Computing,
University of Leeds, UK
d.c.hogg@leeds.ac.uk

Anthony G Cohn
School of Computing,
University of Leeds, UK
a.g.cohn@leeds.ac.uk

ABSTRACT

The success of mobile robots, in daily living environments, depends on their capabilities to understand human movements and interact in a safe manner. This paper presents a novel unsupervised qualitative-relational framework for learning human motion patterns using a single mobile robot platform. It is capable of learning human motion patterns in real-world environments, in order to predict future behaviours.

This previously untackled task is challenging because of the limited field of view provided by a single mobile robot. It is only able to observe one location at any time, resulting in incomplete and partial human detections and trajectories. Central to the success of the presented framework is mapping the detections into an abstract qualitative space, and then characterising motion invariant to exact metric position.

This framework was used by a physical robot autonomously patrolling an office environment during a six week deployment. Experimental results from this deployment demonstrate the effectiveness and applicability of the system.

1. INTRODUCTION

A key factor for the success of intelligent mobile robots, deployed in human populated environments, is their ability to understand human motion. This allows for safer and more effective navigation in populated spaces. Such robot systems perceive and represent the world through a range of sensor modalities, often maintaining abstract representations that allow them to make inferences and decisions. How to best represent knowledge about the world is still a major challenge in the field of intelligent robotics. This problem is magnified on mobile robot platforms where on-board sensors provide only a partial and noisy view of the world.

In this paper, we investigate the problem of how an intelligent mobile robot can learn and predict human motion behaviours in real-world daily living environments (e.g. office areas) from partial and noisy observations of the inhabitants. As such, the problem to be solved is to learn from partial human motions and generalise to underlying motion behaviours.

Appears in: *Proceedings of the 15th International Conference on Autonomous Agents and Multiagent Systems (AAMAS 2016), J. Thangarajah, K. Tuyls, C. Jonker, S. Marsella (eds.), May 9–13, 2016, Singapore.*

Our autonomous mobile robot has a limited field of view due to sensor limitations and occlusions. It detects humans within range of its sensors and uses a robust human tracking algorithm [12] to stitch together detected human positions based on their chronology. We define a *pose* as an xy Cartesian coordinate of a detected human. For each human, our tracking algorithm produces a sequence of poses that we call a *trajectory*. However, these trajectories are always incomplete, representing only a section of the person's motion.

Our assumption is that human motion *relative to key objects* is highly informative of recurrent motion patterns and relates to everyday activities. For example, standing up and walking from a desk towards the printer to collect a printout, is a motion pattern which occurs in many offices, irrespective of the exact xy locations of both the desk and the printer. For all offices, it is difficult to generically express this behaviour in the Cartesian map-plane using a metric approach. However, it is simple to describe this behaviour in relative terms, across offices. Qualitative spatial calculi [6] are well suited to this task as they are able to abstract specific details of observations, extracting similarities whilst preserving qualitative differences. We therefore represent trajectories as a sequence of qualitative spatial-temporal relations (QSTRs) between the human and reference objects. This allows us to abstract away from absolute Cartesian coordinates into a more structured qualitative space. The trajectories we detect have a variable number of metric poses. However, our framework compares their qualitative representations making it highly tolerant to different lengths of trajectories, and suitable for a mobile robot.

The key novelty and contribution of this paper is an unsupervised framework based on qualitative relations that learns and predicts human motion behaviours from a mobile robot's limited view of the world. This approach is able to utilise incomplete and noisy detections, generalising them in a manner that extracts a set of motion behaviour classes.

In the next section we discuss related work, followed by a description of qualitative representations used in this paper. A detailed explanation of our methodology is given in Section 4. We present experiments and results from a six week robot deployment at the UK offices of the G4S security company in Section 5 and 6, followed by our conclusions in Section 7.

2. RELATED WORK

A number of approaches to predict human motion behaviours have been developed particularly in the domain of surveillance. For example, statistical approaches [18, 16, 2], neural networks [17], clustering [22, 21], goal-based state machines [10], etc. The key difference to our framework is that these works use data collected from static cameras with a fixed frame of reference and a wide field of view, which allows them to observe long and complete trajectories. These static camera approaches make no predictions outside their field of view and therefore have limited use outside a surveillance setting, such as in mobile robotics where the field of view is narrow, and often occluded. Motion behaviours over a transportation network have also been learned and predicted from GPS data [20]. Here, similar techniques to the surveillance setting can be used since a person's motion is detected over the entire network. They make no predictions outside of the field of view, and therefore can be considered similar to static camera approaches.

Recent work on trajectory analysis using mobile robots includes [5, 7, 4]. These works have used multiple robots to detect human trajectories. However, their robots are positioned *statically* such that they cover almost the complete region resulting in fully observable trajectories. This requires prior knowledge of where these interesting areas are and pre-defining the robot positioning to obtain the complete trajectories. Furthermore, since they cover the entire region with laser scanners, they segment complete trajectories between 'resting points'. This equates to pre-defining the start and end poses of trajectories, and therefore of potential motion patterns. This is in contrast to our work where a trajectory has arbitrary length and the start can be detected at any point in the global map, which might not be the actual source location of a motion behaviour.

More recently, [19] used a support vector machine to learn trajectory features: speed, area covered, etc. The system is heavily reliant on detecting complete trajectories via a large grid of laser sensors and requires pre-defining feature classes which is not possible in our unsupervised setting.

In this paper we make none of the assumptions found in the papers discussed above. We let our single autonomous mobile robot patrol its operational environment and perform other tasks whilst capturing human detections.

Aside from motion behaviour literature, there is a range of previous work which uses qualitative spatio-temporal relational frameworks similar to those in this paper. These include unsupervised learning of events and event classes using a static camera approach [24], learning activities and classifying online using an egocentric vision approach [3], learning object place arrangements [13], and in a robotic setting using qualitative abstractions in a RoboCup soccer simulator [26]. These works use qualitative frameworks to generalise observations and learn models, each for a different purpose. It is this ability to generalise metric observations into more general models that we draw upon in our work.

3. QUALITATIVE REPRESENTATIONS

Our approach is to characterise movements of people in terms of the qualitative relationships they exhibit with a number of fixed reference points, e.g. doorways, desks, printers, etc. Our framework, based upon qualitative spatial-temporal relations (QSTRs), allows us to keep qualitative information about relative locations, whilst ignoring exact metric location. For example, a qualitative prediction of 'approaching the printer' only needs to state that a person gets closer to the printer over consecutive observations, but does not need to predict precise (and therefore potentially inaccurate) metric changes in position. This notion of 'approaching' provides enough information to allow a robot to reason about its own future actions (e.g. avoiding the region between the human and the printer), and can generalise across printers anywhere in a global coordinate frame. Next we present background work in qualitative representations used throughout this paper, and build upon it in the following sections.

3.1 Qualitative spatio-temporal relations

Given their ability to capture information about trajectories, the following three qualitative relational calculi were considered for our task. All three were computed using a publicly available ROS library we developed [14]:

1. Qualitative Distance Calculus (QDC) [8, 15]
2. Qualitative Trajectory Calculus (QTC) [11]
3. Allen's interval algebra (IA) [1]

QDC: expresses the qualitative Euclidean distance between two points depending on defined region boundaries. In this paper the thresholds are defined as: 'touch' [0-1m], 'near' (1-2m], 'medium' (2-4m], 'far' (4-8m] and 'ignore' (>8m]. The intuition behind using QDC is based on the assumption that human motion can be partially explained using distance relative to key objects. i.e. a set of QDC relations localises a person with respect to reference objects, and changes in these relations can be used to explain relative motion.

QTC: a calculus to represent the relative motion of two points with respect to the reference line connecting them. In this paper, we use the QTC_{B11} variant [11], which relies upon two time points per relation. It defines the following three qualitative spatial relations between two objects $o1, o2$: $o1$ is moving towards $o2$ (represented by the symbol $-$), $o1$ is moving away from $o2$ $(+)$, and $o1$ is neither moving towards or away from $o2$ (0). Since our reference objects are static, we only need to represent the relation between $o1$ and $o2$ rather than the inverse also (as in the full QTC_{B11}). QTC represents relative motion between two objects in a qualitative manner [25] and is considered appropriate for our task. Intuitively people often move towards objects that are of interest and relevant to their motion, whilst objects they directly depart from can also be informative. For example, someone who wants to print a document will most likely follow a motion behaviour *towards* $(-)$ a printer.

The two qualitative spatial calculi introduced above complement each other well. QDC describes relative distance between objects, while QTC_{B11} encodes relative motion.

Allen's interval algebra (IA): is a calculus for reasoning with temporal intervals. IA defines 13 qualitative relations corresponding to seven temporal situations; for example for two intervals A, B the possible temporal relations are: *A before B*, *A after B*, *A meets B*, *A overlaps B*, etc. (for a complete list of relations and interpretation refer to [1]).

The benefit of using IA is that it allows us to encode temporal information about states of our chosen qualitative representations abstracted away from an exact instance in time. This allows us to generalise experiences to compare them. We do this by using qualitative spatio-temporal activity graphs explained in the next section.

3.2 Qualitative spatio-temporal activity graphs

For each trajectory, we abstract the sequence of xy poses into a qualitative space using the representations introduced above, and generalise by computing a *Qualitative Spatio-Temporal Activity Graph* (QSTAG) [24]. This abstraction allows whole trajectories to be compared qualitatively. The necessary steps are explained here.

QSR episodes:

Prior to detecting the first trajectory, we manually annotate the global map with semantically meaningful objects, i.e. doorways, desks, printers, etc. An example of a semantic object map, where each object type is a different colour, can be seen in Figure 1 (left). This becomes our set of reference objects O, of known, fixed locations.

Formally, we represent a trajectory, m, as a list of xy Cartesian coordinates, known as *poses*, $P_m = [p_1, p_2, \dots]$. For each trajectory, we generate a set of lists of qualitative spatial relations, where each list encodes the relations between the m poses and a reference object in O, yielding the sequence of QSTRs $Q_{m,O}$. E.g. for a single object in the region, $O = \{desk\}$, we obtain one list of qualitative spatial relations $Q_{m,O} = \{[q_1, q_2, \dots]\}$, where q_i contains one relation from each qualitative calculus used (in our case QDC and QTC_{B11}). Adjacent sequences of identical q_i are compressed to form a QSR *episode* (labelled with the start and end time points). For example, if a trajectory relative to a desk yields the following five combined (QDC, QTC_{B11}) relations:

$$Q_{m,O} = \{[\{Touch, +\}, \{Touch, +\}, \{Near, +\}, \{Near, 0\}, \{Near, 0\}]\}$$

then we can compress them, maintaining a set of spatial relations and an interval of time over which they hold:

$$Q'_{m,O} = \{[[\{Touch, +\}, (1,2)], [\{Near, +\}, (3,3)], [\{Near, 0\}, (4,5)]]\}.$$

This compression maintains ordinal information about the relations and their durations, without keeping every time point of the observation in memory. The above example can be interpreted as a person initially *touching* the desk, *moving away* until they are *near* the desk, finally *stopping* (with respect to the desk) at a distance of *near*.

We define a QSR episode as a tuple containing the following information: an object pair (a unique trajectory ID and one reference object); the set of qualitative spatial relations, (each belonging to a different qualitative calculus); and an interval of time the relations hold over. For example, the sequence of QDC and QTC_{B11} states above can be represented as three QSR episodes, $E_{m,O} = [e_1, e_2, e_3]$, where:

$$e_1 = (traj\_id, desk, \{Touch, +\}, (1, 2)),$$
$$e_2 = (traj\_id, desk, \{Near, +\}, (3, 3),$$
$$e_3 = (traj\_id, desk, \{Near, 0\}, (4, 5)).$$

Each trajectory observed by the robot is compressed into a list of QSR episodes of variable length, where the length depends upon the number of qualitative spatial relation changes the trajectory experiences with the reference objects. Figure 2 represents the example sequence of qualitative spatial relations as a time-line, where the $x-$axis represents time.

For a region containing j reference objects we obtain $E_{m,O} = [E_{m,o_1}, \dots, E_{m,o_j}]$ representing the set of QSR episodes between the trajectory and each of the objects. Using the entire set of $E_{m,O}$ we generate a corresponding QSTAG g_m, described in the next section.

Figure 1: (left) Global map with semantic objects and regions annotated. (right) RGB-image of one region of the deployment map. (Best viewed in colour)

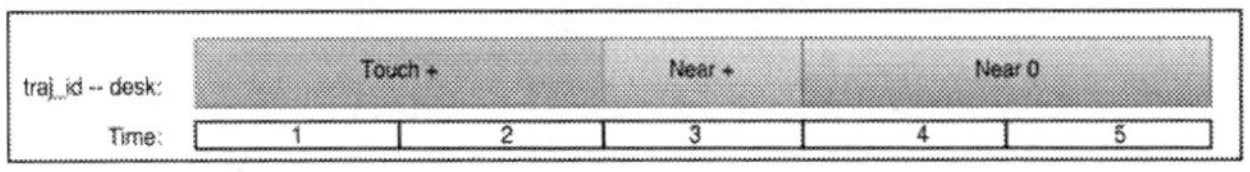

Figure 2: Time-line representation of a trajectory's QSR episode list.

QSTAG:

To generate a Qualitative Spatio-Temporal Activity Graph (QSTAG), from a trajectory, we combine the entire sequence of QSR episodes, $E_{m,O}$. This aggregates the collection of qualitative relations over multiple objects. We do this by generalising the temporal interval of the QSR episodes using Allen's interval algebra. Given $E_{m,O}$ (a list of QSR episodes) as above, an IA relation is computed between every pair of QSR episodes by comparing their intervals, e.g. in the working example, $(1, 2)$ occurs 'before' $(4, 5)$, therefore we say, e_1 occurs 'before' e_3. A QSTAG representing a trajectory ID and a single object can only contain 'meets' and 'before' IA relations, because only one set of spatial relations can hold at any one time between the trajectory and the object. However, a QSTAG representing a trajectory ID and many objects can contain up to seven different IA relations (assuming the arguments to the relations are ordered so as to avoid the six IA inverse relations).

The structure of a QSTAG is composed of nodes partitioned into three layers, and a directed edges set:

- The *objects layer*, contains one node representing the human, and one node per unique object o_j in the list of QSR episodes, where $E_{m,o_j} \in E_{m,O}$. i.e. one node for the human, and a node for each object in O.
- The *spatial episode layer*, contains one node per QSR episode e_i in $E_{m,O}$, where the node encodes the set of spatial relations which hold during that episode.
- The *Allen temporal relations layer*, contains one node per pair of QSR episodes and encodes the IA relation that holds between the two QSR episodes. i.e. a node for each pair, e_i, e_j, where $e_i, e_j \in E_{mO}$.

The QSTAG for the working example is shown in Figure 3. In general, qualitative spatial calculi contain relations which are asymmetric, therefore we encode the argument order using directed edges (indicated with arrows).

A QSTAG provides a compact and efficient graph structure to represent both qualitative spatial information between moving objects, and the temporal information about those relationships. This facilitates the use of standard graph comparison techniques discussed next.

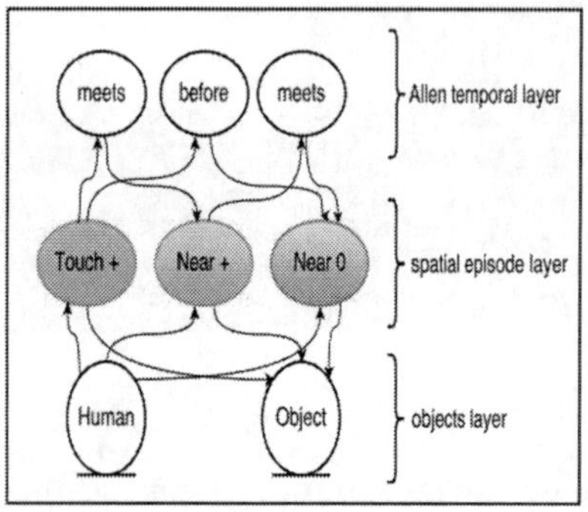

Figure 3: Qualitative Spatio-Temporal Activity Graph between a human and a single object. Directed edges indicate the relations argument order.

Graphlets:

We generate a QSTAG g_m for each detected trajectory m. By comparing multiple QSTAGs we are able to draw conclusions about similarities of the encoded trajectories. A standard technique to compare graphs (such as QSTAGs) is to split each graph into sub-graphs and compare the occurrence of the sub-graphs [9]. However, this requires criteria to be defined on the size and structure of sub-graphs.

We split the QSTAG into a set of overlapping sub-graphs. We restrict the entire set of sub-graphs by defining properties that must hold. This has the effect of restricting the total number of sub-graphs, making the problem tractable, and also only selects sub-graphs that relate to relationships that temporally coincide within a QSTAG. We define a *graphlet* as a connected sub-graph that satisfies the following properties:

i) it maintains the layer structure of a QSTAG;

ii) the objects layer must contain the human node and only one other object node;

iii) the spatial episode layer contains up to three QSR episode nodes which together form a connected interval, this allows the sub-graphs to temporally overlap;

iv) the temporal layer contains up to three IA relation nodes (this is guaranteed by restricting to at most three spatial episode nodes).

This allow us to represent the QSTAG g_m as a bag of overlapping graphlets, $[\gamma_1, \gamma_2, \dots]$, where each graphlet, γ_i, obeys the four properties. The working example QSTAG can be represented as a set of six graphlets, all shown in Figure 4. It can easily be seen that criteria i, ii, and iv hold for each. The third property requires further explanation. A graphlet is restricted to a maximum of three spatial episode nodes to minimise the set of all possible graphlets, whilst allowing them to overlap within the QSTAG. e.g. in the working example, both graphlets γ_2 and γ_3 contain the spatial episode node relating to e_2. Also, a graphlet is said to have a valid duration if it encodes QSR episodes which form a connected temporal interval. e.g. in the example, e_1 and e_2 form a continuous duration over timepoints (1,3) and hence a valid graphlet, γ_2, is created using these two QSR episodes. The two QSR episodes; e_1 and e_3 do not have a continuous duration, since there is a break at timepoint 3, and therefore there is no graphlet containing spatial episode nodes e_1 and e_3 alone. It is worth noting that γ_1, in the example, is itself g. A QSTAG can be a valid graphlet of itself if it maintains the criteria. The valid duration criteria would become more important if condition (ii) were relaxed to allow more than two object nodes in each graphlet. In that more general case, seven different IA relations would be possible, and the continuous duration property holds for graphlets that encode overlapping QSTRs between multiple object pairs.

The set of all possible unique valid graphlets for a QSTAG depends upon the cardinality of the qualitative spatial calculi being used and the number of objects in the QSTAG.

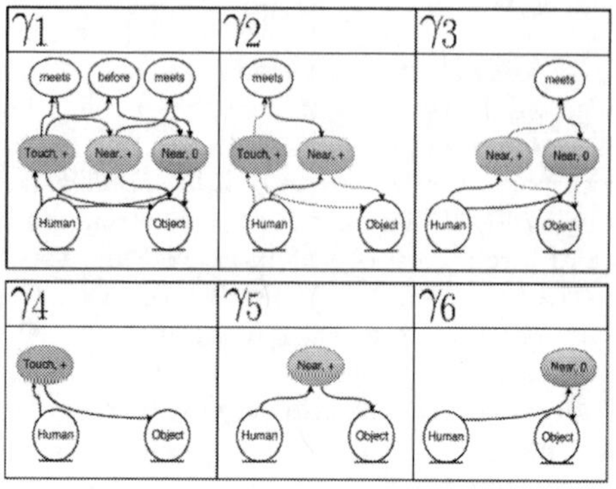

Figure 4: The working example complete bag of graphlets, $[\gamma_1, \dots, \gamma_6]$.

This section presented the theory of QSTAGs and how to extract a set of unique graphlets from a human trajectory. In the next section we explain our methodology for learning human motion behaviours using this representation.

4. METHODOLOGY

The main components of our unsupervised learning framework are shown in Figure 5. It comprises of two phases: training phase only (top layer), and classification phase only (bottom layer). Components common to both phases are shown in the middle layer. More details on these two phases are presented next, followed by a formal description of the framework.

Training Phase:

In the training phase we create a list of QSR episodes for each observed trajectory. i.e. for each trajectory m in our dataset of observed trajectories M, we create E_m, O between the trajectory poses and the reference objects in O. We only encode QSR episodes between the person and the closest n (in this case 5) reference objects (based upon Euclidean distance at the time of detection). This allows us to efficiently capture a spread of relations throughout the region without having to fix the set of reference objects in advance.

For each $m \in M$, a QSTAG g_m is built from the QSR episodes as described in Section 3.2. A set of valid graphlets, $[\gamma_1, \gamma_2, \dots]$ is then extracted from g_m and stored in a database. Therefore, we obtain one QSTAG and corresponding set of graphlets, per observed trajectory.

For all observed trajectories we express the QSTAGs as a set, $G = \{g_1, \dots, g_M\}$, of length $|M|$, where each g_m has a corresponding set of graphlets. We then apply a technique

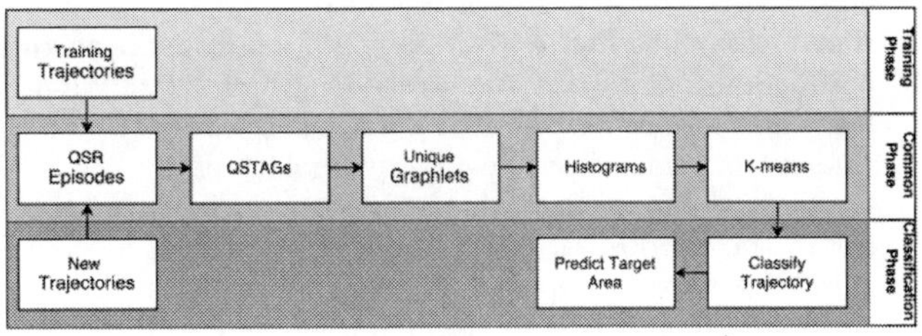

Figure 5: Flowchart of the qualitative unsupervised learning and classification framework (the top layer blocks are for the training phase, the bottom layer blocks are for the classification phase, and the middle layer blocks are common to both phases).

similar to bag-of-words (BoW) to compare the QSTAGs, where each unique graphlet can be thought of as a unique word. This is done by obtaining the set of unique graphlets in all $g_m \in G$, generating a *code book* of words (graphlets) denoted C_G. The code book is incrementally learned and updated over time, depending upon the the training data.

For each QSTAG in G, we count the occurrence of each graphlet code word and create a histogram representation over the code book. i.e. for $g_m \in G$, we compute a histogram h_{g_m} of length $l = |C_G|$. Therefore we represent each QSTAG as a histogram, and generate a set H, where:

$$H = \{h_{g_m} : g_m \in G, m \in M\}.$$

Each histogram in H can be thought of as a feature vector, where each unique graphlet is a unique feature. Using this representation, the exact temporal ordering of each graphlet is lost. However, graphlets that contain two or three spatial episode nodes can overlap within their QSTAG, and therefore maintain ordinal information about the qualitative states within a QSTAG. Further, the representation facilitates the use of unsupervised clustering techniques on H, meaning we can draw comparisons between trajectories in M.

We unit-normalise the histograms in H. We do this because we desire any two histograms with a similar relative proportion of each code word to be considered 'close' in high dimensional space. i.e. if we double every bin of a histogram, after normalisation, the two histograms will be the same. This is a desirable property since different length trajectories can have a different number of QSR episodes and therefore a larger count of graphlets (which tend to be in proportion for the same motion behaviours). However, it is worth noting that a trajectory with fewer poses does not imply fewer QSR episodes. This number depends upon the number of spatial relational changes with the reference objects.

The unsupervised training phase is completed by clustering the dataset of histograms into k clusters, using the k-means algorithm. This produces a model, Θ, with a set of cluster centres, $[\theta_1, \ldots, \theta_k]$, where each θ_i represents a motion behaviour. We determine the value of k, i.e. the number of learned motion behaviours, using the Silhouette Coefficient (SC) [23]. This technique automatically determines k that generates the best model for the data. It uses the mean intra-cluster distance, a, and the mean nearest-cluster distance, b, for each data sample to calculate $SC = (b - a)/\max(a, b)$. The SC value is in the range of $[-1, 1]$, with higher values an indication of better, non-over-fitted, models. As such, with SC we avoid the model over-fitting the data.

Classification Phase:

In the classification phase, the aim is to understand the motion of a newly detected human as quickly as possible. This allows the robot to make a prediction about where that person might be going and alter its behaviour accordingly. The classification process involves comparing a new detection to the learned motion behaviour model, Θ, and as such, is bound by availability of new poses. The people tracker we use groups xy Cartesian coordinates of a person into sub-sequences of poses, to check chronology, where a sub-sequence is a buffer of $0.4s$ of detections and approximately 10 xy coordinates (given a $25Hz$ sampling rate). The classification processes is then repeated for each new sub-sequence of poses.

Once the k-means model is trained and a new trajectory is being observed, the trajectory sub-sequences are available incrementally for the duration of time the human is within sensor range. Given the first sub-sequence, $\approx$10 poses, the common phase steps in Figure 5 are repeated to represent the poses as a QSTAG and as a histogram of unique graphlets. The histogram is unit-normalised and classified into one of k cluster centres, θ_i. This allows the robot to generalise the first sub-sequence, and make an initial behaviour classification using only $0.4s$ of the observed trajectory. It then updates this classification as more trajectory becomes available.

We define the set of data points (training histograms, h_{g_m}) as 'belonging' to their closest cluster centre, θ_i, such that $h_{g_m} \in H_{\theta_i}$, and $H = [H_{\theta_1}, \ldots, H_{\theta_k}]$. Then we can interpret the cluster centre θ_i as the mean histogram of H_{θ_i}, i.e. for $h_{g_m} \in H_{\theta_i}$, θ_i represents the 'influence' of each graphlet γ in the motion behaviour, θ_i. Therefore, when a new trajectory is being observed and is classified into a cluster centre, we use the cluster centre values to extrapolate the trajectory and make a prediction of the QSTRs that we predict to observe in the near future from that motion behaviour.

From the classified cluster centre, the predicted collection of QSTRs are each mapped back onto the metric map plane using the xy coordinates of the reference objects and the QDC relations. This results in aggregating the QSTR predictions over the region, creating a probabilistic *target area* that the robot can use. In practice, this is achieved by maintaining an occupancy grid for each of the k learned cluster centres. The predicted target area is then defined as the most likely occupied group of cells in the grid under a particular motion behaviour. i.e. the target area α_i is predicted from occupancy grid Y_{θ_i}, corresponding to the classified cluster centre θ_i. An example occupancy grid, Y_{θ_i}, is shown in Figure 6.

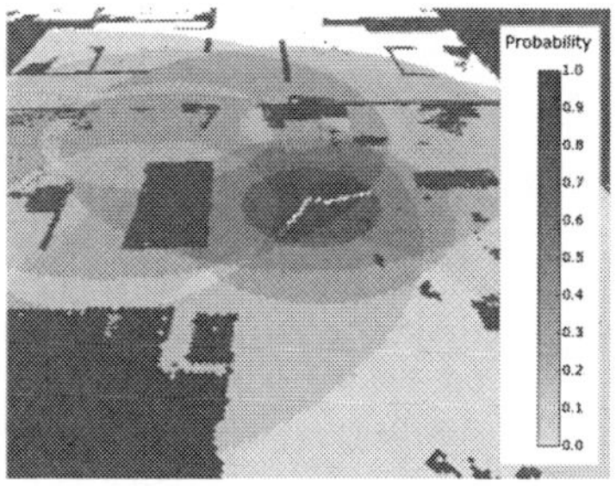

Figure 6: Occupancy grid and predicted target area (yellow-red) from a learned motion behaviour. One trajectory overlaid (green-white) showing sub-sequences of xy coordinates. (Best viewed in colour).

Our training and classification framework presented in this section allows our mobile robot to qualitatively predict human movements within the region of space it is patrolling. The robot can make a decision on which are the most likely qualitative relations a human will achieve with reference objects, continually updating this decision whilst the human is observed. These relations are projected onto the map plane so the robot can either approach the target area to intercept the person, or move away, depending upon the setting.

5. EXPERIMENTS

5.1 Data collection

Data collection took place during a six week deployment at offices of the G4S security company, using a Metralabs Scitos A5 mobile robot. It was equipped with a laser range finder and an RGB-D camera, both of which were used to collect human detections and trajectories. The dataset collected, along with meta-data, is available at: http://doi.org/10.5518/34.

The robot followed a pre-specified schedule during the deployment period which involved patrolling, stationary observation, and object search tasks during weekday working hours (Mon-Fri, 9am-5pm). It was stationary at its charge station during weekends and public holidays. Whilst on its charge station, the robot could perform tasks such as database backups and batch learning, which is when the unsupervised k-means was performed.

During its patrolling and observation operations the robot was detecting and tracking humans. The laser sensor has a 180 degree field of view, however, it was often occluded by obstacles in the environment and fast moving people were only detected briefly. During the six week deployment we recorded approximately $42,000$ trajectories and each was stored as 2D Cartesian poses in a database. Of those, the framework filtered out any with a maximum displacement of less than $1m$, which were considered stationary people or noise. Detections in certain locations were very common (caused by obstacles), i.e. table legs and chairs, being misdetected by the implemented leg detector. After filtering, the average length of a trajectory used in the training phase was 2.2m (median: 1.8m and range: 1m−6.5m). This is in contrast to capturing the complete motion of a person, e.g. a person walking down the approximately 25m long corridor.

The patrolled area was segmented into semantic room regions, each with manually annotated key objects such as desks, bookcases, printers, etc., as shown in Figure 1. In the first week, the robot was predominantly in a particular region that was used for the experimental analysis, resulting in a higher number of trajectories in this region than the following five weeks. This experimental region is the left-most region of the global semantic map in Figure 1 (left).

During the deployment, the robot's behaviour was altered when an observed trajectory was significantly different (based upon a distance threshold), to the learned motion behaviours. The robot would approach the observed person and request them to swipe their security badge.

5.2 Experimental procedure

We evaluate our unsupervised qualitative relational framework using analyses designed to assess the classification and the predicted target area for a new trajectory. Results are presented in Section 6 for the experimental region, which was the most frequently and considered the most interesting region. After filtering, we obtain $1,232$ trajectories in the experimental region with an average length of 2.2m. We use cross-validation of the collected data, where each CV-fold is a different calendar week during the deployment.

One key point is that there is no ground truth with respect to the purpose of a trajectory. Obtaining this would require the robot to either interrupt and ask the human their intention, or an elaborate motion-capture set-up where intention could be inferred from destinations. Neither of these were feasible due to the operational conditions of the deployment. This is a further advantage of the unsupervised framework which learns common motion behaviours which can be post-associated to meaningful activities.

As discussed above, a common problem faced in real world robotic deployments, such as this one, is not being able to perceive complete trajectories from their source locations. This problem is compounded when required to make real-time predictions about a human's future movement, using only the initially observed poses. The people tracker groups the xy poses into sub-sequences as discussed in Section 4. The trajectory poses are stored in the database along with these sub-sequence identifiers. This allows for post-analysis of the trajectories, as if they were being observed live. We use these sub-sequence identifiers during the evaluation to mimic the real-time system.

In our first analysis, we investigate real-time classification metrics to evaluate how well the system classifies a newly observed trajectory into one of the learned motion behaviours θ_i. To do this, for each trajectory, m, in the test set, a QSTAG g_m is generated using only the first sub-sequence poses (≈ 10). The formulation steps are repeated to obtain a histogram representation $h_{g_m}^{[1:10]}$ for this sub-sequence; this is classified into a motion behaviour $\theta_i^{[1:10]}$ and compared against the classification result of the final trajectory θ_m, where all xy poses are used.

In our second analysis, we use the trajectories to evaluate the classification of the k-means model against the prediction of the target area. Here, a previously unseen trajectory, m, is classified into a motion behaviour θ_m as above, and a predicted area is calculated on the metric map using the occupancy grid Y_{θ_m}. An occupancy likelihood score is calculated by taking the average of the occupancy cells corresponding to the xy coordinates of the trajectory. We then check if the likelihood score generated using the classified motion behaviour model θ_m is greater than (or equal to) the likelihood calculated using any other motion behaviour $\theta_i, \forall i \in K \backslash \{m\}$.

Finally, we investigate the effect of adding additional training data into the system. This aims to mimic the live deployed robotic system as it accumulates data over time. Here, we use the final week of data to evaluate, and the first five weeks are incrementally added into the training phase.

6. RESULTS AND DISCUSSION

Figure 7 shows the trajectories that belong to three of k learned motion behaviours in our experimental region. It can be seen that the trajectories belonging to these clusters express specific human behaviours, which we can associate to intent or meaningful activities. For example, the trajectories in the left most image can be interpreted as movements of one specific employee who was present throughout the entire deployment, and whose desk is situated at the source of the trajectories in this image. It shows that this employee

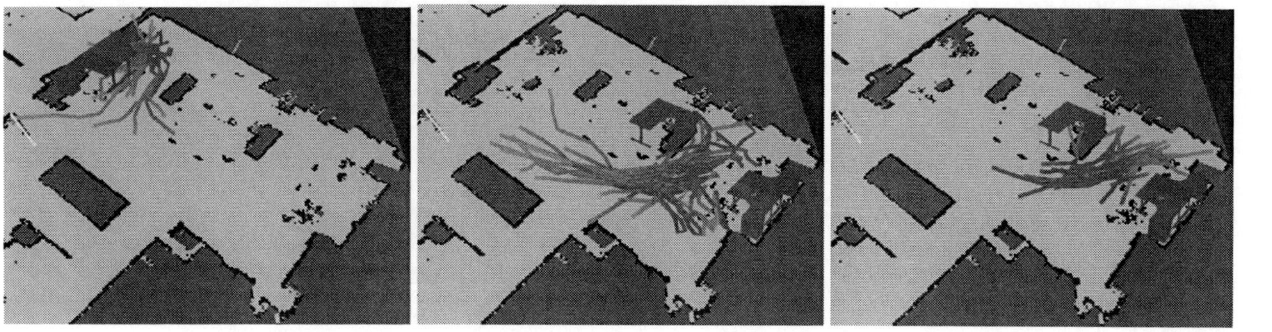

Figure 7: Trajectories belonging to three of the learned k-means clusters in one region, (direction of motion is red to green). Region door showed in yellow. (Best viewed in colour).

commonly walks from behind their desk towards the door (shown in yellow), and we learn this as a common motion behaviour in this region. The centre and right images show there are common motions behaviours towards (right image) and away from (centre image) the collection of desks in the right hand corner of the region. These common behaviours can also be interpreted as employees walking towards and away from their desks. These behaviours enhance our mobile robot's knowledge of the region and each can be translated into a navigation behaviour to approach or avoid the predicted target area when a new trajectory is observed and classified into these motion behaviours.

We evaluate how well the system classifies a newly observed trajectory into one of the learned motion behaviours θ_i. The mean values of recall r, precision p and $F1$-score are calculated after observing increasing percentages of sub-sequences. The results of this first analysis are presented in Figure 8, and were generated using 6-fold cross-validation where each fold is a calendar week of data. The classification process was performed using both QDC and QTC_{B11} relations together, and when using only QDC relations. (QTC_{B11} was not used alone because the QDC relations are needed to predict a target area.) To compare these two classifiers, we collate the data over all percentage-splits and are interested in comparing the number of correctly classified instances (true positives (TP)) with the incorrectly classified instances (false positives (FP)). A 2x2 contingency table is presented in Table 1, where *Test 1* is the classifier based on combined calculi (QDC and QTC_{B11}) and *Test 2* is the classifier based on QDC only relations.

	Test 2 TP	Test 2 FP	Total
Test 1 TP	5498	1640	7138
Test 1 FP	1278	658	1936
Total	6776	2298	9074

Table 1: Contingency table comparing two classifiers based on different QSR calculi.

The graphs in Figure 8 show all metrics are higher for the combination of the two calculi. Further, we perform a McNemar's significance test with null hypothesis that the two classifiers have the same probability of predicting a correctly classified instance. Using a two-tailed test, and a significance level (alpha) of 0.05, we achieve a Z statistic of 6.7, and therefore reject the null hypothesis. This means that the marginal proportions are significantly different from each other and validating our initial belief that QTC_{B11} complements QDC very well. i.e. QDC provides qualitative knowledge about relative distances of the trajectories to objects in the region, whilst QTC_{B11} provides qualitative knowledge about the relative direction of motion.

It can also be seen from the graphs that once 20% of a trajectory is observed, the system has recall $r \approx 0.7$ ($p \approx F1 \approx 0.7$), which demonstrates that even when only a very small section of a trajectory is observed the system is able to perform well. The metrics remain more or less at these values between $20 - 40\%$ of observed trajectory. From 40% and above the metrics increase until all the sub-sequences have been observed.

The results of our second analysis are presented in Table 2. The average scores of recall $r = 0.53$ ($p = 0.67$ and $F1 = 0.55$) demonstrate that, for more than half of new trajectories, the predicted target area generates the highest likelihood score when compared to the other learned motion behaviours. Given the challenging nature of the data (something which is revealed below by the implementation of a previously published algorithm) these results show good performance. This implies that our unsupervised qualitative learning k-means framework is able to express the human motion behaviours that emerge in this environment and predict reasonably well the expectancy of the trajectories using the generated occupancy grids from the cluster centres.

Furthermore, the average recall of the system increases to $r = 70\%$ ($p = 0.80$ and $F1 = 0.72$) if we consider the

cv-fold	k	recall	prec	$F1$
week 0 (342)	13	0.48	0.59	0.48
week 1 (169)	9	0.56	0.80	0.62
week 2 (196)	12	0.48	0.65	0.51
week 3 (104)	10	0.63	0.75	0.67
week 4 (205)	11	0.53	0.53	0.52
week 5 (216)	11	0.48	0.67	0.51
Avg:	11	0.53	0.67	0.55
Std:	–	0.06	0.01	0.08
Random:	–	0.08	0.10	0.08
ZeroR:	–	0.21	0.04	0.07

Table 2: Maximum occupancy likelihood score (testing all k motion models Θ) matching the classified motion.

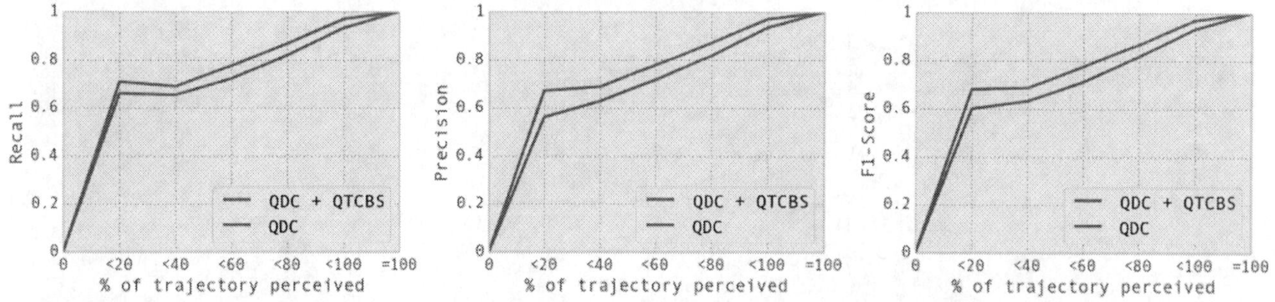

Figure 8: Recall, precision and F1-score presented for the prediction of the final cluster of a new trajectory, given a percentage of its sub-sequences.

highest two occupancy likelihood scores. This is particularly relevant because the predicted target area, given by the occupancy grid Y_{θ_m}, is computed using QDC relations only. However two occupancy grids could appear similar, when their underlying motion behaviour differs due to different QTC_{B11} relations. For example the two motion behaviours, centre and right, in Figure 7 are overlapping with respect to distance relations (QDC) only, but are qualitatively different when considering the direction of motion relations (QTC_{B11}), they are opposite directions.

Finally, we investigate the effect of accumulating training data in a live deployment-like setting. We repeat the previous experiment, but accumulate the training data over five weeks, and test on the sixth. Table 3 shows that as more training data is used, the system is better able to classify new trajectories into motion behaviours. This is further emphasised considering week 0 contained more trajectories than any of the other five weeks.

Training Weeks (M)	k	recall	prec	$F1$
week 0 (342)	9	0.24	0.72	0.29
weeks 0-1 (511)	12	0.43	0.54	0.44
weeks 0-2 (707)	12	0.43	0.56	0.43
weeks 0-3 (811)	10	0.43	0.71	0.49
weeks 0-4 (1016)	14	0.48	0.63	0.53

Table 3: Maximum occupancy likelihood score (testing all k motion models Θ) matching the classified motion, using cumulative training data.

A comparison between our framework and the popular quantitative approach presented in the literature [5], was made by implementing their *Expectation Maximisation* framework to predict motion behaviours. As specified in the abstract of the paper, their objectives appear similar to ours: "This paper proposes an algorithm that learns collections of typical trajectories that characterize a person's motion patterns." It attempts to fit Gaussian Mixture Models (GMMs) over the exact xy locations of trajectories of equal length.

Our training dataset of trajectories were extrapolated to the maximum trajectory length, which in our experiments was 420 xy poses, equivalent to roughly 16 seconds in the robot's field of view. However, the published algorithm was unable to successfully model our data, due to its incomplete and noisy nature. Even using a subset of the training dataset (of 1232 instances) failed to converge in reasonable time, when initialised with a starting number of Gaussian Mixtures. The iterative procedure continued to add a motion model due to low data likelihood, then remove one, due to low motion model utility. This comparison highlights the shortcomings with scalability of quantitative approaches, and the difficulty of clustering real world trajectory data, with no user input.

7. CONCLUSIONS

This paper presented a novel unsupervised learning framework based on qualitative spatio-temporal relations. A qualitative framework that abstracts observations in to a qualitative space is necessary on a mobile robot to generalise incomplete observations. The key challenge was learning motion behaviours and classifying new trajectories given the robot's limited view of the world.

In a high level description, our framework encodes human trajectories into qualitative spatio-temporal activity graphs. Using a BoW-like approach we produce a set of histogram features (which relate to qualitative sub-graphs with certain properties). A k-means algorithm is then trained and queried.

The training and test data were collected over a 6 week deployment of a mobile robot at offices of the G4S security company. Experimental results demonstrate the effectiveness of the system in terms of being able to learn unsupervised meaningful motion behaviours from incomplete trajectories. Analysis using different qualitative spatial calculi showed QDC and QTC_{B11} complement each other well for this task, and provide different modalities of qualitative information about human motions. We also demonstrated that the system is capable of predicting the likely area to be occupied of a newly observed trajectory. Finally, it was shown that the performance increases as it accumulates knowledge.

Future work aims at integrating QTC_{B11} relations into the target area prediction, so a more narrow location can be predicted from the detected human trajectory. Generalising objects to their object types or affordance would allow our system to transfer knowledge between regions. Finally, a challenge is to integrate evaluation metrics to run automatically so that the robot control can benefit from the learned behaviours, forming a closed loop system.

8. ACKNOWLEDGMENTS

We thank colleagues in the School of Computing Robotics lab and in the STRANDS project consortium (http://strands-project.eu) for their input. We also acknowledge the financial support provided by EU FP7 project 600623 (STRANDS).

REFERENCES

[1] J. F. Allen. Maintaining knowledge about temporal intervals. *Communications of the ACM*, 26(11):832–843, 1983.

[2] A. Basharat, A. Gritai, and M. Shah. Learning object motion patterns for anomaly detection and improved object detection. In *IEEE Conf. on Computer Vision and Pattern Recognition (CVPR)*, 2008.

[3] A. Behera, D. C. Hogg, and A. G. Cohn. Egocentric activity monitoring and recovery. In *Asian Conference on Computer Vision (ACCV)*, 2012.

[4] M. Bennewitz, W. Burgard, G. Cielniak, and S. Thrun. Learning motion patterns of people for compliant robot motion. *International Journal of Robotics Research*, 24:31–48, 2005.

[5] M. Bennewitz, W. Burgard, and S. Thrun. Using EM to learn motion behaviors of persons with mobile robots. In *IEEE Conf. on Intelligent Robots and Systems (IROS)*, 2002.

[6] J. Chen, A. G. Cohn, D. Liu, S. Wang, J. Ouyang, and Q. Yu. A survey of qualitative spatial representations. *The Knowledge Engineering Review*, 30:106–136, 2015.

[7] G. Cielniak, M. Bennewitz, and W. Burgard. Where is ...? learning and utilizing motion patterns of persons with mobile robots. In *International Joint Conf. on Artificial Intelligence (IJCAI)*, 2003.

[8] E. Clementini, P. D. Felice, and D. Hernández. Qualitative representation of positional information. *Artificial Intelligence*, 95(2):317 – 356, 1997.

[9] D. Conte, P. Foggia, C. Sansone, and M. Vento. Thirty years of graph matching in pattern recognition. *International Journal of Pattern Recognition and Artificial Intelligence*, 18:265–298, 2004.

[10] H. Dee and D. C. Hogg. Detecting inexplicable behaviour. In *Proc. of British Machine Vision Conference (BMVC2014)*, 2004.

[11] M. Delafontaine, A. G. Cohn, and N. Van de Weghe. Implementing a qualitative calculus to analyse moving point objects. *Expert Systems with Applications*, 38(5):5187 – 5196, 2011.

[12] C. Dondrup, N. Bellotto, F. Jovan, and M. Hanheide. Real-time multisensor people tracking for human-robot spatial interaction. In *Workshop on Machine Learning for Social Robotics at IEEE Conf. on Robotics and Automation (ICRA)*, 2015.

[13] K. S. Dubba, M. R. d. Oliveira, G. H. Lim, H. Kasaei, L. S. Lopes, and A. Tome. Grounding language in perception for scene conceptualization in autonomous robots. In *AAAI Spring Symposium Series*, 2014.

[14] Y. Gatsoulis, P. Duckworth, C. Dondrup, P. Lightbody, and C. Burbridge. QSRlib: A library for qualitative spatial-temporal relations and reasoning, Jan 2016. qsrlib.readthedocs.org.

[15] Y. Gatsoulis et al. QSRlib: A library for qualitative spatial-temporal relations and reasoning. *In preparation.*

[16] W. Hu, X. Xiao, Z. Fu, D. Xie, and T. Tan. A system for learning statistical motion patterns. *IEEE Trans. on Pattern Analysis and Machine Intelligence*, 28:1450–1464, 2006.

[17] W. Hu, D. Xie, and T. Tan. A hierarchical self-organizing approach for learning the patterns of motion trajectories. *IEEE Trans. on Neural Networks*, 15:135–144, 2004.

[18] N. Johnson and D. C. Hogg. Learning the distribution of object trajectories for event recognition. In *Proc. British Machine Vision Conference (BMVC)*, 1995.

[19] T. Kanda, D. Glas, M. Shiomi, and N. Hagita. Abstracting people's trajectories for social robots to proactively approach customers. *IEEE Trans. on Robotics*, 25:1382–1396, 2009.

[20] L. Liao, D. J. Patterson, D. Fox, and H. Kautz. Learning and inferring transportation routines. *Artificial Intelligence*, 171:311–331, 2007.

[21] M. Luber, L. Spinello, J. Silva, and K. Arras. Socially-aware robot navigation: A learning approach. In *IEEE Conf. on Intelligent Robots and Systems (IROS)*, 2012.

[22] C. Piciarelli, G. L. Foresti, and L. Snidaro. Trajectory clustering and its applications for video surveillance. In *IEEE Conf. on Advanced Video and Signal Based Surveillance*, 2005.

[23] P. W. Rousseeuw. Silhouettes: a graphical aid to the interpretation and validation of cluster analysis. *Journal of Computational and Applied Mathematics*, 20:53–65, 1987.

[24] M. Sridhar, A. G. Cohn, and D. C. Hogg. Unsupervised learning of event classes from video. In *Association for the Advancement of Artificial Intelligence (AAAI)*, 2010.

[25] N. Van de Weghe, A. G. Cohn, P. De Maeyer, and F. Witlox. Representing moving objects in computer-based expert systems: The overtake event example. *Expert Systems with Applications*, 29:977–983, 2005.

[26] J. Young and N. Hawes. Learning by observation using qualitative spatial relations. In *IEEE Conf. on Autonomous Agents and Multiagent Systems*, 2015.

Directing Policy Search with Interactively Taught Via-Points

Yannick Schroecker
College of Computing
Georgia Tech
Atlanta, GA 30332, USA
yschroecker3@gatech.edu

Heni Ben Amor
Interactive Robotics Lab
Arizona State University
Tempe, AZ 85282, USA
hbenamor@asu.edu

Andrea Thomaz
Department of ECE
University of Texas at Austin
Austin, TX 78701, USA
athomaz@ece.utexas.edu

ABSTRACT

Policy search has been successfully applied to robot motor learning problems. However, for moderately complex tasks the necessity of good heuristics or initialization still arises. One method that has been used to alleviate this problem is to utilize demonstrations obtained by a human teacher as a starting point for policy search in the space of trajectories. In this paper we describe an alternative way of giving demonstrations as soft via-points and show how they can be used for initialization as well as for active corrections during the learning process. With this approach, we restrict the search space to trajectories that will be close to the taught via-points at the taught time and thereby significantly reduce the number of samples necessary to learn a good policy. We show with a simulated robot arm that our method can efficiently learn to insert an object in a hole with just a minimal demonstration and evaluate our method further on a synthetic letter reproduction task.

Keywords

Reinforcement Learning, Learning from Demonstration, Reinforcement Learning for Motor Skills, Dynamic Movement Primitives, Keyframe Demonstrations

1. INTRODUCTION

Robotics research in recent years has been working towards employing robots in unknown and often unstructured environments. However, controlling a robot in these environments poses major difficulties as the robot has to adapt its actions to the environment and needs to perform tasks with incomplete knowledge of the domain. Reinforcement learning and policy search methods in particular have shown great promise for autonomous learning of motor skills as trajectories. However, due to the high dimensionality and size of the state-action space, the required amount of samples can be prohibitive. A prominent approach to overcome this challenge is to use Learning from Demonstration to obtain an initial trajectory and to ensure that the learning process will quickly converge to the right optimum, see e.g. [15, 18, 4]. Unfortunately, this approach suffers from three major issues: First, providing trajectories as demonstrations can be difficult due to the available input modalities. Recording the desired trajectories using teleoperation or kinesthetic demonstration can be difficult for the user and thus often leads to undesirable pauses, sprints or imperfections. Second, providing full trajectories as demonstrations does not allow the user to put focus on critical segments and limits exploration for segments that the user cannot demonstrate as well as other parts of the trajectory. Third, demonstrations are typically only provided as an initialization of the policy search process. Refining a learned policy and removing undesirable effects usually requires a repeated recording of the entire demonstration and cannot be limited to specific aspects of the task. This problem is amplified if the policy search process has already been started as the learned policy can usually not be combined with new demonstrations.

To address these issues, we propose a method that uses soft via-points to initialize and interactively shape the policy search process. Recent research [1] has shown that via-point based representations can be efficiently obtained by a human teacher in the form of demonstrations and provide the teacher with a more natural way of teaching the desired trajectory. This kind of demonstration can achieve smoother trajectories by separating the act of moving the robot as a teacher from the intended trajectory that the robot should follow. Furthermore, it allows the teacher to focus on the most important aspects of the trajectory. In this paper, we introduce a method to use demonstrations in this form with policy search methods based on Dynamic Movement Primitives. More specifically, we look at policy search methods that can optimize DMP parameters and thereby improve the policy by evaluating parameters sampled around the current best estimate of the optimal policy. This class of policy search algorithms has shown great promise and includes methods such as PoWER [14], REPS [20], policy search based on CMA-ES [8, 22] and PI^2 [24]. By combining these two approaches we allow the teacher to demonstrate the salient points of a trajectory in a natural way while autonomously learning and improving the shape of the trajectory between those via-points. Our method achieves this goal by learning a single and smooth trajectory that adheres to the demonstrated via-points. Furthermore, we introduce a method to modify existing policy distributions by selecting the most likely trajectories based on the provided demonstration. Modifying the trajectory distribution in this way allows the user to provide corrections to existing policies and thereby shape the learning process. These corrections can be applied to policies learned by demonstration, either continuous demonstrations or via-point based demonstrations,

Appears in: *Proceedings of the 15th International Conference on Autonomous Agents and Multiagent Systems (AAMAS 2016), J. Thangarajah, K. Tuyls, C. Jonker, S. Marsella (eds.), May 9–13, 2016, Singapore.*

as well as to policies learned during the autonomous learning process. Finally, we propose to use models of via-points to handle variations of tasks that differ in parameters such as the position and orientation of key-objects in a manipulation task. We show that this facilitates efficient contextual policy search [13, 16] and allows to learn classes of tasks.

2. RELATED WORK

The work presented in this paper is focusing on policy search for robotics. For a survey of this topic, see Deisenroth et al. [6]. Specifically, we are looking at utilizing policy search methods for learning Dynamic Movement Primitives [10] that share the characteristic that they are sampling directly from the current estimate of the optimal policy. One example for this is the Covariance Matrix Adaption Evolution Strategy (CMA-ES) which has been used in [22] in order to learn dynamic movement primitives based on a reward signal. In [14], Kober et al. propose Policy Learning by Weighting Exploration with the Returns (PoWER) which uses regression weighted by rewards in order to obtain a new policy. Another method in this class is PI^2 [24] which uses path integrals to improve on the current policy.

In our evaluation, we use Episodic Relative Entropy Policy Search (REPS) [20] as the underlying policy search method. Peters et al. derive a sample based approximation of the optimal distribution of DMP parameters given trajectory- and reward samples as well as a bound on the KL-divergence between the optimized distribution and the distribution from which the trajectories were sampled. Using this approximation, the mean can iteratively be updated using weighted linear regression over the sampled DMP parameters and the variance can be updated by the weighted sample variance. The proper weights can be calculated by solving a convex optimization problem based on the bound on the KL-divergence and the sampled parameters and rewards. We refer to [20] for details.

In this paper, we consider an approach based on directing the policy search with demonstrations obtained by a human teacher. The field of Learning from Demonstration(LfD) has been extensively covered in [4] and LfD methods have successfully been combined with policy search for Dynamic Movement Primitives [15, 18]. In particular, we are looking at recording partial demonstrations in the form of via-points which have a long history in trajectory generation. Teaching via-points by demonstrations is also known as keyframe demonstration and has been shown to constitute a user-friendly and efficient way to obtain demonstrations [1]. Wada et al. extract via-points from a continuous demonstration and show that these can be used to create a trajectory that minimizes torque change [25]. Miyamoto et al. extend this approach and apply it to learning robot motor skills [17]. Bitzer et al. introduce an approach that combines keyframe demonstrations with reinforcement learning by learning a lower-dimensional manifold to simplify the state-space for a non-episodic reinforcement learner [3]. This method differs from our approach in that it only learns a simpler state-space representation and does not learn a heuristic for specific trajectories. Utilizing corrections in order to change a policy learned from demonstration has been introduced by Argall et al. who propose to use tactile corrections [2]. While this approach is interesting, it cannot be straight-forwardly integrated into autonomous policy search algorithms such as the ones utilized in our approach.

Utilizing feedback from human teachers has been investigated in the field of interactive reinforcement learning. Knox and Stone [12] introduce TAMER+RL, a reinforcement learning framework that utilizes a reward signal obtained by a human teacher in order to learn a regression model that can fulfill a role similar to a Q-function. Another example is given by Griffith et al. [7] who have introduced Policy Shaping. Policy shaping is utilizing rewards obtained by a human teacher in order to learn a separate policy. This policy can then be combined with the policy learned by standard reinforcement learning methods. Judah et al. [11] propose an integrated approach which optimizes a modified objective function based on the reward as well as on human feedback in the form of binary labels. All three methods utilize feedback provided by a human teacher but are different from our approach in that the feedback takes the shape of a reward-like signal instead of demonstrations. One can see both, the learning from demonstration based approach as well as the interactive reinforcement learning approach as belonging to a generalized class of algorithms that utilize insight obtained by a human teacher in order to improve the policy. In this view, the interactive reinforcement learning is online and less structured whereas the classical learning from demonstration based approach is offline and utilizes structured feedback. Our approach is structured as well but can be used in an offline manner as well as online.

Another representation of distributions over trajectories that can be restricted to go through specified via points is called Probabilistic Movement Primitives and has been proposed in [19]. Probabilistic Movement Primitives define feed-forward trajectories directly as combination of basis-functions and define operations on Gaussian distributions over such trajectories. The conditioning operation defined in this approach is similar to the operation for distributions over DMPs introduced in section 3.2. However, while it is likely that Probabilistic Movement Primitives could also be used with our approach, we are focusing on Dynamic Movement Primitives as they are more popular and better understood.

3. APPROACH

In this paper, we want to utilize a human teacher in order to provide corrections and suggestions before and during the learning process. Our goal is to use this information to help the learning algorithm converge to a better solution after seeing fewer samples. Specifically, we propose a setup where the teacher is observing the reinforcement learning process and can, before starting the learning process or in-between iterations, inspect the current estimate of the best policy and provide suggestions by physically or remotely moving the robot. Suggestions are recorded as soft via-points y^* that the trajectories have to pass through at a specified time t^*. In the case of corrections, the time t^* can be naturally recorded by having the user stop the robot during an execution in order to provide the correction. This process is illustrated in Algorithm 1. In the case of initial demonstrations, the time t^* can be estimated manually based on domain knowledge. While choosing the right t^* in this case may require some thought, we have found that simple heuristics such as distributing via-points equally in time or choosing t^* to be proportional to the spatial distance of the via-point are usually sufficient.

We base our method on episodic policy search in the space

of trajectories represented as Dynamic Movement Primitives (DMPs) [10, 21] which we describe in detail in section 3.1. These algorithms optimize the parameters of the DMP w.r.t. a given reward function, often by a weighted average with weights obtained based on a transformation of the rewards. The parameters of the DMP uniquely define a policy and thus, we loosely refer to the parameters $\boldsymbol{\theta}$ as policy and to the distribution over parameters $\pi(\boldsymbol{\theta})$ as policy distribution. To incorporate demonstrations and corrections into this framework, we use the given via-points as a heuristic to guide the learning process to the solution without directly modifying the given objective function. To this end, we obtain a modified policy distribution and sample only trajectories that are close to the demonstrated via-points. By modifying the policy directly, the effects of demonstrations and corrections are immediate and the learning process never samples trajectories that are far from the demonstrated via-points. This leads to faster convergence and safer samples. As we modify the policy directly, we require policy search methods that improve upon the given policy in independent iterations based on samples obtained directly from the policy such as PoWER [14], REPS [20] and CMA-ES [22] which obtain a new policy based on a weighted average of the samples obtained from the old policy distribution as well as PI^2 [24].

In many cases it can be desirable to consider parameterized tasks as this allows us to learn variations of a task instead of optimizing for a single trajectory. For example, the optimal trajectory in a manipulation task may depend on the location of key objects. One way to solve tasks such as these is to learn a linear model of the parameters $\mu_\pi = A_\pi \boldsymbol{\Phi}$ for some features $\boldsymbol{\Phi}$ to serve as the mean of the policy distribution [16]. To handle parameterized tasks, we generalize our notion of via-points to models that are linear in $\boldsymbol{\Phi}$, i.e. $y^* = B\boldsymbol{\Phi}$ where B is either derived from domain knowledge or learned with linear regression.

Algorithm 1 Policy search with interactive demonstrations

```
Initialize π^(0)(θ) ← N(θ; μ_π(0), Σ_π(0))
Obtain initial via-points y*, t* from demonstration
for y*, t* ← y*, t* do
    π^(0)(θ) ← p(θ|y*, t*, μ_π(0), Σ_π(0)) (see Eqs. 18-21)
end for
for k ← 1 to N iterations do
    π^(k)(θ) ← POLICY_SEARCH_ITERATION(π^(k))
    Execute trajectory defined by mean parameters μ_π(k)
    while teacher stops execution do
        Record stop time t*
        Let teacher move the robot, obtain correction y*
        π^(k)(θ) ← p(θ|y*, t*, μ_π(k), Σ_π(k))
        Execute mean trajectory defined by μ_π(k)
    end while
end for
```

3.1 Dynamic Movement Primitives

Policy search relies on optimizing the parameters of a parametric policy representation. One such policy representation are Dynamic Movement Primitives which have been introduced by Ijspeert et al. in [10]. DMPs are given as dynamical systems that are attracted by a goal position while following a superimposed trajectory. As such they have the property that they can adjust the goal position of the trajectory separately from the shape of the trajectory. Furthermore, DMPs have the concept of a phase which is a function of time which can be adapted by changing the time-scale. This is meant to reduce the dependency on the time. DMPs are defined as

$$\ddot{y} = \tau^2 \alpha \left(\beta (g - y) - \frac{\dot{y}}{\tau} \right) + \tau^2 f_{\mathbf{w}}(z), \tag{1}$$

$$\dot{z} = -\tau \alpha_z z. \tag{2}$$

where τ is the time scaling parameter and α_z is a parameter that shapes the phase function. α and β are parameters that are analogous to the gains of a PD-controller and define how the system is drawn to the goal of the trajectory which is defined by g. $f_{\mathbf{w}}(z)$ is the forcing function which determines the shape of the trajectory and is defined as a mixture of radial basis functions with parameters $K \in \mathbb{N}, \mathbf{c}, \mathbf{h} \in \mathbb{R}^K$

$$f_{\mathbf{w}}(z) \doteq \frac{\sum_{i=1}^{K} \varphi_i(z) w_i}{\sum_{i=1}^{K} \varphi_i(z)} z, \tag{3}$$

$$\varphi_i(z) \doteq \exp\left(-\frac{1}{2} \frac{(z - c_i)^2}{h_i} \right). \tag{4}$$

Commonly, the weights $w_i; 0 \leq i < K$ are taken as the parameters of the DMP that are learned by demonstration or autonomously whereas the other parameters are given as hyper-parameters. However, in some cases the goals are not known. We therefore include the goal position in the parameters $\boldsymbol{\theta} \doteq \left(\begin{smallmatrix} g \\ \boldsymbol{w} \end{smallmatrix}\right)$. K then determines the dimensionality of the parameter-space. In this paper, we are utilizing Gaussian distributions over DMP parameters as policy distributions and optimize this distribution with respect to the reward. The mean of this distribution π will be given as a linear function of the features of the task parameters: $\pi(\boldsymbol{\theta}) = \mathcal{N}(\boldsymbol{\theta}, A_\pi \boldsymbol{\Phi}, \Sigma_\pi)$.

3.2 Obtaining a Sample Distribution

Assuming that we have via-points obtained from demonstration as described above, we derive a modified policy distribution for the underlying policy search that passes close to this via-point at the specified time t^*:

$$\pi_H(\boldsymbol{\theta}) \doteq p(\boldsymbol{\theta}|t^*, y^*) \propto p(y^*|t^*, \sigma_y \boldsymbol{I}, \boldsymbol{\theta}) p(\boldsymbol{\theta}|t^*). \tag{5}$$

The latter distribution over parameters $\boldsymbol{\theta}$ denotes the prior of where we assume that the human teacher would want the samples to lie. A possible prior is the current policy $\mathcal{N}(\boldsymbol{\theta}|\mu_{\pi(k)}, \Sigma_{\pi(k)})$ where $\mu_{\pi(k)} = A_{\pi(k)} \boldsymbol{\Phi}$. This prior is reasonable as we want our samples to still follow the current policy where no via points are given. The modified sampling distribution then depends on the previous policy distribution and is given by

$$\begin{aligned} \pi_H(\boldsymbol{\theta}) &= p(\boldsymbol{\theta}|t^*, y^*, A_{\pi(k)}, \Sigma_{\pi(k)}) \\ &\propto p(y^*|t^*, \sigma_y \boldsymbol{I}, \boldsymbol{\theta}) \pi(\boldsymbol{\theta}|A_{\pi(k)}, \Sigma_{\pi(k)}). \end{aligned} \tag{6}$$

The former distribution $p(y^*|t^*, \sigma_y \boldsymbol{I}, \boldsymbol{\theta})$ denotes the probability of a given DMP going through the specified via point with a specified variance σ_y. This distribution is dependent on the trajectory that the DMP is following. As DMPs are defining accelerations as a linear differential equation, they can be solved for y given a starting position and velocity in order to obtain an estimate of the position at any given time. Note that the solution will not be exact as a real robotic system always has noise and the DMP will react to that noise

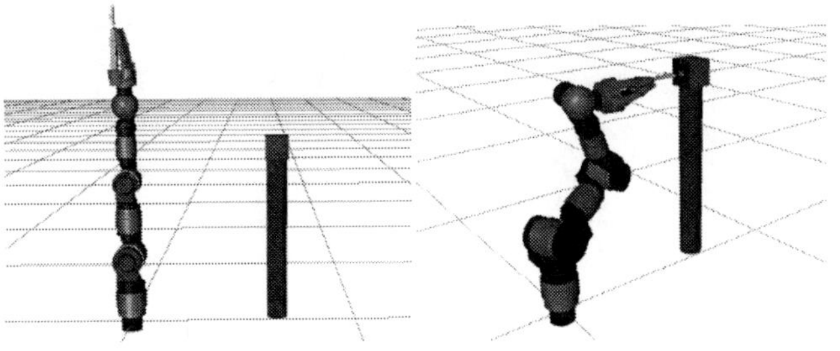

(a) (b)

Figure 1: **a)** Rest position of the robot. The robot has to find a trajectory that puts the object in the box. **b)** Via-point with the key placed in front of the hole, as it was given to the robot. All trajectories have to be close to this via-point which gives significant aid for finding the opening in the box.

as well as inaccuracies in the underlying controller. Only the goal position is being tracked exactly. However, using this estimate is reasonable as long as the noise of the estimate is significantly smaller than the inaccuracies introduced by the human teacher when recording a demonstration. Assuming that we start from a rest position where the position y_0 and velocity $\dot{y}_0$ are zero (we make this assumption for the sake of simplicity. See the appendix for a derivation of the sampling distribution for arbitrary y_0 and $\dot{y}_0$), the dynamical system can be solved for the position y using Duhamel's principle [23]:

$$\begin{pmatrix} y \\ \dot{y} \end{pmatrix} = \int_0^t h_t(s) \begin{pmatrix} 0 \\ \tau^2(\alpha\beta g + \boldsymbol{\Psi}(z(s))^T \boldsymbol{w}) \end{pmatrix} ds, \qquad (7)$$

where

$$h_t(s) \doteq e^{(t-s)\begin{pmatrix} 0 & 1 \\ -\tau^2\alpha\beta & -\tau\alpha \end{pmatrix}}, \qquad (8)$$

$$z(t) \doteq e^{-\tau\alpha_z t}, \qquad (9)$$

$$\boldsymbol{\Psi}_i(z) \doteq \frac{\varphi_i(z) z}{\sum_{j=0}^{K} \varphi_j(z)}. \qquad (10)$$

This equation is linear w.r.t the parameters $\boldsymbol{\theta}$ and can therefore be written as:

$$\boldsymbol{y} = \begin{pmatrix} 1 & 0 \end{pmatrix} \left(\int_0^t h_t(s) \begin{pmatrix} 0 \\ \tau^2(\alpha\beta g + \boldsymbol{\Psi}(z(s))^T \boldsymbol{w}) \end{pmatrix} ds \right) \qquad (11)$$

$$= \begin{pmatrix} 1 & 0 \end{pmatrix} \left(g\alpha\beta \int_0^t h_t(s) \begin{pmatrix} 0 \\ \tau^2 \end{pmatrix} ds \qquad (12) \right.$$

$$\left. \sum_{i=0}^{N} w_i \int_0^t \Psi_i(z(s)) h_t(s) \begin{pmatrix} 0 \\ \tau^2 \end{pmatrix} ds \right)$$

$$= \boldsymbol{M}_t \boldsymbol{\theta}, \qquad (13)$$

where

$$\boldsymbol{M}_t = \begin{pmatrix} m_0 & m_1 & \cdots & m_{N+1} \end{pmatrix}, \qquad (14)$$

$$m_0 = \int_0^t \alpha\beta h_t(s) \begin{pmatrix} 0 \\ \tau^2 \end{pmatrix} ds, \qquad (15)$$

$$m_{i;0<i<N+1} = \int_0^t \Psi_{i-1}(z(s)) h_t(s) \begin{pmatrix} 0 \\ \tau^2 \end{pmatrix} ds. \qquad (16)$$

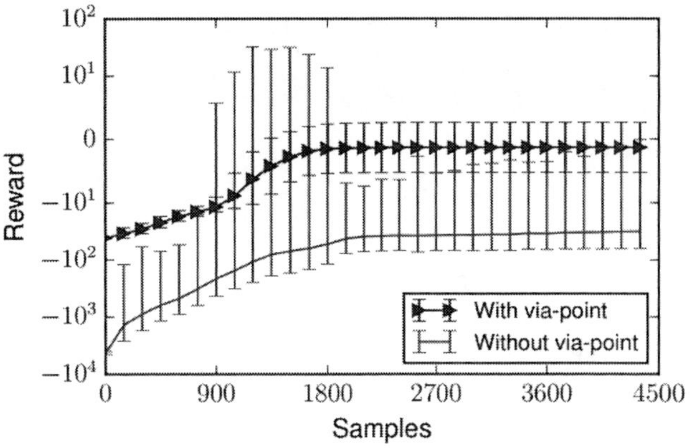

Figure 2: Rewards obtained over 20 trials during the learning process with and without via-points, plotted on a scale that is linear from -10 to 10 and logarithmic outside of that span. In 18 out of 20 trials, the learner with the via-point finds the opening in the box and obtains a reward close to zero. This results in a low standard deviation (error bars). Without the via-point the learning process converges to a local optimum.

Note that this equation is for a single dimension but can straightforwardly be extended to multiple dimensions by extending $\boldsymbol{M}$ diagonally and adding rows to $\boldsymbol{\theta}$ such that

$$\boldsymbol{y} = \begin{pmatrix} \boldsymbol{M}_t & \boldsymbol{0} & \cdots \\ \boldsymbol{0} & \boldsymbol{M}_t & \cdots \\ \vdots & \vdots & \ddots \end{pmatrix} \begin{pmatrix} \boldsymbol{\theta}_0 \\ \boldsymbol{\theta}_1 \\ \vdots \end{pmatrix},$$

where $\boldsymbol{\theta}_j$ denotes the parameters of the DMP for dimension j. Therefore for DMPs, we can write the likelihood distribution $p(y^*|t^*, \sigma_y \boldsymbol{I}, \boldsymbol{\theta})$ as

$$p(y^*|t^*, \sigma_y \boldsymbol{I}, \boldsymbol{\theta}) = \mathcal{N}(y^*|\boldsymbol{M}_{t^*}\boldsymbol{\theta}, \sigma_y \boldsymbol{I}). \qquad (17)$$

Now we can calculate the sampling distribution as the posterior distribution of the likelihood $p(y^*|t^*, \sigma_y \boldsymbol{I}, \boldsymbol{\theta})$, encoding information about the via-point, and the prior distribution π which consists of the previously learned policy. For Gaussian distributions, the sampling distribution is therefore given as

$$\pi_H(\boldsymbol{\theta}) = \mathcal{N}(\boldsymbol{\theta}|A_H \boldsymbol{\Phi}, \Sigma_H), \qquad (18)$$

$$\Sigma_H \doteq \left(\Sigma_{\pi(k)}^{-1} + \boldsymbol{M}_{t^*}^T \sigma_y^{-1} \boldsymbol{I} \boldsymbol{M}_{t^*} \right) \qquad (19)$$

$$= \Sigma_{\pi(k)} - \Sigma_{\pi(k)} \boldsymbol{M}_{t^*}^T (\sigma_y \boldsymbol{I} + \qquad (20)$$

$$\left. \boldsymbol{M}_{t^*} \Sigma_{\pi(k)} \boldsymbol{M}_{t^*}^T \right)^{-1} \boldsymbol{M}_{t^*} \Sigma_{\pi(k)},$$

$$A_H \doteq \Sigma_H \left(\boldsymbol{M}_{t^*}^T \sigma_y^{-1} \boldsymbol{I} B + \Sigma_{\pi(k)}^{-1} A_{\pi(k)} \right). \qquad (21)$$

Where the application of the Woodbury matrix identity in Eq. 20 allows for numerically stable computation of Σ_H. This sampling distribution can then be used in place of the policy in order to obtain the samples used in the next iteration of the policy search as described in Algorithm 1.

4. EXPERIMENTS

In section 3, we showed how to derive a modified sampling distribution based on via-points with timing information that are provided by a human demonstration. In this section, we first utilize a simulated robot arm to show that

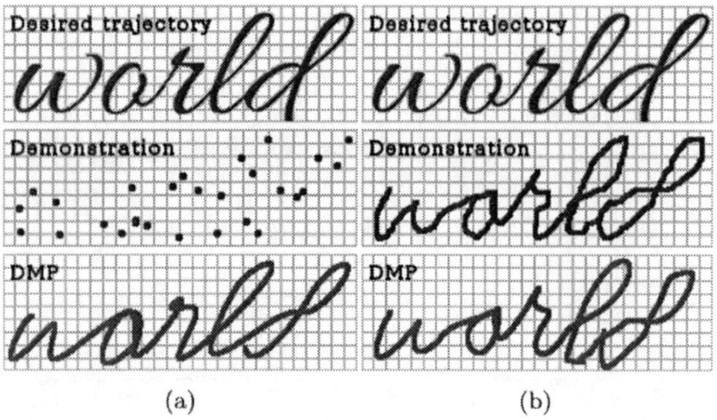

Figure 3: **a)** Mean trajectory of initial policy (bottom) derived from via-points (center). The trajectory is smooth and barely deviates from the desired trajectory (top) even in-between via-points. **b)** Mean trajectory (bottom) of initial policy derived from a continuous demonstration (center). Especially the last letter shows how the trajectory mimics imperfections of the demonstration.

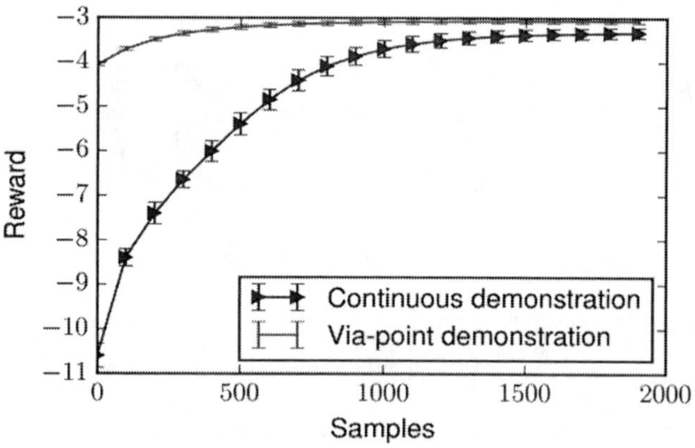

Figure 4: Comparison of reward obtained within 2000 samples, averaged over 30 trials. Error bars are showing the standard deviation. The reward function is defined as the minimum squared distance to the goal position. Learning initialized with via-points consistently outperforms the learning process initialized with a continuous demonstration.

such a modified sampling distribution can drastically improve the outcome of a reinforcement learner by having it learn how to insert an object in a hole while requiring only minimal information from the user. We then utilize a word reproduction task in order to provide a comparison to continuous demonstrations and to exhaustively analyze the key-properties of our algorithm.

4.1 Object Insertion with a Robot Arm

In our first experiment, we are evaluating the influence of a small number of demonstrated via-points on the reinforcement learning process and show that it can drastically improve the convergence of the policy search. To this end, we are utilizing a simulated 7 DoF robot arm and have it learn how to insert an object into a hole without any knowledge about the environment. We provide a single via-point (see Figure 1b) and show that this is sufficient to lead the learning process to the right solution which cannot reliably be found without a demonstration. To learn this task, we are utilizing our method with REPS as the underlying policy search algorithm to optimize the distribution over trajectories. These trajectories are represented by 7 Dynamic Movement Primitives with 6-dimensional weights leading to a 49-dimensional action vector $\boldsymbol{\theta}$. For evaluation, the outcome of the learning process is averaged over 20 trials with 30 policy search iterations per trial and 150 samples for each iterations. As can be seen in Figure 2, the reward curve observed by using the via-point is converging to a value close to 0 and therefore the distance of the trajectory to the goal position is converging to 0 as well. The learning process initialized with a zero mean policy, on the other hand, is converging to different values. This can easily be explained by the local optima that arise around the box, i.e. the robot is converging to solutions where the end-effector is pressing against the middle of other the sides of the box in order to get closer to the goal position. As a consequence, it stops exploring the box and does not find the opening. Note that the learning process always exceeds the initial reward obtained by our approach as the reinforcement learner always finds at least the closest points outside of the box which cannot be derived by the provided via-point alone, i.e. the provided via-point is further away from the box than the local optima.

4.2 Letter Writing

To further investigate the properties of this algorithm we are evaluating our approach on a letter reproduction task as well. Variations of this task have been used in the past to evaluate different properties of Dynamic Movement Primitives as it has many similarities with learning trajectories for robot arms while allowing for intuitive visualization, easy recording of demonstrations and thus good conditions for a comparison to conventional demonstrations as well as fast execution [10, 9]. The objective of the letter reproduction task is to learn trajectories for both dimensions which, when followed by a simulated pen, can accurately reproduce a sequence of letters. We are representing those trajectories as DMPs with a 60 dimensional weight-vector for each dimension and initialize the policy by a continuous demonstration or via-points before optimizing it using REPS. For the policy search, we defined the reward function as the number of overlapping black pixels: $-\frac{10^4}{\#IntersectingPixels+1}$. Note that solving this task requires the learning algorithm to learn trajectories that are far more complex than in the previous task while utilizing a sparser reward signal. First, we will compare our algorithm to learning trajectories from continuous demonstrations as a baseline, then we will evaluate the use of corrections after the learning process has started and finally we will show that linear models of via-points can be used to learn policies that can reproduce trajectories with different rotation and scaling factors.

4.2.1 Comparison to Continuous Demonstrations

The first instance of the letter reproduction task compares learning initialized with a normal distribution around a continuous demonstration to learning initialized on a fixed set of via-points at equi-distant points in time. In this experiment we show that despite the lack of information between via-points, our approach will converge to a more accurate solution in fewer iterations. To obtain an initial policy from a continuous demonstration, we use standard least squares

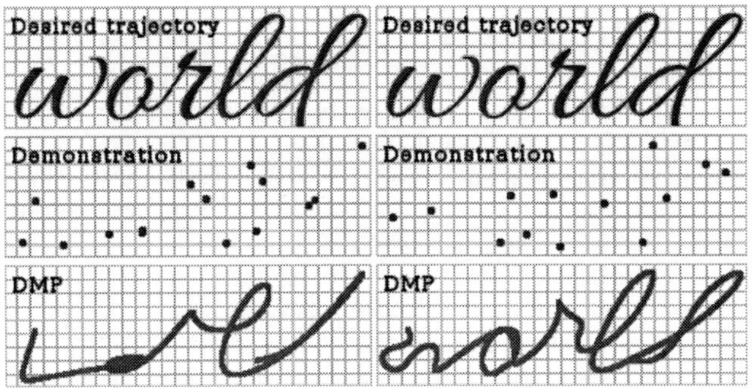

(a) (b)

Figure 5: **a)** Mean trajectory of the initial policy (bottom) derived by using only every second via-point (center). This trajectory omits whole letters when compared to the desired trajectory (top). **b)** Trajectory after 3 iterations (bottom), when the second half of the via-points have been added (center). The policy now shows the desired word and can be improved in future iterations. The "r" is not fully formed immediately after the correction due to learned behavior.

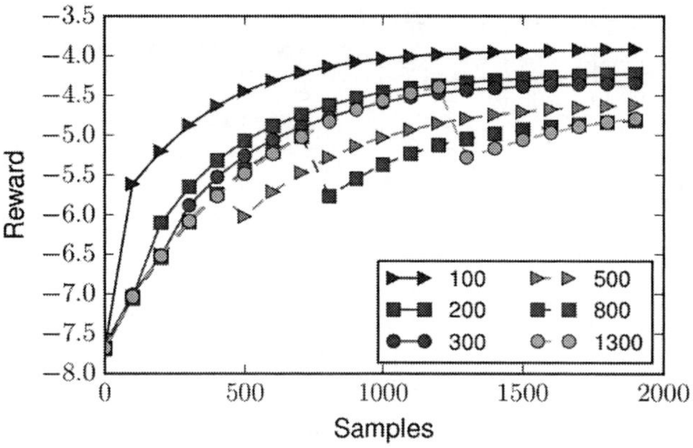

Figure 6: Comparison of rewards obtained with the rest of the via-points added after different numbers of samples. Early demonstrations are clearly better than late demonstrations but late demonstrations can still be effective.

to learn the mean and then add an initial variance of 10^3 for the weights and 5 for the goals of the DMPs. We have found these values to yield the best result in the continuous case. For policy search initialized with via-points, we start with a multivariate normal distribution with mean 0 and a variance of 10^5 for the weights and 500 for the goal positions. Note that the higher initial variance is necessary as conditioning on the via-points will otherwise lead to an overly narrow distribution with each added via-point decreasing the variance of the policy. This initial distribution is then used as the prior distribution to obtain a modified initial policy based on the via-points that can be seen in Figure 3a. In Figures 3a and b, it can be seen that the initial policy derived from the via-points is very smooth whereas the initial policy derived from a continuous demonstration mirrors the imperfections of that demonstration. Note that these imperfections are often much larger in practice as policy search is unnecessary in domains where given demonstrations already solve the task perfectly. Furthermore, the figures show that the errors introduced by missing information between the via-points is of the same order as the errors that can be introduced by linear regression and that the mean of the initial policy is already describing a good trajectory which leads to a fast learning process. Finally, Figure 4 shows that our approach yields both, higher initial reward as well as higher final reward and therefore better trajectories before and after the learning process, when compared to the baseline. Note that the higher initial reward is tied to the amount of exploration that is necessary in the beginning and can, in many cases, be a desirable property when it comes to safe exploration. While our approach only explores the areas in-between the via-points, a reinforcement learner that has been initialized with a continuous demonstration has to explore around the full trajectory. It is possible to reduce the exploration around the continuous demonstrations; however this would also reduce the final reward that can be obtained.

4.2.2 Active Corrections

One important aspect of the approach presented in this paper is that via-points can be provided at any time and can be used to modify an already trained policy. This is especially useful in situations where the optimal trajectory is not immediately apparent to the user. To investigate the impact of providing via-points at later iterations we are looking at a variation of the letter writing task where only every second of the initial via-points are provided from the start. Figure 5a shows that this constitutes a far worse initial policy and that we would expect large gains by providing the second half of the via-points. As can be seen in Figure 5b as well as in the reward curve in Figure 6, via-points provided at a later point can indeed improve the policy significantly.

However, while giving the via-points after some number of iterations can still cause a significant jump in reward, the size of this jump decreases for later iterations. After some time, the modified sample distribution will even decrease the performance of the learning process. This effect can be attributed to a mismatch of the chosen prior distribution, i.e. the current policy, with the optimal prior distribution which is the unknown policy according to which the human teacher is sampling his via-points. As the learning process converges to a sub optimal policy, it is impossible to sample trajectories that adhere to both, the learned policy as well as the specified via-points. Depending on the value of the variance parameter, the learner can then either sam-

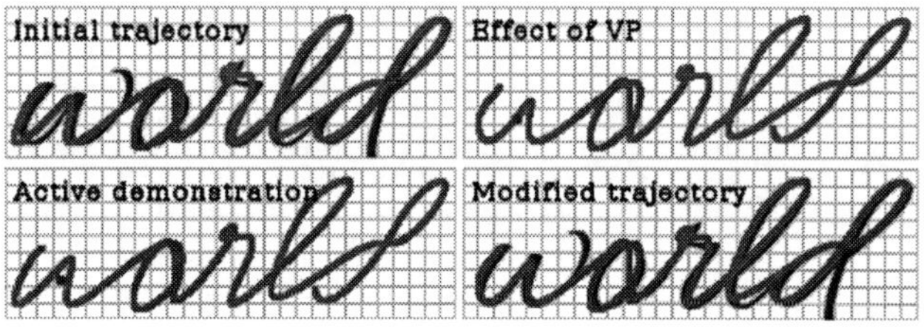

(a) (b)

Figure 7: Example of giving via-points interactively. **a)** Original policy in comparison to the desired trajectory (top) and the via-point that has been provided as a correction (bottom). **b)** Mean of the modified policy. The trajectory goes through the via-point (top) and thereby matches the desired trajectory more closely (bottom).

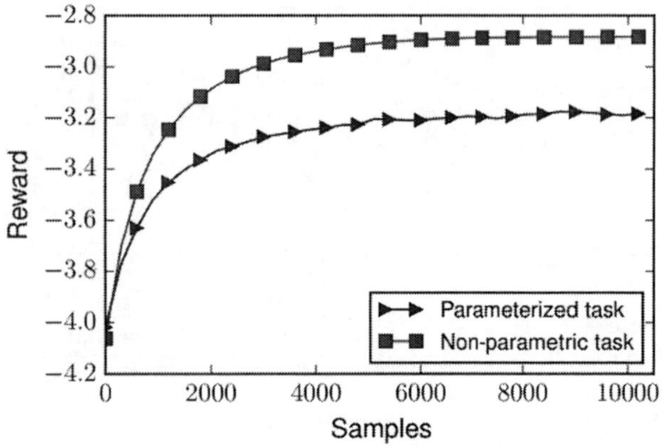

Figure 8: Reward obtained by contextual REPS shows that via-point models are an effective initialization. Rewards on the non-parametric task are displayed for comparison. The initial reward is identical due to the linear model and is improved upon significantly in both cases.

ple degenerate trajectories from low-probability areas of the current policy or ignore the given suggestion. The variance parameter is thus a measure of safety and specified how far the new policy can stray from the learned policy in order to adhere to the correction. To avoid this effect, via-points should always be given while the uncertainty in the current policy is relatively high in comparison to the deviation of the via-points from this policy. Note that in this experiment, the via-points are already known from the start even if the agent doesn't utilize them. This allowed us to analyze the effect of giving late demonstrations without having to account for the human factor. However, in practice, late demonstrations should be given depending on trajectories sampled from the current policy. This way, the user can actively shape the trajectory and guide the learning process to the right solution. We illustrate the process of providing via-points interactively and show the impact of a correction in Figure 7.

4.2.3 *Evaluation of Learning with Linear Models*

For the third experiment, we investigated the properties of learning a parametric generalization of the above task with a linear via-point model. We are looking at learning a model that can recreate words with respect to rotation and scaling of the target image. Note that similar kinds of parametric tasks can be found in practice, where the parameters often denote the location and orientation of an object. We are assuming that good features are known as this would be a necessity for obtaining a via-point model in practice. In this case we are using the feature vector $(s_x cos(\theta), s_y cos(\theta), s_x sin(\theta), s_y sin(\theta), 1)$ with s_x and s_y representing the scaling and lie between 0.6 and 1.4 whereas θ represents the rotation of the target image which lies between -45 and 45 degrees. The linear via-point models are then given w.r.t. these features and are used for learning a linear Gaussian policy using locally linear weighted regression and contextual REPS. Figure 8 shows that the initial policy adapts to the task parameters and that it can be used in conjunction with contextual REPS to obtain a similar reward curve for arbitrary rotations and scaling as for a single instance of the task.

5. CONCLUSION

In this paper we introduced an approach to utilize partial demonstrations to interactively guide the policy search process. We have shown that our approach of using soft via-points significantly outperforms continuous demonstrations when used to initialize the learning process. Furthermore, our results show that our approach can be used to guide the learning process in an interactive way, utilizing the knowledge gained from observing the robot to change specific aspects of the policy. Finally, we have shown that we can use linear models of via-points to generalize over variations of a task.

One key insight is that when applying our method during the learning process, the results are largely dependent on the covariance of the already learned policy. While sampling completely new trajectories ensures that the robot continues exploration and does not return to the original trajectory after reaching the via-point, it also requires a prior distribution that specifies sensible trajectories. In our approach, this distribution is given by the policy search. In the future, we plan to investigate other prior distributions based on different models of how humans give via-points to allow providing corrections to already converged policies. Furthermore, for each via-point the user is required to specify an exact point in time. We plan to relax this assumption and allow the user to specify distributions in time as the importance of preserving the timing is heavily dependent on the task. Finally, the method presented in this paper is based on the assumption that the policy is a Gaussian distribution. While this can be a reasonable assumption, there are cases where other distributions would be preferable. Multi-modal policies, for example, can be used to learn tasks with multiple solutions [5]. In the future, we would like to explore this avenue and extend our approach to different types of policies.

Acknowledgments

This work was conducted as a part of the OpenLabs project 1436618 sponsored by PSA Peugeot and partially funded under ONR grant number N000141410003.

APPENDIX

A. DERIVING $\pi_H(\theta)$ FOR ARBITRARY INITIAL POSITIONS AND VELOCITIES

In section 3, we derived a sampling distribution under the assumption that $y_0 = 0$ and $\dot{y}_0 = 0$. However, while $y_0 = 0$ can be assumed w.l.o.g., $\dot{y}_0 = 0$ is only true for trajectories that start from a rest position. Here, we derive an equivalent sampling distribution for the general case. In the general case, the closed form for dynamic movement primitives is given by

$$\begin{pmatrix} \boldsymbol{y} \\ \dot{\boldsymbol{y}} \end{pmatrix} = \int_0^t e^{(t-s)\begin{pmatrix} 0 & 1 \\ -\tau^2\alpha\beta & -\tau\alpha \end{pmatrix}} \begin{pmatrix} 0 \\ \tau^2(\alpha\beta g + \Psi(z(s))^T \boldsymbol{w}) \end{pmatrix} ds + e^{t\begin{pmatrix} 0 & 1 \\ -\tau^2\alpha\beta & -\tau\alpha \end{pmatrix}} \begin{pmatrix} y_0 \\ \dot{y}_0 \end{pmatrix}. \quad (22)$$

And therefore

$$\boldsymbol{y} = \boldsymbol{M}_t \boldsymbol{\theta} + c \quad (23)$$

where

$$c \doteq \begin{pmatrix} 1 & 0 \end{pmatrix} e^{t\begin{pmatrix} 0 & 1 \\ -\tau^2\alpha\beta & -\tau\alpha \end{pmatrix}} \begin{pmatrix} y_0 \\ \dot{y}_0 \end{pmatrix}. \tag{24}$$

The sampling distribution $p(\boldsymbol{\theta}|t^*, y^*) = \mathcal{N}(\boldsymbol{\theta}|A_H\boldsymbol{\Phi}, \Sigma_H)$ is then computed with the modified likelihood distribution

$$p(y^*|t^*, \boldsymbol{\theta}) = \mathcal{N}(y^*|\boldsymbol{M}_{t^*}\boldsymbol{\theta} + c, \sigma_y \boldsymbol{I}). \tag{25}$$

The mean of this distribution differs slightly from the distribution derived in section 3 so that

$$A_H\boldsymbol{\Phi} = \Sigma_H \left(\boldsymbol{M}_{t^*}^T \sigma_y^{-1} \boldsymbol{I} \left(B\boldsymbol{\Phi} - c\right) + \Sigma_{\pi(k)}^{-1} A_{\pi(k)} \boldsymbol{\Phi}\right). \tag{26}$$

Note that we can assume w.l.o.g. that $\boldsymbol{\Phi}$ is of the form $\boldsymbol{\Phi} = \begin{pmatrix} \Phi_1 & \Phi_2 & \cdots & 1 \end{pmatrix}^T$. The sampling distribution is then defined by

$$\Sigma_H \doteq \Sigma_{\pi(k)} - \Sigma_{\pi(k)} \boldsymbol{M}_{t^*}^T \left(\sigma_y \boldsymbol{I} + \boldsymbol{M}_{t^*} \Sigma_{\pi(k)} \boldsymbol{M}_{t^*}^T\right)^{-1} \boldsymbol{M}_{t^*} \Sigma_{\pi(k)}, \tag{27}$$

$$A_H \doteq \Sigma_H \left(\boldsymbol{M}_{t^*}^T \sigma_y^{-1} \boldsymbol{I} \left(B - \begin{pmatrix} 0 & \ldots & 0 & c \end{pmatrix}\right) + \Sigma_{\pi(k)}^{-1} A_{\pi(k)}\right). \tag{28}$$

REFERENCES

[1] B. Akgun, M. Cakmak, J. W. Yoo, and A. L. Thomaz. Trajectories and keyframes for kinesthetic teaching: a human-robot interaction perspective. In *International Conference on Human-Robot Interaction*, pages 391–398, 2012.

[2] B. Argall, E. Sauser, and A. Billard. Policy adaptation through tactile correction. In *Annual Convention of the Society for the Study of Artificial Intelligence and Simulation of Behaviour (AISB)*, 2010.

[3] S. Bitzer, M. Howard, and S. Vijayakumar. Using dimensionality reduction to exploit constraints in reinforcement learning. In *International Conference on Intelligent Robots and Systems (IROS)*, pages 3219–3225, 2010.

[4] S. Chernova and A. L. Thomaz. Robot learning from human teachers. *Synthesis Lectures on Artificial Intelligence and Machine Learning*, 8(3):1–121, 2014.

[5] C. Daniel, G. Neumann, and J. Peters. Hierarchical relative entropy policy search. In *International Conference on Artificial Intelligence and Statistics (AISTATS)*, 2012.

[6] M. P. Deisenroth, G. Neumann, and J. Peters. A survey on policy search for robotics. *Foundations and Trends in Robotics*, 2(1-2):1–142, 2013.

[7] S. Griffith, K. Subramanian, J. Scholz, C. Isbell, and A. L. Thomaz. Policy shaping: integrating human feedback with reinforcement learning. In *Advances in Neural Information Processing Systems (NIPS)*, pages 2625–2633, 2013.

[8] N. Hansen and A. Ostermeier. Adapting arbitrary normal mutation distributions in evolution strategies: the covariance matrix adaptation. In *International Conference on Evolutionary Computation (ICEC)*, pages 312–317, 1996.

[9] A. J. Ijspeert, J. Nakanishi, H. Hoffmann, P. Pastor, and S. Schaal. Dynamical movement primitives: learning attractor models for motor behaviors. *Neural Computation*, 25(2):328–373, 2013.

[10] A. J. A. Ijspeert, J. Nakanishi, and S. Schaal. Learning attractor landscapes for learning motor primitives. In *Advances in Neural Information Processing Systems (NIPS)*, pages 1547–1554, 2002.

[11] K. Judah, S. Roy, A. Fern, and T. G. Dietterich. Reinforcement Learning Via Practice and Critique Advice. *AAAI*, 2010.

[12] W. B. Knox and P. Stone. Reinforcement learning from simultaneous human and MDP reward categories and subject descriptors. In *Autonomous Agents and Multiagent Systems (AAMAS)*, pages 475–482, 2012.

[13] J. Kober, E. Oztop, and J. Peters. Reinforcement learning to adjust robot movements to new situations. In *Robotics: Science and Systems (RSS)*, 2010.

[14] J. Kober and J. Peters. Policy search for motor primitives in robotics. In *Advances in Neural Information Processing Systems (NIPS).*, pages 849–856, 2008.

[15] P. Kormushev, S. Calinon, and D. G. Caldwell. Robot motor skill coordination with EM-based reinforcement learning. In *Intelligent Robots and Systems (IROS)*, pages 3232–3237, 2010.

[16] A. G. Kupcsik, M. P. Deisenroth, J. Peters, and G. Neumann. Data-Efficient Generalization of Robot Skills with Contextual Policy Search. In *AAAI Conference on Artificial Intelligence (AAAI)*, 2013.

[17] H. Miyamoto, S. Schaal, F. Gandolfo, H. Gomi, Y. Koike, R. Osu, E. Nakano, Y. Wada, and M. Kawato. A Kendama learning robot based on bi-directional theory. *Neural Networks*, 9(8):1281–1302, 1996.

[18] K. Mülling, J. Kober, O. Kroemer, and J. Peters. Learning to select and generalize striking movements in robot table tennis. *International Journal of Robotics Research*, 32(3):263–279, 2013.

[19] A. Paraschos, C. Daniel, J. Peters, and G. Neumann. Probabilistic movement primitives. In *Advances in Neural Information Processing Systems (NIPS)*, pages 2616–2624, 2013.

[20] J. Peters, K. Mülling, and Y. Altun. Relative Entropy Policy Search. In *AAAI Conference on Artificial Intelligence (AAAI)*, pages 1607–1612, 2010.

[21] S. Schaal. Dynamic movement primitives - a framework for motor control in humans and humanoid robotics. In *Adaptive Motion of Animals and Machines*, pages 261–280. Springer Tokyo, 2003.

[22] F. Stulp and O. Sigaud. Path integral policy improvement with covariance matrix adaptation. In *International Conference on Machine Learning (ICML)*, pages 281–288, 2012.

[23] G. Teschl. *Ordinary differential equations and dynamical systems*, volume 140. American Mathematical Soc., 2012.

[24] E. Theodorou, J. Buchli, and S. Schaal. Learning policy improvements with path integrals. In *International Conference on Artificial Intelligence and Statistics (AISTATS)*, pages 828–835, 2010.

[25] Y. Wada, Y. Koike, E. Vatikiotis-Bateson, and M. Kawato. A computational model for cursive handwriting based on the minimization principle. In *Advances in Neural Information Processing Systems (NIPS)*, pages 727–734, 1993.

Inverse Reinforcement Learning from Failure

Kyriacos Shiarlis
Informatics Institute
University of Amsterdam
Science Park 904
Amsterdam, Netherlands
k.c.shiarlis@uva.nl

Joao Messias
Informatics Institute
University of Amsterdam
Science Park 904
Amsterdam, Netherlands
j.messias@uva.nl

Shimon Whiteson
Dept. of Computer Science
University of Oxford
Wolfson Building, Parks Rd
Oxford, United Kingdom
shimon.whiteson@cs.ox.ac.uk

ABSTRACT

Inverse reinforcement learning (IRL) allows autonomous agents to learn to solve complex tasks from successful demonstrations. However, in many settings, e.g., when a human learns the task by trial and error, *failed* demonstrations are also readily available. In addition, in some tasks, purposely generating failed demonstrations may be easier than generating successful ones. Since existing IRL methods cannot make use of failed demonstrations, in this paper we propose *inverse reinforcement learning from failure* (IRLF) which exploits both successful and failed demonstrations. Starting from the state-of-the-art *maximum causal entropy IRL* method, we propose a new constrained optimisation formulation that accommodates both types of demonstrations while remaining convex. We then derive update rules for learning reward functions and policies. Experiments on both simulated and real-robot data demonstrate that IRLF converges faster and generalises better than maximum causal entropy IRL, especially when few successful demonstrations are available.

Keywords

Inverse reinforcement learning, learning from demonstration, social navigation, robotics, machine learning.

1. INTRODUCTION

In *inverse reinforcement learning* (IRL) [10], an *apprentice* aims to learn a policy for acting in an environment, typically modelled as a *Markov decision process* (MDP), for which the reward function is not available, but successful demonstrations provided by an *expert* performing the task are given instead. An IRL algorithm tries to find a reward function that leads the apprentice to behave similarly to the expert while generalising well to situations for which expert data is not available.

Numerous IRL methods have been proposed. In [14] a structured prediction formulation using maximum margin is developed and applied to mobile robotics. In [12], a Bayesian formulation is proposed along with approximations necessary for computational tractability. Other work considers nonlinear representations of the reward function using Gaussian processes [8] or decision trees [13]. IRL has also been applied to a wide range of applications, from autonomous driving [1, 7] to socially appropriate navigation [6, 18] and training parsers for natural language processing [9].

Existing IRL algorithms learn only from successful demonstrations, i.e., from data gathered by an expert performing the task well. This is consistent with the main motivation of IRL since it allows learning in tasks where the reward cannot be trivially hard-coded. For example, the reward function that allows an agent to perform complicated manoeuvres while flying a helicopter cannot be trivially determined, but example demonstrations are easy to obtain from an expert.

In many realistic scenarios, failed demonstrations are also readily available. Consider for example tasks such as driving a car. Since humans also learn this task by trial and error, demonstrations of both successful and failed behaviour are available. Although hand-coding a reward function for this task would be infeasible, labelling each trial as successful or failed is straightforward. In addition, in many tasks, it may be easier to demonstrate failure than success. If expert demonstrations are scarce but a safe simulator is available, a non-expert can often easily demonstrate multiple failure modes, yielding data that complements the scarce successful demonstrations. This idea is explored in [16], where a robot learns to avoid people using simulations of failed avoidance. Finally, failed demonstrations may be used to explore the state-action space, an idea previously leveraged in learning from demonstration [5].

In existing IRL methods, failed demonstrations have been treated as noise [19] and filtered out in order to improve robustness. However, such methods do not actually use such demonstrations for learning.

In this paper, we introduce *inverse reinforcement learning from failure* (IRLF), which is to our knowledge the first IRL algorithm that can learn from both successful and failed demonstrations. In doing so, we address a key difficulty in IRL: the problem is typically under-constrained since many reward functions are consistent with the expert's behaviour. By exploiting failed demonstrations, our method reduces this ambiguity, resulting in faster and better learning.

To derive IRLF, we start from the state-of-the-art *maximum causal entropy IRL* [22, 20] method, which is also related to [2]. We propose a new constrained optimisation formulation that accommodates both successful and failed demonstrations while remaining convex. We then derive update rules for learning policies and reward functions.

We evaluate our algorithm on the task of social navigation for a mobile robot, using both simulated and real-robot

Appears in: *Proceedings of the 15th International Conference on Autonomous Agents and Multiagent Systems (AAMAS 2016), J. Thangarajah, K. Tuyls, C. Jonker, S. Marsella (eds.), May 9–13, 2016, Singapore.*

data, as well as the *Factory* problem, a well known decision making benchmark. On the simulated scenarios, our results demonstrate that IRLF generalises better than maximum causal entropy IRL when successful demonstrations are scarce, with little additional computational cost. On the real-robot data, IRLF also outperforms this baseline.

2. BACKGROUND

Most IRL methods formalise the underlying decision-making problem as a *Markov decision process* (MDP), a model of a discrete-time process wherein an agent's actions may stochastically influence its environment. In an MDP, at step t, the system (which includes the agent and its environment) is known to be in a *state* $s_t \in \mathcal{S}$; the agent selects an action $a_t \in \mathcal{A}$ and is awarded a real-valued *reward*; and the system jumps to state s_{t+1} with probability $P(s_{t+1}|s_t, a_t)$. Formally, an MDP is a tuple $\langle \mathcal{S}, \mathcal{A}, T, R\rangle$, where $\mathcal{S}$ and $\mathcal{A}$ are sets of discrete states and actions respectively, $T : \mathcal{S}\times\mathcal{A}\times\mathcal{S} \to [0, 1]$ is a transition function such that $T(s, a, s') = P(s'|s, a)$, and $R : \mathcal{S} \times \mathcal{A} \to \mathbb{R}$ is the reward function. Optimally solving an MDP involves finding a policy $\pi : \mathcal{S} \times \mathcal{A} \to [0, 1]$ with $\pi(s, a) = P(a \,|\, s)$, that maximises the expected sum of rewards over a fixed number of decisions h. This expectation can be expressed as the *value* of policy π:

$$V^{\pi}(s) := E\{\sum_{t=1}^{h} R(s_t, a_t) \,|\, s_1 = s\}. \quad (1)$$

Given data obtained from interacting with an MDP, RL methods seek a policy that maximises this expectation for a given reward function. By contrast, given data obtained from *expert* interactions with an MDP, IRL seeks the reward function that the expert was maximising. IRL is useful in the many situations in which the expert cannot easily formalize her objectives as a reward function. Instead, the *learner*, an autonomous agent, can learn the reward function from the expert's behaviour and use it to imitate her.

IRL is formalised as an 'incomplete' MDP $\langle \mathcal{S}, \mathcal{A}, T\rangle$, also known as an MDP/R. Though initially unknown, the reward function is parametrised by K *feature functions*, $\phi_k(s, a)$:

$$R(s, a) = \sum_{k=1}^{K} w_k \phi_k(s, a), \quad (2)$$

where $w = [w_1\, w_2 \,\dots\, w_k]^T$ is the weight vector that IRL aims to learn.

Since w is independent of states and actions, (1) and (2) imply a parametric form of the value function:

$$V^{\pi}(s) = \sum_{k=1}^{K} w_k \left(E\{\sum_{t=1}^{h} \phi_k(s_t, a_t) \,|\, s_1 = s\} \right) \quad (3)$$

$$=: \sum_{k=1}^{K} w_k \mu_k^{\pi,1:h}|_{s_1=s}, \quad (4)$$

where $\mu_k^{\pi,1:h}|_{s_1=s}$, the *feature expectation*, is the expected accumulation of instances of feature ϕ_k between steps 1 and h under policy π given that $s_1 = s$. The step indices are omitted for simplicity when this expectation is over the full horizon $\{1, \dots, h\}$.

The learner learns from a dataset of N trajectories, $\mathcal{D} = \{\tau_1, \tau_2, \dots\tau_N\}$. Each trajectory $\tau_i = \langle (s_1^{\tau_i}, a_1^{\tau_i}), (s_2^{\tau_i}, a_2^{\tau_i}), \dots, (s_h^{\tau_i}, a_h^{\tau_i})\rangle$ is a state-action sequence of length h generated by the expert. Given $\mathcal{D}$, the learner can compute the *empirical feature expectation*, the average accumulated instances of each feature in $\mathcal{D}$:

$$\widetilde{\mu}_k^{\mathcal{D}} := \frac{1}{N} \sum_{\tau\in\mathcal{D}} \sum_{t=1}^{h} \phi_k(s_t^{\tau}, a_t^{\tau}). \quad (5)$$

Note that $\widetilde{\mu}_k^{\mathcal{D}}$ is state independent and implicitly estimates an expectation across the expert's initial state. To fairly compare the feature expectation of some policy π to $\widetilde{\mu}_k^{\mathcal{D}}$, we obtain an analogously state-independent measure of π's feature expectation by marginalising out s_1:

$$\mu_k^{\pi}|_{\mathcal{D}} := \sum_{s\in\mathcal{S}} P_{\mathcal{D}}(s_1 = s)\mu_k^{\pi}|_{s_1=s}, \quad (6)$$

where $P_{\mathcal{D}}(s_1 = s) = N_1(s)/N$ is the maximum likelihood estimate of the expert's initial state distribution, given that $N_1(s)$ is the number of trajectories with $s_1 = s$.

The learner aims to find w such that the distance between the vectors $\widetilde{\mu}^{\mathcal{D}} = [\widetilde{\mu}_1^{\mathcal{D}} \dots \widetilde{\mu}_k^{\mathcal{D}}]^T$ and $\mu^{\pi}|_{\mathcal{D}} = [\mu_1^{\pi}|_{\mathcal{D}} \dots \mu_k^{\pi}|_{\mathcal{D}}]$ is minimised according to some metric, while also generalising well to unseen initial conditions.

IRL methods are typically iterative. An initial guess for w is fed to a planner that produces a policy π that is optimal given w. Using π, trajectories are generated from the same initial states as in $\mathcal{D}$ to compute $\mu^{\pi}|_{\mathcal{D}}$, which is then compared to $\widetilde{\mu}^{\mathcal{D}}$. Finally, w is updated to reduce to distance between the two expectations, and the process repeats.

The task of finding w can be formulated as an optimisation problem that requires the expert trajectories to have maximal value [1] or that do so by some margin [14]. Alternatievely one may employ Bayesian inference [12, 4] to compute a posterior distribution over the weights. In this paper, we concentrate on methods that learn maximum-entropy policies [22, 20]. A maximum-entropy approach is attractive because it is probabilistic and thus robust to noise and randomness in the actions of the expert, and results in convex optimisation problems. The methods work by solving the following constrained optimisation problem:

$$\text{find:} \quad \max_{\pi} H(\mathcal{A}^h||\mathcal{S}^h) \quad (7)$$

$$\text{subject to:} \quad \widetilde{\mu}_k^{\mathcal{D}} = \mu_k^{\pi}|_{\mathcal{D}} \quad \forall k \quad (8)$$

$$\text{and:} \quad \sum_{a\in\mathcal{A}} \pi(s, a) = 1 \quad \forall s \in \mathcal{S} \quad (9)$$

$$\text{and:} \quad \pi(s, a) \geq 0 \quad \forall s \in \mathcal{S}, a \in \mathcal{A}, \quad (10)$$

where $H(\mathcal{A}^h||\mathcal{S}^h)$, the *causal entropy*, is the conditional entropy of the action sequence $\mathcal{A}^h$, causally conditioned on the state sequence $\mathcal{S}^h$:

$$H(\mathcal{A}^h||\mathcal{S}^h) = -\sum_{t=1}^{h} \sum_{\substack{s_{1:t}\in\mathcal{S}^t \\ a_{1:t}\in\mathcal{A}^t}} P(a_{1:t}, s_{1:t}) \log(P(a_t|s_t)), \quad (11)$$

where:

$$\begin{aligned} P(a_{1:t}, s_{1:t}) &= P(s_{1:t-1}, a_{1:t-1})P(s_t|s_{t-1}, a_{t-1})P(a_t|s_t) \\ &= P(s_{1:t-1}, a_{1:t-1})T(s_{t-1}, a_{t-1}, s_t)\pi(s_t, a_t). \end{aligned}$$

The constraints require that π consists of proper probability distributions that match the empirical feature expectations.

The optimisation problem is solved using the method of Lagrange multipliers. First, the equality constraint (8) is relaxed, yielding a Lagrangian:

$$\mathcal{L}(\pi, w) := H(\mathcal{A}^h||\mathcal{S}^h) + \sum_{k=1}^{K} w_k(\mu_k^\pi|_\mathcal{D} - \widetilde{\mu}_k^\mathcal{D}), \tag{12}$$

and in turn a less constrained optimisation problem:

$$\text{find: } \min_w \left\{\max_\pi (\mathcal{L}(\pi, w))\right\} \tag{13}$$

$$\text{subject to: } \sum_{a\in\mathcal{A}} \pi(s,a) = 1 \quad \forall s \in \mathcal{S} \tag{14}$$

$$\text{and: } \pi(s,a) \geq 0 \quad \forall s \in \mathcal{S}, a \in \mathcal{A}, \tag{15}$$

Differentiating $\mathcal{L}(\pi, w)$ with respect to π at time t results in [20, p. 186]:

$$\nabla_{\pi(s_t,a_t)}\mathcal{L}(\pi, w) = P(s_{1:t}, a_{1:t-1})\Bigg(- \log(\pi(a_t, s_t)) + H(\mathcal{A}^{t+1:h}||\mathcal{S}^{t+1:h}) + \sum_{k=1}^{K} w_k E\left\{\sum_{\tau=1}^{h} \phi_k(s_t, a_t)|s_{1:t}, a_{1:t-1}\right\}\Bigg). \tag{16}$$

Setting the gradient to zero and solving for π gives:

$$\pi(s_t, a_t) \propto \exp\left(H(\mathcal{A}^{t:h}||\mathcal{S}^{t:h}) + \sum_{k=1}^{K} w_k \mu_k^{\pi,t:h}|_{s_t,a_t}\right). \tag{17}$$

Due to (4), the rightmost term in (17) is a measure of value for a given state and action, parameterised by w. [20] showed that solving (17) while satisfying (14) and (15) amounts to solving a soft Bellman equation:

$$\begin{aligned} Q_w(s,a)^{soft} &= \sum_{k=1}^{K} w_k\phi_k(s,a) + \sum_{s'} T(s,a,s')V_w(s'), \\ V_w(s)^{soft} &= \log \sum_a exp(Q_w(s,a)), \\ \pi(s,a) &= \exp(Q_w(s,a) - V_w(s)). \end{aligned} \tag{18}$$

Once π is computed for a given w, w is updated via gradient descent, by noting that:

$$\nabla_w \mathcal{L}(\pi, w) = \mu^\pi|_\mathcal{D} - \widetilde{\mu}^\mathcal{D}, \tag{19}$$

where $\mu^\pi|_\mathcal{D}$ is computed by rolling out policy π from the initial state distribution $P_\mathcal{D}(s_1)$ over h steps, and taking an expectation over the features accumulated at each step. The optimisation process terminates once the weight vector converges to the optimal solution.

3. METHOD

In this section, we propose *inverse reinforcement learning from failure* (IRLF), a novel IRL algorithm that exploits failed demonstrations. IRLF is applicable in settings where the apprentice has access to a dataset $\mathcal{F}$ of failed demonstrations, in addition to a dataset $\mathcal{D}$ of successful ones.

A critical challenge in developing such a method is deciding how to interpret failed trajectories. While successful trajectories may not be optimal, it is clear that the agent should try to imitate them, which in our case means matching feature expectations. By contrast, a failed trajectory is more ambiguous because it is unclear what about it is wrong: was the entire trajectory incorrect, or was it almost correct but wrong with respect to one particular feature? A key characteristic of the method we propose is that it works well in both these cases.

The first step is to formulate a new constrained optimisation problem analogous to (7)–(10). In addition to requiring that the feature expectations of the learned policy match the empirical expectations of $\mathcal{D}$, we now also want those feature expectations to be *dissimilar* to the empirical expectations of $\mathcal{F}$. Although successful and failed demonstrations are semantic opposites, incorporating the latter into IRL proves to be nontrivial.

A straightforward approach is to add inequality constraints to the optimisation problem:

$$|\widetilde{\mu}_k^\mathcal{F} - \mu_k^\pi|_\mathcal{F}| > \alpha_k \quad \forall k, \tag{20}$$

where $\widetilde{\mu}_k^\mathcal{F}$ is the empirical expectation of feature k according to $\mathcal{F}$, computed analogously to (5), and α_k is a variable to be maximised as part of the optimisation objective, which becomes:

$$\max_{\pi,\alpha} H(\mathcal{A}^h||\mathcal{S}^h) + \sum_{k=1}^{K} \alpha_k. \tag{21}$$

However, this formulation is problematic because (20) is not a convex constraint. In fact, this approach is equivalent to maximising the L_1 norm of $\widetilde{\mu}^\mathcal{F} - \mu^\pi|_\mathcal{F}$, which is nonconvex.

A convex relaxation of the above approach can be formulated by removing the extra constraint in (20) and instead adding to the objective the inner product of a parameter vector $\theta = [\theta_1 \ \ldots \ \theta_k]^T$ and the difference in feature expectations, yielding the following objective function:

$$\max_{\pi,\theta} H(\mathcal{A}^h||\mathcal{S}^h) + \sum_{k=1}^{K} \theta_k(\mu_k^\pi|_\mathcal{F} - \widetilde{\mu}_k^\mathcal{F}). \tag{22}$$

However, this approach is also problematic because it complicates the maximisation of the Lagrangian. We now need to find a critical point with respect to *both* π and θ, which is analytically involved and numerically expensive, since it requires calculating $\mu^\pi|_\mathcal{F}$ each time that π is updated via the soft Bellman backup in (18).

To avoid these difficulties, we propose a different formulation. The main idea is to create new equality constraints of the form $\mu_k^\pi|_\mathcal{F} - \widetilde{\mu}_k^\mathcal{F} = z_k$ with $z_k \in \mathbb{R}$, and introduce the z_k variables as terms in the optimisation objective. The complete constrained optimisation problem is thus:

$$\max_{\pi,\theta,z} \quad H(\mathcal{A}^h||\mathcal{S}^h) + \sum_{k=1}^{K} \theta_k z_k - \frac{\lambda}{2}||\theta||^2 \tag{23}$$

$$\text{subject to:} \quad \mu_k^\pi|_\mathcal{D} = \widetilde{\mu}_k^\mathcal{D} \quad \forall k \tag{24}$$

$$\text{and:} \quad \mu_k^\pi|_\mathcal{F} - \widetilde{\mu}_k^\mathcal{F} = z_k \quad \forall k \tag{25}$$

$$\text{and:} \quad \sum_{a\in\mathcal{A}} \pi(s,a) = 1 \quad \forall s \in \mathcal{S} \tag{26}$$

$$\text{and:} \quad \pi(s,a) \geq 0 \quad \forall s \in \mathcal{S}, a \in \mathcal{A}, \tag{27}$$

where λ is a constant. Intuitively, the first term in the objective seeks to maximise π's causal entropy, while the second term balances this against maximising dissimilarity between π's feature expectations and the empirical expectations in $\mathcal{F}$; the third term regularises to discourage large values of θ.

The main advantage of this formulation is that π and θ become decoupled for a given z, making maximisation of the

Lagrangian feasible while preserving convexity. Specifically, the new Lagrangian is:

$$\mathcal{L}(\pi,\theta,z,w^{\mathcal{D}},w^{\mathcal{F}}) = H(\mathcal{A}^h||\mathcal{S}^h) - \frac{\lambda}{2}||\theta||^2 + \sum_{k=1}^{K}\theta_k z_k + \sum_{k=1}^{K} w_k^{\mathcal{D}}(\mu_k^{\pi}|_{\mathcal{D}} - \widetilde{\mu}_k^{\mathcal{D}}) + \sum_{k=1}^{K} w_k^{\mathcal{F}}(\mu_k^{\pi} - \widetilde{\mu}_k^{\mathcal{F}}|_{\mathcal{F}} - z_k). \tag{28}$$

The less constrained optimisation problem of (13)–(15) remains unchanged except that maximisation of the Lagrangian is now with respect to π, θ, and z. Next, we differentiate the new Lagrangian with respect to the primal variables, beginning with θ and z:

$$\nabla_{\theta_k}\mathcal{L}(\pi,\theta,z,w^{\mathcal{D}},w^{\mathcal{F}}) = z_k - \lambda\theta_k, \tag{29}$$

$$\nabla_{z_k}\mathcal{L}(\pi,\theta,z,w^{\mathcal{D}},w^{\mathcal{F}}) = \theta_k - w_k^{\mathcal{F}}. \tag{30}$$

Setting both derivatives to zero yields:

$$z_k = \lambda w_k^{\mathcal{F}} \text{ and } \theta_k = w_k^{\mathcal{F}}. \tag{31}$$

Plugging this back into the Lagrangian gives:

$$\max_{z,\theta}\mathcal{L}(\pi,\theta,z,w^{\mathcal{D}},w^{\mathcal{F}}) =: \mathcal{L}_{z,\theta}(\pi,w^{\mathcal{D}},w^{\mathcal{F}}) = H(\mathcal{A}^h||\mathcal{S}^h) - \frac{\lambda}{2}||w^{\mathcal{F}}||^2 + \sum_{k=1}^{K} w_k^{\mathcal{F}}(\mu_k^{\pi}|_{\mathcal{F}} - \widetilde{\mu}_k^{\mathcal{F}} - \lambda w_k^{\mathcal{F}}) + \sum_{k=1}^{K} w_k^{\mathcal{D}}(\mu_k^{\pi}|_{\mathcal{D}} - \widetilde{\mu}_k^{\mathcal{D}}). \tag{32}$$

Finally, we differentiate $\mathcal{L}_{z,\theta}$ with respect to π:

$$\nabla_{\pi(s_t,a_t)}\mathcal{L}_{z,\theta}(\pi,w^{\mathcal{D}},w^{\mathcal{F}}) = P(s_{1:t},a_{1:t-1})\big(-\log(\pi(a_t,s_t)) + H(\mathcal{A}^{t+1:h}||\mathcal{S}^{t+1:h}) + \sum\nolimits_{k=1}^{K}(w_k^{\mathcal{D}}+w_k^{\mathcal{F}})E\{\sum\nolimits_{\tau=1}^{h}\phi_k(s_t,a_t)|s_{1:t},a_{1:t-1}\}\big) \tag{33}$$

$$\pi(s_t,a_t) \propto \exp\left(H(\mathcal{A}^{t:h}||\mathcal{S}^{t:h}) + \sum_{k=1}^{K}(w_k^{\mathcal{D}}+w_k^{\mathcal{F}})\mu_k^{\pi,t:h}|_{s_t,a_t}\right). \tag{34}$$

Intuitively, (34) implies that the value of π now depends on *both* Lagrangian multipliers $w^{\mathcal{D}}$ and $w^{\mathcal{F}}$. We can maximise with respect to π using a soft backup method analogous to (18) with the crucial difference that the reward function is now $\sum_{k=1}^{K}(w_k^{\mathcal{D}}+w_k^{\mathcal{F}})\phi_k(s,a)$. Using the resulting policy π^*, we can define the dual objective:

$$L^*(w^{\mathcal{D}},w^{\mathcal{F}}) := \max_{\pi,\theta,z}\left(\mathcal{L}(\pi,\theta,z,w^{\mathcal{D}},w^{\mathcal{F}})\right) = H^{\pi^*}(\mathcal{A}^h||\mathcal{S}^h) - \frac{\lambda}{2}||w^{\mathcal{F}}||^2 + \sum_{k=1}^{K} w_k^{\mathcal{D}}(\mu_k^{\pi^*}|_{\mathcal{D}} - \widetilde{\mu}_k^{\mathcal{D}}) + \sum_{k=1}^{K} w_k^{\mathcal{F}}(\mu_k^{\pi^*}|_{\mathcal{F}} - \widetilde{\mu}_k^{\mathcal{F}} - \lambda w_k^{\mathcal{F}}). \tag{35}$$

Finally, to solve the dual, i.e., minimise L^*, we differentiate it with respect to $w^{\mathcal{D}}$ and $w^{\mathcal{F}}$:

$$\nabla_{w_k^{\mathcal{D}}}L^*(w^{\mathcal{D}},w^{\mathcal{F}}) = \mu_k^{\pi^*}|_{\mathcal{D}} - \widetilde{\mu}_k^{\mathcal{D}}, \tag{36}$$

$$\nabla_{w_k^{\mathcal{F}}}L^*(w^{\mathcal{D}},w^{\mathcal{F}}) = \mu_k^{\pi^*}|_{\mathcal{F}} - \widetilde{\mu}_k^{\mathcal{F}} - \lambda w_k^{\mathcal{F}}. \tag{37}$$

Setting (37) to zero yields:

$$w_k^{\mathcal{F}} = \frac{\mu_k^{\pi^*}|_{\mathcal{F}} - \widetilde{\mu}_k^{\mathcal{F}}}{\lambda}. \tag{38}$$

(36) implies that $w_k^{\mathcal{D}}$ can be updated using gradient descent, since the value of $\mu_k^{\pi^*}|_{\mathcal{D}}$ will change in the next iteration. The minimising solution for $w_k^{\mathcal{F}}$ is found analytically. (38) shows how IRLF pushes the apprentice away from the failed demonstrations. If $\mu_k^{\pi^*}|_{\mathcal{F}} - \widetilde{\mu}_k^{\mathcal{F}}$ is positive, then $w_k^{\mathcal{F}}$ will also be positive. Since $w^{\mathcal{F}}$ is part of the reward function, on the next iteration, this will encourage a new π^* that increases $\mu_k^{\pi^*}|_{\mathcal{F}} - \widetilde{\mu}_k^{\mathcal{F}}$ further. The reverse occurs when $w^{\mathcal{F}}$ is negative.

A key characteristic of IRLF is that it also handles cases where the failed trajectories are only 'partial' failures, i.e., when the failed trajectories are similar to the successful ones with respect to some features and dissimilar with respect to others. For example, suppose there are only two features and $\widetilde{\mu}_1^{\mathcal{D}}$ is similar to $\widetilde{\mu}_1^{\mathcal{F}}$ but $\widetilde{\mu}_2^{\mathcal{D}}$ is dissimilar to $\widetilde{\mu}_2^{\mathcal{F}}$. It might seem that the updates to $w_k^{\mathcal{D}}$ and $w_k^{\mathcal{F}}$ with respect to the first feature would cancel each other out, thereby preventing IRLF from successfully imitating the successful trajectories with respect to that feature. However, that is not the case.

As IRLF iterates, the gradient descent update on $w_1^{\mathcal{D}}$ will bring the model and the data closer with respect to the first feature. Due to the similarity between $\widetilde{\mu}_1^{\mathcal{D}}$ and $\widetilde{\mu}_1^{\mathcal{F}}$, the analytical update on $w_1^{\mathcal{F}}$ will be smaller. Therefore, the inluence of the failed demonstrations with respect to that feature will be small. The opposite will happen with respect to the second feature. Since, $\widetilde{\mu}_2^{\mathcal{D}}$ and $\widetilde{\mu}_2^{\mathcal{F}}$ are disimilar, the update $w_2^{\mathcal{F}}$ will have an increasingly greater influence on the overall reward associated with that feature. Thus, with respect to the second feature, IRLF will be pulled towards the successful trajectories and pushed away from the failed ones. At the same time, this will not prevent IRLF from being pulled towards the successfull trajectories with respect to the first feature. Our experiments in the next section empirically validate this characteristic of IRLF.

Another convenient characteristic of IRLF is that it does not require the feature sets for successful and failed demonstrations that make up $\mu^{\pi^*}|_{\mathcal{F}}$ and $\mu^{\pi^*}|_{\mathcal{D}}$ to be the same. A designer is therefore free to represent failed demonstrations with a different feature set that is more informative than the one used for succesful demonstrations. Exploiting this property in practice is an interesting direction for future work.

However, a potential problem with IRLF is that, because (36) is updated incrementally while (38) is solved analytically, performance may oscillate, as small changes in w_k^s may be accompanied by large changes in w_k^f. This is especially true because the feature expectations of π are influenced by the updates on both $w^{\mathcal{D}}$ and $w^{\mathcal{F}}$. Fortunately, we can make IRLF more stable by annealing λ across iterations. Specifically, we start with a large value of λ, meaning that failed demonstrations are essentially ignored, and decrease it by a factor of α_λ on each iteration until a user-specified floor λ_{min} is reached. Intuitively, IRLF begins by ignoring the failed demonstrations and gradually takes them into account more and more.

Algorithm 1 describes IRLF procedurally. First, we compute the empirical feature expectations (lines 1-2) for both datasets $\mathcal{D}$ and $\mathcal{F}$ using (5). The initial state distributions are also computed (lines 3-4) by taking the normalised counts of the initial states in the two datasets. Then, we initialise the reward function (lines 5-8) used to find a policy (line 9). Using this policy, the model feature expectations are calculated as described by [21]. Next, we perform the updates following (36) and (38) (lines 12-13). Finally, we incrementally reduce λ (lines 14-15) to improve stability.

Algorithm 1 IRLF($\mathcal{S}, \mathcal{A}, T, \phi, \mathcal{D}, \mathcal{F}, \alpha, \alpha_\lambda, \lambda, \lambda_{min}$)

1: $\widetilde{\mu}^{\mathcal{D}} \leftarrow$ `empiricalFE`($\mathcal{D}$) {using (5)}
2: $\widetilde{\mu}^{\mathcal{F}} \leftarrow$ `empiricalFE`($\mathcal{F}$)
3: $P^{s_1}_{\mathcal{D}} \leftarrow$ `initialStateDistribution`($\mathcal{D}$)
4: $P^{s_1}_{\mathcal{F}} \leftarrow$ `initialStateDistribution`($\mathcal{F}$)
5: $w^{\mathcal{F}}_k \leftarrow 0 \quad \forall k \in \{1, \ldots, K\}$
6: Initialize $w^{\mathcal{D}}$ randomly
7: **repeat**
8: $\quad R(s,a) \leftarrow (w^{\mathcal{D}} + w^{\mathcal{F}})^T \phi(s,a) \quad \forall s \in \mathcal{S}, a \in \mathcal{A}$
9: $\quad \pi \leftarrow$ `softPlan`($\mathcal{S}, \mathcal{A}, T, R$) {using (18)}
10: $\quad \mu^{\pi}|_{\mathcal{D}} =$ `calculateFE`($\pi, T, P^{s_1}_{\mathcal{D}}$)
11: $\quad \mu^{\pi}|_{\mathcal{F}} =$ `calculateFE`($\pi, T, P^{s_1}_{\mathcal{F}}$)
12: $\quad w^{\mathcal{D}} \leftarrow w^{\mathcal{D}} - \alpha(\mu^{\pi}|_{\mathcal{D}} - \widetilde{\mu}^{\mathcal{D}})$
13: $\quad w^{\mathcal{F}} \leftarrow \frac{(\mu^{\pi}|_{\mathcal{F}} - \widetilde{\mu}^{\mathcal{F}})}{\lambda}$
14: $\quad$ **if** $\lambda > \lambda_{min}$ **then**
15: $\qquad \lambda \leftarrow \alpha_\lambda \lambda$
16: $\quad$ **end if**
17: **until** convergence
18: **return** R, π

4. EXPERIMENTS

To evaluate IRLF, we consider three domains. Two of these concern the task of navigating a mobile robot in a social environment, a key challenge problem in social robotics [11]. Because social rules are difficult to quantify, IRL is well suited to this task [6, 18]. We first consider learning in a simulated navigation domain and then repeat the process using data gathered from experiments on a real telepresence robot.[1]

Our third domain is the *Factory* problem, a well known decision-theoretic benchmark domain[3]. We compare IRLF to the original *maximum casual entropy IRL* [22], which we henceforth refer to simply as IRL.

4.1 Simulated Navigation Domain

First, we consider a simulated navigation domain, shown in Figure 1, in which a robot (blue) navigates its environment to reach a target (red) while avoiding a moving obstacle (green). The state space contains all possible combined (x, y) positions of the obstacle and the robot as well as five possible orientations for the obstacle, with one of them being stopped. The action space is $\mathcal{A} = \{up, down, left, right, stay\}$. Binary state features are computed by discretising the displacement between the (x, y) coordinates of the robot to both the obstacle and the target into five possible values for each of the four dimensions, yielding a complete feature vector $\phi(s) \in \{0, 1\}^{20}$ for any $s \in \mathcal{S}$. The transition model for this world is deterministic. The action chosen by the robot results in the agent moving to that direction with probability 1. The moving obstacle maintains its initial orientation throughout the episode. When the obstacle moves beyond the edge of the grid, it reappears on the opposite side, while the robot remains in the same cell until a valid action is chosen.

[1]Code to replicate the experiments in Sections 4.1 and 4.2 can be found at : `https://github.com/KyriacosShiarli/IRLF_aamas2016_Replicate.git`.

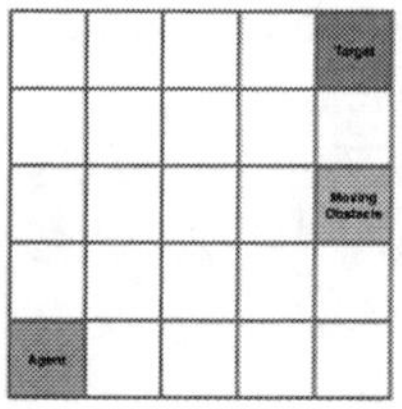

Figure 1: Simulated social navigation task.

We first manually define two ground truth reward functions, $R^{\mathcal{D}^*} = w^{\mathcal{D}^*} \phi(s,a)$, $R^{\mathcal{F}^*} = w^{\mathcal{F}^*} \phi(s,a)$, described further below. Then, we sample initial test states from a uniform distribution over the state space, over which we define $P^{s_1}_{test}$, for all experimental runs. These initial conditions, along with the optimal maximum-entropy policies for $R^{\mathcal{D}^*}$ and $R^{\mathcal{F}^*}$, allow us to compute feature expectations $\widetilde{\mu}^{\mathcal{D}_{test}}$ and $\widetilde{\mu}^{\mathcal{F}_{test}}$ respectively. For each experimental run, we then sample a set of initial training states, over which we define $P^{s_1}_{train}$, and generate the respective feature expectations $\widetilde{\mu}^{\mathcal{D}_{train}}$, $\widetilde{\mu}^{\mathcal{F}_{train}}$. These feature expectations are used to learn reward functions and their corresponding policies using each algorithm under evaluation. Each learned policy π^* is then executed from initial states sampled from $P^{s_1}_{test}$ to determine $\mu^{\pi^*}|_{test}$, the feature expectations for the policy at those initial conditions. Finally, we compute the values of each policy, at those initial conditions, with respect to the two reward functions, $V^{\pi^*}_{\mathcal{D},test} = (w^{\mathcal{D}^*})^T \mu^{\pi^*}|_{test}$, $V^{\pi^*}_{\mathcal{F},test} = (w^{\mathcal{F}^*})^T \mu^{\pi^*}|_{test}$. A good algorithm will yield a high $V^{\pi^*}_{\mathcal{D},test}$ and a low $V^{\pi^*}_{\mathcal{F},test}$.

Within this domain, we consider three scenarios that differ in how $R^{\mathcal{D}^*}$ and $R^{\mathcal{F}^*}$ are defined. In the *contrasting scenario*, $w^{\mathcal{D}^*}$ rewards reaching the target and avoiding the obstacle, while $w^{\mathcal{F}^*}$ rewards being in the same cell as the obstacle. This scenario examines the value of completely failed demonstrations when the successful demonstrations already show the complete desired behaviour.

In the *overlapping scenario*, $w^{\mathcal{D}^*}$ is as before but $w^{\mathcal{F}^*}$ rewards not only colliding with the obstacle, but also reaching the target. This scenario examines the value of failed demonstrations when they are similar in some respects to the successful demonstrations.

In the *complementary scenario*, $w^{\mathcal{D}^*}$ rewards only reaching the target, while $w^{\mathcal{F}^*}$ only rewards hitting the obstacle. This scenario examines the value of failed demonstrations when the successful demonstrations do not fully disambiguate the desired behaviour.

Figures 2a and 2d compare the performance of IRLF, with and without incremental updates to λ, to that of IRL in the contrasting scenario. Both versions of IRLF successfully utilise failed demonstrations to learn better and faster than IRL in terms of $V^{\pi^*}_{\mathcal{D},test}$. They achieve similar performance to IRL in terms of $V^{\pi^*}_{\mathcal{F},test}$.

Figures 2b and 2e show results for the overlapping scenario. Even in this challenging setting, IRLF learns better than IRL, demonstrating the resilience of our method to the fact that some successful and failed trajectories might be similar and showing that our method can exploit the additional data found in failed trajectories without negative side effects.

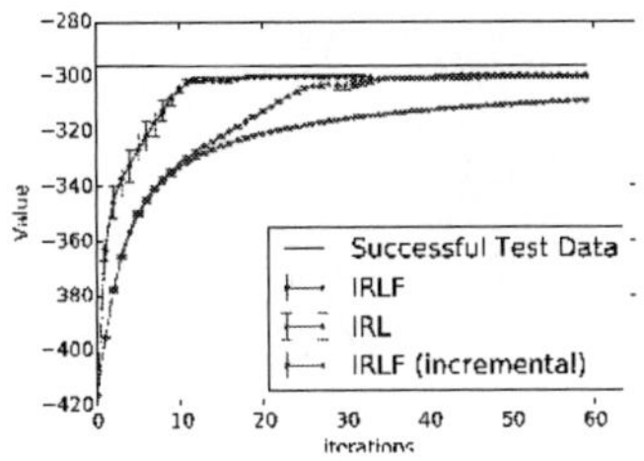

(a) Contrasting w.r.t. $w^{\mathcal{D}^*}$

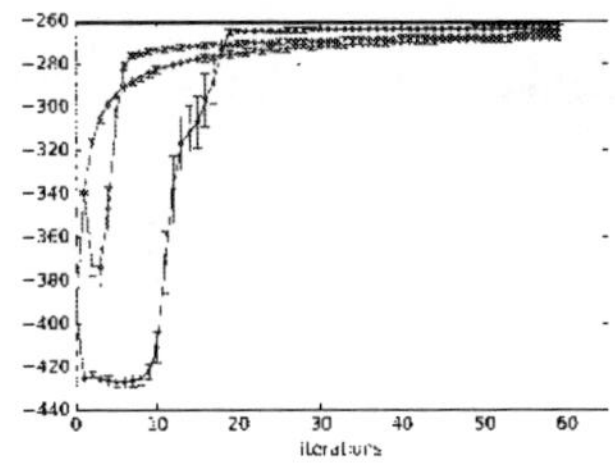

(b) Overlapping w.r.t. $w^{\mathcal{D}^*}$

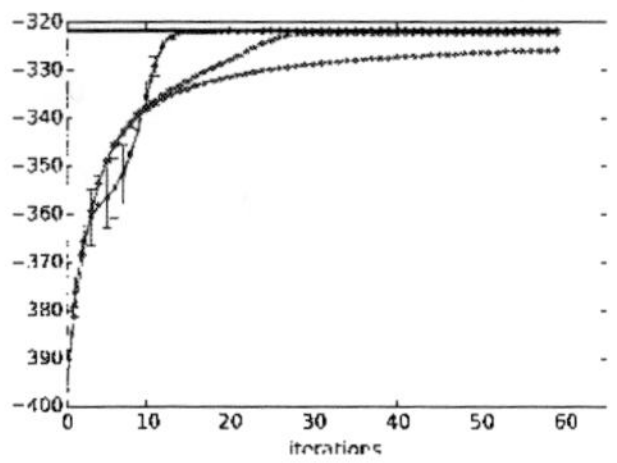

(c) Complementary w.r.t. $w^{\mathcal{D}^*}$

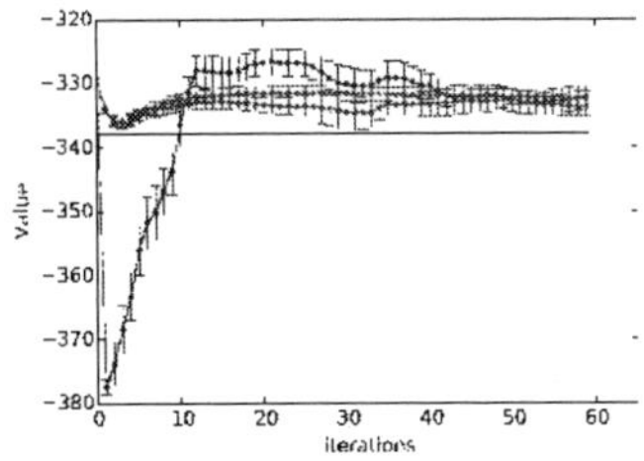

(d) Contrasting w.r.t. $w^{\mathcal{F}^*}$

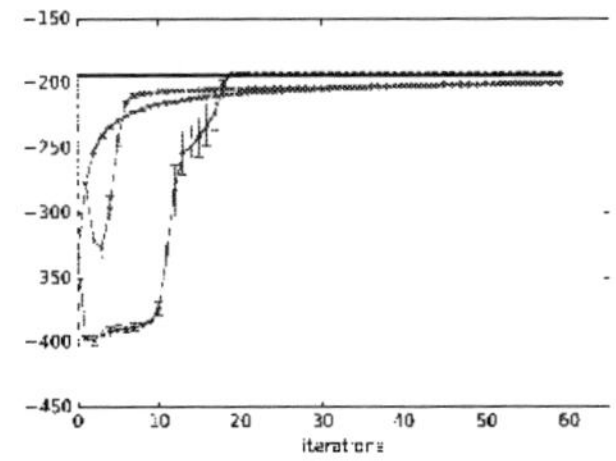

(e) Overlapping w.r.t. $w^{\mathcal{F}^*}$

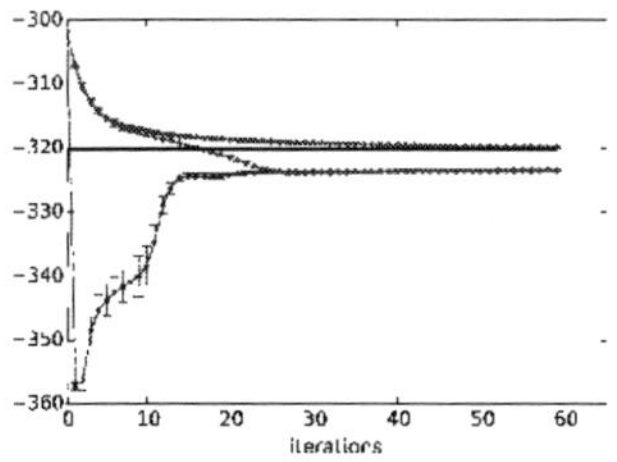

(f) Complementary w.r.t. $w^{\mathcal{F}^*}$

Figure 2: Value over 60 iterations, for 20 runs in contrasting, complementary and overlapping simulated domains w.r.t. $w^{\mathcal{D}^*}$ and $w^{\mathcal{F}^*}$.

Finally, Figures 2c and 2f show similar results for the complementary scenario. The IRLF methods again perform better in terms of $V^{\pi^*}_{\mathcal{D},test}$ but now also perform better in terms of $V^{\pi^*}_{\mathcal{F},test}$. In fact, they outperform even the successful data in terms of $V^{\pi^*}_{\mathcal{F},test}$, a consequence of the complementary nature of the reward functions.

IRLF's performance with respect to $V^{\pi^*}_{\mathcal{F},test}$ (Figure 2 bottom row) illustrates how the algorithm gives priority to successful demonstrations when necessary. For the contrasting scenario, the probability of approaching the obstacle is already low for $w^{\mathcal{D}^*}$; therefore, IRL and IRLF behave similarly with respect to $w^{\mathcal{F}^*}$. In the ovelapping scenario, IRLF gives priority to reaching the target quickly, since this matches the behavior in the successful demonstrations (even though it is discouraged from doing so by the failed demonstrations). Doing so means accumulating more value in terms of $V^{\pi^*}_{\mathcal{F},test}$. In the complementary scenario, since it is possible to satisfy both objectives simultaneously (reaching the target and avoiding obstacles), IRLF finds a reward function that performs well with respect to the succesful demonstrations while at the same time having a lower value with respect to the failed demonstrations.

In all scenarios, IRLF is more stable with incremental updates than without. In the contrasting and complementary scenarios, IRLF with incremental updates learns more slowly, while in the overlapping scenario it learns faster initially but plateaus slightly lower.

In the experiments above, all methods received successful and failed demonstrations from five initial states. Hence, the results do not address how the number of succesful demonstrations given to the two learners affects their performance on the test set. In the complementary scenario, failed demonstrations are obviously important regardless of how many succesful demonstrations are available. In the other scenarios, however, it is not clear whether failed demonstrations are still useful even when successful demonstrations are abundant.

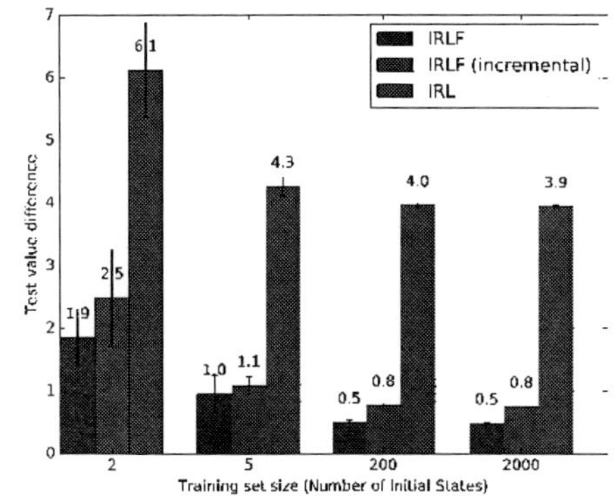

Figure 3: Performance of all three methods in the constrasting scenario for different numbers of initial states.

To test this, we repeated our experiments in the constrasting scenario but with 5, 50, 200 and 2000 initial states for successful demonstrations, while keeping the failed demonstrations to 5. For each algorithm, we plot $(w^{\mathcal{D}^*})^T \tilde{\mu}^{\mathcal{D}_{test}}$ - $V^{\pi^*}_{\mathcal{D},test}$ after 60 iterations of the algorithm. The smaller this value, the closer the learner comes to replicating the expert on the test set of initial states. The results, shown in Figure 3, demonstrate that IRLF maintains its superiority over IRL even if the number of initial states for which demonstrations are given rises significantly.

To shed more light on IRLF's behaviour, Figure 4 plots the original and learned reward functions for IRL and IRLF for the contrasting scenario. In the original reward function $w^{\mathcal{D}^*}$ (Figure 4a), the obstacle is in cell [2,2] and the goal in cell [4,4], which explains the dips and spikes in those locations. The reward function learned by IRL (Figure 4c) is flat in the area of the obstacle. However, IRLF, by employing $w^{\mathcal{F}^*}$ (Figure 4b) learns a reward function (4d) that properly assigns a low reward to the obstacle and its surroundings. The reward function resulting from IRLF can therefore generalise better to unseen initial conditions and environments.

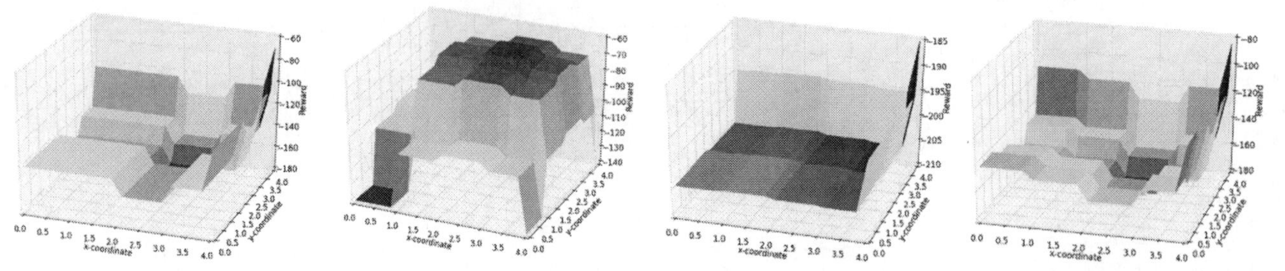

(a) $w^{\mathcal{D}^*}$ (b) $w^{\mathcal{F}^*}$ (c) IRL (d) IRLF

Figure 4: The original reward and learned reward functions for the two algorithms. Obstacle is static at [2,2]

4.2 Simulated Factory Domain

Our second simulated domain is the *Factory* benchmark problem proposed by Dearden & Boutilier [3]. In this domain, an autonomous agent is tasked with building an object according to specifications, which involves some sequence of shaping, painting, cleaning and assembly operations on its parts. Each individual operation costs some time and may have a probabilistic outcome, possibly resulting in unwanted side effects on the condition of each of the parts. Furthermore, there are precedence conditions on some of these operations – for instance, parts must be shaped before they can be assembled. The goal of this domain is to produce the object in the most cost-efficient way.

While this problem has been previously tackled from the perspective of off-line decision-theoretic planning, it is a suitable domain to demonstrate the applicability of learning from demonstration, and in particular of IRLF. In a real manufacturing problem, human demonstrations on how to properly execute the manufacturing task, as well as failed demonstrations, in which the resulting object did not meet the quality specifications, would be readily available. Furthermore, consider a situation where the conditions in the factory problem may be subject to changes (for example, in the shapes or sizes of the parts) which may affect the optimal manufacturing policy. Learning a reward function, as opposed to learning a policy from demonstration, would make it easier for an autonomous agent to adapt to these changes.

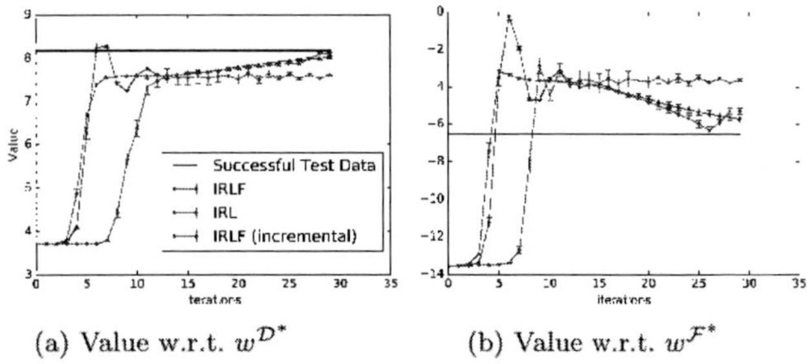

(a) Value w.r.t. $w^{\mathcal{D}^*}$ (b) Value w.r.t. $w^{\mathcal{F}^*}$

Figure 5: Value over 30 iterations, for 15 runs of learning in the Factory domain.

Our instantiation of the Factory problem follows Dearden & Boutilier's description [3] (*c.f.* Section A.2). It has 512 states, factored into 9 binary variables, and 10 actions. The expert demonstrations were drawn from the optimal policy for that domain according to its original additive rewards

Feature Index i	Proposition	$w_i^{\mathcal{D}^*}$	$w_i^{\mathcal{F}^*}$
1	AClean	0.1	1
2	BClean	0.1	-0.1
3	APainted	0.2	0.4
4	BPainted	0.2	0
5	Joined	0.4	-2

Table 1: Reward functions for the Factory domain.

($w_i^{\mathcal{D}^*}$, Table 1), while the failed demonstrations were drawn from a policy derived from a different reward function ($w_i^{\mathcal{F}^*}$, Table 1). Note that we consider only 5 features, corresponding to those state factors that have non-zero rewards. Each demonstration starts from random initial conditions and the evaluation proceeds in an identical manner to Section 4.1.

Figure 5 shows the results, which are consistent with our previous observations. Figure 5a shows that the reward function learned using IRLF is capable of yielding a policy that achieves a higher $V^{\pi^*}_{\mathcal{D},test}$ than IRL, and very close to that of the original policy. Furthermore, Figure 5b shows that IRLF is capable of achieving lower $V^{\pi^*}_{\mathcal{F},test}$ than IRL. These results not only demonstrate the stability and reliability of IRLF, but further confirm the usefulness of failed demonstrations in inverse reinforcement learning.

4.3 Real Navigation Domain

We also evaluate the performance of IRLF on a social navigation dataset gathered using is a commercially available telepresence robot that has been augmented with extra sensors and processors. The collected dataset consists of 47 trajectories of an expert navigating the robot towards an interaction target while avoiding a moving or standing person in a socially appropriate way. The positions of the people and the robot were accurately recorded using a motion capture system covering an area of $5m \times 5m$. A sample of the collected trajectories are shown in Figure 6.

For safety reasons, the failed dataset $\mathcal{F}$, which consists of 59 trajectories, was collected by driving the robot in a simulator in a way that intentionally violates social norms, e.g., running into, following, or standing next to people.

To model this domain as an MDP, we define a state space S consisting of discretised positions for both the obstacle and the robot, as well as the discretised orientation of the obstacle, yielding a total of 837,808 states. The action space consists of eight possible directions for robot movement, and an action that stops the robot. Using $\mathcal{D}$, we learned a fac-

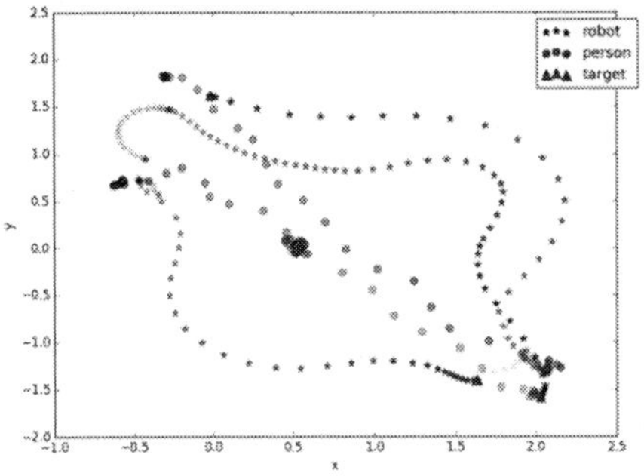

Figure 6: A sample of trajectories from the real navigation domain data set. Darker dots occur later in time.

tored stochastic transition function T. Furthermore, we defined a feature set $\phi(s,a)$ of 1401 binary features, encoding the relative position of the robot from both the target and the obstacle, as well as their relative orientations.

Applying IRL and IRLF to this domain is straightforward. However, measuring performance is not, because we do not have access to the ground truth reward function needed to compute a policy's value. In previous work on IRL, researchers have taken multiple approaches to evaluation. Some have considered simulated domains [8, 17, 15] as in our results above, where a ground truth reward function is available. Others have considered real-world data but relied on qualitative evaluation [14], domain-specific performance measures [9] or ad-hoc performance measures [18].

Since none of these approaches is entirely satisfactory, we adopt a different approach. First, we apply IRL to both $\mathcal{D}$ and $\mathcal{F}$ and derive reward functions, $R^{\mathcal{D}}$ and $R^{\mathcal{F}}$ and their respective weights $w^{\mathcal{D}^*}$ and $w^{\mathcal{F}^*}$, which we thereafter treat as ground truth. Because MDPs are generative models, we can use these two separate reward functions to generate data while preserving access to the ground-truth reward functions that are so essential to evaluation. We are therefore able to conduct an evaluation analogous to the done in the simulated navigation domain, with the key difference that the $w^{\mathcal{D}^*}$ and $w^{\mathcal{F}^*}$ are learned from real data.

Figure 7, which shows example trajectories generated by these reward functions, confirms that $w^{\mathcal{D}^*}$ produces human-like trajectories, while $w^{\mathcal{F}^*}$ generates inappropriate behaviour. These two reward functions can therefore be considered to be two separate agents whose demonstrations IRLF uses in order to learn a single reward function in a principled manner.

Figure 8 shows the results of our experiments on the real data, averaged across 6 independent runs. These results demonstrate that both versions of IRLF substantially outperform IRL with respect to $w^{\mathcal{D}^*}$. The performance of all methods is similar with respect to $w^{\mathcal{F}^*}$, which suggests that, in this domain, imitating good behaviour is sufficient to score very low with respect to $w^{\mathcal{F}^*}$. IRLF without incremental updates to λ clearly oscillates, as expected, but still converges, while IRLF with incremental updates is stable and achieves a higher value than IRL. Overall, the consistency of these results with those of the simulated domain provides further confirmation that failed demonstrations are useful for IRL, allowing it to generalise better to new initial conditions. Furthermore, IRLF is a useful method for exploiting this data.

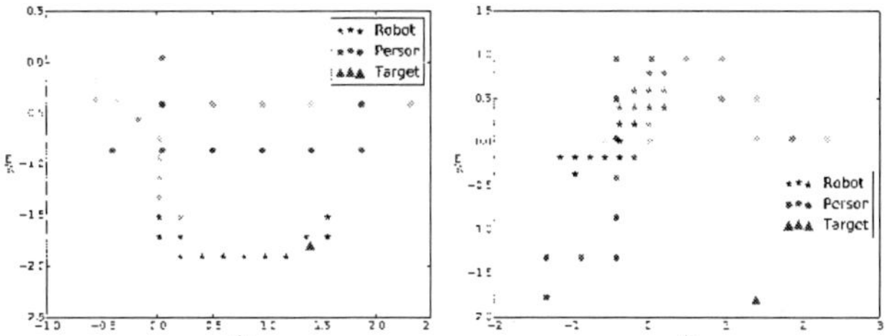

Figure 7: Sample trajectories from $w^{\mathcal{D}^*}$ (top) and $w^{\mathcal{F}^*}$ (bottom). Darker dots occur later in time.

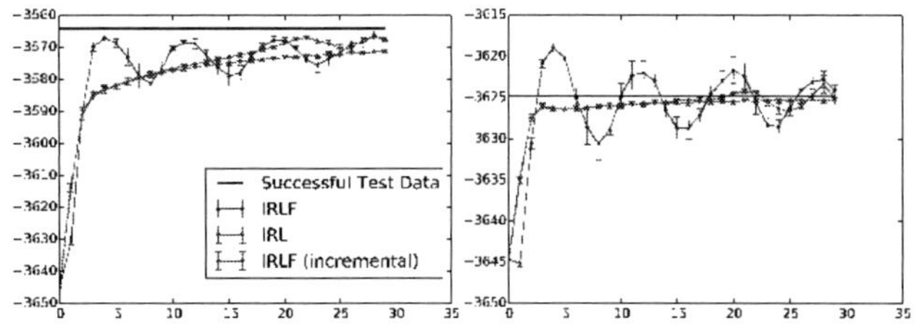

(a) Value w.r.t. $w^{\mathcal{D}^*}$ (b) Value w.r.t. $w^{\mathcal{F}^*}$

Figure 8: Value over 30 iterations, for 6 runs on real data.

5. CONCLUSIONS AND FUTURE WORK

This paper introduced IRLF, the first inverse reinforcement learning algorithm that can learn from successful as well as failed demonstrations simultaneously. Starting from the maximum causal entropy IRL method, we proposed a new constrained optimisation formulation that accommodates both types of demonstrations while remaining convex and derived update rules for learning reward functions and policies. Our simulated navigation experiments investigated the properties of IRLF in cases where the succesful and failed demonstrations are either constrasting, overlapping, or complementary. The results in the overlapping scenario show that IRLF works even if the failed demonstrations are similar to the successful ones. We also presented results on a simulated factory domain as well as on real robot data from a social navigation task. These results clearly suggest that IRLF consistently learns faster and generalises better than the original IRL algorithm in consideration. In future work, we aim to investigate whether other IRL methods can also be extended to exploit failed demonstrations. In addition, we plan to conduct more experiments with real robots, including deploying an IRLF-learned policy on a robot.

6. ACKNOWLEDGEMENTS

This work is funded by the EC-FP7 under grant agreement no. 611153 (TERESA). We would like to thank the Social Robotics group of University Pablo Olavide (UPO) for their help in collecting and processing the data used in the experiments.

REFERENCES

[1] P. Abbeel and A. Y. Ng. Apprenticeship learning via inverse reinforcement learning. In *Proceedings of the twenty-first International Conference on Machine Learning (ICML)*, page 1. ACM, 2004.

[2] M. Babes, V. Marivate, K. Subramanian, and M. L. Littman. Apprenticeship learning about multiple intentions. In *Proceedings of the 28th International Conference on Machine Learning (ICML-11)*, pages 897–904, 2011.

[3] R. Dearden and C. Boutilier. Abstraction and approximate decision-theoretic planning. *Artificial Intelligence*, 89(1):219–283, 1997.

[4] C. Dimitrakakis and C. A. Rothkopf. Bayesian multitask inverse reinforcement learning. In *Recent Advances in Reinforcement Learning*, pages 273–284. Springer, 2012.

[5] D. H. Grollman and A. Billard. Donut as i do: Learning from failed demonstrations. In *Robotics and Automation (ICRA), 2011 IEEE International Conference on*, pages 3804–3809. IEEE, 2011.

[6] P. Henry, C. Vollmer, B. Ferris, and D. Fox. Learning to navigate through crowded environments. In *Proceedings of the IEEE International Conference on Robotics & Automation (ICRA)*, pages 981–986. IEEE, 2010.

[7] M. Kuderer, S. Gulati, and W. Burgard. Learning driving styles for autonomous vehicles from demonstration. In *Proceedings of the IEEE International Conference on Robotics & Automation (ICRA), Seattle, USA*, volume 134, 2015.

[8] S. Levine, Z. Popovic, and V. Koltun. Nonlinear inverse reinforcement learning with gaussian processes. In *Advances in Neural Information Processing Systems*, pages 19–27, 2011.

[9] G. Neu and C. Szepesvári. Training parsers by inverse reinforcement learning. *Machine learning*, 77(2-3):303–337, 2009.

[10] A. Y. Ng, S. J. Russell, et al. Algorithms for inverse reinforcement learning. In *Proceedings of the International Conference on Machine Learning (ICML)*, pages 663–670, 2000.

[11] E. Pacchierotti, H. I. Christensen, and P. Jensfelt. Embodied social interaction for service robots in hallway environments. In *Field and Service Robotics*, pages 293–304. Springer, 2006.

[12] D. Ramachandran and E. Amir. Bayesian inverse reinforcement learning. *Urbana*, 51:61801, 2007.

[13] N. Ratliff, D. Bradley, J. A. Bagnell, and J. Chestnutt. Boosting structured prediction for imitation learning. *Robotics Institute*, page 54, 2007.

[14] N. D. Ratliff, J. A. Bagnell, and M. A. Zinkevich. Maximum margin planning. In *Proceedings of the 23rd international conference on Machine learning*, pages 729–736. ACM, 2006.

[15] C. A. Rothkopf and C. Dimitrakakis. Preference elicitation and inverse reinforcement learning. In *Machine Learning and Knowledge Discovery in Databases*, pages 34–48. Springer, 2011.

[16] C. Sungjoon, K. Eunwoo, L. Kyungjae, and O. Songhwai. Leveraged non-stationary gaussian process regression for autonomous robot navigation. In *Proceedings of the IEEE International Conference on Robotics & Automation (ICRA)*, 2015.

[17] U. Syed and R. E. Schapire. A game-theoretic approach to apprenticeship learning. In *Advances in neural information processing systems*, pages 1449–1456, 2007.

[18] D. Vasquez, B. Okal, and K. O. Arras. Inverse reinforcement learning algorithms and features for robot navigation in crowds: An experimental comparison. In *Proceedings of Intelligent Robots and Systems (IROS 2014)*, pages 1341–1346. IEEE, 2014.

[19] J. Zheng, S. Liu, and L. M.-S. Ni. Robust bayesian inverse reinforcement learning with sparse behavior noise. In *Proceedings of the National Conference on Artificial Intelligence, 28th AAAI Conference on Artificial Intelligence, AAAI 2014, 26th Innovative Applications of Artificial Intelligence Conference, IAAI 2014 and the 5th Symposium on Educational Advances in Artificial Intelligence, EAAI 2014, Quebec City, Canada*, page 2198, 2014.

[20] B. D. Ziebart. *Modeling purposeful adaptive behavior with the principle of maximum causal entropy*. PhD thesis, Carnegie Mellon University, 2010.

[21] B. D. Ziebart, J. A. Bagnell, and A. K. Dey. The principle of maximum causal entropy for estimating interacting processes. *Information Theory, IEEE Transactions on*, 59(4):1966–1980, 2013.

[22] B. D. Ziebart, A. L. Maas, J. A. Bagnell, and A. K. Dey. Maximum entropy inverse reinforcement learning. In *AAAI*, pages 1433–1438, 2008.

Planning with Resource Conflicts in Human-Robot Cohabitation

Tathagata Chakraborti[1], Yu Zhang[1], David E. Smith[2], Subbarao Kambhampati[1]
[1]Department of Computer Science, Arizona State University, AZ
[2]Autonomous Systems & Robotics Intelligent Systems Division, NASA Ames Research Center, CA
tchakra2@asu.edu, yzhan442@asu.edu, david.smith@nasa.gov, rao@asu.edu

ABSTRACT

In order to be acceptable members of future human-robot ecosystems, it is necessary for autonomous agents to be respectful of the intentions of humans cohabiting a workspace and account for conflicts on shared resources in the environment. In this paper we build an integrated system that demonstrates how maintaining predictive models of its human colleagues can inform the planning process of the robotic agent. We propose an Integer Programming based planner as a general formulation of this flavor of "human-aware" planning and show how the proposed formulation can be used to produce different behaviors of the robotic agent, showcasing compromise, opportunism or negotiation. Finally, we investigate how the proposed approach scales with the different parameters involved, and provide empirical evaluations to illustrate the pros and cons associated with the proposed style of planning.

1. INTRODUCTION

In environments where multiple agents are working independently, but utilizing shared resources, it is important for these agents to model the intentions and beliefs of other agents so as to act intelligently and prevent conflicts. In cases where some of these agents are human, as in the case of assistive robots in household environments, these are required (rather than just desired) capabilities of robots in order for them to be considered "socially acceptable" - this has been one of the important objectives of "human-aware" planning, as evident from existing literature in human-aware path planning [13, 10] and human-aware task planning [5, 9, 3, 15]. An interesting aspect of many of these scenarios, is the presence of many of the aspects of multi-agent environments, but absence of typical assumptions often made in explicit teaming scenarios between humans and robots, as pointed out in [4]. Probabilistic plan recognition plays an important role in this regard, because by not committing to a plan, that presumes a particular plan for the other agent, it might be possible to minimize suboptimal (in terms of redundant or conflicting actions performed during the execution phase) behavior of the autonomous agent.

Here we look at possible ways to minimize such suboptimal behavior by ways of *compromise*, *opportunism* or *negotiation*. Specifically, we ask the question, what information can be extracted from the predicted plans, and how this information can be used to guide the behavior of the autonomous agent. There has been previous work [1, 6] on some of the modeling aspects of the problem, in terms of planning with uncertainty in resources and constraints. In this paper we provide an integrated framework (shown in Figure 1) for achieving these behaviors of the autonomous agent, particularly in the context of stigmergic coordination of human-robot cohabitation. To this end, we modularize our architecture so as to handle the uncertainty in the environment separately with the planning process, and show how these individual modules interact with each other by the way of usage profiles of the concerned resources.

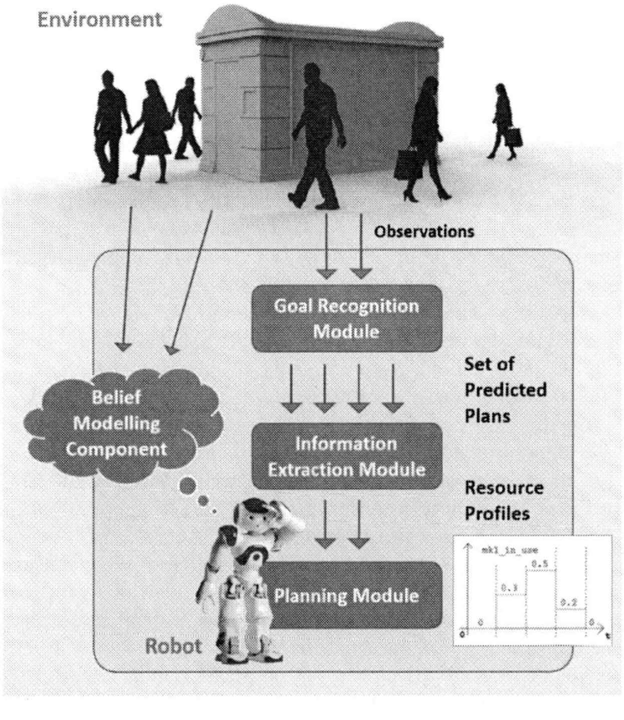

Figure 1: Schematic diagram of our integrated system for belief modeling, goal recognition, information extraction and planning. The robot maintains a belief model of the environment, and uses observations from the environment to extract information about how the world may evolve, which is then used to drive its own planning process.

Appears in: *Proceedings of the 15th International Conference on Autonomous Agents and Multiagent Systems (AAMAS 2016), J. Thangarajah, K. Tuyls, C. Jonker, S. Marsella (eds.), May 9–13, 2016, Singapore.*

The general architecture of the system is shown in Figure 1. The autonomous agent, or the robot, is acting (with independent goals) in an environment co-habited with other agents (humans), who are similarly self-interested. The robot has a model of the other agents acting independently in its environment. These models may be partial and hence the robot can only make uncertain predictions on how the world will evolve with time. However, the resources in the environment are limited and are likely to be constrained by the plans of the other agents. The robot thus needs to reason about the future states of the environment in order to make sure that its own plans do not produce conflicts with respect to the plans of the other agents.

With the involvement of humans, however, the problem is more skewed against the robot, because humans would expect a higher priority on their plans - robots that produce plans that clash with those of the humans, without any explanation, would be considered incompatible for such an ecosystem. Thus the robot is expected to follow plans that preserve the human plans, rather than follow a globally optimal plan for itself. This aspect makes the current setting distinct from normal human robot teaming scenarios and produces a number of its own interesting challenges. *How does the robot model the human's behavior? How does it plan to avoid friction with the human plans? If it is possible to communicate, how does it plan to negotiate and refine plans?* These are the questions that we seek to address in this work. Our approach models human beliefs and defines resource profiles as abstract representations of the plans predicted on the basis of these beliefs. The robot updates its beliefs upon receiving new observations, and passes on the resultant profiles onto its planner, which uses an IP-formulation to minimize the overlap between these resource profiles and those produced by the human's plans.

The contribution of our paper is thus three-fold, we (1) propose *resource profiles* as a concise mode of representing different types of information from predicted plans; (2) develop an IP-based planner that can utilize this information and provide different modalities of conformant behavior; and (3) provide an integrated framework that supports the proposed mode of planning - the modular approach also provides an elegant way to handle different challenges separately (e.g. uncertainty and/or nested beliefs of humans leaves the planner). The planner, as a consequence of these, has properties not present in existing planners - for example, the work that probably comes closest is [9] that models a specific case of compromise only, while the formulation is also likely to blow up in presense of large hypothesis sets due to absence of concise representation techniques like the profiles. We will discuss the trade-offs and design choices in more detail in the evaluation sections.

The rest of the paper is organized as follows. We will start with a brief introduction of the agent models that comprise the belief component, and describe how it facilitates plan recognition. Then, in Sections 2.3 and 2.4, we are going to go into details of how resource profiles may be used to represent information from predicated plans, and describe how our planner converts this information into constraints that can be solved as an integer program during the plan generation process. In Section 3 we will demonstrate how the planner may be used to produce different modes of autonomous behavior. Finally in Section 4 we will provide empirical evaluations of the planner's internal properties.

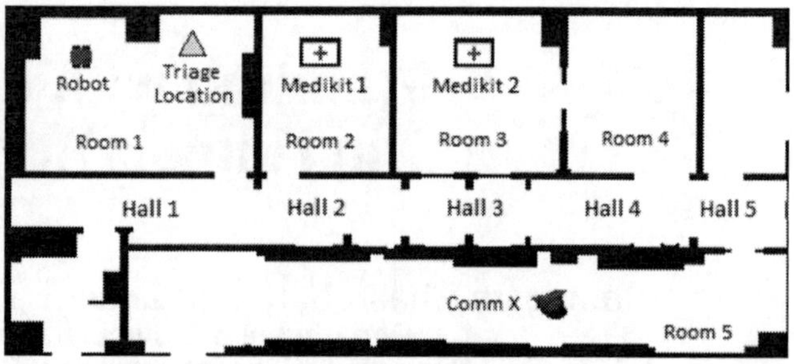

Figure 2: Use case - Urban Search And Rescue (USAR).

2. PLANNING WITH CONFLICTS ON SHARED RESOURCES

We will now go into details about each of the modules shown in Figure 1. The setting (adopted from [14]) involves a commander `CommX` and a robot in a typical USAR (Urban Search and Rescue) task illustrated in Figure 2. The commander can perform triage in certain locations, for which he needs the medkit. The robot can also fetch medkits if requested by other agents (not shown) in the environment. The shared resources here are the two medkits - some of the plans the commander can execute will lock the use of and/or change the position of these medkits, so that from the set of probable plans of the commander we can extract a probability distribution over the usage (or even the position) of the medkit over time based on the fraction of plans that conform to these facts. These *resource availability profiles* (i.e. the distribution over the usage or position of the medkit evolving over time) provide a way for the agents to minimize conflicts with the other agents. Before going into details about the planner that achieves this, we will first look at how the agents are modeled and how these profiles are computed in the next section.

2.1 The Belief Modeling Component

The notion of modeling beliefs introduced by the authors in [14] is adopted in this work. Beliefs about state are defined in terms of predicates $bel(\alpha, \phi)$, where α is an agent with belief $\phi = true$. Goals are defined by predicates $goal(\alpha, \phi)$, where agent α has a goal ϕ. The set of all beliefs that the robot ascribes to α together represents the perspective for the robot of α. This is obtained by a belief model Bel_α of agent α, defined as $\{ \phi \mid bel(\alpha, \phi) \in Bel_{self} \}$, where Bel_{self} are the first-order beliefs of the robot (e.g., $bel(self, at(self, room1))$). The set of goals ascribed to α is similarly described by $\{goal(\alpha, \phi) | goal(\alpha, \phi) \in Bel_{self}\}$.

Next, we turn our attention to the domain model D_α of the agent α that is used in the planning process. We use PDDL [11] style agent models for the rest of the discussion, but most of the analysis easily generalizes to other related modes of representation. Formally, a planning problem $\Pi = \langle D_\alpha, \pi_\alpha \rangle$ consists of the domain model D_α and the problem instance π_α. The domain model of α is defined as $D_\alpha = \langle T_\alpha, V_\alpha, S_\alpha, A_\alpha \rangle$, where T_α is a set of object types; V_α is a set of variables that describe objects that belong to types in T_α; S_α is a set of named first-order logical predicates over the variables V_α that describe the state; and A_α is a set of operators available to the agent. The action models $a \in A_\alpha$ are represented as $a = \langle \mathbb{N}, \mathbb{C}, \mathbb{P}, \mathbb{E} \rangle$ where $\mathbb{N}$ denotes the name of that action; $\mathbb{C}$ is the cost of that action; $\mathbb{P} \subseteq S_\alpha$ is the list of pre-conditions that must hold for the action a to be applicable in a particular state $s \subseteq S_\alpha$ of the environment; and $\mathbb{E}_a = \langle eff^+(a), eff^-(a) \rangle$, $eff^\pm(a) \subseteq S_\alpha$ is a tuple that contains the add and delete effects of applying the action to a state. The transition function $\delta(\cdot)$ determines the next state after the application of action a in state s as $\delta(a,s) \models \bot$ if $\exists f \in \mathbb{P}$ s.t. $f \notin s; \delta(a,s) \models (s \setminus eff^-(a)) \cup eff^+(a)$ otherwise.

The belief model, in conjunction with beliefs about the goals / intentions of another agent, will allow the robot to instantiate a planning problem $\pi_\alpha = \langle \mathbb{O}_\alpha, \mathbb{I}_\alpha, \mathbb{G}_\alpha \rangle$, where $\mathbb{O}_\alpha$ is a set of objects of type $t \in T_\alpha$; $\mathbb{I}_\alpha$ is the *initial state* of the world, and $\mathbb{G}_\alpha$ is a set of *goals*, which are both sets of the predicates from S_α initialized with objects from $\mathbb{O}_\alpha$. First, the initial state $\mathbb{I}_\alpha$ is populated by all of the robot's initial beliefs about the agent α, i.e. $\mathbb{I}_\alpha = \{\phi \mid bel(\alpha, \phi) \in Bel_{robot}\}$. Similarly, the goal is set to $\mathbb{G}_\alpha = \{\phi \mid goal(\alpha, \phi) \in Bel_{robot}\}$. Finally, the set of objects $\mathbb{O}_\alpha$ consists of all the objects that are mentioned in either the initial state, or the goal description: $\mathbb{O}_\alpha = \{o \mid o \in (\phi \mid \phi \in (\mathbb{I}_\alpha \cup \mathbb{G}_\alpha))\}$. The solution to the planning problem is an ordered sequence of actions or *plan* given by $\pi_\alpha = \langle a_1, a_2, \ldots, a_{|\pi_\alpha|} \rangle$, $a_i \in A_\alpha$ such that $\delta(\pi_\alpha, \mathbb{I}_\alpha) \models \mathbb{G}_\phi$, where the cumulative transition function is given by $\delta(\pi, s) = \delta(\langle a_2, a_3, \ldots, a_{|\pi|} \rangle, \delta(a_1, s))$. The cost of the plan is given by $C(\pi_\alpha) = \sum_{a \in \pi_\alpha} \mathbb{C}_a$ and the optimal plan π^*_α is such that $C(\pi^*_\alpha) \leq C(\pi_\alpha)\ \forall \pi_\alpha$ with $\delta(\pi_\alpha, \mathbb{I}_\alpha) \models \mathbb{G}_\alpha$. This planning problem instance (though not directly used in the robot's planning process) enables the goal recognition component to solve the compiled problem instances. More on this in the next section.

2.2 The Goal Recognition Component

For many real world scenarios, it is unlikely that the goals of the humans are known completely, and that the plan computed by the planner is exactly the plan that they will follow. We are only equipped with a *belief* of the likely goal(s) of the human - and this may not be a full description of their actual goals. Further, in the case of an incompletely specified goal, there might be a set of *likely* plans that the human can execute, which brings into consideration the idea of incremental goal recognition over a possible goal set given a stream of observations.

2.2.1 Goal Extension

To begin with, it is worth noting that the robot might have to deal with multiple plans even in the presence of completely specified goals (even if the other agents are fully rational). For example, there may be multiple optimal ways of achieving the same goal, and it is not obvious beforehand which one of these an agent is going to end up following. In the case of *incompletely* specified goals, the presence of multiple likely plans become more relevant. To accommodate this, we extend the robot's current belief of an agent α's goal, $\mathbb{G}_\alpha$, to a *hypothesis goal set* Ψ_α. The computation of this goal set can be done using the planning graph method [2]. In the worst case, Ψ_α corresponds to all possible goals in the final level of the converged planning graph. Having further (domain-dependent) knowledge (e.g. in our scenario, information that `CommX` is only interested in triage-related goals) can prune some of these goals by removing the goal conditions that are not typed on the triage variable.

2.2.2 Goal / Plan Recognition

In the present scenario, we thus have a set Ψ_α of goals that α may be trying to achieve, and observations of the actions α is currently executing. At this point we refer to the work of Ramirez and Geffner who in [12] provided a technique to compile the problem of plan recognition into a classical planning problem. Given a sequence of observations θ, we recompute the probability distribution Θ over $G \in \Psi_\alpha$ by using a Bayesian update $P(G|\theta) \propto P(\theta|G)$, where the likelihood is approximated by the function $P(\theta|G) = 1/(1 + e^{-\beta\Delta(G,\theta)})$ where $\Delta(G,\theta) = C_p(G - \theta) - C_p(G + \theta)$. Here $\Delta(G,\theta)$ gives an estimate of the difference in cost C_p of achieving the goal G without and with the observations, thus increasing $P(\theta|G)$ for goals that explain the given observations. Thus, solving two compiled planning problems, with goals $G - \theta$ and $G + \theta$, gives us the required posterior update for the distribution Θ over possible goals of α. The details of the approach is available at [12].

The specific problem we will look at now is how to inform the robot's own planning process from the recognized goal set Ψ_α. In order to do this, we compute the optimal plans for each goal in the hypothesis goal set Ψ_α, and associate them with the probabilities of these goals from the distribution thus obtained. Information from these plans is then represented concisely in the form of resource profiles.

Notes on the Recognition Module

For our plan recognition module we use a much faster variation [7] of the above approach that exploits cost and interaction information from plan graphs to estimate the goal probabilities. This saves on the computational effort of having to solve two planning problems per goal. Also, note that while computing the plan to a particular goal G, we use a compiled problem instance with the goal $G + \theta$ to ensure that the predicted plan conforms to the existing observations. Details on the compilation is available at [12].

Also, the output of the planner does not need to be associated with probabilities - this is just the most general formulation. If we want to deal with just a set of plans that the robot needs to be aware of, we can treat the plan set either with a uniform distribution and/or by requiring exactly zero conflicts in the objective of the planner (this will become clearer in Section 2.4) depending on the preference.

Perhaps the biggest computational issue here is the need to compute optimal plans. While we still do it for our domain, as we will note later in Section 2.3, this might not be necessary, and suboptimal plans may be used in larger domains where computation is an issue.

2.3 Resources and Resource Profiles

As we discussed previously, since the plans of the agents are in parallel execution, the uncertainty introduced by the commander's actions cannot be mapped directly between the commander's final state and the robot's initial state. However, given the commander's possible plans, the robot can extract information about at what points of time the shared resources in the environment are likely to be locked by the commander. This information can be represented by *resource usage profiles* that capture the expected (over all the recognized plans) variation of probability of usage or availability over time. The robot can, in turn, use this information to make sure that the profile imposed by its own plan has minimal conflicts with those of the commander's.

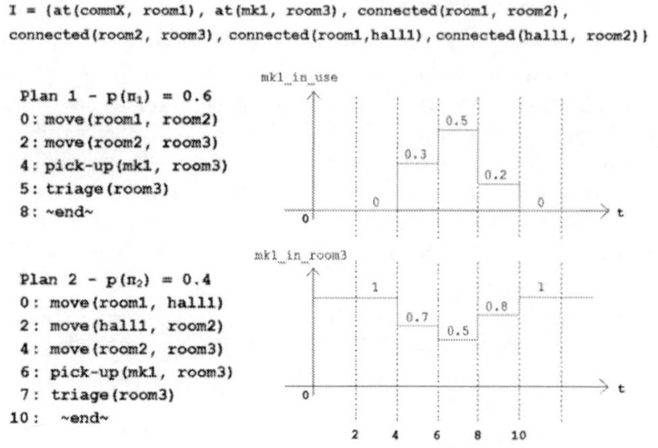

Figure 3: Different types of resource profiles.

Formally, a profile is defined as a mapping from time step T to a real number between 0 and 1, and is represented by a set of tuples as follows $\mathcal{G} : \mathbb{N} \rightarrow [0,1] \equiv \{(t,g) : t \in \mathbb{N}, g \in [0,1],$ such that $G(t) = g$ at time step $t\}$.

The concept of resource profiles can be handled at two levels of abstraction. Going back to our running example, shared resources that can come under conflict are the two (locatable typed objects) medkits, and the profiles over the medkits can be over both usage and location, as shown in Figure 3. These different types of profiles can be used (possibly in conjunction if needed) for different purposes. For example, just the usage profile shown on top is more helpful in identifying when to use the specific resource, while the resource when bound with the location specific groundings, as shown at the bottom can lead to more complicated higher order reasoning (e.g. the robot can decide to wait for the commander's plans to be over, as he inadvertently brings the medkit closer to it with high probability as a result of his own plans). We will look at this again in Section 3.

Let the domain model of the robot be $D_R = \langle T_R, V_R, S_R, A_R \rangle$ with the action models $a = \langle \mathbb{N}, \mathbb{C}, \mathbb{P}, \mathbb{E} \rangle$ defined in the same way as described in Section 2.1. Also, let $\Lambda \subseteq V_R$ be the set of shared resources and for each $\lambda \in \Lambda$ we have a set of predicates $f^\lambda \subseteq S_R$ that are *influenced* (as determined by the system designer) by λ, and let $\Gamma : \Lambda \rightarrow \mathcal{P}(\xi)$ be a function that maps the resource variables to the set of predicates $\xi = \cup_\lambda f^\lambda$ they influence. Without any external knowledge of the environment, we can set $\Lambda = V_\alpha \cap V_R$ and $\xi = S_\alpha \cap S_R$, though in most cases these sets are much smaller. In the following discussion, we will look at how the knowledge from the hypothesis goal set can be modeled in terms of resource availability graphs for each of the constrained resources $\lambda \in \Lambda$.

Consider the set of plans Ψ_α^P containing optimal plans corresponding to each goal in the hypothesis goal set, i.e. $\Psi_\alpha^P = \{\pi_G^* = \langle a_1, a_2, \ldots a_t \rangle \mid \delta(\pi_G^*, \mathbb{I}_\alpha) \models G,\ a_i \in A_\alpha \forall i,\ G \in \Psi_\alpha\}$ and let $l(\pi)$ be the likelihood of the plan π modeled on the goal likelihood distribution $\forall\ G \in \Psi_\alpha,\ p(G) \sim \Theta$ as $l(\pi_G) = c|\pi_G| \times p(G)$, where c is a normalization constant.

At each time step t, a plan $\pi \in \Psi_\alpha^P$ may lock one or more of the resources λ. Each plan thus provides a profile of usage of a resource with respect to the time step t as $\mathcal{G}_\pi^\lambda : \mathbb{N} \rightarrow \{0,1\} = \{(t,g) \mid t \in [1, |\pi|]$ and $g = 1$ if λ is locked by π at step t, 0 otherwise$\}$ such that $\mathcal{G}_\pi^\lambda(t) = g\ \forall\ (t,g) \in \mathcal{G}_\pi^\lambda$. The resultant usage profile of a resource λ due to all the plans in Ψ_α^P is obtained by summing over (weighted by the individual likelihoods) all the individual profiles as $\mathcal{G}^\lambda : \mathbb{N} \rightarrow [0,1] = \{(t,g) \mid t \in \{1, max_{\pi \in \Psi_\alpha^P}|\pi|\}$ and $g \propto \frac{1}{|\Psi_\alpha^P|} \sum_{\pi \in \Psi_\alpha^P} \mathcal{G}_\pi^\lambda(t) \times l(\pi)\}$.

Similarly, we can define profiles over the actual groundings of a variable (shown in the lower part of Figure 3) as $\mathcal{G}_\pi^{f^\lambda} = \{(t,g) \mid t \in [1, |\pi|]$ and $f^\lambda = 1$ at step t of plan π, 0 otherwise$\}$, and the resultant usage profile due to all the plans in Ψ_α^P is obtained as before as $\mathcal{G}^{f^\lambda} = \{(t,g) \mid t = 1, 2, \ldots, \max_{\pi \in \Psi_\alpha^P} |\pi|$ and $g \propto \frac{1}{|\Psi_\alpha^P|} \sum_{\pi \in \Psi_\alpha^P} \mathcal{G}_\pi^{f^\lambda}(t) \times l(\pi)\}$. These profiles are helpful when actions in the robot's domain are conditioned on these variables, and the values of these variables are conditioned on the plans of the other agents in the environment currently under execution.

One important aspect of this formulation that should be noted here is that the notion of "resources" is described here in terms of the subset of the common predicates in the domain of the agents ($\xi \subseteq S_\alpha \cap S_R$) and can thus be used as a generalized definition to model different types of conflict between the plans between two agents. In as much as these predicates are descriptions (possibly instantiated) of the typed variables in the domain and actually refer to the physical resources in the environment that might be shared by the agents, we will stick to this nomenclature of calling them *"resources"*. We will now look at how an autonomous agent can use these resource profiles to minimize conflicts during plan execution with other agents in its environment.

Notes on Usefulness of Profile Computation

One interesting aspect of computing resource profiles is that it provides a powerful interface between the belief on the environment and the planner. On the one hand, note that the input from the previous stage (goal/plan recognition module) is as generic as possible - a set of plans possibly associated with probabilities. Given any changes in preceding stages, e.g. modeling stochasticity or more complex belief models, still yields a set of plans that the robot needs to be aware of. Thus the plan set and resource profiles provide a surprisingly simple yet powerful way of abstracting away relevant information for the planner to use.

The profiles may also be leveraged to address different modalities of conformant behavior, for example with multiple humans and their relative importance, by (1) weighing the contributions from individual profiles by the normalized priority of the human, which would cause the planner to avoid conflicts with these profiles more than with those with lower priorities; or (2) requiring zero conflicts on a subset of profiles which would cause the planner to avoid a subset of conflicts at all costs, while minimizing the rest.

A somewhat implicit advantage of using profiles is its ability to form *regions of interest* given the possible plans. This will become clear later in Section 4.2 when we show that the predicted conflicts provide well-informed guidance to avoiding real conflicts during execution (as evident by the robustness in performance with just 1-3 observations, and zero actual conflicts in low probability areas in the computed profiles). Right now this has the implication that we need not necessarily compute perfect plan costs and goal distributions to get good plans.

2.4 Conflict Minimization

The planning problem of the robot - given by $\Pi = \langle D_R, \pi_R, \Lambda, \{G^\lambda | \forall \lambda \in \Lambda\}, \{G^{f^\lambda} \mid \forall f \in \Gamma(\lambda), \forall \lambda \in \Lambda\}\rangle$ - consists of the domain model D_R and the problem instance $\pi_R = \langle \mathbb{O}_R, \mathbb{I}_R, \mathbb{G}_R\rangle$ similar to that described in section 2.3, and also the constrained resources and all the profiles corresponding to them. This is because the planning process must take into account both goals of achievement as also conflict of resource usages as described by the profiles. Traditional planners provide no direct way to handle such profiles within the planning process. Note here that since the execution of the plans of the agents is occurring in parallel, the uncertainty is evolving at the time of execution, and hence the uncertainty cannot be captured from the goal states of the recognized plans alone, and consequently cannot be simply compiled away to the initial state uncertainty for the robot and solved as a conformant plan. Similarly, the problem does not directly compile into action costs in a metric planning instance because the profiles themselves are varying with time. Thus we need a planner that can handle these resource constraints that are both stochastic and non-stationary due to the uncertainty in the environment. To this end we introduce the following IP-based planner (partly following the technique for IP encoding for state space planning outlined in [16]) as an elegant way to sum over and minimize overlaps in profiles during the plan generation process. The following formulation finds such T-step plans in case of non-durative or instantaneous actions.

For action $a \in A_R$ at step t we have an action variable:

$$x_{a,t} = \begin{cases} 1, & \text{if action a is executed in step t} \\ 0, & \text{otherwise;} \quad \forall a \in A_R,\ t \in \{1, 2, \ldots, T\} \end{cases}$$

Also, for every proposition f at step t a binary state variable is introduced as follows:

$$y_{f,t} = \begin{cases} 1, & \text{if proposition is true in plan step t} \\ 0, & \text{otherwise;} \quad \forall f \in S_R,\ t \in \{0, 1, \ldots, T\} \end{cases}$$

Note here that the plan computed by the robot introduces a resource consumption profile itself, and thus one optimizing criterion would be to minimize the overlap between the usage profile due to the computed plan with those established by the predicted plans of the other agents in the environment. Let us introduce a new variable to model the resource usage graph imposed by the robot as follows:

$$g_{f,t} = \begin{cases} 1, & \text{if } f \in \xi \text{ is locked at plan step } t \\ 0, & \text{otherwise;} \quad \forall f \in \xi,\ t \in \{0, 1, \ldots, T\} \end{cases}$$

Further, for every resource $\lambda \in \Lambda$, we divide the actions in the domain of the robot into three disjoint sets -

$\Omega_f^+ = \{a \in A_R \text{ such that } x_{a,t} = 1 \implies y_{f,t} = 1\}$,
$\Omega_f^- = \{a \in A_R \text{ such that } x_{a,t} = 1 \implies y_{f,t} = 0\}$, and
$\Omega_f^o = A_R \setminus (\Omega_f^+ \cup \Omega_f^-), \forall f \in \xi$.

These then specify respectively those actions in the domain that lock, free up, or do not affect the use of a particular resource, and are used to calculate $g_{f,t}$ in the IP. Further, we introduce a variable $h_{f,t}$ to track preconditions required by actions *in the generated plan* whose success is conditioned on the influence of the plans of the other agents on the world (e.g. position of the medkits are changing, and the action `pickup` is conditioned on it) as follows:

$$h_{f,t} = \begin{cases} 1, & \text{if } f \in \mathbb{P}_a \text{ and } x_{a,t+1} = 1 \\ 0, & \text{otherwise;} \quad \forall f \in \xi,\ t \in \{0, 1, \ldots, T-1\} \end{cases}$$

Then the solution to the IP should ensure that the robot only uses these resources when they are in fact most expected to be available (as obtained by maximizing the overlap between $h_{f,t}$ and G^{f^λ}). These act like *demand profiles* from the perspective of the robot. We also add a "no-operation" action $A_R \leftarrow A_R \cup a_\phi$ so that $a_\phi = \langle \mathbb{N}, \mathbb{C}, \mathbb{P}, \mathbb{E}\rangle$ where $\mathbb{N} = \texttt{NOOP}$, $\mathbb{C} = 0$, $\mathbb{P} = \{\}$ and $\mathbb{E} = \{\}$.

The IP formulation is given by:

$$min\ k_1 \sum_{a\in A_R} \sum_{t\in\{1,2,\ldots,T\}} \mathbb{C}_a \times x_{a,t}$$
$$+k_2 \sum_{\lambda\in\Lambda} \sum_{f\in\Gamma(\lambda)} \sum_{t\in\{1,2,\ldots,T\}} g_{f,t} \times G^\lambda(t)$$
$$-k_3 \sum_{\lambda\in\Lambda} \sum_{f\in\Gamma(\lambda)} \sum_{t\in\{0,1,\ldots,T-1\}} h_{f,t} \times G^{f^\lambda}(t)$$

$$y_{f,0} = 1\ \forall f \in \mathbb{I}_R \setminus \xi \quad (1)$$
$$y_{f,0} = 0\ \forall f \notin \mathbb{I}_R \text{ or } f \in \xi \quad (2)$$
$$y_{f,T} = 1\ \forall f \in \mathbb{G}_R \quad (3)$$
$$x_{a,t} \le y_{f,t-1}\ \forall a\ s.t.\ f \in \mathbb{P}_a, \forall f \notin \xi, t \in \{1, \ldots, T\} \quad (4)$$
$$h_{f,t-1} = x_{a,t}\ \forall a\ s.t.\ f \in \mathbb{P}_a, \forall f \in \xi, t \in \{1, \ldots, T\} \quad (5)$$
$$y_{f,t} \le y_{f,t-1} + \sum_{a\in add(f)} x_{a,t}$$
$$\text{s.t. } add(f) = \{a | f \in eff^+(a)\}, \forall f, t \in \{1, \ldots, T\} \quad (6)$$
$$y_{f,t} \le 1 - \sum_{a\in del(f)} x_{a,t}$$
$$\text{s.t. } del(f) = \{a | f \in eff^-(a)\}, \forall f, t \in \{1, \ldots, T\} \quad (7)$$
$$\sum_{a\in A_R} x_{a,t} = 1, t \in \{1, 2, \ldots, T\} \quad (8)$$
$$\sum_{a\in\Omega_f^+} \sum_t x_{a,t} \le 1\ \forall f \in \xi, t \in \{1, 2, \ldots, T\} \quad (9)$$
$$g_{f,t} = \sum_{a\in\Omega_f^+} x_{a,t} + (1 - \sum_{a\in\Omega_f^+} x_{a,t} - \sum_{a\in\Omega_f^-} x_{a,t}) \times g_{f,t-1}$$
$$\forall f \in \xi, t \in \{1, \ldots, T\} \quad (10)$$
$$h_{f,t} \times G^{f^\lambda}(t) \ge \epsilon\ \forall f \in \xi, t \in \{0, 1, \ldots, T-1\} \quad (11)$$
$$y_{f,t} \in \{0, 1\}\ \forall f \in S_R, t \in \{0, 1, \ldots, T\} \quad (12)$$
$$x_{a,t} \in \{0, 1\}\ \forall a \in A_R, t \in \{1, 2, \ldots, T\} \quad (13)$$
$$g_{f,t} \in \{0, 1\}\ \forall f \in S_R, t \in \{0, 1, \ldots, T\} \quad (14)$$
$$h_{f,t} \in \{0, 1\}\ \forall f \in S_R, t \in \{0, 1, \ldots, T-1\} \quad (15)$$

where k_1, k_2, k_3 are constants determining the relative importance of the optimization criteria and ϵ is a constant.

Here, the objective function minimizes the sum of the cost of the plan and the overlap between the cumulative resource usage profiles of the predicted plans and that imposed by the current plan of the robot itself while maximizing the validity of the demand profiles. Constraints (1) through (3) model the initial and goal conditions, while the value of the constrained variables are kept uninitialized (and are determined by their profiles). Constraints (4) and (5), depending on the particular predicate, enforces the preconditions, or produces the demand profiles respectively, while (6) and (7) enforces the state equations that maintain the add and delete effects of the actions. Constraint (8) imposes non concurrency on the actions, and (9) ensures that the robot does not repeat the same action indefinitely to increase its utility. Constraint (10) generates the resource profile of the current plan, while (11) maintains that actions are only executed if there is at least a small probability ϵ of success. Finally (12) to (15) provide the binary ranges of the variables.

Note on Temporal Expressivity

At this point it is worth acknowledging the implications of having durative actions in our formulation. Note that our approach does *not* discretize time, but rather uses time points as steps in the plan - that can be easily augmented with their own durations. So in order to handle durative actions, the only (somewhat minor) change required in the formulation is in the way the conflicts are integrated (instead of summed) over in the objective function. Further, uncertainty in action durations is always a big issue in human interactions; though resource profiles cannot directly handle uncertain durations, it only affects the way the profiles are calculated, and the way in which information is expressed in it remains unchanged (i.e. expectations over action durations add an extra expectation to the already probabilistic profile computation). As noted before in Section 2.3, the ability of profiles to form regions of interest is crucial in handling such scenarios implicitly.

3. MODULATING BEHAVIOR OF THE ROBOT

The planner is implemented on the IP-solver **gurobi** and integrates [7] and [8] respectively for goal recognition and plan prediction for the recognized goals. We will now illustrate how the formulation can produce different behaviors of the robot by appropriately configuring the parameters of the planner. For this discussion we will limit ourselves to a singleton hypothesis goal set in order to observe the robot's response more clearly.

3.1 Compromise

Let us now look back at the environment we introduced in Figure 1. Consider that the goal of the commander is to perform triage in `room1`. The robot computes the human's optimal plan (which ends up using `medkit1` at time steps 7 through 12) and updates the resource profiles accordingly. If it has its own goal to perform triage in `hall3`, the plan that it comes up with given a 12 step lookahead is shown below. Notice that the robot opts for the other medkit (`medkit2` in `room3`) even though its plan now incurs a higher cost in terms of execution. The robot thus can adopt a policy of *compromise* if it is possible for it to preserve the commander's (expected) plan.

```
01 MOVE_ROBOT_ROOM1_HALL1
02 MOVE_ROBOT_HALL1_HALL2
03 MOVE_ROBOT_HALL2_HALL3
04 MOVE_ROBOT_HALL3_HALL4
05 MOVE_REVERSE_ROBOT_HALL4_ROOM4
06 MOVE_REVERSE_ROBOT_ROOM4_ROOM3
07 PICK_UP_MEDKIT_ROBOT_MK2_ROOM3
08 MOVE_ROBOT_ROOM3_ROOM4
09 MOVE_ROBOT_ROOM4_HALL4
10 MOVE_REVERSE_ROBOT_HALL4_HALL3
11 CONDUCT_TRIAGE_ROBOT_HALL3
12 DROP_OFF_ROBOT_MK2_HALL3
```

3.2 Opportunism

Notice, however, that the commander is actually bringing the medkit to `room1` as predicted by the robot, and this is a favorable change in the world, because robot can use this `medkit` once the commander is done and achieve its goal at a much lower cost. The robot, indeed, realizes this once we give it a bigger time horizon to plan with, as shown above (on the right). Thus, in this case, the robot shows *opportunism* based on how it believes the world state will change.

```
01 NOOP
02 NOOP
   ...
13 NOOP
14 PICK_UP_MEDKIT_ROBOT_MK1_ROOM1
15 MOVE_ROBOT_ROOM1_HALL1
16 MOVE_ROBOT_HALL1_HALL2
17 MOVE_ROBOT_HALL2_HALL3
18 CONDUCT_TRIAGE_ROBOT_HALL3
19 DROP_OFF_ROBOT_MK1_HALL3
```

3.3 Negotiation

In many cases, the robot will have to eventually produce plans that will have potential points of conflict with the expected plans of the commander. This occurs when there is no feasible plan with zero overlap between profiles (specifically $\sum g_{f,t} \times G^{\lambda}(t) = 0$) or if the alternative plans for the robot are too costly (as determined by the objective function). If, however, the robot is equipped with the ability to communicate with the human, then it can *negotiate* a plan that suits both. To this end, we introduce a new variable $H^{\lambda}(t)$ and update the IP as follows:

$$\begin{aligned} &min\; k_1 \textstyle\sum_{a \in A_R} \sum_{t \in \{1,2,\ldots,T\}} \mathbb{C}_a \times x_{a,t} \\ &+k_2 \textstyle\sum_{\lambda \in \lambda} \sum_{f \in \Gamma^{-1}(\lambda)} \sum_{t \in \{1,2,\ldots,T\}} g_{f,t} \times H^{\lambda}(t) \\ &-k_3 \textstyle\sum_{\lambda \in \Lambda} \sum_{f \in \Gamma^{-1}(\lambda)} \sum_{t \in \{0,1,\ldots,T-1\}} h_{f,t} \times G^{f^{\lambda}}(t) \\ &+k_4 \textstyle\sum_{\lambda \in \Lambda} \sum_{t \in \{0,1,\ldots,T\}} ||G^{\lambda}(t) - H^{\lambda}(t)|| \end{aligned}$$

$$y_{f,T} \geq h_{f,t-1}\; \forall\, a\; s.t.\; f \in \mathbb{P}_a, \forall f \in \xi, t \in \{1,\ldots,T\} \tag{5a}$$

$$H^{\lambda}(t) \in [0,1]\; \forall \lambda \in \Lambda, t \in \{0,1,\ldots,T\} \tag{16}$$

$$H^{\lambda}(t) \leq G^{\lambda}(t)\; \forall \lambda \in \Lambda, t \in \{0,1,\ldots,T\} \tag{17}$$

Constraint (5a) now complements constraint (5) from the existing formulation, by promising to restore the world state every time a demand is made on a variable. The variable $H^{\lambda}(t)$, maintained by constraints (16) and (17), determine the desired deviation from the given profiles. The objective function has been updated to reflect that overlaps are now measured with the desired profile of usage, and there is a cost associated with the deviation from the real one. The revised plan now produced by the robot is shown below.

```
01 MOVE_ROBOT_ROOM1_HALL1
02 MOVE_ROBOT_HALL1_HALL2
03 MOVE_REVERSE_ROBOT_HALL2_ROOM2
04 PICK_UP_MEDKIT_ROBOT_MK1_ROOM2
05 MOVE_ROBOT_ROOM2_HALL2
06 MOVE_ROBOT_HALL2_HALL3
07 CONDUCT_TRIAGE_ROBOT_HALL3
08 MOVE_REVERSE_ROBOT_HALL3_HALL2
09 MOVE_REVERSE_ROBOT_HALL2_ROOM2
10 DROP_OFF_ROBOT_MK1_ROOM2
```

Notice that the robot restores the world state that the human is believed to expect, and can now communicate to him *"Can you please not use* `medkit1` *from time 7 to 9?"* based on how the real and the ideal profiles diverge, i.e. t such that $H^{\lambda}(t) < G^{\lambda}(t)$ for each resource λ.

Notes on Adaptive Behavior Modeling

One might note here that people are often adaptive and it is very much possible that they may be willing to change their goals based on observing the robot or are even unwilling to negotiate if their plans conflict. Hence the policies of compromise and opportunism for the robot are complementary to negotiation in the event the latter fails. Thus, for example, the robot might choose to communicate a negotiation strategy to the human, but fall back on a compromise if that fails. It is a merit of such a simple formulation to be able to handle such interesting adaptive behaviors.

4. EVALUATION

The power of the proposed approach lies in the modular nature in which it tackles several complicated problems that are separate research areas in their own rights. As we saw throughout the course of the discussion, approaches used in the individual modules may be varied with little to no change in the rest of the architecture. For example the expressivity of the belief modeling or goal recognition component is handled separately as the planner used information from a generic plan set. Again the representation technique introduced in terms of resource profiles provide properties in terms of computational independence with respect to size of the hypothesis set and number of agents (which gets manifested in complexity in number of resources) that general planners do not have. So it becomes a design choice depending on which metric needs to be optimized.

For empirical evaluations, we simulated the USAR scenario on 360 different problem instances, randomly generated by varying the specific (as well as the number of probable) goals of the human, and evaluated how the planner behaved with the number of observations it can start with to build its profiles. We fix the domain description, location and goal of the agents, and the position of the resources, and consider randomly generated hypothesis goal sets of size 2-11. The goals of the commander were assumed to be known to be triage related, but the location of the triage was allocated randomly (one of which was again picked at random as the real goal). Finally for each of these problems, we generate 1-5 observations by simulating the commander's plan over the real goal, and use these observations known *a priori* the robot's plan generation process. The experiments were conducted on an Intel Xeon(R) CPU E5-1620 v2 3.70GHz×8 processor with a 62.9GiB memory.

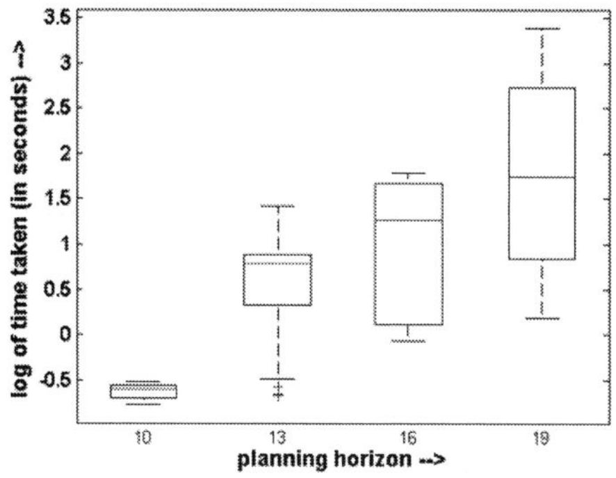

(a) w.r.t. T ($|\Lambda| = 2$)

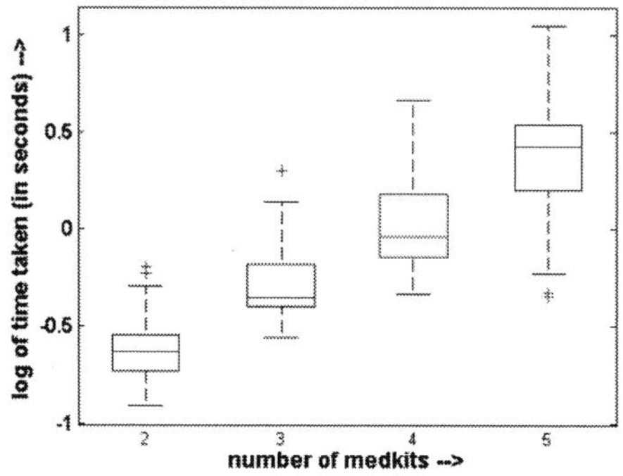

(b) w.r.t. #medkits ($T = 10$)

Figure 4: Performance of the planner w.r.t. planning horizon T and number of constrained resources (medkits).

4.1 Scaling Up

Our primary contribution is the formulation for planning with resource profiles, while the goal recognition component can be any off-the-shelf algorithm, and as such we compare scalability with respect to the planning component only.

- *w.r.t. Length of the Planning Horizon*

The performance of the planner with respect to the planning horizon is shown in Figure 4a. This is, as expected, the bottleneck in computation due to exponential growth of the size of the IP. It is however not prohibitively expensive, and the planner is still able to produce plans of length 20 (steps, not durations) for our domain in a matter of seconds.

- *w.r.t. Number of Resources*

The performance of the planner with respect to the number of constrained resources (medkits, in the context of the current discussion) is shown in Figure 4b. Evidently, the computational effort is dominated by that due to the planning horizon. This reiterates the usefulness of abstracting the information in predicted plans in the form of resource profiles, thus isolating the complexities of the domain with that of the underlying planning algorithm.

- *w.r.t. the Number of Agents and Goals*

The planning module (i.e. the IP formulation) is by itself independent of the number of agents being modeled. In fact, this is one of the major advantages of using abstractions like resource profiles in lieu of actual plans of each of the agents. On the other hand, the time spent on recognition, and on calculating the profiles, is significantly affected. However, observations on multiple agents are asynchronous, and goal recognition can operate in parallel, so that this is not a huge concern beyond the complexity of a single instance. Similarly the performance is also unaffected by the size of the hypothesis set Ψ_α, as shown in Figure 5, which shows increase in the number of the possible goals does not complicate the profiles to an extent to affect the complexity.

4.2 Quality of the Plans Produced

We define U as the average conflicts per plan step when a demand is placed on a resource by the robot, and S as the success probability per plan step that the demand is met. C is the cost of a plan. F is the percentage of times there was an actual conflict during execution (distinct from U which estimates the possible conflict that may occur per plan step). We observe the quality of the plans produced by the planner by varying the ratio of parameters k_1 and k_3 from the objective function and the length of the planning horizon T. Similar results can be produced by varying k_1/k_2.

From Table 1, as k_1/k_3 decreases, the planner becomes more conservative (to maximize success probability) and thus plans become costlier. At the same time the *expected* success rate of actions are also increased (with simultaneous increase in usage conflict), as reflected by a higher failure rate due to actual execution time conflicts.

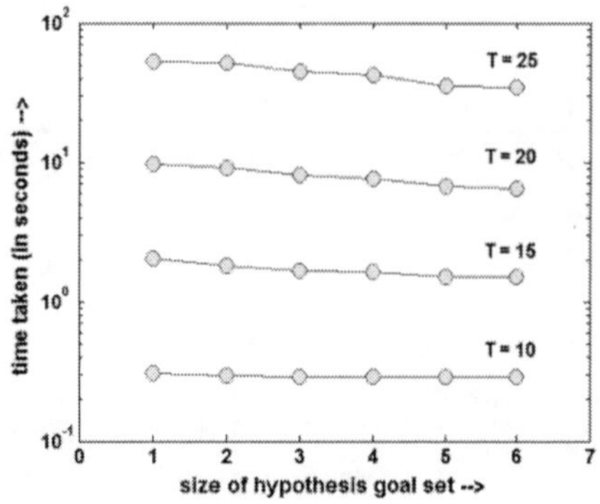

Figure 5: Performance of the planner w.r.t. size of the goal set. As expected, computational complexity is not affected.

k_1/k_3	0.05	0.5	5.0
C	9.47	6.37	6.31
U	0.18	0.17	0.17
S	0.85	0.579	0.578
F	27.5	23.0	21.3

Table 1: Quality of plans produced w.r.t. k_1/k_3. Conservative plans result in lowered utility.

Also note, from Table 2 the impact of the planning horizon T on the types of behaviors we discussed in the previous section. As we increase T, the plan cost falls below the optimal, indicating opportunities for opportunistic behavior on the part of the robot. The expected conflict also falls to almost 0. However the expected success rate of actions also decreases, the ratio k_1/k_2 determines how daring the robot is, in choosing between cheap versus possibly invalid plans. Note, however, the actual execution time conflict is extremely low with increasing T, for even sufficiently conservative estimates of S.

Thus we see that the robot is successfully able to navigate conflicts and find in many cases plans even cheaper than the original optimal plan, thus highlighting the usefulness of the approach. Finally, we look at the impact of the parameters in the plan recognition module in Figure 6. As expected, with bigger hypothesis sets, the success rate goes down. Interestingly, the plan cost also shows a downward trend which might be because the bigger variety in possible goals give a better idea of which medkits are generally more useful for that instance at what points of time. With more observations, as expected, the success rate goes up and the expected conflict goes down. The cost, however, increases a little as the planner opts for more conservative options.

5. CONCLUSIONS

In this paper we investigate how plans may be affected by conflicts on shared resources in an environment cohabited by humans and robots, and introduce the concept of resource profiles as a means of representation for concisely modeling the information pertaining to the usage of such resources, contained in predicted behavior of the agents. We propose a general formulation of a planner for such scenarios and show how the planner can be used to model different types of behavior of the robot by appropriately configuring the objective function and optimization parameters. Finally, we provide an end-to-end framework that integrates belief modeling, goal recognition and an IP-solver that can enforce the desired interaction constraints. One interesting research direction would be to consider nested beliefs on the agents; after all, humans are rarely completely aloof of other agents in its environment. Such interactions should have to consider evolution of beliefs with continued interactions and motivate further exploration of the belief modeling component. The modularity of the proposed approach allows for focused research on each (individually challenging) subtask without significantly affecting the others.

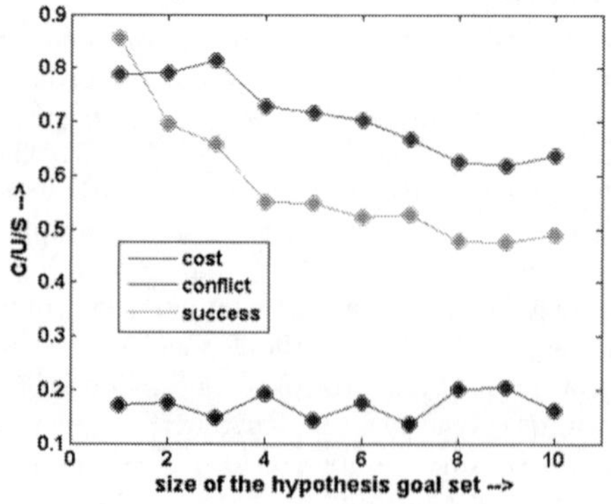

(a) w.r.t. $|\Psi_\alpha|$

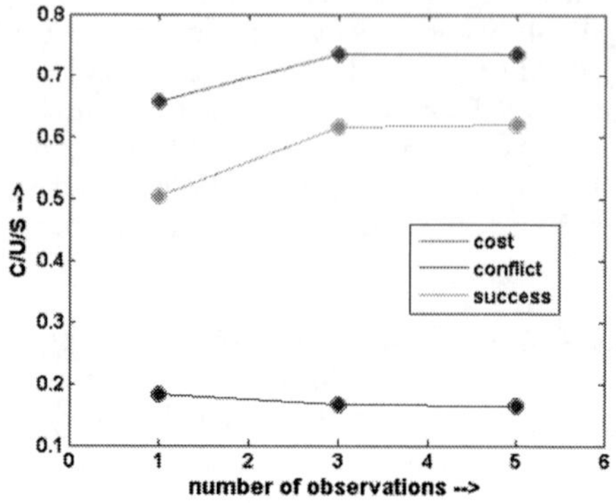

(b) w.r.t. #obs

Figure 6: Performance of the planner w.r.t. size of goal set and number of observations ($k_1/k_3 = 0.5, T = 16$).

T	10	13	16	Optimal
C	9.0	5.6	4.53	9.0
U	0.46	0.04	≈0	n/a
S	1.0	0.48	0.25	n/a
F	53.3	11.9	6.6	53.3

Table 2: Quality of plans produced w.r.t. T. Opportunities for opportunism explored, conflicts minimized.

Acknowledgment

This research is supported in part by the ONR grants N00014-13-1-0176, N00014-13-1-0519 and N00014-15-1-2027, and the ARO grant W911NF-13-1-0023.

REFERENCES

[1] E. Beaudry, F. Kabanza, and F. Michaud. Planning with concurrency under resources and time uncertainty. In *Proceedings of the 2010 Conference on ECAI 2010: 19th European Conference on Artificial Intelligence*, pages 217–222, Amsterdam, The Netherlands, The Netherlands, 2010. IOS Press.

[2] A. Blum and M. L. Furst. Fast planning through planning graph analysis. In *IJCAI*, pages 1636–1642, 1995.

[3] F. Cavallo, R. Limosani, A. Manzi, M. Bonaccorsi, R. Esposito, M. Di Rocco, F. Pecora, G. Teti, A. Saffiotti, and P. Dario. Development of a socially believable multi-robot solution from town to home. *Cognitive Computation*, 6(4):954–967, 2014.

[4] T. Chakraborti, G. Briggs, K. Talamadupula, Y. Zhang, M. Scheutz, D. Smith, and S. Kambhampati. Planning for serendipity. In *IEEE/RSJ International Conference on Intelligent Robots and Systems (IROS)*, 2015.

[5] M. Cirillo, L. Karlsson, and A. Saffiotti. Human-aware task planning for mobile robots. In *Proc of the Int Conf on Advanced Robotics (ICAR)*, 2009.

[6] M. Cirillo, L. Karlsson, and A. Saffiotti. Human-aware task planning: An application to mobile robots. *ACM Trans. Intell. Syst. Technol.*, 1(2):15:1–15:26, Dec. 2010.

[7] Y. E.-Martín, M. D. R.-Moreno, and D. E. Smith. A fast goal recognition technique based on interaction estimates. In *Proceedings of the Twenty-Fourth International Joint Conference on Artificial Intelligence, IJCAI 2015, Buenos Aires, Argentina, July 25-31, 2015*, pages 761–768, 2015.

[8] M. Helmert. The fast downward planning system. *CoRR*, abs/1109.6051, 2011.

[9] U. Koeckemann, F. Pecora, and L. Karlsson. Grandpa hates robots - interaction constraints for planning in inhabited environments. In *Proc. AAAI-2010*, 2014.

[10] M. Kuderer, H. Kretzschmar, C. Sprunk, and W. Burgard. Feature-based prediction of trajectories for socially compliant navigation. In *Proceedings of Robotics: Science and Systems*, Sydney, Australia, July 2012.

[11] D. Mcdermott, M. Ghallab, A. Howe, C. Knoblock, A. Ram, M. Veloso, D. Weld, and D. Wilkins. Pddl - the planning domain definition language. Technical Report TR-98-003, Yale Center for Computational Vision and Control,, 1998.

[12] M. Ramirez and H. Geffner. Probabilistic plan recognition using off-the-shelf classical planners. In *In Proc. AAAI-2010*, 2010.

[13] E. Sisbot, L. Marin-Urias, R. Alami, and T. Simeon. A human aware mobile robot motion planner. *Robotics, IEEE Transactions on*, 23(5):874–883, Oct 2007.

[14] K. Talamadupula, G. Briggs, T. Chakraborti, M. Scheutz, and S. Kambhampati. Coordination in human-robot teams using mental modeling and plan recognition. In *Intelligent Robots and Systems (IROS 2014), 2014 IEEE/RSJ International Conference on*, pages 2957–2962, Sept 2014.

[15] S. Tomic, F. Pecora, and A. Saffiotti. Too cool for school - adding social constraints in human aware planning. In *Proc of the International Workshop on Cognitive Robotics (CogRob)*, 2014.

[16] T. Vossen, M. O. Ball, A. Lotem, and D. S. Nau. On the use of integer programming models in ai planning. In T. Dean, editor, *IJCAI*, pages 304–309. Morgan Kaufmann, 1999.

Iterated Multi-Robot Auctions for Precedence-Constrained Task Scheduling

Mitchell McIntire
University of Minnesota
200 Union St. SE
Minneapolis, MN 55455
mcint286@cs.umn.edu

Ernesto Nunes
University of Minnesota
200 Union St. SE
Minneapolis, MN 55455
enunes@cs.umn.edu

Maria Gini
University of Minnesota
200 Union St. SE
Minneapolis, MN 55455
gini@cs.umn.edu

ABSTRACT

We consider the multi-robot task scheduling problem with precedence constraints, and introduce a general algorithm to approximate a solution to this problem. Our algorithm utilizes an iterated auction scheme, in which a batch of tasks that are pairwise unconstrained is selected in each iteration and scheduled using a modified sequential single-item auction. This algorithm also gains flexibility by allowing the use of task prioritization to order the scheduling process. We demonstrate the effectiveness of this iterated auction scheme empirically using existing 100- and 1000-task data sets that we have modified to include precedence constraints.

1. INTRODUCTION

The basic task scheduling problem has been studied in many variations and in many domains, with applications in operations research, parallel processing, and robot routing. The last of these in particular often requires robots to travel to a specified location in order to complete a task; the resulting problems are typically NP-hard and therefore intractable in general. As a result, scheduling heuristics and approximation algorithms are used.

In robot routing, auction-based algorithms have risen to prominence, providing a strong decentralized approach to task scheduling. Auctions have the advantage of being naturally decentralized (offloading most of the computation into each robot's calculation of its bids), as well as being flexible to different team objectives and problem types.

Here we study the precedence-constrained multi-robot task allocation problem with homogeneous robots (henceforth PC-MRTA), which is NP-hard (it is shown in [16] that a special case of PC-MRTA is NP-hard). This problem falls under the XD[ST-SR-TA] category of the MRTA taxonomy given in [14], since precedence constraints impose cross-schedule dependencies, robots can execute at most one task at a time, tasks are assigned to single robots, and multiple tasks can be assigned to each robot (so the problem is time-extended). Unlike many other MRTA problems, this problem (in the general form, allowing arbitrary precedence constraints) has not been thoroughly studied, perhaps due in part to its complexity even for approximation.

In this paper, we develop an auction-based algorithm which gives a decentralized method of approximate solution for PC-MRTA and generalize this algorithm to make use of methods for task prioritization. We analyze this algorithm's complexity, prove its soundness and completeness, and demonstrate its performance empirically using modified versions of the Solomon [25] and Gehring-Homberger [5] data sets for the vehicle routing problem with time windows.

Appears in: *Proceedings of the 15th International Conference on Autonomous Agents and Multiagent Systems (AAMAS 2016), J. Thangarajah, K. Tuyls, C. Jonker, S. Marsella (eds.), May 9–13, 2016, Singapore.*

2. RELATED WORK

Multiprocessor Scheduling

The problem of task scheduling with precedence constraints is well-studied within the parallel processing literature. Graham [7] gives a $(2-\frac{1}{m})$-approximation algorithm for scheduling under precedence constraints with the minimum-makespan objective. However, this problem is substantially simpler than ours, in which robots must travel between tasks.

Multiprocessor scheduling algorithms often make use of linear programming (LP) relaxations; in [9], a 7-approximation is given for precedence-constrained problems with release dates (i.e. earliest start times) using task completion times in the LP-relaxed schedule to order tasks for simple list scheduling. Chekuri et al. [1] improve this bound, and it has been shown that using LP midpoints to order the tasks gives a 4-approximation for the more general constraint of precedence delays [22]. This result in particular is enticing; precedence delays specify an amount of time that must elapse before each task can begin after its predecessors, which evokes a comparison with travel time. Unfortunately, precedence delays are not general enough to incorporate travel time, which varies based on a robot's prior location.

Another important aspect that is lacking (for our purposes) in these methods is a decentralized approach. List scheduling algorithms can often be adapted into an auction framework, but in general multiprocessor scheduling algorithms are not designed with this goal in mind. In MRTA, however, auction-based approaches are desirable due to their flexibility, decentralized nature, and robustness to failure.

Multi-robot Task Allocation and Scheduling

For the simple case of the MRTA problem in which robots are homogeneous and need only to visit tasks in order to complete them, the sequential single-item (SSI) auction from [15] gives a 2-approximation for the total sum-cost of the resulting schedule and a 2m-approximation for the makespan [16]. The SSI auction has been shown both effective and computationally inexpensive compared to other auction schemes [13].

A more general approach using a mixed integer LP (MILP) model similar to ours was taken by [6], but this model was strictly centralized. In [10] a decentralized method is introduced that performs well, but for a problem variant that is not sufficiently general to extend to PC-MRTA.

Luo, Chakraborty, and Sycara [17] recently introduced an auction-based algorithm for multi-robot assignment of tasks for a particular special case of PC-MRTA, in which precedence constraints are in a form called *set* precedence constraints (SPCs). The SPC problem partitions tasks into sets with size at most equal to the number of robots. These sets are strictly ordered, giving a precedence relationship. The resulting problem is similar to ours, but heavily constrains the space of allowable precedence graphs. In particular, if we view the precedence graph by layers (described in more detail later), SPCs require that every task in a layer has a precedence constraint between it and every task in the next layer. This is equivalent to saying that the topological ordering of an SPC precedence graph is unique up to changing the order of tasks within each set. They also require that robots complete at most one task per set. This method is therefore too restrictive to apply to our problem.

In [24], a distributed solution to a problem similar to ours is presented. However, this solution computes essentially a greedy schedule initially, and then adapts this schedule during task execution. Our goal by contrast is to compute the entire schedule initially, which does not require communication during task execution.

Distributed Constraint Optimization

Distributed Constraint Optimization Problem (DCOP) [19] models and algorithms offer an alternative framework for PC-MRTA. However, solving DCOP exactly is NP-hard and impractical even for unconstrained MRTA problems [11]. Thus, approximate methods such as Max-Sum [4] have been used for task allocation in sensor networks and in RoboCup Rescue [23].

Various other methods have been proposed for solving varieties of DCOP [23, 18, 3, 27]. However, despite the wealth of literature on DCOP models and solutions, we are unaware of any work that has extended DCOP to handle general precedence constraints.

3. PROBLEM DEFINITION

We are given $\mathcal{T}$, a set of n tasks with precedence constraints. The precedence constraints can be encoded with a precedence graph, i.e. a directed graph $G_\mathcal{P} = (\mathcal{T}, E)$, where if $t_1 \prec t_2$ (or equivalently, if $(t_1, t_2) \in E$), then the task t_1 is a predecessor of t_2 and must be completed before any robot begins executing t_2. It is straightforward to see that $G_\mathcal{P}$ must be acyclic for a valid schedule to exist. We allow any valid precedence constraints on the tasks; i.e. $G_\mathcal{P}$ may be any directed acyclic graph (DAG) over the tasks.

Additionally, we have $\mathcal{R}$, a set of m robots, each with an initial location. This initial location is allowed to differ from robot to robot, but $\mathcal{R}$ is otherwise homogeneous. Each task has a location associated with it that a robot must be at to execute the task.

A valid schedule for PC-MRTA consists of a partitioning of $\mathcal{T}$ across $\mathcal{R}$ (allocation) and a schedule for each robot which specifies the time at which each allocated task is executed. These robot schedules must collectively respect the precedence constraints on $\mathcal{T}$. The makespan of a schedule S is defined as the latest finish time of any task in S, i.e. the maximum robot finish time. Our goal is to minimize this value, which is similar to the MiniMax team objective in e.g. [16, 26, 28].

The mathematical model for this problem is described in Figure 1. The model adds a set of dummy tasks $\mathcal{T}_d$ at the robots' initial locations to represent their starting positions. The decision variables include the continuous and nonnegative start (S_{t_j}) and finish (F_{t_j}) time variables for each task, the makespan variable Z, the binary assignment variables $A_{t_j}^{r_i}$, $Y_{t_j}^{r_i}$, and the precedence ordering variables $X_{t_j,t_k}^{r_i}$. The variable $A_{t_j}^{r_i}$ is 1 if task t_j is allocated to robot r_i, $Y_{t_j}^{r_i}$ is 1 if t_j is the last task for r_i, and $X_{t_j,t_k}^{r_i}$ is 1 if

$$\text{minimize:} \quad Z \tag{2}$$
$$\text{subject to:} \quad Z \geq F_{t_j}, \ \forall t_j \in \mathcal{T} \tag{3}$$
$$\sum_{r_i \in \mathcal{R}} A_{t_j}^{r_i} = 1, \ \forall t_j \in \mathcal{T} \cup \mathcal{T}_d \tag{4}$$
$$\sum_{t_j \in \mathcal{T}_d} A_{t_j}^{r_i} = 1, \ \forall r_i \in \mathcal{R} \tag{5}$$
$$\sum_{t_j \in \mathcal{T}} Y_{t_j}^{r_i} = 1, \ \forall r_i \in \mathcal{R} \tag{6}$$
$$\sum_{t_j \in \mathcal{T} \cup \mathcal{T}_d, t_j \neq t_k} X_{t_j,t_k}^{r_i} = A_{t_j}^{r_i}, \ \forall t_k \in \mathcal{T}, r_i \in \mathcal{R} \tag{7}$$
$$\sum_{t_k \in \mathcal{T}, t_j \neq t_k} X_{t_j,t_k}^{r_i} + Y_{t_j}^{r_i} = A_{t_j}^{r_i}, \ \forall t_j \in \mathcal{T} \cup \mathcal{T}_d, \ r_i \in \mathcal{R} \tag{8}$$
$$F_{t_j} + d(t_j, t_k) - M(1 - X_{t_j,t_k}^{r_i}) \leq S_{t_k} \ \forall t_j, t_k \in \mathcal{T}, \ r_i \in \mathcal{R} \tag{9}$$
$$0 \leq S_{t_j} \leq \infty, \ \forall t_j \in \mathcal{T}_d \tag{10}$$
$$0 \leq F_{t_j} \leq \infty, \ \forall t_j \in \mathcal{T} \cup \mathcal{T}_d \tag{11}$$
$$F_{t_j} - S_{t_j} \geq \text{dur}(t_j), \quad \forall t_j \in \mathcal{T} \tag{12}$$
$$S_{t_k} - F_{t_j} \geq 0, \ \forall (t_j, t_k) \in \mathcal{T}_{prec} \tag{13}$$
$$A_{t_j}^{r_i} \in \{0, 1\}, \ \forall t_j \in \mathcal{T} \cup \mathcal{T}_d, \ r_i \in \mathcal{R} \tag{14}$$
$$Y_{t_j}^{r_i} \in \{0, 1\}, \ \forall t_j \in \mathcal{T}, \ r_i \in \mathcal{R} \tag{15}$$
$$X_{t_j,t_k}^{r_i} \in \{0, 1\}, \ \forall t_j, t_k \in \mathcal{T} \cup \mathcal{T}_d, \ r_i \in \mathcal{R} \tag{16}$$

Figure 1: Mixed Integer Program for PC-MRTA

robot r_i performs task t_j followed by t_k. The model accounts for the time robots spend traveling between tasks, $d(t_j, t_k)$, and the duration of tasks, $\text{dur}(t_j)$.

The model variable Z is a continuous positive variable that replaces the optimization objective in Equation 1. We linearize the optimization objective by making Z the upper bound for all finish times across all tasks, i.e.

$$Z = \max_{t_j \in \mathcal{T}} F_{t_j} \tag{1}$$

In this model, constraint (2) defines the makespan as the latest finish time of any task. Constraints (3-4) ensure that each task is assigned to exactly one robot, and that each robot has a dummy task; constraints (5-7) limit the number of final tasks for each robot to one and ensure that all tasks that are not scheduled first or last have predecessors or successors respectively. Constraints (8-11) are temporal constraints that enforce that robots have time to travel between and execute their tasks, and constraint (12) establishes a relationship between start times of dependent tasks ($\mathcal{T}_{prec}$), such that a task never starts before its predecessors. In constraint (8) M is a large value, which is part of the big-M formulation for mixed integer program constraints.

4. THE ITERATED AUCTION ALGORITHM

Our algorithm is in the form of an iterated auction, which repeatedly uses a modified version of the sequential single-item (SSI) auction to schedule tasks in batches. In particular, batches of tasks are selected such that the tasks are pairwise independent, so that they can be scheduled without regard for when the other tasks in the batch are scheduled. This task independence is the main assumption of the SSI auction. The batch selection and auctioning process is managed by an auctioneer, while robots serve as bidders.

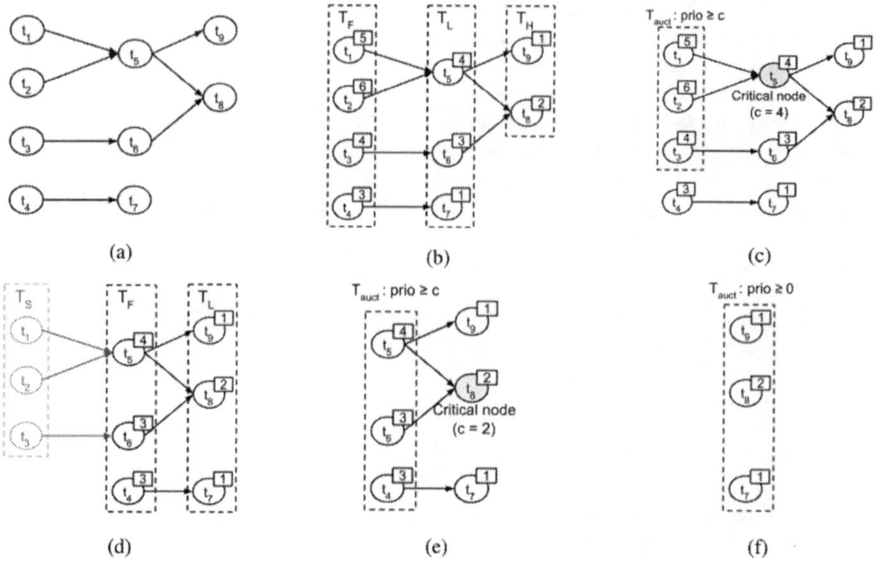

Figure 2: A demonstration of the iterated auction. The number in a square next to each node in (b)-(f) represents that task's priority. Priorities have been assigned arbitrarily to illustrate the batch selection process. (a) The initial task precedence graph. (b) The labeling of the precedence graph by layers. (c) The identification of the critical node, and batch selection for the first iteration of pIA. (d) The new labels for the precedence graph after the first iteration. (e) Batch selection for the second iteration. (f) The remaining tasks are scheduled in the final iteration.

Henceforth we will use the term 'free' to describe task nodes with no parents, and for a set of tasks A we let free(A) be the set of tasks in A which have no predecessors in A. In explaining the operation of the iterated auction algorithm, it is helpful to visualize the task precedence graph $G_{\mathcal{P}}$ as a DAG with nodes grouped into layers, as shown in Figure 2b. The first layer, T_F, is the set of tasks with no predecessors, i.e. $T_F = \text{free}(\mathcal{T})$. The second layer is then $T_L = \text{free}(\mathcal{T} \setminus T_F)$, and so on for successive layers. In our notation, T_H is the set of tasks which are not in $T_F \cup T_L$, i.e. the 'hidden' tasks which are not free or second-layer. We refer to T_H as 'hidden' tasks because in a given iteration the tasks in T_H do not affect the scheduling process.

It is important to note that no precedence constraints exist between tasks in any layer of $G_{\mathcal{P}}$. To see this, just consider that if a constraint did exist within a layer, then the child node would not be free, which contradicts the layer selection process (see Figure 2b). This allows us to use the modified SSI auction, since the tasks in each layer can be scheduled in any order with respect to each other without violating constraints.

4.1 The Simple Iterated Auction

We will refer to the simplest iterated auction algorithm as the Simple Iterated Auction (sIA). In sIA, the batches of tasks to be auctioned are the layers of $G_{\mathcal{P}}$. In each iteration, the auctioneer selects the top layer of tasks, T_F, and sends them to each robot; the robots then compute and send bids to the auctioneer, which selects the robot with the lowest bid and assigns the corresponding task to it (as in an SSI auction; see e.g. [15, 16] for a more detailed description). The pseudocode for sIA is given in Algorithms 1-4 if all tasks are taken to have priority zero. Alternatively, one obtains full pseudocode for sIA by removing line 5 from Algorithm 1 and replacing line 6 with $T_{auct} = T_F$ (so that the entire first layer is auctioned). Since the algorithm presented in the next section is more general than sIA in this sense, we defer the full description of the process to the following sections.

4.2 The Iterated Auction with Prioritization

The simplicity of sIA is appealing, and allows the iterated auction process to be easily visualized as peeling layers from the task precedence graph. By adding a precomputation step in which tasks are assigned a numerical priority (which we discuss later), we can guide the scheduling process. Put simply, in each iteration only the tasks in T_F that are high-priority with respect to the tasks in T_L are scheduled, as shown in Figure 2c. This allows less important first-layer tasks to be delayed so that important tasks not in T_F can be completed sooner. We call this the Iterated Auction with Prioritization (pIA).

The pseudocode for the auctioneer's role in pIA is given in Algorithm 1. In lines 1-2, tasks are partitioned into T_S, T_F, T_L, and T_H based on whether they have been scheduled, are free, are second-layer, or are 'hidden'; this is shown in Figure 2b. In line 3, the arrays F and PC are initialized; F stores the latest finish time of tasks that have been scheduled, while PC stores the earliest valid start time for tasks whose preconditions have been scheduled. Note that the tasks initially in T_F can be started at any time, so the values of zero in PC are appropriate for these tasks.

In each iteration (starting in line 4), the auctioneer finds the 'critical value' c, which is the maximum priority of any second-layer task (shown in line 5 of Algorithm 1; in this paper, we use the convention that $\max_{\emptyset}(x) \equiv 0$ for all x). We will occasionally refer to a task in T_L with priority c as a critical node in the context of the task precedence graph. In line 6, the first-layer tasks with priority at least as high as the critical value (see Figure 2c) are then selected as T_{auct}. The tasks in T_{auct} are then auctioned in line 7 using the same modified SSI auction as in sIA. The robots' algorithm for this auction is shown in Algorithm 3.

In the modified SSI auction, the auctioneer sends T_{auct} to each robot along with the earliest start times for the tasks in PC. In parallel, the robots each find the task in T_{auct} for which their bid is lowest and submit this (task, bid) pair to the auctioneer (lines 2-12 of Algorithm 3). The auctioneer then sends the (robot, task) pair

Algorithm 1 Auctioneer's algorithm for pIA

Input: Precedence graph $G_{\mathcal{P}} = (\mathcal{T}, E)$, robots $\mathcal{R}$
1: $T_S = \emptyset$, $T_F = \text{free}(\mathcal{T})$
2: $T_L = \text{free}(\mathcal{T} \setminus T_F)$, $T_H = \mathcal{T} \setminus (T_F \cup T_L)$
3: Initialize arrays F, PC to zero
4: **while** $|T_S| < n$ **do**
5: $\quad c = \max_{t \in T_L}(\text{prio}(t))$
6: $\quad T_{auct} = \{t \in T_F : \text{prio}(t) \geq c\}$
7: $\quad$ModifiedSSI(T_{auct}, PC)
8: $\quad$ReceiveFinishTimes($\mathcal{R}$,F)
9: $\quad$**for all** $t \in T_{auct}$ **do**
10: $\quad\quad$UpdatePrecGraph(t, PC, $G_{\mathcal{P}}$)
11: $\quad$**end for**
12: **end while**
13: **return** F

Algorithm 2 UpdatePrecGraph

Input: Task t, array PC, precedence graph $G_{\mathcal{P}}$
1: Move $t : T_F \rightarrow T_S$
2: **for all** $t' \in T_L \cap$ children(t) **do**
3: $\quad$**if** parents(t') $\subset T_S$ **then**
4: $\quad\quad$Move $t' : T_L \rightarrow T_F$
5: $\quad\quad PC[t'] = \max_{t'' \in \text{parents}(t')}(F[t''])$
6: $\quad\quad$**for all** $t'' \in T_H \cap$ children(t') **do**
7: $\quad\quad\quad$**if** parents(t'') $\subset T_S \cup T_F$ **then**
8: $\quad\quad\quad\quad$Move $t'' : T_H \rightarrow T_L$
9: $\quad\quad\quad$**end if**
10: $\quad\quad$**end for**
11: $\quad$**end if**
12: **end for**

Algorithm 3 Robot r's algorithm for each auction

Input: Set of tasks T_{auct}, earliest start times PC
Output: Vector of finishing times F
1: **while** $|T_{auct}| > 0$ **do**
2: $\quad b = \infty$
3: $\quad t_{bid} = \varnothing$
4: $\quad$**for all** $t \in T_{auct}$ **do**
5: $\quad\quad$**for all** positions p in current schedule S **do**
6: $\quad\quad\quad$Insert t in S at p to get S'
7: $\quad\quad\quad$**if** isValid(S') and bid(S') $< b$ **then**
8: $\quad\quad\quad\quad b$ = bid(S'), $t_{bid} = t$
9: $\quad\quad\quad$**end if**
10: $\quad\quad$**end for**
11: $\quad$**end for**
12: $\quad$sendBid(b, t_{bid})
13: $\quad r_{win}, t_{win}$ = receiveWinner()
14: $\quad$**if** $r = r_{win}$ **then**
15: $\quad\quad$Insert t_{win} in S at best valid position
16: $\quad$**end if**
17: $\quad T_{auct} = T_{auct} \setminus t_{win}$
18: **end while**
19: TightenSchedule(F)
20: return F

Algorithm 4 TightenSchedule

Input: Vector of finishing times F,
Vector of robot's internal constraints on latest finish times, LF
1: **for all** tasks t in current schedule S **do**
2: $\quad$Compute earliest finish time f for task t
3: $\quad$Set task finish time to return to auctioneer: $F[t] = f$
4: $\quad$Introduce temporal constraint on STN: $LF[t] = f$
5: **end for**

with the lowest bid to each robot, shown in line 13 of Algorithm 3. In lines 14-16, the winning robot updates its schedule to include the new task. The auction continues in this way until all of T_{auct} has been scheduled. In line 19 of Algorithm 3, each robot calls 'TightenSchedule' (Algorithm 4), which updates the finish times in F and imposes constraints on the tasks the robot has scheduled so that they cannot be delayed. This is done to ensure precedence constraints are satisfied, and is discussed in more detail below.

After the modified SSI auction finishes, the auctioneer collects the finish times for T_{auct} and updates F, shown in line 8 of Algorithm 1. The last step in each iteration is the call to 'UpdatePrecGraph', in which the auctioneer maintains the labeling of tasks as e.g. second-layer. The value $PC[t]$ for each task t that has been freed in the current iteration is also set during this step to the latest finish time of any parent of t. This allows robots to enforce that a task is not begun before its predecessors finish.

4.3 Robot Scheduling and Bidding

We have until now glossed over the mechanisms by which robots maintain their schedules and compute bids, mainly because it is more complicated than the rest of the discussion. In the basic SSI auction, the robots simply receive tasks from the auctioneer, compute the cheapest insertion of each task into their existing schedules (this is called the insertion heuristic), and place a bid (usually either the cost of insertion or the makespan after insertion). The winning robot then inserts the corresponding task into its schedule.

Since our goal is to minimize the makespan, our robots bid the makespan of the new schedule (which prevents overencumbered robots from being assigned more tasks if other robots can help). Note that a robot's bid is a function only of its current schedule and the additional task under consideration; robots are not aware of task prioritization. In the iterated auction scheme, we must introduce additional complexity to ensure that precedence constraints are not violated. This yields the modified SSI auction described above, written in Algorithm 1 as 'ModifiedSSI(T_{auct}, PC)'. The auctioneer's role in this auction is essentially the same as in an SSI auction. However, instead of inserting tasks arbitrarily into their schedules, robots instead check for the validity of schedules, and 'tighten' their schedule between iterations. Pseudocode for the robots' scheduling process is given in Algorithm 3, and for 'TightenSchedule' in Algorithm 4. We will discuss the 'TightenSchedule' procedure shortly.

In a robot's schedule, to represent timing constraints and check whether a task insertion is valid, we use a Simple Temporal Network [2]. The STN is a graph-like data structure in which events (task start and finish times in our case) are nodes. Timing constraints are represented as edges; an edge between nodes constrains their relative time of occurrence (e.g. an edge between task start and task finish enforcing that the duration of the task elapses between them). Constraints can also be added with respect to absolute time, so that events occur in a specific time window.

In 'TightenSchedule' (Algorithm 4), the robot adds constraints so that its currently scheduled tasks cannot be delayed by tasks in a later iteration. This ensures that precedence constraints are not violated, while maintaining the robots' privacy, i.e. robots are only aware of their tasks and the timing constraints on those tasks. The STN also allows us to check that a schedule is feasible, or can be completed by the robot without violating any constraints; this is done via 'isValid' in Algorithm 3, which utilizes the tasks' earliest start times in PC. See [2] for a more detailed description of managing temporal constraints using STNs, and [21] for an example of their application in a similar setting.

The similarity of 'ModifiedSSI' to the SSI auction is possible due to the lack of precedence constraints between tasks in T_{auct}. This allows us to, despite the constraints in the overall problem, approach each iteration with a independent-task scheduling method, and gain some of the benefit of the insertion heuristic (as discussed in [25, 16]) in each iteration based on how large T_{auct} is. In particular, the finish times in F are not set until the end of the iteration, since these are malleable until the end of the iteration. This allows tasks to be inserted into schedules in the most efficient manner possible. When 'TightenSchedule' is called additional constraints are added to each robot's internal STN to ensure that no currently scheduled task can be delayed.

5. PRIORITY ASSIGNMENT

The question of how to prioritize tasks is critical to the performance of pIA; with the flexibility of controlling the order in which tasks are scheduled comes the potential to either worsen or improve the resulting schedule. In this paper, we use a simple heuristic to assign priorities based on the shape of the precedence graph.

We define $U(t)$ and $L(t)$ for $t \in \mathcal{T}$ to be the length of the longest path in $G_{\mathcal{P}}$ rooted at t, respectively with and without travel time between tasks. More precisely, we let

$$L(t) = \text{dur}(t) + \max_{t' \in \text{children}(t)} (L(t')) \,,$$

$$U(t) = \text{dur}(t) + \max_{t' \in \text{children}(t)} (d(t,t') + U(t')) \,,$$

where we use the convention that $\max_{\emptyset}(x) \equiv 0$, so that $L(t) = U(t) = \text{dur}(t)$ if the task t has no children. Then we let

$$\text{prio}_{\alpha}(t) = (1-\alpha)L(t) + \alpha U(t) \,,\; 0 \leq \alpha \leq 1.$$

In this way our priority assignment is a heuristic for the total length of the precedence graph, or the total time to completion for the maximum-duration chain of tasks rooted at the given task. The value $U(t)$ represents the total time this chain would take to be executed by a single robot (in the absence of other constraints), while $L(t)$ is the least possible time required to execute these tasks (since it is the sum of their durations, and the tasks are constrained and must be completed sequentially).

The parameter α can be thought of roughly as the proportion of travel time that is accounted for in task priorities. If α is high, then the priority of a task t is approximately $U(t)$, or the longest path to completion including travel time. Similarly, $\alpha \approx 0$ yields $\text{prio}_{\alpha}(t) \approx L(t)$, which is the longest path to completion including only the duration of the tasks. Since the task nodes along the longest path to completion may change as α changes, our intuition for α as the proportion of travel time accounted for should be taken more as a rough intuition and not as a definition.

Formulating the priorities in this way allows the possibility of adaptively choosing α for each task based on the structure of the graph or other factors, or changing the value of α during the iterated auction based on robot locations, etc. Though we do not use adaptive choices for α in this paper, it is possible that practical use cases for our algorithm will find this flexibility useful. We will use α to refer specifically to our method for priority assignment throughout this paper. In most cases, intuiting it as a proportion of travel time accounted for is appropriate.

Note that we can compute these priorities in time linear in the size of the precedence graph $G_{\mathcal{P}}$ by using dynamic programming. This can be achieved by computing priorities bottom-up, beginning with the tasks that have no children. Thus each task node is iterated over once when its priority is computed and each edge is iterated over once when a parent node checks the priority of each of its children.

This system of prioritization is inspired by critical path scheduling methods, introduced in [12]. These methods identify the longest task chain in a DAG and schedule tasks so as to minimize delays on that chain. Adapting this critical path approach to the PC-MRTA problem is difficult, however. We use the priority system above to account for the ability of other robots to continue a task chain and thereby lessen the cost of travel time.

Our method of prioritization is a somewhat naive heuristic, since it does not always correctly account for travel time and fails to consider the location of future tasks; for example, a robot may ignore a conveniently located, easy-to-complete task in favor of higher-priority tasks, and thereby worsen its schedule when it must return to complete this task. Heuristics which explicitly consider task location (and not just the length of a task chain) may be more successful.

As an open question, we conjecture that a non-heuristic prioritization scheme based on an LP relaxation may be very successful in pIA. It was shown in [22] that using task midpoints from a schedule produced via LP relaxation to order tasks for a list scheduling algorithm gives a 4-approximation for the general problem of multiprocessor scheduling with precedence delays; we suspect that a similar approach for prioritization could outperform many heuristic methods in the pIA scheme for PC-MRTA.

6. ANALYSIS

In this section, we provide arguments for the complexity, soundness, and completeness of the iterated auction.

6.1 Complexity Analysis

Here we provide a sketch for the complexity of the complete iterated auction procedure. We will assume the average case, in which tasks are assigned in roughly equal number to the different robots. This assumption seems strong, but is actually well-founded; a robot's bid is the total time taken to complete its current schedule, so robots with more tasks will tend to make higher bids and be assigned fewer tasks.

First consider the 'ModifiedSSI' procedure called in line 11 of Algorithm 1. Let $n_{auct} = |T_{auct}|$ be the number of tasks to be auctioned. The auctioneer sends T_{auct} and PC to each robot for m total messages of size $\mathcal{O}(n_{auct})$. Let n_{pre} be the total number of tasks scheduled in previous iterations. Then in iteration i of Algorithm 3's while loop, any given robot will have on average $\frac{n_{pre}+i}{m}$ positions for insertion of a task in its current schedule. On average there will therefore be $\mathcal{O}((n_{auct}-i)(\frac{n_{pre}+i}{m}))$ attempted insertions in any robot's schedule (line 6 of Algorithm 3). Validity checking using the robot's STN has average time complexity of $\mathcal{O}((\frac{n_{pre}+i}{m})^3)$ [2], and thus the total time taken in a scheduling iteration is $\mathcal{O}((n_{auct}-i)(\frac{n_{pre}+i}{m})^4)$, along with $2m$ messages (one sent and one received by each robot) of size $\mathcal{O}(1)$. Since this procedure is repeated n_{auct} times, this gives us a total complexity

$$\sum_{i=1}^{n_{auct}} (n_{auct}-i)(\frac{n_{pre}+i}{m})^4 = \mathcal{O}(\frac{n_{auct}^2}{m^4}(n_{auct}^4 + n_{pre}^4)) \,.$$

Note that this complexity for the 'ModifiedSSI' procedure is (typically) asymptotically dominant in each iteration; the only other consideration is the n_{auct} calls to 'UpdatePrecGraph', which will on average be relatively inexpensive. To see this, observe that the total work done during the entire iterated auction by 'UpdatePrecGraph' is to move all n tasks into T_S, layer by layer. This requires

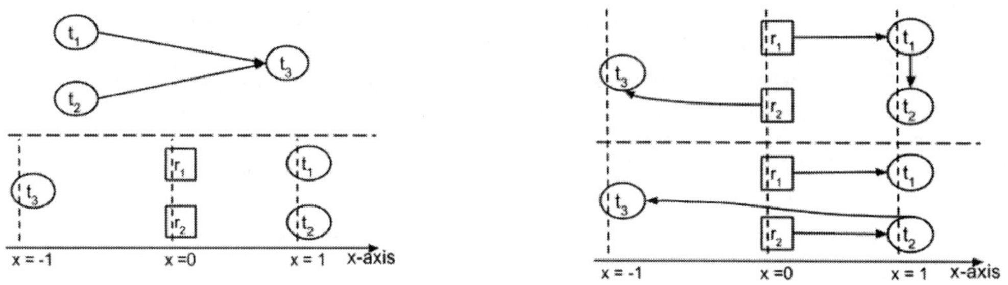

(a) (b)

Figure 3: A simple worst-case example demonstrating the vulnerability of the iterated auction to certain mistakes. In (a), the example is defined by three tasks with the precedence graph shown on the top of the figure, and with task locations and initial robot locations shown below. In (b), the optimal allocation is shown on top, while the iterated auction allocation (for any prioritization) is shown on the bottom.

at most three movements per task (from T_H to T_L, then to T_F, then to T_S), and thus the total work done by 'UpdatePrecGraph' is $\mathcal{O}(n)$. The complexity of the modified SSI auction is therefore asymptotically dominant.

Now consider the complexity of the overall algorithm. Roughly, we have two extremes - either for each iteration $n_{auct} = \mathcal{O}(1)$, or $n_{auct} = \Omega(n)$. In the former case, the above complexity for each iteration evaluates to $\mathcal{O}((\frac{i}{m})^4)$ for iteration i, which gives us a total complexity of

$$\sum_{i=1}^{\mathcal{O}(n)} (\frac{\mathcal{O}(i)}{m})^4 = \mathcal{O}(\frac{n^5}{m^4}) .$$

In the latter case, we have $\mathcal{O}(1)$ iterations, with total complexity $\mathcal{O}(\frac{n^6}{m^4})$. Thus if we assume that tasks are evenly distributed among robots, the iterated auction algorithm has complexity

$$\mathcal{O}(\frac{n^5}{m^4}) \leq T(n,m) \leq \mathcal{O}(\frac{n^6}{m^4}) .$$

It is interesting to note that this result implies that pIA is more efficient than sIA, since prioritization reduces the average value of n_{auct}. Note also that this is often a fairly loose upper bound, since in particular many of the checks made by robots for their schedules' validity will be resolved more quickly than the asymptotic bound.

6.2 Soundness and Completeness

We will now show that the iterated auction algorithm will always produce a valid schedule if one exists. Note that we allow general precedence constraints, and so any set of tasks whose precedence graph is a DAG is valid. Furthermore, a valid schedule will always exist in this case, since we can simply assign every task to a single robot, which can complete the tasks in any topological ordering of the precedence graph. For the rest of this section, we will assume that the problem instance is valid, with a directed acyclic precedence graph. We therefore only need to show that the iterated auction algorithm produces a valid schedule in this case. We will prove this for pIA, since sIA is equivalent to pIA for a given priority assignment. We assume that priorities are nonnegative and that the priority of every task is at least as high as that of any of its successors in the precedence graph.

First, we show that pIA will successfully schedule all the tasks and terminate. The relevant pseudocode is the while loop beginning on line 4 of Algorithm 1. We will argue that in every iteration $|T_{auct}| > 0$, and therefore that the number of tasks scheduled, $|T_S|$, increases in every iteration until all tasks are scheduled.

To see this, first suppose for a given iteration that T_L, the set of second-layer tasks, is nonempty. Then the critical value c will be set to the priority of a task in T_L, and by definition of T_L that task must have a parent in the set of free tasks T_F. Since the priority of a task is at least that of its successors, this task in T_F has priority at least c and will be included in T_{auct}.

Now assume instead that T_L is empty. Then c will be set to zero. If T_L is empty there must be at least one task in T_F, as otherwise every task would already have been scheduled. Since we assume that priorities are nonnegative, every task in T_F will be added to T_{auct}, and so T_{auct} will be nonempty. Thus in every iteration at least one task is scheduled, and so the algorithm terminates.

Next, we must show that the schedule produced by the algorithm is valid. It is only invalid if precedence constraints are violated. Consider tasks t_1, t_2 with $t_1 \prec t_2$. Note that the tasks scheduled in any given iteration are pairwise independent, so since $t_1 \prec t_2$, t_1 must have been scheduled in an earlier iteration than t_2.

When t_1 was scheduled, the robot to which it was assigned returned t_1's finish time in F (Algorithm 1, line 8 and Algorithm 3, line 20). This followed the robot's call to 'TightenSchedule', which set $F[t_1]$ as the latest valid finish time for t_1. When t_2 was moved into T_F by 'UpdatePrecGraph' (Algorithm 2) after all of its predecessors were scheduled, $PC[t_2]$ was set to the maximum completion time of any of its predecessors; since $t_1 \prec t_2$, we therefore know that $PC[t_2]$ is at least the finish time of t_1. But then when t_2 is auctioned, $PC[t_2]$ is passed to each robot as the earliest start time for t_2 (Algorithm 1, line 7). The robot that wins t_2 in the auction adds it to its schedule in line 15 of Algorithm 3; in particular, t_2 is inserted into the robot's schedule in the best *valid* position, i.e. the position which respects all of the earliest start times in PC and yields the cheapest schedule of all such insertion positions. Validity is checked using robots' STNs, the data structure in which timing constraints are managed (discussed above). Since t_2 is inserted into only valid positions, and no other task insertion is allowed if it results in t_2 beginning before $PC[t_2]$, t_2 will start no earlier than $PC[t_2]$. Since the finish time of t_1 is at most $F[t_1] \leq PC[t_2]$, this implies that the precedence constraint $t_1 \prec t_2$ is satisfied.

6.3 Weaknesses of the Iterated Auction

In Figure 3, an example problem is shown that the iterated auction performs poorly for. Refer to Figure 3b. If each task has duration δ, the optimal allocation sends the robots in different directions, so task t_1 is completed at time $1+\delta$, task t_2 at time $1+2\delta$, and task t_3 at time $1+3\delta$. However, the iterated auction attempts to free t_3 for scheduling as soon as possible, resulting in both robots being sent to $x = 1$. In this case, both $t1$ and $t2$ are completed at time $1+\delta$, but t_3 is not completed until time $3+2\delta$.

This example exploits the primary weakness of the iterated auction. Since pIA does not explicitly consider future task locations, robots may be mispositioned with respect to future iterations if task locations oscillate between extremes from iteration to iteration. In such cases, the entire robot team may be enlisted to help in each location in consecutive iterations, depending on the lengths of their partial schedules. This can result in relatively poor performance with respect to the optimal schedule.

To improve performance in such cases, a modified bidding scheme could be used in which robots place bids that are based in part on distance traveled. This would result in an optimal solution of the example in Figure 3: when the robots are bidding for task t_2 in the first iteration, the first robot's bid (using our bidding scheme) is its new makespan, $1 + 2\delta$, while the other robot bids $1 + \delta$. If the fact that the latter robot would travel an entire unit is taken into account, however, its bid would be higher, and the first robot would complete both t_1 and t_2. See e.g. [21] for more details on such a bidding scheme.

7. EXPERIMENTS

Our experiments were conducted via simulation, using an implementation of the pIA algorithm in C++. We utilized existing data sets from the vehicle routing problem (VRP) literature [25, 5], using the time windows for task completion in these problems to loosely order generation of precedence constraints. This was necessary due to the lack of current research on PC-MRTA; we were unable to find more relevant problem instances.

Each of the above data sets is split into six parts: C1, C2, R1, R2, RC1, and RC2. The C instances have tasks which are spatially clustered, while the R instances have tasks which are randomly distributed. The RC instances are a mixture of R and C, with some tasks clustered and others randomly placed. Each Solomon instance has 100 tasks, while each Gehring-Homberger (G-H) instance has 1000 tasks.

Since these data sets are for research on the VRP with time windows, we must modify them in order to use them for PC-MRTA. To this end, we use the method of [20] to generate a precedence graph uniformly at random on the tasks in each instance. In this we respect the time windows of the original data; if a task's time window closes before another's in the original data, we do not allow the latter task to precede the former in our precedence structure.

In addition to imposing a loose ordering on the precedence graph, we also restrict the density of the graph. Without density limits, a random DAG will have on average $\frac{n^2}{4}$ edges [20], which is overconstrained for a scheduling problem: a Solomon instance with 100 tasks would have roughly 2500 constraints. To remedy this, we generate for each original data instance eight random precedence graphs, four of which are sparse (limited to at most $\frac{n}{2}$ edges) and four of which are denser (limited to at most $2n$ edges). In all cases, we average across all four of the random graphs for each instance and level of density to reduce the effects of chance.

For the clustered (C) and partially clustered (RC) data sets, we reasoned that random constraints on a clustered set of tasks would de-emphasize the clustered nature of the tasks. We therefore imposed additional restrictions on the precedence structure in these sets. The generation process selects random pairs of nodes and inserts an edge between them if it is valid (or removes the edge if it already exists); for the C and RC data instances, we randomly decline edges that pass between clusters with a probability of 0.8. This yields a precedence graph in which the majority of constraints respect the clustered structure of the original data, and task clusters are sparsely connected by constraints.

7.1 Results and Discussion

Our results were gathered by running our implementation of pIA on each of our data sets to get the makespan of the iterated auction schedule on each instance, using ten robots for the sparse Solomon data and five for the dense Solomon data, with ten times this number for the G-H data. We gathered results for sIA and for pIA with $\alpha \in \{0.1, 0.3, 0.5, 0.7, 0.9\}$. For comparison, we also used a simple greedy algorithm that selects a task at random from T_F and allocates it to the robot that can finish it soonest. As mentioned above, each instance's result (e.g. Solomon instance C101 with sparse precedence constraints) is averaged across four random graphs.

Additionally, we used Gurobi [8] with the model in Figure 1 to compute optimal results for three small instances based on Solomon data. For all three, pIA ($\alpha = 0.5$) performed within about 10% of the optimal, and sIA somewhat worse. The paths for a 16 task, 4 robot problem are shown in Figure 4. For this problem, the optimal makespan was 109.4, while the pIA and sIA makespans were 121 and 149 respectively.

Our results are shown in Table 1. Each entry is averaged over approximately 80 trials: there are about 20 instances in the Solomon and G-H data sets for each problem type, and we generate four random precedence graphs for each instance. A distributed implementation of each algorithm runs in ≈ 0.25 seconds on the Solomon problems and less than 10 seconds on the 1000-task G-H problems.

First, we see that the iterated auctions significantly outperform the greedy auction in almost every case. For the Solomon data, sIA produces schedules that beat the greedy schedule by about 20% or more for every type of problem and level of sparsity, with pIA performing slightly worse than sIA in most cases.

For the G-H data, the results are less uniform; on the dense precedence graphs, either sIA or pIA achieve about a 20% improvement on the greedy schedule. However, on the sparse graphs, this improvement is less substantial, with sIA achieving a 12% improvement on the R data, about a 5% improvement on the RC data, and actually performing slightly worse than the greedy algorithm on the C data. In each of these cases, there is a value of α such that pIA is about 12% better than the greedy algorithm, however ($\alpha = 0.1$ for the C and RC data, and $\alpha = 0.9$ for the R data).

We can see that in addition to outperforming the greedy algorithm, sIA also performs as well as or slightly better than pIA in most cases. The only cases in which pIA offers significant improvement over sIA are on the C and RC sets from the G-H data. This is due to two separate effects: the increasing effectiveness of prioritization for larger numbers of tasks, and the improving performance of our priority assignment scheme for more clustered data. We will discuss the former effect first.

With any reasonable priority assignment scheme, we expect pIA to become more effective on larger problems. This is because sIA puts the maximum number of tasks into each auction, making extensive use of the insertion heuristic to order the tasks and exploit pathing synergies between them. Prioritization attempts to ensure that high-priority tasks are completed sooner, but sacrifices this full-sized auction and reduces use of the insertion heuristic. For the 1000-task G-H problems, there are still enough tasks in the auction to benefit from the insertion heuristic, and using the task information encoded in the priorities becomes relatively more valuable.

Second, we see that our method of priority assignment tends to perform much better for clustered data. For the Solomon problems, pIA performs marginally better than sIA only on the C instances, while on the G-H problems, pIA performs much better than sIA on the C instances and somewhat better on the RC instances. This reflects on our particular priority assignment scheme; on the R data, priorities are assigned based on the random positions of the tasks,

Data Set	Problem Type	Sparsity		Greedy	sIA	pIA				
						$\alpha = 0.1$	$\alpha = 0.3$	$\alpha = 0.5$	$\alpha = 0.7$	$\alpha = 0.9$
Solomon	R	Sparse	μ	376.80	**295.23**	306.66	303.39	302.34	302.38	301.35
			σ	9.72	6.82	8.24	6.36	7.33	5.50	6.89
		Dense	μ	812.47	**645.85**	666.70	655.49	652.45	652.77	651.68
			σ	13.89	12.01	10.49	13.59	11.40	13.78	15.37
	C	Sparse	μ	440.12	349.76	341.84	**339.24**	345.96	344.09	342.79
			σ	12.80	8.41	8.67	9.02	13.88	10.34	14.26
		Dense	μ	946.56	743.04	741.84	**739.31**	739.79	743.91	749.10
			σ	21.57	19.13	25.54	21.03	26.96	23.36	20.87
	RC	Sparse	μ	455.44	**346.70**	358.06	355.80	356.72	355.16	358.23
			σ	9.49	8.51	6.07	8.02	11.24	9.12	9.24
		Dense	μ	1001.6	**770.19**	798.95	789.41	791.75	786.75	792.64
			σ	17.17	23.16	17.06	20.95	16.75	14.08	16.83
G-H	R	Sparse	μ	868.13	**761.15**	784.51	782.10	776.05	771.19	765.85
			σ	14.68	10.01	32.31	39.38	27.90	29.39	22.66
		Dense	μ	1777.0	**1407.6**	1463.6	1468.2	1473.2	1490.7	1488.7
			σ	17.99	26.84	24.55	31.49	28.17	27.70	26.02
	C	Sparse	μ	763.04	789.66	**674.84**	688.01	686.43	687.31	689.08
			σ	22.83	19.91	41.95	40.13	37.06	44.44	46.30
		Dense	μ	1498.5	1305.9	**1208.1**	1236.7	1237.7	1252.5	1239.3
			σ	54.85	31.24	43.17	46.74	40.12	38.92	39.70
	RC	Sparse	μ	828.24	788.23	**722.53**	726.16	726.09	729.70	725.48
			σ	11.69	13.67	36.27	37.48	34.92	38.58	38.53
		Dense	μ	1628.1	1354.8	**1297.4**	1311.3	1315.9	1333.7	1332.8
			σ	35.87	22.54	40.96	45.84	38.62	49.55	45.50

Table 1: Makespan results for sparse and dense precedence graphs comparing the pIA and sIA auctions, and a greedy method.

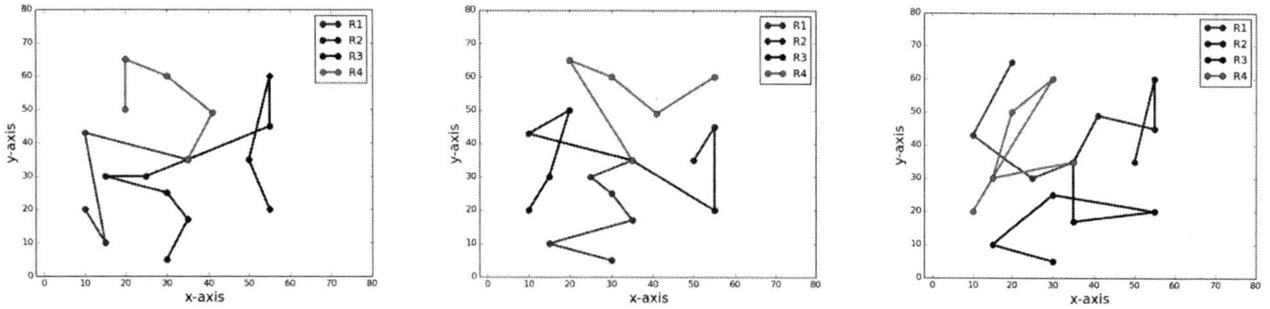

Figure 4: Routes produced by the optimal (left; makespan 109.4), pIA (middle; makespan 121) and sIA (right; makespan 149) methods for a Solomon instance with 16 tasks and four robots.

and may not accurately reflect the proper ordering of the tasks, as discussed above. For clustered data, low priority tasks that are available for scheduling are likely to be located in clusters that have lower average priority; since the task is free, it has no parents within the cluster and is therefore topologically highest, limiting the priority of its children. Due to the higher density of constraints within clusters, this provides a strong indication that the entire cluster is of lower priority. This shows that heuristic priority assignments can exploit synergies within data sets, which is desirable; in general we expect precedence-constrained data to be nonrandom, and to have some type of relationship between task constraints and locations. We expect that in specific applications, prioritization methods may be tailored to exploit the relationships between task locations and constraints for further improvement.

8. CONCLUSIONS AND FUTURE WORK

We introduced the iterated auction scheme for PC-MRTA and demonstrated substantial improvements over simple greedy scheduling. Our results indicate that at least for some problem types, priority assignment can improve on the performance of sIA. In particular, pIA performs well for large problem sizes with clustered or semi-clustered task groups. We also found that pIA performed within 10% of optimal for several small problems.

Since we used simple methods of prioritization, we expect that more sophisticated methods might yield further improvements. As mentioned previously, in practice precedence constraints are often related somehow to task location, so for a specific application certain priority schemes might provide strong performance by exploiting the specific structure of the problem. For example, if constrained tasks are always east of their parent tasks, a priority scheme that assigns more priority to western tasks may be successful by preventing robots from backtracking.

As we discussed in the section on priority assignment, we believe that using priorities derived from an LP relaxation as in [22] may provide excellent performance for a wide variety of problem types. This method of prioritization may work well in more general settings, when relationships between task locations and precedence constraints are not well understood. It may be also be that low-priority tasks are easier to identify than high-priority tasks; another approach to approximating PC-MRTA might use the sIA method and prune low-priority tasks in each iteration.

REFERENCES

[1] C. Chekuri, R. Motwani, B. Natarajan, and C. Stein. Approximation techniques for average completion time scheduling. *SIAM Journal on Computing*, 31(1):146–166, 2001.

[2] R. Dechter, I. Meiri, and J. Pearl. Temporal constraint networks. *Artificial Intelligence*, 49, 1991.

[3] A. Farinelli, L. Iocchi, D. Nardi, and V. Ziparo. Assignment of dynamically perceived tasks by token passing in multirobot systems. *Proceedings of the IEEE*, 94(7):1271 –1288, 2006.

[4] A. Farinelli, A. Rogers, A. Petcu, and N. R. Jennings. Decentralised coordination of low-power embedded devices using the Max-Sum algorithm. In *Int'l Conf. on Autonomous Agents and Multi-Agent Systems*, pages 639–646, 2008.

[5] H. Gehring and J. Homberger. A parallel hybrid evolutionary metaheuristic for the vehicle routing problem with time windows. In *Proceedings of EUROGEN99*, 1999.

[6] M. Gombolay, R. Wilcox, and J. Shah. Fast scheduling of multi-robot teams with temporospatial constraints. In *Robotics: Science and Systems (RSS)*, 2013.

[7] R. L. Graham. Bounds on multiprocessing timing anomalies. *SIAM Journal on Applied Mathematics*, 17(2), 1969.

[8] I. Gurobi Optimization. Gurobi optimizer reference manual, 2014.

[9] L. A. Hall, A. S. Schulz, D. B. Shmoys, and J. Wein. Scheduling to minimize average completion time: Offline and online approximation algorithms. *Mathematics of Operations Research*, 22(3), 1997.

[10] E. G. Jones, M. B. Dias, and A. Stentz. Time-extended multi-robot coordination for domains with intra-path constraints. In *Robotics: Science and Systems (RSS)*, 2009.

[11] R. Junges and A. L. C. Bazzan. Evaluating the performance of DCOP algorithms in a real world, dynamic problem. In *Int'l Conf. on Autonomous Agents and Multi-Agent Systems*, pages 599–606, 2008.

[12] J. E. Kelley Jr. and M. R. Walker. Critical-path planning and scheduling. In *Proceedings of the Eastern Joint Computer Conference*, 1959.

[13] S. Koenig, C. Tovey, M. Lagoudakis, V. Markakis, D. Kempe, P. Keskinocak, A. Kleywegt, A. Meyerson, and S. Jain. The power of sequential single-item auctions for agent coordination. In *Proc. AAAI Conf. on Artificial Intelligence*, 2006.

[14] G. A. Korsah, A. Stentz, and M. B. Dias. A comprehensive taxonomy for multi-robot task allocation. *The International Journal of Robotics Research*, 32(12):1495–1512, 2013.

[15] M. G. Lagoudakis, M. Berhault, S. Koenig, P. Keskinocak, and A. J. Kleywegt. Simple auctions with performance guarantees for multi-robot task allocation. In *Proc. IEEE/RSJ Int. Conf. on Intelligent Robots and Systems*, 2004.

[16] M. G. Lagoudakis, E. Markakis, D. Kempe, P. Keskinocak, A. Kleywegt, S. Koenig, C. Tovey, A. Meyerson, and S. Jain. Auction-based multi-robot routing. In *Robotics: Science and Systems (RSS)*, 2005.

[17] L. Luo, N. Chakraborty, and K. Sycara. Multi-robot assignment algorithm for tasks with set precedence constraints. In *Proc. IEEE Int'l Conf. on Robotics and Automation*, 2011.

[18] K. S. Macarthur, R. Stranders, S. D. Ramchurn, and N. R. Jennings. A distributed anytime algorithm for dynamic task allocation in multi-agent systems. In *Proc. AAAI Conf. on Artificial Intelligence*, pages 701–706, 2011.

[19] R. T. Maheswaran, M. Tambe, E. Bowring, J. P. Pearce, and P. Varakantham. Taking dcop to the real world: Efficient complete solutions for distributed multi-event scheduling. In *Int'l Conf. on Autonomous Agents and Multi-Agent Systems*, pages 310–317, 2004.

[20] G. Melançon, I. Dutour, and M. Bousquet-Mélou. Random generation of directed acyclic graphs. *Electronic Notes in Discrete Mathematics*, 10, 2001.

[21] E. Nunes and M. Gini. Multi-robot auctions for allocation of tasks with temporal constraints. In *Proc. AAAI Conf. on Artificial Intelligence*, 2015.

[22] M. Queyranne and A. S. Schulz. Approximation bounds for a general class of precedence constrained parallel machine scheduling problems. *SIAM Journal on Computing*, 35(5), 2006.

[23] S. Ramchurn, A. Farinelli, K. Macarthur, M. Polukarov, and N. Jennings. Decentralised coordination in RoboCup Rescue. *The Computer Journal*, 53(9):1–15, 2010.

[24] S. Sariel, T. Balch, and N. Erdogan. Incremental multi-robot task selection for resource constrained and interrelated tasks. In *Proc. IEEE/RSJ Int. Conf. on Intelligent Robots and Systems*, pages 2314–2319, Oct 2007.

[25] M. M. Solomon. Algorithms for the vehicle routing and scheduling problems with time window constraints. *Operations Research*, 35(2), 1987.

[26] C. Tovey, M. Lagoudakis, S. Jain, and S. Koenig. The generation of bidding rules for auction-based robot coordination. In L. Parker, F. Schneider, and A. Schultz, editors, *Multi-Robot Systems. From Swarms to Intelligent Automata Volume III*, pages 3–14. Springer Netherlands, 2005.

[27] Y. Xu, P. Scerri, B. Yu, S. Okamoto, M. Lewis, and K. Sycara. An integrated token-based algorithm for scalable coordination. In *Int'l Conf. on Autonomous Agents and Multi-Agent Systems*, pages 407–414, 2005.

[28] X. Zheng, S. Koenig, and C. Tovey. Improving sequential single-item auctions. In *Proc. IEEE/RSJ Int. Conf. on Intelligent Robots and Systems*, 2006.

Distributed Formation Control of Quadrotors under Limited Sensor Field of View*

Duarte Dias[1,2], Pedro U. Lima[2], Alcherio Martinoli[1]
[1]Distributed Intelligent Systems and Algorithms Laboratory, EPFL, Lausanne, Switzerland
[2]Institute for Systems and Robotics, IST, Universidade de Lisboa, Lisboa, Portugal
[1,2]duarte.dias@epfl.ch

ABSTRACT

This work tackles the problem of quadrotor formation control, using exclusively on-board resources. Local inter-robot localization systems are typically characterized by limited sensing capabilities, either in range or in the field of view. Most of the existing literature on the subject uses inter-robot communication to obtain the unavailable information, but problems such as communication delays and packet loss can seriously compromise the system stability, especially when the system shows fast dynamics such as that of quadrotors. This work focuses on the sensor field of view limitation: it proposes a formation control algorithm that extends the existing methods to allow each quadrotor to control the occupied area of its sensor field of view, while moving to the right place in the formation. This decreases the situations when necessary inter-robot information is unavailable through local sensing, thus reducing the communication requirements. The system is proven to be stable when this algorithm is applied. Results, both using simulated and real quadrotors, show the correct behavior of the algorithm without the use of communications, even when each robot can only sense a subset of the robots in the group.

General Terms

Algorithms, Experimentation, Performance

Keywords

Quadrotors, Formation Control, Limited Field of View

1. INTRODUCTION

The use of Unmanned Aerial Vehicles (UAVs) has been substantially increasing because their design has been simplified and their control techniques made more robust, ultimately enabling for vehicles of smaller size. A Smaller vehicle size allows for a more convenient exploration of multi-UAV systems in confined spaces, and at close range. Quadrotors are typically chosen due to their high maneuverability in such confined spaces. Additionally, through vehicle coordination, the geometry of these systems can be explored to minimize the impact of each vehicle limitations. For example, UAVs can organize to pick and transport heavier objects with a specific shape, or to direct their limited on-board cameras so that their combined images provide full 3D environment coverage. This coordination is achieved through formation control algorithms.

Formation control is a widely studied topic, both in 2D and 3D configurations, with an extensive literature. Formation control laws typically require that each robot knows the relative positions between itself and its neighbors. In most common approaches, the robots obtain this information by sharing via a communication channel their absolute positions with respect to an environment, computed using Global Navigation Satellite Systems (GNSSs) [20] in outdoor environments, Motion Capture Systems (MCS) [19, 1, 9] in indoor environments, or even Montecarlo or SLAM methods [16, 15], if the required on-board positioning sensors and environment conditions allow to do so.

Other approaches use the on-board sensors to directly extract the relative positions between robots, without the need for communication or external systems. However, these sensors have limited capabilities, either on accuracy or Field Of View (FOV). This is especially true for the 3D case, because of the challenging sensing design, either due to the fact that the robot body represents an obstacle for the sensor itself, or because there is a compromise between the sensing area that needs to be covered, and the resolution of the sensor. For example, in [18, 6], on-board cameras extract accurate relative bearing information, which is then used in a formation control algorithm. However, since the cameras are characterized by a limited FOV, the information required from the neighbors that are not directly observed has to be provided also through communication. In [17], the proposed framework uses both range and bearing information collected by each quadrotor to reduce the amount of required observed neighbors per quadrotor. However, if the required neighbors are not observed, communication is still needed to acquire the missing information.

Since high control rates are necessary to stabilize the highly dynamical system formed by these vehicles, all previous approaches become fragile to packet loss or latency in communication links. This is particularly important for short range inter-robot interactions, requiring faster reaction times. To keep communication to a minimum, the sensor constraints must be directly addressed. This was done mostly for ground vehicles, and for sensor range constraints, using potential

*This work has been partially supported by ISR/LARSyS Strategic Funds from FCT [UID/EEA/5009/2013] and FCT SFRH/BD/51928/2012.

Appears in: *Proceedings of the 15th International Conference on Autonomous Agents and Multiagent Systems (AAMAS 2016), J. Thangarajah, K. Tuyls, C. Jonker, S. Marsella (eds.), May 9–13, 2016, Singapore.*

field algorithms that include specialized terms to guarantee that neighbor behavior will not compromise this type of constraint [8, 12]. FOV constraints have also been considered, but just for leader-follower formations, where each follower controls its FOV in a way to maximize the observation of its leader [11, 10, 21]. However, since only one neighbor is considered inside the sensor FOV, the multi-robot system is bounded to a limited number of inter-robot connections, compromising the number of geometries achievable for formation control. Additionally, less connections means reduced system reactivity.

This work tackles these last issues. Sensor range limitations are left aside, and for the experiments, it was made sure that all the necessary inter-robot positions were smaller than the sensor range limits. Also, sensor FOV constraints are considered to be on the horizontal dimension, as typical quadrotor formations simply lie on horizontal planes. With the previous assumptions, the work proposes an algorithm, applicable to quadrotors or any robot with similar dynamics. In particular, we extend the algorithm presented in [5] for a second order holonomic robot dynamics, where each quadrotor uses an additional term to control the critical angle formed between the two neighbors closest to sensor FOV limits. This is performed by making the quadrotor moving closer or further away from the neighbors, depending if the angle needs to increase or decrease respectively. Additionally, this angle is also centered in the FOV to optimize the sensor safety margins.

The algorithm provides two contributions. Firstly, quadrotor trajectories become constrained to cope with the vehicle's sensor limitations when observing multiple neighbors. Secondly, by also controlling angles, this algorithm is able to tackle configurations not achievable by some of the previous algorithms (as the one in [5]) in presence of sensor FOV constraints. This work shows that the terms added in the algorithm do not compromise the system stability. Also, although no discussion is provided about the system initial conditions or disturbances for which the FOV constraints are still maintained, results (simulated and real) show that for typical situations, these constraints are effectively controlled. Thus, the proposed algorithm allows for formation control without the use of inter-robot communication.

This paper is organized as follows. Section 2 provides basic definitions and assumptions about the quadrotor dynamics and its sensing capabilities. Based on those definitions, Section 3 formally introduces the FOV constraints and discusses how to built valid geometric formation configurations. Section 4 presents the formation control algorithm, along with its stability properties. In Section 5, a set of simulation and real experiments are performed to show the correct behavior of the algorithm, and some modifications are designed to cope with real world disturbances. The work concludes with some remarks in Section 6.

2. BASIC DEFINITIONS

This work considers a group of N quadrotors, forming at any time a geometric configuration, defined by a full network graph $\mathcal{G} := (\mathcal{V}, \mathcal{E})$. In this graph, $\mathcal{V}$ is the set of N nodes, each one representing a quadrotor, described in a 3D environment by a position $\mathbf{x}_i \in \mathbb{R}^3$, a velocity, $\mathbf{v}_i \in \mathbb{R}^3$, and an attitude, given by the roll ϕ_i, pitch θ_i, and yaw ψ_i, angles. Each quadrotor is considered to have an on-board auto-pilot and inertial sensors, which allows for the control

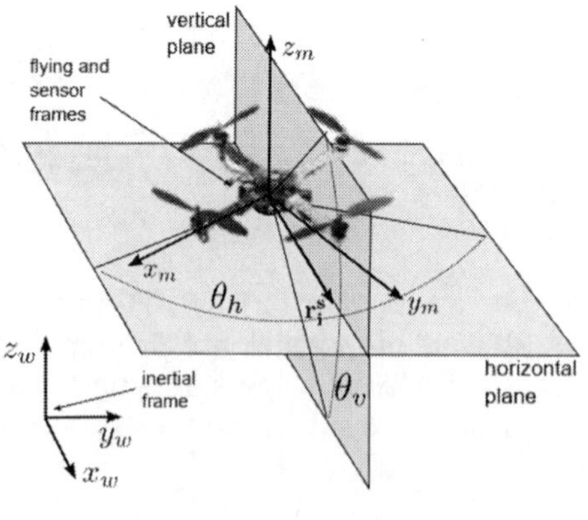

Figure 1: Description of the quadrotor flying frame (x_m, y_m, z_m), with respect to the inertial frame. The quadrotor is placed horizontally for illustrative purposes, but it can have non-zero roll and pitch. Note the sensor horizontal (θ_h) and vertical (θ_v) FOV.

of the vehicle thrust together with the estimation and control of its attitude. This enables the quadrotor to move to any desired 3D position, so it can be considered has an almost perfectly holonomic vehicle. Note that only roll and pitch control together with the thrust control are needed to move the vehicle on the three position axes, leaving the yaw control free to be used for independent purposes (as it will be discussed later). Therefore, we split the pose control of the quadrotor into 3D position control, with a double integrator model, and yaw control with a single integrator dynamics:

$$\ddot{\mathbf{x}}_i = \mathbf{u}_i, \qquad \dot{\psi}_i = u_i^{\psi}, \tag{1}$$

where $\mathbf{u} = (u_i^x, u_i^y, u_i^z)$ and u_i^{ψ} are the desired control inputs for the quadrotor 3D position and yaw angle respectively. The single integrator on the yaw angle is a feature commonly provided by the on-board auto-pilots of quadrotors.

The set of all $N(N-1)/2$ edges of $\mathcal{G}$ is represented by $\mathcal{E}$, where each edge represents relative kinematic information between two quadrotors, namely relative position, $\mathbf{x}_{ij} = \mathbf{x}_j - \mathbf{x}_i = (x_{ij}, y_{ij}, z_{ij})^T$ and, as derived quantity, relative velocity $\mathbf{v}_{ij} = \mathbf{v}_j - \mathbf{v}_i = (v_{ij}^x, v_{ij}^y, v_{ij}^z)^T$. To control $\mathcal{G}$, the quadrotors need to collect information represented by a subset of the previous edges, using their on-board sensors. The information that can be obtained at any time is described by a sensing graph, defined by $\mathcal{G}_S := (\mathcal{V}, \mathcal{E}_S)$, with $\mathcal{E}_S$ representing the set of edges of $\mathcal{G}$, for which the relative positions between the respective quadrotors can be measured using the on-board sensors.

Each quadrotor i is considered to have an on-board sensor, measuring the position $\mathbf{x}_{ij}$ and the velocity $\mathbf{v}_{ij}$, in a reference frame described in Fig. 1. The frame origin is the same as the quadrotors, and the z-axis is aligned with the inertial frame (vertical). In the remainder of this paper, we will call this frame the *flying frame*; it has an attitude of $(\phi, \theta, \psi) = (0, 0, \psi_i)$ with respect to the inertial frame. The sensor has its FOV center in the horizontal xy-plane, considered to be the sensor direction, $\mathbf{r}_i^s$. The FOV is represented by its horizontal, θ_h, and vertical, θ_v, components, defined with respect to the previous described horizontal plane, and a vertical plane formed by $\mathbf{r}_i^s$ and the z-axis of the flying frame. This can be assumed as quadrotors usually move using low roll and pitch values, and the distances between the center of the robot and the sensor are small. In case the

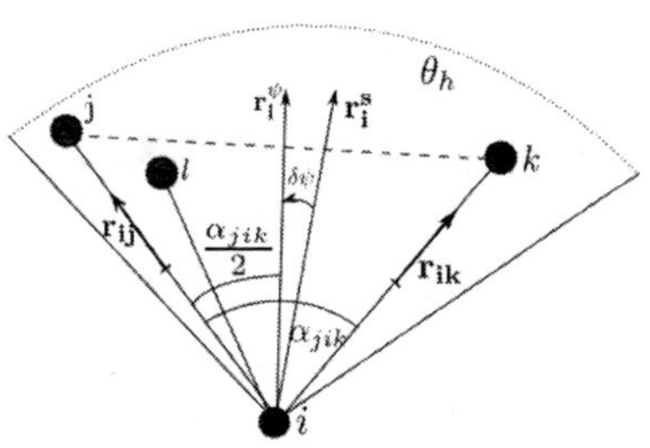

Figure 2: Inter-edge aperture between the edges connecting nodes j and k, to node i, both within the FOV of node i. Apertures formed by different node pairs, for example using node l, are contained inside it. Note the optimal sensor direction, $\mathbf{r}_i^\psi$, equally dividing the occupied area on both sides of the FOV.

quadrotor and the sensors are tilted, the measures extracted on the sensor frame can be transformed into the flying frame, using the ϕ_i and θ_i values acquired from the inertial sensors.

Since the z-axis of the flying frame is the same for all quadrotors, it is useful to decouple the formation control into horizontal and vertical components (as explained later in Section 4). For this reason, the previous relative kinematic information is divided into horizontal components, $\mathbf{x}_{ij}^{h} = (x_{ij}, y_{ij})^T$ and $\mathbf{v}_{ij}^{h} = (v_{ij}^x, v_{ij}^y)^T$, and vertical components, z_{ij} and v_{ij}^z. The horizontal position component can be transformed into polar coordinates $(e_{ij}^h, \mathbf{r}_{ij}^h)^T$, where e_{ij}^h is the absolute distance between quadrotors i and j, and $\mathbf{r}_{ij}^h$ is a unitary vector defining the direction between i and j. The next section formally introduces the FOV constraints for each quadrotor, and discusses the type of geometric configurations considered in this work.

3. FIELD OF VIEW CONSTRAINTS

The sensor FOV constraints can be mathematically described through the concept of inter-edge aperture. Given two nodes j and k connected to node i, the inter-edge aperture of the respective connection edges, α_{jik}, is defined by the angle between the relative position vectors represented by those edges, as shown in Fig. 2. This concept is divided into horizontal and vertical components, by projecting the edges in the respective planes defined in Fig. 1. Therefore, the inter-edge aperture of every pair of edges belonging to $\mathcal{G}_S$ for a given quadrotor i must be smaller than θ_h in the horizontal case, or θ_v in the vertical case. Only the biggest aperture for each quadrotor needs to be considered, because if this value is smaller than the FOV limit, all the others apertures will be also smaller, as illustrated in Fig. 2. Our algorithm operates on the FOV constraints by directly controlling these apertures, as explained in the next section.

Note that if the FOV constraints are verified, there is always a quadrotor yaw ψ_i, describing the sensor direction, $\mathbf{r}_i^s$, that allows all neighbors to be observed. In fact, it is possible to define an optimal sensor direction r_i^ψ, illustrated in Fig. 2, defined so that it equally distributes the sensing area around the center of the largest inter-edge aperture, optimizing the measurement safety margins.

A targeted geometric configuration is defined by a graph $\mathcal{G}$ whose edges correspond to desired inter-robot positions $\mathbf{x}_{ij}^d = (x_{ij}^d, y_{ij}^d, z_{ij}^d)$, and zero velocity. From this information, all the desired apertures between sets of three nodes, α_{jik}^d can be obtained. To control this configuration, a formation control graph $\mathcal{G}_F := (\mathcal{V}, \mathcal{E}_F)$ is defined, where each edge in $\mathcal{E}_F$ corresponds to a controlled inter-robot distance. The configuration is controllable if the following two conditions are verified: $\mathcal{G}_F$ is rigid, so that it has a unique solution (the reader is referred to [14] for more details about graph rigidity); $\mathcal{G}_S$ must contain enough information to enable the control of all edges in $\mathcal{G}_F$. This work assumes $\mathcal{G}_S$ and $\mathcal{G}_F$ fixed and defined a priori. Note that, in order to achieve the desired $\mathcal{G}_S$, the robots need to start the algorithm in positions that are already respecting the FOV constraints.

Note that the previous section described the sensor direction, $\mathbf{r}_i^s$ to be always directed and controlled horizontally. Therefore, this work assumes geometric configurations where all quadrotors have the same height, or smaller than the vertical FOV, avoiding therefore vertical FOV violations. Additionally, this work considers the edges in $\mathcal{E}_S$ and $\mathcal{E}_F$ to be bi-directional. For $\mathcal{E}_S$ edges, this concretely means that the quadrotors forming any given edge can mutually sense each other. For $\mathcal{E}_F$ edges, this concretely means that both quadrotors forming the edge actively participate on the control of the mutual distance. These bi-directionality assumptions are made to reduce the distance instability between quadrotors, caused by possible delays in the vehicle perception-to-action loop.

The previous assumptions can limit the formation configurations that can be considered, as the number of robots increases. This work focuses on the simplest type of formations, placing the robots on the convex hull of the target formation shape. Robots can also be placed inside the convex hull, at different heights to avoid sensor occlusion. Their neighbors can be selected randomly as long as the largest inter-neighbor aperture respects the sensor FOV constraints, as explained above. However, should the previous edge bi-directionality assumptions be kept, since robots inside the convex hull observe a reduced neighbor set, the number of inter-robot connections achievable by the other robots is also reduced. Uni-directional edges can be used if the overall formation rigidity is kept, but this case is left for future work. The next section introduces the formation control algorithm, and how it provides sufficient controllability to establish $\mathcal{G}_F$.

4. CONTROL ALGORITHM

The algorithm leverages two distinct components: the control of the inter-robot distance and the maintenance of FOV visibility. To control the inter-robot distances, each distance is given a weight, describing how strongly the quadrotor controls it. The weighting information can be elegantly represented using a Laplacian matrix, $\mathbf{L}$, where the element $\mathbf{L}_{ij}$ defines the control weight for the distance between neighbors i and j. This matrix is positive definite, the sum of the elements of each line sum to zero, and $\mathbf{L}_{ii} = -\sum_{j \neq i} \mathbf{L}_{ij}$. If $\mathbf{L}_{ij} = 0$, the distance between quadrotors i and j is not directly controlled. In this work, $\mathbf{L}$ is constant, since $\mathcal{G}_F$ is assumed constant. Each quadrotor controls distances using inter-robot position information measured by its on-board sensors, in the flying frame. Since the z-axis of this frame is the same for all quadrotors, and equal to the z-axis of the inertial frame, this dimension is controlled with a simple consensus equation, similarly to [3, 13], as follows:

$$u_i^z = k_p \sum_{j=1}^{N} \mathbf{L}_{ij} \left(z_{ij}^d - z_{ij} \right) + k_v \sum_{j=1}^{N} \mathbf{L}_{ij} v_{ij}^z, \qquad (2)$$

where u_i^z is the desired vertical acceleration for quadrotor i, k_p and k_v are gain parameters for the position and the velocity components of the controller. To control the horizontal dimension, the range and bearing controller proposed in [5] is used, but extended for a double integrator case and simplified to the case of holonomic vehicles:

$$\mathbf{u_i^h} = k_p \sum_{j=1}^{N} \mathbf{r_{ij}^h L_{ij}} \left(e_{ij}^h - e_{ij}^d \right) + k_v \sum_{j=1}^{N} \mathbf{L_{ij} v_{ij}^h}, \tag{3}$$

where $\mathbf{u_i^h} = (u_i^x, u_i^y)^T$ is the desired horizontal input in the flying frame for quadrotor i and e_{ij}^d is the desired horizontal distance between quadrotors i and j, obtained from $||(x_{ij}^d, y_{ij}^d)||$. In both the previous equations, the position component aims at achieving the formation requirements, while the velocity component stabilizes the second order dynamic system. Distances controlled in this way allow the edges representing them to be added into $\mathcal{G}_F$. To control these distances, the respective relative position information is needed, which means these control edges must also belong to $\mathcal{E}_S$.

The second component of the algorithm controls the FOV constraints, which can happen as the formation rotates around its z axis, or when quadrotors move to their desired positions. To solve this issue, two new terms are included, allowing each quadrotor to additionally control the largest observed inter-edge aperture, and the sensor direction, $\mathbf{r_i^s}$, in the horizontal plane. A simple yaw controller is used to derive $\mathbf{r_i^s}$ to the optimal direction defined in the previous section, $\mathbf{r_i^\psi}$. This is done by computing the angle between the two vectors, $\delta\psi$, illustrated in Fig. 2. Note that $\mathbf{r_i^s}$ is always known, and $\mathbf{r_i^\psi}$ is computed by averaging $\mathbf{r_{ij}}$ and $\mathbf{r_{ik}}$. The obtained $\delta\psi$ is given as the control input of the yaw controller and driven to zero:

$$u_i^\psi = -k_\psi \delta\psi_i, \tag{4}$$

where u_i^ψ is the yaw control input defined in Eq. 1, and k_ψ is a control gain. The biggest inter-edge aperture observed by quadrotor i, α_{kij}, is controlled by adding a term to Eq. 3, as follows:

$$\mathbf{u_i^{h*}} = \mathbf{u_i^h} + k_\alpha(\alpha_{kij}^d - \alpha_{kij})(K\mathbf{r_i^c} + K_\perp \mathbf{r_i^{c\perp}}), \tag{5}$$

where α_{kij}^d is the desired aperture between quadrotor i and neighbors j and k currently defining the biggest aperture, k_α is a control gain, and K and $K_\perp$ will be chosen according to the stability analysis presented in Proposition 1. Vector $\mathbf{r_i^c}$, illustrated in Figs. 3 and 4, is a unitary vector defining the direction between quadrotor i and the averaged formation center, $\mathbf{C_i}$. This center is defined for each quadrotor, and its displacement from the robot is computed using the first term of Eq. 3:

$$\mathbf{r_i^c} e_i = \sum_{j=1}^{N} \mathbf{r_{ij}^h L_{ij}} e_{ij}^h, \tag{6}$$

where e_i is the distance between quadrotor i and $\mathbf{C_i}$. The distance between a neighbor j and $\mathbf{C_i}$ is defined as e_i^j. Note that $\mathbf{r_i^c}$ is always in between the neighbors closer to the FOV edges. Therefore, if α_{kij} is too large, robot i generates a force pointing backwards, in a direction that will always decrease α_{kij}. The contrary occurs when α_{kij} is too small. This corresponds to a direct control of the sensor FOV constraint during the algorithm's operation.

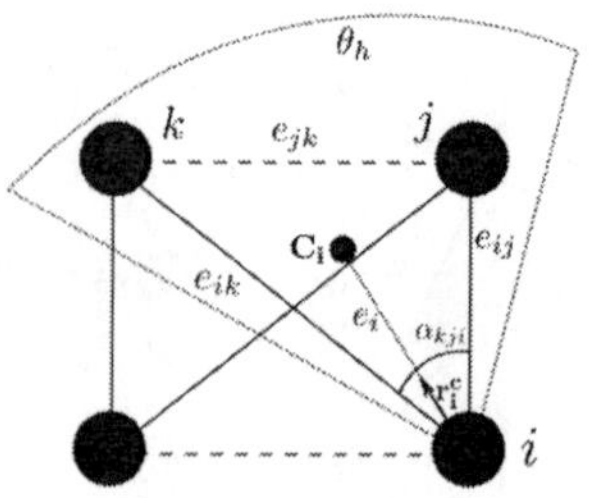

Figure 3: Possible $\mathcal{G}_F$ for a square formation and an horizontal FOV of less than 90°. Filled edges correspond to direct distance control. Dashed edges are included if aperture control is activated. Note quadrotor i's weighted formation center.

With the additional control terms, each quadrotor also indirectly controls the distances between the neighbors themselves, without them knowing the respective relative position information. Consider the example in Fig. 3, when the FOV is less than 90°. The most complete $\mathcal{G}_S$ possible with these constraints is the one shown in the figure (excluding the dashed lines). So, with just direct distance control, no rigid graph can be defined. However, if quadrotor i additionaly controls α_{jik}, one can see that e_{jk} is fully expressed in terms of the direct controlled quantities, e_{ij}, e_{ik}, and α_{jik}. So, the edge between neighbors j and k is automatically included in $\mathcal{E}_F$, which does not need to belong to $\mathcal{G}_S$. Each quadrotor can control an additional edge in this way, allowing the establishment of rigid, or even fully connected, formation graphs that could not possibly be formed before.

The next proposition shows that the new proposed terms do not compromise the system stability. The algorithm can be easily extended to control more than one inter-edge aperture for each quadrotor, but the presented stability properties are related to the largest. Additionally, it is not clear that these properties hold if the neighbors forming the aperture changes in time. Since the previous case is rare, in this paper we focus on characterizing the algorithm behavior when the inter-edge aperture remains the same during operation, and leave the previous issue for future work.

PROPOSITION 1. *As long the necessary FOV constraints are not violated, the multi-robot system, with each quadrotor i described by the dynamics in Eq. (1) and applying the controller presented in Eqs. (2), (3), (4), and (5), is stable, for any chosen set of weights described in $\mathbf{L}$, and any k_p, k_v, K and $K^\perp$ greater than zero.*

PROOF. Note that [13] already proved convergence properties for vertical controller components Eq. (2). Also,the component in Eq. (4) is independent from the actual formation control. Therefore, if the formation converges, $\mathbf{r_i^\psi}$ converges as well, allowing the yaw controller to stabilize $\delta\psi_i$ to zero, since it is a proportional control applied to a single integrator system.

The proof for the horizontal controller components of $\mathbf{u_i^{h*}}$ follows the reasoning of [5], which performs the analysis separately for each robot, and its neighbors are assumed to have fixed positions, and then combines the results at the end. To simplify the proof, the bias terms (α_{kij}^d and e_{ij}^d) are set to zero, but the stability still holds for non-zero terms (such terms would only change the equilibrium point).

Let us assume the case for quadrotor i, described in Fig. 4, representative of the horizontal control components. Quadro-

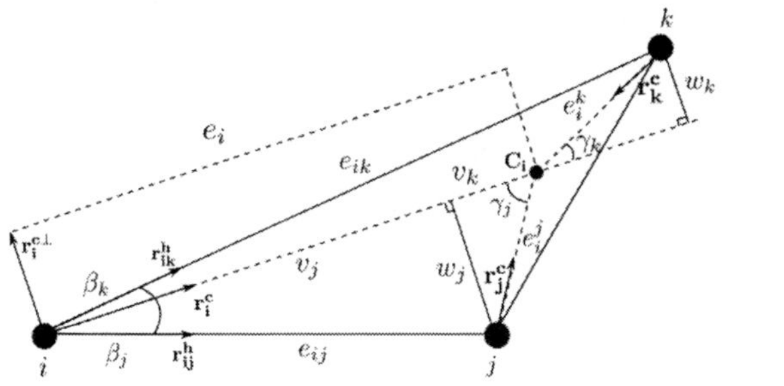

Figure 4: Horizontal formation control formulation.

tors j and k correspond to quadrotor i neighbors forming the largest aperture in its FOV. The position of quadrotor i's formation center, $\mathbf{C_i}$, can be expressed in the inertial frame as $\mathbf{x_i} + \mathbf{r_i^c} e_i$, where the second term comes from Eq. 6. This expression does not depend on $\mathbf{x_i}$ if $\sum_{j \neq i} \mathbf{L_{ij}} = 1$, which means $\mathbf{C_i}$ doesn't change with quadrotor i's movements. If the neighbors are assumed to have fixed positions, their distances to $\mathbf{C_i}$, e_i^j and e_i^k, are constant. The axes of quadrotor i's reference frame are changed to $\mathbf{r_i^c}$ and $\mathbf{r_i^{c\perp}}$, representing respectively the radial and orthogonal axis with respect to $\mathbf{C_i}$. The velocity of $\mathbf{C_i}$ in this new frame is decomposed on the radial, $\dot{e}_i$ and orthogonal, $\dot{e}_i^\perp$, axes. Note that this velocity corresponds to the second term of Eq. 3, and that $\dot{e}_i$ is the velocity of e_i, representing the distance between quadrotor i and $\mathbf{C_i}$. From the previous definitions, a simple Lyapunov function is chosen to analyze the stability of the system for quadrotor i:

$$V_i(\alpha_{kij}, e_i, \dot{e}_i, \dot{e}_i^\perp) = \frac{1}{2}(k_\alpha \alpha_{kij}^2 + k_p e_i^2 + (\dot{e}_i)^2 + (\dot{e}_i^\perp)^2),$$

which is greater than zero except in $V_i(0,0,0,0)$. The four components were considered because they represent the states that are being controlled (aperture, distance, and radial and orthogonal velocity). The derivative of V_i with respect to time can be expressed as:

$$\dot{V}_i = k_\alpha \alpha_{kij} \dot{\alpha}_{kij} + k_p e_i \dot{e}_i + \dot{e}_i \ddot{e}_i + \dot{e}_i^\perp \ddot{e}_i^\perp,$$

where $\ddot{e}_i$ and $\ddot{e}_i^\perp$ can be expressed from the $\mathbf{u_i^{h*}}$ terms in Eqs. 3 and 5, projected into the radial and orthogonal components respectively:

$$\begin{aligned} \ddot{e}_i &= K k_\alpha \alpha_{kij} - k_p e_i - k_v \dot{e}_i, \\ \ddot{e}_i^\perp &= K_\perp k_\alpha \alpha_{kij} - k_v \dot{e}_i^\perp. \end{aligned}$$

Therefore, $\dot{V}_i$ can be simplified, by removing the equal terms in its expression, to:

$$\dot{V}_i = k_\alpha \alpha_{kij} \dot{\alpha}_{kij} + k_\alpha \alpha_{kij}(\dot{e}_i K + \dot{e}_i^\perp K_\perp) - k_v(\dot{e}_i)^2 - k_v(\dot{e}_i^\perp)^2.$$

The last two terms are always negative, which leaves the study of the first component. From Fig. 4, the aperture α_{kij} can be divided into $\beta_j + \beta_k$, where $\beta_{(*)} = \arctan(w_{(*)}/v_{(*)})$, and $(*)$ is either j or k. By differentiating $\beta_{(*)}$, $\dot{\alpha}_{kij}$ can be defined as:

$$\dot{\alpha}_{kij} = \frac{v_j \dot{w}_j - \dot{v}_j w_j}{e_{ij}^2} + \frac{v_k \dot{w}_k - \dot{v}_k w_k}{e_{ik}^2}.$$

From the figure, on can define $v_{(*)} = e_i - e_i^{(*)} \cos(\gamma_{(*)})$ and $w_{(*)} = e_i^{(*)} \sin(\gamma_{(*)})$, where $\gamma_{(*)}$ is the angle going from $\mathbf{r_{(*)}^c}$ to $\mathbf{r_i^c}$. Recalling that neighbors have fixed positions with respect to $\mathbf{C_i}$, $\gamma_{(*)}$ only depends on $\dot{e}_i^\perp$, according to the linear-to-angular velocity equation, $\dot{e}_i^\perp = \dot{\gamma}_{(*)} e_i$. Using the previous result for $\dot{\gamma}_{(*)}$, and recalling that $e_i^{(*)}$ is constant, the derivatives of the previous expressions for $v_{(*)}$ and $w_{(*)}$ are as follows:

$$\dot{v}_{(*)} = \dot{e}_i + \dot{e}_i^\perp \sin(\gamma_{(*)}) \frac{e_i^{(*)}}{e_i}, \quad \dot{w}_{(*)} = \dot{e}_i^\perp cos(\gamma_{(*)}) \frac{e_i^{(*)}}{e_i}.$$

From the previous result, and noting that the alternative definitions $w_{(*)} = e_{i(*)} \sin(\beta_{(*)})$ and $v_{(*)} = e_{(*)} \cos(\beta_{(*)})$, the previous expression for $\dot{\alpha}_{kij}$ can be re-arranged, to isolate the terms in $\dot{e}_i^\perp$ and $\dot{e}_i$, as follows:

$$\begin{aligned} \dot{\alpha}_{kij} = \dot{e}_i^\perp &\left(\frac{e_j}{e_i} \frac{\cos(\gamma_j + \beta_j)}{e_{ij}} + \frac{e_k}{e_i} \frac{\cos(\gamma_k + \beta_k)}{e_i e_{ik}} \right) \\ -\dot{e}_i &\left(\frac{\sin(\beta_j)}{e_{ij}} + \frac{\sin(\beta_k)}{e_{ik}} \right). \end{aligned}$$

One can now choose K and $K_\perp$ of the aperture controller to eliminate the previous components, ending with the following result:

$$\begin{aligned} K &= \left(\frac{\sin(\beta_j)}{e_{ij}} + \frac{\sin(\beta_k)}{e_{ik}} \right) \\ K_\perp &= -\left(\frac{e_j}{e_i} \frac{\cos(\gamma_j + \beta_j)}{e_{ij}} + \frac{e_k}{e_i} \frac{\cos(\gamma_k + \beta_k)}{e_{ik}} \right) \\ \dot{V}_i &= -k_v(\dot{e}_i)^2 - k_v(\dot{e}_i^\perp)^2. \end{aligned}$$

Note that $\dot{V}_i \leq 0$, and therefore using the Lyapunov theorem, the system with the proposed controller is stable and converges to a subset of the state-space defined by $\dot{V}_i = 0$. This can be extended to all quadrotors, by setting $V = V_1 + ... + V_N$, where V_i is the previous Lyapunov function but for each quadrotor. $V > 0$ except in $V(0) = 0$, and $\dot{V} <= 0$, and therefore, the system as a whole is also stable. Finally, note that $k_p \sum_{j \neq i} \mathbf{L_{ij}}$ can always be transformed into $k_p^* \sum_{j \neq i} \mathbf{L_{ij}^*}$ for each quadrotor, where $\sum_{j \neq i} \mathbf{L_{ij}^*} = 1$, necessary to guarantee that $\mathbf{C_i}$ does not depend on robot i's movement. This allows the use of any Laplacian matrix in this system, regardless of k_p. □

The system is stable, but it converges to the set described as $\dot{V} \leq 0$, which, from the previous proof, only guarantees that the quadrotor velocities are zero. Deadlocks can occur, especially if the configuration is ill defined, i.e. the set of desired ranges and apertures correspond to an impossible configuration. In this case, the system will converge to a situation where the aperture controller will counter-act the distance controller, creating the deadlock. The study of deadlocks is considered to be future work. However, note that those already existed in [5], referenced as local minima.

Finally, the gains K and $K_\perp$ found for the aperture controller are analyzed. The value of K is related to the controller radial component. Its value is intuitive, saying that it is always bigger than zero, as $\beta_{(i)} \leq \pi$, and it is bigger as the angle increases to $\pi/2$, corresponding to the point of maximum influence of the controller in the angle. Also, as e_{ij} decreases, the gain increases since the influence on the aperture also increases. The value of $K_\perp$ is related to the controller orthogonal component, and it is less intuitive. However, note that it uses cosine instead of sine functions, indicating that it is controlling an axis orthogonal to the one K controls. For example, if all quadrotors are found in a line, $K = 0$, since moving on the line does not control the aperture, but $K_\perp \neq 0$, since moving orthogonally to the line increases the aperture. For simplicity, and due to time constraints, this work considers $K_\perp = 0$, but the experiments show that the system can converge without this component.

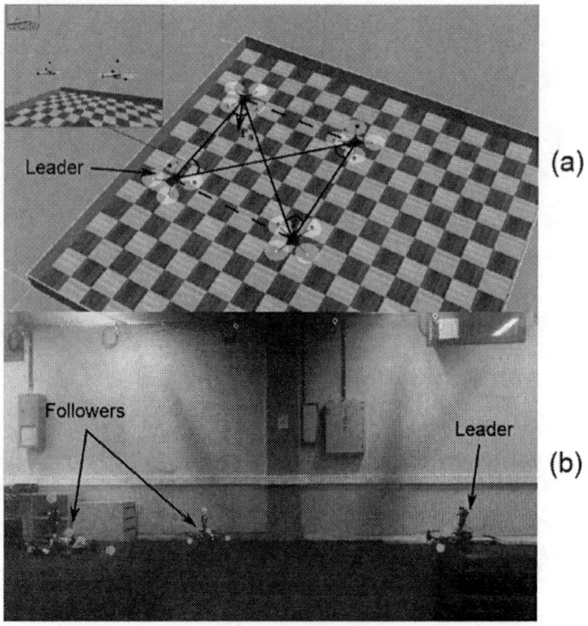

Figure 5: Experimental setups. (a) Webots simulator using a square formation - note that only two quadrotors are visible from the simulated camera sensor view (upper left corner). (b) Triangle formation in the flying arena endowed with a MCS, manufactured by Motion Analysis Inc. and composed of 20 Osprey cameras able to track the quadrotors using a set of reflective markers in an useful volume of 4x7x2.5 m. Note the static leader on the right.

Future work will include experiments done with a non-zero value of $K_\perp$ in the controller.

5. EXPERIMENTS

The algorithm was tested through a set of experiments conducted using the platforms described in Fig. 5. Both simulation (Fig. 5 (a)) and real (Fig. 5 (b)) environments were considered. In reality, Hummingbird quadrotors, manufactured by Ascending Technologies[1], were used. Each quadrotor was equipped with a set of active markers. An on-board camera with a 320x240 pixel frame and an horizontal FOV of 90° was used to detect the active markers on the neighbors, and extract their relative positions using an algorithm similar to the one presented in [4]. After calibration, the sensor noise had a standard deviation of 13 cm at a 3 meter range. The high-fidelity robotic simulator Webots[2] was used as the simulating environment, with a standard quadrotor model, not tuned to match the real quadrotors. The markers were simulated as colored blobs, and an ideal camera sensor was simulated with the same FOV. Perturbations were added on the simulated images to achieve the same noise levels measured in reality. Although in reality sensor noise decreases at smaller distances, in simulation it was kept with the same intensity at all distances. Finally, the actuation noise in reality was not measured, and in simulation it was set to be zero. A positioning ground truth is provided in reality through the MCS presented in Fig. 5. Additional details about the real setup and the system composed of the camera and active markers can be found in [2].

[1]http://www.asctec.de/

[2]https://www.cyberbotics.com/

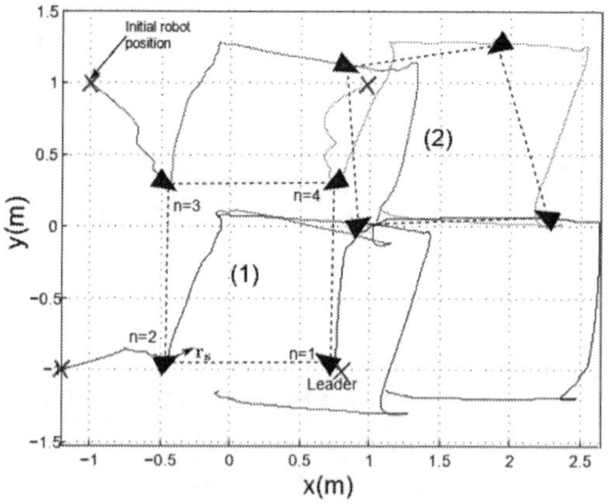

Figure 6: Evolution of the quadrotor trajectories performed in simulation using the formation control algorithm and the defined leader goal following strategy. Each robot is represented by a black triangle, and each color illustrates a trajectory of a specific quadrotor. The triangle orientation is the same as $\mathbf{r}_i^s$. (1) and (2) represent snapshots, when the formation is respectively stable and distorted.

The formation task was performed using four and three quadrotors, in simulation and real environments, respectively. Although not needed for the formation control, a leader was selected with the objective of anchoring the formation in the environment, and for the simulation experiments, to move the formation. The simulation experiments use a square formation configuration, depicted in Fig. 5 (a), and also described in Fig. 3, to assess rigidity issues. The square sides measured 1.2 m, and each quadrotor observed other two quadrotors, controlling an aperture of 45° between them. The formation leader was chosen at random. The real experiments use a triangle formation configuration, depicted in Fig. 5 (b), where the leader was static in the environment. The desired distances were 1.5 m between the leader and the followers, and 2.12 m between the followers. The desired aperture for each follower was also 45°. Both graphs, if the aperture control is included, are fully connected and rigid. The desired relative heights between the quadrotors in both scenarios were set to zero.

To move the leader in simulation, an extra term is added to the vertical and horizontal formation control laws in Eqs. (5) and (2), as follows:

$$u_i^{hl} = k_f u_i^{h*} + k_g k_v (\mathbf{v_i^h} - \mathbf{v^d}),$$
$$u_i^{zl} = k_f u_i^z + k_g k_v (v_i^z - v_i^{zd}),$$

where k_f and k_g regulate the importance of formation cohesion and goal following behaviors, both set to 0.5, indicating equal importance. The values of k_p, k_v and k_α were set to 1.6, 2.2 and 1.0 respectively. Therefore, the leader performs both goal following and formation cohesion, similar to the work presented in [7], and followers perform just the formation cohesion. The Laplacian weights between the leader and the followers were set to 1, as opposed to the weights between the followers, always chosen to be $\frac{1}{N_i}$, where N_i is the number of neighbors of robot i. This is because, in contrast to the leader, follower movements do not translate directly

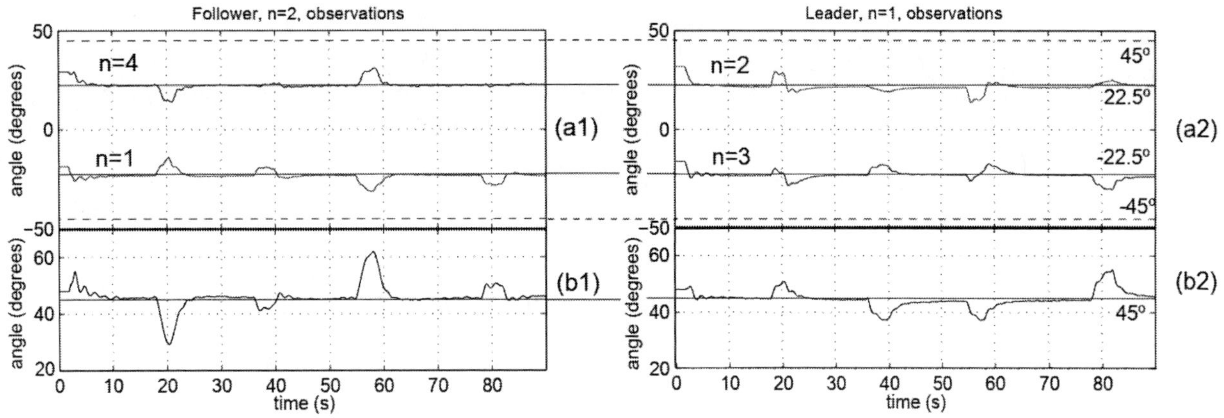

Figure 7: Controlled bearings (a) and aperture (b) values, observed from quadrotors n=2, and n=1. Desired bearing and apertures depicted using horizontal lines, with respected values shown on the right. The neighbor to which each bearing line corresponds, is indicated in text on the left. FOV limits shown with dashed lines.

the behavior that is desired for the robot, but rather a response to other neighbor changes, that can either have lag, noise, or be wrong. Therefore, these behaviors should be averaged. The next sections describe separately the results obtained in each environment.

5.1 Simulation Results

The formation stability, rigidity, and correct maintenance of the sensor FOV constraint were tested by moving the square formation through leader commands with a certain velocity in the x and y dimensions separately, as shown in Fig. 6 (the z velocity is set to zero). The used velocity value was of 0.5 m/s. The initial quadrotor positions were set so that all necessary FOV constraints were initially met. The proposed algorithm was then activated, so that the quadrotors could converge to the desired configuration. For one experimental run, Fig. 8 shows the progress of all the horizontal distance errors between two pairs of quadrotors, and Fig. 7 shows the neighbor bearings and apertures observed by the leader $n = 1$ and the follower $n = 2$ (numbers described in Fig. 6). The bearings are defined with respect to the camera FOV center, $\mathbf{r}_i^s$, illustrated in Fig. 5 (a).

Fig. 8 shows that the formation always converges to the right configuration, even after the perturbation caused by leader movements, showing its rigidity and stability. Note that, when the leader moves, the configuration is distorted (also observed in Fig. 6), and with higher intensity on the y axis (observed by the higher distance errors). The distortions happen because only the leader has the knowledge of the desired velocity and the followers simply follow the leader. The distortion is bigger on the y axis, because that is the direction where the leader is aligned with the follower $n = 4$, that only relies on other followers for information. This will generate a bigger movement delays between the leader and that follower, creating a bigger distance and aperture errors.

Fig. 7 shows similar perturbations on the bearing and aperture values. However, Fig. 7 (a), shows the convergence of neighbor bearings, in both leader and follower cases, to symmetric values with respect to $\mathbf{r}_i^s$, meaning that the yaw controller described in Eq. (4) optimizes the sensor FOV. Additionally, Fig. 7 (b) confirms, for the leader and follower cases, the convergence of the aperture to the desired values, which in combination with results presented in Fig. 8, shows the correct behavior of the horizontal controller proposed in Eqs. (2), (3), and (5), and the correct maintenance of the FOV constraints. The aperture distortions are also higher for movements on the y axis, for the same reasons as before.

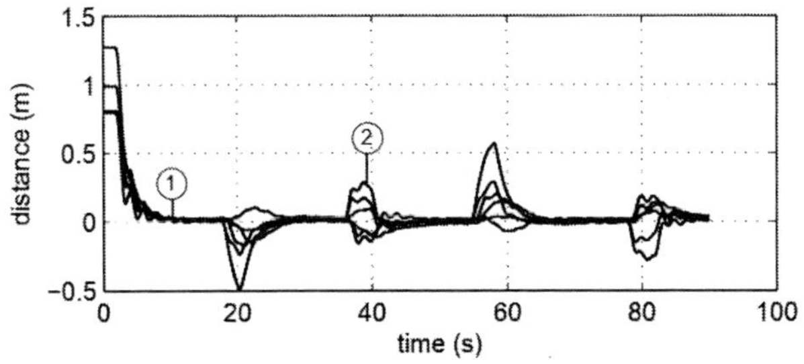

Figure 8: Horizontal distance errors between two pairs of quadrotors, during the experiment run corresponding to Fig. 6. The two snapshots described on that figure are highlighted here using circles.

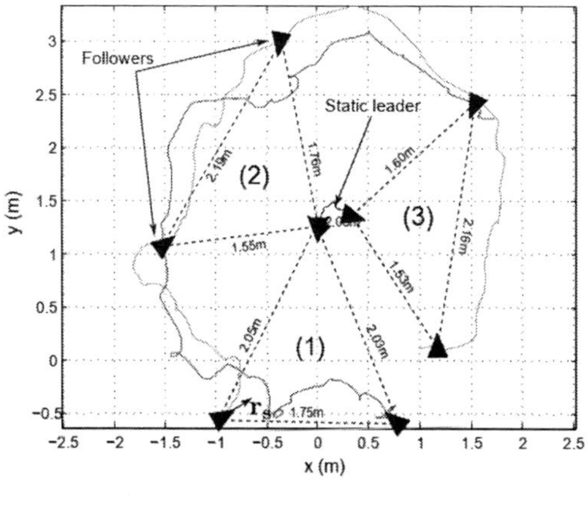

Figure 9: Real quadrotor trajectories tracked by the MCS, during a run of the algorithm. Note that the leader is static. Each color represents one quadrotor. Vector $\mathbf{r}_i^s$ is defined by the orientation of the described triangles. (1), (2), and (3) represent three snapshots of the formation, where (1) corresponds to the initial follower positions.

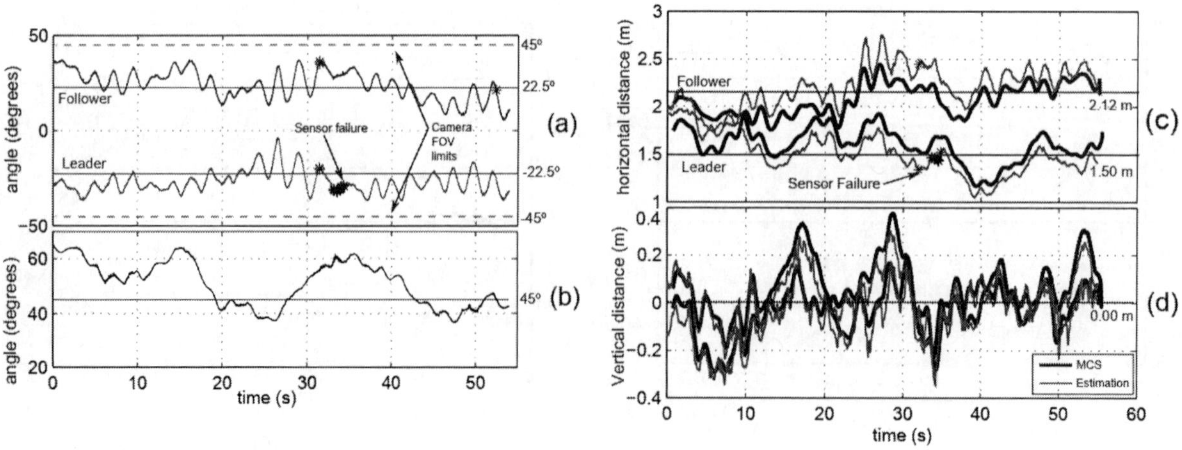

Figure 10: Neighbor bearings (a), aperture (b), and distances observed in the local frame of one of the followers for a real experiment. The distance is divided into horizontal (c) and vertical (d) components. Desired bearings, apertures, and distances are depicted on the respective plot using horizontal lines, with their values written on the right. The neighbor to which each bearing or horizontal distance line corresponds is indicated in text on the left of the line. Vertical ranges of both neighbors indistinguishable since they are both close to zero. The aperture is related to both neighbors. All values are tracked using the MCS, but on the distance plots, the values estimated from the sensor data are also shown. Black dots on the lines signal moments where the follower stopped receiving sensor data of the respective neighbor for more than 100 ms.

5.2 Real Experiments

Similar experiments were performed using the triangle formation described above, using the real setup depicted in Fig. 5 (b). The leader was placed in the environment, and it remains static through all the experiment. The followers were teleoperated into their initial positions using the MCS position feedback, in order to guarantee that their on-board cameras FOV initially cover their neighborhood. The algorithm was then activated, running exclusively on-board, using the camera for sensor feedback, until a stop and land command was broadcast. The resulting trajectories for each quadrotor, from the start of the algorithm to the end of one experiment, are shown in Fig. 9. The neighbor bearing, aperture, and distance information was tracked throughout the experiment for one of the followers, and shown in Fig. 10. For the bearing and aperture, the results show that, although the followers rotate around the leader, their values remain close to the desired, as in the simulated results, showing the correct behavior of the controller. This allowed loss of sensor data to be kept to a minimum, as shown in the figure. Note that, because of follower rotations, the leader had to be also rotated by hand, so that the followers would keep observing the leader.

Follower rotations happen due to biases present on actuation and on sensing. Fig. 10 (c) shows an example of a sensor bias on the horizontal plane, observed by the differences between MCS and on-board estimations of the tracked relative positions. These biases create unwanted forces competing with the formation control algorithm. Since the algorithm forces are tangent to the edge between quadrotors, the algorithm becomes weak on the radial axis, allowing relatively small forces to still be able to generate rotation movements. The biases can be different for each quadrotor, it could happen that they generate rotations in different directions, that would lead to a steady increase of the follower aperture observed by the leader. In this case, the leader would perform aperture control, going backwards to maintain the desired value. If these biases are constant, the system would move backwards until the end of the experiment. However, these biases can be minimized using integrators, included on the range control on each edge. Note that more than one edge is needed to compensate the bias, as range control on an edge is tangential to that edge. An integrator was also included in the height controller. This can generate low frequency oscillations around the desired relative displacements, which is possible to observe in Fig. 10, in both vertical, with a maximum of 40 cm, and horizontal components, with a maximum of 30 cm. However, despite those oscillations, the algorithm was still successfully maintaining the desired formation.

6. CONCLUSIONS

This work proposed a distributed formation control algorithm for quadrotors, that actively controls the system to satisfy the FOV constraints of the robot on-board sensors, for multiple observed neighbors. This allows for more complex and dynamic formation configurations with minimal or no communication requirements. Results show that the system is stable and that the FOV constraints are satisfied in both simulation and reality.

As future work, the previously discussed deadlocks will be investigated, together with the inclusion of goal following control for formation guidance. These experiments are to be performed with the orthogonal component of the aperture control activated. Furthermore, the sensing and control edge bi-directionality assumptions will be relaxed in order to consider additional formation configurations, paying special attention to how this might impact the formation stability. The results reported in this paper also outline that it is relevant to reproduce, in simulation, the real sensing and actuation mismatches, to further study the bias effects. This algorithm can be strengthened if the stability properties are found for the control of multiple apertures, and if the initial conditions that guarantee the FOV maintenance during the system operation are investigated.

REFERENCES

[1] F. Augugliaro, A. P. Schoellig, and R. D'Andrea. Generation of collision-free trajectories for a quadrocopter fleet: A sequential convex programming approach. In *International Conference on Intelligent Robots and Systems*, pages 1917–1922, 2012.

[2] D. Dias, R. Ventura, P. U. Lima, and A. Martinoli. On-board vision-based 3d relative localization system for multiple quadrotors. In *International Conference on Robotics and Automation*, 2016 (to appear).

[3] M. Egerestedt. Graph-theoretic methods for multi-agent coordination. In *ROBOMAT*, 2007.

[4] M. Faessler, E. Mueggler, K. Schwabe, and D. Scaramuzza. A monocular pose estimation system based on infrared leds. In *IEEE International Conference on Robotics and Automation*, 2014.

[5] R. Falconi, S. Gowal, and A. Martinoli. Graph-based distributed control of non-holonomic vehicles endowed with local positioning information engaged in escorting missions. In *International Conference on Robotics and Automation*, pages 3207–3214, 2010.

[6] A. Franchi, C. Masone, V. Grabe, M. Ryll, H. Bülthoff, and P. Giordano. Modeling and control of uav bearing formations with bilateral high-level steering. *International Journal of Robotics Research*, 31(12):1504–1525, 2012.

[7] D. Goldin and J. Raisch. Controllability of second order leader-follower systems. In *IFAC Workshop on Distributed Estimation and Control in Networked Systems*, pages 223–238, 2010.

[8] M. Ji and M. Egerstedt. Connectedness preserving distributed coordination control over dynamic graphs. In *American Control Conference*, pages 93–98, 2005.

[9] N. M. M. Turpin and V. Kumar. Decentralized formation control with variable shapes for aerial robots. In *IEEE International Conference on Robotics and Automation*, pages 23–30, 2012.

[10] D. Panagou and V. Kumar. Maintaining visibility for leader-follower formations in obstacle environments. In *IEEE International Conference on Robotics and Automation*, pages 1811–1816, 2012.

[11] D. Panagou and K. Kyriakopoulos. Cooperative formation control of underactuated marine vehicles for target surveillance under sensing and communication constraints. In *IEEE International Conference on Robotics and Automation*, pages 1871–1876, 2013.

[12] G. Pereira, A. K. Das, V. Kumar, and M. Campos. Formation control with configuration space constraints. In *IEEE International Conference on Intelligent Robots and Systems*, pages 2755 – 2760, 2003.

[13] W. Ren and E. Atkins. Second-order consensus protocols in multiple vehicle systems with local interactions. In *Guidance, Navigation, and Control Conference*, 2005.

[14] R. O. Saber and R. M. Murray. Graph rigidity and distributed formation stabilization of multi-vehicle systems. In *IEEE International Conference on Decision and Control*, pages 2965–2971, 2002.

[15] D. Scaramuzza, M. Achtelik, L. Doitsidis, F. Friedrich, E. Kosmatopoulos, A. Martinelli, M. Achtelik, M. Chl, S. Chatzichristofis, L. Kneip, D. Gurdan, L. Heng, H. Gim, S. Lynen, M. Pollefeys, A. Renzaglia, R. Siegwart, J. Stumpf, P. Tanskanen, C. Troiani, S. Weiss, and L. Meier. Vision-controlled micro flying robots: from system design to autonomous navigation and mapping in gps-denied environments. *IEEE Robotics & Automation Magazine*, 21(3):26–40, 2014.

[16] S. Shen, Y. Mulgaonkar, N. Michael, and V. Kumar. Vision-based state estimation and trajectory control towards high-speed flight with a quadrotor. In *Robotics: Science and Systems*, 2013.

[17] G. Stacey, R. Mahony, and P. Corke. A bondgraph approach to formation control using relative state measurements. In *European Control Conference*, pages 1262–1267, 2013.

[18] R. Tron, J. Thomas, G. Loianno, J. Polin, V. Kumar, , and K. Daniilidis. Vision-based formation control of aerial vehicles. In *Robotics: Science and Systems*, 2014.

[19] M. Turpin, N. Michael, and V. Kumar. Trajectory design and control for aggressive formation flight with quadrotors. *Autonomous Robots*, 33(1-2):143–156, 2012.

[20] G. Vásárhelyi, C. Virágh, G. Somorjai, N. Tarcai, T. Szorényi, T. Nepusz, and T. Vicsek. Outdoor flocking and formation flight with autonomous aerial robots. In *International Conference on Intelligent Robots and Systems*, pages 3866–3873, 2014.

[21] C. Verginis, C. Bechlioulis, D. Dimarogonas, and K. Kyriakopoulos. Decentralized 2-d control of vehicular platoons under limited visual feedback. In *IEEE International Conference on Intelligent Robots and Systems*, 2015.

Custard: Computing Norm States over Information Stores

Amit K. Chopra
School of Computing and Communications
Lancaster University
Lancaster, LA1 4WA, UK
a.chopra1@lancaster.ac.uk

Munindar P. Singh
Department of Computer Science
North Carolina State University
Raleigh, NC 27695-8206, USA
mpsingh@ncsu.edu

ABSTRACT

Norms provide a way to model the social architecture of a sociotechnical system (STS) and are thus crucial for understanding how such a system supports secure collaboration between principals, that is, autonomous parties such as humans and organizations. Accordingly, an important challenge is to compute the state of a norm instance at runtime in a sociotechnical system.

Custard addresses this challenge by providing a relational syntax for schemas of important norm types along with their canonical lifecycles and providing a mapping from each schema to queries that compute instances of the schema in different lifecycle stages. In essence, Custard supports a norm-based abstraction layer over underlying information stores such as databases and event logs. Specifically, it supports deadlines; complex events, including those based on aggregation; and norms that reference other norms.

We prove important correctness properties for Custard, including stability (once an event has occurred, it has occurred forever) and safety (a query returns a finite set of tuples). Our compiler generates SQL queries from Custard specifications. Writing out such SQL queries by hand is tedious and error-prone even for simple norms, thus demonstrating Custard's practical benefits.

1. INTRODUCTION

A sociotechnical system (STS) involves social elements or *principals*, such as autonomous humans or organizations, and technical elements such as IT resources. We understand an agent as a software entity that acts on behalf of a principal in an STS.

Norms provide a standard of correctness for interactions among the principals, thereby capturing the social architecture of an STS [37]. Specifically, a norm captures how the principals ought to interact: it provides a social-level, yet computational, encoding of an integrity or security (for simplicity, including privacy) requirement regarding their collaboration. An example norm would be that a physician is prohibited by the hospital from disclosing identifying information about a patient. Such a norm helps characterize security at the social level independently of the implementation. Therefore, representing norms is crucial for an agent to determine how to act; and how to evaluate compliance and accountability of others.

We distinguish norm schemas from instances. A norm schema or specification describes a norm in general terms, such as a prohibition against disclosing information about a patient. A norm instance would specify the specific patient whose information has been received. Some instances of a norm may be violated and some satisfied. We consider important norm types from the literature, namely, commitment, authorization, prohibition, and power [4, 22, 26, 36]. Each of these norm types involves a canonical lifecycle [36], discussed in Figure 3, in which a norm instance may be created, expired, detached, discharged, or violated.

Norms as *institutional facts* are elements of social reality in the sense of Searle [31] and as such are realized through and reflected in *brute facts* [3], that is, low-level information. In our setting, brute facts are recorded in databases and event logs; often, these events correspond to messages sent and received. However, Searle's claims about mental representation are inapplicable here [7, 16, 30, 32].

An important challenge in realizing norms, therefore, is how to compute norm instances from brute facts. To this end, we treat (1) norms on par with information schemas and (2) database relations as stores of norm instances in various lifecycle stages. For example, an information store may indicate which instances of a prohibition are expired and which are violated. In general, we would like to specify nested norms—for example, a commitment to inform patients of the violation of a prohibition on disclosing their private information. Figure 1 illustrates our approach in conceptual terms.

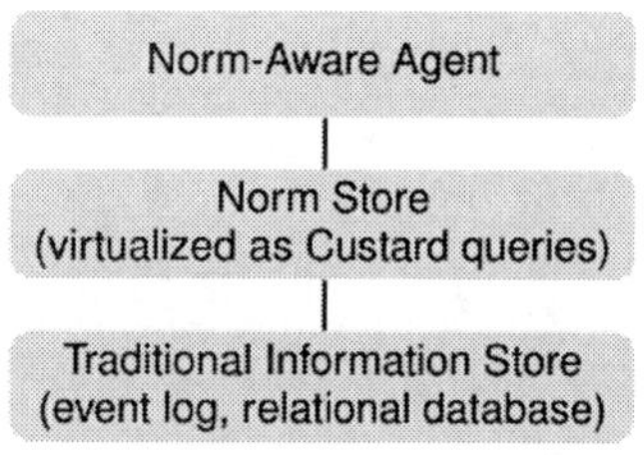

Figure 1: Custard realizes norms over information stores. An agent can query a virtual norm store for norm instances; Custard computes and retrieves such instances based on events in the underlying information store.

Our contributions are as below. First, we propose *Custard*, a language for specifying information-based norms, including *commitments*, *authorizations*, *prohibitions*, and *powers*. Custard is event-based: important stages in the lifecycle of a norm instance, specifically, its creation, detachment, expiration, discharge, and violation, are event instances and inferred from event instances recorded in the underlying information store. Custard supports complex event expressions involving logic operators, aggregation operators, relative time intervals within which events should occur, and nested norms. We give the semantics of Custard via queries in the tuple relational calculus (TRC) [15]. Effectively, for every norm specified in Custard, we define a query (expression) for each stage in the norm's canonical lifecycle, which yields all instances of the norm in that stage. The benefit of using the TRC is that it maps well to underlying representations and paves the way for easy implementation in widely used query languages such as SQL.

Appears in: *Proceedings of the 15th International Conference on Autonomous Agents and Multiagent Systems (AAMAS 2016), J. Thangarajah, K. Tuyls, C. Jonker, S. Marsella (eds.), May 9–13, 2016, Singapore.*

Second, we formulate and prove two desirable properties for Custard. *Stability* is monotonicity over time: once an event instance has occurred, it stays occurred forever. For example, a prohibition instance violated at one moment remains violated at all future moments. Ensuring stability requires a correct treatment of time. *Safety* captures the idea that queries map to finite sets.

Third, because of Custard's support for specifying the nonoccurrence of an event, aggregation, and expressive time intervals, the TRC queries for a norm turn out to be nontrivial. As Section 4 shows, even a simple Custard specification yields SQL queries that are complex and an order of magnitude longer. Writing such queries by hand would be highly tedious, time-consuming, and error-prone. To demonstrate the practical benefits of Custard, we implemented a compiler that generates SQL queries from Custard specifications.

2. SAMPLING CUSTARD IN PRIVACY

We demonstrate the effectiveness of Custard by modeling a real-world privacy consent scenario being considered by Health Level Seven (HL7) [18], which is a leading standardization body for health information systems. A patient signs up with a cloud-based health vault provider to store and manage access to its private health information (PHI). This information may include records of the patient's vital signs such as blood pressure and blood sugar, for example, as monitored by wearable devices and uploaded to the vault. The patient may authorize third parties, such as a health coach, to receive the PHI from the vault by indicating consent. A patient may revoke an authorization. The overseeing jurisdictional authority empowers the patient to grant or revoke such authorizations. In general, third parties authorized by the patient to access information are prohibited from forwarding the information they receive to yet other parties. Parties may be sanctioned for violating this prohibition.

Listing 1 shows an information schema for this healthcare setting. It describes a number of event specifications as relations, each annotated with its key and timestamp attributes. No two instances of an event (specification) may have identical bindings for the key; for every instance, the timestamp attribute records the time of occurrence of the instance. The key of one event may occur in another. For example, accID occurs in Allowed. Such foreign keys enable correlation: every Allowed instance can be correlated by a Signedup instance via the binding for accID in the former. In general, correlations may be effected via chaining of foreign keys. For example, a Revoked instance is correlated with an Allowed instance by discID, and, therefore, with Signedup via accID.

Notice that there can be at most one SentCred instance for an Allowed instance as their keys are identical. For every disclosure to a third party, there can be zero or more requests for data from that party to the vault provider (ReqData). For every request, there can be at most one access (Accessed). A third party may forward data that it has accessed via a request to other parties zero or more times (Forwarded). Every Forwarded instance is correlated with a Signedup instance via a chain of correlations (forID to reqID to discID to accID).

We exclude methodologies for designing the appropriate information schemas from our present scope and expect such methodologies can build on known data and ontology modeling techniques.

Listing 1: Example schema for the healthcare scenario.

```
schema
 //Patient pID registers in jurisdiction jID
  Registered(pID, jID, resID, council)
  key resID time t

 //pID signs up with health vault provider hID
 Signedup(pID, hID, accID)
  key accID time t

 //pID allows disclosure to third party tpID
 Allowed(pID, hID, discID, accID, tpID, info)
  key discID time t

 //pID revokes disclosure for tpID
 Revoked(pID, hID, discID)
  key discID time t

 //hID sends creds to tpID if disclosure allowed
 SentCred(hID, tpID, discID, credentials)
  key discID time t

 //tpID requests patient data from hID
 ReqData(tpID, hID, reqID, discID, request)
  key reqID time t

 //tpID gets access to the requested data
 Accessed(tpID, hID, reqID, response)
  key reqID time t

 //tpID forwards data to party otherID
 Forwarded(tpID, otherID, forID, reqID, response)
  key forID time t

 //hID sanctions tpID for mishandling information
 Sanction(hID, tpID, discID, details)
  key discID time t
```

We build on recent work that understands norm types such as commitment, authorization, prohibition, and power as directed *social expectations* between agents [36,37]. Figure 2 shows important elements of our conceptual model.

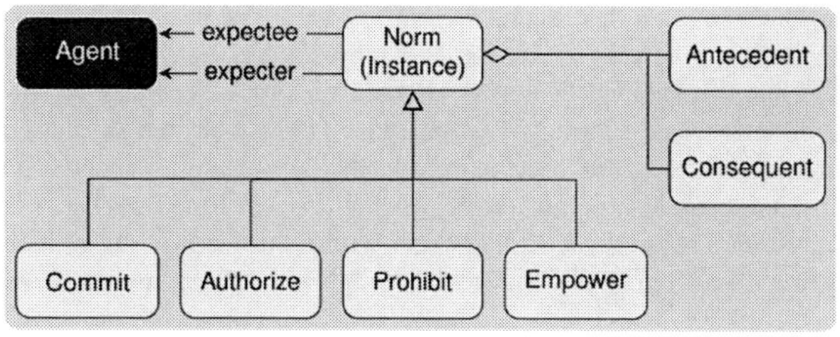

Figure 2: Simplified metamodel for norms (based on [36]).

In Figure 2, each (created) norm instance is a conditional expectation, whose *antecedent* states the condition under which the force of the norm, given by the *consequent*, applies. The expector and expectee represent the *privileged* and *liable* parties, respectively. Crucially, this formulation yields a basis for accountability in STSs: the *expectee* is accountable to the *expector* for the satisfaction of the expectation. Conversely, the expector has *standing* and may legitimately demand that the expectee give an account of the status of the expectation. As Example 1 illustrates, doing so helps understand accountability independently of implementation.

EXAMPLE 1. A commitment from a hospital to encrypt sensitive private health information (PHI) represents the patient's expectation that the hospital will do just that—and that the patient has a basis for demanding an account from the hospital about whether his or her PHI has been encrypted. A failure to encrypt PHI would be a violation, for which the hospital may be sanctioned.

Viewing norms as expectations leads to interesting questions that have not received adequate attention in the literature. For example, when is an authorization violated? And, who is accountable to whom for the violation? We now discuss possible lifecycles for the norm types, as in Figure 3, and conventions about accountability.

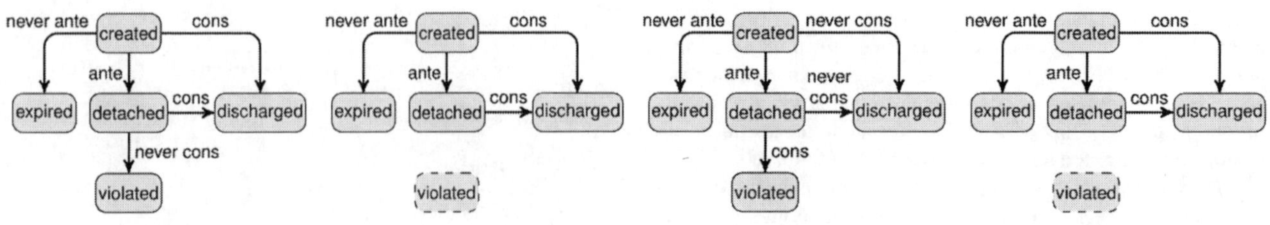

(a) Commitment (b) Authorization (c) Prohibition (d) Power

Figure 3: Lifecycles for the various norms. For each norm type, each box refers to a lifecycle event (not a state). The transitions refer to events as well—the occurrence or the impossibility of occurrence of the antecedent and consequent events.

2.1 Commitment

Our notion of commitment corresponds to the standard one in the literature [33]: the debtor commits to the creditor to bring about a condition (the consequent) if some condition (the antecedent) holds. We give an example from the foregoing scenario.

EXAMPLE 2. When a patient signs up, the health vault provider commits to the patient that if the patient grants access to a third party, the vault provider will authorize that party within a day.

Listing 2 shows a commitment listing in Custard. DisclosureCom is a name for the schema. The commitment is from hID to pID; it is created upon the occurrence of a Signedup instance; detached upon the occurrence of a correlated Allowed disclosure instance, provided that disclosure has not been Revoked (this allows modeling situations where patients may change their minds); it is discharged when a correlated instance of DisclosureAuth (an authorization, see Listing 3) is created. The detach and discharge clauses represent the antecedent and the consequent, respectively. In an expression of the form $E[l, r]$, $[l, r]$ is a time interval; the expression says that E should occur within this interval. To reduce clutter, we often omit l and r when they are 0 and ∞, respectively.

Listing 2: Captures Example 2.

```
commitment DisclosureCom hID to pID
 create Signedup
 detach Allowed except Revoked
 discharge created DisclosureAuth[0, Allowed+1]
```

Figure 3a shows the lifecycle of a created commitment instance. The instance is violated if the antecedent occurs but the consequent cannot; it expires if the antecedent cannot occur; and it is discharged if the consequent occurs. For simplicity, a commitment instance may be both expired and discharged: when its antecedent can no longer occur (as after a time out) but the consequent occurs.

2.2 Authorization

An agent authorizes another to bring about its consequent provided its antecedent holds.

EXAMPLE 3. The health vault provider authorizes a party by sending it credentials assuring it that patient data will be available for access any time between one and ten days after its request.

Listing 3: An authorization in Custard.

```
authorization DisclosureAuth tpID by hID
 create SentCred
 detach ReqData
 discharge Accessed[ReqData+1, ReqData+10]
```

In authorizations, we treat the authorizing party as the expectee and the authorized party as the expector. Thus, in Listing 3, the expector is tpID and the expectee is the vault. Specifically, tpID *expects* access to patient information if it has been authorized to obtain it. This agrees with the intuition that an authorization is the authorized party's privilege, not a liability. The authorization instance would be violated if the patient had authorized disclosure to a specific party, but the vault provider blocks that party from accessing the patient's information.

Although, in principle, an authorization may be violated as above, we make an architectural assumption and adopt a convention that the violation of an authorization is impossible [36]. Specifically, we assume that authorizations are regimented [20] by the agent, for example, via authentication and access control mechanisms. That is, access to a patient's record is controlled via a mechanism that allows access by all who are authorized. Figure 3b captures the authorization lifecycle. It makes the *violated* event unreachable to capture the doctrine that authorizations cannot be violated.

2.3 Prohibition

An agent prohibits another from bringing about the consequent if its antecedent has occurred. In contrast with authorizations, we apply prohibitions to cases where events are either not easily regimented or not desired to be regimented. For example, it is in general impossible to regiment a system to make disclosure of confidential information impossible. We capture the undesirability of such behaviors by placing prohibitions on them. Example 4 demonstrates a prohibition followed by its formal encoding in Listing 4.

EXAMPLE 4. The health vault provider prohibits any party who accesses patient information from forwarding that information to other parties.

Listing 4: A prohibition in Custard.

```
prohibition DisclosureProh tpID by hID
 create discharged DisclosureAuth
 violate Forwarded
```

Figure 3c captures the prohibition lifecycle. A prohibition is violated if the antecedent and the consequent have both occurred. In a prohibition, the expectee and expector are the prohibited and prohibiting parties, respectively.

2.4 Power

An agent empowers another to bring about certain states of affairs by simply "saying so" provided some conditions hold [5, 19]. We adopt Jones and Sergot's distinction between power and authorization [20]. In our setting, power is the ability of an agent to modify norms among other agents whereas authorization is the ability to access resources [36]. In addition, as discussed above, we treat authorizations as regimented via technical mechanisms.

EXAMPLE 5. The jurisdictional authority empowers the patient to authorize any party to receive the patient's information from the vault provider by simply filling out the appropriate form.

Listing 5 captures Example 5. It says that a patient who is registered in a jurisdiction and who has signed up with a vault provider after becoming a resident has the power to authorize disclosure to other parties—and to revoke such authorizations.

Listing 5: A power in Custard.

```
power ConsentPower pID by jID
 create Registered
 detach Signedup[Registered ,]
 discharge Allowed[Signedup ,] and Revoke[Signedup ,]
```

In a power instance, the empowered agent is the privileged party, that is, the expector. The empowering agent is the liable party, that is, the expectee. For simplicity, we adopt the view that a power cannot be violated for the simple reason that "saying so" under the right conditions is enough to fully exercise the power. The effects of a power may be realized through other norms. In Example 5, the effect of the power is realized through the vault provider becoming committed to authorizing parties who are allowed by the patient to receive information. Of course, the vault provider may refuse to comply, thus violating the above-mentioned commitment. If the antecedent would never not hold, then the power expires. Figure 3d captures the lifecycle of power.

2.5 Aggregation

Norms can naturally involve aggregation, as Example 6 illustrates. Such norms capture key performance indicators in business settings as well as levels of infraction by various agents.

EXAMPLE 6. The vault provider commits to the patient to declare a third party as "out of compliance" if in the year following the patient authorizing the party to receive information, it violates the prohibition to forward information to others more than twice.

Listing 6 captures Example 6. The aggregation syntax is based on the standard one in databases: specify the attribute to aggregate over (forID), the expression in which the attribute appears (violated DisclosureProh), how to group the tuples of the expression (by discID), and the attribute that holds the aggregated value (numViol). The aggregate event occurs when the count of forID over the specified interval is greater than two.

Listing 6: A norm involving aggregation in Custard.

```
commitment SanctionCom hID to pID
 create Signedup
 detach count forID of violated DisclosureProh as
     numViol group by discID > 2
     [Signedup , Signedup+365]
 discharge Sanction[,detached SanctionCom+10] where
     details="Out of compliance"
```

3. TECHNICAL FRAMEWORK

Let $\mathcal{D} = \{\mathcal{D}_1 \dots \mathcal{D}_n\}$ be a set of domains where $\mathcal{T} \in \mathcal{D}$ is the domain of time instants; in particular, $\mathcal{T} = \mathbb{N} \cup \{\infty\}$, where $\mathbb{N}$ is the set of natural numbers and ∞ is an infinitely distant time instant. Below, $\mathcal{A}$ and $\mathbb{R}$ are the sets of agent names and the real numbers, respectively. Table 1 defines the syntax of Custard.

Expr yields complex events. The foregoing Custard listings use a surface syntax in which we (1) write and, or, and except for $\sqcap$, $\sqcup$, and $\ominus$ respectively; (2) omit lower and upper instants in time intervals when they are, respectively, 0 and ∞; (3) omit the detach clause for unconditional norms; and (4) label norms to simplify writing nested commitments. For instance, Listing 2 equals the following Spec expression: commitment(hID, pID, SignedUp[0,∞], Allowed[0,∞] $\ominus$ Revoked[0,∞], created authorization(tpID, hID, SentCred[0,∞], ReqData[0,∞], Accessed[ReqData+1, ReqData+10])[0,Allowed+1]).

Spec	$\longrightarrow$	Norm($\mathcal{A}$, $\mathcal{A}$, Expr, Expr, Expr)
Norm	$\longrightarrow$	commitment | prohibition | authorization | power
Expr	$\longrightarrow$	Event[Time, Time] | Expr where φ | Expr EvOp Expr
Event	$\longrightarrow$	Base | Life | Aggr
Life	$\longrightarrow$	created Spec | detached Spec | discharged Spec expired Spec | violated Spec
EvOp	$\longrightarrow$	$\sqcap$ | $\sqcup$ | $\ominus$
Aggr	$\longrightarrow$	Func $\mathcal{D}$ of Event as $\mathcal{D}$ group by GSpec Comp $\mathbb{R}$
GSpec	$\longrightarrow$	$\mathcal{D}$ | GSpec,$\mathcal{D}$
Time	$\longrightarrow$	Event–$\mathcal{T}$ | Event + $\mathcal{T}$ | $\mathcal{T}$
Func	$\longrightarrow$	sum | count | min | max | avg
Comp	$\longrightarrow$	> | >= | < | <= | = | !=

Table 1: Syntax of Custard. Spec is the start symbol.

3.1 Semantics

As Definition 1 describes, an *information schema* is a nonempty set of event schemas, each modeled as a relation with a key and a distinguished timestamp column. Informally, these correspond to Base events in our syntax (Table 1). The relation for each event schema records (positive) events. That is, no event that has occurred ever goes away.

Below, we assume that the timestamp does not feature in a key since it has no semantic force as such. $\mathcal{N}$ is a set of event names.

DEFINITION 1. *For convenience, we identify a domain with its set of possible values. (Treating each attribute as unique with its own domain simplifies the notation without loss of generality.)*

An information schema I *over* $\mathcal{D}$ *is a partial mapping from event names to attributes and keys; it includes precisely the events of interest. That is,* $I : \mathcal{N} \to \mathcal{D} \times \mathcal{D}$. *Specifically,* $I(E) = \langle A, K\rangle$, *where* $A \subseteq \mathcal{D}$, $\mathcal{T} \in A \setminus K$, *and* $K \subseteq A$. *For brevity, we write* $E = \langle A, K\rangle$ *below.*

Definition 2 gives the intension, the set of possible extensions, of an event schema with respect to a universe. A universe captures the possible combinations of attribute values under consideration.

DEFINITION 2. *Let* $E = \langle\{A_1 \dots A_m\}, K\rangle$. *The* universe over E, $U_E = A_1 \times \dots \times A_m$.

The intension of E *is the powerset of* U_E *restricted to sets that satisfy the key constraint of the event schema. That is, any two* E *instances that agree on the key attributes must agree on every attribute (that is, they are the same instance). That is,* $\langle\!| E |\!\rangle = \{Y | Y \subseteq U_E \text{ and } (\forall u_i, u_j \in Y\text{: if } u_i||K = u_j||K, \text{ then } u_i = u_j)\}$, *where* $||$ *indicates projection to the specified set of attributes.*

An extension of E *is any member of its intension.*

Let I_E be the set of event schemas defined in an information schema I. Definition 3 states that a model of an information schema determines an extension for each of its event schemas.

DEFINITION 3. *A model* M *of an information schema,* I, *maps each of* I*'s event schemas to its extension. Let* $E = \langle A, K\rangle \in I_E$. *Then the extension of* E *in* M *is any member of* E*'s intension: that is,* $[\![E]\!]^M \in \langle\!| E |\!\rangle$. *(We omit* M *when it is understood.)*

The model defines $[\![Ev]\!]$ for Base event Ev. The semantic postulates below lift $[\![\,]\!]$ to all expressions in Custard via the TRC. In the TRC, quantification is over tuples; for a tuple τ, $\tau.a$ gives the value of attribute a of τ. Below, t is the distinguished timestamp attribute of all event schemas; $\{c, d\} \subseteq \mathcal{T}$; $E, F, \ldots$ are expressions of type Event; $X, Y, \ldots$ are expressions of type Expr; l and r are Time expressions; $\oplus$ is either '+' or '−'; $\rhd$ is any Comp operator; N is a Norm expression; g is a GSpec expression.

We use the following auxiliary definitions. The function att produces the nontimestamp attributes of an event schema; and cmn the common nontimestamp attributes of two event schemas. The predicate eq takes two tuples and a set of attributes and returns true if and only if the tuples are equal for each of those attributes; nul takes a tuple and a set of attributes and returns true if and only if each attribute's value is null in that tuple; and $holds$ takes a constraint and a tuple and returns true iff the tuple satisfies the constraint. The function $sumf$ works like the conventional sum operator in database theory: it takes four inputs, a relation S, an attribute col (in S) which needs to be summed, a set of columns g to group S by, and an attribute colsum whose value will be the sum and produces a set of tuples with the attributes g and colsum. That is, it produces a relation whose attributes are g and colsum and whose values are what it computes. We would need analogous functions $maxf$, $minf$, $countf$, and $avgf$ for tackling the corresponding constructs in Custard. The functions $maxt$ and $mint$ compute max and min of timestamps.

D_1. $[\![E[c,d]]\!] = \{\tau | \tau \in [\![E]\!] \wedge c \leqslant \tau.t < d\}$. Select all events in E that occur after (including at) c but before d.

D_2. $[\![E[F \oplus c, d]]\!] = \{\tau | \exists \tau'\ \tau \in [\![E]\!] \wedge \tau' \in [\![F]\!] \wedge eq(\tau, \tau', cmn(E, F)) \wedge \tau'.t \oplus c \leqslant \tau.t < d\}$. Select E if F occurs and E occurs after (or before, depending upon what $\oplus$ is) c moments of F's occurrence but before d.

D_3. $[\![E[c, F \oplus d]]\!] = \{\tau | \exists \tau'\ \tau \in [\![E]\!] \wedge \tau' \in [\![F]\!] \wedge eq(\tau, \tau', cmn(E, F)) \wedge c \leqslant \tau.t < \tau'.t \oplus d\}$. Select E if F occurs and E occurs after c but before d moments have passed since F's occurrence (or at least d moments before F's occurrence, depending upon what $\oplus$ is).

D_4. $[\![E[F \oplus c, G \oplus d]]\!] = \{\tau | \tau \in [\![E[F \oplus c, \infty]]\!] \wedge \tau \in [\![E[0, G \oplus d]]\!]\}$. Combines D_2 and D_3.

We give definitions for aggregate events involving sum. We skip the analogous definitions for the other Func expressions (min, max, count, avg) for brevity.

D_5. $[\![$sum col of E as $colsum$ group by $g \rhd n\ [l, d]]\!] = \{\tau | \exists \tau' \in sumf([\![E[l,d]]\!], col, colsum, g) \wedge \tau'.colsum \rhd n \wedge eq(\tau, \tau', g \cup \{colsum\}) \wedge \tau.t = d\}$. Compute all E instances between l and d and sum them up grouped by g over column col. If the sum for some g is $\rhd n$, then the event has occurred with a timestamp of d.

D_6. $[\![$sum col of E as $colsum$ group by $g \rhd n\ [l, F \oplus d]]\!] = \{\tau | \exists \tau' \in sumf([\![E[l, F \oplus d]]\!], col, colsum, g) \wedge \tau'.colsum \rhd n \wedge eq(\tau, \tau', g \cup \{colsum\}) \wedge (\exists \tau'' \in [\![F]\!] \wedge eq(\tau', \tau'', att(F)) \wedge \tau.t = \tau'' \oplus d)\}$. Analogous to D_5 except that the timestamp of the sum event is relative to a corresponding F event.

D_7. $[\![X \sqcap Y]\!] = \{\tau | \exists \tau' \in [\![X]\!] \wedge (\exists \tau'' \in [\![Y]\!] \wedge eq(\tau, \tau', att(X)) \wedge eq(\tau, \tau'', att(Y)) \wedge \tau.t = maxt(\tau'.t, \tau''.t))\}$. Select ($X$, Y) pairs where both have occurred; the timestamp of this composite event is the greater of the two.

D_8. $[\![X \sqcup Y]\!] = \{\tau | (\exists \tau' \in [\![X]\!] \wedge (\exists \tau'' \in [\![Y]\!] \wedge eq(\tau, \tau', att(X)) \wedge eq(\tau, \tau'', att(Y)) \wedge \tau.t = mint(\tau'.t, \tau''.t))) \vee$

$(\exists \tau' \in [\![X]\!] \wedge eq(\tau, \tau', att(X)) \wedge \tau.t = \tau'.t \wedge nul(\tau, att(Y)) \wedge (\forall \tau'' \in [\![Y]\!] \rightarrow \neg eq(\tau, \tau'', att(Y)))) \vee$

$(\exists \tau' \in [\![Y]\!] \wedge eq(\tau, \tau', att(Y)) \wedge \tau.t = \tau'.t \wedge nul(\tau, att(X)) \wedge (\forall \tau'' \in [\![X]\!] \rightarrow \neg eq(\tau, \tau'', att(X))))\}$.

Select (X, Y) pairs where at least one has occurred. The timestamp of this composite event is the smaller of the two, if both have occurred, or equal to the timestamp of the one that has occurred.

The interpretation of $X \ominus Y$ is that X should have occurred but the (corresponding) Y should not have occurred. But what is the time of nonoccurrence of an event? Consider $X \ominus E[l, d]$. Here, $E[l, d]$ (corresponding to X) has not occurred if E (corresponding to X) has not occurred between l and d. Thus if E occurs before l, say at b, then the time of the nonoccurrence of $E[l, d]$ is b; if E does not occur before d, then the time of nonoccurrence of $E[l, d]$ is d, which could be ∞. The time of occurrence of the $X \ominus E[l, d]$ is the maximum of the timestamps of X and $E[l, d]$.

D_9. $[\![X \ominus E[l, d]]\!] = \{\tau | (\exists \tau' \in [\![X]\!] \wedge eq(\tau, \tau', att(X)) \wedge \tau.t = maxt(\tau'.t, d) \wedge (\forall \tau'' \in [\![E[0, d]]\!] \rightarrow \neg eq(\tau', \tau'', cmn(X, E)))) \vee$

$(\exists \tau' \in [\![X]\!] \wedge eq(\tau, \tau', att(X)) \wedge (\exists \tau'' \in [\![E[0, l]]\!] \wedge eq(\tau', \tau'', cmn(X, E)) \wedge \tau.t = maxt(\tau'.t, \tau''.t)))\}$.

The definition of $[\![X \ominus E[c, F \oplus d]]\!]$ follows along the same lines except to account for the difference that the right timepoint refers to an event (F) instead of being a constant. As before, we want X if E occurs too soon (before c). In addition, we want X if E occurs too late, in this case, after $f \oplus d$, where f is the value of F's timestamp. We will give this nonoccurrence of E the timestamp $f \oplus d$. But what if F itself has not occurred? Then, we would not have a value for f. But in this case, we would not want X anyway because without the occurrence of F, it is not possible to determine the appropriateness of the occurrence of E.

D_{10}. $[\![X \ominus E[l, F \oplus d]]\!] = \{\tau | (\exists \tau' \in [\![X]\!] \wedge (\exists \tau'' \in [\![F]\!] \wedge eq(\tau, \tau', att(X)) \wedge eq(\tau', \tau'', cmn(X, F)) \wedge \tau.t = maxt(\tau'.t, \tau''.t \oplus d) \wedge (\forall \tau''' \in [\![E[0, F \oplus d]]\!] \rightarrow \neg eq(\tau, \tau''', cmn(X, E))))) \vee$

$(\exists \tau' \in [\![X]\!] \wedge eq(\tau, \tau', att(X)) \wedge (\exists \tau'' \in [\![E[0, l]]\!] \wedge eq(\tau', \tau'', cmn(X, E)) \wedge \tau.t = maxt(\tau'.t, \tau''.t)))\}$.

D_{11}. $[\![X$ where $\varphi]\!] = \{\tau | \tau \in [\![X]\!] \wedge holds(\tau, \varphi)\}$.

D_{12}–D_{15} transform complex expressions involving $\ominus$ to those where $\ominus$ has an event of the form $E[l, r]$ as its right hand side operand.

D_{12}. $[\![X \ominus (Y \sqcap Z)]\!] = [\![(X \ominus Y) \sqcup (X \ominus Z)]\!]$.

D_{13}. $[\![X \ominus (Y \sqcup Z)]\!] = [\![(X \ominus Y) \sqcap (X \ominus Z)]\!]$.

D_{14}. $[\![X \ominus (Y \ominus Z)]\!] = [\![(X \ominus Y) \sqcup (X \sqcap Z)]\!]$.

D_{15}. $[\![X \ominus (Y$ where $\varphi)]\!] = [\![(X \ominus Y) \sqcup T]\!]$, where $T = \{\tau | \exists \tau' \in [\![X \sqcap Y$ where $\neg\varphi]\!] \wedge eq(\tau, \tau', att(X)) \wedge \tau.t = \tau'.t\}$.

Below, we write $N(c, r, u)$ where the definition applies uniformly to all kinds of norms. For brevity, we omit the expectee and expecter agents.

D_{16}. $[\![\mathsf{created}\ N(c,r,u)]\!] = [\![c]\!]$. An norm instance is created when its create event occurs.

D_{17}. $[\![\mathsf{detached}\ N(c,r,u)]\!] = [\![c \sqcap r]\!]$. A norm instance is detached when its create and detach events both occur.

D_{18}. $[\![\mathsf{expired}\ N(c,r,u)]\!] = [\![c \ominus r]\!]$. A norm instance is expired when its create event has occurred but its detach fails to occur within the specified interval.

D_{19}. $[\![\mathsf{discharged\ commitment}(c,r,u)]\!] = [\![(c \sqcap u) \sqcup (r \sqcap u)]\!]$. A commitment is discharged when its discharge event has occurred along with either its create or detach event.

D_{20}. $[\![\mathsf{discharged\ authorization}(c,r,u)]\!] = [\![c \sqcap r \sqcap u]\!]$. An authorization is discharged when its discharge event has occurred along with its create and detach event.

D_{21}. $[\![\mathsf{discharged\ power}(c,r,u)]\!] = [\![c \sqcap r \sqcap u]\!]$. A power is discharged when its discharge event has occurred along with its create and detach event.

D_{22}. $[\![\mathsf{discharged\ prohibition}(c,r,u)]\!] = [\![(c \sqcap r) \ominus u]\!]$. A prohibition is discharged when its create and detach events occur but the violate event fails to occur.

D_{23}. $[\![\mathsf{violated\ commitment}(c,r,u)]\!] = [\![(c \sqcap r) \ominus u]\!]$. A commitment is violated when its create and detach events occur but the discharge event fails to occur.

D_{24}. $[\![\mathsf{violated\ authorization}(c,r,u)]\!] = \emptyset$ (the empty set). No authorization can be violated.

D_{25}. $[\![\mathsf{violated\ power}(c,r,u)]\!] = \emptyset$. No power can be violated.

D_{26}. $[\![\mathsf{violated\ prohibition}(c,r,u)]\!] = [\![c \sqcap r \sqcap u]\!]$. A prohibition is violated when its create, detach, and violate events all occur.

3.2 Properties

Stability is the idea that once an event is determined to have occurred, then at all future time instants, it should continue to be determined to have occurred. In other words, an event that has occurred cannot later unoccur. For example, a message that been sent cannot be unsent. Stability of events is a fundamental assumption in reasoning about distributed systems.

We would like to extend this notion of stability to norm lifecycle event instances. Thus, for example, if a prohibition instance is determined to have been violated at a time instant, then at all future instants, it should be determined violated. Stability would be highly desirable in business settings as it would give stakeholders confidence in the status of things.

A Base event is by definition stable, since the model defines its extension. However, stability for complex events, including lifecycle events, does not automatically follow from the stability of Base events. Two features, in particular, demand careful consideration.

First, let us consider $\ominus$, the except operator. Imagine an event specification of the form $X \ominus E[0,100]$. Let us say an expression is evaluated at time 50, before which some X instance has occurred but the corresponding E instance has not occurred. Then one may assume that the corresponding $X \ominus E[0,100]$ instance has occurred. However, doing so would be premature: the E instance could yet occur, say at time 55, and a later query would determine the $X \ominus E[0,100]$ instance to have not occurred. In essence, we would have switched the status of the event from occurred to not occurred.

Second, let us consider aggregation operators. A sum event determined to have occurred at an instant may at future instants be determined to have not occurred as additional events occur. For example, if the sum over a number of events was required to be greater than some value, it may hit that value after observing, say, five events. However, future events may lower the sum (if the attribute which is being summed can take negative values) and cause it to dip below the required value.

We have built the semantics so that stability is guaranteed for all events and the above-described scenarios do not occur. We can treat all observations up to a time as forming a model. Thus as a computation progresses and additional events occur, a model corresponding to additional observations would extend a prior model.

DEFINITION 4. *Let L and M be two models for information schema I. Then M* expands on *L if and only if for each event in I_E, $[\![E]\!]^L \subseteq [\![E]\!]^M$.*

Theorem 1 states that the result obtained by evaluating an expression would persist through expansions of models, thereby ensuring stability of Custard.

THEOREM 1. *Let L and M be models where M expands on L. Let X be any Expr expression. Then, $[\![X]\!]^L \subseteq [\![X]\!]^M$.*

Proof Sketch. The proof is by induction on the syntax. Specifically, an expression X maps to a tree of height h where the leaf nodes are Base events and the root is the expression itself.

The expressions at the leaves represent the base case for the induction. The model defines $[\![Ev]\!]$ if Ev is a Base event. We obtain $[\![Ev]\!]^L \subseteq [\![Ev]\!]^M$ immediately from our assumption regarding Base events. Consider an expression at height k ($0 < k \leqslant h$). Assume that the property holds for its children. The expression must correspond to one of the postulates in D_1–D_{26}. We must show that the stability property holds for them.

D_1. From the inductive hypothesis, we know that $[\![E]\!]^L \subseteq [\![E]\!]^M$. It follows from D_1 that $[\![E[c,d]]\!]^L \subseteq [\![E[c,d]]\!]^M$. Reasoning for D_2–D_4 is analogous.

D_5. If $\tau \in [\![\mathsf{sum}\ col\ \mathsf{of}\ E\ \mathsf{as}\ colsum\ \mathsf{group\ by}\ \gamma \rhd n[l,d]]\!]^L$, then from the fact that $\tau.t = d$, we know all relevant E instances, that is, those that happen in $[\![E[l,d]]\!]$ have been considered. Further, $[\![E[l,d]]\!]^L = [\![E[l,d]]\!]^M$. Therefore, stability holds. D_6 is analogous.

D_7. Follows from $[\![X]\!]^L \subseteq [\![X]\!]^M$ and $[\![Y]\!]^L \subseteq [\![Y]\!]^M$. D_8 is analogous.

D_9. Two subcases. One, $\tau \in [\![X \ominus E[l,d]]\!]^L$ and τ occurs at some time k but E does not occur in $[0,d]$. In this case, stability of the sum event follows from the fact that $[\![E[0,d]]\!]^L = [\![E[0,d]]\!]^M$ and $[\![X]\!]^L \subseteq [\![X]\!]^M$. Two, $\tau \in [\![X \ominus E[l,d]]\!]^L$ because X and $E[0,l]$ have both occurred. In this case, stability of the sum event follows from the fact that $[\![E[0,l]]\!]^L = [\![E[0,l]]\!]^M$ and $[\![X]\!]^L \subseteq [\![X]\!]^M$. D_{10} is analogous.

D_{11}. Follows from the fact that $[\![X]\!]$ is stable.

D_{12}–D_{15}. An expression of these forms reduces to an expression where the right hand side of every $\ominus$ operand is a base event, lifecycle event, or aggregation event qualified by a time interval. Such expressions are stable. Their combinations with other expressions is also stable.

D_{16} Follows from the fact that $[\![c]\!]$ is stable. D_{17}–D_{26} are analogous.

Safety is a well-known correctness criterion for database queries [15]. Definition 6 describes safety as the idea that the result of any query evaluated over a finite database is finite. Here, a query is an expression that we evaluate using a database.

DEFINITION 5. *Let M be a model over information schema I. Then M is a* finite model *if and only if for each event E occurring in I_E, $[\![E]\!]^M$, is finite.*

DEFINITION 6. *Let Q be an Expr expression. Then, Q is* safe *if and only if given any finite model M of I, the extension of Q relative to M, $[\![Q]\!]^M$, is finite.*

Negation-like operators such as $\ominus$ have the potential to compromise safety if their usage is not restricted adequately. For example, imagine that we had a unary negation operator $\ominus_u$ and the create clause for some commitment were simply $\ominus_u E$ (assume E is Base). This would amount to considering created infinitely many commitment instances, one for each E instance that is *not* present in $[\![E]\!]$. A technique that is commonly employed to avoid such conclusions is to guard such negation-like operators, as we do in Custard: $\ominus$ is a binary operator, the extension of whose left operand circumscribes the extension of its right operand. Theorem 2 and its proof sketch below capture the foregoing discussion.

THEOREM 2. *Let Q be any Expr expression in Custard. Then Q is safe.*

Proof sketch. The proof is by induction on the height of the syntax tree. The expressions at the leaves represent the base case. We know that they have finite extensions because a finite model defines finite extensions for Base events. Assume finiteness for every expression at height k and show finiteness for every expression at height $k+1$. For brevity, we illustrate only the crucial cases, which involve $\ominus$, as motivated above. Suppose an expression at $k+1$ is $X \ominus E[l, d]$. By the inductive hypothesis, we know that both X and $E[l, d]$ have finite extensions. According to the definition of $[\![X \ominus E[l, d]]\!]$ (D_9), there are two subcases to consider, corresponding to the disjunction. In both cases, though, we are selecting tuples from finite extensions of X and E (specifically, from $E[0, d]$ and $E[0, l]$). Hence, $[\![X \ominus E[l, d]]\!]$ is finite. The other cases involving $\ominus$ are analogous.

4. IMPLEMENTATION

We implemented a Custard compiler in Java using the Eclipse XText language definition and parsing library (version 2.8.3). The compiler reads in one or norm schemas along with an information schema, such as the one in Listing 1, and outputs (1) SQL table creation statements corresponding to the information schema and (2) SQL queries, one for each lifecycle event for each specified norm schema. We adopt the widely used MySQL dialect of SQL. Listing 7 shows some of the table creation statements generated for the information schema in Listing 1.

Listing 7: Generated SQL Create Table statements.

```
CREATE TABLE SentCred (
  hID VARCHAR(10), tpID VARCHAR(10), discID
      VARCHAR(10), credentials VARCHAR(10),
  t DATETIME,
  PRIMARY KEY(discID)
);

CREATE TABLE ReqData (
  hID VARCHAR(10), tpID VARCHAR(10), discID
      VARCHAR(10), reqID VARCHAR(10), request
      VARCHAR(10),
  t DATETIME,
  PRIMARY KEY(reqID)
);

CREATE TABLE Accessed (
  hID VARCHAR(10), tpID VARCHAR(10), reqID
      VARCHAR(10), response VARCHAR(10),
  t DATETIME,
  PRIMARY KEY(reqID)
);
```

For the authorization specification in Listing 3, the compiler generates four SQL queries corresponding to the created, expired, detached, and discharged instances (recall that in our model, authorizations cannot be violated). Listing 8 shows the SQL query that returns the created instances of the authorization at time NOW (the current time). That is, it shows $[\![\text{created } \mathit{DisclosureAuth}]\!]^{NOW}$—rendered into SQL. Although, in the current implementation all queries are automatically evaluated for NOW, we are working on an extension where the user could input a time value. This would allow the user to run retrospective queries such as *How many instances of this authorization were created two months ago?* and hypothetical queries such as *Given the current state of the database, augmented with some hypothetical events, how many instances of DisclosureCom commitments will be violated?*

Listing 8: Generated SQL for created instances of DisclosureAuth.

```
SELECT hID, tpID, discID, credentials, t
FROM (SELECT hID, tpID, discID, credentials, t
      FROM SentCred) AS Query0
WHERE t < NOW();
```

Listing 8 contains a nested SQL query. The query is simple and could be easily rewritten without nesting. Listing 9, which shows the SQL query for the discharged instances of the authorization, is far more complex, and contains several levels of unavoidable nesting. Such a query would be practically impossible to write by hand—which demonstrates the significant practical benefits of Custard.

Listing 9: Generated SQL for the discharged instances. The SQL DATETIME values '1000-01-01 00:00:00' and '9999-12-31 23:59:59' correspond to the 0th and the infinitely distant time instants, respectively, in our implementation. The unit of time is day.

```
SELECT
  hID, tpID, discID, credentials, reqID,
      response, t
FROM
  (SELECT
      hID, tpID, discID, credentials, reqID,
          response,
         GREATEST(Query21.t, Query28.t3) AS t
   FROM
      (SELECT
      hID, tpID, discID, credentials, t
   FROM
      SentCred) AS Query21
   NATURAL JOIN (SELECT
      hID, tpID, reqID, response, t AS t3
   FROM
      (SELECT
      hID, tpID, reqID, response,
         GREATEST(Query30.t, Query32.t4) AS t
   FROM
      (SELECT
      hID, tpID, reqID, response, discID,
          request,
         GREATEST(Query22.t, Query34.t5) AS t
   FROM
      (SELECT
      hID, tpID, reqID, response, t
   FROM
      Accessed) AS Query22
   NATURAL JOIN (SELECT
      hID, tpID, discID, reqID, request, t AS t5
   FROM
```

```
        (SELECT
        hID, tpID, discID, reqID, request, t
    FROM
        ReqData) AS Query23) AS Query34
    WHERE
        Query34.t5 + INTERVAL 0 DAY <= Query22.t
            AND Query22.t < '9999-12-31 23:59:59')
                AS Query30
    NATURAL JOIN (SELECT
        hID, tpID, reqID, response, t AS t4
    FROM
        (SELECT
        hID, tpID, reqID, response, discID,
            request,
            GREATEST(Query22.t, Query36.t6) AS t
    FROM
        (SELECT
        hID, tpID, reqID, response, t
    FROM
        Accessed) AS Query22
    NATURAL JOIN (SELECT
        hID, tpID, discID, reqID, request, t AS t6
    FROM
        (SELECT
        hID, tpID, discID, reqID, request, t
    FROM
        ReqData) AS Query24) AS Query36
    WHERE
        '1000-01-01 00:00:00' <= Query22.t
            AND Query22.t < Query36.t6 + INTERVAL
                10 DAY) AS Query31) AS Query32) AS
                Query25) AS Query28) AS Query26
WHERE
    t < NOW();
```

5. DISCUSSION

Custard is a language for specifying norms over low-level information schemas and evaluating norm instances over information stores. Custard supports subtle features that are important in real-world settings, such as nonoccurrence of events, nesting, and aggregation. Custard's novelty lies not only in that it raises norm specifications to the level of information schemas but also in how it describes a general approach to formalizing norm lifecycles. Specifically, our formalization can readily support alternative semantics for norm lifecycles—for example, considering an authorization as violated when its consequent occurs without the antecedent having occurred. The implementation of Custard to generate SQL queries is evidence of its practical value in combating complexity. SQL queries corresponding to even a simple norm turn out to complex, running in tens of lines. Thus Custard offer benefits in dealing with complexity by saving a modeler significant effort.

Custard follows a recent trend toward increasingly explicit information modeling in commitments [10, 27]. It is specifically informed by advances reported in Cupid [10], which presents an information-based language for commitments. Whereas Custard adopts Cupid's basic style and approach, it goes significantly beyond Cupid in expressiveness. Cupid supports only commitments and does not support aggregation. Cupid formulates the query extensions in terms of relational algebra whereas Custard defines them in terms of the TRC, which yields cleaner and more direct set-based formulations. The formulation and proof of stability (over model expansions) is novel to Custard.

Norms are widely studied in multiagent systems from different perspectives. Custard leverages work on first-order event-based representations of commitments and, more generally, norms [4, 25, 39, 40, 43]. These representations often emphasize different aspects, for example, reasoning about operations on norms, richer content, and deadlines. Through being first order, these approaches naturally support distinguishing norm schemas and instances. Where Custard goes beyond existing languages is in bringing together important modeling concerns in a single expressive language with a clear information-based semantics. Features such as nesting and aggregation are not supported in any of the existing languages.

Custard may be applied toward specifying security policies. There is a significant conceptual difference from traditional approaches for specifying security policies, for instance, in languages such as XACML [28]. In such languages, one specifies the actions to be taken by the computer system upon a security-pertinent event ("obligations") or the actions that must be blocked by the system ("prohibitions"). In other words, the policies are implemented and executed by the computer system. These approaches are not sociotechnical in that they do not represent or reason about any of the social aspects. Specifically, they talk about computer systems and not sociotechnical systems. By contrast, with Custard, one may capture requirements via norms among autonomous agents. Custard leaves it to each agent, in light of its autonomy, to decide whether to satisfy or violate a norm. Singh emphasizes these distinctions, crucial for achieving secure collaboration, in greater depth in recent work on norms and cybersecurity [36, 37].

In the literature on normative multiagent system, important overlapping themes relevant to Custard concern (1) modeling institutions and contracts [4, 22, 24]; (2) how to develop sociotechnical system specifications given stakeholder requirements [8, 12] and a low-level information schema; (3) protocol specifications specified in information-based languages such as BSPL [34, 35]; (4) formulating alignment of commitment states across asynchronously communicating autonomous agents [9, 11]; (5) norm reasoning and conflicts [17, 29, 42]; (6) monitoring and reasoning about agent compliance with norms [1, 26, 41]; and (7) programming norm-aware intelligent agents that reason about norms in deciding upon a course of action [2, 6, 13, 21, 23, 25, 41].

Future Work. Custard represents an initial effort to represent norms in an information-oriented framework. It opens up many interesting directions of work. These include improvements to Custard to accommodate valuable ideas from the literature as well as enhancements to address particular needs of real-life problems, such as in healthcare or business.

The following are some particularly important and interesting directions for future research. One, formalizing norms in higher-level database logics, such as 4QL, which are beginning to be applied in settings of collaborative agents [14] as well as defeasible reasoning. Two, extending Custard to enable capturing settings where there is uncertainty associated with the occurrence of events [38] and therefore the states of the norm instances. Three, developing an enhanced agent-oriented API to support runtime monitoring of norms and their incorporation in the agent deliberation cycle. Four, creating a catalog of norm patterns that arise in real-life settings and attempting to encode them in Custard. This exercise would point to directions in which Custard would need to be extended. Five, developing a tool-supported methodology for writing Custard specifications, including well-formedness criteria for specifications, for example, relating to the specification of time intervals and keys. Six, relating Custard specifications to alignment for ensuring that multiple Custard stores remain adequately synchronized.

Acknowledgments

We thank the anonymous reviewers for their helpful comments on a previous version of this paper. Munindar Singh thanks the US Department of Defense for partial support under the Science of Security Lablet.

REFERENCES

[1] N. Alechina, N. Bulling, M. Dastani, and B. Logan. Practical run-time norm enforcement with bounded lookahead. In *Proceedings of the 14th International Conference on Autonomous Agents and Multiagent Systems*, pages 443–451. IFAAMAS, 2015.

[2] N. Alechina, M. Dastani, and B. Logan. Programming norm-aware agents. In *Proceedings of the 11th International Conference on Autonomous Agents and Multiagent Systems (AAMAS)*, pages 1057–1064, Valencia, 2012. IFAAMAS.

[3] G. E. M. Anscombe. On brute facts. *Analysis*, 18(3):69–72, Jan. 1958.

[4] A. Artikis, M. J. Sergot, and J. V. Pitt. Specifying norm-governed computational societies. *ACM Transactions on Computational Logic*, 10(1):1:1–1:42, Jan. 2009.

[5] J. L. Austin. *How to Do Things with Words*. Clarendon Press, Oxford, 1962.

[6] M. Baldoni, C. Baroglio, and F. Capuzzimati. A commitment-based infrastructure for programming socio-technical systems. *ACM Transactions on Internet Technologies*, 14(4):23:1–23:23, Dec. 2014.

[7] A. K. Chopra, A. Artikis, J. Bentahar, M. Colombetti, F. Dignum, N. Fornara, A. J. I. Jones, M. P. Singh, and P. Yolum. Research directions in agent communication. *ACM Transactions on Intelligent Systems and Technology (TIST)*, 42(2):20:1–20:23, Mar. 2013.

[8] A. K. Chopra, F. Dalpiaz, F. B. Aydemir, P. Giorgini, J. Mylopoulos, and M. P. Singh. Protos: Foundations for engineering innovative sociotechnical systems. In *Proceedings of the 18th IEEE International Requirements Engineering Conference (RE)*, pages 53–62, Karlskrona, Sweden, Aug. 2014. IEEE Computer Society.

[9] A. K. Chopra and M. P. Singh. Multiagent commitment alignment. In *Proceedings of the 8th International Conference on Autonomous Agents and MultiAgent Systems (AAMAS)*, pages 937–944, Budapest, May 2009. IFAAMAS.

[10] A. K. Chopra and M. P. Singh. Cupid: Commitments in relational algebra. In *Proceedings of the 29th Conference on Artificial Intelligence (AAAI)*, pages 2052–2059, Austin, Texas, Jan. 2015. AAAI Press.

[11] A. K. Chopra and M. P. Singh. Generalized commitment alignment. In *Proceedings of the 14th International Conference on Autonomous Agents and MultiAgent Systems (AAMAS)*, pages 453–461, Istanbul, May 2015. IFAAMAS.

[12] A. K. Chopra and M. P. Singh. From social machines to social protocols: Software engineering foundations for sociotechnical systems. In *Proceedings of the 25th International World Wide Web Conference*, pages 1–12, Montréal, Apr. 2016. ACM.

[13] F. Dignum. Autonomous agents with norms. *Artificial Intelligence and Law*, 7(1):69–79, Mar. 1999.

[14] B. Dunin-Kęplicz and A. Strachocka. Tractable inquiry in information-rich environments. In *Proceedings of the 24th International Joint Conference on Artificial Intelligence*, pages 281–300, Buenos Aires, Aug. 2015.

[15] R. Elmasri and S. B. Navathe. *Fundamentals of Database Systems*. Benjamin Cummings, 2nd edition, 1994.

[16] D. Fitzpatrick. Searle and collective intentionality: The self-defeating nature of internalism with respect to social facts. *American Journal of Economics and Sociology*, 62(1):45–66, Jan. 2003.

[17] K. V. Hindriks and M. B. V. Riemsdijk. A real-time semantics for norms with deadlines. In *Proceedings of the 12th International Conference on Autonomous agents and Multiagent Systems*, pages 507–514, St. Paul, Minnesota, 2013. IFAAMAS.

[18] HL7. Consent directive use cases. http://wiki.hl7.org/index.php?title=Consent_Directive_Use_Cases.

[19] W. N. Hohfeld. *Fundamental Legal Conceptions as Applied in Judicial Reasoning and other Legal Essays*. Yale University Press, New Haven, Connecticut, 1919. A 1919 printing of articles from 1913.

[20] A. J. I. Jones and M. J. Sergot. On the characterisation of law and computer systems: The normative systems perspective. In J.-J. C. Meyer and R. J. Wieringa, editors, *Deontic Logic in Computer Science: Normative System Specification*, chapter 12, pages 275–307. John Wiley and Sons, Chichester, UK, 1993.

[21] Ö. Kafalı, A. Günay, and P. Yolum. GOSU: Computing goal support with commitments in multiagent systems. In *Proceedings of 21st European Conference on Artificial Intelligence*, pages 477–482, 2014.

[22] T. C. King, T. Li, M. D. Vos, V. Dignum, C. M. Jonker, J. Padget, and M. B. van Riemsdijk. A framework for institutions governing institutions. In *Proceedings of the 14th International Conference on Autonomous Agents and Multiagent Systems*, pages 473–481. IFAAMAS, 2015.

[23] F. Meneguzzi and M. Luck. Norm-based behaviour modification in BDI agents. In *Proceedings of the 8th International Conference on Autonomous Agents and Multiagent Systems*, pages 177–184. IFAAMAS, 2009.

[24] F. Meneguzzi, S. Miles, M. Luck, C. Holt, and M. Smith. Electronic contracting in aircraft aftercare: A case study. In *Proceedings of the 7th International Conference on Autonomous Agents and Multiagent Systems (AAMAS) Industry Track*, pages 63–70, Estoril, Portugal, May 2008. IFAAMAS.

[25] F. Meneguzzi, P. R. Telang, and M. P. Singh. A first-order formalization of commitments and goals for planning. In *Proceedings of the 27th Conference on Artificial Intelligence (AAAI)*, pages 697–703, Bellevue, Washington, July 2013. AAAI Press.

[26] S. Modgil, N. Oren, N. Faci, F. Meneguzzi, S. Miles, and M. Luck. Monitoring compliance with E-contracts and norms. *Artificial Intelligence and Law*, 23(2):161–196, 2015.

[27] M. Montali, D. Calvanese, and G. D. Giacomo. Verification of data-aware commitment-based multiagent system. In *Proceedings of the 13th International Conference on Autonomous Agents and Multiagent Systems*, pages 157–164, Paris, May 2014. IFAAMAS.

[28] OASIS. eXtensible Access Control Markup Language (XACML) version 3.0 specification document. *OASIS Standard*, Aug. 2010. http://docs.oasis-open.org/xacml/3.0/xacml-3.0-core-spec-cs-01-en.pdf.

[29] A. Rotolo, G. Governatori, and G. Sartor. Deontic defeasible reasoning in legal interpretation: Two options for modelling interpretive arguments. In *Proceedings of the 15th International Conference on Artificial Intelligence and Law*, pages 99–108. ACM, 2015.

[30] M. Sbisá. How to read Austin. *Pragmatics*, 17(3):461–473, Sept. 2007.

[31] J. R. Searle. *The Construction of Social Reality*. Free Press, New York, 1995.

[32] M. P. Singh. Agent communication languages: Rethinking the principles. *IEEE Computer*, 31(12):40–47, Dec. 1998.

[33] M. P. Singh. An ontology for commitments in multiagent systems: Toward a unification of normative concepts. *Artificial Intelligence and Law*, 7(1):97–113, Mar. 1999.

[34] M. P. Singh. Information-driven interaction-oriented programming: BSPL, the Blindingly Simple Protocol Language. In *Proceedings of the 10th International Conference on Autonomous Agents and MultiAgent Systems (AAMAS)*, pages 491–498, Taipei, May 2011. IFAAMAS.

[35] M. P. Singh. Semantics and verification of information-based protocols. In *Proceedings of the 11th International Conference on Autonomous Agents and MultiAgent Systems (AAMAS)*, pages 1149–1156, Valencia, Spain, June 2012.

[36] M. P. Singh. Norms as a basis for governing sociotechnical systems. *ACM Transactions on Intelligent Systems and Technology (TIST)*, 5(1):21:1–21:23, Dec. 2013.

[37] M. P. Singh. Cybersecurity as an application domain for multiagent systems. In *Proceedings of the 14th International Conference on Autonomous Agents and MultiAgent Systems (AAMAS)*, pages 1207–1212, Istanbul, May 2015. IFAAMAS. Blue Sky Ideas Track.

[38] A. Skarlatidis, A. Artikis, J. Filippou, and G. Paliouras. A probabilistic logic programming event calculus. *Theory and Practice of Logic Programming*, 15(02):213–245, 2015.

[39] N. A. M. Tinnemeier, M. Dastani, and J.-J. C. Meyer. Programming norm change. In *Proceedings of the 9th International Conference on Autonomous Agents and MultiAgent Systems (AAMAS)*, pages 957–964, Toronto, 2010. IFAAMAS.

[40] P. Torroni, F. Chesani, P. Mello, and M. Montali. Social commitments in time: Satisfied or compensated. In *Proceedings of the 7th International Workshop on Declarative Agent Languages and Technologies (DALT)*, volume 5948 of *Lecture Notes in Computer Science*, pages 228–243. Springer, 2009.

[41] M. B. van Riemsdijk, L. A. Dennis, M. Fisher, and K. V. Hindriks. Agent reasoning for norm compliance: A semantic approach. In *Proceedings of the International Conference on Autonomous Agents and Multiagent Systems*, pages 499–506. IFAAMAS, 2013.

[42] W. W. Vasconcelos, M. J. Kollingbaum, and T. J. Norman. Normative conflict resolution in multi-agent systems. *Journal of Autonomous Agents and Multi-Agent Systems (JAAMAS)*, 19(2):124–152, Oct. 2009.

[43] P. Yolum and M. P. Singh. Flexible protocol specification and execution: Applying event calculus planning using commitments. In *Proceedings of the 1st International Joint Conference on Autonomous Agents and MultiAgent Systems (AAMAS)*, pages 527–534, Bologna, July 2002. ACM Press.

Ethical Judgment of Agents' Behaviors in Multi-Agent Systems

Nicolas Cointe
Institut Henri Fayol, EMSE
LabHC, UMR CNRS 5516
F-42000, Saint-Etienne, France
nicolas.cointe@emse.fr

Grégory Bonnet
Normandie University
GREYC, CNRS UMR 6072
F-14032 Caen, France
gregory.bonnet@unicaen.fr

Olivier Boissier
Institut Henri Fayol, EMSE
LabHC, UMR CNRS 5516
F-42000, Saint-Etienne, France
olivier.boissier@emse.fr

ABSTRACT

The increasing use of multi-agent technologies in various areas raises the necessity of designing agents that judge ethical behaviors in context. This is why several works integrate ethical concepts in agents' decision making processes. However, those approaches consider mainly an agent-centered perspective, letting aside the fact that agents are in interaction with other artificial agents or human beings that can use other ethical concepts. In this article, we address the problem of producing ethical behaviors from a multi-agent perspective. To this end, we propose a model of ethical judgment an agent can use in order to judge the ethical dimension of both its own behavior and the other agents' behaviors. This model is based on a rationalist and explicit approach that distinguishes theory of good and theory of right. A proof-of-concept implemented in Answer Set Programming and based on a simple scenario is given to illustrate those functionalities.

General Terms

Theory

Keywords

Multi-Agent Systems, Ethical Judgment, Computational Ethics

1. INTRODUCTION

The increasing presence of autonomous agents in various fields as health care, high-frequency trading, transportation and so on, may rise many issues if these agents are not able to consider and follow some rules, and adapt their behavior. These rules can be some simple constraints as a communication protocol or prohibition of certain behaviors, or some more complex ones as preferences of the user or the description of a code of deontology. For instance, the understanding of codes of conduct may ease the cooperation between a practitioner and a medical agent or a patient, considering some concepts as medical secrecy or dignity respect. Even if some works propose implementations of action restrictions [34], simple prohibitions or obligations [7], some codes of conducts use more complex notions such as moral values or ethical principles, and need further work. An explicit implementation of such concepts, like generosity or altruism, needs specific structures and processes in the architecture of the agent. Consequently, the interest in designing ethical autonomous agents has recently been raised in the Artificial Intelligence community [29] as highlighted by numerous articles [20, 23, 25, 26] and conferences[1]. However, all these works consider ethics in an individual – single-agent – point of view whereas numerous real-world applications such as transportation or high-frequency trading involve multiple agents, enforcing the need to consider the collective – multi-agent – point of view.

An individual point of view can be enough for an agent to act ethically within an agent organization. However, to evaluate the behavior of another agent (e.g. to collaborate with or to punish), agents need to be able to judge the ethics of the others. In this article, we are interested in the question of ethical judgment, i.e. the assessment of appropriateness or not of agents' behavior with respect to moral convictions and ethical principles. We propose a generic model for the judgment of behaviors that can be used by an agent both to decide on its behavior and to judge the behavior of others.

The remainder of the article is organized as follows. Section 2 introduces some key concepts of moral philosophy and a short state of the art on common approaches in computational ethics. We detail in Section 3 our ethical judgment model. Section 4 then illustrates the use of this model by an agent while interacting with other agents. Section 5 offers a proof of concept in ASP (Answer Set Programming). We compare our work to existing approaches in Section 6 and conclude in Section 7 by pointing out the importance of computational ethics for multi-agent systems, and by giving some perspectives about the next steps of our work.

2. ETHICS AND AUTONOMOUS AGENTS

We introduce first in Section 2.1 moral philosophy concepts on which we base our approach and review in section 2.2 existing autonomous agent architectures that propose ethical behaviors. Finally, Section 2.3 points out the principles of our approach.

Appears in: *Proceedings of the 15th International Conference on Autonomous Agents and Multiagent Systems (AAMAS 2016), J. Thangarajah, K. Tuyls, C. Jonker, S. Marsella (eds.), May 9–13, 2016, Singapore.*

[1]Symposium on Roboethics - www.roboethics.org, International Conference on Computer Ethics and Philosophical Enquiry - philevents.org/event/show/15670, Workshop on AI and Ethics, AAAI conference - www.cse.unsw.edu.au/~tw/aiethics, International Conference on AI and Ethics - wordpress.csc.liv.ac.uk/va/2015/02/16/.

2.1 Moral philosophy concepts

From ancient philosophers to recent works in neurology [10] and cognitive sciences [16], many studies have been interested in the capability of human beings to define and distinguish between the fair, rightful and good options and the invidious, iniquitous and evil options. From the various discussions in moral philosophy on concepts like *morals*, *ethics*, *judgment* or *values*, we consider the following definitions:

Definition 1. Morals consists in a set of moral rules which describes the compliance of a given behavior with mores, values and usages of a group or a single person. These rules associate a good or bad value to some combinations of actions and contexts. They could be specific or universal, i.e. related or not to a period, a place, a folk, a community, etc.

Everyone knows many moral rules as "Lying is evil", "Being loyal is good" or "Cheating is bad". This kind of rules grounds our ability to distinguish between good and evil. Morals can be distinguished from law and legal systems in the sense that there is not explicit penalties, officials and written rules [15].

Moral rules are often supported and justified by some moral values (e.g. freedom, benevolence, wisdom, conformity). Psychologists, sociologists and anthropologists almost agree that moral values are central in the evaluation of actions, people and events [31].

A set of moral rules and moral values establishes a *theory of the good* which allows humans to assess the goodness or badness of a behavior and *theories of the right* which define some criteria to recognize a fair or, at least, acceptable option (also respectively named *theory of values* and *theories of right conduct* [32]). For example even if stealing can be considered as immoral (regarding a theory of the good), some philosophers agree that it is acceptable for a starving orphan to rob an apple in a supermarket (regarding a theory of the right). Humans commonly accept many situations where it is right and fair to satisfy needs or desires, even if it is not acceptable from a set of moral rules and values. The description of this conciliation is called *ethics* and, relying on some philosophers as Paul Ricoeur [28], we admit the following definition:

Definition 2. Ethics is a normative practical philosophical discipline of how humans should act and be toward the others. Ethics uses *ethical principles* to conciliate morals, desires and capacities of the agent.

Philosophers proposed various ethical principles, such as Kant's Categorical Imperative [18] or Thomas Aquinas' Doctrine of Double Effect [24], which are sets of rules that allow to distinguish an ethical option from a set of possible options. Traditionally, three major approaches are considered in the literature:

- **Virtue ethics**, where an agent is ethical if and only if he[2] acts and thinks according to some values as wisdom, bravery, justice, and so on [17].
- **Deontological ethics**, where an agent is ethical if and only if he respects obligations and permissions related to possible situations [2].
- **Consequentialist ethics**, where an agent is ethical if and only if he weighs the morality of the consequences of each choice and chooses the option which has the most moral consequences [33].

[2]In this section, we consider agents in terms of philosophy, not only in terms of computer sciences.

However, in some unusual situations, an ethical principle is unable to give a different valuation (a preference) between two options. Those situations, called *dilemmas*, are choices between two options, each supported by ethical reasons, given that the execution of both is not possible [22]. Each option will bring some regret. Many famous dilemmas, such as the trolley problem [12], are perceived as failures in morals or ethics or, at least, as an interesting question in the human ability to judge ethically and to provide a rational explanation of this judgment. In this article, we consider dilemma as a choice for which an ethical principle is not able to indicate the best option, regarding a given theory of good. When facing a dilemma, an agent can consider several principles in order to find a suitable solution. That is why an autonomous artificial agent must be able to understand a broad range of principles, and must be able to judge which principle leads to the most satisfying decision.

Indeed, the core of ethics is the judgment. It is the final step to make a decision and it evaluates each choices, with respect to the agent's desires, morals, abilities and ethical principles. Relying on some consensual references [1] and our previous definitions, we consider the following definition:

Definition 3. Judgment is the faculty of distinguishing the most satisfying option in a situation, regarding a set of ethical principles, for ourselves or someone else.

If an agent is facing two possible choices with both good and/or bad effect (e.g. kill or be killed), the ethical judgment allows him to make a decision in conformity with a set of ethical principles and preferences.

2.2 Ethics and autonomous agents

Considering all these notions, many frameworks have been developed in order to design autonomous agents embedded with an individual ethics. They are related to *ethics by design*, *ethics by casuistry*, *logic-based ethics* and *ethical cognitive architecture*.

Ethics by design consists in designing an ethical agent by an a priori analysis of every situation the agent may encounter and by implementing for each situation a way to avoid potential unethical behaviors. This approach can be a direct and safe implementation of rules (e.g. the military rules of engagement for an armed drone [4]). Its main drawback is the lack of explicit representation of any generic ethical concepts (as morals, ethics, etc). Moreover, it is not possible to measure a kind of similarity or distance between two ethics by design because they are not explicitly described. As a result, conceiving cooperative heterogeneous agents with different desires and principles, but without an explicit representation of ethics, is difficult and only permits the implementation of a strict deontological principle by a direct implementation of rules.

Casuistry aims first at inferring ethical rules from a large set of ethical judgment examples produced by some experts and second at using these rules to produce an ethical behavior [3]. Even if this approach offers a generic architecture for every application field, the human expertise is still necessary to describe many situations. Moreover, the agent's ethical behavior is still not guaranteed (due to under- or over-learning). The agent's knowledge is still not explicitly described and ethical reasoning is made by proximity and not deduction. Consequently, cooperation between heterogeneous agents with different desires and principles is still difficult.

Logic-based ethics is the direct translation of some well-known and formally defined ethical principles (as Kant's Categorical Imperative or Thomas Aquinas' Doctrine of Double Effect) into logic programming [13, 14, 30]. The main advantage of this method is the formalization of theories of the right, even if theories of good are commonly simply considered as parameters. Consequently, it only permits to judge an option with respect to a single ethical principle.

Finally, *cognitive ethical architectures* consist in full explicit representations of each component of the agent, from the classical beliefs (information on the environment and other agents), desires (goals of the agent) and intentions (the chosen actions) to some concepts as heuristics or emotional machinery [5, 8, 9]. Even this kind of agent is able to use explicit norms and to justify its decisions, explicitly reasoning on other agents' ethics is not implemented.

2.3 Requirements for judgment in MAS

The approaches presented in the previous section propose interesting methods and models to design a single ethical autonomous agent. However in a multi-agent system, agents may need to interact and work together to share resources, exchange data or perform actions collectively. Previous approaches often consider other agents of the system as environmental elements whereas, in a collective perspective, agents need to represent, to judge and to take into account the other agents' ethics. We identify two major needs to design ethical agents in MAS:

- Agents need an explicit representation of ethics as suggested by the theory of mind. Indeed, the ethics of others can only be understood through an explicit representation of individual ethics [19]. In order to express an conciliate as many moral and ethical theories as possible, we propose both to split their representations in several parts and to use preferences on ethical principles. Thus, we propose to represent both theories of the good, split between moral values and moral rules, and theories of the right, split between ethical principles and the agents' ethical preferences. Such representations also ease the agents' configuration by non-specialists of artificial intelligence and ease the communication with other agents, including humans.

- Agents need an explicit process of ethical judgment in order to allow them both individual and collective reasoning on various theories of good and right. According to previous definitions, we consider judgment as an evaluation of the conformity of a set of actions regarding given values, moral rules, ethical principles and preferences, and we propose different kinds of judgment based on the ability to substitute the moral or the ethics of an agent by another one. Thus, we propose that agents use judgment both as a decision making process as in social choice problems [21], and as the ability to judge other agents according to their behaviors.

In the sequel, we describe the generic model we propose to enable agents to judge the ethical dimension of behaviors being themselves or the others.

3. ETHICAL JUDGMENT PROCESS

In this section we introduce our generic judgment architecture. After a short global presentation, we detail each function and explain how they operate.

3.1 Global view

As explained in Section 2.1, ethics consists in conciliating desires, morals and abilities. To take these dimensions into account, the generic ethical judgment process (EJP) use *evaluation*, *moral* and *ethical* knowledge. It is structured along *Awareness*, *Evaluation*, *Goodness* and *Rightness* processes (see components in Fig. 1). In this article, we consider it in the context of a BDI model, using also mental states such as *beliefs* and *desires*. For simplicity reasons, we only consider ethical judgment reasoning on short-term view by considering behaviors as actions. This model is only based on mental states and is not dependent on a specific architecture.

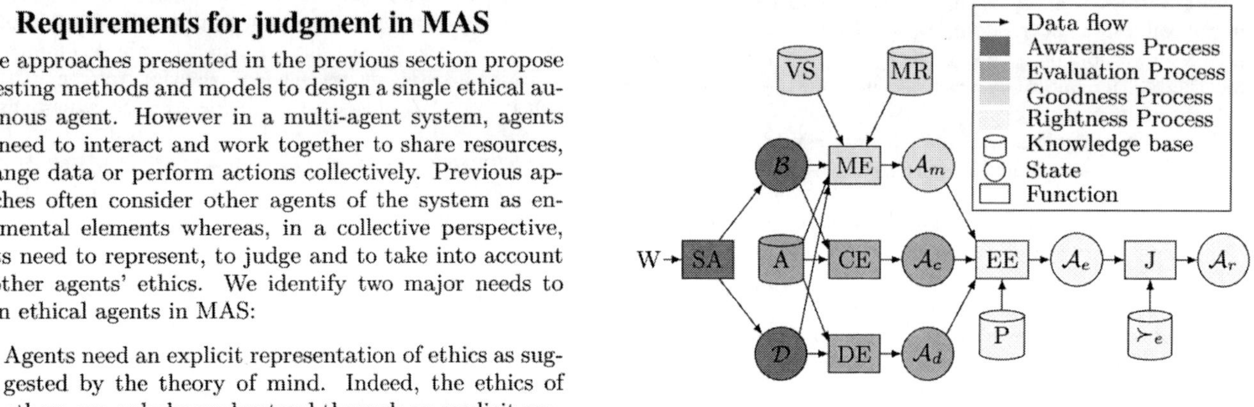

Figure 1: Ethical judgment process

Definition 4. An *ethical judgment process* EJP is defined as a composition of an Awareness Process (AP), an Evaluation Process (EP), a Goodness Process (GP), a Rightness Process (RP), an Ontology $\mathcal{O}$ ($\mathcal{O} = \mathcal{O}_v \cup \mathcal{O}_m$) of moral values ($\mathcal{O}_v$) and moral valuations ($\mathcal{O}_m$). It produces an assessment of actions from the current state of the world W with respect to moral and ethical considerations.

$$EJP = \langle AP, EP, GP, RP, \mathcal{O} \rangle$$

This model should be considered as a global scheme, composed of abstract functions, states and knowledge bases. These functions can be implemented in various ways. For instance, moral valuations from $\mathcal{O}$ may be discrete such as { good, evil } or continuous such as a degree of goodness.

3.2 Awareness and evaluation processes

In this process, agents must first assess the state of the world in terms of beliefs and desires through an awareness process.

Definition 5. The *awareness process* AP generates the set of beliefs that describes the current situation from the world

W, and the set of desires that describes the goals of the agent. It is defined as:

$$AP = \langle \mathcal{B}, \mathcal{D}, SA \rangle$$

where $\mathcal{B}$ is the set of beliefs that the agent has about W, $\mathcal{D}$ is the set of the agent's desires, and SA is a situation assessment function that updates $\mathcal{B}$ and $\mathcal{D}$ from W:

$$SA : W \rightarrow 2^{\mathcal{B} \cup \mathcal{D}}$$

From its beliefs $\mathcal{B}$ and desires $\mathcal{D}$ states, an agent executes the evaluation process EP to assess both desirable actions (i.e. actions that allow to satisfy a desire) and executable actions (i.e. actions that can be applied according to the current beliefs about the world).

Definition 6. The *evaluation process* EP produces desirable actions and executable actions from the set of beliefs and desires. It is defined as:

$$EP = \langle A, \mathcal{A}_d, \mathcal{A}_c, DE, CE \rangle$$

where A is the set of actions (each action is described as a pair of conditions and consequences bearing on beliefs and desires), $\mathcal{A}_d \subseteq A$ and $\mathcal{A}_c \subseteq A$ are respectively the sets of desirable and feasible actions, desirability evaluation DE and capability evaluation CE are functions such that:

$$DE : 2^{\mathcal{D}} \times 2^{A} \rightarrow 2^{\mathcal{A}_d}$$

$$CE : 2^{\mathcal{B}} \times 2^{A} \rightarrow 2^{\mathcal{A}_c}$$

The desirability evaluation is the ability to deduce the interesting actions to perform regarding the desires and knowledge on conditions and consequences of actions. Having defined the awareness and evaluation processes, we can turn now to the core of the judgment process that deals with the use of moral rules (resp. ethical principles) for defining the goodness process (resp. the rightness process).

3.3 Goodness Process

As seen in the state of the art, an ethical agent must assess the morality of actions given a situation assessment. To that purpose, we define the goodness process.

Definition 7. A *goodness process* GP identifies moral actions given the agent's beliefs and desires, the agent's actions and a representation of the agent's moral values and rules. It is defined as:

$$\mathrm{GP} = \langle VS, MR, \mathcal{A}_m, ME \rangle$$

where VS is the knowledge base of value supports, MR is the moral rules knowledge base, $\mathcal{A}_m \subseteq A$ is the set of moral actions[3]. The moral evaluation function ME is:

$$ME : 2^{\mathcal{D}} \times 2^{\mathcal{B}} \times 2^{A} \times 2^{VS} \times 2^{MR} \rightarrow 2^{\mathcal{A}_m}$$

In order to realize this goodness process, an agent must first be able to associate a finite set of moral values to combinations of actions and situations. The execution of the actions in these situations promotes the corresponding moral values. We consider several combinations for each moral value as, for instance, honesty could be both "avoiding telling something when it is incompatible with our own beliefs" (because it is lying) and "telling our own beliefs to someone when he believes something else" (to avoid lying by omission).

Definition 8. A *value support* is a tuple $\langle s, v \rangle \in VS$ where $v \in \mathcal{O}_v$ is a moral value, and $s = \langle a, w \rangle$ is the support of this moral value where $a \subseteq A$, $w \subset \mathcal{B} \cup \mathcal{D}$.

The precise description of a moral value relies on the language used to represent beliefs, desires and actions. For instance, from this definition, generosity supported by "giving to any poor agent" and honesty supported by "avoiding telling something when it is incompatible with our own beliefs" may be represented by:

$$\langle\langle give(\alpha), \{belief(poor(\alpha))\}\rangle, generosity\rangle$$

$$\langle\langle tell(\alpha, \phi), \{belief(\phi)\}\rangle, honesty\rangle$$

where α represents any agent, $poor(\alpha)$ (resp. ϕ) is a belief representing the context for which executing the action $give(\alpha)$ (resp. $tell(\alpha, \phi)$) supports the value *generosity* (resp. *honesty*).

In addition to moral values, an agent must be able to represent and to manage moral rules. A moral rule describes the association of a moral valuation (for instance in a set such as {moral, amoral, immoral}) to actions or moral values in a given situation.

Definition 9. A *moral rule* is a tuple $\langle w, o, m \rangle \in MR$ where w is a situation of the current world described by $w \subset \mathcal{B} \cup \mathcal{D}$ interpreted as a conjunction of beliefs and desires, $o = \langle a, v \rangle$ where $a \in A$ and $v \in V$, and $m \in \mathcal{O}_m$ is a moral valuation described in $\mathcal{O}_m$ that qualify o when w holds.

Some rules are very common such as "killing a human is immoral" or "being honest with a liar is quite good". For instance, those rules can be represented as follows:

$$\langle\{human(\alpha)\}, \langle kill(\alpha), \_\rangle, immoral\rangle$$

$$\langle\{liar(\alpha)\}, \langle \_, honesty\rangle, quite\ good\rangle$$

A moral rule can be more or less specific depending on the situation w or on the object o. For instance "Justice is good" is more general (having less combinations in w or o, thus applying in a larger number of situations) than "To judge a murderer, considering religion, skin, ethnic origin or political opinion is bad". Classically, moral theories are classified in three approaches (refer to Section 2.1). Using both moral values and moral rules as defined above, we can represent such theories.

- A *virtuous* approach uses general rules based on moral values (e.g. "Being generous is good"),
- A *deontological* approach classically considers specific rules concerning actions in order to describe as precisely as possible the moral behavior (e.g. "Journalists should deny favored treatment to advertisers, donors or any other special interests and resist internal and external pressure to influence coverage"[4]),
- A *consequentialist* approach uses both general and specific rules concerning states and consequences (e.g. "Every physician must refrain, even outside the exercise of his profession, any act likely to discredit it"[5]).

[3] $\mathcal{A}_m \not\subseteq \mathcal{A}_d \cup \mathcal{A}_c$ because an action might be moral by itself even if it is not desired or feasible.

[4] Extract of [27], section "Act Independently".

[5] French code of medical ethics, article 31.

3.4 Rightness process

From the sets of possible, desirable and moral actions, we can introduce the rightness process aiming at assessing the rightful actions. As shown in Section 2, an ethical agent can use several *ethical principles* to conciliate these sets of actions.

Definition 10. A *rightness process RP* produces rightful actions given a representation of the agent's ethics. It is defined as:

$$RP = \langle P, \succ_e, \mathcal{A}_r, EE, J \rangle$$

where P is a knowledge base of ethical principles, $\succ_e \subseteq P \times P$ an ethical preference relationship, $\mathcal{A}_r \subseteq A$ the set of rightful actions and two functions EE (evaluation of ethics) and J (judgment) such that :

$$EE : 2^{\mathcal{A}_d} \times 2^{\mathcal{A}_p} \times 2^{\mathcal{A}_m} \times 2^P \rightarrow 2^{\mathcal{E}}$$

where $\mathcal{E} = A \times P \times \{\perp, \top\}$

$$J : 2^{\mathcal{E}} \times 2^{\succ_e} \rightarrow 2^{\mathcal{A}_r}$$

An ethical principle is a function which represents a philosophical theory and evaluates if it is right or wrong to execute a given action in a given situation regarding this theory.

Definition 11. An *ethical principle* $p \in P$ is a function that describes the rightness of an action evaluated in terms of capabilities, desires and morality in a given situation. It is defined as:

$$p : 2^A \times 2^{\mathcal{B}} \times 2^{\mathcal{D}} \times 2^{MR} \times 2^V \rightarrow \{\top, \perp\}$$

The ethics evaluation function EE returns the evaluation of all desirable ($\mathcal{A}_d$), feasible ($\mathcal{A}_p$) and moral ($\mathcal{A}_m$) actions given the set P of known ethical principles.

For instance, let us consider three agents in the following situation inspired by the one presented by Benjamin Constant to counter the Immanuel Kant's categorical imperative. An agent A hides in an agent B's house in order to escape an agent C, and C asks B where is A to kill C, threatening to kill B in case of non-cooperation. B's moral rules are "prevents murders" and "don't lie". B's desires are to avoid any troubles with C. B knows the truth and can consider one of the possible actions: tell C the truth (satisfying a moral rule and a desire), lie or refuse to answer (both satisfying a moral rule). B knows three ethical principles (which are abstracted in P by functions):

P1 If an action is possible, motivated by at least one moral rule or desire, do it,

P2 If an action is forbidden by at least one moral rule, avoid it,

P3 Satisfy the doctrine of double effect[6].

B's evaluation of ethics return the tuples given in Table 1 where each row represents an action and each column an ethical principle.

[6]Meaning doing an action only if the four following conditions are satisfied at the same time: the action in itself from its very object is good or at least indifferent; the good effect and not the evil effect are intended (and the good effect cannot be attained without the bad effect); the good effect is not produced by means of the evil effect; there is a proportionately grave reason for permitting the evil effect [24].

Action \ Principle	P1	P2	P3
tell the truth	$\top$	$\perp$	$\top$
lie	$\top$	$\perp$	$\perp$
refuse	$\top$	$\top$	$\top$

Table 1: Ethical evaluation of agent B's actions

Given a set of actions issued of the ethic evaluation function $\mathcal{E}$, the judgment J is the last step which selects the rightful action to perform, considering a set of ethical preferences (defining a partial or total order on the ethical principles).

To pursue the previous example, let us suppose that B's ethical preferences are P3 $\succ_e$ P2 $\succ_e$ P1 and J uses a tie-breaking rule based on a lexicographic order. Then "refusing to answer" is the rightful action because it satisfies P3 whereas "lying" doesn't. Even if "telling the truth" satisfies the most preferred principle, "refusing to answer" is righter because it satisfies also P2. Let us notice that judgment allows dilemma: without the tie-breaking rule both "telling the truth" and "refusing to answer" are the rightest actions.

4. ETHICAL JUDGMENT OF OTHERS

The judgment process described in the previous section is useful for an agent to judge it's own behavior, namely one action considering its own beliefs, desires and knowledge. However, it can also judge the behaviors of other agents in a more or less informed way by putting itself at their place, partially or not.

Given an EJP defined in the previous section, the states $\mathcal{B}$, $\mathcal{D}$, $\mathcal{A}_d$, $\mathcal{A}_p$, $\mathcal{E}$, $\mathcal{A}_m$ and knowledge of actions (A), goodness knowledge – *theory of good* – (MR, VS) and rightness knowledge – *theory of right* – (P, $\succ_e$) may be shared between the agents. The ontology $\mathcal{O}$ is assumed as common knowledge, even if we could consider in future works having several ontologies. The way they are shared can take many forms such as common knowledge, direct communications, inferences, and so on that are beyond the scope of this article. In any cases, we distinguish three categories of ethical judgments:

- *Blind ethical judgment* where the judgment of the judged agent is realized without any information about this agent, except a behavior,
- *Partially informed ethical judgment* where the judgment of the judged agent is realized with some information about this agent,
- *Fully informed ethical judgment* where the judgment of the judged agent is realized with a complete knowledge of the states and knowledge used within the judged agent's judgment process.

In all kinds of judgment, the judging agent reasons on its own beliefs or those of the judged one. This kind of judgment can be compared to the role of the human theory of mind [19] in the human judgment (the ability for a human to put himself in the place of another). Then, the judging agent uses its EJP and compares the resulting $\mathcal{A}_r$ and $\mathcal{A}_m$ to the behavior of the judged agent. If the action performed by the judged agent is in $\mathcal{A}_r$, it means that it is a rightful behavior, and if it is in $\mathcal{A}_m$, it means that is a moral behavior (being in both is stated as a rightful and moral behavior).

Both statements have to be considered with respect to the context of the situation, the theory of good and the theory of right that are used to judge. We consider that this ethical judgment is always relative to the states, knowledge bases and ontology used to execute the judgment process.

4.1 Blind ethical judgment

The first kind of judgment an agent can make is without any information about morals and ethics of the judged agent (for instance when agents are unable or do not want to communicate). Consequently, the judging agent a_j uses its own assessment of the situation ($\mathcal{B}_{a_j}$ and $\mathcal{D}_{a_j}$)[7], its own theory of good $\langle MR_{a_j}, VS_{a_j}\rangle$ and theory of right $\langle P_{a_j}, \succ_{e,a_j}\rangle$ to evaluate the behavior of the judged agent a_t. This is an *a priori* judgment and a_t is judged as not considering rightful actions, or moral actions if the action $\alpha_{a_t} \notin \mathcal{A}_{r,a_j}$ or $\alpha_{a_t} \notin \mathcal{A}_{m,a_j}$.

4.2 Partially informed ethical judgment

The second kind of judgment that an agent can do is grounded on partial information about the judged agent in case the judging agent is able to acquire parts of the knowledge of the judged agent (e.g. by perception or communication). Three partial ethical judgments can be considered knowing either (i) the situation (i.e. $\mathcal{B}_{a_t}$, $\mathcal{D}_{a_t}$, A_{a_t}) either (ii) the theory of good (i.e. $\langle VS_{a_t}, MR_{a_t}\rangle$) and A_{a_t}[8] or (iii) the theory of right (i.e.$\langle P_{a_t}, \succ_e, a_t\rangle$) of the judged agent.

Situation-aware ethical judgment.

Firstly, if the judging agent a_j knows the beliefs $\mathcal{B}_{a_t}$ and desires $\mathcal{D}_{a_t}$ of the judged agent a_t, a_j can put itself in the position of a_t and can judge if the action α executed by a_t belongs to $\mathcal{A}_{r,a_j}$, considering its own theories. Firstly, a_j is able to evaluate the morality of α by generating $\mathcal{A}_{m,a_t}$ from A_{a_t} and qualify the morality of a_t's behavior (i.e. if α is or not in $\mathcal{A}_{m,a_t}$). The agent a_j can go a step further by generating $\mathcal{A}_{r,a_t}$ from the generated $\mathcal{A}_{m,a_t}$ to check if α is conform to the rightness process, i.e. belongs to $\mathcal{A}_{r,a_t}$.

Theory-of-good-aware ethical judgment.

Secondly, if the judging agent is able to obtain the moral rules and values of the judged one, it is possible to evaluate the actions in a situation (shared or not), regarding these rules. From a simple moral evaluation perspective, the judging agent can compare the theories of the good by checking if moral values MV_{a_t} or moral rules MR_{a_t} are consistent with its own theory of good (i.e. the same definition as a_j's one or at least no contradiction). For a moral judgment perspective, the judging agent can evaluate the morality of a given action from the point of view of the judged one. Interestingly, this judgment allows to judge an agent that has different duties (due to a role or some special responsibilities for instance) as human being can judge a physician on the conformity between its behavior an a medical code of deontology.

Theory-of-right-aware ethical judgment.

Thirdly, let us now consider the case of a judging agent able to reason on ethical principles and preferences of other agents, considering a situation (shared or not) and a theory of good (shared or not)[9]. It allows to evaluate how the judged agent a_t conciliates its desires, moral rules and values in a situation by comparing the sets of rightful actions $\mathcal{A}_r, a_j$ and $\mathcal{A}_r, a_t$ respectively generated by the use of P_{a_j}, $\succ_{e,a_j}$ and P_{a_t}, $\succ_{e,a_t}$. For instance, if $\mathcal{A}_r, a_j = \mathcal{A}_r, a_t$ with an unshared theory of good, it shows that their theories of right produce the same conclusions in this context. This judgment can be useful for an agent to estimate how another can judge it with a given goodness process.

4.3 Fully informed judgment

Finally, a judging agent can consider both goodness and rightness process to judge another agent. This kind of judgment needs information about all the internal states and knowledge bases of the judged agent. This kind of judgment is useful to check the conformity of the behavior of another agent with the judge's information about its theories of good and right.

5. PROOF OF CONCEPT

In this section we illustrate how each part of the model presented in the previous sections works through a multi-agent system implemented in Answer Set Programming (ASP). The complete source code is downloadable on a cloud service[10]. This agent illustrates an example of ethical agent in a multi-agent system where agents have beliefs (about richness, gender, marital status and nobility), desires, and their own judgment process. They are able to give, court, tax and steal from others or simply wait. We mainly focus on an agent named `robin_hood`.

5.1 Awareness Process

In this example, the situation awareness function SA is not implemented and the beliefs are directly given in the program. The following code represents a subset of the beliefs of `robin_hood`:

```
agent(paul).                  -man(marian).
agent(prince_john)            rich(prince_john).
agent(marian).                man(prince_john).
-poor(robin_hood).            noble(prince_john).
-married(robin_hood).         poor(paul).
```

The set of desires $\mathcal{D}$ are `robin_hood`'s desires. In our implementation we consider two kinds of desires: desires to accomplish an action (`desirableAction`) and desires to produce a state (`desirableState`).

```
desirableAction(robin_hood,robin_hood,court,marian).
desirableAction(robin_hood,robin_hood,steal,A):-
  agent(A), rich(A).
desireState(prince_john,rich,prince_john).
-desireState(friar_tuck,rich,friar_tuck).
```

The two first desires concern actions: `robin_hood` desires to court `marian` and to steal from any rich agent. The next two desires concern states: `prince_john` desires to be rich, and `friar_tuck` desires to stay in poverty, regardless the action to perform.

[7]We use the subscript notation to denote the agent handling the represented set of information.

[8]In this case, A_{a_t} is necessary as, contrary to ethical principles, the moral rules can explicitely refer to specific actions.

[9]If both the situation and the theory of good are shared, it is a fully informed judgment (see 4.3).

[10]http://depositfiles.com/files/g2msnfncq

5.2 Evaluation Process

The agents' knowledge about actions A is described as labels associated to sets (possibly empty) of conditions and consequences. For instance, the action give is described as:

```
action(give).
condition(give,A,B):-
  agent(B), agent(A), A!=B, not poor(A).
consequence(give,A,B,rich,B):- agent(A), agent(B).
consequence(give,A,B,poor,A):- agent(A), agent(B).
```

A condition is a conjunction of beliefs (here the fact that A is not poor). The consequence of an action is a clause composed of the new belief generated by the action and the agent concerned by this consequence. The desirability evaluation DE (see Definition 6) deduces the set of actions $\mathcal{A}_d$. An action is in A_d if it was directly desired (in $\mathcal{D}$) or if its consequences are a desired state:

```
desirableAction(A, B, X, C):-
  desireState(A,S,D), consequence(X,B,C,S,D).
```

The capability evaluation CE (see Definition 6) evaluates from beliefs and conditions the set of actions $\mathcal{A}_c$. An action is possible if its conditions are satisfied.

```
possibleAction(A,X,B):- condition(X,A,B).
```

5.3 Goodness Process

In the goodness process, value supports VS are implemented as (for instance):

```
 generous(A,give,B) :- A != B, agent(A), agent(B).
-generous(A,steal,B):- A != B, agent(A), agent(B).
-generous(A,tax,B)  :- A != B, agent(A), agent(B).
```

Then, we can express the agents' moral rules for each ethical approaches (see Sections 2.1 and 3.3). An example of moral rule in a virtuous approach is:

```
moral(robin_hood,A,X,B):-
  generous(A,X,B), poor(B), action(X).
```

The morality evaluation ME gives the set of moral actions $\mathcal{A}_m$ (see Section 3.3):

```
moralAction(A,X,B):- moral(A,A,X,B).
-moralAction(A,X,B):- -moral(A,A,X,B).
```

and produces as results:

```
moralAction(robin_hood,give,paul)
-moralAction(robin_hood,tax,paul)
```

In this example, we only present a virtuous approach. However, examples of deontological and consequentialist approaches are also given in our downloadable code.

5.4 Rightness Process

In order to evaluate each action, we define several naive ethical principles that illustrate priorities between moral and desirable actions. For instance, here is the perfAct (for perfect, i.e. a moral, desirable and possible action) principle:

```
ethPrinciple(perfAct,A,X,B):-
  possibleAction(A,X,B),
  desirableAction(A,A,X,B),
  not -desirableAction(A,A,X,B),
  moralAction(A,X,B),
  not -moralAction(A,X,B).
```

Intention \ Principle	perfAct	dutNR	desNR	dutFst	nR	desFst
give,paul	$\bot$	$\top$	$\bot$	$\top$	$\top$	$\bot$
give,little_john	$\bot$	$\bot$	$\bot$	$\bot$	$\top$	$\bot$
give,marian	$\bot$	$\bot$	$\bot$	$\bot$	$\top$	$\bot$
give,prince_john	$\bot$	$\bot$	$\bot$	$\bot$	$\top$	$\bot$
give,peter	$\bot$	$\bot$	$\bot$	$\bot$	$\top$	$\bot$
steal,little_john	$\bot$	$\bot$	$\bot$	$\bot$	$\top$	$\bot$
steal,marian	$\bot$	$\bot$	$\bot$	$\bot$	$\top$	$\bot$
steal,prince_john	$\bot$	$\bot$	$\top$	$\bot$	$\top$	$\top$
steal,peter	$\bot$	$\bot$	$\top$	$\bot$	$\top$	$\top$
court,marian	$\bot$	$\bot$	$\top$	$\bot$	$\top$	$\top$
wait,robin_hood	$\bot$	$\bot$	$\bot$	$\bot$	$\top$	$\bot$

Figure 2: Ethical evaluation $\mathcal{E}$ of the actions

If paul is the only poor agent, marian is not married and robin_hood is not poor, robin_hood obtains the evaluation given in Figure 2.

All principles are ordered with respect to robin_hood's preferences:

```
prefEthics(robin_hood,perfAct,dutNR).
prefEthics(robin_hood,dutNR,desNR).
prefEthics(robin_hood,desNR,dutFst).
prefEthics(robin_hood,dutFst,nR).
prefEthics(robin_hood,nR,desFst).

prefEthics(A,X,Z):-
  prefEthics(A,X,Y), prefEthics(A,Y,Z).
```

The five first lines describe the order on the ethical principles. The last lines define transitivity for the preference relationship (here perfAct $\succ_e$ dutNR $\succ_e$ desNR $\succ_e$ dutFst $\succ_e$ nR $\succ_e$ desFst).

Finally, the judgment J is implemented as:

```
existBetter(PE1,A,X,B):-
  ethPrinciple(PE1,A,X,B),
  prefEthics(A,PE2,PE1),
  ethPrinciple(PE2,A,Y,C).

ethicalJudgment(PE1,A,X,B):-
  ethPrinciple(PE1,A,X,B),
  not existBetter(PE1,A,X,B).
```

Consequently, the rightful action a_r for robin_hood is give,paul which complies with dutNR.

5.5 Multi-agent ethical judgment

In order to allow a blind judgment, we introduce a new belief about the behavior of another agent:

```
done(little_john,give,peter).
```

Then robin_hood compares its own rightful action and this belief to judge little_john with:

```
blindJudgment(A,ethical,B):-
  ethicalJudgment(_,A,X,C), done(B,X,C), A!=B.

blindJudgment(A,unethical,B):-
```

```
not blindJudgment(A,ethical,B),
agent(A), agent(B),
done(B,_,_), A!=B.
```

In this example, the action give to peter was not in $\mathcal{A}_r$ for robin_hood. Then little_john is judged unethical by robin_hood.

For a partial-knowledge judgment, we replace a part of robin_hood's knowledges ans states by those of little_john. With the beliefs of little_john (which believes that peter is a poor agent and paul is a rich one), robin_hood judged him ethical.

Finally, for a full-knowledge judgment, we replace all the beliefs, desires and knowledge bases of the agent robin_hood by little_john's one. Then, robin_hood is able to reproduce the whole Ethical Judgment Process of little_john and compare both judgments of a same action.

6. RELATED WORKS

We adopt in this article a full rationalist approach (based on reasoning, not emotions) but some other works propose other close approaches [34, 6]. The main specificity of our work is the avoidance of any representation of emotions to be able to justify the behavior of an agent in terms of moral values, moral rules and ethical principles to ease the evaluation of its conformity with a code of deontology or any given ethics.

On the first hand, [6] is an full intuitionistic approach which evaluates plans from emotional appraisal. The values are only source of emotions, and influence the construction of plans by an anticipatory emotional appraisal. In our point of view, values and goals (desires) must be separated because agents must be able to distinguish desires from moral motivations and may explain how to conciliate them.

On the other hand, [34] is a logic-based approach of modeling moral reasoning with deontic constraints. This model is a way to implement a theory of good and is used to implement model checking of moral behavior [11]. However, ethical reasoning is only considered in [34] as meta-level reasoning and is only suggested as the adoption of a less restrictive model of behavior. In this perspective, our work precisely focuses on the need of representing theory of the right as a set of principles to address the issue of moral dilemmas.

7. CONCLUSION

In order to act collectively in conformity with a given ethics an moral, an autonomous agent needs to be able to evaluate the rightness/goodness of both its own behavior and those of the others. Based on concepts in moral philosophy, we proposed in this article a generic judgment ability for autonomous agents. This process uses explicit representations of elements such as moral values, moral rules and ethical principles. We illustrated how this model allows to compare ethics of different agents. Moreover, this ethical judgment model has been designed as a module to be plugged on existing architectures to provide an ethical layer in an existing decision process. As this judgment process can be used with information on moral values, moral rules, ethical principles and preferences which are shared by a collective of agents, our approach defines a guideline for a forthcoming definition of collective ethics.

Even if this article presents a framework to implement a given ethics and to use it to provide judgment, the model is still based on a qualitive approach. Whereas we can define several moral valuations, there is neither degrees of desires, neither degrees of capability, nor degrees of rightfulness. Moreover, ethical principles need to be more precisely defined in order to capture the various set of theories suggested by philosophers.

Thus, our future works will be first directed towards exploring various uses of this ethical judgment through the implementation of existing codes of conduct (e.g. medical and financial deontologies) in order to assess the genericity of our approach. Secondly, we intend to extend our model to quantitative evaluations in order to assess how far from rightfulness or goodness a behavior is. Indeed, such extension would be useful to define a degree of similarity between two morals or two ethics to facilitate the distinction between different ethics from an agent perspective.

Acknowledgements

The authors acknowledge the support of the French Agence Nationale de la Recherche (ANR) under reference ANR-13-CORD-0006.

REFERENCES

[1] Ethical judgment. Free Online Psychology Dictionary, August 2015.

[2] L. Alexander and M. Moore. Deontological ethics. In Edward N. Zalta, editor, *The Stanford Encyclopedia of Philosophy*. Spring edition, 2015.

[3] M. Anderson and S.L. Anderson. Toward ensuring ethical behavior from autonomous systems: a case-supported principle-based paradigm. *Industrial Robot: An International Journal*, 42(4):324–331, 2015.

[4] R. Arkin. *Governing lethal behavior in autonomous robots*. CRC Press, 2009.

[5] K. Arkoudas, S. Bringsjord, and P. Bello. Toward ethical robots via mechanized deontic logic. In *AAAI Fall Symposium on Machine Ethics*, pages 17–23, 2005.

[6] C. Battaglino, R. Damiano, and L. Lesmo. Emotional range in value-sensitive deliberation. In *12th International Conference on Autonomous agents and multi-agent systems*, pages 769–776, 2013.

[7] G. Boella, G. Pigozzi, and L. van der Torre. Normative systems in computer science - Ten guidelines for normative multiagent systems. In *Normative Multi-Agent Systems*, Dagstuhl Seminar Proceedings, 2009.

[8] H. Coelho and A.C. da Rocha Costa. On the intelligence of moral agency. *Encontro Português de Inteligência Artificial*, pages 12–15, October 2009.

[9] H. Coelho, P. Trigo, and A.C. da Rocha Costa. On the operationality of moral-sense decision making. In *2nd Brazilian Workshop on Social Simulation*, pages 15–20, 2010.

[10] A. Damasio. *Descartes' error: Emotion, reason and the human brain*. Random House, 2008.

[11] L.A. Dennis, M. Fisher, and A.F.T. Winfield. Towards verifiably ethical robot behaviour. In *1st International Workshop on AI and Ethics*, 2015.

[12] P. Foot. The problem of abortion and the doctrine of the double effect. *Oxford Review*, pages 5–15, 1967.

[13] J.-G. Ganascia. Ethical system formalization using

non-monotonic logics. In *29th Annual Conference of the Cognitive Science Society*, pages 1013–1018, 2007.

[14] J.-G. Ganascia. Modelling ethical rules of lying with Answer Set Programming. *Ethics and information technology*, 9(1):39–47, 2007.

[15] B. Gert. The definition of morality. In Edward N. Zalta, editor, *The Stanford Encyclopedia of Philosophy*. Fall edition, 2015.

[16] J. Greene and J. Haidt. How (and where) does moral judgment work? *Trends in cognitive sciences*, 6(12):517–523, 2002.

[17] R. Hursthouse. Virtue ethics. In Edward N. Zalta, editor, *The Stanford Encyclopedia of Philosophy*. Fall edition, 2013.

[18] R. Johnson. Kant's moral philosophy. In Edward N. Zalta, editor, *The Stanford Encyclopedia of Philosophy*. Summer edition, 2014.

[19] K.-J. Kim and H. Lipson. Towards a theory of mind in simulated robots. In *11th Annual Conference Companion on Genetic and Evolutionary Computation Conference*, pages 2071–2076, 2009.

[20] P. Lin, K. Abney, and G.A. Bekey. *Robot ethics: the ethical and social implications of robotics*. MIT press, 2011.

[21] W. Mao and J. Gratch. Modeling social causality and responsibility judgment in multi-agent interactions. In *23rd International Joint Conference on Artificial Intelligence*, pages 3166–3170, 2013.

[22] T. McConnell. Moral dilemmas. In Edward N. Zalta, editor, *The Stanford Encyclopedia of Philosophy*. Fall edition, 2014.

[23] D. McDermott. Why ethics is a high hurdle for AI. In *North American Conference on Computing and Philosophy*, 2008.

[24] A. McIntyre. Doctrine of double effect. In Edward N. Zalta, editor, *The Stanford Encyclopedia of Philosophy*. Winter edition, 2014.

[25] B.M. McLaren. Computational models of ethical reasoning: Challenges, initial steps, and future directions. *IEEE Intelligent Systems*, 21(4):29–37, 2006.

[26] J.M. Moor. The nature, importance, and difficulty of machine ethics. *IEEE Intelligent Systems*, 21(4):18–21, 2006.

[27] Society of Professional Journalists. Code of ethics, September 2014.

[28] P. Ricoeur. *Oneself as another*. University of Chicago Press, 1995.

[29] S. Russell, D. Dewey, M. Tegmar, A. Aguirre, E. Brynjolfsson, R. Calo, T. Dietterich, D. George, B. Hibbard, D. Hassabis, et al. Research priorities for robust and beneficial artificial intelligence. 2015. avaible on futureoflife.org/data/documents/.

[30] A. Saptawijaya and L. Moniz L. Moniz Pereira. Towards modeling morality computationally with logic programming. In *Practical Aspects of Declarative Languages*, pages 104–119. 2014.

[31] S.H. Schwartz. Basic human values: Theory, measurement, and applications. *Revue française de sociologie*, 47(4):249–288, 2006.

[32] M. Timmons. *Moral theory: an introduction*. Rowman & Littlefield Publishers, 2012.

[33] S.A. Walter. Consequentialism. In Edward N. Zalta, editor, *The Stanford Encyclopedia of Philosophy*. Winter edition, 2015.

[34] V. Wiegel and J. van den Berg. Combining moral theory, modal logic and MAS to create well-behaving artificial agents. *International Journal of Social Robotics*, 1(3):233–242, 2009.

Personalised Automated Assessments

Patricia Gutierrez[1], Nardine Osman[1], Carme Roig[2], Carles Sierra[1]
[1]IIIA-CSIC, Campus de la UAB, Barcelona, Spain
{patricia,nardine,sierra}@iiia.csic.es
[2]INS Torras i Bages, L'Hospitalet de Llobregat, Spain
mroig112@xtec.cat

ABSTRACT

Consider a person who needs to assess a large amount of information. For instance, think of a teacher of a massive open online course with thousands of enrolled students, or a senior program committee member in a large conference who needs to decide what are the final marks of reviewed papers, or a buyer in an e-commerce scenario who needs to build up her opinion about products. When assessing a large number of objects, sometimes it is simply unfeasible to evaluate them all and very often one needs to rely on the opinions of others. In this paper, we provide a model that uses peer assessments (assessments made by others) in an online community to approximate the assessments that a particular member of the community would generate given the occasion to do so (e.g. the tutor, the SPC member or the buyer—we refer to this person as the *leader*). Furthermore, we provide a measure of the uncertainty of the computed assessments and a ranking of the objects that should be assessed next. The model, although inspired by human societies is thought to be used in the organisation of agent communities.

Keywords

Trust and reputation, Collective intelligence, Community Assessment, Educational Applications

1. INTRODUCTION

Consider a person who needs to assess a large amount of information. For instance, think of a teacher of a massive open online course with thousands of enrolled students, or a senior program committee member in a large conference who needs to decide what are the final marks of reviewed papers, or a buyer in an e-commerce scenario who needs to build up her opinion about products. When assessing a large number of objects, sometimes it is simply unfeasible to evaluate them all and very often one needs to rely on the opinions of others. In the process of building up one's opinion, there are some questions that need to be answered, such as: How much should I trust the opinion of a peer? What should I believe given a peer's opinion? What should I believe when many peers give divergent opinions? Which objects should I assess next, such that the certainty of my beliefs improves? This paper seeks answers to these questions through the Personalised Automated ASsessment model (PAAS).

PAAS uses peer assessments (assessments made by others) in an online community to approximate the assessments that a particular member of the community would generate given the occasion to do so (e.g. the tutor, the SPC member or the buyer). The computed peer-based assessment of objects aims at matching the perspective/view/opinion of a specific community member. We will call this person the *community leader* or simply the *leader*. PAAS aggregates peer assessments giving more weight to those peers that are trusted by the leader. How much a leader trusts a peer is based on the similarity between her (past) assessments and the peer's (past) assessments over the same objects.[1] When such a trust measure between the leader and a peer cannot be obtained—that is, when no object was assessed by both of them—, an indirect trust measure is built based on the reputation of the peer within the community, where this reputation is computed from the perspective of the leader. That is, the closer the peer's opinions to the leader's opinions the higher her reputation. As such, our objective, differently from most previous approaches, is not consensus building.

Finally, we are also able to provide a measure of the uncertainty of PAAS's computed assessments and a ranking of the objects that should be assessed next by the leader in order to decrease the overall uncertainty of those calculated assessments.

This paper is based on the work carried out in [3]. We take from [3] the idea of biasing evaluations with respect to a leader. However, the method described in this paper is completely new. In particular, our improvements with respect to [3] include: (1) the use of information theory: trust and assessments are represented as probability distributions and not as just ordinal numbers; (2) the use of the Eigentrust algorithm to calculate indirect trust instead of a graph search; (3) the increased efficiency as we do not need to maintain and update a graph of trust relations; and (4) the computation of the uncertainty of the automated assessments generated, helping suggesting which objects should be evaluated next.

This paper is structured as follows. In Section 2 we do a quick review of previous work. In Section 3 we present the model with associated algorithms in Section 4. We experimentally evaluate the model in Section 5. Finally, we conclude in Section 6.

2. RELATED WORK

Previous works have proposed different methods for generating assessments based on peer assessments.

CrowdGrader [1] is a framework which defines a crowdsourcing algorithm for peer evaluation. The authors claim that, when performing evaluations, relying on a single person is often impractical and can be perceived as unfair. Their method aggregates the as-

Appears in: *Proceedings of the 15th International Conference on Autonomous Agents and Multiagent Systems (AAMAS 2016), J. Thangarajah, K. Tuyls, C. Jonker, S. Marsella (eds.), May 9–13, 2016, Singapore.*

[1]We could extend the approach by using semantic similarity and thus using past experiences evaluating *similar* objects. This has been explored in previous works [5, 11] and PAAS could be easily extended to cover this case.

sessments of an assignment made by several students into an overall assessment for the assignment, relying on a reputation system. The reputation of each student (or their *accuracy degree* as they call it) is measured by comparing the student's assessments with the assessments of their fellow students for the same assignments. In other words, the reputation of a student describes how far are her assessments from those of her fellow students. The overall assessment (consensus grade) is calculated by aggregating all student assessments weighted by the reputation of the students providing them. The algorithm executes a fixed number of iterations using the consensus grade to estimate the reputation (or accuracy degree) of students, and in turn uses the updated student's reputation to compute more precise suggested assessments.

PeerRank [13] is based on the idea that the grade of an agent is constructed from the grades it receives from other agents, and the grade an agent gives to another agent is weighted by the grading agent's own grade. Thus, the grade of each agent α is calculated as a weighted average of the grades of the agents evaluating α, and thus the grades of α's evaluators are themselves weighted averages of the grades of other agents evaluating them, and so on. The final grades are defined as a fixed point of an equation, similar to the PageRank method where web-pages are ranked according to the ranks of the web-pages that link to them.

Piech et al [6] proposes a method to estimate student reliability and to correct student biases in an online learning scenario, presenting results over two Coursera courses. They assume the existence of a true score for every assignment, which is unobserved and to be estimated. Every grader is associated with a bias, which reflects the grader's tendency to inflate or deflate her assessments with respect to the true score. Also, graders are associated with a reliability which reflects how close the grader's assessments tend to land near the corresponding true score, after having them corrected for bias. Authors infer the values of these unobserved variables using known approximated inference methods such as Gibbs sampling. The model proposed is therefore probabilistic and is compared to the grade estimation algorithm used on Coursera's platform, which does not take into account individual biases and reliability.

Wu et al [14] investigates consensus building between a group of experts in a trust network. New trust relationships are derived from the trust network and the trust scores of such relationships are calculated using an averaging operator that aggregates trust/distrust values from multiple trust paths in the network. The trust score is used to distinguish the most trusted expert from the group and, ultimately, to drive the aggregation of the individual opinions in order to arrive at a group consensual decision making solution. This work also includes a visual consensus model to identify discordant opinions, to produce recommendations to those experts that are furthest from the group, and to show future consensus status if experts are to follow the recommendations.

Collaborative Filtering (CF) [9] is a classical social information filtering algorithm that recommends content to users based on their previous ratings, exploiting the similarities between the tastes of different users. The basic idea is as follows:

1. The system maintains a user profile, which is a record of the user ratings over specific items.
2. Then, the system computes a similarity measure among users' profiles.
3. Finally, the system recommends items to users with a rating that is a weighted average of the ratings on that item given by other users. The weights are the similarity measures between the profiles of users rating the item and the profile of the user receiving the recommendation.

What is fundamentally different between our PAAS model and these works is that the computation of our automated assessments is tuned to the perspective of a specific community member, a leader. We clarify that our target is not consensus building to provide assessments, but to accurately estimate those unknown assessments *from the leader's point of view*. Furthermore, PAAS aggregates peer assessments giving more weight to those peers that are trusted by the leader. Such trust metrics are built, as we will see shortly, using probability distributions based on the history of past assessments between the leader and his/her peers, rather than using aggregations.

Some models allow agents to adapt the opinions expressed by others when aggregating those to compute an overall trust value. For instance, BLADE [7] is a Bayesian model that enables a buyer agent to interpret the ratings of other buyers (aka advisors) over sellers. Each buyer uses the advisors' ratings to build a model of the evaluation function of the advisor. Then, it adjusts the ratings by comparing the advisor's evaluation function and its own evaluation function. Similarly, HABIT [12] is another Bayesian trust model which builds a two-layer hierarchical model in which the opinions of different reputation sources are represented at the bottom level, and their correlation with the actual trustee's behaviour is computed at the top level. Then, information sources with a low correlation with the actual behaviour are considered unreliable and filtered out from the reputation computation. Similarly to these models, we reinterpret the opinions given by peers. However, in our case, the reinterpretation is made based on the relation between the opinions and a gold standard provided by an opinion leader in the community and not by the observation of actual behaviour. Also, differently from them, we use an approach based on information theory and entropy measures to build trust, where with every new observation the uncertainty of the model decreases.

In the experimental evaluation of our system, we compare PAAS to CF since CF is the only one that biases the final computation towards the opinion of a particular member of the community. Furthermore, CF has been widely adopted by the industry. Typical recommendation services, as the ones provided by Amazon, Youtube or Last.fm, are based on the CF algorithm.

3. THE PAAS MODEL

3.1 Notation and Problem Definition

Let ϵ represent the leader who needs to assess a large set of objects $\mathcal{I}$, and let $\mathcal{P}$ be a set of peers able to assess objects in $\mathcal{I}$.

We define a peer assessment e^{α}_{μ} (also referred to as evaluation or opinion) as an element from an ordered discrete evaluation space $\mathcal{E}$, where $\alpha \in \mathcal{I}$ is the object being evaluated and $\mu \in \{\epsilon\} \cup \mathcal{P}$ is the evaluating peer. We define an automated assessment e^{α}_{-} for object α as a metric (which could be the mean, the median, the maximum, etc.) built from a probability distribution $\mathbb{P}$ over the evaluation space $\mathcal{E}$. We say $\mathbb{P}=\{x_1 \mapsto v_1, \ldots, x_n \mapsto v_n\}$, where $\{x_1, \ldots, x_n\}=\mathcal{E}$ and $v_i \in [0,1]$ represents the value assigned to each element $x_i \in \mathcal{E}$, with the condition that $\sum_{0<i\leq|\mathcal{E}|} v_i = 1$.

For example, one can define the evaluation space of the quality of an English classroom homework as $\mathcal{E}=\{poor, good, excellent\}$. The distribution $\{poor \mapsto 0, good \mapsto 0, excellent \mapsto 1\}$ would represent the best possible assessment, whereas the distribution $\{poor \mapsto 0, good \mapsto 1/2, excellent \mapsto 1/2\}$ would represent that the quality of the homework is most probably between good and excellent, and so on.

Finally, we define $\mathcal{H}$ as the history of all assessments performed, and $\mathcal{O}^{\alpha} \subset \mathcal{H}$ as the set of past peer assessments over the object α.

The ultimate goal of our model is to compute the probability distribution of ϵ's evaluation over a certain object α, given the evaluations of several peers over that same object α. In other words, what is the probability that ϵ's evaluation of α is x given the set of peers' evaluations $\mathcal{O}^\alpha$? Such expectation can be formalized with the following conditional probability: $p(X^\alpha{=}x \mid \mathcal{O}^\alpha)$. To calculate the above conditional probability, we take into account every particular evaluation in $\mathcal{O}^\alpha$. In other words, expectations (or probabilities) are calculated for *each* individual evaluation in $\mathcal{O}^\alpha$, before those expectations are aggregated into $p(X^\alpha{=}x \mid \mathcal{O}^\alpha)$. The probability that ϵ's assessment is x given a particular evaluation $e_\mu^\alpha \in \mathcal{O}^\alpha$ is $p(X^\alpha{=}x \mid e_\mu^\alpha)$ and then, $p(X^\alpha{=}x \mid \mathcal{O}^\alpha)$ is defined as an aggregation of these individual probabilities, where our particular aggregation is presented in Section 3.4.

We base the computation of the individual conditional probabilities on the notion of *trust* between peers built from previous experiences, where trust is understood as the similarity between the assessments made by those peers for the same objects. In other words, our intuition is that we expect ϵ will tend to agree with μ's assessment on an object if her trust on μ is high. Otherwise, ϵ's evaluation will probably be different. To build a trust measure between ϵ and μ we perform a sort of analogical reasoning: if in the past μ gave opinions that were similar to ϵ's opinions to a certain degree (trust), then ϵ is likely to coincide with μ's opinion again now to the same degree.

The remainder of this section is divided as follows. We first describe in detail how the measure of trust between peers is calculated (Section 3.2). Then, we illustrate how to calculate ϵ's assessment of an object α given μ's assessment of α and ϵ's trust on μ's assessments (Section 3.3), that is, we present our approach to calculate the individual probability $p(X^\alpha{=}x \mid e_\mu^\alpha)$. We then illustrate how to combine these probabilities to build the probability distribution of ϵ's assessments given the assessments of several peers (Section 3.4), that is, we present an approach for calculating the probability $p(X^\alpha{=}x \mid \mathcal{O}^\alpha)$. Finally, we provide a measure of the uncertainty of the computed assessments and a ranking of the objects that should be assessed next by ϵ in order to decrease that uncertainty (Section 3.5).

3.2 Step 1. How much should I trust a peer?

ϵ needs to decide how much can she trust the assessment of a peer μ. We base this trust measure on two intuitions. First, if ϵ and μ have both assessed the same object in the past, then the similarity of their assessments for that object can give a hint on how close their judgments/thinking are. When there are no objects evaluated by both ϵ and μ, ϵ would not know how much to trust μ's assessments. Second, and to cover this latter situation, we approximate the unknown trust between ϵ and μ by transitivity over the path with direct trust links between ϵ and μ In the following, we make these two intuitions concrete through two different types of trust relations: *direct trust* and *indirect trust*.

3.2.1 Direct Trust

Direct trust is the trust relation that emerges between two people or two agents that have already assessed the same objects in the past. Our approach is to compute such relation as an aggregation of their evaluations' similarity. For instance, let the set $A_{i,j} = \{\alpha \mid e_i^\alpha, e_j^\alpha \in \mathcal{H}\}$ be the set of objects that have been assessed by agents i and j. Then, different definitions for the direct trust between i and j can be adopted based on different similarity functions over objects in $A_{i,j}$, such as:

- The average of the similarities: $\dfrac{\sum_{\alpha \in A_{i,j}} sim(e_i^\alpha, e_j^\alpha)}{|A_{i,j}|}$
- The conjunction of the similarities: $\bigwedge_{\alpha \in A_{i,j}} sim(e_i^\alpha, e_j^\alpha)$
- The linear correlation between i and j:
$$\frac{\sum_{\alpha \in A_{i,j}} sim(e_i^\alpha, \bar{e}_i) \cdot sim(e_j^\alpha, \bar{e}_j)}{\sqrt{\sum_{\alpha \in A_{i,j}} sim(e_i^\alpha, \bar{e}_i)^2}\sqrt{\sum_{\alpha \in A_{i,j}} sim(e_j^\alpha, \bar{e}_j)^2}},$$
where $\bar{e}_i$, $\bar{e}_j$ are the means of the evaluations performed over the set $A_{i,j}$ by i and j, respectively.

However, when we calculate such aggregations we loose relevant information. For instance, we are not able to tell if j usually under rates with respect to i, if it usually over rates, or neither. We are also not able to tell if the dissimilarities between i and j's evaluations are highly variable or not.

To cope with such loss of information, we will define the direct trust between two peers i and j as a probability distribution $\mathbb{T}_{i,j}$ over evaluation differences built from the historical data of previous evaluations performed by i and j.

Definition 3.1. *We define the* evaluation difference *between two assessments performed by i and j as:*

$$diff(e_i^\alpha, e_j^\alpha) = e_i^\alpha - e_j^\alpha \quad (1)$$

We use the euclidean distance between assessments as the measure of dissimilarity, as it is the most used distance in the literature on similarity in metric spaces. If $diff(e_i^\alpha, e_j^\alpha){=}0$, it means that i and j provide the same evaluation for α. If $diff(e_i^\alpha, e_j^\alpha) > 0$, it means that i *over rates* α with respect to j, if $diff(e_i^\alpha, e_j^\alpha) < 0$, it means that i *under rates* α with respect to j. Note that $diff(e_i^\alpha, e_j^\alpha) \neq diff(e_j^\alpha, e_i^\alpha)$.

When defining $\mathbb{T}_{i,j}$, we are interested in maintaining information about whether a peer under rates or over rates with respect to another peer. As such, the support of the distribution representing i's direct trust on j (i.e. the x-axis of $\mathbb{T}_{i,j}$) consists of the possible evaluation difference values between i and j. Trust distribution $\mathbb{T}_{i,j}(x)$ then describes the probability that i and j would assess an object with an evaluation difference x. Therefore, the distribution $\mathbb{T}_{i,j}(0) = 1$ represents a trust distribution where i *fully* trusts on j's opinion, since the probability that their assessments are the same is 1.

Definition 3.2. *Given a numeric evaluation space $\mathcal{E} = [0, b]$, a* Trust Distribution *is any probability distribution over the differences in $\mathcal{E}$, that is over the interval $[-b, b]$.*

In what follows, we explain how we build direct trust distributions computationally, based on previous experiences. We use an information theory approach where the behavior of the studied phenomenon is modeled by probability distributions which are updated with every new observation. This approach is inspired by [2].

Initially, the direct trust distribution between any two peers i and j is the distribution describing ignorance (i.e. the uniform distribution). Then, whenever j evaluates an object α that was already evaluated by i we update $\mathbb{T}_{i,j}$ as follows:

1. We find the element x in $\mathbb{T}_{i,j}$'s support whose probability needs to be adjusted: $x{=}diff(e_i^\alpha, e_j^\alpha)$.

2. We increase the probability of x in $\mathbb{T}_{i,j}$ as follows:

$$p(X^\alpha{=}x) = p(X^\alpha{=}x) + \gamma \cdot (1 - p(X^\alpha{=}x)) \quad (2)$$

The update is based on increasing the current probability $p(X^\alpha = x)$ by a fraction $\gamma \in [0, 1]$ of the total potential increase $(1 - p(X^\alpha{=}x))$. For instance, if the probability of x is 0.6 and γ is 0.1, then the new probability of x becomes $0.6+0.1\cdot(1-0.6) = 0.64$. We note that the ideal value of γ should be closer to 0 than to 1 so that one single experience does not result in considerable changes in the distribution. In other words, a *single* assessment cannot result in a *significant* change in the probability distribution.

3. We normalize $\mathbb{T}_{i,j}$ by following the entropy based approach of [10]. The entropy-based approach updates $\mathbb{T}_{i,j}$ such that: (1) the value $p(X^\alpha{=}x)$ is maintained and (2) the resulting distribution has a minimal relative entropy with respect to the previous one. In other words, we look for a distribution that contains the updated probability value $p(X^\alpha{=}x)$ and that is at a minimal distance from the previous $\mathbb{T}_{i,j}$:

$$\mathbb{T}_{i,j}(X) = \arg\min_{\mathbb{P}'(X)} \sum_{x'} p(X^\alpha{=}x') \log \frac{p(X^\alpha{=}x')}{p'(X^\alpha{=}x')} \quad (3)$$
$$\text{such that} \quad \{p(X^\alpha{=}x) = p'(X^\alpha{=}x)\}$$

where $p(X^\alpha{=}x')$ is a probability value in the original distribution, $p'(X^\alpha{=}x')$ is a probability value in the potential new distribution $\mathbb{P}'$, and $\{p(X^\alpha{=}x) = p'(X^\alpha{=}x)\}$ specifies the constraint that needs to be satisfied by the resulting distribution.

3.2.2 Indirect Trust

Indirect trust is the trust relation that is deduced between peers when they have not assessed any objects in common and thus a direct trust relation cannot be computed. The notion of indirect trust is inspired in the eigentrust algorithm for reputation management [4]. Eigentrust proposes a reputation system that aggregates the local trust values of users in a peer-to-peer network, based on the notion of transitive trust, that is: a peer i will have a high opinion of those peers who have had a trustworthy behaviour. If they are honest in their behaviour they are also likely to be honest in reporting their local trust values, so peer i is likely to trust them. Local trust values are reported to i by community members. Then, the trust that i places on a peer k is based on the trust values reported by the community members and weighted by the trust i has on each community member.

In eigentrust the transitivity in trust is based on products and additions of positive real numbers. However, in our case we need to define operators to compute the transitive trust distribution from two distributions. That is, what is $\mathbb{T}_{i,k}$ given $\mathbb{T}_{i,j}$ and $\mathbb{T}_{j,k}$. The idea is that differences have to be combined in an additive way. We define this next.

If we want to compute the distance distribution between the leader and a peer α via an intermediary peer β we need to combine the probability distribution representing the evaluation difference between β and α with the probability distribution representing the evaluation difference between the leader and β. Thus, for a difference in opinion x between peers β and α and a difference in opinion y between β and the leader, the overall difference between the leader and α is $z = x + y$, as we are in an ordinal space. When we move to probabilities, we then say that $P(z) = P(x) * P(y)$, as we assume independence between opinions. Following this intuition, we define the combined distance distribution between two peers as follows.

DEFINITION 3.3. *Given Trust Distributions $\mathbb{P}$ and $\mathbb{Q}$ over the numeric interval $[-b, b]$ we define their* Combined Distance Distribution, *noted $\mathbb{R} = \mathbb{P} \otimes \mathbb{Q}$, as:*

$$r(X = x) = \begin{cases} \sum_{x_1+x_2=x} p(X = x_1) * q(X = x_2) & \text{if } x \in (-b, b) \\ \sum_{x_1+x_2\leq -b} p(X = x_1) * q(X = x_2) & \text{if } x \leq -b \\ \sum_{x_1+x_2\geq b} p(X = x_1) * q(X = x_2) & \text{if } x \geq b \end{cases} \quad (4)$$

This operation can be nicely applied to our case of evaluation differences as the transitive trust is nothing else than the aggregation (addition) of the combined probability (product) of given evaluation differences happening.

The $\leq$ and $\geq$ are used to maintain the range of the evaluation distance within the $[-b, b]$ limits. For example, assume $\mathbb{P} = \{0, 0, 1\}$ and $\mathbb{Q} = \{1, 0, 0\}$, over the support (x-axis) [-1,1]. Now assume we need to calculate $\mathbb{R}(-1)$. We say $\mathbb{R}(-1)$ should aggregate the product of the probabilities of $\mathbb{P}(-1)$ and $\mathbb{Q}(0)$ (since $(-1) + 0 = -1$), the product of the probabilities of $\mathbb{P}(0)$ and $\mathbb{Q}(-1)$ (since $0 + (-1) = -1$), as well as the product of the probabilities of $\mathbb{P}(-1)$ and $\mathbb{Q}(-1)$ (since $(-1) + (-1) = -2$, and -2 is outside the limits of the numeric interval of the evaluation distance).

Note that this operator, $\otimes$, is commutative. Its neutral element is the distribution $\mathbb{O}$ for the ideal (or optimal) distribution where the probability that the evaluation difference between two peers is 0 is equal to 1, that is $p(X = 0) = 1$.

The other important operation needed is how to aggregate combined distances calculated from different sources (different peers). In this case, from several distance distributions, we select the one that is closer to $\mathbb{O}$, that is, the one that makes the leader and the student closer in their judgments. In the eigentrust algorithm, this would be equivalent to selecting the maximum combination (modeled as the product of the values in the links) instead of the used weighted sum of all the combinations. We note that other operators could be used here, for instance selecting the distribution with minimum entropy. In the following we define this operator.

DEFINITION 3.4. *Given probability distributions $\mathbb{P}$ and $\mathbb{Q}$ over the numeric interval $[a, b]$ we define $\mathbb{P} \oplus \mathbb{Q}$, as:*

$$\mathbb{P} \oplus \mathbb{Q} = \arg \min_{\mathbb{T}\in\{\mathbb{P},\mathbb{Q}\}} (emd(\mathbb{T}, \mathbb{O})) \quad (5)$$

with emd standing for the earth mover's distance [8].

Note that this operator, $\oplus$, is commutative and associative so the order in which we combine the trust distributions is irrelevant.

Next, we show how we use these operators following a similar approach to eigentrust. First, we store the direct trust distributions between ϵ's peers in a matrix C, where at the position (i, j) we store the current probability distribution between peers i and j: $\mathbb{T}_{i,j}$. We store the indirect trust distributions between the leader ϵ and each community member in a vector t_ϵ, where at each position i we have $\mathbb{T}_{\epsilon,i}$. Initially, t_ϵ contains the probability distributions describing ignorance (i.e. the flat equiprobable distribution $\mathbb{F}$) in all rows. Let us call this initial vector t_ϵ^0. The t_ϵ vector is updated as follows:

$$t_\epsilon^{k+1} = C^T t_\epsilon^k \quad (6)$$

until $\|t_\epsilon^{k+1} - t_\epsilon^k\| < \eta$, where η is a specified threshold to determine that we have reached a fix point. As in the eigentrust algorithm, the trust vector t_ϵ converges after a certain amount of iterations. In this way, the trust that ϵ has on i is built aggregating the direct trust distributions between community members and peer i weighted by the trust (initially ignorance) that ϵ has on each community member. The product between matrix C^T and t_ϵ^k is defined, recalling previous definitions, as follows:

$$t_{\epsilon,j}^{k+1} = \bigoplus_{0<i\leq n} \mathbb{T}_{i,j} \otimes \mathbb{T}_{\epsilon,i}^k \quad (7)$$

Finally, if a direct trust distribution is already built between ϵ and j, $\mathbb{T}_{i,j}$, then after each step of the algorithm, $t_{\epsilon,j}^{k+1}$ is overwritten with $\mathbb{T}_{i,j}$, since we prefer to preserve direct trust distributions, which are built from the history of assessments.

3.2.3 Information Decay

An important notion in our proposal is the *decay* of information. We say the integrity of information decreases with time. In other words, the information provided by a trust probability distribution should lose its value over time and decay towards a default value. We refer to this default value as the *decay limit distribution* $\mathbb{D}$. For instance, $\mathbb{D}$ may be the ignorance distribution, which would mean that trust information learned from past experiences tends to ignorance over time.

Information in a probability distribution $\mathbb{T}$ decays from t to t' (where $t' > t$) as follows:

$$\mathbb{T}^{t \rightsquigarrow t'} = \Lambda(\mathbb{D}, \mathbb{T}^t) \quad (8)$$

where Λ is the *decay function* satisfying the property: $\lim_{t' \to \infty} \mathbb{T}^{t \rightsquigarrow t'} = \mathbb{D}$. One possible definition for Λ could be:

$$\mathbb{T}^{t \rightsquigarrow t'} = \nu^{\Delta_{t,t'}} \cdot \mathbb{T}^t + (1 - \nu^{\Delta_{t,t'}})\mathbb{D} \quad (9)$$

where ν is the decay rate, and:

$$\Delta_{t,t'} = \begin{cases} 0 & \text{, if } t' - t < \omega \\ 1 + \dfrac{t'-t}{t_{max}} & \text{, otherwise} \end{cases}$$

The definition of $\Delta_{t,t'}$ above serves the purpose of establishing a minimum *grace* period, determined by the parameter ω, during which the information does not decay, and that once reached the information starts decaying. The parameter t_{max}, which may be defined in terms of multiples of ω, controls the *pace of decay*. The main idea behind this is that after the grace period, the decay happens very slowly; in other words, $\Delta_{t,t'}$ decreases very slowly.

To implement such a decay mechanism in our model, we need to:

1. Record all evaluations $e_\mu^\alpha \in \mathcal{H}$ made at time t with a timestamp t, noted $e_\mu^{\alpha^t}$.
2. Record all direct trust distributions $\mathbb{T}_{i,j}$ with a timestamp t, noted $\mathbb{T}_{i,j}^t$, where t is the timestamp of the last evaluation that modified the trust distribution (recall that direct trust distributions may be modified when a new assessment occurs). The first time $\mathbb{T}_{i,j}$ is modified, t is the timestamp of the evaluation involved in the modification. Then, every time a new evaluation with timestamp $t' > t$ is considered to update $\mathbb{T}_{i,j}^t$, $\mathbb{T}_{i,j}^t$ is first decayed from t to t' before the distribution is modified.
3. Record all indirect trust distributions $\mathbb{T}_{i,j}$ with a timestamp t, noted $\mathbb{T}_{i,j}^t$. Every time $\mathbb{T}_{i,j}$ is calculated, all probability distributions involved in this calculation will first be decayed to the time of calculation t, which will be the resulting timestamp of $\mathbb{T}_{i,j}$.

3.3 Step 2: What to believe when a peer gives an opinion?

Given a peer assessment e_μ^α, the question now is how to compute the probability distribution of ϵ's evaluation. In other words, what is the probability that ϵ's evaluation of α is x given that μ evaluated α with e_μ^α. As illustrated earlier, this is expressed as the conditional probability:

$$\mathbb{P}(X^\alpha{=}x \mid e_\mu^\alpha)$$

To calculate this conditional probability, the intuition is that ϵ would tend to agree with μ's evaluation if his trust on μ is high (that is, the expected evaluation difference between their assessments is close to 0). Otherwise, ϵ's evaluation would probably be different. We perform then a sort of analogical reasoning: if in the past μ gave assessments with a certain evaluation difference with respect to ϵ, then this will probably happen again now.

We thus calculate the above conditional probability simply as:

$$p(X^\alpha{=}x \mid e_\mu^\alpha) = \begin{cases} \sum\limits_{y \leq diff(x, e_\mu^\alpha)} \mathbb{T}_{\epsilon,\mu}(y) & if\, x = 0 \\ \sum\limits_{y \geq diff(x, e_\mu^\alpha)} \mathbb{T}_{\epsilon,\mu}(y) & if\, x = b \\ \mathbb{T}_{\epsilon,\mu}(diff(x, e_\mu^\alpha)) & otherwise \end{cases} \quad (10)$$

Observe that in two cases the probabilities are computed as the summation of the probability mass of $\mathbb{T}_{\epsilon,\mu}$ for points below or over the difference between the new opinion and the point x under consideration. This is done to cope with the fact that we cannot under rate or over rate more as we are at the extremes already and consider that for instance past cases where we under rated more should be taken into account when we are determining the probability that the leader gives a 0 in the assessment. Similarly for b. For example, assume μ's assessment is 2 when the maximum mark is 3, we are calculating the probability of ϵ's assessment, and ϵ usually over rates μ by 2 marks. The probability of ϵ's assessment being 2 will essentially be $\mathbb{T}(0)$ (since the difference $2 - 2 = 0$). However, the probability of ϵ's assessment being 3, cannot simply be $\mathbb{T}(1)$ (since the difference $3 - 2 = 1$), because it is the maximum value of the evaluation space and so it also needs to consider all the over rating possibilities described by $\mathbb{T}(2)$ and $\mathbb{T}(3)$ as well. As such, the probability of ϵ's assessment being 3 aggregates $\mathbb{T}(1)$, $\mathbb{T}(2)$, and $\mathbb{T}(3)$.

3.4 Step 3: What to believe when many give opinions?

In the previous section we computed $\mathbb{P}(X^\alpha \mid e_\mu^\alpha)$. That is, the probability distribution of ϵ's evaluation on α given the evaluation of a peer μ on α. But what does ϵ do when there is more than one peer assessing α?

Given the set of opinions $\mathcal{O}^\alpha = \{e_{\mu_1}^\alpha, e_{\mu_2}^\alpha, \ldots, e_{\mu_n}^\alpha\}$ of a group of peers over the object α, we define the probability of ϵ's assessment being x as follows:

$$p(X^\alpha{=}x \mid \mathcal{O}^\alpha) = \begin{cases} \bigvee_{i=1}^{n} (\mathbb{I}(\mathbb{T}_{\epsilon,\mu_i}) \cdot p(X^\alpha{=}x \mid e^\alpha_{\mu_i})) & \sum_{i=1}^{n} \mathbb{I}(\mathbb{T}_{\epsilon,\mu_i}) > \delta \\ 1/n & \text{otherwise} \end{cases} \quad (11)$$

where $\vee$ is an operator that combines probabilities assuming the sources are independent:[2] $a \vee b = a + b - a * b$, and $\mathbb{I}(\mathbb{T}_{\epsilon,\mu})$ measures the information content of the probability distribution $\mathbb{T}_{\epsilon,\mu}$ as the earth mover's distance to the ignorance distribution (the uniform distribution $\mathbb{F}$). In other words, the probability of ϵ's assessment being x given the set of opinions $\mathcal{O}^\alpha$ is a disjunction of the probabilities of ϵ's assessment being x given each evaluation $e^\alpha_{\mu_i} \in \mathcal{O}^\alpha$ and diminished by the information content of the evaluation distributions $\mathbb{I}(\mathbb{T}_{\epsilon,\mu_i})$. We diminish the probability derived from a particular opinion when that opinion is actually not very informative and thus very close to ignorance. In the case that most opinions are close to ignorance, $\sum_{i=1}^{n} \mathbb{I}(\mathbb{T}_{\epsilon,\mu_i}) \leq \delta$, the result of such combination might be too close to zero (for a small δ) and thus we prefer to assume ignorance, $1/n$, for the probability value.

Finally, for several purposes (give a mark to a student, rank objects to purchase, ...) it is practical to 'summarise' distributions $\mathbb{P}(X^\alpha \mid \mathcal{O}^\alpha)$ into a number. From the several methods that can be used (centre of gravity, mean, median, ...) in the experiments we use the mode value of the distribution.

3.5 Step 4: What should be evaluated next?

The previous three steps allow to compute assessments of objects that have not been assessed by ϵ, based on peers opinions. The level of uncertainty of the assessments so generated by our method can be calculated as the uncertainty of the probability distribution $\mathbb{P}(X^\alpha \mid \mathcal{O}^\alpha)$. A classical method to measure this uncertainty is the the distribution's entropy:

$$\mathbb{H}(\mathbb{P}(X^\alpha \mid \mathcal{O}^\alpha)) = \sum_{x \in X^\alpha} p(X^\alpha{=}x \mid \mathcal{O}^\alpha) \cdot \ln p(X^\alpha{=}x \mid \mathcal{O}^\alpha) \quad (12)$$

We will explore in the experiments a heuristic that aims at reducing the number of assessments made by the leader. In other words, what object should be assessed next by ϵ in order to maximally decrease the overall uncertainty? For example, what assignments and in which order should a tutor evaluate so that the uncertainty of the computed assessments, i.e. the uncertainty on the students' marks, becomes *acceptable*. The heuristic is simple: we suggest that ϵ evaluates objects by decreasing value of the entropy of their assessment distribution, that is the next object α that the leader should assess is:

$$\alpha = arg \max_{\alpha} \mathbb{H}(\mathbb{P}(X^\alpha \mid \mathcal{O}^\alpha)$$

4. ALGORITHM

In this section we provide the pseudo-code of PAAS, which is a straightforward implementation from the equations defined in Section 3.

Algorithm 1 defines the method to apply when a new assessment is performed. In lines 1-14 direct trust distributions are updated in matrix C and vector t_ϵ, as discussed in subsection 3.2.1. In lines 15-22, indirect trust distributions are updated using the adapted eigentrust method, as discussed in subsection 3.2.2. Algorithm 2 is the method that updates direct trust distributions given a new opinion. Line 1 decays the distribution from time stamp t to t'. Line 2 updates the value in the distribution for the point representing the distance in the observation. Line 3 normalizes this distribution by computing the distribution with minimum relative entropy with respect to the distribution before the observation and that respects the updated value. Algorithm 3 deduces the overall assessment values (i.e. $\mathbb{P}(X^\alpha \mid \mathcal{O}^\alpha)$ after a number of assessments have been made.

[2]This assumption is not very restrictive for the scenarios we are considering: peer assessments in online education or e-commerce as opinions are expressed by people that do not know each other.

Algorithm 1 $newAssessment(e_i^{\alpha^t})$

Require: $\mathcal{H} = \{\}$ ▷ This is the history of assessments
Require: $\mathbb{F}$ ▷ This is a trust probability distribution describing ignorance
Require: t'_ϵ ▷ This is a vector where ϵ's direct trust distributions are stored
1: **for all** $e_j^\alpha \in \mathcal{H}$ **do** ▷ Ordered by their timestamps
2: $diff_{i,j} = e_i^\alpha - e_j^\alpha$
3: $diff_{j,i} = e_j^\alpha - e_i^\alpha$
4: **if** $i = \epsilon$ **then**
5: $updateDirectDistribution(t_\epsilon[j], t, diff_{i,j})$
6: $t'_\epsilon = t'_\epsilon \cup t_\epsilon[j]$
7: **else if** $j = \epsilon$ **then**
8: $updateDirectDistribution(t_\epsilon[j], t, diff_{j,i})$
9: $t'_\epsilon = t'_\epsilon \cup t_\epsilon[j]$
10: **else**
11: $updateDirectDistribution(C_{i,j}, t, diff_{i,j})$
12: $updateDirectDistribution(C_{j,i}, t, diff_{j,i})$
13: **end if**
14: **end for**
15: $t_\epsilon^0 = \mathbb{F}$
16: **repeat**
17: $t_\epsilon^{k+1} = C^T t_\epsilon^k$ ▷ Equations 6 and 7
18: $error = \|t_\epsilon^{k+1} - t_\epsilon^k\|$
19: $t_\epsilon^{k+1} = t_\epsilon^k$
20: $t_\epsilon^{k+1} \leftarrow t'_\epsilon$ ▷ Overwrite distributions for those peers with direct trust
21: **until** $error < \eta$
22: $\mathcal{H} = \mathcal{H} \cup \{e_i^{\alpha^t}\}$

Algorithm 2 $updateDirectDistribution(\mathbb{T}^{t'}, t, x)$

Require: Λ ▷ This is the decay function
Require: $\mathbb{D}$ ▷ This is the default distribution
1: $\mathbb{T}_{i,j}^{t' \leadsto t} = \Lambda(\mathbb{D}, \mathbb{T}_{i,j}^t)$ ▷ Equations 8 and 9
2: $\mathbb{T}(X{=}x) = \mathbb{T}(X{=}x) + \gamma \cdot (1 - \mathbb{T}(X{=}x))$
3: $\mathbb{T}(X) = \arg\min_{\mathbb{P}'(X)} \sum_{x'} p(X{=}x') \log \frac{p(X{=}x')}{p'(X{=}x')}$ such that $\{p(X{=}x) = p'(X{=}x)\}$

5. EVALUATION

We present experiments performed over real data coming from two English language classrooms (30 14-years old students). Two different tasks were given to the classroom: an English composition task and a song vocabulary task. A total of 71 assignments were submitted by the students and marked by the teacher (our leader).

Students assessed their fellow students during a 1 hour period. A total of 168 student assessments were completed by the students (each student assessed on average 2.4 assignments). Marks vary from 1 (very bad) to 4 (very good). Students evaluated different criteria from the assignments: *focus, coherence, grammar* in the composition task and *in-time submission, requirements, lyrics* in the song vocabulary task.

Algorithm 3 $calculateAssessments()$

Require: $\mathcal{I}$ ▷ This is the set of objects to be assessed
Require: $\mathcal{H}$ ▷ This is the history of assessments
$result = \{\}$
for all $\alpha \in \mathcal{I}$ **do**
  if $e^{\alpha}_{\epsilon} \in \mathcal{H}$ **then**
    $result = result \cup e^{\alpha}_{\epsilon}$
  else
    $O^{\alpha} = \{e^{\alpha}_{\mu} | e^{\alpha}_{\mu} \in \mathcal{H}\}$
    $e^{\alpha}_{\_} = \{x | \mathbb{P}(X^{\alpha} = x \mid O^{\alpha}) \text{ is maximum}\}$ ▷ Equations 11 and 10
    $result = result \cup e^{\alpha}_{\_}$
  end if
end for
return $result$

Thus, $\mathcal{E} = \{1, 2, 3, 4\}$, and the x-axis of our trust distributions is $\{-4, -3, -2, -1, 0, 1, 2, 3, 4\}$ (which are the possible evaluation distance values between peers in this setting). We calculate the error of the generated assessments, noted as $e^{\alpha}_{\_}$, as the average difference between them and the tutor assessments, that is:

$$error = \frac{\sum_{\alpha \in \mathcal{I}} \| e^{\alpha}_{\_} - e^{\alpha}_{\epsilon} \|}{|\mathcal{I}|}$$

In addition to the error, we are also interested in plotting the number of deduced assessments. We note that when there is no peer or tutor assessment for a particular assignment, an automated mark for that assignments can not be generated.

In the first experiment where we compare our model with the well known Collaborative Filtering (CF) algorithm [9]. As discussed in Section 2, CF is a social information filtering algorithm that recommends content to users based on their previous preferences. CF biases the final computation towards a particular member: the person being recommended, as our algorithm does.

In this experiment, we randomly select a subset of 6 teacher assessments to use as the leader's opinion in both PAAS and CF (this subset represents 8.4% of the total number of assessments, the rest of teacher assessments are used to calculate the error). Then, several iterations are performed, one for each student assessment. On each iteration:

- One student assessment is selected randomly from the set of student assessments and added to PAAS and CF
- Automated assessments are generated by PAAS and CF and the error is calculated. To calculate the error, our groundtruth is the set of all tutor assessments.

Results are averaged over 50 executions. When an assessment for a particular assignment could not be deduced, a default mark (ignorance) 2 is given, since this value is situated more or less in the middle of the evaluation space. Default marks are used in both PAAS and CF error calculations.

Figure 1 shows the results of PAAS and CF on three cases. As the assignments are different with different evaluation criteria we choose a criterion per group, necessarily different, so that we can have a larger number of assignments in the experiments. Three such pairings of criteria are shown in the figure. It is clear in the three cases the remarkable improvement of PAAS over CF considering the number of final marks generated (see the right column of graphics in the figure). PAAS has an added capability with respect to CF in using indirect trust measures to generate assessments. In CF the opinion of someone without any similarity in her profile with the leader (in our case, without any common assignment being assessed) cannot be used to suggest a recommendation (an assessement). Thus, PAAS is capable of generating many more assessments, specially once the graph of indirect trust relationships becomes more and more connected. This highlights PAAS's first point of strength: *PAAS increases the number of assessments that can be calculated.* On the left, we show the improvement of PAAS over CF in terms of the error with respect to the ground truth that we know (the actual teacher assessments). The error is calculated over the entire set of assignments, including assignments that receive the default mark. This highlights PAAS's second point of strength in outperforming CF: *PAAS decreases the error of the assessments calculated.* We note that when the number of peer assessments increases PAAS and CF's error get closer because the effect of indirect trust diminishes. However, we are much better than CF for a small effort per peer (for instance, think of 5 or 6 assessments per peer instead of hundreds).

We perform a second experiment where we assess the impact of using the heuristic that informs the teacher of which assignment to select next to assess, see section 3.5 for details. In this case, we designed an experiment where we simulate a classroom of 200 students with 200 submitted assignments, where each assignment is evaluated by 5 students (1000 peer assessments performed). To show a critical case, we simulate that half of the assignments are evaluated accurately by half of the students (that is, those students provided the same mark as the tutor) and the other half of the assignments are evaluated poorly (that is, randomly) by the other half of the students. In the simulation, we have two instances of the PAAS model: PAAS Random and PAAS Ranking. First, all the student assessments are added to both instances of the PAAS model. Then, several iterations are performed, one for each tutor assessment. On each iteration:

- We randomly select a tutor assessment for an assignment that has not been assessed yet, and we add this tutor assessment to PAAS Random.
- We select a tutor assessment for an assignment not yet assessed following the suggestion of the entropy heuristic, and we add this tutor assessment to PAAS Ranking.
- Automated assessments are generated by PAAS Random and PAAS Ranking and the error is calculated.

Figure 2 (a) shows the error which of course decreases with every new tutor assessment. We also see how ranking the assessments with the entropy heuristic decreases the error faster. Figure 2 (b) shows the same experiments but with the real data. In this case, there is no clear advantage in ranking assessments over simply assessing randomly. This is an indicator that the students from these two groups where closely aligned with the tutor's opinion. In other words, all the assignments where performed with more or less the same quality (in contrast with the scenario presented in (a) with simulated data). Figure 2 (c) shows the same experiment presented in (b) but in this case the assessments of half of the assignments were overwritten providing a random mark. Such noise introduced, even in this rough manner, produces that the ranking strategy becomes slightly more effective. We also highlight the fact that the error of the PAAS model does not change drastically when noise is introduced, since PAAS is able to distinguish which assessments are trustworthy and which are not very quickly. We conclude from this second experiment that although in some cases, e.g. when the students are good 'recommenders', the heuristic may not be needed, in general it can improve the results when such recommendation quality is missing.

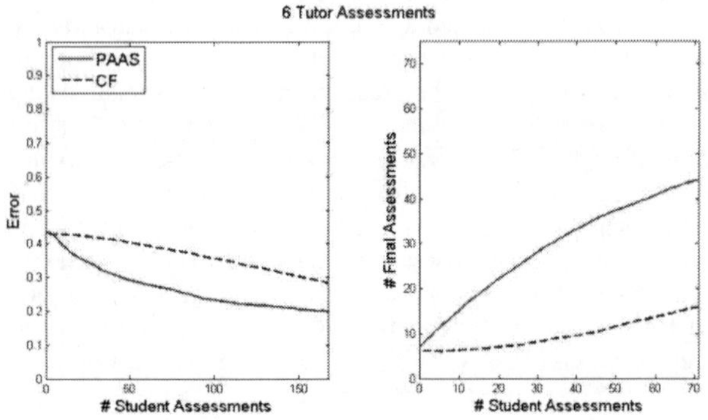

(a) focus and in-time submission criteria

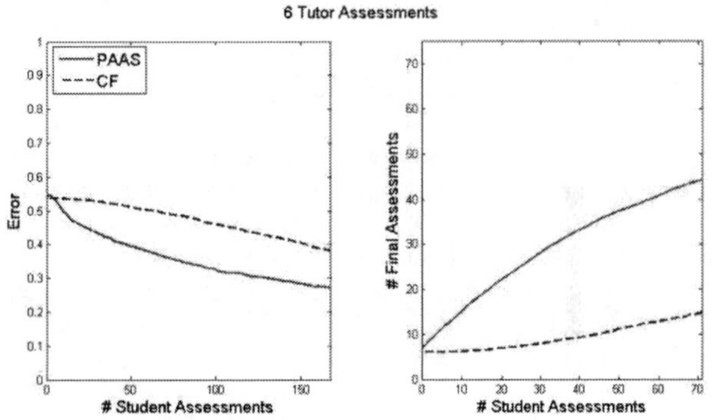

(b) coherence and requirements criteria

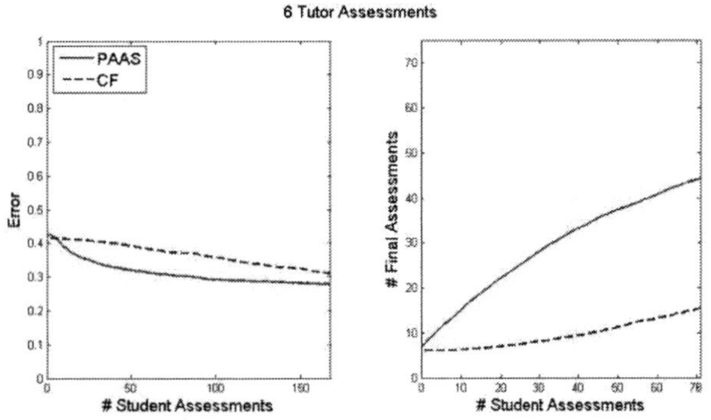

(c) grammar and lyrics criteria

Figure 1: Experiments with Real Data: PAAS vs CF. We show the results for opinions on two criteria, one for each assignment. For instance in (a) we combine opinions on focus in the composition task and submission on time in the song vocabulary task.

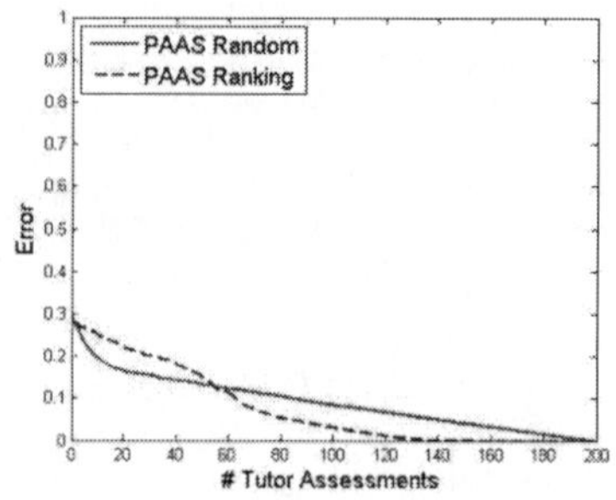

(a) Synthetic data

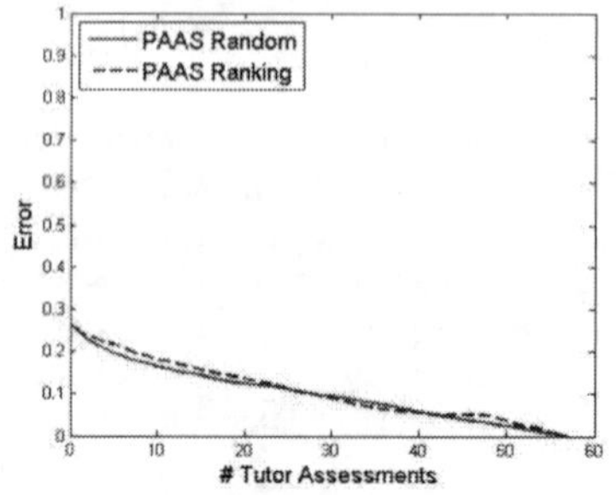

(b) Real data

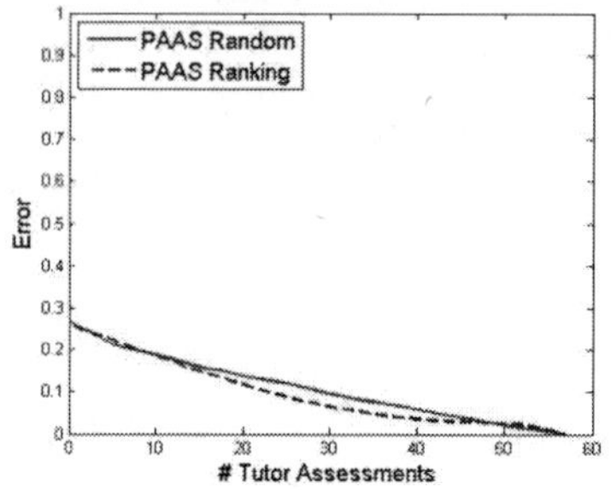

(c) Randomised Real data

Figure 2: Experiments considering the entropy heuristic

6. CONCLUSIONS AND FUTURE WORK

In this paper we have presented the Personalised Automated ASsessments model (PAAS), a trust-based assessment service that helps compute automated assessments from the perspective of a specific community member: a community leader. This computation essentially aggregates peer assessments, giving more weight to those peers that are trusted by the leader. How much the leader trusts a peer is based on the similarity between her (past) assessments and the peer's (past) assessments over the same objects. The application of this model is specially useful in the context of online communities, where community members interact providing feedback or when the number of objects to be assessed is so large that it would be very costly to assess them on an individual basis.

We have experimentally shown that the algorithm works well in a real setting, and outperforms the well-known CF algorithm in two different ways: (1) by remarkably increasing the number of assessments that can be calculated, and (2) by remarkably decreasing the error of the assessments calculated.

Plans for future work include: 1) evaluating the model with more extensive real datasets that are currently being collected; 2) testing the model in real settings by a company specialised in online learning solutions; and 3) applying the model to a domain other than online learning, where the direct and indirect trust relations can help community members decide who to trust in a given context. Another question to study is how the results would change when other similarity measures for the differences between peers are used.

Acknowledgments

This work is supported by the CollectiveMind project (funded by the Spanish Ministry of Economy and Competitiveness, under grant number TEC2013-49430-EXP).

REFERENCES

[1] L. de Alfaro and M. Shavlovsky. Crowdgrader: Crowdsourcing the evaluation of homework assignments. *Thech. Report 1308.5273, arXiv.org*, 2013.

[2] J. Debenham and C. Sierra. Trust and honour in information-based agency. *Proceedings of Fifth International Joint Conference on Autonomous Agents and Multi Agent Systems*, pages 1225–1232, 2006.

[3] P. Gutierrez, N. Osman, and C. Sierra. Trust-based community assessment. *Pattern Recognition Letters*, submitted for publication.

[4] S. Kamvar, M. Schlosser, and H. Garcia-Molina. The eigentrust algorithm for reputation management in p2p networks. *Proceedings of the 12th international conference on World Wide Web*, pages 640–651, 2003.

[5] N. Osman, C. Sierra, F. McNeill, J. Pane, and J. K. Debenham. Trust and matching algorithms for selecting suitable agents. *ACM TIST*, 5(1):16, 2013.

[6] C. Piech, J. Huang, Z. Chen, C. Do, A. Ng, and D. Koller. Tuned models of peer assessment in moocs. *Proc. of the 6th International Conference on Educational Data Mining (EDM 2013)*, 2013.

[7] K. Regan, P. Poupart, and R. Cohen. Bayesian reputation modeling in e-marketplaces sensitive to subjectivity, deception and change. *Proceedings of 21st national conference on Artificial intelligence*, pages 1206–1212, 2006.

[8] Y. Rubner, C. Tomasi, and L. J. Guibas. A metric for distributions with applications to image databases. In *Proceedings of the Sixth International Conference on Computer Vision (ICCV 1998)*, ICCV '98, pages 59–, Washington, DC, USA, 1998. IEEE Computer Society.

[9] U. Shardanand and P. Maes. Social information filtering: Algorithms for automating "word of mouth". pages 210–217. ACM Press, 1995.

[10] C. Sierra and J. Debenham. An information-based model for trust. In *Proceedings of the Fourth International Joint Conference on Autonomous Agents and Multiagent Systems*, AAMAS '05, pages 497–504, New York, NY, USA, 2005. ACM.

[11] C. Sierra and J. K. Debenham. Information-based agency. In M. M. Veloso, editor, *IJCAI 2007, Proceedings of the 20th International Joint Conference on Artificial Intelligence, Hyderabad, India, January 6-12, 2007*, pages 1513–1518, 2007.

[12] W. T. L. Teacy, M. Luck, A. Rogers, and N. R. Jennings. An efficient and versatile approach to trust and reputation using hierarchical bayesian modelling. *Artificial Intelligence*, pages 149–185, 2012.

[13] T. Walsh. The peerrank method for peer assessment. In T. Schaub, G. Friedrich, and B. O'Sullivan, editors, *ECAI 2014 - 21st European Conference on Artificial Intelligence, 18-22 August 2014, Prague, Czech Republic - Including Prestigious Applications of Intelligent Systems (PAIS 2014)*, volume 263 of *Frontiers in Artificial Intelligence and Applications*, pages 909–914. IOS Press, 2014.

[14] J. Wu, F. Chiclana, and E. Herrera-Viedma. Trust based consensus model for social network in an incompletelinguistic information context. *Applied Soft Computing*, 2015.

Personalized Hitting Time for Informative Trust Mechanisms Despite Sybils

Brandon K. Liu
Paulson School of Engineering
Harvard University
brandon.k.liu@gmail.com

David C. Parkes
Paulson School of Engineering
Harvard University
parkes@eecs.harvard.edu

Sven Seuken
Department of Informatics
University of Zurich
seuken@ifi.uzh.ch

ABSTRACT

Informative and scalable trust mechanisms that are robust to manipulation by strategic agents are a critical component of multi-agent systems. While the global hitting time mechanism (GHT) introduced by Hopcroft and Sheldon [9] is more robust to manipulation than PageRank, strategic agents can still benefit significantly under GHT by performing sybil attacks. In this paper, we introduce the *personalized hitting time mechanism* (PHT), which we show to be significantly more robust to sybil attacks than GHT. Specifically, if an agent has already cut all of its outlinks under PHT (which only leads to a negligible benefit), then adding sybils leads to no additional benefit. We provide an experimental analysis which demonstrates that, in the presence of strategic agents that create sybils, PHT dominates GHT (as well as PageRank and personalized PageRank) in terms of informativeness. We find the large dominance of PHT over GHT particularly surprising given the small difference between the two mechanisms. Finally, we provide a Monte Carlo algorithm to compute approximate PHT scores at scale, and we show that PHT retains its robustness to manipulation when used with approximate scores.

CCS Concepts

•Applied computing → Economics; •Information systems → Reputation systems;

Keywords

Trust Mechanisms; Reputation Mechanisms; Mechanism Design; Sybils; Informativeness

INTRODUCTION

With the continued emergence of market-based systems (consider Uber and Airbnb) we get closer to the vision of agent-mediated commerce [15], with automated software agents negotiating and trading on behalf of a network of individuals who know very little about each other. Problems of trust are of the utmost importance: in identifying trustworthy counter-parties with whom to transact (who to take a ride with) and with the knock-on effect of promoting trustworthy behavior (clean cars, direct routes).

A *trust mechanism* takes reports about the experiences agents have with others, aggregates this information, and shares it in some form with the agents. An effective trust mechanism must be scalable and robust against manipulation in the presence of strategic agents who are willing to misreport trust to improve their own score or reduce the score of others. Ultimately we care about a mechanism that is informative, able to generate trust scores that discriminate between low quality and high quality agents. Specifically, we care about informativeness in the presence of strategic agents.

Some trust mechanisms are *global mechanisms*, which assign a single trust score to each agent, reflecting an aggregate view of the agent's trustworthiness based on all reports. Other trust mechanisms are *personalized* and may assign the same agent different trust scores depending on the viewpoint taken; e.g., agent v_k's score from the perspective of v_i may not be the same as v_k's score from the perspective of v_j. We model this as a graph-theoretic problem: agents are nodes; agents' reports are weighted directed edges indicating trust; and trust mechanisms are graph-based algorithms.

The PageRank algorithm is a global mechanism originally developed to identify reputable web pages [14]. PageRank is known to be easily manipulated by *sybil attacks* [4], in which an agent introduces and controls the reports of a number of fake agents (the sybils). PageRank, for example, is vulnerable to a "two-loop attack," in which an agent indicates trust in its sybils, and its sybils indicate trust in the agent. Sybil attacks have been a concern in many multi-agent systems (e.g., in auction-based systems [19]).

In response to this concern, Hopcroft and Sheldon [9] (HS) introduced the *global hitting time mechanism* (GHT). GHT is closely related to PageRank. In fact, a transformed GHT score for an agent v_k can be computed via PageRank on a modified graph with all of v_k's out-edges removed. This difference is crucial. Whereas a PageRank score for agent v_k may depend on its own as well as others reports, a GHT score is independent of an agent's own reports. Although this removes the two-loop attack, GHT remains vulnerable to sybils through a "restart-capture attack."[1] HS point this out, stating GHT can be "heavily swayed" in the extreme of a large number of sybils. These authors also suggest the idea of "limiting the restart probability granted to new nodes" and point to personalized variations on PageRank [7], as well as variations of PageRank that use pre-trusted nodes for restart [8] (see also Kamvar et al. [10]).

HS provide a limiting analysis, pointing out that sybils can boost a trust score by a large additive amount, reflecting the probability of restart. But HS leave open the question as to the practical implication of restart recapture in GHT, especially its effectiveness relative to other manipulations, its consequences for GHT relative

[1]Restart-capture refers to the role of sybils in capturing probability when the random walk used to define GHT scores restarts and jumps to a new node selected at random.

Appears in: *Proceedings of the 15th International Conference on Autonomous Agents and Multiagent Systems (AAMAS 2016), J. Thangarajah, K. Tuyls, C. Jonker, S. Marsella (eds.), May 9–13, 2016, Singapore.*

to other mechanisms, and its effect on the informativeness of GHT. This paper closes this gap.

We study the *personalized hitting time* (PHT) mechanism, which does not appear to have been discussed or studied in the prior literature. We make the following contributions:

- We prove that the optimal manipulation strategy under PHT only involves cutting outlinks, but does not involve adding sybils. In comparison, the optimal manipulation strategies under PageRank, GHT and a personalized variation of PageRank all require sybils.
- Through a detailed experimental analysis, we quantify the extent to which PHT, GHT, PageRank, and personalized PageRank are vulnerable to sybil attacks. We demonstrate that sybil attacks are especially powerful in global mechanisms (GHT and PageRank) and also effective in personalized PageRank. We show that PHT is very robust to sybil attacks, which translates into a large improvement in informativeness relative to GHT and other mechanisms. The dominance of PHT over GHT is particularly surprising given the small difference between the two mechanisms.
- We provide a Monte Carlo algorithm to compute PHT scores and bound the error as a function of the number of samples. Furthermore, we show that an approximate version of the PHT mechanism retains robustness against sybil manipulations by strategic agents.

Related Work

Trust mechanisms have been proposed for various applications, including the efficient identification of web spam [8], searching for trusted web pages on the Internet [14], and identifying good peers [10, 12]. Yu et al. [22] give an extensive survey of the wide range of trust mechanisms and trust management systems in the literature.

Although Cheng and Friedman's [3] conception of a successful sybil manipulation differs slightly from our own (since they allow an agent to transact as a sybil), and although they only consider sybil attacks in isolation from other manipulations, their main result is relevant here— non-trivial global trust mechanisms are susceptible to sybil attacks while personalized trust mechanisms can be robust against sybils.

Hopcroft and Sheldon [9] introduce GHT and provide a theoretical treatment of its manipulation-resistance in regard to both dropping trust reports and using sybils. But as discussed above, they do not explore in simulation the remaining vulnerability of GHT to sybil attacks, study a personalized variation, or consider informativeness.

Tang et al. [18] show that max-flow and a shortest-path based mechanism are less informative than PageRank and GHT in the absence of strategic agents. Based on this, we restrict our attention to mechanisms based on random-walks in the style of PageRank and GHT.

Seuken et al. [17] have studied trust-based mechanisms for work accounting systems, where the goal is to incentivize users to contribute as much as they consume over time. Recently, Seuken and Parkes [16] have proven that it is impossible to design accounting mechanisms that use transitive trust (like PageRank and hitting time) and are are also sybil-proof. While their framework is slightly different from ours, their results demonstrate the challenges that using a notion of transitive trust imply for achieving robustness towards sybil attacks.

One way to achieve certain robustness against sybil attacks is to leverage external trust information. Unlike methods such as SybilGuard [21] and SybilLimit [20] that assume access to additional information such as pre-existing social links on social networks, we limit inputs to voluntary reports from agents.

PRELIMINARIES

Let V denote a set of agents, with cardinality $|V| = n$, and let $v_i, v_j \in V$ denote individual agents. In our model, agents engage in transactions with each other. One agent is the initiator and one is the provider. Transactions are risky and may succeed or fail. Each agent v_i has a (latent) *type* $\theta_i \in [0, 1]$. This defines how trustworthy the agent is. A transaction initiated by v_j with provider v_i succeeds with probability θ_i, depending on the type of the provider.

At any point in time, let V_i denote the set of agents with whom agent v_i has initiated a transaction. Following a transaction, we assume that an agent updates its belief about the type of the provider, e.g., by considering its prior and the success or failure of the transaction. We do not model this update explicitly for our theoretical model, but rather use $\beta_{ij} \in [0, 1]$ to denote agent v_i's belief about an agent $v_j \in V_i$ with which it has transacted.

A trust mechanism takes a report from each agent. The report from agent v_i is a claim (perhaps untruthful) about the trustworthiness of each agent $v_j \in \hat{V}_i \subseteq V_i$, where $\hat{V}_i$ is the set of other agents about which it makes reports. Let $\hat{w}_{ij} \in [0, 1]$ denote its report about agent v_j, and let $\hat{w}_i$ denote the complete set of reports from v_i. We assume that an agent can only make reports about agents with which it has initiated one or more transactions.

A *trust graph* $G = (V, E, \beta)$ is a weighted directed graph (digraph) with a set V of vertices, a set E of directed edges, and edge weights $\beta : E \mapsto \mathbb{R}_{\geq 0}$. We slightly abuse notation, using V for both the set of agents and the set of vertices. A trust graph is constructed from a set of reports in the natural way, with agents corresponding to vertices, and a weighted directed edge from (the vertex corresponding to) agent v_i to agent v_j with weight $\hat{w}_{ij}$, for report $\hat{w}_{ij}$ from v_i about v_j.

A *trust mechanism* takes a set of reports and returns a *trust score* $x_{ij} \in \mathbb{R}_{\geq 0}$ for every pair of agents $v_i, v_j \in V$ with $v_i \neq v_j$; this is the trust for v_j from the viewpoint of v_i. In a global trust mechanism, we have $x_{ij} = x_{kj}$ for all agents v_j, and all v_i, v_k. In this case, we let x_j denote the score of agent v_j. In a personalized trust mechanism, we may have $x_{ij} \neq x_{kj}$, with the score of agent v_j depending on whether the viewpoint is that of v_i or v_k.

The hitting time mechanisms are defined in terms of a random walk on a trust graph. This is a sequence of random variables $(X_0, X_1, \ldots)$, where each $X_i \in V$, and

$$\mathbb{P}(X_{t+1} = v_j | X_t = v_i) = \frac{\beta_{ij}}{\sum_{(i,j') \in E} \beta_{ij'}}. \quad (1)$$

In defining this walk, a self-loop is added to any vertex that has no out-edges. Depending on the context, vertex X_0 may be fixed, or sampled according to some *restart distribution* F_q. The *hitting time* of vertex v_j is $H(v_j) = \min\{t : X_t = v_i \mid X_0 \sim F_q\}$. An *$\alpha$-terminating random walk*, for some $\alpha \in [0, 1]$, is a finite random walk $(X_0, X_1, \ldots, X_\tau)$ where the walk length is a random variable, $\tau \sim \text{Geom}(1 - \alpha)$. In effect, the random walk terminates with probability α in each step. Let $(X_t)_{t=0}^{\tau}$ denote the sequence of vertices visited by an α-terminating random walk.

DEFINITION 1 (GLOBAL HITTING TIME MECH. (GHT)). *Given a reported trust graph, parameter $\alpha \in [0, 1]$, and restart distribution F_q, the global hitting-time score $x_{\text{GHT},j}$ of agent v_j is the probability that an α-terminating random walk initiated at a vertex sampled from F_q visits v_j before it restarts, i.e., $x_{\text{GHT},j} = \mathbb{P}(v_j \in (X_t)_{t=0}^{\tau} \mid X_0 \sim F_q)$.*

This is equivalent to defining the GHT score as $\mathbb{P}(H(v_j) \leq \tau)$, where τ is the distribution on path length before restart.

We assume that distribution F_q puts some probability on sybils in our theoretical analysis, and take it to be uniform in our simulations. Given access to a fixed set of pre-trusted vertices, then restart can be limited to these vertices. Personalized hitting time is a special case, where the pre-trusted set is simply the agent itself.

DEFINITION 2 (PERSON. HITTING TIME MECH. (PHT)). *Given a reported trust graph and parameter $\alpha \in [0, 1]$, the personalized hitting time score $x_{\text{PHT},ij}$ of agent v_j as viewed from agent v_i is the probability that an α-terminating random walk that starts from v_i visits v_j before it restarts, i.e., $x_{\text{PHT},ij} = \mathbb{P}(v_j \in (X_t)_{t=0}^{\tau} \mid X_0 = v_i)$.*

This is equivalent to defining the PHT score for v_j as viewed by v_i as $\mathbb{P}(H(v_j) \leq \tau \mid X_0 = v_i)$, which denotes the probability that a random walk initiated at v_i will visit v_j before terminating.

DEFINITION 3 (PAGERANK MECHANISM). *Given a reported trust graph, parameter $\alpha \in [0, 1]$, and restart redistribution F_q, the global PageRank score $x_{\text{PR},j}$ of agent v_j is the steady-state probability that an α-terminating random walk initiated at a vertex sampled from F_q spends at v_j.*

DEFINITION 4 (PERSONALIZED PAGERANK MECH. (PPR)). *Given a reported trust graph and parameter $\alpha \in [0, 1]$, the personalized PageRank score $x_{\text{PPR},ij}$ of agent v_j as viewed from agent v_i is the steady-state probability that an α-terminating random walk that starts (and restarts) from v_i spends at v_j.*

Collectively, we call these the *random-walk family* of trust mechanisms.

Motivated by the ubiquity of related schemes in social and economic platforms, we also adopt the *average-score mechanism* (AS) as a simple baseline. This computes $x_{\text{AS},j}$ as the average of reports about v_j by others. As we will show, AS turns out to have interesting properties. In particular, it is less manipulable than GHT and PageRank, and is relatively informative for scenarios where the agents are collectively well-informed about each other.

THEORETICAL ANALYSIS

In this section, we analyze the robustness of PHT to manipulation and compare this with the other mechanisms.

A *strategic agent* is interested in increasing its own score and decreasing the scores of others (because such manipulations may lead to other agents initiating more transactions with this agent). One strategy is to *misreport* other agents as untrustworthy, which in the random-walk family of mechanisms is equivalent to dropping reports (and hence also known as *cutting outlinks*). A strategic agent v_j can also execute a *sybil attack* by creating one or more sybils and arbitrary trust reports among itself and its sybils. Following previous research (e.g., Tang et al. [18]), we assume no trust reports from other agents to v_j's sybils.[2]

We characterize the optimal combination of misreports and sybil attacks for each of our mechanisms.[3]

[2]In practice, obtaining a positive trust report for a sybil should be similarly costly as obtaining a trust report for oneself, but the latter should be at least as beneficial for one's reputation.

[3]The results for PageRank and PPR follow from Bianchini et al. [2] and Cheng and Friedman [4]. The results for GHT follow from Hopcroft and Sheldon [9]. The analysis for PHT is new. We provide a self-contained proof of the theorem for completeness.

THEOREM 1. *The optimal manipulations for a strategic agent v_j with access to one or more sybils are:*

- *GHT: Drop all trust reports about other agents. Add as many sybils as possible and have each sybil report trust 1 for v_j.*
- *PHT: Drop all trust reports about other agents. Do not add any sybils.*
- *PageRank: Drop all trust reports about other agents. Add as many sybils as possible with "two-loops" such that v_j reports trust 1 for each sybil, and each sybil reports trust 1 for v_j.*
- *PPR: Drop all trust reports about other agents. Add one sybil and one two-loop with this sybil.*
- *AS: Report zero trust for every agent in set V_j.[4] Add as many sybils as possible and have each sybil report trust 1 for v_j.*

PROOF. • GHT: Dropping all trust reports to others is strictly dominant because a random walk (r.w.) at v_j has already hit v_j and an out-edge from v_j can make it possible for the r.w. to also hit another agent. Thus, an out-edge leaves v_j's own score unchanged while increasing the score of others. Consider adding a sybil s. A r.w. at v_j has already hit v_j and thus adding an edge to s does not change the score of v_j. But sybil s is useful for capturing a restarted r.w. and sending it in a single hop (the shortest possible) to v_j, thus improving the score of v_j. For this, s has an out-edge (with weight 1) to v_j and no other edges.[5]

• PHT: Consider v_j and the viewpoint from some other agent v_i. The analysis in regard to dropping reports of other agents is the same as for GHT. In regard to a sybil s, it remains irrelevant to add an edge to s. In addition, s no longer captures restart probability (except for trust scores as viewed from s), since all restart for the trust scores from the viewpoint of v_i occurs at v_i.[6]

• PageRank: Adding a sybil s with a two-loop from v_j to s and back to v_j sends a r.w. at v_j back to v_j as quickly as possible (at least as effectively as if the r.w. visits some other vertex), increasing the visit probability at v_j. A sybil also captures restart probability, and a two-loop sends a r.w. that starts at s to v_j as quickly as possible. To maximize both effects it is optimal to have as many sybils as possible, each with two-loops to provide the shortest path possible back to v_j. Given one or more two-looped sybils, it is optimal for v_j to drop all trust reports to other agents. An out-edge from v_j to v_i allows a r.w. at v_j to also visit v_i, increasing the score of v_i. With one or more two-loops, there is no need to use v_i to allow the r.w. to return to v_j because v_j's sybils already provide the shortest-possible return path.[7]

[4]Reporting zero is different from dropping a report in AS because reports are averaged, and the absence of information is different from a report of zero.

[5]If it wasn't already optimal for v_j to drop trust reports about others, there is an additional role for sybils in GHT. Beyond capturing restart probability, a sybil can divert a r.w. at v_j away from other agents and reduce the score of these other agents. For this, v_j would want to introduce a large number of sybils s' with an edge from v_j to s', along with sybils s that have an edge from s to v_j. A similar observation can be made for PHT, where without dropping trust reports about others then it would be useful to introduce sybils s' with an edge from v_j to each s'.

[6]Similar to the analysis for GHT, if v_j cannot drop reports, there is a role to play for sybils. However, a sybil attack without dropping reports is strictly less effective than dropping all reports. Consider an agent v_k with outlinks to some sybils and without dropping any reports. A r.w. at v_k has a non-zero probability of taking an outlink to another agent, whereas a r.w. at v_j has a *zero* probability of doing so.

[7]Without sybils, it can sometimes be beneficial to keep an out-edge with an agent who reports trust in v_j. This depends on a balance

• PPR: The analysis is similar, but reveals that only one sybil is required. A single sybil s with a two-loop from v_j to s and back to v_j sends a r.w. at v_j back to v_j as quickly as possible (at least as effectively as if the r.w. visits some other vertex), increasing the visit probability at v_j. But now a sybil does not capture restart probability, and thus the second effect in PageRank is not present, and only one sybil is required. The rest of the analysis is unchanged, and dropping reports of other agents is optimal together with a two-loop with a sybil.

• AS: A trust report of 0 about another agent v_i maximally decreases the trust score of v_i. Having a sybil s report high trust for v_j increases v_j's score. A trust report by v_j about s has no effect on the score of v_j. □

Theorem 1 tells us that sybils do not bring new manipulation ability to a strategic agent in PHT who is already able to misreport trust about others. This property is unique to PHT amongst these mechanisms.

Sybils are useful for restart-capture in the global mechanisms, even when an agent is already dropping reports about others. Sybils with two-loops are useful in PageRank and PPR, and even when an agent is already dropping reports about others. Sybils are useful in AS.

Following Hopcroft and Sheldon [9], we can also quantify the effect of manipulation in PHT and compare this with GHT. Let $\rho = \sum_{s \in S} q(s)$, where S is the set of sybils introduced by agent v_j and $q(s)$ the restart probability (given by distribution F_q). This is the total probability captured by v_j's sybils. Let $\mathit{infl}(j, k) = \mathbb{P}[H(v_j) < H(v_k) \leq \tau]$ denote the *influence* of v_j on v_k (where $H(v_j)$ and $H(v_k)$ may be correlated). Without sybils, the impact of strategic behavior on v_k is equal to the change in influence of v_j on v_k. For PHT, let $\mathit{infl}(j, k \mid i) = \mathbb{P}[H(v_j) < H(v_k) \leq \tau \mid X_0 = v_i]$ denote the *influence* of v_j on v_k's trust score, as determined from the viewpoint of v_i. We have

$$\begin{aligned} \mathit{infl}(j, k \mid i) &= \mathbb{P}[H(v_j) \leq \tau \mid X_0 = v_i] \\ &\quad \cdot \mathbb{P}[H(v_j) < H(v_k) \leq \tau \mid X_0 = v_i, H(v_j) \leq \tau] \\ &= x_{\mathrm{PHT},ij} \cdot \mathbb{P}[H(v_k) \leq \tau' \mid X_0 = v_j] \\ &= x_{\mathrm{PHT},ij} \cdot x_{\mathrm{PHT},jk}, \end{aligned} \tag{2}$$

where $\tau' \sim \mathrm{Geom}(1 - \alpha)$. The influence of v_j on the score of v_k in PHT, viewed from v_i, depends on the score v_j gives to v_k, but dampened through the score v_i gives to v_j. Let x and x' denote trust scores computed on the basis of true inputs and following manipulation by v_j, respectively.

THEOREM 2 (FOLLOWING HOPCROFT & SHELDON (2007)). *The effect on trust scores of manipulation by a strategic agent v_j with access to sybils is:*

- *In GHT:*
  (i) $x'_{\mathrm{GHT},j} \leq (1 - \rho)x_{\mathrm{GHT},j} + \rho$, *and*
  (ii) $x'_{\mathrm{GHT},k} \geq (1 - \rho)(x_{\mathrm{GHT},k} - \mathit{infl}(j, k)), \forall v_k \neq v_j$.
- *In PHT: for any observer $v_i \neq v_j$,*
  (i) $x'_{\mathrm{PHT},ij} = x_{\mathrm{PHT},ij}$, *and*
  (ii) $x'_{\mathrm{PHT},ik} \geq x_{\mathrm{PHT},ik} - \mathit{infl}(j, k \mid i), \forall v_k \notin \{v_i, v_j\}$.

The properties for GHT are stated as Theorem 4.10 (i) and (ii) in Hopcroft and Sheldon [9]. The properties for PHT follow from Corollary 4.7 (i) and (ii) in Hopcroft and Sheldon [9], using our Theorem 1 to reduce the properties of PHT with strategic behavior in the presence of sybils to the properties of GHT with strategic behavior in the absence of sybils.

PHT with sybils enjoys the same analytic results in regard to strategic behavior as those for GHT in a system where sybils are precluded by assumption. From properties (i), whereas an agent in GHT may be able to increase its own score by as much as ρ, it cannot change its own score in PHT. From properties (ii), whereas an agent in GHT may be able to both remove the effect of its influence on the score of another agent and further dampen this by a factor $(1 - \rho)$, the second factor goes away in PHT.

between allowing a r.w. to visit this other agent, thus increasing the other agent's score, while also bringing the r.w. back to v_j, increasing v_j's own score. A similar observation can be made for PPR.

COMPUTING PHT TRUST SCORES

Large-scale applications of trust mechanisms require algorithms that can quickly compute trust scores. We will now first present an exact method for computing PHT, which is based on solving a system of linear equations that relate hitting time values to each other, but that runs in in $\mathcal{O}(n^4)$. In a second step we will then present a Monte Carlo approximation method.

An Exact Algorithm for Computing PHT

ALGORITHM 1 (EXACT). *Given a weighted digraph G, let $\vec{x}(j)$ be the vector of PHT scores from every vertex to v_j, i.e., $\vec{x}_i(j) = x_{\mathrm{PHT},ij}$. Set parameter α. Let P denote the transition matrix of G. Solving the system of linear equations defined by*

$$\vec{x}(j) = (1 - \alpha)P(j)\vec{x}(j) + \vec{e}_j \tag{3}$$

yields the values for $\vec{x}(j)$, where $P(j)$ is a modified transition matrix of G where $P_{jk}(j) = 0$ for all k, and $\vec{e}_j$ is the standard basis vector.

THEOREM 3. *The exact algorithm correctly computes the PHT scores in $\mathcal{O}(n^4)$ time.*

PROOF. Let $(X_t)_{t=0}^{\tau}$ be a finite sequence of random variables representing the sequence of states that are visited by an α-terminating random walk on a weighted digraph G. Then the PHT score $x_{\mathrm{PHT},ij}$ is

$$x_{\mathrm{PHT},ij} = \mathbb{P}(v_j \in (X_t)_{t=0}^{\tau} \mid X_0 = v_i).$$

Conditioning on X_1 and expanding by the law of total probability yields

$$\sum_k \mathbb{P}(v_j \in (X_t)_{t=0}^{\tau} | X_0 = v_i, X_1 = v_k) \cdot \mathbb{P}(X_1 = v_k | X_0 = v_i).$$

When $i \neq j$, we can simplify the first term to $x_{\mathrm{PHT},kj}$ by the Markov property. The second term simplifies to the product of the survival probability $1 - \alpha$ and the transition probability P_{ik}, where P is the transition matrix of G. This yields

$$x_{\mathrm{PHT},ij} = (1 - \alpha) \sum_k P_{ik} \cdot x_{\mathrm{PHT},kj}.$$

Let $P(j)$ be a modified transition matrix with the same entries as P but with $P_{jk}(j) = 0$ for all k. We can now vectorize this expression for $x_{\mathrm{PHT},ij}$ with j fixed, taking care to ensure that $x_{\mathrm{PHT},jj} = 1$. We make use of $P(j)$ and the standard basis vector $\vec{e}_j$ to produce the vectorization

$$\vec{x}(j) = (1 - \alpha)P(j)\vec{x}(j) + \vec{e}_j.$$

To find all n^2 PHT scores, we must solve n systems of these linear equations. As solving a system of n linear equations in n variables takes time $\mathcal{O}(n^3)$, the total algorithm takes $\mathcal{O}(n^4)$ time. □

Although each system of equations can be solved in parallel, and computation can be accelerated further by methods in parallel numerical linear algebra [6], the $\mathcal{O}(n^4)$ time complexity is likely to remain prohibitive in practical applications. For this reason, we will next present a significantly faster, albeit *approximate* approach for computing PHT.

A Monte Carlo Method for Computing PHT

A simple Monte Carlo approximation would simulate α-terminating random walks between every pair of vertices, and estimate $x_{\text{PHT},ij}$ as the proportion of walks starting at v_i that reach v_j before terminating. We improve on this, by introducing the following *multi-walk algorithm*.

ALGORITHM 2 (MULTI-WALK). *Given a trust graph $G = (V, E, \beta)$ (and $|V| = n$), initiate a total of m α-terminating random walks, with $m_i = m/n$ walks initiated at each vertex v_i. Let Z_{ij} be the number of walks that include a subsequence that visits v_i and subsequently v_j. Let Y_i be the number of walks for which v_i is visited (including those started at v_i). Estimate PHT scores by $\hat{x}_{\text{PHT},ij} = Z_{ij}/Y_i$.*

The multi-walk algorithm improves on the simple approach by (1) using a random walk (r.w.) from v_i to estimate the trust score from v_i to multiple other vertices; and (2) using a subsequence of a r.w. started at some vertex v_i', to estimate the trust score from v_i' to multiple other vertices. In order to avoid bias and keep samples independent, we must take care not to use a subwalk from a vertex that has already been visited on the current r.w.

THEOREM 4. *The estimate computed by the multi-walk algorithm is unbiased and consistent.*

PROOF. Consider all r.w.s that visit vertex v_i (there are Y_i of these). For such a random walk $(X_t)_{t=0}^{\tau}$, let H_i denote the step (or hitting time) at which this first occurs. The estimator $\hat{x}_{\text{PHT},ij}$ is given by the proportion of these walks that subsequently visit v_j. The probability that the r.w. visits v_j is $\mathbb{P}(v_j \in (X_t)_{t=H_i}^{\tau} | v_i \in (X_t)_{t=0}^{\tau})$. Using the time-homogeneous and Markovian property of the random walk, this is just $\mathbb{P}(v_j \in (W_t)_{t=0}^{\tau'} | W_0 = v_i)$, where $(W_t)_{t=0}^{\tau'} = (X_t)_{t=H_i}^{\tau}$ and $\tau' = \tau - H_i$. Due to the memoryless property of the geometric distribution, it also holds that $\tau' \sim \text{Geom}(1-\alpha)$. This is exactly the quantity $x_{\text{PHT},ij}$. Thus the proportion of random walks that succeed can be modeled as the average of Y_i Bernoulli trials, each of which succeeds independently with probability $x_{\text{PHT},ij}$. Hence, $\hat{x}_{\text{PHT},ij} \sim \frac{1}{Y_i}\text{Binom}(Y_i, x_{\text{PHT},ij})$, and is an unbiased and consistent estimator for $x_{\text{PHT},ij}$. □

THEOREM 5. *For $\delta, \epsilon > 0$, obtaining an estimate $\hat{x}_{\text{PHT},ij}$ for which $\mathbb{P}(|Y_i(\hat{x}_{\text{PHT},ij} - x_{\text{PHT},ij})| \geq \epsilon Y_i x_{\text{PHT},ij}) \leq \delta$ requires $Y_i \geq \frac{3\ln(2/\delta)}{\epsilon^2 x_{\text{PHT},ij}}$, where Y_i is the number of random walks that visit v_i.*

PROOF. The proof follows from a standard two-sided Chernoff bound analysis: Given K independent random variables $X_1, \ldots, X_K$ with $\mathbb{E}[X_i] = \mu$ and $0 \leq X_i \leq 1$ for all i, let $\overline{X}$ be their mean. Then for any ϵ, the Chernoff bound is given by:

$$\mathbb{P}(|\overline{X} - \mu| \geq \epsilon\mu) \leq 2\exp\left(-\frac{\epsilon^2}{3}K\mu\right). \tag{4}$$

Given ϵ and $0 < \delta < 1$, call $\overline{X}$ an (ϵ, δ)-approximation if $\mathbb{P}(|\overline{X} - \mu| \geq \epsilon\mu) \leq \delta$. For this, the Chernoff bound tells us we must have $K \geq \frac{3\ln(2/\delta)}{\epsilon^2\mu}$. Instantiating to the multi-walk algorithm (where the mean is $x_{\text{PHT},ij}$) yields the result. □

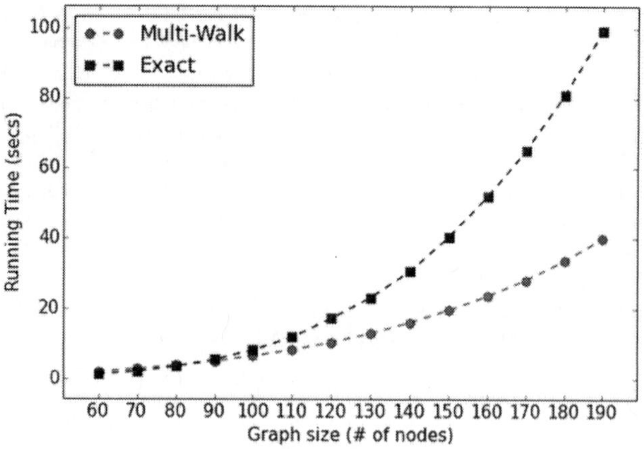

Figure 1: Run-time of the exact and multi-walk algorithms for computing PHT scores as a function of graph size n.

We now compare the run-time of the exact and approximate methods on preferential-attachment graphs [1], which are graphs that have a power-law degree distribution and replicate some of the statistical regularities seen in real-world social and economic networks [5]. Figure 1 provides the run-time of the exact and multi-walk algorithms on increasing graph sizes. We vary the number n of vertices, and set the number of edges so that there are $n/10$ edges per vertex, with edge weights sampled $uniform(0, 1)$.[8] The multi-walk algorithm is faster for large graphs, with the cross-over occurring for systems with as few as 100 agents. Moreover, the multi-walk algorithm can be easily parallelized in a map-reduce environment.[9]

PROPOSITION 1. *The strategic properties of the approximate-PHT mechanism are the same as with the PHT mechanism.*

PROOF. In regard to the characterization (Theorem 1), the argument is based on the property of an individual r.w. and its role in determining trust scores, and does not depend on the number of r.w.s used (and thus the accuracy of the estimate). This also provides Theorem 2 (i) for approximate PHT. In regard to Theorem 2 (ii) for approximate PHT, the argument in Hopcroft and Sheldon [9] generalizes, just replacing $\mathit{infl}(i, k \mid j) = x_{\text{PHT},ji} \cdot x_{\text{PHT},ik}$ with $\mathit{infl}(i, k \mid j) = \hat{x}_{\text{PHT},ji} \cdot \hat{x}_{\text{PHT},ik}$. □

The important consequence of this result is that this random-sample based approximation approach can be used to scale the computation while obtaining the same strategic properties of the mechanism.

EMPIRICAL ANALYSIS

In this section, we present the results of a quantitative study of the effect of manipulation in each mechanism, both in terms of the benefit it brings to an agent and the effect it has on informativeness.

[8]We scale the total number of walks in multi-walk as $20N^2$, which keeps the Spearman correlation between approximate and exact trust ranks between 0.99 and 0.995. The Spearman correlation between the rank order induced by approximate scores $(\hat{x}_{\text{PHT},i1}, \ldots, \hat{x}_{\text{PHT},iN})$ with exact scores $(x_{\text{PHT},i1}, \ldots, x_{\text{PHT},iN})$ is averaged over all agents.

[9]The exact and Monte Carlo algorithms were both implemented in Python for a fair comparison; there was no dependency on lower-level C or FORTRAN libraries. In practice (and in our other experiments), FORTRAN linear algebra routines can be used to substantially speed up the exact algorithm.

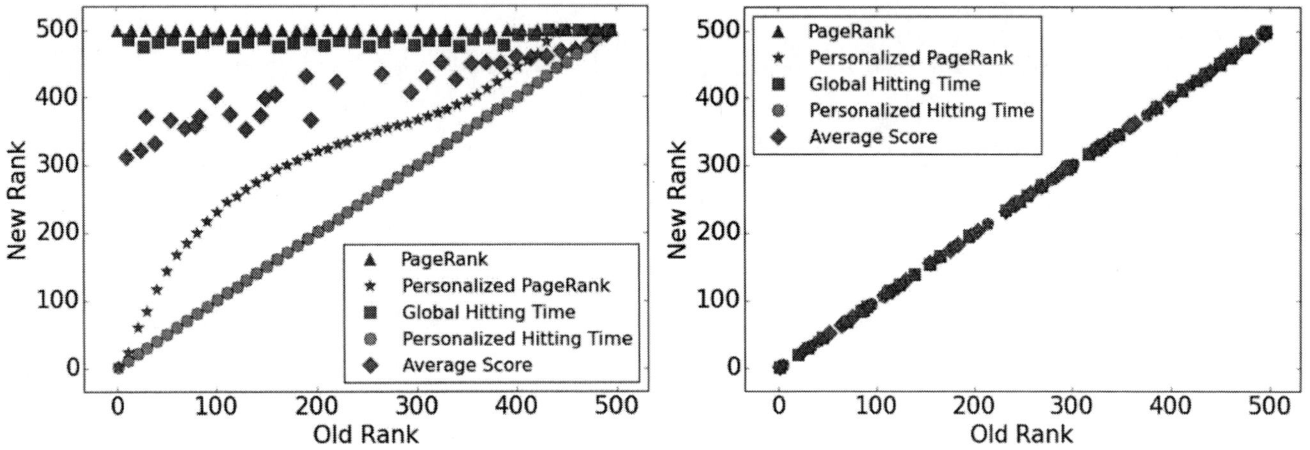

(a) with 50 Sybils

(b) without Sybils

Figure 2: The effect of strategic behavior by a single agent, with $n = 500$ non-sybil agents, leading to graphs with up to $N = 550$ agents in total. (a) New rank vs old rank, with 50 sybils. (b) New rank vs old rank, with 0 sybils.

Experimental Set-up

Throughout, we compute exact trust scores and set $\alpha = 0.15$ for the random-walk based mechanisms, as is standard in the literature [9]. We let $\theta_i \sim uniform[0, 1]$.[10] The process of generating a trust graph captures the idea of transitivity: the higher the type of an agent v_i, the more likely v_i has good information about other agents (i.e., the more likely v_i actually trusts other trustworthy agents), and the more likely other agents are to trust v_i.

Concretely, this process is parameterized by integers $d > 0$ (the "out-neighborhood size") and $t > 0$ (the "transaction count"). The set V_i of agents (size $|V_i| = d$) with whom agent v_i initiates transactions is determined as follows. Until d agents have been selected: with probability θ_i, select some agent $v_j \in V$ according to soft-max probability $p_j = \exp(\theta_j/z)/\sum_{j'} \exp(\theta_{j'}/z)$ (we use $z = 0.05$); with probability $1 - \theta_i$, select some agent $v_j \in V$ uniformly at random.

Eventually, agent v_i initiates a transaction with each $v_j \in V_i$. The belief that agent v_i forms about the type of agent v_j is defined as the average of t independent Bernoulli trials, each succeeding with probability θ_j (we use $t = 8$, unless otherwise stated). This is then used as the edge weight β_{ij} from v_i to v_j in the resulting trust graph.

Across our experiments, we vary the out-neighborhood size (i.e., d), the fraction of strategic agents, and the number of sybils available to each strategic agent.[11] Throughout, we let n denote the non-sybil agents (strategic and non-strategic), which we vary between $n = 100$ and $n = 500$. We let N denote the total number of agents in the graph (including the sybil agents created by the strategic agents), which varies between $N = 100$ and $N = 1100$.

Effect of Manipulation

We first investigate the ability for an agent to change its rank in each mechanism. For this, we fix $n = 500$ and $d = 50$, so that each agent has transacted with 1/10 of the agents, and vary the number of sybils available to agents.[12]

For a fixed trust graph, we compute the effect on each agent's rank as if it were the only strategic agent and employed the optimal manipulation in the presence of sybils (following Theorem 1). If a strategic agent does not have any sybils, then it only drops all trust reports (or reports zero trust about others, in the case of AS).[13] For a personalized mechanism, we define the rank of an agent to be the average rank in all of its personalized rankings (excluding its own).

Figures 2(a) and (b) show the effect of manipulation on rank in each mechanism (500 is best, 1 is worst), where we have subsampled the results for better readability. Strategic agents have access to 50 sybils in (a), but we exclude sybils in (b). The results are averaged over three trials; e.g., the agent with "old rank" 20 has a rank of 20 without manipulation, and its "new rank" is the average of the ranks attained through manipulation in each of three trust graphs. We observe the following:

- From Figure 2(a) we observe that PHT is robust to manipulation, even in the presence of sybils, while the global mechanisms are more vulnerable to sybils. PPR is more robust than the global mechanisms, but more manipulable than PHT.
- From Figure 2(b) we observe that the mechanisms are all very robust to manipulation when agents cannot use sybils (i.e., when they can only cut outlinks). Note that cutting outlinks can only harm other agents' trust scores, and cannot boost one's own trust score. In reasonably well-connected graphs (which characterize our generated graphs), the capacity to harm others' trust scores in random walk-based mechanisms is limited, because the removal of one agent's edges has a negligible effect on the reachability of other agents.

As we can see, the mechanisms differ primarily in their ability to handle sybils. The restart-capture effect in the global mechanisms is very powerful. The two-loop effect in PPR is also powerful relative to just dropping reports (compare Figure 2(a) and Figure 2(b)).

[10] We have also experimented with truncated Normal(0.5, 0.5), and Beta(2, 2), and they provide qualitatively similar results.

[11] We assume that the majority of the agents are non-strategic. This recognizes that some participants in real-world systems may be altruistic, but more importantly, that strategic behavior may be costly, and that strategic behavior could be identified and punished.

[12] The results are qualitatively the same for $n = 100, d = 5, d = 20, t = 2$ and $t = 32$.

[13] This is the optimal, no-sybil manipulation for all mechanisms except PageRank and PPR, where it may sometimes be useful to retain a single report. Because of this, the analysis of PageRank and PPR mechanisms in the special case of no sybils provides a lower-bound on the effect of optimal manipulation.

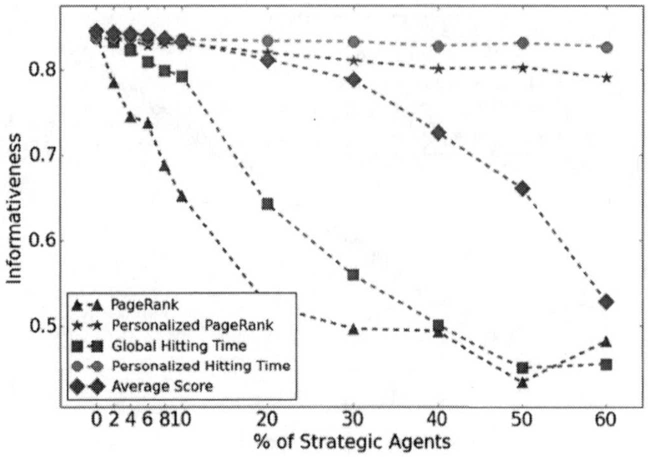

(a) Dense Graphs

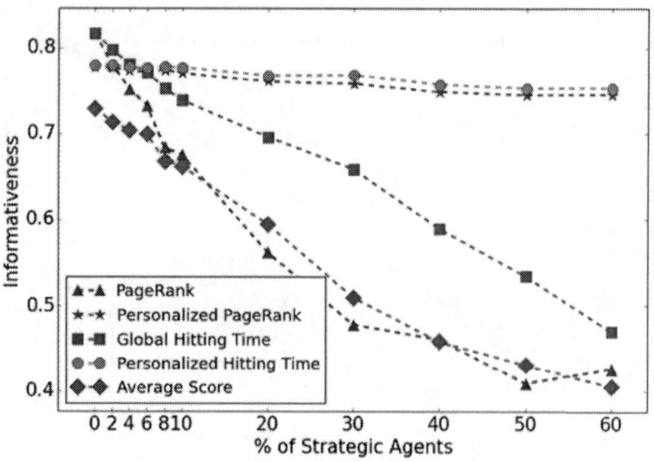

(b) Sparse Graphs

Figure 4: The effect of strategic behavior on the informativeness of each mechanism, with $n = 100$ non-sybil agents, leading to graphs with up to $N = 700$ agents in total. (a) Informativeness vs. fraction of strategic agents in dense graphs ($d = 30$) with 10 sybils per strategic agent. (b) Informativeness vs. fraction of strategic agents in sparse graphs ($d = 5$) with 10 sybils per strategic agent.

In Figure 3, we vary the number of sybils available to the strategic agent and plot the increase in rank through strategic behavior, averaged across five strategic agents evenly distributed in initial ranking (initial ranks are 0, 100, 200, 300, and 400). Thus, the best possible average increase in rank is 300, which would occur if every agent achieved a new rank of 500. We see that sybils already have a large effect in all mechanisms except PHT even when an agent can only use a single sybil. The global mechanisms consistently perform worse than the personalized mechanisms because of restart-capture, and PageRank and PPR perform worse than the corresponding hitting time-based mechanisms because of two-loops. A strategic agent in PPR only requires a single sybil, and hence the two-loop manipulation explains well the difference between PPR and PHT, and also between PageRank and GHT (notice the similar differences between the corresponding curves in Figure 3).[14]

[14]This does not imply that restart-capture is "stronger" than two-loops. The effectiveness of restart-capture depends on the proportion of nodes that are sybils, while the effectiveness of a two-loop depends on the "original" reputation of the node, since two-loops have a "multiplicative" effect. Whether one is more effective than the other depends on the parameters of the particular graph.

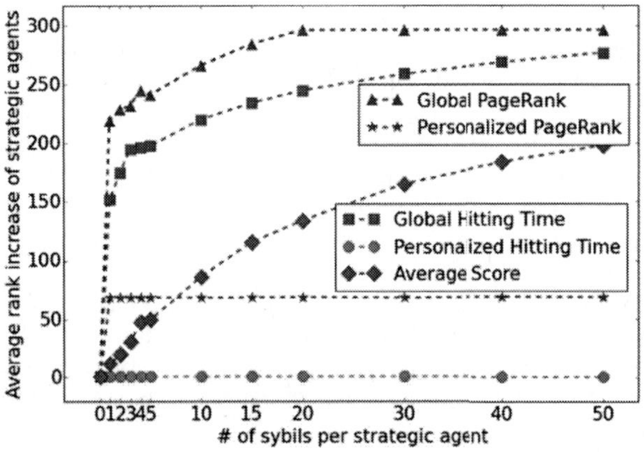

Figure 3: The effect of strategic behavior with $n = 500$ non-sybil agents, leading to graphs with up to $N = 750$ agents in total. Shown is the average increase in rank vs. number of sybils available (averaged across 5 strategic agents).

Effect on Informativeness

Informativeness measures the effectiveness of a mechanism in allowing an agent to discriminate between high type and low type agents when initiating transactions. To measure this, we follow earlier work by Tang et al. [18]: We determine the fraction of transactions initiated by non-strategic agents that succeed, assuming that the counter-party is chosen as the agent with the highest trust score from a set of candidate agents, where this set comprises 5% of all agents selected uniformly at random. Our results are robust to the size of this set of candidate agents with whom the agents transact.

We focus on non-strategic agents because strategic agents receive no useful information from the personalized mechanisms, since the random walk initiated at such an agent cannot follow any edges. Furthermore, we are mainly interested in how cooperative agents are affected by manipulation by strategic agents.

For the following experiment, individual agents are designated to be *strategic* with probability $1 - \theta_i$ (such that agents with lower type are more likely to be strategic), capturing the intuition that lower type agents have more to gain from manipulating. However, the sampling is repeated until the desired number of strategic agents is achieved. The reported results are averaged over three trials.

We first consider the effect of varying the number of strategic agents, each of whom has access to 10 sybils. We use $n = 100$ non-sybil agents here, as the presence of the large number of strategic agents with 10 sybils each will lead to graphs with a maximum number of $N = 700$ total agents in Figure 4(a) and (b), and $N = 1100$ total agents in Figure 5.

We consider dense ($d = 30$) and sparse ($d = 5$) trust graphs, in Figure 4(a) and (b) respectively. The effect of graph density is to vary the amount of information available. We observe the following:

- PHT is the most informative mechanism when more than 4% and 10% of agents are strategic, in sparse and dense trust graphs respectively. With a very small number of strategic agents we

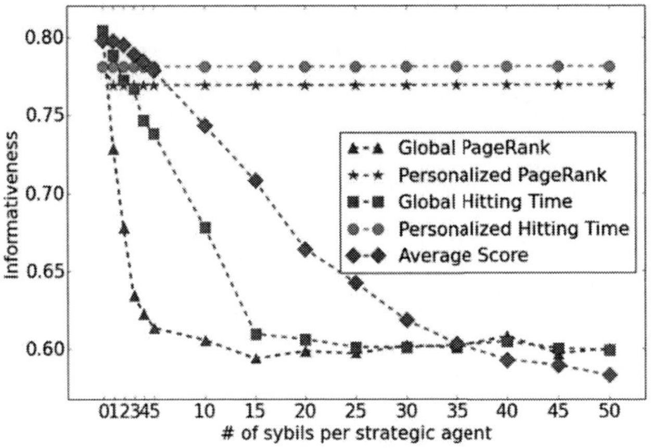

Figure 5: The effect of strategic behavior on the informativeness of each mechanism, in systems with $n = 100$ non-sybil agents, leading to graphs with up to $N = 1100$ agents in total. Shown is the informativeness vs. number of sybils per strategic agent ($d = 20$ and 20 strategic agents).

see that PageRank and GHT have a slight advantage for sparse graphs, with AS best-performing for dense graphs.[15]

- A large gap in performance opens up between the personalized trust mechanisms and the global mechanisms, even with as few as 10% of strategic agents.
- PHT is more informative than PPR, with its advantage getting larger as graphs become more dense and as the number of strategic agents increases.

Figure 5 shows how the informativeness changes when the number of sybils per strategic agent is varied, here using $d = 20$ and with 20% of the agents being strategic. PHT is better than the other random-walk mechanisms for just two sybils per agent. The AS mechanism's performance again dominates that of the global, random-walk based mechanisms for this relatively dense trust graph. The PHT mechanism has better informativeness than AS with four or more sybils per strategic agent.

In summary, Figures 4(a), 4(b), and Figure 5 clearly show the dominance of PHT over the other mechanisms in terms of informativeness. However, note that a comparison at any fixed percentage of strategic agents must be considered a lower bound on the difference we would expect to observe in practice. As the analysis in the previous section on "manipulation" has shown, under all mechanisms except PHT, the agents have a large incentive to become strategic. Consider again Figure 3, where a single sybil per strategic agent is enough to increase the rank of a strategic agent under PPR by roughly 70. Thus, in equilibrium, we should expect a large number of strategic agents when using GHT, PR, PPR, while we should expect no strategic agents when using PHT. Thus, for the ultimate comparison of informativeness, we must compare the performance of PHT in Figures 4(a) and (b) with 0% strategic agents with the performance of the other mechanisms with a larger percentage of strategic agents. This elevates the difference in informativeness between PHT and the other mechanisms even further.

[15]Two factors are at play. First, the locality of AS (just averaging local information) means that the effect of strategic behavior is isolated (just dropping reports from strategic agents and adding fake reports to these same agents). Second, AS is effective in dense graphs because the average score is accurate, consisting of an average over 8×30 unbiased samples ($t = 8$ and $d = 30$).

CONCLUSION

In this paper, we have presented the first study of the *personalized hitting time (PHT)* trust mechanism. We have made three main contributions. First, we have provided a Monte Carlo approximation algorithm to compute PHT scores efficiently, with good theoretical bounds on its approximation error. Second, we have shown formally that PHT is significantly more robust against sybil attacks than all other mechanisms we have studied. In particular, we haven proven that the optimal manipulation under PHT only involves dropping outlinks, but does not involve adding sybils. Furthermore, we have shown that PHT retains this robustness to sybil attacks when PHT scores are approximated. Third, and most importantly, we have provided an empirical evaluation, showing the impact that strategic agents (that can create sybils) have on PHT, global PageRank, personalized PageRank, and global hitting time (GHT). Our experimental results are striking in demonstrating the devastating effect that sybils have on the manipulability and the informativeness of existing mechanisms, even with just a few sybils per agent. This is particularly true for the global mechanisms, including GHT, whose informativeness rapidly declines as the number of strategic agents, or the number of sybils per strategic agents grows. In contrast, because adding sybils is not beneficial under PHT, it remains highly informative, even in the presence of a large number of strategic agents. We found this large dominance of PHT over GHT particularly surprising, given the small difference between the two mechanisms. The high manipulability and low informativeness of GHT raises doubts about the applicability of the GHT mechanism in practice, and leads us to suggest PHT as a building block for multi-agent systems. Future research should experiment on real-world networks (e.g., leveraging some network data at KONECT [11] or SNAP [13]), validating the robustness, informativeness and computational properties of PHT at a larger scale.

Acknowledgements

We are very grateful for the feedback we have received from reviewers on previous versions of this paper.

REFERENCES

[1] A.-L. Barabási and R. Albert. Emergence of Scaling in Random Networks. *Science*, 286(5439):509–512, Oct. 1999.

[2] M. Bianchini, M. Gori, and F. Scarselli. Inside pagerank. *ACM Transactions on Internet Technology*, 5(1):92–128, 2005.

[3] A. Cheng and E. Friedman. Sybilproof reputation mechanisms. In *Proceedings of the 2005 ACM SIGCOMM Workshop on Economics of Peer-to-Peer Systems*, pages 128–132. ACM, 2005.

[4] A. Cheng and E. Friedman. Manipulability of PageRank under sybil strategies. In *First Workshop on the Economics of Networked Systems*, 2006.

[5] A. Clauset, C. R. Shalizi, and M. E. J. Newman. Power-Law Distributions in Empirical Data. *SIAM Review*, 51(4):661–703, Nov. 2009.

[6] J. W. Demmel, M. T. Heath, and H. A. van der Vorst. Parallel numerical linear algebra. *Acta Numerica*, 2:111–197, 1993.

[7] D. Fogaras, B. Rácz, K. Csalogány, and T. Sarlós. Towards scaling fully personalized PageRank: Algorithms, lower bounds, and experiments. *Internet Mathematics*, 2(3):333–358, 2005.

[8] Z. Gyöngyi, H. Garcia-Molina, and J. Pedersen. Combating Web Spam with TrustRank . In *Proceedings of the 30th International Conference on Very Large Databases*, pages 576–587, Mar. 2004.

[9] J. Hopcroft and D. Sheldon. Manipulation-resistant reputations using hitting time. In *Algorithms and Models for the Web-Graph*, pages 68–81, 2007.

[10] S. D. Kamvar, M. T. Schlosser, and H. Garcia-Molina. The Eigentrust algorithm for reputation management in P2P networks. In *Proceedings of the 12th International Conference on World Wide Web*, pages 640–651, 2003.

[11] J. Kunegis. The koblenz network collection (KONECT), 2015. Accessed on August 30, 2015, `http://konect.uni-koblenz.de/`.

[12] R. Landa, D. Griffin, R. G. Clegg, E. Mykoniati, and M. Rio. A sybilproof indirect reciprocity mechanism for peer-to-peer networks. In *INFOCOM 2009*, pages 343–351, 2009.

[13] J. Leskovec. Stanford network analysis project, 2015. Accessed on August 30, 2015, `http://snap.stanford.edu/index.html`.

[14] L. Page, S. Brin, R. Motwani, and T. Winograd. The PageRank citation ranking: Bringing order to the web. Technical report, Stanford InfoLab, 1999.

[15] J. S. Rosenschein and G. Zlotkin. Designing conventions for automated negotiation. *AI Magazine*, 15(3):29, 1994.

[16] S. Seuken and D. C. Parkes. Sybil-proof accounting mechanisms with transitive trust. In *Proceedings of the 13th International Conference on Autonomous Agents and Multiagent Systems (AAMAS)*, Paris, France, 2014.

[17] S. Seuken, J. Tang, and D. C. Parkes. Accounting mechanisms for distributed work systems. In *Proceedings of the 24th Conference on Artificial Intelligence (AAAI)*, Atlanta, GA, 2010.

[18] J. Tang, S. Seuken, and D. C. Parkes. Hybrid transitive trust mechanisms. In *Proceedings of the 9th International Conference on Autonomous Agents and Multiagent Systems*, pages 233–240, 2010.

[19] M. Yokoo, Y. Sakurai, and S. Matsubara. The effect of false-name bids in combinatorial auctions: new fraud in internet auctions. *Games and Economic Behavior*, 46(1):174–188, 2004.

[20] H. Yu, P. B. Gibbons, M. Kaminsky, and F. Xiao. Sybillimit: A near-optimal social network defense against sybil attacks. *Security and Privacy*, pages 3–17, 2008.

[21] H. Yu, M. Kaminsky, P. B. Gibbons, and A. Flaxman. Sybilguard: Defending against sybil attacks via social networks. *ACM SIGCOMM Computer Communication Review*, 36(4):267–278, 2006.

[22] H. Yu, Z. Shen, C. Leung, C. Miao, and V. R. Lesser. A survey of multi-agent trust management systems. *IEEE Access*, pages 35–50, 2013.

A Framework for Organization-Aware Agents
(JAAMAS Extended Abstract)

Andreas Schmidt Jensen
DTU Compute
Technical University of Denmark
Kongens Lyngby, Denmark
ascje@dtu.dk

Virginia Dignum
Delft University of Technology
Faculty of Technology, Policy and Management
Delft, The Netherlands
m.v.dignum@tudelft.nl

Jørgen Villadsen
DTU Compute
Technical University of Denmark
Kongens Lyngby, Denmark
jovi@dtu.dk

ABSTRACT
This short paper introduces and summarizes the AORTA reasoning framework that can be integrated into BDI-agents to enable organizational decision-making. This work has recently been published in the Journal of Autonomous Agents and Multi-Agent Systems (JAAMAS), as [3].

Keywords
Autonomous Agents; Multi-Agent Systems; Organizations; Operational Semantics

1. INTRODUCTION
Open systems are characterized by the presence of a diversity of heterogeneous and autonomous agents that act according to private goals. Organizations, such as those existing in the real-world to structure human activities, can also be used to describe and regulate the agents' behavior space. The success of an agent's participation in an open system depends on its ability to understand and reason about the system organization (roles, rules and ontologies). Assuming an environment where agents are developed independently of the organizational structures, it is necessary to endow those agents with information and functionalities that enables them to reason about the organization so that they can deliberate about their own actions, act within the expected boundaries, and work towards the objectives of the organization. AORTA provides "organization-ignorant" agents with capabilities that allow them to perform organizational reasoning, such that they understand the organizational model of a system, can reason about participation and are able to choose whether or not to comply with the expectations that stem from the role(s) they enact. Such agents are *organization-aware*.

The main contributions of [3], which we highlight in the remainder of this short paper, are:

1. The operational semantics, based on temporal logic, that enable agents to make organizational decisions in order to coordinate and cooperate without explicit coordination mechanisms within the agents.
2. The organizational metamodel that enables to handle organizational models developed with different frameworks. The AORTA metamodel supports the notions of roles and role enactment, objectives and objective dependencies, capabilities, and conditional obligations.

Appears in: *Proceedings of the 15th International Conference on Autonomous Agents and Multiagent Systems (AAMAS 2016), J. Thangarajah, K. Tuyls, C. Jonker, S. Marsella (eds.), May 9–13, 2016, Singapore.*

2. THE AORTA FRAMEWORK
Organizational models describe expectations and requirements or goals of an organization. In itself, an organizational model is just a structural description, and provides no central control over the agents and no specific mechanisms to ensure the fulfilment of the expectations. Moreover, agents joining the organization may be designed by distinct designers, which leads to uncertainty about the agents' motives and actions. Organizational reasoning concerns the capabilities that enable agents to decide about entering and exiting an organization, reasoning about which roles to enact, whether to comply or violate certain norms and how to coordinate tasks with other members of the organization. Agents that are able to perform organizational reasoning are called *organization-aware* agents [4]. In the following, we define what we mean by organizational reasoning and compare our approach to related work on organizational reasoning. Considering the three dimensions of organizational reasoning presented in [4], our work can be positioned as follows: (i) AORTA takes a top-down approach, assuming an existing model and providing agents with the means to reason about this model. (ii) AORTA provides agents with the possibility to understand organizational specifications, and assumes that agents understand the domain ontology used in the organizational model. (iii) AORTA provides reasoning rules that allow agents to successfully move through the phases of participation: entering the organization, playing roles in the organization and leaving the organization.

The focus of AORTA is on the second dimension: to provide agents with the possibility to understand organizational specifications. This understanding, combined with organizational reasoning rules, allows agents to successfully move through the phases of participation: entering the organization, playing roles in the organization and leaving the organization.

AORTA assumes a pre-existing organization, is independent from the agent, and focuses on reasoning rules that specify how the agent reasons about the organization. The organization is completely separated from the agent, meaning that the architecture of the agent is independent from the organizational model, and the agent is free to decide

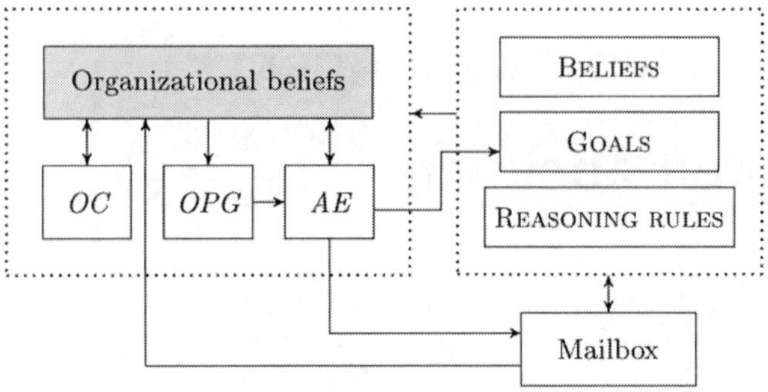

Figure 1: The AORTA component.

on how to use AORTA in its reasoning. The separation is possible because AORTA is based on an organizational metamodel, to which other organizational models can be translated. Figure 1 shows the AORTA component and the flow of information. Organizational reasoning in AORTA divided into three phases: *obligation check* (OC), *option generation* (OPG) and *action execution* (AE). The OPG-phase uses the organizational state to generate possible organizational options. The OC-phase uses the agent's mental state and organizational state to determine if obligations are activated, satisfied or violated, and updates the organizational state accordingly. The agent considers these options in the AE-phase using reasoning rules, which can alter the organizational state, the agent's intentions or send messages to other agents.

Each individual agent will use its own AORTA component. This means that agents can decide by themselves how to use the component, making AORTA suitable for many different kinds of agents. It may, however, also lead to agents holding different views about the organization, leading to inconsistency among them. However, this is not different from what happens in real-life, where actors in an environment may very well have different views about the world state, and contributes therefore to the realism of the approach.

3. AORTA METAMODEL

The AORTA metamodel supports the notions of roles and role enactment, objectives and objective dependencies, and conditional obligations and is defined by the following predicates:

- role(*Role*, *Objs*), where *Role* is the role name, and *Objs* is a set of objectives, where each *Obj* is a partial state description.
- obj(*Obj*, *SubObjs*), where *Obj* is the name of an objective, and *SubObjs* is a set of sub-objectives.
- dep($Role_1$, $Role_2$, *Obj*), where role $Role_1$ depends on role $Role_2$ for completion of objective *Obj*.
- rea(*Ag*, *Role*), where agent *Ag* enacts role *Role*.
- cond(*Role*, *Obj*, *Deadline*, *Cond*), where there is a conditional obligation for role *Role* to complete *Obj* before *Deadline* when *Cond* holds.
- obl(*Ag*, *Role*, *Obj*, *Deadline*), where there is an obligation for agent *Ag* playing role *Role* to complete *Obj* before *Deadline*.
- viol(*Ag*, *Role*, *Obj*), where agent *Ag* playing role *Role* has violated the obligation to complete *Obj*.

4. AORTA SEMANTICS

The framework is founded in formal operational semantics that precisely define how the agent can reason about an organization. Firstly, using temporal logic, we have formalized the intended behavior of organization-aware agents. Secondly, we defined the operational semantics of executing agents in the AORTA framework using a transition system, which consists of a set of transition rules that define the transformation from one configuration to another. The semantics of the deontic aspects of the domain are based on LAO [1] extended with the ability to deal with obligations, which also enables us to capture the fact that the agents and the organization reside in an environment, which none of them fully control. For details and proofs on the AORTA semantics, we refer the reader to [3]. Note that there is currently no formal connection between these semantic models, and future work is needed in order to establish the correctness of the operational semantics with respect to the semantics of obligations.

Using transition rules, the component can activate obligations, detect violations and suggest role enactment or objective commitments, all based on the agent's current state. The agents act upon this using organizational actions, allowing to following the suggestions – enact roles or commit to objectives – or to coordinate their actions with other agents in the system.

5. CONCLUSIONS

AORTA can be seen as an add-on component to cognitive agents, providing them with organizational reasoning capabilities. [3] provides an initial evaluation of the framework using a tender process scenario, demonstrating that, given agents with the capabilities to fulfil the roles in such a scenario, AORTA made it possible for them to coordinate their tasks and detect and act upon violations of the obligations imposed upon the agents. The framework has been partially implemented in Java and integrated in the *Jason* platform [2]. We plan to extend that work with the complete and updated operational semantics presented in the paper [3]. This would make it possible to execute and evaluate larger scenarios, and to, e.g., test how agents are able to recover from violations of obligations.

REFERENCES

[1] V. Dignum and F. Dignum. A logic of agent organizations. *Logic Journal of the IGPL*, 20(1):283–316, Oct. 2011.

[2] A. S. Jensen, V. Dignum, and J. Villadsen. The AORTA architecture: Integrating organizational reasoning in *Jason*. In Dalpiaz, et al., editor, *Engineering Multi-Agent Systems - 2nd International Workshop, EMAS*, volume 8758 of *LNCS*, pages 127–145. Springer, 2014.

[3] A. S. Jensen, V. Dignum, and J. Villadsen. A framework for organization-aware agents. *Autonomous Agents and Multi-Agent Systems*, 2016.

[4] M. B. van Riemsdijk, K. Hindriks, and C. Jonker. Programming organization-aware agents. In *ESAW '09*. Springer, 2009.

Discovering Underlying Plans Based on Distributed Representations of Actions

Xin Tian
Dept of Computer Science
Sun Yat-Sen University
Guangzhou, China. 510006
tianxin1860@gmail.com

Hankz Hankui Zhuo*
Dept. of Computer Science
Sun Yat-Sen University
Guangzhou, China. 510006
zhuohank@mail.sysu.edu.cn

Subbarao Kambhampati
Dept. of Computer Sci. & Eng.
Arizona State University
Tempe, Arizona, US
rao@asu.edu

ABSTRACT

Plan recognition aims to discover target plans (i.e., sequences of actions) behind observed actions, with history plan libraries or domain models in hand. Previous approaches either discover plans by maximally "matching" observed actions to plan libraries, assuming target plans are from plan libraries, or infer plans by executing domain models to best explain the observed actions, assuming complete domain models are available. In real world applications, however, target plans are often not from plan libraries and complete domain models are often not available, since building complete sets of plans and complete domain models are often difficult or expensive. In this paper we view plan libraries as corpora and learn vector representations of actions using the corpora; we then discover target plans based on the vector representations. Our approach is capable of discovering underlying plans that are not from plan libraries, without requiring domain models provided. We empirically demonstrate the effectiveness of our approach by comparing its performance to traditional plan recognition approaches in three planning domains.

1. INTRODUCTION

As computer-aided cooperative work scenarios become increasingly popular, human-in-the-loop planning and decision support has become a critical planning chellenge (c.f. [5, 6, 17]). An important aspect of such a support [13] is recognizing what plans the human in the loop is making, and provide appropriate suggestions about their next actions [1]. Although there is a lot of work on plan recognition, much of it has traditionally depended on the availability of a complete domain model [21, 31]. As has been argued elsewhere [13], such models are hard to get in human-in-the-loop planning scenarios. Here, the decision support systems have to make themselves useful without insisting on complete action models of the domain. The situation here is akin to that faced by search engines and other tools for computer supported cooperate work, and is thus a significant departure for the "planning as pure inference" mindset of the automated planning community. As such, the problem calls for plan recognition with "shallow" models of the domain (c.f. [11]), that can be easily learned automatically.

There has been very little work on learning such shallow models to support human-in-the-loop planning. Some examples include the work on Woogle system [6] that aimed to provide support to humans in web-service composition. That work however relied on very primitive understanding of the actions (web services in their case) that consisted merely of learning the input/output types of individual services.

In this paper, we focus on learning more informative models that can help recognize the plans under construction by the humans, and provide active support by suggesting relevant actions. To drive this process, we need to learn shallow models of the domain. We propose to adapt the recent successes of word-vector models [18] in language to our problem. Specifically, we assume that we have access to a corpus of previous plans that the human user has made. Viewing these plans as made up of action words, we learn word vector models for these actions. These models provide us a way to induce the distribution over the identity of each unobserved action. Given the distributions over individual unobserved actions, we use an expectation-maximization approach to infer the joint distribution over all unobserved actions. This distribution then forms the basis for action suggestions.

We will present the details of our approach, and will also empirically demonstrate that it does capture a surprising amount of structure in the observed plan sequences, leading to effective plan recognition. We further compare its performance to traditional plan recognition techniques, including one that uses the same plan traces to learn the STRIPS-style action models, and use the learned model to support plan recognition.

2. PROBLEM DEFINITION

A plan library, denoted by $\mathcal{L}$, is composed of a set of plans $\{p\}$, where p is a sequence of actions, i.e., $p = \langle a_1, a_2, \ldots, a_n \rangle$ where a_i, $1 \leq i \leq n$, is an action name (without any parameter) represented by a string. For example, a string *unstack-A-B* is an action meaning that *a robot unstacks block A from block B*. We denote the set of all possible actions by $\bar{\mathcal{A}}$ which is assumed to be known beforehand. For ease of presentation, we assume that there is an empty action, ϕ, indicating an unknown or not observed action, i.e., $\mathcal{A} = \bar{\mathcal{A}} \cup \{\phi\}$. An observation of an *unknown* plan $\tilde{p}$ is denoted by $\mathcal{O} = \langle o_1, o_2, \ldots, o_M \rangle$, where $o_i \in \mathcal{A}$, $1 \leq i \leq M$, is either an action in $\bar{\mathcal{A}}$ or an empty action ϕ indicating the corresponding action is missing or not observed. Note that $\tilde{p}$ is not necessarily in the plan library $\mathcal{L}$, which makes the plan recognition problem more challenging, since matching the observation to the plan library will not work any more.

We assume that the human is making a plan of at most length M. We also assume that at any given point, the planner is able to observe $M - k$ of these actions. The k unobserved actions might either be in the suffiix (i.e., yet to be formed part) of the plan, or in the middle (due to observational gaps). Our aim is to suggest, for

*Corresponding author.

Appears in: *Proceedings of the 15th International Conference on Autonomous Agents and Multiagent Systems (AAMAS 2016), J. Thangarajah, K. Tuyls, C. Jonker, S. Marsella (eds.), May 9–13, 2016, Singapore.*

each of the k unobserved actions, m possible choices–from which the user can select the action. (Note that we would like to keep m small, ideally close to 1, so as not to overwhelm the user). Accordingly, we will evaluate the effectiveness of the decision support in terms of whether or not the user's best/intended action is within the suggested m actions.

Specifically, our recognition problem can be represented by a triple $\Re = (\mathcal{L}, \mathcal{O}, \mathcal{A})$. The solution to $\Re$ is to discover the unknown plan $\tilde{p}$ that best explains $\mathcal{O}$ given $\mathcal{L}$ and $\mathcal{A}$. An example of our plan recognition problem in the *blocks*[1] domain is shown below.

Example: A plan library $\mathcal{L}$ in the *blocks* domain is assumed to have four plans as shown below:

plan 1: *pick-up-B stack-B-A pick-up-D stack-D-C*
plan 2: *unstack-B-A put-down-B unstack-D-C put-down-D*
plan 3: *pick-up-B stack-B-A pick-up-C stack-C-B pick-up-D stack-D-C*
plan 4: *unstack-D-C put-down-D unstack-C-B put-down-C unstack-B-A put-down-B*

An observation $\mathcal{O}$ of action sequence is shown below:

observation: *pick-up-B* ϕ *unstack-D-C put-down-D* ϕ *stack-C-B* ϕ ϕ

Given the above input, our DUP algorithm outputs plans as follows:

pick-up-B stack-B-A unstack-D-C put-down-D pick-up-C stack-C-B pick-up-D stack-D-C

Although the "plan completion" problem seems to differ superficially from the traditional "plan recognition" problem, we point out that many earlier works on plan recognition do in fact evaluate their recognition algorithms in terms of completion tasks, e.g., [22, 28, 31]. While these earlier efforts use different problem settings, taking either a plan library or action models as input, they share one common characteristic: they all aim to look for a plan that can best explain (or complete) the observed actions. This is exactly the same as our problem we aim to solve.

3. OUR DUP ALGORITHM

Our DUP approach to the recognition problem $\Re$ functions by two phases. We first learn vector representations of actions using the plan library $\mathcal{L}$. We then iteratively sample actions for unobserved actions o_i by maximizing the probability of the unknown plan $\tilde{p}$ via the EM framework. We present DUP in detail in the following subsections.

3.1 Learning Vector Representations of Actions

Since actions are denoted by a name string, actions can be viewed as words, and a plan can be viewed as a sentence. Furthermore, the plan library $\mathcal{L}$ can be seen as a corpus, and the set of all possible actions $\mathcal{A}$ is the vocabulary. We thus can learn the vector representations for actions using the Skip-gram model with hierarchical softmax, which has been shown an efficient method for learning high-quality vector representations of words from unstructured corpora [18].

The objective of the Skip-gram model is to learn vector representations for predicting the surrounding words in a sentence or document. Given a corpus $\mathcal{C}$, composed of a sequence of training words $\langle w_1, w_2, \ldots, w_T \rangle$, where $T = |\mathcal{C}|$, the Skip-gram model maximizes the average log probability

$$\frac{1}{T}\sum_{t=1}^{T}\sum_{-c\leq j\leq c, j\neq 0} \log p(w_{t+j}|w_t) \tag{1}$$

where c is the size of the training window or context.

[1]http://www.cs.toronto.edu/aips2000/

The basic probability $p(w_{t+j}|w_t)$ is defined by the hierarchical softmax, which uses a binary tree representation of the output layer with the K words as its leaves and for each node, explicitly represents the relative probabilities of its child nodes [18]. For each leaf node, there is an unique path from the root to the node, and this path is used to estimate the probability of the word represented by the leaf node. There are no explicit output vector representations for words. Instead, each inner node has an output vector $v'_{n(w,j)}$, and the probability of a word being the output word is defined by

$$p(w_{t+j}|w_t) = \prod_{i=1}^{L(w_{t+j})-1} \Big\{\sigma(\mathbb{I}(n(w_{t+j}, i+1) = child(n(w_{t+j}, i))) \cdot v_{n(w_{t+j},i)} \cdot v_{w_t})\Big\}, \tag{2}$$

where

$$\sigma(x) = 1/(1+\exp(-x)).$$

$L(w)$ is the length from the root to the word w in the binary tree, e.g., $L(w) = 4$ if there are four nodes from the root to w. $n(w, i)$ is the ith node from the root to w, e.g., $n(w, 1) = root$ and $n(w, L(w)) = w$. $child(n)$ is a fixed child (e.g., left child) of node n. v_n is the vector representation of the inner node n. v_{w_t} is the input vector representation of word w_t. The identity function $\mathbb{I}(x)$ is 1 if x is true; otherwise it is -1.

We can thus build vector representations of actions by maximizing Equation (1) with corpora or plan libraries $\mathcal{L}$ as input. We will exploit the vector representations to discover the unknown plan $\tilde{p}$ in the next subsection.

3.2 Maximizing Probability of Unknown Plans

With the vector representations learnt in the last subsection, a straightforward way to discover the unknown plan $\tilde{p}$ is to explore all possible actions in $\bar{\mathcal{A}}$ such that $\tilde{p}$ has the highest probability , which can be defined similar to Equation (1), i.e.,

$$\mathcal{F}(\tilde{p}) = \sum_{k=1}^{M}\sum_{-c\leq j\leq c, j\neq 0} \log p(w_{k+j}|w_k) \tag{3}$$

where w_k denotes the kth action of $\tilde{p}$ and M is the length of $\tilde{p}$. As we can see, this approach is exponentially hard with respect to the size of $\bar{\mathcal{A}}$ and number of unobserved actions. We thus design an approximate approach in the Expectation-Maximization framework to estimate an unknown plan $\tilde{p}$ that best explains the observation $\mathcal{O}$.

To do this, we introduce new parameters to capture "weights" of values for each unobserved action. Specifically speaking, assuming there are X unobserved actions in $\mathcal{O}$, i.e., the number of ϕs in $\mathcal{O}$ is X, we denote these unobserved actions by $\bar{a}_1, ..., \bar{a}_x, ..., \bar{a}_X$, where the indices indicate the order they appear in $\mathcal{O}$. Note that each $\bar{a}_x$ can be any action in $\bar{\mathcal{A}}$. We associate each possible value of $\bar{a}_x$ with a weight, denoted by $\bar{\Gamma}_{\bar{a}_x,x}$. $\bar{\Gamma}$ is a $|\bar{\mathcal{A}}| \times X$ matrix, satisfying

$$\sum_{o\in\bar{\mathcal{A}}} \bar{\Gamma}_{o,x} = 1,$$

where $\bar{\Gamma}_{o,x} \geq 0$ for each x. For the ease of specification, we extend $\bar{\Gamma}$ to a bigger matrix with a size of $|\bar{\mathcal{A}}| \times M$, denoted by Γ, such that $\Gamma_{o,y} = \bar{\Gamma}_{o,x}$ if y is the index of the xth unobserved action in $\mathcal{O}$, for all $o \in \bar{\mathcal{A}}$; otherwise, $\Gamma_{o,y} = 1$ and $\Gamma_{o',y} = 0$ for all

$o' \in \bar{\mathcal{A}} \wedge o' \neq o$. Our intuition is to estimate the unknown plan $\tilde{p}$ by selecting actions with the highest weights. We thus introduce the weights to Equation (2), as shown below,

$$p(w_{k+j}|w_k) = \prod_{i=1}^{L(w_{k+j})-1} \Big\{\sigma(\mathbb{I}(n(w_{k+j}, i+1) = child(n(w_{k+j}, i))) \cdot av_{n(w_{k+j},i)} \cdot bv_{w_k})\Big\}, \quad (4)$$

where $a = \Gamma_{w_{k+j},k+j}$ and $b = \Gamma_{w_k,k}$. We can see that the impact of w_{k+j} and w_k is penalized by weights a and b if they are unobserved actions, and stays unchanged, otherwise (since both a and b equal to 1 if they are observed actions). We redefine the objective function as shown below,

$$\mathcal{F}(\tilde{p}, \Gamma) = \sum_{k=1}^{M} \sum_{-c \leq j \leq c, j \neq 0} \log p(w_{k+j}|w_k), \quad (5)$$

where $p(w_{k+j}|w_k)$ is defined by Equation (4). The only parameters needed to be updated are Γ, which can be easily done by gradient descent, as shown below,

$$\Gamma_{o,x} = \Gamma_{o,x} + \delta \frac{\partial \mathcal{F}}{\partial \Gamma_{o,x}}, \quad (6)$$

if x is the index of unobserved action in $\mathcal{O}$; otherwise, $\Gamma_{o,x}$ stays unchanged, i.e., $\Gamma_{o,x} = 1$. Note that δ is a learning constant.

With Equation (6), we can design an EM algorithm by repeatedly sampling an unknown plan according to Γ and updating Γ based on Equation (6) until reaching convergence (e.g., a constant number of repetitions is reached).

An overview of our DUP algorithm is shown in Algorithm 1. In Step 2 of Algorithm 1, we initialize $\Gamma_{o,k} = 1/M$ for all $o \in \bar{\mathcal{A}}$, if k is an index of unobserved actions in $\mathcal{O}$; and otherwise, $\Gamma_{o,k} = 1$ and $\Gamma_{o',k} = 0$ for all $o' \in \bar{\mathcal{A}} \wedge o' \neq o$. In Step 4, we view $\Gamma_{\cdot,k}$ as a probability distribution, and sample an action from $\bar{\mathcal{A}}$ based on $\Gamma_{\cdot,k}$ if k is an unobserved action index in $\mathcal{O}$. In Step 5, we only update $\Gamma_{\cdot,k}$ where k is an unobserved action index. In Step 6, we linearly project all elements of the updated Γ to between 0 and 1, such that we can do sampling directly based on Γ in Step 4. In Step 8, we simply select $\bar{a}_x$ based on

$$\bar{a}_x = \arg\max_{o \in \bar{\mathcal{A}}} \Gamma_{o,x},$$

for all unobserved action index x.

Algorithm 1 Framework of our DUP algorithm

Input: plan library $\mathcal{L}$, observed actions $\mathcal{O}$
Output: plan $\tilde{p}$

1: learn vector representation of actions
2: initialize $\Gamma_{o,k}$ with $1/M$ for all $o \in \bar{\mathcal{A}}$, when k is an unobserved action index
3: **while** the maximal number of repetitions is not reached **do**
4: sample unobserved actions in $\mathcal{O}$ based on Γ
5: update Γ based on Equation (6)
6: project Γ to [0,1]
7: **end while**
8: select actions for unobserved actions with the largest weights in Γ
9: **return** $\tilde{p}$

Our DUP algorithm framework belongs to a family of policy gradient algorithms, which have been successfully applied to complex problems, e.g., robot control [19], natural language processing [3]. Our formulation is unique in how it recognizes plans, in comparison to the existing methods in the planning community.

Note that our current study shows that even direct application of word vector learning methods provide competitive performance for plan completion tasks. We believe we can further improve the performance by using the planning specific structural information in the EM phase. In other words, if we are provided with additional planning structural information as input, we can exploit the structural information to filter candidate plans to be recognized in the EM procedure.

4. EXPERIMENTS

In this section, we evaluate our DUP algorithms in three planning domains from International Planning Competition, i.e., blocks[1], depots[2], and driverlog[2]. To generate training and testing data, we randomly created 5000 planning problems for each domain, and solved these planning problems with a planning solver, such as FF[3], to produce 5000 plans. We then randomly divided the plans into ten folds, with 500 plans in each fold. We ran our DUP algorithm ten times to calculate an average of accuracies, each time with one fold for testing and the rest for training. In the testing data, we randomly removed actions from each testing plan (i.e., $\mathcal{O}$) with a specific percentage ξ of the plan length. Features of datasets are shown in Table 1, where the second column is the number of plans generated, the third column is the total number of words (or actions) of all plans, and the last column is the size of vocabulary used in all plans.

Table 1: Features of datasets

domain	#plan	#word	#vocabulary
blocks	5000	292250	1250
depots	5000	209711	2273
driverlog	5000	179621	1441

We define the accuracy of our DUP algorithm as follows. For each unobserved action $\bar{a}_x$ DUP suggests a set of possible actions S_x which have the highest value of $\Gamma_{\bar{a}_x,x}$ for all $\bar{a}_x \in \bar{\mathcal{A}}$. If S_x covers the *truth* action a_{truth}, i.e., $a_{truth} \in S_x$, we increase the number of correct suggestions g by 1. We thus define the accuracy acc as shown below:

$$acc = \frac{1}{T} \sum_{i=1}^{T} \frac{\#\langle correct\text{-}suggestions\rangle_i}{K_i},$$

where T is the size of testing set, $\#\langle correct\text{-}suggestions\rangle_i$ is the number of correct suggestions for the ith testing plan, K_i is the number of unobserved actions in the ith testing plan. We can see that the accuracy acc may be influenced by S_x. We will test different size of S_x in the experiment.

State-of-the-art plan recognition approaches with plan libraries as input aim at finding a plan from plan libraries to best explain the observed actions [9], which we denote by MatchPlan. We develop a MatchPlan system based on the idea of [9] and compare our DUP algorithm to MatchPlan with respect to different percentage of unobserved actions ξ and different size of suggestion set S_x. Another baseline is action-models based plan recognition approach [22] (denoted by PRP, short for Plan Recognition as Planning). Since we do not have action models as input in our DUP algorithm, we exploited the action model learning system ARMS [26] to learn action models from the plan library and feed the action models to the PRP approach. We call this hybrid plan recognition approach ARMS+PRP. To learn action models, ARMS requires

[2]http://www.cs.cmu.edu/afs/cs/project/jair/pub/volume20/long03a-html/JAIRIPC.html

[3]https://fai.cs.uni-saarland.de/hoffmann/ff.html

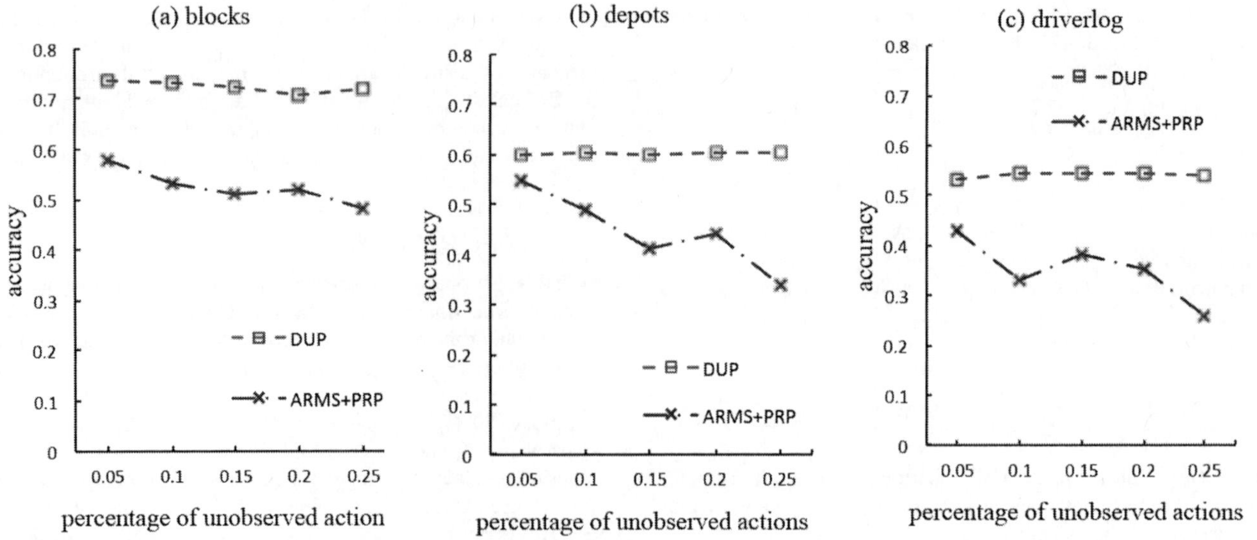

Figure 1: Accuracies of DUP and ARMS+PRP with respect to different percentage of unobserved actions

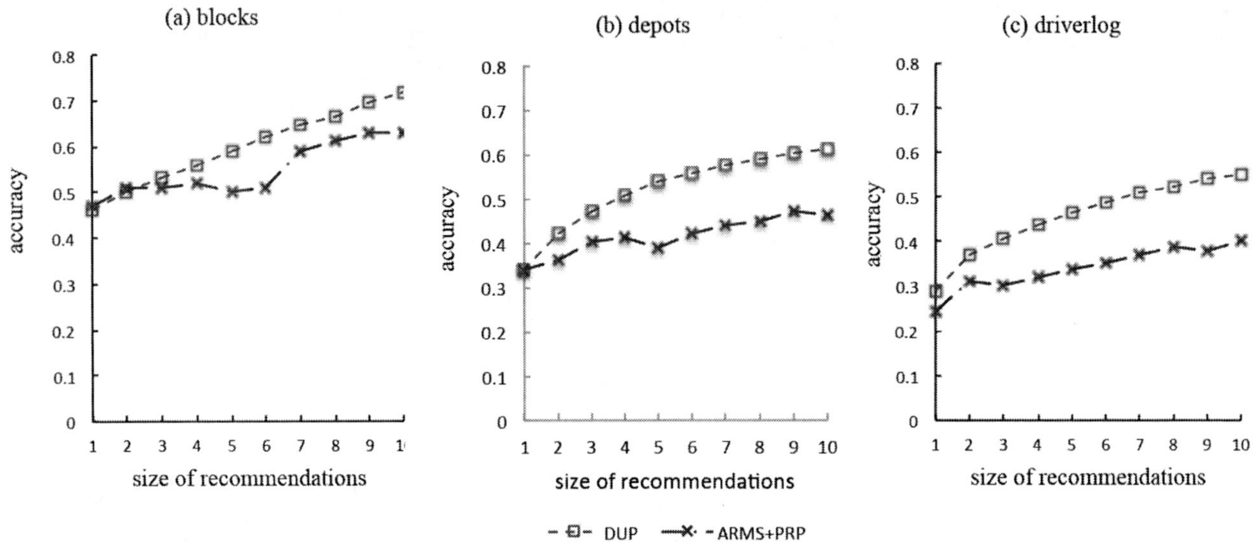

Figure 2: Accuracies of DUP and ARMS+PRP with respect to different size of recommendations

state information of plans as input. We thus added extra information, i.e., initial state and goal of each plan in the plan library, to ARMS+PRP. In addition, PRP requires as input a set of candidate goals $\mathcal{G}$ for each plan to be recognized in the testing set, which was also generated and fed to PRP when testing. In summary, the hybrid plan recognition approach ARMS+PRP has more input information, i.e., initial states and goals in plan library and candidate goals $\mathcal{G}$ for each testing example, than our DUP approach.

4.1 Comparison between DUP and ARMS+PRP

We first compare our DUP algorithm to ARMS+PRP to see the advantage of DUP. We varied the percentage of unobserved actions and the size of recommended actions to see the change of accuracies, respectively. The results are shown below.

4.1.1 Varying Percentage of Unobserved Actions

In this experiment we would like to see the change of accuracies of both our DUP algorithm and ARMS+PRP with respect to ξ in $\mathcal{O}$. We set the window of training context c in Equation (1) to be three, the number of iterations in Algorithm 1 to be 1500, the size of recommendations to be ten, and the learning constant δ in Equation (6) to be 0.1. For ARMS+PRP, we generated 20 candidate goals for each testing example including the ground-truth goal which corresponds to the ground-truth plan to be recognized. The results are shown in Figure 1.

From Figure 1, we can see that in all three domains, the accuracy of our DUP algorithm is generally higher ARMS+PRP, which verifies that our DUP algorithm can indeed capture relations among actions better than the model-based approach ARMS+PRP. The rationale is that we explore global plan information from the plan library to learn a "shallow" model (distributed representations of actions) and use this model with global information to best explain the observed actions. While ARMS+PRP tries to leverage global plan information from the plan library to learn action models and uses the models to recognize observed actions, it enforces itself to extract "exact" models represented by planning models which are often with noise. When feeding those noisy models to PRP, since PRP that uses planning techniques to recognize plans is very sensitive to noise of planning models, the recognition accuracy is lower than DUP, even though ARMS+PRP has more input information (i.e., initial states and candidate goals) than our DUP algorithm.

Looking at the changes of accuracies with respect to the percentage of unobserved actions, we can see that our DUP algorithm performs fairly well even when the percentage of unobserved action reaches 25%. In contrast, ARMS+PRP is sensitive to the percentage of unobserved actions, i.e., the accuracy goes down when more actions are unobserved. This is because the noise of planning models induces more uncertain information, which harms the recognition accuracy, when the percentage of unobserved actions becomes larger. Comparing accuracies of different domains, we can see that our DUP algorithm functions better in the *blocks* domain than the other two domains. This is because the ratio of #word over #vocabulary in the *blocks* domain is much larger than the other two domains, as shown in Table 1. We would conjecture that increasing the ratio could improve the accuracy of DUP. From Figure 1 (as well as Figure 3), we can see that it appears that the accuracy of DUP is not affected by increasing percentages of unobserved actions. The rationale is (1) the percentage of unobserved actions is low, less than 25%, i.e., there is at most one unobserved action over four continuous actions; (2) the window size of context in DUP is set to be 3, which ensures that DUP generally has "stable" context information to estimate the unobserved action when the percentage of unobserved actions is less than 25%, resulting in the stable accuracy in Figure 1 (likewise for Figure 3).

4.1.2 Varying Size of Recommendation Set

We next evaluate the performance of our DUP algorithm with respect to the size of recommendation set S_x. We evaluate the influence of the recommendation set by varying the size from 1 to 10. The size of recommendation set is much smaller than the complete set. For example, the size of complete set in the blocks domain is 1250 (shown in Table 1). It is less than 1% even though we recommend 10 actions for each unobserved action. We set the context window c used in Equation (1) to be three, the percentage of unobserved actions to be 0.25, and the learning constant δ in Equation (6) to be 0.1. For ARMS+PRP, the number of candidate goals for each testing example is set to 20. ARMS+PRP aims to recognize plans that are optimal with respect to the cost of actions. We relax ARMS+PRP to output $|S_x|$ optimal plans, some of which might be suboptimal. The results are shown in Figure 2.

From Figure 2, we find that accuracies of the three approaches generally become larger when the size of the recommended set increases in all three domains. This is consistent with our intuition, since the larger the recommended set is, the higher the possibility for the *truth* action to be in the recommended set. We can also see that the accuracy of our DUP algorithm are generally larger than ARMS+PRP in all three domains, which verifies that our DUP algorithm can indeed better capture relations among actions and thus recognize unobserved actions better than the model-learning based approach ARMS+PRP. The reason is similar to the one given for Figure 1 in the previous section. That is, the "shallow" model learnt by our DUP algorithm is better for recognizing plans than both the "exact" planning model learnt by ARMS for recognizing plans with planning techniques. Furthermore, the advantage of DUP becomes even larger when the size of recommended action set increases, which suggests our vector representation based learning approach can better capture action relations when the size of recommended action set is larger. The possibility of actions correctly recognized by DUP becomes much larger than ARMS+PRP when the size of recommendations increases.

4.2 Comparison between DUP and MatchPlan

In this experiment we compare DUP to MatchPlan which is built based on the idea of [9]. Likewise we varied the percentage of unobserved actions and the size of recommended actions to see the change of accuracies of both algorithms. The results are exhibited below.

4.2.1 Varying Percentage of Unobserved Actions

To compare our DUP algorithm with MatchPlan with respect to different percentage of unobserved actions, we set the window of training context c in Equation (1) of DUP to be three, the number of iterations in Algorithm 1 to be 1500, the size of recommendations to be ten, and the learning constant δ in Equation (6) to be 0.1. To make fair the comparison (with MatchPlan), we set the matching window of MatchPlan to be three, the same as the training context c of DUP, when searching plans from plan libraries $\mathcal{L}$. In other words, to estimate an unobserved action $\bar{a}_x$ in $\mathcal{O}$, MatchPlan matches previous three actions and subsequent three actions of $\bar{a}_x$ to plans in $\mathcal{L}$, and recommends ten actions with the maximal number of matched actions, considering observed actions in the context of $\bar{a}_x$ and actions in $\mathcal{L}$ as a successful matching. The results are shown in Figure 3.

From Figure 3, we find that the accuracy of DUP is much better than MatchPlan, which indicates that our DUP algorithm can better learn knowledge from plan libraries than the local matching approach MatchPlan. This is because we take advantage of global plan information of the plan library when learning the "shallow" model, i.e., distributed representations of actions, and the model with global information can best explain the observed actions. In contrast, MatchPlan just utilizes local plan information when matching the observed actions to the plan library, which results in lower accuracies. Looking at all three different domains, we can see that both algorithms perform the best in the *blocks* domain. The reason is similar to the one provided in the last subsection (for Figure 1), i.e., the number of words over the number of vocabulary in the *blocks* domain is relatively larger than the other two domains, which gives us the hint that it is possible to improve accuracies by increasing the ratio of the number of words over the number of vocabularies.

4.2.2 Varying Size of Recommendation Set

Likewise, we also would like to evaluate the change of accuracies when increasing the size of recommended actions. We used the same experimental setting as done by previous subsection. That is, we set the window of training context c of DUP to be three, the learning constant δ to be 0.1, the number of iterations in Algorithm 1 to be 1500, the matching window of MatchPlan to be three. In addition, we fix the percentage of unobserved actions to be 0.25. The results are shown in Figure 4.

We can observe that the accuracy of our DUP algorithm are generally larger than MatchPlan in all three domains in Figure 4, which suggests that our DUP algorithm can indeed better capture relations among actions and thus recognize unobserved actions better

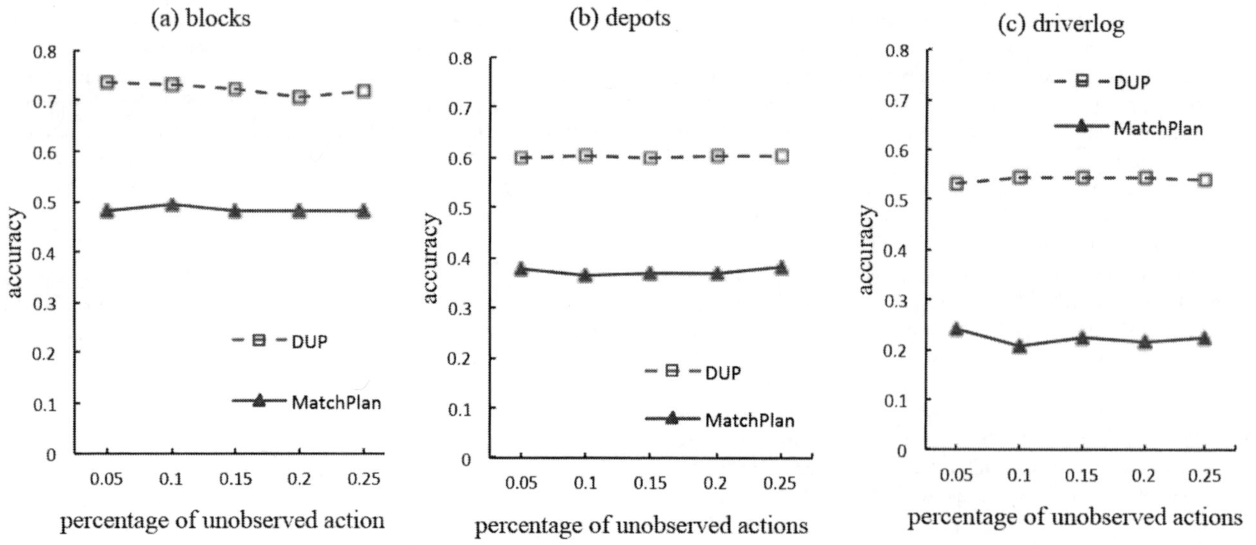

Figure 3: Accuracies of `DUP` and `MatchPlan` with respect to different percentage of unobserved actions

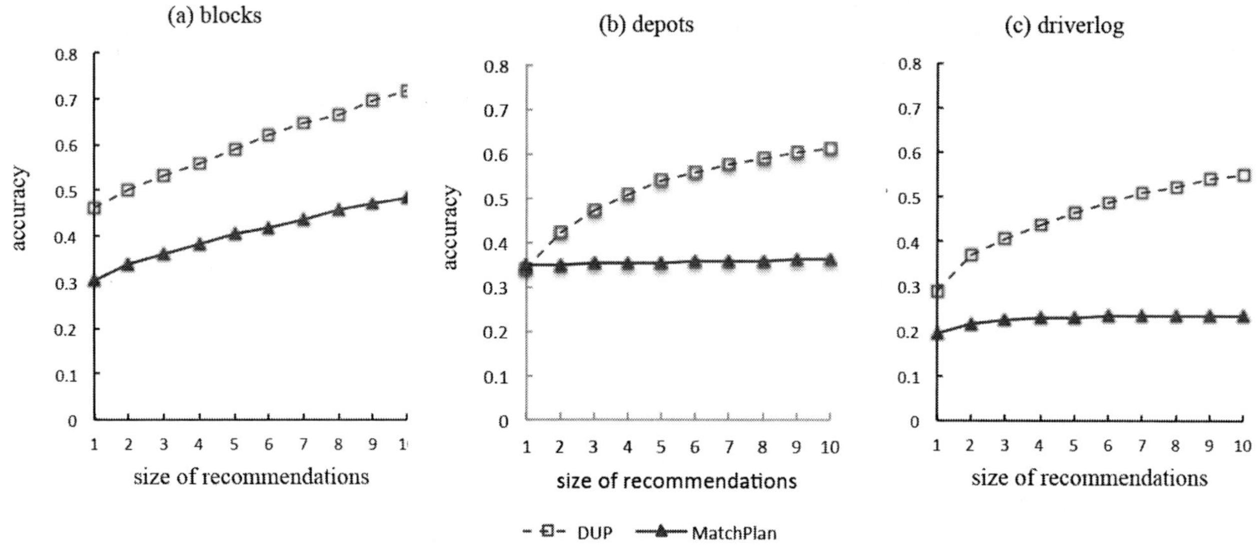

Figure 4: Accuracies of `DUP` and `MatchPlan` with respect to different size of recommendations

than the matching approach `MatchPlan`. The reason behind this is similar to previous experiments, i.e., the global information captured from plan libraries by `DUP` can indeed better improve accuracies than local information exploited by `MatchPlan`. In addition, looking at the trends of the curves of both `DUP` and `MatchPlan`, we can see the performance of `DUP` becomes much better than `MatchPlan` when the size of recommendations increases. This indicates the influence of global information becomes much larger when the size of recommendations increasing. In other words, larger size of recommendations provides better chance for "shallow" models learnt by `DUP` to perform better.

4.2.3 Varying Size of Training Set

To see the effect of size of training set, we ran both `DUP` and `MatchPlan` with different size of training set. We used the same setting as done by last subsection except fixing the size of recommendations to be 10, when running both algorithms. We varied the size of training set from 2500 to 4500. The results are shown in Figure 5.

We observed that accuracies of both `DUP` and `MatchPlan` generally become higher when the size of training set increases. This is consistent with our intuition, since the larger the size of training set is, the richer the information is available for improving the ac-

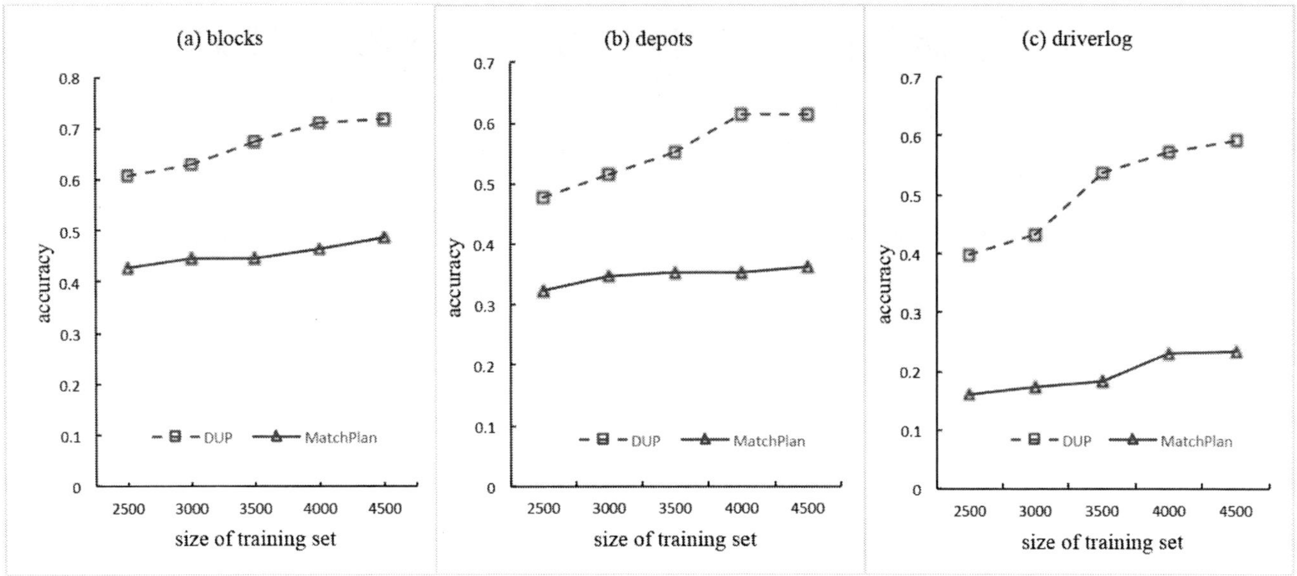

Figure 5: Accuracies of DUP and MatchPlan with respect to different size of training set

curacies. Comparing the curves of DUP and MatchPlan, we can see that DUP performs much better than MatchPlan. This further verifies the benefit of exploiting global information of plan libraries when learning the shallow models as done by DUP.

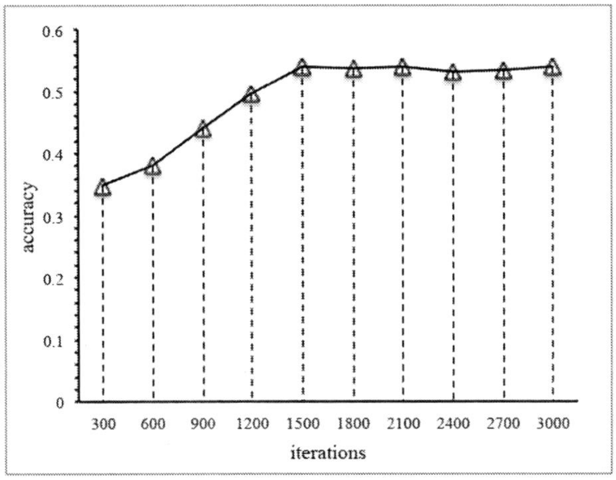

Figure 6: Accuracy with respect to different number of iterations in the blocks domain

4.3 Accuracy w.r.t. Iterations

In the previous experiments, we set the number of iterations in Algorithm 1 to be 1500. In this experiment, we would like to see the influence of iterations of our DUP algorithm when running the EM-style procedure. We changed the number of iterations from 300 to 3000 to see the trend of accuracy. We exhibit the experimental result in the *blocks* domain (the results of the other two domains are similar) in Figure 6.

From Figure 6, we can see the accuracy becomes higher at the beginning and stays flat when reaching the size of 1500. This exhibits that the EM procedure converges and has stable accuracies after the iteration reaches 1500. Similar results can also be found in the other two domains.

5. RELATED WORK

Our work is related to planning with incomplete domain models (or model-lite planning [12, 29]). Figure 7 shows the schematic view of incomplete models and their relationships in the spectrum of incompleteness. In a full model, we know exactly the dynamics of the model (i.e., state transitions). Approximate models are the closest to full models and their representations are similar except that there can be incomplete knowledge of action descriptions. To enable approximate planners to perform more (e.g., providing robust plans), planners are assumed to have access to additional knowledge circumscribing the incompleteness [25]. Partial models are one level further down the line in terms of the degree of incompleteness. While approximate models can encode incompleteness in the precondition/effect descriptions of the individual actions, partial models can completely abstract portions of a plan without providing details for them. In such cases, even though providing complete plans is infeasible, partial models can provide "planning guidance" for agents [27]. Shallow models are essentially just a step above having no planning model. They provide interesting contrasts to the standard precondition and effect based action models used in automated planning community. Our work in this paper belongs to the class of shallow models. In developing shallow models, we are interested in planning technology that helps humans develop plans, even in the absence of any structured models or plan traces. In such cases, the best that we can hope for is to learn local structures of the planning model to provide planning support, similar to providing spell-check in writing. While some work in web-service composition (c.f. [7]) did focus on this type of planning support, they were hobbled by being limited to simple input/output type comparison. In contrast, we expect shallow models to be useful in "critiquing" the plans being generated by the humans (e.g. detecting that an action introduced by the human is not consistent with the model), and "explaining/justifying" the suggestions generated by humans.

Our work is also related to plan recognition. Kautz and Allen proposed an approach to recognizing plans based on parsing observed actions as sequences of subactions and essentially model this knowledge as a context-free rule in an "action grammar" [14].

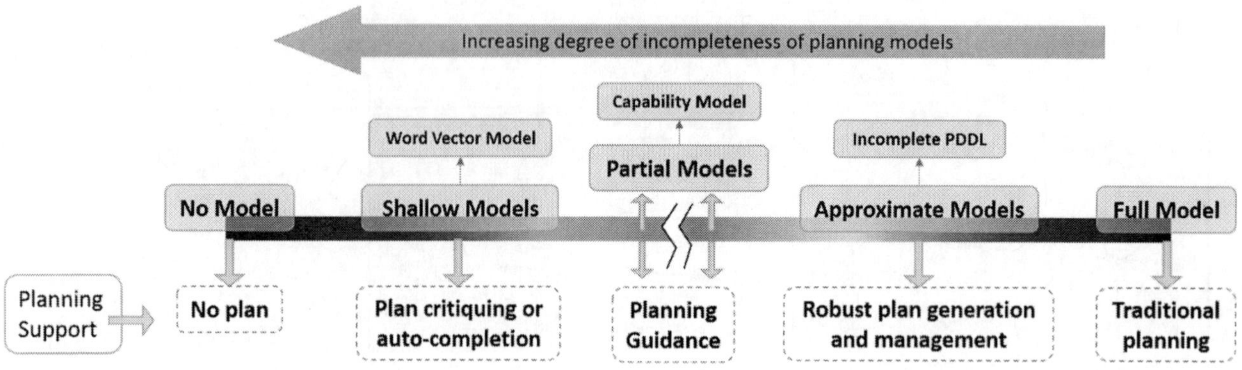

Figure 7: Schematic view of incomplete models and their relationships in the spectrum of incompleteness

All actions, plans are uniformly referred to as goals, and a recognizer's knowledge is represented by a set of first-order statements called event hierarchy encoded in first-order logic, which defines abstraction, decomposition and functional relationships between types of events. Lesh and Etzioni further presented methods in scaling up activity recognition to scale up his work computationally [16]. They automatically constructed plan-library from domain primitives, which was different from [14] where the plan library was explicitly represented. In these approaches, the problem of combinatorial explosion of plan execution models impedes its application to real-world domains. Kabanza and Filion [10] proposed an anytime plan recognition algorithm to reduce the number of generated plan execution models based on weighted model counting. These approaches are, however, difficult to represent uncertainty. They offer no mechanism for preferring one consistent approach to another and incapable of deciding whether one particular plan is more likely than another, as long as both of them can be consistent enough to explain the actions observed. Although we exploit a library of plans in our DUP approach, we aim to learning shallow models and utilize the shallow models to recognize plans that are not necessarily in the plan library, which is different from previous approaches that assume the plans to be recognized are from the plan library.

Instead of using a library of plans, Ramirez and Geffner [22] proposed an approach to solving the plan recognition problem using slightly modified planning algorithms, assuming the action models were given as input (note that action models can be created by experts or learnt by previous systems [26, 30]). Except previous work [14, 4, 8, 22] on the plan recognition problem presented in the introduction section, Saria and Mahadevan presented a hierarchical multi-agent markov processes as a framework for hierarchical probabilistic plan recognition in cooperative multi-agent systems [24]. Amir and Gal addressed a plan recognition approach to recognizing student behaviors using virtual science laboratories [2]. Ramirez and Geffner exploited off-the-shelf classical planners to recognize probabilistic plans [23]. Different from those approaches, we do not require any domain model knowledge provided as input. Instead, we automatically learn shallow domain models from previous plan cases for recognizing unknown plans that may not be identical to previous cases.

6. CONCLUSION AND DISCUSSION

In this paper we present a novel plan recognition approach DUP based on vector representation of actions. We first learn the vector representations of actions from plan libraries using the Skip-gram model which has been demonstrated to be effective. We then discover unobserved actions with the vector representations by repeatedly sampling actions and optimizing the probability of potential plans to be recognized. We also empirically exhibit the effectiveness of our approach.

While we focused on a one-shot recognition task in this paper, in practice, human-in-the-loop planning will consist of multiple iterations, with DUP recognizing the plan and suggesting action addition alternatives; the human making a selection and revising the plan. The aim is to provide a form of flexible plan completion tool, akin to auto-completers for search engine queries. To do this efficiently, we need to make the DUP recognition algorithm "incremental."

The word-vector based domain model we developed in this paper provides interesting contrasts to the standard precondition and effect based action models used in automated planning community. One of our future aims is to provide a more systematic comparison of the tradeoffs offered by these models. Although we have focused on the "plan recognition" aspects of this model until now, and assumed that "planning support" will be limited to suggesting potential actions to the humans. In future, we will also consider "critiquing" the plans being generated by the humans (e.g. detecting that an action introduced by the human is not consistent with the model learned by DUP), and "explaining/justifying" the suggestions generated by humans. Here, we cannot expect causal explanations of the sorts that can be generated with the help of complete action models (e.g. [20]), and will have to develop justifications analogous to those used in recommendation systems.

Another potential application for this type of distributed action representations proposed in this paper is social media analysis. In particular, work such as [15] shows that identification of action-outcome relationships can significantly improve the analysis of social media threads. The challenge of course is that such action-outcome models have to be learned from raw and noisy social media text containing mere fragments of plans. We believe that action vector models of the type we proposed in this paper provide a promising way of handling this challenge.

Acknowledgements

Tian and Zhuo thank National Natural Science Foundation of China (No. 61309011) and Key Lab of Machine Intelligence and Advanced Computing, Ministry of Education of China for the support of this research. Kambhampati's research is supported in part by the ARO grant W911NF-13-1-0023, the ONR grants N00014-13-1-0176, N00014-09-1-0017 and N00014-07-1-1049, and the NSF grant IIS201330813.

REFERENCES

[1] S. V. Albrecht and S. Ramamoorthy. Are you doing what I think you are doing? criticising uncertain agent models. In *Proceedings of the Thirty-First Conference on Uncertainty in Artificial Intelligence*, pages 52–61, 2015.

[2] O. Amir and Y. K. Gal. Plan recognition in virtual laboratories. In *Proceedings of IJCAI*, pages 2392–2397, 2011.

[3] S. Branavan, N. Kushman, T. Lei, and R. Barzilay. Learning high-level planning from text. In *Proceedings of ACL-12*, 2012.

[4] H. H. Bui. A general model for online probabilistic plan recognition. In *Proceedings of IJCAI*, pages 1309–1318, 2003.

[5] P. R. Cohen, E. C. Kaiser, M. C. Buchanan, and S. L. et al. Sketch-thru-plan: a multimodal interface for command and control. *Commun. ACM*, 58(4):56–65, 2015.

[6] X. Dong, A. Y. Halevy, J. Madhavan, E. Nemes, and J. Zhang. Simlarity search for web services. In *(e)Proceedings of the Thirtieth International Conference on Very Large Data Bases*, pages 372–383, 2004.

[7] X. Dong, A. Y. Halevy, J. Madhavan, E. Nemes, and J. Zhang. Simlarity search for web services. In *Proceedings of VLDB*, pages 372–383, 2004.

[8] C. W. Geib and R. P. Goldman. A probabilistic plan recognition algorithm based on plan tree grammars. *Artificial Intelligence*, 173(11):1101–1132, 2009.

[9] C. W. Geib and M. Steedman. On natural language processing and plan recognition. In *IJCAI 2007, Proceedings of the 20th International Joint Conference on Artificial Intelligence, Hyderabad, India, January 6-12, 2007*, pages 1612–1617, 2007.

[10] F. Kabanza, J. Filion, A. R. Benaskeur, and H. Irandoust. Controlling the hypothesis space in probabilistic plan recognition. In *IJCAI*, 2013.

[11] S. Kambhampati. Model-lite planning for the web age masses: The challenges of planning with incomplete and evolving domain models. In *Proceedings of the Twenty-Second AAAI Conference on Artificial Intelligence*, pages 1601–1605, 2007.

[12] S. Kambhampati. Model-lite planning for the web age masses: The challenges of planning with incomplete and evolving domain theories. In *Proceedings of AAAI*, pages 1601–1605, 2007.

[13] S. Kambhampati and K. Talamadupula. Human-in-the-loop planning and decision support. 2015. rakaposhi.eas.asu.edu/hilp-tutorial.

[14] H. A. Kautz and J. F. Allen. Generalized plan recognition. In *Proceedings of AAAI*, pages 32–37, 1986.

[15] E. Kıcıman and M. Richardson. Towards decision support and goal achievement: Identifying action-outcome relationships from social media. In *Proceedings of the 21th ACM SIGKDD International Conference on Knowledge Discovery and Data Mining*, pages 547–556. ACM, 2015.

[16] N. Lesh and O. Etzioni. A sound and fast goal recognizer. In *IJCAI*, pages 1704–1710, 1995.

[17] L. Manikonda, T. Chakraborti, S. De, K. Talamadupula, and S. Kambhampati. AI-MIX: using automated planning to steer human workers towards better crowdsourced plans. In *Proceedings of the Twenty-Eighth AAAI Conference on Artificial Intelligence*, pages 3004–3009, 2014.

[18] T. Mikolov, I. Sutskever, K. Chen, G. S. Corrado, and J. Dean. Distributed representations of words and phrases and their compositionality. In *NIPS*, pages 3111–3119, 2013.

[19] A. Y. Ng, H. J. Kim, M. I. Jordan, and S. Sastry. Autonomous helicopter flight via reinforcement learning. In *Proceedings of NIPS-03*, 2003.

[20] C. J. Petrie. Constrained decision revision. In *Proceedings of the 10th National Conference on Artificial Intelligence. San Jose, CA, July 12-16, 1992.*, pages 393–400, 1992.

[21] M. Ramírez and H. Geffner. Plan recognition as planning. In *IJCAI 2009, Proceedings of the 21st International Joint Conference on Artificial Intelligence, Pasadena, California, USA, July 11-17, 2009*, pages 1778–1783, 2009.

[22] M. Ramirez and H. Geffner. Plan recognition as planning. In *Proceedings of IJCAI*, pages 1778–1783, 2009.

[23] M. Ramirez and H. Geffner. Probabilistic plan recognition using off-the-shelf classical planners. In *Proceedings of AAAI*, pages 1121–1126, 2010.

[24] S. Saria and S. Mahadevan. Probabilistic plan recognitionin multiagent systems. In *Proceedings of AAAI*, 2004.

[25] M. D. Tuan Nguyen, Subbarao Kambhampati. Synthesizing robust plans under incomplete domain models. In *Proc. AAAI Workshop on Generalized Planning*, 2011.

[26] Q. Yang, K. Wu, and Y. Jiang. Learning action models from plan examples using weighted MAX-SAT. *Artificial Intelligence Journal*, 171:107–143, February 2007.

[27] Y. Zhang, S. Sreedharan, and S. Kambhampati. Capability models and their applications in planning. In *Proceedings of AAMAS*, pages 1151–1159, 2015.

[28] H. H. Zhuo and L. Li. Multi-agent plan recognition with partial team traces and plan libraries. In *Proceedings of IJCAI*, pages 484–489, 2011.

[29] H. H. Zhuo, T. A. Nguyen, and S. Kambhampati. Model-lite case-based planning. In *AAAI*, 2013.

[30] H. H. Zhuo, Q. Yang, D. H. Hu, and L. Li. Learning complex action models with quantifiers and implications. *Artificial Intelligence*, 174(18):1540–1569, 2010.

[31] H. H. Zhuo, Q. Yang, and S. Kambhampati. Action-model based multi-agent plan recognition. In *Proceedings of NIPS*, pages 377–385, 2012.

Optimal Target Assignment and Path Finding for Teams of Agents

Hang Ma
Department of Computer Science
University of Southern California
hangma@usc.edu

Sven Koenig
Department of Computer Science
University of Southern California
skoenig@usc.edu

ABSTRACT

We study the TAPF (combined target-assignment and path-finding) problem for teams of agents in known terrain, which generalizes both the anonymous and non-anonymous multi-agent path-finding problems. Each of the teams is given the same number of targets as there are agents in the team. Each agent has to move to exactly one target given to its team such that all targets are visited. The TAPF problem is to first assign agents to targets and then plan collision-free paths for the agents to their targets in a way such that the makespan is minimized. We present the CBM (Conflict-Based Min-Cost-Flow) algorithm, a hierarchical algorithm that solves TAPF instances optimally by combining ideas from anonymous and non-anonymous multi-agent path-finding algorithms. On the low level, CBM uses a min-cost max-flow algorithm on a time-expanded network to assign all agents in a single team to targets and plan their paths. On the high level, CBM uses conflict-based search to resolve collisions among agents in different teams. Theoretically, we prove that CBM is correct, complete and optimal. Experimentally, we show the scalability of CBM to TAPF instances with dozens of teams and hundreds of agents and adapt it to a simulated warehouse system.

Categories and Subject Descriptors

I.2.8 [**Artificial Intelligence**]: Problem Solving, Control Methods, and Search—*graph and tree search strategies, heuristic methods*; I.2.11 [**Artificial Intelligence**]: Distributed Artificial Intelligence—*intelligent agents, multiagent systems*

General Terms

Algorithms, Performance, Experimentation

Keywords

heuristic search; Kiva (Amazon Robotics) systems; multi-agent path finding; multi-robot path finding; network flow; path planning; robotics; target assignment; team work; warehouse automation

Appears in: *Proceedings of the 15th International Conference on Autonomous Agents and Multiagent Systems (AAMAS 2016), J. Thangarajah, K. Tuyls, C. Jonker, S. Marsella (eds.), May 9–13, 2016, Singapore.*

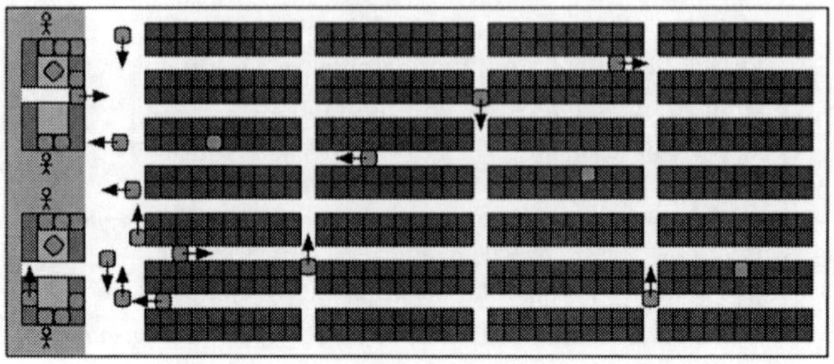

Figure 1: A typical Kiva warehouse system [22].

1. INTRODUCTION

Teams of agents often have to assign targets among themselves and then plan collision-free paths to their targets. Examples include autonomous aircraft towing vehicles [12], automated warehouse systems [22], office robots [19] and game characters in video games [15]. For example, in the near future, autonomous aircraft towing vehicles might tow aircraft all the way from the runways to their gates (and vice versa), reducing pollution, energy consumption, congestion and human workload. Today, autonomous warehouse robots already move inventory pods all the way from their storage locations to the inventory stations that need the products they store (and vice versa), see Figure 1.

We therefore study the **TAPF (combined target-assignment and path-finding) problem** for teams of agents in known terrain. The agents are partitioned into teams. Each team is given the same number of unique targets (goal locations) as there are agents in the team. The TAPF problem is to assign agents to targets and plan collision-free paths for the agents from their current locations to their targets in a way such that each agent moves to exactly one target given to its team, all targets are visited and the makespan (the earliest time step when all agents have reached their targets and stop moving) is minimized. Any agent in a team can be assigned to a target of the team, and the agents in the same team are thus exchangeable. However, agents in different teams are not exchangeable.

1.1 Related Work

The TAPF problem generalizes the anonymous and non-anonymous MAPF (multi-agent path-finding) problems:

- The **anonymous MAPF problem** (sometimes called goal-invariant MAPF problem) results from the TAPF problem if only one team exists (that consists of all agents). It is called "anonymous" because any agent can be assigned to a target, and the agents are thus exchangeable. The anonymous MAPF problem can be solved optimally in polynomial time [23]. Anonymous MAPF solvers use, for example, the polynomial-time **max-flow algorithm** on a time-expanded network [23] (an idea that originated in the operations research literature [1]) or graph-theoretic algorithms [11].

- The **non-anonymous MAPF problem** (often just called MAPF problem) results from the TAPF problem if every team consists of exactly one agent and the number of teams thus equals the number of agents. It is called "non-anonymous" because only one agent can be assigned to a target (meaning that the assignments of agents to targets are pre-determined), and the agents are thus non-exchangeable. The non-anonymous MAPF problem is NP-hard to solve optimally and even NP-hard to approximate within any constant factor less than 4/3 [10]. Non-anonymous MAPF solvers use, for example, reductions to problems from satisfiability, integer linear programming or answer set programming [24, 6, 17] or optimal, bounded suboptimal or suboptimal search algorithms [16, 8, 20, 14, 3, 9, 5, 2, 4], such as the optimal **CBS (conflict-based search) algorithm** [13].

Research so far has concentrated on these two extreme cases. Yet, many real-world applications fall between the extreme cases because the number of teams is larger than one but smaller than the number of agents, which is why we study the TAPF problem in this paper. The TAPF problem is NP-hard to solve optimally and even NP-hard to approximate within any constant factor less than 4/3 if more than one team exists [10]. It is unclear how to generalize anonymous MAPF algorithms to solving the TAPF problem. Straightforward ways of generalizing non-anonymous MAPF algorithms to solving the TAPF problem have difficulties with either scalability (due to the resulting large state spaces), such as searching over all assignments of agents to targets to find optimal solutions, or solution quality, such as assigning agents to targets with algorithms such as [18, 26] and then planning collision-free paths for the agents with non-anonymous MAPF algorithms (perhaps followed by improving the assignment and iterating [21]) to find sub-optimal solutions.

1.2 Contribution

We present the **CBM (Conflict-Based Min-Cost-Flow) algorithm** to bridge the gap between the extreme cases of anonymous and non-anonymous MAPF problems. CBM solves the TAPF problem optimally by simultaneously assigning agents to targets and planning collision-free paths for them, while utilizing the polynomial-time complexity of solving the anonymous MAPF problem for all agents in a team to scale to a large number of agents. CBM is a hierarchical algorithm that combines ideas from anonymous and non-anonymous MAPF algorithms. It uses CBS on the high level and a min-cost max-flow algorithm [7] on a time-expanded network on the low level. Theoretically, we prove that CBM is correct, complete and optimal. Experimentally, we show the scalability of CBM to TAPF instances with dozens of teams and hundreds of agents and adapt it to a simulated warehouse system.

2. TAPF

In this section, we formalize the TAPF problem and show how it can be solved via a reduction to the integer multi-commodity flow problem on a time-expanded network.

2.1 Definition and Properties

For a TAPF instance, we are given an undirected connected graph $G = (V, E)$ (whose vertices V correspond to locations and whose edges E correspond to ways of moving between locations) and K teams $team_1 \dots team_K$. Each *team* $team_i$ consists of K_i agents $a^i_1 \dots a^i_{K_i}$. Each agent a^i_j has a unique *start vertex* s^i_j. Each team $team_i$ is given unique *targets* (goal vertices) $g^i_1 \dots g^i_{K_i}$. Each agent a^i_j must move to a unique target $g^i_{j'}$. An *assignment* of agents in team $team_i$ to targets is thus a one-to-one mapping φ^i, determined by a permutation on $1 \dots K_i$, that maps each agent a^i_j in $team_i$ to a unique target $g^i_{j'} = \varphi^i(a^i_j)$ of the same team. A *path* for agent a^i_j is given by a function l^i_j that maps each integer time step $t = 0 \dots \infty$ to the vertex $l^i_j(t) \in V$ of the agent in time step t. A *solution* consists of paths for all agents that obey the following conditions:

1. $\forall i, j : l^i_j(0) = s^i_j$ (each agent starts at its start vertex);
2. $\forall i, j$ $\exists$a minimal T^i_j $\forall t \geq T^i_j$: $l^i_j(t) = \varphi^i(a^i_j)$ (each agent ends at its target);
3. $\forall i, j, t$: $(l^i_j(t) = l^i_j(t+1)$ or $(l^i_j(t), l^i_j(t+1)) \in E)$ (each agent always stays at its current vertex or moves to an adjacent vertex);
4. $\forall a^i_j, a^{i'}_{j'}, t$ with $a^i_j \neq a^{i'}_{j'}$: $l^i_j(t) \neq l^{i'}_{j'}(t)$ (there are no vertex collisions since different agents never occupy the same vertex at the same time);
5. $\forall a^i_j, a^{i'}_{j'}, t$ with $a^i_j \neq a^{i'}_{j'}$: $(l^i_j(t) \neq l^{i'}_{j'}(t+1)$ or $l^{i'}_{j'}(t) \neq l^i_j(t+1))$ (there are no edge collisions since different agents never move along the same edge in different directions at the same time).

Given paths for all agents in team $team_i$, the *team cost* of team $team_i$ is $\max_j T^i_j$ (the earliest time step when all agents in the team have reached their targets and stop moving). Given paths for all agents, the *makespan* is $\max_{i,j} T^i_j$ (the earliest time step when all agents have reached their targets and stop moving). The task is to find an *optimal solution*, namely one with minimal makespan. Note that a (non-anonymous) MAPF instance can be obtained from a TAPF instance by fixing the assignments of agents to targets. Any solution of a TAPF instance is thus also a solution of a (non-anonymous) MAPF instance on the same graph for a suitable assignment of agents to targets. Since the makespan of any optimal (non-anonymous) MAPF solution is bounded by $O(|V|^3)$ [25], the makespan of any optimal TAPF solution is also bounded by $O(|V|^3)$.

We define a collision between an agent agent a^i_j in team $team_i$ and a different agent $a^{i'}_{j'}$ in team $team_{i'}$ to be either a *vertex collision* ($team_i$, $team_{i'}$, l, t) [if $l = l^i_j(t) = l^{i'}_{j'}(t)$ and thus both agents occupy the same vertex at the same time] or an *edge collision* ($team_i$, $team_{i'}$, l_1, l_2, t) [if $l_1 = l^i_j(t) = l^{i'}_{j'}(t+1)$ and $l_2 = l^{i'}_{j'}(t) = l^i_j(t+1)$ and thus both agents move along the same edge in different directions at the same time]. Likewise, we define a constraint to be either a *vertex*

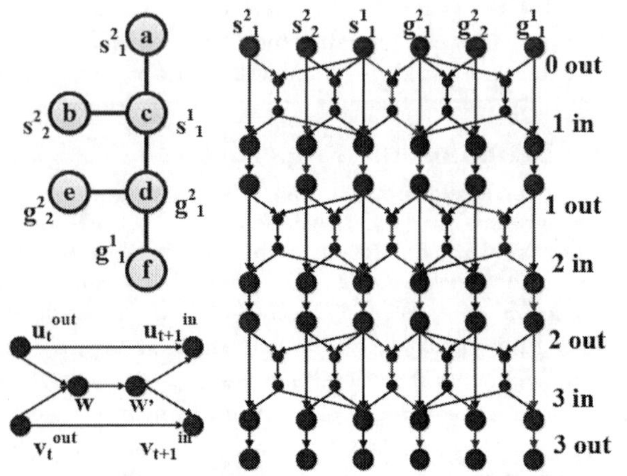

Figure 2: An example of constructing and finding a feasible integer multi-commodity flow for a 3-step time-expanded network. The TAPF instance consists of two teams. Team 1 consists of agent $\{a_1^1\}$ with target $\{g_1^1\}$. Team 2 consists of agents $\{a_1^2, a_2^2\}$ with targets $\{g_1^2, g_2^2\}$. The red edges represents a flow for commodity type 1, which corresponds to a path for the agent in Team 1. The blue edges represent a flow for commodity type 2, which corresponds to paths for the two agents in Team 2. The flow thus corresponds to an assignment of agent a_1^1 to target g_1^1, agent a_1^2 to target g_2^2 and agent a_2^2 to target g_1^2 as well as the (optimal) solution $\{\langle c, d, f, f\rangle\}$ and $\{\langle a, c, d, e\rangle, \langle b, b, c, d\rangle\}$.

constraint ($team_i$, l, t) [that prohibits any agent in $team_i$ from occupying vertex l in time step t] or an *edge constraint* ($team_i$, l_1, l_2, t) [that prohibits any agent in team $team_i$ from moving from vertex l_1 to vertex l_2 between time steps t and $t+1$].

2.2 Solution via Reduction to Flow Problem

Given a TAPF instance on undirected *graph* $G = (V, E)$ and a limit T on the number of time steps, we construct a T-step time-extended network using a reduction that is similar to that from the (non-anonymous) MAPF problem to the integer multi-commodity flow problem [24] (the idea of which is an extension of [23]). A *T-step time-extended network* is a directed network $\mathcal{N} = (\mathcal{V}, \mathcal{E})$ with vertices $\mathcal{V}$ and directed edges $\mathcal{E}$ that have unit capacity. Each vertex $v \in V$ is translated to a vertex $v_t^{out} \in \mathcal{V}$ for all $t = 0 \ldots T$ (which represents vertex v at the end of time step t) and a vertex $v_t^{in} \in \mathcal{V}$ for all $t = 1 \ldots T$ (which represents vertex v in the beginning of time step t). There is a supply of one unit of commodity type i at vertex $(s_j^i)_0^{out}$ and a demand of one unit of commodity type i at vertex $(g_j^i)_T^{out}$ for all $i = 1 \ldots K$ and $j = 1 \ldots K_i$. Each vertex $v \in V$ is also translated to an edge $(v_t^{out}, v_{t+1}^{in}) \in \mathcal{E}$ for all $t = 0 \ldots T-1$ (which represents an agent staying at vertex v between time steps t and $t+1$). Each vertex $v \in V$ is also translated to an edge $(v_t^{in}, v_t^{out}) \in \mathcal{E}$ for all $t = 1 \ldots T$ (which prevents vertex collisions of the form $(*, *, v, t)$ among all agents since only one agent can occupy vertex v between time steps t and $t+1$). Each edge $(u, v) \in E$ is translated to a *gadget* of vertices in $\mathcal{V}$ and edges in $\mathcal{E}$ for all $t = 0 \ldots T-1$, which consists of two auxiliary vertices $w, w' \in \mathcal{V}$ that are unique to the gadget (but have no subscripts here for ease of readability) and the edges $(u_t^{out}, w), (v_t^{out}, w), (w, w'), (w', u_{t+1}^{in}), (w, v_{t+1}^{in}) \in \mathcal{E}$. This gadget prevents edge collisions of the forms $(*, *, u, v, t)$ and $(*, *, v, u, t)$ among all agents since only one agent can move along the edge (u, v) in any direction between time steps t and $t+1$. Figure 2 shows a simple example. The following theorem holds by construction and can be proved in a way similar to the one for the reduction of the (non-anonymous) MAPF problem to the integer multi-commodity flow problem [24]:

Theorem 1. *There is a correspondence between all feasible integer multi-commodity flows on the T-step time-extended network of a number of unit that equals the number of agents and all solutions of the TAPF instance with makespans of at most T.*

An optimal solution can therefore be found by starting with $T = 0$ and iteratively checking for increasing values of T whether a **feasible integer multi-commodity flow** of a number of units that equals the number of agents exists for the corresponding T-step time-expanded network (which is an NP-hard problem), until an upper bound on T is reached (such as the one provided in [25]). Each T-step time-expanded network is translated in the standard way into an ILP (integer linear program), which is then solved with an ILP algorithm. We evaluate this ILP-based TAPF solver experimentally in Section 4.1. The anonymous MAPF problem results from the TAPF problem if only one team exists (that consists of all agents). The following corollary thus follows from [23]:

Corollary 2. *The TAPF problem can be solved optimally in polynomial time if only one team exists.*

3. CONFLICT-BASED MIN-COST FLOW

In this section, we present the **CBM (Conflict-Based Min-Cost-Flow) algorithm**, a hierarchical algorithm that solves TAPF instances optimally. On the high level, CBM considers each team to be a meta-agent. It uses CBS to resolve collisions among meta-agents, that is, agents in different teams. CBS is a form of best-first search on a tree, where each node contains a set of constraints and paths for all agents that obey these constraints, move all agents to unique targets of their teams and result in no collisions among agents in the same team. On the low level, CBM uses a polynomial-time min-cost max-flow algorithm [7] on a time-expanded network to assign all agents in a single team to unique targets of the same team and plan paths for them that obey the constraints imposed by the currently considered high-level node and result in no collisions among the agents in the team. Since the running time of CBS on the high level can be exponential in the number of collisions that need to be resolved [13], CBM uses edge weights on the low level to bias the search so as to reduce the possibility of creating collisions with agents in different teams.

The idea of biasing the search on the low level has been used before for solving the (non-anonymous) MAPF problem with CBS [2]. Similarly, the idea of grouping some agents into a meta-agent on the high level and planning paths for each group on the low level has been used before for solving the (non-anonymous) MAPF problem with CBS

Algorithm 1: High-Level Search of CBM

```
1  Root.constraints ← ∅;
2  Root.paths ← ∅;
3  for each team_i do
4      if Lowlevel(team_i, Root) returns no paths then
5          return No solution exists;
6      Add the returned paths to Root.paths;
7  Root.key ← Makespan(Root.paths);
8  Priorityqueue ← {Root};
9  while Priorityqueue ≠ ∅ do
10     N ← Priorityqueue.pop();
11     if Findcollisions(N.paths) returns no collisions then
12         return Solution is N.paths;
13     Collision ← earliest collision found;
14     for each team_i involved in Collision do
15         N' ← Newnode() /* with parent N */;
16         N'.constraints ← N.constraints;
17         N'.paths ← N.paths;
18         Add one new constraint for team_i to N'.constraints;
19         if Lowlevel(team_i, N') returns paths then
20             Update N'.paths with the returned paths;
21             N'.key ← max(Makespan(N'.paths), N.key);
22             Priorityqueue.insert(N');
23 return No solution exists;
```

[13] but faces the difficulty of having to identify good groups of agents. The best way to group agents can often be determined only experimentally and varies significantly among MAPF instances. On the other hand, grouping all agents in a team into a meta-agent for solving the TAPF problem is a natural way of grouping agents since the assignments of agents in the same team to targets and their paths strongly depend on each other and should therefore be planned together on the low level. For example, if an agent is assigned to a different target, then many of the agents in the same team typically need to be assigned to different targets as well and have their paths re-planned. Also, the lower level can then use a polynomial-time max-flow algorithm on a time-expanded network to assign all agents in a single team to targets and find paths for them due to the polynomial-time complexity of the corresponding anonymous MAPF problem.

3.1 High-Level Search of CBM

On the high level, CBM performs a best-first search on a binary tree, see Algorithm 1. Each node N contains constraints *N.constraints* and paths for all agents *N.paths* that obey these constraints, move all agents to unique targets of their teams and result in no collisions among agents in the same team. All nodes are stored in a priority queue. The priority queue initially consists of only the root node *Root* with no constraints and paths for all agents that move all agents to unique targets of their teams, result in no collisions among agents in the same team and minimize the team cost of each team [Lines 1-8]. If the priority queue is empty, then CBM terminates unsuccessfully [Line 23]. Otherwise, CBM always chooses a node N in the priority queue with the smallest key [Line 10]. The key of a node is the makespan of its paths. (Ties are broken in favor of the node whose paths have the smallest number of colliding teams.) If the paths of node N have no colliding agents, then they are a solution and CBM terminates successfully with these paths [Lines 11-12]. Otherwise, CBM determines all collisions between two agents (which have to be in different teams) and then resolves a collision *Collision* whose time step t is smallest [Line 13]. (We have evaluated different ways of prioritizing the collisions, including the one suggested in [3], but have not observed significant differences in the resulting running times of CBM.) Let the two colliding agents be in $team_i$ and $team_{i'}$. CBM then generates two child nodes N_1 and N_2 of node N, both of which inherit the constraints and paths from their parent node [Lines 15-17]. If the collision is a vertex collision $(team_i, team_{i'}, l, t)$ or, equivalently, $(team_{i'}, team_i, l, t)$, then CBM adds the vertex constraint $(team_i, l, t)$ to the constraints of node N_1 and the vertex constraint $(team_{i'}, l, t)$ to the constraints of node N_2 [Line 18]. If the collision is an edge collision $(team_i, team_{i'}, l_1, l_2, t)$ or, equivalently, $(team_{i'}, team_i, l_2, l_1, t)$, then CBM adds the edge constraint $(team_i, l_1, l_2, t)$ to the constraints of node N_1 and the edge constraint $(team_{i'}, l_2, l_1, t)$ to the constraints of node N_2 [Line 18]. For each of the two new nodes, say node N_1, the low-level search is called to assign all agents in team $team_i$ to unique targets of the same team and find paths for them that obey the constraints of node N_1 and result in no collisions among the agents in the team. If the low-level search successfully returns such paths, then CBM updates the paths of node N_1 by replacing the paths of all agents in team $team_i$ with the returned ones, updates the key of node N_1 and inserts it into the priority queue [Lines 19-22]. Otherwise, it discards the node.

3.2 Low-Level Search of CBM

On the low level, Lowlevel($team_i$,N) assigns all agents in team $team_i$ to unique targets of the same team and finds paths for them that obey all constraints of node N (namely all vertex constraints of the form $(team_i, *, *)$ and all edge constraints of the form $(team_i, *, *, *)$) and result in no collisions among the agents in the team.

Given a limit T on the number of time steps, CBM constructs the T-step time-expanded network from Section 2.2 with the following changes: a) There is only a single commodity type i since CBM considers only the single team $team_i$. There is a supply of one unit of this commodity type at vertex $(s_j^i)_0^{out}$ and a demand of one unit of this commodity type at vertex $(g_j^i)_T^{out}$ for all $j = 1 \ldots K_i$. b) To obey the vertex constraints, CBM removes the edge (l_t^{in}, l_t^{out}) from $\mathcal{E}$ for each vertex constraint of the form $(team_i, l, t)$. c) To obey the edge constraints, CBM removes the edges $((l_1)_t^{out}, w)$ and $(w', (l_2)_{t+1}^{in})$ from $\mathcal{E}$ for all gadgets that correspond to edge $(l_1, l_2) \in E$ for each edge constraint of the form $(team_i, l_1, l_2, t)$. Let $\mathcal{V} = \mathcal{V}'$ be the set of (remaining) vertices and $\mathcal{E}'$ be the set of remaining edges.

Similar to the procedure from Section 2.2, CBM iteratively checks for increasing values of T whether a feasible integer single-commodity flow of K_i units exists for the corresponding T-step time-expanded network, which can be done with the polynomial-time max-flow algorithm that finds a **feasible maximum flow**. CBM can start with T being the key of the parent node of node N since it is a lower bound on the new key of node N due to Line 21. (For N = *Root*, CBM starts with $T = 0$.) During the earliest iteration when the max-flow algorithm finds a feasible flow of K_i units, the call returns successfully with the paths for the agents in the team that correspond to the flow. If T reaches an upper bound on the makespan of an optimal solution (such as the one provided in [25]) and no feasible flow of K_i units was found, then the call returns unsuccessfully with no paths.

CBM actually implements Lowlevel($team_i$,N) in a more sophisticated way to avoid creating collisions between agents in team $team_i$ and agents in other teams by adding edge weights to the T-step time-expanded network. CBM sets the weights of all edges in $\mathcal{E}'$ to zero initially and then modifies them as follows: a) To reduce vertex collisions, CBM increases the weight of edge $(v_t^{in}, v_t^{out}) \in \mathcal{E}'$ by one for each vertex $v = l_{j'}^{i'}(t) \in V$ in the paths of node N with $i' \neq i$ to reduce the possibility of an agent of team $team_i$ occupying the same vertex at the same time step as an agent from a different team. b) To reduce edge collisions, CBM increases the weight of edge $(v_t^{in}, w) \in \mathcal{E}'$ by one for each edge $(u = l_{j'}^{i'}(t), v = l_{j'}^{i'}(t+1)) \in E$ in the paths of node N with $i' \neq i$ (where w is the auxiliary vertex of the gadget that corresponds to edge (u, v) and time step t) to reduce the possibility of an agent of team $team_i$ moving along the same edge in a different direction but at the same time step as an agent from a different team.

CBM uses the procedure described above, except that it now uses a min-cost max-flow algorithm (instead of a max-flow algorithm) that finds a **flow of minimal weight among all feasible maximal flows**. In particular, it uses the successive shortest path algorithm [7], a generalization of the Ford-Fulkerson algorithm that uses Dijkstra's algorithm to find a path of minimal weight for one unit of flow. The complexity of the successive shortest path algorithm is $O(U(|\mathcal{E}'| + |\mathcal{V}'| \log |\mathcal{V}'|))$, where $O(|\mathcal{E}'| + |\mathcal{V}'| \log |\mathcal{V}'|)$ is the complexity of Dijkstra's algorithm and U is the value of the feasible maximal flow, which is bounded from above by K_i. The number of times that the successive shortest path algorithm is executed is bounded from above by the chosen upper bound on the makespan of an optimal solution, which in turn is bounded from above by $O(|V|^3)$. Thus, each low-level search runs in polynomial time.

3.3 Analysis of Properties

We use the following properties to prove that CBM is correct, complete and optimal.

Property 1. *There is a correspondence between all feasible integer flows of K_i units on the T-step time-extended network constructed for team $team_i$ and node N and all paths for agents in team $team_i$ that a) obey the constraints of node N, b) move all agents from their start vertices to unique targets of their team, c) result in no collisions among agents in team $team_i$ and d) result in a team cost of team $team_i$ of at most T.*

Reason. The property holds by construction and can be proved in a way similar to the one for the reduction of the (non-anonymous) MAPF problem to the integer multi-commodity flow problem [24]:
Left to right: Assume that a flow is given that has the stated properties. Each unit flow from a source to a sink corresponds to a path through the time-extended network from a unique source to a unique sink. Thus, it can be converted to a path for an agent such that all such paths together have the stated properties: Properties a and d hold by construction of the time-extended network; Property b holds because a flow of K_i units uses all supplies and sinks; and Property c holds since the flows neither share vertices nor edges.
Right to left: Assume that paths are given that have the stated properties. If necessary, we extend the paths by letting the agents stay at their targets. Each path now corresponds to a path through the time-extended network (due to Properties a and d) from a unique source to a unique sink (due to Property b) that does not share directed edges with the other such paths (due to Property c). Thus, it can be converted to a unit flow such that all such unit flows together respect the unit capacity constraints and form a flow of K_i units.

Property 2. *CBM generates only finitely many nodes.*

Reason. The constraint added on Line 18 to a child node is different from the constraints of its parent node since the paths of its parent node do not obey it. Overall, CBM creates a binary tree of finite depth since only finitely many different vertex and edge constraints exist and thus generates only finitely many nodes.

Property 3. *Whenever CBM inserts a node into the priority queue, its key is finite.*

Reason (by induction). The property holds for the root node. Assume that it holds for the parent node of some child node. The key of the child node is the maximum of the key of the parent node and the team costs of all teams for the paths of the child node. The key of the parent node is finite due to the induction assumption. The low level returned the paths for each team successfully at some point in time and all team costs are thus finite as well.

Property 4. *Whenever CBM chooses a node on Line 10 and the paths of the node have no colliding agents, then CBM correctly terminates with a solution with finite makespan of at most the value of its key.*

Reason. The key of the node is finite according to Property 3, and the makespan of its paths is at most the value of its key due to Line 21.

Property 5. *CBM chooses nodes on Line 10 in non-decreasing order of their keys.*

Reason. CBM performs a best-first search, and the key of a parent node is most the key of any of its child nodes due to Line 21.

Property 6. *The smallest makespan of any solution that obeys the constraints of a parent node is at most the smallest makespan of any solution that obeys the constraints of any of its child nodes.*

Reason. The solutions that obey the constraints of a parent node are a superset of the solutions that obey the constraints of any of its child nodes since the constraints of the parent node are a subset of the constraints of any of its child nodes.

Property 7. *The key of a node is at most the makespan of any solution that obeys its constraints.*

Reason (by induction). The property holds for the root node. Assume that it holds for the parent node N of any child node N' and that the paths for team $team_i$ were updated in the child node. Let x be the smallest makespan of any solution that obeys the constraints of the parent node and y be the smallest makespan of any solution that obeys the constraints of the child node. We show in the following that the key of the parent node and the team costs of all teams for the paths of the child node are all at most y. Then, the key of the child node is also at most y since it is the maximum of all these quantities, and the property holds. First, consider the key of the parent node. The key of the parent node is at most x due to the induction assumption, which in turn is at most y due to Property 6. Second, consider any team different from team $team_i$. Then, the team cost of the team for the paths of the child node is equal to the team cost of the team for the paths of the parent node (since the paths were not updated in the child node and are thus identical), which in turn is at most the key of the parent node (since the key of the parent node is the maximum of several quantities that include the team cost of the team for the paths of the parent node), which in turn is at most y (as shown directly above). Finally, consider team $team_i$. When the low level finds new paths for team $team_i$, it starts with T being the key of the parent node, which is at most y (as shown directly above). Thus, the max-cost min-flow algorithm on a T-step time-expanded network constructed for team $team_i$ and the child node finds a feasible integer flow of K_i units for $T \leq y$ since there exists a solution with makespan y that obeys the constraints of the child node. The team cost of the corresponding paths for team $team_i$ is at most T due to Property 1.

Theorem 3. *CBM is correct, complete and optimal.*

Proof. Assume that no solution to a TAPF instance exists and CBM does not terminate unsuccessfully on Line 5. Then, whenever CBM chooses a node on Line 10, the paths of the node have colliding agents (because otherwise a solution would exist due to Property 4). Thus, the priority queue eventually becomes empty and CBM terminates unsuccessfully on Line 23 since it generates only finitely many nodes due to Property 2.

Now assume that a solution exists and the makespan of an optimal solution is x. Assume, for a proof by contradiction, that CBM does not terminate with a solution with makespan x. Thus, whenever CBM chooses a node on Line 10 with a key of at most x, the paths of the node have colliding agents (because otherwise CBM would correctly terminate with a solution with makespan at most x due to Property 4). A node whose constraints the optimal solution obeys has a key of at most x due to Property 7. The root note is such a node since the optimal solution trivially obeys the (empty) constraints of the root node. Whenever CBM chooses such a node on Line 10, the paths of the node have colliding agents (as shown directly above since its key is at most x). CBM thus generates the child nodes of this parent node, the constraints of at least one of which the optimal solution obeys and which CBM thus inserts into the priority queue with a key of at most x. Since CBM chooses nodes on Line 10 in non-decreasing order of their keys due to Property 5, it chooses infinitely many nodes on Line 10 with keys of at most x, which is a contradiction with Property 2. □

4. EXPERIMENTS

In this section, we describe the results of four experiments on a 2.50 GHz Intel Core i5-2450M PC with 6 GB RAM. First, we compare CBM to four other TAPF or MAPF solvers. Second, we study how CBM scales with the number of agents in each team. Third, we study how CBM scales with the number of agents. Fourth, we apply CBM to a simulated warehouse system.

4.1 Experiment 1: Alternative Solvers

We compare our optimal TAPF solver CBM to two optimal (non-anonymous) MAPF solvers, namely a) the CBS solver provided by the authors of [13] and b) the ILP-based MAPF solver provided by the authors of [24], and two optimal TAPF solvers, namely a) an unweighted version of CBM that runs the polynomial-time max-flow algorithm on a time-expanded network without edge weights (instead of the min-cost max-flow algorithm on a time-expanded network with edge weights) on the low level and b) an ILP-based TAPF solver (based on the ILP-based MAPF solver) that casts a TAPF instance as a series of integer multi-commodity flow problems as described in Section 2.2, each of which it models as an ILP and solves with the ILP solver Gurobi 6.0 (www.gurobi.com).

For Experiment 1, each team consists of 5 agents but the number of agents varies from 10 to 50, resulting in $2 \ldots 10$ teams. For each number of agents, we generate 50 TAPF instances from the same 50 30×30 4-neighbor grids with 10% randomly blocked cells by randomly assigning unique start cells to agents and unique targets to teams. For the MAPF solvers, we convert each TAPF instance to a (non-anonymous) MAPF instance by randomly assigning the agents in each team to unique targets of the same team.

Table 1 shows the success rates as well as the means of the makespans and running times (in seconds) over the instances that are solved within a time limit of 5 minutes each. Red entries indicate that some instances are not solved within the time limit, while dashed entries indicate that all instances are not solved within the time limit. CBM solves all TAPF instances within the time limit.

4.1.1 CBS and the ILP-Based MAPF Solver

Both MAPF solvers solve most of the MAPF instances within the time limit. The running times of CBM and CBS are similar because, on the low level, both the min-cost max-flow algorithm of CBM (for a single team) and the A* algorithm of CBS (for a single agent) are fast. Optimal solutions of the TAPF instances have smaller makespans than optimal solutions of the MAPF instances due to the freedom of assigning agents to targets for the TAPF instances rather than assigning them randomly for the MAPF instances.

4.1.2 Unweighted CBM

Unweighted CBM solves less than half of all TAPF instances within the time limit if the number of agents is larger than 10 due to the large number of collisions among agents in different teams produced by the max-flow algorithm on the low level in tight spaces with many agents, which results in a large number of node expansions by CBS on the high level. We conclude that biasing the search on the low level is important for CBM to solve all TAPF instances within the time limit.

4.1.3 ILP-Based TAPF Solver

The ILP-based TAPF solver solves less than half of all TAPF instances within the time limit if the number of

Table 1: Results on 30×30 4-neighbor grids with randomly blocked cells for different numbers of agents.

	CBM (TAPF)			Unweighted CBM (TAPF)			ILP (TAPF)			CBS (MAPF)			ILP (MAPF)		
agts	mkspn	time	success	mkspn	time	success	mkspn	time	success	mkspn	time	success	mkspn	time	success
10	22.34	0.34	1	22.08	0.41	0.72	22.34	18.24	1	36.36	0.03	1	36.36	8.66	1
15	23.88	0.57	1	24.64	1.06	0.44	23.88	35.44	1	37.32	0.05	1	37.32	15.31	1
20	25.06	0.78	1	23.73	2.06	0.22	24.74	62.85	0.94	39.84	0.55	1	39.84	30.30	1
25	25.20	1.07	1	22.25	1.58	0.08	24.76	88.55	0.82	40.44	0.12	1	40.44	43.76	1
30	26.26	1.71	1	31	6.73	0.02	24.70	108.75	0.66	41.92	0.21	1	41.92	65.86	1
35	26.50	1.92	1	-	-	0	24.65	121.99	0.46	42.50	1.55	1	42.50	81.83	1
40	27.60	2.95	1	-	-	0	25.29	152.98	0.14	43.69	4.82	0.98	43.53	115.53	0.98
45	27.20	3.66	1	-	-	0	24.29	161.52	0.14	42.41	2.60	0.92	42.37	133.47	0.98
50	27.90	5.32	1	-	-	0	24.50	161.95	0.04	43.96	7.95	0.96	42.86	166.99	0.86

K	mkspn	time
2	11.1	2.75
4	15.9	4.30
5	17.12	2.56
10	23.04	5.53
20	29.32	6.06
25	30.88	6.44
50	39.76	12.15

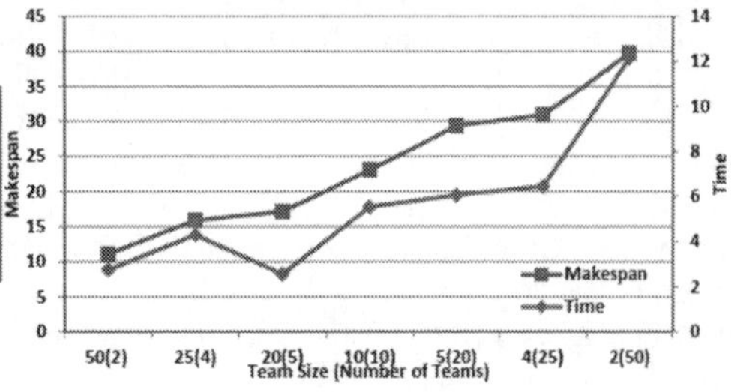

Figure 3: Results on 30×30 4-neighbor grids with randomly blocked cells for different team sizes. (K is the number of teams.)

agts	mkspn	time	success
100	30.10	6.14	1
150	29.67	8.10	0.96
200	32.09	12.97	0.94
250	31.05	15.56	0.86
300	32.09	25.42	0.7
350	33.03	32.59	0.6
400	34.19	59.69	0.42
450	35.80	101.47	0.1

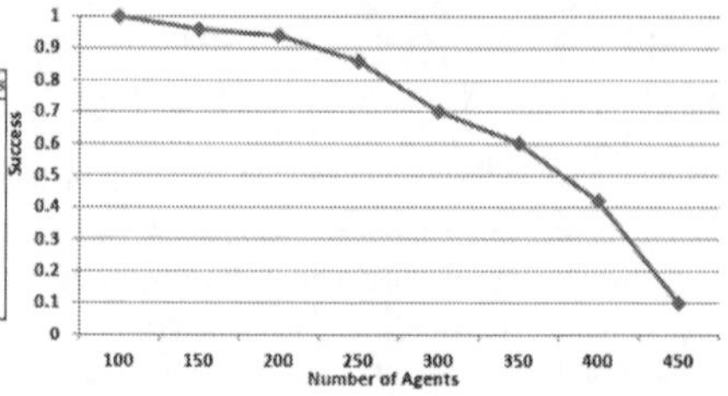

Figure 4: Results on 30×30 4-neighbor grids with randomly blocked cells for different numbers of agents.

agents is larger than 30, and its running time is much larger than that of CBM. The success rates and running times of the the ILP-based TAPF solver tend to be larger than those of the ILP-based MAPF solver even though the ILP formulation of a TAPF instance has fewer variables than that of the corresponding MAPF instance (since the number of commodity types equals the number of teams for the TAPF instance but the number of agents for the MAPF instance). However, the variables in the ILP formulation of the MAPF instance are Boolean variables while those in the ILP formulation of the TAPF instance are integer variables. Furthermore, the ILP-based MAPF solver uses the maximum over all agents of the length of a shortest path of each agent as the starting value of T for the time-expanded network while the ILP-based TAPF solver solves the LP formulation of the max-flow problem that finds paths for each team (ignoring other teams) and then uses the maximum over all teams of the team costs of the paths as the starting value T for the time-expanded network.

4.2 Experiment 2: Team Size

For Experiment 2, there are 100 agents but the number of agents in a team (team size) varies from 50 to 2, resulting in $K = 2 \dots 50$ teams. For each team size, we generate 50 TAPF instances as described before.

Table 3 shows the means of the makespans and running times (in seconds) over the instances that are solved within a time limit of 5 minutes each. CBM solves all TAPF instances within the time limit. For large team sizes and thus small numbers of teams, the makespans are small because CBM has more freedom to assign agents to targets. The running times are also small because the min-cost max-flow algorithm on the low level is fast even for large numbers of agents while CBS on the high level is fast because it needs to resolve collisions among agents in different teams but there are only a small number of teams. Thus, it is advantageous for teams to consist of as many agents as possible.

4.3 Experiment 3: Number of Agents

For Experiment 3, each team consists of 5 agents but the number of agents varies from 100 to 450, resulting in $20 \dots 90$ teams. For each number of agents, we generate 50 TAPF instances as described before.

Table 3 shows the success rates as well as the means of the makespans and running times (in seconds) over the instances that are solved within a time limit of 5 minutes each. For 250 agents or fewer, the success rate is larger than 85%. Current (non-anonymous) MAPF algorithm are not able to handle instances of this scale. As the number of agents increases, the success rates decrease and the makespans and running times increase due to the increasing number of collisions among agents in different teams produced by the min-cost max-flow algorithm on the low level. For 450 agents, for example, more than half of the unblocked cells are occupied by agents and thus many start cells of agents are also targets for other agents.

4.4 Experiment 4: Warehouse System

We now apply CBM to a simulated **Kiva (now: Amazon Robotics) warehouse system** [22]. Figure 1 shows a typical grid layout with *inventory stations* on the left side and *storage locations* in the *storage area* to the right of the inventory stations. Each inventory station has an entrance (purple cells) and an exit (pink cells). Each storage location (green cell) can store one *inventory pod*. Each inventory pod consists of a stack of trays, each of which holds bins with products. The autonomous warehouse robots are called *drive units*. Each drive unit is capable of picking up, carrying and putting down one inventory pod at a time. As a team, the drive units need to move inventory pods all the way from their storage locations to the inventory stations that need the products they store (to ship them to customers) and then back to the same or different empty

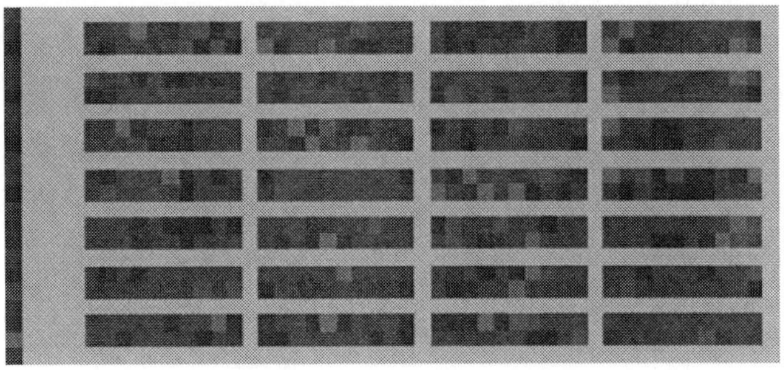

Figure 5: A randomly generated Kiva instance. CBM returns a solution with makespan 65 in 25.97 seconds. The length of the shortest path for both green drive units near the top-right corner to the green inventory station in the bottom-left corner is 64. Thus, at least one of them has to wait for at least one time step to enter the green inventory station and the solution found by CBM is optimal.

storage locations. After a drive unit enters an inventory station, the requested product is removed from its inventory pod by a worker. Once drive units have delivered all requested products for one shipment to the same inventory station, the worker prepares the shipment to the customer.

Figure 5 shows a randomly generated Kiva instance. The light grey cells are free space. The dark grey cells are storage locations occupied by inventory pods and thus blocked. There are 7 inventory stations on the left side. The red cells are their exits, and the other 7 cells with graduated blue-green colors are their entrances. Drive units can enter and leave the inventory stations one at a time through their entrances and exits, respectively. The cells with graduated blue-green colors in the storage area are occupied by drive units. Each drive unit needs to carry the inventory pod in its current cell to the inventory station of the same color.

For Experiment 4, we generate 50 TAPF instances. Each instance has 420 drive units. 210 "incoming" drive units start at randomly determined storage locations: 30 drive units each need to move their inventory pods to the 7 inventory stations. In order to create difficult Kiva instances, we generate the start cells of these drive units randomly among all storage locations rather than cluster them according to their target inventory stations. 210 "outgoing" drive units start at the inventory stations: 30 drive units each need to move their inventory pods from the 7 inventory stations to the storage locations vacated by the incoming drive units. The task is to assign the 210 outgoing drive units to the vacated storage locations and plan collision-free paths for all 420 drive units in a way such that the makespan is minimized. The incoming drive units that have the same inventory station as target are a team (since they can arrive at the inventory station in any order), and all outgoing drive units are a team.

So far, we have assumed that, for any TAPF instance, all start vertices are unique, all targets are unique and each of the teams is given the same number of targets as there are agents in the team but these assumptions are not necessarily satisfied here. 1) The outgoing drive units that start at the same inventory station all start at its exit. In this case, we change the construction of the T-step time-extended network for the team of outgoing drive units so that there is a supply of one unit at vertex $v_t^{out} \in \mathcal{V}'$ for all $t = 0 \dots 29$ and all vertices $v \in V$ that correspond to exits of inventory stations. This construction forces the outgoing drive units that start at the same inventory station to leave it one after the other during the first 30 time steps. No further changes are necessary. 2) The incoming drive units that have the same inventory station as target all end at its entrance. In this case, we change the construction of the T-step time-extended network for each team of incoming drive units so that there is an auxiliary vertex with a demand of 30 units and vertex $v_t^{out} \in \mathcal{V}'$ for all $t = 0 \dots T$ is connected to the auxiliary vertex with an edge with unit capacity and zero edge weight, where $v \in V$ corresponds to the entrance of the inventory station. This construction forces the incoming drive units to enter the inventory station at different time steps. No further changes are necessary. 3) There could be more empty storage locations than outgoing drive units. In this case, no changes are necessary.

CBM finds solutions for 40 of the 50 Kiva instances within a time limit of 5 minutes each, yielding a success rate of 80%. The mean of the makespan over the solved Kiva instances is 63.73, and the mean of the running time is 91.61 seconds. Since early Kiva warehouse systems typically had about 200 drive units in more spacious (and thus less challenging) warehouses and even bounded-suboptimal (non-anonymous) MAPF algorithms that were specifically designed for simulated Kiva warehouse systems do not scale well to hundreds of agents [4], we conclude that CBM is a promising TAPF algorithm for applications of real-world scale.

5. CONCLUSIONS

In this paper, we studied the TAPF (combined target-assignment and path-finding) problem for teams of agents in known terrain to bridge the gap between the extreme cases of anonymous and non-anonymous MAPF problems, as required by many applications. We presented CBM, a hierarchical algorithm that is correct, complete and optimal for solving the TAPF problem. CBM outperforms (non-anonymous) MAPF algorithms in terms of both scalability and solution quality in our experiments. It also generalizes to applications with dozens of teams and hundreds of agents, which demonstrates its promise.

6. ACKNOWLEDGMENTS

We thank Jingjin Yu for making the code of their ILP-based MAPF solver and Guni Sharon for making the code of their CBS solver available to us. Our research was supported by NASA via Stinger Ghaffarian Technologies as well as NSF under grant numbers 1409987 and 1319966 and a MURI under grant number N00014-09-1-1031. The views and conclusions contained in this document are those of the authors and should not be interpreted as representing the official policies, either expressed or implied, of the sponsoring organizations, agencies or the U.S. government.

REFERENCES

[1] J. E. Aronson. A survey of dynamic network flows. *Annals of Operations Research*, 20(1-4):1–66, 1989.

[2] M. Barer, G. Sharon, R. Stern, and A. Felner. Suboptimal variants of the conflict-based search algorithm for the multi-agent pathfinding problem. In

Annual Symposium on Combinatorial Search, pages 19–27, 2014.

[3] E. Boyarski, A. Felner, R. Stern, G. Sharon, D. Tolpin, O. Betzalel, and S. E. Shimony. ICBS: improved conflict-based search algorithm for multi-agent pathfinding. In *International Joint Conference on Artificial Intelligence*, pages 740–746, 2015.

[4] L. Cohen, T. Uras, and S. Koenig. Feasibility study: Using highways for bounded-suboptimal multi-agent path finding. In *Annual Symposium on Combinatorial Search*, pages 2–8, 2015.

[5] B. de Wilde, A. W. ter Mors, and C. Witteveen. Push and rotate: Cooperative multi-agent path planning. In *International Conference on Autonomous Agents and Multi-agent Systems*, pages 87–94, 2013.

[6] E. Erdem, D. G. Kisa, U. Oztok, and P. Schueller. A general formal framework for pathfinding problems with multiple agents. In *AAAI Conference on Artificial Intelligence*, pages 290–296, 2013.

[7] A. V. Goldberg and R. E. Tarjan. Solving minimum-cost flow problems by successive approximation. In *Annual ACM Symposium on Theory of Computing*, pages 7–18, 1987.

[8] M. Goldenberg, A. Felner, R. Stern, G. Sharon, N. R. Sturtevant, R. C. Holte, and J. Schaeffer. Enhanced partial expansion A*. *Journal of Artificial Intelligence Research*, 50:141–187, 2014.

[9] R. Luna and K. E. Bekris. Push and swap: Fast cooperative path-finding with completeness guarantees. In *International Joint Conference on Artificial Intelligence*, pages 294–300, 2011.

[10] H. Ma, C. Tovey, G. Sharon, T. K. S. Kumar, and S. Koenig. Multi-agent path finding with payload transfers and the package-exchange robot-routing problem. In *AAAI Conference on Artificial Intelligence*, 2016.

[11] P. MacAlpine, E. Price, and P. Stone. SCRAM: Scalable collision-avoiding role assignment with minimal-makespan for formational positioning. In *AAAI Conference on Artificial Intelligence*, pages 2096–2102, 2015.

[12] R. Morris, C. Pasareanu, K. Luckow, W. Malik, H. Ma, S. Kumar, and S. Koenig. Planning, scheduling and monitoring for airport surface operations. In *AAAI-16 Workshop on Planning for Hybrid Systems*, 2016.

[13] G. Sharon, R. Stern, A. Felner, and N. R. Sturtevant. Conflict-based search for optimal multi-agent pathfinding. *Artificial Intelligence*, 219:40–66, 2015.

[14] G. Sharon, R. Stern, M. Goldenberg, and A. Felner. The increasing cost tree search for optimal multi-agent pathfinding. *Artificial Intelligence*, 195:470–495, 2013.

[15] D. Silver. Cooperative pathfinding. In *Artificial Intelligence and Interactive Digital Entertainment*, pages 117–122, 2005.

[16] T. S. Standley. Finding optimal solutions to cooperative pathfinding problems. In *AAAI Conference on Artificial Intelligence*, pages 173–178, 2010.

[17] P. Surynek. Reduced time-expansion graphs and goal decomposition for solving cooperative path finding sub-optimally. In *International Joint Conference on Artificial Intelligence*, pages 1916–1922, 2015.

[18] C. Tovey, M. Lagoudakis, S. Jain, and S. Koenig. The Generation of Bidding Rules for Auction-Based Robot Coordination. In L. Parker, F. Schneider, and A. Schultz, editors, *Multi-Robot Systems. From Swarms to Intelligent Automata*, volume 3, chapter 1, pages 3–14. Springer, 2005.

[19] M. Veloso, J. Biswas, B. Coltin, and S. Rosenthal. CoBots: Robust Symbiotic Autonomous Mobile Service Robots. In *International Joint Conference on Artificial Intelligence*, pages 4423–4429, 2015.

[20] G. Wagner and H. Choset. Subdimensional expansion for multirobot path planning. *Artificial Intelligence*, 219:1–24, 2015.

[21] G. Wagner, H. Choset, and N. Ayanian. Subdimensional expansion and optimal task reassignment. In *Annual Symposium on Combinatorial Search*, pages 177–178, 2012.

[22] P. R. Wurman, R. D'Andrea, and M. Mountz. Coordinating hundreds of cooperative, autonomous vehicles in warehouses. *AI Magazine*, 29(1):9–20, 2008.

[23] J. Yu and S. M. LaValle. Multi-agent path planning and network flow. In E. Frazzoli, T. Lozano-Perez, N. Roy, and D. Rus, editors, *Algorithmic Foundations of Robotics X, Springer Tracts in Advanced Robotics*, volume 86, pages 157–173. Springer, 2013.

[24] J. Yu and S. M. LaValle. Planning optimal paths for multiple robots on graphs. In *IEEE International Conference on Robotics and Automation*, pages 3612–3617, 2013.

[25] J. Yu and D. Rus. Pebble motion on graphs with rotations: Efficient feasibility tests and planning algorithms. In *Algorithmic Foundations of Robotics XI, Springer Tracts in Advanced Robotics*, volume 107, pages 729–746. Springer, 2015.

[26] X. Zheng and S. Koenig. K-swaps: Cooperative negotiation for solving task-allocation problems. In *International Joint Conference on Artifical Intelligence*, pages 373–378, 2009.

Argumentation-Based Multi-Agent Decision Making with Privacy Preserved

Yang Gao
Institute of Software, Chinese Academy of Sciences
gaoyang@iscas.ac.cn

Francesca Toni
Imperial College London, UK
f.toni@imperial.ac.uk

Hao Wang, Fanjiang Xu
Institute of Software, Chinese Academy of Sciences
{wanghao, fanjiang}@iscas.ac.cn

ABSTRACT

We consider multi-agent decision making problems in which agents need to communicate with other agents to make socially optimal decisions but, at the same time, have some private information that they do not want to share. *Abstract argumentation* has been widely used in both single-agent and multi-agent decision making problems, because of its ability for reasoning with incomplete and conflicting information. In this work, we propose an abstract argumentation-based knowledge representation and communication protocol, such that agents can find socially optimal strategies by only disclosing the 'necessary' and 'disclosable' information. We prove that our protocol is sound, efficient, of perfect information security and guaranteed to terminate.

Keywords

Abstract Argumentation; Distributed Constraints Satisfaction; Privacy Preservation; Social Optimality

1. INTRODUCTION

In many *cooperative multi-agent decision making* problems, agents may have limited sensory capabilities and there may exist some restrictions on actions (e.g. some actions cannot be performed in certain states, and some actions need to be performed by a certain number of agents simultaneously); therefore, agents need to communicate with each other, so as to share some information and to coordinate their actions to meet the constraints [27]. Even though these agents are cooperative, they may have some private information that they do not want to share with other agents. This type of problem is interesting not only because many real problems can be viewed as instances thereof, e.g. time scheduling problems [22], freight scheduling problems [19] and sensor networks [34], but also because it involves information sharing, conflict resolution as well as privacy preservation at the same time.

Abstract argumentation frameworks (AFs, c.f. [8, 4]) are natural techniques to model and solve this type of problems in a novel way. Since AFs can naturally represent and reason with conflicting information, they have been widely used to model functionalities in both single-agent (e.g. [3]) and multi-agent (e.g. [14]) decision making problems. Furthermore, because of the dialectic nature of AFs, argumentation dialogue models [23, 9] have been proposed so that agents can jointly resolve conflicts or make decisions by exchanging only the necessary information (see, e.g., [12]). In this paper, inspired by algorithms for solving *distributed constraint satisfaction problems* (DisCSPs; see, e.g., [32]), we propose an AF-based cooperation protocol, which not only uses AFs to represent each agent's beliefs and observations, but also uses AF-based dialogues to regulate communication between agents. We prove that, by using our protocol, after finitely many rounds of communication, agents can find a strategy profile efficiently, by exchanging only the necessary information and limiting the disclosure of private information. The resulting strategy profile is **(i)** 'feasible', i.e. all actions in the strategy profile are 'doable' according to all agents' observations and beliefs; **(ii)** 'acceptable', i.e. meeting all constraints; and **(iii)** socially optimal, i.e. there does not exist another strategy profile that satisfies requirements **(i)** and **(ii)** and makes every agent 'better off'.

Throughout, we use, for illustration, the following motivating scenario, adapted from the *Battle of the Sexes* game in [25] and the meeting scheduling problem in [28].

Example 1. Alice and Bob want to decide on an activity for the day. Alice prefers going to a ballet to watching a football game, while Bob's preference is the opposite. Both Alice and Bob want to go to the same place rather than different ones. This is a simple DisCSP, but where both agents have private concerns they would rather not disclose.

As for Alice, she worries about Bob's ex-wife attending the ballet (we denote this concern by **Ex?**), but she does not want Bob to know about this concern. Caroline, Bob's and his ex-wife's daughter, told Alice earlier that she went hiking today with her mother (denoted by *C:Hiking*). Also, Alice worries about the weather for the day (denoted by *Wea*), but she found from a forecast that it will be sunny (denoted by *Sun*). Alice does not mind disclosing these two pieces of weather-related information. Alice's beliefs and observations can be modelled by the AF in Fig. 1(a), where arrows represent *attacks* (e.g., **Ex?** attacks A:Ballet, since Bob's ex-wife attending the ballet is a reason against Alice and Bob going, in Alice's mind). Note that this AF does not represent preferences (see Sect. 3.2 for more on this).

As for Bob, he worries about whether Alice likes watching sports games (denoted by **LikeSport?**): Alice has told him before, but he forgets and would rather Alice not be aware of this! However, they went to a tennis match last week and Alice enjoyed that (denoted by *EnjoyTennis*). Also, Bob

Appears in: *Proceedings of the 15th International Conference on Autonomous Agents and Multiagent Systems (AAMAS 2016), J. Thangarajah, K. Tuyls, C. Jonker, S. Marsella (eds.), May 9–13, 2016, Singapore.*

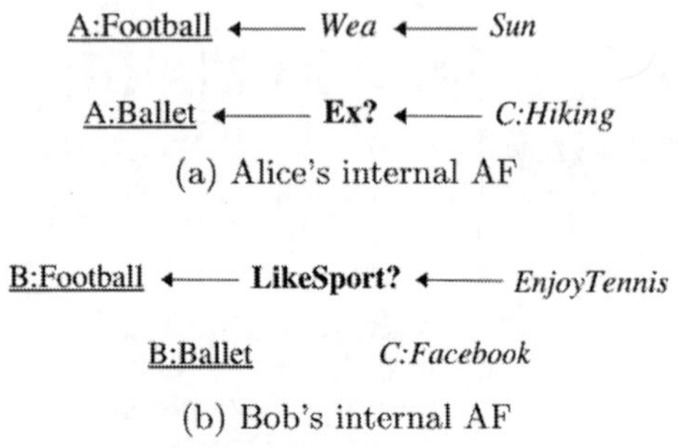

(a) Alice's internal AF

(b) Bob's internal AF

Figure 1: AFs that represent (a) Alice's and (b) Bob's beliefs and observations (respectively).

notices that his daughter Caroline has posted on Facebook 'In the ballet hall now!' (denoted by *C:Facebook*). Bob's beliefs and observations (but, again, not preferences) can be modelled by the AF in Fig. 1(b).

Note that *C:Facebook* is in conflict with *C:Hiking*. However, since Alice and Bob do not know each other's arguments a priori, no attack from *C:Facebook* to *C:Hiking* is present in Fig. 1. However, as soon as they share these arguments, an attack will naturally emerge.

We present a protocol for agents equipped with AFs with private and disclosable beliefs and observations, as in this example, to communicate and coordinate so as to solve DisCSPs, such as the one in this example, so as to guarantee social optimality, taking all agents' preferences into account, while preserving privacy in some sense.

2. BACKGROUND

We summarise abstract argumentation frameworks, argumentation dialogues and distributed constraints satisfaction problems in Sect. 2.1, 2.2 and 2.3, respectively. Finally, we give background on information security in Sect. 2.4. This will be used to characterise our protocol as 'privacy preserving'.

2.1 Abstract Argumentation Frameworks

An *Abstract argumentation Framework* (AF) [8] is a pair (Arg, Att) where Arg is a set of *arguments* and $Att \subseteq Arg \times Arg$ is a binary relation representing the *attacks* between arguments. An AF is typically visualised as a graph, as in Fig 1. A set $S \subseteq Arg$ attacks an argument $b \in Arg$ when some member of S attacks b. A set $S \subseteq Arg$ is *conflict-free* iff no member of S attacks a member of S.

Argumentation semantics are defined as criteria for selecting sets of 'winning' arguments in AFs. The *admissible semantics* is widely used: in $\mathsf{F} = (Arg, Att)$, $S \subseteq Arg$ is *admissible* iff S is conflict-free and attacks any argument in Arg that attacks an argument in S. We say that an argument is admissible (in F) iff it belongs to at least one admissible set.

Although the admissible (and other) semantics can identify sets of 'winning' arguments, it does not 'explain' why an argument belongs to a 'winning' set. To tackle this, the *related-admissible* semantics [13] has been proposed. In (Arg, Att), $S \subseteq Arg$ is *related-admissible* iff S is admissible and $\exists a \in S$ such that every argument in S *defends* a (such a is a *topic* of S), where argument b defends a iff:

- $b = a$; or
- $\exists c \in Arg$ s.t. c attacks a and b attacks c; or
- $\exists c \in Arg$ s.t. c defends a and b defends c.

A related-admissible set S is a *compact explanation of* a iff a is a topic of S and S is the smallest (wrt. $\subseteq$) among all related-admissible sets whose topics include a.

Example 2. Consider Bob's AF in Fig. 1(b). The set {**LikeSport?**, *EnjoyTennis*} is not admissible as it is not conflict-free. The set {*B:Football*, *EnjoyTennis*, *C:Facebook*} is admissible but not related-admissible since *C:Facebook* does not defend *B : Football* or *EnjoyTennis*. {*B : Football*, *EnjoyTennis*} is related-admissible and a compact explanation of *B:Football*. Also, {*B : Ballet*} is a compact explanation of *B : Ballet*.

Similarly, in Alice's AF (Fig. 1(a)), there are two compact explanations: {*C:Hiking*, *A : Ballet*} for argument *A : Ballet*, and {*Sun*, *A:Football*} for argument *A : Football*.

2.2 Argument Games and Disputes

Argumentation semantics define the 'winning' sets of arguments, but do not specify how to obtain them. Inspired by the dialectic nature of argumentation, *argument games* (also known as *dialogues*) are proposed as a proof theory for argumentation semantics (see, e.g., [18, 20]). An argument game involves two players[1]: a *defender* and a *challenger*. The defender starts with an argument to be tested, after which each player must attack the other player's arguments. This process is known as a *dispute*. The *two parties immediate response dispute* (TPI-dispute) [30, 9] is a widely used dialogue model. A player in a TPI-dispute is allowed to present an argument (only in the first move) or present an argument attacking one of the previous arguments of the other player. An argument is said to be *defended* by a TPI-dispute iff this argument is the first move in this TPI-dispute and the defender wins this dispute (as for the definition of 'win', see [30]). An argument is admissible iff it can be defended in every TPI-dispute. When there are finitely many arguments, TPI-disputes are guaranteed to terminate.

2.3 DisCSPs

DisCSPs are problems where knowledge (i.e., domains, variables and constraints) is distributed among communicating agents and cannot be centralized for various reasons (e.g. prohibitive costs of constraint translation or security/privacy issues) [32]. *Chronological synchronous backtracking* (SBT) is one of the simplest while most fundamental algorithms for DisCSPs; many modern algorithms for DisCSPs, e.g. asynchronous backtracking and its variants, have their roots in SBT [32]. SBT requires a static ordering of agents. Following this, agents try to extend a partial solution into a total one by adding consistent assignments for unassigned variables. Agents pass a token among them; the agent who has the token can extend the partial solution and then send the extended partial solution and the token to the next agent. SBT terminates either because all variables are included in the partial solution or because every value for the variable of the first agent has been discarded. In the former case, the partial solution constitutes a solution for the problem, while in the latter case, the problem is unsatisfiable. SBT is guaranteed to terminate and is sound and complete (i.e. it terminates only with correct answers, and it terminates for all problems) [17].

[1]Later in Sect. 5 we will see that the players are different from the agents in the problems we consider.

2.4 Information Entropy and Security

The extent to which a certain secret can be preserved, or the level of *information security*, has been rigorously studied in *information theory* [26, 7]. *Perfect security* is the highest privacy preserving level, in which the information disclosed by an agent does not provide any 'hints' to other agents about the private information of the agent, even when the other agents have unlimited computational resources.

The *(Shannon) entropy* [26] is arguably the most widely used measurement to quantitatively evaluate the information loss and the level of security. Formally, the entropy of a discrete random variable X with possible values $\{x_1, \cdots, x_n\}$ and probability mass function $P(X)$ is defined as

$$H(X) = -\sum_i p(x_i) \cdot \log_2 p(x_i)$$

where $p(x_i)$ is a shorthand for $P(X = x_i)$. Note that when $p(x_i) = 0$ for some i, the value of the corresponding summand is taken to be 0, i.e. $0 \cdot \log_2(0) = 0$. As an extension, the *conditional entropy* of two events X and Y is defined as

$$H(X|Y) = \sum_{i,j} p(x_i, y_j) \cdot \log_2[p(y_j)/p(x_i, y_j)]$$

where $p(x_i, y_j)$ is the probability that $X = x_i, Y = y_j$.

Perfect security can be defined using these notions of entropy, as follows. Suppose *Agent* has a secret message M, and *Agent* discloses information C according to some communication protocol Pr; Pr is of *perfect security wrt.* M iff $H(M) = H(M|C)$, i.e. the prior probability of M is the same as its posteriori probability given the disclosure of C.

3. PROBLEM DEFINITION

We first give a formal definition of the type of DisCSPs we consider in this paper (Sect. 3.1), and then introduce the AFs we use to model each agent (Sect. 3.2). Finally, we define the strategy profiles we are after (Sect. 3.3).

3.1 Problem Description

The problems we consider are tuples (Ag, Act, Con), where $Ag = \{Agent_1, \cdots, Agent_N\}$ is the set of agents ($N \in \mathbb{N}, N \geq 2$), $Act = \{a_1, \cdots, a_M\}$ is the set of available actions for each agent ($M \in \mathbb{N}, M \geq 1$), and $Con : Act \to 2^{\{0,\cdots,N\}}$ is the constraint function. Given an action $a \in Act$, $Con(a) \subseteq \{0, \cdots, N\}$ is the required number of agents to perform this action.[2] For example, if an action a can be performed by no agents or by two agents simultaneously, $Con(a) = \{0, 2\}$. In the reminder, unless stated otherwise, we let i and j range over all agents and all actions, respectively. A *strategy profile* S is a list $\langle ac_1, \cdots, ac_N \rangle$, such that $ac_i \in Act$ is the action of $Agent_i$.

We say that a strategy profile S is *acceptable* for a problem if it satisfies all constraints in the problem. We say that a problem is *satisfiable* if all its constraints can be satisfied by some (acceptable) strategy profile(s). Formally, for a strategy profile S and an action a, let $N(\mathsf{S}, a)$ be the number of agents assigned to perform a in S. Then:

[2]We only consider constraints on the number of agents simultaneously performing an action. More complex constraints in DisCSPs (see, e.g., [6]) are left for future work.

Definition 1. A strategy profile S is *acceptable* for problem (Ag, Act, Con) iff $\forall a \in Act$, $N(\mathsf{S}, a) \in Con(a)$. A problem (Ag, Act, Con) is *satisfiable* if there exists an acceptable strategy profile for it.

Example 3. In Example 1, $N = 2$ because there are two agents (Caroline and her mother are not counted as agents as they do not participate in the decision making). Also, $M = 2$ as there are two actions ('go to the ballet' and 'watch football'). Con('go to the ballet') $=$ Con('watch football') $= \{0, 2\}$ because both agents want to attend these activities together or not at all. This problem is satisfiable, as there are two acceptable strategy profiles: both agents going to the ballet and both agents watching football.

3.2 AFs for Knowledge Representation

We assume that each agent has a complete pre-order expressing a preference on all available actions, and we term $Agent_i$'s preference on actions the *ideal preference* of $Agent_i$, denoted by $\leq^i_{Ideal}$. $<^i_{Ideal}$ is a total order derived from $\leq^i_{Ideal}$, such that for $a_p, a_q \in Act$, $a_p <^i_{Ideal} a_q$ iff $a_p \leq^i_{Ideal} a_q$ and $a_q \not\leq^i_{Ideal} a_p$. This derived total order is used later in Sect. 3.3 when we define social optimality. Also, each agent has information (including beliefs and observations) for or against some actions or other information, represented by *internal AFs*. Agents will share elements of their internal AFs via our cooperation protocol. The *perfect-view internal AF* of an agent includes all arguments that other agents may disclose during cooperation. In this subsection, we define these concepts formally.

Arguments in internal AFs.

In line with some widely used AF-based decision making paradigms [3, 5], we distinguish two categories of arguments: *practical* and *epistemic* arguments. Practical arguments recommend actions to agents. For simplicity, for each action and agent, we allow for one and only one practical argument to recommend this action to the agent. We let A_{ij} denote the (one and only) practical argument recommending action a_j to $Agent_i$, and denote the set of all practical arguments belonging to $Agent_i$ by $pPra_i$ (p is short for 'private', and Pra stands for 'Practical'), i.e. $pPra_i = \{A_{i1}, \cdots, A_{iM}\}$. Practical arguments are *private* since, in our protocol, agents directly inform other agents about their action choices (in line with SBT, see later in Sect. 4) and, thus, they do not need to additionally communicate the reasons for these choices (expressed by the practical arguments).

As for the epistemic arguments, we distinguish two subcategories: *disclosable* and *private* arguments, which an agent is willing and unwilling to disclose to other agents, respectively. We denote $Agent_i$'s disclosable and private epistemic argument sets by $dEpi_i$ (d is short for 'disclosable') and $pEpi_i$, respectively.

We denote $Agent_i$'s argument set by $Arg_i = pPra_i \cup dEpi_i \cup pEpi_i$. We impose that $pPra_i$, $dEpi_i$ and $pEpi_i$ are mutually disjoint and that Arg_i is finite. In Fig. 1, practical arguments are underlined, private epistemic arguments are in boldface and disclosable epistemic arguments are in italic. How to build these arguments from beliefs and raw observations is not the focus of this paper; in principle, any structured argumentation technique, e.g. ABA [29] or ASPIC+ [21], can be used for this purpose.

Internal AFs.

We first discuss attacks within an agent's internal AF. In line with [3], we impose that practical arguments do not attack each other, so as to preserve all relevant information in the decision process (see Sect. 2.3 in [1] for a thorough explanation). Since a practical argument supports an agent to perform an action, while an epistemic argument justifies beliefs and observations on which practical arguments are built, in line with [3], practical arguments are not allowed to attack (private or disclosable) epistemic arguments.

As for attacks between epistemic arguments, since private arguments usually represent agents' private beliefs/concerns, whereas disclosable arguments usually represent observations/facts (see Example 1), and we believe that the latter are 'stronger' than the former, we do not allow private arguments to attack disclosable arguments; we leave the relaxation of this constraint for future work. Finally, each private epistemic argument is attacked by some disclosable (epistemic) arguments. This guarantees that, when negotiating with other agents, other agents can 'indirectly' defend or attack each private epistemic argument by (directly) attacking or defending some disclosable arguments attacking it. This will be further discussed in Sect. 5.

We now define the internal AF for each agent.

Definition 2. $Agent_i$'s internal AF is $AF_i = (Arg_i, Att_i)$, such that $Arg_i = pPra_i \cup dEpi_i \cup pEpi_i$ and

1. $\forall a, b \in pPra_i$, $(a, b) \notin Att_i$;
2. $\forall a \in pPra_i$, $\nexists b \in pEpi_i \cup dEpi_i$ such that $(a, b) \in Att_i$;
3. $\forall a \in pEpi_i$, $\nexists b \in dEpi_i$ such that $(a, b) \in Att_i$; and
4. $\forall a \in pEpi_i$, $\exists b \in dEpi_i$ such that $(b, a) \in Att_i$.

In line with our earlier discussion: condition 1 gives that the set of all practical arguments is conflict-free, condition 2 gives that practical arguments are not allowed to attack epistemic arguments, condition 3 gives that private arguments are not allowed to attack disclosable arguments, and condition 4 gives that each private argument is 'publicly defeasible' during coordination, as discussed earlier.

Example 4. The AF in Fig. 1(a) is an internal AF, as required by Def. 2. Indeed, there are no attacks between practical arguments (condition 1), no attacks from practical arguments to epistemic arguments (condition 2) and no attacks from private arguments to disclosable arguments (condition 3). Also, the only private epistemic argument, **Ex?**, is attacked by the disclosable epistemic argument *C:Hiking*, thus condition 4 holds too. Similarly, it is easy to check that the AF in Fig. 1(b) also satisfies the requirements of Def. 2.

Attacks across internal AFs/Perfect-view internal AFs.

Now we discuss attacks between arguments of different agents. Since an agent cannot know another agent's private arguments, we restrict attacks between agents' arguments only to their disclosable (epistemic) arguments, i.e. given a practical or private epistemic argument of $Agent_i$, this argument cannot attack or be attacked by another agent's arguments. In addition, we assume that agents have a consensus on the attack relation between (disclosable) arguments (irrespective of the agents they belong to). This assumption is in line, e.g., with [25]. Note that with this assumption we do not mean that an agent knows another agent's disclosable epistemic arguments a priori; instead, we mean that if two disclosable arguments are presented in front of an agent, this

	Disclosable?	Allowed to attack which arguments?
$pPra_i$	No	$\emptyset$
$dEpi_i$	Yes	$dEpi\_{_i} \cup Arg_i$
$pEpi_i$	No	$pPra_i \cup pEpi_i$

Table 1: Properties of different kinds of arguments (from $Agent_i$'s perspective).

agent is able to decide the attack relation between them, and this attack relation is agreed by all other agents. We denote the attack relation between different agents' arguments by Att^*, such that $Att^* \subseteq \bigcup_i dEpi_i \times \bigcup_i dEpi_i$.

Let $dEpi\_{_i} = \bigcup_{p \neq i} dEpi_p$, for $p \in \{1, \cdots, N\}$. Namely, $dEpi\_{_i}$ consists of all disclosable epistemic arguments belonging to agents other than $Agent_i$. Properties of different kinds of arguments are summarised in Table 1. We now define the perfect-view internal AF for each agent.

Definition 3. $Agent_i$'s perfect-view internal AF is $AF_i^* = (Arg_i^*, Att_i^*)$, where $Arg_i^* = dEpi\_{_i} \cup Arg_i$ and $Att_i^* = Att_i \cup Att^*$.

Example 5. Alice's perfect-view internal AF (Arg_A^*, Att_A^*) has $Arg_A^* = Arg_A \cup \{EnjoyTennis, C{:}Facebook\}$ and $Att_A^* = Att_A \cup \{(C{:}Facebook, C{:}Hiking)\}$, where (Arg_A, Att_A) is the AF in Fig. 1(a). Bob's perfect-view internal AF can be obtained similarly.

Note that an agent may not be able to know the full contents of its perfect-view internal AF during cooperation. Nevertheless, this notation allows to define desirable properties of the protocol.

3.3 Desirable Properties

We want for the strategy profiles obtained by our protocol to meet the following requirements: **i)** *feasible*, i.e. if a strategy profile assigns action a_j to $Agent_i$, then a_j should be 'doable' for $Agent_i$; **ii)** *acceptable*, i.e. the strategy profiles satisfy all constraints; and **iii)** *socially optimal* wrt. agents' ideal preferences. We have already defined acceptability in Def. 1. Let us now define the other requirements.

Definition 4. An action a_j is *locally feasible* for $Agent_i$ iff argument A_{ij} (the practical argument that recommends a_j to $Agent_i$) is admissible in $Agent_i$'s internal AF.

If an action is not locally feasible for $Agent_i$, it is not supported by the information held by $Agent_i$ and, thus, $Agent_i$ has no incentive to propose it. We say that $Agent_i$'s internal AF is *feasible* iff all actions in *Act* are locally feasible for $Agent_i$. For example, we can see that every practical argument in Fig. 1 is admissible in the internal AF it belongs to. Thus, both Alice's and Bob's internal AFs are feasible. We assume that all agents' internal AFs are feasible; we leave relaxing this restriction for future work.

Definition 5. An action a_j is *(globally) feasible* for $Agent_i$ iff argument A_{ij} is admissible in (Arg_i^*, Att_i^*).

A strategy profile $\mathsf{S} = \langle ac_1, \cdots, ac_N \rangle$ is *feasible* iff, for each $i \in \{1, \cdots, N\}$, action ac_i is globally feasible for $Agent_i$.

Now we define the notion of 'social optimality' as follows:

Definition 6. $\mathsf{S} = \langle ac_1, \cdots, ac_N \rangle$ is *socially optimal* iff:

- S is acceptable and feasible; and
- there is no $\mathsf{S}' = \langle ac_1', \cdots, ac_N' \rangle$ s.t. $\mathsf{S}' \neq \mathsf{S}$, S' is acceptable and feasible, and for any i $ac_i <^i_{Ideal} ac_i'$.

Example 6. As we mentioned in Example 3, there are two acceptable strategy profiles: both agents 'going to the ballet' or 'watching football'. We first check whether <u>*A : Ballet*</u> is feasible, i.e. whether it is admissible in Alice's perfect-view internal AF (given in Example 5). Easily, we can see that <u>*A : Ballet*</u> is not admissible, because it is attacked by **Ex?**, which, in turn, is defended by *C:Facebook*. Thus, the strategy profile wih both agents 'going to the ballet' is not feasible and not a desirable profile we want to obtain. Instead, we can easily verify that both agents 'watching football' is feasible; since this is the only strategy profile that meets the first two requirements, it is socially optimal by Def. 6.

Finally, we want to avoid agents' 'privacy leaks' during coordination. In this paper, this amounts to preventing that agents' private epistemic arguments are disclosed.[3] Thus, we require that **(iv)** our protocol is *of perfect security wrt. agents' private epistemic arguments* (as defined in Sect. 2.4). Next, we propose a protocol that can obtain strategy profiles with all desirable properties identified in this section.

4. THE COORDINATION PROTOCOL

The pseudo code of our protocol is presented in Alg. 1. The overall structure of this protocol is similar to that of SBT (see Sect. 2.3).[4] Without loss of generality, we assume that agents with smaller index numbers are higher in the static agent ordering required by SBT.

Let us walk through this protocol. This is activated by sending the token and a message **ok?**(S) to $Agent_1$. $Agent_1$ initialises S to an empty strategy profile (line 1). *my_act* stores $Agent_i$'s action choice, and is initialised to *null* (line 2). When an agent receives the token (line 3), it iterates over all actions that are equally or less preferred than its current action *my_act* by invoking function GETNEXTBESTACT (line 4). When the input action of GETNEXTBESTACT is *null*, it returns (one of) the agent's most preferred action(s). For the current action a, the agent checks whether it is *consistent*[5] with S and (globally) feasible using function CHECK (line 5), which is detailed later in Alg. 2.

After obtaining a consistent and feasible action a, the agent adds $(Agent_i, a)$ into S, updates *my_act* (line 6), and sends the updated S and the token to the next agent if the agent is not the last (line 8) or returns the obtained full strategy profile otherwise (line 10). If the action being checked is not consistent and feasible, the agent checks the next.

However, if the agent fails to find any consistent and feasible action (lines 14 to 18), it sends message **ngd** (short for 'not good') and the token to the previous agent so as to backtrack (line 15). In particular, if $Agent_1$ cannot find a feasible and consistent action and needs to backtrack, the protocol terminates and no strategy is obtained (line 17).

[3]Preserving other kinds of information may also be of interest in certain applications: for example, the agents may also want to avoid directly informing other agents about their proposed actions, or they may have private constraint functions that they do not want to disclose. Privacy preservation has been widely studied in DisCSPs (e.g. see [16, 6, 28, 31, 33]; more details are given in Sect. 7). We leave the study of further notions of privacy preservation as future work.

[4]More advanced algorithms for DisCSPs can be used as the basis for our protocol; we leave this for future work.

[5]Roughly speaking, assigning action a_j to $Agent_i$ is consistent with a partial strategy profile S if merging this assignment into S does not violate any constraints. Details are given later in this section when defining CHECK.

Algorithm 1 The protocol ($Agent_i$'s perspective).

```
1: Initialise S to an empty strategy profile if i is 1
2: my_act ← null
3: if I have the token then
4:   for a ← GETNEXTBESTACT(my_act) do
5:     if CHECK(a, S, i) == [consistent, feasible] then
6:       update S and my_act
7:       if i < N then
8:         send ok?(S) and token to Agent_{i+1}
9:       else
10:        return S
11:      end if
12:    end if
13:  end for
14:  if i > 1 then
15:    send ngd and the token to Agent_{i-1}
16:  else
17:    return null
18:  end if
19: end if
```

Example 7. We now use Alg. 1 to coordinate Alice and Bob's actions. Suppose Alice is ranked higher in the static agent ordering; thus, she obtains the token first (line 3). Alice checks whether her most preferred action — going to the ballet — is consistent with S (note that S is empty at this stage) and globally feasible, by invoking CHECK (line 5). We omit the checking process here (see Examples 8 and 9), but its result suggests that going to the ballet is not feasible; Alice thus checks her next preferred action: watching football. By invoking CHECK again, Alice finds that watching football is consistent with S and is feasible. So she inserts (Alice,'watch football') into S and lets *my_act* be 'watch football' (line 6). Then she sends **ok?**(S) and the token to Bob (line 8).

Once Bob receives the token and Alice's message (line 3), he begins to propose his own action. Similarly, he starts from his favourite action: watching football (line 4), and he finds that this action is consistent with S (note that S now includes Alice's proposal) and is feasible by invoking CHECK (line 5). Since Bob is the last agent, after he updates S and *my_act* (line 6), he returns the full strategy profile and the whole protocol terminates (line 10).

Now we introduce the function CHECK (invoked in line 5 in Alg. 1), which checks an action's consistency and (global) feasibility. Its pseudo code is given in Alg. 2. It first checks the consistency of assignment $(Agent_i, a)$ wrt. the input partial strategy (line 2), as follows: it first counts the number of agents action a has been assigned to in S (we denote this number by $N(\mathsf{S}, a)$; see Sect. 3.1), and then compares $N(\mathsf{S}, a)$ with $\max Con(a)$, i.e. the maximal number of agents required to perform a (see Sect. 3.1 for the definition of $Con(a)$). When $i \neq N$ (i.e. the current agent is not the last agent), we say that assignment $(Agent_i, a)$ is *consistent* with S iff $N(\mathsf{S}, a) \leq \max Con(a)$; when $i = N$, the assignment is *consistent* with S iff adding this assignment into S generates an acceptable strategy profile (see Def. 1). The function updates *status* accordingly (line 3).

Algorithm 2 CHECK(action a, strategy S, agent $Agent_i$)

1: $status \leftarrow [not\_consistent, not\_feasible]$
2: **if** assignment $(Agent_i, a)$ is consistent with S **then**
3: let the first element in *status* be *consistent*
4: **end if**
5: Obtain all compact reasons $E_1, \cdots, E_K$ for a
6: **for** each E_k, $k = 1, \cdots, K$ **do**
7: **if** *Discussion* suggests that E_k is *successful* **then**
8: let the second element in *status* be *feasible*
9: **end if**
10: **end for**
11: **return** *status*

Example 8. We illustrate how Alice checks the consistency of her first proposed action: going to the ballet. Note that the input strategy profile S is empty at this stage. Since $Con(\text{go to the ballet}) = \{0, 2\}$ (see Example 3), there can be at most two agents performing this action. Because Alice is not the last agent, she only needs to check whether there still exists any allowance for her to perform this action, i.e. she needs to check whether $N(\mathsf{S}, \text{go to the ballet}) \leq \max Con(\text{go to the ballet})$. Because $N(\mathsf{S}, \text{go to the ballet}) = 0$, her proposed action is consistent with S.

To illustrate the last agent's consistency check, we walk through how Bob checks whether his proposed action 'watch football' is consistent. Note that, in this case, the input partial strategy profile S includes Alice's proposal (watch football). After Bob inserts his proposal into S, the new strategy profile is $\mathsf{S}' = \langle\text{watch football, watch football}\rangle$, in which the first and second action are Alice's and Bob's proposed action, respectively. Thus, $N(S', \text{go to the ballet}) = 0$ and $N(S', \text{watch football}) = 2$, both satisfying the constraints (see Example 3); according to Def. 1, this strategy profile is acceptable and Bob's action proposal is thus consistent.

Function CHECK also checks the (global) feasibility of the input action (line 5 to 10). The intuition of this part is as follows: an agent obtains all '*compact reasons*' for the input action (line 5; here we suppose there are $K \in \mathbb{N}$ compact reasons), and '*discusses*' with other agents to see whether there exists any '*successful*' compact reason (line 7); the action is feasible if there exists (at least) one successful compact reason (line 8). In the next section, we detail the concept of 'compact reasons', 'discussion' and 'successful', and prove that the CHECK function is sound and it terminates.

5. EXPLAINING ACTION CHOICES WITH PRIVACY PRESERVED

In this section, we analyse which arguments need to be disclosed so as to check the feasibility of an action without leaking the private arguments. An intuitive method to find which arguments need to be disclosed is to compute the 'reasons' for an action; then the agent can 'discuss' these reasons with other agents, so that other agents only need to disclose their arguments 'relating to' these reasons. We use the related-admissible semantics (see Sect.2.1) to compute the reasons for actions. The next proposition shows that, for each related-admissible set that includes one and only one practical argument, the practical argument is the set's topic (see Sect. 2.1).

PROPOSITION 1. *Given $Agent_i$'s internal AF (Arg_i, Att_i), if $S \subseteq Arg_i$ is related-admissible and $S \cap pPra_i = \{A_{ij}\}$, then A_{ij} is the topic of S.*

PROOF. We prove this by contradiction. Suppose the topic of S is argument A, and $A \neq A_{ij}$. Since A_{ij} is the only practical argument in S, A is an epistemic argument. By condition 2 in Def. 2, practical arguments cannot attack epistemic arguments; thus, A_{ij} cannot defend A (for defend, see Sect. 2.1); however, by assumption, A is the topic of S and every element in S should defend S. Contradiction. □

Given $Agent_i$'s internal AF, if one of its related-admissible sets S includes only one practical argument A_{ij}, we say that *S recommends action a_j to $Agent_i$*. If S recommends a_j to $Agent_i$ and is a compact explanation (see Sect. 2.1) of A_{ij}, we say that $S \setminus \{A_{ij}\}$ is an *$Agent_i$'s compact reason for a_j*. In the next proposition, we prove that each non-empty compact reason includes disclosable arguments.

PROPOSITION 2. *For $Agent_i$'s internal AF (Arg_i, Att_i), if $S \subseteq Arg_i$, S is a compact reason for a_j and $S \neq \emptyset$, then $S \cap dEpi_i \neq \emptyset$.*

PROOF. We prove this by contradiction. Suppose $S \cap dEpi_i = \emptyset$; thus, all epistemic arguments in S are private. However, $\forall a \in S, \exists b \in dEpi_i$ s.t. $(b, a) \in Att_i$ (condition 4 in Def. 2). As private arguments are not allowed to attack disclosable arguments (condition 3 in Def. 2), S cannot attack b and S cannot be a compact reason. Contradiction. □

We say that a compact reason $E \subseteq Arg_i$ for action a_j is *successful* for $Agent_i$ (line 7 in Alg. 2) iff every disclosable argument in E is contained in (at least) one admissible set in $Agent_i$'s perfect-view internal AF (Arg_i^*, Att_i^*) (see Sect. 3.2). In the next proposition, we show that an action is feasible if it has (at least) one successful compact reason.

PROPOSITION 3. *Suppose E is an $Agent_i$'s compact reason for action a_j and it consists of l ($l \in \mathbb{N}, l \geq 1$) disclosable arguments $d_1, \cdots, d_l$. If $\exists S \subseteq Arg_i^*$ such that $\{d_1, \cdots, d_l\} \subseteq S$ and S is admissible, then action a_j is feasible, i.e. argument A_{ij} is admissible in $AF_i^* = (Arg_i^*, Att_i^*)$.*

PROOF. We denote $E \cup \{A_{ij}\}$ by E'. To prove this proposition, we show that $\exists S' \subseteq Arg_i^*$ s.t. $E' \subseteq S'$ and S' is admissible in AF_i^*. $\forall a \in Arg_i^*$ that attacks $b \in E'$:

- If $a \in Arg_i$, since E' is related-admissible, E' attacks a.
- Else, $a \in Arg_i^* \setminus Arg_i$, i.e. $a \in dEpi_{-i}$, then b must be a discloable argument (i.e. $b \in \{d_1, \cdots, d_l\}$) because another agent's arguments are not allowed to attack $Agent_i$'s private arguments (see Table 1). Because S is admissible in AF_i^* and $b \in S$, there exists $c \in S$ such that c attacks a. We prove that $E' \cup \{c\}$ is conflict-free.
  - If $c \in dEpi_i$, suppose $E' \cup \{c\}$ is not conflict-free. Because E' is related-admissible, $\exists d \in \{d_1, \cdots, d_l\}$ such that d attacks c. Because both d and c are in S, S is not conflict-free. Contradiction. Thus, If $c \in dEpi_i$, $E' \cup \{c\}$ is conflict-free.
  - Else, $c \in Arg_i^* \setminus Arg_i$, i.e. $c \in dEpi_{-i}$. Because c is in S, $\{d_1, \cdots, d_l\} \cup \{c\}$ is conflict-free; also, since c is not allowed to be in an attack relation with $Agent_i$'s private arguments, $\{c\} \cup (E' \cap Pri)$, for Pri the set of all $Agent_i$'s private (epistemic and practical) arguments, is conflict-free. Thus, when $c \in dEpi_{-i}$, $\{c\} \cup E'$ is conflict-free.

Thus, for every a that attacks $b \in E'$, there exists some argument c attacking a and $E' \cup \{c\}$ is conflict-free. Therefore, A_{ij} is admissible in AF_i^*. □

Proposition 3 explains lines 6 to 9 in Alg. 2: by checking whether there exists a successful compact reason for action a_j, we can check the feasibility of a_j. However, to check whether a compact reason is successful, an agent needs to obtain some necessary disclosable arguments from other agents. We term this process *Discussion* (line 7 in Alg. 2).

We use a variant of the TPI-dispute (see Sect. 2.2) to implement Discussion. There are two (opponent) players in the dispute: a *defender* and a *challenger*. Note that these two players are different from the agents; instead, they are only used in the dispute to ask agents to provide some of their disclosable arguments, so as to find whether a compact reason is successful. Also, note that even inactive agents (i.e. agents that do not have the token) can disclose their arguments to the players, upon players' requests. Our variant of TPI-dispute, called *compact-reason-oriented TPI-dispute*, is formally defined as follows.

Definition 7. Suppose E is an $Agent_i$'s compact reason for action a_j, and E contains l ($l \in \mathbb{N}, l \geq 1$) disclosable arguments $d_1, \cdots, d_l$. An *E-oriented TPI-dispute* satisfies the following requirements:

- In the first move, the defender puts forward arguments $d_1, \cdots, d_l$.
- After that, players take turns to ask all agents except $Agent_i$ whether they have disclosable arguments attacking one of the arguments presented earlier by the opponent player; if they do, the asking player presents one of these arguments (following the rules given below); otherwise, we say that the player *runs out of moves*.
- Both players are allowed to *backtrack*, i.e. present an argument attacking some earlier argument of the other player, called the *backtracked* argument.
- Both players are allowed to repeat arguments earlier presented by the defender.
- The challenger is allowed to repeat arguments presented earlier by itself iff those repeated arguments are in different *dispute lines*[6] from their earlier uses.
- No other moves are allowed.
- The challenger wins the dispute iff it does an *eo ipso* move (i.e. uses a previous non-backtracked argument of the other player) or the defender runs out of moves. The defender wins iff the challenger cannot win.

Example 9. We illustrate the discussion between Alice and Bob (line 7 in Alg. 2) that checks the feasibility of Alice's actions. Since Alice has two compact explanations (see Example 2), we can easily obtain her compact reasons: {*C:Hiking*} is the compact reason for <u>A : *Ballet*</u>, and {*Sun*} is the compact reason for <u>A : *Football*</u> (since each action has one compact reason, $K = 1$ in line 6, Alg. 2). We walk through the {*C:Hiking*}-oriented TPI-dispute as follows (**D1**/**C1** labels the first step of the defender/challenger, respectively.):

- **D1**: The defender puts forward *C:Hiking*.
- **C1**: The challenger asks Bob whether he has argument(s) attacking *C:Hiking*, and Bob reports *C:Facebook*. Thus, the challenger presents *C:Facebook*.

After step **C1**, since the defender runs out of moves, the challenger wins the dispute and, thus, the compact reason {*C:Hiking*} is not successful and <u>A : *Ballet*</u> is not feasible.

Instead, the compact reason for <u>A : *Football*</u>, i.e. {*Sun*}, is successful, as the challenger cannot make any moves after the defender puts it forward. Thus, <u>A : *Football*</u> is feasible.

Proposition 4. *If E is an $Agent_i$'s compact reason for action a_j, E is successful iff the defender wins in every E-oriented TPI-dispute.*[7]

Proof. (Sketch) We first prove that if the defender wins in every E-oriented TPI-dispute, E is successful. Because the challenger cannot win, the arguments presented by the defender are conflict-free (otherwise, the challenger can perform eo ipso) and can attack every arguments presented by the challenger (otherwise, the defender runs out of moves). Conversely, if E is successful, suppose S is an admissible set and $E \subseteq S$; then the defender can win every dispute by using arguments in S only. □

Since all moves other than the first in our disputes are the same as in standard TPI-disputes, and there are finitely many arguments presented in the first move, we have:

Proposition 5. *If E is an $Agent_i$'s compact reason for action a_j, every E-oriented TPI-dispute terminates.*

6. PROPERTIES OF THE PROTOCOL

Theorem 1. *Alg. 1 is guaranteed to terminate.*

Proof. (Sketch) Function Check employs compact-reason-oriented TPI-disputes (Def. 7) to check whether compact reasons are successful, and the disputes are guaranteed to terminate (Proposition 5); thus, Check terminates. Also, because the basic structure of Alg. 1 is the same as that of SBT, and all functions in Alg. 1 terminate, Alg. 1 is guaranteed to terminate. □

Theorem 2. *Alg. 1 is sound, i.e. the strategy profile obtained by this protocol is socially optimal (see Def. 6).*

Proof. (Sketch) The SBT structure of Alg. 1 ensures that the obtained strategy profile is acceptable. Propositions 3 and 4 ensure that all obtained strategy profiles are feasible. Since agents propose their actions according to their ideal preferences (line 5 in Alg. 1), the obtained strategy is the most preferred feasible and acceptable strategy wrt. agents' ideal preferences. Thus, the strategy profile obtained by Alg. 1 is socially optimal. □

However, note that our current protocol is not complete: it may return no solutions when there exist some. For example, consider a problem consisting of two agents and one action a_1. The constraint is that a_1 should be performed by both agents. For $Agent_1$'s internal AF (Arg_1, Att_1), $Arg_1 = \{A_{11}, d_1, d_2\}$, $dEpi_1 = \{d_1, d_2\}$, $pPra_1 = \{A_{11}\}$ and $Att_1 =$

[6]A dispute line is a dispute where each move replies to the immediately preceding move.

[7]Due to the space limit, we sketch or omit some proofs.

$\{(d_1, A_{11}), (d_2, d_1)\}^8$. For $Agent_2$'s internal AF (Arg_2, Att_2), $Arg_2 = \{A_{21}, d_3, p_1\}$, $pPra_2 = \{A_{21}\}$, $dEpi_2 = \{d_3\}$, $pEpi_2 = \{p_1\}$ and $Att_2 = \{(p_1, A_{21}), (d_3, p_1)\}$. Also, we let d_3 attacks both d_1 and d_2. Thus, $Agent_1$ and $Agent_2$'s compact reason for their practical arguments are $\{d_2\}$ and $\{d_3\}$, respectively. We can see that $Agent_1$'s compact reason is not successful (line 7 in Alg. 2) as d_2 is attacked by d_3, but A_{11} is actually admissible in $Agent_1$'s perfect-view internal AF. Thus, our protocol will return no strategy profile in this example, while 'both agents perform a_1' is actually a strategy profile that meets all our requirements (see Sect. 3.3). We leave improving completeness for future work.

THEOREM 3. *Alg. 1 is of* perfect security *wrt. agents' private epistemic arguments.*

PROOF. For $Agent_i$ and $Agent_h$, $i, h \in \{1, \cdots, N\}$, $i \neq h$, let $\mathbb{P}^i_h = \{a | Agent_h$ believes a may be in $pEpi_i\}$. Because $Agent_h$ has no information about the cardinality of $pEpi_i$ (denoted by $|pEpi_i|$), $|\mathbb{P}^i_h|$ is $+\infty$. Similarly, we let $\mathbb{D}^i_h = \{a | Agent_h$ believes a may be in $dEpi_i\}$; then $|\mathbb{D}^i_h| = +\infty$.

Thus, for any $a \in \mathbb{P}^i_h$, the probability that a is contained in $pEpi_i$ (denoted by $p_h(a \in pEpi_i)$) is $|pEpi_i|/|\mathbb{P}^i_h|$, because each argument in $\mathbb{P}^i_h$ has the same probability to be included in $pEpi_i$. Thus, $p_h(a \in pEpi_i) = 0$. Although $Agent_j$ may be aware of some argument $b \in dEpi_i$, since $p(a \in pEpi_i, b \in dEpi_i) = 0$ and $p(b \in dEpi_i) = |dEpi_i|/|\mathbb{D}^i_h| = 0$, by Eq. (2.4), $H(a \in pEpi_i) = H(a \in pEpi_i | b \in dEpi_i) = 0$. The protocol is thus perfect secure wrt. private arguments. □

Since, in our compact-reason-oriented TPI-disputes, only arguments attacking earlier-presented arguments can be presented, we can easily see that the communication between agents is 'efficient', i.e. only arguments that *defend* (see Sect. 2) the practical arguments are communicated.

THEOREM 4. *For $Agent_i$ to check the feasibility of action a_j using function* CHECK, *if an argument $d \in dEpi_{-i}$ is presented by the defender in a compact-reason-oriented TPI-dispute (Def. 7), d defends argument A_{ij} in AF^*_i.*

7. RELATED WORK

Our work is related to the *distributed constraint optimisation* problems (DisCOPs) [10], in which variables and constraints are distributed among a set of agents who must communicate to find an optimal assignment of values for the variables. The acceptability and social optimality requirements can be represented in DisCOPs, but the feasibility requirement cannot, because agents' domain knowledge (including beliefs and observations) about the feasibility of actions is not considered in DisCOPs.

Some work has investigated the types of privacies and methods to preserve private information in DisCSPs and DisCOPs, e.g. [16, 6, 28, 31, 33]. Two types of privacies are widely identified and studied: i) *constraint privacy*, i.e. the constraints are partially known by each involved agent, and ii) *assignment privacy*, i.e. each agent does not directly let other agents know its own assignment. The privacy we consider is not covered by either of these two types, because we consider the agents' private beliefs information (beliefs and observations). Methods to preserve privacies fall into two categories: i) *privacy enforcement*, i.e. only disclose the necessary information so as to minimise privacy loss; and ii) *encrypted message*, i.e. encrypt some messages so that only certain agents can understand them. Our protocol falls into the privacy enforcement category.

Grant et al. [15] consider a variant of Boolean games, in which agents cannot observe some *environment variables*; a human operator can disclose certain environment variables' values and preserve the others, so as to influence agents' decisions, in the hope of obtaining (socially) optimal strategy profiles. Their work is not as generic as ours, as they focus on Boolean games and propositional logic-based knowledge representation. Also, the privacy they considered is centralised (pertaining only to the environment) while the privacy we consider is distributed (pertaining to every agent).

Amgoud and Devred [2] represented AFs as DisCSPs, and used solvers for DisCSPs to compute 'winning' sets of arguments (wrt. some different semantics). Our work integrates argumentation and DisCSPs in a different way: we use algorithms from DisCSPs to guarantee the acceptability of the strategy profiles, and use argumentation to represent agents' domain knowledge on the feasibility of actions and to regulate communication between agents.

Some work has been devoted to efficient argumentation-based negotiation. Fan and Toni [11] introduced a dialogue protocol based in ABA [29], which does not require agents to put forward all their domain knowledge. Pasquier et al. [24] introduced *interest-based negotiation*, in which agents not only communicate their requirements, but also the reasons (i.e. interests) behind the requirements, so that agents can cooperate to find better alternative solutions. However, none of these works considers agents' private information, e.g. agents' private arguments.

8. CONCLUSION AND FUTURE WORK

We consider a class of cooperative multi-agent decision making problems, and propose an abstract argumentation based knowledge representation and communication protocol that is sound, efficient, guaranteed to terminate and privacy-preserving. Our work suggests that abstract argumentation can be used to represent agents' domain knowledge that includes private information; upon this knowledge representation, agents can communicate and coordinate their actions 'efficiently' and 'securely' (without leaking personal information) by using argumentation-based dialogues. Our work connects argumentation, distributed constraint satisfaction/optimisation and game theory in a novel manner, suggesting that several multi-agent coordination techniques can be used together to tackle complex problems.

We identify two major lines for extending this work: **i)** stick to cooperative multi-agent decision-making problems, and improve the current protocol, e.g. relax some restrictions, improve the completeness of the protocol, or use more advanced DisCSPs algorithms as the basis of the protocol; **ii)** consider more complex problems, and adjust the current framework accordingly; for example, allowing agents to have different action sets, or tuning the 'selfishness' of each agent, so that agents cooperate and compete simultaneously.

Acknowledgements

F. Toni was supported by the EPSRC TRaDAr project *Transparent Rational Decisions by Argumentation*: EP/J020915/1.

[8] For $a, b \in Arg_i$, $(a, b) \in Att_i$ is read 'a attacks b'.

REFERENCES

[1] L. Amgoud and C. Cayrol. Inferring from inconsistency in preference-based argumentation frameworks. *Journal of Automated Reasoning*, 29(2):125–169, 2002.

[2] L. Amgoud and C. Devred. Argumentation frameworks as constraint satisfaction problems. In S. Benferhat and J. Grant, editors, *SUM, LNAI*. Springer, 2011.

[3] L. Amgoud and H. Prade. Using arguments for making and explaining decisions. *Artificial Intelligence*, 173(3):413–436, 2009.

[4] T. J. M. Bench-Capon and P. E. Dunne. Argumentation in artificial intelligence. *Artificial Intelligence*, 171:619–641, 2007.

[5] T. J. M. Bench-Capon and H. Prakken. Justifying actions by accruing arguments. *Frontiers in Artificial Intelligence and Applications*, 144:247, 2006.

[6] I. Brito, A. Meisels, P. Meseguer, and R. Zivan. Distributed constraint satisfaction with partially known constraints. *Constraints*, 2008.

[7] T. M. Cover and J. A. Thomas. *Elements of information theory, 2nd edition.* Wiley-Interscience, 2006.

[8] P. M. Dung. On the acceptability of arguments and its fundamental role in nonmonotonic reasoning, logic programming and n-person games. *Artificial Intelligence*, 77(2):321–357, 1995.

[9] P. E. Dunne and T. J. M. Bench-Capon. Two party immediate response disputes: Properties and efficiency. *Artificial Intelligence*, 149(2):221–250, 2003.

[10] B. Faltings. Distributed constraint programming. In T. Walsh, editor, *Handbook of Constraint Programming*. Elsevier, 2006.

[11] X. Fan and F. Toni. Assumption-based argumentation dialogues. In *Proceedings of International Joint Conferences on Artificial Intelligence*, 2011.

[12] X. Fan and F. Toni. A general framework for sound assumption-based argumentation dialogues. *Artificial Intelligence*, 2014.

[13] X. Fan and F. Toni. On computing explanations in argumentation. In *Proceedings of AAAI Conference on Artificial Intelligence*, 2015.

[14] X. Fan, F. Toni, A. Mocanu, and M. Williams. Multi-agent decision making with assumption-based argumentation. In *Proceedings of Thirteenth International Conference on Autonomous Agents and Multiagent Systems*, 2014.

[15] J. Grant, S. Kraus, M. Wooldridge, and I. Zuckerman. Manipulating games by sharing information. *Studia Logica*, 102:267–295, 2014.

[16] T. Grinshapoun and T. Tassa. A privacy preserving algorithm for distributed constraint optimisation. In *Proceedings of International Conference on Autonomous Agents and Multiagent Systems*, 2014.

[17] P. Harvey. *Solving Very Large Distributed Constraint Problems.* PhD thesis, University of Wollongong, 2009.

[18] H. Jakobovits and D. Vermeir. Dialectic semantics for argumentation frameworks. In *Proceedings of International Conference on Artificial Intelligence and Law*, 1999.

[19] T. Leaute and B. Faltings. Distributed constraint optimization under stochastic uncertainty. In *Proceedings of AAAI Conference on Artificial Intelligence*, 2011.

[20] R. Loui. Process and policy: resource-bounded nondemonstrative reasoning. *Computational Intelligence*, 14(1):1–38, 1998.

[21] S. Modgil and H. Prakken. The ASPIC+ framework for structured argumentation: a tutorial. *Argument and Computation, Special Issue: Tutorials on Structured Argumentation Computation*, 5(1):31–62, 2014.

[22] J. Modi and M. Veloso. Multiagent meeting scheduling with rescheduling. In *Distributed Constraint Reasoning Workshops, DCR*, 2004.

[23] S. Parsons and P. McBurney. Argumentation-based communication between agents. In *Communications in Multiagent Systems.* Springer, 2003.

[24] P. Pasquier, R. Hollands, I. Rahwan, F. Dignum, and L. Sonenberg. An empirical study of interest-based negotiation. *Journal of Autonomous Agents and Multi-Agent Systems*, 2010.

[25] I. Rahwan and K. Larson. Argumentation and game theory. In *Argumentation in Artificial Intelligence.* Springer, 2009.

[26] C. E. Shannon. *The Mathematical Theory of Communication.* University of Illinois Press, 1949.

[27] Y. Shoham and K. Leyton-Brown. *Multiagent Systems: Algorithmic, Game-Theoretic, and Logical Foundations.* Cambridge University Press, 2009.

[28] M. Silaghi and D. Mitra. Distributed constraint satisfaction and optimization with privacy enforcement. In *Proceedings of IEEE/WIC/ACM International Conference on Intelligent Agent Technology (IAT)*, 2004.

[29] F. Toni. A tutorial on assumption-based argumentation. *Argument and Computation, Special Issue: Tutorials on Structured Argumentation*, 5(1):89–117, 2014.

[30] G. Vreeswijk and H. Prakken. Credulous and sceptical argument games for preferred semantics. In *Proceedings of European Conference on Logics in Artificial Intelligence*, 2000.

[31] R. J. Wallace and E. C. Freuder. Constraint-based reasoning and privacy/efficiency tradeoffs in multi-agent problem solving. *Artificial Intelligence*, 161:209–227, 2005.

[32] M. Yokoo and K. Hirayama. Algorithms for distributed constraint satisfaction: A review. *Journal of Autonomous Agents and Multi-Agent Systems*, 2000.

[33] M. Yokoo, K. Suzuki, and K. Hirayama. Secure distributed constraint satisfaction: Reaching agreement without revealing private information. *Artificial Intelligence*, 161:229–245, 2005.

[34] W. Zhang, Z. Xing, G. Wang, and L. Wittenburg. Distributed stochastic search and distributed breakout: properties, comparison and applications to constraints optimization problems in sensor networks. *Artificial Intelligence*, 16:55–87, 2005.

A Value Equivalence Approach for Solving Interactive Dynamic Influence Diagrams

Ross Conroy[*], Yifeng Zeng[*], Marc Cavazza[**], Jing Tang[*], Yinghui Pan[***]
[*]Teesside University, Middlesbrough, UK
{ross.conroy, y.zeng, x9019186}@tees.ac.uk
[**]University of Kent, Kent, UK
m.o.cavazza@kent.ac.uk
[***]Jiangxi University of Finance and Economics, China
panyinghui@jxufe.edu.cn

ABSTRACT

Interactive dynamic influence diagrams (I-DIDs) are recognized graphical models for sequential multiagent decision making under uncertainty. They represent the problem of how a subject agent acts in a common setting shared with other agents who may act in sophisticated ways. The difficulty in solving I-DIDs is mainly due to an exponentially growing space of candidate models ascribed to other agents over time. in order to minimize the model space, the previous I-DID techniques prune behaviorally equivalent models. In this paper, we challenge the minimal set of models and propose a value equivalence approach to further compress the model space. The new method reduces the space by additionally pruning behaviorally distinct models that result in the same expected value of the subject agent's optimal policy. To achieve this, we propose to learn the value from available data particularly in practical applications of real-time strategy games. We demonstrate the performance of the new technique in two problem domains.

Categories and Subject Descriptors

I.2.11 [**Distributed Artificial Intelligence**]: Multiagent systems

General Terms

Algorithms, Experimentation

Keywords

Influence Diagrams, Decision Making, Multiple Agents

1. INTRODUCTION

Interactive dynamic influence diagrams (I-DIDs) [7, 24] provide a general framework for solving sequential multiagent decision making problems under uncertainty. Different from other frameworks, like Dec-POMDPs [19] and multiagent influence diagrams (MAIDs) [10], I-DIDs solve the problem from the perspective of individual agents and do not make a common belief assumption on modeling other agents. Hence I-DIDs become a more general decision model and can be employed to solve both cooperative and competitive multiagent decision problems. Recent research has found some practical applications of I-DIDs [12, 11, 4].

Appears in: *Proceedings of the 15th International Conference on Autonomous Agents and Multiagent Systems (AAMAS 2016), J. Thangarajah, K. Tuyls, C. Jonker, S. Marsella (eds.), May 9–13, 2016, Singapore.*

Algorithms for solving I-DIDs need to compute a large number of candidate models of other agents that represent how the agents optimize their decisions in an uncertain environment. In addition, the I-DID solutions have to track the evolution of all the models as other agents observe, act and update their beliefs over time. Consequently, the computational complexity of solving I-DIDs is mainly due to the exponential growth in the number of models are ascribed to other agents.

Recognizing that only the predicted behavior of other agents matters to the decisions of the subject agents, existing I-DID solutions [24] reduce model space by retaining only those models that exhibit different behavior of other agents. For example, the exact algorithm, called discriminative model update (DMU) [6], clusters models that are *behaviorally equivalent* (BE) - whose behavioral predictions for the other agent are identical - and maintains one representative model from every cluster. Exploiting BE models has become a core technique for reducing the complexity of I-DID solutions. Continuous effort has focused on identifying BE models and resulted in a series of approximate I-DID algorithms [26]. Recently, Chen *et al.* [3] develop an online algorithm that limits the search in the model space by incrementally building the true models of other agents during the agents' interactions. Conroy *et al.* [4] learn behavior of other agents from interaction data and don't need to explicitly model decision making process for other agents. This line of work improves the BE-based I-DID solutions and facilitates the I-DID applications in practice. However, all the previous techniques still rest on the BE principle for reducing the model space of other agents. As a large amount of different behavior always exists for agents, the existing I-DID algorithms are not sufficiently capable to deal with complex decision making problems.

In this paper, we initiate a new approach on compressing model space of other agents in I-DIDs. The behavioral equivalence focuses only on the difference of other agents' behavior and postulates that the difference leads to distinction of the subject agent's decisions. However, it is still safe to assume that the difference of other agents' behavior may only matter if it affects the expected value of the subject agent's optimal policy for their interactions. In other words, what really matters to the subject agent is not the difference of other agents' behavior, but the difference of the received rewards. Inspired by this observation, we redefine the equivalence of other agents' models in terms of their impact on the subject agent's expected value. Models that generate the same expected value of the subject agent's optimal policy are value equivalence (VE) and can be grouped into one VE class. The new VE measurement in comparison to BE will further reduce the model space since distinct behavior of other agents may generate the same expected values to the subject agent and will be clustered. In addition, VE has a direct link with the solution quality, which has been lacking in the previous I-DID techniques.

Without building a complete I-DID, it is not easy to compute expected values of the subject agent. We resort to agents' interaction history and learn the expected values for determining VE of models ascribed to other agents over time. This is particularly useful for applications where interaction data is widely available and will be incrementally added to over time. As demonstrated in recent I-DID applications in computer games [4], the continuously uploaded data that records gaming activities of computer-and-human players facilitates the learning task in the new VE approach. In this context, this paper makes the following contributions:

- We propose a new approach for solving I-DIDs. The VE technique reduces the model space of other agents by considering their behavioral impact on expected values of the subject agent. This provides more reduction than the previous I-DID solutions.
- We focus on learning expected values from agents' interaction data and develop approximate techniques for determining the model equivalence.
- We theoretically analyze computational savings of the new model compression technique compared to BE. Additionally we demonstrate the performance in a set of experiments and focus on practical applications of computer games.

We organize the paper as follows. We briefly review the I-DID framework as well as the BE concept in Section 2. We formulate the new approach of value equivalence and propose a learning technique for determining VE in Section 3. The computational savings and solution quality are theoretically analyzed in Section 4. We empirically analyze the method performance in a scalable UAV (unmanned aerial vehicle reconnaissance problem) simulation testbed and demonstrate applications in a real-time strategy game in Section 5. We discuss related work in Section 6 and conclude this paper with a discussion of the challenges and future work.

2. BACKGROUND: INTERACTIVE DYNAMIC INFLUENCE DIAGRAM

We start with a brief review on the framework of interactive dynamic influence diagrams (I-DIDs) with elaboration in the well-studied multiagent tiger problem [8]. Subsequently, we describe the I-DID solutions based on behavioral equivalence (BE).

2.1 Representation

I-DIDs represent sequential decision making problems for a subject agent who interacts with other agents in an uncertain environment. As other agents act simultaneously, which is not fully observable to the subject agent, I-DID models their predicted behavior by solving all possible models of other agents. Actions of both the agents impact the common environmental states S and rewards R. Fig. 1 shows a level l I-DID for the subject agent i who models other agent j in level $l-1$, where level refers to recursive reasoning between agents and agents in level 0 do not model the others. In addition to regular chance, decision and utility nodes in DID [20], a new type of node called the *model node*, $M_{j,l-1}$, models how other agent j makes its decisions simultaneously at level $l-1$. More explicitly, it contains a set of j's candidate models whose solutions give the predicted behavior A_j, which is represented by a *policy link* (the dashed line) connecting $M_{j,l-1}$ and A_j. Each candidate model of agent j, $m_{j,l-1}$, could be either a level $l-1$ I-DID or a DID at level 0.

The I-DID modeling complexity arises with update of the model node (containing j's models) over time, as represented by the *model*

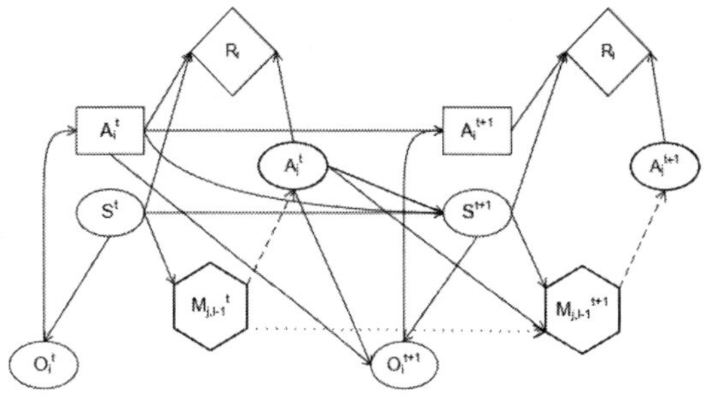

Figure 1: A generic two time-slice level l I-DID for agent i who optimises its decisions A_i given observations O_i.

update link (the dotted arrow from $M^t_{j,l-1}$ to $M^{t+1}_{j,l-1}$ in Fig. 1). As agent j acts and receives observations over time, the models are updated to reflect its changed beliefs. The updated models differ in the beliefs of j's actions and observations. Since agent i needs to track the update of j's models, the number of models grows in a new model node. The number of models in $M^{t+1}_{j,l-1}$ is up to $|\mathcal{M}^t_{j,l-1}||A_j||\Omega_j|$ where $|\mathcal{M}^t_{j,l-1}|$ is the number of models at time step t, and $|A_j|$ and $|\Omega_j|$ are the largest spaces of actions and observations respectively.

We may replace the model nodes and model update links with regular chance nodes and dependency links in I-DID. Subsequently, I-DID becomes a regular DID and any DID technique can be used to solve the converted I-DID. Below we use a two-agent tiger problem to elaborate the I-DID framework.

Figure 2 shows a level 1 I-DID for agent i who considers two models of agent j, $m^{t,1}_{j,0}$ and $m^{t,2}_{j,0}$, at level 0. The converted I-DID is a regular DID in which the chance node $Mod[M_{j,0}]$ represents agent j's possible models. The models differ in j's beliefs about the tiger's location and solving the models obtains optimal decisions for agent j. As indicated by the conditional probability table (CPT) in Fig. 4, agent j's optimal decisions are OL and L respectively when the two models are solved at level 0. The optimal decisions are mapped into the predicted actions in the chance node A^t_j.

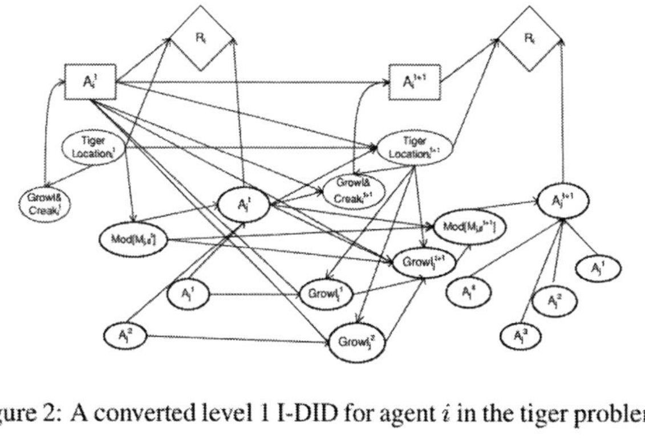

Figure 2: A converted level 1 I-DID for agent i in the tiger problem.

We show the update of $m^{t,1}_{j,0}$ and $m^{t,2}_{j,0}$ in Fig. 3. As agent j may receive one of two observations (either GL or GR), four new models are generated in the model node $M^{t+1}_{j,0}$.

We show the CPT of $Mod[M^{t+1}_{j,0}]$ in Fig. 4. For example, the first row of the CPT shows that $m^{t,1}_{j,0}$ is updated into the model $m^{t+1,1}_{j,0}$ when agent j takes the action OL at time t and observes GL at $t+1$. As neither OR nor L is the optimal decision for $m^{t,1}_{j,0}$, we assign a uniform distribution to indicate that $m^{t,1}_{j,0}$ does not transform into any of the new models for these actions.

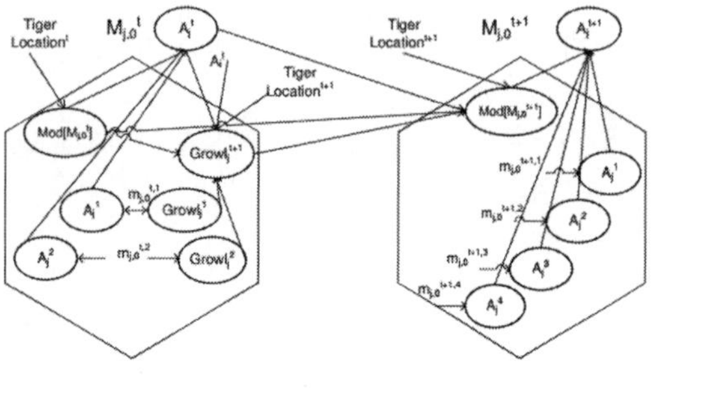

Figure 3: Details of the model update link where two models are expanded into four models in $M_{j,0}^{t+1}$.

Mod[$M_{j,0}^t$]	OL	OR	L
$m_{j,0}^{t,1}$	1	0	0
$m_{j,0}^{t,2}$	0	0	1

CPT of A_j^t

Decisions(A_j)
OL: Open the left door
OR: Open the right door
L: Listen
Observations($Growl_j$)
GL: Growl from the left door
GR: Growl from the right door

<A_j^t, $Growl_j^{t+1}$>	Mod[$M_{j,0}^t$]	$m_{j,0}^{t+1,1}$	$m_{j,0}^{t+1,2}$	$m_{j,0}^{t+1,3}$	$m_{j,0}^{t+1,4}$
<OL, GL>	$m_{j,0}^{t,1}$	1	0	0	0
<OL, GR>	$m_{j,0}^{t,1}$	0	1	0	0
<L, GL>	$m_{j,0}^{t,2}$	0	0	1	0
<L, GR>	$m_{j,0}^{t,2}$	0	0	0	1
<OR, * >	*	1/4	1/4	1/4	1/4
<L, * >	$m_{j,0}^{t,1}$	1/4	1/4	1/4	1/4
<OL, * >	$m_{j,0}^{t,2}$	1/4	1/4	1/4	1/4

CPT of Mod[$M_{j,0}^{t+1}$]

Figure 4: The CPTs of the chance nodes A_j^t and $Mod[M_{j,0}^{t+1}]$.

I-DID EXACT(level $l \geq 1$ I-DID or level 0 DID, horizon T)
Expansion Phase
1. **For** t **from** 0 **to** $T-1$ **do**
2. **If** $l \geq 1$ **then**
Populate $M_{j,l-1}^{t+1}$
3. **For each** m_j^t **in** $\mathcal{M}_{j,l-1}^t$ **do**
4. Recursively call algorithm with the $l-1$ I-DID (or DID) that represents m_j^t and horizon, $T-t$
5. Map the decision node of the solved I-DID (or DID), $OPT(m_j^t)$, to the corresponding chance node A_j
6. $\mathcal{M}_{j,l-1}^t \leftarrow$ **PruneBehavioralEq**($\mathcal{M}_{j,l-1}^t$)
7. **For each** m_j^t **in** $\mathcal{M}_{j,l-1}^t$ **do**
8. **For each** a_j **in** $OPT(m_j^t)$ **do**
9. **For each** o_j **in** O_j (part of m_j^t) **do**
10. Update j's belief, $b_j^{t+1} \leftarrow SE(b_j^t, a_j, o_j)$
11. $m_j^{t+1} \leftarrow$ New I-DID (or DID) with b_j^{t+1}
12. $\mathcal{M}_{j,l-1}^{t+1} \stackrel{\cup}{\leftarrow} \{m_j^{t+1}\}$
13. Add the model node, $M_{j,l-1}^{t+1}$, and the model update link
14. Add the chance, decision, and utility nodes for $t+1$ time slice and the dependency links between them
15. Establish the conditional probability tables (CPTs) for each chance and utility node

Solution Phase
16. **If** $l \geq 1$ **then**
17. Represent the model nodes, policy links and the model update links to obtain the DID
18. Apply the standard look-ahead and backup method to solve the expanded DID

Figure 5: Algorithm for exactly solving a level $l \geq 1$ I-DID or level 0 DID expanded over T time steps.

2.2 Solutions and Behavioral Equivalence

We present the exact I-DID algorithm in Fig. 5. We first transform an I-DID into a regular DID by expanding j's models at level $l-1$ (lines 2-15) and then solve the converted DID (lines 16-18). Lines 4-5 solve j's models to instantiate the policy link. Line 6 invokes techniques for compression of the model space based on *behavioral equivalence* [18], **PruneBehavioralEq** ($\mathcal{M}_{j,l-1}$), and returns representative models of j. Lines 7-15 implement the model update link in the I-DID. Finally, lines 17-18 solve the transformed I-DID using standard DID algorithms.

Previous I-DID techniques focus on implementing BE in either exact or approximate ways. Formally we define behavioral equivalence of agent j's models below.

DEFINITION 1 (BEHAVIORAL EQUIVALENCE). *Two models, m_j and $\hat{m}_j$, of agent j, are behaviorally equivalent if* $\mathsf{OPT}(m_j) = \mathsf{OPT}(\hat{m}_j)$*, where* $\mathsf{OPT}(\cdot)$ *denotes the solution of the model.*

A model solution is the agent's policy and is generally represented by a policy tree. A depth-T policy tree contains a set of policy paths, $\mathcal{T}_j^T = \bigcup h_j^T$ where the policy path, h_j^T, is an action-observation sequence over T planning horizons. We let $h_j^T = \{a_j^t, o_j^{t+1}\}_{t=0}^{T-1}$, where o_j^T is null with no observations following the final action. Notice that a policy tree can either be built by solving an agent's model or be learned from the available data that describes the agent's behavior [4].

Thus, BE models are those whose behavioral predictions for agent j are identical. After compressing the BE models, the procedure **PruneBehavioralEq** ($\mathcal{M}_{j,l-1}$) returns a set of representative models that are behaviorally distinct. The set of behaviorally distinct models, denoted by $\hat{\mathcal{M}}_{j,l-1}^{BE}$, are considered as the minimal set of agent j's behavior [24]. In this paper, we aim to further compress the model space by merging behaviorally distinct models.

3. VALUE EQUIVALENCE APPROACH AND IMPLEMENTATION

Due to the uncertainty of agent j's models, I-DID algorithms are challenged by the exponential growth in the number of the models over time. BE literally compares solutions of j's models and maintains only the behaviorally distinct models that may become a sufficient coverage of j's behavior.

As different behavior of agent j may have the same impact on the subject agent's decisions, grouping behaviorally distinct models may further reduce the model space without compromising the I-DID solution quality. We utilize this insight toward developing a new technique on examining the model equivalence in the I-DIDs.

3.1 Value Equivalence

We assume that models of agent j have identical frames and differ only in their beliefs in I-DID. Our aim is to identify models that are *value equivalence* (VE) from the perspective of the subject agent i.

The expected value of level l agent i's optimal policy given by the I-DID for T time steps is computed in Eq. 1.

$$V^T(m_{i,l}) = \rho(b_{i,l}, a_i^*) + \sum_{o_i} Pr(o_i|b_{i,l}, a_i^*) V^{T-1}(m'_{i,l}) \quad (1)$$

where $\rho(b_{i,l}, a_i^*) = \sum_{s, m_{j,l-1}} b_{i,l}(s, m_{j,l-1}) \sum_{a_j} R_i(s, a_i^*, a_j) \times Pr(a_j|m_{j,l-1})$. Here, $b_{i,l}(s, m_{j,l-1})$ is the agent i's belief over the physical states and possible models of j at level $l-1$, a_i^* is i's optimal action and $m'_{i,l}$ is the updated model of agent i containing the updated belief at the next time step.

Let $m_{j,l-1}, \hat{m}_{j,l-1} \in \mathcal{M}_{j,l-1}$ be two candidate models of agent j at level $l-1$, and $\bar{\mathcal{M}}_{j,l-1}$ be the set of j's candidate models

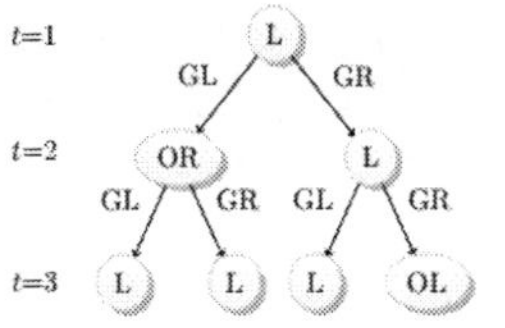

(a) Agent j's policy tree by solving m_j^0

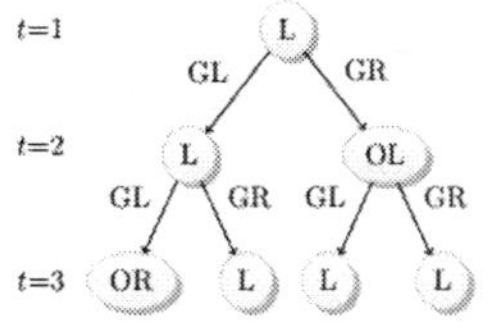

(b) Agent j's policy tree by solving m_j^1

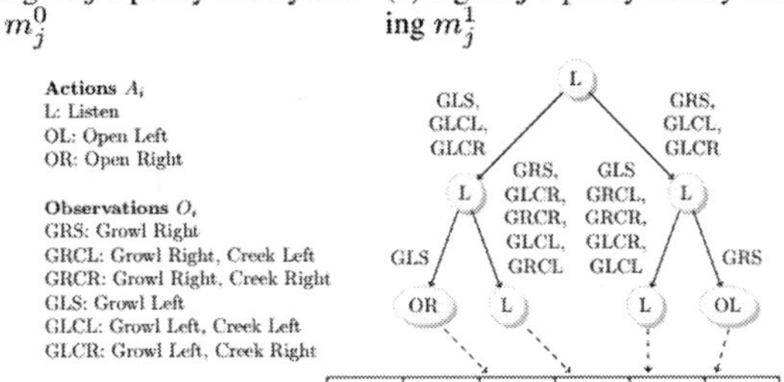

m_j^0	Pr(·)	0.20225	0.30255	0.3026	0.1926
-	EV(·)	1.351	-0.8682	-0.8691	1.695
m_j^1	Pr(·)	0.19455	0.30335	0.3032	0.1989
-	EV(·)	1.494	-0.798	-0.798	1.469

(c) Agent i's policy given by the I-DID

Figure 6: Agent i has the same expected value of the optimal policy (c) for different j's models: m_j^0 (a) and m_j^1 (b).

excluding $m_{j,l-1}$ and $\hat{m}_{j,l-1}$, e.g. $\bar{\mathcal{M}}_{j,l-1} = \mathcal{M}_{j,l-1}/(m_{j,l-1}, \hat{m}_{j,l-1})$. The two models are value equivalence if enclosing either of them in the I-DID will result in the same expected value for agent i. Let $V^T(m_{i,l}|m_{j,l-1})$ (or $V^T(m_{i,l}|\hat{m}_{j,l-1})$) be i's expected value when the model $m_{j,l-1}$ (or $\hat{m}_{j,l-1}$), together with other models $\bar{\mathcal{M}}_{j,l-1}$, are included in the I-DID and are subsequently expanded over T time steps. Formally we define the value equivalence (VE) of two models below.

DEFINITION 2 (VALUE EQUIVALENCE). *Two models of agent j, $m_{j,l-1}$ and $\hat{m}_{j,l-1}$, are value equivalence if $V^T(m_{i,l}|m_{j,l-1}) = V^T(m_{i,l}|\hat{m}_{j,l-1})$, where $V^T(m_{i,l}|m_{j,l-1})$ and $V^T(m_{i,l}|\hat{m}_{j,l-1})$ are as defined above.*

In other words, VE models are those that induce identical expected values for agent i when the I-DID is expanded using any of the models. Thus, the VE models do not enforce the behavioral equivalence of the models. We elaborate it below.

EXAMPLE 1. *Assume that three j's models are expanded in an I-DID of three time steps in the two-agent tiger problem. Fig. 6(a) and (b) show the policy trees for two models with different initial beliefs. The models are not behaviorally equivalent since they have different actions except those at t=1. As shown in the table, agent j's behaviors from different models induce different probabilities ($Pr(h_i)$) over agent i's action-observation sequences every one of which is a policy branch in the tree. However, each of which generate the same expected value of agent i's optimal policy given by the I-DID, which is the sum of the expected values for all policy paths ($EV(h_i)$). Thus, the two models are VE. For the case of I-DIDs with 5 planning horizons, using VE can reduce more than half of behaviorally distinct models of agent j.*

Given the set of agent j's candidate models, $\mathcal{M}_{j,l-1}$, we can group the models that are confirmed to be VE, and then pick a representative model while pruning others from the group. The representative models from the different groups are value difference and partition the entire model space of agent j. Immediately we may introduce an approximate version of VE in Definition 3. A larger value of ϵ groups more value difference models thereby resulting in less model space of agent j.

DEFINITION 3 (ϵ-VE). *Two models of agent j, $m_{j,l-1}$ and $\hat{m}_{j,l-1}$, are ϵ-VE if $|V^T(m_{i,l}|m_{j,l-1}) - V^T(m_{i,l}|\hat{m}_{j,l-1})| \leqslant \epsilon$.*

Similarly to the BE approaches, the procedure **PruneBehavioralEq** ($\mathcal{M}_{j,l-1}$) can be replaced with the one using VE to prune the models in the model node. Recall that agent i assigns some probability mass to each model in the model node ($Mod[M_j^t]$). When the VE models are pruned, we transfer over from the probability mass over the pruned models to the representative models that are retained in the model node. This avoids introducing errors in the I-DID solution quality due to the loss of probability mass over j's candidate models.

3.2 Value Computation

To determine VE of agent j's models, we need to compute the expected value of agent i's optimal policy given by the I-DID that will be constructed with the expansion of all j's models. This seems to be a paradox since we need to first prune the VE models and then expand the I-DID accordingly. A potential method that interleaves VE determination with a partial I-DID expansion could be developed, which will be discussed in Section 7.

In this paper, we focus on learning VE from available domain data. This is partially motivated by the I-DID practical applications in a real-time strategy game (RTS) where game replay data is continuously supplied by the growing gamer community [4]. Without explicitly building decision making models for agents, we can learn their policies/behaviors from the data. We compute VE from input data instead of candidate models, because computing VE from candidate models would require all such models to be solved as part of the I-DID expansion. I-DID expansion can be time consuming especially for larger time horizons, sometimes impossible due to computational and memory limitations. Computing VE from data avoids this computational complexity allowing for a reduced candidate set of models to be created without I-DID expansion. We will present the VE learning technique in the computer game context, which is also applicable in the setting where agents' interaction data is available.

3.2.1 Value of the Learned Policy

In the context of RTS games, we build an I-DID from the perspective of a non-player character (NPC, or one human-player, denoted by agent i) that models human-players (agent j) at a low level. The NPC aims to optimize its policy upon predicting behavior of human-players. Since it is rather difficult to explicitly model the decision making process of human-players through specific decision models, like IDs or DIDs, we learn their behavior from replay data. Each type of behavior is corresponding to one possible model of human-players. By doing this, we don't need to build the descriptive models of human-players and then solve the models to obtain their behavior. As different types of human-players exist in the game community, the learned behaviors could be many and the I-DID for the NPC cannot include all types of the behavior. We will reduce the behavioral space directly through the VE approach. In a popular RTS game, namely *StarCraft* [1], we elaborate the computation of the expected value of agent i in the VE approach.

Table 1 shows a portion of replay data publicly available in *StarCraft*. The data records the game time-stamp, unit identifier and type, units' rewards in the current game state and so on. The units

[1]http://eu.blizzard.com/en-gb/games/sc/

Time	Unit ID	Type	...	Obs	Action	Util
1	216	Goliath	...	3	escape	0
1	212	Goliath	...	3	escape	0
			...			
5	216	Goliath	...	1	attack	1

Table 1: Sample of *StarCraft* replay data recording activities of various units during the gameplay.

are controlled by either the NPC or human-players. As presented in [4], the behavior of each unit over T time steps can be built as a policy tree in which the probability of each policy path is calculated accordingly. The probability is computed as the occurring frequency of an action-observation sequence in the interaction activities.

Let $Pr(h_i^T)$ be the probability of a policy path in the tree, and $U(h_i^T)$ be the rewards that are gathered by the agent executing the action-observation sequence. We can compute $U(h_i^T)$ by summing immediate rewards received by the agent over the entire planning horizon. Subsequently, we can calculate the expected value of agent i's policy as follows.

$$V^T(\mathcal{T}_i) = \sum_{h_i^T \in \mathcal{T}_i} Pr(h_i^T)U(h_i^T) \tag{2}$$

Given sufficient interaction data, the learned behavior becomes the optimal policy of agents. The expected value of the learned behavior can be counted as the expected value as it is computed by solving its corresponding model, e.g., $V^T(m_{i,l}) = V^T(\mathcal{T}_i)$. Without differentiating whether the policy is obtained by either solving the agent's models or learning the behavior from the data, we denote the expected value as $V^T(m_{i,l} \sim \mathcal{T}_i)$.

As shown in [4], we can still learn the agent's policy from limited data that is sufficiently good to be used in the I-DIDs. With the increasing set of interaction data, the learned policy approaches the optimal policy for agents. The quality of the I-DID solutions can be bounded with a probabilistic guarantee, which may in turn ensure the quality of the VE determination.

3.2.2 *Implementation*

We build a level l I-DID, $m_{i,l}$, for an NPC (agent i) where the variables (including states, observations, actions and rewards) are retrieved from the data and follow gaming knowledge. Since the set of variables are obtained by following a unique type of unit, we can learn the agent i's policy, $\mathcal{T}_i$, from the replay data. As the policy is interleaving with various types of human-players (agent j), we compute its expected value for each type of j's behavior, e.g., $V^T(m_{i,l} \sim \mathcal{T}_i|\mathcal{T}_{j,l-1})$. Consequently, we can obtain a set of the expected values, $\{V^T(m_{i,l} \sim \mathcal{T}_i|\mathcal{T}_{j,l-1}^1), \cdots, V^T(m_{i,l} \sim \mathcal{T}_i|\mathcal{T}_{j,l-1}^n)\}$, each of which quantifies the impact of one type of human-players' behavior on the NPC's policy. By comparing the expected values, we can identify VE of human-players' behavior and prune the behavioral space. The reduced set of agent j's behavior is used to expand the I-DID $m_{i,l}$, as developed in the expansion phase of the I-DID algorithm in Fig. 5.

4. SAVINGS AND SOLUTION QUALITY

As with the previous I-DID techniques, the primary complexity of solving I-DIDs is due to the exponentially growing number of j's models over time. At time step t, there could be $|\mathcal{M}_{j,l-1}^0|(|A_j||\Omega_j|)^t$ many models of the other agent j, where $|\mathcal{M}_{j,l-1}^0|$ is the number of models considered initially. The previous BE methods have reduced the model set into the minimal set, $\hat{\mathcal{M}}_{j,l-1}^{BE}$, that is much smaller than $\mathcal{M}_{j,l-1}^0$. Since VE further clusters behaviorally distinct models, it results in less model space. Let $\hat{\mathcal{M}}_{j,l-1}^{VE}$ be the largest set of value difference models. Then, the following proposition holds.

PROPOSITION 1 (CARDINALITY). *The set $\hat{\mathcal{M}}_{j,l-1}^{VE}$ resulting from the VE approach is not larger than the behaviorally distinct set $\hat{\mathcal{M}}_{j,l-1}^{BE}$ from the BE approach.*

PROOF. BE requires that models have the same optimal actions given observations for each time step. As indicated in the value computation in Eq. 2, the BE models will result in the same expected value. Thus, the BE models naturally become the VE models. Meanwhile, as discussed previously, the behavioral difference could be mediated by the receiving rewards of agent i in the value computation. Thus, the behaviroally distinct models may result in the same expected value and are further classified as VE models. The VE approach may filter out more models than BE does. □

The BE techniques fail to measure the quality of I-DID solutions, which are agent i's policy given by the I-DID, since BE literally compares j's policies that have no direct links with i's policy. In contrast, the VE approach conducts the model reduction by comparing the model influence on the expected value of i's policy. Hence the method can directly bound solution errors if approximation is introduced in the VE determination. Let $\hat{V}^T(m_{i,l})$ be expected value of i's optimal policy given by the I-DID in which the model $m_{j,l-1}$ is replaced with the representative VE model. Evidently, according to Def. 3, the ϵ-VE approach bounds the I-DID solution error not larger than ϵ. Thus, Proposition 2 holds.

PROPOSITION 2 (QUALITY). $|V^T(m_{i,l}) - \hat{V}^T(m_{i,l})| \leqslant \epsilon$

5. EXPERIMENTAL RESULTS

We implemented the VE approach by learning the expected values from the data. The implementation replaces the procedure **PruneBehavioralEq** ($\mathcal{M}_{j,l-1}$) in Fig. 5 to prune agent j's models in the I-DID. Meanwhile, we implemented the ϵ-VE method for the comparison purpose. We compare the variants of the VE approach to the exact BE technique (DMU) [6] and report their performance in two problem domains. The first domain is the multi-unmanned aerial vehicle reconnaissance problem (UAV), which is the largest problem setting so far used in the recent I-DID development [24]; while the second one is the RTS game of *StarCraft* in the I-DID practical applications. We show that, (a) in comparison to DMU, the VE approach further reduces the model space of other agents in the I-DID and achieves better scalability; (b) the quality of solutions provided by the VE methods improves upon more available data; (c) the VE technique can be effectively adapted in an online I-DID solution and outperforms the recently developed online I-DID solution [3].

5.1 UAV Problem Domain

We assume that the UAV scenario is played out in a 5×5 grid of sectors ($|S|$=81, $|A_i|$=$|A_j|$=5, $|\Omega_i|$=$|\Omega_j|$=5), as illustrated in Fig. 7. We build the level 1 I-DID for UAV I modelling J using level 0 DIDs. We consider 20 models of UAV J that differ in the beliefs on its initial position in the grid.

We solve the I-DID using the DMU approach and obtain the optimal policy for UAV I. To generate the data for the VE approach, we let UAV I play with J for N times in which a model of J is randomly picked in the interaction. Given the data of N plays, we

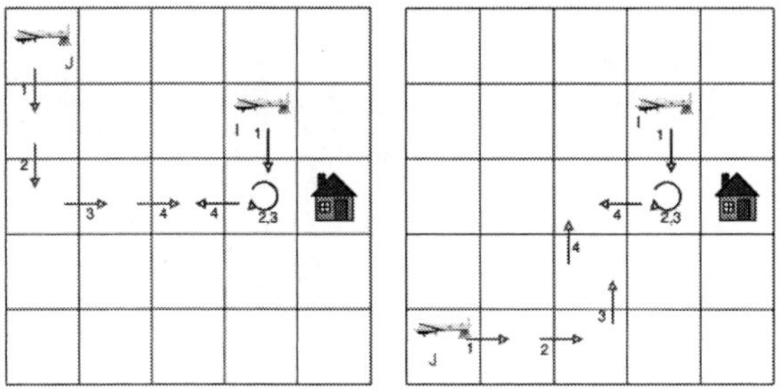

Figure 7: UAV I is tasked with intercepting J before the latter raids the allied base. Two example trajectories show the different behavior of UAV J, which results in the same interception strategy for UAV I. The numbers denote the policy steps of the two UAVs that move continuously and concurrently in the simulation.

proceed to learn J's behavior as well as I's policy, and use VE to prune the behavioral space. Subsequently, we build a new I-DID using the J's behavior reduced by the VE approach. Solving the I-DID results in the new I's optimal policy.

In Fig. $8(a)$-(b), we show the average rewards received by UAV I over 200 runs when it plays with J by executing the policies obtained by either DMU or VE approaches. Since DMU can't solve the I-DIDs for the horizon of 7 [2], its performance is not shown in Fig. $8(b)$. When more interaction data is available for learning the values, determining VE becomes more accurate and the performance approaches that of the DMU method. The ϵ-VE methods perform as expected for the solution quality when the ϵ values are varied in the experiments. We notice that the VE approach even outperforms DMU given more accumulated data. This is because the DMU approach considers the entire space of UAV J's distinct behavior with a uniform probability distribution while VE concentrates on a small set of J's behavior that avoids more randomness in I's prediction.

Fig. $8(c)$ confirms our intuition that VE leads to fewer model classes compared to DMU. A larger ϵ value allows the grouping of more VE models resulting in more compressed model space at each time step. We show two examples of selected trajectories of UAVs I and J using the two methods for a horizon of 4 in Fig. 7. Although UAV J exhibits rather different strategies on approaching the allied base, the distinction does not lead to a different policy to I intercepting J before J initiates the attack. Note that the two example trajectories represent some typical raid behavior of UAV J, which belongs to solutions of J's different models differing in its initial beliefs.

Since VE leads to a smaller model space, it achieves a better scalability than DMU and can solve the I-DID for a larger horizon up to 10 [3]. We don't report their time efficiency in solving the I-DIDs since DMU and VE employ different schemes to obtain J's policies. But we observe in the experiments that learning behavior from data is much more efficient than solving decision models ascribed to J. Solving the I-DIDs that are expanded with the reduced number of models for other agents is very efficient.

We take a further step to adapt VE in the online I-DID solutions, namely OPIAM (online plan, interact and adapt models), as developed in [3]. OPIAM starts with a small set of J's models and uses BE to adapt the model space in the online interactions. In the version of OnlineVE, we adapt the model space by choosing the models that result in larger expected values to I during the interactions. In this set of experiments, we let UAV I choose a set of 5 models (from 20 models) of J to build an initial I-DID, and adapt the I-DID online. Fig. 9 shows that the OnlineVE progresses much better than OPIAM over interactions. OnlineVE benefits from directing I's prediction on J's behavior to I's rewards during immediate interactions. We are optimistic that VE may be well integrated into the development of other I-DID solutions.

5.2 StarCraft Application

The real world domain we choose to model and test the VE approach is *StarCraft*. We choose *StarCraft* because it has partial observability as to the true battle state, as well as the availability of human vs human replay files from sources such as Gosu Gamers [4] and Team Liquid [5]. From these replay files states, observations, actions and rewards can be extracted such as shown in Table 1 from which we can learn policies of human players.

StarCraft games are incredibly complex with players having to focus on areas such as resource gathering, build orders, combat and scouting. To simplify this domain for the purposes of this paper we focus on a typical combat scenario between groups of units. Specifically for testing we use a 3 vs 3 unit scenario. Fig $10(a)$ shows the complexity of games between two human players and the typical scenario we have broken this down into. We mine for data from replays by observing in the data where small groups of units are close together and record their states, actions, observations and rewards for these battles. A battle is considered over when either one of the groups of units are all killed or units have moved far enough away from enemy units to no longer engage in battle.

We build level 1 I-DID for player i modelling j of sectors ($|S|$=16, $|A_i|$=$|A_j|$=3, $|\Omega_i|$=$|\Omega_j|$=4) using data from replay files. Policies of player j are learned from replay data and pruned through either DMU or VE approaches. In Fig. $10(b)$ we show a small sample tree of typical behavior in the aforementioned scenario taken from a much larger and complex policy. The behavior shown is a typical defensive behavior where a player may be defending an area or unit by only attacking when confident there is a low number of enemy units to prevent loss, standing ground both when there is nothing close-by to attack, and when there is a larger number close-by standing ground to defend whatever the units may be defending.

Fig. 11 shows results of experiments of simulated battles between players i and j where i is controlled by the polices by solving the above I-DIDs for varying amounts of mined replay data and j executes a random policy from those learned from the mined data, average rewards are calculated over approximately 100 battles. In Fig. $11(a)$-(b), we compare DMU methods of reducing j's model space with reduction of j's model space by VE and VE with varying ϵ values (0.25 and 0.3) for planning horizons T=5 and T=7. For the larger horizon of T=7 where more data is available a greater number of j's behavior are learned increasing the size of the I-DID model space. This causes the model to no longer be solvable by DMU methods due to memory limitations; however, we find that reduction by VE methods reduces the model space by approximately 20-30%, enough for the I-DID to be solved where DMU fails. We also find that for a larger ϵ such as 0.3 for VE methods can introduce unpredictability into the quality of policies calculated for i due to over-reducing the known behavior of j preventing accurate predictions of their behavior. On the other hand, VE performs better and more stable when more data is supplied.

[2] We use the approximate BE technique (ϵ-BE [24]) to generate the data.

[3] We use ϵ-BE to generate a sufficiently large set of data that result in reliable policies.

[4] `http://www.gosugamers.net/`

[5] `http://www.teamliquid.net/`

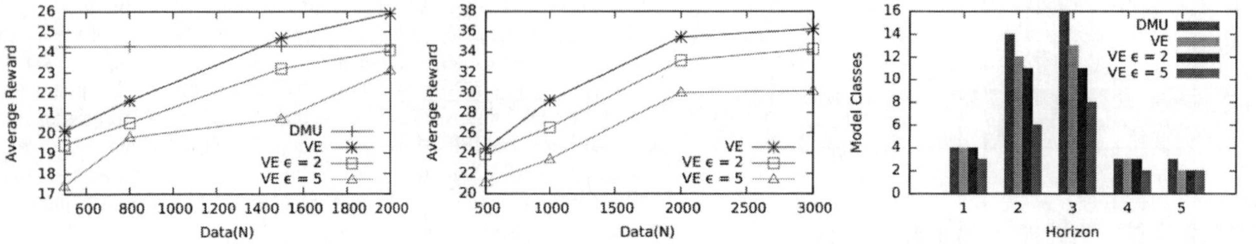

(a) Average reward for T=5

(b) Average reward for T=7

(c) Number of models at each time step for T=5

Figure 8: Performance profile for the UAV problems obtained by solving level 1 I-DID through either DMU or VE approaches.

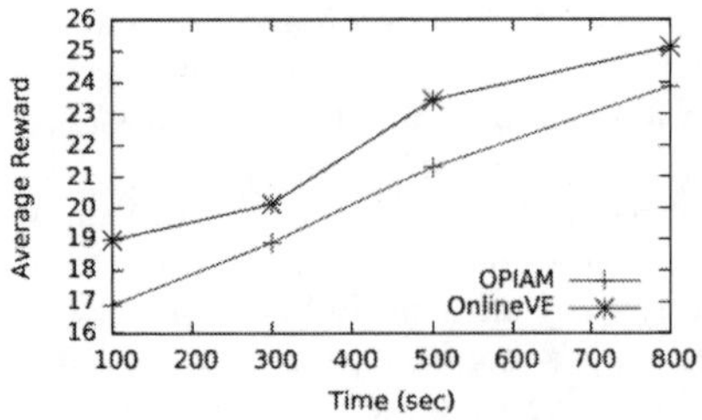

Figure 9: Average rewards received by UAV I interacting with J online. UAV I adapts the model space every 200-300 seconds.

6. RELATED WORK

I-DIDs generalize influence diagrams to multiagent settings facilitating decision making in the presence of other sophisticated decision makers of uncertain types. They are viewed as graphical counterparts of finitely-nested interactive partially observable Markov decision processes (I-POMDPs) [8].

As we mentioned before, a predominant factor in the complexity of I-DIDs is due to an exponential growth in candidate models of other agents. Exploiting BE to reduce the model space is a mainstream research on addressing I-DID solution challenges [24]. Notably, by discriminating between model updates, the DMU approach [6] generates a minimal set of models in each non-initial model node. It may pre-emptively avoid expanding models that will turn out to be BE to others in the next time step. Meanwhile, much effort has been invested into determining BE models efficiently by investigating the development of policy trees. Zeng *et al.* [25, 5, 23] sought to cluster models by comparing only a partial set of paths in the policy trees. Chen *et al.* [3] initiated the study of online I-DID solutions by developing true behavior of other agents during their interactions. Conroy *et al.* [4] focused on learning agents' behavior from available data, which provides prior knowledge on refining model space in I-DIDs. The BE based techniques have improved the usability of I-DIDs and driven potential real-world applications [12, 11, 4], which contributes into the learning techniques in computer games [2].

While graphical models remain as yet unexplored in the context of cooperative decision making models using frameworks such as decentralized POMDPs [19], factored representations of the state space are becoming prevalent [13]. The factored representations facilitate solutions to decentralized POMDPs with many agents by exploiting the interaction structure among the agents [14]. Pajarinen and Peltonen [16] utilized factored representations in a dynamic Bayesian network to project agents' beliefs forward, and applied expectation-maximization to learn stochastic finite-state controllers. Meanwhile, Witwicki and Durfee [22] used influence-

(a) *StarCraft* battles are very complex and we focus on a commonly occurring scenario where two groups of units are battling in the field.

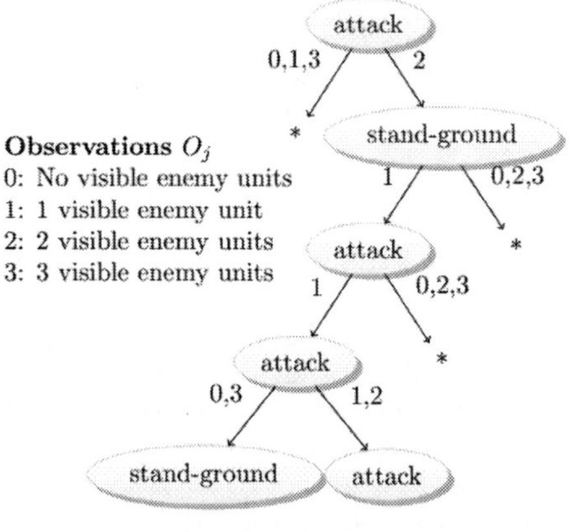

(b) Sample section of a policy tree learned for agent j for a typical type of gaming behavior.

Figure 10: Applications of I-DIDs in *StarCraft* where behavior of players can be learned from replay data.

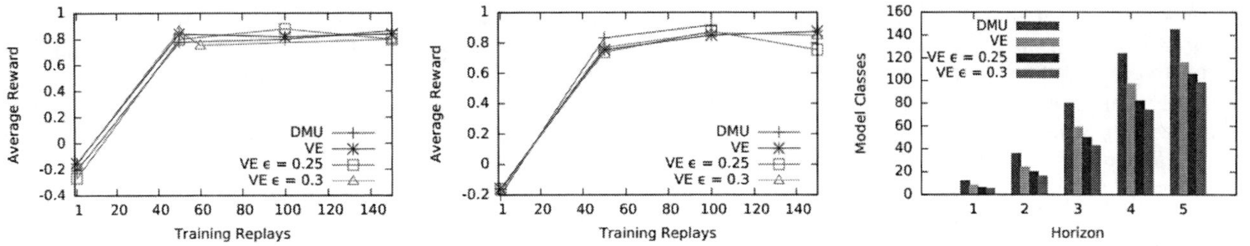

(a) Average reward for T=5 (b) Average reward for T=7 (c) Model reduction for T=5 from 150 replays

Figure 11: Performance profile of the VE approach in *StarCraft* where we learn behavior of player j from replay data.

based abstraction to decouple local agents' interactions in decentralized POMDPs, which is further generalized to quantify the complexity of multiagent planning [15].

Specifically, exploiting structure of value functions has been a useful technique for improving solutions to agents' planning [21]. This research attempts to reduce the complexity of belief updates by approximating the value functions, e.g., through a set of basis functions [9]. With the exploitation of stochastic transition and observation functions, the value function approximation results in very efficient solutions to decentralized POMDPs with many agents [17]. Recently, Amato and Oliehoek [1] used search methods to facilitate the decomposition of interacted values in multiagent planning. The VE technique shows significant improvement on solution scalability and enjoys theoretical guarantee.

7. DISCUSSION AND CONCLUSION

We show how we exploit behavioral impact to further determine the model equivalence and apply it to scale up solutions of I-DIDs. Our insight is that comparing the expected value induced by other agents is likely sufficient for grouping more models than previously clustered by BE approaches. We formulate a principled VE technique to decide the model equivalence and implement it through the value learning task. We empirically examine the VE approach from multiple facets in two selected problem domains.

While we demonstrate the utility of VE in a comprehensive set of experiments, we still face the challenge of computing the expected value of the subject agent without fully expanding the I-DID. As indicated in the experiments, learning values from data can serve to compose an initial model space that will be refined in the new interactions. This could be particularly useful in the areas of game playing and user modeling where either data or domain knowledge can be accessed. Pynadath and Marsella [18] demonstrated an application of utility equivalence techniques in a social simulation setting related to class bullying. Here, both the teacher and the bully maintain a limited number of mental models of each other without suffering a loss in expected utility.

Interleaving VE determination with expanding I-DIDs is another way to solve I-DID in a more general decision making setting. We evaluate VE while expanding the I-DID with a partial set of candidate models, and prune the models in an incremental way. The issue is about selection of candidates so that the solution quality could be guaranteed in the VE approach. This is in line with our future research.

REFERENCES

[1] C. Amato and F. A. Oliehoek. Scalable planning and learning for multiagent POMDPs: Extended version. In *Proceedings of the Twenty-Ninth AAAI Conference on Artificial Intelligence (AAAI)*, pages 1995–2002, 2015.

[2] K. T. Andersen, Y. Zeng, D. D. Christensen, and D. Tran. Experiments with online reinforcement learning in real-time strategy games. *Applied Artificial Intelligence: An International Journal*, 23:855–871, 2009.

[3] Y. Chen, P. Doshi, and Y. Zeng. Iterative online planning in multiagent settings with limited model spaces and pac guarantees. In *Proceedings of the Fourteenth Internationl Conference on Autonomous Agents and Multiagents Systems Conference (AAMAS)*, pages 1161–1169, 2015.

[4] R. Conroy, Y. Zeng, M. Cavazza, and Y. Chen. Learning behaviors in agents systems with interactive dynamic influence diagrams. In *International Joint Conference on Artificial Intelligence (IJCAI)*, pages 39–45, 2015.

[5] P. Doshi, M. Chandrasekaran, and Y. Zeng. Epsilon-subject equivalence of models for interactive dynamic influence diagrams. In *WIC/ACM/IEEE Conference on Web Intelligence and Intelligent Agent Technology (WI-IAT)*, 2010.

[6] P. Doshi and Y. Zeng. Improved approximation of interactive dynamic influence diagrams using discriminative model updates. In *Eighth Internationl Conference on Autonomous Agents and Multiagents Systems Conference (AAMAS)*, pages 907–914, 2009.

[7] P. Doshi, Y. Zeng, and Q. Chen. Graphical models for interactive pomdps: Representations and solutions. *Journal of Autonomous Agents and Multi-Agent Systems (JAAMAS)*, 18(3):376–416, 2009.

[8] P. Gmytrasiewicz and P. Doshi. A framework for sequential planning in multiagent settings. *Journal of Artificial Intelligence Research (JAIR)*, 24:49–79, 2005.

[9] M. Hauskrecht. Value-function approximations for partially observable markov decision processes. *Journal of Artificial Intelligence Research (JAIR)*, 13:33–94, 2000.

[10] D. Koller and B. Milch. Multi-agent influence diagrams for representing and solving games. In *International Joint Conference on Artificial Intelligence (IJCAI)*, pages 1027–1034, 2001.

[11] J. Luo, H. Yin, B. Li, and C. Wu. Path planning for automated guided vehicles system via interactive dynamic influence diagrams with communication. In *9th IEEE International Conference on Control and Automation (ICCA)*, pages 755 –759, 2011.

[12] B. Ng, C. Meyers, K. Boakye, and J. Nitao. Towards applying interactive POMDPs to real-world adversary modeling. In *Innovative Applications in Artificial Intelligence (IAAI)*, pages 1814–1820, 2010.

[13] F. Oliehoek, M. Spaan, S. Whiteson, and N. Vlassis.

Exploiting locality of interaction in factored Dec-POMDPs. In *Seventh International Conference on Autonomous Agents and Multiagent Systems (AAMAS)*, pages 517–524, 2008.

[14] F. A. Oliehoek, S. Whiteson, and M. T. Spaan. Approximate solutions for factored Dec-POMDPs with many agents. In *Proceedings of the 2013 international conference on Autonomous agents and multi-agent systems (AAMAS)*, pages 563–570, 2013.

[15] F. A. Oliehoek, S. J. Witwicki, and L. P. Kaelbling. Influence-based abstraction for multiagent systems. In *Twenty-Sixth AAAI Conference on Artificial Intelligence (AAAI)*, pages 1422–1428, 2012.

[16] J. Pajarinen and J. Peltonen. Efficient planning for factored infinite-horizon Dec-POMDPs. In *International Joint Conference on Artificial Intelligence (IJCAI)*, pages 325–331, 2011.

[17] J. Pajarinen and J. Peltonen. Efficient planning for factored infinite-horizon Dec-POMDPs. In *Proceedings of the Twenty-Second international joint conference on Artificial Intelligence (IJCAI)*, pages 325–331, 2011.

[18] D. Pynadath and S. Marsella. Minimal mental models. In *Twenty-Second Conference on Artificial Intelligence (AAAI)*, pages 1038–1044, Vancouver, Canada, 2007.

[19] S. Seuken and S. Zilberstein. Formal models and algorithms for decentralized decision making under uncertainty. *Journal of Autonomous Agents and Multi-agent Systems*, pages 190–250, 2008.

[20] J. A. Tatman and R. D. Shachter. Dynamic programming and influence diagrams. *IEEE Transactions on Systems, Man, and Cybernetics*, 20(2):365–379, 1990.

[21] T. Veiga, M. T. J. Spaan, and P. U. Lima. Point-based pomdp solving with factored value function approximation. In *Twenty-Eighth AAAI Conference on Artificial Intelligence (AAAI)*, pages 2513–2519, 2014.

[22] S. J. Witwicki and E. H. Durfee. Influence-based policy abstraction for weakly-coupled dec-pomdps. In *International Conference on Automated Planning and Scheduling (ICAPS)*, pages 185–192, 2010.

[23] Y. Zeng, Y. Chen, and P. Doshi. Approximating behavioral equivalence of models using top-k policy paths (extended abstract). In *International Conference on Autonomous Agents and Multi-Agent Systems (AAMAS)*, pages 1229–1230, 2011.

[24] Y. Zeng and P. Doshi. Exploiting model equivalences for solving interactive dynamic influence diagrams. *Journal of Artificial Intelligence Research (JAIR)*, 43:211–255, 2012.

[25] Y. Zeng, P. Doshi, Y. Pan, H. Mao, M. Chandrasekaran, and J. Luo. Utilizing partial policies for identifying equivalence of behavioral models. In *Twenty-Fifth AAAI Conference on Artificial Intelligence*, pages 1083–1088, 2011.

[26] Y. Zeng, H. Mao, Y. Pan, and J. Luo. Improved use of partial policies for identifying behavioral equivalence. In *Proceedings of the Eleventh Internationl Conference on Autonomous Agents and Multiagents Systems Conference (AAMAS)*, pages 1015–1022, 2012.

Regular Strategies and Strategy Improvement: Efficient Tools for Solving Large Patrolling Problems

Antonín Kučera*
Faculty of Informatics, Masaryk University
Botanická 68a, 60200 Brno
Czech Republic
kucera@fi.muni.cz

Tomáš Lamser
Faculty of Informatics, Masaryk University
Botanická 68a, 60200 Brno
Czech Republic

ABSTRACT

In patrolling problems, the task is to compute an optimal strategy for a patroller who moves among vulnerable targets and aims at detecting possible intrusions. Previous approaches to this problem were mostly based on non-linear programming, and the solution space was restricted to positional strategies or to strategies dependent on a bounded history of patroller's moves. In this paper, we extend the solution space to *regular* strategies, and show that regular strategies are *strictly more powerful* than strategies dependent on a bounded history. Further, we design a *strategy improvement* technique for regular strategies which completely avoids the use of non-linear programming. Intuitively, we start with *some* regular strategy, and then repeatedly *improve* this strategy by incorporating a solution of a certain *linear* program. Our experiments demonstrate that the proposed approach can quickly produce strategies of very good quality even for quite large patrolling problems.

Keywords

Robotic patrolling; Security of Agent Systems; Stackelberg Equilibrium; Strategy Synthesis

1. INTRODUCTION

Game theoretic approaches to patrolling problems have received a considerable amount of attention in recent years (see, e.g., [15, 4] for an everview). The task is to design an optimal strategy (policy) for a patroller who moves among a given set of vulnerable targets and aims at detecting possible intrusions. Since the intruder can observe the moves of the patroller but the patroller has no knowledge about the plans and actions of the intruder, the solution concepts used in this setting are mostly based on Stackelberg equilibrium [17]. That is, the patroller's strategy for visiting the targets should maximize his expected utility against all best responses of the intruder.

Most of the existing algorithms for solving patrolling problems (see Section 2) are based on mathematical programming. This approach has to deal with two fundamental difficulties: First, some of the constraints are (inevitably) *non-linear.* Second, the encoding is usually restricted to *positional* patroller's strategies, where the decision depends only on the current patroller's position. That is, the solution encoded by the program is actually optimal only among the subset of positional strategies. It has been argued in, e.g., [8, 5], that the patroller can achieve a better expected utility when his decisions depend on the last K visited positions, where $K \geq 1$ is a suitable constant (such strategies are called *last-K strategies* in this paper). Although one can modify the programs constructed for positional strategies so that they work for *last-K* strategies, the size of the modified programs grows *exponentially* in K. Even for small instances (say, 10 targets and $K = 3$), one may thus obtain non-linear programs with more than 1000 variables. Hence, this approach does not scale with increasing K.

Our contribution. We consider a special class of *regular* patroller's strategies that utilize deterministic finite-state automata to collect some information about the history of patroller's moves. The patroller's decision after a history $v_1, \ldots, v_n$ of visited positions then depends not only on the current position v_n, but also on the state of the automaton entered after reading the word $v_1 \cdots v_n$. We show that regular strategies are *strictly more powerful* (i.e., can achieve a strictly better expected utility for the patroller) than all strategies of $\bigcup_{K=1}^{\infty}$ *last-K*. Further, we design a *strategy improvement* technique for regular strategies which completely avoids the use of non-linear programming. Intuitively, we start with *some* regular strategy, and then try to *improve* this strategy by performing a given number of *rounds*, where each round consists of three steps: (1) we construct a linear program whose coefficients depend on the regular strategy computed in the previous round. The size of this program is *linear* in the size of the patrolling problem and the size of the automaton used by the regular strategy; (2) we solve the linear program; (3) we construct a new regular strategy by taking a suitable "combination" of the strategy from the previous round and the solution of the linear program. Compared to the existing methods, our approach is applicable to patrolling problems of considerably larger size, which is witnessed by the experiments presented in Section 5.

2. RELATED WORK

Existing approaches to protecting the targets against intrusions are based either on optimizing static allocation of available resources to the targets in order to discover the

*Supported by the Czech Science Foundation, grant No. 15-17564S.

Appears in: *Proceedings of the 15th International Conference on Autonomous Agents and Multiagent Systems (AAMAS 2016), J. Thangarajah, K. Tuyls, C. Jonker, S. Marsella (eds.), May 9–13, 2016, Singapore.*

intruder, or by computing an optimal movement strategy for a mobile patroller. The first model, also known as *security games*, has been studied in [11, 12]. The earlier works [14] concentrated on finding an allocation that minimizes the chance for penetrating an unprotected target. Later, the main task was extended with a requirement that the allocation needs to satisfy some extra constraints [16].

In the second model, also known as *patrolling games*, the focus was primarily on finding locally optimal strategies for robotic patrolling units either on restricted graphs (e.g., on circles in [2, 3]), or arbitrary graphs with weighted preference on the targets [5, 6]. Alternatively, the work focused on some novel aspects of the problem, such as variants with moving targets [8, 10], multiple patrolling units [7], or movement of the intruder on the graph [6] and reaction to alarms [13]. Most of the existing literature assumes that the patroller is following a memoryless (Markov) strategy that depends solely on the current position of the patroller in the graph and they seek for a solution using mathematical programming. Few exceptions include duplicating each node of the graph to distinguish internal states of the patroller (e.g., in [2] authors consider a direction of the patrolling robot as a specific state; in [9], this concept is further generalized), or seeking for higher-order strategies in [5]. In [1], an algorithm for computing an ε-optimal strategy for the patroller is designed, but this algorithm is of exponential complexity.

The model considered in this paper is the same as in [5]. That is, we allow for an arbitrary topology of the game graph, we assume that the time needed to complete an intrusion can be different at each target, and the importance of the individual targets can be different for the patroller and the intruder.

3. REGULAR STRATEGIES

A *patrolling problem* is a tuple $\mathcal{G} = (V, E, T, d)$, where V is a finite set of *vertices* (patroller's positions), $E \subseteq V \times V$ are admissible moves, $T \subseteq V$ is a set of *targets*, and d assigns to every $t \in T$ the number $d(t) > 0$ of time units needed to complete the intrusion at t. We require that the directed graph (V, E) is strongly connected. It can be safely assumed that the patroller spends one unit of time in each vertex, because longer stays can be modeled by inserting auxiliary vertices and edges. A *history* is a finite path in $\mathcal{G}$, and a *walk* is an infinite path in $\mathcal{G}$. Note that a history h can also be seen as a (non-empty) finite word over the alphabet V. The set of all histories is denoted by $\mathcal{H}$.

A *finite-state observer for* $\mathcal{G} = (V, E, T, d)$ is a deterministic finite-state automaton $\mathcal{A} = (S, \delta)$, where S is a finite set of *states* and $\delta : S \times V \to S$ is a total transition function. We extend δ to histories in the expected way. Further, we require that the state space of $\mathcal{A}$ is *strongly connected*, i.e., for all $s, s' \in S$ where $s \neq s'$ there exists a history h such that $\delta(s, h) = s'$. An *$\mathcal{A}$-regular patroller's strategy* is a triple $\sigma = (\hat{v}, \hat{s}, \kappa)$, where $\hat{v} \in V$ is the *initial vertex*, $\hat{s} \in S$ is the *initial state*, and κ is a function which to every pair $(v, s) \in V \times S$ assigns a probability distribution μ over V such that $\mu(v') > 0$ only if $(v, v') \in E$. The set of all $\mathcal{A}$-regular patroller's strategies is denoted by $\Sigma_{\mathcal{A}}$. Given a history h ending in a vertex v, the next vertex is selected randomly according to the distribution $\kappa(v, s)$, where $s = \delta(\hat{s}, h)$. The state s represents the information collected by $\mathcal{A}$ after reading h. Thus, σ determines a unique probability measure $\mathcal{P}^{\sigma}$ over all patroller's walks in $\mathcal{G}$ initiated in $\hat{v}$.

An *intruder's strategy* is a function $\pi : \mathcal{H} \to \{\mathit{wait}, \mathit{enter}_t \mid t \in T\}$ which says whether the intruder should wait or try to penetrate a target t after observing a given history of patroller's moves. The intruder is allowed to attack at most once along a patroller's walk, which means that if $\pi(h) = \mathit{enter}_t$ for some $t \in T$, then $\pi(h') = \mathit{wait}$ for all proper prefixes h' of h. The set of all intruder's strategies is denoted by Π. Given a strategy $\pi \in \Pi$ and a patroller's walk $w = v_0, v_1, v_2, \ldots$, we say that the intruder *waits along* w if $\pi(h) = \mathit{wait}$ for every finite prefix h of w. If there is $j \geq 0$ such that $\pi(v_0, \ldots, v_j) = \mathit{enter}_t$, then we say that the intruder *enters* t *along* w, and he is either *captured* in t or *penetrates* t, depending on whether t appears among the vertices $v_j, \ldots, v_{j+d(t)-1}$ or not, respectively. Given an $\mathcal{A}$-regular patroller's strategy $\sigma = (\hat{v}, \hat{s}, \kappa)$ and an intruder's strategy π, the probability of all walks w initiated in $\hat{v}$ such the intruder waits along w, is captured in t, and penetrates t, is denoted by $\mathcal{P}^{\sigma}(\mathit{noattack}^{\pi})$, $\mathcal{P}^{\sigma}(\mathit{capture}^{\pi}_t)$, and $\mathcal{P}^{\sigma}(\mathit{penetrate}^{\pi}_t)$, respectively.

In general, the patroller and the intruder may regard the importance of each outcome differently, and hence there are separate families of *utilities* $U^P_c(t)$, $U^P_p(t)$ to the patroller and $U^I_c(t)$, $U^I_p(t)$ to the intruder if the outcome is $\mathit{capture}_t$ and $\mathit{penetrate}_t$, respectively. Without restrictions, we assume that both players receive 0 for the outcome *noattack*, and require that $U^P_p(t) \leq 0 \leq U^P_c(t)$ and $U^I_c(t) \leq 0 \leq U^I_p(t)$ for every target t. Given a pair of strategies σ, π, the *expected patroller's utility* is defined by

$$\mathrm{EU}^{\sigma,\pi}_P = \sum_{t \in T} \mathcal{P}^{\sigma}(\mathit{capture}^{\pi}_t) \cdot U^P_c(t) + \mathcal{P}^{\sigma}(\mathit{penetrate}^{\pi}_t) \cdot U^P_p(t)$$

The *expected intruder's utility* $\mathrm{EU}^{\sigma,\pi}_I$ is defined in the same way, but $U^I_c(t)$, $U^I_p(t)$ are used instead of $U^P_c(t)$, $U^P_p(t)$.

For each $\sigma \in \Sigma_{\mathcal{A}}$, we define the set $\mathrm{BR}(\sigma)$ of all $\pi^* \in \Pi$ such that $\mathrm{EU}^{\sigma,\pi^*}_I = \sup_{\pi \in \Pi} \mathrm{EU}^{\sigma,\pi}_I$, i.e., π^* is a *best response to* σ. A pair of strategies $(\sigma^*, \pi^*) \in \Sigma_{\mathcal{A}} \times \Pi$ is a *Stackelberg equilibrium* if the following conditions are satisfied:

(a) π^* is a best response to σ^*;

(b) π^* maximizes the expected patroller's utility among all best responses, i.e., $\mathrm{EU}^{\sigma^*,\pi^*}_P = \sup_{\pi \in \mathrm{BR}(\sigma)} \mathrm{EU}^{\sigma^*,\pi}_P$;

(c) the patroller is not motivated to change his strategy, i.e., $\mathrm{EU}^{\sigma^*,\pi^*}_P = \sup_{\sigma \in \Sigma_{\mathcal{A}}} \sup_{\pi \in \mathrm{BR}(\sigma)} \mathrm{EU}^{\sigma,\pi}_P$.

THEOREM 1. *For every patrolling problem $\mathcal{G}$, every finite-state observer $\mathcal{A}$, and all $U^P_c, U^P_p, U^I_c, U^I_p$, there exists a Stackelberg equilibrium.*

PROOF SKETCH. First we show that for every $\sigma \in \Sigma_{\mathcal{A}}$, the set $\mathrm{BR}(\sigma)$ is non-empty. The argument crucially depends on the regularity of σ, which guarantees that the patroller plays in one of the finitely many ways after re-visiting a given vertex. Then, we show that there exists a strategy $\pi^* \in \mathrm{BR}(\sigma)$ which maximizes the expected patroller's utility among all best responses. Finally, we prove there exists at least one $\sigma^* \in \Sigma_{\mathcal{A}}$ satisfying the condition (c) above. This is achieved by considering an infinite sequence $\sigma_0, \sigma_1, \ldots$ of strategies such that $\sup_{\pi \in \mathrm{BR}(\sigma_i)} \mathrm{EU}^{\sigma_i,\pi}_P$ converges monotonically to $\sup_{\sigma \in \Sigma_{\mathcal{A}}} \sup_{\pi \in \mathrm{BR}(\sigma)} \mathrm{EU}^{\sigma,\pi}_P$ as $i \to \infty$, and showing that σ^* can be chosen as the limit of a converging subsequence of $\sigma_0, \sigma_1, \ldots$ □

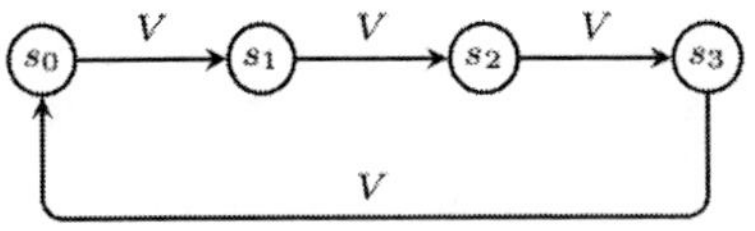

Figure 1: A finite-state observer $\mathcal{A}$.

Due to Theorem 1, we can also define the *Stackelberg value* achievable by $\mathcal{A}$-regular strategies in $\mathcal{G}$ by

$$Val(\mathcal{G}, \mathcal{A}) \;=\; \mathrm{EU}_P^{\sigma^*,\pi^*}$$

where (σ^*, π^*) is a Stackelberg equilibrium. Further, for every $\sigma^* \in \Sigma_{\mathcal{A}}$, we define the *value of* σ^* *in* $\mathcal{G}$ by

$$Val(\sigma^*, \mathcal{G}) \;=\; \sup_{\pi \in \mathrm{BR}(\sigma)} \mathrm{EU}_P^{\sigma^*,\pi}.$$

We say that $\sigma^* \in \Sigma_{\mathcal{A}}$ is *$\mathcal{A}$-optimal* if $Val(\sigma^*, \mathcal{G}) = Val(\mathcal{G}, \mathcal{A})$.

In the special case of *zero-sum* patrolling problems, where the utilities also satisfy $U_c^P(t) + U_c^I(t) = U_p^P(t) + U_p^I(t) = 0$ for all $t \in T$, the intruder maximizes his expected utility iff he minimizes the expected patroller's utility. Further, every $\pi \in \mathrm{BR}(\sigma)$ achieves the same (and hence the maximal) expected patroller's utility. Thus, for zero-sum patrolling problems we obtain that

$$Val(\sigma^*, \mathcal{G}) \;=\; \inf_{\pi \in \Pi} \mathrm{EU}_P^{\sigma^*,\pi}$$

$$Val(\mathcal{G}, \mathcal{A}) \;=\; \sup_{\sigma \in \Sigma_{\mathcal{A}}} \inf_{\pi \in \Pi} \mathrm{EU}_P^{\sigma,\pi}$$

EXAMPLE 1. *To get some intuition about the efficiency of regular strategies, consider a (zero-sum) patrolling problem $\mathcal{G}$ where*

- $V = \{v_1, \ldots, v_{30}\}$
- $E = V \times V, \quad T = V,$
- $d(v_i) = 3$ *for all* $1 \le i \le 10$, *and* $d(v_j) = 5$ *for all* $11 \le j \le 30$,
- $U_c^P(t) = U_c^I(t) = 0,\ U_p^P(t) = -1,\ U_p^I(t) = 1$ *for all* t.

Consider a finite-state observer $\mathcal{A}$ of Fig. 1. Further, let V_0, V_1 be a partition of $\{v_1, \ldots, v_{10}\}$ into two subsets of 5 elements, and U_0, U_1, U_2, U_3 be a partition of $\{v_{11}, \ldots, v_{30}\}$ into four subsets of 5 elements. Also observe that for all $(\sigma, \pi) \in \Sigma_{\mathcal{A}} \times \Pi$, we have that $1 + \mathrm{EU}_P^{\sigma,\pi}$ is the probability of all walks where the intruder is captured or waits forever. Hence, the patroller/intruder actually aims at maximizing/minimizing this probability.

Let $\sigma = (v_1, s_3, \kappa)$ be an $\mathcal{A}$-regular strategy such that $\kappa(v, s_i)$ is a uniform distribution over the set $V_j \cup U_k$, where $j = (i+1) \bmod 2$ and $k = (i+1) \bmod 4$. Then, one can easily confirm that $Val(\sigma, \mathcal{G}) = -9/10$. That is, if the patroller uses the strategy σ, the probability of all walks where the intruder is either captured or waits forever is at least $1/10$ (for every intruder's strategy). Intutively, this seems quite close to the optimum, because in the first 4 moves, each vertex of $\{v_1, v_{11}, \ldots, v_{30}\}$ should be visited at least once, and each vertex of $\{v_2, \ldots, v_{10}\}$ should be visited "about twice on average". Hence, the probability of all walks where the intruder is captured or waits forever is bounded by a number close to $4/(21 + 2 \cdot 9) = 4/39$. The "periodicity" of σ captured by $\mathcal{A}$ is essential for achieving the efficiency of σ, and it cannot be mimicked by any strategy which depends just on some finite suffix of the history.

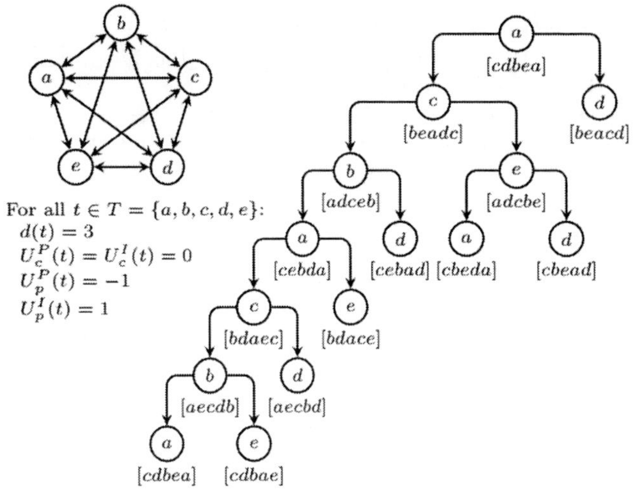

Figure 2: A zero-sum patrolling problem.

Now we give a rigorous proof that regular strategies can be strictly better than all strategies of $\bigcup_{K=1}^{\infty}$ *last-K* (see Section 1), even for zero-sum patrolling problems with fully connected environment where all vertices are targets, $d(t)$ is the same for all targets, and the patroller/defender aims just at maximizing/minimizing the probability of all walks where the intruder is either captured or waits forever. First, observe that *last-K* strategies can be seen as $\mathcal{A}_K$-regular strategies, where the finite-state observer $\mathcal{A}_K$ "remembers" the sequence of the last K visited vertices in its state-space (hence, $\mathcal{A}_K$ needs $(|V| + 1)^K$ control states). We have the following:

THEOREM 2. *Let $\mathcal{G}$ be the zero-sum patrolling problem of Fig. 2 (left). Then there exists a finite-state observer $\mathcal{A}$ such that $Val(\mathcal{G}, \mathcal{A}) > Val(\mathcal{G}, \mathcal{A}_K)$ for all $K \ge 1$.*

PROOF SKETCH. The set of states of $\mathcal{A}$ are all permutations of $\{a, b, c, d, e\}$ which encode the information about the current vertex, and about two previously visited vertices and their immediate successors. For example, the permutation $[cebda]$ says that the current vertex is a, the vertex visited before a was b and the other successor of b was d, and the vertex visited before b was c and the other successor of c was e. The transition function of $\mathcal{A}$ is defined as follows. For every state (permutation) $[x_1, x_2, x_3, x_4, x_5]$ we put $\delta([x_1, x_2, x_3, x_4, x_5], x_1) = [x_3, x_4, x_5, x_2, x_1])$ and $\delta([x_1, x_2, x_3, x_4, x_5], x_2) = [x_3, x_4, x_5, x_1, x_2])$. For the other y such that $x_1 \ne y \ne x_2$ we define $\delta([x_1, x_2, x_3, x_4, x_5], y)$ arbitrarily. Further, for every vertex x and every state of the form $[y_1, y_2, y_3, y_4, x]$ we put $\kappa(x, [y_1, y_2, y_3, y_4, x]) = \mu(y_1, y_2)$, where $\mu(y_1, y_2)$ selects between y_1 and y_2 with probability $1/2$. For the other arguments, κ is defined arbitrarily. Let us consider an $\mathcal{A}$-regular strategy $\sigma^* = (a, [aecdb], \kappa)$. A fragment of this strategy is shown in Fig. 2 (right), together with the states of $\mathcal{A}$ entered after reading the history associated to the nodes. One can easily verify that $\inf_{\pi \in \Pi} \mathrm{EU}_P^{\sigma^*,\pi} = -1/2$. That is, if the patroller uses the strategy σ, the probability of all walks where the intruder is either captured or waits forever is at least $1/2$ (for every intruder's strategy). Further, for *every* finite-state observer $\mathcal{B}$ and *every* $\mathcal{B}$-regular strategy σ we have that this probability is at most $1/2$, because σ is obliged to visit four vertices in at most two steps, which means that some of them is inevitably visited with probability at most 1/2. Hence, $Val(\mathcal{G}, \mathcal{A}) = -1/2$.

Now we prove that for an arbitrarily large $K \geq 1$ we have that $Val(\mathcal{G}, \mathcal{A}_K) < -1/2$. For the sake of contradiction, assume that $Val(\mathcal{G}, \mathcal{A}_K) \geq -1/2$, which implies that $Val(\mathcal{G}, \mathcal{A}_K) = -1/2$ by using the same argument as above. The core of the argument reveals that every optimal $\mathcal{A}_K$-regular strategy must, from certain point on, behave identically as the $\mathcal{A}$-regular strategy σ constructed above. This is because whenever a vertex x is visited, each of the four remaining vertices must be visited *exactly* with probability 1/2 in the next two steps. This very soon enforces the regularity captured by $\mathcal{A}$. However, $\mathcal{A}_K$-regular strategies cannot behave like the strategy σ. Consider the leftmost branch in the tree of Fig. 2 (right). This branch is an infinite sequence of vertices obtained by repeating the sequence *acb* infinitely often. The behaviour of σ along this branch depends on the length of the history modulo 6, which cannot be deduced from an arbitrarily long suffix of the history. □

4. STRATEGY IMPROVEMENT

A Stackelberg equilibrium for a given patrolling problem and a given finite-state observer is hard to compute in general. In this section, we consider a slightly relaxed variant of this task: Compute a pair of strategies (σ^*, π^*) such that

(a) π^* is a best response to σ^*;

(b) π^* maximizes the expected patroller's utility among all best responses to σ^*;

(c) $\mathrm{EU}_P^{\sigma^*,\pi^*}$ is as large as possible.

Hence, the intruder is still not motivated to change his strategy, and the patroller may still be satisfied with his expected utility.

Our approach to computing (σ^*, π^*) is based on *strategy improvement*. Intuitively, we start with *some* regular strategy for a given patrolling problem, and then improve this strategy in a finite number of rounds by repeatedly constructing and solving a "small" linear program. In the end, we obtain a pair (σ^*, π^*) satisfying the above requirement, together with the associated $\mathrm{EU}_P^{\sigma^*,\pi^*}$.

For the rest of this section, we fix a patrolling problem $\mathcal{G} = (V, E, T, d)$, a finite-state observer $\mathcal{A} = (S, \delta)$, and utility functions $U_c^P, U_p^P, U_c^I, U_p^I$.

4.1 Zero-Sum Patrolling Problems

For simplicity, we first assume that our patrolling problem is *zero-sum*, i.e., $U_c^P(t) + U_c^I(t) = U_p^P(t) + U_p^I(t) = 0$ for all $t \in T$. General utility functions are discussed in Section 4.2.

Before describing the algorithm, we need to introduce further notions. Let $C \subseteq V \times S$. A *selector for* C is a function $sel : C \to 2^V$ such that, for every $(v, s) \in C$, the set $sel(v, s)$ is non-empty and contains only vertices that are immediate successors of v (i.e., if $v' \in sel(v, s)$, then $(v, v') \in E$). A *consistent path* in (C, sel) is a finite sequence $(v_0, s_0), \ldots, (v_n, s_n)$ such that $(v_i, s_i) \in C$ for all $i \leq n$, and $v_{i+1} \in sel(v_i, s_i)$, $s_{i+1} = \delta(s_i, v_{i+1})$ for all $i < n$. We say that (C, sel) is an *end component* if the following conditions are satisfied:

- C is closed under sel, i.e., if $(v, s) \in C$ and $v' \in sel(v, s)$, then $(v', s') \in C$, where $s' = \delta(s, v')$.
- For all $(v, s), (v', s') \in C$, there is a finite consistent path from (v, s) to (v', s') in (C, sel).

Let $\sigma = (\hat{v}, \hat{s}, \kappa)$ be an $\mathcal{A}$-regular strategy. Then κ determines a selector sel_κ for $V \times S$ where $sel_\kappa(v, s)$ consists of all $v' \in V$ such that $\kappa(v, s)(v') > 0$. Let C_σ be the set of all $(v, s) \in V \times S$ which can be reached from $(\hat{v}, \delta(\hat{s}, \hat{v}))$ via a consistent path in $(V \times S, sel_\kappa)$. Further, let sel_σ be a selector for C_σ obtained by restricting sel_κ to C_σ. We say that σ *stays* in an end component (C, sel) if $C_\sigma \subseteq C$ and $sel_\sigma(v, s) \subseteq sel(v, s)$ for all $(v, s) \in C$.

THEOREM 3. *For every $\mathcal{A}$-regular strategy $\sigma = (\hat{v}, \hat{s}, \kappa)$ there exist $\bar{v} \in V$ and $\bar{s} \in S$ such that the $\mathcal{A}$-regular strategy $\bar{\sigma} = (\bar{v}, \bar{s}, \kappa)$ satisfies $Val(\bar{\sigma}, \mathcal{G}) \geq Val(\sigma, \mathcal{G})$ and $(C_{\bar{\sigma}}, sel_{\bar{\sigma}})$ is an end component.*

PROOF SKETCH. Let $\to_\sigma$ be a binary relation on $V \times S$ such that $(v, s) \to_\sigma (v', s')$ iff $\kappa(v, s)(v') > 0$ and $s' = \delta(s, v')$. Let D be a bottom strongly connected component (BSCC) of $(V \times S, \to_\sigma)$. For every $(v, s) \in D$ and $t \in T$, let $U_\sigma[(v, s), t]$ be the expected patroller's utility when the strategy σ is changed into (v, s', κ) where $\delta(s', v) = s$, and the intruder's strategy π satisfies $\pi(v) = enter_t$. Further, let $Val(D) = \min\{U_\sigma[(v, s), t] \mid (v, s) \in D, t \in T\}$ and let $\bar{D}$ be a BSCC of $(V \times S, \to_\sigma)$ such that $Val(\bar{D}) \geq Val(D)$ for every BSCC D of $(V \times S, \to_\sigma)$. Let $(v, s) \in \bar{D}$. We put $\bar{v} = v$ and set $\bar{s}$ so that $\delta(\bar{s}, v) = s$. One can easily verify that $Val(\bar{\sigma}, \mathcal{G}) \geq Val(\sigma, \mathcal{G})$. Further, $(C_{\bar{\sigma}}, sel_{\bar{\sigma}})$ is an end component because $\bar{D}$ is a BSCC of $(V \times S, \to_\sigma)$. □

For the rest of this subsection, we fix an *initial* $\mathcal{A}$-regular strategy $\sigma = (\hat{v}, \hat{s}, \kappa)$. Due to Theorem 3, we may safely assume that (C_σ, sel_σ) is an end component.

When improving σ, it may happen that the original selector sel_σ is extended. However, we constrain such extensions by choosing an end component (C, sel) such that (C_σ, sel_σ) is (componentwise) contained in (C, sel); the $\mathcal{A}$-regular strategy computed by our strategy improvement algorithm is then guaranteed to stay in (C, sel). This is particularly useful in situations when we want to restrict the scope of our algorithm to strategies that do not assign positive probabilities to some edges of E when $\mathcal{A}$ is in certain states. If we do not want to implement any such restrictions, we set (C, sel) to the *largest* end component subsuming (C_σ, sel_σ), which is guaranteed to exist and is easy to compute. For the rest of this section, we fix some end component (C, sel) that subsumes (C_σ, sel_σ).

For all $(v, s) \in C$ and $t \in T$, we define the set $CP[(v, s), t]$ of *t-capturing paths* consisting of all consistent paths $(v_0, s_0), \ldots, (v_n, s_n)$ in (C, sel) such that $(v_0, s_0) = (v, s)$, $v_n = t$, $n < d(t)$, and $v_i \neq t$ for all $i < n$. A *probability assignment* for (C, sel) is a function λ that assigns to each $(v, s) \in C$ a probability distribution over $sel(v, s)$. Now consider the non-linear program of Fig. 3 constructed for (C, sel). The variables $x[(v, s), v']$ encode a probability assignment for (C, sel) (constraints (1) and (2)). The auxiliary variables $c[(v, s), t]$ encode the probability of capturing the intruder entering t when the patroller visits v and $\mathcal{A}$ is in the state s after reading the current history (constraint (3)). The variable z encodes the expected utility of the patroller against the "best attack" of the intruder (assuming that the patroller plays according to the probability assignment encoded by the variables $x[(v, s), v']$).

max z
subject to:

$\forall (v,s) \in C,\ \forall t \in T:$

$$
\begin{aligned}
0 &\leq x[(v,s),v'] \qquad \forall v' \in sel(v,s) & (1)\\
1 &= \sum_{v' \in sel(v,s)} x[(v,s),v'] & (2)\\
c[(v,s),t] &= \sum_{\substack{(v_0,s_0),\ldots,(v_n,s_n)\\ \in CP[(v,s),t]}} \prod_{i=0}^{n-1} x[(v_i,s_i),v_{i+1}] & (3)\\
z &\leq c[(v,s),t] \cdot U_c^P(t) + (1 - c[(v,s),t]) \cdot U_p^P(t) & (4)
\end{aligned}
$$

Figure 3: A non-linear program $\mathrm{NLP}[(C, sel)]$**.**

Solving the program of Fig. 3 is computationally difficult. Nevertheless, the program can be used to *improve* an existing probability assignment λ for (C, sel) in the following way: We construct a *linear* program $\mathrm{LP}[(C, sel), \lambda])$ by replacing the righ-hand side of the non-linear constrains (3) with

$$\sum_{\substack{(v_0,s_0),\ldots,(v_n,s_n)\\ \in CP[(v,s),t]}} \left(x[(v_{n-1}, s_{n-1}), v_n] \cdot \prod_{i=0}^{n-2} \lambda(v_i, s_i)(v_{i+1}) \right).$$

That is, the variables $x[(v_i, s_i), v_{i+1}]$ for $0 \leq i \leq n-2$ are replaced with the corresponding constants of λ. By solving $\mathrm{LP}[(C, sel), \lambda])$, we obtain concrete values for all variables $x[(v,s),v']$, where $(v,s) \in C$ and $v' \in sel(v,s)$, that minimize the objective z. These values form another probability assignment for (C, sel) denoted by $Solve(\mathrm{LP}[(C, sel), \lambda])$. Now, we compute an "improved" probability assignment by taking a suitable combination $Combine(\lambda, \alpha)$ of λ and $\alpha = Solve(\mathrm{LP}[(C, sel), \lambda])$. As we shall see in Section 5, even a simple convex combination works quite well in practice; however, *Combine* can be a more complicated function in general. Our strategy improvement algorithm (i.e., Algorithm 1) performs N such rounds, starting with the unique probability assignment λ_σ satisfying the following conditions:

- $\lambda_\sigma(v,s)(v') = \kappa(v,s)(v')$ for all $(v,s) \in C_\sigma$ and $v' \in sel_\sigma(v,s)$.
- For all $(v,s) \in C \smallsetminus C_\sigma$, $\lambda_\sigma(v,s)$ is the uniform distribution on $sel(v,s)$.

Let λ be the probability assignment for (C, sel) obtained after completing the **repeat-until** loop at lines 3–7 of Algorithm 1. For every pair $(v,s) \in C$, the assignment λ determines an $\mathcal{A}$-regular strategy $\sigma[(v,s),\lambda] = (v, \bar{s}, \bar{\lambda})$, where $\bar{s} \in S$ is a state satisfying $\delta(\bar{s}, v) = s$ and $\bar{\lambda}$ is (some) extension of λ to all elements of $V \times S$ (since (C, sel) is an end component, the choice of $\bar{\lambda}(v', s')$ for $(v', s') \notin C$ is actually irrelevant). One may be tempted to think that $Val(\sigma[(v,s),\lambda], \mathcal{G})$ is the same for all $(v,s) \in C$. However, this is generally not true, and we need to invest some extra computational effort to identify an "optimal" pair (v,s) and compute the associated $Val(\sigma[(v,s),\lambda], \mathcal{G})$. This is achieved by the procedure $Evaluate(\lambda)$ at line 8 of Algorithm 1, which is described in the next paragraphs.

Let $\rightarrow_\lambda \subseteq C \times C$ be a relation defined by $(v,s) \rightarrow_\lambda (v', s')$ iff $\lambda(v,s)(v') > 0$ and $s' = \delta(s, v')$. Further, let $D \subseteq C$ be a bottom strongly connected component (BSCC) of the directed graph $(C, \rightarrow_\lambda)$. For every $(v,s) \in D$ and $t \in T$, let $c_\lambda[(v,s),t]$ be the probability of capturing the intruder entering t when the patroller visits v and $\mathcal{A}$ is in the state s after reading the current history. That is,

$$c_\lambda[(v,s),t] = \sum_{\substack{(v_0,s_0),\ldots,(v_n,s_n)\\ \in CP[(v,s),t]}} \prod_{i=0}^{n-1} \lambda(v_i, s_i)(v_{i+1}).$$

We also use $U_\lambda[(v,s),t]$ to denote the associated expected patroller's utility, i.e.,

$$U_\lambda[(v,s),t] = c_\lambda[(v,s),t] \cdot U_c^P(t) + (1 - c_\lambda[(v,s),t]) \cdot U_p^P(t).$$

Finally, we put

$$enter_D = \min\{U_\lambda[(v,s),t] \mid (v,s) \in D, t \in T\}$$

and $Val(D) = \min\{0, enter_D\}$. We claim that for all $(v,s) \in D$ we have that $Val(\sigma[(v,s),\lambda], \mathcal{G}) = Val(D)$. To see this, first realize that if $enter_D > 0$, then the optimal strategy for the intruder against $\sigma[(v,s),\lambda]$ is to *wait* forever, because otherwise his expected utility only decreases. Hence, $Val(\sigma[(v,s),\lambda], \mathcal{G}) = 0$ in this case. Otherwise, the intruder should *wait* until the patroller enters a vertex v so that $\mathcal{A}$ is in a state s where $U_\lambda[(v,s),t] = enter_D$ for some $\in T$, and then *enter* the target t. Such a situation must eventually occur with probability one, because D is a BSCC of $(C, \rightarrow_\lambda)$. Thus, the intruder achieves his (optimal) expected utility $-Val(D)$.

Let D be a BSCC of $(C, \rightarrow_\lambda)$ such that $Val(D) \geq Val(D')$ for every BSCC D' of $(C, \rightarrow_\lambda)$. Then, for every $(v,s) \in C$ we clearly have that $Val(\sigma[(v,s),\lambda], \mathcal{G}) \leq Val(D)$. Hence, the patroller should stick to $\sigma[(v,s),\lambda]$ where $(v,s) \in D$, and the value of this strategy is equal to $Val(D)$. The procedure $Evaluate(\lambda)$ returns $(\sigma[(v,s),\lambda], \pi)$, $Val(D)$, where π is the intruder's strategy achieving the expected utility $-Val(D)$ described in the previous paragraph.

Algorithm 1: Strategy improvement for $\mathcal{G}$, $\mathcal{A}$, U_c^P, U_p^P

```
  input  : σ, (C, sel), N
  output : (σ*, π*), Val(σ*, G)
1 λ ← λ_σ
2 i ← 0
3 repeat
4   | α ← Solve(LP[(C, sel), λ])
5   | λ ← Combine(λ, α)
6   | i ← i + 1
7 until i = N
8 (σ*, π*), Val(σ*, G) ← Evaluate(λ)
```

4.2 Non-Zero-Sum Patrolling Problems

In this subsection, we show how to extend the results of Section 4.1 to non-zero-sum patrolling problems. Recall that our aim is to compute a pair of strategies (σ^*, π^*) such that π^* is a best response to σ^* maximizing the expected patroller's utility among all best responses, and the expected utility of the patroller is as large as possible.

Here we restrict ourselves to a subset of $\mathcal{A}$-regular strategies σ such that (C_σ, sel_σ) is an end component, because

max $u^P[(v^*, s^*), t^*]$, where $((v^*, s^*), t^*)$ is a fixed element of R.
subject to:

$\forall(v,s) \in C,\ \forall((\bar{v},\bar{s}),\bar{t}) \in R,\ \forall t \in T:$

$$0 < x[(v,s),v'] \qquad \forall v' \in sel(v,s) \quad (5)$$

$$1 = \sum_{v' \in sel(v,s)} x[(v,s),v'] \quad (6)$$

$$c[(v,s),t] = \sum_{\substack{(v_0,s_0),\ldots,(v_n,s_n) \\ \in CP[(v,s),t]}} \prod_{i=0}^{n-1} x[(v_i,s_i),v_{i+1}] \quad (7)$$

$$u^I[(v,s),t] = c[(v,s),t] \cdot U_c^I(t) + (1-c[(v,s),t]) \cdot U_p^I(t) \quad (8)$$

$$u^P[(\bar{v},\bar{s}),\bar{t}] = c[(\bar{v},\bar{s}),\bar{t}] \cdot U_c^P(\bar{t}) + (1-c[(\bar{v},\bar{s}),\bar{t}]) \cdot U_p^P(\bar{t}) \quad (9)$$

$$u^I[(v,s),t] < u^I[(v^*,s^*),t^*] \quad \text{where } ((v,s),t) \notin R \quad (10)$$

$$u^I[(\bar{v},\bar{s}),\bar{t}] = u^I[(v^*,s^*),t^*] \quad (11)$$

$$u^P[(\bar{v},\bar{s}),\bar{t}] = u^P[(v^*,s^*),t^*] \quad (12)$$

Figure 4: A non-linear program NLP$[(C, sel), R]$.

then we can easily classify intruder's best responses (see Theorem 4).

For the rest of this section, we fix an end component (C, sel). Let $\sigma = (\hat{v}, \hat{s}, \kappa)$ be an $\mathcal{A}$-regular strategy such that $(C_\sigma, sel_\sigma) = (C, sel)$. Further, let $R \subseteq C \times T$. We say that an intruder's strategy π is *R-compatible* if the following conditions are satisfied:

- If $\pi(h) = enter_t$ where h ends in a vertex v, then $((v,s),t) \in R$ where $s = \delta(\hat{s}, h)$.
- $\mathcal{P}^\sigma(noattack^\pi) = 0$.

Let MBR$(\sigma) \subseteq$ BR(σ) be the set of best responses to σ that maximize the patroller's expected utility. The next theorem gives a characterization of MBR(σ).

THEOREM 4. *Let σ be an $\mathcal{A}$-regular strategy such that $(C_\sigma, sel_\sigma) = (C, sel)$. Then there are two possibilities:*

- MBR$(\sigma) = \{\pi\}$ *where $\pi(h) = wait$ for every history h;*
- MBR$(\sigma) = \{\pi \in \Pi \mid \pi$ *is R-compatible*$\}$ *for some $R \subseteq C \times T$.*

PROOF SKETCH. For every $(v,s) \in C$ and $t \in T$, let $u^I[(v,s),t]$ and $u^P[(v,s),t]$ be the expected intruder's utility and the expected patroller's utility when the strategy σ is changed into (v, s', κ) where $\delta(s', v) = s$, and the intruder's strategy π satisfies $\pi(v) = enter_t$. Further, let $Val^I = \max\{u^I[(v,s),t] \mid (v,s) \in C, t \in T\}$. If $Val^I \leq 0$, then the intruder cannot gain anything by entering any target, and his (only) optimal response to σ is the strategy π such that $\pi(h) = wait$ for every history h. Now assume $Val^I > 0$. Let BR $= \{((v,s),t) \mid u^I[(v,s),t] = Val^I\}$, and let $Val^P = \max\{u^P[(v,s),t] \mid ((v,s),t) \in \text{BR}\}$. Finally, we put $R = \{((v,s),t) \in \text{BR} \mid u^P[(v,s),t] = Val^P\}$. Clearly, for every R-compatible intruder's strategy π we have that $\text{EU}_I^{\sigma,\pi} = Val^I$ and $\text{EU}_P^{\sigma,\pi} = Val^P$, which proves the claim. □

The characterization of MBR(σ) given in Theorem 4 is implemented in the non-linear program of Fig. 4. This program covers the second possibility when MBR(σ) consists of all R-compatible intruder's strategies (the other possibility is discussed below). The variables $x[(v,s),v']$ encode a probability assignment for (C, sel), i.e., some $\mathcal{A}$-regular strategy σ (constraints (5) and (6)). We require that all of these probabilities are positive (constraint (5)), which implements the assumption $(C_\sigma, sel_\sigma) = (C, sel)$. The auxiliary variables $c[(v,s),t]$ encode the probability of capturing the intruder entering t when the patroller visits v and $\mathcal{A}$ is in the state s after reading the current history (constraint (7)). The variables $u^I[(v,s),t]$ encode the expected intruder's utility for σ and a $\{((v,s),t)\}$-compatible intruder's strategy (constraint (8)). Similarly, the $u^P[(\bar{v},\bar{s}),\bar{t}]$ variables, where $((\bar{v},\bar{s}),\bar{t}) \in R$, encode the expected patroller's utility for σ and a $\{((\bar{v},\bar{s}),\bar{t})\}$-compatible intruder's strategy (constraint (9)). Constraints (10) and (11) guarantee that MBR(σ) consists of R-compatible strategies. The $((v^*,s^*),t^*)$ is a fixed element of R (chosen arbitrarily).

Note that the possibility when MBR$(\sigma) = \{\pi\}$, where $\pi(h) = wait$ for every history h, can be encoded by a simpler program consisting of the constraints (5)–(8) and $u^I[(v,s),t] \leq 0$. The objective of this program is irrelevant, we require just feasibility.

Now, for a given probability assignment λ for (C, sel), we can replace the right-hand sides of the non-linear constrains (7) with

$$\sum_{\substack{(v_0,s_0),\ldots,(v_n,s_n) \\ \in CP[(v,s),t]}} \left(x[(v_{n-1},s_{n-1}),v_n] \cdot \prod_{i=0}^{n-2} \lambda(v_i,s_i)(v_{i+1}) \right)$$

and thus obtain a linear program LP$[(C, sel), R, \lambda]$. Given some initial strategy σ (and the associated probability assigment λ_σ for (C, sel)), we can again "improve" λ_σ by Algorithm 1 where LP$[(C, sel), R, \lambda]$ is used instead of LP$[(C, sel), \lambda]$. Observe that on top of choosing the "right" (C, sel) and the initial strategy σ, we also need to choose a suitable R. Although there are exponentially many candidates for the "right" R, a reasonable option is to try out all singletons first and then possibly proceed with larger subsets of C depending on the obtained results.

5. EXPERIMENTS

In this section we experimentally evaluate the strategy improvement algorithm designed in Section 4. For simplicity, we restrict our attention to zero-sum patrolling problems where $U_c^P(t) = U_c^I(t) = 0$, $U_p^P(t) = -1000$, and $U_p^I(t) = 1000$ for all $t \in T$. For every finite-state observer $\mathcal{A}$ and all $(\sigma, \pi) \in \Sigma_\mathcal{A} \times \Pi$, let $\mathcal{P}^\sigma(defend^\pi)$ be the probability of all walks where the intruder is captured or waits forever. That is,

$$\mathcal{P}^\sigma(defend^\pi) = \mathcal{P}^\sigma(noattack^\pi) + \sum_{t \in T} \mathcal{P}^\sigma(capture_t^\pi).$$

We have that

$$1000 + \text{EU}_P^{\sigma,\pi} = 1000 \cdot \mathcal{P}^\sigma(defend^\pi).$$

Hence, the patroller/intruder actually aims at maximizing/minimizing $\mathcal{P}^\sigma(defend^\pi)$. Since this quantity appears more intuitive than $\text{EU}_P^{\sigma,\pi}$, we also define the *defending value* of a given $\mathcal{A}$-regular strategy σ by $DVal(\sigma, \mathcal{G}) = 1000 + Val(\sigma, \mathcal{G})$, and we use $DVal(\sigma, \mathcal{G})$ instead of $Val(\sigma, \mathcal{G})$ when presenting the performance of the computed strategies. Hence, if $DVal(\sigma, \mathcal{G}) = 250$, then the patroller defends all targets with probability at least 0.25 against all intruder's strategies, and there exists an intruder's strategy π such that

Table 1: The Outcomes of the 1st Comparison.

$\|V\|$	$\|V_4\|$	$\|V_7\|$	$DVal(\sigma_{\mathcal{A}})$, $N \leq 20$	$DVal(\sigma_{\mathcal{B}})$, $N \leq 20$
9	3	6	500.00000	448.78190
11	6	5	345.47092	337.56432
13	5	8	328.80138	316.48640
15	8	7	257.93970	252.89687
17	7	10	246.77666	241.28626
19	10	9	204.66290	202.02953
21	9	12	200.00000	194.72047
23	12	11	168.63060	168.15142
25	11	14	163.13892	162.93894
26	11	15	160.06754	158.73937
27	14	13	145.73724	143.98550
31	16	15	127.24003	125.88467
31	13	18	136.05868	133.96578
35	18	17	112.46766	111.82252
36	15	21	117.34851	115.87416
39	20	19	101.47058	100.58408
41	17	24	103.35841	102.08437
43	22	21	092.00802	091.39703
46	19	27	092.11294	091.22598
47	24	23	084.01209	083.74692

the probability of defending all targets against π is exactly 0.25.

Note that Algorithm 1 is parameterized by the choice of (C, sel), the initial strategy σ, the number of iterations N, and the function *Combine* invoked at line 5. In all of our experiments, we use $Combine(\lambda, \alpha) = 0.5 \cdot \lambda + 0.5 \cdot \alpha$. The number of iterations is typically set to 20. The choice of (C, sel) and σ substantially influences the quality of the strategy produced by Algorithm 1. In principle, (C, sel) and σ can be constructed either "manually" in some ad-hoc way, or synthesized automatically by inspecting the topological properties of the underlying directed graph of $\mathcal{G}$. We compare two such methods. The first one is simple; we construct a trivial finite-state observer $\mathcal{B}$ with just one state s such that $\delta(s, v) = s$ for every vertex v. The associated end component is the unique maximal end component of $V \times \{s\}$ (recall that the directed graph of $\mathcal{G}$ is strongly connected), and the initial strategy is a strategy which selects uniformly among all vertices.

The second method works as follows. Let $\mathcal{G} = (V, E, T, d)$ be a patrolling problem where $T = V$ and $d(t) \geq 2$ for all $t \in T$. Further, let $D(\mathcal{G}) = \{d(v) \mid v \in V\}$, and for every $d \in D(\mathcal{G})$, let V_d be the set of all $v \in V$ such that $d(v) = d$. As a running example, consider the case when $D(\mathcal{G}) = \{3, 4, 7, 13\}$. For simplicity, let us first assume that $\mathcal{G}$ has a full topology, i.e., $E = V \times V$. Then, we can partition each V_d into d pairwise disjoint subsets

$$V_d[0], \ldots, V_d[d{-}2], V_d[d{-}1]$$

so that each $V_d[i]$, where $0 \leq i \leq d-2$, has $|V_d|$ div $(d{-}1)$ elements, and $V_d[d{-}1]$ has $|V_d|$ mod $(d{-}1)$ elements. For example, if $d = 4$ and V_4 consists of 11 vertices, we obtain the sets $V_4[0], V_4[1], V_4[2], V_4[3]$ such that each $V_4[i]$, where $0 \leq i \leq 2$, contains 3 vertices, and $V_4[3]$ contains the two remaining vertices.

Table 2: Some cases when $\mathcal{A}$ outperforms $\mathcal{B}$.

$D(\mathcal{G})$	$DVal(\sigma_{\mathcal{A}})$, $N \leq 20$	$DVal(\sigma_{\mathcal{B}})$, $N \leq 20$
$\{6, 9\}$	500.00000	433.27517
$\{8, 9\}$	500.00000	426.33215
$\{12, 14\}$	500.00000	413.44493
$\{14, 15\}$	500.00000	409.91645
$\{22, 25\}$	500.00000	403.87134

Let k be the least common multiple of all $d - 1$ such that $d \in D(\mathcal{G})$. In our running example, k is the least common multiple of 2, 3, 6, 12, which is 12. Now we construct a finite-state observer $\mathcal{A}$ with states $\{s_0, \ldots, s_{k-1}\}$ such that, for every $v \in V$, $\delta(s_i, v) = s_j$ where $j = (i + 1) \bmod k$.

Further, we construct an end component (C, sel) in the following way: For every $i \in \{0, \ldots, k - 1\}$, let

$$M_i = \bigcup_{d \in D(\mathcal{G})} V_d[i \bmod (d{-}1)] \cup V_d[d{-}1]$$

In our running example, we obtain, e.g.,

$$M_8 = V_3[0] \cup V_3[2] \cup V_4[2] \cup V_4[3] \cup V_7[2] \cup V_7[6] \cup V_{13}[8] \cup V_{13}[12]$$

The set C consists of all pairs (v, s_i) such that $0 \leq i < k$ and $v \in M_i$. Further, for each $(v, s_i) \in C$, we define $sel(v, s_i) = M_i \setminus \{v\}$.

Intuitively, (C, sel) is constructed so that, for every $d \in D(\mathcal{G})$, the vertices of $V_d[0], \ldots, V_d[d{-}2]$ are visited precisely once in $d - 1$ steps after every history h, where the only possible exception is the vertex where h ends. Since it is not clear how the remaining vertices of $V_d[d{-}1]$ should be visited, (C, sel) allows to visit all of them "any time". The initial strategy σ is defined by $\sigma = (\hat{v}, s_{k-1}, \kappa)$, where $\hat{v}$ is a fixed vertex of some $V_d[0]$, and $\kappa(v, s)$ is the uniform distribution over $sel(v, s)$.

Note that the above construction requires the existence of edges only among the vertices of M_i and $M_{(i+1) \bmod k}$. Hence, it is applicable also to patrolling problems where E is a proper subset of $V \times V$, but E must be "dense" in the sense that it contains the required edges.

For simplicity, in our experiments we consider only patrolling problems with fully connected topology where all vertices are targets, i.e., $E = V \times V$ and $T = V$.

In our first experiment, we examine the case when $D(\mathcal{G}) = \{4, 7\}$ for various (almost random) instances. The outcomes are summarized in Table 1. The columns $DVal(\sigma_{\mathcal{A}})$, $N \leq 20$, and $DVal(\sigma_{\mathcal{B}})$, $N \leq 20$ show the defending values of the best $\mathcal{A}$-regular and $\mathcal{B}$-regular strategies obtained by Algorithm 1 in at most 20 rounds. Note that $\sigma_{\mathcal{A}}$ always outperforms $\sigma_{\mathcal{B}}$, but the difference is not so significant as one might expect. This is because the numbers in $D(\mathcal{G})$ are still relatively small. In Table 2, we show the outcomes (obtained after 20 rounds) for some specific cases where $|V_d| = d-1$ for every $d \in D(\mathcal{G})$. For example, for the patrolling problem considered in the first line of Table 2 we have that $|V_6| = 5$ and $|V_9| = 8$. Here, $DVal(\sigma_{\mathcal{A}})$ is always equal to 500, but $DVal(\sigma_{\mathcal{B}})$ decreases as the numbers in $D(\mathcal{G})$ increase.

An interesting feature of Algorithm 1 revealed by our experiments is that the outcomes can "oscillate" among better and worse strategies as N increases. This behaviour is documented in Table 3, where we consider the case $D(\mathcal{G}) = \{3, 4, 7, 13\}$, and show the defending values for the strategies

Table 3: The Outcomes of the 2nd Comparison.

$\|V\|$	$\|V_3\|$	$\|V_4\|$	$\|V_7\|$	$\|V_{13}\|$	$DVal(\sigma_{\mathcal{A}})$, $N = 10$	$DVal(\sigma_{\mathcal{A}})$, $N = 15$	$DVal(\sigma_{\mathcal{A}})$, $N = 20$
25	4	3	6	12	200.00000	200.00000	200.00000
29	5	4	7	13	164.31373	164.36930	164.37348
33	6	5	8	14	136.23451	137.11697	137.73950
37	7	6	9	15	120.24780	115.83532	118.51474
41	8	7	10	16	105.64002	105.81254	105.50371

$\|V\|$	$\|V_3\|$	$\|V_4\|$	$\|V_7\|$	$\|V_{13}\|$	$DVal(\sigma_{\mathcal{B}})$, $N = 10$	$DVal(\sigma_{\mathcal{B}})$, $N = 15$	$DVal(\sigma_{\mathcal{B}})$, $N = 20$
25	4	3	6	12	197.03123	197.11447	197.11542
29	5	4	7	13	162.85415	162.90246	162.90214
33	6	5	8	14	138.67156	138.70364	138.70487
37	7	6	9	15	120.69474	120.71614	120.71646
41	8	7	10	16	106.81787	106.83392	106.83405

obtained after 10, 15, and 20 rounds. The mentioned oscillation is present in several lines (for both observers). It can be influenced by changing the mixing ratio used by *Combine*. The two finite-state observers $\mathcal{A}$ and $\mathcal{B}$ do comparably well on the presented instances. This is mainly because $|V_d|$ is not much larger than d, and hence the size of $V_d[d-1]$ is comparable to the size of $V_d[j]$ for $j \leq d-2$.

All of our results have been obtained by a naive implementation of Algorithm 1 in Python that was run on an average Intel 64 PC with 4GB RAM. We used the PuLP package to solve the linear programs (all of our instances were solved in less then two minutes, often is seconds). Despite this lightweight implementation, we were able to analyze patrolling problems with about 100 vertices. We believe that a more serious implementation can easily handle substantially larger instances.

6. CONCLUSIONS

We designed a strategy improvement algorithm for regular strategies which avoids the use of non-linear programming. This algorithm is applicable to patrolling problems of realistic size, and it can quickly produce quite efficient strategies.

There is a lot of space for improvement, and we believe that the main ideas presented in this paper can be further developed and refined into an even more efficient framework. The strategy improvement technique is generic and possibly applicable also to other problems that have so far been tackled using non-linear programming and other computationally costly methods. We see all of these possibilities as great challenges for future work.

REFERENCES

[1] M. Abaffy, T. Brázdil, V. Řehák, B. Bošanský, A. Kučera, and J. Krčál. Solving adversarial patrolling games with bounded error. In *Proceedings of AAMAS 2014*, pages 1617–1618, 2014.

[2] N. Agmon, S. Kraus, and G. A. Kaminka. Multi-robot perimeter patrol in adversarial settings. In *Proceedings of ICRA 2008*, pages 2339–2345, 2008.

[3] N. Agmon, V. Sadov, G. A. Kaminka, and S. Kraus. The impact of adversarial knowledge on adversarial planning in perimeter patrol. In *Proceedings of AAMAS 2008*, pages 55–62, 2008.

[4] N. Basilico, N. Gatti, and F. Amigoni. Patrolling security games: Definition and algorithms for solving large instances with single patroller and single intruder. *Artificial Intelligence*, 184–185:78–123, 2002.

[5] N. Basilico, N. Gatti, and F. Amigoni. Leader-follower strategies for robotic patrolling in environments with arbitrary topologies. In *Proceedings of AAMAS 2009*, pages 57–64, 2009.

[6] N. Basilico, N. Gatti, T. Rossi, S. Ceppi, and F. Amigoni. Extending algorithms for mobile robot patrolling in the presence of adversaries to more realistic settings. In *WI-IAT*, pages 557–564, 2009.

[7] N. Basilico, N. Gatti, and F. Villa. Asynchronous Multi-Robot Patrolling against Intrusion in Arbitrary Topologies. In *AAAI*, 2010.

[8] B. Bosansky, V. Lisy, M. Jakob, and M. Pechoucek. Computing Time-Dependent Policies for Patrolling Games with Mobile Targets. In *Proceedings of AAMAS 2011*, 2011.

[9] B. Bosansky, O. Vanek, and M. Pechoucek. Strategy Representation Analysis for Patrolling Games. In *AAAI Spring Symposium*, 2012.

[10] F. Fang, A. X. Jiang, and M. Tambe. Optimal Patrol Strategy for Protecting Moving Targets with Multiple Mobile Resources. In *Proceedings of AAMAS 2013*, 2013.

[11] M. Jain, E. Karde, C. Kiekintveld, F. Ordóñez, and M. Tambe. Optimal defender allocation for massive security games: A branch and price approach. In *Workshop on Optimization in Multi-Agent Systems at AAMAS*, 2010.

[12] C. Kiekintveld, M. Jain, J. Tsai, J. Pita, F. Ordóñez, and M. Tambe. Computing optimal randomized resource allocations for massive security games. In *Proceedings of AAMAS 2009*, pages 689–696, 2009.

[13] E. Munoz de Cote, R. Stranders, N. Basilico, N. Gatti, and N. Jennings. Introducing alarms in adversarial patrolling games: extended abstract. In *Proceedings of AAMAS 2013*, pages 1275–1276, 2013.

[14] J. Pita, M. Jain, J. Marecki, F. Ordónez, C. Portway, M. Tambe, C. Western, P. Paruchuri, and S. Kraus. Deployed ARMOR protection: The application of a game theoretic model for security at the Los Angeles Int. Airport. In *Proceedings of AAMAS 2008*, pages 125–132, 2008.

[15] M. Tambe. *Security and Game Theory: Algorithms, Deployed Systems, Lessons Learned.* Cambridge University Press, 2011.

[16] J. Tsai, S. Rathi, C. Kiekintveld, F. Ordóñez, and M. Tambe. IRIS—a tool for strategic security allocation in transportation networks categories and subject descriptors. In *Proceedings of AAMAS 2009*, pages 37–44, 2009.

[17] Z. Yin, D. Korzhyk, C. Kiekintveld, V. Conitzer, and M. Tambe. Stackelberg vs. Nash in security games: Interchangeability, equivalence, and uniqueness. In *Proceedings of AAMAS 2010*, pages 1139–1146, 2010.

Multi-Valued Verification of Strategic Ability

Wojciech Jamroga
Institute of Computer Science,
Polish Academy of Sciences
ul. Jana Kazimierza 5
01-248 Warsaw, Poland
wojciech.jamroga@ipipan.waw.pl

Beata Konikowska
Institute of Computer Science,
Polish Academy of Sciences
ul. Jana Kazimierza 5
01-248 Warsaw, Poland
beata.konikowska@ipipan.waw.pl

Wojciech Penczek*
Institute of Computer Science,
Polish Academy of Sciences
ul. Jana Kazimierza 5
01-248 Warsaw, Poland
wojciech.penczek@ipipan.waw.pl

ABSTRACT

Some multi-agent scenarios call for the possibility of evaluating specifications in a richer domain of truth values. Examples include runtime monitoring of a temporal property over a growing prefix of an infinite path, inconsistency analysis in distributed databases, and verification methods that use incomplete anytime algorithms, such as bounded model checking. In this paper, we present *multi-valued ATL** (mv-ATL$^*_{\preccurlyeq}$), an expressive logic to specify strategic abilities in multi-agent systems. We show that our general method for model-independent translation from multi-valued to two-valued model checking cannot be directly extended to mv-ATL$^*_{\preccurlyeq}$. We also propose two ways of overcoming the problem. Firstly, we identify constraints on mv-ATL$^*_{\preccurlyeq}$ formulas for which the model-independent translation can be suitably adapted. Secondly, we present a model-dependent reduction that can be applied to all formulas of mv-ATL$^*_{\preccurlyeq}$. We show that, in all cases, the complexity of verification increases only polynomially when new truth values are added to the evaluation domain. We also consider several examples that show possible applications of mv-ATL$^*_{\preccurlyeq}$ and motivate its use for model checking MAS.

Keywords

model checking, multi-valued verification, alternating-time logic

1. INTRODUCTION

The alternating-time temporal logic ATL* and its less expressive variant ATL [3] are probably the most popular logics that allow for reasoning about agents' abilities in strategic encounters. ATL combines features of temporal logic and basic game theory, encapsulated in the main language construct of the logic, $\langle\langle A\rangle\rangle\gamma$, which can be read as "the group of agents A has a strategy to enforce γ". Property γ can include operators X ("next"), G ("always"), F ("eventually") and/or U ("until"). Much research on ATL* has focused on the way it can be used for verification of multi-agent systems, including theoretical studies on the complexity of model checking, as well as practical verification algorithms.

Typically, model checking is a yes/no problem. However, it is sometimes convenient to consider the output of verification in a richer domain of values. This can be due to two reasons. First, our model of the system can be only partially conclusive with respect to properties of the system. A good example is runtime monitoring of temporal properties, where a temporal formula (interpreted with an infinite time horizon in mind) is checked on a finite but constantly growing sequence of events, observed so far. Consider for instance specification Fp. If p has already occurred then the formula is clearly true whatever happens next. What if it has not occurred? Then, the formula may still turn out true (because p may occur in subsequent steps), but it can also turn out false; effectively, the truth value is unknown in our current model. Likewise, formula Gp can be only proved false in the course of monitoring, or the model is inconclusive regarding its value. Indeed, well known approaches to runtime monitoring use multi-valued interpretation of temporal formulas in finite runs [7, 8].

Secondly, even if the model is complete and faithful, the verification procedure can be only partially conclusive. For instance, in bounded model checking [10, 47], a full transition system is given but the formula is checked on runs of length at most n. Now, again, Fp is clearly true if we find p to occur on every path in up to n steps. Otherwise, the output is inconclusive (because p might or might not occur in subsequent steps). The case of Gp is analogous. A more sophisticated motivating example is presented below.

EXAMPLE 1 (ANYTIME STATE ABSTRACTION). *Let M be a transition system that models the behavior of k agents operating in a common environment (e.g., autonomous vehicles at a busy intersection). The following ATL formula specifies a sensible requirement on the system: $\langle\langle a\rangle\rangle$G$\mathsf{safe}_a$. Suppose further that the state of each agent is determined by m binary variables. It is easy to see that the system has $O(2^{k\cdot m})$ global states, which makes straightforward model checking, and even explicit generation of the whole model problematic for large values of k.*

State abstraction *is a technique that consists in "clustering" global states into* abstract states *according to an equivalence relation $\mathcal{R}$. For example, $q\mathcal{R}q'$ iff q, q' coincide on the variables of agent a. Such states will end up in the same abstract state $[q]_{\mathcal{R}}$. However, it can happen that the value of a proposition (e.g., safe_a) varies across $[q]_{\mathcal{R}}$. Then, the most reasonable value for safe_a in the abstract state is "conflicting" or "inconsistent". Moreover, if we use an* anytime *algorithm, it may be stopped before it computes the truth of safe_a in some of the new states. Then, the value of the proposition can be set to "uncomputed" or "undecided". Consequently, we will have to manipulate at least four truth values when model checking the formula $\langle\langle a\rangle\rangle$G$\mathsf{safe}_a$ in the abstract model.*

In this paper, we study model checking for a multi-valued variant of ATL* over arbitrary lattices of logical values. We call the new logic mv-ATL$^*_{\preccurlyeq}$. Our approach extends previous work on temporal model checking: similarly to [38, 39], we do not propose dedicated

*Also affiliated with: Institute of Informatics, University of Natural Sciences and Humanities, Siedlce, Poland.

Appears in: *Proceedings of the 15th International Conference on Autonomous Agents and Multiagent Systems (AAMAS 2016), J. Thangarajah, K. Tuyls, C. Jonker, S. Marsella (eds.), May 9–13, 2016, Singapore.*

algorithms for mv-ATL$^*_\preccurlyeq$. Instead, we look for general efficient translations from the multi-valued case to the 2-valued case. We (i) prove that no model-independent translation exists for the whole language of mv-ATL$^*_\preccurlyeq$, (ii) identify a broad subclass of formulas for which such a translation can be obtained, and (iii) propose a recursive model-dependent translation that works for all instances of the problem. We also show that all the results easily extend to verification of strategies under imperfect information.

Related work. Multi-valued interpretation of modal formulas has been used in multiple approaches to verification. The main idea was proposed by Fitting [22, 23] already 25 years ago. In the 2000s, a number of works adapted it to verification of distributed and multi-agent systems. A variant of CTL* for models over finite quasi-boolean lattices was proposed in [38], together with a general translation scheme that reduced multi-valued model checking of CTL* specifications to the standard 2-valued case. This was later extended to multi-valued modal μ-calculus [26, 12, 51, 46], and to multi-valued modal μ-calculus with knowledge [39]. Our paper follows this line of work, and extends the techniques to strategic operators of ATL*.[1] We also enrich the language with the "comparison" operators $\preccurlyeq$ and $\cong$, which provide: (i) the notions of material implication and biconditional, useful in specifying general properties of multi-valued models; (ii) a way of model checking "threshold properties" analogous to probabilistic temporal logics behind PRISM [40]. As it turns out, the new operators require non-trivial treatment, significantly different from [38, 26, 12, 51, 39].

Model checking methods for the special case of 3-valued temporal logics were discussed in [25, 28, 30]. Related approaches include runtime verification, which often uses 3-valued [7] or 4-valued interpretation [8, 26] of temporal formulas. Moreover, 4-valued semantics has been used to evaluate database queries [44, 45]. 3-valued semantics of strategic abilities was considered in [6] for alternating μ-calculus and, recently, in [43] for ATL. In both cases the main aim was to verify abstractions of multi-agent systems. Note that, while the agenda of our paper comes close to that of [43], our semantics differs from [43] even in the 3-valued case.

A quite different but related strand of research concerns real-valued logics over probabilistic models for temporal [20, 41, 32] and strategic specifications [33]. We also mention the research on probabilistic model checking of temporal and strategic logics [29, 5, 40, 14, 18] that evaluates specifications in the 2-valued domain but recognizes different degrees of success and the need to aggregate them over available strategies and possible paths.

2. PRELIMINARIES

We begin by presenting the basics of alternating-time temporal logic and quasi-boolean domains of truth values.

2.1 What Agents Can Achieve

Alternating-time temporal logic [3] generalizes branching-time temporal logic CTL* by replacing path quantifiers E, A with *strategic modalities* $\langle\langle A\rangle\rangle$. Informally, $\langle\langle A\rangle\rangle\gamma$ says that a group of agents A has a collective strategy to enforce temporal property γ. Similarly to CTL* and CTL, we consider two syntactic variants of the alternating-time logic, namely ATL* and ATL.

Let $\mathcal{A}$ be a finite set of agents, and $Prop$ a countable set of atomic propositions. The language of ATL* is defined as follows:

$$\varphi ::= \mathsf{p} \mid \neg\varphi \mid \varphi\wedge\varphi \mid \langle\langle A\rangle\rangle\gamma,$$

[1]Note that, despite having "games" in the title, [51] was not concerned with strategic specifications. "Games" were used there only in the technical sense, to define the semantics of μ-calculus. However, [4] deals with game applications of [51].

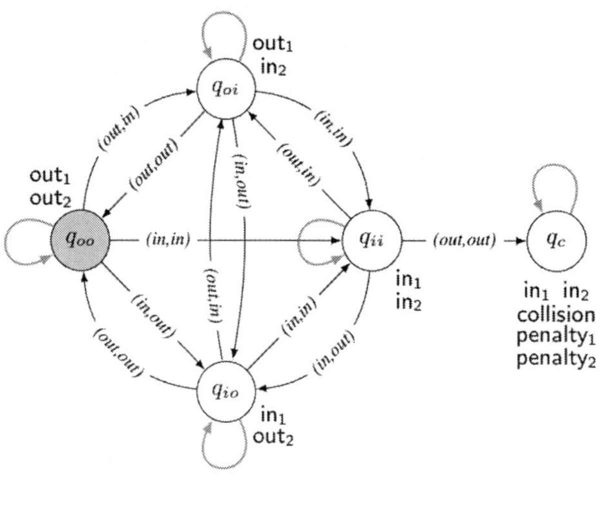

Figure 1: Autonomous vehicles at the intersection: model M_1

$$\gamma ::= \varphi \mid \neg\gamma \mid \gamma\wedge\gamma \mid \mathsf{X}\,\gamma \mid \gamma\,\mathsf{U}\,\gamma.$$

where $A \subseteq \mathcal{A}$ and $\mathsf{p} \in Prop$. Derived boolean connectives and constants ($\vee, \top, \bot$) are defined as usual. "Sometime", "weak until", and "always from now on" are defined as $\mathsf{F}\gamma \equiv \top\,\mathsf{U}\,\gamma$, $\gamma_1\,\mathsf{W}\,\gamma_2 \equiv \neg((\neg\gamma_2)\,\mathsf{U}\,(\neg\gamma_1\wedge\neg\gamma_2))$, and $\mathsf{G}\gamma \equiv \gamma\,\mathsf{W}\,\bot$. Also, we can use $\overline{\langle\langle A\rangle\rangle}\,\gamma \equiv \neg\langle\langle A\rangle\rangle\gamma$ to express that, for each strategy of A, property γ fails on some paths.[2]

ATL (without "star") is the syntactic variant in which strategic and temporal operators are combined into compound modalities:

$$\varphi ::= \mathsf{p} \mid \neg\varphi \mid \varphi\wedge\varphi \mid \langle\langle A\rangle\rangle\mathsf{X}\,\varphi \mid \langle\langle A\rangle\rangle\varphi\,\mathsf{U}\,\varphi \mid \langle\langle A\rangle\rangle\varphi\,\mathsf{W}\,\varphi.$$

Semantics. The semantics of ATL* is defined over a variant of synchronous multi-agent transition systems.

Definition 1 (CGS). *A* concurrent game structure (CGS) *is a tuple $M = \langle\mathcal{A}, St, Act, d, t, Prop, V\rangle$ which includes nonempty finite sets of: agents $\mathcal{A} = \{1,\ldots,k\}$, states St, actions Act, atomic propositions $Prop$, and a propositional valuation $V : St \to 2^{Prop}$. The function $d : \mathcal{A}\times St \to 2^{Act}$ defines availability of actions. The (deterministic) transition function t assigns a successor state $q' = t(q, \alpha_1,\ldots,\alpha_k)$ to each state $q \in St$ and any tuple of actions $\alpha_i \in d(i,q)$ that can be executed by $\mathcal{A}$ in q.*

A pointed CGS *is a pair (M, q_0) consisting of a concurrent game structure M and an initial state q_0 in M.*

Example 2 (Driving agents). *Consider an intersection with k autonomous vehicles around it. Each vehicle is modeled as a separate agent, whose local state is characterized by either the proposition* out_i *(when the vehicle is outside the intersection) or* in_i *(when the vehicle is inside it). The available actions are: in ("drive in" or "stay in", depending on the current state) and out ("drive out" or "stay out"). When both agents are in and decide to leave at the same time, a collision occurs* ($\mathsf{collision}$)*, and the guilty party – or parties – have to pay a penalty* ($\mathsf{penalty}_i$)*.*

Figure 1 presents a pointed CGS modeling the scenario for $k = 2$. The combinations of actions that are not displayed in the graph do not change the state of the system.

[2]In some papers, $[\![A]\!]\gamma \equiv \neg\langle\langle A\rangle\rangle\neg\gamma$ is used as the dual strategic operator. We use $\overline{\langle\langle A\rangle\rangle}\,\gamma$ instead for technical convenience, to avoid negations of path subformulae when transforming to NNF.

A *path* $\lambda = q_0q_1q_2\dots$ in a CGS is an infinite sequence of states such that there is a transition between each q_i, q_{i+1}. $\lambda[i]$ denotes the ith position on λ and $\lambda[i,\infty]$ the suffix of λ starting with i.

A *perfect recall strategy* (or *IR*-strategy) for agent a is a function $s_a : St^+ \to Act$ such that $s_a(q_0q_1\dots q_n) \in d(a, q_n)$. A *collective strategy* for agents $A = \{a_1, \dots, a_r\}$ is a tuple of individual strategies $s_A = \langle s_{a_1}, \dots, s_{a_r}\rangle$. The set of such strategies is denoted by Σ_A^{IR}. The "outcome" function $out(q, s_A)$ returns the set of all paths that can occur when agents A execute strategy s_A from state q onward. The semantics of ATL* is defined as follows:

$M, q \models \mathsf{p}$ iff $q \in V(\mathsf{p})$, for $\mathsf{p} \in Prop$;

$M, q \models \neg\varphi$ iff $M, q \not\models \varphi$;

$M, q \models \varphi_1 \wedge \varphi_2$ iff $M, q \models \varphi_1$ and $M, q \models \varphi_2$;

$M, q \models \langle\!\langle A\rangle\!\rangle\gamma$ iff there is a strategy $s_A \in \Sigma_A^{IR}$ such that, for each path $\lambda \in out(q, s_A)$, we have $M, \lambda \models \gamma$.

$M, \lambda \models \varphi$ iff $M, \lambda[0] \models \varphi$;

$M, \lambda \models \neg\gamma$ iff $M, \lambda \not\models \gamma$;

$M, \lambda \models \gamma_1 \wedge \gamma_2$ iff $M, \lambda \models \gamma_1$ and $M, \lambda \models \gamma_2$;

$M, \lambda \models \mathsf{X}\,\gamma$ iff $M, \lambda[1,\infty] \models \gamma$; and

$M, \lambda \models \gamma_1\, \mathsf{U}\, \gamma_2$ iff there is an $i \in \mathbb{N}_0$ such that $M, \lambda[i,\infty] \models \gamma_2$ and $M, \lambda[j,\infty] \models \gamma_1$ for all $0 \le j < i$.

EXAMPLE 3 (DRIVING AGENTS, CTD.). *For model M_1, we have $M_1, q_{oo} \models \langle\!\langle 1\rangle\!\rangle\mathsf{G}\neg\mathsf{penalty}_1$: agent 1 can avoid the penalty forever (the obvious strategy is to never enter the crossroads). On the other hand, the agent cannot make sure it will get the penalty even if it wants to: $M_1, q_{oo} \not\models \langle\!\langle 1\rangle\!\rangle\mathsf{F}\,\mathsf{penalty}_1$. This can only be ensured if the agents cooperate: $M_1, q_{oo} \models \langle\!\langle 1,2\rangle\!\rangle\mathsf{F}\,\mathsf{penalty}_1$. Moreover, $M_1, q_{oo} \models \langle\!\langle 1\rangle\!\rangle\mathsf{F}\,\mathsf{in}_1 \wedge \langle\!\langle 2\rangle\!\rangle\mathsf{F}\,\mathsf{in}_2$: each agent is able to enter the intersection. Still, it cannot successfully drive through the crossroads on its own (e.g., $M_1, q_{oo} \not\models \langle\!\langle 1\rangle\!\rangle\mathsf{F}(\mathsf{in}_1 \wedge \mathsf{F}\,\mathsf{out}_1)$).*

Negation Normal Form. Formulas of ATL* can be equivalently transformed so that negation is only applied to atomic propositions. For this, the set of primitive operators must be extended as follows:

$$\varphi ::= \mathsf{p} \mid \neg\mathsf{p} \mid \varphi\wedge\varphi \mid \varphi\vee\varphi \mid \langle\!\langle A\rangle\!\rangle\gamma \mid \overline{\langle\!\langle A\rangle\!\rangle}\,\gamma,$$
$$\gamma ::= \varphi \mid \gamma\wedge\gamma \mid \gamma\vee\gamma \mid \mathsf{X}\,\gamma \mid \gamma\,\mathsf{U}\,\gamma \mid \gamma\,\mathsf{W}\,\gamma.$$

The Negation Normal Form for ATL is constructed analogously.

2.2 Quasi-Boolean Lattices

We will use quasi-boolean and De Morgan algebras [11] to interpret formulas of our multi-valued logics.

DEFINITION 2. *A* lattice *is a partial order $\mathcal{L} = (L, \le)$, where every pair of elements $x, y \in L$ has the greatest lower bound (called* meet *and denoted by $x \cap y$) and the least upper bound (called* join *and denoted by $x \cup y$).*[3]

In what follows, we only consider finite lattices. We denote the least and the greatest elements of $\mathcal{L}$ by $\bot, \top$, respectively. Also, we write (i) $x_1 < x_2$ iff $x_1 \le x_2$ and $x_1 \ne x_2$, and (ii) $x_1 \bowtie x_2$ iff neither $x_1 \le x_2$ nor $x_2 \le x_1$. Moreover, let:

- $\uparrow x = \{y \in L \mid x \le y\}$ denote the upward closure of x, and
- $\downarrow x = \{y \in L \mid y \le x\}$ denote the downward closure of x.

[3]It follows from antisymmetry of $\le$ that both the greatest lower bound and the least upper bound of x, y are uniquely determined.

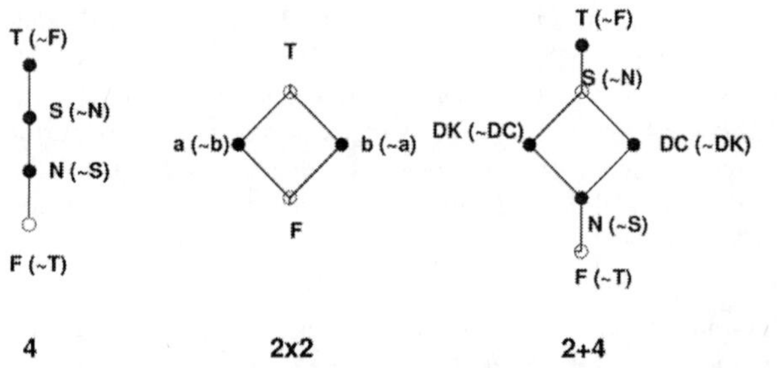

Figure 2: De Morgan algebras and join-irreducible elements

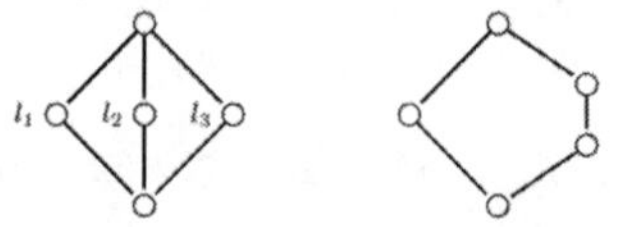

Figure 3: Non-distributive lattices M5 and N5

DEFINITION 3. *$\mathcal{L} = (L, \le, \sim)$ is a* quasi-boolean (QB) algebra *if $(L, \le)$ is a lattice and $\sim$ is a unary operator (called* complement*) such that, for any $x, y \in L$: (i) $\sim(x \cap y) = \sim x \cup \sim y$, (ii) $\sim(x \cup y) = \sim x \cap \sim y$, (iii) $x \le y$ iff $\sim y \le \sim x$, (iv) $\sim\sim x = x$.*

DEFINITION 4. *A lattice $\mathcal{L} = (L, \le)$ is distributive if, for any $x, y, z \in L$, the following two conditions hold: (i) $z \cup (x \cap y) = (z \cup x) \cap (z \cup y)$, (ii) $z \cap (x \cup y) = (z \cap x) \cup (z \cap y)$. A distributive QB algebra is called a* De Morgan *algebra, shortly:* DM algebra.

EXAMPLE 4. *Figure 2 presents three DM algebras with applicability motivated by clear practical intuitions: the total order* **4** *for representing uncertainty, lattice* **2** $\times$ **2** *for representing disagreement, and lattice* **2** + **4** *for representing both uncertainty and disagreement. In our view, lattice* **2** + **4** *seems especially useful, as it provides truth values for both inconsistent and inconclusive evidence. The usual interpretation of its logical elements is: $\bot$ - must not (absolute falsity),* **N** *- should not,* **DC** *- do not care,* **DK** *- do not know,* **S** *- should, $\top$ - must (absolute truth). In this paper, we will use a somewhat different notation, writing* **i** *("inconsistent") instead of* **DC** *and* **u** *("undecided") instead of* **DK**.
Example non-distributive QB lattices are shown in Figure 3. Note that a lattice is distributive iff it contains neither M5 nor N5 [11].

DEFINITION 5. *Let $\mathcal{L} = (L, \le)$ be a lattice. An element $l \in L$ is called* join-irreducible *iff $l \ne \bot$ and, for any $x, y \in L$, if $l = x \cup y$, then either $l = x$ or $l = y$.*
The set of all join-irreducible elements of $\mathcal{L}$ is denoted by $\mathcal{JI}(\mathcal{L})$.

It is well known [19] that every element of a finite distributive lattice can be uniquely decomposed into the join of all join-irreducible elements in its downward closure, i.e.

$$x = \bigcup(\mathcal{JI}(\mathcal{L}) \cap \downarrow x) \tag{1}$$

EXAMPLE 5. *The join-irreducible elements of the DM algebras in Figure 2 are marked with black dots. In the lattice* **2** + **4***, the element S, which is not join-irreducible, can be decomposed into the join of the join-irreducible elements DK and DC.*

The characterization (1) is used to define translations from multi-valued to standard model checking using the following theorem.

THEOREM 1 ([39]). *Let $\mathcal{L}$ be a finite DM algebra, and let $l \in \mathcal{JI}(\mathcal{L})$. Then the function $f_l : L \longrightarrow \{\bot, \top\}$ defined by $f_l(\uparrow l) = \top$, $f_l(L \setminus \uparrow l) = \bot$ preserves arbitrary bounds.*

REMARK 1. *The above does not hold for lattices which are not distributive. To see this, consider the element l_1 of* **M5**, *which is join-irreducible. However, f_{l_1} does not preserve join, as $f_{l_1}(l_2 \cup l_3) = f_{l_1}(\top) = \top$ whereas $f_{l_1}(l_2) \cup f_{l_1}(l_3) = \bot \cup \bot = \bot$.*

3. MULTI-VALUED STRATEGIC LOGIC

In this section we extend the syntax and semantics of ATL* to allow for multi-valued reasoning.

3.1 Multi-Valued ATL*

Domain of interpretation. We propose a variant of ATL* where formulas are interpreted in a quasi-boolean algebra $\mathcal{L} = (\mathrm{L}, \leq, \sim)$, see Section 2.2 for details.

DEFINITION 6 (INTERPRETED QB ALGEBRAS). *Let $\mathcal{C}$ be a countable set of symbols. An interpreted QB algebra over $\mathcal{C}$ (*IQB *algebra, for short) is a pair $\mathcal{L}^+ = (L, \sigma)$, where $\mathcal{L} = (L, \leq, \sim)$ is a QB algebra and $\sigma : \mathcal{C} \to L$ is an interpretation of the symbols in $\mathcal{C}$ as truth values in L.*

Syntax. Logical operators can often be naturally interpreted as either maximizers or minimizers of the truth values. For example, disjunction ($\varphi \vee \psi$) can be understood as a maximizer ("the most that we can make of either φ or ψ), and conjunction as a minimizer. This extends to existential quantification (maximizing) and universal quantification (minimizing) over paths, strategies, moments in time, etc. Since multi-valued negation is problematic, we will use the syntactic variant of ATL* in *negation normal form*. Moreover, valuation will be given explicitly for all literals and not only atoms. To increase the expressive power of the language, we allow for the use of symbols in $\mathcal{C}$. Finally, we add the operator $\preccurlyeq$ representing the lattice order, useful for comparing truth values of formulas. The resulting logic is called mv-ATL$^*_{\preccurlyeq}$ and has the following syntax:

$$\varphi ::= c \mid \mathsf{p} \mid \neg\mathsf{p} \mid \varphi \wedge \varphi \mid \varphi \vee \varphi \mid \langle\!\langle A \rangle\!\rangle\gamma \mid \overline{\langle\!\langle A \rangle\!\rangle}\,\gamma \mid \varphi \preccurlyeq \varphi,$$
$$\gamma ::= \varphi \mid \gamma \wedge \gamma \mid \gamma \vee \gamma \mid \mathsf{X}\,\gamma \mid \gamma\,\mathsf{U}\,\gamma \mid \gamma\,\mathsf{W}\,\gamma.$$

where $\mathsf{p} \in \mathit{Prop}$, $A \subseteq \mathcal{A}$, and $c \in \mathcal{C}$. In what follows, by an *order formula* we shall mean any formula of the form $\varphi_1 \preccurlyeq \varphi_2$. Additionally, we define $\varphi_1 \cong \varphi_2 \equiv (\varphi_1 \preccurlyeq \varphi_2) \wedge (\varphi_2 \preccurlyeq \varphi_1)$.

Semantics. The semantics is provided over concurrent game structures with multi-valued interpretation of literals.

DEFINITION 7 (MULTI-VALUED CGS). *Let $Lit = \{\mathsf{p}, \neg\mathsf{p} \mid \mathsf{p} \in Prop\}$, and let $\mathcal{L}^+ = (\mathcal{L}, \sigma)$ be an IQB algebra with $\mathcal{L} = (L, \leq, \sim)$. A multi-valued concurrent game structure (mv-CGS) over $\mathcal{L}$ is a tuple $M = \langle \mathcal{A}, St, Act, d, t, Prop, V, \mathcal{L}^+ \rangle$, where $\mathcal{A}$, St, Act, d, t, $Prop$ are as before, and $V : Lit \times St \to L$ assigns all literals with truth values of the logical domain L. Note that, for greater generality, we do not require that $V(\neg p, q) = \sim V(p, q)$.*

Let $M = \langle \mathcal{A}, St, Act, d, t, Prop, V, \mathcal{L}^+ \rangle$ be an mv-CGS, with $\mathcal{L}^+ = (\mathcal{L}, \sigma)$.The valuation function $[\cdot]$ is defined as below. We sometimes use $\bigcap_X \{Y\}$ as a shorthand for $\bigcap\{Y \mid X\}$, and similarly for the supremum. For any $q \in St$ and any path λ in M:

$[c]_{M,q} = \sigma(c)$ for $c \in \mathcal{C}$;
$[\mathsf{p}]_{M,q} = V(\mathsf{p}, q)$ and $[\neg\mathsf{p}]_{M,q} = V(\neg\mathsf{p}, q)$ for $\mathsf{p} \in Prop$;
$[\varphi_1 \wedge \varphi_2]_{M,q} = [\varphi_1]_{M,q} \cap [\varphi_2]_{M,q}$;
$[\varphi_1 \vee \varphi_2]_{M,q} = [\varphi_1]_{M,q} \cup [\varphi_2]_{M,q}$;

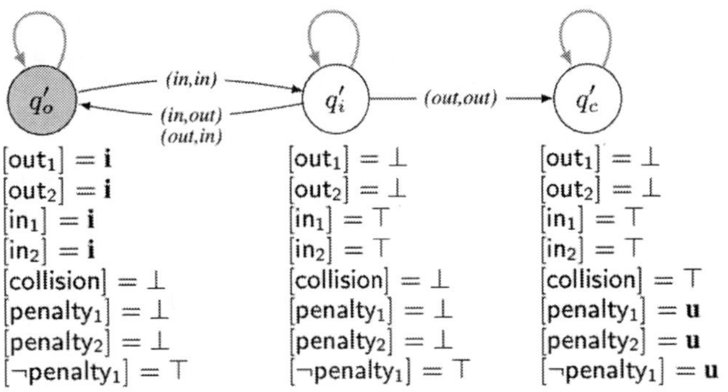

Figure 4: Abstract model of the driving agents: M_2

$[\gamma_1 \wedge \gamma_2]_{M,\lambda}$, $[\gamma_1 \vee \gamma_2]_{M,\lambda}$: analogously;
$[\varphi]_{M,\lambda} = [\varphi]_{M,\lambda[0]}$; $\qquad [\mathsf{X}\,\gamma]_{M,\lambda} = [\gamma]_{M,\lambda[1..\infty]}$;
$[\gamma_1\,\mathsf{U}\,\gamma_2]_{M,\lambda} =$
$\quad \bigcup_{i=0,1,\dots} \{\bigcap\{[\gamma_2]_{M,\lambda[i..\infty]}, [\gamma_1]_{M,\lambda[j..\infty]} \mid 0 \leq j < i\}\}$;
$[\gamma_1\,\mathsf{W}\,\gamma_2]_{M,\lambda} = \bigcap_{i=0,1,\dots}\{[\gamma_1]_{M,\lambda[i..\infty]}\} \cup$
$\quad \bigcup_{i=0,1,\dots} \{\bigcap\{[\gamma_2]_{M,\lambda[i..\infty]}, [\gamma_1]_{M,\lambda[j..\infty]} \mid 0 \leq j < i\}\}$;
$[\langle\!\langle A \rangle\!\rangle\gamma]_{M,q} = \bigcup_{s_A \in \Sigma_A} \bigcap_{\lambda \in out(q,s_A)} \{[\gamma]_{M,\lambda}\}$;
$[\overline{\langle\!\langle A \rangle\!\rangle}\,\gamma]_{M,q} = \bigcap_{s_A \in \Sigma_A} \bigcup_{\lambda \in out(q,s_A)} \{[\gamma]_{M,\lambda}\}$;
$[\varphi_1 \preccurlyeq \varphi_2]_{M,q} = \top$ if $[\varphi_1]_{M,q} \leq [\varphi_2]_{M,q}$ and $\bot$ otherwise.

EXAMPLE 6 (STATE ABSTRACTION FOR DRIVING AGENTS). *We take the CGS of Figure 1 and apply the metod of state abstraction from [42] with the following mapping: $\sigma(q_{oo}) = \sigma(q_{oi}) = \sigma(q_{io}) = q'_o$, $\sigma(q_{ii}) = q'_i$, and $\sigma(q_c) = q'_c$. That is, situations where at least one agent is outside and no collision has happened are represented by the abstract state q'_o, those where both agents are inside are mapped to q'_i etc. The resulting multi-valued CGS over lattice* **2 + 4** *is presented in Figure 4. Note that, e.g., $[\mathsf{out}_1]_{M_2,q'_o} =$* **i** *("inconsistent"), as the truth values of* out$_1$ *in the original states q_{oo}, q_{oi}, q_{io} are in conflict. Moreover, let us assume that the responsibility for the accident is determined by a complex constraint satisfaction problem, involving variables like the trajectory and speed of the vehicles, their technical condition etc., and that the model generating procedure had insufficient time to compute the values of* penalty$_1$ *and* penalty$_2$ *in state q_c (and hence also q'_c). Thus, $[\mathsf{penalty}_1]_{M_2,q'_c} = [\mathsf{penalty}_2]_{M_2,q'_c} =$* **u** *("undecided").*
The valuations of those negated atoms that will appear in further examples are also given.

To explicitly show the connection between the truth values and their names in $\mathcal{C}$, for any IQB algebra $\mathcal{L}^+ = ((\mathrm{L}, \leq, \sim), \sigma)$ and any truth value $x \in \sigma(\mathcal{C})$, we will use the notation $\boxed{x}$ to denote any symbol $c \in \mathcal{C}$ such that $\sigma(c) = x$. In other words, we will always have $\sigma(\boxed{x}) = x$ for all $x \in \sigma(\mathcal{C})$.

EXAMPLE 7 (STATE ABSTRACTION, CTD.). *We evaluate the formulas from Example 3 in our multi-valued model M_2 of Figure 4. For some of them the truth values remain the same, e.g., $[\langle\!\langle 1 \rangle\!\rangle \mathsf{G}\neg\mathsf{penalty}_1]_{M_2,q'_o} = \top$, and $[\langle\!\langle 1 \rangle\!\rangle \mathsf{F}\,\mathsf{penalty}_1]_{M_2,q'_o} = \bot$. We also get $[\langle\!\langle 1,2 \rangle\!\rangle \mathsf{F}\,\mathsf{penalty}_1]_{M_2,q'_o} =$* **u**, *which suggests that the abstraction is too fine-grained with respect to* penalty$_1$ *to verify $\langle\!\langle 1,2 \rangle\!\rangle \mathsf{F}\,\mathsf{penalty}_1$ efficiently. Finally, we get $[\langle\!\langle 1 \rangle\!\rangle \mathsf{F}\,\mathsf{in}_1]_{M_2,q'_o} =$* **i**, *which suggests that the abstraction is too coarse with respect to* in$_1$, *i.e., it loses some information necessary to compute the value of $\langle\!\langle 1 \rangle\!\rangle \mathsf{F}\,\mathsf{in}_1$. The same applies to $\langle\!\langle 2 \rangle\!\rangle \mathsf{F}\,\mathsf{in}_2$.*

We note that most approaches to multi-valued model checking of temporal specifications [38, 26, 39, 51] allow also for *multi-valued transitions* in the models, analogous to probabilistic transitions in Markov chains and Markov Decision Processes. That is, transitions can be assigned with "weights" drawn from the same algebra $\mathcal{L}$. Similarly, most 3-valued approaches to temporal abstraction and model checking implicitly assume 3-valued transitions by distinguishing between *may* and *must* transitions [24, 25, 28, 30]. However, the two approaches differ in how such transitions affect the semantics of formulas with universal quantification (such as "for all paths γ"). In the general multi-valued approach, the "weaker" the path is, the more it decreases the value of the formula. In the 3-valued approach, "weaker" paths have less influence on the overall value. We do not want to engage in this discussion here, and leave a proper treatment of multi-valued transitions for future work.

EXAMPLE 8 (COMPARING TRUTH VALUES). *The "comparison" operators provide several interesting specification patterns. For instance, they allow for specifications that are accepted when the "strength" of a property reaches a given threshold, similarly to the probabilistic approaches of [40, 18]. For example, the formula* $\boxed{u} \preccurlyeq \langle\langle 1\rangle\rangle \mathsf{G}\neg\mathsf{collision}$ *can be used to specify that the truth value of* $\langle\langle 1\rangle\rangle \mathsf{G}\neg\mathsf{collision}$ *is at least* **u** *(intuitively: there is no evidence that the formula is false). Moreover,* $\langle\langle 2\rangle\rangle \mathsf{G}\neg\mathsf{penalty}_2 \preccurlyeq \langle\langle 1\rangle\rangle \mathsf{G}\neg\mathsf{penalty}_1$ *says that assuming the ability of agent 1 to avoid penalty is more reasonable than in the case of agent 2. Finally,* $\langle\langle\emptyset\rangle\rangle \mathsf{G}(\varphi \cong \boxed{\top})$ *expresses that formula* φ *holds in all reachable states of the model.*

Levels of truth. We assume that $\top$ is the single designated value, standing for full logical truth. In consequence, the truth and validity of formulas can be defined in a straightforward way as follows:

DEFINITION 8 (LEVELS OF VALIDITY). *Let M be mv-CGS, q - a state in M, and φ - a state formula of mv-ATL$^*_\preccurlyeq$. Then:*

- *φ is* true *in M, q (written $M, q \models \varphi$) iff $[\varphi]_{M,q} = \top$.*
- *φ is* valid *in M ($M \models \varphi$) iff φ is true in every state of M.*
- *φ is* valid *($\models \varphi$) iff φ is valid in every mv-CGS M.*
- *Additionally, for a path formula γ, we can say that γ holds on run λ in a mv-CGS M (written $M, \lambda \models \gamma$) iff $[\gamma]_{M,\lambda} = \top$.*

3.2 Properties of mv-ATL*

We now show that mv-ATL$^*_\preccurlyeq$ agrees with standard ATL* on 2-valued models, unlike the 3-valued version of ATL* from [43].

THEOREM 2. *The logic mv-ATL$^*_\preccurlyeq$ is a conservative extension of ATL*, i.e. every CGS M for ATL* can be identified with an mv-CGS M' for mv-ATL$^*_\preccurlyeq$ over a two-valued lattice, where, for any ATL* formula φ and any state (path) ι: $M', \iota \models \varphi$ iff $M, \iota \models \varphi$.*

Proof. For any CGS $M = \langle \mathcal{A}, St, Act, d, t, AP, V\rangle$ for ATL*, define mv-CGS $M' = \langle \mathcal{A}, St, Act, d, t, AP, V', \mathcal{L}_2\rangle$, where $\mathcal{L}_2 = (\{\bot, \top\}, \leq, \sim, \sigma)$ with $\sim\bot = \top, \sim\top = \bot$, and $V'(p, q) = \top$ if $q \in V(p)$, $\bot$ otherwise. Then M' is an mv-CGS for mv-ATL$^*_\preccurlyeq$, and, obviously, for any ATL* formula φ, $M', \iota \models \varphi$ iff $M, \iota \models \varphi$.

The following is an immediate consequence:

COROLLARY 1. *Each valid formula of mv-ATL$^*_\preccurlyeq$ which does not contain the operator $\preceq$ is a valid formula of ATL*.*

Note that the converse does not hold, i.e., a valid formula of ATL* need not be valid in mv-ATL$^*_\preccurlyeq$. An example of such a formula is $p \vee \neg p$, which is valid in ATL* but not in mv-ATL$^*_\preccurlyeq$. Some important validities that do carry over from classical ATL are the fixpoint equivalences (which in case of multi-valued models can be seen as analogues of Bellman equations for MDPs [9]):

THEOREM 3 (BELLMAN EQUATIONS FOR MV-ATL$_\preccurlyeq$). *The following formulas of mv-ATL$_\preccurlyeq$ are valid:*

- $\langle\langle A\rangle\rangle \varphi_1 \,\mathsf{U}\, \varphi_2 \cong \varphi_2 \vee \varphi_1 \wedge \langle\langle A\rangle\rangle \mathsf{X}\, \langle\langle A\rangle\rangle \varphi_1 \,\mathsf{U}\, \varphi_2$*;*
- $\langle\langle A\rangle\rangle \varphi_1 \,\mathsf{W}\, \varphi_2 \cong \varphi_2 \vee \varphi_1 \wedge \langle\langle A\rangle\rangle \mathsf{X}\, \langle\langle A\rangle\rangle \varphi_1 \,\mathsf{W}\, \varphi_2$.

Proof. The proof is analogous to [33, Proposition 3], and we omit it due to lack of space.

4. MODEL CHECKING mv-ATL$^*_\preccurlyeq$

Given a mv-CGS M, a state q, and a mv-ATL$^*_\preccurlyeq$ formula φ, the model checking problem consists in computing the value of $[\varphi]_{M,q}$. This can be done in two ways: either by a dedicated algorithm (based e.g. on the fixpoint equations of Prop. 3), or by an efficient reduction to the 2-valued model checking. The latter option has many advantages. First and foremost, it allows us to benefit from the ongoing developments in 2-valued model checking, including symbolic model checking techniques, heuristics, model reduction techniques, etc. In this section, we show how model checking of mv-ATL$^*_\preccurlyeq$ can be reduced to the 2-valued variant of this problem.

4.1 Adapting Translations to mv-ATL$^*_\preccurlyeq$

A key result obtained in [38] was Theorem 1, providing a method for reducing a model for mv-CTL* based on a lattice L of logical values to a model based on a sublattice L' of L. This ultimately allowed us to reduce model-checking mv-CTL* to model checking of (two-valued) CTL*. An analogue of that theorem can be shown to hold for mv-ATL*, i.e., the sublanguage of mv-ATL$^*_\preccurlyeq$ consisting of formulas without the $\preccurlyeq$ operator. That is, we have the following:

THEOREM 4. *Let $\mathcal{L} = (L, \leq, \sim)$ be an arbitrary finite QB algebra, $\mathcal{L}' = (L', \leq', \sim')$ a subalgebra of $\mathcal{L}$, and $f : L \to L'$ a mapping which preserves arbitrary bounds in $\mathcal{L}$, i.e.,*

$$f(\bigcap_{i\in I} x_i) = \bigcap_{i\in I} f(x_i), \qquad f(\bigcup_{i\in I} x_i) = \bigcup_{i\in I} f(x_i) \qquad (2)$$

where I is an arbitrary set of indices. Further, let $\mathcal{L}^+ = (\mathcal{L}, \sigma)$ be an IQB algebra, $M = \langle \mathcal{A}, St, Act, d, t, Prop, \mathcal{V}, \mathcal{L}^+\rangle$ an mv-CGS, and $M' = \langle \mathcal{A}, St, Act, d, t, Prop, \mathcal{V}, \mathcal{L}'^+\rangle$ an mv-CGS obtained out of M by replacing each value $x \in L$ returned by σ or $\mathcal{V}$ in M with $f(x)$, i.e., $\sigma'(c) = f(\sigma(c))$ and $\mathcal{V}'(p, q) = f(\mathcal{V}(p, q))$, for $c \in \mathcal{C}$, $q \in St$, and $p \in Prop \cup \overline{Prop}$.

Then, for any state (path) formula φ of mv-ATL* over $\mathcal{L}$ and any state (resp. path) ι, we have

$$[\varphi]_{M',\iota} = x \text{ iff } [\varphi]_{M,\iota} \in f^{-1}(x) \qquad (3)$$

The proof follows easily from the key result given below:

LEMMA 1. *Let a state or path formula φ be such that*

$$[\varphi]_{M,\iota} = \bigcup_{i\in I} \bigcap_{j_i\in J_i} [\varphi_{j_i}]_{M,\iota_{j_i}} \quad \text{or} \quad [\varphi]_{M,\iota} = \bigcap_{i\in I} \bigcup_{j_i\in J_i} [\varphi_{j_i}]_{M,\iota_{j_i}}$$

for any mv-CGS M, any states and/or paths ι, ι_{j_i} of M, any countable sets I, J_i, and state (resp. path) formulas of mv-ATL* φ_{j_i} for $j_i \in J_i, i \in I$, such that φ_{j_i} satisfy (3). Then φ satisfies (3) too.

Proof. We consider the case $[\varphi]_{M,\iota} = \bigcup_{i\in I} \bigcap_{j_i\in J_i} [\varphi_{j_i}]_{M,\iota_{j_i}}$; the other case follows by symmetry. As f preserves the bounds, by the assumption on φ we have $f([\varphi]_{M,\iota}) = \bigcup_{i\in I} \bigcap_{j_i\in J_i} f([\varphi_{j_i}]_{M,\iota_{j_i}})$.

Each φ_{j_i} satisfies (3), so $f([\varphi]_{M,\iota}) = \bigcup_{i\in I}\bigcap_{j_i\in J_i}[\varphi_{j_i}]_{M',\iota_{j_i}} = [\varphi]_{M',\iota}$, whence $[\varphi]_{M',\iota} = x$ iff $[\varphi]_{M,\iota} \in f^{-1}(x)$, and (3) holds for φ. To prove Theorem 4, it suffices to check that the semantics of each formula of mv-ATL* can be given like in Lemma 1.

4.2 Translating Order Formulas

Unfortunately, Theorem 4 cannot be extended to mv-ATL$^*_{\preccurlyeq}$, i.e. to the language of mv-ATL* extended with order formulas of the form $\varphi_1 \preceq \varphi_2$, where $\preceq$ represents the algebra order — because Equation (3) does not hold for such formulas.

To show a counterexample, we consider the QB algebra $\mathcal{L}_o = (\mathrm{L}_o, \leq, \sim)$, where $\mathrm{L}_o = \{0, ..., k-1, k, ..., 2k-1\}$, $\leq$ is the usual total order on L_o, and $\sim x = (2k-1) - x$. Of course, in $\mathcal{L}_o$ we have $0 = \bot, 2k-1 = \top$ according to our lattice notation. Then the translation $f : \mathrm{L}_o \to \{0, 2k-1\}$ given by $f(x) = 2k-1$ if $x \geq k$, and $f(x) = 0$ if $x < k$ preserves the bounds in $\mathcal{L}_o$.

Now take arbitrary k_1, k_2 such that $0 < k_1 < k_2 < k$, and an mv-CGS M over $\mathcal{L}_o^+ = (\mathcal{L}_o, \sigma)$ for an arbitrary $\sigma : \mathcal{C} \to \mathrm{L}_o$ such that, for some state $q \in St$ of M and atomic propositions $p_1, p_2 \in PV$, we have $V(p_i, q) = k_i$ for $i = 1, 2$.

Next, let $\varphi = p_2 \preceq p_1$. Since $[p_i]_{M,q} = k_i$ for $i = 1, 2$ and $k_2 > k_1$, we have $\neg([p_2]_{M,q} \leq [p_1]_{M,q})$, whence $[\varphi]_{M,q} = 0$.

However, for the model M_1 obtained from M with the translation f we get $[p_i]_{M_1,q} = 0$ for $i = 1, 2$ (as $k_i < k$, $f(k_i) = 0$ for $i = 1, 2$), where $[p_2]_{M_1,q} \leq [p_1]_{M_1,q}$, which implies $[\varphi]_{M_1,q} = 2k-1$. Yet, as $f^{-1}(2k-1) = \{k, k+1, ..., 2k-1\}$ we have $[\varphi]_{M,q} = 0 \notin f^{-1}(2k-1)$, which contradicts Equation (3).

The above result can be generalized as follows:

LEMMA 2. *If $\mathcal{L} = (L, \leq, \sim)$ of Theorem 4 contains a chain or anti-chain of cardinality n, and $\mathcal{L}' = (L', \leq', \sim')$ is a subalgebra of $\mathcal{L}$ of cardinality $n' < n$, then there is no function $f : L \to L'$ satisfying condition (3) if the language under consideration contains order formulas.*

Now we give a necessary and sufficient condition for $f : L \to L'$ as in Theorem 4, preserving bounds in $\mathcal{L}$, to satisfy the translation condition (3) from Theorem 4 also for order formulas.

LEMMA 3. *Let the QB algebra $\mathcal{L} = (L, \leq, \sim)$, its subalgebra $\mathcal{L}' = (L', \leq', \sim')$, a mapping $f : L \to L'$, and mv-CGSs M, M' satisfy the assumptions of Theorem 4. Then, (3) of that Theorem is satisfied for all order formulas iff the following conditions hold:*

C1 $(\forall x_1, x_2 \in L)\ [x_1 < x_2 \Rightarrow f(x_1) < f(x_2)]$

C2 $(\forall x_1, x_2 \in L)\ [x_1 \bowtie x_2 \Rightarrow f(x_1) \bowtie f(x_2)]$

Proof. Note that an order formula is a state formula, and that for any such formula ψ we have $[\psi]_{M,q} \in \{\bot, \top\}$ for any mv-CGS M and any $q \in St$. Thus in order to prove (3) for such formulas, it suffices to show that, for any order formula φ and any state q:

$$[\varphi]_{M',q} = \top \text{ iff } [\varphi]_{M,q} \in f^{-1}(\top) \tag{4}$$

"$\Rightarrow$": We start by proving the necessity of conditions C1,C2. Assume first f satisfies (4) for order formulas. We should prove that f satisfies Conditions C1, C2 for all such formulas. For what follows, denote $\xi = p_1 \preceq p_2, \psi = p_2 \preceq p_1$, where $p_1, p_2 \in PV, p_1 \neq p_2$.

C1: We argue by contradiction. Suppose $x_1, x_2 \in \mathrm{L}, x_1 < x_2$ and $f(x_1) \geq f(x_2)$. Then, as $x_1 < x_2$ implies $x_1 \leq x_2$ and f preserves bounds, we also have $f(x_1) \leq f(x_2)$, which yields $f(x_1) = f(x_2)$.

Now let M be an mv-CGS over $\mathcal{L}$ such that, for some state $q \in St$, we have $V(p_i, q) = x_i$ for $i = 1, 2$, and let M' be the image of M under f. Since $\psi = p_2 \preceq p_1$ and $[p_2]_{M,q} = x_2 > x_1 = [p_1]_{M,q}$, we have $[\psi]_{M,q} = \bot$. However, $[\psi]_{M',q} = \top$, because $[p_2]_{M',q} = f(x_2) = f(x_1) = [p_1]_{M',q}$. As $\bot \notin f^{-1}(\top)$, this contradicts (4).

C2: We again argue by contradiction. Suppose $x_1, x_2 \in L, x_1 \bowtie x_2$ and $\neg(f(x_1) \bowtie f(x_2))$. Without any loss of generality, we can assume that $f(x_1) \leq f(x_2)$. Let mv-CGSs M, M' and state q of M be like in the preceding item. Then, as $[p_1]_{M,q} = x_1 \bowtie x_2 = [p_2]_{M,q}$, we have in particular $[p_1]_{M,q} \not\leq [p_2]_{M,q}$. Since $\xi = p_1 \preceq p_2$, this implies $[\xi]_{M,q} = \bot$. In turn, $[\xi]_{M',q} = \top$, because $[p_1]_{M',q} = f(x_1) \leq f(x_2) = [p_2]_{M',q}$, which again contradicts (4).

"$\Leftarrow$": It remains to prove the sufficiency of conditions C1,C2. We assume that C1, C2 hold, and prove that (4) holds for formulas of the form $\varphi = \varphi_1 \preceq \varphi_2$. We start by proving this result for non-nested order formulas, i.e., we assume that φ_1, φ_2 do not contain $\preceq$. Then, by Theorem 4, (4) holds for φ_1, φ_2, which implies that

$$[\varphi_i]_{M',q} = f([\varphi_i]_{M,q}), \quad i = 1, 2. \tag{5}$$

"$\Rightarrow$": We begin with the forward implication in (4). Assume that $[\varphi]_{M',q} = \top$. Then $[\varphi_1]_{M',q} \leq [\varphi_2]_{M',q}$. By (5), this implies $f([\varphi_1]_{M,q}) \leq f([\varphi_2]_{M,q}$. We show by contradiction that it implies

$$[\varphi_1]_{M,q} \leq [\varphi_2]_{M,q}. \tag{6}$$

Suppose that (6) does not hold, then we have two possible cases:

Case 1: $[\varphi_1]_{M,q} > [\varphi_2]_{M,q}$. Then by C1 we have $f([\varphi_1]_{M,q}) > f([\varphi_2]_{M,q})$, whence from (5) we get $[\varphi_1]_{M',q} > [\varphi_2]_{M_1,q}$ and $[\varphi]_{M',q} = \bot$ — which is a contradiction.

Case 2: $[\varphi_1]_{M,q} \bowtie [\varphi_2]_{M,q}$. Then $f([\varphi_1]_{M,q}) \bowtie f([\varphi_2]_{M,q})$ by C2, whence from (5) we get $\neg([\varphi_1]_{M',q} \leq [\varphi_2]_{M',q})$. Consequently, $[\varphi]_{M',q} = \bot$ — which is again a contradiction.

Thus (6) above holds, whence $[\varphi]_{M,q} = \top \in f_1(\top)$, and the forward implication in (4) holds.

"$\Leftarrow$": The final step is proving the backward implication in (4). Assume that $[\varphi]_{M,q} = f^{-1}(\top)$. As $[\varphi]_{M,q} \in \{\bot, \top\}$ and $f(\bot) \neq \top$ by the preservation of bounds by f and the non-triviality of L, L', we obtain $[\varphi]_{M,q} = \top$, whence $[\varphi_1]_{M,q} \leq [\varphi_2]_{M,q}$. Since f preserves bounds, this implies $f([\varphi_1]_{M,q}) \geq f([\varphi_2]_{M,q})$, whence from (5) we obtain $[\varphi_1]_{M_1,q} \leq [\varphi_2]_{M',q}$. This yields $[\varphi]_{M',q} = \top$, whence the backward implication in (4) holds, too.

Now assume (4) holds for order formulas with $\preceq$ nested at most k times, and assume φ is an order formula with $\preceq$ nested $k+1$ times. Then $\varphi = \varphi_1 \preceq \varphi_2$, where $\preceq$ is nested at most k times in φ_1, φ_2. Consequently, by the inductive assumption (6) holds for φ_1, φ_2, and repeating the proof given above for order formulas without nesting of $\preceq$ we can show that (4) holds for φ too.

This completes the proof of the sufficiency of C1, C2 for all order formulas, and the proof of Lemma 3. From Lemma 3 we can easily derive by induction the following general result:

THEOREM 5. *Let the QB algebra $\mathcal{L} = (L, \leq, \sim)$, its subalgebra $\mathcal{L}' = (L', \leq', \sim')$, $f : L \to L'$, and mv-CGS M, M' satisfy the assumptions of Theorem 4. Then the condition (3) of that Theorem:*

$$[\varphi]_{M',\iota} = x \quad \text{iff} \quad [\varphi]_{M,\iota} \in f^{-1}(x) \tag{7}$$

is satisfied for all formulas of mv-ATL$^*_{\preccurlyeq}$ over $\mathcal{L}$ iff conditions C1, C2 of Lemma 3 hold.

It can be seen that conditions C1, C2 imply that any translation f meeting them must preserve the exact structure of the QB algebra $\mathcal{L}$. An important consequence of that fact is:

COROLLARY 2. *Given a QB algebra $\mathcal{L} = (L, \leq, \sim)$ and its subalgebra $\mathcal{L}' = (L', \leq', \sim')$, any function $f : L \to L'$ preserving the algebra bounds and satisfying the translation condition (3) for all order formulas must be one-to-one.*

Proof. Suppose f satisfies the above assumption, $x_1, x_2 \in L$ and $x_1 \neq x_2$. Then we have one of the following cases:

1. $x_1 < x_2$ or $x_2 < x_1$. Then $f(x_1) \neq f(x_2)$ by C1 of Theorem 5.
2. $x_1 \bowtie x_2$. Then $f(x_1) \bowtie f(x_2)$ by C2 of Theorem 5, which again implies $f(x_1) \neq f(x_2)$.

The meaning of Corollary 2 is that there is no way of reducing n-valued model checking to k-valued model checking for $k < n$, if we want to handle all order formulas. In particular:

COROLLARY 3. *No reduction of mv-ATL$^*_\preccurlyeq$ model checking to 2-valued model checking is possible.*

4.3 Recursive Model Checking of mv-ATL$^*_\preccurlyeq$

The impossibility result in Corollary 3 is due to the fact that order formulas can be used to encode the semantics in the language – including in particular its n-valued character. However, one usually wants to model-check one formula at a time. Then, Theorem 5 can be in many cases modified to provide the desired reduction:

THEOREM 6. *Let $\mathcal{L}$, its subalgebra $\mathcal{L}'$, $f : L \to L'$, and M, M' be as in Theorem 4. Further, let φ be a formula of mv-ATL$^*_\preccurlyeq$ and $Sub(\varphi)$ be the set of all its subformulas. Then φ satisfies the translation condition 7 of Theorem 5 whenever for any order formula $\phi \in Sub(\varphi)$ such that $\phi = \varphi_1 \preceq \varphi_2$ and for $x_i = [\varphi_i]_{M,\iota}, i = 1, 2$, the following conditions hold:*

C1' $x_1 < x_2 \Rightarrow f(x_1) < f(x_2)$

C2' $x_1 \bowtie x_2 \Rightarrow f(x_1) > f(x_2)$

Proof. To prove the thesis, we assume that C1', C2' are satisfied, and show by structural induction that the translation condition holds for any $\psi \in Sub(\varphi)$, i.e.,

$$[\psi]_{M',\iota} = x \quad \text{iff} \quad [\psi]_{M,\iota} \in f^{-1}(x) \tag{8}$$

For atomic or constant ψ, the thesis follows from Theorem 4. Suppose now (8) holds for all subformulas of φ having rank k, and assume ψ is of rank $k + 1$. If ψ is obtained from subformulas of rank at most k using any operator Op other than $\preceq$, the satisfaction of (8) follows from the fundamental Lemma 3.

Thus it remains to consider the case of $\preceq$. Assume $\psi = \psi_1 \preceq \psi_2$, where (8) holds for ψ_1, ψ_2. Since ψ is an order formula, according to what we have already noted in the proof of Lemma 2, proving (8) for ψ reduces to showing

$$[\psi]_{M',q} = \top \quad \text{iff} \quad [\psi]_{M,q} \in f^{-1}(\top) \tag{9}$$

Note that since ψ_1, ψ_2 are in $Sub(\varphi)$, then C1', C2' hold for $x_i = [\varphi_i]_{M,q}, i = 1, 2$. By the inductive assumption, we also have

$$[\psi_i]_{M',q} = f([\psi_i]_{M,q}), \quad i = 1, 2 \tag{10}$$

"$\Rightarrow$": We begin with the forward implication in (9). Assume that $[\psi]_{M',q} = \top$. Then $[\psi_1]_{M',q} \leq [\psi_2]_{M',q}$. By (10), this implies $f([\psi_1]_{M,q}) \leq f([\psi_2]_{M,q})$. We show by contradiction that it implies

$$[\psi_1]_{M,q} \leq [\psi_2]_{M,q} \tag{11}$$

Suppose that (11) does not hold, then we have two possible cases:

Case 1: $[\psi_1]_{M,q} > [\psi_2]_{M,q}$. Then by condition C1' we have $f([\psi_1]_{M,q}) > f([\psi_2]_{M,q})$, whence from (10) we get $[\psi_1]_{M',q} > [\psi_2]_{M',q}$ and $[\psi]_{M',q} = \bot$, which is a contradiction.

Case 2: $[\psi_1]_{M,q} \bowtie [\psi_2]_{M,q}$. Then $f([\psi_1]_{M,q}) > f([\psi_2]_{M,q})$ by condition C2', which again leads to a contradiction by what we have already proved for Case 1.

Thus (11) above holds, whence $[\psi]_{M,q} = \top \in f^{-1}(\top)$, and the forward implication in (9) holds.

"$\Leftarrow$": The final step consists in proving the backward implication in (9). Assume that $[\psi]_{M,q} = f^{-1}(\top)$. As $[\psi]_{M,q} \in \{\bot, \top\}$ and $f(\bot) \neq \top$ by the preservation of bounds by f and the non-triviality of $\mathcal{L}, \mathcal{L}'$, we get $[\psi]_{M,q} = \top$, and consequently $[\psi_1]_{M,q} \leq [\psi_2]_{M,q}$. Since f preserves bounds, this implies $f([\psi_1]_{M,q}) \leq f([\psi_2]_{M,q})$, whence from (10) we obtain $[\psi_1]_{M',q} \leq [\psi_2]_{M',q}$. This yields $[\psi]_{M',q} = \top$, whence the backward implication in (9) holds, too.

REMARK 2. *Notice that Condition C2' is necessary, but C1' is not. Moreover, both are necessary iff φ is symmetric w.r.t. to $\preceq$, i.e., $(\varphi_2 \preceq \varphi_1) \in Sub(\varphi)$ whenever $(\varphi_1 \preceq \varphi_2) \in Sub(\varphi)$.*

Assume that our mv-CGSs are defined over DM algebras, i.e., distributive QB algebras. We can show that the translation method based on join irreducible elements ($\mathcal{JI}(\mathcal{L})$) [26, 12, 38, 37] can be applied to a formula φ of mv-ATL$^*_\preccurlyeq$ and an mv-CGS M, provided the assumptions of Theorem 6 are satisfied.

By (1), for each $x \in$ L we have $x = \bigcup(\mathcal{JI}(\mathcal{L}) \cap \downarrow x)$. Let M^l be the model obtained using the translation f_l. Therefore, according to Theorem 6: $[\varphi]_{M_1,\iota} = x$ iff $[\varphi]_{M,\iota} \in f_l^{-1}(x)$ whence $[\varphi]_{M_1,\iota} = \top$ iff $[\varphi]_{M,\iota} \in \uparrow l$. Thus,

$$[\varphi]_{M,\iota} = \bigcup\{l \in \mathcal{JI}(\mathcal{L}) \mid [\varphi]_{M_1,\iota} = \top\}. \tag{12}$$

In case the assumptions of Theorem 6 are not satisfied for M and φ, we cannot translate model checking of mv-ATL$^*_\preccurlyeq$ to model checking of ATL*. Then, the simplest solution is to replace all the subformulas of φ which are order formulas by fresh atomic propositions, and then apply our translation method to the resulting formula φ' of mv-ATL* and the new model M' which extends M by the valuation of the new atomic propositions.

The algorithm is recursive. For each order subformula $\psi = \psi_1 \leq \psi_2$ of φ such that $\psi_1, \psi_2 \in$ mv-ATL*, we define a fresh propositional variable p_ψ. Then, for each state q of model M' we have $V'(p_\psi, q) = \top$ iff $[\psi_1]_{M,q} \leq [\psi_2]_{M,q}$, and $V'(\neg p_\psi, q) = \bot$ iff $\neg([\psi_1]_{M,q} \leq [\psi_2]_{M,q})$, where $[\psi_i]_{M,q}$ for $i \in \{1, 2\}$ is computed using our translation method. Next, when all order subformulas have been replaced with fresh propositions, we compute $[\varphi']_{M,q}$ using the translation method defined.

The main disadvantage of the above method compared to the direct translation method is that it requires computing the values of the new atomic propositions for all states of the model M. The method can be improved if we assume that a specific symbolic model checking method for two valued mv-ATL$^*_\preccurlyeq$ is used. We leave a study of this subject for future work. Nevertheless, the algorithm has two important consequences. First, it provides a general polynomial-time reduction from model checking mv-ATL$^*_\preccurlyeq$ (resp. mv-ATL$_\preccurlyeq$) to model checking standard 2-valued ATL* (resp. ATL). We state it formally as follows.

THEOREM 7. *Multi-valued verification of ATL* incurs only polynomial increase in the complexity compared to the 2-valued case. Specifically, model checking mv-ATL$_\preccurlyeq$ is* **P***-complete, and model checking mv-ATL$^*_\preccurlyeq$ is* **2EXPTIME***-complete in model size, formula length, and number of logical values.*

Secondly, we note that correctness of the translation does not depend on the type of strategies being used in the semantics of mv-ATL$^*_{\preccurlyeq}$. As it is, the translation provides a model checking reduction to the *IR* variant of ATL* (perfect information + perfect recall). If we used memoryless strategies of type $s_a : St \to Act$ instead of perfect recall, the translation would yield reduction to the *Ir* variant of ATL* (perfect information + imperfect recall [50]). Since the *IR* and *Ir* semantics coincide in 2-valued ATL, we get the following.

THEOREM 8. *For mv-ATL$_{\preccurlyeq}$, memory is irrelevant, i.e., its semantics can be equivalently given by memoryless strategies.*

5. IMPERFECT INFORMATION

It can be argued that realistic multi-agent systems always include some degree of limited observability [50, 31, 1, 36, 2, 34, 49]. However, model checking of ATL with imperfect information is hard – more precisely, $\mathbf{\Delta_2^P}$- to **PSPACE**-complete for agents playing memoryless strategies [50, 35, 13] and undecidable for agents with perfect recall [21]. Furthermore, the imperfect information semantics of ATL does not admit fixpoint equivalences [15], which makes incremental synthesis of strategies cumbersome if not impossible. Practical attempts at the problem have emerged only recently [48, 16, 27, 17], and do not go far beyond checking each of the exponentially many strategies. The experimental results show that this is feasible only for very small models.

To such hard problems, state abstraction can be successfully applied, but it must be very coarse (clustering many concrete states together into a single abstract state) in order to reduce the model sufficiently. This can lead to a substantial reduction in the complexity, though possibly at the expense of introducing inconsistent or inconclusive labeling of propositions at some abstract states. In consequence, multivalued model checking can be extremely useful when reasoning about strategies under uncertainty. We formalize this by the following extension of mv-ATL$^*_{\preccurlyeq}$.

Multivalued ATL* with imperfect information. Let us extend mv-CGS with indistinguishability relations $\sim_1, \dots, \sim_k$, one per agent in $\mathcal{A}$. Memoryless strategies with imperfect information (*ir* strategies, for short) are functions $s_a : St \to Act$ such that $q \sim_a q'$ implies $s_a(q) = s_a(q')$. Perfect recall strategies with imperfect information (shortly: *iR* strategies) are functions $s_a : St^+ \to Act$ st. $q_0 \sim_a q_0', \dots, q_n \sim_a q_n'$ implies $s_a(q_0 \dots q_n) = s_a(q_0' \dots q_n')$. Again, collective strategies for $A \subseteq \mathcal{A}$ are tuples of individual strategies for $a \in A$. We denote them by Σ_A^{ir} and Σ_A^{iR}, respectively.

The semantics of mv-ATL$^*_{\mathfrak{S}\preccurlyeq}$, parameterized by the type of strategies $\mathfrak{S} = IR, Ir, ir, iR$, can be defined by replacing the clause for $\langle\langle A\rangle\rangle\gamma$ from Section 3.1 as follows:

$$[\langle\langle A\rangle\rangle\gamma]_{M,q} = \bigsqcup_{s_A\in\Sigma_A^{\mathfrak{S}}} \bigsqcap_{\lambda\in out(q,s_A)}\{[\gamma]_{M,\lambda}\}.^4$$

EXAMPLE 9 (ABSTRACTION FOR IMPERFECT INFO). *Take model M_1 from Example 2, and assume that agent 2 does not see the location of vehicle 1. This can be modeled by the following indistinguishability relation: $q_{oo} \sim_2 q_{io}$ and $q_{oi} \sim_2 q_{ii}$. If we further apply the state abstraction σ of Example 6, we obtain model M_3 that adds $q_o' \sim_2 q_i'$ to the mv-CGS M_2. Now, e.g., $[\langle\langle 1,2\rangle\rangle \mathsf{F}(\mathsf{penalty}_1)]_{M_3,q_o'} = \bot$, as the only winning strategy for coalition $\{1,2\}$ (play (in,in) at state q_o' and (out,out) at q_i') is not executable for agent 2 under imperfect information. On the other hand, we still have that $[\langle\langle 2\rangle\rangle \mathsf{F}\mathsf{in}_2]_{M_3,q_o'} = \mathbf{i}$.*

[4]This corresponds to the notion of *objective ability*, cf. the semantic definitions of the logics ATL$^*_{i_or}$ and ATL$^*_{i_oR}$ in [15]. *Subjective ability* requires additional quantification over indistinguishable states; we omit the formal treatment for lack of space.

THEOREM 9. *mv-ATL$^*_{ir\preccurlyeq}$ is a conservative extension of ATL$^*_{i_or}$, i.e. every imperfect information CGS M can be identified with an imperfect information mv-CGS M' over a two-valued lattice, where, for any ATL* formula φ and any state or path ι, we have that $M', \iota \models \varphi$ iff $M, \iota \models \varphi$.*

Similarly, mv-ATL$^*_{iR\preccurlyeq}$ is a conservative extension of ATL$^*_{i_oR}$.

Translations of model checking and the complexity of multivalued verification. We emphasize again that the techniques proposed in Section 4 *do not depend on the actual definition of strategy sets Σ_A*. In consequence, they carry over to the imperfect information case, and can be applied *in exactly the same way* to obtain model checking reductions from mv-ATL$^*_{\mathfrak{S}\preccurlyeq}$ to the corresponding 2-valued cases. Specifically, Theorems 4, 5, and 6, as well as Corollaries 2 and 3, hold for translations from model checking of mv-ATL$^*_{ir\preccurlyeq}$ (resp. mv-ATL$^*_{iR\preccurlyeq}$) to classical model checking of ATL$^*_{i_or}$ (resp. ATL$^*_{i_oR}$). This demonstrates the power of the translation method that can be directly applied to a vast array of possible semantics for ATL. Combining the observation with the existing complexity results [13], we get the following as immediate consequences:

THEOREM 10. *Model checking mv-ATL$_{ir\preccurlyeq}$ is* **P**-*complete, and model checking mv-ATL$^*_{ir\preccurlyeq}$ is* **PSPACE**-*complete in the size of the model and the formula, and the number of logical values.*

THEOREM 11. *Model checking mv-ATL$^*_{iR\preccurlyeq}$ and mv-ATL$_{iR\preccurlyeq}$ is undecidable in general. For the fragment of mv-ATL$_{iR\preccurlyeq}$ with singleton coalitions only, model checking is* **EXPTIME**-*complete in the model size, formula length, and number of logical values.*

6. CONCLUSIONS

In this paper, we study a variant of alternating-time temporal logic, called mv-ATL$^*_{\preccurlyeq}$, where the truth values are drawn from an arbitrary De Morgan algebra. We also argue that multivalued model checking of mv-ATL$^*_{\preccurlyeq}$ specifications can be useful, especially for systems whose models cannot be fully analyzed due to their complexity and/or inaccessibility of the relevant information. Examples include verification of distributed databases and abstraction-based model checking of massive multi-agent systems, especially for specifications of strategies under imperfect information.

We prove that our multivalued semantics of ATL* provides a conservative extension of the classical 2-valued variant. Even more importantly, we propose efficient (i.e., polynomial-time) translations from multivalued model checking to the 2-valued case. The proposed techniques are elegant enough so that they can be directly applied to other semantic variants of strategic ability, for example ones that refer to imperfect information scenarios. Other results comprise analogues of Bellman equations and positionality of winning strategies for mv-ATL$_{\preccurlyeq}$ in perfect information scenarios.

Our translation method for mv-ATL$^*_{\preccurlyeq}$ formulas allows us to benefit from the efficient 2-valued model checking algorithms. If a translation for a formula φ cannot be defined, our model checking method becomes less efficient, as it requires replacing all the order subformulas of φ with propositions and computing their values in a given mv-CGS.

In the future, we plan to have a closer look at state and action abstractions of complex models, including an appropriate semantic interpretation of multi-valued transitions.

Acknowledgements. Wojciech Jamroga acknowledges support of the 7th Framework Programme of the European Union under the Marie Curie IEF project ReVINK (PIEF-GA-2012-626398).

REFERENCES

[1] T. Ågotnes. A note on syntactic characterization of incomplete information in ATEL. In *Procedings of Workshop on Knowledge and Games*, pages 34–42, 2004.

[2] T. Ågotnes. Action and knowledge in alternating-time temporal logic. *Synthese*, 149(2):375–407, 2006.

[3] R. Alur, T. A. Henzinger, and O. Kupferman. Alternating-time Temporal Logic. *Journal of the ACM*, 49:672–713, 2002.

[4] A. M. B. Aminof, O. Kupferman. Improved model checking of hierarchical systems. *Information Computation*, 210:68–86, 2012.

[5] C. Baier, M. Kwiatkowska, and G. Norman. Computing probability bounds for linear time formulas over concurrent probabilistic systems. *Electronic Notes in Theoretical Computer Science*, 21(19), 1999.

[6] T. Ball and O. Kupferman. An abstraction-refinement framework for multi-agent systems. In *Proceedings of LICS*, pages 379–388. IEEE Computer Society, 2006.

[7] A. Bauer, M. Leucker, and C. Schallhart. Monitoring of real-time properties. In *Proceedings of FSTTCS*, volume 4337 of *Lecture Notes in Computer Science*, pages 260–272. Springer, 2006.

[8] A. Bauer, M. Leucker, and C. Schallhart. The good, the bad, and the ugly, but how ugly is ugly? In *Proceedings of RV*, volume 4839 of *Lecture Notes in Computer Science*, pages 126–138. Springer, 2007.

[9] R. Bellman. A Markovian decision process. *Journal of Mathematics and Mechanics*, 6:679–684, 1957.

[10] A. Biere, A. Cimatti, E. Clarke, and Y. Zhu. Symbolic model checking without BDDs. In *Proceedings of TACAS*, volume 1579 of *Lecture Notes in Computer Science*, pages 193–207. Springer, 1999.

[11] G. Birkhoff. *Lattice Theory (2nd edition)*. American Mathematical Society, 1948.

[12] G. Bruns and P. Godefroid. Model checking with multi-valued logics. In *ICALP*, pages 281–293, 2004.

[13] N. Bulling, J. Dix, and W. Jamroga. Model checking logics of strategic ability: Complexity. In M. Dastani, K. Hindriks, and J.-J. Meyer, editors, *Specification and Verification of Multi-Agent Systems*, pages 125–159. Springer, 2010.

[14] N. Bulling and W. Jamroga. What agents can probably enforce. *Fundamenta Informaticae*, 93(1-3):81–96, 2009.

[15] N. Bulling and W. Jamroga. Comparing variants of strategic ability: How uncertainty and memory influence general properties of games. *Journal of Autonomous Agents and Multi-Agent Systems*, 28(3):474–518, 2014.

[16] S. Busard, C. Pecheur, H. Qu, and F. Raimondi. Improving the model checking of strategies under partial observability and fairness constraints. In *Formal Methods and Software Engineering*, volume 8829 of *Lecture Notes in Computer Science*, pages 27–42. 2014.

[17] P. Cermak, A. Lomuscio, F. Mogavero, and A. Murano. MCMAS-SLK: A model checker for the verification of strategy logic specifications. In *Proc. of CAV'14*, volume 8559 of *LNCS*, pages 525–532. Springer-Verlag, 2014.

[18] T. Chen, V. Forejt, M. Kwiatkowska, D. Parker, and A. Simaitis. PRISM-games: A model checker for stochastic multi-player games. In *Proceedings of TACAS*, volume 7795 of *LNCS*, pages 185–191. Springer, 2013.

[19] B. A. Davey and H. A. Priestley. *Introduction to Lattices and Order*. Cambridge University Press, 1990.

[20] L. de Alfaro, M. Faella, T. Henzinger, R. Majumdar, and M. Stoelinga. Model checking discounted temporal properties. *Theoretical Computer Science*, 345:139–170, 2005.

[21] C. Dima and F. Tiplea. Model-checking ATL under imperfect information and perfect recall semantics is undecidable. *CoRR*, abs/1102.4225, 2011.

[22] M. Fitting. Many-valued modal logics. *Fundamenta Informaticae*, 15(3-4):335–350, 1991.

[23] M. Fitting. Many-valued modal logics II. *Fundamenta Informaticae*, 17:55–73, 1992.

[24] P. Godefroid and R. Jagadeesan. Automatic abstraction using generalized model checking. In *Proceedings of CAV*, volume 2404 of *Lecture Notes in Computer Science*, pages 137–150. Springer, 2002.

[25] P. Godefroid and R. Jagadeesan. On the expressiveness of 3-valued models. In *Proceedings of VMCAI'03*, volume 2575 of *LNCS*, pages 206–222. Springer-Verlag, 2003.

[26] A. Gurfinkel and M. Chechik. Multi-valued model checking via classical model checking. In *Proceedings of CONCUR*, volume 2761 of *LNCS*, pages 266–280. Springer-Verlag, 2003.

[27] X. Huang and R. van der Meyden. Symbolic model checking episte- mic strategy logic. In *Proceedings of AAAI*, pages 1426–1432, 2014.

[28] M. Huth, R. Jagadeesan, and D. A. Schmidt. A domain equation for refinement of partial systems. *Mathematical Structures in Computer Science*, 14:469–505, 2004.

[29] M. Huth and M. Z. Kwiatkowska. Quantitative analysis and model checking. In *Logic in Computer Science*, pages 111–122, 1997.

[30] M. Huth and S. Pradhan. Consistent partial model checking. In *Proc. of the Workshop on Domains VI*, volume 73 of *ENTCS*, pages 45–85. Elsevier, 2004.

[31] W. Jamroga. Some remarks on alternating temporal epistemic logic. In B. Dunin-Keplicz and R. Verbrugge, editors, *Proceedings of FAMAS*, pages 133–140, 2003.

[32] W. Jamroga. A temporal logic for Markov chains. In *Proceedings of AAMAS'08*, pages 697–704, 2008.

[33] W. Jamroga. A temporal logic for stochastic multi-agent systems. In *Proceedings of PRIMA'08*, volume 5357 of *LNCS*, pages 239–250, 2008.

[34] W. Jamroga and T. Ågotnes. Constructive knowledge: What agents can achieve under incomplete information. *Journal of Applied Non-Classical Logics*, 17(4):423–475, 2007.

[35] W. Jamroga and J. Dix. Model checking abilities of agents: A closer look. *Theory of Computing Systems*, 42(3):366–410, 2008.

[36] W. Jamroga and W. van der Hoek. Agents that know how to play. *Fundamenta Informaticae*, 63(2–3):185–219, 2004.

[37] B. Konikowska and W. Penczek. Reducing model checking from multi-valued CTL* to CTL*. In *Proceedings CONCUR*, volume 2421 of *LNCS*, pages 226–239. Springer-Verlag, 2002.

[38] B. Konikowska and W. Penczek. Model checking for multi-valued computation tree logics. In M. Fitting and E. Orłowska, editors, *Beyond Two: Theory and Applications of Multiple Valued Logic*, pages 193–210. Physica-Verlag, 2003.

[39] B. Konikowska and W. Penczek. Model checking of multivalued logic of knowledge and time. In *Proceedings of AAMAS*, pages 169–176. ACM, 2006.

[40] M. Kwiatkowska, G. Norman, and D. Parker. PRISM: probabilistic symbolic model checker. In *Proceedings of TOOLS*, volume 2324 of *Lecture Notes in Computer Science*, pages 200–204. Springer, 2002.

[41] A. Lluch-Lafuente and U. Montanari. Quantitative μ-calculus and CTL based on constraint semirings. *Electr. Notes Theor. Comput. Sci.*, 112:37–59, 2005.

[42] A. Lomuscio and J. Michaliszyn. An abstraction technique for the verification of multi-agent systems against ATL specifications. In *Proceedings of KR*. AAAI Press, 2014.

[43] A. Lomuscio and J. Michaliszyn. Verifying multi-agent systems by model checking three-valued abstractions. In *Proc. of the 2015 Inter. Conf. on Autonomous Agents and Multiagent Systems, (AAMAS 2015)*, pages 189–198, 2015.

[44] J. Maluszynski and A. Szalas. Logical foundations and complexity of 4QL, a query language with unrestricted negation. *Journal of Applied Non-Classical Logics*, 21(2):211–232, 2011.

[45] J. Maluszynski and A. Szalas. Partiality and inconsistency in agents' belief bases. In *Proceedings of KES-AMSTA*, volume 252 of *Frontiers in Artificial Intelligence and Applications*, pages 3–17. IOS Press, 2013.

[46] H. Pan, Y. Li, Y. Cao, and Z. Ma. Model checking Computation Tree Logic over finite lattices. *TCS*, to appear, 2015.

[47] W. Penczek and A. Lomuscio. Verifying epistemic properties of multi-agent systems via bounded model checking. In *Proceedings of AAMAS'03*, pages 209–216, New York, NY, USA, 2003. ACM Press.

[48] J. Pilecki, M. Bednarczyk, and W. Jamroga. Synthesis and verification of uniform strategies for multi-agent systems. In *Proceedings of the 15th Workshop on Computational Logic in Multi-Agent Systems CLIMA XV*, volume 8624 of *LNCS*, pages 166–182. Springer, 2014.

[49] H. Schnoor. Strategic planning for probabilistic games with incomplete information. In *Proceedings of AAMAS'10*, pages 1057–1064, 2010.

[50] P. Y. Schobbens. Alternating-time logic with imperfect recall. *Electr. Notes in Theoretical Computer Science*, 85(2):82–93, 2004.

[51] S. Shoham and O. Grumberg. Multi-valued model checking games. *J. Comput. Syst. Sci.*, 78(2):414–429, 2012.

Automatic Verification of Multi-Agent Systems in Parameterised Grid-Environments

Benjamin Aminof
Technische Universität Wien, Austria
benj@forsyte.at

Aniello Murano, Sasha Rubin
Università di Napoli Federico II, Italy
aniello.murano@unina.it
sasharubin@unina.it

Florian Zuleger
Technische Universität Wien, Austria
zuleger@forsyte.at

ABSTRACT

We present a framework for modeling and analysing multiple mobile agents on grid-environments such as finite mazes and labyrinths. Agents are modeled as automata, and the grid-environments are parameterised by their size and the relative positions of the obstacles. We study the verification problem, i.e., whether given agents complete a given task on a given (possibly infinite) set of grid-environments. We identify restrictions on the agents and on the environments for which the verification problem is decidable (and in PSPACE). These assumptions are: i) there are a bounded number of obstacles, and ii) the agents are not allowed to issue commands like "increase my x-coordinate by 1" but can only issue commands that change their relative positions, e.g., "increase my x-coordinate until I go past this wall".

We prove PSPACE-hardness already for the verification problem of a single agent on singleton parameterised environments with no obstacles. It is therefore remarkable that the PSPACE-upper bound also holds for the verification problem with multiple agents, parameterised environments and multiple obstacles. We prove that weakening either of restrictions i) or ii) results in undecidability. The importance of this work is that it is the first to give a sound and complete decision procedure for the verification problem on parameterised grid-like environments. Previous work either involved only a single grid, restricted the scheduling of the agents, or excluded grids altogether.

General Terms

Theory, Verification

Keywords

Computational Models; Autonomous Mobile Agents; Distributed Robot Systems; Grids; Parameterised Verification

1. INTRODUCTION

Physical multiagent systems are designed to move in space. Thus 2D or 3D space, or their abstractions into grids [41, 7, 25, 26, 3], are the canonical environments for modeling multiagent systems. In some cases, e.g., if the environment is too dangerous or expensive to be reached by humans, we may assume that agents initially only have partial information about the environment. For instance, they may not know the exact size of the space or the extent of the obstacles, but they may know the relative positions of obstacles. Thus, agents should be designed so that they operate correctly on all possible grids that are consistent with their information [44, 43, 7, 31, 19, 25, 3]. In this paper we study the verification problem for such multiagent systems that have partial information about the environment.

Model checking is one of the main paradigms for automatic verification: the system is modeled as a finite structure M, the specification is expressed as a formula ϕ in a suitable logical formalism, and a model checking algorithm is used to verify if the structure M satisfies the formula ϕ [13]. The main obstacle to using this paradigm in our setting is that, since the environment is not completely-known, we have to model check many (potentially infinitely many) structures M. There are two main approaches to overcoming this problem, abstraction [13] and parameterised model-checking [6]. We pursue the second approach.

Motivating Scenario: Navigating Manhattan. Suppose you are arrive at Grand Central Station (GCS) in midtown Manhattan and want to get to a certain landmark, say Carnegie Hall (CH), by walking along the streets and avenues. Perhaps you already know (because you have a crude map drawn on a piece of paper) the relative positions of some of the major landmarks,[1] e.g., Times Square (TS) is west of GCS, somewhere between TS and GCS is a point, North of which is the Museum of Modern Art (MOMA), and CH is North of MOMA. Can you use this information to reach CH? Any algorithm that you use to navigate will probably have primitives of the form "walk east until you reach landmark X", or "walk east for a while, and stop at some point to look at your map again". Now, suppose you have a generic algorithm for navigating, given the relative positions of landmarks. Is your algorithm always guaranteed to succeed? This is the parameterised verification problem. It is parameterised because you do not want to test your algorithm only on this particular part of Manhattan, but on all, potentially infinitely many, such environments.

We believe that there are many scenarios of multi-agent systems where navigating using exact positioning is not possible or desirable. On the one hand, precise positioning requires complicated hardware (such as GPS receivers, servo

Appears in: *Proceedings of the 15th International Conference on Autonomous Agents and Multiagent Systems (AAMAS 2016), J. Thangarajah, K. Tuyls, C. Jonker, S. Marsella (eds.), May 9–13, 2016, Singapore.*

[1]Even if one has a map which is to scale, one probably does not navigate by measuring or calculating the distance one travels.

mechanisms, etc.), and on the other hand, even if the agent knows its exact location, many times it does not have this information for other objects in the environment, e.g., if a complete to-scale map of the environment is not available, and only a partial schematic exists (such as a "map" drawn on a napkin), or if there is no map at all.

Aims and Contributions. In order to capture the motivating example above, as well as many other scenarios, the aim of this work is to provide a formal framework for reasoning mathematically and computationally about multiple mobile-agents in grid-environments, having some tasks to perform. We model agents as finite-state machines that walk on grids containing obstructions. The agents can move along the axes, e.g., in two dimensions they can move horizontally and vertically but not diagonally. Agents maintain a fixed number of beacons which they can place on the grid to remember positions they have been to, and can be used for navigation or coordination with other agents. Grid-environments are parameterised by their size and the relative positions of the obstacles on the grid. Tasks are formalised in a suitable linear-time logic that extends LTL by adding the ability to talk about the relative positions of the agents and obstacles at different points in time. In particular, it can express tasks like gathering, border patrol, and line-formation. Agents move asynchronously according to an optional scheduling policy; this is motivated by the assumption that agents have no common notion of time since they have different internal clocks [40, 2, 6].

We prove that the verification problem is decidable (and in PSPACE) under two restrictions: i) there is a bounded number of obstacles, and ii) the agents are not allowed to issue commands like "increase my x-coordinate by 1" but can only issue commands that change their relative positions, e.g., "increase my x-coordinate until I go past this wall". We prove PSPACE-hardness already for the verification problem of a single agent on singleton parameterised environments with no obstacles and no beacons. We therefore find it remarkable that the PSPACE-upper bound also holds for the verification problem with multiple agents, beacons, parameterised environments and multiple obstacles.

In stark contrast, we prove that verification is undecidable, even for very simple tasks (such as reachability), if either of these two conditions is relaxed. E.g., even on empty grids, thus i) holds, if agents can issue commands with absolute distances then verification is undecidable; and, if ii) holds, but there is no bound on the number of obstacles, then verification is undecidable even on simple "Avenues-and-Street" grids.[2]

The importance of this work is that it is the first to give a sound and complete decision procedure for the verification problem on parameterised grid-like environments. Previous work either involved abstractions [37], only a single environment [36], parameterised environments but with schedulings that restricted the number of turns [2], or parameterised environments but excluded grids altogether [45]. Thus, completely new ideas are needed.

Our work is based on the insight that the ability to move precisely in a coordinate system results in undecidability, and that methods from formal methods can shed light on weakened agents that still retain the ability of moving relative to other objects. In this way we obtain a powerful new paradigm for modelling multi agent systems.

Related work. The parameterised model-checking problem has been considered in the verification community for models of (typically immobile) processes — see [6] for a survey. On the other hand, the distributed-computing literature consideration of mobile robots (i.e., automata walking on graphs) is mostly mathematical rather than algorithmic, but naturally (and interestingly) provides theorems that are parameterised (in, e.g., the number of robots, the number of internal states of the robots, etc.) [8, 38, 28, 20, 15, 14, 27].

The main tool we exploit for decidability is a spatio temporal logic called constraint LTL that was originally defined for the verification of counter machines [17, 18].

Our paper considers qualitative tasks. In contrast, [43] studies the shortest path problem in a 2D model that bares some similarity to ours: obstacles are non-intersecting rectangles with sides parallel to the axes, and obstacles that are in a straight line of sight can be seen, and also measured.

Our beacons are reminiscent of pebble automata [21, 4] which themselves are related to extensions of first-order logic with transitive closure; we remark that in our model there is no stack-like restriction on the orders that beacons can placed or retrieved, and yet we still achieve decidability.

Our paper considers verification. A related problem is synthesis with partially known environments, also known as generalised planning, which typically considers one dimensional environments [16, 32, 34, 35].

Besides navigation in known environments, the AAMAS community has studied distributed solutions to navigation tasks in unknown environments, and in contrast to our work, most studies were experimentally verified: [33] contains a technique for computationally sophisticated robots to solve the multi-robot coverage task problem using Voronoi partitioning; In [12], computationally and memory limited agents are studied using coalition logic to manage team-formation; in [29], the agents communicate by exchanging messages with a predefined set of other agents, whose task is to reach a goal state in weighted planar graphs where robots discover adjacent nodes to visited nodes; [24] contains a variation of the A^* algorithm for finding optimal paths in partially known graphs, i.e., where robots discover nodes adjacent to visited ones; and the authors of [11], motivated by reducing deployment time, consider intelligent cameras and autonomous robots for a museum guiding service.

2. NOTATION AND BACKGROUND

Notation. Let $\mathbb{N}$ denote the integers, and $\mathbb{N}_0$ be $\mathbb{N} \cup \{0\}$. For $N \in \mathbb{N}$, write $[N]$ for the set $\{1, 2, \ldots, N\}$. Fix an infinite set var of variables (that vary over $\mathbb{N}$). Fix, once and for all, a dimension $D \in \mathbb{N}$ for the grids (e.g., if $D = 1$ then the agents move on a line, if $D = 2$ then they move on planar grids, etc). Write ϵ_i for the D-tuple $(0, \ldots, 0, 1, 0, \ldots, 0)$ that is 0 everywhere except for the ith co-ordinate which is 1. Write $\overline{0}$ for the D-tuple $(0, \ldots, 0)$. Write $\overline{x}[i \leftarrow a]$ for the tuple $\overline{x}$ with the value of the ith co-ordinate replaced by the a, e.g., $(0,0,1)[2 \leftarrow 1]$ is $(0,1,1)$. Throughout, we freely interchange between functional notation $f(i) = b$ and vector notation $(\ldots, b, \ldots)$. For an infinite sequence σ, write σ_i for the ith element of σ.

[2]Moreover, we get undecidability even if the absolute placement of the obstacles is not fixed, e.g., the width of the avenues may vary.

Two-counter Machines. Our undecidability proofs proceed by reducing the halting problem of two counter machines to the verification problem. An *input-free 2-counter machine* (2CM) [42] is a deterministic program manipulating two nonnegative integer counters using commands that can increment a counter by 1, decrement a counter by 1, and check whether a counter is equal to zero. We refer to the "line numbers" of the program code as the "states" of the machine. One of these states is called the *halting state*, and once it is entered the machine *halts*. The *non-halting problem for 2CMs*, which is known to be undecidable [42], is to decide given a 2CM M whether it does not halt.

Constraint linear-temporal logic (C-LTL). Linear temporal logic (LTL) is nowadays a well-established logic for reasoning about reactive systems. We recall the definition of constraint linear-temporal logic (C-LTL) introduced in [18]. C-LTL is a spatio-temporal logic that has been introduced for the verification of constraint automata, a class of automata that can be viewed as abstractions of counter-automata. It is the main tool that allows us to achieve decidability of the verification problem for multi-agent systems on grids.

A *term* t is either an element of $\mathbb{N}_0$ or an expression of the form $\mathsf{O}^i(x)$ ($x \in \mathsf{var}$ and $i \in \mathbb{N}_0$). We identify $\mathsf{O}^0(x)$ with x. An *atomic constraint* R is an expression of the form $t \bowtie t'$ where t, t' are terms and $\bowtie$ is one of $=, <, \equiv^b_a$ ($0 \leq a < b \in \mathbb{N}_0$). Here $=, <$ are interpreted as usual on $\mathbb{N}_0$, and $\equiv^b_a$ is the modulo unary relation, i.e., $\equiv^b_a (x)$ iff $x = a \mod b$. E.g., $\mathsf{O}^2(x) < \mathsf{O}^1(y)$ is an atomic constraint. Informally, it means that the value of x two time steps ahead is less than the value of y one time step ahead. A *constraint* is a Boolean combination of atomic constraints. A *number constraint* is a constraint that only involves elements of $\mathbb{N}_0$ and variables, i.e., no terms of the form $\mathsf{O}^i(x)$ for $i > 0$.

The syntax of C-LTL is given by: $\varphi ::= R \,|\, \neg\varphi \,|\, (\varphi \vee \varphi) \,|\, \mathsf{O}\,\varphi \,|\, \varphi\,\mathsf{U}\,\varphi$ where R is an atomic constraint. A *valuation* is a function $\mathsf{var} \to \mathbb{N}_0$. Models of C-LTL formulas are infinite sequences of valuations, i.e., $\sigma = \sigma_0\sigma_1\ldots$ where each σ_j is a valuation. The semantics of C-LTL follows:

$$
\begin{array}{ll}
(\sigma, i) \models R & \text{iff } \sigma_{i+l}(x) \bowtie \sigma_{i+m}(y) \text{ and} \\
& \quad R = \mathsf{O}^l(x) \bowtie \mathsf{O}^m(y) \\
(\sigma, i) \models \neg\varphi & \text{iff } (\sigma, i) \not\models \varphi \\
(\sigma, i) \models \varphi \vee \psi & \text{iff } (\sigma, i) \models \varphi \text{ or } (\sigma, i) \models \psi \\
(\sigma, i) \models \mathsf{O}\,\varphi & \text{iff } (\sigma, i+1) \models \varphi \\
(\sigma, i) \models \varphi\,\mathsf{U}\,\psi & \text{iff } \exists j \geq i : (\sigma, j) \models \psi \text{ and} \\
& \quad \forall l \in [i, j) : (\sigma, l) \models \varphi
\end{array}
$$

Write $\sigma \models \varphi$ if $(\sigma, 0) \models \varphi$. We use the usual derived operators $\mathsf{F}\,\varphi := \mathsf{true}\,\mathsf{U}\,\varphi$, its dual $\mathsf{G}\,\varphi := \neg\,\mathsf{F}\,\neg\varphi$, and $\varphi_1\,\mathsf{R}\,\varphi_2$ which is the dual of U, i.e., $\neg(\neg\varphi_1\,\mathsf{U}\,\neg\varphi_2)$, as well as the short-hands $\bigwedge$ and $\bigvee$. For example, $\mathsf{G}(x < \mathsf{O}^1(x))$ means that "globally the value of x at the current point of time is smaller than the value of x at the next point of time", which simply means that x is always strictly increasing.

We mention the following important facts about C-LTL, see [18]. First, recall that linear-temporal logic (LTL) has the same syntax as C-LTL except that instead of atomic constraints it has atomic propositions such as p and q; and LTL formulas are interpreted over infinite sequences of sets of atomic propositions. Now, C-LTL generalizes LTL (the idea is to associate to each atom p a unique variable x, and replace p by the constraint $x = 1$ and replace $\neg p$ by the constraint $x = 0$). Second, the satisfiability problem (and thus also the validity problem) for C-LTL (i.e., given a C-LTL formula φ, decide if there exists σ such that $\sigma \models \varphi$) is decidable, and in fact has the same complexity as for LTL, i.e., it is PSPACE-complete.

3. ENVIRONMENTS AND AGENTS

Environments. We model environments as grids of arbitrary, but fixed, dimension containing obstacles whose faces are parallel to the axes. A (finite or infinite) set of environments of interest is called a *parameterised environment*. Comparisons between points of $\mathbb{N}^D$ are taken point-wise, e.g., $\overline{v} \leq \overline{w}$ means that $v_i \leq w_i$ for $i \leq d$. We describe various subsets of $\mathbb{N}^D$. A *rectangle* is a subset of $\mathbb{N}^D$ of the form $\{\overline{a} \in \mathbb{N}^D : \overline{v} \leq \overline{a} \leq \overline{w}\}$, where $\overline{v} \leq \overline{w} \in \mathbb{N}^D$. The points $\overline{v}$ and $\overline{w}$ are called the *SW- and NE-corners* of the rectangle, respectively.[3] The *interior* of a rectangle R, whose SW and NE corners are $\overline{v}$ and $\overline{w}$, is the set $R^{int} := \{\overline{a} \in \mathbb{N}^D : \overline{v} < \overline{a} < \overline{w}\}$.

A *K-obstruction* $M = \langle M_1, \ldots, M_k \rangle$ is a tuple of K many rectangles. Given $L \in \mathbb{N}$, and a K-obstruction M such that all rectangles in M are contained in $[L]^D$, the (L, M)-*environment* is the graph $G = (V, E)$ whose vertex set $V = [L]^D \backslash (\bigcup_i M^{int})$ (i.e., it is the rectangle with corners $(0, \ldots, 0)$ and $(L, \ldots, L)$, and the interiors of the rectangles in M removed), and whose edge relation $E \subset V \times V$ consists of pairs $(\overline{v}, \overline{w})$ such that for some i we have $|v_i - w_i| = 1$ and for $j \neq i$ we have $v_i = w_i$ (i.e., horizontally- or vertically-adjacent vertices are joined with an edge). Environments are also called finite labyrinths [30]. A *parameterised environment* is some finite or infinite set of environments.

Since only the interiors of the obstructing rectangles are removed, agents are allowed to move along the "walls" of an obstacle. Observe that this has the effect that if, for example, two rectangles (or a rectangle and a boundary of the grid) have a common edge/face, agents can still walk between them "along the adjoining wall". If one wants to ensure, that agents cannot walk between two rectangles, one can specify that the rectangles overlap. We add that overlapping rectangles can be used to build obstacles of different shapes than rectangles. For example, one can build a non-rectangular obstacle such as an "L" by using two rectangles and specifying that they have the same SW-corner, and that one rectangle is thinner and higher and the other rectangle is broader and more shallow. We finally add, that if one wants to remove the points common to a rectangle and a boundary of the grid[4] this could be accomplished by adding a second type of rectangle with the desired behaviour. For ease of exposition we refrain from doing so.

Agents. Agents are modeled as finite-state machines that can move along the axes of the grid. E.g., in a 2-dimensional grid, each single move is in direction north, south, east or west, but not diagonally. More formally, an agent A is tuple (Q, I, δ) where Q is a finite set of *states* (we usually assume

[3]Note that even though our grids are not necessarily 2-dimensional this is perhaps the most common case, and we find it assists in imagining things if we use 2-dimensional terms like "NE".

[4]This can be used also to simulate a grid with sides of different length by positioning suitable obstacles along the boundaries.

w.l.o.g. that $Q = [|Q|]$); $I \subseteq Q$ is a set of *initial states*; $\delta \subset Q \times \text{GC} \times Q$ is a finite *transition relation*. Elements of GC are called *guarded commands* and are of the form $(d, guard)$ where $d \in [D]$ is the axis along which the agent should move, and *guard* is a condition specifying some restriction that the path taken by the agent during this move must satisfy for the move to be possible. For example, the guard may specify that the agent moves exactly one step in the positive direction of the axis. There are many possible definitions for the types of guards that can be used, and these choices determine the "power" the agents have, and we will consider a few possible definitions of GC in later sections. In all cases, we assume that the guard can test whether the agent is at a boundary of the grid. Observe that we implicitly assume[5] that i) the path taken by an agent in a single command does not collide with any other agent (in more detail, an agent may start and end in the same position as another agent, but it may not "pass-through" an agent in a single move); and ii) the path taken does not use positions occupied by an obstruction. Note that the guard may be such that it does not fully specify the end position of a move, in which case the system nondeterministically chooses it (in a way which satisfies the guard).

4. UNDECIDABILITY RESULTS

In this section we give two simple undecidability results that direct our choice of model for agents in parameterized grid environments, presented in the next section.

A common assumption is that agents have the ability to exactly know and/or control their position [41, 27, 38, 39, 36]. This assumption abstracts real-world situations of agents that, for example, are equipped with a global positioning system (GPS). Unfortunately, as demonstrated by the following theorem, it is very easy to show that making this assumption leads to undecidability of the verification problem with respect to even the simplest tasks and parameterized grid environments. It is worth noting that this assumption can be made, without leading to undecidability, in many cases where the environments of interest are not grids, e.g., environments with bounded tree-width [45, 2].

Say that an agent has *precise positioning* if GC contains (directly or indirectly) commands of the form $(d, x_d = x'_d + j)$, with $j \in \{0, -1, 1\}$, where x_d, x'_d are the positions of the agent along the d axis at the start and end of the move, and guards that allow the agent to test its position, in particular whether it is on the bottom or left boundary of the grid.

THEOREM 1. *The following problem is undecidable: given a single agent with precise positioning, and a state h of the agent, verify that for all obstacle-free finite 2-dimensional grids no run of the agent ever enters state h.*

PROOF. The proof is by reduction from the non-halting problem of 2-counter machines. Given a 2CM M, we build an agent A that has the same states as the 2CM plus an additional `overflow` state. The agent simulates the 2CM by using its position (x, y) to encode a configuration of M where the first counter has value x and the second counter has value y. The agent begins by going to the origin of the grid (south as far as possible then west as far as possible). Incrementing (resp. decrementing) a counter is done by simply moving one step in the correct direction. A test for zero amounts to the agent checking that it has collided with the bottom or left boundary of the grid. If the agent wants to go right or up (to simulate an increment), but hits the boundary, it enters the special `overflow` state and discontinues the simulation.

It is easy to see that, on an $L \times L$ grid, the agent can simulate any prefix of the computation of the 2CM in which the values of both counters never go above n. Thus, M does not halt iff, for all $L \in \mathbb{N}$ the agent A doesn't enter the halting state in the $L \times L$ grid. □

Observe that it is simple to modify Theorem 1 and obtain that, if one wishes to consider grids of unbounded size, verifying any non-trivial task for an agent with precise positioning is undecidable. Hence, if we wish to be able to automatically verify that the agent performs its task on a families of grids of unbounded size we must limit the agent's ability to precisely control/know its location.

In our quest for a model for describing agents in parameterized grid environments we are motivated by the example from the introduction of a person navigating in an unknown city using a schematic map, or instructions from a GPS unit. Note that one is usually *not* using the precise positioning information available to the GPS, but one is simply following instructions such as "turn left at the next corner". All that is needed to follow such an instruction is the ability to detect the next corner. Let us consider then a model for the agent where the guarded command can specify a guard that expresses (directly or indirectly) that the end position $\overline{x}'$ of the move is a vertex of some obstacle in the environment, and no point strictly between the start point and the end point is a vertex of an obstacle.[6] This is arguably a very basic way of detecting a corner, as one is doing it "by feel" (reminiscent of how a blind person uses a white cane). We call agents with this ability agents with *next corner detection.*

For the following theorem, given $L \in \mathbb{N}$, let the L-regular-city be the 2-dimensional grid environment of length $2L+1$, in which for every $i, j \in \{0, \ldots, L\}$ there is a 1×1 obstacle whose SW corner is located at $(2i, 2j)$.

THEOREM 2. *The following problem is undecidable: given a single agent with next corner detection, and a state h of the agent, verify that for all $L \in \mathbb{N}$, no run of the agent ever enters state h while navigating the L-regular-city.*

PROOF. The proof is very similar to that of Theorem 1. Unlike Theorem 1, we do not assume that the agent has precise positioning, and thus it can not encode the counters of the 2CM directly by its position. However, it can do so indirectly as follows: it encodes the value of the first counter by the number of obstacles that are strictly to the west of it (at the same y coordinate as it is), and the value of the second counter by the number of obstacles that are strictly to the south of it (at the same x coordinate). The main difference with the agent in the proof of Theorem 1, is that incrementing (resp. decrementing) a counter is done by moving to the SW corner of the next obstacle in the correct direction, which takes two moves. For example, if q is an increment of the first counter, the agent moves twice to the next corner to the east: the first move takes it from the SW corner of the current obstacle to its SE corner (and to state

[5]In other words, an instruction can be taken only if these extra conditions are satisfied.

[6]If one wishes, one can further assume that if no such $\overline{x}'$ exists then the agent walks as far as it can.

q'), and the next move takes it to the SW corner of the next obstacle (and the next state of the 2CM).

It follows that, in an L-regular-city, the agent can simulate any prefix of the computation of M in which the counter values don't exceed L. Thus, M does not halt iff, for all $L \in \mathbb{N}$, the agent never enters the halting state of M. □

As was the case with Theorem 1, one can modify the proof above to obtain undecidability for any non-trivial task. The proof goes through unchanged even if the definition of an L-regular-city is modified to allow the obstacles and the gaps between them to have different sizes, as long as the general structure of aligned streets and avenues is maintained.

5. A MODEL OF MAS ON GRIDS

In this section we present a model of multiple agents operating asynchronously in unbounded parameterized grid environments with a bounded number of obstacles. We also define a way to specify the tasks for these agents.

The theorems in the previous section imply that if we want to be able to decide whether our agents achieve their specified tasks on grid environments of unbounded size, and still maintain the agents' ability to detect corners of obstacles, we should disallow the agents from precisely specifying the distance they travel as well as bound the number of obstacles in a parameterized environment. However, we place no bounds on the sizes and positions of the obstacles.

Informally, the guarded commands of the agents do not allow them to specify absolute positions or step sizes, and only allow one to express relative positioning with respect to other objects in the environment. In order to regain some of the power lost by this relative positioning, agents are also allowed to place some *fixed* number of smart markers, called *beacons* (similar to non-directional radio beacons used in air and marine navigation), in the environment. At any point in time, and from any point in the environment, an agent can test whether its position along any of the D axes is smaller, equal, or larger than that of any other agent, corner of an obstacle, or any beacon (of any agent). A beacon can also be remotely retrieved by the agent that owns it (i.e., without going back to it) and deposited at the current location of the agent. Agents are also able to query other agents as to their current local state.

Note that the beacons allow the agents to perform certain operations that would otherwise be impossible with relative positioning, e.g., such as marking a position an agent can later return precisely to, or to draw a virtual line in the town square such that the agents later gather in the square with half of them on each side of the line. The beacons can be implemented, for example, by making the following (limited) use of a GPS system and memory registers: placing a beacon number i of agent j in the current position is *simulated* by j recording, in its i'th register, the current position as indicated by the GPS. Comparing an agent's position to that of the beacon is done by querying the GPS system as to whether some coordinate d of the current location is smaller, larger, or equal, to the value in the corresponding register. Retrieving the beacon is done by simply overwriting the value in the register. Obviously, not all the power of this model may be needed or possible to implement by a real system. For example, our agents can see through walls (I.e., they are in a "smart city" where the corners of each obstacle broadcast radio signals), and one is welcome to not make use of any unnecessary feature (E.g., limit the agents to not see through obstacles).

For the rest of the paper fix the number B of beacons, the number N of agents, and the number K of obstacles.

Variables. We define the following variables (i.e., elements of var), that will be used later to define other important concepts such as guards, runs, etc.:

- *agent variables* $\mathsf{avar} := \{x_{n,d} : n \in [N], d \in [D]\}$;
- *primed agent variables* $\mathsf{avar}' := \{x'_{n,d} : n \in [N], d \in [D]\}$;
- *beacon variables* $\mathsf{bvar} := \{b^j_{n,d} : n \in [N], d \in [D], j \in [B]\}$;
- *primed beacon variables* $\mathsf{bvar}' := \{b'^j_{n,d} : n \in [N], d \in [D], j \in [B]\}$;
- *agent local-state variables* $\mathsf{svar} := \{s_n : n \in [N]\}$;
- *obstruction variables* $\mathsf{ovar} := \{u_{k,d}, v_{k,d} : k \in [K], d \in [D]\}$;
- the *size variable* l, and the *turn variable* $turn$.

The values of each variable have the following meanings. $\overline{x}_n := (x_{n,1}, \ldots, x_{n,d})$, is the current position of agent n, and the primed version $\overline{x}'_n$ is the next position of agent n; the position of the j'th beacon of agent n is $\overline{b}^j_n := (b^j_{n,1}, \ldots, b^j_{n,d})$, and its next position is $\overline{b}'^j_n := (b'^j_{n,1}, \ldots, b'^j_{n,d})$. The value of s_n is the current local state of the nth agent. The variables $\overline{u}_k$ and $\overline{v}_k$ are the SW- and NE-corners of the kth obstacle; l is the length of the grid; and $turn$ is which agent's turn it is (used to define schedules). For simplicity, we assume that the values of l and variables in ovar do not change over time, i.e., that the size of the grid and the positions of obstacles are fixed throughout a run of a system.

Parameterised environments with a fixed number of obstacles. An *environment constraint* is a number constraint ϕ over variables $\mathsf{ovar} \cup \{l\}$. It determines a set of environments $\mathcal{G}_\phi$ as follows. Every (L, M)-environment G with $M = \langle M_1, \ldots, M_K \rangle$ determines a valuation σ_G over $\mathsf{ovar} \cup \{l\}$ as follows: σ_G maps variable l to L, and for each $i \in [K]$, σ_G maps $\overline{u}_i$ (resp. $\overline{v}_i$) to the SW-corners (resp. NE-corner) of the rectangle M_i. Thus, a number constraint ϕ determines the set $\mathcal{G}_\phi$ of environments G such that the valuation σ_G satisfies ϕ. E.g., for $d = 2, K = 1$, and 2-tuples of variables $(u_1, u_2), (v_1, v_2)$ representing the inner rectangle, the constraint $l \geq 10 \wedge \bigwedge_{i=1,2} 0 < u_i < v_i < l$ determines the set of rectangular "race-tracks" of size at least 10.

Note that by constraining the variable l, we may specify environments of a single size (e.g., $l = 4$), a finite set of sizes (e.g., $l = 4 \vee l = 5$ or $l < 10$), or infinitely many sizes (e.g., $l > 10$ or $\equiv^2_0 (l)$).

Agents. Recall from Section 3 that an agent A is tuple (Q, I, δ) where Q is a finite set of states, $I \subseteq Q$ is a set of initial states, and $\delta \subset Q \times \textsc{gc} \times Q$ is a finite transition relation, where the guarded commands $\textsc{gc}$ are of the form $(d, guard)$ where $d \in [D]$. It remains to define the possible values of $guard$. We let $guard$ be any number constraint over $\mathsf{avar} \cup \mathsf{avar}' \cup \mathsf{bvar} \cup \mathsf{bvar}' \cup \mathsf{ovar} \cup \{l\}$. Note that a transition specifies that beacon j of agent n is retrieved and dropped in the new location of the agent by specifying in the guard that $\overline{x}'_n = \overline{b}'^j_n$. An *agent ensemble* is a tuple of agents $\mathcal{A} = \langle A_1, \cdots, A_N\rangle$ (such that all the agents' commands use the same N, K and B).

Configurations, Schedules, Runs. Let $G = (V, E)$ be an (L, M)-environment with K obstacles, and let $\mathcal{A}$ be an agent ensemble. A *configuration* of $\mathcal{A}$ on G is a tuple $c := (loc, locb, state)$, where $loc : [N] \to V$ maps an agent to its location; $locb : [N] \times [B] \to V$ maps a beacon to its location; and $state : [N] \to \cup_j Q_j$, such that $state(j) \in Q_j$ (for $j \in [N]$), maps an agent to its current local state. Say that c is an *initial* configuration if $state(j) \in I_j$ (for $j \in [N]$).

We can think of c as a valuation val_c over variables avar $\cup$ bvar $\cup$ ovar $\cup$ svar that (for $n \in [N], j \in [B], k \in [K]$): maps $\overline{x}_n$ to $loc(n)$, maps $\overline{b}^j_n$ to $locb(n, j)$, maps $\overline{u}_k$ (resp. $\overline{v}_k$) to the SW-corner (resp. NE-corner) of the kth obstruction M_k of the environment G; and maps s_n to $state(n)$. Similarly, if we are given a second configuration c', we can further extend val_c to get a valuation $val_{c,c'}$ that maps $\overline{x}'_n$ to $loc'(n)$ and $\overline{b}'^j_n$ to $locb'(n, j)$.

For configurations $c = (loc, locb, state)$ and $c' = (loc', locb', state')$, and $n \in [N]$, write $c \vdash_n c'$ if agent n can, by taking one transition, change the configuration from c to c'. Formally, $c \vdash_n c'$ if there exists $(q, (d, guard), q') \in \delta_n$ and $\alpha \in \mathbb{Z}$ such that:

1. $state(n) = q$, and $state' = state[n \leftarrow q']$ (i.e., the agent changes state from q to q');
2. $loc' = loc[n \leftarrow loc(n) + \alpha e_d]$ (i.e., the agent moves some distance $\alpha \in \mathbb{Z}$ along the dth axis);
3. For every $m \in [N], j \in B$, either $locb'(m, j) = locb(m, j)$, or $m = n$ and $locb'(m, j) = loc'(n)$; (i.e., the agent can transfer any of its beacons to its new location);
4. $\sigma_{loc,loc'} \models guard$ (i.e., the guard holds);
5. for every $\overline{v} \in \mathbb{N}_0^D$ strictly between $loc(n)$ and $loc'(n)$: $\overline{v} \in V$ (i.e., no obstruction) and $\overline{v} \neq loc(j)$ for all $j \in [N] \setminus \{n\}$ (i.e., no collision).

An *schedule* κ is an element of $[N]^\omega$. A set S of schedulers is called a *scheduler*. A *scheduler constraint* is a C-LTL formula ω over the variable $\{turn\}$. It induces the set of schedules κ such that there exists $\sigma \models \omega$ such that $\sigma_i \models (turn = \kappa_i)$ for all $i \in \mathbb{N}$.[7]

Example 1. *Round-robin of N agents may be expressed as the N-scheduler consisting of the schedules $(\pi(1) \ldots \pi(N))^\omega$ such that π is a bijection of $[N]$. To express this scheduler in* C-LTL *one may use the formula $\bigvee_\pi \mathsf{G} \bigwedge_n (turn = n) \to \mathsf{O}(turn = \pi(\pi^{-1}(n) + 1))$ where the disjunction is over all bijections π of $[N]$.*

Example 2. *Fair scheduling of N agents may be expressed as the set of schedules satisfying $\bigwedge_n \mathsf{G}\,\mathsf{F}(turn = n)$.*

A *run ρ of $\mathcal{A}$ on G according to scheduler S* is an infinite sequence $\rho = \rho_1\rho_2\rho_3 \cdots$ of configurations such that ρ_1 is initial and there exists $\kappa \in S$ such that $\rho_i \vdash_{\kappa_i} \rho_{i+1}$, for all i. The *agent locations of the run* is the sequence $loc(\rho_1)loc(\rho_2)\ldots$, the *beacon locations of the run* is the sequence $locb(\rho_1)locb(\rho_2)\ldots$, and the *states of the run* is the sequence $state(\rho_1)state(\rho_2)\ldots$. To every run $\rho = \rho_1\rho_2\ldots$ we associate $val(\rho)$, which is the sequence of valuations $val_{\rho_1} val_{\rho_2} \ldots$.

[7]It is also possible to define more powerful schedulers by C-LTL formulae over the variables $\{turn\}$ $\cup$ svar $\cup$ avar $\cup$ bvar $\cup$ ovar $\cup$ $\{l\}$. For ease of exposition we refrain from doing so.

Agent Tasks. Agents should achieve some task in their environment. A *task* is a C-LTL formula τ over variables avar $\cup$ svar $\cup$ bvar $\cup$ ovar $\cup$ $\{l\}$. The ensemble $\mathcal{A}$ *achieve the task τ in environment G according to scheduler S* if for all runs ρ of $\mathcal{A}$ on G according to scheduler S, the sequence of valuations $val(\rho)$, satisfies τ. Note that the task may, if one wishes, restrict the initial states and positions of the agents. For example, agents may be required to start at the corners of the grid, etc.

Example 3. *Agents* gather *if eventually they arrive at the same, not previously determined, location [39]. This task can be expressed by the* C-LTL *formula $\mathsf{F} \bigwedge\{x_{n,d} = x_{m,d} : n, m \in [N], d \in [D]\}$.*

Example 4. *The* Line Formation *task requires the set of agents to form a line, an example of a pattern-formation task [25]. This can be expressed by the* C-LTL *formula: $\mathsf{F}\, Line$ where $Line := \bigvee_{d\in[D]} \bigwedge\{x_{n,d} = x_{m,d} : n, m \in [N]\}$. A variation asks that the agents repeatedly form a line, and can be written $\mathsf{G}\,\mathsf{F}\, Lin$.*

The following is inspired by the task of a guard making sure that the doors of all buildings on campus are locked.

Example.

We consider the task of **border patrol** for a **single agent**. This task consists of moving through the grid such that every border, in our encoding *every edge* of *every obstacle*, is traversed at least once by the agent. Below we will give a specification for border patrol and describe a protocol for an agent that achieves border patrol. Our main positive result (Theorem 3) means that one can automatically verify this protocol against this specification for every parameterized grid environment satisfying the constraints of Theorem 3. For ease of exposition, we consider the 2-D setting where all obstacles are disjoint (disjointness can be encoded by a C-LTL-formula which is quadratic in the number of obstacles).

Specification for border patrol. We consider an obstacle described by SW corner (x_1, y_1) and NE (x_2, y_2). For the edge between (x_1, y_1) and (x_1, y_2) (the bottom edge of the rectangle) we can encode by an *eventually formula* the agent arrives at the corner (x_1, y_1) or (x_1, y_2). Then we can describe by an *until formula* that the agent will eventually reach the other corner of the edge while not leaving the edge on the way. Border control is specified by a conjunction of formulae as described above for every edge of every obstacle.

Protocol for border control. We assume that the agent starts at the origin (where the security personnel office is located), i.e., the SW corner of the grid. When the agent is at the left side of the grid it places a beacon on its position. Then the agent moves from the left of the grid to the right of the grid circling around every obstacle encountered on its way. After circling around an obstacle the agent uses the beacon to stay on the horizontal line defined by the coordinates of the beacon. When the agent has arrived at the right hand side of the grid it returns to the beacon. Then the agent moves upwards until it on the same height with the next obstacle, i.e, the agent and the SW corner of the first obstacle in the whole environment whose SW corner is at a larger y coordinate then its current position. The agent repeats this behavior until it reached the NE corner of the grid. This completes the description of the agent. It is interesting to note that the described agent can be implemented by a finite automaton with a single beacon whose size only depends linearly on the number of obstacles.

Observe that in the description above, the agent's move up until aligned with the SW corner of the next obstacle cannot be directly implemented in a model where the agent can only use vision to navigate (since that corner may be obstructed by other obstacles that are horizontally between the agent and that corner), and the example illustrates the power of our model. As noted before, one can obviously limit the agents to not use the full power of the model, and one can come up with border patrol protocols for vision/touch limited agents as well.

6. PARAMETERISED VERIFICATION

We first formalise the parameterised verification problem (PVP) for agents on parameterized grids with a bounded number of obstacles (as defined in the previous section) and show that it is decidable. The PVP depends on formulas for tasks, environments, and schedulers. Recall that $\mathcal{G}_\phi$ is the (possibly infinite) set of environments determined by ϕ, and S_ω is the set of schedules determined by ω.

DEFINITION 1. *The* ***parameterised verification problem of Sliding Robots on Grids****, written* PVP*, is the following decision problem: given an agent ensemble $\mathcal{A}$, a task τ for the agents, an environment constraint ϕ describing a parameterized grid environment, and scheduler constraint ω, decide whether for every $G \in \mathcal{G}_\phi$, the agents $\mathcal{A}$ achieve task τ on environment G according to scheduler S_ω.*

THEOREM 3. *The* PVP *is in* PSPACE.

PROOF. We show this by reducing the PVP to satisfiability of C-LTL which is in PSPACE [18]. I.e., we effectively transform the agent-ensemble $\mathcal{A} = \langle A_1, \ldots, A_N \rangle$, environment constraint ϕ, and scheduler constraint ω, into a C-LTL formula $\psi_{\mathcal{A},\phi,\omega}$ whose models code all, and only, the runs of $\mathcal{A}$ on environments $G \in \mathcal{G}_\phi$ according to the scheduler S_ω. Then we check that the C-LTL formula $\psi_{\mathcal{A},\phi,\omega} \to \tau$ is valid, or equivalently, that $\neg(\psi_{\mathcal{A},\phi,\omega} \to \tau)$ is not satisfiable.

Here are the details of the transformation. Say $A_n = (Q_n, I_n, \delta_n)$, and w.l.o.g. assume, for $n \in [N], j \in Q_n$, that $Q_n = [|Q_n|]$. The formula $\psi_{\mathcal{A},\phi}$ has variables $\mathsf{avar} \cup \mathsf{ovar} \cup \{l\} \cup \{s_i : i \in [N]\} \cup \{turn\}$ and uses constants from the set $\{0, 1, \cdots, \max_n |Q_n|\}$. We first define some helper formulas:

- $In(\overline{x}, \overline{u}, \overline{v})$ is $\bigwedge_d u_d \leq x_d \leq v_d$ (position $\overline{x}$ is within the rectangle determined by $\overline{u}$ and $\overline{v}$);
- $NotObstructed$ is $\bigwedge_n \bigwedge_k \neg In(\overline{x}_n, \overline{u}_k, \overline{v}_k)$ (no agent is inside any rectangle obstruction);
- $Btwn_d(\overline{x}, \overline{y}, \overline{z})$ is $(x_d < y_d < z_d \vee z_d < y_d < x_d) \wedge \bigwedge_{e \neq d} z_e = y_e = x_e$ (position $\overline{y}$ is between positions $\overline{x}$ and $\overline{z}$ and lie parallel to axis d);
- $\mathsf{O}^1(\overline{z})$ is $(\mathsf{O}^1(z_1), \ldots, \mathsf{O}^1(z_n))$.

Define $\psi_{\mathcal{A},\phi,\omega}$ as the conjunction of:

- $\mathsf{G}\, NotObstructed$ (agents are unobstructed);
- $\phi \wedge \mathsf{G}[l = \mathsf{O}^1(l) \wedge \bigwedge_k \overline{u}_k = \mathsf{O}^1(\overline{u}_k) \wedge \overline{v}_k = \mathsf{O}^1(\overline{v}_k)]$ (obstructions satisfy the environment constraint and do not change over time);
- $\bigwedge_n \bigvee_{j \in I_n} s_n = j$ (each agent starts in an initial state);
- $\omega \wedge \mathsf{G} \bigwedge_n (turn \neq n) \to (\overline{x}_n = \mathsf{O}^1(\overline{x}_n) \wedge s_n = \mathsf{O}^1(s_n))$ (agents take turns according to a schedule in ω);
- $\mathsf{G} \bigwedge_n \bigwedge_{i \in B} (turn \neq n) \to (\overline{b}^i_n = \mathsf{O}^1(\overline{b}^i_n))$ (only beacons of the agent whose turn it is can be moved);
- $\bigwedge_{n,j} \mathsf{G}[turn = n \wedge s_n = j \to \bigvee_{t \in \delta_n} Next_t]$ (agents follow their protocols),

where $Next_t$, for t of the form $(j, (d, guard), j')$, is

$$guard' \wedge move \wedge \mathsf{O}^1(s_n) = j' \wedge nocollide \wedge beacon$$

where $guard'$ is $guard$ with every primed agent variable $x'_{m,e}$ (resp. beacon variable $b^i_{m,e}$) is replaced by $\mathsf{O}^1(x_{m,e})$ (resp. $\mathsf{O}^1(b^i_{m,e})$); $move$ is $\bigwedge_{e \neq d} x_{n,e} = \mathsf{O}^1(x_{n,e})$; $nocollide$ is $\bigwedge_{m \neq n} \neg Btwn_d(\overline{x}_n, \overline{x}_m, \mathsf{O}^1(\overline{x}_n))$; and $beacon$ is $\bigwedge_i \overline{b}^i_n \neq \mathsf{O}^1(\overline{b}^i_n) \to \mathsf{O}^1(\overline{b}^i_n) = \mathsf{O}^1(\overline{x}_n)$ (the agent can move a beacon only to its new location).

It is not hard to check that for every sequence σ of valuations, $\sigma \models \psi_{\mathcal{A},\phi,\omega}$ if and only if there exists $G \in \mathcal{G}_\phi$ and a run ρ of $\mathcal{A}$ on G according to scheduler S_ω such that *(i)* $\sigma \restriction \mathsf{avar}$ is equal to $loc(\rho)$; *(ii)* $\sigma \restriction \{s_n : n \in [N]\}$ is equal to $state(\rho)$; *(iii)* $\sigma \restriction \mathsf{ovar} \cup \{l\}$ is a sequence of identical valuations, each satisfying ϕ.

Thus, $\psi_{\mathcal{A},\phi,\omega} \to \tau$ is not valid if and only if there exists a sequence σ satisfying $\psi_{\mathcal{A},\phi,\omega} \wedge \neg\tau$ if and only if there exists $G \in \mathcal{G}_\phi$ and a run ρ of $\mathcal{A}$ on G according to scheduler S_ω such that the sequence $val(\rho)$ of valuations of the run ρ satisfies $\neg\tau$ if and only if the agents $\mathcal{A}$ do not achieve the task τ according to scheduler S_ω on all environments from $\mathcal{G}_\phi$. This completes the proof. □

Before presenting a PSPACE lower-bound for the PVP, we need some definitions and a lemma.

Let AP be a set of atomic propositions, and let $\mathsf{AP}_{ig} := \mathsf{AP} \cup \{ignore\}$, where $ignore$ is a new atomic proposition not in AP. Let $\Sigma := 2^{\mathsf{AP}}$ and $\Sigma_{ig} := 2^{\mathsf{AP}_{ig}}$. Given a word $w' \in \Sigma^\omega_{ig}$, let $sub(w)$ be the word obtained by deleting all letters in w that are not in Σ (i.e., which contain $ignore$).

LEMMA 1. *Let ϕ be an* LTL *formula over atomic propositions* AP. *One can compute in polynomial time an* LTL *formula ϕ' over AP_{ig}, such that for every $w' \in \Sigma^\omega_{ig}$ we have that $w' \models \phi'$ iff $sub(w)$ is infinite and models ϕ.*

PROOF. W.l.o.g., we assume that ϕ is in positive normal form (i.e., negations are pushed to the atoms). The required formula is the conjunction of two formulas: the first requires that $\neg ignore$ holds infinitely often (thus ensuring that if $w' \models \phi'$ then $sub(w)$ is infinite), and the second "simulates" ϕ on the points where $\neg ignore$ holds (and "skipping" the points in which $ignore$ holds). Formally, $\phi' := \widehat{\phi} \wedge \mathsf{G}\,\mathsf{F}(\neg ignore)$, where $\widehat{\phi}$ is constructed by induction on the structure of ϕ as follows:

- if $\phi := t$, where t is an atomic proposition or its negation, then $\widehat{\phi} := ignore\, \mathsf{U}(\neg ignore \wedge t)$;

- if $\phi := \phi_1 \bowtie \phi_2$, where $\bowtie \in \{\vee, \wedge\}$, then $\widehat{\phi} := \widehat{\phi_1} \bowtie \widehat{\phi_2}$;
- if $\phi := \mathsf{O}\,\phi_1$ then $\widehat{\phi} := ignore\,\mathsf{U}(\neg ignore \wedge \mathsf{O}\,\widehat{\phi_1})$;
- if $\phi := \phi_1 \,\mathsf{U}\, \phi_2$ then $\widehat{\phi} := (ignore \vee \widehat{\phi_1})\,\mathsf{U}(\neg ignore \wedge \widehat{\phi_2})$;
- if $\phi := \phi_1 \,\mathsf{R}\, \phi_2$ then $\widehat{\phi} := (\neg ignore \wedge \widehat{\phi_1})\,\mathsf{R}(ignore \vee \widehat{\phi_2})$.

This completes the proof. □

THEOREM 4. PVP *is* PSPACE*-hard already for the case of a single agent on singleton parameterized environments with no obstacles and no beacons.*

PROOF. We reduce the problem of validity of LTL formulas, which is PSPACE-hard, to the PVP. Let ϕ be an LTL formula over the atomic propositions (w.l.o.g.) $\mathsf{AP} := \{1, \ldots, D\}$. Consider the parameterized environment G containing the single D-dimensional grid with sides of length 1 (i.e., the discrete d-dimensional unit hypercube), with no obstacles. Note that every position on this grid is a vector $\overline{x} \in \{0,1\}^D$. Consider a single agent A with two states $\top, \bot$. The transition relation allows the agent, from each state $\top, \bot$, to transition to either $\top, \bot$ while moving in any direction (or staying in the same place).

A configuration c of A on G encodes a set $X \in \Sigma_{ig}$ of atomic propositions in AP_{ig} as follows: $i \in [D]$ is in X iff the i'th coordinate of the location of A is 1, and $ignore \in X$ iff the local state of A is $\bot$. Hence, by the definition of A, for every word $w' \in \Sigma_{ig}^{\omega}$ there is some run of A on G that encodes w', and vice-versa. Also, using the same encoding (of atomic propositions of AP_{ig} as constraints on the location/state of the agent) we can write, with a linear blowup, a task τ that is a C-LTL formula that encodes the LTL formula ϕ' we obtain from ϕ using Lemma 1.

By Lemma 1, ϕ is valid iff ϕ' is valid. By the reasoning above, the later is true iff the output of the PVP is true on the input: agent A, a formula describing the hypercube G, and the task τ (and the unrestricted scheduler true). □

Observe that, in the proof above, the location of the robot encodes the values of all atomic propositions in parallel, which is the reason D dimensions are used. However, we can make do instead with a single dimension if we encode the values in serial. I.e., if we partition the positions (over time) of the robot into blocks of length D, and let the j position inside a block encode the value of the j'th atomic proposition at the time corresponding to the block number. I.e., for $i \in \mathbb{N}_0$, and $1 \leq j \leq D$, the position of the robot at time $iD+j$ encodes the value of atomic proposition number i at time j. By suitably modifying ϕ' and $\widehat{\phi}$ to this new encoding we can deduce that the problem remains PSPACE-hard also in the interesting cases of 2 and 3-dimensional grids.

7. DISCUSSION

Parameterized verification of multi-agent systems is a hard problem, and the case of most interest, i.e., that of 2 and 3-dimensional grids, even more so. Indeed, in [2] it is shown that (for agents with precise positioning) while the problem is decidable for many parameterized environments it is undecidable even for agents working on a 1-D grid with only collision-detection abilities. In this work we gave one way to regain decidability. We have presented a model for describing multiple agents moving in parameterised grid environments of arbitrary size with a fixed number of obstacles of arbitrary sizes. We have shown that relaxing the requirement that agents can not specify exact absolute positioning or step size, or the requirement of having a bounded number of obstacles, results in undecidability of the verification problem of very simple tasks of even a single agent. Our model of agents is very powerful (without becoming undecidable), and it generalises many other models (such as vision and touch based agents).

Many works in the past reason about environments by using all kinds of abstractions into graphs [9, 10, 44, 46]. Our approach avoids such abstractions (except for discretising space) by directly reasoning about the grid environments. We believe that our choice of using C-LTL as a logic for specifying both agents, parameterised environments, and tasks, allows one to encode things in a direct and natural way, and yields an elegant automatic verification algorithm. We draw an analog to the case of timed-automata, which are extremely popular because they provide users with direct and natural modeling formalism. Indeed, timed-automata can be verified by a sound and complete "region abstraction" to finite graphs [1, 22, 23], but working directly with these graphs is not convenient. A similar abstraction possibly exists for our framework, although it is not immediately clear or obvious how to define an abstraction with multiple agents, especially since they can stop "in the middle" of edges, and one can speak of their relative positions. Many forms of abstraction are not sound/complete. Thus, they do not allow one to map the border between decidability and undecidability as we do. Also, because an abstraction "throws away information", it must be tailor-made depending on the property to be verified.

Future Work. As mentioned above, one possible task is to try and come up with a form of "region abstraction" of our framework that is both sound and complete.

It is interesting to note that one can modify Theorem 1 to the case that the agent has access to absolute positioning with some error (i.e., $\pm\epsilon$, as would be provided by a real-world GPS system). However, it is not clear if it can be modified to the case of an agent that has no global positioning but can measure its step size with some error. This suggests that one may come up with a model for such agents that has a decidable parameterised verification problem (with or without relative positioning).

Two other natural directions of future work are the following. First, one can investigate in practice the actual performance of the presented framework by implementing the proposed algorithms. Although the complexity is PSPACE in general, one can hope — as it is with many algorithms in formal verification — that in many natural cases the algorithm may exhibit acceptable performance. Another possible direction is to try to extend this framework to get decidability results (with reasonable complexity) for multi-robot system scenarios that are rich enough to capture protocols found in the distributed computing literature, e.g., [5, 25, 26, 38].

Acknowledgments

B. Aminof and F. Zuleger are supported by the Austrian National Research Network S11403-N23 (RiSE) of FWF and by WWTF through grant ICT12-059. S. Rubin is a Marie Curie fellow of the Istituto Nazionale di Alta Matematica. A. Murano is partially supported by the GNCS 2016 project: Logica, Automi e Giochi per Sistemi Auto-adattivi.

REFERENCES

[1] R. Alur, C. Courcoubetis, and D. L. Dill. Model-checking in dense real-time. *Inf. Comput.*, 104(1):2–34, 1993.

[2] B. Aminof, A. Murano, S. Rubin, and F. Zuleger. Verification of asynchronous mobile-robots in partially-known environments. In *PRIMA*, LNCS 9387, pages 185–200, 2015.

[3] E. M. Barrameda, S. Das, and N. Santoro. Uniform dispersal of asynchronous finite-state mobile robots in presence of holes. In *ALGOSENSORS*, LNCS 8243, pages 228–243, 2013.

[4] M. A. Bender, A. Fernandez, D. Ron, A. Sahai, and S. Vadhan. The power of a pebble: Exploring and mapping directed graphs. *I & C*, 176(1):1–21, 2002.

[5] M. A. Bender and D. K. Slonim. The power of team exploration: Two robots can learn unlabeled directed graphs. Technical report, MIT, 1995.

[6] R. Bloem, S. Jacobs, A. Khalimov, I. Konnov, S. Rubin, H. Veith, and J. Widder. *Decidability of Parameterized Verification*, volume 6 (1) of *Synthesis Lectures on Distributed Computing Theory*. 2015.

[7] A. Blum, P. Raghavan, and B. Schieber. Navigating in unfamiliar geometric terrain. *SIAM J. Comput.*, 26(1):110–137, 1997.

[8] M. Blum and C. Hewitt. Automata on a 2-dimensional tape. *SWAT (FOCS)*, pages 155–160, 1967.

[9] R. Brafman, J. Latombe, Y. Moses, and Y. Shoham. Applications of a logic of knowledge to motion planning under uncertainty. *J.ACM*, 44(5):633–668, 1997.

[10] W. Burgard, M. Moors, C. Stachniss, and F.Schneider. Coordinated multi-robot exploration. *IEEE Transactions on Robotics*, 21(3):376–386, 2005.

[11] A. Canedo-Rodríguez, V. Alvarez-Santos, C. V Regueiro, X. M. Pardo, and R. Iglesias. Multi-agent system for fast deployment of a guide robot in unknown environments. *Journal of Physical Agents*, 6(1):31–41, 2012.

[12] K. Cheng and P. Dasgupta. Coalition game-based distributed coverage of unknown environments by robot swarms. In *AAMAS*, pages 1191–1194, 2008.

[13] E. Clarke, O. Grumberg, and D. Peled. *Model Checking*. MIT, 2002.

[14] R. Cohen, P. Fraigniaud, D. Ilcinkas, A. Korman, and D. Peleg. Label-guided graph exploration by a finite automaton. In *Automata, Languages and Programming*, LNCS 3580, pages 335–346. 2005.

[15] S. Das. Mobile agents in distributed computing: Network exploration. *Bull. EATCS*, 109:54–69, 2013.

[16] G. De Giacomo, P. Felli, F. Patrizi, and S. Sardiña. Two-player game structures for generalized planning and agent composition. In *AAAI*, 2010.

[17] S. Demri and D. D'Souza. An automata-theoretic approach to constraint LTL. *Inform. and Comp.*, 205(3):380 – 415, 2007.

[18] S. Demri and R. Gascon. Verification of qualitative Z constraints. *Theor. Comput. Sci.*, 409(1):24–40, 2008.

[19] A. Dessmark and A. Pelc. Optimal graph exploration without good maps. In *ESA*, LNCS 2461, pages 374–386. Springer, 2002.

[20] K. Diks, P. Fraigniaud, E. Kranakis, and A. Pelc. Tree exploration with little memory. *Journal of Algorithms*, 51(1):38–63, 2004.

[21] J. Engelfriet and H. J. Hoogeboom. Nested pebbles and transitive closure. In *STACS*, pages 477–488, 2006.

[22] M. Faella, S. La Torre, and A. Murano. Dense real-time games. In *LICS*, pages 167–176. IEEE Computer Society, 2002.

[23] M. Faella, S. La Torre, and A. Murano. Automata-theoretic decision of timed games. *Theor. Comput. Sci.*, 515:46–63, 2014.

[24] A. Felner, R. Stern, and S. Kraus. PHA*: performing A* in unknown physical environments. In *AAMAS*, pages 240–247. ACM, 2002.

[25] P. Flocchini, G. Prencipe, and N. Santoro. Computing by mobile robotic sensors. In *Theoretical Aspects of Distributed Computing in Sensor Networks*, EATCS, pages 655–693. 2011.

[26] P. Flocchini, G. Prencipe, and N. Santoro. *Distributed Computing by Oblivious Mobile Robots*. Synthesis Lectures on Distributed Computing Theory. 2012.

[27] P. Fraigniaud, D. Ilcinkas, G. Peer, A. Pelc, and D. Peleg. Graph exploration by a finite automaton. *Theoretical Computer Science*, 345:331–344, 2005.

[28] L. Gasieniec and T. Radzik. Memory efficient anonymous graph exploration. In *Graph-Theoretic Concepts in Computer Science*, LNCS 5344, pages 14–29. Springer, 2008.

[29] A. Gilboa, A. Meisels, and A. Felner. Distributed navigation in an unknown physical environment. In *AAMAS*, pages 553–560, 2006.

[30] F. Hoffmann. One pebble does not suffice to search plane labyrinths. In *Fundamentals of Computation Theory*, LNCS 117, pages 433–444. 1981.

[31] T. Hsiang, E. M. Arkin, M. A. Bender, S. P. Fekete, and J. S. B. Mitchell. Algorithms for rapidly dispersing robot swarms in unknown environments. In *WAFR*, Springer Tracts in Advanced Robotics, vol. 7, pages 77–94. Springer, 2002.

[32] Y. Hu and G. De Giacomo. Generalized planning: Synthesizing plans that work for multiple environments. In *IJCAI*, pages 918–923, 2011.

[33] K. Hungerford, P. Dasgupta, and K. R. Guruprasad. Distributed, complete, multi-robot coverage of initially unknown environments using repartitioning. In *AAMAS*, pages 1453–1454. IFAAMAS, 2014.

[34] A. Khalimov, S. Jacobs, and R. Bloem. PARTY parameterized synthesis of token rings. In *CAV*, LNCS 8044, pages 928–933, 2013.

[35] A. Khalimov, S. Jacobs, and R. Bloem. Towards efficient parameterized synthesis. In *VMCAI*, LNCS 7737, pages 108–127, 2013.

[36] P. Kouvaros and A. Lomuscio. Automatic verification of parameterised multi-agent systems. In *AAMAS*, pages 861–868, 2013.

[37] P. Kouvaros and A. Lomuscio. A counter abstraction technique for the verification of robot swarms. In *AAAI*, pages 2081–2088, 2015.

[38] E. Kranakis, D. Krizanc, and S. Rajsbaum. Mobile agent rendezvous: A survey. In *SIROCCO*, LNCS 4056, pages 1–9, 2006.

[39] E. Kranakis, D. Krizanc, and S. Rajsbaum.

Computing with mobile agents in distributed networks. In *Handbook of Parallel Computing: Models, Algorithms, and Applications. Chapter 8.* 2007.

[40] N. A. Lynch. *Distributed Algorithms.* Morgan Kaufmann, 1996.

[41] D. K. M. Blum. On the power of the compass (or, why mazes are easier to search than graphs). In *FOCS*, pages 132–142, 1978.

[42] M. L. Minsky. *Computation: finite and infinite machines.* Prentice-Hall, Inc., 1967.

[43] C. H. Papadimitriou and M. Yannakakis. Shortest paths without a map. *Theor. Comput. Sci.*, 84(1):127–150, 1991.

[44] N. Rao, S. Kareti, W. Shi, and S. Iyengar. *Robot navigation in unknown terrains: Introductory survey of non-heuristic algorithms.* Jul 1993.

[45] S. Rubin. Parameterised verification of autonomous mobile-agents in static but unknown environments. In *AAMAS*, pages 199–208, 2015.

[46] K. Senthilkumar and K. Bharadwaj. Multi-robot exploration and terrain coverage in an unknown environment. *Robotics and Autonomous Systems*, 60(1):123–132, 2012.

Formal Verification of Opinion Formation in Swarms

Panagiotis Kouvaros
Department of Computing
Imperial College London
p.kouvaros@imperial.ac.uk

Alessio Lomuscio
Department of Computing
Imperial College London
a.lomuscio@imperial.ac.uk

ABSTRACT

We investigate the formal verification of consensus protocols in swarm systems composed of arbitrary many agents. We use templates to define the behaviour of the agents in an opinion dynamics setting and formulate their verification in terms of the associated parameterised model checking problem. We define a finite abstract model that we show to simulate swarms of any size, thereby precisely encoding any concrete instantiation of the swarm. We give an automatic procedure for verifying temporal-epistemic properties of consensus protocols by model checking the associated finite abstract model. We present a toolkit that can be used to generate the abstract model automatically and verify a given protocol by symbolic model checking. We use the toolkit to verify the correctness of majority rule protocols in arbitrary large swarms.

1. INTRODUCTION

Robotic swarm systems have been put forward as a robust alternative to single-robots in a variety of domains, e.g., remote exploration, maintenance of industrial plants, etc. Typically a swarm is a collection of agents running the same simple program. The physical agents in a swarm are often relatively low-powered devices with limited sensing and communication capabilities. Even if their capabilities are limited by physical and computational constraints, their collective ability can be significant. For example, simple protocols can ensure robotic swarms perform flocking behaviour, or other collective properties [3, 28, 29].

Consensus, or opinion formation, protocols [7, 13, 18, 19, 22, 30, 31, 32] are of particular significance in the context of robot swarms since they can be used as the basis for coordination. The aim of a consensus protocol is for the agents in the system to agree on a particular outcome, e.g., which area to move to collectively as a swarm. Before being applied and developed for swarms, they were initially introduced in distributed computing [9, 12] and also used for reasoning about social, economic, and natural sciences problems and scenarios.

In an opinion formation protocol agents maintain a state encoding their present opinion on the issue they need to converge upon. The opinion is associated with an action that an agent may perform. For example, if the agents need to agree on a destination, this may simply be the direction of travel. An agent's opinion is updated at each time step following observations and communication with the agent's peers.

A key issue with opinion formation protocols is to investigate their convergence. In this paper we put forward a formal methodology that can be applied to analyse consensus protocols that follow the majority rule. In these protocols the agents in the system update their opinions simply by considering the opinions of their neighbours and adopting the one that is favoured by the simple majority of these. While this mechanism appears simple, a large number of applications including collective transport [7], task sequencing [23], and the best-of-n decision problem [32] rely on the majority rule or simple variations of it. For example, variations of the rule have been put forward to account for *latency* or *nesting*. In latency models agents do not change their opinion for a time that is proportional to the quality of their current opinions [7]. In nesting models the process of opinion formation only takes place in a nest, where the agents with opinions of better quality spend proportionally more time [32].

The analysis of these systems is normally conducted by means of two techniques. Optimisation techniques can provide assurances of the behaviour of the swarm; these use differential equations on continuous domains and assume an infinite number of agents in the system [30, 31]. In contrast, simulation techniques compute the actual evolution but only for a swarm of a given size [7, 32]. However, an ideal analysis of a swarm should give guarantees of a behaviour of the system irrespective of the number of agents in the system when it is deployed. A key essence of protocol verification is, indeed, that conclusions ought to be drawn independently from or with minimal assumptions on the number of agents in the system.

Parameterised model checking has previously been applied for the analysis of generic swarm systems of an arbitrary number of components [16]. In this paper we extend the methodology put forward in [16] to model consensus protocols following the majority rule. The results that we report indicate that under limited assumptions the methodology here presented can be used to analyse any consensus protocol in this class. We are not aware of other automated model checking techniques that can provide formal guarantees on the outcome of consensus protocols irrespective of the number of agents in the system.

The rest of the paper is organised as follows. In Sec-

Appears in: *Proceedings of the 15th International Conference on Autonomous Agents and Multiagent Systems (AAMAS 2016), J. Thangarajah, K. Tuyls, C. Jonker, S. Marsella (eds.), May 9–13, 2016, Singapore.*

tion 2 we introduce a specialised template-based semantics for consensus protocols in swarm systems, and we present the syntax of the temporal-epistemic language that we will use to analyse the protocols. In Section 3 we introduce a class of abstract models that can be used to reason about the infinitely many instantiations of a given consensus protocol. In Section 4 we present an implementation of the theoretical results in the form of a novel toolkit that we use to validate a majority rule protocol. We conclude in Section 5 by discussing related work.

2. OPINION FORMATION SEMANTICS

In this section we introduce an opinion formation semantics for robotic swarms. In line with the standard treatment of robot swarms, the semantics here introduced accounts for an unbounded collection of behaviourally identical agents [3, 28]. Each agent interacts with its peers through local exchanges, realised by the repeated application of the majority-rule, that enable the swarm to reach consensus on a certain opinion.

In its simplest form, a majority-rule protocol is described as follows [18]. At each time step a team of three randomly picked agents is formed. Each agent can be in one of two states; each state is associated with one of two opinions. The members of a team adopt the opinion held by the majority of the members in team. This process is repeated until consensus is reached on one of the two opinions. Studies have shown that a collective agreement is eventually established on the opinion with the highest initial density [18].

Several extensions to the simple protocol above have been proposed. For example, [7, 19] introduce the concept of *latency*. Latency refers to a period of time in which the agents do not engage in the opinion formation procedure. Specifically, following the adoption of an opinion, an agent enters a latent state from which the agent does not interact with other agents. The time in which the agent remains in the latent state depends on the quality of the recently adopted opinion. As a result, simulation studies indicate that the swarm collectively adopts the opinion characterised by the shortest latency period [7]. For instance, if opinions represent actions, the swarm converges on the action requiring less time to perform. For example, a swarm may decide to take the shortest path to a destination [7, 30], the best site to explore [13, 32], and so forth. In these cases the majority-rule protocol is often used as a decision making mechanism to solve the best-of-n decision problem [22, 32], i.e., the problem of establishing consensus on the opinion with the highest quality among a set of n opinions.

In the rest of this section we introduce a formal semantics for reasoning about the temporal-epistemic properties of opinion formation protocols based on the majority-rule.

2.1 Semantics

We begin by specifying a generic *agent template* modelling the agents in a swarm. The concrete system of n agents is constructed from the template by providing the number $n \geq 1$ of actual agents in the swarm.

The models we define are loosely based on interpreted systems [11] and parameterised interpreted systems [15, 16]. They are, however, specialised and extended to the modelling of opinion formation protocols. The agent template is defined as follows.

DEFINITION 2.1 (AGENT TEMPLATE). *An agent template is a tuple $\mathcal{A} = (O, h, \alpha, t)$, where:*

- *O is a nonempty and finite set of opinions;*
- *$h : O \to \mathbb{N}$ is a mapping from the set of opinions into the set natural numbers, where $h(o)$ represents the quality of opinion o. O and h define a set*
$$L = \{(o, v, l) : o \in O, 0 \leq v \leq \max(h(o) : o \in O), \\ l \in \{\mathit{false}, \mathit{true}\}\}$$
of local states, where each triple (o, v, l) encodes an opinion o, a latent value v, and whether or not the template is into latent state ($l = \mathit{true}$, and $l = \mathit{false}$, respectively);
- *$\alpha \in \mathbb{N}$ is the size of the neighbourhood for the template at any given time step;*
- *$t : L \times O \to L$ is a transition function that returns the next local state given the current local state and the majority opinion held by neighbouring agents.*

Note that a local state is built from an observable component representing an opinion, and a non-observable component associated with a latent value and the latent status. The domain of the latent value depends on the opinions' maximum quality. Intuitively, different behaviours are associated with different opinions. For instance, as we exemplify in Section 4, the latent value can be used to keep track of the time an agent is engaged in the protocol before it goes into latent state; this period of time is proportional to its currently held opinion. For a local state l, we write $\mathit{opinion}(l)$, $\mathit{value}(l)$, and $\mathit{latent}(l)$ to denote the opinion, the latent value, and the latent status, respectively, encoded in l. We assume that whenever $\mathit{latent}(l) = \mathit{false}$ and $t(l, o) = l'$, then $\mathit{opinion}(l') = o$; i.e, at each time step, an agent switches to the majority opinion in its neighbourhood if not in latent state.

Note the special case of the majority rule in which an agent's neighbourhood is equally split among opinions. This is typically resolved by either considering neighbourhoods of an odd number of agents, or by withholding the currently held opinion, or by randomly adopting an opinion [18, 32]. This can be easily added to the framework without altering any of the technical details presented in this paper.

An agent template describes an unbounded family of *concrete opinion formation systems*; each system is obtained by instantiating the template with the actual number of agents in the system. In other words, given $n \geq 1$, the concrete system $\mathcal{S}_{\mathcal{A}}(n)$ is the result of composing precisely n concrete agents participating in the opinion formation system. Each concrete agent is represented in the interpreted systems formalism [11], a standard semantics for multi-agent systems. That is, a concrete agent i is associated with a set of local states L_i, a set of actions Act_i, a protocol P_i that governs which actions may be performed in a given local state, and a transition function t_i that determines the temporal evolution of the agent.

DEFINITION 2.2 (CONCRETE AGENT). *Given an agent template $\mathcal{A} = (O, h, \alpha, t)$ and $n \geq 1$, the concrete agent A_i, with $1 \leq i \leq n$, is a tuple $A_i = (L_i, I_i, Act_i, P_i, t_i)$, where:*

- *$L_i = L$ is the set of local states for agent i;*

- $I_i = \{(o, v, l) : o \in O, v = h(o), l = \mathit{false}\}$ *is the set of initial states for agent* i;
- $Act_i = \{act_o : o \in O\}$ *is the set of actions for agent* i;
- *the local protocol* $P_i : L_i \to \mathcal{P}(Act_i)$ *for agent* i *is defined for each* $l \in L_i$ *as follows:*
  - $P_i(l) = \{act_{opinion(l)}\}$ *if* $latent(l) = \mathit{true}$;
  - $P_i(l) = Act_i$ *if* $latent(l) = \mathit{false}$;
- *the local transition function* $t_i : L_i \times Act_i \to L_i$ *for agent* i *is such that* $t_i(l, act_o) = l'$ *iff* $t(l, o) = l'$.

So, a concrete agent inherits from its template the set of local states and its local transition function. The agent is initially active and it holds an arbitrary opinion. For each opinion o, the agent admits a corresponding action act_o that is enabled by the protocol whenever the agent holds the opinion; intuitively, act_o represents the majority opinion in its neighbourhood upon which the agent acts. Whenever the agent is in latent state, its protocol only enables the action associated with its currently held opinion; i.e, an agent does not engage in the opinion formation protocol when it is in latent state in that it can only update its latent value and status independently of the other agents' opinions.

We now describe the overall system. A global state $g = (l_1, \ldots, l_n)$ is a tuple of local states for all the agents in the system; g describes the configuration of the system at a particular instant of time. Given a global state g, we write $g.i$ for the local state l_i of agent A_i in g. Given an opinion o, we write $\#(g, o)$ to denote the number of agents with opinion o in g. By $\#^{\mathit{false}}(g)$, we mean the number of agents that are not in latent state in g. We use $\#^{\mathit{false}}(g, o)$ to express the number of agents with opinion o that are not in latent state in g, and $\#^{\mathit{true}}(g, o)$ for the number of agents with opinion o that are in latent state in g.

Following the application of the majority rule at a global state g, an agent updates its current opinion to opinion o if there are at least $mj(g)$ agents with opinion o in its neighbourhood, where $mj(g)$ is equal to the following:

$$mj(g) = \left\lceil \frac{\alpha}{|\{o : \exists i.\, opinion(g.i) = o \wedge latent(g.i) = \mathit{false}\}|} \right\rceil$$

The probability $P(g, o)$ that an agent will adopt opinion o when applying the majority rule at state g is calculated as follows:

$$P(g, o) = \sum_{r=mj(g)}^{\min(\alpha, \#^{\mathit{false}}(g,o))} \frac{\binom{\alpha}{r}\binom{\#^{\mathit{false}}(g)-\alpha}{\#^{\mathit{false}}(g,o)-r}}{\binom{\#^{\mathit{false}}(g)}{\#^{\mathit{false}}(g,o)}}$$

We now define the concrete semantics, i.e, the notion of a concrete opinion formation system.

Definition 2.3 (Concrete System). *Given an agent template* $\mathcal{A} = (O, h, \alpha, t)$ *and* $n \geq 1$, *the* concrete opinion formation system *(OFS) with* n *agents is a tuple* $\mathcal{S}_{\mathcal{A}}(n) = (G(n), I(n), R(n), V(n))$, *where:*

- $G(n) \subseteq L_1 \times \ldots \times L_n$ *is the set of global states reachable via* $R(n)$ *from the set of initial global states* $I(n) = I_1 \times \ldots \times I_n$;
- $R(n) \subseteq G(n) \times G(n)$ *is the global transition relation that is defined as* $(g, g') \in R(n)$ *iff the following hold:*
  - *for all* $o \in O$, *we have that*
  $$\#(g', o) = [\#^{\mathit{false}}(g).\, P(g, o)] + \#^{\mathit{true}}(g, o)$$
  where $[x]$ *denotes the nearest integer to* x *plus-minus 1 such that* $\sum_{o \in O} \#(g', o) = n$;
  - *there is a joint action* $(a.1, \ldots, a.n) \in Act_1 \times \ldots \times Act_n$ *such that for all* $1 \leq i \leq n$, *we have that* $t_i(g.i, a.i) = g'.i$;
- $V(n) : G(n) \to \mathcal{P}(AP)$ *is a labelling function for a set* $AP = \{p(o) : o \in O\}$ *of atomic propositions that is defined as follows:* $p(o) \in V(n)(g)$ *iff* $opinion(g.i) = o$ *for every* $1 \leq i \leq n$.

A path is a sequence $\pi = g^0 g^1 g^2 \ldots$ with $(g^i, g^{i+1}) \in R(n)$, for every $i \geq 0$. Given a path π we write $\pi(i)$ for the i-th state in π. The set of all paths originating from a state g is denoted by $\Pi(g)$.

Following the above definition, an agent template generates a family of systems; each system is composed of a different number of agents. The concrete transition relation $R(n)$ is such that whenever $(g, g') \in R(n)$, the density of each opinion o in g' corresponds to the probability that an agent will have said opinion in the next time step. Note that our analysis is not probabilistic, since we do not consider transitions that reflect every possible outcome of a given probability distribution; but it is qualitative in the sense that it aims to establish the correctness of a given protocol w.r.t its average behaviour on an infinite number of rounds. Further, note that $R(n)$ does not explicitly depend on the neighbourhood of each agent. Indeed, we abstract away the spatial position for a robot and, in line with existing literature [7, 18], we assume a random neighbourhood for each agent at any instant of time.

The labelling function assigns an atomic proposition $p(o)$ on a state iff all the agents agree on opinion o in the state. As we explain below, this will enable us to define consensus specifications which can be interpreted on a concrete system.

2.2 Specifications

We express OFSs specifications in ACTLK, the universal fragment of the temporal-epistemic logic CTLK [24]. CTLK has long been used to express temporal-epistemic properties of the agents in a multiagent system. We fix the notation below; we refer to [25] for more details. Given a set *Agents* of agents and a set AP of atomic propositions, ACTLK formulae are defined by the following BNF grammar:

$$\phi ::= p(o) \mid \neg p(o) \mid \phi \wedge \phi \mid \phi \vee \phi \mid AX\phi \mid A(\phi U \phi) \mid A(\phi R \phi) \mid K_{A_i}\phi \mid E_\Gamma \phi \mid C_\Gamma \phi$$

where $p(o) \in AP$, $A_i \in \mathit{Agents}$, and $\Gamma \subseteq \mathit{Agents}$. The epistemic modality $K_{A_i}\phi$ is read as "agent A_i knows that ϕ"; $E_\Gamma\phi$ encodes "every agent in group Γ knows that ϕ"; and $C_\Gamma\phi$ expresses "it is common knowledge in Γ that ϕ" [11]. The temporal modality $AX\phi$ represents "for all paths, ϕ holds at the next step"; $A(\phi U \psi)$ stands for "for all paths, at some point ψ holds and before then ϕ is true along the path"; and $A(\phi R \psi)$ denotes "for all paths, ψ holds along the path up to and including the point when ϕ becomes true in the path". The interpretation of ACTLK formulae on an OFS $\mathcal{S}_{\mathcal{A}}(n)$ is given as usual: the temporal modalities are interpreted by means of the global transition relation [6], and the epistemic modalities are interpreted by using the epistemic possibility relations [11]. The epistemic possibility relation for an agent $A_i \in Agents$ is defined as follows:

$$\sim_{A_i} = \{(g, g') \in G(n) \times G(n) : g.i = g'.i\}.$$

We write $(\mathcal{S}(n), g) \models \phi$ to mean that a formula ϕ is true at state g in $\mathcal{S}_\mathcal{A}(n)$. If $\mathcal{S}_\mathcal{A}(n)$ is clear, then we simplify the notation to $g \models \phi$.

Definition 2.4 (Satisfaction of ACTLK). *Given an OFS $\mathcal{S}_\mathcal{A}(n)$, the satisfaction relation $\models$ is inductively defined as follows:*

$g \models p(o)$	*iff*	$p(o) \in V(n)(g)$ *for any* $p(o) \in AP$;
$g \models \neg p(o)$	*iff*	$g \not\models p(o)$;
$g \models \phi \wedge \psi$	*iff*	$g \models \phi$ *and* $g \models \psi$;
$g \models \phi \vee \psi$	*iff*	$g \models \phi$ *or* $g \models \psi$;
$g \models AX\phi$	*iff*	*for every* $\pi \in \Pi(g)$, *we have that* $\pi(1) \models \phi$;
$g \models A(\phi U \psi)$	*iff*	*for every* $\pi \in \Pi(g)$, *there is* $i \geq 0$ *such that* $\pi(i) \models \psi$ *and* $\pi(j) \models \phi$ *for all* $0 \leq j < i$;
$g \models A(\phi R \psi)$	*iff*	*for every* $\pi \in \Pi(g)$ *and for all* $i \geq 0$, *if* $\pi(j) \not\models \phi$, *for all* $0 \leq j < i$, *then* $\pi(i) \models \psi$;
$g \models K_{A_i}\phi$	*iff*	*for all* $g' \in G(n)$, $g \sim_{A_i} g'$ *implies* $g' \models \phi$;
$g \models E_\Gamma\phi$	*iff*	*for all* $g' \in G(n)$, $g \sim_{E,\Gamma} g'$ *implies* $g' \models \phi$;
$g \models C_\Gamma\phi$	*iff*	*for all* $g' \in G(n)$, $g \sim_{C,\Gamma} g'$ *implies* $g' \models \phi$.

In the definition above, the relation $\sim_{E,\Gamma}$ is defined as the union of the epistemic relations for all the agents in Γ: $E\phi \triangleq \bigcup_{A_i \in \Gamma} \sim_i$, and the relation $\sim_{C,\Gamma}$ is defined as the transitive closure of $\sim_{E,\Gamma}$. An ACTLK formula ϕ is said to be true in $\mathcal{S}_\mathcal{A}(n)$, denoted as $\mathcal{S}_\mathcal{A}(n) \models \phi$, if $(\mathcal{S}_\mathcal{A}(n), g) \models \phi$ for every $g \in I(n)$. The customary abbreviations of *truth* and *falsity* are assumed: $\top \triangleq p(o) \vee \neg p(o)$, $\bot \triangleq p(o) \wedge \neg p(o)$. Further, we define $AF\phi \triangleq A(\top U \phi)$ representing "for all paths, ϕ eventually becomes true", and $AG\phi \triangleq A(\bot R \phi)$ standing for "for all paths, ϕ is globally true".

We now express some specifications of interest. We are interested in verifying whether an OFS will eventually reach consensus on a certain opinion. Observe that consensus ought to be stable, i.e., it should not be violated at future points. This is expressed by the following formula:

$$\phi_1 \triangleq AF \bigvee_{o \in O} AGp(o)$$

Further, a typical requirement of opinion formation protocols is that the swarm will eventually agree on the opinion of the highest quality:

$$\phi_2 \triangleq AFAGp(\boldsymbol{o}),$$

where $\boldsymbol{o}$ denotes an opinion with $h(\boldsymbol{o}) \geq h(o)$ for all $o \in O$. Additionally, we would like to check whether every agent knows the above properties and whether the swarm has common knowledge of the above properties:

$$\phi_3 = E_\Gamma\phi_1 \quad \phi_4 = E_\Gamma\phi_2 \quad \phi_5 = C_\Gamma\phi_1 \quad \phi_6 = C_\Gamma\phi_2$$

where $\Gamma = Agents$. Finally, we are interested in assessing whether it is always the case that individual knowledge of consensus implies group and common knowledge of consensus, as expressed by the following formulae:

$$\phi_7 = AG(K_{A_i}\phi_1 \to E_\Gamma\phi_1) \qquad \phi_8 = AG(K_{A_i}\phi_2 \to E_\Gamma\phi_2)$$
$$\phi_9 = AG(K_{A_i}\phi_1 \to C_\Gamma\phi_1) \qquad \phi_{10} = AG(K_{A_i}\phi_2 \to C_\Gamma\phi_2)$$

where $A_i \in Agents$ and $\Gamma = Agents$. Following the unbounded nature of OFSs, for the rest of the paper we restrict ACTLK to specifications ϕ in which:

1. for each K_{A_i} appearing in ϕ, we have $i = 1$. Thus, the epistemic modalities appearing in a formula ϕ can only refer to agent A_1. Note, however, that ϕ can be read as referring to any agent of any concrete system. Indeed, studies on the inherent symmetry present in systems of homogeneous agents have shown the following [17]: the interpretation of ϕ on a concrete system $\mathcal{S}_\mathcal{A}(n)$ is equivalent to the interpretation of ϕ^i on $\mathcal{S}_\mathcal{A}(n)$, where ϕ^i is obtained from ϕ by replacing each epistemic modality K_{A_1} with K_{A_i}.

2. for each E_Γ and C_Γ appearing in ϕ, Γ denotes the set of all concrete agents in the system on which the modalities are interpreted.

3. PARAMETERISED VERIFICATION FOR OPINION FORMATION SYSTEMS

In this section we put forward a verification procedure for the analysis of OFSs independently of the number of agents in the system. Our technique is based on previous work in the literature aimed to solve the *parameterised model checking problem* [5, 10, 15]; but it is extended and adapted to opinion formation protocols. In the context of OFSs, we define the decision problem as follows.

Definition 3.1 (PMCP). *Given an agent template $\mathcal{A}$ and an ACTLK formula ϕ, the parameterised model checking problem (PMCP) is the decision problem of determining whether the following holds:*

$$\mathcal{S}_\mathcal{A}(n) \models \phi \text{ for every } n \geq \alpha.$$

Obviously the PMCP involves checking an unbounded number of systems. Consequently, the problem cannot by solved by traditional model checking techniques for finite state systems. Indeed, the problem is known to be undecidable in general [2]. However, we observe that any real-world swarm system obeys the *small neighbourhood property* defined below; this enables us not only to show the problem is decidable but also to give a finite abstraction that allows us to solve the PMCP for the case under analysis.

We begin by formulating the small neighbourhood property. Given an agent template $\mathcal{A}$ defined on a neighbourhood size $\alpha \in \mathbb{N}$, we say that an OFS $\mathcal{S}_\mathcal{A}(n)$ satisfies the small neighbourhood property if at each time step the number of agents not in latent state is much greater than the neighbourhood size. By "much greater" we mean that for any given global state g and opinion o, we have that $\left(\frac{\#^{false}(g,o)}{\#^{false}(g)}\right)^\alpha = \left(\frac{\#^{false}(g,o)-\alpha}{\#^{false}(g)-\alpha}\right)^\alpha \pm \epsilon$, for some small constant ϵ. We write $n \gg \alpha$ to denote this. Since swarms are typically made of very large numbers of agents each interacting with very few neighbours, all systems of interest satisfy the small neighbourhood property. Given this, we formally restate the

PMCP defined above as one that assumes small neighbourhoods.

Definition 3.2 (PMCP for small neighbourhoods). *The PMCP for OFSs with small neighbourhoods of size α concerns establishing whether the following holds:*

$$\mathcal{S}_{\mathcal{A}}(n) \models \phi_i \text{ for every } n \gg \alpha.$$

In the following we will assume that the OFSs that we consider obey the small neighbourhood property and present a solution for the PMCP for small neighbourhoods.

3.1 Weighted abstraction

To solve the PMCP we introduce the notion of *weighted abstraction*. By means of a weighted abstraction we build an abstract model that represents every concrete system. An abstract state is a set of pairs of weights and template local states in $\mathbb{R} \times L$; it represents every concrete state in which the ratio of agents in each local state to all the agents approximates the weight associated with the state. Note that every local state that does not appear in an abstract state is assumed to be associated with a weight equal to 0.

We now describe the construction of the abstract model. Given an abstract state γ and an opinion o, we write $\%(\gamma, o)$ to denote the sum of the weights associated with o, i.e, $\%(\gamma, o) = \sum_{(w,l)\in\gamma, opinion(l)=o} w$. By $\%^{false}(\gamma)$, we mean the sum of weights corresponding to local states that have the latent status set to *false*. We use $\%^{false}(\gamma, o)$ to express the sum of weights corresponding to local states that have the latent status set to *false* and have opinion o, and $\%^{true}(\gamma, o)$ for the sum of weights corresponding to local states that have the latent status set to *true* and have opinion o.

A concrete agent in a global state represented by γ updates its current opinion to opinion o if there are at least $\hat{mj}(\gamma)$ agents with opinion o in its neighbourhood, where $\hat{mj}(\gamma)$ is equal to the following:

$$\left\lceil \frac{\alpha}{|\{o : \exists (w,l) \in \gamma \text{ s.t. } opinion(l) = o \wedge latent(l) = false\}|} \right\rceil$$

In the previous section we have defined the probability $P(g, o)$ that a concrete agent in a state g will update its current opinion to opinion o. We now calculate $P(g, o)$ from an abstract state γ that represents g. If g is a state of n agents, then $P(g, o)$ can be expanded as follows:

$$\sum_{r=\hat{mj}(\gamma)}^{\min(\alpha, \#^{false}(g,o))} \binom{\alpha}{r} \frac{\#^{false}(g,o)}{\#^{false}(g)} \frac{\#^{false}(g,o)-1}{\#^{false}(g)-1} \cdots$$
$$\frac{\#^{false}(g,o)-r+1}{\#^{false}(g)-r+1} \frac{n-\#^{false}(g,o)}{\#^{false}(g)-r} \cdots$$
$$\frac{n-\#^{false(g,o)}-\alpha+r+1}{\#^{false}(g)-\alpha+1}$$

From the above and the small neighbourhood assumption it is easy to show that $\hat{P}(\gamma, o) = P(g, o) \pm \epsilon$, where $\hat{P}(\gamma, o)$ is given by the following:

$$\hat{P}(\gamma, o) = \sum_{r=\hat{mj}(\gamma)}^{\alpha} \left(\binom{\alpha}{r} \left(\%^{false}(\gamma, o)\right)^r \right.$$
$$\left. \left(\%^{false}(\gamma) - \%^{false}(\gamma, o)\right)^{\alpha-r} \right)$$

$\hat{P}$ provides a means to represent concrete transitions that are enabled from any concrete state represented by a given abstract state. The following definition makes this precise.

Definition 3.3 (Weighted Abstraction). *Given an agent template $\mathcal{A} = (O, h, \alpha, t)$, assume a finite uniformly discrete set W in the metric space $[0, 1]$. The abstract model is a tuple $\hat{\mathcal{S}_{\mathcal{A}}} = \left(\hat{G}, \hat{I}, \hat{R}, \hat{V}\right)$, where:*

- *$\hat{G} \subseteq \mathcal{P}(W \times L)$ is the set of abstract states;*
- *$\hat{I} = \{X : X = \{(w, (o, h(o), false) : o \in O\}\}$ is the set of initial abstract states such that $\sum_{(w,l)\in X} w = 1$ for each $X \in \hat{I}$.*
- *$\hat{R} \subseteq \hat{G} \times \hat{G}$ is the abstract transition relation that is defined as $(\gamma, \gamma') \in \hat{R}$ iff the following hold:*
  - *for all $o \in O$, we have that*
  $$\%(\gamma', o) = [\%^{false}(\gamma). \hat{P}(\gamma, o)] + \%^{true}(\gamma, o)$$
  where $[x]$ denotes the nearest weight to x such that $\sum_{o\in O} \%(\gamma', o) = 1$;
  - *for every $(w, l) \in \gamma$ there is $(w', l') \in \gamma'$ with $t(l, o') = l'$, where $o' = opinion(l')$;*
  - *for every $(w', l') \in \gamma'$ there is $(w, l) \in \gamma$ with $t(l, o') = l'$, where $o' = opinion(l')$;*
- *$\hat{V} : \hat{G} \to \mathcal{P}(AP)$ is the abstract labelling function defined as $p(o) \in \hat{V}(\gamma)$ iff for all $(w, l) \in \gamma$ we have that $opinion(l) = o$.*

Thus, the set of initial abstract states represents any possible initial density of opinions in a concrete system. The abstract transition relation is such that whenever $(\gamma, \gamma') \in \hat{R}$, the density of each opinion in γ' corresponds to the probability that a concrete agent in a state represented by γ will have said opinion in the next time step. Finally, the abstract labelling function assigns an atomic proposition $p(o)$ on a state iff the opinion o is the only opinion encoded in the state.

While weighted abstraction provides a natural way to interpret temporal formulae built from global atomic propositions, it does not allow for the interpretation of epistemic modalities. This is because the individual agents' behaviours are not encoded in the abstract model. Therefore, although, as we show below, the abstract model can be used to check temporal specifications, the verification of epistemic specifications is problematic. To circumvent this, we perform weighted abstraction on the concrete space modulo one agent. In other words, we compose the abstract model with one concrete agent. In this setting an abstract state is built from a concrete component and an abstract component. The abstract component is an abstract state as given in Definition 3.3; it represents the local states for the agents $A_2, \ldots, A_n$ in a concrete state g with n agents. The concrete component corresponds to the local state of agent A_1 in g. Given an abstract state γ, we write $\gamma.c$ for the concrete component in γ, and $\gamma.\hat{a}$ for the abstract component in γ.

Definition 3.4 (Partial Weighted Abstraction). *Given an agent template $\mathcal{A} = (O, h, \alpha, t)$, the composition of the abstract model with one concrete agent is a tuple $\hat{\mathcal{S}_{\mathcal{A}}}(1) = \left(\hat{G}(1), \hat{I}(1), \hat{R}(1), \hat{V}(1)\right)$ where:*

- $\hat{G}(1) = L_1 \times \hat{G}$;
- $\hat{I}(1) = I_1 \times \hat{I}$;
- $\hat{R}(1) \subseteq \hat{G}(1) \times \hat{G}(1)$ *is defined as* $(\gamma, \gamma') \in \hat{R}(1)$ *iff* $(\gamma.\hat{a}, \gamma'.\hat{a}) \in \hat{R}$ *and* $(\gamma.c, opinion(\gamma'.c)) = \gamma'.c$;
- $\hat{V}(1) : \hat{G}(1) \rightarrow \mathcal{P}(AP)$ *is defined as* $p(o) \in \hat{V}(1)(\gamma)$ *iff* $opinion(\gamma.c) = o$ *and* $p(o) \in \hat{V}(\gamma.\hat{a})$.

Finally, we consider group and common knowledge. Since the abstract model is composed of exactly one agent and a concrete system is composed of arbitrarily many agents, it is easy to see that the group and common knowledge modalities are not necessarily preserved from a concrete system to the abstract model. To alleviate this problem, we abstract the satisfaction relation for $\sim_{E_\Gamma}$ and $\sim_{C_\Gamma}$ as follows.

DEFINITION 3.5 (ABSTRACT $\sim_{\hat{E_\Gamma}}$). *The abstract relation for group knowledge* $\sim_{\hat{E_\Gamma}} \subseteq \hat{G}(1) \times \hat{G}(1)$ *is defined as* $(\gamma, \gamma') \in \sim_{\hat{E_\Gamma}}$ *iff either one of the following holds:*

- $\gamma \sim_{A_1} \gamma'$;
- *there is a template local state* $l \in L$ *such that* $(w, l) \in \gamma$ *and* $(w', l) \in \gamma'$ *for some weights* w, w'.

Intuitively, two abstract states are $\sim_{\hat{E_\Gamma}}$-related iff they have concrete representatives that are $\sim_i$-related for an arbitrary agent A_i.

DEFINITION 3.6 (ABSTRACT $\sim_{\hat{C_\Gamma}}$). *The abstract relation for common knowledge* $\sim_{\hat{C_\Gamma}} \subseteq \hat{G}(1) \times \hat{G}(1)$ *is defined as the transitive closure of* $\sim_{\hat{E_\Gamma}}$.

The abstract satisfaction relation $\models_{ab}$ is defined for group knowledge as $(\hat{\mathcal{S}_\mathcal{A}}, \gamma) \models_{ab} E_\Gamma \phi$ iff for all γ' with $\gamma \sim_{\hat{E_\Gamma}} \gamma'$, we have that $(\hat{\mathcal{S}_\mathcal{A}}, \gamma') \models_{ab} \phi$; for common knowledge it is defined as $(\hat{\mathcal{S}_\mathcal{A}}, \gamma) \models_{ab} C_\Gamma \phi$ iff for all γ' with $\gamma \sim_{\hat{C_\Gamma}} \gamma'$, we have that $(\hat{\mathcal{S}_\mathcal{A}}, \gamma') \models_{ab} \phi$; $\models_{ab}$ is defined for the other cases as in Definition 2.4.

We now establish a correspondence between the concrete systems and the abstract model. Specifically, we show that the abstract model simulates every concrete system. Additionally, we show that there is a concrete system that simulates the abstract model. By means of the former result, the satisfaction of an ACTLK formula on the abstract model entails the satisfaction of the formula on every concrete system. Conversely, by means of both results, the falsification of an ACTLK formula on the abstract model implies the existence of a concrete system that falsifies the formula. Consequently, the PMCP is reduced to checking the abstract model against a given specification. We begin by defining a notion of simulation between a concrete system and the abstract model.

DEFINITION 3.7 (SIMULATION). *A relation* $\mathcal{R} \subseteq G(n) \times \hat{G}(1)$ *is a simulation between a concrete system* $\mathcal{S}_\mathcal{A}(n)$ *and the abstract model* $\hat{\mathcal{S}_\mathcal{A}}(1)$ *if the following conditions hold:*

1. *For every* $g \in I(n)$, *there is a* $\gamma \in \hat{I}(1)$ *with* $(g, \gamma) \in \mathcal{R}$;

Whenever $(g, \gamma) \in \mathcal{R}$, *then*

2. $V(n)(g) = \hat{V}(1)(\gamma)$;
3. *If* $(g, g') \in R(n)$ *for some* $g' \in G(n)$, *then there is a* $\gamma' \in \hat{G}(1)$ *such that* $(\gamma, \gamma') \in \hat{R}(1)$ *and* $(g', \gamma') \in \mathcal{R}$;
4. *If* $g \sim_{A_1} g'$ *for some* $g' \in G(n)$, *then there is a* $\gamma' \in \hat{G}(1)$ *such that* $\gamma \sim_{A_1} \gamma'$ *and* $(g', \gamma') \in \mathcal{R}$.
5. *If* $g \sim_{A_i} g'$ *for some* i *with* $2 \leq i \leq n$ *and some* $g' \in G(n)$, *then there is a* $\gamma' \in \hat{G}(1)$ *such that* $\gamma \sim_{\hat{E_\Gamma}} \gamma'$ *and* $(g', \gamma') \in \mathcal{R}$.

We say that the abstract model $\hat{\mathcal{S}_\mathcal{A}}(1)$ simulates a concrete system $\mathcal{S}_\mathcal{A}(n)$ if there is a simulation relation between $\mathcal{S}_\mathcal{A}(n)$ and $\hat{\mathcal{S}_\mathcal{A}}(1)$. ACTLK formulae are preserved from the abstract model to the concrete system being simulated.

LEMMA 3.8. *Assume that* $\hat{\mathcal{S}_\mathcal{A}}(1)$ *simulates* $\mathcal{S}_\mathcal{A}(n)$. *Then,* $\hat{\mathcal{S}_\mathcal{A}}(1) \models_{ab} \phi$ *implies* $\mathcal{S}_\mathcal{A}(n) \models \phi$, *for any ACTLK formula* ϕ.

PROOF SKETCH. Assume a simulation relation $\mathcal{R}$ between $\mathcal{S}_\mathcal{A}(n)$ and $\hat{\mathcal{S}_\mathcal{A}}(1)$. We show that

$$(g, \gamma) \in \mathcal{R}, \gamma \models_{ab} \phi \text{ implies } g \models \phi$$

by induction on ϕ. $\phi \in AP$: from simulation requirement 2; $\phi = AX\psi$, $\phi = A(\phi U \psi)$, $\phi = A(\phi R \psi)$: from requirement 3 [4]; $\phi = K_{A_1}\phi$: from requirement 4; $\phi = E_\Gamma \psi$: from requirements 4 and 5. Let $\phi = C_\Gamma \psi$ and assume $\gamma \models_{ab} \phi$. We have to show that $g \models \phi$. Let g' with $g \sim_{C_\Gamma} g'$. Then, there is a sequence $g^1 g^2 \ldots g^k$ such that $g = g^1, g' = g^k$ and for all i with $1 \leq i < k$, there is an agent $A_j \in \Gamma$ such that $g^i \sim_{A_j} g^{i+1}$. By requirements 4 and 5, there is sequence $\gamma^1 \gamma^2 \ldots \gamma^k$ such that $\gamma = \gamma^1$ and for all i with $1 \leq i < k$, $\gamma^i \sim_{\hat{E_\Gamma}} \gamma^{i+1}$. Hence, $\gamma \sim_{\hat{C_\Gamma}} \gamma^k$, and therefore $\gamma^k \models_{ab} \psi$. By the inductive hypothesis, $g' \models \psi$, and thus $g \models \phi$.

By the conclusion of the above induction and by simulation requirement 1, the lemma is entailed. □

A simulation relation between the abstract model and a concrete system is defined similarly to Definition 3.7, but by swapping the LHS with the RHS in each of the clauses. We say that a concrete system $\mathcal{S}_\mathcal{A}(n)$ simulates the abstract model $\hat{\mathcal{S}_\mathcal{A}}(1)$ if there is a simulation relation between $\hat{\mathcal{S}_\mathcal{A}}(1)$ and $\mathcal{S}_\mathcal{A}(n)$.

LEMMA 3.9. *Assume that* $\mathcal{S}_\mathcal{A}(n)$ *simulates* $\hat{\mathcal{S}_\mathcal{A}}(1)$. *Then,* $\mathcal{S}_\mathcal{A}(n) \models \phi$ *implies* $\hat{\mathcal{S}_\mathcal{A}}(1) \models_{ab} \phi$, *for any ACTLK formula* ϕ.

PROOF. The proof is similar to the proof of Lemma 3.8. □

A concrete system $\mathcal{S}_\mathcal{A}(n)$ and the abstract model $\hat{\mathcal{S}_\mathcal{A}}(1)$ are said to be simulation equivalent if $\mathcal{S}_\mathcal{A}(n)$ simulates $\hat{\mathcal{S}_\mathcal{A}}(1)$ and $\hat{\mathcal{S}_\mathcal{A}}(1)$ simulates $\mathcal{S}_\mathcal{A}(n)$.

LEMMA 3.10. *Assume that* $\hat{\mathcal{S}_\mathcal{A}}(1)$ *simulates* $\mathcal{S}_\mathcal{A}(n)$ *and* $\mathcal{S}_\mathcal{A}(n)$ *simulates* $\hat{\mathcal{S}_\mathcal{A}}(1)$. *Then,* $\hat{\mathcal{S}_\mathcal{A}}(1) \models_{ab} \phi$ *iff* $\mathcal{S}_\mathcal{A}(n) \models \phi$, *for any ACTLK formula* ϕ.

PROOF. ($\Rightarrow$) Lemma 3.8. ($\Leftarrow$) Lemma 3.9. □

We now show that the abstract model simulates every concrete system, and we prove the existence of a concrete system that simulates the abstract model.

LEMMA 3.11. *Given an agent template $\mathcal{A}$ and an ACTLK formula ϕ, the following hold:*

1. *for all $n \gg \alpha$, $\hat{\mathcal{S}_{\mathcal{A}}}(1)$ simulates $\mathcal{S}_{\mathcal{A}}(n)$;*

2. *there is $n \gg \alpha$ such that $\mathcal{S}_{\mathcal{A}}(n)$ simulates $\hat{\mathcal{S}_{\mathcal{A}}}(1)$.*

PROOF SKETCH.

(1) Assume $n \gg \alpha$. Define a mapping $\delta_n : G(n) \to \hat{G}(1)$ from concrete states to abstract states as follows: $\delta_n(g) = (g.1, X)$, where

$$X = \left\{(w, l) : \exists i. 2 \leq i \leq n, g.i = l \text{ and } w \approx \frac{\#(g, l)}{n}\right\},$$

$w \approx x$ whenever w is the nearest weight to x, and $\#(g, l)$ denotes the number of agent in local state l in g. Assume the relation $\mathcal{R} = \{(g, \gamma) : \delta_n(g) = \gamma\}$. We show that $\mathcal{R}$ is a simulation relation between $\mathcal{S}_{\mathcal{A}}(n)$ and $\hat{\mathcal{S}_{\mathcal{A}}}(1)$. Simulation requirement 1 follows from the definitions of the initial states for the two models. Let $(g, \gamma) \in \mathcal{R}$ be arbitrary. We show simulation requirements 2, 3, 4, 5.

- Requirement 2. From the definition of $\mathcal{R}$.

- Requirement 3. Assume $(g, g') \in R(n)$ for some $g' \in G(n)$. From the small neighbourhood assumption we have that $\hat{P}(\gamma, o) = P(g, o) \pm \epsilon$, for each opinion o. Therefore,

$$\frac{\#(g', o)}{n} \approx [\%^{false}(\gamma). \hat{P}(\gamma, o)] + \%^{true}(\gamma, o)$$

  for each opinion o. That is, the above two expressions have the same nearest weight. The latter entails $(\gamma, \delta_n(g')) \in \hat{R}(1)$. Also, $(g', \delta_n(g')) \in \mathcal{R}$. Therefore the requirement is satisfied.

- Simulation requirement 4. Assume $g \sim_{A_1} g'$ for some $g' \in G(n)$. Let π be a path in $\mathcal{S}_{\mathcal{A}}(n)$ such that $\pi(i) = g$, for some $i \geq 0$. By simulation requirements 1 and 3, there is a path $\hat{\pi}$ in $\hat{\mathcal{S}_{\mathcal{A}}}(1)$ with $\hat{\pi}(i) = \delta_n(\pi(i))$. As such, we have that $\gamma \sim_{A_1} \hat{\pi}(i)$. Consequently the requirement is satisfied.

- Simulation requirement 5. Assume $g \sim_{A_i} g'$ for some i with $2 \leq i \leq n$ and some $g' \in G(n)$. From simulation conditions 1 and 3, $\delta_n(g') \in \hat{G}(1)$. By definition of $\sim_{\hat{E_\Gamma}}$, $\gamma \sim_{\hat{E_\Gamma}} \delta_n(g')$. Obviously, $(g', \delta_n(g')) \in \mathcal{R}$. Hence the requirement is satisfied.

(2) Pick $n \gg \alpha$ such that $\mathcal{S}_{\mathcal{A}}(n)$ admits every initial density of opinions that is represented by the set of abstract initial states. Define $\mathcal{R}$ as above. Then the proof proceeds along the same lines with the proof in (1). □

A consequence of the above is the following.

THEOREM 3.12. *Given an agent template $\mathcal{A}$ and an ACTLK formula ϕ, the following hold:*

1. *$\hat{\mathcal{S}_{\mathcal{A}}}(1) \models \phi$ implies $\forall n \gg \alpha. \mathcal{S}_{\mathcal{A}}(n) \models \phi$.*

2. *$\hat{\mathcal{S}_{\mathcal{A}}}(1) \not\models \phi$ implies $\exists n \gg \alpha. \mathcal{S}_{\mathcal{A}}(n) \not\models \phi$.*

PROOF. **(1)** By (1) of Lemma 3.11 and by Lemma 3.8. **(2)** From Lemma 3.11 there is $n \gg \alpha$ such that $\mathcal{S}_{\mathcal{A}}(n)$ and $\hat{\mathcal{S}_{\mathcal{A}}}(1)$ are simulation equivalent. Therefore the thesis follows from Lemma 3.10. □

Theorem 3.12 is our main theoretical result. The theorem provides a constructive methodology for solving the PMCP by checking the abstract model against a given specification.

4. APPLICATIONS

We implemented the weighted abstraction methodology presented earlier in `MCMAS-OFP`, an experimental toolkit that we built from `MCMAS-P`, an open-source model checker for the verification of unbounded multi-agent systems [15]. We designed the input language for `MCMAS-OFP`, called `ISPL-OFP`, to allow for the semantic structures considered here. The language closely follows the modular structure of an agent template. In particular, a template's declaration includes declarations of the template's opinions and their qualities, its transition function, and its neighbourhood size. Figure 4.1 exemplifies `ISPL-OFP` on the protocol described below.

Given an input description for an agent template, `MCMAS-OFP` constructs the abstract model which it encodes symbolically. The base model-checker `MCMAS` [20] is then called to verify the abstract model against the given specifications. Following this, the user can conclude, as per Theorem 3.12, whether the specifications hold on a swarm of any size that satisfies the small neighbourhood assumption. We refer to [21] for more details.

4.1 A majority rule protocol

To evaluate the approach, we consider a majority rule protocol put forward to solve the best-of-n decision problem [32]. The protocol assumes two opinions where each opinion corresponds to a spatial area (site) associated with certain resources that determine its quality. Upon exploring a site, an agent determines the site's quality. Then the agent returns to the *nest* where it engages in the opinion formation protocol. According to the protocol, the agents can either be in a *dissemination state* or in an *exploration state*. In the former case, the agents move around the nest while maintaining a well-mixed spatial distribution. Additionally, they broadcast their opinions by means of wireless sensors of limited range. The time an agent spends in this state is proportional to the quality of the opinion it currently holds. Before an agent goes into the exploration state, it updates its opinion according to the majority rule. In the exploration state, the agent leaves the nest to explore the site associated with its current opinion. The site is explored for a period of time that is proportional to its quality. Afterwards, the agent returns to the nest.

We encode the above scenario in the formalism of OFSs. We represent the dissemination state by means of template states with the latent status set to *false*, and we express the exploration state by using template states with the latent status set to *true*. The ratio of the qualities for the sites, as well as the neighbourhood size given below correspond to the robot experiments performed in [32]. The agent template $\mathcal{A} = (O, h, \alpha, t)$ is defined as follows: $O = \{A, B\}$, where A, B represent the two sites; $h(A) = 8$, $h(B) = 4$ (thus, site A is twice as good as site B); $\alpha = 25$. Finally, the template transition relation $t : L \times O \to L$ is defined by:

- $t((o, v, \mathit{false}), o') = (o', v - 1, \mathit{false})$ if $v > 0$;
- $t((o, v, \mathit{false}), o') = (o', h(o'), \mathit{true})$ if $v = 0$;
- $t((o, v, \mathit{true}), o) = (o, v - 1, \mathit{true})$ if $v > 0$;
- $t((o, v, \mathit{true}), o) = (o, h(o), \mathit{false})$ if $v = 0$.

So, whenever the template changes its latent status, the latent value is set to the quality of the currently held opinion. It then decreases at each time step until it reaches 0 at

```
Agent Template
 Opinions = {A,B};
 Qualities = {A->8, B->4};
 NeighbourhoodSize = 25;
 Evolution:
  opinion = majority and lvalue = lvalue-1 if
                     lvalue>0 and latent=false;
  opinion = majority and lvalue = 8 and
            latent=true if opinion=A and lvalue=0
            and latent=false;
  opinion = majority and lvalue = 4 and
            latent=true if opinion=B and lvalue=0
            and latent=false;
  lvalue = lvalue-1 if lvalue>0 and latent=true;
  lvalue = 8 and latent = false if opinion=A and
                     lvalue=0 and latent=true;
  lvalue = 4 and latent = false if opinion=B and
                     lvalue=0 and latent=true;
 end Evolution
end Template
```

Figure 1: ISPL-OFP snippet.

which point the template switches its latent status. Thus, the period of time an agent spends in the dissemination (exploration, respectively) state is here modelled by the number of time steps the template is in non-latent (latent, respectively) state.

We used MCMAS-OFP to verify the above protocol against the specifications introduced in Section 2. By means of these results we conclude not only that the protocol reaches a consensus, but it also reaches a consensus on the opinion with the highest quality, namely site A. Additionally, not only every agent knows this, but it is also common knowledge among the swarm that consensus is eventually reached.

The construction of the abstract model and its verification against all formulae took approximately 5 seconds on an Intel Core i7 machine clocked at 3.4 GHz, with 7.7 GiB cache, running 64-bit Fedora 20, kernel 3.16.6. MCMAS-OFP and the ISPL-OFP file encoding the scenario are available at [21].

5. CONCLUSIONS AND RELATED WORK

In this paper we investigated the formal verification of consensus protocols in swarms. We put forward templates to model the behaviour of the agents in an opinion dynamics setting, and we formulated their verification in terms of the associated parameterised model checking problem. While this is undecidable in general, we built a finite abstract model that we showed to simulate any swarm of any size under very permissive conditions. As we proved, the abstract model encodes any concrete instantiation of the swarm and can be used to verify its properties. We presented a toolkit that can be used to generate said abstract model automatically and verify opinion formation protocols. Indeed, we used the toolkit to verify the correctness of a majority rule protocol in swarms.

The key aspect of this work is that it operates at protocol level and not at system level. In other words, we do not just assess a particular system instantiation; but evaluate the whole class of swarm instances following a consensus protocol. We are not aware of other work in the swarm systems literature that is based on parameterised model checking. As stated in the introduction, swarm protocols, including consensus protocols, are typically analysed either via simulation [7, 32] or via optimisation methods [30, 31]. By means of optimisation techniques one can typically evaluate the behaviour of the system with very large number of components; whereas simulation approaches are limited by the size of the population under analysis. Equally, model checking techniques for swarm systems are typically limited by the number of agents in the swarm [1, 8, 14, 27, 26, 33]. In this paper we set out to overcome some of these limitations by providing a first formal, yet completely automatic, approach to the problem. The model we put forward is general enough to model all consensus protocols that follow various forms of the majority rule. While these protocols are normally defined in probabilistic terms, we showed that a purely discrete analysis that merely accounts for the possible evolutions of the system can provide considerable insight in the protocol.

The results here presented build upon recent work in which the foundations of parameterised verification for multi-agent systems were laid out [16]. This paper differs from that work in several key aspects. Firstly, we here investigate concrete protocols and not just arbitrary multi-agent interactions. This requires the definition of novel, specialised models and appropriate templates. Secondly, given the different semantics, the cut-off results presented in [16] cannot be here applied; instead we used an ad-hoc construction of an abstract model to simulate all possible behaviours of the system. Thirdly, while the toolkit we released is based on MCMAS-P and we reuse its routines for parsing the files and performing symbolic model checking operations, the key aspect of the implementation that we presented is its support for the automatic construction of the abstract model. This has correspondences with work in counter-abstraction, including [15], but the technical details of the abstract model are different.

In the future we intend to work on other swarm protocols in order to ascertain whether they can also be analysed by means of parameterised model checking and appropriate abstractions.

6. ACKNOWLEDGMENTS

This research was funded by the EPSRC under grant EP/I00520X/1 and a Doctoral Prize Fellowship.

REFERENCES

[1] B. Aminof, A. Murano, S. Rubin, and F. Zuleger. Verification of asynchronous mobile-robots in partially-known environments. In *PRIMA 2015: Principles and Practice of Multi-Agent Systems*, pages 185–200. Springer, 2015.

[2] K. Apt and D. C. Kozen. Limits for automatic verification of finite-state concurrent systems. *Information Processing Letters*, 22(6):307–309, 1986.

[3] E. Bonabeau, M. Dorigo, and G. Theraulaz. *Swarm intelligence.* Oxford University Press, 1999.

[4] M. C. Browne, E. M. Clarke, and O. Grumberg. Characterizing finite Kripke structures in propositional temporal logic. *Theoretical Computer Science*, 59:115–131, 1988.

[5] E. Clarke, O. Grumberg, and M. Browne. Reasoning about networks with many identical finite state processes. *Information and Computation*, 81(1):13–31, 1989.

[6] E. M. Clarke, O. Grumberg, and D. A. Peled. *Model Checking*. The MIT Press, Cambridge, Massachusetts, 1999.

[7] M. de Oca, , E. Ferrante, A. Scheidler, C. C. Pinciroli, M. Birattari, and M. Dorigo. Majority-rule opinion dynamics with differential latency: a mechanism for self-organized collective decision-making. *Swarm Intelligence*, 5(3-4):305–327, 2011.

[8] C. Dixon, A. Winfield, M. Fisher, and C. Zeng. Towards temporal verification of swarm robotic systems. *Robotics and Autonomous Systems*, 60(11):1429–1441, 2012.

[9] D. Dolev, C. Dwork, and L. Stockmeyer. On the minimal synchronism needed for distributed consensus. *Journal of the ACM (JACM)*, 34(1):77–97, 1987.

[10] E. A. Emerson and K. S. Namjoshi. Automatic verification of parameterized synchronous systems. In *Proceedings of the 8th International Conference one Computer Aided Verification (CAV96)*, volume 1102 of *Lecture Notes in Computer Science*, pages 87–98. Springer, 1996.

[11] R. Fagin, J. Y. Halpern, Y. Moses, and M. Y. Vardi. *Reasoning about Knowledge*. MIT Press, Cambridge, 1995.

[12] M. Fischer, N. Lynch, and M. Paterson. Impossibility of distributed consensus with one faulty process. *Journal of the ACM (JACM)*, 32(2):374–382, 1985.

[13] S. Garnier, J. Gautrais, M. Asadpour, C. Jost, and G. Theraulaz. Self-organized aggregation triggers collective decision making in a group of cockroach-like robots. *Adaptive Behavior*, 17(2):109–133, 2009.

[14] S. Konur, C. Dixon, and M. Fisher. Analysing robot swarm behaviour via probabilistic model checking. *Robotics and Autonomous Systems*, 60(2):199–213, 2012.

[15] P. Kouvaros and A. Lomuscio. A counter abstraction technique for the verification of robot swarms. In *Proceedings of the 29th AAAI Conference on Artificial Intelligence (AAAI15)*, pages 2081–2088. AAAI Press, 2015.

[16] P. Kouvaros and A. Lomuscio. Verifying emergent properties of swarms. In *Proceedings of the 24th International Joint Conference on Artificial Intelligence (IJCAI15)*, pages 1083–1089. AAAI Press, 2015.

[17] P. Kouvaros and A. Lomuscio. Parameterised verification for multi-agent systems. *Artificial Intelligence*, 234:152–189, 2016.

[18] P. Krapivsky and S. Redner. Dynamics of majority rule in two-state interacting spin systems. *Physical Review Letters*, 90(23):238701, 2003.

[19] R. Lambiotte, J. Saramäki, and V. Blondel. Dynamics of latent voters. *Physical Review E*, 79(4):046107, 2009.

[20] A. Lomuscio, H. Qu, and F. Raimondi. MCMAS: A model checker for the verification of multi-agent systems. In *Proceedings of the 21th International Conference on Computer Aided Verification (CAV09)*, volume 5643 of *Lecture Notes in Computer Science*, pages 682–688. Springer, 2009.

[21] MCMAS-OFP. Model Checking Opinion Formation Protocols `http://vas.doc.ic.ac.uk/software/extensions`, 2016.

[22] C. Parker and H. Zhang. Cooperative decision-making in decentralized multiple-robot systems: The best-of-n problem. *IEEE/ASME Transactions on Mechatronics*, 14(2):240–251, 2009.

[23] C. Parker and H. Zhang. Collective unary decision-making by decentralized multiple-robot systems applied to the task-sequencing problem. *Swarm Intelligence*, 4(3):199–220, 2010.

[24] W. Penczek and A. Lomuscio. Verifying epistemic properties of multi-agent systems via bounded model checking. *Fundamenta Informaticae*, 55(2):167–185, 2003.

[25] W. Penczek and A. Lomuscio. Verifying epistemic properties of multi-agent systems via bounded model checking. In *Proceedings of the 2nd International Joint Conference on Autonomous Agents and Multi-agent systems (AAMAS03)*, pages 209–216. IFAAMAS, 2003.

[26] C. R. r, A. Vanderbilt, M. Hinchey, W. Truszkowski, and J. Rash. Properties of a formal method for prediction of emergent behaviors in swarm-based systems. In *Proceedings of the 2nd International Conference on Software Engineering and Formal Methods (SEFM04)*, pages 24–33. IEEE, 2004.

[27] S. Rubin. Parameterised verification of autonomous mobile-agents in static but unknown environments. In *Proceedings of the 14th International Conference on Autonomous Agents and Multiagent Systems (AAMAS15)*, pages 199–208. IFAAMAS, 2015.

[28] E. Şahin. Swarm robotics: From sources of inspiration to domains of application. In *Proceedings of the 2004 international conference on Swarm Robotics (SAB04)*, volume 3342 of *Lecture Notes in Computer Science*, pages 10–20. Springer, 2005.

[29] E. Şahin and A. Winfield. Special issue on swarm robotics. *Swarm Intelligence*, 2(2):69–72, 2008.

[30] A. Scheidler. Dynamics of majority rule with differential latencies. *Physical Review E*, 83(3):031116, 2011.

[31] G. Valentini, H. Hamann, and M. Dorigo. Self-organized collective decision making: The weighted voter model. In *Proceedings of the 14th International Conference on Autonomous Agents and Multiagent Systems*, pages 45–52. IFAAMAS Press, 2014.

[32] G. Valentini, H. Hamann, and M. Dorigo. Efficient decision-making in a self-organizing robot swarm: On the speed versus accuracy trade-off. In *Proceedings of the 14th International Conference on Autonomous Agents and Multiagent Systems*, pages 1305–1314. IFAAMAS Press, 2015.

[33] A. Winfield, J. Sa, M. Fernández-Gago, C. Dixon, and M. Fisher. On formal specification of emergent behaviours in swarm robotic systems. *International journal of advanced robotic systems*, 2(4):363–370, 2005.

Verifying Security Properties in Unbounded Multiagent Systems

Ioana Boureanu
Department of Computing
Imperial College London, UK
i.boureanu@ic.ac.uk

Panagiotis Kouvaros
Department of Computing
Imperial College London, UK
p.kouvaros@ic.ac.uk

Alessio Lomuscio
Department of Computing
Imperial College London, UK
a.lomuscio@ic.ac.uk

ABSTRACT

We study the problem of analysing the security for an unbounded number of concurrent sessions of a cryptographic protocol. Our formal model accounts for an arbitrary number of agents involved in a protocol-exchange which is subverted by a Dolev-Yao attacker. We define the parameterised model checking problem with respect to security requirements expressed in temporal-epistemic logics. We formulate sufficient conditions for solving this problem, by analysing several finite models of the system. We primarily explore authentication and key-establishment as part of a larger class of protocols and security requirements amenable to our methodology. We introduce a tool implementing the technique, and we validate it by verifying the NSPK and ASRPC protocols.

1. INTRODUCTION

Formalisms grounded in the multi-agent systems (MAS) paradigm have made a significant contribution to the development of a wide range of applications, including search and rescue [19], automatic negotiation [13], and security [9]. For the MAS paradigm to continue to drive the sound development of forthcoming topical applications, the underlying MAS formalisms need to evolve to capture and solve the theoretical challenges that arise in these applications.

The "internet of things" (IoT) is an important area of current and future growth, where MAS can play a leading role. In current IoT applications networked objects equipped with sensors and computing capabilities exchange data over the Internet. It is expected that some of these objects will become autonomous and will independently cooperate and negotiate with their peers while representing the needs of a human user or an organisation. Security and privacy aspects of IoT applications remain a concern. Users may not be willing to adopt the technology if the data being exchanged can be directly traced back to them, or tampered with by unauthorised third parties. It is therefore important to guarantee that the protocols run by IoT applications are robust and cannot be hijacked by attackers. One important property is the correctness of the underlying authentication and key-establishment procedures.

Of course these have long been the object of research in security. Several noteworthy protocols, including versions of secure RPC [30] discussed herein, have been analysed by a variety of methods, including model checking [5]. However, these results cannot in general be applied to IoT. This is because verification of security protocols traditionally analyses a bounded number of interacting principals. In contrast, IoT's unbounded connectivity intrinsically calls for the need to verify an arbitrary number of protocol executions.

The aim of this paper is to put forward a novel methodology for the unbounded verification of a class of security protocols. A key feature of our work is that, similarly to [7], we also capture the epistemic properties of the principals in a secure exchange. To do so we develop a Dolev-Yao threat model in a MAS setting (Section 2); we define and solve the parameterised model checking problem for these systems (Section 3); we present a tailored verification toolkit for the automatic verification of protocols described in a new, security-oriented language (Section 4); and we showcase the methodology on NSPK [27] and ASRPC [30]. In doing so, we answer the open question of model-checking an unbounded number of protocol executions against temporal-epistemic properties.

Appears in: *Proceedings of the 15th International Conference on Autonomous Agents and Multiagent Systems (AAMAS 2016), J. Thangarajah, K. Tuyls, C. Jonker, S. Marsella (eds.), May 9–13, 2016, Singapore.*

2. PARAMETERISED SECURITY MODEL

High-level protocol descriptions.

Consider the following high-level description of the well-known Neeham-Shroeder public-key (NSPK) protocol [27]. At step 1, A encrypts the concatenation of her identity and a nonce n_A with the public key of B and sends this to B. At step 2, upon receipt and decryption, B concatenates a new nonce n_B to the received n_A, encrypts this with the public key of A and sends the overall result to A. The rest follows similarly. We refer to the full representation of A's variables and actions as the *A-role*.

`The High-Level Description of NSPK`

`Protocol:`
1. $A \rightarrow B: enc((A, n_A); pub_B)$
2. $B \rightarrow A: enc((n_A, n_B); pub_A)$
3. $A \rightarrow B: enc(n_B; pub_B)$

`Longterm Vars:` $priv_A; pub_A; A; priv_B; pub_B; B;$
`Prot. Vars:` $n_A, n_B : nonce;$
n_A `bound` A; n_B `bound` B
`Goals: A:B:auth(`A, n_A, pub_A`); secret(`n_A`);`

In protocol executions, high-level roles are embodied by *parties* with concrete credentials. If a party acts according to an A-role, we call it an A-*party*. `Longterm Vars` refer to data belonging to parties and not varying with protocol executions: an A-party called *alice* has $skey_{alice}$ as her long-term secret key. In turn, the `Prot. Vars` part contains sub-messages which are freshly generated in each new, correct session: e.g., n_A is a nonce. It originates from an A-party, as "n_A `bound` A" stipulates. So, we say that n_A is *bound* to the A-role. Contrarily, n_B is *free* in the A-role, as n_B is *bound* to the B-role. `NSPK`'s `goals` here amount to two security requirements. By "`A:B:auth`(A, n_A, pub_A)" it is meant that in any session, the B-party is convinced of communicating to a specific A-party on the basis of A, n_A, and pub_A, and that it was this party who sent the data. By "`secret`(n_A)", it is intended that in any one session, n_A should only become known to the two participating A- and B-parties.

Intermediate level protocol description.

Any protocol Pr can be described algebraically by considering: 1) a set S of sorts (e.g., $Keys$, $Nonces$); 2) a sort-indexed set of variables $X = (X_s \mid s \in S)$ – in `NSPK`, for $s{=}Nonces$, $X_s = \{n_A, n_B\}$; 3) a signature Σ over X, which then gives a set $T_{\Sigma,X}$ of terms to symbolise the protocol-messages, e.g., $enc((A, n_A); pub_B)$ for `NSPK`; 4) a universal algebra $\mathbb{A}$ with *infinitely countable* support-sets A_s, used to interpret Σ; 5) a term algebra $\mathbb{T}$; 6) a set or theory E of equations over terms encoding the cryptographic operations on them.

Assignments δ of variables into the algebra $\mathbb{A}$ and their homomorphic extension to terms, actions and roles model protocol executions. At the start, parties ignore the values of variables free in their role (like n_B for `NSPK`'s A-role). To denote this, we use *null values* denoted $\bot$ or $\bot_s$ for a specific sort $s \in S$. We extend $\mathbb{A}$ to the algebra $\mathbb{A}_\bot$, which has $A_{s\bot}{=}A_s \cup \{\bot_s\}$ as support-sets and all operations over null values returning null values.

Shorthands & building blocks.

We call a protocol *receiver-transparent* if receivers can decipher messages down to variables upon their receipt. `NSPK` and many other authentication and key-agreement protocols [31] are receiver-transparent.

As in protocol-descriptions, we differentiate between longterm variables ($\mathcal{LT}$), free variables ($\mathcal{F}_R$) and bound variables ($\mathcal{B}_R$) in some role R. This extends naturally to terms (i.e., if a term contains a free variable it is free in that role, otherwise it is bound to that role). On this, we give the range of a term homomorphically, as follows.

Definition 2.1 (Range of a term for role). *The range* $Range_R(t)$ *of a term* $t \in T_{\Sigma,X}$ *for a role* R *is as follows:* $Range_R(t)=$

$$\begin{cases} A_s & \text{if } t \in (\mathcal{B}_R)_s \cap X_s \\ A_{s\bot} & \text{if } t \in (\mathcal{F}_R)_s \cap X_s \\ (A_{s_1} \times \ldots \times A_{s_n}) \cup A_s & \text{if } t \in (\mathcal{B}_R)_s, t = \sigma(t_1, \ldots, t_n), \\ & \sigma \in \Sigma_{(s_1,\ldots,s_n),s}, t_i \in T_{\Sigma,X,s_i} \\ (A_{s_1} \times \ldots \times A_{s_n}) \cup A_{s\bot} & \text{if } t \in (\mathcal{F}_R)_s, t = \sigma(t_1, \ldots, t_n), \\ & \sigma \in \Sigma_{(s_1,\ldots,s_n),s}, t_i \in T_{\Sigma,X,s_i} \end{cases}$$

The *maximal range of a term* t, written $Range(t)$, is defined as the union of $Range_R(t)$ over all the roles R. Ranges of long-term variables do not vary with roles: for $t \in \mathcal{LT}$, $Range(t) = A_\omega$, where $\omega \in S^*$ is the type of t. We consider a variable called *step* of sort $Steps$, to encode the actual protocol steps. Ranges $Range_R(step)$ of steps for a given role R are finite and in line with the protocol description.

Let $Msg \subsetneq T_{\Sigma,X}$ denote strictly the protocol-messages. For a protocol-role R, let the sets $SentMsg_R \subsetneq Msg$ and $RecvMsg_R \subsetneq Msg$ respectively denote the messages sent and received by R. We introduce a functional symbol *out* of type $(SentMsg_R; Steps)$, which is interpreted as the particular protocol-step at which a message is sent. We write $out(t) = x$ to denote that a message t is sent at step x, i.e., in `NSPK`, $out(enc((A, n_A); pub_B)){=}1$. Similarly, let *in* be a functional symbol of type $(RecvMsg_R; Steps)$ which is interpreted as the protocol-step at which a concrete message is to be received.

Let $Sub(t)$ be the set of proper sub-terms of t and $Vars(t)$ denote the variables in t. In `NSPK`, $Vars(enc((A, n_A); pub_B))$ $=\{A, n_A, pub_B\}$ and $(A, n_A) \in Sub(enc((A, n_A); pub_B))$.

Templates and parameterised systems for security.

Interleaved interpreted system (IIS) [23] are a multi-agent system semantics in which agents synchronise on one sole action to be performed at each point in time. IIS components can be described in a parametric way via *templates* [21]. The *instances* of these templates, also called *agents*, unravel an actual, *concrete system*. Next, we will present a security model based on templates.

Definition 2.2 (Template (adapted from [21])). *A template is a tuple* $T{=}(X, L, \iota, Act, P, t)$, *where* X *is a set of variables,* $L \subseteq X \times A$ *is a set of local states describing variables* X *with their values in the support sets of the algebra* $\mathbb{A}$, $\iota \in L$ *is a unique initial local state,* Act *is a nonempty set of actions defined over* X, $P : L \to Act$ *is a protocol function dictating which action can be performed at a local state,* tr: $L \times Act \to L$ *is a local evolution function specifying state-updates caused by actions. A "null" action* $\lambda \in Act$ *can be performed at any state and yields no state update.*

Templates here differ from [21] in that they have an algebraic nature, with sorted variables and ranges over infinitely countable sets of a term-algebra. We will also partition these sets driven by a security semantics. This will then open for new techniques of instantiating templates into agents. For instance, agents herein will be able to share variables and their ranges.

We say that an action is *executable* in a template if given a concrete, local state of some arbitrary instance of this template, this action can take place at that local state.

We say that an executable action is *setting* in a template if once this action is performed at a local state of some arbitrary instance of this template, then that local state is consequently updated.

Protocol roles to templates.

Let R be a protocol-role in a receiver-transparent protocol Pr. We will map each such protocol-role R into a *template for* R, written T-R.

T-R's variables. These are described by the set $X_{T\text{-}R}{=}$ $\{\mathcal{LT} \cup \mathcal{F}_R \cup \mathcal{B}_R\}$.

So, T-R's variables distinguish between those free and those bound in R, as well as longterm variables.

The local states of T-R. These are described by the relation $L_{T\text{-}R}{=}(t{::}Range_R(t) \mid t \in X_{T\text{-}R})$ between terms and their respective ranges for the R-role.

The local states for the T-A in `NSPK` are as follows: $(step{::}$ $\mathbb{N}, n_A{::}\mathbb{N}, n_B{::}\mathbb{N}_\bot, pub_B{::}Keys_\bot, A{::}ID)$, where $step, n_A \in \mathcal{B}_A$, $n_B, B \in \mathcal{F}_A$ and $A \in \mathcal{LT}$.

In the *initial state* ι *of the T-R*, we assign bound and long-term variables to arbitrary non-null values over their ranges, free variables to null, and all steps are set to 1.

Actions for templates for roles. The actions of the T-R template are given by:
$Act_{T\text{-}R} = \{send\_intercept(t_1), receive\_transmit(t_2), \lambda\}$, for all $t_1 \in SentMsg_R$ and $t_2 \in RecvMsg_R$.

So, templates's actions encode the sending and receiving of abstract messages, or perform the empty action λ. For the operational semantics, we need a 'handle' to concrete values and template-instances. This is as follows.

Representative values in T-R. Let $t \in T_{\Sigma,X}$. A *representative value for* t *in* T-R, written $val_{T\text{-}R}(t)$ or simply $val(t)$, is the value in $Range_R(t)$ held for t in an arbitrary instance of T-R at a given point.

We now give the operational semantics of T-R'a actions.

Operational sending actions. Let $t \in SentMsg_R$. An *action* $send\_intercept(t)$ *is executable in* T-R if $val(v) \neq \perp$, for all $v \in Vars(t)$.

In other words, an instance of T-A in NSPK needs to have non-null values for n_B, i.e., $val(n_B) \neq \perp$, in order to send the NPSK's third message m_3. Its initial state appears as $(step = 1, n_A = n, n_B = \perp, \ldots)$; the $send\_intercept(m_3)$ action is enabled only once it is in a state $(step = 1, n_A = n, n_B = n' \ldots)$, with $n, n' \in \mathbb{N}$.

Operational receiving actions. Let $t \in RecvMsg_R$. An *action* $receive\_transmit(t)$ *is executable in* T-R if the following holds: for each $v \in Vars(t)$, if $val(v) \neq \perp$ then $val(v) = \delta(t)|_v$, where $\delta(t)$ is a concrete value for t now being sent to an instance of T-R and $\delta(t)|_v$ returns the value of v within $\delta(t)$.

An executable action $receive\_transmit(t)$ is *setting in* T-R if for all $v \in Vars(t)$ such that $val(v) = \perp$, the application of $receive\_transmit(t)$ changes $val(v)$ to $\delta(t)|_v$.

Thus, a receive-transmit action is executable if any value received at some point is consistent with data held previously and locally. This is in line with the matching receiving semantics in [29]. In NSPK, when an A-party receives a value $\delta(enc((n_A, n_B); pub_A))$ for the second message, she checks that her previously used value $val(n_A)$ for n_A matches the n_A-value $\delta(enc((n_A, n_B); pub_A))|_{n_A}$ sent via $\delta(enc((n_A, n_B); pub_A))$. An executable receive-transmit action is *setting* if it causes variable-updates in concrete instances of templates. In NSPK, a local value for n_B would be extracted out of the received $\delta(enc((n_A, n_B); pub_A))$ and $val(n_B)$ would be consequently updated.

Local protocol for T-R. Let l be a local state of T-R, $t_1 \in SentMsg_R$, $t_2 \in RecvMsg_R$. Then, the local protocol function $P_R : L_{T\text{-}R} \to Act_R$ is defined as follows:

$$\begin{cases} P_R(l) = send\_intercept(t_1), & \text{if } v(step) = out(t_1), \\ & send\_intercept(t_1) \\ & \text{is executable in } T\text{-}R; \\ P_R(l) = receive\_transmit(t_2), & \text{if } v(step) = in(t_2), \\ & receive\_transmit(t_2) \\ & \text{is executable in } T\text{-}R. \end{cases}$$

If an action a is such that $a \in P_R(l)$, we say that a *is enabled (at l) in T-R*.

So, any T-R instance is able to perform an action if she is at the right protocol step for it and if the action is executable (i.e., all values to send are non-null and values to receive are consistent with those already held).

Local evolution for T-R. Let $a_1, a_2 \in Act_R$ such that $a_1 = send\_intercept(t_1)$ and $a_2 = receive\_transmit(t_2)$. Let l be an arbitrary local state of T-R and $val(\cdot)$ denote values held by some arbitrary instance of T-R at their instance of l.

The local evolution function is tr_R: $L_{T\text{-}R} \times Act_R \to L_{T\text{-}R}$ with $tr_R(l, a_i) = l'$ if $a_i \in P_R(l)$ (for $i \in \{1, 2\}$) and the following holding:

$$\begin{cases} val(step) + +, & \text{if } a_i = a_1 \quad (1) \\ val(step) + + \text{ and } a_2 \text{ is setting}, & \text{if } a_i = a_2 \quad (2), \end{cases}$$

where $val(\cdot)$ denotes values held at l'.

The above says that enabled actions, once performed, update the current local state with incremented protocol-steps, and receiving actions may set new values.

The Environment template.

We will now present a special template called the *Environment template* and written T-Env. It models the outer network hosting both the honest parties' from the adversary. In a concrete multi-agent system, T-Env is instantiated into *concrete Environment* which we denote by Env.

Local states for T-Env. These are defined by a series of variables, emulating the following map for each role R: $log[t, \{v :: val \mid v \in Vars(t)\}]$ with $t \in SentMsg_R$, and $val \in Range(v) \cup \{\perp\}$.

That is, T-Env tracks the values of the variables v inside each protocol-message t. For $enc((A, n_A); pub_B)$ in NSPK, T-Env stores three variables for A, n_A, and pub_B.

In *T-Env's initial states* all the log are set to null-values: i.e., $log[t][v] := \perp$, for all $v \in Vars(t)$, for all $t \in Msg$, denoting that no tracking has yet occurred.

The concrete environment Env contains in fact several copies of a $log[t, \cdot]$ map, one reserved for each instance of T-R having emitted a value for t, as depicted below.

Representative values in T-Env. Let $t \in SentMsg_R$. *Representative values for t in T-Env* are the set of arbitrary values in $2^{Range(t) \cup \perp}$ held in Env for $Vars(t)$ under the handle t^{rep} of t, written $log[t^{rep}, \{v \mid v \in Vars(t)\}]$.

So, if an instance rep of T-A sends NSPK's m_1 as some $\delta(enc((A, n_A); pub_B))$, then Env sets $log[m_1^{rep}][n_a]$ to $\delta(m_1)|_{n_a}$, sets $log[m_1^{rep}][A]$ to $\delta(m_1)|_A$, etc., where $log[\cdot^{rep}][\cdot]$ is a rep-reserved' copy of $log[\cdot][\cdot]$.

Actions for T-Env. These are given by the set $Act_{T\text{-}Env} = Act_{T\text{-}R} \cup \{tamper\_log(t)\}$, for all R-roles, for all $t \in RecvMsg_R$.

The $tamper\_log(t)$ actions refer to the threat model; we will describe these later in the section. The other actions are in tandem with T-R: if T-R sends something, then T-Env intercepts it, and if T-R receives something it is because T-Env transmits it.

Let $t \in SentMsg_R$, $t' \in RecvMsg_R$ be as above. Let rep be an arbitrary instance of T-R at a given point.

Operational intercept. The *action* $send\_intercept(t)$ *is executable in* T-Env at any local state of T-Env.

An *action* $send\_intercept(t)$ *is setting in* T-Env in that $log[t^{rep}][v]$ becomes $\delta(t)|_v$, for all $v \in Vars(t)$, where $\delta(t)$ is the arbitrary concrete value for t sent within rep and $\delta(t)|_v$ returns the value of v within $\delta(t)$.

The second part of the above says that all send-intercept actions are setting: they make the corresponding logs of *Env*'s take the respective values from the messages sent.

Operational transmit. The *action* $receive\_transmit(t')$ *is executable in* T-Env if $log[t'][v] \neq \bot$, for all $v \in Vars(t')$.

A receive-transmit action is executable in T-Env if all the necessary sub-parts of the message to be received by a T-R instance have been logged by T-Env, symbolising that the concrete message is present over the network.

The *local protocol or local evolution function for* T-Env are implicitly specified by the operational semantics above.

The Intruder Template.

We will now present a special template called the *Intruder template*, written T-In, which encapsulates a Dolev-Yao (DY) threat model [14]. We instantiate the T-In template by one agent only which we call $Intr$ or *concrete intruder*.

T-In's local states. These are defined by the following:
1) a set of variables, emulating the maps $constr[t, \{v :: val \mid v \in Vars(t)\}]$, for each role R, with $t \in SentMsg_R$, and $val \in Range(v) \cup \{\bot\}$;
2) a series of boolean variables $poss(val)$, for each $val \in Range(v) \backslash \{\bot\}$, for each $v \in Vars(t)$, for each $t \in Msg$;

The T-In's *constr*-variables capture the protocol's messages as formed by the attacker. The *poss*-variables denote the intruder's data-possessions. I.e., $poss(alice) = .T.$ denotes that the intruder knows the name *alice* to be a protocol participant; $poss(300) = .F.$ encodes that the intruder cannot use 300 as a fresh value.

Representatives for T-In. Let *rep* be an arbitrary instance of T-R. All term t linked to *rep* that the intruder tracks or manipulates w.r.t. to this instance is referred to as t^{rep}.

Like with *Env*, the concrete $Intr$ would replicate $constr[t, \cdot]$ into $constr[t^{rep}, \{v :: val \mid v \in Vars(t)\}]$ for each *rep*.

In T-In*'s initial states*, all the *constr*-variable are set to null-values; some of the *poss*-variables are set to *true*, some are set to *false* denoting the intruder initial knowledge. This is done in such a way that T-Rs and T-In share no value for variables that are not long-term.

Actions for T-In. The actions of the T-In template are given by: $Act_{Intr} = \{DY(t_1), tamper\_log(t_2), \lambda\}$, for all R-roles, for all $t_1 \in SentMsg_R$, for all $t_2 \in RecvMsg_R$.

We introduce a shortcut to intercepts by the intruder: the $Intr$ is allowed conceptual access to the values of messages inside any arbitrary instance of T-R. He performs closure of DY-analysis and DY-synthesis [28] of these messages. This is formalised below.

Operational DY actions. Let *rep* be an arbitrary instance of T-R, $t \in SentMsg_R$, $val(t)$ be the homomorphically composed value of t within *rep*, $t_1 \in RecvMsg_{R'}$, and rep_2 be an arbitrary instance of T-R'.

An *action* $DY(t)$ *is executable in* T-In if $constr[t^{rep}][v] = \bot$, for all $v \in Vars(t)$.

An executable $DY(t)$ action *is setting in* T-In if the following is the case:

$$\begin{cases} poss[x] = .T., & \text{if } x \in analz(val(t), poss),\ x \neq \bot \ (1) \\ constr[t_1^{rep_2}][v] := y, & \text{if } y \in \overline{synth(analz(poss), t_1)},\ y \neq \bot \ (2) \end{cases}$$

By point (1) above, once a DY action is performed, it sets values in *poss* upon analysis of the value of t inside T-R's instance *rep*. As per (2) above, the values in *poss* are then used to try and compose a value for message t_1: i.e., $\overline{synth(analz(poss), t_1)}$ denotes closure of DY synthesis and analysis over all $Intr$ possessions, for the construction of t_1. If successful, the synthesised value y is recorded in that $constr[t_1^{rep_2}][v] := y$.

We took $DY(t)$-action to be executable if $constr[t^{rep}][v]$ is $\bot$; so, we see now that this equates to $Intr$ decomposing values of messages t that he has not formed himself. For example, let instance *rep* of T-A for NSPK have a local value $\delta(m_1)$ for the first message $enc((A, n_A); pub_B)$ such that for the value $\delta(m_1)|_{pub_B}$, $Intr$'s *poss* has $\delta(m_1)|_{priv_B}$ set to true. Then $Intr$ can decrypt $\delta(m_1)$ and, according to (1) above, $poss(v_1)$ becomes $.T.$, where $v_1 = \delta(m_1)|_{n_a}$. Next, according to (2), the DY action is such that $constr[t'^{rep_2}][n_a] := v_1$, where rep_2 is another instance of T-A and $Intr$ is now constructing a message replaying in it the value of n_a as per rep_1 possibly purporting to be from rep_2.

The operational semantics for the *tamper_log*-actions in T-In and in T-Env follows.

Operational tampering actions. Let $t \in SentMsg_R$. An *action* $tamper\_log(t)$ *is executable in* T-In if $constr[t][v] \neq \bot$, for all $v \in Vars(t)$.

An *action* $tamper\_log(t)$ *is executable in* T-Env at any local state of T-Env.

Let *rep* be an arbitrary instance of T-R. An executable *action* $tamper\_log(t)$ *is setting in* T-Env in that $log[t^{rep}][v]$ becomes $constr[t^{rep}][v]$ in *Env*, for all $v \in Vars(t)$.

The operational semantics of tampering actions stipulates that $Intr$ is able to perform a $tamper\_log(t)$-action if it has constructed all the parts needed in t, i.e., it holds a value $v \neq \bot$, for all the variables of t. In T-Env, these actions are executable at any point and have as effect the injection of the intruder's constructions in *constr* in *Env*'s the log-vars.

The *local protocol or local evolution function for* T-In are specified implicitly via the operational semantics above.

DEFINITION 2.3 (PARAMETERISED SECURITY SYSTEM). *A* parameterised security system (PSS) *for a protocol* Pr *is a tuple* $S = (\mathcal{T}, T\text{-}Intr, T\text{-}Env)$, *where* $\mathcal{T} = \bigcup_{R\text{-}role\ in\ Pr} \{T\text{-}R\}$, *with the components defined as above.*

3. UNBOUNDED SECURITY IN MAS

A *concrete instance of template* T-R is defined constructively and inductively based on the instances who already 'joined' a concrete system modelled by a PSS. A non-basic step of this inductive definition is given below. For the next two definitions, we assume w.l.o.g. that there are two roles R and R' in the protocol Pr.

Concrete agents.

DEFINITION 3.1 (CONCRETE ROLE-AGENTS). *Let* R *be an arbitrarily fixed role and* $T\text{-}R = (X = \mathcal{B}_R \cup \mathcal{F}_R \cup \mathcal{LT}, L \subseteq X \times A, \iota, Act, P, tr)$ *as above. Let* $m \geqslant 1$ *be the total number of instances present in the system. Let* $n \geqslant 1$ *be the total number of instances of* T-R *present in the system. Let* i *with* $1 \leqslant i \leqslant n$. *The* (i, n, m)-concrete instance of T-R, *written* ag_R^i *or for simplicity* ag, *is defined by the* $(X^{ag}, L^{ag}, \iota^{ag}, Act^{ag}, P^{ag}, tr^{ag})$ *tuple as follows:*
I. X^{ag} *is a multi-copy of* X, *where:*

1). If $x \in \mathcal{B}_R$, then $x^{ag} \in X^{ag}$;
2). If $y \in \mathcal{F}_R \cap \mathcal{B}_{R'}$, then $y_1^{ag}, \ldots, y_{m-n}^{ag} \in X^{ag}$;
3). If $z \in \mathcal{LT}$, then $z_1^{ag}, \ldots, z_m^{ag} \in X^{ag}$.
II. $L^{ag} \subseteq X^{ag} \times 2^{Range(X)}$ is as follows:
1). Let $x \in \mathcal{B}_R \cup \mathcal{LT}$. Then, $(x, Range_{ag}(x)) \in L^{ag}$ where $Range_{ag}(x)$ is a subset of $Range_R(x)$ with $|Range_{ag}(x)|=n+1$ such that $Range_{ag'}(x) \supsetneq Range_{ag}(x)$, where ag' is the (i, n', m')-concrete instance of T-R and $n' > n$;
2). Let $x \in X_{Steps}$. Then, $(x, Range_R(x)) \in L^{ag}$.
III. Act^{ag} is a multi-copy of Act, as local terms are expanded over X^{ag};
• *Any $a \in Act$ is send_intercept(t) or receive_transmit(t), with $t \in Msg$. Then, $a_1^{ag}, \ldots, a_s^{ag} \in Act^{ag}$, where $s = |Range_{ag}(t)|$ with $Range_{ag}(t) = \times_{x \in Vars(t)} Range_{ag}(x)$.*
IV. ι^{ag}, P^{ag} and tr^{ag} are defined as on T-R expanded over X^{ag}, L^{ag}, Act^{ag} above and homomorphically instantiated.

Point I.1 in Definition 3.1 says that the agent keeps just one single local copy of each variables bound to its role. By I.2, for each party that may provide ag with a value for a variable free in its role, ag holds a separate copy of that variable. Indeed, an A-party in NSPK may receive n_b's for all the B-parties that she engages with. Finally, I.3 describes the fact that long-term values may be associated to all m parties in the system, i.e., the agent has public-keys of all the parties she communicates to. Point II shows that we capture a truly unbounded system and we expand the ranges of variables on-the-fly, as more instances 'join' the system. Point II.1 expresses that constructing a new instance of T-R makes the ranges of its bound variables grow: at the i-th instance, this range has a size of $n + 1$ (as n could cause logic omniscience). Point II.2 stipulates that protocol-steps do not vary with instances. And, upon point III, an agent will have send or receive actions over all the possible values (in $Range_{ag}(t)$) derived homomorphicaly from the variables x in t and their ranges defined as per point II.

Definition 3.2 (Concrete (n, m)-intruder). *Let T-Intr $= (X, L \subseteq X \times A, \iota, Act, P, tr)$ as above. Let $m \geqslant 1$ be the number of all role-agents present in the system. For an arbitrary role R, let all $n \geqslant 1$ instances of T-R therein define the set Ag.* The concrete (n, m)-intruder $Intr(n, m)$, *or simply Intr, follows the definition of T-In, where:*
I. X^{Intr} is a multi-copy of X expanded by Ag:
1). For each $t \in SentMsg_R$, for each $v \in Vars(t)$, for each ag, we have that $x \in X^{Intr}$, where $x = constr[t^{ag}][v]$;
Then, let $Range_{Intr}(x)$ be $\bigcup_{ag \in Ag} Range_{ag}(v) \cup \mathcal{R}_1 \cup \mathcal{R}_2$, where $\mathcal{R}_1 \subseteq \{Range(v) \backslash \{\bigcup_{ag \in Ag} Range_{ag}(v)\} | v \notin \mathcal{LT}\}$ and $|\mathcal{R}_1| = n$, $\mathcal{R}_2 \subseteq \{Range(v) \backslash \{\bigcup_{ag \in Ag} Range_{ag}(v)\} | v \in \mathcal{LT}\}$ and $|\mathcal{R}_2| = m$.
2). Let $x' \in X^{Intr}, x' = constr[t][v]$ as above. For each val in $Range_{Intr}(x')$, let $x = poss[val]$. Then, $x \in X^{Intr}$; Also, let $Range_{Intr}(x)$ be $\{true, false\}$.
II. $L^{Intr} \subseteq X^{Intr} \times 2^{Range(X)}$ where $(x, Range_{Intr}(x)) \in L^{ag}$ for each $x \in X^{Intr}$ as above.
III. Act^{Intr} is a multi-copy of Act, as local terms and their values are homomorphically expanded over $x \in X^{Intr}$ and $Range_{Intr}(x)$. The resulting $DY(\cdot)$ actions are denoted Act-DY^{Intr}.
IV. ι^{Intr}, P^{Intr} and tr^{Intr} are as in T-Intr expanded over X^{Intr}, L^{Intr}, Act^{Intr} and homomorphically instantiated.

Point I.1 in Definition 3.2 shows that the intruder can compose and decompose messages over all the respective values inside the role-agents present in the system. Then, by the set $\mathcal{R}_1$, we see that for each role-agent that "joins" the system, $Intr$ gets a new possible value for each variable that is not long-term; so, he could inject all needed fresh values in each session. The set $\mathcal{R}_2$ shows that he can get long-term values for all instances; so, he could potentially be a party in any session using appropriate long-term keys. The rest is self-explained or explained in the template T-$Intr$.

Definition 3.3 (Concrete (n, m)-environment). *Let T-Env $= (X, L \subseteq X \times A, \iota, Act, P, tr)$ as above. Let $m \geqslant 1$ be the number all role-agents present in the system. For an arbitrary role R, let all $n \geqslant 1$ instances of T-R therein define the set Ag. Then, the concrete (n, m)-environment $Env(n, m)$ follows the definition of T-Env such that:*
• *X^{Env} is a multi-copy of X, where for each $t \in SentMsg_R$, for each $v \in Vars(t)$, for each ag instance of T-R, we have that $x \in X^{Env}$, with $x = log[t^{ag}][v]$;*
Let $Range_{Env}(x)$ be $Range_{Intr}(x)$;
• *$L^{Env} \subseteq X^{Env} \times 2^{Range(X)}$ where $(x, Range_{Env}(x)) \in L^{ag}$ for each $x \in X^{Env}$.*
• *Act^{Env} is $\bigcup_{ag \in Ag} Act^{ag} \cup$ Act-DY^{Intr}.*
• *ι^{Env}, P^{Env} and tr^{Env} are defined as on T-Env expanded over X^{Env}, L^{Env}, Act^{Env} and homomorphically instantiated.*

Iteration of instances and their systems.

Let $R, R', R'', \ldots$ be all protocol roles in the system. Assume $n_R, n_{R'}, n_{R''}, \ldots$ to be the number of instances of T-R, T-R', T-R'',..., respectively, present in the system. Consider m to be the total numbers of role-agents in the system. Then, the interactions over all agents $i \leqslant n_R$ of the (i, n_R, m)-concrete instances of T-R with a (n_R, m)-concrete environment and a (n_R, m)-concrete intruder, for each protocol-role T-R, define a concrete or product system of size $\overline{n} = (n_R, n_{R'}, n_{R''}, \ldots)$. This contains a concrete environment and a concrete intruder, which we denote $Env(\overline{n})$ and $Intr(\overline{n})$, respectively.

Atomic propositions for templates and agents.

Role and agent predicates. Let T-$R = (X, L \subseteq X \times A, \iota, Act, P, t)$ as above. Let AP_R be a set of atomic propositions over X and $\mathcal{V}_R : L \rightarrow \mathcal{P}(AP_R)$ be a valuation function of these atoms in T-R. Let ag be an instance of T-R. The above construction of ag over T-R induces a set AP_R^{ag} of atomic propositions over X^{ag}. Let $\mathcal{V}_R^{ag} : L^{ag} \rightarrow \mathcal{P}(AP_R^{ag})$ be a valuation function of these atoms in ag.

Let T-$Intr = (X', L' \subseteq X' \times A', \iota', Act', P', t')$ be as above. Let $AP_{T\text{-}Intr}$ be a set of atomic propositions over X'. From the definition of $Intr(n_R, m)$, we derive $AP^{Intr(n_R,m)}$ and $\mathcal{V}^{Intr(n_R,m)} : L^{Intr(n_R,m)} \rightarrow \mathcal{P}(AP^{Intr(n_R,m)})$. We do the same for $Env(n_R, m)$. On a concrete system, these are extended to $Env(\overline{n})$ and $Intr(\overline{n})$.

Let a product system be built as above and AP be the union of all its resulting atoms. Then, let $\mathcal{V}(\overline{n}) : \times_{1 \leqslant i \leqslant n_R} L^i \times \ldots \times L^{Intr(\overline{n})} \times L^{Env(\overline{n})} \rightarrow \mathcal{P}(AP)$ be defined as $\mathcal{V}(\overline{n})((l^1, \ldots, l^{Intr(\overline{n})}, l^{Env(\overline{n})})) = \{p \,|\, p \in V^a(l^a)\}$, for $a \in \{1, \ldots, Intr(\overline{n}), Env(\overline{n})\}$.

Concrete systems.

Definition 3.4 (Concrete security system). *Let R be a role, S be a PSS, and $\overline{n}$ be as above. A* concrete security system (CSS) of size $\overline{n}$ *for S is the tuple $S(\overline{n}) = (((ag_R^i)_{i \in \{1,\ldots,n_R\}})_R, Intr(\overline{n}), Env(\overline{n}), \mathcal{V})$.*

The tuple $S(\overline{n})$ given above is an interleaved interpreted system whose components are defined as in Sections 2 and 3.

The product of local objects (e.g., states, actions) in a CSS define global objects. The *unwound CSS* $\mathbb{S}(\overline{n})$ is the underlining Kripke structure obtained from a given CSS. The global actions and the global transition function induce paths over the global states of a CSS, as usually [16]. The indistinguishability relations over global states are: $\sim_{ag^i_R}$ for agents, $\sim_{Intr(\overline{n})}$ for the intruder, $\sim_{Env(\overline{n})}$ for the environment. These are defined on local equalities: $g \sim_j g'$ iff $g_j = g'_j$ where $j \in \{ag^i_R, Intr(\overline{n}), Env(\overline{n})\}$, and g_j is the local state of j in the global state g. This indistinguishability relation is correct cryptographically due to the fact that we model receiver-transparent protocols.

Specification language.

System properties are expressed in a variant of CTLK [16], stemming from the following BNF:

$$\phi ::= p \mid \neg\phi \mid \phi \vee \phi \mid EX\phi \mid E(\phi U \phi) \mid EG\phi \mid K_i\phi$$

where $i \in T\text{-}R, T\text{-}Intr$ and $p \in AP_R \cup AP_{Intr}$. Dual temporal modalities and the universal path quantifier A ("for all paths") are defined as usual [18]. These formulae are interpreted over any unwound interpreted system, like CSSs, as expected [16]; for formula satisfaction, we write $\mathbb{S}(\overline{n}) \models \phi$.

Since variables and atoms are indexed by roles, we now introduce a variant of *indexed CTLK*; we will use the *AG*-fragment of this.

Formula-schemata. We use abstract formula-schemata specified over a PSS. Applying instantiations to these, produces concrete formulae in the corresponding CSSs, irrespective of the numbers of concrete agents within. With our models, we only use formulae generated upon this *schema*:

$$[T\text{-}R : \vec{x}, \vec{u}, \ldots, T\text{-}Intr : \vec{w}]^{+} AG(\phi(p(x,u), \ldots, p'(w), \ldots)),$$

where $\vec{x}$, $\vec{u}$, $\vec{w}$ are lists of variables, $x \in \vec{x}$, $u \in \vec{u}$, $w \in \vec{w}$, $p \in AP_R$, $p' \in AP_{T\text{-}Intr}$, ϕ is formed with the atoms p, p'. The values of the variables in $\vec{x}$ will iterate over the names of $T\text{-}R$ instances, and elements of $\vec{u}$ and $\vec{w}$ will span values of variables inside atoms in AP_R and $AP_{T\text{-}Intr}$, respectively.

Concrete formulae. An *expansion of a schema inside a CSS* is the conjunction over all the 'names' a of agents iterated over with $\vec{x}$s, over all the values b inside their atoms iterated over with $\vec{u}$s, over all references to values c in atoms of $Intr$ iterated over with $\vec{w}$:

$$\bigwedge_{\vec{x}=\vec{a}, \vec{u}=\vec{b}, \ldots, \vec{w}=\vec{c}} AG(\phi(p^{ag}(a,b), \ldots, p^{I}(c), \ldots),$$

where $p^{ag} \in AP^{ag}_R$, $p^I \in AP^{Intr}$.

Indexed specifications. A formula following the above schema is called a *$\vec{v}$-indexed formula*, where $\vec{v}$ is called the *index* of the formula; it denotes all lists of variables bound to templates as per the schema. We use $\forall_{\vec{v}} AG\phi(\vec{v})$ to denote both an indexed schema in a PSS or its expansion in a CSS. By $\#(\vec{v})$ we refer to the vector $\#(\vec{v}) = (m_R, m_{R'}, \ldots)$ denoting the number m_R of variables in $\vec{v}$ bound to each template $T\text{-}R$; we assume w.l.o.g that $m_R \geqslant 1$ for each $T\text{-}R$.

Parameterised model checking and cut-offs of PSS.

Parameterised MC problem [21]. Given a PSS and an $\vec{v}$-indexed formula $\forall_{\vec{v}} AG\phi(\vec{v})$, the parameterised model checking problem (PMCP) concerns answering whether

$$\forall \overline{n} \geqslant \#(\vec{v}), \mathbb{S}(\overline{n}) \models \forall_{\vec{v}} AG\phi(\vec{v}),$$

The PMCP is undecidable [3] over general unbounded transition systems. For systems with communication patterns [21] similar to those of PSSs, the problem can be decided by finding a *cut-off*. This is the number of system components that suffices to be considered when evaluating a given specification.

DEFINITION 3.5 (PSS CUTOFF). *Let S be a PSS and $\vec{v}$ be an arbitrary index in an indexed formula. Let $\overline{c} = (c_R, c_{R'}, \ldots)$ be a vector of size equal to the number of protocol-roles R, R' in PSS, with $c_R, c'_R \geqslant 1$. The vector $\overline{c}$ is said to be a* PSS cutoff *if the following holds:*

$\mathbb{S}(\overline{c}) \models \forall_{\vec{v}} AG\phi(\vec{v})$ *iff* $\forall \overline{n} > \overline{c}. (\mathbb{S}(\overline{n}) \models \forall_{\vec{v}} AG\phi(\vec{v}))$,
where $\mathbb{S}(\overline{n})$ is S's unwound CSS of size $\overline{n} = (n_R, n_{R'}, \ldots)$.

To give a cut-off for PSS, we need the following notion. A *trivial assignment of variables for an index $\vec{v}$* assigns different variables of the same sort (e.g., different nonces) to different values in their ranges. We can map these values to indices or natural numbers, since our ranges or our algebra support sets are infinitely countable; we use this in the next proofs. For $\forall_{\vec{v}} AG\phi(\vec{v})$ under a trivial assignment, we write $AG\phi(\vec{\epsilon})$.

THEOREM 3.1 (SYMMETRY REDUCTION). *Let S be a PSS and $\vec{v}$ be an arbitrary index in an indexed formula. For a $\vec{v}$-indexed formula $\forall_{\vec{v}} \phi(\vec{v})$, we have that*

$\mathbb{S}(\overline{n}) \models \forall_{\vec{v}} \phi(\vec{v})$ *iff* $\mathbb{S}(\overline{n}) \models AG\phi(\vec{\epsilon})$,
where $\mathbb{S}(\overline{n})$ is S's unwound CSS of size $\overline{n} = (n_R, n_{R'}, \ldots)$

Proof. We adapt [15] for S, poising on receiver-transparency.

This lemma reduces the size of the formulae to check, making it sufficient to consider exactly one value from the domains of each of the variables. This is exploited next.

Finding cut-offs for PSSs.

Consider $\overline{c} = (c_R, c_{R'}, \ldots)$, where each c_R denotes as many agents as the number of variables admitted by T-R and appear in $\forall_{\vec{v}} AG\phi(\vec{v})$, plus 1 special agent; i.e., if $(m_R, m_{R'}, \ldots) = \#(\vec{v})$, then $c_R = m_R + 1$ for each protocol-role $T\text{-}R$. We show that $\overline{c}$ is a cutoff. To do this, we establish a relation between the CSS $\mathbb{S}(\overline{c})$ and an arbitrary CSS $\mathbb{S}(\overline{n})$ with $\overline{n} \geqslant \overline{c}$. More specifically, we define a function ζ_c that maps a path in $\mathbb{S}(\overline{c})$ to a path in $\mathbb{S}(\overline{n})$, and a function ζ_n that maps a path in $\mathbb{S}(\overline{n})$ to a path in $\mathbb{S}(\overline{c})$. Since the transition function in each system is triggered by one precise action at a time, any sequence $ga^1a^2\ldots$, where g is a concrete initial state and $a^1, a^2 \ldots$ are concrete actions, specifies a well-defined path. We begin with ζ_n which is defined as $\zeta_n(ga^1a^2\ldots) = g'a'^1a'^2\ldots$, where

- g' is any initial state in $\mathbb{S}(\overline{c})$ such that the intruder's *poss*-variables that refer to a concrete (special) agent $ag^{c_R}_R$, for any role R, are set to *true*;
- for each $i \geqslant 1$, if $a_i \in Act^{ag^x_R}$, where $x \geqslant c_R$, then a'_i is the null action;
- for each $i \geqslant 1$, if $a_i \in Act^{ag^x_R}$, where $x < c_R$, then a'_i is the action obtained from a_i by replacing each variable with index greater than c_R with c_R;
- for each $i \geqslant 1$, if a_i is an intruder's action, then a'_i is the action obtained from a_i by replacing each variable with index greater than c_R with c_R.

We now define ζ_c by $\zeta_c(g'a'^1a'^2\dots) = ga^1a^2\dots$, where
• g is an initial state in $\mathbb{S}(\overline{n})$ such that an intruder's *poss*-variable is set to *true* iff the variable is admitted by the intruder in $\mathbb{S}(\overline{c})$ and it is set to *true* in $\mathbb{S}(\overline{c})$;
• for each $i \geqslant 1$, $a^i = a'^1$.

On PSSs, we imposed that agents synchronise on actions. This is the core of the mappings above, which entail the following theorem, showing $\overline{c}$ to be our cutoff.

THEOREM 3.6. *$\mathbb{S}(\overline{c}) \models \forall_{\vec{v}} AG\phi(\vec{v})$ iff $\mathbb{S}(\overline{n}) \models \forall_{\vec{v}} AG\phi(\vec{v})$ for any $\overline{n} \geqslant \overline{c}$.*

PROOF. ($\Rightarrow$) Assume $\mathbb{S}(\overline{c}) \models \forall_{\vec{v}} AG\phi(\vec{v})$ and choose $\overline{n} \geqslant \overline{c}$. By Theorem 3.1, $\mathbb{S}(\overline{c}) \models AG\phi(\vec{\epsilon})$. Let π be an arbitrary path in $\mathbb{S}(\overline{c})$ originating from an initial state. We have that $(\mathbb{S}(\overline{c}), g) \models \phi(\vec{\epsilon})$ for every g in π. Consider $\zeta_c(\pi)$. By definition of ζ_c, $(\mathbb{S}(\overline{n}), g) \models \phi(\vec{\epsilon})$ for every g in $\zeta_c(\pi)$. Therefore, $\mathbb{S}(\overline{n}) \models AG\phi(\vec{\epsilon})$.

($\Leftarrow$) As above, but using ζ_n. □

The above provides a methodology to solve the PMCP for PSSs by checking every concrete systems up to the cutoff.

4. IMPLEMENTATION

We implemented the theoretical grounds of verifying parameterised security systems (PSS) in *MCMAS-S*, as an extension of the MCMAS-P model-checker [20]. We designed the input language for *MCMAS-S*, *SISPL*, tailored to our semantics.

A MAS-specification language for security protocols. Next, we use SISPL snippets. We start with an SISPL excerpt for the *A-role* in NSPK. Template for roles in SISPL include types of variables with denotation and range as per the security semantics:

```
Template Role_A
Protocol Vars: -- bound to the A-role
   ...
   n_a  :    {null,atom_a};
end Vars
Log Vars:  -- free in the A-role
   n_b  logs Role_B.n_b; ...
end Vars
Longterm Vars:   -- longterm data
   a    :    {null,alice}; ...
end Vars
```

Under Log Vars, *n_b* models the n_b free variable in NSPK's *A-role*. So, concrete values for *n_b* depend on the ranges defined in the *B*-role template (i.e., n_b logs Role_B.n_b). In a concrete system, with each new instance i of *Role_A*, a new value $atom\_a_i$ is added to the growing range of n_a, and each such instance will hold as many copies of n_b as there are instances of *Role_B*. To encode the operational semantics of actions, we designed several, overloaded shorthands to be used in a part called Messaging Actions:

```
... Messaging Actions ...
  receive_byTransmit_msg2 composes (+n_a-,-n_b+,+a-);...
```

The keyword composes denotes that the concrete messages to be sent or received have ranges homomorphically defined via the ranges of the variables within. Then, the sign '+' in front of a variable denotes that the concrete agent has to have a non-null value for that variable in order for the action to be enabled or executable (see Section 2). A sign '-' in front of a variable stipulates that the action is executable irrespective of the value of this variable; due to composes (...,-n_b...,), a *Role_A* agent in NSPK would receive the second message no matter the value of *n_b*. For this action, the '+' preceding *n_a* is used to implement matching-receive semantics: an instance of *Role_A* would not accept the second message in NSPK unless its inner value for n_a coincided with her a-priori value of *n_a*. Lastly, the sign '+' after a variable implements the setting nature of actions (see Section 2): composes (...,n_b+...,) denotes that the receipt of NSPK's second message by an instance of *Role_A* will assign a concrete value for *n_b* accordingly. The specification of protocol and evolution functions is minimalistic (as per Section 2) and uses PISPL [21] syntax, i.e., as in the MCMAS-P model-checker that we extended..

We now discuss the environment's SISPL specification.

```
Template Environment
Log Vars:
   a_log_protocol_msg1   logs Role_A.a;
   n_a_log_protocol_msg1 logs Role_A.n_a; ...
end Vars
Messaging Actions ...
-- A sends msg1, Env intercepts
sent_intercept_msg1   composes
   (-a_log_protocol_msg+,-n_a_log_protocol_msg1+,
    -b_log_protocol_msg1+);
-- Env's logs might be rewritten by Intr
tamper_log_msg1 composes
   (-a_log_protocol_msg1+,-n_a_log_protocol_msg1+,
    -b_log_protocol_msg1+); ...
```

The *Log Vars* part is inline with *T-Env* discussed in Section 2: in an instance-by-instance fashion, the environment stores the values for all the messages exchanged. In the Messaging Actions part, by the preceding '-' signs, we mean that the environment does not need any particular value to intercept messages; this will set all due values (i.e., the suffix + signs). The tamper_log_msg1 lines show the *Env-Intr* synchronisation, where *Env*'s intercepted logs may be overwritten by Dolev-Yao compositions.

Now consider a snippet from the Intruder template:

```
... Messaging Actions ...
analz_msg_1_as_enc_pair composes
(-a_in_protocol_msg1+,-n_a_in_protocol_msg1+,
+b_in_protocol_msg1+);...
```

It is a part of the Dolev-Yao analysis on a NSPK message: if *Intr* knows the decrypting key (i.e., "+b_in_protocol_msg1"), then his variables will be set to the inner-values of this message (i.e., n_a_in_protocol_msg1+).

The specification of logical formulae is as in PISPL [21].

MCMAS-S: a prototype model checker for security protocols given as MAS specifications. The input to MCMAS-S is a PSS S and a set of logical formulae in indexed CTLK following our schemata, written as SISPL file. The model checker solves the PMCP for PSS. MCMAS-S is based on the same core parameterised model checking techniques as MCMAS-P [21]. In other words, it implements the techniques in Section 3, exploiting agent-environment synchronisation and symmetry reductions to find cut-offs as in Theorem 3.6. Once a cut-off $\overline{c}$ is calculated, the reachable state-space of $\mathbb{S}(\overline{c})$ is computed and encoded symbolically. Then, the formulae are checked on this and a result is presented.

MCMAS-S differs from MCMAS-P primarily in that agents can share variables and ranges. Like in MCMAS-P, the construction of these ranges is done on-the-fly, as larger systems and formulae up to the cut-off $\overline{c}$ are being considered; however, the semantics in Section 3 implies that in MCMAS-S we expand these ranges differently with a security-driven fine-tuning in mind.

The C++ implementation of MCMAS-S is available at [1].

5. EXPERIMENTAL RESULTS

We evaluated our theoretical results and the implementation by verifying two authentication and key-establishment protocols: NSPK [27], presented in Section 2, and ARSPC [30]. The PSSs and the indexed CTLK formulas to express their respective authentication and secrecy goals were coded in a SISPL file.

Following Section 2, NSPK's authentication goal is

$$AG(end_A(\vec{u}, \vec{v}) \wedge end_B(\vec{u'}, \vec{v'}) \rightarrow agree\_naAB(\vec{u}, \vec{u'}, \vec{v}, \vec{v'}, \vec{w}, \vec{w'})),$$

where $end_A \in AP_A$ denotes that template T-A of A-role is at the end-step of the protocol, $\vec{u}$ and $\vec{v}$ range over instances of T-A, $agree\_naAB$ is a conjunction of atoms in AP^A and AP^B expressing that the values of A, n_A and B are the same in (instances of) T-A and T-B, and $\vec{w}$ iterates over the values of A, n_A and B inside T-A. Similarly, $\vec{u'}$, $\vec{v'}$ span instances of T-B and $\vec{w'}$ ranges over the values of the cited variables inside T-B.

Following Section 2, NSPK's secrecy goal is

$$AG(end_A(\vec{u}, \vec{v}) \wedge end_B(\vec{u'}, \vec{v'}) \rightarrow$$
$$\neg K_{Intr}(holds\_na(\vec{u}, \vec{u'}, \vec{v}, \vec{v'}\vec{w}, \vec{w'}))),$$

where $holds\_na$ is a conjunction of atoms in AP_A and AP_B expressing that the value of n_A is the same in (instances of) T-A and T-B, and the rest is as previously explained.

By using MCMAS-S, we obtain a cut-off of $(2, 2)$ underpinning an attack which refuted the first formula above. This attack consists of two A-parties and two B-parties, with the intruder tampering with the sessions of these parties.

Indeed, for the first formula, we also find a counterexample emulating the famous Lowe-attack [24] on NSPK. For the second formula, MCMAS-S offers us a longer counterexample but analogous to that of Lowe's attack, showing that the intruder learns the value of n_a in an instance of T-A and replays it to an instance of T-B, with $\neg K_{Intr}(holds\_na(\ldots))$ failing therein.

Many authentication and key-establishment protocols have inter-session attacks similar to Lowe's attack in NSPK. Indeed, ARSPC (Andrew Secure RPC) [30] is a key-establishment protocol where two concurrent sessions can be exploited in this way [25]. To avoid this, Lowe proposed [25] a strengthening [22] of ARSPC.

We used MCMAS-S to check this version of ARSPC against a CTLK formula similar to NSPK's authentication-requirement but expressed for the key established in ARSPC. We found a cut-off of $(2, 2)$ as above; by checking the concrete models, we were able to establish that Lowe's version of ARSPC is correct in the unbounded setting.

On a PC with an Intel(R) Core(TM)2 Quad CPU Q8200 2.33GHz, with 4GB of total memory, running Ubuntu 3.13.0-55-generic, it takes approximately 5 seconds to find the cut-offs above and to check the corresponding systems. The SISPL files for these tests are available together with MCMAS-S at [1].

6. CONCLUSIONS

Forthcoming pervasive applications in the IOTcall for the deployment of MAS to be secure. To this end, this paper puts forward a technique to verify whether the security protocols underlying these applications are correct in a provable way. Concretely, we introduced a semantics that accounts for an unbounded number of protocol sessions and unbounded size data-exchanges under a Dolev-Yao threat and we defined the parameterised model checking problem for these. Though the problem is generally undecidable, in our case we solved it by analysing a finite number of bounded systems. This was possible due to our models enjoying agent-environment synchronisations and a certain symmetry, which is in part down to he class of protocols considered. We mechanised these in MCMAS-S: a model checker which verifies parameterised MAS modelling security protocols against requirements given a fragment of CTLK. We verified versions of the NSPK and ASRPC authentication and key-establishment protocols [31], and we proved their (in)security in an unbounded-session setting.

Related Work. We built upon [20, 21], where the parameterised model checking problem for MAS and the model checker MCMAS-P were introduced. However, neither the semantics nor the tool in [20] can account for security models. For instance, in [20] there is no support for multiple templates, partitioned variables in templates, or for unbounded variables and ranges inside the agents; these are needed to express protocol-roles and the unbounded ranges of, e.g., long-term keys.

The Dolev-Yao-based [14] security semantics is widely adopted in security-verification [5, 29, 12]. But few of these [7] support agent-driven models and temporal-epistemic specifications. Unlike [7], we consider an unbounded number of protocol sessions and agents therein, and so we check a protocol in general terms rather than just draw conclusions for a specific number of principals and sessions of its exchanges.

ProVerif and Tamarin are tools for security-verification in unbounded settings [26, 6], based on methods other than model-checking. They are semidecidable, halting only when an attack is found. This is not the case of MCMAS-S, which ascertains both correctness and incorrectness of unbounded systems. Moreover, those tools generally cannot handle state-based properties in unbounded-size models. And even when they can do so in the bounded setting [4], their requirements cannot pertain to agency-based logics, so they cannot reason on the epistemic states of the principals explicitly, as we do here. As such, it has often been argued that using primitives on agents' knowledge can simplify and clarify specifications of security protocols [2, 17, 11]. Indeed, note that the epistemic formulae we verify, $\neg K_{Intr}(\ldots))$, can be used à la [8] to express privacy requirements via the attacker's ignorance w.r.t. to facts spanning the whole state-space of the systems.

Future Work. We will extend the approach to other classes of protocols and exhibit the analysis of privacy requirements, given their intrinsic epistemic nature.

7. ACKNOWLEDGEMENTS

This research was funded by the European Union's Horizon 2020 research and innovation programme under the Marie Skłodowska-Curie grant agreement No 661362 and by the EPSRC under grant EP/I00520X and a Doctoral Prize Scholarship.

REFERENCES

[1] MCMAS-S. `http://vas.doc.ic.ac.uk/software/extensions/`, 2016.

[2] M. Abadi and M. R. Tuttle. A semantics for a logic of authentication. In *Proc. of the 10th Annual ACM Symposium on Principles of Distributed Computing (PODC'91)*, pages 201–216, 1991. ACM Press.

[3] K. Apt and D. Kozen. Limits for automatic verification of finite-state concurrent systems. *Information Processing Letters*, 22(6):307–309, 1986.

[4] D. Basin, J. Dreier, and R. Sasse. Automated symbolic proofs of observational equivalence. In *Proc. of the 22nd ACM SIGSAC Conference on Computer and Communications Security (CCS'15)*, pages 1144–1155, 2015. ACM.

[5] D. Basin, S. Modersheim, and L. Vigano. OFMC: A symbolic model checker for security protocols. *International Journal of Information Security*, 4(3):181–208, 2005.

[6] B. Blanchet. An efficient cryptographic protocol verifier based on prolog rules. In *Proc.of the 14th IEEE Workshop on Computer Security Foundations (CSFW'01)*, pages 82, 2001. IEEE Computer Society.

[7] I. Boureanu, M. Cohen, and A. Lomuscio. A compilation method for the verification of temporal-epistemic properties of cryptographic protocols. *Journal of Applied Non-Classical Logics*, 19(4):463–487, 2009.

[8] I. Boureanu, A. V. Jones, and A. Lomuscio. Automatic verification of epistemic specifications under convergent equational theories. In *Proc. of the 11th International Conference on Autonomous Agents and Multi-Agent systems (AAMAS'12)*, pages 1141–1148. IFAAMAS Press, 2012.

[9] M. Brown, B. An, C. Kiekintveld, F. Ordóñez, and M. Tambe. An extended study on multi-objective security games. *Autonomous Agents and Multi-Agent Systems*, 28(1):31–71, 2014.

[10] M. Burrows, M. Abadi, and R. Needham. A logic of authentication. *ACM Transactions on Computer Systems*, 8(1):18–36, 1990.

[11] R. Chadha, S. Delaune, and S. Kremer. Epistemic logic for the applied pi calculus. In *Formal Techniques for Distributed Systems*, volume 5522 of *LNCS*, pages 182–197. Springer Berlin Heidelberg, 2009.

[12] B. Conchinha, D. Basin, and C. Caleiro. FAST: an efficient decision procedure for deduction and static equivalence. In *Proc. of the 22nd International Conference on Rewriting Techniques and Applications (RTA'11)*, pages 11–20, 2011.

[13] J. Dickerson, J. Goldman, J. Karp, A. Procaccia, and T. Sandholm. The computational rise and fall of fairness. In *Proc. of the 28th AAAI Conference on Artificial Intelligence*, pages 1405–1411, 2014.

[14] D. Dolev and A. Yao. On the Security of Public-Key Protocols. *IEEE Transactionson Information Theory 29*, 29(2):198–208, 1983.

[15] E. Emerson and A. Sistla. Symmetry and model checking. *Formal methods in system design*, 9(1):105–131, 1996.

[16] R. Fagin, J. Y. Halpern, Y. Moses, and M. Y. Vardi. *Reasoning about Knowledge*. MIT Press, Cambridge, 1995.

[17] J. Y. Halpern and R. Pucella. Modeling Adversaries in a Logic for Security Protocol Analysis. In *Proc. of the Workshop on Formal Aspects of Security (FASec02)*, volume 2629 of *LNCS*, pages 115–132. Springer-Verlag, 2002.

[18] M. R. A. Huth and M. D. Ryan. *Logic in Computer Science: Modelling and Reasoning about Systems (2nd edition)*. Cambridge University Press, Cambridge, England, 2004.

[19] J. Jennings, G. Whelan, and W. Evans. Cooperative search and rescue with a team of mobile robots. In *Proc. of the 8th International Conference on Advanced Robotics (ICAR'97)*, pages 193–200, 1997.

[20] P. Kouvaros and A. Lomuscio. A cutoff technique for the verification of parameterised interpreted systems with parameterised environments. In *Proc. of the 23rd International Joint Conference on Artificial Intelligence (IJCAI'13)*, pages 2013–2019. AAAI Press, 2013.

[21] P. Kouvaros and A. Lomuscio. Parameterised verification for multi-agent systems. *Artificial Intelligence*, 234:152–189, 2016.

[22] Laboratoire Spécification et Vérification (LSV), École Normale Supérieure Cachan. Lowe's version of the ARSPC protocol. A Library of Cryptographic Protocols Descriptions.

[23] A. Lomuscio, W. Penczek, and H. Qu. Partial order reductions for model checking temporal-epistemic logics over interleaved multi-agent systems. *Fundamenta Informaticae*, 101(1):71–90, 2010.

[24] G. Lowe. An attack on the Needham-Schroeder public-key authentication protocol. *Information Processing Letters*, 56(3):131–133, Nov. 1995.

[25] G. Lowe. Some new attacks upon security protocols. In *Proc. of the 9th IEEE Workshop on Computer Security Foundations (CSFW'96)*, pages 162, 1996. IEEE Computer Society.

[26] S. Meier, B. Schmidt, C. Cremers, and D. Basin. The TAMARIN Prover for the Symbolic Analysis of Security Protocols. In *Proc. of the 25th International Conference on Computer Aided Verification (CAV'13)*, pages 696–701, Berlin, Heidelberg, 2013. Springer-Verlag.

[27] R. Needham and M. Schroeder. Using Encryption for Authentication in Large Networks of Computers. *ACM Communications*, 21(12):993–999, Dec. 1978.

[28] L. Paulson. The Inductive Approach to Verifying Cryptographic Protocols. *Journal of Computer Security*, 6(1-2):85–128, Jan. 1998.

[29] M. Rusinowitch and M. Turuani. Protocol Insecurity with Finite Number of Sessions is NP-complete. *Proc. of the 21st IEEE Symposium on Security and Privacy (S&P'01)*, 2001.

[30] M. Satyanarayanan. Integrating security in a large distributed system. *ACM Trans. Comput. Syst.*, 7(3):247–280, Aug. 1989.

[31] SPORE. Security protocols open repository. http://www.lsv.ens-cachan.fr/spore.

A Lazy Approach to Temporal Epistemic Logic Model Checking

Alessandro Cimatti
Fondazione Bruno Kessler
Trento, Italy
cimatti@fbk.eu

Marco Gario
Fondazione Bruno Kessler
Trento, Italy
gario@fbk.eu

Stefano Tonetta
Fondazione Bruno Kessler
Trento, Italy
tonettas@fbk.eu

ABSTRACT

Temporal Epistemic Logic is used to reason about the evolution of knowledge over time. A notable example is the temporal epistemic logic KL_1, which is used to model what a reasoner can infer about the state of a dynamic system by using available observations. Applications of KL_1 span from security (verification of cryptography protocols and information flow) to diagnostic systems (fault detection and diagnosability).

In this paper, we tackle the verification of KL_1 properties under observational semantics, by proposing an effective approach that is able to deal with both finite and infinite state systems. The denotation of the epistemic atoms is computed in a lazy way, driven by the counter-examples obtained from model checking an abstraction of the property. We analyze the approach on a comprehensive set of finite- and infinite-state benchmarks from the literature, evaluate the effectiveness of various optimizations, and demonstrate that our approach outperforms existing approaches.

Keywords

Temporal Epistemic Logic; KL_1; Model Checking; Infinite State; IC3

1. INTRODUCTION

Temporal Epistemic Logic (TEL) is a modal logic combining operators for the evolution of time, and the representation of knowledge. TEL is gaining interest from the practical standpoint. Several works [10, 22, 1, 8] use temporal epistemic logic to model and analyze the knowledge of a perfect reasoner (or agent) that can observe (or sense) a part of a running system. The most common example is in the context of information security [1], or cryptographic protocols verification [8], where we are interested in guaranteeing that some information will remain private, even if some public information is shared. Another interesting example comes from the domain of diagnostic system design [10]. In this domain, we are interested in showing that a diagnoser can detect the occurrence of some non-observable situation (e.g., a fault) by only using the information provided by the available sensors. If the faults are monitored by multiple diagnosers, possibly sharing the available sensors, we obtain a multi-agent characterization of the problem, in which we can study whether one agent is able to detect more faults than another. In several works [19, 30, 10, 24, 4, 23, 4], in these domains, properties are expressed in KL_1 [21], which is an extension of LTL [27] including the knowledge operator K_A, with the restriction that no nesting of knowledge operators occurs.

To properly capture the target domains of cryptograpthic protocols and physical systems, infinite state models are needed. At the same time, infinite state model-checking for transition systems has become a consolidated area of research in the formal verification community [17, 6, 13], where efficient SAT/SMT [2] based algorithms have been developed. Although, in the general case, this is an undecidable problem, these algorithms (e.g., IC3 [15]) are able, in practice, to deal with infinite state models. Moreover, when these techniques are applied to finite state models, they usually exhibit better scalability than BDD-based [12] algorithms.

Our goal is to show how to exploit existing verification algorithms (e.g., IC3) to model-check KL_1 over finite/infinite state transition systems.

Contribution

In this work, we propose an effective approach for KL_1 model-checking of both finite and infinite state transition systems, under observational semantics. This is the first approach to model checking of temporal epistemic logic over infinite state systems that does not rely on the abstraction of the system.

Our solution is characterized by a *lazy* approach. The computation of the denotation of epistemic subformulae of the property is not carried out up-front. Rather, we delay it as much as possible, relying on a counter-example guided abstraction refinement (CEGAR) of the property. Similarly to the lazy approach in Satisfiability Modulo Theories, the epistemic atoms are initially treated as Boolean variables, and incrementally axiomatized as a result of proving the spuriousness of the counterexamples.

This idea makes it possible to deal with infinite state systems, where it might not be possible to compute the reachable state set, and yields a unified approach for both finite and infinite state systems. Moreover, the technique is independent from the underlying model-checking algorithm, and thus we can apply modern verification techniques (e.g., IC3 [11]) and leverage the impressive advancements achieved in the formal verification community.

We propose a number of optimizations to the basic algorithm, and identify a fragment of the logic (*InvKL*$_1$) that has practical interest and for which significant improvements can be achieved. We experimentally evaluate the approach, analyzing the effectiveness of the proposed optimizations, and comparing against an *eager* version of the approach, where the characterization of the epistemic subformula is computed upfront. Additionally, we compare the approach on the benchmarks that can be processed by the competitor systems (thus limited to finite state). The evaluation demonstrates that our approach can dramatically outperform existing approaches.

Appears in: *Proceedings of the 15th International Conference on Autonomous Agents and Multiagent Systems (AAMAS 2016), J. Thangarajah, K. Tuyls, C. Jonker, S. Marsella (eds.), May 9–13, 2016, Singapore.*

Related Work

Decidability and complexity of model checking temporal epistemic logic in the context of infinite state system, has been explored in the context of Artifact Centric Systems [5, 3]. In those works, restrictions on the system are imposed in order to be able to reduce it to a finite state one. Thus, conceptually, one could apply existing finite state techniques. Our work differs in several aspects. First, we deal with transition systems, which are a common formalism to model physical systems and programs, and are typically used as underlying semantics for higher-level design specification languages. Second, we implement and evaluate our technique against both infinite and finite examples. Finally, and maybe most importantly, we use effective and well-known techniques for infinite state model checking as a black-box. In this way, we can automatically benefit from the improvements that are occurring in the area. To the best of our knowledge, [5, 3] are limited to the theoretical aspects, and no implementation is available.

Techniques for model-checking temporal epistemic logic for linear time and observational semantics for finite state systems are mostly based on BDDs. Unfortunately, BDDs are not able to deal with industrial size designs that can easily overcome 10^{200} states. For this reason, we are interested in applying SAT/SMT based algorithms.

From the algorithmic point of view, BDD-based techniques rely on the upfront, eager computation of the denotation, i.e., the set of states that satisfy a formula. In principle, it is possible to perform the eager computation of the denotation using SAT/SMT approaches but, as shown by the experimental evaluation in Section 7, this simple approach does not scale in practice. Instead, we rely on a lazy computation of the denotation.

In terms of underlying technology, we present an approach that is independent from the underlying model-checking technique. In our experimental evaluation, we implement it on top of an IC3-based verification engine for infinite-state transition systems.

MCMAS [26] and MCK [20] represent the state of the art in model checking temporal epistemic logic, and they both mostly rely on BDD-based techniques. In terms of expressiveness, we focus on *KL*$_1$, the fragment of the logic without nesting of epistemic operators and common knowledge, while MCK and MCMAS support both arbitrary nesting and common knowledge; on the other hand, the technique proposed here deals also with infinite state systems.

A few works (including MCK) use Bounded Model Checking techniques, for fragments of the logic in which the epistemic operator does not appear negated [31]. Apart from the syntactical limitation, these approaches are incomplete, since bounded model checking is, in general, an incomplete technique.

Our work is very related also to [29]. In [29] the temporal epistemic model checking problem is reduced to temporal model checking, by introducing (expressions on) variables local to an agent that are satisfied if and only if the corresponding epistemic expression is satisfied. In that work, however, the identification of such variables, called local propositions, is performed manually and up-front. Our approach provides an effective and fully automated technique to obtain an expression over the observable variables that characterizes the epistemic expression; additionally, we show that our approach works, in practice, also for infinite state transition systems.

Structure of the paper

The paper is structured as follows. Section 2 provides some necessary background. Section 3 formalizes the logic *KL*, the fragment *InvKL*$_1$, and defines the problem of model checking *KL* on a transition system. Section 4 presents an eager approach at solving the problem, while Section 5 presents the basic version of our lazy approach. Optimizations are discussed in Section 6. In Section 7 we provide a detailed experimental analysis of the approach. Section 8 concludes with directions for future work.

2. BACKGROUND

Our setting is quantifier-free first order logic. We use the standard notions of theory, satisfiability, validity, logical consequence. We denote formulas with $\phi, \varphi, \psi, I, T$, variables with v, x, y, and sets of variables with V. We refer to 0-arity predicates as Boolean variables, and to 0-arity uninterpreted functions as (theory) variables. If $V_1, \ldots, V_n$ are a sets of variables and φ is a formula, we might write $\varphi(V_1, \ldots, V_n)$ to indicate that all the variables occurring in φ are elements of $\bigcup_{i=1}^{n} V_i$. For each variable x, we assume that there exists a corresponding variable x' (the *primed version* of x). If V is a set of variables, V' is the set obtained by replacing each element x with its primed version ($V' = \{x' \mid x \in V\}$). Given an assignment s to variables in V, we denote with s' the assignment to the variables V' such that $s'(v') = s(v)$ for every $v \in V$. Given a formula φ, φ' is the formula obtained by adding a prime to each variable occurring in φ. Given a theory $\mathcal{T}$, we write $\varphi \models_{\mathcal{T}} \psi$ (or simply $\varphi \models \psi$) to denote that the formula ψ is a logical consequence of φ in the theory $\mathcal{T}$. Given a finite set V of variables with a (potentially) infinite domain, we denote with $\Sigma(V)$ the set of assignments to V.

A *transition system* (TS) S is a tuple $S = (V, I, T)$, where V is a set of (state) variables, $I(V)$ is a formula representing the initial states, and $T(V, V')$ is a formula representing the transitions. A state $s \in \Sigma(V)$ of S is an assignment to the variables V. A [finite] trace σ of S is an infinite [resp., finite] sequence of states $\sigma = s_0, s_1, \cdots$ such that $s_0 \models I$ and $\forall i.\ (s_i, s'_{i+1}) \models T$. We use $\sigma[i]$ to denote the state s_i of a trace, while we use σ^i to denote the prefix $\sigma[0], \sigma[1], \cdots, \sigma[i]$ of σ. A state s is reachable iff there is a finite trace σ such that $\sigma[i] = s$ for some i. We use $Reach$ to denote the set of reachable states. Without loss of generality, we assume the system to be deadlock free, i.e., that for all $s \in Reach$, there exists s' such that $s, s' \models T(V, V')$.

The infinite characterization of these systems is given by the infinite domain of the variables, i.e., in each state we have a finite number of variables that can potentially have an infinite domain. For example, we can have integer or rational values, and use the theory of arithmetic [18] to define the transition relation.

Given a transition system S and a property φ expressed, for example, in LTL [27], the model-checking problem asks whether all the traces of S satisfy φ, i.e., $S \models \varphi$. Let S be a transition system and let U be a set of parameters, we define the *parametric transition system* $P = (V, U, I_U, T_U)$, where $I(V, U)$ and $T(V, U, V')$ are now defined on both the state variables and parameters. Given a valuation for the parameters ($\gamma \in \Sigma(U)$), and a formula ψ we denote by $\gamma(\psi)$ the formula obtained by substituting in ψ every occurrence of u with $\gamma(u)$ for every parameter u in U. Given a parametric transition system P and a valuation for the parameters γ, we can compute the *induced* transition system, by replacing the parameters with their valuation: $P_\gamma = (V, \gamma(I_U), \gamma(T_U))$. Given an LTL property ϕ expressed over the state variables and parameters of a parametric transition system P, the *parameter synthesis* problem consists in finding the set of assignments to the parameters, called parameter region ω, s.t. the property is satisfied by every trace of the induced system, formally: $\omega = \{\gamma \mid P_\gamma \models \gamma(\phi)\}$

In this work, we rely on off-the-shelf tools for LTL model-checking and parameter synthesis for infinite-state systems [13].

3. MODEL CHECKING KL_1

Let A be an agent from a set $\mathcal{A}\}$ of possible agents. We want to talk about the possible knowledge of A assuming that it is a perfect reasoner. A *partially observable transition system* (POTS) is a transition system equipped with a set of observable variables $O \subseteq V$, i.e., $M = (V, I, T, O)$. We associate to each observer A a set of observable variables of the POTS M: $O_A \subseteq O$. Given an observer, we define the observation function $obs_A : \Sigma(V) \to \Sigma(O_A)$ as the projection on the observable variables of A for a given state. A *KL* formula has the following syntax:

$$\varphi := p \mid \varphi \wedge \varphi \mid \neg\varphi \mid X\varphi \mid Y\varphi \mid \varphi U \varphi \mid \varphi S \varphi \mid K_A\varphi$$

where p is a predicate, and $A \in \mathcal{A}\}$ is an observer. We define the Boolean operators $\vee, \to$, and the temporal operators globally (G), finally (F), once (O) and historically (H) as usual [25]. When dealing with only one observer, we simply write $K\varphi$.

The semantics of *KL* is defined recursively on points of traces and observation functions of the system M. Given a trace $\sigma = s_0, \cdots, s_n, \cdots$ of M, and $n \geq 0$ we have that:

- $(M, \sigma, n) \models p$ iff $\sigma[n] \models p$
- $(M, \sigma, n) \models \neg\varphi$ iff $(M, \sigma, n) \not\models \varphi$
- $(M, \sigma, n) \models X\varphi$ iff $(M, \sigma, n+1) \models \varphi$
- $(M, \sigma, n) \models Y\varphi$ iff $n > 0$ and $(M, \sigma, n-1) \models \varphi$
- $(M, \sigma, n) \models \varphi U \psi$ iff there exists $i \geq n$ such that $(M, \sigma, i) \models \psi$ and for all $j, n \leq j < i$, $(M, \sigma, j) \models \varphi$
- $(M, \sigma, n) \models \varphi S \psi$ iff there exists $i \leq n$ such that $(M, \sigma, i) \models \psi$ and for all $j, i < j \leq n$, $(M, \sigma, j) \models \varphi$
- $(M, \sigma, n) \models K_A\varphi$ iff for all traces σ' of M and integers $m \geq 0$ s.t. $obs_A(\sigma[n]) = obs_A(\sigma'[m])$ it holds that $(M, \sigma', m) \models \varphi$.

We say that a system M satisfies a formula φ ($M \models \varphi$) if every trace of M satisfies φ. The semantics that we use for K_A is called *observational semantics*. To evaluate the validity of this formula, the observer can use only the information available in the current time-point (i.e., no-memory). Although this looks quite limited, the observer can reason about past and future behaviors of the system, since it knows the model of the system. For example, imagine a counter from 0 to 10; when the observer sees the value of the counter being 10, it knows that previously it was 5. Another important reason for using observational semantics is the possibility of encoding *bounded recall*. If the observer can remember the last w observations, we just extend the system with a queue of observations, in which we store the last w observations.

Due to the observational semantics, if $(M, \sigma, n) \models K_A\varphi$, then $(M, \sigma', m) \models K_A\varphi$ for every trace σ' of M such that $obs_A(\sigma[n]) = obs_A(\sigma'[m])$. In this sense, the satisfaction of the formula $K_A\varphi$ in (σ, n) depends only on the state $\sigma[n]$. Thus, we define the denotation of $K_A\varphi$ in M (written $[\![K_A\varphi]\!]_M$) as:

$$[\![K_A\varphi]\!]_M = \{\overline{s} \in Reach \mid \forall\sigma, \forall n.\ obs_A(\sigma[n]) = obs_A(\overline{s}) \Rightarrow (M, \sigma, n) \models K_A\varphi\}.$$

So, for every σ, for every $n \geq 0$, $(M, \sigma, n) \models K_A\varphi$ iff $\sigma[n] \in [\![K_A\varphi]\!]_M$. KL_n is the syntactic fragment of *KL* in which the deepest nesting of K operators contains at most n K's: KL_1 is the fragment of *KL* without nesting of K, and KL_0 is LTL. We allow multiple agents, and thus we have potentially many K operators (multi-modal). For example, given the observers A and B, the formula $K_Ap \wedge K_B\neg p$ is in KL_1, while the formula K_AK_Bp is not, since there is a nesting of the epistemic operator.

We call *epistemic invariants* of KL_1 ($InvKL_1$) the properties that fall into the following syntactic fragment (ϕ):

$$\phi := G\psi, \quad \psi := p \mid \psi \wedge \psi \mid \neg\psi \mid K_A\gamma$$
$$\gamma := p \mid \gamma \wedge \gamma \mid \neg\gamma \mid X\gamma \mid Y\gamma \mid \gamma U \gamma \mid \gamma S \gamma$$

Notice that, apart from the top-level G, all other temporal operators can occur only within the K (i.e., γ). KL_1 (and $InvKL_1$) are widely used fragments, despite their simplicity. The following are just a few examples of properties in the literature that are not only in KL_1 but in $InvKL_1$:

- Muddy Children [19]:
  $$G(((K_i muddy_i) \vee (K_i \neg muddy_i)) \to says_i)$$
- Dining Cryptographers [30]:
  $$G([(K_1\neg paid_1) \wedge (K_1\neg paid_2) \wedge (K_1\neg paid_3)] \vee$$
  $$[K_1(paid_1 \vee paid_2 \vee paid_3) \wedge \neg(K_1 paid_2) \wedge \neg(K_1 paid_3)])$$
- FDI maximality [10]: $G(KOfault \to Alarm)$
- Card Games [24]: $G(allred \to K_{Player1}F(win_1))$

and more examples include the Faulty Train Gate Controller [4], the Gossip Protocol [4], and goals in planning problems [23].

Voters Example

A group of people are called to express a vote. The vote is represented by an unbounded integer value bigger than 0. The vote is secret, but the jury can access the sum of all votes (observable). This model can be captured by the following transition system:

$$Vars : \{guess \in \mathbb{N}, vote_i \in \mathbb{N}, voted \in \mathbb{B}\}$$
$$Init : \neg voted$$
$$Trans : (result' = vote_0 + \cdots + vote_n) \wedge$$
$$voted' \wedge guess' = guess \wedge vote_i' = vote_i$$

Can the jury know what somebody voted? More formally, can the jury know what the first voter voted, i.e., if $M \models G(voted \to \neg K_{\{jury\}} vote_1 = guess)$, where $guess$ is an integer variable, and $jury = \{result, guess\}$ is the set of observable variables for the jury. Intuitively, for every possible guess, it is not possible for the jury to know that the first voter's vote matches the guess. The counter-example to this specification is a corner case: if everybody votes 0, the jury knows what everybody voted.

4. EAGER ALGORITHM

A simple way of solving the model-checking problem for KL_1, consists in computing the denotation of the epistemic atoms upfront. By replacing the epistemic atoms with their denotation, the KL_1 property can then be reduced to an LTL property. This is similar to what is done by BDD-based techniques, and we call it *eager* approach. We use the definition of denotation to compute it. In particular, we first compute the set of reachable states of the system, and then partition it based on observations. Finally, we consider only those sets of states with the same observations s.t. all of them satisfy β (e.g., for $[\![K_A\beta]\!]$). Given the set of reachable states, the denotation can be symbolically computed by performing quantifier-elimination.

A similar approach to obtain the denotation can be defined as a parameter synthesis problem [14]. The intuition is that the parameters are indicators of which states belong to the denotation. We experimented with this idea by building it on top of an IC3-based parameter synthesis engine. However, this yielded limited scalability (more details in Section 7). The intuition behind the limited performances is the following. Consider the property $G(K_A\beta \rightarrow \alpha)$ (every-time that the observer knows β, then α holds). To disprove this property, eager approaches need to compute the denotation of $K_A\beta$ and then intersect it with the denotation of $\neg\alpha$. The intersection might represent only a small set of states. Therefore, a lot of the computation performed up-front might not be needed (e.g., if α is always true). Moreover, in the case of infinite state systems, it might not be possible to represent the set of states of the denotation. For this reason, we develop the lazy approach, in which we compute only an approximation of the denotation that is sufficient to verify the property.

5. LAZY ALGORITHM

For a system to violate a property, we need a counter-example trace. We model-check an abstract version of the property, in which we treat all epistemic subformulas as propositional atoms. If we find a counter-example for this abstract property, we need to verify whether the counter-example satisfies all epistemic subformulas or whether it is spurious. If it is not spurious, we are done and the property is not satisfied. Otherwise, we need to refine our abstracted property, by learning additional constraints, and repeat. This flow is similar to the typical CEGAR [16] loop, with the significant difference that we do not refine the model but the property. The approach is divided into four main phases (Figure 1):

1. KL_1 to LTL abstraction
2. LTL Verification
3. Spuriousness check
4. Property Refinement.

```
1: function VERIFY(M, φ)
2:     φ_ρ, placeholders := BOOL_ABSTRACTION(φ)
3:     M_ρ := EXTEND(M, placeholders)
4:     loop
5:         cex := M_ρ ⊨ φ_ρ
6:         if not cex then
7:             return "Satisfied"
8:         end if
9:         if IS_SPURIOUS(M, cex, placeholders) then
10:            φ_ρ := LEARN_LEMMA(M, cex, placeholders, φ_ρ)
11:        else
12:            return cex
13:        end if
14:    end loop
15: end function
16:
17: function IS_SPURIOUS(M, cex, placeholders)
18:    for state ∈ cex do
19:        for ρ_{K_Aβ} ∈ placeholders do
20:            p_value := ρ_{K_Aβ}(state)
21:            if not ((state ∈ [[K_Aβ]]) ↔ p_value) then
22:                return True // Spurious!
23:            end if
24:        end for
25:    end for
26:    return False
27: end function
```

Figure 1: Lazy Algorithm Pseudo-Code

Property Abstraction

For every epistemic subformula $K_A\beta$, we introduce a fresh *placeholder variable* $\rho_{K_A\beta}$ and obtain the abstracted property $\varphi_\rho = \varphi[K_A\beta/\rho_{K_A\beta}]$ by replacing each epistemic formula with the corresponding placeholder (Line 2 – BOOL_ABSTRACTION). The system is extended by adding the placeholder variables, that are initially unconstrained (Line 3). This corresponds to the most general abstraction of the property: in any state the placeholder can be true or false. Counter-examples to the abstract property, represents assignments for the epistemic subformulas that can violate the property. For example, if a state of a counter-example contains a placeholder set to true, it means that in that state we want the epistemic subformula to hold. After this step, we have a property φ_ρ that is purely LTL, and an extended transition system (M_ρ) that contains all the variables of M plus the (unconstrained) placeholder variables.

LTL Verification

The main loop (Line 4) of the algorithm checks whether $M_\rho \models \varphi_\rho$. If we verify the abstract property on the system, then also the original property is satisfied. However, the converse is not true, due to spurious counter-examples, i.e., a counter-example trace that is not consistent from the epistemic point of view. For example, there is a state where the epistemic subformula holds, but that does not belong to the denotation of the epistemic formula. We iterate until a valid counter-example is found, or the property is shown to hold ($M_\rho \models \varphi_\rho$). If no counter-example is found (Lines 6-7), then the model satisfies the abstracted property, and therefore we can terminate: on some systems we are able to terminate without ever checking the epistemic part. If a counter-example exists, we need to check whether it is spurious (Line 9). If this is the case, we can exclude the counter-example, otherwise we have found a valid counter example.

Spuriousness Check and Refinement

To check the spuriousness of a counter-example, we need to check that each state of the counter-example satisfies the epistemic part. This is implemented in the function IS_SPURIOUS (Line 17). Each state can be checked in isolation because the transition relation is independent from the epistemic part. For each state of the counter-example, and for each epistemic subformula (Lines 18-19), we extract the value of the placeholder (p_value, Line 20), and check whether the state belongs to the denotation. If p_value is true but the state does not belong to the denotation or, viceversa, p_value is false and the state belongs to the denotation, then we are in a spurious state, and we can exclude the counter-example. If we validated all epistemic formulas in all the states, then the counter-example is a real counter-example (Line 26).

To know whether a state s belongs to $[\![K_A\beta]\!]$, ($s \in [\![K_A\beta]\!]$) we perform the following model-checking query:

$$M \models G(\bigwedge_{x \in O_A} x = s(x) \rightarrow \beta)$$

intuitively, we ask whether each reachable state that has the same observation of s, satisfies the formula β. If M satisfies the property (positive case), we learn the lemma $\bigwedge_{x \in O_A} x = s(x) \rightarrow \rho_{K_A\beta}$, otherwise (negative case) we learn $\bigwedge_{x \in O_A} x = s(x) \rightarrow \neg\rho_{K_A\beta}$

(these are the lemmas returned by the LEARN_LEMMA function at Line 10). These lemmas impose additional constraints between all the states with the given observation and the placeholder variables, thus characterizing the epistemic atoms. In particular, if the counter-example is spurious, then we exclude it. Lemmas are learned by updating φ_ρ (Line 12), i.e., learned lemmas (λ_i) become preconditions to to φ_ρ. Thus in each iteration i, we have $\varphi_\rho^i := \lambda_i \rightarrow \varphi_\rho^{i-1}$.

InvKL$_1$

If $\varphi \in$ *InvKL*$_1$, the property rewriting step gives us a formula $G(\psi)$ where ψ is purely propositional. Since we are assuming deadlock freedom, this encodes an invariant over reachable states and we can take advantage of this fact, by using ad-hoc reachability algorithms, instead of a full LTL algorithm. This provides us with a performance boost and, more importantly, guarantees us that the counter-example will be a finite trace ending in a state that violates ψ. During the validation of the counter-example we need to validate only the last state of the trace, thus obtaining significant speed-ups, since the validation phase does not depend anymore on the length of the counter-example traces.

Example

We apply the algorithm on the property $\varphi = G(K\beta \rightarrow \alpha)$. We first rewrite it as LTL, and introduce the placeholder variable: $\varphi_\rho = G(\rho_{K\beta} \rightarrow \alpha)$. The transition system $M = (V, I, T, O)$ is extended by adding the unconstrained placeholder variable $M_\rho = (V \cup \{\rho_{K\beta}\}, I, T, O)$. The main-loop of the procedure checks whether $M_\rho \models \varphi_\rho$. Let us assume that the answer is negative, and we get the trace:

$$(o_1, \alpha, \beta, \rho_{K\beta}), (\neg o_1, \neg\alpha, \beta, \rho_{K\beta})$$

that violates the abstract property, since the last state requires the epistemic formula to hold, but α does not hold. We check whether this is a spurious counter-example, by checking the consistency of each state of the trace. In particular, we want to know if the first state belongs to the denotation of $K\beta$, since the state has observation o_1, we verify whether : $M \models G(o_1 \rightarrow \beta)$. Let us assume that this query has a positive outcome then we check the next state, and whether $M \models (G\neg o_1 \rightarrow \beta)$. Let us assume that this query has a negative outcome then we modify our property to include this lemma: $\varphi'_\rho = (\neg o_1 \rightarrow \neg\rho_{K\beta}) \rightarrow \varphi_\rho$. Since this is a spurious state, the counter-example is considered spurious, and we need to find another counter-example. We check $M_\rho \models \varphi'_\rho$ and no counter-example is found. Thus, we conclude that $M \models G(K\beta \rightarrow \alpha)$. Notice that the property is an *InvKL*$_1$ property, therefore it would have been sufficient to only verify the last.

5.1 Correctness

The following two lemmas show that the lazy approach is correct, i.e., $M \models \varphi$ iff the lazy algorithm does not produce a counter-example:

LEMMA 1. *Given M and φ, and the associated M_ρ, φ_ρ, we have that if $M_\rho \models \varphi_\rho$ then $M \models \varphi$.*

DEFINITION 1 (SPURIOUS STATE). *Let σ_ρ be a trace of M_ρ and σ be its projection on the variables of M. The state $\sigma_\rho[n]$ is* spurious *iff: for all $K_A\beta$ occurring in φ, $(M_\rho, \sigma_\rho, n) \models \rho_{K_A\beta}$ iff $\sigma[n] \in [\![K_A\beta]\!]_M$.*

LEMMA 2. *Let σ_ρ be a trace of M_ρ and σ be its projection on the variables of M. If $(M_\rho, \sigma_\rho) \models \neg\varphi_\rho$ and, for all $n \geq 0$. $\sigma_\rho[n]$ is not spurious , then $(M, \sigma) \models \neg\varphi$.*

Lemma 2 requires that the counter-example is not spurious, and in particular, that we are able to check whether a state belongs to the denotation. Therefore, we need to prove that the model-checking query that we use to check whether a state belongs (or not) to the denotation is correct:

THEOREM 1. *Given a reachable state s of M, the following three statements are equivalent:*

1. $s \in [\![K_A\beta]\!]_M$
2. $M \models G(\bigwedge_{x\in O_A} x = s(x) \rightarrow \beta)$
3. $M \models G(\bigwedge_{x\in O_A} x = s(x) \rightarrow K_A\beta)$

PROOF. 1 $\Leftrightarrow$ 3) By the definition of KL_1, $M \models G(\bigwedge_{x\in O_A} x = s(x) \rightarrow \beta)$ iff for all σ, for all n, if $obs_A(\sigma[n]) = obs_A(s)$, then $(M, \sigma, n) \models K_A\beta$. Then, by the definition of $[\![K_A\beta]\!]_M$, the condition 1 holds iff s is reachable and 2 holds.

2 $\Rightarrow$ 3) Consider a trace σ and an integer n such that $obs_A(\sigma[n]) = obs_A(s)$. Since the condition 2 holds, then for all σ', for all n', if $obs_A(\sigma'[n']) = obs_A(s)$, then $(M, \sigma', n') \models \beta$; thus, for all σ', for all n', if $obs_A(\sigma'[n']) = obs_A(\sigma[n])$, then $(M, \sigma', n') \models \beta$. Thus, $(M, \sigma, n) \models K_A\beta$.

3 $\Rightarrow$ 2) The condition 2 follows directly from 3 and the fact that $K_A\beta \rightarrow \beta$ is a tautology for all β (Axiom of knowledge **T**). □

THEOREM 2. *Given a reachable state s of M, the following three statements are equivalent:*

1. $s \notin [\![K_A\beta]\!]_M$
2. $M \not\models G(\bigwedge_{x\in O_A} x = s(x) \rightarrow \beta)$
3. $M \models G(\bigwedge_{x\in O_A} x = s(x) \rightarrow \neg K_A\beta)$

PROOF. 1 $\Leftrightarrow$ 3) follows from Theorem 1 by contraposition.

2 $\Rightarrow$ 3) Consider a trace σ and an integer n such that $obs_A(\sigma[n]) = obs_A(s)$. Since the condition 2 holds, then there exists σ' and n' such that $obs_A(\sigma'[n']) = obs_A(s)$ and $(M, \sigma', n') \not\models \beta$; thus, it is not true that for all σ', for all n', if $obs_A(\sigma'[n']) = obs_A(\sigma[n])$, then $(M, \sigma', n') \models \beta$. Thus, $(M, \sigma, n) \models \neg K_A\beta$.

3 $\Rightarrow$ 2) Suppose by contradiction that $M \models G(\bigwedge_{x\in O_A} x = s(x) \rightarrow \beta)$. Thus, by Theorem 1, $M \models G(\bigwedge_{x\in O_A} x = s(x) \rightarrow K_A\beta)$. Since s is reachable, then there exists σ and n such that $\sigma[n] = s$. Thus $(M, \sigma, n) \models K_A\beta$ and, by the condition 3, $(M, \sigma, n) \models \neg K_A\beta$, which is a contradiction. □

Finally, we need to show that the lemmas that we are adding to exclude a spurious counter-example are correct, i.e., the abstract model-checking problem is still a sound over-approximation of the concrete model-checking problem. More precisely, if we use the lemma to restrict the abstract state space and the abstract model checking passes, then we can still conclude that $M \models \varphi$:

THEOREM 3. *(Positive case) Assume that $M \models G(\bigwedge_{x\in O} \overline{o}(x) = x \rightarrow \beta)$ and $M_\rho \models G(\bigwedge_{x\in O} \overline{o}(x) = x \rightarrow \rho_{K\beta}) \rightarrow \varphi_\rho$ Then $M \models \varphi$.*

PROOF. (Positive case) If $M_\rho \models G(\bigwedge_{x\in O} \overline{o}(x) = x \rightarrow \rho_{K\beta}) \rightarrow \varphi_\rho$, then i) $M \models G(\bigwedge_{x\in O} \overline{o}(x) = x \rightarrow K\beta) \rightarrow \varphi$ (by Theorem 1). If $M \models G(\bigwedge_{x\in O} \overline{o}(x) = x \rightarrow \beta)$, then ii) $M \models G(\bigwedge_{x\in O} \overline{o}(x) = x \rightarrow K\beta)$ (by Theorem 1). From i) and ii), we can deduce that $M \models \varphi$.
□

THEOREM 4. *(Negative case) Assume that* $M \not\models G(\bigwedge_{x\in O}\overline{o}(x) = x \rightarrow \beta)$ *and* $M_\rho \models G(\bigwedge_{x\in O}\overline{o}(x) = x \rightarrow \neg\rho_{K\beta}) \rightarrow \varphi_\rho$ *Then* $M \models \varphi$.

PROOF. (Negative case) If $M_\rho \models G(\bigwedge_{x\in O}\overline{o}(x) = x \rightarrow \neg\rho_{K\beta}) \rightarrow \varphi_\rho$, then i) $M \models G(\bigwedge_{x\in O}\overline{o}(x) = x \rightarrow \neg K\beta) \rightarrow \varphi$ (by Theorem 1). If $M \not\models G(\bigwedge_{x\in O}\overline{o}(x) = x \rightarrow \beta)$, then ii) $M \models G(\bigwedge_{x\in O}\overline{o}(x) = x \rightarrow \neg K\beta)$ (by Theorem 2). From i) and ii), we can deduce that $M \models \varphi$. □

We mentioned that if the property falls within the *InvKL*$_1$ fragment, then it is possible to validate only the last state of the counter-example.

THEOREM 5. *Let* M *be a system,* $G\varphi$ *an InvKL*$_1$ *property, and* M_ρ *and* $G\varphi_\rho$ *the corresponding abstractions. If there exists a trace* σ_ρ *of* M_ρ *of size* n *s.t.* $\sigma_\rho[n] \not\models \varphi_\rho$ *and* $\sigma_\rho[n]$ *is not spurious, then* $M \not\models G\varphi$.

PROOF. Let σ be the projection of σ_ρ on the variables of M. From the Definition 1, we know that if $\sigma_\rho[n] \not\models \varphi_\rho$ then $\sigma[n] \not\models \varphi$. Therefore, the invariant property is violated. □

5.2 Termination

System	*InvKL*$_1$	*KL*$_1$
Finite	Complete	Complete
Infinite w/ Finite Domain Obs.	Relative Complete	Incomplete
Infinite w/ Infinite Domain Obs.	Incomplete	Incomplete

Figure 2: Completeness

Our algorithm is guaranteed to terminate on finite state systems, since there is a finite number of possible values for observations and placeholders. Model checking for infinite state systems is in general undecidable, therefore we have the problem that the internal model-checking calls might not terminate. In practice, model-checkers for infinite state systems (e.g., UPPAAL [6], SAL [17], nuXmv [13]) can terminate on particular instances or classes of models. We call *relative complete* an algorithm that terminates assuming that all the model-checking queries terminate. Our approach is relative complete for infinite state systems only if we have both finite domain observations, and finite counter-examples (as in the case of *InvKL*$_1$). Otherwise, the algorithm is incomplete, since we might need to enumerate infinitely many observations, or validate infinitely many states. Figure 2 summarizes the result. Despite the theoretical result, we will show in Section 7, that our approach is able in practice to verify many models of interest.

6. OPTIMIZATIONS

Static Learning

The placeholder variables are initially unconstrained. However, there are some facts that we can learn by looking at the property, for example, the axioms of epistemic logic. First, we know that $K\beta \rightarrow \beta$. This translates into the constraint: $\rho_{K\beta} \rightarrow \beta$. This ensures that we never need to validate a counter example in which $\rho_{K\beta}$ and $\neg\beta$. Moreover, if o is a Boolean observable for A, then $K_A o \leftrightarrow o$. Thus, we add the constraints $\rho_{Ko} \leftrightarrow o$ for each observable variable of the observer A.

Lemma Generalization

During refinement we learn something about a single observation. We generalize this to cover a bigger space of the observations, relating multiple observations to the value of the placeholder. For a state s and an observation $\overline{o}$, we generalize the lemma $\overline{o} \rightarrow \rho_{K\beta}$ into $\overline{o}_1 \vee \cdots \vee \overline{o}_n \rightarrow \rho_{K\beta}$ (similarly for the negative case).

The main technique that we use to perform the generalization is parameter synthesis. Given the observation $\overline{o}$, we remove some element, and perform the parameter synthesis starting from a partial assignment. We partition the set of observables in the ones we fix and the one we parameterize: $O = O_F \cup O_P$, $O_F \cap O_P = \emptyset$. For $K\beta$ we solve the following parameter synthesis problem:

$$\omega = \{\overline{o}' \mid M \models G((\bigwedge_{x\in O_F} \overline{o}(x) = x \wedge \bigwedge_{x\in O_P} \overline{o}'(x) = x) \rightarrow \beta)\}$$

where $\overline{o}'$ is an assignment to the O_P variables. In practice, we obtain the region ω of assignments to O_P that (toghether with $\overline{o}$) imply β. Since the region is maximal, all other assignments to O_P do not entail β. Therefore, we learn the lemma: $\overline{o} \rightarrow (\omega \leftrightarrow \rho_{K\beta})$.

Choosing the partition into O_F and O_P is an interesting point of research, which we leave as future work. We propose a simple baseline heuristic, in which we randomly select a number w of observable variables. The choice of w is also heuristic, since a small value will cause overhead without gaining much generalization, while a big value will quickly lead to too many parameters. Indeed, picking $O_P = O$ (i.e., using all observable variables as parameters) is equivalent to solving the problem using the *eager* approach. In our implementation, we pick w as the logarithm of the iterations performed so far.

Dual-Rail Encoding

Validating a long counter-example is expensive. However, not all states might need to be validated. Let us consider the property: $a \wedge Xa \wedge XXKb$. A counter-example to this might be the trace: $(a, b, \rho_{Kb}), (a, b, \neg\rho_{Kb}), (a, \neg b, \neg\rho_{Kb})$. The satisfaction of the epistemic subformula in the first two states is irrelevant. We would like the model-checker to identify those states so that we can skip them. Thus, we provide a way for the counter-example to contain *don't care* information, transforming the trace above to:

$$(a, b, -), (a, b, -), (a, \neg b, \neg\rho_{Kb})$$

This saves us from checking the first two states, and can be a significant saving when the traces are long. We use the Dual-Rail encoding [28] to encode three values: *True*, *False* and *Don't Care*. For a placeholder ρ_i we introduce the variables ρ_i^{True} and ρ_i^{False}, that are mutually exclusive. If ρ_i^{True} is true, then the placeholder is true; if ρ_i^{False} is true, then the placeholder is false; if both are false, then the placeholder has a do not care value. We then modify the IS_SPURIOUS function (Figure 1) to handle the special case in which the placeholder is set to *don't care*, by considering the epistemic subformula as satisfied.

Positive Generalization via UNSAT-Cores

For epistemic atoms encoding safety properties, we can perform a more aggressive lemma generalization in case of a positive outcome from the placeholder query. If β is a safety property, when showing that $M \models G(\overline{o} \rightarrow \beta)$ holds, an IC3-based model-checker will also provide us with an *inductive invariant* ι as witness. Since ι is an inductive invariant, $\iota \rightarrow (\overline{o} \rightarrow \beta)$. We use unsat-core extraction to obtain a subset of the observations $\overline{o}$ that make the above unsatisfiable. In fact, $\iota \wedge \overline{o} \wedge \neg\beta$ is unsatisfiable, and we obtain an unsat-core expressed over the observable variables that justifies the unsatisfiability [7]. Let us call $\overline{o}'$ such an unsat core. By definition, we have that $\iota \wedge \overline{o}' \rightarrow \beta$. Therefore, $\overline{o}'$ is a generalization of $\overline{o}$. Moreover, the unsat core extraction is a purely combinational problem, that can be efficiently handled by a SAT or SMT solver.

Voters Example

In the voters example (Section 3), there are infinitely many voting combinations that constitute a counter-example. The positive lemma UNSAT-Core generalization can help us quickly find the problem, by generating the lemma:

$$(result = 0 \wedge guess = 0) \rightarrow \rho_K$$

that justifies the counterexample. Let us assume that at least one voter did not vote 0. We rewrite the property as:

$$M \models G(voted \wedge (\bigvee_{v \in voter} vote_v \neq 0) \rightarrow \neg K_{jury} vote_1 = guess)$$

To show that no other counter-example exists, we would need to check all possible values of the votes, that are infinitely many. The negative generalization based on parameter synthesis allows us to terminate, by showing that any other voting is good.

7. EXPERIMENTAL ANALYSIS

7.1 Setup

We implemented a prototype on top of an IC3 model-checker for infinite state systems using the theory of Linear Rational Arithmetic [18]. We evaluated the scalability of the approach on infinite state models for both KL_1 and $InvKL_1$ properties, and compared the different optimizations to identify a competitive configuration. Finally, we compared our approach against the latest versions of two state-of-the-art model checkers: MCK [20] and MCMAS [26]. Both tools implement BDD-based techniques for model-checking temporal epistemic logic with observational semantics (including common knowledge operator, that we do not consider). Experiments were executed on a 2.5Ghz Intel Xeon CPU, with a timeout of 1 hour; tools, and benchmarks are available online[1].

Benchmarks

The *Battery-Sensor* model (described in [10]) encodes a typical subsystem found in aerospace designs, in which a set of redundant sensors are powered by a redundant power supply unit containing batteries that are modeled using real-valued variables. We study multiple properties related to faults in the system, for example:

$$G(fault\_gen_1 \rightarrow K fault\_gen_1)$$
$$G(K(gen_1.off \wedge gen_2.off) \rightarrow KX^{10}(\neg device.on))$$
$$G(fault\_psu \rightarrow FKO(fault\_psu))$$

The second benchmark is a set of *magicboxes* [9], where a ball moves through a predefined pattern defined on a bi-dimensional grid. The external observer can only perform row and column observations, where row observation do not provide information on the column (and viceversa). The reasoner needs to consider the predefined path inside the magicbox and the available row and column information to try to identify the location of the ball. Scaling the size of the magicbox enables stressing the algorithms. For each magicbox we generate also an MCK and MCMAS model and test whether it is possible to know that the ball is in a given cell: $G(target\_cell \rightarrow K target\_cell)$.

[1] https://es.fbk.eu/people/gario/aamas16/

The *Dining Cryptographers* is a well studied problem in temporal epistemic logic [30]. We generated instances also for MCMAS and MCK, for an increasing number of cryptographers (up to 400) and verify whether if one cryptographer paid, he knows that nobody else did: $G((done \wedge paid_1) \rightarrow K_1 \neg(\bigvee_{i \in [2..n]} paid_i))$, and whether if a cryptographer paid it can eventually know that somebody else paid: $paid_1 \rightarrow XF(K_1 paid_2)$.

7.2 Results

Optimizations Evaluation

We studied the impact of all optimizations on the complete benchmark set, and identified two main configurations. For full KL_1, we perform static learning, generalization and use the dual-rail encoding. For $InvKL_1$, we also perform static learning and generalization, but disable dual-rail encoding. Moreover, for $InvKL_1$, we only perform the validation of the last state of the trace. To study the quality of these configurations, we proceed as follows. We compare our chosen configuration (Lazy Best) against all other possible configurations (i.e., for $InvKL_1$, we have 16 configurations in total). For each benchmark problem, we select the best configuration that is different from Lazy Best. We call that configuration Virtual Second Best Solver (VSBS). We compare Lazy Best and VSBS in Figure 3. Lazy Best times out in only 10 instances out of 349, while the VSBS times out in 20. Generalization sometimes adds significant overhead. We also compare the strategy of validating the whole trace vs. the last state (Figure 4): the latter can significantly pay off. The exceptions are cases in which a single counter-example is sufficient to learn everything needed to prove the property.

Generalization is fundamental to be able to solve the Dining Cryptographers benchmarks. In fact (Figure 5), applying generalization we are able to solve all DC problems (up-to 400 cryptographers), while without generalization our approach times out when reaching 13 cryptographers.

For the infinite state benchmark (Battery Sensor), we considered problems with increasing bounded recall. Increasing the recall, increases the size of the model and the number of observables (Figure 6). Without any optimization, the algorithm times out with recall 6 ($\sim$80 obs. variables), while with our chosen configuration, we can verify up to recall 40 (i.e., an infinite state model with 20 Real-valued variables and more than 500 Boolean variables).

Eager Approach

We implemented the eager approach on top of an IC3-based parameter synthesis engine, and compared it against the lazy approach. In Figure 7, we can see that the eager approach does not scale when increasing the problem size, i.e., for a recall of 5 the eager approach reaches the timeout of 1 hour, while the lazy approach terminates in less than a minute.

Finite State

In the finite case, we get excellent performances when compared to MCK and MCMAS. The comparison on all finite state problems (magicboxes and dining cryptographers) for MCK and MCMAS is given in Figures 8 and 9. In many cases our approach can provide up-to two orders of magnitude improvement, and solves all the 118 instances, while MCMAS times out on 20, and MCK on 66. We highlight the results for the dining cryptographers benchmark in Figure 10. In which MCMAS is able to verify models only up-to 240 dining cryptographers (MCK is not included because it times-out at 20). The lazy approach can verify problem with 400 cryptographers in slighly more than 10 minutes.

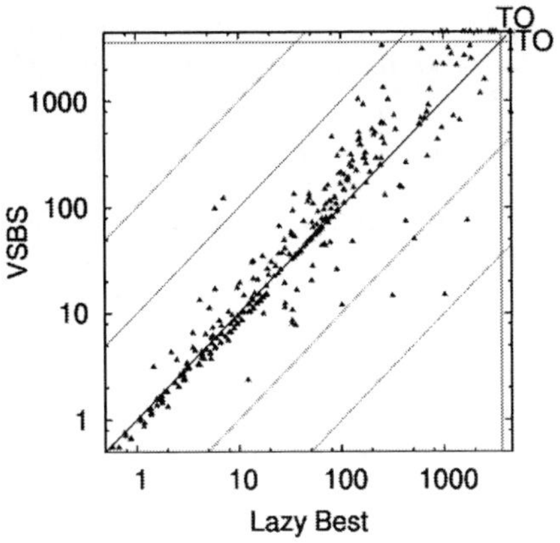

Figure 3: Comparing configurations.

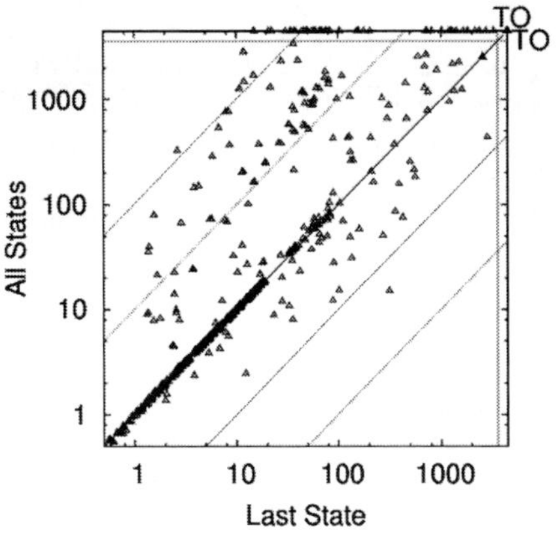

Figure 4: *InvKL*$_1$ Optimization.

#DC	Lazy w/o Gen.	Lazy w/ Gen.
3	0.26	0.15
5	1.01	0.15
7	6.07	0.13
9	58.03	0.15
11	1358.11	0.15
13	TO	0.15

Figure 5: DCs *InvKL*$_1$ properties (sec.)

Recall	#Obs	Lazy Basic	Lazy Best
0	11	3.28	1.46
5	66	3536.17	52.72
10	121	TO	103.47
20	231	TO	288.31
40	451	TO	981.11

Figure 6: Bounded Recall BS: Optimizations Impact (sec.)

Recall	Eager	Lazy
0	3.38	1.46
1	29.48	2.18
2	153.16	5.15
3	661.28	10.24
4	3028.94	13.44
5	T.O.	52.72

Figure 7: Bounded Recall BS: Eager vs Lazy (sec.)

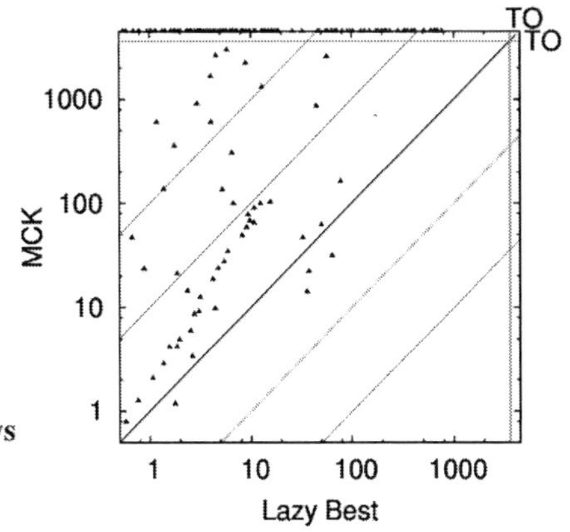

Figure 8: Lazy vs MCK (66/118 T.O.)

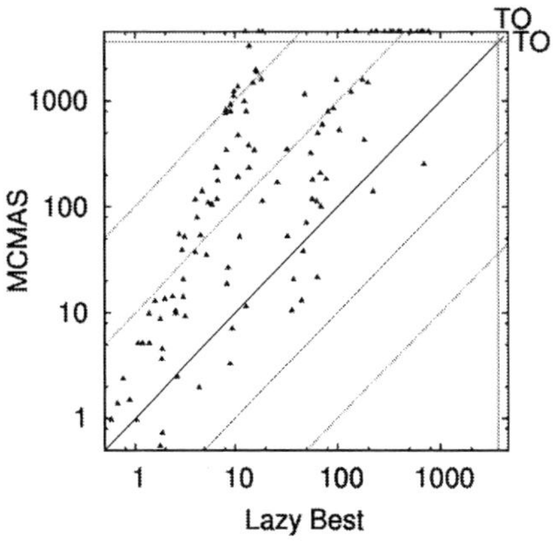

Figure 9: Lazy vs MCMAS (20/118 T.O.)

#DC	MCMAS	Lazy
40	3.66	1.83
80	26.57	8.54
120	169.43	25.9
160	322.45	55.2
200	528.42	104.02
240	1582.68	174.86
280	T.O.	287.06
320	T.O.	391.57
360	T.O.	598.4
400	T.O.	765.96

Figure 10: DCs Runtime for *KL*$_1$ properties (sec.)

8. CONCLUSIONS

KL_1 is a temporal epistemic logic that is extensively used in the literature. In this paper, we presented an efficient model checking approach for KL_1 under observational semantics. This is the first approach for KL_1 model checking over infinite state transition systems. The use of modern model-checking techniques, together with our lazy refinement approach and several optimizations (i.e., static learning, generalization, and dual-rail encoding) enables reasoning on models of considerable size. The experimental evaluation shows orders of magnitude improvements over existing approaches.

As future work, we plan to generalize the technique for perfect recall semantics. Moreover, it would be interesting to extend our lazy approach to reason about Artifact-Centric Systems. Finally, we would like to apply the approach on more industrial case-studies from diagnoser design.

Acknowledgements

We would like to thank Ron van der Meyden and Xiaowei Huang for providing us with an internal up-to-date version of MCK, and Franco Raimondi for providing us with a Dining Cryptographers generator for MCMAS.

REFERENCES

[1] M. Balliu, M. Dam, and G. Le Guernic. Epistemic temporal logic for information flow security. In *Proceedings of the ACM SIGPLAN 6th Workshop on Programming Languages and Analysis for Security*, PLAS '11, pages 6:1–6:12, New York, NY, USA, 2011. ACM.

[2] C. W. Barrett, R. Sebastiani, S. A. Seshia, and C. Tinelli. Satisfiability modulo theories. *Handbook of satisfiability*, 185:825–885, 2009.

[3] F. Belardinelli, D. Grossi, and A. Lomuscio. Finite abstractions for the verification of epistemic properties in open multi-agent systems. In *Proceedings of the 24th International Conference on Artificial Intelligence*, pages 854–860. AAAI Press, 2015.

[4] F. Belardinelli, A. V. Jones, and A. Lomuscio. Model checking temporal-epistemic logic using alternating tree automata. *Fundamenta Informaticae*, 112(1):19–37, 2011.

[5] F. Belardinelli, A. Lomuscio, and F. Patrizi. Verification of agent-based artifact systems. *Journal of Artificial Intelligence Research (JAIR)*, 51:333–376, 2014.

[6] J. Bengtsson, K. Larsen, F. Larsson, P. Pettersson, and W. Yi. *UPPAAL a tool suite for automatic verification of real-time systems*. Springer, 1996.

[7] B. Bittner, M. Bozzano, A. Cimatti, M. Gario, and A. Griggio. Towards Pareto-optimal parameter synthesis for monotonic cost functions. In *Proceedings of the 14th Conference on Formal Methods in Computer-Aided Design*, pages 23–30. FMCAD Inc, 2014.

[8] I. Boureanu, M. Cohen, and A. Lomuscio. Automatic verification of temporal-epistemic properties of cryptographic protocols. *Journal of Applied Non-Classical Logics*, 19(4):463–487, 2009.

[9] M. Bozzano, A. Cimatti, M. Gario, and S. Tonetta. Formal Specification and Synthesis of FDI through an Example. In *Workshop on Principles of Diagnosis (DX'13)*, pages 174–179, 2013. Available at URL http://www.dx-2013.org/dx13-proceedings.pdf.

[10] M. Bozzano, A. Cimatti, M. Gario, and S. Tonetta. Formal design of asynchronous FDI components using temporal epistemic logic. *Logical Methods in Computer Science*, 2015.

[11] A. R. Bradley. SAT-based model checking without unrolling. In *Verification, Model Checking, and Abstract Interpretation*, pages 70–87. Springer, 2011.

[12] R. Bryant. Graph-based algorithms for boolean function manipulation. *Computers, IEEE Transactions on*, 100(8):677–691, 1986.

[13] R. Cavada, A. Cimatti, M. Dorigatti, A. Griggio, A. Mariotti, A. Micheli, S. Mover, M. Roveri, and S. Tonetta. The nuxmv symbolic model checker. In *Computer Aided Verification*, pages 334–342. Springer, 2014.

[14] A. Cimatti, A. Griggio, S. Mover, and S. Tonetta. Parameter synthesis with IC3. In *Formal Methods in Computer-Aided Design (FMCAD), 2013*, pages 165–168. IEEE, 2013.

[15] A. Cimatti, A. Griggio, S. Mover, and S. Tonetta. Ic3 modulo theories via implicit predicate abstraction. In *Tools and Algorithms for the Construction and Analysis of Systems*, pages 46–61. Springer, 2014.

[16] E. Clarke, O. Grumberg, S. Jha, Y. Lu, and H. Veith. Counterexample-guided abstraction refinement. In *Computer aided verification*, pages 154–169. Springer, 2000.

[17] L. De Moura, S. Owre, H. Rueß, J. Rushby, N. Shankar, M. Sorea, and A. Tiwari. Sal 2. In *Computer aided verification*, pages 496–500. Springer, 2004.

[18] B. Dutertre and L. De Moura. A fast linear-arithmetic solver for DPLL (T). In *Computer Aided Verification*, pages 81–94. Springer, 2006.

[19] R. Fagin, Y. Moses, J. Y. Halpern, and M. Y. Vardi. *Reasoning about knowledge*. MIT press, 2003.

[20] P. Gammie and R. V. D. Meyden. MCK: Model checking the logic of knowledge. *Computer Aided Verification*, pages 256–259, 2004.

[21] J. Halpern and M. Vardi. The complexity of reasoning about knowledge and time. lower bounds. *Journal of Computer and System Sciences*, 38(1):195–237, 1989.

[22] X. Huang. Diagnosability in concurrent probabilistic systems. In *Proceedings of the 2013 international conference on Autonomous agents and multi-agent systems*, pages 853–860. International Foundation for Autonomous Agents and Multiagent Systems, 2013.

[23] F. Kominis and H. Geffner. Beliefs in multiagent planning: From one agent to many. In *Proc. ICAPS Workshop on Distributed and Multi-Agent Planning*, 2014.

[24] M. Kwiatkowska, A. Lomuscio, and H. Qu. Parallel model checking for temporal epistemic logic. In *European Conference on Artificial Intelligence*, 2010.

[25] O. Lichtenstein, A. Pnueli, and L. Zuck. The glory of the past. In R. Parikh, editor, *Logics of Programs*, volume 193, pages 196–218. Springer Berlin Heidelberg, 1985.

[26] A. Lomuscio, H. Qu, and F. Raimondi. MCMAS: A model checker for the verification of multi-agent systems. In *Computer Aided Verification*, pages 682–688. Springer, 2009.

[27] A. Pnueli. The temporal logic of programs. In *FOCS*, pages 46–57, 1977.

[28] J.-W. Roorda and K. Claessen. SAT-based assistance in abstraction refinement for symbolic trajectory evaluation. In *Computer Aided Verification*, pages 175–189. Springer, 2006.

[29] W. Van Der Hoek, M. Wooldridge, and S. van Otterloo. Model checking knowledge and time via local propositions: Cooperative and adversarial systems. 2004.

[30] R. Van der Meyden and K. Su. Symbolic model checking the knowledge of the dining cryptographers. In *17th IEEE Computer Security Foundations Workshop*, 2004.

[31] B. Woźna, A. Lomuscio, and W. Penczek. Bounded model checking for knowledge and real time. In *Proceedings of the fourth international joint conference on Autonomous agents and multiagent systems*, pages 165–172. ACM, 2005.

Action-Level Intention Selection for BDI Agents

Yuan Yao
School of Computer Science
University of Nottingham
Nottingham, UK
yvy@cs.nott.ac.uk

Brian Logan
School of Computer Science
University of Nottingham
Nottingham, UK
bsl@cs.nott.ac.uk

ABSTRACT

Belief-Desire-Intention agents typically pursue multiple goals in parallel. However the interleaving of steps in different intentions may result in conflicts, e.g., where the execution of a step in one plan makes the execution of a step in another concurrently executing plan impossible. Previous approaches to avoiding conflicts between concurrently executing intentions treat plans as atomic units, and attempt to interleave plans in different intentions so as to minimise conflicts. However some conflicts cannot be resolved by appropriate ordering of plans and can only be resolved by appropriate interleaving of steps within plans. In this paper, we present *SA*, an approach to intention selection based on Single-Player Monte Carlo Tree Search that selects which intention to progress at the current cycle at the level of individual plan steps. We evaluate the performance of our approach in a range of scenarios of increasing difficulty in both static and dynamic environments. The results suggest *SA* out-performs existing approaches to intention selection both in terms of goals achieved and the variance in goal achievement time.

1. INTRODUCTION

In Belief-Desire-Intention-based (BDI) agent programming languages, e.g., [4, 9], the behaviour of an agent is specified in terms of beliefs, goals, and plans. *Beliefs* represent the agent's information about the environment (and itself). *Goals* represent desired states of the environment the agent is trying to bring about. *Plans* are the means by which the agent can modify the environment in order to achieve its goals. Plans are composed of *steps* which are either *primitive actions* that directly change the agent's environment or *subgoals* which are in turn achieved by other plans. For each top-level goal, the agent selects a plan which forms the root of an *intention*, and commences executing the steps in the plan. If the next step in an intention is a subgoal, a (sub)plan is selected to achieve the subgoal and added to the intention, and the steps in the (sub)plan are then executed and so on. This process of repeatedly choosing and executing plans is referred to as the agent's *deliberation cycle*.

In many BDI agent architectures, the plans comprising the agent's intentions are executed in parallel, e.g., by executing one step of an intention at each cycle in round robin fashion [4, 30]. Interactions between interleaved steps in different intentions may result in conflicts, i.e., the execution of a step makes it impossible to execute a step in another concurrently executing intention. For example, consider a Mars Rover which has a goal to perform a rock experiment, r, and a goal to upload some image data, u. The plan to perform a rock experiment consists of two actions: collecting a sample, a_1, and analysing the sample, a_2. $a1$ has precondition p (being at the appropriate location) and a_2 has the postcondition $\neg q$ (overwriting the current contents of the rover's data buffer). The plan to upload image data also consists of two steps: compressing the image, b_1, and transmitting the compressed data, b_2. b_1 has precondition q (the image currently in the data buffer), and b_2 has postcondition $\neg p$ (the rover must be reoriented for transmission). Even if p and q have been established by previous steps in the intentions for r and u, it is clear that r and u cannot both be achieved without an appropriate interleaving of plan steps.

Appears in: *Proceedings of the 15th International Conference on Autonomous Agents and Multiagent Systems (AAMAS 2016), J. Thangarajah, K. Tuyls, C. Jonker, S. Marsella (eds.), May 9–13, 2016, Singapore.*

A number of approaches to reasoning about possible interactions between intentions have been proposed in the literature. Thangarajah et al. [22, 21] describe an approach based on *summary information* that avoids conflicts by reasoning about necessary and possible pre- and post-conditions of different ways of achieving a goal. They give algorithms for computing summary information at compile time, and for dynamically updating it at run-time. They also present mechanisms to determine whether a newly adopted (sub)goal will definitely be safe to execute without conflicts, or will definitely result in conflicts, or may result in conflicts. If the goal cannot be executed safely, execution of the intention is deferred. Yao et al. [31] present a stochastic approach based on Single-Player Monte-Carlo Tree Search (SP-MCTS) in which pseudorandom simulations of different interleavings of the plans in each intention are used to determine which intention to progress. However these approaches are limited to interleaving intentions at the plan level, i.e., execution of another intention is only possible when a subgoal is posted and steps in different plans are not interleaved, and they have only been evaluated in a static environment. Waters et al. [27, 28] present a *coverage-based* approach to intention selection proposed by [23], in which the intention with the lowest coverage, i.e., the highest probability of becoming non-executable due to changes in the environment, is selected for execution. Unlike Thangarajah et al. and Yao et al. [23, 31], they evaluate their approach in a dynamic environment; however intention selection is again limited to the plan level, and their experimental evaluation assumes that there are no conflicts between intentions.

In this paper, we introduce *SA*, a new approach to avoiding conflicts between intentions. *SA* extends the stochastic scheduling approach of Yao et al. [31] in two ways. First, we allow the interleaving of primitive actions in different intentions. Second, we change the function used to select the 'best' intention to progress at this cycle to take both the dynamism of the environment and the fairness of the interleaving into account. We evaluate the performance of *SA* and compare it to that of round robin (RR), first in first out (FIFO), summary information-based (SI) and coverage-based (C) intention selection in static and dynamic environments, both in synthetic domains and a more realistic scenario based on the Miconic-10 elevator domain [14]. Our results suggest *SA* out-performs RR, FIFO, SI, and C both in terms of goals achieved and/or the variance in goal achievement time, and is capable of successfully interleaving intentions so as to achieve their top-level goals even when the number of potential conflicts between intentions is high. Moreover, in the scenarios considered, the computational overhead of *SA* is modest.

2. GOAL-PLAN TREES

We use the notion of *goal-plan trees* [22, 21] to represent the relations between goals, plans and actions, and to reason about the interactions between intentions. The root of a goal-plan tree is a top-level goal (goal-node), and its children are the plans that can be used to achieve the goal (plan-nodes). Plans may in turn contain subgoals (goal nodes), giving rise to a tree structure representing all possible ways an agent can achieve the top-level goal. In [22, 21] goal-plan trees contain only goals and plans. To support action-level intention selection, we extend the definition of goal-plan trees to allow primitive actions in plans in addition to subgoals as in [32].

To allow reasoning about interactions between intentions, each goal plan tree records information about the conditions necessary to achieve a (sub)goal or successfully execute a plan or an action in the form of pre-, in- and post-conditions associated with goal, plan and action nodes. *Preconditions* are conditions that must be true in order to execute a plan or an action. *In-conditions* are conditions that must hold during the pursuit of a goal or plan; if an in-condition becomes false during the execution of a goal or plan, the goal or plan is dropped with failure. *Postconditions* are conditions that are made true by executing a plan or an action or by achieving a goal (in addition to achieving the goal itself).

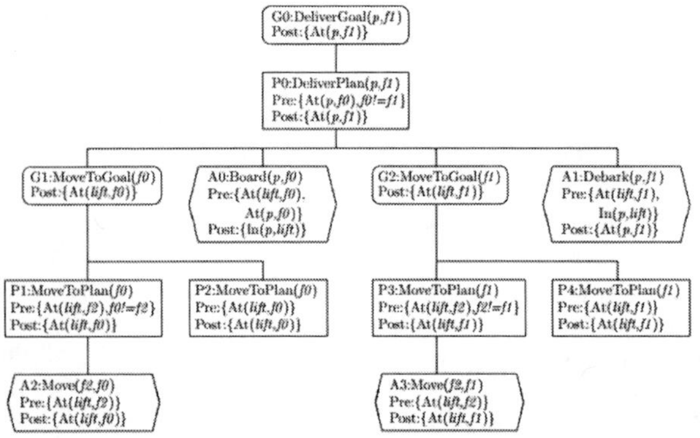

Figure 1: A goal-plan tree for the elevator domain

Figure 1 shows a simple goal-plan tree for the elevator domain [14]. The top level goal, G0, is to deliver passengers *p* to floor *f1*. There is a single plan, P0, to achieve G0. P0 consists of two subgoals, G1 and G2 and two actions, A0 and A1. Each subgoal may be achieved by two subplans (P1 and P2 for G1 and P3 and P4 for G2). The pre- and postconditions of plans and actions are shown in the figure; for example, the action A0:Board(*p, f0*), has precondition that both the *lift* and passengers *p* are at floor *f0*, and postcondition that the passengers are in the lift.

In addition to defining the relationships between goals, plans and actions, goal-plan trees can be used to define several notions that characterise the robustness of an agent program in a given environment (and hence the likelihood that a particular interleaving of two goal plan trees will result in conflicts). The *coverage* of a goal-plan tree is the percentage of world states for which there is some applicable plan for any subgoal within an intention. The *overlap* of a goal-plan tree is the percentage of world states in which two or more plans for a goal are applicable [23]. A preparatory-effect or *p-effect* occurs when a plan or action establishes the precondition of a later step (subplan or action) in the same goal-plan tree [22]. (Note that we extend the notion of p-effect in [22] to include the establishment of the precondition of an action by a previous action in the same plan.) For example, in Figure 1, a precondition of action A0, At(*lift, f0*), is established by executing plans P1 or P2. At(*lift, f0*) is therefore a p-effect which needs to be protected until action A0 is executed. We define the *size of a p-effect* as the number of possible interleaving points between the plan or action that establishes a precondition and the later step which requires the p-effect as its precondition. For example, the size of the p-effect At(*lift, f0*) is 1, as there is only one point at which a step from another intention can be interleaved. Like coverage and overlap, p-effect size is a measure of an intention's robustness: the greater size of the p-effects, the more likely interleaving steps from other intentions will destroy (clobber) the established precondition.

In a dynamic environment, *SA* takes the coverage of each goal-plan tree into account when choosing which intention to progress. We also use coverage, overlap and p-effect size to characterise the difficulty of the evaluation scenarios in Section 6.

3. SELECTING INTENTIONS

We represent the agent's intentions as a set of goal-plan trees $T = \{t_1, \dots, t_n\}$ corresponding to the agent's top-level goals. The progression of an intention to achieve a top-level goal amounts to choosing a path through the corresponding goal-plan tree. Each path corresponds to a different way of achieving the top level goal forming the root of the tree. The path specifies a sequence of plans, actions, subgoals and sub-plans that, if executed successfully, will achieve the top-level goal. The execution of an agent program thus corresponds to an interleaving of paths through each of the goal-plan trees corresponding to the agent's current intentions.

An inappropriate interleaving of plans or primitive actions in different goal-plan trees can give rise to conflicts. We say the progression of a set of intentions is *conflict free*, if the choice of path through each goal-plan tree, and the interleaving of the steps in these paths, ensure that the preconditions of each plan and action on a path are true when the plan or action are executed, and that any in-conditions required by a goal or plan are true during the achievement of the goal or execution of the plan.

To minimise conflicts (and hence maximise the number of goals achieved),[1] an intention selection mechanism must be able to appropriately interleave the execution of steps in an agent's intentions. In many cases, the interleaving of intentions is also desirable in its own right, e.g., to ensure more predictable response times for users or other agents. We therefore prefer interleavings that maximise *fairness*. We say an interleaving is more fair if it minimises the variance in the elapsed time of each successful intention (subject to achieving as many goals as possible). The elapsed time, r, of an intention is defined as $r = d_f - d_a$, where d_a is the cycle at which the top-level goal of the intention is adopted by the agent, and d_f is the cycle at which the goal is achieved. The *variance in elapsed time*, v, of a set of n intentions with elapsed times $r_1, \dots, r_n$ is given by $v = \sum_{i=1}^{n}(r_i - \overline{r})^2/n$, where $\overline{r}$ is the average elapsed time. Fairness is then defined as $1/v$.

[1]We implicitly assume that goals are of equal importance; it is straightforward to modify our approach to handle cases where some goals are more important than others.

The *intention selection problem* is the problem of choosing an intention to progress at the current deliberation cycle, such that the progression of the set of intentions is conflict free. To make the problem precise, we introduce the notion of the current step, s_i, and next step, $succ(s_i)$, of a goal-plan tree t_i representing an intention. s_i is a pointer to the current step in t_i, which may be a primitive action or a subgoal. The path from the root of the goal-plan tree to the current step represents the choices made (and steps executed) so far in achieving the top-level goal. When an agent adopts an intention for a new top-level goal g_i, the current step of the goal-plan tree rooted at g_i is initially set to g_i itself. The next step $succ(s_i)$ specifies how t_i is to be progressed following s_i. If the current step is a primitive action, the next step is the primitive action or subgoal following that action in the same plan. If the current step is a subgoal, advancing the current step involves choosing a plan for the subgoal, and setting the next step to be the first action or subgoal of the selected plan. The intention selection problem can now be stated as: given a set of goal plan trees and their current step pointers $I = \{(t_1, s_1), \ldots, (t_n, s_n)\}$ corresponding to the agent's current intentions, and a set of condition variables E representing the current state of the agent's environment, return a next step $succ(s_i)$ of an intention $(t_i, s_i) \in I$ to be executed at the current deliberation cycle. We further require that $succ(s_i)$ maximises the number of goals achieved and fairness of the interleaving, subject to achieving as many goals as possible. That is, there is no $(t_j, s_j) \in I, j \neq i$ such that progressing t_j would achieve more goals than progressing t_i, or if progressing t_j and t_i achieve the same number of goals, progressing t_j results in an interleaving that is at least as fair.

4. SA ALGORITHM

Our approach to intention scheduling is based on Single-Player Monte-Carlo Tree Search (SP-MCTS) [18]. SP-MCTS is a best-first search in which pseudorandom simulations are used to guide expansion of the search tree. It was originally developed to solve single-player puzzles (games against the environment) [18], however it has also been used successfully to solve reentrant scheduling problems [15].

Algorithm 1 Return the action be executed at this cycle

1: $I \leftarrow \{(t_1, s_1), \ldots, (t_n, s_n)\}$
2: **procedure** *SA*$(E, e, \delta, \alpha, \beta)$
3: $\quad n_0 \leftarrow node_0(I, E)$
4: $\quad$ **for** $i \leftarrow 1, \alpha$ **do**
5: $\quad\quad n_e \leftarrow$ MAX-UCT-LEAF-NODE(n_0)
6: $\quad\quad children(n_e) \leftarrow$ EXPAND(n_e)
7: $\quad\quad n_s \leftarrow$ RANDOM-CHILD$(children(n_e))$
8: $\quad\quad S \leftarrow \emptyset$
9: $\quad\quad$ **for** $j \leftarrow 1, \beta$ **do**
10: $\quad\quad\quad S \leftarrow S \cup \{$SIMULATE$(n_s)\}$
11: $\quad\quad v_g(n_s), v_f(n_s) \leftarrow \max_{<_{g,f}}(S)$
12: $\quad\quad$ BACKUP(n_s)
13: $\quad$ **if** $e > \delta$ **then**
14: $\quad\quad n_b \leftarrow \max_{<_{g,c,f}} children(n_0)$
15: $\quad$ **else**
16: $\quad\quad n_b \leftarrow \max_{<_{g,f}} children(n_0)$
17: $\quad I \leftarrow gpt(n_b)$
18: $\quad$ **return** (n_0, n_b)

The *SA* algorithm updates the set of goal plan trees and their current step pointers $I = \{(t_1, s_1), \ldots, (t_n, s_n)\}$ corresponding to the agent's current intentions. It takes five parameters as input: the current state of the agent's environment, E, the average number of environment changes per deliberation cycle, e, the dynamism threshold, δ, the number of iterations to be performed, α, and the number of simulations to be performed at each iteration, β; and returns a next step of an intention in I for execution at this cycle (see Algorithm 1). The parameters δ, α and β allow the agent developer to configure *SA* for a particular application: δ specifies the mean number of environment changes per deliberation cycle at which the agent should favour more robust (higher coverage) plans; α and β determine the effort expended on intention selection.

Starting from a root node n_0 representing the current progression of the agent's intentions I and state of the environment E, the algorithm iteratively builds a search tree. Each node in the search tree represents an interleaving of steps from the goal-plan trees in I that is consistent with the order of steps in each tree. The node records the state of the agent's environment resulting from the execution of this interleaving, the current step in each goal-plan tree, the start time of all top-level goals and the completion time for the goals achieved by the interleaving. In addition, the node also contains a record of the number of times it has been visited, the value of the node, and the best simulation performed from the node (described below). Edges represent the selection of a plan for a subgoal or the execution of primitive action in a plan.

Each iteration of the main loop (lines 4–12) consists of 4 phases: selection, expansion, simulation and back-propagation. In the *selection* phase, a leaf node, n_e, is selected for expansion (line 5). A node may be expanded if it represents a non-terminal state (a state in which it is possible to execute the next step of a goal-plan tree). n_e is selected using a modified version of Upper Confidence bounds applied to Trees (UCT) [18], which models the choice of node as a k-armed bandit problem. Starting from the root node n_0, we recursively follow child nodes with highest UCT value until a leaf node n_e is reached.

In the *expansion* phase, nodes representing the environment state (and the current step of each goal-plan tree) resulting from executing each next step of a goal-plan tree that is executable the state represented by n_e are added as children of n_e (line 6). Each child node corresponds to a different choice of which intention to execute at this cycle. One of the newly created child nodes, n_s, is then selected at random for simulation (line 7).

In the *simulation* phase, the value of n_s is estimated by performing β pseudorandom simulations (lines 8–11). The *value* of a node consists of two components: the maximum number of goals that can be achieved from this node, v_g, and the fairness of the interleaving, v_f. Each simulation starts in the environment represented by n_s. A next step of a goal-plan tree that is executable in the environment state represented by n_s is randomly selected and executed, and the environment and the current step of the selected goal-plan tree updated. We keep choosing executable next steps and updating the environment until a terminal state is reached in which no next steps can be executed or all top-level goals are achieved. The value of the simulation is taken to be the values of v_g and v_f in the terminal state. The simulation with the highest value is returned as the value of n_s ($<_{g,f}$ is a lexicographic order on v_g and v_f, i.e., v_f is used to break ties when child nodes have the same v_g value).

Finally, the simulation value is *back-propagated* from n_s to all nodes on the path to the root node n_0 (line 12).

As the search tree is expanded by iteration of the main loop, the random part of the interleaving represented by leaf nodes becomes shorter, and we obtain better estimates of v_g and v_f. After α iterations, the step that leads to the best child n_b of the root node n_0 is returned, and the goal-plan trees and their associated current step pointers (one of which has been updated) are assigned to I for use at the next deliberation cycle (lines 13–18). (The function gpt returns the goal-plan trees and their associated current step pointers represented by the node n_b.) Which step is considered best depends on the degree of dynamism of the environment. If the mean number of environment changes observed by the agent is less than the dynamism threshold set by the agent developer, δ, *SA* selects steps using $<_{g,f}$, i.e., first on the number of top-level goals achieved, and, where two or more steps result in the achievement of the same number of goals, it prefers steps that also maximise fairness. If the dynamism exceeds the threshold, *SA* selects steps using the order $<_{g,c,f}$, i.e., first on the number of goals achieved, secondly on coverage (intentions with lower coverage are preferred) and thirdly which maximise fairness.

SA therefore adopts a similar approach to [23, 27, 28] in dynamic environments, in prioritising intentions which are more likely to become unexecutable due to changes in the environment. However, unlike previous coverage-based approaches, it selects the intention to be progressed at the action, rather than plan level, interleaving actions in a manner that is most likely to achieve the largest number of goals, and adaptively prioritises fairness in low dynamism environments. Our use of SP-MCTS to sample the space of possible interleavings is similar to [31], but that work interleaves intentions at the plan level and does not take the coverage of intentions or fairness into account.

5. SA AND THE DELIBERATION CYCLE

SA implies some modifications to the standard BDI deliberation cycle. In this section we briefly sketch these changes and some obvious optimisations of our approach.

The standard BDI deliberation cycle consists of three phases [5, 16]:

1. select one or more events to process at this cycle;
2. for each selected goal event, select a relevant applicable plan to achieve the goal;
3. finally, select one or more intentions, and execute one or more steps of each selected intention.

Particular BDI languages may subdivide one or more of these phases. However some instantiation of this basic deliberation cycle is found in most BDI agent languages and platforms.

SA effectively merges elements of phase 1 and phases 2 and 3 of the standard deliberation cycle into a single process which is responsible for determining both which plan to adopt for a particular (sub)goal, and which step of which intention to execute at this cycle. Only the choice of which top-level goals to adopt falls outside the scope of *SA*: once a top-level goal is adopted, *SA* determines which plans to execute and how these plans should be interleaved so as to maximise the number of goals achieved and minimise the variance in elapsed time. If the intention selected for execution at the previous cycle posted a subgoal, *SA* explores, through sampled pseudorandom simulation, the implications of intending all relevant applicable plans for the subgoal (and the possible subplans of those plans) and their possible interleavings with all possible ways of achieving the agent's other intentions, for the number of goals achieved and the elapsed time.

As such it assumes responsibility for decisions that some agent platforms traditionally leave to the developer, e.g., the S_O and S_I selection functions of Jason [4] allow a developer to customise Jason's plan and intention selection for a particular application domain. While such customisation may be necessary or desirable for some problems, it requires specialist expertise on part of the developer to program at the level of the interpreter rather than writing BDI agent code.[2] In addition, the developer no longer has to anticipate and control possible interactions between intentions using atomic constructs. On the other hand, *SA* does entail additional developer effort in defining the pre- and postconditions of actions. However alternative approaches to avoiding conflicts between intentions, e.g., SI, require similar information in the form of pre- and postconditions of plans and goals. (Note that in *SA*, pre- and postconditions of plans are derived from the pre- and postconditions of the actions comprising the plan.) Some BDI programming languages already require the developer to specify the pre- and postconditions of actions, e.g., actions in GOAL [13], belief-update actions in 2APL [9]. For languages such as Jason, our experimental results indicate the kinds of scenarios where the additional effort of specifying the pre- and postconditions of actions would be worthwhile in terms of increased agent performance.

We conclude this section by briefly outlining some simple optimisations of our current implementation. As described in Section 4, *SA* builds a search tree at each deliberation cycle. As we show below, in many cases *SA* is able to find an interleaving that achieves all the agent's goals. If the environment does not change, the next step in this interleaving can simply be returned at subsequent deliberation cycles without further computation. It is only necessary to build a new search tree when the environment changes or the agent adopts a new top-level goal. In low dynamism environments, this means the already small overhead of *SA* (see Section 6.3) can be amortised over multiple execution steps.

6. EVALUATING SA

In this section we compare the performance of *SA* with existing approaches to intention selection used in practical implementations of agent programming languages (first in first out, round robin), and from the theoretical literature (summary information, coverage-based). We consider both static and dynamic environments in synthetic domains, and a more realistic scenario based on the Miconic-10 elevator domain [14].

First in first out (FIFO) executes each of the agent's intentions to completion (the goal is achieved or the next step in the intention cannot be executed) before starting to execute the next intention (this is termed a *non-interleaved execution strategy* in [2]). FIFO minimises interactions between intentions, however it has the disadvantage that the achievement of some goals may be significantly delayed compared to other goals.

Round robin (RR) attempts to ensure 'fairness' between intentions by executing a fixed number of steps of each intention in turn. A disadvantage of round robin is that it increases the number of possible conflicts between intentions: the interleaving of steps in different intentions may destroy a precondition established by a step in another intention before the action that requires the precondition is executed.[3] Round robin is the default intention selection function used by Jason [4]; some platforms, such as JACK [30] allow the developer to choose between round robin and first in first out.

In *Summary Information*-based intention selection (SI), summary information about pre-, in- and postconditions is propagated up each goal-plan tree to allow reasoning about interactions between trees. For example, if there are two possible plans for a goal g which both have p as a postcondition, then it is possible to infer

[2]*SA* could be extended to allow customisation of the value function(s) that determine which interleavings are preferred; however our current implementation does not support this.

[3]The same problems occur if the agent executes a step of each intention in parallel at each cycle as in, e.g., 2APL [9].

that p will definitely occur as a result of achieving g, and that any other goal that brings about $\neg p$ may cause a conflict. SI uses this information to protect active p-effects and in-conditions. If adopting a new goal will result in a conflict, i.e., a postcondition of the new goal destroys an active p-effect or in-condition, then progression of the intention containing the new goal is delayed until the p-effect or in-condition is no longer active.

Coverage-based intention selection (C) is based on the notions of *coverage* and *overlap* defined in Section 2. It prioritises the progression of intentions with lowest coverage, as they are more likely to fail due to changes in the environment. Waters et al. [27, 28] implemented and evaluated the approach proposed in [23] (which they call c0), and a preemptive variant of c0 which they call c1. c0 executes the progressable intention with lowest coverage and maintains focus as long as possible. Only when the current intention is finished or blocked will c0 recalculate coverage for all intentions and change focus to the progressable intention with lowest coverage. In c1, whenever a sub-goal is posted, the coverage of each intention is recalculated and its progressibility determined. As a result, c1 will change focus to a lower coverage progressable intention, even if the current intention is progressable.

FIFO does not interleave the execution of intentions. SI and C interleave intentions at the plan level. RR and *SA* interleave intentions at the action level.

FIFO, RR, SI and C implicitly prioritise different criteria. FIFO prioritises minimisation of conflicts at the expense of 'fairness'. Round robin introduces more potential for conflicts, but is more fair. Summary information based and coverage-based intention selection lie somewhere in between. We therefore evaluate the performance of each approach on two criteria: the number of goals achieved, and the variance in elapsed time (see Section 4).[4] In Sections 6.1.1 and 6.1.2, we only report variance results where the number goals achieved is > 8; as the number of intentions which complete successfully decreases, the variance value conflates the ability to achieve goals with the fairness of intention selection. For example, intentions that fail increase the variance of RR and decrease the variance of FIFO.

6.1 Synthetic Domains

In the interests of generality, our first evaluation is based on sets of randomly-generated, synthetic goal-plan trees representing the current intentions of an agent in a simple environment. By controlling the characteristics of the trees, and the dynamism of the environment, we can evaluate the performance of each scheduling algorithm under different conditions.

The environment is defined by a set of propositions that may appear as pre-, in- or postconditions of a goal-plan tree. Each environment variable is modelled as a Poisson process with specified mean, allowing the frequency with which the environment changes the value of the variable to be controlled. For a static environment, the means of all Poisson processes are set to 0. For the experiments reported below, the environment consists of 20 propositions.

Each synthetic goal-plan tree is specified by five parameters: the depth of the goal-plan tree, the plan branching factor (the maximum number of plans that can be used to achieve a goal), the goal branching factor (the maximum number of sub-goals a plan may have), the maximum number of actions in a plan and the number of environment variables that may appear in the tree.

For the experiments reported below, we assume there are at most two plans for each goal, and that each plan has a single environment variable as its precondition. The precondition may either depend on

[4] An alternative definition of fairness is used as an evaluation criterion in [28].

the current state of the environment or be established by the postcondition of a previous step in the goal-plan tree, i.e., by a p-effect. Where the preconditions of the plans for a goal g are not established by p-effects (e.g., top-level goals), a proposition p is chosen randomly from the set of environment variables, and one plan for g has the precondition p and the other plan has precondition $\neg p$. Each plan consists of a number of actions followed by a single subgoal. The first action in the plan has the plan's precondition as its own precondition. The remaining actions either have the plan precondition as their own precondition or their precondition is established by a previous action in the plan. The postcondition of an action is selected randomly from the set of environment variables. The constraints ensure that: (a) each plan is well formed (the plan can be successfully executed in some environment), and (b) taken individually, each goal-plan tree is executable (there is at least one way to achieve the top-level goal in all (static) environments).

These parameters generate trees similar to those used in previous evaluations of SI [21] and C [27, 28]. The main differences are that: unlike [21] goals do not have postconditions and plans and goals do not have in-conditions (for compatibility with [27, 28]); and, unlike [27, 28], environment variables are shared by all goal-plan trees (for compatibility with [21]).

6.1.1 Static Environment

Our first set of experiments evaluated the performance of FIFO, RR, SI and *SA* in a static environment. (C is designed primarily for dynamic environments and is considered in Section 6.1.2.) For each experiment, we generated 50 sets of 10 goal-plan trees using the parameters specified above (depth 5, plan branching factor of at most 2, goal branching factor 1). Other parameters of the trees were varied in each experiment as detailed below. The environment consisted of 20 variables, all of which can be chosen for pre- and postconditions in each tree. *SA* was configured with a dynamism threshold $\delta = 0.1$, and to perform 100 iterations ($\alpha = 100$) and 10 random simulations at each iteration ($\beta = 10$).

We first consider two parameters which influence the number of potential conflicts between intentions: the number of plan preconditions established by p-effects and the coverage of the goal plan trees. These parameters were varied to create intention selection scenarios of increasing difficulty.

Experiment 1 In the first experiment we varied the percentage of plan preconditions established by p-effects from 33% to 100%. Goal-plan trees with lower % p-effects have higher coverage (plans whose precondition is not established by a p-effect have have preconditions p and $\neg p$, and hence no overlap), and therefore less potential for conflicts (whatever the value of p the agent has an applicable plan). We set the average p-effect size at level 5 to be 3 (i.e., on average, the precondition of a plan is established by an action executed three steps earlier, in the parent plan), and each plan contained three actions.

% p-effects	FIFO	RR	SI	*SA*
33%	10 (1856)	3.04	10 (291)	10 (17)
66%	10 (1856)	3.02	9.88 (320)	10 (20)
100%	10 (1856)	2.82	9.72 (373)	10 (19)

Table 1: Goals & variance with increasing % p-effects

Table 1 shows the average number of goals achieved and variance in goal achievement time (in brackets, smaller numbers are better) for each scheduling algorithm for each percentage of p-effects considered. (Recall that we only report variance results where the number goals achieved is > 8.) As can be seen, RR is able to achieve only 3.04 goals on average when 33% of plan preconditions are established by p-effects. This is because, even though 67% of subgoals have 100% coverage, there are still many points at which an action from another intention can destroy the precondition of a plan or an action. With 33% p-effects SI is able to achieve all 10 goals, however as the percentage of p-effects increases, the number of goals achieved decreases slightly. FIFO and *SA* are able to achieve all 10 goals even with 100% p-effects. However the variance in completion time is much higher with FIFO (1856) than with *SA* (20).

Experiment 2 We investigated the effect of reducing coverage. When generating the goal-plan trees, we varied the probability of a goal having only a single plan. 25% 1-plan means that with probability 0.25 only one plan is generated for a goal, and so on. Increasing the probability that a goal has only one plan reduces coverage, and increases the likelihood of conflicts between intentions. The percentage of plan preconditions established by p-effects was 100% (i.e., all plans to achieve subgoals have their preconditions established by preceding actions); other parameters were as in Experiment 1.

% 1-plan	FIFO	RR	SI	*SA*
0%	10 (1856)	2.82	9.72 (373)	10 (19)
25%	8.92 (1603)	2.76	9.24 (455)	10 (22)
50%	7.92	2.44	8.88 (475)	10 (27)
75%	7.36	2.12	8.52 (489)	10 (28)

Table 2: Goals & variance with increasing % 1-plan (100% p-effects)

The results are shown in Table 2. As can be seen, for FIFO, RR and SI, as coverage decreases, the average number of goals achieved also decreases. This effect is particularly marked in the case of FIFO (if a top-level goal has only one plan, the postcondition of an action in a previously executed intention which destroys the precondition of the plan will make the intention unexecutable). *SA* is able to achieve 10 goals at all coverage levels. For *SA* and SI variance increases as coverage decreases. However *SA* has significantly lower variance than SI for all coverage levels, as SI approximates FIFO when protecting p-effects.

Next we investigated the performance of each approach when intentions are more complex and hence the likelihood of negative interactions is greater. In these experiments, we varied the p-effect size, and the number of actions in each plan.

Experiment 3 We investigated the effect of increasing p-effect size. We generated trees in which the precondition of each plan is chosen from environment variables appearing in the postcondition of any preceding action in the tree. For trees of depth 5, this gives an average p-effect size of 5 at level 5 (i.e., on average, the precondition of a plan is established by an action executed five steps earlier, in the parent of the parent of the plan). As in Experiment 2, we varied the probability of a goal having only a single plan from 0% to 75%; all other parameters are the same as in Experiment 2.

% 1-plan	FIFO	RR	SI	*SA*
0%	10 (1856)	2.68	9.32 (374)	10 (19)
25%	9.08 (1617)	2.64	9.04 (460)	10 (22)
50%	7.94	2.2	8.6 (471)	10 (25)
75%	6.94	2	8.34 (490)	10 (27)

Table 3: Goals & variance with increasing % 1-plan (100% p-effects, average p-effect size 5)

The results are shown in Table 3. With a larger p-effect size, FIFO, RR and SI perform slightly worse in terms of goals achieved than in Experiment 2, while *SA* is still able to achieve 10 goals in all cases. The variance for all approaches is essentially the same as in Experiment 2.

Experiment 4 We increased the number of actions in each plan to 5. As in Experiment 2, we varied the probability of a goal having only a single plan from 0% to 75%; all other parameters are the same as in Experiment 2.

% 1-plan	FIFO	RR	SI	*SA*
0%	10 (5156)	1.64	9.28 (544)	10 (40)
25%	8.92 (4564)	1.56	9 (755)	10 (58)
50%	7.36	1.36	8.52 (843)	10 (63)
75%	6.52	1.32	8.3 (874)	10 (66)

Table 4: Goals & variance with increasing % 1-plan (100% p-effects, each plan contains 5 actions)

The results are shown in Table 4. As can be seen, the performance of FIFO, RR and SI decrease when plans have 5 actions, with a more marked decline in the case of RR. SI shows a significant increase in variance. However, *SA* still achieves all 10 goals, and while the variance is increased, it is much smaller than that for the other approaches.

6.1.2 *Dynamic Environment*

Our second set of experiments evaluated the performance of FIFO, RR, *SA*, and two variants of C from [27, 28], c0 and c1, in a dynamic environment. In the dynamic case, all the Poisson processes controlling the environment variables have the same non-zero mean. (In reality, different environment variables will change value at different rates, however for random trees we believe this is a reasonable approximation.) The larger the mean, the greater the probability an environment variable will change value (from p to $\neg p$ or vice versa). We used three values for the mean: 0.01, which results in an average of 0.2 events (changes in the value of an environment variable) per deliberation cycle, 0.05 (which gives an average of 0.97 events per cycle), and 0.1 (which gives 1.91 events per cycle). In the dynamic case, the environment is first updated to reflect the execution of the next step of the selected intention (as in the static case). The Poisson processes controlling the environment variables are then evaluated, possibly resulting in additional changes to the environment. The resulting environment state is then 'sensed' by the agent at the beginning of the next deliberation cycle. For each experiment, we generated 50 sets of 10 goal plan trees using the same parameters as in the static experiments. As before, $\delta = 0.1$, $\alpha = 100$ and $\beta = 10$.

We first consider the effect of increasing dynamism and reduced coverage.

Experiment 5 In the fifth experiment, we used the same parameters as in first row in Table 2, i.e., all plans have two goals (0% 1-plan), %p-effects was 100%, each plan has 3 actions and the p-effect size at level 5 was 3. The means of Poisson process was varied from 0.01 to 0.1.

Dyn	FIFO	RR	c0	c1	*SA*
0.01	8.92 (1625)	2.24	9.52 (1849)	8.88 (96)	9.82 (95)
0.05	5.40	1.06	8.62 (1830)	8.64 (94)	9.40 (95)
0.10	3.28	1	8.16 (1962)	8.56 (97)	9.08 (95)

Table 5: Goals & variance with increasing dynamism (100% p-effects, 0% 1-plan)

The results are shown in Table 5. As can be seen, for all approaches, as the means of Poisson processes increase, the average number of goals achieved decreases. This effect is particularly marked in the case of FIFO. c0 performs better than c1 when the Poisson mean is small, and c1 has a better performance than c0 when Poisson means are larger. *SA* outperforms the other approaches in terms of the number of goals achieved. The variance in goal achievement time of *SA* is similar to c1 and significantly lower than c0.

Experiment 6 We set the probability of a goal having only a single plan to be 0.25 (i.e., the second row in Table 2); the means of the Poisson processes varied from 0.01 to 0.1; all other parameters are the same as in Experiment 2.

Dyn	FIFO	RR	c0	c1	*SA*
0.01	7.90	1.82	9.12 (1877)	8.40 (116)	9.74 (114)
0.05	4.74	1.14	7.98	8.26 (118)	9.28 (120)
0.10	2.54	0.72	7.64	8.22 (124)	8.94 (123)

Table 6: Goals & variance with increasing dynamism (100% p-effects, 25% 1-plan)

The results are shown in Table 6. As can be seen, for all approaches and levels of dynamism, with reduced coverage (25% 1-plan) the average number of goals achieved decreases and the variance in completion time increases. However, *SA* still achieves the highest number of goals of any of any approach (between 8%–16% better than c1), and its variance in goal achievement time is comparable to c1.

We then investigated the effect of increasing dynamism when intentions are more complex.

Experiment 7 We increased the p-effect size to 5 at level 5. All other parameters were as in the first row in Table 2, and we again varied the means of Poisson process from 0.01 to 0.1.

Dyn	FIFO	RR	c0	c1	*SA*
0.01	8.88 (1641)	2	9.42 (1863)	8.6 (100)	9.8 (96)
0.05	5.34	1.02	8.48 (1876)	8.54 (108)	9.32(97)
0.10	3.12	0.94	8.02(1978)	8.48 (110)	8.98 (96)

Table 7: Goals & variance with increasing dynamism (100% p-effects, p-effect size 5)

The results are shown in Table 7. Compared to Experiment 5, the performance of c0, c1 decreases as we increase the p-effect size. However, *SA* still outperforms other approaches on the number of goals achieved and its variance in completion time is slightly lower than that of c1.

Experiment 8 We increased the number of actions in each plan to 5; other parameters were same as the first row in Table 2, and the means of the Poisson process were varied from 0.01 to 0.1.

Dyn	FIFO	RR	c0	c1	*SA*
0.01	8.4 (4664)	1.08	9.22 (4605)	8.32 (360)	9.52 (346)
0.05	3.76	0.62	8.18 (4765)	8.26 (387)	9.08(367)
0.10	1.84	0.42	7.88	8.18 (382)	8.72 (386)

Table 8: Goals & variance with increasing dynamism (100% p-effects, each plan contains 5 actions)

The results are shown in Table 8. As can be seen, compared to Experiment 5, the performance of FIFO, RR, c0, c1 and *SA* decreases as we increase the number of actions in each plan. However, *SA* still outperforms other approaches on the number of goals achieved and has a similar variance to c1.

Overall, *SA* outperforms FIFO, RR and SI on the number of goals achieved in static environments. In simpler scenarios, FIFO and SI are able to achieve all 10 goals. However, as the scenarios become more challenging, their performance declines (FIFO more markedly than SI). *SA* also has a significantly lower variance in elapsed time (particularly compared to FIFO), as it allows interleaving at the action level. In dynamic environments, *SA* outperforms FIFO, RR, c0 and c1 in terms of the number of goals achieved. The variance in elapsed time time of *SA* is comparable to that of c1, and significantly lower than that of c0. While the relative performance advantage of *SA* in a dynamic environment is smaller than in a static environment, it consistently outperforms c1 in terms of number of goals achieved by between 5% and 10%.

6.2 Miconic-10 Elevator Domain

In this section we evaluate the performance of *SA* in a more realistic scenario based on the Miconic-10 elevator domain [14].[5] Unlike traditional elevators, the Miconic-10 elevator allows passengers to enter their destination floor when calling the elevator using a 10-digit keypad installed in each elevator lobby. In the scenario, the Miconic-10 elevator is controlled by a BDI agent program. Using standard techniques for translating HTN planning problems into BDI agent programs, e.g., [10], we translated the methods and operators in the Miconic-10 Elevator HTN planning domain given in [14], to goals, plans and actions in a BDI agent program. The goal-plan tree for the resulting BDI program is shown in Figure 1.

In our experiments, there is a single Miconic-10 elevator installed in a 10 floor building. Passengers may move from floor to floor using the elevator. Requests to travel to a particular floor give rise to top-level goals (one for each request) which are achieved by the BDI agent program. For simplicity, we assume there is no limitation on the number of passengers that can be in the elevator at any one time.

We evaluated the performance of *SA* in two scenarios. In the first experiment, all goals (elevator requests) are given at deliberation cycle 0 (corresponding to the static environment in the synthetic domains). We generated 50 sets of 10 goals to travel between two randomly chosen distinct floors. *SA* was configured as in Section 6.1.1, i.e., $\delta = 0.1$, $\alpha = 100$ and $\beta = 10$.

FIFO	RR	SI	*SA*
10 (123)	1.10	10 (33)	10 (28)

Table 9: Goals & variance for 10 goals

The number of goals achieved and variance in elapsed time (in parentheses) for FIFO, RR, SI and *SA* are shown in Table 9. As can be seen, with the exception of RR, all approaches achieve 10 goals. However FIFO has significantly higher variance than SI and *SA*, as FIFO executes the intentions sequentially.

In our second experiment, we use a more realistic model in which elevator requests arrive over time. As before, a total of 10 top-level goals must be achieved. However, in this scenario two goals are given at deliberation cycle 0, and the remaining top-level goals are posted during the progression of the agent's current intentions. We varied $\#g$, the number of new top-level goals generated after executing each primitive action, from 0.33 to 3. When $\#g = 0.33$, a new top-level goal is posted after every 3 primitive actions; when $\#g = 3$, 3 new top-level goals are posted after executing each primitive action. The *SA* search configuration was the same as in the first scenario.

$\#g$	FIFO	RR	c0 & c1	*SA*
0.33	10 (14)	2.16	10 (14)	10 (1)
0.50	10 (36)	1.56	10 (36)	10 (1)
1	10 (71)	1.20	10 (71)	10 (9)
2	10 (95)	1.10	10 (95)	10 (18)
3	10 (102)	1.10	10 (102)	10 (21)

Table 10: Goals & variance with decreasing time between goals

[5] An elevator controller written in GOAL is evaluated in [1].

The results are shown in Table 10. As in the first scenario, with the exception of RR, all approaches achieve 10 goals. However in the dynamic setting, c0 and c1 have the same variance as FIFO (as the *MoveTo* subgoal has 100% coverage, achieving a *MoveTo* subgoal does not change the coverage of the current intention and so both c0 and c1 behave like FIFO). In contrast *SA* has significantly lower variance (i.e., the waiting times for passengers is 'fairer'), as it is able to interleave actions in different intentions without destroying preconditions.

6.3 Computational Overhead of SA

The computational overhead of *SA* depends on the search configuration: how many iterations of the algorithm are performed α and how many random simulations are performed at each node β. With the search configuration used for the experiments above ($\alpha = 100$ and $\beta = 10$), *SA* requires 35 milliseconds to compute a complete interleaving of actions in 10 synthetic goal-plan trees (150 primitive actions). In a static environment, this interleaving only needs to be recomputed when the agent adopts a new top-level goal, so in the best case (no new top-level goals during the execution of the current intentions) the overhead of *SA* is effectively amortised over the execution of all 10 intentions, and the amortised CPU time required to selection an intention is approximately 0.2 milliseconds per deliberation cycle. In a dynamic environment, the interleaving must be recomputed whenever the agent's beliefs change, so the cost of intention selection will be correspondingly higher.

7. RELATED WORK

In addition to the work of Thangarajah et al. [22, 21, 23], Waters et al. [27, 28] and Yao et al. [31] discussed above, a number of other approaches to scheduling intentions to avoid conflicts have been proposed in the literature.

Shaw and Bordini have proposed approaches to intention selection based on Petri nets [19] and constraint logic programming [20]. As in [22, 21, 23, 27, 28, 31]), the plans and sub-goals in a goal-plan tree are regarded as basic steps, and interleaving is at the level of sub-plans and subgoals. They do not consider interactions between actions in plans.

The TÆMS (Task Analysis, Environment Modelling, and Simulation) framework [11] together with Design-To-Criteria (DTC) scheduling [26] have been used in agent architectures such the Soft Real-Time Agent Architecture [25] and AgentSpeak(XL) [3] to schedule intentions. TÆMS provides a high-level framework for specifying the expected quality, cost and duration of of methods (actions) and relationships between tasks (plans). DTC decides which tasks to perform, how to perform them, and the order in which they should be performed, so as to satisfy hard constraints (e.g., deadlines) and maximise the agent's objective function. DTC can produce schedules which allow interleaved or parallel execution of tasks and can be used in an anytime fashion. In the work closest to that presented here, DTC was used to schedule execution of AgentSpeak intentions at the level of individual plans [3]. The TÆMS relations between plans required to generate a schedule (*enables*, *facilitates* and *hinders*) were specified as part of the agent program. In contrast *SA* interleaves intentions at the level of actions, and information about possible conflicts between intentions is extracted automatically from goal-plan trees generated from the agent program.

In [17] Sardina et al. show how an HTN planner can be integrated into a BDI agent architecture. However their focus is on finding a hierarchical decomposition of a plan that is less likely to fail by avoiding incorrect decisions at choice points, and they do not take into account interactions with other concurrent intentions.

In [29], Wilkins et al. present the Cypress architecture which combines the the PRS-CL reactive executor and the SIPE-2 look-ahead planner. A Cypress agent uses PRS-CL to pursue its intentions using a library of procedures (plans). If a failure occurs during the execution of the plan due to an unanticipated change in the agent's environment, the executor calls SIPE-2 to produce a new plan to achieve the goal, and continues executing those portions of plans which are not affected. However, their approach focuses on the generation of new plans to recover from plan failures, rather than interleaving intentions so as to avoid conflicts.

In [32], Yao et al. present an approach to recovering from execution failures in BDI agent programs that relies on progressing executable intentions so as to (re)establish the precondition of the next step in an unexecutable intention as a 'side effect'. As in the work presented here, they interleave intentions at the action level. However the focus of their work is on minimising backtracking (trying an alternative plan when an intention becomes unexecutable), rather than coverage and fairness. Moreover, their approach is based on MCTS (rather than SP-MCTS), and their evaluation is limited to static domains.

There has also been work on avoiding conflicts in a multi-agent setting. For example, Clement and Durfee [6, 7, 8] propose an approach to coordinating concurrent hierarchical planning agents using summary information and HTN planning. However in this work, summary information is used to identify when conflicts may arise between two or more agents rather than to avoid conflicts between the intentions of a single agent. Moreover, it is assumed that the agents plan offline in a static environment. In [12], Ephrahi et al. present an approach to planning and interleaving the execution of tasks by multiple agents. The task of each agent is assigned dynamically, and the execution of all tasks achieves a global goal. They show how conflicts between intentions can be avoided by appropriate scheduling of the actions of the agents.

8. DISCUSSION & FUTURE WORK

We presented *SA*, an extension of the stochastic scheduling approach proposed in [31], that allows the interleaving of primitive actions in different intentions, and which takes both the dynamism of the environment and fairness into account when choosing which intention to progress. Action level intention selection allows conflicts that cannot be resolved by scheduling at the plan level to be avoided. We evaluated the performance of *SA* in static and dynamic environments, both in synthetic domains and a more realistic scenario based on the Miconic-10 elevator domain. Our results indicate that our approach out-performs RR, FIFO SI, and C, and is capable of successfully scheduling intentions so as to achieve their top-level goals even when the number of potential conflicts between intentions is high. Moreover, in the scenarios considered, the computational overhead of *SA* is modest.

Our approach has a number of limitations. When the agent's beliefs or goals change, our current implementation simply regenerates the SP-MCTS search tree from scratch, rather than merging belief and goal updates into the search tree from the previous deliberation cycle. A direction for future work is therefore to investigate ways of re-using an existing SP-MCTS search tree when the interleaving must be recomputed. Another line of future work is to consider intention selection where top-level goals are associated with deadlines as in, e.g., [24].

Acknowledgments

We would like to thank John Thangarajah for many helpful discussions relating to the work presented here.

REFERENCES

[1] N. Alechina, T. Behrens, M. Dastani, K. Hindriks, J. Hubner, B. Logan, H. Nguyen, and M. van Zee. Multi-cycle query caching in agent programming. In M. desJardins and M. Littman, editors, *Proceedings of the Twenty-Seventh AAAI Conference on Artificial Intelligence (AAAI 2013)*, volume 1, pages 32–38, Bellevue, Washington, July 2013. AAAI, AAAI Press.

[2] N. Alechina, M. Dastani, B. Logan, and J.-J. C. Meyer. Reasoning about agent deliberation. In G. Brewka and J. Lang, editors, *Proceedings of the Eleventh International Conference on Principles of Knowledge Representation and Reasoning (KR'08)*, pages 16–26, Sydney, Australia, September 2008. AAAI.

[3] R. Bordini, A. L. C. Bazzan, R. d. O. Jannone, D. M. Basso, R. M. Vicari, and V. R. Lesser. AgentSpeak(XL): Efficient intention selection in BDI agents via decision-theoretic task scheduling. In *Proceedings of the First International Conference on Autonomous Agents and Multiagent Systems (AAMAS'02)*, pages 1294–1302, 2002.

[4] R. H. Bordini, J. F. Hübner, and M. Wooldridge. *Programming multi-agent systems in AgentSpeak using Jason*. Wiley Series in Agent Technology. Wiley, 2007.

[5] M. E. Bratman, D. J. Israel, and M. E. Pollack. Plans and resource-bounded practical reasoning. *Computational Intelligence*, 4(4):349–355, 1988.

[6] B. J. Clement and E. H. Durfee. Theory for coordinating concurrent hierarchical planning agents using summary information. In J. Hendler and D. Subramanian, editors, *Proceedings of the Sixteenth National Conference on Artificial Intelligence (AAAI'99)*, pages 495–502, Orlando, Florida, USA, July 1999. AAAI Press / The MIT Press.

[7] B. J. Clement and E. H. Durfee. Performance of coordinating concurrent hierarchical planning agents using summary information. In *Proceedings of the 4th International Conference on Multi-Agent Systems*, pages 373–374, Boston, MA, USA, July 2000. IEEE Computer Society.

[8] B. J. Clement, E. H. Durfee, and A. C. Barrett. Abstract reasoning for planning and coordination. *Journal of Artificial Intelligence Research*, 28:453–515, 2007.

[9] M. Dastani. 2APL: a practical agent programming language. *Autonomous Agents and Multi-Agent Systems*, 16(3):214–248, 2008.

[10] L. de Silva and L. Padgham. A Comparison of BDI Based Real-Time Reasoning and HTN Based Planning. In G. I. Webb and X. Yu, editors, *AI 2004: Advances in Artificial Intelligence, Proceedings of the 17th Australian Joint Conference on Artificial Intelligence*, volume 3339, pages 1167–1173, Cairns, Australia, December 2004. Springer.

[11] K. S. Decker and V. R. Lesser. Quantitative modeling of complex environments. *International Journal of Intelligent Systems in Accounting, Finance and Management*, 2:215–234, 1993.

[12] E. Ephrati and J. S. Rosenschein. A framework for the interleaving of execution and planning for dynamic tasks by multiple agents. In C. Castelfranchi and J. Müller, editors, *From Reaction to Cognition, Proceedings of the 5th European Workshop on Modelling Autonomous Agents (MAAMAW'93)*, pages 139–153, Neuchatel, Switzerland, August 1993. Springer.

[13] K. V. Hindriks. Programming rational agents in GOAL. In A. El Fallah Seghrouchni, J. Dix, M. Dastani, and R. H. Bordini, editors, *Multi-Agent Programming: Languages, Tools and Applications*, pages 119–157. Springer, 2009.

[14] J. Koehler and K. Schuster. Elevator Control as a Planning Problem. In S. Chien, S. Kambhampati, and C. A. Knoblock, editors, *Proceedings of the Fifth International Conference on Artificial Intelligence Planning Systems*, pages 331–338, Breckenridge, CO, USA, April 2000. AAAI.

[15] S. Matsumoto, N. Hirosue, K. Itonaga, N. Ueno, and H. Ishii. Monte-Carlo tree search for a reentrant scheduling problem. In *40th International Conference on Computers and Industrial Engineering (CIE)*, pages 1–6, Awaji, 2010. IEEE.

[16] A. S. Rao and M. P. Georgeff. An abstract architecture for rational agents. In C. Rich, W. Swartout, and B. Nebel, editors, *Proceedings of Knowledge Representation and Reasoning (KR&R-92)*, pages 439–449, 1992.

[17] S. Sardiña, L. de Silva, and L. Padgham. Hierarchical planning in BDI agent programming languages: a formal approach. In H. Nakashima, M. P. Wellman, G. Weiss, and P. Stone, editors, *Proceedings of the Fifth International Joint Conference on Autonomous Agents and Multiagent Systems (AAMAS 2006)*, pages 1001–1008, Hakodate, Japan, May 2006. ACM.

[18] M. P. D. Schadd, M. H. M. Winands, M. J. W. Tak, and J. W. H. M. Uiterwijk. Single-player Monte-Carlo tree search for SameGame. *Knowledge-Based Systems*, 34:3–11, 2012.

[19] P. H. Shaw and R. H. Bordini. Towards alternative approaches to reasoning about goals. In M. Baldoni, T. C. Son, M. B. van Riemsdijk, and M. Winikoff, editors, *Proceedings of the Fifth International Workshop on Declarative Agent Languages and Technologies (DALT 2007)*, volume 4897, pages 104–121, Honolulu, HI, USA, May 2007. Springer.

[20] P. H. Shaw and R. H. Bordini. An alternative approach for reasoning about the goal-plan tree problem. In H. Coelho, R. Studer, and M. Wooldridge, editors, *Proceedings of the 19th European Conference on Artificial Intelligence (ECAI 2010)*, volume 215, pages 1035–1036, Lisbon, Portugal, August 2010. IOS Press.

[21] J. Thangarajah and L. Padgham. Computationally effective reasoning about goal interactions. *Journal of Automated Reasoning*, 47(1):17–56, 2011.

[22] J. Thangarajah, L. Padgham, and M. Winikoff. Detecting & avoiding interference between goals in intelligent agents. In G. Gottlob and T. Walsh, editors, *Proceedings of the Eighteenth International Joint Conference on Artificial Intelligence (IJCAI-03)*, pages 721–726, Acapulco, Mexico, August 2003. Morgan Kaufmann.

[23] J. Thangarajah, S. Sardina, and L. Padgham. Measuring plan coverage and overlap for agent reasoning. In W. van der Hoek, L. Padgham, V. Conitzer, and M. Winikoff, editors, *Proceedings of the 11th International Conference on Autonomous Agents and Multiagent Systems (AAMAS 2012)*, pages 1049–1056. IFAAMAS, June 2012.

[24] K. Vikhorev, N. Alechina, and B. Logan. Agent programming with priorities and deadlines. In K. Turner, P. Yolum, L. Sonenberg, and P. Stone, editors, *Proceedings of the Tenth International Conference on Autonomous Agents and Multiagent Systems (AAMAS 2011)*, pages 397–404, Taipei, Taiwan, May 2011.

[25] R. Vincent, B. Horling, V. Lesser, and T. Wagner. Implementing soft real-time agent control. In *Proceedings of*

the Fifth International Conference on Autonomous Agents (AGENTS'01), pages 355–362, 2001.

[26] T. Wagner, A. Garvey, and V. Lesser. Criteria-directed heuristic task scheduling. *International Journal of Approximate Reasoning*, 19:91–118, 1998.

[27] M. Waters, L. Padgham, and S. Sardina. Evaluating coverage based intention selection. In A. Lomuscio, P. Scerri, A. Bazzan, and M. Huhns, editors, *Proceedings of the 13th International Conference on Autonomous Agents and Multi-agent Systems (AAMAS 2014)*, pages 957–964. IFAAMAS, 2014.

[28] M. Waters, L. Padgham, and S. Sardiña. Improving domain-independent intention selection in BDI systems. *Autonomous Agents and Multi-Agent Systems*, 29(4):683–717, 2015.

[29] D. E. Wilkins, K. L. Myers, J. D. Lowrance, and L. P. Wesley. Planning and reacting in uncertain and dynamic environments. *Journal of Experimental and Theoretical Artificial Intelligence*, 7(1):121–152, 1995.

[30] M. Winikoff. JACK intelligent agents: An industrial strength platform. In R. H. Bordini, M. Dastani, J. Dix, and A. E. Fallah-Seghrouchni, editors, *Multi-Agent Programming: Languages, Platforms and Applications*, pages 175–193. Springer, 2005.

[31] Y. Yao, B. Logan, and J. Thangarajah. SP-MCTS-based intention scheduling for BDI agents. In T. Schaub, G. Friedrich, and B. O'Sullivan, editors, *Proceedings of the 21st European Conference on Artificial Intelligence (ECAI-2014)*, pages 1133–1134, Prague, Czech Republic, August 2014. ECCAI, IOS Press.

[32] Y. Yao, B. Logan, and J. Thangarajah. Robust execution of BDI agent programs by exploiting synergies between intentions. In *Proceedings of the Thirtieth AAAI Conference on Artificial Intelligence (AAAI-16)*, Phoenix, USA, February 2016. AAAI, AAAI Press. (In press).

Automating Failure Detection in Cognitive Agent Programs

Vincent J. Koeman
Delft University of Technology
Mekelweg 4, 2628CD
Delft, The Netherlands
v.j.koeman@tudelft.nl

Koen V. Hindriks
Delft University of Technology
Mekelweg 4, 2628CD
Delft, The Netherlands
k.v.hindriks@tudelft.nl

Catholijn M. Jonker
Delft University of Technology
Mekelweg 4, 2628CD
Delft, The Netherlands
c.m.jonker@tudelft.nl

ABSTRACT

Debugging is notoriously difficult and extremely time consuming but also essential for ensuring the reliability and quality of a software system. In order to reduce debugging effort and enable automated failure detection, we propose an *automated testing framework* for detecting failures in cognitive agent programs. Our approach is based on the assumption that modules within such programs are a natural unit for testing. We identify a minimal set of temporal operators that enable the specification of test conditions and show that the test language is sufficiently expressive for detecting all failures in an existing failure taxonomy. We also introduce an approach for specifying *test templates* that supports a programmer in writing tests. Furthermore, empirical analysis of agent programs allows us to evaluate whether our approach using test templates detects all failures.

Keywords

multi-agent systems; testing; verification

1. INTRODUCTION

Debugging is notoriously difficult and extremely time consuming [23] but also essential for ensuring the reliability and quality of a software system. Manual testing, using, for example, a debugger for single-step execution to identify differences between observed and intended behaviour, however, is not an efficient failure detection method and heavily relies on the programmer to identify the failure. In order to reduce debugging effort and enable automated failure detection, we propose an *automated testing framework for cognitive agent programs.* Automated testing yields a reduction in the effort needed to detect a failure and is more effective than code inspection methods [24]. In addition, it also facilitates running tests repeatedly at no additional costs.

The aim of this paper is to introduce and develop a test framework that supports *automated failure detection* for programs written in rule-based agent programming languages that use a logic for representing the cognitive state of the agent, including e.g. its beliefs. A *failure* is an event in which a system does not perform a required function within specified limits [16]. Failures thus are manifestations of undesired behaviour. They are caused by a *fault*, an incorrect step, process, or data definition in a program [16] or mistake in a program [27]. Upon detecting a failure, a programmer needs to locate and correct the fault that causes the failure. Our focus is on automating the detection of failures and on dynamic analysis, i.e., the process of evaluating a system or component based on its behaviour during execution [16]. We will see, however, that the test framework introduced also provides support for fault localization.

The main contribution of this paper is an *automated test framework* for cognitive agent programs that provides support for detecting frequently occurring failure types. As a first step towards such a framework, we argue that program modules instead of the top-level agent program are the most natural unit for testing, and that test conditions should be associated with modules. Second, we introduce two basic temporal operators that in practice are sufficient for specifying test conditions to detect failures. Third, using this generic framework, we propose test templates for failure types that have been identified in a previously developed taxonomy in [27]. Finally, we introduce a test approach for deriving test templates given some initial functional requirements. In order to empirically evaluate and demonstrate that our framework is expressive enough to detect all failure types, we verify that we can reproduce and identify all failures found in the sample used in [27]. The test templates that we introduce can be considered as a refinement of the failure taxonomy proposed in [27]. We show that by automating testing, we are able to identify more failures. We also show that our work is not biased towards this sample by demonstrating that the same test approach is also able to identify all failures in different samples of programs.

The paper is organized as follows. Section 2 discusses related work. Section 3 introduces our automated test framework. Section 4 introduces the test templates and approach. Section 5 evaluates the test framework. Section 6 concludes.

2. RELATED WORK

In general, different techniques for detecting failures of program code are available, ranging from *inspection* of source code and logs to automated *testing* tools [24]. The need for debugging techniques and test approaches for agent-oriented programming has been broadly recognized [2, 9, 10]. Techniques for agent-oriented programming need to be based on the underlying agent paradigm [21, 28]. However, this is a significant challenge, as they should for example take into account that agents execute a specific decision cycle and operate in non-deterministic environments [1, 4, 14].

Appears in: *Proceedings of the 15th International Conference on Autonomous Agents and Multiagent Systems (AAMAS 2016), J. Thangarajah, K. Tuyls, C. Jonker, S. Marsella (eds.), May 9–13, 2016, Singapore.*

To facilitate code inspection, a (source-level) debugger that supports single-step execution of an agent can be used. [19], for example, provides a useful tool for detecting failures in a program. Debugging is particularly useful for zooming in on a bug of which the location is already more or less clear; it requires a programmer to go through the execution steps of an agent program one-by-one and to observe any mistakes in the program manually. This method of code inspection is not only inefficient, but also subjective, as it depends on observations made by a programmer. It requires the same effort repeatedly since, after correcting an identified fault, a programmer needs to manually evaluate program behaviour again to verify that a fix does not introduce new defects. Automated testing offers a method that is complementary to debugging, able to find different kinds of failures, and thus increasing the overall number of detected failures [23, 24]. Moreover, debugging techniques that support the localization of the fault that causes a failure that has been identified by automated tests are still needed. Such techniques include state inspection, mechanisms for browsing and searching (historical) agent states, etcetera [7, 19].

Five levels of testing a multi-agent system (MAS) are distinguished in [20]: *unit*, *agent*, *integration*, *system*, and *acceptance*. In this classification, unit testing targets components that are part of an agent. Testing an agent means to test the integration of these components as well as its ability to interact with its environment. Integration testing focuses on agent interaction and communication protocols, system testing concerns the target operating environment, and acceptance testing takes the customer's perspective into account. The focus of this paper is on unit and agent testing.

Testing can target different artifacts [24]. The test framework of [28], for example, targets Prometheus design models. The paper presents a mechanism for generating suitable test cases. Similarly, the methodology of [12] is based on specific 'meta-models' and 'protocol descriptions'. Other methods focus on the interaction between agents specifically, often using 'mock agents' to check if specific interaction has taken place [6, 18]. The concept of a 'mock agent', i.e., a specific agent that is used for testing, is also used in the work of [5] to test an agent's behaviour based on 'agent stories'. Most of these approaches consider an agent to be the smallest possible artifact to test. Other approaches target more specific artifacts like plans ([22, 25]) or goals ([11]). In this work, however, we argue that modules are the most suitable target artifact. This is partly motivated by the work of [15], which states that techniques that rely heavily on formal methods or sophisticated program analysis are valuable, but difficult to apply in practice, and thus not always effective in finding real bugs. *Bug patterns* (code idioms that are often errors) can be used to facilitate the development of simple detectors (e.g., test templates) that facilitate efficient bug detection in real applications. Therefore, unlike these existing methods, we focus on *how to create tests that can detect specific bug patterns in cognitive agents.*

3. AUTOMATED TESTING FRAMEWORK

We introduce an automated test framework for rule-based agent programming languages that use some knowledge representation (KR) for representing the cognitive state of an agent. We aim for a framework that is as generic as possible, but in order to introduce a concrete framework we need to make a number of assumptions about these languages. First, agents have a *perception processing component* that they use for processing received percepts, which are simple facts that we denote by $p(\vec{t})$ (or simply p if parameters do not matter). We assume that percepts are stored each agent cycle when received from an environment for further processing. Second, we assume that the KR used supports a *negation* operator, denoted by not. Third, we assume that the cognitive state includes a *belief state* that can be queried and which allows to make percepts persistent. Fourth, we assume that agents somehow can represent *goals* that they want to achieve as part of their state; agents can do this, for example, by means of events, plans, or declarative goals. Otherwise, the structure of an agent's cognitive state depends of the specifics of the agent programming language, which almost always includes more, e.g., also events, messages, and/or plans. Fifth, we assume that the language provides support for aggregating or encapsulating basic language elements such as knowledge, goals, plans, and/or rules in what we call *modules* in this paper. Finally, we assume that an agent has a top-level module, which enables associating test conditions with the agent itself.

Three important design questions need to be addressed to define an automated test framework for cognitive agent programs. First, we need to specify what the *basic unit or program component* is that tests are performed on or are associated with. Second, we need to define a *test language* for specifying test conditions. And, third, we need to specify an *infrastructure that automates running tests.*

3.1 Modules Basic Unit for Testing

An important question that we need to address when setting up a test framework is what the *target unit* for testing is in an agent-oriented program. We argue that a test framework for agent programs should not focus on knowledge bases to avoid reinventing the wheel, but developers should rather re-use existing (unit) test frameworks for the underlying KR technology of an agent programming language. For example, a language that uses SWI Prolog for KR should aim at re-using the available unit test framework [26]. We have also found that, in practice, testing at the level of individual goals, plans, or rules is too fine-grained and not that useful. Writing tests at the level of individual rules, for example, would not only result in more test than source code, but even worse, would not focus on the failures that need to be detected. A more suitable level is the aggregate level that collects multiple goals, plans, and/or rules in a single unit. We call such units *modules* and assume agent programming languages provide some level of support for modules. We will therefore *associate test conditions with modules* and introduce a test language that supports this.

Modules thus can be perceived of as components in an agent program that set goals or plans and generate actions to be executed, much like individual basic actions but at a higher level of abstraction. A module thus provides an execution unit smaller than the agent program itself but larger than other basic language elements. By using modules as targets for testing, we provide a developer with some additional control over which behaviour of the agent program is tested, as only the behaviour generated by the module will be evaluated. This allows a developer to write tests that target only specific parts of an agent program.

An agent enters a module when it starts executing the module and exits the module again when module execu-

test	:=	[*timeout*] *moduletest** *agenttest*$^+$
timeout	:=	`timeout` = *integer* .
agenttest	:=	*id* (, *id*)* { *testaction*$^+$ }
testaction	:=	`do` (*action* | *id*) [`until` ψ] .
moduletest	:=	`test` *id* `with`
		[`pre{` ψ `}`] [`in` { χ^+ }] [`post{` ψ `}`]
ψ	:=	*stateop*(ϕ) | `done(`*action*`)` | $\psi \wedge \psi$
χ	:=	`never` ψ | ψ `leadsto` ψ .

Table 1: Test Language Grammar

tion is finished. These execution points provide two natural places for introducing test conditions. We will associate *pre-conditions* and *post-conditions* with a module that is evaluated, respectively, when entering and when exiting the module. Although useful, in practice pre- and post-conditions are not sufficient for monitoring the trace, i.e., behaviour and states, generated while a module is executed. To be able to evaluate a module's behaviour, we therefore also introduce so-called *in-conditions* that are associated with a module. An in-condition is a temporal property evaluated on the trace generated by a module. These conditions allow the detection of failures that occur during module execution. These conditions also provide better support for fault localization as a test is terminated upon a failure at the code location where the failure was detected.

3.2 Test Language

A test language should provide support for two main tasks: *setting up a test* and *specifying* which *test conditions* should be evaluated. To this end, we introduce the test language in Table 1. We have developed a test framework[1] that, when provided with a *test* program as specified by the grammar, will initialize and set up the infrastructure for running an agent system and (external) environment in which test will be automatically performed. A *timeout* can be specified to ensure termination of the test after a specified time. A timeout is global and specifies how many time (in seconds) is allowed to pass before the entire test should have been completed. If a timeout happens, the test is aborted.

Test Setup The agents that are part of a test need to be referenced explicitly in a test program by means of their *id*'s. These agents are launched when the test is started and automatically connected to an environment, if available, to receive percepts from and perform actions in that environment. The fact that agents are launched, however, does not mean that the program code of these agents is executed. Instead, the *testactions* that are specified in an *agenttest* clause (see Table 1) are performed when the test is run. Test actions can be preparatory actions `do` *action* for, e.g., initializing an agent's state, where *action* can be a sequence of actions that are available in an agent language. Test actions can also be instructions `do` *id* to execute a module, with *id* the module's name. Note that it is possible to run an agent itself by executing its top-level module (each agent is assumed to have one). Finally, an `until` ψ condition can be associated with a module (or, less usefully, an action) that terminates execution when a state condition ψ holds. An agent test thus determines which actions and modules are executed and when they should be terminated. An agent test can be shared by multiple agents, but it is also possible to define different actions for different agents, which will then be executed in parallel.

[1]The source and implementation of the test framework are available at `http://goalhub.github.io/eclipse`

The environment that agents operate in is not explicitly referenced in our test language because the specifics of starting an external environment are very different for each agent language. Here, we simply assume that a language-specific mechanism is used for connecting agents to an environment.

Test Conditions As explained, test conditions are associated with modules. Which conditions should be evaluated when a module is executed is specified by a `test` *id* `with` statement, where *id* is a module name. Optionally, a pre-condition `pre{` ψ `}`, a post-condition `post{` ψ `}`, and an in-condition `in` { χ^+ } can be associated with the module. The pre-condition of a module is a state condition ψ that should hold when a module is entered (otherwise, the test fails). Similarly, a post-condition is a state condition that should hold when a module is exited (terminated). An in-condition is a temporal condition that specifies which behaviour is expected of a module.

A state condition ψ is a condition of the form *stateop*(ϕ) on the cognitive state of an agent, where ϕ is an expression in a KR language, or a condition of the form `done(`α`)` on the action α that an agent has just performed. The state conditions *stateop*(ϕ) that are supported will be different for each agent language, as they each use a specific cognitive state structure and associated state operators *stateop* for inspecting that state. Querying the beliefs of an agent, for example, may be written as ϕ? in one language and as bel(ϕ) in another.

A temporal property or condition is a statement of the form `never` ψ or ψ `leadsto` ψ. Conditions `never` ψ can be used to specify safety conditions, i.e., things that never should occur. Conditions ψ `leadsto` ψ can be used to specify liveness conditions, i.e., things that are supposed to occur sooner or later after something else has happened [3].

Our test language is based only on the two basic temporal operators `never` and `leadsto`. Most importantly, this is so because it turns out to be sufficient for detecting failures (as we show below as well). We also do not want to complicate our test language more than strictly necessary, as we aim for our language to be used by trained agent programmers. We therefore want to minimize the level of acquaintance with concepts from temporal logic that is needed. In particular, we want to avoid nesting of temporal operators because conditions would quickly become difficult to read in that case. Finally, we note that some temporal operators such as `always` ψ can be introduced as syntactic sugar for `never` `not(`ψ`)`. Note that this assumes, however, that the `not` can be applied to a state condition or moved inwards into the KR expressions used in the state condition, which is not the case in most agent languages. Similarly, `eventually` ψ can be introduced as shorthand for `true` `leadsto` ψ.

Although it is outside the scope of this paper to provide a formal semantics of the test conditions, we briefly introduce the basic semantic model that we assume informally. A run or trace of an agent program consists of a (finite or potentially infinite) sequence of cognitive states of the agent. Test conditions associated with a module are evaluated on (partial) traces generated by that module. For testing purposes, these conditions are assigned one of three values: *undetermined*, *passed*, or *failed*. Initially, all test conditions of a module have the value *undetermined*. The pre-condition of a module, if specified, is evaluated on the current state when

P1:	failure to deal with percept
P2:	other incorrect percept processing
G1:	failure to add a goal that should be added
G2:	failure to drop a goal that should be dropped
G3:	adding a goal that shouldn't be added
G4:	incorrectly adding a second goal of the same type
G5:	dropping a goal that shouldn't be dropped
A1:	selecting the wrong (user-defined) action
A2:	beliefs not updated correctly when action performed
A3:	action selected when should be doing nothing
A4:	action interface mismatch
O:	other failure not classified above

Figure 1: Failure Taxonomy of [27]

entering the module and assigned *passed* when the condition succeeds, and *failed* otherwise. Similarly, the post-condition is evaluated on the current state when a module is exited or terminated. The value of in-conditions is (re-)evaluated every time the cognitive state of the agent changes while the module is being executed. The temporal operator of the condition determines whether the value is updated:

- `never` ψ: the value is changed to *failed* if ψ holds in the state; the value is changed to *passed* if the module (or test) is terminated and the value still is *undetermined*; otherwise, its value remains *undetermined*.
- ψ `leadsto` ψ': if the module (or test) is terminated, the value is changed to *passed* if every state where ψ holds has been followed by a state where ψ' holds (and vacuously so if ψ did never hold); otherwise, the value is changed to *failed*. If the module (or test) has not been terminated yet, the value is *undetermined*.

A test is aborted as soon as a condition is assigned the value *failed*. In that case, the entire test is regarded as failed, indicating that something needs to be fixed. Note that when a test is terminated (whether aborted or not), all conditions will have been assigned the value *passed* or *failed*. If a test is terminated because of a timeout, this does not always imply that the test is a failure; if all conditions are passed, the test is considered to have passed as well. Finally, our test framework keeps track of the last code instruction in an agent program that is executed and points at the corresponding code location when testing is terminated (aborted), which is useful for fault localization.

4. TESTING FOR FAILURES

In order to verify that we can detect all failures in agent programs with our framework, we show that we can detect the same failures that were identified by [27] in a given agent program sample that was used to define the failure taxonomy of Figure 1. We provide a systematic approach for detecting failures by introducing test templates that target specific types of failures in the taxonomy, and a systematic method for using these templates for testing.

4.1 Test Templates

A test template consists of one or more templates for individual test conditions. We provide test templates for each failure type in the taxonomy, except for *A4*, which calls for another detection method and raises a specific design issue for test frameworks. We note that a test condition specifies expected behaviour, and a violation indicates a failure.

P1, P2: Failure to process percept (correctly).

In order to define test conditions for percept processing, we assume a state operator percept(p), indicating that p is perceived, that can be used to inspect the contents of a percept store. This does not mean that these conditions must be supported in the programming language itself, but only that it should be possible to somehow inspect which percepts have been received.

In order to support various options for percept processing, we distinguish four percept types and associate specific test templates with each type. Although in theory alternatives can easily be conceived of, we have specified test templates below based on the assumption that the percept information needs to be made persistent in the agent's belief state, which worked well in practice. We also assume that test conditions for percepts can be associated with a percept processing module called *ppm*, and we can write test statements of the form `test` *ppm* `with in {` χ^+ `}`. Each agent language provides some kind of support for this, although perhaps not in the language itself but 'under the hood'. It is important that test conditions for percepts are associated with and evaluated while executing the percept processing module. Because this module is executed once each cycle of the agent, in order to not violate the test conditions, percepts must have been processed and beliefs updated accordingly at the end of percept processing.

Template *P-once*: concerns percepts that are only received *once*, typically when the agent is launched to inform about static information such as locations on maps. The test template expects that after receiving the percept, it will be made persistent such that the agent believes it.

```
percept(p) leadsto bel(p)
```

Template *P-always*: concerns percepts about facts p that are *always* received when p is the case, meaning that not receiving the percept implies that p does not hold. The test template consists of two test conditions. The first is identical to the one for ***P-once***; the second condition expects that not perceiving p, which would indicate that p does not hold, should lead to removing the belief p (if present).

```
percept(p) leadsto bel(p)
not(percept(p)) ∧ bel(p) leadsto not(bel(p))
```

Template *P-on-change*: concerns percepts that are sent only when parameters change. A percept *loc*(*place*), for example, is sent each time when an agent's location changes.

```
percept(p(t⃗)) leadsto bel(p(t⃗))
percept(p(t⃗))∧bel(p(t⃗')) ∧ t⃗ ≠ t⃗' leadsto not(bel(p(t⃗')))
```

Template *P-on-change-with-negation*: concerns percepts p that are received once when p becomes true, and percepts *not*(p) that are received once when p becomes false (again). For example, *in*(*room*) is received when an agent enters a room, and not(*in*(*room*)) is received when it leaves again.

```
percept(p) leadsto bel(p)
percept(not(p)) leadsto not(bel(p))
```

G1: Failure to add a goal that should be added.

The taxonomy in Fig. 1 includes five failure categories related to goal handling. We therefore assume that a state operator goal is available for checking for the presence or absence of a goal. Each of these failure categories, with the exception of *G4*, suggest that a *reason* for (not) having a goal has not been adequately taken into account.

Template *G-adopted*: concerns a goal ϕ that the agent is expected to adopt because of some (sufficient) reason ψ.

```
ψ leadsto goal(φ)
```

G2: Failure to drop a goal that should be dropped.

The failure to drop a goal is taken here as an indication that the agent did not adequately reconsider the goals that it has. As one would expect an agent to reconsider its goals if the environment has changed outside the control of that agent, these failures would most likely only occur in dynamic environments or in a multi-agent context.

Template *G-reconsideration*: concerns a goal that should be reconsidered and dropped as a result for some reason ψ.

```
ψ leadsto not(goal(φ))
```

G3: Adding a goal that should not be added.

The counterpart of *G1*, reflected by the fact that we use a safety (`never`) instead of liveness (`leadsto`) condition here.

Template *G-incorrect*: concerns a situation in which there is a reason ψ for not adopting (having adopted) the goal.

```
never goal(φ) ∧ ψ
```

G4: Adding a second goal of the same type.

Some goals should only occur once and it should never be the case that the goal is instantiated twice. For example, an agent might have a goal of visiting a room but should never have two of those goals simultaneously.

Template *G-duplicate*: concerns a single-instance goal that should be instantiated at most once.

```
never goal(φ(t⃗)) ∧ goal(φ(t⃗')) ∧ t⃗ ≠ t⃗'
```

G5: Dropping a goal that should not be dropped.

Similar to *G3*, *G5* is the counterpart of *G2*.

Template *G-maintain*: concerns a situation in which ψ is a reason why an agent should have a goal, and should maintain it for that reason.

```
never not(goal(φ)) ∧ ψ
```

A1: Failure to select an action.

Fig. 1 includes four failure categories related to actions. Categories *A1* and *A3* suggest that a *reason* for (not) selecting an action has not been adequately taken into account.

Template *A-selected*: concerns an action α that the agent is expected to have selected because of some reason ψ.

```
ψ leadsto done(α)
```

A2, A3: Incorrect action (selection).

We provide one test template for categories *A*2 and *A*3, which both suggest that something happened that should (never) have happened, and thus can be viewed as the counterpart of *A*1. *A*2 indicates that beliefs should not have been updated the way they are, and *A*3 indicates there is a situation in which an action should never have been selected.

Template *A-incorrect*: concerns an action α that should never be (immediately) followed by ψ (*A*2), or a situation ψ in which an action should never have been selected (*A*3).

```
never done(α) ∧ ψ
```

A4: Action interface mismatch.

This failure concerns an agent that attempts to perform an action in an environment that is not supported by that environment. An environment is expected to raise an exception or use another event-mechanism to indicate this issue. To detect these failures, rather than providing a test template, the test framework should abort testing immediately after receiving the exception or event. Aborting upon receiving an exception is a general principle that is supported in our framework.

4.2 Taxonomy Refinement

The test templates that we have introduced do not offer a perfect match with the failure categories, but provide a refinement of the taxonomy in Fig. 1. Instead of two categories *P1*,*P2* for percept processing failures, we introduced four templates (***P-once***, etc.). The main reason for this difference is that in a test approach we should specify what kind of percept is expected, instead of indicating that no processing was done at all (*P1*) or something went wrong (*P2*). For a similar reason, we renamed *A1* from 'selecting the wrong action' to 'failure to select an action', which also highlights the similarity with the template for *G1*. We merged *A2* and *A3* which are covered by a single test template; note again the structural similarity with the template for ***G-incorrect*** (*G3*). As discussed, we do not have a corresponding template for *A4*, as tests should rather be aborted when this failure happens. Finally, we have no templates for the 'other' category; our empirical results suggest there is no need for an additional template, as we show below.

4.3 Test Approach

In order to test and use the test templates, we need a *systematic test approach* that tells us what to do (steps) and, more specifically, provides clues on how to instantiate the templates for a specific application. An important question, for example, is how to find reasons to instantiate the ψ conditions that occur in the ***G***- and ***A***-templates. Table 2 lists information resources that are particularly useful for testing.

Source	Type of Information
Agent program (comments)	Clues for reasons & design
Agent trace (screen, logs)	Observable behaviour
Agent design & specification	Functional requirements
Environment (documentation)	Percepts, actions available

Table 2: Information sources for testing

Step 1: Defining success.

The first step is to identify functional requirements from available agent design documentation (Table 2). These requirements define success and provide a concrete method for checking that a program does what it is supposed to do. A program can be considered free of failures if it meets requirements. In order to automatically check this, functional requirements must also be specified in the test language. Typically, these requirements will be associated with the top-level module, called `main` here, that is executed by the agent, and we can specify them as pre-, post-, or in-conditions of that module using `test main with` statements or by using a statement `do main until` ψ. The latter is particularly useful for checking that some overall objective ψ is realized (and, if so, the test will be automatically terminated; a `timeout` should be specified to guarantee termination if this is not the case). For example, the requirement or objective to pickup and deliver n packages, which was used in [27] and below will be used to reproduce results, can be specified by `do main until` bel($delivered(n)$).

Step 2: Testing cognitive state updating.

It is important to test that updating of an agent's cognitive state works as expected. The state conditions used in test conditions are evaluated on this state and will fail for unclear reasons when state updating has not been implemented correctly. For example, a condition `never` done($putDown$) $\wedge$ not(bel($in(Room)$)), which expresses that a package should never be put down when not in a room, could simply fail because beliefs about *in(Room)* were not updated correctly.

Identify percepts, actions, and goals used As a preparatory step, it is useful to collect and list all percepts, including their type (*once*, etc.), that may be received and the actions that may be performed from environment documentation (Table 2). Similarly, all goals that an agent may have should be collected from the agent program code.

Validating percept processing The most basic step is to instantiate the appropriate test templates ***P-once***, etc. for each percept according to type. The resulting test conditions should be associated as in-conditions with the percept processing module, and the test framework used to evaluate these conditions. Tests should be repeated sufficiently often as percepts generated will differ per run, if only because environments are more often than not non-deterministic. To gain confidence that percepts are correctly handled, it is important to check against the list of actions created above whether a sufficient variation of actions has been performed during runs, as different actions often yield other percepts.

Check single-instance goals Based on design, and intended use of goals in comments in a program (Table 2), for example, and using the goal list created, the subset of goals that are single-instance goals should be identified. For each of these goals, the test template ***G-duplicate*** should be instantiated and associated as an in-condition with the module where the goal is adopted.

We note that Step 2 can be performed by almost mechanically instantiating templates once relevant information has been collected. If these initial tests succeed, therefore, this will give a high level of confidence that cognitive states are updated correctly. For all templates other than those used above, however, a state condition ψ needs to be derived using insights gained from the design and behaviour of an agent.

Step 3: Classifying failures.

After testing state updating and checking that failures still are present (see Step 1), there are two approaches for classifying those failures. A bottom-up approach would start with the action and goal list created and try to instantiate templates for all these actions and goals, using the agent program itself as the main source of information. A top-down approach would rather start by analysing agent traces (Table 2) and observing agent behaviour in order to identify which action should (not) have been performed or goal should (not) have been added. Although a top-down approach suggests to start with testing goals, this order is not fixed and testing might just as well proceed with actions.

Failures concerning actions In order to instantiate ***A***-templates, apart from the action, a state condition should be identified that provides a reason ψ for (not) selecting it. For ***A-selected*** (resp. ***A-incorrect***), the question is in which situations ψ an action should (never) be executed. The instantiated conditions should be associated as in-conditions with the module(s) where the action might (not) be selected.

There are two basic approaches for identifying ψ:

1. By inspecting the agent program, clues may be obtained for useful test conditions ψ. In particular, the triggering conditions of rules can be useful, as they typically indicate reasons for selecting an action. For example, a condition bel($in('DropZone') \wedge holding(Block)$) that triggers execution of an action *putDown* suggests that an agent should execute *putDown* when it is holding a block in the $'DropZone'$. By simply using this condition for ψ we can instantiate ***A-selected*** as follows: bel($in('DropZone') \wedge holding(Block)$) `leadsto` done($putDown$). This simple approach can already detect failures, e.g., in case the rule order prevents the rule for *putDown* to ever be applied. Similarly, by simply negating conditions found in a program, we can instantiate ***A-incorrect***. This assumes that the condition must hold for the action to be selected. Although these assumptions may be too strong, they provide a useful starting point and can be weakened or strengthened based on further analysis.

2. If an action failure is suspected because, for example, a functional requirement is not satisfied, observing an agent's behaviour may provide clues for identifying a useful condition ψ for instantiating a test template for that action. Suppose a requirement bel($in(Room)$) `leadsto` not(bel($in(Room)$)) fails, i.e., an agent does not always leave a room after entering it. By observing that the *goTo* action is never performed, a failure to select this action is suggested. To test for this, the ***A-selected*** template can be instantiated by instantiating ψ with the reason for leaving and α with the *goTo* action, which yields: bel($in(Room) \wedge Room \neq OtherRoom$) `leadsto` done($goTo(OtherRoom)$). This process can be continued until the root cause has been identified.

Failures concerning goals The approach for instantiating ***G***-templates, apart from identifying the goal that might cause the failure, is similar to that for ***A***-templates. The associated questions for the templates are, for ***G-adopted***: for which ψ should the goal be added?; for ***G-reconsideration***: for which ψ should the goal be dropped?; ***G-incorrect***: for which ψ should a goal never be added?; and for ***G-maintain***: for which ψ should a goal never be removed. The approach for identifying ψ above also applies for goals. The instantiated conditions should be associated as in-conditions with the module(s) that are related to the goal.

We illustrate a test for a goal $in(Room)$ that is adopted in a rule with a triggering condition bel($room(Place)$) $\wedge$ not(bel($visited(Place)$)), i.e., indicating that an agent should adopt (multiple) $in(Room)$ goals when it knows about a room that it has not visited before. By simply using this condition for ψ we can instantiate ***G-adopted*** as follows: bel($room(Place)$) $\wedge$ not(bel($visited(Place)$)) `leadsto` goal($in(Place)$. Again, this simple approach can already detect failures, e.g., in case the rule order prevents the rule

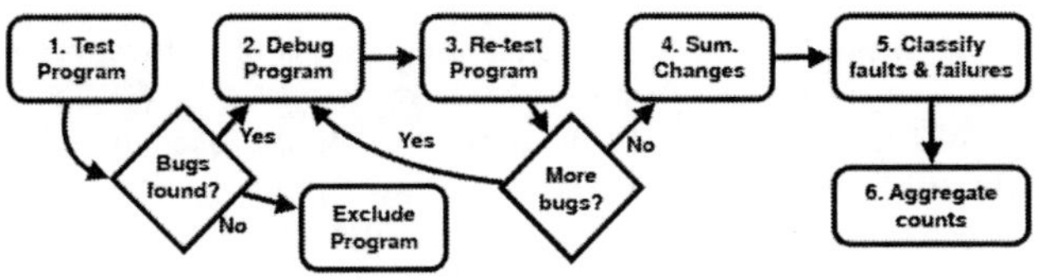

Figure 2: The methodology used in [27]

from ever being applied. Similarly, by simply negating conditions found in a program, we can instantiate ***G-incorrect***. This assumes that the condition must hold for the goal to be adopted, e.g., we never want to go to rooms we have visited before. A similar approach can be used for the ***G-reconsideration*** and the ***G-maintain*** templates.

5. EVALUATION

In this section, we first evaluate whether our automated approach is able to detect all failures in a specific set of agent programs. Next, we evaluate whether we are able to detect all failures in a different set of agents operating in the same environment, but with additional functional requirements. Finally, we evaluate this for a single agent program sample that operates in a different environment.

5.1 Comparing the Approaches

To establish the effectiveness of our automated test framework and test approach, we evaluate here whether the automated test framework, using the test templates introduced above, is able to detect the failures that were detected by manual inspection in [27]. We aim to show that our framework can be used to detect failures to obtain failure-free programs, meaning that functional requirements are met.

Methodology We used the agent program sample and the methodology for testing, debugging, and classifying failures of Fig. 2 that was also used by [27]. Only step 1 and 3 were replaced by tests performed using our test framework instead of manual inspection of logs and traces. We also used the same 'success criteria', i.e., the requirement formulated at the end of Step 1 of our approach. As we want to demonstrate that failures detected in [27] can also be detected automatically, we used a bottom-up approach for writing tests and created test templates for all percepts, actions, and goals in a program to ensure as large a coverage as possible. Upon detecting a failure (bug), we applied the same fixes as [27], which we obtained from the author, and re-ran our tests. We verified that the same bug was found by our tests, e.g., by checking that the code location where the test was terminated corresponds with the code location where a fix was applied. If we could not match a failure found by automated testing with one found originally by manual inspection, this failure was registered separately, the corresponding test conditions were removed, and the evaluation was continued.

Results We analysed and wrote a large set of test conditions for 20 agent programs. The results in terms of number of failures found are summarized in Table 3. Each individual failure found was counted and included in the Table. Note that we used taxonomy of Fig. 1 for classification, and not our refinement, to allow for comparison. We were able to reproduce every failure found by [27] ('Orig.' column in Table 3) and often found more ('Difference' column). In particular, we were able to automatically verify that all programs were failure-free after fixing buggy programs by testing that they met the requirement, indicating success.

We were able to detect 88% of the original failures by performing automated tests. So even though we were able to fully automatically establish that a program was failure-free, detecting some problems that were originally classified as failures required manual inspection (counts between brackets in Table 3). After analysis, it turned out that all these failures only occur when agent's cycles are delayed indefinitely while an environment may continue running. This can happen when a developer manually pauses an agent. As an example, an agent that runs at normal speed and is connected to the environment BW4T [17], which we used in our sample, would never simultaneously receive the percepts not(*in(room(a1))* and *in(room(a2))*. This is because it takes time to move from *a1* to *a2*, and an agent running at normal speed would first receive the first and only later receive the second percept. If an agent is paused, because the environment continues running both percepts may be queued and received simultaneously when the agent is resumed. When we run tests with agents using the automated test framework, we do not detect such 'failures' because agents are never paused. Our finding thus highlights that it is important to take timing issues into account. We also note that no *G5* failures were found (confirmed after discussion with the author of [27]), but we did find such a failure in the sample we discuss in Section 5.

We identified 24% more failures, most of which (70%) were detected by means of the percept test templates (*P1*, *P2*) and the template ***G-duplicate*** (*G4*). Interestingly, these templates are used in Step 2 of our test approach. This suggests that manual inspection is biased more towards a top-down approach in Step 3. As we argued, developing and testing a program is facilitated, however, if confidence is gained first that state updating is free of failures. One likely other reason that explains why we found more failures is that we were able to perform many test runs, as the test framework facilitates performing repeated test runs, and each run may produce different failures because of non-determinism.

A particularly interesting result is that we found that 63 from the 82 (77%) failures detected by automated tests immediately pointed at the code location of the fault. This, of course, makes it easier for a developer to fix a bug, and is a clear indication of the value that automating testing can have for agent programming. Fault locations are hardly ever pointed at, however, when a wrong action is performed (***A-selected***, *A1*), suggesting that locating faults for such failures may require a different approach.

We now show that our approach is also able to detect all failures in sample programs other than those used to reproduce the results of [27]. The test templates that we proposed have been based on the failure taxonomy of [27] which was derived from an analysis of the sample used in the previous section. We aim to provide additional support that shows that our set of test templates is complete and our approach is not biased towards a particular sample by looking at other sample programs.

5.2 Different Agent Program Sample

We selected a new sample of 10 agent programs that were written for the BW4T environment but by different programmers. Moreover, these programs were supposed to satisfy several more functional requirements instead of only one.

Failure	Manual [27]	Automated	Difference
P1	14	17 (3)	3
P2	11	16 (1)	5
A1	29	30 (5)	1
A2	3	4 (0)	1
A3	4	5 (0)	1
A4	1	1 (0)	0
G1	5	5 (0)	0
G2	3	3 (0)	0
G3	7	10 (1)	3
G4	5	11 (0)	6
G5	0	0 (0)	0
Totals	82	102 (10)	20

Table 3: Comparison of results (5.1)

Failure	Count
P-failure (P1,P2)	10
A-selected (A1)	11
A-incorrect (A2,3)	7
G-adopted (G1)	4
G-reconsideration (G2)	1
G-incorrect (G3)	16
G-duplicate (G4)	3
G-maintain (G5)	1
Total	53

Table 4: Results of the performed evaluation (5.2)

Agents were required, for example, to not do any redundant tasks: "An agent should go directly to the drop zone when it is holding a block", formalized as never done($goTo(Room)$) $\wedge$ $Room \neq 'DropZone'$ $\wedge$ bel($holding(Block)$), and "An agent should not go to the drop zone without holding a block", formalized as never done($goTo('DropZone')$) $\wedge$ not(bel($holding(Block)$)). These additional requirements also pose a greater challenge for our test approach, as a program is considered failure-free only if all requirements are satisfied, increasing the difficulty of detecting all failures.

All failures found could be classified using our refined taxonomy; Table 4 presents counts per type. We did not find any *A4* failures but did find a ***G-maintain*** (*G5*) failure. Failures that were detected were fixed using the same approach as [27]. We thus were able to successfully generate failure-free agents that satisfy all functional requirements.

A larger set of functional requirements facilitated the use of a top-down approach (Section 4) rather than a bottom-up approach, as was used for reproduction. An interesting finding is that this lead to a decrease in the amount of test failures that pointed directly at code locations of corresponding faults (25%, 13 out of 53, as opposed to 77% before). More work is needed to explain this finding.

5.3 Different Environment

Finally, we performed an evaluation whether the test framework and approach would detect failures in a single agent program sample that operates in a different environment. We chose an environment called the Vacuum World to this end [8]. In this world, squares in a grid can be either clean, dusty, or contain an obstacle that the robot should move around, thus requiring the agent to also successfully navigate the robot over the grid. A robot is able to move to any neighbouring clean or dusty square and clean up (vacuum) the square it is currently on (removing the dust).

For the evaluation, we used an agent program sample that was developed to meet the requirement that all dusty squares in a grid have been cleaned. This initial agent program did not meet the functional requirement specified, and we thus applied our test approach to detect failures.

Four failures were detected in the agent program, which is similar to the average of about four or five failures that were found for all other sample programs. Two percept failures were detected using the ***P*** templates, and two failures related to action selection were detected using the ***A-selected*** template. After fixes were applied for these failures, the agent did meet its requirement. Consistent with earlier results, percept failures indicated code locations for corresponding faults, whereas the action failures required more debugging effort for fault localization.

6. CONCLUSION

In this paper, we proposed and defined an *automated testing framework* for cognitive agent programs, facilitating automated failure detection and reducing debugging effort that is required from a developer. We argue that modules are a natural unit for testing, and associate test conditions with modules of an agent program. We also introduced a test language that we used to specify test templates for detecting failure types. These test templates refine a failure taxonomy introduced in [27]. A test approach has also been specified that explains how to instantiate test templates and derive test conditions for specific failure types. The main steps of this approach are (i) to define success in terms of functional requirements, (ii) to test cognitive state updating, and (iii) to classify failures that concern actions and goals.

The test language proposed is minimal in the sense that only two temporal operators are provided. We showed by analysing different agent program samples that the language is nevertheless sufficient for detecting all failures in these programs. In particular, we were able to reproduce and detect all failures that were manually identified in [27] using our automated test framework. Interestingly, in about 77% of failures found in this reproduction, the test framework also pointed to the code location of the corresponding fault. We demonstrated that our approach is not biased towards a specific sample of agent programs by applying the framework to other sample programs, and in a different environment. We were able to detect all failures by means of the automated test framework, i.e., all agents eventually met all functional requirements after fixing the detected failures.

Our work points to several issues that need more work. The focus of our work has been on automatically detecting failures. Even though our results are encouraging in that fault localization was facilitated by the test framework, more work is needed for locating faults that correspond with these failures. In particular, we found that faults related to actions that are performed but should not have been performed are difficult to locate. Tools that can explain why these actions were performed might be useful here [13].

Finally, further evaluation of the test framework is needed in more environments. Because of non-deterministic environments and other agents that act in the same environment, failures that occur in one run may not occur in the next. More work is needed to identify how often a test should be repeated in order to find all failures in an agent program. Measures of the variation one should expect in a given environment could be useful here.

Acknowledgments

We would like to thank Michael Winikoff for sharing his experiment data and providing valuable insights on this work.

REFERENCES

[1] R. Bordini, M. Dastani, and M. Winikoff. Current Issues in Multi-Agent Systems Development. In *Engineering Societies in the Agents World VII*, volume 4457, pages 38–61. 2007.

[2] R. H. Bordini, L. Braubach, J. J. Gomez-sanz, G. O. Hare, A. Pokahr, and A. Ricci. A survey of programming languages and platforms for multi-agent systems. *Informatica*, 30:33–44, 2006.

[3] T. Bosse, C. M. Jonker, L. van der Meij, and J. Treur. Leadsto: A language and environment for analysis of dynamics by simulation. In T. Eymann, F. Klügl, W. Lamersdorf, M. Klusch, and M. N. Huhns, editors, *Multiagent System Technologies*, volume 3550 of *Lecture Notes in Computer Science*, pages 165–178. Springer Berlin Heidelberg, 2005.

[4] G. Caire, M. Cossentino, and A. Negri. Multi-agent systems implementation and testing. In *Proc. of the 4th From Agent Theory to Agent Implementation Symposium, AT2AI-4*, 2004.

[5] A. Carrera, C. A. Iglesias, and M. Garijo. Beast methodology: An agile testing methodology for multi-agent systems based on behaviour driven development. *Information Systems Frontiers*, pages 1–14, July 2013.

[6] R. Coelho, U. Kulesza, A. von Staa, and C. Lucena. Unit testing in multi-agent systems using mock agents and aspects. In *Proceedings of the 2006 international workshop on Software engineering for large-scale multi-agent systems - SELMAS '06*, page 83, New York, New York, USA, 2006. ACM Press.

[7] R. Collier. Debugging agents in agent factory. In R. H. Bordini, M. Dastani, J. Dix, and A. El Fallah Seghrouchni, editors, *Programming Multi-Agent Systems*, volume 4411 of *Lecture Notes in Computer Science*, pages 229–248. Springer Berlin Heidelberg, 2007.

[8] R. Collier and J. Howell. Vacuum world. `https://github.com/eishub/vacuumworld`. Accessed: 2015-11-17.

[9] M. Dastani. Programming multi-agent systems. *The Knowledge Engineering Review*, 30:394–418, 9 2015.

[10] J. Dix, K. V. Hindriks, B. Logan, and W. Wobcke. Engineering Multi-Agent Systems (Dagstuhl Seminar 12342). *Dagstuhl Reports*, 2(8):74–98, 2012.

[11] E. Ekinci, A. Tiryaki, v. Çetin, and O. Dikenelli. Goal-oriented agent testing revisited. In M. Luck and J. J. Gomez-Sanz, editors, *Agent-Oriented Software Engineering IX*, volume 5386 of *Lecture Notes in Computer Science*, pages 173–186. Springer Berlin Heidelberg, 2009.

[12] J. Gómez-Sanz, J. Botía, E. Serrano, and J. Pavón. Testing and debugging of MAS interactions with INGENIAS. In *Agent-Oriented Software Engineering IX*, pages 199–212, 2009.

[13] K. V. Hindriks. Debugging is explaining. In I. Rahwan, W. Wobcke, S. Sen, and T. Sugawara, editors, *PRIMA 2012: Principles and Practice of Multi-Agent Systems*, volume 7455 of *Lecture Notes in Computer Science*, pages 31–45. Springer Berlin Heidelberg, 2012.

[14] Z. Houhamdi. Multi-Agent System Testing: A Survey. *International Journal of Advanced Computer Science and Applications*, 2(6):135–141, 2011.

[15] D. Hovemeyer and W. Pugh. Finding bugs is easy. *SIGPLAN Notices*, 39(12):92–106, Dec. 2004.

[16] ISO. ISO/IEC/IEEE 24765:2010 systems and software engineering - vocabulary. Technical report, Institute of Electrical and Electronics Engineers, Inc., 2010.

[17] M. Johnson, C. Jonker, B. van Riemsdijk, P. J. Feltovich, and J. M. Bradshaw. Joint activity testbed: Blocks world for teams (bw4t). In H. Aldewereld, V. Dignum, and G. Picard, editors, *Engineering Societies in the Agents World X*, volume 5881 of *Lecture Notes in Computer Science*, pages 254–256. Springer Berlin Heidelberg, 2009.

[18] M. A. Khamis and K. Nagi. Designing multi-agent unit tests using systematic test design patterns-(extended version). *Engineering Applications of Artificial Intelligence*, 26(9):2128–2142, Oct. 2013.

[19] V. J. Koeman and K. V. Hindriks. Designing a source-level debugger for cognitive agent programs. In Q. Chen, P. Torroni, S. Villata, J. Hsu, and A. Omicini, editors, *PRIMA 2015: Principles and Practice of Multi-Agent Systems*, volume 9387 of *Lecture Notes in Computer Science*, pages 335–350. Springer International Publishing, 2015.

[20] M. Moreno, J. Pavón, and A. Rosete. Testing in agent oriented methodologies. In S. Omatu, M. P. Rocha, J. Bravo, F. Fernández, E. Corchado, A. Bustillo, and J. M. Corchado, editors, *Distributed Computing, Artificial Intelligence, Bioinformatics, Soft Computing, and Ambient Assisted Living*, volume 5518 of *Lecture Notes in Computer Science*, pages 138–145. Springer Berlin Heidelberg, 2009.

[21] C. D. Nguyen, A. Perini, C. Bernon, J. Pavón, and J. Thangarajah. Testing in Multi-Agent Systems. In *Agent-Oriented Software Engineering X*, volume 6038, pages 180–190. Springer Berlin Heidelberg, 2011.

[22] L. Padgham, Z. Zhang, J. Thangarajah, and T. Miller. Model-based test oracle generation for automated unit testing of agent systems. *Software Engineering, IEEE Transactions on*, 39(9):1230–1244, Sept 2013.

[23] C. Parnin and A. Orso. Are automated debugging techniques actually helping programmers? In *Proceedings of the 2011 International Symposium on Software Testing and Analysis*, ISSTA '11, pages 199–209, New York, NY, USA, 2011. ACM.

[24] P. Runeson, C. Andersson, T. Thelin, A. Andrews, and T. Berling. What do we know about defect detection methods? *Software, IEEE*, 23(3):82–90, May 2006.

[25] A. M. Tiryaki, S. Öztuna, O. Dikenelli, and R. C. Erdur. SUnit: a unit testing framework for test driven development of multi-agent systems. In *Proceedings of the 7th international conference on Agent-oriented software engineering VII*, pages 156–173, 2007.

[26] J. Wielemaker, T. Schrijvers, M. Triska, and T. Lager. Swi-prolog. *Theory and Practice of Logic Programming*, 12:67–96, 2012.

[27] M. Winikoff. Novice programmers' faults & failures in goal programs. In *Proceedings of the 2014 International Conference on Autonomous Agents and Multi-agent Systems*, AAMAS '14, pages 301–308, Richland, SC, 2014. International Foundation for Autonomous Agents and Multiagent Systems.

[28] Z. Zhang, J. Thangarajah, and L. Padgham. Model based testing for agent systems. *Software and Data Technologies*, 22:399–413, 2008.

Requirements Specification in The Prometheus Methodology via Activity Diagrams

(JAAMAS Extended Abstract)

Yoosef Abushark
RMIT University
Melbourne, Australia
yoosef.abushark@rmit.edu.au

John Thangarajah
RMIT University
Melbourne, Australia
johnt@rmit.edu.au

Tim Miller
University of Melbourne
Melbourne, Australia
tmiller@unimelb.edu.au

Michael Winikoff
University of Otago
Dunedin, New Zealand
michael.winikoff@otago.ac.nz

James Harland
RMIT University
Melbourne, Australia
james.harland@rmit.edu

ABSTRACT

In this work we extend a popular agent design methodology, Prometheus, and improve the understandability and maintainability of requirements by automatically generating UML activity diagrams from existing requirements models; namely scenarios and goal hierarchies. The approach is general to all the methodologies that support similar notions in specifying requirements.

Keywords

AOSE Methodology; Goal-Oriented Requirements

1. INTRODUCTION

The agent-oriented software engineering field has a number of methodologies that assist developers in the development process, including the Prometheus methodology [2]. A fundamental aspect of all agent-oriented software engineering methodologies is the specification of requirements. We base our approach on Prometheus, however, it can be generalised to all the methodologies that support similar notions in specifying requirements.

We use the trading agent system [2] to illustrate this specification process. In Prometheus, the system is specified via scenarios, goals and interfaces to the environment. A scenario is similar to a use case [1] and describes a particular run of the system as a sequence of steps (Figure 1). These step types include percepts, actions or goals. Goals can be decomposed into sub-goals, using a goal-tree. There are three types of goal decompositions (only two are shown in Figure 2): disjunctive, undirected conjunctive or directed conjunctive. The disjunctive decomposition (denoted by OR) implies that a parent goal is realised if any of its children is realised. The undirected conjunctive decomposition (denoted by AND) implies that a parent goal is realised if all its children are realised in some, unspecified, order. The directed conjunctive decomposition (denoted by AND with dashed arrows between the children) implies that a parent goal is realised if all its children are realised in the specified order. The combination of the scenarios together with the goal trees forms part of the requirements for the system.

Appears in: *Proceedings of the 15th International Conference on Autonomous Agents and Multiagent Systems (AAMAS 2016), J. Thangarajah, K. Tuyls, Marsella, C. Jonker, S. Marsella (eds.), May 9–13, 2016, Singapore.*

Type		Name	Role
1	Percept	Store_Opening	Seller
2	Goal	Send_Item_List	Seller
3	Goal	Select_Item	Buyer
4	Goal	Send_Item_Price	Seller
5	Goal	Make_Payment	Buyer
6	Goal	Validate_Card	Banker
7	Goal	Notify_Participants	Banker
8	Goal	Send_Item	Seller

Figure 1: Sale Transaction Scenario Description

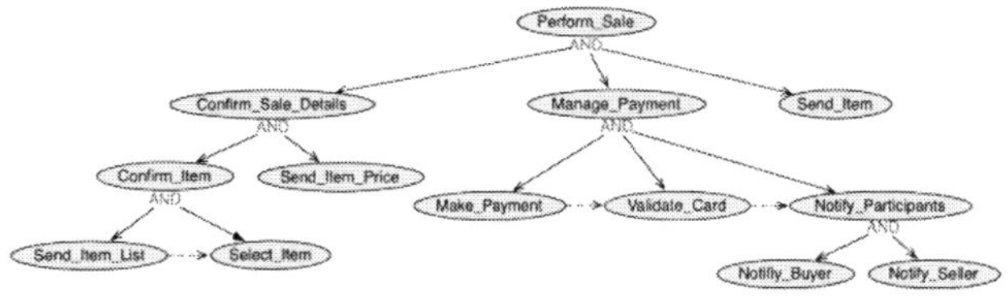

Figure 2: Goal Overview Diagram for the Trading Agent System

Although a scenario is a single sequence of steps there may be different ways to realise the same scenario. This is because when there are goal steps, the goals may also be realised (and hence, the requirement specified) through its children from the goal overview diagram. For example, the goal step "Notify Participants" in Figure 1 could be implemented through the step itself, the step with its children, or just the children, ("Notify Buyer" and "Notify Seller", see Figure 2).

Our approach aims to provide agent-based software designers with an automatically constructed activity diagram that complements the scenario and goal overview diagram by modelling the possible paths in a given scenario, with consideration of information from the goal overview diagram relevant to that scenario. The activity diagram includes alternatives of the goal steps in the scenario according to the goal overview diagram.

2. METHOD

The construction process of the activity diagram of the specified scenario involves two phases:

1. *step-wise activity diagram generation*: this phase takes one step – of a given scenario – at a time, and constructs its

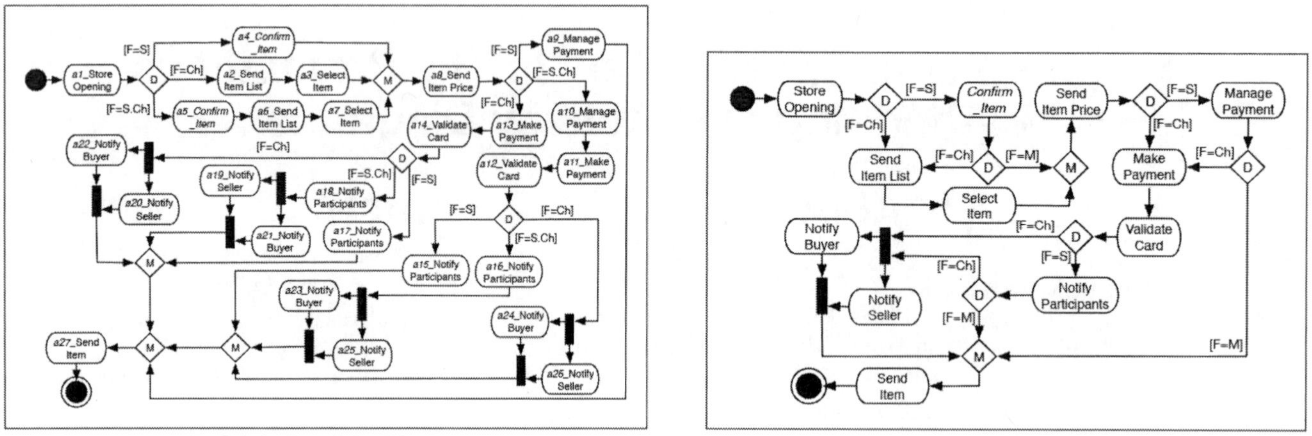

(a) Original Activity Diagram

(b) Reduced Activity Diagram

Figure 3: Activity diagram that merges the scenario in Figure 1 with the goal tree in Figure 2 (F:Flow, S:Goal Step, Ch: Children, P: Parent)

equivalent activity diagram structure. Such a description reflects the transformation of the steps in a given scenario into activity diagram control fragments. Actions and percepts are transformed into sequential control fragments. The goal steps are transformed into combination of alternative, parallel, and sequential control fragments, depending on the decomposition of these goal steps in the goal overview diagram. Then, the different structures are concatenated to form the complete activity diagram corresponding to the specified scenario (Figure 3a).

2. *activity diagram reduction*: the generation phase results in an activity diagram with duplicate nodes. As it is shown in Figure 3a, the diagram includes several duplicate nodes, and in some cases, duplicate sub-graphs, which affects its readability. Duplicate nodes are semantically equivalent, that is, they refer to the same event, but are prefixed with unique identifiers This phase intends to reduce these duplicates, if possible, while preserving the semantics of the original activity diagram (Figure 3b).

We have implemented the mapping from scenario and goal overview diagram to activity diagram as an eclipse plug-in that integrates with the Prometheus Design Tool (PDT). The tool applies a set of rules that merge the specified scenario with its relevant information from the goal overview diagram to generate the abstract description. Then, it uses the abstract description to generate a DOT Graph source script, which Graphviz can then use to generate a graphical depiction of the activity diagram.

3. EVALUATION

We conducted a controlled experimental evaluation to measure the usefulness of activity diagram as a complementary artefact in Prometheus. We recruited fifteen participants with varying levels of experience in Prometheus, and gave them several tasks to complete on simple requirements documents, measuring aspects of their performance. A pre-evaluation questionnaire was used to measure the experience of the participants. Then, each participant was given several tasks to perform. The tasks asked participants to manipulate a set of requirements models for two simple systems. The presence or absence of the additional activity diagram in the requirements provided was the independent variable. After the tasks had been completed, participants were asked to complete a post-evaluation questionnaire, asking about their experience, and their perception of the usefulness of activity diagrams..

Table 1: Summary of the total results in both approaches (CI: confidence interval value at a confidence level of 95%)

	Activity Diagam		Non-Activity	
	Scores (out of 9)	Time (in minutes)	Scores (out of 9)	Time (in minutes)
Mean	8.4	7:55	5.8	10:29
CI	0.373	1:41	0.96	2:20
Upper confidence bound	8.77	9:36	6.76	12:49
Lower confidence bound	8.02	6:13	4:84	8:08

We measured two dependent variables: time and correctness. For time we simply measured the clock time from start to completion for each task as a proxy for both maintainability and understandability; that is, how much the activity diagram aids software engineers to come up to speed with the semantics of the requirements models, and to modify them. There were no time limits on tasks. For correctness we assessed the participants' answers to each task to determine whether they had completed the task correctly. This is also used as a proxy for measuring maintainability and understandability; that is, how much the activity diagram impacts the ability to understand and modify the requirements models correctly.

The results in Table 1 shows that including activity diagrams leads to better understanding of the specification by giving a more holistic view on what the intended system is meant to achieve and how it should behave, and provides assistance when performing maintenance on the system. Also, participants in our experiment unanimously agreed, through the post-evaluation questionnaire, that the inclusion of the activity diagram improved their ability to understand the requirements models. Given this, we recommend the Prometheus methodology, and indeed other AOSE methodologies, to include activity diagrams as an integrated feature in the methodology.

REFERENCES

[1] I. Jacobson. *Object-oriented software engineering: a use case driven approach.* ACM Press Series. ACM Press, 1992.

[2] L. Padgham and M. Winikoff. *Developing intelligent agent systems: A practical guide.* John Wiley & Sons, Chichester, 2004.

GPU Delegation: Toward a Generic Approach for Developping MABS using GPU Programming

Emmanuel Hermellin
LIRMM - CNRS - University of Montpellier
161 rue Ada
34095 Montpellier - France
hermellin@lirmm.fr

Fabien Michel
LIRMM - CNRS - University of Montpellier
161 rue Ada
34095 Montpellier - France
fmichel@lirmm.fr

ABSTRACT

Using Multi-Agent Based Simulation (MABS), computing resources requirements often limit the extent to which a model could be experimented. As the number of agents and the size of the environment are constantly growing in these simulations, using General-Purpose Computing on Graphics Units (GPGPU) appears to be very promising as it allows to use the massively parallel architecture of the GPU (Graphics Processing Unit) to do High Performance Computing (HPC). Considering the use of GPGPU for developing MABS, the conclusions of Perumalla and Aaby's work [25] in 2008 was twofold: (1) data parallel execution capabilities of GPU can be used effectively in MABS and afford excellent speedup on models and (2) effective use of data parallel execution requires resolution of modeling and execution challenges at the cost of a decrease in modularity, ease of programmability and reusability. In this paper, we propose to study through experiments if the conclusions and issues outlined by Perumalla and Aaby are still true despite the evolution of GPGPU and MABS. To this end, we use the *GPU environmental delegation* principle on four models in order to compare CPU and GPU implementations. Then, we discuss and analyze the results from both a conceptual and a performance point of view.

Keywords

MABS, GPGPU, CUDA, Hybrid architecture

1. INTRODUCTION

Multi-Agent Based Simulations (MABS) are used to study complex systems in many research domains (collective robotics, biology, economy, urban management, etc.) [20]. Experimenting with MABS, performances often represent a major issue limiting the extent to which an Agent-Based Model (ABM) could be studied [22]. Especially, it is interesting to not be too limited by the size of the environment or the number of agents, which may require a lot of computing resources.

That is why High Performance Computing (HPC) is more and more considered as a relevant way of speeding up MABS thanks to functional solutions that use Central Processing Unit (CPU) clusters, computational grids, etc. A flagship example of this trend is the Repast HPC platform[1] [7], which allows to simulate millions of agents using CPU clusters.

Among HPC technologies, Graphics Processing Units (GPU) have been proved to be excellent computational platforms able to perform general-purpose computations [21]. General-Purpose computing on Graphics Processing Units (GPGPU) is thus a technology which relies on using the massively parallel architecture of usual PC graphics cards for accelerating very significantly the performance of programs (applications can be up to 100 times faster)[2] [6]. So, GPGPU is a cheap HPC solution which could be now used on almost every PC.

In 2008, Perumalla and Aaby's work [25] (P&A for short) was one of the first that studied the use of GPGPU in the context of MABS. The purpose of this work was to evaluate the advantages and drawbacks of this technology by implementing several representative ABM. So, P&A compared the runtime speed of GPU-based models against CPU-based implementations and showed that impressive speedup could be achieved (up to x40 in the paper). However, one major conclusion of this work was that this increase of performance could only be done at the expense of programmability, modularity and reusability. Indeed, it turns out that implementing ABM using GPGPU is very challenging because GPU programming relies on a highly specialized hardware architecture. Especially, usual object oriented features, which are common in ABM, are no longer available using GPGPU.

Since this study, graphic cards and their programming interfaces have dramatically evolved so that GPGPU is now recognized as a very efficient HPC solution in many domains. Still, considering GPGPU for MABS, it is worth noting that, despite some important milestones, very few works have been done: Implementing ABM using GPGPU remains very challenging and P&A's conclusions still hold [17, 10, 28, 2]. Moreover, research works that only focus on performances are too hard to reuse, which does not ease the adoption of GPGPU in the MABS community.

Among the few works dealing with accessibility issues and that do not only focus on performance gains, almost all seek to hide GPGPU through a transparent use of this technology [27, 29, 15]. However, this approach cannot take into account all the cases and needs that the implementations of MABS with GPGPU could require. Indeed, it is hard to create a framework or universal solution because of the wide variety of models.

In this paper, we present a completely different approach

Appears in: *Proceedings of the 15th International Conference on Autonomous Agents and Multiagent Systems (AAMAS 2016), J. Thangarajah, K. Tuyls, C. Jonker, S. Marsella (eds.), May 9–13, 2016, Singapore.*

[1] *e.g.* http://repast.sourceforge.net/repast_hpc.php
[2] *e.g.* https://developer.nvidia.com/about-cuda

to these works: Instead of focusing on accessibility by means of transparency, we show that it is more interesting to use a design principle which transforms or adapts a model because it is thus possible to take into account a wider variety of models. To this end, we use *GPU environmental delegation* [18] as a way to implement MABS with GPGPU. Based on an hybrid approach (the execution is shared between the CPU and the GPU), this principle put forward reusability rather than transparency [12]. The idea is to identify in the model some computations which can be transformed into environmental dynamics and then translated into GPU modules. The purpose of this article is to study the interest of this principle and show that it helps to address some of the problems outlined by P&A.

This paper is organized as follows: Section 2 introduces the evolution of the GPGPU technology in the MABS domain and presents the GPU environmental delegation. Section 3 presents the models used for the experimentation and describes the adaptation process and implementations of these models using the GPU environmental delegation principle. Section 4 proposes a performance study and analyses the results of the experimentations while answering the questions expressed in this paper. Section 5 summarizes the work we have done and outlines our future researches.

2. GPGPU FOR MABS

2.1 Related Works

In 2008, the implementation made by P&A used graphical features of the card to perform generic computations. Indeed, at this time, using a specialized programming interface dedicated to GPU programming was not widespread, due to the youth of these tools. So, the few people interested by this technology had to divert the primary use of GPU by tinkering with graphical functions [9, 27].

However, the release of two programming interface dedicated to GPGPU, CUDA[3] (Compute Unified Device Architecture, 2007) and OpenCL[4](Open Computing Language, 2008), have greatly simplified this technology while offering better support and improving its accessibility. GPGPU thus became a very appealing alternative for many domains in which computation time is critical. Consequently, the number of MABS using GPGPU has increased and new tools and frameworks have emerged.

Flame GPU [29] is a flagship example of the possibilities offered by the rise of specialized GPU programming tools. However, the majority of the existing works still start from scratch and put all their attention on acquiring the best computational gains without considering the accessibility, reusability and modularity. This is especially true in the scope of works that address the study of flocking models [10, 13], crowd [28], traffic simulations [32] or autonomous navigation and path planning algorithms [5, 8].

However, as pointed out in [2], implementing a model on GPU does not necessarily imply an increase of performances, notably in the field of MABS where many different and heterogeneous architectures can be conceived. Considering this issue, [2] clearly shows the influence of implementation choices on the results and performances. So, despite the release of frameworks such as CUDA, achieving an efficient implementation still requires to take into account the specific programming model that comes with GPU. That is why, most of the previous cited works were realized in an *ad hoc* way and only offer one-off solutions.

Before 2011, most of works used an approach that consist in executing completely the model on the GPU (*all-in-GPU*). This approach is useful when the main objective is to accelerate the simulation's execution. But from a software engineering point of view, this approach is not adapted because all development efforts are lost. In such a case, the implementation is designed for a specific model and therefore cannot be reused in other contexts. There is no possibility to generalize and reuse the work.

Considering these issues, hybrid systems begin to appear in 2011 and represent a very attractive alternative because they consist in sharing the execution of the MABS between the CPU and the GPU according to the nature of the computations. Despite the fact that an all-in-GPU implementation is more efficient than an hybrid implementation, the hybrid approach has many advantages.

Firstly, hybrid approaches enable a step further toward the achievement of more complex MAS models because one can choose what is executed on the GPU. It is thus possible to use agents with complex and heterogeneous architectures (*e.g.* [16]). Moreover, they are inclined toward modularity, and for instance ease to concretely implement independently the agents and the environment (*e.g.* [18] [23]).

So, even if genericness is not necessarily an explicit objective of hybrid systems, such approaches actualy exhibit a software architecture promoting modularity and thus reusability. The MCMAS library [15] is a recent and good example of this trend. Moreover, by removing the programming constraints related to all-in-GPU systems, hybrid approaches are by definition more flexible and open to other technologies so that accessibility is greatly increased [16, 18].

2.2 Analyzing the Evolution of MABS and GPGPU

In their work, P&A concluded that the data parallel execution capabilities of GPU are very useful to speed up simulation of agent-based models. The empirical results from their experiments show that high simulation speeds can be achieved especially with very large agent populations (million of agents). The runtime speeds on the GPU are roughly two to three orders of magnitude higher than those of existing ABM toolkits. However, the excellent speedup obtained on simple models comes at the expense of modularity, ease of programmability and reusability.

From this overview, it is clear that the conclusions set out by P&A have been taken into account to some extent. But, research works are still divided into two distinct categories: (1) Works that are only interested in performance gains and (2) works that try to answer the issues raised by P&A about modularity, ease of programmability and reusability. The works of this second category are mostly based on hybrid systems, which is clearly the most promising approach to address such issues. However, these works propose solutions that only focus on a transparent use of GPGPU in MABS. But, because of the wide variety of MAS models, making the use of GPGPU transparent cannot be generic enough and take into account all the cases and needs that MABS implementations with GPGPU could require.

So, the stated problems were not clearly resolved and the lack of reusability, accessibility and modularity are still

[3] *e.g.* https://developer.nvidia.com/what-cuda
[4] *e.g.* http://www.khronos.org/opencl

present (despite work such as Flame GPU [29] or [16, 15]). This is especially true considering that the proportion of works dealing with the use of GPGPU in MABS is still very small compared to the number of MABS-based publications and while the need in computing resources is strong and always increasing.

2.3 GPU Environmental Delegation

The purpose of the work presented in this article is to determine whether the conclusions stated by P&A in 2008 are still relevant today despite the evolution of GPGPU and its use in MABS. To this end, the *GPU Environmental Delegation principle* (GPU delegation for short) is used. Based on an hybrid approach, this design principle aims at easing the integration of GPGPU in MABS models rather than making its use transparent, in contrary to the works previously mentioned.

2.3.1 Overview of the Principle

GPU delegation is inspired by an Agent-Oriented Software Engineering (AOSE) trend which consists in using the environment as a first class abstraction in MAS [1]. This idea is today well accepted and has proved to be a relevant approach for modeling and developing MAS [33]. Especially, it could help to enhance the efficiency of agent interactions or simplify the behavioral process of the agents thanks to the environment that produce high level percepts. Therefore, at a high level, such an approach allows to design MAS with a clear separation of concerns.

So, at the implementation level, GPU delegation has to be related to other research works that consider the environment as a core concept of MAS and which reify parts of the agents' computations in external structures. Related examples are EASS (Environment As Active Support for Simulation) [3], IODA (Interaction Oriented Design of Agent simulations) [14], environment-centered approach for MABS [24] and the artifact approach [26]. In the scope of our work, considering the environment as a first class entity enables us to keep the programming accessibility of the agent model in a GPU context and be able to scale up both the number of agents and the size of the environment.

Proposed in [18], the GPU delegation principle is based on the fact that it is very difficult to deport all the behavior of agents on graphics cards (that is why it is especially reactive agents who evolve in simulations which use an all-in-GPU approach [27]). So, this principle consists in making a clear separation between the agent behaviors, managed by the CPU, and environmental dynamics, handled by the GPU. Especially, one major idea underlying this principle is to identify some computations (such as agent-level perceptions) which can be transformed into environmental dynamics.

2.3.2 GPU Delegation in Practice

GPU delegation has been used for the first time on a model of Multi-Level Emergence (MLE) [4] of complex structures [18]. This very simple model relies on a unique behavior which allows to generate complex structures which repeat in a fractal way. The agent behavior is extremely simple and based on the perception, spread and reaction to pheromones. So, in this work, GPU modules dedicated to the perception and the spread of pheromones were proposed.

A second experimentation was proposed in [12] which further trials GPU Delegation by testing its feasibility and genericness on a classic ABM, namely Reynolds's boids[5]. [12] especially shows that applying GPU delegation not only speeds up boids simulations but also produces an ABM which is easy to understand, thanks to a clear separation of concerns.

For both of these works, the integration of GPU computations was performed in the TurtleKit platform[6] [19]. TurtleKit is a generic spatial ABM, implemented with Java, wherein agents evolve in a 2D environment discretized in cells. The proposed hybrid approach integrated in TurtleKit focuses on modularity. In this context, this allows to achieve three objectives: (1) maintaining accessibility in the agent model while using GPGPU, (2) being able to scale and work with large number of agents on large environment sizes and (3) promoting reusability in the particular context of GPU programming.

2.3.3 Evolution of GPU Delegation

With respect to the underlying hybrid approach, GPU Delegation is about identifying specific behaviors which can be turned into environmental dynamics. Especially, GPU delegation states that agent perception computations that do not involve the agent's states could be translated into environmental dynamics and thus into a GPU module performing the computation.

However, the flocking model experimentation [12] shows that, according to the model used, GPU delegation could be extended with the aim at finding more computations to be delegated. So, the GPU delegation principle has evolved in order to be applied on a larger number of models and could be now stated as follows: If computations made within the behavior of the agent do not involve or do not modify the agent's states, they could be translated into environmental dynamics.

3. MODELS AND IMPLEMENTATIONS

To provide a comparison between the study conducted by P&A in 2008 and solutions available in 2015, especially hybrid systems, we use GPU Delegation to adapt and implement four models: Two already done by P&A (Conway's Game of Life and Schelling's segregation) and two taken from the Netlogo models library [31] (Fire model and DLA model). In this section, we present the associated technology and describe the implementation's process.

3.1 GPGPU Implementation with CUDA

To program on the graphics card and exploit its GPGPU capabilities, we use CUDA which is the GPGPU programming interface provided by Nvidia. The associated programming model relies on the following philosophy[7]: The CPU is called the *host* and plays the role of scheduler. The *host* manages data and triggers *kernels*, which are functions specifically designed to be executed by the GPU, which is called the *device*. The GPU part of the code really differs from sequential code and has to fit the underlying hardware architecture. More precisely, the GPU device is programmed to proceed the parallel execution of the same procedure, the *kernel*, by means of numerous *threads*. These *threads* are

[5] `http://www.lirmm.fr/~hermellin/Website/Reynolds_Boids_With_TurtleKit.html`
[6] *e.g.* http://www.turtlekit.org
[7] *e.g.* http://docs.nvidia.com/cuda/

organized in *blocks* (the parameters *blockDim.x*, *blockDim.y* characterize the size of these blocks), which are themselves structured in a global grid of blocks. Each *thread* has unique 3D coordinates (*threadIdx.x*, *threadIdx.y*, *threadIdx.z*) that specifies its location within a *block*. Similarly, each *block* also has three spatial coordinates (respectively *blockIdx.x*, *blockIdx.y*, *blockIdx.z*) that localize it in the global *grid*. Figure 1 illustrates this organization for the 2D case. So each *thread* works with the same *kernel* but uses different data according to its spatial location within the grid[8]. Moreover, each *block* has a limited *thread* capacity according to the hardware in use.

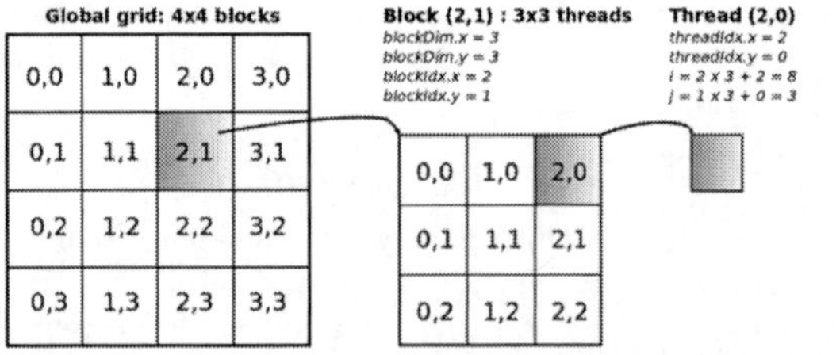

Figure 1: Thread, blocks, grid organization

For using GPGPU in the TurtleKit platform, we use the JCUDA library which allows to use CUDA through Java[9].

3.2 Models and Application of GPU Delegation

In this section, the four selected models and their implementation are introduced. Then, the application of the GPU delegation on each of these models is described.

3.2.1 Game of Life

The first model, which was also in P&A study, is the Conway's Game of Life [11]. This famous model shows that complex patterns can emerge from the implementation of simple rules. While this model does not contain agents (it is a cellular automaton), it defines an environmental dynamics which is representative of those encountered in MAS.

The environment of the Game of Life is a cellular automaton made of a two dimensional grid of square cells, each of which being in one of two possible states: Dead or alive. Each cell interacts with its eight neighbors according to the following rules: (1) Any living cell with less than two or more than three alive neighbors dies, (2) any living cell with two or three living neighbors stays alive and (3) any dead cell with exactly three living neighbors becomes alive.

In our experiments, the grid is initialized randomly[10]. At each time step, all the cells are updated according to the previous rules. Figure 2 illustrates the simulation steps.

Applying GPU Delegation.

The main computational part of the model is located in step (1) which consists in computing a sequential loop: It calculates the new state of each cell for the next step of the simulation. So, the more the environment is large, the more this computation is long. It may therefore be advantageous to transform this computation into a GPU module.

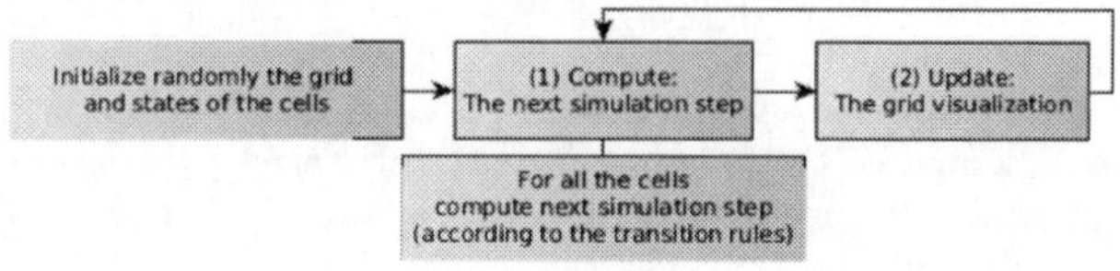

Figure 2: Game of Life simulation

To create the GPU module correctly, it is necessary to focus on the representation of data. Especially, to avoid expensive transfers between CPU and GPU, the data need to be sent only once at each step. To this end, each cell write its state value (1 for alive and 0 for dead) in a 2D array (matching the size of the environment) according to its position. Then, this array is sent to the GPU. This module does the sum of the states (more precisely the sum of the number of alive cells) of all Moore neighborhood cells for each cell of the grid and stores the result in the 2D result array. Thus, each cell of the result array contains a value between 0 (no cell alive) and 8 (all neighbors are alive). The result array is then used to update the grid and compute the next simulation step according to the transition rules. Algorithm 1 presents an implementation of the corresponding GPU kernel.

Algorithm 1: Alive cells *Kernel*

input : $width$, $height$, $statesArray$
output: $resultArray$ (the number of alive neighbors)
$i = blockIdx.x * blockDim.x + threadIdx.x$;
$j = blockIdx.y * blockDim.y + threadIdx.y$;
$sumOfState = 0$;
if $i < width$ *and* $j < height$ **then**
  | $sumOfState =$ getNeighborsState($statesArray[i, j]$);
end
$resultArray[i, j] = sumOfState$;

3.2.2 Schelling's Segregation

The second model is a variant of the Schelling's Segregation model [30]. This project models the behavior of two types of agents in a neighborhood: Red agents and green agents. These agents are scattered across a two dimensional grid. Their purpose is to be happy by staying near like-colored agents (each red agent wants to live near at least some red agents, and the same holds for the green agents). If they are dissatisfied at their position, the agents attempt to move to a new random vacant location for finding a better place according to their objective of happiness.

The simulation shows how these individual preferences ripple through the neighborhood, leading to large-scale patterns. In our experiments, green and red agents are scattered with the same proportion, and distributed randomly over the environment. Figure 3 illustrates the simulation steps.

Applying GPU Delegation.

The most intensive computations are in step (2) and (3) which consist, for each agent, in recovering a neighbor list

[8] *Thread* is similar to the concept of task: A *thread* may be considered as an instance of the *kernel* which is performed on a restricted portion of the data depending on its location in the global grid (its identifier).
[9] *e.g.* http://www.jcuda.org
[10] The probability for the cell to be dead or alive is the same.

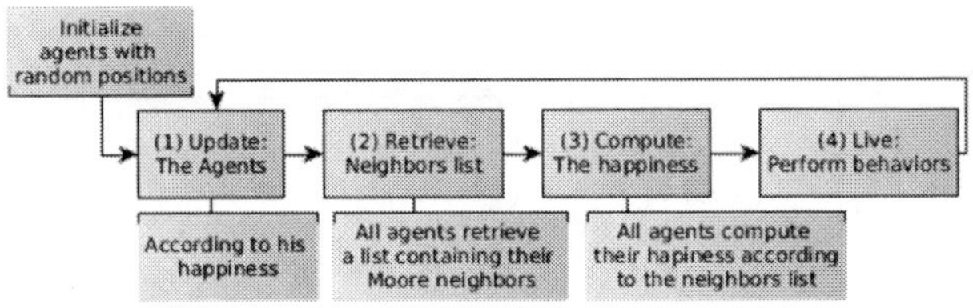

Figure 3: Segregation simulation

and then computing its happiness according to the list. So, many sequential loops have to be done at each time step, and the required computation time clearly increases depending on the number of agents. According to the GPU delegation, the happiness computation can be deported into an environmental dynamics because these computations do not modify agents' states.

In the CPU model, the computation of happiness is done by testing the color of the agents present in the list of neighbors and counting the number of agents in each community according to their state: 1 for green agents and -1 for red agents. However, if we want to deport this computation, the data structure sent to the GPU needs to be adapted. So, at each time step, agents write in a 2D array (matching the size of the environment) their states depending on their position. This table is sent to the GPU that computes the sum of the neighboring states and returns in a result array the values for each cell of the environment. This result array thus contains values between -8 (all agents around are red) and 8 (all agents around are green). The agents then recover the value in the result array with respect to their position and act accordingly. Algorithm 2 presents an implementation of the corresponding GPU kernel.

Algorithm 2: Hapiness *Kernel*

```
input : width, height, communityArray
output: resultArray (agent's type around)
i = blockIdx.x * blockDim.x + threadIdx.x ;
j = blockIdx.y * blockDim.y + threadIdx.y ;
sumOfCommunityState = 0 ;
if i < width and j < height then
    for agent in getNeighborsCommunity() do
        agentCommunityState =
        communityArray[i, j];
        if agentCommunityState == 1 then
            sumOfCommunityState + +;
        end
        else if agentCommunityState == −1 then
            sumOfCommunityState − −;
        end
    end
end
resultArray[i, j] = sumOfCommunityState ;
```

3.2.3 *Fire*

Inspired by a model from the Netlogo library, this third model is called *Fire* and simulates the spread of a fire through a forest. It shows that the fire's chance of affecting the most possible number of trees in the forest depends critically on the density of trees.

In our model, all the trees are agents placed randomly in the environment (a two dimensional grid). Trees can be alive, burned or dead. When it burns, a tree releases heat which spreads in the environment. This heat can ignite other trees around: A tree ignites when the temperature is above a defined threshold. The threshold of each agent is randomly set within a range of values. A tree dies when its life reaches zero: The life of the tree decreases when it burns. Figure 4 illustrates the simulation steps.

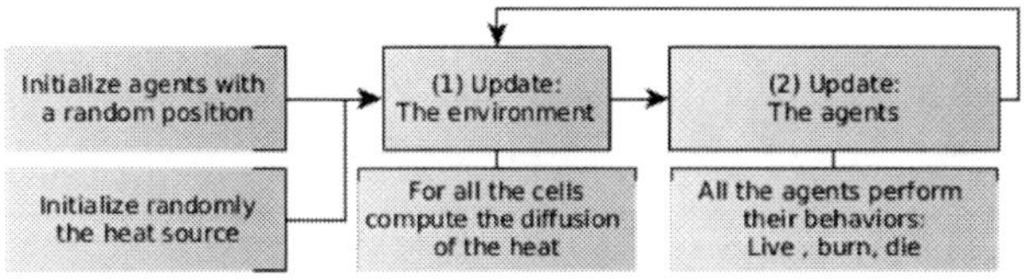

Figure 4: Fire simulation

Applying GPU Delegation.
The most greedy computation loop of this model is in step (1). Indeed, the environment must compute the heat diffusion which requires making a global sequential loop over all the cells. Thus, the computation time increases very quickly according to the size of the environment. Because the heat diffusion is already an environmental dynamics, the delegation of this computation is very easy because it can be directly translated into a GPU module.

So, in the GPU model, the heat diffusion is done as follows: At each time step, agents add in a 2D array (matching the size of the environment) the heat that they release according to their state (alive, burn or dead). Then, this array is sent to the GPU module that compute the sum of heat values from neighboring cells (Moore neighborhood here) for each cell of the environment. More precisely, the sum consists in adding the heat values already present in the environment (from the previous steps) and the heat generated by the agents, all modulated by a diffusion variable. Once the computation performed, the agents recover the heat value in the array with respect to their position and act accordingly. Algorithm 3 presents an implementation of the corresponding GPU kernel.

Algorithm 3: Heat diffusion *Kernel*

```
input : width, height, heatArray, radius
output: resultArray (the quantity of heat)
i = blockIdx.x * blockDim.x + threadIdx.x ;
j = blockIdx.y * blockDim.y + threadIdx.y ;
sumOfHeat = 0 ;
if i < width and j < height then
    sumOfHeat =
    getNeighborsHeat(heatArray[i, j], radius);
end
resultArray[i, j] = sumOfHeat * heatAdjustment ;
```

3.2.4 *DLA*

The last model is also inspired from a Netlogo model and is called *DLA*. DLA demonstrates diffusion-limited aggregation, in which randomly moving particles stick together to form beautiful treelike branching fractal structures. There are many patterns found in nature that resemble the patterns produced by this model: Crystals, coral, fungi, lightning, and so on.

In this model, particles are agents (initialy red), that move in a random way over the all environment (a two dimensional grid). Randomly, one of the agents stops and stays at the same position and in turn changes its color to green. Then, when a moving red agent encounters a motionless green agent, it stops and changes its color to green while the other agents continue to move in a random way. Figure 5 illustrates the simulation steps.

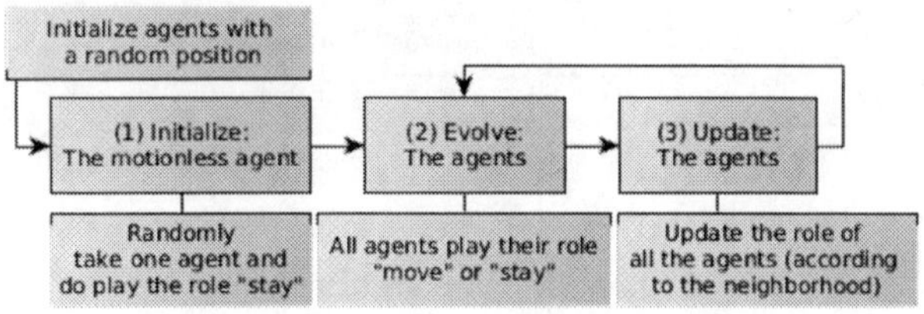

Figure 5: DLA simulation

Applying GPU Delegation.

The most greedy computations are in step (2) and (3) which consist for each agent in recovering a neighbor list and then searching within this list the nearest neighbors. So, the computation time of this model greatly increases according to the number of agents. According to GPU delegation, the agent action which consists in checking if one of the neighbor agents is green (motionless) can be converted into an environmental dynamics and then performed by a GPU kernel because this computation do not modify agents' states.

However, it is necessary to adapt the data structure to enable this transformation. Thus, all agents report, according to their position, their presence in a 2D array (matching the size of the environment): 1 if an agent occupies the cell, 0 otherwise. This array is sent to the GPU that calculates for each cell if there are agents around it. All the cells of the result array thus contain a value representing the number of neighbor agents (0 for an empty cell, 1 or more means there are neighbors around). So, the agents only have to recover the result value in the array and adjust their behavior accordingly. Algorithm 4 presents an implementation of the corresponding GPU kernel.

Algorithm 4: Presence detection *Kernel*

```
input  : width, height, presenceArray
output: resultArray (the number of neighbors around)
i = blockIdx.x * blockDim.x + threadIdx.x ;
j = blockIdx.y * blockDim.y + threadIdx.y ;
sumOfAgents = 0 ;
if i < width and j < height then
    sumOfAgents =
    getNeighborsPresence(presenceArray[i, j]);
end
resultArray[i, j] = sumOfAgents ;
```

4. EXPERIMENTATIONS AND ANALYSIS

In this section, the main idea is not only to evaluate the performance of the experiments but to reflect on the accessibility, modularity and ease of use of the GPU delegation principle (the conceptual part of these implementations).

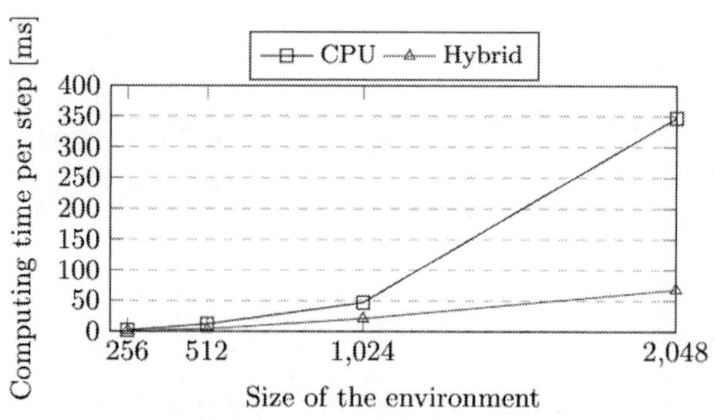

Figure 6: Results for the Game of Life model

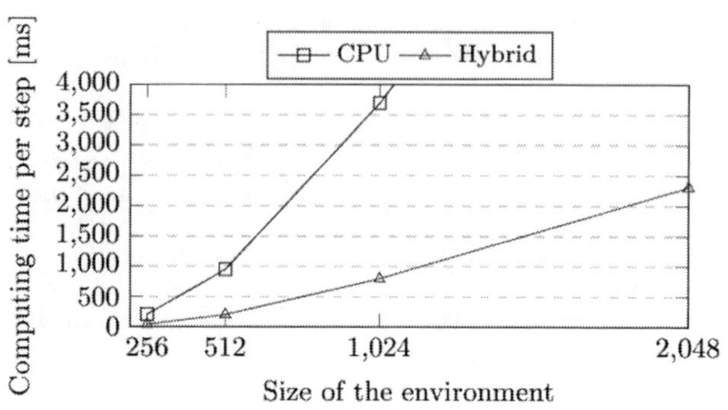

Figure 7: Results for the Segregation model

4.1 Experimentations

The GPU delegation principle produces implementations which are very different from those made by P&A. Moreover, the hardware and associated tools have also greatly evolved since P&A's work. So, we cannot directly compare the performance results of P&A with the experiences that we conduct here.

To test the performance of our implementations, each model is simulated in its CPU and hybrid (CPU + GPU) versions. Moreover, each model is simulated for different environment sizes and various densities of agents. Each simulation is executed several times over a period of 10,000 time steps. We average then the execution time for an iteration (lower execution time is better) allowing to compare the execution performance of each implementation.

For those tests, the configuration is composed of an Intel i7-4770 processor (Haswell generation, 3.40 GHz) and an Nvidia K4000 graphics card (Kepler architecture, 768 CUDA cores). Here is the list of experimentations (with setup) conducted and their results:

- Game Of Life (Figure 6): Environment size 256, 512, 1 024, 2 048; Fixed density of agents: 50%.
- Segregation (Figure 7): Environment size 256, 512, 1 024, 2 048; Fixed density of agents: 90%.
- Fire (Figure 8): Environment size 256, 512, 1 024, 2 048; Density of agents ranging from 10% to 100%.
- DLA (Figure 9): Environment size 256, 512, 1 024, 2 048; Density of agents ranging from 10% to 90%.

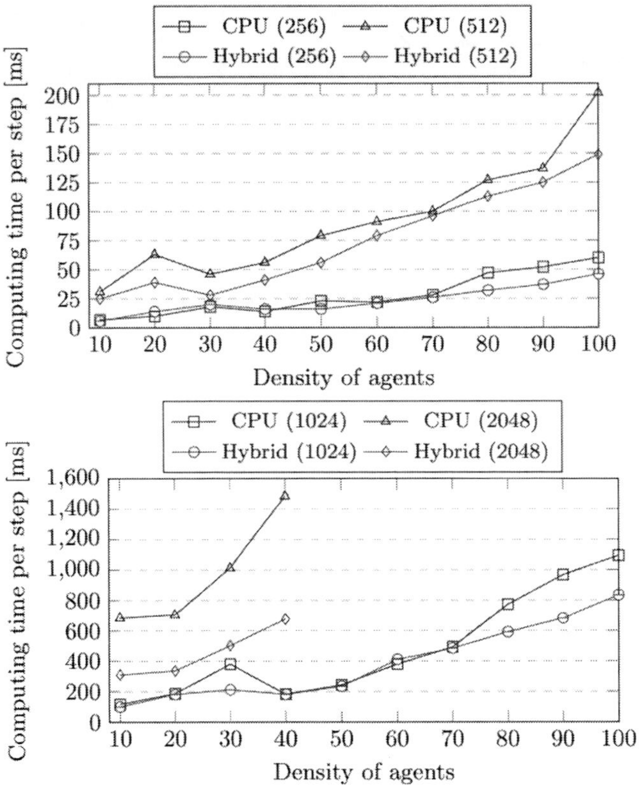

Figure 8: Results for the Fire model

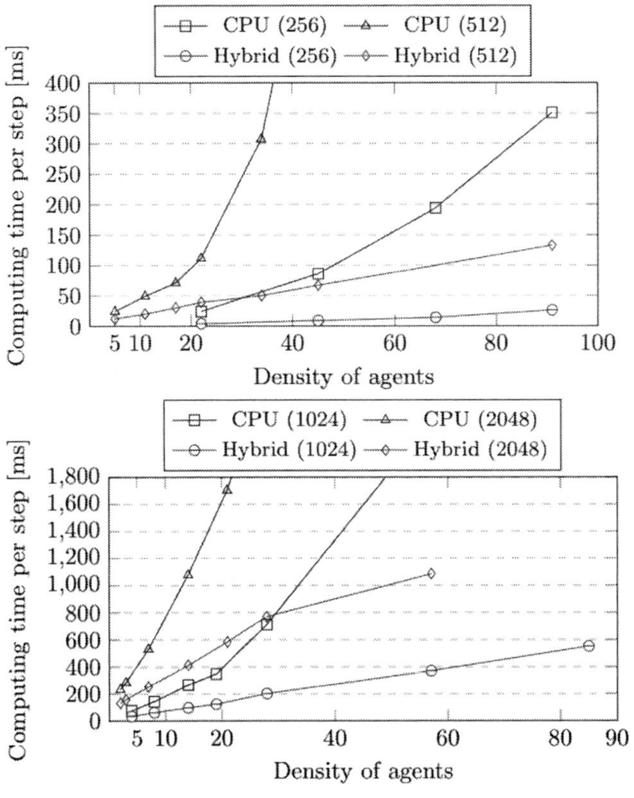

Figure 9: Results for the DLA model

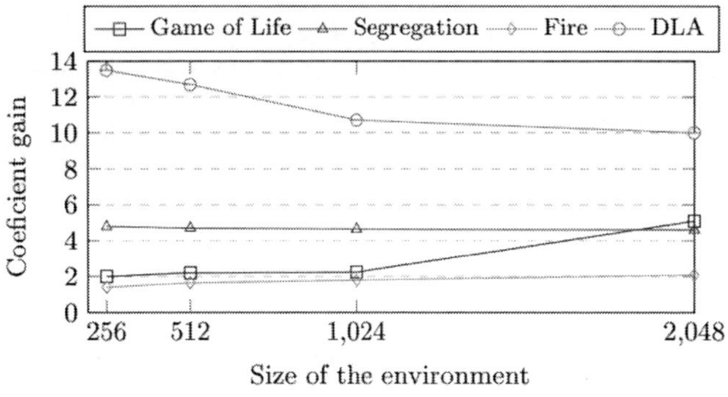

Figure 10: Coefficient of acceleration (between CPU and CPU+GPU versions)

4.2 Analysis

In this section, we analyze the results from both a performance and a conceptual perspective by taking into account accessibility, genericness and ease of use of GPU delegation.

4.2.1 *Performances*

From Figure 10, we notice that performance gains vary significantly depending on the simulated model and the size of the environment. With GPU delegation, the gain can reach x14 but is more likely between x2 and x5 which is still a good result. Concerning the DLA model, the performance decreases when increasing the size of the environment (which is the opposite of what can be seen with the other models). This decrease is explained by the consumption of resource by the agents that slows the simulation.

P&A's implementations are much more efficient and allow to have greater performance gains that can reach x40 (particularly for the Game of Life model) but generally the gain is around x15 [25]. The differences are huge but must be put in perspective because we have no informations about how the models and CPU implementations were created. Nonetheless, the order of magnitude of performance gains cannot be ignored. This difference is explained by the implementation technique used by P&A. Indeed, they used an all-in-GPU approach that consists in running entirely the model on the GPU with the objective of obtaining maximum performances. GPU delegation offers less impressive performances but brings other significant benefits.

4.2.2 *Genericness, Modularity and Reusability*

GPU delegation brings more genericness thanks to its hybrid conception. Especially, the created GPU modules can be reused in other simulations. That is the case here: The module created for the Game of Life model was reused in the DLA model. Only the data sent have been adapted. This is a major difference compared to the work and implementations of P&A, and more generally with works using an all-in-GPU approach. Indeed, with such works, the model used is completely redesigned and reprogrammed to run entirely on the GPU and thus cannot be easily reused. Therefore, the solution created is only punctual, which is not satisfying from a software engineering perspective.

On the contrary, more genericness could be obtained with an hybrid approach. This is especially the case with GPU delegation because it allows to reuse the created GPU modules, thus saving a lot of development time.

From an accessibility perspective, GPU delegation increases GPGPU accessibility because it promotes a modular design of the model that produces very simple kernels requiring only very little GPGPU knowledge. Moreover, by deporting only a specific part of the agent computations, it is thus possible to take advantage of the computing power of GPGPU without changing the agent model.

Finally, this modular design allows to choose what is run on the CPU and executed by the GPU. The strategy put forward by GPU delegation is to identify in the model the computations that can be transformed into environmental dynamics and thus translated into GPU modules. Considering the difficulties faced when implementing the behavior of agent on GPU or providing generic tools to do it, this approach greatly eases the use of GPGPU in MABS context.

4.2.3 Toward a Dedicated Methodology

The application of GPU delegation as generic approach for using GPU programming in MABS has shown many advantages whether in [18] or [12]. The experiment conducted in this article confirms it. However, in view of these studies, there are still some open questions such as the difficulty of implementation for a new GPGPU user and the types of models on which GPU delegation could be applied.

Indeed, for now, we have only tested GPU delegation on models that we know compatible. This type of model has the following features: The agents are reactive and operate in a discretized environment. These agents communicate and exchange informations through the environment. Next step will be to consider models with continuous environments or agents having cognitive abilities.

About the implementation difficulties, GPU delegation aims at easing the integration of GPGPU in MABS models by promoting a real delegation strategy that ends with very simple kernels wich are easy to implement and require only very little GPGPU knowledge. However, it will be necessary to improve the support around this approach.

But more generally, our objective is to offer a generic approach which can be applied on a wide variety of models and that eases the use of GPGPU. An approach that is also able to define if the model can benefit from GPGPU power before starting the adaptation process and could determine whether there is an interest in applying the GPGPU delegation on the selected model.

From the previous experiment, a recurring process has appeared during the application of GPU delegation. We have indeed followed an iterative process that allows us to apply our approach on each model. Once formalized, we believe that this process can become a methodology dedicated to GPGPU for MABS. A methodology that would (1) help potential users to decide if they could benefit from GPGPU considering their models and (2) support the translation of MABS model into GPU programming without hiding the underlying technology. And finally such a methodology would help to spread the GPGPU in the MABS community.

5. SUMMARY AND FUTUR WORKS

In this paper, we proposed to study through experiments if the conclusions and issues outlined by P&A in 2008 are still true despite the evolution of GPGPU and MABS. This paper was motivated by the fact that there are actually only very few publications dealing with the use of GPGPU in a MABS context, despite the computing power that these simulations require.

To address some of the challenges that remains when using GPGPU for MABS, we apply GPU delegation on four models and show that it helps to solve some of the problems outlined by P&A. Based on a hybrid approach, GPU delegation proposes to identify in the model what are the computations that can be transformed into environmental dynamics and then translated into GPU modules.

Instead of focusing on accessibility by hiding the use of GPGPU, GPU delegation aims at easing the direct integration of GPU programming in MABS models. So, GPU delegation helps he user during the adaptation process contrary to some solutions which seek to make transparent the use of GPGPU.

This principle was applied on four models and an experimentation which compares the GPU-based runtime speed with the speed of equivalent CPU-based models was conducted. The results of experiments and analysis were then proposed.

From a performance perspective, GPU delegation offers less significant performance gains compared to all-in-GPU solutions. As highlighted by P&A, this performance gap can only be obtained at the expense of the accessibility, modularity and genericity and reflects of a totally different use of the GPU architecture.

From a conceptual point of view, we have seen that GPU delegation improves genericity (reusability of the created GPU modules), provides a more modular design (with the hybrid approach) and enhances accessibility thanks to the fact that we are no longer using an all-in-GPU approach. More precisely, its reusability and design ease the direct use of GPGPU in a MABS context. Given that GPU does not run the entire simulation but only some parts, the adaptation of the model is more simple and the knowledge required is less important. Indeed, the reusability allows to save the time invested and the efforts done to use this technology because it concretely relies on an AOSE perspective thate promotes a clear separation of concerns, and thus modularity and reusability.

Thanks to the evolution of both the GPGPU field and associated tools, GPU delegation shows that it can be easy to implement and efficient while providing significant conceptual advantages. The next step is to develop the user support so that GPU delegation can be simple to use. To this end, it is now necessary to formalize its use and all conception steps.

Especially, during implementation of the four models, we identified some repetitions in the application of the principle. Moreover, some patterns and similarities in the source code can be observed. So, an iterative process begin to appear: A list of the steps necessary to transform the model in order to use GPGPU through GPU delegation.

Based on this work, our next objective is to create a comprehensive design methodology for GPGPU in a MABS context based on the GPU delegation principle. This methodology will allow to take a model and then will help in every step necessary in the translation process in order to let the model takes advantage of GPGPU power. Such a methodology should allow to use GPU programming on a wide variety of models and spread this technology in the MABS community.

REFERENCES

[1] 4th International Workshop, E4MAS 2014 - 10 Years Later, Paris, France, May 6, 2014, Revised Selected and Invited Papers. In D. Weyns and F. Michel, editors, *Agent Environments for Multi-Agent Systems IV*, volume 9068 of *LNCS*. Springer, 2015.

[2] B. G. Aaby, K. S. Perumalla, and S. K. Seal. Efficient Simulation of Agent-based Models on multi-GPU and Multi-core Clusters. In *Proceedings of the 3rd International ICST Conference on Simulation Tools and Techniques*, SIMUTools '10, pages 29:1–29:10, ICST, Brussels, Belgium, 2010. ICST (Institute for Computer Sciences, Social-Informatics and Telecommunications Engineering).

[3] F. Badeig, F. Balbo, and S. Pinson. A contextual environment approach for multi-agent-based simulation. In *ICAART'2010, 2nd International Conference on Agents and Artificial Intelligence*, pages pp 212–217, Spain, June 2010. ICAART.

[4] G. Beurier, O. Simonin, and J. Ferber. Model and Simulation of Multi-Level Emergence. In *ISSPIT'02*, Apr. 2008.

[5] A. Bleiweiss. Multi agent navigation on the GPU. *Games Developpement Conference*, 2009.

[6] S. Che, M. Boyer, J. Meng, D. Tarjan, J. W. Sheaffer, and K. Skadron. A performance study of general-purpose applications on graphics processors using CUDA. *Journal of Parallel and Distributed Computing*, 68(10):1370–1380, 2008. General-Purpose Processing using Graphics Processing Units.

[7] N. Collier and M. North. *Repast HPC: A Platform for Large-Scale Agent-Based Modeling*, pages 81–109. John Wiley and Sons, Inc., 2012.

[8] A. Demeulemeester, C.-F. Hollemeersch, P. Mees, B. Pieters, P. Lambert, and R. Van de Walle. Hybrid Path Planning for Massive Crowd Simulation on the GPU. In J. Allbeck and P. Faloutsos, editors, *Motion in Games*, volume 7060 of *Lecture Notes in Computer Science*, pages 304–315. Springer Berlin Heidelberg, 2011.

[9] R. M. D'Souza, M. Lysenko, and K. Rahmani. SugarScape on steroids: simulating over a million agents at interactive rates. *Proceedings of Agent 2007 conference*, 2007.

[10] U. Erra, B. Frola, V. Scarano, and I. Couzin. An Efficient GPU Implementation for Large Scale Individual-Based Simulation of Collective Behavior. In *High Performance Computational Systems Biology, 2009. HIBI '09. International Workshop on*, pages 51–58, Oct 2009.

[11] M. Gardner. Mathematical games: The fantastic combinations of John Conways new solitaire game life. *Scientific American*, 223(4):120–123, 1970.

[12] E. Hermellin and F. Michel. GPU Environmental Delegation of Agent Perceptions: Application to Reynolds's Boids. In *Multi-Agent-Based Simulation XVI - International Workshop, MABS 2015, Istanbul, Turkey, May 5*.

[13] A. V. Husselmann and K. A. Hawick. Simulating Species Interactions and Complex Emergence in Multiple Flocks of Boids with GPUs. In *International Conference on Parallel and Distributed Computing and Systems*, pages 100–107. IASTED, 2011.

[14] Y. Kubera, P. Mathieu, and S. Picault. IODA: an interaction-oriented approach for multi-agent based simulations. *Autonomous Agents and Multi-Agent Systems*, 23(3):303–343, 2011.

[15] G. Laville, K. Mazouzi, C. Lang, N. Marilleau, B. Herrmann, and L. Philippe. MCMAS: A Toolkit to Benefit from Many-Core Architecure in Agent-Based Simulation. In D. an Mey, M. Alexander, P. Bientinesi, M. Cannataro, C. Clauss, A. Costan, G. Kecskemeti, C. Morin, L. Ricci, J. Sahuquillo, M. Schulz, V. Scarano, S. Scott, and J. Weidendorfer, editors, *Euro-Par 2013: Parallel Processing Workshops*, volume 8374 of *Lecture Notes in Computer Science*, pages 544–554. Springer Berlin Heidelberg, 2014.

[16] G. Laville, K. Mazouzi, C. Lang, N. Marilleau, and L. Philippe. Using GPU for Multi-agent Multi-scale Simulations. In *Distributed Computing and Artificial Intelligence*, volume 151 of *Advances in Intelligent and Soft Computing*, pages 197–204. Springer Berlin Heidelberg, 2012.

[17] M. Lysenko and R. M. D'Souza. A Framework for Megascale Agent Based Model Simulations on Graphics Processing Units. *Journal of Artificial Societies and Social Simulation*, 11(4):10, 2008.

[18] F. Michel. Translating Agent Perception Computations into Environmental Processes in Multi-Agent-Based Simulations: A means for Integrating Graphics Processing Unit Programming within Usual Agent-Based Simulation Platforms. *Systems Research and Behavioral Science*, 30(6):703–715, 2013.

[19] F. Michel, G. Beurier, and J. Ferber. The TurtleKit Simulation Platform: Application to Complex Systems. In A. Akono, E. Tonyé, A. Dipanda, and K. Yétongnon, editors, *Workshops Sessions of the Proceedings of the 1st International Conference on Signal-Image Technology and Internet-Based Systems, SITIS 2005, November 27 - December 1, 2005, Yaoundé, Cameroon*, pages 122–128. IEEE, november 2005.

[20] F. Michel, J. Ferber, and A. Drogoul. Multi-Agent Systems and Simulation: a Survey From the Agents Community's Perspective. In Adelinde Uhrmacher and Danny Weyns, editors, *Multi-Agent Systems: Simulation and Applications*, Computational Analysis, Synthesis, and Design of Dynamic Systems, pages 3–52. CRC Press - Taylor & Francis, June 2009.

[21] J. D. Owens, D. Luebke, N. Govindaraju, M. Harris, J. Kruger, A. E. Lefohn, and T. J. Purcell. A Survey of General-Purpose Computation on Graphics Hardware. *Computer Graphics Forum*, 26(1):80–113, 2007.

[22] H. Parry and M. Bithell. Large scale agent-based modelling: A review and guidelines for model scaling. In A. J. Heppenstall, A. T. Crooks, L. M. See, and M. Batty, editors, *Agent-Based Models of Geographical Systems*, pages 271–308. Springer Netherlands, 2012.

[23] R. Pavlov and J. Muller. Multi-Agent Systems Meet GPU: Deploying Agent-Based Architectures on Graphics Processors. In L. Camarinha-Matos, S. Tomic, and P. Graca, editors, *Technological*

Innovation for the Internet of Things, volume 394 of *IFIP Advances in Information and Communication Technology*, pages 115–122. Springer Berlin Heidelberg, 2013.

[24] D. Payet, R. Courdier, N. Sébastien, and T. Ralambondrainy. Environment as support for simplification, reuse and integration of processes in spatial MAS. In *Proceedings of the 2006 IEEE International Conference on Information Reuse and Integration, IRI - 2006: Heuristic Systems Engineering, September 16-18, 2006, Waikoloa, Hawaii, USA*, pages 127–131. IEEE Systems, Man, and Cybernetics Society, 2006.

[25] K. S. Perumalla and B. G. Aaby. Data parallel execution challenges and runtime performance of agent simulations on GPUs. *Proceedings of the 2008 Spring simulation multiconference*, pages 116–123, 2008.

[26] A. Ricci, M. Piunti, and M. Viroli. Environment programming in multi-agent systems: an artifact-based perspective. *Autonomous Agents and Multi-Agent Systems*, 23(2):158–192, 2011.

[27] P. Richmond and D. M. Romano. Agent based GPU, a real-time 3d simulation and interactive visualisation framework for massive agent based modelling on the GPU. In *In Proceedings International Workshop on Super Visualisation (IWSV08)*, 2008.

[28] P. Richmond and D. M. Romano. A High Performance Framework For Agent Based Pedestrian Dynamics On GPU Hardware. *European Simulation and Modelling*, 2011.

[29] P. Richmond, D. Walker, S. Coakley, and D. M. Romano. High performance cellular level agent-based simulation with FLAME for the GPU. *Briefings in bioinformatics*, 11(3):334–47, 2010.

[30] T. C. Schelling. *Micromotives and Macrobehavior*. W. W. Norton, revised edition, Sept. 1978.

[31] E. Sklar. NetLogo, a Multi-agent Simulation Environment. *Artificial Life*, 13(3):303–311, 2007.

[32] D. Strippgen and K. Nagel. Multi-agent traffic simulation with CUDA. In *High Performance Computing Simulation, 2009. HPCS '09. International Conference on*, pages 106–114, June 2009.

[33] D. Weyns, H. Dyke Parunak, F. Michel, T. Holvoet, and J. Ferber. Environments for Multiagent Systems State-of-the-Art and Research Challenges. In D. Weyns, H. Dyke Parunak, and F. Michel, editors, *Environments for Multi-Agent Systems*, volume 3374 of *Lecture Notes in Computer Science*, pages 1–47. Springer Berlin Heidelberg, 2005.

Engineering Commitment-based Business Protocols with the 2CL Methodology

(Extended Abstract)

Matteo Baldoni
University of Torino

Cristina Baroglio
University of Torino

Elisa Marengo
University of Bozen-Bolzano

Viviana Patti
University of Torino

Federico Capuzzimati
University of Torino

General Terms: Design.
Keywords: Commitment-based business protocols, regulations, methodologies, risk, accountability.

1. INTRODUCTION

Business protocols are a means for specifying the interaction of a set of autonomous parties with heterogeneous software designs and implementations. They have a normative value in that parties are expected to behave accordingly. Often the reality in which parties operate is characterized by a *high degree of regulation*. This is, for instance, the case of banking and of trading services. As new regulations are issued, there is the need of adapting business protocols to the new dictates, which usually restrict – e.g. by adding new commitments and new constraints – the possible interactions, or require the combination of different protocols. When this happens, it is important for those organizations, whose conducts are affected by the new regulation, to have the means for identifying their *exposure to risks of violation*.

The commitment-based approach (e.g. [7, 5]) allows expressing interaction in terms of actions, whose social meaning is shared by the interacting parties. The execution of such actions affects the world and can either cause the creation of social commitments between the parties or the manipulation of already existing ones (e.g. by delegating, canceling, assigning them). Thus, commitment-based approaches naturally capture the contractual relationships among the partners rather than strictly encoding the order in which messages are to be exchanged. 2CL [2, 4] extends classical commitment-based protocols with the possibility to express temporal *constraints among commitments*.

The article introduces 2CL Methodology, a *software engineering methodology* for the business protocol language 2CL, by which business protocols are specified in a declarative way by means of social commitments. Besides supporting 2CL protocol specification, 2CL Methodology includes specific guidelines for the *composition* and the *specialization* of protocols. The latter is used in the case in which a protocol must take in a new regulation or, as we say, a regulation is to be *grafted* upon an existing protocol [3, 1]. As an example of usage, the article applies the 2CL Methodology to the Markets in Financial Instruments Directive (MiFID) which is an important example of EU regulation having an impact on trading procedures. The article also describes an integrated set of software tools, that support the design and the analysis of 2CL business protocols.

2. BACKGROUND

We maintain that *commitments* and *constraints* supply the right abstractions for capturing the intents of the specification without being overly prescriptive: the former, by capturing contractual engagements between the interacting parties, the latter, by expressing agreements, norms, conventions, habits and such like on the evolution of the interaction. So, we build upon 2CL and introduce 2CL Methodology, a modeling methodology aimed at harnessing the complexity of the analysis and the design of evolving business protocols. 2CL Methodology is an enhanced version of the Amoeba methodology [6], which is specifically thought for realizing commitment-based business protocols, either designing them from scratch or by adapting already existing ones. The version that we propose is conceived for tackling not only commitments but also temporal constraints, the two chief components of 2CL specifications. It also includes steps that are conceived for performing the *composition* and the *specialization* of business protocols, the latter of which is used for performing the grafting of regulations.

A 2CL business protocol models business interactions based on the two main notions of *commitment* and of *constraint*. It is an aggregation of various elements:

- *Role*: conceptualizes a possible actor in a protocol. Roles are played by specific actors when protocols are enacted;
- *Domain Element*: is an element of the *universe of discourse*;
- *Initial State*: is a set of items belonging to *Domain Element* and represents the initial state of an interaction that respects the business protocol;
- *Action*: represents a move that players of roles may execute. It conceptualizes the "counts as" relationship between the move at issue and its social meaning, given in terms of modifications to the social state;
- *Constraint*: conceptualizes an interaction pattern that is to be respected.

Appears in: *Proceedings of the 15th International Conference on Autonomous Agents and Multiagent Systems (AAMAS 2016), J. Thangarajah, K. Tuyls, C. Jonker, S. Marsella (eds.), May 9–13, 2016, Singapore.*

Actions and constraints are both defined based on *facts* and *commitments* which are part of a set of *Domain Elements*. Facts are positive or negative propositions that do not concern commitments and which contribute to the social state.

3. THE 2CL METHODOLOGY

Due to lack of space we sketch only the part of the methodology that concerns proocol specification, the parts for protocol composition and specialization can be found in the paper [1]. When defining a 2CL protocol, the designer should identify a set of roles, a set of domain elements, the content of the initial state, a set of actions, and a set of constraints.

***M1:* Roles Identification.** The set of roles of a protocol is obtained, first, by identifying the set of participants to the interaction that it is of interest to represent; second, by abstracting from players the roles they play in the protocol.

***M2:* Contractual Relationships Identification.** This step is structured in three substeps which basically aim at determining:

M2.1 the domain elements (or universe of discourse) on which the protocol relies;

M2.2 the contractual relationships and conditions of interest that are involved in the interaction;

M2.3 the contractual relationships and conditions of interest that exist prior to the interaction and that belong to the initial state.

***M3:* Identify Actions Social Meanings.** The analyst considers the set of commitments and facts individuated at the previous step. By following the extracted information on their creation, satisfaction and manipulation, she determines which actions have an impact (and which) on the set of domain elements. Accordingly, she associates to each action a meaning, given in terms of operations on commitments or assertion of facts, and if necessary also a context.

***M4:* Identify Constraints.** The analyst is expected to identify a set of temporal requirements, or co-occurrence relations, the interaction is desired to respect and to find a suitable representation in terms of 2CL constraints.

4. GRAFTING

We describe how the MiFID regulation that applies to the offer of investment services off-site, i.e., the case when a bank promotes and sells financial products with the help of external collaborators (intermediaries), can be grafted on a previously existing financial product sale protocol. Notice that if an intermediary buys a financial product for a client, *violating* some of the constraints imposed by MiFID, the sale is however valid, the client results to be the owner of the product. This happens because MiFID does not define "sale" (sale is defined by a different regulation) but dictates how the interaction with the client should be carried on by adding a new layer of regulations on top of existing ones. So, the violation of some constraint does not affect the sale directly but creates both a risk of sanction and a risk of exposure for the intermediary. The article shows how such risks can be identified by way of the tools we developed, and how, by following the steps of the methodology that were devised for protocol specialization, it is possible to upgrade the business protocols in a way that accounts for the new regulation.

5. 2CL TOOLS

We developed a suite of tools that enable the verification of exposure to risk on the graph of the possible executions, and support taking decisions about how to behave (or how to modify the protocol) so to avoid such a risk. The realized system, an Eclipse plug-in (java-based and open source IDE), is available at the URL `http://di.unito.it/2CL`. Its functionalities can be grouped into three components: design, reasoning and visualization. The *design component* supports the definition of business protocols. It supplies the action (textual) editor, and the constraint (graphical) editor. Constraints graphical representation can be converted into a textual one, that can be used to generate a Prolog program. The *reasoning component* allows generating all the possible interactions, which are allowed by a protocol actions, labelling them as legal or not according to the protocol constraints. The program is realized in tuProlog and builds upon the enhanced commitment machine by Winikoff et al. Annotations account for all the regulative aspects concerning both commitments and constraints. So each illegal state of the graph has a set of labels that capture the violation of some constraints, the presence of pending conditions, or the presence of unsatisfied active commitments. The *Graph Explorer* supplies many functionalities, among which: the visualization of the shortest path between two states, the visualisation of legal (or illegal) paths only, hand-made addition or deletion of a node in a path, the search of all the states that contain a certain fact or commitment, the exploration of the graph one state at a time, by choosing which node to expand, the incremental construction of the graph.

REFERENCES

[1] M. Baldoni, C. Baroglio, E. Marengo, V. Patti, and F. Capuzzimati. Engineering commitment-based business protocols with 2CL methodology. *J. of Autonomous Agents and Multi-Agent Systems*, 28(4):519–557, 2014.

[2] M. Baldoni, C. Baroglio, E. Marengo, and V. Patti. Constitutive and Regulative Specifications of Commitment Protocols: a Decoupled Approach. *ACM Trans. on Intelligent Systems and Technology, Spec. Iss. on Agent Communication*, 4(2):22:1-22:25, 2013.

[3] M. Baldoni, C. Baroglio, V. Patti, and E. Marengo. Supporting the Analysis of Risks of Violation in Business Protocols: the MiFID Case Study. In *Information Systems: Crossroads for Organization, Management, Accounting and Eng.* Springer, 2012.

[4] M. Baldoni, C. Baroglio, and E. Marengo. Behavior-Oriented Commitment-based Protocols. In *Proc. of ECAI*, volume 215 of *Frontiers in AI and Applications.* IOS Press, 2010.

[5] A. K. Chopra, A. Artikis, J. Bentahar, M. Colombetti, F. Dignum, N. Fornara, A. J. I. Jones, M. P. Singh, and P. Yolum. Research directions in agent communication. *ACM TIST*, 4(2), 2013.

[6] N. Desai, A. K. Chopra, and M. P. Singh. Amoeba: A Methodology for Modelling and Evolving Cross-Organizational Business Processes. *ACM Trans. on Soft. Eng. and Methodology*, 19(2), 2009.

[7] P. Yolum and M. P. Singh. Flexible protocol specification and execution: applying event calculus planning using commitments. In *Proc. of AAMAS* 2002.

Commitments and Interaction Norms in Organisations (JAAMAS Extended Abstract)

Mehdi Dastani
Utrecht University
The Netherlands
m.m.dastani@uu.nl

Leendert van der Torre
University of Luxembourg
Luxembourg
leon.vandertorre@uni.lu

Neil Yorke-Smith
American University of Beirut
Lebanon
nysmith@aub.edu.lb

ABSTRACT

In an organisational setting such as an online marketplace, an entity called the 'organisation' or 'institution' defines interaction protocols, monitors agent interaction, and may intervene to enforce the interaction protocols. This extended abstract summarises our JAAMAS article [10]. In the article we generalise over application-specific protocols and consider commitment lifecycles as generic interaction protocols. We model interaction protocols by explicitly-represented norms, operationalise the enforcement of protocols by means of norm enforcement, and analyse the protocols by a logical analysis of the norms. We adopt insights and methods from commitment-based approaches to agent interaction as well as from norm-based approaches to agent behaviour governance. First, we show how to use explicitly-represented norms to model commitment dynamics (lifecycles). Second, we introduce an operational semantics to operationalise norm enforcement. Third, we show how to logically analyse interaction protocols by means of commitment dynamics and norm enforcement. The model, operational semantics, and logical analysis are illustrated by a running example from a vehicle insurance domain.

1. BACKGROUND AND MOTIVATION

A sizeable body of literature has developed theories about organisations, interaction protocols, commitments, and norms. For example, an organisational setting is manifest in the finance and accounting literature, where regulatory bodies monitor or audit firms, and may fine violations of regulations or statues and failures in corporate governance [6].

Andrighetto et al. [1] provide a survey of work in the multi-agent systems literature. This work studies decision making and agent organisations, as modelled by norms, interaction protocols and commitments. A central challenge in this literature is to investigate the relationships between *commitment-based approaches* and *norm-based approaches*. The JAAMAS article [10] contributes to this challenge by modelling dynamics of commitments (often explained as variety in commitment lifecycle) using an explicit representation of norms.

The fact that a commitment lifecycle and a norm set can both be seen as constituting an interaction protocol suggests a fundamental relation between commitment lifecycle and norms. This relation, which forms the main focus of our article, can be explained by viewing a commitment cycle from a normative stance and by viewing it as a set of norms that governs the dynamics of commitments which in turn can be used to regulate the agents' interaction. Following this relation, we propose a formal framework where a commitment lifecycle is modelled as a set of explicitly represented interaction norms. This framework allows us to operationalise commitment lifecycles, and to logically analyse and compare them.

2. CONTRIBUTIONS

Multi-agent systems in an organisational setting typically possess an entity defining interaction protocols, monitoring agent interaction, and enforcing interaction norms by means of regulation policies. We call this entity the 'organisation' or 'institution'. For our purposes, an organisation consists of two main processes: the *monitoring process* checks for conformance of agents' behaviour to protocols or norms, while the *enforcement process* ensures the coordination by means of enforcing the regulation policies.

In the article, we propose to model the interaction protocols of the organisation by explicitly-represented interaction norms. This norm representation has two advantages. The first advantage is that we can operationalise the enforcement of protocols by means of norm enforcement, and the second advantage is that we can analyse the protocol by a logical analysis of the norms. To make this idea more precise, we adopt insights and methods from commitment-based approaches as well as from norm-based approaches.

First, we show how to use explicitly represented norms to model variety in the commitment lifecycle. From the organisation's viewpoint, agent interactions affect the state of the institutional facts, in particular the commitments, while regulation policy is responsible for updating the organisation state as a consequence of detected violations. By modelling the interaction protocols of the organisation as a set of explicitly represented norms, to which the agents' interaction should adhere, we are able to generalise interaction protocols to represent, for example, which agents can detach or satisfy commitments, whether commitments can be satisfied before they are detached or not, and temporal conditions such as whether a commitment which is fulfilled exactly at the moment of the deadline, counts as violated or not.

Second, we introduce an operational semantics to operationalise protocol enforcement. In this way, we show how to operationalise the enforcement of protocols by means of

Appears in: *Proceedings of the 15th International Conference on Autonomous Agents and Multiagent Systems (AAMAS 2016), J. Thangarajah, K. Tuyls, C. Jonker, S. Marsella (eds.), May 9–13, 2016, Singapore.*

norm enforcement. An organisational state consists of a set of brute facts, a set of institutional facts, a set of contexts, a set of norms and a set of regulation policies. Given a way to define the set of applicable rules in a context, two transition rules define how the brute and institutional facts should be updated. In the same way, we could add rules for changing the contexts, norms and policies.

Third, we show how to analyse interaction protocol of the organisation and thus commitment cycles by logically analysing the norms and norm enforcement. Since the norms are represented explicitly, and the system dynamics depends on the norms, we can use techniques and insights from deontic logic [12]. Temporal properties show that we can formally check that the operational semantics corresponds to the commitment lifecycle. Moreover, we can analyse interference between distinct commitments, which is often seen as a source of problems in protocol analysis. Finally, redundancy of norms tells us whether the protocol behaves as expected. For example, if an agent makes an offer, it is redundant for it to make the same offer again, or to make an offer which is strictly worse for the other party.

Hence, the contribution of the article is the systematic methodology to formally model and analyse commitment lifecycles in terms of norms and regulation policies that govern the creation and dynamics of commitments emerged during agents' interaction. Our proposed framework is based on a generic operational semantics that operationalise the enforcement of norms and regulation policies, and thereby operationalise the dynamics of commitments. The proposed framework is generic in that it allows formal instantiation and comparison of different approaches to commitment dynamics and commitment lifecycles.

The scope of the article is on monitoring agents' interaction in an organisational setting. Other organisation attributes and processes, such as environmental interaction, or roles, entities, and the relationships between them, are orthogonal to our purpose. We also do not consider other issues discussed in the literature, such as explicit temporal references in the commitments [13], roles of the agents [2, 3], teams and groups, organisational dynamics, procedural norms [4] and culture.

3. METHODOLOGICAL INNOVATION

Throughout the article, we emphasise the methodological innovation of our approach. We address the usual questions regarding agent communication, coordination and monitoring, and we adopt the usual formal methods like constitutive norms [14, 11, 5, 7, 1]. However, the way we establish our formal framework is different from all prior work, as we do not constrain ourselves to one particular commitment lifecycle. Of course, this does not mean that any set of norms and policies defined in our framework will behave well. It is part of our methodology that the behaviour of the organisation is left to the system designer, who defines the norms and policies. The properties we establish show that the commitment cycle we use in the main part of our discussion is well behaved. Whether other norms or policies are as well behaved has to be checked independently.

Acknowledgements. We thank the JAAMAS reviewers, the participants of the COIN'12 workshop at AAMAS'12 [9], and the reviewers of the AAMAS'12 conference [8]. Thanks to Amit Chopra, Steven McNamara and Paolo Torroni. NYS acknowledges award number 102853 from the University Research Board, American University of Beirut, and thanks the Operations group at the Cambridge Judge Business School and the fellowship at St Edmund's College, Cambridge.

REFERENCES

[1] G. Andrighetto, G. Governatori, P. Noriega, and L. van der Torre, editors. *Normative Multi-Agent Systems*, volume 4 of *Dagstuhl Follow-Ups*, Dagstuhl, Germany, 2013. Schloss Dagstuhl–Leibniz-Zentrum fuer Informatik.

[2] M. Baldoni, G. Boella, and L. van der Torre. Roles as a coordination construct: Introducing powerJava. *Electronic Notes in Theoretical Computer Science*, 150(1):9–29, 2006.

[3] G. Boella and L. van der Torre. The ontological properties of social roles in multi-agent systems: definitional dependence, powers and roles playing roles. *Artificial Intelligence and Law*, 15(3):201–221, 2007.

[4] G. Boella and L. van der Torre. Substantive and procedural norms in normative multiagent systems. *Journal of Applied Logic*, 6(2):152–171, 2008.

[5] N. Bulling and M. Dastani. Verifying normative behaviour via normative mechanism design. In *Proc. of IJCAI'11*, pages 103–108, 2011.

[6] J. C. Coffee Jr and H. A. Sale. *Securities Regulation.* Foundation Press, Eagan, MN, 12th edition, 2012.

[7] M. Dastani, J. C. Meyer, and D. Grossi. A logic for normative multi-agent programs. *Journal of Logic and Computation*, 23(2):335–354, 2013.

[8] M. Dastani, L. van der Torre, and N. Yorke-Smith. A programming approach to monitoring commitments in an organisational environment. In *Proc. of AAMAS'12*, pages 1373–1374, 2012.

[9] M. Dastani, L. van der Torre, and N. Yorke-Smith. Monitoring interaction in organisations. In *Coordination, Organizations, Institutions, and Norms in Agent Systems VIII*, LNCS 7756, pages 17–34. Springer, New York, NY, 2013.

[10] M. Dastani, L. van der Torre, and N. Yorke-Smith. Commitments and interaction norms in organisations. *Autonomous Agents and Multi-Agent Systems*, 2016. To appear.

[11] N. Fornara, F. Viganò, and M. Colombetti. Agent communication and artificial institutions. *Autonomous Agents and Multi-Agent Systems*, 14:121–142, 2007.

[12] D. Gabbay, J. Horty, X. Parent, R. van der Meyden, and L. van der Torre, editors. *Handbook of Deontic Logic and Normative Systems.* College Publications, London, UK, 2013.

[13] E. Marengo, M. Baldoni, C. Baroglio, A. K. Chopra, V. Patti, and M. P. Singh. Commitments with regulations: Reasoning about safety and control in REGULA. In *Proc. of AAMAS'11*, pages 467–474, 2011.

[14] M. P. Singh. A social semantics for agent communication languages. In *Issues in Agent Communication 2000*, LNCS 1916, pages 31–45. Springer, New York, NY, 2000.

Dynamically Generated Commitment Protocols in Open Systems

(JAAMAS Extended Abstract)

Akın Günay
School of Computer Eng.
Nanyang Technological University
Singapore
akingunay@ntu.edu.sg

Michael Winikoff
Department of Information Science
University of Otago
Dunedin, New Zealand
michael.winikoff@otago.ac.nz

Pınar Yolum
Department of Computer Engineering
Bogazici University
Istanbul,Turkey
pinar.yolum@boun.edu.tr

ABSTRACT

This extended abstract presents our work "Dynamically Generated Commitment Protocols in Open Systems" that appeared in the Journal of Autonomous Agents and Multi-Agent Systems [1].

Keywords

Commitment Protocol; Generation; Ranking

Protocols are used in multiagent systems to regulate interactions of agents. Typically, protocols are developed at design-time and embedded into the implementations of the agents. However, there are three shortcomings of this approach in open systems: (1) New types of agents, which do not comply with all the requirements of the design-time protocols, may join to an open system. (2) The environment of an open systems may evolve, and as a result, the design-time protocols may become insufficient to allow agents to achieve their goals in the changing environment. (3) Preferences of the agents may change over time, and accordingly the design-time protocols may fail to satisfy the new preferences of the agents.

For these reasons, we argue that agents in an open multiagent system should be able to derive new protocols at run-time, rather than completely relying on the design-time protocols. The ability to derive new protocols at run-time requires a formalism to define protocols, which can be interpreted by the agents. We define protocols in terms of *social commitments* [2], rather than sequences of message exchanges that are embedded into the implementations of the agents. The use of commitment protocols allow agents to reason about their situation, and carry out their interactions in a flexible manner while preserving their autonomy [3]. This paper proposes run-time generation of commitment-based interaction protocols.

Our contribution is not just a mechanism for creating a commitment protocol at run-time, but also a framework for the life-cycle of such protocols. To this end, we develop a complete agent process that defines how an agent can generate a set of candidate commitment protocols that allow the agent to achieve its goals, rank the candidate protocols according to the agent's preferences, and reach agreement with other agents on a suitable candidate protocol for enactment. Our main contributions are: (1) We develop two algorithms for the generation of commitment protocols, which

Appears in: *Proceedings of the 15th International Conference on Autonomous Agents and Multiagent Systems (AAMAS 2016), J. Thangarajah, K. Tuyls, C. Jonker, S. Marsella (eds.), May 9–13, 2016, Singapore.*

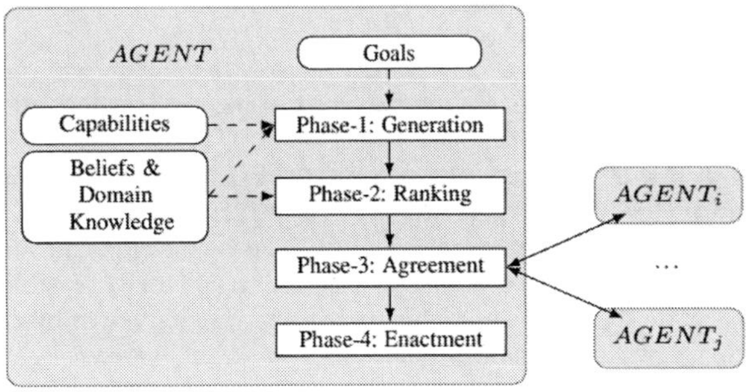

Figure 1: Process of an agent for run-time protocol enactment.

use the agent's own capabilities, and also its knowledge of other agents' services and incentives to generate a set of candidate commitment protocols that support the agent's goals. (2) We develop a novel metric, namely risk-discounted utility, that combines utility and trust concepts for ranking the candidate commitment protocols. (3) We define a procedure that can be used by the agents to reach agreement on a suitable candidate protocol for enactment.

We present the four-phase agent process that we propose in Figure 1. The first phase of the process is the *generation* of a set of candidate commitment protocols by an agent that aims to achieve a certain goal state. All of the candidate protocols ensure that the agent reaches its goal state. Furthermore, the candidate protocols also take into account the goals and services of the other agents to create incentive and ensure their collaboration. In the second phase, the generating agent evaluates the candidate protocols, and *ranks* them according to its preferences. This ranking is subjective by nature, and different parties may prefer different protocols over others. After the ranking, in the third phase, the generating agent engages in negotiation with the other agents in order to reach *agreement* on a candidate protocol for enactment. Finally, in the last phase, the chosen candidate protocol is *enacted* by the agents.

Generation: We propose the algorithms ProtocolBased and GoalBased for generating a set of commitment protocols that allow the generating agent to achieve its goals. The algorithms use the generating agent's capabilities in conjunction with its beliefs about the other agents, which define the services that they provide, and also what they may expect for the provision of their services. The core criterion of our algorithms is to establish the necessary *support* for the goals of the generating agent. We say that an agent supports a goal, if either the goal can be achieved by the agent itself using its own capabilities, or there are established commitments

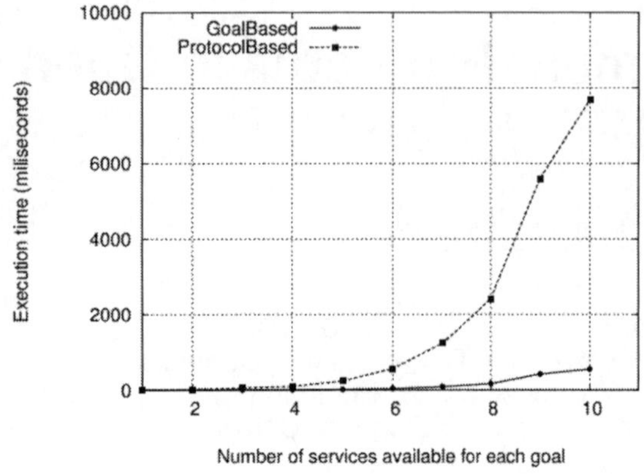

Figure 2: Execution times of PROTOCOLBASED and GOALBASED according to the number of available services.

from the other agents for the provision of the services that allow the agent to achieve its goal.

Our first algorithm PROTOCOLBASED is a direct recursive implementation of the support definition using depth-first search. The algorithm starts from an empty protocol. At each step it considers one goal from the generating agent's goal set, and tries to establish support for it either by using the agent's own capabilities, or by creating a new commitment to utilize a service of another agent. As a result of this step, new goals may be generated, which represent the intermediary conditions that should be achieved by the generating agent to use her own capabilities (e.g., preconditions of the capabilities), and also to create incentive on other agents to provide their services (e.g., the expectations of the other agents in return for the provision of their services). The base case is reached if the agent can support a goal using her own capabilities in an unconditional manner. This procedure generates a tree structure, where each path from the root to a leaf node, in which the base case is supported, corresponds to a candidate commitment protocol.

PROTOCOLBASED provides us a baseline algorithm. However, it is inefficient and suffers from lack of scalability, mainly because it finds support for a goal multiple times, if the goal is involved in the context of different candidate protocols. To overcome this drawback, we develop an efficient algorithm using the divide-and-conquer strategy, which we call GOALBASED. This algorithm considers goals independently from the candidate protocols. Accordingly, for each individual goal of the agent the algorithm generates a set of sub-protocols that support only that goal. Then these sub-protocol are merged to build a complete protocol to support all the goals of the agent. This modular approach allows us to reuse the sub-protocols that are generated in the context of different candidate protocols. Hence, the algorithm generates sub-protocols for each goal only once and avoids redundant computation.

We conducted experiments to evaluate efficiency and scalability of our proposed algorithm. In the experiments, we used a data set that we generated systematically according to several parameters, such as the number of available services to support a goal, and the number of preconditions required for using the agent's capabilities. We show the execution times of our algorithms with respect to the number of available services to support a goal in Figure 2, which shows the efficiency and scalability of GOALBASED.

Ranking: After the generation of the candidate protocols, the next phase is to evaluate and rank the candidate protocols to reflect the generating agent's preferences. To this end, we develop a metric for ranking commitment protocols, namely *risk-discounted utility*, that combines *utility* and *trust* concepts. The *utility* of a protocol for an agent reflects how much an agent would gain by enacting the protocol. The utility is basically the difference between the benefit of the protocol and its cost ($utility = benefit - cost$). Intuitively, each agent would want to maximize its utility, given that two protocols achieve the same goals. There may also be some protocols that are not acceptable to a given agent, i.e., protocols with negative utility. The *risk-discounted utility* extends utility by also considering risk. Some of the agents that enact a protocol may fail to fulfill their commitments, and accordingly the expected benefit of the protocol may not be realized. We therefore extend the definition of utility by *discounting* the benefits of a protocol based on the risk of the protocol due to other agents failures. The risk of a protocol is based on how trustworthy the agents enacting the protocol are for the various services that they provide in the context of the protocol. If all the agents are completely trustworthy, then there is no risk associated with a protocol. However, if any agent in the protocol is somewhat untrustworthy, then the protocol would be in risk, and the expected utility of the protocol may be jeopardized.

Agreement & Enactment: After the ranking of the candidate protocols, the next phase is to reach agreement between the agents on the enactment of one of the candidate protocols. To achieve this we develop a procedure that is led by the generating agent using the monotonic concession concept as follows. First, the generating agent selects the candidate protocol that it prefers most (e.g., the protocol that has the best risk-discounted utility). Then, it proposes creation of the candidate protocol's commitments to the corresponding debtors. If all the debtors accept to create the proposed commitments, an agreement is established over the protocol. Otherwise, the generating agent selects another candidate protocol that it prefers less (e.g., the protocol that is ranked next to the last offered protocol in terms of risk-discounted utility), and repeats the procedure. Note that in this phase, the debtors only accept to create the commitments, but they do not actually create the commitments. Actual creation of the commitments happens in the enactment phase, which follows the agreement phase. Enactment of a commitment protocol is system specific, hence we do not consider the details of this phase, and assume that enactment can be done in the targeted system. Note that our agreement procedure is independent from the ranking of protocols. Hence, alternative ranking metrics to risk-discounted utility can also be used for agreement.

In conclusion, in this paper we develop an agent process that defines how an agent can generate a set of candidate commitment protocols to support its goals, rank the candidate protocols according to its preferences, and reach agreement with other agents on a candidate protocol for enactment. This process allows agents of an open multiagent system to create and enact new protocols at run-time according to their changing needs and preferences, and reduces their dependency on the design-time protocols.

REFERENCES

[1] A. Günay, M. Winikoff, and P. Yolum. Dynamically generated commitment protocols in open systems. *Autonomous Agents and Multi-Agent Systems*, 29(2):192–229, 2015.

[2] M. P. Singh. An ontology for commitments in multiagent systems: Toward a unification of normative concepts. *Artificial Intelligence and Law*, 7(1):97–113, 1999.

[3] P. Yolum and M. P. Singh. Flexible protocol specification and execution: Applying event calculus planning using commitments. In *Proceedings of the First International Joint Conference on Autonomous Agents and Multiagent Systems*, pages 527–534, 2002.

Decision Theoretic Norm-Governed Planning (Extended Abstract)

Luca Gasparini, Timothy J. Norman, Martin J. Kollingbaum
Dept. of Computing Science
University Of Aberdeen, UK

Liang Chen
School of Computing and Engineering
University of West London, UK

ABSTRACT

We propose Normative Dec-POMDPs, a model of collective decision making in the presence of complex norms, with violations of norms classified according to their relative severity. We extend the PBPG algorithm in order to solve Normative Dec-POMDPs and propose a heuristic that improves its scalability without affecting the policy quality.

Categories and Subject Descriptors

I.2.11 [**Distributed Artificial Intelligence**]: Coherence and coordination

Keywords

Norms, Coordination, Decision Theory

1. INTRODUCTION

Existing approaches to norm-directed collective decision making often consider limited representations of norms, such as labelling of states with violations. This is insufficient even for some of the most common types of norms, such as separation and binding of duties, and obligations with deadlines. Compliance with these norms must be evaluated based on an execution history, rather than on a single state. Moreover, violations are often modelled as a loss of utility on a real scale. This leaves the way open to significant fallacies in reasoning. Consider, for example, confidentiality levels for documents and assume that a punishment for disclosing a "Top Secret" document would be ten times as costly as that for the disclosure of a "Secret" document. Should we infer that 10 disclosures of secret documents is as severe as that of a top secret one? A more natural means to model norm violations in these cases is as a partial order, where violations lie at different qualitative levels of severity.

We develop mechanisms that enable a coalition of agents to coordinate their activity in order to maximize their compliance level. We represent this problem as an extension of the Decentralized Partially Observable MDP (Dec-POMDP), denoted as Normative Dec-POMDP (N-Dec-POMDP), which allows us to reason about decision making in the presence of complex norms with violations of varying severity.

Appears in: *Proceedings of the 15th International Conference on Autonomous Agents and Multiagent Systems (AAMAS 2016), J. Thangarajah, K. Tuyls, C. Jonker, S. Marsella (eds.), May 9–13, 2016, Singapore.*

2. NORMATIVE DEC-POMDPS

Dec-POMDPs model distributed decision making problems where multiple agents, each with a different view of the environment, must coordinate in order to maximise a joint-reward [3]. A Dec-POMDP is as a tuple, $\langle I, S, b^0, \{A_i\}, P, \{\Omega_i\}, O, R\rangle$ where I is a set of agents, and S a set of states; b^0 is a probability distribution over possible initial states; A_i the actions available to agent i and $\vec{a} = \langle a_1, \dots, a_n\rangle$ a joint-action, one action for each agent; $P(s_j|s_i, \vec{a})$ is the probability that taking $\vec{a}$ in s_i will result in a transition to s_j; Ω_i are observations available to agent i and $\vec{\Omega}$ is the set of joint observations $\vec{o}$, one observation for each agent; $O(\vec{o} \mid \vec{a}, s_j)$ is the probability of observing $\vec{o}$ when taking $\vec{a}$ and transitioning to s_j; $R(s_i, \vec{a})$ is the reward obtained by performing $\vec{a}$ in s_i. A policy for agent i maps sequences of interleaved local actions and observations to local actions. Solving a Dec-POMDP means finding a joint-policy (one policy per agent) that maximises the expected total reward. Algorithms to approximately solve Dec-POMDPs rely on the fact that the transition probability depends only on the current state and joint-action (*Markovian property*). As discussed above, the evaluation of some complex norms depends on the execution history and is, therefore, non-Markovian. A number of norm formalisms (e.g. [2]) rely on a *normative configuation* to keep track of the evolution of norm instances (activation, expiration, etc.) as the system evolves. Algorithm 1 extends the state of a Dec-POMDP to include a normative configuration (nc_i) so that norm evaluation becomes Markovian. Let $\langle s_i, nc_i\rangle$ denote a normative state, consisting of the state of a Dec-POMDP (the factual state) and a normative configuration. We assume a function $viol(ns_i)$ that returns the violations detected in ns_i and a function upd_η that updates the normative configuration after a transition of the factual state. Let s^t and nc^t denote, respectively, the factual state and the normative configuration at time t, and η a set of norms. $upd_\eta(s^t, s^{t+1}, nc^t)$ denotes the normative configuration nc^{t+1} of the system after a transition from $\langle s^t, nc^t\rangle$ to a normative state with factual state s^{t+1}. The implementation of upd_η will depend on the chosen normative fomalism. We consider each possible execution, starting from every possible state (with an initial configuration nc_0), and update the configuration as we transition between states. We assume that observations depend only on factual states.

We now specify a partial order among norms and use it to define a utility function that captures the norms and their severity. Given two norms nd_k and nd_l, $nd_k \succ_n nd_l$ means that a violation of nd_k is more severe than any number of violations of nd_l. Let ϕ_k denote a violation of nd_k, and Φ_i

Algorithm 1 Generation of a N-Dec-POMDP

```
Input: I, S, {A_i}, P, {Ω_i}, O, η
Output: NS_*, P_*, O_*
toProc = ∅ , NS_* = ∅
for all s_i ∈ S do
    add ⟨s_i, upd_η(s_i, s_i, nc_0)⟩ to NS_* and toProc
end for
while toProc is not empty do
    ns_i = ⟨s_i, nc_i⟩ ← remove first element of toProc
    for all a⃗_j ∈ A_0 × ··· × A_n do
        for all s_k ∈ S s.t. P(s_k|s_i, a⃗_j) > 0 do
            ns_l ← ⟨s_k, upd_η(s_i, s_k, nc_i)⟩
            P_*(ns_l|ns_i, a⃗_j) ← P(s_k|s_i, a⃗_j)
            if ns_l ∉ NS_* then
                toProc ← toProc ∪ {ns_l} ; NS_* ← NS_* ∪ {ns_l}
            end if
        end for
        for all o⃗_m ∈ Ω_0 × ··· × Ω_n do
            O_*(o⃗_m|a⃗_j, ns_i) ← O(o⃗_m|a⃗_j, s_i)
        end for
    end for
end while
```

a violation set. We use this partial order to partially order violation sets. Φ_i is more severe than Φ_j ($\Phi_i \succ_v \Phi_j$) iff:

$$\exists \phi_k \in \Phi_i : \phi_k \notin \Phi_j \text{ and } \forall \phi_l \in \Phi_j : \phi_l \in \Phi_i \text{ or } nd_k \succ_n nd_l$$

Let Rk be a function that takes a violation set and gives its position in a ranking from the least to the most severe: (i) $Rk(\Phi_i) = 1$ if there is no $\Phi_j \in 2^{\Phi}$ such that $\Phi_i \succ_v \Phi_j$. (ii) $Rk(\Phi_i) = max\{Rk(\Phi_j) : \Phi_i \succ_v \Phi_j\} + 1$, otherwise. We refer to $Rk(ns_i) := Rk(viol(ns_i))$ as the *severity level* of ns_i. Bonet and Pearl [1] developed a qualitative theory of MDPs based on an order of magnitude approximation for utilities and probabilities. Given that ϵ represents a small unknown quantity, they define extended reals $\psi \in \Psi$ as infinite series $\psi = \sum_k c_k \epsilon^k$. They define operations over Ψ and, given a large parameter ρ, the magnitude of an extended real as $\|\psi^i\|_\rho := \sum_k |c_k| \rho^{-k}$. We use Ψ to represent the cost of a set of violations. Let mS be the maximum severity level. Equation 1 can be interpreted as the agents incurring in a higher cost for visiting states with higher severity.

$$\forall\ ns_i \in NS, \vec{a}_j \in \vec{A} : R(ns_i, \vec{a}_j) = -\epsilon^{mS - Rk(ns_i)} \quad (1)$$

3. SOLVING N-DEC-POMDPS

PBPG [3] may be adapted to solve N-Dec-POMDPs with extended reals rewards. PBPG heuristically identifies the beliefs that are most likely to be encountered and optimises policies against them. We propose the Most-Critical-States (MCS) heuristics that rely on the utility function structure to further restrict these beliefs and improve scalability. Given an initial state ns_i, MCS simulates the execution of the centralized MDP policy in order to identify reachable states ($R^t_{MDP}(ns_i)$) and estimate the probability of reaching each state ns_j ($pr_{ns_i}(ns_j)$). We use the MDP value function (V_{MDP}) to estimate what states are likely to lead to severe violations. Given a threshold $th \in \Psi$ and an initial state ns_i, $mc^{ns_i}_{th}$ is the set of $ns_j \in R^t_{MDP}(ns_i)$ s.t. the product of $V_{MDP}(ns_j)$ and $pr_{ns_i}(ns_j)$ is less than th. MdpMCS is the heuristics that selects beliefs b according to Equation 2. An improved heuristics (MixedMcs) uses a joint-policy to sample reachable states and V_{MDP} to evaluate them.

$$b(ns_j) = \begin{cases} \frac{pr_{ns_i}(ns_j)}{\sum_{ns_k \in mc^{ns_i}_{th}} pr_{ns_i}(ns_k)} & \text{if } ns_j \in mc^{ns_i}_{th} \\ 0 & \text{otherwise} \end{cases} \quad (2)$$

Table 1: Generation and Policy Computation

		Standard		MCS		Generation		
Ag	**B**	**Value**	**Time[s]**	**Value**	**Time[s]**	**DP**	**NDP**	**Time[s]**
Initial Step								
2	2	-4.89e-4± 1.37e-3	34± 1	-4.89e-4± 1.37e-3	31± 1	223	2128	18
2	3	-1.98e-4± 3.38e-4	1415± 142	-3.32e-5± 1.23e-4	1041± 97	781	28360	738
3	2	-4.11e-6± 8.42e-6	1155± 81	-4.28e-6± 1.11e-5	794± 61	1141	8445	250
Improvement Step								
2	2	-1.79e-20± 2.91e-21	43± 1	-1.79e-20± 2.91e-21	37± 1	223	2128	18
2	3	-2.73e-20± 1.24e-23	1184± 143	-2.73e-20± 1.23e-23	813± 50	781	28360	738
3	2	-1.44e-21± 7.58e-24	1172± 65	-1.44e-21± 7.58e-24	827± 35	1141	8445	250

We evaluated our approach on the sea-guard scenario presented in [2], where a set of agents must surveil a restricted area and intercept any unauthorized access before a deadline. Four norms, specified in CÒIR [2], are included in the scenario. Agents observe their locations and, by monitoring the area, increase their chances of detecting unauthorized boats. Table 1 presents results for different instantiations of the scenario, with varying number of agents (**Ag**) and unauthorized boats (**B**). **Generation** shows the state-space size before (**DP**) and after (**NDP**) the expansion and the execution time for the generation. The left part of the table compares MCS with heuristics that do not use the severity-based pruning. The table shows average (over 20 runs) time for the computation of a policy and the magnitude ($\rho = 10^5$) of their values. **Initial Step** compares MdpMCS with a standard Mdp-based heuristics and **Improvement Steps** uses the same policy to evaluate MixedMcs against a standard Dec-POMDP based heuristics on the same scenarios. We tested these results for significance and observed significant difference in the execution times but not in the values.

4. CONCLUSION

We have presented N-Dec-POMDP, a formalism for modelling collective decision making in the presence of complex norms of varying severity. We represent norm violations using a qualitative decision theory, and adapted PBPG to solve N-Dec-POMDPs. Our heuristic, MCS, increases PBPG scalability while preserving policy quality.

Acknowledgements

This research was sponsored by Selex ES.

REFERENCES

[1] B. Bonet and J. Pearl. Qualitative mdps and pomdps: An order-of-magnitude approximation. In *Proc. of the 18th conference on Uncertainty in artificial intelligence*, pages 61–68. Morgan Kaufmann Publishers Inc., 2002.

[2] L. Gasparini et al. CÒIR : Verifying normative specifications of complex systems. In *Proc. of the 18h International Workshop on Coordination, Organisations, Institutions and Norms*, 2015.

[3] F. Wu, S. Zilberstein, and X. Chen. Point-based policy generation for decentralized POMDPs. In *Proc. of the 9th International Conference on Autonomous Agents and Multiagent Systems*, pages 1307–1314, 2010.

Egalitarianism of Random Assignment Mechanisms (Extended Abstract)

Haris Aziz
Data61 and UNSW
Sydney, Australia
haris.aziz@nicta.com.au

Aris Filos-Ratsikas
University of Oxford
Oxford, UK
Aris.Filos-Ratsikas@cs.ox.ac.uk

Jiashu Chen
UNSW
Sydney, Australia
jiashu.chen@student.unsw.edu.au

Simon Mackenzie   Nicholas Mattei
Data61 and UNSW
Sydney, Australia
{simon.mackenzie,nicholas.mattei}@nicta.com.au

ABSTRACT

We consider the egalitarian welfare of random assignment mechanisms when agents have unrestricted cardinal utilities over the objects. We define and give bounds on how well different random assignment mechanisms approximate the *optimal egalitarian value (OEV)* and investigate the effect that different well-known properties like ordinality, envy-freeness, and truthfulness have on the achievable egalitarian value. Finally, we conduct detailed experiments analyzing the tradeoffs between efficiency with envy-freeness or truthfulness using two prominent random assignment mechanisms — random serial dictatorship and the probabilistic serial mechanism — for different classes of utility functions and distributions.

Keywords

Algorithms; Economics; Social Choice; Game Theory

1. INTRODUCTION

We explore the tradeoffs between fairness and efficiency for randomized mechanisms for the *assignment problem.* Specifically, we consider settings where n agents express preferences (cardinal or ordinal) over a set of m indivisible objects. The objective is to assign the objects to agents in a fair and mutually beneficial manner [1, 3]. This general setting has a number of important and significant applications including the assignment of tasks to cores in cloud computing, kidneys to patients in organ exchanges, runways to airplanes in transportation, and students to seats in schools. We consider the classic assumption that irrespective of whether agents are asked to report ordinal or cardinal preferences, they have an underlying utility structure, where each agent assigns real or cardinal valuations to the objects.

A well-established criterion for fairness is the Rawlsian concept of maximizing the happiness of the least satisfied agent [4]. Following the spirit of this idea, we quantify the fairness of an allocation in terms of its *egalitarian value*: the minimum ratio of the value of objects assigned to an agent to his total valuation for all the objects. The *optimal egalitarian value (OEV)* for a valuation profile of all agents is the best egalitarian value achievable over all assignments. The optimal egalitarian value is well-grounded for a number of reasons. If each agent has a total utility of one for the set of all objects (a standard assumption in the literature [5]), it is equivalent to the maximum egalitarian welfare. The OEV does not change if agents scale their relative values for the objects, unlike other metrics. Furthermore, if the egalitarian value of each agent is $1/n$, then the well-known proportionality requirement [4] is satisfied.

The egalitarian value is not the only criterion for desirable allocation mechanisms. Allocation mechanisms may have other goals and requirements such as envy-freeness or truthfulness. Crucially, both these properties are incompatible with optimizing the egalitarian value.Thus, it is natural to examine the *tradeoffs* between optimizing the egalitarian value and achieving other desirable properties. Evaluating these tradeoffs also motivates the study of how established mechanisms with other desiderata perform in terms of the egalitarian value. For a given mechanism J, we examine the approximation ratio $guar(J)$, which is the minimum ratio (among all valuation profiles) of the egalitarian value of an allocation returned by the mechanism to the OEV.

We study randomized assignment mechanisms for which achieving ex ante fairness is easier compared to deterministic mechanisms. Thus, to evaluate the performance of the mechanisms, we compare their egalitarian value with the OEV achieved by any randomized allocation. Note that computing the allocation with the optimal egalitarian value is an NP-hard problem when we restrict ourselves to deterministic allocations [4]. On the other hand, when we consider randomized allocations, the optimal egalitarian value can be computed in polynomial time via a linear program.

We give extra consideration to two randomized assignment mechanisms — *random serial dictatorship (RSD)* and *probabilistic serial (PS)*, which are probably the best-known and most-studied mechanisms in the random assignment literature [3].In RSD,[1] a permutation over the agents is se-

Appears in: *Proceedings of the 15th International Conference on Autonomous Agents and Multiagent Systems (AAMAS 2016), J. Thangarajah, K. Tuyls, C. Jonker, S. Marsella (eds.), May 9–13, 2016, Singapore.*

[1]The original definition of RSD is for n agents and n objects; the definition here is an adaptation for $n < m$.

lected uniformly at random and each agent in the permutation picks the most preferred m/n units of object that are not yet allocated [3]. In PS, each object is considered to have an infinitely divisible probability weight of one. To compute an allocation, agents simultaneously and with the same speed eat the probability weight of their most preferred object which has not been completely consumed. Once an object has been completely eaten by a subset of agents, each of these agents moves on to eat their next most preferred object that has not been completely eaten. The procedure terminates after all the objects have been eaten. The random allocation of an agent by PS is the amount of each object he has eaten [3]. PS satisfies stochastic dominance (SD) envy-freeness (envy-freeness with respect to all cardinal utilities consistent with the ordinal preferences). We also define a mechanism which we refer to as *Optimal Egalitarian and Envy-Free Mechanism (OEEF)*, which maximizes the egalitarian value of an allocation under the constraint that the allocation is envy-free. Allocations under this mechanism can be computed in polynomial time via linear programming since envy-freeness can be captured by linear constraints.

2. THEORETICAL RESULTS

We present novel theoretical and empirical results regarding fairness in randomized mechanisms. Our main theoretical contributions are: (1) For *any* SD envy-free mechanism J: $guar(J) = O(n^{-1})$. (2) For *any* envy-free mechanism J: $guar(J) = \Omega(n^{-1})$ and $guar(J) = O(n^{-1/5})$. (3) For *any* truthful-in-expectation mechanism J: $guar(J) = O(n^{-1/5})$. (4) For *any* ordinal mechanism J: $guar(J) = O(n^{-1})$.

The first three results apply to mechanisms that may be cardinal mechanisms. As a result of our general bounds, we also get asymptotically tight bounds of $\Theta(n^{-1})$ for RSD and PS. As a result of our general bounds for envy-free mechanisms, we obtain bounds for well-known envy-free mechanisms such as *competitive equilibrium with equal incomes (CEEI)* [7] and the *pseudo-market* mechanism [6]. Since a random assignment of indivisible objects can also be interpreted as a fractional assignment of divisible objects, *our results apply as well to fair allocation of divisible objects.* The constructions that provide the upper bounds for the *guar* values can be considered as extreme examples that may not be common in real-life scenarios.

3. EMPIRICAL RESULTS

In order to better understand how the mechanisms may perform in practice, we consider the approximation ratio achieved by RSD and PS. We also examine the effect of imposing the envy-freeness constraint on the overall allocation. To study this, we generate ordinal profiles via a Mallows model for different levels of dispersion ϕ from a common reference ranking of objects, assigning cardinal utilities via the Borda and exponential scoring functions. Sweeping ϕ from 0, where all agents have the same preference, to 1.0, where all preference orders are equally likely (the Impartial Culture), allows us to make statements regarding situations where agent preferences are more or less correlated.

Overall, there is a negligible difference between the minimum and average achievable approximation ratios for PS and RSD under Borda utilities. While PS performs slightly better than RSD when agents have more extreme (exponential) utilities, both mechanisms perform strictly worse when agents' valuations are more similar, as they are under Borda utilities. When we require envy-freeness (as in OEEF) with exponential utilities, as ϕ increases towards 1.0 (i.e. Impartial Culture) the achievable approximation ratio first decreases slightly and then increases. Hence, as agents value more disparate objects highly, satisfying envy-freeness does not impose as stiff a penalty on the achievable approximation ratio. In our experiments, the requirement of envy-freeness as a constraint in itself (as in the OEEF mechanism) does not have a large impact on the OEV. However, since PS returns an SD envy-free (envy-free for all cardinal utilities consistent with the ordinal preferences) allocation, its achievable approximation ratio is strictly less than OEEF.

4. CONCLUSION

We present theoretical and experimental results concerning how well different randomized mechanisms approximate the optimal egalitarian value. It has been well-known that egalitarianism can be incompatible with envy-free or truthfulness. In this paper, we quantified how much egalitarianism is affected by such properties. For details including full proofs and comprehensive coverage of the experiments, please see the our full technical report [2].

Acknowledgments

Data61 is funded by the Australian Government through the Department of Communications and the Australian Research Council through the ICT Centre of Excellence Program. Aris Filos-Ratsikas was supported by the ERC Advanced Grant 321171 (ALGAME).

REFERENCES

[1] H. Aziz, S. Gaspers, S. Mackenzie, and T. Walsh. Fair assignment of indivisible objects under ordinal preferences. In *Proc. of 13th AAMAS Conference*, pages 1305–1312, 2014.

[2] H. Aziz, J. Chen, A. Filos-Ratsikas, S. Mackenzie, and N. Mattei. Egalitarianism of random assignment mechanisms. Technical Report arXiv:1507.06827, arXiv.org, 2015.

[3] A. Bogomolnaia and H. Moulin. A new solution to the random assignment problem. *Journal of Economic Theory*, 100(2):295–328, 2001.

[4] S. Bouveret and M. Lemaître. Characterizing conflicts in fair division of indivisible goods using a scale of criteria. In *Proc. of 13th AAMAS Conference*, pages 1321–1328. IFAAMAS, 2014.

[5] A. Filos-Ratsikas, S. K. S. Frederiksen, and J. Zhang. Social welfare in one-sided matchings: Random priority and beyond. In *Proc. of 7th International Symposium on Algorithmic Game Theory (SAGT)*, pages 1–12, 2014.

[6] A. Hylland and R. Zeckhauser. The efficient allocation of individuals to positions. *The Journal of Political Economy*, 87(2):293–314, 1979.

[7] V. V. Vazirani. Combinatorial algorithms for market equilibria. In N. Nisan, T. Roughgarden, É. Tardos, and V. Vazirani, editors, *Algorithmic Game Theory*, chapter 5, pages 103–134. Cambridge University Press, 2007.

Strategy-Proof Data Auctions with Negative Externalities*
(Extended Abstract)

Xiang Wang†, Zhenzhe Zheng†, Fan Wu†, Xiaoju Dong†, Shaojie Tang§, and Guihai Chen†
†Shanghai Key Laboratory of Scalable Computing and Systems
Department of Computer Science and Engineering
Shanghai Jiao Tong University, China
§Department of Information Systems, University of Texas at Dallas, USA

ABSTRACT

Data has appeared to be a new kind of commodity with distinctive characteristics, which make it fundamentally different from physical goods as well as traditional digital goods. Therefore, new trading mechanisms for data need to be designed. In this paper, we model the data market as an auction with negative externalities, and design practical mechanisms for data trading. Specifically, we propose a family of Data auctIons in CompetiTive mArkets, namely DICTA. DICTA contains two mechanisms, including DICTA-FUL and DICTA-PAR. DICTA-FUL is a direct revelation auction mechanism in full competition markets, achieving strategy-proofness and optimal social welfare. In the partial competition markets, we show that the allocation problem is NP-hard. Therefore, we present an approximation algorithm for winner determination. By carefully integrating this approximation allocation algorithm and a charging scheme, DICTA-PAR achieves both strategy-proofness and d-approximation, where d is the maximum degree of the underlying undirected graph of the competition graph.

General Terms

Algorithms, Theory, Economics

Keywords

Data Market, Auction, Externality

1. INTRODUCTION

In recent years, data has become a new kind of commodity that can be traded on the Internet. For example, Xignite sells financial data, Gnip vends data from social networks, and Sabre trades consumers' booking and searching data on travel. To facilitate online data marketing, several plantforms have emerged, *e.g.*, Azure Data Marketplace, Infochimps, and Dataexchange. These centralized plantforms let data owners upload and sell their data, and let data consumers discover and purchase the data needed.

However, data as a kind of commodity is fundamentally different from physical goods, since data exhibits a distinctive characteristic, *i.e.*, once produced, the data can be duplicated for any number of copies with low or no cost. Digital goods are also in unlimited supply, but for traditional digital goods, such as electronic books, audio files, and pay-per-view movie, the negative externalities do not exist. However, data buyers may want to possess the data exclusively or to limit the distribution of data copies to their competitors. According to a recent survey on data market [3], out of all vendors in the research, 87% of offered data is in business contexts. Buyers, who are mostly companies, purchase their interested data in order to gain advantages in their business against their competitors. Such advantages can be undermined, if their competitors also get the same data, called negative externalities. Therefore, a buyer's valuation on the data not only depends on whether she can get the data set, but also on the data allocation to her competitors.

There indeed exist some works studying negative externalities in share-averse digital good auctions [1, 2]. However, there are huge differences between our auction model and theirs. A major difference is that, in share-adverse auctions, externality only depends on the number of buyers sharing the item, which is just like the complete competition scenario in our paper. However, in the partial competition scenario, each buyer can submit her set of competitors. Yet, another major difference is that they all assume the externality function being a common knowledge. However, in our model, the information about externality, specifically, tolerance bound and set of competitor, is private information.

In this paper, we conduct an in-depth study on designing strategy-proof data auctions. We propose a family of Data auctIons in CompetiTive mArkets (DICTA). DICTA contains two mechanisms, namely DICTA-FUL and DICTA-PAR. Specifically, DICTA-FUL is for an ideal but meaningful setting, *i.e.*, full competition markets, where any pair of buyers compete with each other. In this scenario, we propose a computationally tractable algorithm to calculate an optimal allocation, so that Vickrey-Clarke-Groves (VCG) mechanism can be applied to achieve both efficiency and strategy-proofness. We further consider a more practical

*This work was supported in part by the State Key Development Program for Basic Research of China (2012CB316201), in part by China NSF grant 61422208, 61472252, 61272443 and 61133006, in part by Shanghai Science and Technology fund 15220721300, in part by CCF-Tencent Open Fund, in part by the Scientific Research Foundation for the Returned Overseas Chinese Scholars, and in part by Jiangsu Future Network Research Project No. BY2013095-1-10. The opinions, findings, conclusions, and recommendations expressed in this paper are those of the authors and do not necessarily reflect the views of the funding agencies or the government.

Appears in: *Proceedings of the 15th International Conference on Autonomous Agents and Multiagent Systems (AAMAS 2016), J. Thangarajah, K. Tuyls, C. Jonker, S. Marsella (eds.), May 9–13, 2016, Singapore.*

scenario, *i.e.*, partial competition markets, in which each buyer just competes with a subset of the buyers instead of all. In this setting, the VCG mechanism is no longer appropriate due to computational intractability of searching for the optimal allocation. Therefore, we turn to design an approximation algorithm that finds a sub-optimal allocation, and incorporate it with a simple but effective pricing scheme to achieve strategy-proofness.

2. RESULTS

We consider a one shot sealed bid data auction with a trusted auctioneer and a set of n buyers $\mathbb{N} = \{1, 2, 3, \cdots, n\}$. There is a single set of data that can be duplicated to any number of copies, and then be sold to different interested buyers. Each buyer $i \in \mathbb{N}$ is interested in a single copy of the data set.

Each buyer has a set of business competitors $S_i \subseteq \mathbb{N} \setminus \{i\}$, and can only tolerate up to t_i competitors sharing the same set of data. If the buyer i wins the data set and there are no more than t_i competitors winning at the same time, then she has a valuation v_i on the data set. Otherwise, the valuation of the data set to the buyer i becomes 0. The triple $\theta_i = (S_i, t_i, v_i)$ is the private information of buyer i, and is widely known as type in the literature. In the data auction, each buyer i proposes a bid $b_i = (\hat{S}_i, \hat{t}_i, \hat{v}_i)$, which can differ from her type.

After collecting the bids from the buyers, the auctioneer constructs a directed *competition graph* G, in which each vertex represents a buyer, and each edge $(i, j), i, j \in \mathbb{N}$ indicates that buyer j is in buyer i's competitor set. Then, the auctioneer determines a set of winners $\mathbb{W} \subseteq \mathbb{N}$ and calculates a payment p_i for each winner.

2.1 FULL COMPETITION MARKETS

In this section, we present data auction mechanism DICTA-FUL for the full competition markets, in which any pair of buyers compete with each other, *i.e.*, the competition graph is a complete graph.

In this scenario, we can design a polynomial time algorithm to compute the optimal allocation, and thus can apply the celebrated Vickrey-Clarke-Groves (VCG) mechanism to achieve strategy-proofness. Therefore, we focus on algorithm design of allocation rule in this section.

In the data set allocation algorithm, we first sort all the buyers in a non-increasing order of their declared valuations, and denote the sorted list by Γ.

$$\Gamma : \hat{v}_1' \geq \hat{v}_2' \geq \cdots \geq \hat{v}_n'.$$

If there exists a tie, we break it arbitrarily. We note that $\hat{v}_i'$ may not be equal to $\hat{v}_i$ after sorting, and we will apply the allocation algorithm to the buyers according to the order in the sorted list.

Since any pair of buyers compete with each other in the full competition markets, for each winner, the number of her winning competitors is equal to the number of all the winners minus one. Thus, we can traverse every possible number of winners from 1 to n. For each number $m \in \{1, 2, \cdots, n\}$, we pick top m buyers whose tolerance bounds are no less than $m - 1$ from the sorted list Γ, and calculate their social welfare. If the number of qualified buyers is less than m, we simply select all of them without filling out the quota. Finally, we locate the m achieving the maximal social welfare, and output the corresponding set of winners as $\mathbb{W}$.

2.2 PARTIAL COMPETITION MARKETS

In this section, we present data auction mechanism DICTA-PAR for partial competition markets, in which each buyer competes with a subset of the buyers. The previously studied full competition markets are special cases of the partial competition markets.

Due to the hardness of allocating in partial competition markets, we here present our computationally efficient algorithm for data set allocation achieving d-approximation ratio.

Same as before, we first sort all the buyers in a non-increasing order of their declared valuations, and denote the sorted list by Γ. If there exists a tie, we break it arbitrarily.

Following the sequence specified in Γ, we visit each buyer i one by one, and check whether she can be allocated the data set without violating the following two constraints.

► The first constraint is that allocating the data set to buyer i should not breach any of the previously selected winners' tolerance bounds, *i.e.*,

$$\forall j \in \left\{k | k \in \mathbb{W} \wedge i \in \hat{S}_k'\right\}, \hat{t}_j' > \left|\hat{S}_j' \cap \mathbb{W}\right|.$$

► The second constraint is that the number of previously selected winning competitors of buyer i should not exceed her tolerance bound, *i.e.*,

$$\hat{t}_i' \geq \left|\hat{S}_i' \cap \mathbb{W}\right|.$$

If both the above constraints are satisfied, we allocate the data set to buyer i; Otherwise, we deny buyer i's bid.

Since DICTA-PAR follows a greedy allocation rule, we adopt the concept of critical bid to determine the payment for each of the buyers. Given the distinctive characteristics of the binary valuation function in our data auction, we achieve strategy-proofness by adopting critical bid.

3. CONCLUSIONS

In this paper, we have modeled the data trading market as an auction with negative externalities. We have studied two different but connected market scenarios, including full competition markets and partial competition markets. For full competition markets, we have designed DICTA-FUL to compute the optimal allocation, and integrate it with the celebrated VCG mechanism. Thus, DICTA-FUL achieves both strategy-proofness and optimal social welfare. For partial competition markets, we have shown that finding the optimal allocation is NP-hard, and also hard to approximate. In this scenario, we have designed DICTA-PAR, which is a combination of a d-approximation allocation algorithm and a carefully designed charging scheme.

REFERENCES

[1] J. Pei, D. Klabjan, and W. Xie. Approximations to auctions of digital goods with share-averse bidders. *Electronic Commerce Research and Applications*, 13(2):128–138, 2014.

[2] M. Salek and D. Kempe. Auctions for share-averse bidders. In *WINE*, volume 8, pages 609–620. Springer, 2008.

[3] F. Schomm, F. Stahl, and G. Vossen. Marketplaces for data: An initial survey. *ACM SIGMOD Record*, 42(1):15–26, 2013.

Expectedness in Human-Robot Collaboration

(Extended Abstract)

Mahni Shayganfar, Charles Rich, Candace L. Sidner
Worcester Polytechnic Institute
100 Institute Road
Worcester, Massachusetts
mshayganfar, rich, sidner@wpi.edu

ABSTRACT

We have investigated the mutual influences of affective and collaborative processes in a cognitive theory to support interaction between humans and robots or virtual agents. We build primarily on the *cognitive appraisal* theory of emotions and the *SharedPlans* theory of collaboration to investigate the structure, fundamental processes and functions of emotions in a collaboration. We have developed the *expectedness* appraisal algorithm as part of a new overall computational model. We have evaluated our implemented algorithm by conducting an online user study.

Categories and Subject Descriptors

I.2.11 [**Artificial Intelligence**]: Distributed Artificial Intelligence—*Intelligent agents*

General Terms

Algorithms, Design, Human Factors, Experimentation

Keywords

Algorithms; Appraisal; Human-Robot Collaboration

1. INTRODUCTION

This work is implemented as part of a larger effort to build robots capable of generating and recognizing emotions in order to be better collaborators. Our contribution is to ground general appraisal concepts in the specific context of collaboration. In this paper, we report on the specific problem of appraising the expectedness of events within a collaboration (see Figure 1). This work is part of the development of *Affective Motivational Collaboration Theory* [3] which is built on the foundations of the *SharedPlans* theory of collaboration [2] and the *cognitive appraisal* theory of emotions [1]. We believe appraisal plays a key role in collaboration due to its regulatory and evaluative nature. Also, collaboration induces some changes to underlying appraisal processes due to its unique nature. Yet, collaboration and emotion theories have never been combined, as they are in our work. Therefore, a systematic integration of collaboration theories and appraisal theory can help explain the underlying processes of collaboration structure.

Appears in: *Proceedings of the 15th International Conference on Autonomous Agents and Multiagent Systems (AAMAS 2016), J. Thangarajah, K. Tuyls, C. Jonker, S. Marsella (eds.), May 9–13, 2016, Singapore.*

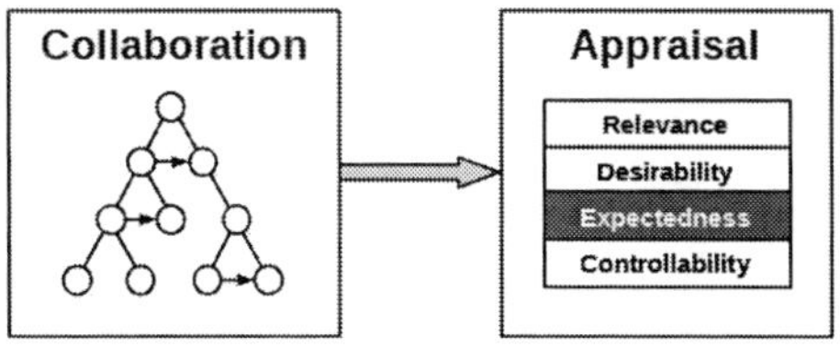

Figure 1: Influence of Collaboration on Appraisal (mechanisms in our framework).

2. COLLABORATION

The Collaboration mechanism constructs a hierarchy of goals associated with tasks in a hierarchical task network (see Figure 2), and maintains the constraints and other required details of the collaboration including the inputs and outputs of individual tasks, the preconditions, and the postconditions. Collaboration also monitors the focus of attention, which determines the salient objects at each point, and shifts the focus of attention during the interaction.

- *recognizeGoal(ε_t)* returns the unique goal to which the given event (e.g., action) directly contributes; it is only one goal since the robot can only do one primitive action at a time in our collaboration model. [1]
- *getTopLevelGoal(g_t)* returns g_t's top level goal.
- *isLive(g_t)* returns *true* if all the predecessors of g_t are ACHIEVED and all the preconditions are SATISFIED, i.e., PENDING or IN PROGRESS goals; otherwise returns *false*.
- *isFocusShift(g_t)* returns *true* if the given goal is not the previous focus (top of the stack); otherwise returns *false*.
- *isNecessaryFocusShift(g_t)* returns *true* if the status of the previous focus was ACHIEVED; otherwise returns *false*.
- *isPath(g_1, g_2)* returns *true* if there is a path between g_1 and g_2 in a plan tree structure; otherwise returns *false*.

3. EXPECTEDNESS IN COLLABORATION

Expectedness is the extent to which the truth value of a state could have been predicted from causal interpretation of an event. In the collaboration context the expectedness of an event evaluates the congruency of the event with respect to the existing knowledge about the shared goal. Thus, expectedness underlies a collaborative robot's attention. The collaboration mechanism uses expectedness to maintain the robot's attention and subsequently its mental state with respect to the shared goal. Reciprocally, the appraisal mechanism uses the underlying information of the collaboration structure to evaluate the expectedness of an event.

[1]Ambiguity introduces some extra complexities which are beyond scope of this paper.

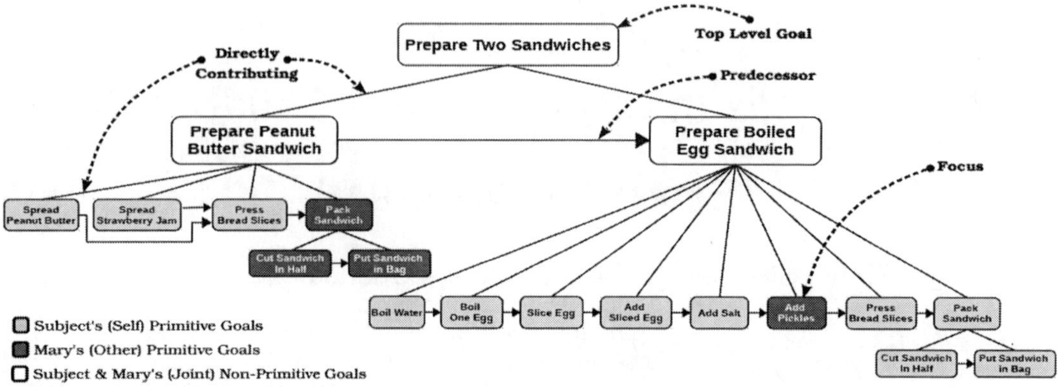

Figure 2: Example of collaboration structure (also used as task model for the evaluation).

In Algorithm 1 we provide the process of computing the expectedness based on the shared plan and status of the shared goal. The key point in this algorithm is the status of the current shared goal (g_t), which is associated with the event ε_t and its relationship with the top level goal (g_{top}).

The intuition captured here is that one expects the current goal to be finished before undertaking another activity, but the goals that can be the next focus of attention are also to be expected. Therefore, if the goal is live, the algorithm checks whether the goal has not changed, or whether the interpretation of the last event results in a necessary focus shift. Shifting the focus to a new goal is necessary when the former goal is achieved and a new goal is required. Consequently the new event is the MOST-EXPECTED one. However, even if the focus shift is not necessary, the new event can be considered as EXPECTED, since the corresponding goal is already live. For goals that have not yet been started (that is, are not live), the algorithm must determine how unexpected it would be to pursue one now; if the goal is at least in the plan, i.e., on the path to the top level goal, it is just UNEXPECTED while any others are MOST-UNEXPECTED.

Algorithm 1 (Expectedness)

function IsEventExpected(Event ε_t)
  $g_t \leftarrow recognizeGoal(\varepsilon_t)$
  $g_{top} \leftarrow getTopLevelGoal(g_t)$
  if ($isLive(g_t)$) **then**
    if ($\neg isFocusShift(g_t)$ **or**
      $isNeccessaryFocusShift(g_t)$) **then**
      return MOST-EXPECTED
    else
      return EXPECTED
  else
    if ($isPath(g_t, g_{top})$) **then**
      return UNEXPECTED
    else
      return MOST-UNEXPECTED

4. EVALUATION

We conducted a between-subject user study using an online crowdsourcing website – CrowdFlower[2] – to test our hypothesis that humans will provide similar answers to questions related to our expectedness algorithm. There were originally 40 subjects. We had a questionnaire with 12 questions (including 2 test questions). Test questions were included to check the sanity of the answers. We eliminated subjects providing wrong answers to our sanity questions, and subjects with answering times less than 2 minutes.

[2]http://www.crowdflower.com

To minimize the background knowledge necessary for our test subjects, we used a simple example of preparing a peanut butter and jelly sandwich, and a hard boiled egg sandwich. We provided textual and graphical instructions for the questionnaire; Figure 2 shows the corresponding task model which was also the input to our algorithm. The instructions presented a sequence of hypothetical collaborative tasks to be carried out by the test subject and an imaginary friend, Mary. We also provided a simple definition for the expectedness appraisal variable. The questions introduced specific situations related to the shared plan, which included blocked tasks and failure or achievement of a shared goal.

Each question had 3 answers; therefore, a random distribution would result in a ratio of 0.33 agreement with our algorithm's output. However, average results and standard deviation of the ratio of subjects answers agreeing with our algorithm's output was 0.785 and 0.120, respectively. Our results indicate that people largely performed as our hypothesis predicted. The p-value obtained based on a one-tailed z-test shows the probability of human subjects' answers being generated from a random set. The very small p-value (<0.001) indicates that the data set is not random; in fact, the high percentage of similarity confirms our hypothesis and shows that the algorithm can help us to model expectedness as an appraisal in collaboration.

5. CONCLUSION

According to the collaboration theories (e.g., SharedPlans), collaborators are required to commit to their shared plan or intentions to successfully collaborate and achieve a shared goal. This commitment requires them to appraise their environment based on the shared plan structure. In our next step, we want to test our appraisal algorithms and their influence on action selection during collaboration. This study will be conducted between a KUKA youbot and human subjects on a different task model.

REFERENCES

[1] J. Gratch and S. C. Marsella. A domain-independent framework for modeling emotion. *Cognitive Systems Research*, 5(4):269–306, 2004.

[2] B. J. Grosz and C. L. Sidner. Plans for discourse. In P. R. Cohen, J. Morgan, and M. E. Pollack, editors, *Intentions in Communication*, pages 417–444. MIT Press, Cambridge, MA, 1990.

[3] M. Shayganfar, C. Rich, and C. L. Sidner. An overview of affective motivational collaboration theory. In *Proceedings of AAAI Workshop on Symbiotic Cognitive Systems, Phoenix, Arizona*, 2016.

How Testable are BDI Agents? An Analysis of Branch Coverage

(Extended Abstract)

Michael Winikoff
Department of Information Science, University of Otago
Dunedin, New Zealand
michael.winikoff@otago.ac.nz

ABSTRACT

In this paper we extend our understanding of the feasibility of testing BDI agent programs by analysing their testability with respect to the *all edges* test adequacy criterion, and comparing with previous work that considered the *all paths* criterion. Our findings extend the earlier analysis with respect to the all paths criterion to give a more nuanced understanding of the difficulty of testing BDI agents.

Keywords

Verification and validation; agent-based systems

1. INTRODUCTION

When any software system is deployed, it is important to have assurance that it will function as required. Traditionally, this assurance is obtained by testing. However, there is a general intuition that agents exhibit behaviour that is complex. Given this complexity, a key question is whether agent systems are harder, and possibly even infeasible, to assure by testing.

The only work that we are aware of that considers the question of testability is the recent work by Winikoff & Cranefield [3, 4], which investigates the testability of Belief-Desire-Intention (BDI) agent programs with respect to the *all paths* test adequacy criterion. They concluded that BDI agent programs do indeed give rise to a very large number of possible paths (see left part of Table 1). They therefore conclude that whole BDI programs are likely to be infeasible to assure via testing. They also compared BDI programs with procedural programs, and found that BDI programs are *harder* to test than equivalently sized procedural programs. However, they do acknowledge that the all paths criterion is known to be overly conservative, i.e. it requires a very large number of tests. Indeed, the all paths criterion *subsumes* a wide range of other criteria, including all edges.

In this paper we consider the testability of BDI agent programs with respect to the *all edges* [2] test adequacy criterion. Whereas the all paths criterion used by Winikoff & Cranefield is conservative, the all edges criterion is optimistic: it is regarded as *"the generally accepted minimum"* [1]. The contribution of this paper is to extend the previous work to obtain a better understanding of, and a tighter bound on, the testability of BDI agent programs.

Appears in: *Proceedings of the 15th International Conference on Autonomous Agents and Multiagent Systems (AAMAS 2016), J. Thangarajah, K. Tuyls, C. Jonker, S. Marsella (eds.), May 9–13, 2016, Singapore.*

2. ALL-EDGE COVERAGE ANALYSIS

Given a program and a *test adequacy criterion* (e.g. *all paths*, *all edges*), we consider the testability of a program to be the smallest number of tests[1] that would be required to satisfy the criterion. The *all paths* criterion is satisfied iff the set of tests in the test suite T cover all *paths* in the program's control flow graph. The *all edges* criterion (also referred to as "branch coverage") is satisfied iff the set of paths in the test suite T covers all *edges* in the control-flow graph [2].

We define a BDI program P using the grammar:

$$P ::= a \mid g^{\{P^*\}} \mid P_1;P_2 \mid P_1 \triangleright P_2$$

where a is an action, $g^{\mathcal{P}}$ is a (sub-)goal with associated applicable plans $\mathcal{P} = \{P_1, \ldots, P_n\}$, $P_1; P_2$ is a sequence, and $P_1 \triangleright P_2$ represents a "backup plan": if P_1 succeeds, then nothing else is done (i.e. P_2 is ignored), but if P_1 fails, then P_2 is used.

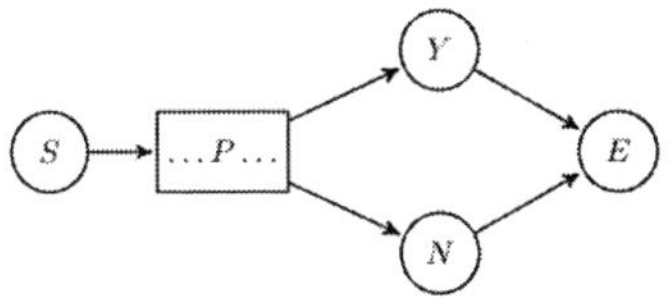

One important feature of BDI programs is that the execution of a BDI program (or sub-program) can either succeed or fail. A failed execution triggers failure handling. We represent this by mapping a program P to a graph that is reachable from the start node S, and that has *two* outgoing edges: to Y (corresponding to a successful execution) and to N (corresponding to a failed execution).

We have derived equations (details omitted, results in Figure 1) that calculate the smallest number of paths from S to E required such that all edges appear at least once in the set of paths. In order to do this, it turns out that we need to also capture how many of these paths correspond to successful executions (go via Y) and how many go via N. We define $\mathrm{p}(P)$ to be the number of paths required to cover all edges in the graph corresponding to program P. We also define $\mathrm{y}(P)$ (respectively $\mathrm{n}(P)$) to be the number of these paths that go via Y (respectively N). By construction we have that $\mathrm{p}(P) = \mathrm{y}(P) + \mathrm{n}(P)$.

3. RESULTS

We now use the derived equations (Figure 1) to compare the all edges criterion against the all paths criterion. We know that the all paths criterion requires more tests to be satisfied, but how many more? Since comparing (complex) formulae is not easy, we follow the approach of Winikoff & Cranefield, and instantiate the formulae with a range of plausible values, to obtain actual numbers that can

[1] A single test corresponds to a path through the program's control-flow graph from its starting node to its final node.

Parameters			Number of ...			All Paths		All Edges	All Edges
j	k	d	goals	plans	actions	$n^{\checkmark}(g)$	$n^{\times}(g)$	$\mathrm{p}(g)$	$\mathrm{q}(Q)$
2	2	3	21	42	62 (13)	6.33×10^{12}	1.82×10^{13}	78	62
3	3	3	91	273	363 (25)	1.02×10^{107}	2.56×10^{107}	2,961	363
2	3	4	259	518	776 (79)	1.82×10^{157}	7.23×10^{157}	808	776
3	4	3	157	471	627 (41)	3.13×10^{184}	7.82×10^{184}	4,767	627

Table 1: Comparison of All Paths and All Edges analyses. The first number under "actions" (e.g. 62) is the number of actions in the tree, the second (e.g. 13) is the number of actions in a single execution where no failures occur.

$$
\begin{aligned}
\mathrm{p}(a) &= 2 \quad \mathrm{y}(a) = 1 \quad \mathrm{n}(a) = 1\\
\mathrm{p}(P_1; P_2) &= \mathrm{n}(P_1) + \max(\mathrm{y}(P_1), \mathrm{p}(P_2))\\
\mathrm{y}(P_1; P_2) &= \mathrm{y}(P_2) + \epsilon_1\\
\mathrm{n}(P_1; P_2) &= \mathrm{n}(P_1) + \mathrm{n}(P_2) + \epsilon_2\\
&\quad \text{where } \epsilon_1 + \epsilon_2 = \max(0, \mathrm{y}(P_1) - \mathrm{p}(P_2))\\
\mathrm{p}(P_1 \rhd P_2) &= \mathrm{y}(P_1) + \max(\mathrm{n}(P_1), \mathrm{p}(P_2))\\
\mathrm{y}(P_1 \rhd P_2) &= \mathrm{y}(P_1) + \mathrm{y}(P_2) + \epsilon_3\\
\mathrm{n}(P_1 \rhd P_2) &= \mathrm{n}(P_2) + \epsilon_4\\
&\quad \text{where } \epsilon_3 + \epsilon_4 = \max(0, \mathrm{n}(P_1) - \mathrm{p}(P_2))\\
\mathrm{p}(g^{\{P\}}) &= \mathrm{p}(P)\\
\mathrm{y}(g^{\{P\}}) &= \mathrm{y}(P)\\
\mathrm{n}(g^{\{P\}}) &= \mathrm{n}(P)\\
\mathrm{p}(g^{\mathcal{P}}) &= \sum_{P_i \in \mathcal{P}} \mathrm{y}(P_i) + \max(\mathrm{n}(P_i), \mathrm{p}(g^{\mathcal{P} \setminus \{P_i\}}))\\
\mathrm{y}(g^{\mathcal{P}}) &= \sum_{P_i \in \mathcal{P}} \mathrm{y}(P_i) + \mathrm{y}(g^{\mathcal{P} \setminus \{P_i\}}) + \epsilon_i\\
\mathrm{n}(g^{\mathcal{P}}) &= \sum_{P_i \in \mathcal{P}} \mathrm{n}(g^{\mathcal{P} \setminus \{P_i\}}) + \epsilon_i'\\
&\quad \text{where } \epsilon_i + \epsilon_i' = \max(0, \mathrm{n}(P_i) - \mathrm{p}(g^{\mathcal{P} \setminus \{P_i\}}))
\end{aligned}
$$

Figure 1: Equations to calculate $\mathrm{p}(P)$, $\mathrm{y}(P)$ and $\mathrm{n}(P)$

be compared. We use the same scenarios (i.e. parameters) that they used, and compare "uniform" BDI programs [3, Section 4]

Table 1 contains the results for these illustrative comparison cases (ignore the rightmost column for now). The left part of the Table (Parameters, Number of goals, plans, and actions, and All Paths) are taken from the all paths analysis of Winikoff & Cranefield [3]. The right part (All Edges, $\mathrm{p}(g)$) is the new numbers from this work.

As expected, the number of tests required to adequately test a given BDI program P with respect to the all edges test adequacy criterion is lower than the number of tests required with respect to the all paths criterion. However, what is interesting is that the numbers are very much lower. Indeed, the number of tests required with respect to the all edges criterion is sufficiently small to be feasible. For instance, in the third case ($j = 2$, $k = 3$, $d = 4$) where the (uniform) BDI program has 259 goals and 518 plans, corresponding to a non-trivial agent program, the number of required test cases is less than 1000. However, it is worth emphasising that the all edges criterion, even for traditional software, is regarded as a *minimum*. Additionally, it can be argued that agents, which are situated in an environment that is typically non-episodic, might be more likely than traditional software to be affected by the history of their interaction with the environment [3, Section 1.1], and therefore the all paths criterion would be more appropriate.

We also considered the question of whether testing BDI agent programs is *harder*. We did this by comparing the number of tests required to adequately test a BDI agent program (with respect to the all edges criterion) with the number of tests required to adequately test an equivalent-sized (abstract) procedural program.

Following Winikoff & Cranefield [3] we define an abstract procedural program as $Q ::= s \mid Q + Q \mid Q; Q$ where the base case is a statement s, and a compound program can be a combination of programs either in sequence ($Q_1; Q_2$), or as an alternative choice ($Q_1 + Q_2$). We then consider how many tests (i.e. paths) are required to cover all edges in the graph corresponding to a procedural program Q. We denote this number by $\mathrm{q}(Q)$.

The rightmost column of Table 1 shows the number of tests (paths) required to test a procedural program Q of the same size[2] as the BDI program in question for that row. Although in some cases $\mathrm{p}(g)$ is quite close to $\mathrm{q}(Q)$ (e.g. 78 vs. 62 in the first row), in other cases there is a significant difference (e.g. 4767 vs. 627). In essence, the more plans there are per goal (j), the bigger the difference. Overall, we conclude that where goals have multiple plans available, then testing a BDI agent program is indeed harder than testing an equivalently-sized procedural program. This lends strength to the earlier result of Winikoff & Cranefield, who found that BDI agent programs were harder to test than equivalently sized procedural programs with respect to the all paths criterion.

In conclusion, we analysed the testability of BDI programs with respect to the all edges criterion. Our findings extend the earlier analysis with respect to the all paths criterion to give a more nuanced understanding of the difficulty of testing BDI agents. We conclude that the number of required tests to satisfy the all edges criterion is not just lower, as expected, but very much lower. We also conclude that, as is the case for all paths, testing BDI agents is harder than testing equivalently-sized procedural programs.

REFERENCES

[1] P. Jorgensen. *Software Testing: A Craftsman's Approach*. CRC Press, second edition edition, 2002.

[2] A. P. Mathur. *Foundations of Software Testing*. Pearson, 2008. ISBN 978-81-317-1660-1.

[3] M. Winikoff and S. Cranefield. On the testability of BDI agent systems. *Journal of Artificial Intelligence Research (JAIR)*, 51:71–131, 2014.

[4] M. Winikoff and S. Cranefield. On the testability of BDI agent systems (extended abstract). In *Journal track of the International Joint Conference on Artificial Intelligence (IJCAI)*, pages 4217–4221, 2015.

[5] H. Zhu, P. A. V. Hall, and J. H. R. May. Software unit test coverage and adequacy. *ACM Computing Surveys*, 29(4):366–427, Dec. 1997.

[2] i.e. number of actions in the BDI program = number of statements in the procedural program

Simulation of Agent-rescuer Behaviour in Emergency Based on Modified Fuzzy Clustering

(Extended Abstract)

Armen L. Beklaryan and Andranik S. Akopov
National Research University Higher School of Economics
20 Myasnitskaya str., Moscow, 101000, Russian Federation
{aakopov, abeklaryan}@hse.ru

ABSTRACT

Although there are various methods and models of agent's behaviour in emergencies, the problem of the synthesis of the optimal control systems, which can support best evolution strategies for agent-rescuers in emergency characterized by a high level of an uncertainty, is still needed. We developed the simulation of agent-rescuers behaviour in emergencies and proposed an effective modified fuzzy procedure for dynamical clustering of the crowd in order to define the optimal values of control parameters for agent-rescuers (such as speed of agents, time of waiting, distribution types of agents-rescuers between crowd clusters, etc.).

Categories and Subject Descriptors

I.2.8 [**Artificial Intelligence**]: Problem Solving, Control Methods, and Search—*dynamic programming*; I.2.11 [**Artificial Intelligence**]: Distributed Artificial Intelligence—*intelligent agents, multiagent systems*

General Terms

Algorithms, Experimentation

Keywords

intelligent agents; fuzzy means clustering; crowd behavior

1. INTRODUCTION

In recent years, there has been a line of research (e.g., [1, 2, 5]) on human crowd behaviour in emergencies. Many works focused on the problem of the psychology and social aspects of the human crowd behaviour. For instance, in the pioneer work [6] the reasons of the formation and distribution of a human panic are described in detail. Many studies are based on the hypothesis that the personal behaviour significantly differs from the human behaviour in a crowd [7] because of such effects as the "crowd crash" and the "crowd turbulence" [1] which can be caused by a panic, rumors and the reaction of the growth of crowd density. There has been a line of research of Dirk Helbing [5, 6, 7] in which the author investigated the pedestrian crowds in normal and evacuation situations. Helbing in his work [6], published in Nature, firstly reconstructed some important phenomenons such as formation of traffic jams, involvement of new people in a panic and others with the help of mathematical modeling. Further, the discrete choice models of pedestrian walking behavior based on Helbing's results was created and described in the work [3].

This research focused on the problem of designing the crowd simulation system for agent-rescuers, based on the suggested modified fuzzy clustering algorithm of the crowd dynamics in emergencies, estimating of the probability of best evacuation routings, and forming optimal dynamics of agent-rescuers (number of agents, speed, routes, etc.).

2. SIMULATION OF AGENT BEHAVIOUR

The developed simulation model is based on the earlier developed phenomenological model of human crowd behaviour suggested in works [1, 2]. The dynamics of agent-rescuers are described by the systems of ordinary differential equations for each agent-rescuer and for each usual agent with simulating of the attracting process of usual agents toward agent-rescuers and evacuation exits. The model was implemented in the *AnyLogic* simulation system.

The main problem is trying to maximize the number of evacuated agents. To reach this purpose, optimal control parameters (waiting times, number of agent-rescuers, speeds of agent-rescuers, and types of distributions between crowd clusters) should be set.

PROBLEM A. *The need to maximize the number of evacuated agents through the set of control parameters* $\{K(t), s_k(t), \tau_k(t), g_c\}$*:*

$$\max_{\{K(t),s_k(t),\tau_k(t),g_c\}} \left[\sum_{t=t_0+1}^{t_0+T_{ev}} \sum_{i=1}^{I(t)} st_i(t) - st_i(t-1) \right]$$

under different constraints having a clear sense.

Here, t – the simulation time, $t \in [t_0, t_0 + T_{ev}]$ (t_0 – the start time); T_{ev} – the limit of evacuation time); $i = \overline{1..I(t)}$ – indexes of usual agents; $st_i(t) \in \{0, 1\}$ – the status of the ith-agent ($st_i(t) = 1$ – the ith-agent is evacuated, else $st_i(t) = 0$); $K(t)$ – the number of agent-rescuers, which are required for the evacuation of agents, $\bar{K}$ – the maximum number of agent-rescuers in the system (resource limit); $g_c \in \{1, 2, 3\}$ – the control parameter, which defines matching between the cth-crowd cluster and the appropriate group clusters having the fixed distribution type (one of three possible) for the

Appears in: *Proceedings of the 15th International Conference on Autonomous Agents and Multiagent Systems (AAMAS 2016), J. Thangarajah, K. Tuyls, C. Jonker, S. Marsella (eds.), May 9–13, 2016, Singapore.*

destination of agent-rescuers as well as the strategy of the distribution of agent-rescuers between clusters; τ_k – waiting time of the kth-agent-rescuers in crowd clusters and on exits.

3. MODIFIED FUZZY CLUSTERING

It should be noted that the convergence of the fuzzy C-means clustering algorithm was firstly showen in the work [4]. Additional internal restrictions and parameters were included into the standard fuzzy C-means procedure in order to take into account natural restrictions for the evacuation such as wall, obstacles, etc., which can isolate individuals from their clusters. Also, an initial partition matrix, as opposed to the standard implementation, is chosen not by chance, but based on the modification results of the agglomerative algorithm with Ward's distance.

The developed modified fuzzy clustering algorithm is implemented for each agent. This algorithm is used for recognition of the centers of clusters of crowd by agent-rescuers for the purpose of increase of efficiency of procedure of evacuation through the distribution of agent-rescuer between crowd clusters. The algorithm aims to minimize an objective function:

$$J = \sum_{c=1}^{C(t)} \sum_{i \in I(t)} (m_{ci})^w e^{B\frac{\alpha_{ci}}{\pi}} d(v_c, x_i),$$

where $c = \overline{1..C(t)}$ – indexes of clusters; m_{ci} – degree of belonging of ith-agent to c^{th}-cluster; w – fuzzifier; v_c – c^{th}-cluster center coordinate; x_i – i^{th}-agent coordinate; α_{ci} – angle between the direction of ith-agent movement and the direction from the ith-agent to the cth-cluster center; B – weight coefficient.

4. RESULTS OF THE SIMULATION

The results of the simulation are represented in the Figure 1 for the case study of emergency in the Domodedovo airport (Moscow, 2011 year). The *genetic algorithm* was applied for solving the main optimization problem. The combined chart reflects the dynamics of agent-rescuers and evacuated agents during the evacuation time, as well as the dynamics of crowd clusters, taking into account the sequence of their disappearing. It should be noted that the *verification of the developed simulation of agent-rescuers behaviour* was completed with the help of *video-data*, which were obtained from the Domodedovo airport after the emergency.

5. CONCLUSIONS

The simulation of agent-rescuers behaviour in emergencies using the developed fuzzy clustering algorithm and the suggested procedure of bypassing around dynamical obstacles for the optimal control of agent-rescuers behaviour was represented. The approach allows increasing the number of evacuated agents with the help of limited number of agent-rescuers in the condition of an appearance of dynamical obstacles.

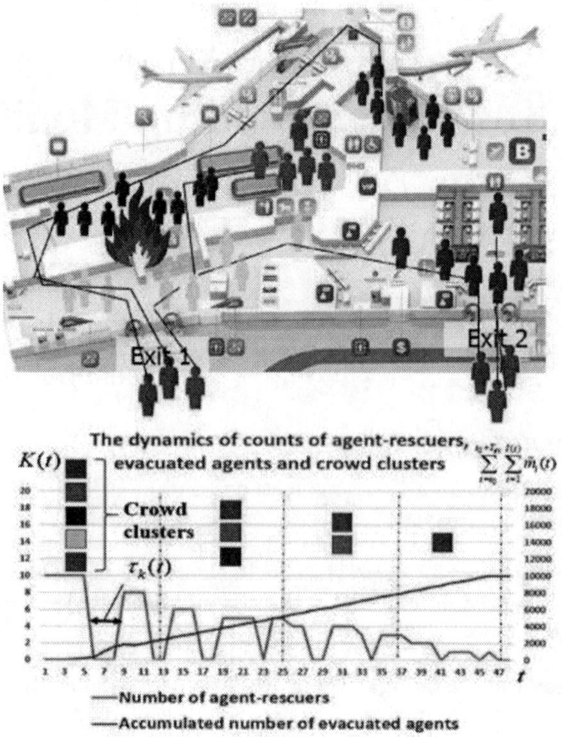

Figure 1: The results of the simulation and clustering.

Acknowledgments

The reported study was partially supported by RFBR, research project No. 15-37-20265 mol_a_ved.

REFERENCES

[1] A. S. Akopov and L. A. Beklaryan. Simulation of human crowd behavior in extreme situations. *International Journal of Pure and Applied Mathematics*, 79(1):121–138, 2012.

[2] A. S. Akopov and L. A. Beklaryan. An agent model of crowd behavior in emergencies. *Automation and Remote Control*, 76(10):1817–1827, 2015.

[3] G. Antonini, M. Bierlaire, and M. Weber. Discrete choice models of pedestrian walking behavior. *Transportation Research Part B*, 40(8):667–687, 2006.

[4] J. C. Bezdek. *Pattern Recognition with Fuzzy Objective Function Algorithms.* Kluwer Academic Publishers, Norwell, Mass., 1981.

[5] D. Helbing, I. J. Farkas, P. Molnar, and T. Vicsek. Simulation of pedestrian crowds in normal and evacuation situations. *Pedestrian and evacuation dynamics*, 21(2):21–58, 2002.

[6] D. Helbing, I. J. Farkas, and T. Vicsek. Simulating dynamical features of escape panic. *Nature*, (407):487–490, 2000.

[7] D. Helbing, A. Johansson, and H. Z. Al-Abideen. Dynamics of crowd disasters: An empirical study. *Physical review E*, 75(4):046109–1–046109–7, 2007.

Digital Good Exchange

(Extended Abstract)

Wenyi Fang, Pingzhong Tang, and Song Zuo
Institute for Interdisciplinary Information Sciences
Tsinghua University, Beijing, China
{fwy13@mails., kenshin@, zuos13@mails.}tsinghua.edu.cn

ABSTRACT

Over the past decade, computer-automated barter exchange has become one of the most successful applications at the intersection of AI and economics. Standard exchange models, such as house allocation and kidney exchange cannot be applied to an emerging industrial application, coined *digital good exchange*, where an agent still possesses her initial endowment after exchanging with others. However, her valuation toward her endowment decreases as it is possessed by more agents.

We put forward game theoretical models tailored for digital good exchange. In the first part of the paper, we first consider a natural class of games where agents can choose either a subset of other participants' items or no participation at all. It turns out that this class of games can be modeled as a variant of congestion games. We prove that it is in general NP-complete to determine whether there exists a non-trivial pure Nash equilibrium where at least some agent chooses a nonempty subset of items. However, we show that there exist non-trivial Pure Nash equilibria for subsets of games and put forward efficient algorithms to find such equilibria.

In the second part of the paper, we investigate digital good exchange from a mechanism design perspective. We ask if there is a truthful mechanism in this setting that can achieve good social welfare guarantee. To this end, we design a randomized fixed-price-exchange mechanism that is individually rational and truthful, and for two-player case yields a tight log-approximation with respect to any individually rational allocation.

Keywords

Barter Exchange; Digital Good Exchange; Congestion Games; Mechanism Design

1. INTRODUCTION

In the stylized model of barter exchanges, agents enter the exchange with some endowments and exchange their endowments for better allocations without monetary transfers. However, standard models of barter exchanges [5, 1, 3, 4] have certain limitations. For one, agents lose ownerships of their endowments once the exchange takes place. This is not the case with exchanges of digital goods, in which case agents still possess one copy of their endowments even though the exchange has taken place. In addition, agents have negative externality for other agents to own their items, namely, an agent's valuation towards her endowment decreases as more agents possess her item. A representative type of digital good is data. The owner can produce as many copies of data as possible, however, it is commonly believed that her value of data decreases as it is owned by more agents, due to the fact that her market power on possessing data decreases as it is shared with more agents.

Over the past few years, digital good exchange has become a common industrial practice, as a part of the *sharing economy tsunami*. As Bloomberg reports, "A market for data swaps is rapidly emerging. Factual, a Los Angeles-based startup, has put together a database that houses location data and details on retailers and restaurants. Access to the database costs companies money, but they can accrue discounts by agreeing to contribute some of their own information."[1] Another successful example of data exchange is `www.datatang.com`, which encourages individual data owners to share their data in a centralized database and in return awards them a discount, or limited-time free access for obtaining other data sets in their wish lists.

To our best knowledge, there has been no theoretical model tailored for this domain. In this paper, we put forward several game-theoretical models for digital good exchange and investigate their properties. Our goal is to model and analyze existing digital exchange mechanisms, as well as to provide theoretical and practical guidelines for designing new mechanisms in this domain.

2. MODEL

Let $A = \{a_1, \ldots, a_n\}$ be a set of n agents, and $D = \{d_1, \ldots, d_n\}$ be the corresponding set of digital goods (or simply goods), where d_i is initially owned by agent a_i.

Let $\mathbf{x}_j = (x_{1j}, ..., x_{nj}) \in \{0, 1\}^n$ be a deterministic allocation of good d_j over all agents and $v_{ij}(\mathbf{x}_j)$ be the valuation of agent a_i over allocation $\mathbf{x}_j$, in this way, we let agent a_i's valuation over good d_j explicitly depend on the allocation of d_j. All agents have *additive, quasi-linear utility* functions,

$$u_i = \sum_{j \in [n]} v_{ij}(\mathbf{x}_j) - p_i, \ \forall i \in [n],$$

where p_i is the monetary transfer from agent a_i to anybody else. In this paper, we consider barter exchanges, so $p_i = 0$.

[1] `http://www.bloomberg.com/bw/articles/2012-11-15/data-bartering-is-everywhere`

Appears in: *Proceedings of the 15th International Conference on Autonomous Agents and Multiagent Systems (AAMAS 2016), J. Thangarajah, K. Tuyls, C. Jonker, S. Marsella (eds.), May 9–13, 2016, Singapore.*

As mentioned, agents never lose ownerships of their endowments, so the feasibility constraint, $x_{ii} = 1$, is imposed on each deterministic allocation.

Besides, an agent's valuation toward a digital good decreases as it is owned by more agents. Let $\mathsf{Supp}(\mathbf{x}_j) = \{i|x_{ij} = 1\}$. The valuation functions satisfy the following

$$\begin{cases} v_{ij}(\mathbf{x}_j) = 0, & i \notin \mathsf{Supp}(\mathbf{x}_j) \\ v_{ij}(\mathbf{x}_j) \geq v_{ij}(\mathbf{x}'_j), & i \in \mathsf{Supp}(\mathbf{x}_j) \subseteq \mathsf{Supp}(\mathbf{x}'_j) \end{cases}.$$

3. DIGITAL EXCHANGE GAME

The following game captures the interesting feature of the data exchange websites mentioned in the introduction: agents share their own goods to exchange for the rights to download others' data.

DEFINITION 1 (DIGITAL EXCHANGE GAME). *The game $G = (A, \mathcal{S}, u)$ is defined as follows,*

- *The* ***set of actions*** *S_i of agent a_i is to either choose a subset S_i (must include d_i) of the goods, or exit this game (denoted by $S_i = \perp$). The goods allocated to a_i, is either the intersection of S_i and the goods whose owners do not exit this game, if $S_i \neq \perp$; or $\{d_i\}$, otherwise.*
- *The* ***utility function*** *u_i of agent a_i is the sum of the values from the allocation of each item, $u_i(\mathbf{x}) = \sum_j v_{ij}(\mathbf{x}_j)$, where $\mathbf{x}$ is the allocation induced by the game play.*

The above game has an interesting congestion-game interpretation, so we coin this game as "player-specific congestion game with endowments".

3.1 The Pure Nash Equilibria

First of all, non-participation for all agents forms a PNE. However, determining whether there is a non-trivial PNE, where at least one agent participates, is hard.

CLAIM 1. *The game always has a trivial PNE, where each $S_i = \perp$. Meanwhile, $S_i = A$ always weakly dominates any other subsets (except for $\perp$).*

THEOREM 1. *Given an instance of the digital exchange game, determining if there is a non-trivial PNE is NP-complete.*

COROLLARY 1. *Even if each agent is limited to choosing at most two goods, or each agent has strictly positive valuation over goods, the determination problem is still NP-hard.*

3.2 Two Cases for Efficiently Computable PNEs

We derive positive results for two special cases: ordered agents and single-minded agents with unit demand.

DEFINITION 2 (ORDERED AGENTS). *The agents in A are ordered under game G, if there is an order $a_1, \ldots, a_n$, such that for $i < j$, and any PNE S where $S_i = \perp$ and $S_j \neq \perp$, then $S^{(i,j)}$ is also a PNE, where $S^{(i,j)}$ is obtained by switching each appearance of i and j.*

THEOREM 2. *If the agents are ordered under game G, then we can find a non-trivial PNE in poly-time. In particular, if all the agents have identical valuation functions, we can find a non-trivial PNE in poly-time.*

For single-minded agents with unit demand, where each agent has positive valuation towards exactly one item besides its own endowment, we consider *efficient* PNEs.

We use $\delta(i) = j$ for agent a_i desires good d_j. Then *efficient* means that in the PNE, $S = (S_1, \ldots, S_n)$,

$$\forall a_i \in A, \delta(i) = j, \ S_i \in \{\{a_i, a_j\}, \{a_i\}, \perp\},$$

and at least one exchange is performed.

THEOREM 3. *For single-minded agents with unit demand case, there is a dynamic program based algorithm to find or prove non-existence of* efficient *PNEs in poly-time.*

4. MECHANISM DESIGN

We put forward a direct mechanism coined "Randomized FPE Mechanism" (RFPE), which is the expectation of parametric *fixed-price-exchange* (FPE) mechanisms with parameters drawn from some pre-specified distribution.

The FPE mechanism is a simplified version of *fixed-price-trading* [2]. In our case, each agent only has one type of endowment, and the exchange is conducted according to one single fixed exchange rate (fixed-price). The exchange amount is determined in an incentive compatible (utility maximizing) way.

MECHANISM 1 (RANDOMIZED FPE MECHANISM). *Given distribution $\mathcal{F}$ of fixed-price ($\mathcal{F}$ specified prior to the mechanism) the randomized FPE mechanism is defined as follows,*

$$\mathsf{RFPE}^{\mathcal{F}}(\{\nu_{ij}\}_{i,j=1}^{n}) = \mathbf{E}_{\Pi \sim \mathcal{F}} \mathsf{FPE}^{\Pi}(\{\nu_{ij}\}_{i,j=1}^{n}).$$

THEOREM 4. *Any RFPE mechanism is IC and IR.*

Particularly, for two-agent case, there is a tight bound of the social welfare approximation ratio against the optimal IR allocation.

Acknowledgments

This work was supported by the National Basic Research Program of China Grant 2011CBA00300, 2011CBA00301, the Natural Science Foundation of China Grant 61033001, 61361136003, 61303077, 61561146398, a Tsinghua Initiative Scientific Research Grant and a China Youth 1000-talent program.

REFERENCES

[1] D. J. Abraham, A. Blum, and T. Sandholm. Clearing algorithms for barter exchange markets: Enabling nationwide kidney exchanges. In *Proceedings of the 8th ACM conference on Electronic commerce*, pages 295–304. ACM, 2007.

[2] S. Barberà and M. O. Jackson. Strategy-proof exchange. *Econometrica: Journal of the Econometric Society*, pages 51–87, 1995.

[3] Y. Liu, P. Tang, and W. Fang. Internally stable matchings and exchanges. In *AAAI Conference on Artificial Intelligence (AAAI)*, pages 1433–1439, 2014.

[4] S. Luo and P. Tang. Mechanism design and implementation for lung exchange. In *Proceedings of the International Joint Conference on Artificial Intelligence (IJCAI)*, pages 209–215, 2015.

[5] A. E. Roth, T. Sönmez, and M. Ünver. Kidney exchange. *The Quarterly Journal of Economics*, 119(2):457–488, 2004.

Distributed Search for Pure Nash Equilibria in Graphical Games

(Extended Abstract)

Omer Litov
Department of Computer Science
Ben-Gurion University of the Negev
Beer-Sheva, 84-105, Israel
litov@cs.bgu.ac.il

Amnon Meisels
Department of Computer Science
Ben-Gurion University of the Negev
Beer-Sheva, 84-105, Israel
am@cs.bgu.ac.il

ABSTRACT

Graphical games introduce a compact representation, where agents' outcomes depend only on their neighbors. A distributed search algorithm for pure Nash equilibria of graphical games is presented. The algorithm uses the analogy of graphical games with asymmetric distributed constraints optimization problems (ADCOPs). The proposed algorithm includes three components - an admissible pruning heuristic; a back-checking mechanism; and a pseudo tree representation of the game. An experimental evaluation of the components of the proposed search algorithm is presented for randomly generated networks of multiple agents. The major speedup over a naive search algorithm is shown to arise from the use of a pseudo tree representation. A simple assessment method of the privacy loss due to back-checking is presented and is shown to result in a tradeoff between the performance of the complete algorithm and its privacy loss.

Categories and Subject Descriptors

I.2.11 [**Distributed artificial intelligence**]: Multi-agent systems

General Terms

Algorithms

Keywords

Distributed problem solving; DCOP; Nash equilibrium; Privacy

1. INTRODUCTION

In many Multi Agent situations, agents interact with one another to achieve some goal. For cooperative agents, this goal may be a global objective such as the minimization of total cost in distributed constraints reasoning. For selfish agents, attempting to maximize their personal gains, Game Theory predicts that the outcome will be a stable state (e.g., an equilibrium) from which every agent will not wish to deviate.This notion of stability is a fundamental concept in game theory and has been a major focus of work in the field of Multi Agent Systems.

Graphical Games have been proposed as a compact representation of normal form games played over a graph [3]. It is a model that exploits the locality of interactions between agents and enables one to specify payoffs in terms of neighbors rather than in terms of the entire population of agents. Several algorithms have been proposed for finding an approximate **mixed** strategy equilibrium of graphical games, the most recent being ANT [2].

In a pure Nash equilibrium (PNE), which may not always exist, every agent chooses a single pure strategy. It is a clear solution concept for a multi-agent situation since it is deterministic in nature (unlike mixed Nash equilibria in which every agent is eventually required to draw its selected strategy from the probability distribution of its mixed strategy). Centralized solvers have been proposed (Gambit [4] and more recently ConGa [6]), although centralized algorithms may not be appropriate when privacy of gains is an issue, since it requires complete revelation of information from all of the agents.

The present paper focuses on finding Pure Nash Equilibria in a distributed environment and is based on modeling graphical games as (Asymmetric) Distributed Constraints Optimization Problems (DCOPs) [5]. Several tools for finding stable points are presented and are then combined into a complete algorithm. The model uses Asymmetric DCOPs (ADCOPs) [1], which are an extension of standard DCOPs. The proposed search algorithms for finding a PNE combines two well known DCOP techniques – a back checking procedure and a pseudo-tree.

An extensive experimental evaluation (abbreviately shown in figure 1) shows the improvement in performance of both run-time and network load, over a distributed version of the Gambit solver and over any of the algorithmic tools separately. An upper bound on the loss of privacy is calculated, to present the tradeoff between performance and privacy conservation. An improvement in performance of a factor 10 in speedup in exchange for an upper bound of 7% loss of privacy.

The next section describes the main concepts of the proposed algorithm.

2. FINDING A PURE NASH EQUILIBRIUM

Every graphical game with a finite set of strategies can be represented as an ADCOP in the following way: The set of players is represented by the set of agents $\mathcal{A}$, where each agent A_i has exactly one variable X_i. The set of strategies of A_i is represented by its domain D_i. The cost/payoff of every interaction between players in a given neighborhood (i.e., connected by edges in the graph of the game) is represented as an asymmetric constraint. Standard ADCOP algorithms search for the Social Welfare solution [1]. The present study focuses on search for pure Nash equilibria (PNEs), which will be addressed next.

Appears in: *Proceedings of the 15th International Conference on Autonomous Agents and Multiagent Systems (AAMAS 2016), J. Thangarajah, K. Tuyls, C. Jonker, S. Marsella (eds.), May 9–13, 2016, Singapore.*

2.1 Back Checking algorithm

For simplicity, we start by describing a partial algorithm, which uses a back checking procedure, without the structure of a pseudo-tree. The proposed back checking algorithm is based on distributed backtracking search, and uses the following messages.

1. **CPA** - Current Partial Assignment.
2. **Backtrack**
3. **Check_PNE** - A request to check whether the value assignment $v_{i_k} \in CPA$ has the potential to be a best response.
4. **Response** - A response to a **Check_PNE** message.

The algorithm has each agent assign a value synchronously on the **CPA** message according to a predefined complete order of all the agents. After agent A_i assigns a value to its variable, and before it sends a **CPA** message to the next agent, it sends a **Check_PNE** message to every constrained agent before it. When an agent that is constrained with A_i receives a **Check_PNE** message it will check for the pruning criteria according to the heuristic defined below. Next, it will send back a **Response** message that states whether the current CPA can be continued. Only when agent A_i receives back all of the **Response** messages from its constrained predecessors it will proceed, either by pruning its value or by sending forward a **CPA**. When the last agent has received a positive **Response** message from all of its constrained ancestor a Pure Nash Equilibrium solution has been reached.

We must now define the method to identify obsolete value assignments, which can be pruned. We will define the following two heuristics.

$$LB(v_{i_k}) = CurrentCost(CPA, v_{i_k}) + \sum_{A_j \notin CPA} \min_{v_{j_q} \in D_j} Cost_i(v_{i_k}, v_{j_q}) \quad (1)$$

$$UB(v_{i_k}) = CurrentCost(CPA, v_{i_k}) + \sum_{A_j \notin CPA} \max_{v_{j_q} \in D_j} Cost_i(v_{i_k}, v_{j_q}) \quad (2)$$

where $Cost_i(v_{i_k}, v_{j_q})$ is defined to be the cost for agent A_i for the constraint between A_i's value v_{i_k} and A_j's value v_{j_q}, and $CurrentCost(CPA, v_{i_k}) = \sum_{v_j \in CPA} Cost_i(v_{i_k}, v_j)$.

It is possible to see that $LB(v_{i_k})$ (and $UB(v_{i_k})$) is a lower bound (and upper bound) on the cost of agent A_i for assigning v_{i_k}, respectively. It follows that if $\exists v_{i_q} \neq v_{i_k} : UB(v_{i_q}) < LB(v_{i_k})$, then the value v_{i_k} can be pruned from the search. This check is performed in two places: when an agent receives the **CPA** and attempt to assign a new value, and when an agent receives a **Check_PNE** (in order to inform the sending agent to prune its own value).

2.2 Using a Pseudo-Tree

The main component of the proposed search algorithm for a PNE uses a very well known tool for DCOP search algorithms – a Pseudo-Tree [5]. The pseudo-tree defines a partial order over the agents (unlike the total order used before), starting from the root down to the leafs. When an agent with more than one child needs to send forward a **CPA**, it sends it concurrently to every one of its children. Each leaf acts as a last agent in its branch and since there are multiple leaves the possible solutions must propagate up the tree to the root. This presents a problem for agents with more than one child. An agent may receive several **Check_PNE** messages from each sub-tree, and the solution may be any combination of the partial assignments of those messages.

In order to solve the problem described above one needs to define a new type of message – **Sub_Problem_PNE**. When a leaf agent receives a positive **Response** from all of its constrained agents it sends a **Sub_Problem_PNE** message to $Splitter(A_i)$. We define the $Splitter(A_i)$ agent to be the closest ancestor of agent A_i who has more than one child. $Branch(A_i)$ is defined to be the set of ancestors of agent A_i up to (and excluding) the $Splitter(A_i)$ agent. The **Sub_Problem_PNE** message contains a Partial Assignment PA. The assignment of every agent $A_j \in Branch(A_i)$ in PA is a best response. This is due to the fact that all agents sent a positive **Response** to the leaf for the given PA, in which all of their constrained agents are already assigned. The leaf agent continues the search, because it is not waiting for any response to that message. Agent A_i tries to combine the partial assignment from the **Sub_Problem_PNE** with every other partial assignment received from the other sub-trees, and check whether any one of the combinations is a possible PNE. For any Partial Assignment PA constructed from a combination of assignments received by **Sub_Problem_PNE** messages, if value assignment of A_i is a best response then PA may possibly be extended into a PNE for the entire problem and thus should be propagated up the tree. Agent A_i propagates every such PA by sending every agent $A_j \in Branch(A_i)$ a **Check_PNE** message and if all **Responses** are positive it then sends a **Sub_Problem_PNE** to $Splitter(i)$.

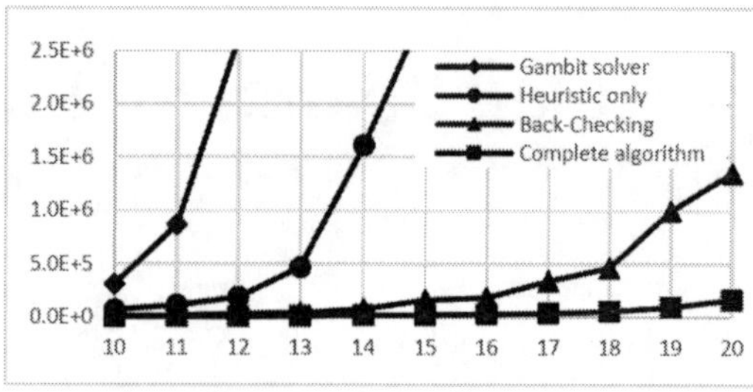

Figure 1: NCCC for variable number of agents

REFERENCES

[1] T. Grinshpoun, A. Grubshtein, R. Zivan, A. Netzer, and A. Meisels. Asymmetric distributed constraint optimization problems. *Journal of Artificial Intelligence Research*, pages 613–647, 2013.

[2] A. Grubshtein and A. Meisels. Finding a nash equilibrium by asynchronous backtracking. In *Principles and Practice of Constraint Programming - 18th International Conference, CP 2012, Québec City, QC, Canada, October 8-12, 2012. Proceedings*, pages 925–940, 2012.

[3] M. J. Kearns, M. L. Littman, and S. P. Singh. Graphical models for game theory. In *UAI '01: Proceedings of the 17th Conference in Uncertainty in Artificial Intelligence, University of Washington, Seattle, Washington, USA, August 2-5, 2001*, pages 253–260, 2001.

[4] R. D. McKelvey, A. M. McLennan, and T. L. Turocy. Gambit: Software tools for game theory, version 14.1.0. `http://www.gambit-project.org`, 2014.

[5] P. J. Modi, W. Shen, M. Tambe, and M. Yokoo. ADOPT: asynchronous distributed constraints optimization with quality guarantees. *Artificial Intelligence*, 161:1-2:149–180, January 2005.

[6] T. Nguyen and A. Lallouet. A complete solver for constraint games. In *Principles and Practice of Constraint Programming - 20th International Conference, CP 2014, Lyon, France, September 8-12, 2014. Proceedings*, pages 58–74, 2014.

Neuro-Evolution for Multi-Agent Policy Transfer in RoboCup Keep-Away

(Extended Abstract)

Sabre Didi, Geoff Nitschke
Department of Computer Science
University of Cape Town
Cape Town, South Africa
sabredd0@gmail.com, gnitschke@cs.uct.ac.za

ABSTRACT

An objective of transfer learning is to improve and speed-up learning on target tasks after training on a different, but related source tasks. This research is a study of comparative *Neuro-Evolution* (NE) methods for transferring evolved multi-agent policies (behaviors) between multi-agent tasks of varying complexity. The efficacy of five variants of two NE methods are compared for multi-agent policy transfer. The NE method variants include using the original versions (search directed by a fitness function), behavioural and genotypic diversity based search to replace objective based search (fitness functions) as well as hybrid objective and diversity (behavioral and genotypic) maintenance based search approaches. The goal of testing these variants to direct policy search is to ascertain an appropriate method for boosting the task performance of transferred multi-agent behaviours. Results indicate that an indirect encoding NE method using hybridized objective based search and behavioral diversity maintenance yields significantly improved task performance for policy transfer between multi-agent tasks of increasing complexity. Comparatively, NE methods not using behavioral diversity maintenance to direct policy search performed relatively poorly in terms of efficiency (evolution times) and quality of solutions in target tasks.

Keywords

Machine Learning; Policy Transfer; Neuro-Evolution

Neuro-Evolution for Policy Transfer

This study presents a comparative evaluation of various neuro-evolution methods for multi-agent policy (behavior) transfer, where *Keep-Away RoboCup Soccer* is the experimental case study. This study ascertains the most appropriate method for transfer between tasks of increasing complexity.

We use the *Neuro-Evolution for Augmenting Topologies* (NEAT) [6] and HyperNEAT [5] methods for transfer learning in multi-agent keep-away tasks of varying complexity. These methods were selected in order to test the efficacy of a direct encoding (NEAT) versus an indirect encoding method (HyperNEAT) for multi-agent policy transfer, where such methods have been widely demonstrated as effective for controller design in various multi-agent tasks [8], [1]. Whilst many studies support the efficacy of objective-based search approaches in transfer learning [9], [7], [8], the impact of *genotypic* and *behavioral diversity maintenance* on transfer learning remains unexplored.

Five variants of both NEAT and HyperNEAT for directing the policy search process were tested. *Variant 1* tests unmodified versions of these methods. In *variant 2* behavioral diversity maintenance (*Novelty Search* [3]) replaced the objective (fitness) function. *Variant 3* used a hybrid of objective based search and novelty search. *Variant 4* used a hybrid of objective based search and genotypic diversity maintenance. In *Variant 5* genotypic diversity maintenance replaced the fitness function.

This study investigates how behavioral and genotypic diversity maintenance, non-objective and objective search impacts policy transfer using direct (NEAT) and indirect encoding (HyperNEAT) methods to evolve behaviors. Also, these methods extend previous work on *inter-task mappings for policy search* [7] to facilitate transfer learning [8].

Hypothesis 1 is that, given related policy transfer results [8], NEAT and HyperNEAT are appropriate policy (multi-agent behavior) search methods for enabling policy transfer where transferred behaviors yield a significantly higher task performance and efficiency compared to those without policy transfer (*evolved from scratch*). Hypothesis 2 is that, given behavioral diversity maintenance results [4], [2], if novelty search is hybridized with objective based search in the tested policy search methods, this will yield a significantly higher *task performance* for all source and target tasks, compared to the other method variants tested.

Experiments

Experiments were run in a source keep-away task, where populations evolved after 20 generations (using NEAT or HyperNEAT), were transferred to a target task and evolved for a further 50 generations. Results were compared to those where no policy transfer took place, but rather where NEAT or HyperNEAT evolved keep-away behaviours from *scratch* in target tasks. For both NEAT and HyperNEAT, each genotype (agent team) was evaluated over 30 task trials per generation. Each task trial tested different (random) agent positions. Average fitness per genotype was computed over these 30 task trials. Policy transfer occurred between a

Appears in: *Proceedings of the 15th International Conference on Autonomous Agents and Multiagent Systems (AAMAS 2016), J. Thangarajah, K. Tuyls, C. Jonker, S. Marsella (eds.), May 9–13, 2016, Singapore.*

Experiment	4vs3 Keep-Away	5vs3 Keep-Away	6vs4 Keep-Away
No Policy Transfer			
NEAT	0.438 (0.037)	0.473 (0.052)	0.419 (0.057)
HyperNEAT	0.587 (0.059)	0.765 (0.050)	0.533 (0.044)
Variant 1			
Fitness Policy Transfer			
NEAT	0.482 (0.059)	0.580 (0.069)	0.464 (0.033)
HyperNEAT	0.729 (0.089)	0.873 (0.089)	0.632 (0.038)
Variant 2			
NS Policy Transfer			
NEAT	0.470 (0.03)	0.505 (0.039)	0.460 (0.03)
HyperNEAT	0.707 (0.027)	0.827 (0.033)	0.605 (0.024)
Variant 3			
Fitness + NS Policy Transfer			
NEAT	0.545 (0.047)	0.638 (0.0048)	0.520 (0.036)
HyperNEAT	0.752 (0.054)	0.943 (0.029)	0.697 (0.032)
Variant 4			
Fitness + GD Policy Transfer			
NEAT	0.442 (0.012)	0.456 (0.018)	0.436 (0.016)
HyperNEAT	0.482 (0.041)	0.509 (0.039)	0.468 (0.035)
Variant 5			
GD Policy Transfer			
NEAT	0.432 (0.018)	0.453 (0.029)	0.426 (0.025)
HyperNEAT	0.475 (0.038)	0.497 (0.029)	0.452 (0.025)

Table 1: Average normalized maximum fitness (over 20 runs) for the three experimental setups. Values are portions of the maximum possible hold time (possession of the ball) for the team of keepers. *NS:* Novelty Search. *GD:* Genotype Diversity. Standard deviations are shown in parentheses.

source and incrementally complex target tasks. The source task was three keepers versus two takers (*3vs2*) in a 20 x 20 virtual field[1]. Evolved behaviors (policies) were transferred (and evolution continued) in one of three target tasks, four keepers versus three takers (*4vs3*), five keepers versus three takers (*5vs3*) or six keepers versus four takers (*6vs4*).

Table 1 presents the average normalized maximum fitness attained by teams evolved with no policy transfer and each policy transfer variant. These results have important implications for current transfer learning research, specifically multi-agent policy transfer where neuro-evolution is used to evolve multi-agent behaviors in source and target tasks. Supported by related research [8], results indicated significant *task performance* benefits (Mann-Whitney U test, p-value < 0.05) of policy transfer for increasingly complex versions of *Keep-away RoboCup Soccer*. Also, results supported the efficacy of using an objective-novelty search hybrid (highest performing variant with statistical significance) to direct NEAT and HyperNEAT behavior evolution for policy transfer. This is similarly supported by previous research demonstrating the benefits of hybrid objective-novelty search approaches over pure novelty search [2].

Future work will compare neuro-evolution methods with well established *reinforcement learning* methods in more complex keep-away soccer tasks, as well as testing these methods for policy transfer between different but related multi-agent tasks such as keep-away to multi-agent predator-prey [1].

[1]All experiments were run in *RoboCup Keep-Away version 6* [7]. Source code and executables can be found at: http://people.cs.uct.ac.za/~gnitschke/KeepAway/

Acknowledgements

This research was funded by a PhD Research Fellowship from the Science Faculty at the University of Cape Town and the National Research Foundation of South Africa (NRF).

REFERENCES

[1] D. D'Ambrosio and K. Stanley. Scalable multiagent learning through indirect encoding of policy geometry. *Evolutionary Intelligence Journal*, 6(1):1–26, 2013.

[2] J. Gomes, P. Urbano, and A. Christensen. Evolution of swarm robotics systems with novelty search. *Swarm Intelligence*, 7:115–144, 2013.

[3] J. Lehman and K. Stanley. Abandoning objectives: Evolution through the search for novelty alone. *Evolutionary computation*, 19(2):189–223, 2011.

[4] J. Mouret and S. Doncieux. Encouraging behavioral diversity in evolutionary robotics: An empirical study. *Evolutionary Computation*, 20(1):91–133, 2012.

[5] K. Stanley, D. D'Ambrosio, and J. Gauci. A hypercube-based indirect encoding for evolving large-scale neural networks. *Artificial Life*, 15(2):185–212, 2009.

[6] K. Stanley and R. Miikkulainen. Evolving neural networks through augmenting topologies. *Evolutionary Computation*, 10(2):99–127, 2002.

[7] M. Taylor, P. Stone, and Y. Liu. Transfer learning via inter-task mappings for temporal difference learning. *Journal of Machine Learning*, 8(1):2125–2167, 2010.

[8] P. Verbancsics and K. Stanley. Evolving static representations for task transfer. *Journal of Machine Learning Research*, 11(1):1737–1763, 2010.

[9] S. Whiteson and P. Stone. Evolutionary function approximation for reinforcement learning. *Journal of Machine Learning Research*, 7(1):877–917, 2006.

Wheeled Robots playing Chain Catch: Strategies and Evaluation

(Extended Abstract)

Garima Agrawal
International Institute of Information Technology
Hyderabad, India
garima.agrawal@research.iiit.ac.in

Kamalakar Karlapalem
IIIT Hyderabad/ IIT Gandhinagar
India
kamal@iiit.ac.in

ABSTRACT

Robots playing games that humans are adept in is a challenge. We studied robotic agents playing Chain Catch game as a Multi-Agent System (MAS). Chain Catch is a combination of two challenges - pursuit domain and robotic chain formation. In this paper, we present a Chain Catch simulator that allows us to incorporate game rules, design strategies and simulate the game play. We developed cost model driven strategies for each of Escapee, Catcher and Chain. Our results, simulation and robots implementation show that Sliding slope strategy is the best strategy for Escapees whereas Tagging method is the best method for chain′s movement in Chain Catch.

General Terms

Design, Algorithms, Experimentation, Performance

Keywords

Strategies, Multi-agent games, Simulation, Robots, Heuristics

1. INTRODUCTION

We implement robotic agents playing Chain Catch, which is a common multi-player playground game that requires strategic decision making and cooperation among chain members to stay together (as a chain) while catching another player whereas other players to compete with chain to escape from getting caught. Simulating robot games like Robosoccer and Robot pursuit evasion games have been a topic of extensive research in the field of Multi-Robot systems [6]. Our game starts as simple Catch-Catch or "tag" game that falls under pursuit domain problems. In our Chain Catch game (i) the Catcher Catches one of the Escapees, (ii) the Catcher and caught Escapee form a chain to Catch other Escapees and (iii) step (ii) is repeated until all Escapees are caught and become one chain. Chain Catch requires complex and efficient strategies for the Escapee and chain, we also developed techniques for robotic chain formation and movement suitable in game scenario. Our Chain Catch agents are autonomous and compute their strategy in a decentralized manner.

Appears in: *Proceedings of the 15th International Conference on Autonomous Agents and Multiagent Systems (AAMAS 2016), J.Thangarajah, K.Tuyls, C.Jonker, S.Marsella (eds.), May 9–13, 2016, Singapore.*

Strategy name	Cost function Description with respect to Catcher
Max distance	maximize their distance
K circle	Form a circle with radius equal to "K"
K circle with rotation	form a K circle and rotate around it
Sliding slope	K circle strategy along with sliding slopes at the corners

Table 1: Summarizing strategies for Escapees.

1.1 Related Work

Korf suggested a standard solution to the pursuit problem [4], which is a motivation behind Max Distance strategy for our Escapees. Game theoretical approaches can also be used for prey-predator games [3]. But however this approach is centralized unlike our decentralized multi-agent system. Robot control aspects of forming chain is discussed in [5].

2. AGENT STRATEGIES

We use a cost model to develop strategies for each of Escapee, Catcher and Chain. Lesser the cost of a cell, better it is for the agent to move into it. Catcher's strategy is based on computing the cell closest to the nearest Escapee. Escapees' strategies involve maintaining safe distance from the Catcher/chain while achieving an implicit formation among fellow Escapees. Table 1 summarizes all strategies designed for Escapee agents . Member agents of the chain have dual objectives- (i) Catch an Escapee (ii) maintain chain formation. We have designed two strategies (Table 2) for chain members keeping the two objectives under consideration.

3. ROBOT SIMULATION

We use production quality Nex Robotics platforms Fire Bird- V ATMEGA2560 with Xbee API module. Our robotic setup does not have localization mechanism therefore, we implement virtual localization through communication. These robots are similar in terms of size, speed (same and constant) and behavior. Users have to place the robots onto the specified starting location to begin the game. Once the game begins, the robots compute the best move possible depending upon information it has about other agents and by using its Strategy Engine module. We have six robots; and imple-

Strategy name	Description
Tagging method (CC)	Leader moves towards nearest Escapee. Other members tag themselves to their neighbour in direction of Leader and move to the cell closest to it
Variance method (CC)	All members try to attain different *variance* distances from Escapee to surround it while maintaining safe distance R_c from their neighbours
Tagging method (AC)	Leader moves towards nearest Escapee. Other members to its left and right tag themselves to their neighbour in direction of Leader
Variance method (AC)	All members try to attain different *variance* (as defined for case-2) distance from Escapee while maintaining R_c from neighbours

Corner catch = CC, Any one catch = AC

Table 2: Chain strategies

mented Catcher, Escapee and Chains algorithms on these robots in different scenarios and examined the performance (see Figure 1).

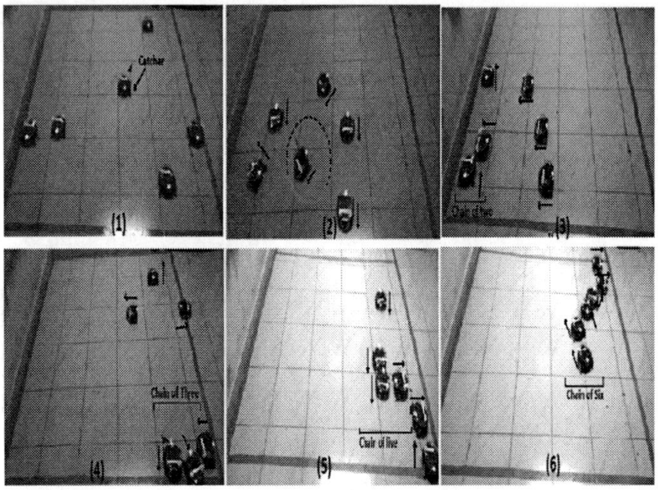

Figure 1: Robot simulation of Chain game with chains Tagging method and Escapees moving with K circle strategy. (1) Initial condition. (2) K circle around Catcher. (3) First Catch (4) Chain of three (5) Chain of five. (6) Chain completion

Live videos of some of the game play experiments can be found in reference section [1].

4. EXPERIMENTAL RESULTS

We built a front-end simulator to design and experiment with various Chain Catch game strategies. Total time (T_c), is the time taken till the last Escapee gets caught. Chain aims to lower T_c while Escapees aim at higher T_c. We performed over 100 empirical experiments, with varying number of agents from 3 to 100, and different starting locations of agents in each case. Transition table shown in Table 3 gives overall analysis of game results as average number and standard deviation of steps taken for the complete chain formation. The data >3000 implies that the strategy is insignificant; as it takes more than maximum possible steps (3000) to finish the game. Sliding slope is the best strategy for Escapees while Tagging method is the best strategy for chain.

chain \ escapee	Naive strategy	K circle strategy without rotation	K circle strategy with rotation	Sliding slope strategy	Random strategy
Tagging strategy (CC)	197.39 ± 88.44	566.17 ± 314.88	290.6 ± 124.29	673.6 ± 323.98	139.41 ± 79.09
Variance strategy (CC)	308.78 ± 277.42	720.25 ± 307.62	503.66 ± 246.02	837.38 ± 278.22	249.89 ± 200.12
Random strategy	>3000	>3000	>3000	>3000	962.44 ± 639.91
Tagging strategy (AC)	136.9 ± 107.73	475.6 ± 300.33	250.14 ± 114.83	553.17 ± 320.14	110 ± 89.23
Variance strategy (AC)	240.17 ± 151.14	613.5 ± 289.24	449.66 ± 203.34	710.44 ± 249.78	200.2 ± 144.53

Corner catch = CC, Any one catch = AC

Table 3: Average number and standard deviation of steps (T_c) taken.

5. SUMMARY

We built a Multi-robot system where robotic agents are capable to play Catch-Catch and Chain Catch. We implemented the system both as simulation framework and in physical environment with real robots. An example of Chain Catch is where, to trap a terrorist the robots might have to form a chain and move in a coordinated fashion or even surround it with a circular formation as done by our chain and escapees. [2] is the extended version of this work.

REFERENCES

[1] Simulation and robot implementation of various game strategies. *https://goo.gl/8nIyBG*, 2015.

[2] G. Agrawal and K. Karlapalem. Wheeled robots playing chain catch: Strategies and evaluation (full paper - arxiv). *http://arxiv.org/abs/1602.06460*, 2016.

[3] R. E. Korf. A game theoretic approach to the pursuit problem. In *Working Papers of the 11th International Workshop on Distributed Artificial Intelligence*, pages 195–213.

[4] R. E. Korf. A simple solution to pursuit games. In *Working Papers of the 11th International Workshop on Distributed Artificial Intelligence*, pages 183–194, 1992.

[5] R. Mead, J. B. Weinberg, , and J. R. Croxell. A demonstration of a robot formation control algorithm and platform. *22nd National Conference on Artificial Intelligence, Vancouver, BC*, 2007.

[6] F. L. Wurtz. Ai in prey predator domain. Master's thesis, Technical University of Denmark, 2008.

Hierarchical Approach to Transfer of Control in Semi-Autonomous Systems

(Extended Abstract)

Kyle Hollins Wray Luis Pineda Shlomo Zilberstein
College of Information and Computer Sciences
University of Massachusetts Amherst
{wray,lpineda,shlomo}@cs.umass.edu

ABSTRACT

Semi-Autonomous Systems (SAS) describe a class of systems that are explicitly controlled by both human and agent actors, incorporating the distinct capabilities of each. They are designed for domains that require quick and safe transfer of control between the agent and human, and embed control transfer decisions in the overall high-level plan. We formally define SAS as a hierarchical model and its properties. We discuss how micro-level transfer of control and macro-level path planning can be solved together. Finally, we explore how SAS can be applied to semi-autonomous vehicles.

1. INTRODUCTION

Purely autonomous systems have been applied to a wide range of domains ranging from water reservoir control [3] to energy-conserving smart environments [7]. Almost all applications, however, require human intervention as part of their standard operating procedure. Few models actively incorporate this collaboration, and instead use hard-coded default behaviors [2]. Semi-Autonomous Systems (SAS) are models that explicitly model the collaboration of actors, in order to proactively utilize their respective capabilities [11].

New challenges arise in semi-autonomous systems due to the inherent uncertainty and complexity of human behavior. We consider semi-autonomous driving [10] as our target application. Within this domain, vehicles can only operate autonomous on a subset of the roads (e.g., only well-mapped roads). For longer routes, the vehicle requires the human to occasionally take control during execution. This transfer of control process requires second to second monitoring as the vehicle messages the driver to change the vehicle's controlling entity. It may be unsuccessful due to the state of the human (e.g., distracted) or simply time limitations.

The proposed collaborative multiagent framework is quite distinct from other models such as Shared Plans [4], Teamwork [9], and Dec-POMDPs [1]. First, SAS requires exactly one actor in control at a time. Second, transfer of control must be explicitly modeled. Finally, SAS must proactively leverage each actor's capabilities (or lack thereof) as it efficiently moves through the sate space.

Appears in: *Proceedings of the 15th International Conference on Autonomous Agents and Multiagent Systems (AAMAS 2016), J. Thangarajah, K. Tuyls, C. Jonker, S. Marsella (eds.), May 9–13, 2016, Singapore.*

2. SEMI-AUTONOMOUS SYSTEMS

Semi-Autonomous Systems (SAS) rely on collaboration between a human and an agent in order to achieve some goals while maintaining a measure of safety [11]. We consider semi-autonomy within the context of automated planning, extending a Markov Decision Process (MDP) to support semi-autonomy, as formally defined below.

DEFINITION 1. *A* ***semi-autonomous system*** *is represented by a tuple* $\langle \mathcal{A}, S_+, A_+, T_+, C_+, G, L\rangle$.

- $\mathcal{A}$ *is a set of actors (controlling entities).*
- $S_+ = S \times \mathcal{A}$ *is a set of factored states: a standard state set* S *and the current controlling actor* $\mathcal{A}$.
- $A_+ = A \times \mathcal{A}$ *is a set of factored actions: a standard action set* A *and the next desired actor* $\mathcal{A}$.
- $T_+ : S_+ \times A_+ \to \triangle^{|S_+|}$ *is a transition function, comprised of a state transition* $T_\mathbf{a} : S \times A \to \triangle^{|S|}$ *for each actor* $\mathbf{a} \in \mathcal{A}$, *and control transfer function* $\rho : S_+ \times \mathcal{A} \to \triangle^{|\mathcal{A}|}$.
- $C_+ : S_+ \times A_+ \to \mathbb{R}^+$ *is a cost function.*
- $G \subseteq S_+$ *is a set of goal states.*
- $L \subseteq S_+$ *is a set of live states, such that for actor capability function* $\psi : S \to 2^{\mathcal{A}}$, $L = \{\langle s, \mathbf{a}\rangle | \mathbf{a} \in \psi(s)\}$.

The actors $\mathcal{A}$ of the system describe controlling entities, which include at a minimum a human λ and an autonomous agent ν; we focus in this paper on situations involving these specific two actors. The states must record who is in control at any given time, and the actions must record intentions to switch control to new actors. In SAS, we cannot always assume that transfer of the control has a flawless execution. Hence our T_+ is factored into two components: $T_\mathbf{a}$ and ρ.

The first component, an **actor state transition function** denoted as $T_\mathbf{a} : S \times A \to \triangle^{|S|}$, describes how an actor $\mathbf{a} \in \mathcal{A}$ can operate in the world when in control (n-simplex $\triangle^n$). The second component, a **control transfer function** denoted as $\rho : S_+ \times \mathcal{A} \to \triangle^{|\mathcal{A}|}$, describes the result of attempting to transfer control from the current actor in a given state. Combining these two functions, we define the **SAS state transition function** T_+ for any state $s_+ = \langle s, \mathbf{a}\rangle$, action $a_+ = \langle a, \hat{\mathbf{a}}\rangle$, and successor $s'_+ = \langle s', \mathbf{a}'\rangle$:

$$T_+(s_+, a_+, s'_+) = \begin{cases} T_\mathbf{a}(s, a, s'), & \text{if } \mathbf{a}{=}\hat{\mathbf{a}}{=}\mathbf{a}' \\ T_\mathbf{a}(s, a, s')\rho(s_+, \hat{\mathbf{a}}, \mathbf{a}'), & \text{if } \mathbf{a}{\neq}\hat{\mathbf{a}} \\ 0, & \text{otherwise} \end{cases} \quad (1)$$

In Equation 1, the first component corresponds to keeping the current actor, which simply follows the actor's state transition. The second component describes the actor still in control but seeking to switch to a different actor at the next state. Finally, the third component indicates that it is impossible to take away control from an actor without the desire to transfer control. The separation of macro-level planning and micro-level transfer of control denotes is hierarchical approach, as a type of *option* [8].

The **actor capability function** ψ defines which actors can act in each state. In the semi-autonomous driving domain, $\psi(s)$ always contains the human λ, but only includes the vehicle ν on a subset of the roads on which it can operate. This function induces the set of **live states** L (Definition 1). Live states describe states in which the system is *alive* or *safe*. We impose **live state constraints** that guarantee non-live states are unable to reach any goal state, also called *dead ends* [6]. We characterize both *policies* and *systems* based on their ability to maintain live state. Specifically, if a policy guarantees live state, then we call it **strong**; otherwise, it is **weak**. A SAS is called **strong** if its optimal policy is strong, and **weak** otherwise. In practice, this requires that we prove the transfer of control ρ is well-behaved.

3. DESIGN AND APPLICATION

Designing semi-autonomous systems first requires creating the transfer of control process, then defining the SAS itself.

3.1 Transfer of Control

Transfer of Control (TOC) is the critical method that enables effective and safe transference of the controlling entity in the system. TOC considers the sequences of messages to the human (or other actors) that preserves the human's amiable perception of the agent (e.g., aggregated annoyance) while still effectively conveying the desired intentions. We assume this process can always be aborted safely. For example, in semi-autonomous driving, the vehicle will pull over to the side of the road.

This process can be modeled as a POMDP [5]. States encode time remaining, information regarding the last message sent, and a notion of the human state. Actions are the TOC messages and an abort action. Observations encode noisy sensors within the SAS that monitor the human. The state transition and observation functions capture the uncertainty regarding the human's response to messages.

3.2 Semi-Autonomous Vehicles

The application of our TOC model produces a ρ, based on its performance in transferring control in various scenarios. A SAS for Semi-Autonomous VEhicles (SAVE) can be created using a weighted directed graph of roads with start and end vertexes. Each vertex corresponds to an intersection. Edge weights denote the time spent on each road following the speed limit. This SAVE graph is represented as the standard states S in the SAS. The standard actions A are directions to take at intersections. The state transitions $T_{\mathbf{a}}$ follow from the graph, only entering dead ends when the vehicle ν enters a road in which it cannot drive.

The transfer of control process can be used to effectively notify the user with ever-increasing persistence (Figure 1). This transfer process is captured in the SAVE transition, using pre-solved instances of the TOC POMDP model as a kind of option, thus behaving as a hierarchical model.

Figure 1: Semi-autonomous vehicle simulator: System requests to transfer control to a busy driver.

4. CONCLUSION

We present a new multiagent model for semi-autonomous systems. It enables explicit modeling of agents (actor), including humans, each with their own capabilities. We show how a POMDP can be used to solve the transfer of control problem, enabling a safe change of the controlling entity. Finally, we state how semi-autonomous vehicles may be modeled as a SAS.

Acknowledgments. This work was supported in part by the National Science Foundation grant number IIS-1405550.

REFERENCES

[1] D. S. Bernstein, R. Givan, N. Immerman, and S. Zilberstein. The complexity of decentralized control of Markov decision processes. *Mathematics of Operations Research*, 27(4):819–840, 2002.

[2] J. Biswas and M. M. Veloso. Localization and navigation of the CoBots over long-term deployments. *International Journal of Robotics Research (IJRR)*, 32(14):1679–1694, 2013.

[3] A. Castelletti, F. Pianosi, and R. Soncini-Sessa. Water reservoir control under economic, social and environmental constraints. *Automatica*, 44(6):1595–1607, 2008.

[4] B. J. Grosz and S. Kraus. Collaborative plans for complex group action. *Artificial Intelligence*, 86(2):269–357, 1996.

[5] L. P. Kaelbling, M. L. Littman, and A. R. Cassandra. Planning and acting in partially observable stochastic domains. *Artificial Intelligence*, 101(1):99–134, 1998.

[6] A. Kolobov, Mausam, and D. Weld. A theory of goal-oriented MDPs with dead ends. In *Proceedings of the 28th Annual Conference on Uncertainty in Artificial Intelligence (UAI)*, pages 438–447, Corvallis, Oregon, August 2012.

[7] J.-Y. Kwak, P. Varakantham, R. Maheswaran, M. Tambe, F. Jazizadeh, G. Kavulya, L. Klein, B. Becerik-Gerber, T. Hayes, and W. Wood. SAVES: A sustainable multiagent application to conserve building energy considering occupants. In *Proccedings of the 11th International Conference on Autonomous Agents and Multiagent Systems (AAMAS)*, pages 21–28, Valencia, Spain, 2012.

[8] R. S. Sutton, D. Precup, and S. Singh. Between MDPs and semi-MDPs: A framework for temporal abstraction in reinforcement learning. *Artificial Intelligence*, 112:181–211, 1999.

[9] M. Tambe. Towards flexible teamwork. *Journal of Artificial Intelligence Research*, 2:83–124, 1997.

[10] K. H. Wray and S. Zilberstein. Multi-objective POMDPs with lexicographic reward preferences. In *Proceedings of the 24th International Joint Conference of Artificial Intelligence (IJCAI)*, pages 1719–1725, July 2015.

[11] S. Zilberstein. Building strong semi-autonomous systems. In *Proceedings of the 29th Conference on Artificial Intelligence (AAAI)*, pages 4088–4092, Austin, Texas, 2015.

A Hybrid Approach for Detecting Fraudulent Medical Insurance Claims

(Extended Abstract)

Chenfei Sun[1], Yuliang Shi[1], Qingzhong Li[1], Lizhen Cui[1], Han Yu[2], Chunyan Miao[2]
[1]School of Computer Science and Technology, Shandong University, Jinan, China
[2]Joint NTU-UBC Research Centre of Excellence in Active Living for the Elderly (LILY),
Nanyang Technological University, 50 Nanyang Avenue, Singapore 639798
sun.chenfei@163.com, {shiyuliang, lqz, clz}@sdu.edu.cn, {han.yu, ascymiao}@ntu.edu.sg

ABSTRACT

Medical insurance frauds are causing huge losses for public healthcare funds in many countries. Detecting medical insurance frauds is an important and difficult challenge. Because of the complex granularity of data, existing fraud detection approaches tend to be less effective in terms of recalling fraudulent claim behaviours. In this paper, we propose a Hybrid Fraud Detection Approach (HFDA) to address this problem, which is compared with four state-of-the-art approaches using a real-world dataset. Extensive experiment results show that the proposed approach is significantly more effective and efficient.

Keywords

Behaviour patterns; outliers; evidence theory; fraud

1. INTRODUCTION

In today's world, population aging has brought new challenges to the healthcare system [1]. As many people live longer, governments around the world are increasing their spending on healthcare. Medical insurance fraud is a serious threat to public funds and public trust [5]. This has motivated many researchers to develop fraud detection technologies.

As more and more healthcare insurance systems move online, many claim-related activities take place over the Internet and can thus be tracked by the claim system. Therefore, the combination of behaviour trajectory big data and machine learning techniques offer promising solutions to the medical insurance fraud problem. The granularity of behaviours, represented by mathematical symbols, can be very fine-grained. This can result in some behaviours belonging to the same category being represented by different sets of symbols. Due to the curse of cardinality, existing pattern recognition based fraud detection methods cannot accurately identity latent patterns which are more effectively identified at a coarser behaviour granularity [3].

In this paper, we propose a Hybrid Fraud Detection Approach (HFDA) which can detect both unusual categories of claim behaviours and unusual frequencies of claim behaviours simultaneously. Our proposed approach is compared against four state-of-the-art approaches using a large-scale real-world dataset containing more than 40 million medical claim activity records from over 40,000 users of the medical insurance claim system used in Zibo, Shandong, China. Extensive experiments show that the proposed hybrid approach is significantly more effective and efficient.

Appears in: *Proceedings of the 15th International Conference on Autonomous Agents and Multiagent Systems (AAMAS 2016), J. Thangarajah, K. Tuyls, C. Jonker, S. Marsella (eds.), May 9–13, 2016, Singapore.*

2. THE PROPOSED APPROACH

In a medical insurance claim system, there can be millions of transactions from a large number of users. In order to make better sense of the users' actions, it is advantageous to organize the transactions into behaviour sequences.In this paper, we use the term *behaviour*, b, to refer to an activity, a, performed by a subject, s, at a given point in time, t. Thus, $b = \langle s, a, t \rangle$. An example behaviour b_1 can be ⟨"ID123456", "received asthma medications","2012/10/15 14:30:08"⟩. A *behaviour sequence* refers to a collection of behaviours carried out by the same subject in chronological order over a given period of time. It is can be represented conceptually as $BS = (b_1 \rightarrow b_2 \rightarrow \ldots \rightarrow b_m)$, where $b_1, b_2, \ldots, b_m$ represent different behaviours from the same subject.

We denote a behaviour sequence as a weighted behaviour graph, $G(V, E, W)$, where V, E and W represent the set of vertices, edges and weights of the graph, respectively. Every vertex represents a distinct behaviour. Vertex i corresponds to b_i and vertex j corresponds to b_j in a set of behaviours. $d(i,j)$ represents the distance between vertices i and j in a behaviour sequence. An edge e_{ij} between two vertices i and node j only exists if $d(i,j) < r$ more than once across multiple behaviour sequences in a behaviour sequence set $\mathbf{\Phi}$. In this case, r is a predefined threshold for neighbors to be regarded as relevant. The weight of the edge between vertices i and j is defined as $w_{ij} = \sum_{\forall BS_n, 1 \le n \le N} \frac{1_{[d(i,j)<r]}}{N}$ where N is the number of behaviour sequences in a behaviour sequence set $\mathbf{\Phi}$. $1_{[\text{condition}]}$ is a function which evaluates to 1 if [condition] is true. Otherwise, it evaluates to 0. The larger the value of w_{ij}, the more often b_i and b_j appear close to each other in the behaviour sequences. Thus, w_{ij} indicates the closeness between behaviours b_i and b_j across multiple behaviour sequences.

Based on original behaviour sequences alone, it is hard to define the distances between the sequences or extract useful features. When the behaviour sequences are composed of a large number of behaviours, it is difficult to cluster the behaviour sequences. One way to tackle this problem is to

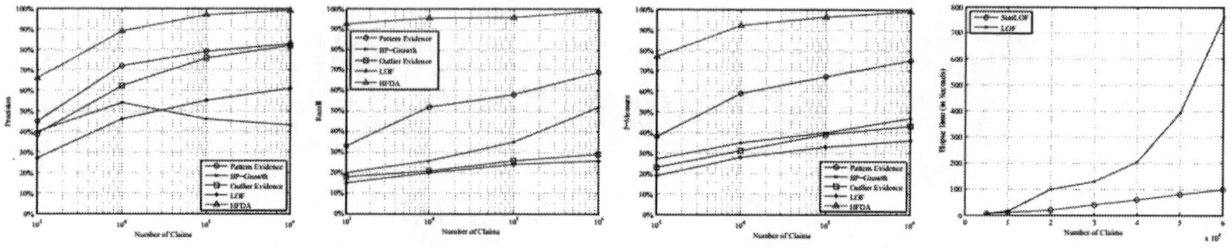

(a) precision (b) recall (c) f-measure (d) time cost

Figure 1: Experiment Results.

represent the behaviour sequences by behaviour classes. By denoting the behaviour sequences in the form of behaviour classes, repeated subsequences can be observed more clearly and sequential features can be more meaningful.

In order to reduce the dimensionality of the myriad of behaviours in a typical medical insurance claim system, we need to embed the behaviours into a lower dimension. Manifold learning [2] is the process of estimating a low-dimensional structure which underlies a collection of high-dimensional data. To carry out the embedding, we take advantage of the manifold embedding of a graph.

As medical insurance claim data for each individual user tend to be sparse, peer group comparison is favoured over self-comparison when it comes to outlier-based fraud detection. The outlier based fraud probability, p', for an incoming claim, c, can be obtained by computing the density of known fraudulent claims which share some features with c. The top K nearest neighbors of c in the historical claims data (i.e., $x_1, x_2, ..., x_K$) are selected for the calculation as $density(c) = \frac{1}{K}\sum_{i=1}^{k} p(x_i)$ where $p(x_i)$ is the probability density function of x_i.

Through this process, we obtain two sources of evidence to determine if an incoming claim is fraudulent: 1) *behaviour pattern-based evidence*, which represents unusual categories of behaviours; and 2) *outlier-based evidence*, which represents unusual frequencies of behaviours. In order to combine these two sources of evidence, we leverage on the Dempster-Shafer Evidence Theory [4]. Since the two sources of evidence are independent from each other, we base our proposed approach on Dempster's Rule of Combination [7].

3. EXPERIMENTAL EVALUATIONS

In this section, we evaluate the performance of the proposed approach using a real-world dataset. The dataset used in this experiment is collected from the Dareway Medical Insurance Claim System which is currently used in Zibo City, Shandong Province, China. The dataset contains medical insurance claim activities from over 40,000 users.

We adopt *precision*, *recall*, *f-measure* and *time cost* to evaluate how effectively each approach identifies fraudulent medical insurance claims. It can be observed from Figures 1(a), 1(b) and 1(c) that the proposed approach, which combines pattern-based evidence and outlier-based evidence, can achieve significantly better performance than other comparison approaches. BP-Growth proposed optimizing strategies for association rule mining for behaviour pattern analysis. However, because of the curse of cardinality, BP-Growth is not effective in mining large-scale frequent itemsets consisting of more than two types of behaviours. The proposed approach is significantly more efficient, too (Figure 1(d)).

4. CONCLUSIONS AND FUTURE WORK

In this paper, we propose a hybrid approach to detect both unusual categories of claim behaviours and unusual frequencies of claim behaviours simultaneously. The proposed approach is evaluated against four state-of-the-art approaches using a large-scale real-world dataset. Extensive experiments show that the proposed approach is significantly more effective and efficient than existing approaches. In future, we will infuse human factors such as computational curiosity [6, 8] into the approach to build decision support agents.

Acknowledgements

This research is supported, in part, by the National Natural Science Foundation of China under Grant No. 61572295, 61573212, 61272241; the Natural Science Foundation of Shandong Province of China under Grant No. ZR2014FM031, ZR2013FQ014; the Shandong Province Independent Innovation Major Special Project No. 2015ZDXX0201B03; the Shandong Province key research and development plan No. 2015GGX101015, 2015GGX101007; the Fundamental Research Funds of Shandong University No. 2015JC031; the National Research Foundation Singapore under its Interactive Digital Media (IDM) Strategic Research Programme; and the Lee Kuan Yew Post-Doctoral Fellowship Grant.

REFERENCES

[1] Y. Cai, Z. Shen, S. Liu, H. Yu, *et. al.* An agent-based game for the predictive diagnosis of Parkinson's disease. In *AAMAS*, pages 1663–1664, 2014.

[2] C.-C. Chiu and S. Marsella. Gesture generation with low-dimensional embeddings. In *AAMAS*, pages 781–788, 2014.

[3] J. Liu, E. Bier, A. Wilson, T. Honda, *et. al.* Graph analysis for detecting fraud, waste, and abuse in healthcare data. In *IAAI*, pages 3912–3919, 2015.

[4] G. Shafer. *A Mathematical Theory of Evidence.* Princeton University Press, 1976.

[5] Z. Shen, H. Yu, C. Miao, and J. Weng. Trust-based web service selection in virtual communities. *Web Intelligence and Agent Systems*, 9(3):227–238, 2011.

[6] Q. Wu, X. Han, H. Yu, Z. Shen, and C. Miao. The innovative application of learning companions in virtual singapura. In *AAMAS*, pages 1171–1172, 2013.

[7] R. R. Yager. On the dempster-shafer framework and new combination rules. *Information Sciences*, 41(2):93–137, 1987.

[8] H. Yu, Z. Shen, C. Miao, and A.-H. Tan. A simple curious agent to help people be curious. In *AAMAS*, pages 1159–1160, 2011.

Reinforcement Learning Algorithms for Regret Minimization in Structured Markov Decision Processes

(Extended Abstract)

Prabuchandran K. J.
Indian Institute of Science
Bangalore 560012, India
prabu.kj@csa.iisc.ernet.in

Tejas Bodas
Indian Institute of Technology
Mumbai, 400076, India
tejaspbodas@ee.iitb.ac.in

Theja Tulabandhula
Xerox Research Centre India
Bangalore 560103, India
Theja.Tulabandhula@xerox.com

ABSTRACT

A recent goal in the Reinforcement Learning (RL) framework is to choose a sequence of policy to minimize the regret incurred in *a finite time horizon*. For several RL problems in operation research and optimal control, the optimal policy of the underlying Markov Decision Process (MDP) is characterized by a known structure. The state of the art algorithms do not utilize this known structure of the optimal policy while minimizing regret. In this work, we develop new RL algorithms that exploit the structure of the optimal policy to minimize regret. Numerical experiments on MDPs with structured optimal policies show that our algorithms have better performance and are easy to implement.

Categories and Subject Descriptors

G.3 [**Probability & Statistics**]: Markov processes, Renewal theory

General Terms

Algorithms, Performance, Experimentation, Theory

Keywords

Multi-arm Bandit, Markov Decision Processes, UCB, Thompson Sampling, Renewal Reward Processes, Optimal threshold Policy.

1. INTRODUCTION

Optimal sequential decision problems are common in artificial intelligence, operation research and various other scientific disciplines. These problems are modeled using the framework of MDPs where a goal is to find a policy that maximizes the long run average reward collected. In an important subclass of these problems, one can characterize the structure of the optimal policy that maximizes this long run average reward. For example, the multi-period (s, S) policy in inventory control management [5] and the multi-threshold policies in queueing systems [3] are MDP problems where the optimal policy is characterized by a special structure. For such problems, one can develop efficient algorithms to obtain the optimal policy by restricting the search over such structured policies.

In this paper, our aim is to minimize the cumulative regret in a finite time horizon for the class of RL problems where the structure of the optimal policy is known. We provide two algorithms, *pUCB and pThompson*, that treat 'structured policies' as arms of a corresponding multi-arm bandit (MAB) problem [2] and then compare their performances with state of the art PSRL [4] algorithm.

Appears in: *Proceedings of the 15th International Conference on Autonomous Agents and Multiagent Systems (AAMAS 2016), J. Thangarajah, K. Tuyls, S. Marsella, C. Jonker (eds.), May 9–13, 2016, Singapore.*

2. PRELIMINARIES

Let us consider a finite unichain MDP [5] setting. Let P and R correspond to the transition probabilities and reward functions of the MDP. In our setting, we assume reward function is bounded by 1. A stationary deterministic policy (SDP) π specifies the action ($\pi(i)$) that needs to be chosen in state i. For each policy π, the long-run average reward is $\rho(\pi) = \lim_{T\to\infty} \frac{\mathbb{E}\left[\sum_{t=1}^{T} R(s_t, \pi(s_t), s_{t+1})\right]}{T}$. Let π^* correspond to the optimal policy that maximizes the long-run average reward among the finite set of SDPs.

In many modern RL settings, the goal is to find a sequence of policy $\{\pi_t\}$ that minimizes the expected *regret* in a given horizon T. Here, the expected regret when started from state s_{start} is $\mathcal{R}_{s_{start}}(T) = \rho(\pi^*)T - \sum_{t=1}^{T}\mathbb{E}[R(s_t, \pi_t(s_t), s_{t+1})]$, where π_t represents the policy chosen at time t.

In this paper we are concerned with minimizing regret when there exists some structure for π^*. Such structure exists in a wide collection of MDPs. Now using this structure in the optimal policy, one can create a smaller subset of policies that satisfies this structure. We can search for a policy that minimizes regret using this set as compared to searching in the complete policy space.

In our algorithms, we directly maintain a belief on the average reward $\rho(\pi)$ for each policy. Note that this has the advantage that we can reuse ideas from the UCB [2] and the Thompson sampling algorithms [1], which are the state-of-the-art algorithms in the multi-armed bandit setting. Another particularly attractive feature is that we can work directly with average reward of policies rather than the underlying transition probabilities and reward function.

One of the *key innovations* that we provide is *the way the beliefs on the average rewards $\rho(\pi)$ will be updated.* For this we use the Renewal-Reward Theorem ([6]). Under a given policy π, by fixing the return times to a fixed state s_{start} as renewal times, the MDP becomes a renewal reward process. Now one can estimate $\rho(\pi)$ by estimating the reward collected in a cycle (starting from s_{start} and returning to s_{start}) and the duration of the cycle.

3. ALGORITHMS

In our algorithms, we consider policies that has same structure as of the optimal policy. Let K denote the number of such policies.

In pUCB, we maintain an estimate of the long-run average reward obtained under each policy π_k as $\hat{\rho}(k)$. At the end of a cycle,

Algorithm 1: pUCB algorithm (pUCB)

1: **Input:** $T, \Pi = \{\pi_k : k = 1, \ldots, K\}, s_{start}, \tau$
2: **Output:** CR_T (Cumulative reward in T rounds)
3: **for** $k = 1$ to K **do**
4: $\quad \hat{\rho}(k) = 1,\ n(k) = 0$
5: $\quad R_{arm}(k) = 0$ (Running sum of rewards for policy π_k)
6: $\quad T_{arm}(k) = 0$ (Running sum of number of rounds for π_k)
7: **end for**
8: $s = s_{start},\ t' = 0, r = 0,\ k \sim \text{rand}(1, K)$
9: **for** $t = 1$ to T **do**
10: $\quad$ **if** $(t \neq 1$ **and** $s = s_{start})$ **or** $t' \geq \tau$ **then**
11: $\quad\quad R_{arm}(k) = R_{arm}(k) + r,\ T_{arm}(k) = T_{arm}(k) + t'$
12: $\quad\quad \hat{\rho}(k) = \frac{R_{arm}(k)}{T_{arm}(k)},\ c(k) = \sqrt{\frac{2 \log t}{n(k)}}$
13: $\quad\quad n(k) = n(k) + 1,\ k = \underset{j=1,\ldots,K}{\arg\max}\left\{\hat{\rho}(j) + c(j)\right\}$
14: $\quad\quad t' = 0,\ r = 0$
15: $\quad$ **end if**
16: $\quad s_{next} \sim P(\cdot \mid s, \pi_k(s)), r = R(s, a, s_{next})$
17: $\quad t' = t' + 1,\ s = s_{next}$
18: **end for**
19: $CR_T = \sum_{j=1}^{K} R_{arm}(j)$

we update $\hat{\rho}(k)$ using r and t' as shown in line number 11 in Algorithm 1. This is justified using the renewal-reward theorem as discussed in Section 2. In the next cycle, we follow the policy that has the highest values of the sum of the average reward estimate $\hat{\rho}(k)$ and the confidence bonus $\sqrt{\frac{2 \log t}{n(k)}}$. Here $n(k)$ tracks the count of the number of times policy k has been picked by round t.

Algorithm 2: pThompson algorithm (pThompson)

1: **Input:** $T, \Pi = \{\pi_k : k = 1, \ldots, K\}, s_{start}, \tau$
2: **Output:** CR_T (Cumulative reward in T rounds)
3: **for** $k = 1$ to K **do**
4: $\quad CR_T = 0, S(k) = 0,\ F(K) = 0$
5: **end for**
6: $s = s_{start},\ t' = 0,\ r = 0,\ k \sim \text{rand}(1, K)$
7: **for** $t = 1$ to T **do**
8: $\quad$ **if** $(t \neq 1$ **and** $s = s_{start})$ **or** $t' \geq \tau$ **then**
9: $\quad\quad CR_T = CR_T + r$
10: $\quad\quad S(k) = S(k) + r,\ F(k) = F(k) + t' - r$
11: $\quad\quad$ **for** $k = 1$ to K **do**
12: $\quad\quad\quad \theta(k) \sim Beta(S(k), F(k))$
13: $\quad\quad$ **end for**
14: $\quad\quad k = \underset{j=1,\ldots,K}{\arg\max}\left\{\theta(j)\right\},\ t' = 0, r = 0$
15: $\quad$ **end if**
16: $\quad s_{next} \sim P(\cdot \mid s, \pi_k(s)),\ r = R(s, a, s_{next})$
17: $\quad t' = t' + 1,\ s = s_{next}$
18: **end for**

In pThompson, we maintain a different set of internal estimates. In particular, for each policy π_k, it maintains two estimates $S(k)$ and $F(k)$. These two estimates parameterize a Beta distribution that encodes our beliefs on the average reward of policy π_k. The cumulative reward in a cycle is added to the running estimate $S(k)$ (line 10) of the current policy k and an update of the form $t - r$ is added to $F(k)$. This update step is critical and ensure that the mean of the Beta distribution is an unbiased estimate of average reward $\rho(k)$. Then for the new policy selection, we draw a realization

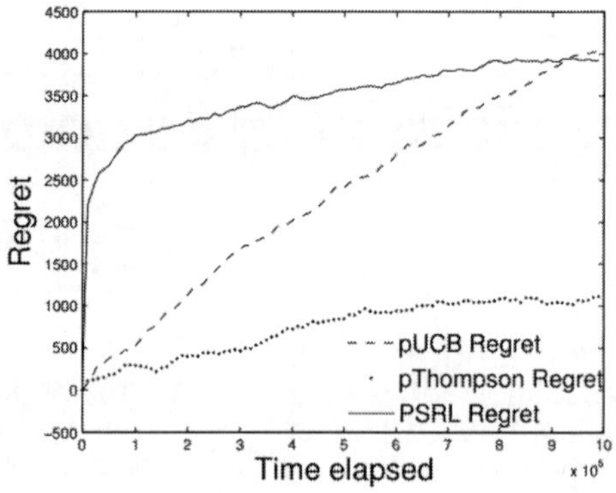

Figure 1: Regret as a function of number of rounds for the slow server problem.

for each of the K Beta distributions and pick that policy whose realization value is the highest.

Note that the PSRL algorithm maintain $O(M^2N)$ estimates. This is significantly higher compared to our algorithms, that typically maintain $O(M)$ estimates (as seen in many problem instances).

4. NUMERICAL RESULTS

We consider the slow server problem [3] and assume that we do not know the service rate parameters themselves in this setting but know that $\mu_1 > \mu_2$. Let the buffer size be $B < \infty$. Note that for this setting, the optimal policy is of the threshold type. For our experiment, we chose $\lambda = \frac{12}{31}$, $\mu_1 = \frac{18}{31}$ and $\mu_2 = \frac{1}{31}$. The buffer length of the queue was chosen to be 20 (thus leading to a number of states equal to 80). We ran 10 Monte Carlo simulations. As shown in Figure 1, pUCB and pThompson perform much better than PSRL from the very outset. This clearly illustrates the advantage of using knowledge of the optimal policy structure.

5. CONCLUDING REMARKS

We have built on the well established, easy to use UCB and Thompson sampling algorithms to provide competitive regret minimizing RL algorithms (making novel modifications for getting unbiased estimated of the long run average reward $\rho(k)$ and the number of rounds that each policy π_k needs to be applied). Such direct use of structural information is not easily possible for the state of the art PSRL algorithm. The algorithms presented are simple and better than state-of-the-art methods for cumulative regret minimization in RL settings. They have significant advantage in terms of computation and sampling costs.

REFERENCES

[1] S. Agrawal and N. Goyal. Analysis of thompson sampling for the multi-armed bandit problem. *arXiv preprint arXiv:1111.1797*, 2011.

[2] P. Auer, N. Cesa-Bianchi, and P. Fischer. Finite-time analysis of the multiarmed bandit problem. *Machine learning*, 47(2-3):235–256, 2002.

[3] W. Lin and P. Kumar. Optimal control of a queuing system with two heterogeneous servers. *IEEE Trans. on Automatic Control*, 29:696–703, 1984.

[4] I. Osband, D. Russo, and B. Van Roy. (more) efficient reinforcement learning via posterior sampling. pages 3003–3011, 2013.

[5] M. L. Puterman. *Markov decision processes: discrete stochastic dynamic programming*. John Wiley & Sons, 2014.

[6] S. M. Ross. *Stochastic processes*, volume 2. John Wiley & Sons New York, 1996.

Game-theoretic Modeling of Transmission Line Reinforcements with Distributed Generation

(Extended Abstract)

Merlinda Andoni
Heriot-Watt University
Edinburgh, UK
ma146@hw.ac.uk

Valentin Robu
Heriot-Watt University
Edinburgh, UK
v.robu@hw.ac.uk

ABSTRACT

Favourable sites for renewable generation are often remote locations (such as islands) where installed capacity, e.g. from wind turbines, exceeds local aggregate demand. We study the effect that curtailment mechanisms - applied when there is excess generation - have on the incentives to build additional capacity and the profitability of the generators. Next, for a two-location setting, we study the combined effect that curtailment schemes and line access rules have on the decision to invest in transmission expansion. In particular, for "common access" rules, this leads to a Stackelberg game between transmission and local generation capacity investors, and we characterise the equilibrium of this game. Finally, we apply and exemplify our model to a concrete problem of a grid reinforcement project, between Hunterston and the Kintyre peninsula, in western Scotland, and we determine a mechanism for setting transmission charges that assures both the profitability of the line and local renewable investors.

Keywords

generation incentives, renewable energy, transmission investment, Stackelberg game

1. INTRODUCTION

Integrating energy generated from renewable sources into existing grids is one of the key challenges for ensuring a sustainable, carbon-free energy future [1, 5]. A plethora of incentives have led fast increases of installed renewable generation capacity. However, a key problem is that locations which are best suited for installing new generation capacity (due to favourable resources or social approval), such as large wind turbines, are typically remote locations, such as islands far from population/industry centres of high electricity demand. At these areas, a substantial amount of generated energy might be subject to *curtailment*, as it cannot be absorbed by the grid, because of low local demand or insufficient grid capacity to transport it elsewhere. In practice, each location's curtailment level and crucially the curtailment policy applied are very significant factors affecting the decision of investors to build new generation capacity [4]. Apart from technical, regulatory and legal implications, covered by the power systems literature [3], the curtailment schemes can play a crucial role in generation and transmission expansion, the study of which is the prime objective of our work.

Integration of renewable generation requires substantial transmission investment, traditionally performed by distribution network or transmission system operators (DNOs/ TSOs), often associated with prohibitive costs. For this reason, incentivising privately built lines [2] would be highly desirable from a public policy standpoint. New power lines could be built under a *"common access"* principle, where private line investors are required to allow access to third parties, by setting a payment mechanism per unit of energy transmitted, the level of which is subject to a cap set by the regulator. In this work, we use game-theoretical models to examine the interplay of curtailment mechanisms and line access rules and we show this leads to a complex *Stackelberg game*, between the line investor and local generators, and we determine the expected generation and profits at equilibrium. Finally, we apply our theoretical results to a real-life project.

2. CURTAILMENT STRATEGIES AND GENERATION INCENTIVES

The most widely used curtailment schemes can be summarised as last-in-first out (LIFO) and Pro Rata schemes. In *LIFO*-based curtailment, generators are curtailed based on the inverse order in which they were granted the right to connect to the grid. By contrast, *Pro Rata* shares curtailment equally among installed generators proportionally to the rated capacity or actual power output, at the time of curtailment. Our work shows that LIFO displays a clear market advantage for early connections, leading to lower capacity factors for "late" generators than Pro Rata, which is detrimental both for the viability of existing and future investment. Given an area where curtailment is imposed, we determine an upper level of tolerable curtailment, which enables renewable capacity investment to be profitable, which depends on the relation of the generation cost with the Feed in Tariff (FiT) price. Moreover, since the curtailment scheme is usually chosen by a regulatory authority or the local DNO, we show that given a single location and a perfectly competitive setting (Cournot analysis), the local generation capacity is maximised under proportional curtailment schemes, which share curtailment equally amongst generators.

Appears in: *Proceedings of the 15th International Conference on Autonomous Agents and Multiagent Systems (AAMAS 2016), J. Thangarajah, K. Tuyls, C. Jonker, S. Marsella (eds.), May 9–13, 2016, Singapore.*

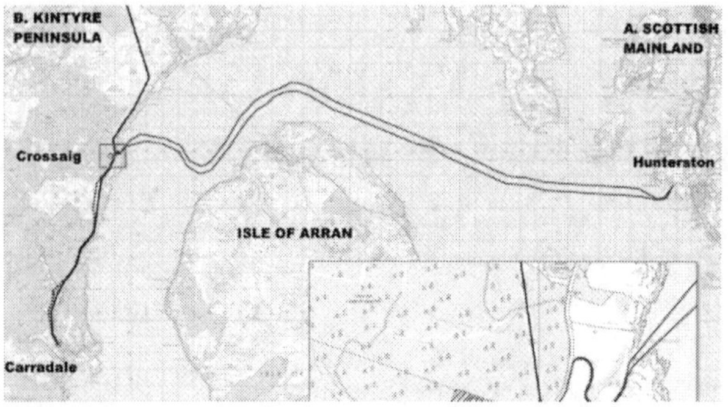

Figure 1: Transmission line connecting Scottish mainland to the Kintyre peninsula

3. TRANSMISSION INVESTMENT

Next we consider two locations, where excess generation and demand are not co-located: location A is a net consumer (e.g. a mainland location with industry or significant population density) and B is a net energy producer (e.g. a remote region rich in wind resource). Moreover, we consider two players: a line investor interested in building the $A - B$ transmission link and additional renewable generation capacity at B and a local player, who represents other renewable generators or investors located at B.

Crucially, in this setting, the line investor has a "first mover" advantage, as only he can build the grid infrastructure, which is expensive and technically challenging and only a limited set of investors (such as DNO-approved or DNOs themselves), have the technical expertise and regulatory approval to carry it out. The line investor (or leader) can assess and evaluate the reaction of other investors to determine his strategy, namely the capacity of the power line and the level of renewable capacity to be installed, with ultimate goal to influence the equilibrium price and maximise his profits. Local investors (or follower) can only act after observing the leader's strategy. This two-stage process is analysed as a Stackelberg game and its equilibrium is found through backward induction. We determine the expected generation and profits for both players, for LIFO and Pro Rata. Equilibrium results depend on the FiT price, transmission fee, generation costs and the demand at A. We show that under a LIFO scheme the line investor is protected from any curtailment, hence he can build all generation capacity to cover demand at A himself. On the other hand, a proportional scheme leads to larger volumes of generation capacity being built than actual demand, subject to an upper level of curtailment.

4. NETWORK UPGRADE CASE-STUDY

Next, the theoretical model was applied to the concrete case-study of the Kintyre-Hunterston transmission link, in Western Scotland[1] (see Fig. 1). The power grid in the Kintyre peninsula, originally designed to serve a rural area, proved insufficient to accommodate the large amounts of wind generation built in the area. SSE (the local DNO) proceeded in a £$230m$ network upgrade project, which includes a sub-sea link, creating headroom for additional 150 MW of renewable capacity. Based on the parameters of this project, we determine the capacity built and the profits of the line and local investors for a Stackelberg game.

[1]https://www.ssepd.co.uk/KintyreHunterston/

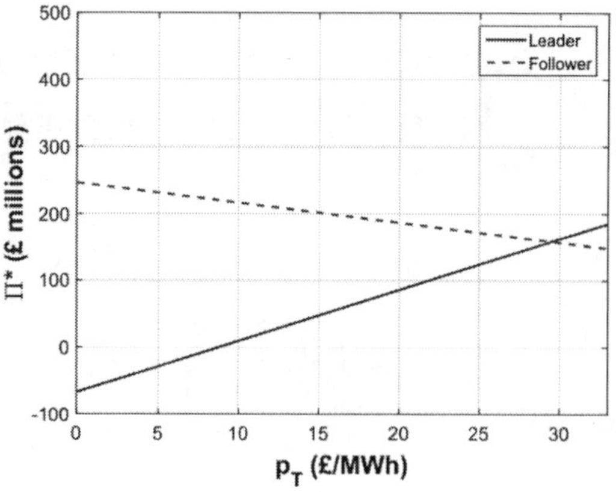

Figure 2: Effect of transmission fee on profits at Stackelberg equilibrium

In Fig. 2, we show the effect of the transmission fee p_T on the profits Π of the players. The transmission charges, agreed by the line investor and the regulatory authority, have to be set within a specific range. Low values of p_T may lead to the investment being aborted (i.e. when the leader's profits are above 0 – in our case, transmission charges need to be at least £$0.08/kWh$) and high values might discourage additional investment from local community investors. Regulatory authorities, who seek renewable facilitation can promote grid infrastructure expansion, not only by providing subsidies or technical support, but by allowing "common access" rules, as a tool to attract private investment and improve the profitability of line investors. To our knowledge, this is the first work examining the combined effects of curtailment strategies and transmission access rules on generation capacity investment and foremost network expansion.

REFERENCES

[1] G. Chalkiadakis, V. Robu, R. Kota, A. Rogers, and N. R. Jennings. Cooperatives of distributed energy resources for efficient virtual power plants. In *10th International conference on Autonomous Agents and Multi-Agent Systems*, pages 787–794, Taipei, May 2011. AAMAS.

[2] P. Joskow and J. Tirole. Merchant transmission investment. *The Journal of Industrial Economics*, 53(2):233–264, June 2005.

[3] L. Kane and G. Ault. Evaluation of wind power curtailment in active network management schemes. *IEEE Transactions on Power Systems*, 30(2):672–679, 2015.

[4] A. Laguna Estopier, E. Crosthwaite Eyre, S. Georgiopoulos, and C. Marantes. FPP low carbon networks: Commercial solutions for active network management. In *CIRED*, Stockholm, 2013.

[5] V. Robu, R. K. Ramachandra, G. Chalkiadakis, A. Rogers, and N. R. Jennings. Cooperative virtual power plant formation using scoring rules. In *26th Conference on Artificial Intelligence*, pages 370–376, Toronto, July 2012. AAAI.

Covering Number: Analyses for Approximate Continuous-state POMDP Planning*

(Extended Abstract)

Zongzhang Zhang
Soochow University
zzzhang@suda.edu.cn

Quan Liu
Soochow University
quanliu@suda.edu.cn

ABSTRACT

To date, many theoretical results on discrete POMDPs have not yet been extended to continuous-state POMDPs, due to the infinite dimensionality of the belief space in a continuous-state case. In this paper, we define a distance in the ℓ_n-metric space with respect to a partitioning representation of the continuous-state space, and formalize the size of the search space reachable under inadmissible heuristics via the covering number concept. Together with existing proof techniques in discrete POMDPs, we use the covering number to analyze the computational complexity of approximate planning for some types of continuous-state POMDPs.

Keywords

POMDP; Continuous-state Space; Complexity Theory

1. INTRODUCTION

Recent developments in approximate solutions, e.g., point-based methods and online heuristic algorithms, have drastically improved the speed of discrete POMDP planning. On the theortical front, the covering number of a search space has been used to quantify the complexity of approximate discrete POMDP planning [2, 4]. However, most real world POMDP problems are naturally modeled by continuous-state spaces. In this case, the dimensionality of the belief space is infinite. Thus, simple generalizations of known approaches and complexity results for discrete-state models to continuous-state domains are not appropriate.

To find approximate solutions, existing approaches first approximately represent beliefs in the infinite-dimensional space by a low-dimensional discrete representation. Some of them share the idea to represent beliefs in the infinite-dimensional continuous belief space by a parametric form and solve the approximate POMDP on the parametric space. The algorithm recently proposed in Brechtel et al. [1] is similar to ours, in that they also automatically learn a low-dimensional, discrete representation of the continuous-state space during the process of solving. The insight exploited in [1] is that states which are close in the continuous-state space will usually lead to similar outcomes and thus have similar α-vectors in most problems. Motivated by the work of [1], we propose a disjunct space representation, namely, space partitioning, with piecewise constant beliefs and α-functions. Then, we define a distance in the ℓ_n-metric space with respect to the space partitioning and use it to formalize the size of the search space reachable under inadmissible heuristics. Thus, we can use the covering number proof techniques in discrete POMDPs to analyze the computational complexity of approximate planning for some types of continuous-state POMDP from the covering number viewpoint.

*The work was supported in part by National Natural Science Foundation of China (61502323, 61272005, 61472262).

Appears in: *Proceedings of the 15th International Conference on Autonomous Agents and Multiagent Systems (AAMAS 2016), J. Thangarajah, K. Tuyls, C. Jonker, S. Marsella (eds.), May 9–13, 2016, Singapore.*

2. DEFINITIONS

Formally, a POMDP is a tuple (S, A, Z, T, R, Ω), where S, A, and Z, respectively, denote a state space, action space and observation space; T, R, and Ω are transition, reward, and observation functions, respectively. In continuous-state POMDPs, S is continuous, but A and Z are discrete.

The knowledge about the system's state is represented by a belief b in the belief space $\mathcal{B}$ with $b : S \to \mathbb{R}_{\geq 0}$ and $\int_{s \in S} b(s)ds = 1$. The initial belief b_0 is assumed to be known. After taking action a in belief b, the agent reaches the next belief $b^{a,z}$, computed by the Bayesian updating formula.

The goal of a POMDP solver is to find a policy $\pi : \mathcal{B} \to A$ maximizing the value $V : \mathcal{B} \to \mathbb{R}$ for b_0. The value associated with a policy π is given by $\mathbf{E}\left[\sum_{t=0}^{\infty} \gamma^t R(b_t, \pi(b_t))\right]$. The optimal value function $V^*(b)$ satisfies the Bellman equation: $V^*(b) = \max_{a \in A} Q^*(b, a)$, where $Q^*(b, a) = R(b, a) + \sum_{z \in Z} Pr(z|b, a)V^*(b^{a,z})$. So, $\pi^*(b) = \arg\max_{a \in A} Q^*(b, a)$. Additionally, $V^*(b)$ can be approximated arbitrary well by a peicewise-linear and convex function: $V^*(b) \approx \max_{\alpha \in \Gamma^*}(\alpha \cdot b) = \max_{\alpha \in \Gamma^*} \int_{s \in S} b(s)\alpha(s)ds$ with $S \subseteq \mathbb{R}^n$ and $\alpha : S \to \mathbb{R}^n$, where Γ^* is the finite set of linear α-functions.

We use V^L and V^U to represent the lower and upper bounds of V^*, respectively. Both V^L and V^U are assumed to be uniformly improvable. We also assume that we are provided with heuristics, f and y, that can provide initial values V_f^L to the lower bound of V^* and V_y^U to the upper bound of V^*. The function $y(b)$ may not be the true upper bound. That is, $y(b)$ is allowable to be less than $V^*(b)$ for some b in the belief space $\mathcal{B}$. Similarly, Q^L, Q^U, Q_f^L and Q_y^U are used for the corresponding bounds of Q^*.

A search space B is a subspace of $\mathcal{B}$ and can be represented as a belief tree $\mathcal{T}_B$ rooted at the initial belief b_0. The reachable belief space under inadmissible heuristics, $\mathcal{R}_{f,L}^{y,U}(b_0)$, is defined as the set of beliefs that are reachable from b_0 by going through action branches a that satisfy

$Q_y^U(b,a) \geq V^*(b)$ and observation branches z that satisfy $V_y^U(b) - V_f^L(b) - \frac{\epsilon}{\gamma^{d_b}} > 0$.

To split the continuous-state space into finite and abstraction states, we adopt the following definition of a state-space partitioning. Such a kind of partitioning works well in bounding the error between the value function of the induced discrete POMDP and the true value function of the original continuous-state POMDP.

DEFINITION 1. *A μ-partitioning of a continuous-state space S, $\mathcal{K}_\mu = \{K_\mu^1, K_\mu^2, \cdots K_\mu^{|\mathcal{K}_\mu|}\}$, satisfies that*

1. $S \subseteq \bigcup_{i=1}^{|\mathcal{K}_\mu|} K_\mu^i$;
2. $K_\mu^i \bigcap K_\mu^j = \emptyset$, *where* $i, j \in \{1, 2, \cdots, |\mathcal{K}_\mu|\}$ *and* $i \neq j$;
3. *for any* $s_i, s_j \in K_\mu^m$ *and any* $\alpha \in \Gamma^*$, $|\alpha(s_i) - \alpha(s_j)| \leq \mu$, *where* $i, j \in \{1, 2\}$ *and* $m = \{1, 2, \cdots, |\mathcal{K}_\mu|\}$.

The partitioning $\mathcal{K}_\mu$ induces an ℓ_n-distance metric on the belief space $\mathcal{B}$, as below:

DEFINITION 2. *Suppose that $\mathcal{K}_\mu$ be a μ-partitioning of the continuous-state space S. The distance between any two beliefs b and b' in the infinite-dimensional ℓ_n-metric space $\mathcal{B}$ with respect to $\mathcal{K}_\mu$ is*

$$d_{n,\mathcal{K}_\mu}(b,b') = \Big(\sum_{K \in \mathcal{K}_\mu} \Big| \int_{s\in K} b(s)ds - \int_{s \in K} b'(s)ds \Big|^n \Big)^{\frac{1}{n}}.$$

The new metric measures the difference in probability mass for subsets of states rather than individual states. The mathematical definition of the *covering number* of a set of points in the ℓ_n-metric space with respect to the space partitioning $\mathcal{K}_\mu$ is recapitulated as follows:

DEFINITION 3. *Given an infinite-dimensional ℓ_n-metric space $\mathcal{X}$, a δ-cover of a set $B \subseteq \mathcal{X}$ is a set of points $C \subseteq \mathcal{X}$ such that for every point $b \in B$, there is a point $c \in C$ with $d_{n,\mathcal{K}_\mu}(b,c) \leq \delta$. The δ-covering number of B, denoted by $\mathcal{C}_B(\delta)$, is the size of the smallest δ-cover of B.*

Intuitively, the covering number of a space B is equal to the minimum number of balls of radius δ needed to cover B. We denote $\mathcal{C}_{f,L}^{y,U}(\delta)$ as the δ-covering number of $\mathcal{R}_{f,L}^{y,U}(b_0)$.

3. COMPLEXITY RESULTS

The following Lipschitz condition is satisfied by the optimal value function on the ℓ_n-metric space with respect to the space partitioning $\mathcal{K}_\mu$.

LEMMA 1. *Let $\mathcal{K}_\mu$ be a μ-partitioning of the continuous-state space S, and let $\mathcal{B}$ be the corresponding belief space over S in the ℓ_n-metric space. For any b, $b' \in \mathcal{B}$, if $d_{n,\mathcal{K}_\mu}(b,b') \leq \delta$, then $|V^*(b) - V^*(b')| \leq \frac{R_{\max}}{1-\gamma}\rho_n\delta + 2\mu$. Here*

$$\rho_n = \begin{cases} 1 & n = 1 \\ \sqrt{|\mathcal{K}_\mu|} & 1 < n \leq 2 \\ |\mathcal{K}_\mu| & 2 < n \leq \infty. \end{cases} \quad (1)$$

The effect of the μ-partitioning over the state space in Lemma 1 is to obtain a finite-dimensional belief representation and constrain the error caused by dimensional reduction, that is, the difference of optimal values between two beliefs in the same μ-region splitted by $\mathcal{K}_\mu$, is no more than 2μ.

Lemma 1 is fundamental here because it provides a way of connecting the covering number to POMDP planning complexity: for any two beliefs in an infinite-dimensional space of continuous probability distributions, if their distance in the ℓ_n-metric space with respect to $\mathcal{K}_\mu$ is small, then their optimal values are also similar.

Using Lemma 1, we can establish a theoretical connection between the covering number and the planning complexity of continuous-state POMDPs, as below:

THEOREM 1. *Assume that $\mathcal{K}_\mu$ be a μ-partitioning of the continuous-state space S, where $\mu \leq \frac{(1-\gamma)\epsilon}{6\gamma}$. Suppose that the computational complexity of $\int_{s\in K} b(s)ds$ for any $K \in \mathcal{K}_\mu$ is $O(1)$. For any $b_0 \in \mathcal{B}$, let $\mathcal{C}_{f,L}^{y,U}(\delta)$ be the δ-covering number of $\mathcal{R}_{f,L}^{y,U}(b_0)$ in the ℓ_n-metric space with respect to $\mathcal{K}_\mu$. Define $\zeta = \max\{0, \max_{b\in\mathcal{R}(b_0)}[V^*(b_0) - V_y^U(b)]\}$. Given constant $\epsilon > 0$, an approximation $V(b_0)$ of $V^*(b_0)$, with error $|V^*(b_0) - V(b_0)| \leq 2\epsilon + \gamma\zeta$, can be found in time $O\Big(h \cdot \mathcal{C}_{f,L}^{y,U}(\delta/2)^2\Big)$, where $h = \log_\gamma \frac{(1-\gamma)\epsilon}{3R_{\max}}$, $\delta = \frac{(1-\gamma)^2\epsilon}{3\gamma\rho_n R_{\max}}$, V_f^L is used as an initial lower bound, and the inadmissible heuristic function V_y^U is used for the initial upper bound. Here, ρ_n is defined as Equation 1.*

The theorem provides insights in the three aspects: (1) under some conditions an approximately optimal solution over the ℓ_n-metric space with respect to $\mathcal{K}_\mu$ can be computed in time at most quadratic polynomial in the covering number of $\mathcal{R}_{f,L}^{y,U}(b_0)$; (2) prior knowledge can be used as heuristics to reduce the search space size to make POMDP problems easier to solve; and (3) a near optimal policy is still computable when using an inadmissible heuristic as the upper bound of V^*. These insights might be helpful in designing more efficient methods for continuous-state POMDPs.

Finally, we discuss the two conditions in Theorem 1. The first one is that the computational complexity of finding a μ-partitioning of the continuous-state space is $O\big(h \cdot \mathcal{C}_{f,L}^{y,U}(\delta/2)^2\big)$. This is satisfiable under the assumption: there exists a positive constant θ such that, for any two states s and s' satisfying $|s - s'| \leq \theta$, we have $|\alpha(s) - \alpha(s')| \leq \mu$. We think such an assumption can be met in most continuous-state problems. When $|s - s'| < +\infty$, $|\mathcal{K}_\mu|$ equals to $\lceil 1/\epsilon * \max_{s,s'} |s - s'| \rceil$ in this case. The second one that requiring $\int_{s\in K} b(s)ds$ to be computed in $O(1)$ is satisfiable when the beliefs can be represented by Gaussian mixtures [3]. In this case, the integral $\int_{s\in K} b(s)ds$, for a continuous region K, has a closed form.

REFERENCES

[1] S. Brechtel, T. Gindele, and R. Dillmann. Solving continuous POMDPs: Value iteration with incremental learning of an efficient space representation. In *Proc. ICML-13*, pages 370–378, 2013.

[2] D. Hsu, W. Lee, and N. Rong. What makes some POMDP problems easy to approximate. In *Proc. NIPS-07*, pages 689–696, 2007.

[3] J. Porta, N. Vlassis, M. Spaan, and P. Poupart. Point-based value iteration for continuous POMDPs. *Journal of Machine Learning Research*, 7:2329–2367, 2006.

[4] Z. Zhang, D. Hsu, and W. Lee. Covering number for efficient heuristic-based POMDP planning. In *Proc. ICML-14*, pages 28–36, 2014.

Trust Management for Composite Services in Distributed Multi-agent Systems with Indirect Ratings

(Extended Abstract)

Tung Doan Nguyen
Auckland University of Technology, New Zealand
tung.nguyen@aut.ac.nz

Quan Bai
Auckland University of Technology, New Zealand
quan.bai@aut.ac.nz

Categories and Subject Descriptors

I.2.11 [**Artificial Intelligence**]: Distributed Artificial Intelligence—*Intelligent agents, Multi-agent systems*

Keywords

Trust management, reputation, composite service, rating distribution

1. INTRODUCTION

So far, trust evaluation models depend highly on collected evidences, which are mainly in the form of ratings, to produce trust values [3]. However, many situations require agents to form groups to provide more complicated services (composite services); meanwhile, consumers rate the quality of a composite service as a whole rather than individual group members [2]. Namely, all providers, who are in charge of the sub-services, are not rated individually. The lack of effective rating distribution mechanism has produced a gap in trust management systems since it causes the missing evidence of the members joined in composite services; thus, it can affect the robustness of trust evaluation models.

To distribute a group rating is a non-trivial problem, especially when the given ratings could damage agents' reputation. The subjective and indivisible nature of ratings restricts the use of fair-division [1] approaches in finding a solution. Under uncertainty assumption of members' contribution and group structures, self-interest members could argue that they performed well and lay the blame on others for any undesirable rating of the group. To distribute group rating while reducing the conflict of interest of members, this paper proposes an evidence-based approach, considers supporting facts related to the performance of members to distribute the group rating. Firstly, we develop a communication protocol to cope with collecting evidence in distributed environment. We form the performance graph from the social relations of members and then distribute group ratings based on obtained graph characteristics.

2. THE EVIDENCE-BASED APPROACH

Under uncertainty, the distributed ratings of members are influenced by its base performance (the performance of agent when ignoring the current environmental factors, denoted as $QoS_{base}(p_i)$) adjusted by the uncertainty factor (Δ_u) of the current group:

$$QoS(p_i) = QoS_{base}(p_i) + \Delta_u\,(p_i \mid G) \tag{1}$$

To find the base performance of each agent, this paper introduces an extended evidence space, which includes current group G as an evidence to historical transactions provided by all members of group G. This approach can assure the space always has at least one evidence. Each group member will then form a performance graph, which comprises a set V of nodes (representing providers) together with a set of undirected weighted edges, i.e., E, indicating the degree of the performance relationship between two nodes. Edges contain two coefficients: distance and pairwise performance. The distance of two nodes is calculated by using:

$$d_{p_ip_j} = \frac{1}{1+\log(k)} \tag{2}$$

, where k is the number of evidence that contain both p_i and p_j; $d_{p_ip_j}$ has value in (0, 1]. Smaller distance means two agents work together more frequently. The pairwise performance of the agent p_i and agent p_j is calculated using

$$r_{p_ip_j} = \frac{\sum_{l=1}^{n} r_{\{G_n|G_n\in H_i\}}.\delta_l}{\sum_{l=1}^{n}\delta_l} \tag{3}$$

, where δ_l is the discount factor that control the weight of evidence based on timestamp. The evidential performance of the p_i in G is calculated from all provided evidence containing p_i. With the presence of other members in group G, the evidential performance of p_i is:

$$ep(p_i|G) = \frac{\sum_{j=1}^{j=n} d_{p_ip_j}^{-1} r_{p_ip_j}}{\sum_{j=1}^{j=n} d_{p_ip_j}^{-1}} \tag{4}$$

, where $ep(p_i|G)$ can be considered as the base performance of in the environment of group G. Next, the uncertainty can give a member a rating reward or punishment based on the evidence relevancy, which is the similarity of common features in feature set f_G between two groups:

$$Sim(G_i, G_j) = \frac{|f_{G_i} \cap f_{G_j}|}{|f_{G_i} \cup f_{G_j}|} \tag{5}$$

, where $0 \leq Sim_i(f_{G_i}, f_{G_j}) \leq 1$. The unaccountability of the extended evidence of p_i and the current group G:

$$UA(p_i|G) = 1 - \frac{\sum_{j=1}^{k} Sim(G, G_{ij})}{k} \tag{6}$$

Appears in: *Proceedings of the 15th International Conference on Autonomous Agents and Multiagent Systems (AAMAS 2016), J. Thangarajah, K. Tuyls, C. Jonker, S. Marsella (eds.), May 9–13, 2016, Singapore.*

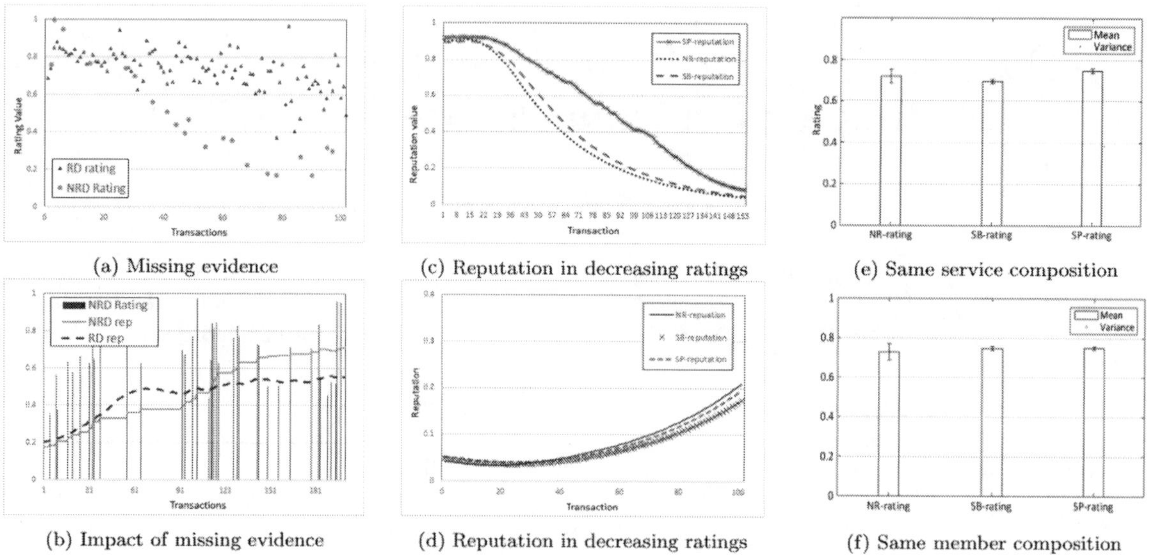

(a) Missing evidence
(b) Impact of missing evidence
(c) Reputation in decreasing ratings
(d) Reputation in decreasing ratings
(e) Same service composition
(f) Same member composition

Figure 1: Some experimental results of rating distribution in different settings

, where G_{ij} is group containing p_i. In case that member p_j has no historic transaction, the extended evidence space makes $UA(p_i|G) = 0$. Apply Equation 4 and 6 to Equation 1, the rating distribution for each p_i in a group:

$$R(p_i|G) = \begin{cases} ep_{p_i} + (1 - UA(p_i|G)) \cdot (r_G - ep_{p_i}) & \text{if } ep_i \leq r_G \\ ep_{p_i} + UA(p_i|G) \cdot (r_G - ep_{p_i}) & \text{if } ep_i > r_G \end{cases}$$

Some properties of the distribution (without proof): (1) Members with no evidence (or new comers) receive the same rating as group rating; (2) Members with smaller unaccountability receive less reward or punishment, and likewise.

3. EXPERIMENTAL RESULTS

Several experiments have been conducted to evaluate the consistency of reputation system and the satisfaction of members over distributed ratings. We consider that agents are honest and there is no collusion to manipulate the evidence. Providers were created with various performance profiles and a provider can join only one group at a time. The comparison of two systems, one with (RD) and one without a rating distribution method (NRD), shows that NRD system suffers from the missing evidence problem when the number of composite services increases (Fig.1a). Consequently, the NRD system is less reliable than RD since NRD calculates reputation values based on incomplete evidence (see Fig.1b).

The satisfaction is analysed by comparing our distribution (SP method) with two other methods, namely, service similarity based (SB method [2]) and a naive distribution (NR), which gives the same group rating to all members. Fig.1c and Fig.1d show the reputation under decreasing and increasing group ratings respectively. Both SB and SP methods show additional adjustments for ratings compared to NR method because the unaccountability factor makes reputation resist to sudden changes of group rating to evidential performance. As a consequence, the reputation of NR and SB changed relatively fast compared to SP method. Obviously, the rated members have better satisfaction under receiving low group ratings. In another experiment with more randomised ratings, the SP method outperformed the others two since it can keep the reputation of provider relatively high and stable. Finally, we investigated the effect of service composition to distribution in two cases. First, when providers join a group with same service composition (members can be different), statistical results show that the SB method has smallest rating variation amongst the three (see Fig.1e). It is because SB approach considers only the service similarity while ignoring the difference in members composition. However, in the case of groups with same member composition, SP approach has the least variation in both rating and reputation (see Fig.1f). These results also indicate that SP method can give better reputation protection for providers who frequently work together. They are less likely to receive unexpected ratings than other methods because the accountability factor is smaller than other.

4. CONCLUSIONS

This paper has investigated the indirect ratings in the context of groups and proposed an efficient method to distribute group rating to its members while diminishing the conflict of interest. The approach can be integrated easily into any reputation system to enhance the consistency and accuracy by adding performance evidence for trust evaluation.

REFERENCES

[1] S. J. Brams and A. D. Taylor. *Fair Division: From cake-cutting to dispute resolution.* Cambridge University Press, 1996.

[2] T. D. Nguyen and Q. Bai. Accountable individual trust from group reputations in multi-agent systems. In *PRICAI 2014: Trends in Artificial Intelligence*, volume 8862 of *Lecture Notes in Computer Science*, pages 1063–1075. Springer International Publishing, 2014.

[3] H. Yu, Z. Shen, C. Leung, C. Miao, and V. Lesser. A survey of multi-agent trust management systems. *IEEE Access*, 1:35–50, 2013.

Social Welfare in One-Sided Matching Mechanisms (Extended Abstract)

George Christodoulou
University of Liverpool
Ashton Street, Liverpool, U.K.
gchristo@liv.ac.uk

Aris Filos-Ratsikas
University of Oxford
Parks Road, Oxford, UK
aris.filos-ratsikas@cs.ox.ac.uk

Søren Kristoffer Stiil Frederiksen
Aarhus University
Abogade 34, Aarhus, DK
sorensf@gmail.com

Paul W. Goldberg
University of Oxford
Parks Road, Oxford, UK
paul.goldberg@cs.ox.ac.uk

Jie Zhang
University of Oxford
Parks Road, Oxford, UK
jie.zhang@cs.ox.ac.uk

Jinshan Zhang
University of Oxford
Ashton Street, Liverpool, UK
jinshan.zhang@liv.ac.uk

ABSTRACT

We study the Price of Anarchy of mechanisms for the well-known problem of one-sided matching, or house allocation, with respect to the social welfare objective. We consider both ordinal mechanisms, where agents submit preference lists over the items, and cardinal mechanisms, where agents may submit numerical values for the items being allocated. We present a general lower bound of $\Omega(\sqrt{n})$ on the Price of Anarchy, which applies to *all* mechanisms and we show that a very well-known mechanisms, Probabilistic Serial achieves a matching upper bound. We extend our lower bound to the Price of Stability of a large class of mechanisms that satisfy a common proportionality property.

Keywords

One-sided matching, probabilistic serial, truthfulness, price of anarchy, Nash equilibrium

1. INTRODUCTION

One-sided matching (also called the house allocation problem) is the fundamental problem of assigning items to agents, such that each agent receives exactly one item, which has numerous applications. In this setting, agents are often asked to provide *ordinal preferences*, i.e. preference lists, or rankings of the items. We assume that underlying these ordinal preferences, agents have numerical values specifying how much they value each item [7]. In game-theoretic terms, these are the agents' von Neumann-Morgenstern utility functions [12] and the associated preferences are often referred to as *cardinal preferences*.

A *mechanism* is a function that maps agents' valuations to matchings. However, agents are rational strategic entities that might not always report their valuations truthfully; they may misreport their values if that results in a better matching (from their own perspective). Assuming the agents report their valuations strategically to maximize their utilities, it is of interest to study the *Nash equilibria* of the induced game, i.e. strategy profiles from which no agent wishes to unilaterally deviate.

A natural objective for the designer is to choose the matching that maximizes the *social welfare*, i.e. the sum of agents' valuations for the items they are matched with, which is the most prominent measure of aggregate utility in the literature. Given the strategic nature of the agents, we are interested in mechanisms that maximize the social welfare *in the equilibrium*. We use the standard measure of equilibrium inefficiency, the *Price of Anarchy* [8], that compares the maximum social welfare attainable in any matching with the *worst-case* social welfare that can be achieved in an equilibrium.

We evaluate the efficiency of a mechanism with respect to the Price of Anarchy of the induced game. We study both deterministic and randomized mechanisms: in the latter case the output is a probability mixture over matchings, instead of a single matching. We are interested in the class of *cardinal* mechanisms, which use cardinal preferences, and generalize the ordinal mechanisms.

Note that our setting involves no monetary transfers and generally falls under the umbrella of *approximate mechanism design without money* [10]. In general settings without money, one has to fix a canonical representation of the valuations. A common approach in the literature is to consider the *unit-sum* normalization, i.e. each agent has a total value of 1 for all the items.

Our main contributions

Our main contribution can be summarized by the following theorem.

THEOREM 1. *The Price of Anarchy of Probabilistic Serial is $O(\sqrt{n})$ and the Price of Anarchy of any mechanism is $\Omega(\sqrt{n})$. This implies that Probabilistic Serial is (asymptotically) optimal among all mechanisms for the problem.*

The upper bound of the theorem holds with respect to the very general equilibrium notion, the *coarse correlated equilibrium*, as well as the *Bayes-Nash equilibrium*, when agents have incomplete information about the preference orderings of other agents.

We extend the lower bound of Theorem 1 to the the *Price of Stability*, a more optimistic measure of efficiency, for all

Appears in: *Proceedings of the 15th International Conference on Autonomous Agents and Multiagent Systems (AAMAS 2016), J. Thangarajah, K. Tuyls, C. Jonker, S. Marsella (eds.), May 9–13, 2016, Singapore.*

mechanisms that satisfy a simple *proportionality* property, which requires that any agent can report some preference list that guarantees her an allocation at least as good as an equal split (in terms of probability) of each item, regardless of the reports of the other agents. This property is satisfied by most mechanisms in literature, including Probabilistic Serial.

Finally, for deterministic mechanisms, we prove that no mechanism can achieve a Price of Anarchy smaller than $\Omega(n)$, proving that randomization is essential for non-trivial guarantees to be achievable. The proofs to our results can be found in the full version of the paper [5].

Discussion

The one-sided matching problem was introduced in [7] and has been studied extensively ever since, with various desirable objectives related to truthfulness, fairness and economic efficiency. The objective of social welfare maximization for one-sided matching problems has been studied before in the literature, for mechanisms that are truthful [6]. The authors in [6] prove that Random Priority, a well-known truthful mechanism, achieves an approximation ratio of $O(\sqrt{n})$, which is asymptotically optimal among all *truthful* mechanisms. Our lower bounds are more general, since they apply to *all* mechanisms, not just truthful ones. In particular, our lower bound on the Price of Anarchy of all mechanisms generalizes the corresponding bound for truthful mechanisms in [6].

We establish the tightness of the bounds in Theorem 1, by bounding the inefficiency of perhaps the most popular one-sided matching mechanism, Probabilistic Serial. The mechanism was introduced in [3] and since then, it has been in the center of attention of the matching literature, with related work on characterizations, strategic aspects and hardness of manipulation. Somewhat surprisingly, the Nash equilibria of the mechanism were only recently studied [1].

A somewhat different recent branch of study considers ordinal measures of efficiency instead of social welfare maximization, under the assumption that agents' preferences are only expressed through preference orderings over items [2, 9, 4]. While interesting, these measures of efficiency do not accurately encapsulate the socially desired outcome the way that social welfare does, especially since an underlying cardinal utility structure is part of the setting [3, 7, 12]. Our results actually suggest that in order to achieve the optimal welfare guarantees, one does not even need to elicit this utility structure; agents can only be asked to report preference orderings, which is arguably more appealing.

Finally, we point out that our work is in a sense analogous to the literature that studies the Price of Anarchy in item-bidding auctions for settings without money. Furthermore, the extension of our results to very general solution concepts (coarse correlated equilibria) and settings of incomplete information (Bayes-Nash equilibria) is somehow reminiscent of the *smoothness* framework [11] for games. While our results are not proven using the smoothness condition, our extension technique is similar in spirit.

Acknowledgements

G. Christodoulou, P.W. Goldberg and Jinshan Zhang were supported by the EPSRC grant EP/K01000X/1. P.W. Goldberg was supported by COST Action IC1205. A. Filos-Ratsikas and Jie Zhang were supported by the ERC Advanced Grant 321171 (ALGAME). A. Filos-Ratsikas and S.K.S. Frederiksen acknowledge support from the Danish National Research Foundation and The National Science Foundation of China (under the grant 61061130540) for the Sino-Danish Center for the Theory of Interactive Computation, within which part of this work was performed and support from the Center for Research in Foundations of Electronic Markets (CFEM), supported by the Danish Strategic Research Council. The authors would like to thank Piotr Krysta for useful discussion.

REFERENCES

[1] H. Aziz, S. Gaspers, S. Mackenzie, N. Mattei, N. Narodytska, and T. Walsh. Equilibria under the probabilistic serial rule. *arXiv preprint arXiv:1502.04888*, 2015.

[2] A. Bhalgat, D. Chakrabarty, and S. Khanna. Social Welfare in One-Sided Matching Markets without Money. In *APPROX-RANDOM*, pages 87–98, 2011.

[3] A. Bogomolnaia and H. Moulin. A New Solution to the Random Assignment Problem. *Journal of Economic Theory*, 100:295–328, 2001.

[4] D. Chakrabarty and C. Swamy. Welfare maximization and truthfulness in mechanism design with ordinal preferences. In *Proceedings of the 5th Conference on Innovations in Theoretical Computer Science*, pages 105–120, 2014.

[5] G. Christodoulou, A. Filos-Ratsikas, S. K. S. Frederiksen, P. W. Goldberg, J. Zhang, and J. Zhang. Social Welfare in One-sided Matching Mechanisms. *arXiv preprint arXiv:1502.03849*, 2015.

[6] A. Filos-Ratsikas, S. K. S. Frederiksen, and J. Zhang. Social welfare in one-sided matchings: Random priority and beyond. In *7th International Symposium on Algorithmic Game Theory (SAGT)*, pages 1–12, 2014.

[7] A. Hylland and R. Zeckhauser. The Efficient Allocation of Individuals to Positions. *The Journal of Political Economy*, 87(2):293–314, 1979.

[8] E. Koutsoupias and C. Papadimitriou. Worst-case equilibria. In *STACS 99*, pages 404–413. Springer, 1999.

[9] P. Krysta, D. Manlove, B. Rastegari, and J. Zhang. Size versus truthfulness in the House Allocation problem. In *Proceedings of the 15th ACM Conference on Economics and Computation*, pages 453–470. ACM, 2014.

[10] A. D. Procaccia and M. Tennenholtz. Approximate mechanism design without money. In *Proceedings of the 10th ACM Conference on Electronic Commerce*, pages 177–186. ACM, 2009.

[11] T. Roughgarden. Intrinsic robustness of the price of anarchy. In *Proceedings of the forty-first annual ACM symposium on Theory of computing*, pages 513–522. ACM, 2009.

[12] J. Von Neumann and O. Morgenstern. *Theory of games and economic behavior (60th Anniversary Commemorative Edition)*. Princeton university press, 2007.

Bribery in k-Approval and k-Veto Under Partial Information (Extended Abstract)

Dirk Briskorn
Schumpeter School of Business and Economics
Bergische Universität Wuppertal
Wuppertal, Germany
briskorn@uni-wuppertal.de

Gábor Erdélyi and Christian Reger
School of Economic Disciplines
University of Siegen
Siegen, Germany
{erdelyi, reger}@wiwi.uni-siegen.de

ABSTRACT

In bribery an external agent tries to alter the outcome of an election by changing some voters' votes. Usually, when investigating bribery problems, full information is assumed, i.e., that the manipulative agent knows the set of candidates, each voter's votes and the voting rule used. In this paper, we formally introduce different structures of partial information, we show the connections between them and existing notions, define bribery under partial profiles, and examine the complexity of bribery under partial information for the k-Approval and k-Veto rules.

Categories and Subject Descriptors

I.2.11 [**Artificial Intelligence**]: Distributed Artificial Intelligence—*Multiagent systems*

General Terms

Algorithms, Theory, Economics

Keywords

Computational Social Choice, Voting Rules, Bribery

1. INTRODUCTION

Voting provides a useful method for collective decision-making and preference aggregation, and as such has applications in politics, economics, and computer science. In many applications in computer science we are dealing with huge data volumes. Thus, it is worth studying the computational aspects of problems related to voting. For over two decades now, many have investigated the complexity of voting problems (such as the winner problem, manipulation, bribery, or electoral control) in different settings. Traditionally, the complexity of voting problems is studied under the full information assumption; in the bribery problem for instance, it is assumed that the briber knows the set of candidates, the set of voters, each voter's full preferences over the candidates, and the voting rule used. However, recognizing that in many real-world settings we simply lack full information, a new research line is concerned with the complexity analysis of voting problems under some kind of uncertainty. Following this approach, in this paper we present a systematic study of the complexity of bribery in k-Approval and k-Veto in settings where the briber has only partial information regarding the voters' preferences. Furthermore, we introduce three new notions of partial information and show the connections between these and existing models from the literature.

Appears in: *Proceedings of the 15th International Conference on Autonomous Agents and Multiagent Systems (AAMAS 2016), J. Thangarajah, K. Tuyls, C. Jonker, S. Marsella (eds.), May 9–13, 2016, Singapore.*

2. OUR RESULTS

In this section we introduce and motivate different types of partial information models followed by a discussion on how these types relate to each other. At the end of the section we present our results on bribery under partial information.

For each of the types of partial information introduced in the following we specify the structure of data given and how the set of potential rankings is specified. We let $m = |C|$ be the number of candidates.

Gaps (GAPS): Our first partial information model covers the case, where the briber only knows fractions of each vote, i.e., there are some blocks in each vote that are fully ranked and there are some blocks, where the briber knows which candidates there are in that block, but has no information on how they are ranked. Formally, for each vote v we have a partition $C_1^v, \dots, C_{2m+1}^v$ of the set of candidates and a total order for each C_k^v with k even. Note that possibly $C_k^v = \emptyset$ for some k. A ranking of candidates is in the information set if and only if for each (c, c') with $c \in C_k^v$ and $c' \in C_{k'}^v$, $k' > k$, c is preferred to c' and candidates in C_k^v, k even, are ranked according to the total order given for C_k^v. Note that if $C_k^v = C_{k+1}^v = \emptyset$ we can drop both partite sets without changing the information set. Therefore, we can restrict ourselves to at most $2m + 1$ partite sets.

One Gap (1GAP): A similar model was introduced by Baumeister et al. [1] as doubly-truncated preferences, where in each vote there are subsets of candidates ranked at the top and at the bottom of the votes, and there is a gap between the top and bottom ranked candidates. We adopt this notion and extend it in a way that we allow the top or bottom ranked candidate set to be empty. Formally, 1GAP refers to the special case of GAPS with $C_k^v = \emptyset$, for each $k \in \{1, 5, 6, \dots, 2m + 1\}$, for each voter v.

Top-truncated Orders (TTO): TTO was introduced by Baumeister et al. [1] and refers to the special case of 1GAP where $C_4^v = \emptyset$ for each voter v.

Bottom-truncated Orders (BTO): BTO was also introduced by Baumeister et al. [1] and refers to the special case of 1GAP where $C_2^v = \emptyset$ for each voter v.

Complete or empty votes (CEV): As suggested by Konczak and Lang [4], we introduce CEV as a special case of

Voting rule	FI	Gaps	FP	TOS	PC	CEV	1TOS	1Gap	TTO	BTO
Plurality	P	**NPC**	**NPC**	**NPC**	**NPC**	**P**	**P**	**NPC**	**P**	**NPC**
2-Approval	P	**NPC**	**NPC**	**NPC**	**NPC**	**P**	**P**	**NPC**	**P**	**NPC**
k-Approval, $k \geq 3$	NPC	*NPC*	*NPC*	*NPC*	*NPC*	*NPC*	*NPC*	*NPC*	*NPC*	*NPC*
Veto	P	**P**	**P**	**P**	**P**	**P**	**P**	**P**	**P**	**P**
2-Veto	P	**P**	**P**	**P**	**P**	**P**	**P**	**P**	**P**	**P**
3-Veto	P	**P**	**P**	**P**	**P**	**P**	**P**	**P**	**P**	**P**
k-Veto, $k \geq 4$	NPC	*NPC*	*NPC*	*NPC*	*NPC*	*NPC*	*NPC*	*NPC*	*NPC*	*NPC*

Table 1: Summary of the complexity results for bribery under partial information. P stands for element of P, NPC stands for NP-complete.

TTO with either $C_2^v = \emptyset$ or $C_3^v = \emptyset$ for each voter v. Note that this is equivalent to the special case of BTO with either $C_1^v = \emptyset$ or $C_2^v = \emptyset$ for each voter v.

Fixed Positions (FP): For each vote v we have a subset of candidates C^v with distinct positions in range between 1 and m assigned. A ranking of candidates is in the information set if and only if each candidate in C^v has the assigned position.

Pairwise Comparisons (PC): PC is probably the most natural way of displaying partial preferences. It has been introduced by Konczak and Lang [4] and has been used in many papers since. Formally, for each vote v we have a subset Π^v of $C \times C$. A ranking of candidates is in the information set if and only if for each $(c, c') \in \Pi^v$ c is preferred to c'. Note that we may restrict Π^v to be asymmetric and transitive for matters of convenience.

Totally Ordered Subset of Candidates (TOS): For each voter the briber has the information in a form of a totally ordered subset (for each voter a possibly different subset). Formally, for each vote v we have a subset C^v of candidates and a total order for C^v. A ranking of candidates is in the information set if and only if c is preferred to c' for each pair of candidates (c, c') with $c, c' \in C^v$ and c is preferred to c' according to the given order.

Unique Totally Ordered Subset of Candidates (1TOS): 1TOS was first suggested by Konczak and Lang [4] and formally defined by Chevaleyre et al. [2]. 1TOS refers to the special case of TOS where each voter v ranks the same subset of candidates, i.e., $C^v = C'$ for each voter v.

The following theorem shows the relations between the partial information models discussed in this paper.

THEOREM 2.1. *The following relations hold:*

(1) 1TOS ⊂ TOS.
(2) CEV ⊂ TOS.
(3) CEV ⊂ TTO.
(4) CEV ⊂ BTO.
(5) TTO ⊂ 1GAP.
(6) BTO ⊂ 1GAP.
(7) 1GAP ⊂ GAPS.
(8) 1GAP ⊂ FP.
(9) TOS ⊂ PC.
(10) GAPS ⊂ PC.

This list is complete in the following sense: Relations that are not listed here and that do not follow from transitivity do not hold in general.

An *n-voter profile* P on C consists of n strict linear orders $P = (v_1, \ldots, v_n)$. Let P' be a partial profile and let $I(P')$ denote the *information set*, which is the set of all complete n-voter profiles which are not contradicted by P'.

In the classic bribery problem (with full information about votes and a voting rule given) the question is whether a briber can change a given number of votes such that his favorite candidate is a winner. We carry over this idea to partial information models. Given an election, a designated candidate c, a non-negative integer ℓ and a partial profile P' according to one of the partial information models. We ask if it is possible to make c a winner of the election under a given voting rule for each complete profile in $I(P')$ by changing up to ℓ votes?

Table 1 shows the results on the complexity of bribery under partial information in k-Approval and k-Veto. Column FI displays the results for the case with full information due to Faliszewski et al. [3] and Lin [5]. Results in italic are hardness results that follow from already existing hardness results for full information. Results in boldface are new. Each NP-hardness result was achieved by a reduction from the NP-complete problem EXACT COVER BY 3-SETS.

3. CONCLUSIONS

We introduced three new partial information models (Fixed Positions, Gaps, and Totally Ordered Subsets of Candidates) and studied six known models. We showed the relations of all nine partial information models discussed in this paper. Furthermore, we defined bribery under partial information. We obtained a number of results on the complexity of this problem with respect to two important families of voting rules, namely k-Approval and k-Veto. We refer the reader to Table 1 for an overview.

Acknowledgments

The second and third author were supported in part by the DFG under grant ER 738/2-1.

REFERENCES

[1] D. Baumeister, P. Faliszewski, J. Lang, and J. Rothe. Campaigns for lazy voters: Truncated ballots. In *Proceedings of the 11th International Joint Conference on Autonomous Agents and Multiagent Systems*, pages 577–584. IFAAMAS, June 2012.

[2] Y. Chevaleyre, J. Lang, N. Maudet, and J. Monnot. Possible winners when new candidates are added: The case of scoring rules. In *Proceedings of the 24th AAAI Conference on Artificial Intelligence*, pages 762–767. AAAI Press, July 2010.

[3] P. Faliszewski, E. Hemaspaandra, and L. A. Hemaspaandra. How hard is bribery in elections? *Journal of Artificial Intelligence Research*, 35:485–532, 2009.

[4] K. Konczak and J. Lang. Voting procedures with incomplete preferences. In *Proceedings of IJCAI-05 Multidisciplinary Workshop on Advances in Preference Handling*, pages 124–129, 2005.

[5] A. Lin. The complexity of manipulating k-approval elections. In *Proceedings of the 3rd International Conference on Agents and Artificial Intelligence*, pages 212–218, 2011.

Local Search on Trees and a Framework for Automated Construction Using Multiple Identical Robots*

(Extended Abstract)

Trevor Cai
Computer Science Dept.
Univ. of Southern California
tcai@usc.edu

David Y. Zhang
Google
New York City
dzhang21@gmail.com

T. K. Satish Kumar
Computer Science Dept.
Univ. of Southern California
tkskwork@gmail.com

Sven Koenig
Computer Science Dept.
Univ. of Southern California
skoenig@usc.edu

Nora Ayanian
Computer Science Dept.
Univ. of Southern California
ayanian@usc.edu

ABSTRACT

We present an algorithmic framework for automated construction using multiple identical robots. Our approach is based on the principle of tree-based dynamic programming and a concomitant idea of local search on trees to improve the quality of the generated plans. Inspired by the TERMES project of Harvard University, robots in this domain are required to gather construction blocks from a reservoir and coordinate with each other in building user-specified structures much larger than themselves. While the robots are roughly of the same size as the blocks, they can scale greater heights by using temporarily constructed ramps in the substructures. Our algorithm employs an inner loop in which the planning problem is solved by performing dynamic programming on a tree that spans the footprint of the user-specified structure. The outer loop of the algorithm furnishes a good tree for the inner loop. We show how we can search for a good tree in the outer loop using local search methods that yield significant improvements in plan quality. Synchronization rules are then applied to parallelize the execution of the generated plan for multiple identical robots.

General Terms

Algorithms, Performance, Experimentation

Keywords

Automated Construction, Multiple Identical Robots

1. INTRODUCTION

The Harvard TERMES project is intended to investigate how small reliable robots can cooperate in teams to build user-specified 3D structures much larger than themselves [2]. The hardware system consists of small autonomous mobile robots and a reservoir of passive "building blocks". The robots and blocks are endowed with mechanical features that make the system very reliable. Moreover, the robots are of roughly the same size as the blocks themselves; and yet, they can manipulate these blocks one at a time to build tall structures by stacking the blocks on each other and building ramps to scale greater heights. Multiple robots should be able to work with each other in a team to build a user-specified structure as cost-effectively and as fast as possible.

In [1], a polynomial-time tree-based algorithm is presented to solve planning problems in the TERMES domain. In particular, given a user-specified structure, the algorithm yields a cost-effective plan that attempts to minimize the number of pickup and drop-off operations on blocks. The inner loop of the algorithm solves the planning problem by conducting dynamic programming on a tree that spans the footprint of the user-specified structure. The outer loop of the algorithm furnishes a good tree for the inner loop. Put together, the algorithm exploits the *locality principle*: "distant substructures of a building are only loosely related to each other".

While the algorithm in [1] exploits the locality principle, it does not fully explore the space of all trees in the outer loop. Instead, it uses specific trees like the *minimum spanning tree* (MST) or its *reweighted* version (RMST). We show how we can search for a good tree in the outer loop using local search methods that yield significant improvements in plan quality. A second problem with the algorithm in [1] is that it generates a sequential plan meant to be executed by a single robot. In this paper, we also show how we can parallelize the generated plan using proper synchronization rules to make it viable for multiple robots. We henceforth use basic concepts and terminology introduced in [1].

*NSF 1409987, 1319966; MURI N00014-09-1-1031

Appears in: *Proceedings of the 15th International Conference on Autonomous Agents and Multiagent Systems (AAMAS 2016), J. Thangarajah, K. Tuyls, C. Jonker, S. Marsella (eds.), May 9–13, 2016, Singapore.*

2. LOCAL SEARCH ON TREES

Given a spanning tree T, the procedure 'Compute-Tree-Score' in Algorithm 1 calculates the cost of the construction plan generated by the inner loop if it conducted dynamic programming on T. Procedure 'Local-Search-on-Trees' in Algorithm 2 presents the local search procedure on the space of spanning trees. It takes as input a candidate spanning tree *seedTree* that acts as the starting point of the local search. Here, the graph G is a graphical representation of

Algorithm 1: Procedure Compute-Tree-Score

Input: a spanning tree T of the workspace graph G
Output: the *score* of T

(1) Initialize *total* to 0.
(2) Generate markers on tree T.
(3) For each node N in T:
(a) Let $L_N = \{m_{(N,1)}, m_{(N,2)} \dots m_{(N,|L_N|)}\}$ be N's list of markers.
(b) For $i = 1, 2 \dots |L_N| - 1$:
(b1) $total = total + |m_{(N,i+1)} - m_{(N,i)}|$.
(4) Return *total*.

Algorithm 2: Procedure Local-Search-on-Trees

Input: a starting tree *seedTree* spanning G; the maximum number of flips *maxFlips*; the cycle length filter c
Output: an improved tree based on conducting local search on the space of spanning trees of G within the parameters *maxFlips* and c

(1) Set *currentTree* to *seedTree*.
(2) Set *minScore* to Compute-Tree-Score(*currentTree*).
(3) Set *flips* to 0.
(4) While *flips* < *maxFlips*:
(a) Let (u, v) be an edge in $G \backslash currentTree$ such that $dist_{currentTree}(u, v) < c$.
(b) Let graph H be *currentTree* $\cup\{(u, v)\}$.
(c) Let C be a cycle in H.
(d) Set lists *improvedList* and *equalsList* to empty lists.
(e) For each edge $e \neq (u, v)$ in C:
(e1) Let T be the tree $H \backslash \{e\}$.
(e2) If Compute-Tree-Score(T) < *minScore*, add e to list *improvedList*.
(e3) If Compute-Tree-Score(T) == *minScore*, add e to list *equalsList*.
(f) If *improvedList* is not empty, select an edge e' randomly from *improvedList*.
(g) Else if *equalsList* is not empty, select the least recently used edge e' from *equalsList* breaking ties randomly.
(h) Else with probability $0.5e^{-\frac{flips}{1000}}$, select a random edge $e' \neq (u, v)$ in C.
(i) If e' is still not defined from (f), (g) or (h), continue.
(j) *currentTree* = *currentTree* $\cup\{(u, v)\} \backslash \{e'\}$.
(k) Set *minScore* to Compute-Tree-Score(*currentTree*).
(l) Mark (u, v) and e' as being used in iteration number *flips*.
(m) Increment *flips*.
(5) Return *currentTree*.

the workspace matrix[1] with nodes corresponding to cells in the matrix and edges corresponding to adjacent cells. The procedure outputs an improved spanning tree that has a lower score than the starting tree.

Table 1 shows the significant benefits of our local search algorithm. Rows with 0 iterations indicate that no local search was done. The other rows indicate the score of the tree returned after 10000 (*maxFlips*) iterations starting from the specified *seedTree* with no cycle length filter. The '%Empty' column indicates the percentage of empty cells—cells where no towers stand—in the input matrix. We report only on the 30% empty and 70% empty cases due to space restrictions. We ran our experiments on input matrices of different sizes. Due to space restrictions, we report only on a 100 15×15 input matrices each with a maximum height of 15. The same trends are also observed in more elaborate data.

3. MULTIPLE IDENTICAL ROBOTS

The sequential plan generated by the algorithm in [1] is in the form of *waves*. Every odd numbered wave adds blocks and every even numbered wave removes blocks. After the successful parallelization of a set of steps $s_{i+1}, s_{i+2} \dots s_{i+l_1}$ in the plan, the next set of steps $s_{i+l_1+1}, s_{i+l_1+2} \dots s_{i+l_1+l_2}$ for parallelization is heuristically chosen by examining the steps $s_{i+l_1+1}, s_{i+l_1+2} \dots$ one at a time and stopping when one of three rules for synchronization becomes effective. Here, $s_{i+l_1+l_2+1}$ is the first step after s_{i+l_1+1} such that either: (a) it belongs to a different wave compared to s_{i+l_1+1}, or (b) l_2 is equal to the maximum number of available robots, or (c) it is causally dependent on s_{i+l_1+j} for some $1 \leq j \leq l_2$. An action(step) a_2 with target node n_2 depends on an action a_1 with target node n_1 for its precondition in the plan only if a_1 occurs before a_2 and n_1 is an ancestor of n_2 in the tree along which the dynamic programming is carried out. Robots executing parallel actions traverse the spanning tree from the root to their target nodes (or vice versa) in parallel with the robot having to traverse the longest path starting first and all robots waiting until the last one is done.

Table 2 shows the number of parallel time steps needed for plan completion by different numbers of identical TERMES robots on models of world-famous buildings used in [1]. Experiments on random instances show similar patterns.

[1]input matrix padded with additional '0's on the boundary using a conservative estimate of how much space we need for constructing ramps [1]

%Empty	Iterations	*seedTree*	Field	Score
30	0	RBR	mean	7984.89
30	0	RBR	std	548.49
30	0	MST	mean	3900.07
30	0	MST	std	284.56
30	0	RMST	mean	3805.69
30	0	RMST	std	278.26
30	10000	RBR	mean	3412.73
30	10000	RBR	std	222.37
30	10000	MST	mean	3412.73
30	10000	MST	std	222.37
30	10000	RMST	mean	3412.73
30	10000	RMST	std	222.37
70	0	RBR	mean	4899.76
70	0	RBR	std	486.25
70	0	MST	mean	3173.90
70	0	MST	std	340.54
70	0	RMST	mean	2430.26
70	0	RMST	std	201.83
70	10000	RBR	mean	2119.50
70	10000	RBR	std	184.87
70	10000	MST	mean	2119.50
70	10000	MST	std	184.87
70	10000	RMST	mean	2119.50
70	10000	RMST	std	184.87

Table 1

Building Model	1 Agent	2 Agents	3 Agents
Eiffel Tower	9064	6758	6110
Empire State	5068	3740	3278
Giza Pyramid	5190	3344	2958
Taj Mahal	8064	5448	4756

Table 2

REFERENCES

[1] T. K. S. Kumar, S. Jung, and S. Koenig. A tree-based algorithm for construction robots. In *Proceedings of the Twenty-Fourth International Conference on Automated Planning and Scheduling (ICAPS-2014)*, 2014.

[2] K. Petersen, R. Nagpal, and J. Werfel. Termes: An autonomous robotic system for three-dimensional collective construction. In *Proceedings of Robotics: Science and Systems (RSS-2011)*, 2011.

Multi-Agent Continuous Transportation with Online Balanced Partitioning

(Extended Abstract)

Chao Wang[†], Somchaya Liemhetcharat[§], Kian Hsiang Low[†]
Department of Computer Science, National University of Singapore, Singapore[†]
Institute for Infocomm Reserach, Agency for Science, Technology and Research, Singapore[§]
{wangchao, lowkh}@comp.nus.edu.sg[†], liemhet-s@i2r.a-star.edu.sg[§]

ABSTRACT

We introduce the concept of *continuous transportation* task to the context of multi-agent systems. A continuous transportation task is one in which a multi-agent team visits a number of fixed locations, picks up objects, and delivers them to a transportation hub. The goal is to maximize the rate of transportation while the objects are replenished over time . In this extended abstract, we present a hybrid of centralized and distributed approaches that minimize communications in the multi-agent team. We contribute a novel online partitioning-transportation algorithm with information gathering in the multi-agent team.

Keywords

Multi-agent system; Partitioning; Transportation; Cooperation

1. INTRODUCTION

We are interested in multi-agent coordination and continuous transportation, where agents visit locations in the environment to transport objects (passengers or items) and deliver them to a transportation hub. The objects replenish over time, and we consider Poisson model of object replenishment. Poisson model is suitable for scenarios with independently-occurring objects, such as passengers appear at the transit stops. Thus, the continuous transportation task is general and applicable to many real-life scenarios, e.g., first/last mile problem, package or mail collection and delivery.

The most similar work has been done is in multi-robot foraging and delivery problem [2, 3]. A multi-robot team forages resources from environment to a home location or delivers items to locations on request while the resources replenish over time. The goal of continuous foraging is to maximize the rate of resource foraging. Thus, continuous foraging has similarities to continuous transportation, and thus we compare our algorithms with that of [2, 3].

In addition, continuous area sweeping (e.g., [1]) problem has similarities to continuous transportation, with the main difference being that the agents have a carrying capacity and must periodically return to the transportation hub. Hence, we compare to the benchmark of [1]. Besides, [1] uses area partitioning algorithm that relies on communications and negotiations among robots. Thus, it is prone to message loss and inconsistency. In contrast, our approach does not require communications among agents, and the partitioning is conducted separately. Hence, we present a hybrid of centralized and distributed approaches, and the efficacy is demonstrated in the evaluation section.

Appears in: *Proceedings of the 15th International Conference on Autonomous Agents and Multiagent Systems (AAMAS 2016), J. Thangarajah, K. Tuyls, C. Jonker, S. Marsella (eds.), May 9–13, 2016, Singapore.*

2. PROBLEM AND APPROACH

In this section, we formally define the multi-agent continuous transportation problem in detail, and give an overview of our approach. In a continuous transportation task, a multi-agent team visits a number of fixed locations and transport objects to a transportation hub.

2.1 Formal Problem Definition

The multi-agent continuous transportation problem can be defined as follows:

- $\mathcal{A} = \{a_1, ..., a_k\}$ is the set of transportation agents, e.g., the autonomous vehicles.
- s_i, c_i, and y_i ($\leq c_i$) denote agent a_i's speed, maximum capacity, and current load, i.e., the number of objects carried.
- $\mathcal{L} = \{l_1, ..., l_n\}$ is the set of locations, where l_0 is the transportation hub.
- $v_{j,t}$ denotes the number of objects avaliable at location l_j at time step t, e.g., the number of passengers appear at the transit stop l_j.
- $\hat{v}_{j,t}^{(i)}$ denotes a_i's estimate of $v_{j,t}$ at time step t.
- o_j denotes the observation made at location l_j. When a transportataion agent a_i arrives at a location l_j ($j > 0$), $\min(v_{j,t},\ c_i - y_i)$ objects at l_j are picked up by a_i, and a_i makes an observation o_j of the number of objects remaining. When a_i arrives at l_0, all y_i objects carried by a_i are transferred to l_0.
- $D : \mathcal{L} \times \mathcal{L} \to \mathbb{R}^+$ is the distance function of the locations.
- $t(a_i, l_j, l_k) = \left\lceil \frac{D(l_j, l_k)}{s_i} \right\rceil$ is the time steps taken for an agent a_i to move from location l_j to l_k.

The goal is to maximize the rate of objects delivered to the transportation hub l_0 within T time steps, i.e., maximize $\frac{v_{0,T}}{T}$.

2.2 Our Approach

Our approach for solving the continuous transportation problem is:

- We assume that $v_{j,t}$ follows a known model — in this paper, we assume that $v_{j,t}$ follows the Poisson model, where the number of objects replenished every time step follows a Poisson distribution with mean λ_j. However, the parameters of the models (i.e., λ_j) are not known in advance;
- The estimates $\hat{v}_{j,t}^{(i)}$ are updated using the model and observations from transportation agents a_i visiting location l_j;
- Following [2], the transportation agents do not share their models $\hat{v}_{j,t}^{(i)}$ since it could be expensive subject to the communication bandwidth and team size. Different from [2], in our approach, the sharing of destination and load among agents are not required.

We contribute an online algorithm that partition the locations based on their 2D-position and estimated replenishment rate, and controls the transportation agents a_i, that use $\hat{v}_{j,t}^{(i)}$ to plan their next destination within the cluster of locations assigned. The algorithm dynamically repartitions locations based on information gathered by the multi-agent team.

3. ALGORITHM AND EVALUATION

Our Online Balanced Partitioning (OBP) algorithm begins with statically partition the locations into clusters based on 2D-position of locations with k-means algorithm. The algorithm is inspired by algorithms proposed for continuous foraging [2]. The main difference is that the agents replan destinations in the cluster of locations assigned, instead of all the locations. The replanning of destination within each cluster is based on Greedy Rate [2], i.e., maximizing the transportation rate. Further, due to partitioning, communications of destinations and loads are not required.

By only considering the 2D-position of locations, the workload of each agent might not be balanced, i.e., the total replenishment rate of some clusters could be so high that the agents cannot afford it, while some other agents are idle. On the other hand, the result of standard k-means algorithm depends on the choice of initial centroid which is randomly generated. In this case, we introduce online balanced partitioning, i.e., balance estimated total replenishment rate of each cluster with information gathering. The replenishment rate is not known in advance. The agents use preset estimated replenishment rate to update its estimated number of objects. The estimate can only be corrected when they visit the location and make an observation. Since we focus on Poisson replenishment model, where number of objects replenished per time step follows a mean value, we believe that estimated replenishment rate can be corrected with continuous observations, i.e., the total number of objects replenished divided by time steps elapsed.

Our online partitioning algorithm dynamically corrects the estimated replenishment rate by visiting a location and making observation. Once the deviation of total replenishment rate of clusters are greater than a preset threshold, repartitioning will be done immediately.

Figure 1 shows the performance of our Online Balanced Partitioning (OBP) algorithm when the capacities of the agents are 10 and the number of locations are 20. In order to demonstrate the effectiveness of OBP, we compared OBP with GR+EO [2] which requires the presence of a reconnaissance agent. The solid red, blue, and gray lines show Online Balanced Partitioning (OBP), Greedy Rate with Expected Observation (GR+EO), and Random Transportation (R), and the shaded areas show the standard deviations of these algorithms.

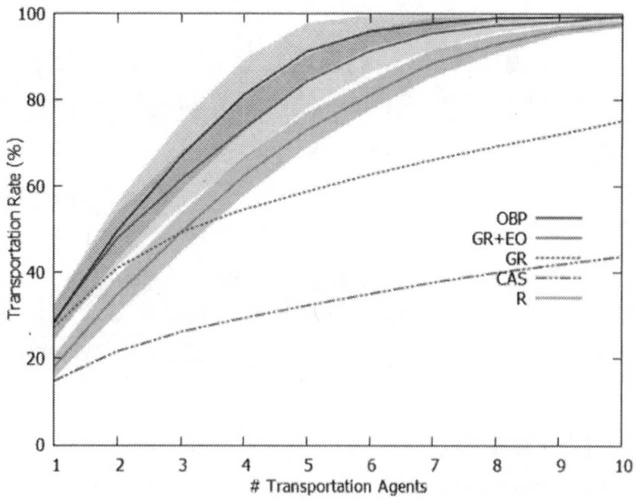

Figure 1: Comparison of our Online Balanced Partitioning (OBP) algorithm against the benchmark of Greedy Rate with Expected Observation (GR+EO) and Continuous Area Sweeping (CAS) algorithm.

As the number of agents increase, OBP outperforms all other algorithms, even GR+EO ($p = 3 \times 10^{-23}$), primarily because of the dynamic partitioning with information gathering by the multi-agent team. It clearly illustrates the efficacy of our OBP algorithms over GR. Without the use of reconnaissance agent and communications among agents, our OBP algorithm can still outperform GR+EO algorithm.

Acknowledgments

This work was supported by NUS Computer Center through the use of its high performance computing facilities.

REFERENCES

[1] M. Ahmadi and P. Stone. A multi-robot system for continuous area sweeping tasks. In *Robotics and Automation, 2006. ICRA 2006. Proceedings 2006 IEEE International Conference on*, pages 1724–1729. IEEE, 2006.

[2] S. Liemhetcharat, R. Yan, and K. P. Tee. Continuous foraging and information gathering in a multi-agent team. In *Proceedings of the 2015 International Conference on Autonomous Agents and Multiagent Systems*, pages 1325–1333. International Foundation for Autonomous Agents and Multiagent Systems, 2015.

[3] S. Liemhetcharat, R. Yan, K. P. Tee, and M. Lee. Multi-robot item delivery and foraging: Two sides of a coin. *Robotics*, 4(3):365–397, 2015.

Single Item Auctions with Discrete Action Spaces (Extended Abstract)

Yicheng Liu
Institute for Interdisciplinary Information Sciences,
Tsinghua University, China
liuyicheng13@mails.tsinghua.edu.cn

Pingzhong Tang
Institute for Interdisciplinary Information Sciences,
Tsinghua University, China
kenshin@mail.tsinghua.edu.cn

1. INTRODUCTION

An implicit assumption in truthful mechanism design is that revelation of one's true type is always feasible. Indeed, this is not a problem in standard mechanism design setups, where it is up to the designer to determine the action spaces. However, this assumption fails to hold in many practical scenarios, where there are natural, exogenous constraints on the set of possible actions. For example, in combinatorial auctions [5] where bidders have combinatorial preferences on bundles of items, truthful revelation of such a preference requires a bidder to communicate a value on each subset of items, results in an exponential blow up in communication complexity. A practical combinatorial auction often imposes constraints on the number of package bids a bidder can place. The above observations motivate an active line of research that concerns the *expressiveness* of mechanisms [1, 2, 3, 4].

We consider a practical single-item auction design setting with restricted expressiveness. In particular, the action space of all bidders is restricted to a set of discrete *bid levels*, while the values are in continuous spaces. With this interface, truth revelation is not feasible and the revelation principle fails to hold (We will address this point later).

Tailored for this setting, we put forward an auction, coined the *extended second price auction* (ESP). Our auction resembles the second price auction when there are multiple winners tied at the highest bid; however, when there is a unique winner, our auction charges a bit more than the second price auction. We show that, our auction satisfies the following desirable properties:

- Anonymity: if we replace the bids of any two bidders, their winning probability and payments (if win) will also be replaced.
- Truthfulness: each bidder finds in her best interests to bid the highest bid level below her true type;
- Not dominated in welfare: there exists no other auction that can dominate our auction in welfare for every possible type profile;
- Not dominated in revenue: there exists no other ex-post individually rational (IR) truthful auction that can dominate our auction in revenue for every possible type profile;

In our setting, truthfulness is different from standard definition because of the restriction on expressiveness. However, similar to the other settings, in a truthful mechanism, it is "straightforward" for bidders to decide their bids and their bids truthfully (partially in our setting) reveal their values. An equivalent understanding of our truthfulness is as follows. The bid levels separate the value space into many intervals, such that two consecutive intervals are separated by a bid level. Let *value intervals* denote these intervals. A mechanism is truthful if each bidder finds in her best interests to report the value intervals she belongs to.

2. THE SETTINGS

We consider a setting that is built upon the standard independent private value (IPV) setting. In an IPV setting, there is a seller who has an indivisible item for sale. Her valuation of the item is zero. There is a set M of m bidders that are interested in the item. The degree of interest is expressed by a number called valuation. Each bidder i knows her own valuation v_i. Other bidders, denoted by $-i$, treat v_i as a random variable that is distributed according to some distribution function $F_i(v_i)$ that is positive everywhere on $[0, v_{max}]$. v_i is independent of v_j for any $i \neq j$. An (direct) auction then solicits bids from the bidders, allocates the item to the bidders according to its allocation rule and charges payments according to its payment rule.

Distinct from the standard IPV setting, which places no restrictions on the set of bids to report, our setting only allows bidders to select bids from a given list of *bid levels* $\mathcal{B} = \{l_1, l_2, \ldots, l_n\}$ such that $v_{max} > l_1 > \ldots, l_n = 0$. $b_i \in \mathcal{B}$ denotes agent i's bid. Distinct from the standard IPV setting, in our setting the seller does not have any knowledge about valuation distribution. Therefore, our setting effectively excludes cases such as full-information setting where the seller knows the exact value of each bidder, as well as Myerson's standard setting of optimal Bayesian auction design. The utility of bidder i is $u_i = v_i - p_i$.

3. EXTENDED SECOND PRICE AUCTION

In cases where there are several highest bids tied at some bid level. The ESP is exactly the same as SP. However, when the highest bid is different from the second highest, the winner needs to pay a bit more than what they pay in SP, i.e., the second highest bid. The winner's payment is independent from their own bid, which ensures the truthful-

Appears in: *Proceedings of the 15th International Conference on Autonomous Agents and Multiagent Systems (AAMAS 2016), J. Thangarajah, K. Tuyls, C. Jonker, S. Marsella (eds.), May 9–13, 2016, Singapore.*

ness of the auction. The detailed description of ESP is as follows.

Mechanism 1 The ESP auction

Input: Bid levels $\mathcal{B}$ and a bidding profile $(b_1, b_2, \ldots, b_n)$.

Output: Price profile $P = \{p_1, p_2, \ldots, p_n\}$ where p_i is the price for bidder i; the winner w ($w \in \{1, 2, \ldots, n\}$).

1: Let b^* denote the highest bid, b' denote the second highest bid.
2: **if** $b^* = b'$ **then**
3: Uniformly randomly pick one bidder who bids b^* as the winner w.
4: $p_w = b^*$. For $i \neq w$, $p_i = 0$.
5: **else**
6: w is the bidder who bids b^*.
7: Let $n(b)$ be the number of bidders who bid b. b'' denotes the lowest bid level above b'. $p_w = \frac{n(b')b''+b'}{n(b')+1}$; For $i \neq w$, $p_i = 0$.
8: **end if**

Remark:
(b', b'', b^*) can also be (l_k, l_{k-1}, l_i). The $\frac{n(b')b''+b'}{n(b')+1}$ is in fact an indifference point. If we charge more than this amount, the winner has incentive to underbid; otherwise, some bidder may have incentive to overbid.

It can be proved that ESP can obtain great properties as follows.

THEOREM 1. *The ESP auction is truthful.*

PROOF. Our proof will discuss two cases. First, we show that agents cannot benefit from overbidding. Then, we show that they cannot benefit from underbidding either.

We consider an arbitrary bidder i, whose type is v_i and the highest bid level under v_i is b_i^*. In the following discussion, we compare to the truthful case where i bids b_i^* and show that overbidding or underbidding cannot increase i's utility.

- First, we argue that i cannot benefit from reporting higher than b_i^*.
  - If i is the only possible winner[1], reporting a higher bid will not reduce her payment.
  - If someone else bid b' higher than v_i, i needs to bid at least b' to be possible to get the item, and pay at least b'. As $b' > v_i$, i will lose money.
  - If i is tied with $k (k \geq 1)$ bidders at the top bid, i gets $(v_i - b_i^*)/(k+1)$ in expectation. If i reports higher, i will be the winner, but charged $(b_i' k + b_i^*)/(k+1)$, where b_i' is the level closest above b_i^*. It results in a lower utility since
$$v_i - (b_i' k + b_i^*)/(k+1) < (v_i - b_i^*)/(k+1).$$
- Then we argue that i cannot benefit from reporting lower than b_i^*.
  - If i is not the only possible winner, underbid disqualifies i as a winner. Since obviously i gets non-negative utility whenever she is a winner, underbid will not increase her utility in this case.
  - Now, we consider the case where i is the only possible winner. If i reports less but higher than the second highest bid. i's utility remains the same. If i reports less than the second highest bid, i will no longer get the item. If i bid the same as the second highest bid, i's utility will become $(v_i - b_{sec})/(k+1)$, which is less than the original utility $v_i - (b'_{sec} k + b_{sec})/(k+1)$. Here, b_{sec} is the second highest bid, k is the number of bidders who bid b_{sec}. b'_{sec} is the bid level closest above b_{sec}

To sum up, we have shown that overbid or underbid does not increase the utility of an agent. □

[1] i bids strictly higher than the second highest bidder.

THEOREM 2. *The ESP auction is not dominated on social welfare.*

THEOREM 3. *The ESP auction is not dominated in revenue among all truthful, ex-post IR auctions.*

THEOREM 4. *Given the distributions of bidders' types are i.i.d. and all the bidders truthfully report, the revenue of ESP can be at most $\frac{1}{e}MG$ more than SP, where MG is the difference between the highest and the lowest bid levels.*

4. ACKNOWLEDGMENTS

This work was supported by the National Basic Research Program of China Grant 2011CBA00300, 2011CBA00301, the Natural Science Foundation of China Grant 61033001, 61361136003, 61303077, 61561146398, a Tsinghua Initiative Scientific Research Grant and a China Youth 1000-talent program.

REFERENCES

[1] M. Benisch, N. M. Sadeh, and T. Sandholm. A theory of expressiveness in mechanisms. In *Proceedings of the Twenty-Third AAAI Conference on Artificial Intelligence, AAAI 2008, Chicago, Illinois, USA, July 13-17, 2008*, pages 17–23, 2008.

[2] V. Conitzer and T. Sandholm. Computing optimal outcomes under an expressive representation of settings with externalities. *Journal of Computer and System Sciences*, 78:2–14, 2012. Special issue on Knowledge Representation and Reasoning. Early version in AAAI-05.

[3] P. Dhangwatnotai. Multi-keyword sponsored search. In *Proceedings 12th ACM Conference on Electronic Commerce (EC-2011), San Jose, CA, USA, June 5-9, 2011*, pages 91–100, 2011.

[4] D. C. Parkes and T. Sandholm. Optimize-and-dispatch architecture for expressive ad auctions. In *Proceedings of the Workshop on Sponsored Search Auctions*, 2005.

[5] T. Sandholm. Algorithm for optimal winner determination in combinatorial auctions. *Artificial Intelligence*, 135(1-2):1–54, 2002.

An Adaptive Learning Framework for Efficient Emergence of Social Norms

(Extended Abstract)

Chao Yu
School of Computer Science and Technology
Dalian University of Technology
Dalian, 116024, China
cy496@dlut.edu.cn

Hongtao Lv
School of Computer Science and Technology
Dalian University of Technology
Dalian, 116024, China
lvhongtao@mail.dlut.edu.cn

Sandip Sen
Department of Mathematical & Computer Sciences
The University of Tulsa
Tulsa, Oklahoma 74104, United States
sandip-sen@utulsa.edu

Jianye Hao
School of software
Tianjin University
Tianjin, 300072, China
jianye.hao@tju.edu.cn

Fenghui Ren
School of Computer Science and Software Engineering
University of Wollongong
Wollongong, 2500, Australia
fren@uow.edu.au

Rui Liu
School of Computer Science and Technology
Dalian University of Tech.
Dalian, 116024, China
913917030@qq.com

ABSTRACT

This paper investigates how norm emergence can be facilitated by agents' adaptive learning behaviors. A general learning framework is proposed, in which agents can dynamically adapt their learning behaviors through social learning of their individual learning experience. Experimental results indicate that the proposed framework outperforms the static learning framework in various comparison criteria.

Keywords

Norm Emergence; Reinforcement Learning; Social Networks

1. INTRODUCTION

Learning from individual experience has been shown to be a robust mechanism to facilitate norm emergence in multiagent systems (MASs). A great deal of work has studied norm emergence achieved through agent learning behaviors [1, 2, 3]. The focus of these existing studies is to examine general mechanisms behind efficient emergence of norms while agents interact with each other using basic learning (particularly reinforcement learning) methods. These mechanisms include the social learning strategy [1], the collective interaction protocol [3, 4], and the utilization of topological knowledge [2], etc. Learning parameters in these studies, however, are often fine-tuned by hand and thus cannot be adapted according to the varying norm emerging situations. A key question then arises that how agents can adapt their learning behaviors dynamically during the process of norm emergence, and how this kind of adaptive learning behaviors can influence the final emerging outcomes?

Appears in: *Proceedings of the 15th International Conference on Autonomous Agents and Multiagent Systems (AAMAS 2016), J. Thangarajah, K. Tuyls, C. Jonker, S. Marsella (eds.), May 9–13, 2016, Singapore.*

This paper provides another perspective in the research of norm emergence by simply focusing on the role of learning itself in affecting the process of norm emergence. A double-layered adaptive learning framework is proposed, in which agents interact with each other using basic Reinforcement Learning (RL) methods in the local layer learning, and generate guiding policies by exploiting historical learning experience in the upper layer learning. To generate guiding policies, the historical learning experience of each agent is synthesized into a strategy that competes with other strategies in the population based on the principle of Evolutionary Game Theory (EGT). The generated guiding policies are then passed down to the local layer learning in order to adapt agents' learning behaviors based on the consistency between agents' behaviors and the guiding policies. Experiments show that the proposed framework enables norms to emerge more efficiently and with higher convergence levels than the static learning framework, and some critical parameters such as norm spaces and network topologies can have significant influences on norm emergence.

2. THE PROPOSED FRAMEWORK

Each agent is equipped with a capability to memorize a certain period of learning experience in terms of the chosen action and the corresponding reward. Agent i then synthesizes its past learning experience into two tables $TA_i^t(a)$ and $TR_i^t(a)$. $TA_i^t(a)$ denotes the frequency of choosing action a in the last M steps and $TR_i^t(a)$ denotes the overall reward of choosing action a. The past learning experience in terms of table $TA_i^t(a)$ and $TR_i^t(a)$ indicates how successful the strategy of choosing action a is in the past. The upper layer learning makes use of this information in order to generate a supervision policy for local layer learning. To realize the supervision policy generation, each agent learns from other agents by comparing their learning experience. The motivation of this comparison comes from the EGT, which provides a powerful methodology to model how strategies evolve overtime based on their performance. Two different approaches are proposed in this paper to realize the EGT concept in the upper layer learning process, depending on how to define the competing strategy and the corresponding performance evaluation criteria (i.e., fitness) in EGT. In the *reward-based approach*, the strategy in EGT is represented by the most profitable action, and the fitness is represented by the corresponding reward of that action; On the contrary, the *action-based approach* considers the action which has been most adopted in the past to be the strategy in EGT, and the corresponding reward of that action to be the fitness in EGT. After synthesizing the historical learning experience, agent i then gets an action strategy of a_i' and its corresponding fitness of $TR(a_i')$. It then interacts with other agents through social learning (i.e., imitation rule) in EGT.

The new strategy a_i' indicates the most successful strategy in the neighborhood and therefore should be integrated into the local layer learning in order to entrench its influence. By comparing its action at time step t, a_i^t, with the supervision strategy a_i', agent i can evaluate whether it is performing well or not so that its learning behavior can be dynamically adapted to fit the supervision strategy. The concept of "winning" or "losing" in the well-known Multi-Agent Learning (MAL) algorithm WoLF (Win-or-Learn-Fast) [5] is elegantly borrowed to indicate whether an agent's behavior is consistent with the guiding policy. According to the "winning" or "losing" situation, agents then can dynamically adapt their learning behaviors (in terms of learning and/or exploration rate) in the local layer learning.

3. EXPERIMENTS AND RESULTS

We compare the proposed learning framework with the static social learning framework [1] in order to demonstrate the merits of adaptive learning behavior of agents. The three adaptive learning approaches under the proposed framework are: (1) *Supervision-α* (adapting learning rate), *Supervision-ϵ* (adapting exploration rate), and *Supervision-both* (adapting learning rate and the exploration rate at the same time). The performance of the four different approaches in the corresponding learning frameworks is plotted in Figure 1(a)-1(c). The results show that the three adaptive learning approaches outperform the static social learning approach in all three networks in terms of a higher level of convergence and a faster convergence speed. Through dynamically adapting their learning behaviors, agents are able to reach an agreement more easily, and thus norms can emerge more quickly to a higher level of convergence in the proposed framework. Result in Figure 1(d) shows that norms emerge faster with the action-based approach in the beginning. As the process moves on, the reward-based approach catches up with the action-based approach, and then brings about a higher level of norm emergence afterwards.

We also investigate the influence of several key factors on norm emergence under the proposed framework: (1) In terms of norm space size, a larger number of available actions results in a delayed convergence of norms; (2) The norm emergence process is hindered as the population is growing larger; (3) Network topologies such as network diameter and cluster coefficient can have significant influences on norm emergence. It is more efficient for a norm to emerge in a network with smaller network diameter (i.e., higher network randomness), and norm emergence is steadily promoted when cluster coefficient of network is increased (i.e., larger average number of neighbors). In all cases, the adaptive learning approaches can bring about more robust and efficient norm emergence than the social learning approach.

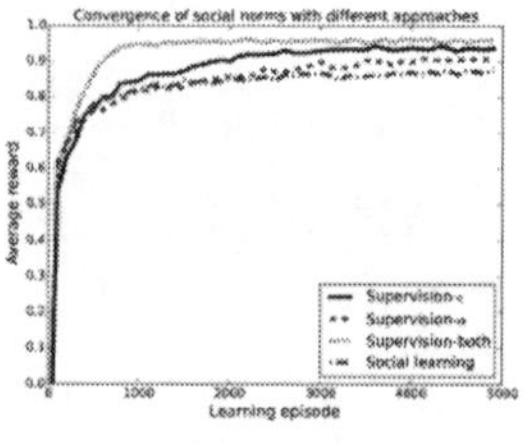

(a) Grid

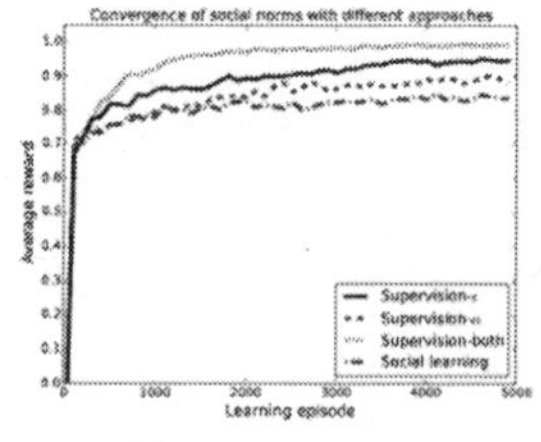

(b) Small-world

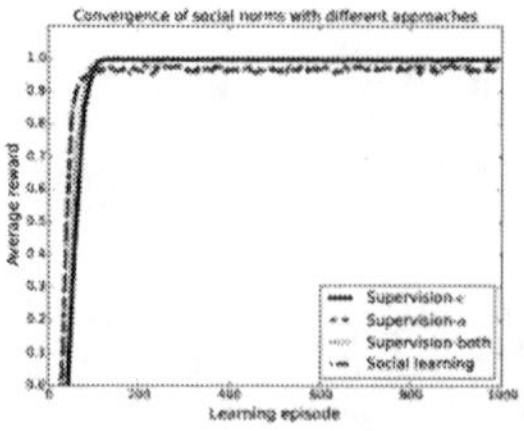

(c) Scale-free

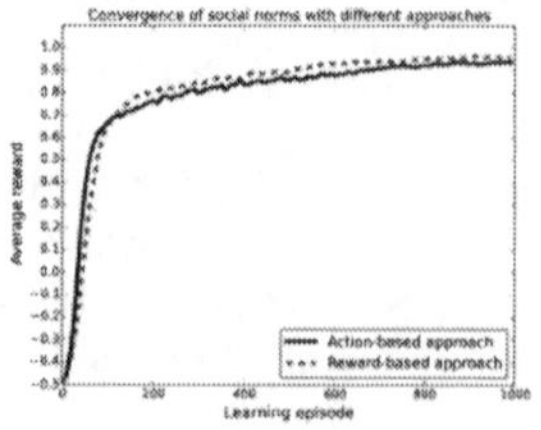

(d) Ensemble method

Figure 1: Performance of norm emergence.

4. CONCLUSION AND FUTURE WORK

In this paper, a novel learning framework was proposed to investigate how agents' adaptive learning behaviors can facilitate norm emergence. The highlight of the framework is the integration of social learning into the local individual learning in order to dynamically adapt agents' learning behaviors for a better performance of norm emergence. Experimental results illustrated that this kind of interplay between individual learning and social learning is indeed helpful in facilitating the emergence of social norms among agents.

Acknowledgments

This work is supported by the National Natural Science Foundation of China (No. 61502072), Post-Doctoral Science Foundation of China (No. 2014M561229 and 2015T80251), and National Undergraduate Training Programs for Innovation and Entrepreneurship (No. 2015101410154).

REFERENCES

[1] S. Sen and S. Airiau. Emergence of norms through social learning. In *Proc. of 20th IJCAI*, pages 1507–1512, 2007.

[2] D. Villatoro, J. Sabater-Mir, and S. Sen. Social instruments for robust convention emergence. In *Proc. of 22nd IJCAI*, pages 420–425, 2011.

[3] C. Yu, M. Zhang, F. Ren, and X. Luo. Emergence of social norms through collective learning in networked agent societies. In *Proc. of AAMAS2013*, pages 475–482, 2013.

[4] C. Yu, M. Zhang, and F. Ren. Collective learning for the emergence of social norms in networked multiagent systems. *IEEE Transactions on Cybernetics*, 44(12):2342–2355, 2014.

[5] M. Bowling and M. Veloso. Multiagent learning using a variable learning rate. *Artificial Intelligence*, 136:215–250, 2002.

Learning from the Wizard: Programming Social Interaction through Teleoperated Demonstrations EXTENDED ABSTRACT

W. Bradley Knox, Samuel Spaulding, and Cynthia Breazeal
Massachusetts Institute of Technology
wbradleyknox@gmail.com, samuelsp@media.mit.edu, and cynthiab@media.mit.edu

ABSTRACT

This paper considers the question of whether robots can be effectively programmed for autonomous social interaction through learning from demonstrations recorded via Wizard-of-Oz teleoperation. We present a novel LfW system for educational play between young children and a robot and results from a randomized experiment comparing a teleoperated robot and a robot with autonomous behavior derived by LfW. Across numerous metrics, the teleoperated robot and the autonomous robot programmed by LfW elicit similar behavior from their human interaction partners. Additionally, when children were asked whether the robot was human-controlled or autonomous, approximately half in each condition thought it was human-controlled.

1. INTRODUCTION

In human-computer interaction research, a Wizard-of-Oz scenario involves a human interacting with some machine interface—such as a socially expressive robot—that is secretly controlled by a human teleoperator. We define **learning from the wizard** (LfW) as a subtype of learning from demonstration in which the training demonstrations are derived from records of Wizard-of-Oz interaction and are used to learn policies for interacting autonomously with humans. Previous work on LfW exists but until now has lacked a unifying name and has not been extended learn tasks of social human-robot interaction.

This paper focuses on validating LfW by answering *whether learning from the wizard can retain the interaction benefits of a teleoporated robot.* To this end, we conducted an evaluation of robot LfW in an educational domain with young children aged 4–8 years.

2. RELATED WORK

There exist related LfW projects that involve human-interaction tasks, social tasks, or rigorous evaluations of learned behavior [5, 10, 7, 8, 11, 4, 3], but to our knowledge only Breazeal et al.'s work [1] involves all three *on a robot.* However, though their nearly autonomous robot could effectively complete simple, single-agent tasks, its social behaviors—communicating and coordinating with the human—were considered unsuccessful by the authors, leaving open the question of whether LfW can effectively program socially interactive robot behavior.

Appears in: *Proceedings of the 15th International Conference on Autonomous Agents and Multiagent Systems (AAMAS 2016), J. Thangarajah, K. Tuyls, C. Jonker, S. Marsella (eds.), May 9–13, 2016, Singapore.*

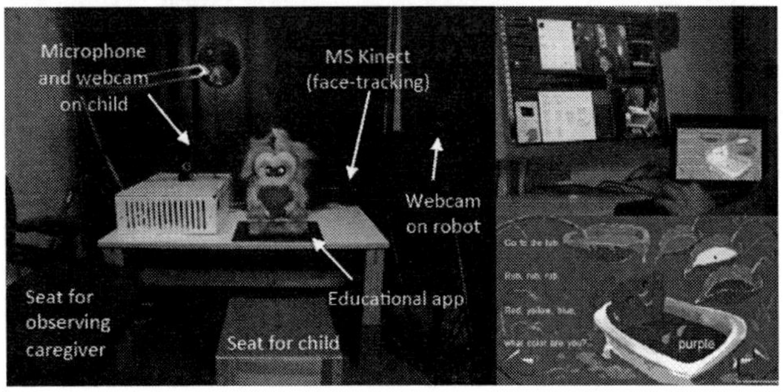

Figure 1: Clockwise from left: Interaction setting; experimenter interface; color-mixing app, from the Tinkrbook e-book.

3. LfW FOR AN EDUCATIONAL DOMAIN

To explore the potential of LfW for social tasks, we developed a robotic learning companion for young children. This section describes the educational domain and integrated system.

Figure 1 shows the interaction setting. Children aged 4–8 sat across from a squash-and-stretch robot that was designed for social interaction with young children. Between the robot and child was a tablet with an educational app designed to teach color-mixing and reading concepts to young children. Children could tap on leaves to add color to the birdbath and to wash the bath clean. Adding multiple pigments to the birdbath can create secondary colors and brown.

3.1 General system

The system sensors include 2 webcams (one pointed at the child, another at the robot), a Microsoft Kinect, a microphone, and the tablet itself. The tablet reports the start and end of child touches by their locations and times. It also reports time-stamped app events, such as triggering pigment to fall. During each interaction, the various system components communicated via ROS [6]. Time-stamped logs in the form of rosbags were recorded that contained video from the two webcams, app events (human- or robot-triggered), estimates of the child's face location in 3D space (derived from the Kinect), microphone audio, and robot actions.

The final system, used during the experiment, has 30 robot actions in its agent framework. 15 are simple emotional utterances paired with expressive motions. 5 actions cause the robot to lean towards the tablet and trigger app events. 9 actions are prompts to the child, requesting one of eight colors (e.g., "Red?!") or "Now you go." The final action is to not initiate any behavior. Video illustrations of app events, the robot action space, and child-robot interaction can be seen at `https://www.youtube.com/user/LearningFromWizard`.

3.2 Autonomy by learning from the wizard

In this section, we give a brief overview of how we structured teleoperation, training, and learned autonomous behavior. The robot's actions are exclusively determined either by a teleoperator during Wizard-of-Oz interaction or by a learned policy during autonomous interaction, never by a mixture of the two. To create the autonomous behavior model, 122 feature values (e.g., describing the current color of the birdbath, the child's and robot's last actions, time since last child/robot action, etc.) are computed at 100ms time intervals from logs of teleoperated data. Each set of feature values creates a sample for supervised learning, labeled by what action the teleoperator specified over the previous 100ms. Our goal is to learn a model that answers: given a feature vector $\boldsymbol{f}$ drawn from sensory history at time t, for each action a, what is the probability $\pi(\boldsymbol{f}, a)$ that a would have been triggered by a teleoperator within the previous 100ms? For this 30-class learning problem, we created a hierarchical model using binary logistic regression (from Weka [2]) as a base learner, with L2 regularization applied with a scaling parameter of 10 to account for the large number of features. During autonomous interaction, these same features are computed at the start of each 100 ms time step, and a single action is chosen and executed by sampling from the model's output probability distribution over actions, $\pi(\boldsymbol{f}, \cdot)$.

4. STUDY DESIGN

Data from 29 participants' interactions with a teleoperated robot formed the training data. A separate group of 85 participants took part in a subsequent randomized experiment with three conditions, differing in what the child played with: TABLET-ONLY, a control condition without the robot; WoZ-EXPERIMENT, with the teleoperated robot; and AUTONOMY, with the robot acting according to its learned autonomous model.

5. RESULTS AND DISCUSSION

Subjective observations and quantitative analysis are presented below.

5.1 Learned behavior

In the authors' subjective judgement, the robot largely succeeded in learning to emulate the demonstrated interaction heuristics. For instance, the autonomous robot often celebrates when the child creates a robot-requested color. The following section gives objective, quantitative results.

5.2 Behavioral results

Multiple-testing analysis of 11 behavioral metrics—by the Benjamini and Hochberg procedure, with a false discovery rate of 0.05—results in numerous significant differences between TABLET-ONLY and either AUTONOMY or WoZ-EXPERIMENT and *zero* significant differences between the two robot conditions. Significant results include children that interacted with the robots volunteering to play longer, having a higher proportion of color taps result in creating complex colors, smiling more, and looking down at the screen less. Together, these results indicate that the learned autonomous robot preserves the interaction benefits of the teleoperated robot.

5.3 Participants guess: teleoperated or autonomous

As a double-blind question, another experimenter asked participants whether the robot was autonomous or teleoperated by a human. Through this question, the experiment serves as a variant of the Turing test [9], albeit social, embodied, and constrained to 30 possible actions. Counting answers of "undecided" or "both" as half a vote for each option, 52.8% of respondents in the AUTONOMY condition thought the robot was teleoperated. 47.2% in the WoZ-EXPERIMENT condition thought it was teleoperated; the autonomous robot was judged as human-teleoperated marginally more often than the robot that *was* human-teleoperated.

6. CONCLUSION

From the perspective of *how to program autonomous socially interactive robot behavior*, learning from the wizard constitutes a nascent approach that could be instrumental in the much-needed transition of social robots from Wizard-of-Oz control towards autonomy. Evaluating LfW within a playful, educational domain, this paper provides the first validation of the technique to program socially interactive robot behavior, showing that LfW generally retained the statistically significant interaction benefits that a teleoperated robot has over play without the robot.

REFERENCES

[1] C. Breazeal, N. DePalma, J. Orkin, S. Chernova, and M. Jung. Crowdsourcing human-robot interaction: New methods and system evaluation in a public environment. *Journal of Human-Robot Interaction*, 2(1):82–111, 2013.

[2] M. Hall, E. Frank, G. Holmes, B. Pfahringer, P. Reutemann, and I. H. Witten. The weka data mining software: An update. *SIGKDD Explorations*, 11, 2009.

[3] C.-M. Huang and B. Mutlu. Learning-based modeling of multimodal behaviors for humanlike robots. In *Proceedings of the 2014 ACM/IEEE international conference on Human-robot interaction*, pages 57–64. ACM, 2014.

[4] S. Nikolaidis and J. Shah. Human-robot cross-training: Computational formulation, modeling and evaluation of a human team training strategy. In *Proceedings of the IEEE/ACM International Conference on Human-Robot Interaction*, 2013.

[5] M. Okamoto, Y. Yang, and T. Ishida. Wizard of oz method for learning dialog agents. In *Cooperative Information Agents V*, pages 20–25. Springer, 2001.

[6] M. Quigley, K. Conley, B. Gerkey, J. Faust, T. Foote, J. Leibs, R. Wheeler, and A. Y. Ng. Ros: an open-source robot operating system. In *ICRA workshop on open source software*, volume 3, page 5, 2009.

[7] V. Rieser and O. Lemon. Learning human multimodal dialogue strategies. *Natural Language Engineering*, 16(01):3–23, 2010.

[8] J. Schrum, I. V. Karpov, and R. Miikkulainen. UtâĄĄ 2: Human-like behavior via neuroevolution of combat behavior and replay of human traces. In *Computational Intelligence and Games (CIG), 2011 IEEE Conference on*, pages 329–336. IEEE, 2011.

[9] A. M. Turing. Computing machinery and intelligence. *Mind*, pages 433–460, 1950.

[10] J. Williams and S. Young. Using wizard-of-oz simulations to bootstrap reinforcement-learning-based dialog management systems. In *Proceedings of the 4th SIGDIAL Workshop on Discourse and Dialogue*, 2003.

[11] J. Young, K. Ishii, T. Igarashi, and E. Sharlin. Style by demonstration: teaching interactive movement style to robots. In *Proceedings of the 2012 ACM international conference on Intelligent User Interfaces*, pages 41–50. ACM, 2012.

Budget-Constrained Reasoning in Agent Computational Environments

(Extended Abstract)

Stefania Costantini
DISIM, Università di L'Aquila
Via Vetoio, I-67100 L'Aquila, Italy
stefania.costantini@univaq.it

Andrea Formisano
DMI, Università di Perugia — GNCS-INdAM
via Vanvitelli 1, I-06123 Perugia, Italy
formis@dmi.unipg.it

ABSTRACT

In this paper we consider the software-engineering problem of how to empower modular agent architectures with the capability to perform quantitative reasoning in a uniform and principled way.

Keywords

Multi-Context Systems; Quantitative Reasoning; Agent-Oriented Software Engineering

1. INTRODUCTION

There are many examples in agent-based applications where data might be potentially accessible or activities might be performed on the web, but agents are constrained by the available budget since access to knowledge bases is subject to costs. The work [8] identifies the problem that an agent faces when it has limited budget and costly queries to perform, and proposes a special resource-aware modal logic for deriving possible courses of actions, which however for complexity reasons can hardly be used in practice.

In this paper we consider the software-engineering problem of how to practically empower agents with the capability to perform such kind of reasoning in a uniform and principled way. We consider the adoption of a flexible and reasonably efficient reasoning device that enables an agent which has costly objectives: (i) to establish which are the alternative possibilities within the available budget; (ii) to select, based upon its preferences, the goals to achieve and the resources to spend; (iii) to implement its choice. We illustrate the proposed approach via a realistic case study.

2. RESOURCE-BASED REASONING

In this paper, for quantitative reasoning we adopt RASP (Resource-based Answer Set Programming) [4, 5], which is an extension of ASP (Answer Set Programming), a well-established logic programming paradigm (cf., among many, [7]). RASP has been proven in [6] to be equivalent to an interesting fragment of Linear Logic, specifically an Horn fragment empowered however via the ASP default negation that Linear Logic does not provide. RASP explicitly introduces in ASP the notion of *resource*, and supports both formalization and quantitative reasoning on consumption and production of amounts of resources.

Appears in: *Proceedings of the 15th International Conference on Autonomous Agents and Multiagent Systems (AAMAS 2016), J. Thangarajah, K. Tuyls, C. Jonker, S. Marsella (eds.), May 9–13, 2016, Singapore.*

3. ENHANCING THE ACE FRAMEWORK

An enhanced Agent Computational Environment (ACE) [2] is defined as a tuple $\langle A, M_1, \ldots, M_r, C_1, \ldots, C_s, R_1, \ldots, R_q \rangle$ where module A is the "basic agent", i.e., an agent program written in any agent-oriented language. The "overall" agent is obtained by equipping the basic agent with the following facilities. The M_is are "Event-Action modules", which are special modules aimed at Complex Event Processing. The R_js (new addition w.r.t. [2]) are "Reasoning modules", which are specialized in specific reasoning tasks. The C_ks are contexts in the sense of MCSs (Multi-Context Systems, cf. [1]), i.e., external data/knowledge sources that the agent is able to locate and to query about some subject, but upon which it has no further knowledge and no control.

Interaction among ACE's components occurs via *bridge rules*, inspired by those of MCSs. However, here bridge rules become (via a smooth formal integration into ACE's semantics) *bridge rule patterns* of the following form:
$s \leftarrow (\mathcal{C}_1 : p_1), \ldots, (\mathcal{C}_j : p_j), not\,(\mathcal{C}_{j+1} : p_{j+1}), \ldots, not\,(\mathcal{C}_m : p_m).$
where each $\mathcal{C}_i$ can be either a constant indicating a context name, or a term of the form $m_i(k_i)$ that we call *context designator*, which indicates the *kind* of context (rather than the specific one) to be queried, to be specified before bridge-rule execution. Such a rule, once context designators have been instantiated to actual context names, is *applicable* (and s can thus be added to the consequences of a module's knowledge base) whenever each p_r, $r \leq j$, belongs to the consequences of module $\mathcal{C}_r$ while instead each p_w, $j < w \leq m$, does not belong to the consequences of $\mathcal{C}_w$.

In an ACE basic agent we adopt for bridge rules the agent-oriented modalities of DACMACSs [3]. First, bridge rules are applied proactively upon specific conditions, via *trigger rules* of the form Q **enables** $A(\hat{x})$, where: Q is a query to agent's internal knowledge-base and $A(\hat{x})$ is the conclusion of one of agent's bridge rules, which is "fired" whenever Q evaluates to *true*. Second, the result returned by a bridge rule with head $A(\hat{x})$ will be exploited via a *bridge-update rule* of the form **upon** $A(\hat{x})$ **then** $\beta(\hat{x})$ where $\beta(\hat{x})$ specifies the elaboration to be applied for $\hat{x}$ to be incorporated into the agent's knowledge base.

4. CASE STUDY

As a case study we consider a student, represented by an agent which can be seen as her "personal assistant agent". Upon completing the secondary school, she wishes to apply for enrollment to an US university. Each application has a cost, and the tuition fee will have to be paid in case of admission and enrollment. The student has an allotted maximum budget for both. The example deals with two aspect of quantitative reasoning: (i) the cost of knowledge, as in practical terms a student applies in order *to know* whether she is admitted; (ii) reasoning under budget limits, as a student may send an application only if: she can afford the fees related to the application; in case of admission, she can then afford the tuition fees. The student has a list of preferred universities, and within such list she would apply only to universities whose ranking is higher than a threshold. Additionally, since she likes basketball, all other things being equal (*ceteris paribus*) she would prefer universities with the best rankings of the basketball team.

Without any pretension to precision, we consider the following steps a student has to undergo: pass the general SAT test; pass the specific SAT test for the subject of interest; in case of foreign students, pass the TOEFL test; fill the general application on the application website (that we call collegeorg); send the SAT results to the universities of interest; complete the application for such universities. All steps are subject to the payment of fees, which are fixed (independent of the university where one applies) for the first four steps and depend upon each university for the last two steps.

In the case study, the agent will activate the following bridge rule, where *rasp_mod* is a RASP quantitative reasoning module which computes the list *Sel_UnivL* of the universities where it is possible to apply given the available budget:

$$chooseU(Universities, Budget, Sel\_UnivL) \leftarrow$$
$$chooseU(Universities, Budget, Sel\_UnivL) : rasp\_mod$$

The corresponding bridge-update rule will, given the preferred subject, instantiate and trigger a bridge rule pattern to perform the general tests, among which, if needed, the TOEFL test, and fill the general part of the application. It will then, given *Sel_UnivL*, generate for each element an instance of the following bridge rule pattern, to send test results and complete the application:

$$apply(Univ, ResponseUniv) \leftarrow test\_res(R1, R2, R3),$$
$$send\_test\_results(R1, R2, R3) : myuniv(Univ),$$
$$complete\_application(ResponseUniv) : myuniv(Univ)$$

Finally, the student will choose where to enroll among the universities that return a positive answer (code not shown here).

5. RASP IMPLEMENTATION

Below we shortly illustrate the main features of the RASP module *rasp_mod*. (The full code and the RASP solver for its execution can be found at `www.dmi.unipg.it/formis/raspberry/`) As facts, we have the universities to which the students is interested, the SAT subjects (in general), and the SAT subjects available at each university.

```
% Universities
university(theBigUni).  university(theSmallUni).
university(thePinkUni).  university(theBlueUni).
% SAT subjects
sat_subject(mathematics).    ...
% SAT subjects in each University
availableSubject(theBigUni, S) :- sat_subject(S).
availableSubject(theSmallUni, mathematics).
...
```

Then we have: the tuition fees and the maximum fee allowed; the university rankings and the minimum required; the basketball team ranking, and the budget available for the applications (where notation "#" indicates a resource quantity, here money).

```
% Tuition fees
tuitionFee(theBigUni, 21000).    ...
% Tuition fee cannot exceed this threshold
maxTuition(22000).
% University reputation ranking R
reputation(theBigUni, 100).    ...
% Reputation must be higher than this threshold
reputationThrs(70).
% BasketballTeam Ranking
extraRank(theSmallUni, 10).    ...
% Budget for the application procedure
dollar#1500.
```

Then, the subject(s) of interest and (if applicable) the status as foreign student are indicated. The universities where to potentially apply (`canApply(Univ,Subject)`) are derived according to the preferred subject (`canApplyForSubject(Subject)`) and to the constraints concerning the university ranking and tuition fee. If any is found, then `canApply` becomes true. The RASP rules below perform quantitative reasoning, by considering the fees for the different kinds of tests.

```
% 1) General SAT test, feel fixed
testSATfeeGen :- dollar#300, canApply.
% 2) Disciplinary SAT test, fee2 fixed
testSATfeeSbj(mathematics) :-
    dollar#170, canApplyForSubject(mathematics).
...
% 3) For foreign student, TOEFL fee3 fixed
testTOEFLfee :- dollar#200, foreign, canApply.
% 4) Collegeorg application, fee4 fixed
testCollegeOrg :- dollar#130, canApply.
```

If the available budget is too low, no applications can be issued. Otherwise, the costs related to potential applications and the remaining amount (if any) are computed. Clearly, this code performs a quantitative evaluation and does not execute actual actions, which are left to the agent (and to the user). The RASP solver can compute all solutions which maximize the number of applications given the constraints. Here, the best-preferred solution involves applying to thePinkUni and theBigUni, with a second-best solution which involves applying to thePinkUni and theSmallUni.

6. CONCLUDING REMARKS

In this paper we have demonstrated by means of a practical example how quantitative reasoning can be performed in modular agent-based frameworks. The approach of this paper is fairly general and novel, as no significant related work can be found so far.

REFERENCES

[1] G. Brewka, T. Eiter, and M. Fink. Nonmonotonic multi-context systems. In *Logic Programming, Knowledge Representation, and Nonmonotonic Reasoning*, Springer LNCS 6565, 2011.

[2] S. Costantini. ACE: a flexible environment for complex event processing in logical agents. In *Post-Proceedings of EMAS 2015 (Revised Selected Papers)*, Springer LNCS 9318, 2015.

[3] S. Costantini. Knowledge acquisition via non-monotonic reasoning in distributed heterogeneous environments. In *Proc. of LPNMR 2015*, Springer LNCS 9345, 2015.

[4] S. Costantini and A. Formisano. Modeling preferences and conditional preferences on resource consumption and production in ASP. *J. of Algorithms in Cognition, Informatics and Logic*, 64(1), 2009.

[5] S. Costantini and A. Formisano. Answer set programming with resources. *J. of Logic and Computation*, 20(2), 2010.

[6] S. Costantini and A. Formisano. RASP and ASP as a fragment of linear logic. *J. of Applied Non-Class. Logics*, 23(1-2), 2013.

[7] M. Gelfond. Answer sets. In *Handbook of Knowledge Representation*. Chapter 7. Elsevier, 2008.

[8] P. Naumov and J. Tao. Budget-constrained knowledge in multiagent systems. In *Proc. of AAMAS 2015*. ACM, 2015.

Relaxation for Constrained Decentralized Markov Decision Processes

(Extended Abstract)

Jie Xu
University of Miami
1251 Memorial Drive
Coral Gables, FL 33146
jiexu@miami.edu

ABSTRACT

This paper studies a class of decentralized multi-agent stochastic optimization problems. In these problems, each agent has only a partial view of the world state, and a partial control of the actions but must cooperatively maximize the long-term system reward. The state that an agent observe consists of two parts - a common public component and an agent-specific private component. Importantly, taking actions incurs costs and the actions that the agents can take are subject to an overall cost constraint in each interaction period. We formulate this problem as an infinite time horizon Decentralized Markov Decision Process (DEC-MDP) with resource constraints and develop efficient approximate algorithms that allow decentralized computation of the agent policy based on Lagrangian relaxation.

Keywords

decentralized MDP, Lagrangian relaxation

1. INTRODUCTION

Decentralized MDP (DEC-MDP) [4] [8] [3] has emerged as an important framework for cooperative multi-agent decision making problems in which each agent has only a partial view of the world and a partial control of the actions but must cooperatively maximize the system reward. This paper studies an important variant of DEC-MDP in which the actions that agents can take are subject to resource constraints. The considered DEC-MDPs operate in an infinite time horizon and are almost independent among agents but their decision making is coupled via the resource constraints imposed in each interaction period. There are numerous applications where this problem class can be useful, such as wireless multi-user communications and distributed intrusion detection. To solve this type of constrained DEC-MDP, we develop efficient decentralized solutions based on Lagrange relaxation [9] [1] [6] [5]. Iterative approaches based on Lagrange multipliers are widely adopted in myopic optimization problems [6] [5], but the stochastic version is much more complicated since the objective function is about foresighted rewards and the resource constraint is state-specific. Standard Lagrange relaxation methods fail to decompose the problem because agents need the knowledge of the stochastic environment and policies of other agents to solve their own subproblems. In this paper, we develop a novel method that enables efficient problem decomposition by using Lagrange multipliers that depend on only the public component of agent states. We prove the correctness of such decomposition - agents can solve their own subproblems without knowing other agents' subproblems and solutions. Moreover, we derive closed-form solutions for the subgradients of the decomposed as well as the overall relaxed problems, thereby enabling a decentralized implementation of the policy computation based on the subgradient method. We note that the joint policy derived by our method may still be suboptimal since the relaxation is approximate due to the use of only public state-dependent multipliers rather than joint state-dependent multipliers. However, compared to existing Lagrange relaxation methods based on uniform multipliers, we theoretically prove and experimentally demonstrate the superiority of our method to existing method that relies on a uniform multiplier [9][1].

Appears in: *Proceedings of the 15th International Conference on Autonomous Agents and Multiagent Systems (AAMAS 2016), J. Thangarajah, K. Tuyls, C. Jonker, S. Marsella (eds.), May 9–13, 2016, Singapore.*

2. PROBLEM FORMULATION

An infinite time horizon N-agent constrained DEC-MDP is defined by a tuple $\langle I, S, A, P, R, C, B\rangle$, where I is the set of agents; S is a finite set of states, with a distinguished initial state s^0; $A = \times_{i\in I} A_i$ is a finite set of joint actions; $P: S\times A\times S \to [0,1]$ is the transition function; $R: S\times A \to \mathbb{R}$ is a reward function; $C: S\times A \to \mathbb{R}$ is a resource cost function; $B: S \to \mathbb{R}$ is a resource budget function for each joint state. The constrained DEC-MDP requires that, for each state, $C(s, \boldsymbol{a}) \leq B(s), \forall s$. Without loss of generality, we can let $B(s) = 1, \forall s$ after a normalization and hence $C(s, \boldsymbol{a}) \leftarrow C(s, \boldsymbol{a})/B(s)$.

As a common assumption in the DEC-MDP literature [2][3], we study factored DEC-MDP (i.e. the state can be factored into $N+1$ components, $S = S_0 \times S_1 \times ... \times S_N$). Such a factorization allows a separation of features of the world state that belong to one agent from those of the others and from the external features. In this definition, S_0 refers to public external states which all agents can observe but cannot affect. S_i refers private internal state features for agent i. These features can only be observed by agent i and only affect agent i's rewards. A stationary local policy π for agent i is a mapping from its local states to local actions, i.e. $\pi : S_0 \times S_i \rightarrow A_i$. A joint policy $(\pi_1, ..., \pi_N)$ is the combination of local policies. The long-term discounted reward of the system is $U(s^0, \pi) = \mathbb{E}\left\{(1-\delta)\sum_{t=0}^{\infty}(\delta^t \cdot R^t)\right\}$ where $\delta \in (0,1)$ is the discount factor. The system objective is to maximize the long-term discounted reward while satisfying the resource constraint by determining the joint policy. Formally

$$\max_{\pi_1,\ldots,\pi_N} U(s^0, \pi) \quad \text{s.t. } C^t \leq 1, \forall t \tag{1}$$

We identify a subclass of infinite-horizon DEC-MDP with resource constraints that is amenable to problem decomposition. In particular, we consider DEC-MPDs that are transition independent (i.e. there exist P_0 through P_N such that $P(s_i'|s, \boldsymbol{a}) = P_0(s_0'|s_0)$, if $i = 0$; $P(s_i'|s, \boldsymbol{a}) = P_i(s_i'|s_0, s_i, a_i)$, if $i \neq 0$), reward independent (i.e. $R(s, \boldsymbol{a}) = \sum_{i=1}^{N} R_i(\hat{s}_i, a_i)$) and cost independent ($C(s, \boldsymbol{a}) = \sum_{i=1}^{N} C_i(\hat{s}_i, a_i)$). If there were no resource budget constraint, then these DEC-MDPs would be fully independent and hence, the agents can solve their local problems in a fully decentralized manner. However, due to the resource budget constraint, agents' decision making is still coupled and hence requires careful coordination. Weakly-coupled multi-agent MDP studied in [9][1][7] can be considered as a special case of this class where S_0 is a singleton.

3. DECENTRALIZED SOLUTION

The central idea of our method is as follows. Instead of associating each joint state s with a Lagrange multiplier λ_s, we associate each public external state $s_0 \in S_0$ with a Lagrange multiplier μ_{s_0}. We use the boldface symbol $\boldsymbol{\mu}$ to denote the set of all such Lagrange multipliers. Then the Lagrangian of (1) becomes $L(s; \boldsymbol{\mu}) = \max_{\boldsymbol{a}}[\sum_i R_i(\hat{s}_i, a_i) - \mu_{s_0}(\sum_i C_i(\hat{s}_i, a_i) - 1) + \delta \sum_{s'} P(s'|s, \boldsymbol{a}) L(s'; \boldsymbol{\mu})]$. We aim to solve $L^{*,p}(\boldsymbol{s}^0) = \min_{\boldsymbol{\mu} \geq \mathbf{0}} L(s^0, \boldsymbol{\mu})$. The advantages of using only public state-dependent multipliers are many-fold. Firstly, this problem is now scalable. The number of dual variables is a constant $|S_0|$ that does not depend on the number of agents. Secondly, this problem can be decoupled, thereby enabling decentralized solutions. Specifically, for any joint state s, given $\boldsymbol{\mu}$, we have

$$L(s; \boldsymbol{\mu}) = \sum_i L_i(\hat{s}_i; \boldsymbol{\mu}) + \mathbf{e}_{s_0}^T (\mathbf{I} - \delta P)^{-1} \boldsymbol{\mu} \tag{2}$$

where $\mathbf{e}^T$ denotes a row vector of size $|S_0|$ with the element corresponding to public state s_0 being 1 and other elements being 0, $\mathbf{I}$ is the identity matrix of size $|S_0|$ and $L_i(\hat{s}_i; \boldsymbol{\mu}) = \max_{a_i}\{R_i(\hat{s}_i, a_i) - \mu_{s_0} C_i(\hat{s}_i, a_i) + \delta \sum_{\hat{s}_i} P(\hat{s}_i'|\hat{s}_i, a_i) L_i(\hat{s}_i; \boldsymbol{\mu})$. Thirdly, solving the optimal $\boldsymbol{\mu}$ becomes much easier. We can provide closed-form solutions for the subgradient $\nabla_{\boldsymbol{\mu}} L(s^0, \boldsymbol{\mu})$. Specifically, one subgradient $\nabla_{\boldsymbol{\mu}} L_i(\hat{s}_i; \boldsymbol{\mu})$ for agent i's problem is $\forall s_0'$, $\nabla_{\mu_{s_0'}} L_i(\hat{s}_i; \boldsymbol{\mu}) = -\mathbf{e}_{\hat{s}_i}^T (\mathbf{I}_i - \delta \hat{P}_{i,\boldsymbol{\mu}})^{-1} \mathbf{D}_{i,\boldsymbol{\mu},s_0'}$ where $\mathbf{e}_{\hat{s}_i}^T$ is a row vector of size $|\hat{S}_i|$ with the element corresponding to $\hat{s}_i$ being 1 and other elements being 0, $\mathbf{I}_i$ is the identity matrix of size $|\hat{S}_i|$.

Based on these results, we develop a decentralized algorithm for solving the N-agent constrained DEC-MDP. The algorithm is an iterative algorithm with an optional centralized coordinator. In each iteration, the agents exchange limited messages with each other or with the optional coordinator. First, given the current $\boldsymbol{\mu}$, each agent solves its own Bellman equation using value iteration or policy iteration. Each agent also computes the local subgradient $\nabla_{\boldsymbol{\mu}} L_i(\hat{s}_i; \boldsymbol{\mu})$. Next, agents exchange their local subgradients. Then the coordinator or the agent themselves combine the local subgradients to obtain the overall subgradient. The Lagrange multipliers $\boldsymbol{\mu}$ are then updated using the subgradient method according to $\boldsymbol{\mu}^{k+1} \leftarrow [\boldsymbol{\mu}^k - \gamma^k \nabla_{\boldsymbol{\mu}} L(s; \boldsymbol{\mu})]^+$ where γ^k is the step size in iteration k. The iteration terminates when $\|\nabla_{\boldsymbol{\mu}} L(s; \boldsymbol{\mu})\|$ is sufficiently small.

We can prove that $L^{*,u}(s^0) \geq L^{*,p}(s^0) \geq L^*(s^0) \geq U^*(s^0)$ where $L^{*,u}(s^0)$ is the solution by using a uniform multiplier and $L^{*,p}(s^0)$ is the solution by the proposed public state-dependent multiplier. Therefore, we achieve a tighter solution bound than existing work. Numerical results under a multiarmed bandit problem setting to validate the efficacy of our proposed method are reported in Table 1.

Table 1: Simulation Results

N	$\lvert S_0\rvert$	$\lvert S_i\rvert$	δ	$L^{*,p}$	$L^{*,u}$	U^p	U^u
4	2	4	0.95	14.74	15.06	13.24	12.95
4	2	4	0.8	3.73	3.83	3.40	3.36
4	2	8	0.95	14.33	14.57	12.78	12.59
4	2	8	0.8	3.79	3.88	3.41	3.37
8	3	4	0.95	16.76	17.11	14.65	14.11
8	3	4	0.8	4.35	4.44	3.88	3.76
8	3	8	0.95	16.70	16.93	14.48	14.08
8	3	8	0.8	4.34	4.42	3.83	3.75

REFERENCES

[1] D. Adelman and A. J. Mersereau. Relaxations of weakly coupled stochastic dynamic programs. *Operations Research*, 56(3):712–727, 2008.

[2] R. Becker, S. Zilberstein, V. Lesser, and C. V. Goldman. Transition-independent decentralized markov decision processes. In *Proceedings of the second international joint conference on Autonomous agents and multiagent systems*, pages 41–48. ACM, 2003.

[3] R. Becker, S. Zilberstein, V. Lesser, and C. V. Goldman. Solving transition independent decentralized markov decision processes. *Journal of Artificial Intelligence Research*, pages 423–455, 2004.

[4] D. S. Bernstein, R. Givan, N. Immerman, and S. Zilberstein. The complexity of decentralized control of markov decision processes. *Mathematics of operations research*, 27(4):819–840, 2002.

[5] D. P. Bertsekas. Nonlinear programming. 1999.

[6] S. Boyd and L. Vandenberghe. *Convex optimization.* Cambridge university press, 2004.

[7] F. Fu and M. van der Schaar. A systematic framework for dynamically optimizing multi-user wireless video transmission. *Selected Areas in Communications, IEEE Journal on*, 28(3):308–320, 2010.

[8] C. V. Goldman and S. Zilberstein. Decentralized control of cooperative systems: Categorization and complexity analysis. *J. Artif. Intell. Res.(JAIR)*, 22:143–174, 2004.

[9] J. T. Hawkins. *A Langrangian decomposition approach to weakly coupled dynamic optimization problems and its applications.* PhD thesis, Massachusetts Institute of Technology, 2003.

A Bayesian Approach for Learning and Tracking Switching, Non-Stationary Opponents

(Extended Abstract)

Pablo Hernandez-Leal
Instituto Nacional de Astrofísica, Óptica y Electrónica
Puebla, México
pablohl@ccc.inaoep.mx

Benjamin Rosman
Council for Scientific and Industrial Research, and the University of the Witwatersrand, South Africa
brosman@csir.co.za

Matthew E. Taylor
Washington State University, Pullman, Washington, USA
taylorm@eecs.wsu.edu

L. Enrique Sucar
Instituto Nacional de Astrofísica, Óptica y Electrónica
Puebla, México
esucar@inaoep.mx

Enrique Munoz de Cote
Instituto Nacional de Astrofísica, Óptica y Electrónica
Puebla, México
jemc@inaoep.mx

ABSTRACT

In many situations, agents are required to use a set of strategies (behaviors) and switch among them during the course of an interaction. This work focuses on the problem of recognizing the strategy used by an agent within a small number of interactions. We propose using a Bayesian framework to address this problem. In this paper we extend Bayesian Policy Reuse to adversarial settings where opponents switch from one stationary strategy to another. Our extension enables online learning of new models when the learning agent detects that the current policies are not performing optimally. Experiments presented in repeated games show that our approach yields better performance than state-of-the-art approaches in terms of average rewards.

Categories and Subject Descriptors

I.2.11 [**Distributed Artificial Intelligence**]: Multiagent Systems

Keywords

Policy reuse; non-stationary opponents; repeated games

1. INTRODUCTION

A core problem in multiagent systems and human-computer interaction is being able to identify the behaviors of other (target) agents. When such a problem is tackled correctly, it allows an agent to derive an optimal policy against such behavior [1]. Consider, for example, a poker player whose behavior has been identified by the opponent player. Then, the opponent can act optimally against such player, anticipating every move. Another example are service robots. They need to interact with persons that have not one but a set of different behaviors (strategies) depending, for example, on factors such as personality or physical capabilities. Moreover, it is desirable that robots learn new tasks and learn how to optimize those.

The target opponent agents that we focus on use a fix (stationary) strategy for an unknown number of interactions, switching to another fixed strategy and repeating this switching to different strategies. There has been some literature addressing this problem [2, 3, 5], however, no work has focused on the problem of reusing previously seen strategies to boost learning speeds.

The Bayesian policy reuse (BPR) framework [7] has been proposed to determine *quickly* the best policy to select when faced with an unlabeled (but previously seen) task. However, standard BPR assumes knowledge of all possible tasks and optimal policies from the start. Our contribution, BPR+, is an extension to BPR for adversarial settings against non-stationary opponents. In particular, we relax the assumption of knowing all opponent strategies *a priori* by providing an online learning approach for incorporating models of new strategies when current policies perform suboptimally.

2. BPR+

Our proposal BPR+ handles non-stationary opponents and learns new models in an online manner. BPR was presented in a single agent environment facing different tasks (represented by MDPs). BPR+ extends to a multiagent setting. Now the tasks correspond to opponent strategies and the policies correspond to optimal policies against those stationary strategies. To cope with these new type of environment, some considerations need to be taken.

(i) An exploration for switch detection is added: drift exploration. Against non-stationary opponents, exploration cannot be terminated. Strategy switches can be difficult to

Appears in: *Proceedings of the 15th International Conference on Autonomous Agents and Multiagent Systems (AAMAS 2016), J. Thangarajah, K. Tuyls, C. Jonker, S. Marsella (eds.), May 9–13, 2016, Singapore.*

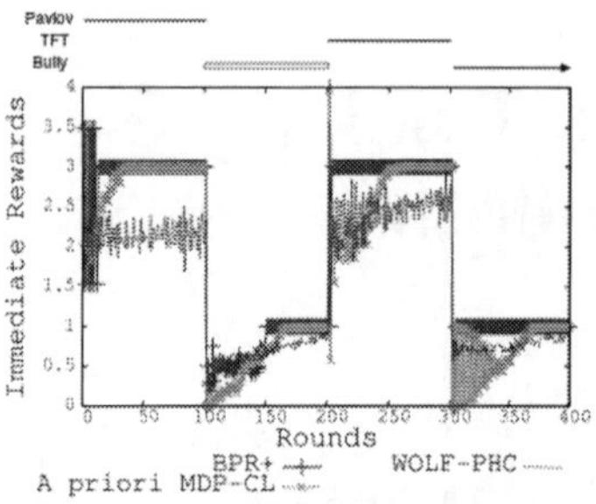

Figure 1: BPR+ and other approaches against a non-stationary opponent (thick line on top of the figure means a unknown strategy to BPR+).

Table 1: Average rewards with std. dev. (±) of the learning agents (average of 100 trials). The opponent changes strategies randomly. Agents can have initial information about the opponent strategies (*Known* column) or start without any information (*Unknown* column), $*, \dagger$ represent statistical significance with *a priori* MDP-CL and WOLF-PHC respectively.

	Opponent strategies	
Learning agent	*Known*	*Unknown*
Omniscient	2.53 ± 0.00	2.32 ± 0.00
BPR+	**2.24 ± 0.30** $*\dagger$	**2.17 ± 0.27** $*\dagger$
A priori MDP-CL	2.18 ± 0.31	2.11 ± 0.24
WOLF-PHC	1.71 ± 0.27	1.77 ± 0.19

detect, particularly if the strategies in question are very similar. Such similarities can produce a "shadowing" effect [4] in the agent's perception — an agent's optimal policy π^* will produce an ergodic set of states against some opponent strategy, but if the opponent's switching strategy induces a similar MDP where the policy π^* produces the same ergodic set, the agent will not detect something has changed (unless some exploration occurs).

(ii) A method for detecting when an unknown opponent strategy appears is needed. This scenario is identified through receiving a sequence of rewards which are unlikely given the known opponent models. Two parameters are needed, ρ measures how different the probabilities need to be (compared to the known opponent strategies) and n controls the number of rounds needed before consider learning a new opponent strategy.

(iii) A method for learning the new opponent strategy (and a new optimal policy). The opponent behavior is modeled trough an MDP, $\mathcal{M}_{new}$ [1]. To learn its parameters an exploratory phase is needed. We assume the opponent will not change of strategies during the learning phase (a number of rounds) after which an MDP representing the opponent strategy is obtained. Since the rewards are deterministic, solving the MDP is done through value iteration, obtaining an optimal policy π^*_{new}.

(iv) An algorithm to update the known models to add the the recently learned model, $\mathcal{M}_{new}$, is needed.

3. EXPERIMENTS

Our approach is evaluated in the context of repeated games, in particular using the iterated prisoner's dilemma. Well-known strategies in this domain are Tit-for-Tat (TFT), Pavlov and Bully [6].

We show the behavior of BPR+ against a switching opponent which uses known and unknown strategies. BPR+ only has information about TFT and Pavlov strategies. However, the opponent will also use Bully. Figure 1 depicts rewards for BPR+, *a priori* MDP-CL [5], and WOLF-PHC [2]. For the known opponents (TFT and Pavlov) BPR+ takes about 4 rounds to reach the optimal reward. From round 100 the opponent uses Bully which is unknown to BPR+. Then, BPR+ detects this as a new opponent strategy and starts a learning phase which finishes approximately at round 160. Now, BPR+ computes and uses an optimal policy against Bully and updates its models to cope with future switches (round 300).

We evaluated BPR+ against an opponent that switches randomly among the three mentioned strategies. Table 1, under column *Known*, shows the average rewards with standard deviations for the three learning approaches and the Omniscient player against an opponent that switches strategies randomly every 200 rounds. Both BPR+ and *a priori* MDP-CL know the strategies the opponent may use but not the order or the switching times (the opponent should use all strategies at least once). Lastly, we tested the approaches without any prior information, this is shown under column *Unknown*. Results show that BPR+ obtained statistically significant score improvements over the other approaches.

4. CONCLUSIONS

We propose a Bayesian approach to cope with non-stationary opponents (that change from one stationary strategy to another) in repeated games. Our approach, BPR+, exploits information of how the policies behave against different strategies in order to asses the best policy faster than any algorithm in literature. We also provided BPR+ with an online learning algorithm for adding models to its library.

Acknowledgments

This research has taken place in part at the Intelligent Robot Learning (IRL) Lab, Washington State University. IRL research is supported in part by grants AFRL FA8750-14-1-0069, AFRL FA8750-14-1-0070, NSF IIS-1149917, NSF IIS-1319412, USDA 2014-67021-22174, and a Google Research Award.

REFERENCES

[1] B. Banerjee and J. Peng. Efficient learning of multi-step best response. In *Proceedings of the 4th AAMAS*, pages 60–66, Utretch, Netherlands, 2005. ACM.

[2] M. Bowling and M. Veloso. Multiagent learning using a variable learning rate. *Artificial Intelligence*, 136(2):215–250, 2002.

[3] B. C. Da Silva, E. W. Basso, A. L. Bazzan, and P. M. Engel. Dealing with non-stationary environments using context detection. In *Proceedings of the 23rd ICML*, pages 217–224, Pittsburgh, Pennsylvania, 2006.

[4] N. Fulda and D. Ventura. Predicting and Preventing Coordination Problems in Cooperative Q-learning Systems. In *Proceedings of the 20th IJCAI*, pages 780–785, Hyderabad, India, 2007.

[5] P. Hernandez-Leal, E. Munoz de Cote, and L. E. Sucar. Using a priori information for fast learning against non-stationary opponents. In *Advances in Artificial Intelligence – IBERAMIA*, pages 536–547, Santiago de Chile, 2014.

[6] M. L. Littman and P. Stone. Implicit Negotiation in Repeated Games. *ATAL '01: Revised Papers from the 8th International Workshop on Intelligent Agents VIII*, 2001.

[7] B. Rosman, M. Hawasly, and S. Ramamoorthy. Bayesian Policy Reuse. *Machine Learning*, (in press) 2016.

Posting Prices for a Perishable Item (Extended Abstract)

Bo Zheng
Tsinghua University
Beijing, China
zhengb06science@gmail.com

Li Xiao
University of California, Irvine
Irvine, CA 92697
lxiao4@uci.edu

Guang Yang
Tsinghua University
Beijing, China
guang.research@gmail.com

Tao Qin
Microsoft Research
Beijing, China
taoqin@microsoft.com

ABSTRACT

In this paper, we study the problem of posting take-it-or-leave-it prices for a perishable item to maximize the seller's expected revenue. Agents arrive independently over time, and each of them makes a purchase decision according to the price. We study the case that the seller has no prior information about agents' valuations, whereas the benchmark in the competitive analysis is an optimal mechanism that knows the value distribution. We propose a mechanism Γ_1 which obtains constant competitive ratios under various valuation models. We also conduct numerical simulations and validate the empirical performance of Γ_1.

CCS Concepts

•Theory of computation → Computational pricing and auctions; *Online algorithms;* **•Computing methodologies → Multi-agent systems;**

Keywords

online mechanism design; revenue maximization; competitive analysis; detail-free mechanism

1. INTRODUCTION

Imagine a scenario, where you intend to transfer a ticket for a given concert. You post the information on campus BBS and set a price for the ticket. Potential agents arrive online and each has a valuation for the ticket. As a senior user of the campus BBS, you are familiar with the visiting traffic and estimate it as a Poisson process. However, you have no information about how potential agents would value the ticket, except from a range of reasonable valuations. The price can be updated at any time, and the target is to maximize the expected revenue.

Posted-price mechanism in such a scenario combines multiple challenges: (i) Challenge of *detail-free* mechanism design [4], which does not use any information about the value distribution. (ii) Challenge of *online* mechanism design [5], which needs to deal with uncertainty about future arrivals. (iii) Challenge of *finite time* horizon, which constitutes a period of validity for the mechanism. In this work, we design posted-price mechanisms with revenue guarantees for selling a single item in a finite time period.

In a typical posted-price mechanism, the seller presents a take-it-or-leave-it price for each buyer, and the buyer makes a purchase decision with respect to that price. Posted-price mechanisms show many advantages over traditional auction-style mechanisms. It is shown that more and more *eBay* transactions are made by posting prices rather than auctions [2].

Detail-free mechanisms are desirable since having knowledge of value distributions is costly or unrealistic in many practical scenarios [1]. We evaluate the performance of such a mechanism by *competitive analysis* [3], which compares the revenue implemented by the mechanism (without any knowledge of value distributions) with the optimal one (with the knowledge of value distributions).

We study posted-price mechanism design in an online fashion, i.e. prices are posted immediately after every agent arrives without knowledge of future agents. This online condition reflects our real lives, because the decision problems in many buying and selling domains are inherently dynamic rather than static [6]. We assume that the seller is able to build an accurate model to predict the distribution of agents' arrivals, as it is not difficult for the seller to measure "footfall" of a shop or "visiting traffic" of a webpage.

In this work, we consider the item for sale is perishable, i.e. only available for a limited period. It is easy to think of examples in real life, such as a concert/movie ticket, or a time-limited coupon.

2. MODELS, MECHANISM, AND ANALYSIS

Suppose there is a seller who is interested in selling a single item, within a finite period T. At any time $t \in [0, T]$, the seller offers a take-it-or-leave-it price. Agents arrive online according to a Poisson process with known intensity λ.

Two valuation models are studied in this paper:

- **Identical Valuations:** Agents have a unified valuation v for the item, that is, all agents' valuations are the same.
- **Random Valuations:** Agents' valuations are independently drawn from a fixed distribution.

The valuations[1] of agents for the item are independently and identically drawn from a distribution function F. The seller does

[1]As the identical-valuation model can be seen as a special case of the random-valuation model, we formulate the problem in the language of the random-valuation model.

Appears in: *Proceedings of the 15th International Conference on Autonomous Agents and Multiagent Systems (AAMAS 2016), J. Thangarajah, K. Tuyls, C. Jonker, S. Marsella (eds.), May 9–13, 2016, Singapore.*

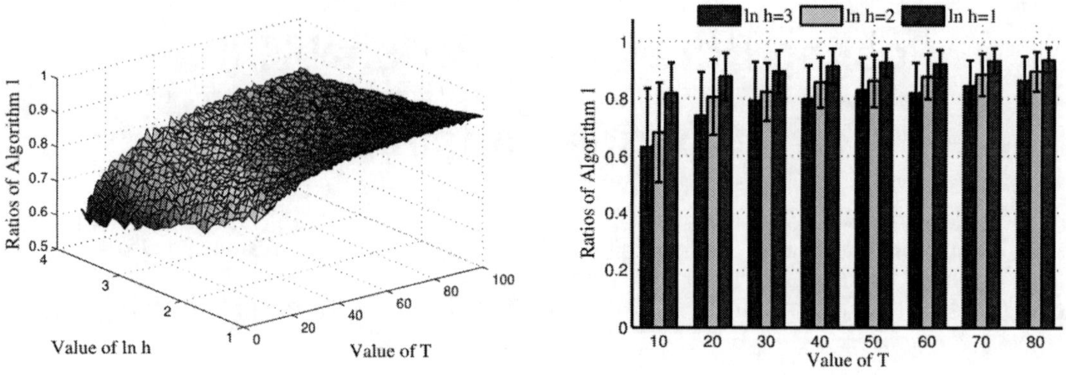

Figure 1: Uniform Distribution Samples

not know F, but knows that F belongs to the distribution family $\mathcal{F}$ with support $[v_{\min}, v_{\max}]$. $v_{\min}$ and $v_{\max}$ can be estimated by the seller. For simplicity, we normalize the range as $[1, h]$ for $h = v_{\max}/v_{\min} \geq 1$.

We use $p(t) : [0, T] \to \mathbb{R}_{\geq 0}$ to denote the *pricing strategy* of the seller. The agent who arrives at t, buys the item if and only if her valuation $v(t) \geq p(t)$, and in case she buys the item, she pays the price $p(t)$. Clearly, the posted-price mechanism is incentive compatible. Note that in the posted-price mechanism, the seller never learns the exact valuation of any arrived agent, but only observes the agent's decision: buy it or leave it.

First, we prove that the non-increasing pricing strategy (i.e., $p(t)$ is non-increasing with time t) is a dominant strategy for the seller. What's more, such a pricing strategy must maintain a bottom price (i.e., price 1) for the last period of the time horizon.

Second, we study the identical-valuation model. We present a deterministic posted-price mechanism Γ_1, which posts exponential decreasing prices (from the highest price h to the bottom price 1), and maintains the bottom price from time t_0 to deadline T. t_0 is a parameter to be optimized. In Γ_1, we define t_0 as the unique positive real root of the equation $\frac{\lambda t_0}{\ln h} = e^{\lambda(T-t_0)} - 1$. We show that Γ_1 has a competitive ratio of $\frac{1-e^{-\lambda(T-t_0)}}{1-e^{-\lambda T}}$.

Third, we study the random-valuation model. We assume value distributions satisfy the non-decreasing monotone hazard rate property, i.e., the hazard rate $H(x) = \frac{f(x)}{1-F(x)}$ is non-decreasing, where $F(x)$ is the cumulative distribution function and $f(x) = dF(x)/dx$ is the probability density function. We show that Γ_1 still achieves a good revenue compared to the benchmark. Specifically, Γ_1 has a competitive ratio of $\frac{1-\epsilon}{\kappa e}$, where $0 < \epsilon < 1$, and κ is a parameter depending on λT and h.

3. SIMULATION RESULTS

We conduct simple simulations to evaluate Γ_1 under illustrative value distributions and Poisson arrival models. We focus on examining the performance of Γ_1 on revenue compared with the *offline optimal revenue*. Fig.1 shows the simulation results of our mechanism under uniform distributions.

The empirical performances of Γ_1 is much better than the worst-case bounds (as indicated by competitive ratio). For example, when $T = 30$, $\lambda = 1$ and $\ln h = 2$, the empirical result of Γ_1 gives ratio 0.833, while the competitive analysis gives a ratio around 0.132. It can also be seen that the ratio of Γ_1 increases with T but decreases with h (the opposite for standard deviation), which consists with the worst case analysis since the competitive ratio is an increasing function of T and an decreasing function of h.

4. CONCLUSIONS

In this paper, we studied the online posted-price mechanisms for selling a single item in a finite time horizon. We designed a detail-free mechanism with revenue that is close to the optimal revenue. We proved in the identical-valuation model that Γ_1 achieves the optimal competitive ratio among all the deterministic posted-price mechanisms. In the random-valuation model, we showed that Γ_1 achieves constant competitive ratio if the valuation distributions are MHR (Monotone Hazard Rate).

Furthermore, we conjecture that $1/e$ is the tight upper bound for the competitive ratio in the random-valuation model. It remains open to study posted-price mechanism in conjunction with auctions and multiple item settings.

5. ACKNOWLEDGEMENTS

This research was supported by the National Basic Research Program of China Grant 2011CBA00300, 2011CBA00301, the Natural Science Foundation of China Grant 61033001, 61361136003, 61303077, 61561146398, 61170062, 61222202, 61433014, a Tsinghua Initiative Scientific Research Grant and a China Youth 1000-talent program.

REFERENCES

[1] S. Chawla, J. D. Hartline, D. L. Malec, and B. Sivan. Multi-parameter mechanism design and sequential posted pricing. In *Proceedings of the forty-second ACM symposium on Theory of computing*, pages 311–320. ACM, 2010.

[2] L. Einav, C. Farronato, J. D. Levin, and N. Sundaresan. Sales mechanisms in online markets: What happened to internet auctions? Technical report, National Bureau of Economic Research, 2013.

[3] A. V. Goldberg, J. D. Hartline, A. R. Karlin, M. Saks, and A. Wright. Competitive auctions. *Games and Economic Behavior*, 55(2):242–269, 2006.

[4] J. D. Hartline and T. Roughgarden. Optimal mechanism design and money burning. In *Proceedings of the fortieth annual ACM symposium on Theory of computing*, pages 75–84. ACM, 2008.

[5] R. Lavi and N. Nisan. Competitive analysis of incentive compatible on-line auctions. In *Proceedings of the 2nd ACM conference on Electronic commerce*, pages 233–241. ACM, 2000.

[6] D. C. Parkes. Online mechanisms. In *Algorithmic Game Theory*, pages 411–439. Cambridge University Press, 2007.

Modeling Team Formation in Self-assembling Software Development Teams

Mehdi Farhangian, Martin K.Purvis,
Maryam Purvis, Bastin Tony Roy Savarimuthu
Information Science Department, University of Otago, Dunedin, New Zealand
{mehdi.farhangian, martin.purvis, maryam.purvis,tony.savarimuthu}@otago.ac.nz

ABSTRACT

Many contemporary project teams are self-assembling, with potential team members operating as individual agents that self-select their own teams. Some examples include software development teams, crowdsourcing platforms, and the formation of scientific collaborative teams. In many such cases, team formation is significantly influenced by the makeup of participants' personalities and temperaments (even without considering the technical skills possessed by individuals). In this paper, we develop a model to help explain team formation processes and predict future team compositions by considering these personality aspects. We have used agent-based modeling to test a number of hypotheses on the team-formation mechanism with respect to a specific context by comparing the model's operation with data drawn from the Python Enhancement Proposal (PEP) process, an open-source software development process. In PEP operations, developers are free to select their fellow team members. We predict the future team composition of self-assembly teams by first inferring potential teammates' MBTI personalities based on analyzing their written texts expressed on social-networking sites. Once the personalities of PEP developers were identified, we simulated the team-formation process using agent-based simulation. The results were analyzed using factor analysis to examine the contribution of our hypotheses in the prediction of future team-assembly. The results indicated that a combination of four personal characteristics (knowledge of previous team performance, previous familiarity with people involved in the new team, and the degrees to which an agent is an MBTI perceiving personality and an MBTI feeling personality) improves the accuracy of the team composition prediction.

Keywords
Multi-agent Systems, Social Simulation, Personality, Team Formation, Self-assembling Teams.

1. INTRODUCTION

In recent years, the importance of focusing on teams of people rather than individuals in a team is widely being acknowledged. Today a vast proportion of teams are classified as project teams, since they are ad-hoc groups of distributed collaborators. Project teams are time-bound and are often assembled one-off and produce one-time outputs [1]. Some examples include crowdsourcing platforms, scientific collaboration teams, and open-source software development teams. In spite of their importance, there is little understanding about how these teams are assembled [2].

Appears in: *Proceedings of the 15th International Conference on Autonomous Agents and Multiagent Systems (AAMAS 2016), J. Thangarajah, K. Tuyls, C. Jonker, S. Marsella (eds.), May 9{13, 2016, Singapore.*

In this paper, we posit that personality types of individuals play an important role in the success of team work, and we consider them explicitly in the team-assembly process. Thus a model is developed on the basis of theoretical and empirical literature on personalities and team behavior. This conceptual model is then implemented as an agent-based computer simulation consisting of simple rules.

2. THE MODEL

In our model agents are of two types: requestors and contributors. Requestors send invitations to join their team to chosen contributors. Contributors choose among invitations received to join a team. The model has six factors hypothesized as important characteristics of the team assembly process: 1) the effect of familiarity of other team members on teammate selection, 2) the effect of past performance on the teammate selection, 3) the effect of the MBTI thinking-feeling personality dimension on familiarity, 4) the effect of the MBTI intuitive-sensing personality dimension on assessing past performance, 5) the effect of the MBTI extraverted-introverted personality dimension on familiarity likelihood, and 6) the effect of the MBTI perceiving-judging personality dimension on team-changing behavior.

3. DATA SET

We have chosen a specific application domain and investigated a real case study by extracting data from the Python Enhancement Proposal (PEP) process. Since the MBTI personalities of PEPs developers are not accessible, we have used techniques similar to [3] to determine the personality of people from their written texts. In this connection we developed a model to relate linguistic styles and personality.

Our method for extracting insights about the relationship between Python developers and their personality consisted of 3 main steps: 1) gathering the data; 2) finding relationships between personality and text usage; and 3) establishing the personalities of PEPs developers from the relationships found in step 2. These three steps are explained below.

Firstly we gathered texts written by users who reported their personalities in three social networking websites: Quora (393 users), Reddit (39 users), and College Confidential (185 users). In the second step, we extracted the text of the Quora users from their responses to other questions. Users' texts were analysed with the Linguistic Inquiry and Word Count (LIWC) tool [3], and the values for all the 80 LIWC dimensions were identified for each user. Secondly, after generating the value of all the variables in our Quora samples, we measured correlations between personality types and these variables. These correlations were then used to develop a computational model that can be used to determine the personalities of people from their texts. For validation, this formula was cross-tested with our Reddit and College Confidential data, and the results showed 73% and 60% accuracy, respectively. Thirdly, we applied the same formulae on the text written by Python developers involved in the creation of Python Enhancement Proposals (PEPs), which were developed in a team setting. The texts written by the team members were gathered from the PEPs' public activities on the Internet. This resulted in the identification of the personality type of the PEP developers.

4. SIMULATION AND RESULTS

By using an agent-based simulation, we investigated the hypotheses of our proposed model. The main research question is to what extent those hypotheses explain the behavioral outcome in the PEPs data. Experiments have been conducted using NetLogo [4].

In order to evaluate our model, we used a cross-validation procedure. A similar approach for validation of agent-based model can be seen in [5] and [6]. Our simulations start with 10 percent of teams; so among 78 PEP teams, the compositions of the 8 first teams are known and the model predicts the composition of the remaining 70 teams. The performance of the model is evaluated by counting the number of correctly predicted teams. The next iteration of the process occurs by selecting the first 9 PEPs teams to predict the remaining 69 teams. We continue with this process until the final step, when only the last two teams are unknown. The accuracy of the model is then the average of all of the experimental iterations.

The performance of the model is evaluated by counting the number of correctly predicted teams. We compared our simulation results with the real data from PEPs. Our model in average predicted 8.3% of the teams, correctly. When the proposed model is not employed and we ask the requestors and the contributors to randomly select each other, correctly chosen teams only occur 2.9% of the time. That shows the potential of the model to be used for prediction of compositions of self-assembled teams.

Furthermore, we test each hypothesis separately, to investigate the influence of each factor on the final results. Each of these factors either does or does not have an effect on the team formation, resulting in $2^6 (i.e. 64)$ separate conditions. Each condition was modelled as a separate experiment and was repeated 100 times. A factor analysis on the average performance of experiments reveals the contribution of each factor on the results. The results show that four factors appear to significantly affect the team formation mechanisms. These are 1) previous performance 2) teammate familiarity 3) MBTI feeling personality and 4) MBTI perceiving personality. The other factors did not have significant effects on the team formation in this particular context. In other words, including factors such as the effect of extraversion on the familiarity connections and the effect of sensing on the previous performance, though plausible from a psychological context, did not improve the accuracy of the model in connection with PEP team formation.

5. CONCLUSIONS

This paper offers a contribution to the relatively unexplored area of using simulation to study the impact of personality while forming self-assembly teams. We have developed an agent-based model to explore how different variables (e.g. personality types, familiarity of team members, and past team performance experience), impact the formation of self-assembly teams, using PEPs as a concrete example. To achieve that, we created a computational model to determine the relationship between MBTI personality and the LIWC dimensions.

Using simulation results, we found certain characteristics (i.e. previous performance of teams, familiarity of members in a team, and the impact of feeling personality dimension on the familiarity and the impact of perceiving dimension personality on the likelihood of changing teams) helped to predict future team compositions in PEPs, better than teams that are formed randomly. This highlights the potential of simulation for understanding team formation.

Note that our results are representative of PEPs, and we urge caution about over-generalizing our model for other data. With our application, we were working with a limited number of developers' teams in a particular domain. In addition our approach for predicting personality from text use also has some limitations. The LIWC tool has a bias against individuals whose first language is not English, and we did not separate non-English users and developers. Social roles, gender, age, and other demographic factors which are not covered in this study might be involved in the linguistic styles. Further experiments and validations should be performed before our correlations and results can be generalized.

6. REFERENCES

[1] S. G. Cohen, "What Makes Teams Work: Group Effectiveness Research from the Shop Floor to the Executive Suite," J. Manage., vol. 23, no. 3, pp. 239–290, Jun. 1997.

[2] N. Contractor, "Some assembly required: leveraging Web science to understand and enable team assembly.," Philos. Trans. A. Math. Phys. Eng. Sci., vol. 371, no. 1987, p. 20120385, Mar. 2013.

[3] J. Pennebaker and L. King, "Linguistic styles: language use as an individual difference.," Journal of personality and social psychology, 1999.

[4] S. Tisue and U. Wilensky, "NetLogo : Design and Implementation of a Multi-Agent Modeling Environment," in Proceedings of Agent, 2004.

[5] P. G. and R. Crutzen, "An Agent-Based Social Network Model of Binge Drinking Among Dutch Adults." JASSS, 31-Mar-2013.

[6] P. J. Giabbanelli, A. Alimadad, V. Dabbaghian, and D. T. Finegood, "Modeling the influence of social networks and environment on energy balance and obesity," J. Comput. Sci.,vol.3,no.1–2,pp.17–27,Jan.2012.

Analysis of Condition for the Cooperation Achievement on Arbitrary Networks

(Extended Abstract)

Shohei USUI
Graduate School of Engineering,
The University of Tokyo
7-3-1, Hongo, Bunkyo-ku
Tokyo, Japan 113-8656
usui@crimson.q.t.u-tokyo.ac.jp

Fujio TORIUMI
Graduate School of Engineering,
The University of Tokyo
7-3-1, Hongo, Bunkyo-ku
Tokyo, Japan 113-8656
tori@sys.t.u-tokyo.ac.jp

ABSTRACT

We analyze relations between evolution of cooperation on networks and network structures. Most researchers have used simple networks, such as scale-free networks and random networks. We performed decision tree analysis on various networks. The decision tree is constructed from cooperation degree and five network feature. Here, these five network features are selected from a lot of network features. We estimate their cooperation degree by SVR. As a result, estimation is successful because estimation values are correlated with measurement values strongly in the correlation coefficient of 0.8. Therefore, it is said that cooperation degree can be explained by five network features. The decision tree is constructed with cooperation degree and five network features, and then analyzed. We found that the conditions for achieving cooperation are having few hub nodes, being not very disassortative, and having a short average shortest-path length.

Keywords

prisoner's dilemma; complex network; network model; network feature

1. INTRODUCTION

Our goal is to understand the relation between network structure and cooperation. Most researchers approached this problem under limited conditions, it cannot be said that general knowledge about it has been obtained so far. For example, Rong et al. [3] studied cooperation focusing on assortativity. They generated scale-free networks with assortativity $r = 0.0 - 0.3$ by the Xulvi-Sokolov algorithm, and observed the relation between assortativity and cooperation. However there is a correlation between assortativity and average shortest-path length of the networks, and it is unclear which features affect cooperation degree. From the above reasons, it cannot be analyzed sufficiently without a compound analysis of the structure feature.

In this paper, we make clear which network features affect evolution of cooperation by the analysis of a decision tree. We simulate SPD games on various networks, and construct a decision tree. However, there are not enough guarantees to explain evolution of cooperation by adopted explanatory variables. Therefore, we estimate the achievement degree of the cooperation (cooperation degree) from explanatory variables. If it is possible to estimate at a high level, it shows that cooperation degree is explained sufficiently by these features.

Appears in: *Proceedings of the 15th International Conference on Autonomous Agents and Multiagent Systems (AAMAS 2016), J. Thangarajah, K. Tuyls, C. Jonker, S. Marsella (eds.), May 9–13, 2016, Singapore.*

2. NETWORK FEATURES THAT CAN EXPLAIN COOPERATION

In this paper, 5 network features adopted as explanatory variables to exlain cooperation degree. However there are not enough guarantees to explain their cooperation degree. Then, we estimate cooperation degree from network structures. If cooperation degree can be estimated, it can be said that the adopted network features are sufficient to explain cooperation. In this paper, we employ support vector regression (SVR).

2.1 Estimation setting

Analyzed features are the following: average shortest-path length L, cluster coefficient C, assortativity r, α of Beta distribution, β of Beta distribution. We construct decision trees using five explanatory variables.

Cooperation degree P_c is defined as an objective variable of the decision tree. In this paper, Spatial Prisoner's dilemma is adopted [3]. Payoff matrix is defined as follows:

$$\begin{pmatrix} R & S \\ T & P \end{pmatrix} = \begin{pmatrix} 1.0 & 0.0 \\ 1.2 & \epsilon \end{pmatrix}, \tag{1}$$

where ϵ is a minimum value.

2.2 DataSet

In this paper, 4,000 networks are generated as the network dataset. Table 1 shows statistics of the network dataset. It is said values of each feature are various values. Therefore, the dataset includes networks with various network structures.

2.3 Estimation Result

We try to estimate cooperation degree P_c from explanatory variables by SVR. A gauss kernel is used for the kernel function of SVR. We perform 8-division cross validation, and the parameters are optimized by simulated annealing [2].

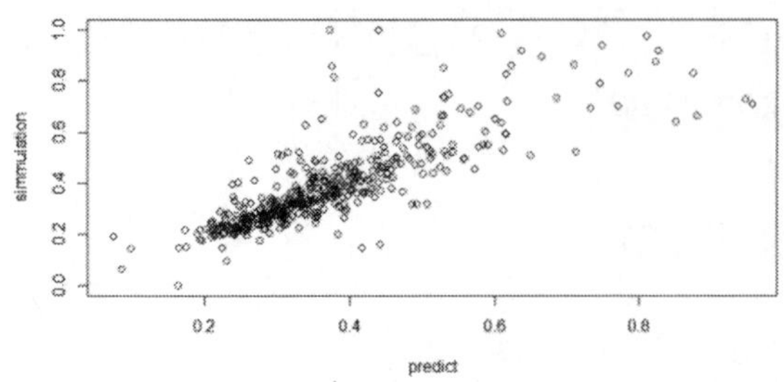

Figure 1: Estimation result

Figure 1 shows the estimation values calculated by SVR and measurement values calculated by the SPD game simulation. It is said that estimation succeeded because estimation values correlated with measurement values strongly in the correlation coefficient of 0.824. Therefore, cooperation degree can be estimated from the adopted network features uniquely; that is, cooperation degree can be explained with adopted explanatory variables.

3. ANALYSIS OF CONDITION WHERE COOPERATION BECOMES DOMINANT

3.1 Result of Analysis

In this section, we analyze how and which features affect cooperation degree. A decision tree is constructed for analyzing them. The cross validation error of the decision tree is 0.325.

There are three conditions in which the cooperator becomes the majority, as shown in Table 2. We consider the condition of highest cooperation degree. It is suggested that the lower average shortest-path length L leads to high cooperation degree. However, if average shortest-path length L is high, the cooperation degree can be high, as shown in the second highest condition. In the second highest condition, the condition in which α of degree distribution is low is added instead of the condition in which average shortest-path length L is low. The networks with high α have a lot of low degree nodes. Therefore, nodes with small degree are required for achievement of cooperation.

Next, not so low assortativity $r \geq -0.261$ leads to cooperation achievement. It is common to the second- and third-highest condition. Therefore, it can be said that disassortative networks cannot keep cooperators. In addition, in the third-highest condition, very high assortativity r leads to low cooperation degree. It is suggested that very disassortative networks and very assortative networks cannot keep cooperators.

Finally, high β leads to high cooperation degree. It is common to three conditions. The degree distribution with high β has a long tail. It is suggested that cooperation degree is affected by a long tail.

Table 1: Statistics of network dataset.

	Range	Average	Standard diviation	Max	Min
L	$1 \leq L$	3.49	1.07	6.08	2.23
C	$0 \leq C \leq 1$	0.291	0.201	0.793	0.00357
r	$-1 \leq r \leq 1$	0.0647	0.325	0.887	-0.562
α	$0 \leq \alpha$	2.14	1.38	7.97	0.723
β	$0 \leq \beta$	21.4	13.4	89.7	4.17

Table 2: Condition in highest and lowest networks

	Highest	2nd highest	3rd highest
P_c	0.769	0.621	0.612
L	$L < 2.65$	$L \geq 2.65$	-
C	-	-	$C < 0.559$
r	$r \geq -0.261$	$r \geq -0.159$	$-0.146 \leq r < 0.339$
α	-	$\alpha < 2.90$	$\alpha < 3.05$
β	$\beta \geq 24.2$	$\beta \geq 24.2$	$15.0 \leq \beta < 24.2$

3.2 Discussion

First, we found that not very disassortative and very assortative networks keep cooperators. Rong et al. [3] showed that disassortative networks are needed for cooperation. However, they analyzed the networks with assortativity $r \geq 0$. We analyzed the networks with assortativity $r < 0$, and we found very disassortative networks cannot keep cooperators. Therefore, the condition does not contradict their findings.

Second, there is almost no influence by the cluster coefficient in this research. Assenze et al. [1] showed that the networks with a high cluster coefficient lead to cooperation achievement. However, they analyzed only cluster coefficient, and did not analyze the features that may correlate with a cluster coefficient. A cluster coefficient is likely to be correlated with average shortest-path length in the networks generated by the HK model. It is suggested that average shortest-path length is related cooperation, and the correlation between cluster coefficient and cooperation is a spurious correlation.

Finally, it can be said that the distributions with high β and low α lead to high cooperation. These distributions are power-law distributions. That is, the scale-free networks (those with power-law degree distributions) are required to achieve cooperation. The average of cooperation degree in $R^2 \geq 0.5$ is 0.331 and that in $R^2 \leq 0.5$ is 0.505. It suggests that the power-low distributions lead to higher cooperation.

4. CONCLUSION

In this paper, we analyzed the relation between cooperation degree and each network feature statistically by simulating the SPD game on generated networks with various structures. First, we estimated the cooperation degree from network features to show that they are sufficient to explain cooperation. Second, we clarified how and which features affect cooperation by decision tree analysis.

REFERENCES

[1] S. Assenza, J. Gómez-Gardeñes, and V. Latora. Enhancement of cooperation in highly clustered scale-free networks. *Phys. Rev. E*, 78:017101, Jul 2008.

[2] S. Kirkpatrick, C. D. Gelatt, and M. P. Vecchi. Optimization by simulated annealing. *SCIENCE*, 220(4598):671–680, 1983.

[3] Z. Rong, X. Li, and X. Wang. Roles of mixing patterns in cooperation on a scale-free networked game. *Phys. Rev. E*, 76:027101, Aug 2007.

Achieving Sustainable Cooperation in Generalized Prisoner's Dilemma with Observation Errors*

(Extended Abstract)

[1]Fuuki Shigenaka, [1]Shun Yamamoto, [1]Motohide Seki,
[2]Tadashi Sekiguchi, [3]Atsushi Iwasaki, and [1]Makoto Yokoo
1: Kyushu University, {shigenaka@agent., syamamoto@agent., seki@, yokoo@}inf.kyushu-u.ac.jp
2: Kyoto University, sekiguchi@kier.kyoto-u.ac.jp
3: University of Electro-Communications, iwasaki@is.uec.ac.jp

ABSTRACT

A repeated game is a formal model for analyzing cooperation in long-term relationships. The case where each player observes her opponent's action with some observation errors (imperfect private monitoring) is difficult to analyze, and existing works show that cooperative relations can be sustainable only in ideal situations. We deal with a generic problem that can model both the prisoner's dilemma and the team production problem. We examine a situation with an additional action that is dominated by another action. By adding this seemingly irrelevant action, players can achieve sustainable cooperative relations far beyond the ideal situations. Moreover, for a two-player case, the obtained welfare matches a theoretical upper bound.

Keywords

Game theory, Repeated games, Private monitoring, Prisoner's dilemma, Belief-free equilibrium

1. INTRODUCTION

A repeated game, where players repeatedly play the same stage game over an infinite time horizon, is a formal model for analyzing cooperation in long-term relationships and has received considerable attention in MAS and economics literature. The case of perfect monitoring, where each player can observe other players' actions, is now well understood. There is also a large body of literature on the *imperfect monitoring* case, where players' actions are only imperfectly observed through some signals. Such imperfect monitoring cases are further classified into *public* and *private monitoring* cases. If *all* players observe the same set of signals that imperfectly indicate players' actions, we have an *imperfect public monitoring* case. In contrast, suppose that each player observes her opponent's action with some observation errors. Assume that each player chooses cooperation (C) or defection (D), and a signal, which determines a player's outcome, can be either good (g) or bad (b). If the opponent plays C, a player usually observes g, but she may observe b with a small probability. An important feature of this model is that a player's observation is her private information that is not known to the opponent. This is an example of repeated games with *imperfect private monitoring*, where each player privately receives signals about the actions of other players. Then, players do not share a common understanding about whom to punish and when punishment should start (and end). Hence constructing effective punishment, which sustains cooperation and is voluntarily followed by players, is substantially more difficult than in the public monitoring case. Verifying an equilibrium becomes hard since we need to check that no player has an incentive to deviate under any possible belief she might have on the past histories of other players.

On the other hand, a special type of an equilibrium called *belief-free* equilibrium is identified, where checking whether a profile of strategies forms such an equilibrium is more tractable [1, 3]. However, these existing works show that cooperative relations can be sustainable only in ideal cases where the discount factor (δ) is close to 1 and/or the observation error rate (ϵ) is close to 0.

We deal with a generic problem that can model both the repeated Prisoner's Dilemma (PD) game and the team production problem (in which alternating (C, D) and (D, C) maximizes players' welfare). Furthermore, we introduce an additional action that we call C' as well as an associated observation g' for this action. This action is dominated by another action, and playing it decreases the players' total welfare. Thus, adding it is irrelevant in a one-shot game. To our surprise, it turns out that by adding this action, players can achieve sustainable cooperative relations far beyond the ideal cases identified in existing works. More specifically, we identify a class of strategies called one-shot punishment strategy that constitutes a belief-free equilibrium in a wide range of δ and ϵ. Moreover, when the number of players is two, we show that the sum of the discounted average payoffs achieved by the one-shot punishment strategies is actually theoretically *optimal*, i.e., it matches a theoretical upper bound for any belief-free equilibrium.

2. TWO-PLAYER MODEL

Let us explain only the case with two players due to space limitations, though our results have been generalized to cases

*This work was partially supported by JSPS KAKENHI Grant Number 24220003 and 26280081.

Appears in: *Proceedings of the 15th International Conference on Autonomous Agents and Multiagent Systems (AAMAS 2016), J. Thangarajah, K. Tuyls, C. Jonker, S. Marsella (eds.), May 9–13, 2016, Singapore.*

Table 1: Stage game payoff

	$a_2 = C$	$a_2 = D$	$a_2 = C'$
$a_1 = C$	1	$-y$	$1 - \alpha$
$a_1 = D$	$1 + x$	0	$1 + x - \alpha$
$a_1 = C'$	1	$-y$	$1 - \alpha$

with an arbitrary number of players. There exists a set of players $N = \{1, 2\}$. Two players repeatedly play the same stage game over an infinite horizon $t = 0, 1, 2, \ldots$. In each period, player i takes an action $a_i \in A = \{C, D, C'\}$, and her expected payoff in that period is given by stage game payoff function $u_i(\boldsymbol{a})$, where $\boldsymbol{a} = (a_1, a_2) \in A^2$ is an action profile in that period.

The stage game payoff is shown in Table 1. Here, we only show player 1's payoff since the game is symmetric. We assume x, y, and $\alpha > 0$. Here, the payoff for playing C' is identical to C for the player who plays it. On the other hand, the player can hurt the other player (by α) by playing C' instead of C. Since action C' is dominated by D, adding it is irrelevant when the stage game is played only once. When $x < y + 1$, this stage game corresponds to the well-known PD game, where (C, C) is the outcome that maximizes the total payoff of two players. When $x > y + 1$, this stage game corresponds to the team production problem [2], where the outcome that maximizes the total payoff of two players is either (C, D) or (D, C).

Within each period, player i observes her private signal $\omega_i \in \Omega = \{g, b, g'\}$ that is related to the opponent's action. Here, g (or b, g') is the "correct" signal for C (or D, C'). Let a_{-i} denote the opponent's action, and $o(\omega_i \mid a_{-i})$ denote the marginal distribution of ω_i given a_{-i}. We set $o(\omega_i \mid a_{-i})$ to $1 - 2\epsilon$ when ω_i is the correct signal for a_{-i}, and otherwise to ϵ. We assume $0 < \epsilon < 1/3$, i.e., a correct signal is more likely to be observed. Player i's *realized* payoff is denoted as $\pi_i(a_i, \omega_i)$. Hence, her expected payoff is given by $\sum_{\omega_i \in \Omega} \pi_i(a_i, \omega_i) \cdot o(\omega_i \mid a_{-i})$. This formulation ensures that realized payoff π_i conveys no more information than a_i and ω_i. Player i's expected discounted payoff from a sequence of action profiles $\boldsymbol{a}^0, \boldsymbol{a}^1, \ldots$ is $\sum_{t=0}^{\infty} \delta^t u_i(\boldsymbol{a}^t)$, with discount factor $\delta \in (0, 1)$. The (expected) discounted *average payoff* (payoff per period) is defined as $(1 - \delta) \sum_{t=0}^{\infty} \delta^t u_i(\boldsymbol{a}^t)$.

3. ONE-SHOT PUNISHMENT STRATEGY

We define *one-shot punishment* strategies. The strategy profile $\boldsymbol{\sigma}^{L^*}$ is defined by an FSA (Finite-State Automaton). Here, $L^* \in \{1, 2\}$ represents the number of players who are supposed to play C in each period. Each player basically follows a prescribed cycle of two states. When $L^* = 2$, the actions of both states are C. When $L^* = 1$, the action of one prescribed state is C, and the action of the other state is D.

Figure 1(a) shows an FSA where $L^* = 2$. Player 1 starts from W_1 and player 2 starts from W_2. Here, the upper-side cycle of W_1 and W_2 is the prescribed cycle. When player 1 is at W_1, player 2 should be at W_2 (or P_2) and should play C (or C'). If player 1 observes b, she punishes player 2 in the next period by moving to P_2. Then player 2 should be at W_1 (or P_1). If player 1 observes b again, she punishes player 2 again in the next period by moving to P_1. Otherwise, she returns to the prescribed cycle, i.e., moves to W_1.

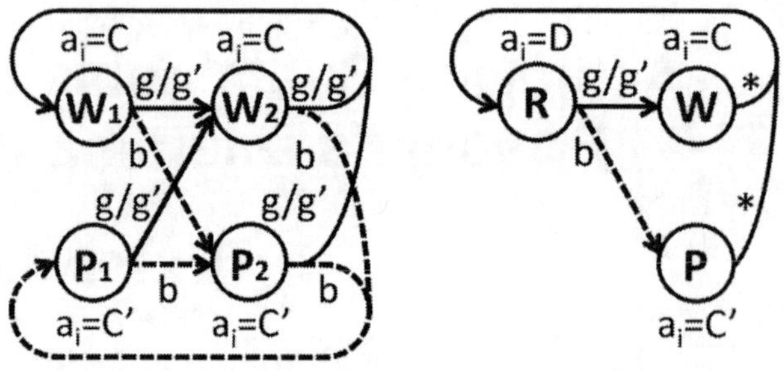

(a) $L^* = 2$ (b) $L^* = 1$

Figure 1: One-shot punishment strategy

Figure 1(b) shows an FSA where $L^* = 1$. Here, the prescribed cycle has two states: W and R. Therefore, only one punishment state P exists.

THEOREM 1. *A one-shot punishment strategy profile $\boldsymbol{\sigma}^{L^*}$ forms a belief-free equilibrium if and only if the following Inequality* (1) *holds:*

$$\alpha \geq w/[\delta(1 - 3\epsilon)]. \tag{1}$$

Where $w = x$ for $L^* = 2$, and $w = y$ for $L^* = 1$.

Note that we can extend the one-shot punishment strategy for cases with an arbitrary number of players and have successfully identified the equilibrium condition.

Let $E_N(\boldsymbol{s})$ denote the sum of all the players' discounted average payoffs given by a strategy profile $\boldsymbol{s}$. Let $E_N^*(\boldsymbol{\sigma}^{L^*})$ denote the maximum of E_N by varying α in the range where Inequality (1) is satisfied. This value is actually optimal for any belief-free equilibria; the following theorem holds.

THEOREM 2. *For any given δ, x, y, and ϵ, if a profile of strategies $\boldsymbol{s}$ forms a belief-free equilibrium, then the following Inequality* (2) *holds:*

$$E_N(\boldsymbol{s}) \leq \max(E_N^*(\boldsymbol{\sigma}^2), E_N^*(\boldsymbol{\sigma}^1), 0). \tag{2}$$

4. CONCLUSIONS

We introduced a generic problem that can model both the repeated PD game and the team production problem, and examined a situation where seemingly irrelevant action C' is added. We identified one-shot punishment strategy, which can constitute a belief-free equilibrium in a wide range of parameters. Moreover, when the number of players is two, we showed that the obtained welfare of this equilibrium matches the theoretical upper bound.

Our future works include applying a similar idea to different settings, e.g., C' requires an additional cost, a player can choose the level of punishment, and so on.

REFERENCES

[1] J. C. Ely and J. Välimäki. A robust folk theorem for the prisoner's dilemma. *Journal of Economic Theory*, 102(1):84–105, 2002.

[2] H. Kobayashi, K. Ohta, and T. Sekiguchi. Repeated partnerships with decreasing returns. Public Economics Seminar, Keio University, October 2014.

[3] M. Piccione. The repeated prisoner's dilemma with imperfect private monitoring. *Journal of Economic Theory*, 102(1):70–83, 2002.

A Novel Incentive Mechanism for Truthful Performance Assessments of Cloud Services

(Extended Abstract)

Lie Qu
Macquarie University
Sydney, NSW 2109, Australia
lie.qu@mq.edu.au

Yan Wang
Macquarie University
Sydney, NSW 2109, Australia
yan.wang@mq.edu.au

Mehmet A. Orgun
Macquarie University
Sydney, NSW 2109, Australia
mehmet.orgun@mq.edu.au

ABSTRACT

The performance evaluation of cloud services usually relies on continual assessments from cloud users. In order to elicit continual and truthful assessments, an effective incentive mechanism should allow users to provide uncertain assessments when they are not sure about the real performance of cloud services, rather than providing untruthful or arbitrary assessments. This paper a novel uncertain-assessment-aware incentive mechanism. Under this mechanism, a rational user not only has sufficient incentives to continually provide truthful assessments, but also would prefer providing uncertain assessments over untruthful or arbitrary assessments since uncertain assessments can bring more benefits than untruthful or arbitrary assessments.

Keywords

Incentive Mechanism, Uncertain Assessments, Cloud Services

1. INTRODUCTION

In cloud environments, service performance may vary substantially and frequently due to the dynamic nature of cloud services. Thus, continual assessments over time are needed to effectively reflect the dynamic performance of services. However, eliciting continual and truthful assessments from self-interested cloud users is still a challenging problem.

To motivate users, an effective incentive mechanism should be designed. A common solution is that a cloud user can be paid if he/she provides assessments on schedule. The monetary rewards may be provided by some professional cloud evaluation organizations, such as CloudReviews[1], the aim of which is to provide cloud selection services to potential cloud consumers based on cloud users' assessments and therefore earn profits from the potential consumers. However, such a simple mechanism cannot prevent a user from "free-riding" (i.e., providing arbitrary assessments) [2, 3]. Moreover, sometimes an honest user could also provide arbitrary assessments in order to obtain monetary rewards when he/she does not really know the real performance of cloud services. Such arbitrary assessments may be erroneous and misleading. To avoid the submission of such arbitrary assessments, an effective incentive mechanism should allow honest users to provide uncertain assessments to express their uncertainty about service performance when necessary.

In this paper, we propose an uncertain-assessment-aware incentive mechanism for eliciting continual and truthful assessments of cloud services. Under this mechanism, a user can receive monetary rewards from a *broker* for regularly providing assessments on schedule, where truthful assessments would bring the most rewards; uncertain assessments would bring less rewards; untruthful or arbitrary assessments would bring the very least rewards. Through our mechanism, a rational user would choose his/her best option, i.e., providing truthful assessments. Once he/she is not sure about service performance, there still exists a second-best option, i.e., providing uncertain assessments.

[1]www.cloudreviews.com

Appears in: *Proceedings of the 15th International Conference on Autonomous Agents and Multiagent Systems (AAMAS 2016), J. Thangarajah, K. Tuyls, C. Jonker, S. Marsella (eds.), May 9–13, 2016, Singapore.*

2. THE PROPOSED MECHANISM

2.1 The Uncertain-assessment-aware Assessment Scheme

A cloud user can give his/her assessments for different performance aspects of cloud services. For any type of an assessment system, an uncertain state can be added into the system to express users' uncertainty about service performance. For example, if a rating scheme consists of three states: "good", "fair" and "poor", the uncertain-assessment-aware assessment scheme is composed of four states, i.e., "good", "fair", "poor" and "uncertain", where the first three are considered as the *certain* assessments.

2.2 Game Setup

A broker requires cloud users to provide continual assessments at regular time intervals. A user can get paid if he/she provides an assessment in a scheduled time window. In each time window, the broker must pay each user no matter what kind of an assessment (certain or uncertain assessment) the user gives. The amount of payment has two levels. If a user gives a certain assessment, he/she would get a payment P regardless of the value of the assessment. Conversely, if a user gives an uncertain assessment, he/she would get a discounted payment λP for $\lambda \in [0, 1]$ since uncertain assessments cannot benefit the broker but the user still tells the truth. Thus, the payment from the broker in our framework can be considered "*ex-ante*" [3] with two amount levels. Here,

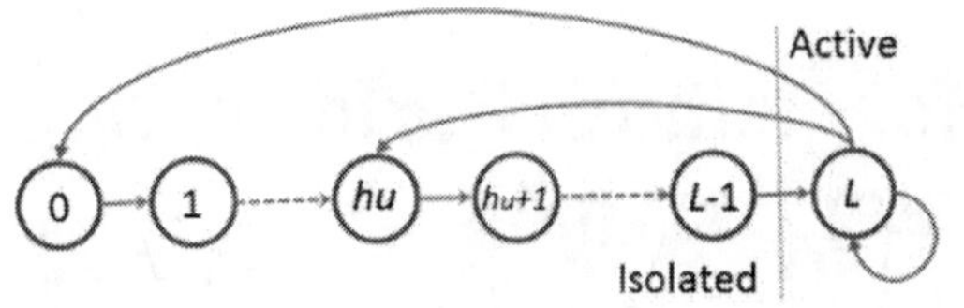

Figure 1: The Assessment Scoring Scheme

such compulsory payments aim to prevent the broker from "false-reporting" [1].

2.3 The Assessment Scoring Scheme

In order to make a user's dominant strategy cooperation (i.e., providing truthful assessments), we propose an assessment scoring scheme to control users' participation in the transactions of selling their assessments. A user has an assessment score to determine if he/she can sell his/her assessments to the broker in a time window. An assessment score θ is a positive integer from a nonempty finite set Θ ($\theta \in \Theta = \{0, 1, 2, \cdots, L\}$), where L is the largest score.

At the end of each time window, the broker can judge whether an assessment is truthful or untruthful by employing an approach such as the majority opinion. According to the broker's reports and users' current assessment scores, a user' score would be updated at the end of each time window. However, there may exist an error probability α of the broker falsely reporting without intention, e.g., a truthful assessment is reported as an untruthful one, and vice versa.

Let $\tau(\theta, b)$ denote the assessment scoring scheme, and the new score of a user at the end of a time window is computed as follows:

$$\tau(\theta, b) = \begin{cases} L, & \text{if } \theta = L \text{ and } b = T, \\ h_U, & \text{if } \theta = L \text{ and } b = U, \\ 0, & \text{if } \theta = L \text{ and } b = UT, \\ \theta + 1, & \text{if } \theta < L, \end{cases} \quad (1)$$

where θ is a user's current score and b is his/her reported behavior. h_U can be considered as a punishment level for users providing uncertain assessments. A user can be reported as having three types of behaviors, i.e., providing *truthful* (T), *uncertain* (U) or *untruthful* (UT) assessments. Figure 1 shows the scoring scheme. All users can be classified into two groups: active users and isolated users. If a user is considered to give a/an uncertain or untruthful assessment, he/she would be punished by being prohibited from selling assessments for a period of time. If a user is not be able to behave cooperatively for some reason, he/she has a second-best option, i.e., giving uncertain assessments, since $0 < h_U < L$.

2.4 Effective Incentive Mechanism Design

In order to build an effective incentive mechanism, we need to analyze the long-term expected payoffs that an "honest" user can obtain and find out what values of L and h_U are necessary for an effective incentive mechanism.

Let $p(\theta'|\theta)$ denote the transition probability of an honest user's assessment scores between two adjacent time windows, where θ represents the user's current score and θ' is the user's new score. Suppose that α is the error probability of the broker making a false judgement about the user's assessment, and β is the probability of the user giving an uncertain assessment in a time window. Hence, an honest user's long-term expected payoff in a time window can be computed by solving the following recursive equation:

$$v^{\infty}(\theta) = v(\theta) + \delta \sum_{\theta'} p(\theta'|\theta) v^{\infty}(\theta'), \text{for all } \theta \in \Theta, \quad (2)$$

where $v^{\infty}(\theta)$ denotes a user's long-term payoff when he/she has the assessment score θ in a time window; $v(\theta)$ denotes the user's instant payoff after giving his/her assessment in the current time window; and $\delta \in (0, 1)$ represents a user's patience about his/her future payoffs. A larger δ means that the user cares more about its future payoffs, and vice versa.

Suppose γ is the probability that a free-riding user guesses the right result of cloud performance. P is the full payoff a user can obtain by giving a certain assessment. C is the cost of the effort for a user providing a truthful assessment, where $P > C$.

We study an active user's long-term expected payoff. If a user provides a *truthful* (T) assessment in a time window, and then his/her long-term expected payoff can be computed as follows:

$$v_T^{\infty}(L) = P - C + \delta[(1 - \alpha)v^{\infty}(L) + \alpha v^{\infty}(0)]. \quad (3)$$

And if a user provides an *uncertain* (U) assessment, his/her payoff can be computed as follows:

$$v_U^{\infty}(L) = \lambda P + \delta[v^{\infty}(h_U)]. \quad (4)$$

If a user provides an *untruthful* (UT) assessment, his/her payoff can be computed as follows:

$$v_{UT}^{\infty}(L) = P + \delta[\alpha v^{\infty}(L) + (1 - \alpha)v^{\infty}(0)]. \quad (5)$$

Likewise, the long-term payoff a free-riding user can obtain is computed as follows:

$$\begin{aligned} v_F^{\infty}(L) = P + \delta\{&\gamma[(1 - \alpha)v^{\infty}(L) + \alpha v^{\infty}(0)] + \\ &(1 - \gamma)[\alpha v^{\infty}(L) + (1 - \alpha)v^{\infty}(0)]\}. \end{aligned} \quad (6)$$

Hence, in order to determine the unique dominant strategy and the second-best strategy, an effective incentive mechanism in our framework should satisfy the constraints:

$$v_T^{\infty}(L) > v_U^{\infty}(L), v_U^{\infty}(L) > v_F^{\infty}(L), v_U^{\infty}(L) > v_{UT}^{\infty}(L). \quad (7)$$

3. CONCLUSION

This paper has proposed a novel incentive mechanism for eliciting continual and truthful assessments of cloud services, the main novelty of which is to consider uncertain assessments. Through an assessment scoring scheme, a user would have a dominant strategy (giving truthful assessments) and a second-best strategy (giving uncertain assessments). Hence, our proposed mechanism can protect a user's honesty of providing assessments in unavoidable situations.

REFERENCES

[1] M. Feldman, C. H. Papadimitriou, J. Chuang, and I. Stoica. Free-riding and whitewashing in peer-to-peer systems. *IEEE Journal on Selected Areas in Communications*, 24(5):1010–1019, 2006.

[2] D. Lopez-Pintado. The spread of free-riding behavior in a social network. *Eastern Economic Journal*, 34(4):464–479, 2008.

[3] Y. Zhang and M. van der Schaar. Reputation-based incentive protocols in crowdsourcing applications. In *IEEE INFOCOM*, pages 2140–2148, 2012.

Truthful Team Formation for Crowdsourcing in Social Networks

(Extended Abstract)

Wanyuan Wang, Zhanpeng He, Peng Shi, Weiwei Wu and Yichuan Jiang*
School of Computer Science and Engineering, Southeast University, Nanjing, China,
{wywang.seu, zphe.seu}@gmail.com, {pengshi, weiweiwu, yjiang}@seu.edu.cn

ABSTRACT

We study complex task crowdsourcing by team formation in social networks (SNs), where the requester wishes to hire a group of socially close workers that can work together as a team. The workers are selfish that can manipulate the crowdsourcing system by providing unreal private information, which will discourage other workers from participation and is unprofitable for the requester. This paper develops two efficient truthful mechanisms for the small- and large-scale social team crowdsourcing applications, to guarantee each worker's profit is optimized by behaving truthfully.

Keywords

Mechanism design, team crowdsourcing, social networks

1. INTRODUCTION

This paper studies team/group crowdsourcing, where the requester wishes to hire a group of workers that can work together as a team for the complex task completion [1]. Social networks (SNs) provide good opportunities to address the team crowdsourcing problem, where the social connections among workers are often good indicator of effective collaboration [3]. This social team crowdsourcing can be implemented by a reverse auction model, where the requester, first announces his task's skill requirements and each worker then bids to sell his skill services associated with his working cost and social relationships. Based on the workers' bids, the crowdsourcing system aims to form the optimal feasible (i.e., professional and collaborative) team of workers that requires the minimal working cost for the requester. However, the workers are selfish that can lie about their private information [2], which will discourage other workers from participation and increase the requester's budget. Therefore, it is essential to design truthful social team crowdsourcing mechanisms, where each worker's optimal bidding strategy is to declare his private information truthfully [5].

Directly extending existing social team formation approach [3] is not applicable, because it cannot guarantee truthfulness. Moreover, the VCG type mechanism [4], well-known for guaranteeing truthfulness while maximizing social welfare, is not applicable neither, because this social team crowdsourcing problem is NP-hard. Against this background, we propose a novel fixed-parameter time truthful mechanism for the small-scale applications, which works by first transforming a social network to a binary tree network, and then a dynamic programming-based optimal mechanism is developed in the transformed tree, and a novel polynomial time mechanism for the large-scale applications, which works by selecting the team members greedily based on their social structure as well as on their skills and working cost.

Appears in: *Proceedings of the 15th International Conference on Autonomous Agents and Multiagent Systems (AAMAS 2016), J. Thangarajah, K. Tuyls, C. Jonker, S. Marsella (eds.), May 9–13, 2016, Singapore.*

* Corresponding author

2. PROBLEM DESCRIPTION

There is a task T=<V_T,O_T>, where V_T is the profit of T and $O_T = \{s_1, s_2, \dots, s_k\}$ is T's skill requirements. We model the team crowdsourcing paradigm as a reverse auction framework, where the requester announces its task skill requirements O_T and then each worker a_i submits its bid B_i=(R_i,$\tilde{c}_i$,N_i), consisting of the skills $R_i = \{s_1, s_2, \dots, s_l\}$ it can provide, the working cost $\tilde{c}_i$, representing the minimum reward a_i wishes to be paid and its neighbors/collaborative partners N_i. After receiving these workers' bids, the crowdsourcing platform can determine the workers' social network SN=<A,E>, where A={$a_1, a_2, \dots, a_n$} denotes the collection of agents/workers and $\forall(a_i, a_j) \in E$ represents the existence of a connection between a_i and a_j.

A mechanism $\mathcal{M} = (X, Pay)$ consists of a team formation function X and a payment function Pay. The team formation function $X = \{x_1, x_2, \dots, x_n\}$ determines whether an agent a_i is selected as a winner (x_i=1) or not (x_i=0). Let $S = \{a_i | x_i = 1\}$ be the winner team. To complete task T successfully, the formed team S must satisfy 1) ***Professional:*** each skill $s_j \in O_T$ must be satisfied by at least one team member and 2) ***Collaborative:*** the subgraph induced by the team members S must be connected. The payment function $Pay = \{p_1, p_2, \dots, p_n\}$ determines the reward paid to each winner. The utility u_i of each winner $a_i \in S$ then is u_i=p_i-c_i, equals p_i-$\tilde{c}_i$ under truthful bidding. The requester's utility then is $u_T = V_T - \sum_{a_i \in S} p_i$. The social welfare W_T of the crowdsourcing system is the sum of the requester's utility and the agents' aggregate utility, i.e., $W_T = V_T - \sum_{a_i \in S} p_i + \sum_{a_i \in S}(p_i - \tilde{c}_i) = V_T - \sum_{a_i \in S} \tilde{c}_i$. This paper considers maximizing social welfare.

Each agent is strategic for maximizing its own utility, such an objective of maximizing social welfare alone will encourage the strategic agents to lie about its working cost information [1]. This paper designs truthful mechanisms to elicit the agents to report their working cost truthfully.

[1]Regarding why workers cannot manipulate their skills and social relationships: Over-report the skills that a worker cannot provide might make task failure, which can be detected during task execution. Each social relationship depends on two workers and once a worker reports the nonexistent relationships, it can also be detected.

3. TRUTHFUL SOCIAL TEAM CROWDSOURCING MECHANISMS

Towards Small-Scale Applications. The small-scale-oriented mechanism consists of the following three phases.

- **Tree Network Extraction.** We first extract a tree network Γ from the original network SN=<A,E> such that Γ preserves as much social connection information as that in SN. The proposed tree extraction algorithm is $\frac{1}{D}$-approximation on maximizing network closeness, where network closeness $CL(SN)$ is defined as how socially close these agents A connect with each other in network SN, i.e., $CL(SN)$=$\sum_{a_i \in A}\sum_{a_j \neq a_i}\frac{1}{d(a_i,a_j,SN)}$ and D is the diameter of the network SN.
- **Binary Tree Transformation.** We then transform the tree Γ to the binary tree Γ^{β}. We start from the root agent a_r of Γ. Suppose that a_r has l children $\{a_1, a_2, \ldots, a_l\}$ and we replace a_r and a_r's children with a binary tree of depth $\lceil log_2 l \rceil$+1, where the root agent still is a_r and the leaf agents are $\{a_1, a_2, \ldots, a_l\}$. The newly-added auxiliary agents between a_r and $\{a_1, a_2, \ldots, a_l\}$ in this binary tree neither have any skill nor require any working cost. Moreover, once their parent agent is selected as a winner, they will also be selected as winners. This transformation repeats recursively for all of the other none-leaf agents down a_r and finally the binary tree Γ^{β} is constructed.
- **Optimal Truthful Mechanism in Binary Tree.** For each agent a_i in Γ^{β}, let $S(a_i,1,U)$ be the optimal team formed to satisfy the skills $U \subseteq O_T$ in the subtree $\Gamma^{\beta}_{a_i}$, where a_i is selected as a winner. Let $W(a_i,1,U)$ be the welfare of $S(a_i,1,U)$. Similarly, let $W(a_i,0,U)$ be the welfare of the optimal team $S(a_i,0,U)$ formed in $\Gamma^{\beta}_{a_i}$ without selecting a_i. Let $l(a_i)$ and $r(a_i)$ denote a_i's left and right child. The following dynamic programming is then implemented recursively for each agent a_i.

$$W(a_i,1,U) = \max \begin{cases} W(r(a_i),1,U \backslash R_i) - \tilde{c}_i; \\ W(l(a_i),1,U \backslash R_i) - \tilde{c}_i; \\ \max\limits_{U' \subseteq U \backslash R_i} W(r(a_i),1,U') + \\ \quad W(l(a_i),1,U \backslash U') - \tilde{c}_i - V_T. \end{cases} \tag{1}$$

and

$$W(a_i,0,U) = \max\{W(r(a_i),1,U), W(r(a_i),0,U), W(l(a_i),1,U), W(l(a_i),0,U)\}. \tag{2}$$

The initial conditions of this dynamic programming approach are: $W(\emptyset,0,\emptyset)$=V_T, and $\forall a_i \in A$, $W(a_i,1,\emptyset)$=V_T-$\tilde{c}_i$ and $\forall U \neq \emptyset$, $W(\emptyset,0,U)$=0. Finally, the optimal team formed in Γ^{β} is returned from function $\max\{W(a_r,0,O_T)$, $W(a_r,1,O_T)\}$. Denoted by the optimal team and its welfare as S_{Γ_β} and W_{Γ_β}, then the VCG-based threshold payment p_i for each winner agent $a_i \in S_{\Gamma^\beta}$ is defined as:

$$p_i = (W_{\Gamma^\beta} + \tilde{c}_i) - \max\{W_{\Gamma^\beta_{r(a_i)}}, W_{\Gamma^\beta_{l(a_i)}}, W_{\Gamma^\beta \backslash \Gamma^\beta_{a_i}}\} \tag{3}$$

The value $W_{\Gamma^\beta_{r(a_i)}}$=$V_T$-$\sum_{a_j \in S_{\Gamma^\beta_{r(a_i)}}}\tilde{c}_j$ is the welfare of $S_{\Gamma^\beta_{r(a_i)}}$, where $S_{\Gamma^\beta_{r(a_i)}}$ is the optimal team returned from a_i's right subtree $\Gamma^\beta_{r(a_i)}$. The other terms have the similar meanings.

Towards Large-Scale Applications. We present a polynomial time truthful mechanism for the large-scale applications, which includes the monotonously greedy team formation algorithm and the threshold payment algorithm.

- **Greedy Team Formation.** We first locate the agent a_i that has the largest marginal contribution-per-cost value as team root, where agent a_i's marginal contribution-per-cost value with respect to the skill set $U \in O_T$ is $\epsilon(a_i,U)$= $|U \bigcap R_i|/\tilde{c}_i$. Then, we select the team's best neighbor agent $a^* = \arg\max_{a_i \in I}\epsilon(a_i,O_T)$ with the largest marginal contribution-per-cost to join this team, where $I = \bigcup_{a_i \in Q}\{a_x | a_x \in N_i : \epsilon(a_x,O_T) > 0|\}$. We proceed to select the desirable team neighbors round by round until the team is professional.
- **Threshold Payment.** We adapt the threshold payment technique of Singer [5] to achieve the threshold payment p_{a_i} for each winner a_i such that p_{a_i} is the maximal value a_i can bid and still be selected by the greedy team formation.

4. EXPERIMENTS

We collect 928 workers data from a popular crowdsourcing website Guru. These workers are interconnected by the scale-free network structure. We also collect the tasks on Guru and observe that most of the tasks require less than 30 kinds of skills. For each task T, we assume its profit V_T is draw from the range [300, 400] randomly. We compare the proposed mechanisms, i.e., optimal mechanism in a tree network **OPT-Tree** and the greedy mechanism **Greedy** with the benchmark optimal mechanism **OPT** on social welfare.

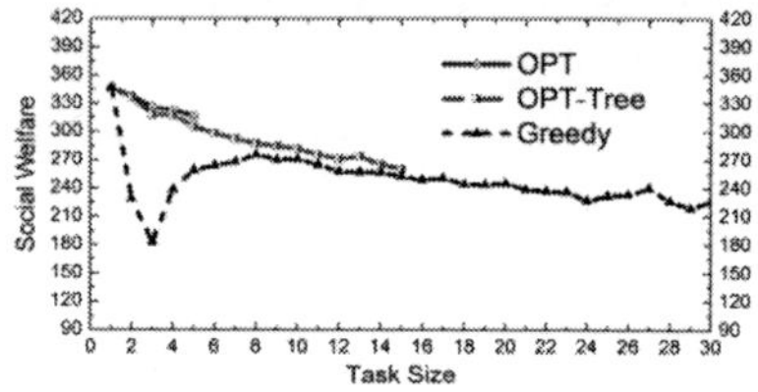

The right figure shows the social welfare of the these mechanisms. For the small-scale applications where task size $k \leq 5$, OPT-Tree performs very close to OPT. Greedy performs worse when task size grows up from 1 to 3. However, as task size ranges from 3 to 8, the social welfare of Greedy grows up. Interestingly, when task size becomes larger further, i.e., $\geq$8, the social welfare of Greedy deceases again. Although OPT can always form the optimal team with the maximum social welfare, its exponential time complexity on task size limits itself to be applicable to the small-scale applications (i.e., $k \leq 5$) only, while Greedy scales well to various scale applications.

Acknowledgments

This work was supported by the National Natural Science Foundation of China (No. 61170164, No. 61472079 and No. 71201077), the Funds for Distinguished Young Scholars of the Natural Science Foundation of Jiangsu Province (No. BK2012020), and the Program for Distinguished Talents of Six Domains in Jiangsu Province (No. 2011-DZ023).

REFERENCES

[1] J. Chamberlain. Groupsourcing: Distributed problem solving using social networks. In *HCOMP'14*, 2014.

[2] Y. Jiang and J. C. Jiang. Understanding social networks from a multiagent perspective. *Parallel and Distributed Systems, IEEE Transactions on*, 25(10):2743–2759, 2014.

[3] T. Lappas, K. Liu, and E. Terzi. Finding a team of experts in social networks. In *KDD '09*, 2009.

[4] N. Nisan and A. Ronen. Algorithmic mechanism design. *Games and Economic Behavior*, 35(1-2), 2001.

[5] Y. Singer. Budget feasible mechanisms. In *FOCS '10*, 2010.

Convergence and Quality of Iterative Voting Under Non-Scoring Rules

(Extended Abstract)

Aaron Koolyk
The Hebrew University
Jerusalem, Israel
aaron.koolyk@mail.huji.ac.il

Omer Lev
University of Toronto
Toronto, Canada
omerl@cs.toronto.edu

Jeffrey S. Rosenschein
The Hebrew University
Jerusalem, Israel
jeff@cs.huji.ac.il

ABSTRACT

Iterative voting is a social choice mechanism whereby voters are allowed to continually make strategic changes to their stated preferences until no further change is desired. We study the iterative voting framework for several common voting rules and show that, for these rules, an equilibrium may never be reached. We also consider several variations of iterative voting and show that with these variations equilibrium likewise may not be reached. Finally, we present an empirical analysis of the quality of candidates elected through iterative voting.

Keywords

Social Choice; Equilibrium; Iterative Voting

1. INTRODUCTION

The topic of voting, that is, how to aggregate diverse individual preferences into a collective decision, is of great importance in many automated agent scenarios; it has thus been the topic of much research in multiagent systems. One innovative voting model that was recently proposed is that of *iterative voting* [3]. Classic voting protocols terminate with the announcement of a winner following a single round of ballot submission; in iterative voting, on the other hand, as long as some voter wishes to change their vote, they may do so (when multiple voters wish to change their votes simultaneously, an arbitrary voter is chosen). The process terminates when no voter wishes to change their vote.

Iterative voting thus embraces the inevitable manipulability of voting, and considers agents' uniform ability to vote strategically as a collective opportunity. But in addition to being an intriguing method for reaching consensus, iterative voting has been proposed as a formal solution concept for voting games. Standard Nash equilibria are of limited utility in voting scenarios in which the group outcome is generally robust to changes in any single voter's action. The set of iterative voting equilibria, however, is a subset of Nash equilibria, and in particular those iterative voting equilibria reachable from the truthful profile could be considered a more natural (or meaningful) solution concept.

Appears in: *Proceedings of the 15th International Conference on Autonomous Agents and Multiagent Systems (AAMAS 2016), J. Thangarajah, K. Tuyls, C. Jonker, S. Marsella (eds.), May 9–13, 2016, Singapore.*

The most salient questions regarding iterative voting thus have two interpretations. Regarding iterative voting as a method for reaching consensus: does the process terminate? And does it arrive at "good" conclusions? In parallel, regarding iterative voting as a solution concept: do solutions exist? And what is their "price of stability/anarchy"?

2. CYCLICITY

We consider the convergence of several common non-scoring voting rules under the following iterative dynamics.

BR: An ordered pair of profiles is in the *best response* dynamic if the preferences of all voters but one are identical; the voter whose preferences change prefers the outcome of the second profile to that of the first profile; and of all possible changes to his preferences, the outcome under the second profile is preferred at least as much as the outcome under any other possible change.

TOP: In this dynamic, a changed vote necessarily assigns the candidate which the voter will make the winner the top spot in the new preference order. In many of the voting rules we consider (and in any weakly-monotone rule) this dynamic is a subset of the best-response dynamic, and, indeed, it generalizes the dynamic used in [3].

TB: This dynamic requires the new winner to be at the top of the new ballot, and the previous winner to be at the bottom. While in many scoring rules (e.g., plurality and veto) this is a subset of best response moves (and generalizes those used in [2, 5]), this is not true in general, and particularly in the voting rules we study in this work.

KT: This dynamic restricts best response to those moves with minimum Kendall-Tau distance from the previous vote.

SWAP: This restrictive dynamic, allows only changes of a single adjacent swap (a new vote is of a KT distance of one from the previous vote; a notion referred to as a 'swap' in the literature on bribery).

The following result establishes that neither best response iterative voting nor any of the four variations on iterative voting can be guaranteed to converge for a number of well-studied voting rules; see [1, 4].

THEOREM 1. *Maximin, Copeland, Bucklin, STV, Second Order Copeland, and Ranked Pairs with linear order tie-breaking do not converge under BR, TOP, TB, KT or SWAP.*

3. QUALITY

In this section, we present simulations of best-response-iterative voting for the six rules we have studied. Simulations were run for each rule with four candidates and both ten voters and twenty five voters. 10,000 initial (truthful) profiles were sampled uniformly. Each profile evolved under best response dynamics and was run to completion (or detection of a cycle) 20 times. Each step was made by uniformly sampling a voter and a best-response move.

For all of the rules, cycles occur quite rarely; see Table 1. So although we have shown that all these rules *can* cycle, the frequency with which they do is very low.

	Number of Cycles	Initial winner re-selected
Maximin 10	180 (0.09%)	28,244 (14.12%)
Maximin 25	55 (0.03%)	19,036 (9.52%)
Copeland 10	1132 (0.57%)	34,641(17.32%)
Copeland 25	107 (0.05%)	23,540 (11.77%)
Bucklin 10	545 (0.27%)	33,932 (16.97%)
Bucklin 25	191 (0.10%)	34,834 (17.42%)
STV 10	79 (0.04%)	10,518 (5.26%)
STV 25	25 (0.01%)	13,777 (6.89%)
SOC 10	943 (0.47%)	33,715 (16.86%)
SOC 25	110(0.06%)	22,607 (11.30%)
Ranked Pairs 10	226 (0.11%)	26,493 (12.25%)
Ranked Pairs 25	40 (0.02%)	17,967 (8.98%)

Table 1: Statistics of the 200,000 Paths.

The rarity of cycles suggest that perhaps iterative voting could be considered even with these rules and best response dynamics. In the rare case of a cycle, the situation could be deferred to a cycle-breaking rule. The election could be run again, or a profile within the cycle (or an outcome among the cycle's outcomes) could be randomly chosen, for instance.

With regard to the quality of the outcomes, first note that quite often iterative voting leads to the original outcome. Many such instances are the result of original profiles which are non-manipulable. But many are also the result of manipulations, whose equilibrium reverted to the original winner; see Table 1 with respect to the latter.

Next, we assess the change in Borda score and Condorcet efficiency. The change between the Borda score of the original winner (in the original profile) and the Borda score of the equilibrium winner (in the original/truthful profile) is shown in Table 2.

With regard to Condorcet efficiency, we consider, for each of the 10,000 profiles (of which a Condorcet Winner existed in 4764 and 8413, respectively), whether the CW is selected by the voting rule, and whether it is selected in equilibrium. The latter is presented in Table 2 in terms of efficiency (out of 10,000) after aggregating equilibria over non-cycling paths.

Of the two rules that are not Condorcet consistent, Bucklin and STV actually improve their efficiency under iterative voting. These two rules also fared well under Borda criteria, suggesting that iterative Bucklin and iterative STV could be considered improvements on their static counterparts.

4. CONCLUSIONS

We have shown that for a number of common non-scoring voting rules, iterative voting under best response dynamics does not always converge. Even after restricting the dynamics to allow voters only limited changes to their ballots—

	Percent increase of avg. BS	Initial winner is CW	Equilibrium winner is CW
Maximin 10	-0.84	4764	0.47
Maximin 25	-0.34	8413	0.82
Copeland 10	-0.48	4764	0.47
Copeland 25	-0.10	8413	0.81
Bucklin 10	2.10	3717	0.45
Bucklin 25	2.19	4461	0.58
STV 10	0.40	4610	0.47
STV 25	0.32	7795	0.83
SOC 10	-0.46	4764	0.47
SOC 25	-0.17	8413	0.81
Ranked Pairs 10	-0.40	4764	0.47
Ranked Pairs 25	-0.35	8413	0.82

Table 2: Borda Score and Condorcet Efficiency at Equilibrium

whether by constraining the positioning of affected candidates, or by prioritizing minor ballot changes—they still do not always converge.

On the other hand, we have shown empirically that cycles occur quite infrequently for all these rules. Given the sparsity of cycles and the possibility of detecting and overcoming them, it would seem that best response iterative voting could be considered even for rules that do not always converge. The quality of the outcome of iterative voting is never much worse, and sometimes better, than non-iterative voting.

Acknowledgments

This research has been partly funded by Microsoft Research through its PhD Scholarship Program, and by Israel Science Foundation grant #1227/12.

REFERENCES

[1] A. Koolyk. Iterative voting: Convergence, cyclicality, and quality. Master's thesis, Hebrew University, 2015.

[2] O. Lev and J. S. Rosenschein. Convergence of iterative voting. In *The Eleventh International Joint Conference on Autonomous Agents and Multiagent Systems*, pages 611–618, Valencia, Spain, June 2012.

[3] R. Meir, M. Polukarov, J. S. Rosenschein, and N. Jennings. Convergence to equilibria of plurality voting. In *The Twenty-Fourth National Conference on Artificial Intelligence*, pages 823–828, Atlanta, Georgia, July 2010.

[4] S. Obraztsova, E. Markakis, M. Polukarov, Z. Rabinovich, and N. R. Jennings. On the convergence of iterative voting: How restrictive should restricted dynamics be? In *Proceedings of the Twenty-Ninth AAAI Conference on Artificial Intelligence*, pages 993–999, Austin, Texas, January 2015.

[5] R. Reyhani and M. C. Wilson. Best reply dynamics for scoring rules. In *The 20th European Conference on Artificial Intelligence (ECAI 2012)*, pages 138–144, Montpellier, France, August 2012.

A Hyper-Heuristic Framework for Agent-Based Crowd Modeling and Simulation

(Extended Abstract)

Jinghui Zhong
School of Computer Engineering
Nanyang Technological University
Singapore, 639798
jinghuizhong@ntu.edu.sg

Wentong Cai
School of Computer Engineering
Nanyang Technological University
Singapore, 639798
ASWTCAI@ntu.edu.sg

ABSTRACT

This paper proposes a hyper-heuristic crowd modeling framework to generate realistic crowd dynamics that can match video data. In the proposed framework, motions of agents are driven by a high-level heuristic (HH) which intelligently selects way-points for agents based on the current situations. Three low-level heuristics are defined and used as building blocks of the HH. Based on the newly defined building blocks and fitness evaluation function, the Self-Learning Gene Expression Programming (SL-GEP) is utilized to automatically evolve a suitable HH. To test its effectiveness, the proposed framework is applied to learn suitable HHs based on real video data. The best HH learned is then applied to generate crowd simulations and the simulation results demonstrate that the proposed method is effective to generate realistic crowd dynamics.

Categories and Subject Descriptors

I.2.11 [**Artificial Intelligence**]: Distributed Artificial Intelligence, Intelligent agents

General Terms

Algorithms

Keywords

Agent-Based Modeling; Crowd Simulation; Genetic Programming

1. INTRODUCTION

A fundamental and challenging issue in crowd modeling and simulations is to generate realistic crowd dynamics. To solve this problem, various methods have been proposed over the years. Exiting methods generally can be classified into two groups. The first group focus on designing crowd models manually by experts [1, 3]. This group of methods require a great amount of manual efforts and domain knowledge. The second group of methods, namely, the data-driven modeling methods [2, 4], focus on automatically learning patterns from crowd data and utilizing patterns to update the movement of agents in particular situations. The data-driven modeling approaches have shown great potential to generate realistic crowd dynamics. One limitation of the existing data-driven approaches is that the knowledge learned is not generic enough to be applied to different scenarios.

In this paper, a novel data-driven crowd modeling approach based on hyper heuristic is proposed. The key idea is to construct a generic high-level heuristic (HH) which consists of multiple low-level heuristics (LHs) to drive agents' movement. A recent published genetic programming (GP) variant named Self-Learning Gene Expression Programming (SL-GEP) [6] is utilized to evolve a suitable HH. The simulation results demonstrate that the proposed method is effective to generate realistic crowd dynamics in comparison with several simulation models.

2. HYPER-HEURISTIC FRAMEWORK

In this paper, we focus on simulating crowd dynamics on a common scenario where there are several destination regions. Each agent tries to reach one of the destinations by following a series of way-points. To generate the candidate way-points of agents, we divide the entire simulation region into discrete grids. The centre points of each discrete grids is considered as a candidate way-point. At each time step, an agent will choose a next way-point from multiple alternative way-point options by using a high-level heuristic (HH). Our objective is to automatically construct a suitable HH to select the next way-points of agents so that the simulation can match those observed in videos. To achieve this goal, a hyper-heuristic framework that consists of two parts is proposed.

In the first part, three low-level heuristics (LHs) are defined and used as building blocks to construct the HH. Given a destination and a candidate way-point, a low-level heuristic can return a score value of the candidate way-point. The higher the score, the better the way-point. The first LH (labelled as D) is related to the distance between the destination and the candidate way-point. The second LH (labelled as R) is related to the density of Pedestrians in the Opposite Direction (PODs). The third LH (labelled as T) is related to the density of historical trajectories. After the LHs are defined, the SL-GEP is utilized to evolve HHs. During the evolution process of the SL-GP, the fitness of each newly generated HH is evaluated by using simulation results where way-points of agents are selected by the HH. In this paper, two macroscopic features are defined to evaluate the simulated results. The first feature measures the similarity in terms of the density distributions of pedestrians that have the same destinations. The second feature measures the similarity in terms of the mean speed of pedestrians moving towards their goals.

In the second part, a crowd simulation is generated by using the given HH (denoted as Φ) to guide the motions of agents. At

Appears in: *Proceedings of the 15th International Conference on Autonomous Agents and Multiagent Systems (AAMAS 2016), J. Thangarajah, K. Tuyls, C. Jonker, S. Marsella (eds.), May 9–13, 2016, Singapore.*

each time step of the simulation, all agents sense the environment features and calculate the values of LHs. Then the scores of alternative way-point options of each agent are evaluated by the HH. The one with the highest score is selected as the next way-point of the agent. After the next way-points of all agents are determined, a collision avoidance model (e.g., the RVO2) is utilized to update the positions and velocities of all agents.

3. EXPERIMENT STUDIES

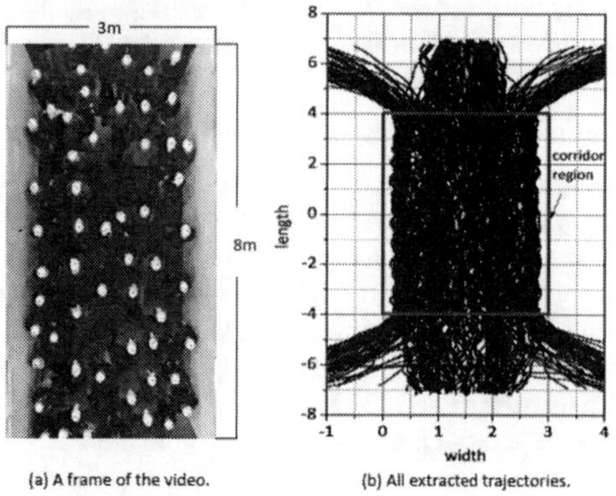

Figure 1: Corridor dataset. (a) A frame of the video; (b) All extracted trajectories in this scenario.

First, the proposed framework is applied to learn a suitable HH based on a real trajectory dataset. The dataset contains trajectories of 219 pedestrians which are walking through a corridor[1]. The trajectory points are annotated at 16 fps (i.e., with a time step of 0.0625 seconds). Fig. 1(a) shows a sample frame of the video and Fig. 1(b) plots all extracted trajectories in the dataset. The parameter settings of SL-GEP are set as follows: $NP = 20$, $h = 20$, $h' = 5$, $K = 3$, maximum generation = 200, $L1 = 3$, $L2 = 6$. The SL-GEP is performed for 20 independent runs with different random seeds. The best HH found by the SL-GEP is as follow:

$\Phi = (pow(fabs((G_1((D-T),D) * G_0(D,D))),$
$((R/pow(fabs(R),R)) + T)) * G_1(G_1(R, G_1(G_1(D,T),R)),D));$
$G_0(t_1,t_2) = (t_1 * ((t_1/t_2) + t_1))$
$G_1(t_1,t_2) = (t_1 * t_2)$
$G_2(t_1,t_2) = (pow(fabs(t_1),(t_1/t_1))/(t_1/t_2))$

The best HH is then applied to simulate the crowd behaviors in the corridor scenario as shown in Fig. 1. To facilitate description, the simulation model with the best HH is denoted as HH-RVO2. Six other simulation models are used for comparison. The first model is the commonly used RVO2 model. The second model is the same as HH-RVO2 except that it uses D as the heuristic. We denote the second model as D-RVO2. Similarly, we define the third and the four models (denoted as T-RVO2 and R-RVO2) by using T and R as the heuristic respectively. The fifth model is denoted as DRT-RVO2 which uses $D \cdot R \cdot T$ as the heuristic. The last model is a recently published data-driven approach named D-ABC [5], which learns velocity fields from video to determine the next way-points of agents.

We adopt the average speed over time as the performance metric. For each simulation model, 20 independent runs with different random seeds are performed and the average speed over time is used for comparison. Fig. 2 shows the simulation results. It can be observed that the curve of HH-RVO2 is the most similar to

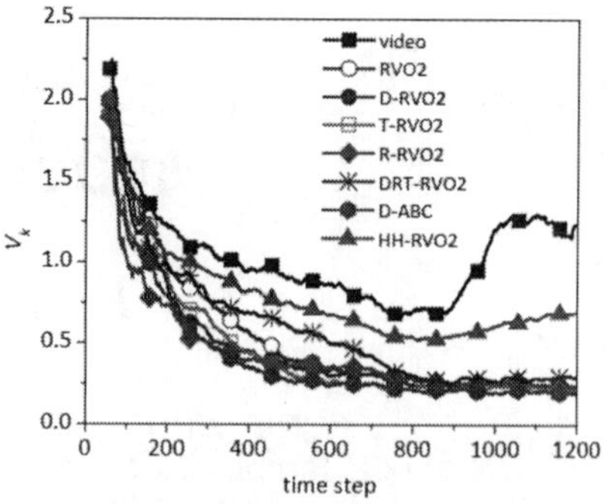

Figure 2: Speed over time.

that of the video, which indicates that the proposed method is more effective to generate realistic crowd dynamics in this corridor scenario.

4. CONCLUSIONS

This paper has proposed a hyper-heuristic framework for agent-based crowd modeling. The key idea is to use high-level heuristic (HH) to guide agents' motions and use genetic programming to automatically evolve the HH so that the simulated crowd dynamics can match those observed in the video. The simulation results have demonstrated that the simulation model using the learned HH (HH-RVO2) can offer better performance than other six models when it is applied to the same corridor scenario.

Acknowledgments

The research reported in this paper is financially supported by the Tier 1 Academic Research Fund (AcRF) under project Number RG23/14.

REFERENCES

[1] D. Helbing and P. Molnar. Social force model for pedestrian dynamics. *Physical review E*, 51(5):4282, 1995.

[2] K. H. Lee, M. G. Choi, Q. Hong, and J. Lee. Group behavior from video: a data-driven approach to crowd simulation. In *Proceedings of the 2007 ACM SIGGRAPH/Eurographics symposium on Computer animation*, pages 109–118. Eurographics Association, 2007.

[3] M. Moussaïd, D. Helbing, and G. Theraulaz. How simple rules determine pedestrian behavior and crowd disasters. *Proceedings of the National Academy of Sciences*, 108(17):6884–6888, 2011.

[4] M. Zhao, S. J. Turner, and W. Cai. A data-driven crowd simulation model based on clustering and classification. In *2013 IEEE/ACM 17th International Symposium on Distributed Simulation and Real Time Applications (DS-RT)*, pages 125–134. IEEE, 2013.

[5] J. Zhong, W. Cai, L. Luo, and Y. Haiyan. Learning behavior patterns from video: a data-driven framework for agent-based crowd modeling. In *Proceedings of the 2015 international conference on Autonomous agents and multi-agent systems (AAMAS'15)*. International Foundation for Autonomous Agents and Multiagent Systems, 2015.

[6] J. Zhong, Y.-S. Ong, and W. Cai. Self-learning gene expression programming. *IEEE Transactions on Evolutionary Computation*, PP(99):1–1, 2015.

[1]The video and extracted trajectories are downloaded from `http://www.asim.uni-wuppertal.de/datenbank/own-experiments/corridor/2d-bidirectional.html`

Emergence of Cooperation in Complex Agent Networks Based on Expectation of Cooperation

(Extended Abstract)

Ryosuke Shibusawa, Tomoaki Otsuka, and Toshiharu Sugawara*

Deptartment of Computer Science and Communications Engineering
Waseda University, Tokyo 169-8555, Japan
{r.shibusawa, t.otsuka}@isl.cs.waseda.ac.jp, sugawara@waseda.jp

ABSTRACT

This paper proposes a behavioral strategy called expectation of cooperation strategy with which cooperation in the prisoner's dilemma game emerges in agent networks by incorporating Q-learning. The proposed strategy is simple and easy to implement but nevertheless can evolve and maintain cooperation in all agent networks under certain conditions. We conducted a number of experiments to clarify these conditions, and the results indicate that cooperation emerged.

Categories and Subject Descriptors

I.2.11 [**Artificial Intelligence**]: Distributed Artificial Intelligence—*Multiagent systems*

General Terms

Experimentation

Keywords

Norm, Complex networks, prisoner's dilemma

1. INTRODUCTION

Humans are basically self-interested and individually rational but often pursue social benefits on the basis of, for example, altruism and indirect reciprocity. This kind of behavior is selected to avoid/resolve social dilemmas such as conflicts between (groups of) humans and the existence of free riders. Agents' decisions made only from the self-interested and local viewpoints often result in non-cooperative behavior resulting in conflicts that may result in loss for both sides. To avoid such conflicts, agents should take into account not only local benefits but also social benefits; such socially cooperative behavior may be the non-best choice from a short-term and local viewpoint but will bring better results eventually in the long term.

A number of studies have been conducted, and socially cooperative behavior as a norm has emerged in which Nash equilibria are not appropriate from social viewpoint [2, 3, 1]. However, these studies did not succeed in the emergence of cooperation in social dilemma in some agent networks or it is not obvious to implement in the actual systems.

The contribution of this paper is the proposal of the simple behavioral strategy called *expectation of cooperation* with which (the norm of) cooperation in the prisoner's dilemma (PD) games emerges under a certain condition. We then experimentally show that the expectation of cooperation strategy fosters cooperation in the whole networks, although it is simple and easy to implement.

2. PROPOSED METHOD

2.1 PD Games with Ensemble Strategy

For a given agent network $G = (A, E)$, we assume that all pairs of agents in E play the PD game once in a single round in random order. Agent i decides its strategy by the *ensemble strategy decision with Q-value* or simply the *ensemble decision* with ε-greedy method for all neighbors. More specifically, i has the Q-value, $Q^i(s, j)$, for the strategy $s \in S_{tr}$ and neighbor agent $j \in N_i$ at the t-th round, and it is updated by

$$Q^i_t(s,j) = (1-\alpha_i)\cdot Q^i_{t-1}(s,j) + \alpha_i \cdot r^i_j(t-1),$$

where $r^i_j(t-1)$ is the payoff received after the latest PD game with j at round $t-1$, and α_i is the parameter for the learning rate of agent i.

At the beginning of the t-th round, agent i identifies its strategy, $s^i(t)$, so that the following condition is satisfied.

$$s^i(t) = \arg\max_{s\in S_{tr}} p^i(s), \tag{1}$$

where $p^i(s)$ is the preference function for ensemble decision. In our experiments, we define it as a plurality, i.e.,

$$p(s) = \sum_{j\in N_i} \delta(s, s^i_j(t-1)) \tag{2}$$

$$s^i_j(t-1) = \arg\max_{s\in S_{tr}} Q^i_{t-1}(s,j), \tag{3}$$

where $\delta(s, s') = 1$ if $s = s'$; otherwise it is zero. Then, i selects strategy $s^i(t)$ with probability $1-\varepsilon$ and selects it randomly from S_{tr} with probability ε. We call strategy $s^i(t)$ as the *preferred strategy* of i at the t-th round.

*This work is supported by KAKENHI (25280087).

Appears in: *Proceedings of the 15th International Conference on Autonomous Agents and Multiagent Systems (AAMAS 2016), J. Thangarajah, K. Tuyls, C. Jonker, S. Marsella (eds.), May 9–13, 2016, Singapore.*

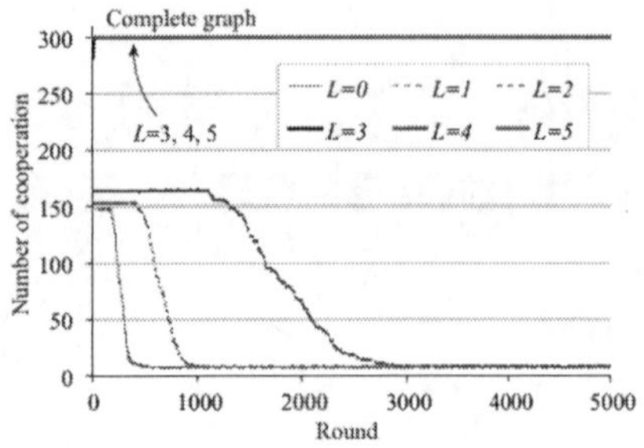

Figure 1: Ratios of cooperation per round.

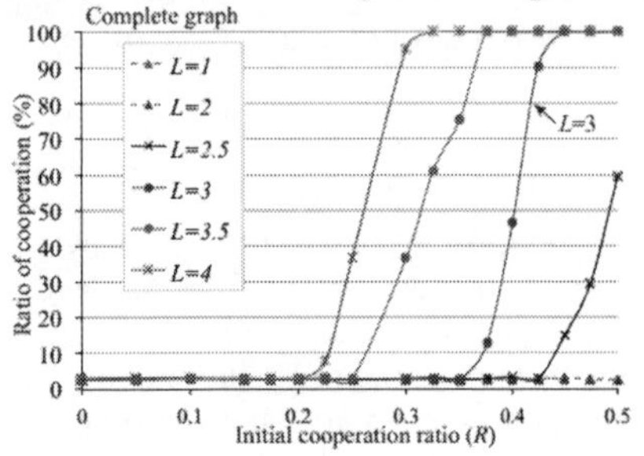

Figure 2: Ratios of cooperation.

2.2 Expectation of Cooperation Strategy

Agents with the proposed behavioral strategy, called the *expectation of cooperation strategy*, are assumed to know that social cooperative behavior is better than defection, so they expect (hope for) it when interacting with their neighbors, but they also know that it is fruitless if other local agents do not cooperate. Furthermore, agents can observe others' strategies only when they interact. We introduce the positive integer, L, which represents *cooperation persistence*. Agent i also has the parameter $l_i(\geq 0)$ to express the remaining term for persisting cooperation, i.e., when $l_i = 0$, i selects the preferred strategy, but while $l_i > 0$, i causes cooperation persistence in the hope of cooperation in the local environment. The initial value of l_i is set to zero.

If agents i and j mutually select cooperation, (C, C), occasionally, they will individually set l_i and l_j to L and enter the term for persisting cooperation in the hope of (local) emergence of cooperation. Thus, i and j persist cooperation in at least the next L PD games (not rounds) with their neighbors, and l_i is decremented by one after each game. However, if i encounters joint (C, C) again, l_i is set to L and the term of persisting cooperation is prolonged.

It is obvious that if the cooperation persistence, L, is large, agents continue to select C, and if $L = 0$, it is the PD games with normal Q-learning, so all agents tend to select D, which is the Nash equilibrium. We are interested in the smallest value of L that leads to (almost) total cooperation.

3. EXPERIMENTAL RESULT

We evaluated our strategy using the agent network of compete graph. The payoff matrix for PD game is defined as

	C	D
C	3, 3	0, 5
D	5, 0	1, 1

The learning rate α $(= \alpha_i$ for $\forall i \in A)$ is set to 0.1, and ε for the ε-greedy strategy is set to 0.05. The number of agents $|A|$ is three hundred. The data described below is the mean values of 20 independent trials.

Figure 1 plots the ratios of agents that select cooperation, C, per round. Note that the initial values of $Q_0^i(s, j)$ for $\forall i \in A$ and $\forall j \in N_i$ is set to 0. We can see that when $L \leq 2$, cooperation could not emerge in the society of agents with the expectation of cooperation strategy but did emerge (thus the preferred strategy, $s^i(t)$, converged to C for $\forall i \in A$) when $L \geq 3$. Note that we also conducted the same experiment for the agents with only expectation of cooperation strategy without the ensemble strategy decision with Q-values, so agent i selects D with probability $1 - \varepsilon$ and C or D randomly with probability ε when $l_i = 0$. In this case, no cooperation emerged even when $L = 5$.

The ratios of cooperation seemed to depend on the ratios of cooperation in the first round (initial strategies) due to the characteristics of expectation of cooperation behavioral strategy since the joint action (C, C) by a pair of agents forced them to cooperate individually for the next L rounds. In the experiment described above, $Q(C) = Q(D) = 0$, so fifty percent of the agents preferred cooperation ($s^i(0) = C$), and the other agents preferred defection ($s^i(0) = D$) on average. Thus, we set the Q-values, $Q(C) = Q(D) = 0$, like in the previous experiment, but we assumed that agents selected C as the initial preferred strategy, $s^i(0)$, with probability R $(0 \leq R \leq 0.5$, so the other agents selected D with probability $1 - R)$.

Figure 2 plotted the ratios of cooperation at the 5000th round when R was varied. The ratios of cooperation sharply increase to 100% with increasing initial cooperation rate, R. For example, the curve for $L = 3$ indicated that all agents selected C after all when $R = 0.45$, but approximately half of the agents and none of the agents selected C when $R = 0.40$ and $R = 0.35$, respectively.

When the initial cooperation ratio was small, the experiment started from the situation in which many agents preferred D. Furthermore, since agents were tightly connected to each other in the complete graph, relatively larger cooperation persistence, L, was necessary to overturn the situation where D was the majority strategy, but the overturn was immediate if R reached a sufficiently large number.

4. CONCLUSION

We proposed the strategy called expectation of cooperation in which agents continue to cooperate for $L > 0$ times after mutual cooperation. We also conducted other types of networks, such BA and CNN, and if agents select C or D randomly, $L = 3$ seems the minimal number for this strategy from our experiments.

REFERENCES

[1] N. Masuda. Evolution of cooperation driven by zealots. *Nature Scientific Reports*, 2(646), 2012.

[2] K. Moriyama, S. Kurihara, and M. Numao. Evolving subjective utilities: Prisoner's dilemma game examples. In *Proc. of AAMAS 2011 - Vol. 1*, pages 233–240, 2011.

[3] D.-M. Shi, H.-X. Yang, M.-B. Hu, W.-B. Du, B.-H. Wang, and X.-B. Cao. Preferential Selection Promotes Cooperation in a Spatial Public Goods Game. *Physica A: Statistical Mechanics and its Applications*, 388(21):4646 – 4650, 2009.

Market Share Analysis with Brand Effect (Extended Abstract)

Zhixuan Fang
Tsinghua University
Beijing, China
fzx13@mails.tsinghua.edu.cn

Longbo Huang
Tsinghua University
Beijing, China
longbohuang@tsinghua.edu.cn

ABSTRACT

We investigate the effect of brand in market competition by proposing a variant Hotelling model, with an additional brand effect term modeled by a function of its market area of the form $-\beta\cdot(\text{Market Area})^q$, where β captures the brand influence and q captures how market share affects the brand. We show that at equilibrium, a company's price is proportional to its market area over the competition intensity with its neighbors, a result that quantitatively reconciles the common belief of a company's pricing power. We also study an interesting "wipe out" phenomenon that only appears when $q > 0$, which is similar to the "undercut" phenomenon in the Hotelling model, where companies may suddenly lose the entire market area with a small price increment. Our results offer novel insight into market pricing and positioning under competition with brand effect.

Keywords

Game theory; Market share; Brand effect

1. INTRODUCTION

Both market area and brand name effect have been subjects with extensive studies, as showed in [2] [4] [7] [6]. However, there are limited works on analyzing the relationship between brand name effect and market share. We use a variant Hotelling model (see [3] [1] [5]) to analyze how brand name and market area affects each others.

2. MODEL AND PRELIMINARIES

Consider an abstract market modeled by the K-dimensional Euclidean space $\mathcal{M} = \mathbb{R}^K$, where each axis represents one feature of the products in consideration. For simplicity, we assume that all companies produce products different only in features we consider, with zero cost and no limit on production capacity. Without loss of generality, we assume that there exists infinitely many companies and they are placed all over the market. Meanwhile, customers are assumed to be uniformly distributed among the space with equal demand of the products. Let $\mathcal{N}$ denotes the set of companies that we consider, all of whose locations $\mathbf{x}_i$ are inside the square of $\{\mathbf{x} \mid \|\mathbf{x}\|_\infty \leq B/2\}$. Companies in $\mathcal{N}$ can decide their own mill prices, while other companies are assumed to have fixed mill prices. On the other hand, customers at $\mathbf{x}$ will choose to buy products from the seller with lowest aggregate price:

$$P_i\{\mathbf{x}\} = P_i + D(\mathbf{x}, \mathbf{x}_i) - \beta S_i^q, \quad \beta, q \geq 0, \quad \forall i \in \mathcal{N}, \tag{1}$$

where (i)P_i is i's mill price; (ii) $D(\mathbf{x}, \mathbf{x}_i)$ is the distance function between $\mathbf{x}$ and $\mathbf{x}_i$; (iii) S_i is i's market area, or market share under normalization, q denotes how the market share contributes to the brand name, and β represents the degree to which customers consider the brand names when making decisions.

A company i's market area is the volume of the market space where all customers inside choose to buy from i, which is proven to be a convex polyhedron. For tractability and without loss of generality, we adopt the commonly used quadratic form distance function between customer and company (see [1]) in (1) here, i.e., $D(\mathbf{x}, \mathbf{x}_i) = \|\mathbf{x} - \mathbf{x}_i\|_2^2$.

3. MARKET EQUILIBRIUM WHEN $Q = 0$

We present our results when $q = 0$ in this section.

THEOREM 1. *In the 1D market with $q = 0$, Nash equilibrium always exists, and when market is at equilibrium, we must have:*

$$P_i = \frac{2d_i d_{i-1}}{d_i + d_{i-1}} S_i, \forall i \in \mathcal{N}, \tag{2}$$

where $d_i = x_{i+1} - x_i$ is the distance between $\mathbf{x}_{i+1}$ and $\mathbf{x}_i$.

The existence of equilibrium is proved by showing the utility function of a company is exactly a parabola. Equation (2) tells us that a company's price at equilibrium is proportional to its market area. The coefficient $\frac{2d_i d_{i-1}}{d_i + d_{i-1}}$ is a constant for a company since their locations are fixed. Denote $\frac{1}{\gamma} = \frac{2d_i d_{i-1}}{d_i + d_{i-1}}$, or $\gamma = \frac{1}{2}(\frac{1}{d_i} + \frac{1}{d_{i-1}})$. Notice that with bigger d_i, d_{i-1} values, γ becomes smaller, which implies higher equilibrium prices with the same market area. Therefore, γ can be viewed as the *competition intensity*, i.e., farther distance between companies mitigates the competition and increase company profit. This is similar to the maximal differentiation principle [1], which states that companies should not choose similar positions in the market, i.e., larger d_i values. The simple form in Theorem 1 that equilibrium price is determined by market area over competition intensity matches our intuition that companies with more market share or less competition in products usually have more pricing power.

Appears in: *Proceedings of the 15th International Conference on Autonomous Agents and Multiagent Systems (AAMAS 2016), J. Thangarajah, K. Tuyls, C. Jonker, S. Marsella (eds.), May 9–13, 2016, Singapore.*

Figure 1: From (a) to (b), company in blue colour suffers from decrease of market area and neighbors due to price increment.

We now turn to the 2D case. The biggest challenge in analyzing the 2D market is that companies' neighbors may change when prices vary (Figure 1), while in the 1D market, company i's neighbors remain unchaged. Due to the change in neighbors, each company's utility function will be piecewise continuous (Figure 2), i.e., it changes every time a neighbor comes or goes. Moreover, since companies' locations are arbitrary, the shape of a company's market area may be irregular, which makes the analysis more difficult, even proving existence of equilibrium is non trivial.

THEOREM 2. *In the 2D market with $q = 0$, Nash equilibrium always exists, and when the market is at Nash equilibrium, we have:*

$$P_i = \frac{1}{\sum_{j \in \mathcal{NR}(i)} \frac{l_{ij}}{2d_{ij}}} S_i, \quad \forall i \in \mathcal{N}. \tag{3}$$

where l_{ij} is the length of border line between i, j and d_{ij} is the distance between i, j.
Similarly to the 1D case, the factor $\gamma = \sum_{j \in \mathcal{NR}(i)} \frac{l_{ij}}{2d_{ij}}$ represents the competition intensity. For a company i, farther distance to competitors (bigger d_{ij}) can reduce the competition intensity, while longer contiguous border (bigger l_{ij}) increases it.

4. MARKET EQUILIBRIUM WHEN $Q = 1$

In this section, we discuss the situation when $q = 1$, i.e., when the market area has a linear relationship with the brand name. We show that the interesting "wipe out" phenomenon appears when $q > 0$.

The "wipe out" phenomenon substantially increases the difficulty in analyzing the problem, because in this case a company's market area can suddenly shrinks to zero after some threshold price. In this case, its neighbors' utility functions are not continuous. This is exactly the same problem as in the classic Hotelling model, where "undercut" destroys the continuity of the utility function, and therefore leads to the non-existence of equilibrium.

THEOREM 3. *Nash equilibrium always exists in the 1D market with $q = 1$.*
Note that proving the existence of equilibrium under the possibility of "wipe out" is highly non-trivial, since any "sudden death" company may lead to chain reaction of all companies' pricing strategies. In fact, we can show that for any company i, the necessary and sufficient condition of surviving in the market is $\beta < \frac{2d_i d_{i-1}}{d_i + d_{i-1}}$. In another world, companies can survive better with farther distances to neighbors (greater d_i, d_{i-1}) or in a market with less brand effect (smaller β). Moreover, we can also show results similar to Theorem 2, but due to the "wipe-out" phenomenon, companies' strategies will be more conservative, and equilibrium prices will be lower than those under $q = 0$.

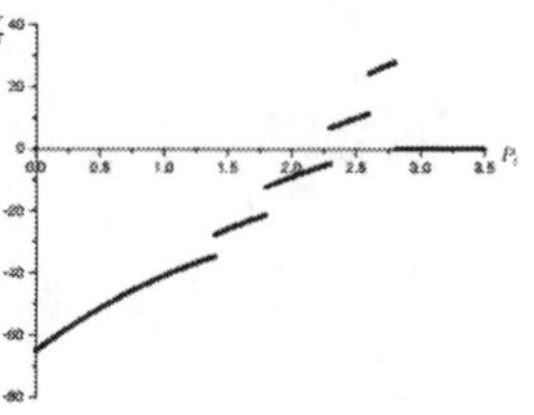

Figure 2: An example of second order derivative of the utility function. Each piece is a fragment from an increasing downward parabola.

5. CONCLUSION

In this paper, we study equilibrium properties based on a variant Hotelling model, considering brand name effect in the market by including a market area term into customers' aggregate price. We prove the existence of Nash equilibrium in single-feature and dual-feature market, and also derive explicit characterizations of equilibrium prices and market areas. Our results reconcile the common belief that company's pricing power is proportional to its market area over competition intensity, and offer insight into pricing under brand name effect and market positioning.

Specifically, our results offer the following insight: (i) When there is no brand effect or equivalent brand effect, i.e., β or q is zero, the equilibrium price of a company is proportional to its market area (market power) over the competition intensity with its neighbors (boundary over distance). (ii) When brand name has a positive effect in attracting customers, it is important to lower the price and seize more market area. (iii) New companies should try to avoid markets where the brand factor is large, and to avoid positioning at market points where competition is intense, because they can be "wiped out".

Acknowledgments

This work was supported in part by the National Basic Research Program of China Grant 2011CBA00300, 2011CBA00301, the National Natural Science Foundation of China Grant 61361136003, 61303195, Tsinghua Initiative Research Grant, Microsoft Research Asia Collaborative Research Award, and the China Youth 1000-talent Grant.

REFERENCES

[1] C. d'Aspremont, J. J. Gabszewicz, and J.-F. Thisse. On hotelling's" stability in competition". *Econometrica: Journal of the Econometric Society*, pages 1145–1150, 1979.

[2] F. A. Fetter. The economic law of market areas. *The Quarterly Journal of Economics*, pages 520–529, 1924.

[3] H. Hotelling. Stability in competition. *The Economic Journal*, 39(153):pp. 41–57, 1929.

[4] C. D. Hyson and W. P. Hyson. The economic law of market areas. *The Quarterly Journal of Economics*, pages 319–327, 1950.

[5] E. Veendorp and A. Majeed. Differentiation in a two-dimensional market. *Regional Science and Urban Economics*, 25(1):75–83, 1995.

[6] J. M. Villas-Boas. Consumer learning, brand loyalty, and competition. *Marketing Science*, 23(1):134–145, 2004.

[7] B. Wernerfelt. Brand loyalty and market equilibrium. *Marketing Science*, 10(3):229–245, 1991.

Argumentation-Based Reasoning Using Preferences over Sources of Information

(Extended Abstract)

Victor S. Melo, Alison R. Panisson, and Rafael H. Bordini
Pontifical Catholic University of Rio Grande do Sul (PUCRS)
Postgraduate Programme in Computer Science – School of Informatics (FACIN)
Porto Alegre, RS – Brazil
{victor.melo.001, alison.panisson}@acad.pucrs.br, r.bordini@pucrs.br

ABSTRACT

Argumentation-based reasoning plays an important role in agent reasoning and communication. In this work, we extend an argumentation-based reasoning mechanism to take into account preferences over arguments supporting contrary conclusions. Such preferences come from elements that are present or can be more easily obtained in the context of practical multi-agent programming platforms, such as multiple sources from which the information (used to construct the arguments) was acquired, as well as varying degrees of trust on them. Further, we introduce different agent profiles by varying the way certain operators are applied over the various information sources. Unlike previous approaches, our approach accounts for multiple sources for a single piece of information and is based on an argumentation-based reasoning mechanism implemented on a multi-agent platform.

Categories and Subject Descriptors

I.2.11 [**Distributed Artificial Intelligence**]: Multiagent systems, intelligent agents

Keywords

Argumentation-Based Reasoning, Trust

1. INTRODUCTION

An important topic of research in argumentation for autonomous agents is argumentation-based reasoning, and recent work has brought this to the context of agent-oriented programming languages [4]. In that context, agents need to reason about possible arguments in order to make decisions and to communicate. Further, argumentation-based reasoning includes the capability of agents to construct arguments in the face of uncertainty (i.e., incomplete and incorrect information). Therefore, it is important that the agents are able to construct arguments using the most precise pieces of information available to them, based on the most trustworthy sources, in order to avoid as much as possible elements of doubt in the arguments used, hence improving their decisions and therefore their actions (in particular interactions). With these issues in mind, we propose an approach to combine argumentation-based reasoning and preferences over sources of information, for example using information about trust on the agents who provided the information used to construct arguments. This combination allows the agents to make decisions in situations where they would not have been able to make a clear choice, for example because of undecided conflicts in argumentation-based reasoning mechanisms without such preferences.

Differently from previous approaches, we here consider that an agent might have various different sources for the same piece of information. This is in fact often the case in multi-agent systems developed on agent-programming platforms, such as Jason [1], where beliefs are annotated with all known sources of that information. Furthermore, elaborate trust systems have been studied [6] in the context of multi-agent systems which could provide reliable trust information about each such source.

2. REASONING MECHANISM

We here use the work presented in [4] as argumentation-based reasoning mechanism, so arguments are constructed using strict and defeasible inferences rules. In [4], conflict between arguments are of two types[1]: (i) an argument $\langle S_1, c_1\rangle$ *rebuts* the argument $\langle S_2, c_2\rangle$ if $c_1 \equiv \overline{c_2}$, and (ii) an argument $\langle S_1, c_1\rangle$ *undercuts* $\langle S_2, c_2\rangle$ if $c_1 \equiv \overline{c_3}$ with $c_3 \in S_2$.

An argument attacking another does not necessarily mean that it defeats the other. Defeat is a "successful" attack, and it considers the set of arguments that defend each other, including preferences between the conflicting arguments [8]. In [4], the set of acceptable arguments from an agent's knowledge base is defined in terms of the *defeasible semantics* introduced in [2], which considers some basic preferences over arguments. Clearly, strict arguments are stronger than defeasible arguments, so they always have priority, i.e., when arguments are in conflict, strict arguments always defeat defeasible ones. Considering only defeasible arguments, the work in [4] considers two types of priority[2]: (i) priority by specificity, where more specific conclusions are preferred over more general ones, and (ii) the explicit declaration of priority between defeasible rules, using a special predicate `sup(Rule1,Rule2)`, indicating that `Rule1` has priority over (i.e., is superior to) `Rule2`.

[1]We use '$\neg$' for strong negation and an overline as a *contrary* operation, thus $\overline{\varphi} \equiv \neg\varphi$ and $\overline{\neg\varphi} \equiv \varphi$.
[2]Originally from Nute's defeasible logic [3].

Appears in: *Proceedings of the 15th International Conference on Autonomous Agents and Multiagent Systems (AAMAS 2016), J. Thangarajah, K. Tuyls, C. Jonker, S. Marsella (eds.), May 9–13, 2016, Singapore.*

Although the approach presented in [4] provides some means for dealing with conflicting information (arguments in particular), when conflicts cannot be resolved considering only the set of arguments, that approach proves limited. Therefore, we propose that when an agent has conflicting arguments that cannot be decided upon by specificity or explicit declaration of preference, the agent can use meta-information such as which of the arguments was constructed using more trustworthy information.

3. TRUST ON BELIEFS

There are many approaches to models of trust in the agents literature [5, 6, 7]. Often a function $tr(Ag_i, Ag_j)$ returning a value between 0 and 1 is used to represent how much agent Ag_i trusts agent Ag_j[3]. However, an agent can obtain information from different sources (e.g., from other agents and from perceiving the environment). Therefore, we expand the trust function to have as input an agent and the possible sources of information, so function $tr(Ag_i, Ag_j)$ is generalised to $tr(Ag_i, s_j)$, where s_j represents one of the sources of information for agent Ag_i.

In order to define how much Ag_i trusts in some information φ (denoted by $trb_i(\varphi)$), we consider the tr value associated with each source of φ for Ag_i. To this end, we introduce two agent profiles for calculating trust values over beliefs: (i) **credulous agents** consider only the most trustworthy source of information, i.e., $trb_i(\varphi) = max\{tr(Ag_i, s_1), ..., tr(Ag_i, s_n)\}$, where $\{s_1, ..., s_n\}$ is the set of sources that informed φ to Ag_i, and (ii) **sceptical agents** consider all the sources from which they received the information as well as the trust value of each such source in order to have some form of social trust value, i.e., $trb_i(\varphi) = \frac{\sum_{s \in S^+_\varphi} tr(Ag_i, s)}{|S^+_\varphi| + |S^-_\varphi|}$, where $S^+_\varphi = \{s_1, ..., s_n\}$ is the set of n different sources of φ and S^-_φ is the set of sources for $\overline{\varphi}$.

4. TRUST ON ARGUMENTS

In order to enable agents to make decisions over those still undecided conflicts between arguments, we combine the argumentation-based reasoning mechanism from [4] and the trust value for beliefs introduced above. The approach presented here is applicable to both premises and inference rules as used in [4]. This is possible because the inference rules are represented using special predicates in the format of AgentSpeak beliefs. The trust value on an argument depends on the values of each element in its support.

Definition 1 (Trust on Arguments). *The trust on an argument is based on the trust value of its support. For an argument $\langle S, c\rangle$, its trust value is given by the trust on its support S, i.e., $tra(\langle S, c\rangle) = trb(\varphi_1) \otimes^{tra} \ldots \otimes^{tra} trb(\varphi_n)$ where $S = \{\varphi_1, \ldots, \varphi_n\}$ is the support set for that argument.*

Considering the agent profiles we introduced, the generic operator $\otimes^{tra}$ can be defined as follows: (i) **credulous agents** use $\otimes^{tra}$ as the maximum trust value (the highest trust value present in the argument's support), i.e., $tra(\langle S, c\rangle) = \max\{trb(\varphi_1), \ldots, trb(\varphi_n)\}$; and (ii) **sceptical agents** use $\otimes^{tra}$ as the minimum trust value, i.e., $tra(\langle S, c\rangle) = \min\{trb(\varphi_1), \ldots, trb(\varphi_n)\}$. When agent Ag_i has multiple arguments for a conclusion c, it can opt for the argument that has the highest trust value, i.e., $tra(\langle S, c\rangle) = \max\{tra(\langle S_1, c\rangle), \ldots, tra(\langle S_n, c\rangle)\}$. Therefore, when it has an undecided conflict between two arguments, it can resolve the conflict by looking at the trust values.

Definition 2 (Rebutting Defeat using Trust). *Let $\langle S_1, c_1\rangle$ and $\langle S_2, c_2\rangle$ be two conflicting arguments, with $c_1 \equiv \overline{c_2}$. We say that $\langle S_1, c_1\rangle$* rebuts *$\langle S_2, c_2\rangle$ iff $tra(\langle S_1, c_1\rangle) > tra(\langle S_2, c_2\rangle)$.*

Definition 3 (Undercutting Defeat using Trust). *Let $\langle S_1, c_1\rangle$ and $\langle S_2, c_2\rangle$ be two conflicting arguments, where $c_1 \equiv \overline{c_3}$ with $c_3 \in S_2$. We say that $\langle S_1, c_1\rangle$* undercuts *$\langle S_2, c_2\rangle$ iff $tra(\langle S_1, c_1\rangle) > tra(\langle S_2, c_2\rangle)$.*

Although we introduced only two simple agent profiles above, clearly other profiles and instantiations for the generic operators could be used, as suggested in [5, 7].

5. FINAL REMARKS

We showed how an argumentation-based reasoning mechanism, implemented in an agent-oriented programming language, can be extended to take into account trust over the sources of information. Trust on such sources is used to generate trust values for beliefs by combining the trust on the multiple sources for the same piece of information. Our approach allows agents to have a *social* perspective on the information they use to construct arguments. For example, more trustworthy sources could have less influence over the final trust value for a belief if there are more sources asserting the contrary. As the trust values for beliefs are then used to calculate trust values for arguments, the agents can decide upon conflicting arguments based on such values. Further, we have introduced some agent profiles that can be used to model different attitudes towards aggregating the trust on multiple sources of information. The profile choice for an agent is arguably domain dependent.

REFERENCES

[1] R. H. Bordini, J. F. Hübner, and M. Wooldridge. *Programming Multi-Agent Systems in AgentSpeak using Jason (Wiley Series in Agent Technology)*. John Wiley & Sons, 2007.

[2] G. Governatori, M. J. Maher, G. Antoniou, and D. Billington. Argumentation semantics for defeasible logic. *J. Log. Comp.*, 14(5):675–702, 2004.

[3] D. Nute. Defeasible logic. In *Handbook of Logic in Artificial Intelligence and Logic Programming*, pages 353–395. Oxford University Press, 2001.

[4] A. R. Panisson, F. Meneguzzi, R. Vieira, and R. H. Bordini. An Approach for Argumentation-based Reasoning Using Defeasible Logic in Multi-Agent Programming Languages. In *ArgMAS*, 2014.

[5] S. Parsons, Y. Tang, E. Sklar, P. McBurney, and K. Cai. Argumentation-based reasoning in agents with varying degrees of trust. In *AAMAS*, 2011.

[6] I. Pinyol and J. Sabater-Mir. Computational trust and reputation models for open multi-agent systems: a review. *Artificial Intelligence Review*, 40(1):1–25, 2013.

[7] Y. Tang, K. Cai, P. McBurney, E. Sklar, and S. Parsons. Using argumentation to reason about trust and belief. *J. Log. Comp.*, page 38, 2011.

[8] D. Walton, C. Reed, and F. Macagno. *Argumentation Schemes*. Cambridge University Press, 2008.

[3]We refer to [5] for further details about the trust framework.

Real-time Robot Path Planning Using Experience Learning From Common Obstacle Patterns

(Extended Abstract)

Olimpiya Saha
University of Nebraska at Omaha
6001 Dodge St
Omaha, NE 68182
osaha@unomaha.edu

Prithviraj Dasgupta
University of Nebraska at Omaha
6001 Dodge St
Omaha, NE 68182
pdasgupta@unomaha.edu

ABSTRACT

In this paper we investigate the problem of online robot path planning in an environment. Our main hypothesis in this paper is that the path planning times for a robot can be significantly reduced if it can refer to previous maneuvers it used to avoid collisions with common obstacles during earlier missions, and adapt that information to avoid obstacles during its current navigation. To verify this hypothesis, we propose an online path planning algorithm called LearnerRRT. Our algorithm utilizes a pattern matching technique called Sample Consensus Initial Alignment (SAC-IA) in combination with an experience based learning technique to adapt to the current scenario. We have conducted several experiments in simulations to verify the performance of LearnerRRT and compared it with a sampling-based planner Informed RRT*. Our results show that LearnerRRT performs much better than Informed RRT* in terms of planning time and total time to solve a given navigation task. When navigation times and distances traveled are explicitly compared, LearnerRRT takes slightly more navigation time and distance than Informed RRT*.

Categories and Subject Descriptors

Computing methodologies, Machine Learning, Artificial Intelligence

General Terms

Algorithms, Performance, Reliability

Keywords

Experience learning, Real-time robot path planning, Obstacle feature matching

1. INTRODUCTION

Autonomous navigation is one of the fundamental problems in robotics used in several real life applications such as unmanned search and rescue, autonomous exploration and surveillance, and domestic applications such as automated waste cleanup or vacuum cleaning. We consider the navigation problem for a robot in an unstructured environment where the location and geometry of obstacles are initially unknown or known only coarsely. To navigate in such an environment, the robot has to find a collision-free path in real-time, by determining and dynamically updating a set of waypoints that connect the robot's initial position to its goal position. While there are several state-of-the-art path planners available for robot path planning [1], these planners usually replan the path to the goal from scratch every time the robot encounters an obstacle that obstructs its path to the goal - an operation that can consume considerable time (order of minutes or even hours), if the environment is complex, with many obstacles. Excessively expended path planning time also reduces the robot's energy (battery) to perform its operations, and aggravates the overall performance of the robot's mission. To address this problem, in this paper, we propose an algorithm LearnerRRT based on the insight that, although obstacles could be geometrically dissimilar in nature, yet there exists some generic features that are common across most obstacles. If a robot can be trained to navigate around obstacles with some basic geometric patterns, it can adapt and synthesize these movements to navigate around more complex obstacles without having to learn the motion around those obstacles from scratch. In this manner, navigation can be learned incrementally by a robot, without having to be trained independently for each new environment it is placed in. The features of the obstacles perceived by the robot's sensors and its movements or actions to avoid the obstacles are stored in summarized format within a repository maintained inside the robot. Our results illustrate that the state-of-the-art sampling-based planner Informed RRT* takes significantly more planning time and total time when compared to the time taken by our algorithm to solve the same navigation tasks. With respect to navigation times and distances traveled LearnerRRT on average takes marginally more navigation time and distance to solve a given task. However, we believe this difference is trivial when compared to the significant improvements observed in planning time and total time taken by the robot to achieve its navigation task in real-time.

2. SOLUTION APPROACH

Consider a wheeled robot situated within a bounded environment having obstacles. The objective of the robot in navigation tasks is to find a sequence of actions that guarantees a collision free navigation path connecting the start location to the goal location. In other words, no action along the navigation path should take the robot to a configuration that is in collision with an obstacle.The LearnerRRT algorithm first creates a library of obstacle patterns and robot actions and reuses the learned actions to navigate around obstacles. The proposed algorithm proceeds in two steps which are described below.

Appears in: *Proceedings of the 15th International Conference on Autonomous Agents and Multiagent Systems (AAMAS 2016), J. Thangarajah, K. Tuyls, C. Jonker, S. Marsella (eds.), May 9–13, 2016, Singapore.*

2.1 Library Creation

The robot is first trained to find a collision-free path for navigating around obstacles that have different but well-defined geometries. Each navigation task used for training is called a source task. We assume that the environments in which the robot will perform navigation tasks later on will have obstacles with significant similarities in their boundary patterns with respect to the source tasks, although the orientation and dimensions of individual obstacles in the later environments might vary. We consider four well-defined obstacle geometry patterns as source tasks - cave, column or passage, corner and block. To construct the action library, L, for a source task corresponding to an obstacle with label lab, the robot is initially placed in front of the obstacle in such a way that the robot's range sensor can perceive the obstacle's entire boundary facing the robot. A set of goal locations, G_{lab}, corresponding to positions where the robot will have avoided the obstacle are specified. The robot internally constructs the obstacle boundary from the range data as a set of 2D coordinates $LS_{lab} = \{(\hat{x}, \hat{y})\}$ and uses the Informed RRT* path planner [2] to plan a path to each of the goal locations. The path returned by Informed RRT* along with LS_{lab} are stored in the library.

2.2 Obstacle Avoidance Using Learned Navigation Actions

After learning actions for avoiding common obstacle patterns, the robot is given a navigation task. Note that the new navigation task can be given in a different environment than the one in which the action library was created. The general scheme that the robot uses after constructing its action library is to reuse actions from its action library, after suitable adaptations, when it encounters an obstacle while navigating towards the goal. When the robot encounters an obstacle obs it first records the proximity data from the obstacle, as a set of coordinates in the 2D plane $LS_{obs} = \{(\hat{x}, \hat{y})\}$. The robot first preprocesses the data to scale it approximately to match LS_{lab}. It then uses a state-of-the-art algorithm for aligning object features called Sample Consensus Initial Alignment(SAC-IA) algorithm [3], to match LS_{obs} with the obstacle proximity data for the different obstacles recorded in the action library L. The algorithm returns the corresponding transformation between the proximity data and the library data. The extent of match between LS_{obs} and LS_{lab} calculated by SAC-IA is measured by analyzing their Jaccard Index JI, which reflects the extent of overlap between two geometric shapes. Once the best obstacle match in the action library lab_{match} has been determined, the robot retrieves the set of paths from the library, applies the transformation to each of them, followed by applying the same scaling factor calculated during preprocessing. It then selects the adapted path which minimizes the distance to the goal. Finally, the robot does two post-processing steps to correct and optimize the selected path.

3. EXPERIMENTAL SETUP AND RESULTS

We have verified the performance of the LearnerRRT algorithm using simulated Corobot robots on the Webots version 6.3.2 simulator and compared the performance with Informed RRT*. For comparing the performance of our algorithm with Informed RRT*, we have primarily used three main measures- the planning time to predict the path to be undertaken by the robot, the total time that the robot requires in order to traverse the entire arena and lastly we also compared the total distance that the robot navigated in each of the cases in order to reach the goal. Different test cases have been created by selecting different start-goal pairs in the simulated environments. We have selected the start-goal pairs for our test cases in

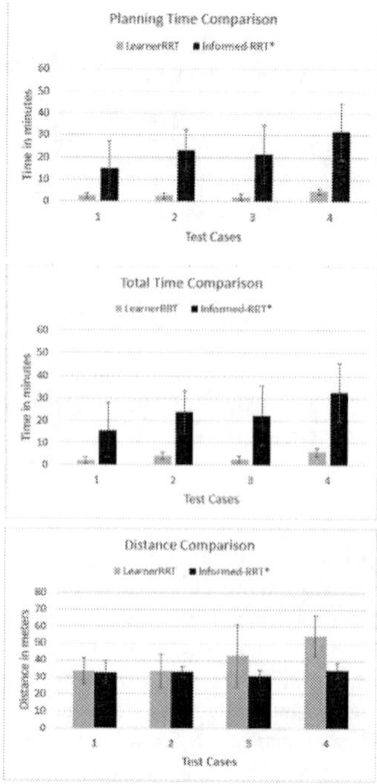

Figure 1: Planning time, total time and distances traveled for the test cases

such a manner that the direct path connecting the start to the goal contains maximum number of obstacles in it. This means that the robot had to replan its path multiple times while navigating from the start to the goal. In order to make the test cases representative, we have selected start and goal locations from different regions of the environments. Figure 1 shows the comparative planning time, total time and distance traveled by the robot for solving the test cases by following our LearnerRRT algorithm and Informed RRT*. From our experimental results it can be observed that the planning time and total time taken by LearnerRRT is much lesser when compared to Informed RRT*. When compared with the mean of the planning times and total times for all the test cases across all environments, LearnerRRT was found to beat Informed RRT* approximately by a factor of 10 for planning time and a factor of 7 for total time.

REFERENCES

[1] H. Choset, W. Burgard, S. Hutchinson, G. Kantor, L. E. Kavraki, K. Lynch, and S. Thrun. *Principles of Robot Motion: Theory, Algorithms, and Implementation*. MIT Press, June 2005.

[2] J. Gammell, S. Srinivasa, and T. Barfoot. Informed rrt*: Optimal sampling-based path planning focused via direct sampling of an admissible ellipsoidal heuristic. In *Intelligent Robots and Systems (IROS 2014), 2014 IEEE/RSJ International Conference on*, pages 2997–3004, Sept 2014.

[3] R. Rusu, N. Blodow, and M. Beetz. Fast point feature histograms (fpfh) for 3d registration. In *Robotics and Automation, 2009. ICRA '09. IEEE International Conference on*, pages 3212–3217, May 2009.

Can't Do or Won't Do? Social Attributions in Human–Agent Cooperation

(Extended Abstract)

Philipp Kulms
Bielefeld University (Germany)
pkulms@techfak.uni-bielefeld.de

Nikita Mattar
Bielefeld University (Germany)
nmattar@techfak.uni-bielefeld.de

Stefan Kopp
Bielefeld University (Germany)
skopp@techfak.uni-bielefeld.de

ABSTRACT

We highlight how human–agent cooperation is linked to the attribution of critical qualities like trustworthiness and competence to the cooperation partner. To investigate these aspects in a systematic fashion, we devise a novel paradigm of an interactive cooperation game that goes beyond commonly adopted economic scenarios. Our results indicate how a less skillful agent that shows little appreciation for its human partner's suggestions regarding the next action is ascribed negative trustworthiness, but also positive competence. This suggests that perceived competence and cooperativeness interact with each other in important ways that can be studied jointly in an interactive cooperation game scenario.

1. INTRODUCTION

Agents are social actors and are hence perceived in ways similar to how we perceive humans. In human–human interaction and cooperation, humans interpret the behavior of others in terms of two underlying universal dimensions of social cognition, namely, warmth and competence [1]. We hypothesize that these mechanisms transfer to human–agent cooperation. That is, we assume that artificial agents engaged in cooperative interaction with human partners elicit the perception and attribution of qualities similar to warmth and competence, and this assessment is important for future cooperative behavior.

Researchers in HCI, robotics and artificial intelligence have been investigating the social dimensions of human–agent interaction. Considering the effects of even minimal social cues [6], it is clear that addressing only task-related aspects is insufficient to understand human–agent cooperation. Agents must also be willing and trusted to act toward the joint cooperative goal. This adds an important social dimension on which agents need to assess and affect their partners. To this date, there is no framework that describes how complex goal-directed behavior of two agents and social outcome variables evolve and interact over time. Standard cooperative games as used in behavioral game theory are limited when it comes to studying qualities like warmth and competence and how they evolve, since problem solving is translated to the decision between cooperation and non-cooperation based on reasoning about the other agent's corresponding intention. The possibility to include and manipulate qualities like task competence or the willingness to cooperate is very limited in such models. In this paper, we present work towards a more comprehensive account of the relevant *perceived* qualities of intelligent agents in human–agent cooperation. Based on related work in human–human and human–agent interaction, we hypothesize that the attribution of competence, trustworthiness and cooperativeness are important in human–agent cooperation. For example, seemingly non-cooperative behavior can be due to a lack of cooperativeness and/or a lack of competence. Likewise, competent behavior is necessary for attaining goals but in itself is not sufficient in cooperative settings, in which decisions about whom to entrust a certain, potentially crucial task are needed. We hence take trustworthiness to be an important and relevant sub-concept of warmth, and we aim to study how perceived competence and trustworthiness are interlinked with each other, and how they are differentially related to cooperativeness. Our results demonstrate that both the quality of task-related action as well as (non-)compliance with recommendations of the partner affect how humans perceive *both* competence and trustworthiness of an autonomous agent, and this differentially correlates with the attribution of cooperativeness.

2. METHOD

We devise an interaction framework in which we manipulate and analyze key characteristics of cooperative behavior systematically. We focus on how an autonomous agent in a cooperative interaction is perceived in terms of its competence and trustworthiness, and how this is related to attributed cooperativeness. The interaction paradigm is a turn-based scenario in which two partners solve a puzzle cooperatively. The setting involves two players working together to place two kinds of Tetris-like blocks in a manner that minimizes required space. The game allows us to easily manipulate the agent's task-related behavior and thus its perceived competence. Moreover, we can induce both individual (as individual payoff for a block) and cooperative goals (as joint payoff added to the individual payoff for completed rows). Two different player roles are introduced: a human block recommender and an agent decider (see [3] for more details). The recommender suggests the next block for the agent to choose. The agent then decides whether it accepts the offer or picks the other block. Importantly, in each round, both blocks are drawn by the players from an urn without replacement.

Appears in: *Proceedings of the 15th International Conference on Autonomous Agents and Multiagent Systems (AAMAS 2016), J. Thangarajah, K. Tuyls, C. Jonker, S. Marsella (eds.), May 9–13, 2016, Singapore.*

Both players receive points individually for every block they place. There are two kinds of blocks: a T-shaped block and a U-shaped block that is harder to place. The U-block yields twice as many points than the T-block, leading to an individual benefit in placing more U-blocks. In addition, both players obtain bonus points when a certain amount of rows are completed horizontally. We refer to this as cooperative or joint goal, since it can only be achieved if the players act cooperatively by recommending and choosing blocks that maximize the number of completed rows and by placing the blocks well. The interactive cooperation game paradigm was designed with the goal in mind to enable the study of *perceived* competence, trustworthiness, and cooperation. These factors are operationalized as follows:

Cooperation: The two players attain the cooperative goal by alternately placing blocks in a coordinated efficient manner. Additionally, the agent accepts or rejects the human's suggestion for its next block. Cooperative actions are thus based on the context in which they occur, there is no action that is universally cooperative. Participants are asked to assess agent cooperativeness.

Competence: An agent is competent if it places blocks skillfully, that is, in a way that maximizes the likelihood of completed rows. We manipulate this skill using two different heuristics and assess the extent to which participants think the agent is competent.

Trustworthiness: An agent that is perceived as socially warm is perceived as friendly, helpful, having positive intentions and, as a recurrent factor in the literature, trustworthy [1]. We assume that trustworthiness more clearly pertains to the perception of cooperative artifacts than the broad warmth concept and use this sub-term instead. Trustworthiness, then, is an agent's ability to signal integrity, benevolence, and ability (i.e., competence) [5]. Participants are asked to assess agent trustworthiness.

3. RESULTS AND CONCLUSION

We conducted an exploratory study to answer the following RQ: How does the behavior of an agent player influence its perceived trustworthiness and competence, and how are trustworthiness and competence related to perceived cooperativeness? We investigated how human recommenders judge decider agents with varying degrees of task skill ("I am able") and compliance ("I adopt your strategy") regarding the human's suggestion. The study had a 2 (Heuristic: maximize occupied space by blocks [*MS*] vs. random next move [*R*]) X 2 (Compliance: high [*HC*] vs. low [*LC*]) between-subjects design. Seventy-seven participants took part in the experiment.

A number of significant differences emerged. First, the agent was more competent given *MS* vs. *R*, and given *LC* vs. *HC*. Second, the agent was more trustworthy given *HC* vs. *LC*, and given *MS* vs. *R*. Third, during *R* conditions, competence was judged significantly higher for *LC* vs. *HC*. Fourth, cooperativeness correlated strongly with trustworthiness and moderately with competence (competence and trustworthiness were uncorrelated). These patterns converge to an overall importance of skill and compliance in our game, each influencing both perceived competence and trustworthiness, as well as a modulation effect of compliance on competence such that unskilled behavior was perceived as competent.

In conclusion, the interactive cooperation game paradigm allows us to frame the perceived qualities of trustworthiness, competence, and cooperativeness into a picture that is grounded in social cognition research and theorizing in human–centered HCI. Our results indicate that competence alone does not ensure an overall favorable assessment of an agent, although competence was a necessary condition of goal attainment. Perceived trustworthiness and competence – attributions that are crucial for social interactions – were affected both by an agent's compliance and competence. This shows that in cooperation, humans are very sensitive to the agent's cooperativeness in light of its competence, and vice versa. The unskilled agent, when it only chose the high-value option, was rated nearly as competent as the actual competent agents, although it played much worse in comparison. Participants apparently assumed intentionality behind this behavior [4] and felt that the agent is able to enact its goals. Competence is self-profitable [7], the agent was thus perceived as competent enough to act selfishly. Our next steps further address the issue of how intelligent agents should be designed for cooperative settings. Given conflicting human–agent goals, agents need to consider the trade-off between individual and joint payoff [2]. While the former benefits from competence, the latter builds on trustworthiness. We attempt to interrelate the behaviors and judgments occurring in our game with established measures on the cooperation spectrum and investigate how social cues facilitate trustworthiness in the game.

4. ACKNOWLEDGEMENTS

This research was supported by the German Federal Ministry of Education and Research (BMBF) within the Leading-Edge Cluster 'it's OWL', managed by the Project Management Agency Karlsruhe (PTKA), as well as by the Deutsche Forschungsgemeinschaft (DFG) within the Center of Excellence 277 'Cognitive Interaction Technology' (CITEC).

REFERENCES

[1] S. T. Fiske, A. J. C. Cuddy, and P. Glick. Universal dimensions of social cognition: warmth and competence. *Trends in Cognitive Sciences*, 11(2):77–83, 2007.

[2] G. Klein, D. Woods, J. Bradshaw, R. Hoffman, and P. Feltovich. Ten challenges for making automation a "team player" in joint human-agent activity. *IEEE Intelligent Systems*, 19(06):91–95, 2004.

[3] P. Kulms, N. Mattar, and S. Kopp. An interaction game framework for the investigation of human–agent cooperation. In W.-P. Brinkman, J. Broekens, and D. Heylen, editors, *Intelligent Virtual Agents*, volume 9238, pages 399–402. Springer, Berlin, Heidelberg, 2015.

[4] B. F. Malle and J. Knobe. The folk concept of intentionality. *Journal of Experimental Social Psychology*, 33(2):101–121, 1997.

[5] R. C. Mayer, J. H. Davis, and F. D. Schoorman. An integrative model of organizational trust. *The Academy of Management Review*, 20(3):709–734, 1995.

[6] C. Nass and Y. Moon. Machines and mindlessness: Social responses to computers. *Journal of Social Issues*, 56(1):81–103, 2000.

[7] G. Peeters. Relational and informational patterns in social cognition. In W. Doise and S. Moscovici, editors, *Current Issues in European Social Psychology*, pages 201–237. Cambridge University Press, Cambridge, 1983.

Computational Models of Emotion, Personality, and Social Relationships for Interactions in Games

(Extended Abstract)

Andry Chowanda*, Peter Blanchfield, Martin Flintham, Michel Valstar
School of Computer Science, The University of Nottingham, UK
{psxac6, peter.blanchfield, martin.flintham, michel.valstar}@nottingham.ac.uk

Keywords

Game Environment, Computational Models, Social Relationships, Social Interactions

1. INTRODUCTION

We present a novel computational model of emotion, personality and social relationships, implemented and evaluated in an existing commercial game (The Elder Scrolls V: Skyrim). We argue that Non Player Characters (NPCs) with such capabilities will accommodate a new experience in playing games and provide evidence supporting this. Applying the ERiSA Framework [1, 2] to the Skyrim Creation Kit, we designed a simple quest and 2 unique NPCs to interact with. When the ERiSA framework is used, players reported significant changes in their social relationship with the two NPCs compared to the baseline. Most importantly, the results further indicate that the models provide a new experience in playing games. In particular, players report enhanced emotional attachment to the NPCs and appear to forge relationships with the NPCs. Finally, the implemented models result in significant changes in the game engagement and the game immersion score.

2. COMPUTATIONAL MODELS

Fig 1 illustrates how in our models emotion, personality and social relationships (SR) interact with each other in influencing the NPCs' behaviour. We distinguish internal emotions that the NPCs actually "felt" from what they displayed. This is because some aspects, such as an social relationships, cultural display rules and the current situation can influence people to mask their emotions [3].

The model of personality we adopt here is based on the OCEAN model [5], represented as:

$$\mathcal{P}_{(p)} = \{O, C, E, A, N\} \in [-1, 1]^5 \quad (1)$$

Our emotion model is based on the most classic and common classification system: the six universal emotions, pro-

*A. Chowanda is also with Bina Nusantara University, ID

Appears in: *Proceedings of the 15th International Conference on Autonomous Agents and Multiagent Systems (AAMAS 2016), J. Thangarajah, K. Tuyls, C. Jonker, S. Marsella (eds.), May 9–13, 2016, Singapore.*

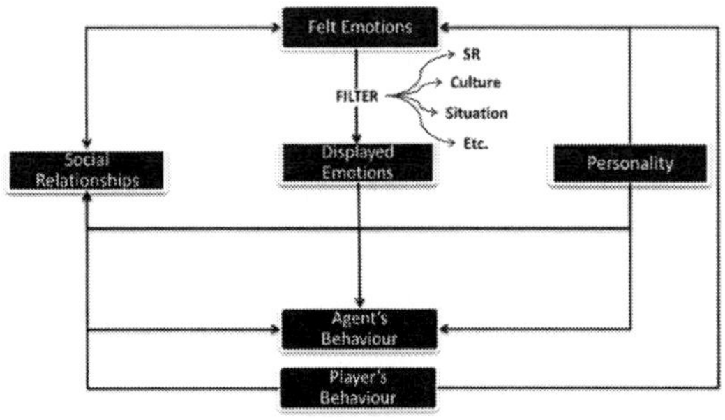

Figure 1: Models of Personality, Emotions, and SR

posed by Paul Ekman [3]. In our models it is encoded as:

$$ve = \begin{cases} \{anger, disgust, fear, sadness, surprise\} \in [-1, 0]^4 \\ \{happiness, surprise\} \in [0, 1]^2 \end{cases} \quad (2)$$

In our models, the NPC's personality sets the basic value of their emotion threshold ($\theta_{(v)}$). In addition, the emotions' threshold at time t is dynamically changed depending on the social relationship between i and j. Equation 3 represents the model of emotion threshold $\mathcal{T}_{(v,i,j,t)}$:

$$\mathcal{T}_{(v,i,j,t)} = \theta_{(v)} \times \mathcal{R}_{(i,j,t-1)} \quad (3)$$

A decay function is applied in our work, causing emotion to gradually return to the rest state over a period of time. The emotion intensity will depreciate below the level of the threshold, thus disappearing unless it is re-activated. We based our decay function on a sigmoid function with r as the decay rate and $\mu = ln(2)/r$. The intensity of emotion v at time t (see Equation 4 and 5) depends on the emotion triggered by the NPC as result of the event $Ev_{(v,t)}$, the importance of the event [4] ($\mathcal{M}_{(v,t)}$), the personality $\mathcal{P}_{(p)}$ of the NPC and how strong the personality influences the intensity of emotions ($\mathcal{W}_{(p)}$) at time t.

$$\mathcal{I}_{(v,i,j,t+1)} = \begin{cases} min(1, max(0, \mathcal{I}_{(v,i,j,t+1)} + \mathcal{I}_{(v,i,j,t)})) & v \geq 0 \\ max(-1, min(0, \mathcal{I}_{(v,i,j,t+1)} + \mathcal{I}_{(v,i,j,t)})) & v < 0 \end{cases} \quad (4)$$

where

$$\mathcal{I}_{(v,i,j,t)} = \begin{cases} \frac{\sum_v^n Ev_{(v,t)} \times \mathcal{M}_{(v,t)} + (\mathcal{P}_{(E)} \times \mathcal{W}_{(p)})}{1+e^{(t-\mu)r}} - \mathcal{T}_{(v,i,j,t)} & Ev \geq 0 \\ \frac{\sum_v^n Ev_{(v,t)} \times \mathcal{M}_{(v,t)} - (\mathcal{P}_{(N)} \times \mathcal{W}_{(p)})}{1+e^{(t-\mu)r}} - \mathcal{T}_{(v,i,j,t)} & Ev < 0 \end{cases} \quad (5)$$

We adopt the two dimensional social relationship model for NPCs in games based on [1, 2] with the familiarity in the x-axis and affinity in the y-axis. The model dynamically interacts with the game states and rules, creating a dynamic game play based on the social relationship as well as the NPCs' personality and emotional states. Affinity at time t denotes the degree of liking between the person i and j ($\mathcal{A}_{(i,j,t)}$), while familiarity at time t indicates how intimate the person i is to person j ($\mathcal{F}_{(i,j,t)}$), given by the number of interactions and time spent between two individuals. The models are represented as :

$$\mathcal{R}_{(i,j,t)} = \frac{\mathcal{F}_{(i,j,t)} \times \mathcal{A}_{(i,j,t)} \times \mathcal{N}_{(i,j,t)}}{1 + e^{(t-\mu)r}} \in [-1, 1] \qquad (6)$$

where

$$\mathcal{F}_{(i,j,t)} = \frac{\mathcal{NI}_{(i,j,t)}}{maxFamiliarity} \in [0, 1] \qquad (7)$$

and

$$\mathcal{A}_{(i,j,t)} = \mathcal{A}_{(i,j,t-1)} + (\mathcal{SF}_{(i,j)} \times I_{(v,t-1)}) \in [-1, 1] \qquad (8)$$

The value of familiarity in our social relationship model is governed by the frequency of the interactions characterised by time spent together by two entities. Research shows the frequency of interactions has a strong correlation with the social relationship strength. The value of affinity is driven by the emotion intensity perceived by the NPC during event $Ev_{(v,t)}$ and the level of significance of this event to the relationship between persons i and j ($\mathcal{SF}_{(i,j)}$), aggregated to the affinity of time $t-1$. In addition, Relationships Intention from person i to person j at time t is denoted by $\mathcal{N}_{(i,j,t)}$.

3. THE SKYRIM GAME

Parts of the ERiSA Framework [1] are implemented to perceive and interpret the player's emotions, conveyed by their facial expression [6] and recorded by camera. We then integrated our models into the Agent Components of ERiSA. The Dialogue Manager proposes NPC's actions and a set of possible dialogues for the player to choose depending on the player's and NPC's internal states from the Interpreter Components, processed with our proposed models. Finally, the output is sent to the Skyrim Game Engine. A player's facial expressions also regulates their dialogue options when interacting with an NPC. For example, the option for the player to make their avatar express happiness will only be available when the Facial Expression Recognition Module interprets the real user's emotion as happy.

For evaluation, we designed two characters with opposite personality to interact with, Stella Erisa ($P_{(E,N)} = \{0.5, 0\}$, $\theta_{(v-)} = -0.3$ and $\theta_{(v)} = 0.2$) and Max Erisa($P_{(E,N)} = \{0, 0.5\}$, $\theta_{(v-)} = -0.2$ and $\theta_{(v)} = 0.3$), emotion decay rate $r = -0.5$, $maxFamiliarity = 200$, $\mathcal{W}_{(p)} = 0.2$, SR decay rate $r = -0.25$ and $\mathcal{SF}_{(i,j)} = 0.02$.

To evaluate the models, we recruited 15 participants (60% female, 73.33 % Asian, AVG age = 24.6) to play the game. All participants were familiar with the RPG Game Genre, and one-third had played Skyrim previously. A total of sixty interactions were evaluated in 18.16 hours (AVG = 1.3 hours, MAX = 51.8 mins, MIN = 1.85 mins). Each participant interacted with both NPCs, both in a baseline without the ERiSA framework and with our models implemented.

To avoid order bias, the sessions were randomized for all players. All interactions were video and audio recorded, the player, NPCs' internal states and the player's choices were also saved. The players were asked to complete a 5-point Likert scale questionnaire every time they finished a session of the game to evaluate: the NPC's personality perceived by the player, the social relationships between them, their feelings when they interacted with the NPC during the quest and their experience during the game based on the Game Engagement Questionnaire. Selected participants were invited to discuss their experience.

4. CONCLUSIONS AND FUTURE WORK

A Wilcoxon Signed-rank indicated that with the model implemented, the characteristics which constitute both NPCs personality, are evidently perceived by players ($p < 0.01$) in addition to a significant change in the relationship score ($p < 0.01$). The favourite strategy to build relationships with the NPCs was giving favourable items to them, with exploring Skyrim world together as the second choice.

Stella is perceived as a person who is positive thinking, generates a lot of enthusiasm, is considerably outgoing and sociable, is relaxed and handles stress well, is emotionally stable, not easily upset, and is polite to others, in contrast with Max. Most of the participants (87%) judge Max as an extremely unpleasant person. 40% of players realised that it was easier to have a negative relationship thus decided to build a negative relation with Max as a winning strategy, even if they already gained a positive relation with him.

Moreover, the models provide a new experience in playing games to the player ($p < 0.02$), particularly in relation to the emotional attachment to the NPCs and how they build a social relationship with them. The models provide a more realistic manner to interact with NPCs and forge relationships with them. The results indicate the players are more engaged and emotionally immersed when the models were implemented ($p < 0.02$). The players were also interested to see how the game's event would progress ($p < 0.01$).

As a future research direction with these models, additional variation for interactions with the NPCs (e.g. accomplishing a quest together and more conversational topics) can be added to enhance the user experience when playing.

Acknowledgments

The work by A. Chowanda and M. Valstar is partly funded by European Union's Horizon 2020 research and innovation programme under grant agreement No 645378.

REFERENCES

[1] A. Chowanda, P. Blanchfield, M. Flintham, and M. Valstar. Erisa: Building emotionally realistic social game-agents companions. In *IVA*, volume 8637 of *LCNS*, pages 134–143. Springer, 2014.

[2] A. Chowanda, P. Blanchfield, M. Flintham, and M. Valstar. Play smile game with erisa: A user study on game companions. In *Workshop on ESIVA*, 2015.

[3] P. Ekman. *Emotions revealed: Recognizing faces and feelings to improve communication and emotional life.* Macmillan, 2007.

[4] N. H. Frijda. The laws of emotion. *American psychologist*, 43(5):349, 1988.

[5] G. Saucier and L. R. Goldberg. The language of personality: Lexical perspectives on the five-factor model. pages 21–50. New York: Guilford, 1996.

[6] M. Valstar. Automatic facial expression analysis. In *Understanding Facial Expressions in Communication*, pages 143–172. Springer, 2015.

Multi-Objective Dynamic Dispatch Optimisation using Multi-Agent Reinforcement Learning*

(Extended Abstract)

Patrick Mannion
National University of Ireland Galway
p.mannion3@nuigalway.ie

Karl Mason
National University of Ireland Galway
k.mason2@nuigalway.ie

Sam Devlin
University of York
UK
sam.devlin@york.ac.uk

Jim Duggan
National University of Ireland Galway
jim.duggan@nuigalway.ie

Enda Howley
National University of Ireland Galway
ehowley@nuigalway.ie

ABSTRACT

In this paper, we examine the application of Multi-Agent Reinforcement Learning (MARL) to a Dynamic Economic Emissions Dispatch problem. This is a multi-objective problem domain, where the conflicting objectives of fuel cost and emissions must be minimised. We evaluate the performance of several different MARL credit assignment structures in this domain, and our experimental results show that MARL can produce comparable solutions to those computed by Genetic Algorithms and Particle Swarm Optimisation.

Keywords

Multi-objective; Reinforcement Learning; Reward Shaping; Difference Rewards; Multi-Agent Systems; Smart Grid

1. INTRODUCTION

In a Multi-Agent System (MAS), multiple autonomous agents act independently in a common environment. The majority of MAS research focuses on optimising systems with respect to a single objective, despite the fact that many real world problems are inherently multi-objective in nature. This is the issue addressed by multi-objective optimisation (MOO) approaches: the requirement to make a trade-off between competing objectives. MOO approaches typically seek to approximate the true Pareto front of a problem, i.e. the set of solutions that are incomparable, where each solution is not dominated by any of the others on every objective.

Multi-Agent Reinforcement Learning (MARL) has proven to be successful in developing suitable joint policies in numerous complex single-objective problems, but research into its application to multi-objective problems is still at a very early stage. MARL problems may be formalised using the Stochastic Game (SG) framework. A SG is defined as a tuple $< S, A_{1...n}, T, R_{1...n} >$, where n is the number of agents, S is the set of states, A_i is the set of actions for agent i (and A is the joint action set), T is the transition function, and R_i is the reward function for agent i. In MARL, agents learn to maximise the return from R, and thus the design of R directly affects the joint policies learned. R may be augmented by an additional shaping reward F, in order to provide additional feedback to the agents. Reward shaping has been investigated as a method to improve learning speed and/or the final joint policy learned in MARL problems [3]. Potential-Based Reward Shaping (PBRS) is a form of reward shaping which has been proven not to alter the set of Nash equilibria of a MAS [2]. In PBRS the shaping term is of the form $F(s, s') = \gamma\Phi(s') - \Phi(s)$, where $\Phi(s)$ is a potential function which represents preferences for agents to reach certain system states.

Two typical MARL reward functions exist: **local rewards** (L_i) based on the utility of the part of a system that agent i can observe directly, and **global rewards** (G) based on the utility of the entire system. A **difference reward** (D_i) is a shaped reward signal that aims to quantify each agent's individual contribution to the system performance, with $R = G$ and $F = -G(z_{-i})$. The global utility for a theoretical system without the contribution of agent i is represented by the counterfactual $G(z_{-i})$. Here z is a general term that may represent states or state-action pairs.

Counterfactual as Potential (CaP) [3], is an automated method of generating multi-agent potential functions using the same knowledge represented by D. CaP automatically assigns potentials to states using counterfactuals, so that $\Phi(s) = G(z_{-i})$. Here $R = G$, and F is calculated as normal in PBRS. CaP preserves the guarantee of consistent Nash equilibria when using PBRS, while incorporating knowledge based on D in an automated manner.

2. DYNAMIC ECONOMIC EMISSIONS DISPATCH (DEED)

In the DEED problem a number of electricity generators must be scheduled to meet a specified customer demand over a period of time, while minimising the conflicting objectives of fuel cost and emissions. Basu [1] analysed DEED as a multi-dimensional optimisation problem, with each dimension in the problem space representing the power output of

*A full version of this paper is available at `endahowley.ie`

Appears in: *Proceedings of the 15th International Conference on Autonomous Agents and Multiagent Systems (AAMAS 2016), J. Thangarajah, K. Tuyls, C. Jonker, S. Marsella (eds.), May 9–13, 2016, Singapore.*

a generator at a given time. Approaches such as Genetic Algorithms (GA) [1] and Particle Swarm Optimisation (PSO) [4] have previously been applied to DEED.

In our MARL approach, each agent $i \in \{2, ..., N\}$ controls the power output of a generator $n \in N$ at each hour $m \in M$, and the first generator is a slack generator. The local cost $f_c^L(n,m)$ and emissions $f_e^L(n,m)$ terms for generator n over hour m are calculated as:

$$f_c^L(n,m) = a_n + b_n P_{nm} + c_n (P_{nm})^2 + |d_n sin\{e_n(P_n^{min} - P_{nm})\}| \quad (1)$$

$$f_e^L(n,m) = E(\alpha_n + \beta_n P_{nm} + \gamma_n (P_{nm})^2 + \eta \exp \delta P_{nm}) \quad (2)$$

where a_n, b_n, c_n, d_n and e_n are the cost coefficients for each generator, α_n, β_n, γ_n, η_n and δ_n are the emission coefficients for each generator, P_{nm} is the power output from generator n at time m, P_n^{min} is the minimum permissible power output of generator n, and $E = 10$ is the emissions scaling factor.

The global cost and emissions for hour m may then be calculated as the summation of $f_c^L(n,m)$ and $f_e^L(n,m)$ respectively over the $N = 10$ generators in the system. To discourage violations of system operating limits, a global penalty function f_p^G is used, which returns the total number of constraint violations multiplied by 10^6. The counterfactual versions of the global cost, emissions and violations terms for agent i are calculated by assuming that the agent chose the same action as in the previous timestep.

We combine the reward signals L_o, G_o, D_o and CaP_o for each objective $o \in O$ into single reward signals, using two different scalarisation techniques: linear scalarisation (+) and hypervolume scalarisation (λ). The objective weights used for the linear scalarisation are: $w_c = 0.45$, $w_e = 0.55$, and $w_p = 1.0$. The agents receive one of these scalarised reward signals while learning: $L(+)$, $L(\lambda)$, $G(+)$, $G(\lambda)$, $D(+)$, $D(\lambda)$, $CaP(+)$ or $CaP(\lambda)$. Note that all reward signals given to agents are negative, as this is a minimisation problem. We apply multiple individual Q-learners with ϵ-greedy exploration to DEED, learning using the reward functions above for 20,000 episodes. Each episode comprises $M = 24$ hours. The learning parameters for all agents are: $\alpha = 0.10$, $\gamma = 0.75$, $\epsilon = 0.05$. All values for cost coefficients, emission coefficients, ramp limits, generator capacity limits, power demands and transmission line loss coefficients can be found in the work of Basu [1].

3. RESULTS AND DISCUSSION

The average results over 50 statistical runs for the MARL approaches tested are presented in Table 1. All claims of statistical significance are supported by two-tailed t-tests assuming unequal variances, with $p = 0.05$ selected as the threshold for significance. As expected, L performs poorly here, encouraging agents to greedily minimise their own fuel cost and emissions without considering the utility of the system as a whole. D converges to a stable policy most quickly with both scalarisations, while both variants of G learn good policies, but at a slower rate than D. CaP initially learns more quickly than G for both scalarisations; increased learning speed is a typical characteristic of PBRS. However, the final joint policies learned by CaP are not as good as those learned by G or D.

No statistical difference was found between the final performance of the scalarisation approaches for $G(+)$ and $G(\lambda)$, or for $CaP(+)$ and $CaP(\lambda)$. The differences in the means between $D(+)$ and $D(\lambda)$ were statistically insignificant for the cost objective, but were significant for the emissions objective ($p = 1.19 \times 10^{-8}$). The differences in the mean final performance of $D(+)$ and $G(+)$ were found to be significant for both the cost objective ($p = 5.01 \times 10^{-22}$), and the emissions objective ($p = 3.20 \times 10^{-10}$). Overall, $D(+)$ offered the best performance of all the MARL approaches tested.

GA results reported by Basu [1] and PSO results reported by Mason [4] are included in Table 1 for comparison purposes. Our experiments show that MARL produces results that are comparable to those produced by GA and PSO based approaches, although not quite as good. For example, Basu's NSGA-II [1] has 4.2% lower costs, and 6.8% lower emissions than $D(+)$ on average in this problem. However, MAS is arguably a more interesting paradigm to use when studying these types of optimisation problems, due to the ability to modify simulation parameters while learning online, and the possibility of modelling system disturbances (e.g. generator failure). MAS are inherently suited to distributed control and optimisation problems like DEED, and we intend to investigate further applications of MAS and MARL to these types of problems in the future.

Table 1: DEED Average solutions

	Cost (\$ $\times 10^6$)	Emissions (lb $\times 10^5$)
$L(+)$	4.1127	28.8266
$L(\lambda)$	4.1149	17.6606
$CaP(+)$	2.8777	7.4774
$CaP(\lambda)$	2.8919	9.6431
$G(+)$	2.7647	3.9098
$G(\lambda)$	2.7607	3.9788
$D(+)$	2.6641	3.3255
$D(\lambda)$	2.6748	3.8980
NSGA-II [1]	2.5226	3.0994
PSO-AWL [4]	2.5463	2.9455

Acknowledgments

Patrick Mannion is funded by the Irish Research Council.

REFERENCES

[1] M. Basu. Dynamic economic emission dispatch using nondominated sorting genetic algorithm-ii. *International Journal of Electrical Power & Energy Systems*, 30(2):140–149, 2008.

[2] S. Devlin and D. Kudenko. Theoretical considerations of potential-based reward shaping for multi-agent systems. In *Proceedings of the 10th International Conference on Autonomous Agents and Multiagent Systems (AAMAS)*, pages 225–232, 2011.

[3] S. Devlin, L. Yliniemi, D. Kudenko, and K. Tumer. Potential-based difference rewards for multiagent reinforcement learning. In *Proceedings of the 13th International Conference on Autonomous Agents and Multiagent Systems (AAMAS)*, pages 165–172, 2014.

[4] K. Mason. Avoidance techniques & neighbourhood topologies in particle swarm optimisation. Master's thesis, National University of Ireland Galway, 2015.

Sequential Plan Recognition

(Extended Abstract)

Paper ID ex260

ABSTRACT

Plan recognition algorithms need to maintain all candidate hypotheses which are consistent with the observations, even though there is only a single hypothesis that is the correct one. Unfortunately, the number of possible hypotheses can be exponentially large in practice. This paper addresses the problem of how to disambiguate between many possible hypotheses that are all consistent with the actions of the observed agent. One way to reduce the number of hypotheses is to consult a domain expert or the acting agent directly about its intentions. This process can be performed sequentially, updating the set of hypotheses during the recognition process. The paper specifically addresses the problem of how to minimize the number of queries made that are required to find the correct hypothesis. It adapts a number of probing techniques for choosing which plan to query, such as maximal information gain and maximum likelihood. These approaches were evaluated on a domain from the literature using a well known plan recognition algorithm. The results showed that the information gain approach was able to find the correct plan using significantly fewer queries than the maximum likelihood approach as well as a baseline approach choosing random plans. Our technique can inform the design of future plan recognition systems that interleave the recognition process with intelligent interventions of their users.

Keywords

Plan Recognition; Activity Recognition; Human-Aware AI

1. INTRODUCTION

Plan recognition, the task of inferring agents' plans based on their observed actions, is a fundamental problem in AI, with a broad range of applications, such as advising in health care [1], or recognizing activities in gaming and educational software [4]. Many real world domains are ambiguous, in the sense that there are many possible hypotheses that are consistent with an observed agent's activities. Consider for example an e-learning software for chemistry education. Students' interactions in the lab consist of building models of chemical reactions, running the models, and analyzing the results. There can be many possible solution strategies that students can use to solve problems, and variations within each due to exploratory activities and mistakes carried out by the student. Given a set of actions performed by the student, one hypothesis may relate a given action to the solution of the problem, while another may relate this action to a failed attempt or a mistake. In general, the size of the hypothesis space can be very large. We focus on domains in which agents may pursue several goals at the same time. Thus a hypothesis includes a set of plans, one for each goal that the agent is pursuing.

In many domains it is possible to query the observed agent itself or a domain expert about certain aspects of the correct hypothesis. The query can be performed in real time (for example, the student may be asked about her solution strategy to a problem during her interaction with educational software), or offline after all observations were collected (for example, a system administrator observing suspicious behavior that can ask a cyber security expert for her opinion of these actions). Answers for such queries allow to reduce the set of possible hypotheses in a way that does not impede the completeness of the recognition process. Our approach is to query whether a given plan in one of the hypotheses is correct, and update all hypotheses in which this plan appears (or does not appear, depending on the answer to the query).

We evaluated these approaches in several domains from the plan recognition literature. We considered candidate plans to query that maximize the information gain as well as the likelihood of the resulting hypotheses given the expected query result. These approaches significantly decreased the number of queries compared to a baseline technique. In addition, once the number of hypotheses is large enough, the number of queries performed by the information-gain approach was significantly smaller than the other approaches. The potential impact of this work is to show how existing recognition systems can be extended to disambiguate the hypothesis space by intelligently querying their potential users in a way that minimizes the disruption and overhead.

2. SEQUENTIAL PLAN RECOGNITION

We define the sequential plan recognition process (SPRP) as a process with two stages: First, a plan recognizer receives a set of observations and returns a set of hypotheses that describe the observations. Second, the query process receives the set of hypotheses as input and sequentially chooses a plan p from the hypotheses set, to query whether it is part of the agent's plans. According to the answer of the query,

Appears in: *Proceedings of the 15th International Conference on Autonomous Agents and Multiagent Systems (AAMAS 2016), J. Thangarajah, K. Tuyls, C. Jonker, S. Marsella (eds.), May 9–13, 2016, Singapore.*

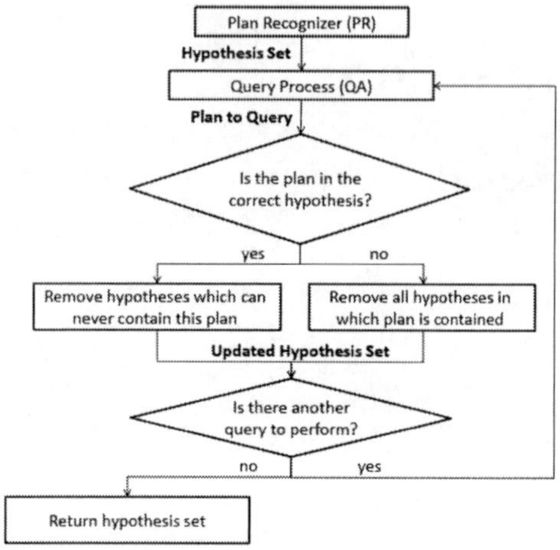

Figure 1: The SPRP Process

the set of hypotheses needs to be updated.

Querying about p means that we wish to know if the agent is executing a set of plans that include p. In SPRP, querying about p might also return True if p is a partial plan in the agent's set: $QA(p)$=True if there exists a plan p' in the agent's true set of plans such that p can be extended to p' if the agent executes additional actions. Accordingly, if the result of the query is True, we cannot discard all hypotheses that do not contain p, but only those which will never contain p, no matter what future actions will be taken. Similarly, if a query about p returns False, we can discard all plans that equal to p or extend it.

The query process continues until there are no more plans to query about in the remaining hypotheses set. The complete SPRP process is described in Figure 1.

Using SPRP, we can define the *sequential plan recognition problem*: how to minimize the set of queries required to reach the correct hypothesis.

We propose several heuristic methods for generating a policy that aim to minimize the number of queries required to achieve the minimal set of hypotheses that are consistent with the observations. These methods rely on the standard assumption that each hypothesis h is associated with a probability $P(h)$ that is assigned by the PR (such as PHATT [2]).
Most Probable Hypothesis (MPH). Choose a plan from the hypothesis h that is associated with the highest probability and was not yet queried about.
Most Probable Plan (MPP). Choose the plan that is associated with the highest cumulative probability across all hypotheses: $\text{argmax}_{t \in T} P(t)$, where T is the union set of all plans in all of the hypotheses H, and $P(t)$ denotes the cumulative probability assigned to all hypotheses that contain the plan t.
Minimal Entropy. Choose the plan with the maximal information gain (or minimal entropy) given the resulting hypothesis set.

We show an evaluation of the probing approach on the simulated domain used by Kabanza et al. [3]. This domain includes 100 instances with a fixed number of actions, 10 identified goals, and a branching factor of 3 for rules in the grammar. We used the Most Probable Plan (MPP), the Most Probable Hypothesis (MPH) and the Minimal Entropy (Entropy) approaches, as well as a baseline approach that

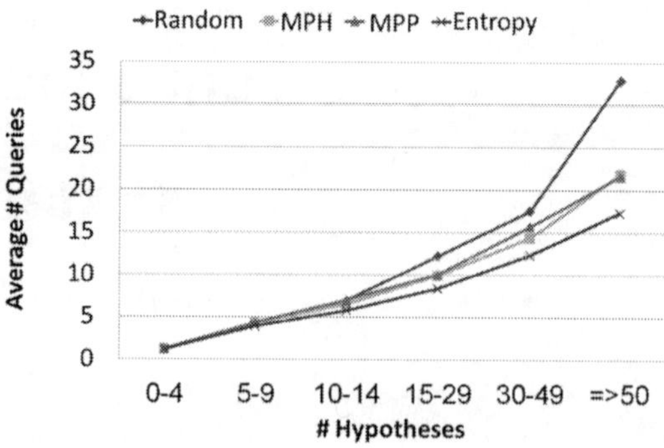

Figure 2: Queries until convergence given explanations for simulated domain

picked a tree to query at random. For the plan recognition process, we used the PHATT algorithm [2].

Figure 2 shows the average number of queries until converging to the single correct hypothesis in both of the domains, as a function of the number of hypotheses. As shown by the figure, in both domains, the random baseline generated significantly more queries than did the other approaches.

In particular, the number of queries needed for convergence grew exponentially for the random approach in the VirtualLabs domain. At first there is not enough ambiguity between the different explanations to make the insights from the queries useful, thus no method is significantly better than the others. As we increase the number of hypotheses, we see a difference between the more informed query approaches. As shown by the figure, although there is a monotonous increase in the number of queries required by all approaches, the growth rate of the Entropy query approach is the smallest. In total, the number of queries that were generated by the Entropy approach were significantly less than the number of queries generated by the MPP and MPH approaches (two-sided t-test $p < 0.05$).

Acknowledgments

This work was supported in part by EU FP7 FET project, Grant agreement n.600854, and the Israeli Science Foundation Research Grant no. 1276/12.

REFERENCES

[1] J. Allen, G. Ferguson, N. Blaylock, D. Byron, N. Chambers, M. Dzikovska, L. Galescu, and M. Swift. Chester: Towards a personal medication advisor. *Journal of Biomedical Informatics*, 39(5):500 – 513, 2006. Dialog Systems for Health Communications.

[2] C. Geib and R. Goldman. A probabilistic plan recognition algorithm based on plan tree grammars. *Artificial Intelligence*, 173(11):1101–1132, 2009.

[3] F. Kabanza, J. Filion, A. R. Benaskeur, and H. Irandoust. Controlling the hypothesis space in probabilistic plan recognition. In *IJCAI*, pages 2306–2312, 2013.

[4] O. Uzan, R. Dekel, and Y. Gal. Plan recognition for exploratory domains using interleaved temporal search. In *Proceedings of the 16th International Conference on Artificial Intelligence in Education (AIED)*, 2013.

Strategyproof Matching with Minimum Quotas and Initial Endowments*

(Extended Abstract)

Naoto Hamada, Ryoji Kurata, Suguru Ueda, Takamasa Suzuki, and Makoto Yokoo
Kyushu University
Motooka 744, Fukuoka, Japan
{nhamada@agent.,kurata@agent.,ueda@,tsuzuki@,yokoo@}inf.kyushu-u.ac.jp

ABSTRACT

Although minimum quotas are important in many real-world markets, existing strategyproof mechanisms require an unrealistic assumption that all students consider all schools acceptable (and vice-versa). We develop a strategyproof matching mechanism called Priority-List based Deferred Acceptance mechanism with Minimum Quotas (PLDA-MQ), which works under more realistic assumptions: (i) a student considers (at least) one particular school, which we call her initial endowment school, acceptable, and vice-versa, and (ii) the initial endowments satisfy all the minimum quotas. We require a matching to respect initial endowments; each student must be assigned to a school that is at least as good as her initial endowment. PLDA-MQ obtains the student-optimal matching within all matchings that respect minimum quotas/initial endowments and satisfies a stability requirement called Priority-List based (PL-) stability.

CCS Concepts

•**Computing methodologies** → **Multi-agent systems;**
•**Applied computing** → *Economics;*

Keywords

Two-sided matching; Deferred acceptance algorithm; Minimum quotas

1. INTRODUCTION

The theory of matching has been extensively developed for markets in which schools have maximum quotas that cannot be exceeded [4]. However, in many real-world markets, *minimum* quotas are also present [2]. In existing works, to guarantee that mechanisms obtain feasible matchings (which respect minimum quotas), it is required that all students consider all schools *acceptable* and vice-versa. This requirement seems unrealistic in many applications. For example, in a public school choice program, it is not likely that a student is willing to attend a public school located very far away from her residence, unless the school offers some very appealing characteristics.

In this paper, we develop a mechanism that works under much more realistic assumptions. We require that a student considers at least one particular school acceptable, which we call her initial endowment school. We assume each school can consider some students unacceptable. However, we require that each school consider its initial endowment students acceptable. We also assume that the matching corresponds to the initial endowments is feasible, i.e., it satisfies all minimum/maximum quotas.

In general, fairness and standard nonwastefulness, both of which compose stability, are incompatible when minimum quotas are imposed [1]. Thus, in this paper, we introduce alternative definitions called Priority-List based (PL-) fairness and PL-nonwastefulness. They compose PL-stability.

We set our research goal to develop a strategyproof mechanism that improves students' welfare while satisfying the required properties. Our newly developed mechanism obtains the *student-optimal* matching within all matchings that satisfy these properties.

2. MODEL

A matching market is given by $(S, C, X, \omega, \succ_S, \succ_C, \succ_{PL}, q_C, p_C)$. $S = \{s_1, s_2, \dots, s_n\}$ is a finite set of students. $C = \{c_1, c_2, \dots, c_m\}$ is a finite set of schools. $X \subseteq S \times C$ is a finite set of contracts. Contract $x = (s, c) \in X$ represents that student s is assigned to school c. For any $X' \subseteq X$, let X'_s denote $\{(s, c) \in X' \mid c \in C\}$. Also, let X'_c denote $\{(s, c) \in X' \mid s \in S\}$. $\omega : S \to C$ is an initial endowment function. $\omega(s)$ returns $c \in C$, which is s's initial endowment. Let X^* denote $\bigcup_{s \in S}\{(s, \omega(s))\}$, i.e., X^* is the set of contracts, where each element is a contract between a student and her initial endowment school.

$\succ_S = (\succ_{s_1}, \succ_{s_2}, \dots, \succ_{s_n})$ is a profile of the students' preferences. For each student s, $\succ_s$ represents the preference of s over X_s. We assume $\succ_s$ is strict for each s. We say $(s, c) \in X_s$ is acceptable for s if $(s, c) \succ_s (s, \omega(s))$ or $c = \omega(s)$ holds. $\succ_C = (\succ_{c_1}, \succ_{c_2}, \dots, \succ_{c_m})$ is a profile of the schools' priorities. For each school c, $\succ_c$ represents the priority of c over $X_c \cup \{(\phi, c)\}$, where (ϕ, c) represents an outcome such that c is unmatched. We assume $\succ_c$ is strict for each c. Contract (s, c) is acceptable for c if $(s, c) \succ_c (\phi, c)$ or $\omega(s) = c$ holds. We assume each contract x in X_c is acceptable for c. This is without loss of generality because if some contract is unacceptable to a school, we assume it is not included in X. $\succ_{PL}$ is a serial order over X called *priority list (PL)*,

*This work was partially supported by JSPS KAKENHI Grant Number 24220003 and 15K16058.

Appears in: *Proceedings of the 15th International Conference on Autonomous Agents and Multiagent Systems (AAMAS 2016), J. Thangarajah, K. Tuyls, C. Jonker, S. Marsella (eds.), May 9–13, 2016, Singapore.*

which represents a tie-breaking order among contracts. We assume $\succ_{PL}$ respects the initial endowments, i.e., for each $x \in X^*$ and $x' \in X \setminus X^*$, $x \succ_{PL} x'$ holds. Also, we assume $\succ_{PL}$ respects $\succ_C$, i.e., for any $(s,c),(s',c) \in X \setminus X^*$, $(s,c) \succ_{PL} (s',c)$ holds iff $(s,c) \succ_c (s',c)$ holds.

$q_C = (q_{c_1}, q_{c_2}, \ldots, q_{c_m})$ is a vector of the schools' maximum quotas. Also, $p_C = (p_{c_1}, p_{c_2}, \ldots, p_{c_m})$ is a vector of the schools' minimum quotas. We assume $\sum_{c \in C} p_c \leq n \leq \sum_{c \in C} q_c$ holds.

X' is *feasible* if it satisfies the following conditions: (i) for all $s \in S$, $X'_s = \{x\}$ and x is acceptable for s, and (ii) for all $c \in C$, $p_c \leq |X'_c| \leq q_c$ holds. We call a feasible set of contracts a *matching*. We assume X^* is feasible, i.e., for each $c \in C$, $p_c \leq |X^*_c| \leq q_c$ holds.

For set of matchings $\mathcal{X}$, $X' \in \mathcal{X}$ is *student-optimal* within $\mathcal{X}$ if it satisfies the following condition: for all $X'' \in \mathcal{X}$ and for all $s \in S$, where $X'_s = \{x'\}$ and $X''_s = \{x''\}$, either $x' \succ_s x''$ or $x' = x''$. There is a chance that no student-optimal matching exists in $\mathcal{X}$. If a student-optimal matching does exist in $\mathcal{X}$, it must be unique.

A *mechanism* is a function that takes a profile of students' preferences as input and returns a matching. We say a mechanism is *strategyproof* if no student ever has any incentive to misreport her preference, regardless of what the other students report.

We say student s has justified envy toward $s' \neq s$ in matching X', where $(s,c) \in X'$, $(s',c') \in X' \setminus X^*$, and $(s,c') \in X \setminus X'$, if $(s,c') \succ_s (s,c)$ and $(s,c') \succ_{c'} (s',c')$ hold. We say student s has justified envy toward $s' \neq s$ in matching X' based on PL, where $(s,c),(s',c') \in X'$ and $(s,c'') \in X \setminus X'$, if $(s,c'') \succ_s (s,c)$, $|X'_{c''}| < q_{c''}$, $|X'_{c'}| > p_{c'}$, and $(s,c'') \succ_{PL} (s',c')$ hold. Matching X' is *PL-fair* if no student has justified envy or justified envy based on PL.

Student s claims an empty seat of c' in matching X' based on PL, where $(s,c) \in X'$ and $(s,c') \in X \setminus X'$, if $(s,c') \succ_s (s,c)$, $|X'_{c'}| < q_{c'}$, $|X'_c| > p_c$ and $(s,c') \succ_{PL} (s,c)$ hold. Matching X' is *PL-nonwasteful* if no student claims an empty seat based on PL.

We say a matching is *PL-stable* if it is PL-fair and PL-nonwasteful. We say a mechanism is PL-stable if it always gives a PL-stable matching.

3. PRIORITY-LIST BASED DEFERRED ACCEPTANCE MECHANISM WITH MINIMUM QUOTAS (PLDA-MQ)

PLDA-MQ is built upon choice functions $Ch_S : 2^X \to 2^X$ and $Ch_C : 2^X \to 2^X$. Ch_S is a choice function of students S, which is a union of individual choice functions, i.e., $Ch_S(X') := \bigcup_{s \in S} Ch_s(X')$. Let $\widehat{X}'_s$ denote $\{x \in X'_s \mid x$ is acceptable for $s\}$. $Ch_s(X')$ returns $\{(s,c)\}$, where (s,c) is s's most preferred contract in $\widehat{X}'_s$ (or $\emptyset$ if $\widehat{X}'_s$ is $\emptyset$).

Ch_C is a choice function of schools C, which is defined as follows.

DEFINITION 1 (CHOICE FUNCTION OF SCHOOLS C). *$Ch_C(X')$ is defined as follows:*

1. *$Y \leftarrow \emptyset$.*
2. *Remove (s,c) from X' such that (s,c) has the highest priority based on PL in X'. If there exists no such contract, terminate the procedure and return Y. Otherwise, $Z \leftarrow Y \cup \{(s,c)\}$.*
3. *If $|Z_c| \leq q_c$ and $\sum_{c' \in C} \max(|Z_{c'}|, p_{c'}) \leq n$, then $Y \leftarrow Z$. Go to 2.*

The PLDA-MQ is one instance of the generalized Deferred Acceptance mechanism presented in [3], which is defined as follows.

DEFINITION 2 (PLDA-MQ).

Step 1 *$Re \leftarrow \emptyset$.*

Step 2 *$X' \leftarrow Ch_S(X \setminus Re)$, $X'' \leftarrow Ch_C(X')$.*

Step 3 *If $X' = X''$, then return X', otherwise, $Re \leftarrow Re \cup (X' \setminus Ch_C(X'))$, go to Step 2.*

Here Re represents the rejected contracts. A student cannot choose a contract in Re. First, students propose a set of contracts X' that are most preferred and not rejected so far. Then schools choose X'', which is a subset of X'. If no contract is rejected, the mechanism terminates. Otherwise, the rejected contracts are added to Re, and the mechanism repeats the same procedure.

From Definition 1, it is clear that PLDA-MQ respects q_C. Also, since $n - \sum_{c' \neq c} |Z_{c'}| \geq p_c$ holds, at least p_c students will be allocated to c. Furthermore, a student is never rejected by her initial endowment school. Thus, the outcome of PLDA-MQ is always feasible.

About PLDA-MQ, the following theorems hold.

THEOREM 1. *PLDA-MQ obtains a feasible set of contracts.*

THEOREM 2. *PLDA-MQ is strategyproof, PL-stable, and obtains the student-optimal matching within all the PL-stable matchings.*

4. CONCLUSIONS

In this paper, we developed a new strategyproof mechanism called PLDA-MQ that can work under more realistic assumptions than existing mechanisms. PLDA-MQ satisfies required properties (respecting minimum quotas/initial endowments, PL-stability), and obtains the student-optimal matching within all matchings that satisfy the required properties. Our future works include developing a mechanism that respects minimum quotas/initial endowments and is more efficient than PLDA-MQ, although it may not be fair.

REFERENCES

[1] L. Ehlers, I. E. Hafalir, M. B. Yenmez, and M. A. Yildirim. School choice with controlled choice constraints: Hard bounds versus soft bounds. *Journal of Economic Theory*, 153:648–683, 2014.

[2] D. Fragiadakis, A. Iwasaki, P. Troyan, S. Ueda, and M. Yokoo. Strategyproof matching with minimum quotas. *ACM Transactions on Economics and Computation*, 4(1):6:1–6:40, 2015.

[3] J. W. Hatfield and P. R. Milgrom. Matching with contracts. *American Economic Review*, 95(4):913–935, 2005.

[4] A. E. Roth and M. A. O. Sotomayor. *Two-Sided Matching: A Study in Game-Theoretic Modeling and Analysis (Econometric Society Monographs)*. Cambridge University Press., 1990.

Incorporating Observation Error when Modeling Trust between Multiple Robots Sharing a Common Workspace

(Extended Abstract)

Shreyasha Paudel
Department of Aeronautics and Astronautics
Stanford University
Stanford, CA
spaudel2@stanford.edu

Christopher M. Clark
Department of Engineering
Harvey Mudd College
Claremont, CA
clark@hmc.edu

ABSTRACT

Most multi-robot systems assume all robots are programmed to cooperate and complete tasks without consideration of dishonest robots seeking to maximize their own benefit. The work presented here develops and analyzes a distributed trust estimation framework that allows robots to estimate the trustworthiness of other robots in the community, and share these estimates to enable cooperative trust estimation. Our previous work has shown that when observation errors were ignored, the trust-estimation error converges to a steady state value over time. We extend this previous work, by now considering the effects of observation error and proving that trust-estimation error converges.

Keywords

Cooperation, Multi-robot systems,Trust and Reputation

1. INTRODUCTION & RELATED WORK

In Multi-Robot Systems (MRS), it is common for robots to communicate and share information. However, it is not always clear if robots can trust the information being shared by another robot, especially if that robot was deployed by a different and possibly competing organization. To model and establish the trust between robots in this context, a framework was presented in [4], (see Fig. 1). Building on this previous work, proposed here is the addition of observation error. With this new addition comes the following contributions of this work: 1) introduction of observation error into the trust framework, and 2) analysis of the effects of observation error on trust estimation error convergence.

MRS have been developed for a wide variety of applications, often involving cooperative search and mapping [1, 2]. These systems typically use wireless communication and information sharing to minimize the individual robot path lengths required to complete the exploration of a workspace [2]. Lacking has been the ability to determine if the information shared between robots can be trusted.

Within the field of multi-*agent* systems, as opposed to MRS, reputation and trust models have become an integral part of the systems [6, 5]. Previous works range from simple online reputation models [6] which simply classify positive, neutral and negative to a sophisticated model such as FIRE [3] and TRAVOS [9] which computes a trust value for each agent and a reliability measure taking into account both direct experience, witness information and third party certification. Recently, the work in [8, 7] used an observation based trust model for detecting unreliable team members in a multi-robot patrolling task. While our work is similar to [8] in that we consider a binary observation model, our model does not require a dedicated observer to detect false observations. Our work also differs in that it considers cases in which some robots attempt to provide false information.

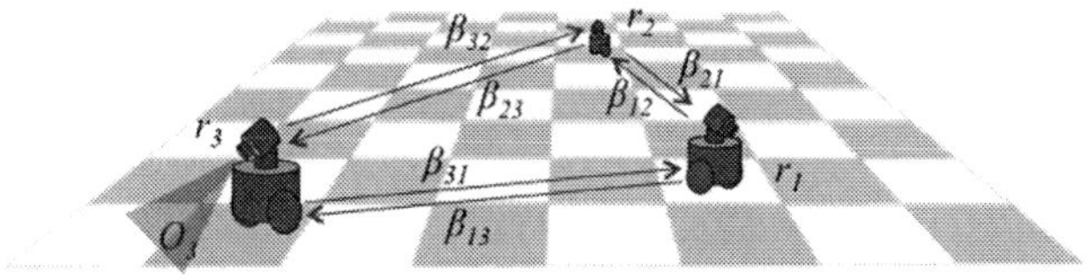

Figure 1: Illustration of the trust framework. Each robot r_i estimates the likelihood $\beta_{i,j}$ that robot r_j broadcasts the true value of its observations $O_{j,k,t}$ of cell k at time t.

2. PROBLEM DEFINITION

Given: There exists a set $R = \{r_1, r_2, ..., r_n\}$ of n robots sharing a common workspace. Each robot's goal is to estimate a set of K binary variables of interest $p_k \in \{0,1\}, k = 1..K$. Each variable has an associated workspace position X_k. Each robot r_i is equipped with the neccessary sensors to take observations $O_{i,k,t} \in [0,1]$ of p_k at time t when within distance d of X_k.

Using inter-robot communication, robots can share observations, and reduce the number of locations to visit in the workspace. However, each robot r_i may not always send truthful information, i.e. it only broadcasts the actual set of mean measurements $\bar{O}_{i,k,t}$ with probability β_i. Otherwise, it broadcasts 1-$\bar{O}_{i,k,t}$ with probability 1-β_i. To accommodate this, each robot must determine how much they trust shared observations by estimating the likelihood β_j that each robot j sends its actual set of mean observations. Specifically, we say that robot r_i's estimate of β_j at time t is $\hat{\beta}_{i,j,t}$.

If robots also share estimates of $\hat{\beta}_{i,j,t}$ through wireless

Appears in: *Proceedings of the 15th International Conference on Autonomous Agents and Multiagent Systems (AAMAS 2016), J. Thangarajah, K. Tuyls, C. Jonker, S. Marsella (eds.), May 9–13, 2016, Singapore.*

communication, they can more quickly estimate β_j values. We must introduce $\hat{\beta}'_{i,j,t}$ as the value robot r_i broadcasts to other robots as its estimate of β_j. Note that, $\hat{\beta}'_{i,j,t} = \hat{\beta}_{i,j,t}$ only if robot r_i is truthful. Deceiving robots inflate (or deflate) $\hat{\beta}'_{i,j,t}$ by $\epsilon_{\beta,i}$. That is $\hat{\beta}'_{i,j,t} = \hat{\beta}_{i,j,t} + \epsilon_{\beta,i}$.

Given this scenario, each robot r_i in R must calculate an estimate $\hat{\beta}_{i,j,t}$ of the likelihood that each of the other robot r_j is broadcasting truthful observations at every time step t.

3. TRUST FRAMEWORK

In this framework, trust values are estimated by using two pieces of information - 1) trust values $\hat{\beta}'_{k,j,t}$ broadcasted by other robots and 2) individual robot measurements of truthfulness of broadcasted messages $z_{i,j,t}$. This information is incorporated into the proposed discrete time update rule:

$$\hat{\beta}_{i,j,t+1} = \frac{1}{n}\sum_{k=1}^{n}\hat{\beta}'_{k,j,t} + K_\beta(z_{i,j,t} - \frac{1}{n}\sum_{k=1}^{n}\hat{\beta}'_{k,j,t}) \quad (1)$$

In (1), n is the number of robots in R, K_β is a constant proportional gain hereafter referred as the trust constant. The variable $z_{i,j,t}$ is robot r_i's measurement of the fraction of robot r_j's statements that are true. The first term averages the trust estimates shared by all robots in R and is used as a predictive element. The second term uses the robot's individual observations as a corrective element.

A binary measurement system is assumed in which the ith robot makes an observation $O_{i,k,t} \in \{0,1\}$ of some variable $p_k \in \{0,1\}$. The observation is subject to sensing errors $\epsilon_{s01,i}$ and $\epsilon_{s10,i}$. The framework incorporates the possibility of robots misinforming one another. Specifically, a robot r_j broadcasts to all other robots its mean estimated observation value $\bar{O}_{j,k,t}$ with a likelihood of β_j, and conversely $1 - \bar{O}_{j,k,t}$ with a likelihood of $1 - \beta_j$.

It can be shown that for constant β_j values, mean inflation error $\bar{\epsilon}_\beta$, and sensing errors ϵ_{s10i}, ϵ_{s01i}, the steady state error in robot r_i's trust estimation of robot r_j using the proposed framework converges over time and is equal to:

$$\hat{\beta}_{i,j,t\to\infty} = \beta_j + \frac{1 - K_\beta}{K_\beta}\bar{\epsilon}_\beta + \epsilon_{s10,i} + \epsilon_{s10,j}(1 - 2\beta_j) \quad (2)$$

4. VALIDATION VIA SIMULATION

The trust framework was simulated within an exploration task. A square grid map of K cells was defined where each cell C_k was assigned a value $p_k \in \{0,1\}$. The $n = 4$ robots in R were tasked with estimating p_k for all the map cells. Each robot was assigned a $\beta_i \in [0,1]$. At each timestep, each robot broadcasted a message stating the mean observation value $\bar{O}_{i,k,t}$ of the cell C_k that it currently occupies. A robot r_i broadcasts its true observation with probability β_i. The robots also broadcasted truth estimates $\hat{\beta}'_{i,j,t}$ of all the robots in R.

Eq. (2) was validated with simulations where a set of robots were placed in the single cell and shared their observations of p_k where $k = 1$. Simulations were run for 20000 iterations, (i.e. time steps) with various values of β_i, K_β, $e_{s01,i}$, $e_{s10,i}$, and $\epsilon_{\beta,i}$. Figure 2 shows a plot of $\hat{\beta}_{i,j,t}$ vs Timestep for one of the single cell estimation simulations with sensing error $\epsilon_{s01,i} = \epsilon_{s10,i} = 0.1$ and β inflation $\epsilon_{\beta,i} = 0.05$ $\forall i$. As expected, $\hat{\beta}_{i,j,t}$ converges to the theoretical prediction.

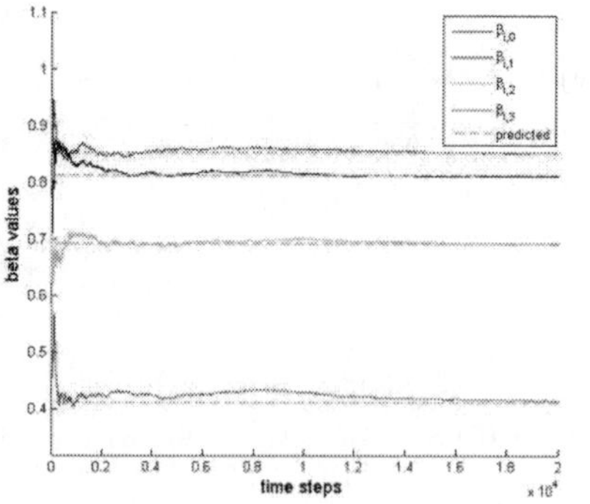

Figure 2: Trust estimate vs timestep for varying beta values in a simulation of single cell map. β estimates converge to theoretical prediction over time.

5. CONCLUSION

This work proposes a method for robots to identify trustworthy robots in a workspace where deceptive robots might be present. By monitoring the information communicated by robots, the level of trust in each robot can be estimated. The estimation of a robot's truthfulness is shown to converge to a bounded error, despite errors in sensing.

REFERENCES

[1] A. Birk and S. Carpin. Merging occupancy grid maps from multiple robots. *Proceedings of the IEEE*, 94(7):1384–1397, July 2006.

[2] W. Burgard, M. Moors, C. Stachniss, and F. Schneider. Coordinated multi-robot exploration. *Robotics, IEEE Transactions on*, 21(3):376–386, June 2005.

[3] T. D. Huynh, N. R. Jennings, and N. R. Shadbolt. An integrated trust and reputation model for open multi-agent systems. *Autonomous Agents and Multi-Agent Systems*, 13(2):119–154, 2006.

[4] K. T. Mantel and C. M. Clark. Trust networks in multi-robot communities. In *Robotics and Biomimetics (ROBIO), 2012 IEEE International Conference on*, pages 2114–2119. IEEE, 2012.

[5] Z. Noorian and M. Ulieru. The state of the art in trust and reputation systems: a framework for comparison. *Journal of theoretical and applied electronic commerce research*, 5(2):97–117, 2010.

[6] I. Pinyol and J. Sabater-Mir. Computational trust and reputation models for open multi-agent systems: a review. *Artificial Intelligence Review*, 40(1):1–25, 2013.

[7] C. Pippin and H. Christensen. Trust modeling in multi-robot patrolling. In *Proceedings of the IEEE International Conference on Robotics and Automation (ICRA 2014)*, 2014.

[8] C. E. Pippin, H. Christensen, and L. Weiss. Dynamic, cooperative multi-robot patrolling with a team of uavs. volume 8741, pages 874103–874103–8, 2013.

[9] W. L. Teacy, J. Patel, N. R. Jennings, and M. Luck. Travos: Trust and reputation in the context of inaccurate information sources. *Autonomous Agents and Multi-Agent Systems*, 12(2):183–198, 2006.

Towards Learning from Implicit Human Reward (Extended Abstract)

Guangliang Li*, Hamdi Dibeklioğlu†, Shimon Whiteson‡ and Hayley Hung†
*Ocean University of China, Qingdao, China & University of Amsterdam, Amsterdam, The Netherlands
†Delft University of Technology, Delft, The Netherlands
‡University of Oxford, Oxford, UK
g.li@uva.nl, {h.dibeklioglu, h.hung}@tudelft.nl, shimon.whiteson@cs.ox.ac.uk

ABSTRACT

The *TAMER* framework provides a way for agents to learn to solve tasks using human-generated rewards. Previous research showed that humans give copious feedback early in training but very sparsely thereafter and that an agent's competitive feedback — informing the trainer about its performance relative to other trainers — can greatly affect the trainer's engagement and the agent's learning. In this paper, we present the first large-scale study of TAMER, involving 561 subjects, which investigates the effect of the agent's competitive feedback in a new setting as well as the potential for learning from trainers' facial expressions. Our results show for the first time that a TAMER agent can successfully learn to play Infinite Mario, a challenging reinforcement-learning benchmark problem. In addition, our study supports prior results demonstrating the importance of bi-directional feedback and competitive elements in the training interface. Finally, our results shed light on the potential for using trainers' facial expressions as reward signals, as well as the role of age and gender in trainer behavior and agent performance.

Categories and Subject Descriptors

I 2.6 [**Artificial Intelligence**]: Learning

General Terms

Performance, Human Factors, Experimentation

Keywords

Reinforcement learning; human agent interaction

1. INTRODUCTION

Socially intelligent autonomous agents have the potential to become our high-tech companions in the family of the future. The ability of these intelligent agents to efficiently learn from non-technical users to perform a task in a natural way will be key to their success. Therefore, it is critical to develop methods that facilitate the interaction between these non-technical users and agents, through which they can transfer task knowledge effectively to such agents.

Learning from human reward, i.e., evaluations of the quality of the agent's behavior, has proven to be a powerful technique for facilitating the teaching of artificial agents by their human users [2, 8, 4]. Compared to learning from demonstration [1], learning from human reward does not require the human to be able to perform the task well herself; she needs only to be a good judge of performance. Nonetheless, agent learning from human reward is limited by the quality of the interaction between the human trainer and the agent.

Previous research shows that the interaction between the agent and the trainer should ideally be bi-directional [5, 6, 7] and that if an agent informs the trainer about the agent's past and current performance and its performance relative to others, the trainer will provide more feedback and the agent will ultimately perform better. This paper presents the results of the first large-scale study of TAMER—a popular method for enabling autonomous agents to learn from human reward [4]—by implementing it in the Infinite Mario domain. Our study was conducted at a science museum in Amsterdam using 561 museum visitors as subjects and investigates the effect of the agent's socio-competitive feedback in a new setting. In addition, we also study the potential of using facial expressions as reward signals, since several TAMER studies have shown that humans give copious feedback early in training but very sparsely thereafter [3, 5].

Our experimental results show for the first time that a TAMER agent can successfully learn to play Infinite Mario, a challenging reinforcement learning benchmark problem. Moreover, our study provides large-scale support of the results of Li et al. [5, 6] demonstrating the importance of bi-directional feedback and competitive elements in the training interface and sheds light on the potential for using trainers' facial expressions as reward signals, as well as the role of age and gender in trainer behavior and agent performance.

2. EXPERIMENT CONDITIONS

In our study at the science museum in Amsterdam involving 561 subjects, we test two independent variables: 'competition'—whether the agent will inform the competitive feedback to the trainer, and 'facial expression'—whether trainers were told that their facial expressions would be used in addition to key presses to train the agent. The main idea of the facial expression condition is to examine the effect that the additional modality of facial expressions could have on the cognitive load of trainers and whether this varies depending on age or gender.

We investigate how 'competition' and 'facial expression' affect the agent's learning performance and trainer's facial expressiveness in four experimental conditions in our study: the *control condition*—without 'competition' or 'facial expression', the *facial expression condition*—without 'compe-

Appears in: *Proceedings of the 15th International Conference on Autonomous Agents and Multiagent Systems (AAMAS 2016), J. Thangarajah, K. Tuyls, S. Marsella, C. Jonker (eds.), May 9–13, 2016, Singapore.*

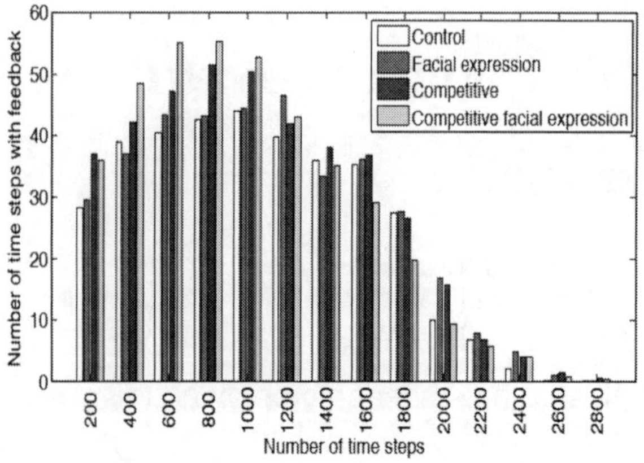

Figure 1: Mean number of time steps with feedback per 200 time steps for all four conditions during the training process.

tition' but with 'facial expression', the *competitive condition*—with 'competition' but without 'facial expression', and the *competitive facial expression condition*—with both. We hypothesize that 'competition' will result in better performing agents, and 'facial expression' will result in worse agent performance. In addition, we expect that both 'competition' and 'facial expression' will increase the trainer's facial expressiveness.

3. EXPERIMENTAL RESULTS

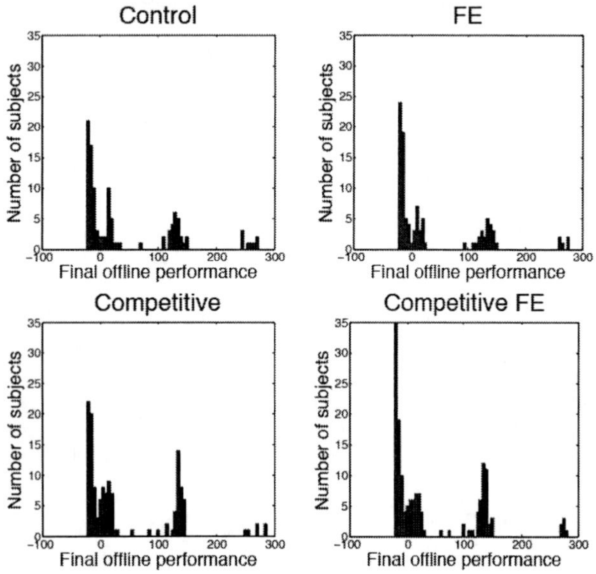

Figure 2: Distribution of final offline performance across the four conditions. FE=Facial Expression.

Figure 1 shows how feedback was distributed per 200 time steps over the learning process for the four conditions. From Figure 1 we can see that the number of time steps with feedback received by agents in the four conditions increased at the early training stage and decreased dramatically afterwards, which supports previous studies [3, 5] and our motivation for investigating methods of enabling agents to learn from the trainer's facial expressions. In addition, it shows that the agent's competitive feedback can increase the number of feedback given by the trainer before 1000 time steps. Figure 2 shows histograms of the distribution of the final offline performance for the four conditions. Further analysis with n-way ANOVA shows that 'competition' can significantly improve agent learning ($p = 0.035$) and help the best trainers the most ($p = 0.01$). In addition, our results suggest that 'facial expression' has a significantly negative effect on agent training by female subjects, especially those who are less than 13 years old ($p = 0.008$) and cannot train agents to perform well ($p = 0.01$).

Furthermore, our analysis shows that telling trainers to use facial expressions makes them inclined to exaggerate their expressions, resulting in higher accuracy for predicting positive and negative feedback using facial expressions. Competitive conditions also elevated facial expressiveness and further increased predicted accuracy. This has significant consequences for the design of agent learning systems that wish to take into account a trainer's spontaneous facial expressions as a reward signal. Further investigation into the nature of spontaneous and posed facial expressions is needed, in particular in terms of their relation to feedback quality and quantity.

Acknowledgments

This research was part of Science Live, the innovative research programme of Science Center NEMO in Amsterdam that enables scientists to carry out real, publishable, peer-reviewed research using NEMO visitors as volunteers. Science Live is partially funded by KNAW and NWO.

REFERENCES

[1] B. D. Argall, S. Chernova, M. Veloso, and B. Browning. A survey of robot learning from demonstration. *Robotics and autonomous systems*, 57(5):469–483, 2009.

[2] C. Isbell, C. R. Shelton, M. Kearns, S. Singh, and P. Stone. A social reinforcement learning agent. In *Proceedings of the fifth international conference on Autonomous agents*, pages 377–384. ACM, 2001.

[3] W. B. Knox, B. D. Glass, B. C. Love, W. T. Maddox, and P. Stone. How humans teach agents. *International Journal of Social Robotics*, 4(4):409–421, 2012.

[4] W. B. Knox and P. Stone. Interactively shaping agents via human reinforcement: The TAMER framework. In *Proceedings of the fifth international conference on Knowledge capture*, pages 9–16. ACM, 2009.

[5] G. Li, H. Hung, S. Whiteson, and W. B. Knox. Using informative behavior to increase engagement in the TAMER framework. In *Proceedings of the 2013 international conference on Autonomous agents and multi-agent systems*, pages 909–916, 2013.

[6] G. Li, H. Hung, S. Whiteson, and W. B. Knox. Learning from human reward benefits from socio-competitive feedback. In *Proceedings of the Fourth Joint IEEE International Conference on Development and Learning and on Epigenetic Robotics*, pages 93–100, 2014.

[7] G. Li, S. Whiteson, W. B. Knox, and H. Hung. Using informative behavior to increase engagement while learning from human reward. *Autonomous Agents and Multi-Agent Systems*, pages 1–23, 2015.

[8] A. L. Thomaz and C. Breazeal. Teachable robots: Understanding human teaching behavior to build more effective robot learners. *Artificial Intelligence*, 172(6):716–737, 2008.

Influence-Based Opinion Diffusion

(Extended Abstract)

Laurence Cholvy
ONERA
Toulouse, France
laurence.cholvy@onera.fr

Keywords

Opinion diffusion, belief merging

1. INTRODUCTION

Understanding the dynamics of opinion among agents is an important question which has recently received large attention in the community of autonomous agents and multi-agent systems [2, 3, 4, 5, 6, 7, 8, 9]. It requires to model several parameters such as the different relations which exist between agents, the opinions agents have and the way they make them evolve. This present work inspires from [9] and propose a formal model of opinion diffusion in a population of agents by assuming that: (i) opinions are propositional formulas or, equivalently, sets of propositional interpretations; (ii) the population of agents is structured according to a binary relation of influence which relates two agents when one influences the other; (iii) any agent orders its influencers (i.e. agents which influence it) according to the strength of the influence relation; (iv) any agent changes its opinion by merging the opinions of its influencers, from the most influential one to the least; (v) there is a special formula, called *integrity constraint* which expresses something true in the world and which has to be taken into account by the merging operator.

2. INFLUENCE-BASED BELIEF REVISION GAMES

Consider a finite propositional language L. If φ is a formula of L, $Mod(\varphi)$ denotes the set of models of φ i.e., the set of interpretations in which φ is true. A multi-set of formulas $\{\varphi_1, ..., \varphi_n\}$ equipped with a total order $\prec$ s.t. $\varphi_i \prec \varphi_{i+1}$ $(i = 1...n-1)$ is called *an ordered multi-set of formulas* and denoted $\varphi_1 \prec ... \prec \varphi_n$.

DEFINITION 1 (IMPORTANCE-BASED MERGING OPERATOR). *An Importance-Based Merging Operator, is a function Δ, which associates a formula μ and a non empty ordered multi-set of consistent formulas $\varphi_1 \prec ... \prec \varphi_n$ with a formula denoted $\Delta_\mu(\varphi_1 \prec ... \prec \varphi_n)$ so that:*

$$Mod(\Delta_\mu(\varphi_1 \prec ... \prec \varphi_n)) = Min_{\leq_{d,\varphi_1 \prec ... \prec \varphi_n}} Mod(\mu)$$

with:

- $w \leq_{d,\varphi_1 \prec ... \prec \varphi_n} w'$ *iff* $[D(w,\varphi_1), ..., D(w,\varphi_n)] \leq_{lex} [D(w',\varphi_1), ..., D(w',\varphi_n)]$
- $[D(w,\varphi_1), ..., D(w,\varphi_n)]$ *is a vector whose* k^{th} *element is* $D(w,\varphi_k)$
- $D(w,\varphi) = min_{w' \in Mod(\varphi)} d(w,w')$*, w and w' being two interpretations and d is a pseudo-distance between interpretations.*
- $\leq_{lex}$ *is a lexicographic comparison of vectors of reals defined by:* $[v_1, ...v_n] \leq_{lex} [v'_1, ...v'_n]$ *iff (i)* $\forall k \ v_k = v'_k$ *or (ii)* $\exists k \ v_k < v'_k$ *and* $\forall j < k \ v_j = v'_j$

By definition, Importance-Based Merging Operators are Distance-Based Merging Operators [1].

In the following, we introduce Influence-Based Belief Revision Games and Influence-Based Belief Sequences. These definitions are adapted from [9].

DEFINITION 2 (INFLUENCE-BASED BELIEF REVISION GAME). *An Influence-Based Belief Revision Game (IBRG) is a quadruplet $G = (A, \mu, B, Inf)$ where: $A = \{1, ..., n\}$ is a finite set of agents; μ is a consistent formula of L; B is a function which associates any agent i of A with a consistent formula of L denoted for short B_i such that $B_i \models \mu$; Inf is a function which associates any agent i of A with a non-empty set of agents $\{i_1, ...i_{n_i}\}$ equipped with a total order $\prec_i$ s.t. $i_k \prec_i i_{k+1}$ for $i = 1...(n_i - 1)$. For short, we denote $Inf(i) = \{i_1 \prec_i ... \prec_i i_{n_i}\}$.*

A is the finite set of agents. The formula μ represents the information which is true in the world. It is called *integrity constraint*. For any agent i, the formula B_i represents its initial beliefs. It is called the *initial belief state of i*. We assume that agents are rational and thus that B_i is consistent and satisfies the integrity constraint μ. For any agent i, $Inf(i)$ is the non-empty set of agents i considers as influent i.e., i considers that its own opinion is influenced by the opinions of agents in $Inf(i)$. With the total order $\prec_i$, i ranks its influencers according to their degree of influence: for any agents j and k in $Inf(i)$, $j \prec_i k$ means that, according to i, its own opinion is more influenced by j's opinion than by k's opinion. Notice that i may or may not belong to $Inf(i)$.

DEFINITION 3 (INFLUENCE-BASED BELIEF SEQUENCE). *Consider an (IBRG) $G = (A, \mu, B, Inf)$ and an agent $i \in A$ with $Inf(i) = \{i_1 \prec_i ... \prec_i i_{n_i}\}$. The Influence-Based Belief*

Appears in: *Proceedings of the 15th International Conference on Autonomous Agents and Multiagent Systems (AAMAS 2016), J. Thangarajah, K. Tuyls, C. Jonker, S. Marsella (eds.), May 9–13, 2016, Singapore.*

Sequence of i, denoted $(B_i^s)_{s\in\mathbb{N}}$*, is defined by:* $B_i^0 = B_i$ *and* $\forall s \in \mathbb{N}$, $B_i^{s+1} = \Delta_\mu(B_{i_1}^s \prec \ldots \prec B_{i_{n_i}}^s)$.

The Influence-Based Belief Sequence (or Belief Sequence for short) of agent i, $(B_i^s)_{s\in\mathbb{N}}$, represents i's belief state all along the game: B_i^0 is the initial belief state of i; B_i^s is the belief state of i after s moves i.e., the opinion of i after s steps. The evolution of i's opinion is done according to the importance-based merging operator Δ_μ: i's opinion at step s is the result of Δ_μ applied to the ordered multi-set of opinions: $B_{i_1}^s \prec \ldots \prec B_{i_{n_i}}^s$.

PROPOSITION 1. *In an (IBRG), the belief sequence of any agent is cyclic i.e., the belief sequence of any agent i is characterized by an initial segment* $B_i^0 \ldots B_i^{b-1}$ *and a belief cycle,* $Cyc(B_i) = B_i^b \ldots B_i^e$ *which will be repeated up as infinitum.*

DEFINITION 4. *An (IBRG)* $G = (A, \mu, B, Inf)$ *converges iff* $\forall i \in A \quad | Cyc(B_i) |= 1$.

DEFINITION 5. *Let* $G = (A, \mu, B, Inf)$ *be an (IBRG) and* φ *a formula of L.* φ *is accepted by agent i of A iff for all* $B_i^s \in Cyc(B_i)$*, we have* $B_i^s \models \varphi$. φ *is unanimously accepted in G iff* φ *is accepted by all i in A.* φ *is majoritary accepted if the number of agents who accept it is strictly greater than the number of agents who do not.*

Let us now introduce three more definitions related to (IBRG). The first one is adapted from [8], the two others are original.

DEFINITION 6 (DAG WITH LOOPS). *From any (IBRG)* $G = (A, \mu, B, Inf)$*, we can build a graph whose nodes are agents of A and edges are* $i \to j$ *iff* $i \in Inf(j)$*. We say that G is a DAG with loops if this graph is a directed graph where the only permitted cycles are of type* $i \to i$.

DEFINITION 7 (DOGMATIC AGENT). *Consider the (IBRG)* $G = (A, \mu, B, Inf)$ *and* $i \in A$*. i is a dogmatic agent iff* $Inf(i) = \{i\}$.

An agent is dogmatic when it is not influenced by other agents. As a consequence, a dogmatic agent i never changes its opinion i.e., $\forall s \geq 0 \; B_i^s = B_i^0$.

DEFINITION 8 (SPHERE OF INFLUENCE OF AN AGENT). *Let* $G = (A, \mu, B, Inf)$ *an IBRG. Let* $i \in A$. $Sphere(i) = \{j : Inf(j) = \{i \prec \ldots\}\} \cup \{j_k : \exists j_0 \ldots j_{k-1} \; \forall m = 1 \ldots (k-1) \; Inf(j_m) = \{j_{m-1} \prec \ldots\} \text{ and } j_0 = i\}$

The following proposition identifies a case where IBRG converge.

PROPOSITION 2. *DAG with loops converges.*

The following proposition identifies some sufficient conditions for accepting a given formula.

PROPOSITION 3. *Let G be an IBRG and i a dogmatic agent. If* $Sphere(i) = A$ *then* B_i *is unanimously accepted. If* $| Sphere(i) |> \frac{|A|}{2}$ *then* B_i *is majoritary accepted.*

Obviously, if an agent is the most infuential one for any agent in the population, then its initial opinion is unanimously accepted. If an agent is the most infuential one for more than a half population, then its initial opinion is majoritary accepted.

3. CONCLUDING REMARKS

This work suggested to model influence-based diffusion of opinion with Influenced-Based Belief Revision Games. It also presented some conditions on the Influence-Based Revision Game which guarantee the convergence of the diffusion process or the emergence of a majoritary or unanimous opinion. This work can be extended in several directions.

First, it could be interesting to change our assumption about the way agents orders their influencers. In this present work, we have assumed that agents order their influencers according to a strict order. Thus, two agents cannot be considered as equally influential for a given agent. Changing this assumption will lead us to consider preorders instead of orders. Defining a merging operator which takes into account preorders is an open question.

Secondly, an interesting extension is to consider that there is no global integrity constraint but only some local ones, shared by the agents who, in some way, belong to a commn community. Studying the acceptability in such a context is challenging.

Finally, to make this work more realistic, we have to consider the fact that an agent may influence another one not for any type of information but for only some kind of information, related to a given topic. Extending this work to topic-dependent influence is the next step of our research.

REFERENCES

[1] S. Konieczny, J. Lang, P. Marquis: *DA2 merging operators.* Artificial Intelligence, 157(1-2), pp 49-79 (2004).

[2] O. Pryymak, A. Rogers, N. Jennings. *Efficient Opinion Sharing in Large Decentralised Teams.* Proc. of AAMAS 2012. W. van der Hoek, L. Padgham, V. Conitzer, M. Winikoff (eds).

[3] C. Crawford, L. Brooks, S. Sen. *Opposites Repel: The Effect of Incorporating Repulsion on Opinion Dynamics in the Bounded Confidence Model.* Proc. of AAMAS 2013. M. Gini, O. Shehory, T. Ito, C. Jonker (eds).

[4] S. Chatterjee, F.M Hafizoglu, S. Sen. *Predicting Migration and Opinion Adoption Patterns in Agent Communities.* Proc. of AAMAS 2013. M. Gini, O. Shehory, T. Ito, C. Jonker (eds).

[5] H.F. Chau, C.Y. Wong, F.K. Xhow, C.F Fung. *Social Judgment theory based model on opinion formation, polarization and evolution.* Physica A 415, pp 133-140, Elsevier, 2014.

[6] A. Tsang, K. Larson. *Opinion dynamics of skeptical agents.* Proce. of AAMAS 2014, A. Bazzan, M. Huhns, A. Lomuscio, P. Scerri (eds).

[7] Z. Christoff, J. U. Hansen *A logic for diffusion in social networks* Journal of Applied Logic 13, pp 48-77, 2015.

[8] U. Grandi, E. Lorini, L. Perrussel. *Propositional Opinion Diffusion.* Proc. of AAMAS 2015. G. Weiss, P. Yolum, R. Bordini, E. Elkind (eds).

[9] N. Schwind, K. Inoue, G. Bourgne, S. Konieczny, P. Marquis. *Belief Revision Games.* Proc. of AAAI 2015. B. Bonet, S. Koenig (eds).

Applying DCOP_MST to a Team of Mobile Robots with Directional Sensing Abilities

(Extended Abstract)

Harel Yedidsion and Roie Zivan,
Department of Industrial Engineering and Management,
Ben-Gurion University of the Negev,
Beer-Sheva, Israel
{yedidsio,zivanr}@bgu.ac.il

ABSTRACT

DCOP_MST is an extension of the DCOP framework for representing and solving dynamic multi-agent applications that include teams of mobile sensing agents. Local search algorithms, enhanced with exploration methods were recently found to produce high quality solutions for DCOP_MST in software simulations. Applying DCOP_MST to robots with directed sensors (e.g., cameras) requires addressing limitations, which were not part of the original design of the DCOP_MST model, e.g., limited angle of the field of vision, collisions between robots etc.

In this paper we contribute to the ongoing effort of applying DCOPs to real world applications by addressing the challenges one faces when applying the DCOP_MST model to a team of mobile sensing robots with directed sensors. We integrate the required adjustments into a new model, DCOP_MST^R, which is the modified version of DCOP_MST for such a real world robot application with directed sensors. The proposed revised model was implemented and evaluated both in software simulations and on a team of robots carrying cameras. Our evaluation of existing algorithms revealed the need to combine actions that change the location of a robot with actions that change its sensing direction in order to achieve effective exploration when solving DCOP_MST^R.

1. INTRODUCTION

Multi-agent systems that include teams of mobile sensing agents have been previously modeled using the Distributed Constraint Optimization Problem (DCOP) framework by representing mobile sensors as agents that need to select locations and their tasks/targets as constraints [2]. Recently, Zivan et al. [5, 3] proposed a model (DCOP_MST) and corresponding local search algorithms for representing and solving such scenarios, particularly focusing on teams of mobile sensing agents that need to select a deployment for the sensors in order to cover a partially unknown environment. DCOP_MST is an extension of the DCOP model that allows agents to adjust their location in order to adapt to dynamically changing environments. The local distributed search algorithms that were proposed for solving DCOP_MST, were adjustments of standard local search techniques, such as Distributed Stochastic Algorithm (DSA) [4], to the model, enhanced by specifically designed exploration methods [5]. Nevertheless, prior to this work, the DCOP_MST model and its corresponding algorithms were only tested on a software simulator and not on a mobile robot team. The task of designing a distributed model for a team of hardware robots is most challenging. Thus, there exists only a handful of studies in which DCOP models were actually used to represent real mobile robots [1, 2]. Inspired by the pioneering work of [1, 2], our paper continues the effort to advance the research on realistic implementations of distributed constraint models and algorithms by applying the DCOP_MST model to a team of hardware robots carrying cameras. We analyzed the challenges that are raised when shifting to a hardware simulation, adjusted the existing models to represent these challenges, designed an algorithm that copes with the adjustments better than existing algorithms and empirically evaluated the model and algorithm both on hardware and software simulations.

Our results indicate that algorithms that performed best when solving standard DCOP_MST problems are not as effective for solving DCOP_MST^R scenarios. Therefore, we designed an algorithm (DSA_PDMR^R) with enhanced exploration abilities, inspired by the *Periodic Double Mobility Range* (PDMR) exploration method proposed by [5]. This algorithm outperformed existing algorithms both in our hardware implementations and in software simulations of DCOP_MST^R.

2. DCOP_MST^R

In order to face the discrepancies between the DCOP_MST model and the realistic scenario we discussed above, we propose the DCOP_MST^R model (R stands for realistic/robots), whose details are specified next:

- For each agent A_i, Dir_i is the direction in which its camera is currently pointing at.
- The assignment of agent A_i is a pair that includes its position Cur_Pos_i and the direction Dir_i.
- The domain of agent A_i includes all possible moves, e.g, a change of location, or a change of direction.
- For each agent A_i, $Ang_i \in (0, 360]$ defines its angle of vision. A_i can monitor a target T_j only if the distance of target T_j from Cur_Pos_i is not larger than A_i's sensing range (SR_i) and the angle between the line of sight to T_j and Dir_i is smaller than or equal to $Ang_i/2$.
- The reduction in credibility resulting from the distance between the agent A_i and target T_j is determined by the *Linear Credibility Reduction Function* ($lin_{i,j}$).

Appears in: *Proceedings of the 15th International Conference on Autonomous Agents and Multiagent Systems (AAMAS 2016), J. Thangarajah, K. Tuyls, C. Jonker, S. Marsella (eds.), May 9–13, 2016, Singapore.*

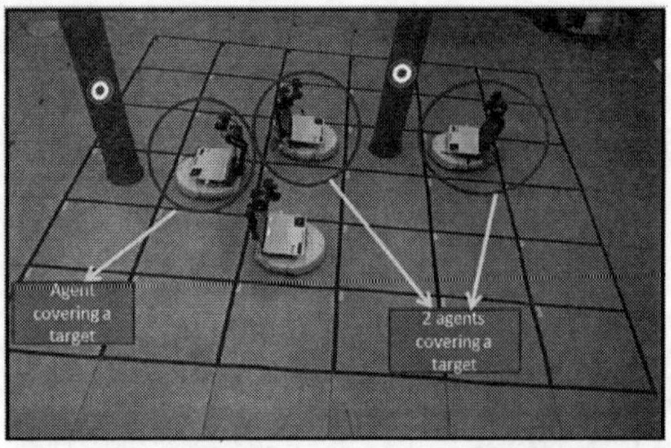

Figure 1: A team of mobile robots with directional sensing equipment covering targets (orange cons).

- Similarly, the reduction in credibility as a result of the angle between the direction the sensor is pointed at and the line of sight between agent A_i and target T_j is specified by the *Lateral Credibility Reduction Function* ($lat_{i,j}$).
- Agents sense a target only if there is no other agent or target in the line of sight between them.
- The effective credibility of agent A_i to target T_j, $Cred_{i,j} = Cred_i \cdot lin_{i,j} \cdot lat_{i,j}$
- Agents are not allowed to be located at the same position.

3. ALGORITHMIC ADJUSTMENTS

The most effective exploration method found in software simulations for DCOP_MST was Periodic Increment of Largest Reduction (PILR), which allows agents to periodically choose a sub-optimal assignment, escape local minima and achieve better coverage [5]. Our empirical results indicate that this method does not perform as well when used to solve DCOP_MST^R. The reasons for this difference partly stem from the difference in the domains' content. In DCOP_MST^R a single move changes a relatively smaller part of the local environment. In addition, due to the dependency on the direction, the exploration must be more accurate. Finally, the discretization of turn angles requires a combination of action to be taken to achieve optimal coverage in certain cases.

Thus, we propose an adjusted version of the PDMR exploration method described in [5] for DCOP_MST^R. In DCOP_MST, PDMR allows agents to periodically consider assignments within twice their mobility range (MR). In DCOP_MST^R we adjust PDMR so that agents consider a combination of up to two actions e.g., a move forward and a turn assignment.

4. EXPERIMENTAL SECTION

We conducted experiments both on a team of hardware robots and on a software simulation of the model. The robots chosen for this system were iRobot Creates mounted with Asus laptops equipped with PrimeSense sensors (Figure 1). The setting for the hardware experiment included 6 agents. The agents along with 3 targets were randomly located on a 10 by 10 grid. The targets had importance of 100 and the agents had credibility of 60. The algorithms ran for 15 iterations while at the 7th iteration we simulated a target movement. Each reported result in the graphs in Figure 2 is an average over 10 runs of the algorithm on different randomly generated problems. The results in Figure 2 indicate clearly that DSA_PILR does not have the same level of success as it had when solving standard DCOP_MST [5]. On the other hand DSA_PDMR^R offers a significant improvement over both DSA and DSA_PILR.

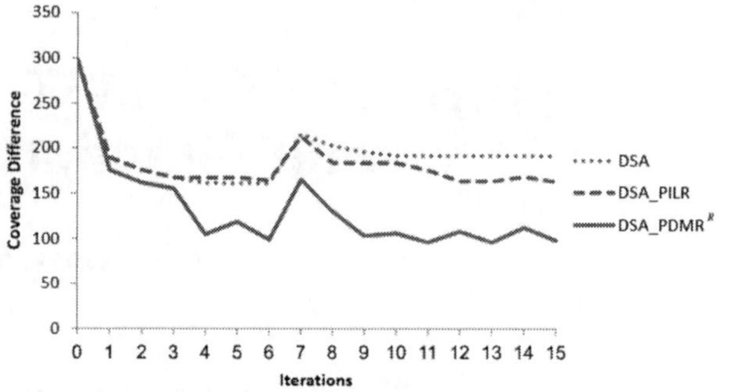

Figure 2: A comparison of the algorithms' performance on the robots. 3 targets, 6 robots.

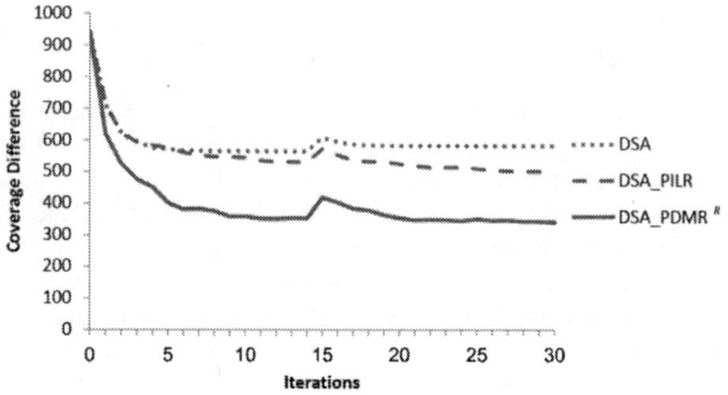

Figure 3: A comparison of the algorithms' performance on the simulator. 10 target, 20 agents.

Software simulations allowed the investigation of larger scenarios. The experiments in Figure 3 included 20 agents and 10 targets that were randomly located on a 20 by 20 grid. Each reported result is an average over 50 runs of the algorithm on different randomly generated problems. it is apparent that, like in the hardware experiment, DSA_PILR offers a very small improvement over DSA for DCOP_MST^R. The DSA_PDMR^R version that we proposed in this paper offers a more significant improvement.

Acknowledgments

The research was partially supported by the Helmsley Charitable Trust through the Agricultural, Biological and Cognitive Robotics Initiative of Ben-Gurion University of the Negev.

REFERENCES

[1] M. Jain, M. E. Taylor, M. Yokoo, and M. Tambe. Dcops meet the real world: Exploring unknown reward matrices with applications to mobile sensor networks. In *IJCAI*, 2009.

[2] R. Stranders, A. Farinelli, A. Rogers, and N. R. Jennings. Decentralised coordination of mobile sensors using the max-sum algorithm. In *IJCAI*, 2009.

[3] H. Yedidsion, R. Zivan, and A. Farinelli. Explorative max-sum for teams of mobile sensing agents. In *AAMAS*, 2014.

[4] W. Zhang, Z. Xing, G. Wang, and L. Wittenburg. Distributed stochastic search and distributed breakout: properties, comparishon and applications to constraints optimization problems in sensor networks. *Artificial Intelligence*, 2005.

[5] R. Zivan, H. Yedidsion, S. Okamoto, R. Glinton, and K. P. Sycara. Distributed constraint optimization for teams of mobile sensing agents. *JAAMAS*, 29, 2015.

Tracking Performance and Forming Study Groups for Prep Courses Using Probabilistic Graphical Models

(Extended Abstract)

Yoram Bachrach
yobach@microsoft.com
Microsoft Research

Yoad Lewenberg
yoadlew@cs.huji.ac.il
Hebrew Univ. of Jerusalem

Jeffrey S. Rosenschein
jeff@cs.huji.ac.il
Hebrew Univ. of Jerusalem

Yair Zick
yairzick@cs.cmu.edu
Carnegie Mellon Univ.

ABSTRACT

Efficient tracking of class performance across topics is an important aspect of classroom teaching; this is especially true for psychometric general intelligence exams, which test a varied range of abilities. We develop a framework that uncovers a hidden thematic structure underlying student responses to a large pool of questions, using a probabilistic graphical model.

General Terms

Experimentation, Theory

Keywords

Probabilistic Graphical Models, Bayesian PCA, Education

1. INTRODUCTION

When teaching a class, students often exhibit varied abilities across topics; this is especially evident when a curriculum is diverse. Preparatory courses for psychometric entrance exams such as the SAT or GMAT tutor students on various topics including mathematics, writing skills, and logical puzzles. Naturally, student proficiency across topics is not uniform: a student may be a math whiz, but have poor writing skills. Prep courses try to ensure that students perform well on all topics. This requires the teachers to shift focus based on class performance: if students are doing poorly in logical puzzles, additional practice on this sub-topic is required.

Our Contribution: We develop a framework for *course personalization* that uncovers a hidden thematic structure underlying students' responses to a large pool of questions. Our framework identifies abstract skills required to correctly answer the different questions in the pool.

Further, our model provides educators a way to keep track of students' overall course performance and offer personalized assistance on the course and individual student level. Using a form of Bayesian Principal Component Analysis, akin to other Bayesian matrix factorization methods [4], we recover latent abilities that explain student performance. We show that these latent abilities offer a *meaningful interpretation* of the data, as they match the actual sub-topic divisions in the case of the verbal and English sub-topics.

A key application of our framework is a method for dividing students into *study groups*, consisting of students with similar difficulties in the different skills tested in the exam. Our system automatically identifies the different skills tested in the exam, and the students' proficiency levels in these areas. We use this information to partition the students into student sets with homogeneous proficiencies in topics. We show that our latent ability-based clustering method has better performance than a baseline clustering method based directly on the observed responses. Our method for clustering students results in study groups that are more homogeneous, the student in every group have roughly the same skill level in each topic, and share the same difficulties.

Appears in: *Proceedings of the 15th International Conference on Autonomous Agents and Multiagent Systems (AAMAS 2016), J. Thangarajah, K. Tuyls, C. Jonker, S. Marsella (eds.), May 9–13, 2016, Singapore.*

2. SLAB MODEL

We are interested in identifying an underlying reason for students' performance; to do so, we introduce a model of Student Latent ABilities (SLAB, for short). For a fixed dimension K, the model assumes there are K latent abilities tested by a topic (K is assumed to be much smaller than the number of students and questions). Therefore every student s and question q are represented by a K-dimensional latent vector $\vec{x}_s \in \mathbb{R}^K$ and $\vec{y}_q \in \mathbb{R}^K$, respectively, where $(\vec{x}_s)_i$ is student s's proficiency in ability i and $(\vec{y}_q)_i$ is the level that q requires in ability i.

For every student s and question q we denote by $X_{s,q}$ the random variable that represents the performance of s on question q; $C_{s,q}$ is the Boolean random variable that equals "True" if the student s gave the correct answer to the question q, and "False" otherwise. We assume $X_{s,q}$ is normally distributed with mean $\vec{x}_s^T \vec{y}_q + b$ and standard deviation β, where b is the student and question bias. We assume that $\Pr[C_{s,q} = \text{True}] = \Pr[X_{s,q} > 0]$. This model resembles other Bayesian models for matrix factorization (e.g., [1, 4]).

SLAB's input is a set of student responses to questions (correct\incorrect). Based on the observed data, and using the Infer.NET [2] framework for graphical models and the Expectation Propagation algorithm [3], the model infers the values of the vector of each student and question.

	st_1	st_2	st_3
st_1	**59 (20)**	3 (36)	33 (39)
st_2	4 (14)	**76 (47)**	41 (60)
st_3	1 (2)	18 (14)	**29 (32)**

(a) English

	st_1	st_2	st_3	st_4
st_1	**48 (34)**	1 (7)	8 (18)	11 (8)
st_2	0 (24)	**20(0)**	13 (7)	0 (2)
st_3	26 32	10 6	**51 (35)**	1 (15)
st_4	15 23	0 2	2 23	**47 (16)**

(b) Verbal

	st_1	st_2	st_3	st_4
st_1	**15 (21)**	7 (5)	29 (4)	39 (24)
st_2	14 18	**10 (7)**	32 (41)	27 (17)
st_3	7 (22)	10 (4)	**47 (48)**	28 (18)
st_4	6 (13)	13 (4)	12 (34)	**44 (24)**

(c) Quantitative

Table 1: Confusion matrices of subtopic (st) labels for all topics, based on the latent-abilities vectors (response vectors)

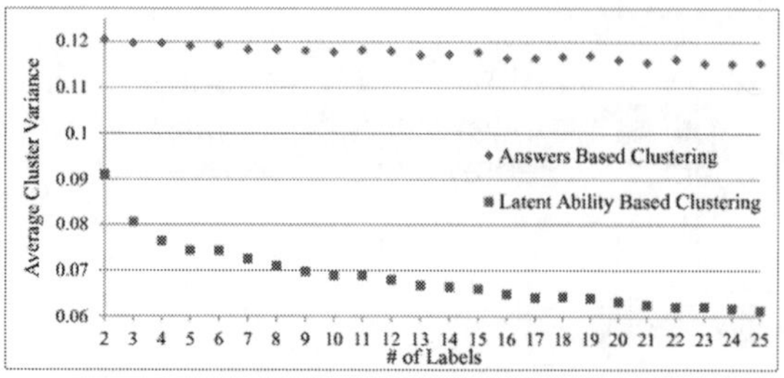

Figure 1: The average cluster variance for answers and latent abilities clustering

3. RESULTS

The Data: Our dataset consists of student responses to mock Israeli Psychometric Entrance Tests (PET), provided by a private company that administers PET prep courses. Questions are labeled according to topic (English, Verbal and Quantitative) and subtopic, as well as the correct answers to the questions. The database had 345 Verbal questions, 340 Quantitative questions, and 352 English questions. A total of 5874 students took the exam.

Eliciting Latent Problem-Solving Abilities: Using the SLAB model, we are able to use the latent ability vectors to recover the sub-topic divisions with relatively high accuracy. To demonstrate this, we do the following: each question q is associated with a vector of latent abilities $\vec{y}_q$. We cluster the questions to a number of clusters equal to the number of subtopics using k-means; now, each question has a label. To assess how well these labels match the actual divisions of the questions into sub-topics, we produce a *confusion matrix* for each subtopic. A confusion matrix C is a $k \times k$ matrix, where the C_{ij} are the number of times that a question of type j was labeled as a question of type i. A confusion matrix with a high trace is one which indicates that the prediction was accurate. Using k means clustering puts us at a disadvantage; performing k-means clustering may output a labeling that will perfectly match the original labels *up to a permutation.* In other words, it may assign the label 3 to all questions from topic 1, the label 2 to all questions from topic 3 and the label 1 to all questions from topic 2. To overcome this difficulty, once a latent-ability based labeling is produced, we permute the labels until we find a permutation that offers the highest trace for the confusion matrix. To benchmark our clustering method, we compare it to response-based clustering. The resulting confusion matrices are presented in Tables 1a, 1b and 1c. The tables show that clustering by latent abilities recovers questions well in the English and Verbal topics, but does not do well for the quantitative section. Nevertheless, in every topic latent-abilities clustering outperformed response-based clustering.

Focus Groups via Latent Abilities: The latent abilities elicited by our model can be effectively used in order to group students into focus groups. Grouping similar students is important: one would want to have students facing similar difficulties working together, in order to make effective use of time. In our dataset, we know the type of each question — the questions in each section have a distinct, known type — thus we can cluster students based on their competence in each sub-topic. However, this is not always the case; questions do not always belong to a specific type, which would pose a challenge for educators who wish to offer personalized tutoring to their students.

Our approach is simple: for each student s, we infer a vector of latent abilities, $\vec{x}_s$; next, we cluster the student body based on the student ability vectors. To assess the effectiveness of our latent ability based clustering, we measure the mean-squared variance in student subtopic proficiency within each cluster. If our methodology works, then all students from the same cluster should have similar capabilities in terms of their abilities to correctly answer questions from various sub-topics. We benchmark our latent ability clustering method by comparing it to response-based clustering. Our results are summarized in Figure 1. This is an encouraging finding; it further establishes that different latent abilities are needed to answer questions in each sub-topic; furthermore, ability-based clustering presents educators with an effective method of grouping students when there is no clear sub-topic division.

4. CONCLUSIONS AND FUTURE WORK

We have utilized probabilistic graphical models to elicit course metrics. Our framework can be extended to settings where there are no preset correct answers; an immediate use is in guiding experts towards tasks they do better, by assigning them problems at which they show higher proficiency. By eliciting latent abilities required by the tasks and those of the workers, we can better match tasks to experts. Our framework can also be used to make predictions about future student success.

Acknowledgements

This research has been partly funded by Microsoft Research through its PhD Scholarship Program, and by Israel Science Foundation grant #1227/12.

REFERENCES

[1] D. Agarwal and B.-C. Chen. flda: matrix factorization through latent dirichlet allocation. In *Proceedings of WSDA 2010*, pages 91–100. ACM, 2010.

[2] T. Minka, J. Winn, J. Guiver, S. Webster, Y. Zaykov, B. Yangel, A. Spengler, and J. Bronskill. Infer.NET 2.6, 2014. Microsoft Research Cambridge.

[3] T. P. Minka. Expectation propagation for approximate bayesian inference. In *Proceedings of UAI 2001*, pages 362–369. Morgan Kaufmann Publishers Inc., 2001.

[4] D. H. Stern, R. Herbrich, and T. Graepel. Matchbox: large scale online bayesian recommendations. In *Proceedings of WWW 2009*, pages 111–120. ACM, 2009.

Argumentation for Resolving Privacy Disputes in Online Social Networks

(Extended Abstract)

Nadin Kökciyan
Department of Computer Engineering
Bogazici University
34342 Bebek, Istanbul, Turkey
nadin.kokciyan@boun.edu.tr

Nefise Yaglikci
Department of Computer Engineering
Bogazici University
34342 Bebek, Istanbul, Turkey
ngyaglikci@gmail.com

Pınar Yolum
Department of Computer Engineering
Bogazici University
34342 Bebek, Istanbul, Turkey
pinar.yolum@boun.edu.tr

Categories and Subject Descriptors

I.2.1 [**Artificial Intelligence**]: Distributed Artificial Intelligence *Multiagent systems*

General Terms

Algorithms, Design

Keywords

Privacy; Online Social Networks; Argumentation

1. INTRODUCTION

Preserving privacy of users in online social networks is important. Usually, users specify their privacy constraints and the online social network is expected to enforce them. However, many times a piece of content is related to a number of users, whose privacy constraints might be incompatible. For example, when a user shares a party photo, her privacy constraints are enforced on the picture but the privacy constraints of the people in the picture are not. One way to deal with this problem is to enable collaborative policies to be written per content [5]. However, composing privacy policies from scratch is extremely time consuming. Further, it is difficult to overcome conflicts among users. Another way of dealing with this problem is to use agent-based approaches such that agents represent their users and employ agreement techniques to reach a conclusion on whether a content should be shared or not [3, 4]. Following this line of work, we advocate an agent-based approach where each user in the social network is represented by an agent that manages its user's privacy constraints. Each agent represents its domain knowledge using an ontology and its user's privacy constraints as semantic rules. When a user wants to post a content, her agent contacts the relevant agents (e.g., agents of tagged users in the content) to request permission. Upon receiving the request, these agents evaluate it using their own rules. If any of the agents has a concern; i.e., its privacy constraint is violated, then the agents engage in an argumentation session. The argumentation is done in a distributed manner where agents take turns to provide evidence as to why the content should be shared or vice verse. The evidence is generated from the agent's ontology and semantic rules on demand based on what the other agents have proposed. At the end of the argumentation, winning arguments are computed, leading to a decision on whether the content should be shared or not.

Appears in: *Proceedings of the 15th International Conference on Autonomous Agents and Multiagent Systems (AAMAS 2016), J. Thangarajah, K. Tuyls, C. Jonker, S. Marsella (eds.), May 9–13, 2016, Singapore.*

2. TECHNICAL DETAILS

We represent a social network user with an agent. The main goal of an agent is to manage its user's privacy constraints. For this, an agent is equipped with an ontology to represent the social network domain, the content being shared, the relationships of its user, and the privacy constraints of its user (e.g., not disclose location information). Each privacy constraint is represented as a semantic rule in the user's ontology.

2.1 Assumption-based Argumentation

We use Assumption-based Argumentation (ABA)[1] to generate arguments from information provided by the agents. In an ABA framework, there are four main constructs: (i) the language to describe information, (ii) a set of rules to derive arguments, (iii) a set of assumptions to represent non-factual information, and (iv) a set of contraries to disprove validity of assumptions. In ABA, an argument is of the form $S \vdash^R \sigma$, where S (the support) is a set of assumptions, R is a set of rules and σ is the claim of the argument inferred by the use of R. Assumptions are the weak points of arguments and can be refuted by other arguments. An argument a_1 can attack another argument a_2 if the claim of a_1 is the contrary of one of the assumptions in a_2. In ABA, various semantics can be used to compute winning (acceptable) arguments. In this work, we use the credulous admissible semantics. Hence, an argument that is not attacked by any other argument or it is attacked but defended by other arguments in ABA is a winning argument. In a recent work, Fan *et al.* [2] propose an approach for multiple agent decision making as we do here. Our work is different in that: (i) Agents are equipped with ontologies to represent knowledge (the social network domain and the privacy constraints). (ii) Agents generate arguments by using their ontologies. (iii) Agents can consult other agents to enrich their knowledge base if they have missing information in their ontologies.

2.2 Distributed Argumentation

Prior to sharing a post, an agent starts an argumentation with other agents relevant to this post request. The initial assumption is that the post can be shared. During the argumentation, agents send *messages* to each other in a turn taking fashion to provide their arguments and to convince other agents. A message consists of rules, facts, assumptions and their contraries. After an agent sends a post request, relevant agents to this post request evaluate it by creating a post request instance in their ontologies. As a result of ontological reasoning, agents infer more information about this post request (e.g., the context). In another words, agents evaluate a given post request regarding the privacy constraints of their users; they make use of their ontologies to accept or reject a post request. If any of the agents rejects the post request, that agent provides new information (rules, facts, assumptions and contraries), and updates the ongoing message to attack other agents' assumptions. In order to formulate arguments, agents can use their own ontologies or consult other agents in their social network to collect information. This is similar to real life where people consult others if they do not have enough information about a topic. The argumentation session terminates when agents cannot provide new information and update the message. At the end of the argumentation, the initiator agent gives the final message to an ABA engine and queries its initial assumption. If the initial assumption is a winning argument, then the post is shared by the initiator agent. Otherwise, the post is not shared.

2.3 Running Example

Consider a scenario where Bob wants to share a photo of Alice. Bob would like to consult Alice before sharing it since this content could violate Alice's privacy constraints. For this, Bob starts an argumentation session with Alice. It creates an initial message where he puts information about the post request. Moreover, Bob's agent `:bob` has an initial assumption that the post can be shared (A_{B_1}). Alice rejects any post request, which includes a photo taken abroad since she does not want other users to know when she is abroad. This privacy concern is represented as a privacy rule in Alice's ontology (R_{A_1}). Upon receiving the message, her agent `:alice` assumes that the photo is taken abroad (A_{A_1}). If an agent can prove that the photo is taken in Alice's home country, that would oppose A_{A_1}. Bob has two rules in his ontology. The first rule states that a country is the home country of a person if this person was born in a city of that country (R_{B_1}). The second rule states that if the photo is taken in a country, which is the home country of an agent, then the photo is taken in the home country of this agent (R_{B_2}). Bob also has an assumption about which country the photo was taken in (A_{B_2}).

Initially, `:bob` prepares a message where it puts factual information about the post request (e.g., tagged agents) and its initial assumption A_{B_1}, and it sends the message to `:alice`. In its turn, `:alice` evaluates the post request in its ontology. The post request violates the privacy rule R_{A_1} since `:alice` has the assumption A_{A_1}, `:alice` rejects the post request. `:alice` updates the message by adding R_{A_1} to the rule set and A_{A_1} to the assumption set of the message. Next, `:bob` receives the message and evaluates the message in its ontology. `:bob` knows the city where Alice was born hence it uses R_{B_1} to infer the home country of Alice. Moreover, it has the assumption A_{B_2} and the rule R_{B_2}. It turns out that the photo is taken in the home country of Alice hence `:bob` proves the contrary of A_{A_1}. `:bob` updates the message and sends it to `:alice`. When `:alice` receives the message again, it checks whether it can attack A_{B_2}. Since it has no supporting knowledge in its ontology, it consults `:carol` (a friend of `:alice`) to gather extra information for attacking A_{B_2}. `:carol` cannot provide any information either. The argumentation session terminates since `:alice` and `:bob` cannot update the message with new information. `:bob` uses the final message to compute winning arguments in an ABA engine. For this, it queries its initial assumption A_{B_1}, which results in a winning argument. Thus, `:bob` shares the photo in the online social network. In this scenario, `:bob` has convinced `:alice` to share the photo by providing information that `:alice` was not aware of. If there would not be such environment for agents to challenge each others' arguments, the post would not be shared; i.e., `:bob` would not share the photo to protect `:alice`'s privacy.

3. DIRECTIONS

Our current approach assumes all the agents are trustworthy since they are connected to each other in the social network. However, it would be interesting to study situations where the rules and assumptions are added to the argumentation based on the trustworthiness of the agents. It would also be interesting to study the formal properties of the decisions that are reached through argumentation as well as analyze the performance of our approach when multiple agents engage in argumentation.

Acknowledgments

This work has been supported by TUBITAK under grant 113E543.

REFERENCES

[1] P. M. Dung, R. A. Kowalski, and F. Toni. Assumption-based argumentation. In *Argumentation in Artificial Intelligence*, pages 199–218. Springer, 2009.

[2] X. Fan, F. Toni, A. Mocanu, and M. Williams. Dialogical two-agent decision making with assumption-based argumentation. In *International Conference on Autonomous Agents and Multi-agent Systems (AAMAS)*, pages 533–540, Richland, SC, 2014.

[3] R. Fogues, P. Murukanniah, J. Such, A. Espinosa, A. Garcia-Fornes, and M. Singh. Argumentation for multi-party privacy management. In *The Second International Workshop on Agents and CyberSecurity (ACySe)*, pages 3–6, 2015.

[4] Y. Mester, N. Kökciyan, and P. Yolum. Negotiating privacy constraints in online social networks. In F. Koch, C. Guttmann, and D. Busquets, editors, *Advances in Social Computing and Multiagent Systems*, volume 541 of *Communications in Computer and Information Science*, pages 112–129. Springer, 2015.

[5] R. Wishart, D. Corapi, S. Marinovic, and M. Sloman. Collaborative privacy policy authoring in a social networking context. In *Proceedings of the IEEE International Symposium on Policies for Distributed Systems and Networks (POLICY)*, pages 1–8, 2010.

Methods for Finding Leader-Follower Equilibria with Multiple Followers

(Extended Abstract)

Nicola Basilico
University of Milan
Milan, Italy
nicola.basilico@unimi.it

Stefano Coniglio
University of Southampton
Southampton, UK
s.coniglio@soton.ac.uk

Nicola Gatti
Politecnico di Milano
Milan, Italy
ngatti@elet.polimi.it

ABSTRACT

Leader-follower (LF) equilibria play a central role in several applications of game theory. In spite of this, the literature only presents sporadic results for the case with two or more followers. In this work, we address the problem of computing LF equilibria in this setting, assuming that the followers play a Nash Equilibrium after the leader's commitment.

Categories and Subject Descriptors

I.2.11 [**Artificial Intelligence**]: Multi-agent systems

Keywords

Game Theory (cooperative and non-cooperative); Equilibrium computation; Multi-Follower Stackelberg Games; Experimentation

1. INTRODUCTION

Leader-Follower equilibria (LFEs) have been much studied for the case of a single follower who, in an equilibrium, is known to play w.l.o.g. a pure strategy [6]. In this case, computing an LFE is easy with complete information, whereas it becomes $\mathcal{FNP}$-hard for Bayesian games [2]. In the case of multiple followers, the literature shows that, if the followers play a correlated equilibrium, an LFE can be found in polynomial time [1] whereas, if they play sequentially, the problem is $\mathcal{FNP}$-hard [2].

In this work, we address the fundamental case where, after the leader's commitment, the followers play a Nash Equilibrium (NE). It is relevant in many applications, such as *social planning* (e.g., urban traffic plans) or *monetary economics* (e.g., monetary policies of central banks). We refer to the corresponding LFE as *Leader-Follower Nash Equilibrium* (LFE-N). Depending on the leader's assumption on the followers' compliance, we define an *optimistic* and a *pessimistic* variant of the problem where the followers select an NE which either maximizes or minimizes the leader's utility.

2. PROBLEM ANALYSIS

We outline few hardness results of LFE-Ns computation:

Appears in: *Proceedings of the 15th International Conference on Autonomous Agents and Multiagent Systems (AAMAS 2016), J. Thangarajah, K. Tuyls, C. Jonker, S. Marsella (eds.), May 9–13, 2016, Singapore.*

PROPOSITION 1. *Computing an optimistic or pessimistic LFE-N is $\mathcal{FNP}$-hard and it is not in Poly-$\mathcal{APX}$ unless $\mathcal{P} = \mathcal{NP}$, even for polymatrix games.*

PROPOSITION 2. *Deciding whether one of the leader's actions is played with strictly positive probability in an optimistic LFE-N is $\mathcal{NP}$-hard.*

In general, the computation of an LFE-N amounts to solving a *bilevel program*. In the first level, we look for a leader's strategy δ while, in the second level and for the given δ, we look for followers' strategies $\rho_1, \rho_2, \ldots, \rho_{n-1}$ forming an NE which either maximizes (optimistic case) or minimizes (pessimistic case) the leader's utility. If we assume the convexity of the second level problem, bilevel programs can be cast as (compact) single-level programs by substituting for the second level their KKT conditions [4]. This is not needed for optimistic LFE-Ns, as we can turn the second level problem into one of pure feasibility over which the leader has full control: he looks for a strategy δ and, given δ, also for an NE in the followers' game such that his utility is maximized. This allows for the exact solution of the problem via (nonlinear) mathematical programming. For pessimistic LFE-Ns, we cannot get rid of the second level objective function as the leader cannot control which NE the followers choose. Moreover, KKT conditions do not yield a compact reformulation, as even the sole feasible region of the second level (the set of NEs of a game parameterized by δ) is highly nonconvex. For this case, we investigate the use of (heuristic) black-box optimization techniques, which only assure a lower bound on the leader's utility in an optimal LFE-N.

3. COMPUTING LFE-NS

In the following, we consider both Normal-Form (NF) and PolyMatrix (PM) games, randomly generated with GAMUT.

3.1 Optimistic variant

To compute optimistic LFE-Ns, we propose different exact mathematical programming formulations, tailored for both NF and PM games, which we test with two global optimization solvers, SCIP and BARON. Let us first introduce our notation. Let $N = \{1, \ldots, n\}$ be the set of agents and, for each $i \in N$, let A_i be the corresponding set of actions, with $m_i = |A_i|$. For each agent $i \in N$, let $x_i \in [0,1]^{m_i}$, with $e^T x_i = 1$ (where e is the all-one vector), be his *strategy*, where each component x_i^a represents the probability that action $a \in A_i$ is played. Let $U_i \in \mathbb{R}^{m_1 \times \ldots \times m_n}$ denote, for each agent $i \in N$, his multidimensional payoff matrix, where each component $U_i^{a_1,\dots,a_n}$ is the utility of agent i when the agents play actions $a_1,\dots,a_n$. Let agent n be the leader, whom we relabel as ℓ, and $F = N\setminus\{\ell\}$ be the set of followers. While we assume $n = 3$ ($F = \{1,2\}$) and $m_\ell = m_1 = m_2$, the generalization to $n > 3$ and general m_is is straightforward. For all $f \in F$, we adopt the notation $f' := F \setminus \{f\}$ and denote x_ℓ, x_1, x_2 by δ, ρ_1, ρ_2, respectively. The following formulation is the one which turned out to be the most efficient (when solved with SCIP):

$$\max_{\substack{\delta,\rho_1,\rho_2,v_f\geq 0\\ u_f,r_f,y_f,z\geq 0\\ s_f\in\{0,1\}}} \sum_{i\in A_\ell}\sum_{j\in A_1}\sum_{k\in A_2} z^{ijk}U_\ell^{ijk} \quad \text{s.t.} \tag{1}$$

$$u_f^j = \sum_{i\in A_\ell}\sum_{k\in A_{f'}} y_{f'}^{ik}U_f^{ijk} \quad \forall f\in F, j\in A_f \tag{2}$$

$$y_f^{ij} = \delta^i\rho_f^j \ \forall i\in A_\ell, f\in F, j\in A_f \tag{3}$$

$$z^{ijk} = y_1^{ij}\rho_2^k \ \forall i\in A_\ell, j\in A_1, k\in A_2 \tag{4}$$

$$\sum_{i\in A_\ell}\sum_{j\in A_f} y_f^{ij} = 1, y_f \geq 0 \quad \forall f\in F \tag{5}$$

$$\sum_{i\in A_\ell}\sum_{j\in A_1}\sum_{k\in A_2} z^{ijk} = 1, z\geq 0 \tag{6}$$

$$e^T\delta = 1, e^T\rho_1 = 1, e^T\rho_2 = 1 \tag{7}$$

$$v_f \geq u_f^j \quad \forall f\in F, j\in A_f \tag{8}$$

$$r_f^j = v_f - u_f^j \quad \forall f\in F, j\in A_f \tag{9}$$

$$\rho_f^j \leq 1 - s_f^j \quad \forall f\in F, j\in A_f \tag{10}$$

$$r_f^j \leq M_f s_f^j \quad \forall f\in F, j\in A_f. \tag{11}$$

Overall, the formulation contains $2m^2+m^3$ quadratic constraints and a linear objective function. Solving it with SCIP, we obtain average optimality gaps $< 30\%$ ($< 35\%$ in the worst-case) for $m \leq 40$. This formulation may thus constitute a valid (empirical) approximation algorithm, yielding a $\frac{6.5}{10}$-approximation.

The average (over 10 random instances) computing times, which we report as a function of n and m for both NF and PF games in the following two tables, show that we can tackle instances comparable, in size, to the largest ones used in [5] for NE finding algorithms, in spite of our problem being more general. They also show how, in the PF case, the formulation (which contains fewer nonlinearities in this case) allows for a substantial reduction of the computing times.

Normal-form games

	$m=2$	$m=3$	$m=4$	$m=5$
$n=3$	0.06	0.20	0.92	23.79
$n=4$	0.19	8.274	142.66	1304.45
$n=5$	278.06	409.78	2016.97	-
$n=6$	172.90	2350.95	2212.95	-

Polymatrix games

	$m=5$	$m=6$	$m=7$	$m=8$	$m=9$	$m=10$
$n=3$	0.24	2.17	1.87	7.31	24.45	194.71
$n=4$	4.84	10.85	121.57	247.84	622.72	1947.54
$n=5$	7.51	90.83	332.04	1982.77	2396.01	2175.29
$n=6$	10.31	1169.50	2062.75	-	-	-

3.2 Pessimistic variant

For the pessimistic case, we introduce a Black-Box approach (BB) based on a Radial Basis Function (RBF) estimation, relying on the solver RBFOpt [3]. The idea is of exploring the leader's strategy space (variables δ) with a direct search which, iteratively, builds an RBF approximation of the objective function, relying on the solution of an *oracle formulation* for the objective function evaluation. Given an incumbent value $\hat{\delta}$, the oracle solves the (NF or PM) pessimistic second level problem (where the leader's utility is minimized) with the following exact mathematical programming formulation, with δ fixed to $\hat{\delta}$:

$$\min_{\substack{\rho_1,\rho_2,v_f\geq 0\\ u_f,r_f,y\geq 0\\ s_f\in\{0,1\}}} \sum_{i\in A_\ell}\sum_{j\in A_1}\sum_{k\in A_2} \hat{\delta}^i y^{jk}U_\ell^{ijk} \quad \text{s.t.} \tag{12}$$

$$u_f^j = \sum_{i\in A_\ell}\sum_{k\in A_{f'}} \hat{\delta}^i\rho_{f'}^k U_f^{ijk} \quad \forall f\in F, j\in A_f \tag{13}$$

$$y^{jk} = \rho_1^j\rho_2^k \quad \forall j\in A_1, k\in A_2 \tag{14}$$

$$\sum_{j\in A_1}\sum_{k\in A_2} y_f^{jk} = 1 \tag{15}$$

$$\text{Constraints (7)–(11).} \tag{16}$$

In Fig. 1 (a), we compare BB (also in the optimistic setting) to the exact (optimistic) formulation. On the instances with $m \leq 5$ (for which, being solved to optimality by SCIP, we know the optimal solution value), we see that the gap between optimistic and pessimistic LFE-Ns is rather small, suggesting that, in the pessimistic case, the leader could force the followers to play a strategy providing him with a utility not dramatically smaller than that which he would obtain in the optimistic setting. The figure also shows the limit of the approach, indicating that, for $m \geq 15$, the time needed to solve the oracle formulation becomes too high for the method to be practical.

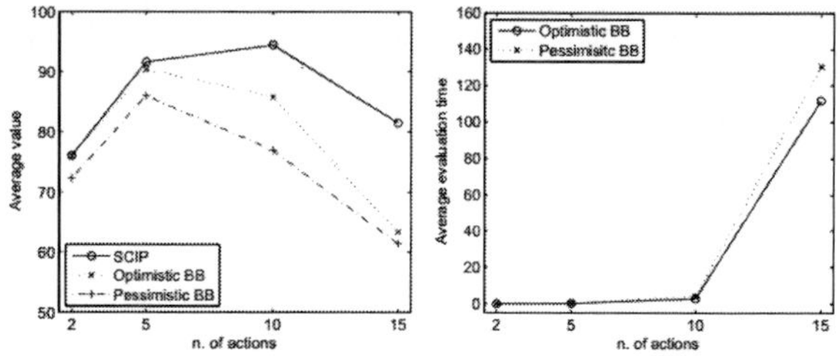

(a) Average objective (b) Average oracle time

Figure 1: Black-Box approach.

REFERENCES

[1] V. Conitzer and D. Korzhyk. Commitment to correlated strategies. In *Proc. of the 25th AAAI Conference on Artificial Intelligence AAAI*, 2011.

[2] V. Conitzer and T. Sandholm. Computing the optimal strategy to commit to. In *ACM Conference on Electronic Commerce*, pages 82–90, 2006.

[3] A. Costa, G. Nannicini, T. Schroepfer, and T. Wortmann. Black-box optimization of lighting simulation in architectural design. In *Complex Systems Design & Management Asia*, pages 27–39. 2015.

[4] S. Dempe. *Foundations of bilevel programming.* Springer Science & Business Media, 2002.

[5] R. Porter, E. Nudelman, and Y. Shoham. Simple search methods for finding a nash equilibrium. *Games and Economic Behavior*, 63(2):642–662, 2008.

[6] B. von Stengel and S. Zamir. Leadership games with convex strategy sets. *Games and Economic Behavior*, 69:446–457, 2010.

Multi-Agent Mechanism for Efficient Cooperative Use of Energy

(Extended Abstract)

Romain Caillière
Univ Lyon
LIRIS, UMR 5205
F-69622, Lyon, France
romain.cailliere@univ-lyon1.fr

Samir Aknine
Univ Lyon
LIRIS, UMR 5205
F-69622, Lyon, France
samir.aknine@univ-lyon1.fr

Antoine Nongaillard
Univ. Lille
CNRS, Centrale Lille, UMR 9189 - CRIStAL (SMAC)
F-59000 Lille, France
antoine.nongaillard@univ-lille1.fr

ABSTRACT

Promoting the development of renewable energies and the efficient and intelligent use of energy could be achieved through making adaptive consumer demands to energy supply. In this paper, we propose a mechanism based on three time scales, year, day and hour and three sets of agents, consumers, aggregators and providers to adapt consumption to production. We propose to use in this model the breakthroughs in energy : grouping consumers to reduce deviation in aggregated demand, *Time-of-Use* and *Prediction-of-Use* tariff schemes, storage capacities, shifting and the possibility for consumers to produce energy.

CCS Concepts

•**Computing methodologies** → **Multi-agent systems;** *Multi-agent planning;*

Keywords

Negotiation; Multiagent; Protocol; Energy Management

1. INTRODUCTION

Today, research on energy focuses on energy supply and mix, whereas consumption should be raised first. Indeed, the technological progress allows buildings to be equipped with generator units, as well as optimization and monitoring tools of their consumption. The use of the new storage capacities (Electric vehicles, household batteries) in the home looks promising to manage this complexity. The new meters allow sending and receiving data, allowing to balance supply and demand given new tariff scheme. Indeed, the current tariff schemes are insufficiently flexible to adapt the supply and demand on a continuous way. Lots of tariff schemes have been created [2] to address this issue. One of the most studied, *Time-of-Use* (TOU) is founded on slot of energy demand and gives different prices according to the slot. The tarification *Prediction-of-Use* (POU) [7] is based on a forecast base demand that the consumer gives to his provider. Every deviation from this base demand involves the payment of a penalty. On one side, the TOU scheme allows proposing a tariff according to the demand but doesn't take into account the forecast aspects. On the other side, the POU scheme incites consumers to forecast exactly their demand but doesn't propose a tariff which depends on the supply and the demand. Moreover, other works study the coalition formation or agent cooperatives with the aim to reduce energy costs [6, 1, 5, 4]. This reduction is often reached by the transmission of a price signal which incites consumers to buy energy when prices are low and shift consumptions when prices are high. In this paper, we propose a multi-agent architecture which allows combining both tariff schemes. In this architecture three kinds of agents are modeled, consumers, providers and aggregators and three time scales are considered. We consider that consumers can produce their energy, have storage capacities and group into cooperatives. The aggregator agent role is to locally match the production and the consumption of the cooperative by pooling local information and productions. We propose a negotiation model which relies on three interaction levels according to three time scales : the first level supports interactions between providers and aggregators for the annual contract negotiation. The second level supports interactions between aggregators and consumers for the daily contract, allowing coordination between agents. Last level is dedicated to the hourly contracts including an amount of energy and a tariff. The POU properties should be preserved : not be incited to consume to avoid penalties and not consuming should be viewed as the best option. The respective commitments for consumers (to respect some consumption limits) and providers (the tariffs never exceed a maximum price) guarantee a band of price for the consumers and a band of demand for the providers. The model based on cooperatives should incite the agents to join a cooperative with regard to views on final profit they will earn.

Appears in: *Proceedings of the 15th International Conference on Autonomous Agents and Multiagent Systems (AAMAS 2016), J. Thangarajah, K. Tuyls, S. Marsella, C. Jonker (eds.), May 9–13, 2016, Singapore.*

2. MODEL OF THE AGENTS

We consider three sets $\mathcal{A}_U, \mathcal{A}_A, \mathcal{A}_F \in \mathcal{A}$ of agents where $\mathcal{A}_U$ represents the set of consumers, $\mathcal{A}_P$ the set of providers and $\mathcal{A}_A$ the set of aggregators which manage interactions between providers and cooperatives of consumers.

The behaviour of an aggregator agent: an aggregator agent manages the energy stream within a cooperative. This agent contracts with providers to meet internal demand of the cooperative. We differentiate three kinds of contracts: (i)-the annual contract sets the maximum tariff applicable by a provider and the maximal and minimal demand requested by the cooperative at each slot. (ii)-

The daily contract concerns a set of hourly contracts and applies the TOU tariff scheme. (iii)-The hourly contract is composed of a tariff, an amount of energy and the number of slots. POU tariff scheme is applied on hourly contracts taking as baseline what have been negotiated in the daily contract.

Optimization model of a consumer agent : let a_u be an agent representing consumer u and $\mathcal{T}$ the set of slots. We assume that a_u is represented by a tuple $<\mathcal{Q}^{min}, \mathcal{Q}^{max}, b, q, s, soc, \alpha, p^{max}, p, \sigma^b, \sigma^p>$, with : $\mathcal{Q}^{min}$ (resp. $\mathcal{Q}^{max}$), the minimum (resp. maximum) amount of energy requested by a_u whatever the slot t. b, is the energy amount a_u needs at slot t, $q \in [\mathcal{Q}^{min}, \mathcal{Q}^{max}]$, is the energy amount requested by a_u at slot t. q may differ from b since the needs may partially be compensated by the stored energy and the produced energy, etc. s is the storage capacity of a_u. soc_- represents the state of charge and soc_+ represents the remaining storage capacity, $soc_- + soc_+ = s$. p represents the energy produced by a_u renewable generator, $p \leq p^{max}$. σ^b is the forecast mean error of the consumer consumption. The deviation between the forecast of consumer's needs and the real needs follows a normal law $\mathcal{N}(b, \sigma^b)$ (see [3]). σ^p is the forecast mean error of the consumer production. The deviation between the forecast of consumer's production and the real production follows the normal law $\mathcal{N}(p, \sigma^p)$. Every day, consumer agent minimizes formula (1) (under some constraints, not detailed here) :

$$\min \sum_{t=1}^{24} tr_t.q_t \quad (1)$$

With tr_t, the tariff at slot t and q_t the energy requested at slot t.

Decision model of provider agents: Each provider agent $a_f \in \mathcal{A}_F$ has a production capacity $p_f^t \in [0; p_i^{MAX}]$ where p_f^{MAX} is the maximum production capacity of the agent. We also suppose that each agent has an optimal production capacity p_f^{OPT} which allows him to maximize profit, with $0 < p_f^{OPT} < p_f^{MAX}$. The tariffs proposed by the provider tend to be low when the energy demand is close to his optimal production p_f^{OPT}. The tariffs become higher as the demand moves away from the optimal production. Providers make consumers pay a subscription. The coefficients A_f and pen_f represent the subscription and the penalty costs of provider f. Moreover, each provider has a maximal tariff tr_{MAX} above which nobody is willing to buy his energy. The provider agent uses a function $\mathcal{F}$ which returns a tariff according to an amount of energy, $\mathcal{F} : \mathcal{Q} \rightarrow \mathcal{T}r$ where $\mathcal{Q}$ is an amount of energy and $\mathcal{T}r$ a tariff.

$$\mathcal{F}_f(q_a^{tot}) = tr_f^{OPT} + tr_a^{max}(1 - e^{(\frac{-|p_f^{OPT} - q_a^{tot}|}{tr_a^{max}})}) \quad (2)$$

tr_f^{OPT} is the minimal tariff proposed by the provider when $p_f^{OPT} = q_f^{tot}$ and $tr_f^{max} \in [0, tr_{MAX}]$ is the coefficient negotiated in the annual contract.

Optimization model of aggregator agents Aggregator agents have to manage the negotiations of the different contracts with providers, which can be formulated as a linear program (3). The goal is to get the lower energy price.

$$\min \sum_{f \in \mathcal{F}} A_f.x_a + pen_f.\sigma_{coop}.\mathcal{H}.y_a \quad (3)$$

With x_a the maximal amount of energy requested by the aggregator agent to provider f, $y_a = \mathcal{Q}^{max} - \mathcal{Q}^{min}$, $\mathcal{H}$ is the number of hours in a year and σ_{coop} the mean deviation consumption of the cooperative. x_a affects the subscription costs and y_a affects the penalty cost.

3. NEGOTIATION MECHANISM

The multilevel mechanism we propose takes into account information feedback from one level to another. The first level, Annual, interacts with the two other levels, Daily and Hourly levels.

Negotiation of the annual contract : the distribution of the demand according to the different offers of the providers results from (3). We choose to apply the MCP but our model allows to use other protocols: (i)-Each consumer agent sends his consumption profile to the aggregator. (ii)-The aggregator computes the cooperative profile and the distribution of the demands between the providers. He submits the annual contract proposals. (iii)- The provider accepts or counters proposals. (iv)- The negotiation between the agents continues following the MCP protocol.

Negotiation of the daily contract : (i) each consumer agent sends its profile of the day $<q_{ps}^t, \ldots, q_{ps}^{t+n}>$, (ii) the aggregator computes the profile of the cooperative $<\sum_{ps \in Coop} q_{ps}^t, \ldots, \sum_{ps \in Coop} q_{ps}^{t+n}>$ and requests providers, (iii) Providers send their tariff profile $<tr_{pv}^t, tr_{pv}^{t+1}, \ldots, tr_{pv}^{t+n}>$, (iv) Aggregators transfer pricing signal (consumers can reschedule their planning to reduce their bill), (v) Go to step (ii) if there are reschedules.

The hourly contract: There are no negotiations for the hourly contract. Agents pay for their consumption with penalties according to their deviation.

4. CONCLUSION

In this paper, we combine progresses in energy and multi-agent systems to attack the problem of designing a sustainable mechanism for energy management in smart grids. The mechanism we present allows grouping consumers into cooperatives to reduce uncertainty in aggregated deviation, taking into account a new tariff scheme, storage capacities and shifting in consumers model. Our experiments show that consumers take advantage being in a cooperative and adapt their demand to dynamic tariffs.

5. ACKNOWLEDGMENT

This work was supported by the Région Rhône Alpes, within the program "Communautés de Recherche Académique (ARC) 4".

REFERENCES

[1] C. Akasiadis and G. Chalkiadakis. Agent cooperatives for effective power consumption shifting. In *AAAI*, 2013.

[2] M. H. Albadi and E. El-Saadany. A summary of demand response in electricity markets. *Electric Power Systems Research*, 78(11):1989–1996, 2008.

[3] M. Hazewinkel. Theory of errors. *Encyclopedia of mathematics*, 2001.

[4] S. D. Ramchurn, P. Vytelingum, A. Rogers, and N. R. Jennings. Agent-based homeostatic control for green energy in the smart grid. *ACM Transactions on Intelligent Systems and Technology (TIST)*, 2(4):35, 2011.

[5] A. Veit, Y. Xu, R. Zheng, N. Chakraborty, and K. P. Sycara. Multiagent coordination for energy consumption scheduling in consumer cooperatives. In *AAAI*, 2013.

[6] M. Vinyals, F. Bistaffa, A. Farinelli, and A. Rogers. Stable coalition formation among energy consumers in the smart grid. In *Proceedings of the 3rd International Workshop on Agent Technologies for Energy Systems (ATES 2012)*, 2012.

[7] M. Vinyals, V. Robu, A. Rogers, and N. Jennings. *Prediction-of-use games: a cooperative game theory approach to sustainable energy tariffs*, pages 829–836. ACM, 2014.

A Dialogue Protocol to Support Meaning Negotiation (Extended Abstract)

Gabrielle Santos, Valentina Tamma, Terry R. Payne, Floriana Grasso
University of Liverpool, Liverpool L69 3BX, UK
{G.S.J.Santos, V.Tamma, T.R.Payne, floriana}@liverpool.ac.uk

ABSTRACT

Despite numerous efforts, the problem of dynamically reconciling heterogeneity within open distributed multi-agent systems is far from solved. As different systems often use their own vocabularies to express the content of communication messages (*ontologies*), semantic reconciliation requires some form of agreement over a shared model, obtained through an alignment whereby concepts in the requester's ontology are *mapped* (translated) into concepts in the respondent's one. This paper presents a dialogue that allows agents to reach an agreement over a correspondence between two entities in their respective ontologies in a decentralised fashion, without requiring prior knowledge over their ontological models.

Keywords

Ontology Matching & Alignment; Meaning Negotiation; Dialogues

1. INTRODUCTION

The emergence of annotated data and sophisticated mechanisms for representing formal data models has promoted the proliferation of agents that typically commit to their own knowledge model (*ontologies*). The success of agent interactions therefore depends on an agent's ability to successfully make sense of the intended meaning of the messages exchanged with other agents. To overcome the resulting ontological heterogeneity, semantic reconciliation is needed to facilitate seamless interaction, which relies on finding an agreement on the choice of *mappings* that translate concepts from a source ontology to a target ontology. This problem has been investigated by numerous research efforts [1, 2]; however these approaches require sharing the ontological model in part or fully, without guaranteeing if such mappings could be determined. If two vocabularies have no overlapping intended models, the mappings calculated are unlikely to support the meaningful translation of requests between agents, potentially hindering interoperation.

We address the reconciliation problem using negotiation, exploring how dialogue protocols can be used to determine mappings that satisfy the agents requirements and strategies. The use of dialogical models allows the agents to state their position over the correctness of a mapping in an asynchronous and distributed fashion, whilst maintaining control over the type of knowledge (class labels vs. ontological axioms) disclosed. We investigate reaching an agreement that facilitates the translation of one term to another in different vocabularies. These translations are computed opportunistically (*anytime*), and limit the information exchange only to what is pertinent, thus supporting a specific translation. Our main contribution is a dialogue based negotiation protocol that allows agents to propose a viable lexical mapping, and support this proposal with evidence in the form of ontological fragments. These are shared on a per-need basis, and hence the mechanism is purely opportunistic.

Appears in: *Proceedings of the 15th International Conference on Autonomous Agents and Multiagent Systems (AAMAS 2016), J. Thangarajah, K. Tuyls, C. Jonker, S. Marsella (eds.), May 9–13, 2016, Singapore.*

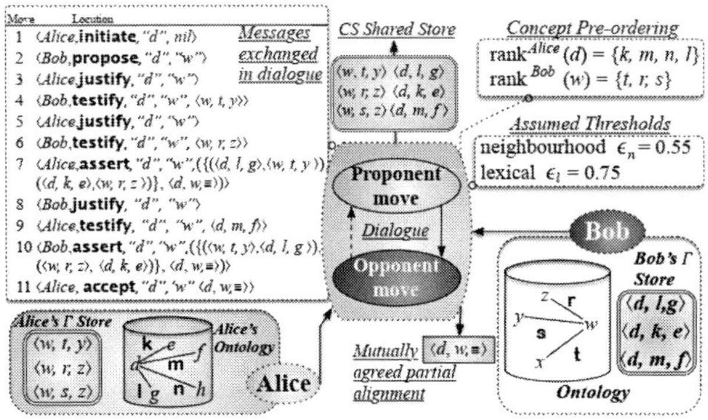

Figure 1: Dialogue Architecture using *Alice* and *Bob* described in the walkthrough example (Section 3).

2. DIALOGUE MODULE SYSTEM

The proposed dialogue consists of a sequence of *moves*, $\mathcal{M}$, between the participating agents [3], where a move is a message exchanged between two agents x (the sender, or agent making the move), and $\hat{x}$ (the recipient) at time s, and $m_s = \langle x, \tau, e, e' \rangle$. We denote τ as the move type s.t $\tau \in \mathcal{T}$, where $\mathcal{T} = \{$*initiate, propose, assert, accept, reject, testify, justify, fail*$\}$; e is the source entity being discussed (defined within the *initiate* move); e' is the candidate target entity (*i.e.* the entity that could be mapped to from e) or nil where there is no entity specified (in the case of the *initiate* and *fail* moves). The moves are presented in Table 1, complete with a description of their informal semantics. Both agents manage a public, joint knowledge base, or *Commitment Store*, CS, containing a trace of the moves uttered [3]; whereas, each agent manages its own private knowledge base, (*Gamma Store*, Γ), which stores knowledge regarding the ontological entities acquired from the other agent.

3. WALKTHROUGH EXAMPLE

In this section, we present an example dialogue between two agents, *Alice* and *Bob*. Each agent posesses a private ontological fragment (see Fig. 1), that models the entities they use to com-

Table 1: The set $\mathcal{M}$ of legal moves permitted by the dialogue.

Move	Pre-condition	Post-condition
$\langle x$, *initiate*, e, nil, nil$\rangle$	*initiate* is uttered when a correspondence is desired for e, which must be in x's ontology; and has not previously appeared in an *initiate* move.	The only permissible moves are *propose* (*i.e.* the opponent has a potential match for the entity e), or *fail* (*i.e.* no potential match for e can be found).
$\langle x$, *propose*, $e, e'\rangle$	The *propose* move is uttered when the sender x has some previously undisclosed entity e' in its ontology which is a *lexically viable* match for e.	Permissible moves: *justify* - the opponent seeks evidence to support the candidacy of $\langle e, e', \equiv\rangle$; *assert* - the opponent has sufficient evidence for the candidacy); or *reject* - there is no evidence to support the candidacy.
$\langle x$, *assert*, $e, e', A\rangle$	The sender has a candidate correspondence between e and e'; if i) the two entities are believed to be a *lexically viable* match; and ii) if the premise of the previously undisclosed argument A is considered *acceptable*; *i.e.* its aggregate similarity score is greater than or equal to the threshold ϵ_n.	Permissible moves: *accept* if the opponent accepts the correspondence in the claim given its own assessment of the support; or *justify* when the opponent rejects the support, and thus seeks additional or alternative evidence to support the claim.
$\langle x$, *justify*, $e, e'\rangle$	The sender x believes the opponent/proponent has undisclosed knowledge supporting the candidacy of $\langle e, e', \equiv\rangle$, and that a *lexically viable* match between e and e' exists, but does not have sufficient evidence to assert it.	The only permissible move is *testify*.
$\langle x$, *testify*, $e, e', \varphi\rangle$	The *testify* move is uttered in response to a *justify* move requesting evidence to support the candidacy of some correspondence between e and e' which is believed to be a *lexically viable* match.	The value of φ will be a new triple supporting $\langle e, e', \equiv\rangle$ (if this exists), otherwise no triple (i.e. $\varnothing$) will be returned. The triple is added to the recipient's (Γ). Permissible moves: *justify*, *assert* or *reject*
$\langle x$, *accept*, $e, e', A\rangle$	The sender x believes a candidate correspondence $\langle e, e', \equiv\rangle$ is *lexically viable* and there is sufficient evidence to support it. The argument A is the one appearing in the previous move (which should be an *assert* move).	Once the move has been made, the argument is added to the commitment store. The only move that is permissible following a *accept* move is an *initiate* move, whereby a new source entity is considered.
$\langle x$, *reject*, $e, e'\rangle$	Although x believes that there could be a *lexically viable* match between the two entities e and e', it does not have sufficient evidence to assert a correspondence; and it no longer believes the other agent has undisclosed knowledge that could support its candidacy.	Permissible moves: If x is the opponent, the proponent can either *assert* an alternate argument for the correspondence, or seek further evidence using *justify*. If x is the proponent, it can utter *propose* if another entity could match e, or *fail* if it is no longer possible to find a correspondence for e.
$\langle x$, *fail*, e, nil$\rangle$	Sender x can't find a undisclosed target entity e' in its ontology that is a *lexically viable* match for e. Thus no possible match for e could be found.	The only move that is permissible following a *fail* move is an *initiate* move, whereby a new source entity is considered.

municate. We assume they use the same metric, σ_n, to assess the similarity of the neighbourhood of a concept, expressed in terms of triples, and the same lexical[1] similarity σ_l. Agents generate a pre-ordering of properties for each concept e, using some private function rank(). Each agent attempts to identify a *premise*, Pr, which consists of pairs of triples believed to be structurally similar. A neighbourhood similarity metric $\sigma_n(Pr)$ was chosen that calculates the average structural similarity $\bar{\sigma}_s$ of the triple pairs in some premise Pr, with a coefficient increasing asymptotically as the cardinality of Pr increases; i.e. $\sigma_n(Pr) = \bar{\sigma}_s \times (1 - \frac{1}{2(|Pr|+1)})$. We assume a neighbourhood threshold $\epsilon_n = 0.55$ and a lexical threshold $\epsilon_l = 0.75$. This example dialogue is presented in (Fig. 1).

Move 1: *Alice* utters an *initiate* move stating she wants to discuss a possible match for concept d. **Move 2:** *Bob* agrees to cooperate by identifying w as the most (lexically) similar concept to d in his ontology, with a lexical similarity $\sigma_l^{Bob}(\text{“}d\text{”}, \text{“}w\text{”}) = 0.82$, which is above threshold ϵ_l. He therefore responds with $\langle Bob$, *propose*, “d”, “w”$\rangle$. **Move 3:** *Alice* now knows that $\langle d, w, \equiv\rangle$ is a potential correspondence c (based on *Bob's* lexical similarity claim). She checks that the lexical similarity is above threshold ($\sigma_l^{Alice}(d, w) = 0.79$), and asks *Bob* to justify the candidacy of c. So far, no agents has support for c; i.e. $Pr = \varnothing$. **Move 4:** *Bob* determines the next property with w as the subject that has not yet been disclosed, and thus is not in the CS. As his ranking for w is $\text{rank}^{Bob}(w) = \{t, r, s\}$, *Bob* shares the highest ranked property t relating w to y. **Move 5:** *Alice* determines if there is sufficient support for c. She realises that $\langle d, l, g\rangle$ is the most similar triple she has to the one *Bob* disclosed in move 4, where $\sigma_s^{Alice} = 0.66$. She calculates that the premise $Pr = \{(\langle d, l, g\rangle, \langle w, t, y\rangle)\}$ has a neighbourhood similarity $\epsilon_n = 0.495$. She will only *assert* an argument for c if this is above the threshold $\epsilon_n = 0.55$. However, as this not the case, she requests additional evidence to justify c.

Move 6: *Bob's* next highest undisclosed property with the subject w is r, and so he shares $\langle w, r, z\rangle$. **Move 7:** *Alice* checks to see if she has a similar triple to this; and finds two candidates. She selects $\langle d, k, e\rangle$ as the similarity is higher than $\langle d, n, h\rangle$. She adds this to Pr and calculates the neighbourhood similarity which is $\sigma_n^{Alice} = 0.5\dot{6}$, which (from *Alice's* perspective) is above threshold. She therefore *asserts* the correspondence $c = \langle d, w, \equiv\rangle$, given the premise $Pr = \{(\langle d, l, g\rangle, \langle w, t, y\rangle), (\langle d, k, e\rangle, \langle w, r, z\rangle)\}$.

Move 8: *Bob* can either *accept* this premise if $\sigma_n^{Bob}(Pr)$ is above threshold or request further evidence for c. He calculates the neighbourhood similarity (from his perspective), and finds that $\sigma_n^{Bob} = 0.5\dot{3}$, which is below threshold. *Bob* is also aware other triples for the concept w that do not appear in Pr, and asks *Alice* for further evidence. **Move 9:** *Alice* shares $\langle d, m, f\rangle$ as m is her highest ranked, non-disclosed property for the domain concept d (property k was ranked higher but has already been disclosed). **Move 10:** *Bob* recalculates the mean similarity for the new support (inclusive of the triple shared in Move 9): $\sigma_n^{Bob} = 0.551$, now above threshold, *Bob* accepts the candidacy of c. He can now *assert* the new argument for c given the new premise Pr. **Move 11:** *Alice* confirms from her perspective, $\sigma_n^{Alice} = 0.59$, which is also above threshold, and accepts the candidacy of the correspondence $\langle d, w, \equiv\rangle$.

4. CONCLUSIONS

We present our initial work on a dialogue based mechanism that allows agents to reach an agreement in a decentralised fashion over a correspondence between two entities in their respective ontologies, without having any prior information over the ontological structures that the agents commit to. This work is part of an ongoing effort over a larger dialogical framework that identifies a number of (potentially synergistic) correspondences between two ontologies, thus dynamically forming agreement on an alignment.

REFERENCES

[1] S. Bailin and W. Truszkowski. Ontology negotiation: How agents can really get to know each other. In *Innovative Concepts for Agent-Based Systems*, pages 320–334. 2003.

[2] E. Jiménez-Ruiz, T. R. Payne, A. Solimando, and V. Tamma. Limiting logical violations in ontology alignment through negotiation. In *Proc. KR'16*, 2016.

[3] D. Walton and E. Krabbe. *Commitment in Dialogue: Basic Concepts of Interpersonal Reasoning*. SUNY series in Logic and Language. State University of New York Press, 1995.

[1]The metrics σ_n and σ_l may exploit lexical similarity of labels for concepts and roles, but are not defined here. In addition, the concept and role names have replaced by single character identifiers.

How is Cooperation/collusion Sustained in Repeated Multimarket Contact with Observation Errors?

(Extended Abstract)

Atsushi Iwasaki[1], Tadashi Sekiguchi[2], Shun Yamamoto[3], and Makoto Yokoo[3]
[1]University of Electro-Communications, Tokyo 182-8585, Japan, iwasaki@is.uec.ac.jp
[2]Kyoto University, Kyoto 606-8501, Japan, sekiguchi@kier.kyoto-u.ac.jp
[3]Kyushu University, Fukuoka 819-0395, Japan, {syamamoto@agent., yokoo@}inf.kyushu-u.ac.jp

ABSTRACT

This paper analyzes repeated multimarket contact with observation errors where two players operate in multiple markets simultaneously. Multimarket contact has received much attention in economics, management, and so on. Despite vast empirical studies that examine whether multimarket contact fosters cooperation or collusion, little is theoretically known as to how players behave in an equilibrium when each player receives a noisy and different observation or signal indicating other firms' actions (*private* monitoring). To the best of our knowledge, we are the first to construct a strategy designed for multiple markets whose per-market equilibrium payoffs exceed one for a single market, in our setting. We first construct an entirely novel strategy whose behavior is specified by a non-linear function of the signal configurations. We then show that the per-market equilibrium payoff improves when the number of markets is sufficiently large.

Keywords

Game theory, repeated games, belief-free equilibrium

1. INTRODUCTION

This paper analyzes repeated multimarket contact with observation errors where two players operate in multiple markets simultaneously, e.g., [1]. A firm, e.g., Uber, provides its taxi service in multiple distinct markets (areas) and determines its price or allocation in each area, facing an oligopolistic competition, which is often modeled as a prisoners' dilemma (PD). To improve profits, it is inevitably helpful to realize how the firm's rival should behave in an equilibrium. However, despite vast empirical studies that have examined whether multimarket contact fosters cooperation or collusion, little is theoretically known as to how players behave in an equilibrium when each player receives a noisy observation or signal of other firms' actions.

This paper considers a realistic noisy situation where players do not share common information on each other's past history, i.e., *private* monitoring where each player may observe a different signal. For example, although a firm cannot directly observe its rival's action, e.g., prices, it can observe a noisy signal, e.g., its own sales amounts. Analytical studies on this class of games have not been very successful.

To the best of our knowledge, we are the first to construct a strategy designed for multiple markets whose per-market equilibrium payoffs exceed one for a single market. We construct an entirely novel strategy whose behavior is specified by a nonlinear function of the signal configurations.

2. MODEL

Two players play M PDs simultaneously in each period. In each PD, each player chooses either C (cooperation) or D (defection). The players can choose different actions over the M PDs, so that each player's action set in each period is $\{C, D\}^M$. In each PD, each player receives either a good signal g or a bad signal b. The pair of signals they privately receive in each PD follows a common symmetric probability distribution that depends entirely on the action pair of that PD. We denote it by $o(\omega_1, \omega_2|a_1, a_2)$, where $(\omega_1, \omega_2) \in \{g, b\}^2$ and $(a_1, a_2) \in \{C, D\}^2$. Since the signal distributions are described by one parameter, there exists $p \in (1/2, 1)$ such that for any i, (ω_1, ω_2), and (a_1, a_2),

$$\sum_{\omega_i \in \{g,b\}} o(\omega_i, \omega_j|a) = \begin{cases} p & \text{if } (a_i, \omega_j) \in \{(C, g), (D, b)\}, \\ 1-p & \text{otherwise.} \end{cases}$$

In each PD, player i's payoff depends only on his action and the signal of that PD. The payoff function is common to all PDs, denoted by $\pi_i(a_i, \omega_i)$. We are more interested in the expected payoff function

$$g_i(a_1, a_2) = \sum_{(\omega_1,\omega_2)} \pi_i(a_i, \omega_i) o(\omega_1, \omega_2|a_1, a_2).$$

Their expected payoff functions are represented by the following payoff matrix:

	C	D
C	$1, 1$	$-y, 1+x$
D	$1+x, -y$	$0, 0$

We assume $x > 0$, $y > 0$ and $1 > x - y$, so that it indeed represents a PD.

All M PDs are played infinitely, in periods $t = 0, 1, 2, \ldots$. Player i's *private history* at the beginning of period $t \geq 1$ is an element of $H_i^t \equiv \left[\{C, D\}^M \times \{g, b\}^M\right]^t$. Let H_i^0 be an arbitrary singleton, and let $H_i = \cup_{t \geq 0} H_i^t$ be the set of player i's all private histories. Player i's strategy of this repeated game is a mapping from H_i to the set of all probability distributions over $\{C, D\}^M$. If the actual play of the repeated game is such that the action pair $\left(a_1^m(t), a_2^m(t)\right)$ is

Appears in: *Proceedings of the 15th International Conference on Autonomous Agents and Multiagent Systems (AAMAS 2016), J. Thangarajah, K. Tuyls, C. Jonker, S. Marsella (eds.), May 9–13, 2016, Singapore.*

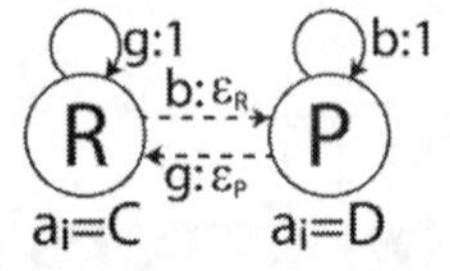

Figure 1: EV strategy

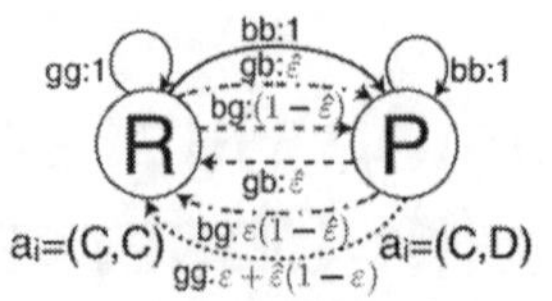

Figure 2: NTPD strategy

played in the m-th PD in period t for each m and t, player i's normalized average payoff is

$$(1-\delta)\sum_{t=0}^{\infty}\delta^t\sum_{m=1}^{M}g_i\left(a_1^m(t),a_2^m(t)\right),$$

where $\delta\in(0,1)$ is their common discount factor. Let us herein focus on *belief-free equilibria*, which is a subclass of a *sequential equilibrium* [2]. A strategy pair is a belief-free equilibrium if for any $t\geq 0$, $h_1^t\in H_1^t$ and $h_2^t\in H_2^t$, each player i's continuation strategy given h_i^t is optimal against player j's continuation strategy given h_j^t.

Among belief-free equilibria, a benchmark strategy, which we call EV, is found by Ely and Välimäki [3] and is depicted in Figure 1. It is parameterized by two numbers, $\varepsilon_R\in[0,1]$ and $\varepsilon_P\in[0,1]$. A player first cooperates at state R, but after observing a bad signal, she defects at the next period with probability ϵ_R, or keep cooperation with $1-\epsilon_R$. Likewise, after she defects at P, if she observes a good signal, she returns cooperation with ϵ_P, or keep defection with $1-\epsilon_P$. They identify a sufficient condition for the existence of ε_R and ε_P in an equilibrium and derive the average payoff starting from state R is $V_R=1-\frac{(1-p)x}{2p-1}$.

3. NONLINEAR TRANSITION, PARTIAL DEFECTION STRATEGY

Let us introduce a novel class of strategies, which we call the *nonlinear transition, partial defection* (NTPD) strategy.

DEFINITION 1 (NTPD STRATEGY). *Given M PDs, an NTPD strategy for $M(\geq 2)$ PDs is a two-state automaton strategy, parameterized by an integer M_A such that $1\leq M_A<M$ and two numbers $\varepsilon\in[0,1]$ and $\hat{\varepsilon}\in[0,1]$. Let $A=\{1,2,\ldots,M_A\}$ and $B=\{M_A+1,M_A+2,\ldots,M\}$.*

- *The state space is $\{R,P\}$, and R is the initial state.*
- *At state R, the player is prescribed to choose C in all PDs. At state P, she is prescribed to choose C in all PDs in A and D in all PDs in B.*
- *Suppose the current state is R and k is an integer between 0 and $M_B=M-M_A$. Then*
  1. *if b is observed among **all PDs in A** and there are k bad signals among the PDs in B, then the state shifts to P with probability $1-(M_B-k)\hat{\varepsilon}$ (and stays at R with the remaining probability).*
  2. *if g is observed among **some PD in A** and there are k bad signals among the PDs in B, then the state shifts to P with probability $k\hat{\varepsilon}$ (and stays R with the remaining probability).*
- *Suppose the current state is P and k is an integer between 0 and M_A. Then*
  1. *if g is observed among **all PDs in B** and there are k bad signals among the PDs in A, then the state shifts to R with probability $\varepsilon+\hat{\varepsilon}\{(1-\varepsilon)M_A-k\}$ (and stays P with the remaining probability).*
  2. *if b is observed among **some PD in B** and there are k bad signals among the PDs in A, then the state shifts to R with probability $(M_A-k)\hat{\varepsilon}$ (and stays P with the remaining probability).*

Figure 2 illustrates NTPD for two PDs. A player cooperates in all PDs in A at state P. Then, she always cooperates in all PDs in A whichever state she is in. For example, the transition probabilities from P to R are specified as follows. Their increase is constant for the number of bad signals from PDs in B. If she observes at least one bad signal from B, it is zero, otherwise, $\varepsilon-\hat{\varepsilon}\varepsilon M_A$. The transition probabilities decrease by $\hat{\varepsilon}$ in the number of bad signals k in A. For k bad signals from A, the transition probability from P to R is specified as $(M_A-k)\hat{\varepsilon}$ if she observes some b in B, or $\varepsilon+\hat{\varepsilon}\{(1-\varepsilon)M_A-k\}$ otherwise. We here mix $1-k\hat{\varepsilon}$ with $(M_A-k)\hat{\varepsilon}$ by the last parameter ε.

THEOREM 1 (NTPD FOR M PDS). *There exist ε and $\hat{\varepsilon}$ such that the NTPD strategy pair is a belief-free equilibrium if*

$$\delta\Big[x(1-s^{M_A})+s^{M_A-1}\Big\{M_B(p-s)-x(M_A-M_B)p-\frac{s^{M_B}(p-s)M_By}{p^{M_B}-s^{M_B}}\Big\}\Big]\geq x(1+s^{M_A-1}M_B)\ \text{and}$$

$$\delta\Big[(p^{M_B}-s^{M_B})\{M_B(p-s)+(M_A-M_B)x(s-s^{M_A})\}+M_By(p-s)(1-s^{M_A}-s^{M_B})\Big]$$

$$\geq M_Ax(p^{M_B}-s^{M_B})+M_By(p-s)$$

hold. The average payoff starting from R is

$$V_R=M-\frac{\delta s^{M_A}(p-s)(M-V_P)+(1-\delta)(s-s^{M_A})M_Bx}{(p-s)\{1-\delta(1-s^{M_A})\}},$$

where $V_P=M_A+\frac{pM_Ax}{p-s}+\frac{s^{M_B}M_By}{p^{M_B}-s^{M_B}}$.

We herein refer to $1-p$ as s for simplicity. Then, let us show that, if the numbers of PDs are sufficiently large, NTPD achieves a greater payoff than EV.

COROLLARY 1. *Fix x, y, and p. Suppose both M_A and M_B are sufficiently large and satisfy*

$$M_Apx-(M_B-1)\{2p-1-(1-p)x\}\geq(1-p)y.$$

Then if NTPD is an equilibrium for sufficiently large δ, EV is equilibrium, but its payoff is smaller than that of NTPD.

In addition, our numerical analysis supports this result with a given discount factor ($\delta<1$) and suggests that the transition probabilities to specify the behavior can still be improved. In future work, we would like to improve NTPD and to characterize an optimal equilibrium strategy class.

Acknowledgments

This research was partially supported by KAKENHI 24220003 and 26280081.

REFERENCES

[1] B. D. Bernheim and M. D. Whinston. Multimarket Contact and Collusive Behavior . *RAND Journal of Economics*, 21(1):1–26, 1990.

[2] J. C. Ely, J. Horner, and W. Olszewski. Belief-free equilibria in repeated games. *Econometrica*, 73(2):377–415, 2005.

[3] J. C. Ely and J. Välimäki. A robust folk theorem for the prisoner's dilemma. *Journal of Economic Theory*, 102(1):84–105, 2002.

Structural Control in Weighted Voting Games*

Anja Rey and Jörg Rothe
Heinrich-Heine-Universität Düsseldorf
40225 Düsseldorf, Germany
{rey, rothe}@cs.uni-duesseldorf.de

ABSTRACT

Inspired by the study of control scenarios in elections and complementing manipulation and bribery settings in cooperative games with transferable utility, we introduce the notion of structural control in weighted voting games. We model two types of influence, adding players to and deleting players from a game, with goals such as increasing a given player's Shapley–Shubik power index in relation to the original game. We study the complexity of the problems of whether such structural changes can achieve the desired effect.

Keywords

Game theory; computational social choice; computational complexity; structural control

1. INTRODUCTION

A major task in computational social choice is the complexity analysis of the question of whether a certain form of influence (such as manipulation, bribery, and control) is possible in an election under some voting rule (see, e.g., [11, 2]). Whenever successful manipulative actions are generally possible, a high computational complexity may provide some protection against them. Similar ideas have been adapted to other fields, such as judgment aggregation (again, see, e.g., [11, 2]). In algorithmic game theory, the question of influencing the outcome of a game has also been studied extensively. For example, the complexity of manipulation by merging, splitting, and annexation has been studied in weighted voting games (WVGs) [1, 6, 9], as well as manipulation of the quota [13]. In dynamic WVGs [5], the quota changes dynamically over time. Bribery has been studied for path-disruption games [10].

Inspired by the notion of control in elections, we consider control scenarios in WVGs. We define the problems of whether it is possible to change the structure of a game by either *adding* or *deleting* players so as to achieve certain goals. One could, for instance, think of a committee able to decide upon an issue with a certain quota of votes. In order to increase the significance of some participant, an organizer might invite further participants or choose a meeting schedule to make sure that others are excluded. Structural changes could also be viewed as a change of participation over time without malicious intentions. Goals include *increasing* and *decreasing* a distinguished player's power in relation to the original game. Moreover, if an *exact* number of players is to be added, it might be desirable to *maintain* an original player's power index. All defined control types are possible in WVGs, we therefore analyze the complexity of whether structural control can be successful in a given game. The complexity depends on the control type, the goal, and on whether the number of players that can be added or deleted is fixed or given in the problem instance.

2. PRELIMINARIES

A simple game $\mathcal{G} = (N, v)$ can be compactly represented as a *weighted voting game* $\mathcal{G} = (w_1, \dots, w_n; q)$, where w_i is player i's *weight*, q is a *quota*, and a coalition $C \subseteq N$ *wins* if $\sum_{i \in C} w_i \geq q$ and otherwise it *loses*. To measure player i's significance in $\mathcal{G}$, power indices such as the *probabilistic Penrose–Banzhaf index (PBI)* [4] and the *Shapley–Shubik index (SSI)* [12] can be used:

$$\mathrm{PBI}(\mathcal{G}, i) = 2^{1-n} \sum_{C \subseteq N \smallsetminus \{i\}} (v(C \cup \{i\}) - v(C)) \text{ and}$$

$$\mathrm{SSI}(\mathcal{G}, i) = \frac{1}{n!} \sum_{C \subseteq N \smallsetminus \{i\}} \|C\|!(n-1-\|C\|)(v(C \cup \{i\}) - v(C)).$$

For more background on cooperative game theory, see, e.g., [3]. We use the standard notions of *hardness* and *completeness* for a complexity class (e.g., NP or coNP) with respect to *many-one polynomial-time reducibility*. #P is the class of all functions that give the number of solutions of a problem in NP. Probabilistic polynomial time, PP, is the class of all decision problems X for which there exist a function $f \in \#\mathrm{P}$ and a polynomial p such that for all instances x, $x \in X \iff f(x) \geq 2^{p(|x|)-1}$. It is considered to be a rather large complexity class, since it is known that $\mathrm{PH} \subseteq \mathrm{P}^{\mathrm{PP}}$.

3. CONTROL TYPES AND GOALS

We define control by adding and by deleting players in WVGs. For each control type, we consider goals, such as increasing or decreasing a distinguished player's power, in relation to the original game. We first define how adding and deleting a player affects the coalitional function for WVGs: For control by adding players, from a given WVG $\mathcal{G} = (w_1, \dots, w_n; q)$ with $N = \{1, \dots, n\}$ and a set $M = \{n+1, \dots, n+m\}$ of m unregistered players with weights $w_{n+1}, \dots, w_{n+m}$, we obtain a new game $\mathcal{G}_{\cup M} = (w_1, \dots, w_{n+m}; q)$. For example, for control by adding players to increase a power index PI we ask: Given a WVG $\mathcal{G}$, a set M of unregistered players with weights $w_{n+1}, \dots, w_{n+m}$, a distinguished player p, $1 \leq p \leq n$, and a positive integer k, can at most k players $M' \subseteq M$ be added to $\mathcal{G}$ such that for the new game $\mathcal{G}_{\cup M'}$ it holds that $\mathrm{PI}(\mathcal{G}_{\cup M'}, p) > \mathrm{PI}(\mathcal{G}, p)$? Analogously, we can ask whether the game can be controlled so as to decrease a certain player's index; or whether it is possible to add players to a game without changing the distribution of power among the original players. Deleting a subset

*This work was supported in part by DFG grant RO-1202/14-2.

Appears in: *Proceedings of the 15th International Conference on Autonomous Agents and Multiagent Systems (AAMAS 2016), J. Thangarajah, K. Tuyls, S. Marsella, C. Jonker (eds.), May 9–13, 2016, Singapore.*

$M \subseteq N$ of m players from a WVG $\mathcal{G} = (w_1, \ldots, w_n; q)$ yields a WVG $\mathcal{G}_{\setminus M} = (w_{j_1}, \ldots, w_{j_{n-m}}; q)$ with $\{j_1, \ldots, j_{n-m}\} = N \setminus M$. We ask whether at most k players $M' \subseteq N \setminus \{p\}$ can be deleted from $\mathcal{G}$ to reach some goal for p. If a player i is deleted from a WVG, any other player j gains the same amount of power that i would gain if j were deleted [7]. After deleting a subset $M \subseteq N \setminus \{i\}$ of size $m \geq 1$ from a WVG $\mathcal{G}$, player i's PBI changes by at most $1 - 2^{-m}$ and by at least $-1 + 2^{-m}$; her SSI changes by at most $1 - {}^{(n-m+1)!}/_{2n!}$ and by at least $-1 + {}^{(n-m-1)!}/_{2(n-2)!}$.

4. IN- AND DECREASING AN INDEX

Similarly to control by adding or deleting voters or candidates in elections, adding and deleting players are not merely inverse operations, as when adding players all original players are guaranteed to be part of the game before and after the structural change, whereas when deleting players each player except the distinguished one can be removed from the game. Hardness in terms of complexity can be seen as a shield to prevent a game from being controlled to improve or worsen a player's significance.

4.1 Control by Adding Players

We show PP-hardness via techniques inspired by related work [9, 6, 13]: For a #P-parsimonious-complete function F, COMPARE-$F = \{(x,y) \mid F(x) > F(y)\}$ is PP-complete. In this manner, COMPARE-#SUBSETSUM is PP-complete. We reduce from a PP-hard restricted variant of this problem, COMPARE-#SUBSETSUM-RR: Given a set $A = \{1, \ldots, n\}$ and a function $a : A \to \mathbb{N} \setminus \{0\}$, $i \mapsto a_i$, with $\alpha = \sum_{i=1}^{n} a_i$, is the number of subsets of A with values that sum up to $(\alpha/2) - 2$ greater than the number of those summing up to $(\alpha/2) - 1$? The results can be adapted to the SSI by means of a transformation from X3C allowing constant solution sizes.

THEOREM 1. *Control by adding a given number of players in order to increase (decrease) a player's PBI or SSI is* PP-*hard.*

An upper bound of $\mathrm{NP}^{\mathrm{PP}}$ can be established whenever the number of players to be added is given. If the number of players to be added is fixed, we even obtain a PP upper bound.

THEOREM 2. *Control by adding a fixed number of players in order to increase (decrease) a player's PBI or SSI is* PP-*complete.*

4.2 Control by Deleting Players

We have the following two initial results.

THEOREM 3. *1. Control by deleting players to increase a player's SSI is* NP-*hard (even if only one player is deleted).*

2. Control by deleting players to decrease a player's PBI is coNP-*hard (even if only one player is deleted).*

NP-hardness holds by a reduction from SUBSETSUM with constant solution sizes. Our coNP-hardness result can be shown by a reduction from the complement of PARTITION.

5. MAINTAINING AN INDEX

In addition to constructive or destructive goals, we now consider situations with the goal of maintaining a player's index when an exact number of players is added. It may, for instance, happen that legislative bodies such as the EU Commission, national parliaments, or the United Nations Security Council, have to be expanded by adding a certain number of new members. Then, an old member may be interested in maintaining power. This goal is not only differently motivated but also different in its algorithmic nature. Note that here we require an *exact* (fixed or given) number of players to be added to or deleted from the game to avoid the trivial case of adding or deleting none of *at most* a number of players. While PP-hardness is also valid for control by adding a given number of players to maintain a player's PBI or SSI, PP-hardness for a fixed number of players to be added cannot immediately be deduced. However, we have a PP upper bound in this case (as PP is closed under complement) and a coNP-hardness lower bound.

THEOREM 4. *1. Control by adding a fixed number of players to maintain a player's PBI or SSI is* coNP-*hard and in* PP.

2. Control by deleting players in order to maintain a player's PBI is coNP-*hard (even if only one player can be deleted).*

6. CONCLUSIONS AND FUTURE WORK

The complexity of some control problems is left open; interesting gaps remain, e.g., between NP-hardness and PP as well as PP-hardness and $\mathrm{NP}^{\mathrm{PP}}$. So far we have studied goals in *relation to the original game*. Alternatively, one might think of a situation where the goal is to increase a player's power in *comparison to the other players*; or where a player is required to exceed a certain *constant index*. We might also study obtaining an exact value. There may be different ways to reasonably model the new game, e.g., similar to weighted majority games, where players do not make an absolute but a relative contribution to the game. Studying a change of players dynamically over time is an interesting task for future work.

There seems to be a close connection to the notion of *synergies* in cooperative games (see, e.g., [8]), and it will be interesting to have a closer look at related results here. Other classes of games might also be affected by control scenarios.

REFERENCES

[1] H. Aziz, Y. Bachrach, E. Elkind, and M. Paterson. False-name manipulations in weighted voting games. *Journal of Artificial Intelligence Research*, 40:57–93, 2011.

[2] F. Brandt, V. Conitzer, U. Endriss, J. Lang, and A. Procaccia, editors. *Handbook of Computational Social Choice*. Cambridge University Press, 2016. To appear.

[3] G. Chalkiadakis, E. Elkind, and M. Wooldridge. *Computational Aspects of Cooperative Game Theory*. Morgan & Claypool, 2011.

[4] P. Dubey and L. Shapley. Mathematical properties of the Banzhaf power index. *Mathematics of Operations Research*, 4(2):99–131, 1979.

[5] E. Elkind, D. Pasechnik, and Y. Zick. Dynamic weighted voting games. In *Proc. AAMAS'13*, pages 515–522. IFAAMAS, 2013.

[6] P. Faliszewski and L. Hemaspaandra. The complexity of power-index comparison. *Theoretical Computer Science*, 410(1):101–107, 2009.

[7] R. Myerson. Conference structures and fair allocation rules. *International Journal of Game Theory*, 9(3):169–182, 1980.

[8] T. Rahwan, T. Michalak, and M. Wooldridge. A measure of synergy in coalitions. Technical Report arXiv:1404.2954.v1 [cs.GT], CoRR, Apr. 2014.

[9] A. Rey and J. Rothe. False-name manipulation in weighted voting games is hard for probabilistic polynomial time. *Journal of Artificial Intelligence Research*, 50:573–601, 2014.

[10] A. Rey, J. Rothe, and A. Marple. Path-disruption games: Bribery and a probabilistic model. *Theory of Computing Systems*. To appear.

[11] J. Rothe, editor. *Economics and Computation. An Introduction to Algorithmic Game Theory, Computational Social Choice, and Fair Division*. Springer-Verlag, 2015.

[12] L. Shapley and M. Shubik. A method of evaluating the distribution of power in a committee system. *American Political Science Review*, 48(3):787–792, 1954.

[13] M. Zuckerman, P. Faliszewski, Y. Bachrach, and E. Elkind. Manipulating the quota in weighted voting games. *Artificial Intelligence*, 180–181:1–19, 2012.

Robots Reasoning with Cuts and Connections: Creating and Removing Entities

(Extended Abstract)

Mihai Pomarlan and Michael Beetz
{blandc, beetz}@cs.uni-bremen.de *

ABSTRACT

Several tasks that autonomous service robots will be expected to do involve changing material objects by cutting or separating parts, then rearranging them to obtain assemblages satisfying certain properties. In this paper we describe a system to represent and reason about entities that disappear or are created by the robot through such actions. Entities are grounded in objects that the robot can perceive and manipulate, and reasoning provides specific parameters for the robot's actions. For this paper, our system has knowledge only of geometric aspects related to cutting and rearrangement of objects. We test our system in simulation, but also discuss how it can be connected to a robot's perception and control.

General Terms

Algorithms, Languages, Theory

Keywords

Reasoning in agent-based systems; Robot planning (including action selection, motion and path planning and manipulation); Robotic agent languages, middleware and formal methods for robot systems

1. MOTIVATION

As robotic agents become more capable the range of manipulation tasks they are to perform becomes also more varied. Consider robots intended for household tasks; they will have to tackle actions such as wiping, cutting, spreading, and scooping. Also, objects often have to be rearranged in ways that satisfy given constraints, which the robot should be able to represent and reason about.

Performing such actions competently requires physics and geometric reasoning to capture their continuous effects on the material objects around the robot. There is also the problem of making the respective knowledge actionable; the robots have to choose the positions where to scoop from, the trajectory of end effectors etc.

In contrast to robot control, most action representations used for agent control are inspired by the STRIPS formalism. Many variations exist, including probabilistic STRIPS and STRIPS with resources, but their common limitation for robot control is the treatment of action as a black box, which doesn't express the causal relation between *how an action is executed* and *what effects it causes*.

*The authors are with the Institute for Artificial Intelligence, Universität Bremen, Am Fallturm 1, 28359 Bremen, Germany.

Appears in: *Proceedings of the 15th International Conference on Autonomous Agents and Multiagent Systems (AAMAS 2016), J. Thangarajah, K. Tuyls, C. Jonker, S. Marsella (eds.), May 9–13, 2016, Singapore.*

Figure 1: Robot preparing to cut out a crustless slice of pizza.

Here, we investigate representation and reasoning mechanisms to enable robotic agents to plan and execute cutting actions. Consider a robot with a collection of pizzas with assorted toppings sprinkled unevenly on their surfaces, and a set of customers, each with their own preferences for toppings. The robot must cut out slices, then regroup slices onto plates; there are constraints on how slices can be arranged before delivery. Though seemingly contrived, this is a problem a human would tackle with ease, even if it contains various subproblems that are current and interesting for robotics. The robot needs to have a way to represent the pizzas and where the toppings are; it needs to cope with the fact that pizzas will be cut and slices rearranged– objects pop in and out of existence as a consequence of the robot's actions.

We show a system able to represent and reason about entities that disappear or are created by the robot. The reasoning tackles the sub-symbolic level as well, to give the robot specific descriptions of the actions needed to obtain a given outcome. Currently, our system only treats geometric aspects of cutting and rearrangement of objects, not physics. Our contributions are:

- (○) A world state representation with entities that can be destroyed or created by removing or adding parts
- (○) Managing the interaction between entities created by manipulating physical parts and entities asserted as task goals
- (○) A grammar for object arrangements, integrated into a planner
- (○) Integrated reasoning about cuts into a robot planning system
- (○) Grounding a fragment of common-sense reasoning into robot percepts and actions

We build and showcase our system around the pizza cutting and distributing scenario described above, but we argue that the lessons learned and concepts developed here improve a robot's competence in acting on the world, and the methods we provide can generalize beyond the specific showcase application. We work in simulation here, but with consideration of how to proceed on a real robot: what inputs our system needs from a robot's perception, and the procedures to clean up perception data. The output our system provides is usable by constraint-based controller similar to [1] to perform the motion on an actual robot.

2. OVERVIEW

Though our chosen problem domain is simple, it illustrates interesting robotics topics. First, our system must describe cutting out a part, and the connection types in its problem domain, from a logical level (asserting that a connection exists) down to spatial relations between physical objects.

Second, our system must capture structural constraints on arrangements and the implications of cutting actions. Our robot needs to know that pizzas can be cut into slices of a given shape, that slices cannot be put together into a pizza again, but that we do consider them an "Assembly" if they lie in a fan pattern on a plate.

Third, we need to track what entities exist in the robot's environment. Some entities are physical objects (for example slices), but it is convenient to consider arrangements of objects as being entities as well: for example, a fan of pizza slices, all lying on the same plate, are an "Assembly" that the robot can deliver to a customer.

Fourth, the problem of object identity after changes in form. For example, after cutting out the first slice, we still think of the resulting object as the same pizza. Another aspect of this problem is handling violations on structural constraints on arrangements. Removing the middle slice from an Assembly changes it into another arrangement type (in an Assembly, the slices should make up a fan).

Finally, the results of the robot's reasoning queries must produce action parameters: where to cut, where to put an object.

Fig. 2 shows a sketch of our system. A geometric level handles queries about obtaining trajectories for cutting, checking connection types between objects, obtaining object poses to establish a connection type. This level also defines some auxiliary annotations to assist in its reasoning. The mereotopologic layer handles queries about what cuts are necessary to separate parts out of physical objects, and about arrangements of physical objects and the structural constraints on them. It uses a spatial grammar to describe arrangements in terms of part and connection types. The task level receives the customer orders, and issues queries to the underlying levels in order to generate plans and actions for the robot.

The world state is described by the poses of the physical objects that the robot can perceive; these are the primitive entities. Further entities can be asserted by the task and mereotopological layers. The task layer asserts "ghost" entities that are needed to fulfill an order (they need not be initially associated to physical objects). The mereotopological layer asserts entities when physical objects are arranged in certain ways; to avoid proliferation, it only asserts an entity when it is maximal. Either layer can vote to remove an asserted entity when it is no longer needed (task layer) or no longer embodied in a collection of physical objects (mereotopological layer), but both must agree before removal occurs.

3. RELATED WORK

Learning control parameters for cuts, given a quality measure such as time taken, was tackled by [2]. Cut location, or deciding whether a cut is necessary, was not in the scope of that research.

Cutting as a "microworld" for common-sense reasoning appears in [3], which gives two formal theories for the cutting of solid objects. Formal theories of parthood and connection (mereotopology) are overviewed in [4], spatial grammars in [5]. We extend the previous work by insisting on action parameter production for a robot, and on spatial grammar parsing and its application to planning.

Our approach is related to general purpose common-sense reasoning, which includes reasoning about geometric and physical properties and interactions [6], and that formal methods applied to reasoning about assemblies have seen application for automatic generation of customizable furniture models [7].

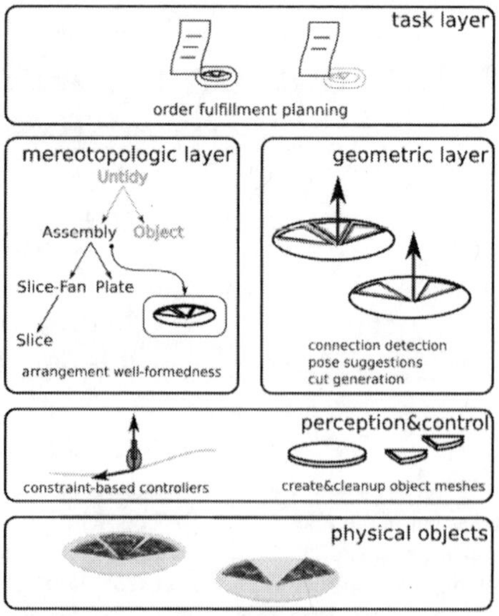

Figure 2: The layers of our system. The geometric layer annotates models of objects with information useful to analyze connections and suggest placements and cuts. The mereotopologic layer ensures arrangements of objects obey structural constraints. The task layer creates plans to fulfill customer orders and queries underlying levels.

4. CONCLUSION

We describe a robotic system able to reason about generating new parts out of materials it has at its disposal, and arrange those parts into assemblages that obey structural constraints.

Acknowledgements

This work is supported by the EU FP7 project *RoboHow* (Grant Agreement Number 288533).

REFERENCES

[1] G. Bartels, I. Kresse, and M. Beetz, "Constraint-based movement representation grounded in geometric features," in *Procs. of the IEEE-RAS Intern. Conference on Humanoid Robots*, October 2013.

[2] R. Lioutikov, O. Kroemer, J. Peters, and G. Maeda, "Learning manipulation by sequencing motor primitives with a two-armed robot," in *Procs. of the 13th Intern. Conference on Intelligent Autonomous Systems*, ser. Advances in Intelligent Systems and Computing, vol. 302. Springer, 2014.

[3] E. Davis, "The kinematics of cutting solid objects," *Ann. Math. Artif. Intell.*, vol. 9, no. 3-4, pp. 253–305, 1993.

[4] A. G. Cohn and J. Renz, "Qualitative spatial representation and reasoning," *Handbook of knowledge representation*, vol. 3, pp. 551–596, 2008.

[5] A. McKay, S. Chase, K. Shea, and H. H. Chau, "Spatial grammar implementation: From theory to useable software," *AI EDAM*, vol. 26, no. Special Issue 02, pp. 143–159, 2012.

[6] E. Davis and G. Marcus, "Commonsense reasoning and commonsense knowledge in artificial intelligence," *Commun. ACM*, vol. 58, no. 9, pp. 92–103, 2015.

[7] J. Shrivastava and M. Grüninger, "Developing an ontology for joints in furniture design," in *Formal Ontologies Meet Industry*, ser. Lecture Notes in Business Information Processing, R. Cuel and R. Young, Eds. Springer International Publishing, 2015, vol. 225, pp. 88–99.

Minimising the Rank Aggregation Error

(Extended Abstract)

Mathijs M. de Weerdt
Delft University of Technology, Netherlands
m.m.deweerdt@tudelft.nl

Enrico H. Gerding
University of Southampton, UK
eg@ecs.soton.ac.uk

Sebastian Stein
University of Southampton, UK
ss2@ecs.soton.ac.uk

ABSTRACT

Rank aggregation is the problem of generating an overall ranking from a set of individual votes which is as close as possible to the (unknown) correct ranking. The challenge is that votes are often both noisy and incomplete. Existing work focuses on the most likely ranking for a particular noise model. Instead, we focus on minimising the error, i.e., the expected distance between the aggregated ranking and the correct one. We show that this results in different rankings, and we show how to compute local improvements of rankings to reduce the error. Extensive experiments on both synthetic data based on Mallows' model and real data show that Copeland has a smaller error than the Kemeny rule, while the latter is the maximum likelihood estimator.

Keywords

Economic paradigms: Social Choice Theory

1. INTRODUCTION

Marquis de Condorcet [6] said that voting or rank aggregation may be regarded as a way of uncovering the ground truth. There are many practical examples of rank aggregation, including websites that produce rankings of restaurants, books and movies based on crowdsourced contributions from their users, and scientific communities that use votes from their members to select which project proposals to fund or which papers to accept [2]. In these settings votes are not only noisy, but also incomplete since typically only a subset of the alternatives is ranked by any single individual.

To find a ranking close to the ground truth, most current work assumes a probabilistic noise model such as Mallows [4, 7], and then aims to find the aggregate ranking with the highest likelihood of being the true ranking. For Mallows' model, it has been shown that the Kemeny rule is the maximum likelihood estimator (MLE) [7]. However, in most settings the aim should be to find a ranking that gives the best results when used in subsequent decision making. When votes are noisy and incomplete, many rankings may have a likelihood of similar magnitude, and the probability of any of these being the true ranking is small. In addition, the likelihood does not account for the distance to the true ranking when the chosen ranking is not the true one. Therefore, we argue that, instead, the aim should be to minimise the *expected distance* of an aggregate ranking to the true ranking, which we term the *error*. In contrast to MLEs, to date, it is still unknown what voting rules perform best regarding this objective.

Appears in: *Proceedings of the 15th International Conference on Autonomous Agents and Multiagent Systems (AAMAS 2016), J. Thangarajah, K. Tuyls, C. Jonker, S. Marsella (eds.), May 9–13, 2016, Singapore.*

2. MODEL AND THEORETICAL RESULTS

Let $A = \{1, 2, \ldots, m\}$ denote a set of alternatives and $N = \{1, 2, \ldots, n\}$ the set of agents. We define a vote by agent k as a linear order over an $A_k \subseteq A$, denoted by $\sigma_k : A_k \to \{1, 2, \ldots, |A_k|\}$. Here, $\sigma_k(i)$ defines the rank of alternative i (lower is better). We also use $i \succ_{\sigma_k} j$ to denote $\sigma_k(i) < \sigma_k(j)$. Furthermore, we use D to denote the set of all votes.

The Kendall-tau distance K counts the pairs of alternatives that are differently ordered by σ than by τ.

$$K(\sigma, \tau) = |\{\{i, j\} \subseteq A : i \succ_\sigma j \text{ and } i \prec_\tau j\}| \quad (1)$$

We assume noise according to the well-known Mallows' model for a probability $p > 0.5$. Given this model, the likelihood of observing the votes D given that the true ranking is τ is given by:

$$\mathcal{L}(\tau|D) = \frac{1}{Z_1} \prod_{\{i,j\} \subseteq A : i \succ_\tau j} p^{n_a(i,j|D)}(1-p)^{n_d(i,j|D)}, \quad (2)$$

where Z_1 is a (normalisation) constant. It has been shown that the Kemeny rule — which minimises the sum of Kendall-tau distances to all votes — is an MLE [7]. We extend this model to incomplete rankings by introducing a probability q of missing an alternative:

$$\mathcal{L}'(\tau|D) = \mathcal{L}(\tau|D) \frac{1}{Z_2} \prod_{k \in N} (1-q)^{|\sigma_k|} q^{m-|\sigma_k|}. \quad (3)$$

It is easy to see that Kemeny optimal still maximises the likelihood, irrespective of the value of q.

Given a set of all rankings T, we define the *rank aggregation error* as the *expected Kendall-tau distance*, formally:

$$\text{KT-error}(\tau) = \sum_{\tau' \in T} K(\tau, \tau') \cdot \mathcal{L}'(\tau'|D). \quad (4)$$

The following example shows that minimising this error produces a single natural ranking, whereas multiple rankings maximise the likelihood.

EXAMPLE 1. *Let three alternatives a, b, c be given, and one agent with vote $a \succ_{\sigma_1} b$. The Kemeny rule is indifferent between the three possible aggregate rankings without noise. The expected Kendall-tau distances, however, differ:*

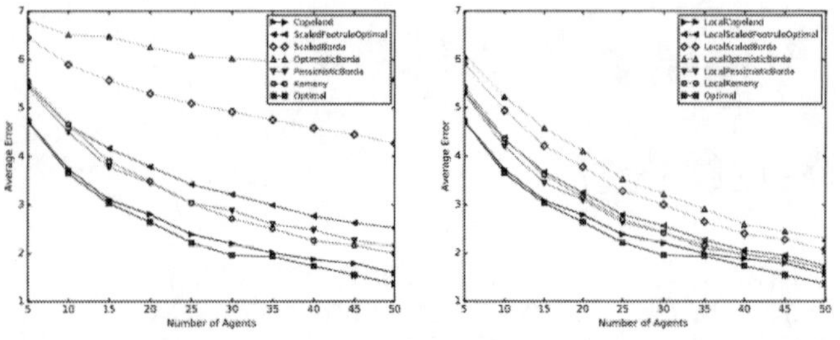

Figure 1: Results for synthetic data with $m = 6$, $p = \frac{2}{3}$ and $q = 0.7$. The right graph shows results after applying local Kemenisation (same for Figure 2).

τ_i	*ranking*	$\mathcal{L}(\tau_i \mid \{\sigma_1\})$	$K(\tau_i, \tau_j)$			*KT-error*(τ_i)
τ_1	$a \succ b \succ c$	$\frac{1}{3}$	0	1	2	1
τ_2	$a \succ c \succ b$	$\frac{1}{3}$	1	0	1	$\frac{2}{3}$
τ_3	$c \succ a \succ b$	$\frac{1}{3}$	2	1	0	1

Because the distance of $a \succ c \succ b$ to each of the other rankings is only 1, it has a lower expected error.

Similarly, we can construct examples with complete votes where the rankings maximising the likelihood do not minimise the KT-error.

Hardness. Finding the ranking with the largest likelihood (i.e., Kemeny) is NP-complete [3]. Towards establishing the computational complexity of finding an aggregate ranking with the minimum error, we can show that the problem of computing the error of a (single) aggregate ranking is #P-hard (even) when there is no noise in the data D.

THEOREM 1. *Even without noise, determining the expected error of an aggregate ranking π is #P-hard.*

The proof is by reduction from computing the number of linear extensions of a partial order, which is #P-complete [1].

Local Search. Although computing the error does not seem to be feasible, we can improve a ranking by making local adjustments. In particular, given a ranking τ, it is easy to determine if, by swapping two adjacent alternatives, we can improve the KT-error.

THEOREM 2. *Let τ_{ab} and τ_{ba} be two equal rankings except that two adjacent alternatives, a and b, are swapped. That is, $a \succ_{\tau_{ab}} b$ and $b \succ_{\tau_{ba}} a$. Then: KT-error$(\tau_{ab}) <$ KT-error(τ_{ba}) iff $n_a(a, b|D) > n_a(b, a|D)$.*

It turns out that repeatedly applying this rule until a local optimum is found has been termed local Kemenisation [2]. Our result adds that this is locally minimising the KT-error as well. Note that, although the proof assumes Mallows' model, it seems intuitive for *any* noise model to swap adjacent alternatives if one is ranked more often above the other.

3. EXPERIMENTAL RESULTS

We consider experiments using synthetic data, and real data from the Dots experiments (PrefLib library [5]). In Figures 1 and 2 we compare extensions of Spearman's Footrule (Scaled Footrule Optimal) and Borda for incomplete votes [2], Copeland, the Kemeny rule and an Optimal rule that minimises the KT-error assuming Mallows' model. As expected, having more agents decreases the average distance to the true ranking for all rules. We also observe that the Kemeny rule is indeed not optimal, with around 0.5 inversions more than Optimal on average. Interestingly, Copeland performs significantly better than Kemeny, and at times on par with Optimal. Even more striking is the significant improvement of most rules by local Kemenisation. Surprisingly, similar results hold for the Dots data set, despite the fact that this is not generated using Mallow's model.

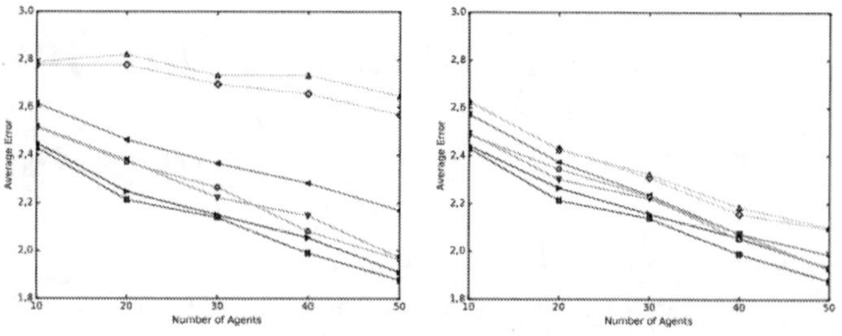

Figure 2: Results using the Dots dataset and $q = 0.7$

4. CONCLUSIONS

We have shown that voting rules which maximise the likelihood of a ranking do not necessarily minimise the expected distance to the true ranking. Specifically, for rank aggregation with noise and missing votes, maximising the likelihood can result in a significantly higher error than computationally simpler methods such as Copeland. This discrepancy can occur even when votes are complete. Furthermore, we have shown that Optimal performs best in both synthetic and real data settings, even when we do not know the noise parameter exactly. For Mallows' model we have shown that computing this error is hard. Furthermore, we proved that an efficient procedure called local Kemenisation, which is known to improve the likelihood, also reduces the error, and that this leads to a significant performance improvement.

Acknowledgments. This work has been partly supported by COST Action IC1205 on Computational Social Choice.

REFERENCES

[1] G. Brightwell and P. Winkler. Counting linear extensions is #P-complete. In *23rd ACM Symposium on Theory of Computation*, pages 175–181, 1991.

[2] C. Dwork, R. Kumar, M. Naor, and D. Sivakumar. Rank aggregation methods for the web. In *10th Int. Conf. on World Wide Web*, pages 613–622. ACM, 2001.

[3] E. Hemaspaandra, H. Spakowski, and J. Vogel. The complexity of Kemeny elections. *Theoretical Computer Science*, 349(3):382–391, 2005.

[4] C. L. Mallows. Non-null ranking models. I. *Biometrika*, pages 114–130, 1957.

[5] A. Mao, A. Procaccia, and Y. Chen. Better Human Computation Through Principled Voting. In *AAAI*, 2013.

[6] M. Nicolas de Condorcet. *Essai sur l'application de l'analyse à la probabilité des décisions rendues à la pluralité des voix.* L'imprimerie royale, 1785.

[7] P. Young. Optimal voting rules. *The Journal of Economic Perspectives*, 9(1):51–64, 1995.

Moving Target Defense for Web Applications using Bayesian Stackelberg Games

(Extended Abstract)

Satya Gautam Vadlamudi, Sailik Sengupta, Marthony Taguinod, Ziming Zhao, Adam Doupé, Gail-Joon Ahn, Subbarao Kambhampati
Department of Computer Science, Arizona State University
{gautam, sailik.sengupta, mtaguino, zmzhao, doupe, gahn, rao}@asu.edu

ABSTRACT

Vulnerabilities in web applications allow hackers to access and/or modify restricted data. Here the hackers have the opportunity to perform reconnaissance so as to gain knowledge about the web application layout before launching an attack, whereas the defender (administrator of the web application) must secure the application even with its potential vulnerabilities. In order to mask such vulnerabilities which are primarily associated with different individual configurations, Moving Target Defense systems were proposed wherein the defender switches between various configurations thereby making it difficult to attack with success, while maintaining a seamless experience for the genuine users. In this paper, we present a way to find effective switching strategies by modeling this ecosystem as a Bayesian Stackelberg game with the administrator as the leader and the hackers as the followers, which as we show succinctly captures various aspects of the Moving Target Defense systems. Furthermore, we propose ways to find the most critical vulnerabilities and the most sensitive attacker types, which are key issues in such scenarios.

Keywords

Cyber security; Web applications; Moving target defense; Bayesian Stackelberg games

1. INTRODUCTION

Web application vulnerabilities pose risks to the security and privacy of both businesses and users. Several techniques and tools based on static analysis (white-box) and dynamic analysis (black-box) have been proposed to discover the vulnerabilities in web applications, so that the vulnerabilities can be removed before the attackers discover and exploit them. However, such efforts are not enough due to the increasing complexity of modern web applications and the limited development and deployment time, whereas the attackers can perform reconnaissance and attack. To address these challenges, a Moving Target Defense (MTD) based approach was proposed in [2] to secure web applications, which complements the aforementioned vulnerability analysis techniques through a defense-in-depth mechanism.

Appears in: *Proceedings of the 15th International Conference on Autonomous Agents and Multiagent Systems (AAMAS 2016), J. Thangarajah, K. Tuyls, C. Jonker, S. Marsella (eds.), May 9–13, 2016, Singapore.*

The MTD based approach dynamically configures and shifts systems over time, at different layers of the web application stack, to increase the uncertainty and complexity for the attackers with their probing and attacking, while ensuring that the system is available for legitimate users.

In this paper, we focus on the design of effective policies for movement in the MTD system that maximize the resilience of the web application, given the set of components and configurations of the system which can be "moved around." We show that many of the features of this problem such as attacker reconnaissance and attacker type uncertainty can be captured effectively by modeling it as a Bayesian Stackelberg Game (BSG). Our main contributions are: 1) An effective way to model MTD as BSG, 2) Showcase how the modeling leads to finding better MTD policies, 3) A methodology to find most critical vulnerabilities, and 4) A methodology to find most sensitive attacker types. To the best of our knowledge, this is the first work that models Moving Target Defense as a Bayesian Stackelberg game. The full version of this extended abstract is available as a technical report [3].

2. MODELING MOVING TARGET DEFENSE AS BAYESIAN STACKELBERG GAME

A Stackelberg game consists of a leader who commits to a strategy first, and then a follower adopts a strategy which maximizes its own reward based on the leader's strategy. Here the leader has an advantage because she gets to make the first move (choose a strategy and commit), and therefore can restrict the moves of the follower in a sense. A Bayesian game contains a set of n agents ($n = 2$ in this case, leader and follower) where each agent i could be of any of the T_i types. Here, each agent i has a set of strategies available to it S_i and a reward/utility function $R_i : T_1 \times T_2 \times S_1 \times S_2 \rightarrow \mathbb{R}$. The objective then is to find an optimal mixed strategy for the leader to commit to (one which maximizes her rewards), given that the follower(s) may know that strategy when choosing their strategy.

The defender in MTD can be modeled as the leader in BSG, and the attacker- as the follower. Whereas the defender (web application) is of a single type, clearly the attacker could be of multiple types consistent with our formulation of Bayesian Stackelberg games above. Note that, the movements of the defender can be viewed as choosing strategies as follows: different moves in MTD would lead to different configurations at different layers (we call each set of valid configurations as a 'combination'). So, a move in

MTD from one particular combination to another combination could be modeled as a strategy in BSG. And, each of the attack options of the attacker in MTD could be viewed as a strategy for the follower in BSG. Note that, each attacker type in MTD has a set of attack options which may or may not be overlapping with other attacker types.

Whether a particular attacker type has access to a given attack option is dependent on (and hence formulated based on) the following criteria:

- The difficulty of carrying out the action/attack.
- The popularity of the target technology, as more popular implementations of services result in higher chance of exploits and wider array of available tools.

The choice of reward values for the defender and the attacker are guided by the following considerations:

- The effect of the action/attack on the target website. Note that, the "effect" here is dependent on the particular website, since a very complex and clever attack may sometimes only be able to uncover data which is less critical to the defender (website). Also, it is dependent on how much an attacker can leverage out of the data acquired. Therefore, the rewards here are based on both the defender (the criticality of various data/functionality) and the attacker type (ability to leverage the success of various attacks).
- Whether the attack leads to detection of the attacker, which may in-turn depend on aspects such as the number of exploits they target in each attack.

The uncertainty in the attacker types is captured by associating probabilities with each of them that serve as relative estimates of each of such attackers attacking the web application under consideration. Once the attacker types, the associated probabilities, their attack options, and the reward values for the defender and the attacker types are decided for each attack, an optimal mixed strategy for the defender could be obtained by using any BSG solver such as [1].

In our experiments comparing the BSG based strategy with the uniform mixed strategy (UMS) on a representative example, we observed that, on an average (and also in most cases), the UMS results in a negative reward value of -0.50 for the defender, whereas the BSG based mixed strategy results in a positive reward value of 1.14, demonstrating its clear advantage (winning as opposed to losing). For more details on the methodology and results, please see [3].

3. FINDING CRITICAL VULNERABILITIES

We formulated and solved the problem of finding most critical vulnerabilities in web applications, which is a much needed feature for defenders, since they usually have to put their limited time and energy to harden the weakest link in their system once the system is deployed (or even before the system is deployed). In this scenario, it is useful to focus on those vulnerabilities or attacks first which are not effectively masked by the optimal mixed strategy with which the system is deployed. These are the most critical vulnerabilities for the current deployment of the system.

We consider the generic problem of finding k-most critical vulnerabilities where k is an input that can be chosen based on the resources available to work on them simultaneously. Our approach works by performing posterior analysis of addressing various vulnerabilities thereby knowing which subset of them would have led to larger gains. For more details on the methodology and results, please see [3].

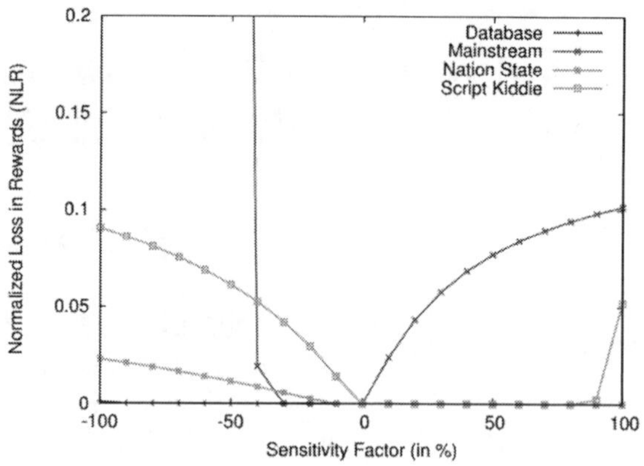

Figure 1: NLR values for various attacker types when their probabilities are modified ranging from -100% to 100%.

4. FINDING SENSITIVE ATTACKER TYPES

It is often the case that the web application administrator (defender) does not know accurately the probability with which a particular type of attacker might attack the system. Therefore, we have formulated and solved the problem of finding the most sensitive attacker types. This is important since a change in their probability will influence the optimal reward for defenders the most, which in-turn helps in knowing which probabilities are to be estimated with as high precision as possible for an effective MTD deployment.

We propose a methodology to find a real-valued quantity $\in [0, 1]$ called the *Normalized Loss in Rewards (NLR)* to measure the sensitivity of different attacker types. The attacker types for which the loss (NLR value) is higher than the rest are the most sensitive attacker types. Figure 1 shows the results obtained on an example with four attacker types: database, mainstream, nation state and script kiddie, in which the mainstream hacker and the script kiddie turn out to be the most sensitive ones.

5. SUMMARY

We have shown how MTD can be effectively modeled as BSG. For more details on the modeling, solving BSGs, working examples, criticality and sensitivity analysis, and experimental results, please see [3].

Acknowledgments

This work was partially supported by the grants from ONR N00014-13-1-0176, N00014-13-1-0519 and N00014-15-1- 2027, the ARO grant W911NF-13- 1-0023, the NSF grant NSF-SFS-1129561 and the Center for Cybersecurity and Digital Forensics at ASU.

REFERENCES

[1] P. Paruchuri, J. P. Pearce, J. Marecki, M. Tambe, F. Ordonez, and S. Kraus. Playing games for security: An efficient exact algorithm for solving bayesian stackelberg games. In *Proceedings of the 7th AAMAS-Volume 2*, pages 895–902, 2008.

[2] M. Taguinod, A. Doupé, Z. Zhao, and G.-J. Ahn. Toward a Moving Target Defense for Web Applications. In *Proceedings of 16th IEEE International Conference on Information Reuse and Integration (IRI)*, 2015.

[3] S. G. Vadlamudi, S. Sengupta, S. Kambhampati, M. Taguinod, Z. Zhao, A. Doupé, and G.-J. Ahn. Moving Target Defense for Web Applications using Bayesian Stackelberg Games. *CoRR*, abs/1602.07024, 2016.

Water Resources Systems Operations via Multiagent Negotiation

(Extended Abstract)

Francesco Amigoni
Politecnico di Milano
Piazza Leonardo da Vinci 32
20133 Milano, Italy
francesco.amigoni@polimi.it

Andrea Castelletti
Politecnico di Milano
Piazza Leonardo da Vinci 32
20133 Milano, Italy
andrea.castelletti@polimi.it

Paolo Gazzotti
Politecnico di Milano
Piazza Leonardo da Vinci 32
20133 Milano, Italy
paolo.gazzotti@mail.polimi.it

Matteo Giuliani
Politecnico di Milano
Piazza Leonardo da Vinci 32
20133 Milano, Italy
matteo.giuliani@polimi.it

Emanuele Mason
Politecnico di Milano
Piazza Leonardo da Vinci 32
20133 Milano, Italy
emanuele.mason@polimi.it

ABSTRACT

The operations of water resources infrastructures, like dams and diversions, often involve multiple conflicting interests and stakeholders. Agent-based approaches have recently attracted an increasing attention to design optimal operating policies for these systems. In this paper we contribute a general monotonic concession negotiation protocol that allows the stakeholders-agents of a regulated lake to reach agreements on the amount of water to release daily, balancing control of lake floods and water supply to agricultural districts downstream.

Keywords

Water resources systems; Negotiation

1. INTRODUCTION

Agent-based approaches have been recently proposed to represent the variety of stakeholders and decision makers in the operations of water resources infrastructures. To better capture the conflicting nature of the stakeholders' interactions, few works have attempted to model such interactions as negotiations [1,6]. Yet, they introduce strong and somehow unrealistic assumptions, like the necessity for each agent to know the preferences of all other agents.

In this paper, we propose to use a general *monotonic concession negotiation* framework that allows the stakeholders-agents of a regulated lake to periodically reach agreements on the lake operating policy that determines the amount of water to release daily. The agreements mimic the outcomes of the decision-making process of the lake regulator, who has to balance different goals. In our approach, a mediator coordinates the negotiation process, without the need for agents (including the mediator) to know all their preferences.

Appears in: *Proceedings of the 15th International Conference on Autonomous Agents and Multiagent Systems (AAMAS 2016), J. Thangarajah, K. Tuyls, C. Jonker, S. Marsella (eds.), May 9–13, 2016, Singapore.*

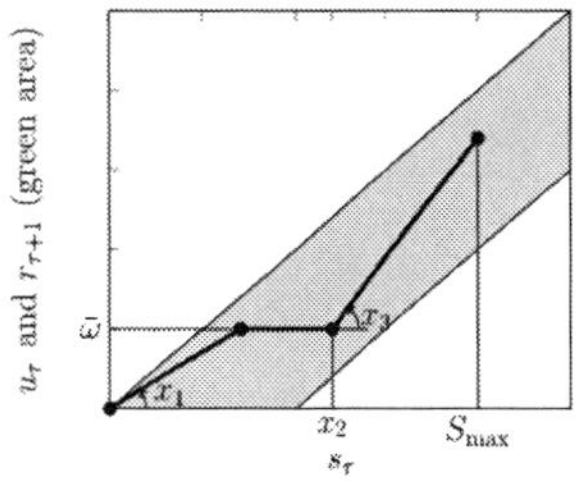

Figure 1: The control law and the feasible regulation region.

2. THE CASE STUDY

We consider a realistic test case inspired by a real world context, the Lake Como system, in Northern Italy, which is a regulated lake dammed on the outlet. The lake dam is operated to supply water downstream mostly for irrigation and to control floods on the lake shores.

The dam is operated with a control law $\pi()$ mapping the lake storage s_τ (expressed in m^3) at day τ into the release decision u_τ (expressed in m^3/day): $u_\tau = \pi(s_\tau)$. When actuated, u_τ produces the actual release $r_{\tau+1}$ (expressed in m^3/day) according to the physical constraints over the actuation (see green area in Fig. 1). As a control law $\pi()$, we consider the piecewise linear function of Fig. 1, known as the Standard Operating Policy, which depends on three parameters: x_1, x_2, and x_3. Note that $\bar{\omega}$ is the (constant) water request for irrigation and $S_{\max}$ is the maximum storage the lake can reach.

We consider the conflicting interests of the lake regulator that operates the dam as two agents. The *city agent* represents the communities living on the lake shores, who are worried about floods that happen when the water level is above a given threshold. The *irr agent* represents the farmers in the downstream irrigation districts that need $\bar{\omega}$ water supply to grow their crops. Different agents have different preferences on the values of the parameters x_1, x_2, and x_3 of the release policy. While the city agent prefers to maximize the release at every water level, the irr agent wants the release to satisfy the fixed demand and to not waste water that can be used in the future. Hence, values of x_1, x_2, and x_3 are the issues that are negotiated with the protocols illustrated below.

3. THE NEGOTIATION PROTOCOLS

We assume n agents that negotiate over m variables that can take real values (in our application, $n = 2$ and $m = 3$). An agent i makes its best proposal (that maximizes its utility function $\mathcal{U}_i : \mathbb{R}^m \mapsto \mathbb{R}$)[1] p_i^0 at the first negotiation step $t = 0$. It then proposes $p_i^{t+1} = \mathcal{F}_i(p_i^t, a^t)$ at later steps according to its strategy function that takes into account the counter-proposal a^t of mediator at step t. The mediator receives the proposals of the agents, calculates the counter-proposal according to its agreement function $a^t = \mathcal{A}(\{p_1^t, p_2^t, \ldots, p_n^t\})$, and sends it to the agents. The negotiation process can terminate with an agreement over the values of the m variables or with a *conflict deal*.

The first protocol is called *point-based*, has been originally presented in [2], and considers proposals as vectors of m elements: $p_i^t = [x_1, x_2, \ldots, x_m] \in \mathbb{R}^m$, with the meaning that p_i^t contains the values that agent i would like to assign to the m variables at step t (in our application, a proposal is the release policy that agent i would like to adopt). The strategy function of agent i is:

$$p_i^{t+1} = \mathcal{F}_i(p_i^t, a^t) = p_i^t + \alpha_i \cdot (a^t - p_i^t)$$

where $\alpha_i \in (0, 1]$ is called *concession coefficient* and represents the rigidity of agent i to move toward the counter-proposal received from the mediator. The agreement function $\mathcal{A}(\{p_1^t, p_2^t, \ldots, p_n^t\})$ averages the proposals p_i^t of the n agents and, in a way, expresses the aggregated preferences of all agents. If, at some t, all p_i^t are equal to the same value $\bar{p}$, then the final agreement is reached.

The second protocol is called *set-based* and has been originally introduced in [4]. Let call $\mathcal{P}_i(\Gamma_i^t) = \{x \in \mathbb{R}^m \mid \mathcal{U}_i(x) \geq \Gamma_i^t\}$ the set of proposals that agent i accepts given an *acceptability threshold* Γ_i^t. Namely, $\mathcal{P}_i(\Gamma_i^t)$ contains all the combinations of values for the m variables that give agent i an utility that is at leastΓ_i^t. In the set-based protocol the proposals are defined as: $p_i^t = \mathcal{P}_i(\Gamma_i^t)$, namely agent i, at each step t of the negotiation, proposes the set of *all* the combinations of values for the m variables that it can accept (in our application, a proposal is the set of release policies that agent i can adopt). The strategy function of agent i updates the acceptability thresholdΓ_i^t in order to concede, namely in order to have$\Gamma_i^{t+1} < \Gamma_i^t$, for example:$\Gamma_i^{t+1} = \Gamma_i^t - c_i$, where $c_i > 0$ is called *concession step*. The agreement function $\mathcal{A}(\{p_1^t, p_2^t, \ldots, p_n^t\})$ used by the mediator is:

$$a^t = \bigcap_{i=1}^{n} p_i^t = \bigcap_{i=1}^{n} \mathcal{P}_i(\Gamma_i^t)$$

If, at some step t, $a^t \neq \emptyset$, then an agreement is found.

[1]Note that the negotiation protocols are presented referring to utility functions $\mathcal{U}_i$ for uniformity with relevant literature, but in our application we consider cost functions. The two representations are trivially related.

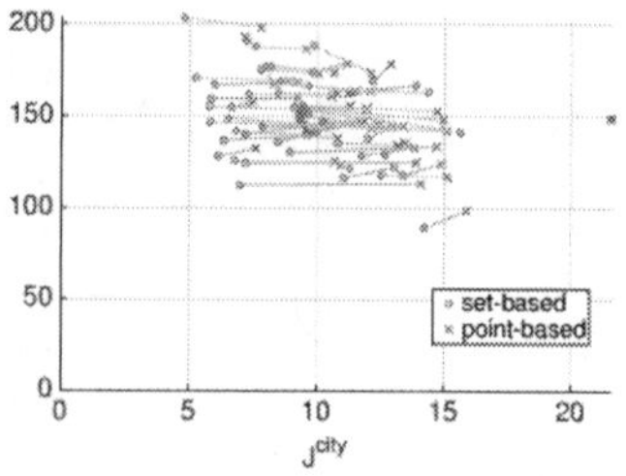

Figure 2: Actual costs incurred by the agents.

4. SIMULATIONS

We have implemented the two protocols in MATLAB. We assume a linear relation between inflow q_τ and water storage: $s_{\tau+1} = s_\tau + q_{\tau+1} - r_{\tau+1}$. Values for q_τ are stochastically generated from a normal distribution $q_\tau \sim N(\mu_q, \sigma_q)$ with $\mu_q = 40$ m^3/day and $\sigma_q = 10$ m^3/day. We generate time series of 5,000 samples (one sample per day) and divide them in blocks $B_1, B_2, \ldots, B_j, \ldots$ of $b = 90$ days each. A negotiation is performed every b days. Cost functions of the city and irr agents are derived from [3, 5]. For the negotiation relative to block B_{j+1}, the cost functions of agents are calculated by considering the cost incurred by the agents over block B_j.

We report experiments showing that the set-based protocol consistently produces Pareto optimal agreements, which are not reached in many cases when using the point-based protocol. Fig. 2 shows the *actual* costs incurred by the two agents for the policies corresponding to the agreements found over all the blocks with the point-based (green) and the set-based (orange) protocols. Agreements relative to the same block are connected with a line segment that is orange if the policy found by the set-based protocol dominates that found by the point-based protocol, green if the opposite happens, and grey if the the two policies are not dominated.

REFERENCES

[1] G. Adams, G. Rausser, and L. Simon. Modelling multilateral negotiations: An application to California water policy. *J Econ Behav Organ*, 30(1):97–111, 1996.

[2] F. Amigoni and N. Gatti. A formal framework for connective stability of highly decentralized cooperative negotiations. *Auton Agent Multi-Ag*, 15(3):253–279, 2007.

[3] D. Anghileri, A. Castelletti, F. Pianosi, R. Soncini-Sessa, and E. Weber. Optimizing watershed management by coordinated operation of storing facilities. *J Water Res Pl-ASCE*, 139(5):492–500, 2013.

[4] C. Badica and A. Badica. A set-based approach to negotiation with concessions. In *Proc. BCI*, pages 239–242, 2012.

[5] A. Castelletti, S. Galelli, M. Restelli, and R. Soncini-Sessa. Tree-based reinforcement learning for optimal water reservoir operation. *Water Resour Res*, 46(9), 2010.

[6] S. Thoyer, S. Morardet, P. Rio, L. Simon, R. Goodhue, and G. Rausser. A bargaining model to simulate negotiations between water users. *JASSS-J Artif Soc S*, 4(2), 2001.

Learning to be Fair in Multiplayer Ultimatum Games (Extended Abstract)

Fernando P. Santos, Francisco C. Santos, Francisco Melo, Ana Paiva
INESC-ID and Instituto Superior Técnico, Universidade de Lisboa
Taguspark, Av. Prof. Cavaco Silva
2780-990 Porto Salvo, Portugal

Jorge M. Pacheco
CBMA and Departamento de Matemática e Aplicações, Universidade do Minho
Campus de Gualtar
4710-057 Braga, Portugal

fernando.pedro@tecnico.ulisboa.pt

ABSTRACT

We study a multiplayer extension of the well-known Ultimatum Game (UG) through the lens of a reinforcement learning algorithm. Multiplayer Ultimatum Game (MUG) allows us to study fair behaviors beyond the traditional pairwise interaction models. Here, a proposal is made to a quorum of Responders, and the overall acceptance depends on reaching a threshold of individual acceptances. We show that learning agents coordinate their behavior into different strategies, depending on factors such as the group acceptance threshold and the group size. Overall, our simulations show that stringent group criteria trigger fairer proposals and the effect of group size on fairness depends on the same group acceptance criteria.

Categories and Subject Descriptors

I.2.11 [**Artificial Intelligence**]: Distributed Artificial Intelligence—*multiagent systems*; J.4 [**Social and Behavioral Sciences**]: Economics

Keywords

Fairness, Groups, Ultimatum Game, Learning, Multiagent systems

1. INTRODUCTION

The evidence of fairness in decision-making has for long captured the attention of academics and the subject comprises a fertile ground of multidisciplinary research [1]. In this context, UG stands as a simple interaction paradigm that is capable to synthesize the clash between rationality and fairness [2]. In its original form, two players interact acquiring two distinct roles: Proposer and Responder. The Proposer is endowed with some resource and has to propose a division (p) to the second player. After that, the Responder has to state her acceptance or rejection, based on a threshold of acceptance (q). If the proposal is rejected ($p < q$), none of the players earns anything. If the proposal is accepted ($p \geq q$), they will divide the resource as it was proposed: the Proposer keeps $1 - p$ and the Responder earns p. A fair outcome is defined as an egalitarian division, $p = 0.5$, in which both the Proposer and the Responder earn a similar reward.

A large set of works address the dynamics of agents playing UG in its original two-player formulation. There are, however, many group interactions in which fairness also plays a fundamental role [7, 4, 3], and which cannot be captured by means of the traditional 2-player UG. Consider, for instance, the cases of democratic institutions, economic and climate summits, collective bargaining, group buying, auctions, or the ancestral activities of proposing divisions regarding the loot of group hunts and fisheries. Here we analyze a group version of UG that allows us address the interactions in which proposals are made to groups and the groups should decide, through suffrage, about its acceptance or rejection [7]. In MUG, proposals are made (p), yet now each of the Responders states acceptance ($p \geq q$) of rejection ($p < q$) and the overall acceptance depends on an aggregate of these individual decisions: if the number of acceptances equals or exceeds a threshold M, the proposal is accepted by the group. In this case, the Proposer keeps what she did not offered, $1 - p$, and the offer is evenly divided by all the Responders, $p/(N-1)$; otherwise, if the number of acceptances remain bellow M, the proposal is rejected by the group an no one earns anything. The interesting values of M range between 1 and $N - 1$. If $M < 1$ all proposals would be accepted and having $M > N - 1$ would dictate unrestricted rejections. If $N = 2$ and $M = 1$ we recover the traditional 2-person UG, described above [2].

2. LEARNING MODEL AND RESULTS

We use the Roth-Erev algorithm [6] to analyse the outcome of a population of learning agents playing MUG in groups of size N. In this algorithm, at each time-step t, the decision-making of each agent k is implemented by a propensity vector $Q_k(t)$ that, as we will see, translates the prob-

Appears in: *Proceedings of the 15th International Conference on Autonomous Agents and Multiagent Systems (AAMAS 2016), J. Thangarajah, K. Tuyls, C. Jonker, S. Marsella (eds.), May 9–13, 2016, Singapore.*

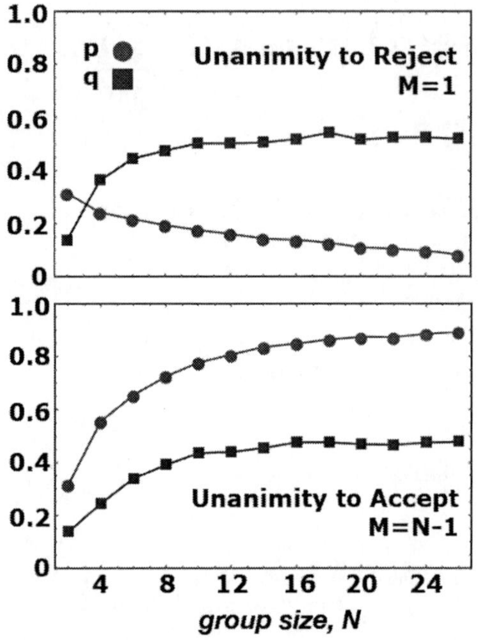

Figure 1: Average values of p and q for different combinations of group sizes, N, and group decision criteria, M when population size $Z = 50$

ability of using each strategy. This vector will be updated considering the payoff gathered in each play. This way, successfully employed actions will have high probability of being repeated in the future. We consider that games take place within a population of size $Z > N$ of adaptive agents. To calculate the payoff of each agent, we sample random groups without any kind of preferential arrangement (well-mixed assumption). We consider MUG with discretised strategies. We round the possible values of p (proposed offers) and q (individual threshold of acceptance) to the closest multiple of $1/D$, where D measures the granularity of the strategy space considered. We map each pair of decimal values p and q into an integer representation, thereafter $i_{p,q}$ is the integer representation of strategy (p, q) and p_i (or q_i) designates the p (q) value corresponding to the strategy with integer representation i. The core of the learning algorithm takes place in the update of the propensity vector of each agent, $Q(t+1)$, after a play at time-step t. Denoting the set of possible actions by $A, a_i \in A : a_i = \{p_i, q_i\}$ and the population size by Z, the propensity matrix, $Q(t) \in \mathbb{R}_+^{Z\times|A|}$ is updated following the base rule

$$Q_{ki}(t+1) = \begin{cases} Q_{ki}(t) + \Pi(p_i, q_i, p_{-i}, q_{-i}) & \text{if } k \text{ played } i \\ Q_{ki}(t) & \text{otherwise} \end{cases} \tag{1}$$

When an agent is called to pick an action, she will do so following the probability distribution dictated by her normalised propensity vector.

Following the traditional game theoretical equilibrium assumptions, the strategy picked by each agent would always be that of unconditional acceptance and minimal offer (subgame perfect equilibrium [5]). Given this prediction, even considering MUG, proposals would always be accepted ($q \rightarrow 0$) and Proposers would always keep the largest share of payoff ($p \rightarrow 0$). This conclusion rules out any possible effect played by group sizes (N) or group acceptance criteria (M). Notwithstanding, through the implemented learning model, we show that larger groups induce individuals to rise their average acceptance threshold (Figure 1). Indeed, it is reasonable to assume that, as the group of Responders grow and as they have to divide the offers between more individuals, the pressure to learn optimal low q values is alleviated. This way, the values of q should increase, on average, approaching the 0.5 value. Differently, the proposed values exhibit a dependence on the group size that is conditioned on M. For mild group acceptance criteria (low M), having a big group of Responders is synonym of having a proposal easily accepted. In these circumstances, Proposers tend to offer less without risking having their proposals rejected, keeping this way more for themselves and exploiting the Responders. Oppositely, when groups agree upon stricter acceptance, having a big group of Responders means that more persons need to be convinced of the advantages of a proposal. This way, Proposers have to adapt, increase the offered values and sacrifice their share in order to have their proposals accepted. Contrarily to the sub-game perfect equilibrium played by fully rational agents, learning agents, under the proper group configurations, can indeed learn to be fair.

Acknowledgments

This research was supported by Fundação para a Ciência e Tecnologia (FCT) through grants SFRH/BD/94736/2013, PTDC/EEI-SII/5081/2014, PTDC/MAT/STA/3358/2014 and by multi-annual funding of CBMA and INESC-ID (under the projects UID/BIA/04050/2013 and UID/CEC/50021/2013 provided by FCT).

REFERENCES

[1] U. Fischbacher, C. M. Fong, and E. Fehr. Fairness, errors and the power of competition. *Journal of Economic Behavior & Organization*, 72(1):527–545, 2009.

[2] W. Güth, R. Schmittberger, and B. Schwarze. An experimental analysis of ultimatum bargaining. *Journal of Economic Behavior & Organization*, 3(4):367–388, 1982.

[3] R. J. Kauffman, H. Lai, and C.-T. Ho. Incentive mechanisms, fairness and participation in online group-buying auctions. *Electronic Commerce Research and Applications*, 9(3):249–262, 2010.

[4] D. M. Messick, D. A. Moore, and M. H. Bazerman. Ultimatum bargaining with a group: Underestimating the importance of the decision rule. *Organizational Behavior and Human Decision Processes*, 69(2):87–101, 1997.

[5] M. J. Osborne. *An introduction to game theory.* Number 3. Oxford University Press New York, 2004.

[6] A. E. Roth and I. Erev. Learning in extensive-form games: Experimental data and simple dynamic models in the intermediate term. *Games and Economic Behavior*, 8(1):164–212, 1995.

[7] F. P. Santos, F. C. Santos, A. Paiva, and J. M. Pacheco. Evolutionary dynamics of group fairness. *Journal of Theoretical Biology*, 378:96–102, 2015.

Verifying Conflicts among Multiple Norms in Multi-agent Systems

(Extended Abstract)

Eduardo Augusto Silvestre
Federal Fluminense University (UFF)
Av. Gal. Milton Tavares de Souza, sem nro
24210-346, Niterói, Brazil
eduardosilvestre@iftm.edu.br

Viviane Torres da Silva
IBM Research, Brazil (on leave from UFF)
Av. Gal. Milton Tavares de Souza, sem nro
24210-346, Niterói, Brazil
vivianetorressilva@gmail.com

ABSTRACT

Norms represent the expected behavior of an agent in a multi-agent system. Generally, norms describe the actions that can be performed, must be performed, and cannot be performed in the system. Due to the number of norms defined to govern a multi-agent systems (MAS), norms may conflict with each other. Norms are in conflict when the fulfillment of one norm violates the other and vice-versa. There are several works that analyze the conflicting norms. However, to the best of our knowledge, these works only analyze conflicts between pairs of norms. There are situations that conflict can only be detected when we analyze several norms together. This work presents an approach to check for conflicts among multiple norms and a strategy to minimize the complexity of this NP-hard problem.

Keywords

Multi-agent systems; normative multi-agent systems; normative conflict

1. INTRODUCTION

Multi-agent systems (MAS) have been gaining great importance in the development of various applications. MAS are autonomous, and heterogeneous societies that can work to achieve common or different goals [5].

In order to deal with the autonomy and diversity of interests among different members, the behavior of agents is governed by a set of norms specified to regulate their actions [1]. The norms govern the behavior of agents by defining obligations (stating the actions that the agents must perform), prohibitions (stating the actions that the agents must not perform) or permissions (stating the actions that the agents can perform). An important challenge when implementing normative MAS is that the set of norms can be in conflict. Conflicts occur when norms regulating the same behavior are activated and are inconsistent [3]. In such cases, the agent is unable to fulfill all the activated norms.

Although there are several works that deal with normative conflicts, to the best of our knowledge, all those approaches check for conflicts by analyzing the norms in pairs. However, there are conflicts that can only be detected when we consider several norms together. For instance, let's consider a conflict that can only be detected if norms N1, N2 and N3 are analyzed together. N1 obliges agent A to dress red shirt. N2 forbids agent A to dress red pant. N3 obliges agent A to dress pant and shirt of the same color. There are no conflicts between the pairs N1-N2, N2-N3 and N1-N3, but when the three norms are analyzed together, we can figure out the conflict.

Since several authors in literature have proved that the analysis of multiple norms is a NP-complete problem [3], we have developed an strategy to minimize the complexity of such problem. Our conflict checker starts by filtering the set of norms and grouping the norms in subsets of norms that may be in conflict. The analysis of conflicts is in fact applied to such subsets. The main contributions of this work are: (i) a more expressive representation of norms; (ii) a normative conflict checker algorithm able to check for conflicts among multiple norms; and (iii) a Java application.

Appears in: *Proceedings of the 15th International Conference on Autonomous Agents and Multiagent Systems (AAMAS 2016), J. Thangarajah, K. Tuyls, C. Jonker, S. Marsella (eds.), May 9–13, 2016, Singapore.*

2. BACKGROUND

The norm definition is based on [2] but our representation is more complex and expressive. A norm n $\in N$ is a tuple of the form {deoC, c, e, a, ac, dc} where deoC is a deontic concept from the set {O(obligation), F(prohibition) or P(permission)}, c $\in C$ is the context where the norm is defined, e $\in E$ is the entity whose action is being regulated, a $\in B$ is the action being regulated, ac $\in Cd$ indicates the condition that activates the norm and dc $\in Cd$ is the condition that deactivates the norm.

An action is defined by the name of the action and, optionally, its attributes and their values, an object where the action will be executed and a list of attributes (with their values). Thus, in this paper we define four different ways to represent the action: (i) {action}; (ii) {action object}; (iii) {action (attr1=value1,…,attrN=valueN)}; and (iv) {action object (attr1=value1,…,attrN=valueN)}. In order to exemplify these four ways to describe a action, let's consider the following four prohibition norms: Na = forbids agent A to get dressed, Nb = forbids agent A to dress pant, Nc = forbids agent A to dress red clothes and Nd forbids agent A to dress red pants. The action of the norms can be represented as: (i) Na: {to dress}; (ii) Nb: {to dress pant}; (iii) Nc: {dress (color={red})}; and (iv) Nd : {dress pant (color={red})}.

3. CONFLICT CHECKER

Our conflict checker algorithm is divided in three steps. First, all norms are transformed into permissions (details in [4]) in order to facilitate the analysis. Since all norms are permissions, the analysis made by the conflict checker is very simple, it checks if the norms intersects. Two or more norms intersects if there is at least one possible situation where the agent is able to fulfill all norms being analyzed.

In order to apply the transformation, we assume that if an agent is obliged to execute an action, it needs to be permitted. Therefore, the transformation from an obligation norm to a permission norm is direct. A prohibition is converted into a permission by (i) negating the execution of the action being prohibited, (ii) negating the execution of the action over the object, (iii) and (iv) by inverting the values of the attributes. The second step of our conflict checker is responsible to filter the norms by including them into bags of similar norms. In order to do so, such step uses 3 filters. The filters separate into bags the norms that apply in the same context, govern the same entity and regulate the same action. After applying all filters, only the norms stored in the same bag are the ones that may be in conflict. Norms stored in different bags apply in different contexts, govern different entities or actions. The analyzes of the conflict is executed in the third step of the algorithm. The algorithm checks if the norms in each bag are in conflict. It starts by checking the norms by pairs of norms and then consider all possible group of k-norms until k be equal to the number of norms in the bag. At the end, the algorithm is checking for conflicts among all the norms of the bag at the same time.

For instance, let's consider the three norms described in Section 1. Since norm N3 is a complex norm (a norm applied over two objects), we have splited it in two norms: N3a (obliges agent A to dress pants of color X) and N3b (obliges agent A to dress shirts of color X), where X is a generic color. In the first step of the algorithm, it transforms the three obligations into permissions. Then, in the second step, the algorithm groups all norms in the same bag since they are applied in the same context (we are omitting the context for simplicity), govern the same entity (agent A) and regulate the same action (to dress). In the third and last step, it verifies that there is a conflict among these three norm. The conflict exists because there is not an intersection among the norms, i.e., agent A is unable to dress a red shirt, a pant that is not red, and a shirt and a pant of the same color.

Analysing the most expensive operation of the algorithm, the cost of the algorithm in the best case is O(1). The best case occur when each bag stores exactly one norm, i.e., the norms apply in different contexts and regulate different entities of different actions, and, therefore, are never in conflict. In such case, there is not a need to execute the third step. The worst case occurs when all norms are stored in one bag. It can happen if all norms apply in the same context, govern the same entity and regulate the same action. The cost of the algorithm in the worst case is $O(2^n)$, where n is the number of norms. The cost of the medium case, $O(2^k)$, where k is the number of norms in the bigger bag, we are unable to calculate. Such evaluation depends on the application domain, i.e., it depends on the number of different contexts, entities and actions found in the norms. Although it is not possible to calculate the medium case, we strongly believe (Section 4) that the use of filters can drastically reduce the cost of the conflict checker.

4. VALIDATION

The main purpose of the validation section is to ensure that our approach is able to detect all conflicting norms and ensure that the technique is computationally feasible. We have developed a tool to randomly generate norms based on the norms of type (iv) in order to focus on the checking of multiple conflicts. This test explores the worst scenario, i.e., all 14 norms generated have the same context, entity and action and, therefore, are stored in the same set. In this case, the time spent by the algorithm to check a small set of 14 norms is tremendous. On the other hand, a more feasible scenario where a set of 14 norms is also generated, but now considering different contexts, entities and actions have a execution time extremely smaller than the time spent when all norms are in the same bag. These test cases also demonstrate the applicability of the filter we have defined.

5. CONCLUSIONS AND FUTURE WORK

Despite significant research in the area, there are still many challenges to be considered. We presented an approach able to checker for conflicts among multiple norms that uses transformations and filters to minimize the computational cost. We have implemented our strategy in Java; the source can be accessed in https://goo.gl/CqXR4Z.

A direct consequence of this work is the investigation of how the conflicts among multiple norms should be solved. Can the techniques used to solve conflicts between pairs of norms be used to solve conflicts among multiple norms? An initial approach should investigate the applicability of famous techniques found in literature used to solve conflicts between pairs of norms, such as, lex posterior, lex superior and lex specialis.

In this work, we have not considered indirect conflicts. The algorithm presented in this paper does only check for direct conflicts, i.e., conflicts among norms that have the same entities, contexts and actions. An important and necessary extension of our work is the identification of indirect conflict among multiple norms

REFERENCES

[1] V. T. da Silva. From the specification to the implementation of norms: an automatic approach to generate rules from norms to govern the behavior of agents. *Autonomous Agents and Multi-Agent Systems*, 17(1):113–155, 2008.

[2] K. da Silva Figueiredo, V. T. da Silva, and C. de O. Braga. Modeling norms in multi-agent systems with normml. In *Coordination, Organizations, Institutions, and Norms in Agent Systems VI - COIN 2010 International Workshops, COIN@AAMAS 2010, Toronto, Canada, May 2010, COIN@MALLOW 2010, Lyon, France, August 2010, Revised Selected Papers*, pages 39–57, 2010.

[3] W. Vasconcelos, M. Kollingbaum, and T. Norman. Normative conflict resolution in multi-agent systems. volume 19, pages 124–152. Springer US, 2009.

[4] G. H. von Wright. Deontic logic. *Mind*, 60(237):1–15, 1951.

[5] M. Wooldridge. *An Introduction to MultiAgent Systems*. Wiley Publishing, 2nd edition, 2009.

A Truthful Mechanism with Biparameter Learning for Online Crowdsourcing

(Extended Abstract)

Satyanath Bhat, Divya Padmanabhan, Shweta Jain, Yadati Narahari
Indian Institute of Science, Bangalore 560012, India
{satyanath.bhat, divya.padmanabhan, jainshweta, hari}@csa.iisc.ernet.in

General Terms

Algorithms, Economics, Theory

Keywords

Strategic Agents, Mechanism Design

1. INTRODUCTION

Consider the motivating example of crowdsourcing of a sequence of large translation jobs which arrive online. Each job has to be completed within a deadline and with an assured level of accuracy. To accomplish this, the requester could split such a job into tasks and allocate each task to a crowd worker. A worker, if employed for a long duration, might commit errors. We refer to the duration until which an agent works without committing any error as the time to failure (TTF). The time taken by a worker to complete the job all by himself is called the job completion time (JCT) of that worker. Each worker incurs a certain cost to complete the entire job. Note that the workers are heterogeneous in terms of their costs and stochastic parameters JCT and TTF. Importantly, the crowd workers are strategic and may misrepresent their costs in the hope of gaining higher utility.

In this work, we consider jobs which (a) arrive online, (b) are divisible (into tasks), (c) have strict completion deadlines, and (d) are to be completed with an assured accuracy. We propose a multi-armed bandit (MAB) mechanism which learns the two parameters (mean job completion time (MJCT) and mean time to failure (MTTF)) of the workers while eliciting their privately held costs truthfully [1].

2. THE MODEL

Let $N = \{1, \ldots, n\}$ denote the set of crowd workers (agents) available to the requester. A sequence of T homogeneous jobs arrives at the platform, one at a time. Following are some of the design issues of the requester.

Job Parameters: *(a) Deadline*: We use D to denote the deadline on each job starting from the arrival of that job, before which the job is required to be completed in expectation. *(b) Task creation*: The requester can divide a current job t $(t = 1, \ldots, T)$ into a certain number of tasks to meet deadline D. We use $x_i^{(t)}$ to denote the fraction of the job t assigned as a task to the worker i. We call an allocation x_i *feasible* when $0 \leq x_i^{(t)} \leq 1$ and $\sum_{i=1}^{n} x_i^{(t)} = 1$. *(c) Threshold on probability of failure*: We say a worker has failed when he commits an error. We use ε to denote (the common) threshold on probability of failure for any task.

Worker Parameters: *(a) Job Completion Time (JCT)*: A worker has a stochastic job completion time, which is the time he requires to complete the entire job by himself. JCT for a worker is a random variable with a fixed but unknown mean. We refer to the mean job completion time (MJCT) of worker i as ρ_i, which the requester wishes to learn. The task allocation $x_i^{(t)}$ will meet the deadline constraint in expectation if $x_i^{(t)} \times \rho_i \leq D$. *(b) Time to Failure (TTF)*: A worker is also characterized by a stochastic time to failure, which denotes the duration for which a worker would work without a failure. Like JCT, TTF also has a fixed yet unknown mean (MTTF). Let F_i be the CDF of TTF for agent i, the requirement on threshold probability error dictates $F_i(x_i^{(t)} \times \rho_i) \leq \varepsilon$. Like MJCT, a requester also seeks to learn MTTF. *(c) Cost Incurred*: Worker i has a privately held cost $c_i \in [\underline{c}, \bar{c}]$ which represents the cost incurred by worker i to complete the job entirely on his own. Therefore, the cost involved to complete $x_i^{(t)}$ fraction of the job by the worker i is $c_i x_i^{(t)}$.

Goal of the Optimization Problem: The constraints on deadline and task accuracy, which in turn depend on MJCT and MTTF, have to be met in a cost optimal way for every online job t. Thus, this problem is a biparameter learning problem.

We model the JCT of a worker as a log-normal distribution with unknown mean $\rho_i \in [\underline{\rho}, \bar{\rho}]$ while the TTF is modelled an exponential distribution with mean $\beta_i \in [\underline{\beta}, \bar{\beta}]$. If the parameters c_i, ρ_i, and β_i are known, the requester's optimization problem is given by eq. (1).

$$\min_{\substack{\text{Feasible } x_i \\ x_i \in [0,1]}} \sum_{i=1}^{n} c_i x_i, \text{ s.t. } , \rho_i x_i \leq \min\left(D, \beta_i \ln\left(\frac{1}{1-\varepsilon}\right)\right) \; \forall i \in N. \tag{1}$$

In practice, ρ_i and β_i are unknown and need to be learnt.

2.1 Difficulty in Learning β_i

In learning of ρ_i, every allocation contributes a single sample. However, for estimating β_i, each input sample must correspond to a failure, but this is not practical as we do not observe failure at every instance of allocation. To handle this difficulty, we propose to use a surrogate random vari-

Appears in: *Proceedings of the 15th International Conference on Autonomous Agents and Multiagent Systems (AAMAS 2016), J. Thangarajah, K. Tuyls, C. Jonker, S. Marsella (eds.), May 9–13, 2016, Singapore.*

able. Consider the experiment where a worker i is allocated a task on which the worker spends a duration of at least δ. The experiment is deemed to have failed if the worker i fails in the first δ duration of allocation, otherwise it is deemed to be a success. Let $N_\delta^{(i)}$ be the number of such independent experiments until a failure is encountered. We propose to use the random variable $\beta'_{\delta,i} = \delta \times N_\delta^{(i)}$ to construct a sample from exponential(β_i). The expectation of the surrogate random variable in the limit coincides with β_i(MTTF).

2.2 Non strategic workers: SW-GREEDY

For learning MTTF and MJCT, we use the Robust UCB technique [2] with truncated empirical mean as the estimator. Let $\hat{\rho}_i^+$ and $\hat{\beta}_i^+$ denote the upper confidence indices while $\hat{\rho}_i^-$ and $\hat{\beta}_i^-$ denote the lower confidence indices of MJCT and MTTF, respectively, obtained from Robust UCB. $\hat{\rho}_i$ and $\hat{\beta}_i$ are the empirical estimates of MJCT and MTTF, respectively, for worker i. The workers are indexed in increasing order of their costs and each worker i is allocated the largest possible fraction x_i^{PST} which does not violate the constraints in eq. (1) until all tasks of the job are allocated. A higher value of ρ_i enforces a lower allocation to worker i compared to when a lower value of ρ_i is used. Hence we refer to $\hat{\rho}_i^+$ as a pessimistic estimate for ρ_i. Similarly, we refer to $\hat{\beta}_i^-$ as the pessimistic estimate for β_i. The use of pessimistic estimates ensures that even with the true values of underlying means, the constraint in eq. (1) is satisfied. We refer to the above allocation as SW-GREEDY (Algorithm 1). Every worker i is paid an amount equal to the cost incurred, i.e. $x_i^{\text{PST}}(t) \times c_i$.

3. STRATEGIC WORKERS: TD-UCB

Here, before an allocation is performed, the agents announce their bids. We denote the bid profile by (b_i, b_{-i}). We introduce a mechanism TD-UCB for which we use the same allocation rule as SW-GREEDY .

3.1 Payment Scheme

Let ξ_t denote a tuple of allocation and performance of the allocated workers for the job t. The learning until job t is captured in the history $h_t = \{\xi_k\}_{k=0}^t$. We denote the externality imposed by agent i on j as $x_{i,j}^{\text{EXT}}(b_i, b_{-i}; h_t, t)$, which signifies the additional fraction of the job allocated to the agent j in the absence of agent i. The externality for the job t depends on the bid profile (b_i, b_{-i}) as well as the history till job t. Let $\overline{k_t}$ be the agent with the largest reported bid in the worker set chosen by the allocation scheme.

$$x_{i,j}^{\text{EXT}}(b_i, b_{-i}; t) = \begin{cases} 0 & \text{if } j < \overline{k_t} \text{ or } i > \overline{k_t}, \\ Z_1 & \text{if } j = \overline{k_t}, \\ Z_2 & \text{if } j > \overline{k_t}, \quad \text{where,} \end{cases} \tag{2}$$

$$Z_1 = \min\left(\frac{1}{\hat{\rho}_j^+} \min\left(D, \hat{\beta}_j^- \log\left(\frac{1}{1-\epsilon}\right)\right) - x_j^{\text{PST}}(t), x_i^{\text{PST}}(t)\right),$$

$$Z_2 = \min\left(\frac{1}{\hat{\rho}_j^+} \min\left(D, \hat{\beta}_j^- \log\left(\frac{1}{1-\epsilon}\right)\right), x_i^{\text{PST}}(t) - \sum_{s=\overline{k}_t}^{j-1} x_{i,s}^{\text{EXT}}(t)\right)$$

We now propose a payment structure in eq. (3).

$$p_i(b_i, b_{-i}; t) = \begin{cases} 0 & \text{if } i > \overline{k_t}, \\ Z_3 & \text{otherwise,} \quad \text{where,} \end{cases} \tag{3}$$

ALGORITHM 1: SW-GREEDY Allocation Algorithm

Input: Set of workers N, number of jobs T, deadline D, accuracy level ε, input cost vector: $c_1 \le c_2 \le \ldots \le c_n$ (By re-indexing N)

Initialize
$\forall i \in N$, $\hat{\rho}_i = \bar{\rho}$, $\hat{\rho}_i^+ = \bar{\rho}$, $\hat{\rho}_i^- = \underline{\rho}$, $N_{i,t=0}$
$\hat{\beta}_i = \underline{\beta}$, $\hat{\beta}_i^+ = \bar{\beta}$, $\hat{\beta}_i^- = \underline{\beta}$, $N_{i,t}^\beta = 0$,
$\eta_\delta^{(i)} = 0$

for *Online job arrival* $t = 1, \ldots, T$ **do**
  Pessimistic Selection
  $x^{\text{PST}}(t) = \{x_1^{\text{PST}}(t), \ldots, x_n^{\text{PST}}(t)\} = \{0, \ldots, 0\}$
  $i = 1$
  while $\sum_{j=1}^n x_j^{\text{PST}}(t) < 1$ **do**
    $x_i^{\text{PST}}(t) = \frac{1}{\hat{\rho}_i^+} \min\left(D, \hat{\beta}_i^- \ln\left[\frac{1}{1-\varepsilon}\right]\right)$
    if $1 - \sum_{j=1}^{i-1} x_j^{\text{PST}}(t) < x_i^{\text{PST}}(t)$ **then**
      $x_i^{\text{PST}}(t) = 1 - \sum_{j=1}^{i-1} x_j^{\text{PST}}(t)$
    $i = i + 1$
  Define $\bar{k}_t = \max\{i : x_i^{\text{PST}} > 0\}$
  Allocate the job t as per x_i^{PST}
  Observe $\tilde{\tau}_i$, the time of completion of x_i^{PST} by i
  $\forall i \in \{1, \ldots, \bar{k}_t\}, N_{i,t} = N_{i,t-1} + 1$
  $\hat{\rho}_i = \left(N_{i,t-1} \times \hat{\rho}_i + \frac{\tilde{\tau}_i}{x_i^{\text{PST}}(t)}\right) \times \frac{1}{N_{i,t}}$
  Updates for Surrogate of β_i
  for $i \in \{1, \ldots, \bar{k}_t\}$ **do**
    if *Worker i made an error during δ* **then**
      $\hat{\beta}_i = \frac{\hat{\beta}_i \times N_{i,t-1}^\beta + (\delta \times \eta_\delta^{(i)})}{N_{i,t-1}^\beta + 1}$
      $N_{i,t}^\beta = N_{i,t-1}^\beta + 1$
      $\eta_\delta^{(i)} = 0$
    else
      $\eta_\delta^{(i)} = \eta_\delta^{(i)} + 1$
      $N_{i,t}^\beta = N_{i,t-1}^\beta$

$$Z_3 = \sum_{s=\overline{k}_t}^{n} \left[x_{i,s}^{\text{EXT}}(t) \times b_s\right] + \left(x_i^{\text{PST}}(t) - \sum_{s=\overline{k}_t}^{n} x_{i,s}^{\text{EXT}}(t)\right) \times \bar{c}$$

4. PROPERTIES OF TD-UCB MECHANISM

THEOREM 1. *The TD-UCB mechanism is Dominant Strategy Incentive Compatible and Individually Rational.*

DEFINITION 1. *Optimal worker set: For a problem instance with all the parameters known, in the solution to the optimization problem of eq. (1), we refer to the set of agents allocated a non-zero fraction of the job as the the optimal worker set.*

THEOREM 2. *The TD-UCB mechanism selects an optimal worker set after the job $t' \in O(\log T)$.*

THEOREM 3. *The average regret of TD-UCB mechanism approaches zero asymptotically.*

References

[1] S. Bhat, D. Padmanabhan, S. Jain, and Y. Narahari. A truthful mechanism with biparameter learning for online crowdsourcing. *arXiv preprint arXiv:1602.04032*, 2016.

[2] S. Bubeck, N. Cesa-Bianchi, and G. Lugosi. Bandits with heavy tail. *IEEE Transactions on Information Theory*, 59(11):7711–7717, 2013.

Probably Approximately Correct Greedy Maximization (Extended Abstract)

Yash Satsangi
University of Amsterdam
y.satsangi@uva.nl

Shimon Whiteson
University of Oxford
shimon.whiteson@cs.ox.ac.uk

Frans A. Oliehoek
University of Liverpool
University of Amsterdam
frans.oliehoek@liverpool.ac.uk

ABSTRACT

Submodular function maximization finds application in a variety of real-world decision-making problems. However, most existing methods, based on greedy maximization, assume it is computationally feasible to evaluate F, the function being maximized. Unfortunately, in many realistic settings F is too expensive to evaluate exactly even once. We present *probably approximately correct greedy maximization*, which requires access only to cheap anytime confidence bounds on F and uses them to prune elements. We show that, with high probability, our method returns an approximately optimal set. We propose novel, cheap confidence bounds for *conditional entropy*, which appears in many common choices of F and for which it is difficult to find unbiased or bounded estimates. Finally, results on a real-world dataset from a multi-camera tracking system in a shopping mall demonstrate that our approach performs comparably to existing methods, but at a fraction of the computational cost.

Keywords

Submodularity; Greedy maximization; Sensor scheduling; Planning.

1. INTRODUCTION

Submodularity is a property of set functions that formalizes the notion of *diminishing returns*. Many real-world problems involve maximizing submodular functions, e.g., summarizing text, image collection summarization, or selecting sensors to minimize uncertainty about a hidden variable. Formally, given a ground set $\mathcal{X} = \{1, 2 \ldots n\}$, a set function $F : 2^{\mathcal{X}} \to \mathbb{R}$, is submodular if for every $\mathcal{A}_M \subseteq \mathcal{A}_N \subseteq \mathcal{X}$ and $i \in \mathcal{X} \setminus \mathcal{A}_N$, $\Delta_F(i|\mathcal{A}_M) \geq \Delta_F(i|\mathcal{A}_N)$, where $\Delta_F(i|\mathcal{A}) = F(\mathcal{A} \cup i) - F(\mathcal{A})$ is the *marginal gain* of adding i to A. Typically, the aim is to find an $\mathcal{A}^*$ that maximizes F subject to certain constraints. Here, we consider a constraint on $\mathcal{A}^*$'s size: $\mathcal{A}^* = \arg\max_{\mathcal{A} \in \mathcal{A}^+} F(\mathcal{A})$, where $\mathcal{A}^+ = \{\mathcal{A} \subseteq \mathcal{X} : |\mathcal{A}| \leq k\}$.

As n increases, the $\binom{n}{k}$ possibilities for $\mathcal{A}^*$ grow rapidly, rendering naive maximization intractable. Instead, *greedy maximization* finds an approximate solution $\mathcal{A}^G$ faster by iteratively adding to a partial solution the element that maximizes the marginal gain. Nemhauser et. al. [4] showed that the value obtained by greedy maximization is close to that of full maximization, i.e., $F(\mathcal{A}^G) \geq (1 - e^{-1})F(\mathcal{A}^*)$, if F is submodular, non-negative and monotone.

Appears in: *Proceedings of the 15th International Conference on Autonomous Agents and Multiagent Systems (AAMAS 2016), J. Thangarajah, K. Tuyls, C. Jonker, S. Marsella (eds.), May 9–13, 2016, Singapore.*

Most of the existing methods [3] assume it is computationally feasible to exactly compute F, and thus the marginal gain. In many settings, this is not the case. For example, consider a surveillance task [6] in which an agent aims to minimise uncertainty about a hidden state by selecting a subset of sensors that maximise *information gain*. Computing information gain is computationally expensive, especially when the hidden variable can take many values, as it involves an expectation over the entropy of posterior beliefs about the hidden variable. When surveilling large areas like shopping malls, exactly computing the entropy of a single posterior belief becomes infeasible, let alone an expectation over them.

In this paper, we present a new algorithm called *probably approximately correct greedy maximization*. Rather than assuming access to F itself, we assume access only to confidence bounds on F that are cheaper to compute than F and are *anytime*, i.e., we can tighten them by spending more computation time, e.g., by generating additional samples. Our method uses confidence bounds to prune elements, thereby avoiding the need to further tighten their bounds. We provide a PAC analysis that shows that, with high probability, our method returns an approximately optimal set.

Given an unbiased estimator of F, it is possible to use concentration inequalities like Hoeffding's inequality to obtain the confidence bounds needed by PAC greedy maximization. Unfortunately, many applications, such as sensor placement and decision tree induction require information-theoretic definitions of F such as information gain that depend on computing entropy over posterior beliefs, which are impossible to estimate in unbiased way [5]. The absence of an unbiased estimator makes it hard to obtain computationally *cheap* confidence bounds on conditional entropy [2]. Therefore, in this paper, we propose novel, cheap confidence bounds on conditional entropy.

Finally, we apply PAC greedy maximization with these new confidence bounds to a real-life dataset collected a multi-camera tracking system employed in a shopping mall. Our empirical results demonstrate that our approach performs comparably to greedy and *lazier* greedy maximization, but at a fraction of the computational cost, leading to much better scalability.

2. METHOD & ANALYSIS

In this section, we propose *probably approximately correct greedy maximization*. We assume U and L be set functions such that for $\mathcal{A} \in \mathcal{A}^+$, with probability $1 - \delta_u$, $U(\mathcal{A}) \geq F(\mathcal{A})$ and for each $\mathcal{A} \in \mathcal{A}^+$, with probability $1 - \delta_l$, $F(\mathcal{A}) \geq L(\mathcal{A})$. The main idea is to use U and L to prune elements that with high probability do not maximize marginal gain.

PAC greedy maximization works by initializing a partial solution $\mathcal{A}^P$ as $\emptyset$ and adding at each iteration the element i^P, which maximizes the marginal gain for that iteration to $\mathcal{A}^P$ until $|\mathcal{A}^P|$

equals k. Algorithm 1 shows the main subroutine for finding i^P. Algorithm 1 maintains a queue of unpruned elements prioritized by their upper bound. In each iteration of the outer while loop, the algorithm examines each of these elements and prunes it if its upper bound is not at least ϵ_1 greater than the max lower bound found so far. In addition, the element with the max lower bound is never pruned. If an element is not pruned, then its bounds are tightened.

Algorithm 1 $\texttt{pac-max}(U, L, \mathcal{A}^P, \epsilon_1, t)$

$i^P \leftarrow 0$ % element with max lower bound
for $i \in \mathcal{X} \setminus \mathcal{A}^P$ **do**
  $\rho.\texttt{enqueue}(i, U(\mathcal{A}^P \cup i))$ % initialize priority queue
  $i^P \leftarrow \arg\max_{j \in \{i, i^P\}} L(\mathcal{A}^P \cup j))\}$
end for
while $\rho.\texttt{length}() > 1 \vee$ change in U & L is $> t$ **do**
  $\rho' \leftarrow$ empty queue
  while $\neg\rho.\texttt{empty}()$ **do**
    $i \leftarrow \rho.\texttt{dequeue}()$
    if $i = i^P \vee U(\mathcal{A}^P \cup i) >= L(\mathcal{A}^P \cup i^P) + \epsilon_1$ **then**
      $\texttt{tighten}(\mathcal{A}^P \cup i)$
      $i^P \leftarrow \arg\max_{j \in \{i, i^P\}} L(\mathcal{A}^P \cup j)$
      $\rho'.\texttt{enqueue}(i, U(\mathcal{A}^P \cup i))$
    end if
  end while
  $\rho \leftarrow \rho'$
end while
return i^P.

Assumption 1. pac-max always terminates with $\rho.length() = 1$.

In other words, we assume that U and L can be tightened enough to disambiguate i^P. Using this assumption we show that PAC greedy maximization with high probability achieves the same guarantees as regular greedy maximization minus a constant term.

Theorem 1. *If F is non-negative, monotone and submodular in $\mathcal{X}$ and if Assumption 1 holds then, with probability $1 - \delta$,*

$$F(\mathcal{A}^P) \geq (1 - e^{-1})F(\mathcal{A}^*) - \epsilon, \quad (1)$$

where $\mathcal{A}^P$ is the solution returned by PAC greedy maximization, $\mathcal{A}^* = \arg\max_{\mathcal{A} \in \mathcal{A}^+} F(\mathcal{A})$, $\delta = k(\delta_u + \delta_l)$, and $\epsilon = k\epsilon_1$.

Proof. See [7]. □

Our main focus is on settings where F has information-theoretic definitions like *information gain, entropy* or *conditional entropy*, for which computationally cheap upper and lower bounds are not easy to find in absence of an unbiased estimator. In the sensor selection task, given a set of n sensors $\mathcal{X}$, the aim is to find $\mathcal{A}^* = \arg\max_{\mathcal{A} \in \mathcal{A}^+} [-H_b^{\mathcal{A}}(s|\mathbf{z})]$. Here s denotes a hidden variable, $b(s)$ denotes the prior probability distribution over s, $\mathbf{z} = \langle z_1, z_2 \ldots z_n \rangle$ denotes the observation vector, z_i stands for the observation about s from sensor i and $H_b^{\mathcal{A}}(s|\mathbf{z}) = \mathbb{E}_{\mathbf{z}|b,\mathcal{A}}[H_{b_{\mathbf{z}}^{\mathcal{A}}}(s)]$ is the conditional entropy [5] of s given $\mathbf{z}$, which is the *expected* value for the *entropy* $H_{b_{\mathbf{z}}^{\mathcal{A}}}(s)$ [5] of the posterior probability distribution $b_{\mathbf{z}}^{\mathcal{A}}(s)$.

The upper bound on $F(\mathcal{A}) = -H_b^{\mathcal{A}}(s|\mathbf{z})$ can be obtained by simply approximating the entropy of $b_{\mathbf{z}}^{\mathcal{A}}$, $H_{b_{\mathbf{z}}^{\mathcal{A}}}(s)$ with its *maximum likelihood estimates* $H_{\hat{b}_{\mathbf{z}}^{\mathcal{A}}}(s)$, that is, $U(\mathcal{A}) = -\mathbb{E}_{\mathbf{z}|b,\mathcal{A}}[H_{\hat{b}_{\mathbf{z}}^{\mathcal{A}}}(s)] + \eta$ [7]. The lower bound, which is rather difficult to find, is obtained by using $\mathbf{r} = \langle r_1, r_2 \ldots, r_n \rangle$ in place of $\mathbf{z}$, which is a crude approximation of $\mathbf{z}$, e.g., obtained by clustering z_i into d clusters deterministically and r_i denotes the cluster z_i belongs to. $L(\mathcal{A})$ is defined as $L(\mathcal{A}) = -[H_{\hat{b}}^{\mathcal{A}}(s|\mathbf{r}) + \eta + \log(1 + \frac{1}{M}(\psi_b(s) - 1))]$, where $\psi_b(s)$ is the support of $b(s)$. [7] provides the proofs and details that show, with probability $1 - \delta_u$, $U(\mathcal{A}) \geq F(\mathcal{A})$ and with probability $1 - \delta_l$, $L(\mathcal{A}) \leq F(\mathcal{A})$ with exact definitions of δ_u, δ_l, η and M. The following theorem ties our results together to show that for $F(\mathcal{A}) = -H_b^{\mathcal{A}}(s|\mathbf{z})$, PAC greedy maximization with above definitions of U and L, computes $\mathcal{A}^P$ such that $F(\mathcal{A}^P)$ has bounded error with respect to $F(\mathcal{A}^*)$, and achieves the same guarantees as greedy maximization minus a constant term.

Theorem 2. *For the above described definitions of F, U and L, if Assumption 1 holds and if $\mathbf{z}$ is conditionally independent given s, then with probability $1 - \delta$, (1) is true.*

Proof. See [7]. □

3. EXPERIMENTS & RESULTS

We evaluated PAC greedy maximization on the problem of tracking multiple people using a multi-camera system. The problem was extracted from a real-world dataset [1] collected in a shopping mall using 13 CCTV cameras for over 4 hours. To evaluate a given algorithm, a trajectory was sampled randomly. The goal is to select a subset of cameras at each time step that induce a low-entropy belief about the person's location that can be used to predict those locations. As a baseline, we tested against greedy maximization which simply uses an approximation based on the MLE estimates of posterior beliefs and lazier greedy maximization [3] which, in each iteration, samples a subset of size $\mathcal{R}$ from $\mathcal{X}$ and selects i from $\mathcal{R}$ that maximizes marginal gain.

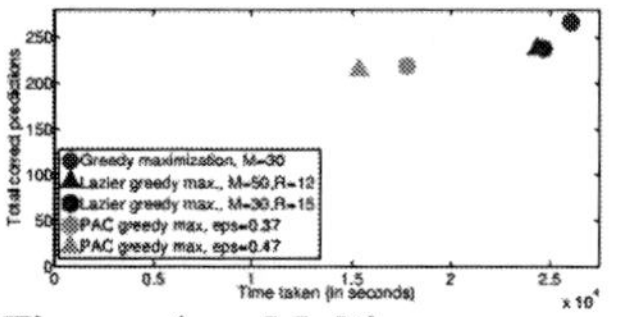

Figure 1: Multi-person tracking for $n = 20$ and $k = 3$.

Figure 1 shows the number of correct predictions (y-axis) against the runtime (x-axis) of each method. Thus, the top left is the most desirable region. PAC greedy maximization performs nearly as well as the greedy maximization and lazier greedy maximization but does so at lower computational cost leading to much better scalability.

Acknowledgments

This research is supported by the Dutch Technology Foundation STW (project #12622) and NWO Innovational Research Incentives Scheme Veni #639.021.336. We thank Henri Bouma and TNO for providing us with the dataset used in our experiments and the STW User Committee for its useful input.

REFERENCES

[1] H. Bouma, J. Baan, S. Landsmeer, C. Kruszynski, G. van Antwerpen, and J. Dijk. Real-time tracking and fast retrieval of persons in multiple surveillance cameras of a shopping mall. 2013.

[2] P.-L. Loh and S. Nowozin. Faster hoeffding racing: Bernstein races via jackknife estimates. In *Algorithmic Learning Theory*, 2013.

[3] B. Mirzasoleiman, A. Badanidiyuru, A. Karbasi, J. Vondrák, and A. Krause. Lazier than lazy greedy. In *AAAI*, 2015.

[4] G. Nemhauser, L. Wolsey, and M. Fisher. An analysis of approximations for maximizing submodular set functions. *Mathematical Programming*, 1978.

[5] L. Paninski. Estimation of entropy and mutual information. *Neural computation*, 2003.

[6] Y. Satsangi, S. Whiteson, and F. Oliehoek. Exploiting submodular value functions for faster dynamic sensor selection. In *AAAI*, 2015.

[7] Y. Satsangi, S. Whiteson, and F. Oliehoek. Probably approximately correct greedy maximization. *ArXiv e-prints*, Feb. 2016. http://arxiv.org/abs/1602.07860.

Analysis of Lane Level Dynamics for Emergency Vehicle Traversal

(Extended Abstract)

Akash Agarwal
Center for Data Engineering
IIIT Hyderabad, Gachibowli
Hyderabad 500032, India
akash.agarwal@research.iiit.ac.in

Praveen Paruchuri
Center for Data Engineering
IIIT Hyderabad, Gachibowli
Hyderabad 500032, India
praveen.p@iiit.ac.in

ABSTRACT

Slow moving traffic in heavily populated cities, can many times result in loss of lives due to emergency vehicles not being able to reach their destination hospitals on time. In this paper, we assume the usage of inter vehicular communication to optimize the lane level dynamics for an Emergency Vehicle Agent (EVA), traversing a multi lane stretch of road in an urban traffic setting. In particular, we present the Fixed Lane Strategy (FLS) and the Best Lane Strategy (BLS) for EVA traversal. FLS is a simple strategy that acts as a good baseline while BLS is a sophisticated strategy that can adapt to varying traffic patterns.

Keywords

Lane Level Dynamics, Emergency Vehicles, Traffic Simulation, Intelligent Transportation Systems, SUMO - Simulation of Urban Mobility

1. INTRODUCTION

Recent advances in the field of **Intelligent Transportation Systems (ITS)** makes it increasingly likely that vehicles in the near future will be equipped with advanced systems that allow inter vehicular communication. This is being made possible using VANETS (vehicular ad hoc networks), a key component of ITS. Vehicle to vehicle (V2V) communication will allow for several innovative methods of urban traffic management. In this paper, we will study one application of this technology that can improve the traversal time of Emergency Vehicles (EVs). Note that we only assume usage of inter-vehicular communication system (V2V) but not the usage of any other road side infrastructure. We perform our analysis using a free and open microscopic traffic simulation suite named **Simulation of Urban MObility (SUMO)** [1]. We use its rich feature set to simulate a variety of realistic traffic scenarios, introduce the EV modeled as an Agent (EVA) into the environment and allow its behavior to play out in the simulation.

Much of the previous work on this topic has focused on developing techniques to identify better lanes for vehicles in general. There are lane changing models that are used by vehicles in microscopic traffic simulation suites like SUMO [3]. However they do not focus on EVAs, which need specialized routing strategies to take advantage of the fact that other vehicles make way for EVAs and also to account for the accurate information about other vehicles such as speed, vehicle position, etc., available due to ITS assumptions.

The works that do focus on better routing of EVAs, describe the best path to be taken by the EVA but do not describe the actual traversal details (like lane selection/ changing), once a stretch of road in the path is identified. In this paper, we focus specifically on the lane level dynamics for an EVA. In particular, we describe the **Fixed Lane Strategy (FLS)** and **Best Lane Strategy (BLS)**, and the improvements they provide. While FLS is a simple strategy that acts as a good baseline, BLS is a sophisticated strategy that can adapt to varying traffic patterns. Unlike prior works, where the decision to traverse on a lane(s) is based on the presence of a faster leader(s), BLS uses a utility function which by including average speeds, slowest speeds and normalized free space considers both the possibility of an immediate faster lane and the clearing time of other vehicles.

Appears in: *Proceedings of the 15th International Conference on Autonomous Agents and Multiagent Systems (AAMAS 2016), J. Thangarajah, K. Tuyls, S. Marsella, C. Jonker (eds.), May 9–13, 2016, Singapore.*

2. THE STRATEGIES

We now describe the FLS and BLS strategies that would enable an EVA to handle better lane level dynamics while traversing on a multi-lane stretch of road. These strategies only specify the lane that the EVA should travel in while the low-level dynamics of traversal namely speed, acceleration/deceleration and the dynamics involved in changing the lane for the EVA are handled by SUMO. Another task these strategies perform is to identify the appropriate vehicles to send lane change requests.

2.1 The SUMO strategy

For purposes of modeling EVA traversal behavior using SUMO, we perform the following extension: In real-world, EVAs have sirens and lights to indicate other vehicles to make way. To model this into SUMO, we add communication on top of the SUMO default strategy. This will allow EVA to send lane change requests to vehicles on its current lane up to a distance, c_d in front of it. We assume that all lane change requests sent will reach the intended vehicles and vehicles will try to clear immediately upon receiving them. Similar communication facility is assumed for FLS and BLS strategies (not to model the effect of sirens/lights but) due to the availability of V2V communication. Availability of communication in SUMO provides an advantage to the EVA since in real traffic scenarios sirens may not always be heard or drivers may not always know the lane to clear until the EVA is in sight. Also, the SUMO strategy includes the simulator's state of the art lane change model which has been shown to compare favorably against other competing models described in [3]. Hence, the SUMO strategy we use for bench-marking is expected to be favorable to the EVA in terms of travel time.

2.2 The Fixed Lane Strategy (FLS)

FLS is a baseline strategy that is based on the following idea: the EVA identifies the lane, that is fastest on an average, based on prior information and picks that as the fixed lane for its entire journey. Assuming a right handed driving system, in most cases leftmost lane is the fastest, as faster vehicles tend to move on the left lanes while the slower ones move on the right lanes (the vice-verse typically holds true for left handed driving systems). When using FLS the EVA therefore moves to the leftmost lane from its current position and then tries to clear out the vehicles from that lane.

2.3 The Best Lane Strategy (BLS)

In BLS, the EVA calculates the utilities of the current lane and the other lanes using the utility computation function described below and then takes a decision to switch if it is beneficial to do so. Similar to FLS the EVA tries to clear out vehicles from the lane it currently is in. Also, the EVA can get the information about the speed and position of vehicles upto the **communication distance** (c_d).

We envision utility u_l, of a lane l, to be a function of the following factors: (a) Normalized speed of the slowest vehicle, calculated as (speed/maximum possible speed) and denoted by $\frac{a}{m}$ (since traffic on a lane eventually moves at speed of the slowest vehicle). (b) Normalized average speed (many times a vehicle(s) might be temporarily slow since it is just about to change a lane or near an intersection i.e., give some weight to average rather than decide entirely on temporary phenomenon), $\frac{b}{m}$, calculated as (average speed/maximum possible speed), and (c) Normalized free space (since not all vehicles may be able to switch lanes immediately after a clear lane message is received), an approximation computed as $\frac{n-c}{n}$, where c is the number of vehicles present on the lane l upto distance c_d, and n is the maximum number of vehicles that can be on the lane upto c_d. To compute n we assume an average length for vehicles which makes the computation an approximation. Here, m , maximum possible speed, is the speed limit of the road (different lanes can have additional speed restrictions). Combining the terms:

$$u_l = w_a * \frac{a}{m} + w_b * \frac{b}{m} + w_c * \frac{n-c}{n} \quad (1)$$

where w_a, w_b, w_c are the weights of each of the terms. At the beginning of the simulation an EVA starts on the lane with maximum value of u_l. Utilities are recomputed every t seconds and lane changes happen when the utility of the best lane u_b, exceeds the utility of the current lane u_c, by at least δ to compensate for lane switching overheads:

$$u_b - u_c > \delta \text{ (} \textit{Condition for lane change} \text{)}$$

In addition to the above described strategies, we also model the **Empty road baseline (ERB)** strategy. The ERB strategy acts as a lower bound on the EVA traversal time and captures the time taken by the EVA when there are 0 vehicles on the road apart from the EVA.

3. EXPERIMENTAL RESULTS

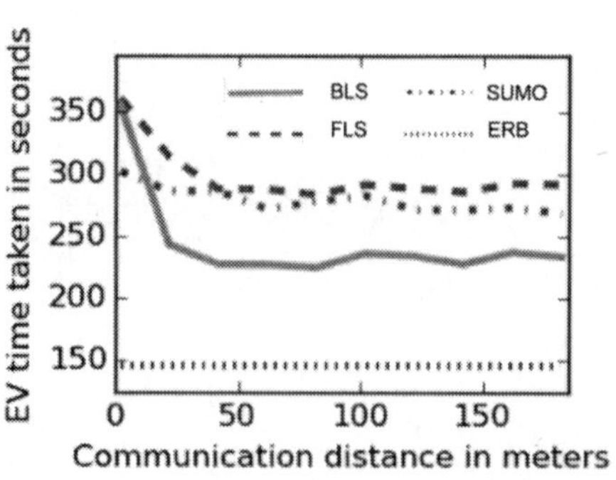

Figure 1: Variation with communication distance, c_d

For purposes of this experiment, we modeled an urban traffic environment corresponding to a densely populated city namely New York City. We tested on a wide range of lane speeds, calibrated using data from a data set providing us with actual traffic speeds of a comprehensive set of roads in New York city available from the City of New York Department of Transportation [2]. Our results in Figure 1 are an average of our simulations for a 2 km representative stretch of a road. The experiment shows how the four different strategies ERB, SUMO, FLS and BLS perform when c_d changes. The figure shows the different values picked for the parameter c_d on the x-axis (in meters) and the time taken by the EVA on the y-axis (in seconds).

FLS, BLS and SUMO strategies gain advantage from an increase in c_d as the EVA can send lane change requests to farther vehicles. BLS gains additional advantage as it also uses the information about speed and position of other vehicles present in different lanes upto distance c_d, to compute better lanes. However, increasing the distance to greater than say 75 meters, does not lead to much better computation of utilities since additional vehicles may not add much to the existing information. Overall we can conclude that, for realistic distances involving single hop communication, BLS performs significantly better than FLS and SUMO strategies (e.g., 18.90% and 16.42% improvement at $c_d = 100$ meters).

REFERENCES

[1] D. Krajzewicz, J. Erdmann, M. Behrisch, and L. Bieker. Recent development and applications of sumo–simulation of urban mobility. *International Journal On Advances in Systems and Measurements*, 5(3&4), 2012.

[2] City of New York Department of Transportation. Real-time traffic speed data. `https://data.cityofnewyork.us/Transportation/Real-Time-Traffic-Speed-Data/xsat-x5sa`, Oct. 2015.

[3] M. Rahman, M. Chowdhury, Y. Xie, and Y. He. Review of microscopic lane-changing models and future research opportunities. *Intelligent Transportation Systems, IEEE Transactions on*, 14(4):1942–1956, 2013.

Strategic Disclosure of Opinions on a Social Network

(Extended Abstract)

Umberto Grandi
IRIT, University of Toulouse
France
Umberto.Grandi@irit.fr

Emiliano Lorini
IRIT-CNRS
University of Toulouse, France
Emiliano.Lorini@irit.fr

Laurent Perrussel
IRIT, University of Toulouse
France
Laurent.Perrussel@irit.fr

ABSTRACT

We study the strategic aspects of social influence in a society of agents linked by a trust network, introducing a new class of games called games of influence. A game of influence is an infinite repeated game with incomplete information in which, at each stage of interaction, an agent can make her opinions visible (public) or invisible (private) in order to influence other agents' opinions. The influence process is mediated by a trust network, as we assume that the opinion of a given agent is only affected by the opinions of those agents that she considers trustworthy (i.e., the agents in the trust network that are directly linked to her). Each agent is endowed with a goal, expressed in a suitable temporal language inspired from linear temporal logic (LTL). We show that games of influence provide a simple abstraction to explore the effects of the trust network structure on the agents' behaviour, by considering solution concepts from game-theory such as Nash equilibrium, weak dominance and winning strategies.

1. INTRODUCTION

At the micro-level, social influence can be conceived as a process where an agent forms her opinion on the basis of the opinions expressed by other agents in the society. Social influence depends on trust since an agent can be influenced by another agent, so that her opinions are affected by the expressed opinions of the other, only if she trusts her. At the macro-level, social influence is the basic mechanism driving the diffusion of opinions in human societies: certain agents in the society influence other agents in the society towards a given view, and these agents, in turn, influence other agents to acquire the same view, and so on. In other words, social influence can be seen as the driving force of opinion diffusion in human and human-like agent societies. This view is resonant of existing studies in social sciences and social psychology which emphasize the role of interpersonal processes in how people construe and form their perceptions, judgments, and impressions.

Recent work in multi-agent systems [3, 1] proposed a formal model of opinion diffusion that combined methods and techniques from social network analysis with methods and techniques from belief merging and judgment aggregation.

Appears in: *Proceedings of the 15th International Conference on Autonomous Agents and Multiagent Systems (AAMAS 2016), J. Thangarajah, K. Tuyls, C. Jonker, S. Marsella (eds.), May 9–13, 2016, Singapore.*

The two models aim at studying how opinions of agents on a given set of issues evolve over time due to the influence of other agents in the population. The basic component of these models is the trust network, as it is assumed that the opinions of a certain agent are affected only by the opinions of the agents that she trusts (i.e., the agents in the trust network that are directly linked to her). Specifically, the opinions of a certain agent at a given time are the result of aggregating the opinions of the trustworthy agents at the previous time.

In this work we build on these models to look at social influence from a strategic perspective. We do so by introducing a new class of games, called games of influence. Games of influence provide a simple abstraction to explore the effects of the trust network structure on the agents' behaviour. Specifically, a game of influence is an infinite repeated game with incomplete information in which, at each stage of interaction, an agent can make her opinions visible (public) or invisible (private) to the other agents. Incompleteness of information is determined by the fact that an agent has uncertainty about the private opinions of the other agents, as she cannot see them. At each stage of the game, every agent is influenced by the *public* opinions of the agents she trusts (i.e., her neighbors in the trust network) and changes her opinions on the basis of the aggregation criterion she uses.

Following the representation of agents' motivations given in [2], in a game of influence each agent is identified with the goal that she wants to achieve. This goal is represented by a formula of a variant of linear temporal logic (LTL), in which we can express properties about agents' present and future opinions. For example, an agent might have the achievement goal that at some point in the future there will be consensus about a certain proposition p (i.e., either everybody has the opinion that p is true or everybody has the opinion that p is false), or the maintenance goal that two different agents will always the same opinion about p.

2. BASIC DEFINITIONS

Let $\mathcal{I} = \{p_1, \ldots, p_m\}$ be a finite set of propositions or issues and let $\mathcal{N} = \{1, \ldots, n\}$ be a finite set of individuals or agents. In this section we provide some of the basic definitions of our setting, starting from the modelling of private and public opinions of individuals in $\mathcal{N}$ about the issues in $\mathcal{I}$, presenting then a model of opinion diffusion based on aggregation, together with a suitable logical language to express temporal goals of the individuals, and finally giving a general definition of influence games.

2.1 Private and public opinions

Agents have opinions about all issues in $\mathcal{I}$ in the form of a propositional evaluations:

DEFINITION 1 (PRIVATE OPINION). *The private opinion of agent i is a function $B_i : \mathcal{I} \to \{1, 0\}$.*

We also assume that each agent has the possibility of declaring or hiding her private opinion on each of the issues.

DEFINITION 2 (VISIBILITY FUNCTION). *The visibility function of agent i is a map $V_i : \mathcal{I} \to \{1, 0\}$.*

By combining the private opinion with the visibility function of an agent we can build her public opinion as a three-valued function on the set of issues.

DEFINITION 3 (PUBLIC OPINION). *Let B_i be agent i's opinion and V_i her visibility function. The public opinion induced by B_i and V_i is a function $P_i : \mathcal{I} \to \{1, 0, ?\}$ s.t.:*

$$P_i(p) = \begin{cases} B_i(p) & \text{if } V_i(p) = 1 \\ ? & \text{if } V_i(p) = 0 \end{cases}$$

Observe that an agent can only hide or declare her opinion about a given issue, but is not allowed to lie.

2.2 Opinion diffusion through aggregation

First, we assume that individuals are connected by an *influence network* which we model as a directed graph $E \subseteq \mathcal{N} \times \mathcal{N}$. We interpret $(i, j) \in E$ as "agent j is influenced by agent i". Given a profile of public opinions and an influence network E, we model the process of opinion diffusion by means of an aggregation function, which shapes the private opinion of an agent by taking into consideration the public opinions of her influencers.

DEFINITION 4 (AGGREGATION PROCEDURE). *An aggregation procedure for agent i is a class of functions*

$$F_i : \mathcal{B} \times \mathcal{P}_J \longrightarrow \mathcal{B} \text{ for each } J \subseteq \mathcal{N} \setminus \{i\}$$

that maps agent i's individual opinion and the public opinions of a set of agents J to agent i's individual opinion.

2.3 A language for goals

We introduce a logical language based on a combination of simple version of multi-agent epistemic logic and linear temporal logic (LTL) that can be interpreted over histories of influenced opinions. In line with our framework, term *epistemic state* should be interpreted as *private opinion*. Goals in our perspective consists of targeting an epistemic state: typically "agent i wants that agent j has private opinion φ in the future".

We call ELTL–I the following logic, from epistemic linear temporal logic of influence. Its language, denoted by $\mathcal{L}_{\mathsf{ELTL\text{-}I}}$, is defined by the following BNF:

$$\begin{array}{rcl} \alpha & ::= & \mathsf{op}(i,p) \mid \mathsf{vis}(i,p) \mid \neg\alpha \mid \alpha_1 \wedge \alpha_2 \mid \mathsf{K}_i\alpha \\ \varphi & ::= & \alpha \mid \neg\varphi \mid \varphi_1 \wedge \varphi_2 \mid \mathsf{X}\varphi \mid \varphi_1 \mathsf{U} \varphi_2 \end{array}$$

where i ranges over $\mathcal{N}$ and p ranges over $\mathcal{I}$. $\mathsf{op}(i,p)$ has to be read "agent i's opinion is that p is true" while$\neg\mathsf{op}(i,p)$ has to be read "agent i's opinion is that p is true" (since we assume that agents have binary opinions). $\mathsf{vis}(i,p)$ has to be read "agent i's opinion about p is visible". Finally, $\mathsf{K}_i\alpha$ has to be read "agent i knows that α is true". $\mathsf{X}\varphi$ and U are the standard LTL operators 'next' and 'until'.

The operator K_i is rather peculiar, and should not be interpreted as a classical individual epistemic operator. It mixes public and private opinions of our model. Operator K_i reading is rather "agent i is uncertain about other agents private opinion as this opinion is not visible" and $\mathsf{K}_i\alpha$ stands for agent i knows α despite this uncertainty.

2.4 Influence games

We are now ready to give the following definition:

DEFINITION 5 (INFLUENCE GAME). *An influence game is a tuple $IG = (\mathcal{N}, \mathcal{I}, E, F_i, S_0, \gamma_1, \ldots, \gamma_n)$ where $\mathcal{N}$, $\mathcal{I}$, E and S_0 are, respectively, a set of agents, a set of issues, an influence network, and an initial state, F_i are aggregation procedures, and $\gamma_i \in \mathcal{L}_{\mathsf{ELTL\text{-}I}}$ is agent i's goal.*

Strategies, best-responses and Nash equilibria, can be defined according to the relevant literature.

3. SUMMARY OF RESULTS

We inquire into the multiple aspects of the relation between the structure of the influence network, and the existence of well-known game-theoretic solution concepts. such as Nash equilibrium and weak dominance. For instance, we show that if the trust network is fully connected and every agent wants to reach a consensus about a certain proposition p, then there always exists a least one Nash equilibrium.

Moreover, we study how the relative position of an agent in the trust network determines her influencing power, that is, her capacity to influence opinions of other agents, no matter what the others decide to do (which corresponds to the concept of uniform strategy).

We are also able to show that model checking for our language, as well as the problem of checking whether a given profile is a Nash equilibrium, is in PSPACE, hence no harder than the linear temporal logic on which our language is based.

Acknowledgments

This work was partially supported by the project "Social Choice on Networks" of Labex CIMI ANR-11-LABX-0040-CIMI within the program ANR-11-IDEX-0002-02.

REFERENCES

[1] U. Grandi, E. Lorini, and L. Perrussel. Propositional opinion diffusion. In *Proceedings of the 14th International Joint Conference on Autonomous Agents and Multiagent Systems (AAMAS-2015)*, 2015.

[2] J. Gutierrez, P. Harrenstein, and M. Wooldridge. Iterated boolean games. *Information and Computation*, 242:53–79, 2015.

[3] N. Schwind, K. Inoue, G. Bourgne, S. Konieczny, and P. Marquis. Belief revision games. In *Proceedings of the Twenty-Ninth AAAI Conference on Artificial Intelligence (AAAI-2015)*, 2015.

Preference Elicitation in Matching Markets via Interviews: A Study of Offline Benchmarks

(Extended Abstract)

Baharak Rastegari
School of Computing Science
University of Glasgow
Glasgow, UK
baharak.rastegari@glasgow.ac.uk

Paul Goldberg
Dept. of Computer Science
University of Oxford
Oxford, UK
paul.goldberg@cs.ox.ac.uk

David Manlove
School of Computing Science
University of Glasgow
Glasgow, UK
david.manlove@glasgow.ac.uk

ABSTRACT

In this paper we study *two-sided matching markets* in which the participants do not fully know their preferences and need to go through some costly deliberation process in order to learn their preferences. We assume that such deliberations are carried out via *interviews*, thus the problem is to find a good strategy for interviews to be carried out in order to minimize their use, whilst leading to a stable matching. One way to evaluate the performance of an interview strategy is to compare it against a naïve algorithm that conducts all interviews. We argue however that a more meaningful comparison would be against an optimal offline algorithm that has access to agents' preference orderings under complete information. We show that, unless P=NP, no offline algorithm can compute the optimal interview strategy in polynomial time. If we are additionally aiming for a particular stable matching, we provide restricted settings under which efficient optimal offline algorithms exist.

Keywords

Two-sided matching; preferences; interviews

1. INTRODUCTION

Two-sided matching markets model many practical settings, such as corporate hiring and university admission [6, 3]. In the classical *stable marriage problem* participants are partitioned into two disjoint sets, and each participant on one side of the market wishes to be matched to a candidate from the other side of the market and has preferences over potential matches. A matching is called stable if no pair of participants would prefer to leave their assigned partners to pair with each other. Gale and Shapley's seminal paper [1] proposed a polynomial-time algorithm for finding a stable matching; a rich literature has developed since.

A key assumption in much of this literature is that all market participants know their full preference orderings. However, as markets grow large (e.g., in the hospital-resident matching market or college admission market [1, 3]) it quickly becomes impractical for participants to assess their precise preference rankings. Instead, participants usually start out with some partial knowledge about their preferences and need to perform some deliberation in order to learn their precise preference ordering. In this paper we assume that deliberations are carried out via *interviews*. Interviews are usually costly, therefore we wish to minimize their usage.

Any interviewing strategy leads to refinements of the partial orders contained in the original problem instance that represented uncertainty over the true preferences. A key aim could be to carry out sufficient interviews so as to arrive at an instance that admits a super-stable matching μ. Informally speaking, super-stability ensures that μ will be stable regardless of how the remaining uncertainty is resolved. The original instance need not admit a super-stable matching (see [2] for an example) but we are guaranteed that a super-stable matching is always achievable (e.g., by conducting all possible interviews). We seek a good strategy that conducts as few interviews as possible so as to obtain a refined instance that admits a super-stable matching. In general any such strategy will be an online algorithm, since the next interview to be carried out might depend on the results of previous ones.

2. PRELIMINARY DEFINITIONS

SMP, SMTI *and* SMT.

In an instance of the *Stable Marriage problem with Partially ordered preferences (*SMP*)*, there are two sets of agents, namely a set of men M and a set of women W. Each agent a finds a subset of agents on the opposite side of the market acceptable – we refer to these as *a's acceptable candidates*. An agent a's preferences over his/her acceptable candidates need not be strict. That is, given two candidates, a might be indifferent between them. We denote by I an instance of SMP, and by p_a the partial orders that represent the preference ordering of agent a. A *matching* μ is a pairing of men and women such that each man is paired with at most one woman and vice versa, and no agent is matched to an unacceptable partner. A well studied special case of SMP is the *Stable Marriage problem with Ties and Incomplete lists (*SMTI*)*. In SMTI, each agent has a partition of acceptable candidates into *ties* such that he or she is indifferent between the candidates in the same tie but has a strict preference ordering over the ties. The *Stable Marriage problem with Ties (*SMT*)* is the special case of SMTI in which each man finds each woman acceptable and vice versa.

Appears in: *Proceedings of the 15th International Conference on Autonomous Agents and Multiagent Systems (AAMAS 2016), J. Thangarajah, K. Tuyls, C. Jonker, S. Marsella (eds.), May 9–13, 2016, Singapore.*

Interviews to refine the partial orders.

In a given instance I of SMP in this paper, we assume that the partial preference ordering profile represents the agents' initial information state. That is, agents may not have enough information initially in order to rank their acceptable candidates in strict order. However each agent a has a strict preference ordering $\succ_a$ over his or her acceptable candidates, although s/he may not initially be aware of this entire ordering. We let $\succ_{M,W}$ denote the *strict (true underlying) preference ordering profile of all agents.* The task of the agents is to learn enough information about their acceptable candidates in order to refine their preferences, in a manner consistent with $\succ_{M,W}$, to obtain an SMP instance I' that admits a super-stable matching μ (thus μ will be stable with respect to $\succ_{M,W}$).

Following the model introduced in [4], we assume that instances can be refined through *interviews.* Each interview pairs one man m with one woman w. An interview is informative to both parties involved. When agent a interviews ℓ candidates, this results in a new refined SMP instance which is exactly the same as I except that a now has a strict preference ordering over the ℓ interviewed candidates.

Note that not all refinements of I can be reached by a set of interviews. We say that an SMP instance I' is an *interview-compatible refinement* of I if I' can be refined from I using interviews. We define the *cost* of I' to be the minimum number of interviews required to refine I into I'.

Definitions of the interview minimization problems.

The motivating problem is as follows: given an instance I of SMP, find an interview-compatible refinement I' of minimum cost such that I' admits a super-stable matching. Since the result of one interview might influence which interview/s to carry out next, any strategy for carrying out interviews should be regarded as an online algorithm. Towards computing bounds for the competitive ratio of an online algorithm, the offline scenario is of interest, and that is what we consider in what follows. In the offline case, the mechanism designer is given $\succ_{M,W}$, the strict (true underlying) preference ordering profile of the agents, and would like to compute an optimal interviewing schedule, i.e., an interview-compatible refinement I' of I, such that $\succ_{M,W}$ refines I'. This is reflected in the definition of the following problem, named MIN-ICR, which is an abbreviation for "Minimum-cost Interview Compatible Refinement problem".

DEFINITION 1. *An instance of* MIN-ICR *comprises a tuple $(I, \succ_{M,W})$, where I is an instance of* SMP *and $\succ_{M,W}$ is a strict preference ordering profile that refines I. The problem is to find an interview-compatible refinement I' of I such that (i) $\succ_{M,W}$ refines I', (ii) I' admits a super-stable matching, and (iii) I' is of minimum cost amongst interview-compatible refinements that satisfy (i) and (ii).*

It is sometimes the case that we aim for a particular matching, stable under $\succ_{M,W}$, that has some desirable properties, for example it is preferred to every other stable matching by women. The offline problem can then be viewed as a restricted variant of MIN-ICR where, in addition to I and $\succ_{M,W}$, we are also equipped with a matching μ. This is reflected in the definition of the following problem, named MIN-ICR-EXACT, which is an abbreviation for "Minimum-cost Interview Compatible Refinement problem with Exact matching".

DEFINITION 2. *An instance of* MIN-ICR-EXACT *comprises a tuple $(I, \succ_{M,W}, \mu)$, where I is an instance of* SMP, *$\succ_{M,W}$ is a strict preference ordering profile that refines I, and μ is a matching that is weakly stable w.r.t. $\succ_{M,W}$. The problem is to find an interview-compatible refinement I' of I, such that (i) $\succ_{M,W}$ refines I', (ii) μ is super-stable in I', and (iii) I' is of minimum cost amongst interview-compatible refinements of I that satisfy (i) and (ii).*

3. RESULTS

In the full version of this paper [5], we prove that MIN-ICR and MIN-ICR-EXACT are NP-hard even if I is an instance of SMTI in which each tie is of size at most 3. Further, we prove that both problems are NP-hard even for SMT instances, and even if all men are indifferent between all women. The hardness proofs are by reduction from the Vertex Cover problem (VC).

We then explore the tractability of MIN-ICR-EXACT under various restricted settings, using a reverse reduction from MIN-ICR-EXACT to VC to prove our claims. We show that MIN-ICR-EXACT is solvable in polynomial time under three different restrictions: (i) if one side has fully known strict preference ordering, (ii) if I is an instance of SMTI in which ties are of size at most 2, and (iii) if I is an instance of of SMTI in which all men are endowed with the same ties, as well as all women.

4. FUTURE WORK

The main direction is to investigate the online case, where the true underlying preferences are not known to the mechanism designer, with respect to measures such as the competitive ratio. Furthermore, an important question is whether MIN-ICR is polynomial-time solvable under some restricted setting. Extending the known results on interviewing in stable marriage markets to many-to-one markets such as college admission is another important future direction. It is also interesting to study online algorithms in a setting where elicitation is taking place via comparison queries.

Acknowledgments. We thank Rob Irving and Piotr Krysta for the useful discussions and their valuable feedback. This work was supported by EPSRC grants EP/K01000X/1 and EP/K010042/1, and COST Action IC1205.

REFERENCES

[1] D. Gale and L. S. Shapley. College admissions and the stability of marriage. *Amer. Math. Monthly*, 69:9–15, 1962.

[2] R. W. Irving. Stable marriage and indifference. *Discrete Applied Math.*, 48(3):261–272, 1994.

[3] D. F. Manlove. *Algorithmics of Matching Under Preferences.* World Scientific, 2013.

[4] B. Rastegari, A. Condon, N. Immorlica, and K. Leyton-Brown. Two-sided matching with partial information. In *Proc. EC '13*, pp. 733–750. ACM, 2013.

[5] B. Rastegari, P. Goldberg and D. Manlove. Preference elicitation in matching markets via interviews: A study of offline benchmarks. CoRR abs/1602.04792, 2016.

[6] A. Roth and M. Sotomayor. *Two-Sided Matching: A Study in Game-Theoretic Modeling and Analysis.* Cambridge University Press, 1990.

Robust Influence Maximization

(Extended Abstract)

Meghna Lowalekar, Pradeep Varakantham, Akshat Kumar
School of Information Systems, Singapore Management University
meghnal.2015@phdis.smu.edu.sg,{pradeepv,akshatkumar}@smu.edu.sg

ABSTRACT

Influence Maximization [2] is the problem of finding a fixed size set of nodes, which will maximize the expected number of influenced nodes in a social network. The number of influenced nodes is dependent on the influence strength of edges that can be very noisy. The noise in the influence strengths can be modeled using a random noise or adversarial noise model. It has been shown that all random processes that independently affect edges of the graph can be absorbed into the activation probabilities themselves and hence random noise can be captured within the independent cascade model.

On the other hand, similar to He *et al.* [1], we consider the adversarial noise where influence strength for an edge can belong to any point in the interval: $[\check{p}_{u,v}, \hat{p}_{u,v}]$ and the exact values are chosen by an adversary from this interval. The problems of evaluating robustness of a given solution and computing robust optimal solutions have received scant attention in the literature and are of key interest in this paper. Specifically, we aim to minimize (over all available seed sets) the maximum (over all instantiations of influence strengths) regret. Concretely, the key contributions are: **(1)** We show that maximum regret for a given solution is attained when influence strength on each of the edges is set to one of the extreme values of the influence strength intervals on edges. **(2)** We provide a novel way of considering samples that accounts for the noise in influence strength on all edges. **(3)** We develop a framework which provides an approach to get an optimal regret solution and more importantly a metric to evaluate robustness of a given solution based on the regret optimal solution. **(4)** Finally, we show results on evaluating the robustness of the well known greedy approach. Surprisingly, even without considering noise in influence strengths explicitly, greedy approach achieves highly robust solutions on small-medium scale social network instances.

Keywords

Influence Maximization, Regret, Optimization

1. ROBUST INFLUENCE MAXIMIZATION

The value of influence strength, $p_{u,v}$ from u to v can not be observed directly and is generally inferred from observed behavior which is inherently very noisy. We assume that the actual influence strength for an edge can belong to any point in the interval: $[\check{p}_{u,v}, \hat{p}_{u,v}]$. Our goal is to compute a robust seed set of M nodes that will minimize the maximum regret over the interval noise in influence strengths. Let $\mathbb{S}$ denote the set of all possible node sets of size M and let $\mathcal{P} = \{[\check{p}_e, \hat{p}_e]\}_{e \in E}$ represent the noise in influence strengths. We define regret, maximum regret and minimax regret using the following equations:

$$\delta(S, \mathbf{p}) = \max_{S' \in \mathbb{S}} \ \sigma_{\mathbf{p}}(S') - \sigma_{\mathbf{p}}(S) \quad (1)$$

$$\delta^{\mathbf{MR}}(S, \mathcal{P}) = \max_{p \in \mathcal{P}} \ \delta(S, \mathbf{p}) \quad (2)$$

$$\delta^{\mathbf{MMR}}(\mathcal{P}) = \min_{S \in \mathbb{S}} \ \delta^{\mathbf{MR}}(S, \mathcal{P}) \quad (3)$$

where S' and S are seed sets of size M and $\sigma_{\mathbf{p}}(S)$ is the expected influence value of set S for the probability values $\mathbf{p}$. We can then show that maximum regret for any set S is obtained when all edge probabilities are at extreme values.

The proposed optimization model for calculating $\mathbf{MMR}(\mathcal{P})$ is extended on the one by Sheldon *et al.* [3]. The constraints in the formulation ensure that for a given seedset, regret is higher than maximum possible regret over all influence strength vectors in set $\mathcal{P}$ and the objective ensures the computation of least maximum regret over all possible seedsets. Since the set of extreme influence strength vectors grows exponentially with the number of edges, the optimization formulation is not scalable. We address this challenge by using constraint generation.

The key idea is to decompose the formulation of $\mathbf{MMR}(\mathcal{P})$ into two components that are run iteratively until convergence: **(1)** A master component, $\mathbf{MMR}(\mathcal{P}_{sub})$ that computes minimax regret solution, S for a discrete subset, $\mathcal{P}_{sub}$ of probability vectors.**(2)** A slave component, $\mathbf{MR}(S, \mathcal{P})$ that computes the probability vector, p^*, which yields maximum regret given $\mathcal{P}$ and S. If $\mathbf{MR}(S, \mathcal{P}) \leq \mathbf{MMR}(\mathcal{P}_{sub})$, then we stop the process and return S, otherwise p^* is added to $\mathcal{P}_{sub}$ for the master component to compute a new S. The key novelty of the slave formulation is in identifying a probability vector (with extreme values for each edge) for a given seed set that maximizes regret. Unlike in traditional influence maximization and in master component, the activation of an edge is not generated before hand (outside optimization model) based on uniform random numbers, but in the formulation as we have an interval of influence strengths for each edge. Given the influence strength interval, $[\check{p}_e, \hat{p}_e]$ for an edge e, constraints ensure that edge is active with a min-

Appears in: *Proceedings of the 15th International Conference on Autonomous Agents and Multiagent Systems (AAMAS 2016), J. Thangarajah, K. Tuyls, C. Jonker, S. Marsella (eds.), May 9–13, 2016, Singapore.*

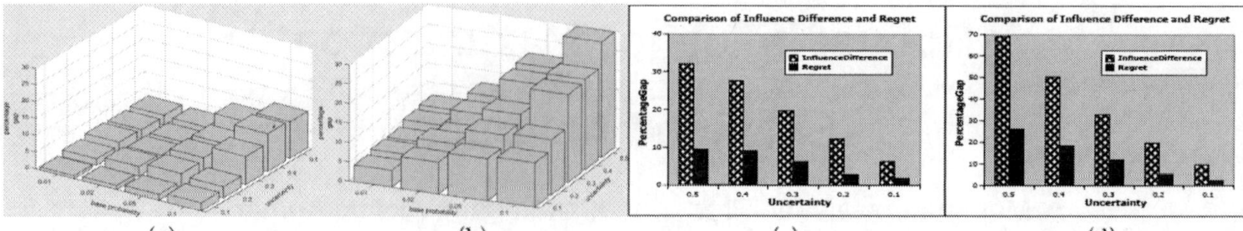

(a) (b) (c) (d)

Figure 1: Percentage gap of greedy solution (a) SmallW (b) NetScience. In (a) Number Of Samples($|\Xi|$) = 200 and (b) $|\Xi|$ =110. Comparison of Influence Difference and Regret on (c) SmaGri Network; and (d) CSPhD Network.

imum probability of $\check{p}_e$ and a maximum probability of $\hat{p}_e$.

Evaluating Robustness of a Given Solution We now describe a method to compute percentage gap of a given solution from the optimal minimax regret for a given set of samples. We denote $\hat{\mathbf{R}}$ and $\check{\mathbf{R}}$ as the upper and lower bound on regret, if the algorithm is stopped before convergence. We can provide a bound on the difference from regret optimal influence value. Let $\sigma_{\mathbf{p}}(S^*)$ be the optimal influence value for any influence strength vector $\mathbf{p}$,then for the current solution S, the upper and lower bound of influence at $\mathbf{p}$ are:

$$\hat{\sigma}_{\mathbf{p}}(S) = \sigma_{\mathbf{p}}(S^*) - \check{\mathbf{R}}, \check{\sigma}_{\mathbf{p}}(S) = \sigma_{\mathbf{p}}(S^*) - \hat{\mathbf{R}}$$

The percentage gap, Δ for S and $\mathbf{p}$ is given by

$$\Delta_{\mathbf{p}}(S) = \frac{\hat{\sigma}_{\mathbf{p}}(S) - \check{\sigma}_{\mathbf{p}}(S)}{\hat{\sigma}_{\mathbf{p}}(S)} * 100 = \left(1 - \frac{1}{1 + \frac{\hat{\mathbf{R}} - \check{\mathbf{R}}}{\sigma_{\mathbf{p}}(S^*) - \hat{\mathbf{R}}}}\right) * 100 \quad (4)$$

The above expression will be maximum when $\sigma_{\mathbf{p}}(S^*)$ is minimum and the influence value will be minimum when all the edges are at minimum probability. So we calculate $\Delta_{\mathbf{p}}(S)$ at $\mathbf{p} = \{\check{p}_{u,v}, \forall u, v\}$ to obtain $\Delta(S)$ (the worst case percentage gap). In summary, $\Delta(S)$ gives us one number to evaluate the robustness of a given solution S by comparing it against our approach.

2. EXPERIMENTAL RESULTS

In this section, we evaluate the percentage gap of the well known greedy algorithm [2] for varying levels of uncertainty. We are able to demonstrate that percentage gap for greedy is low (<30%) even at very high uncertainty levels (20%-50%). We also show that the existing metric of influence difference proposed by [1] is not suitable to evaluate robustness of solution. We employ the settings used by [1], and vary the base probability to take on the values $\{0.01, 0.02, 0.05, 0.1\}$. The uncertainty interval for an edge (u, v) is: $[(1 - \varepsilon) * p_{u,v}, (1 + \varepsilon) * p_{u,v}]$, where $p_{u,v}$ is the observed base probability and ε is the uncertainty parameter which takes on the values $\{10\%, 20\%, 30\%, 40\%, 50\%\}$.

We first demonstrate the percentage gap values for greedy heuristic provided by the regret metric. We calculate the maximum regret of this greedy solution S^g by using MaxRegret linear program. Let $\mathbf{R}^g$ be the regret of greedy solution, then we calculate the percentage gap of the greedy solution, $\Delta(S^g)$ from the regret optimal solution by substituting $\mathbf{R}^g$ in place of $\hat{\mathbf{R}}$ in equation (4). The detailed percentage gap results for the greedy algorithm on the 2 data sets [1] are given in Figure 1(a-b). Each 3D graph has base probability on the X-axis, uncertainty interval on the Y-axis and the percentage gap of the greedy based compared to regret optimal (or regret lower and upper bounds) on the Z-axis.

We also observe that as the base probability and uncertainty increases the percentage gap from the optimal solution increases. This is because for higher base probability and uncertainty value convergence is slower. So the percentage gap of greedy solution will improve if we can compute the exact value of optimal regret solution.

For adversarial noise model, the only other metric that has been proposed is by He *et al.* [1]. While "influence difference maximization" is employed to measure the stability of an instance and not robustness of a solution, "influence difference for a given solution" can be employed to evaluate robustness of a solution. Influence difference value for a given solution S is calculated using equation 1 in [1](by fixing the solution S and base probability, θ), i.e., $\lambda(S) = max_{\mathbf{p} \in \mathcal{P}} |\sigma_{\mathbf{p}}(S) - \sigma_{\theta}(S)|$

Specifically, we calculate the percentage gap generated by the greedy solution (for base probability) using both the metrics. Let $\lambda(S^g)$ be the influence difference of greedy solution, S^g. We substitute the value $\lambda(S^g)$ in place of $\hat{\mathbf{R}}$ in equation (4), to calculate percentage gap of solution S^g by using influence difference. Figure 1(c)-(d) shows the comparison of percentage gap of S^g by using influence difference and regret metrics for 2 networks for 0.1 base probability and different uncertainty values. By using regret in place of influence difference, we were able to reduce the bounds by almost 60%. In other words, if influence difference indicates that a solution is not-robust, that may not be correct as it is an upper bound on regret. This shows that our method is able to more accurately evaluate robustness of a solution.

Acknowledgments This research is supported by Singapore National Research Foundation under its International Research Centre @Singapore Funding Initiative and administered by the IDM Programme Office, Media Development Authority (MDA).

[1]http://vlado.fmf.uni-lj.si/pub/networks/data/

REFERENCES

[1] X. He and D. Kempe. Stability of influence maximization. *CoRR*, abs/1501.04579, 2015.

[2] D. Kempe, J. Kleinberg, and E. Tardos. Maximizing the spread of influence through a social network. In *Proceedings of the Ninth ACM SIGKDD International Conference on Knowledge Discovery and Data Mining*, KDD '03, pages 137–146, New York, NY, USA, 2003. ACM.

[3] D. Sheldon, B. N. Dilkina, A. N. Elmachtoub, R. Finseth, A. Sabharwal, J. Conrad, C. P. Gomes, D. B. Shmoys, W. Allen, O. Amundsen, and W. Vaughan. Maximizing the spread of cascades using network design. In *UAI, Proceedings of the Twenty-Sixth Conference on Uncertainty in Artificial Intelligence, Catalina Island, CA, USA, July 8-11, 2010*, pages 517–526.

Multi-Agent Cooperative Area Coverage: Case Study Ploughing

(Extended Abstract)

Alireza Janani
Sheffield Hallam University
Howard Street
Sheffield, UK
ajanani@my.shu.ac.uk

Lyuba Alboul
Sheffield Hallam University
Howard Street
Sheffield, UK
l.alboul@shu.ac.uk

Jacques Penders
Sheffield Hallam University
Howard Street
Sheffield, UK
j.penders@shu.ac.uk

ABSTRACT

We present two cooperative strategies in area coverage that are aimed to be applied in agricultural robotics domain. Current strategies in this domain rely on explicit forms of communication for task allocation and coordination. One issue with these approaches is the loss of communicating signal. This paper presents two approaches (FIFO, and LIFO) for task allocation and coordination that relies only on local information of the robots.

Keywords

Multi-robot Area Coverage; Multi-agent System; Agricultural Robotics; Cooperative Behaviour

1. INTRODUCTION

In area coverage, a team of robots has to cooperatively sweep the entire area, possibly containing obstacles. The goal is to build an efficient path for each robot which jointly ensure that every single point in the environment can be visited by the robots. Many real world applications require systematic area coverage including search in forested area, demining, distribution of beacons and line searching. In this paper we focus on the application of agricultural robotics and in particular ploughing.

Ploughing is seedbed preparation process and it is carried out by dragging a ploughing mouldboard across the field. The ploughing mouldboard digs deep into the soil and disperses the soil in one direction. Ploughing creates a two-part pattern: (1) A narrow trench which is called *furrow*, and (2) a hill-top soil which is called *ridge*.

Ploughing has four main restrictions: (I) The target locations have to be ploughed only once. (II) Furrows have to be created consecutively so that a furrow is accompanied by a ridge. (III) Two consecutive furrows cannot be created simultaneously. (IV) The order of field processing (which part of the field to be ploughed next) depends on the attached ploughing mouldboards. There are various types of mouldboards roughly classified into reversible and conventional. With reversible mouldboards, the field can be processed consecutively. In this method, ploughing starts from one side of the field and ends on the other side. Whereas with conventional mouldboards, the field can only be processed in a loop. In this ploughing method, the field is processed from sides and ends in the middle. In this paper, it is assumed that robots are equipped with reversible mouldboards.

Ploughing by a team of robots has to be strongly coordinated with real-time task allocation. Current approaches in agricultural robotic domain achieve this level of coordination and real-time task allocation using base-station ([2], [3]) and direct robot negotiations [1]. These approaches require explicit forms of communication (e.g. using WiFi, Bluetooth, Sonar) which are susceptible to the loss of communicating signal or the base station.

The aim of the proposed strategy is to develop a decentralised scalable distributed self-organising robotic system that would require minimum computational effort, no central-based control and communication, and at the same time high-efficient and adaptable to various agricultural tasks and fields.

2. COOPERATIVE STRATEGY

The proposed strategy is based on the principle of indirect communication. As a result of ploughing, the state of the soil changes. This is detectable using image processing and it is being used for navigation purposes [4]. Alternatively, this information could be interpreted differently. In the proposed strategy the problem of task allocation is resolved by real-time ordering of robots.

Initially, robots approach ploughing locations in a fixed order (e.g. $f_1 \rightarrow f_n$) to analyse the state of the soil. The index of the first detected unploughed location becomes the rank of the robot. Once this location is identified, the robot initiate ploughing right away.

In order to assure that robots obtain a linear order, robots approach the field from a unique and single location. This location is referred to as α and it is located outside of the field and near the first ploughing location.

Once the robot enters the field (in linear order), it needs to identify which locations to plough next. However, since furrows have to be created consecutively, $f_i \rightarrow f_{i+1}$, robots have to assure that the targeted location is next to a created furrow. This requires that robots standby somewhere outside of the field. This waiting area is referred to as *Headland*. At the start and end of the field a headland is required. It is an untreated area allowing to position the robot and the

Appears in: *Proceedings of the 15th International Conference on Autonomous Agents and Multiagent Systems (AAMAS 2016), J. Thangarajah, K. Tuyls, S. Marsella, Jonker (eds.), May 9–13, 2016, Singapore.*

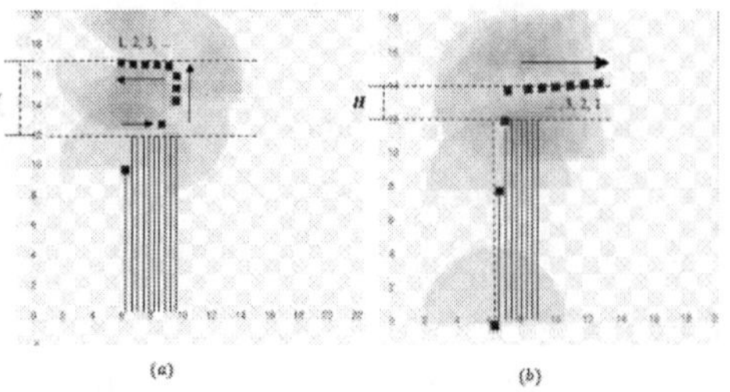

Figure 1: Stage simulation environment: (a) FIFO in a team of 10 robots. (b) LIFO in a team of 10 robots.

plough at the start allowing transitions at the end of a furrow. Headlands are uncultivable as they are not ploughed, and therefore the productivity of the field is affected by the width of headland: *the wider the headland, the less productive the field.* The productivity of a field can be expressed as follows:

$$PR = \frac{l_p}{L} \times 100 \quad (1)$$

Where L is the length of the field, and l_p is the length of the ploughed furrow. l_p can be obtained from $l_p = L - h_1 - h_2$. In here, h_1 and h_2 are the width of the headlands on both sides of the field.

Robots have to standby in headland areas to avoid congestion and to maintain the designated order while the productivity of the field is kept as high as possible. For this we proposed two cooperative models: (I) FIFO: First In First Out, and (II) LIFO: Last In First Out. In FIFO, robots aim at maintaining the original order by queuing behind the first robot (see Fig. 1(a)). In this strategy, robots are lined-up in a fixed width ($n \times f_d$: where n is the number of robots and f_d is the distance between two ploughing locations) but in variable length which affects the width of the headlands. In FIFO, the required width of the headland depends on the team size and it can be evaluated as follows:

$$H_{FIFO} = (\lambda + \epsilon)(n - \lfloor \frac{d_f(2n-1)}{\lambda + \epsilon} \rfloor) \quad (2)$$

In this strategy, ploughing restarts by r_1 whenever it detected that r_n is out of its field of view. This is carried out using image analysis on teammate modelling. In here, we used color detection as robots are homogeneous and look alike.

In LIFO, the original order is reversed on each round of furrow transitioning. In here, the advantage is to increase the productivity of the field by reducing the required headland. Robots line-up in front of each other and move reversely to avoid collision while in the queue (see Fig. 1(b)). While waiting, robots utilise their camera to observe and to predict the behaviour of the front robot. Ploughing restarts whenever the last robot, which becomes the first robot for the next round, completes its current ploughing. In-depth analysis of LIFO reveals that this method requires less headland area.

$$H_{LIFO} = \zeta + \lambda \quad (3)$$

The result obtained from simulation and mathematical numeric visualisations of various team sizes approve that the

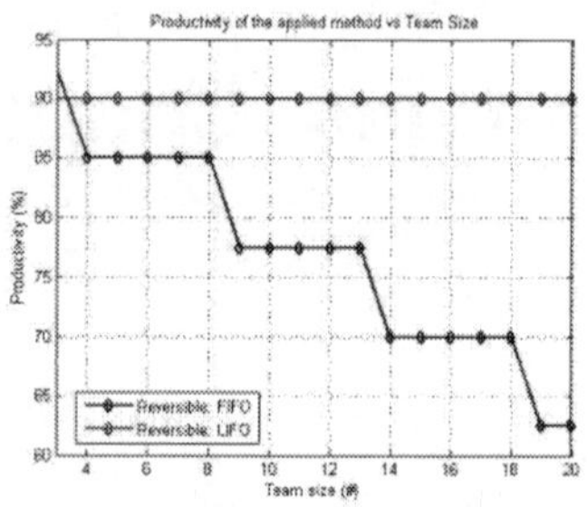

Figure 2: Stage simulation environment: (Blue) FIFO in a team of 10 robots. (Green) LIFO in a team of 10 robots.

LIFO is more productive since headland navigation strategy is independent of the team size (see Fig. 2).

3. CONCLUSION AND FUTURE WORK

In this paper, we addressed the problem of area coverage in the case of ploughing, a fundamental task in agriculture. In the described solutions, task allocation is based on indirect communication between robots. This consists of detecting changes in the soil pattern at particular locations. For cooperative behaviour and coordination, two strategies are proposed: FIFO and LIFO. The approaches are different in terms of required headland for traffic handling by which the productivity of the field will be affected. In FIFO, the productivity of the field is affected as number of participating robots increases. Whereas in LIFO, the productivity of the field remains as constant.

The proposed approaches are only applicable if the robots are equipped with reversible mouldboards, but reversible mouldboards are not always available. Alternatively, robots may be equipped with conventional mouldboards which disperse soil in a fixed direction. In that case, a different strategy is needed to be developed.

Ploughing is a special case in which robots can interact with each other through changes created in the soil. However, in other agricultural tasks, spraying in particular, this facility does not exist. Spraying does not have long term impact on the soil, hence different approach is required.

REFERENCES

[1] H. Anil, K. Nikhil, V. Charitra, and B. Gurusharan. Revolutionizing farming using swarm robotics. *6th International Conference on Intelligent Systems, Modelling and Simulation*, 19(3):141–147, 2015.

[2] D. Drenjanac, S. Tomic, L. Klausner, and E. Kuhn. Harnessing coherence of area decomposition and semantic shared spaces for task allocation. *In Information Processing in Agriculture*, pages 23–34, 2014.

[3] C. Liu and A. Kroll. Memetic algorithms for optimal task allocation in multi robot systems for inspection problems with cooperative tasks. *Journal of Soft Computing*, 19(3):567–584, 2014.

[4] D. Liu, J. Wnag, T. Yan, and B. Chen. Fast detection of furrows based on machine vision on autonomous mobile robot. *Transactions of the Chinese Society for Agricultural Machinery*, 37(4):87–90, 2006.

Decentralised Norm Monitoring in Open Multi-Agent Systems

(Extended Abstract)

Natasha Alechina
University of Nottingham
nza@cs.nott.ac.uk

Joseph Y. Halpern*
Cornell University
halpern@cs.cornell.edu

Ian A. Kash
Microsoft Research
iankash@microsoft.com

Brian Logan
University of Nottingham
bsl@cs.nott.ac.uk

ABSTRACT

We propose an approach to norm monitoring in open multi-agents systems (MAS) in which monitoring is performed by the agents comprising the MAS. Using ideas from *scrip systems*, we show how to design mechanisms where agents are incentivised to monitor the actions of other agents for norm violations. Crtically, the cost of providing incentives is not borne by the MAS. Instead, monitoring incentives come from (scrip) fees for accessing the services provided by the MAS. In some cases perfect monitoring (and hence enforcement) can be achieved: no norms will be violated in equilibrium. In other cases, we show that, while it is impossible to achieve perfect enforcement, we can get arbitrarily close; we can make the probability of a norm violation in equilibrium arbitrarily small.

1. INCENTIVISING MONITORING

We propose an approach to norm monitoring in open multi-agents systems (MAS) in which the monitoring of agent actions is performed by the agents comprising the MAS. We focus on norms which prohibit certain actions (or the state resulting from an action). The novelty of our approach is that the MAS does not bear the cost of monitoring; nor does it levy fines on violating agents to pay for monitoring as in, for example, [1]. (Levying fines is not possible in many open systems as the agents can always leave the system and rejoin later under a different identity.) Instead, monitoring incentives come from (scrip) fees [2] for accessing the services provided by the MAS.

As a simple example, consider a MAS where agents want to post content on the web. There are norms regarding what may be posted; for example, copyrighted images should not be posted, and comments should not be abusive or defamatory. We assume that agents may occasionally submit posts that violate the norm. If such content appears on the web, the MAS loses significant utility (e.g., it can be fined or sued). It is therefore in the MAS's interest that submitted posts are checked for compliance with the norm before they appear on the web. We assume that it is possible to check objectively if a particular item of content violates the norm. (For simplicity, we assume that if a post that violates the norm is checked, the violation will be detected. We can easily modify our approach to handle the case where there is some probability ρ of the violation being caught.) Checking whether a post is 'bad' (violates the norm) requires some work, and incurs a small utility cost. Although checking requires some resources, we assume that if a violation is found, evidence of the violation can be provided that can be checked in negligible time (so we do not need to deal with disputes about whether content violates the norm). If the content does violate the norm, the post is discarded and no violation occurs. We would like to distribute the monitoring of posts among the agents that use the system. Just as for the MAS, monitoring incurs a small negative utility for an agent. This means that agents must be appropriately incentivised to monitor. The scenario we describe applies to a wide range of normative multi-agent systems. The only requirement is that norms apply to single actions, actions can be checked in advance, and their execution prevented if they are found to violate the norm. Examples other than web postings include bids for jobs and bookings of facilities.

We formalise the posting and monitoring of content for norm violations as a non-cooperative game. This scenario (and the resulting game) is similar to that considered by Friedman et al. [2], but differs in several key respects. As in [2], we adopt the idea of using *tokens* as payment for posting and as a reward for monitoring.

2. UNINTENTIONAL VIOLATION

We first consider a scenario in which bad posts are unintentional, and happen with a constant probability b. In this scenario, agents are unaware that they are violating the norm when they post something inappropriate. The game in the inadvertent scenario is described by the following parameters:

- a finite set of n agents $1, \dots, n$;
- the time between rounds is $1/n$;
- at each round t an agent is picked at random to submit a post (we implicitly assume that agents always have something that they want to post);
- probability of a post being bad: b;
- utility of posting (to the agent doing the posting): 1
- disutility of monitoring (to the agent doing the monitoring): $-\alpha$ (where $0 < \alpha < 1$);
- discount rate: $\delta \in (0, 1)$.

*Supported in part by NSF grants IIS-0534064, IIS-0812045, IIS-0911036, and CCF-1214844, and by AFOSR grants FA9550-08-1-0438, FA9550-09-1-0266, and FA9550-12-1-0040, and ARO grant W911NF-09-1-0281.

Appears in: *Proceedings of the 15th International Conference on Autonomous Agents and Multiagent Systems (AAMAS 2016), J. Thangarajah, K. Tuyls, C. Jonker, S. Marsella (eds.), May 9–13, 2016, Singapore.*

The game runs forever. As is standard in the literature, we assume that agents discount future payoffs (this allows us to compute the total utility derived by an agent in the infinite game).

We need some additional notation to describe what happens:

- $p^t \in \{1, \dots, n\}$ is the agent chosen to submit a post at t;
- $v^t \in \{0, \dots, n\} \setminus \{p^t\}$; $v^t = j$ if agent $j \neq p^t$ is chosen to monitor at t, and $v^t = 0$ if no one is chosen to monitor; at t;
- $f^t \in \{0, 1\}$; $f^t = 0$ if the content posted at t is good, $f^t = 1$ if it is bad.

Given that good and bad posts have the same utility (namely, 1), the utility of an agent i in round t is:

$$u_i^t = \begin{cases} 1 & \text{if } i = p^t \text{ and either } v^t = 0 \text{ or } f^t = 0; \\ -\alpha & \text{if } v^t = i; \\ 0 & \text{otherwise.} \end{cases}$$

The total utility U_i for agent i is $\Sigma_{t=0}^{\infty} \delta^{t/n} u_i^t$, where δ is the discount factor.

To incentivise agents to monitor posts, we use tokens as payment for posting and as a reward for monitoring. Agents must pay one token to post and are rewarded with tokens if they detect a bad post. We argue below that in order for the system to function successfully (agents being able to post, and some agents always available for monitoring), the 'right' amount to pay for finding a bad posting is $1/b$. This means, in expectation, an agent gets one token for finding a bad posting. Thus, the price of a posting is equal to the expected cost of checking a posting.

Paying agents $1/b$ for finding a bad posting makes the situation similar to that in [2], where the agent wanting work done pays one token, and the agent doing the work gets one token. However, the fact that in our setting payment is made only if a problem is found complicates matters. Specifically, the agents cannot simply pay the MAS to post, or the MAS pay the agents for finding a bad post. If monitors have a long run of "bad luck" and do not find postings that violate the norm, there will be very few tokens left in the system; on the other hand, if monitors get lucky, and find quite a few postings that violate the norm, the MAS will end up pumping quite a few tokens into the system. Having both too few or too many tokens in the system causes problems [2]. Intuitively, with too many tokens in the system, (almost) all agents will have plenty of tokens, so no one will volunteer to monitor; with too few tokens in the system, it will often be the case that the agent who wants to post will not have a token to pay for it.

To ensure that the number of tokens in "circulation" remains constant, the agents rather than the MAS perform the role of the "bank". We assume that all agents follow a *threshold strategy* when deciding whether to monitor. There is a fixed threshold k such that agents volunteer iff they have fewer than k tokens. If an agent i has at least one token and is chosen to submit a post ($i = p^t$), p^t gives a randomly chosen agent with fewer than $k + 1/b$ tokens one more. The posting agent p^t than asks for volunteers to act as monitor. All agents with fewer than k tokens volunteer. If at least one agent volunteers, one, v^t, is chosen at random to act as monitor. If v^t confirms that the post conforms to the norm, it is posted. If v^t detects a violation of the norm, then the post is discarded, and a randomly chosen agent with at least $1/b$ tokens gives v^t $1/b$ tokens.

THEOREM 1. *For all $\epsilon > 0$, there exist a δ sufficiently close to 1 and an n sufficiently large such that if all n agents have a discount factor $\delta' \geq \delta$, then there exists a k such that the mechanism above with all agents using a threshold of k is an ϵ-Nash equilibrium.*

All proofs, together with additional details and intuitions, are available at arxiv.org/1602.06731. Note that in the equilibrium the existence of which is stated in Theorem 1, we get perfect enforcement; all bad posts will be detected.

3. STRATEGIC VIOLATION

We now consider the scenario in which violations are strategic. When an agent is chosen to submit a post, it can either submit something good (i.e., that does not violate the norm) or something bad. The parameters of the game are the same as in Section 2, except that there is no longer a probability b of a posting being bad (the quality of a posting now becomes a strategic decision), and the utility of a bad posting is no longer 1, but $\kappa > 1$. (We must assume $\kappa > 1$ here, otherwise no agent would ever post anything bad: the utility of doing so is no higher than that of posting something good, and the violation may be detected.) As before, monitoring agents get paid only if they find a bad post.

With these assumptions, it is not hard to show that there does not exist an equilibrium with perfect enforcement.

THEOREM 2. *In the setting of strategic violations, there can be no equilibrium with perfect enforcement.*

Although we cannot achieve perfect enforcement in the strategic setting, we can make the probability of a bad posting as low as we want. More precisely, for all $\epsilon, \epsilon' > 0$, there is an ϵ-Nash equilibrium such that the probability of a bad post is ϵ'.

We have the following mechanism, given a threshold k. If an agent is chosen to post, it submits bad content with probability β^* and good content with probability $1 - \beta^*$. After the agent has decided what to post and made the posting available, the MAS decides whether the posting will be monitored. For an initial period (say 1,000 rounds), a posting is monitored with probability $1 - 1/\kappa$; afterwards, if the fraction of postings that have been discovered to be bad due to monitoring is β and β is more than (say) two standard deviations from β^*, then monitoring occurs with probability $1 - \beta^*/(\beta\kappa)$. If the decision has been made to monitor and the posting agent has at least one token (so that a post can be made), the posting agent asks for volunteers and all agents with fewer than k tokens volunteer to monitor and one is chosen to be the monitor. As in the case of unintentional violations, if at least one agent volunteers, then the posting agent gives a randomly chosen agent with less than $k + 1/\beta^*$ tokens one more. If the monitor approves the posting, it is posted. If the monitor finds a problem with the posting, then a randomly chosen agent with at least $1/\beta^*$ tokens gives the monitor $1/\beta^*$ tokens.

THEOREM 3. *For all $\epsilon > 0$, there exist a δ sufficiently close to 1 and an n sufficiently large such that if all n agents use a discount factor $\delta' \geq \delta$, then there exists a k such that the mechanism above with all agents using a threshold of k is an ϵ-Nash equilibrium.*

Note that, in the equilibrium whose existence is stated in Theorem 3, the probability of a bad posting is β^*, as desired.

REFERENCES

[1] M. S. Fagundes, S. Ossowski, and F. Meneguzzi. Analyzing the tradeoff between efficiency and cost of norm enforcement in stochastic environments. In *21st European Conference on Artificial Intelligence (ECAI 2014)*, pages 1003–1004. 2014.

[2] E. J. Friedman, J. Y. Halpern, and I. A. Kash. Efficiency and nash equilibria in a scrip system for P2P networks. In *Proceedings 7th ACM Conference on Electronic Commerce (EC 2006)*, pages 140–149. 2006.

Integrating Run-Time Incidents in a Large-Scale Simulated Urban Environment

(Extended Abstract)

Steven de Jong*, Alex Klein, Ruben Smelik, and Freek van Wermeskerken
Department of Modeling, Simulation and Gaming, TNO, The Netherlands

ABSTRACT

Motivated by many potential applications within the domain of Defense, Safety & Security, we present an approach for the injection of *incidents* (e.g., an arrest following a shoplifting) in a running, large-scale urban simulation. Incidents are generated within desired user constraints such as what should happen, where, and when. We believe that this approach offers an intuitive and extendable way to create scenario-specific exceptions to daily behavior patterns.

Keywords

Run-Time Incidents, Scenario Generation, Urban Simulation

1. INTRODUCTION

Within the domain of Defense, Safety & Security, state-of-the-art simulation environments can help reduce the time and costs needed to organize large-scale training events or rehearsals. Moreover, they can provide scenarios and situations that are not easily experienced in a real-world setting. However, instructors often experience a lack of control over the flow of scenarios, especially since the behavior of both virtual and real humans involved in these scenarios can be highly unpredictable [3]. For example, a trainee may choose a different route than the one the instructor prepared for.

We present an approach that allows instructors to more directly control and adjust the flow of a running scenario by injecting *incidents* at run-time, to facilitate learning moments or cope with unforeseen behavior. Incidents in our approach specify the instructor's *intent*, i.e. what should happen, where, and when [2]. An efficient planning and sampling algorithm translates the intent to one or more parallel sequences of actions, to be performed by virtual humans (agents) at specific locations and moments in time. Actions, relations and constraints are represented in a modular library, allowing incidents to be automatically composed of building blocks.

To demonstrate our approach, we developed a prototype, which simulates the inhabitants and daily behavior in the Dutch municipality of Rijswijk, driven by GIS and census data. Daily behavior is simulated by relatively simple models, adapting to environmental conditions such as time of day or season. Within this urban setting, we are able to seamlessly inject elaborate incidents at run-time.

2. INJECTING INCIDENTS

To introduce a new incident in the simulation, users specify a small number of high-level parameter settings. Some of these are defined explicitly, e.g., an incident is to take place at a certain location and time. Others are automatically derived based on incidents' definitions, e.g., which types of agents are required to participate in the incident.

Based on these settings, we derive what is needed to make the given incident happen at the desired time, in several phases, detailed below. Instead of directly generating a plan that includes actions, agents and locations, we restrict the size of the planning problem to the number of actions, by creating an abstract plan with a number of unassigned variables, instead of concrete agents and locations. Then, we instantiate the abstract plan by assigning agents and locations to the variables. We adopted a phased approach to overcome the issue that planning problems are PSPACE-complete in the size of the input.

As a running example in the text below, we will use an incident "Arrest an Offender", in which one or more offenders are arrested by one or more police officers at a specified location and time.

Roles and actions. In the first phase, we create an *action plan* to cause the incident. We prepare agents involved for their *roles* in the incident by giving them a suitable sequence of *actions*. Actions and associated concepts, detailed below, are all defined in a modular library. In this way, quite elaborate incidents can be automatically composed by the planner, without the need for extensive scripting.

Actions are placeholders with a number of variables, i.e. an actor variable, an optional target variable, and a location/time variable, each with possible constraints. In the planning phase, these variables are not given a concrete value yet; instead, the planner makes a plan where the variables are correctly linked. In addition to variables, any action may define preconditions concerning roles that are required for actor or target agents, and postconditions specifying the roles the actor or target agents will have after the action is performed. Finally, any action has an underlying model, which controls the behavior of the agents involved while the action is performed. We note that such a model may affect agents that are nearby via area triggers.

Initially, the planner investigates the enabling action of the incident. In the running example, the enabling action is Arrest, which shows one or more police officers arresting one or more offenders. The planner resolves any role preconditions that need to be satisfied to allow the enabling action. For the action Arrest, the actor must have the role Police Officer, while the target must have the role Offender. In case of a generic role, such as Offender, the planner also considers its specializations, such as Shoplifter. Searching for actions that give an actor or target the role Shoplifter, the action Shoplift might be found and added to the plan before the action Arrest; in this case, the actor variable of Shoplift is linked to the target variable of Arrest. Similarly, when resolving the role precondition concerning the Police Officer role, the planner may insert an action Activate Police before the action Arrest to create the required police officers. In this case, the actor variables of the two actions are linked.

Whenever new actions are added to the plan, the planner recursively resolves any role preconditions for these actions in the manner described above. This results in a plan in which all role preconditions for the enabling action of the desired incident are resolved.

* Corresponding author: steven.dejong@tno.nl.

Appears in: *Proceedings of the 15th International Conference on Autonomous Agents and Multiagent Systems (AAMAS 2016), J. Thangarajah, K. Tuyls, S. Marsella, C. Jonker (eds.), May 9–13, 2016, Singapore.*

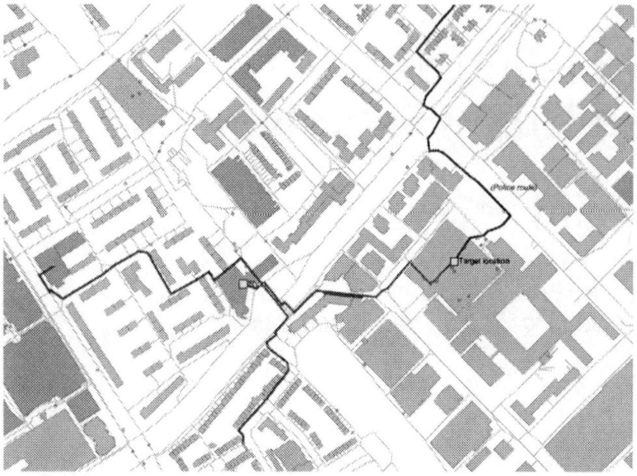

(a)

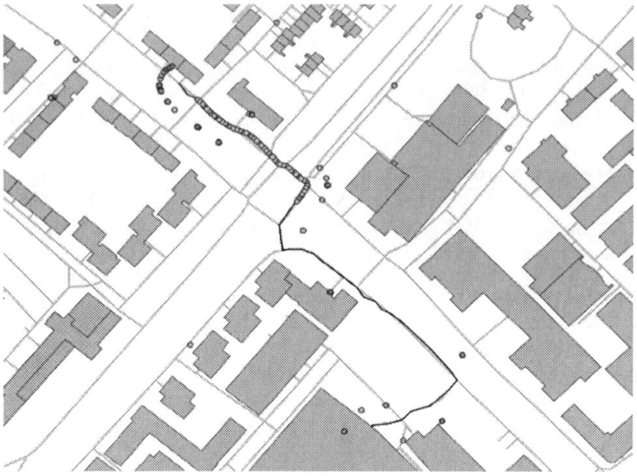

(b)

Figure 1: Examples of run-time injected incidents: (a) an arrest of two shoplifters (red routes) by a police officer (blue route) occurs at the specified location, (b) an improvised protest march (green circles represent participants), which attracts some passers-by (gray circles) using an area trigger.

Movement between actions. Once a plan has been created that resolves all role preconditions, the planner enables agents to travel between locations. For this, the planner introduces movement actions, inserted before each action in the plan. The algorithm for inserting suitable moves takes into account two aspects. First, agents may have acquired a certain role as a result of actions they performed earlier (e.g., Police Officer or Shoplifter). Therefore, we need to select a type of movement that fits this role. The second aspect considered when inserting suitable move actions is the target of the action we move towards, e.g. a police officer should choose Pursuit over Flee or Walk for movement towards an offender. Once the most fitting move action is chosen, it is inserted in the plan.

Assigning agents and locations. The result of the planning algorithm described above is a sequence of actions (i.e., a plan), with correctly linked variables that can be instantiated by assigning agents and locations that are present in the environment. An algorithm based on sampling and iterative improvement now finds such agents and locations, and ensures that the plan can be executed within the requested time constraints (i.e., the enabling action of the plan happens exactly when the user wants it to).

Intuitively, the algorithm works by first sampling a random valid assignment for the locations and agent variables in the plan. A valid assignment takes into account any constraints on the variables. For example, a shoplifting needs to take place in a shop, as represented in a constraint on the location/time variable of the Shoplift action.

Then, while the plan still takes too long to execute, a number of improvement steps are performed, in which (1) the critical path in the plan is found, i.e. the sequence of actions that takes most time, and (2) one variable for a chosen action on the critical path will be assigned differently, in such a way that the plan is expected to take less time. Whenever there is an action preceding the chosen action on the critical path, the current location of this preceding action is apparently too far away from the location of the chosen action. Therefore, the value of the location/time variable of this preceding action needs to be adjusted such that it refers to a valid location closer to the chosen action. If there is no preceding action, the chosen action involves one or more agents that are too far away from the location the chosen action will take place at, and we need to find valid agents that are closer to this location.

If a fixed number of improvement iterations does not yield a plan that fits the time constraints, the algorithm is restarted with a new random valid assignment of the variables in the plan. After a number of failed restarts, the algorithm concludes that planning the incident within the required time is not feasible. The user is then presented with the best plan found so far, and can choose whether s/he wants to have the incident happen at the corresponding time instead.

3. DISCUSSION AND FUTURE WORK

Our contribution. We present an approach for injecting incidents into an urban scenario at run-time, interrupting daily activities and temporarily promoting selected background agents to play a specific role in the sequence of events. Examples are shown in Figure 1. Because incidents are planned on-the-fly based on a library of available actions and associated pre- and postconditions, new incidents can build upon content that is already present.

In addition to run-time incidents, the prototype system also implements a simulation of daily patterns-of-life, based on real-world census data. Individuals in the simulation are given daily activities (such as work, leisure, shopping, having dinner) that match their properties (such as age, gender, and household). We designed the prototype system such that it can be easily extended to include more daily activities, behavior models and different modalities.

Future work. At the moment, the prototype system supports population models at a fixed level of detail. When, for example, trainee interaction with an individual population member is a scenario requirement, more detailed models are needed. Due to the computational complexity of such models, it is not feasible to have this level of detail for the entire population all the time. Instead, the system must be able to dynamically adapt to the level of detail required.

Other work could focus e.g. on including other traffic modalities than pedestrians, or on allowing users to specify population behavior on the level of intent as well, e.g. by drawing a morning rush hour on a specific street, which influences population attributes such as residence and place of work to create the desired dense traffic.

Online repository. The current prototype system is available as open source [1].We encourage others to experiment with the framework and to extend it with novel models and algorithms.

References

1. Population Modelling with Run-Time Incidents. URL `https://github.com/TNOCS/idsa`.

2. M. O. Riedl and R. M. Young. An intent-driven planner for multi-agent story generation. In *AAMAS 2004: The Third International Joint Conference on Autonomous Agents and Multi Agent Systems*, 2004.

3. G. Zacharias, J. MacMillan, and S. Van Hemel, editors. *Behavioral modeling and simulation: from individuals to societies*. National Academies Press, 2008.

Learning Better Trading Dialogue Policies by Inferring Opponent Preferences

(Extended Abstract)

Ioannis Efstathiou
Interaction Lab
Heriot-Watt University
ie24@hw.ac.uk

Oliver Lemon
Interaction Lab
Heriot-Watt University
o.lemon@hw.ac.uk

ABSTRACT

Negotiation dialogue capabilities have been identified as important in a variety of application areas. In prior work, it was shown how Reinforcement Learning (RL) agents can learn to use implicit and explicit manipulation moves in dialogue to manipulate their adversaries in non-cooperative trading games. We now show that trading dialogues are more successful when the RL agent builds an opponent model – an estimate of the (hidden) goals and preferences of the adversary – and learns how to exploit them. We explore a variety of state space representations for the preferences of trading adversaries, including one based on Conditional Preference Networks (CP-NETS), used for the first time in RL. We show that representing adversary preferences leads to significant improvements in trading success rates.

1. INTRODUCTION

Work on automated conversational systems has been focused on cooperative dialogue. However, non-cooperative dialogues, where an agent may act to satisfy its own goals rather than those of other participants, are also of practical and theoretical interest [5]. For example, it may be useful for a dialogue agent not to be fully cooperative when trying to gather information from a human, or when trying to persuade, argue, or debate, or when trying to sell something, or when trying to detect illegal activity, or in the area of believable characters in video games and educational simulations [5]. Another important area in which non-cooperative dialogue behaviour is desirable is in negotiation [8].

Recently it has been shown that when given the ability to perform both cooperative and non-cooperative (manipulative) dialogue moves, an agent can learn to bluff and to lie so as to win games more often, under various conditions such as risking penalties for being caught in deception – against a variety of adversaries [3]. Here we investigate the converse problem: can we develop a negotiator that models its adversaries' preferences and goals, and can learn how to use such models to improve its trading performance?

2. THE TRADING GAME "CATAN"

Appears in: *Proceedings of the 15th International Conference on Autonomous Agents and Multiagent Systems (AAMAS 2016), J. Thangarajah, K. Tuyls, C. Jonker, S. Marsella (eds.), May 9–13, 2016, Singapore.*

To investigate trading dialogues in a controlled setting we used a 2-player version of the board game "Catan", discussed in [4]. We call the 2 players the "adversary" and the "Reinforcement learning agent" (RLA). Trade occurs through proposals that may lead to acceptance or rejection from the adversary. In an agent's proposal (turn) only one 'give 1-for-1' or 'give 1-for-2' trading proposal may occur, or nothing.

State space for adversary preferences.
To overcome issues related to long training times and high memory demands, we implemented a state encoding mechanism that converts all of our trading game states to a significantly smaller number of states in a compressed representation, as discussed in [4]. The new state representation consists of 10 slots, and the first 5 (for resources) are encoded. The subsequent 5 state slots are used to refer to the adversary's inferred preferences. One of the two RLAs uses 2 different symbols to represent whether or not the adversary wants a particular resource (i.e. accepts it), and the other RLA uses 3 symbols because it also considers resources that the adversary does not want (i.e. it rejects that resource).

3. THE RLAS AND THE ADVERSARY

The **Adversary** sets a random goal. Hence its preferences (and therefore its responses to the RLA's proposals) will change according to the goal. We assume that its resources are infinite[1]. The RLAs are: **the Baseline RLA (BRLA),** which does not keep track of the adversarial preferences, **the Positive Preferences RLA (PPRLA),** which keeps track of the preferences and estimates the adversary's goal based on what resources the adversary has accepted in the trading dialogue so far, and **the Negative-Positive Preferences RLA (NPRLA),** which is as the previous but it represents rejected resources too.

4. EXPERIMENTS AND RESULTS

All agents are compared in respect of the percentage of trading games in which they achieve their goal (i.e. to get the resources required to build a city), within a sequence of 7 trading moves.

BRLA vs. Adversary: (Baseline).
The Baseline RLA (i.e. with no opponent modelling) played 250K games against the Adversary. The agent then played 20K testing games and scored a 28.1% success rate.

[1]Experiments conducted against the adversary with finite resources showed similar results but with lower scores.

PPRLA vs. Adversary .

We also trained the Positive Preferences RLA against the Adversary for 250K games, achieving a 44.2% success rate.

NPRLA vs. Adversary .

Likewise, the NPRLA achieved a success rate of 52.5%.

RLA Name	Success Rate
BRLA	28.1%
PPRLA	44.2%*
NPRLA	52.5%*

Table 1: ***Results (*= $p < 0.05$ over BRLA)***

5. CONDITIONAL PREFERENCE MODELS

We now extend the previous experiments to the cases where the RLA uses a CP-NET [1] to model preferences.

5.1 New extended state representation

The RLA has now a state representation which consists of 25 features: 5 for the resources (encoded) and 20 for the CP-NET adversarial preferences. An example of such a feature (preference) might be $s \to r$, that is the adversary's preference for sheep over rocks. We use again 3 characters to represent the RLA's knowledge about the adversary's preference for each of the CP-NET's 20 possibilities.

CPNET RLA vs. Adversary.

We first trained the CP-NET RLA against the adversary over 250K games. After 20K testing games this RLA achieved a success rate of 36.1%. The performance is better than that of the BRLA (28.1%), proving that the CP-NET improves the RL procedure, but it is worse than that of the PPRLA (44.2%) and that of the NPRLA (52.5%) The reason was the significantly larger state representation. Hence we ran another experiment for 1.5 million training games, and in the following 20k testing games the CP-NET RLA's performance increased to 46.9%. That result was better than that of the PPRLA in 250K training games but not as high as that of the NPRLA in 250k training games. Thus we ran another experiment for 2.5m training games. The performance of the CP-NET RLA was 50.3%. We ran a final experiment for 5 million training games, which resulted in a similar performance (52.4%) to that of the NPRLA.

6. MULTIPLAYER JSETTLERS

The experiments of this Section are all conducted using JSettlers [7] (full multi-player version of "Catan"). The goal is now to win the overall game (via building), rather than succeed in each trading dialogue. Here we tested the NPRLA policy against expert hand-crafted rule-based agents (which we call "Bots") which use complex heuristics to trade and to build pieces on the board. These Bots are the "benchmark" agents described in [6], and show strong performance, for example when compared to human play.

6.1 Our trained NPRLA Settlers agents

Both of our trained NPRLA agents are in fact a Bot modified so as to make offers based on the NPRLA learned policies, instead of using those of the Bot. The NPRLA maintains a history of all the opponents' (Bots) resource preferences during the game, treating them all as one adversary.

NPRLA vs. 3 Settlers Bots.

Our trained agent played 50K games versus the Bots and resulted in a win rate (in a 4-player game) of 25.19%, while those of the 3 Bots were 24.96%, 25.24% and 24.61% respectively. In 10K games the performances were 24.98% for the NPRLA, and 24.8%, 24.4% and 25.82% for the 3 Bots. The similarity of the results suggests that our agent knows how to trade towards a particular goal, like the Bots, even though it was not trained specifically to beat them.

7. CONCLUSIONS

We show that RL trading agents which track adversarial preferences outperform agents which don't. Furthermore, a RLA who considers the positive and negative preferences outperforms one which considers only the accepted trades by 8.3% success rate. Note that these preferences are inferred during learning since the beginning of each new game. We also extended this approach by using CP-NETs [1] showing that it results in a positive difference of 8% compared to the winning performance of the RLA who doesn't have preference information. We also evaluated the performance of our best trader (NPRLA) in the full multi-agent game of Settlers, compared to expert hand-crafted rule-based agents [6]. We found that our trained trading policies performed as well as these hand-crafted agents, suggesting that data-driven policy training can result in very competitive trading strategies, without expert hand-crafting. We also suggest that bilateral training environments may suffice for multilateral non-cooperative trading scenarios for effective RL, providing that efficient selection of the state representation and of the actions has been made. Deep Reinforcement Learning is also a promising research direction [2].

Acknowledgments

This work is funded by the ERC grant no. 269427 (STAC).

REFERENCES

[1] C. Boutilier, R. Brafman, C. Domshlak, H. Hoos, and D. Poole. CP-nets : A Tool for Representing and Reasoning with Conditional *Ceteris Paribus* Preference Statements. *Journal of AI Research*, 21:135–191, 2004.

[2] H. Cuayahuitl, S. Keizer, and O. Lemon. Strategic Dialogue Management via Deep Reinforcement Learning. In *Proc. NIPS*, 2015.

[3] I. Efstathiou and O. Lemon. Learning to manage risks in non-cooperative dialogues. In *Proc. SemDial*, 2014.

[4] I. Efstathiou and O. Lemon. Learning non-cooperative dialogue policies to beat opponent models: "the good, the bad and the ugly". In *Proc. SemDial*, 2015.

[5] K. Georgila and D. Traum. Reinforcement learning of argumentation dialogue policies in negotiation. In *Proc. INTERSPEECH*, 2011.

[6] M. Guhe and A. Lascarides. Game Strategies in *The Settlers of Catan*, booktitle = Proc. IEEE Conference on Computational Intelligence in Games. 2014.

[7] R. Thomas and K. Hammond. Java settlers: a research environment for studying multi-agent negotiation. In *Proc. of IUI '02*, pages 240–240, 2002.

[8] D. Traum. Extended abstract: Computational models of non-cooperative dialogue. In *Proc. of SIGdial Workshop on Discourse and Dialogue*, 2008.

Efficient Boolean Games Equilibria: A Scalable Approach (Extended Abstract)

Zohar Komarovsky
Ben-Gurion University
Be'er-Sheva, Israel
zoharkom@cs.bgu.ac.il

Vadim Levit
Ben-Gurion University
Be'er-Sheva, Israel
levitv@cs.bgu.ac.il

Tal Grinshpoun
Ariel University
Ariel, Israel
talgr@ariel.ac.il

Amnon Meisels
Ben-Gurion University
Be'er-Sheva, Israel
am@cs.bgu.ac.il

ABSTRACT

The present study focuses on a family of Boolean games whose agents' interactions are defined by a social network. The task of finding social-welfare-maximizing outcomes for such games is NP-hard. Moreover, such optimal outcomes are not necessarily stable. Therefore, our aim is to devise a procedure that finds stable outcomes with an as high as possible social welfare. To this end, we construct a quadratic-time procedure, by which any initial outcome of a game in this family can be transformed into a stable solution by the use of side payments. The resulting stable outcome is ensured to be at least as efficient as the initial outcome. Considering the fact that this procedure applies for any initial state, one may use good search heuristics to find an outcome of high social welfare, and then apply the procedure to it. This naturally leads to a scalable process that finds desirable efficient and stable solutions.

Keywords

Boolean games; side payments; efficient equilibria

1. INTRODUCTION

One of the major research challenges in Boolean games [1], as well as in game theory in general, is stabilization, i.e., securing the existence of a *pure-strategy Nash equilibrium* (PNE). However, a *stable* outcome from which no agent wants to unilaterally deviate, is not necessarily an *efficient* outcome. Herein, we relate to *social welfare*, which is a common notion of efficiency representing the sum of agents' utilities. In that sense, an outcome that maximizes social welfare is considered efficient.

In this study we address the problematic tradeoff between stability and efficiency in the context of a family of Boolean games, in which the interactions of agents are defined by some underlying social network. This family of Boolean games is inspired by the well-studied class of network games known as "best-shot" public goods games [2, 3]. There, the action that each agent takes (or avoids) is associated with an investment in some local public good (e.g., buying a book or some other product that is easily lent from one agent to another). Each agent wants that the action will be taken by at least one agent in its neighborhood, including itself. However, there is a cost associated with taking the action, so if any of its neighbors take the action then the agent prefers to avoid taking it.

Contemplating on the tradeoff between stability and efficiency, it is important to note that finding a social-welfare-maximizing outcome is equivalent in our settings to finding a minimal dominating set, which is known to be NP-hard. Moreover, such optimal solutions are not necessarily PNEs. Therefore, our objective is to reach efficient (yet not necessarily optimal) and stable solutions, while still remaining scalable. For this purpose we construct a quadratic-time procedure that works on any initial arbitrary outcome of the games at focus. We use the *side payments* mechanism [5] in order to ensure stability. However, not necessarily every outcome can be transformed to a stable state by the use of side payments [4]. Thus, we move, if needed, to a different outcome that *can* be stabilized using side payments. The new outcome is ensured to be at least as efficient as the original outcome. Finally, the new outcome is transformed, if needed, to a PNE by the use of side payments.

Considering the fact that the above procedure applies for any arbitrary state, one may use good search heuristics to find a state with some desirable properties. Using a run-time-efficient heuristic in the initial stage, combined with the quadratic-time procedure that follows, leads to a scalable process that finds desirable efficient and stable solutions.

2. PUBLIC GOODS BOOLEAN GAMES

A *public goods Boolean Game* (PGBG) is defined according to some underlying graph that describes the agents' interactions network. Each vertex represents an agent $i \in A$ in the corresponding Boolean game, and edges represent the interaction structure of the game. The set of i's neighbors is denoted by N_i; these are the agents whose actions may impact i's payoff (by enabling/disabling i's ability to achieve its personal goal). The *neighborhood* of i is the set $\{i\} \cup N_i$.

This study assumes that each agent i possesses a single Boolean variable $a_i \in \Phi$, which denotes i's chosen strategy: $a_i = \top$ (for performing an action), or $a_i = \bot$ (for avoiding it). The personal goal γ_i of agent i is a disjunction of all

Appears in: *Proceedings of the 15th International Conference on Autonomous Agents and Multiagent Systems (AAMAS 2016), J. Thangarajah, K. Tuyls, C. Jonker, S. Marsella (eds.), May 9–13, 2016, Singapore.*

Boolean variables possessed by agents in i's neighborhood. This definition of personal goal implies that each participant's primary aim is that at least one agent in its neighborhood will perform an action. Consequently, each agent can ensure the achievement of its personal goal by performing the action. The strategic nature of the game comes from the fact that performing the action involves costs. More formally, the cost function $c : \Phi \times \mathbb{B} \to \mathbb{R}_{\geq}$ defines a zero cost for choosing $\perp$ ($\forall i \in A : c(a_i, \perp) = 0$), and some positive cost $\mathcal{C}_i > 0$ for choosing $\top$ ($\forall i \in A : c(a_i, \top) = \mathcal{C}_i$).

Given an outcome of the game $v \in V$, the possible *states* of an agent $i \in A$, denoted by $State(i, v)$, can be divided into the next four distinct types:

1. $\mathbb{TT}$: $v(a_i) = \top$ and $\exists j \in N_i : v(a_j) = \top$
2. $\mathbb{TF}$: $v(a_i) = \top$ and $\forall j \in N_i : v(a_j) = \perp$
3. $\mathbb{FT}$: $v(a_i) = \perp$ and $\exists j \in N_i : v(a_j) = \top$
4. $\mathbb{FF}$: $v(a_i) = \perp$ and $\forall j \in N_i : v(a_j) = \perp$

We say that agent i *depends* on agent j under outcome v, denoted by $i <^v j$, if the achievement of i's personal goal depends only on j's choice at outcome v.

3. SIDE PAYMENTS

Side payments enable Boolean games to be transformed from the inside, by endowing agents with the possibility of sacrificing part of their payoff in order to convince other agents to play a certain strategy. This incentive mechanism inherently fits the PGBG scenario, since it is in the best interest of an agent to sacrifice part of its payoff in order to convince one of its neighbors in the network to take the action (invest in the public good). We adopt the Boolean transfer functions $\beta_i : V \times A \to \mathbb{R}_{\geq}$ of Turrini [5].

Since the use of side payments is mainly motivated by the attempt to secure a stable state (PNE) with certain properties, it is required to differentiate between outcomes that can be transformed to a PNE and those that can not.

Definition 1. An outcome v in a Boolean game G is *side payments enforceable* (SPE) if there exists a transfer function β, such that: $\forall i \in A, \forall v'_i \in V_i : u_i^\beta(v_i, v_{-i}) \geq u_i^\beta(v'_i, v_{-i})$, where $u_i^\beta(v)$ denotes the utility of agent i from outcome v under transfer function β.

4. STABILITY ENFORCING PROCEDURE

Starting from an initial outcome v, the first stage of the procedure finds an improved outcome v^* that is guaranteed to be SPE. The second stage applies the side payments mechanism to transform the improved outcome to a stable one. We restrict our attention to cases where all costs ($\mathcal{C}_i$) are identical, namely all costs equal $\mathcal{C}$.

First Stage. The first stage consists of two loops, each of which deals with one unstable state ($\mathbb{FF}$ or $\mathbb{TT}$). Starting at some outcome v, the first loop ensures that no agent will stay in state $\mathbb{FF}$, by changing the choice of each such agent from $\perp$ to $\top$. After the first loop, each agent is in one of three states: $\mathbb{TF}$, $\mathbb{FT}$ or $\mathbb{TT}$. The second loop ensures that each agent in state $\mathbb{TT}$ will have at least one other agent that depends on it, or otherwise the agent changes its choice from $\top$ to $\perp$. Such dependence enables compensating the agent by the use of side payments, and thus stability can be enforced. Applying these loops results in outcome v^*.

PROPOSITION 1. *For every outcome $v \in V$ it holds that v^* is side payments enforceable.*

PROPOSITION 2. *For every outcome $v \in V$, the utility of any agent in v^* is not lower than its utility in v.*

All proofs are omitted due to space limitation. Since Proposition 2 ensures that the utility of every agent is non-decreasing, then so is the sum of all agents' utilities.

COROLLARY 3. *For every outcome $v \in V$, the social welfare of v^* is greater than or equal to that of v.*

Second Stage. Here we apply a transfer function β that incentivizes only agents in state $\mathbb{TT}$ and only in outcome v^*:

$$\beta_j(v^*, i) := \begin{cases} \frac{\mathcal{C}}{d_i(v^*)}, & \text{if } State(i, v^*) = \mathbb{TT} \wedge j <^{v^*} i \\ 0, & \text{otherwise} \end{cases} \quad (1)$$

where $d_i(v^*)$ denotes the number of agents in A that depend on i in outcome v^*. Note that for all other outcomes $v' \neq v^*$ no payments are transferred (i.e., $\forall j, i \in A : \beta_j(v', i) = 0$).

PROPOSITION 4. *The stability enforcing procedure runs in quadratic time.*

5. CONCLUSIONS

We have introduced a stability enforcing procedure. Applying it on an initially efficient outcome, e.g., of maximal social welfare, results in an efficient equilibrium, as desired. However, finding an outcome of maximal social welfare is NP-hard, thus it is applicable only for relatively small networks. A more widely applicable approach would be to use a heuristic in order to find an initial outcome v with relatively high (yet not necessarily optimal) social welfare, and then apply the stability enforcing procedure to it. Using a runtime-efficient heuristic, combined with the quadratic runtime complexity of the procedure (Proposition 4), results in a scalable process for securing an efficient equilibrium. To conclude, the process consists of the following stages:

1. Applying a heuristic that returns an initial outcome v.
2. Transforming v to v^* according to the first stage.
3. Securing stability using the β transfers of Equation 1.

Acknowledgments

This study was supported by the Lynn and William Frankel center for Computer Sciences.

REFERENCES

[1] P. Harrenstein, W. van der Hoek, J.-J. Meyer, and C. Witteveen. Boolean games. In *TARK*, pages 287–298, 2001.

[2] J. Hirshleifer. From weakest-link to best-shot: The voluntary provision of public goods. *Public choice*, 41(3):371–386, 1983.

[3] M. O. Jackson and Y. Zenou. Games on networks. *Handbook of game theory*, 4, 2014.

[4] V. Levit, Z. Komarovsky, T. Grinshpoun, and A. Meisels. Tradeoffs between incentive mechanisms in Boolean games. In *IJCAI*, pages 68–74, 2015.

[5] P. Turrini. Endogenous Boolean games. In *IJCAI*, pages 390–396, 2013.

Coordinating Wind Turbines and Flexible Consumers with Cooperative and Competitive Agents

(Extended Abstract)

Kristof Coninx
iMinds-DistriNet KULeuven
kristof.coninx@cs.kuleuven.be

Tom Holvoet
iMinds-DistriNet KULeuven
tom.holvoet@cs.kuleuven.be

Keywords

Multi-agent systems, smart grids, renewable energy

1. INTRODUCTION AND PROBLEM

Meeting the 20-20-20 objectives put forward by the European Commission to increase the share of renewable energy production in Belgium to 13% of the gross final energy consumption, requires the installation of large wind farms both on- and offshore. Integrating these wind farms into existing distribution infrastructure is challenging because of potential congestion caused by imbalance between wind turbine energy production and consumers' energy offtake.

One technical constraints that needs to be considered is guaranteeing that existing cables can cope with the increased wind energy injection into the grid. Adding energy production elements to existing grids can cause power rates to increase past the rates that would ensure safe cable operation. Upgrading existing cable infrastructure to cope with increased power rates would lead to a costly replacement of existing cables. Experience in industrial projects shows that this is an actual problem DSO's are facing when incorporating wind turbines into existing distribution infrastructure. Considering that these excessive power rates only occur occasionaly, alternative remedies are investigated.

Literature describes ANM techniques for dealing with these forms of increased power production related current congestion in a more cost effective manner [3]. Active Network Management (ANM) techniques describe a class of techniques for actively performing steering actions in distribution network management to minimize congestion problems from excessive wind power production.

This work focuses on DSM as an ANM technique to resolve the problem of upstream current congestion. The distinction is made between two phases and we propose algorithms for both phases. The first phase deals with an ahead of time planning phase where grid investment or reinforcement has to be outweighed against demand-side management (DSM) [3]. A second phase considers a real time situation for online allocation of ANM resources based on local wind production forecasts. For online power flexibility allocation, two mechanisms, a cooperative contract-net based mechanisms and a competitive qualitative Vickrey auction (QVA) are implemented and compared in terms of allocative efficiency.

Appears in: *Proceedings of the 15th International Conference on Autonomous Agents and Multiagent Systems (AAMAS 2016), J. Thangarajah, K. Tuyls, C. Jonker, S. Marsella (eds.), May 9–13, 2016, Singapore.*

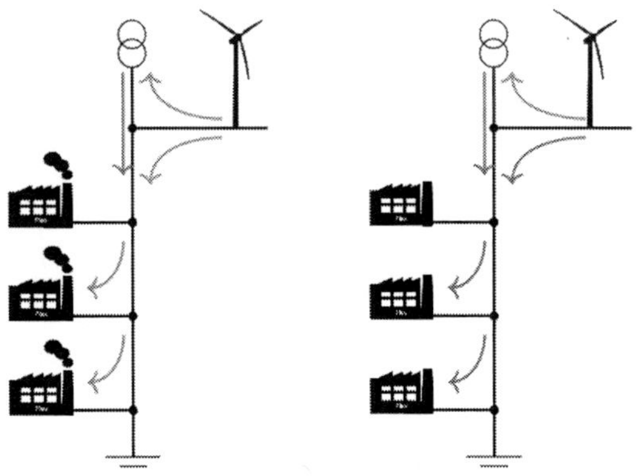

Figure 1: Example scenario for upstream current congestion. Left: Energy flows from wind turbine to factories downstream and all excess production flows upstream towards the TSO transformer for grid injection. Right: Factories downstream are inactive and all energy flows upstream towards the TSO transformer causing upstream current congestion.

2. REMEDYING CONGESTION

We focus on tertiary reserve under a dynamic profile (R3DP) as the closest matching real-world strategic reserve product that is relevant to this work because of its focus on flexible DSO-connected grid users. The flexibility product description that is used in this work is therefore proposed for DSO-connected grid users that offer consumption increase flexibility according to the following constraints, which are similar to the R3DP activation constraints specified by Elia, the belgian TSO:

- A maximum of 40 activations/year is allowed.
- All activations last max. 2 hours.
- The time between 2 consecutive activations should be at least 12 hours.

2.1 Offline Allocation

Primarily, an offline optimal solution can provide an upper bound on the maximum allocative efficiency that is attainable for given wind profiles and flexibility in the system, constrained by activation such as described in the previous section.

Optimally solving the allocation problem is done by solving a MIP model to maximize the remedied congestion over time $s(t)$ to maximize the efficiency of the allocation of the flexibility activation.

2.2 Online Allocation

For solving the real-time problem we study two different approaches to the flexibility allocation problem. A cooperative setting relating to current practice in industry is modeled. DSM participation is currently often regulated by contracts and these contracts are enforced with significant fines and complete exclusion from DSM programs. In response to state-of-art proof of concept cases, modeling flexibility market mechanisms where all parties act as market participants, a strategy proof, Qualitative Vickrey Auction (QAV) is implemented as a counterpart to the cooperative setting. Both approaches are evaluated in terms of allocative efficiency which is defined as the amount of excess energy that is actually reduced by a DSM activation. Any activation that leads to more energy reduced than the amount that was causing congestion is considered inefficient. Both mechanisms are implemented to follow a similar message protocol. Every time period of 15 minutes, the center agent evaluates whether forecasts show that congestion will occur and if so, will send out a *call for proposals* to all agents. Agents then respond with a bid depending on their capabilities at that time and the winning bid is sent an activation signal.

In the cooperative mechanism, the winner is determined by a social choice function $\mathcal{F}(R^n)$ which favors the closest bid that could resolve most of the congestion among all the bids. This function is defined in (1) where $C(t)$ is the function representing the congestion over time and $\epsilon(x)$ represents the allocative efficiency for that bid.

$$\mathcal{F}(R^n) = \arg\max_{y \in R^n}(\epsilon(y)) \tag{1}$$

$$\epsilon(x) = \int_{x_{start}}^{x_{end}} \min(C(t), x_p)dt \tag{2}$$

In the competative mechanism, contract auctions are implemented. Contract auctions are an application of Qualitative Vickrey Auctions (QVA) [2], which are known to be the only mechanisms that are individually rational, dominant strategy proof and capable of selecting stable, Pareto efficient outcomes given the assumption of weakly transferable utility [1]. The assumption of weakly transferable utility does not hold because the center has single (positively) peaked preferences which introduces a local maximum. Inspired by the work in [1], a fixed and publicly announced tie-breaking rule is used to guarantee strategy proofness in the absence of weakly transferable utility. In this case, however, Pareto efficient outcomes cannot be guaranteed, however.

3. EVALUATION AND DISCUSSION

The optimal full knowledge allocation approach can deliver very efficient allocations in general. The main drawback is that optimally allocating agent power flexibility over a one year time horizon in 15 minute increments, leads to very high resource requirements, in both CPU time and memory for the branch-and-bound technique used for solving MIP problems.

The first result is that attaining totally efficiency allocations is not possible in even the simplest case with 1 flexibility provider, using the optimal allocation algorithm. The observed mean efficiency from repeated simulations with 1 provider was 98.96% with no provider attaining 100%. Simulations with more provider yielded lower efficiency rates. Further study into the flexibility required to solve these specific current congestion problems is needed because currently available flexibility products can not be used to attain 100% efficient allocations in the best case scenario.

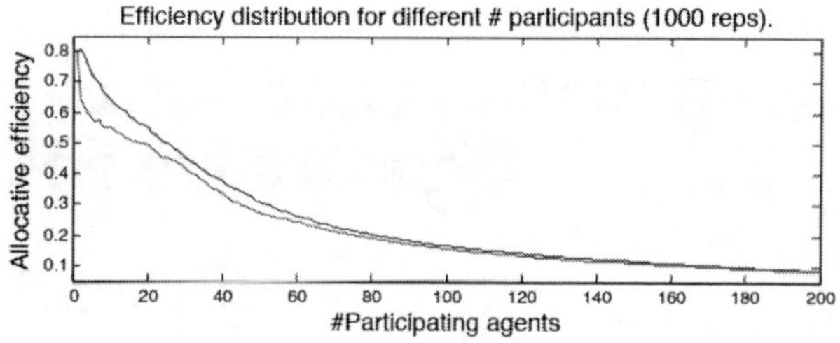

Figure 2: Results for up to 200 participating agents show higher mean allocative efficiency of the cooperative (blue/higher) setting when compared to the competitive (red/lower) solution.

The second result in Figure 1 shows that the cooperative approach manages to attain a higher allocative efficiency than the competitive approach. These results also indicate that the difference in mean efficiency between both approaches decreases significantly as the number of participating agents increases making the difference between the two approaches negligible in terms of result when many agents participate. Assuming that more than 10 agents would be located in such a way that they can all be used to resolve congestion is, however, unreasonable because all agents need to be connected to the same feeder, as is illustrated in Figure 1.

4. CONCLUSION

This work presents initial findings in a study to apply cooperative and competitive MAS techniques to the problem of upstream current congestion. Further results analysing different metric and different wind profiles are underway.

Further work is necessary to specify the exact flexibility product requirements that are necessary for dealing with these current congestion problems. In future work we will also analyse investmentment costs and compare these costs to other ANM techniques such as storage.

Acknowledgment

This research is partially funded by the Research Fund KU Leuven.

REFERENCES

[1] M. M. De Weerdt, P. Harrenstein, and V. Conitzer. Strategy-proof contract auctions and the role of ties. *Games and Economic Behavior*, 86:405–420, 2014.

[2] B. P. Harrenstein, M. M. de Weerdt, and V. Conitzer. A Qualitative Vickrey Auction Categories and Subject Descriptors. In *Proceedings of the 10th ACM conference on Electronic commerce*, pages 197–206, 2009.

[3] L. Van Halewyck, J. Verstraeten, M. Strobbe, C. Develder, L. V. Halewyck, J. Verstraeten, M. Strobbe, and C. Develder. Economic evaluation of active network management alternatives for congestion avoidance: the DSO perspective. In *Europe 2014, the 5e IEEE PES Innovative Smart Grid Technologies European Conference (ISGT-2014)*, pages 1–6. IEEE, 2014.

Approximate Plutocratic and Egalitarian Nash Equilibria *

(Extended Abstract)

Artur Czumaj, Michail Fasoulakis, Marcin Jurdziński
Department of Computer Science and Centre for Discrete Mathematics and its Applications (DIMAP)
University of Warwick
{A.Czumaj, M.Fasoulakis, M.Jurdzinski}@warwick.ac.uk

ABSTRACT

We pose the problem of computing approximate Nash equilibria in bimatrix games with two simultaneous criteria of optimization: minimization of the incentives to deviate from a strategy profile and maximization of a measure of quality of the strategy profile. We consider two natural measures of quality: the maximum and the minimum of the payoffs of the two players. Maximizing the former yields *plutocratic Nash equilibria*, and maximizing the latter yields *egalitarian Nash equilibria*. We give polynomial-time algorithms that compute ε-Nash equilibria for $\varepsilon \geq \frac{3-\sqrt{5}}{2} \approx 0.382$, and that *approximate the quality of plutocratic and egalitarian Nash equilibria* to various degrees.

1. INTRODUCTION

The fundamental problem in game theory is to study properties of equilibria in noncooperative games. By the classical result of Nash [10], we know that every finite game has at least one Nash equilibrium. However, in many natural scenarios one is not only interested in finding or characterizing any equilibrium, but in fact, one wants to find equilibria that have some desirable properties, one wants to find "best" or "fairest" equilibria. While we understand quite well various properties of the set of all Nash equilibria, if we consider also the quality of a solution sought and aim at characterizing the "best" Nash equilibria, then our knowledge is limited.

The situation is even more challenging if we take into account the computational complexity of the task. For example, even in two-player games, the problem of finding an arbitrary Nash equilibrium is known to be PPAD-complete and the problem of finding a Nash equilibrium with almost any additional constraint is NP-hard [3, 6], and thus, it is likely to be computationally even more difficult. In fact, it is even NP-hard to approximate (to any positive ratio) the maximum social welfare, or the maximum egalitarian payoffs, or the maximum plutocratic payoffs, obtained in an exact Nash equilibrium, even in symmetric two-player games [3, Corollaries 6–8].

In recent years, the computational hardness of finding (exact) Nash equilibria led to an increasing interest in the study of *approximate Nash equilibria* (ε-Nash equilibria) that are strategy profiles in which each player has the incentive to deviate to another strategy limited by $\varepsilon > 0$. In this paper we study the fundamental problem of *computing approximate Nash equilibria* in bimatrix games, for which a certain measure of quality is close to the best value of that measure among all Nash equilibria in the game. We naturally focus on values of ε for which polynomial-time algorithms are already known for computing (approximate) ε-Nash equilibria, and we aim to develop polynomial-time algorithms for computing such approximate equilibria which are also "approximately best."

There have been some investigations aiming to efficiently find approximate Nash equilibrium that also approximate well the *social welfare* (the total payoff of the players), see Section 1.3. However in this paper, we consider equilibria focusing on other objectives: instead of aiming to maximize the social welfare, or, in short, expected payoff of the players, we will study the scenarios where one wants to maximize the smallest of the payoffs, or that one wants to maximize the largest of the payoffs. That is, we consider two natural settings to describe the notion of the "best Nash equilibrium":

- *plutocratic Nash equilibrium*—that *maximizes the expected maximum* of the payoffs of the players;
- *egalitarian Nash equilibrium*—that *maximizes the expected minimum* of the payoffs of the players.

1.1 Notation

Consider a bimatrix game (R, C) played by the *row* and the *column player*. Each player has n pure strategies at her disposal and the payoff matrix is in $[0,1]^{n\times n}$. If the row player plays a strategy i and the column player plays a strategy j, then the row player receives payoff R_{ij} and the column player receives payoff C_{ij}. The players can randomize over their pure strategies, and a *mixed strategy* x is a probability distribution over the set of all pure strategies. If the row player plays a mixed strategy x and the column player plays a mixed strategy y, then the *expected payoff of the row player* is $x^T Ry$ and the *expected payoff of the column player* is $x^T Cy$.

A *Nash equilibrium* (NE) is a strategy profile (x^*, y^*) such that: x^* is a best response to y^* (i.e., $\forall i\; x^{*T} Ry^* \geq e_i^T Ry^*$) and y^* is a best response to x^* (i.e., $\forall i\; x^{*T} Cy^* \geq x^{*T} Ce_i$), where e_i is a column vector with all 0s except for a 1 in the ith coordinate.

An *ε-Nash equilibrium* (ε-NE) is a strategy profile (x^*, y^*) such that: x^* is an ε-best response to y^* (i.e., $\forall i\; x^{*T} Ry^* \geq e_i^T Ry^* - \varepsilon$) and y^* is an ε-best response to x^* (i.e., $\forall i\; x^{*T} Cy^* \geq x^{*T} Ce_i - \varepsilon$).

In this paper, our goal is to find ε-NE that are close to a "best" NE. We consider two very natural versions of a best NE:

A **plutocratic NE** is a NE that maximizes the following:

$$u^*_{max} \stackrel{\text{def}}{=} \max\left\{ \max\{x^T Ry, x^T Cy\} : (x, y) \text{ is a NE} \right\} .$$

An **egalitarian NE** is a NE that maximizes the following:

$$u^*_{eg} \stackrel{\text{def}}{=} \max\left\{ \min\{x^T Ry, x^T Cy\} : (x, y) \text{ is a NE} \right\} .$$

---

*Research partially supported by the Centre for Discrete Mathematics and its Applications (DIMAP) and by the EPSRC awards EP/D063191/1 and EP/G069034/1.

Appears in: *Proceedings of the 15th International Conference on Autonomous Agents and Multiagent Systems (AAMAS 2016), J. Thangarajah, K. Tuyls, C. Jonker, S. Marsella (eds.), May 9–13, 2016, Singapore.*

We extend these notions to approximate Nash equilibria.

DEFINITION 1. *An **(additive) ρ-plutocratic** ε-NE is an ε-NE (x, y) such that $u^*_{max} - \max\{x^T Ry, x^T Cy\} \le \rho$. If a strategy profile (x, y) is a 0-plutocratic ε-NE then it is a **plutocratic** ε-NE.*

DEFINITION 2. *An **(additive) ρ-egalitarian** ε-NE is an ε-NE (x, y) such that $u^*_{eg} - \min\{x^T Ry, x^T Cy\} \le \rho$. A **relative ρ-egalitarian** ε-NE is an ε-NE (x, y) with $\rho \cdot u^*_{eg} \le \min\{x^T Ry, x^T Cy\}$.*

1.2 New results

For all $\varepsilon \ge \frac{3-\sqrt{5}}{2} \approx 0.382$, we give polynomial-time algorithms for computing ε-Nash equilibria, which approximate what plutocratic and egalitarian Nash equilibria optimize.

THEOREM 3. *There is a polynomial-time algorithm that computes a plutocratic $\frac{1}{2}$-NE.*

THEOREM 4. *Let $\frac{3-\sqrt{5}}{2} \le \varepsilon < \frac{1}{2}$. There is a polynomial-time algorithm that computes an additive $\frac{1-2\varepsilon}{1-\varepsilon}$-plutocratic ε-NE.*

THEOREM 5. *There is a polynomial-time algorithm that computes a relative $\frac{1}{2}$-egalitarian $\frac{1}{2}$-NE.*

THEOREM 6. *Let $\frac{3-\sqrt{5}}{2} \le \varepsilon < \frac{1}{2}$. There is a polynomial-time algorithm that computes an additive $\frac{1}{2}$-egalitarian ε-NE.*

The results are obtained by first showing the existence of such approximate Nash equilibria adapting the method of Daskalakis et al. [5] and by carefully maintaining the tradeoff between the payoffs of the players. Once the existence of an appropriate approximate NE is given, we apply an LP-based approach to find them efficiently.

Observe that our analysis assumes that $\varepsilon \ge \frac{3-\sqrt{5}}{2} \approx 0.382$, which covers almost the entire range for which ε-Nash equilibria are currently known to be computable in polynomial time. Indeed, the smallest value of ε for which a polynomial-time algorithm is known that computes an ε-Nash equilibrium is $\varepsilon \approx 0.3393$ [11].

1.3 Related works

The tradeoff between minimizing incentives to deviate and the quality of the solution found has been studied in the past, though the main focus of the research was on the goal of finding approximate Nash equilibria that approximate the optimal *social welfare*. There have been two strands of these investigations, one comparing the social welfare to the optimal social welfare of the game and one comparing it to the optimal social welfare in any NE.

It is known that the social welfare of a NE can be arbitrarily far from the optimal social welfare in a bimatrix game [4]. Motivated by this result, there have been recent studies aiming to find an approximate NE with the social welfare close to the best possible (optimal social welfare of the game, not necessarily in a NE). It was shown in [4] that for every fixed $\varepsilon > 0$, every bimatrix game has an ε-NE with the social welfare at least a constant factor of the optimum. E.g., for any $\varepsilon \ge \frac{1}{2}$, there is always an ε-NE whose social welfare is at least $2\sqrt{\varepsilon} - \varepsilon \ge 0.914$ times the optimal social welfare, and this bound is tight. Furthermore, these results are algorithmic, and for every fixed $0 \le \varepsilon^* < \varepsilon$, if one can find an ε^*-NE in polynomial time, then one can find in polynomial time an ε-NE with the social welfare at least a constant factor of the optimum.

There has been also some research aiming to efficiently find an approximate NE that *approximates well the social welfare in any NE*. (Observe that if an ε-NE approximates well the optimal social welfare, as in [4], then it also approximates well the social welfare in any NE.) It has been noted that the quasi-polynomial-time algorithm for approximating NE by Lipton et al. [9] not only finds an ε-NE for arbitrary $\varepsilon > 0$, but also the social welfare of the equilibrium found is an ε-approximation of the social welfare in any NE. In other words, in time $n^{O(\log n/\varepsilon^2)}$ we can find an arbitrarily good approximate NE with social welfare near to the best NE. (Further, we note that it is straightforward to extend the quasi-polynomial-time algorithm from [9] to find an ε-NE whose plutocratic (or egalitarian) payoff is no more than ε smaller than the maximum plutocratic (or egalitarian, respectively) payoff of a NE in the game.)

While this result raised a hope that it may be possible to extend it to design a polynomial-time ε-approximation algorithm, recent hardness results [1, 2, 8] showed that it is unlikely. Braverman et al. [2] showed that assuming the deterministic Exponential Time Hypothesis, there is a constant $\varepsilon > 0$ such that any algorithm for finding an ε-NE whose social welfare is at least $(1 - \varepsilon)$ times the optimal social welfare of a NE of the game, requires $n^{\Omega(\log n)}$ time (see also [1, 8] for related results that assume hardness of finding a large planted clique). These hardness results show that it is unlikely to obtain a polynomial-time approximation scheme that for every constants ε and ε' would construct in polynomial time an ε-NE whose social welfare is at least $(1 - \varepsilon')$ times the optimal social welfare of a NE of the game. (Austrin et al. [1] showed that many similar variants of the bicriteria approximation are similarly hard.)

On the other hand, the results from [4] can be combined with the polynomial-time algorithm finding an ε^*-NE in any bimatrix game with $\varepsilon^* \approx 0.3393$ [11], to obtain a polynomial-time algorithm that for any $\varepsilon > \varepsilon^*$ finds an ε-NE whose social welfare is at least $(1 - \sqrt{\frac{1-\varepsilon}{1-\varepsilon^*}})^2$ times the optimal social welfare of a NE of the game; for $\varepsilon \ge \frac{1}{2}$, the approximation bound can be made at least $2\sqrt{\varepsilon} - \varepsilon \ge 0.914$ times the optimal social welfare.

REFERENCES

[1] P. Austrin, M. Braverman, and E. Chlamtac. Inapproximability of NP-complete variants of Nash equilibrium. *Theory Comput.*, 9:117–142, 2013.

[2] M. Braverman, Y. K. Ko, and O. Weinstein. Approximating the best Nash equilibrium in $n^{o(\log n)}$-time breaks the exponential time hypothesis. *26th SODA*, pp. 970–982, 2015.

[3] V. Conitzer and T. Sandholm. New complexity results about Nash equilibria. *Games Econom. Behav.*, 63:621–641, 2008.

[4] A. Czumaj, M. Fasoulakis, and M. Jurdziński. Approximate Nash equilibria with near optimal social welfare. *Proc. 24th IJCAI*, pp. 504–510, 2015.

[5] C. Daskalakis, A. Mehta, and C. Papadimitriou. A note on approximate Nash equilibria. *Theoret. Comput. Sci.*, 410(17):1581–1588, 2009.

[6] I. Gilboa and E. Zemel. Nash and correlated equilibria: Some complexity considerations. *Games Econom. Behav.*, 1(1):80–93, 1989.

[7] A. Greenwald and K. Hall. Correlated Q-learning. *Proc. 20th ICML*, pp. 242–249, 2003.

[8] E. Hazan, R. Krauthgamer. How hard is it to approximate the best Nash equilibrium? *SIAM J. Comput.*, 40:79–91, 2011.

[9] R. Lipton, E. Markakis, and A. Mehta. Playing large games using simple strategies. *Proc. 4th EC*, pp. 36–41, 2003.

[10] J. Nash. Non-cooperative games. *Ann. of Math.*, 54(2):286–295, 1951.

[11] H. Tsaknakis and P. G. Spirakis. An optimization approach for approximate Nash equilibria. *Internet Math.*, 5(4):365–382, 2008.

A Core Task Abstraction Approach to Hierarchical Reinforcement Learning

(Extended Abstract)

Zhuoru Li†, Akshay Narayan† and Tze-Yun Leong†§
School of Computing, National University of Singapore†
School of Information System, Singapore Management University§
{lizhuoru, anarayan, leongty}@comp.nus.edu.sg

ABSTRACT

We propose a new, *core task abstraction* (CTA) approach to learning the relevant transition functions in model-based hierarchical reinforcement learning. CTA exploits contextual independences of the state variables conditional on the task-specific actions; its promising performance is demonstrated through a set of benchmark problems.

Keywords

hierarchical reinforcement learning; core task abstraction

1. INTRODUCTION

In hierarchical reinforcement learning (HRL), a complex problem is solved by recursively decomposing the problem into smaller subtasks at different levels of details. Most model-based methods derived from the benchmark MAXQ framework [2] solve HRL problems by learning the individual task transition dynamics in a task hierarchy of the problem space. We propose a new learning algorithm that can efficiently compute the task transition functions in the hierarchy. For instance, Figure 1 shows the MAXQ task hierarchy for a taxi problem, where the objective for the agent is to pick up and deliver a passenger to the destination. The root problem is decomposed into the *Get* and *Put* tasks, which can be further decomposed into navigation subtasks and primitive actions. Recent improvements to MAXQ include integrating directed exploration [4], using Bayesian priors [1] and Monte-Carlo simulation [6]. One major problem of the MAXQ based methods is that many similar subtasks that potentially share the same transition dynamics are created. For example, in Figure 1 there are four navigation subtasks, one for each possible destination. These subtasks are independent, hence more exploration is needed to learn a good policy. Our approach aims to avoid the redundant work by reusing the common "knowledge".

We introduce the concept of *fragments* (partial structures shared across tasks) that supports simultaneously learning multiple task transition functions. For example, all the navigation subtasks in Figure 1 that share the same transition dynamics but differ in terminal states and local reward functions can be captured using a single navigation fragment. We also exploit the contextual independences of state variables conditional on the action executed, i.e. the state variables will have different sets of parents, depending on the action executed.

Our method assumes given information on safe state abstraction (i.e. ignoring the features that do not affect the values of the states), as in current MAXQ based methods. Based on our algorithm, however, an agent's experience in learning one task would help speed up learning all the other tasks with similar features. This leads to better empirical performance as compared with existing methods. Such abstraction information can be interactively or automatically learned in future.

Appears in: *Proceedings of the 15th International Conference on Autonomous Agents and Multiagent Systems (AAMAS 2016), J. Thangarajah, K. Tuyls, C. Jonker, S. Marsella (eds.), May 9–13, 2016, Singapore.*

2. CORE TASK ABSTRACTION

Consider the hierarchy in Figure 1. Each non-leaf node in this hierarchy is a task. A "task" is a unit of execution, similar to an option [5]. It has an input set I and terminating states G. It is a well-defined factored Markov decision process (MDP) representation of a single problem— it has a set of state variables or features F, a set of actions A, a transition function T and a reward function R. Here, F and A are given, T and R are to be learned.

DEFINITION 1. *A fragment j is a tuple $\langle F_j, A_j, T_j\rangle$ where F_j is the set of relevant features, A_j is the set of applicable actions and T_j is the local transition function.*

Unlike a task, a fragment does not have an input set, terminating states and a local reward function, and thus is not a well-defined MDP. A fragment corresponds to multiple similar tasks that share the same transition dynamics, but differ in the terminating states and local reward functions. Learning a fragment allows the agent to perform well in all the tasks by sharing the learned knowledge across tasks. We can redefine the MAXQ hierarchy in Figure 1 using fragments for navigation, which is common to both *Get* and *Put*. For simplicity of exposition, we use the term *node* to refer both task and fragment. We use N to denote the set of all non-root nodes and X to denote a subset of N.

To obtain the transition function using CTA, we identify the features unique to a subset of nodes under consideration. We define a unique function to do this as follows. $Uni(\bigcap_{i\in X} F_i) = \bigcap_{i\in X} F_i - \bigcup_{j\in \overline{X}} F_j$, where the first term is a set of features relevant to X, and the second term is not.

THEOREM 1. *Let $X_a = \{i | i \in N \wedge a \in A_i\}$ represent the set of nodes where action a is applicable. The transition*

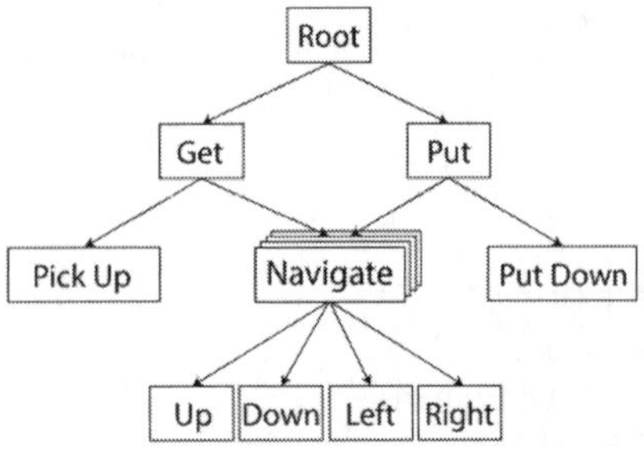

Figure 1: Task hierarchy for the taxi problem. There are four navigation subtasks, which can be represented using a single fragment.

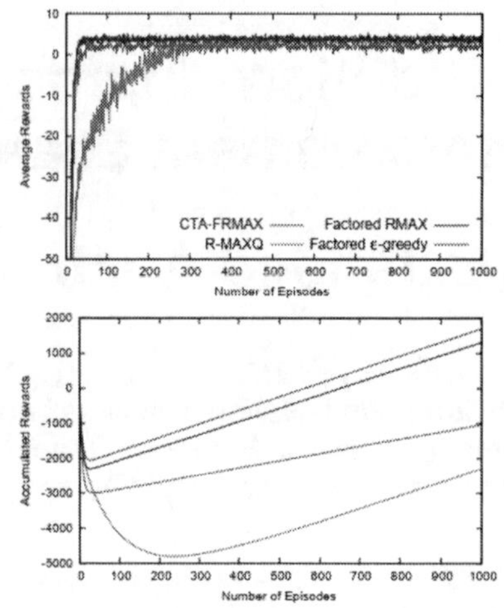

Figure 2: Results on MAXQ taxi.

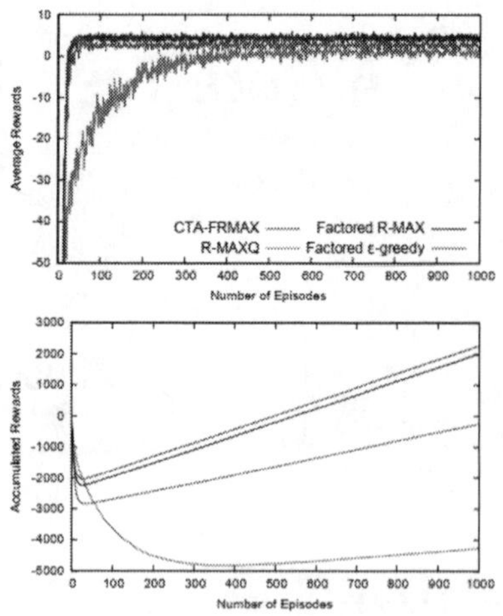

Figure 3: Results on fickle taxi.

model for node i is given by,

$$P(F'_i|F_i,a) = \prod_{Y:Y\subseteq N \wedge i\in Y} P\left(Uni(\bigcap_{j\in Y} F'_j) \mid \bigcap_{j\in X_a\cap Y} F_j, a\right)$$

The theorem states that the transition function is a product of factors where, the parent set of $Uni(\bigcap_{j\in Y} F'_j)$ depends on the action being executed. This is captured in the relation $\bigcap_{j\in X_a\cap Y} F_j$.

The direct outcome of the theorem is a reduced feature set for learning. We combine the safe state abstraction information and contextual independence to eliminate the maximum number of features from the parent set to improve the learning efficiency.

We introduce the CTA-FRMAX algorithm by combining efficient transition function learning in Theorem 1 with RMAX style exploration in factored spaces [3]. CTA-FRMAX maintains an exploration count on each factor in Theorem 1. If the count is smaller than a threshold, the agent transits to a fictitious state and receives maximum reward.

3. RESULTS

We test the performance of CTA-FRMAX in the original MAXQ taxi and the fickle taxi benchmark problems [2]. The experimental setup involves a 5×5 grid-world with four landmarks. The passenger location and destination must be one of the landmarks. There are six actions: *navigate* along the four directions, *pickup* and *putdown* as shown in Figure 1. In the fickle taxi variant the passenger may change the destination with probability 0.3. The episode ends if passenger reaches the destination or 1000 time steps elapse.

CTA-FRMAX computes the transition function for both *Get* and *Put*, and executes *Get* when the passenger is not on board and *Put* otherwise. Navigation is modeled as a fragment. We compare the performance of CTA-FRMAX against R-MAXQ [4], Factored RMAX [3] and Factored ϵ-greedy. The latter two methods are given the full dynamic Bayesian network (DBN) representation of the transition functions for both the *Get* and *Put*. We set the exploration threshold m to be 1 for both CTA-FRMAX and Factored RMAX. Since R-MAXQ does not converge with $m = 1$, we use $m = 5$ like other methods [4, 1].

As shown in Figure 2 and Figure 3, CTA-FRMAX outperforms all the other methods. In terms of number of episodes, CTA-FRMAX converges in about 50 episodes whereas R-MAXQ takes about 500 episodes to converge due to the delayed exploration—it is unable to explore *putdown* unless it completes the current navigation task. Also, R-MAXQ fails to converge to the optimal policy in the fickle taxi experiment, since it treats each subtask like a primitive action; it cannot immediately react to a change of destination until its current subtask completes. CTA-FRMAX also has better cumulative reward than Factored RMAX, despite that it only requires the relevant features for each task to be specified, while Factored RMAX requires the complete DBN structure of task transition dynamics.

Acknowledgments

This research is supported by a SMART Grant: Enhancing the Care for Elderly through Robotic Aides and Academic Research Grant: T1 251RES1211 from the Ministry of Education in Singapore.

REFERENCES

[1] F. Cao and S. Ray. Bayesian Hierarchical Reinforcement Learning. In *NIPS-12*, pages 73–81, 2012.

[2] T. G. Dietterich. The MAXQ Method for Hierarchical Reinforcement Learning. In *ICML-98*, pages 118–126, 1998.

[3] C. Guestrin, R. Patrascu, and D. Schuurmans. Algorithm-directed Exploration for Model-based Reinforcement Learning in Factored MDPs. In *ICML-02*, pages 235–242, 2002.

[4] N. K. Jong and P. Stone. Hierarchical Model-based Reinforcement Learning: R-MAX + MAXQ. In *ICML-08*, pages 432–439. ACM, 2008.

[5] R. Sutton, D. Precup, and S. Singh. Between MDPs and Semi-MDPs: A Framework for Temporal Abstraction in Reinforcement Learning. *Artificial Intelligence*, 112:181–211, 1999.

[6] N. A. Vien and M. Toussaint. Hierarchical Monte-Carlo Planning. In *AAAI-15*, 2015.

Role Assignment for Game-Theoretic Cooperation (Extended Abstract)

Catherine Moon
Duke University
Durham, NC, USA
csm17@duke.edu

Vincent Conitzer
Duke University
Durham, NC, USA
conitzer@cs.duke.edu

ABSTRACT

In multiagent systems, often agents need to be assigned to different *roles*. Multiple aspects should be taken into account for this, such as agents' skills and constraints posed by existing assignments. In this paper, we focus on another aspect: when the agents are self-interested, careful role assignment is necessary to make cooperative behavior an equilibrium of the repeated game. We formalize this problem and provide an easy-to-check necessary and sufficient condition for a given role assignment to induce cooperation. However, we show that finding whether such a role assignment exists is in general NP-hard. Nevertheless, we give two algorithms for solving the problem. The first is based on a mixed-integer linear program formulation. The second is based on a dynamic program, and runs in pseudopolynomial time if the number of agents is constant. Minor modifications of these algorithms also allow for determination of the minimal subsidy necessary to induce cooperation. In our experiments, the IP performs much, much faster.

Keywords

role assignment, cooperation, repeated games

1. INTRODUCTION

In this paper, we study the *game-theoretic* ramifications in role assignment when agents are self-interested. A careful assignment of roles might induce cooperation whereas a careless assignment may result in incentives for an agent to defect. Specifically, we consider a setting where there are multiple *minigames* in which agents need to be assigned roles. These games are then infinitely repeated, and roles cannot be reassigned later on. It is well known, via the folk theorem, that sometimes cooperation can be sustained in infinitely repeated games due to the threat of future punishment. Nevertheless, some infinitely repeated games, in and of themselves, do not offer sufficient opportunity to punish certain players for misbehaving. If so, cooperation may still be attained by the threat of punishing the defecting agent in *another* (mini)game. But for this to be effective, the defecting agent needs to be assigned the right role in the other minigame.

Appears in: *Proceedings of the 15th International Conference on Autonomous Agents and Multiagent Systems (AAMAS 2016), J. Thangarajah, K. Tuyls, C. Jonker, S. Marsella (eds.), May 9–13, 2016, Singapore.*

Our work contrasts with much work in game theory in which the model zooms in on a single setting without considering its broader strategic context. In such models, firms make production and investment decisions based on competition in a single market; teammates decide on how much effort to put in on a single project; and countries decide whether to abide by an agreement on, for instance, reducing pollution. In reality, however, it is rare to have an isolated problem at hand, as the same agents interact with each other in other settings as well. Firms often compete in several markets (e.g., computers and phones); members of a team usually work on several projects simultaneously; and countries interact with each other in other contexts, say trade agreements, as well.

Looking at a problem in such an isolated manner can be limiting. There are games where a player has insufficient incentive to play the "cooperative" action, as the payoff from that action and the threat of punishment for defection are not high enough. In such scenarios, putting two or more games with compensating asymmetries can leave hope for cooperation. A firm may allow another firm to dominate one market in return for dominance in another; a team member may agree to take on an undesirable task on one project in return for a desirable one on another; and a country may agree to a severe emissions-reducing role in one agreement in return for being given a desirable role in a trade agreement.

2. MOTIVATING EXAMPLE

Consider two individuals (e.g., faculty members or board members) who together are to form two distinct committees. Each of the committees needs a chair and another member; these are the roles we need to assign to the two individuals. Each committee's chair can choose to behave selfishly or cooperatively. Each committee's other member can choose to sabotage the committee or be cooperative. The precise payoffs differ slightly across the two committees because of their different duties. (For example, acting selfishly as the chair of a graduate admissions committee is likely to lead to different payoffs than acting selfishly as the chair of a faculty search committee.)

Chair \ Member	sabotage	cooperate
selfish	2, 1	3, 0
cooperate	1, 1	2, 2

Chair \ Member	sabotage	cooperate
selfish	2, 1	4, 0
cooperate	0, 1	2, 3

Let us first consider each of these two minigames separately. If the minigame is only played once, the chair has a strictly dominant strategy of playing selfishly (and hence, by iterated dominance, the other member will sabotage the committee). Even if the game is repeated (with a discount factor $\delta < 1$), we cannot sustain the (cooperate, cooperate) outcome forever. This is because the chair would receive a payoff of 2 in each round from this outcome—but defecting to playing selfishly would give her an immediate utility of 3 or 4 in that round after which she can still guarantee herself a utility of at least 2 in each remaining round by playing selfishly.

Now let us consider the minigames together. If the same agent is assigned as chair in each minigame, again we could not sustain the (cooperate, cooperate) outcome in both minigames, because the chair would gain $3+4$ immediately from defecting and still be able to obtain $2+2$ in each round forever after. On the other hand, if each agent is chair in one game, then with a reasonably high discount factor, (cooperate, cooperate) can be sustained. For suppose the chair of the second committee deviates by acting selfishly in that committee. This will give her an immediate gain of $4-2=2$. However, the other agent can respond by playing selfishly on committee 1 and sabotaging committee 2 forever after. Hence in each later round the original defector can get only $1+2=3$ instead of the $2+2=4$ from both agents cooperating, resulting in a loss of 1 in each round relative to cooperation. Hence, if δ is such that $2 \leq \delta/(1-\delta)$, the defection does not benefit her in the long run. This shows that linking the minigames allows us to attain cooperative behavior where this would not have been possible in each individual minigame separately. It also illustrates the importance of assigning the roles carefully in order to attain cooperation.

One may wonder what would happen if we link the minigames in a single-shot (i.e., not repeated) context. This would correspond to the case $\delta = 0$, so that the above formula indicates that cooperation is not attained in this case. In fact, linking minigames cannot help in single-shot games in general: in a single-shot model, any equilibrium of the (linked) game must consist simply of playing an equilibrium of each individual minigame. (Otherwise, a player could improve her overall payoff by deviating in a minigame where she is not best-responding.) Linking becomes useful only when the game is repeated, because then one's actions in one minigame can affect one's future payoffs in other minigames, by affecting other players' future actions. This is why the repeated game aspect is essential to our model.

3. THEORETICAL OUTLINE

We are interested in how to assign roles within minigames (of which there are two in the example above, corresponding to the two committees) to assess whether a particular outcome can be sustained in repeated play. For this question, the key issue is which roles (from different minigames) are bundled together, rather than which particular agent is assigned this bundle of roles.

Using the ideas behind the folk theorem, we can analyze whether our problem has a solution or not. We show that whether it does comes down to a single number per minigame role. The intuition that allows us to show this is as follows. To determine whether a given agent i will defect (i.e., play something other than the target action in some role assigned to her), by the folk theorem, we may assume that all other agents will play their target actions until some defection has taken place, after which they maximally punish agent i (in *all* minigames, not just the ones in which she defected). Thus, in the round in which agent i defects, she may as well play the single-round best-response to the target actions in every role assigned to her; afterwards, she will forever receive the best she can do in response to maximal punishment. (Since we only consider Nash equilibrium, we do not have to worry about multiple agents deviating.) The net effect of the defection on i's utility may be positive or negative for any given role; whether i will defect depends solely on the sum of these effects.

Because it is straightforward to compute the net effect of the defection on agent utilities, the problem of *finding* a role assignment reduces to a computational problem. We show that this problem is weakly NP-complete even in an extremely restricted special case, and strongly NP-complete for n player games. The problem can be solved in pseudopolynomial time using dynamic programming when there are at most a constant number of agents, though an integer programming approach performs much better empirically.

4. CONCLUSION

We believe that there are many other important directions that can be studied in the context of game-theoretic role assignment. Our model can be extended to allow (perhaps costly) reassignment of roles as time progresses; different agent types that value roles differently, and preferences not only over roles but also over which type of agent one is matched with (providing connections to matching [3] and hedonic games [1]); side payments between agents (providing connections to matching with contracts [2]); not every minigame being played in each round; generalizing from repeated games to stochastic or arbitrary extensive-form games; and so on. We believe that our paper provides a good foundation for such follow-up work.

Acknowledgments

We are thankful for support from ARO under grants W911NF-12-1-0550 and W911NF-11-1-0332, NSF under awards IIS-1527434, IIS-0953756, CCF-1101659, and CCF-1337215, and a Guggenheim Fellowship. This work was done in part while Conitzer was visiting the Simons Institute for the Theory of Computing. We thank the anonymous referees for their comments and suggestions.

REFERENCES

[1] H. Aziz and R. Savani. Hedonic games. In F. Brandt, V. Conitzer, U. Endriss, J. Lang, and A. D. Procaccia, editors, *Handbook of Computational Social Choice*, chapter 15. Cambridge University Press, 2015.

[2] J. W. Hatfield and P. R. Milgrom. Matching with contracts. *American Economic Review*, 95(4):913–935, September 2005.

[3] B. Klaus, D. Manlove, and F. Rossi. Matching under preferences. In F. Brandt, V. Conitzer, U. Endriss, J. Lang, and A. D. Procaccia, editors, *Handbook of Computational Social Choice*, chapter 14. Cambridge University Press, 2015.

Conveying Social Relations in Virtual Agents Through an Emotion Sharing and Response Model

(Extended Abstract)

Nuno Salvador, João Dias, Samuel Mascarenhas, Ana Paiva
Universidade de Lisboa, Instituto Superior Técnico, INESC-ID
Taguspark, Av. Prof. Cavaco Silva
2780-990 Porto Salvo, Portugal
nuno.c.salvador@ist.utl.pt,{joao.dias,samuel.mascarenhas,ana.paiva}@inesc-id.pt

1. INTRODUCTION

The impact of social relationships in human behavior is a complex topic but it is an important aspect to consider when creating believable agents. To achieve more believable social relations, we focus on a phenomenon of human interaction that is tightly coupled to social relationships but has been overlooked in most agent models of emotions: the "social sharing of emotions". It corresponds to a common daily event where a person, the sharer, tells another, the listener, about an emotional episode he experienced in the past. This phenomenon happens on a daily basis and it is important for social relationships as it signals some level of intimacy. Therefore, we propose an agent model that endows agents with the capability to speak about their past emotional experiences, and provide a supportive response in case they are the listeners.

For evaluation purposes, we developed a case study that consists in a simulation of a distressful situation in a 3D environment involving three autonomous characters. Two variations of this situation were designed: one in which our model causes a character to share the negative emotion it experiences and another where the character does not share any emotion. An user study was then conducted to assess the impact of the emotional sharing concerning the characters' believability and perceived relationship with each other.

2. EMOTION SHARING AND RESPONSE MODEL

Our model, as presented in Figure 1, considers both the sharer of an emotional episode and the listener of the episode itself. Whenever a new perception is sensed, the *Perceive-Appraisal Emotional Storage* process decides how that event will affect the agent's internal state. The main responsibility of this process is to store emotional memories in autobiographic memory and strengthen existing ones based on emotional cues, leading them to be shared later.

Subsequently, the *Emotion Sharing Activation* process will then decide if it is appropriate to share an emotional episode in the current situation. It will decide with who, when and what will be shared. The choice of the emotional episode to

Appears in: *Proceedings of the 15th International Conference on Autonomous Agents and Multiagent Systems (AAMAS 2016), J. Thangarajah, K. Tuyls, C. Jonker, S. Marsella (eds.), May 9–13, 2016, Singapore.*

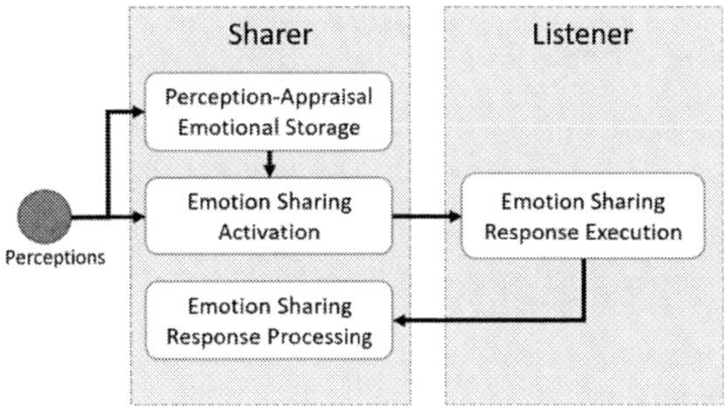

Figure 1: Emotion Sharing and Response Model

share from the autobiographic memory is done by favoring negative memories over positive ones, and later by finding the one who has the strongest event associated. Concerning the target that will be chosen to share, the choice is based on the agent's current social relations. More precisely, the chosen agent will be the one that is liked the most among the agents that have a positive relationship score. This decision is in line with the findings that indicate that people choose to share with who they have strong bonds [6]. If the emotion sharing process is enabled, the agent will share the emotional episode chosen with the target verbally, through a dialogue mechanism that is based on templates (see [1] for more details). Moreover, the act of sharing will make the agent remember the eliciting emotions regarding the episode.

On the listener side, the shared episode will activate the *Emotion Sharing Response Execution* process. First, the listener agent uses an *Empathic Appraisal* mechanism, based on the one described in [5], to generate an empathic emotion. If the listener has a negative social relationship with the sharer, then the listener will reject support, otherwise the listener will provide support. There are two types of supporting strategies that the listener agent might follow: (1) socio-affective or (2) cognitive work stimulation. A socio-affective response is performed if the shared emotion is positive or, in case it is negative, if it emphatically affected the listener agent. This is performed by expressing the empathic emotion and by generating a speech act such as "oh, that was really bad.". Otherwise, a cognitive work stimulation strategy such as resignation will be applied. If the shared episode is negative and contains one event corresponding to the activation or failure of a listener's goal then the listener will perform a generic speech act such as "Nevermind that, there's nothing you can do about it". The number of episodes an episode has been shared is used as a modulation factor for the emphatic process. This is very important to allow the emotion sharing response to change accordingly. The first time a listener hears a new episode it will more likely choose to perform a socio-affective response. However, if the sharer continues sharing the same emotional episode, is because the initial response was not appropriate to provide emotion recovery, and thus a more complex cognitive strategy should be provided.

The final phase is performed by the sharer of the emotional episode when it receives the listener's response. In case of a rejection response, the social relation towards the listener drops and a new negative emotion that concerns the failure of the emotion sharing process is created. When it comes to a support sharing response the social relation towards the listener increases and a new positive emotion is created. If the support response is of the cognitive work stimulation type, the autobiographic memory will be affected by decreasing the emotion value associated. When the emotion value becomes below a certain level, the event will then be removed from memory.

3. CASE STUDY AND EVALUATION

The proposed model was integrated into an the emotional agent architecture FAtiMA[2]. The resulting architecture was then used to drive the behavior of three different characters (the Ticket Inspector, John and Peter) in a social simulation that takes place in a virtual train. Two versions of this simulation were built, one in which both John and Peter have the emotion sharing model and another version in which they do not.

In the first part of the narrative the Ticket Inspector asks for John's ticket. Without knowing, John presents him a ticket that has a different destination for where he wants to go. Ticket Inspector notices the mistake and forces John to pay a fine (making John sad). Afterwards, Peter (John's friend) appears in the train. He sits right next his friend, starting a conversation with him. Now, in the version with the emotion sharing model, John decides to share the fine situation with Peter. Peter then chooses to support him socio-affectively (since John is his friend and it is the first time he shares that situation with him). This part ends by having them going to the train bar. In the final part, John and Peter return to their places and continue talking with each other. At some point in time, the Ticket Inspector will pass by in front of them. John will recognize the Ticket Inspector, which will revive the fine situation felt and make him share again. Given that it is the second time the same episode is shared the intensity of the emphatic emotion is much lower and so Peter decides to adopt a cognitive work stimulation strategy of type resignation.

Using the case study an evaluation was conducted to measure the impact of the proposed model in the perception of the characters' believability and the characters' social relations in the train scenario. The evaluation was performed through the online Mechanical Turk platform[1]. Participants were randomly assigned to watch a video of the version of the simulation with the emotion sharing model or a video of the version without. They were then asked to fill out a questionnaire about the characters. Concerning the questions of the survey, they were divided in two groups: believability, and Friendship Attachment. The believability questions were based on the work of Gomes [3]. The friendship attachment questions quantity the relationship between John and Peter in the eyes of the user. For this section, we adjusted McGill Friendship Questionnaire (MFQ) [4].

In total, 60 participants responded to our questionnaire. 34 participants were male while 26 were female. Only 6 of the participants were under 26 years old, while the rest were between 26 and 40. Given that the data did not follow a normal distribution, we applied the Mann Whitney U test and found statistically significant effect for the following variable: Friendship attachment of John towards Peter, $p=0.000$ with $r = 0.49$ (effect close to strong). There was no statistically significant difference for all the other variables tested. The results show that users indeed perceived John as having a stronger relationship towards Peter in the version with the Emotion Sharing and Response Model.

The fact that there were no differences in the user's perception of Peter towards John can be explained by the fact that in the version without the model there was no opportunity to illustrate an unsupportive behaviour by Peter, since there was no Emotion Sharing process by John in the first place. As such, to properly evaluate the response part of the model, we would need a third scenario where John performs Emotion Sharing but Peter responds negatively. Regarding believability, users found both versions equally believable. On hindsight, it seems that it was not clear to the users the exact degree of friendship, and thus both versions portrayed behaviour that was considered reasonable by users.

Acknowledgments

This work was supported by national funds through Fundação para a Ciência e a Tecnologia (FCT) with reference UID/CEC/50021/2013.

[1]https://www.mturk.com/mturk

REFERENCES

[1] J. Dias, W. C. Ho, T. Vogt, N. Beeckman, A. Paiva, and E. André. I know what i did last summer: Autobiographic memory in synthetic characters. In *Affective computing and intelligent interaction*, pages 606–617. Springer, 2007.

[2] J. Dias, S. Mascarenhas, and A. Paiva. Fatima modular: Towards an agent architecture with a generic appraisal framework. In *Proceedings of the International Workshop on Standards for Emotion Modeling*, 2011.

[3] P. F. Gomes, C. Martinho, and A. Paiva. I've been here before!: location and appraisal in memory retrieval. In *The 10th International Conference on Autonomous Agents and Multiagent Systems-Volume 3*, pages 1039–1046. International Foundation for Autonomous Agents and Multiagent Systems, 2011.

[4] M. J. Mendelson and F. E. Aboud. Measuring friendship quality in late adolescents and young adults: Mcgill friendship questionnaires. *Canadian Journal of Behavioural Science/Revue canadienne des sciences du comportement*, 31(2):130, 1999.

[5] S. H. Rodrigues, S. Mascarenhas, J. Dias, and A. Paiva. A process model of empathy for virtual agents. *Interacting with Computers*, page iwu001, 2014.

[6] E. Zech, B. Rimé, F. Nils, et al. Social sharing of emotion, emotional recovery, and interpersonal aspects. *The regulation of emotion*, pages 157–185, 2004.

Exclusion Method for Finding Nash Equilibrium in Multi-Player Games

(Extended Abstract)

Kimmo Berg
Aalto University School of Science
Dept. of Mathematics and Systems Analysis
kimmo.berg@aalto.fi

Tuomas Sandholm
Carnegie Mellon University
Computer Science Department
sandholm@cs.cmu.edu

ABSTRACT

We present a complete algorithm for finding an ϵ-Nash equilibrium, for arbitrarily small ϵ, in games with more than two players. The best prior complete algorithm has significantly worse complexity and has, to our knowledge, never been implemented. The main components of our tree-search-based method are a node-selection strategy, an exclusion oracle, and a subdivision scheme. The node-selection strategy determines the next region to be explored—based on the region's size and an estimate of whether the region contains an equilibrium. The exclusion oracle provides a provably correct sufficient condition for there not to exist an equilibrium in the region. The subdivision scheme determines how the region is split if it cannot be excluded. Unlike well-known incomplete methods, our method does not need to proceed locally, which avoids it getting stuck in a local minimum that may be far from any actual equilibrium. The run time grows rapidly with the game size, and this suggests a hybrid scheme where one of the relatively fast prior incomplete algorithms is run, and if it fails to find an equilibrium, then our method is used.

Keywords

Nash equilibrium; multi-player games; noncooperative games

1. INTRODUCTION

Finding a Nash equilibrium is an important and well-studied problem. Finding (even an approximate) Nash equilibrium in a multi-player game is PPAD-complete [2, 3]. Several techniques have been proposed: simplicial subdivision [10], homotopy [4, 5], mixed-integer programming [9], support enumeration [8], and differential evolution methods. The only prior complete method for finding an approximate Nash equilibrium is an exhaustive grid search in the space of probabilities [1], and it had not been implemented.

We present a complete method that improves the best-known upper bound for computing an approximate Nash equilibrium. It is guaranteed to find an ϵ-Nash equilibrium, for arbitrarily small ϵ, in finite time that depends on ϵ.

Appears in: *Proceedings of the 15th International Conference on Autonomous Agents and Multiagent Systems (AAMAS 2016), J. Thangarajah, K. Tuyls, C. Jonker, S. Marsella (eds.), May 9–13, 2016, Singapore.*

2. NORMAL-FORM GAMES

Let $N = \{1, .., n\}$ be the set of players and $A_i = \{a_1, .., a_m\}$ is the set of pure actions for player i. The function $u_i : A \mapsto \mathbf{R}$ gives player i's payoff. Each player i assigns a probability $p_i(a_j) \geq 0$ for each pure action $a_j \in A_i$ such that $\sum_{k=1}^{m} p_i(a_k) = 1$. A strategy p^* is a Nash equilibrium if $u_i(a_j, p^*_{-i}) \leq u_i(p^*_i, p^*_{-i})$ for all $a_j \in A_i$ and $i \in N$. At least one Nash equilibrium always exists in these finite games [6].

We can define player i's regret of action a_j as $r_i(a_j, p) = u_i(a_j, p_{-i}) - u_i(p)$. The regret of player i is $r_i(p) = \max_{a_j \in A_i} r_i(a_j, p)$ and $r(p) = \max_{i \in N} r_i(p)$. A strategy p^* is an ϵ-Nash equilibrium if the regret is small enough: $r(p^*) = \epsilon$.

3. TREE-SEARCH-BASED METHOD

We propose a tree-search-based method for finding a Nash equilibrium in multi-player games. It splits the space of strategy probabilities into smaller regions until a solution is found, that is, when the regrets are small enough.

3.1 Region selection (node-selection strategy)

An important choice in the method is the order in which the regions are examined. We propose a ranking function $g(R, p^0)$ that uses the size of the region $d(R)$, the regret, and its gradient evaluated at one point $p^0 \in R$:

$$g(R, p^0) = \max_{i \in N} r_i(p^0)/(d(R) \cdot M_i(p^0)), \qquad (1)$$

$$M_i(p^0) = \max_{a_j \in A_i(p^0)} \|\nabla r_i(a_j, p^0)\|_\infty \qquad (2)$$

is the maximum derivative at p^0 of player i's regret over all the variables in p' and $d(R) = \max_{q \in R} \|q - p^0\|$.

3.2 Exclusion oracle

An exclusion oracle can detect that a Nash equilibrium cannot be in the region. If this is the case, the region can be excluded, and otherwise the region is subdivided. We determine a global upper bound for the gradient of the regret:

$$M_i^* = \max_{p \in P'} \max_{a_j \in A_i(p)} \|\nabla r_i(a_j, p)\|_\infty.$$

THEOREM 3.1. *A p^0-centered ball with radius s cannot contain 0-Nash if*

$$r_i(p^0) > s \cdot M_i^*, \quad \textit{for some } i \in N. \qquad (3)$$

Table 1: Results for the random general-sum games.

n	m	Dim	Avg Time	Median	Timeout %	Avg ϵ at timeout
3	2	3	0.04	0.02	0	-
3	3	6	18.2	0.8	1	0.0028
3	5	12	900	900	100	0.07
4	2	4	21.5	0.47	1	0.0026
4	3	8	343	96	27	0.003
5	2	5	110	27	7	0.0038
5	3	10	576	652	49	0.003

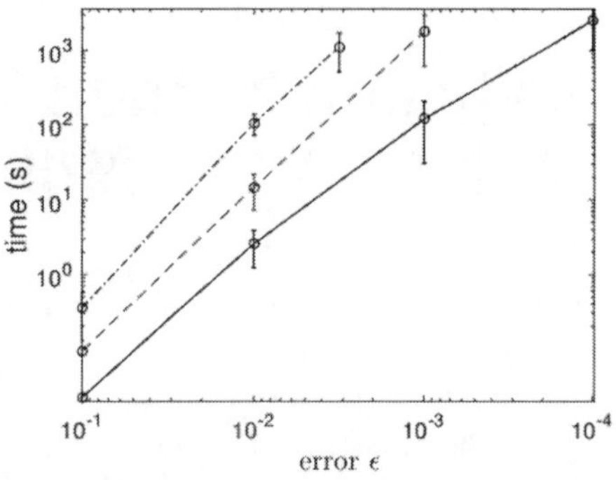

Figure 1: 3 to 5-player games with 3 actions.

3.3 Subdivision of the region

There are many ways how the search space can be subdivided. In this paper, we use hyperrectangles which makes the memory requirement linear in dimension. It is also easy to compute the middle point p^0 in the hyperrectangle and the maximum distance d to the corner points:

$$p^0_x = (u_x + l_x)/2,$$

$$d = 1/2 \cdot \sqrt{\sum_{x \in p'} (u_x - l_x)^2},$$

where l_x and u_x are the lower and upper bounds of the hyperrectangle in dimension x. We use a bisection method and split the hyperrectangle along the longest edge.

Algorithm 1
Repeat until the stopping condition is met
1. Select the region with minimal value of g in Eq. (1).
2. Compute $r(p^0)$. If Eq. (3) holds, exclude and goto 1.
3. Bisect the region.

THEOREM 3.2. *Any bisection algorithm excludes all points with* $r(p) \geq \epsilon$ *within* $2^{(m-1)n\lceil \log\left(\frac{2M^*}{\epsilon}\right)/\log(2)\rceil} - 1$ *iterations, where* $M^* = \max_{i \in N} M_i^*$.

The only prior complete algorithm is an exhaustive grid search by Babichenko et al. [1]. It is slower: it runs in $(k+1)^{nm}$ iterations, where $k > 8(\log m + \log n - \log \epsilon + \log 8)/\epsilon^2$.

THEOREM 3.3. *The number of iterations required by any bisection algorithm (with small enough* ϵ *and large enough* m *and* n*) is smaller than* $(k+1)^{mn}$.

4. EXPERIMENTS

We tested the algorithms on randomly generated normal-form games (time limit 900s) and on GAMUT games [7]; we used target accuracy $\epsilon = 10^{-3}$. One can see from the results that the running times grow rapidly as the search space dimension increases.

Figure 1 shows the computation times for different ϵ in three-player (black solid line), four-player (red dashed line) and five-player (blue dash-dotted line) games, with three actions per player. Moreover, we have tested different node-selection strategies: depth-first, breadth-first and random search order, and they were slower than the presented one.

5. CONCLUSION

Our aim was not to develop the fastest incomplete method but a method that is guaranteed to find an ϵ-Nash equilibrium on all instances. In contrast, the homotopy methods, e.g., are often much faster in practice as they improve the current solution locally, but they may not find a solution. That suggests a hybrid scheme where one runs some relatively fast incomplete method first, and if it fails to find an equilibrium, then one runs our algorithm. That achieves the best of both worlds: the speed of the prior algorithms and the completeness of ours. It would also be extremely interesting to develop improvements to each of the three component techniques used in our tree search.

Acknowledgments

This material is based on work supported by the NSF under grants 1320620 and 1546752.

REFERENCES

[1] Y. Babichenko, S. Barman, and R. Peretz. Simple approximate equilibria in large games. EC '14, p. 753–770, 2014.

[2] X. Chen, X. Deng, and S.-H. Teng. Settling the complexity of computing two-player Nash equilibria. *Journal of the ACM*, 56(3), 2009.

[3] C. Daskalakis. On the complexity of approximating a Nash equilibrium. *ACM Trans. on Alg.*, 9(3), 2013.

[4] S. Govindan and R. Wilson. A global Newton method to compute Nash equilibria. *JET*, 110:65–86, 2003.

[5] P. J.-J. Herings and A. van den Elzen. Computation of the Nash equilibrium selected by the tracing procedure in n-person games. *GEB*, 38:89–117, 2002.

[6] J. Nash. Equilibrium points in n-person games. *PNAS*, 36:48–49, 1950.

[7] E. Nudelman, J. Wortman, Y. Shoham, and K. Leyton-Brown. Run the gamut: A comprehensive approach to evaluating game-theoretic algorithms. AAMAS '04, p. 880–887, 2004.

[8] R. Porter, E. Nudelman, and Y. Shoham. Simple search methods for finding a Nash equilibrium. *GEB*, 63:642–662, 2008.

[9] T. Sandholm, A. Gilpin, and V. Conitzer. Mixed-integer programming methods for finding Nash equilibria. *AAAI*, p. 495–501, 2005.

[10] G. van der Laan, A. Talman, and L. van der Heyden. Simplicial variable dimension algorithms for solving the nonlinear complementarity problem on a product of unit simplices using a general labelling. *Math of OR*, 12(3):377–397, 1987.

Sum-Product-Max Networks for Tractable Decision Making (Extended Abstract)

Mazen Melibari
University of Waterloo
Waterloo, Ontario, Canada
mmelibar@uwaterloo.ca

Pascal Poupart
University of Waterloo
Waterloo, Ontario, Canada
ppoupart@uwaterloo.ca

Prashant Doshi
University of Georgia
Athens, GA, USA
pdoshi@cs.uga.edu

1. INTRODUCTION

Influence diagram (ID) has been the graphical language of choice for probabilistically modeling decision-making problems [5]. IDs extend the probabilistic inference of Bayesian networks with decision and utility nodes to allow the computation of expected utility and decision rules. However, unlike Bayesian networks that have witnessed a rich portfolio of algorithms to automatically learn their structure from data, no algorithms exist to the best of our knowledge for learning the structure and parameters of IDs from data.

Recent investigations into new models for tractable probabilistic inference such as arithmetic circuits [2] and sum-product networks [4] that are suited to learn models from large datasets could help fill this gap. Specifically, approaches to directly learn a network polynomial that is graphically represented as a network of sum and product nodes from data have been devised [3]. Evaluations of the polynomial provide the joint or conditional distributions as desired and are performed in time that is *linear* in the size of the network. Thus, arithmetic circuits and sum-product networks represent a tractable class of inference models compared to the generally intractable inferencing of Bayesian networks.

Motivated by tractable inference, we generalize sum-product networks to a new class of problems that involve probabilistic decision making, in this paper. To enable this, we introduce two new types of nodes: *max* nodes to represent the maximization operation over different possible values of a decision variable, and *utility* nodes to represent the utility values. We refer to the resulting network as a sum-product-max network (SPMN), whose solution provides a decision rule that maximizes the expected utility in linear time. The semantics of the max node is that its output is the decision that leads to the maximal value among all decisions. Analogously to sum-product networks, we introduce a set of properties that guarantee the validity of the SPMN, such that the solution will correspond to the expected utility obtained from a valid embedded probabilistic model and utility function that are encoded by the network.

We present a first method to learn the structure and parameters of valid SPMNs from decision-theoretic data. Such data not only consists of instances of the random state variables but also possible decision(s) and the corresponding valuation(s). This is a significant advance because it brings machine learning to decision making, which has so far relied on handcrafted expert models.

2. SUM-PRODUCT-MAX NETWORKS

Appears in: *Proceedings of the 15th International Conference on Autonomous Agents and Multiagent Systems (AAMAS 2016), J. Thangarajah, K. Tuyls, C. Jonker, S. Marsella (eds.), May 9–13, 2016, Singapore.*

2.1 Definition and Solution

SPMNs generalize SPNs [4] by introducing two new types of nodes to an SPN: max and utility nodes. We begin by defining an SPMN.

DEFINITION 1 (SPMN). *An SPMN over decision variables $D_1, \ldots, D_m$ and random variables $X_1, \ldots, X_n$ is a rooted directed acyclic graph. Its leaves are either binary indicators of the random variables or utility nodes. An internal node of an SPMN is either a sum, product or max node. Each max node corresponds to one of the decision variables and each outgoing edge from a max node is labeled with one of the possible values of the corresponding decision variable. The value of a max node i is $\max_{j \in Children(i)} v_j$, where $Children(i)$ is the set of children of i, and v_j is the value of the subgraph rooted at child j. The sum and product nodes are defined as in the SPN.*

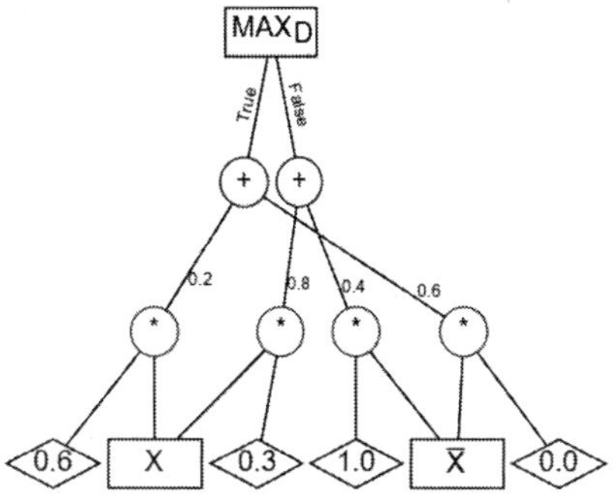

Figure 1: An SPMN for one decision and random variable.

Figure 1 shows a generic example SPMN for a decision-making problem with a single decision D_1 and binary random variable X_1. Indicator nodes $X_1 = T$ and $X_1 = F$ return a 1 and 0 respectively, when the random variable X_1 is true, and vice versa if X_1 is false.

Next, we define a set of properties to ensure that a SPMN encodes a function that computes the maximum expected utility (MEU) given some partial order between the variables and utility function U.

DEFINITION 2 (COMPLETENESS OF SUM NODES). *An SPMN is sum-complete iff all children of the same sum node have the same scope.*

The scope of a node is the set of all random variables associated with indicators and decision variables associated with max nodes that appear in the SPMN rooted at that node.

DEFINITION 3 (DECOMPOSABILITY OF PRODUCT NODES). *An SPMN is decomposable iff no variable appears in more than one child of a product node.*

DEFINITION 4 (COMPLETENESS OF MAX NODES). *An SPMN is max-complete iff all children of the same max node have the same scope, where the scope is as defined previously.*

DEFINITION 5 (UNIQUENESS OF MAX NODES). *An SPMN is max-unique iff each max node that corresponds to a decision variable D appears at most once in every path from root to leaves.*

Together, these properties allow us to define a valid SPMN.

DEFINITION 6 (VALIDITY). *A SPMN is valid if every sum node in the network is complete, every product node is decomposable, and each max node is complete and unique.*

Evaluation An SPMN is evaluated by setting the indicators that are consistent with the evidence to 1 and the rest to 0. Then, we perform a bottom-up pass of the network during which operators at each node are applied to the output values of its children. The optimal decision rule is found by tracing back (i.e., top-down) through the network and choosing the edges that maximize the decision nodes.

2.2 Structure Learning

Our method for learning SPMNs labeled as LearnSPMN generalizes LearnSPN [3], which is a recursive top-down learning method for SPNs. This allows automated learning of computational models of decision-making problems from appropriate data. LearnSPMN extends LearnSPN to generate the two new types of nodes introduced in SPMNs: max and utility nodes. Equally important, the generalization also requires modifying a core part of LearnSPN so that the learned structure respects the constraints that are imposed by the partial order $\mathcal{P}^{\prec}$ on variables involved in the decision problem. Algorithm 1 describes the structure-learning method.

Algorithm 1: LearnSPMN

input :$\mathcal{D}$:data,$\mathbf{V}$: set of variables,i:infoset index,$\mathcal{P}^{\prec}$: partial order
output:
if $|\mathbf{V}| = 1$ **then**
  if *the variable V in $\mathbf{V}$ is a utility* **then**
    $u \leftarrow estimate\ \mathrm{Pr}(V = True)$ from $\mathcal{D}$;
    return *a utility node with the value u*
  else
    return *smoothed univariate distribution over V*
else
  $rest \leftarrow \mathcal{P}^{\prec}[i+1...]$;
  if $\mathcal{P}^{\prec}[i]$ *is a decision variable* **then**
    for $v \in$ *decision values of* $\mathcal{P}^{\prec}[i]$ **do**
      $\mathcal{D}^v \leftarrow$ subset of $\mathcal{D}$ where $\mathcal{P}^{\prec}[i] = v$
    return MAX_v LearnSPMN$(\mathcal{D}^v, \mathrm{rest}, \mathrm{i}+1, \mathcal{P}^{\prec})$
  else
    Try to partition $\mathbf{V}$ into independent subsets $\mathbf{V}_j$ while keeping $rest$ in one partition;
    if *a partition is found* **then**
      return $\prod_j$ LearnSPMN$(\mathcal{D}, \mathbf{V}_j, \mathrm{i}, \mathcal{P}^{\prec})$
    else
      partition $\mathcal{D}$ into clusters $\mathcal{D}^j$ of similar instances;
      return $\sum_j \frac{|\mathcal{D}^j|}{|\mathcal{D}|} \times$ LearnSPMN$(\mathcal{D}^j, \mathbf{V}, \mathrm{i}, \mathcal{P}^{\prec})$

LearnSPMN takes as input a dataset $\mathcal{D}$ and a partial order $\mathcal{P}^{\prec}$. Each utility variable in the data is first converted into a binary random variable, say U, independent from other utility variables by using the well-known Cooper transformation [1]. Specifically, $\mathrm{Pr}(U = true|Parents(U)) = \frac{u - u_{min}}{u_{max} - u_{min}}$ where u_{min} and u_{max} are the minimum and maximum values for that utility variable and $Parents(U)$ is a joint assignment of the variables that U depends on. This step has an added benefit in that it allows for stochastic utility functions as well such as in bandit problems. Next, we duplicate each instance a fixed number of times and replace the utility value of each instance by an i.i.d. sample of *true* or *false* from the corresponding distribution over U. Consequently, utility variables may be treated as traditional random variables in the learning method. Algorithm 1 iterates through the partial order $\mathcal{P}^{\prec}$. For each decision variable D, a corresponding max node is created. For each set $\mathcal{V}$ of random variables in an information set of the partial order, the algorithm constructs an SPN of sum and product nodes by recursively partitioning the random variables in non-correlated subsets and by partitioning the data into clusters of similar instances. As in LearnSPN, LearnSPMN can be implemented using any suitable method such as a pairwise χ^2 or G-test to partition the variables and instances. Clustering algorithms such as EM and K-means can be used to partition the data into clusters of similar instances.

3. EXPERIMENTS

We evaluate LearnSPMN by applying it to a small test bed of 3 data sets whose attributes consist of state and decision variables and corresponding utility values. These datasets were created by simulating a randomly generated directed acyclic graph of nodes whose conditional probability tables and utility tables were populated by values from symmetric Dirichlet distributions. Table 1 gives some descriptive statistics for these data sets.

Dataset	#Dec_var	|ID|	|Dataset|	|SPMN|
Random-ID 1	3	116	100K	730
Random-ID-2	5	283	100K	922
Random-ID 3	8	580	100K	2940

Table 1: Synthetic datasets and learned model statistics. #Dec_var is the number of decisions variables in the problem, |ID| is the total representational size of the ID (total clique size + sepsets), |Dataset| is the size of the dataset, and |SPMN| is the size of the learned SPMN.

The last column of Table 1 reports on the size of the SPMN that was learned for each dataset. While the size is usually larger than the total representational complexity of the corresponding ID, we emphasize that the run time complexity of SPMN is *linear* in the size of the network. For the top two datasets, SPMN yields an identical MEU as that from the IDs and the third dataset exhibits a 10.3% difference in the MEU from the SPMN.

Acknowledgments

This research is supported in part by grants from NSERC and ONR #N000141310870.

REFERENCES

[1] G. F. Cooper. A method for using belief networks as influence diagrams. 1998.
[2] A. Darwiche. A differential approach to inference in bayesian networks. In *UAI*, pages 123–132, 2000.
[3] R. Gens and P. Domingos. Learning the structure of sum-product networks. In *Proceedings of The 30th International Conference on Machine Learning*, pages 873–880, 2013.
[4] H. Poon and P. Domingos. Sum-product networks: A new deep architecture. In *Proc. 12th Conf. on Uncertainty in Artificial Intelligence*, pages 2551–2558, 2011.
[5] R. D. Shachter. Evaluating influence diagrams. *Operations Research*, 34(6):871–882, 1986.

Knowledge-Enabled Robotic Agents for Shelf Replenishment in Cluttered Retail Environments

(Extended Abstract)

Jan Winkler, Ferenc Bálint-Benczédi,
Thiemo Wiedemeyer, Michael Beetz
Institute for Artificial Intelligence
University of Bremen, Germany

Narunas Vaskevicius,
Christian A. Mueller, Tobias Fromm,
Andreas Birk
Robotics, CS & EE
Jacobs University Bremen, Germany

ABSTRACT

Autonomous robots in unstructured and dynamically changing retail environments have to master complex perception, knowledge processing, and manipulation tasks. To enable them to act competently, we propose a framework based on three core components: (∘) a knowledge-enabled perception system, capable of combining diverse information sources to cope with occlusions and stacked objects with a variety of textures and shapes, (∘) knowledge processing methods produce strategies for tidying up supermarket racks, and (∘) the necessary manipulation skills in confined spaces to arrange objects in semi-accessible rack shelves. We demonstrate our framework in an simulated environment as well as on a real shopping rack using a PR2 robot. Typical supermarket products are detected and rearranged in the retail rack, tidying up what was found to be misplaced items.

General Terms

Algorithms, Experimentation

Keywords

robot perception; knowledge-based reasoning;

1. INTRODUCTION

Robotic agents that are embodied and can manipulate the world in order to accomplish human-scale manipulation tasks in open and realistic environments are still a largely unresolved challenge.

Lately robotic solutions for retail environments are becoming more and more popular. Common tasks include refilling product shelves, and putting misplaced products back to where they belong. Retail scenarios are semi-structured, but unpredictable in details, products might be missing, requirements of where to place which item change, or products and shelves are partially obstructed. The products are placed such that they can be easily seen, the front side is typically visually distinctive but they also constitute challenges as identical items are placed directly next to each other, complicating object segmentation as well as manipulating objects without causing side effects on the neighboring items. The tasks that the robotic agents are to accomplish include loading an empty rack, restocking sold items, cleaning up unordered shelves, rearranging product configurations, etc.

Figure 1: Retail environment showing the used robot next to the perceived objects of an example scene

In this paper, we outline our systematic solution for robotic agents that perform a limited kind of shelf reordering. The robotic agent takes a qualitative spatial description of how the items in a shelf should be re-ordered, such as the cereal should be placed to the right of the coffee. The robotic agent then tessellates the target region of the items into variable size grid cells that are allocated for the individual product groups. The items are to be placed in the respective grid cell, next to each others and facing the front.

The solution presented herein is unique on the first hand in the way that objects can be recognized and grasped even if they are subject to heavy occlusion, or similar objects are stacked or aligned with each other (see Fig. 1). Multiple instances per object are not a limitation either. Second, our approach focuses on reasoning about objects' semantics which is crucial for everyday scenarios where the requirement is to achieve a certain final object configuration. Additionally, since we want to avoid to accidentally clear up the whole shelf, awareness and avoidance of clutter objects are a central requirement in such a scenario.

2. SYSTEM OVERVIEW

Addressing the problems stated in this paper would not be possible without a tight integration between specific modules that are needed by an autonomous robotic agent.

Three main components were used to build up the system, each of them introduced recently, mainly because they are open-source software and because they meet the required needs of being modular and easy to extend: (∘) CRAM [2] – a high-level robot planning

Appears in: *Proceedings of the 15th International Conference on Autonomous Agents and Multiagent Systems (AAMAS 2016), J. Thangarajah, K. Tuyls, S. Marsella, C. Jonker (eds.), May 9–13, 2016, Singapore.*

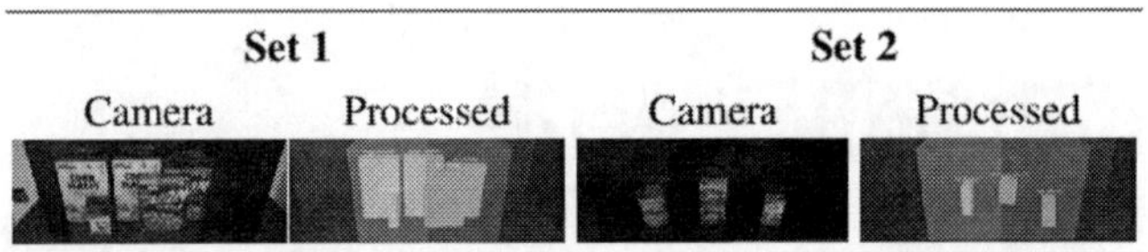

Figure 2: Example experiment arrangements of objects in a shopping rack. The left images show the source camera data. The right images depict the processed object instances recognized by the perception system.

and reasoning system (◦) KnowRob [4] – a centralized knowledge processing and inference framework (◦) RoboSherlock [1] – a knowledge-enabled robotic perception framework.

Furthermore, RoboSherlock was extended with two essential perception components and tasked with the gist of the recognition process: a texture [5] and a shape-based [3] recognition system.

The entry point to the system is a generalized plan for rearranging the shelf, generated by CRAM and the target arrangement of the shelves in a specific aisle defined in our knowledge base. As a first step, RoboSherlock is queried for the detected items. At this point, using knowledge about the environment stored in the semantic map of KnowRob, the raw data is filtered in order to contain only the regions of interest for the current task, that is, the respective shelf. Based on the filtered images, the instance and shape recognition then hypothesize about possible products and their locations, and transmit these back to CRAM through RoboSherlock.

Internally, the plan generation evaluates different strategies for executing the rearrangement task, which are ranked based on their intrinsic cost as calculated by an A*-based planner implemented in CRAM. The best ranked strategy is then chosen to be executed.

Once the best strategy has been chosen, the actual manipulation plan is generated and executed by the robot. In case of failures that occur during the manipulation (e.g. unable to grasp object, dropped object, unable to plan manipulation trajectory, etc.), control is handed back to CRAM where the contingency is resolved and an alternative plan is generated.

3. RESULTS

To evaluate the importance of harmonizing the different system components of our approach when dealing with complex shopping rack scenarios, we present a series of example cases. In these, we demonstrate the effects of slight variations in perception data on the output of the planning algorithm, and thus, in the manipulation.

Figure 2 depicts two examples of 20 shopping rack situations we created, separated into two qualitatively different series with varying pose, obstacles, unknown objects and stacking of similar and different objects. In some cases, objects were not or wrongly detected. The planner's goal was to group the available objects and evenly distribute them over two of the rack's shelves.

The cost shown in Table 1 represents the accumulated cost of all individual actions inside of a planned sequence as used by A*. Picking and placing are rather simple actions, while moving the robot's torso takes quite some time. As execution time is a quality criterion while tidying up shopping racks, it is more expensive. Moving the robot's base is rather fast, and handing over an object from one hand to the other takes longer than picking and placing.

As experiments suggest, the cost does not exceedingly increase when meeting difficulties, such as obstructions, or stacked objects.

Failures in perception are therefore not directly reflected in the planner's output. In one case, two stacked objects were identified as only one object, leading to a simpler, and wrong plan. In another case, both lower objects on the stacks are not detected at all, also resulting in a wrong configuration. In these cases, we rely on the failure detection and recovery mechanisms which are implemented in CRAM. After every manipulation action, the performing robot re-perceived and validated the current scene, and re-plans its strategy if inconsistencies are detected. The video we created in the course of this work[1] shows the system being executed on a PR2 robot.

	Time [s]	# Pick	# Place	# Move Torso	# Move Base	Cost
Set 1	5.35	4	4	6	2	23.6
	(18.6±37.8)	(4.4±0.5)	(4.4±0.5)	(5.6±1.6)	(1.2±1.0)	(23.0±2.7)
Set 2	4.3	4.5	4.5	5.0	2.0	22.0
	(20.0±32.5)	(4.5±0.8)	(4.5±0.8)	(5.3±1.3)	(1.4±1.0)	(22.8±3.9)

Table 1: Summary of details from action sequences as generated based on the data from two qualitatively different sets, with 10 scenes each. "Time" is the time taken to plan the action sequence, "Cost" is the accumulated cost of all individual actions (top: median, bottom: mean ± standard deviation).

4. CONCLUSION

We have shown a novel application of knowledge-based manipulation in an everyday retail scenario which requires extended perception and reasoning capabilities.

In the current state of the art it is hard to measure the competence of full robotic systems other than evaluating individual components. In our experiments we show how the results of visual perception reflect in the generation of manipulation plans for robotic agents. Having a quantifiable connection between beliefs about the real world and the quality of the plans for the robotic agents allows for further investigation of other modalities for improving the robot behavior.

Acknowledgements

This work was partly supported by the EU FP7 project *RoboHow* (Grant Agreement Number 288533).

REFERENCES

[1] M. Beetz, F. Balint-Benczedi, N. Blodow, D. Nyga, T. Wiedemeyer, and Z.-C. Marton. RoboSherlock: Unstructured Information Processing for Robot Perception. In *International Conference on Robotics and Automation*, 2015.

[2] M. Beetz, L. Moesenlechner, and M. Tenorth. CRAM – A Cognitive Robot Abstract Machine for Everyday Manipulation in Human Environments. In *International Conference on Intelligent Robots and Systems*, 2010.

[3] C. Mueller, K. Pathak, and A. Birk. Object shape categorization in RGBD images using hierarchical graph constellation models based on unsupervisedly learned shape parts described by a set of shape specificity levels. In *International Conference on Intelligent Robots and Systems*, 2014.

[4] M. Tenorth and M. Beetz. KnowRob: A knowledge processing infrastructure for cognition-enabled robots. *International Journal of Robotics Research*, 32(5):566–590, 2013.

[5] N. Vaskevicius, K. Pathak, A. Ichim, and A. Birk. The Jacobs robotics approach to object recognition and localization in the context of the ICRA'11 Solutions in Perception Challenge. In *International Conference on Robotics and Automation*, 2012.

[1] `https://youtu.be/xFwinZAHrnA`

Communicating Intentions for Coordination with Unknown Teammates

(Extended Abstract)

Trevor Santarra and Arnav Jhala
University of California Santa Cruz
{tsarratt,jhala}@soe.ucsc.edu

ABSTRACT

Ad hoc multiagent teamwork introduces the challenge of coordinating with a variety of potential teammates, including teammates with unknown behavior. We examine the communication of policy information for enhanced coordination between such agents. The proposed decision-theoretic approach examines the uncertainty within a model of an unfamiliar teammate, identifying and acquiring policy information valuable to the collaborative effort.

Categories and Subject Descriptors

I.2.11 [**Distributed Artificial Intelligence**]: Cooperation and coordination

General Terms

Experimentation

Keywords

Ad Hoc Teams; Teamwork; Coordination

1. INTRODUCTION

Coordinating a team of autonomous agents necessitates that agents must act in such a way that progresses toward the achievement of a goal while avoiding conflict with their teammates. In traditional multiagent systems literature, these teams of agents share an identical design for reasoning, planning, and executing actions, allowing perfect modeling of teammates. Ad hoc teamwork [4] further complicates this problem by introducing a variety of teammates with which an agent must coordinate. In these scenarios, one or more agents within a team can be unfamiliar, having unknown planning capabilities guiding their behavior.

Much of the existing ad hoc teamwork research focuses on reinforcement learning and decision theoretic planning. Agents employ models of known behavior to predict teammates' actions, using decision theory to maximize expected utility in instances where the predicted actions are uncertain [1]. Online learning refines these models with observations of behaviors during execution, increasing the accuracy of the models' predictions, permitting the team to coordinate more effectively [2, 3].

Our approach addresses the problem of planning under teammate behavior uncertainty by incorporating intentional multiagent communication within ad hoc teams. In partially observable multiagent domains, agents must share information regarding aspects of the environment such that uncertainty is reduced across the team, permitting better coordination. Similarly, we consider how communication may be utilized within ad hoc teams to resolve behavioral uncertainty. Querying a teammate for its intended actions in various states allows an agent to adjust its predictions of the teammate's course of action. With more accurate predictions of team behavior, an agent can better select its actions to support team cohesion. In contrast to traditional multiagent communication applications where communicative acts are few in number, we allow the agent to consider the entire set of states encountered when planning. In short, an ad hoc agent coordinating with an unknown teammate can identify uncertainties within its own predictive model of teammate behavior then request the appropriate policy information, allowing the agent to adapt its individual policy.

2. APPROACH

Having complete knowledge of a teammate's intended behavior would allow optimal planning on the part of the coordinating agent. However, online learning of a complete model of a teammate's behavior within relatively complex domains with thousands or millions of states is infeasible during limited instances of coordination. As Barrett et al. [1] observed, ad hoc agents can often collaborate effectively when observing the behavior of an unknown team in a comparatively small, recurring section of the domain's state space. This is particularly true in cases where the team attempts repeated trials with static initial conditions. It is, however, beneficial for agents to reason over what information about teammates they already possess and evaluate what subset of the team's behavior would be beneficial to know when coordinating in uncommon states.

Decision theory provides a mechanism for determining the expected change in expected utility for acquiring new information, as shown by Equation 1. During evaluation of communicative acts, for each potential response for an intention query, the agent reevaluates its expected utility (denoted by V') for both its original policy, π, as well as an updated policy, π', constructed under the new information. The difference in these two utilities is the increase in expected utility the agent would receive given the information in advance,

Appears in: *Proceedings of the 15th International Conference on Autonomous Agents and Multiagent Systems (AAMAS 2016), J. Thangarajah, K. Tuyls, C. Jonker, S. Marsella (eds.), May 9–13, 2016, Singapore.*

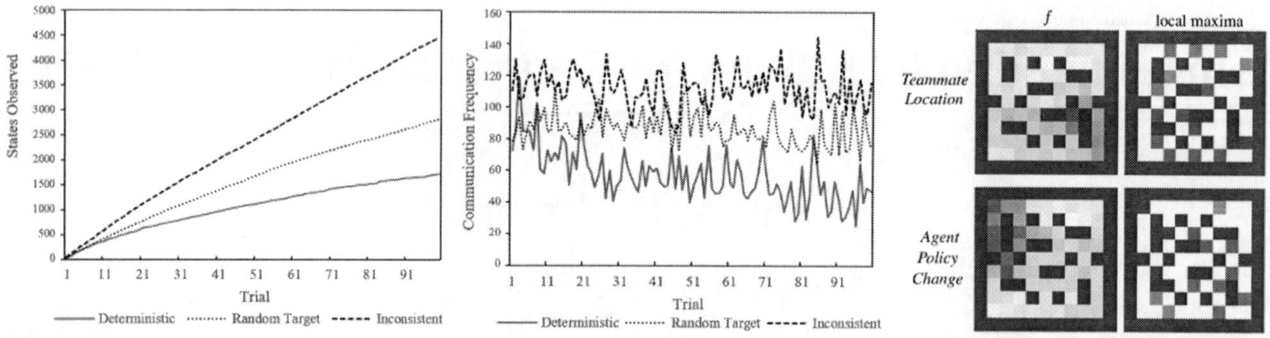

(a) Unique states encountered across successive trials.

(b) Average query frequency across successive trials.

(c) A heatmap of query frequencies, depicting the teammate's location and the corresponding location of the change in the agent's policy.

allowing the agent to preemptively adapt its policy.

$$U_{Comm}(s_t) = \sum_{a \in A_{s_t}} Pr(a|s_t)\left(V'_{\pi'|a}(s_0) - V'_{\pi|a}(s_0)\right) \quad (1)$$

3. SELECTED EXPERIMENTS

We test the communicating ad hoc agent in a variant of the multiagent pursuit domain, where a team of agents coordinate to trap one of several fleeing prey within a maze. The ad hoc agent in the team possesses a basic observation-based learning capacity, initially uniformly predicting the actions of its teammate. This model is updated by observing the teammate and predicting future actions with probability proportional to the frequency count with Laplace smoothing. In order to ensure a degree of uncertainty in the paired teammate's behavior, we test the coordinating ad hoc agent with a range of teammate types, varying in degrees of consistency of behavior, as follows:

1. Deterministic - This teammate consistently selects its target across trials and pursues it in an identical, deterministic manner each round.
2. Random Target - Here, the teammate begins each trial by uniformly sampling which target it will pursue.
3. Inconsistent - This agent periodically chooses an action at random as well as occasionally switches targets.

In contrast to existing work where unknown teammates may have largely deterministic behaviors from static initial conditions, we observe that more varied teammate behavior has a significant impact on the quantity of unique states encountered by the team. Uncommon states are consequently unlikely to have sufficient observations for the learned model to accurately predict teammate behavior. Analysis of the communication frequency to resolve intention uncertainty found that over time coordination attempts with the deterministic and random target teammate types resulted in decreased communication over successive trials. However, when the ad hoc agent coordinated with the inconsistent teammate, communication frequency was, on average, greater than for other teammate types and did not exhibit a statistically significant decline over time.

Furthermore, the relative frequencies of states queried for the teammate's intended actions demonstrate a bias toward states nearer to the initial state, where intention resolution may dictate which of three prey should be pursued. In addition, the local maxima of the state illustrate the agent correctly identifies branches within the maze as more commonly valuable to communicate over non-branch positions.

Teammate	Spearman's ρ	p
Deterministic	-0.627	<0.001
Random Target	-0.295	0.003
Inconsistent	-0.130	0.196

Table 1: Monotonicity of communicative frequency.

4. CONCLUSION

When cooperating with unknown teammates, agents with the capability to query policy information can act in a proactive manner, acquiring valuable team behavior information. Restricting an agent to learning purely through observation requires either a sufficient number of observations of teammate behavior or the ability to generalize predictions from prior experience [2]. The communication of intentional information complements learning agents, as such communicative behavior both requires a reflective analysis of the uncertainty within an existing teammate model as well as proactively expands the information an agent possesses about its teammates.

REFERENCES

[1] S. Barrett, P. Stone, and S. Kraus. Empirical evaluation of ad hoc teamwork in the pursuit domain. In *The 10th International Conference on Autonomous Agents and Multiagent Systems-Volume 2*, pages 567–574. International Foundation for Autonomous Agents and Multiagent Systems, 2011.

[2] S. Barrett, P. Stone, S. Kraus, and A. Rosenfeld. Teamwork with limited knowledge of teammates. In *AAAI*, 2013.

[3] T. Sarratt and A. Jhala. Tuning belief revision for coordination with inconsistent teammates. In *Eleventh Artificial Intelligence and Interactive Digital Entertainment Conference*, 2015.

[4] P. Stone, G. A. Kaminka, S. Kraus, J. S. Rosenschein, et al. Ad hoc autonomous agent teams: Collaboration without pre-coordination. In *AAAI*, 2010.

OWLS: Observational Wireless Life-enhancing System (Extended Abstract)

Hanzhong Zheng
Allegheny College
520 North Main Street
Allegheny, PA
zhengh@allegheny.edu

Janyl Jumadinova
Allegheny College
520 North Main Street
Allegheny, PA
jjumadinova@allegheny.edu

ABSTRACT

Socially assistive robotics technologies for individuals, who have been affected by age-related disabilities and similar types of disorders, have become popular options for facilitating natural independence and uninterrupted mobility. Wireless wearable sensor systems enable proactive personal health management and the ubiquitous monitoring of vital signs to keep an active watch on immediate health conditions. In this paper, we develop a system, called OWLS, where multiple wearable sensors, software agents, robots and health analysis technology, have been integrated into a single personal therapy solution (SPTS). Our system uses a reinforcement learning algorithm to make decisions about the user's current health conditions, and to take appropriate actions, as necessary (i.e, contacting outside parties). We show that the approach of non-invasive monitoring, when combined with an alert system, makes this a desirable SPTS in future health care.

1. INTRODUCTION

There is an increasing need for the personalized care to allow people with physical limitations or disabilities to continue functioning independently.Robotic systems have been used for various therapies such as movement training, wrist and arm rehabilitation, and others [3]. Recently, wearable sensors, have been used to also assist humans to monitor health conditions [4] and to enable proactive and ubiquitous personal health management. In this paper, we present an *Observational Wireless Life-enhancing System*, which we call OWLS, composed of multiple robots, sensors, and software agents, to provide uninterrupted personalized monitoring of a user's current health in his or her own environment. Similar to an owl who watches uninterruptedly in the wild, by unintrusive observation, the robots and sensors in our system collect data to ascertain the general health conditions and well-being of the user. A reinforcement learning algorithm is used to decide on the condition of the monitored user and take an appropriate action. At regular intervals, the OWLS prepares a compiled report of all the processed information to keep a person's caregiver (i.e., doctors, family, etc.) informed of any changes in the health status of the monitored individual. If an analysis of the user's well-being determines a form of threat or the likelihood of a threat in the future (developing illness, worsening conditions, etc.), then the system is equipped to immediately notify the appropriate caregivers. The experimental results show that OWLS is accurate in determining the user's condition and taking an appropriate action. Reinforcement learning algorithm used by OWLS is also shown to outperform a baseline algorithm used for comparison.

Appears in: *Proceedings of the 15th International Conference on Autonomous Agents and Multiagent Systems (AAMAS 2016), J. Thangarajah, K. Tuyls, C. Jonker, S. Marsella (eds.), May 9–13, 2016, Singapore.*

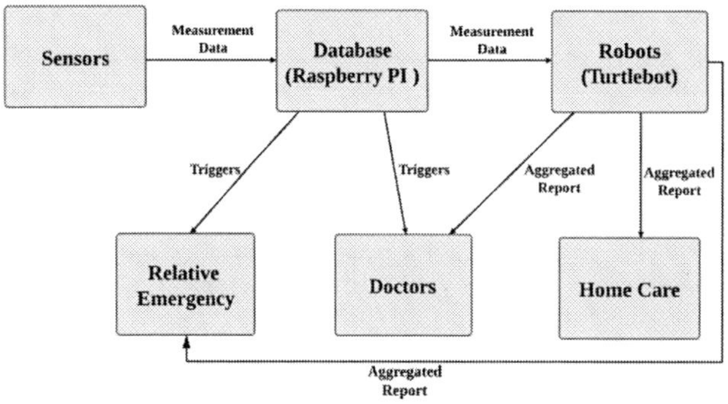

Figure 1: The diagram of the OWLS interactions.

2. REINFORCEMENT LEARNING-BASED MONITORING ALGORITHM

Figure 1 shows the interactions between various components of our system. A person employs multiple wearable sensors to collect data regarding his or her activity levels or other vital conditions (i.e., temperature, heart rate, altitude, magnitude, angle, etc.). This data is then stored in a database, which contains triggers for emergency situations. The robots monitor the person's movements and motion using a technique similar to [2].

The algorithm used by OWLS for the decision making in our system is the reinforcement learning using Q-learning technique. This learning paradigm relies on agents choosing an action and then receiving a scalar reward based on how the state of the environment changes. In our system, the state of the environment correlates to the condition of the monitored user. Each individual robot collects data from its own observation of the user and also collects the latest raw sensor data from the database. For the data that is competitive, where the same type of data is collected by both the robot and the sensor, the robot uses Kalman Filter [1] to aggregate it. The complementary data is also processed to extract relevant information to be added to the report. The robots then use simple decision rules to take all of the aggregated data and obtain a current observation value.

During reinforcement learning, one of four policies is chosen to maximize the potential reward. These policies are designed to apply a simple change to the action to produce the anticipated next state. The expected reward is calculated for each policy, and the policy yielding the most favorable reward is chosen along with the corresponding action. By using the reward-based learning process each agent incorporates feedback from its own historical experience through the local observation and also from the other agents' by considering the global observation value when calculating the reward. By maintaining historical data on the reward given for each action performed, we can design our robotic agents to seek the most optimal reward possible based on both short-term and long-term goals. This type of agent learning was chosen due to the lack of existing monitored data for the scenarios tested in the scope of user health monitoring. Without such reference data, we needed a way to determine the validity of each robot's decision; and reinforcement learning provided a reliable solution to the problem.

3. EXPERIMENTAL RESULTS

We conducted experiments using two Turtlebot II robots, and several wearable sensors using Flora - wearable electronic platform, including GPS, accelerometer, compass, gyroscope, temperature sensors, among others. Turtlebot II robots use a 3D Kinect sensor to monitor and record the movements of the person, including the distance that the person travels. The robots and sensors are tasked with monitoring a person's behavior over a period of time. This simple experiment allows us to test our model in a controlled environment.

The information generated by the robots is related to a user's movement and motion data (i.e. the distance, altitude, magnitude and the acceleration of user movement in a 3D space). Each robot determines its observational value based on the aggregated sensor data and its own data, which is sent to the central computer, where OWLS aggregates (averages) the robots' observational values and selects an action based on this analysis. The report is then sent remotely to three different machines: the user's own machine, the doctor's machine and that of the caregiver (or relatives). In our experiments, we restricted the possible aggregated observational values to the set $\{0, 1, 2, 3\}$, corresponding to the following actions, {"just send the report for a normal situation", "notify the caregiver", "notify the doctor, emergency"}. We ran the experiments for 1 hour, with data readings each second, where one of the co-authors wore the sensor system and imitated various situations, including sitting, standing, walking, quick fall, slow fall, running (slow and fast). To vary the temperature, an ice packet and then a heat wrap was applied to the user to imitate the decrease and increase in temperature, correspondingly. Our experimental results have shown that the reinforcement learning algorithm developed with our system allows the robots to accurately detect immediate signs for the correct determination of the health conditions in monitored users.

We also compared our reinforcement learning techniques with multiple robots and sensors to a decision-making method without a multi-robot system present. In our baseline comparison technique, the action chosen by the system was purely dependent on the data produced by wearable sensors. The same simple decision rules were used as the ones used by OWLS. Table 3 shows the accuracy percentages, which were calculated by comparing the calculated observation values and chosen actions by the two techniques against the manually recorded "events" (e.g. the time step at which the drastic fall or temperature rise occurred). Overall, our comparison experiments supported that OWLS, which utilizes both a multi-robot and a multi-sensor system, performed better than a basic multi-sensor system.

State	Baseline	OWLS
Normal	90%	99%
Slightly abnormal (notify caregiver)	87%	93%
Abnormal (notify doctor)	92%	96%
Very abnormal (emergency)	95%	100%

Table 1: Accuracy of the OWLS vs. the baseline technique that utilizes only sensor data.

We also noted that the final observation values, obtained using 3 and 4 robots, were similar to the previous results and therefore, these results have not been included in this paper. In summary, we conclude that our multi-robot, multi-sensor system with learning support is able to efficiently learn the conditions of its users to be able to make the necessary notifications regarding their well-being.

4. CONCLUSION

In this paper we have described a single personal therapy solution (SPTS) that uses reinforcement learning based multi-robot and multi-sensor well-being monitoring system, called OWLS. Our experimental results have shown that the reinforcement learning algorithm developed with our system allows the robots to accurately detect immediate signs for the correct determination of the health conditions in monitored users. OWLS, using multiple robots and wearable sensors was able to outperform the system that only relies on the wearable sensor data. In the future we plan to conduct more experiments with our system for more complex and continuous health monitoring tasks. In particular, we plan to use more medically relevant sensors, such as a blood pressure and sugar level detecting sensors. We also plan to do statistical comparison of our results with other commonly used learning methods.

REFERENCES

[1] S. Chen. Kalman filter for robot vision: a survey. *Industrial Electronics, IEEE Transactions on*, 59(11):4409–4420, 2012.

[2] E. Machida, M. Cao, T. Murao, and H. Hashi. Human motion tracking of mobile robot with kinect 3d sensor. In *SICE Annual Conference*, pages 2207–2211, 2012.

[3] T. Nef and R. Riener. Armin-design of a novel arm rehabilitation robot. In *Rehabilitation Robotics. ICORR.*, pages 57–60. IEEE, 2005.

[4] A. Pantelopoulos and N. G. Bourbakis. A survey on wearable sensor-based systems for health monitoring and prognosis. *IEEE Transactions on Systems, Man, and Cybernetics, Part C: Applications and Reviews,*, 40(1):1–12, 2010.

Supporting Group Plans in the BDI Architecture using Coordination Middleware*

(Extended Abstract)

Stephen Cranefield
Department of Information Science,
University of Otago, Dunedin, New Zealand
stephen.cranefield@otago.ac.nz

ABSTRACT

This paper investigates the use of group plans and goals as programming abstractions that encapsulate the communication needed to coordinate collaborative behaviour. It presents an extension of the BDI agent architecture to include explicit constructs for goals and plans that involve coordinated action by groups of agents. Formal operational semantics for group goals are outlined, and an implementation of group plans and goals for the Jason agent platform, based on integration with the ZooKeeper coordination middleware, is described.

Keywords

BDI agents; Group plans and goals; Coordination middleware

1. INTRODUCTION

Belief-Desire-Intention (BDI) agent programming is a powerful and popular model for developing software that is goal-oriented, adaptive to its circumstances, and equipped with pre-existing domain knowledge in the form of plans. However, when multiple agents need to coordinate their actions over sustained interactions, especially in interdependent activities such as working together towards a common team goal, manual implementation of the required communication actions can be complex and error prone. It can also compromise scalability and other desirable properties of distributed systems, such as robustness against network partitions.

Our aim in this work is to raise the level of abstraction when programming groups of BDI agents so that explicit coordination is no longer necessary, but rather is handled implicitly by robust industry-grade coordination middleware. This paper investigates the potential of group goals and plans to provide such a programming abstraction.

2. GROUP GOALS

We define a group goal as one requiring coordinated action by a group of agents. In this paper, we focus on conjunctive group goals, in which each agent has a specific *local* subgoal to achieve, and the group goal is satisfied only when *all* the subgoals are individually satisfied. We consider that the group goal becomes active when one or more agents begin working towards it, and can then eventually fail or succeed. However, to avoid agents waiting indefinitely for other agents to complete their subgoals, we allow a group goal to fail due to a "join timeout" or a "completion timeout". A join timeout occurs when some agents do not begin working on their subgoals within a certain interval after the earliest start of any of the other agents' subgoals. A completion timeout occurs when the result of some subgoals are still unknown within a certain interval since the last agent began work on its subgoal.

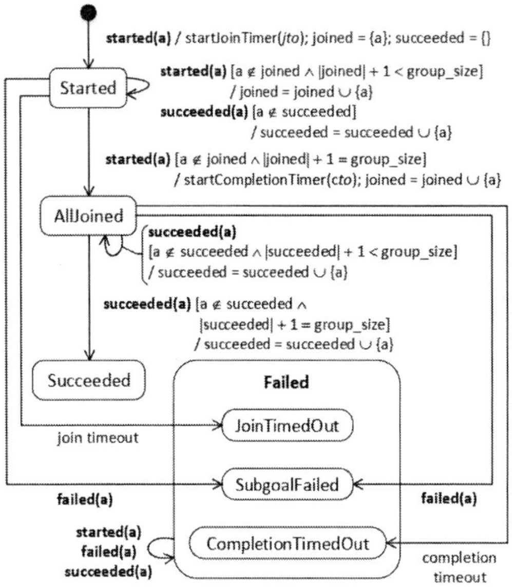

Figure 1: State diagram for a group goal

Figure 1 shows the lifecycle of a group goal as a UML state diagram. The variables *joined* and *succeeded* record the agents that have begun work and completed their subgoals.

3. GROUP PLANS

We conceptualise a group plan as one that defines a collective view of coordinated action amongst a group of agents, and rely on group goals to provide this coordination. We thus define a group plan as one in which all goals are group goals. A group plan is supported by a set of individual plans for each agent to achieve its local subgoals. These individual plans could be known by all agents, or they could be kept private, as the application requires.

In this paper we restrict our attention to group plans in which each group goal involves *all* agents in the group. However, any

*Full paper: http://hdl.handle.net/10523/6232

Appears in: *Proceedings of the 15th International Conference on Autonomous Agents and Multiagent Systems (AAMAS 2016), J. Thangarajah, K. Tuyls, C. Jonker, S. Marsella (eds.), May 9–13, 2016, Singapore.*

```
{ include("group_plans.asl") }
// Group plan
+!pincer(a1,a2,l1,l2,l3) <-
   !gg(surround, [loc(l1)[agent(a1)],
                  loc(l2)[agent(a2)]]);
   !gg(converge, [loc(l3)[agent(a1)],
                  loc(l3)[agent(a2)]]).

// Example local plan for a group goal
+!loc(L)[agent(a1), gg(surround)] <-
  move_to(L);
  ?loc(L).
```

Figure 2: An example group plan

agent's subgoal may be a trivial "do-nothing" goal (one having a plan that immediately succeeds), and BDI agents may have multiple goals (intentions) active at the same time. Thus it is possible for an agent to work towards its own local goals while waiting for the other agents to complete their work towards a group goal. We can also model sequential turn-taking behaviour by a sequence of group goals in which all agents except one have a do-nothing goal.

Figure 2 shows a group plan for two agents, a_1 and a_2, to perform a pincer attack on an enemy at location l_3, with a_1 moving to one side of the enemy (location l_1), and a_2 moving to the other side (location l_2), before they both converge on location l_3. This is expressed in the Jason platform's version of AgentSpeak [1]. The `include` directive loads a set of plans for maintaining the state of group goals via an integration between Jason and the Apache ZooKeeper coordination middleware. The group plan above comprises a sequence of two group goals, but group plans may include any control structures provided by the BDI programming language. However, we do not currently address the use of context conditions.

4. SEMANTICS OF GROUP GOALS

We have defined a set of inference rules stating how the operation of each agent's underlying BDI platform is extended to take account of the shared state of group goals. We model the combined goal states of the agents as a set comprising *goal trees* labelled with agent names. Each goal tree records a top-level goal for an agent as the root of a tree of subgoals, generated by a stack of currently executing plan bodies. There can be multiple goal trees for each agent. The inference rules then define the valid transitions on a triple comprising this set of labelled goal trees, a set of group goal state machines, and a time stamp. A *local computation* rule allows local agent goal-tree transitions to proceed as usual, if they do not involve an immediate local subgoal of a group goal that the agent has not yet joined. A *join goal* rule allows an agent to begin a subgoal of a non-failed group goal, and updates the state machine for that group goal as defined in Figure 1. *Local failure* and *local success* rules ensure that failure or success of an agent's local subgoal causes the state machine for the parent group goal to be updated. Finally, *group failure* and *group success* rules react to a group goal's state machine reaching the failure or success state by marking each agent's local subgoal for that group goal as having failed or succeeded. This allows the agents' local computation to handle this failure or success.

Using LTL model checking in Maude [2], we verified for the two-agent case the desired relationships between individual subgoal and group goal failures and successes.

5. IMPLEMENTATION

We have implemented our semantics in a distributed setting by using Apache ZooKeeper [4] to provide Jason agents, potentially running on different hosts, with an eventually consistent view of the state of their group goals. ZooKeeper is a high performance coordination middleware system that maintains data objects replicated across a set of servers. The data objects, known as *znodes* are organised into a hierachical namespace like a file system, and are designed to support the storage of coordination metadata in distributed applications. In our implementation, distributed Jason BDI agents run within containers provided by the camel-agent middleware [3]. This provides the ability for agent action invocations to be delivered as messages to the Apache Camel message routing and mediation engine [5], and for percepts to be delivered back to the agents. Message processing "routes" written in Camel's domain-specific language interpret certain agent actions as ZooKeeper client requests to update the state of group goals, while other routes deliver updates about their state to agents in the form of percepts. The Camel routes collectively manage the representation of the state machines for group goals as a collection of ZooKeeper znodes. In particular, one master route, run repeatedly at a set frequency, checks znodes representing the lists of agents who have begun and completed their subgoals of a group goal, and updates the znode encoding of the state machine's state.

The semantics defined by our inference rules (outlined in Section 4), are implemented by a standard set of plans that can be included in the code defining a group plan (see line 1 in Figure 2). These plans define (i) how to achieve the `gg` goal for beginning a new group goal, (ii) how to handle percepts generated by Camel routes (via camel-agent) to indicate the success or failure of a group goal, and (iii) how to handle the Jason event signalling the failure of an agent's local subgoal for a group goal—this plan performs an action to update ZooKeeper (via Camel) about this failure.

6. CONCLUSION

This paper has presented a model for coordinating the activities of a group of BDI agents by providing them with shared group plans containing group goals. These concepts provide an abstraction layer that removes the need for the programmer to provide explicit communication actions to share information about the agents' failures and successes in pursuit of a larger goal. We defined the lifecycle of group goals as a state machine and described formal operational semantics for the interaction between the individual agents' BDI execution engines and a set of shared state machines for the group goals. We also described an implementation of this model using Jason and the industrial-strength coordination middleware, Apache ZooKeeper.

REFERENCES

[1] R. H. Bordini, J. F. Hübner, and M. Wooldridge. *Programming Multi-Agent Systems in AgentSpeak using Jason*. Wiley, 2007.

[2] M. Clavel, F. Durán, S. Eker, P. Lincoln, N. Martí-Oliet, J. Meseguer, and C. Talcott. The Maude 2.0 system. In *Rewriting Techniques and Applications*, volume 2706 of *Lecture Notes in Computer Science*, pages 76–87. Springer, 2003.

[3] S. Cranefield and S. Ranathunga. Embedding agents in business processes using enterprise integration patterns. In *Engineering Multi-Agent Systems*, volume 8245 of *Lecture Notes in Computer Science*, pages 97–116. Springer, 2013.

[4] P. Hunt, M. Konar, F. P. Junqueira, and B. Reed. ZooKeeper: Wait-free coordination for Internet-scale systems. In *Proceedings of the USENIX Annual Technical Conference*. USENIX Association, 2010.

[5] C. Ibsen and J. Anstey. *Camel in Action*. Manning, 2010.

Reputation-based Provider Incentivisation for Provenance Provision

(Extended Abstract)

Lina Barakat
King's College London
UK, WC2R 2LS
lina.barakat@kcl.ac.uk

Samhar Mahmoud
King's College London
UK, WC2R 2LS
samhar.mahmoud@kcl.ac.uk

Phillip Taylor
University of Warwick
UK, CV4 7AL
phillip.taylor@warwick.ac.uk

Nathan Griffiths
University of Warwick
UK, CV4 7AL
nathan.griffiths@warwick.ac.uk

Simon Miles
King's College London
UK, WC2R 2LS
simon.miles@kcl.ac.uk

ABSTRACT

Knowledge of circumstances under which past service provisions have occurred enables clients to make more informed selection decisions regarding their future interaction partners. Service providers, however, may often be reluctant to release such circumstances due to the cost and effort required, or to protect their interests. In response, we introduce a reputation-based incentivisation framework, which motivates providers towards the desired behaviour of reporting circumstances via influencing two reputation-related factors: the *weights* of past provider interactions, which directly impact the provider's reputation estimate, and the overall *confidence* in such estimates.

Keywords

Reputation; Circumstances; Incentivisation; Provenance

1. INTRODUCTION

A service-oriented marketplace can be seen as a dynamic marketplace where individuals interact to achieve their goals. Besides the outcomes of past interactions, knowledge of the *circumstances* under which interactions took place gives individuals useful (more sufficient) information to support their decision making in selecting a future interaction partner. The PROV standard [3] (published by W3C as a standard for interoperable provenance) provides a suitable solution for exposing information on various circumstances underlying a service provision. A PROV document describes in a queryable form the causes and effects within a particular past process of a system as a directed graph with annotations. The contents of a provenance graph can be collated from data recorded by a set of independent agents, and clients have a standard means to query the data.

Providers are the obvious source of such provenance data, as it is a record of how they provided a service, but they may not be willing to release such records for several reasons. This may be due to the additional burden incurred on the provider side (the process of provenance recording and documentation could be tedious and expensive), or for competitive grounds (e.g. it may be against provider interests to release records showing that they performed poorly). Targeting providers with relevant *incentives* is a promising way to encourage them to release provenance data. In the context of service-oriented marketplaces, *reputation* is a particularly attractive (extrinsic) incentive for service providers since it has a direct effect on their chances of being selected by clients. Based on this, a reputation-based incentivisation framework is investigated in this paper.

Appears in: *Proceedings of the 15th International Conference on Autonomous Agents and Multiagent Systems (AAMAS 2016), J. Thangarajah, K. Tuyls, C. Jonker, S. Marsella (eds.), May 9–13, 2016, Singapore.*

2. INCENTIVISATION FRAMEWORK

To influence a provider towards provision of (true) circumstances reports, the incentivisation mechanism in place (reputation-based in our case) should allow the provider to gain some utility in response. Existing reputation mechanisms provide a reputation score to compare providers, usually estimated from ratings given by past customers. An intuitive approach would thus be to allow the circumstances given by the provider to influence such a score via influencing the *weight* of these ratings. In fact, when circumstances are available, such an approach seems necessary to ensure accurate assessments of provider reputation for clients. In many cases, this also brings benefits to reputation from the provider perspective. Consider a provider who fails to deliver some goods on time on a day when an unexpected transport strike occurs. Such a failure can potentially harm the provider's reputation, but is out of the provider's control. Thus, it is advantageous for the provider to justify this failure via revealing the mitigating circumstances that occurred, to allow for its effect on reputation to be discounted.

Yet, there may be other cases where exposure of circumstances would not benefit a provider's reputation (e.g. the provider consistently delivers a good performance, so reporting circumstances or reporting their absence would only incur an additional cost without additional benefit). Moreover, such an approach (i.e. weighting past ratings by released circumstances) may also motivate providers towards the undesired behaviour of supplying untrue information (e.g. a provider may claim untrue mitigating circumstances in order to justify their occasional poor performance and thus avoid reputation losses).

To discourage these deception opportunities (i.e. omitted or misleading information by providers), a provider's circumstances provision behaviour should have an effect on another reputation related factor. We argue that a plausible factor is the *confidence* in the *weights* assigned to ratings, influencing in turn the *overall confidence* in the reputation score. The intuition behind this is as follows. When the circumstances underlying a rating are withheld, the rating's relevence for the current situation is uncertain, which should be reflected via a low confidence in the weight assigned for the rating. Similarly, if the circumstances report is provided, but is *suspicious* (suspicious reports can be detected by confirming them against those provided by others in the population), the confidence in the respectively calculated weight for the rating should also be reduced. The overall confidence in the reputation score for a provider could have an important impact on the decision making of the client, and a provider with a low confidence could potentially be placed lower in the ranking list despite having a good reputation score.

3. EVALUATION

We conducted an agent-based simulation, which proceeds in rounds, each involving three phases: client reconsideration; service provision; and provider reconsideration. In the *client reconsideration* phase, each client selects an interaction partner for the current round from the n most reputable service providers (with an exploration probability). To determine a provider reputation, the client utilises FIRE [2] as the base reputation mechanism, augmented with the proposed extension, with the overall ranking score of a provider being a combination of the provider's respective reputation and confidence scores. In the *service provision* phase, each client receives a service from the selected provider, and rates this service according to their satisfaction. Here, we consider *freak events* as potential circumstances affecting provision of services, as a result of which providers deliver their services at lower quality levels. In the *provider reconsideration*, each provider observes the profit achieved (in terms of the number of client requests received) in the current round following its previous circumstances provision decision, compares this profit against the cost incurred (0 if no circumstances report is provided, and a negative cost otherwise), and adjusts its action policies accordingly through a form of q-learning [1]. Here, we assume two possible states, *occurrence of a freak event*, denoted by s^+, and no occurrence of freak events, denoted by s^-, with three possible provider actions at each state: reporting correct information (ci), reporting false information (fi), and withholding information (wi). The goal is to push the provider's behaviour towards action ci, which corresponds to reporting a freak event occurrence (for state s^+), and reporting no freak event occurrence (for state s^-).

Figures 1(a) and 1(b) illustrate the results obtained (averaged over 100 simulation runs, each involving 50 service providers and 100 clients, with a duration of 2000 rounds). The proposed incentivisation strategy achieves the desired provider behaviour, increasing the probability of action ci to a high level in both states s^+ and s^-. In particular, in state s^- (Figure 1(a)), withholding information is not a favourable action since it lowers the confidence in the provider's reputation estimate, and consequently decreases the provider's overall ranking. Action fi is not beneficial in this state,

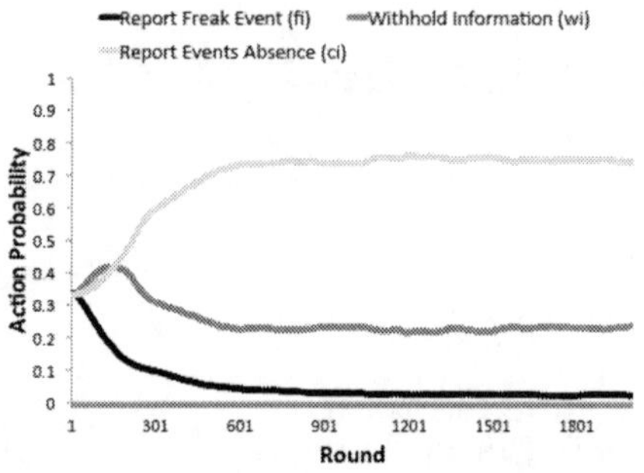

(a) Negative State (No Freak Event)

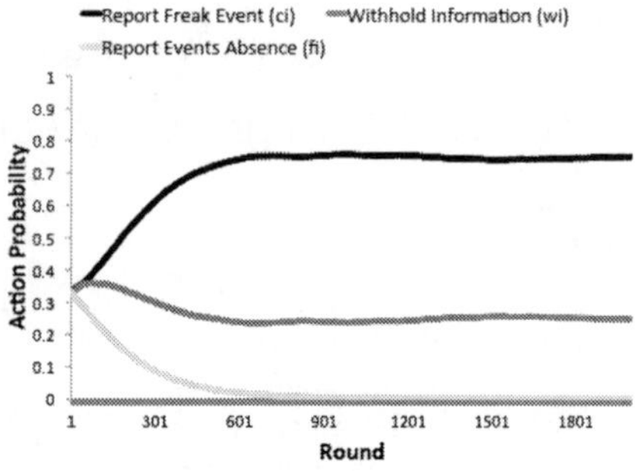

(b) Positive State (Freak Event)

Figure 1: Incentivisation with Circumstance-aware Weighting and Circumstance-aware Confidence

leading to favouring action ci (i.e. reporting freak events absence), where the boost in confidence achieved via reporting correct information (verified by comparing this information with other providers) compensates for the negative utility of information provision. The same applies for state s^+ (Figure 1(b)). Here, the decrease in confidence from chosing actions wi or fi further lowers the ranking (and thus the selection chances) of the provider affected by the freak event, while choosing action ci (i.e. reporting the freak event) provides a double benefit (discounting the impact of affected interactions on reputation, and increasing confidence).

Acknowledgments

This work was part funded by the UK Engineering and Physical Sciences Research Council as part of the Justified Assessments of Service Provider Reputation project, ref. EP/M012654/1 and EP/M012662/1.

REFERENCES

[1] M. Bowling and M. Veloso. Rational and convergent learning in stochastic games. In *Proceedings of the 17th International Joint Conference on Artificial Intelligence*, pages 1021–1026, 2001.

[2] T. D. Huynh, N. R. Jennings, and N. R. Shadbolt. An integrated trust and reputation model for open multi-agent systems. *J. of Autonomous Agents and Multi-Agent Systems*, 13(2):119–154, 2006.

[3] W3C. PROV model primer. http://www.w3.org/TR/prov-primer/, 2013.

The Convergence of Reciprocation
(Extended Abstract)

Gleb Polevoy
Delft University of Technology
Delft, The Netherlands
g.polevoy@tudelft.nl

Mathijs de Weerdt
Delft University of Technology
Delft, The Netherlands
M.M.deWeerdt@tudelft.nl

Catholijn Jonker
Delft University of Technology
Delft, The Netherlands
c.m.jonker@tudelft.nl

ABSTRACT

People often interact repeatedly: with relatives, through file sharing, in politics, etc. Many such interactions are reciprocal: reacting to the actions of the other. In order to facilitate decisions regarding reciprocal interactions, we analyze the development of reciprocation over time. To this end, we propose a model for such interactions that is simple enough to enable formal analysis, but is sufficient to predict how such interactions will evolve. Inspired by existing models of international interactions and arguments between spouses, we suggest a model with two reciprocating attitudes where an agent's action is a weighted combination of the others' last actions (reacting) and either i) her innate kindness, or ii) her own last action (inertia). We analyze a network of repeatedly interacting agents, each having one of these attitudes, and prove that their actions converge to specific limits. Convergence means that the interaction stabilizes, and the limits indicate the behavior after the stabilization. For two agents, we describe the interaction process and find the limit values. For a general connected network, we find these limit values if all the agents employ the second attitude, and show that the agents' actions then all become equal. In the other cases, we study the limit values using simulations. We discuss how these results predict the development of the interaction and constitute the first step towards helping agents decide on their behavior.

Keywords

reciprocal interaction; repeated reciprocation; behavior; convergence; Perron-Frobenius; agent's influence

1. INTRODUCTION

Interaction is central in life, e.g., at school, on the road, and in politics. We aim to facilitate decision support to people and applications that interact, such as a self-driving car. To this end, we need to predict interaction. Instead of being economically rational, people tend to adopt other ways of behavior [6]. Furthermore, people tend to reciprocate, i.e., react on the past actions of others [2]. Some extant work studies how reciprocation has emerged. For example, Axelrod [1] shows that (discrete) reciprocity is rational to egoists, while [3] reasons that people sometimes exhibit irrational reciprocity, and gave explanations of it. Reciprocity seems to be intrinsic [7]. On another avenue, given the reciprocal tendencies, several works analyze why they make interactions develop in certain ways. For instance, [2, 5] define a game where utility depends on reciprocal behavior. Since no analysis considers non-discrete lengthy interactions, caused by reciprocation, we ask how reciprocal interactions evolve with time. This will facilitate decision making by predicting what approach will benefit the agents more.

Consider an interaction network where vertices stand for agents N, and two agents interact if and only if they are neighbors. We model an action by a single number, which represents the value of that action to the recipient. This number is defined to be a convex combination between the inner self and outer influence. Every agent i has her kindness k_i, representing the default value of her action, and a direct and a social reciprocation coefficient, r_i and r'_i, respectively, representing her inclination to react to a given agent and to all the agents she interacts with, respectively. Denote the action of agent i on j at time t by $x_{i,j}(t)$, and the set of the neighboring agents of i by $\mathrm{N}(i)$. We assume that all the agents act on times $T = \{0, 1, \ldots\}$. We define two reciprocation attitudes. In the *fixed* attitude, the action of agent i on j at time t is defined by the kindness, the reaction to the other's action, and the reaction to the average of the actions of the neighbors:

$$(1 - r_i - r'_i) \cdot k_i + r_i x_{j,i}(t-1) + r'_i \frac{\sum_{j \in \mathrm{N}(i)} x_{j,i}(t-1)}{|\mathrm{N}(i)|},$$

In the *floating* attitude, the first term is own action, namely:

$$(1 - r_i - r'_i) \cdot x_{i,j}(t-1) + r_i x_{j,i}(t-1) + r'_i \frac{\sum_{j \in \mathrm{N}(i)} x_{j,i}(t-1)}{|\mathrm{N}(i)|}.$$

Defining action or state by a linear combination of the other side's actions and own actions and qualities is also used to analyze arms race [8] and spouses' interaction [4] (piecewise linear in this case). This model defines an infinite sequence of actions for every agent, and predicting this process would allow setting up efficient reciprocation.

2. PAIRWISE INTERACTION

When only a pair of agents interact, assume w.l.o.g. that $r'_1 = r'_2 = 0$. We prove convergence as time approaches infinity. Convergence means that the interaction stabilizes with time. When both agents are *fixed*, they converge in an oscillating manner (see Figure 1), and $\lim_{t \to \infty} x_{i,j}(t) =$

Appears in: *Proceedings of the 15th International Conference on Autonomous Agents and Multiagent Systems (AAMAS 2016), J. Thangarajah, K. Tuyls, C. Jonker, S. Marsella (eds.), May 9–13, 2016, Singapore.*

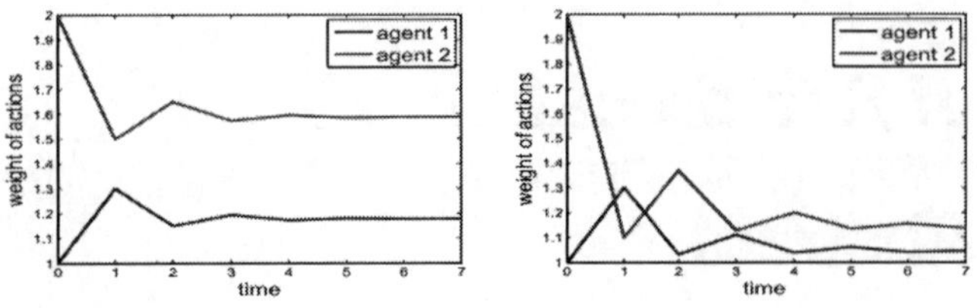

Figure 1: Simulation of actions for $r_1+r_2 < 1$, $r_2 = 0.5$ on the left, and $r_1+r_2 > 1$, $r_2 = 0.9$ on the right. It is a *fixed* - *fixed* reciprocation, with $k_1 = 1, k_2 = 2, r_1 = 0.3$.

$\frac{(1-r_i)k_i+r_i(1-r_j)k_j}{1-r_ir_j}$. When at least one agents is *floating*, they converge to a common limit. If both are *floating*, the limit is $\frac{r_2}{r_1+r_2}k_1 + \frac{r_1}{r_1+r_2}k_2$; if i is *fixed* and j is *floating*, the limit is k_i, and if $r_1 + r_2 \leq 1$, the convergence is monotonic from some moment on. The limits imply that if you consider your kindness while reciprocating (*fixed*), then, asymptotically, your actions values get closer to your kindness than if you consider it only at the outset. Thus, persistence makes the interaction go your way. Another interesting result is that always $k_i \leq k_j \Rightarrow \lim_{t\to\infty} x_{i,j}(t) \leq \lim_{t\to\infty} x_{j,i}(t)$.

3. MULTI-AGENT INTERACTION

For multiple agents, we employ the Perron-Frobenius theorem. When all r'_i are positive, we prove a geometrically fast convergence. We also prove that when at least one agent is *fixed*, every $\lim_{t\to\infty} x_{i,j}(t)$ is a positive combination of the kindnesses of the *fixed* agents. If all the *fixed* agents have the same kindness k, this is also the (common) limit. If all the agents are *floating*, we show that the actions of all the agents converge to a common limit, which is

$$\frac{\sum_{i\in N}\left(\frac{|N(i)|}{r_i+r'_i}\cdot k_i\right)}{\sum_{i\in N}\left(\frac{|N(i)|}{r_i+r'_i}\right)}. \qquad (1)$$

The convergence partially explains personal styles of behavior. The commonality alludes to the formation of organizational (sub)cultures. The limit being a combination of the kindness values of certain agents means that the kindness of an agent has either no influence, or it constitutes a linear term. Observe that when all the agents are *floating*, the influence of an agent on the common limit is proportional to the number of agents on whom she may act, and inversely proportional to her tendency to reciprocate, which may be called stability. This explains that persistence makes an agent more influential on the actions in the interaction.

An interesting example is a regular interaction network, where $|N(i)|$ is the same for all i. This holds, for instance, for cliques, modeling small groups of people or countries, and for cycles, modeling circular computer networks. In this case, Eq. (1) becomes $\frac{\sum_{i\in N}\left(\frac{k_i}{r_i+r'_i}\right)}{\sum_{i\in N}\left(\frac{1}{r_i+r'_i}\right)}$. Another interesting example is a star network, modeling a supervisor of separate entities. Assume w.l.o.g. that agent 1 is the center, and the common limit becomes $\frac{\frac{|N|-1}{r_1+r'_1}\cdot k_1+\sum_{i\in N\setminus\{1\}}\left(\frac{k_i}{r_i+r'_i}\right)}{\frac{|N|-1}{r_1+r'_1}+\sum_{i\in N\setminus\{1\}}\left(\frac{1}{r_i+r'_i}\right)}$.

We show that to maximize the limit value of the actions by setting her r_i (or r'_i), an agent needs an extreme value of her r_i (or r'_i). When all the agents are *floating*, Eq. (1) implies that the dependency of the limits on the extent of reciprocativeness r_i (or on r'_i) is monotonic, so maximizing the limits requires being either completely reciprocal or not at all. To study this when we do not know the limit, we simulate the interaction, obtaining plots like those in Figure 2. In all the considered cases, this dependency is monotonic. For the dependency on r'_i, the obtained graphs are also monotonic.

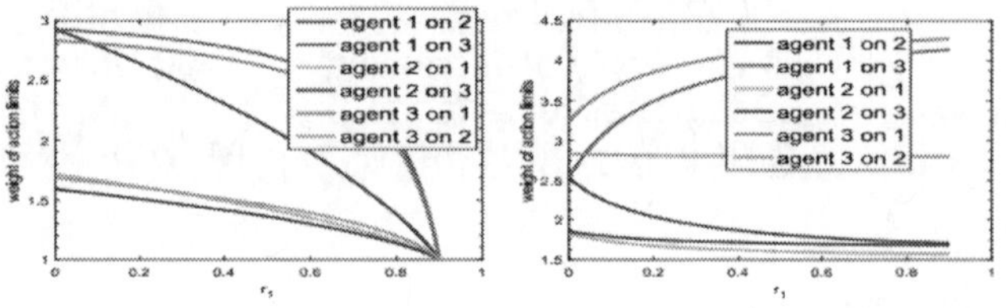

Figure 2: The simulated limits of actions as functions of r_1, for $r_2 = 0.1, r_3 = 0.6, r'_1 = 0.1, r'_2 = 0.4, r'_3 = 0.1$, $k_1 = 3, k_2 = 1, k_3 = 5$. On the left, agent 1 and 2 are the only *fixed* agents, while on the right, 1 is the only *floating* agent.

To advise more constructively about what agents' parameters and attitude are useful, defining utilities and considering choosing one's parameters, so as to maximize own utility is very promising for future work. To summarize, we analyze the interaction process, in order to predict reciprocal interaction and thereby, to facilitate decisions regarding how to reciprocate.

The full version, named "Towards Decision Support in Reciprocation", includes the non-synchronous case and the proofs and appears at `http://arxiv.org/abs/1601.07965`.

Acknowledgments

This work has been supported by the project SHINE, the flagship project of DIRECT (Delft Institute for Research on ICT at Delft University of Technology).

REFERENCES

[1] R. Axelrod. The emergence of cooperation among egoists. *American Political Science Review*, 75:306–318, 1981.

[2] A. Falk and U. Fischbacher. A theory of reciprocity. *Games and Economic Behavior*, 54(2):293 – 315, 2006.

[3] H. Gintis. *Game Theory Evolving: A Problem-centered Introduction to Modeling Strategic Behavior*. Economics / Princeton University Press. Princeton University Press, 2000.

[4] J. Gottman, C. Swanson, and J. Murray. The mathematics of marital conflict: Dynamic mathematical nonlinear modeling of newlywed marital interaction. *Journal of Family Psychology*, 13:3–19, 1999.

[5] M. Rabin. Incorporating fairness into game theory and economics. *The American Economic Review*, 83(5):pp. 1281–1302, Dec. 1993.

[6] A. Rubinstein. *Modeling Bounded Rationality*, volume 1. The MIT Press, 1997.

[7] R. L. Trivers. The evolution of reciprocal altruism. *The Quarterly Review of Biology*, 46:35–57, 1971.

[8] M. D. Ward. Modeling the USA-USSR arms race. *Transactions of The Society for Modeling and Simulation International*, 43:196–203, 1984.

SOBE: Source Behavior Estimation for Subjective Opinions In Multiagent Systems *

(Extended Abstract)

Murat Şensoy[1], Lance Kaplan[2], Geeth de Mel[3], Taha Dogan Gunes[1]
[1]Department of Computer Science, Ozyegin University, Istanbul, Turkey
[2] US Army Research Lab, Adelphi, MD 20783, USA
[3]IBM T. J. Watson Research Center, NY, Hawthorne, US
murat.sensoy@ozyegin.edu.tr

ABSTRACT

In cooperative or hostile environments, agents communicate their subjective opinions about various phenomenon. However, sources of these opinions may not always be competent and honest but more likely erroneous or even malicious. Furthermore, malicious sources may adopt certain behaviors to mislead the decision maker in a specific way. Fortunately, the reports of such misleading sources are correlated to ground truth. In this work, we propose to learn statistically meaningful opinion transformations that represent various behaviors of information sources. Then, we exploit these transformations while fusing opinions from unreliable sources. We show that our approach can be used to determine set of transformations that may lead to more accurate estimation of the truth.

Keywords

Trust, Agents, Fusion

1. INTRODUCTION

In multi-agent systems, agents perceive information about their environment, evaluates the situation, and make decisions to achieve their goals. In partially observable and uncertain environments, agents' own observations and perceptions may be unavailable, incomplete, or inaccurate to make informed decisions. In such settings, agents may gather information from diverse and unreliable sources. However, there is no guarantee that the information collected from these sources are useful or at least not misleading. In this work, we argue that the misleading information from unreliable sources can also be utilized to estimate the truth if the underlying correlations between the truth and the information are estimated correctly and exploited intelligently. Therefore, in this paper, we propose to learn statistically meaningful transformations that represent various behaviors of information sources. This is achieved by applying multi-dimensional Hough transform [1] on the historical data. Then, we exploit the discovered transformations within a statistical framework to estimate the ground truth. The approach proposed in this paper allows agents to estimate the ground truth even when there is no competent source that is consistently honest while sharing information; that is, our approach can estimate the ground truth accurately using only the misleading information.

2. BEHAVIOR DISCOVERY

In this work, agents and information sources represent their opinions about binary propositions using Beta distribution parameters. A binary proposition has two mutually exclusive outcomes such as $true$ and $false$ or yes and no. The Beta distribution has two parameters $\langle \alpha_1, \alpha_2 \rangle$ that defines the likelihood of the probability for each outcome. Ideally, a source may construct its opinions through Bayesian update of a prior distribution (e.g., uniform distribution) using its observations. For instance, if the source observes r positive evidence for and s negative evidence against the proposition, its genuine opinion for the proposition should be constructed as $\langle r+1, s+1 \rangle$ using uniform distribution as prior. The uniform distribution corresponds to a beta distribution with parameters $\langle 1, 1 \rangle$, which means that each outcome is equally likely.

A decision maker may observe a specific correlation between its own opinions and the opinions shared by the sources adopting a specific behavior. Let us assume a competent source provides $\boldsymbol{\alpha_o} = \langle r_o+1, s_o+1 \rangle$ as its opinion for a binary proposition. Similarly, the decision maker has its own opinion $\boldsymbol{\alpha_d} = \langle r_d+1, s_d+1 \rangle$ for the same proposition. The total number of evidence used in these opinions are $n_o = r_o + s_o$ and $n_d = r_d + s_d$, respectively. We use this opinion pair for training if these opinions are certain enough; that is, n_o and n_d are greater than a predefined threshold. Given the opinion pair, the decision maker can easily compute the expected number of positive evidence ($r_{d|o}$) and negative evidence ($s_{d|o}$) if n_o evidence were observed by itself as follows:

$$r_{d|o} = n_o \times \frac{r_d + 1}{r_d + s_d + 2} \quad \text{and} \quad s_{d|o} = n_o \times \frac{s_d + 1}{r_d + s_d + 2}$$

It is obvious that $\boldsymbol{\alpha_d}$ is consistent with the resulting opinion $\boldsymbol{\alpha_{d|o}} = \langle r_{d|o}+1, s_{d|o}+1 \rangle$. However, its consistency with $\boldsymbol{\alpha_o}$ depends on the source's behavior. In this work, we focus on the cases where the decision maker's opinion is consistent with $\langle r'_o + 1, s'_o + 1 \rangle$,

*Research was sponsored by the U.S. Army Research Laboratory and the U.K. Ministry of Defence and was accomplished under Agreement Numbers W911NF-06-3-0001 and W911NF-13-1-0243. The views and conclusions contained in this document are those of the author(s) and should not be interpreted as representing the official policies, either expressed or implied, of the U.S. Army Research Laboratory, the U.S. Government, the U.K. Ministry of Defence or the U.K. Government. The U.S. and U.K. Governments are authorized to reproduce and distribute reprints for Government purposes notwithstanding any copyright notation hereon. Dr. Şensoy thanks to the U.S. Army Research Laboratory for its support under grant W911NF-14-1-0199 and The Scientific and Technological Research Council of Turkey (TUBITAK) for its support under grant 113E238.

Appears in: *Proceedings of the 15th International Conference on Autonomous Agents and Multiagent Systems (AAMAS 2016),*
J. Thangarajah, K. Tuyls, C. Jonker, S. Marsella (eds.),
May 9–13, 2016, Singapore.

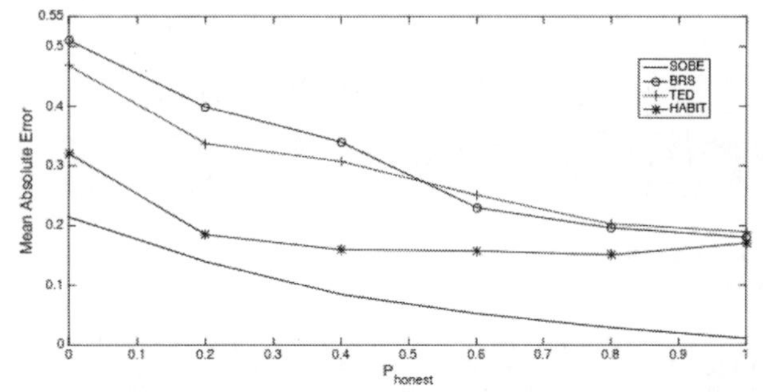

Figure 1: Variation of mean absolute error as P_{honest} varies.

which is calculated using the following linear transformation of the source's original opinion: $[r'_o,\ s'_o] = [r_o,\ s_o,\ 1] \times M$, where M is an 3x2 transformation matrix defined by six parameters: $\left(\begin{smallmatrix} a & b & c \\ d & e & f \end{smallmatrix}\right)^T$. The transformation matrix is determined directly by the behavior adopted by the source. If a source is competent and honestly shares its opinions, M should be $\left(\begin{smallmatrix} 1 & 0 & 0 \\ 0 & 1 & 0 \end{smallmatrix}\right)^T$, hence $r'_o = r_o$ and $s'_o = s_o$. On the other hand, if the source tries to mislead the decision maker by flipping parameters of its opinion, M should be $\left(\begin{smallmatrix} 0 & 1 & 0 \\ 1 & 0 & 0 \end{smallmatrix}\right)^T$, hence $r'_o = s_o$ and $s'_o = r_o$.

While the decision maker does not know about the behaviors of sources, it can discover transformation matrices relevant to these behaviors. For this purpose, the decision maker derives a training set from $\langle \alpha_o^i, \alpha_d^i \rangle$ pairs, each of which includes opinion of a source and opinion of the decision maker for the same proposition i. The derived training set contains $\langle \alpha_o^i, \alpha_{d|o}^i \rangle$ pairs, where $\alpha_{d|o}^i$ is derived as explained before. Using this training set, the decision maker aims to learn meaningful linear transformations that map α_o^i to $\alpha_{d|o}^i$. Each transformation matrix encodes two linear equations:

$$\begin{aligned} r_{d|o} &\simeq a \times r_o + b \times s_o + c \\ s_{d|o} &\simeq d \times r_o + e \times s_o + f \end{aligned} \qquad (1)$$

To discover parameters of arbitrary number of meaningful transformations, we propose to use 3D *Hough transform* in this work [1].

3. FRAMEWORK OVERVIEW

Our framework maintains a history of personal opinions of decision maker as well as opinions from various information sources. Behavior discovery module uses *Hough Transform* [1] to learn various linear transformations that translate misleading opinions from information sources to more informative opinions. Each discovered transformation represents a specific source behavior. Source modeler learns behavior profile of each source, which is represented as a Dirichlet distribution over the probability of adopting discovered behaviors, using Bayesian update. When the decision maker needs opinions related to a proposition, opinion retriever module gathers opinions related to the proposition from various information sources. Using the computed behavior profiles of information sources, information fusion component combines the gathered opinions using moment matching to come up with a single fused opinion. This opinion is used by decision maker as an estimate of the ground truth about the proposition. If the decision maker observes evidence related to the proposition, it can compose its own opinion and stores it in the opinion history as a personal opinion. Later, personal opinions are used, as explained above, to discover new behaviors and update behavior profiles of information sources.

4. EVALUATION

In this section, we compare our approach with existing approaches: BRS [4], HABIT [3], and TED [2]. We conduct a number of simulations to evaluate our approach. Each simulation last 200 time steps, which is enough for convergence of the approaches. At each step, a decision maker is given a binary proposition and it contacts 50 information sources to estimate the ground truth about this proposition. Each source can observe a number of positive and negative evidence about the ground truth. Based on the observed evidence, the sources compose their genuine opinions. Upon decision maker's request, each source adopts one of five behaviors with different probabilities: i) honestly sharing opinion, ii) providing random opinion, iii) flipping the opinion parameters, iv) being optimistic by doubling positive evidence in opinion, v) being pessimistic by doubling negative evidence in opinion. After collecting opinions, the decision maker uses BRS, HABIT, TED, and SOBE — the proposed approach — to fuse these opinions in order to approximate the ground truth. Lastly, the decision maker observes some evidence about the ground truth and composes its own opinion. This opinion is used by these approaches to learn trustworthiness or behaviors of sources. At the end of each step, we compute the *fusion error*, which is defined as the absolute difference of the expectation value of the fused opinion and the ground truth. During simulations, each source changes its identity to whitewash its reputation with probability 0.1 at each step.

In Figure 1, we show how the mean fusion error of the approaches change as we vary the probability that a source predominantly honest (P_{honest}); predominantly honest sources pick the honest behavior among others with probability 0.7. Our results show that SOBE achieves the best performance; its error is slightly above 0.2 when $P_{honest} = 0$, and drops down to 0.02 as P_{honest} increases. HABIT also achieves low fusion error especially when there are some honest sources. Also, as shown on the figure, performances of other approaches improve as P_{honest} increases; their mean absolute errors approach to that of HABIT. SOBE is the only method than can correct for misleading reports and that is why SOBE does much better even when P_{honest} is high.

5. CONCLUSIONS

In this paper, we propose a comprehensive framework for behavior discovery and likelihood estimation for information sources at multi-agent systems. Our approach aims decision makers to exploit information from malicious sources by discovering the underlying correlations between their opinions and the truth perceived by the decision maker. We demonstrate that the proposed approach can successfully estimate the truth when there is no consistently honest source and sources change their identities to blur trust estimations.

REFERENCES

[1] P. Bhattacharya, H. Liu, A. Rosenfeld, and S. Thompson. Hough-transform detection of lines in 3-d space. *Pattern Recognition Letters*, 21(9):843 – 849, 2000.

[2] L. Kaplan, M. Sensoy, and G. de Mel. Trust estimation and fusion of uncertain information by exploiting consistency. In *Proceedings of the 17th International Conference on Information Fusion (FUSION)*, pages 1–8, July 2014.

[3] W. L. Teacy, M. Luck, A. Rogers, and N. R. Jennings. An efficient and versatile approach to trust and reputation using hierarchical bayesian modelling. *Artificial Intelligence Journal*, 193:149–185, 2012.

[4] A. Whitby, A. Jøsang, and J. Indulska. Filtering out unfair ratings in bayesian reputation systems. *The ICFAIN Journal of Management Research*, 4(2):48–64, 2005.

Boolean Satisfiability Approach to Optimal Multi-agent Path Finding under the Sum of Costs Objective

(Extended Abstract)

Pavel Surynek
Charles University Prague
Malostranské náměstí 25
11800, Praha, Czech Republic
pavel.surynek@mff.cuni.cz

Ariel Felner Roni Stern
Ben Gurion University
Beer-Sheva, Israel 84105
felner,sternron@bgu.ac.il

Eli Boyarski
Bar-Ilan University
Ramat-Gan, Israel
eli.boyarski@gmail.com

ABSTRACT

This paper focuses on finding optimal solutions to the *multi-agent path finding* (MAPF) problem over undirected graphs where the task is to find non-colliding paths for multiple agents, each with a different start and goal position. An encoding of MAPF to Boolean satisfiability (SAT) is already known to the *makespan optimal* variant of the problem. In this paper we present the first SAT-solver for minimizing the *sum of costs* enabled by introducing *cardinality constraints* into the SAT encoding. An experimental evaluation on grid graphs indicate promising performance of the new SAT-based method in comparison with the best variants of previous sum-of-costs search solvers.

Keywords

Multi-agent path finding (MAPF), Boolean satisfiability (SAT), sum of costs objective, makespan objective

1. INTRODUCTION AND BACKGROUND

The *multi-agent path finding* (MAPF) problem consists a graph, $G = (V, E)$ and a set of m agents labeled $a_1, a_2, \dots a_m$, where each agent a_i has a start position in V and a goal position in V. Time is discretized into time points. At each time step an agent can either *move* to an adjacent empty location or *wait* in its current location. The task is to find a *valid solution*, i.e., a sequence of move/wait actions for each agent a_i, moving it from the start to the goal position such that agents do not *conflict*, i.e., do not occupy the same location at the same time.

MAPF has many practical applications [3], and can model many real-world problems in games, traffic control, robotics, aviation and more. The scope of this paper is limited to the *centralized setting*, in which we assume that the agents are *fully cooperative* and centrally controlled.

MAPF is usually solved aiming at minimizing a global cumulative cost function. Two such cost functions that are commonly used in the literature are the *sum of costs* [8, 5, 4] and the *makespan* [9, 10]. The *sum of costs* is the summation, over all agents, of the number of time steps required to reach the goal location while the *makespan* is the maximum of the number of times steps over all agents.

Finding makespan optimal and sum-of-cost optimal solutions are both NP-Hard [11, 9] as the state-space grows exponentially with m (# of agents). Therefore, many suboptimal solvers based on rules or relaxed search were developed and are usually used when m is large [6, 1].

The focus of this paper is within the class of *optimal MAPF solvers*. Research on optimal solutions sheds light on the theoretical hardness of the problem and on its attributes and characteristics. Optimal solvers are divided into two main classes.

(1) Reduction-based solvers which reduce MAPF to problems such as CSP [3], SAT, Inductive Logic Programming [10] (ILP) [11] and Answer Set Programming (ASP) [2]. These papers mostly provide and prove a polynomial-time reduction from MAPF to these problems typically for the makespan variant.

(2) Search-based solvers consider all the different ways to place m agents into V vertices, one agent per vertex. Many enhancements of the basic A*-based approach have been developed like *Independence Detection* and *Operator Decomposition* [8]. Another approach is used in the *increasing cost tree search* (ICTS) [5] and *conflict based search* algorithms (CBS, MA-CBS, and ICBS [4]) - they use a two-level framework where the search is divided between a more abstract high-level and low-level which places agents to vertices according to constraints from the high-level.

1.1 Contributions

Most of the search-based algorithms can be easily modified to the makespan variant by modifying the cost function and the way the state-space is represented. By contrast, the reduction-based algorithms are not trivially modified to the sum-of-costs variant and sometimes a completely new reduction is needed.

In this paper we address this challenge and develop the first SAT-based solvers for the sum-of-costs variant which is enabled by integrating so called *cardinality constraint* [7] for bounding the sum-of-costs.

2. OPTIMAL COST MAPF SOLVING

A significant difficulty in applying SAT-based approach to the *sum of costs* metric is the numeric character of this objective function, which contrasts with the modeling abilities of the SAT paradigm where no numeric but only Boolean

Appears in: *Proceedings of the 15th International Conference on Autonomous Agents and Multiagent Systems (AAMAS 2016), J. Thangarajah, K. Tuyls, C. Jonker, S. Marsella (eds.), May 9–13, 2016, Singapore.*

variables are available. Fortunately, the SAT modeling practice offers another technique that can be used for the purpose of calculating and bounding the cost within SAT - *cardinality constraints* [7]. The cardinality constraint bounds the number of propositional variables from the given set that can be set to `TRUE`.

We integrated cardinality constraints into existing SAT-approaches to *makespan optimal* MAPF solving to obtain a *cost optimal* approach. Particularly, we adopted the core concept of a *time expansion graph* (TEG) which is a graphical representation of agents' arrangements at individual time-steps. In TEG, the underlaying graph G is duplicated for all time-steps from 0 up to the given bound. Each *time expansion* in TEG corresponds to adding propositional variables and constraints for a single time-step into the formula so that any of possible arrangement of agents at that time step can be represented. Constraints added as clauses into the formula ensure that the formula is satisfiable if and only if there is a solution of the given MAPF of makespan equal to the number of time expansions.

By the simple strategy, that iteratively increases the number of time expansions [10] (that is, makespans $0, 1, 2, ...$ are tried) until a satisfiable formula is obtained, the optimal makespan can be calculated (the corresponding makespan optimal solution can be extracted from the formula as well).

Furthermore, agent's actions that have non-zero cost are mapped to positive valuations of certain propositional variables. Bounding the number of these variables that are assigned `TRUE` by the cardinality constraint then leads to the desirable bounding of the *sum of costs*. The search for optimal sum-of-costs is done in a similar way as in the case of makespan optimal approach - cost bounds $\xi_0, \xi_0+1, \xi_0+2, ...$ are tried, where ξ_0 is the lower bound of the sum-of-costs calculated as the sum of lengths of shortest path between agent's initial positions and goals. The cost bound increasing strategy needs to be accompanied with increasing the number of time expansions in the TEG (makespan bound) so that any solution of the given cost can be represented in the corresponding TEG.

3. EXPERIMENTAL EVALUATION

We performed experiments on 4-connected grids with randomly placed obstacles, which are a standard MAPF benchmark [6]. Specifically, we experimented on 8×8, 16×16, and 32×32 grids, in which 10% of the vertices are occupied by an obstacle. The initial position of the agents were randomly selected (all vertex had uniform probability).

Two variants of our novel encoding called BASIC-SAT and MDD-SAT with several state-of-the-art search-based techniques, namely the ICTS [5] and ICBS [4] were compared. The MDD-SAT encoding uses the technique of MDD [5] to reduce the size of TEG which consequently reduces the size of the Boolean formulae.

[1] The presented SAT-based approach was implemented in C++. As a SAT solver, we used `Glucose 3.0`. The cardinality constraints were encoded using a standard circuit based encoding called *sequential counter* in [7]. ICTS and ICBS were implemented in C#, based on their original implementation.

For each number of agents, we generated 10 random instances as explained above. Experimental results achieved for the grid 32×32 are presented in Figure 1. We measured the number of problem instances solved by each algorithm under a timeout of 512 seconds and the average runtime over the cases that all the algorithms solved all the 10 instances.

[1]All experiments were performed on a computer with CPU Xeon 2Ghz, 12 Gb of memory, and Linux kernel 3.5.0-48.

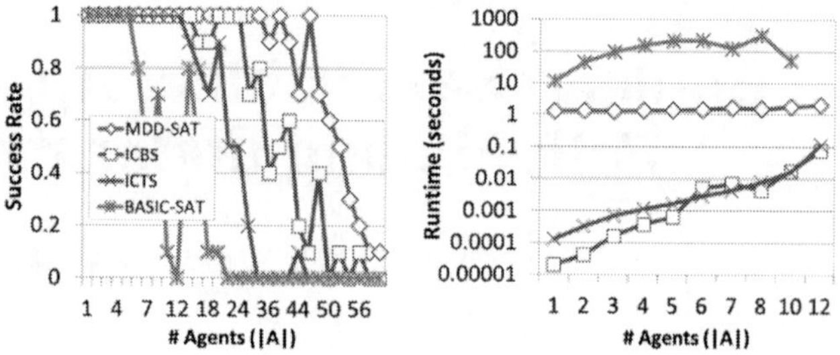

Figure 1: Success rate and runtime on 32×32 grid.

4. DISCUSSION AND CONCLUSIONS

A trend observed in grid experiments is that our MDD-SAT encoding solves more instances and for more agents than all other algorithms. It indicates that SAT-based solvers would be able to scale to denser and harder problems than the search-based algorithms.

The runtime results suggest that while search-based solver may be faster for sparse domains with a small number of agents, the SAT encodings, and in particular MDD-SAT, is expected to be the algorithm of choice for complicated scenarios.

REFERENCES

[1] B. de Wilde, A. W. ter Mors, and C. Witteveen. Push and rotate: cooperative multi-agent path planning. In *AAMAS*, pages 87–94, 2013.

[2] E. Erdem, D. G. Kisa, U. Oztok, and P. Schueller. A general formal framework for pathfinding problems with multiple agents. In *AAAI*, 2013.

[3] M. Ryan. Constraint-based multi-robot path planning. In *ICRA*, pages 922–928, 2010.

[4] G. Sharon, R. Stern, A. Felner, and N. R. Sturtevant. Conflict-based search for optimal multi-agent pathfinding. *Artif. Intell.*, 219:40–66, 2015.

[5] G. Sharon, R. Stern, M. Goldenberg, and A. Felner. The increasing cost tree search for optimal multi-agent pathfinding. *Artif. Intell.*, 195:470–495, 2013.

[6] D. Silver. Cooperative pathfinding. In *AIIDE*, pages 117–122, 2005.

[7] C. Sinz. Towards an optimal CNF encoding of boolean cardinality constraints. In *CP 2005*, pages 827–831, 2005.

[8] T. S. Standley. Finding optimal solutions to cooperative pathfinding problems. In *AAAI*, 2010.

[9] P. Surynek. An optimization variant of multi-robot path planning is intractable. In *AAAI*, 2010.

[10] P. Surynek. Compact representations of cooperative path-finding as SAT based on matchings in bipartite graphs. In *ICTAI*, pages 875–882, 2014.

[11] J. Yu and S. M. LaValle. Structure and intractability of optimal multi-robot path planning on graphs. In *AAAI*, 2013.

What Kind of Stories Should a Virtual Human Swap? (Extended Abstract)

Setareh Nasihati Gilani
USC Institude for Creative Technology
sngilani@ict.usc.edu

Kraig Sheetz
US Military Academy
kraig.sheetz2@usma.edu

Gale Lucas, David Traum
USC Institude for Creative Technology
{lucas,traum}@ict.usc.edu

General Terms

Human Factors,Experimentation

Keywords

Virtual Humans, Story swapping, identity, user studies, rapport

1. INTRODUCTION

Stories are pervasive in conversation between people [5]. They are used to establish identity pass on cultural heritage, and build rapport. Often stories are swapped when one conversational participant will reply to a story with a story.

Stories are also told by virtual humans [1, 6, 2]. In creating or mining stories for a virtual human (VH) to tell, there are a number of considerations that come up about what kinds of stories should be told, and how the stories should be related to the virtual human's identity, such as whether the identity should be human or artificial, and whether the stories should be about the virtual human or about someone else.

We designed a set of virtual human characters who can engage in a simple form of story-swapping. Each of the characters can engage in simple interactions such as greetings and closings and can respond to a set of "ice-breaker" questions, that might be used on a first date or similar "get to know you" encounter. For these questions the character's answer includes a story. We created 4 character response sets, to have all combinations of identity (human or artificial) and perspective (first person stories about the narrator, or third person stories about someone else). We also designed an experiment to try to explore the collective impact of above principles on people who interact with the characters. Participants interact with two of the above characters in a "get to know you" scenario. We investigate the degree of reciprocity where people respond to the character with their own stories, and also compare rapport of participants with the characters as well as the impressions of the character's personality.

2. RELATED WORK

Several virtual agent systems have told, elicited or swapped stories. Many systems tell stories as part of an interaction establishing information about the character. Stories have also been told as part of establishing a long-term relationship and influencing users to adopt behavioral change. Perhaps the first system that allowed a kind of story-swapping with a virtual agent was [6], in which a child character Sam would alternate telling and listening to stories with children.

[2] performed an experiment contrasting first vs third person stories in a health-care application, where an agent told inspiring stories about weight loss, either about the agent (first person) or about someone else (third person). They found that first-person participants reported greater enjoyment, but there was no significant difference in either looking forward to talking or feeling of dishonesty between the groups. However first-person subjects did have a greater probability of talking to the agent. We revisit the question of first vs third person stories, but in a more casual setting, where the agents also use speech input to trigger virtual agent responses, elicit user stories, and including an additional condition of artificial identity.

3. STORY-SWAPPING AGENTS

We created six versions of simple story-swapping agents, using the Virtual Human Toolkit [4]. All were designed to engage with users in a simple "get to know you" dialogue, including reciprocal question answering. Four different sets of character dialogue were created, each being able to answer 20 "ice-breaker" questions, such as "Do you play sports". We created two different characters: Arnold tells first-person stories, while Arron tells third person stories about an acquaintance.

Figure 1: VH and Human Arron and Arnold

For each character, there are two versions of the stories, one in which the character is portrayed as human (Human), and having fully human experiences, and another (VH) in which the character has an artificial identity, and unable to do things like eat, but having experiences in a virtual world. For the human stories, we also have two means of display: virtual human (VH) and video recordings of people (Human). Figure 1 shows the four presentations of VH and Human Aaron and Arnold. We thus have six different

Appears in: *Proceedings of the 15th International Conference on Autonomous Agents and Multiagent Systems (AAMAS 2016), J. Thangarajah, K. Tuyls, C. Jonker, S. Marsella (eds.), May 9–13, 2016, Singapore.*

agents, considering perspective (Arnold-1st or Arron-3rd), identity (Human or VH) and embodiment (Human or VH).

4. EXPERIMENTAL DESIGN

In order to shed light on the best design choices for virtual human stories in story-swapping dialogue, we recruited experimental participants to engage in dialogue with the six agents described in the previous section. We examined independent variables of perspective (first vs 3rd person), identity (human or VH), and presentation (human video or virtual human). We used a partial within-subjects design, where each participant talked to multiple virtual humans. We decided to look at perspective (first vs third) within subjects, and to keep the identity and presentation variables the same for that subject. To control for order effects, half of the participants first talked to Arnold, while the other half first talked to Arron.

4.1 Metrics

The experiment consisted of a 3 (agent: VH-VH vs. VH-Human vs. Human-Human) × 2 (order: 1st then 3rd vs. 3rd then 1st) design. Our 60 participants (38 male, 22 female) were randomly assigned to one of these 6 cells (10 per cell). We measured the following dependent variables for each interaction: a 9-item rapport scale based on [3], a 6-item ancillary rapport scale, two items on subjective sharing of personal information, a set of 30 personality characteristics, length of participant responses and number of participant responses containing stories.

4.2 Protocol

After receiving a general explanation of the system and the procedure of the study, participants gave consent. Prior to starting the interaction with the agent, participants were given the set of questions that were supposed to be the topics of their conversation and 5 minutes to plan their answers. Each conversation consisted of a sequence of sub-dialogue episodes. After the greetings, each episode began with an ice breaking question like 'What was your favorite vacation?" from the participant followed by the agent's answer. The agent responded to the question and told stories according to its assigned perspective and identity. After his answer, the agent prompted the user to reciprocate, using phrases like "What about you?" or "Yourself?".

After going through all the questions, participants were asked to fill out a questionnaire with the subjective items about their experience with the agent. Then, participants went through the same procedure with the second character.

5. RESULTS

On each of the dependent variables, we conducted a 2 (perspective: 1st person vs. 3rd person) × 2 (order: 1st then 3rd vs. 3rd then 1st) × 3 (agent: human-human, VH-VH, vs. VH-human) mixed ANOVA with order and agent as between-subject factors, and perspective as a within-subjects factor. For the Rapport Scale, there was only a marginally significant main effect of perspective, F(1, 53) = 3.21, p = .08, such that users experienced greater rapport with the 1st person agent (M = 3.61, SE = 0.09) than with the 3rd person agent (M = 3.42, SE = 0.09).

For our ancillary rapport measure, we also found a main effect of perspective, $F(1,53) = 4.44, p = .04$, again such that users experienced greater rapport with the 1st person agent ($M = 3.41, SE = 0.12$) than with the 3rd person agent ($M = 3.10, SE = 0.12$). Participants shared significantly more personal information with the 1st person agent ($M = 3.92, SE = 0.12$) than with the 3rd person agent ($M = 3.65, SE = 0.14$) $F(1,53) = 6.88, p = .01$. 1st person agents were also seen as significantly more cheerful and trustworthy and less aloof and (marginally) less rude.

In the VH-human condition, participants overall rated both agents as more "unsympathetic" when they interact first with the 3rd person agent. This was true also for ratings of "unintelligent", but the opposite held for VH-VH and Human-Human conditions. Furthermore, users spent more time speaking with the agents they came across second. We did not witness any other significant differences in the percentage of told stories among the six conditions.

6. CONCLUSIONS

In Summary, like [2], we see a general preference for 1st person over third person stories. On the other hand, we do not see differences in objective measures of user reactions to the stories in dialogue, so it may also be fine to tell third-person stories or have a non-human backstory identity, as long as the stories are interesting and approachable, and the identities are consistent.

There are many ways in which we would like to follow up this study. We can vary the within-subjects variables, look at effects of different genders of virtual humans, and other subject matter. We also want to look at different dialogue protocols, and a mixture of types of stories.

Acknowledgments

The effort described here is supported by the U.S. Army. Any opinion, content or information presented does not necessarily reflect the position or the policy of the United States Government, and no official endorsement should be inferred. We owe special thanks to Anton Leuski, Ed Fast, Arno Hartholt, Abigail Kronenberg, Andrew Jones, Jill Boberg and Rachel Wood for helping us through the course of this project.

REFERENCES

[1] L. Bell and J. Gustafson. Interaction with an animated agent in a spoken dialogue system. In *Proceedings of Eurospeech '99*, pages 1143–1146, 1999.

[2] T. W. Bickmore, D. Schulman, and L. Yin. Engagement vs. deceit: Virtual humans with human autobiographies. In Z. Ruttkay, M. Kipp, A. Nijholt, and H. H. Vilhjálmsson, editors, *IVA*, pages 6–19. 2009.

[3] J. Gratch, N. Wang, J. Gerten, E. Fast, and R. Duffy. Creating Rapport with Virtual Agents. In Proceedings of the 7th *IVA*, 2007.

[4] A. Hartholt, D. Traum, S. C. Marsella, A. Shapiro, G. Stratou, A. Leuski, L.-P. Morency, and J. Gratch. All together now: Introducing the virtual human toolkit. In *IVA* 2013.

[5] N. R. Norrick. *Conversational narrative: Storytelling in everyday talk*, John Benjamins Publishing, 2000.

[6] K. Ryokai, C. Vaucelle, and J. Cassell. Virtual peers as partners in storytelling and literacy learning. *Journal of Computer Assisted Learning*, 19(2):195–208, 2003.

Simultaneous Influencing and Mapping Social Networks (Extended Abstract)

Leandro Soriano Marcolino[1], Aravind Lakshminarayanan[2], Amulya Yadav[1], Milind Tambe[1]
[1]University of Southern California, Los Angeles, CA, 90089, USA
sorianom,amulyaya,tambe@usc.edu
[2]Indian Institute of Technology, Madras, Tamil Nadu, 600036, India
aravindsrinivas@gmail.com

1. INTRODUCTION

Influencing a social network is an important technique, with potential to positively impact society, as we can modify the behavior of a community. For example, we can increase the overall health of a population; Yadav et al. (2015) [4], for instance, spread information about HIV prevention in homeless populations. However, although influence maximization has been extensively studied [2, 1], their main motivation is viral marketing, and hence they assume that the social network graph is fully known, generally taken from some social media network. However, the graphs recorded in social media do not really represent all the people and all the connections of a population. Most critically, when performing interventions in real life, we deal with large degrees of lack of knowledge. Normally the social agencies have to perform several interviews in order to learn the social network graph [3]. These highly unknown networks, however, are exactly the ones we need to influence in order to have a positive impact in the real world, beyond product advertisement.

Additionally, learning a social network graph is very valuable *per se*. Agencies need data about a population, in order to perform future actions to enhance their well-being, and better actuate in their practices [3]. As mentioned, however, the works in influence maximization are currently ignoring this problem. Each person in a social network actually knows other people, including the ones she cannot directly influence. When we select someone for an intervention (to spread influence), we also have an opportunity to obtain knowledge. Therefore, in this work we present for the first time the problem of simultaneously influencing and mapping a social network. We study the performance of the classical influence maximization algorithm in this context, and show that it can be arbitrarily low. Hence, we study a class of algorithms for this problem, performing an experimentation using four real life networks of homeless populations. We show that our algorithm is competitive with previous approaches in terms of influence, and is significantly better in terms of mapping.

2. INFLUENCING AND MAPPING

We consider the problem of maximizing the influence in a social network. However, we start by knowing only a subgraph. Each time we pick a node to influence, it may teach us about subgraphs. Our objective is to spread influence, at the same time learning the network. We call this problem "Simultaneous Influencing and Mapping" (SIAM). We consider a version of SIAM where we only need to map the nodes that compose the network. We assume that we always know all the edges between the nodes of the known subgraph. Formally, let $G := (V, E)$ be a graph with a set of nodes V and edges E. We pick one node at each one of η interventions. The selected node is used to spread influence and map the network. We do not know the graph G, we only know a subgraph $G_k = (V_k, E_k) \subset G$, where k is the current intervention number. G_k starts as $G_k := G_0 \subset G$. For each node v_i, there is a subset of nodes $V^i \subset V$, which will be called "teaching list". Each time we pick a node v_i, the known subgraph changes to $G_k := (V_{k-1} \cup V^i, E_k)$, where E_k contains all edges between the set of nodes $V_{k-1} \cup V^i$ in G. Our objective is to maximize $|V_k|$, given η interventions.

For each v_i, we assume we can observe a number γ_i, which indicates the size of its teaching list. We study two versions: in one γ_i is the number of nodes in V^i that are not yet in G_k (hence, the number of new nodes that will be learned when picking v_i). We refer to this version as "perfect knowledge". In the other, $\gamma_i := |V^i|$, and thus we cannot know how many nodes in V^i are going to be new or intersect with already known nodes in V_k. We refer to this version as "partial knowledge". Note that we may also have nodes with empty teaching lists ($\gamma_i = 0$). The teaching list of a node v_i is the set of nodes that v_i will teach us about once picked, and is not necessarily as complete as the true set of all nodes known by v_i. Some nodes could simply refuse to provide any information. We assume the teaching list and the neighbor list to be independent. That is, a node may teach us about nodes that it is not able to directly influence. For instance, it is common to know people that we do not have direct contact with, or we are not "close" enough to be able to influence. Similarly, a person may not tell us about all her close friends, due to limitations of an interview process, or even "shame" to describe some connections. We consider a probability φ that a node will have a non-empty teaching list.

We also want to maximize the influence over the network. We consider the traditional independent cascade model, with observation, as in Golovin and Krause (2010) [1]. That is, a node may be either influenced or uninfluenced. An uninfluenced node may change to influenced, but an influenced node will never change back to uninfluenced. Each time we pick a node for an intervention, it will change to influenced. When a node changes from uninfluenced to influenced, it will "spread" the influence to its neighbors with some probability. That is, at each edge e there is a probability p_e. When a node v_1 changes to influenced, if there is an edge $e = (v_1, v_2)$, the node v_2 will also change to influenced with probability p_e. Similarly, if v_2 changes to influenced, it will spread the influence to its neighbors by the same process. Influence only spreads in the moment a node changes from uninfluenced to influenced. As in [1], we consider that we have knowledge about whether a node is influenced or not (but in our case, we can only know about nodes in the current known subgraph G_k). Let I_k be the number of influenced

Appears in: *Proceedings of the 15th International Conference on Autonomous Agents and Multiagent Systems (AAMAS 2016), J. Thangarajah, K. Tuyls, C. Jonker, S. Marsella (eds.), May 9–13, 2016, Singapore.*

nodes after k interventions. Our objective is to maximize I_k given η interventions. Influence may spread beyond G_k. We consider I_k as the number of influenced nodes in the full graph G. We denote as σ_i the expected number of nodes that will be influenced when picking v_i (usually calculated by simulations).

We must maximize both $|V_k|$ and I_k. Similarly to previous influence maximization works [2, 1], we study greedy solutions. The fundamental problem of SIAM is whether to focus on influencing or mapping the network. Hence, we propose as a general framework to select the node v_i such that: $v_i = \text{argmax}(c_1 \times \sigma_i + c_2 \times \gamma_i)$. Constants c_1 and c_2 control the balance between influencing or mapping. $c_1 = 1, c_2 = 0$ is the classical influence maximization algorithm (*"influence-greedy"*); $c_1 = 0, c_2 = 1$, on the other hand, only maximizes the knowledge-gain at each intervention (*"knowledge-greedy"*). $c_1 = c_2 = 1$ is an algorithm where both objectives are equally balanced (*"balanced"*). In order to better handle *partial knowledge*, we also propose the *"balanced-decreasing"* algorithm, where c_2 constantly decreases until reaching 0. Hence, we define c_2 as: $c_2 := \begin{cases} c_2' - \frac{1}{d} \times c_2' \times k & \text{if } k \leq d \\ 0 & \text{otherwise} \end{cases}$, where c_2' is the value for c_2 at the very first iteration, and d controls how fast it decays.

We begin by studying *influence-greedy*. It was shown that when picking the node v which $\text{argmax}(\sigma_v)$ at each intervention, we achieve a solution that is a $(1 - 1/e - \epsilon)$ approximation of the optimal, as long as our estimation of σ_v (by running simulations) is "good enough" [2]. However, even though the actual influence spread may go beyond the known graph G_k, we can only run simulations to estimate σ_v in the current G_k. Hence, the previous results are no longer valid. We show with an example that we can obtain arbitrarily low-performing solutions by using *influence-greedy*.

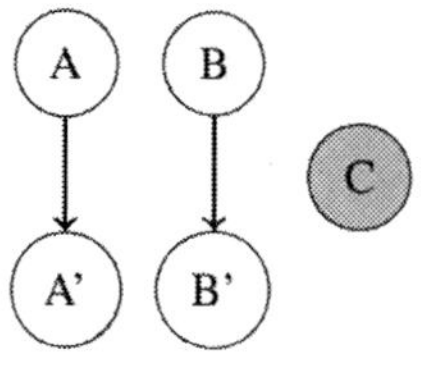

Figure 1: Greedy algorithm has low performance.

Consider the graph in Figure 1, and assume we will run 2 interventions (i.e., pick 2 nodes). There is a probability 1 to spread influence in any edge. Our initial knowledge is $V_0 = \{A, A', B, B', C\}$. A and B can influence A' and B', respectively. However, C cannot influence any node. A, B, A' and B' have empty teaching lists. C, on the other hand, can teach us about a connected graph of z nodes. *Influence-greedy*, by running simulations on the known graph, picks nodes A and B, since each can influence one more node. The optimal solution, however, is to pick node C, which will teach us about the connected graph of z nodes. Then, we can pick one node in that graph, and influence $z + 1$ nodes in total. Hence, the *influence-greedy* solution is only $\frac{4}{z+1}$ of the optimal. As z grows, *influence-greedy* will be arbitrarily far from the optimal solution.

3. RESULTS

We run experiments using four real life social networks of the homeless population of Los Angeles, provided by Eric Rice, from the School of Social Work of the University of Southern California. All the networks are friendship-based social networks of homeless youth who visit a social agency. We run 100 executions per network. At the beginning of each execution, 4 nodes are randomly chosen to compose our initial subgraph (G_0). We noticed similar tendencies in the results across all four social networks. Due to space constraints, we plot here the results considering all networks simultaneously (that is, we average over all the 400 executions). In all graphs, the error bars show the confidence interval, with $\rho = 0.01$.

We measure the percentage of influence in the network ("Influence") and percentage of known nodes ("Knowledge"). We consider

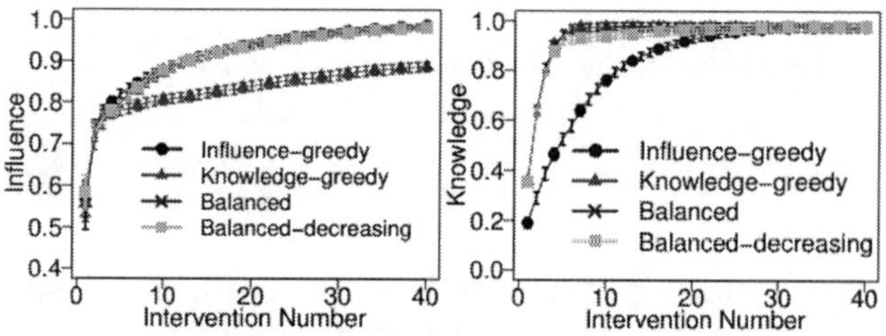

(a) Influence (b) Knowledge

Figure 2: Results in real world networks across many interventions.

balanced-decreasing with $c_2' = 1.0$, and $d = 5$. In order to estimate the expected influence spread (σ_v) of each node, we run 1000 simulations before each intervention. Simulations are run in the current known subgraph G_k, although the actual influence may go beyond G_k (which will be considered when we measure Influence). Concerning γ_v, we consider it to hold the number of *new* nodes that would be learned if v is selected, for *balanced* and *knowledge-greedy* (i.e., perfect knowledge). For *balanced-decreasing*, we consider γ_v to hold the full teaching list size, including nodes that are already known (i.e., partial knowledge). Hence, we evaluate if *balanced-decreasing* approximates well *balanced.*

We simulate the teaching lists, since there are no real world data available yet (we only have data about the connections in the four networks). If a node has a teaching list, we fix its size according to a uniform distribution from 0 to $0.5 \times |V|$. Each node in the graph is also equally likely to be in the teaching list of a node v_i.

Figure 2 shows the result at each intervention for $\varphi = 0.5$ and $p = 0.5$. The Influence obtained by *influence-greedy*, *balanced*, and *balanced-decreasing* are similar. Out of all 40 interventions, their result is not significantly different in any of them (and they are significantly better than *knowledge-greedy* in around 75% of the interventions). This shows that *balanced* is able to successfully spread influence in the network, while at the same time mapping the graph. We also notice that perfect knowledge about the number of new nodes in the teaching lists is not necessary, as *balanced-decreasing* obtained close results to *balanced.* In terms of Knowledge, all algorithms clearly outperform *influence-greedy* with statistical significance. Moreover, the result for *knowledge-greedy*, *balanced* and *balanced-decreasing* are not significantly different in any of the interventions. This shows that we are able to successfully map the network (as well as *knowledge-greedy*), but at the same time spreading influence successfully over the network (as well as *influence-greedy*), even in the *partial knowledge* case.

Acknowledgments: This research was supported by MURI grant W911NF-11-1-0332, and by IUSSTF.

REFERENCES

[1] D. Golovin and A. Krause. Adaptive submodularity: A new approach to active learning and stochastic optimization. In *COLT*, 2010.

[2] D. Kempe, J. Kleinberg, and E. Tardos. Maximizing the spread of influence through a social network. In *KDD*, 2003.

[3] P. V. Marsden. Recent developments in network measurement. In *Models and methods in social network analysis*. Cambridge University Press, 2005.

[4] A. Yadav, L. S. Marcolino, E. Rice, R. Petering, H. Winetrobe, H. Rhoades, M. Tambe, and H. Carmichael. Preventing HIV spread in homeless populations using PSINET. In *IAAI*, 2015.

Collaborative Human Task Assignment for Open Systems (Extended Abstract)

Bin Chen, Adam Eck, and Leen-Kiat Soh
Department of Computer Science and Engineering
University of Nebraska, Lincoln, NE
{bchen, aeck, lksoh}@cse.unl.edu

ABSTRACT

Through gathering information, acting autonomously, learning, and behaving socially, intelligent agents provide useful interfaces between complex systems and human users. For example, agents can interact with people to discover their preferences, skills, and expertise, then find suitable tasks that exploit the users' abilities. We describe modeling environmental openness and human learning in a multiagent system for a human collaborative task assignment problem.

Categories and Subject Descriptors

I.2.11 [**Artificial Intelligence**]: Distributed Artificial Intelligence – *intelligent agents, multiagent systems*

General Terms

Performance, Design, Experimentation, Human Factors.

Keywords

Collaborative Task Assignment; Openness; Human Learning; Emergent Behavior

1. INTRODUCTION

Human collaborative task assignment occurs in environments where there exist human users and tasks that require multiple people to combine their individual skills and expertise to work together towards a common (possibly temporary) goal. As motivation, each participant earns a share of a joint reward if the task is accomplished successfully. For example, the assignment could be used to (1) form temporary teams of freelance workers (e.g., independent software developers or artists) to satisfy contracts from companies lacking the internal expertise to accomplish tasks (e.g., developing particular pieces of software or graphic design), (2) combine the expertise and skills of office workers across divisions within large companies to accomplish tasks needed by the company, or (3) match students to peer-based learning tasks in computer-aided education.

In such a problem, software agents are valuable in assisting human users in identifying appropriate tasks (or subtasks) to complete, as well as in securing such tasks (or subtasks) for their human users. Such agents can first model the abilities of their assigned users, then find and acquire tasks that best benefit their users, with the emergent behavior that the overall system benefits from the task assignment. When modeling a human user, an agent should take into account the impacts of human learning on its human user's expertise and skills, especially so when deciding on which tasks to pursue. This consideration is non-trivial, as the task providing the most immediate reward might not simultaneously provide the greatest opportunity for learning that would improve a human user's expertise and skills and ultimately lead to greater future rewards. Therefore, an agent faces a difficult tradeoff when selecting tasks for its learning-capable human user.

Furthermore, when the environment is open where existing human users may leave while new human users may enter, or existing tasks may disappear and new tasks may appear, modeling human learning and leveraging that in an agent's reasoning become more complicated. In this paper, we focus on modeling openness and human learning in human collaborative task assignment as a first key step towards a solution approach to address this human collaborative task assignment problem.

2. MODELING OPENNESS

We consider two types of openness: (1) agent openness and (2) task openness. Our definition of task openness follows from Chen *et al.* [3] while that of agent openness is a slight variant from [3].

Agent openness represents the phenomenon that human users (who are also intelligent, non-artificial agents) join and leave the environment over time. For example, in a freelance software development environment, individual developers might leave software companies to do independent freelance work instead, whereas others might switch from being freelance workers to working solely for a software company. Likewise, in an office worker environment, the company might hire new employees and let others go over time. As a result of agent openness, various agents (with the number of agents determined by the degree of agent openness) will leave and/or join the environment over time. Thus, the set of human users H (and their corresponding software agents A) is non-stationary and changes over time. To closely model many real-world scenarios, we assume that agents do not necessarily know their peers around them at any point in time, nor how many peers they have. Note that new expertise entering the environment would be helpful for completing collaborative tasks. However, as existing agents leave the environment, they will take their expertise with them, potentially creating a void in important skills or expertise, making it more difficult for collaborative tasks to be completed. This exodus could especially hurt the system since human users' capabilities do improve due to learning over time, so the amount of overall expertise leaving the system due to openness could exceed the amount of expertise joining the system.

Task openness represents the phenomenon that the set of tasks that require collaboration to solve could also change. For example, in a freelance software development environment, changes in programming paradigms and the types of software needed by clients would cause different collaborative tasks to exist over time. Moreover, in an office worker environment, different seasonal

Appears in: *Proceedings of the 15th International Conference on Autonomous Agents and Multiagent Systems (AAMAS 2016), J. Thangarajah, K. Tuyls, C. Jonker, S. Marsella (eds.),* May 9–13, 2016, Singapore.

activities of the company could require different tasks over time. As a result of task openness, a number of tasks will disappear from the environment, while new batches of tasks might be introduced for human users to work on (again, with the numbers of changing tasks being determined by the degree of task openness). Given that different expertise and capabilities are required of users to solve their tasks, task openness will affect the ability of agents to acquire tasks for their users. That is, as easier tasks become available, more users would be qualified to complete tasks, increasing the competition among them. On the other hand, as tasks become more difficult, it would be more difficult for an agent to find a suitable task for its assigned user. Furthermore, new tasks requiring different skills could bring previously unmet opportunities for users to leverage their capabilities.

Of note, our work on agent and task openness within a problem model is similar to and builds upon prior research by Jumadinova *et al.* [5]. In particular, their research explored the impacts of agent and task openness when agents work together in ad hoc teams under the assumption of simple rules for forming teams based on agent capabilities. Here we add principled computational models of human learning based on an extensive literature review to improve how agents reason about the benefits of task accomplishment for human users.

3. MODELING HUMAN LEARNING

Human learning is especially important in the presence of agent and task openness within the collaborative task assignment problem because learning enables human users to gain expertise and skills needed both (1) to replace expertise leaving the environment due to agent openness, as well as (2) to perform a wider range of tasks encountered due to task openness. In particular, we model learning as increases in user capabilities $cap_{h,k} \in [0,1]$ (where h references a particular human user and k represents a particular skill or knowledge). We focus on two particular learning paradigms: (1) learning by doing and (2) learning by observation.

Learning by Doing. One way that humans learn is through experience gained by directly performing tasks. Here, a user h gains capability $cap_{h,k}$ in the skill or knowledge k it uses while participating in a task. To model *learning by doing*, we propose considering *experience curve effects* [4] to derive the learning gain function for a human user performing learning by doing. Different task types may have different learning curves (e.g., power law, exponential, sigmoidal) [6, 7]. For example, Leibowitz *et al.* [6] outline an exponential learning equation for success-based learning:

$$p_n = p_\infty - (p_\infty - p_0) \cdot e^{-\alpha \cdot S_n} \quad (1)$$

where p measures a user's performance, n counts the learning episode such that p_∞ is the maximum infinite-horizon performance achievable, p_0 is the initial performance, S_n is the accumulated sum of all previous performances preceding the n-th episode, and α is a constant rate coefficient. The change in performance, or learning gain, according to Leibowitz *et al.* [6], is:

$$\dot{p} = \alpha p \cdot (p_\infty - p) \quad (2)$$

The constant rate coefficient α caps the amount of learning gain at each episode. The general shape of this curve is a (concave downward) parabola: when a user's expertise is low, it learns a little; as its expertise grows, it starts to learn faster up to a peak rate; after it peaks, its learning slows back down. Thus, for a user's gain via learning by doing with a learning curve capped by α_{do}, using its capability $cap_{h,k}$, we have:

$$\Delta_{do} cap_{h,k} = c\dot{a}p_{h,k} = \alpha_{do} \cdot cap_{h,k} \cdot (1 - cap_{h,k}) \quad (3)$$

Learning By Observation. To model learning by observation, we look to Bandura's social cognitive learning theory [1, 2] containing four stages involved in observational learning: attention, retention or memory, initiation or reproduction, and motivation. In human collaborative task assignment, *attention* implies that a user h learns about $cap_{h,k}$ from observing other users using skill or knowledge k only when they are in the same team collaboratively solving a task. To ensure *retention* (or memory), each user updates its capability after task execution, using Eqs. 4-5 as described later. *Initiation* (or reproduction) requires that "observers must be physically and intellectually capable of producing the act." [2]. That is, when a user h observes another user performing k, h can only learn if its skill is relatively close to what it is observing in order to improve h's capability. As a result, we model the learning gain function of user h observing a teammate performing skill or knowledge k as follows:

$$\Delta_{obs} cap_{h,k} = \begin{cases} \dot{p} & 0 \le obs_k - cap_{i,k} < \beta \\ 0 & otherwise \end{cases} \quad (4)$$

where obs_k is the observed production of k by the teammate, β is the threshold under which $cap_{h,k}$ is close enough to obs_k for learning by observation to take place, and $\dot{p}$ for observational learning is modeled similarly from Eqs. 1-2 above:

$$\dot{p} = \alpha_{obs} \cdot (obs_k - cap_{h,k}) \cdot \left(\beta - (obs_k - cap_{h,k})\right) \quad (5)$$

where α_{obs} refers to the cap for the corresponding learning curve for observational learning for that capability. In summary, gain from learning by observation is zero if a user observes a k being performed that is either (1) too much greater than her current capability ($\ge \beta$), or (2) if the user is more capable that the performance it observes. Finally, we assume that learning-aware human users are always *motivated* to learn, and thus we assume learning by observation to be of no cost to human users.

4. REFERENCES

[1] Bandura, A. 1986. *Social Foundations of Thought and Action: A Social Cognitive Theory*. Prentice-Hall series in social learning theory.

[2] Bandura, A. 2004. Observational learning, in J. H. Byrne (Ed.), *Learning and Memory*. 2nd Ed. New York: Macmillan Reference USA, pp. 482-484.

[3] Chen, B., Chen, X., Timsina, A., and Soh, L.-K. 2015. Considering agent and task openness in ad hoc team formation (Extended Abstract). In *Proc. AAMAS'2015*, 1861-1862.

[4] Henderson, B. 1984. The application and misapplication of the experience curve, *Journal of Business Strategy*, 4(3):3-9.

[5] Jumadinova, J., Dasgupta, P., and Soh, L.-K. 2014. Strategic capability-learning for improved multi-agent collaboration in ad-hoc environments. *IEEE Transactions on Systems, Man, and Cybernetics-Part A*, 44(8):1003-1014.

[6] Leibowitz, N., Baum, B., Enden, G., and Karniel, A. 2010. The exponential learning equation as a function of successful trials results in sigmoid performance. *Journal of Mathematical* Psychology, 54:338-340.

[7] Newell, A. and Rosenbloom P.S. 1993. Mechanisms of skill acquisition and the law of Practice, *The SOAR Papers*, **1**:81-135.

Investigating the Characteristics of One-Sided Matching Mechanisms

(Extended Abstract)

Hadi Hosseini, Kate Larson, and Robin Cohen
Cheriton School of Computer Science
University of Waterloo
Waterloo, Ontario, Canada
{h5hossei,klarson,rcohen}@uwaterloo.ca

ABSTRACT

For one-sided matching problems, two widely studied mechanisms are the Random Serial Dictatorship (RSD) and the Probabilistic Serial Rule (PS). The induced outcomes of these two mechanisms are often incomparable and thus there are challenges when it comes to deciding which mechanism to adopt in practice. Working in the space of general preferences, we provide empirical results on the (in)comparability of RSD and PS and analyze their economic properties.

Keywords

Mechanism Design; Matching; Random Assignment; Probabilistic Serial; Random Serial Dictatorship

1. INTRODUCTION

The problem of assigning a number of indivisible objects to a set of agents, in the absence of monetary transfers, is fundamental in many multiagent resource allocation applications, and has been the center of attention amongst researchers at the interface of artificial intelligence, economics, and mechanism design. Examples include assigning dormitory rooms or offices to students, courses to students, and medical resources to patients.

Two important (randomized) matching mechanisms that only elicit *ordinal preferences* from agents are *Random Serial Dictatorship* (RSD) [1] and *Probabilistic Serial Rule* (PS) [3]. Both mechanisms have important economic properties and are practical to implement. The RSD mechanism has strong truthful incentives but guarantees neither efficiency nor envyfreeness. PS satisfies efficiency and envyfreeness; however, it is susceptible to manipulation. Therefore, there are subtle points to be considered when deciding which mechanism to use. For example, given a particular preference profile, the mechanisms often produce random assignments which are simply incomparable and thus, it is difficult to determine which is the "better" outcome.

We empirically study the comparability of PS and RSD when there is only one copy of each object, and analyze the space of all preference profiles for different combinations of agents and objects. We argue that the theoretical findings on RSD and PS do not necessarily provide enough guidance to a market designer trying to select the correct mechanism for a specific setting. For example, the *sd*-inefficiency of RSD does not mean that PS always outperforms RSD. Similarly, the envy of RSD and the manipulability of PS both depend on the structure of preference profiles, and thus, a compelling question, that justifies the practical implications of deploying a matching mechanism, is to analyze the space of profiles to find the likelihood of inefficient, manipulable, or envious assignments under these mechanisms.

Appears in: *Proceedings of the 15th International Conference on Autonomous Agents and Multiagent Systems (AAMAS 2016), J. Thangarajah, K. Tuyls, C. Jonker, S. Marsella (eds.), May 9–13, 2016, Singapore.*

2. MODEL AND PROPERTIES

Let N denote a set of n agents and M denote a set of m indivisible objects. Each agent $i \in N$ has a private strict preference ordering, $\succ_i$, over M where $a \succ_i b$ indicates that agent i prefers to receive object a over object b. We let $\mathcal{P}$ denote the set of all complete and strict preference orderings over M. A *preference profile* $\succ \in \mathcal{P}^n$ specifies a preference ordering for each agent, and we use the standard notation $\succ_{-i} = (\succ_1, \ldots, \succ_{i-1}, \succ_{i+1}, \ldots, \succ_n)$ to denote preferences orderings of all agents except i and thus $\succ = (\succ_i, \succ_{-i})$.

In one-sided matching, if $m = n$ then each agent will receive exactly one object, however if $m > n$ then some agents may receive multiple objects. An assignment is represented as a matrix A where each element $A_{i,j} \in [0, 1]$ is the probability that agent i is assigned object j. We let $\mathcal{A}$ denote the set of all *feasible* assignments where an assignment $A \in \mathcal{A}$ is *feasible* if and only if $\forall j \in M$, $\sum_{i \in N} A_{i,j} = 1$.

A *matching mechanism*, $\mathcal{M}$, is a mapping from the set of preference profiles, $\mathcal{P}^n$ to the set of feasible assignments, $\mathcal{A}$. In this paper, we focus our attention on two widely studied mechanisms for one-side matching: Random Serial Dictatorship (RSD) [1] and Probabilistic Serial Rule (PS) [3].

RSD randomly chooses a priority ordering of agents where the first agent gets to select its most preferred object from the set of objects, the second agent selects its most preferred object from the remaining objects and so on until no objects remain.[1] PS treats objects as a set of divisible goods and simulates a simultaneous eating algorithm. Each agent starts "eating" its most preferred object, all at the same rate. Once an object is exhausted then the agent starts eating its next preferred object among the remaining objects, until all objects have been "eaten".

[1]For $n < m$, we use a variant of RSD based on *quasi-dictatorial* mechanisms [6, 4].

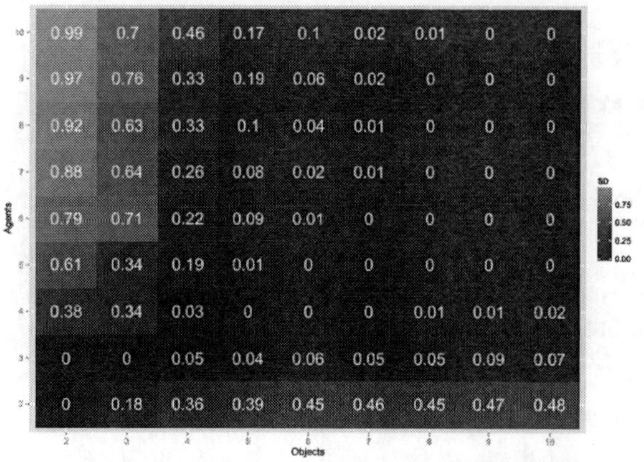

Figure 1: The fraction of preference profiles that PS stochastically dominates RSD.

3. PROPERTIES OF RSD AND PS

To evaluate the quality of a random assignment, we use first-order stochastic dominance [3]. According to our model, given a random assignment A_i, the probability that agent i is assigned an object that is at least as good as object ℓ is defined as $w(\succ_i, \ell, A_i) = \sum_{j \in M: j \succ_i \ell} A_{i,j}$. We say an agent always prefers assignment A_i to B_i, if for each object ℓ the probability of assigning an object at least as good as ℓ under A_i is greater or equal that of B_i, and strictly greater for some object. Formally, A_i *stochastically dominates (sd)* $B_i (\neq A_i)$ if $\forall \ell \in M,\ w(\succ_i, \ell, A_i) \geq w(\succ_i, \ell, B_i)$.

A matching mechanism is *sd*-efficient if at all preference profiles $\succ \in \mathcal{P}^n$, for all agents $i \in N$, the induced random assignment is not stochastically dominated by any other assignment. An important desirable property in matching mechanisms is strategyproofness. A mechanism $\mathcal{M}$ is *sd-strategyproof* if at all preference profiles $\succ \in \mathcal{P}^n$, for all agents $i \in N$, and for any misreport $\succ_i' \in \mathcal{P}^n$, such that $A = \mathcal{M}(\succ)$ and $A' = \mathcal{M}(\succ_i', \succ_{-i})$, we have $\forall \ell \in M,\ w(\succ_i, \ell, A_i) \geq w(\succ_i, \ell, A_i')$. An assignment is *manipulable* if it is not *sd*-strategyproof. If there exists some agent who strictly benefits from the manipulation, then we say the assignment is *sd*-manipulable. Similarly, an assignment is *sd*-envyfree if each agent strictly prefers her random allocation to any other agent's assignment.

The theoretical properties of PS and RSD have been well studied in the literature [3, 5, 2]. PS has been shown to be both *sd*-envyfree and *sd*-efficient. However, it is *sd*-manipulable when $n < m$ [5], and is not *sd*-strategyproof when $n \geq m$. On the other hand, RSD is *sd*-strategyproof, but it does not guarantee *sd-efficiency*.

4. RESULTS

We studied the space of preference profiles and provided empirical results on the (in)comparability of RSD and PS under general and lexicographic preferences. Under lexicographic preferences, any fraction of a more preferred object is preferred to other less preferred objects. The number of all possible preference profiles is super exponential $(m!)^n$. For each combination of n agents and m objects we did a brute force coverage of all possible preference profiles. For the cases of $n = 10$ and $m \in \{9, 10\}$, we randomly generated 1,000 instances by sampling from a uniform preference profile distribution. For each preference profile, we ran both PS and RSD mechanisms and compared their outcomes. Our main results are as follows:

General preferences: In terms of efficiency, the fraction of preference profiles $\succ \in \mathcal{P}^n$ for which PS stochastically dominates RSD converges to zero as $\frac{n}{m} \to 1$. PS is almost 99% manipulable when $n \leq m$ and the fraction of *sd*-manipulable profiles rapidly goes to 1 as $\frac{m}{n}$ grows (Figure 1).

Lexicographic preferences: The fraction of preference profiles $\succ \in \mathcal{P}^n$ for which RSD is lexicographically dominated by PS at $\succ$ converges to zero as $\frac{n}{m} \to 1$. For lexicographic preferences, we also observe that the fraction of preference profiles for which PS assignments strictly dominate RSD-induced allocations goes to 1 when the number of agents and objects diverge. The fraction of preference profiles $\succ \in \mathcal{P}^n$ for which RSD is lexicographically dominated by PS at $\succ$ converges to 1 as $|n - m|$ grows.

5. DISCUSSION

Our work in this paper can be used to help guide designers of multiagent systems who need to solve allocation problems. If a designer strongly requires *sd*-efficiency then the theoretical results of PS indicate that it is better than RSD. However, our results show that PS is highly prone to manipulation for various combinations of agents and objects. This manipulation and the possible gain from manipulation become more severe particularly when agents can receive more than one object, and designers need to take this into consideration. We have also instantiated utility functions for agents under variety of risk attitude models to gain deeper insights on the manipulability, social welfare, and envyfreeness of PS and RSD. Our results show that while RSD does not theoretically guarantee *sd*-efficiency, it tends to do quite well – sometimes even outperforming PS in terms of social welfare. RSD also has the added advantage of being *sd*-strategyproof and thus is not prone to the manipulation problems of PS.

REFERENCES

[1] A. Abdulkadiroğlu and T. Sönmez. Random serial dictatorship and the core from random endowments in house allocation problems. *Econometrica*, 66(3):689–701, 1998.

[2] H. Aziz, S. Gaspers, S. Mackenzie, N. Mattei, N. Narodytska, and T. Walsh. Manipulating the probabilistic serial rule. In *Proceedings of the 14th International Conference on Autonomous Agents and Multiagent Systems (AAMAS 2015)*, pages 1451–1459, 2015.

[3] A. Bogomolnaia and H. Moulin. A new solution to the random assignment problem. *Journal of Economic Theory*, 100(2):295–328, 2001.

[4] H. Hosseini and K. Larson. Strategyproof quota mechanisms for multiple assignment problems. *arXiv preprint arXiv:1507.07064*, 2015.

[5] F. Kojima and M. Manea. Incentives in the probabilistic serial mechanism. *Journal of Economic Theory*, 145(1):106–123, 2010.

[6] S. Pápai. Strategyproof multiple assignment using quotas. *Review of Economic Design*, 5(1):91–105, 2000.

A Multi-Agent System for Resource Privacy: Deployment of Ambient Applications in Smart Environments

(Extended Abstract)

Ferdinand Piette[1,2], Costin Caval[1],
Amal El Fallah Seghrouchni[1], Patrick Taillibert[1] and Cédric Dinont[2]
[1] Sorbonne Universités, UPMC Univ Paris 06, LIP6, Paris, France
{costin.caval, amal.elfallah, patrick.taillibert}@lip6.fr
[2] Institut Supérieur de l'Électronique et du Numérique, Lille, France
{ferdinand.piette, cedric.dinont}@isen-lille.fr

ABSTRACT

In this paper, we present Multi-Agent Systems (MAS) as a well-adapted paradigm for designing software for the configuration, deployment and monitoring of distributed applications in the domain of Ambient Intelligence (AmI). We show how privacy is enhanced by hiding information using the agent architecture and organisation. We introduce privacy policies that can allow or prevent the sharing of resource information. This results in privacy by design.

Keywords

Multi-agent system; Ambient Intelligence; Privacy management; Deployment; Goal-driven agents

1. DEPLOYMENT OF APPLICATIONS

Ambient Intelligence (AmI) research focuses on the improvement of human interactions with smart applications and proposes frameworks and platforms that facilitate the development of context-aware and dynamic applications. In this domain, it is often assumed that an underlying interoperable hardware and energy infrastructure already exists. Meanwhile, the main challenge of the Internet of Things (IoT) is to achieve full interoperability of interconnected devices while enabling advanced services and guaranteeing the trust, privacy and security of communications [1]. Because of the heterogeneity of such systems, it is difficult to have horizontal communication between connected devices. Present applications using connected devices on the IoT infrastructure are vertically connected from the device to a server that collects the data. This approach raises privacy questions and inevitably leads to a Big Brother effect: the user does not own his data any more. To allow horizontal connections between devices, we need mechanisms that reason on the heterogeneity of systems in order to automatically deploy smart applications provided by AmI on an existing hardware infrastructure provided by the IoT. To address these issues, we propose a distributed approach to solve the deployment problem using a multi-agent architecture which, as will be seen, helps to ensure resource privacy.

Appears in: *Proceedings of the 15th International Conference on Autonomous Agents and Multiagent Systems (AAMAS 2016), J. Thangarajah, K. Tuyls, C. Jonker, S. Marsella (eds.), May 9–13, 2016, Singapore.*

2. MULTI-AGENT MODELLING

We identify several necessary specificities to build the deployment software. It has to dynamically deploy and undeploy distributed AmI applications in an environment that is also dynamic. It also has to manage the context, like the location of the user, in order to choose the most relevant devices to deploy applications. Resource and information privacy is an important requirement in the AmI domain. At last, autonomy and robustness of the system are very important specificities. If a part of the system failed, the other parts should continue to work normally. To solve the dynamic deployment problem, we extend our previous work [4] where the available hardware infrastructure and the requirements of the deployable applications are described by graphs. Nodes represent hardware entities or relations between these entities and properties can be attached to each node. A graph matching algorithm can then be used on the available infrastructure graph to find the entities that can support the running of the application. However, this previous solution was centralised, which makes it unsuitable for real systems that need to take into consideration, among others, privacy and scalability. For the other specificities (context management, autonomy, robustness and privacy) of the deployment software, we identified Multi-Agent Systems (MAS) as a suitable solution. This paradigm possesses good properties to facilitate a local processing of the data, guarantee the autonomy of the different parts of the hardware infrastructure and so handle some aspects of privacy. The context management, autonomy and robustness are well studied in the agent literature [3]. In this paper, we focus on the encapsulation of resource privacy, using the restriction of information sharing and agent organisation.

2.1 Classes of Agent

The system is made of four classes of agent:

- An ***Infrastructure Agent*** deals with a part of the global hardware infrastructure which is represented as a graph [4] that is never shared with other agents. The agent uses a graph-matching algorithm to propose complete or partial solutions for the deployment of applications. This class of agent has several goals:

keep the infrastructure graph up to date; propose solutions for the deployment of applications, considering the available hardware infrastructure, but also the sharing and privacy policy (see Sec. 2.2); and deploy or undeploy functionalities of an application.

- An ***Infrastructure Super Agent*** is a representative of a group of *Infrastructure Agents*, acting as a proxy between the group and the other agents.
- An ***Application Agent*** manages an entire application during its runtime. It has a graph-based description of the application. The goals of this class of agent are to guarantee the consistency of the application and deploy or undeploy functionalities of the application if necessary. The functionalities of the application can be deployed on several parts of the infrastructure, managed by associated *Infrastructure Agents* with which the *Application Agent* will need to interact.
- At last, the ***User Agent*** is the interface between the agents of the deployment software and the user. This one can request the deployment or undeployment of applications.

In order to enhance the resource privacy, the agents only have a local view of the system. Indeed the graph representation of the available hardware infrastructure managed by an *Infrastructure Agent* is only known by this agent and is never shared with others. Moreover, the architecture used helps to keep a clear separation between the users, interacting with the associated *User Agents*, the applicative part, managed by the *Application Agents*, and the hardware part, monitored by the *Infrastructure Agents*.

2.2 Organisation and Interactions

Infrastructure Agents can be grouped behind an *Infrastructure Super Agent* which, as stated before, acts as a proxy for the agents of the group. From an outside view, this *Infrastructure Super Agent* is seen as a normal *Infrastructure Agent*, resulting in a multi-scale organisation that helps to improve privacy. It is then easier to abstract groups of agents and make them invisible from the outside.

To improve resource privacy, we also introduced sharing policies to regulate the access of the *User Agents* (and implicitly their users) to the infrastructure. These policies include completely blocking the access by the *Infrastructure Agent* for unknown users. Otherwise, the authorization levels can be, for example : (1) Administrator: the agent has full access to the resources proposed by the *Infrastructure (Super) Agent*, can manage the authorisation levels, reconfigure the *Super Agent* and add or remove *Infrastructure Agents* to the *Super Agent*; (2) Regular user: the agent has access to the resources of the *Infrastructure (Super) Agent* but it cannot reconfigure authorisation levels or agent organisation and; (3) Guest: the agent has a restricted access to the resources. Only the resources considered as non critical by an administrator can be shared. These authorisation levels are not limited to three and can be modified by one of the administrators of the *Infrastructure Agent*. As the *Application Agents* are created by *User Agents*, they both share the same authorisation level.

2.3 Design and Implementation

We used goal-driven agents for gains in the autonomy and robustness of the application. The goal-based representation adopted is the Goal-Plan Separation (GPS) approach [2]. This approach helped handle agent complexity through a multi-level description, from top level abstract behaviours with *goals plans* that describe relationships between goals, to low level *action plans* that detail the sequences of concrete actions.

We developed a demonstration model of the deployment software based on an apartment replica in which we executed various scenarios applied to home care for dependent persons. These scenarios use commercial connected devices tweaked to be horizontally connected, thanks to the deployment software. This realisation helps us asses the difficulties of handling the heterogeneity of hardware entities. We now have a concrete base for the implementation of a complete middleware that handles applications through an AppStore for Smart Homes and deploys automatically these applications in a real environment, using the available hardware devices, and including mechanisms to ensure management of resource privacy.

3. CONCLUSION AND FUTURE WORK

The MAS proposed in this paper contains four classes of goal-directed agent that reason on the deployment of applications on a hardware infrastructure. The use of MAS made it possible to introduce privacy measures at architecture and organisation levels, on top of which we added a user-defined privacy policy mechanism. This was an important criterion for the choice of the agent paradigm since in the AmI domain there are often different infrastructure owners that need to ensure the privacy of their resources. The separation between the applicative and the infrastructure layers, together with the decentralised approach also enhance the robustness of the solution. The clearly delimited entities, with either virtual (the applications) or physical (users, infrastructure elements) correspondents, guided the agentification. The next steps of this work will be to consider data privacy by defining data privacy policies in order to facilitate the local processing and storage of the data, with the user deciding which kinds of data he authorises to come out of his own infrastructure. This will impact the reasoning on the deployment, since the hardware entities have to be chosen in order to comply with this new data privacy policy.

REFERENCES

[1] L. Atzori, A. Iera, and G. Morabito. The internet of things: A survey. *Computer Networks*, 54(15):2787 – 2805, 2010.

[2] C. Caval, A. El Fallah Seghrouchni, and P. Taillibert. Keeping a clear separation between goals and plans. In F. Dalpiaz, J. Dix, and M. van Riemsdijk, editors, *Engineering Multi-Agent Systems*, volume 8758 of *Lecture Notes in Computer Science*, pages 15–39. Springer International Publishing, 2014.

[3] K. Kravari and N. Bassiliades. A survey of agent platforms. *Journal of Artificial Societies and Social Simulation*, 18(1):11, 2015.

[4] F. Piette, C. Dinont, A. El Fallah Seghrouchni, and P. Taillibert. Deployment and configuration of applications for ambient systems. *Procedia Computer Science*, 52:373 – 380, 2015. The 6th International Conference on Ambient Systems, Networks and Technologies (ANT-2015).

Object-Focused Advice in Reinforcement Learning (Extended Abstract)

Samantha Krening
Georgia Institute of Technology
skrening@gatech.edu

Brent Harrison
Georgia Institute of Technology
brent.harrison@cc.gatech.edu

Karen M. Feigh
Georgia Institute of Technology
karen.feigh@gatech.edu

Charles Isbell
Georgia Institute of Technology
isbell@cc.gatech.edu

Andrea Thomaz
Georgia Institute of Technology
athomaz@ece.utexas.edu

ABSTRACT

In order for robots and intelligent agents to interact with and learn from people with no machine-learning expertise, robots should be able to learn from natural human instruction. Many human explanations consist of simple sentences without state information, yet most machine learning techniques that incorporate human guidance cannot use non-specific explanations. This work aims to learn policies from a few sentences that aren't state specific. The proposed Object-focused advice links an object to an action, and allows a person to generalize over an object's state space. To evaluate this technique, agents were trained using Object-focused advice collected from participants in an experiment in the Mario Bros. domain. The results show that Object-focused advice performs better than when no advice is given, the agent can learn where to apply the advice in the state space, and the agent can recover from adversarial advice. Also, including warnings of what not do to in addition to advice of what actions to take improves performance.

CCS Concepts

•Human-centered computing → Text input; •Computing methodologies → *Reinforcement learning;*

Keywords

Advice; Reinforcement Learning; Human Teachers

1. INTRODUCTION

This work focuses on an area of learning from explanations that has been addressed little in previous research - how to learn from human explanations that lack state information. Learning from a few simple sentences is a worthwhile goal because it can decrease the amount of time and effort a human teacher needs to contribute compared to demonstrations or critique. Most forms of machine learning that use human input force the person to provide state-specific information, whether or not that level of detail is reasonable or intuitive, and cannot learn from human sentences that lack state information [1, 4, 2, 6, 5].

Appears in: *Proceedings of the 15th International Conference on Autonomous Agents and Multiagent Systems (AAMAS 2016), J. Thangarajah, K. Tuyls, C. Jonker, S. Marsella (eds.), May 9–13, 2016, Singapore.*

2. OBJECT-FOCUSED HUMAN ADVICE

This work proposes **Object-focused advice**, a method in which human advice is tied to objects instead of specific states and is generalized over the object's state space. Consider this explanation from the popular Super Mario Brothers game: "Mario should jump on enemies." While this advice would easily be understood by a human student, it proves problematic for reinforcement learning agents. The teacher did not specify state information like where the enemy needs to be with respect to Mario and what Mario's velocity should be. Knowing that Mario should jump on an enemy is valuable information, but how can an agent make use of it if no state information is provided?

Object-focused advice addresses this by linking an *object* to an action that should be used around that object. We define this to be **advice** because it tells the agent what actions to take.

> Mario should jump to collect *coins*, and jump over *chasms*.

A person might also provide **warnings** in an explanation to teach the agent what actions to avoid.

> Do not move right into an *enemy*. Do not fall into *chasms*.

Using Object-focused advice that is independent of the object's state allows the person to perform object-level generalization instead of the agent. Generalizing over the entire state space of an object may seem drastic, but it is a way to quickly operationalize human explanations without state information. It is unrealistic to expect people to provide detailed state information when giving advice. A person might say, "Jump on the enemy," but will not say, "Hold the jump key for 10 frames when Mario is within 2.5 horizontal blocks of an enemy with a velocity of 3.2 units/frame." The agent will take the action advice of "Jump on the enemy," and determine to which portions of the state space, if any, the advice applies.

Following advice a set number of times and then relying on experience allows the agent to recover from adversarial advice, which is input that is expected to result in minimal reward. Also, Object-focused advice lets the agent's 'trust' in the human advice vary across the domain. The agent will treat each piece of advice without prejudice; if a person provides one piece of good advice along with eight pieces of bad advice, the agent will use its experience to build policies that reflect the good and ignore the bad.

Advice describes what to do, while warnings describe what not to do. To incorporate warnings, all objects in the state space are taken into account together by summing up the Q-values associated with each action across all objects. Choosing an action by taking multiple objects into account allows us to get an idea of the overall severity of each action.

3. RESULTS

The experiment was conducted in the Mario Bros. domain [7] It is a partially-observable environment in which Mario must collect rewards and avoid being harmed while moving toward the goal. During the experiment, we collected responses from participants in which one action was advised for every object; this advice was used to train agents using Object-focused advice and Object-focused Q-learning [3].

Figure 1 shows an agent trained with adversarial advice quickly recovers and performs as well as no advice, but not as well as good advice. After 400 trials, the best advice from the experiment led to Mario falling into chasms approximately 16% of the time, while the agents using adversarial or no advice fell into chasms 34% of occurrences. The results were averaged over 100 episodes with a sliding window average of width of 25. The parameters used were $\alpha = 0.1$, $\gamma = 0.95$, $\epsilon_0 = 0.8$, and $\epsilon_{min} = 0.15$. ϵ-greedy exploration was used.

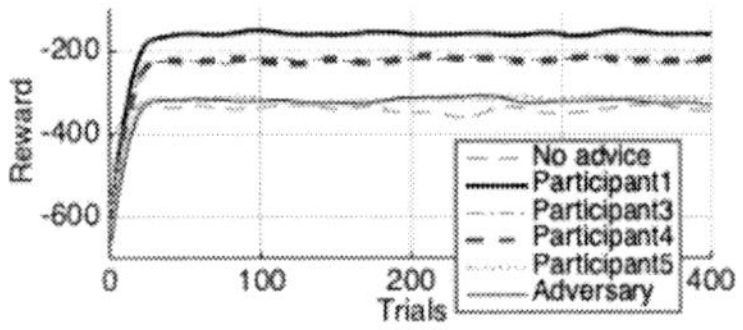

Figure 1: Cumulative Reward for Chasms.

Figure 2 shows the agent learns to which part of the state space the advice applies. The agent was advised to jump to the right when encountering Goombas. The agent learned this was a good policy when the Goomba was to the right of Mario in a 'goldilocks' zone - not too close but not too far away - but was bad advice when the enemy was above Mario.

Incorporating "what not to do" warnings in addition to "what to do" advice approximately doubled the cumulative reward earned by the agent for different objects.

4. CONCLUSIONS

We presented a novel form of human advice and warnings that links objects to actions. Advice and warnings are object-specific, and so do not require people to specify state variables. Using warnings in addition to advice and combining the Q-values from multiple objects improves the agent's performance. Object-focused advice allows people to generalize over an object's state space, which lets agents learn from a few simple sentences with no numbers or particulars

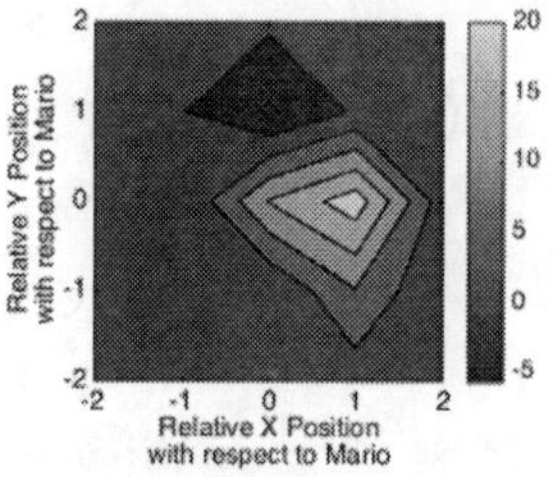

Figure 2: Visualizing Object-level Generalization in a Policy for Goombas. The color scale represents Q-values showing when to jump right.

describing the state. A model-free approach has been described that does not require the intensive construction of formal language translations.

The goal of Object-focused advice is not to capture all the nuances and subtleties of free-form teaching, but rather to make use of human explanations without state information. It is vital to develop methods that use human explanations that aren't state-specific since they reflect much of non-expert instruction.

5. ACKNOWLEDGMENTS

This work was funded under ONR grant number N000141410003.

REFERENCES

[1] B. D. Argall, S. Chernova, M. Veloso, and B. Browning. A survey of robot learning from demonstration. *Robotics and autonomous systems*, 57(5):469–483, 2009.

[2] S. Chernova and A. L. Thomaz. Robot learning from human teachers. *Synthesis Lectures on Artificial Intelligence and Machine Learning*, 8(3):1–121, 2014.

[3] L. C. Cobo, C. L. Isbell, and A. L. Thomaz. Object focused q-learning for autonomous agents. In *Proceedings of the 2013 international conference on Autonomous agents and multi-agent systems*, pages 1061–1068. International Foundation for Autonomous Agents and Multiagent Systems, 2013.

[4] S. Griffith, K. Subramanian, J. Scholz, C. Isbell, and A. L. Thomaz. Policy shaping: Integrating human feedback with reinforcement learning. In *Advances in Neural Information Processing Systems*, pages 2625–2633, 2013.

[5] J. MacGlashan, M. Babes-Vroman, M. desJardins, M. Littman, S. Muresan, S. Squire, S. Tellex, D. Arumugam, and L. Yang. Grounding english commands to reward functions. In *Proceedings of Robotics: Science and Systems*, Rome, Italy, July 2015.

[6] R. Maclin, J. Shavlik, L. Torrey, T. Walker, and E. Wild. Giving advice about preferred actions to reinforcement learners via knowledge-based kernel regression. In *Proceedings of the National Conference on Artificial intelligence*, volume 20, page 819. Menlo Park, CA; Cambridge, MA; London; AAAI Press; MIT Press; 1999, 2005.

[7] J. Togelius, S. Karakovskiy, and R. Baumgarten. The 2009 mario ai competition. In *Evolutionary Computation (CEC), 2010 IEEE Congress on*, pages 1–8. IEEE, 2010.

Reinforcement Learning Framework for Modeling Spatial Sequential Decisions under Uncertainty*

(Extended Abstract)

Truc Viet Le#, Siyuan Liu⋆, and Hoong Chuin Lau#
#School of Information Systems, Singapore Management University
⋆Smeal College of Business, Pennsylvania State University
#{trucviet.le.2012, hclau}@smu.edu.sg; ⋆siyuan@psu.edu

ABSTRACT

We consider the problem of trajectory prediction, where a trajectory is an *ordered* sequence of location visits and corresponding timestamps. The problem arises when an agent makes sequential decisions to visit a set of spatial locations of interest. Each location bears a stochastic utility and the agent has a limited budget to spend. Given the agent's observed *partial* trajectory, our goal is to predict the remaining trajectory. We propose a solution framework to the problem considering both the uncertainty of utility and the budget constraint. We use reinforcement learning (RL) to model the underlying decision processes and inverse RL to learn the utility distributions of the locations. We then propose two decision models to make predictions: one is based on long-term optimal planning of RL and another uses myopic heuristics. We finally apply the framework to predict real-world human trajectories and are able to explain the underlying processes of the observed actions.

Keywords

Reinforcement learning; trajectory prediction; stochastic utility; budget constraint; Markov decision process; sequential decisions.

1. INTRODUCTION

How does one decide to visit a set of locations in space? Assuming there are distinct points of interest (POIs), then the act of visiting them has to happen sequentially. We call it *spatial* sequential decision-making. It is reasonable to assume that each location bears a utility (reward) to the decision-maker that would not be fully realized until it is visited. Until then, utilities remain *uncertain* and reflect the agent's prior preferences. When making sequential decisions, a rational agent should also weigh in the long-term costs of visiting each of the locations in order to make an optimal plan, where "costs" here are assumed proportional to physical distances. Hence, answering the question above would require a model of the agent's sequential decisions for selecting locations, whose utilities remain uncertain and costs are dynamic, and weighing in their long-term consequences into the decision-making process.

*This research is supported by the National Research Foundation of Singapore under its International Research Centre @ Singapore Funding Initiative and administered by the IDM Programme Office, Media Development Authority.

Appears in: *Proceedings of the 15th International Conference on Autonomous Agents and Multiagent Systems (AAMAS 2016), J. Thangarajah, K. Tuyls, C. Jonker, S. Marsella (eds.), May 9–13, 2016, Singapore.*

In many practical situations, the agent typically has a limited amount of resources (e.g., time) to run its plan, which we call *budget*. Such a budget constraint can significantly shape the agent's decision-making process in non-obvious ways. In this paper, we propose a framework based on reinforcement learning [2] to model the agent's spatial sequential decision-making, taking into account the uncertainty of the utilities and the budget constraint. Using the framework, we could discover the underlying processes that drive real-world behaviors such as the conditions for making long-term optimal decisions. Such discoveries give insights into real-world human behaviors and the conditions for rationality that would help bridge the gap between human and machine intelligence [3].

Our motivation comes from the problem of predicting the *next* sequence of location visits (called *trajectory*) of a mobile agent knowing its current trajectory and past observed trajectories of other similar agents. In this paper, we develop on the framework proposed by Le *et al.* [1] for spatial decision modeling. However, we set out to predict an *ordered* sequence of an agent's future locations. Furthermore, our novelty is that we do not rely solely on generative models (e.g., HMMs) to generate sequential actions. Instead, we integrate them into a reinforcement learning framework to model an agent's optimal sequential decision-making. This enables us to explain the underlying processes of the predicted outcomes and the effects of budget constraint on the decision-making.

2. SOLUTION OVERVIEW

We propose an integrated framework to model and predict the next sequence of locations given the observed partial trajectory. The framework consists of two components: learning and prediction. Fig. 1a illustrates the overall proposed framework.

Learning. We first divide agents in the training set $\mathcal{S}$ into K clusters, where each cluster Cl_j $(1 \leq j \leq K)$ represents an agent *type*. Using the agents' observed features and the K clusters as class labels, we train a multi-class classifier (e.g., multinomial logistic regression). We also model the environment that the agents interact with as a finite set of states S, where each state $s \in S$ has a distinct vector of features $\mathbf{f}_s$. We use hidden Markov models (HMMs) to transform the observed trajectories into finite sequences of states. Such a representation can then be modeled as a Markov decision process (MDP). The utility of each action (i.e., location visit) can then be derived via the process of inverse reinforcement learning (IRL) [3] using the agents' observed actions (represented in the transition probability matrix P of the MDP). The final outcomes of IRL are the reward matrices $\mathbf{R}$.

Prediction. Given the observed partial trajectory and features of an agent i in the test set $\mathcal{T}$, we first predict i's type Cl_k^i using the trained classifier above. We then use the Viterbi algorithm to find

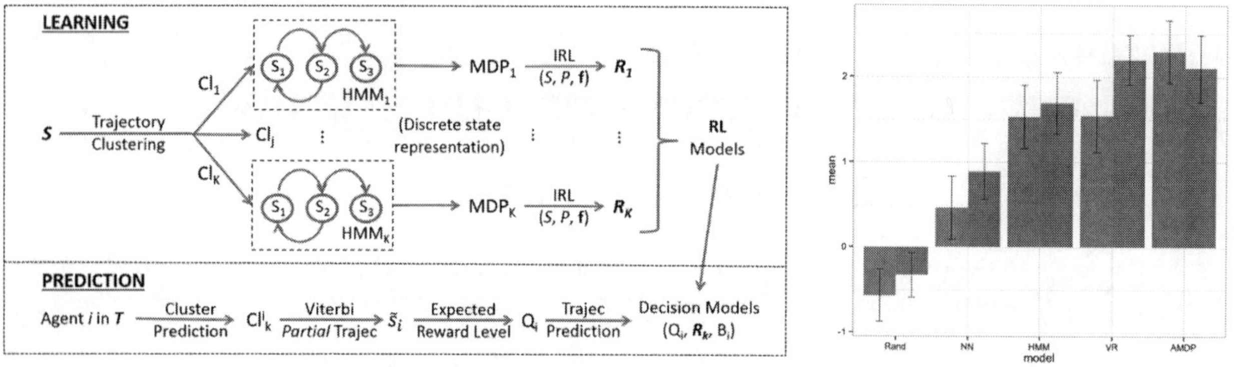

(a)

(b)

Figure 1: (a) The proposed framework to predict the remaining trajectory of test agent $i \in \mathcal{T}$ given observed partial trajectory $\tilde{s}_i$, budget B_i, and trajectories of the agents in the training set $\mathcal{S}$. (b) Similarity measures between the actual and predicted trajectories across the baselines: Random ("Rand"), Nearest Neighbor ("NN"), and HMM; and the proposed models: Value Ratio ("VR") and Adaptive MDP ("AMDP").

the most probable sequence of states $\tilde{s}_i$ for the observed trajectory. We are then able to model i's goal Q_i using the value function and predict the next sequence of visits that can meet this goal within budget B_i. We finally propose two decision models that take into account the uncertainty of the utilities (represented by the matrix $\mathbf{R}_k$ for each type k) and budget B_i. One is based on long-term optimal planning of RL and another uses myopic heuristics.

3. EXPERIMENTS

We collaborated with a large theme park in a major Asian city to conduct experiments and collect data from their visitors from January to April, 2014. The dataset $\mathcal{D}$ contains $3,867$ visitors' trajectories tracked using RFID devices. In the experiments, visitors pay upfront a fixed amount in order to redeem up to 14 attractions (POIs) in the theme park. Visitors can only redeem the attractions during the period from 9 a.m. to 7 p.m. on a chosen day.

We perform 5-fold cross-validation on $\mathcal{D}$. For each fold, the training set $\mathcal{S}$ is used for trajectory clustering and modeling. Our hierarchical clustering results in $K = 2$ clusters. For each agent $i \in T$, let l_i be i's final sequence length. We first predict i's type using its demographic features via a multinomial logistic model. Given i's partial trajectory of length k, we predict i's remaining trajectory while varying $k \in [2, l_i - 1]$. Let s_i^* and $\hat{s}_i$ be i's actual and predicted remaining trajectory, respectively. We use the Levenshtein edit distance to quantify their similarity Each match receives a fixed positive score and each mismatch incurs a negative penalty proportional to the distance between the two locations.

We evaluate two models based on the proposed framework: Adaptive MDP (AMDP), which is based on the long-term optimal planning of MDP, and Value Ratio (VR), which uses a greedy and myopic heuristic to make decisions. The baseline models are the same as in [1]. Our trajectory clustering reveals that the main differences between the two agent types are their temporal behaviors. Agent type 1 tends to arrive earlier and has their peak of visiting activities earlier in the day, and then (their visit frequency) sharply drops off. Whereas, agent type 2 tends to arrive much later and reaches their peak later, and then gradually declines. As a result, we call agent type 1 the "early birds" and agent type 2 the "latecomers".

Fig. 1b summarizes the experimental results, which shows the distributions of the similarity measures (i.e., the means and the 95% confidence bars) across the models. A higher mean similarity implies a more accurate prediction, on average. For type 1, it shows that the AMDP model has the most accurate prediction. The VR and HMM model both have about the same second best average prediction score. The Random baseline model has the least accurate average prediction followed by the NN model. For type 2, the AMDP model performs marginally worse than VR, even though still faring much better than the other baselines. In other words, the VR model makes the most accurate average prediction.

Because type 1 are the early birds and agent type 2 are the latecomers, agent type 1 has a much larger budget than agent type 2. Larger budget means more foresight and better long-term planning, which is what the AMDP model reflects: it embodies the long-term optimal policy of reinforcement learning. This indeed performs better than other short-sighted baselines. On the other hand, a smaller budget, which agent type 2 has, translates into less time for careful planning, which ultimately results in more myopic and suboptimal decisions (i.e., resorting to greedy strategies). This is reflected in the experimental results, where the greedy and myopic Value Ratio (VR) model performs the best for agent type 2.

4. CONCLUSION

In this paper, we address the problem of trajectory prediction using reinforcement learning to model the agent's sequential decisions. By doing so, we have discovered from real-world trajectories how people make decisions: they make more optimal decisions when given enough time to do so. This is perhaps not surprising in retrospect, because it is reasonable that foresighted decisions and careful plans need time to coordinate, while myopic ones do not (as only the immediate rewards are considered). On the other hand, this also validates our framework's ability to model real-world behaviors by finding out what makes reasonable sense in real life.

REFERENCES

[1] T. V. Le, S. Liu, H. C. Lau, and R. Krishnan. Predicting bundles of spatial locations from learning revealed preference data. In *Proceedings of the 2015 International Conference on Autonomous Agents and Multiagent Systems*, pages 1121–1129. International Foundation for Autonomous Agents and Multiagent Systems, 2015.

[2] R. S. Sutton and A. G. Barto. *Reinforcement Learning: An Introduction*. MIT Press, Cambridge, MA, USA, 1998.

[3] B. D. Ziebart, A. L. Maas, J. A. Bagnell, and A. K. Dey. Human behavior modeling with maximum entropy inverse optimal control. In *AAAI Spring Symposium: Human Behavior Modeling*, page 92, 2009.

Simulation Summarization

(Extended Abstract)

Nidhi Parikh, Madhav V. Marathe, Samarth Swarup
Network Dynamics and Simulation Science Lab,
Biocomplexity Institute of Virginia
Virginia Tech,
Blacksburg, VA, USA.
{nidhip,mmarathe,swarup}@vbi.vt.edu

ABSTRACT

As increasingly large-scale multiagent simulations are being implemented, new methods are becoming necessary for concisely summarizing the results of a simulation run. Here we pose this as the problem of simulation summarization: how to extract the causally-relevant states from the trajectories of the agents. We present a simple algorithm to compress agent trajectories through state space by identifying the state transitions which have significant impact on the final outcome of interest. We apply it to a complex simulation of a major disaster in an urban area and present results.

Keywords

simulation summarization, causal states

1. INTRODUCTION

Large-scale multiagent simulations are becoming increasingly common in many domains of scientific interest, including economics, epidemiology, social science, and disaster response. These simulations have complex models of agents, environments, infrastructures, and interactions.

Often the goal is to study a hypothetical situation in a detailed and realistic virtual setting, with the intention of making policy recommendations. However, analyzing results for such simulations pose some challenges:

1. They are computationally too expensive to run enough number of times to obtain the statistical power.
2. Often the kind of interventions to evaluate are not known. Ideally, we would like to run simulation to get some insights that help suggest interventions.
3. Large-scale simulations can generate much more data in each simulation run than goes into the simulation.

As a first step towards addressing these kinds of problems, we introduce the problem of simulation summarization. Our perspective on summarizing a multiagent simulation is that the summary should capture the causally-relevant states of the simulation. By "causally-relevant", we mean agent states that have a measurable impact on outcomes of interest, even if the impact is delayed. In line with this intuition, we adapt the approach of "causal states" for stochastic process.

Appears in: *Proceedings of the 15th International Conference on Autonomous Agents and Multiagent Systems (AAMAS 2016), J. Thangarajah, K. Tuyls, C. Jonker, S. Marsella (eds.), May 9–13, 2016, Singapore.*

2. CAUSAL STATES

Consider a stochastic process as a sequence of random variables X_t, drawn from a discrete alphabet, $\mathcal{A}$. Let $\overleftarrow{X} = X_{-\infty} \dots X_{t-2}X_{t-1}X_t$ and $\overrightarrow{X} = X_{t+1}X_{t+2}\dots X_{\infty}$ denote the *past* and the *future* of the sequence, respectively.

Crutchfield et. al. [1] suggested a simple method for modeling a stochastic process that captures the mutual information that is communicated from the past $\overleftarrow{X}$ to the future $\overrightarrow{X}$ of the sequence: group together all the histories that predict the same future. This gives rise to a state machine, called an ϵ-machine, defined as:

$$\epsilon(\overleftarrow{x}) = \{\overleftarrow{x}' | Pr(\overrightarrow{X}|\overleftarrow{x}) = Pr(\overrightarrow{X}|\overleftarrow{x}')\}. \quad (1)$$

Shalizi et. al. have presented an algorithm for learning ϵ-machine from time series, known as *Causal State Splitting Reconstruction* (CSSR) [4]. It learns an ϵ-machine as a Hidden Markov Model (HMM) in an incremental fashion. The HMM is initialized with one state which consists of null history of length 0. The algorithm tests the distribution over the next symbol given progressively longer past sequences. Let L be the length of the past sequences considered so far. At the next step, it looks at sequences of length $L+1$, e.g., ax^L where x^L is a sequence of length L and $a \in \mathcal{A}$. If ax^L belongs to the same causal state as x^L, then we would have,

$$Pr(X_t|ax^L) = Pr(X_t|\hat{S} = \hat{\epsilon}(x^L)), \quad (2)$$

where $\hat{S}$ is the current estimate of the causal state to which x^L belongs. This hypothesis can be tested using a statistical test such as the Kolmogorov-Smirnov test. If the test shows that the LHS and RHS of equation 2 are statistically significantly different distributions, then CSSR tries to match the sequence ax^L with all the other causal states estimated so far. If $Pr(X_t|ax^L)$ turns out to be significantly different in all cases, a new causal state is created and ax^L is assigned to it. This process is carried out up to some length L_{max}.

3. OUR APPROACH

Our approach adapts the causal state formalism by treating the trajectory of each agent in the simulation as an instance of the same stochastic process. Let N be the number of agents in the simulation. State of an agent a is denoted by a k-dimensional state vector $\mathbf{x_a}(t) = [x_1(t), x_2(t), \dots x_k(t)]^\intercal$, which evolves over time. Let d_i be the number of possible values x_i can take and hence $d = d_1 \times d_2 \times \dots \times d_k$ is the number of ways in which agent state can evolve. Let the outcome variable for agent a be denoted by y_a.

Our goal is to compress the trajectory of each agent through state space to a small number of important states that have a significant impact on the outcomes we care about.

At each time step t, the agent population is devided into a set of clusters, $C(t) = \{C_1(t) \cup C_2(t) \cup \ldots C_m(t)\}$. Initially, all the agents belong to one cluster. At each next time step, the state of each agent can change in d ways. Hence, an arbitrary cluster of agents, $C_i(t)$ can split into up to d groups at time step $t+1$. But not all of these changes may have a significant impact on the outcome. We treat each group derived from $C_i(t)$ as a candidate cluster, $CC_{i,j}(t+1)$, where $j \in 1 \ldots d$. At each step, we compare $Pr(Y|C_i(t))$ with $Pr(Y|CC_{i,j}(t+1)$ using the Kolmogorov-Smirnov test. Our null hypothesis (analogous to equation 2) is,

$$Pr(Y|CC_{i,j}(t+1)) = Pr(Y|C_i(t)). \quad (3)$$

We also introduce a parameter δ, which is a threshold on the "effect size", measured as the KL-divergence between $Pr(Y|C_i(t))$ and $Pr(Y|CC_{i,j}(t+1))$. If the null hypothesis is rejected at a level α (say 0.001) and $D_{KL}(Pr(Y|C_i(t))|| Pr(Y|CC_{i,j}(t+1))) > \delta$, then candidate cluster $CC_{i,j}(t+1)$ is accepted as a new cluster at time $t+1$. If none of the candidate clusters at time step $t+1$ are accepted, then $C_i(t)$ is added to the set of clusters for time step $t+1$.

Thus, the entire simulation is decomposed into a tree structure of agent clusters. Furthermore, each cluster splits only when the corresponding state change is informative about the final outcome of concern. The trajectory of each agent traces a path through this tree structure. We compress the trajectory by retaining only those time steps at which the cluster to which the agent belongs splits off from its parent cluster. The set of compressed agent trajectories constitutes our summary representation of the simulation.

The parameter δ allows to control the number of new clusters formed and consequently, the amount of compression. A high value of δ will retain only the clusters which have a large difference in outcomes from their parent clusters.

4. EXPERIMENTS

We apply our algorithm to a multiagent simulation of a hypothetical improvised nuclear device detonation in Washington DC [3]. Our simulation consists of a large, detailed "synthetic information system" [2] which represents the human population of the region and detailed models of four infrastructures: cell phone communication system, power system, transportation system, and healthcare system.

Agents are defined by a number of state variables. However, for the purpose of summarization, we focus on six variables: health (modeled on a 0 to 7 range where 0 is dead and 7 corresponds to full health), behavior (six behaviors mentioned below, plus categories indicating if agent is in healthcare location or out of the affected area), whether the agent has received an emergency broadcast (EBR), the agent's exposure to radiation, whether the agent has received treatment, and the agent's distance from the ground zero.

Agent behavior is conceptually based on the formalism of decentralized semi-Markov decision process (Dec-SMDP) with communication using the framework of options. High level behaviors are modeled as collection of options. We model six behaviors: household reconstitution (HRO), evacuation, shelter-seeking, healthcare-seeking, panic, and aid & assist. These high level behavior options are policies over low level actions which are to call, text or move. These actions are supported by infrastructural systems. Details of agent design and behavior can be found in [3].

4.1 Results

Due to limitation of space, we only present results from one value of KL-divergence threshold, $\delta = 5$. Compressed trajectories of agents are stored in a database table along with the expected value of final health state which can be used to query any subpopulation of interest.

We evaluate two queries that identify top 10 transitions in first three hours where current health state remains same (so improvement is not due to current health state) but the expected health state is improved or reduced, ordered by expected improvement or reduction in descending order.

Results show that for agents who are close to ground zero and in health state 4 or 5, reaching healthcare location early helps to improve health, even if the exposure level is high. For agents in healthstate 5 to 7, who are far from ground zero though with medium exposure, getting out of the area helps. Also, for agents in health state 7, who are far from ground zero, with medium exposure, and panicking, receiving EBR helps (as it provides information about the event and recommends sheltering).

For agents who are currently in a full health, close to ground zero, and have high exposure level, doing household reconstitution (HRO) reduces their expected outcome. Even if the current health state is good, this accounts for the delayed effect of radiation. For people who are already in low health (health state 3), panicking or seeking healthcare (which makes them travel to healthcare location and get exposed to more radiation) deteriorates expected health state, even if far from ground zero.

Acknowledgments

This work has been supported in part by DTRA CNIMS Contract HDTRA1-11-D-0016-0001, DTRA Grant HDTRA1-11-1-0016, NIH MIDAS Grant 5U01GM070694-11, NIH Grant 1R01GM109718, NSF NetSE Grant CNS-1011769, and NSF SDCI Grant OCI-1032677.

REFERENCES

[1] J. P. Crutchfield and K. Young. Inferring statistical complexity. *Phys Rev Lett*, 63(2):105–108, 1989.

[2] M. Marathe, H. Mortveit, N. Parikh, and S. Swarup. Prescriptive analytics using synthetic information. In W. H. Hsu, editor, *Emerging Trends in Predictive Analytics: Risk Management and Decision Making*. IGI Global, 2014.

[3] N. Parikh, S. Swarup, P. E. Stretz, C. M. Rivers, B. L. Lewis, M. V. Marathe, S. G. Eubank, C. L. Barrett, K. Lum, and Y. Chungbaek. Modeling human behavior in the aftermath of a hypothetical improvised nuclear detonation. In *Proceedings of the International Conference on Autonomous Agents and Multiagent Systems (AAMAS)*, Saint Paul, MN, USA, May 2013.

[4] C. R. Shalizi and K. L. Shalizi. Blind construction of optimal nonlinear recursive predictors for discrete sequences. In M. Chickering and J. Halpern, editors, *Proceedings of the Twentieth Conference on Uncertainty in Artificial Intelligence*, pages 504–511, Banff, Canada, 2004.

An Autonomous Agent for Learning Spatiotemporal Models of Human Daily Activities

(Extended Abstract)

Shan Gao
Interdisciplinary Graduate School
Nanyang Technological University
50 Nanyang Ave, Singapore 639798
gaos0009@e.ntu.edu.sg

Ah-Hwee Tan
School of Computer Engineering
Nanyang Technological University
50 Nanyang Ave, Singapore 639798
asahtan@ntu.edu.sg

ABSTRACT

Activities of Daily Living (ADLs) refer to activities performed by individuals on a daily basis. As ADLs are indicatives of a person's habits, lifestyle, and well being, learning the knowledge of people's ADL routine has great values in the healthcare and consumer domains. In this paper, we propose an autonomous agent, named Agent for Spatia-Temporal Activity Pattern Modeling (ASTAPM), being able to learn spatial and temporal patterns of human ADLs. ASTAPM utilises a self-organizing neural network model named Spatiotemporal - Adaptive Resonance Theory (ST-ART). ST-ART is capable of integrating multimodal contextual information, involving the time and space, wherein the ADL are performed. Empirical experiments have been conducted to assess the performance of ASTAPM in terms of accuracy and generalization.

General Terms

Algorithms, Design, Experimentation

Keywords

Fusion ART, Activity pattern, spatiotemporal features

1. INTRODUCTION

Activities of daily living (ADLs), as used by health care professionals, refers to daily self care activities performed by an individual in his or her place of residence, outdoor, or both. In elderly health care, ADLs are usually used to measure the functional status of elderly. Researchers, e.g. [2] [3], have used the topic model approach to discover activity patterns, wherein topics are pulled from a document using a bag-of-words approach. However, these works mainly study the relationships between low level activities and ADLs. We have proposed ADLART architecture [1] which incorporates the fusion ART (Adaptive Resonance Theory) model [5] to learn ADL sequence patterns. Although ADLART made various applications possible, there are some limitations. Firstly, ADLART could not associate personalized ADL spatial and temporal information to the ADL categories. Secondly, due to its data structure, ADLART uses only the starting time of ADLs and does not capture the ADL duration information.

In this paper, we propose a self-organizing neural model named SpatioTemporal - Adaptive Resonance Theory (ST-ART). ST-ART is capable of learning the personalized spatial temporal information of ADLs by encoding the space, time, and activity information across multimodal pattern channels. With the extended spatiotemporal feature, compared with ADLART, the ST-ART model has a better accuracy on classification in spatiotemporal domains. Based on ST-ART, we propose an autonomous agent named Agent for Spatia-Temporal Activity Pattern Modeling, or ASTAPM, which performs daily ADL pattern learning and spatiotemporal information retrieval.

Appears in: *Proceedings of the 15th International Conference on Autonomous Agents and Multiagent Systems (AAMAS 2016), J. Thangarajah, K. Tuyls, C. Jonker, S. Marsella (eds.), May 9–13, 2016, Singapore.*

2. FUSION ART

Various models of ART and their supervised learning versions are used in the pattern analysis and recognition tasks [4]. Within the family of ART models, there is a group of networks known as Fusion ART [5] or multi-channel adaptive resonance associative map (multi-channel ARAM) [7], which formulates cognitive nodes associating multi-modal patterns across multiple input channels. Fusion ART models can also be used for reinforcement learning. For example, a three channel fusion ART called FALCON is described in [6] [8]. Self-organizing is another important feature of fusion ART. When no learnt node is matched, the network could autonomously use the uncommitted node to represent the new pattern. The architecture of a typical fusion ART model is shown in Figure 1.

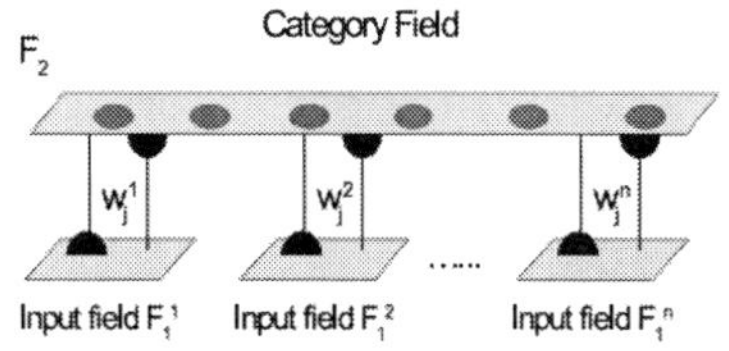

Figure 1: The generic fusion ART architecture.

3. ST-ART ARCHITECTURE

SpatioTemporal - Adaptive Resonance Theory (ST-ART) is a four-layer neural network, as shown in Figure 2. The first layer represents the low level temporal information in two input fields, namely the time field and the day field. The second layer is the ADL spatiotemporal layer, consisting of the ADL type field, temporal field, and spatial field. The third layer is the spatiotemporal ADL (ST ADL) layer, wherein the ST ADL category nodes encode the associations of ADL types and spatiotemporal information. Finally, the highest layer is the ADL routine layer, wherein the ADL routine nodes encode the sets of ST ADLs over a day.

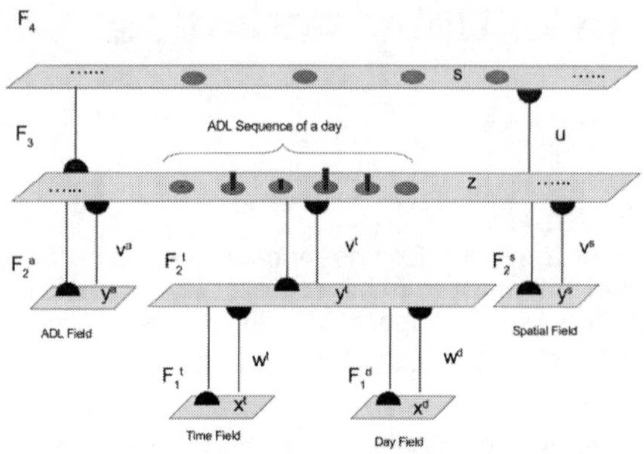

Figure 2: ST-ART model

4. ASTAPM

Based on ST-ART described in Section 3, ASTAPM proactively learns the spatiotemporal patterns of ADLs and ADL daily routines through a training process. At each level, if there is one wining node satisfies the match function, e.g., resonance occurred, related weights will be updated, otherwise a new node is created for the input pattern. The process of learning spatiotemporal patterns and daily routine across the four layers is summarized in Algorithm 1.

Algorithm 1 ASTAPM training process

Require: A sequence of ADLs each in the form of $(\mathbf{x}^t, \mathbf{x}^d, \mathbf{y}^a, \mathbf{y}^s)$
Ensure: Learn an ADL routine
for each input ADL $(\mathbf{x}^t, \mathbf{x}^d, \mathbf{y}^a, \mathbf{y}^s)$ **do**
  Compute activity vector $\mathbf{y}^t$ in F_2^t layer using input patterns $\mathbf{x}^t$ and $\mathbf{x}^d$
  The winning F_2^t node learns a temporal category from $\mathbf{x}^t$ and $\mathbf{x}^d$
  Update activity vector $\mathbf{z}$ in F_3 layer using input patterns $\mathbf{y}^t, \mathbf{y}^a$, and $\mathbf{y}^s$
  The winning F_3 node learns a ST ADL category from $\mathbf{y}^t, \mathbf{y}^a$, and $\mathbf{y}^s$
end for
Update activity vector $\mathbf{s}$ in F_4 layer using input patterns $\mathbf{z}$
The winning F_4 node learns an ADL routine category from $\mathbf{z}$

5. EXPERIMENTS

5.1 Methodology

To evaluate the performance of ST-ART, we designed a simulation environment to conduct experiments. The simulator generates daily ADL samples based on a person's profile over a period of one year. The purpose of the experiment is to study the spatiotemporal ADL categories created in the F_4 layer by using different vigilant values.

5.2 Daily routine categories generation

In this experiment, we look at the learning process from F_3, the ADL category layer containing the learnt spatial temporal ADL categories that a person performed in his daily life, to F_4, the ADL daily routine category layer. This step is to learn ADL daily sequences or ADL daily routines that could be used to describe his personal behaviour or lifestyle. After training with the simulation data of 365 samples, the F_3 layer learnt the spatiotemporal ADL categories. In order to obtain generalized personal daily routine patterns, we aim to identify a low vigilance value, for generating roughly 50 or less ADL routine categories. After conducting experiments with different vigilance values, we found by using a vigilance value of 0.8, ST-ART learnt a total of 46 ADL daily routine categories. The top frequency categories are listed in Table 1.

Table 1: Top frequency ADL daily routines learnt by ST-ART

Index	Count	Routine Interpretation
1	64	Normal Weekday
2	49	Normal Weekend
3	41	Exercise on Weekday
4	28	Outing on Weekend
5	19	No breakfast day

6. CONCLUSION

In this paper, a spatiotemporal fusion ART neural network model (ST-ART) is used to model the spatial and temporal information of human ADLs. The ST-ART model is capable of learning multimodal contextual information. An autonomous agent utilizing the ST-ART model is proposed and named Agent for Spatia-Temporal Activity Pattern Modeling, or ASTAPM. Simulation experiments are conducted to evaluate the ASTAPM agent. In the future, experiments on real data will be conducted.

Acknowledgment

This research is supported by the National Research Foundation Singapore under its Interactive Digital Media (IDM) Strategic Research Programme.

REFERENCES

[1] S. Gao and A.-H. Tan. User daily activity pattern learning: A multi-memory modeling approach. In *2014 International Joint Conference on Neural Networks*, pages 1542–1548, 2014.

[2] T. Huynh, M. Fritz, and B. Schiele. Discovery of activity patterns using topic models. In *Proceedings of the 10th International Conference on Ubiquitous Computing*, pages 10–19, 2008.

[3] E. Kim, S. Helal, and D. Cook. Human activity recognition and pattern discovery. *Pervasive Computing, IEEE*, 9(1):48–53, 2010.

[4] A.-H. Tan. Adaptive resonance associative map. *Neural Networks*, 8(3):437–446, 1995.

[5] A.-H. Tan, G. A. Carpenter, and S. Grossberg. Intelligence through interaction: Towards a unified theory for learning. In *Advances in Neural Networks–ISNN 2007*, pages 1094–1103. Springer, 2007.

[6] A.-H. Tan, N. Lu, and D. Xiao. Integrating temporal difference methods and self-organizing neural networks for reinforcement learning with delayed evaluative feedback. *IEEE Transactions on Neural Networks*, 19(2):230–244, 2008.

[7] A.-H. Tan and H.-S. V. Soon. Concept hierarchy memory model: A neural architecture for conceptual knowledge representation, learning, and commonsense reasoning. *International Journal of Neural Systems*, 7(3):305, 1996.

[8] D. Wang and A.-H. Tan. Creating autonomous adaptive agents in a real-time first-person shooter computer game. *IEEE Transactions on Computational Intelligence and AI in Games*, 7(2):123–138, 2015.

Policy Shaping in Domains with Multiple Optimal Policies (Extended Abstract)

Himanshu Sahni †
himanshu@gatech.edu

Brent Harrison †
brent.harrison@cc.gatech.edu

Kaushik Subramanian †
ksubrama@cc.gatech.edu

Thomas Cederborg †
thomascederborgsemail@gmail.com

Charles Isbell †
isbell@cc.gatech.edu

Andrea Thomaz §
athomaz@ece.utexas.edu

ABSTRACT

In many domains, there exist multiple ways for an agent to achieve optimal performance. Feedback may be provided along one or more of them to aid learning. In this work, we investigate whether humans have a preference towards providing feedback along one optimal policy over the other in two gridworld domains. We find that for the domain with significant risk to exploration, 60% of our participants prefer to discourage the agent's exploration along the risky portion of the state space, while 40% state that they have no preference. We also use the interactive reinforcement learning algorithm Policy Shaping to evaluate the performance of simulated oracles with a number of feedback strategies. We find that certain domain traits, such as risk during exploration and number of optimal policies play an important role in determining the best performing feedback strategy.

Keywords

interactive machine learning; learning from critique; reinforcement learning; policy shaping

1. INTRODUCTION

In real world environments, an expert may not always be at hand to train the behavior of a human guided learning agent. Thus, such agents must be able to learn from feedback by non-expert teachers. Policy Shaping [2] attempts to use feedback directly as policy advise and combine it with standard reinforcement learning approaches such as Bayesian Q-learning. Recently, Policy Shaping has been shown to be robust to noisy and sparse human feedback [1]. Cederborg et al. discovered that human provided critique led to better performance than the simulated teacher on two different pac-man domains. They state that the difference in performance could be because humans seemed to give positive feedback to any strategy that appeared optimal. The simulated teacher, on the other hand, had a single fixed optimal policy that was computed beforehand. It may also be the case that certain optimal policies can be learnt faster and the human teachers were guiding the agent towards them. Their experimental setup was not designed to verify these conjectures, since the finding came as a surprise. In this work, we specifically investigate whether humans employ differing feedback strategies in two different gridworld domains. Knowledge of whether different people chose different optimal policies to teach in the same domain can be used to lend us greater insight into designing algorithms learning from human critique. We conduct a user study in which participants are asked to provide feedback to an agent acting on a pre-determined set of policies. In a post-study interview, we ask the users which, if any, optimal policy they gave preference to during teaching. We find that users do have feedback preferences in one of the domains.

The findings of the user study motivate an in-depth analysis of how learning performance is impacted by choice of feedback strategies over multiple optimal policies. A complicated task in a real-world environment will likely have many ways of solving it. A non-expert, end user critiquing the agent may provide feedback for all of them at the same time. Or they may choose to ignore all but one in order to simplify their task of teaching the agent. A human teacher may also try to adapt their feedback to encourage more of what the agent is already doing correctly. Our hypothesis is that different tasks will have different optimal feedback strategies. Therefore, an understanding of which strategies lead to best performance in which domains is important.

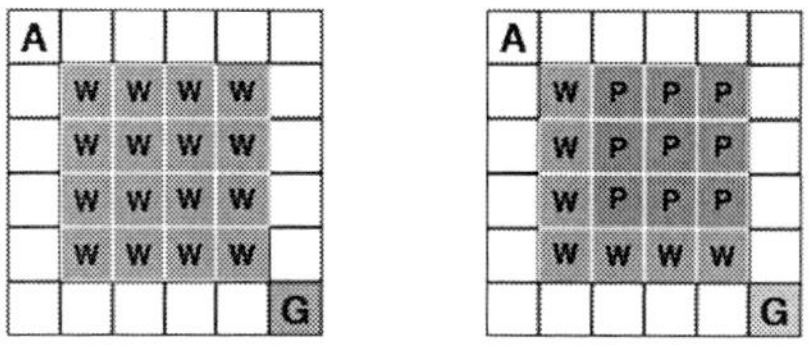

(a) *blocks* domain (b) *pits* domain

Figure 1: The gridworld domains used in user studies and simulated experiments. The *blocks* domain has two identical optimal policies while in *pits* one of them is clearly better for learning in combination with a random exploration strategy.

2. RELATED WORK

Interactive machine learning is emerging as a promising field with many useful applications. In the context of reinforcement learning, prior work has attempted to convert feedback signals into rewards, akin to those coming from the environment. However, human feedback may be noisy, inconsistent, and not easily translated into rewards. An alternative solution has been to use feedback to influence the policy, instead of the reward signal. Policy Shaping [2] ex-

Appears in: *Proceedings of the 15th International Conference on Autonomous Agents and Multiagent Systems (AAMAS 2016), J. Thangarajah, K. Tuyls, C. Jonker, S. Marsella (eds.), May 9–13, 2016, Singapore.*

†College of Computing, Georgia Institute of Technology
§Department of Electrical and Computer Engineering University of Texas at Austin

tracts policy level information directly from feedback and combines it with environment based signals.

This work explores the effects of using Policy Shaping in situations where there are multiple optimal ways of behaving. A modification to Q-learning, $\bar{Q}$-learning, performs optimally when combined with an exploration strategy [3]. John notices that paths along the wall of a gridworld can be faster to learn as a sub-optimal move has less of a chance of sending the agent further away from the goal. Our work explores a similar effect in the setting of learning from critique. We try to answer the question: when there are multiple solutions to a task, all equally optimal, what effect does feedback strategy have over learning performance?

3. HUMAN FEEDBACK PREFERENCE

The goal of our user study was to determine whether people have differing preferences over feedback strategies when faced with multiple optimal policies in the same domain. We recruited 10 participants, all graduate students not familiar with this project, who were presented with an agent acting on the same pre-determined policies in the *pits* and the *blocks* domains (Figure 1). The participants were instructed to provide positive or negative critique (Figure 2).

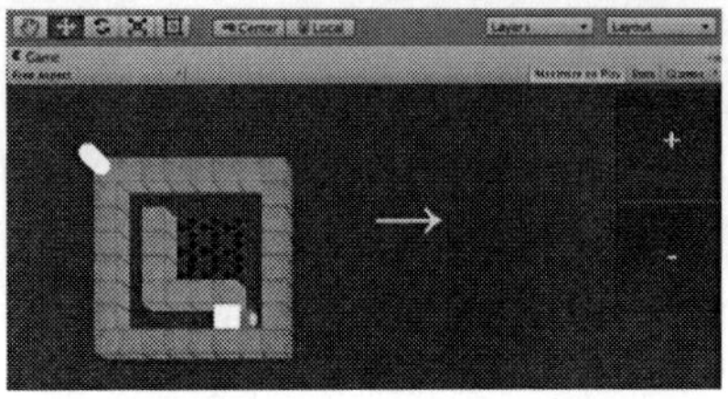

Figure 2: Feedback interface. The agent is represented by the white, the goal by the green and the pits by the red blocks. An arrow indicates the most recent action.

At the end of the study, the subjects are asked a small set of questions about their preferred feedback strategy. In the *pits* domain 6 of our participants said that they preferred the safer path to the goal. The most common reason was that it was "less dangerous" or it had "less chance of [the agent] falling into the pit". The remaining 4 said that they had no preference over the path the agent took. They said, "[I] wanted the agent to reach the goal as fast as possible" or "feedback I was giving was based on its [agent's] first action". Participant 6 said, "I wanted the agent to know more than one path". All participants said that they had no preference between the paths in the *blocks* domain and that "they looked identical". Since users may chose different feedback strategies depending on the domain, this leads us to the question of how this affects learning performance. We explore this using simulated oracles in the next section.

4. ORACLE PERFORMANCE

We study a carefully designed set of teachers that span a range of evaluation behaviors. Automated oracles provide feedback consistent with each behavior and allow us fine control over its frequency. Broadly speaking, we consider four different kinds of feedback strategies. The *all policy* oracle provides positive critique along all optimal policies while the *single policy* oracle does only along one. The *single path* oracle provides positive critique along only one optimal trajectory through the state space. In states not on the trajectory, it does not provide any feedback at all. The *adaptive* oracle is more likely to positively critique optimal actions that the agent has tried before.

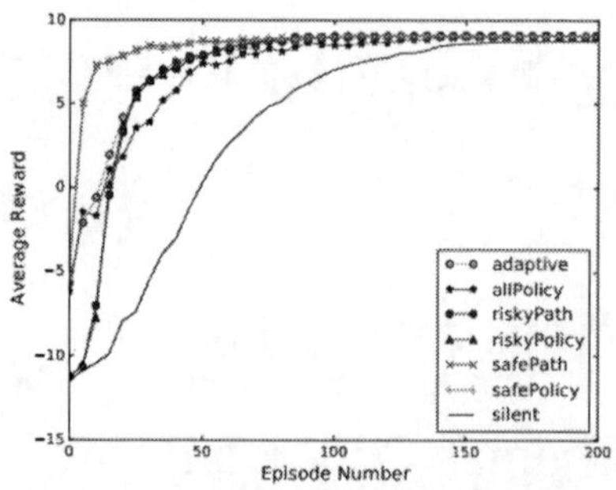

Figure 3: Average rewards (1000 independent trials) obtained by each oracle in the *pits* domain. T-tests are used to ensure statistical significance. *Risky policy* and *risky path* behave as *single path* oracles on the path along the pits.

Figure 3 shows the performance of the oracles and when no feedback is provided (*silent*) in the *pits* domain. As expected, the *safe path* and *safe policy* oracles converge in the least number of episodes. Interestingly, the *risky path* and *risky policy* oracles also converge faster than the *all policy* oracle. A one-sample t-test rejects the null hypothesis that the average reward achieved by *risky policy* oracle is optimal until episode 109 ($p < 0.05$). For *all policy* oracle this occurs at episode 177. The *risky policy* oracle is curtailing the agent's exploration and it learns the *risky policy* faster than it manages to learn a policy over the entire state space. In a larger version of the *blocks* domain with wider corridors, the *single path* oracle is slowest to converge ($p < 0.05$). This may be due to the large number of optimal policies of which only a single path is being critiqued.

5. CONCLUSIONS AND FUTURE WORK

In the *pits* domain, four of our users stated that they have no preference over the two paths. With simulated oracles, we have shown that in fact the *all policy* feedback strategy is slower to achieve optimal reward than any of the *single path* ones. In general, it may be the case that the policy which is easiest to learn is not the one the teacher is interested in providing feedback on. A lot of computational and human effort may be wasted in exploring difficult to learn optimal policies before positive results are seen. In depth exploration of best performing teaching strategies in different domains is a fruitful and important direction of future research.

Acknowledgments

This work was funded under ONR grant number N000141410003

REFERENCES

[1] T. Cederborg, I. Grover, C. L. Isbell, and A. L. Thomaz. Policy Shaping With Human Teachers. In *Proceedings of the Twenty-Fourth International Joint Conference on Artificial Intelligence (IJCAI)*, 2015.

[2] S. Griffith, K. Subramanian, J. Scholz, C. Isbell, and A. L. Thomaz. Policy shaping: Integrating human feedback with reinforcement learning. In *Advances in Neural Information Processing Systems 26*, pages 2625–2633. Curran Associates, Inc., 2013.

[3] G. H. John. When the best move isn't optimal: Q-learning with exploration. In *Proceedings of the Twelfth National Conference on Artificial Intelligence*, page 1464, 1994.

Using Facial Expression and Body Language to Express Attitude for Non-Humanoid Robot

(Extended Abstract)

Mei Si
Department of Cognitive Science
Rensselaer Polytechnic Institute
sim@rpi.edu

Joseph Dean McDaniel
Department of Computer Science
Rensselaer Polytechnic Institute
mcdanj2@rpi.edu

ABSTRACT

This work investigates designing social interactions for robots that are large and sturdy, and whose bodies may be not built proportionally to human. A modified version of Baxter robot was used. We examined the usage of facial expression, social dialogue, and arm movement to make people feel comfortable to interact with the robot. Our results show that body language may play a more important role than facial expressions for such robots, and that the synchronization between speech and body movements is critical.

Categories and Subject Descriptors

J.4 [**Computer Applications**]: Social and Behavioral Sciences

Keywords

Robot Human Interaction

1. INTRODUCTION

In recent years, there has been an increasing interest in designing social robots to interact with people. Most social robots currently being used are light-weight and much smaller in size compared to people, such as Nao, Hanson, and robotic pets. This makes them naturally look non-threatening. In contrast, many robots used by rescue teams, law enforcement, and the military are designed with functionality as a higher priority, and thus, they do not appear very human-like and have limited means to support natural human-robot interaction. They are sometimes referred to as appearance constrained robots [1]. One of the challenges we face in designing the movements of a large and sturdy robot is how to make people feel comfortable interacting with it. To enable long-term natural interaction between robots and users, we strive to not only rely on safe, and dependable robotic movements, but also leverage research studying human-robot interaction and human social interaction to create a positive psychological experience with trust and comfort.

In this work, we started this exploration using a modified version of Baxter, a dual-arm robot by Rethink Robotics [2].

Appears in: *Proceedings of the 15th International Conference on Autonomous Agents and Multiagent Systems (AAMAS 2016), J. Thangarajah, K. Tuyls, C. Jonker, S. Marsella (eds.), May 9–13, 2016, Singapore.*

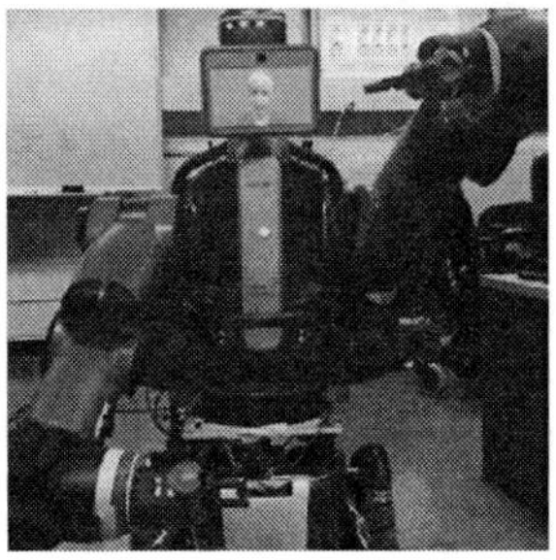

Figure 1: Modified Baxter Robot with Face

The robot by itself is 3'1" in height. Its arms can reach out 41". Though the arms have similar joints as a human's arms, the robot overall has a different upper body proportion from that of a human. Its body looks sturdy, with a weight of 165 lbs. The robot was installed on top of an electronic wheelchair, which makes its actual height similar to an adult. Figure 1 shows a picture of the robot. We conducted an empirical study and examined how using facial expressions, body movement and social dialogue can make people feel more comfortable to interact with the robot. In particular, because the robot's head display may need to be used for purposes other than showing an animated face, we investigated the importance of the robot having a face.

2. PROCEDURE AND IMPLEMENTATION

Each subject interacted with the robot individually. During the interaction, the robot first introduced itself, and then asked the subjects 10 questions about their lives or interests (to which they replied verbally on 7-point scales) and commented on their responses after all the questions had been answered. This part of the interaction lasted approximately 5 minutes. Afterward, the robot prompted the subject to approach it and shake its right hand but assured that they could decline to do so if they felt uncomfortable. If the subject decided to shake its hand, the robot would extend its arm as the subject approached.

The robot used text to speech. Its facial expressions and arm movements were designed by the experimenters to be synchronized with its speech and express a friendly attitude. ROS and Robot Raconteur [4] services were used for controlling the robot's arm movements. The Virtual Human Toolkit [3] was used for controlling the robot's facial expressions. We used the face and voice of a female char-

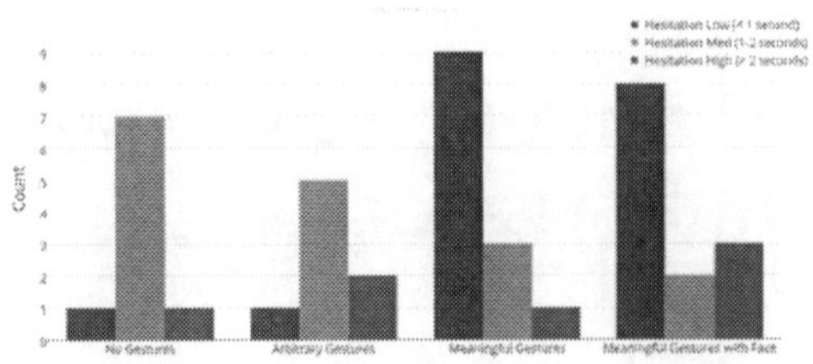

Figure 2: Hesitation to Shake Hands

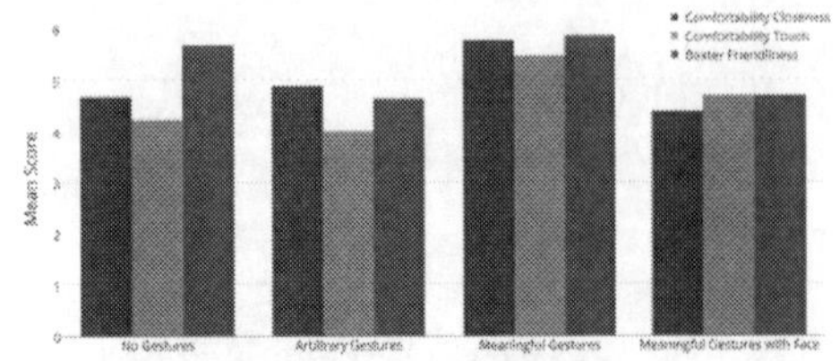

Figure 3: Subjective Ratings of the Robot

acter named Rachel from the toolkit. A Windows Forms application was developed in C#/.NET for communicating with these services and controlling the robot during the interaction. The experiment was conducted in a "Wizard of Oz"-style. When the subjects were asked questions, such as how difficult their schoolwork was or how often they listened to music, the experimenter recorded the answers and sent verbal and non-verbal commands to the robot using the Windows Forms application.

3. EXPERIMENTAL DESIGN

43 undergraduate students were recruited to participate. They were randomly assigned to one of four groups in a between-subjects design. **No Gestures ($N = 9$):** The robot used just voice and had neither arm movement nor facial expression during the interaction. **Arbitrary Gestures ($N = 8$):** The robot moved its arms randomly while speaking. **Meaningful Gestures ($N = 13$):** The robot's arm movements were synchronized with its speech. **Meaningful Gestures with Face ($N = 13$):** The robot's arm movements and facial expressions were both synchronized with its speech.

We measured a categorical dependent variable, **"hesitation,"** which represents how long the subject hesitated before approaching the robot when prompted to shake hands: "low" for less than 1s; "medium" for 1 and 2s, and "high" for more than 2 seconds, or looked to the experimenter for confirmation. After the interaction, all subjects rated on 7-point Likert scales for their comfortability interacting with the robot at a close distance ("comfortability closeness"), and their comfortability letting the robot use its arm to touch them ("comfortability touch"). In addition, for answering one of the questions the subjects rated how friendly the robot seemed ("friendliness"), which was also used as a dependent variable.

4. RESULTS AND DISCUSSION

A chi-square test of independence was conducted to examine the relation between the experiment condition and the amount of hesitation. The test showed a significant relationship, $X^2(6) = 15.46$, $p = 0.02$. No subjects declined to shake hands with the robot, but they differed significantly in the amount of time to approach the robot after the request. Of the standardized residual values, the differences were significant at the 0.05 level between the "Meaningful Gestures" group and "No Gestures" and "Arbitrary Gestures" groups for subjects in the low and medium hesitation categories. Overall, the subjects in the "Meaningful Gestures" group hesitated least in approaching the robot, and the subjects in the "No Gestures" and "Arbitrary Gestures" groups hesitated more often. A comparison of the hesitation measures of all conditions is shown in Figure 2.

Three ANOVA tests were conducted to evaluate the differences between groups on their perceived "comfortability closeness", "comfortability touch", and "friendliness". The mean scores for each condition in all measures can be seen in Figure 3. All ANOVAs were significant at 0.05 level. Post hoc comparisons using the Fisher LSD test were performed. For "comfortability closeness", the "Meaningful Gestures" group was significantly higher than the "No Gestures" and "Meaningful Gestures with Face" groups. For "comfortability touch", again, the "Meaningful Gestures" group was significantly higher than the "No Gestures" and "Arbitrary Gestures" groups. For "friendliness", the "Meaningful Gestures" group was significantly higher than the "Arbitrary Gestures" and "Meaningful Gestures with Face" groups, and the "No Gestures" group was significantly higher than the "Meaningful Gestures with Face" group. There were no significant differences between any other pairing of groups.

In general, the subjects were more likely to approach the robot without hesitation and perceived the robot as more friendly and trustworthy when they witnessed gestural arm movement beforehand, with or without the presence of a human face. Introducing irrelevant, arbitrary arm movement did not help, suggesting that the synchronization between arm movement and speech is critical to expressing attitudes. In a few cases, we observed that having a human-like face hurt the subjects' trust and perceived friendliness of the robot. This could be due to the uncanny valley effect. For future work, we will evaluate the role of facial expressions in more details and also study the effects of having longer term interactions between the robot and the user.

REFERENCES

[1] C. L. Bethel and R. R. Murphy. Survey of non-facial/non-verbal affective expressions for appearance-constrained robots. *Systems, Man, and Cybernetics, Part C: Applications and Reviews, IEEE Transactions on*, 38(1):83–92, 2008.

[2] C. Fitzgerald. Developing baxter. In *Technologies for Practical Robot Applications (TePRA), 2013 IEEE International Conference on*, pages 1–6. IEEE, 2013.

[3] A. Hartholt, D. Traum, S. C. Marsella, A. Shapiro, G. Stratou, A. Leuski, L.-P. Morency, and J. Gratch. All together now. In *Intelligent Virtual Agents*, pages 368–381. Springer, 2013.

[4] J. D. Wason and J. T. Wen. Robot raconteur: A communication architecture and library for robotic and automation systems. In *Automation Science and Engineering (CASE), 2011 IEEE Conference on*, pages 761–766. IEEE, 2011.

Optimal Sample Size for Adword Auctions (Extended Abstract)

Jiang Rong[1], Tao Qin[2], Bo An[3], Tie-Yan Liu[2]
[1]The Key Laboratory of Intelligent Information Processing, ICT, CAS & University of Chinese Academy of Sciences rongjiang13@mails.ucas.ac.cn
[2]Microsoft Research {taoqin, tyliu}@microsoft.com
[3]Nanyang Technological University boan@ntu.edu.sg

ABSTRACT

Generalized Second Price (GSP) mechanism is widely used in ad auctions and reserve price is an effective tool for revenue maximization. The optimal reserve price depends on bidders' value distribution, which, however, is generally unknown to auctioneers. A common practice for auctioneers is to first collect information about the value distribution by a *sampling procedure* and then apply the reserve price estimated with the sampled bids to the following auctions. In order to maximize his/her total revenue over finite GSP ad auctions, it is important for the auctioneer to find a proper sample size to trade off between the cost of the sampling procedure and the optimality of the estimated reserve price. We first propose the revenue bounds during and after sampling. Then we formulate the problem of finding the optimal sample size that maximizes the auctioneer's worse-case total revenue as an constrained optimization problem, the solution of which is independent of the value distribution.

Keywords

Revenue Maximization, Ad Auction, Optimal Reserve Price, Generalized Second Price

1. INTRODUCTION

Ad auctions have become a major monetization channel for Internet economy, including sponsored search auctions [9] and realtime bidding (RTB) [2]. In sponsored search, when a user issues a query[1] to a search engine, in addition to a list of relevant webpages, a selective set of ads related to the query will also be shown to the user. A position auction is used to determine which ads to show and how much to charge the corresponding advertisers. In RTB for display advertising, when a user visits a publisher's website, an ad impression with related information will be sent to the advertisers (or ad networks) through an ad exchange. Then the bids from the advertisers are collected and an auction is used to determine which ad to show and how much to charge the advertiser. In these applications, GSP is the most popularly used auction mechanism and has attracted a lot of research attention in recent years [4, 11].

When bidders' value distribution is known, the auctioneer can compute the optimal reserve price based on the Myerson's theory [7]. However, in the real world, bidders' valuations are private information and are invisible to the auctioneer. In practice, auctioneers usually need to collect information about the value distribution using the auction mechanism with a heuristically set reserve price. With the sampled data, the auctioneer can infer the optimal reserve price and use it in the future auctions. Existing works have neglected the revenue loss during the sampling period. Obviously, more rounds of sampling will lead to a more accurate estimation of the optimal reserve price. However, the sampling process usually cannot achieve the optimal revenue by itself, i.e., there is a "cost" of sampling. On the other hand, fewer samples will make lower revenue loss during the sampling period but lead to worse estimation of the optimal reserve price. In the real world, the auctioneer usually cares for his/her revenue in finite auctions, e.g., one month, one quarter, or one year. Hence, the auctioneer need to determine how many rounds should be used for sampling in order to maximize the overall revenue.

In this paper, we study the trade-off between the cost of sampling and the optimality of the estimated reserve price for revenue maximization, in the context of finite-horizon GSP auctions. Specifically, we first consider the revenue loss for two phases: the sampling period and the period after sampling. Then we formulate the trade-off problem as a constrained optimization problem, which aims to maximize the auctioneer's worse-case total revenue. We show that the optimal sample size is independent of the value distribution.

2. GSP MECHANISM AND OPTIMAL RESERVE PRICE

There are N bidders competing for K ad slots ($K < N$). Each ad slot has a corresponding click-through-rate (CTR). Let v_i denote the value of bidder i's ad and $v = (v_1, v_2, \ldots, v_N)$ represent the value profile. Bidders' values are usually assumed to be independent and identically distributed (i.i.d.) with cumulative distribution function F (probability density function f), which is common knowledge to bidders but unknown to the auctioneer [3, 8].

In the theory of revenue maximization, it is usually assumed that bidders were playing the lowest-revenue envy-free (LREF) equilibrium for GSP [4, 5, 8, 11], which is an efficient Nash Equilibrium. Then according to [6, 7], the auctioneer's expected revenue with respect to the reserve

[1]For simplicity, we only consider the exact match between queries and keywords.

Appears in: *Proceedings of the 15th International Conference on Autonomous Agents and Multiagent Systems (AAMAS 2016), J. Thangarajah, K. Tuyls, C. Jonker, S. Marsella (eds.), May 9–13, 2016, Singapore.*

price r can be written as

$$R(r) = E_v\{\sum_{i=1}^{N} \psi(v_i)x_i^r(v)\},$$

where $\psi(v_i) = v_i - \frac{1-F(v_i)}{f(v_i)}$ is called the *virtual value function* and $x_i^r(v)$ is the CTR bidder i can receive given v and r. The optimal reserve price r^* satisfies that [7]

$$\psi(r^*) = 0.$$

3. PROBLEM FORMULATION

We realistically consider that bidders' value distribution is unknown to the auctioneer who aims to maximize his/her overall revenue for M rounds . The first τ rounds are used for sampling and the reserve price is set as zero in this period in order to observe complete (i.e., non-truncated) value distribution. Note that the auctioneer can only observe bids of the advertisers but not their values. We assume that bidders were playing the LREF equilibrium and compute the values from bids according to the method in [11]. Then we make an estimation of the optimal reserve price, represented as $\overline{r}$, with the sampled data and set it for the remaining $M - \tau$ rounds. The total revenue the auctioneer will get is

$$\tau \cdot R(0) + (M - \tau) \cdot R(\overline{r}).$$

The revenue loss is thus

$$M \cdot R(r^*) - (\tau \cdot R(0) + (M - \tau) \cdot R(\overline{r})),$$

which is equal to

$$M \cdot R(r^*)(1 - (\frac{\tau}{M} \cdot \frac{R(0)}{R(r^*)} + (1 - \frac{\tau}{M}) \cdot \frac{R(\overline{r})}{R(r^*)})).$$

Then minimizing the total loss means that

$$\max_{\tau} \frac{\tau}{M} \cdot \frac{R(0)}{R(r^*)} + (1 - \frac{\tau}{M}) \cdot \frac{R(\overline{r})}{R(r^*)}, \quad (1)$$

$$\text{s.t. } \tau \in \{1, 2, \dots, M\}.$$

4. OPTIMAL SAMPLE SIZE

Further analysis shows that both $\frac{R(0)}{R(r^*)}$ and $\frac{R(\overline{r})}{R(r^*)}$ are related to the density function $f(\cdot)$. As a result, the solution of the problem is a function of $f(\cdot)$. Since the priori $f(\cdot)$ is unknown to the auctioneer, we need to find a solution that is independent of $f(\cdot)$ and has good performance on optimality at the same time. Specifically, inspired by [1] and [3] which proposed the distribution-independent lower bounds of $\frac{R(0)}{R(r^*)}$ and $\frac{R(\overline{r})}{R(r^*)}$ respectively for a simple mechanism where winners pay the same minimal price, we can derive the corresponding bounds for the GSP mechanism. We use l_1 to denote the lower bound of $\frac{R(0)}{R(r^*)}$. Since more samples will lead to a better estimation of the optimal reserve price, the lower bound $l_2(\tau)$ of $\frac{R(\overline{r})}{R(r^*)}$ is a function with respect to τ. Based on this result, we can re-formulate the optimization problem with l_1 and $l_2(\tau)$ as follows:

$$\max_{\tau} \ \widehat{\mathcal{R}}(\tau) = \frac{\tau}{M} l_1 + (1 - \frac{\tau}{M}) l_2(\tau), \quad (2)$$

$$\text{s.t. } \tau \in \{1, 2, \dots, M\}. \quad (3)$$

Since both l_1 and $l_2(\tau)$ do not relay on $f(\cdot)$, the optimal sample size τ^* of the problem defined in Eqs. (2) and (3), which aims to maximize the auctioneer's worse-case total revenue, is robust against any distribution.

5. EXTENSIONS AND FUTURE WORK

This paper is based on the unweighted GSP, but the model can be extended to the weighted GSP [10]. First note that the LREF equilibrium also works in weighted GSP. Then we can follow [10] to assume that $s_i = v_i e_i$ is drawn from an i.i.d. regular distribution F, where e_i is bidder i's ad quality. The optimal reserve price for bidder i is modified as s^*/e_i, where s^* satisfies $\psi(s^*) = 0$. All the equations still hold if we replace v_i with $v_i e_i$. Thus the model can be extended to the weighted GSP.

The model can also be applied to VCG auctions. It is known that bidders' payments are the same for the (dominant) truth-telling equilibrium with VCG mechanism and the LREF equilibrium with GSP mechanism. Hence, if we assume bidders in VCG auctions to have i.i.d. values and bid truthfully, the model can be directly extended to VCG.

In future work, we will derive the tight bounds for $\frac{R(0)}{R(r^*)}$ and $\frac{R(\overline{r})}{R(r^*)}$ and propose efficient algorithms to solve the optimization problem.

REFERENCES

[1] J. Bulow and P. Klemperer. Auctions vs. negotiations. Technical report, National Bureau of Economic Research, 1994.

[2] Y. Chen, P. Berkhin, B. Anderson, and N. R. Devanur. Real-time bidding algorithms for performance-based display ad allocation. In *Proceedings of the 17th ACM SIGKDD international conference on Knowledge discovery and data mining*, pages 1307–1315, 2011.

[3] P. Dhangwatnotai, T. Roughgarden, and Q. Yan. Revenue maximization with a single sample. *Games and Economic Behavior*, 91:318–333, 2015.

[4] B. Edelman, M. Ostrovsky, and M. Schwarz. Internet advertising and the generalized second price auction: Selling billions of dollars worth of keywords. Technical report, National Bureau of Economic Research, 2005.

[5] B. Edelman and M. Schwarz. Optimal auction design and equilibrium selection in sponsored search auctions. *The American Economic Review*, pages 597–602, 2010.

[6] J. Hartline. Lectures on optimal mechanism design. *Lecture notes*, 2006.

[7] R. B. Myerson. Optimal auction design. *Mathematics of operations research*, 6(1):58–73, 1981.

[8] M. Ostrovsky and M. Schwarz. Reserve prices in internet advertising auctions: A field experiment. In *Proceedings of the 12th ACM conference on Electronic commerce*, pages 59–60, 2011.

[9] T. Qin, W. Chen, and T.-Y. Liu. Sponsored search auctions: Recent advances and future directions. *ACM Transactions on Intelligent Systems and Technology*, 5(4):60:1–60:34, 2015.

[10] Y. Sun, Y. Zhou, and X. Deng. Optimal reserve prices in weighted GSP auctions. *Electronic Commerce Research and Applications*, 13(3):178–187, 2014.

[11] H. R. Varian. Position auctions. *international Journal of industrial Organization*, 25(6):1163–1178, 2007.

Multi-Option Descending Clock Auction

(Extended Abstract)

Tri-Dung Nguyen
University of Southampton
Mathematical Sciences and Business School
T.D.Nguyen@soton.ac.uk

Tuomas Sandholm*
Carnegie Mellon University
Computer Science Department
sandholm@cs.cmu.edu

ABSTRACT

A descending clock auction (DCA) is for buying items from multiple sellers. The literature has focused on the case where each bidder has two options: to accept or reject the offered price. However, in many settings—such as the FCC's imminent incentive auction—each bidder may be able to sell one from a *set of options*. We present a multi-option DCA (MDCA) framework where at each round, the auctioneer offers each bidder different prices for different options, and a bidder may find multiple options still acceptable. Setting prices during a MDCA is trickier than in a DCA. We develop a Markov chain model for the dynamics of each bidder's state (which options are still acceptable). We leverage it to optimize the trajectory of price offers to different bidders for different options. This is unlike most auctions which only compute the next price vector. Computing the trajectory enables better planning. We reoptimize the trajectory after each round. Each optimization minimizes total payment while ensuring feasibility in a stochastic sense. We also introduce percentile-based approaches to decrementing prices. Experiments with real FCC incentive auction interference constraint data show that the optimization-based approach dramatically outperforms the percentile-based approach—because it takes feasibility into account in pricing. Both pricing techniques scale to the large.

Keywords

Descending clock auction; incentive auction; spectrum auction; combinatorial auction; auction optimization; planned auction trajectory; pricing

1. INTRODUCTION

A *descending clock auction (DCA)* is for buying items from multiple sellers [2]. The DCA framework is agnostic to how offered prices are decremented across rounds. Doing that well is a key problem for which no solutions had been published until recently. Nguyen and Sandholm recently presented techniques for this [3]. That paper—and, to our knowledge, all other papers on incentive auctions and on the DCA to date [2, 4]—consider the setting where bidders have only two options, that is, either to sell or not.

In contrast, in many settings, each seller may be able to sell *one from a set of options*. The DCA can be generalized to this setting by offering each bidder a separate price for each of her options in each round. However, the problem of decreasing prices appropriately during the DCA is more intricate in this *multi-option DCA (MDCA)* setting.

We present an MDCA framework and price-decrementing techniques for it. The model captures a broad set of applications, including the imminent flagship application of DCAs, the FCC incentive auctions. The FCC announced that a multi-option DCA will be used for the reverse auction [1], but left open the important question of how prices will be decremented across rounds. Ours is, to our knowledge, the first paper on pricing techniques for multi-option DCAs.

We present our MDCA in the domain of the FCC incentive auction, where the number of options per bidder is at most three (plus the option of rejecting all three options), but the techniques can be directly extended to more options. Bidders (stations) that are currently in the UHF band, have four choices: go off-air, go down to LVH, go down to UVH, or reject all of these options. Similarly, stations currently in UVH (LVH) have three (two) choices. Rejecting all options leads to being allocated to a channel in the original band.

In each DCA round, the auctioneer offers each bidder prices for all the options for which the bidder is still active. Each bidder then decides which of those options are still acceptable. As long as a bidder is still active for an option, she enters the next round where the same process will be repeated for the remaining active options. If a bidder becomes inactive for all options, she needs to be allocated to her current band and is not paid anything.

2. SETTING & DECREMENTING PRICES

A key component of a DCA is how the prices offered to active bidders are initialized and decremented across rounds. The auctioneer needs to consider the tradeoff between minimizing payment to the accepted bidders and fulfillment of the target (e.g. repacking feasibility). How the prices are changed across rounds should depend on (a) the estimated value functions of the bidders, (b) the importance of the items for the target to be fulfilled and (c) the desired number of rounds. We provide an optimization model that does this. To this end, we need to calculate the (expected) number of stations that will finally end up in each band—which is non-trivial. We propose using Markov chains to model the dynamic of the station's state throughout the MDCA.

*Corresponding author.

Appears in: *Proceedings of the 15th International Conference on Autonomous Agents and Multiagent Systems (AAMAS 2016), J. Thangarajah, K. Tuyls, C. Jonker, S. Marsella (eds.), May 9–13, 2016, Singapore.*

For each station i and for each option $k \in \{1,2,3\}$, suppose the valuations v_{ik} are drawn from some distribution on support $[l_{ik}, u_{ik}]$. Assume that the auctioneer knows these distributions but not the valuations. We denote by p_{ik}, $k \in \{1,2,3\}$, the offer price to station i for option k and by q_{ik} the probability that station i finds price p_{ik} acceptable for option k. For example, if the valuation distribution is uniform, $q_{ik} = \frac{u_{ik}-p_{ik}}{u_{ik}-l_{ik}}$. For convenience, we regard $\boldsymbol{q}$ as the decision variables that the auctioneer sets.

We define the state of a station to depend on which of the three options are still active. Figure 1 shows our Markov chain for a UHF station's state throughout the MDCA; Markov chains for UVH and LVH stations are analogous but simpler, and are omitted due to limited space.

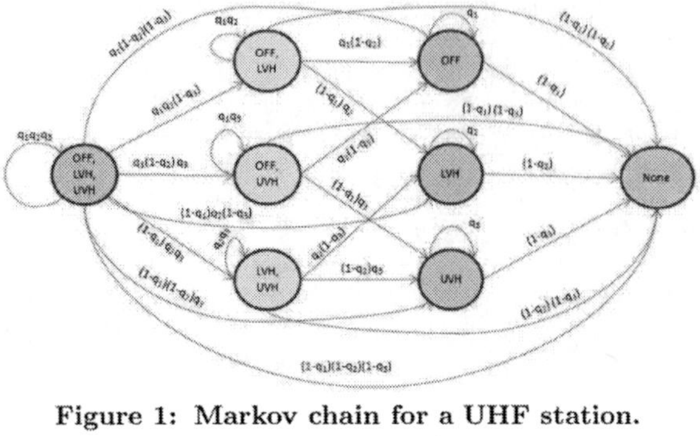

Figure 1: Markov chain for a UHF station.

THEOREM 1. *The state transition of the m-round MDCA with fixed acceptance probabilities (q_1, q_2, q_3) is equivalent to a single-round MDCA with acceptance probabilities q_1^m, q_2^m, q_3^m.*

The significance of Theorem 1 is that, instead of having to keep track of the transitions through m rounds, we can apply the change of variables presented in the theorem, and view the setting as a single-round MDCA. This helps simplify the expression of the state probabilities, and helps tame the complexity of the nonlinear model as we will show.

Optimization approach for price setting: We consider the setting where the auctioneer can offer different acceptance rates to different stations. Instead of seeking the same (q_1, q_2, q_3) for all stations, we aim to find the optimal (q_{i1}, q_{i2}, q_{i3}) for each station i. This gives flexibility and can lead to lower aggregate payment by the auctioneer.

Our OPT-SCHED model for minimizing expected payment while ensuring that the expected number of accepted bidders in each band does not exceed its target is

$$\min_{\boldsymbol{\kappa}} \sum_{i \in \mathcal{N}} f_i(\boldsymbol{\kappa}_i)$$
$$\text{s.t.} \sum_{i \in \mathcal{N}} g_i(\boldsymbol{\kappa}_i) \le C_{UHF}, \sum_{i \in \mathcal{N}} h_i(\boldsymbol{\kappa}_i) \le C_{UVH}, \sum_{i \in \mathcal{N}} u_i(\boldsymbol{\kappa}_i) \le C_{LVH},$$

where $\kappa_{ik} = q_{ik}^m$ and $f_i(\boldsymbol{\kappa}_i)$ is the expected payment to station i and where $g_i(\boldsymbol{\kappa}_i), h_i(\boldsymbol{\kappa}_i), u_i(\boldsymbol{\kappa}_i)$ are the probabilities of station i ending up in UHF, UVH and LVH bands, respectively. The C's are the given targets. Here, we utilized Theorem 1 to transform from decision variable $\boldsymbol{q}$ to $\boldsymbol{\kappa}$ and show that the resulting model has a 4th-order polynomial on the objective function and 3rd-order polynomials on the constraints.

This problem has $3n$ continuous variables. Solving it directly is still not easy due to nonlinearity and nonconvexity. However, the problem has a separable objective and separable constraints. Hence we can apply Lagrangian relaxation.

Percentile-based approach for price setting: A simple way to adjust prices across MDCA rounds is to decrease each price by a given percentage—starting from the upper bound of the support of the station's valuation distribution for each of the options.

3. EXPERIMENTS

We tested our optimization-based price-decrementing technique against the percentile-based method using the real FCC constraint data. Since no incentive auctions have yet been conducted, we had to generate data on the bounds on the bidders' valuations. We did that based on population size covered by each license. (Results for the symmetric setting were very similar and are omitted due to limited space.)

We tried a number of possible acceptance probabilities in the range $\{0.97, 0.975, 0.98, 0.985, 0.99, 0.995, 1\}$ and report the sum of the prices of all active options of the second-to-last (i.e., last feasible) round for the asymmetric setting.[1] Figure 2 shows that OPT-SCHED yields lower final payment than the percentile-based approach—for all choices of the fixed per-round acceptance probability in the latter—on all instances. It results in 25% lower payment on average. It is able to reject high bids by taking into account feasibility considerations. It typically succeeds in proceeding through significantly more rounds before reaching infeasibility by more intelligently taking feasibility into account in the pricing.

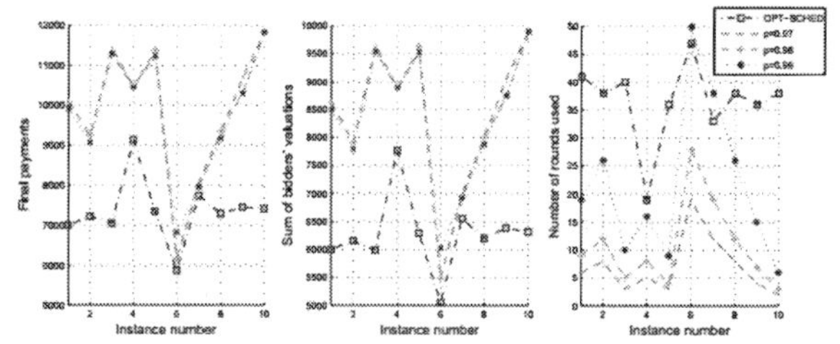

Figure 2: The sum of prices, the bidders' respective valuations, and the number of rounds used.

REFERENCES

[1] FCC. Broadcast incentive auction 101. Technical report, FCC, 2016. http://wireless.fcc.gov/incentiveauctions/learn-program/Broadcast_Incentive_Auction_101_slides.pdf.

[2] P. Milgrom and I. Segal. Deferred-acceptance auctions and radio spectrum reallocation. *ACM Conference on Economics and Computation (EC)*, 2014.

[3] T.-D. Nguyen and T. Sandholm. Optimizing prices in descending clock auctions. *ACM Conference on Economics and Computation (EC)*, pages 93–110, 2014.

[4] V. G. Paul Duetting and T. Roughgarden. The performance of deferred-acceptance auctions. *ACM Conference on Economics and Computation*, 2014.

[1]After the last round where the packing ceases to be feasible, the auctioneer has to decide an outcome for each bidder so as to minimize total payment. We developed a technique for this using decomposition of the station graph (into geographical regions) and Lagrangean relaxation.

Strategy-proof Mechanism Design for Facility Location Games: Revisited *

(Extended Abstract)

Lili Mei
College of Computer Science,
Zhejiang University
meilili@zju.edu.cn

Minming Li
Department of Computer
Science, City University of
Hong Kong
minming.li@cityu.edu.hk

Deshi Ye
College of Computer Science,
Zhejiang University
yedeshi@zju.edu.cn

Guochuan Zhang
College of Computer Science,
Zhejiang University
zgc@zju.edu.cn

ABSTRACT

In facility location games, one aims at designing a mechanism to decide the facility location based on the addresses reported by all agents. In the standard facility location game, each agent wants to minimize the distance from the facility, while in the obnoxious facility game, each agent prefers to be as far away from the facility as possible. In this paper we revisit the two games on a line network by finely defining more reasonable agent cost (utility) functions in terms of their satisfaction degree with respect to the facility location. Namely, a happiness factor within [0, 1] is introduced to measure the difference between the best facility location for an agent and the one given by the mechanism. Agents aim at a largest possible happiness factor while the social satisfaction is to maximize the total factors. For the standard facility location game, we observe that the median mechanism [4] is of 3/2-approximation. We then devise a 5/4-approximation group strategy-proof mechanism. For the obnoxious facility game, we show the majority mechanism [1] is best possible with approximation ratio of two.

Categories and Subject Descriptors

F.7.2 [**Theory of computation**]: Theory and algorithms for application domains—*Algorithmic game theory and mechanism design*

General Terms

Algorithms, Economics, Theory

*This work was partly supported by a grant from the Research Grants Council of the Hong Kong Special Administrative Region, China [Project No. CityU 117913] and the Nature Science Foundation of Zhejiang Province [Project NO. LQ15A010001].

Appears in: *Proceedings of the 15th International Conference on Autonomous Agents and Multiagent Systems (AAMAS 2016), J. Thangarajah, K. Tuyls, C. Marsella, S. Jonker (eds.), May 9–13, 2016, Singapore.*

Keywords

Algorithmic Mechanism Design, Facility Location Game, Happiness Factor, Social Satisfaction

1. INTRODUCTION

Facility location is one of the fundamental optimization problems, that assigns one or several facilities to a given network so that all clients in the network are served and the total cost is minimized. It is assumed that the full information of clients is known as public knowledge. In a game setting, however, the location of each client (we call an agent in the terminology of game theory) is private, that is not known before an algorithm is designed. The system manager (mechanism designer) is required to publicize an algorithm (mechanism) first. Then the agents report their locations (addresses) in the network, based on which the mechanism decides the facility locations. In the standard facility location game, each agent wants to minimize the distance from the facility, while in the obnoxious facility game, each agent prefers to be as far away from the facility as possible. It is of great interests if all agents are willing to tell the truth. The mechanism designer thus aims at strategy-proof mechanisms (where no agents have incentives to lie) maximizing the total utility (or minimizing the total cost) of the agents.

In the literature, the research of the facility location game and the obnoxious facility game has rich history. However, to the best of our knowledge, in both games, the cost or utility of each agent is simply the distance from the agent to the facility location. We observe that for agents at different positions, the best utilities or costs they can achieve from any mechanism will be different. To reflect the relative happiness of each agent compared to the best she can achieve, in this paper, we propose the happiness factor of each agent, which considers the agent's degree of satisfaction for the facility location.

Related results. In the facility location game, each agent wants to minimize the distance from the facility. Moulin [3] and Schummer and Vohra [5] characterized a class of generalized median voter schemes for the single-peak preference on the line and other networks, respectively. The study of approximation mechanism design for facility location games was first introduced by Procaccia and Tennenholtz [4]. They proposed the best possible strategy-proof mechanisms for the facility location game for minimizing the sum of all the agents' costs (minSum) and the maximum cost (minMax).

For the obnoxious facility game, each agent wants to stay far away from the facility. Cheng et al. [1] first proposed and studied the obnoxious facility game for maximizing the sum of all the agents' utilities (maxSum). Ibara and Nagamochi [2] characterized all the strategy-proof mechanisms.

2. PROBLEM STATEMENT

We study the setting where the underlying network is a closed interval $I = [0, 1]$. There are n agents in the interval, denoted as $N = \{1, 2, \ldots, n\}$. Each *agent* i has a location $x_i \in I$, which is private information. Let $\mathbf{x} = (x_1, x_2, \ldots, x_n) \in I^n$ denote the agents' location profile. In our setting, a mechanism f is a function $f : I^n \to I$ where the input is the reported location profile and the output is the facility location. As mentioned before, in this paper, each agent wants to maximize her satisfaction degree, which is named happiness factor in our setting.

Let $y \in I$ denote the facility location. Since our setting is an interval, let $d(y, x_i) = |y - x_i|$ be the distance between *agent* i and the facility. Let $d^i_{max} = \max\{d(0, x_i), d(1, x_i)\}$ denote the longer distance from agent i to two endpoints. For the facility location game, the happiness factor function $h(y, x_i)$ for agent i is $h(y, x_i) = 1 - \frac{d(y,x_i)}{d^i_{max}}$. And for the obnoxious facility game, the happiness factor function is $h(y, x_i) = \frac{d(y,x_i)}{d^i_{max}}$. In our setting, the social satisfaction is the sum of all the agents' happiness factors, *i.e.*, $SH(y, \mathbf{x})$ is $\sum_{i \in N} h(y, x_i)$. In this paper, we aim to design mechanisms to elicit the location profile and maximize the social satisfaction as much as possible.

If a mechanism f elicits the true location profile, we say the mechanism is strategy-proof, *i.e.*, no agent can improve her happiness factor by misreporting. Formally, given any location profile $\mathbf{x}$, we have $h(f(\mathbf{x}), x_i) \geq h(f(x'_i, \mathbf{x}_{-i}), x_i)$ for all $x'_i \in I$, where $\mathbf{x}_{-i} = (x_1, \ldots, x_{i-1}, x_{i+1}, \ldots, x_n)$ is the location profile without agent i. Moreover, a mechanism f is group strategy-proof if no any coalition of agents can improve their happiness factors by misreporting their locations simultaneously, *i.e.*, given any location profile $\mathbf{x}$, for any non-empty subset $S \subseteq N$, there exists $i \in S$ such that $h(f(\mathbf{x}), x_i) \geq h(f(\mathbf{x}'_S, \mathbf{x}_{-S}), x_i)$ for any $\mathbf{x}'_S \in I^{|S|}$, where $\mathbf{x}_{-S}$ is the location profile without agents in S.

Let y^* denote the optimal facility location. A mechanism f is ρ-approximation if $SH(y^*, \mathbf{x}) \leq \rho \cdot SH(f(\mathbf{x}), \mathbf{x})$ for any location profile $\mathbf{x}$.

3. MAIN RESULTS

3.1 The facility location game

We first study the median mechanism in [4], which returns the leftmost median agent's location as the facility location. In their setting, the mechanism gets an optimal solution. However, in our setting, it cannot guarantee optimality any longer.

THEOREM 3.1. *The median mechanism is a group strategy-proof mechanism with approximation ratio 3/2 for maximizing the social satisfaction.*

Then we consider a better mechanism below.

MECHANISM 1. *Given a location profile $\mathbf{x} \in I^n$, without loss of generality, we assume that $x_1 \leq x_2 \leq \cdots \leq x_n$. Mechanism f outputs*

$$f(\mathbf{x}) = \begin{cases} 1/5 & \text{if } med(\mathbf{x}) \in [0, \frac{1}{5}] \\ 4/5 & \text{if } med(\mathbf{x}) \in [\frac{4}{5}, 1] \\ med(\mathbf{x}) & \text{otherwise} \end{cases},$$

where $med(\mathbf{x})$ is the output of the median mechanism.

THEOREM 3.2. *Mechanism 1 is a group strategy-proof mechanism with approximation ratio 5/4 for maximizing the social satisfaction.*

We then consider lower bounds for the facility location game. We obtain the following theorem.

THEOREM 3.3. *Let $N = \{1, 2, \cdots, n\}$, where $n \geq 2$. Any strategy-proof mechanism cannot have an approximation ratio less than $8 - 4\sqrt{3}$ for maximizing the social satisfaction.*

We finally consider a mechanism when there are only two agents. We establish the following group strategy-proof mechanism and the approximation ratio is $8 - 4\sqrt{3}$.

MECHANISM 2. *Given a location profile $\mathbf{x} \in I^2$, if two agents is in different sides of 1/2, mechanism f outputs 1/2; otherwise outputs the one which is closer to 1/2.*

3.2 The obnoxious facility game

In [1], a majority mechanism is presented. If the number of agents in $[0, 1/2]$ is larger than (or equal to) that in $(1/2, 1]$, the mechanism outputs 1, otherwise outputs 0.

THEOREM 3.4. *The majority mechanism is a group strategy-proof mechanism with approximation ratio 2 for maximizing the social satisfaction.*

Now we turn to consider lower bounds and we get the following theorem which implies that the majority mechanism is the best.

THEOREM 3.5. *Let $N = \{1, 2, \cdots, n\}$, where $n \geq 2$. Any strategy-proof mechanisms cannot have an approximation ratio less than $2 - \epsilon$ for maximizing the social satisfaction, where $\epsilon > 0$ is an arbitrary small number.*

REFERENCES

[1] Cheng, Y. and Yu, W. and Zhang, G.: Mechanisms for obnoxious facility game on a path. The 5th Annual International Conference on Combinatorial Optimization and Applications (COCOA), pp. 262–271, 2011.

[2] Ibara, K. and Nagamochi, H.: Characterizing mechanisms in obnoxious facility game. The 6th Annual International Conference on Combinatorial Optimization and Applications (COCOA), pp. 301–311, 2012.

[3] Moulin, H.: On strategy-proofness and single peakedness. Public Choice 35(4), pp 437-455, 1980.

[4] Procaccia, A.D. and Tennenholtz, M.: Approximate mechanism design without money. The 10th ACM conference on Electronic Commerce (EC), pp. 177–186, 2009.

[5] Schummer, J. and Vohra, R.V.: Strategy-proof location on a network. Journal of Economic Theory 104(2), pp 405-428, 2002.

Stochastic Shortest Path with Energy Constraints in POMDPs*

(Extended Abstract)

Tomáš Brázdil
Faculty of Informatics
Masaryk University
Brno, Czech Republic
brazdil@fi.muni.cz

Krishnendu Chatterjee
IST Austria
Klosterneuburg, Austria
kchatterjee@ist.ac.at

Martin Chmelík
IST Austria
Klosterneuburg, Austria
mchmelik@ist.ac.at

Anchit Gupta
IIT Bombay
Mumbai, India
anchit@iitb.ac.in

Petr Novotný
IST Austria
Klosterneuburg, Austria
pnovotny@ist.ac.at

ABSTRACT

We extend the traditional framework of POMDPs to model resource consumption inducing a hard constraint on the behaviour of the model. Resource levels increase and decrease with transitions, and the hard constraint requires that the level remains positive in all steps. We present an algorithm for solving POMDPs with resource levels, developing on existing POMDP solvers. Our second contribution is related to policy representation. For larger POMDPs the policies computed by existing solvers are too large to be understandable, an issue particularly pronounced in POMDPs with resource levels. We present a procedure based on machine learning techniques that extracts important decisions of a policy and outputs its readable representation.

Keywords

POMDP; planning; energy constraints; decision trees

1. INTRODUCTION

Partially observable Markov decision processes (POMDPs) are a powerful framework for solving planning problems under uncertainty. Given a POMDP formulation of a problem, the task is to compute an optimal *policy* in the POMDP: there is a reward or a cost associated with each transition, and the goal is to maximize the aggregated reward (resp. minimize the aggregated cost) over a finite or an infinite horizon. The sequence of rewards (or costs) can be aggregated by considering, e.g. the discounted reward, the average reward, etc. Particularly relevant from the planning point of view is the *indefinite-horizon (or stochastic shortest path, SSP)* objective [1, 2, 4], where the task is to reach a state from a given set of target states T and minimize the expected total cost till T is reached, i.e., the expected sum of costs of all transitions traversed before reaching T.

Most autonomous robotic devices operate under certain *energy constraints*, i.e. they need a steady supply of some resource (e.g. fuel, electricity, etc.) to operate correctly. We extend POMDPs so as to capture these constraints. To a POMDP $\mathcal{M}$ with a given objective we assign a positive integer capacity cap and to each observation-action pair (Z, a) in $\mathcal{M}$ we assign an integer *update* representing the amount of a resource consumed or reloaded by a under observation Z. Such a POMDP starts with some initial resource level (say cap, i.e. the resource is loaded to a full capacity) which is then modified as the system evolves: whenever an action with some update u is taken, the resource level changes from ℓ to $\min\{\ell + u, cap\}$ (discarding any quantity exceeding cap captures the fact that the robot's storage capacity cannot be exceeded). The task is to find a strategy optimizing the original objective under the constraint that the resource level stays positive. Although constrained optimization in POMDPs was already studied, e.g. in constrained POMDPs [7], our approach radically differs from the previous work, since the constraints in constrained POMDPs are *soft*, i.e. they are bounds on the *expected value* of some quantity. In contrast, our resource level must be positive on each individual run, so the constraints we consider are *hard*.

The concept of resource consumption can be put on top of any standard POMDP objective. We focus on SSP-POMDPs with energy constraints, which we call *energy-reachability (ER)* POMDPs for short. That is, our aim is to find a policy ensuring that the resource level is positive till the target set T is reached and among all such policies minimizes the expected total cost before reaching T. We present and evaluate a framework for solving ER-POMDPs that allows us to use off-the-shelf tools to obtain an optimal policy.

Solving ER-POMDPs highlights another issue: policies obtainable from many POMDP solvers are represented as

*The research was partly supported by Austrian Science Fund (FWF) Grant No P23499-N23, FWF NFN Grant No S11407-N23 (RiSE/SHiNE), ERC Start Grant (279307: Graph Games), Czech Science Foundation grant No. P202/12/G061, and the People Programme (Marie Curie Actions) of the European Union's Seventh Framework Programme (FP7/2007-2013) under REA grant agreement No [291734].

Appears in: *Proceedings of the 15th International Conference on Autonomous Agents and Multiagent Systems (AAMAS 2016), J. Thangarajah, K. Tuyls, C. Jonker, S. Marsella (eds.), May 9–13, 2016, Singapore.*

tables storing belief-action pairs, where entry (B, a) signals that an action a should be taken when the agent's belief is close to b. These tables can be very large and not easily readable by humans. But from the engineering point of view it is vital visualize and understand the policy, as witnessed by numerous informal rules for safety-critical system design enforcing "simplicity" and "readability" (e.g. [6]).

Readability of policies is relevant for POMDPs in general, but the issue is especially pronounced in energy-constrained POMDPs, as the standard representation does not reveal which decisions depend on states and which depend on current resource level, an information useful for identifying bottlenecks caused by insufficient storage capacity or exploiting the fact that policy's dependency on resource levels might not be complex (e.g. "when low on fuel, go to a gas station"). We present a general method of obtaining succinct and readable policy representations based on *decision trees*, and we evaluate this approach in the context of ER-POMDPs.

2. OVERVIEW OF RESULTS

We show how to construct, for any POMDP $\mathcal{M}$ with ER objective (given by a target set T and capacity cap) a new SSP-POMDP $\mathcal{M}'$ (without energy constraints) such that finding a policy of value v in $\mathcal{M}'$ yields a policy of value v in $\mathcal{M}$ satisfying the energy constraint. Intuitively, $\mathcal{M}'$ is formed by augmenting the states of $\mathcal{M}$ with the information on the current resource level, i.e. its states are pairs (s, e), where s is a state of $\mathcal{M}$ and $0 \leq e \leq cap$ is an integer.

To compute (near-)optimal policies in $\mathcal{M}'$ (and thus also in $\mathcal{M}$) in practice, any off-the-shelf solver for SSP-POMDPs can be used. We experimented with the algorithm from [4], which is a modification of the RTDP-Bel algorithm [2], on standard benchmarks that were naturally extended with energy levels. The algorithm solved ER-POMDPs in orders of tens of seconds in cases where $\mathcal{M}'$ had ≤ 3000 states and in orders of hundreds of seconds where $\mathcal{M}'$ had ≤ 8000 states.

The algorithm of [4] outputs a policy in a form of a table-represented function which assigns actions to vectors (that represent discretized beliefs). One of the most popular formalisms for succinct representation of functions on vectors are *decision trees* (DTs, see [9]). We explain DTs on an example in Figure 1, which displays a DT representing a policy in an instance of a Hallway benchmark [8]. Edges in the tree are labelled by inequalities between numbers and *variables* that characterize the input belief vector. In Figure 1 there are two variables: one representing the current energy level and one representing the probability (belief) that the current y-coordinate of the agent on the 8×8 grid is 7. Leaves are labelled by actions. To execute the policy the agent maintains (an approximation of) its current belief. In every step it finds the unique path from root to a leaf ℓ in the tree such that all inequalities on the path are satisfied by the current belief, and it then performs the action labelling ℓ.

To obtain a DT from a table-representation of a policy we can employ off-the-shelf DT-learning tools. We experimented with several such tools [5, 11, 10]. For each benchmark we fixed a suitable set V of variables (e.g. for the Hallway benchmark we had variables *Energy*, and $x_0, \ldots, x_h$, $y_0, \ldots, y_w$, where h, w are the height and width of the corresponding grid, respectively) and used each of the tools to learn a DT over V. The advantage of this approach is that the learning tools are often able to identify the crucial decisions made by a policy and encode *only these* decisions in

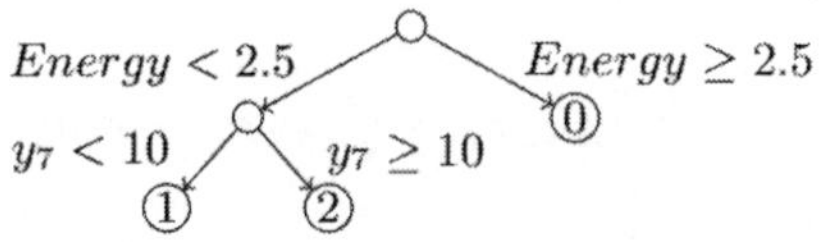

Figure 1: A DT policy for Hallway on an 8x8 grid with $cap = 10$.

the DT, which may result in much more succinct representation without significant loss of the policy's performance. To support this claim we simulated the tree policies to compare them with the original RTDP-Bel policies. In a clear majority of cases at least one tool learned a small DT policy whose value was close to the value of the corresponding RTDP-Bel policy. For instance, for Hallway 8×8 with $cap = 10$ the RTDP-Bel policy had value 21.020 and was represented by a table with 527 entries. The *tree* learning package extracted from this table the 5-node DT in Figure 1, representing a policy with value 52.689, while the *rpart* package learned a 21-node DT with value 26.396. A baseline strategy choosing a random action in each step yielded value 954.160. Similar pattern, where the performance of a DT strategy is very close to the RTDP-Bel strategy (when compared to the baseline strategy), was observed in about 75% of cases. Interestingly, this shows that POMDP policies exhibit a phenomenon known as *Pareto's principle*, where a minority of decisions amount for the majority of optimization effort.

The details of our work are in a technical report [3].

REFERENCES

[1] D. P. Bertsekas. *Dynamic Programming and Optimal Control.* Athena Scientific, 1995. Volumes I and II.

[2] B. Bonet and H. Geffner. Solving POMDPs: RTDP-Bel vs. Point-based Algorithms. In *IJCAI*, pages 1641–1646, 2009.

[3] T. Brázdil, K. Chatterjee, M. Chmelík, A. Gupta, and P. Novotný. Stochastic Shortest Path with Energy Constraints in POMDPs. Technical report. Available at http://arxiv.org/abs/1602.07565.

[4] K. Chatterjee, M. Chmelík, R. Gupta, and A. Kanodia. Optimal cost almost-sure reachability in POMDPs. *Artificial Intelligence*, 234:26–48, 2016.

[5] M. Hall, E. Frank, G. Holmes, B. Pfahringer, P. Reutemann, and I. H. Witten. The WEKA data mining software: an update. *ACM SIGKDD*, 11(1):10–18, 2009.

[6] G. J. Holzmann. The power of 10: rules for developing safety-critical code. *Computer*, 39(6):95–99, 2006.

[7] J. D. Isom, S. P. Meyn, and R. D. Braatz. Piecewise Linear Dynamic Programming for Constrained POMDPs. In *AAAI*, pages 291–296, 2008.

[8] M. L. Littman, A. R. Cassandra, and L. P. Kaelbling. Learning policies for partially observable environments: Scaling up. In *ICML*, 1995.

[9] J. R. Quinlan. Induction of decision trees. *Machine Learning*, 1(1):81–106, 1986.

[10] B. Ripley. *tree: Classification and Regression Trees*, 2015. R package version 1.0-36.

[11] T. Therneau, B. Atkinson, and B. Ripley. *rpart: Recursive Partitioning and Regression Trees*, 2015. R package version 4.1-10.

Using Environmental Patterns to Evaluate Agent Teams Performance

(Extended Abstract)

Mariana R. Franco
Lab. de Técnicas Inteligentes
Escola Politécnica
Universidade de São Paulo
mafranko@usp.br

Gustavo A. L. de Campos
MACC
Universidade Estadual do Ceará
gustavo@larces.uece.br

Jaime S. Sichman
Lab. de Técnicas Inteligentes
Escola Politécnica
Universidade de São Paulo
jaime.sichman@poli.usp.br

ABSTRACT

The design of a rational organization composed by a team of agents is a challenging problem in domains such as collective robotics, war games and military missions. In these domains, a team is designed to confront an opponent team with technical and numerical equivalence, and aiming to conquer areas where there are scarce resources distributed in locations within a territory whose topology is unknown. In these scenarios, it is hard for the agents to do the right thing. In addition to being competitive, the task environments are unknown, partially observable and dynamic. The challenge is how to design a rational team whose members are not ideal rational agents. This work argues that one approach is to implement a suitable organizational specification that fits the task environment, according to some previously defined environmental patterns that include both domain-specific and topological characteristics. In this work, we present an experimental evaluation of these patterns' influence on the performance of teams of agents evolving on the Agents on Mars environment, a well-known agent programming testbed. The results of the evaluation show that organizational specifications that exploit this information perform better than others that don't.

Keywords

Organisations and Institutions; Team Formation; Engineering Multi-Agent Systems; Profiling and Benchmarking of Agent-Based Systems

1. INTRODUCTION

In competitive domains, a challenge that arises is how to design a rational team of agents, each of those not ideally rational. We argue that one way to face this challenge is to implement a suitable Organizational Specification (**OS**) that fits the task environment in each domain. Moreover, we focus on the influence of *environmental patterns* (**EP**) in the performance of a team of agents designed to confront a technical and numerical equivalent opponent, and aiming to conquer areas where there are scarce resources of high economic value (*clusters*), that are distributed in locations within a territory whose topology is unknown. The notion of environmental pattern is defined based on some *clusters'* spatial attributes, whose values are perceived by the teams when they explore the environment.

The agents' team performance evaluation is domain-dependent. In our case, it is based on the testbed provided by the Multi-agent Programming Contest (**MAPC**), more precisely in the *Agents on Mars* (**AoM**) scenario [1]. The results of our evaluation show that **OS**s that exploit this information perform better than others that don't. For example, the number of clusters leads, in some cases, to situations where it may be better for the whole team to occupy a single cluster, while in other cases it may be better to divide the team into smaller squads to try to gain control over multiple clusters in the environment.

Appears in: *Proceedings of the 15th International Conference on Autonomous Agents and Multiagent Systems (AAMAS 2016), J. Thangarajah, K. Tuyls, C. Jonker, S. Marsella (eds.), May 9–13, 2016, Singapore.*

2. EVALUATION SCENARIO

In the **AoM** scenario, the environment is represented by a weighted graph, where the vertices denote water wells and possible locations for the agents, and the edges indicate the possibility of crossing from one vertex to another.

At the beginning of the simulation, the map is unknown to the agents. Each team consists of 28 players that can be of 5 different types: explorers, sentinels, saboteurs, inspectors and repairers. These types define the characteristics of each agent such as life level, maximum energy, and strength. The roles also limit the possible actions that the agent can perform in the environment. For instance, explorers can discover water wells and help to explore the map, while sentinels have long distance sensors and thus can observe larger areas, saboteurs can attack and disable enemies, inspectors can spy opponents, and repairers can repair damaged agents.

We associated the notion of **EP**s in the context of **AoM** to capture the diversity of environments, i.e., how many "valuable areas" (subgraph with high value) appear in the map. In our work, these "valuable areas" are called *clusters*. From the agents' point of view, we define the environmental pattern **EP** = (**N**, **H**, **D**) associated with an environment by three attributes related to its clusters: the number (**N**) of clusters, their homogeneity (**H**) and their dispersion (**D**). Figure 1 shows environments with different cluster patterns.

3. DESIGNING THE ORGANIZATION

In order to design a solution for our problem, we need to solve two related problems: the design of individual cooperative heterogeneous agents and the design of an **OS** for a rational team of these agents. The notion of **OS** in this work is based on Moise organizational modeling language [3], where an organizational specification **OS** = **(SS, FS, DS)** is decomposed in three dimensions. The Structural Specification (**SS**) defines the roles and the groups. The Functional Specification (**FS**) defines as the overall objectives are broken down into goals and missions. The Deontic Specification (**DS**) relates these two dimensions, identifying subsets of missions and goals in **FS** that are permitted and/or required for each role in **SS**.

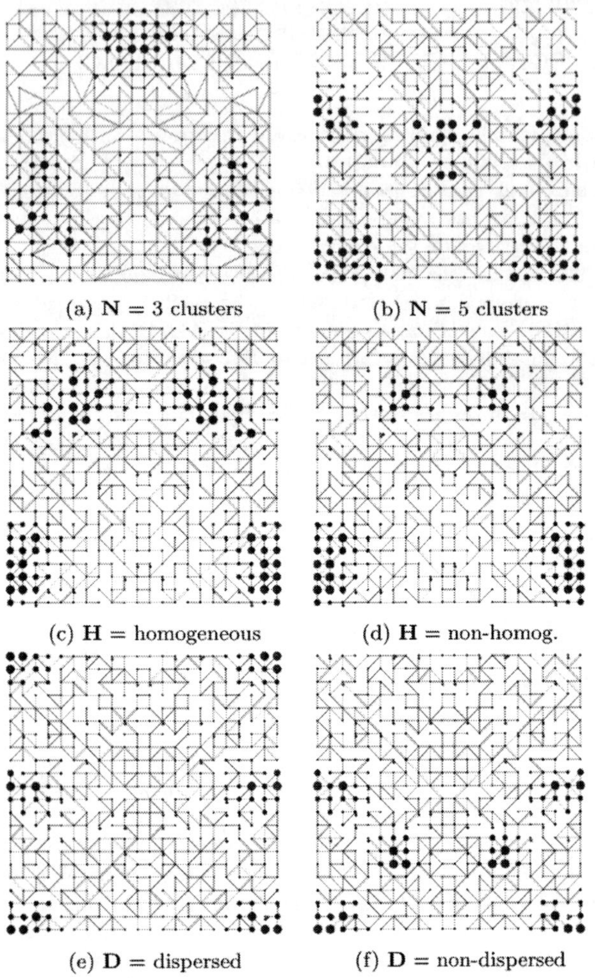

(a) **N** = 3 clusters (b) **N** = 5 clusters (c) **H** = homogeneous (d) **H** = non-homog. (e) **D** = dispersed (f) **D** = non-dispersed

Figure 1: Environments with different patterns.

4. EXPERIMENTAL EVALUATION

The goal of our experiments was to evaluate the impact of the **EP**s over teams' performance, and measuring the performance of two adversary teams composed by the same BDI agents, but with two different **OS**s.

Considering teams' **OS**s, we have fixed the attribute values associated with the **FS** and **DS**, and have just modified the number of squads and the cardinality of each squad in the **SS**. Hence, the experiments consisted of seven different teams that competed each against other for 10 times, using 14 environments with different **EP**s. Each team is composed of a different number of groups called *squads* which are in charge of occupying the best possible clusters they can find in the map [2].

We used the *Wilcoxon T* test as a hypothesis test to define for each match if the 10 simulations were sufficient or not to conclude that a team was better than other in a determined environment.

Regarding **N**, the team must have a number of squads equal or closer to the number of clusters on the map. If the number of squads is smaller than the number of clusters, the team will not cover all good areas, which can then be easily occupied by the opponent.

For **H**, the experiments showed that occupying the clusters with highest values is critical in non-homogeneous environments since the winner ends up by being the team that occupies the bigger clusters. This favours teams with small number of squads, since they can occupy the best clusters, while an opponent with a larger number of squads ends up by spreading its agents in smaller clusters.

Finally, regarding **D**, the results showed that less dispersed clusters help teams with a larger number of squads to form larger areas than they could if the clusters (and the agents) were dispersed.

5. CONCLUSIONS AND FURTHER WORK

Although our results are preliminary ones, we believe that they provide at least two contributions that can be exploited in the design of agents' teams when the task environment is hard, but can be described in terms of **EP**s.

The first contribution is related to the knowledge the designer can learn about these task environments, to assess whether a team will be able to selectively search for solutions. The second one is related to the proper notion of **EP** realized in this work. Considering it as a complementary representation of the state of the environment, and the consistent knowledge that can be provided by a more intensive evaluation of the impact of **EP**s over teams' performance, we believe that two possibilities are generated for the designer (that may be a team agent): (1) to predict the behavior of a team if he knows its goals, its **OS**, and the current **EP**s; (2) to define a team behaviour by designing a suitable **OS** if he knows the current **EP** and team's goal. These are hypotheses that we hope to prove in the near future.

Acknowledgments

Jaime Sichman is partially financed by CNPq, # 303950/2013-7.

REFERENCES

[1] T. Behrens, M. Köster, F. Schlesinger, J. Dix, and J. Hübner. The Multi-agent Programming Contest 2011: A Résumé. In L. Dennis, O. Boissier, and R. Bordini, editors, *Programming Multi-Agent Systems*, volume 7217 of *Lecture Notes in Computer Science*, pages 155–172. Springer Berlin / Heidelberg, 2012.

[2] M. R. Franco. Avaliação Organizacional de Times de Agents para o Multi-Agent Programming Contest. Master's thesis, Escola Politécnica da Universidade de São Paulo, 2014.

[3] J. Hübner, J. Sichman, and O. Boissier. A model for the structural, functional, and deontic specification of organizations in multiagent systems. *Advances in Artificial Intelligence*, 2002.

Estimating Second-Order Arguments in Dialogical Settings (Extended Abstract)

Seyed Ali Hosseini
Department of Informatics
King's College London
ali.hosseini@kcl.ac.uk

Sanjay Modgil
Department of Informatics
King's College London
sanjay.modgil@kcl.ac.uk

Odinaldo Rodrigues
Department of Informatics
King's College London
odinaldo.rodrigues@kcl.ac.uk

ABSTRACT

This paper proposes mechanisms for agents to model other agents' arguments, so that modelling agents can anticipate the likelihood that their interlocutors can constructs arguments in dialogues. In contrast with existing works on "opponent modelling" which treat arguments as abstract entities, the likelihood that an agent can construct an argument is derived from the likelihoods that it possesses the beliefs required to construct the argument. We therefore also address how a modeller can quantify the certainty that its interlocutor possesses beliefs based on previous dialogues, and membership of interlocutors in communities.

Keywords

Opponent modelling, Argumentation-based dialogue

1. INTRODUCTION

In real world models of computational dialogue involving computational and or human participants, one needs to address the strategic choice of locutions and use of enthymemes (i.e. arguments with incomplete logical structures [1]). This requires *opponent modelling* capabilities i.e. agents modelling their interlocutors' arguments. Hence an agent can anticipate the possible counter-arguments in a given dialogue, thus moving an argument that is least susceptible to attack, and avoid sending information in enthymemes that is already known to others. In such setups, in addition to constructing its own arguments from its knowledge-base (*first-order* arguments), an agent can generate a model of its interlocutor's arguments (*second-order* arguments).

In existing works on opponent modelling, agents assign values $[0, 1]$ to abstract arguments, representing the likelihood that they can be constructed by other agents. However, models of second-order *abstract* arguments are incomplete as they do not account for all second-order arguments that can be constructed from constituent beliefs. Furthermore, most existing works do not address the provenance of these values. Here we propose two sources for these values: the information exchanged in dialogues an agent participates in, and (when dialogical data is insufficient) a quantitative measure of similarity amongst all agents in the environment, using the notion of *agent communities*.

Appears in: *Proceedings of the 15th International Conference on Autonomous Agents and Multiagent Systems (AAMAS 2016), J. Thangarajah, K. Tuyls, C. Jonker, S. Marsella (eds.), May 9–13, 2016, Singapore.*

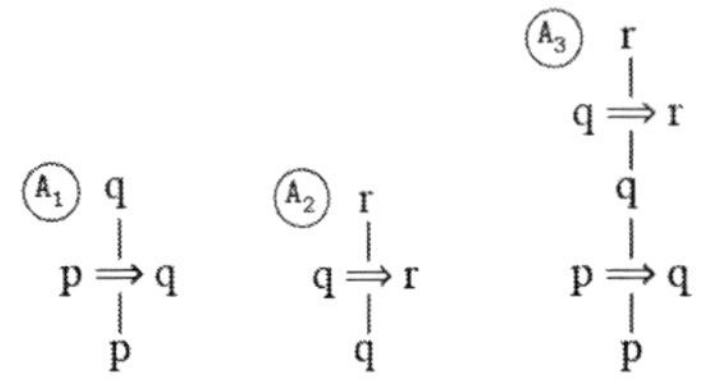

Figure 1: Several arguments

2. THE MODEL

Consider an agent i determining the likelihood that another agent j can construct a certain argument. Unlike existing works [3], we argue that this issue cannot be addressed without explicit access to the constituents of arguments.

Example 1. Suppose j submits only arguments A_1 and A_2 in Figure 1, in distinct dialogues with i. If i treats arguments only as abstract entities, it would believe that j only has arguments A_1 and A_2, and not A_3. It is however clear that j can also construct A_3 because it has the required beliefs to do so.

Hence access to the constituents of arguments is required when valuating the likelihoods of their construction. One common approach, though studied in the context where values denote likelihoods of truth [2], is to derive the values associated with arguments from the those associated with their constituent beliefs. In our context, this would mean that the likelihood that j can construct an argument A is derived from the likelihoods that it has the necessary beliefs to construct A. The next step thus is to address the likelihoods that are associated with second-order beliefs.

We consider two complementary mechanisms for i to evaluate the likelihood that j has a certain belief α. The first is i's history of dialogical interactions. For this, an assignment d_{ij} for any two agents i, j is defined, where given i's history of dialogues and a belief α, it returns a number $[0, 1]$ representing the likelihood that j has α. Additionally, i records the case where dialogical evidence suggests that j does not have α (in which case $d_{ij}(\alpha) = \bot$). By default, for every two agents i, j and belief α, $d_{ij}(\alpha) = 0$, as i has no dialogical data regarding j having α. However, once i receives such evidence in a dialogue, $d_{ij}(\alpha)$ is updated. For example, when j directly commits to α in a dialogue with i, in which case $d_{ij}(\alpha) = 1$, or when i is indirectly informed of j's belief in α, e.g. by another agent k, in which case $d_{ij}(\alpha)$ could correspond to i's level of trust in k. Failed information-seeking dialogues from i to j regarding α would trigger $d_{ij}(\alpha) = \bot$.

In case dialogical data is insufficient to determine whether j has α, i can refer to its dialogical data regarding other

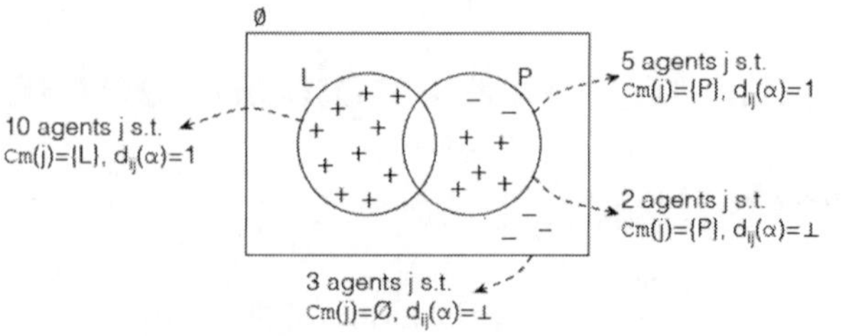

Figure 2: The figure corresponding to Example 2

agents knowing α, while factoring in their relationship with j. This relationship is modelled through the notion of *agent groups* and *communities*.

A *group* of agents is a set of agents sharing a certain property (e.g. organisational roles). A general assumption underpinning this model is that the shared property between the members of a group licenses their sharing of a specific set of beliefs. As agents may have multiple properties, agent groups may intersect, and each of these intersections may themselves license the sharing of a separate set of beliefs between its members. For example, assume a group A of agents all having beliefs $\mathcal{B}_A$ and a group B of agents with $\mathcal{B}_B$. Assuming a monotonic relationship between group membership and having beliefs, for the set $\mathcal{B}_{AB}$ of beliefs shared between agents in AB (i.e. agents in $A \cap B$), we have $\mathcal{B}_{AB} \supseteq \mathcal{B}_A \cup \mathcal{B}_B$, where the set $\mathcal{B}_{AB} \setminus \{\mathcal{B}_A \cup \mathcal{B}_B\}$ is the unique set of beliefs shared amongst AB's members because of their membership to "both A and B". Therefore, given the set $\mathcal{G}$ of all groups, we are interested in $2^{\mathcal{G}}$ where each of its elements is called a *community*. Given communities $\{A\}$ and $\{A, B\}$ (henceforth denoted A and AB), the latter is more *specific* than the former – due to their members having more properties – and the former is more *general* than the latter.[1]

Example 2. Let $\mathcal{G} = \{\mathrm{L}, \mathrm{P}\}$, where L and P respectively denote "lawyers" and "paralegals", and let α be technical legal information. The experience of i after consulting with several legal firms is summarised in Figure 2 which shows agents' community memberships and whether they believe (+) or do not believe (−) α, according to i. In this context, community $\emptyset$, containing all agents, represents "those working in a legal firm" and $\mathtt{Cm}(j)$ is the community j belongs to.

For any belief α and agent i, a set $\mathsf{c}_i(\alpha)$ of tuples $\langle \kappa, p \rangle$ is determined where κ is a community, and $p \in [0, 1]$, called a p-score, is the likelihood that a member of κ believes α according to i. The p-scores can be determined based on standard conditional probability $\sum_{x \in \kappa} \mathsf{d}_{ix}(\alpha) / |\{x \in \kappa \,|\, \mathsf{d}_{ix}(\alpha) \neq 0\}|$. For community $\emptyset$ in Example 2, the p-score would be 15/20, and so $\mathsf{c}_i(\alpha) = \{\langle \mathrm{L}, 1\rangle, \langle \mathrm{P}, 0.71\rangle, \langle \emptyset, 0.75\rangle\}$. However in this approach, some communities (e.g. LP) may not be assigned any p-score, which could for example be due to incomplete data (i.e. agent i not having dialogues with any of their members regarding α). Moreover, some communities (e.g. $\emptyset$) might be assigned superficially high values due to being too general. In the case of $\emptyset$ (i.e. those working in a legal firm), the p-score suggests that there is 0.75 probability that another member of $\emptyset$ believes α. However, a large proportion of this value (10 out of 15 agents contributing to 0.75) is due to agents being lawyers.

[1] In this context, agents in $\emptyset \in 2^{\mathcal{G}}$ do not need to have any specific properties, essentially all agents in the environment, and the beliefs shared amongst them is *common knowledge*.

To remedy these issues, the p-scores are calculated iteratively, which ensures that **a)** those communities without a p-score value inherit the highest value of the most specific communities that are more general (e.g. L and P in the case of LP), and **b)** that each agent contributes only to the p-score of the community whose membership is the most likely reason why it believes α (i.e. the community with the highest $\mathsf{c}_i(\alpha)$ value). In the case of Example 2, in iteration 1 the p-score of L is set to 1 because it has the highest $\mathsf{c}_i(\alpha)$ value. Then from the remaining agents and communities, P will receive 0.71 and $\emptyset$ will receive 0.25, thus at iteration 2, P's p-score is set to 0.71. In iteration 3, from the remaining agents, $\emptyset$ will be assigned 0, as all of its members are in other communities with higher p-score values.

These values are then aggregated in a function $\mathsf{c}_{ic}(\alpha)$ for every agent i, community c, and belief α, representing the likelihood that a member of c believes α according to i. Together with $\mathsf{d}_{ij}(\alpha)$, these functions provide an approximate model of j's beliefs, according to i.

3. CONCLUSION

With our proposed mechanisms, an agent is able to utilise its dialogue history and its knowledge of agents' distribution in communities to determine the likelihood that another agent has certain beliefs, and subsequently derive the likelihood that it can construct arguments from those beliefs.

Suppose now that to persuade j to accept ϕ, i wants to send an argument for ϕ. By anticipating the arguments that j can construct and submit as counter-arguments, i can strategically choose from amongst all its arguments for ϕ, those that are least susceptible to be attacked by j. Let $\mathtt{Poss}(\phi)$ denote the set of all possible arguments claiming ϕ that i can construct. For each argument $\mathtt{A}$ in $\mathtt{Poss}(\phi)$, i must first identify every possible counter-argument to $\mathtt{A}$ along with the likelihoods associated with j being able to construct them. Then for each argument in $\mathtt{Poss}(\phi)$, i would consolidate the number of its counter-arguments and their likelihood values, allowing it to select the argument which is least likely to be attacked by j.

Another application is the use of enthymemes in dialogues. For this, i examines all sub-arguments $\mathtt{A}'$ of an argument $\mathtt{A}$ it wants to send to j, and removes $\mathtt{A}'$ from $\mathtt{A}$ if its likelihood value is higher than a certain threshold.

In the future, we will consider enabling agents to not only anticipate the arguments of other agents, but also what arguments they deem acceptable, which would allow for devising even more sophisticated strategies in dialogues.

REFERENCES

[1] S. A. Hosseini, S. Modgil, and O. Rodrigues. Enthymeme construction in dialogues using shared knowledge. In *Computational Models of Argument*, volume 266 of *Frontiers in Artificial Intelligence and Applications*, pages 325 – 332. IOS Press, 2014.

[2] A. Hunter. A probabilistic approach to modelling uncertain logical arguments. *International Journal of Approximate Reasoning*, 54(1):47 – 81, 2013.

[3] H. Li, N. Oren, and T. Norman. Probabilistic argumentation frameworks. In *Theories and Applications of Formal Argumentation*, volume 7132 of *Lecture Notes in Computer Science*, pages 1–16. 2012.

A Virtual Emotional Freedom Therapy Practitioner (Demonstration)

Hedieh Ranjbartabar
Computing Department, Macquarie University
NSW 2109, Australia
+61(0)2 9850 6344
hedieh.ranjbartabar@students.mq.edu.au

Deborah Richards
Computing Department, Macquarie University
NSW 2109, Australia
+61(0)2 9850 9567
deborah.richards@mq.edu.au

ABSTRACT

The role of virtual humans in a range of health scenarios, including therapy and counselling, are being explored. To help people in managing their emotional health this research project novelly investigates the value of a virtual practitioner to deliver the Emotional Freedom Technique (EFT). EFT, also known as Tapping Method, is a kind of psychological acupressure technique to optimize emotional and physical health. Significantly, we compare two different types of virtual EFT therapists, one that seeks to exhibit empathetic behaviour with another that delivers the therapy in a neutral manner. An initial online semi-interactive study with 37 participants reported benefits for both therapists from baseline emotion, and these improvements increased with a subsequent session, the empathic agent delivered slight but non-significant improvements but did not achieve a higher level of rapport with the human.

Keywords
Intelligent virtual agents; empathic agents; virtual humans; emotional freedom technique.

1. INTRODUCTION

The effectiveness of intelligent virtual agents (IVAs) that act as Virtual Humans (VHs) in a wide range of health and wellbeing roles is being explored. These VHs require social ability, communication skills and appropriate verbal and non-verbal behaviours. Interest is particularly growing in examining the viability and benefits of building long-term relationships with VHs. Rapport has been found to play an important role in establishing and maintaining human relationships [14]. Empathic behaviours are also being used to build a socio-emotional bond between the human and agent [10]. Questions are being raised concerning the extent to which VHs need to be believable or the same as humans (e.g. [3]), particularly when researchers are identifying that VHs might be preferable, such as in anonymous or non-judgmental contexts [5], and provide numerous benefits over their counterparts such as being more available and less variable – while also able to tailor responses according to the situation [8]. Via this demonstration we question whether empathic dialogue, and the associated effort, is always preferable.

The overarching aim of the demonstration was to determine whether an empathic or neutral agent delivered more emotional benefit. In the study reported in this paper, we explore the relative benefits of a virtual therapist that uses empathic behaviours, primarily exhibited via verbal communication, over the same therapist who uses neutral behaviours.

Appears in: Proceedings of the 15th International Conference on Autonomous Agents and Multiagent Systems (AAMAS 2016), J. Thangarajah, K. Tuyls, C. Jonker, S. Marsella (eds.), May 9–13, 2016, Singapore.

2. SCENARIO & TECHNOLOGY USED

Callahan [2] developed a method of tapping on acupressure points (acupoints) for treating mental problems called Thought Field Therapy (TFT) in the 1980s. Gary Craig developed EFT in the mid-1990s as a consequence of his study of TFT. Craig modified and improved Callahan's methodology to a simplified version. EFT is easy to learn and effective [9].

We chose to use EFT because, while it is often guided by an Emotional Freedom Practitioner, the method primarily involves individuals performing the therapy on themselves, as in the case of meditation, but additionally has a physical element also performed by the patient on themselves. Though there is use of acupuncture to treat psychological disorders and claims by energy therapy researchers that acupoint tapping creates unexpectedly strong and rapid clinical outcomes [4], EFT is not recognized as an evidence-based medical therapy. However, our aim was not to treat physical or mental health conditions, but to provide therapy that could be used by anyone to manage their own stresses and provide a testbed for exploring whether tailored empathic dialogue delivered significant benefits to justify the additional complexity and effort required to build an empathic VH.

The EFT process involves first identifying a specific problem to focus on while tapping, eg fear of flashbacks following a recent trauma. Next is to score the level of trouble on a scale of 0-10. After that saying out loud the 'set-up' statement, eg 'Even though I have this fear of the flashbacks I deeply and completely accept myself'. This statement is repeated three times, while tapping on the Karate Chop Point following by tapping gently on a number of meridian points of the head, face and body. Reassessing the level of disturbance and if necessary repeating the whole process [11].

Our virtual EFT practitioner, known as EFFIE the Emotional Freedom FrIEnd, is based on Virtual Human Toolkit components [6]. As seen in Figure 1 for the system to deliver credible and effective communication in real time, we developed a dialogue engine written in C#. Communication between components is done by message passing, which is implemented in ActiveMQ [12]. The dialogue engine sends BML (Behavior Markup Language) message to NVBG (NonVerbal-Behavior-Generator) module containing the line the character will say and for which nonverbal behavior needs to be generated. BML [7] is an XML description language used for controlling the verbal and nonverbal behavior of humanoid embodied conversational agents. The output of NVBG is also BML which are transformed into synchronized sequences of animations by Smartbody character animation system which is a BML realization engine [13].

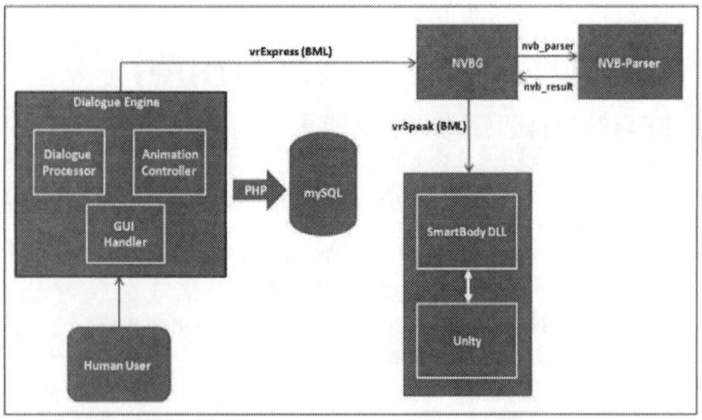

Figure 1: Architecture for virtual EFT practitioner: EFFIE.

We chose to add and execute pre-recorded voice snippets for Effie dialogues rather than use CSLU Toolkit's speech synthesizer to minimize the possible negative influence of an automated voice for the therapy session. For each continuous speech there exist 4 files, a wav file for the audio, an XML file for non verbal behaviour such as smiling or nodding, a BML file for lip synchronising and a text file containing the sentence(s). To create the BML file we used CSLUPhonemeScheduler tool from CSLU Toolkit. The BML files generated by this tool has viseme schedule with detailed timing information for lip-synching and word boundary timing information for synchronization of nonverbal behavior as specified through BML.

The dialogue engine consists of three main parts, a dialogue processor, an animation controller and a GUI handler. These three parts runs simultaneously to achieve synchronizing between dialogues, user interaction and animations. The dialogue processor sends the BML messages to NVBG and is responsible for turn taking. The user interacts with the system through the GUI handler. For each tapping animation there is an animation clip and an animation state. All tapping animation clips are maintained by an animator controller. The controller manages the animation states. Figure 2 shows Mecanim's Animation State Machine created for Effie. Animation Controller uses the state machine parameters to trigger desired animation and simulate the dynamic reasoning process of a real EFT therapist. The information provided by the user during the EFT session is sent to the mySQL database via a PHP command.

Two dialogues (empathic, neutral) were developed and contained two parts (welcome and intro to EFT round 1; followup and intro to round 2). Empathic dialogue sought to be more caring and was tailored to the emotional responses of the user (see video comp.mq.edu.au/~richards/AAMAS16-Demo/EffieVideo.wmv).

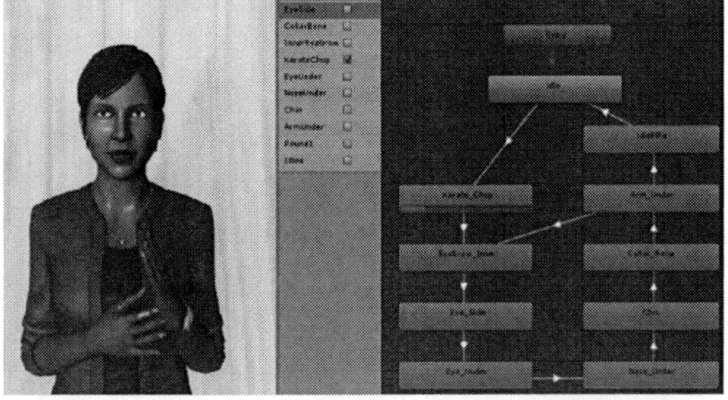

Figure 2: Mecanim's Animation State Machine for Effie.

3. EVALUATION

To explore the research questions of this study, we designed a quasi-experiment consisting of one between-subjects factors (empathic/neutral virtual therapist) and one within-subjects factor (time). A between-subjects design for agent-type was chosen to expose participants to both types, which would allow them to observe any differences and allow us to gather more data, including their preferences, with less participants. Qualtrics randomly assigned participants to groups that received the two types of agent in different orders. Different orders were designed to counterbalance and measure potential order effects. Group 1 interacted with the empathic ECA followed by the neutral ECA. Group 2 interacted with the neutral ECA followed by the empathic ECA. The independent variables (time and agent) were manipulated to measure the effect on the dependent variables: emotional score and sense of rapport.

To run the application written with the Virtual Human Toolkit three 3rd party software tools are required: .NET Framework, DirectX Redistributable and ActiveMQ. These three tools need to be installed on the users' machines and would require downloading of a 400+MB zip file, which unzipped to over 600MB. We did not believe that it was ethical or practical to ask volunteers to download and install the application. To avoid dealing with installing the 3rd party software by the user, we decided to record multiple video simulations (covering the main combinations of responses) of our character with the two scenarios, empathetic virtual therapist and neutral virtual therapist. In response to the users selection we played the corresponding video; providing a semi-interactive session.

A total number of 37 people (22 females, 15 males; mean age=23, SD=4.9) took part in the study. Group 1 (empathic-neutral) had 17 participants and Group 2 (neutral-empathic) had 20 participants. Participants in both groups achieved emotional benefits during the two sessions, with 50% and 46% overall reduction in their negative feeling towards their problem in group 1 and group 2, respectively. Although the achievement for group 1 is higher than group 2, the difference is not significant. This difference may be due to the semi-interactive use of multiple videos which meant we were unable to fully tailor empathic Effie's responses to the individual. Furthermore, the video did not allow participants to experience some aspects of the empathic dialogue, in particular the "empathy for the user" cues where Effie responded to the questions about how the participants day was going or whether their scores were improving or getting worse. This belief is evident in responses to the question "Effie was not empathic towards me" where both versions of Effie were found to be similarly moderately empathic even though empathetic cues derived from the literature [1] were only included in the empathic agent implementation. In summary, EFFIE was able to deliver emotional benefits to participants, however a short empathetic conversation before treatment involving greeting, social dialogue and sharing knowledge does not necessarily deliver better therapeutic benefits than a session that just focuses on EFT.

Initial analysis of results from an onsite study where 26 participants engaged with the character through real-time interaction indicate similar findings and through discussion with an EFT practitioner, it appears that the empathic dialogue does not deliver significant benefits and that differences are only likely if much more tailoring of dialogue and the treatment (i.e. adapting the animations and tapping points) are provided. Thus, as future work we plan to increase EFFIE's functionality, amend dialogues and use camera input to generate appropriate nonverbal behavior in real time based on EFFIE's perceptions.

4. REFERENCES

[1] Bickmore, T., Gruber, A., and Picard, R., 2005. Establishing the computer–patient working alliance in automated health behavior change interventions. *Patient Education and Counseling 59*, 1, 21-30.

[2] Callahan, R.J., 1995. A Thought Field Therapy (TFT) algorithm for trauma. *Traumatology 1*, 1, 2.

[3] De Melo, C.M. and Gratch, J., 2015. Beyond Believability: Quantifying the Differences Between Real and Virtual Humans. In *Intelligent Virtual Agents* Springer, 109-118.

[4] Feinstein, D., 2012. Acupoint stimulation in treating psychological disorders: Evidence of efficacy. *Review of General Psychology 16*, 4, 364.

[5] Gratch, J., Lucas, G.M., King, A.A., and Morency, L.-P., 2014. It's only a computer: the impact of human-agent interaction in clinical interviews. In *Proceedings of the 2014 international conference on Autonomous agents and multi-agent systems* International Foundation for Autonomous Agents and Multiagent Systems, 85-92.

[6] Hartholt, A., Traum, D., Marsella, S.C., Shapiro, A., Stratou, G., Leuski, A., Morency, L.-P., and Gratch, J., 2013. All together now. In *Intelligent Virtual Agents* Springer, 368-381.

[7] Kopp, S., Krenn, B., Marsella, S., Marshall, A.N., Pelachaud, C., Pirker, H., Thórisson, K.R., and Vilhjálmsson, H., 2006. Towards a common framework for multimodal generation: The behavior markup language. In *Intelligent virtual agents* Springer, 205-217.

[8] Lisetti, C.L., 2012. 10 advantages of using avatars in patient-centered computer-based interventions for behavior change. *SIGHIT Record 2*, 1, 28.

[9] Mitchell, M., 2009. Emotional freedom technique. *The practising midwife 12*, 7, 12-14.

[10] Ochs, M., Pelachaud, C., and Sadek, D., 2008. An empathic virtual dialog agent to improve human-machine interaction. In *Proceedings of the 7th international joint conference on Autonomous agents and multiagent systems-Volume 1* International Foundation for Autonomous Agents and Multiagent Systems, 89-96.

[11] Scott, J., 2008. Emotional freedom technique. *Counselling at Work. Winter 9*, 9-12.

[12] Snyder, B., Bosnanac, D., and Davies, R., 2011. *ActiveMQ in action*. Manning.

[13] Thiebaux, M., Marsella, S., Marshall, A.N., and Kallmann, M., 2008. Smartbody: Behavior realization for embodied conversational agents. In *Proceedings of the 7th international joint conference on Autonomous agents and multiagent systems-Volume 1* International Foundation for Autonomous Agents and Multiagent Systems, 151-158.

[14] Tickle-Degnen, L. and Rosenthal, R., 1990. The nature of rapport and its nonverbal correlates. *Psychological inquiry 1*, 4, 285-293.

Multilayered Multiagent System for Traffic Simulation (Demonstration)

Rafik Hadfi
Department of Computer Science and Engineering
Nagoya Institute of Technology
Gokiso, Showa-ku, Nagoya, 466-8555 Japan
rafik.hadfi@nitech.ac.jp

Takayuki Ito
Department of Computer Science and Engineering
Nagoya Institute of Technology
Gokiso, Showa-ku, Nagoya, 466-8555 Japan
ito.takayuki@nitech.ac.jp

ABSTRACT

We propose a multilayered multiagent simulator that can simulate traffic in any urban environment on earth, subject to specific weather conditions. We adopt an agent-based approach for the behaviors of the vehicles and the drivers. We additionally propose a behavioral model to realistically emulate the driving behaviors of humans.

Keywords

Simulation; Multiagent Systems; Traffic Simulation; Geographic Information System; Mobility; Weather Simulation

1. INTRODUCTION

Multiagent systems have inspired an increasing number of researchers from different domains. Their goal is to model the real world in terms of autonomous agents that can purposely interact with their external environment [13]. An agent can basically gather information from the environment using sensors, while attempting to execute its objectives using effectors [12]. In this paper, we propose a multiagent simulator that simulates traffic in an urban area subject to particular weather conditions. An inherent feature of such complex system is its multilayered structure and the nested levels of detail that compose it. Hence, we will model our simulator in terms of multiple independent layers. Each layer processes a particular aspect of the simulation through the interactions of its elements. A layer will therefore be represented by a complex network of interacting agents that communicate within that layer and possibly with other layers. Multiagent traffic simulation has been extensively studied since traffic and transportation management require autonomic, collaborative, and reactive agents [1]. It is within this perspective that we propose to simulate traffic while adopting a multilayered multiagent architecture coupled to behavioral agent simulation. This is in fact a way to refine both microscopic and macroscopic aspects found in many traffic simulators. Additionally, the availability of data collected via sensors and mobile devices allows us to better model human behaviors. For instance, this allows for the analysis of driver behaviors and the underlying decision-making mechanisms [3, 9, 10, 11]. As a result, we can build large-scale simulations by embedding the social interactions and by elaborating fine-grained human behaviors [7]. The resulting multiagent social simulation [2] is well suited to any social context due to its ability to simulate pro-active behaviors, parallel computations [8], and dynamic micro scenarios [6, 4]. Our motivation is to build a simulator that can emulate traffic as well as any environmental factor that effects traffic flow, routing, and even CO_2 emission. Being able to simulate weather is a novel way to approach traffic simulation since it allows the reproduction of real-world scenarios like traffic congestion in natural disaster situations. Such simulator becomes a testbed for general-purpose computational intelligence and can be used for the benchmarking of routing algorithms.

In section 2, we provide the architecture of the simulator. In section 3, we cover the behavioral models. Finally, we discuss the result.

Appears in: *Proceedings of the 15th International Conference on Autonomous Agents and Multiagent Systems (AAMAS 2016), J. Thangarajah, K. Tuyls, C. Jonker, S. Marsella (eds.), May 9–13, 2016, Singapore.*

2. SIMULATOR ARCHITECTURE

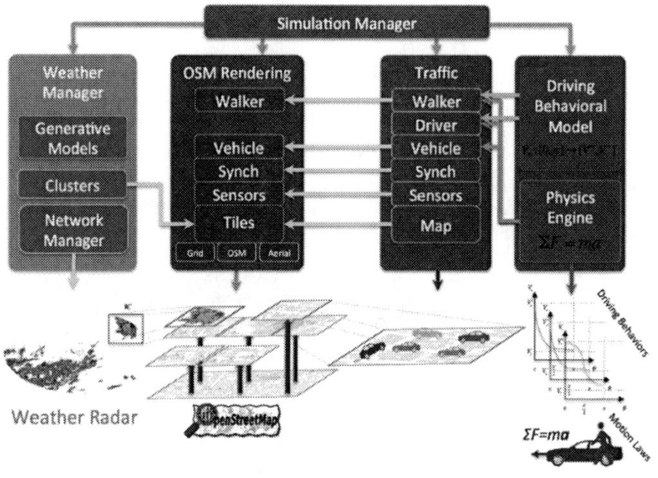

Figure 1: Architecture

The idea is to represent our complex system as a superposition of different layers. Each layer operates autonomously with its internal threads, agents, graphical objects, data, etc. The architecture of the simulator is illustrated in figure 1. We assume that the way vehicles navigate their space is not specific to one particular Geographic Information System (GIS). Particularly, There is an independence between the actual simulation (**Behavioral Models** and **Physical Engine**) and the corresponding GIS rendering. This is important when the renderer is complex, that is, when we are not only rendering vehicles, but weather data, pedestrians, snow, etc. This separation obeys the Dependency Inversion Principle (DIP) in the sense that the physical simulation acts as a high-level, abstract, or mathematical representation of the phenomena we are trying to simulate, while the GIS rendering is one possible way of rendering the traffic simulation. Next, we provide the components of the architecture.

2.1 Physics Engine and Behavioral Models

The **Physics Engine** component provides an approximate simulation of the physics that underly traffic, motion and the interactions between the agents (mostly collision detection). This component performs the simulation in real-time before rendering the result. The **Behavioral Models** component describe the scenarios that govern the motion of the vehicles and the behaviors of the drivers. The flow from the Physics Engine and Behavioral Models towards the OSM renderer is shown in figure 1 using the pink arrows.

2.2 Traffic Module

This module is composed of the 6 components. **Walkers** component relates to the pedestrians and their mobility generation and collision detection. **Drivers** contains routines related to driving, collision prediction, lights and lanes assessment. **Vehicles** is to modulate the acceleration, direction, location, friction, velocity, and breaking. **Synchronization** tier updates the states of the traffic lights. **Sensors** are the motion detectors and **Map** is the space where the motion is generated.

2.3 Weather Module

Weather simulation is the generation of precipitation as if it is detected by a Weather Surveillance Radar (WSR). Additionally, it is possible to download this data in real-time and render it directly onto the map.

2.4 Geographic Module

We adopt OpenStreetMap (OSM) [5] as a geographic referential. The rendering of the map relies on downloading and updating OSM tiles. Such tiles correspond to an area of the map and are loaded dynamically depending on where the simulation is being run. We note that there are two maps: a core map assigned to the physics engine, and a map to represent a real-world referential (OSM in our case). The core map is used to run the simulation in real-time so that the result is later rendered onto the second map (bottom pink arrow in figure 1).

3. BEHAVIORAL MODELING

The behavioral models govern the agents mobility and the actions allowed within the simulator. Herein, we mention two types of behavioral models: driving and vehicle mobility.

3.1 Driving

The main feature that reflects the driving behavior of a human is the velocity and the way it changes as function of the turns. In fact, turns are an important indicator of the driver's mastery of the steering wheel (with angle λ) and its physical effect on the vehicle. Thus, we can look at the turning angle θ comprised between the velocity and direction. For instance, driving in a straight line corresponds to $\theta = 0$ while a right turn corresponds to $\theta = \pi/2$. The minimal and maximal velocities of the vehicle are respectively $\vec{v}^-$ and $\vec{v}^+$, and define the driver's spectrum of physically allowed velocities. A behavioral model is a specific way of mapping θ to a velocity $\vec{v}_\theta$. Figure 2 shows three behavioral models. v_1 corresponds to what is perceived as a reckless driver since he barely decelerates when performing right turns. v_2 shows a conservative driver since he decelerates drastically when reaching right turns. v_3 shows a standard driver. A behavior is invariant beyond π (U-turn), which justifies the interval $[0, \pi]$.

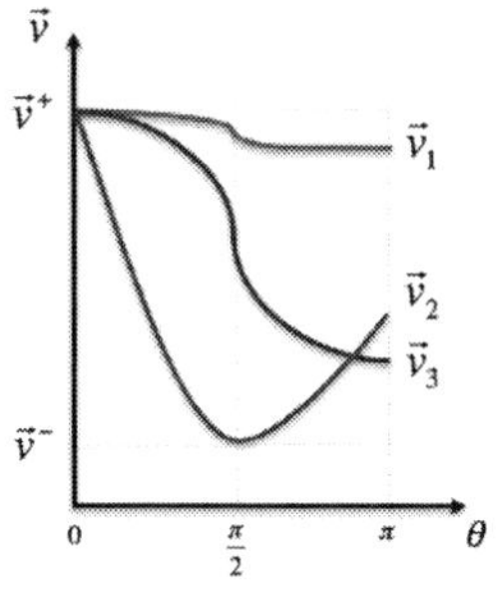

Figure 2: Behavioral Models $\vec{v}_1$, $\vec{v}_2$, and $\vec{v}_3$

3.2 Vehicle Mobility

Moving from point A to point B is reduced to a set of calculations that update the motive force $\vec{F}_m$, friction $\vec{F}_f$, acceleration $\vec{a}$, velocity $\vec{v}$, direction $\vec{d}$, and the location x. $\vec{d}$ is updated to $\alpha_{\vec{d}} + \frac{1}{L}(\|\vec{v}\|\, u_m) sin(\lambda\frac{\pi}{3})p\frac{180}{\pi}$ with λ being the steering wheel angle, L the vehicle wheelbase, u_m the number of units per meter, p the simulation step, and $\alpha_{\vec{d}}$ is the angle of $\vec{d}$. $\vec{v}$ is updated to $\vec{d}\|\vec{v}\| + \vec{a}p$. Based on Newton's second law, $\vec{a}$ is set to $\frac{1}{m}(\vec{F}_m + \vec{F}_f)$. Updating all the forces requires updating the friction force whenever the driver breaks according to $\vec{F}_f \leftarrow -\vec{d}\vec{a}_{max}$ with $\vec{a}_{max}$ being the maximal acceleration. x is updated to $x + \vec{v}u_m p$.

4. DISCUSSION

The user can macroscopically switch between the views (Aerial view, OpenStreetMap view, Grid view) of the simulation by altering the opacity of the layer. It is possible to configure the simulations and specify the desired scenario by providing three XML files. The first file specifies the simulation geographic area. The second file specifies the driving behaviors of each driver by assigning a velocity to a turning angle λ. The third file specifies for each vehicle the starting point, the itinerary, and the driver's type. The separation between the layers allows the simulations to be scalable in the number of vehicles, despite the complexity of their behaviors. Furthermore, running the physical calculations within one monolithic component allows us to render all the results faster than if each layer had to separately perform complex physical computations. The simulator can additionally generate rich datasets corresponding to the vehicles physical processes (location, velocity, predictions), the drivers actions, and the weather effects of the overall traffic simulation.

REFERENCES

[1] B. Chen and H. Cheng. A review of the applications of agent technology in traffic and transportation systems. In *IEEE Transactions on Intelligent Transportation Systems*, pages 485 – 497, 2010.

[2] P. Davidsson. *Multi agent based simulation: beyond social simulation.* Springer, Berlin, Heidelberg, 2001.

[3] H. Dia. An agent-based approach to modelling driver route choice behaviour under the influence of real-time information. *Transportation Research Part C: Emerging Technologies*, 10(5-6):331–349, 2002.

[4] N. Gilbert. *Computer Simulation of Social Processes.* Number 6. Social Research Update, Department of Sociology, University of Surrey, UK, 1994.

[5] M. M. Haklay and P. Weber. Openstreetmap: User-generated street maps. *IEEE Pervasive Computing*, 7(4):12–18, Oct. 2008.

[6] A. Harding. *Microsimulation and Public Policy.* Elsevier, 1996.

[7] H. Hattori, Y. Nakajima, and S. Yamane. Massive multiagent-based urban traffic simulation with fine-grained behavior models. 2011.

[8] J. Misra. *Distributed Discrete-Event Simulation*, volume 18. ACM Computing Surveys (CSUR), 1986.

[9] K. Nagel and F. Marchal. Computational methods for multi-agent simulations of travel behaviour. In *Proceedings of International Association for Travel Behavior Research (IATBR)*, Lucerne, Switzerland, 2003.

[10] R. J. Rossetti, R. H. Bordini, A. L. Bazzan, S. Bampi, R. Liu, and D. Van Vliet. Using bdi agents to improve driver modelling in a commuter scenario. *Transportation Research Part C: Emerging Technologies*, 10(5-6):373–398, 2002.

[11] R. J. Rossetti, R. Liu, H. B. Cybis, and S. Bampi. A multi-agent demand model. In *Proceedings of the 13th Mini-Euro Conference and The 9th Meeting of the Euro Working Group Transportation*, pages 193–198, Bari, Italy, 2002.

[12] S. Russell and P. Norvig. *Artificial intelligence: a modern approach.* 1995.

[13] M. Wooldridge and N. R. Jennings. Intelligent agents: Theory and practice. *The knowledge engineering review*, 10(02):115–152, 1995.

A Treasure Hunt With An Empathic Virtual Tutor (Demonstration)

Mei Yii Lim, Amol Deshmukh, Srinivasan Janarthanam, Helen Hastie, Ruth Aylett
School of Mathematical and Computer Sciences, Heriot-Watt University, Edinburgh, UK
{M.Lim, A.Deshmukh, sc445, H.Hastie, R.S.Aylett}@hw.ac.uk

Lynne Hall
Department of Computing, Engineering and Technology, University of Sunderland, UK
Lynne.hall@sunderland.ac.uk

ABSTRACT

We present a demonstration of a Treasure Hunt Application with an Empathic Virtual Tutor. During the treasure hunt, this empathic agent adapts its interaction based on the affective state of the user to improve learning experience. We demonstrate the application domain; the technology used; and the app focusing on the empathic strategies applied.

Keywords

Treasure Hunt; Empathic Agent; Arousal; Valence; Human-Agent Interaction

1. INTRODUCTION

A central concept in learning is empathy and emotion. Emotions are a part of human essence [2]. On the other hand, empathy is often seen as the capability for perceiving, understanding and experiencing another person's emotions [3]. For empathy to occur in learning, a tutor needs to be able to perceive, model and reason about the affective state experienced by learners and consequently adapt its interaction accordingly [1].

In this demonstration, we present a Treasure Hunt Application (THA) developed for the Heriot-Watt University (HWU) Edinburgh campus[1] with a Halloween Theme, initially based on a local school's annual treasure hunt activity, which forms part of the Geography curriculum [4]. A user has to apply his/her map reading skills while following clues presented by an empathic virtual agent called Emys, to unlock Halloween related treasures (please refer to Figure 2). During the quest, Emys offers advice under different circumstances and these interventions are adapted based on the user's affect determined by valence and arousal [6].

2. TECHNOLOGY USED

The original THA was developed to run on Android tablets for outdoor environment with GPS tracking. However, for the purpose of this demonstration, a Samsung SIII phone and NFC technology [7] are used as shown in Figure 1.

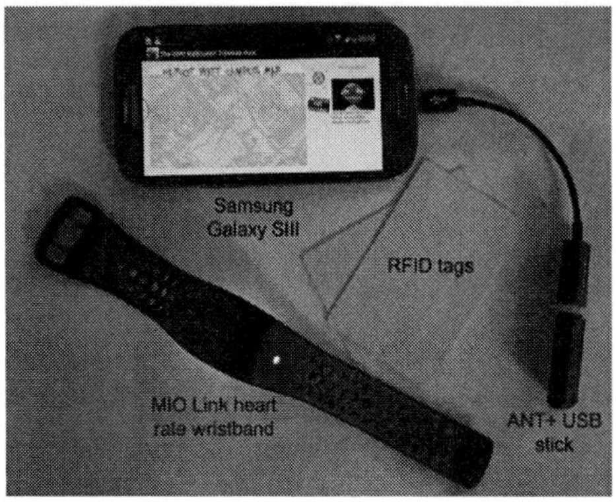

Figure 1: The THA Components

Each treasure point has been replaced by a passive RFID [5] tag which will be picked up by the mobile phone as it is being moved along the paper map. To estimate the user's arousal, his/her heart rate is monitored using a MIO Link heart rate sensor[2]. ANT+[3] device profile is used for sending data between the sensor and the app. Emys voice is from Cereproc[4].

This interactive demo will allow attendees (one user at a time) to try out the treasure hunt by moving the mobile phone on the paper map and tapping on the correct treasure point which is analogous to moving in the real environment. Meanwhile his/her heart rate (which changes as he/she carries out some physical activities) and performance in navigating and unlocking treasures will be monitored so that Emys can offer appropriate advice when necessary (please refer to Section 3.1 for the empathic strategies).

3. THE TREASURE HUNT APPLICATION

The THA displays the empathic agent, Emys; a compass; and a digital map of HWU Edinburgh campus. At each step, Emys presents the directional information and clues to

[1]http://www.hw.ac.uk/student-life/campus-life/edinburgh.htm

[2]http://www.mioglobal.com/en-uk/Mio-Link-heart-rate-monitor-wristband/Product.aspx

[3]https://www.thisisant.com/developer/ant-plus/ant-plus-basics

[4]https://www.cereproc.com/

Appears in: *Proceedings of the 15th International Conference on Autonomous Agents and Multiagent Systems (AAMAS 2016), J. Thangarajah, K. Tuyls, C. Jonker, S. Marsella (eds.), May 9–13, 2016, Singapore.*

a treasure. While the user is on the quest, interventions can occur under 5 circumstances: 1) after a clue has been presented and the user does not start moving - assumes that the user is confused; 2) when the user heads in the wrong direction; 3) when the user has passed the destination; 4) when the user is at the destination but does not start answering questions - assumes that the user can't find the treasure; and 5) when the user thinks s/he is at the destination but is actually not.

When the user thinks s/he has found a treasure, s/he has to press the "Got there!" button shown in Figure 2. Emys either confirms by posing questions related to the newly found treasure or intervenes by telling the user that s/he is not at the destination yet. Emys also provides the user with feedback on the correctness of answers to the questions. Treasures will appear on screen when the user answers all questions correctly.

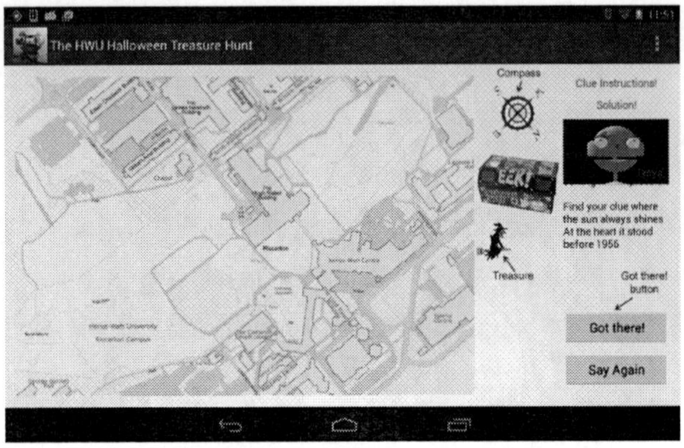

Figure 2: The THA User Interface

3.1 Empathic strategies

Arousal is based on the user's heart rate while valence is based on the user's performances. They are categorised into 3 different levels: low, medium, high and negative, neutral, positive respectively.

Prior to the treasure hunt, the user's baseline heart rate is recorded. As the user walks from one point to another, his/her heart rate is being monitored continuously. When Emys needs to intervene, it will compare the user's current heart rate taking into consideration the baseline to an average range (recorded with 8 people walking the same route). If the resulting range is higher than the average range, then it falls into the category high while if it is less than half of the average range, it falls into the category low. Anything that falls in-between is considered as medium arousal. The same rules apply for categorisation of arousal when the user is stationary (a different average comparison range is used here based on recording 8 people while they are stationary).

Valence is estimated using the user's performance where 3 scores are taken into account: percentage of questions answered correctly, percentage of treasures unlocked and an intervention score. If the user completes a step without any intervention, they will score 5 points while each intervention incurs a penalty point. For example at step 3, the total collectable points would be 15 and if 6 interventions have occurred, the intervention score will be $(15-6)/15 = 0.6$. Please note that it is possible to have a negative intervention score. Valence is the average of these 3 scores, for example, a user who has answered 3 out of 5 questions correctly, unlocked 2 out of 3 treasures and has the above intervention score is assigned a valence of $(0.6+0.67+0.6)/3 = 0.623$. Any value above 0.7 is categorised as positive valence while any value below 0.3 is categorised as negative valence. Any value in between is considered as neutral.

The intervention utterances change under 4 different affective states: 1) frustration: high arousal, negative valence; 2) excitement: high arousal, positive valence; 3) boredom: low arousal, negative valence; and 4) neutral: neutral valence. Example of utterances under different affective states for when the user is going astray is as below:

- Neutral: You are heading off the path, please use the compass to guide you.
- Frustration: I am sorry to tell you that you are heading off the path. Please use the compass to guide you.
- Boredom: Hmm... looks like you are heading off the path. Don't give up, use the compass to guide you.
- Excitement: Wait a minute... you are heading off the path!

4. CONCLUSION

We are currently running an evaluation to explore the effect of these empathic strategies on perception of the virtual agent Emys as well as the overall performance and experience of users carrying out the treasure hunt activity.

Acknowledgments

This work was partially supported by the European Commission (EC) and was funded by the EU FP7 ICT-317923 project EMOTE. The authors are solely responsible for the content of this publication. It does not represent the opinion of the EC, and the EC is not responsible for any use that might be made of data appearing therein.

REFERENCES

[1] G. Castellano, A. Paiva, A. Kappas, R. Aylett, H. Hastie, W. Barendregt, F. Nabais, and S. Bull. Towards empathic virtual and robotic tutors. In *Artificial Intelligence in Education*, pages 733–736, Boston, USA, 2013. Springer Berlin Heidelberg.

[2] A. Damasio. *Descartes' Error: Emotion, Reason and the Human Brain*. Gosset/Putnam Press, New York, 1994.

[3] M. L. Hoffman. *Empathy and moral development: Implications for caring and justice*. Cambridge University Press, Cambridge, 2001.

[4] M. Y. Lim, M. E. Foster, S. Janarthanam, A. Deshmukh, H. Hastie, and R. Aylett. Let's go for a treasure hunt. In *Affective Agents Workshop, 14th International conference on Intelligent Virtual Agents*, Boston, USA, 2014.

[5] C. M. Roberts. Radio frequency identification (rfid). *Computers & Security*, 25(1):18–26, 2006.

[6] J. A. Russell. A circumplex model of affect. *Journal of Personality and Social Psychology*, 39(6):349–355, 1980.

[7] R. Want. Near field communication. *IEEE Pervasive Computing*, (3):4–7, 2011.

A Kinect-based Interactive Game to Improve the Cognitive Inhibition of the Elderly

(Demonstration)

Siyuan Liu[1], Zhiqi Shen[1], Han Yu[1], Han Lin[1], Zhengjin Guo[1], Zhengxiang Pan[1], Chunyan Miao[1], Cyril Leung[1,2]

[1]Joint NTU-UBC Research Centre of Excellence in Active Living for the Elderly
Nanyang Technological University, 50 Nanyang Avenue, Singapore 639798

[2]Department of Electrical and Computer Engineering, The University of British Columbia, Canada

{syliu, zqshen, han.yu, linhan,zjguo, panz0012, ascymiao}@ntu.edu.sg, cleung@ece.ubc.ca

ABSTRACT

Cognitive abilities, including cognitive inhibition, degenerate with the aging process. In this demonstration, we present a Kinect-based interactive game which aims to improve the cognitive inhibition ability of the elderly. The game is designed in the table tennis theme, and the adoption of Kinect makes it convenient for the elderly to use. The players' in-game behaviour data are recorded for the health advisor agent to conduct personalization, analysis, and decision making. A pilot study has been conducted to investigate the relationship between the players' cognitive inhibition abilities and their in-game performance. The study results suggest that the in-game performance can reflect a player's cognitive inhibition ability, and indicate that the game can be used to improve the cognitive inhibition ability of the elderly in the future.

Keywords

Game, Cognitive Inhibition, Elderly, Table Tennis, Kinect

1. INTRODUCTION

It is well-known that human cognitive abilities decline with age [3]. These cognitive skills include *cognitive inhibition* which refers to the ability to tune out the stimuli that are irrelevant to the current mental state [8]. It is a key mechanism in emotion and behavior regulations [9]. Cognitive inhibition deficits can lead to various conditions such as depression [5].

Older adults can maintain and improve their cognitive inhibition abilities through consistent physical exercise [1]. In recent years, interactive games have been found to be helpful in improving general cognitive wellness [14, 15], and rehabilitation for stroke [4] and Parkinson's Disease [2, 6, 7] which require sustained physical exercise. In this demonstration, we present a Kinect-based interactive game – *PingPingPong-Pong* to improve the cognitive inhibition ability of the elderly. The game is incorporated with the traditional Go/No-go tests which require the player to perform an action given certain stimuli [10]. It is implemented in the theme of playing table tennis which the elderly users are generally familiar with. The adoption of Kinect makes it convenient for the elderly to play the game. Driven by each individual player's in-game behaviour trajectory data, a health advisor agent in the game provides feedbacks to the player to recommend suitable exercises for him to train his cognitive inhibition, and determine whether his current condition needs to be brought to the attention of medical professionals. The agents are designed and implemented with our Goal Net Design tools [13]

Appears in: *Proceedings of the 15th International Conference on Autonomous Agents and Multiagent Systems (AAMAS 2016), J. Thangarajah, K. Tuyls, C. Jonker, S. Marsella (eds.), May 9–13, 2016, Singapore.*

2. THE DEMONSTRATION

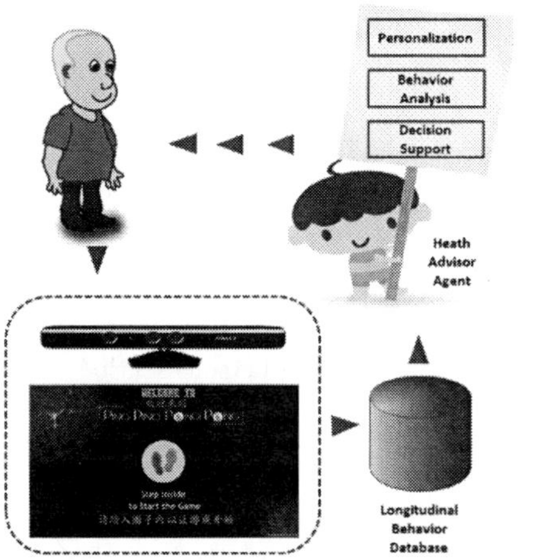

Figure 1: The conceptual framework of the PingPingPongPong game

The game has been infused with familiarity design considerations to improve the adoption by local senior citizens in Singapore [11]. As shown in Figure 1, the player can begin the game through interacting with Kinect with his gestures. After the user logins to the game, his historical playing data will be analysed by the health advisor agent for personalization to calibrate the game difficulty to suit the player's physical and cognitive conditions. The player in-game behavior data will be captured and stored in the longitudinal behavior database to form his personal playing trajectory. After the player completes the game, the agent conducts behavior analysis and makes suggestions to the player according to the analysis results. The data stored in the database will be further used for long-term behavior analysis.

The game is currently designed with 3 tasks, and each includes several sessions (i.e., a session refers to one or multiple table tennis ball(s) being dealt to the player for him to hit it/them back). Figure 2 shows an example session in Task 3.

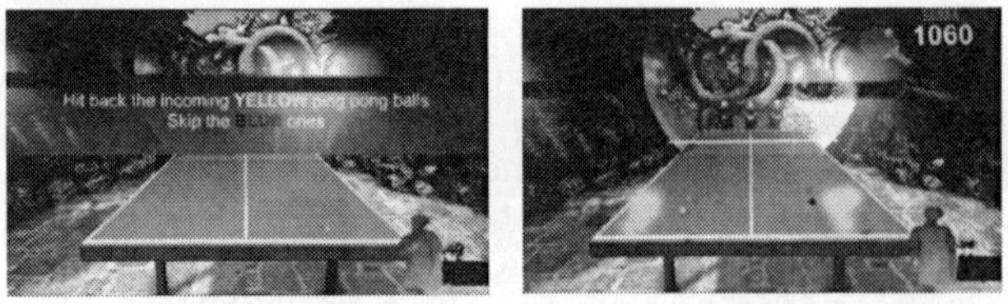

(a) Instructions (b) Session example

Figure 2: Example game scenarios

Task 1 is a single colored task. In each session, there is one colored ball coming out and the player needs to hit the ball in a given color back. For example, the player is asked to only hit the yellow balls back, and should perform nothing when seeing a red ball being dealt to him. The color of the ball in each session is randomized. In this case, color is the stimulus as in the traditional Go/No-go tests. Tasks 2 and 3 are both tasks with two colors. In each session of Task 2, a white ball and a coloured ball are being dealt simultaneously to a player. The player needs to hit the colored ball back. In each session of Task 3, two colored balls are being dealt simultaneously. The color combination of the two balls will not change throughout all sessions. The player needs to hit the ball with a given color back. For example, as shown in Figure 2(a), the instructions ask the player to hit the yellow balls, and skip the blue balls.

The player's in-game behavior data are recorded in the database. Key feature data captured include the spatial locations of key points in a player's skeleton (e.g., hand, elbow, shoulder, hip) at all sampling time steps, the time the balls are dealt, and the session results (i.e., whether the player hits the ball that he should hit). These data are passed to the health advisor agent for real-time analysis and decision making as well as personalization and long-term analysis.

3. PRELIMINARY RESULTS

We conducted a pilot study to investigate the effectiveness of the game in assessing the players' cognitive inhibition abilities. We invited 3 groups of players in the age group of "above 65", "45-55", and "below 20" in the study. Each group includes 50 subjects who completed all the three tasks. We use the following two commonly adopted metrics [12] in the traditional Go/No-go tests to evaluate the players' cognitive inhibition abilities: accuracy (a) and response time (r). They are calculated as follows:

$$a = \frac{N_h}{N}, \quad (1)$$

$$r = \frac{1}{N}\sum_{i=1}^{N}(P_i - C_i), \quad (2)$$

where N is the number of balls being dealt, and N_h is the number of balls hit accurately by the player. C_i is the time that a ball is dealt, and P_i is the time that the player starts movement after he sees the ball. A player with a higher cognitive ability should have a higher accuracy and a lower response time. The average results for the 3 groups of subjects are shown in Figure 3.

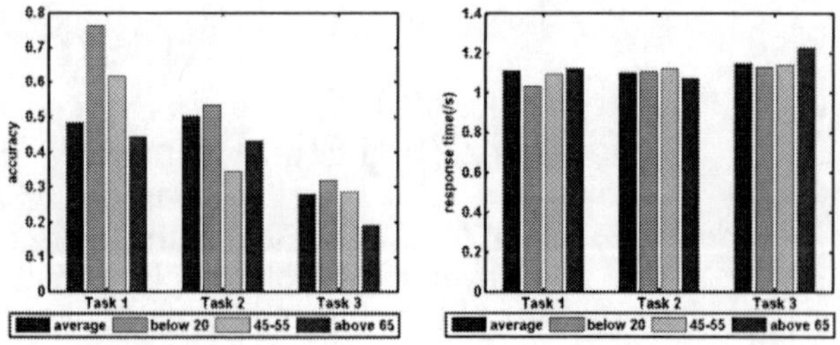

(a) Accuracy (b) Response time

Figure 3: Pilot study results

It can be seen from the results that in Task 1, the accuracy decreases with the increases in players' age. There are some interesting points to note in the results of Task 2. The accuracy for the group of "above 65" is remarkably better than the accuracy of the group of "45-55". The observation may be due to the elderly's difficulty in seeing the white balls. Therefore, they directly hit the coloured balls. The explanation can be further supported by the results of Task 3, where the accuracy for the group of "above 65" is lower than the accuracy for the group of "45-55" as the two balls are both coloured, and the elderly need to take time to differentiate them and hit the correct balls back. The response time for the three tasks present an opposite trend to the accuracy results across the three groups, suggesting that the elderly may need more time to take actions (except for Task 2).

In summary, the pilot study results suggest that the performance of the players in playing the game is correlated with player cognitive inhibition ability (i.e., the older players tend to have lower cognitive inhibition ability, and present lower accuracy and longer response time in playing the game). This implies that the designed game can be used to assess and further improve the cognitive ability of the elderly.

4. CONCLUSIONS

In this demonstration, we proposed a Kinect-based interactive game which targets to improve the cognitive inhibition ability of the elderly. Three tasks are currently designed and implemented. A pilot study has been conducted to investigate the effectiveness of the designed game in assessing the cognitive inhibition ability of the players. The results show that the player behavior reflected in the game is correlated with his cognitive inhibition ability. In subsequent research, we will study the long-term effectiveness of the game in improving the cognitive inhibition ability of the elderly.

Acknowledgements

This research is supported by the National Research Foundation Singapore under its Interactive Digital Media (IDM) Strategic Research Programme; the Interdisciplinary Graduate School, NTU; and the Lee Kuan Yew Post-Doctoral Fellowship Grant.

REFERENCES

[1] J. Buckley, J. D. Cohen, A. F. Kramer, E. McAuley, and S. P. Mullen. Cognitive control in the self-regulation of physical activity and sedentary behavior. *Frontiers in Human Neuroscience*, 8(747), 2014.

[2] Y. Cai, Z. Shen, S. Liu, H. Yu, X. Han, J. Ji, M. J. McKeown, C. Leung, and C. Miao. An agent-based game for the predictive diagnosis of parkinson's disease. In *Proceedings of the 13th International Conference on Autonomous Agents and Multi-agent Systems (AAMAS'14)*, pages 1663–1664, 2014.

[3] R. Engle, M. Kane, and S. Tuholski. Individual differences in working memory capacity and what they tell us about controlled attention, general fluid intelligence, and functions of the prefrontal cortex. *Cambridge University Press*, pages 102–134, 1999.

[4] A. Gazihan, L. Amanda, M. Matt, and K. Caitlin. Towards customizable games for stroke rehabilitation. In *Proceedings of the SIGCHI Conference on Human Factors in Computing Systems*, pages 2113–2122, 2010.

[5] J. Joomann, K. L. Yoon, and U. Zetsche. Cognitive inhibition in depression. *Applied and Preventive Psychology*, 12(3):128–139, 2007.

[6] M. Krause, J. Smeddinck, and R. Meyer. A digital game to support voice treatment for parkinson's disease. In *Proceedings of the CHI'13 Extended Abstracts on Human Factors in Computing Systems (CHI EA'13)*, pages 445–450, 2013.

[7] S. Liu, Z. Shen, M. J. McKeown, C. Leung, and C. Miao. A fuzzy logic based parkinson's disease risk predictor. In *Proceedings of the 2014 IEEE International Conference on Fuzzy Systems (FUZZ-IEEE'14)*, pages 1624–1631, 2014.

[8] C. MacLeod and M. Colin. The concept of inhibition in cognition. *Inhibition in cognition*, pages 3–23, 2007.

[9] A. Mathews and C. MacLeod. Cognitive vulnerability to emotional disorders. *Annual Review of Clinical Psychology*, 1:167–195, 2005.

[10] B. A. Nosek and M. R. Banaji. The go/no-go association task. *Social cognition*, 19(6):625–666, 2001.

[11] Z. Pan, C. Miao, H. Yu, C. Leung, and J. J. Chin. The effects of familiarity design on the adoption of wellness games by the elderly. In *Proceedings of the 2015 IEEE/WIC/ACM International Joint Conference on Web Intelligence and Intelligent Agent Technology (WI-IAT'15)*, pages 387–390, 2015.

[12] T. S. Redick, A. Calvo, C. E. Gay, and R. W. Engle. Working memory capacity and go/no-go task performance: selective effects of updating, maintenance, and inhibition. *Journal of Experimental Psychology: Learning, Memory, and Cognition*, 37(2):308, 2011.

[13] Z. Shen, H. Yu, C. Miao, S. Li, and Y. Chen. Multi-agent system development made easy. In *Proceedings of the 30th AAAI Conference on Artificial Intelligence (AAAI-16)*, 2016.

[14] Q. Wu, X. Han, H. Yu, Z. Shen, and C. Miao. The innovative application of learning companions in virtual singapura. In *Proceedings of the 12th International Conference on Autonomous Agents and Multi-agent Systems (AAMAS'13)*, pages 1171–1172, 2013.

[15] H. Yu, Z. Shen, C. Miao, and A.-H. Tan. A simple curious agent to help people be curious. In *Proceedings of the 10th International Conference on Autonomous Agents and Multiagent Systems (AAMAS'11)*, pages 1159–1160, 2011.

A Decentralised Multi-Agent System for Emergency Resource Allocation in Metropolitan Regions

(Demonstration)

Jihang Zhang, Minjie Zhang, Fenghui Ren
School of Computing and Information Technology
University of Wollongong
NSW, Australia
jz718@uowmail.edu.au, {minjie, fren}@uow.edu.au

Jiakun Liu
School of Mathematics and Applied Statistics
University of Wollongong
NSW, Australia
jiakunl@uow.edu.au

Keywords

Multi-Agent System; Resource Allocation; Emergency Response

1. INTRODUCTION OF THE APPLICATION DOMAIN

Nowadays, emergency departments in many countries still rely on human operators to allocate rescue resources to emergency events. However, with the fast growth of population in metropolitan regions, the frequency of occurrence of emergency events has risen significantly, which imposes tremendous pressure over emergency event operators. Agent and multi-agent systems (MASs) provide potential solutions to address such complicated emergency response problem due to agents ability of autonomous reasoning, adaptive decision making, complex environment modeling and collective group formulation [5]. In recent years, a number of promising agent-based emergency response and simulation systems have been developed to support rescue operations for different emergency situations. Some of the important ones include FireGrid [4], RoboCup Rescue [7], DEFACTO [10], DrillSim [2] and ALADDIN [1]. Nevertheless, most of these systems are limited to simulate and study emergency crises, which do not provide concrete solutions about how to improve the effectiveness of response operations and optimise the resource allocation results.

In this demonstration, we present a MAS for the simulation of emergency rescue response in metropolitan regions, which is implemented based on our previous work in [11]. Our MAS provides a decentralised resource allocation approach to deploy resources to multiple emergency events simultaneously on Google Maps.

2. PROBLEM SCENARIO DESCRIPTION

In metropolitan regions, multiple emergency events could happen concurrently at different locations, which have the five common characteristics, including that (1) these events are hard to be predicted, which makes resources per-allocation become almost impossible; (2) these events usually require multiple resources, which might be distributed over an extensive area with different usage costs, mobilities, availabilities, ownerships and functionalities. This can complicate the resource searching progress; (3) these events have strict time limits for emergency departments to response and allocate rescue resources, which increases the difficulty of finding the optimal resource allocation plan; (4) these events might require same resources at same time during the emergency response, which results in potential resource contention problems and (5) the environments around these events and the events themselves are dynamic, which may introduce many uncertain factors during the emergency resource allocation.

Due to the complexity, unpredictability, dynamic natures and potential resource contention problems among these events, human operators usually have difficulties to efficiently find out the most suitable and effective rescue solution within events' deadlines, which results in the increase of the number of casualties. Our MAS is designed to handle different types of emergency events that require the collaboration responses of multiple emergency departments. Through using a decentralised resource allocation approach, our MAS is more practical to be deployed in real world environments compared with traditional centralised systems. Besides, with the support of the domain transportation theory [9], our MAS can efficiently select the most suitable resources for multiple concurrent emergency events with the objective of minimising the total cost of resources deployment time and money expenditure. In addition to the domain transportation theory, we have also incorporated a resource coordination algorithm into our MAS to dynamically coordinate resources for resource contention events based on their attributes, such as severities and deadlines.

3. OVERVIEW OF THE MAS FRAMEWORK

As described in previous section, in order to maximise the system practicability and extendability, we have applied a decentralised and modular design approach for our MAS, which includes six modules in the system (see Figure 1) — a task identification module, a resource identification module, a proposal generation module, an optimal allocation module,

Appears in: *Proceedings of the 15th International Conference on Autonomous Agents and Multiagent Systems (AAMAS 2016), J. Thangarajah, K. Tuyls, C. Jonker, S. Marsella (eds.), May 9–13, 2016, Singapore.*

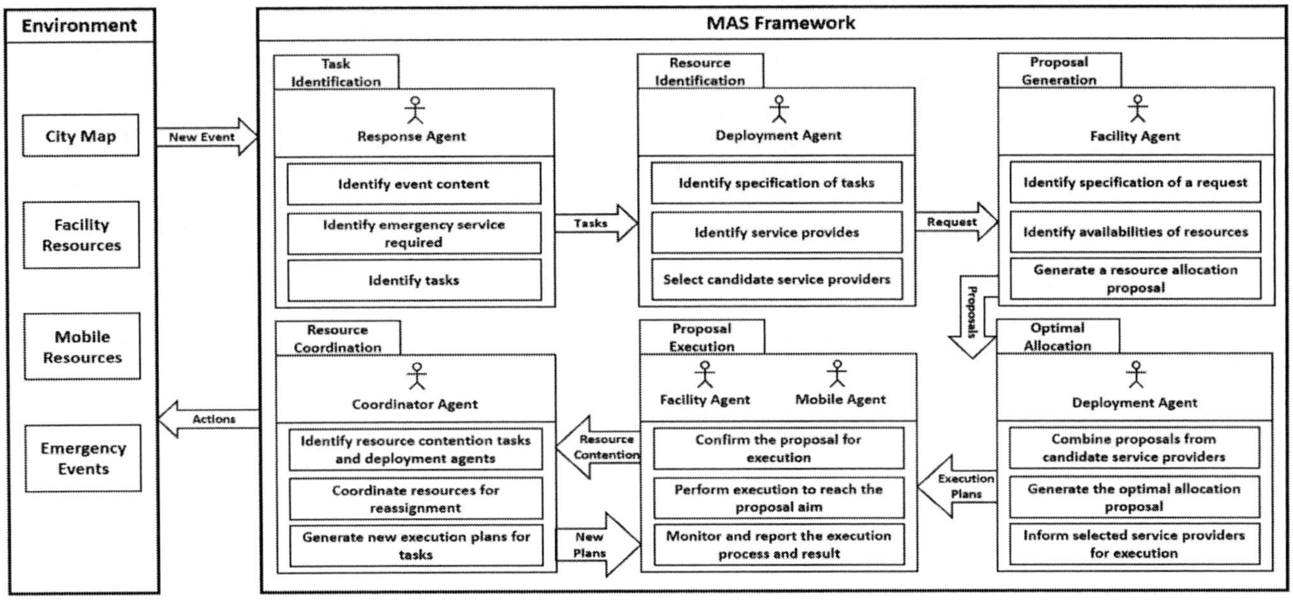

Figure 1: MAS Framework

a proposal execution module and a resource coordination module.

More specifically, when the MAS receives an emergency event, a new system thread will be allocated to process this event. During the resource allocation, the task identification module will be activated first, in which a single response agent is used to identify resource allocation tasks for an emergency event according to the emergency service required by this event. Then, the task identification module passes the resource allocation tasks to the resource identification module, in which a deployment agent generates multiple task processing threads. Each of the task processing threads is used to identify the resource requirements specification in a task and passes this task to relevant candidate service providers (facility agents). After that, in the proposal generation module, each facility agent that has received a resource allocation task will use domain transportation theory to generate a resource allocation proposal based on all resources under its management (i.e. mobile resources). All the generated resource allocation proposals will be passed to the optimal allocation module, in which the deployment agent will combine these proposals and use domain transportation theory to generate a final optimal resource allocation plan for a task. Eventually, this final optimal allocation plan will be passed to the proposal execution module, in which relevant facility agents will confirm the detail of the resource allocation plan. During the execution of resource allocation proposals, if a facility agent finds that if one of its resources is required by two or more different proposals, a new coordination agent will be generated to coordinate the resource dynamically.

4. IMPLEMENTATION AND DEMONSTRATION FEATURES OF THE MAS

Our MAS is implemented as a web-based system with the Model-View-Controller (MVC) architecture [8], which can be accessed from any computer that has web browser and Internet connection. With the MVC architecture design, our system separates the presentation layer from the logic layer, thereby minimising the clutter and the system can be easily extended with new modules in the future. Besides, in order to demonstrate the system capability in solving the resource allocation problems in the real-world environment, we have integrated Google Maps into the View layer of our MAS. By doing so, real-world information regarding to emergency services, routes and live traffic can be easily accessed in our MAS. Furthermore, Java Agent Development Framework (JADE) is used for the implementation of the agents in the Controller layer [3]. The major reason of choosing JADE as the agent platform is that it provides a runtime environment for agent registration and operation, which is extremely important for deploying rescue resources to unexpected emergency events in open and dynamic environments.

With the support of JQuery and Ajax Technologies [6], our web-based MAS provides users with highly interactive demonstration. Generally, our MAS allows users to place any number of emergency events on any city around the world. Users can choose to manually configure the settings of these events or let our system to randomly generate demo settings. During the resource allocation progress, our system will use multiple animations to illustrate how agents interact and coordinate with each other to make decisions, and how rescue resources are moved dynamically on the Google Maps with the effect of live traffic. At the end of the resource allocation progress, our system also provides users with a detail resource allocation report for each event, such as the total cost of the resource allocation, average allocation time and so on.

REFERENCES

[1] N. Adams, M. Field, E. Gelenbe, D. Hand, N. Jennings, D. S. Leslie, D. Nicholson, S. Ramchurn, S. Roberts, and A. Rogers. The aladdin project: intelligent agents for disaster management. In

International Workshop on Robotics for Risky Interventions and Surveillance of the Environment. International Advanced Robotics Programme, 2008.

[2] V. Balasubramanian, D. Massaguer, S. Mehrotra, and N. Venkatasubramanian. *DrillSim: a simulation framework for emergency response drills*. Springer, 2006.

[3] F. L. Bellifemine, G. Caire, and D. Greenwood. *Developing multi-agent systems with JADE*, volume 7. John Wiley & Sons, 2007.

[4] D. Berry, A. Usmani, J. L. Torero, A. Tate, S. McLaughlin, S. Potter, A. Trew, R. Baxter, M. Bull, and M. Atkinson. Firegrid: Integrated emergency response and fire safety engineering for the future built environment. UK e-Science Programme All Hands Meeting, 2005.

[5] F. Fiedrich and P. Burghardt. Agent-based systems for disaster management. *Communications of the ACM*, 50(3):41–42, 2007.

[6] C. Györödi, R. Györödi, G. Pecherle, T. Lorand, and R. Alin. Web 2.0 technologies with jquery and ajax. *Computer Technology and Computer Programming: Research and Strategies*, page 99, 2011.

[7] H. Kitano, S. Tadokoro, I. Noda, H. Matsubara, T. Takahashi, A. Shinjou, and S. Shimada. Robocup rescue: Search and rescue in large-scale disasters as a domain for autonomous agents research. In *1999 IEEE International Conference on Systems, Man, and Cybernetics*, volume 6, pages 739–743. IEEE, 1999.

[8] A. Leff and J. T. Rayfield. Web-application development using the model/view/controller design pattern. In *Enterprise Distributed Object Computing Conference, 2001. EDOC'01. Proceedings. Fifth IEEE International*, pages 118–127. IEEE, 2001.

[9] J. Liu. Regularity of monge–ampère equations in optimal transportation. *Bulletin of the Australian Mathematical Society*, 83(01):173–176, 2011.

[10] J. Marecki, N. Schurr, and M. Tambe. Agent-based simulations for disaster rescue using the defacto coordination system. In *Emergent Information Technologies and Enabling Policies for Counter-Terrorism*, pages 281–297, 2006.

[11] J. Zhang, M. Zhang, F. Ren, and J. Liu. A multiagent-based domain transportation approach for optimal resource allocation in emergency management. In *The Proceedings of the 2 nd International Workshop on Smart Simulation and Modelling for Complex Systems*, page 1.

Using Personality Models as Prior Knowledge to Accelerate Learning About Stress-Coping Preferences*

(Demonstration)

Sebastian Ahrndt
DAI-Labor, Technische Universität Berlin
Ernst-Reuter-Platz 7
10587 Berlin, Germany
sebastian.ahrndt@dai-labor.de

Marco Lützenberger
DAI-Labor, Technische Universität Berlin
Ernst-Reuter-Platz 7
10587 Berlin, Germany
marco.luetzenberger@dai-labor.de

Stephen M. Prochnow
German Turkish Advanced Research Centre for ICT
Ernst-Reuter-Platz 7
10587 Berlin, Germany
stephen.prochnow@gt-arc.com

ABSTRACT

The management of (dis)stress is an important factor for a long and healthy life. Yet, stress affects people differently and everyone manages stress in different ways. In this paper we introduce *PeSA*, the *Personality-enabled Stress Assistant*, an agent-based application that accounts for this individualism. PeSA merges several agent techniques: Reinforcement learning is used to learn about preferences of the users, prior knowledge and knowledge transfer is applied to accelerate the learning process, agent mirroring helps to enable communication and offline functionalities. Based on these mechanisms, PeSA guides through stressful phases by proposing coping strategies that are tailored to the personality of each individual user. Users can assess these advices and thus provide a reward or punishment signal that helps PeSA to improve its suggestions.

Keywords

Human-Agent Teamwork; Human-Behaviour Models; Reinforcement Learning

1. INTRODUCTION

Psychological stress is a well-known trigger for several physical diseases and has a significant impact on our health and health care costs (cf. [5]). The problem that we address with PESA is that the perception of stress is highly individual—as are the actions that may help to relieve stress [2]. PeSA accounts for this very fact by adapting its coping-strategy recommendations to the individuality of the user. In doing so, individual preferences, characteristics, and personalities are supported.

The implementation of this capability is based on a combination of a data-driven and a theory-driven mechanism and directly addresses one of the unsolved human-agent interaction challenges that were described by Prada and Paiva [9]. The theoretical component acts as an accelerator for learning individual preferences and is based on models that were established by human-factor psychology. The data-based component learns by receiving rewards from the users. Knowledge from other PeSA agents is also used to accelerate the learning process, however, to make this work, their users have to have compatible personality models.

PeSA for itself is basically a combination of agent-based software engineering and learning algorithms that use the humans' feedback as reward signals. From a technical perspective, any PeSA instance is a software agent that autonomously collects data, individually detects situations in which stress-relieving actions are required and adapts its recommendations to the personality of its user. To make the learning process faster, we extended the agents' capability to share knowledge with other PeSA agents. The basic idea behind this is that users with similar personalities prefer similar countermeasures (cf. [2, 3]), thus, it is possible that relatively new PeSA agents can learn from agents that have already collected experiences in relieving stress levels—given that their users show similar characteristics.

In our demo, we show how an experienced PeSA agent recommends coping-strategies in order to relieve the stress level of its user and how this agent learns from user feedback. We also show how fresh PeSA agents request knowledge from 'mature' PeSA agents with similar personality profiles in order to become better assistants very quickly. To make this tangible, we show that the user of the new agent is treated in a similar fashion, once the knowledge of an available agent has been transferred and once a stressful situation has been detected. We also show that such knowledge transfer is only done when the personality profiles are actually compatible.

2. PESA IN A NUTSHELL

PeSA was implemented as an application for the Android platform with a cloud-based backend that hosts the multi-agent system. Within the Android container we implemented PeSA as a software agent using the multi-agent-framework *JIAC V* [7]. The backend hosts mirrors of the individual agents, enabling the communication within the agent-system. In more detail: The module that observes a user and triggers actions is separated from the one that communicates to other modules in order to exchange already learned information about how to treat particular person-

*Visit `http://pesa.dai-labor.de` for more information.

Appears in: *Proceedings of the 15th International Conference on Autonomous Agents and Multiagent Systems (AAMAS 2016), J. Thangarajah, K. Tuyls, C. Jonker, S. Marsella (eds.), May 9–13, 2016, Singapore.*

ality profiles. Each module was implemented as a JIAC V agent, such that a PeSA agent actually comprises two agents (one mandatory agent on the Smartphone and one optional agent in the backend). The reason for this design decision is data security. Exchanging information about a user's psychological profile is critical in terms of data security. We offer this feature to accelerate the learning process, yet, only optionally. Agents on the user's Smartphone are capable to learn all required information by themselves. We proceed by explaining how PeSA agents can learn and subsequently elaborate on how they exchange their collected knowledge.

Single Agent – Local learning. To enable the PeSA agent to perform stress management and to adapt its recommendations to the particular requirements of its user, we implemented a reinforcement learning (RL) cycle using classical Q-learning [10] to learn about the action preferences of each user, whereas the actions are the recommended coping-strategies. Since tabula-rasa RL is not fast enough in direct interaction with users, we integrated information about correlations between personality and preferred coping strategies as prior knowledge. These correlations were retrieved from psychological studies [2, 3] and integrated into our PeSA agent as an initial feedback model $\hat{H}$ (henceforth: human-behaviour model) using action biasing [6]. Applying action-biasing adjusts the Q-values only during the action selection, thus, it does not affect the learned Q-values directly. Action-biasing reads as follows: $Q'(s,a) = Q(s,a) + (\beta * \hat{H}(s,a))$, where β is a decaying parameter. In other words, one can say that the personality information is used as an initial heuristic for the action selection. We described this idea in prior work [1]. To complement the human-behaviour model, we determine the personality of the user by means of a questionnaire, which has its roots in human psychology and which aims to assess the *Big-Five* [8] personality traits. In PeSA, we use the determined Q-values to sort the list of available coping-strategies.

Multi-agent system – Knowledge Sharing. To accelerate the learning cycle, we (optionally) allow inexperienced PeSA agents to request knowledge that was already learned by existing agents that assist users with similar personality profiles. If knowledge-sharing is enabled, each PeSA app communicates to one PeSA agent that is running in the backend. Backend agents store information about the learned Q-values and the state of the human-behaviour model. With each new installation, one PeSA agent is deployed in our backend—this agent represents the new user. The agent receives the personality profile from the PeSA app agent after the assessment was completed and broadcasts this information to other available agents in the system, asking for similar personalities and already learned preferences. Responses are collected and ranked for compatible profiles. Therefore, the sum of absolute differences over all measured personality traits is calculated and the one, which is closest to zero but below a certain threshold is selected. Based on this ranking, action preferences are updated for the new user and β is set to the same value that the more experienced agent is using.

3. INTERACTION DETAILS

The goal of the demonstrator is twofold, first, we show how the individual PeSA agent supports a user, secondly, we show how the learning procedure is accelerated when new PeSA agents join an existing PeSA multi-agent system.

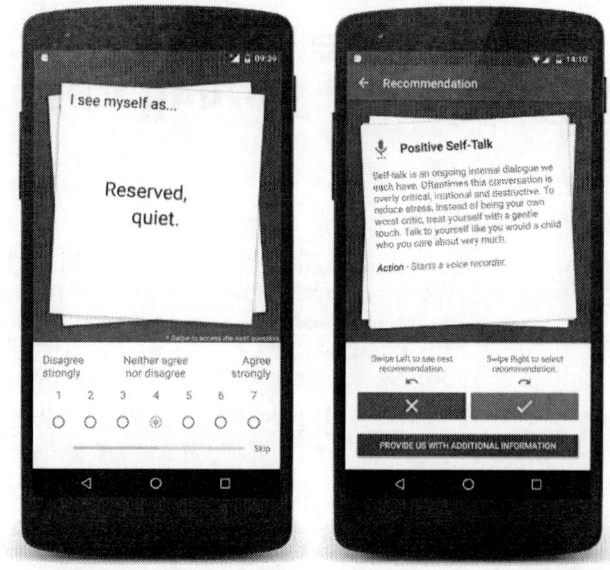

(a) Personality assessment **(b)** Recommendation

Figure 1: Screenshots showing parts of the PeSA app.

In the first step PeSA determines a user's personality using a 10-item personality assessment based on the work of *Gosling et al.* [4]. The personality is measured according to the Big-Five personality theory. Figure 1a shows a screenshot of the questionnaire. Based on the user's answers we calculate the personality profile, which is completed by the sex of the user and which is used to determine the initial strategy. The workflow proceeds with the stress diary, which is the landing page of the PeSA app. Here the user receives information about the goal of PeSA and the history of recorded stress events. If such an event is recognised, PeSA recommends a list of coping strategies. Figure 1b shows a screenshot of the recommendation dialogue; listing a coping-strategy from the cognitive restructuring category that shows a positive correlations with higher extraversion values (cf. [3, p. 1096]). For each advice, the user has the option to accept it (swipe right) or reject it (swipe left). These votes are used as reward signals to learn the actual Q-values for each action (coping-strategy).

To show how new PeSA agents enter the system, we use *ASGARD* [11], a graphical network monitoring tool. ASGARD allows us to show a visualisation of the multi-agent system at runtime. It is able to visualise and analyse the communication between JIAC agents and enables us to analyse the inner processes of PeSA agents.

4. FINAL REMARKS

PeSA combines several agent-techniques in order to help users to manage stress and to live healthy. In doing so, PeSA demonstrates that human-behaviour models improve the interaction with real human beings, i.e. making informed decisions during planning for joint activities.

We are currently evaluating this improvement through the A/B test feature that is provided by the *Google Play-Store*. Our goal is to empirically verify our hypothesis that personality-based information accelerates the learning stage.

REFERENCES

[1] S. Ahrndt, A. Aria, J. Fähndrich, and S. Albayrak. Ants in the OCEAN: Modulating agents with personality for planning with humans. In N. Bulling, editor, *Multi-Agent Systems, 12th European Conference, EUMAS 2014, Prague, Czech Republic, December 18-19, 2014, Revised Selected Papers*, number 8953 in Lecture Notes in Artificial Intelligence, pages 3–18. Springer, April 2015.

[2] C. S. Carver and J. Connor-Smith. Personality and coping. *Annual Review of Psychology*, 61:679–704, January 2010.

[3] J. Connor-Smith and C. Flachsbart. Relations between personality and coping: A meta-analysis. *Journal of Personality and Social Psychology*, 93(6):1080–1107, 2007.

[4] S. D. Gosling, P. J. Rentfrow, and W. B. Swann Jr. A very brief measure of the big-five personality domains. *Journal of Research in Personality*, 37:504–528, 2003.

[5] U. Hapke, U. Maske, C. Scheidt-Nave, L. Bode, R. Schlack, and M. Busch. Chronic stress among adulty in Germany. *Bundesgesundheitsbl*, (5/6):1–5, 2013.

[6] W. B. Knox and P. Stone. Reinforcement learning from simultaneous human and MDP reward. In Conitzer, Winikoff, Padgham, and van der Hoek, editors, *Proceedings of the 11th International Conference on Autonomous Agents and Multiagent Systems (AAMAS 2012)*, pages 475–482. IFAAMAS, 2012.

[7] M. Lützenberger, T. Konnerth, and T. Küster. Programming of multiagent applications with JIAC. In P. Leitao and S. Karnouskos, editors, *Industrial Agents – Emerging Applications of Software Agents in Industry*, pages 381–400. Elsevier, 2015.

[8] R. R. McCrea and O. P. John. An introduction to the five-factor model and its applications. *Journal of Personality*, 60(2):175–215, 1992.

[9] R. Prada and A. Paiva. Human-agent interaction: Challenges for bringing humans and agents together. In *Proc. of the 3rd Int. Workshop on Human-Agent Interaction Design and Models (HAIDM 2014) at the 13th Int. Conf. on Agent and Multi-Agent Systems (AAMAS 2014)*, pages 1–10. IFAAMAS, 2014.

[10] R. S. Sutton and A. G. Barto. *Reinforcement Learning: An Introduction.* Adaptive Computation and Machine Learning. MIT Press, May 1998.

[11] J. Tonn and S. Kaiser. ASGARD – A graphical monitoring tool for distributed agent infrastructures. In Y. Demazeau, F. Dignum, J. M. Corchado, and J. B. Pérez, editors, *Advances in Practical Applications of Agents and Multiagent Systems*, volume 70 of *Advances in Intelligent and Soft Computing*, pages 163–175. Springer, 2010.

A Vision Enriched Intelligent Agent with Image Description Generation (Demonstration)

Li Zhang, Ben Fielding, Philip Kinghorn and Kamlesh Mistry
Department of Computer Science and Digital Technologies
Faculty of Engineering and Environment
Northumbria University
Newcastle, UK, NE1 8ST
{li.zhang; ben.fielding; philip.kinghorn; kamlesh.mistry}@northumbria.ac.uk

ABSTRACT

In this paper, we present an intelligent conversational agent enriched with automatic image understanding and facial expression recognition using state-of-the-art machine learning techniques for the advancement of autonomous interaction with the elderly or infirm. The agent is developed to conduct health and emotion well-being monitoring for the elderly. It is not only capable of conducting question-answering via speech-based interaction, but also able to provide analysis of the user's surroundings, emotional states, hazards and fall actions via visual data. The agent is accessible from a web browser and can be communicated with via voice or text means, with a webcam required for the visual analysis functionality. The system has been evaluated with diverse real-life images to prove its efficiency.

Keywords

Human-agent Interaction; Image Understanding; Agent Architectures

1. INTRODUCTION

We propose an intelligent emotion and health well-being monitoring system for elderly care by incorporating a number of computer vision techniques including scene and object recognition, image description generation, and emotion recognition, with an approachable intelligent conversational 3D humanoid avatar.

The proposed system known as 'Intelligent Chat' provides real-time visual, audial and oral conversation with a number of additional features tailored to the needs of elderly users. It analyzes users' emotional states using an intelligent facial emotion recognition component applied to the user's webcam, integrated in the browser. Moreover the user's environment is analyzed by the proposed system using more advanced vision-based deep learning techniques embedded in a central server, providing analysis of the overall scene, objects, potential hazards around the user, and alerting in the event of a fall. This vision-based analysis, performed on the central server, is used to enhance the conversation with the user to warn hazards and danger, thereby providing an engaging and life-like companionship experience. Intelligent Chat also provides answers to queries on any subject using integration with the popular online encyclopedia Wikipedia, enabling conversation to cover potentially any topic. Empirical results indicate that the proposed system compares favourably with other state-of-the-art related applications in terms of image description generation, facial expression recognition and intelligent health monitoring applications.

Appears in: *Proceedings of the 15th International Conference on Autonomous Agents and Multiagent Systems (AAMAS 2016), J. Thangarajah, K. Tuyls, C. Jonker, S. Marsella (eds.),*
May 9–13, 2016, Singapore.

2. RELATED WORK

2.1 Image Description Generation

Image description generation, or the component parts of such a system, has been the focus of the ImageNet Large Scale Visual Recognition Challenge (ILSVRC) since its conception in 2010. Krizhevsky et al. [1] indicated that deep Convolutional Neural Networks (CNNs) could demonstrate hugely improved, state-of-the-art accuracy when applied to image classification. Following this research finding, a large portion of the entrants and many subsequent state-of-the-art developments have been based on such deep learning architectures with CNNs as encoders. Moreover, Sermanet et al. [2] proposed OverFeat to classify images whilst simultaneously providing localization information and object detection, adding a large amount of information to the output of classification attempts. Their system integrated a CNN with multiscale sliding window processing for object detection. Moreover, there are also other developments in the field using encoder and decoder deep learning architectures for solving diverse complex computer vision tasks [3, 4].

2.2 Facial and Bodily Expression Recognition

Many state-of-the-art research applications have been proposed recently for facial and bodily expression recognition. Neoh et al. [5] developed a facial expression recognition system with direct similarity and Pareto based optimization whereas Zhang et al. [6] developed a novel facial point detector based on unsupervised learning for intensity estimation of facial action units for diverse challenging cases, such as occlusions, rotations and illumination changes. Zhang et al. [7] also proposed a bodily expression recognition system embedded with a particle swarm optimization variant to conduct regression of valence and arousal dimensions.

In comparison to the above state-of-the-art related work, this research employs a novel regional deep learning structure for image description generation to improve existing image captioning techniques, by including regional object detection and recognition, scene classification, and template-based sentence generation. It also incorporates both texture and shape information for facial expression recognition with the attempt to address limitations of single modality based methods. The experimental results proved the superiority of our approach for both image description generation and facial expression recognition.

3. THE PROPOSED SYSTEM

This research proposes a vision enriched 'Intelligent Chat' system for elderly care. The system is developed to conduct facial emotion recognition, object and scene recognition, hazardous object and scene classification, and fall detection. Template-based image description generation is also used to generate sentences based on the above outputs to warn of hazards or generate alarms when falls occur.

We design the system to function as a web-based application with camera equipped devices. The functionality is separated over the client-server architecture in an attempt to make the most of available processing power on both sides. The application is designed to also function as an information retrieval system, enabling users to ask questions which could be answered using the internet as a knowledge base, allowing for limitless knowledge to be accessed through the chat to enhance user experience. The interface of the proposed 'Intelligent Chat' system is shown in Figure 1.

Figure 1. The interface of the 'Intelligent Chat' system

3.1 Conversation Extensions

The conversational functionality forms the core of the system, providing the avatar with a means of prolonging interaction with the user and attempting to maintain a flow of conversation, rather than simply reacting to questions. The conversational aspect is implemented using Artificial Intelligence Markup Language (AIML) [8, 9, 10]. Related APIs have also been implemented to enable speech synthesis and recognition interface developments.

The AIML vocabulary, whilst containing a large amount of information and responses, is noticeably incomplete, due to the restrictions of the AIML language. We have extended the agent's vocabulary monumentally through the implementation of a question-answering system using Wikipedia as a data source. This allows the intelligent agent to answer questions on practically any topic available through collective human knowledge. We also include a new functionality to retrieve and present the user's location using the HTML5 geolocation API. The location is spoken using latitude and longitude co-ordinates with a small map image embedded in the interface to indicate the user's location.

3.2 Image Description Generation

3.2.1 Object Detection & Recognition

The first stage of the image description generation embedded in Intelligent Chat is based upon object detection. The object detector implemented is the Regional Convolutional Neural Network, i.e. R-CNN, from Girschick et al. [11], consisting of 8 learned layers, 5 convolutional layers and 3 fully connected layers. This network is further extended to detect and classify 200 object categories from ImageNet 2013 dataset, collecting selective search data from the whole image. These regions are then each classified by 200 SVMs in order to determine which areas contain a specific object. This object recognition process is also extended to conduct hazardous objects and fall action detection.

3.2.2 Scene Recognition

Scene classification is used to enhance the image description generation by providing an overall context of the setting, which can then be enhanced through the inclusion of detailed object and person description. The classification system used is a CNN trained on the MIT Places dataset [3]. The Places dataset contains over 7 million images from 476 scene categories. The network proposed by Zhou et al [3] was used in our work, which was trained on 2.5 million images, comprised of 205 scene categories.

3.2.3 Facial Emotion Recognition

A facial expression recognition component is also integrated into Intelligent Chat. Active Appearance Model and Neural Networks are used for the recognition of 7 emotions including; happiness, anger, sadness, disgust, surprise, fear and contempt. 3000 images extracted from CK+ are used for the training of AAM [12, 13].

3.2.4 Sentence Construction

To construct a valid descriptive sentence, the recognized object labels, scene context and emotions must be combined in a very natural-sounding manner. In this work, a template-based approach using rule-based reasoning is used to transform these descriptive labels into multiple short sentences that can be concatenated and reported as a single detailed description of the image in question. The scene context identified is also used either as an opening or a closing statement of the generated sentence.

We have tested Intelligent Chat with both real users in real-life settings and hundreds of real-world images. Evaluation results indicate that it achieves 0.389 ROUGE score for image description generation which is impressive and comparable to other state-of-the-art research [14]. Future implementations of this work could be improved by utilising a faster, more efficient object detector such as the Fast R-CNN, and pairing it with a more efficient sentence generation method such as Recurrent Neural Networks [15]. Moreover, the system could be further extended to integrate with disease diagnosis functions [16, 17]. We also aim to conduct substantial system evaluation with elderly users to further prove system efficiency. Demo URL:

https://drive.google.com/file/d/0BxS6ufv4G_TXYmxUSVRiTS1tUUk/view?usp=sharing

4. REFERENCES

[1] Krizhevsky, A., Sutskever, I. and Hinton, G.E. 2012. ImageNet Classification with Deep Convolutional Neural Networks. *Advances in Neural Information Processing Systems*. 1097-1105.

[2] Sermanet, P., Eigen, D., Zhang, X., Mathieu, M., Fergus, R. and LeCun, Y. 2014. OverFeat: Integrated Recognition, Localization and Detection using Convolutional Networks. *International Conference on Learning Representations*.

[3] Zhou, B., Lapedriza, A., Xiao, J., et al. 2014. Learning Deep Features for Scene Recognition using Places Database. *Advances in Neural Information Processing Systems*.

[4] Jia, Y. et al. 2014. Caffe: Convolutional Architecture for Fast Feature Embedding. *Proceedings of MM'14*, 675-678.

[5] Neoh, S.C., Zhang, L., Mistry, K., Hossain, M.A., Lim, C.P., Aslam, N. and Kinghorn, P. 2015. Intelligent Facial Emotion Recognition Using a Layered Encoding Cascade Optimization Model. *Applied Soft Computing*, 34, 72-93.

[6] Zhang, L., Mistry, K., Jiang, M., Neoh, S.C. and Hossain, A. (2015). Adaptive facial point detection and emotion recognition for a humanoid robot. *Computer Vision and Image Understanding*, 140. 93-114.

[7] Zhang, Y., Zhang, L., Neoh, S.C., Mistry, K. and Hossain, A. (2015). Intelligent affect regression for bodily expressions using hybrid particle swarm optimization and adaptive ensembles. *Expert Systems with Applications*, 42. 8678-97.

[8] Wallace, R. 2003. The elements of AIML style.

[9] Zhang, L. and Barnden, J. (2012). Affect Sensing Using Linguistic, Semantic and Cognitive Cues in Multi-threaded Improvisational Dialogue. *Cognitive Computation*. Volume 4, Issue 4, 436-459.

[10] Zhang, L. and Barnden, J.A. (2010). Affect and Metaphor Sensing in Virtual Drama. *International Journal of Computer Games Technology*. Vol. 2010. Article ID 512563.

[11] Girshick, R., Donahue, J., Darrell, T. and Malik, J. 2014. Rich Feature Heirarchies for Accurate Object Detection and Semantic Segmentation. *CVPR*, 580-587.

[12] Zhang, Y., Zhang, L. and Hossain, M.A. (2015). Adaptive 3D facial action intensity estimation and emotion recognition, *Expert Systems with Applications*, 42 (2015).

[13] Zhang, L., Jiang, M., Farid, D. and Hossain, A.M. (2013). Intelligent Facial Emotion Recognition and Semantic-based Topic Detection for a Humanoid Robot. *Expert Systems with Applications*, 40 (2013), 5160-5168.

[14] Lin, D., Kong, C., Fidler, S. and Urtasun, R. (2015). Generating multi-sentence lingual descriptions of indoor scenes. In *British Machine Vision Conference*. UK.

[15] Jozefowicz, R., Zaremba, W. and Sutskever, I. (2015). An Empirical Exploration of Recurrent Network Architectures. In *Proceedings of the 32nd International Conference on Machine Learning (ICML-15)*, 2342-2350.

[16] Bourouis, A., Feham, M., Hossain, M. A. and Zhang, L. (2014). An Intelligent Mobile based Decision Support System for Retinal Disease Diagnosis. *Decision Support Systems*. Elsevier. Volume 59, March 2014, 341–350.

[17] Neoh, S.C., Srisukkham, W., Zhang, L, Todryk, S., Greystoke, B., Lim, C.P., Hossain, A. and Aslam, N. (2015) An Intelligent Decision Support System for Leukaemia Diagnosis using Microscopic Blood Images. *Scientific Reports*, 5 (14938). Nature Publishing Group.

Simulating Drone-be-Gone: Agile Low-Cost Cyber-Physical UAV Testbed (Demonstration)

Mouhyemen Khan[†‡], Sidra Alam[†‡], Amr Mohamed[†], Khaled A. Harras[‡]
[†]Dept. of Computer Science & Engineering, Qatar University, Doha, Qatar
{mouhyemen.khan, sidra.m.alam}@gmail.com, amrm@ieee.org
[‡]School of Computer Science, Carnegie Mellon University, Pittsburgh, USA
kharras@cs.cmu.edu

ABSTRACT

In this paper, we demonstrate Drone-Be-Gone (*DbeG*): a general-purpose, inexpensive, and agile UAV Cyber-Physical System (CPS) testbed. We implement on our testbed 2-D vision-based localization within 5 cm precision, controllability of multiple UAVs, a simulation environment of our testbed in 2-D (named *TeSLA*), and external processing units (EPU). The testbed has the ability to switch between centralized or distributed control and processing due to the addition of EPUs. The simulator will allow users to interact with our testbed virtually and observe its behavior.

Category{I.2.9}: [Cyber-Physical Systems] Sensor Networks, Embedded Systems
Keywords: Autonomous Robots, Simulation

1. INTRODUCTION

Unmanned Aerial Vehicles (UAVs) continue to be the most dynamic sector of the aerospace industry as sensor and automation technologies mature. A sub-domain of UAVs involves the development of testbeds where researchers go beyond theory to more practical implementations. Prior efforts dealing with UAV testbeds typically have a large barrier of entry due to high-cost and extreme customization. Some testbeds are based on expensive motion capture systems [4], or expensive UAVs such as the Hummingbird or Dragan-Flyer [3, 4, 6]. Others include a network of UAVs and Unmanned Ground Vehicles (UGVs) in distributed/centralized fashion [1, 2], and are involved in search and rescue operations or geographical surveillance. Although significant work has been done on testbeds involving UAVs, there has been preliminary efforts in building less expensive testbeds. The Up&Away testbed uses AR.Drone as their UAV and is an initial attempt to build a low-cost CPS testbed [5]. This attempt however has poor localization, lack of distributed control and processing, and coarse-grained navigation of UAVs.

Drone-Be-Gone Testbed: In this paper, we present Drone-Be-Gone (*DbeG*): a general-purpose, inexpensive, and agile Cyber-Physical System (CPS) testbed using off-the-shelf UAVs with centralized or distributed control and processing. *DbeG* has four main features. *1) Vision-based 2-D localization*: Intensity-contour detection and our own Adaptive Tracking Window algorithm detects and distinguishes UAVs respectively inside the testbed. *2) Autonomous navigation for multiple UAVs*: We implement a lightweight navigation routine for controlling AR.Drone 2.0 from Parrot that handles UAV-drift during translational and rotational flights through a feedback control system. *3) Simulation environment of testbed*: We develop an effective simulation environment of our testbed in 2-D for safety testing of algorithms before deploying the actual testbed. The simulator is called ***Te**stbed **S**imulation with **L**ocalization & **A**utonomy (TeSLA)*. *TeSLA* combines our implemented localization and autonomous control of UAVs and serves as a safety pre-cursor before deploying on the real testbed. *4) External processing units (EPUs)*: The addition of EPU enables the groundwork for distributed control and/or processing. Intel Edison is the EPU used in *DbeG*.

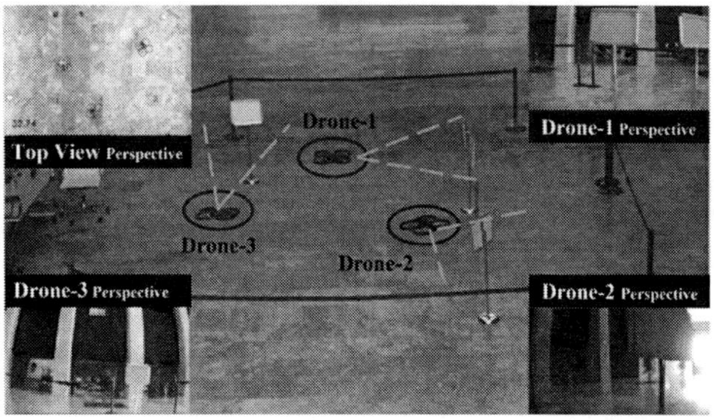

Figure 1: 3-drones (circled in blue) covering their respective targets. Green-dashed lines represent drone-FoV. Within each drone's perspective, the white stands are the targets.

Scenario on our testbed: The scenario depicted in Figure 1 highlights target coverage in a visual-sensor network where the drones are assigned targets to cover within their field-of-view (FoV) autonomously. The top-view perspective, each drone's perspective, and in-action view are shown in Figure 1. Drone-1 covers 2 targets since the targets are adjacent to each other and fit within the FoV of Drone-1. When the third target is introduced, Drone-2 flies to cover it since Drone-1 cannot cover it. The last target elsewhere on the testbed is covered by Drone-3 since Drone-1 and Drone-2 cannot cover the target along with their respective targets.

Drone-be-Gone Architecture: The underlying architecture behind our testbed is depicted in Figure 2a. It comprises of 2 major modules: *Central* and *Client*. Additionally, there is a special module that we call *Multi-homed* module.

Appears in: *Proceedings of the 15th International Conference on Autonomous Agents and Multiagent Systems (AAMAS 2016), J. Thangarajah, K. Tuyls, C. Jonker, S. Marsella (eds.), May 9–13, 2016, Singapore.*

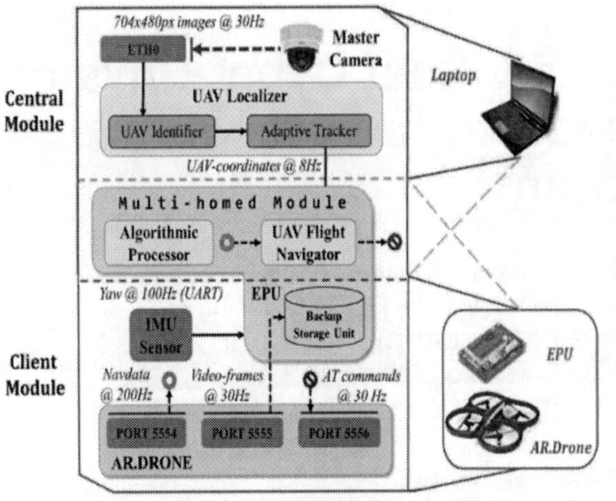

(a) Drone-Be-Gone's Architecture

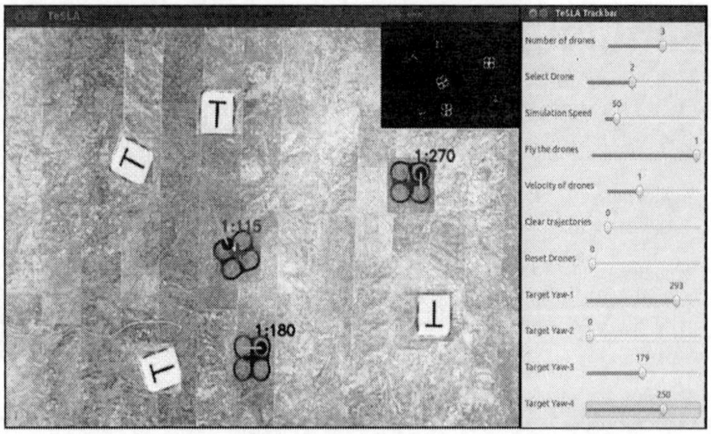

(b) Drone-Be-Gone's simulated version - *TeSLA*

Figure 2: *DbeG's* architecture showing each major module's corresponding hardware location. *TeSLA* allows interactivity through placement of multiple drones, targets, creating individual trajectories for drones, and an interactive trackbar for parameter tuning. *TeSLA* can also be linked with an external algorithm to model the testbed's behavior.

Central and *Client* module has exclusive sub-modules which perform mandatory responsibilities - localization and sensory acquisition respectively. *Multi-homed* module contains sub-modules which can be located in either of the major modules. Based on the location of these sub-modules, the major modules can be tasked with desired responsibilities thereby allowing easy migration between a centralized to distributed platform or vice-versa. The *desired* responsibilities can be algorithmic processing or drone navigation.

2. DEMONSTRATION

This demonstration aims at providing an interactive experience with our testbed through the aid of *TeSLA*. Indeed, it will not be possible to demonstrate the testbed live since the actual localization relies on using a Network Camera overlooking the testbed from above. However, *TeSLA* serves as a handy-tool in demonstrating our testbed's overall performance in a cohesive manner i.e. localization and UAV navigation when integrated with an external CPS application. In addition, we will also present the AR.Drone 2.0 mounted with and controlled by Intel Edison as its EPU. The performance of our testbed, *DbeG*, the simulator, *TeSLA*, and its integration with *DbeG* can be viewed at:

https://youtu.be/rw8rN87tJvA

TeSLA: *TeSLA* simulates *DbeG* in 2-D and incorporates *DbeG's* localization and autonomous navigation routines. However, *TeSLA* goes beyond just the integration of the aforementioned routines. Using *TeSLA*, we are able to observe the performance of our system when integrated with an external CPS application, such as coverage algorithms, on our testbed. The integration of localization, navigation and an external CPS application in action provides us with insights into the nature of our system and serves as an effective safety precursor. It is designed using OpenCV bindings for Python.

Demonstration Setup: For the purposes of our demonstration, we will utilize a laptop running *TeSLA*. Specifically, a Lenovo Y50 laptop will run the simulation and will be made available to the audience to interact with all required modules already installed. A sample coverage algorithm will also be pre-loaded in the laptop in order to demonstrate *TeSLA's* performance.

Audience Interaction: Participants will be able to interact with *TeSLA* as portrayed in Figure 2b. The user will be able to choose the number of drones and also provide individual trajectories for each drone. A trajectory is made up of a destination point and orientation. The user will also be able to place targets anywhere on the testbed and rotate them. The user can also subject *TeSLA* to the coverage algorithm after placing targets anywhere on the testbed to see the drones in action.

3. ACKNOWLEDGMENT

This work was made possible by NPRP grant # 4-463-2-172 from the Qatar National Research Fund (a member of Qatar Foundation).

REFERENCES

[1] C. Fok, A. Petz, D. Stovall, N. Paine, C. Julien, and S. Vishwanath. Pharos: A testbed for mobile cyber-physical systems. *Univ. of Texas at Austin, Tech. Rep. TR-ARiSE-2011-001*, 2011.

[2] O. Lawlor, M. Moss, S. Kibler, C. Carson, S. Bond, and S. Bogosyan. Search-and rescue robots for integrated research and education in cyber-physical systems. In *e-Learning in Industrial Electronics (ICELIE), 2013 7th IEEE International Conference on*, pages 92–97, Nov 2013.

[3] S. Lupashin, A. Schollig, M. Sherback, and R. D'Andrea. A simple learning strategy for high-speed quadrocopter multi-flips. In *Robotics and Automation (ICRA), 2010 IEEE International Conference on*, pages 1642–1648, May 2010.

[4] N. Michael, D. Mellinger, Q. Lindsey, and V. Kumar. The grasp multiple micro-uav testbed. *Robotics Automation Magazine, IEEE*, 17(3):56–65, Sept 2010.

[5] A. Saeed, A. Neishaboori, A. Mohamed, and K. Harras. Up and away: A visually-controlled easy-to-deploy wireless uav cyber-physical testbed. In *Wireless and Mobile Computing, Networking and Communications (WiMob), 2014 IEEE 10th International Conference on*, pages 578–584, Oct 2014.

[6] M. Valenti, B. Bethke, D. Dale, A. Frank, J. McGrew, S. Ahrens, J. How, and J. Vian. The mit indoor multi-vehicle flight testbed. In *Robotics and Automation, 2007 IEEE International Conference on*, pages 2758–2759, April 2007.

TARTARUS: A Multi-Agent Platform for Bridging the Gap between Cyber and Physical Systems

(Demonstration)

Tushar Semwal[1], Nikhil S[2], Shashi Shekhar Jha[3], Shivashankar B. Nair[4]
Department of Computer Science & Engineering
Indian Institute of Technology Guwahati
Guwahati-781039, India
{t.semwal[1], nikhils[2], j.shashi[3], sbnair[4]}@iitg.ernet.in

ABSTRACT

While there are many multi-agent platforms, one that can support the creation of a cyber system (comprising static and mobile soft agents), which in turn can control physical systems, seems grossly missing. In this demonstration, we introduce *Tartarus*, a Prolog based multi-agent platform that can cater to the creation, programming, cloning and termination of both static and mobile agents. *Tartarus* empowers developers to drive both the cyber and physical worlds thereby facilitating the creation and actual deployment of Cyber-Physical Systems (CPS) and Internet of Things (IoT) in the real world.

Keywords

Agent platforms, Multi-Agent Sytems, Cyber-Physical Systems (CPS), Robots

1. INTRODUCTION

For more than a decade, numerous Multi-Agent platforms and software tools have been developed and used for realizing Multi-Agent Systems (MAS) [14]. Except for a few such as Mobile-C [3, 4] which uses a Ch-interpreter to host C/C++ based agents onto embedded devices or JADEX [11] which combines XML and JAVA in order to create intelligent agents with easy binding to WSDL based web services, it is very rare that such platforms or tools are actually used in deploying multi-agent systems in the real world. By real world, we mean the 3-dimensional space where the cyber world intersects its physical counterpart using a communication channel, to culminate in a Cyber-Physical System (CPS) [12]. These systems consist of heterogeneous devices such as laptops, PCs, embedded boards, sensors, robots, cars, etc., connected together either via wired or wireless communication channels.

The distributed nature of a MAS adheres to the requirements of managing various processes within a CPS. An agent which forms the cyber component may sit on top of physical devices such as embedded hardware or robots and make them execute a set of tasks to achieve a goal. We introduce herein, *Tartarus* [13], a multi-agent platform, which, to the best of our knowledge, provides distinctive features that can make the cyber agents access and control the real physical devices with ease. Developed on top of SWI-Prolog [15], *Tartarus* not only provides for the development of static agents but also supports rapid development and deployment of agents with mobility viz. mobile agents. These mobile agents can migrate within a network of nodes and execute programs locally at the concerned node. In addition, *Tartarus* also supports multi-threading and thus caters to concurrent execution of tasks. It currently runs on both Windows and Linux operating systems and can be used in conjunction with Linux based embedded devices such as the Raspberry Pi, Intel® Galileo, etc.

Tartarus and its predecessor *Typhon* [10] have been used in a variety of applications ranging from an agent based Internet of Things (IoT) [6], synchronizing cooperative tasks among robots [7], creating partial green corridors for emergency services in a traffic [2], sharing and learning on-the-fly by a set of distributed nodes in a network [8], etc. These applications involve real time sensing of the environment and consequent decision making to deliver the relevant actuations to the physical side of the system.

2. FEATURES OF TARTARUS

Written in Prolog, *Tartarus*[†] inherently features all the plus points of this language. The platform, however has some salient features, few of which are listed below.

1. Multi-threading: Unlike its predecessor *Typhon*, *Tartarus* uses threaded execution of various processes that allows for concurrent deployment. Threads in *Tartarus* are inherently managed by its core engine, which in turn isolates the developers from the complexities related to mutual exclusion [9].

2. Heterogeneity: *Tartarus* supports a fair degree of heterogeneity in terms of the operating system (Windows/Linux) and the underlying hardware. Agents developed using *Tartarus* on Windows environment can thus communicate with similar agents running on a Linux environment thereby providing reasonable cross-platform communications.

Appears in: *Proceedings of the 15th International Conference on Autonomous Agents and Multiagent Systems (AAMAS 2016), J. Thangarajah, K. Tuyls, C. Jonker, S. Marsella (eds.), May 9–13, 2016, Singapore.*

[†]For the Demonstration Video visit: `https://youtu.be/VeryfhtT5Tk`

3. Hardware-in-the-loop: Unlike most of the available agent platforms, *Tartarus* can be ported on embedded boards that currently include the Raspberry Pi and Intel® Galileo development board. It also comes with an interface for the LEGO® MINDSTORMS® NXT robots. These special interfaces allow developers to access the control systems of the underlying hardware, thus making the job of developers easier.

4. Distributed Control: MASs are well suited in applications which require distributed computations and communications among heterogeneous entities. Agents within *Tartarus* can share information between nodes, migrate from one node to another (mobile agents) and execute the code at a destination node. Agents can even clone to exhibit a certain amount of parallelism within a network.

5. Payloads: Mobile agents can carry a set of programs or data as payload to be either executed on demand at the destination node or be downloaded for use by that node. *Tartarus* provides the necessary execution environment to the agents in order to execute a program based on their defined logic. Agents can also be programmed to shed (offload) or upload payloads during runtime. By modifying payloads, one may even attempt to alter the behaviour of the agent in runtime.

6. Security: Security in *Tartarus* is at the moment naïve and is implemented using a lock and key mechanism. Each *Tartarus* platform has a lock which could be an encrypted code or password. A mobile agent is allowed to enter a *Tartarus* node only if it has the associated key for the same. Better security aids could be developed to make the system secure.

7. Ease of Installation: Installing *Tartarus* is simple and does not require any intricate adjustments such as setting path variables as in the case of Java based platforms.

3. TARTARUS: SOME REAL WORLD APPLICATIONS

Tartarus and its predecessor, Typhon, have been used as a tool for devising various distributed mechanisms in a number of practical applications,¶ some of which are:

1. A Mobile agent based framework for IoT¶ [6]: An IoT is a network of heterogeneous devices such as control boards, sensors, actuator systems, etc., all of which work together to monitor, gather and analyse data and aid us make appropriate decisions. It constitutes a typical distributed system and hence provides a fitting environment for the use of agents in realising it. Mobile agents in *Typhon*, called Typhlets have been used to mitigate the problem of searching for remote resources, monitoring the temperature of an area, making the robot to follow a line, etc.

2. Synchronization of a Sequence of Tasks in a Network of Asynchronous Nodes¶ [7]: A group of entities (such as a set of robots) may be required to perform a set of tasks in a synchronous manner. Synchronizing the movements of robots in a distributed networked system requires a considerable number of messages to be passed on among the participating entities. This results in a large consumption of bandwidth. It also entails problems during real implementation. In this work, a novel technique inspired by the self-organized synchronous behaviour of insect colonies is proposed. The technique uses mobile agents to achieve synchronization through stigmergic communication [1]. The mobile agents, each carrying programs for distinct tasks knit through the robots, communicate using stigmergy and make them perform the tasks in synchronism. They can also handle failures inherently and recover from them. A multi-robot synchronized dance scenario portrayed in the demonstration video† accentuates the use of *Tartarus* in controlling and synchronizing multiple entities.

3. Partial Green Corridors for Emergency Vehicles : A partial green corridor for emergency vehicles [2] is a far better proposition than a full one. Using agents, we demonstrated that the same is feasible and far more efficient. Mobile agents, carrying all information about the vehicle move ahead in a *Tartarus* based Digital Traffic Infrastructure Network (DTIN) to regulate the traffic signals so as to form a few kilometre-long corridor to enable the vehicle to rush through seamlessly. The forward moving corridor is constantly monitored and updated during the vehicle's journey to its destination. The application uses two kinds of mobile agents - a *Map agent* that updates the status of the traffic at each traffic signal and a *Path-finding agent* which creates and maintains the partial green corridor amidst the traffic. Whenever, an emergency vehicle such as an ambulance starts its traversal through the traffic, the partial green corridor created by the *Path-finding agent* aids the ambulance to reach the hospital via the least crowded route. The mechanism also ensures that the adjoining traffic is in no way adversely affected due to the creation of such partial green corridors.

4. *Tartarus* on Embedded Hardware: Currently *Tartarus* has been tested out to work on the Raspberry Pi and Intel® Galileo development boards. Running on Linux, *Tartarus* on such hardware can act as an active wireless node. Agents within these nodes can monitor and act based on the sensors and even send information to remote base stations as has been portrayed in the demonstration video†.

4. CONCLUSIONS

Connecting the cyber world with the physical one is always an arduous task. The use of *Tartarus* alleviates this to quite an extent by empowering agents to actually sense, think and act in the real world. It is envisaged that by 2020, the number of connected devices across the world will reach 20.8 billion [5]. This will result in the creation of an ecosystem comprising different IoT/CPSs working either sequentially or concurrently. While one IoT may be used for weather forecasting and reporting, another could be working to ameliorate agriculture. With the hardware-in-the-loop feature, *Tartarus* will not only be able to handle issues in forecasting and agriculture but also use the derived information to monitor and drive physical devices such as sensors and actuators, used in these scenarios.

Acknowledgments

The authors acknowledge the work done by Manoj Bode and Vivek Singh in the building and testing phases of *Tartarus*.

¶For videos of some of the applications cited herein visit: `http://www.iitg.ernet.in/cse/robotics/?page_id=1936`

REFERENCES

[1] R. Beckers, O. E. Holland, and J.-L. Deneubourg. Fom local actions to global tasks: Stigmergy and collective robotics. In *Prerational Intelligence: Adaptive Behavior and Intelligent Systems Without Symbols and Logic, Volume 1, Volume 2 Prerational Intelligence: Interdisciplinary Perspectives on the Behavior of Natural and Artificial Systems, Volume 3*, pages 1008–1022. Springer, 2000.

[2] M. Bode, S. S. Jha, and S. B. Nair. A Mobile Agent based Autonomous Partial Green Corridor Discovery and Maintenance Mechanism for Emergency Services amidst Urban Traffic. In *The First International Conference on IoT in Urban Space*, pages 13–18, Rome, 2014. Institute for Computer Sciences, Social-Informatics and Telecommunications Engineering.

[3] B. Chen, H. H. Cheng, and J. Palen. Mobile-C: A mobile agent platform for mobile C/C++ agents. *Software: Practice and Experience*, 36(15):1711–1733, 2006.

[4] B. Chen, H. H. Cheng, and J. Palen. Integrating mobile agent technology with multi-agent systems for distributed traffic detection and management systems. *Transportation Research Part C: Emerging Technologies*, 17(1):1 – 10, 2009.

[5] Gartner. Gartner says 6.4 billion connected "things" will be in use in 2016, up 30 percent from 2015, 2015. [Online; accessed 20-February-2016].

[6] W. Godfrey, S. S. Jha, and S. B. Nair. On a mobile agent framework for an internet of things. In *Communication Systems and Network Technologies (CSNT), 2013 International Conference on*, pages 345–350, April 2013.

[7] S. S. Jha, W. W. Godfrey, and S. B. Nair. Stigmergy-Based Synchronization of a Sequence of Tasks in a Network of Asynchronous Nodes. *Cybernetics and Systems*, 45(5):373–406, June 2014.

[8] S. S. Jha and S. B. Nair. On a Multi-agent Distributed Asynchronous Intelligence-Sharing and Learning Framework. *Transactions on Computational Collective Intelligence XVIII*, 9240:166–200, 2015.

[9] L. Lamport. The mutual exclusion problem: Part I: A theory of interprocess communication. *J. ACM*, 33(2):313–326, Apr. 1986.

[10] J. Matani and S. B. Nair. Typhon- A mobile agents framework for real world emulation in Prolog. In *Multi-disciplinary Trends in Artificial Intelligence*, pages 261–273. Springer, 2011.

[11] A. Pokahr, L. Braubach, and W. Lamersdorf. Jadex: A BDI reasoning engine. In *Multi-agent programming*, pages 149–174. Springer, 2005.

[12] R. R. Rajkumar, I. Lee, L. Sha, and J. Stankovic. Cyber-physical systems: The next computing revolution. In *Proceedings of the 47th Design Automation Conference*, DAC '10, pages 731–736, New York, NY, USA, 2010. ACM.

[13] T. Semwal, M. Bode, V. Singh, S. S. Jha, and S. B. Nair. Tartarus: A multi-agent platform for integrating cyber-physical systems and robots. In *Proceedings of the 2015 Conference on Advances In Robotics*, AIR '15, pages 20:1–20:6, New York, NY, USA, 2015. ACM.

[14] W. Van der Hoek and M. Wooldridge. Multi-agent systems. *Handbook of Knowledge Representation*, pages 887–928, 2008.

[15] J. Wielemaker, T. Schrijvers, M. Triska, and T. Lager. SWI-Prolog. *Theory and Practice of Logic Programming*, 12:67–96, 1 2012.

PriGuardTool: A Tool for Monitoring Privacy Violations in Online Social Networks

(Demonstration)

Nadin Kökciyan
Department of Computer Engineering
Bogazici University, 34342 Bebek
Istanbul, Turkey
nadin.kokciyan@boun.edu.tr

Pınar Yolum
Department of Computer Engineering
Bogazici University, 34342 Bebek
Istanbul, Turkey
pinar.yolum@boun.edu.tr

ABSTRACT

In this demonstration, we present PriGuardTool, which is a Web-based tool that can detect privacy violations in online social networks and notify the users accordingly. Our tool comes up with an interface where the users input their privacy concerns. An agent represents a user in the online social network. Each agent is responsible for generating commitments between its user and the system to monitor the social network and check for privacy violations. We demonstrate PriGuardTool by using various real-life scenarios.

Categories and Subject Descriptors

I.2.1 [**Artificial Intelligence**]: Distributed Artificial Intelligence *Multiagent systems*

Keywords

Privacy, Online Social Networks, Commitment, Ontology

1. INTRODUCTION

In online social networks, privacy violations can take place in numerous ways: A user herself may misconfigure the system and reveal unintended content; or a friend of a user can share a content not knowing that the user would not want the content online; or sharing of certain information either by the user or others could lead to other information being unleashed unexpectedly. In all cases, the users seek tools that will help them to preserve their privacy and catch privacy breaches if any, so that they can take an action.

We propose PriGuard model that focuses on: (i) specifying the social network, privacy concerns and privacy violations, (ii) detecting privacy violations in the system, and (iii) notifying the user to take an action. PriGuardTool is a Web-based tool that implements PriGuard model. In this demonstration, we will show how PriGuardTool can deal with various scenarios from the literature.

Appears in: *Proceedings of the 15th International Conference on Autonomous Agents and Multiagent Systems (AAMAS 2016), J. Thangarajah, K. Tuyls, C. Jonker, S. Marsella (eds.), May 9–13, 2016, Singapore.*

2. PRIGUARD APPROACH

PriGuard is a commitment-based model for privacy-aware online social networks. Each user in the social network is represented by an agent. We use commitments [2] to capture the privacy promises done by the social network operator to each user, based on the user's specified privacy expectations. Consider the following example where an online social network user Dennis has requested his location to be hidden from his posts. Later, he shares a picture with friends without knowing that the picture includes a geotag. The geotag includes geographical information that will give away his location. Dennis' privacy agreement with the online social network can be represented with the following commitment: C_1(`:osn`; `:dennis`; *isFriendOf*(`:dennis`,X), *isAbout*(P,`:dennis`), `LocationPost`(P); not(*canSeePost*(X,P))). That is, `:osn` commits to `:dennis` to not show his location posts to the user X if `:dennis` declares X to be a friend.

In PriGuard, the social network domain is formally defined using Description Logics (DL). This domain consists of concepts (e.g.; `Agent`), roles (e.g.; *isFriendOf*) and individuals names (e.g.; `:dennis`). Hence, the relationships and the posts can be semantically described by the use of DL as well. The social network operator operates according to norms (i.e.; semantic rules). In PriGuard, norms are specified as Datalog rules. *sharesPost*(X,P) $\rightarrow$ *canSeePost*(X,P) is a Datalog rule, which states that an agent can see the posts that it shares.

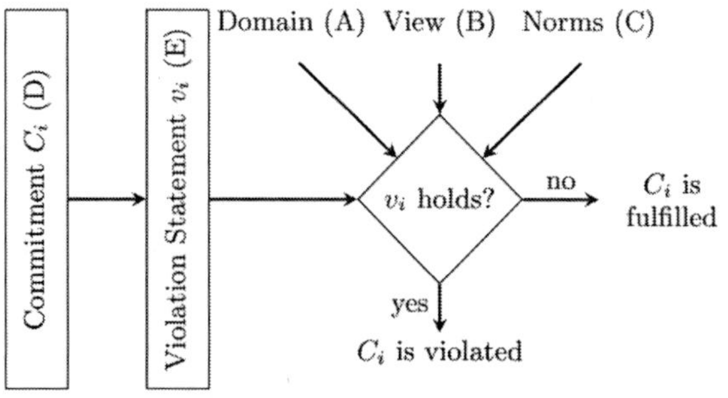

Figure 1: Detection in PriGuard

Detection of Privacy Violations: Figure 1 shows how PriGuard approach works. Recall that there exists a commitment from the social network operator to the user agent to preserve certain privacy conditions. A commitment violation signals a breach of privacy. Hence, the agent computes

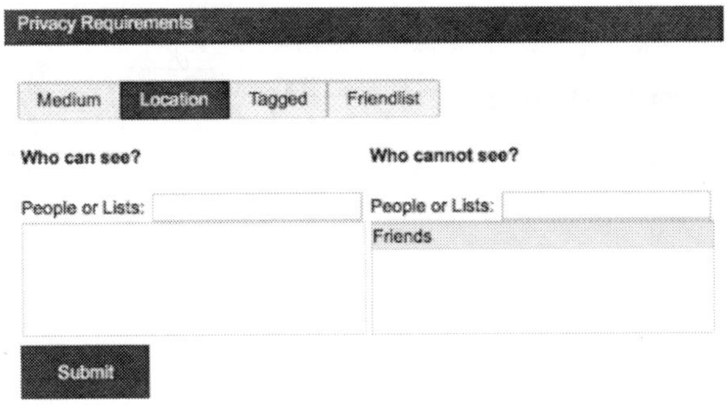

Figure 2: Dennis declaring his friends to not see his location posts.

under which conditions a commitment would be violated [2]. Then, the agent uses the domain information, norms, the view information and the violation statement for detecting privacy violations. A view consists of three sets: a set of agents, a set of relationships and a set of posts. An exact view representation of the social network is the global view of the system. However, an agent can choose to focus on subviews of the exact view. Finally, the agent reports whether there is a privacy violation by checking if a given commitment is violated or not. It depends on the creditor of the commitment (e.g., the user) to take an action accordingly.

3. PRIGUARDTOOL

PriGuardTool is a Web-based tool that implements PriGuard model. Each component in Figure 1 is implemented in PriGuardTool. We use ontologies to capture the domain,, view, and norms of the social network.

Domain (A): The social network domain is represented using PriGuard ontology specified in OWL 2 Web Ontology Language [1]. PriGuard model is a DL model, which can be completely defined in an OWL 2 ontology.

View (B): In PriGuard ontology, a view is a set of class assertions (e.g.; ClassAssertion(`Agent :alice`)) and object property assertions (e.g.; ObjectPropertyAssertion (*isFriendOf* `:dennis :charlie`)).

DL Rules (C): In PriGuard, norms are defined as Datalog rules. OWL 2 is an expressive language to represent some Datalog rules as DL rules. For example, consider this rule: $\texttt{Post} \sqcap \exists hasMedium.\exists hasGeotag.\texttt{Location} \sqsubseteq \texttt{LocationPost}$. This rule states that a post that includes a geotagged picture is an instance of `LocationPost` class in the ontology.

Commitments (D): Users input their privacy concerns via PriGuardTool interface as depicted in Figure 2. The user can specify her privacy concerns regarding medium posts, location posts and posts that the user is tagged in. Moreover, the user can declare who can access her friendlist in the social network. For each category, the user declares two groups of people: one group that can see that category and a group that cannot. If the user specifies conflicting privacy concerns (e.g.; a user is part of both groups), the agent adopts a conservative approach to minimize privacy violations to occur; i.e., it finds conflicting users and move them to the group that cannot see the content.

Violation Statements (E): After all the semantic inferences are made by the use of PriGuard ontology and DL rules, the agent should be able to query this knowledge to monitor privacy violations in the social network. For this, we use SPARQL for querying RDF-based information. Note that ontological axioms can also be seen as RDF triples. In a SPARQL query, there are query variables to retrieve the desired results. We only focus on *SELECT* queries with filter expressions *NOT EXISTS* and *EXISTS* to represent violation statements. The violation statement of C_1 is shown as a SPARQL query in Table 1. The abbreviation P declares a namespace prefix. *osn* prefix shows where to find PriGuard ontology for querying. This *SELECT* query declares two query variables (?x and ?p) to be retrieved. The core part of the query is defined in the *WHERE* block, which consists of four triples (one is used in a filter expression). This query returns friends of Dennis who can see his location posts.

Table 1: The Violation Statement of C_1

```
P rdf: <http://www.w3.org/1999/02/22-rdf-syntax-ns#>
P osn: <http://mas.cmpe.boun.edu.tr/ontologies/osn#>
SELECT ?x ?p WHERE {
        ?x osn:isFriendOf osn:dennis .
        ?p osn:isAbout osn:dennis .
        ?p rdf:type osn:LocationPost .
        FILTER EXISTS {?x osn:canSeePost ?p} }
```

4. DEMO DETAILS

- We will use four real-life scenarios from the literature to demonstrate how PriGuard approach works in PriGuardTool. Each scenario will address a different type of privacy violation, including inference-based and co-privacy violations.
- We will show how a user can use PriGuardTool interface to input her privacy concerns and how the commitments are generated automatically by ensuring that inconsistencies do not arise.
- For each commitment in the system, we will show how the corresponding violation statements are created.
- For each scenario, we will show how the user will check for privacy violations, and how her agent will report the detection results. We will also interpret these results with comparison to existing work.

Our demo video is available online at: `https://youtu.be/9UJ02h-ud0O`.

Acknowledgments

This work is supported by TUBITAK under grant 113E543.

REFERENCES

[1] B. Motik, P. F. Patel-Schneider, B. Parsia, C. Bock, A. Fokoue, P. Haase, R. Hoekstra, I. Horrocks, A. Ruttenberg, U. Sattler, et al. Owl 2 web ontology language: Structural specification and functional-style syntax. *W3C recommendation*, 27(65):159, 2009.

[2] P. Yolum and M. P. Singh. Flexible protocol specification and execution: applying event calculus planning using commitments. In *Proceedings of the First International Joint Conference on Autonomous Agents and Multiagent Systems*, pages 527–534, 2002.

SPECTRE: A Game Theoretic Framework for Preventing Collusion in Security Games

(Demonstration)

Shahrzad Gholami
University of Southern California
941 Bloom Walk
Los Angeles, USA
sgholami@usc.edu

Bryan Wilder
University of Southern California
941 Bloom Walk
Los Angeles, USA
bwilder@usc.edu

Matthew Brown
University of Southern California
941 Bloom Walk
Los Angeles, USA
matthew.a.brown@usc.edu

Arunesh Sinha
University of Southern California
941 Bloom Walk
Los Angeles, USA
aruneshs@usc.edu

Nicole Sintov
University of Southern California
941 Bloom Walk
Los Angeles, USA
sintov@usc.edu

Milind Tambe
University of Southern California
941 Bloom Walk
Los Angeles, USA
tambe@usc.edu

ABSTRACT

Several models have been proposed for Stackelberg security games (SSGs) and protection against perfectly rational and bounded rational adversaries; however, none of these existing models addressed the destructive cooperation mechanism between adversaries. SPECTRE (**S**trategic **P**atrol planner to **E**xtinguish **C**ollusive **ThRE**ats) takes into account the synergistic destructive collusion among two groups of adversaries in security games. This framework is designed for the purpose of efficient patrol scheduling for security agents in security games in presence of collusion and is mainly build up on game theoretic approaches, optimization techniques, machine learning methods and theories for human decision making under risk. The major advantage of SPECTRE is involving real world data from human subject experiments with participants on Amazon Mechanical Turk (AMT).

Keywords

Game Theory, Stackelberg Security Games, Human Behavior Models, Cooperation Mechanism, Collusion

1. INTRODUCTION

Security agencies including the US Coast Guard (USCG), the Federal Air Marshal Service (FAMS) and the Los Angeles Airport (LAX) police are several major domains that have been deploying Stackelberg security games (SSGs) and related algorithms to protect against adversaries strategically [3]. The security games introduced in these domains, mostly, include two players: a defender and an adversary. The interaction between the defender and the attacker was modeled as a single-shot game and the attacker was defined as a perfectly rational player. This well known class of SSGs is sequential, i.e. one player (the leader or the defender) commits to a strategy which can be observed by the other player (the follower or adversary) before choosing his own strategy. On the other hand, SPECTRE deals with the sequential single-shot security games but in which the defender commits to a strategy and the two attackers can either attack individually or cooperatively in terms of sharing the pay-offs. One of the applications of this type of game is in wildlife protection domain which is an active area of research [1], [2].

According to the references, international illegal animal trafficking is increasing incredibly and based on the estimations, it is worth at least $5 billion, annually. The main types of wildlife commodities that are subject to these illegal trades include elephant ivory, rhino horn, tiger parts and caviar, to name a few. These activities have the potential to introduce several threats to the national security and evironment arround the world. Biodiversity loss, potential extinctions, introduction of invasive species and desease transmission into healthy ecosystems, all can impact the environment adveresly. In addition to that, some connections have been observed among wildlife trafficking, organized crime and drug trafficking which means that poor law enforcement, poor patrol scheduling or corrupt rangers at wildlife sources, corrupt governments at transit countries and porous borders can all threaten the national security [4]. Despite the evidence of this illegal exchange between different groups of criminals, the destructive synergistic effect of cooperation among adversaries is unexplored in related literature in security game domain.

To combat this illegal wildlife trade, exploitation and collaboration among criminals and adversaries, SPECTRE is designed, employed within a simulation game in wildlife domain and deployed on Amazon Mechanical Turk (AMT) to demonstrate the concept of collusion in security games. It is worth noting that each of the two adversaries in this type of game can be a representative for either a poacher who is

Appears in: *Proceedings of the 15th International Conference on Autonomous Agents and Multiagent Systems (AAMAS 2016), J. Thangarajah, K. Tuyls, C. Jonker, S. Marsella (eds.), May 9–13, 2016, Singapore.*

directly hunting in the field or a trader who is illegally exchanging the animals or financing other illegal commodities via animal trafficking.

2. HOW TO EXTINGUISH COLLUSION?

SPECTRE system has two main compartments: i) human subject experiment interface (HSI) and ii) the core software for learning the governing model and designing patrol plans. (Demo Link: `https://youtu.be/zRzg2g4PxWA`)

2.1 Human Subject Interface

To see how human adversaries make decisions about cooperating with each other, SPECTRE Human Subject Interface (HSI) was designed in wildlife protection domain. In this software real human subjects are asked to play a game in which two players are involved. In this game, they have the role of a poacher in a national park in Africa. There are different number of hippopotamus distributed over the park which indicates animal density distribution over the area and are considered to visually represent the distribution of wildlife to the players. The entire park area is divided into two sections (right and left) and each human subject can only attack in one section (either right or left); however, they can explore the whole park to find out about reward, penalty and coverage at each sub-region. The other section of the park is only available to another player who is playing the same game. Two players have access to each others' information to make wise decisions about cooperation with each other. Each section of the park is divided into 3×3 grid, i.e. each player has 9 cells (sub-regions) accessible to him to attack. Players are able to choose different sub-regions and all of the information about success and failure likelihood, reward for the attacker (which is animal density in each sub-region) and penalty at each sub-region (either on left or side of park) will be shown to them. To help the human subjects to have a better view of the success/failure percentage (which is defender coverage) over all the sub-regions, we put a heat-map of that overlaid on Google Map view of the park. Also, to help the players to have a better understanding of the cooperation mechanism in this game, we provided a table that summarizes all possible pay-offs for cooperative attacks based on the cooperation bonus considered for each game. The human subjects need to make

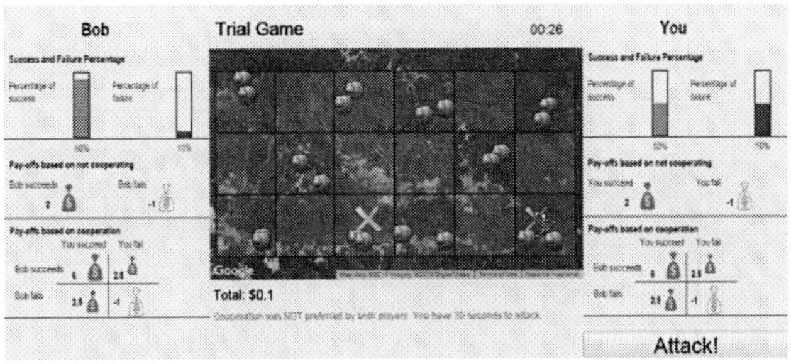

Figure 1: Hunters vs Rangers game interface

decisions about: i)whether they are inclined to cooperate with the other player or not and ii)which region of the park to put their snare (trap) where there is less chance of getting caught and also a high chance of capturing a hippopotamus. So the human subjects may decide to attack "individually and independently" or attack "cooperatively" with the other player. In both situations, they will attack different sections separately but if both of them agree to attack cooperatively, they will share all of their pay-offs with each other, equally (fifty-fifty). To enhance understanding of the game, participants were asked to play one trial game to become familiar with the game interface and procedures. Then we provided a validation game to make sure that the players have read the instructions of the game and are fully aware of the rules and options of the game. Finally, the third game which is the main game is shown to the human subjects and their decisions are recorded. Then we analyze the human subject decisions to derive a more accurate model to describe the human adversary behavior in security games in presence of cooperation mechanism.

2.2 SPECTRE: A Patrol scheduler software

To study how colluding adversaries behave, different payoff structures and defender strategies can be applied to the software. The main output of this software is human decisions about cooperation and the targets they have attacked either in cooperation or individual attack. Figure 2(a) illustrates how SPECTRE functions in human subject experiments analysis.

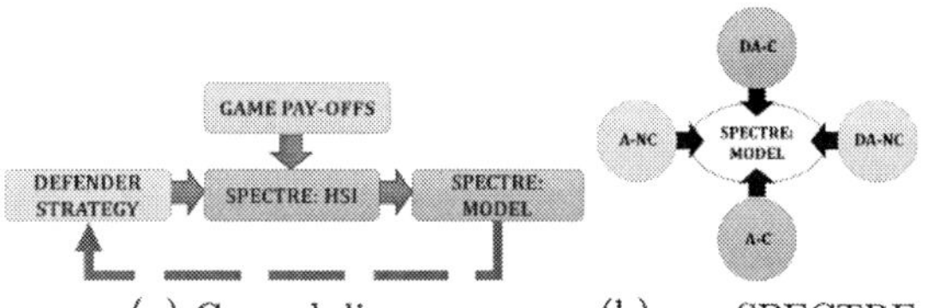

(a) General diagram (b) SPECTRE Components

Figure 2: SPECTRE framework for human adversary analysis

For the initial experiments, SPECTRE HSI starts with rational adversary assumption and generates defender strategies on that basis. After collecting data based on this initial input, new strategies based on bounded rational adversaries are generated and re-applied to the software. The main idea for breaking the cooperation is to put one adversary in a better condition in terms of defender coverage and the other one in a worse condition, then cooperation will not be preferred by one of adversaries and cooperation breaks. So for human behavior analysis, SPECTRE considers four groups of adversaries shown in 2(b): i) a disadvantaged attacker who is inclined to cooperate, DA-C , ii) a disadvantaged attacker who is not inclined to cooperate, DA-NC, iii) an advantaged attacker who is inclined to cooperate, A-C, and iv) an advantaged attacker who is not inclined to cooperate, A-NC. Based on the decisions made by these four groups and human behavior models under risk such as Prospect Theory and SUQR, SPECTRE predicts adversaries behavior and generate an optimal defender strategy which breaks the collusion and maximize the defender utility.

Acknowledgments

This research was supported by MURI Grant W911NF-11-1-0332.

REFERENCES

[1] F. Fang, T. H. Nguyen, R. Pickles, W. Y. Lam, G. R. Clements, B. An, A. Singh, M. Tambe, and A. Lemieux. Deploying paws: Field optimization of the protection assistant for wildlife security. 2016.

[2] F. Fang, P. Stone, and M. Tambe. When security games go green: Designing defender strategies to prevent poaching and illegal fishing. In *International Joint Conference on Artificial Intelligence (IJCAI)*, 2015.

[3] M. Tambe. *Security and game theory: Algorithms, deployed systems, lessons learned.* Cambridge University Press, 2011.

[4] L. S. Wyler and P. A. Sheikh. International illegal trade in wildlife: Threats and us policy. DTIC Document, 2008.

NWin: A Tool for Counting Winning Strategies

Vadim Malvone
Università degli Studi di Napoli
Federico II, Italy
vadim.malvone@unina.it

Aniello Murano
Università degli Studi di Napoli
Federico II, Italy
murano@na.infn.it

Marco Tafuto
Università degli Studi di Napoli
Federico II, Italy
marc.tafuto@gmail.com

ABSTRACT

We present NWin, a tool that allows to count all different winning strategies in two-player turn-based games under the reachability condition. NWin uses a graphical interface to build the game model and collect all acyclic and cyclic winning strategies. By means of benchmarks over random games we show that NWin has a good performance in practice.

Categories and Subject Descriptors

I.2.11 [**Artificial Intelligence**]: Distributed Artificial Intelligence —*Multiagent Systems*

General Terms

Algorithms, Performance

Keywords

Game theory; Reachability condition; Strategic reasoning

1. INTRODUCTION

Game theory is a powerful framework with several applications in MAS [14]. It allows reasoning efficiently about the strategic behavior of reactive systems [2,9,13]. In this paper we consider two-players turn-based games played under the *reachability* condition, i.e, some nodes are declared *target*. Solving such a game amounts to check whether one of the players has a *winning strategy*, i.e., a sequence of moves that lead him to a target node no matter how the opponent acts.

In many cases, knowing how many winning solutions exist is crucial [4,6–8,10,11]. For example, in planning a rescue, it would give to a rescuer some backup plan in case something goes wrong. In solution concepts, this would cope with the *uniqueness* problem in Nash equilibrium (see [1,5,12]).

In this paper we introduce NWin, a tool that addresses the quantitative question of checking how many different strategies a player has to win a two-player reachability game. The tool uses a graphical interface to build the game model and shows all acyclic and cyclic winning strategies. By means of benchmarks over random games we show that NWin has a good performance in practice: it can process 10^8 acyclic strategies plays in less than 10 seconds by a pc.

Appears in: *Proceedings of the 15th International Conference on Autonomous Agents and Multiagent Systems (AAMAS 2016), J. Thangarajah, K. Tuyls, C. Jonker, S. Marsella (eds.), May 9–13, 2016, Singapore.*

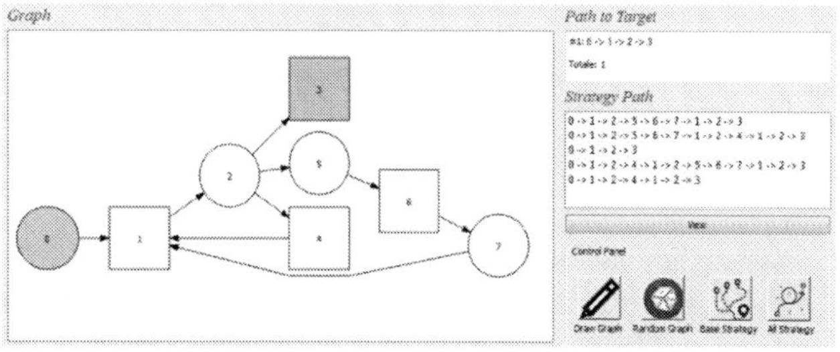

Figure 1: The main window of NWin.

2. THE TOOL

In this section we describe the Graphical User Interface (GUI) of NWin, in the current release (1.0).

Our tool works over two-player turn-based games, played by Player 1 and Player 2, under the reachability condition ($2TG$, for short). These are directed graphs in which the set of nodes (V) is partitioned in two subsets V_1 and V_2. Each V_i contains all nodes owned by Player i. Nodes in V_1 (V_2) are graphically represented by a circle (square). The unique initial node is colored in blue and all target nodes (T) in green. Take a node v, the set of outcoming edges represent all possible moves of the player that owns v. A play is a path starting from the initial node and represents a sequence of performed moves from the players. A strategy for a player is the set of moves he can perform along every prefix of a play. A strategy is *winning* for Player 1 if it induces a play that reaches a target node, no matter which strategy Player 2 uses.

The GUI is depicted in Figure 1. It consists of two parts: the Output Areas (OA) and the Control Panel (CP). The OA is made of three frames. The one on the left side (*Graph*) is used to depict the game graph. The frame on the right upper side (*Path to Target*) shows all *reachable paths* that start at the initial node and end in a target node [1]. Finally, the frame of right lower side (*Strategy Path*) reports all winning strategy plays for Player 1. The CP at the right down corner is composed by four buttons: Draw Graph (DG), Random Graph (RG), Base Strategies (BS), and All Strategies (AS). The DG button is used to build a graph manually. By pressing it, a window pops up in which the user sets the number of nodes and edges of the game graph. Then, another window comes out in which the user decides how the nodes are connected. Finally, he sets in a new window the initial

[1]Formally, these are the reachability paths obtained by looking at the monolithic version of the game graph.

and the set of target nodes. The RG button works similarly to the DG button but after the parameters in the first window are set the game is generated randomly. The BS button works as follows. The first time it is pressed, all reachable paths are shown. At the second press it gives all possible acyclic winning strategy plays in which the Player 1 wins. The AS button works as the BS button, but it also reports the cyclic plays. Finally, if we select a winning strategy play in the frame *Strategy Path* and push the button View (V), in the game graph the path appears in red.

A video demonstration of NWin is on YouTube [2].

3. HOW TO COMPUTE THE STRATEGIES

Given a $2TG$, NWin computes all winning strategies through three main steps. The first two are preliminary and used to partition all nodes in "good" and "bad".

The first step calculates all acyclic reachability paths, *i.e.* the acyclic paths, from the initial node to a target node, that are present in the monolithic version of the game graph. This is done by applying a classic DFS algorithm. Precisely, the algorithm uses two sets of nodes, namely *white* (W) and *black* (B). The set W (B) represents all nodes that can (cannot) reach a target node in T. This step starts with $B = \emptyset$ and $W = T$. For each node v, if it is adjacent to a node in W, then $W = W \cup \{v\}$, otherwise $B = B \cup \{v\}$. The algorithm ends when a fixed point is reached.

The second step works on the nodes in $\{W \cap V_2\} \setminus T$, *i.e.* the nodes of Player 2 that are white but not target nodes. Along this step we remove a node v from W and add it in B iff at least one of the following conditions is satisfied: *(i)* v has a loop; *(ii)* v is adjacent to a node in B; *(iii)* v belongs to a *trap* cycle C for Player 1 (from which he can not go out). Note that, each $v' \in C \cap V_1$ has a single outcome edge.

The third step considers the entire game and in particular the strategies of the players. Given a node $v \in W \cap V_1 \setminus T$, Player 1 has a degree of preference in the mining that, if there exists a node v' adjacent to v and $v' \in W$, then he chooses and moves to v' (even if this node has been already visited). Similarly, given a node $v \in W \cap V_2$, if there exists a node v' adjacent to v and $v' \in B$, then Player 2 chooses v', otherwise he prefers to choose a node that has been already visited, if possible. This step, and thus the algorithm, ends when a target node or a node in B is entered.

It is important to note that, after the first step the tool prints all possible reachability paths. All winning strategy plays are printed only after the third step is completed.

4. CRITICAL ISSUE

To compute all winning strategy plays, we have faced with two main critical issues: all the edges need to be visited in order to discover cycles and nodes require to be visited more than ones whenever they belong to a winning strategy play. The classical DFS is too weak to handle these two points. Indeed, the DFS analyzes all the nodes of the graph, but it does not analyze all edges and so all possible moves of both players. For this reason, we have introduced opportune extensions of the DFS. The first we consider is DFSR, in which it allows the algorithm to *revisit* a node in order to consider all possible edges and all possible acyclic winning strategy plays. In order to retrieve the winning strategy plays for Player 1 that contain also cycles, we have built MDFSR a modified version of the DFSR that is able to collect plays in which there are cycles repeated at most once. We consider only this kind of cycles for two reasons: *(i)* one can pump a cycle an arbitrary number of times to obtain other winning plays, *(ii)* to avoid the algorithm running forever. As last remark it is worth noting that the DFSR is used to visit several times the same node while the MDFSR version is required to visit more than ones the same edge.

[2] www.youtube.com/playlist?list=PL0f6qAJrAYnFBl5PXUbloDMGyj1kif9aF

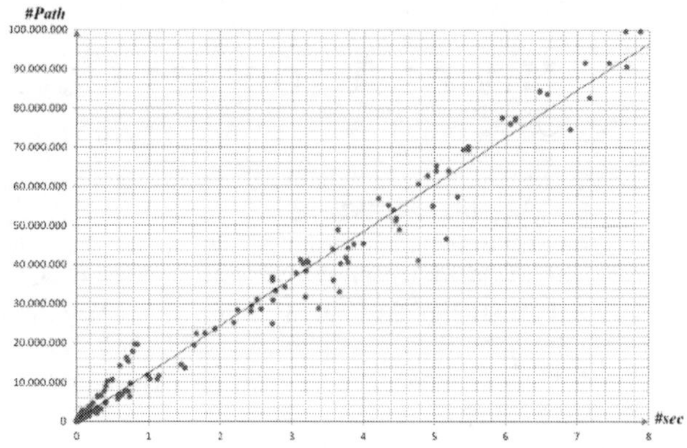

Figure 2: The table of performance.

5. PERFORMANCE

In this section we report on some benchmarks. For the lack of space we only describe those over DSFR. We have run NWin on an i5 processor with 4GB of RAM. We have considered random games evaluated under the RG button by setting as number of nodes $n \in \{2, \ldots, 16\}$ and number of edge $e \in \{n + 1, \ldots, n^2\}$. In particular, we have executed one hundred cases for each n and thus one thousand and five hundred games in total. For each game, we have collected the execution time and the number of paths processed.

The benchmarks are depicted in Figure 2 in which we report the number of paths ($\#Path$) processed per second (s). The graph gives a proportional relationship between the number of paths processed and the seconds that NWin takes to process such paths. In particular, it shows that under 10 seconds NWin can process more than 10^8 paths. It is worth observing that we analyze the number of paths rather than nodes as the former is the fulcrum of NWin.

6. CONCLUSION

In this paper, we have presented NWin a tool that allows to retrieve all possible winning strategy plays in a two-player game under the reachability condition. NWin makes use of a simple but efficient GUI that allows to build the game under two options: random and manual. The tool calculates and reports, upon request, all acyclic and cyclic winning strategy plays. We have reported on some benchmarks on the former case and showed that NWin can calculate more than 10^8 paths in less than 10 seconds. We believe that our tool can be used as a core engine to solve several problems in MAS. As future work we plan to extend this tool in the setting of solution concepts, *e.g.* Nash Equilibrium (NE). In particular, by means of this extension, we aim to solve the uniqueness of NE in practice [3].

REFERENCES

[1] E. Altman, H. Kameda, and Y. Hosokawa. Nash equilibria in load balancing in distributed computer systems. *IGTR*, 4(2):91–100, 2002.

[2] R. Alur, T. Henzinger, and O. Kupferman. Alternating-Time Temporal Logic. *JACM*, 49(5):672–713, 2002.

[3] B. Aminof, V. Malvone, A. Murano, and S. Rubin. Graded Strategy Logic: Reasoning about Uniqueness of Nash Equilibria. In *AAMAS'16*. International Foundation for Autonomous Agents and Multiagent Systems, 2016, (to appear).

[4] P. Bonatti, C. Lutz, A. Murano, and M. Vardi. The Complexity of Enriched muCalculi. *LMCS*, 4(3):1–27, 2008.

[5] R. Cornes, R. Hartley, and T. Sandler. An elementary proof via contraction. *Journal of Public Economic Theory*, 1(4):499–509, 1999.

[6] M. Faella, M. Napoli, and M. Parente. Graded Alternating-Time Temporal Logic. *FI*, 105(1-2):189–210, 2010.

[7] A. Ferrante, A. Murano, and M. Parente. Enriched Mu-Calculi Module Checking. *LMCS*, 4(3):1–21, 2008.

[8] O. Kupferman, U. Sattler, and M. Vardi. The Complexity of the Graded muCalculus. In *CADE'02*, LNCS 2392, pages 423–437. Springer, 2002.

[9] O. Kupferman, M. Vardi, and P. Wolper. Module Checking. *IC*, 164(2):322–344, 2001.

[10] V. Malvone, F. Mogavero, A. Murano, and L. Sorrentino. On the counting of strategies. In *TIME 2015*, pages 170–179, 2015.

[11] V. Malvone, A. Murano, and L. Sorrentino. Games with additional winning strategies. In *CILC 2015*, pages 175–180, 2015.

[12] G. Papavassilopoulos and J. B. Cruz. On the uniqueness of nash strategies for a class of analytic differential games. *Journal of Optimization Theory and Applications*, 27(2):309–314, 1979.

[13] A. Pnueli and R. Rosner. Distributed reactive systems are hard to synthesize. In *FOCS'90*, pages 746–757. IEEE, 1990.

[14] Y. Shoham and K. Leyton-Brown. *Multiagent Systems: Algorithmic, Game-Theoretic, and Logical Foundations*. Cambridge University Press, 2008.

HEALER: POMDP Planning for Scheduling Interventions among Homeless Youth

(Demonstration)

Amulya Yadav, Ece Kamar[1], Barbara Grosz[2], Milind Tambe
University of Southern California, CA 90089 [1]Microsoft Research, WA 98052 [2]Harvard University, MA 02138
{amulyaya, tambe}@usc.edu [1]eckamar@microsoft.com [2]grosz@eecs.harvard.edu

ABSTRACT

Adaptive software agents like HEALER have been proposed in the literature recently to recommend intervention plans to homeless shelter officials. However, generating networks for HEALER's input is challenging. Moreover, HEALER's solutions are often counter-intuitive to people. This demo paper makes two contributions. First, we demonstrate HEALER's Facebook application, which parses the Facebook contact lists in order to construct an approximate social network for HEALER. Second, we present a software interface to run human subject experiments (HSE) to understand human biases in recommendation of intervention plans. We plan to use data collected from these HSEs to build an explanation system for HEALER's solutions.

1. INTRODUCTION

Homeless youth are extremely prone to HIV-AIDS because of their propensity to engage in high-risk behavior such as unprotected sex, sharing needles while using drugs etc. In fact, statistics collected over several years show that homeless youth are 10 times more likely to get HIV infection than stably housed populations [1]. Moreover, HIV is extremely lethal among homeless youth as most youth lack basic resources needed to control and manage the disease (e.g., access to regular medical care, hygienic surroundings).

Therefore, minimizing rates of HIV infection among homeless youth is an extremely important problem. One potential solution is to raise awareness about HIV prevention and treatment measures among homeless youth by conducting intervention programs among youth to raise awareness about HIV prevention and treatment practices [3]. These intervention programs typically consist of day long educational sessions where a select group of homeless youth are trained as "peer leaders" and are given information about how the HIV virus spreads. As "peer leaders", the youth are encouraged to raise awareness about HIV among their social circles via word-of-mouth spread [4]. The homeless shelter conducts several of these intervention programs sequentially. However, due to manpower constraints, the shelter can only intervene upon a small number of youth ($\sim$ 3-6 youth) in each intervention. Therefore, the shelter needs to choose the attendees (or "peer leaders") for each of their interventions. The shelter aims to maximize the number of influenced youth (i.e., those youth who find out about HIV prevention measures) over the course of all the interventions that they conduct [6].

Appears in: *Proceedings of the 15th International Conference on Autonomous Agents and Multiagent Systems (AAMAS 2016), J. Thangarajah, K. Tuyls, C. Jonker, S. Marsella (eds.), May 9–13, 2016, Singapore.*

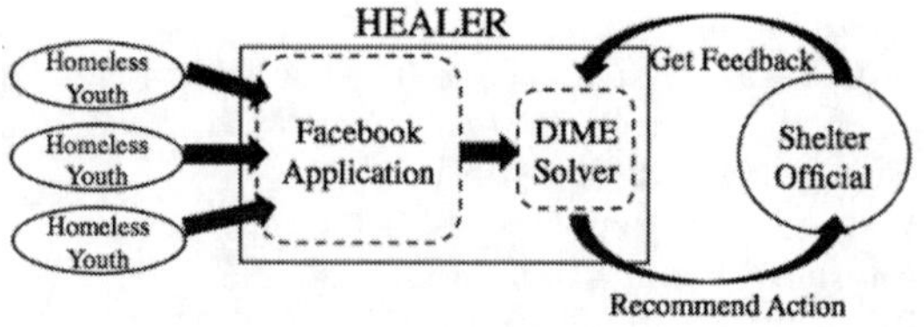

Figure 1: HEALER's Design

This leads to the following *algorithmic question*: Given the friendship based social network of homeless youth, the number of attendees in each intervention (K) and the number of interventions (T) as input, find a sequential plan for choosing K intervention participants for T rounds so that the expected number of people who find about HIV prevention measures (or "get influenced") over the course of T rounds is maximized.

Developed in collaboration with Safe Place for Youth (a homeless shelter which provides food and lodging to homeless youth aged 12-25), HEALER (**H**ierarchical **E**nsembling based **A**gent which p**L**ans for **E**ffective **R**eduction in HIV Spread) is an adaptive software agent which solves the aforementioned algorithmic question by recommending sequential plans for selecting intervention attendees to homeless shelter officials [5]. HEALER uses Partially Observable Markov Decision Process (POMDP) [2] style reasoning to evaluate different choices of intervention attendees over a long time period. HEALER finds the best solution by reasoning about uncertainties in network structure and evolution of influence spread (as both these uncertainties are very common in homeless youth social networks). HEALER is currently being tested in a pilot study with 60 homeless youth at Safe Place for Youth to assess its performance in the field.

Since the optimization problem solved by HEALER involves calculations of long term expectations, the homeless shelter officials found HEALER's solutions very counter-intuitive. This represents a potential barrier to HEALER's widespread acceptability and use. Thus, we propose to build an *explanation system* to justify HEALER's solutions to officials in an intuitive manner.

Against this background, the demonstration presented in this paper introduces two contributions. First, we present HEALER's Facebook application, which parses the Facebook contact lists of homeless youth in order to construct an approximate social network. This social network is fed as input to the DIME solver [5] in order to generate recommendations for intervention attendees. Second, we present a software interface to run human subject experiments (HSE) to understand the way humans make decisions in this domain and evaluate the potential effect of human biases in decision-making. By conducting these HSEs, we can (i) understand

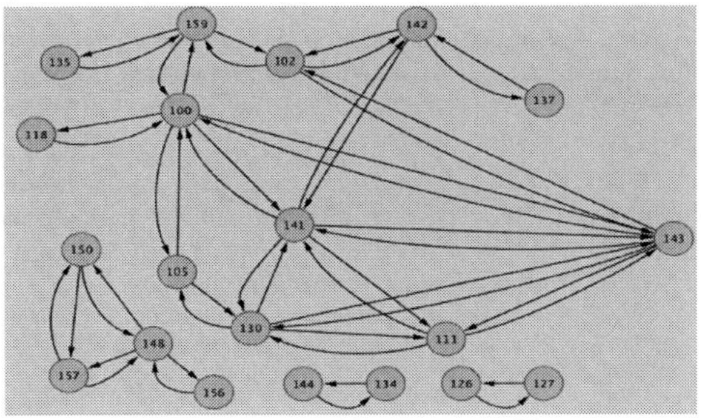

Figure 2: A portion of the raw network generated using HEALER's Facebook application

the intuitions that people (including officials) use while selecting attendees for interventions in social networks and relate them to biases they may have; and (ii) use these intuitions and the understanding of the biases to guide the development of HEALER's explanation system. This paper also presents a short overview of HEALER's design in order to provide proper context.

The demonstration aims to engage audiences by asking them (i) to use HEALER's Facebook application so that they can see the network that connects them and their fellow audience members; and (ii) to participate in the HSEs.

2. HEALER

HEALER consists of: (i) a Facebook application for gathering information about social networks; and (ii) a DIME Solver, which solves the algorithmic question posed in Section 1.

Facebook Application: Homeless youth are asked to register into HEALER's Facebook application. This is reasonable as [3] show that almost 50% of homeless youth are active on Facebook. Once all youth are registered, the application parses the Facebook contact lists of all the registered youth to construct a social network from Facebook friendships between the registered youth. Specifically, the application adds an edge between two youth if (i) they are friends on Facebook; and (ii) they are registered into the application. Figure 4 shows a portion of the actual homeless youth social network that we have generated using HEALER during our pilot study. Each youth (or network node) has a personal identification number (PID) which protects the anonymity of the youth.

DIME Solver: The network generated by the Facebook application is used by HEALER to provide the solution of DIME solver [5] as a series of recommendations (of intervention participants) to homeless shelter officials. Upon the intervention's completion, HEALER *senses* feedback about the conducted intervention from the officials. This feedback includes new observations about the network (e.g., new edges may be found as intervention participants are interviewed by the shelter officials). HEALER uses this feedback to update and improve its future recommendations.

3. THE SIMULATION GAME

Demo: https://www.youtube.com/watch?v=0g4aStj3z9I

We aim to build an explanation system for HEALER that justifies its solutions in an intuitive manner. As a first step, we have built a software interface for conducting HSEs to collect data on how people select intervention attendees in networks. The data collected from these HSEs will help us understand biases and intuitions that people use in selecting intervention participants. We can then use

Figure 3: First Phase of HSE Game

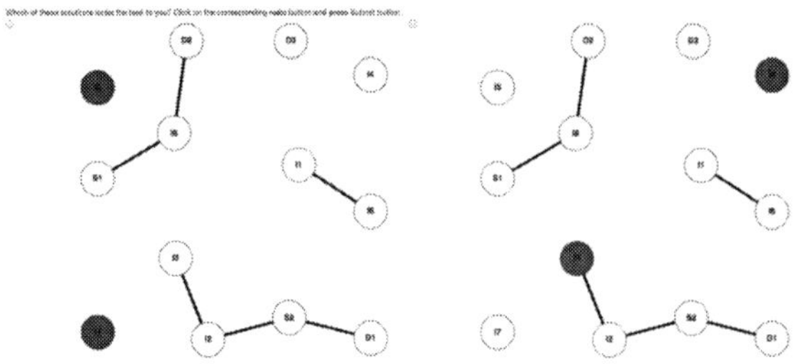

Figure 4: Second Phase of HSE Game

these inferred intuitions to guide the development of our explanation system.

During our demonstration, the audience will be able to directly participate in our HSE. First, they will be presented with a high-level description of the influence spread problem and detailed instructions on how to play the HSE game. Next, they will play the game which consists of two phases.

3.1 First Phase

In the first phase, the audience will be shown eight different networks one by one. For each network, they will be asked to select their choice of 2 most influential nodes. Their choices will be recorded on all 8 networks. This data will help us understand the biases that affect the choice of nodes selected by humans.

3.2 Second Phase

In the second phase, data is collected to find out if people are better at verifying correct solutions than coming up with correct solutions. Recall that in the first phase of our game, each human subject was shown a set of eight different networks and they were asked to select a set of nodes for maximizing influence spread. In the second phase, for each of these eight networks, the audience is shown four different solutions for that network and he/she will be asked to select the solution which they think is best.

Data collected from the second phase will help us in analyzing the need for an explanation system for HEALER. For example, if the collected data shows that people are very good at recognizing that the correct solution (out of the 4 solutions) is HEALER's solution, then that would negate the need for HEALER's explanation system. Thus, using data from the second phase, we plan to empirically validate the need for an explanation system.

3.3 Awards

To promote competition, there will be an award that will be given to the audience member whose solution is closest to the optimal solution in terms of influence spread. A live leaderboard will also be maintained to track the current winner of the award.

4. ACKNOWLEDGEMENTS

This research was supported by MURI Grant W911NF-11-1-0332.

REFERENCES

[1] N. H. Council. HIV/AIDS among Persons Experiencing Homelessness: Risk Factors, Predictors of Testing, and Promising Testing Strategies. www.nhchc.org/wp-content/uploads/2011/09/InFocus_Dec2012.pdf, Dec. 2012.

[2] M. L. Puterman. *Markov Decision Processes: Discrete Stochastic Dynamic Programming*. John Wiley & Sons, 2009.

[3] E. Rice. The Positive Role of Social Networks and Social Networking Technology in the Condom-using Behaviors of Homeless Young People. *Public health reports*, 125(4):588, 2010.

[4] E. Rice, A. Barman-Adhikari, N. G. Milburn, and W. Monro. Position-specific HIV risk in a Large Network of Homeless Youths. *American journal of public health*, 102(1):141–147, 2012.

[5] A. Yadav, H. Chan, A. Jiang, H. Xu, E. Rice, and M. Tambe. Using Social Networks to Aid Homeless Shelters: Dynamic Influence Maximization under Uncertainty - An Extended Version. In *Proceedings of the Fiftienth International Conference on Autonomous Agents and Multiagent Systems (AAMAS 2016)*, 2016.

[6] A. Yadav, L. Marcolino, E. Rice, R. Petering, H. Winetrobe, H. Rhoades, M. Tambe, and H. Carmichael. Preventing HIV Spread in Homeless Populations Using PSINET. In *Proceedings of the Twenty-Seventh Conference on Innovative Applications of Artificial Intelligence (IAAI-15)*, 2015.

Using Automatic Failure Detection for Cognitive Agents in Eclipse

Vincent J. Koeman
Delft University of Technology
Mekelweg 4, 2628CD
Delft, The Netherlands
v.j.koeman@tudelft.nl

Koen V. Hindriks
Delft University of Technology
Mekelweg 4, 2628CD
Delft, The Netherlands
k.v.hindriks@tudelft.nl

Catholijn M. Jonker
Delft University of Technology
Mekelweg 4, 2628CD
Delft, The Netherlands
c.m.jonker@tudelft.nl

1. INTRODUCTION

In order to reduce debugging effort and enable automated failure detection, we proposed an *automated testing framework for cognitive agent programs* that provides support for detecting frequently occurring failure types in [14]. Automated testing yields a reduction in the effort needed to detect a failure and is more effective than manual code inspection methods [16].

A *failure* is an event in which a system does not perform a required function within specified limits [10]. Failures thus are manifestations of undesired behaviour. They are caused by a *fault*, an incorrect step, process, or data definition in a program [10] or mistake in a program [17]. Upon detecting a failure, a programmer needs to locate and correct the fault that causes the failure.

We introduced a test language based on two basic temporal operators, and use this language to specify test templates for detecting failure types. These test templates refine a failure taxonomy introduced previously in [17]. A test approach has also been specified that explains how to instantiate test templates and derive test conditions for specific failure types. The main steps of this approach are (i) to define success in terms of functional requirements, (ii) to test cognitive state updating, and (iii) to classify failures that concern actions and goals.

2. MAIN PURPOSE: THE AUTOMATED TESTING OF COGNITIVE AGENTS

In general, different techniques for detecting failures of program code are available, ranging from *inspection* of source code and logs to automated *testing* tools [16]. The need for debugging techniques and test approaches for agent-oriented programming has been broadly recognized [2, 4, 5]. Techniques for agent-oriented programming need to be based on the underlying agent paradigm [15, 18]. However, this is a significant challenge, as they should for example take into account that agents execute a specific decision cycle and operate in non-deterministic environments [1, 3, 9].

The developed testing framework provides a *systematic approach for detecting failures in cognitive agent programs* by using test templates that target specific types of failures in the taxonomy, and a systematic method for using these templates for testing. Table 1 lists information resources that are particularly useful for testing.

Source	Type of Information
Agent program (comments)	Clues for reasons & design
Agent trace (screen, logs)	Observable behaviour
Agent design & specification	Functional requirements
Environment (documentation)	Percepts, actions available

Table 1: Information sources for testing

3. DEMONSTRATION: TESTING GOAL AGENTS IN THE ECLIPSE IDE

As we have implemented the automated testing framework for GOAL [8], we will use the GOAL agent programming plug-in[1] for Eclipse in our demonstration. This plug-in provides a full-fledged development environment for agent programmers, integrating all agent and agent-environment development tools in a single well-established setting [13]. The Eclipse platform is based on an open architecture that allows for building on top of well-known existing frameworks [6]. By using Eclipse and the DLTK framework [7], for example, a state-of-the-art editor for GOAL has been created, which forms a solid foundation for further tools. The GOAL language itself has been recently updated to use a more modular approach, i.e., better facilitating re-use. In addition, a source-level debugger for agents has been fully implemented in the plug-in based on the work in [12].

The GOAL plug-in for Eclipse contains a fully implemented version of the automated testing framework for GOAL agents. This implementation has been integrated into the source-level debugger, facilitating for example the inspection of an agent's state as soon as a test condition has failed, as illustrated in Figure 1. The new modular approach of the GOAL agent programming language also better facilitates the testing of individual, separate pieces of functionality.

Tests are programs that we write in a *test language*. The test language is built on top of the GOAL programming language and re-uses parts of that language. The test language provides support for two main tasks: *setting up a test* and *specifying* which *test conditions* should be evaluated.

In a test we can execute only part of an agent and even make the agent do things it would not otherwise do. The *testactions* that are specified in the test program are performed

Appears in: *Proceedings of the 15th International Conference on Autonomous Agents and Multiagent Systems (AAMAS 2016), J. Thangarajah, K. Tuyls, C. Jonker, S. Marsella (eds.), May 9–13, 2016, Singapore.*

[1] See `http://goalhub.github.io/eclipse` for a demonstration(video) of the testing framework implementation and instructions on how to install GOAL in Eclipse.

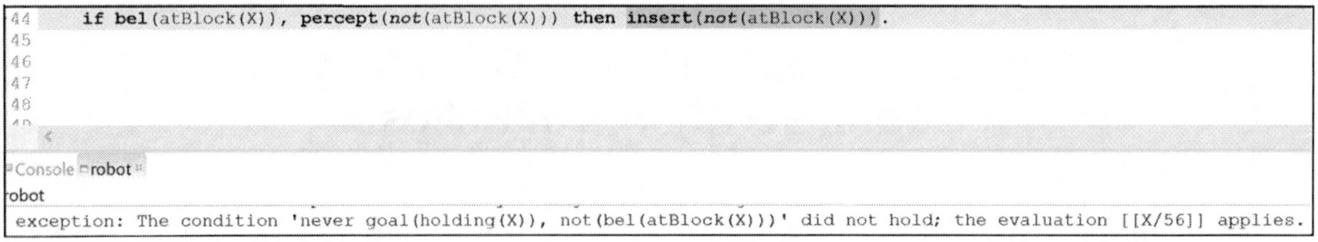

Figure 1: A partial illustration of how test failures are displayed in the source-level agent debugger.

when the test is run. Test actions can be preparatory actions for, e.g., initializing an agent's state, but they can can also be instructions to execute a module. Test conditions are built on top of the cognitive state queries that are used in program rules, like querying the beliefs or goals of an agent. In addition to this, a condition done(*action*) can be used to test whether some action has just been performed. A *test condition* is a temporal condition that expresses that something (i.e. a state query) should happen always, never, eventually, or when some other condition has been true before. Test conditions are associated with a module, and evaluated whilst this module is executed. It is possible to associate a pre-condition, a post-condition, and an in-condition with a module test. The *pre-condition* of a module is a state condition that should hold when a module is entered. Similarly, a *post-condition* is a state condition that should hold when a module is exited. An *in-condition* is a set of temporal test conditions that specify which behaviour is expected of a module while it is executed.

The examples we will use to demonstrate this test framework are some of the educational environments[2] that are developed alongside the GOAL language, like the Blocks World for Teams (BW4T) [11]. In our demonstration, we will show that something we want to happen eventually actually never happens (i.e. detect a failure). For example, an agent should move a block in order to achieve its goal, but it does not do that. We thus want our test to fail. But to show that something will never happen takes a long time. We can instead use a *time out* to ensure termination of the test after a specified time. A time out is global and specifies how much time (in seconds) is allowed to pass before the entire test should be completed. If a time out happens, the test is aborted.

In this example, we want to check whether our agent will move a specific block at some point in time during the execution of its main module (*stackBuilder*). More precisely, we want to know whether at some point in time the agent will perform the action *move(b8,table)*. We can use the **eventually** operator for this. As temporal conditions are specified as in-conditions, and we want to evaluate the *stackBuilder* module, we get the following module test example:

Note that tests should be repeated sufficiently often as states generated will differ per run, if only because environments are more often than not non-deterministic. When a failure is detected, i.e., when running a test it fails at some point, the corresponding fault in the agent program must be located. The program location where the agent is at when the test failed is indicated by the testing framework (when using the debugger). Although it is often the case, it is not always true that this location also is the fault location, i.e., the place of the actual error in the code. If the fault is not located immediately additional debugging is needed. In particular, faults related to actions that are performed but should not have been performed are usually more difficult to locate, as we will show as well.

[2]All (educational) agent environments are freely available at https://github.com/eishub. Most of these projects include an assignment for (novice) agent programmers.

```
use BlocksWorld as mas.
use stackBuilder as module.
timeout = 1.

test stackBuilder with
   in{ eventually done(move(b8,table)). }

stackBuilderAgent {
   do stackBuilder.
}
```

Figure 2: An example of a test that determines whether the *stackBuilderAgent* moves *b8* to the *table* at least once in the *stackBuilder* module.

In this way, we will demonstrate how in practice our test approach (i.e. of [14]) can be used to automatically detect failures and eventually resolve the faults that cause them. In this way, the implementation details of the automated testing framework for GOAL agents will be highlighted, together with the source-level debugger in which it is integrated.

4. CONCLUSION

The main goal of our demonstration, is to show how an automated testing framework for cognitive agents facilitates the detection of failures and aids in the localization of faults. In [14], we have proposed an automated testing framework for cognitive agents and an associated test approach based on test templates for frequently occurring failure types. By using a concrete implementation of the testing framework for the GOAL agent programming language, an integration with the existing source-level debugger was created within the Eclipse environment, thus fully implementing the design within a state-of-the-art setting. This implementation and its source are publicly available, and used in our demonstration in order to illustrate concrete examples of its use, and provide insight into practical implementation details that may be valuable for the adaptation into other agent programming languages.

REFERENCES

[1] R. Bordini, M. Dastani, and M. Winikoff. Current Issues in Multi-Agent Systems Development. In *Engineering Societies in the Agents World VII*, volume 4457, pages 38–61. 2007.

[2] R. H. Bordini, L. Braubach, J. J. Gomez-sanz, G. O. Hare, A. Pokahr, and A. Ricci. A survey of programming languages and platforms for multi-agent systems. *Informatica*, 30:33–44, 2006.

[3] G. Caire, M. Cossentino, and A. Negri. Multi-agent systems implementation and testing. In *Proc. of the 4th From Agent Theory to Agent Implementation Symposium, AT2AI-4*, 2004.

[4] M. Dastani. Programming multi-agent systems. *The Knowledge Engineering Review*, 30:394–418, 9 2015.

[5] J. Dix, K. V. Hindriks, B. Logan, and W. Wobcke. Engineering Multi-Agent Systems (Dagstuhl Seminar 12342). *Dagstuhl Reports*, 2(8):74–98, 2012.

[6] D. Geer. Eclipse becomes the dominant java ide. *Computer*, 38(7):16–18, July 2005.

[7] S. Gomanyuk. An approach to creating development environments for a wide class of programming languages. *Programming and Computer Software*, 34(4):225–236, 2008.

[8] K. V. Hindriks. Programming rational agents in goal. In A. El Fallah Seghrouchni, J. Dix, M. Dastani, and R. H. Bordini, editors, *Multi-Agent Programming: Languages, Tools and Applications*, pages 119–157. Springer US, 2009.

[9] Z. Houhamdi. Multi-Agent System Testing: A Survey. *International Journal of Advanced Computer Science and Applications*, 2(6):135–141, 2011.

[10] ISO. ISO/IEC/IEEE 24765:2010 systems and software engineering - vocabulary. Technical report, Institute of Electrical and Electronics Engineers, Inc., 2010.

[11] M. Johnson, C. Jonker, B. van Riemsdijk, P. J. Feltovich, and J. M. Bradshaw. Joint activity testbed: Blocks world for teams (bw4t). In H. Aldewereld, V. Dignum, and G. Picard, editors, *Engineering Societies in the Agents World X*, volume 5881 of *Lecture Notes in Computer Science*, pages 254–256. Springer Berlin Heidelberg, 2009.

[12] V. J. Koeman and K. V. Hindriks. Designing a source-level debugger for cognitive agent programs. In Q. Chen, P. Torroni, S. Villata, J. Hsu, and A. Omicini, editors, *PRIMA 2015: Principles and Practice of Multi-Agent Systems*, volume 9387 of *Lecture Notes in Computer Science*, pages 335–350. Springer International Publishing, 2015.

[13] V. J. Koeman and K. V. Hindriks. A fully integrated development environment for agent-oriented programming. In Y. Demazeau, K. S. Decker, J. Bajo Pérez, and F. de la Prieta, editors, *Advances in Practical Applications of Agents, Multi-Agent Systems, and Sustainability: The PAAMS Collection*, volume 9086 of *LNCS*, pages 288–291. Springer International Publishing, 2015.

[14] V. J. Koeman, K. V. Hindriks, and C. M. Jonker. Automating failure detection in cognitive agent programs. In *Proceedings of the 2016 International Conference on Autonomous Agents and Multi-agent Systems*, AAMAS '16. International Foundation for Autonomous Agents and Multiagent Systems, 2016.

[15] C. D. Nguyen, A. Perini, C. Bernon, J. Pavón, and J. Thangarajah. Testing in Multi-Agent Systems. In *Agent-Oriented Software Engineering X*, volume 6038, pages 180–190. Springer Berlin Heidelberg, 2011.

[16] P. Runeson, C. Andersson, T. Thelin, A. Andrews, and T. Berling. What do we know about defect detection methods? *Software, IEEE*, 23(3):82–90, May 2006.

[17] M. Winikoff. Novice programmers' faults & failures in goal programs. In *Proceedings of the 2014 International Conference on Autonomous Agents and Multi-agent Systems*, AAMAS '14, pages 301–308, Richland, SC, 2014. International Foundation for Autonomous Agents and Multiagent Systems.

[18] Z. Zhang, J. Thangarajah, and L. Padgham. Model based testing for agent systems. *Software and Data Technologies*, 22:399–413, 2008.

IAGO: Interactive Arbitration Guide Online (Demonstration)

Johnathan Mell
University of Southern California
12015 Waterfront Drive
Los Angeles, CA, USA
mell@ict.usc.edu

Jonathan Gratch
USC Institute for Creative Technologies
12015 Waterfront Drive
Los Angeles, CA, USA
gratch@ict.usc.edu

ABSTRACT

Automated negotiation between two agents has been the subject of much research focused on optimization and efficiency. However, human-agent negotiation represents a field in which real-world considerations can be more fully explored. Furthermore, teaching negotiation and other interpersonal skills requires long periods of practice with open-ended dialogues and partners. The API presented in this paper represents a novel platform on which to conduct human-agent research and facilitate teaching negotiation tactics in a longitudinal way. We present a prototype demonstration that is real-time, rapidly distributable, and allows more actions than current platforms of negotiation.

General Terms & Keywords

Experimentation; Human Factors; Negotiation; Human-Agent Interaction; Virtual Humans

1. INTRODUCTION

Negotiation, specifically multi-issue bargaining, is an important topic in social cognition and interpersonal skill-development [7]. However, most automated negotiation platforms are fine-tuned to attempt to achieve Pareto Optimality (or peak efficiency) among two perfectly rational agents. These platforms therefore do not lend themselves readily to teaching negotiation to human students, nor do they adequately represent a research space for understanding negotiation in the wild.

Human-human negotiation has been studied extensively and found to contain myriad signals beyond simple offer exchanges, from emotional display, to favor-and-ledger-related patter [4], to complex natural language dialogue. Within the agent community, simulating these behaviors is a first step toward developing realistic agents, as well as teaching valuable negotiation skills.

We have developed a platform upon which human-negotiating agents can be adequately developed. Previous efforts have spurred interest and novel research by allowing agent-agent negotiations competitions to be conducted, including at AAMAS. However, recent interest in *human*-agent negotiation requires a new platform that contains features that are necessary for the new domain. Such a platform must also meet practical research goals of being both readily deployable and easy to extend to the particular needs of the study or simulation. IAGO, our Interactive Arbitration Guide Online platform addresses these points. Specifically, IAGO was designed with the following principles in mind:

Appears in: *Proceedings of the 15th International Conference on Autonomous Agents and Multiagent Systems (AAMAS 2016), J. Thangarajah, K. Tuyls, C. Jonker, S. Marsella (eds.),*
May 9–13, 2016, Singapore.

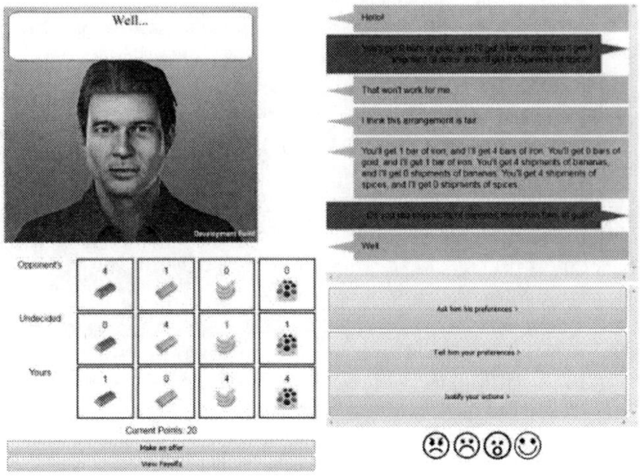

Figure 1: IAGO Screenshot

1. Must support current web-standards and require little to no installation of complex support software on a user's machine.
2. Must deploy a well-defined API that allows both agent designers and negotiation game designers to easily create and specify behaviors for the purposes of competition/research.
3. Must support currently unexamined aspects of human-human negotiation in a human-agent context. Specifically, this must include partial offers, visual representation of emotional signals, and relative preference elicitation/revelation.

2. BACKGROUND

2.1 Human-Human Negotiation Features

The authors have compiled a detailed corpus of human-human negotiation data, including recorded negotiations and annotated transcripts. Several features of human-human negotiation have been examined that are believed to be critical to examine in any negotiation context. Complex forms of signaling intent, such as through emotional reactions to offers or messages, are of critical importance to negotiations [1].

Whereas many negotiation platforms rely on complete offers, many human-human negotiations rarely include complete offers until late in the negotiation. Complete offers represent a full assignment of all items in the multi-issue task to either one party or the other, whereas partial offers omit one or several issues to focus on the remaining issue(s). Furthermore, partial offers are rarely seen as binding until late in a negotiation.

Finally, while preference elicitation remains a core feature of many agent-agent platforms, human-human negotiation contexts (and therefore, human-agent) often showcase relative preferences and utilize natural language to express subtly different meanings. Often, these meanings may be used to hedge and avoid revealing critical information (or often result in outright lies).

Although there are additional features that have been shown to be important to human-agent negotiation, these core features are the focus of IAGO and are, to the authors' knowledge, largely not formalized in human-agent negotiation platforms to date.

2.2 Negotiation Platforms

There have been several different platforms that attempt to facilitate negotiation for various purposes. The GENIUS platform [3] allows a variety of multi-issue bargaining tasks to be completed rapidly between two agents. It has been used in negotiation competitions held at AAMAS and elsewhere for several years[1]. However, as part of its optimization for these types of negotiations, it does not include several key features of human-agent negotiation, such as partial offers, complex preference spaces, non-final offers, favors, and other features. Additionally, the NegoChat agent [6] has attempted to address some of these concerns in a different domain, allowing purely free natural-language information with a chat agent as part of a negotiation.

In IAGO, we create a platform on which future negotiating agents (such as the one implemented by NegoChat) can be built for use in future negotiation competitions. IAGO supports a wide variety of features that have been shown to be critical to realistic human-agent communication. These include partial offers, preference elicitation statements, a customizable set of natural language argumentation phrases (currently based on work by Keenan and Carnevale) [8], and an expressive virtual human agent. The interface also features a full conversational history, the ability to feature non-linear utility structures, and a customizable graphic interface. IAGO exposes a simple API that allows games and agents to be customized with a single template Java class.

3. PLATFORM DESIGN

3.1 Web-Based Interface

IAGO is built to be easily deployed. Human-agent negotiations may be conducted wherever study requirements demand. As IAGO is completely web-based, remote subject platforms such as Amazon's Mechanical Turk may be used as well as traditional methods. No installations are required for IAGO to function; the platform is delivered through HTML5 and OpenGL. JavaScript is used to create web socket communication to the back-end, which is Java-based. Because of these features, IAGO is able to be used on a wide variety of common web browsers with little to no visual distortion. IAGO is also, notably, fully asynchronous. Humans or agents may both choose to take any action at any time and these decisions will be represented in real-time through the interface.

We use under-development aspects of the Virtual Human Toolkit[2] to create the virtual character on screen and simulate the animations, expressions, and backchannels. Users familiar with the VHT can substitute their own models to change the appearance of the virtual human, though IAGO does not require this setup if the standard male agent is acceptable.

3.2 Easy-to-use API

IAGO allows the rapid development of agents by simplifying the communication between agents through a set of pre-specified Events. A core set of Events is listed below:

1. SEND_EXPRESSION – allows for an agent to send or receive an expression from a preset list defined by the game structure. These include prototypical expressions such as Anger, Surprise, Happiness, and Sadness.
2. SEND_MESSAGE – allows for an agent to send or receive a string to be displayed in the chat log. The game can expose the preset list of legal messages that the human can use, simplifying the assumptions if natural language is not the focus of the competition or study.
3. SEND_OFFER – the core of any negotiation, this allows an agent to send or receive an offer (partial or full) that represents some ordering of the issues at hand. An offer will move the items in the offer grid to the desired positions, while a message affects the chat log.
4. TIMING_PROMPT – this allows agents to easily record periods of idleness from their partner, waking after a specified amount of time to take another action (such as reiterating a message, or relenting on a previous offer).

The release version of IAGO will include open-source samples of agents, as well as full documentation of the API.[3]

3.3 Logging Features and History

One critical feature of this system is its ability to provide large amounts of data about the history of the negotiation. This is important both for the users of the system, who will often wish to verify offer or message history, and also for researchers, who require a more detailed description of the logs of a negotiation.

IAGO logs all events along with a timestamp and user identification number, and exports much of its data to files/databases. On the visual side, the full offer history is always available to the user through a scrolling window, as are user preferences and past emotional displays.

3.4 Demonstration Features

The demonstration we have prepared[4] is intended to showcase the core features of IAGO. We have prepared an agent created using the IAGO API that can conduct a simple multi-issue bargaining task featuring four issues at five different levels. The agent utilizes the fixed list of utterances that the human may use, although it has its own set of responses. Our agent attempts to gain the most value for itself in the negotiation by employing several human-negotiation techniques, such as appealing to the principle of fairness by utilizing a fixed-pie lie [1].

The authors anticipate that IAGO will demonstrate the value of a flexible negotiation framework that allows researchers to examine facets of negotiation primarily found within human-agent domains. It will also be a platform upon which human-agent negotiation competitions can be conducted in order to determine which agents are most successful when negotiating with humans—a domain that has not been explored as extensively as the agent-agent competition domain.

4. ACKNOWLEDGMENTS

The authors wish to thank the anonymous reviewers as well as the authors of the GENIUS and NegoChat negotiation platforms for their insight. This work was supported by the National Science Foundation under grant BCS-1419621 and the U.S. Army. Any opinion, content or information presented does not necessarily reflect the position or the policy of the United States Government, and no official endorsement should be inferred.

[1] See information on ANAC, http://web.tuat.ac.jp/~katfuji/ANAC2015/

[2] See https://vhtoolkit.ict.usc.edu/. Some components of VHT are open source.

[3] Please contact the first author for access to development software/documentation.

[4] A short video is available at https://youtu.be/WFs_4YdK5UM

5. REFERENCES

[1] de Melo, C. M., Carnevale, P., & Gratch, J. (2011, May). The effect of expression of anger and happiness in computer agents on negotiations with humans. In The 10th International Conference on Autonomous Agents and Multiagent Systems-Volume 3 (pp. 937-944). International Foundation for Autonomous Agents and Multiagent Systems.

[2] Gratch, J., Nazari, Z., & Johnson, E. (2016). The Misrepresentation Game: How to win at negotiation while seeming like a nice guy. In *Proceedings of the 2016 International Conference on Autonomous Agents and Multiagent Systems*. International Foundation for Autonomous Agents and Multiagent Systems.

[3] Hindriks, K., Jonker, C. M., Kraus, S., Lin, R., & Tykhonov, D. (2009, May). Genius: negotiation environment for heterogeneous agents. In *Proceedings of The 8th International Conference on Autonomous Agents and Multiagent Systems-Volume 2* (pp. 1397-1398). International Foundation for Autonomous Agents and Multiagent Systems.

[4] Keenan, P. A., & Carnevale, P. J. (1989). Positive Effects of Within - Group Cooperation on Between - Group Negotiation1. *Journal of Applied Social Psychology*, *19*(12), 977-992.

[5] Mell, J., Lucas, G., & Gratch, J. (2015, May). An effective conversation tactic for creating value over repeated negotiations. In *Proceedings of the 2015 International Conference on Autonomous Agents and Multiagent Systems*(pp. 1567-1576). International Foundation for Autonomous Agents and Multiagent Systems.

[6] Rosenfeld, A., Zuckerman, I., Segal-Halevi, E., Drein, O., & Kraus, S. (2014, May). NegoChat: a chat-based negotiation agent. In *Proceedings of the 2014 international conference on Autonomous agents and multi-agent systems*(pp. 525-532). International Foundation for Autonomous Agents and Multiagent Systems.

[7] Van Kleef, G. A., De Dreu, C. K., & Manstead, A. S. (2004). The interpersonal effects of emotions in negotiations: a motivated information processing approach. Journal of personality and social psychology, 87(4), 510.

[8] Van Kleef, G. A., De Dreu, C. K., Pietroni, D., & Manstead, A. S. (2006). Power and emotion in negotiation: Power moderates the interpersonal effects of anger and happiness on concession making. *European Journal of Social Psychology*, *36*(4), 557-581.

PRESS: PeRsonalized Event Scheduling recommender System

(Demonstration)

Hoong Chuin Lau, Aldy Gunawan, Pradeep Varakantham, Wenjie Wang
Singapore Management University
80 Stamford Road, Singapore 178902
{hclau, aldygunawan, pradeepv, wjwang}@smu.edu.sg

ABSTRACT

This paper presents a personalized event scheduling recommender system, PRESS, for a large conference setting with multiple parallel tracks. PRESS is a mobile application that gathers personalized information from a user and recommends talks/demos to be attend. The input from a user include a list of keyword preferences and (optionally) preferred talks. We use the MALLET topic model package to analyze the set of conference papers and classify them based on automatically identified topics. We propose an algorithm to generate a list of recommended papers based on the user keywords and the MALLET topics. An optimization model is then applied to obtain a feasible schedule. The recommended set is matched against the selected papers by the user which we obtained from a survey conducted at AAMAS-15 in Istanbul, Turkey. We show that PRESS is able to provide reasonable accuracy, precision and recall rates. PRESS will be deployed live during AAMAS-16 in Singapore.

Keywords: Recommender system; topic model; conference scheduling

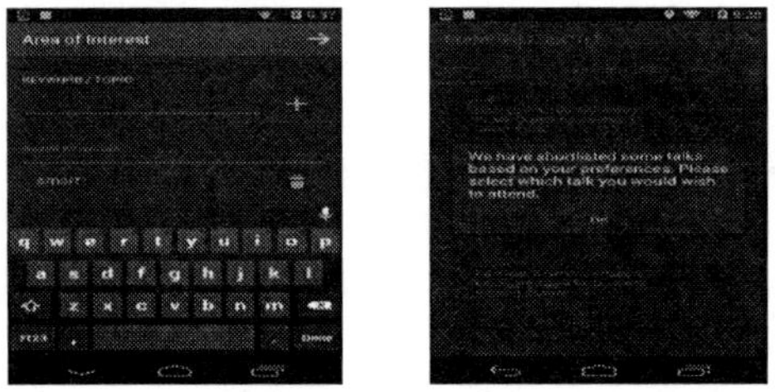

(a) Area of Interest (b) Selected Papers

Figure 1: Screenshots of PRESS

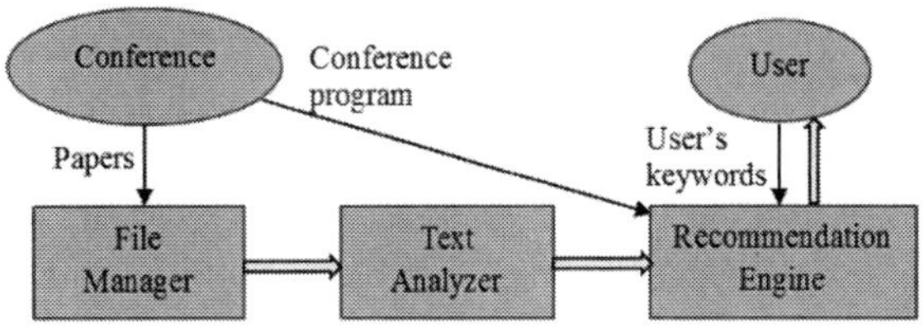

Figure 2: System Architecture

1. INTRODUCTION

In a large conference or tradeshow setting where talks are presented in parallel tracks across multiple days, it is a challenge for a conference attendee to generate a plan of talks/sessions to attend that optimize his/her preferences. And this is particularly cognitively challenging if the conference venue is large, where one may need to consider time to travel between talks. Furthermore, the system will be most helpful if a given talk/session is scheduled in more than one timeslots during the conference, and one has to decide which timeslot is best to attend that talk.

We will present a demo of a personalized recommender system where different people who use the recommender system will expect to get recommendations and plans based on their own preferences [2]. Our personalized recommender system PRESS is realized in an Android mobile application.

PRESS uses the *MA*chine *L*earning for *L*anguag*E* *T*oolkit MALLET [1] that navigates large bodies of information by finding clusters of keywords that frequently appear together, called topics. The underlying idea of topic models is that documents are made up of mixtures of topics, where a topic is a cluster of words that frequently occur together [3]. By using contextual clues, topic models connect words with similar meanings and distinguish between uses of words with multiple meanings. Each document is processed by selecting a distribution over topics, and then generating each keyword at random from a topic by using the selected distribution.

In order to generate personalized recommendations, we first build a topic model using MALLET from the list of papers to be presented at the conference. Then given the profile of a user (which he enters using the app) which consists of his preference keywords and (optionally) a list of selected papers, PRESS generates a list of recommended papers and a feasible (i.e. non-conflicting) schedule for this user that optimizes his utility score. Figure 1 shows the screenshots of PRESS. A demo of this app can be accessed via `http://bit.ly/1R5qV4p`.

Appears in: *Proceedings of the 15th International Conference on Autonomous Agents and Multiagent Systems (AAMAS 2016), J. Thangarajah, K. Tuyls, C. Jonker, S. Marsella (eds.), May 9–13, 2016, Singapore.*

2. ARCHITECTURE AND SYSTEM DESIGN

PRESS consist of three components: file manager, text analyzer and recommendation engine, as shown in Figure 2. The details are given in the following subsections.

A	B	C	D	E	F
0	crowdsourcing	crowdworkers	planner	social games	requester
1	team	dishonest advisors	crowd robotics	attractions	routing
2	complex returns	committee	participation	manipulation	ranks
3	sensor motes	online planning	finite-state controllers	planning	deployment
4	theorem	logic	preference	modal logic	reason
5	customers	opinion	signals	customer	population
6	flock	cybersecurity	fluencing agents	trust	reconnaissance agent
7	advertisers	government	market	dual preference property	bid
8	metrics	antibody	synchronization	virus	maximization
9	learning	reinforcement learning	capability models	state space	policy transfer
10	mechanism design	leader	driver	landfill trash	leader equilibria
11	hedonic games	fractional hedonic games	utility	clustering	pareto efficiency

Figure 3: Screenshot of MALLET output

#doc name topic proportion ...										
0	Paper 1	10	0.821207	15	0.25842	23	0.061721	13	0.03214	0	0.017127
1	Paper 2	10	0.726088	15	0.249853	23	0.082568	18	0.068656	13	0.052124
2	Paper 3	10	0.870099	15	0.226938	3	0.051107	13	0.038831	19	0.010294
3	Paper 4	10	0.797018	15	0.26128	23	0.091565	13	0.047208	17	2.63E-04
4	Paper 5	23	0.737454	10	0.30123	15	0.224803	13	0.033752	17	2.48E-04
5	Paper 6	22	0.839755	15	0.200866	13	0.065629	10	0.053941	17	0.035124
6	Paper 7	24	0.741729	15	0.154617	13	0.075463	23	0.020853	16	0.004314

Figure 4: Screenshot of topic composition

2.1 File Manager

This component is responsible for converting a collection of documents (eg. pdf files) into text files and then tagging the part of speech of words in these text files.

Given a set of papers in the pdf format, the PDFMINER tool extracts the words from each file and output them into a text file. The Illinois Chunker (`https://cogcomp.cs.illinois.edu/page/software_view/Chunker`) is used to identify the semantically related words by assigning different tags. For example, in the noun words "reinforcement learning", the word "reinforcement" is identified as the beginning word of a noun phrase and therefore tagged with B-NP (begins a noun phrase), however, the following word "learning" is identified inside the same noun phrase as "reinforcement" and therefore tagged with I-NP (inside a noun phrase).

2.2 Text Analyzer

The MALLET topic model package [1] is used to extract a set number of topics and the highest frequent words for each topic from the text documents and output the statistics of each extracted topic for each text document. MALLET allows us to filter a standard list of English stop-words from documents before processing. Unfortunately, we cannot edit the contents of this list without modifying code and recompiling. In order to rule out some trivial words, we create an extra-word file containing those trivial words. Figure 3 shows the screenshot of the MALLET output. There are 12 topics generated with 5 keywords for each topic.

The topics that compose each document including the statistics of each topic can be seen in Figure 4. For example, PAPER 1 has topic 10 as its principal topic, at about 82.1%; topic 15 at 25.8 % and so on. The topic model also suggests a connection among documents that might not at first have suspected. Papers 1, 2, 3 and 4 have topic 10 as their principal topic.

2.3 Recommendation Engine

The recommendation engine generates a list of recommended papers based on keywords entered by a user and the MALLET results. It is made up of two key components: the ranking algorithm and the optimization model.

2.3.1 Ranking Algorithm

Based on the MALLET outputs, we calculate the utility score of each paper with respect to the preference keywords provided by a user. We first compare how many keywords are matched with a set of keywords of each topic generated by MALLET. The utility score for each paper is calculated by finding the weighted sum of the number of keywords and utility scores for each topic.

All papers are then sorted in descending order with respect to their utility scores. The recommendation is given from the top x% of papers. This list of papers would be compared with the selected papers by a user. Take note that some papers may clash and we allow user to decide which one(s) would be attended.

2.3.2 Optimization Model

An optimization model is used to generate a feasible schedule. The objective is to maximize the total utility score. By considering the number of days of a conference, time slots and parallel sessions, we ensure that at each time slot, at most one paper presentation is attended. Our model also allow the user to select "must-go" papers and "must-skip" papers. For conferences that span a large geographical space, it is easy to extend our current model in future by considering travel time between talks.

3. RESULTS

In order to verify the goodness of PRESS, a user survey was conducted during the International Conference on Autonomous Agents and Multi-Agent Systems (AAMAS-15) 2015 in Istanbul, Turkey. We managed to collect 45 respondents from the AAMAS-15 participants. Each respondent was asked to specify his/her preference keywords together with the list of talks he/she would be interested to attend. This collection of surveys serve as the ground truth. Due to a short time taken for each survey, we assume that a user will not be able to exhaustively select all preferred papers. Hence, based on a set of selected papers, we include an additional set of selected papers which have high correlation values with those papers (e.g. 0.75). All those papers are considered as the papers selected by a user.

By comparing equal number of user-selected papers and recommended papers generated by PRESS, our experimental results show that the accuracy, precision and recall values of PRESS are 92.2%, 58.6% and 58.6%, respectively, with the cutoff value of top 20% for the recommendation. Interested readers are welcome to visit our demo booth at AAMAS-16, and have their mobile devices deployed with the app.

Acknowledgements

This research is supported by Singapore National Research Foundation under its International Research Centre @ Singapore Funding Initiative as well as its Corp Lab@University scheme. The authors wish to thank people who have contributed to this project: Shih-Fen Cheng, Oi Mei Wong, Chun Pong Fan, Elizabeth Lim, Eng Chye Low, Firmansyah Abd Rahman, Xiang Li, Htar Htar Hlaing & Khin Aye Mon.

REFERENCES

[1] A. K. McCallum. MALLET: A machine learning for language toolkit. http://mallet.cs.umass.edu, 2002.

[2] P. Resnick and H. R. Varian. Recommender systems. *Communications of the ACM*, 40(3), Mar. 1997.

[3] M. Steyvers and T. Griffiths. Probabilistic Topic Models. In *Latent Semantic Analysis: A Road to Meaning*. Hillsdale, NJ: Erlbaum, 2007.

This Page Intentionally Left Blank.

Human-Multi-Robot Team Collaboration using Advising Agents

(Doctoral Consortium)

Ariel Rosenfeld
Bar-Ilan University
Ramat-Gan, Israel
arielros1@gmail.com

ABSTRACT

The number of multi-robot systems deployed in field applications has risen dramatically over the years. Nevertheless, the part of the human operator in these systems has been mostly overlooked. In this work we propose a novel approach for utilizing automated advising agents when assisting an operator to better manage a team of multiple robots in complex environments. We introduce an advice provision methodology and exemplify its implementation using automated advising agents in two real-world human-multi-robot team collaboration tasks: the Search And Rescue (SAR) task and the warehouse operation task. Our intelligent advising agents were evaluated through extensive field trials, with over 100 human operators and both simulated and physical mobile robots, and showed a significant improvement in the team's performance.

Keywords

Human-Robot Interaction; Human-Agent Interaction; Advice Provision

1. INTRODUCTION

In recent years multi-robot systems have been applied to complex tasks which used to be performed by humans alone. Two prominent examples are the Search And Rescue (SAR) [3] and the warehouse operation [2] tasks. In such multi-robot systems the part of the human operator is often assumed to be marginal. Two assumptions are made in this case: the first is that the robots perform relatively smoothly, with the infrequent need for human intervention. Second is that the human operator is only required to perform a single task at any given moment. Reality, however, can be more complicated on both accounts.

The deployment of robots in real-world environments has shown that robots usually face difficulties in completing their tasks. Specifically, failures are common. In such situations, a human operator must get involved in order to solve the problem. Furthermore, human operators may be occupied by numerous tasks at a time. For example, in a warehouse operation setting, the human worker may be employed in packing merchandise, refiling inventory and handling robot malfunctions, all at the same time. The prioritization of the operator's tasks has mostly been overlooked in system design, leaving the prioritization in each operator's hands. Sub-optimal prioritization of the operator's tasks may result in sub-optimal performance by the robot-team and in a high cognitive workload for the operator [8].

Improving the performance of human-multi-robot systems can be done using one of the following approaches: Either (1) Improving the robot's hardware and software, thus relying less on human supervision (making the robots more autonomous): or (2) Improving the efficiency of the Human-Robot Interaction (HRI). Assuming we are given a team of robots and we cannot control the reliability of their hardware or software, our work deals with improving the HRI in order to allow a person to control a team of many (possibly unreliable) robots at once while executing different domain-specific tasks.

In this thesis, we present a novel methodology that enhances operators' performance by using intelligent advising agents. The agents provide advice to the operator regarding which actions she should take and acts as a smart filter between the robots' requests and the human operator. Our methodology is not restricted to any certain hardware or algorithm used by the robots, and we consider these factors constants. Note that intelligent advising agents have been successfully implemented in different domains, for example [6, 1, 5]. However, to the best of our knowledge, this is the first work on utilizing advising agent technology in the HRI field.

We present an optimization heuristic which models the maximization of the human-multi-robot team's performance by selecting when and which advice to provide the operator in a greedy fashion, using a k-steps-lookahead search. We have extensively tested the suggested heuristic in designing advising agents deployed in both simulated environments (using the Gazebo robot simulation toolbox[1]) and physical deployment with more than 100 human operators. Experimental results show that our advising agents were able to significantly enhance the operators' performance when managing a large team of mobile robots in both the SAR and warehouse operation tasks.

The main contribution of this work is in showing, for the first time, that an intelligent agent which supports the human operator can lead to better performance of the human-multi-robot team.

Appears in: *Proceedings of the 15th International Conference on Autonomous Agents and Multiagent Systems (AAMAS 2016), J. Thangarajah, K. Tuyls, C. Jonker, S. Marsella (eds.), May 9–13, 2016, Singapore.*

[1] `http://www.gazebosim.org/`

2. THE SAR TASK

In our SAR task, the operator remotely supervises and controls 10 unmanned mobile ground robots using a computer program. The operator is required to find and correctly classify green objects in a clustered terrain[2]. Our SAR task is conducted in two distinct environments: a real-world office building floor that was investigated in both simulation and physical deployment, and a medium-sized warehouse yard that was investigated in a simulation.

In our SAR task, robots can malfunction. We account for three malfunction types that our physical robots can experience: **Sensing** – where the robot's camera/laser stops working. In such problems, the operator can send the robot back to home base, where the experiment operator can fix it. **Stuck** – where the robot cannot move (for example, due to an obstacle), and needs the operator to help it get loose. In some cases the Stuck malfunction is terminal. **WiFi** – where the robot stops sending and receiving data. In such cases the operator can mark the area as a "no entrance" zone. Upon losing the WiFi signal, the robot is programmed to return to its last point of communication. Furthermore, the operator could perform the following operations: she could **tele-operate** a robot from one place to another, she could order a robot to autonomously **navigate** to a desired point of interest and, once an object is detected by a robot, she could **classify** the object as a ball or a box.

Due to the exponential size of the robots' state space and the relative independence of the operator's possible operations (each operation can be performed regardless of others), we only examined the 1-step-lookahead heuristic.

We have extensively tested the performance of our advising agent, which deployed the 1-step-lookahead heuristic, in a within-subjects experimental design, in both simulation and physical deployment with 44 human subjects.

In our physical deployment, a major **100%** increase in the average number of detected objects was recorded (14.1 vs. 7 objects, $p < 0.001$) when subjects were equipped with our advising agent. An increased average of covered terrain (462 vs. 305 square meters, $p < 0.05$) and a significant decrease in the average time that robots stay idle (2720 vs. 3244 seconds, $p < 0.05$) were also recorded.

Our full results are reported in [4] and a short video[3] summarizing this work is available at `http://vimeo.com/119434903`.

3. WAREHOUSE OPERATION TASK

We focus on a small warehouse acting as a fulfilment center (also known as a packing center) where there is one human worker and 10 mobile ground robots capable of transporting shelves from one place to another over the warehouse floor. At the packing stations, it is the human worker's job to unload products from the arrived shelves. The task is conducted in a simulated warehouse which we built using the Gazebo robot simulation toolbox.

We account for two malfunction types that our simulated robots can experience: **Stuck** – where the robot cannot move (for example, due to a fallen product), and needs the operator to help it get loose. In some cases the Stuck malfunction is terminal. **Path** – where the robot cannot find a feasible path to reach its goal. In such cases, the operator can remove fallen products and tele-operate the different robots to clear the blocked path. Furthermore, the operator could perform the following operations: she could **tele-operate** a robot from one place to another, she could **unload** an item from an arrived shelf, she could direct a robot to **move** a shelf from one place to another and, once all requested items in a customer's order have been unloaded, she could **pack** the order and send it.

Note that the warehouse operator's possible operations are strongly connected and dependent; for example, a worker cannot pack a customer's order before attaining all the requested merchandise. This property necessitates the identification of these connections and their consideration in the advice provision process.

We designed and evaluated 2 advising agents, deploying the 1-step-lookahead and 2-steps-lookahead heuristics. Through an extensive empirical study with 60 human operators, we show that subjects equipped with an advising agent filled significantly more orders compared to subjects using a non-advising agent (Silent) by up to 13% (on average), $p < 0.05$. We further show that our agent that uses the 2-steps-lookahead heuristic, significantly outperforms the agent that uses the 1-step-lookahead heuristic, $p < 0.05$. Surprisingly, subjects equipped with the 1-step-lookahead heuristic agent accepted significantly more pieces of advice compared to subjects equipped with the 2-steps-lookahead heuristic agent. This phenomenon will be investigated in future work.

Our full results are reported in [7] and a short video summarizing this work is available at `http://www.youtube.com/watch?v=rC1a4c6Voco`.

[2]The objects can indicate victims, flames, weapons, etc.
[3]Best Robotics Video - IJCAI 2015.

REFERENCES

[1] A. Azaria, A. Rosenfeld, S. Kraus, C. V. Goldman, and O. Tsimhoni. Advice provision for energy saving in automobile climate-control system. *AI Magazine*, 36(3):61–72, 2015.

[2] E. Guizzo. Three engineers, hundreds of robots, one warehouse. *Spectrum*, 45(7):26–34, 2008.

[3] Y. Liu and G. Nejat. Robotic urban search and rescue: A survey from the control perspective. *Journal of Intelligent & Robotic Systems*, 72(2):147–165, 2013.

[4] A. Rosenfeld, N. Agmon, A. A. Maksimov, Oleg, and S. Kraus. Intelligent agent supporting human-multi-robot team collaboration. In *IJCAI*, 2015.

[5] A. Rosenfeld, A. Azaria, S. Kraus, C. V. Goldman, and O. Tsimhoni. Adaptive advice in automobile climate control systems. In *AAMAS*, pages 543–551, 2015.

[6] A. Rosenfeld and S. Kraus. Providing arguments in discussions based on the prediction of human argumentative behavior. In *AAAI*, pages 1320–1327, 2015.

[7] A. Rosenfeld, A. Noa, O. Maksimov, and S. Kraus. Human-multi-robot team collaboration for efficent warehouse operation. In *Autonomous Robots and Multirobot Systems (ARMS)*, 2016.

[8] P. Squire and R. Parasuraman. Effects of automation and task load on task switching during human supervision of multiple semi-autonomous robots in a dynamic environment. *Ergonomics*, 53(8):951–961, 2010.

An Auction-based Approach for Decentralized Multi-Project Scheduling

(Doctoral Consortium)

Wen Song
Supervisor: Prof. Jie Zhang
Rolls-Royce@NTU Corp Lab, Nanyang Technological University, Singapore
songwen@ntu.edu.sg

ABSTRACT

Many scheduling problems in industry practice are considered as Decentralized Resource-Constrained Multi-Project Scheduling Problem (DRCMPSP). Given its characteristics, the problem must be solved in a decentralized manner while respecting information privacy of projects. However, existing approaches fail in satisfying these requirements, and encounter difficulties in dealing with large cases. To this end, we propose a novel approach based on multi-unit combinatorial auction with greedy resource allocation strategy. A bid modification step is also incorporated to provide chances for project agents to improve utilities. This approach does not require private project information, and scales well to large cases. Experiments show that our approach can obtain better solutions compared to state-of-the-art approaches.

Keywords

Multi-Project Scheduling, Multi-Unit Combinatorial Auction, Resource Allocation

1. INTRODUCTION

To schedule multiple projects under limited resource is a common management activity in most business firms. Each of these projects consists of a set of activities with precedence constraints and resource requirements. Traditionally, all projects are controlled by one decision maker and can be scheduled using certain centralized methods. Nowadays, due to active intra- and inter-firm collaborations, multi-project management has entered a new environment where the projects are controlled by different self-interested decision makers with different individual objectives. Usually, to finish their projects, they need to compete for some shared global resources with limited capacities. On the other hand, some information of the projects may be considered as secret since these decision makers could be potential rivals in the same marketplace. Under this background, the *Decentralized Resource-Constrained Multi-Project Scheduling Problem* (DRCMPSP) is formally proposed in [2] to incorporate these new features to the traditional multi-project scheduling problem. DRCMPSP cases widely exist in industry (e.g. airport ground handling service scheduling, aero repair & overhaul scheduling, and supply chain scheduling).

It is well known that the traditional centralized resource-constrained multi-project scheduling is an NP-hard problem. DRCMPSP, as its decentralized version, exhibits new challenges in that it must be solved in a decentralized manner while respecting the privacy requirements of the decision makers. However, current research fails in providing an approach that can produce high quality solution, maintain information privacy, and scale to large problem cases with tens of projects, thousands of activities in total, and several multi-unit shared resources.

In this work, we develop a decentralized approach based on iterative multi-unit combinatorial auction. To simplify the computational burden of agents, we adopt a greedy resource allocation strategy that grants winning bids in each round of auction. We also incorporate a bid modification step to create chances for decision makers to improve utilities. Our approach does not require private project information, and complexity analysis shows that it can scale to large DRCMPSP cases. Experiment results show that our approach is computationally efficient, and produces better results compared to state-of-the-art decentralized approaches.

2. RELATED WORK

The core problem in DRCMPSP is how to allocate the shared global resources to each decision maker in a decentralized manner. Market-based approach, especially combinatorial auction, is an ideal paradigm for solving decentralized resource allocation problem. In [2], a combinatorial auction based approach is proposed to solve simple DRCMPSP cases with several projects, tens of activities in total and one single-unit global resource. However, as our analysis in [4], this approach suffers from scalability issue. When applied to large case, the computational time becomes very long and the solution quality is relatively low.

Recently, several decentralized approaches have been proposed to solve larger cases which involve tens of projects, thousands of activities in total, and several multi-unit global resources, e.g. [1] [5]. However, most of these approaches are based on activity-level adjustment techniques, which inevitably require activity information from each project. In addition, activity-level adjustments are based on estimated individual objectives, which could lower the solution quality.

3. THE PROPOSED APPROACH

In a DRCMPSP case, a set of N projects sharing some global renewable resources need to be scheduled to minimize

Appears in: *Proceedings of the 15th International Conference on Autonomous Agents and Multiagent Systems (AAMAS 2016), J. Thangarajah, K. Tuyls, C. Jonker, S. Marsella (eds.), May 9–13, 2016, Singapore.*

the *Average Project Delay* (APD), defined as:

$$APD = \frac{\sum_{i=1}^{N} \max\{0, (ct_i - dd_i)\}}{N},$$

where ct_i and dd_i are the finish time and due date of project i, respectively. We model DRCMPSP as a mediated multi-agent system, where each project is represented by a Project Agent (PA) and all PAs are coordinated by a Mediator Agent (MA). To make decisions on global resource allocation, the MA conducts a multi-unit combinatorial auction where the PAs play as bidders and the items for sale are the global resources at each scheduling time slot. A bidder i is associated with a valuation function $v_i(\Lambda)$ for each multiset Λ of items, defined according to the schedule with the lowest delay cost assuming it can obtain the amounts of global resources in Λ. Denote an item allocation as $\Lambda = (\Lambda_1, ..., \Lambda_N)$, the auction objective is to find the allocation Λ^* that maximizes social welfare $SW(\Lambda) = \sum_{i=1}^{N} v_i(\Lambda_i)$. Λ^* can be found by solving a *Winner Determination Problem* (WDP).

It is well known that (multi-unit) combinatorial auction is intractable, since the WDP is NP-complete and communication requirement grows exponentially with the total item capacity. However, when apply combinatorial auction to DRCMPSP, additional complexity is introduced. As we show in [4], to compute the value $v_i(\Lambda)$ of a given multiset Λ is intractable, since it is equivalent to solve an NP-hard single Resource-Constrained Project Scheduling Problem (RCPSP). Given these complexities, it is almost impossible to design an optimal algorithm that can scale to large cases. Hence, in this research we aim at designing an inexact polynomial-time approach instead of a complete algorithm.

To simplify agents' computation, our approach employs an iterative auction process with a greedy resource allocation strategy. In addition, a bid modification step is incorporated to compensate the greedy nature of the approach. To be specific, each round of auction contains two consecutive phases. In the first phase, each participating bidder i is asked to submit a bid $B_i =< \Lambda_i, v_i(\Lambda_i) >$, which includes the multiset Λ_i that can (approximately) maximize its valuation under the current item capacities, along with the value $v_i(\Lambda_i)$. The problem of finding B_i is called the *bidding problem*. Then, the MA solves an initial WDP to determine the initial winners, who are intuitively the most "promising" ones given the current resource capacities. The second phase includes a series of final auctions among the initial winners, who are asked to conduct a bid modification step by submitting a bid $B'_i =< \Lambda'_i, v_i(\Lambda'_i) >$, where Λ'_i is different from Λ but with the same value (i.e. $v_i(\Lambda_i) = v_i(\Lambda'_i)$). The problem of finding Λ'_i is called the *bid modification problem*. The MA solves a final WDP in each round of these auctions, immediately allocates global resources to the final winners, and updates the global resource capacities. The final winners will not participate in any auction in the following rounds.

Here we briefly describe how the aforementioned three types of local problems are formulated and solved. As we show in [4], the bidding problem can be transformed to an RCPSP with time-varying resource constraints, where global resource capacities are equal to the current item capacities. Since RCPSP is NP-hard, we design a polynomial-time algorithm based on the priority rule-based schedule generation approach. In terms of the bid modification problem, we first define a demand ratio vector as the ratio of total demand of initial bids to the corresponding resource capacities. This vector will be calculated and published by the MA before the second phase. We then define the resource index as the dot product of a multiset and demand ratio, and formulate the bid modification problem as an RCPSP with the objective of minimizing resource index. To make sure the bidder's utility will not decrease, an additional hard due date constraint is added. This is also an NP-hard problem, hence we design a polynomial-time algorithm based on flexible activity shifting. Finally, we apply a polynomial-time greedy algorithm in [3] to solve all (initial and final) WDPs.

Our complexity analysis in [4] shows that in the worst case, the total number of bids submitted by the bidders is $O(N^2)$, and the total number of WDPs is $O(N)$. Since all local problems are solved in polynomial time, our approach is in general polynomial-time. We also conduct experiments on public benchmark, and compared our approach with existing ones in [2, 1, 5]. Results show that overall our approach improves the best results by nearly 25%, and the computation is very efficient on large cases which contains tens of projects, thousands of activities in total, and several multi-unit global resources.

4. FUTURE RESEARCH

Our research is based on the DRCMPSP model, which is general and can describe a large class of decentralized scheduling problems. However, in reality the problems could be more complex with more constraints (e.g. hierarchical activity structure and additional resource constraints). Hence an immediate direction is to extend our approach to these more complex real-world cases.

In this research we focus on solving a decentralized resource allocation problem. However, one limitation is that bidders are assumed to be truthful, which may not hold in a decentralized environment that involves multiple self-interested agents. In the future, we aim to address the incentive compatibility issue by seeking theoretical support from mechanism design. An important question to ask is that can we develop a payment scheme, along with the proposed allocation approach, to achieve truthful bidding.

REFERENCES

[1] S. Adhau, M. Mittal, and A. Mittal. A multi-agent system for distributed multi-project scheduling: An auction-based negotiation approach. *Engineering Applications of Artificial Intelligence*, 25(8):1738–1751, 2012.

[2] G. Confessore, S. Giordani, and S. Rismondo. A market-based multi-agent system model for decentralized multi-project scheduling. *Annals of Operations Research*, 150(1):115–135, 2007.

[3] R. Gonen and D. Lehmann. Optimal solutions for multi-unit combinatorial auctions: Branch and bound heuristics. In *Proceedings of the 2nd ACM conference on Electronic Commerce (EC'00)*, pages 13–20, 2000.

[4] W. Song, D. Kang, J. Zhang, and H. Xi. Decentralized multi-project scheduling via multi-unit combinatorial auction. In *Proceedings of the 15th International Conference on Autonomous Agents and Multiagent Systems (AAMAS 2016)*, 2016.

[5] Z. Zheng, Z. Guo, Y. Zhu, and X. Zhang. A critical chains based distributed multi-project scheduling approach. *Neurocomputing*, 143:282–293, 2014.

A Systematic Approach for Detecting Defects in Agent Designs

(Doctoral Consortium)

Yoosef Abushark*
Supervisors: John Thangarajah, James Harland and Tim Miller†
RMIT University
Melbourne, Australia
yoosef.abushark@rmit.edu.au

ABSTRACT

Multi-agent systems are increasingly being used in complex applications due to features such as autonomy, proactivity, flexibility, robustness and social ability. Thus, techniques to detect and avoid defects in such systems are valuable. In particular, it is desirable to detect issues as early as possible in the development lifecycle. This research aims to find ways in which to ensure the correctness of agent design artefacts against different point-of-reference: requirements and interaction protocols. The proposed approach will be applicable at design time not requiring source code or a formal design model.

Keywords

AOSE Methodology, Goal-Oriented Requirements, Interaction Protocol

1. BROADER RESEARCH CONTEXT

Autonomous agents are widely-used for developing systems that are highly dynamic in nature in a broad range of domains [6]. Most existing work on verifying BDI agent systems has focused on formal verification (e.g. [2]), particularly using model checking techniques (e.g. [3]) and theorem proving (e.g. [10]), or on runtime testing (e.g. [8]). Such work tends to focus on the verification of complete agent programs, requiring source code or a formal design model. However, it is long established that early detection and resolution of software defects saves time and money [[1], Page 1466]. Our aim therefore is to develop a suite of lightweight techniques, supported by tools, for detecting defects at the design phase, prior to implementation. One of the barriers to the widespread adoption of the agent technology in the industry is its reliability [4]. In order to increase the trust of such systems, many testing and debugging techniques have been proposed. Some of these techniques (e.g. model-based testing) rely on the design artefacts. As a result, it is vital to check these artefacts and ensure their correctness.

The questions that need to be addressed by this research are as follows:

*Acknowledges King Abdulaziz University for Scholarship.
†University of Melbourne, Melbourne, Australia.

Appears in: *Proceedings of the 15th International Conference on Autonomous Agents and Multiagent Systems (AAMAS 2016), J. Thangarajah, K. Tuyls, C. Jonker, S. Marsella (eds.), May 9–13, 2016, Singapore.*

1. What is the **scope** of the static verification in the context of the **BDI**-model of agency?
   The answer to this question states all possible checkable artefacts in the context of BDI agent-based systems. Also, it identifies the point-of-reference and the design units to be considered in the proposed approach. This question is part of the necessary background knowledge, I consider it as a first step towards the final aim of this research.

2. What is a suitable **executable model** for agent-based design artefacts?
   This question investigates different formalisms with the aim to be used as an executable representation for the point-of-reference artefacts. Since the point-of-reference encompasses two artefacts: requirements and interaction protocols, this question has two sub-questions as follows:

   (a) What is a suitable executable model to represent **requirements**?

   (b) What is a suitable executable model to represent **interaction protocol**?

3. What is a suitable **executable model** to represent **agents' detailed models**?
   It is more likely to have the design of given point-of-reference (requirements specifications or interaction protocol) scattered across multiple agents. In this question, I investigate how to merge all the relevant entities of a given point-of-reference into one coherent structure.

4. How can an **automated checking framework** be developed to **effectively detect design defects**?
   This question is addressed through addressing the following two questions:

   (a) How to extract all possible behavioural runs out of the agent detailed deigns?

   (b) How to check the behavioural runs against the point-of-reference models?

Evaluation of the proposed approach

The evaluation aims to ensure that the effectiveness of the framework proposed through answering the following questions:

(a) Can the framework detect design defects?

(b) What is the level of false positives that are generated by the proposed approach?

(c) How scalable is the proposed checking framework?

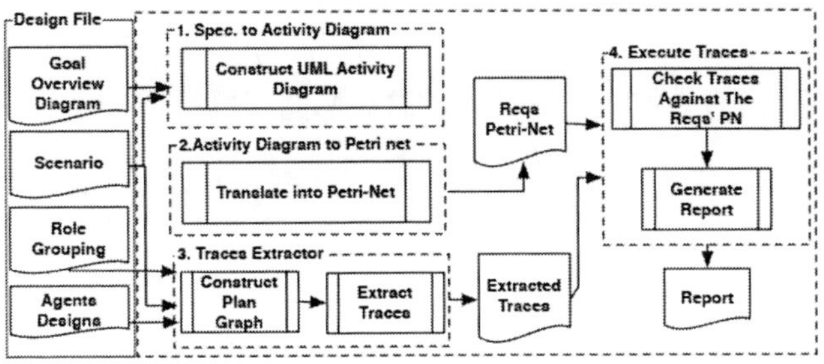

Figure 1: Proposed Framework.

2. METHOD

This research is intended to find a systematic way (Figure 1), supported by algorithms, to ensure the correctness of the detailed design artefacts (events and their associated plans) with respect to the specified point-of-reference (i.e. **requirements** or **interaction protocols**).

In order to verify the design with respect to a given point-of-reference, the point-of-reference should be expressed in a formal notation. Thus, the work of Poutakidis et al. [9] is adopted, as it proposes a way to translate AUML sequence diagrams into more formal representation, *place/transition* Petri-Nets (PN). Then, a plan graph, as proposed in [5], is constructed from the detailed design artefacts of the involved agent in the point-of-reference to act as a coherent structure that merges the designs. The correctness check is performed through running the extracted behavioural runs out of the plan graph over the point-of-reference's PN and logging the existence of any violations.

A plan graph may capture many execution flow fragments including: sequential, selection, loop and parallel. Due to the non-deterministic nature of MAS, plan graphs must be traversed in a way that guarantees that the behavioural runs generated cover all possible combinations. The existing graph traversal algorithms do not fulfil such a purpose. The intention is to transform the plan graph into *place/transition* PN, since it can be used to study and describe systems that have the non-deterministic nature [7]. Then, a reachability graph (RG) for that PN is calculated, since reachability is one of the PN's proprieties that is used for studying its dynamic behaviour [7]. Since that RG captures all possible ways of executing the PN, behavioural runs that cover all possible combinations can be extracted through traversing the RG. The two Petri nets are then compared for similarity through running the behavioural runs extracted from the RG over the point-of-reference's PN. To maintain the computation complexity of the approach, especially in situations when the RG includes too many behavioural runs, the approach considers one run at a time.

3. PROTOTYPE IMPLEMENTATION

I implemented the proposed approach as an eclipse plug-in that integrates with the Prometheus Design Tool (PDT). The tool takes the design file in an XML format, and tokenises the point-of-reference out of the design file. Then it translates them into PNs. Regarding the agent detailed design notations, the tool extracts the entities that are related to the specified point-of-reference. Then, it applies a set of merging rules on the specified point-of-reference to generate the abstract description of the intended plan graph. Then, it uses the abstract description to generate a DOT Graph source script for the plan graph. The tool then extracts all possible behavioural runs and executes them against the specified point-of-reference's PN, and reports any inconsistency.

4. EVALUATION

To the best of my knowledge, there are no existing benchmarks that can be used in evaluating the proposed approach. Thus, the plan was to conduct an empirical evaluation through applying the proposed approach on the artefacts of complete agent-systems (21 cases). Some of these systems were developed as final projects in the Agent-Oriented Programming and Design course, offered at RMIT University, whereas others were developed within the agent group at the university. Also, there are two case studies were included in the evaluation: oil production simulation and an air traffic management system. Regarding the scalability of the approach, a scalability analysis has been conducted on 24 synthesised plan graphs to measure how scalable the approach is. The generation of these plan graphs was systematic with varying the size and the amount of parallelism up until the time taken to extract the traces are still "reasonable". I define "reasonable" to be within 24 hours.

Both analysis methodologies were used: quantitative, by measuring the number of errors detected through applying the proposed framework and qualitative in terms of judging the criticality of the errors and their categories: false and true positives.

The results of the empirical evaluation conducted showed that the proposed approach is able to detect defects in agent designs, with a low number of false positives and generally in a reasonable amount of time. The scalability analysis performed showed that the proposed approach can verify large plan graphs in under 24 hours, despite the exponential explosion in traces as designs get larger.

REFERENCES

[1] B. W. Boehm. Understanding and controlling software costs. *Journal of Parametrics*, 8(1):32–68, 1988.

[2] M. Dastani, K. V. Hindriks, and J.-J. Meyer. *Specification and verification of multi-agent systems*. Springer Science & Business Media, 2010.

[3] L. A. Dennis, M. Fisher, M. P. Webster, and R. H. Bordini. Model checking agent programming languages. *Automated software engineering*, 19(1):5–63, 2012.

[4] N. R. Jennings, K. Sycara, and M. Wooldridge. A roadmap of agent research and development. *Autonomous agents and multi-agent systems*, 1(1):7–38, 1998.

[5] T. Miller, L. Padgham, and J. Thangarajah. Test coverage criteria for agent interaction testing. In *AOSE*, pages 91–105. Springer, 2010.

[6] S. Munroe, T. Miller, R. A. Belecheanu, M. Pechoucek, P. McBurney, and M. Luck. Crossing the agent technology chasm: Lessons, experiences and challenges in commercial applications of agents. *The Knowledge Engineering Review*, 21(04):345–392, 2006.

[7] T. Murata. Petri nets: Properties, analysis and applications. *Proceedings of the IEEE*, 77(4):541–580, 1989.

[8] L. Padgham, Z. Zhang, J. Thangarajah, and T. Miller. Model-based test oracle generation for automated unit testing of agent systems. *Software Engineering, IEEE Transactions on*, 39(9):1230–1244, 2013.

[9] D. Poutakidis, L. Padgham, and M. Winikoff. Debugging multi-agent systems using design artifacts: The case of interaction protocols. In *Proceedings of the first international joint conference on Autonomous agents and multiagent systems: part 2*, pages 960–967. ACM, 2002.

[10] J. Sudeikat, L. Braubach, A. Pokahr, W. Lamersdorf, and W. Renz. Validation of bdi agents. In *Programming Multi-Agent Systems*, pages 185–200. Springer, 2006.

A Novel Approach to Evaluate Robustness of Incentive Mechanism Against Bounded Rationality

(Doctoral Consortium)

Zehong Hu
Rolls-Royce@NTU Corporate Lab, School of Computer Engineering
Nanyang Technological University
Singapore
HUZE0004@e.ntu.edu.sg

ABSTRACT

In this abstract, we first propose a general robustness definition as the upper-bound of the stable region of an equilibrium strategy by generalizing existing bounded rationality models. Then, we develop a robustness evaluation framework, of which a key component is the stability test given a certain level of bounded rationality.

Keywords

Mechanism Design; Bounded Rationality; Robustness

1. INTRODUCTION

Incentive mechanisms are designed to produce desired outcomes through incentivizing agents to perform expected strategies. Incentive is created by inducing a Bayesian game and having the desired outputs as its Nash equilibrium. However, in real-life situations, agents often cannot behave fully rationally, causing mechanisms to fail. To ensure the practical usability of incentive mechanisms, it is crucial to evaluate their robustness. Quite a few qualitative studies have been conducted to judge whether a mechanism is robust. For example, Cabrales [1] and Tumennasan [5] considered robustness from testing the existence of convergent trajectories in all *ex-post* games under the better response learning process and the limited logit quantal response process, respectively.

However, one common limitation of these studies is that they cannot quantitatively evaluate robustness as to what extent an incentive mechanism can be kept under the effects of bounded rationality [3]. Furthermore, most of these studies do not consider precise bounded rationality models, and thus, are not applicable to real-world scenarios where a certain kind of bounded rationality dominates [2]. Besides, the evolutionary processes involved in these studies can only handle the *ex-post* Nash equilibrium with fixed agent's types, while mechanism design is based on Bayesian Nash equilibrium with all agents' types unknown, i.e. the *ex-ante* equilibrium. Thus, we aim to providing a general framework to quantitatively evaluate the robustness of incentive mechanisms against different kinds of bounded rationality.

Appears in: *Proceedings of the 15th International Conference on Autonomous Agents and Multiagent Systems (AAMAS 2016), J. Thangarajah, K. Tuyls, C. Jonker, S. Marsella (eds.), May 9–13, 2016, Singapore.*

2. ROBUSTNESS DEFINITION

To quantitatively evaluate robustness, we need to define robustness at first. However, the literature closely linked to this topic is limited. Thus, we extend the targeted domain of our definition to common Nash equilibrium in arbitrary kinds of games, and enforce it to be consistent with existing ones for correctness. Bounded rationality causes agents to take sub-optimal strategies of the optimal strategy. To depict the strategy variations, the uncertainty set $\mathcal{US}$ is employed to generalize existing bounded rationality models as

$$\mathcal{US}(s_i^*, s_{-i}, \alpha, G) = \{s_i^1, \ldots, s_i^{I_i}\}$$

where G denotes the targeted game and s_{-i} represents the strategy of other agents. s_i^j stands for agent's one strategy which is a probability distribution over all possible actions. I_i represents the total number of possible strategies. Besides, α is a parameter to describe agents' bounded rationality level. To keep consistent among all models, we require $\alpha \in [0,1]$, where $\alpha = 0$ and $\alpha = 1$ denote the cases where agents are fully rational and irrational, respectively. Then, for a game with N players, the uncertainty set involves more than one agent and can be formulated as:

$$\begin{aligned}\mathcal{US}_G(\boldsymbol{s}^*, \alpha_G, G) = \{&\boldsymbol{s} = (s_1, \ldots, s_N)| \\ &s_i \in \mathcal{US}_i(Pr(s_i^*, s_{-i}^*, \alpha_i, G), \boldsymbol{\alpha} \in \Pi(\alpha_G)\}\end{aligned} \tag{1}$$

where $\boldsymbol{\alpha} = (\alpha_1, \ldots, \alpha_N)$ represents the bounded rationality level profile. The parameter $\alpha_G \in [0,1]$, termed as system bounded rationality level, is used to measure agents' bounded rationality from system perspective, and it is required that $\mathcal{US}_G(\boldsymbol{s}^*, 0, G) = \{\boldsymbol{s}^*\}$. $\Pi(\alpha_G)$ denotes all possible bounded rationality level profiles.

The most classical way to define robustness is to measure to what extent parameter variation can make systems unstable. Following this idea, we give a general definition of robustness for Nash equilibrium:

Definition 1. Given a game G with a desired equilibrium $\boldsymbol{s}^E$ and the uncertainty set $\mathcal{US}_G(\boldsymbol{s}^*, \alpha_G, G)$ denoting agents' bounded rationality, the robustness of $\boldsymbol{s}^E$ is R such that

$$R = \frac{Dist\left(\mathcal{US}_G(\boldsymbol{s}^E, 0, G), \mathcal{US}_G(\boldsymbol{s}^E, \alpha_G^M, G)\right)}{Dist\left(\mathcal{US}_G(\boldsymbol{s}^E, 0, G), \mathcal{US}_G(\boldsymbol{s}^E, 1, G)\right)} \tag{2}$$

where α_G^M is determined by the stability function $\mathcal{S}$ as

$$\begin{aligned}\alpha_G^M = \max\{&\alpha_G \in [0,1] | \forall \alpha \in [0, \alpha_G], \\ &\mathcal{S}\left(\alpha, G, \boldsymbol{s}^E, \mathcal{US}_G\right) \leq 0\}\end{aligned} \tag{3}$$

and the distance function $Dist(\cdot)$ is defined as

$$Dist\Big(\mathcal{US}_G(\boldsymbol{s}^E,p,G),\mathcal{US}_G(\boldsymbol{s}^E,q,G)\Big) = \max_{s^p\in\mathcal{US}_G(p)}\max_{s^q\in\mathcal{US}_G(q)}\max_{i\in N}\frac{\|s_i^p - s_i^q\|_1}{2} \quad (4)$$

wherein $\|\cdot\|_1$ denotes the 1-norm function.
In other words, the robustness of a desired Nash equilibrium corresponds to the maximum system bounded rationality level, at which the employed stability function $\mathcal{S}$ can keep non-positive and the game remains stable. This definition provides general guidelines to instantiate more concrete robustness formulations for specific applications.

3. ROBUSTNESS COMPUTATION

An incentive mechanism $\mathcal{M}$ is defined by $\{\boldsymbol{x}(\boldsymbol{a}),\boldsymbol{t}(\boldsymbol{a})\}$, where $\boldsymbol{x}$ and $\boldsymbol{t}$ are the allocation vector and the payoff function, respectively. The Bayesian game induced by $\mathcal{M}$ can be defined as $G = \langle N,\{u_i,\Theta_i,A_i,f_i\}_{i\in N}\rangle$. Here, N denotes the set of n agents. Each agent draws its type $\theta_i \in \Theta_i$ independently from a commonly known distribution over Θ_i with density distribution f_i. The utility of agent i can be calculated as $u_i = v_i(\boldsymbol{x}(\boldsymbol{a}),\theta_i) - t_i(\boldsymbol{a})$, where v_i represents of the value obtained from the allocation $\boldsymbol{x}$. According to Definition 1, given a certain kind of bounded rationality depicted in the form of Equation (1), the remaining two tasks for computing robustness are to: 1) test the stability of the desired equilibrium with a concrete stability function $\mathcal{S}$; 2) solve the maximum value of α_G according to Equation (3). Focusing on the Bayesian game induced by incentive mechanisms, we develop a general robustness evaluation framework:
1) **Robustness Solver** iteratively searches for α_M^G in $[0,1]$. In order to achieve an efficient search, Newton's Dichotomy method is used to skip some useless regions. Specifically, the inputs of our robustness solver include Bayesian game G, the desired action distribution profile $\boldsymbol{s}^E$ and the uncertainty set $\mathcal{US}_G$. At first, the left boundary α_L and right boundary α_R are set to be 0 and 1. The fully irrational case with $\alpha = 1$ is tested. If the test result is stable, we can conclude that the equilibrium is stable for all bounded rationality levels; otherwise, the real boundary should be some value between α_L and α_R. Then, we repeatedly conduct dichotomy and test the middle value $(\alpha_L+\alpha_R)/2$ until the distance between two boundaries is smaller than the acceptable threshold.
2) **Stability Tester** tests the stability of the desired equilibrium at the given level of bounded rationality. To achieve this function, we need to develop a convincing evolutionary process. Those utilized in the literature are not applicable to the *ex-ante* equilibrium. A good alternative is the fictitious play (FP) process which was initially proposed to compute equilibrium in normal-form games. Recently, through introducing new methods to compute the best response, Rabinovich *et al.* [4] used the FP process to compute the pure-strategy Bayesian Nash equilibrium. Although convergence of the FP process cannot be assured for all Bayesian games, it can still be used for our stability test because the divergent case can be used to identify the unstable region. Specifically, our algorithm computes the uncertainty set at first, which acts as the initial belief set of the FP process. Then, the FP process learns the Bayesian Nash equilibrium through gradually updating elements in the belief set with the the best response strategy $s_i^*(a_i)$. The stability function $\mathcal{S}$ is $Dist(\mathcal{US}_t,\{\boldsymbol{s}^E\}) - \epsilon$, where ϵ is the threshold of distance.

3) **Best Response Computing** is the most challenging step in stability tester. Existing methods depend on a specific target domain. To achieve an efficient and general evaluation of different mechanisms, we propose a sampling-based algorithm. Since $\sum_{a_i}\mathbb{E}_{s_{-i}}(a_i|\theta_i)Pr_i(a_i|\theta_i) \le \mathbb{E}_{s_{-i}}(a_i^*|\theta_i)$, the best response for a specific θ_i value should be an action $a_i^*$with the highest expected utility. Thus, the best response computation depends on the comparison between the expected utilities of different actions as $\mathbb{E}_{s_{-i}}[u_i(a_i^l|\theta_i) - u_i(a_i^k|\theta_i)] \ge_\tau \epsilon(l,k)$, where $l,k = 1,\dots,|A_i|$, and $|A_i|$ denotes the number of elements in A_i. Since the accurate comparison is impossible for sampling-based methods, the confidence level τ is introduced, and $a \ge_\tau b$ represents that a is bigger than or equal to b with a probability of τ. Thus, if $a_i^{l^*}$ is the desired best response with probability τ, then $\epsilon(l^*,k) \ge 0$ for $k = 1,\dots,|A_i|$. Furthermore, to compute $\epsilon(l,k)$, bootstrap statistics is employed because it does not rely on explicit assumptions about the shape of a distribution. This feature is useful because nothing is known about the distribution of agent's utility. Specifically, in our algorithm, K samples of opponents' actions are generated at first and the utility for every action $a_i^k \in A_i$ is calculated. Then, the distribution of expectation is computed with bootstrap statistics and the lower bound $\epsilon(l,k)$ is obtained. For those sub-optimal actions, there must exist at least one action that can achieve better utility, and $\{k|\max_{j\in\{1,\dots,|A_i|\}}\epsilon(j,k) \le 0\}$ represents the optimal set. If the size of I is 1, the optimal action is found; otherwise, we need to add another K samples.

4. CONCLUSION AND FUTURE WORK

In this abstract, we proposed a novel framework for evaluating robustness of incentive mechanisms. For future work, we will extend our framework to cover more kinds of bounded rationality and conduct more experiments on various incentive mechanisms to validate the framework.

REFERENCES

[1] A. Cabrales and R. Serrano. Implementation in adaptive better-response dynamics: Towards a general theory of bounded rationality in mechanisms. *Games and Economic Behavior*, 73(2):360–374, 2011.

[2] L. Chen and P. Tang. Bounded rationality of restricted turing machines. In *Proceedings of International Conference on Autonomous Agents and Multiagent Systems (AAMAS)*, pages 1673–1674, 2015.

[3] Y. Liu, J. Zhang, B. An, and S. Sen. A simulation framework for measuring robustness of incentive mechanisms and its implementation in reputation systems. *Autonomous Agents and Multi-Agent Systems*, pages 1–20, 2015.

[4] Z. Rabinovich, V. Naroditskiy, E. H. Gerding, and N. R. Jennings. Computing pure bayesian-nash equilibria in games with finite actions and continuous types. *Artificial Intelligence*, 195:106–139, 2013.

[5] N. Tumennasan. To err is human: Implementation in quantal response equilibria. *Games and Economic Behavior*, 77(1):138 – 152, 2013.

Plan Recognition in Exploratory Domains (Doctoral Consortium)

Reuth Mirsky
Supervisor: Ya'akov (Kobi) Gal
Dept. of Information Systems Engineering
Ben-Gurion University
Beer-Sheva 84105, Israel
dekelr@post.bgu.ac.il

ABSTRACT

My thesis focuses on recognition and interventions of users' activities using open-ended and flexible software. In such *exploratory settings*, users' behavior is characterized by exploration, mistakes and trial-and-error. Exploratory domains provide a flexible and rich interaction environment for their users, but induce challenges for automatic recognition and support of their activities. My thesis focuses on the following three challenges which are central to understanding users' interactions in exploratory settings and to use this understanding in order to provide them with effective support and guidance: (1) Representing and inferring users' interactions in exploratory domains. (2) Disambiguating between possible explanations in order to improve understanding of users' behavior. (3) Producing machine-generated support that adapts to the needs of the users. My research activities combines computational models, algorithms and empirical methodologies to meet the challenges above. They are conducted in the context of various types of exploratory settings. Specifically, I am developing novel plan recognition algorithms for inferring users' interactions in exploratory settings and intervention mechanisms for these environments. I am evaluating my approach in the real world using educational software, medical records and cyber security domains. My results so far include (1) design of a new model for plan recognition; (2) an online plan recognition algorithm that is empirically shown to outperform the state-of-the-art methods in the real world; (3) A sequential process that allows informed disambiguation of possible hypotheses describing an agent's plans. The long term impact of my contribution to computer science will be demonstrated by (1) developing new algorithms for plan recognition, intervention design and adaptation for exploratory settings; (2) showing that these methods generalize to different types of settings that differ widely in they type of interaction that is provided by the users.

Keywords

Human-Aware AI; Activity and Plan Recognition; Model-Based Reasoning; Exploratory Settings

Appears in: *Proceedings of the 15th International Conference on Autonomous Agents and Multiagent Systems (AAMAS 2016), J. Thangarajah, K. Tuyls, C. Jonker, S. Marsella (eds.), May 9–13, 2016, Singapore.*

1. INTRODUCTION

The focus of my thesis is on algorithms and techniques for inferring and guiding agents' behavior in domains in which users engage in exploratory and error-prone behaviors. Developing technology is changing rote and monolithic interaction styles between computers and their users are broken to more flexible types of interactions that allow users to explore and interleave between different activities. Examples include Integrated Development Environments (IDEs), security monitoring software [1], and educational software [9].

One problem I addressed in my thesis online plan recognition in real world exploratory domains [8]. I defined a model for agent's behavior in exploratory domains that is based on a context sensitive grammar with parameterization and free ordering. I augmented an existing state of the art online plan recognition algorithm to be able to consider such domains. I devised several heuristics to make the algorithm run on real-world domains feasible. The heuristics I used are domain dependant, such as the number of future actions expected, and the coherency of the hypotheses. I tried these heuristics on several domains. First, I used the simulated domain generated for a different plan recognition algorithm and compared between them [6]. Second, I used real world logs of students' behavior using educational software [9]. I managed to show that both in the simulated settings and in the real-world domains, the augmented plan recognition algorithm can handle large amount of input and can also output precise explanations of the agent's actions, either simulated or students [3, 4].

Another problem I am tackling is the disambiguation problem in plan recognition. Due to imperfect knowledge about the agent's behavior and the environment, it is often the case that there are multiple hypotheses about an agent's plans that are consistent with the observations, though only one of these hypotheses is correct. My approach assumes the acting agent can be queried about whether a candidate plan in a hypotheses is correct. Only few works exist on interacting with the observed agent as means to disambiguate the hypothesis space during plan recognition [2, 5], but none explicitly reason about the best queries that will maximize the information gain. I defined the sequential plan recognition problem, which seeks to minimize the number of queries made that are required to find the correct hypothesis. In order to address this problem, I propose a process that is performed sequentially and used to update the set of possible hypotheses during the recognition process. Initial results on the same domains as the previous project show that the use of reasoning can decrease significantly the number of queries required to disambiguate between hypotheses.

This thesis will develop more representations and algorithms for building collaborative tools for supporting the participants of exploratory settings that will entail the following capabilities: (1) Automatically recognizing users' activities in real-time during their interaction with the software; (2) Reasoning about the recognized hypotheses and reducing ambiguity of algorithm's output; (3) Producing machine-generated support that adapts to the needs of all participants, including system, users and overseers.

My thesis will combine computational models, algorithms and empirical methodologies that augment existing software to provide capabilities for meeting the desiderata above. My empirical methodology will be conducted on data that is obtained from different types of settings. First, by using data that is obtained from real world exploratory domains, consisting of students' interactions with flexible educational software, traces of users' behavior with operating systems, and medical records. Second, by generating simulated data that allows to control the extent of exploratory activities and provide a benchmark of comparison for my algorithms.

The efficacy and robustness of my approach will be evaluated in several ways: First, by comparing the performance of my recognition and intervention algorithms to a gold standard. Second, by showing the generalizability of my techniques to the different domains. Third, by conducting user studies to compare different visualizations of users' work to overseers (e.g., teachers, researchers); Lastly, by assessing students' performance using the tools I develop.

2. EXPLORATORY GRAMMAR AND CRADLE

In exploratory domains, agents' activities map onto logs of behavior that include switching between activities, extraneous actions, and mistakes. Such settings are prevalent in real world applications such as interaction with open-ended software, collaborative office assistants and integrated development environments. Despite the prevalence of such settings in the real world (e.g., interaction with open-ended software, collaborative office assistants, integrated development environments), there is scarce work in formalizing and inferring agents' behavior in these settings. In my thesis, I developed a formal grammar for describing users' activities in such domains. I also devised a new top-down plan recognition algorithm called CRADLE that uses this grammar to recognize agents' interactions in exploratory domains. I compared the performance of CRADLE with state-of-the-art plan recognition algorithms in experimental settings that use real logs taken from students' interactions with a flexible, open-ended software for chemistry education. My empirical results show that CRADLE was able to output plans in an order of magnitude more quickly than the state-of-the-art without compromising correctness, as determined by domain experts. This approach can form the basis of future systems for providing real-time support to users in a growing class of interesting and challenging domains. My preliminary results of CRADLE were presented in EDM and AAMAS [3, 4].

3. SEQUENTIAL PLAN RECOGNITION

Plan recognition algorithms infer agents' plans from their observed actions. Due to imperfect knowledge about the agent's behavior and the environment, it is often the case that there are multiple hypotheses about an agent's plans that are consistent with the observations, though only one of these hypotheses is correct. I proposed a process to address the problem of how to disambiguate between hypotheses, by querying the acting agent about whether a candidate plan in a hypotheses matches its intentions. This process is performed sequentially and used to update the set of possible hypotheses during the recognition process. I defined the sequential plan recognition problem, which seeks to minimize the number of queries made that are required to find the correct hypothesis. It adapts a number of probing techniques for choosing which plan to query, such as maximal information gain and maximum likelihood. These approaches were evaluated on two domains from the literature using a well known plan recognition algorithm. The results showed that the information gain approach was able to find the correct plan using significantly fewer queries than the maximum likelihood approach as well as a baseline approach choosing random plans. My technique can inform the design of future plan recognition systems that interleave the recognition process with intelligent interventions of their users. Preliminary results are shown in AAMAS16 [7]

REFERENCES

[1] B. Auslander, K. M. Gupta, and D. W. Aha. Maritime threat detection using plan recognition. In *Homeland Security (HST), 2012 IEEE Conference on Technologies for*, pages 249–254. IEEE, 2012.

[2] F. Bisson, F. Kabanza, A. R. Benaskeur, and H. Irandoust. Provoking opponents to facilitate the recognition of their intentions. In *AAAI*, 2011.

[3] R. Dekel and K. Gal. On-line plan recognition in exploratory learning environments. In *EDM (Workshops)*, 2014.

[4] R. Dekel and Y. Gal. Online plan recognition for exploratory domains. In *Workshop on Human-Agent Interaction Design and Models at AAMAS*, 2015.

[5] M. S. Fagundes, F. Meneguzzi, R. H. Bordini, and R. Vieira. Dealing with ambiguity in plan recognition under time constraints. In *Proceedings of AAMAS*, pages 389–396. International Foundation for Autonomous Agents and Multiagent Systems, 2014.

[6] F. Kabanza, J. Filion, A. R. Benaskeur, and H. Irandoust. Controlling the hypothesis space in probabilistic plan recognition. In *Proceedings of IJCAI*, pages 2306–2312. AAAI Press, 2013.

[7] R. Mirsky, Y. Gal, R. Stern, and M. Kalech. Sequential plan recognition. In *Proceedings of AAMAS*, 2016.

[8] O. Uzan, R. Dekel, and Y. Gal. Plan recognition for exploratory domains using interleaved temporal search. In *Proceedings of AIED*, 2013.

[9] D. Yaron, M. Karabinos, D. Lange, J. Greeno, and G. Leinhardt. The ChemCollective–Virtual Labs for Introductory Chemistry Courses. *Science*, 328(5978):584, 2010.

Adapting Plans through Communication with Unknown Teammates

(Doctoral Consortium)

Trevor Santarra
Advisor: Arnav Jhala
University of California Santa Cruz
Santa Cruz, CA 95064
tsarratt@soe.ucsc.edu

Categories and Subject Descriptors

I.2.11 [**Distributed Artificial Intelligence**]: Cooperation and coordination

Keywords

Ad Hoc Teams; Coordination; Multiagent Communication

1. INTRODUCTION

Coordinating a team of autonomous agents is a challenging problem. Agents must act in such a way that makes progress toward the achievement of a goal while avoiding conflict with their teammates. In information asymmetric domains, it is often necessary to share crucial observations in order to collaborate effectively. In traditional multiagent systems literature, these teams of agents share an identical design for reasoning, planning, and executing actions, allowing perfect modeling of teammates. Ad hoc teamwork [10] further complicates this problem by introducing a variety of teammates with which an agent must coordinate. In these scenarios, one or more agents within a team can be unfamiliar, having unknown planning capabilities guiding their behavior.

Much of the existing ad hoc teamwork research focuses on reinforcement learning and decision-theoretic planning. Agents use models of known behavior to predict an ad hoc agent's actions, using decision theory to maximize expected utility in instances where the predicted actions are uncertain. Online learning refines these models with observations of behaviors during execution, increasing the accuracy of the models' predictions, permitting the team to coordinate more effectively [1].

My thesis addresses the problem of planning under teammate behavior uncertainty by introducing the concept of intentional multiagent communication within ad hoc teams. In partially observable multiagent domains, agents much share information regarding aspects of the environment such that uncertainty is reduced across the team, permitting better coordination. Similarly, we consider how communication may be utilized within ad hoc teams to resolve behavioral uncertainty. Transmitting intentional messages allows agents to adjust predictions of a teammate's individual course of action. In short, an ad hoc agent coordinating with an unknown teammate can identify uncertainties within its own predictive model of teammate behavior then request the appropriate policy information, allowing the agent to adapt its personal plan. The main contribution of this work is the characterization of the interaction between learning, communication, and planning in ad hoc teams.

2. INFERENCE OVER BEHAVIORS

Prior experience with a variety of agents can provide a set of known behavior models for future use. Observations of an unknown teammate can then be used to identify a similar existing model as a predictor of its future actions. Our initial work in ad hoc teams considered the case where an agent coordinates with a teammate whose behavior is not represented well by a single model but rather by a composition of modeled behaviors. In this scenario, the teammate may adopt new strategies on the fly, adapting its behavior or pursuing new goals unexpectedly. Traditional probabilistic approaches assume static behavior and do not correct the choice of model in a responsive manner [1]. Furthermore, perfect Bayesian inference would require either known transition probabilities, which are not provided in ad hoc domains, or a mechanism for learning the transition likelihoods. By adopting a technique from on-line learning [2], we demonstrated a computationally lightweight technique for responsively identifying changes in a teammate's behavior, correctly selecting an alternate model that most accurately expresses the post-change observed actions. This approach outperforms the standard Bayesian weight revision method, showing promise for accurately modeling agents of inconsistent behavior as well as agents whose high level strategy can be expressed by a sequence of more simple behaviors [6, 8].

Such model inference approaches, while suitable for a wide range of problems, are not without their limitations, however. The possession of a set of known models requires either prior experience or hand-authored knowledge. Even when complex behavior can be approximated with the composition of known, simple models, the low level behaviors must be available prior to coordination. Initial work in learning a model during coordination has relied on generalization of information across known models to speed up the process [1], and as a result, such transfer learning techniques may not apply to novel conditions in which no prior knowledge is

Appears in: *Proceedings of the 15th International Conference on Autonomous Agents and Multiagent Systems (AAMAS 2016), J. Thangarajah, K. Tuyls, C. Jonker, S. Marsella (eds.), May 9–13, 2016, Singapore.*

available. Furthermore, relying on observations necessitates an act be performed before the information can be utilized to infer or construct an accurate model, a constraint unsuitable for domains with strict limits on potential attempts of completing a task. For this reason, we motivate communicating *in advance* of a point of uncertainty.

3. COMMUNICATION

Across many communicative multiagent frameworks, such as the COM-MTDP model [4] and STEAM [11], communicative actions are often limited to sharing observations. As agents in such systems have complete information regarding the planning capacities of their teammates, they can simply use the shared information to compute precisely how all agents will act. Since the policies of teammates are the source of uncertainty in ad hoc teams, it follows that policy information is a promising target for communicative acts. We introduced this idea in [7].

In early decision-theoretic agent communication literature, various types of communication were theoretically validated in their effect on coordinating multiple agents. These included intentional messages, questions, proposals, threats, imperatives, and statements of propositional attitudes [3]. In each case, providing or requesting information adjusted one or more agents' policies through refining an agent's expectations of either its own policy's likelihood of success or the intentions of another agent acting within the same environment. Analogously, the refinement of predicted action probabilities and, consequently, an improved policy for a coordinating agent is desirable for ad hoc teams.

Whereas the broadcast of the intention of pursuing a goal addresses multiple state-action pairs within an agent's policy computation, we must consider that an unfamiliar teammate may not possess the capability of reasoning with high level abstractions such as joint plans or hierarchical goal decompositions. However, we put forth the observation that all agents involved are universally tasked with assigning actions to states, independent of the particular planning implementation details. From a general perspective, we consider how an ad hoc agent could benefit from obtaining a single state-action pair—the atomic component of a teammate model—from communication.

In our extended abstract to be presented at *AAMAS-16* [9], we have provided an efficient procedure for evaluating potential state-action pairs for communication by examining the uncertainty within a teammate model as well as empirically analyzed various aspects of the communicative capability. For our test domain, we used a variation of the multiagent pursuit domain where two agents attempt to capture a prey within a maze. We were able to show the trade-off between collected information and communication rates and, likewise, the effect of communication costs on query rates and the resulting expected utility of the agent. Finally, our analysis determined that branch points in a maze are commonly communicated more frequently than neighboring cells, indicating that the tested agents determined resolving uncertainty at such states was associated with higher utility.

4. FUTURE WORK

While our previous work has focused on the ability to coordinate with computer agents, we intend to test our approach with human teammates, given the potential applicability of ad hoc team approaches to human-computer teams. Furthermore, over the ensuing year, we intend to transition to a more complex domain, using a slightly simplified form of the real-time strategy game, StarCraft.

An immediate extension to this work is the consideration of communicating multiple state-action pairs without independent evaluation. It is possible for two states to have no utility for communication individually but have non-zero utility when considered together. This opens up a combinatorial space of potential intentional information sets that could be communicated, similar to problem of picking a subset of observations to share within a team, as explored by Roth et al. [5]. Due to the intractable nature of the problem, the authors motivated the exploration of heuristics as approximate solutions. It is yet unclear how states in such collections will be related, though we hypothesize they could take any one of various forms, including sequences of successive states (forming a plan), areas of connected states (a local subspace of the domain), or groups of independently valuable states (such as branch points discussed earlier).

REFERENCES

[1] S. Barrett, P. Stone, S. Kraus, and A. Rosenfeld. Teamwork with limited knowledge of teammates. In *AAAI*, 2013.

[2] O. Bousquet and M. K. Warmuth. Tracking a small set of experts by mixing past posteriors. *The Journal of Machine Learning Research*, 3:363–396, 2003.

[3] P. J. Gmytrasiewicz, E. H. Durfee, and J. Rosenschein. Toward rational communicative behavior. In *AAAI Fall Symposium on Embodied Language*, pages 35–43, 1995.

[4] D. V. Pynadath and M. Tambe. The communicative multiagent team decision problem: Analyzing teamwork theories and models. *Journal of Artificial Intelligence Research*, pages 389–423, 2002.

[5] M. Roth, R. Simmons, and M. Veloso. What to communicate? execution-time decision in multi-agent pomdps. In *Distributed Autonomous Robotic Systems 7*, pages 177–186. Springer, 2006.

[6] T. Sarratt and A. Jhala. Rapid: A belief convergence strategy for collaborating with inconsistent agents. In *Workshops at the Twenty-Ninth AAAI Conference on Artificial Intelligence*, 2015.

[7] T. Sarratt and A. Jhala. The role of models and communication in the ad hoc multiagent team decision problem. In *Proceedings of the Third Annual Conference on Advances in Cognitive Systems Poster Collection*, page 27, 2015.

[8] T. Sarratt and A. Jhala. Tuning belief revision for coordination with inconsistent teammates. In *AIIDE*, 2015.

[9] T. Sarratt and A. Jhala. Communicating intentions for coordination with unknown teammates. In *Workshops at the Thirtieth AAAI Conference on Artificial Intelligence*, 2016.

[10] P. Stone, G. A. Kaminka, S. Kraus, J. S. Rosenschein, et al. Ad hoc autonomous agent teams: Collaboration without pre-coordination. In *AAAI*, 2010.

[11] M. Tambe. Agent architectures for flexible. In *Proc. of the 14th National Conf. on AI, USA: AAAI press*, pages 22–28, 1997.

Curriculum Learning in Reinforcement Learning (Doctoral Consortium)

Sanmit Narvekar
Department of Computer Science
University of Texas at Austin
Austin, TX 78712 USA
sanmit@cs.utexas.edu

ABSTRACT

Transfer learning in reinforcement learning is an area of research that seeks to speed up or improve learning of a complex target task, by leveraging knowledge from one or more source tasks. This thesis will extend the concept of transfer learning to *curriculum learning*, where the goal is to design a sequence of source tasks for an agent to train on, such that final performance or learning speed is improved. We discuss completed work on this topic, including an approach for modeling transferability between tasks, and methods for semi-automatically generating source tasks tailored to an agent and the characteristics of a target domain. Finally, we also present ideas for future work.

General Terms

Algorithms; Performance; Experimentation

Keywords

Reinforcement Learning; Transfer Learning; Curriculum Learning

1. INTRODUCTION

As autonomous agents are called upon to perform increasingly difficult tasks, new techniques will be needed to make learning such tasks tractable. Transfer learning [3, 9] is a recent area of research that has been shown to speed up learning on a complex task by transferring knowledge from one or more easier *source tasks*. Most existing transfer learning methods treat this transfer of knowledge as a one-step process, where knowledge from all the sources are directly transferred to the target. However, for complex tasks, it may be more beneficial (and even necessary) to gradually acquire skills over multiple tasks *in sequence*, where each subsequent task requires and builds upon knowledge gained in a previous task. This is especially important, for example, if the knowledge or experience needed from a source requires prerequisites to obtain.

The goal of this thesis work is to extend transfer learning to the problem of *curriculum learning*. As a motivating example, consider the game of Quick Chess[1] (Figure 1). Quick Chess is a game designed to introduce players to the full game of chess, by using a sequence of progressively more difficult "subgames." For example, the first subgame is a 5x5 board with only pawns, where the player learns how pawns move and about promotions. The second subgame is a small board with pawns and a king, which introduces a new objective: keeping the king alive. In each successive subgame, new elements are introduced (such as new pieces, a larger board, or different configurations) that require learning new skills and building upon knowledge learned in previous games. The final game is the full game of chess.

Figure 1: Different subgames in Quick Chess

The question that motivates this line of work is: can we find an optimal sequence of tasks (i.e. a curriculum) for an agent to play that will make it possible to learn some target task (such as chess) fastest, or at a performance level better than learning from scratch?

Designing an effective curriculum is a complex problem that ties task creation, sequencing, and transfer learning. A good set of source tasks is crucial for having positive transfer. A curriculum designer must be able to suggest source tasks using knowledge of the target domain, and that are tailored to the current abilities of the agent. Second, the tasks must be sequenced in a way that allows new knowledge to be accumulated by the agent along each step. During this process, the agent also needs to know how long it should spend in a source in order to acquire the necessary skills, the kind of knowledge it should obtain for transfer, and how to transfer it to the next stage of the curriculum. In the following sections, we discuss progress made towards some of these objectives, and plans for future work in this direction.

Appears in: *Proceedings of the 15th International Conference on Autonomous Agents and Multiagent Systems (AAMAS 2016), J. Thangarajah, K. Tuyls, C. Jonker, S. Marsella (eds.), May 9–13, 2016, Singapore.*

[1]http://www.intplay.com/uploadedFiles/Game_Rules/P20051-QuickChess-Rules.pdf

2. COMPLETED WORK

There are two pieces of completed work that relate to this thesis. Last year [7], we examined the problem of learning to select which tasks could serve as suitable source tasks for a given target task. Unlike previous approaches, which typically relied on a model of the two task MDPs, or experience (such as sample trajectories) from the two tasks, our approach used a set of meta-level feature descriptors describing each task. We trained a regression model over these feature descriptors to predict the benefit of transfer from one task to another, as measured by the jumpstart metric [9], and showed using a large scale experiment that these descriptors could be used to predict transferability.

This method serves as one way of identifying which task to select as part of a curriculum. However, it assumed that a fixed and suitable set of tasks was provided, which was created using knowledge of the domain. It also only showed successful transfer for a 1-stage curriculum.

At AAMAS 2016, we will present the overall problem of curriculum learning in the context of reinforcement learning [6], and show concrete multi-stage transfer. Specifically, as a first step towards creating a curriculum, we consider how a space of useful source tasks can be generated, using a parameterized model of the domain and observed trajectories of an agent on the target task. We claim that a good source task is one that leverages knowledge about the domain to simplify the problem, and that promotes learning new skills tailored to the abilities of the agent in question. Thus, we propose a series of functions to semi-automatically create useful, agent-specific source tasks, and show how they can be used to form components of a curriculum in two challenging multiagent domains. Particularly, we show that a curriculum is useful and can provide *strong transfer* [9].

The methods we propose are also useful for creating tasks in the classic transfer learning paradigm (1 step curriculum). Past work in transfer learning has typically assumed a fixed set of source tasks are provided, using a static analysis of the domain. This work allows new source tasks to be suggested from a dynamic analysis of the agent's performance.

3. DIRECTIONS FOR FUTURE WORK

In our most recent work [6], we showed how one form of transfer – value function transfer – could be used to transfer knowledge via a curriculum. However, transfer learning literature has shown that alternate forms of transfer are also possible, using options [8], policies [2], models [1], or even samples [5, 4]. Thus, an interesting extension is characterizing what type of knowledge is useful to extract from a task, and whether we can combine multiple forms of transfer for use in a curriculum. For example, it may be that some tasks are more suitable for transferring options, while others are more suitable for transferring samples. Thus, when designing a curriculum, the designer would ask both which task to transfer from, and the type of knowledge to transfer.

Another key question to address is how long to spend on a source task. In our previous work [6, 7], agents trained on source tasks until convergence. However, this is suboptimal for two reasons. First, spending too much time training in a source task can result in overfitting to the source. In curriculum learning, we only care about performance in the target task, and not whether we also achieve optimality in a source. Thus, this excess training can be detrimental. Second, from a practical standpoint, if the necessary skills can be acquired from a source task before reaching convergence, there is no benefit to keep training on it. Doing so would make it harder to show benefits such as strong transfer.

Finally, there is the overall goal of automatically sequencing tasks in the curriculum. Our current work [6] proposed a way of creating a space of tasks, but assumed a separate process (e.g., a human expert) chose which tasks to use. Automating this process completes the loop. Once we have a curriculum for an agent, we can also examine related questions such as how to individualize that curriculum for a new set of agents that have different representations or abilities.

Acknowledgements

This work was done in collaboration with Jivko Sinapov, Matteo Leonetti, and Peter Stone as part of the Learning Agents Research Group (LARG) at the University of Texas at Austin. LARG research is supported in part by NSF (CNS-1330072, CNS-1305287), ONR (21C184-01), AFRL (FA8750-14-1-0070), & AFOSR (FA9550-14-1-0087).

REFERENCES

[1] A. Fachantidis, I. Partalas, G. Tsoumakas, and I. Vlahavas. Transferring task models in reinforcement learning agents. *Neurocomputing*, 107:23–32, 2013.

[2] F. Fernández, J. García, and M. Veloso. Probabilistic policy reuse for inter-task transfer learning. *Robotics and Autonomous Systems*, 58(7):866 – 871, 2010. Advances in Autonomous Robots for Service and Entertainment.

[3] A. Lazaric. Transfer in reinforcement learning: a framework and a survey. In M. Wiering and M. van Otterlo, editors, *Reinforcement Learning: State of the Art*. Springer, 2011.

[4] A. Lazaric and M. Restelli. Transfer from multiple MDPs. In *Proceedings of the Twenty-Fifth Annual Conference on Neural Information Processing Systems (NIPS'11)*, 2011.

[5] A. Lazaric, M. Restelli, and A. Bonarini. Transfer of samples in batch reinforcement learning. In A. McCallum and S. Roweis, editors, *Proceedings of the Twenty-Fifth Annual International Conference on Machine Learning (ICML-2008)*, pages 544–551, Helsinki, Finalnd, July 2008.

[6] S. Narvekar, J. Sinapov, M. Leonetti, and P. Stone. Source task creation for curriculum learning. In *Proceedings of the 15th International Conference on Autonomous Agents and Multiagent Systems (AAMAS 2016)*, Singapore, May 2016.

[7] J. Sinapov, S. Narvekar, M. Leonetti, and P. Stone. Learning inter-task transferability in the absence of target task samples. In *Proceedings of the 2015 ACM Conference on Autonomous Agents and Multi-Agent Systems (AAMAS)*. ACM, 2015.

[8] V. Soni and S. Singh. Using homomorphisms to transfer options across continuous reinforcement learning domains. In *In Proceedings of American Association for Artificial Intelligence (AAAI)*, 2006.

[9] M. E. Taylor and P. Stone. Transfer learning for reinforcement learning domains: A survey. *Journal of Machine Learning Research*, 10(1):1633–1685, 2009.

MAS-based, Scalable Allocation of Resources in Large-scale, Dynamic Environments

(Doctoral Consortium)

Diana Gudu
Karlsruhe Institute of Technology
Karlsruhe, Germany
diana.gudu@kit.edu

ABSTRACT

I study the resource allocation problem, with a focus on computing environments (Cloud, Internet of Things), by employing market mechanisms such as auctions that consider supply and demand, and dynamic pricing in the decision process. However, current approaches face two limitations: (i) *centralisation*, as there is typically a central entity (such as an auctioneer) that holds all the information and decides the allocation based on it, therefore either limiting the size of the auctions that can be handled, or leading to compromises in the quality of the solution, and (ii) *inflexibility*, or inability to deal with heterogeneous, dynamic environments.

In this dissertation I propose a scalable and adaptive approach to overcome these limitations: a market-based, completely decentralised multi-agent system. I investigate techniques to enhance the performance, scalability and quality of the decentralised allocation using insights from centralised approaches.

Keywords

resource allocation; auction; multi-agent system; scalable; distributed; simulation; cloud

1. INTRODUCTION

Resource allocation is a fundamental problem in many fields. Recent trends have replaced traditional resource management techniques with "market-inspired" approaches to achieve a more flexible, economically efficient, and fair allocation. In computing, the Grid has pioneered market-oriented allocation of resources: Broberg et al. [1] surveyed the state-of-the-art and showed how utility computing helped deal with unpredictable or bursty workloads, and how it provided incentives for users to be more flexible in their usage pattern. The advent of cloud computing has taken the concepts of utility computing and market-based resource allocation to the next level due to virtualization, the use of real currency, and better defined services and legal frameworks, sparking new research in already established fields such as combinatorial auctions [3, 8, 6]. A new paradigm in resource allocation is emerging, where self-interested participants, who only try to increase their utility, meet in *ad-hoc* marketplaces, negotiate and finally agree on resource exchanges [1, 2], much as in a free market.

Nevertheless, work on resource allocation so far is either (a) *centralised*: typically a central entity has a global view of user requests and available services, and single-handedly handles the allocation process [7], or (b) *one-sided*: user agents (brokers) analyse a user's various requirements to match them with the providers that can offer the needed resources [4]; at the other end, there are agents acting only on behalf of providers, e.g. holding auctions in order to sell their resources to the highest bidders and maximise provider revenue [9]. At the most, proposed decentralised marketplaces include many independent, competing brokers that mediate the resource exchanges [2], leaving the users with the difficult task of choosing the appropriate broker and optimal market mechanism. Moreover, most resource allocation frameworks only offer specific market mechanisms, exhibiting *inflexibility*, whereas heterogeneous and dynamic environments like the Cloud and the Internet of Things would benefit from higher mechanism diversity.

2. PROPOSED APPROACH

Motivated by the need for scalability and adaptability, I propose a complex, evolving system where independent brokers are replaced by agents that communicate and collaborate to achieve global goals based on local, incomplete information. Such a multi-agent system (MAS) would act as a mediator between providers and users, striving to find the best allocation for all participants, i.e. to maximise the *social welfare*. I aim to off-load most tasks from the client or provider side (including match-making of requirements and resource offers, selection of appropriate market mechanisms) onto the MAS. For heterogeneous, upredictable environments, a plethora of market mechanisms should be made available in the system, each specialised on a certain niche. Prior knowledge of which mechanisms are best suited for certain input patterns, together with learning from past experiences, will be employed to select appropriate mechanisms and improve the overall allocation. The MAS must therefore adapt to the dynamic environment. The inherent decentralisation of the proposed system will contribute to the scalability of the resource allocation.

2.1 Market mechanisms

Most market mechanisms, such as combinatorial auctions, are complex optimisation problems, typically NP-hard [3].

Appears in: *Proceedings of the 15th International Conference on Autonomous Agents and Multiagent Systems (AAMAS 2016), J. Thangarajah, K. Tuyls, C. Jonker, S. Marsella (eds.), May 9–13, 2016, Singapore.*

Various heuristic methods have been developed to solve these problems, inevitably causing some heuristics to give good results for certain problem instances (or use cases) and underperform in others. In a related work, Leyton-Brown et al. [5] propose an approach to identify features that characterise the empirical hardness of combinatorial auctions, by using domain knowledge and machine learning.

I state that a *comprehensive analysis* of centralised market mechanisms aimed at gathering in-depth knowledge for each mechanism is essential in making the multi-agent system more scalable and efficient.

In a paper currently under review, I extensively analysed one such centralised market mechanism, namely a greedy heuristic approach for solving double combinatorial auctions, based on the work of Samimi et al. [6]. I evaluated how metrics such as time, success rate of client requests, resource utilization, average agent utility, and average price per unit of goods sold behave for different inputs, as well as with respect to demand and supply fluctuations. An important finding was that the results for sparse providers (providers specialised on offering disjoint subsets of the possible resource types) were unpredictable and highly sensitive to input, limiting the algorithm to be used only on dense providers and dense client requests. I then analysed the scalability of the same algorithm by distributing it over multiple agents, and found promising speedup results, as well as an expected efficiency loss due to decision making with incomplete information. There is certainly more research to be done in this area, more specifically a thorough analysis and classification of the most suited mechanisms for each use case brought forth, and designing new algorithms where necessary.

2.2 Multi-agent system

I propose a MAS design consisting of three types of agents: *Client Agents*, which deal with customer requests and submit them to an appropriate Matching Agent after a basic analysis; *Resource Agents*, which expose the available providers and their specifications to the appropriate Matching Agents; and finally *Matching Agents*, which use market mechanisms (e.g. auctions, bargaining) to find the best resource allocation for the client requests and provider offers they receive. Each Matching Agent essentially solves an optimisation problem by maximising the sum of all participants' utilities, i.e. the social welfare. This underlines the distributed character of the proposed approach. A participant's utility can include, but is not limited to, the price of resources and associated QoS metrics. However, local optimisation is not sufficient for a globally optimal allocation. Therein lies the intelligent, adaptive behaviour: in the communication between Matching Agents, aimed at finding a trade-off between the amount of information exchanged and the improvement in solution quality (performance vs. efficiency). The communication is based on prior knowledge of market mechanisms (cf. Sec. 2.1) for filtering and forwarding requests based on use cases, as well as learning techniques for a better distribution of requests.

The design expresses the generality of our approach by separating the clients and resource providers on the one hand, and the resource allocation on the other hand. The MAS also provides fair treatment to clients and providers (through social welfare optimisation), as well as incentive for them to participate in a truthful manner (through a careful auction design, more specifically the pricing algorithm).

An ensuing challenge concerns the evaluation of the decentralised system, as well as its comparison with an equivalent centralised one.

2.3 Research question

Essentially, through the proposed thesis, I resolve to address the following research question:

How can one improve the scalability and adaptivity of resource allocation in large-scale, dynamic environments by using a decentralised, market-driven approach?

To that end, the MAS-based approach I proposed encompasses the following: (1) *decentralised decision-making* for increased scalability, (2) *market-driven* allocation and pricing, that is *flexible* and *customised* to the needs of the participants, (3) *fine-grained allocation* of resources, aimed at improving resource utilization for providers, thereby decreasing costs for clients, and (4) *social welfare optimisation*, as opposed to one-sided optimisation which only benefits either the resource providers or the users.

REFERENCES

[1] J. Broberg, S. Venugopal, and R. Buyya. Market-oriented grids and utility computing: The state-of-the-art and future directions. *Journal of Grid Computing*, 6(3):255–276, 2008. doi:10.1007/s10723-007-9095-3.

[2] R. Buyya, C. S. Yeo, and S. Venugopal. Market-oriented cloud computing: Vision, hype, and reality for delivering it services as computing utilities. In *High Performance Computing and Communications, 2008. HPCC'08. 10th IEEE International Conference on*, pages 5–13. IEEE, 2008. doi:10.1109/HPCC.2008.172.

[3] S. De Vries and R. V. Vohra. Combinatorial auctions: A survey. *INFORMS Journal on computing*, 15(3):284–309, 2003. doi:10.1287/ijoc.15.3.284.16077.

[4] F. Jrad. *A service broker for Intercloud computing*. PhD thesis, Karlsruher Institut für Technologie, 2014. urn:nbn:de:swb:90-423243.

[5] K. Leyton-Brown, E. Nudelman, and Y. Shoham. Learning the empirical hardness of optimization problems: The case of combinatorial auctions. In *Principles and Practice of Constraint Programming-CP 2002*, pages 556–572. Springer, 2002. doi:10.1007/3-540-46135-3_37.

[6] P. Samimi, Y. Teimouri, and M. Mukhtar. A combinatorial double auction resource allocation model in cloud computing. *Information Sciences*, 2014. doi:016/j.ins.2014.02.008.

[7] J. Watzl. *A framework for exchange-based trading of cloud computing commodities*. PhD thesis, Ludwig Maximilian University of Munich (LMU), 2014. urn:nbn:de:bvb:19-168702.

[8] S. Zaman and D. Grosu. Combinatorial auction-based allocation of virtual machine instances in clouds. *Journal of Parallel and Distributed Computing*, 73(4):495–508, 2013. doi:10.1016/j.jpdc.2012.12.006.

[9] Q. Zhang, Q. Zhu, and R. Boutaba. Dynamic resource allocation for spot markets in cloud computing environments. In *Utility and Cloud Computing (UCC), 2011 Fourth IEEE International Conference on*, pages 178–185. IEEE, 2011. doi:10.1109/UCC.2011.33.

Learning to Act Optimally in Partially Observable Multiagent Settings

(Doctoral Consortium)

Roi Ceren
Supervisor: Prashant Doshi
THINC Lab, Dept. of Computer Science
University of Georgia
Athens, Georgia, USA
ceren@cs.uga.edu

ABSTRACT

My research is focused on modeling optimal decision making in partially observable multiagent environments. I began with an investigation into the cognitive biases that induce subnormative behavior in humans playing games online in multiagent settings, leveraging well-known computational psychology approaches in modeling humans playing a strategic, sequential game. My subsequent work was in a scalable extension to Monte Carlo exploring starts for POMDPs (MCES-P), where I expanded the theory and algorithm to the multiagent setting. I first introduced a straightforward application with probably approximately correct guarantees (MCESP+PAC), and then introduced a more sample efficient partially model-based framework (MCESIP+PAC) that explicitly modeled the opponent.

Keywords

reinforcement learning; multiple agents; probably approximately correct; partial observability

1. INTRODUCTION

Arriving at optimal policies in single agent partially observable environments can be computationally taxing, but is significantly more so with the introduction of other agents who may have an impact on the environment as well. Exact solutions in all but the simplest domains may be far too intractable with conventional methodologies. I utilize online reinforcement learning (RL) as my departure point for partially observable multiagent settings.

My first investigation into RL was identifying whether humans utilized a reinforcement learning approach when evaluating their prospects of success in strategic, sequential games [1]. As a primary effort, I parameterized Q-learning utilizing known behavioral cognitive biases, including forgetfulness and erroneously ascribing reward to neighboring states. In addition, I implemented subproportional weighting *a la* prospect theory to represent humans misrepresenting probability judgments.

My recent efforts involve generalized frameworks for arriving at optimal policies in partially observable multiagent settings, while additionally providing statistical guarantees via probably approximately correct learning. I extend Monte Carlo Exploring Starts for POMDPs [2] with PAC bounds to the multiagent setting. I then add a partially model-based component explicitly modeling opponent behavior and show it dramatically reduces sample requirements. In addition, I customize ϵ-pruning to improve runtime.

Appears in: *Proceedings of the 15th International Conference on Autonomous Agents and Multiagent Systems (AAMAS 2016), J. Thangarajah, K. Tuyls, C. Jonker, S. Marsella (eds.), May 9–13, 2016, Singapore.*

2. MODELING HUMANS WITH BEHAVIORAL Q-LEARNING

My first work is concerned with the phenomenon of non-normative behavior in human subjects when engaging in strategic environments. I computationally model the effects of three cognitive biases on reinforcement learning: forgetfulness (erroneously discounting previous experience), reward spill over (where subjects attribute experiences in one state to a neighboring state as well), and subproportional weighting (from prospect theory, where probability assessments are categorically under- or over-weighted).

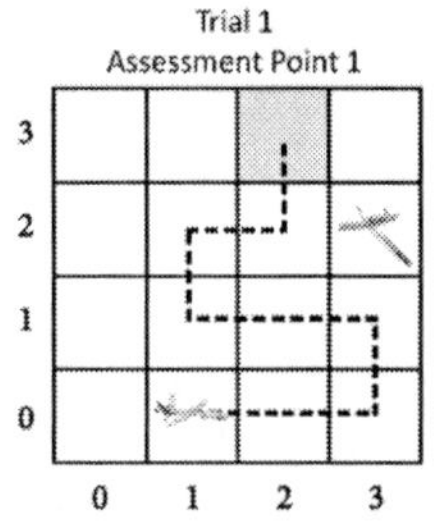

Figure 1: UAV problem domain, with the subject following a predefined path and the predator visible only initially.

In conjunction with the psychology department at my university, we conducted a series of experiments where subjects observed a UAV navigating in a 4x4 grid between a known start and goal sector. However, the environment included a predator UAV who, when arriving in the same sector as the subject UAV, would end the game in a loss. The predator's position is only known in the first step of the game.

I leveraged three parameters in our behavioral reinforcement learning model. α is the learning rate which normally appears in Q-learning. ϕ is an additional depreciation parameter affecting only the previous Q-value. ϵ represents the proportion of the reward that should be equally attributed to neighboring policies, where Eq. 1 represents the proportion given to the sector where the reward was experienced and Eq. 2 are the spilled-over states. Equation 3 is Prelec's one-parameter subproportional weighting. The state in our setting is the joint physical location of the subject and the predator UAVs.

$$Q(s,\pi(s)) = \phi \cdot Q(s,\pi(s)) + \alpha((1-\epsilon)r(s) + \gamma \cdot Q(s',\pi(s')) - \phi \cdot Q(s,\pi(s))) \quad (1)$$

$$Q(s_n,\pi(s)) = \phi \cdot Q(s_n,\pi(s)) + \alpha(\epsilon \cdot r(s) - \phi \cdot Q(s_n,\pi(s))) \quad (2)$$

$$w(p) = e^{-(-ln(p))^{\beta}} \quad (3)$$

I tested the predictive capabilities of the normative and behavioral models using Nelder-Mead downhill simplex with 5-fold cross-validation using 43 participants playing 20 trials each.

Model	total SSD
Behavioral Q-learning + Weighting	401.36
Default Q-learning + Weighting	406.26
Behavioral Q-learning	409.25
Default Q-learning	416.41

Table 1: Behavioral Q-learning with probability weighting shows the best fit and the differences are significant.

3. RL IN PARTIALLY OBSERVABLE MULTIAGENT ENVIRONMENTS

I extend Perkins' Monte Carlo exploring starts for POMDPs [2] (MCES-P) to multiagent domains with public observations of the environment and private observations of other agents' actions. The setting is non-cooperative, akin to the Interactive POMDP [3]. This extension, unlike the majority of the state of the art, does not require communication or collaboration between agents.

I first introduce canonical MCES-P to the multiagent setting, adapting the algorithm to allow private observations, and show that the probably approximately correct bounds also hold, albeit with a larger policy space. MCESP+PAC obtains action-values for policies using sampled trajectories and compares neighboring policies (that is, policies that differ by an action in only one observation sequence) to determine dominating transformations in the local neighborhood. In order to guarantee this transformation dominates, MCESP+PAC requires exactly $k_m \leftarrow \left\lceil 2\left(\frac{\Lambda}{\epsilon}\right)^2 \ln \frac{2N}{\delta_m}\right\rceil$ samples.

samples for each policy, where m is the number of transformations already taken and $\delta_m = 6\delta/(m^2\pi^2)$, and the neighbor must dominate the original policy by at least epsilon. Λ is the range of possible rewards, defined in MCES-P as $2T(R_{max} - R_{min})$. The algorithm can determine a better neighbor in less than k_m samples if, after each policy has p samples after m transformations, the neighbor dominates by $\epsilon(m,p) \leftarrow \Lambda\sqrt{\frac{1}{2p}\ln\frac{2(k_m-1)N}{\delta_m}}$.

MCES for I-POMDPs with PAC bounds (MCESIP+PAC) adds a partially model-based component of explicit models of the opponent and requires dramatically fewer samples than MCES-P for the same configuration and arriving at the same locally-optimal policy. Since MCES-IP maintains a belief over opponent models, the range of rewards is smaller, since it is limited to the rewards achievable for a specific action the opponent takes, which we dub $\Lambda^{\bar{a}_j}$.

Lastly, I provide a custom ϵ-pruning methodology for MCES-P and MCES-IP, referred to as observation sequence pruning, that dramatically reduces the runtime in lieu of introducing bounded regret on the reward lost from foregone transformations. Since sampling some of the observation sequences can be quite costly due to their relative rarity, and since the same observation sequences have limited impact on the reward due to their infrequency, pruning is a powerful technique for speeding up Monte Carlo exploring starts. Given a proportion of allowable regret ϕ (around 15-20% in our experiments), the maximum regret introduced by foregoing transformations cannot exceed ϕ, such that $\sum_{\vec{o}_i \in \mathcal{P}} \bar{regret}_{\vec{o}_i} \leq \phi$.

We ran over 200 trials for two problem domains: the multiagent Tiger problem and a 3x2 Autonomous UAV problem, where the subject is a predator seeking the opponent (prey) before they arrive at the goal sector. In almost every case, MCES-IP arrived at the same policy as MCES-P, but did so in significantly fewer samples.

Method	Policy	Mean # of samples per transform	Mean bound on k_m
MCESP+PAC	Single	102,775 ± 44,468	271,478 ± 28,310
	Mixed	142,137 ± 54,361	262,711 ± 58,315
MCESIP+PAC	Single	50,154 ± 16,979	119,859 ± 11,743
	Mixed	82,940 ± 39,384	118,888 ± 9,283

Method	Policy	Mean # of samples per transform	Mean bound on k_m
MCESP+PAC	Single	48,325 ± 21,694	96,877 ± 8,308
	Mixed	46,210 ± 31,505	108,449 ± 11,314
MCESIP+PAC	Single	14,111 ± 4,488	20,843 ± 1,948
	Mixed	14,191 ± 3,475	19,893 ± 2,007

Table 2: Mean effective sample size and theoretical bound across the stages for the multiagent Tiger problem (top) and the 3×2 AUAV (bottom) problem, stratified over method and opponent model type.

4. FUTURE WORK

My final effort involves first introducing the same PAC bounds and optimal policy search present in MCES-P/MCES-IP to the cooperative Multiagent POMDP (MPOMDP) [4] setting (MCES-IP). In this setting we consider the environment where n agents with private observations of the environment communicate with a centralized controller that iterates and tests a series of joint policies, arriving at a mutually-optimal set of policies for each individual agent. I will then follow up with a work on introducing new sampling techniques in order to further improve the runtime of each framework without impacting the overall optimality of the converged policies.

5. ACKNOWLEDGEMENTS

[1] was supported by a grant from Army RDECOM-#W911NF-09-1-0464 to Prashant Doshi, Adam Goodie, and Dan Hall. Section 3 is supported by grant NSF IIS-0845036 to Dr. Doshi. Thanks to Theodore Perkins for emails clarifying MCESP+PAC and Bikramjit Banerjee for his invaluable advice for MCESIP+PAC. Thanks to Yingke Chen and Junhuan Zhang for assistance in developing theory and problem domains.

REFERENCES

[1] Roi Ceren, Prashant Doshi, Matthew Meisel, Adam Goodie, and David Hall. On modeling human learning in sequential games with delayed reinforcements. In *Systems, Man, and Cybernetics (SMC), 2013 IEEE International Conference on*, pages 3108–3113. IEEE, 2013.

[2] Theodore J Perkins. Reinforcement learning for pomdps based on action values and stochastic optimization. In *AAAI/IAAI*, pages 199–204, 2002.

[3] Piotr J Gmytrasiewicz and Prashant Doshi. A framework for sequential planning in multi-agent settings. *Journal of Artificial Intelligence Research (JAIR)*, pages 49–79, 2005.

[4] Joao V. Messias, Matthijs Spaan, and Pedro U. Lima. Efficient offline communication policies for factored multiagent pomdps. In J. Shawe-Taylor, R. S. Zemel, P. L. Bartlett, F. Pereira, and K. Q. Weinberger, editors, *Advances in Neural Information Processing Systems 24*, pages 1917–1925. 2011.

Strategic Voting and Social Networks
(Doctoral Consortium)

Alan Tsang
Cheriton School of Computer Science
University of Waterloo, Canada
akhtsang@uwaterloo.ca

ABSTRACT

The effects of social networks are pervasive in everyday life, from the subtle effects on mundane, moment-to-moment choices, to political revolutions driven through social media. The last few years have seen a rapid growth of interest in this area from researchers within artificial intelligence and multiagent systems communities. Until recently, relatively little attention has been paid on understanding the effects of these networks on the social aggregation of opinions. My main research question I wish to consider is the impact of social networks on social choice. Specifically, how does communication within social networks affect the strategic voting behavior of the population, and how does it affect the voting outcome?

Keywords

Behavioral game theory, Social choice theory, Social simulation, Agent-based Modeling, Graph theory, Iterative voting, Emergent behavior

1. INTRODUCTION

My current thesis work lays at the intersection of social network and social choice. Social networks have gained tremendous popularity in both research communities and popular media in the last decade. These networks capture the relationships and social structures that define communities both large and small. While early social network research produced theories on how information flows through such a network, and influence is exerted by the popular and powerful, relatively little is known about how this network structure might impact the way in which communities arrive at collective decisions.[1] A social network is typically represented as a graph $G = \{V, E\}$ on a set of vertices V. Each vertex represents an individual, and an edge $(i, j) \in E$ represents a connection between individuals i and j. The graph may be undirected, where $(i, j) \in E$ implies $(j, i) \in E$; or it may be directed. This latter case represents a community where influence (or flow of information) is asymmetric, where i may unilaterally influence j.

Social choice theory is the study of collective decision making within a community. We focus on the topic of voting within social choice, where the community must rank a series of alternatives against each other. Each individual i within the community has her own subjective preferences on the alternatives, and submits a ballot b_i (which may or may not accurately reflect her preferences), and a social choice function maps the set of all ballots $\{b_i\}_{i \in V}$ to a final ordering of the alternatives. When an individual submits a ballot that does not accurately reflect her true preferences, she is voting strategically. One way to model strategic voting behavior is to allow voting to take place in successive rounds (which could be thought of as a series of advanced polls). In each round, the voters observe the results of the previous round and may revise their ballots accordingly. A number of papers have been published recently studying this form of *iterative voting* (such as [4] and [10]). This form of iterative voting makes the assumption that each voter receives complete information on the results of each round of voting; i.e. they see the ballots of all voters within the community. Instead of making this assumption, we assume that the visibility of information for each voter is limited to their social network, which may include not only friends and family, but frequent acquaintances, news outlets, and other forms of mass media. My thesis focuses on relaxing the assumption of information availability and examining the effects this has on strategic voting in the network domain.

2. CURRENT AND PLANNED WORK

My initial work [13] on this topic has been accepted to AAMAS 2016, and is based on Clough's early model [5, 6] in this area, using agent based modeling. While Clough's model was based on a simplistic grid based network, I utilize realistic graph models from random graph theory and opinion dynamics literature. In particular, we focus on networks that feature homophily – the tendency for connections to favor agents of similar opinions. This has a notable effect of reducing both the benefit and frequency of strategic voting behavior, and provides insight into the mechanisms behind the "Echo Chamber Effect" in popular media. We show that while voter dynamics are not guaranteed to converge, they often do so quickly in practice. We also show that these results are robust against variations in tie-breaking and update mechanisms. I plan to extend this paper by exploring additional graph models (see below) and different voting rules, which will require scaling up our simulation to run on more powerful architecture, or using maximum-likelihood methods to speed up computation.

It is clear that in iterative voting and in my social network simulations, voting strategies develop and evolve over time. A number of other papers also study the timing effects of voting. Zou, Meir and Parkes [14] have studied voting patterns in the popular social polling website Doodle, and found later ballots made use of infor-

[1] With the notable exception of Sina et. al's 2015 paper on social network manipulation, which differs from my work in both the model used and the research question being investigated.

Appears in: *Proceedings of the 15th International Conference on Autonomous Agents and Multiagent Systems (AAMAS 2016), J. Thangarajah, K. Tuyls, C. Jonker, S. Marsella (eds.), May 9–13, 2016, Singapore.*

mation available from previous ballots. Alon et al. [2] examines a behavioral model of "herding" behavior where ballots can be entirely decided by the history of previous ballots, if agents derive utility having voted for the winner. As varied as these papers are, none of them address the ability for voters to control the time at which they commit their ballot. This is what I have called *strategizing along the time axis*, where a voter may choose when to cast their ballot, making it publicly visible, so as to maximize its influence on other voters, and is irreversible. This presents a set of interesting new dynamics to explore. In an environment where other voters are also strategic, an early commitment may help establish a favoured candidate as a "lead runner"; while a late commitment will avoid wasted a vote on a hopeless candidate.

I have done some preliminary analytical work in this area by defining a model of voter timing and studying several special cases in the absence of a social network. Consider a scenario where n agents $(1, \ldots n)$ must decide between k alternatives M, each agent having its over preference over the alternatives. Voting proceeds across T rounds. In each round, each voter who has not yet submitted a ballot yet may choose to cast their ballot. This decision is made simultaneously within each round, and their decision and ballot are revealed publicly. Alternatively, a voter may choose to refrain from casting a vote, and wait. In my basic analysis, I have shown that in a 3-player game with circular preferences, there is a subgame perfect Nash Equilibrium where it is in each agent's best interest to vote for their *second* preference with probability 0.2, and to wait with probability 0.8. I suspect this behavior is likely degenerate to small groups with complete knowledge of each others' preferences, and that this "first mover disadvantage" may disappear in larger groups. I hope to be able to extend this work to more general models using either analytical or empirical techniques.

Currently, I also am developing a new random graph model to accurately reflect the evolution of online networks. A central characteristic of human-made networks is that they feature a handful of very high-connected hubs and numerous sparsely connected nodes. This scale-free property was first characterized in the Barabasi-Albert model [1]. Recent work extends this model to directed graphs [3] where communication and influence between nodes may be one-directional, and separately, to feature high clustering coefficients [9] where the two agent sharing a common acquaintance are more likely to be connected to each other. My current work will be the first model to incorporate all three key properties that are found in social networks. I plan to produce both a theoretical analysis of this class of graphs, and to use these graphs to conduct future social choice simulations.

While not part of my thesis work, I have also worked on a related project investigating "should social network structure be taken into account in elections". This is a paper in response to the question posited by Conitzer in his 2012 paper of the same name. While his followup paper [7] answers this in the negative, we propose a more detailed model that answers in the positive. We show that under certain assumptions, we can improve the accuracy of aggregation protocols by up to 20% by using information from the social network of simulated voters. This is joint work with other researchers from my lab [12, 8], which we plan to submit as a journal paper.

In short, the crossroads of computational social choice and social computing is proving to be fruitful grounds for exploration by the AI community. My research has the potential to revolutionize our understanding of online environments, recommender systems, and strategic dynamics in both online and social environments.

REFERENCES

[1] R. Albert and A.-L. Barabási. Statistical mechanics of complex networks. *Reviews of modern physics*, 74(1):47, 2002.

[2] N. Alon, M. Babaioff, R. Karidi, R. Lavi, and M. Tennenholtz. Sequential voting with externalities: herding in social networks. In *EC*, page 36, 2012.

[3] B. Bollobás, C. Borgs, J. Chayes, and O. Riordan. Directed scale-free graphs. In *Proceedings of the fourteenth annual ACM-SIAM symposium on Discrete algorithms*, pages 132–139. Society for Industrial and Applied Mathematics, 2003.

[4] S. Brânzei, I. Caragiannis, J. Morgenstern, and A. Procaccia. How bad is selfish voting? In *Twenty-Seventh AAAI Conference on Artificial Intelligence*, 2013.

[5] E. Clough. Strategic voting under conditions of uncertainty: A re-evaluation of Duverger's law. *British Journal of Political Science*, 37(02):313–332, 2007.

[6] E. Clough. Talking locally and voting globally Duverger's law and homogeneous discussion networks. *Political Research Quarterly*, 60(3):531–540, 2007.

[7] V. Conitzer. The maximum likelihood approach to voting on social networks. In *Allerton*, volume 13, pages 1482–1487, 2013.

[8] J. A. Doucette, H. Hosseini, A. Tsang, R. Cohen, and K. Larson. Voting with social networks: Truth springs from argument amongst friends. 2015.

[9] P. Holme and B. J. Kim. Growing scale-free networks with tunable clustering. *Physical review E*, 65(2):026107, 2002.

[10] O. Lev and J. S. Rosenschein. Convergence of iterative voting. In *Proceedings of the 11th International Conference on Autonomous Agents and Multiagent Systems-Volume 2*, pages 611–618. International Foundation for Autonomous Agents and Multiagent Systems, 2012.

[11] S. Sina, N. Hazon, A. Hassidim, and S. Kraus. Adapting the social network to affect elections. In *Proceedings of the 14th International Conference on Autonomous Agents and Multiagent Systems*, pages 705–713. International Foundation for Autonomous Agents and Multiagent Systems, 2015.

[12] A. Tsang, J. Doucette, and H. Housini. Voting with social influence: Using arguments to uncover ground truth. In *Proceedings of the 14th International Conference on Autonomous Agents and Multiagent Systems*, 2015.

[13] A. Tsang and K. Larson. The echo chamber: Strategic voting and homophily in social networks. In *Proceedings of the 15th International Conference on Autonomous Agents and Multiagent Systems*. International Foundation for Autonomous Agents and Multiagent Systems, 2016.

[14] J. Zou, R. Meir, and D. Parkes. Approval voting behavior in doodle polls.

Planning for Symbiotic Action (Doctoral Consortium)

Tathagata Chakraborti
Advisor: Subbarao Kambhampati
3rd yr PhD Student, Computer Science Department
Arizona State University, Tempe AZ 85281
tchakra2@asu.edu

ABSTRACT

The field of Artificial Intelligence (AI) has become extremely prominent in recent times, with the integration of different intelligent components into devices and services we use in everyday life. As the capabilities of such systems become more and more complex, one branch of AI that becomes relevant is that of *automated planning* or *sequential decision making*, in order for these components to participate in diverse long term tasks. A key aspect of such systems is increased interaction with humans.

Challenges in Human-in-the-Loop Planning (HILP)

Classical planning has traditionally emphasized on the efficiency or accuracy of the plan generation process. However, in real world applications, especially involving humans, planners must deal with typical challenges including uncertainty and partial knowledge, and issues involving priorities and authority. Technologies that become crucial in this context involve abilities to dynamically predict, anticipate and adapt to changing needs while making task plans. My research focuses on such aspects of *"human-in-the-loop planning"*.

Modalities of HILP - My Research Focus

I have looked at two specific ways in which automated planners may interact with humans. First I will describe how planners can enable different types of autonomous behavior of robots sharing their workspace with humans - i.e. interacting with human *colleagues*. Then I will look at possible roles of automated planners in platforms that involve *collaboration* with or among human planners. The aim of my thesis is to provide planning technologies for and motivate well-informed and principled design of complex symbiotic man-machine systems of the future.

Humans as Colleagues

Many of today's robots built for tasks like household assistance or hotel/office service or security guards, do not operate in teams, i.e. they do not have common goals and commitments with humans sharing the environment, and interactions with such agents depart from traditional notions of proximal human-robot teams. Even though these scenarios require significantly different levels of autonomy from the

Appears in: *Proceedings of the 15th International Conference on Autonomous Agents and Multiagent Systems (AAMAS 2016), J. Thangarajah, K. Tuyls, C. Jonker, S. Marsella (eds.), May 9–13, 2016, Singapore.*

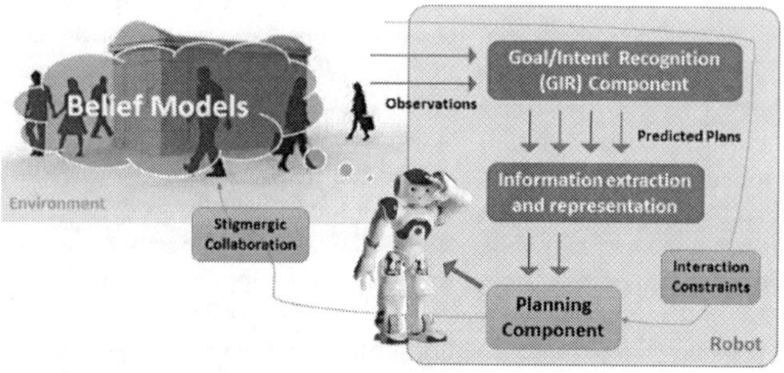

robot, the underlying theme of autonomy in such settings involves the robot achieving some sense of independence of purpose in so much as its existence is not just defined by the goals of the humans around it but is rather contingent on tasks it is supposed to achieve on its own.

Thus the robots in a sense become colleagues rather than teammates. This becomes even more prominent when we consider *inter-team* and *intra-team* interactions between multiple independent teams in a human-robot cohabited environment. We postulate that interaction with the human cohabitants in such cases should be similar to how we interact with our human colleagues rather than teammates. This provides many interesting possibilities in modeling autonomous behavior in these scenarios - the agents must learn modes of passive or *stigmergic* collaboration. In [1, 2, 3, 4] I model such interactions at three levels of granularity - resources, plans and goals - and motivate the need for developing appropriate metrics for quantifying performance in such settings. Much of the challenge in developing such behaviors is in modeling the appropriate interaction constraints (I use integer programming formulations for this purpose). In the following discussion I will briefly introduce two such models.

Planning with Resource Conflicts

In [4], we look at how robots sharing their workspace with humans, and using shared resources, can plan to minimize conflicts on resource usage. We propose a planner that models the intentions of the human colleagues and produces plans that decouple its resource demands with that of the humans'. Note that there is no explicit or direct interaction here between the human and the robot, the interaction is successful inasmuch as the human's plan was successful.

Resource Profiles. We represent information from predicted plans in the form of *resource profiles*, that enables the robot to reason with how the environment will evolve with time, at different levels of abstraction. This way we compile the complexity of accounting for individual predictions into the number of resources being modeled, which makes our approach independent of both the number of agents being modeled and the size of the hypothesis goal set.

Modes of Behavior. We show how our approach models different autonomous behaviors: (1) *compromise* - the robot opts for suboptimal plans to respect the human's plans; (2) *opportunism* - the robot anticipates favorable changes to the world and produces plans even better than the original optimal ones; and (3) *negotiation* - the robot negotiates desired times of use of the resources with the human.

Planning for Serendipity

In [1], we look at how robots can provide assistance to their human colleagues without the latter asking for help, i.e. the robot plans to produce *serendipitous interventions* (which appear as positive exogenous events) during execution of the human's plans. Contrary to the discussion in the previous section, here the robot's actions directly modify the human's plans rather than just effect it indirectly by avoiding potential conflicts. Note that the human, being unaware, cannot plan to exploit these interventions in advance, which imposes several constraints on the plan generation process.

Plan Interruptibility. In order to produce serendipitous interventions, the robot computes parts of the predicted human plan that can be replaced by a (cheaper) plan involving both the human and the robot.

Plan Preservation. But of course all removable sub-plans do not lead to serendipitous interventions, the robot has to ensure additional constraints that involve preserving the prefix of the original human plan and the world state he originally intended to be in after the intervention. A demonstration can be viewed at `http://bit.ly/1Q6tOBW`.

Humans as Collaborators

In this section we will look at the role of automated oversight in human computation tasks - specifically we investigate how an automated planner can contribute to a plan generation process carried out by humans. In order to collaborate with human planners, we postulate that automated planners must be able to perform two fundamental tasks -

Interpretation. In order for the planner to make useful contributions, it must first comprehend the current state of the planning process, as well as the intentions and (often implicit) preferences of the human planners.

Steering. The planner must iteratively refine, validate and critique the planning process, while respecting the authority of the human planners. The goal of this work is to augment the vast domain knowledge of humans with the superiority of automated constraint checking and plan validation.

Crowdsourced Planning - `AI-MIX`

In [5] we investigate how planners can work with a crowd, using extremely shallow models (in tour planning domain). We show how a PDDL domain may be used to support and critique the plan generation process, and how declarative languages like ASP can be used to compile all the constraints to generate the final plan. Our system is the proud winner of the People's Choice Best System Demonstration Award at ICAPS'14. A demonstration of the system is available at `http://bit.ly/1o22ajr`.

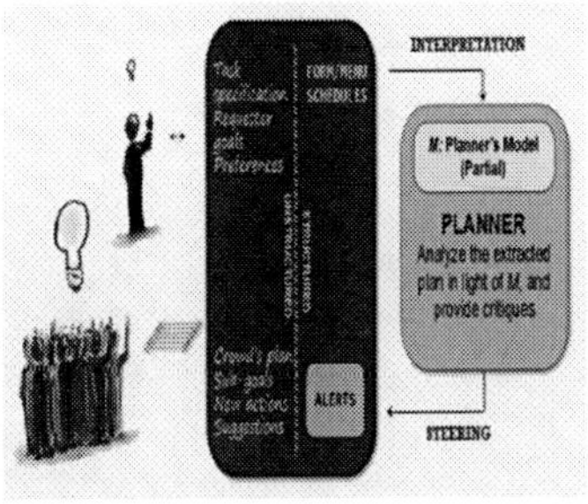

Proactive Decision Support - `RADAR`

We are currently working on a system that can use more complete domain models to collaborate with experts on specialized tasks (like disaster response). An aspirational video is available `http://bit.ly/1KEJZKj`. I am more involved in the planning aspect of the project. Planning applications include plan recognition for preemptive assistance with both the plan generation and the proactive context-based information integration process, and plan validation and refinement using techniques like landmark generation and plan robustness. A preliminary demonstration of these capabilities can be found at `http://bit.ly/1o22ajr`.

Acknowledgments

I would like to take this opportunity to thank the contributions of several people who have made this work possible, including Kartik Talamadupula (IBM T.J. Watson Research Center) and Gordon Briggs (Tufts University) for their early work on coordination in the USAR environment, and David Smith (NASA Ames Research Center) and Matthias Scheutz (Tufts University) for their valuable inputs and support.

Also special thanks to all the funding agencies that have supported my work till now. My research has been funded in part by the ARO grant W911NF-13-1-0023, and the ONR grants N00014-13-1-0176, N00014-13-1-0519, N00014-15-1-2027 and N00014-15-1-2344.

REFERENCES

[1] T. Chakraborti, G. Briggs, K. Talamadupula, Y. Zhang, M. Scheutz, D. Smith, and S. Kambhampati. Planning for serendipity. In *IEEE/RSJ International Conference on Intelligent Robots and Systems (IROS)*, 2015.

[2] T. Chakraborti, V. V. Meduri, V. Dondeti, , and S. Kambhampati. A game-theoretic approach to ad-hoc coalition formation in human-robot societies. In *AAAI 2016 Workshop on Multiagent Interaction without Prior Coordination (MIPC)*, 2016.

[3] T. Chakraborti, K. Talamadupula, Y. Zhang, and S. Kambhampati. A formal framework for studying interaction in human-robot societies. In *AAAI 2016 Workshop on Symbiotic Cognitive Systems (SCS)*, 2016.

[4] T. Chakraborti, Y. Zhang, D. Smith, and S. Kambhampati. Planning with resource conflicts in human-robot cohabitation. In *Proc. of the International Conference on Autonomous Agents and Multiagent Systems (AAMAS)*, 2016.

[5] L. Manikonda, T. Chakraborti, S. De, K. Talamadupula, and S. Kambhampati. AI-MIX: How a Planner Can Help Guide Humans Towards a Better Crowdsourced Plan. In *Innovative Applications of Artificial Intelligence (IAAI) 2014. Winner of People's Choice Best Demonstration Award at ICAPS 2014!*

Author Index